HALLIWELL'S FILM GUIDE

Also edited by John Walker

Halliwell's Filmgoer's Companion
Halliwell's Guide to the Best Children's Films
Halliwell's Guide to the Best Comedies

HALLIWELL'S FILM GUIDE

LESLIE HALLIWELL

10TH EDITION
Revised and Updated

EDITED BY JOHN WALKER

HarperCollins*Publishers*

HarperCollins*Publishers*
77—85 Fulham Palace Road
Hammersmith, London W6 8JB

Tenth edition published by HarperCollins*Publishers* 1994
9 8 7 6 5 4 3 2 1

First published by Granada Publishing 1977
Second edition 1979
Third edition 1981
Fourth edition 1983
Fifth edition 1985
Sixth edition published by Grafton Books 1987
Seventh edition 1989
Eighth edition 1991
Ninth edition published by HarperCollins*Publishers* 1993

ISBN 0 00 638389 0

Set in 7pt Meridien and Gill Sans

Printed in Great Britain by
William Clowes Limited, Beccles, Suffolk

CONTENTS

Introduction to the Tenth Edition   vii

Explanatory Notes   ix

THE FILM GUIDE A–Z   1

Academy Award Winners   1219

Four-Star Films (listed by title)   1227

Four-Star Films (listed by year)   1229

INTRODUCTION

Cinema celebrates its hundredth birthday in 1995, and this tenth edition joins in the festivities by adding another 1,000 entries so that it now contains around 20,000 of the most enduring movies ever made.

It's impossible to date precisely the birth of cinema, although we can say that it was a century ago. The great French film-maker Marcel Pagnol used to insist that it coincided with his birth on 28 February 1895, which was when the Lumière brothers, Louis and Auguste, patented their machine for photographing and projecting motion pictures. They began giving private demonstrations early that year, culminating in the first public showing in Paris on Saturday, 28 December. A month earlier, Max and Emil Skladanowsky had patented their methods and had shown eight films in Berlin. Other public showings swiftly followed, from R. W. Paul in Britain, and C. Francis Jenkins and Thomas Armat in America – and the rest is a notable part of the history of this century.

This edition adds some new features to make this guide an even more complete work of reference. Included are lists, in chronological and alphabetical order, of four-star films – those that, for reasons of excellence or influence, can be accounted among the best that the cinema has produced. Also listed are Oscar-winners in the major categories. And you can now discover, from individual entries, which films have soundtrack albums released on compact disc and which are available on video-cassette, both in Britain and the United States, as well as on laser disc and the newest format, VideoCD.

VideoCD is a standard agreed by all the major electronic companies for releasing, among other things, feature films on compact disc, which can be played either on special consoles or through computers fitted with a CD-ROM drive and a FMV (Full Motion Video) card. The films so far available have been released by Philips to play on its CD-i (Compact Disc Interactive) console and, for reasons best known to Philips, deviate from the agreed standard, although they are also compatible with Commodore's Amiga CD32 console. Several other CD-based video-players are planned and there is at least one special card available for IBM PC and compatible computers which, when linked to a CD-ROM drive, will allow computer users to watch VideoCD.

At the moment, a compact disc can hold about 72 minutes of film, so that, as with many laser discs, two discs are necessary for each film, but it won't be long before single discs are available which can play back an entire film. So far, only a few films have been released on VideoCD, but there are many more on the way. The quality compares favourably with movies on videotape. Visually, the picture is as good, although occasionally movement becomes jerky and the image blurs or breaks up slightly, and the sound is better. Neither matches the quality possible from laser discs.

Information given here on British video releases may not be entirely accurate. At the time of writing, the government has not announced exactly what form its censorship of videos will take when it is included in the forthcoming Criminal Justice Bill, soon to be an Act. But it has agreed in principle to Liberal Democrat MP David Alton's amendment to ban those videos 'containing degrading or gratuitously violent scenes liable to cause psychological damage to a child, or to present a child with an inappropriate role model'. Taken literally, this would mean the disappearance not only of horror movies but of popular comedies, such as *Home Alone*, and of films of far greater artistic importance. Who, after all, would want their child to grow up to be Citizen Kane?

As a consequence of the proposed Act, it is possible that some films currently available on video will be withdrawn and that many others will be available for viewing only in cinemas. The effect on the already floundering British film industry is likely to be catastrophic, not only through loss of revenue but because it will make it more difficult for film-makers to tackle subject-matter that reflects the realities of the age.

Leaving aside the question of whether the best method of protecting children is to ban films intended for adults, there is little doubt that video has become the latest scapegoat of public concern about violence in society as, in the past, have cheap newspapers, music-hall, jazz, rock 'n' roll and horror comics. Indeed, government dislike of popular culture goes back more than 400 years, to laws compelling the licensing of wandering performers, who were similarly blamed for spreading disorder and dissension. As Samuel McKechnie, a historian of entertainment, wrote in the 1930s, 'It is a pity that would-be reformers of entertainments in the past, and in the present, did not have stamped indelibly on their minds the substance of the declaration that "the Drama's laws the Drama's patrons give." If the spectator is reformed the demand for unwholesome fare dies. If the entertainer is suppressed the demand is merely diverted. Soon there is need for the suppression of other entertainers.' Already, Mr Alton is turning his attention to television.

I thank the many readers who have written to me with suggestions and criticisms and Mr John Legard for his loan of a video of a film I should not otherwise have seen. I am especially grateful to William C. Clogston for generously sharing with me his expert knowledge of film, to Valerie Hudson of HarperCollins for her kindness, to my editor Ian Paten for his guidance, to my agents, Gloria Ferris and Rivers Scott, for their sensible advice, to my son Barnaby for cheerfully undertaking some essential, but dull, research, and, above all, to my wife Barbara, for reminding me that there is life to be enjoyed outside the cinema.

John Walker
May 1994

EXPLANATORY NOTES

Alphabetical Order

Unlike some books which take the complete title into account, as though there were no gaps between words, we have always persevered with the old-fashioned word-at-a-time arrangement. Thus, all titles starting with *In*, including *In Which We Serve*, are used up before one goes on to titles beginning *Incredible, Inspector, Intolerance*. Hyphenated or apostrophized words are counted as one word. Compressions such as *Dr* and *St* are treated as though they had been spelled out, as *Doctor* and *Saint*. *Mac* and *Mc* are regarded as interchangeable under *Mac*. Titles consisting of initials, such as *C. C. and Company* or *D.O.A.* are dealt with at the beginning of each alphabetical section, except where they have become acronyms (i.e. pronounceable as one word, e.g. AWOL). In all cases the complete title is given as billed, though the definite and indefinite articles are not counted in the alphabetical arrangement where they occur as the first word of a title. The spelling of the country of origin is used, e.g. *My Favorite Blonde* and not *My Favourite Blonde*.

Individual Entries

All entries follow the same format and the notes are set out below in the order in which they will be encountered.

Publicity tags   These were used in the promotion of the film and, in the manner of trailers, precede the entry.

Ratings   These range from none to four stars. Four stars indicate a film outstanding in many ways, a milestone in cinema history, remarkable for acting, direction, writing, photography or some other aspect of technique. Three stars indicate a very high standard of professional excellence or great historical interest. Or, if you like, three strong reasons for admiring it. Two stars indicate a good level of competence and a generally entertaining film. One star indicates a film not very satisfactory as a whole; it could be a failed giant or a second feature with a few interesting ideas among the dross. No stars at all indicates a totally routine production or worse; such films may be watchable but are at least equally missable.

Country of origin   This is the first item on the second line.

Year of release   This comes after the country of origin and is intended to indicate the year when the film was first shown, which is not necessarily the year that it was made. Dating is sometimes an onerous task, and the result debatable.

Running time   This is given in minutes, signified by 'm'. So far as possible, this is the original release time. Very many films are cut as they appear in different countries, sometimes by twenty minutes or more. An engineering function of British television results in an imperceptible speeding-up of projection and a consequent loss of one minute in every twenty-five. A hundred-minute film, therefore, will run only ninety-six minutes on the box.

Colour   This is indicated by 'bw' for black and white films and 'colour' for the others. The colour process used, such as Technicolor, is given when known.

Other notable points   These are given at the end of the second line, indicating the use of a special process, such as Panavision.

Production credit   This is the central credit on the third line. To the left comes the name of the distributor, which is followed by the production company if different. To the right comes the name or names of the actual producer – in brackets, unless he has a stake in the production, in which case he follows an oblique. These days, many films tend to have more producers of one kind or another than actors. The credit here refers to the person bearing the title of producer rather than to the executive producer, associate producer, production executive and so on.

Video   'V' indicates that the film is available on VHS video-cassette for the British PAL system. 'V (W)' indicates that the film is available on VHS video-cassette for the British PAL system in wide-screen format. 'V (C)' indicates that the film is available on VHS video-cassette for the British PAL system in a computer-colourized version. 'L' indicates that the film is available on laser disc in either American NTSC format or British PAL format. 'V*' indicates that the film is available in the American NTSC format (which is not compatible with the British PAL system). 'CD' indicates that the film is available on Video CD. (See the Introduction for more information on this new format.) 'S' indicates that the film's soundtrack music has been released on compact disc.

Alternative title   This is given on a separate line, usually with a note of the country in which it was used. If no such distinction exists, the formula aka (also known as) is used. Alternative titles are also listed individually, cross-referenced to the main entry for the film to which they belong.

Synopsis   This is a brief description of the film's plot.

Assessment   Again, this is brief and to the point.

Writer credit   (w) This appears first since the script precedes direction and is therefore, at least sometimes, more important than the director credit. The author of the screenplay is given; if this derives from a novel, play, musical, or story, this is given next, together with the original author.

Director credit   (*d*) This follows next. If the director is also the writer, then there will be a combined '*wd*' credit.

Photography credit   (*ph*) This indicates the cinematographer or lighting cameraman, otherwise known as the director of photography, rather than the actual camera operator.

Music credit   (*m*) This means the composer of the background music score. Sometimes there is only a music director (*md*) who orchestrates library or classical music. When noteworthy songs are performed in a film, or are specially written for it, those responsible are indicated by a credit for music and lyrics (*m/ly*) or simply *songs*.

Other credits   These include art director (*ad*), choreographer (*ch*), costume designer (*costume*), film editor (*ed*), production designer (*pd*) and special effects (*sp*). They are given when they seem important and when they can be found. In some cases it has not been possible to track down all the credits one would wish.

Cast   A list of the principal actors is given, roughly in order of importance.

Italics   These denote a contribution of a particularly high standard.

Critical comments   Brief quotes from well-known professional critics are appended to many entries, sometimes because they wittily confirm the assessments and sometimes because they provide alternative opinions. The absence of a quote casts no reflection whatever on the film, only on the difficulty of finding an opinion worth quoting.

Additional notes   Any points of interest about the film are given after the symbol †.

Academy Awards   Awards (AA) and nominations (AAN) are listed for all principal categories, including best picture, acting, direction, photography, music score and songs, and some minor ones, such as sound and make-up, when they seem of interest. British Academy of Film and Television Arts awards follow the abbreviation BFA.

A

A Bout de Souffle ****
France   1960   90m   bw
SNC (Georges de Beauregard)
V, V*, L, S
aka: *Breathless*

A young car thief kills a policeman and goes on the run with his American girlfriend.

Casual, influential, New Wave reminiscence of both *Quai des Brumes* and innumerable American gangster thrillers. (The film is dedicated to Monogram.) One of the first and most influential films of the French New Wave.

w Jean-Luc Godard   story François Truffaut
d Jean-Luc Godard   ph Raoul Coutard   m Martial Solal   ed Cécile Decugis

Jean-Paul Belmondo, Jean Seberg, Daniel Boulanger, Jean-Pierre Melville, Jean-Luc Godard

'A film all dressed up for rebellion but with no real tangible territory on which to stand and fight.' – *Peter John Dyer*

† See also *Breathless*, American remake.

A Double Tour
France/Italy   1959   110m   Eastmancolor
Paris/Panitalia (Robert and Raymond Hakim)
aka: *Web of Passion*

A wealthy wine grower has trouble with his wife, his children, his best friend, and his mistress across the way, who is murdered.

Talented but irritating mixture of Hitchcock and *Les Parents Terribles*; rather an undergraduatish romp.

w Paul Gégauff   novel *La Clé de la Rue Saint-Nicolas*
d Claude Chabrol   ph Henri Decaë   m Paul Misraki

Jacques Dacqmine, Madeleine Robinson, Jean-Paul Belmondo, Bernadette Lafont, Antonella Lualdi, André Jocelyn

A Nos Amours: see *To Our Loves*

A Nous la Liberté ****
France   1931   95m   bw
Tobis
V*
US title: *Freedom for Us*

A factory owner is blackmailed about his past, and helped by an old prison friend, with whom he finally takes to the road.

Operetta-style satirical comedy with leftish attitudes and several famous sequences later borrowed by Chaplin for *Modern Times*. In terms of sheer film flair, a revelation, though the plot has its tedious turns.

wd *René Clair*   ph *Georges Périnal*   m *Georges Auric*
pd *Lazare Meerson*

Raymond Cordy, Henri Marchand, Rolla France, Paul Olivier

'Different from the usual run . . . easily understandable even to those who do not know French.' – *Variety*

'He demonstrates that sound pictures can be as fluid as silents were, and the picture is rightly considered a classic.' – *Pauline Kael, 1970s*

'I was close to the extreme left . . . I wanted to attack the Machine, which led men into starvation instead of adding to their happiness.' – *René Clair*

A Propos de Nice *
France   1930   30m   bw

A satirical documentary on the millionaire's paradise of the French Riviera.

Cheaply made and rather naïve-looking after fifty years, this amusingly belligerent lampoon still has its striking moments.

wd Jean Vigo   ph Boris Kaufman

Aan *
India   1952   190m approx (English version 130m)
    Technicolor
All India Film Corporation/Mehboob Productions
aka: *Savage Princess*

A usurping young prince and his sister are tamed by an athletic peasant and his girlfriend.

One of the few examples to reach the West of Indian costume melodrama with music, spectacle and swashbuckling. Distinctly intriguing, if overpowering.

w Chaudary, Ali Raza   d Mehboob   ph Faredoon A. Irani   m Naushad Dilip

Kumar, Nimmi, Premnath, Nadira

'Disarmingly enthusiastic . . . exotic and yet charmingly naïve.' – *MFB*

De Aanslag: see *The Assault*

Aaron Slick from Punkin Crick *
US   1952   95m   Technicolor
Paramount (William Perlberg, George Seaton)
GB title: *Marshmallow Moon*

A small-town girl is tricked into selling her farm and moving to the city, but eventually marries the simple farmer who rescues her.

Homespun entertainment based on a staple success of the American provincial theatre, with pleasant songs added.

wd Claude Binyon   play Walter Benjamin Hare
ph Charles B. Lang Jnr   m/ly Jay Livingston, Ray Evans   ch Charles O'Curran

Alan Young, Dinah Shore, Robert Merrill, Adele Jergens, Minerva Urecal

Abandon Ship: see *Seven Waves Away*

Abandoned
US   1949   79m   bw
Universal-International

Reporter breaks baby-farming racket.

Competent action thriller for double billing.

w Irwin Gielgud   d Joseph Newman

Dennis O'Keefe, Gale Storm, Raymond Burr (and young Jeff Chandler)

'They're too wild for one world!'
Abbott and Costello Go to Mars
US   1953   76m   bw
U-I (Howard Christie)

Two incompetents accidentally launch a space ship and land first in Louisiana, then on Venus.

Dismal knockabout, badly made.

w John Grant, D. D. Beauchamp   d Charles Lamont
ph Clifford Stine   m Joseph Gershenson

Bud Abbott, Lou Costello, Mari Blanchard, Robert Paige, Martha Hyer

Abbott and Costello in Hollywood *
US   1945   85m   bw
MGM (Martin Gosch)
V*, L

Two agents have hectic adventures in a film studio.

Tolerable star romp on one of their biggest budgets, climaxing in a roller coaster ride.

w Nat Perrin, Lou Breslow   d S. Sylvan Simon
ph Charles Schoenbaum   m George Bassman

Bud Abbott, Lou Costello, Frances Rafferty, Warner Anderson, Robert Z. Leonard

Abbot and Costello in Society: see *In Society*

Abbott and Costello in the Foreign Legion
US   1950   80m   bw
U-I (Robert Arthur)
V*, L

Incompetent legionnaires become heroes to the fury of their sergeant.

Dull star vehicle on ramshackle sets, with no memorable routines.

w John Grant, Leonard Stern, Martin Ragaway
d Charles Lamont   ph George Robinson   m Joseph Gershenson

Bud Abbott, Lou Costello, Patricia Medina, Walter Slezak, Douglass Dumbrille

Abbott and Costello in the Navy: see *In the Navy*

Abbott and Costello Lost in Alaska
US   1952   76m   bw
U-I (Howard Christie)

Two San Francisco firemen take a melancholy prospector back to Alaska to find a gold mine.

Sub-standard comedy vehicle with poor production.

w Martin Ragaway, Leonard Stern   d Jean Yarbrough   ph George Robinson   m Joseph Gershenson

Bud Abbott, Lou Costello, *Tom Ewell*, Mitzi Green, Bruce Cabot

Abbott and Costello Meet Captain Kidd *
US   1952   70m   Supercinecolor
Warner/Woodley (Alex Gottlieb)
V*

Two servants have a treasure map, and a fearsome pirate wants it.

Crude knockabout: the stars are way below their best, and a famous actor is embarrassed.

w Howard Dimsdale, John Grant   d Charles Lamont
ph Stanley Cortez   m Raoul Kraushaar

Bud Abbott, Lou Costello, Charles Laughton, Hillary Brooke, Leif Erickson

Abbott and Costello Meet Dr Jekyll and Mr Hyde *

US   1953   77m   bw
U-I (Howard Christie)
V*

In Victorian London, two rookie policemen catch a monster.

Quite a lively spoof with some well-paced comedy sequences.

w John Grant, Lee Loeb   d Charles Lamont   ph George Robinson   m Hans Salter

7Bud Abbott, Lou Costello, Boris Karloff, Reginald Denny, Craig Stevens, Helen Westcott, John Dierkes

'Gracious Boris Karloff is superior to his surroundings.' – MFB (Though it is doubtful whether he ever got behind the Hyde make-up.)

† In Britain, the film was given an 'X' certificate, though it later played on children's television.

'Jeepers! the creepers are after somebody – and guess who! More howls than you can shake a shiver at!!!'

Abbott and Costello Meet Frankenstein **

US   1948   83m   bw
U-I (Robert Arthur)
V*, L
GB title: Abbott and Costello Meet the Ghosts

Two railway porters deliver crates containing the Frankenstein monster, Dracula, and the Wolf Man.

Fairly lively spoof which put an end to Universal's monsters for a while. Good typical sequences for the stars, a few thrills, and some good lines. Dracula to Costello, lovingly: 'What we need is young blood . . . and brains . . .'

w Robert Lees, Frederic I. Rinaldo, John Grant   d Charles Barton   ph Charles van Enger   m Frank Skinner

Bud Abbott, Lou Costello, Bela Lugosi, Lon Chaney Jnr, Glenn Strange, Lenore Aubert, Jane Randolph

WOLF MAN: 'You don't understand. Every night when the moon is full, I turn into a wolf.'
COSTELLO: 'You and fifty million other guys!'

† Probably the Abbott and Costello film which survives best.

Abbott and Costello Meet the Ghost: see
Abbott and Costello Meet Frankenstein

Abbott and Costello Meet the Invisible Man *

US   1951   82m   bw
U-I (Howard Christie)
V*

A boxer accused of murder makes himself invisible while two detectives clear him.

Quite a bright comedy with good trick effects.

w Robert Lees, Frederic I. Rinaldo, John Grant   d Charles Lamont   ph George Robinson   m Hans Salter

Bud Abbott, Lou Costello, Arthur Franz, Nancy Guild, Adele Jergens, Sheldon Leonard

'When every face wore a custard pie, and vamps broke hearts with a winking eye!'

Abbott and Costello Meet the Keystone Kops *

US   1954   79m   bw
U-I (Howard Christie)

In pioneer film days, two incompetents are sold a dud studio by a con man, but succeed as stunt men.

Flabby comedy which never seems to get going until the chase finale; notable chiefly for a guest appearance by Mack Sennett.

w John Grant   d Charles Lamont   ph Reggie Lanning   m Joseph Gershenson

Bud Abbott, Lou Costello, Lynn Bari, Fred Clark, Frank Wilcox, Maxie Rosenbloom

'More ghoulish glee than when they met Frankenstein!'

Abbott and Costello Meet the Killer, Boris Karloff *

US   1948   84m   bw
U-I (Robert Arthur)
V*, L

Two bellboys help to solve mysterious murders in a remote hotel.

This clumsily titled comedy really does not work until the last sequence in a cavern. Boris Karloff is not the killer and appears very little.

w Hugh Wedlock Jnr, Howard Snyder, John Grant   d Charles Barton   ph Charles van Enger   md Milton Schwarzwald

Bud Abbott, Lou Costello, Boris Karloff, Gar Moore, Lenore Aubert, Alan Mowbray

'It has been said that a man's best friend is his mummy . . .'

Abbott and Costello Meet the Mummy *

US   1955   77m   bw
U-I (Howard Christie)

A missing medallion leads to a lost tomb and a living mummy.

The comedians show their age in this one, but there is some typical if predictable humour and a thrill or two.

w John Grant   d Charles Lamont   ph George Robinson   m Hans Salter

Bud Abbott, Lou Costello, Kurt Katch, Marie Windsor, Michael Ansara, Dan Seymour

'How stupid can you get?' — 'How stupid do you want me to be?'

The Abdication

GB   1974   102m   Technicolor
Warner (Robert Fryer, James Cresson)

17th-century Queen Christina of Sweden journeys to Rome to embrace the Catholic church and falls in love with a cardinal.

Sombre historical fantasia, more irritating than interesting.

w Ruth Wolff   play Ruth Wolff   d Anthony Harvey   ph Geoffrey Unsworth   m Nino Rota

Liv Ullmann, Peter Finch, Cyril Cusack, Paul Rogers, Graham Crowden, Michael Dunn, Lewis Fiander, Harold Goldblatt

'Dainty debauchery and titillating tease straight from twenties women's pulp magazines.' – Variety

'Embalmed in such reverence for its own cultural elevation that it loses all contact with the audience.' – Pauline Kael

The Abductors *

US   1957   80m   bw   Regalscope
TCF/Regal (Ray Wander)

Around 1870, criminals steal Lincoln's body as ransom to effect a convict's release.

Interesting minor melodrama, but not sufficiently well made.

w Ray Wander   d Andrew V. McLaglen   ph Joseph LaShelle   m Paul Glass

Victor McLaglen, Gavin Muir, George Macready

Abdul the Damned *

GB   1935   111m   bw
BIP/Capitol (Max Schach)

In 1900 Turkey, an opera star gives herself to a villainous sultan to protect her fiancé.

Thoroughgoing hokum, well produced, which pleased some people in its day.

w Ashley Dukes, Warren Chetham Strode, Robert Burford   d Karl Grune   ph Otto Kanturek

Fritz Kortner, Adrienne Ames, Nils Asther, John Stuart, Esme Percy, Walter Rilla, Patric Knowles, Eric Portman

Abdulla the Great

GB/Egypt   1954   103m   Technicolor
(Gregory Ratoff)
aka: Abdulla's Harem

A pleasure-loving Egyptian potentate sets his sights on an English girl.

Feeble satire on King Farouk, inept and relentlessly boring.

w George St George, Boris Ingster   d Gregory Ratoff   ph Lee Garmes

Gregory Ratoff, Kay Kendall, Sydney Chaplin

Abdulla's Harem: see Abdulla the Great

Abe Lincoln in Illinois **

US   1940   110m   bw
RKO (Max Gordon)
V*
GB title: Spirit of the People

Episodes in the political and domestic life of Abraham Lincoln.

Pleasant, muted, careful film based on a Broadway success: generally informative and interesting.

w Grover Jones   play Robert E. Sherwood   d John Cromwell   ph James Wong Howe   m Roy Webb

Raymond Massey, Ruth Gordon, Gene Lockhart, Mary Howard, Dorothy Tree, Minor Watson, Howard da Silva

'If you want attitudes, a five gallon hat, famous incidents, and One Nation Indivisible, they're all here. As a picture and as a whole, it just doesn't stick.' – Otis Ferguson

AAN: Raymond Massey, James Wong Howe

Abel **

Netherlands   1985   96m   colour
First Floor Features (Laurens Geels, Dick Maas, Rob Swaab)

A 31-year-old mother's boy, thrown out of home, moves in with his father's mistress.

Witty, neatly plotted black farce of family life.

wd Alex Van Warmerdam   ph Marc Felperlaan   ad Harry Ammerlaan   ed Hans Van Dongen

Alex Van Warmerdam, Henri Garcin, Olga Zuiderhoek, Annet Malherbe, Loes Luca

Abie's Irish Rose

US   1946   96m   bw
UA/Bing Crosby Productions (Edward A. Sutherland)

Flat filming of the twenties Broadway play about Irish girl marrying Jewish boy, leading to a clash of families.

w Anne Nichols   play Anne Nichols   d Edward A. Sutherland   ph William Mellor   m John Scott Trotter

Joanne Dru, Richard Norris, Michael Chekhov, Eric Blore, Art Baker

† There had been a silent version in 1928, and the plot was borrowed, to say the least, for the 1972 TV series Bridget Loves Bernie.

Abilene Town *

US   1946   89m   bw
UA (Jules Levey)
V*

An upright marshal routs crooked cattlemen.

Vigorous, enjoyable Western programmer.

w Harold Shumate   d Edwin L. Marin

Randolph Scott, Ann Dvorak, Rhonda Fleming, Edgar Buchanan, Lloyd Bridges

'Love means never having to say you're ugly!'
The Abominable Dr Phibes *
GB 1971 94m Movielab
AIP (Louis M. Heyward, Ron Dunas)
V, V*, L

A disfigured musical genius devises a series of horrible murders, based on the ten curses of Pharaoh, for the surgeons who failed to save his wife.

Brisk but uninspired treatment of a promising theme, with more unintended nastiness than intended laughs. Some good moments and interesting low-budget thirties sets.

w James Whiton, William Goldstein   d Robert Fuest   ph Norman Warwick   m Basil Kirchen, Jack Nathan   pd Brian Eatwell

Vincent Price, Joseph Cotten, Hugh Griffith, Terry-Thomas, Peter Jeffrey, Virginia North, Aubrey Woods

'The sets are awful, the plot ludicrous and the dialogue inane – what more could a horror freak desire?' – *Motion Picture Guide*

† Sequel: *Dr Phibes Rises Again* (1973).

'See it with someone brave!'
The Abominable Snowman *
GB 1957 91m (85m US) bw RegalScope
Warner/Hammer/Clarion (Aubrey Baring)
US title: *The Abominable Snowman of the Himalayas*

Himalayan explorers are attacked one by one by the Yeti and their own fear.

A thin horror film with intelligent scripting: more philosophizing and characterization than suspense. The briefly glimpsed Yeti are disappointing creations.

w Nigel Kneale,   TV play Nigel Kneale   d Val Guest   ph Arthur Grant   m John Hollingsworth
ad Ted Marshall   ed Bill Lenny

Peter Cushing, Forrest Tucker, Maureen Connell, Richard Wattis, Robert Brown, *Arnold Marle*

About Face
US 1952 96m Technicolor
Warner (William Jacobs)

Moronic remake of *Brother Rat* (qv), shorn of all wit, pace and style.

w Peter Milne   d Roy del Ruth   ph Bert Glennon
m/ly Charles Tobias, Peter de Rose

Eddie Bracken, Gordon Macrae, Dick Wesson, Virginia Gibson, Phyllis Kirk, Joel Grey

About Last Night
US 1986 113m MGM colour
Tri-Star (Jason Brett, Stuart Oken)
V, V*, L, S

The ups and downs of an unmarried relationship.

Smart, slick, up-to-the-minute account of human coupling and uncoupling in the eighties . . . but no plot.

w Tim Kazurinsky, Denise DeClue   play Sexual Perversity in Chicago by David Mamet   d Edward Zwick   ph Andrew Dintenfass   m Miles Goodman
pd Ida Random

Rob Lowe, Demi Moore, Jim Belushi, Elizabeth Perkins, George DiCenzo

'Savvy enough to recognize points of conflict but not daring enough to look beneath the surface.' – *Variety*

About Mrs Leslie *
US 1954 104m bw
Paramount (Hal B. Wallis)

An ageing nightclub singer has a platonic affair with a mysterious wealthy man, who leaves her enough money to buy a boarding house.

Odd, likeable romantic drama tailored for an unusual star; but its plot is too thin and its direction too drab for real success.

w Ketti Frings, Hal Kanter   d Daniel Mann
ph Ernest Laszlo   m Victor Young

Shirley Booth, Robert Ryan, Alex Nicol, Marjie Millar, Eilene Janssen

'This quiet and curious film has an unexpectedly gentle, civilized flavour.' – *Gavin Lambert*

'It's all sunny disposition and sweet sadness for Miss Booth.' – *Judith Crist*

'One is reminded alternately of Chekhov and of *Back Street*.' – *Sight and Sound*

'The love story behind the billion dollar secret!'
Above and Beyond *
US 1952 122m bw
MGM (Melvin Frank, Norman Panama)

The training of Colonel Paul Tibbets, who dropped the first atomic bomb on Japan.

Overstretched flagwaver with laborious domestic interludes. Of little real interest then or now.

w Melvin Frank, Norman Panama   story Beirne Lay Jnr   d Melvin Frank, Norman Panama   ph Ray June   m Hugo Friedhofer

Robert Taylor, Eleanor Parker, James Whitmore, Larry Keating, Larry Gates

AAN: Beirne Lay Jnr, Hugo Friedhofer

Above Suspicion *
US 1943 91m bw
MGM (Victor Saville)
V*

Just before World War II, an Oxford professor on a continental honeymoon is asked to track down a missing agent.

Patchy, studio-bound spy comedy-drama with a couple of good sequences. Notable also for Mr MacMurray's impersonation of a professor who hails a Nazi as 'Hiya, dope!'

w Keith Winter, Melville Baker, Patricia Coleman
novel Helen MacInnes   d Richard Thorpe
ph Robert Planck   m Bronislau Kaper

Fred MacMurray, Joan Crawford, Conrad Veidt, *Basil Rathbone,* Reginald Owen, Felix Bressart, Richard Ainley

'Will need more than strong support for passable biz.' – *Variety*

Above The Law
US 1988 99m Technicolor
Warner (Steven Seagal, Andrew Davis)
V, V*, L
aka: *Nico*

A cop, who is also a martial arts expert, uncovers dirty work in the CIA.

Woodenly acted, violent action movie with an unusual anti-establishment slant.

w Steven Pressfield, Ronald Shusett, Andrew Davis
story Andrew Davis, Steven Seagal   d Andrew Davis   ph Robert Steadman   m David M. Frank
pd Maher Ahmad   sp Art Brewer, Lee Solis
ed Michael Brown

Steven Seagal, Pam Grier, Henry Silva, Daniel Faraldo, Sharon Stone, Nicholas Kusenko

'A story of impudent gallantry!'
Above Us the Waves
GB 1955 99m bw
Rank/London Independent Producers (William Macquitty)
V*

In World War II, midget submarines attack a German battleship in a Norwegian fjord.

Archetypal stiff-upper-lip war drama with disappointing action sequences and jumbled continuity.

w Robin Estridge   d Ralph Thomas   ph Ernest Steward   m Arthur Benjamin

John Mills, John Gregson, Donald Sinden, James Robertson Justice, Michael Medwin, Lee Patterson, Lyndon Brook

'It tells a heroic story without any flowery effects at all.' – *Manchester Guardian*

'The wonder film of the century, about the most romantic figure who ever lived!'
Abraham Lincoln **
US 1930 97m bw
UA/Art Cinema Corporation/D. W. Griffith
V*, L

An account of Lincoln's entry into politics and his years of power.

Rather boring even at the time, this straightforward biopic has the virtues of sincerity and comparative fidelity to the facts.

w Stephen Vincent Benet, Gerrit Lloyd   d D. W. Griffith   ph Karl Struss   m Hugo Riesenfeld
pd William Cameron Menzies

Walter Huston, Una Merkel, Edgar Dearing, Russell Simpson, Henry B. Walthall

'A startlingly superlative accomplishment, one rejuvenating a greatest Griffith . . . one smooth roll of literally pulsating passion, pathos, laughter . . . it should be his greatest contribution to the exhibitor.' – *Variety*

'It brings to us – with a curious finality of disappointment, a sentimental sense of the closing of a chapter – the impression of a director who has nowhere made a valid contact with the condition of the screen today.' – *C. A. Lejeune*

'A treasure trove of magnificent moments.' – *MFB, 1973*

'Dull, episodic, overlong . . . it is difficult to understand why contemporary critics were so impressed.' – *Anthony Slide, 70s*

† There was a silent biopic in 1924 starring George A. Billings, but it lacked cinematic interest. Written by Frances Marion and directed by Phil Rosen, for Rocket/Lincoln/AFN.

'Two roaring Romeos who thought even the dames were on lend lease!'
Abroad with Two Yanks *
US 1944 80m bw
Edward Small
V*

Adventures around the Pacific with two woman-chasing sailors.

This simple-minded farce with its punny title was a great success in its day, and still generates a laugh or two.

w Charles Rogers, Wilkie Mahoney, Ted Sills
d Allan Dwan   ph Charles Lawton   m Lud Gluskin

Dennis O'Keefe, William Bendix, Helen Walker, John Abbott, John Loder

Abschied von Gestern *
West Germany 1966 90m bw
Kairos Film/Independent/Alexander Kluge
aka: *Yesterday Girl*

A Jewish girl escapes from East to West Germany but is disillusioned and gives herself up.

Witty and remarkably light-hearted satirical comedy which can be fully understood only by those living in Germany in the sixties.

wd Alexander Kluge   ph Edgar Reitz, Thomas Mauched   Beata Mainka

Alexandra Kluge, Günther Mack, Hans Korte, Eva Marie Meinecke

Absence of Malice *
US 1981 116m DeLuxe
Columbia/Mirage (Sydney Pollack)
V, V*, L

When a longshoremen's union leader disappears, a lady journalist throws an unfair spotlight on an innocent suspect.

Well-meaning but overwritten attack on journalistic abuses, hampered by unsuitable leading performances.

w Kurt Luedtke *d* Sydney Pollack *ph* Owen Roizman *m* Dave Grusin *pd* Terence Marsh

Paul Newman, Sally Field, Bob Balaban, Melinda Dillon, Luther Adler, Barry Primus

'Pollack seems to be carving out a new niche for himself as an updater of Hollywood's most tried and true methods of sugaring a message.' – *Richard Combs, MFB*

'A thoroughly craftsmanlike movie that never quite delivers on the commercial or the artistic front.' – *Guardian*

'The story is perfunctory and disappointing in a movie that promises but does not deliver.' – *Motion Picture Guide*

AAN: screenplay; Paul Newman; Melinda Dillon

'It's all about a wacky prof who invents an anti-gravity goo that flew!'
The Absent-Minded Professor *
US 1961 97m bw
Walt Disney (Bill Walsh)
V*, L

A lighter-than-air substance called flubber enables its inventor to drive his Model-T through the sky and catch some spies.

Foolishly engaging fantasy comedy with goodish trick effects.

w Bill Walsh *d* Robert Stevenson *ph* Edward Colman *m* George Bruns *sp* Robert A. Mattey, Peter Ellenshaw, Eustace Lycett

Fred MacMurray, Tommy Kirk, Keenan Wynn, Nancy Olson, Leon Ames, Ed Wynn, Edward Andrews

† Sequel: *Son of Flubber* (1963).

AAN: Edward Colman

Absinthe: see *Madame X* (1929)

'Welcome to the world of your dreams!'
Absolute Beginners
GB 1986 107m Rank colour Super Techniscope
Virgin/Goldcrest/Palace (Stephen Woolley, Chris Brown)
V*, L, S

Teen life and pop fashion in 1958 London.

Deafening, mindless, musical, multi-screen pot-pourri of teen culture which sadly needs narrative links not to mention better music and firmer control.

w Richard Burridge, Christopher Wicking, Don MacPherson *novel* Colin MacInnes *d* Julien Temple *ph* Oliver Stapleton *m* David Bowie, Ray Davies, *et al.* *pd* John Beard

Eddie O'Connell, Patsy Kensit, David Bowie, Ray Davies, James Fox, Lionel Blair, Steven Berkoff, Mandy Rice Davies

'All that noise, all that energy, so little governing thought.' – *Time Out*

Absolute Quiet *
US 1936 71m bw
MGM

Interestingly-cast programmer about a murder plot after a planeload of strangers is forced down on a financier's ranch.

w Harry Clork *d* George B. Seitz

Lionel Atwill, Louis Hayward, Raymond Walburn, Stuart Erwin, Wallace Ford, J. Carrol Naish

Absolution *
GB 1978 95m Technicolor
Bulldog (Danny O'Donovan, Elliott Kastner)
V, V*, L
TV title: *Murder by Confession*

A schoolmaster priest at a Roman Catholic boarding school is taunted by a malicious pupil into committing murder.

Interesting and suspenseful, though finally too complicated compromise between a thriller of the *Sleuth* type and a downbeat character study.

w Anthony Shaffer *d* Anthony Page *ph* John Coquillon *m* Stanley Myers

Richard Burton, Dominic Guard, Dai Bradley, Billy Connolly, Andrew Keir

'A dire slice of clever-clever narrative trickery.' – *Paul Taylor, MFB*

'You can't make real bricks from this kind of straw, since a potentially interesting study of character and environment is gradually weakened by the constraints of a second-rate murder mystery.' – *Guardian*

Abwärts: see *Out of Order*

The Abysmal Brute
US 1924 80m approx bw silent
Universal

Remembered more for its title than anything else, this is not a horror film but a comedy about a mild and naïve young mountain man who comes to the big city, becomes a hero of the fight game under the titular pseudonym, and still contrives to make a society marriage.

A star was created, but failed to follow through.

w A. P. Younger *novel* Jack London *d* Hobart Henley

Reginald Denny, Mabel Julienne Scott, Hayden Stevenson, Charles French

The Abyss
US 1989 140m DeLuxe Color
Fox (Gale Anne Hurd)
V, V (W), V*, L, S

Attempting to rescue a nuclear submarine, divers working on underwater drilling encounter aliens.

Despite some clever special effects, a tedious, overlong fantasy that is more excited by machinery than people.

wd James Cameron *ph* Mikael Salomon *m* Alan Silvestri *pd* Leslie Dilley *sp* Laura Buff *ed* Joel Goodman

Ed Harris, Mary Elizabeth Mastrantonio, Michael Biehn, Leo Burmester, Todd Graff, John Bedford Lloyd, J. C. Quinn, Kimberley Scott

'For the most part, as exciting an undersea drama as one could imagine.' – *MFB*

† *The Abyss Special Edition* released on video and Laserdisc contained an extra 27m cut from the original cinema release.

AAN: best cinematography; best art direction

Accattone *
Italy 1961 120m bw
Cino del Duca/Arco (Alfredo Bini)
V, V*, L

A Roman pimp and thief is beset by troubles, and is finally killed escaping from the police.

Sordid and rough-edged but vividly realistic melodrama.

wd Pier Paolo Pasolini *ph* Tonino delli Colli *md* Carlo Rustichelli *ad* Bernardo Bertolucci

Franco Citti, Franca Pasut, Silvana Corsini, Paola Giudi, Roberto Scaringella, Adele Cambria

Accent on Love
US 1941 61m bw
TCF

A real estate executive walks out to become spokesman for his former underprivileged tenants.

Thin Capraesque romantic comedy.

w John Larkin *story* Dalton Trumbo *d* Ray McCarey

George Montgomery, Osa Massen, J. Carrol Naish, Cobina Wright Jnr, Stanley Clements, Thurston Hall, Minerva Urecal

Accent on Youth *
US 1935 77m bw
Paramount (Douglas MacLean)

A secretary falls in love with her middle-aged playwright employer.

Reasonably sparkling comedy from a popular play, later remade as *Mr Music* and *But Not for Me.*

w Herbert Fields, Claude Binyon *play* Samson Raphaelson *d* Wesley Ruggles *ph* Leon Shamroy

Herbert Marshall, Sylvia Sidney, Philip Reed, Astrid Allwyn, Holmes Herbert

'Well adapted, presented and produced for box office satisfaction.' – *Variety*

Accident **
GB 1967 105m Eastmancolor
London Independent Producers (Joseph Losey, Norman Priggen)
V*

An Oxford undergraduate is killed in a car crash; his tutor looks back over the tangle of personal relationships that contributed to his death.

Ascetic drama in which the audience is too often left to observe at length and draw its own conclusions; good characterizations nevertheless.

w Harold Pinter *novel* Nicholas Mosley *d* Joseph Losey *ph* Gerry Fisher *m* John Dankworth

Dirk Bogarde, Stanley Baker, Jacqueline Sassard, Vivien Merchant, Michael York

'The whole thing is such a teapot tempest, and it is so assiduously underplayed that it is neither strong drama nor stinging satire. It is just a sad little story of a wistful don.' – *Bosley Crowther*

'Everything is calm, unruffled, lacquered in a veneer of civilization, yet underneath it all, one gradually begins to realize, the characters are tearing each other emotionally to shreds.' – *MFB*

'Uneven, unsatisfying, but with virtuoso passages of calculated meanness.' – *New Yorker, 1977*

Accidental Hero: see *Hero*

The Accidental Tourist ***
US 1988 121m Technicolor
Warner (Lawrence Kasdan, Charles Okun, Michael Grillo)
V, V*, L, S

Left by his wife, an uptight travel writer falls in love with an exuberant dog-trainer.

A liberating domestic drama, notable for some excellent acting.

w Frank Galati, Lawrence Kasdan *novel* Anne Tyler *d* Lawrence Kasdan *ph* John Bailey *m* John Williams *pd* Bo Welch *ed* Carol Littleton

William Hurt, Kathleen Turner, Geena Davis, Amy Wright, Bill Pullman, Robert Gorman, David Ogden Stiers, Ed Begley Jnr

AA: Geena Davis

AAN: best picture; best adapted screenplay; John Williams

Accidents Will Happen
US   1938   62m   bw
Warner (Bryan Foy)

An insurance claims adjuster takes to crime.

Slack little programmer.

w George Bricker, Anthony Coldeway   *d* William Clemens

Ronald Reagan, Dick Purcell, Gloria Blondell, Addison Richards, Hugh O'Connell

Acción Mutante
Spain   1993   94m   Fuji colour   Cinemascope
Feature Film/El Deseo/CIBY 2000 (Agustin Almodóvar, Pedro Almodóvar)
V

In 2012, a disfigured man leads a group of disabled in a terrorist war against the healthy and perfectly formed for his own advantage.

Bizarre horror that can be taken as a black or sick joke, depending on your attitude to a movie with such characters as a half-dead, half-alive Siamese twin. Whatever, after a brisk beginning, it soon palls and even appals, with its emphasis on the gruesome.

w Jorge Guerricaechevarria, Alex de la Iglesia *d* Alex de la Iglesia   *ph* Carles Gusi   *m* Juan Carlos Cuello   *ad* José Luis Arrizabalaga   *sp* Oliver Gleyze, Yves Domenjoud, Jean-Bapiste Bonetto, Bernard-André le Boetti   *ed* Pablo Blanco

Antonio Resines, Frédérique Feder, Alex Angulo, Juan Viades, Karra Elejalde, Saturnino Garcia, Fernando Guillén, Jaime Blanch

† 'Officially a promising first film, this feels more like a disappointing second one.' – *Empire*

L'Accompagnatrice: see *The Accompanist*

The Accompanist
France   1992   111m   colour
Gala/Film Par Film/De la Boissière Orly/Sedif France/3 Cinema (Jean-Louis Livi)
V (W), S
original title: *L'Accompagnatrice*

In occupied Paris of the early 1940s, a young star-struck woman becomes the accompanist to a fashionable French singer and her rich husband, a reluctant collaborator with the Germans.

The wartime setting is presumably intended to give resonance to this otherwise trite, but charming, tale of self-sacrifice; instead it makes the soul-searching of the central characters seem a luxury and an irrelevance.

w Claude Miller, Luc Béraud   *novel* Nina Berberova
d Claude Miller   *ph* Yves Angelo   *m* Alain Jomy
pd Jean-Pierre Kohut Svelko   *ed* Albert Jurgenson

Richard Bohringer, Elena Safonova, Romane Bohringer, Bernard Verley, Samuel Labarthe, Nelly Borgeaud, Julien Rassam, Jean-Pierre Kohut Svelko

'Dramatically, the movie doesn't cover much ground . . . all he ends up with is the thin old story of a supporting artist who lives by proxy.' – *Michael Sragow, New Yorker*

'The film's uniform visual and narrative dullness does act as a pretty effective anaesthetic. And it also fits a certain, rather unpleasant way of looking at French history in which these stories and images that we've seen a thousand times take on a mythical quality.' – *Martin Bright, Sight and Sound*

According to Mrs Hoyle
US   1951   60m   bw
Monogram

A retired schoolteacher lives in a hotel run by criminals, and becomes involved.

Uninspired sentimental comedy providing a rare star part for a well-liked character actress.

w W. Scott Darling and Barney Gerard   *d* Jean Yarbrough

Spring Byington, Anthony Caruso, Brett King, Tanis Chandler

Account Rendered
GB   1957   60m   bw
Rank/Major Productions (John Temple-Smith)

A detective inspector tracks down the killer of a banker's flirtatious wife.

Indifferent thriller lacking any distinguishing features.

w Barbara S. Harper   *novel* Pamela Barrington
d Peter Graham Scott   *ph* Walter J. Harvey
ad Norman Arnold   *ed* Tom Simpson

Honor Blackman, Griffith Jones, Ursula Howells, Ewen Solon, Robert Raikes, John Van Eyssen

Accused
GB   1936   85m   bw
Criterion/UA

In Paris, a dancer is stabbed and his wife is thought guilty.

Overwrought melodrama chiefly interesting for cast.

w Zoe Akins, George Barraud and Harold French
d Thornton Freeland

Douglas Fairbanks Jnr, Dolores del Rio, Googie Withers, Florence Desmond, Basil Sydney

'The standout suspense triumph of the year!'

The Accused *
US   1948   101m   bw
Paramount (Hal B. Wallis)
aka: *Strange Deception*

In self-defence a lady professor kills a student who has sexually attacked her.

Dullish suspenser with the outcome never in doubt, though the production values are beyond reproach.

w Ketti Frings   *d* William Dieterle   *ph* Milton Krasner   *m* Victor Young

Loretta Young, Robert Cummings, Wendell Corey, Sam Jaffe, Douglas Dick

The Accused *
US   1988   110m   Technicolor
UIP/Paramount (Stanley R. Jaffe, Sherry Lansing)
V, V*, L

A provocatively-dressed woman is raped after performing a sexy dance at a seedy bar.

Unconvincing problem picture that fails to explore the issues it raises.

w Tom Topor   *d* Jonathan Kaplan   *ph* Ralf Bode
m Brad Fiedel   *pd* Richard Kent Wilcox   *ed* Jerry Greenberg, O. Nicholas Brown

Kelly McGillis, Jodie Foster, Bernie Coulson, Ann Hearn, Steve Antin, Tom O'Brien

'Another box-office winner which once again negotiates a fine line between social concern, feminism and exploitation.' – *MFB*

AA: *Jodie Foster*

Accused of Murder
US   1956   76m   Trucolor (and 'Naturama')
Republic

When a crooked lawyer is murdered, his mistress is suspected.

Flat little mystery with unappetizing characters.

w Bob Williams, W. R. Burnett   *novel* Vanity Row by W. R. Burnett   *d* Joe Kane

Vera Ralston, David Brian, Sidney Blackmer, Virginia Grey, Warren Stevens, Lee Van Cleef

Ace Drummond
US   1936   bw   serial: 13 eps
Universal

John King as a civil aviation pioneer hampered by an evil power named The Dragon.

d Ford Beebe, Cliff Smith

Jean Rogers, Noah Beery Jnr, Guy Bates Post

Ace Eli and Roger of the Skies
US   1973   92m   DeLuxe   Panavision
TCF (Robert Fryer, James Cresson)

Adventures of a father-and-son aerial barnstorming act after World War I.

Poorly written melodrama, very tame apart from the flying shots.

w Claudia Salter   *story* Steven Spielberg   *d* John Erman   *ph* David M. Walsh, Bill Birch, Don Morgan   *m* Jerry Goldsmith

Cliff Robertson, Pamela Franklin, Eric Shea, Rosemary Murphy, Bernadette Peters, Alice Ghostley

'A tediously inane flop. Nostalgia isn't what it used to be.' – *Variety*

Ace High (dubbed)
Italy   1968   137m   colour   Techniscope
Crono (Giuseppe Colizzi, Bino Cicogna)
V, V*
original title: *I Quattro dell'Ave Maria*; aka: *Revenge at El Paso*

A gunman is hired to track down the gang who robbed a bank.

Stolid spaghetti Western, poorly dubbed and notable mainly for bringing together Hill and Spencer for the first time.

wd Giuseppe Colizzi   *ph* Marcello Masciocchi

Terence Hill (Mario Girotti), Bud Spencer (Carlo Pedersoli), Eli Wallach, Brock Peters, Kevin McCarthy, Livio Lorenzon, Steffen Zacharias

† Versions of the film also exist that run for 123m and 103m.

Ace in the Hole ***
US   1951   111m   bw
Paramount (Billy Wilder)
aka: *The Big Carnival*

In order to prolong the sensation and boost newspaper sales, a self-seeking journalist delays the rescue of a man trapped in a cave.

An incisive, compelling melodrama taking a sour look at the American scene; one of its director's masterworks.

w Billy Wilder, Lesser Samuels, Walter Newman   *d* Billy Wilder   *ph* Charles B. Lang Jnr   *m* Hugo Friedhofer

Kirk Douglas (Chuck Tatum), Jan Sterling (Lorraine), Porter Hall (Boot), Bob Arthur (Herbie), Richard Benedict (Leo), Ray Teal (Sheriff), Frank Cady (Federber)

LORRAINE to Tatum: 'I've met some hard-boiled eggs, but you – you're twenty minutes!'
LORRAINE: 'I don't go to church. Kneeling bags my nylons.'
TATUM to editor: 'I've done a lot of lying in my time. I've lied to men who wear belts. I've lied to men who wear suspenders. But I'd never be so stupid as to lie to a man who wears both belt and suspenders.'
TATUM, dying, to editor: 'How'd you like to make a thousand dollars a day, Mr Boot? I'm a thousand-dollar-a-day newspaperman. You can have me for nothing.'

'Few of the opportunities for irony, cruelty and horror are missed.' – *Gavin Lambert*

'Style and purpose achieve for the most part a fusion even more remarkable than in *Sunset Boulevard*.' – *Penelope Houston*

'As stimulating as black coffee.' – *Richard Mallett, Punch*

'Americans expected a cocktail and felt I was giving them a shot of vinegar instead.' – *Billy Wilder*

'Some people have tried to claim some sort of satirical brilliance for it, but it's really rather nasty, in a sociologically pushy way.' – *New Yorker, 1980*

'A brilliant arrangement of cause and effect . . . unique as a mirror of the morbid psychology of crowds . . . revolting but incontrovertibly true.' – *New York Times*

† Locations were at Gallup, New Mexico.

AAN: script

Ace of Aces *
US   1933   76m   bw
RKO
V*

On the outbreak of World War I an American sculptor is branded a coward when he does not immediately enlist; but he disappears and turns up in France a hero, though with a sour taste in his mouth.

Melodrama of disillusion, dated in many respects but interesting to compare with *The Dawn Patrol* and *The Last Flight*.

w John Monk Saunders, H. W Hannemann   *story* Bird of Prey by John Monk Saunders   *d* J. Walter Ruben

Richard Dix, Elizabeth Allan, Theodore Newton, Ralph Bellamy, Joseph Sawyer, Frank Conroy, William Cagney

'It's the fine photography and crashes that provide the thrills.' – *Variety*

The Ace of Scotland Yard
US   1929   bw   serial: 10 eps
Universal

The first talking serial: Blake of the Yard thwarts a jewel thief called The Queen of Diamonds.

d Ray Taylor

Crauford Kent, Grace Cunard, Florence Allen

Ace Ventura, Pet Detective
US   1994   93m   colour
Warner/Morgan Creek (James G. Robinson)

A private eye who recovers missing pets is hired to recover the Miami Dolphins' dolphin mascot.

Featuring a relentlessly mugging comedian who makes Jerry Lewis seem as restrained as Buster Keaton, this is an extraordinarily inept comedy, with feeble jokes parodying other movies, feebler slapstick and much homophobia and misogyny; it also provides Sean Young with the most demeaning role of her career.

w Jack Bernstein, Tom Shadyac, Jim Carrey   *d* Tom Shadyac   *ph* Julio Macat   *m* Ira Newborn   *pd* William Elliott   *ed* Don Zimmerman

Jim Carrey, Courtenay Cox, Sean Young, Dan Marino, Noble Winningham, Troy Evans, Udo Kier, Tone Loc

'Doesn't display the comic pedigree needed for the rubber-faced-and-limbed comedian to collar breakthrough dollars. That said, dumb good times still wield a strong lure for the Saturday night date crowd.' – *Variety*

† The film was an unexpected hit in America, earning more than $65m at the box-office and raising Jim Carrey's price per picture from $350,000 to a reported $7m.

Aces High *
GB   1976   114m   Technicolor
EMI/S. Benjamin Fisz/Jacques Roitfeld
V

In the air force during World War I, young pilots are needlessly sacrificed.

Spirited if rather unnecessary remake of *Journey's End* transposed to the air war, which makes it almost identical to *The Dawn Patrol.*

w Howard Barker   *d* Jack Gold   *ph* Gerry Fisher, Peter Allwork   *m* Richard Hartley

Malcolm McDowell, Christopher Plummer, Simon Ward, Peter Firth, John Gielgud, Trevor Howard, Richard Johnson, Ray Milland

'Their Best and Final Mission.'
Aces: Iron Eagle III
US   1992   98m   CFI colour
New Line/7 Arts (Ron Samuels)
V*, S

Veteran fighter pilots battle against South American drug barons.

Energetic but mindless action, with a little slapstick thrown in, and featuring muscle-woman Rachel McLish.

w Kevin Elders   *d* John Glen   *ph* Alec Mills   *m* Harry Manfredini   *pd* Robb Wilson King   *sp* John Richardson   *ed* Bernard Gribble

Louis Gossett Jnr, Rachel McLish, Paul Freeman, Horst Buchholz, Christopher Cazenove, Sonny Chiba, Fred Dalton Thompson, Mitchell Ryan

Across 110th Street **
US   1972   102m   DeLuxe
UA/Film Guarantors (Fouad Said, Ralph Serpe)
V, V*

Police and the Mafia go after three blacks disguised as cops who rob a Harlem numbers bank and kill its operators.

Tough, clever thriller, set within a well-observed society of violence and deprivation.

w Luther Davis   *novel* Wally Ferris   *d* Barry Shear   *ph* Jack Priestley   *m* J. J. Johnson   *ad* Perry Watkins   *ed* Bryan Brandt

Anthony Quinn, Yaphet Kotto, Anthony Franciosa, Paul Benjamin, Ed Barnard, Richard Ward, Antonio Fargas

† The film was cut to 99m on its British release.

Across the Bridge *
GB   1957   103m   bw
Rank/IPF (John Stafford)
V*

A fugitive financier kills his pursuer, finds he was a murderer, and tries to hide out across the Mexican border.

This star *tour de force* is unconvincing in detail and rather unattractive to watch (British films never could cope with American settings), but the early sequences have suspense.

w Guy Elmes, Denis Freeman   *novel* Graham Greene   *d* Ken Annakin   *ph* Reg Wyer   *m* James Bernard

Rod Steiger, David Knight, Marla Landi, Noel Willman, Bernard Lee

Across the Pacific ***
US   1942   99m   bw
Warner (Hal B. Wallis)
V*, L

Just before Pearl Harbor, an army officer is cashiered by arrangement in order to contact pro-Japanese sympathizers.

Hasty, easy-going and very enjoyable hokum, partly ship-set and successfully reteaming three stars of *The Maltese Falcon.*

w Richard Macauley   *serial* Aloha Means Goodbye by Robert Carson   *d* John Huston   *ph* Arthur Edeson   *m* Adolph Deutsch

Humphrey Bogart (Rick Leland), *Mary Astor* (Alberta Marlow), *Sydney Greenstreet* (Dr Lorenz), Sen Yung (Joe

Totsuiko); and Charles Halton, Monte Blue, Richard Loo, Chester Gan, Kam Tong

'A spy picture which tingles with fearful uncertainties and glints with the sheen of blue steel.' – *Bosley Crowther*

† Huston was called up before the film was completed, and allegedly reshaped the script before leaving in order to put the hero in an impossible situation. Direction was eventually completed by Vincent Sherman.
†† Monte Blue, who has a tiny last-reel part as the heroine's drunken father, starred in a 1926 silent film with the same title but a totally different plot. He played an army officer fighting Philippine guerrillas. Darryl F. Zanuck wrote the script, and Roy del Ruth directed, for Warner.

Across the Tracks
US   1991   100m   CFI colour
Desert Productions (Dale Rosenbloom)
V, V*

Two athletic brothers of differing temperaments become rivals.

A well-intentioned movie about teenage problems that may appeal to adolescents but not to adults.

wd Sandy Tung   *ph* Michael Delahoussaye   *m* Joel Goldsmith   *pd* Thomas Meleck   *ed* Farrel Levy

Rick Schroder, Brad Pitt, Carrie Snodgress, David Anthony Marshall, Thomas Mikel Ford, John Linton

Across the Wide Missouri *
US   1951   77m   Technicolor
MGM (Robert Sisk)
V*

In the 1820s, a trapper marries an Indian girl and lives with her people.

Promising credits produce an unsatisfactory Western: despite honest efforts, the elements do not jell into a convincing whole.

w Talbot Jennings   *d* William Wellman   *ph* William C. Mellor   *m* David Raksin

Clark Gable, Ricardo Montalban, John Hodiak, Adolphe Menjou, Maria Elena Marques, J. Carrol Naish, Jack Holt, Alan Napier, Howard Keel (narrator)

Act of Love *
US   1954   104m   bw
UA/Benagoss (Anatole Litvak)

In Paris in 1944, an American with the liberation army falls in love with a French girl, who commits suicide when he is posted and cannot make their rendezvous.

Cheerless romantic drama, rather thin and unmemorable despite the efforts of all concerned.

w Irwin Shaw   *novel* The Girl on the Via Flaminia by Alfred Hayes   *d* Anatole Litvak   *ph* Armand Thirard   *m* Michael Emer, Joe Hajos   *pd* Alexander Trauner

Kirk Douglas, Dany Robin, Barbara Laage, Robert Stauss, Gabrielle Dorziat, Gregoire Aslan, Fernand Ledoux, Serge Reggiani, Brigitte Bardot

† Made in France, an early Hollywood foreign location film.

An Act of Murder *
US   1948   90m   bw
U-I (Jerry Bresler)
aka: *Live Today for Tomorrow*

A judge insists on being tried for the mercy killing of his incurably ill wife.

Earnest social drama which despite excellent acting can only reach an inconclusive ending.

w Michael Blankfort, Robert Thoeren   *novel* The Mills of God by Ernst Lothar   *d* Michael Gordon   *ph* Hal Mohr   *m* Daniele Amfitheatrof

Fredric March, Florence Eldridge, Edmond O'Brien, Geraldine Brooks

Act of Murder **
GB   1964   62m   bw
Merton Park (Jack Greenwood)

A couple arrange a holiday by swapping houses with strangers, and a complex plot ensues.

Slick, superior example of the Edgar Wallace second feature series.

w Lewis Davidson   d Alan Bridges   ph James Wilson   m Bernard Ebbinghouse

John Carson, Anthony Bate, Justine Lord, Duncan Lewis, Dandy Nichols

'This uncommonly intelligent little thriller is just the sort of film which is likely to arouse critical sneers for reaching too high on a low budget.' – *Tom Milne*

Act of the Heart
Canada   1970   103m   colour
Universal (Paul Almond)

A country girl falls in love with a monk after she goes to the big city to sing in a choir.

Intense drama of an unlikely affair that is likely to lose the sympathy of its audience long before its unconvincing end.

wd Paul Almond   ph Jean Boffety   m Harry Freedman   ad Anne Pritchard   ed James D. Mitchell

Geneviève Bujold, Donald Sutherland, Monique Leyrac, Bill Mitchell, Suzanne Langlois, Sharon Acker

'Bujold has some lovely bits, but the masochistic feminine-fantasy material forces her to fall back on the old fragile, incandescent child-woman shtick.' – *Pauline Kael*

Act of Violence **
US   1948   82m   bw
MGM (William Wright)

After the war, an ex-GI tracks down a prison camp informer.

Moody, glossy melodrama with tension well sustained, though the sentimental ending is a cop-out.

w Robert I. Richards   story Collier Young   d Fred Zinnemann   ph Robert Surtees   m Bronislau Kaper

Van Heflin, Robert Ryan, Janet Leigh, Mary Astor

'Strong characterization, fine direction and good photography combine to put this film high among its kind.' – *MFB*

'An effortless narrative control and a real power to maintain tension.' – *Richard Winnington*

Act One *
US   1963   110m   bw
Warner (Dore Schary)

Poor Brooklyn boy Moss Hart rises to Broadway eminence via his writing partnership with George S. Kaufman.

Incredibly stilted film version of an excellent autobiography, notable only for fragments of acting and the fact that a film so totally uncommercial was made at all.

wd Dore Schary   ph Arthur J. Ornitz   m Skitch Henderson

George Hamilton (Hart), Jason Robards Jnr (Kaufman), Jack Klugman, Sam Levene, George Segal, Ruth Ford, Eli Wallach

'From the moment young Hart takes pencil in hand, we have nowhere to go except to that happy ending; and despite all the painstaking detail, we don't believe a word of it.' – *Judith Crist*

Action for Slander *
GB   1937   83m   bw
London Films/Saville (Victor Saville)

A bankrupt officer, accused of cheating at cards, defends his honour with a writ.

Lively melodrama of the old school.

w Ian Dalrymple, Miles Malleson   novel Mary Borden   d Tim Whelan   ph Harry Stradling   md Muir Mathieson

Clive Brook, Ann Todd, Margaretta Scott, Arthur Margetson, Ronald Squire, Athole Stewart, Percy Marmont, Frank Cellier, Morton Selten

'Hollywood in its most lavish spurt of extravagance never went to such pains to assemble a cast . . . general run of patrons however will chafe under the lack of physical movement.' – *Variety*

Action in Arabia
US   1944   75m   bw
Maurice Geraghty/RKO
V*

Nazis and Frenchmen of both persuasions clash in the Damascus desert.

Formula war melodrama using stock footage originally shot by Cooper and Schoedsack.

w Philip MacDonald and Herbert Biberman   d Leonide Moguy

George Sanders (as an American war correspondent), Virginia Bruce, Lenore Aubert, Gene Lockhart, Robert Armstrong, H. B. Warner, Alan Napier, André Charlot, Marcel Dalio

Action in the North Atlantic *
US   1943   127m   bw
Warner (Jerry Wald)
V*, V* (C)

An American convoy bound for Russia comes under U-boat attack.

Efficient propaganda potboiler; studio bound, but still works as a war actioner.

w John Howard Lawson   story Guy Gilpatric   d Lloyd Bacon   ph Ted McCord   m Adolph Deutsch

Humphrey Bogart, Raymond Massey, Alan Hale, Julie Bishop, Ruth Gordon, Sam Levene, Dane Clark

'The production has interludes of tremendous power. What is lacking is dramatic cohesion.' – *Howard Barnes*

'Directly in line of descent from *The Perils of Pauline*.' – *Time*

'The American equivalent of our war documentaries . . . tough, exciting, with no concession to flim flam.' – *New Statesman*

'I cannot think I have ever seen such realistic battles, or lived so intimately with the characters who comprise the crew.' – *Evening Standard*

AAN: Guy Gilpatric

Action Jackson
US   1988   96m   Metrocolor
Guild/Lorimar (Joel Silver)
V*, L, S

A maverick cop is framed for a murder while investigating the killings of union officials.

Violent action movie, with spectacular deaths and car chases, a ludicrous plot and a hissable villain.

w Robert Reneau   d Craig R. Baxley   ph Matthew F. Leonetti   m Herbie Hancock, Michael Kamen   ad Virginia Randolph   ed Mark Helfrich

Carl Weathers, Craig T. Nelson, Vanity, Sharon Stone, Thomas L. Wilson, Bill Duke, Robert Davi

Action of the Tiger
GB   1957   93m   Technicolor   Cinemascope
MGM/Claridge (Kenneth Harper)

An adventurer helps a French girl to rescue her brother from political imprisonment in Albania.

Dull and poorly constructed action melodrama.

w Robert Carson   novel James Wellard   d Terence Young   ph Desmond Dickinson   m Humphrey Searle

Van Johnson, Martine Carol, Herbert Lom, Gustavo Rocco, Anthony Dawson, Helen Haye, Sean Connery

Actors and Sin *
US   1952   91m   bw
UA/Sid Kuller (Ben Hecht)
V*

Two short stories. When an unsuccessful actress commits suicide, her father makes it look like murder so that for once she shall get attention.

The authoress of a romantic script bought by Hollywood is discovered to be a horrid little 9-year-old.

Interesting but incompetent compendium which descends almost to the home movie level and leaves the actors struggling.

wd Ben Hecht   ph Lee Garmes   m George Antheil

Edward G. Robinson, Marsha Hunt, Dan O'Herlihy, Rudolph Anders, Eddie Albert, Alan Reed, Jenny Hecht

'A depressing double bill.' – *Lindsay Anderson*

An Actor's Revenge *
Japan   1963   113m   Daieicolor   Daieiscope
Daiei (Masaichi Nagata)
V
original title: *Yukinojo Henge*

In the early 19th century, a touring actor comes upon the rich merchant who had ruined his parents, and his revenge involves several deaths.

Complex, fascinating period melodrama, both rich and strange, with strong echoes of Jacobean melodrama.

w Daisuke Ito, Teinosuke Kinugasa, Natto Wada   novel Otokichi Mikami   d Kon Ichikawa   ph Setsuo Kobayashi   m Yasushi Akutagawa

Kazuo Hasegawa, Fujiko Yamamoto, Ayako Wakao, Ganjiro Nakamura

The Actress *
US   1928   90m approx (24 fps)   bw   silent
MGM
GB title: *Trelawny of the Wells*

A young Victorian actress marries a rich admirer.

Pleasing, well-cast version of a celebrated play.

w Albert Lewin, Richard Schayer   play Sir Arthur Wing Pinero   d Sidney Franklin   ph William Daniels

Norma Shearer, Ralph Forbes, O. P. Heggie, Owen Moore, Roy D'Arcy

'A thoughtful, rounded and provocative entertainment.' – *New York Times*

† Opening attraction at London's Empire Theatre, Leicester Square.

The Actress
US   1953   91m   bw
MGM (Lawrence Weingarten)

Ruth Jones becomes an actress against the wishes of her stubborn seafaring father.

Episodes from Ruth Gordon's early life, based on her Broadway play *Years Ago*, make a pleasant though scarcely engrossing film: it is all a shade too discreet and wanly winning, and the few key events take place offscreen.

w Ruth Gordon   d George Cukor   ph Harold Rosson   m Bronislau Kaper   ad Cedric Gibbons, Arthur Lonergan

Jean Simmons, Spencer Tracy, Teresa Wright, Anthony Perkins, Ian Wolfe, Mary Wickes

Ada *

US 1961 109m Metrocolor Cinemáscope
MGM/Avon/Chalmar (Lawrence Weingarten)

A political candidate marries a call girl who becomes
his strong right arm and weathers a threat to reveal
her past.

Indecisive romantic drama which pulls too many
punches but has interesting background detail.

w Arthur Sheekman, William Driskill novel Ada
Dallas by Wirt Williams d Daniel Mann
ph Joseph Ruttenberg m Bronislau Kaper

Susan Hayward, Dean Martin, Wilfrid Hyde-White,
Ralph Meeker, Martin Balsam

'A bonanza for connoisseurs of perfectly awful
movies.' – Judith Crist

'Its characterizations are sketchy, its political setting
routine and symbolic.' – New York Herald Tribune

Adalen 31 **

Sweden 1969 115m Technicolor Techniscope
Svensk Filmindustri

A prolonged strike at a small-town paper mill ends in
tragedy when the troops move in.

Effective period piece which emphasizes the idyllic
qualities of the backgrounds rather than the
foreground terrors.

wd Bo Widerberg ph Jorgen Persson

Peter Schildt, Kerstin Tidelius, Roland Hedlund,
Stefan Feierbach, Anita Bjork

AAN: best foreign film

Adam and Eva *

US 1923 83m approx bw silent
Paramount/Cosmopolitan

An extravagant girl reforms when her father goes
bust.

Moral comedy with a happy ending: a hit of its day.

w Luther Reed play Guy Bolton and George
Middleton d Robert G. Vignola

Marion Davies, T. Roy Barnes, Tom Lewis, William
Norris, Percy Ames

Adam and Evelyne

GB 1949 92m bw
Rank/Two Cities (Harold French)

A society playboy adopts his dead friend's daughter,
and falls in love with her.

Undernourished romantic drama, a mild variation on
Daddy Longlegs.

w Noel Langley, Lesley Storm, George Barraud,
Nicholas Phipps d Harold French ph Guy Green
m Mischa Spoliansky

Stewart Granger, Jean Simmons, Helen Cherry,
Edwin Styles, Beatrice Varley, Wilfrid Hyde-White

Adam at 6 A.M. *

US 1970 100m colour
National General (Robert Christiansen, Rick Rosenberg)
V*

A disillusioned Californian university professor
returns to Missouri and takes a labouring job.

Interesting and unconventional drama of a liberal
kind.

w Stephen Karpf, Elinor Karpf d Robert Scheerer
ph Charles Rosher ad Dale Hennessey ed Jack
McSweeney

Michael Douglas, Lee Purcell, Joe Don Baker,
Grayson Hall, Charles Aidman, Louise Latham, Meg
Foster

Adam Had Four Sons *

US 1941 81m bw
Columbia (Robert Sherwood)
V*

A widower's family is cared for by a governess.

Modest magazine fiction which established Ingrid
Bergman as an American star.

w Michael Blankfort, William Hurlbut novel Legacy
by Charles Bonner d Gregory Ratoff ph Peverell
Marley m W. Franke Harling

Warner Baxter, Ingrid Bergman, Susan Hayward,
Richard Denning, Fay Wray

Adam's Rib *

US 1922 86m bw silent
Paramount (Cecil B. de Mille)

By offering herself in her stead, an American girl tries
to prevent her mother's adultery with a European ex-
monarch.

One of its director's 'sin in high life' melodramas,
which packed 'em in at the time, this has nothing but
decoration to offer to a modern audience.

w Jeanie MacPherson d Cecil B. de Mille

Milton Sills, Elliott Dexter, Theodore Kosloff, Anna
Q. Nilsson, Pauline Garon, Julia Faye

Adam's Rib **

US 1949 101m bw
MGM (Lawrence Weingarten)
V*, L

Husband and wife lawyers are on opposite sides of an
attempted murder case.

A superior star vehicle which also managed to
introduce four promising personalities; slangily
written and smartly directed, but perhaps a shade less
funny than it once seemed.

w Ruth Gordon, Garson Kanin d George Cukor
ph George J. Folsey m Miklos Rozsa

Spencer Tracy, Katharine Hepburn, David Wayne, Tom
Ewell, Judy Holliday, Jean Hagen, Hope Emerson,
Clarence Kolb

'Hepburn and Tracy are again presented as the ideal
US Mr and Mrs of upper-middle income. This time, as
well as being wittily urbane, both are lawyers.' – Time

'It isn't solid food but it certainly is meaty and juicy
and comically nourishing.' – Bosley Crowther

† A 1972 TV series of the same title provided a boring
imitation, with Ken Howard and Blythe Danner.

AAN: Ruth Gordon and Garson Kanin

Adam's Woman

Australia 1970 115m colour Panavision
Warner/EMI/SBP Films (Louis F. Edelman)

In the 1840s an American finds himself a prisoner in
an antipodean penal colony, and schemes to get out.

Oddball period drama, unreleased in Britain.

w Richard Fielder d Philip Leacock

Beau Bridges, Jane Merrow, James Booth, John Mills

Adamson of Africa: see The Killers of Kilimanjaro

'Creepy. Kooky. Spooky. Ooky.'
The Addams Family *

US 1991 99m DeLuxe
Columbia TriStar/Paramount/Orion (Scott Rudin)
V, V*, L, S

An impostor turns up at the Addams family mansion,
claiming to be a long-lost elder brother.

Owing more to the TV series of the 1960s than to the
macabre wit of the original New Yorker cartoons, an ill-
conceived, coarse-grained comedy that nevertheless
was a success at the box-office.

w Caroline Thompson, Larry Wilson cartoons based
on characters created by Charles Addams d Barry
Sonnenfeld ph Owen Roizman m Marc Shaiman
pd Richard MacDonald sp visual effects supervisor
Alan Munro, Chuck Comisky ed Dede Allen, Jim
Miller

Anjelica Huston, Raul Julia, Christopher Lloyd, Dan
Hedaya, Elizabeth Wilson, Judith Malina, Carel
Struycken, Dana Ivey, Paul Benedict, Christopher
Hart (whose hand appears as The Thing)

'Plays like a collection of sitcom one-liners augmented
by feature-film special effects – a combination that is
stretched well beyond its limits.' – Variety

'Misguided graveyard slapstick.' – New Yorker

'Motherhood just got a little stranger.'
Addams Family Values *

US 1993 94m colour
UIP/Paramount (Scott Rudin)
V, V*, L, S

The Addams's children try to kill the new baby, but
he is damage-proof; while their parents hire a nanny
who is also a serial killer.

This is less a movie and more a sequence of gags set in
an elongated sit-com, of which few are inspired and
most too ordinary to amuse, but it has its moments.

w Paul Rudnick d Barry Sonnenfeld ph Donald
Peterman m Marc Shaiman pd Ken Adam
ed Arthur Schmidt, Jim Miller

Angelica Huston, Raul Julia, Christopher Lloyd, Joan
Cusack, Christina Ricci, Carol Kane, Jimmy Workman,
Carel Struycken, David Krumholtz, Christopher Hart

'It's the kind of wicked delicious comedy one can
savor without adding the proviso of guilty pleasure.' –
Variety

'The film does not know when to stop, has little idea
of how to begin, and moves forward by a process of
"Quick, who's got the next gimmick" jolts and
nudges.' – Nigel Andrews, Financial Times

'The storyline is almost too slim to recall and the cast
simply earn their bread and butter doing revue turns.'
– Derek Malcolm, Guardian

AAN: Ken Adam

The Adding Machine *

GB 1968 99m Technicolor
Universal/Associated London (Jerome Epstein)

Downtrodden clerk Mr Zero rebels against society by
murdering his boss. Tried and executed, he spends
thirty years in heaven before being 'laundered' and
sent back to start again as another nonentity.

Elmer Rice's satirical fantasy of the twenties is here
robbed of its expressionist staging and presented
naturalistically, a fatal error from which the film never
for one moment recovers.

wd Jerome Epstein ph Walter Lassally m Mike
Leander, Lambert Williamson

Phyllis Diller, Milo O'Shea, Billie Whitelaw, Sydney
Chaplin, Julian Glover, Raymond Huntley, Phil
Brown, Libby Morris

Addio, Fratello Crudele: see 'Tis Pity She's a
Whore

Address Unknown **

US 1944 72m bw
Columbia (William Cameron Menzies)

A German-American becomes a Nazi and is
incriminated by false letters from his one-time friend.

Reasonably engrossing, cheaply-made adaptation of a
slim little thriller which was widely read during
World War II.

w Kressman Taylor, Herbert Dalmass
novel Kressman Taylor d William Cameron
Menzies ph Rudolph Maté m Ernst Toch
ad Lionel Banks, Walter Holscher

Paul Lukas, Carl Esmond, Peter Van Eyck, Mady
Christians, Emory Parnell

AAN: Ernst Toch; art direction

Adieu Philippine *
France/Italy   1962   106m   bw
Unitec/Alpha/Rome-Paris (Georges de Beauregard)

A young TV cameraman is torn between two girls.

Flimsy but attractive romantic comedy, slightly
marred by New Wave improvisation with consequent
rough edges.

w Michèle O'Glor, Jacques Rozier   d Jacques Rozier
ph René Mathelin   m various

Jean-Claude Aimini, Yveline Céry, Stefania Sabatini,
Vittorio Caprioli

Adios, Sabata: see The Bounty Hunters

Adj Kiraly Katonat: see The Princess

'Sex . . . Power . . . Obsession.'
The Adjuster *
Canada   1991   102m   colour
Metro/Ego Film Arts/Téléfilm Canada/Ontario Film
    Development Corp. (Atom Egoyan)
V (W), V*

An insurance loss adjuster becomes involved in the
sexual activities of his clients.

Offbeat movie that takes an oblique approach to the
relationship between cinema and voyeurism.

wd Atom Egoyan   ph Paul Sarossy   m Mychael
Danna   pd Linda Del Rosario, Richard Paris
ed Susan Shipton

Elias Koteas, Arsinée Khanjian, Maury Chaykin,
Gabrielle Rose, Jennifer Dale, Devis Hemblen, Rose
Sarkisyan, Armen Kokorian

'Utterly compelling, a visual treat and, above all, a
fiercely intelligent piece of work.' – Empire

The Admirable Crichton *
GB   1957   93m   Technicolor   Vistavision
Columbia/Modern Screenplays (Ian Dalrymple)
US title: Paradise Lagoon

Lord Loam and his family are shipwrecked on a desert
island, where his manservant proves the undisputed
leader.

Few laughs are to be had from this blunt, sentimental
version of a famous play, but the photography and
decor are excellent.

w Vernon Harris   play J. M. Barrie   d Lewis
Gilbert   ph Wilkie Cooper   m Douglas Gamley,
Richard Addinsell   ad William Kellner
costumes Bernard Nevill   devices Emmett

Kenneth More, Cecil Parker, Sally Ann Howes, Diane
Cilento, Martita Hunt, Jack Watling, Peter Graves,
Gerald Harper

'Barrie's play now seems more remote than Gammer
Gurton.' – David Robinson

The Admiral Was a Lady
US   1950   87m   bw
Roxbury (Albert S. Rogell, Jack M. Warner)
V*

Four ex-airmen and an ex-Wac try to live on their
wits.

Unappealing comedy which gives the impression that
it has tried to find a new style, and failed.

w Sidney Salkow, John O'Dea   d Albert S. Rogell
ph Stanley Cortez

Edmond O'Brien, Wanda Hendrix, Rudy Vallee,
Johnny Sands, Steve Brodie, Richard Erdman, Hillary
Brooke, Richard Lane

The Adolescent
France/West Germany   1979   93m   colour
Janus (Phillipe Dussart)
original title: L'Adolescente

In France in 1939, a 12-year-old girl is infatuated with
a young Jewish doctor.

A solidly acted but otherwise uninspired account of
the stirrings of adolescent angst.

w Henriette Jelinek, Jeanne Moreau   d Jeanne
Moreau   ph Pierre Gautard   m Philippe Sarde
ed Albert Jurgenson

Simone Signoret, Laetitia Chauveau, Edith Clever,
Jacques Weber, Francis Huster

Adolf Hitler – My Part in His Downfall *
GB   1972   102m   Technicolor
UA/Norcon (Gregory Smith, Norman Cohen)

Episodes in the life of a conscript at the beginning of
World War II.

Lumbering anarchic comedy based on Spike
Milligan's own sidesplitting memoirs; an enfeebled
British M*A*S*H.

w Johnny Byrne   d Norman Cohen   ph Terry
Maher   m Wilfred Burns

Jim Dale, Spike Milligan (as his own father), Arthur
Lowe, Bill Maynard, Windsor Davies, Pat Coombs,
Tony Selby, Geoffrey Hughes

'A convincing period shabbiness and sleaziness
which are endearing when they're not being
overstated.' – MFB

Adorable *
US   1933   85m   bw
Fox

A Ruritanian princess falls in love with a naval officer.

Charming, lightweight romance of the old school.

w George Marion Jnr, Jane Storm   story Paul Frank,
Billy Wilder   d William Dieterle   ph John Seitz
m/ly Werner Richard Heymann, George Marion,
Richard Whiting

Janet Gaynor, Henri Garat, C. Aubrey Smith, Herbert
Mundin, Blanche Friderici, Hans von Twardowski

'Not strong b.o. . . . even the neighbourhood fans have
caught up with the musical comedy kingdom idea.' –
Variety

† The film was remade from German-French originals
under a title which translated as Her Majesty Commands.
The German version starred Kaethe von Nagy and
Willy Fritsch, the French Lillian Harvey and Henri
Garat.

Adorable Creatures
France   1952   105m   bw
Sirius/Jacques Roitfeld

A Paris fashion executive recalls his love affairs.

A collection of four short sex comedies which did well
on the heels of La Ronde.

w Charles Spaak, Jacques Companeez   d Christian-
Jaque   ph Christian Matras   m Georges Van Parys

Daniel Gélin, Danielle Darrieux, Edwige Feuillère,
Antonella Lualdi, Martine Carol, Marilyn Buferd

Adorable Julia
Austria/France   1962   97m   bw
Wiener Mundus/Etoile
V*
GB title: The Seduction of Julia

A middle-aged actress takes on a lover.

Moderately pleasing sex comedy, rather more heavily
directed than Maugham would have liked.

w Johanna Sibelius, Eberhard Keindorff
novel Theatre by Somerset Maugham   d Alfred
Weidenmann

Lilli Palmer, Charles Boyer, Jean Sorel, Jeanne Valeri

Adorable Lies **
Cuba   1991   100m   colour
ICAIC (Evelio Delgado)
original title: Adorables Mentiras

A married, unsuccessful scriptwriter pretends to be a

film director in his efforts to seduce a woman he
fancies, who turns out to be a frustrated actress
married to a corrupt government official.

A deft and witty farce of false identities that makes
fun of marriage, desire and ideologically correct
cinema. Not surprisingly, it ran into censorship
problems in Cuba and was hardly seen there.

w Senel Paz   d Gerardo Chijona   ph Julio Valdes
m Edesio Alejandro, Gerardo Garcia   pd Onelio
Larralde   ed Jorge Abello

Isabel Santos, Luis Alberto Garcia, Mirtha Ibarra,
Thais Valdes, Carlos Cruz, Silvia Planas, Santiago
Alvarez

'Combines comedy and melodrama with uneven
results. At times it seems to be a tongue-in-cheek soap
opera, but in other scenes its tones becomes too dark.
While there are some funny moments, this Cuban
sudser goes on too long and eventually grows tiring.'
– Variety

Adorables Mentiras: see Adorable Lies

Adua e le Compagne
Italy   1960   150m   bw
Zebra Film
GB title: Hungry for Love

When brothels in Italy are officially closed, four of the
old girls open a restaurant.

Immensely overlong comedy drama whose rewards
come entirely from the actors.

w Ruggero Maccari, Ettore Scola, Antonio Pietrangeli,
Tullio Pinelli   d Antonio Pietrangeli

Simone Signoret, Marcello Mastroianni, Sandra Milo,
Emmanuelle Riva, Gina Rovere

'The script becomes increasingly episodic, and clichés
abound.' – MFB

Advance to the Rear *
US   1964   97m   bw   Panavision
MGM/Ted Richmond
GB title: Company of Cowards?

After the Civil War, a troop of misfits is sent west out
of harm's way, but manages to capture a rebel spy and
save a gold shipment.

Semi-satirical Western action comedy with a farcical
climax; quite sharply made.

w Samuel A. Peeples, William Bowers   d George
Marshall   ph Milton Krasner   m Randy Sparks

Glenn Ford, Melvyn Douglas, Stella Stevens, Jim
Backus, Joan Blondell, Andrew Prine, Alan Hale,
James Griffith, Preston Foster

'Gable's back and Garson's got him!'
Adventure *
US   1945   126m   bw
MGM (Sam Zimbalist)

A roughneck sailor marries a librarian, but only
settles down to love her when their child is born.

Uniquely embarrassing (and fascinating) mishmash of
pretentious dialogue and cardboard characters.

w Frederick Hazlitt Brennan, Vincent Lawrence
novel Clyde Brion Davis   d Victor Fleming
ph Joseph Ruttenberg   m Herbert Stothart

Clark Gable, Greer Garson, Thomas Mitchell, Joan
Blondell, John Qualen, Richard Haydn

'MGM proudly announce Adventure as the meeting of
a red-blooded man with a blue-blooded woman. Its
impact on the bloodstream of your critic was a chilling
one. Fifty years of the cinema, he thought, and this is
where we've landed.' – Richard Winnington

Adventure for Two: see The Demi-Paradise

Adventure in Baltimore
US 1949 89m bw
RKO (Richard H. Berger)
GB title: *Bachelor Bait*

In 1905, a young society girl becomes a suffragette.

Inconsequential period comedy which did nothing for its young star's fading career.

w Lionel Houser *story* Christopher Isherwood, Lesser Samuels *d* Richard Wallace *ph* Robert de Grasse *m* Frederick Hollander

Shirley Temple, Robert Young, John Agar, Albert Sharpe, Josephine Hutchinson, Johnny Sands, John Miljan, Norma Varden

Adventure in Diamonds
US 1940 76m bw
Paramount (George Fitzmaurice)

A British adventurer in South Africa falls in love with a lady diamond thief.

Acceptable romantic comedy-drama.

w Leonard Lee, Franz Schultz *d* George Fitzmaurice *ph* Charles Lang *m* Leo Shuken

George Brent, Isa Miranda, John Loder, Nigel Bruce, Elizabeth Patterson, Matthew Boulton, Cecil Kellaway, Ernest Truex, E. E. Clive

Adventure in Iraq
US 1943 65m bw

Wartime second feature about Americans who fall into Nazi-Arab hands.

Interesting only as a remake of *The Green Goddess*, with Paul Cavanagh in the George Arliss role.

w George Bilson and Robert E. Kent *d* D. Ross Lederman

Paul Cavanagh, John Loder, Ruth Ford

Adventure in Manhattan
US 1936 73m bw
Columbia
GB title: *Manhattan Madness*

An actress helps an ace reporter to foil a bank robbery by a master criminal.

Flat romantic mystery comedy which wastes a good cast.

w Sidney Buchman, Harry Sauber, Jack Kirkland *d* Edward Ludwig *ph* Henry Freulich

Jean Arthur, Joel McCrea, Thomas Mitchell, Reginald Owen, Herman Bing

Adventure in Washington
US 1941 82m bw
Columbia

A Senate page sells government secrets in Wall Street.

Unlikely melodrama with senators getting together to hush up a scandal.

w Lewis R. Foster, Arthur Caesar *d* Alfred E. Green

Herbert Marshall, Virginia Bruce, Gene Reynolds, Samuel S. Hinds, Ralph Morgan, Vaughan Glaser

Adventure Island
US 1947 67m Cinecolor
Paramount
V*

Seafarers chance on an uncharted island, ruled by a deadly fanatic.

Hokum rehash of Stevenson's *Ebb Tide*, with Paul Kelly as the madman.

w Maxwell Shane *d* Peter Stewart (Sam Newfield)

Paul Kelly, Rory Calhoun, Rhonda Fleming

The Adventure of Sherlock Holmes' Smarter Brother
GB 1975 91m DeLuxe
TCF/Jouer (Richard A. Roth)
V*

More by good luck than good management, Sherlock's younger brother solves one of his cases.

Infuriating parody with little sense of the original and a hit-or-miss style all of its own. Amusing moments fail to atone for the general waste of opportunity.

wd Gene Wilder *ph* Gerry Fisher *m* John Morris *pd* Terry Marsh

Gene Wilder, Marty Feldman, Madeline Kahn, Leo McKern, Dom DeLuise, Roy Kinnear, John Le Mesurier, Douglas Wilmer, Thorley Walters

'Like a compilation of the kind of numbers actors like to do at parties.' – *Howard Kissel*

'He has bitten off more than he can chew or I can swallow.' – *John Simon*

'A few stray chuckles but nothing more.' – *Sight and Sound*

'There's no mystery, and since you can't have a parody of a mystery without a mystery, there's no comic suspense.' – *New Yorker, 1980*

The Adventurer ***
US 1917 21m approx (24 fps) bw silent
Mutual

An escaped convict rescues two wealthy women from drowning and is invited to their home.

Hilarious early Chaplin knockabout, with his physical gags at their most streamlined.

wd *Charles Chaplin* *ph* William C. Foster, Rollie Totheroh

Charles Chaplin, Edna Purviance, Eric Campbell, Henry Bergman

The Adventurers
GB 1950 86m bw
Rank/Mayflower (Maxwell Setton, Aubrey Baring)
V*
US title: *The Great Adventure*; aka: *Fortune in Diamonds*

In 1902, two Boers and a cashiered English officer set out to recover stolen diamonds.

Lethargic South African Western in the wake of *Treasure of the Sierra Madre;* clumsy and unconvincing, with cardboard characters.

w Robert Westerby *d* David MacDonald *ph* Oswald Morris *m* Cedric Thorpe Davie

Dennis Price, Jack Hawkins, Siobhan McKenna, Peter Hammond, Bernard Lee, Grégoire Aslan

The Adventurers *
US 1970 170m Technicolor Panavision
Paramount/Avco Embassy/Adventurers Film (Lewis Gilbert)
V*

A sensualist brought up amid Europe's luxuries returns to his Central American homeland to take vengeance on the brutal security chief who raped and murdered his mother.

Sprawling, sexy, bloodstained extravaganza from a Harold Robbins novel. Expensive to look at and riddled with sensation, but that's about all.

w Michael Hastings, Lewis Gilbert *d* Lewis Gilbert *ph* Claude Renoir *m* Antonio Carlos Jobim *pd* Tony Masters

Bekim Fehmiu, Alan Badel, Candice Bergen, Ernest Borgnine, Olivia de Havilland, Rossano Brazzi, Charles Aznavour, Sidney Tafler, Fernando Rey, Leigh Taylor-Young, Thommy Berggren, John Ireland

'A three-hour slog through every imaginable cliché of writing and direction . . . in addition to an abundance of flaccid sex and violence, it offers drugs, sadism, orchids, fireworks, orgies, lesbianism, a miscarriage, a private torture chamber, and the hell of several

fashion shows with loud pop music accompaniment. This might well be described as the film with everything; trouble is, it is difficult to imagine anybody wanting any of it.' – *MFB*

'Lovers of rotten movies and close-up violence can revel in it.' – *Judith Crist*

Adventures in Babysitting: see *Night On the Town*

Adventures of a Rookie
US 1943 64m bw
RKO

Modest attempt to launch a new comedy team in a threadbare army farce.

w Edward James, William Bowers, M. Coates Webster *d* Leslie Goodwins

Wally Brown, Alan Carney, Erford Gage, Richard Martin

'Sufficiently corny to get through the subsequent duals where the customers are not too particular.' – *Variety*

Adventures of a Taxi Driver
GB 1975 89m Eastmancolor
Alpha/Salon (Peter Long, Stanley Long)
V, V*

A taxi driver finds that his sex life is both busy and confusing.

Lamentable British comedy, in which a cast of reliable performers are allowed to embarrass themselves and their audience.

w Suzanne Mercer *d* Stanley Long *ph* Peter Sinclair *ed* Jo Gannon

Barry Evans, Judy Geeson, Adrienne Posta, Diana Dors, Liz Fraser, Ian Lavender, Stephen Lewis, Robert Lindsay, Henry McGee, Brian Wilde

'A crass, lobotomised production, with no discernible style, humour or purpose.' – *MFB*

Adventures of a Young Man: see *Hemingway's Adventures of a Young Man*

The Adventures of Arsène Lupin *
France/Italy 1956 103m Eastmancolor
Chavane-SNE-Gaumont/Lambor-Costellazione (Robert Sussfeld)

In 1912, the famous jewel thief conducts several successful robberies and outwits the Kaiser.

The most stylish Lupin film, though not based on the original stories.

w Jacques Becker, Albert Simonin, based on the character created by Maurice Leblanc *d* Jacques Becker *ph* Edmond Séchan *ad* Rino Mondellini

Robert Lamoureux, Lisolotte Pulver, Otto Hasse, Henri Rolland

The Adventures of Baron Munchausen
(1943): see *Münchausen*

Adventures of Baron Munchausen **
GB/West Germany 1989 126m Eastmancolor
Prominent Features/Laura Film/Columbia-Tri Star (Thomas Schühly)
V, V*, L, S

A German soldier tells tall stories of his escapades.

Ambitious, extravagant fantasy in which some of the parts are better than the whole.

w Charles McKeown, Terry Gilliam *story* Rudolph Erich Raspe *d* Terry Gilliam *ph* Giuseppe Rotunno *m* Michael Kamen *pd* Dante Ferretti *sp* Richard Conway *ed* Peter Hollywood

John Neville, Eric Idle, Sarah Polley, Oliver Reed, Charles McKeown, Winston Dennis, Jack Purvis, Valentina Cortese, Jonathan Pryce, Bill Paterson, Peter Jeffrey, Uma Thurman

'Munchausen's inability to get into gear rather defeats what would seem the point of the picture: whereas the source is adroit at slipping between fantasy and reality, Gilliam's fiction can't even handle a flashback.' – *MFB*

AAN: best art direction; best costume design; best makeup

The Adventures of Barry Mackenzie *
Australia   1972   114m   Eastmancolor
Columbia/Longford (Philip Adams)

A sex-hungry Australian gets into all kinds of trouble on a visit to the Old Country.

Occasionally funny, defiantly crude and tasteless, but poorly produced comedy-misadventure from the *Private Eye* comic strip. Australian slang combines with bad sound recording to make much of the film unintelligible.

w Barry Humphries, Bruce Beresford   *d* Bruce Beresford   *ph* Don McAlpine   *m* Peter Best

Barry Crocker, Barry Humphries (as Dame Edna Everage), Peter Cook, Spike Milligan, Dennis Price, Avice Landone, Dick Bentley, Joan Bakewell, William Rushton

'A wildly uneven concoction of antipodean bad taste, probably only fully appreciated by Earls Court exiles.' – *Sight and Sound*

† Sequel 1974: *Barry Mackenzie Holds His Own*

The Adventures of Buckaroo Banzai Across the Eighth Dimension *
US   1984   102m   colour
Sherwood (Neil Canton/W. D. Richter)
V, V*, L

A Renaissance man – physicist, surgeon and rock star – crashes into the eighth dimension and releases evil aliens.

Genial spoof of science fiction and other movie genres.

w Earl MacRauch   *d* W. D. Richter   *ph* Fred J. Koenekamp   *m* Michael Boddicker   *pd* J. M. Riva   *ed* Richard Marks, George Bowers

Peter Weller, John Lithgow, Ellen Barkin, Jeff Goldblum, Christopher Lloyd

The Adventures of Bullwhip Griffin *
US   1965   110m   Technicolor
Walt Disney (Bill Anderson)
V*

In the 1849 California Gold Rush, two aristocrats and their butler head west.

Rather splendid spoof Western with careful attention to detail and comedy pointing, well above the average Disney standard.

w Lowell S. Hawley   *novel By the Great Horn Spoon* by Sid Fleischman   *d* James Neilson   *ph* Edward Colman   *m* George Bruns   *titles* Ward Kimball

Roddy McDowall, Suzanne Pleshette, Bryan Russell, Karl Malden, Harry Guardino, Richard Haydn, Mike Mazurki, Hermione Baddeley, Cecil Kellaway

Adventures of Captain Africa
US   1955   bw   serial: 15 eps
Columbia

A wild animal trapper combats rebels who have kidnapped an African prime minister.

Routine hokum.   *d* Spencer Bennet

John Hart, Rick Vallin, Ben Welden

The Adventures of Captain Fabian
US   1951   100m   bw
Republic/Silver (William Marshall)
V*

A sea captain returns to New Orleans to revenge himself on the family which had defrauded his father.

Stilted, old-fashioned *Monte Cristo*ish melodrama with some curiosity value but little verve in the playing or production. An awful warning to independent producers.

w Errol Flynn   *novel Fabulous Ann Medlock* by Robert Shannon   *d* William Marshall   *ph* Marcel Grignon   *m* René Cloerec

Errol Flynn, Micheline Presle, Agnes Moorehead, Vincent Price, Victor Francen, Jim Gerald

† Made in France.

Adventures of Captain Marvel *
US   1941   bw   serial: 12 eps
Republic

When a scientific expedition goes to Siam, the assistant radio operator is endowed by the mysterious Shazam with the power to transform himself into Captain Marvel, and to defeat the evil Scorpion.

Modest classic serial, good for more than a few laughs.   *d* William Witney, John English

Tom Tyler, Frank Coghlan Jnr, William Benedict, Louise Currie

Adventures of Casanova
US   1948   83m   bw
Eagle-Lion

Casanova returns to Sicily and helps overthrow the tyrannical rule of the King of Naples.

Robin Hood transplanted, with a few amorous asides; but this is a totally stilted production which fails to entertain.

w Crane Wilbur, Walter Bullock, Ken de Wolf   *d* Roberto Gavaldon

Arturo de Cordova, Lucille Bremer, Turhan Bey

The Adventures of Don Juan **
US   1949   110m   Technicolor
Warner (Jerry Wald)
V, V*, L
GB title: *The New Adventures of Don Juan*

A reformed 17th-century rake saves his queen from the machinations of her first minister.

Expensive, slightly uneasy, but generally very entertaining swashbuckler with elements of self-spoofery. Flynn's last big-budget extravaganza.

w George Oppenheimer, Harry Kurnitz   *d* Vincent Sherman   *ph* Elwood Bredell   *m* Max Steiner   *ad* Edward Carrere

Errol Flynn, Viveca Lindfors, Romney Brent, Robert Douglas, Alan Hale, Ann Rutherford, Robert Warwick, Jerry Austin, Douglas Kennedy, Una O'Connor, Aubrey Mather, Raymond Burr

'A lavish film on a truly magnificent scale.' – *The Times*

AAN: art direction

Adventures of Ford Fairlane
US   1990   104m   DeLuxe   Panavision
TCF (Joel Silver, Steve Perry)
V, V*, L

A conceited rock 'n' roll detective solves the murder of a Los Angeles disc jockey.

Drearily vulgar comedy, featuring one of the more obnoxious stand-up comedians of the 90s and about as entertaining as stepping in something nasty in the street. It was a flop at the box-office, resulting in Fox's decision not to release Clay's concert film *Dice Rules* (qv).

w Daniel Waters, James Cappe, David Arnott   *story* based on characters created by Rex Weiner   *d* Renny Harlin   *ph* Oliver Wood   *m* Yello   *pd* John Vallone   *ed* Michael Tronick

Andrew Dice Clay, Wayne Newton, Priscilla Presley, Morris Day, Lauren Holly, Maddie Corman, Robert Englund, Ed O'Neill

'Surprisingly funny and expectedly rude.' – *Variety*

'What can you say about a movie whose comic highlight is the hanging of a koala bear?' – *Empire*

Adventures of Frank and Jesse James
US   1948   bw   serial: 13 eps
Republic

Supposed outlaws pay back the money their gang has stolen.

A new but not very interesting twist on history.   *d* Fred Brannon, Yakima Canutt

Clayton Moore, Steve Darrell, Noel Neill

Adventures of Frank Merriwell
US   1936   bw   serial: 12 eps
Universal

A star baseball pitcher, armed with a mysterious ring, goes in search of his missing father.

Ho-hum adventures with sporting asides.   *d* Cliff Smith

Don Briggs, Jean Rogers, Don King

The Adventures of Gallant Bess
US   1948   71m   Cinecolor
Eagle Lion
V*

The master of a trained rodeo horse becomes a range wanderer.

Easy-going animal interest saga with a pleasant ending.

w Matthew Rapf   *d* Lew Landers

Cameron Mitchell, Audrey Long, Fuzzy Knight, James Millican, Ed Gargan

The Adventures of Gerard *
GB   1970   91m   DeLuxe   Panavision
UA/Sir Nigel Films (Peter Beale)

A hussar of Napoleon becomes involved in a double spy game but comes out trumps and wins a fair lady.

A lighthearted historical spoof of military pomp, with plenty of attractive elements which unfortunately fail to jell into a satisfying film.

w H. A. L. Craig and others   *stories* Arthur Conan Doyle   *d* Jerzy Skolimowski   *ph* Witold Sobocinski   *m* Riz Ortolani

Peter McEnery, Claudia Cardinale, Eli Wallach, Jack Hawkins, Mark Burns, Norman Rossington, John Neville

'Enormously graceful and witty . . . picks its way with amazing delicacy through the reefs of facetiousness.' – *Tom Milne*

The Adventures of Hajji Baba *
US   1954   93m   DeLuxe   Cinemascope
Allied Artists/Walter Wanger

In ancient Arabia, a barber helps and falls in love with an escaping princess.

A reasonably dashing sword and sandal romp which no one takes very seriously.

w Richard Collins   *d* Don Weis   *ph* Harold Lipstein   *m* Dimitri Tiomkin   *pd* Gene Allen

John Derek, Elaine Stewart, Thomas Gomez, Amanda Blake, Paul Picerni, Rosemarie Bowe

The Adventures of Huckleberry Finn: see
Huckleberry Finn (1960)

The Adventures of Ichabod and Mr Toad: see
Ichabod and Mr Toad

Adventures of Kitty O'Day
US   1944   63m   bw
Monogram (Lindsley Parsons)
GB title: *Detective Kitty O'Day*

A snoopy phone operator solves three murders before the police get started.

Predictable stuff, but tolerable and bright in its way.

w Tim Ryan, George Callahan, Victor Hammond
d William Beaudine

Jean Parker, Peter Cookson, Tim Ryan, Ralph Sanford

The Adventures of Marco Polo *
US   1938   100m   bw
Samuel Goldwyn
V

The medieval Italian explorer discovers China, fireworks, and a beautiful maiden.

One gets the impression that this began as a standard adventure and that during production it switched to comedy; whatever the cause, lively and amusing scenes fail to add up to more than a thinly scripted pantomime.

w Robert E. Sherwood   *d* Archie Mayo
ph Rudolph Maté   *md* Alfred Newman   *m* Hugo Friedhofer   *ad* Richard Day

Gary Cooper, Sigrid Gurie, Basil Rathbone, Ernest Truex, Binnie Barnes, Alan Hale, George Barbier

'In spite of its elaborate settings and the presence of Gary Cooper, it never quite lives up to its promises.' – *New York Sun*

'Goldwyn's most ambitious endeavour . . . deserves and will get enthusiastic exhibitor plugging. Sherwood's more concerned with entertainment than with history.' – *Variety*

† Release prints were in sepiatone.

The Adventures of Mark Twain **
US   1944   130m   bw
Warner (Jesse L. Lasky)

The life of America's foremost humorous writer, from a Mississippi riverboat to his becoming an honorary fellow of Oxford University.

Conventional biopic, quite watchable and with unusual side turnings, but eventually lacking the zest of the subject.

w Harold M. Sherman, Alan le May, Harry Chandler
d Irving Rapper   *ph* Sol Polito   *m* Max Steiner
ad John J. Hughes

Fredric March, Alexis Smith, Donald Crisp, Alan Hale, C. Aubrey Smith, John Carradine, William Henry, Robert Barrat, Walter Hampden

'It's not that it's much worse than most cinematized biographies, because it does have its good moments. It's just that once more biographical inaccuracy is rampant, and once more the best dramatic possibilities have been overlooked, so it's hard to think of anything new, in the line of protest, to say.' – *David Lardner, New Yorker*

AAN: Max Steiner; John J. Hughes

The Adventures of Martin Eden
US   1942   87m   bw
Columbia (B. P. Schulberg)

An American seaman fights a brutal captain and wins better conditions for his comrades.

Routine actioner based on what are virtually the author's memoirs.

w W. L. River   *story* Jack London   *d* Sidney Salkow

Glenn Ford, Evelyn Keyes, Claire Trevor, Stuart Erwin, Dickie Moore

Adventures of Milo and Otis (dubbed) *
Japan   1986   75m   Eastmancolor   Panavision
Virgin/Fuji (Hisashi Hieda)
V, V*, L
original title: *Koneko Monogatari*

A puppy leaves a farm to search for his friend, a kitten, who has floated downriver in a box.

Innocuous adventure, using real animals, that may appeal to the very young.

w Mark Saltzman   *story* Masanori Hata
d Masanori Hata   *ph* Hideo Fuji, Shinji Tomita
m Michael Boddicker   *ad* Takeharu Sakahuchi
ed Chizuko Osada

Dudley Moore (narrator)

'Youngsters and pet lovers will adore this film. Grown-ups with a less positive attitude to the animal kingdom are well advised to stay away.' – *Empire*

† The film was the second most popular ever made in Japan.

The Adventures of Quentin Durward: see
Quentin Durward

Adventures of Red Ryder
US   1940   bw   serial: 12 eps
Republic

Our hero forms an organization to drive gunfighters out of Santa Fe.

Unsurprising serialized shenanigans.   *d* William Witney, John English

Don Barry, Noah Beery Jnr, Tommy Cook, William Farnum

Adventures of Rex and Rinty
US   1935   bw   serial: 12 eps
Mascot

A stolen prize horse teams up with a wandering dog to help oust various villains.

Slightly unusual chapter play with 'the king of wild horses' and 'Rin Tin Tin Jnr'.   *d* Ford Beebe, B. Reeves Eason

Kane Richmond, Mischa Auer, Norma Taylor, Smiley Burnette

'Only the rainbow can duplicate its brilliance!'
The Adventures of Robin Hood ****
US   1938   102m   Technicolor
Warner (Hal B. Wallis)
V, V*, L, S

Rebel outlaw Robin Hood outwits Guy of Gisbourne and the Sheriff of Nottingham, and saves the throne for the absent King Richard.

A splendid adventure story, rousingly operatic in treatment, with dashing action highlights, fine comedy balance, and incisive acting all round. Historically notable for its use of early three-colour Technicolor; also for convincingly recreating Britain in California.

w Seton I. Miller, Norman Reilly Raine   *d* William Keighley, Michael Curtiz   *ph* Tony Gaudio, Sol Polito, W. Howard Greene   *m* Erich Wolfgang Korngold   *ad* Carl Jules Weyl   *ed* Ralph Dawson

Errol Flynn (Sir Robin of Locksley), *Basil Rathbone* (Sir Guy of Gisbourne), *Claude Rains* (Prince John), Olivia de Havilland (Maid Marian), *Alan Hale* (Little John), Patric Knowles (Will Scarlet), *Eugene Pallette* (Friar Tuck), *Ian Hunter* (King Richard), *Melville Cooper* (Sheriff of Nottingham), Una O'Connor (Bess), Herbert Mundin (Much the Miller's Son), Montagu Love (Bishop of Black Canons), Howard Hill (Captain of Archers)

PRINCE JOHN: 'Any objections to the new tax, from our Saxon friends?'
ROBIN to Gisbourne during duel: 'Did I upset your plans?'
GISBOURNE: 'You've come to Nottingham once too often!'
ROBIN: 'When this is over, my friend, there'll be no need for me to come again!'
PRINCE JOHN: 'Ho, varlets, bring Sir Robin food! Such insolence must support a healthy appetite!'
ROBIN: 'It's injustice I hate, not the Normans!'

'Magnificent, unsurpassable . . . the film is lavish, brilliantly photographed, and has a great Korngold score.' – *NFT, 1974*

'Mostly the picture is full of movement, some of it dashing in fine romantic costume style, some of it just sprightly. The excitement comes from fast action – galloping steeds, men swinging Tarzan-like from the trees, hurling tables and chairs, rapid running swordplay, the sudden whiz of Robin's arrows coming from nowhere to startle his enemies – more than from any fear that Robin might be worsted. Somehow the whole thing has the air of being a costume party, a jolly and rather athletic one, with a lot of well-bred Englishmen playing at being in the greenwood.' – *James Shelley Hamilton, National Board of Review*

† At the time of its release this was Warner's most expensive film, costing more than two million dollars. Chico, California, stood in for Sherwood Forest; the archery contest was shot at Busch Gardens, Pasadena. Curtiz took over direction when it was felt that the action lacked impact.

AA: Erich Wolfgang Korngold; Carl Jules Weyl; Ralph Dawson

AAN: best picture

The Adventures of Robinson Crusoe ***
Mexico   1953   89m   Pathecolor
Tepeyac (Oscar Dancigers, Henry F. Ehrlich)

A 17th-century mariner is shipwrecked on an uninhabited tropical island.

Fascinating version of a famous story, with only one character on screen until the belated arrival of Friday and the escape to civilization. Subtle and compelling, with only the colour unsatisfactory.

w Luis Buñuel, Phillip Roll   *novel* Daniel Defoe
d Luis Buñuel   *ph* Alex Phillips   *m* Anthony Collins

Dan O'Herlihy, Jaime Fernandez

'A film of which the purity, the tense poetic style, evokes a kind of wonder.' – *Gavin Lambert*

'Free of that deadly solicitude which usually kills off classics.' – *New Yorker, 1977*

AAN: Dan O'Herlihy

The Adventures of Sadie: see *Our Girl Friday*

The Adventures of Sherlock Holmes **
US   1939   83m   bw
TCF (Gene Markey)
V, V*, L
GB title: *Sherlock Holmes*

Moriarty sends Holmes on a false trail while he plots to steal the Crown jewels.

An engaging piece of pseudo-Victoriana: all elements smooth save an unconvincing plot.

w Edwin Blum, William Drake   *d* Alfred Werker
ph Leon Shamroy   *m* Cyril Mockridge

Basil Rathbone (Holmes), *Nigel Bruce* (Dr Watson), *George Zucco* (Moriarty), Ida Lupino (Ann Brandon), Alan Marshal (Jerrold Hunter), Terry Kilburn (Billy), E. E. Clive (Inspector Bristol), Henry Stephenson (Sir Ronald Ramsgate), Mary Gordon (Mrs Hudson)

The "elementary my dear Watson" type of dialogue is soft-pedalled for more modern phrases or understandable patter.' – *Variety*

'Told with more movie art per foot than seven reels of anything the intellectual men have been finding good this whole year or more.' – *Otis Ferguson*

† This was the second and last of Rathbone's costume outings as Holmes, and the one in which he sang a comic song in disguise.

Adventures of Sir Galahad
US   1949   bw   serial: 15 eps
Columbia

King Arthur's knight goes in search of the missing magic sword Excalibur.

Predictably stiff-necked medieval goings-on with American accents. *d* Spencer Bennet

George Reeves, Charles King, William Fawcett

Adventures of Smilin' Jack
US 1943 bw serial: 12 eps
Universal

On an Eastern island, an American adventurer helps the Chinese to prevent a Japanese takeover.

Standard rough stuff with a rather interesting cast. *d* Ray Taylor, Lewis D. Collins

Tom Brown, Marjorie Lord, Philip Ahn, Sidney Toler, Turhan Bey, Rose Hobart, Keye Luke, Nigel de Brulier

The Adventures of Tartu *
GB 1943 103m bw
MGM (Irving Asher)
US title: *Tartu*

During World War II, a British spy goes to Czechoslovakia to dismantle a poison gas factory.

Halting and artificial comedy-thriller, saved only by a graceful star performance.

w Howard Emmett Rogers, John Lee Mahin, Miles Malleson *d* Harold S. Bucquet *ph* John J. Cox *md* Louis Levy *m* Hubert Bath

Robert Donat, Valerie Hobson, Walter Rilla, Glynis Johns, Martin Miller

'You are seeing all it has, and bald spots as well, first time around, whereas with a good Hitchcock or even a good Carol Reed, the pleasures visible at a first seeing stand up, or intensify, at a third or a fifth.' – *James Agee*

Adventures of the Flying Cadets
US 1943 bw serial: 13 eps
Universal

Flying students fight a Nazi agent called the Black Hangman.

Spirited thick ear with a competent cast. *d* Ray Taylor, Lewis D. Collins

Johnny Downs, Bobby Jordan, Ward Wood, Robert Armstrong, Eduardo Ciannelli, Billy Benedict, Regis Toomey

Adventures of the Wilderness Family
US 1975 101m colour
Pacific International
V*

An urban family runs into trouble when it takes to the wilds.

Naïve little four-wall family movie in which the pretty scenery (Utah and the Canadian Rockies) and the animals compensate for the dramatic inadequacies.

wd Stewart Raffil

Robert Logan, Susan Damante Shaw

† *Further Adventures of the Wilderness Family* appeared in 1977.

The Adventures of Tom Sawyer ***
US 1938 91m Technicolor
David O. Selznick (William H. Wright)
V*, L

Small-town Mississippi boy tracks down a murderer, Injun Joe.

Set-bound but excellent version of the children's classic by Mark Twain.

w John Weaver *d* Norman Taurog *ph* James Wong Howe, Wilfrid Cline *m* Max Steiner *ad* Lyle Wheeler

Tommy Kelly (Tom), *May Robson* (Aunt Polly), Walter Brennan (Muff Potter), Victor Jory (Injun Joe), Victor Kilian (Sheriff), Jackie Moran (Huckleberry Finn), Ann Gillis (Becky Thatcher), Donald Meek (Sunday School Superintendent), Margaret Hamilton (Mrs Sawyer), Marcia Mae Jones (Mary Sawyer)

'The familiar characters emerge in all their old amiability, the atmosphere is there and so is the excitement.' – *MFB*

'Should make Mark Twain circulate in his grave like a trout in a creel.' – *Otis Ferguson*

'Another Selznick International box office clean-up . . . that there exists a broad audience for films whose essential appeal is to the family trade has always been true. *Snow White* touched a source of almost unlimited audience draw: *Tom Sawyer* follows to the same customers.' – *Variety*

AAN: Lyle Wheeler

The Adventuress: see *I See a Dark Stranger*

Advice to the Lovelorn *
US 1933 62m bw
TCF/Darryl F. Zanuck

A reporter is demoted to the lonelyhearts column and becomes absorbed in it.

Springy vehicle for Lee Tracy.

w Leonard Praskins *novel Miss Lonelyhearts* by Nathanael West *d* Alfred Werker

Lee Tracy, Sally Blane, Sterling Holloway, Isabel Jewell, Jean Adair

† Compare the Paul Muni vehicle *Hi Nellie.* It was remade in 1958 as *Lonelyhearts* (qv).

'Are the men and women of Washington really like this?'
Advise and Consent **
US 1962 139m bw Panavision
Columbia/Alpha-Alpina/Otto Preminger
V*, V* (C)

The President's choice of an unpopular secretary of state leads to divisions in the Senate and the blackmail and suicide of a senator.

Absorbing political melodrama from a novel which aimed to lift the lid off Washington. Many character actors make their mark, but the harsh-contrast photography seems misjudged.

w Wendell Mayes *novel* Allen Drury *d* Otto Preminger *ph* Sam Leavitt *m* Jerry Fielding *titles* Saul Bass

Don Murray, *Charles Laughton,* Henry Fonda, Walter Pidgeon, Lew Ayres, Edward Andrews, Burgess Meredith, Gene Tierney, Franchot Tone, George Grizzard, Paul Ford, Peter Lawford, Inga Swenson, Will Geer

'The result is supremely ambivalent, a battle between fascinatingly real props and procedures and melodramatically unreal characters and situations.' – *Peter John Dyer*

'The parade of people helps to take one's mind off the overwrought melodrama.' – *New Yorker, 1980*

Aelita *
USSR 1924 70m approx bw silent
Mezhrabpom

Two Russian rocket pioneers land on Mars and start a revolution against the planet's queen.

Notable early space fiction, with footage of twenties Moscow as well as interesting set designs.

w Fedor Ozep, Alexei Faiko *novel* Alexei Tolstoy *d* Yakov Protazanov *ph* Yuri Zhelabuzhsky *pd* Sergei Kozlovsky

Yulia Solntseva, Nikolai Batalov, Igor Ilinsky

Aerial Gunner
US 1943 78m bw
Paramount (William H. Pine, William G. Thomas)

A US air force pilot in hospital thinks back to his training and his young brother's problems.

A watered-down *Wings* (with process footage to match) which also starred Arlen.

w Maxwell Shane *d* William H. Pine, William G. Thomas

Richard Arlen, Chester Morris, Jimmy Lydon, Lita Ward, Dick Purcell

Aerograd **
USSR 1935 81m bw
Mosfilm/Ukrainfilm
aka: *Frontier*

Guards keep Japanese spies out of Siberia, where an airport is being built.

An action film with style and pretensions.

wd Alexander Dovzhenko *ph* Edouard Tissé, Mikhail Gindin *m* Dmitri Kabalevsky

Semyon Shagaida, Stepan Shkurat, Sergei Stolyarov

Affair at the Villa Fiorita: see *The Battle of the Villa Fiorita*

Affair in Monte Carlo: see *Twenty-Four Hours of a Woman's Life*

Affair in Trinidad *
US 1952 98m bw
Columbia/Beckworth (Vincent Sherman)
V*

A nightclub singer whose husband is killed by gangsters works undercover for the police and routs the gang with the help of her husband's brother.

A tired tropical melodrama intended to follow up the success of *Gilda,* but without the verve. Some routine pleasures, though.

w Oscar Saul, James Gunn *d* Vincent Sherman *ph* Joseph Walker *m* Morris Stoloff, George Duning

Rita Hayworth, Glenn Ford, Alexander Scourby, Torin Thatcher, Valerie Bettis, Steve Geray, Karel Stepanek, George Voskovec

'Improbable, foolish, but glossy.' – *Penelope Houston*

An Affair to Remember **
US 1957 114m Eastmancolor Cinemascope
TCF (Jerry Wald)
V*, L, S

An ex-nightclub singer falls in love with a wealthy bachelor on a transatlantic liner, but an accident prevents her from attending their subsequent rendezvous.

Remake of *Love Affair,* a surprisingly successful mixture of smart lines, sentiment and tears, all applied with style and assurance.

w Delmer Daves, Leo McCarey *d* Leo McCarey *ph* Milton Krasner *m* Hugo Friedhofer

Cary Grant, Deborah Kerr, Cathleen Nesbitt, Richard Denning, Neva Patterson

'A lush slice of Hollywood romanticism.' – *MFB*

'90 masterly minutes of entrancing light comedy and 25 beastly minutes of beastly, melodramatic, pseudo-tragic guff.' – *Paul Dehn*

AAN: Milton Krasner; Hugo Friedhofer; title song (*m* Harry Warren, *ly* Harold Adamson, Leo McCarey)

Affair with a Stranger *
US 1953 87m bw
RKO (Robert Sparks)

Five friends reminisce about a marriage which seems about to break up.

This would-be-smart comedy has a good idea unsatisfactorily worked out, and could have used a more sparkling cast.

w Richard Flournoy *d* Roy Rowland *ph* Harry J. Wild *m* Roy Webb

Jean Simmons, Victor Mature, Mary Jo Tarola, Monica Lewis, Jane Darwell, Nicholas Joy, Wally Vernon, Dabbs Greer

L'Affaire est dans le Sac *
France 1932 47m bw
Pathé/Nathan
aka: It's in the Bag

Two would-be kidnappers end up (a) married to and (b) employed by their intended victims.

Semi-professional nonsense comedy with political jokes.

w Jacques Prévert d Pierre Prévert ph A. Giboury, Eli Lotar m Maurice Jaubert

J.-P. Le Chanois, Jacques Brunius, Etienne Decroux, Lucien Raimbourg, Julien Carette, Lora Hays

Affairs of a Gentleman
US 1934 68m bw
Universal

A novelist who has used all his love affairs in his novels holds a reunion.

Mild star vehicle which wastes an amusing idea.

w Cyril Hume, Peter Ruric, Milton Krims d Edwin L. Marin

Paul Lukas, Leila Hyams, Onslow Stevens

Affairs of a Rogue: see The First Gentleman

The Affairs of Anatol *
US 1921 95m approx (24 fps) bw silent
Famous Players-Lasky/de Mille-Paramount

A socialite interrupts his honeymoon to go looking for romance.

Dated but historically very interesting sophisticated farce from a time when Hollywood was aping Viennese naughtiness.

w Jeanie MacPherson, Beulah Marie Dix, Lorna Moon, Elmer Harris from Granville Barker's paraphrase of the play Anatol by Arthur Schnitzler d Cecil B. de Mille ph Alvin Wyckoff, Karl Strussed Anne Bauchens

Wallace Reid, Gloria Swanson, Bebe Daniels, Elliott Dexter, Monte Blue, Wanda Hawley, Theodore Roberts

'Should be enormously popular, especially with those who think Schnitzler is a cheese.' – Robert E. Sherwood

'The man who doesn't sell out for every performance of a double run should turn his show shop into a Quaker meeting house.' – Motion Picture Herald

The Affairs of Annabel *
US 1938 69m bw
RKO (Lee Marcus, Lou Lusty)

A crackpot Hollywood press agent sends his star to jail as a publicity stunt.

An amusing frenetic comedy of its time, successful enough to warrant a sequel, Annabel Takes a Tour, in the same year.

w Bert Granet, Paul Yawitz d Lew Landers ph Russell Metty m Roy Webb

Lucille Ball, Jack Oakie, Ruth Donnelly, Bradley Page, Fritz Feld, Thurston Hall, Elizabeth Risdon, Granville Bates, James Burke

The Affairs of Cellini *
US 1934 90m bw
Twentieth Century (Darryl F. Zanuck)

The complex amours of a 16th-century Florentine rake.

Lively period bedroom farce somewhat hampered by censorship.

w Bess Meredyth play The Firebrand by Edwin Justus Mayer d Gregory La Cava ph Charles Rosher m Alfred Newman ad Richard Day

Fredric March, Constance Bennett, Frank Morgan, Fay Wray, Vince Barnett, Louis Calhern, Jessie Ralph

'Gay and entertaining though whipped up synthetically like circus ice cream.' – Variety

AAN: Charles Rosher; Frank Morgan; Richard Day

The Affairs of Dobie Gillis
US 1953 74m bw
MGM (Arthur M. Loew Jnr)

Adventures of an indolent and accident-prone university student.

Scatty comedy with good talent and musical numbers encased in a tatty production.

w Max Shulman d Don Weis ph William Mellor md Jeff Alexander

Bobby Van, Debbie Reynolds, Hans Conried, Barbara Ruick, Bob Fosse

The Affairs of Martha
US 1942 66m bw
MGM
GB title: Once Upon a Thursday

A servant writes a scandalous book about her employers.

Fairly amusing comedy with an ingratiating cast.

w Isobel Lennart, Lee Gold d Jules Dassin

Marsha Hunt, Richard Carlson, Spring Byington, Allyn Joslyn, Frances Drake, Margaret Hamilton, Melville Cooper, Virginia Weidler, Ernest Truex, Marjorie Main

Affairs of Sally: see The Fuller Brush Girl

'She's so romantic she drives four men frantic!'
The Affairs of Susan **
US 1945 110m bw
Paramount (Hal B. Wallis)

Four men in Susan's life see her differently.

Occasionally witty comedy designed as a champagne vehicle for its star. It seemed quite good at the time.

w Richard Flournoy story Laszlo Gorog, T. Monroe d William A. Seiter ph David Abel m Frederick Hollander

Joan Fontaine, George Brent, Walter Abel, Don Defore, Dennis O'Keefe

'The cast enters into the irresponsibilities with gusto.' – MFB

'A bright thing, a bit too long.' – Richard Mallett, Punch

AAN: Laszlo Gorog, T. Monroe

Affectionately Yours
US 1941 88m bw
Warner (Mark Hellinger)

A foreign correspondent hurries home when he hears that his wife plans to divorce him.

Thin lightweight comedy, unsuitably cast.

w Edward Kaufman d Lloyd Bacon ph Tony Gaudio m Heinz Roemheld

Merle Oberon, Dennis Morgan, Rita Hayworth, George Tobias, Ralph Bellamy, James Gleason, Hattie McDaniel

Afraid of the Dark *
GB/France 1992 91m colour
Rank/Sovereign/Telescope/Les Films Ariane/Cine Cinq (Simon Bosanquet)
V, V*

A near-sighted 11-year-old boy with a blind mother worries about the identity of the slasher who is attacking blind women.

A thriller that turns out to be not what it seems, but the twist is ultimately an uninteresting one, though the film does work up a degree of terror.

wd Mark Peploe ph Bruno de Keyzer m Richard Hartley pd Caroline Ames ed Scott Thomas

James Fox, Fanny Ardant, Paul McGann, Clare Holman, Ben Keyworth

'A rather stiff and self-conscious film, not without its pretensions, but also informed by considerable intelligence.' – Derek Malcolm, Guardian

Africa Screams
US 1949 79m bw
UA (Edward Nassour)

Two dumbbells go on safari with a treasure map.

Lower-case comedy.

w Earl Baldwin d Charles Barton

Bud Abbott, Lou Costello, Hillary Brooke, Max Baer, Shemp Howard

Africa Texas Style *
GB 1967 109m Eastmancolor
Paramount/Vantors (Andrew Marton)

A Kenyan settler hires two Texas cowboys to help in his scheme of wild game ranching.

Excellent location sequences are dragged down by a very boring script, but it's a good family film nevertheless.

w Andy White d Andrew Marton ph Paul Beeson m Malcolm Arnold

John Mills, Hugh O'Brian, Nigel Green, Tom Nardini, Adrienne Corri, Ronald Howard

† Forerunner of TV series, Cowboy in Africa.

African Fury: see Cry the Beloved Country

'They never dreamed of being in each other's arms, yet the mystic spell of the jungle swept them to primitive, hungry embrace! The greatest adventure a man ever had … with a woman!'
The African Queen ***
GB 1951 103m Technicolor
IFD/Romulus-Horizon (Sam Spiegel)
V, V*, L

In 1915, a gin-drinking river trader and a prim missionary make odd companions for a boat trip down a dangerous river, culminating in an attack on a German gunboat.

Despite some unfortunate studio sets mixed in with real African footage achieved through great hardship by all concerned, this is one of those surprising films that really work, a splendidly successful mixture of comedy, character and adventure.

w James Agee novel C. S. Forester d John Huston ph Jack Cardiff m Allan Gray

Humphrey Bogart (Charlie Allnutt), Katharine Hepburn (Rose Sayer), Robert Morley (The Rev. Samuel Sayer), Peter Bull (Captain), Theodore Bikel (2nd Officer)

  ROSE: 'I never dreamed that any experience could be so stimulating!'

'Entertaining but not entirely plausible or original.' – Robert Hatch

'The movie is not great art but it is great fun, essentially one long, exciting, old-fashioned movie chase.' – Time

'A Technicolor Cook's Tour of jungle wonders, enriched by performances unmatched by anything Hepburn or Bogart have yet contributed to the screen.' – Cue

† Peter Viertel's book, White Hunter Black Heart, filmed by Clint Eastwood, is basically about Huston during the making of this film. In 1987 Katharine Hepburn wrote a book about her experiences, entitled The Making Of The African Queen, or How I went to Africa with Bogart, Bacall and Huston and almost lost my mind.

AA: Humphrey Bogart

AAN: James Agee; John Huston; Katharine Hepburn

Afrodite Dea Dell'Amore: see *Aphrodite, Goddess of Love*

'Seduced Beyond The Limits Of Deception. Betrayed Beyond The Limits Of Desire.'

After Dark, My Sweet
US 1990 111m colour
Virgin/Avenue (Ric Kidney, Bob Redlin)
V, V*, L, S

A disturbed young drifter becomes involved with an alcoholic widow and a former policeman in a plan to kidnap a child.

Wildly melodramatic thriller with dull performances.

w Bob Redlin *novel* Jim Thompson *d* James Foley *ph* Mark Plummer *m* Maurice Jarre *ad* Kenneth A. Hardy *ed* Howard Smith

Jason Patric, Rachel Ward, Bruce Dern, George Dickerson, James Cotton

After Eight Hours: see *Society Doctor*

'When it's after midnight in New York City, you don't have to look for love, laughter and trouble. They'll all find you!'

After Hours **
US 1985 97m DuArt Color
Warner/Geffen/Double Play (Amy Robinson, Griffin Dunne, Robert F. Colesberry)
V, V*, L

Through a chapter of accidents, a mild-mannered computer programmer has a bad time in the night streets of New York.

An unsettling kind of black comedy with moments of malaise: nobody denies its touches of brilliance, but few people want to see it again.

w Joseph Minion *d* Martin Scorsese *ph* Michael Ballhaus *m* Howard Shore *pd* Jeffrey Townsend *ed* Thelma Schoonmaker

Griffin Dunne, Rosanna Arquette, Verna Bloom, Thomas Chong, Teri Garr, Cheech Marin

'The cinema of paranoia and persecution reaches an apogee . . . would have been pretty funny if it didn't play like a confirmation of everyone's worst fears about contemporary urban life.' – *Variety*

'A film so original, so particular, that one is uncertain from moment to moment exactly how to respond to it. Interesting.' – *Roger Ebert*

After Midnight (1950): see Captain Carey USA

After Midnight
Ireland 1990 100m colour
Lazer/Channel 4/Dublin Cinema Group (Maxine Julius)

An alcoholic nightwatchman in a Dublin hotel redeems himself with the help of a new assistant.

Despite the valiant efforts of Jaffrey, a broad farce that fails to amuse and sticks instead to clichéd characters and situations.

wd Shanis Grewal *ph* Jack Conroy *m* Mickey Gallagher *pd* Brien Vahey *ed* Carl Thomson

Saeed Jaffrey, Hayley Mills, Ian Dury, Dhirendra, Vladek Sheybal

After Office Hours
GB 1932 78m bw
British International

A bird's-eye view of life in a City of London office.

Popular film version of a popular play which would now seem almost Dickensian.

w Thomas Bentley, Frank Launder *play London Wall* by John Van Druten *d* Thomas Bentley

Frank Lawton, Heather Angel, Viola Lyel, Garry Marsh, Eileen Peel, Frank Royde, Katie Johnson

After Office Hours *
US 1935 75m bw
MGM (Bernard H. Hyman)

A newspaperman and his socialite reporter solve a murder mystery.

Crisply-written, fast-moving comedy melodrama; good stuff of its time and type.

w Herman J. Mankiewicz *d* Robert Z. Leonard *ph* Charles Rosher

Clark Gable, Constance Bennett, Stuart Erwin, Billie Burke, Harvey Stephens, Katherine Alexander, Henry Travers, Henry Armetta

'One of the best balanced pix of the season; it has practically everything.' – *Film Daily*

'Mildly satisfactory entertainment . . . story deficiencies are surprising . . . Gable and Bennett will have to carry this one.' – *Variety*

After the Ball *
GB 1957 89m Eastmancolor
IFD/Beaconsfield (Peter Rogers)

The life and loves of music-hall singer Vesta Tilley, who married into the nobility.

Adequate if uninspired biopic with entertaining detail and songs.

w Hubert Gregg *d* Compton Bennett *ph* Jack Asher *md* Muir Mathieson *ad* Norman Arnold

Pat Kirkwood, Laurence Harvey, Clive Morton, Jerry Verno, June Clyde

After the Fox *
US/Italy 1966 103m Technicolor Panavision
UA/Nancy/CCM (John Bryan)
V*

The Fox escapes from jail to execute a gold bullion caper and save his young sister from the streets.

Unlikeable and unfunny farce which sets its star among excitable Italians and hopes for the best, adding a few wild stabs at satire on movie-making styles.

w Neil Simon, Cesare Zavattini *d* Vittorio de Sica *ph* Leonida Barboni *m* Burt Bacharach

Peter Sellers, *Victor Mature* (agreeably sending up his old image), Britt Ekland, Lilia Brazzi, Paola Stoppa, Akim Tamiroff, Martin Balsam

'Never even begins to get off the ground.' – *MFB*

After the Rehearsal **
Sweden 1984 72m colour
Svenskfilmindustri/SV2
V*

After a rehearsal for Strindberg's *Dream Play,* the director sits and remembers the circumstances surrounding an earlier production.

Typical but satisfyingly unpretentious Bergman piece of the second rank.

wd Ingmar Bergman

Erland Josephson, Ingrid Thulin, Lena Olin

'What we are left with is the very strong sense of an artist who has sacrificed many lives for the sake of his art, and now wonders if perhaps one of those lives was his own.' – *Roger Ebert*

After the Thin Man **
US 1936 113m bw
MGM (Hunt Stromberg)
V*, L

Nick and Nora Charles, not forgetting Asta, solve another murder.

Overlong but well-carpentered sequel to *The Thin Man,* developing the thesis that a married couple, even if they are detectives and drink too much, can be interesting and lovable.

w Frances Goodrich, Albert Hackett *d* W. S. Van Dyke II *ph* Oliver T. Marsh *m* Herbert Stothart, Edward Ward

William Powell, Myrna Loy, James Stewart, Elissa Landi, Joseph Calleia, Jessie Ralph, Alan Marshal, Sam Levene

'It is evident that it was almost impossible to make a better mystery comedy than *The Thin Man.* Early speed would have helped, but . . . few films this season have contained more risibles.' – *Variety*

AAN: Frances Goodrich; Albert Hackett

After Tomorrow
US 1932 70m bw
Fox

Family troubles and small salaries prevent a young couple from getting married.

Rather curious drama which was sold on the fact that it retained the sex discussion from its stage original.

w Sonya Levien *play* John Golden, Hugh Stange *d* Frank Borzage

Charles Farrell, Marian Nixon, Minna Gombell, Josephine Hull, William Collier Snr, William Pawley

'In several sequences it pioneers for the picture business. That financial success is doubtful is rather unfortunate.' – *Variety*

After Tonight
US 1933 71m bw
RKO
GB title: *Sealed Lips*

During World War I a Russian lady spy falls for an Austrian officer.

Tediously talky romantic vehicle which barely gets started before it bogs down.

w Jane Murfin *d* George Archainbaud

Constance Bennett, Gilbert Roland, Edward Ellis, Mischa Auer

Agaguk: see *Shadow of the Wolf*

Against a Crooked Sky
US 1975 89m colour
Doty/Dayton

Two Westerners set out to find the sister of one of them, who has been kidnapped by Indians.

Very ordinary variation on *The Searchers,* which in itself was a bit tedious at times.

w Douglas G. Stewart, Eleanor Lamb *d* Earl Bellamy

Richard Boone, Stewart Petersen, Geoffrey Land, Jewel Blanch, Henry Wilcoxon

Against All Flags *
US 1952 83m Technicolor
U-I (Howard Christie)
V*, L

A daring British seaman routs Spanish ships at the request of the king.

Standard pirate yarn, almost Flynn's last swashbuckler; production below par.

w Aeneas Mackenzie, Joseph Hoffman *d* George Sherman *ph* Russell Metty *m* Hans Salter

Errol Flynn, Maureen O'Hara, Anthony Quinn, Mildred Natwick

† Remade as *The King's Pirate* (qv).
†† Though Flynn did most of his own stunts for this picture, he balked at the one involving sliding down through a sail on a rapier blade, which was originated by Douglas Fairbanks in *The Black Pirate;* it was performed by a stunt double.

Against All Odds

US 1984 121m Metrocolor
Columbia/Delphi (Jerry Bick)
V, V*, L, S

An unemployed football player is hired by a bookmaker to find his missing wife.

Complex and lugubrious remake of *Out of the Past* (qv), which long outstays its welcome.

w Eric Hughes   d Taylor Hackford   ph Donald Thorin, E. Pershing Flynn   m Michel Colombier, Larry Carlton   ad Richard James Lawrence

Jeff Bridges, Rachel Ward, James Woods, Richard Widmark, Jane Greer (from the original cast), Alex Karras, Dorian Harewood, Swoosie Kurtz

'It has so many convoluted double crosses that each time you are told what was really going on behind the scene you just witnessed, you care less.' – *Time Out*

'A tedious concatenation of narrative twists.' – *MFB*

'The best thing to do is accept the plot, then disregard it, and pay attention to the scenes of passion.' – *Roger Ebert*

AAN: title song (Phil Collins)

Against the Wind *

GB 1947 96m bw
Ealing (Sidney Cole)
V

In London during World War II, men and women are trained as saboteurs, and one of them is a traitor.

Thoughtful, well-made spy thriller with good performances; but a bit dour.

w T. E. B. Clarke, Michael Pertwee   d Charles Crichton   ph Lionel Banes   m Leslie Bridgewater

Simone Signoret, Robert Beatty, Jack Warner, Gordon Jackson, Paul Dupuis, Gisele Preville, John Slater, Peter Illing, James Robertson Justice

Agantuk **

India/France 1991 120m colour
Artificial Eye/National Film Development Corporation of India/
    Erato/DD/Soprofilms/Canal+ (Satyajit Ray)
aka: *The Stranger*

A Calcutta family suspect that a long-lost uncle who comes to stay may be an impostor.

A charming and humorous examination of cultural differences and ingrained prejudices.

wd Satyajit Ray   ph Barun Raha   m Satyajit Ray   ed Dulal Dutt

Dipankar De, Mamata Shankar, Deepankar De, Bikram Bhattacharya, Utpal Dutt, Dhritiman Chatterjee, Rabi Ghosh, Subrata Chatterjee

'A wise, witty and benevolent work, a worthy sign-off from a great film-maker.' – *Philip Kemp, Sight and Sound*

'Mitra, in Utpal Dutt's performance, combines, as Ray himself did, a powerful intellect and an unsentimental insight into human behaviour with a generosity of spirit and genuine humility.' – *Philip French, Observer*

† It was Ray's last film.

Agatha *

GB 1979 105m Technicolor
Warner/First Artists/Sweetwall/Casablanca (Jarvis Astaire, Gavrik Losey)
V, V*

In 1926, Agatha Christie disappears after marital difficulties and tries to commit suicide in a Harrogate hotel under a pseudonym.

Lushly recreated but still imaginary and unconvincing solution to a real-life disappearance, complete with romantic encounter with an American newspaperman.

w Kathleen Tynan, Arthur Hopcraft   d Michael Apted   ph Vittorio Storaro   m Johnny Mandel   pd Shirley Russell

Vanessa Redgrave, Dustin Hoffman, Timothy Dalton, Helen Morse, Timothy West, Tony Britton, Alan Badel

'With its shadowy characters, paucity of plot, and an abundance of stylistic red herrings, one doubts whether *Agatha* would have met Mrs Christie's own requirements for a thriller, though she may well have enjoyed its sumptuous recreation of hotel interiors in the 1920s.' – *Geoff Brown, MFB*

'It has a general air of knowingness, but seems to be missing the scenes which would explain why it was made.' – *New Yorker*

'There is no suspense, no tension and not even one good scene in this preposterous and ostentatious mess.' – *Motion Picture Guide*

L'Age d'Or **

France 1930 63m bw
Vicomte de Noailles

A collection of strange events satirizing religion and the social order.

Deliberately shocking and possibly quite meaningless, this truly surrealist film is chiefly interesting now for its flashforwards to Buñuel's later work.

w Luis Buñuel, Salvador Dali   d Luis Buñuel   ph Albert Dubergen   m Georges van Parys   ed Luis Buñuel

Gaston Modot, Lya Lys, Max Ernst, Pierre Prévert, Jacques Brunius

'In some way the juxtaposition of images causes in almost every spectator a train of reactions of unprecedented violence.' – *Basil Wright, 1972*

'The story is also a sequence of moral and surrealist aesthetic. The sexual instinct and the sense of death form its substance.' – *Luis Buñuel*

'It retains its outrageous anarchic vitality, as though unwilling to admit its age.' – *Observer 1980*

The Age for Love

US 1931 81m bw
UA/Howard Hughes

A wife does not want children; her husband leaves her and marries a woman who does.

Shapeless and would-be shocking, this forgotten film was written off as soon as it was made.

w Robert E. Sherwood, Frank Lloyd, Ernest Pascal   novel Ernest Pascal   d Frank Lloyd   m Alfred Newman

Billie Dove, Adrian Morris, Charles Starrett, Lois Wilson, Edward Everett Horton, Mary Duncan

'Everybody makes mistakes, and this is one by Howard Hughes.' – *Variety*

Age of Consent *

Australia 1969 103m Technicolor
Columbia/Nautilus (James Mason, Michael Powell)

An artist seduces the granddaughter of a drunken harridan with whom he shares a Barrier Reef island.

Mildly likeable but self-conscious and overlong South Pacific idyll.

w Peter Yeldham   novel Norman Lindsay   d Michael Powell   ph Hannes Staudinger   m Stanley Myers

James Mason, Helen Mirren, Jack McGowran, Neva Carr-Glyn, Frank Thring

Age of Indiscretion

US 1935 80m bw
MGM

A high-minded publisher finds that his wife is unfaithful.

Tolerable marital drama about child custody.

w Otis Garrett, Leon Gordon   story Lenore Coffee   d Edward Ludwig

Paul Lukas, Helen Vinson, May Robson, Madge Evans, Ralph Forbes

Age of Innocence

US 1934 71m bw
RKO

In the 1870s, a young attorney's career is threatened when he falls in love with a divorcee.

Dated romantic drama, rather thinly performed and presented.

w Sarah Y. Mason, Victor Heerman   novel Edith Wharton   d Philip Moeller

Irene Dunne, John Boles, Lionel Atwill, Laura Hope Crews, Helen Westley, Julie Haydon

'It will take smart selling to protect it at the box office, especially away from the social registers of the land.' – *Variety*

Age of Innocence

Canada/GB 1977 101m Eastmancolor
Judson/Willoughby (Henning Jacobsen)

After World War I, an English teacher in Canada develops pacifist views which stir up local resentment and lead to violence.

Rather uninteresting melodrama which never really comes to the boil despite care all round.

w Ratch Wallace   d Alan Bridges   ph Brian West   m Lucio Agostini

David Warner, Honor Blackman, Trudy Young, Cec Linder, Tim Henry, Lois Maxwell, Robert Hawkins

The Age of Innocence **

US 1993 138m Technicolor Super 35mm
Columbia (Barbara de Fina)
V, V*, L, S

In New York in the 1870s, a wealthy and conventional lawyer falls in love with his wife's cousin, a woman of dubious reputation.

A deft study of a repressed society with some effective set-pieces, let down by an insufficiently dramatized narrative; the emotional weight of the film is carried not by the actors, but by the voice-over, which severely limits its impact.

w Jay Cocks, Martin Scorsese   novel Edith Wharton   d Martin Scorsese   ph Michael Ballhaus   m Elmer Bernstein   pd Dante Ferretti   ed Thelma Schoonmaker

Daniel Day-Lewis, *Michelle Pfeiffer*, Winona Ryder, Richard E. Grant, Alec McCowen, Geraldine Chaplin, Mary Beth Hurt, Stuart Wilson, Miriam Margolyes, Sian Phillips, Michael Gough, Alexis Smith, Jonathan Pryce, Robert Sean Leonard

'Scorsese has met most of the challenges inherent in tackling such a formidable period piece, but the material remains cloaked by the very propriety, stiff manners and emotional starchiness the picture delineates in such copious detail.' – *Variety*

'The great virtue of the film is that it takes the past seriously and sets about the task of bringing it to life detail by detail, without false immediacy.' – *Adam Mars-Jones*

'For those whose idea of bliss is watching handsome people in a well-told story of love and denial, this is ecstasy from scene one.' – *Angie Errigo, Empire*

AAN: Winona Ryder; Jay Cocks, Martin Scorsese; Elmer Bernstein; Dante Ferretti; costume design (Gabriella Pescucci)

Agency

Canada 1981 94m colour
Farley
V*

An advertising agency gets into political hands which send out messages through special TV packs.

Faded melodrama which did nothing for anyone involved in it.

w Noel Hynd novel Paul Gottlieb d George Kaczender

Robert Mitchum, Lee Majors, Valerie Perrine, Saul Rubinek, Alexandra Stewart

Agent 8¾: see *Hot Enough for June*

Agent for Harm

US 1966 84m colour
Universal (Joseph F. Robertson)

A Washington agency prevents the Russians from abducting a scientist.

Spy spoof somewhat below the level of the TV *UNCLE* films.

w Blair Robertson d Gerd Oswald

Wendell Corey, Mark Richman, Martin Kosleck, Carl Esmond, Barbara Bouchet

Aggie Appleby Maker of Men

US 1933 73m bw
RKO
GB title: *Cupid in the Rough*

An eccentric girl can't decide between a wimp she has turned into a roughneck and a tough guy she has turned into a sissy.

Dim comedy which doesn't seem to know its own mind.

w Humphrey Pearson, Edward Kaufman play Joseph Kesselring d Mark Sandrich

Wynne Gibson, Charles Farrell, William Gargan, Betty Furness, Blanche Friderici, ZaSu Pitts

The Agitator *

GB 1944 98m bw
British National (Louis H. Jackson)

An embittered mechanic becomes a loud-mouthed union spokesman, but fate eventually takes him into management.

Fairly absorbing, modest narrative of the flaws of socialism.

w Edward Dryhurst novel *Peter Pettinger* by William Riley d John Harlow ph James Wilson

William Hartnell (then being built into a star), Mary Morris, John Laurie, Moore Marriott, George Carney, Edward Rigby, Elliot Mason, Frederick Leister, Cathleen Nesbitt, Moira Lister

Agnes of God *

US 1985 98m Metrocolor
Columbia/Delphi IV (Patrick Palmer, Norman Jewison)
V, V*, L, S

A young nun is accused of giving birth and then killing her baby.

Heavy hysterical weather with no clear solution, but a field day for three actresses.

w John Pielmeier play John Pielmeier d Norman Jewison ph Sven Nykvist m Georges Delerue pd Ken Adam ed Antony Gibbs

Jane Fonda, Anne Bancroft, Meg Tilly

'Predictably, religion and reason play to something like a draw.' – *Variety*

AAN: Anne Bancroft; Meg Tilly (supporting actress); music

Agonia: see *Agony*

Agony **

USSR 1975 148m colour/bw
Mosfilm/Second Film Group
V*
original title: *Agonia*; aka: *Rasputin*

As discontent at the rule of the Tsar increases, and revolution looms in Russia, the monk Rasputin becomes the power behind the throne.

A gripping account of the downfall of the Romanovs and the extraordinary life and death of Rasputin, mixing drama and contemporary newsreels; at times it comes near to being a history lesson, but it fascinates for all that. Nine years in the making, it was banned for ten years by the Soviet authorities.

w Semyon Lungin, Ilya Nusinov d Elem Klimov ph Leonid Kalashnikov md Eri Klas m Alfred Schittke

Alexei Petrenko, Anatoly Romashin, Velta Line, Alisa Freindlikh

† The film also exists in a version that runs for 107m.

The Agony and the Ecstasy *

US 1965 140m DeLuxe Todd-AO
TCF/International Classics Inc (Carol Reed)
V*, L, S

Pope Julius II persuades Michelangelo to leave his sculptures and paint the ceiling of the Sistine Chapel.

Dully reverent comic strip approach to art and history; generally heavy going, but good looking.

w Philip Dunne novel Irving Stone d Carol Reed ph Leon Shamroy m Alex North pd John DeCuir

Charlton Heston, Rex Harrison, Diane Cilento, Harry Andrews, Alberto Lupo, Adolfo Celi

JULIUS: 'You dare to dicker with your pontiff?'

'The vulgarity of the whole concept has none of the joyfully enthusiastic philistinism of a de Mille; rather its tone is a dry, almost cynical, condescension.' – *Brenda Davies*

'All agony, no ecstasy.' – *Judith Crist*

'Not a strong and soaring drama but an illustrated lecture of a slow artist at work.' – *Bosley Crowther*

'Heston hits the ceiling.' – *New York Times*

† The film is said to have cost 12 million dollars and earned 4.
†† Michelangelo was apparently both a dwarf and a homosexual. He is played by Charlton Heston.

AAN: Leon Shamroy; Alex North

Aguirre, Wrath of God ****

West Germany 1972 95m colour
Hessicher Rundfunk/Werner Herzog
V, V*, S

In 1560, one of Pizarro's lieutenants takes a party of forty down river by raft, and succumbs to megalomania.

Absorbing conquistador melodrama, vividly assembled and impossible to forget.

wd Werner Herzog ph Thomas Mauch m Popol Vuh

Klaus Kinski, Ruy Guerra, Helena Rojo, Cecilia Rivera

'It ingeniously combines Herzog's gift for deep irony, his strong social awareness, and his worthy ambition to fashion a whole new visual perspective on the world around us via mystical, evocative, yet oddly direct imagery. It is a brilliant cinematic achievement.' – *David Skerritt, Christian Science Monitor*

Ah! Les Belles Bacchantes: see *Femmes de Paris*

'The play that startled the nation!'
Ah, Wilderness **

US 1935 101m bw
MGM (Hunt Stromberg)
V*

Problems of a small-town family at the turn of the century.

Well-acted, affectionately remembered version of a play later musicalized as *Summer Holiday*. The

commercial success of this film led to the Hardy family series.

w Albert Hackett, Frances Goodrich play Eugene O'Neill d Clarence Brown ph Clyde de Vinna m Herbert Stothart

Wallace Beery, Lionel Barrymore, Eric Linden, Spring Byington, Mickey Rooney, Aline MacMahon, Charley Grapewin, Cecilia Parker, Frank Albertson, Bonita Granville

'A job of picture making, in craftsmanship and feeling, that is wonderful to see.' – *Otis Ferguson*

'That it is a fine artistic effort will not be denied anywhere, but for the public at large it will need all the boosting it can get.' – *Variety*

A-Haunting We Will Go *

US 1942 68m bw
TCF (Sol M. Wurtzel)
V

Gangsters dupe Laurel and Hardy into escorting a coffin, which is accidentally switched with one used in a magic act.

Nothing whatever to do with haunting: a poor comedy with no typical material for the stars, but interesting as a record of the touring show of Dante the Magician.

w Lou Breslow d Alfred Werker ph Glen MacWilliams m Emil Newman

Stan Laurel, Oliver Hardy, *Dante*, Sheila Ryan, John Shelton, Elisha Cook Jnr

'The comedians' lack of enthusiasm for their material is rather evident.' – *William K. Everson, 1967*

Ai No Corrida **

France/Japan 1976 105m Eastmancolor
Argos/Oshima/Shibata (Anatole Dauman)
French title: *L'Empire des Sens*
aka: *Empire of the Passions; Empire of the Senses*

A sexually complicated servant girl has an intense affair with the master of the house, and finally murders and mutilates him.

Strong but stylish stuff, a kind of Japanese *Last Tango in Paris*. Those who like this kind of thing will like it a lot.

wd Nagisa Oshima ph Hideo Ito m Minoru Miki

Tatsuya Fuji, Eiko Matsuda, Aoi Nakajima, Meika Seri

'By the final sequence, we are all implicated in the continuing social system which makes such love impossible. It is not Sade, but the censor in all of us who ultimately wields the knife.' – *Jan Dawson, MFB*

† The film was not given a certificate by the BBFC or a cinema release in Britain until 1991, although it had been shown in cinema clubs.

Aida

Italy 1953 95m Ferraniacolor
Oscar Film (Ferrucio de Martino, Federico Teti)

A young Egyptian army officer loves the captive princess of the Ethiopians.

Stuffy, over-dressed, pantomimish version of the opera, with some pretension to cinematic vitality.

w various opera Verdi d Clemente Fracassi ph Piero Portalupi ad Flavio Mogherini

Sophia Loren (sung by Renata Tebaldi), Lois Maxwell, Luciano della Marra

Aimez-Vous les Femmes?: see *Do You Like Women?*

Ain't Misbehavin' *

US 1955 81m Technicolor
U-I (Samuel Marx)

A young millionaire marries a cabaret girl, who determines to improve her mind and manners.

Lively American version of *Pygmalion*, with musical numbers and some bright lines.

w Edward Buzzell, Philip Rapp, Devery Freeman d Edward Buzzell ph Wilfrid Cline m Joseph Gershenson ch Kenny Williams, Lee Scott

Rory Calhoun, *Piper Laurie, Reginald Gardiner,* Jack Carson, Barbara Britton, Mamie Van Doren

Air America
US 1990 118m DeLuxe
Guild/Indieprod/Carolco (Daniel Melnick)
V, V*, L, S

CIA pilots indulge in illicit activities in Laos.

Frenetic mix of action and comedy – and unsuccessful at both.

w John Eskow, Richard Rush book Christopher Robbins d Roger Spottiswoode ph Roger Deakins m Charles Gross pd Allan Cameron ed John Bloom, Lois Freeman-Fox

Mel Gibson, Robert Downey Jnr, Nancy Travis, Ken Jenkins, David Marshall Grant, Lane Smith, Art La Fleur, Ned Eisenberg, Marshall Bell

'Are you going to let that boy go up alone?'
Air Cadet
US 1951 94m bw
Universal-International
GB title: *Jet Men of the Air*

Problems of an air force flight instructor.

Routine flagwaver.

w Robert L. Richards d Joseph Pevney

Stephen McNally, Alex Nicol, Gail Russell, Richard Long, Charles Drake, Rock Hudson

Air Force *
US 1943 124m bw
Warner (Hal B. Wallis)
V*

A Flying Fortress and its crew see action in Manila, Pearl Harbor and the Coral Sea.

Propaganda piece concentrating on the characters of the crew members, with action set-pieces largely provided by newsreel; but skilled direction still conveys plenty of punch.

w Dudley Nichols d Howard Hawks ph James Wong Howe, Elmer Dyer, Charles Marshall m Franz Waxman ed George Amy

John Garfield, Gig Young, Arthur Kennedy, Charles Drake, John Ridgley, Harry Carey, George Tobias, Stanley Ridges, Moroni Olsen, Edward Brophy

'Maybe the story is high-flown, maybe it overdraws a recorded fact a bit. We'd hate to think it couldn't happen – or didn't – because it leaves you feeling awfully good.' – *Bosley Crowther*

'The film is one crisis after another, and the director stages the air battles handsomely, but for the rest it helps if you're interested in the factors involved in getting a bomber somewhere and back.' – *Pauline Kael, 70s*

AA: George Amy

AAN: Dudley Nichols; James Wong Howe, Elmer Dyer, Charles Marshall

Air Hawks
US 1935 68m bw
Columbia

Two aviation firms battle for airmail contracts.

Routine low-budget action drama inspired by the stratosphere cross-continent flights of Wiley Post (who appears as himself and was killed later in the year along with Will Rogers).

w Griffin Jay and Grace Neville d Albert Rogell

Ralph Bellamy, Wiley Post, Tala Birell, Douglass Dumbrille, Victor Kilian

'Word-of-mouth bally should help in face of marquee weakness.' – *Variety*

Air Mail *
US 1932 84m bw
Universal

Brash young pilot effects a daring rescue and gets the mail through.

Moderate actioner of its time.

w Dale Van Every, Frank Wead d John Ford

Pat O'Brien, Ralph Bellamy, Russell Hopton, Gloria Stuart, Lillian Bond, Slim Summerville

'Far short of a smash . . . it has no sock name, it is weak on the romantic side and the story material is directed at men.' – *Variety*

† There was also a good silent version in 1925, with Warner Baxter and Douglas Fairbanks Jnr, written by James Shelley Hamilton and directed by Irvin Willat; both had remarkable similarities to *Only Angels Have Wings* (1938).

Air Raid Wardens
US 1943 67m bw
MGM (B. F. Zeidman)
V, V*

Rejected by the armed services, two incompetent air raid wardens accidentally round up Nazi spies.

Well below par star comedy: their incomparable dignity has disappeared.

w Jack Jevne, Martin Rackin, Charles Rogers, Harry Crane d Edward Sedgwick ph Walter Lundin m Nathaniel Shilkret

Stan Laurel, Oliver Hardy, Edgar Kennedy, Jacqueline White, Stephen McNally, Nella Walker, Donald Meek

The Airmail Mystery
US 1932 bw serial: 12 eps
Universal

An airmail pilot owns a gold mine which interests the evil Black Hawk.

Reasonably lively fisticuff saga in which the villain has devised an 'aerial catapult' for launching planes. d Ray Taylor

James Flavin (later familiar as an Irish cop), Lucile Browne, Wheeler Oakman, Walter Brennan

Airplane **
US 1980 88m Metrocolor
Paramount/Howard W. Koch (Jon Davison)
V, V*, L

A former pilot gets his nerve back when called upon to land a passenger plane because the crew all have food poisoning.

Arthur Hailey's play *Flight into Danger* and the film *Zero Hour* which was made from it get the zany parody treatment in this popular movie which is often funny but sometimes merely crude. It rang the box-office bell more loudly than most expensive epics of its year.

wd Jim Abrahams, David and Jerry Zucker ph Joseph Biroc m Elmer Bernstein pd Ward Preston

Robert Stack, Lloyd Bridges, Robert Hays, Julie Hagerty, Peter Graves, Leslie Nielsen, Lorna Patterson, Ethel Merman, Kareem Abdul-Jabbar

'Parody may be the lowest form of humour, but few comedies in ages have rocked the laugh meter this hard.' – *Variety*

'It keeps going, like a dervish with skids on.' – *Derek Malcolm, Guardian*

'Proof that the cinema is alive and well and bursting with ingenuity.' – *David Hughes, Sunday Times*

'It's compiled like a jokebook and has the kind of pacing that goes with a laugh track.' – *Pauline Kael*

'All pretty juvenile really, though the relentless pace and sheer poor taste make up for a lack of originality.' – *Time Out, 1984*

'Practically a satirical anthology of movie clichés . . . it compensates for its lack of original comic invention by its utter willingness to steal, beg, borrow and rewrite from anywhere.' – *Roger Ebert*

'Just when you thought it safe to go back into the departure lounge'
Airplane II: The Sequel
US 1982 85m Metrocolor
Paramount (Howard W. Koch)
V, V*, L

A space shuttle gets into trouble but is rescued in the nick of time.

Palsied sequel to a funny film, with some of the same cast and some of the same jokes.

wd Ken Finkleman ph Joe Biroc m Elmer Bernstein pd William Sandell ed Dennis Virkler

Robert Hays, Julie Hagerty, Lloyd Bridges, Peter Graves, William Shatner, Chad Everett, Steven Stucker, Sonny Bono, Raymond Burr, Chuck Connors, Rip Torn, John Dehner, Kent McCord, John Vernon

'All the pleasure lies in the humour's weakness.' – *Observer*

Airport ***
US 1970 136m Technicolor Todd-AO
Universal/Ross Hunter (Jacque Mapes)
V, V*, L, S

Events of one snowy night at a midwestern international airport, culminating in airborne melodrama when a mad bomber is killed and the damaged plane has to be talked down.

Glossy, undeniably entertaining, all-star version of a popular novel, with cardboard characters skilfully deployed in Hollywood's very best style.

w George Seaton novel Arthur Hailey ph Ernest Laszlo m Alfred Newman ed Stuart Gilmore

Burt Lancaster, Dean Martin, Jean Seberg, *Helen Hayes,* Van Heflin, Jacqueline Bisset, George Kennedy, Maureen Stapleton, Barry Nelson, Dana Wynter, Lloyd Nolan, Barbara Hale, Gary Collins, Jessie Royce Landis

'The best film of 1944.' – *Judith Crist*

'For sheer contentment there is nothing to beat the sight of constant catastrophe happening to others.' – *Alexander Walker*

'A *Grand Hotel* in the sky . . . every few years or so some more show-biz types would crowd onto a plane that would threaten to crash, collide with another, meet with terrorists, or otherwise be subjected to the perils of Pauline.' – *Les Keyser, Hollywood in the Seventies*

† The film cost 10 million dollars and earned 45.

AA: Helen Hayes

AAN: best picture; George Seaton (as writer); Ernest Laszlo; Alfred Newman; Maureen Stapleton; editing; costumes (Edith Head)

'Something hit us . . . the crew is dead . . . help us, please, please help us!'
Airport 1975
US 1974 105m Technicolor Panavision
Universal (Jennings Lang, William Frye)
V*

A private aircraft collides with a jet plane and kills or immobilizes its crew, so a stewardess has to manoeuvre the jumbo to safety.

Inept airborne suspenser loaded with stars who do nothing and marred by continuity lapses and boring dialogue.

w Don Ingalls d Jack Smight ph Philip Lathrop m John Cacavas

Charlton Heston, *Karen Black*, George Kennedy, Helen Reddy, Efrem Zimbalist Jnr, Susan Clark, Myrna Loy, Gloria Swanson, Linda Blair, Dana Andrews, Roy Thinnes, Sid Caesar, Ed Nelson, Nancy Olson, Martha Scott

'Aimed squarely for the yahoo trade.' – *Variety*

'Processed schlock. One can have a fairly good time laughing at it, but it doesn't sit too well as a joke, because the people on the screen are being humiliated.' – *Pauline Kael, New Yorker*

'Good exciting corny escapism, and the kind of movie you would not want to watch as an inflight film.' – *Roger Ebert*

Airport '77

US 1977 114m Technicolor Panavision
Universal (William Frye)
V, V*, L

A private airliner loaded with guests and art treasures hits an oil rig and settles underwater on a sandbank.

Hysteria, rescue, and guest stars with nothing to do; the mixture as before.

w Michael Scheff, David Spector *d* Jerry Jameson *ph* Philip Lathrop *m* John Cacavas *pd* George C. Webb

Jack Lemmon, James Stewart, Brenda Vaccaro, Joseph Cotten, Olivia de Havilland, Lee Grant, Darren McGavin, Christopher Lee, Robert Foxworth, Robert Hooks, Monte Markham, Kathleen Quinlan, James Booth

'Neither as riveting as it should be, nor as much fun as its absurd plotline would suggest.' – *Verina Glaessner, MFB*

† See also: *The Concorde – Airport '79.*

Airport '80: The Concorde: see *The Concorde: Airport '79*

Akahige: see *Redbeard*

Akasen Chitai: see *Street of Shame*

Åke and His World *

Sweden 1984 103m colour
Sandrew/Svenska Film Institute/Scentext
original title: *Åke Och Hans Värld*

In the 1930s the six-year-old son of a Swedish country doctor observes the lives and deaths of his father's patients.

Charming, episodic, gently nostalgic account of childhood.

wd Allan Edwall *ph* Jörgen Persson *m* Thomas Lindahl *ad* Anna Asp *ed* Lars Hagström

Martin Lindstrom, Loa Falkman, Gunnel Fred, Katja Blomquist, Ulla Sjöblom, Suzanne Ernrup, Björn Gustafson, Allan Edwall

Akenfield *

GB 1974 98m Techniscope
Angle Films/LWT (Peter Hall, Rex Pyke)

Semi-dramatized film version of a book which documented a Suffolk village by interviewing its older inhabitants.

An interesting venture ruined by imprecision, misty photography, lack of narrative drive or any compensating detail, and the appalling error of using a cheap wide screen process.

w Ronald Blythe *book* Ronald Blythe *d* Peter Hall *ph* Ivan Strasberg *m* Michael Tippett *ad* Ian Whittaker, Roger Christian

Garrow Shand, Peggy Cole, Barbara Tilney, Lyn Brooks, Ida Page, Ted Dedman, Peter Tuddenham

'One of the best films – certainly the most unusual – made in England and about England.' – *Alexander Walker*

'A parochial drama-documentary, commercially dubious but otherwise an impressive achievement.' – *Variety*

'About the impact of the leading players, the beauty of the Edwardian scenes and the triumphantly enhancing use of music, there need be no reservations at all.' – *Michael Ratcliffe*

Akira (dubbed) **

Japan 1987 124m colour
ICA/Akira Committee (Ryohei Suzuki, Shunzo Kato)
V, V*, L, S

In a future neo-Tokyo, filled with revolutionaries, terrorists and warring government factions, a young biker becomes the subject of experiments to create a super-being.

Brilliantly animated film, based on a comic-book, that eschews cartoon violence for the more realistic style of action movies. The narrative, which begins as fantasy and shifts into mysticism, is less enthralling.

w Katsuhiro Otomo, Izo Hashimoto *comic* Katsuhiro Otomo *ph* Katsuji Misawa *m* Shoji Yamashiro *ad* Toshiharu Mizutani *ed* Takeshi Seyama

'Probably the first animated feature with a genuinely novelistic density of incident and character.' – *Tony Rayns, MFB*

Akira Kurosawa's Dreams *

US 1990 119m colour
Warner/Akira Kurosawa USA (Hisao Kurosawa, Mike Y. Inoue)
V, V*, L

Eight dream sequences, concerning animals, ghosts, spirits and nuclear destruction, the most successful of which involves entering the paintings of Van Gogh.

A lesser work of a master: visually fascinating, though too often trite in content.

wd Akira Kurosawa *ph* Takao Saito, Masaharu Ueda *m* Shinichiro Ikebe *ad* Yoshiro Muraki, Akira Sakuragi *ed* Tome Minami

Mitsuko Baisho, Toshihiko Nakano, Mitsunori Isaki, Mie Suzuki, Akira Terao, Mieko Harada, Yoshitaka Zushi, Martin Scorsese, Chosuke Ikariya, Chishu Ryu

'His is not to shock us into surrendering to his visions but to seduce our consent to them. And this he does in one of the most lucid dreamworks ever placed on film.' – *Richard Schickel, Time*

Al Capone **

US 1959 105m bw
Allied Artists (John H. Burrows, Leonard J. Ackerman)
V, V*

An account of Chicago's most famous gangster, up to his arrest for income tax evasion.

Only slightly overplayed, semi-documentary retelling of a larger-than-life true story.

w Malvin Wald, Henry Greenberg *d* Richard Wilson *ph* Lucien Ballard *m* David Raksin

Rod Steiger (a clever impersonation on the border of caricature), Fay Spain, Murvyn Vye, Nehemiah Persoff, Martin Balsam, James Gregory, Joe de Santis

'The most remarkable thing about it is its truth.' – *Daily Telegraph*

'This powerful production may turn out to be the definitive gangster film of all time.' – *Film Daily*

Al Jennings of Oklahoma

US 1950 78m Technicolor
Columbia

A lawyer becomes a Western outlaw.

Tolerable co-feature which strays from the truth.

w George Bricker *d* Ray Nazarro

Dan Duryea, Gale Storm, Dick Foran, Gloria Henry, Guinn Williams

'Imagine if you had three wishes, three hopes, three dreams and they all could come true.'

Aladdin ****

US 1992 90m Technicolor
Buena Vista/Walt Disney (John Musker, Ron Clements)

An urchin with a magic lamp falls in love with a runaway princess.

Another brilliant return to classic form from Disney, notable for its quick-change genie to match the exuberance of Robin Williams' characterisation, and some innovative computer animation.

wd John Musker, Ron Clements, Ted Elliott, Terry Rossio *m* Alan Menken *pd* R. S. Vander Wende *m/ly* Alan Menken, Howard Ashman, Tim Rice *ed* H. Lee Peterson

voices of Scott Weinger, Brad Kane (Aladdin's singing), Robin Williams, Linda Larkin, Lea Salonga (Jasmine's singing), Jonathan Freeman, Frank Welker, Gilbert Gottfried, Douglas Seale

'Floridly beautiful, shamelessly derivative and infused with an irreverent, sophisticated comic flair.' – *Variety*

'A rollicking, bodaciously choreographed fantasy right out of Busby Berkeley.' – *Washington Post*

AA: Alan Menken (score); song: 'Whole New World' (*m* Alan Menken, *l* Tim Rice)

AAN: song: 'Friends like Me' (*m* Alan Menken, *l* Howard Ashman); sound; sound effects editing

Alakazam the Great *

Japan 1960 88m Eastmancolor
Toei (Hiroshi Okawa)
V*
original title: *Saiyu-ki*

The arrogant monkey king of the animals is sent by his human master on a pilgrimage; he defeats evil King Gruesome and returns a hero.

Smartly animated, Disney-inspired cartoon based on the same legend as *Monkey*, translated by Arthur Waley.

w Osamu Tezuka, Keinosuke Uekusa *d* Taiji Yabushita

'The Mission That Became A Fortress ... The Fortress That Became A Shrine ...'

The Alamo *

US 1960 193m Technicolor Todd-AO
UA/Batjac/John Wayne
V, V (W), V*, L, S

In 1836 a small southern fort becomes the centre of Texas' fight for independence, but it is suddenly annihilated by a Mexican raid, and all its defenders killed.

Sprawling historical epic with many irrelevant episodes and distracting changes of mood.

w James Edward Grant *d* John Wayne *ph* William H. Clothier *m* Dimitri Tiomkin *ed* Stuart Gilmore

John Wayne (as Crockett), Richard Widmark (Bowie), Laurence Harvey (Travis), Richard Boone (Houston), Frankie Avalon, Patrick Wayne, Linda Cristal, Chill Wills, Joseph Calleia

CROCKETT: 'Republic. I like the sound of the word. It means people can live free, talk free, go or come, buy or sell, be drunk or sober, however they choose. Some words give you a feeling. Republic is one of those words that makes me tight in the throat – the same tightness a man gets when his baby takes his first step or his first baby shaves and makes his first sound like a man. Some words can give you a feeling that makes your heart warm. Republic is one of those words.'

'Its sole redeeming feature lies in one of those crushing climaxes of total massacre which Hollywood can still pull off thunderingly well.' – *Peter John Dyer*

AAN: best picture; William H. Clothier; Dimitri Tiomkin; Chill Wills; song 'The Green Leaves of Summer' (*m* Dimitri Tiomkin, *ly* Paul Francis Webster); editing

Alamo Bay

US   1985   98m   Metrocolor
Tri-Star/Delphi III (Louis and Vincent Malle)
V, V*, L

Fisherfolk in Galveston Bay resent the intrusion of refugee Vietnamese.

Unsympathetic, slow-paced melodrama which ends up seeming pointless despite a Ku Klux Klan confrontation.

w Alice Arlen   *d* Louis Malle   *ph* Curtis Clark
m Ry Cooder   *pd* Trevor Williams   *ed* James Bruce

Amy Madigan, Ed Harris, Donald Moffat, Rudy Young, Ho Nguyen

'A failed piece of social consciousness.' – *Variety*

Alaska Highway

US   1943   66m   bw
Paramount/Pine-Thomas

Engineer brothers blaze a trail for the Army Engineer Corps, and fall for the same girl.

Routine sock-it-to-me adventure romance with process photography.

w Maxwell Shane, Lewis R. Foster   *d* Frank McDonald

Richard Arlen, Jean Parker, Ralph Sanford, Bill Henry

Alaska Seas

US   1953   78m   bw
Paramount (Mel Epstein)

Alaska fishermen oppose the crooked owner of the local cannery.

Insipid remake of *Spawn of the North* (qv).

w Geoffrey Homes, Walter Doniger   *d* Jerry Hopper
ph William C. Mellor   *md* Irvin Talbot

Robert Ryan, Gene Barry, Jan Sterling, Brian Keith, Richard Shannon

The Alaskan *

US   1924   80m approx   bw
Famous Players/Paramount

An Alaskan defies robber barons intent on corrupting the new state.

Tough, effective and straightforward action drama, one of its star's best roles.

w Willis Goldbeck   *novel* James Oliver Curwood
d Herbert Brenon

Thomas Meighan, Estelle Taylor, John Sainpolis, Anna May Wong

L'Albatross (dubbed)

France   1971   90m   Eastmancolor
Antony Balch/Balzac/Profilm/Belstar (Jean-Pierre Mocky, Jacques Dorfmann, Frédérick Dorfmann)
GB title: *Love Hat*

After escaping from prison, a man accused of murder goes on the run, taking as hostage the daughter of a left-wing politician.

Complex romantic and political thriller, with an atmosphere ruined by its insensitive dubbing.

w Jean-Pierre Mocky, Claude Veillot, Raphael Delpard   *d* Jean-Pierre Mocky   *ph* Marcel Weiss
m Léo Ferré   *ad* Jacques Flamand, Jacques Dor
ed Marguerite Renoir

Jean-Pierre Mocky, Marion Game, André Le Gall, Paul Muller, Francis Terzian

Albert RN **

GB   1953   88m   bw
Dial (Daniel M. Angel)
US title: *Break to Freedom*

Prisoners of war construct a lifelike dummy to cover the absence of escaping prisoners.

Competent, entertaining version of a successful play: an archetypal POW comedy drama.

w Guy Morgan, Vernon Harris   *play* Guy Morgan, Edward Sammis   *d* Lewis Gilbert   *ph* Jack Asher
m Malcolm Arnold

Jack Warner, Anthony Steel, Robert Beatty, William Sylvester, Anton Diffring, Eddie Byrne, Guy Middleton, Paul Carpenter, Frederick Valk

Albuquerque

US   1947   89m   Cinecolor
Pine-Thomas/Paramount
GB title: *Silver City*

The nephew of a town tyrant steps in to save an independent wagon line.

Formula Western with adequate action.

w Gene Lewis and Clarence Upson Young
novel Luke Short   *d* Ray Enright

Randolph Scott, Barbara Britton, George 'Gabby' Hayes, George Cleveland, Lon Chaney Jnr, Russell Hayden

Alcatraz Island

US   1937   64m   bw
Warner/Cosmopolitan

The federal government decides to build a top-security prison on a rock in San Francisco Bay.

Cheap routine treatment of what might have been an interesting subject.

w Crane Wilbur   *d* William McGann

Ann Sheridan, Mary Maguire, Dick Purcell, Addison Richards, *George E. Stone*, Doris Lloyd, John Litel

'Should about complete the Warner file on prisons.' – *Variety*

The Alchemist

US   1981   84m   DeLuxe
Video Form/Ideal Films (Lawrence Applebaum)
V*

A beautiful woman cures a man of his century-old curse.

Low-budget amalgam of horror movie clichés, inexpertly combined.

w Alan J. Adler   *d* Charles Band   *ph* Andrew W. Friend   *m* Richard H. Band   *pd* Dale A. Pelton
ad Pam Warner   *ed* Ted Nicolaou

Robert Ginty, Lucinda Dooling, John Sanderford, Viola Kate Stimpson, Robert Glaudini

Alex and the Gypsy

US   1976   99m   DeLuxe
TCF (Richard Shepherd)

A cynical California bailbondsman involved in illicit activities chooses romantic freedom with a gypsy girl.

Incoherent hardbitten romance with an unconvincing set of characters.

w Lawrence B. Marcus   *novel* The Bailbondsman by Stanley Elkin   *d* John Korty   *ph* Bill Butler
m Henry Mancini

Jack Lemmon, Geneviève Bujold, James Woods, Gino Ardito, Robert Emhardt

'Even if it were well done (which it is not) it would be banal, predictable and cloying.' – *Frank Rich*

'Off the beaten track, but that's just about the only thing you can give it points for.' – *Pauline Kael*

Alex in Wonderland

US   1970   109m   colour
MGM (Larry Tucker)

A Hollywood director finds life tedious.

So did the small paying audiences who saw this pale imitation of Fellini. (Some wags called it *One and a Half*.)

w Paul Mazursky, Larry Tucker   *d* Paul Mazursky
ph Laszlo Kovacs   *m* Tom O'Horgan   *pd* Pato Guzman   *ed* Stuart H. Pappe

Donald Sutherland, Jeanne Moreau, Ellen Burstyn, Federico Fellini

'The Fellini elements are laid onto the film and don't quite sink in . . . but the human story does work, remarkably well.' – *Roger Ebert*

Alexander Hamilton *

US   1931   73m   bw
Warner

The life of America's 18th-century financier.

Star biopic, highly satisfying in its day.

w Julian Josephson, Maude Howell, George Arliss
d John G. Adolfi   *ph* James Van Trees

George Arliss, Doris Kenyon, Montagu Love, Dudley Digges, Lionel Belmore, Ralf Harolde, Alan Mowbray

Alexander Nevsky ****

USSR   1938   112m   bw
Mosfilm
V, V*, L

In 1242, Prince Alexander Nevsky defeats the invading Teutonic Knights in a battle on the ice of Lake Peipus.

A splendid historical pageant which shows the director at his most inventively pictorial and climaxes in a superb battle sequence using music instead of natural sound.

w Pyotr Pavlenko, Sergei Eisenstein   *d Sergei Eisenstein*   *ph Edouard Tissé*   *m* Prokofiev   *ad* I. Shpinel, N. Soloviov, K. Yeliseyev

Nikolai Cherkassov, Nikolai Okhlopkov, Andrei Abrikosov, Dmitri Orlov

'The picture will meet with good results wherever its political sentiments find established adherents. Otherwise it's almost nil for general appeal.' – *Variety*

'Superb sequences of cinematic opera that pass from pastoral to lamentation and end in a triumphal cantata.' – *Georges Sadoul*

'The colossus who conquered the world! The most colossal motion picture of all time!'

Alexander the Great *

US   1956   135m   Technicolor   Cinemascope
UA/Robert Rossen
V*, L, S

The life and early death at 33 of the Macedonian warrior who conquered the entire known world.

Dour impassive epic which despite good intelligent stretches makes one long for Hollywood's usual more ruthless view of history.

wd Robert Rossen   *ph* Robert Krasker   *m* Mario Nascimbene   *ad* Andrei Andreiev

Richard Burton, Fredric March, Danielle Darrieux, Claire Bloom, Barry Jones, Harry Andrews, Peter Cushing, Stanley Baker, Michael Hordern, Niall MacGinnis

'Not a scene is held for a second longer than it is worth; greatness is pictured in constant dissolve.' – *Alexander Walker*

'Rossen has aimed for greatness and lost honourably.' – *Andrew Sarris*

Alexander's Ragtime Band ***

US   1938   106m   bw
TCF (Darryl F. Zanuck, Harry Joe Brown)
V*

Between 1911 and 1939, two songwriters vie for the affections of a rising musical comedy star.

Archetypal chronicle musical with 26 songs: well-paced, smartly made, and bursting with talent.

w Kathryn Scola, Lamar Trotti, Richard Sherman d Henry King ph Peverell Marley md Alfred Newman m/ly Irving Berlin ad Bernard Herzbrun, Boris Leven ed Barbara McLean

Tyrone Power, Alice Faye, Don Ameche, Ethel Merman, Jack Haley, Jean Hersholt, Helen Westley, John Carradine, Paul Hurst, Wally Vernon, Ruth Terry, Eddie Collins, Douglas Fowley, Chick Chandler

'A grand filmusical which stirs and thrills, finding response in the American heart to memories of the exciting, sentimental and patriotic moments of the past quarter of a century.' – Variety

AA: Alfred Newman

AAN: best picture; Irving Berlin (for original story); Irving Berlin (for song, 'Now It Can Be Told'); art direction; editing

Alf, Bill and Fred *
GB 1964 8m Eastmancolor
Biographic 4 (Bob Godfrey)

A man, a duck and a dog enjoy bouncing together.

Bittersweet cartoon fable which pleases much more than its synopsis might suggest.

w Stan Hayward d Bob Godfrey

† Animation by Bob Godfrey.

The Alf Garnett Saga
GB 1972 90m colour
Columbia/Associated London Films (Ned Sherrin, Terry Glinwood)

Bigoted Alf is exasperated by his council flat, his son-in-law, and the possibility that his daughter is pregnant by a black man.

Second inflation of the TV series, Till Death Us Do Part, even cruder and less funny than the first; listlessly written and developed.

w Johnny Speight d Bob Kellett ph Nic Knowland m Georgie Fame

Warren Mitchell, Dandy Nichols, Adrienne Posta, Mike Angelis, John Le Mesurier, Joan Sims, John Bird, Roy Kinnear

'One long, repetitive and unfunny diatribe.' – MFB

Alfie **
GB 1966 114m Techniscope
Paramount/Sheldrake (Lewis Gilbert)
V*

A Cockney Lothario is proud of his amorous conquests, but near-tragedy finally makes him more mature.

Garish sex comedy, an immense box-office success because of its frankness and an immaculate performance from its star.

w Bill Naughton, play Bill Naughton d Lewis Gilbert ph Otto Heller m Sonny Rollins

Michael Caine, Vivien Merchant, Shirley Anne Field, Millicent Martin, Jane Asher, Julia Foster, Shelley Winters, Eleanor Bron, Denholm Elliott

'A film exceptionally well made; never boring; composed of remarkable performances, scenes sharply observed and music neatly attuned.' – Dilys Powell

'Paramount thought it was a good bet because it was going to be made for 500,000 dollars, normally the sort of money spent on executives' cigar bills.' – Lewis Gilbert

AAN: best picture; Bill Naughton; Michael Caine; Vivien Merchant; title song (m Burt Bacharach, ly Hal David)

Alfie Darling
GB 1975 102m Technicolor
EMI/Signal (Dugald Rankin)
V, V*

Further repetitive amorous exploits of the Cockney Lothario, now a continental truck driver.

Soft porn adventures quite unworthy of the writer-director, and tedious to sit through; the touch of tragedy at the end only makes matters worse.

wd Ken Hughes ph Ousama Rawi m Alan Price

Alan Price, Jill Townsend, Paul Copley, Joan Collins, Sheila White, Annie Ross, Hannah Gordon, Rula Lenska

Alfred the Great *
GB 1969 122m Metrocolor Panavision
MGM/Bernard Smith

In AD 871 Alfred takes over kingship from his weak elder brother.

A 'realistic' youth-oriented view of history: blood and four-letter words alternate with cliché to make a dispiriting, disunified whole, though the background detail is interesting and the battle scenes vivid.

w Ken Taylor, James R. Webb d Clive Donner ph Alex Thomson m Ray Leppard pd Michael Stringer

David Hemmings, Michael York, Prunella Ransome, Colin Blakely, Julian Glover, Ian McKellen, Alan Dobie

Alfredo Alfredo
Italy/France 1971 110m Technicolor
CIC/RPA/Rizzoli/Francoriz (Pietro Germi)
V*

A bank clerk, determined to divorce his sexually insatiable wife, recalls his courtship and their difficult marriage.

A laboured and inane comedy of marital misunderstanding; it's possible that you need to be Italian to find it at all interesting.

w Leo Benvenuti, Piero de Bernardi, Tullio Pinelli, Pietro Germi d Pietro Germi ph Aiace Parolin m Carlo Rustichelli ad Carlo Egidi ed Sergio Montanari

Dustin Hoffman, Stefania Sandrelli, Carla Gravina, Clara Colosimo, Daniele Patella

'It simply limps on and on and on to no point or purpose.' – Tom Milne, MFB

† The version released in Britain ran for 98m.

Alf's Button
GB 1930 96m bw
Gaumont

Not the first version (there was one in 1920 with Leslie Henson) but the first in sound of W. A. Darlington's play about a soldier whose button, when rubbed, summons an all-powerful genie. It even had a colour sequence.

w L'Estrange Fawcett d W. P. Kellino

Nervo and Knox (see below), with Tubby Edlin, Alf Goddard, Nora Swinburne and Polly Ward

Alf's Button Afloat **
GB 1938 89m bw
Gainsborough (Edward Black)

Six itinerants encounter a genie, whose granting of their wishes brings riches and embarrassment.

Archetypal music hall farce descending at moments into surrealism (the lovers are eaten by a bear). All concerned are on top form.

w Marriott Edgar, Val Guest, Ralph Smart, novel Alf's Button by W. A. Darlington d Marcel Varnel ph Arthur Crabtree md Louis Levy

Bud Flanagan, Chesney Allen, Jimmy Nervo, Teddy Knox, Charles Naughton, Jimmy Gold (the six original members of the Crazy Gang), Alastair Sim, Wally Patch, Peter Gawthorne

Algiers **
US 1938 95m bw
Walter Wanger
V*

A romantic Casbah thief makes the mistake of falling in love.

Seminal Hollywood romantic drama based closely on a French original, Pepe le Moko; laughed at for years because of the alleged line 'Come with me to the Casbah' (which is never actually said), it holds up remarkably well in its fashion.

w John Howard Lawson, James M. Cain d John Cromwell ph James Wong Howe m Vincent Scotto, Mohammed Igorbouchen

Charles Boyer, Hedy Lamarr, Sigrid Gurie, Gene Lockhart, Joseph Calleia, Alan Hale, Johnny Downs

'A quality of sustained suspense and excitement . . . there is nothing makeshift about the production.' – Variety

'Few films this season, or any other, have sustained their mood more brilliantly.' – New York Times

'The general tone is that of the decent artistry we must demand and enjoy in pictures, which should someday be as respectable as books, only more near and vivid.' – Otis Ferguson

'This version is pure Hollywood, sacrificing everything to glamour, and the heavy make-up and studio lighting make it seem so artificial one can get giggly.' – New Yorker, 1977

† Remake: Casbah (qv).

AAN: James Wong Howe; Charles Boyer; Gene Lockhart

'Wild nights of sheer delights! Burning days of bold adventure! When beauty was the booty and the prize of all was love!'

Ali Baba and the Forty Thieves *
US 1943 87m Technicolor
Universal (Paul Malvern)

A deposed prince pretending to be a bandit regains his rightful throne.

Absurd but likeable wartime pantomime without much humour: a typical big-budget production of its studio and period.

w Edmund L. Hartmann d Arthur Lubin ph George Robinson m Edward Ward

Jon Hall, Maria Montez, Scotty Beckett, Turhan Bey, Frank Puglia, Andy Devine, Kurt Katch

† Remake: Sword of Ali Baba, which over twenty years later used much of the same footage.

Ali Baba and the Forty Thieves *
France 1954 90m Eastmancolor Films du Cyclope

Ali Baba is sent to buy a new wife for his master, and accidentally finds a thieves' treasure cave . . .

Sporadically amusing but finally disappointing version of the Arabian Nights story; it looks hasty.

w Jacques Becker, Marc Maurette, Maurice Griffe d Jacques Becker ph Robert Le Fèbvre m Paul Misraki

Fernandel, Samia Gamal, Dieter Borsche, Henri Vilbert

Ali Baba Goes to Town *
US 1937 81m bw
TCF (Lawrence Schwab)

A hobo falls off a train into a film set and thinks he is back in the Arabian Nights.

Rather flat star vehicle with a few compensations.

w Harry Tugend, Jack Yellen   *d* David Butler
ph Ernest Palmer   *m* Louis Silvers   *m/y* Mack
Gordon, Harry Revel   *ch* Sammy Lee

Eddie Cantor, Tony Martin, Roland Young, John
Carradine, June Lang

'An elaborately produced filmusical which satirizes
the New Deal policies, politicians and politics.' –
Variety

AAN: Sammy Lee

Alias a Gentleman
US   1947   76m   bw
MGM

An ex-convict tries to find his daughter and go
straight.

Sudsy star vehicle.

w William Lipman   *d* Harry Beaumont

Wallace Beery, Gladys George, Tom Drake, Leon
Ames

Alias Bulldog Drummond: see *Bulldog Jack*

Alias French Gertie
US   1934   68m   bw
RKO
GB title: *Love Finds a Way*

A 'French maid' and her accomplice work a high
society racket.

Faded society comedy drama with a rare teaming of
its stars before their exile to England.

w Bayard Veiller   *d* George Archainbaud

Bebe Daniels, Ben Lyon

Alias Jesse James *
US   1958   92m   DeLuxe
Hope Enterprises (Jack Hope)

An incompetent insurance salesman sells a policy to
Jesse James and has to protect his client until he can
get it back.

Ho-hum star comedy saved by a climax in which
Hope is protected by every cowboy star in Hollywood.

w William Bowers, D. D. Beauchamp   *d* Norman Z.
McLeod   *ph* Lionel Lindon   *m* Joseph J. Lilley

Bob Hope, Rhonda Fleming, Wendell Corey, Jim
Davis, Will Wright

Alias Jimmy Valentine
US   1928   75m   bw
MGM

Crook comedy drama previously made in 1920.

This version is notable only as the first MGM sound
film.

w Sarah Y. Mason, A. P. Younger   *d* Jack Conway

William Haines, Karl Dane, Lionel Barrymore

Alias John Preston
GB   1956   66m   bw
The Danzigers

A stranger with amnesia arrives in a small
community, only to find that his frequent nightmares
have a sinister reason.

Watchable second feature.

w Paul Tabori   *d* David MacDonald

Christopher Lee, Alexander Knox, Betta St John,
Patrick Holt, Sandra Dorne, Betty Anne Davies, John
Stuart, John Longden, Bill Fraser

Alias 'La Gringa' *
Peru/Spain   1991   100m   colour
Perfo/Spain Española/Channel 4 (Andres Malatesta, Emilio
Salomon)

A criminal returns to jail to rescue the university

professor who, in the middle of a riot by terrorists,
saved his life.

Harsh exposé of prison life, inspired by a true story,
and providing a little insight into Peruvian life and
politics.

w Alberto Durant, José Watanabé, José María
Salcedo   *d* Alberto Durant   *ph* Mario García Joya
m Pochi Marambio   *pd* Matanabé   *ed* Gianfranco
Annichini

Germano Gonzales, Elsa Oliveros, Orlando Sacha,
Juan Manuel Ochoa, Enrique Victoria, Gonzalo de
Miguel

'Basically action for undemanding Latino auds, but on
its own terms it's efficiently and briskly handled.' –
Variety

Alias Mary Dow
US   1935   65m   bw
Universal

A millionaire persuades a chorus girl to pose as his
long-lost kidnapped daughter, to satisfy his wife.

Obvious audience-pleaser of its time.

w Gladys Unger, Rose Franken, Arthur Caesar
d Kurt Neumann

Ray Milland, Sally Eilers, Henry O'Neill, Katherine
Alexander

'Not a bad picture . . . small towns should like it best.'
– *Variety*

'No man ever held more terrible power over women than
    this tall dark handsome stranger from nowhere! The
    shock-filled story of a man whose love was more
    dangerous than a loaded gun!'
Alias Nick Beal ***
US   1949   93m   bw
Paramount (Endre Bohem)
GB title: *The Contact Man*

A politician is nearly corrupted by a mysterious
stranger offering wealth and power.

Highly satisfactory modern version of *Faust*, done in
gangster terms but not eschewing a supernatural
explanation. Acting, photography and direction all in
the right key.

w Jonathan Latimer   *story* Mindret Lord   *d* John
Farrow   *ph* Lionel Lindon   *m* Franz Waxman

Ray Milland, Thomas Mitchell, Audrey Totter, George
Macready, Fred Clark

Alias the Deacon
US   1940   74m   bw
Ben Pivar/Universal

A sentimental cardsharp is mistaken by smalltown
folk for their new deacon.

Modest rural comedy from a well-worn play.

w Nat Perrin, Charles Grayson   *play* John B. Hymer,
Leroy Clemens   *d* Christy Cabanne

Bob Burns, Mischa Auer, Peggy Moran, Dennis
O'Keefe, Edward Brophy, Thurston Hall, Jack Carson

† Remake of *Half A Sinner* (qv).

Alias the Doctor
US   1932   70m   bw
First National/Warner

A natural man of the soil tries to follow his mother's
wish that he should become a doctor.

Dated drama of family sentiment.

w Benjamin McGill, Houston Branch   *play* Emric
Foldes   *d* Lloyd Bacon

Richard Barthelmess, Laura la Plante, Marian Marsh,
Norman Foster, Oscar Apfel

'It misses big league rating, but will satisfy on the
average programme.' – *Variety*

Alibi *
US   1929   90m   bw
Roland West

An ex-convict marries a policeman's daughter and
uses her in his plan for the perfect murder.

Early talkie drama, mostly risible now but with
interesting fragments of technique and imagination.

w Roland West, C. Gardner Sullivan   *play Nightstick*
by Elaine Sterne Carrington, John Wray, J. C. Nugent
d Roland West   *ph* Ray June   *m* Hugo Riesenfeld
ad William Cameron Menzies

Chester Morris, Eleanor Griffith, Regis Toomey, Mae
Busch, Harry Stubbs

AAN: best picture; Chester Morris; William Cameron
Menzies

Alibi
GB   1931   75m   bw
Twickenham

Hercule Poirot proves that an apparent suicide was
murder.

Tame adaptation, without the narrative gimmick of
Agatha Christie's *The Murder of Roger Ackroyd*.

w H. Fowler Mear   *d* Leslie Hiscott

Austin Trevor, Franklyn Dyall, Elizabeth Allan, J. H.
Roberts, Mary Jerrold

Alibi *
GB   1942   82m   bw
Corona (Josef Somlo)

A nightclub mindreader forces the lady owner to give
him a murder alibi.

Interesting but disappointing minor suspenser copied
from a sharper French original.

w uncredited   *novel* Marcel Achard   *d* Brian
Desmond Hurst   *ph* Otto Heller   *m* Jack Beaver

Margaret Lockwood, Hugh Sinclair, James Mason,
Raymond Lovell, Enid Stamp-Taylor, Hartley Power,
Jane Carr, Rodney Ackland, Edana Romney,
Elizabeth Welch, Olga Lindo, Muriel George

† The French film, *L'Alibi*, was made in 1939 by B-N
Films. The girl was Jany Holt, with Erich von
Stroheim as the villain and Louis Jouvet as the
inspector. Pierre Chenal directed.

Alibi Ike *
US   1935   73m   bw
Warner (Edward Chodorov)

A baseball pitcher gets involved in all kinds of
trouble.

Above average star comedy vehicle.

w William Wister Haines   *story* Ring Lardner
d Ray Enright   *ph* Arthur Todd   *md* Leo F.
Forbstein

Joe E. Brown, Olivia de Havilland, Ruth Donnelly,
Roscoe Karns, William Frawley

Alice ***
GB/Switzerland/West Germany   1988   85m
    Eastmancolor
Condor-Hessisches/SRG/Film Four (Peter-Christian Fueter)
V, L
original title: *Neco z Alenky*

A young girl follows a rabbit through a broken glass
case into Wonderland.

A free, sometimes disturbing interpretation with
surrealist overtones, of Lewis Carroll's masterpiece by
a great animator that, with its mix of live actors and
animation, comes closer than any other to conjuring
the curious atmosphere of the original.

wd Jan Svankmajer   novel Alice in Wonderland by Lewis
Carroll   *ph* Svatoluk Maly   *ad* Eva Svankmerova,
Jiri Blaha   *ed* Marie Drvotova

Kristyna Kohoutova

Alice *
US 1990 106m Duart
Orion/Jack Rollins, Charles H. Joffe
V, V*, L

A bored housewife indulges in a fantasy life.

Moderately amusing comedy of a search for individuality.

wd Woody Allen ph Carlo di Palma pd Santo Loquasto ad Speed Hopkins

Mia Farrow, Joe Mantegna, Alec Baldwin, Blythe Danner, Judy Davis, William Hurt, Keye Luke, Bernadette Peters, Cybill Shepherd, Gwen Verdon

'A likable little pic that will please his fans.' – Variety

AAN: best original screenplay

Alice Adams **
US 1935 99m bw
RKO (Pandro S. Berman)

A social-climbing small-town girl falls in love.

Dated but interesting star vehicle with good production values.

w Dorothy Yost, Mortimer Offner, Jane Murfin novel Booth Tarkington d George Stevens ph Robert de Grasse m Max Steiner, Roy Webb

Katharine Hepburn, Fred MacMurray, Evelyn Venable, Frank Albertson, Fred Stone, Ann Shoemaker, Charles Grapewin, Grady Sutton, Hedda Hopper

'Sturdy cinematic substance, virtually audience proof.' – Variety

'A nice middle-class film, as trivial as a schoolgirl's diary, and just about as pathetically true.' – C. A. Lejeune

'What was in 1922 a biting and observant novel emerges in 1935 as a bitingly satiric portrait of an era.' – Time

AAN: best picture; Katharine Hepburn

Alice au Pays de Merveilles: see Alice in Wonderland (1951)

'A picture for anyone who has ever dreamed of a second chance!'
Alice Doesn't Live Here Any More **
US 1974 112m Technicolor
Warner (David Susskind, Audrey Maas)
V (W), V*, L

A widow sets off with her young son for Monterey and a singing career.

Realistically squalid and foul-mouthed but endearing look at a slice of America today, with firm handling and excellent performances in a surprisingly old-fashioned theme.

w Robert Getchell d Martin Scorsese ph Kent L. Wakeford md Richard La Salle m various pd Toby Carr Rafelson

Ellen Burstyn, Alfred Lutter, Kris Kristofferson, Billy Green Bush, Diane Ladd, Lelia Goldoni, Jodie Foster

'What Scorsese has done is to rescue an American cliché from the bland, flat but much more portentous naturalism of such as Harry and Tonto and restore it to an emotional and intellectual complexity through his particular brand of baroque realism.' – Richard Combs

'Full of funny malice and breakneck vitality.' – New Yorker

'A tough weepie, redeemed by its picturesque locations and its eye for social detail.' – Michael Billington, Illustrated London News

AA: Ellen Burstyn

AAN: Robert Getchell; Diane Ladd

Alice in the Cities
West Germany 1974 110m bw
Filmverlag der Autoren
V, V*

original title: Alice in den Städten

A German journalist in America reluctantly escorts a small girl back to Germany.

Interesting but overlong collection of modern metaphors, occasionally reminiscent of Paper Moon.

wd Wim Wenders ph Robby Müller, Martin Schäfer m Irmin Schmid, Can ed Peter Przygodda

Rüdiger Vogler, Yella Röttlander, Lisa Kreuzer, Edda Köchel

Alice in Wonderland **
US 1933 75m bw
Paramount (Louis D. Lighton)

Intriguing but disappointing version of the nonsense classic, keeping to the Tenniel drawings by dressing an all-star cast in masks, thereby rendering them ineffective.

w Joseph L. Mankiewicz, William Cameron Menzies novel Lewis Carroll d Norman Z. McLeod ph Henry Sharp, Bert Glennon m Dimitri Tiomkin

Charlotte Henry, W. C. Fields (Humpty Dumpty), Cary Grant (Mock Turtle), Gary Cooper (White Knight), Edward Everett Horton (Mad Hatter), Edna May Oliver (Red Queen), Jack Oakie (Tweedledum), Leon Errol (Uncle), Charles Ruggles (March Hare), May Robson (Queen of Hearts), Louise Fazenda (White Queen), Ned Sparks (Caterpillar), Alison Skipworth (Duchess)

'Nothing grows out of anything else in this phantasmagoria. It's like reading a whole volume of separate four-line gags.' – Variety

'Lavishly produced, with great care given to costumes and settings and make-up, but the spirit is missing.' – New Yorker, 1977

† Ida Lupino was brought from the UK for the title role, but not used.

Alice in Wonderland *
US 1951 75m Technicolor
Walt Disney
V, V*, L

Fully animated cartoon version which has good moments but modernizes and Americanizes the familiar characters.

w various d Clyde Geronimi, Hamilton Luske, Wilfred Jackson supervisor Ben Sharpsteen m Oliver Wallace

voices of Kathryn Beaumont, Ed Wynn, Richard Haydn, Sterling Holloway, Jerry Colonna, Verna Felton, Bill Thompson

AAN: Oliver Wallace

Alice in Wonderland *
USA/France/Great Britain 1951 83m Ansco-color
UGC/Rank/Lou Bunin
aka: Alice au Pays de Merveilles

Often interesting if sometimes crude version with Bunin's puppets, filmed in Nice; the simultaneous Disney cartoon version effectively kept it off the world's screens.

Carol Marsh, Stephen Murray (as Lewis Carroll), Pamela Brown (as Queen Victoria), Felix Aylmer (as Dr Liddell)

Alice, Sweet Alice: see Communion (1978)

Alice's Adventures in Wonderland *
GB 1972 101m Eastmancolor Todd-AO
TCF/Josef Shaftel (Derek Horne)

Live-action version which starts amiably enough but soon becomes flat and uninventive, with a star cast all at sea and tedium replacing the wit of the original.

wd William Sterling ph Geoffrey Unsworth m John Barry pd Michael Stringer

Fiona Fullerton, Michael Crawford (White Rabbit), Robert Helpmann (Mad Hatter), Dudley Moore (Dormouse), Spike Milligan (Gryphon), Peter Sellers (March Hare), Dennis Price (King of Hearts), Flora Robson (Queen of Hearts), Rodney Bewes (Knave of Hearts), Peter Bull (Duchess), Michael Hordern (Mock Turtle), Ralph Richardson (Caterpillar), etc

Alice's Restaurant *
US 1969 110m DeLuxe
UA/Florin (Harold Levanthal)
V*, S

Folk singer Arlo Guthrie, on the verge of being drafted, gets some varied experience of life among the drop-outs of Montana, Massachusetts and New York.

Typical of the freakish, anti-Vietnam, do-as-you-please movies which splurged from Hollywood in the wake of Easy Rider; this has the minor benefits of good production values and a few jokes.

w Venable Herndon, Arthur Penn d Arthur Penn ph Michael Nebbia m/songs Arlo Guthrie

Arlo Guthrie, Pat Quinn, James Broderick, Michael McClanathan, Geoff Outlaw

'A subtle, funny, tender and original movie that may not perhaps increase Arthur Penn's present high standing but will certainly do nothing to diminish it.' – Philip French, Sight and Sound

AAN: Arthur Penn

'In space, no one can hear you scream!'
Alien ****
GB 1979 117m Eastmancolor Panavision
TCF/Brandywine (Walter Hill, Gordon Carroll, David Giler)
V, V (W), V*, L, S

Astronauts returning to Earth visit an apparently dead planet and are infected by a violent being which has unexpected behaviour patterns and eliminates them one by one.

Deliberately scarifying and highly commercial shocker. On its own terms, a classic of suspense – and art direction.

w Dan O'Bannon d Ridley Scott ph Derek Vanlint, Denys Ayling m Jerry Goldsmith chief designer H. R. Giger

Tom Skerritt, Sigourney Weaver, John Hurt, Veronica Cartwright, Harry Dean Stanton, Ian Holm, Yaphet Kotto

'A sort of inverse relationship to The Thing invites unfavourable comparisons.' – Sight and Sound

'Empty bag of tricks whose production values and expensive trickery cannot disguise imaginative poverty.' – Time Out

'It was not, as its co-author admitted, a think piece. The message he intended was simple: Don't close your eyes or it will get ya.' – Les Keyser, Hollywood in the Seventies

† It was followed by two sequels, Aliens and Alien³.

AA: visual effects (H. R. Giger, Carlo Rambaldi and others)

Alien Nation
US 1988 94m DeLuxe
Fox (Gale Anne Hurd, Richard Kobritz)
V, V*, L

A detective, one of a despised minority of aliens stranded on Earth, is partnered with a bigoted human cop to solve a murder.

What begins as an interestingly oblique look at the problems of racism soon turns into a lacklustre action movie.

w Rockne S. O'Bannon d Graham Baker
ph Adam Greenberg m Curt Sobel pd Jack T.
Collis

James Caan, Mandy Patinkin, Terence Stamp

'The Bitch Is Back.'
Alien³
US 1992 115m Rank colour Panavision
TCF/Brandywine (Gordon Carroll, David Giler, Walter Hill)
V, V*, L

Ripley crash-lands on a mining planet inhabited by
convicts and discovers that she has brought an alien
with her.

Grim, grey sequel that struggles, and fails, to add
something new to the now familiar story.

w David Giler, Walter Hill, Larry Ferguson Vincent
Ward d David Giler ph Alex Thomson m Elliot
Goldenthal pd Norman Reynolds sp George
Gibbs, Richard Edlund ed Terry Rawlings

Sigourney Weaver, Charles S. Dutton, Charles Dance,
Paul McGann, Brian Glover, Ralph Brown, Danny
Webb, Christopher John Fields, Lance Henriksen

'A muddled effort offering little more than visual
splendor to recommend it.' – Variety

'In space, no one can hear you snore.' – Andy Klein,
Los Angeles Reader

AAN: Visual effects

Aliens *
US 1986 137m DeLuxe
TCF/Brandywine (Gale Anne Hurd)
V, V*, L, S

The sole survivor of the space team in Alien goes back
with another team to the mystery planet, and finds
more monsters.

Frightening but mechanical sequel with none of the
half-assed poetry of the original.

w James Cameron, Walter Hill, David Giler
d James Cameron ph Adrian Biddle m James
Horner pd Peter Lamont ed Ray Lovejoy

Sigourney Weaver, Carrie Henn, Michael Biehn, Paul
Reiser

'Audiences will be riveted to their seats with drooling
dread in anticipation of the next horrifying attack.' –
Variety

'I'm giving the movie a high rating for its skill and
professionalism, and because it does the job it says it
will do. I am also advising you not to eat before you
see it.' – Roger Ebert

† A special edition was released on video running for
154m.

AA: special visual effects (Robert Skotak, Stan
Winston, John Richardson, Suzanne Benson)

AAN: music; production design; Ray Lovejoy;
Sigourney Weaver

Alive
US 1992 127m Technicolor
UIP/Paramount (Robert Watts, Kathleen Kennedy)
V, V*, L, S

Members of a South American rugby team whose
plane crash-lands on an inaccessible mountain-top are
forced to eat their dead in order to survive.

Efficient re-telling of a true story, but one that adds
little to the sum of human knowledge or happiness.

w John Patrick Shanley book Piers Paul Read
d Frank Marshall ph Peter James m James
Newton Howard pd Norman Reynolds
ed Michael Kahn, William Goldenberg

Ethan Hawke, Vincent Spano, Josh Hamilton, Bruce
Ramsay, John Haymes Newton, David Kriegel, Kevin
Breznahan, Sam Behrens

'Neither the exploitative gross-out teens might be
looking for nor quite the rousing adventure it needs to
be.' – Variety

† In 1976 the story was filmed in Mexico by director
Rene Cardona as Survive! (qv).

Alive and Kicking *
GB 1958 94m bw
ABP (Victor Skutezky)

Three old ladies escape from a home to an Irish island.

Agreeable minor comedy, a showcase for its elderly
but vigorous stars.

w Denis Cannan d Cyril Frankel ph Gilbert
Taylor m Philip Green

Sybil Thorndike, Kathleen Harrison, Estelle Winwood,
Stanley Holloway, Joyce Carey, Eric Pohlmann, Colin
Gordon

'The most provocative picture of the year!'
All About Eve ***
US 1950 138m bw
TCF (Darryl F. Zanuck)
V, V*, L

An ageing Broadway star suffers from the hidden
menace of a self-effacing but secretly ruthless and
ambitious young actress.

A basically unconvincing story with thin characters is
transformed by a screenplay scintillating with savage
wit and a couple of waspish performances into a
movie experience to treasure.

wd Joseph L. Mankiewicz ph Milton Krasner m Alfred
Newman ad Lyle Wheeler, George Davis
ed Barbara McLean

Bette Davis (Margo Channing), George Sanders (Addison
de Witt), Anne Baxter (Eve), Celeste Holm (Karen
Richards), Thelma Ritter (Birdie), Gary Merrill (Bill
Sampson), Hugh Marlowe (Lloyd Richards), Gregory
Ratoff (Max Fabian), Marilyn Monroe (Miss
Caswell), Barbara Bates (Girl at Mirror), Walter
Hampden (Speaker at dinner)

MARGO: 'Fasten your seat belts, it's going to be a
bumpy night!'
ADDISON: 'That I should want you at all suddenly
strikes me as the height of improbability . . . you're an
improbable person, Eve, but so am I. We have that in
common. Also a contempt for humanity, an inability
to love or be loved, insatiable ambition – and talent.
We deserve each other.'
BIRDIE: 'The bed looks like a dead animal act.'
ADDISON: 'That's all television is, dear – just
auditions.'
BIRDIE: 'What a story! Everything but the
bloodhounds snappin' at her rear end!'
ADDISON: 'I have lived in the theatre as a Trappist
monk lives in his faith. In it I toil not, neither do I
spin. I am a critic and a commentator. I am essential to
the theatre – as ants to a picnic, as the boll weevil to a
cotton field.'

'The wittiest, the most devastating, the most adult and
literate motion picture ever made that had anything to
do with the New York Stage.' – Leo Mishkin

'The dialogue and atmosphere are so peculiarly
remote from life that they have sometimes been
mistaken for art.' – Pauline Kael, 1968

'Plenty of surface cynicism, but no detachment, no
edge and no satire. Boiled down it is a plush
backstage drama.' – Richard Winnington

'Long, but continuously, wonderfully entertaining in
a way I had almost forgotten was possible for films.' –
Richard Mallett, Punch

'Someone remarked of this witty, exaggerated, cruel
and yet wildly funny film that the secret of its success
was the extreme bad taste shown throughout by all
concerned (though I hope they didn't mean to include
Milton Krasner's tactful camerawork in this).' – Basil
Wright, 1972

'The picture seemed long – though it was not by
today's standards of length – and the crispness of the
dialogue was not matched by equally crisp editing.' –
Hollis Alpert, 1962

† The idea for the film came from a short story, 'The
Wisdom of Eve', by Mary Orr.

AA: best picture; Joseph L. Mankiewicz (as writer);
Joseph L. Mankiewicz (as director); George Sanders

AAN: Milton Krasner; Alfred Newman; Bette Davis;
Anne Baxter; Celeste Holm; Thelma Ritter; art
direction; editing

All Ashore
US 1952 80m Technicolor
Columbia (Jonie Taps)

Three sailors on shore leave work their passage to
Catalina.

Very lightweight musical, no rival for On the Town.

w Blake Edwards, Richard Quine d Richard Quine
ph Charles Lawton Jnr m Morris Stoloff, George
Duning ly Robert Wells

Mickey Rooney, Dick Haymes, Ray McDonald, Peggy
Ryan, Barbara Bates, Jody Lawrance

All at Sea: see Barnacle Bill

All Coppers Are . . .
GB 1972 87m colour
Rank/Peter Rogers (George H. Brown)

A crook and a cop both fancy the same girl.

Pointlessly titled lowlife melodrama with no style
whatever; any episode of Z Cars would be vastly
preferable.

w Allan Prior d Sidney Hayers

Nicky Henson, Martin Potter, Julia Foster, Ian Hendry

All Creatures Great and Small *
GB 1974 92m Eastmancolor
EMI/Venedon (David Susskind, Duane Bogie)
V*

The pre-war Yorkshire life of a country vet.

Simple-minded popular entertainment of a long-
forgotten kind, oddly sponsored by American TV in
the shape of Readers' Digest and the Hallmark Hall of
Fame.

w Hugh Whitemore novel James Herriot
d Claude Whatham ph Peter Suschitzky
m Wilfred Josephs

Anthony Hopkins, Simon Ward, Lisa Harrow, Freddie
Jones, Brian Stirner, T. P. McKenna, Brenda Bruce,
John Collin

† 1976 sequel: It Shouldn't Happen to a Vet.

All Dogs Go To Heaven
Eire 1989 85m Technicolor
Rank/Sullivan Bluth/Goldcrest/Don Bluth, Gary Goldman, John
  Pomeroy
V, V*, L, S

A dead dog returns to Earth to seek revenge on the
vicious gangster dog who had him killed.

Skilful animation goes to waste in a confused and
confusing narrative.

w David N. Weiss d Dan Kuenster, Gary Goldman
m Ralph Burns pd Don Bluth, Larry Leker
m/ly Charles Strouse, T. J. Kuenster, Al Kasha/Joel
Hirschhorn/Michael Lloyd

voices of Burt Reynolds, Vic Tayback, Judith Barsi,
Dom DeLuise, Loni Anderson, Melba Moore, Charles
Nelson Reilly

All Fall Down *
US 1962 111m bw Panavision
MGM (John Houseman)
V*

A young man reveres his ne'er-do-well elder brother

but determines to shoot him when he causes a girl's death.

Another gallery of middle American failures, competently portrayed by a writer and actors very practised at this sort of thing.

w William Inge novel James Leo Herlihy d John Frankenheimer ph Lionel Lindon m Alex North

Warren Beatty, Brandon de Wilde, Angela Lansbury, Karl Malden, Eva Marie Saint

'That strange area of nostalgic Americana where the familiar is the Freudian grotesque.' – New Yorker, 1982

All for Mary *
GB   1955   82m   Eastmancolor
Rank/Paul Soskin

Two rivals for the hand of the pretty daughter of a Swiss hotelier are struck down by chicken pox and cared for by the old nanny of one of them.

Simple-minded farce in which two grown men quail like children before a forceful old lady; on the strength of the latter characterization and a few funny lines the original play was a considerable West End success.

w Peter Blackmore, Paul Soskin play Harold Brooke, Kay Bannerman d Wendy Toye ph Reg Wyer m Robert Farnon

Kathleen Harrison, Nigel Patrick, David Tomlinson, Jill Day, David Hurst, Leo McKern

All Good Citizens: see All My Good Countrymen

All Hands on Deck
US   1961   98m   DeLuxe   Cinemascope
TCF (Oscar Brodney)

Romantic and farcical adventures of sailors on leave.

Tired musical comedy romp with a second team cast.

w Jay Sommars novel Donald R. Morris
d Norman Taurog ph Leo Tover m Cyril Mockridge m/y Jay Livingston, Ray Evans

Pat Boone, Buddy Hackett, Dennis O'Keefe, Barbara Eden, Warren Berlinger, Gale Gordon, Joe E. Ross

All I Desire
US   1953   79m   bw
U-I (Ross Hunter)

A woman who had deserted her husband and family for a life on the stage returns for her daughter's graduation and is reconciled.

Resilient star melodrama with all stops out.

w James Gunn, Robert Blees d Douglas Sirk
ph Carl Guthrie m Joseph Gershenson

Barbara Stanwyck, Richard Carlson, Lyle Bettger, Maureen O'Sullivan, Richard Long, Lori Nelson

'How Far Would You Go To Make A Wish Come True?'
All I Want For Christmas
US   1991   92m   Technicolor
Paramount (Marykay Powell)
V, V*, L, S

The Christmas wish of two children is that their divorced parents should get together again.

Dim comedy that even the season of good-will cannot make palatable.

w Thom Eberhardt, Richard Kramer d Robert Lieberman ph Robbie Greenberg m Bruce Broughton pd Herman Zimmerman ed Richard Berger, Dean Goodhill

Ethan Randall, Thora Birch, Harley Jane Kozak, Jamey Sheridan, Lillian Brooks, Lauren Bacall

All In
GB   1936   71m   bw
Gainsborough

A young man whose rich aunt opposes gambling

finds himself the owner of a wrestling arena as well as a racing stable.

w Leslie Arliss, Val Guest play Tattenham Corner by Bernard Merivale, Brandon Fleming d Marcel Varnel

Ralph Lynn, Gina Malo, Jack Barty, Claude Dampier, Sydney Fairbrother, Garry Marsh

All in a Night's Work
US   1961   94m   Technicolor
Paramount/Hal B. Wallis-Joseph Hazen
V, V*

A publishing heir falls for a girl he suspects of having been his uncle's mistress.

Unpolished and not very amusing comedy which falters after an intriguing start.

w Edmund Beloin, Maurice Richlin, Sidney Sheldon
d Joseph Anthony ph Joseph LaShelle m André Previn

Shirley Maclaine, Dean Martin, Charles Ruggles, Cliff Robertson, Norma Crane, Gale Gordon, Jerome Cowan, Jack Weston

'Tame and aimless sex-and-big-business comedy.' – MFB

All Men Are Enemies
US   1934   78m   bw
Rocket/Fox

Sweethearts parted by the war are reunited at last, despite another woman.

Tedious romantic drama which failed to make a Hollywood star of its British lead.

w Samuel Hoffenstein, Lenore Coffee novel Richard Aldington d George Fitzmaurice

Hugh Williams, Helen Twelvetrees, Mona Barrie, Herbert Mundin, Henry Stephenson, Walter Byron, Una O'Connor, Halliwell Hobbes

All Mine To Give *
US   1956   102m   Technicolor   RKOscope
RKO (Sam Wiesenthal)
GB title: The Day They Gave Babies Away

In 1856, a pioneer couple in Wisconsin train their children to carry on the family after their own deaths.

Weird sentimental sob story, even odder under its English title. Surprisingly, some of it works quite well.

w Dale and Katherine Eunson (apparently about their own ancestors) d Allen Reisner ph William Skall
m Max Steiner

Glynis Johns, Cameron Mitchell, Patty McCormack, Rex Thompson, Ernest Truex, Hope Emerson, Alan Hale

'A strong mood of folksy western reminiscence.' – MFB

All My Good Countrymen **
Czechoslovakia   1968   126m   colour
Filmove Studio Barrandov (Jaroslav Jilovec)
original title: Všichni Dobří Rodáci; aka: All Good Citizens

Life and death among seven friends caught in the turmoil following the Second World War and the rise of the Communist party.

Lyrical and moving account of political expediency and corruption and the human sacrifice it entails. Awarded the best director prize at the Cannes Film Festival in 1969, it was then banned by the Czech government and its director went into exile.

wd Vojtěch Jasný ph Jaroslav Kučera
m Svatopluk Havelka ed Oldřich Mach

Vlastimil Brodský, Radoslav Brzobohatý, Vladimir Mensik, Waldemar Matuška, Drahomira Hofmanová, Pavel Pavlovský

All My Sons *
US   1948   94m   bw
U-I (Chester Erskine)

A young man establishes that his father sold defective airplanes during the war.

Heady family melodrama from a taut and topical stage play. The film is well-meaning but artificial and unconvincing.

w Chester Erskine play Arthur Miller d Irving Reis ph Russell Metty m Leith Stevens

Edward G. Robinson, Burt Lancaster, Mady Christians, Howard Duff

All Neat in Black Stockings
GB   1969   99m   Eastmancolor
Anglo Amalgamated/Miton (Leon Clore)

Sex adventures of an amorous window cleaner.

Modish comedy drama with surface entertainment of a sort, but no depth.

w Jane Gaskell, Hugh Whitemore d Christopher Morahan ph Larry Pizer m Robert Cornford

Victor Henry, Susan George, Jack Shepherd, Anna Cropper, Clare Kelly, Terence de Marney

All Night *
US   1918   57m approx   bw   silent
Bluebird Films

A bright young entrepreneur throws a dinner for would-be investors.

Theatrical farce, with most characters pretending to be what they're not, this must have worked better on the stage but by all accounts did pretty well on film.

w Fred Myton d Paul Powell

Rudolph Valentino, Carmel Myers, Charles Dorian, Mary Warren

All Night Long *
GB   1961   95m   bw
Rank/Bob Roberts (Michael Relph, Basil Dearden)

Because of rumour set about by a jealous rival, a jazz trumpeter at an all-night party tries to strangle his wife.

Cheeky updating of Othello with jazz accompaniment, played a shade too grimly by an excellent cast. An interesting misfire.

w Nel King, Peter Achilles d Basil Dearden
ph Ted Scaife m Philip Green

Patrick McGoohan, Richard Attenborough, Keith Michell, Betsy Blair, Marti Stevens, Paul Harris, Bernard Braden; and on the sound track Dave Brubeck, Tubby Hayes, Johnny Dankworth etc

All Night Long
US   1981   87m   Technicolor
Universal (Leonard Goldberg, Jerry Weintraub)

The wife of the night manager of a supermarket has a hyperactive sex life.

Curiously misjudged and outdated farce which offers very few laughs.

w W. D. Richter d Jean-Claude Tramont
ph Philip Lathrop m Ira Newborn, Richard Hazard
pd Peter Jamison

Barbra Streisand, Gene Hackman, Diane Ladd, Dennis Quaid, Kevin Dobson, William Daniels, Ann Doran

'Neither screenplay nor direction seem very clear what they're trying to say, and large chunks of it make no sense at all.' – Daily Mail

'There are two kinds of women, but only one kind of love!'
All of Me
US   1934   70m   bw
Paramount (Louis Lighton)

An engineering professor on his way to Boulder Dam finds his life affected by the problems of a criminal.

Confused and uninteresting romantic melodrama with a good cast all at sea.

w Sidney Buchman, Thomas Mitchell *play Chrysalis* by Rose Porter d James Flood ph Victor Milner m/ly Ralph Rainger, Leo Robin

Fredric March, Miriam Hopkins, George Raft, Helen Mack, Nella Walker, William Collier Jnr, Gilbert Emery, Blanche Friderici, Edgar Kennedy

'The most startling glorification of criminals that even the movies have ever dared.' – *New York Sun*

'The gags aren't thought out visually in terms of the L.A. locations, and the film has the bland ugliness of sitcoms.' – *Pauline Kael, New Yorker*

All of Me
US 1984 91m Technicolor
Thorn-EMI/Kings Road/Universal (Stephen Friedman)
V, V*, L

A guru accidentally transfers a woman's soul after death into her lawyer's body.

Curiously vulgar sitcom with a familiar team trying and failing to go one better on *The Man With Two Brains*.

w Phil Alden Robinson *novel Me Two* by Ed Davis d Carl Reiner ph Richard H. Kline m Patrick Williams pd Edward Carfagno ed Bud Molin

Steve Martin, Lily Tomlin, Victoria Tennant, Madolyn Smith, Dana Elcar

All Over Town
US 1937 62m bw
Republic

A pair of vaudevillians with a trained seal save a theatre on the skids.

Routine knockabout comedy.

w Jack Townley, Jerome Chodorov d James Horne

Ole Olsen, Chic Johnson, Mary Howard, Harry Stockwell, James Finlayson, Franklin Pangborn

All Over the Town *
GB 1949 88m bw
Rank/Wessex (Ian Dalrymple)

Two reporters revivify a West of England local newspaper, and expose local corruption.

Fresh, agreeable romantic comedy on sub-Ealing lines.

w Derek Twist and others d Derek Twist ph C. Pennington-Richards m Temple Abady

Norman Wooland, Sarah Churchill, Fabia Drake (as a local gorgon), Cyril Cusack, James Hayter

All Quiet on the Western Front ****
US 1930 130m approx bw
Universal (Carl Laemmle Jnr)
V*, L

In 1914, a group of German teenagers volunteer for action on the Western Front, but they become disillusioned, and none of them survives.

A landmark of American cinema and Universal's biggest and most serious undertaking until the sixties, this highly emotive war film with its occasional outbursts of bravura direction fixed in millions of minds the popular image of what it was like in the trenches, even more so than *Journey's End* which had shown the Allied viewpoint. Despite dated moments, it retains its overall power and remains a great pacifist work.

w Lewis Milestone, Maxwell Anderson, Del Andrews, George Abbott *novel* Erich Maria Remarque (in a manner reminiscent of Eisenstein and Lang) ph Arthur Edeson m David Broekman

Lew Ayres (Paul Baumer), Louis Wolheim (Katczinsky), Slim Summerville (Tjaden), John Wray (Himmelstoss), Raymond Griffith (Gerard Duval),

Russell Gleason (Muller), Ben Alexander (Kemmerick), Beryl Mercer (Mrs Baumer)

TJADEN: 'Me and the Kaiser, we are both fighting. The only difference is, the Kaiser isn't here.'
KATCZINSKY: 'At the next war let all the Kaisers, Presidents and Generals and diplomats go into a big field and fight it out first among themselves. That will satisfy us and keep us at home.'
PAUL: 'We live in the trenches out there. We fight. We try not to be killed, but sometimes we are. That's all.'

'A magnificent cinematic equivalent of the book . . . to Mr. Milestone goes the credit of effecting the similitude in united and dynamic picture terms. The sound and image mediums blend as one, as a form of artistic expression that only the motion screen can give.' – *National Board of Review*

'Nothing passed up for the niceties; nothing glossed over for the women. Here exhibited is war as it is, butchery. The League of Nations could make no better investment than to buy up the master-print, reproduce it in every language to be shown to every nation every year until the word war is taken out of the dictionaries.' – *Variety*

'A trenchant and imaginative audible picture . . . most of the time the audience was held to silence by its realistic scenes.' – *New York Times*

AA: best picture; Lewis Milestone (as director)

AAN: Lewis Milestone, Maxwell Anderson, Del Andrews, George Abbott; Arthur Edeson

'Together again . . . surpassing their performances in "Magnificent Obsession"'

All That Heaven Allows
US 1955 89m Technicolor
U-I (Ross Hunter)

A sad widow falls in love with the gardener at her winter home, and marries him despite local prejudice.

Standard tearjerker in the tradition of *Magnificent Obsession*, reuniting the same stars, producer and director in the same rich musical and photographic sauce.

w Peg Fenwick d Douglas Sirk ph Russell Metty m Frank Skinner

Jane Wyman, Rock Hudson, Agnes Moorehead, Conrad Nagel, Virginia Grey, Charles Drake

'As laboriously predictable as it is fatuously unreal.' – *MFB*

All That Jazz **
US 1979 123m Technicolor
COL/TCF (Robert Alan Aurthur, Daniel Melnick)
V, V*, L

A stage musical director pushes himself too hard, and dies of a surfeit of wine, women and work.

Self-indulgent, semi-autobiographical tragi-comic extravaganza complete with heart operations and a recurring angel of death. Flashes of brilliant talent make it a must for Fosse fans.

w Robert Alan Aurthur, Bob Fosse d Bob Fosse ph Giuseppe Rotunno m Ralph Burns pd Philip Rosenberg, Tony Walton ed Alan Heim

Roy Scheider, Jessica Lange, Ann Reinking, Leland Palmer, Ben Vereen, Cliff Gorman

'Egomaniacal, wonderfully choreographed, often compelling . . . more an art item than a broad commercial prospect.' – *Variety*

'An improbable mixture of crass gags, song 'n' dance routines and open heart surgery. Not for the squeamish.' – *Time Out*

'By the end I felt I'd learned more about Fosse than I actually cared to know.' – *Daily Mail*

'High cholesterol hokum. Enjoyable, but probably not good for you.' – *Pauline Kael, New Yorker*

AA: art direction; editing; musical adaptation; costume design (Albert Wolsky)

AAN: best picture; Bob Fosse; Roy Scheider; Giuseppe Rotunno; script

BFA: cinematography; editing; sound

All That Money Can Buy ****
US 1941 106m bw
RKO/William Dieterle (Charles L. Glett)
V*
aka: *The Devil and Daniel Webster; Daniel and the Devil; Here Is a Man*

A hard-pressed farmer gives in to the Devil's tempting, but is saved from the pit by a famous lawyer's pleading at his 'trial'.

A brilliant Germanic *Faust* set in 19th-century New Hampshire and using historical figures, alienation effects, comedy asides and the whole cinematic box of tricks which Hollywood had just learned again through *Citizen Kane*. A magic act in more ways than one.

w Dan Totheroh *story* The Devil and Daniel Webster by Stephen Vincent Benet d William Dieterle ph Joseph August m Bernard Herrmann ad Van Nest Polglase sp Vernon L. Walker

Walter Huston ('Mr Scratch', a great performance), James Craig, Anne Shirley, Simone Simon, *Edward Arnold* (Daniel Webster), Jane Darwell, Gene Lockhart, John Qualen. H. B. Warner

MR SCRATCH: 'A soul. A soul is nothing. Can you see it, smell it, touch it? No. Think of it – this soul – your soul – a nothing, against seven whole years of good luck! You will have money and all that money can buy.'

'Some of those in the movie industry who saw it restively called it a dog; but some of them cried it was another catapult hurling the cinema up to its glorious destiny.' – *Cecilia Ager*

AA: Bernard Herrmann

AAN: Walter Huston

All the Brothers Were Valiant *
US 1953 94m Technicolor
MGM (Pandro S. Berman)

Rivalry between brothers on a whaling schooner.

Remake of a silent melodrama with predictable vengefulness and formula heroism, capably but unmemorably portrayed.

w Harry Brown *novel* Ben Ames Williams d Richard Thorpe ph George Folsey m Miklos Rozsa

Stewart Granger, Robert Taylor, Ann Blyth, Betta St John, Keenan Wynn, James Whitmore, Kurt Kasznar, Lewis Stone

AAN: George Folsey

All the Fine Young Cannibals
US 1960 122m Metrocolor Cinemascope
MGM/Avon (Pandro S. Berman)

The son of a country clergyman loves the daughter of another clergyman; they both find the realities of life in New York a horrid shock.

The glum joys of sex and dope in the big city are revealed in this boring rather than daring farrago which is not even unintentionally funny.

w Robert Thom *novel* The Bixby Girls by Rosamond Marshall d Michael Anderson ph William H. Daniels m Jeff Alexander

Robert Wagner, Natalie Wood, Pearl Bailey, Susan Kohner, George Hamilton, Jack Mullaney, Onslow Stevens, Anne Seymour

All the King's Horses
US 1935 87m bw
Paramount

A Hollywood star revisiting his native Langenstein turns out to be a double of the king, and finds himself romancing the queen.

Operetta-style entertainment grafted onto the plot of *The Prisoner of Zenda*; by no means unacceptable even now.

w Frank Tuttle, Frederick Stephani   *play* Lawrence Clark, Max Giersberg   *d* Frank Tuttle*ch* Leroy Prince

Carl Brisson, Mary Ellis, Edward Everett Horton, Eugene Pallette, Katherine de Mille

AAN: Leroy Prince

'He thought he had the world by the tail – till it exploded in his face, with a bullet attached!'

All the King's Men ***
US   1949   109m   bw
Columbia (Robert Rossen)
V, V*, L

An honest man from a small town is elected mayor and then governor, but power corrupts him absolutely and he ruins his own life and those of his friends before being assassinated.

Archetypal American political melodrama based on the life of southern senator Huey Long. The background is well sketched in and there are excellent performances, but the overall narrative is rather flabby.

w Robert Rossen   *novel* Robert Penn Warren   *d* Robert Rossen   *ph* Burnett Guffey   *m* Louis Gruenberg   *ad* Sturges Carne   *ed* Robert Parrish, Al Clark

Broderick Crawford, John Ireland, Mercedes McCambridge, Joanne Dru, John Derek, Anne Seymour, Shepperd Strudwick

'More conspicuous for scope and worthiness of intention than for inspiration.' – *Gavin Lambert*

'The film is like one of those lifeless digests, designed for people who cannot spare the time to read whole books. Perhaps that accounts for its popularity.' – *Lindsay Anderson*

'A superb pictorialism which perpetually crackles and explodes.' – *Bosley Crowther*

'Realism comes from within as well as without and the core of meaning that might have made this film a step forward from *Boomerang* does not exist amid all the courageous camera-work.' – *Richard Winnington*

'Broderick Crawford's Willie Stark might just make you feel better about the President you've got . . . By no means a great film, but it moves along.' – *Pauline Kael, New Yorker*

AA: best picture; Broderick Crawford; Mercedes McCambridge

AAN: Robert Rossen (as writer); Robert Rossen (as director); John Ireland; editing

All the Marbles . . .
US   1981   113m   Metrocolor
MGM/Aldrich Company (William Aldrich)
V*
GB title: *The California Dolls*

Problems of a women's wrestling team in the midwest.

Tasteless and tedious exploitation comedy with just a few flashes of the director's old flair.

w Mel Frohman   *d* Robert Aldrich   *ph* Joseph Biroc   *m* Frank de Vol   *pd* Carl Anderson   *ed* Irving C. Rosenblum, Richard Lane

Peter Falk, Vicki Frederick, Laurene Landon, Burt Young, Tracy Reed

'The most devastating detective story of the century!'

All the President's Men ****
US   1976   138m   Technicolor
Warner/Wildwood (Robert Redford, Walter Coblenz)
V, V*

A reconstruction of the discovery of the White House link with the Watergate affair by two young reporters from the *Washington Post*.

An absorbing drama from the headlines which despite its many excellences would have been better with a more audible dialogue track, less murky photography and a clearer introduction of the characters concerned. The acting however is a treat.

w William Goldman   *book* Carl Bernstein, Bob Woodward   *d* Alan J. Pakula   *ph* Gordon Willis   *m* David Shire   *pd* George Jenkins

Robert Redford, Dustin Hoffman, Jason Robards Jnr, Martin Balsam, Hal Holbrook, Jack Warden, Jane Alexander, Meredith Baxter

'It works as a detective thriller (even though everyone knows the ending), as a credible (if occasionally romanticized) primer on the prosaic fundamentals of big league investigative journalism, and best of all, as a chilling tone poem that conveys the texture of the terror in our nation's capital during that long night when an aspiring fascist regime held our democracy under siege.' – *Frank Rich, New York Post*

AA: William Goldman; Jason Robards Jnr

AAN: best picture; Alan J. Pakula; Jane Alexander

All the Right Moves
US   1983   91m   colour
Fox (Stephen Deutsch)
V, V*, L

An ambitious high school football star is helped to get an athletics scholarship.

Rather dislikeable melodrama with specifically American atmosphere.

w Michael Kane   *d* Michael Chapman   *ph* Jan de Bont   *m* David Campbell   *ad* Mary Ann Biddle   *ed* David Garfield

Tom Cruise, Craig T. Nelson, Lea Thompson, Charles Cioffi, Christopher Penn

All the Right Noises *
GB   1969   91m   Eastmancolor
(TCF) Trigon (Anthony Hope)

The electrician of a touring company has an affair with a 15-year-old actress, but finally returns to his wife.

Sharp, sensible treatment of a cliché situation, as watchable as a superior television play.

wd Gerry O'Hara   *ph* Gerry Fisher   *m* John Cameron

Tom Bell, Judy Carne, Olivia Hussey, John Standing

'Built on a solid framework of disciplined direction and animated performances.' – *MFB*

All the Vermeers in New York
US   1990   87m   TVC colour
Complex Corporation (Henry S. Rosenthal)
V*, L

A Wall Street trader begins a relationship with a French woman he meets at the Metropolitan Museum of Art.

A desultory, minimalist film that proceeds in a haphazard fashion, picking up and then dropping the threads of the story.

wd Jon Jost   *ph* Jon Jost   *m* Jon A. English   *ed* Jon Jost

Emmanuelle Chaulet, Stephen Lack, Grace Phillips, Laurel Kiefer, Gordon Joseph Weiss, Katherine Bean, Gracie Mansion, Roger Ruffin

'Love is not a thing that grows only in the dark!'

All the Way Home **
US   1963   107m   bw
Paramount/Talent Associates (David Susskind)

In 1916 Tennessee, the beloved father of a family is killed in a car crash, and after the trauma wears off, mother helps the children to rebuild their lives.

Tactful, charming though finally depressing slice of small town period Americana, with generally eloquent performances.

w Philip Reisman Jnr   *play* Tad Mosel   *novel A Death in the Family* by James Agee   *d* Alex Segal   *ph* Boris Kaufman   *m* Bernard Green

Robert Preston, Jean Simmons, Aline MacMahon, Pat Hingle, Michael Kearney

'A heart-wrenching blend of nostalgia and sorrow.' – *Judith Crist*

'Terribly earnest, pictorial, and well intentioned. And a terrible mistake.' – *Pauline Kael, New Yorker*

All the Way Up *
GB   1970   97m   Technicolor
Granada/EMI (Philip Mackie)

Social-climbing Dad makes his way by treachery and blackmail, but gets his come-uppance when his son takes after him.

Crudely farcical adaptation of a thoughtful comedy of its time; the treatment works in fits and starts but leaves one in no mood for the talkative finale.

w Philip Mackie   *play Semi Detached* by David Turner   *d* James MacTaggart   *ph* Dick Bush   *m* Howard Blake

Warren Mitchell, Pat Heywood, Elaine Taylor, Kenneth Cranham, Vanessa Howard, Richard Briers, Adrienne Posta, Bill Fraser

All the Young Men
US   1960   87m   bw
Columbia (Hall Bartlett/Jaguar)
V*

A marine patrol in Korea is commanded by a black man, and racial tensions take precedence over fighting the enemy.

Simple-minded, parsimoniously-budgeted war melodrama.

wd Hall Bartlett   *ph* Daniel Fapp   *m* George Duning

Alan Ladd, Sidney Poitier, Ingemar Johansson, Glenn Corbett, James Darren, Mort Sahl

'Strenuously engaged in exploiting the entertainment values of nostalgia, fear, suspense, hatred and sex.' – *MFB*

All the Youthful Days: see *The Boys from Fengkuei*

All These Women: see *Now About All These Women . . .*

All This and Glamour Too: see *Vogues of 1938*

All This and Heaven Too **
US   1940   143m   bw
Warner (Jack L. Warner, Hal B. Wallis)
V, V*

A 19th-century French nobleman falls in love with his governess and murders his wife.

Romantic, melodramatic soap opera from a mammoth best seller; well made for those who can stomach it, with excellent acting and production values.

w Casey Robinson   *novel* Rachel Field   *d* Anatole Litvak   *ph* Ernest Haller   *m* Max Steiner

Charles Boyer, Bette Davis, Barbara O'Neil, Virginia Weidler, Jeffrey Lynn, Helen Westley, Henry Daniell, Harry Davenport, Walter Hampden, George Coulouris, Janet Beecher, Montagu Love

'Deserves extended runs and upped admissions . . . completely shorn of spectacle, but replete with finely drawn characters in absorbingly dramatic situations.' – *Variety*

'Litvak had it all on paper: he planned every move. There is not the spontaneity or flexibility.' – *Bette Davis*

AAN: best picture; Ernest Haller; Barbara O'Neil

All This and Money Too: see *Love is a Ball*

All This and World War Two *
US   1977   88m   DeLuxe/bw
Fox/Lou Reizner Productions

Wartime newsreels are interwoven with pop songs and clips from feature films.

A messy mélange with obvious items of interest, but totally confusing and uninformative for the young historian.

w no writer credit   *d* Susan Winslow

'Desperately straining to make any kind of sense, it is reduced to making parallels that are either glib or facetious.' – *MFB*

'Killer Bogart takes the Gestapo for a ride!'
All Through the Night *
US   1942   107m   bw
Warner (Jerry Wald)
V*

Gangsters help to track down fifth columnists in World War II New York.

Highly entertaining muddle of several styles which somehow works well and allows several favourites to do their thing.

w Leonard Spigelgass, Edwin Gilbert   *d* Vincent Sherman   *ph* Sid Hickox   *m* Adolph Deutsch

Humphrey Bogart, Conrad Veidt, Peter Lorre, Karen Verne, Judith Anderson, Jane Darwell, Frank McHugh, Jackie Gleason, William Demarest, Phil Silvers

'Exciting slaphappy stuff.' – *Kine Weekly*

'The thrills and the jokes have both been sharpened to a pin point.' – *New Statesman*

The All-American
US   1932   73m   bw
Universal
GB title: *Sport of a Nation*

A college football star finds his fame of little use to him in the outside world.

Lively drama of its day, but with little permanent interest.

w Frank Wead, Ferdinand Reyher, Richard Schayer, Dale Van Every   *d* Russell Mack

Richard Arlen, Andy Devine, Gloria Stuart, James Gleason, Preston Foster

'A pleaser for all audiences, having more than the football stuff to recommend it.' – *Variety*

The All-American
US   1952   83m   bw
U-I (Aaron Rosenberg)
GB title: *The Winning Way*

When his parents are killed on the way to a match, a college football hero rejects sport for the groves of *academe*.

Very modest formula drama.

w D. D. Beauchamp   *d* Jesse Hibbs   *ph* Maury Gertsman   *m* Joseph Gershenson

Tony Curtis, Mamie Van Doren, Lori Nelson, Gregg Palmer, Richard Long, Paul Cavanagh

The All-American Boy
US   1973   118m   colour   Panavision
Warner

A young boxer has got to the top too fast, and is depressed by the future.

Uninteresting character study.

wd Charles Eastman

Jon Voight, Carol Androsky, Anne Archer

Allan Quatermain and the Lost City of Gold
US   1987   99m   colour   JDC
Cannon (Menahem Golan, Yoram Globus)
V*, S

A mysterious old gold piece sends Quatermain looking for his brother, missing in Africa after seeking a lost white race.

Abysmal follow-up to 1985's ghastly *King Solomon's Mines*.

w Gene Quintano   *d* Gary Nelson   *ph* Alex Phillips, Frederick Elmes   *m* Michael Linn   *pd* Trevor Williams, Leslie Dilley   *ed* Alain Jakubowicz

Richard Chamberlain, Sharon Stone, James Earl Jones, Henry Silva, Robert Ronner

'The embarrassing screenplay jettisons Haggard's enduring fantasy and myth-making in favour of a back-of-the-envelope plotline and anachronistic jokes about Cleveland.' – *Daily Variety*

Allegheny Uprising
US   1939   98m   bw
RKO (P. J. Wolfson)
GB title: *The First Rebel*

A young frontiersman smashes liquor traffic with the Indians.

Modestly efficient Western with an impressive cast.

w P. J. Wolfson   *story* Neil Swanson   *d* William A. Seiter   *ph* Nicholas Musuraca

John Wayne, Claire Trevor, Brian Donlevy, George Sanders, Wilfrid Lawson, Robert Barrat, Moroni Olsen, Eddie Quillan, Chill Wills

'Long on horsemanship and action, short on romance and suspense.' – *Variety*

Allegro Ma Troppo *
France   1963   16m   Eastmancolor
Films Je Vois Tout

One night in Paris viewed through accelerated motion.

An amusing if not original conceit, smartly executed.

w/d/ph Paul de Roubaix   *m* François de Roubaix   *ed* Robert Enrico

Allegro Non Troppo *
Italy   1977   74m   colour/bw
Essential/Bruno Bozzetto
V*, L

A mix of live action and animation to create a modernistic version of *Fantasia*, e.g. Ravel's 'Bolero' is danced by a Coca-Cola bottle.

w Bruno Bozzetto, Guido Manuli, Maurizio Nichetti   *d* Bruno Bozzetto   *ph* Mario Masini   *md* Herbert von Karajan, Hans Stadlmair, Lorin Maazel   *m* Debussy, Dvorak, Ravel, Sibelius, Vivaldi, Stravinsky

Maurizio Nichetti, Nestor Garay, Maurizio Micheli, Maria Luisa Giovanni

Alligator *
US   1980   91m   DeLuxe
Group 1/Alligator Associates (Brandon Chase)
V, V*

A pet baby alligator is flushed down the toilet and later, grown to enormous size, goes on the rampage.

Jaws-type monster movie made tolerable by occasional flashes of humour but not otherwise remarkable.

w John Sayles   *d* Lewis Teague   *ph* Joseph Mangine   *m* Craig Hundley   *sp* Richard O. Helmer

Robert Forster, Robin Ryker, Michael Gazzo, Dean Jagger, Jack Carter, Henry Silva

'Hair raising, funny, shrewdly scripted and politically telling.' – *Margaret Hinxman, Daily Mail*

Alligator II: The Mutation
US   1991   90m   DeLuxe   Panavision
Golden Hawk (Brandon Chase)
V, V*

After an unscrupulous property developer dumps toxic waste in the city sewers, a monstrous man-eating alligator emerges to terrorize the town.

Uninvolving sequel that follows a familiar and predictable pattern and lacks the wit and pace of the original.

w Curt Allen   *d* Jon Hess   *ph* Joseph Mangine   *m* Jack Tillar   *pd* George Costello   *ed* Marshall Harvey, Chris Ellis

Joseph Bologna, Dee Wallace Stone, Richard Lynch, Woody Brown, Holly Gagnier, Bill Dailey, Steve Railsback, Brock Peters

An Alligator Named Daisy
GB   1955   88m   Technicolor   Vistavision
Rank (Raymond Stross)

A young songwriter finds himself saddled with a pet alligator.

The ultimate in silly animal comedies, this does score a few laughs.

w Jack Davies   *novel* Charles Terrot   *d* J. Lee-Thompson   *ph* Reg Wyer   *m* Stanley Black

Donald Sinden, Diana Dors, Jean Carson, James Robertson Justice, Stanley Holloway, Roland Culver, Margaret Rutherford, Avice Landone, Richard Wattis, Frankie Howerd, Jimmy Edwards, Gilbert Harding

'Apart from a fairly Kafkaesque scene in which Daisy is discovered in an upright piano, the situation is treated with little wit or comic invention.' – *MFB*

'Nerve-Shattering Terror'
'Her Honeymoon Turned Into A Nightmare Of Horror!'
The Alligator People
US   1959   73m   bw   Cinemascope
TCF (Jerry Wald)

A doctor uses a revolutionary serum which unfortunately turns patients into the alligators from which it was derived.

Moderately inventive 'B' chiller.

w Orville H. Hampton   *d* Roy del Ruth   *ph* Karl Struss   *m* Irving Gertz

George Macready, Frieda Inescort, Beverly Garland, Bruce Bennett, Lon Chaney Jnr

The Allnighter
US   1987   94m   CFI colour
Universal/Aurora (Tamar Simon Hoffs)
V*

Three girls party during their final days at college.

Unbelievably crass teen pic that is enough to put an entire generation off higher education – or sex, for that matter.

w M. I. Kessler, Tamar Simon Hoffs   *d* Tamar Simon Hoffs   *ph* Joseph Urbanczyk   *m* Charles Bernstein   *pd* Cynthia Sowder   *ed* Dan M. Rich

Susanna Hoffs, Dedee Pfeiffer, Joan Cusack, Michael Ontkean, Pam Grier, James Anthony Shanta, John Terlesky

Almonds and Raisins *
GB   1983   90m   bw
Willowgold/Brook Productions and the National Center for Jewish Film

The story of the Yiddish cinema in thirties New York.

Interesting documentary compilation majoring in the work of Edgar G. Ulmer.

w Wolf Mankowitz   *d* Russ Karel

Almost a Bride: see *A Kiss for Corliss*

Almost an Angel

US   1990   95m   DeLuxe
UIP/Paramount (John Cornell)
V, V*, L, S

A petty crook returns to Earth as a good angel.

Trite comedy with little substance and fewer laughs.

w Paul Hogan   d John Cornell   ph Russell Boyd
m Maurice Jarre   pd Henry Bumstead   ad Bernie
Cutler   ed David Stiven

Paul Hogan, Elias Koteas, Linda Kozlowski, Doreen
Lang, Robert Sutton, Travis Venable, Douglas Seale,
Ruth Warshawsky

Almost Angels

US   1962   93m   colour
Buena Vista
V*

A boy joins the Vienna Boys' Choir.

The singing outweighs the story in this overlong but
often pleasing filler.

w Vernon Harris   story R. A. Stemmle   d Steven
Previn

Vincent Winter, Peter Weck, Sean Scully, Hans Holt

Almost Married

US   1932   50m   bw
TCF

An insane Bolshevik breaks out of hospital when he
hears of his wife's bigamous marriage.

Oddly-titled melodrama with flashes of interest,
previously filmed by MGM in 1919.

w Wallace Smith   novel Devil's Triangle by Andrew
Soutar   d William Cameron Menzies

Violet Heming, Ralph Bellamy, Alexander Kirkland,
Alan Dinehart

An Almost Perfect Affair *

US   1979   93m   DeLuxe
Paramount/Terry Carr

A young film producer at the Cannes Festival falls for
the wife of an Italian impresario.

Lively detail lifts many scenes of this eccentric
romance, but the routine plot is a downer.

w Walter Bernstein, Don Peterson   d Michael Ritchie
ph Henri Decae   m Georges Delerue

Keith Carradine, Monica Vitti, Raf Vallone, Christian
de Sica

Almost Summer

US   1978   88m   colour
Universal (Rob Cohen)

High-school students hold an election for their new
president.

Mercifully short farcical comedy, aimed at a teenage
audience.

w Judith Berg, Sandra Berg, Martin Davidson, Marc
Reid Rubel   d Martin Davidson   ph Stevan Larner
m Ron Altbach, Charles Lloyd   ad William F. Hiney
ed Lynzee Klingman

John Friedrich, Bruno Kirby, Lee Purcell, Didi Conn,
Thomas Carter, Tim Matheson, Patronia Paley

Aloha Bobby and Rose

US   1975   89m   Metrocolor
Warner/Cine Artists International (Fouad Said)
V*

A Los Angeles motor mechanic becomes unwittingly
involved in crime and finds himself fleeing for the
Mexican border with a girlfriend.

Warmed-over retread of They Live By Night, not badly
done but of no abiding interest.

wd Floyd Mutrux   ph William A. Fraker

Paul Le Mat, Dianne Hull, Tim McIntire, Leigh
French, Noble Willingham, Robert Carradine

'As accurate a picture of Southern California as I've
yet seen.' – Guardian

Aloha Summer

US   1988   97m   CFI colour
Hanauma Bay (Mike Greco)
V*, L

An American teenager holidaying in Hawaii learns
about racial prejudice, sex and violence.

Typical teen picture, directed with a heavy hand.

w Mike Greco   d Tommy Lee Wallace   ph Steven
Poster   m Jesse Frederick, Bennet Salvay
ad Donald Harris   ed James Coblentz, Jack Hofstra,
Jay Cassidy

Chris Makepeace, Yuji Okumoto, Don Michael Paul,
Tia Carrere, Sho Kosugi, Lorie Griffin

'Pagan love – in an exotic, exciting tropic paradise!'

Aloma of the South Seas

US   1941   77m   Technicolor
Paramount (Monta Bell)

A young Polynesian chieftain returns to quell trouble
on his island after being educated in the US.

Hoary goings-on in gory colour, a remake of a silent
epic devised to display the star's sarong and the
backlot's expensive volcano.

w Frank Butler, Seena Owen, Lillie Hayward
d Alfred Santell   ph Karl Struss, Wilfrid M. Cline,
William Snyder   m Victor Young   sp Gordon
Jennings

Dorothy Lamour, Jon Hall, Lynne Overman, Philip
Reed, Katherine de Mille, Fritz Leiber, Dona Drake,
Esther Dale

'The mountain has the privilege of belching when it is
dissatisfied, which is something no well-bred critic
should do.' – C. A. Lejeune

† A silent version in 1926 had starred Gilda Gray.
Directed by Maurice Tourneur, it adhered more
closely to the original play (by John B. Hymer and
Leroy Clemens).

AAN: Karl Struss, Wilfrid M. Cline, William Snyder

Alone in the Dark

US   1982   93m   Cineffects
New Line/Masada
V*

Maximum-security prisoners in a mental hospital are
liberated by a power failure.

Pretentious but incompetent horror flick of the
Halloween school with a plot partly borrowed from
Spellbound.

wd Jack Sholder

Jack Palance, Donald Pleasence, Martin Landau,
Dwight Schultz, Deborah Hedwall

Alone on the Pacific **

Japan   1963   104m   Eastmancolor   Cinemascope
Ishihara-Nikkatsu (Akira Nakai)
original title: Taiheiyo Hitoribochi

A young man crosses from Osaka to San Francisco in
a small yacht.

Fascinating Robinson-Crusoe-like exercise, with
flashbacks to life on dry land.

w Natto Wada, based on the experiences of Kenichi
Horie   d Kon Ichikawa   ph Yoshihiro Yamazaki
m Yasushi Akatagawa, Tohru Takemitsu

Yujiro Ishihara, Masayuki Mori, Kinuyo Tanaka,
Ruriko Asaoko

'Wonderfully comic moments emerge, but they never
overshadow the film's sheer pictorial value.' – Brenda
Davies, MFB

Along Came Jones *

US   1945   90m   bw
UA/Cinema Artists Corporation (Gary Cooper)
V*

Two cowboys are mistaken for killers.

Very mild Western comedy melodrama, with the star
at his most self-effacing and production only
mediocre.

w Nunnally Johnson   novel Alan le May   d Stuart
Heisler   ph Milton Krasner   m Charles Maxwell,
Arthur Lange, Hugo Friedhofer

Gary Cooper, Loretta Young, William Demarest, Dan
Duryea, Russell Simpson

Along Came Sally: see Aunt Sally

Along the Great Divide

US   1950   88m   bw
Warner (Anthony Veiller)
V*

A marshal prevents an old man from being hanged for
murder, and eventually discovers the real culprit.

Adequate, modest Western with an unusual detective
element.

w Walter Doniger, Lewis Meltzer   d Raoul Walsh
ph Sid Hickox   m David Buttolph

Kirk Douglas, Virginia Mayo, Walter Brennan, John
Agar, Ray Teal

The Alphabet Murders

GB   1965   90m   bw
MGM (Ben Arbeid)
V*

Hercule Poirot solves a series of murders by an
apparent lunatic choosing his victims in alphabetical
order.

Ruination of a classic whodunnit novel, misguided
both in its attempt to mix slapstick with detection and
in its terrible central performance.

w David Pursall, Jack Seddon   novel The ABC
Murders by Agatha Christie   d Frank Tashlin
ph Desmond Dickinson   m Ron Goodwin

Tony Randall, Robert Morley, Anita Ekberg, Maurice
Denham, Guy Rolfe, James Villiers, Clive Morton

Alphaville *

France/Italy   1965   98m   bw
Chaumiane/Filmstudio (André Michelin)
V, V*

A special agent travels across space to find out what
happened to his predecessor, and finds himself in a
loveless society.

A rather chill futuristic fantasy on the lines of 1984 but
with an outer space background and a hero borrowed
from Peter Cheyney. Interesting but not endearing.

wd Jean-Luc Godard   ph Raoul Coutard   m Paul
Misraki

Eddie Constantine, Anna Karina, Akim Tamiroff,
Howard Vernon, Laszlo Szabo

'One surrenders to an experience which is the more
disturbing for being so near the recognisable normal.'
– Dilys Powell

Alpine Fire **

Switzerland   1985   117m   colour
Electric/SRG/WDR/Rex/Bernard Lang
Hohenfeuer

A sister and her deaf-mute brother, isolated on an
Alpine farm, embark on an incestuous relationship.

Unsensational and austere, it creates an atmosphere
all its own.

wd Fredi M. Murer   novel Fredi M. Murer   ph Pio
Corradi   m Mario Beretta   ed Helena Gerber

Thomas Nock, Johanna Lier, Dorothea Moritz, Rolf Illig, Tilli Breidenbach, Joerg Odermatt

Älskande Par: see *Loving Couples*

Altered States *
US 1980 102m Technicolor
Warner/Howard Gottfried, Daniel Melnick
V, V*, L, S

A psychophysiologist uses a sensory deprivation tank to hallucinate himself back into primitive states of human evolution, in which guise he emerges to kill . . .

Amusing elaboration of Jekyll and Hyde, not to mention the Karloff mad doctor second features of the forties. All very po-faced now, and certainly impeccably done.

w Sidney Aaron (Paddy Chayevsky) *novel* Paddy Chayevsky *d* Ken Russell *ph* Jordan Cronenweth *m* John Corigliano *pd* Richard McDonald

William Hurt, Blair Brown, Bob Balaban, Charles Haid

'Russell clomps from one scene to the next, the psychedelic visions come at you like choppy slide shows, and the picture has a dismal, tired, humanistic ending.' – *Pauline Kael, New Yorker*

'A feast for special effects lovers and drugged philosophy majors only.' – *Roger Ebert*

AAN: John Corigliano

'A herd of cattle against a herd of cannon!'
Alvarez Kelly
US 1966 116m Technicolor Panavision
Columbia/Ray David (Sol C. Siegel)
V*

The owner of a herd of 2500 cattle finds himself between two sides in the American Civil War.

Unusual if rather tepid Western which balances historical interest against social conscience and throws in a variety of other elements.

w Franklin Coen *d* Edward Dmytryk *ph* Joseph MacDonald *m* John Green

William Holden, Richard Widmark, Janice Rule, Patrick O'Neal, Victoria Shaw, Roger C. Carmel, Richard Rust

'One of the soppiest and sloppiest of Civil War cow-operas to have come our way in years.' – *Judith Crist*

Alvin Purple
Australia 1973 97m colour
Hexagon (Tim Burstall)

A young man who finds himself irresistible to women finally lands a job . . . as gardener in a convent.

Dismal sex farce which nevertheless helped to start the present world-wide popularity of Australian cinema. It took over a million dollars at the Australian box-office.

w Alan Hopgood *d* Tim Burstall

Graeme Blundell, Abigail, Lynette Curran, Christine Amor, Dina Mann

† A sequel *Alvin Rides Again* (qv) followed.

Alvin Rides Again
Australia 1974 89m colour
Hexagon (Tim Burstall)

Alvin continues to be irresistible to women.

Dire sequel to dim comedy, but one that failed to find an appreciative audience.

w Alan Hopgood *d* David Bilcock, Robin Copping

Graeme Blundell, Alan Finney, Frank Thring, Chantal Contouri, Abigail

Always *
US 1989 123m DeLuxe
UIP/Amblin/Steven Spielberg, Frank Marshall, Kathleen Kennedy
V, V*, L, S

A dead pilot returns as a ghost to aid a romance between another flyer and his girl-friend.

Sentimental remake of the 1944 movie *A Guy Named Joe*.

w Jerry Belson, Diane Thomas *d* Steven Spielberg *ph* Mikael Salomon *m* John Williams *pd* James Bissell *ed* Michael Kahn

Richard Dreyfuss, Holly Hunter, Brad Johnson, John Goodman, Audrey Hepburn, Roberts Blossom, Keith David, Ed Van Nuys

Always Goodbye
US 1931 62m bw
Fox

A much-jilted girl finally believes she has met Mr Right.

Fairly pointless romantic comedy which must have pleased some people in the early days of talkies.

w Kate MacLaurin *d* William Cameron Menzies, Kenneth MacKenna

Elissa Landi, Lewis Stone, Paul Cavanagh, John Garrick, Frederick Kerr

Always Goodbye
US 1938 75m bw
TCF (Raymond Griffith)

An unwed mother gives up her baby and later wants it back.

Tired sentimental warhorse, a remake of *Gallant Lady* (qv).

w Kathryn Scola, Edith Skouras *d* Sidney Lanfield *ph* Robert Planck *md* Louis Silvers

Barbara Stanwyck, Herbert Marshall, Ian Hunter, Cesar Romero, Lynn Bari, Binnie Barnes

'A fair summer attraction . . . should do satisfactorily on the strength of its cast.' – *Variety*

Always in My Heart *
US 1942 92m bw
Warner (Walter McEwen, William Jacobs)

A convict returns home to find his daughter a stranger and his wife about to marry again.

Well acted sentimental drama.

w Adele Commandini *play* Fly Away Home by Dorothy Bennett, Irving White *d* Joe Graham *ph* Sid Hickox *m* Heinz Roemheld

Walter Huston, Kay Francis, Gloria Warren, Frankie Thomas, Sidney Blackmer, Una O'Connor

AAN: title song (*m* Ernest Lecuona, *ly* Kim Gannon)

Always Leave Them Laughing *
US 1949 116m bw
Warner (Jerry Wald)

A vaudeville comedian craves the spotlight at the expense of his private life.

Raucous backstage vehicle, crammed with sentimental and melodramatic cliché but affording tantalizing glimpses of the stage acts of its two stars.

w Jack Rose, Mel Shavelson *d* Roy del Ruth *ph* Ernest Haller *ly* Sammy Cahn *md* Ray Heindorf

Milton Berle, Bert Lahr, Virginia Mayo, Ruth Roman, Alan Hale, Jerome Cowan

Always Together *
US 1947 78m bw
Warner

Dying millionaire bequeaths his all to a working girl, then recovers and tries to retrieve it.

Oddball comedy about a girl who has film fantasies, killed by dull title.

w Henry and Phoebe Ephron, I. A. L. Diamond *d* Frederick de Cordova

Joyce Reynolds, Robert Hutton, Cecil Kellaway, Ernest Truex; guest appearances by Bogart and Flynn (among others)

Ama
GB 1991 100m colour
Artifical Eye/Efiri Tete (Kwesi Owusu, Kwate Nee-Owoo)

A young girl, who learns by means of a computer disk that she is an ancestral messenger of the Asante, is warned that disaster will overtake her brother and father unless they change their plans.

Confused story, overloaded with fantasy, of Africans living unhappily in London.

w Kwesi Owusu *d* Kwesi Owusu, Kwate Nee-Owoo *ph* Jonathan Collinson, Roy Cornwall *m* Kwesi Owusu, Vico Mensah *ad* Ruhi Chaudry, Nigel Ashby, Keith Khan *ed* Justin Hrish

Thomas Baptiste, Anima Misa, Roger Griffiths, Nii Oma Hunter, Joy Elias Rilwan, Georgina Ackerman

'The film's nostalgia for the past, like all forms of sentimentality, implies an unwillingness to engage in reality.' – *Sight and Sound*

'The Man . . . The Music . . . The Madness . . . The Murder . . . The Motion Picture . . . Everything You've Heard Is True.'
Amadeus ***
US 1984 160m Technicolor Panavision
Saul Zaentz
V, V*, L, S

Dying in 1823, the jealous composer Salieri claims to have murdered Mozart.

A musical legend performed with success and economy on stage now becomes an exciting baroque film, like an opera in high-pitched dialogue. Great to look at, and only the American accents jar the ear.

w Peter Shaffer *play* Peter Shaffer *d* Milos Forman *ph* Miroslav Ondricek *md* Neville Marriner *pd* Patrizia Van Brandenstein *ed* Nena Danevic, Michael Chandler

F. Murray Abraham, Tom Hulce, Elizabeth Berridge, Simon Callow, Roy Dotrice, Christine Ebersole

AA: best picture; direction; F. Murray Abraham; adapted screenplay; make-up

AAN: Tom Hulce; photography; editing; art direction

BFA: Miroslav Ondricek

'She gave her innocence, her passion, her body. The one thing she couldn't give was her love.'
L'Amant *
GB/France 1992 115m colour
Guild/A2/Burrill/Giai Phong Film (Claude Berri, Timothy Burrill)
V, V*, L, S
aka: *The Lover*

A 15-year-old French girl in Vietnam begins an obsessive affair with a wealthy Chinese man.

Lushly romantic drama that exerts a certain charm.

w Gérard Brach, Jean-Jacques Annaud *novel* Marguerite Duras *d* Jean-Jacques Annaud *ph* Robert Fraisse *m* Gabriel Yared *ad* Thanh At Hoang *ed* Noëlle Boisson

Jane March, Tony Leung, Frédérique Meininger, Arnaud Giovaninetti, Melvil Poupaud, Lisa Faulkner, Jeanne Moreau (as narrator)

'Lacks the distinctive voice and ambiance of the book, but the abundant sex – soft-core and tasteful – and the splendid sets make up for the film's banal style.' – *Variety*

'Duras's subtle portrait of festering colonialism is brought to the screen with some resource by Annaud . . . But neither Leung nor Marsh, given a difficult role in her first film and certainly looking more fetching than she sounds, can provide a truly holding centre.' – *Derek Malcolm, Guardian*

'Touching, clear-eyed, utterly unsentimental, produced lavishly but with such discipline that the exotic locale never gets in the way of the minutely detailed drama at the center.' – *Vincent Canby, New York Times*

AAN: Robert Fraisse

Amantes: see *Lovers*

Les Amants **
France   1958   88m   bw   Dyaliscope
Nouvelles Editions (Louis Malle)
V
aka: *The Lovers*

A rich provincial wife has a secret life in Paris, but finds real satisfaction in an affair with a young man.

A passionate romance which had some censorship difficulties at the time, this rather gloomy film never quite whirls one away as it should, and it doesn't have the eye for detail of *Brief Encounter*.

w Louis Malle, Louise de Vilmorin   *novel Point de Lendemain* by Dominique Vivant   d Louis Malle   ph Henri Decaë   m Brahms   ad Jacques Saulnier, Bernard Evein   ed Léonide Azar

Jeanne Moreau, Alain Cuny, Jean-Marc Bory, Judith Magre

Les Amants de Montparnasse: see *The Lovers of Montparnasse*

Les Amants du Pont-Neuf
France   1991   125m   colour
Artificial Eye/Christian Fechner
V
aka: *Lovers on the Pont-Neuf*

An artist, who fears she is going blind, takes to the streets and ends up on the Pont-Neuf, inhabited by an old tramp and a young fire-eating drop-out, with whom she has an affair.

An anti-romantic love story: grim, grey and ultimately boring with its uninteresting characters upstaged by the locations.

wd Leos Carax   ph Jean-Yves Escoffier   m Benjamin Britten, Johann Strauss and others   ad Michael Vandestien   ed Nelly Quettier

Juliette Binoche, Denis Lavant, Klaus-Michael Gruber

'Neo-Godardian new wave: lazy in script, crazy in characterisation, wilfully disjunctive but undeniably powerful in performance and visual panache.' – *Ian Johnstone, Sunday Times*

'One of the most visually exhilarating and surprising films of recent years, a true "cinema of attractions" with music, colour, dazzling camerawork, melodramatic coincidences and tour de force performances.' – *Ginette Vincendeau, Sight and Sound*

'One has to admire the audacity, even if the result could be considered mere flim-flam.' – *Derek Malcolm, Guardian*

† The film, originally budgeted at 32 million francs (£3.2 million), became one of the most expensive of French films; its cost soared to between 100—160 million francs (£10—16 million) owing to building an elaborate set recreating the Pont-Neuf and its environs.

Les Amants de Vérone *
France   1948   110m   bw
CICC (Raymond Borderie)
aka: *The Lovers of Verona*

In modern Venice a film is being made of *Romeo and Juliet*, and the stand-ins for the stars feel they are re-enacting the old story.

A superbly stylish if rather empty piece, the dazzling detail being much more interesting than the main story.

w André Cayatte, Jacques Prévert   d André Cayatte   ph Henri Alekan   m Joseph Kosma   ad Moulaert

Pierre Brasseur, Serge Reggiani, Anouk Aimée, Louis Salou, Marcel Dalio

'Visually exciting, immaculately made.' – *Penelope Houston*

Les Amants du Tage: see *The Lovers of Lisbon*

Amarcord **
Italy/France   1973   123m   Technicolor
FC Produzione/PECF (Franco Cristaldi)
V*, S

Memories of a small Italian town during the fascist period.

A bizarre, intriguing mixture of fact, fantasy and obscurity, generally pleasing to watch though hardly satisfying. The title means 'I remember'.

w Federico Fellini, Tonino Guerra   d Federico Fellini   ph Giuseppe Rotunno   m Nino Rota   ad Danilo Donati

Puppela Maggio, Magali Noel, Armando Brancia, Ciccio Ingrassia

'A rich surface texture and a sense of exuberant melancholia.' – *Michael Billington, Illustrated London News*

'Peaks of invention separated by raucous valleys of low comedy.' – *Sight and Sound*

'Some idea of attitudes within the film business may be conveyed by the fact that this witty, tender, humane, marvellously photographed picture has been booked into a cinema with 132 seats.' – *Benny Green, Punch*

'Hitchcock once said that he wanted to play his audiences like a piano. Fellini requires the entire orchestra.' – *Roger Ebert*

AA: best foreign film

AAN: script; direction

The Amateur
US   1982   111m   Technicolor
TCF/Joel B. Michaels, Garth B. Drabinsky
V*

A computer expert goes into action on his own account when his girlfriend is killed in the Munich consulate and the CIA takes no reprisals.

Ho-hum espionage adventure which has its moments but barely got released.

w Robert Littell, Diana Maddox   *novel* Robert Littell   d Charles Jarrott   ph John Coquillon   m Ken Wannberg

John Savage, Christopher Plummer, Marthe Keller, Arthur Hill, Ed Lauter

'Ill constructed and largely implausible, with occasional atmospheric touches.' – *Guardian*

Amateur Daddy
US   1932   71m   bw
Fox

A promise to a dying friend leaves a construction engineer with four orphans to look after.

Sentimental drama of the *Daddy Longlegs* school, with backwoods atmosphere which makes it seem even more dated than it is.

w William Conselman, Doris Malloy and Frank Dolan   *novel Scotch Valley* by Mildred Cram   d John Blystone

Warner Baxter, Marian Nixon, Rita LaRoy, William Pawley, David Landau

'Strikes a strong human interest note . . . more than often very agreeable entertainment.' – *Variety*

The Amateur Gentleman *
GB   1936   102m   bw
Criterion (Marcel Hellman, Douglas Fairbanks Jnr)

A Regency innkeeper's son poses as a travelling pugilist in order to clear his father's name of theft.

Dated but rather fascinating period adventure, quite a lively production of its time.

w Clemence Dane, Edward Knoblock, Sergei Nolbandov   *novel* Jeffrey Farnol   d Thornton Freeland   ph Gunther Krampf   m Richard Addinsell

Douglas Fairbanks Jnr, Elissa Landi, Gordon Harker, Basil Sydney, Hugh Williams, Irene Browne, Margaret Lockwood, Coral Browne, Frank Pettingell, Athole Stewart, Esmé Percy

Amator: see *Camera Buff*

'Growing! growing! growing! When will it stop?'
The Amazing Colossal Man *
US   1957   80m   bw
AIP/Malibu (Bert I. Gordon)
V, V*
GB title: *The Terror Strikes*

A plutonium explosion causes an army colonel to grow at the rate of ten feet a day.

Modest, quite well written sci-fi let down by shaky trick work.

w Bert I. Gordon, Mark Hanna   d Bert I. Gordon   ph Joe Biroc   m Albert Glasser

Glenn Langan, Cathy Downs, William Hudson, James Seay

† Sequel: *War of the Colossal Beast*.

The Amazing Dobermans
US   1977   96m   colour
Golden (David Chudnow)
V*

A con man with five trained dogs helps a treasury agent get the better of a gangster.

So-so doggedly doggy comedy.

w Michael Kraike, William Goldstein, Richard Chapman   d Byron Chudnow   ph Jack Adams   m Alan Silvestri   ed James Potter

Fred Astaire, James Franciscus, Barbara Eden, Jack Carter, Billy Barty, Parley Baer

The Amazing Dr Clitterhouse **
US   1938   87m   bw
Warner (Robert Lord)

A criminologist researcher joins a gangster's mob and becomes addicted to crime.

Amusing, suspenseful, well acted comedy-melodrama.

w John Huston, John Wexley   *play* Barre Lyndon   d Anatole Litvak   ph Tony Gaudio   m Max Steiner

Edward G. Robinson, Humphrey Bogart, Claire Trevor, Allen Jenkins, Gale Page, Donald Crisp, Maxie Rosenbloom

'An unquestionable winner . . . the picture inculcates a bit of the sherlocking theme and modified romance.' – *Variety*

'The story is ingenious, but Anatole Litvak and his producing-acting crew have so thoroughly kept the larky mood of it while setting up the necessary mood of interest and suspense that it is hard to see where conception leaves off and the shaping of it into motion begins.' – *Otis Ferguson*

The Amazing Dr X
US   1948   78m   bw
Eagle-Lion (Ben Stoloff)
GB title: *The Spiritualist*

A widow seeks comfort from a fraudulent medium.

An interesting subject for a thriller is muffed by naïve handling.

w Muriel Roy Bolton, Ian McLellan Hunter *story* Crane Wilbur *d* Bernard Vorhaus *ph* John Alton *m* Alexander Laszlo

Lynn Bari, Richard Carlson, Turhan Bey, Cathy O'Donnell

Amazing Grace and Chuck
US 1987 115m colour
Tri-Star/Rastar (David Field)
V*, L, S
GB title: *Silent Voice*

On both sides of the Iron Curtain, a weird selection of public personalities stand up in favour of the elimination of nuclear weapons.

Expensive but inept propaganda apparently motivated by Ted Turner.

w David Field *d* Mike Newell *ph* Robert Elswit *m* Elmer Bernstein *pd* Dena Roth *ed* Peter Hollywood

Jamie Lee Curtis, Alex English, Gregory Peck, William L. Petersen, Joshua Zuehike

'As amazingly bad as it is audacious.' – *Daily Variety*

The Amazing Mr Beecham: see *The Chiltern Hundreds*

The Amazing Mr Blunden **
GB 1972 99m Eastmancolor
Hemdale/Hemisphere (Barry Levinson)
V*

In 1918, a widow and her two children meet a kindly gentleman who offers them work in his old mansion. Here they meet two ghost children, discover that he is a ghost too, and travel a hundred years back in time to right a wicked wrong.

Involved ghost story for intellectual children, made generally palatable by oodles of period charm and good acting.

wd Lionel Jeffries *story* *The Ghosts* by Antonia Baker *ph* Gerry Fisher *m* Elmer Bernstein *pd* Wilfrid Shingleton

Laurence Naismith, Diana Dors, James Villiers, David Lodge, Lynne Frederick, Dorothy Alison, Rosalyn Lander, Marc Granger

'Easy period charm . . . fills every crevice.' – *Clyde Jeavons*

The Amazing Mr Forrest: see *The Gang's All Here* (1939)

The Amazing Mr Williams *
US 1939 86m bw
Columbia (Everett Riskin)

About-to-be-marrieds investigate a murder.

Brisk comedy-thriller on *Thin Man* lines.

w Dwight Taylor, Sy Bartlett, Richard Maibaum *d* Alexander Hall *ph* Arthur Todd *md* Morris Stoloff

Melvyn Douglas, Joan Blondell, Ruth Donnelly, Clarence Kolb, Ed Brophy, Donald MacBride, Don Beddoe

The Amazing Mrs Holliday
US 1943 98m bw
Universal (Bruce Manning, Frank Shaw)

Torpedoed in mid-Pacific, a missionary's daughter arrives in San Francisco with eight Chinese orphans.

Unusual sentimental vehicle for its star; of no particular interest or merit in itself, but with the usual interludes for song.

w Frank Ryan, John Jacoby *d* Bruce Manning *ph* Elwood Bredell *md* Charles Previn *m* Hans Salter, Frank Skinner

Deanna Durbin, Edmond O'Brien, Frieda Inescort, Barry Fitzgerald, Arthur Treacher, Harry Davenport, Grant Mitchell

'Timely drama with human interest angles.' – *Variety*

AAN: Hans Salter, Frank Skinner

The Amazing Quest of Ernest Bliss
GB 1936 80m bw
Garrett – Klement (Robert Garrett, Otto Klement)
V*
US title: *Romance and Riches*; aka: *Amazing Adventure*

A millionaire accepts a wager that he can live independently of his riches for one year.

Formulary comedy drama of its era on the theme that money isn't everything. Very dated.

w John L. Balderston *novel* E. Phillips Oppenheim *d* Alfred Zeisler *ph* Otto Heller

Cary Grant (on home leave after his first Hollywood success), Mary Brian, Henry Kendall, Leon M. Lion, Garry Marsh, Moore Marriott, Peter Gawthorne, Ralph Richardson

Amazon Women on the Moon
US 1987 85m colour
Universal (Robert K. Weiss)
V*, L

A parody of a 1950s low-budget science fiction movie is interrupted by a series of supposedly comic sketches.

While the parody is precise and amusing, the surrounding material, which occupies the majority of the film, is weak and silly.

w Michael Barrie, Jim Mulholland *d* Joe Dante, Carl Gottlieb, Peter Horton, John Landis, Robert K. Weiss *ph* Daniel Pear *led* Bert Lovitt, Marshall Harvey, Malcolm Campbell

Rosanna Arquette, Ralph Bellamy, Carrie Fisher, Griffin Dunne, Steve Guttenberg, Michelle Pfeiffer

The Ambassador
US 1984 95m TVC colour
Cannon/Northbrook (Isaac Kol)
V*

An American ambassador to Israel gets in the line of fire with the Arabs; meanwhile his wife is having an affair with a man who is secretly a leader of the PLO.

Aged stars go gloomily through some tasteless paces in this politically unwise pseudo-thriller.

w Max Jack *novel* *52 Pick Up* by Elmore Leonard *d* J. Lee Thompson *ph* Avi Karpik, Ofer Yanov, Rami Siman Tov *m* Dov Seltzer

Robert Mitchum, Ellen Burstyn, Rock Hudson, Fabio Testi, Donald Pleasence

'Not wild enough to be funny.' – *Sight and Sound*

† Not much more than a year later, the original novel was filmed under its own title in its original setting.

Ambassador Bill
US 1931 68m bw
Fox
V*

An Oklahoma cattle man is appointed US ambassador to a foreign country ruled by a regency.

Poorly tailored star vehicle.

w Guy Bolton *story* Vincent Sheean *d* Sam Taylor

Will Rogers, Marguerite Churchill, Greta Nissen, Gustav von Seyffertitz, Ray Milland

'Wilting yarn, illogical hoke.' – *Variety*

The Ambassador's Daughter *
US 1956 102m Technicolor Cinemascope
UA/Norman Krasna
V*

An American senator in Paris decides that the presence of US forces in Paris constitutes a moral danger. The ambassador's daughter decides to investigate.

Thin comedy of the old-fashioned type: smart lines and intimate playing not helped by the vast screen.

wd Norman Krasna *ph* Michael Kelber *m* Jacques Metehen

Olivia de Havilland, John Forsythe, Edward Arnold, Adolphe Menjou, Myrna Loy, Francis Lederer, Tommy Noonan, Minor Watson

'An experienced cast approach the story's frivolities with poise and style.' – *MFB*

The Ambulance
US 1990 95m DeLuxe Panavision
Epic/Sarlui/Diamant (Moctesuma Esparta, Robert Katz)
V, V*

Aided by an old reporter, a photographer investigates the disappearance of people from the streets of New York.

Absurd thriller, with rather better acting than it deserves.

wd Larry Cohen *ph* Jacques Haitkin *m* Jay Chatterway *pd* Lester Cohen *ed* Arnold Lebowitz, Claudia Finkle

Eric Roberts, James Earl Jones, Megan Gallagher, Richard Bright, Janine Turner, Eric Braeden, Red Buttons

'A seamless thriller with top-notch thrills.' – *Empire*

Ambush *
US 1938 62m bw
Paramount

A girl proves her brother innocent and brings gangsters to book.

Brisk second feature with an unexpected writing credit.

w S. J. and Laura Perelman *d* Kurt Neumann

Gladys Swarthout, Lloyd Nolan, Ernest Truex

'Hard hitting, fast moving and at all times plausible.' – *Variety*

Ambush *
US 1949 89m bw
MGM (Armand Deutsch)

An army scout leads a posse to capture an Indian chief who is holding a white woman hostage.

Good, clean, robust Western, well produced and acted.

w Marguerite Roberts *d* Sam Wood *ph* Harold Lipstein *m* Rudolph Kopp

Robert Taylor, John Hodiak, Arlene Dahl, Don Taylor, Jean Hagen, Leon Ames

'One man against the west!'
Ambush at Tomahawk Gap
US 1953 73m Technicolor
Columbia (Wallace MacDonald)
V*

Four ex-convicts seek hidden loot in a ghost town.

Standard co-feature Western with rather more violence than usual for its date.

w David Lang *d* Fred F. Sears *ph* Henry Freulich *m* Ross Di Maggio

John Hodiak, John Derek, David Brian, Maria Elena Marques, Ray Teal, John Qualen

Ambush Bay
US 1966 109m DeLuxe
UA/Aubrey Schenck

In 1944, nine Marines try to escape from a Japanese-held island.

Routine, lengthy, sub-standard heroics for action addicts.

w Marve Feinberg, Ib Melchior d Ron Winston ph Emanuel Rojas m Richard La Salle

Hugh O'Brian, Mickey Rooney, James Mitchum, Tisa Chang, Harry Lauter

The Ambushers
US 1967 102m Technicolor
Columbia/Meadway/Claude (Irving Allen)
V*, L

An experimental flying disc disappears on a test run, and the trail leads Matt Helm to the Mexican jungle.

The third Matt Helm adventure had such a stupid script that all concerned decided to send it up, unfortunately with too obvious a tendency to smirk at their own bravado.

w Herbert Baker d Henry Levin ph Burnett Guffey, Edward Colman m Hugo Montenegro

Dean Martin, Senta Berger, Janice Rule, Kurt Kasznar, James Gregory, Albert Salmi

'Plot, jokes and gadgets all well below par.' – *MFB*

'Love of tender girlhood! Passionate deeds of heroes! A rushing, leaping drama of charm and excitement!'
America *
US 1924 122m (24 fps) bw silent
(UA) D. W. Griffith

Various characters experience the Revolutionary War.

The Birth of a Nation, one war back. Much of interest, but nothing new; Griffith was basically repeating himself.

w John Pell d D. W. Griffith ph Billy Bitzer, Hendrick Sartow, Marcel le Picard, Hal Sintzenich

Neil Hamilton, Carol Dempster, Lionel Barrymore, Erville Alderson

'Here is the romance of one hundred million people, told in heartthrobs!' – *D. W. Griffith*

† As the English were the villains, the film was banned in Britain, but later released under the title *Love and Sacrifice*.

America, America *
US 1963 177m bw
Warner/Athena Enterprises (Elia Kazan)
V
GB title: *The Anatolian Smile*

In 1896 Turkey, a young Greek dreams of emigrating to America, and finally does so.

A massive piece of self-indulgence by a one-man band, fascinating for his family circle but so poorly constructed as to be of very limited interest elsewhere.

wd Elia Kazan ph Haskell Wexler m Manos Hadjidakis

Stathis Giallelis, Frank Wolff, Harry Davis, Elena Karam, Estelle Hemsley, Lou Antonio

'Kazan has failed to film the adventure implicit in his material, and a potentially exciting story has gone to waste.' – *MFB*

'If he sinks his teeth in a scene or a sequence that he enjoys, the audience can just sit around and be damned.' – *Stanley Kauffmann*

'Every episode, almost every shot, has its own beginning, middle and end, and the numberless playlets are cemented together into a strip which after the first two hours threatens to stretch grimly into eternity.' – *Robert Hatch, The Nation*

AAN: best picture; Elia Kazan (as writer); Elia Kazan (as director)

The American Beauty: see *La Belle Américaine*

American Blue Note *
US 1989 97m Technicolor
Vested Interests/Fakebook (Ralph Toporoff)
L
aka: *Fakebook*

In the 1960s the leader of a jazz quintet struggles to find an audience for his music.

Gentle, well-observed off-beat film with a sense of humour.

w Gilbert Girion d Ralph Toporoff ph Joey Forsyte m Larry Schanker pd Charles Lagola ed Jack Haigis

Peter MacNicol, Carl Capotorto, Tim Guinee, Bill Christopher-Myers, Jonathan Walker, Charlotte D'Amboise, Trini Alvarado

An American Dream
US 1966 103m Technicolor
Warner (William Conrad)
GB title: *See You in Hell, Darling*

A TV commentator is goaded into murdering his wife, becomes involved with gangsters and, tortured by guilt, allows them to kill him for shielding the girlfriend of one of them.

Ludicrously heavy-handed version of a semi-surrealist book which presumably had something to say about modern America, at least in its author's mind. Nothing comes through but relentless boredom at watching sordid and unlikely events, and sympathy for those involved.

w Mann Rubin novel Norman Mailer d Robert Gist ph Sam Leavitt m Johnny Mandel

Stuart Whitman, Janet Leigh, Eleanor Parker (in a one-scene role of screaming bitchery that has to be seen to be believed), J. D. Cannon, Lloyd Nolan, Barry Sullivan, Murray Hamilton

'An idiotic melodrama laced with the salacious syndromes and little-boy nastiness that are the hallmark of today's "mature film".' – *Judith Crist*

AAN: song, 'A Time for Love' (m Johnny Mandel, ly Paul Francis Webster)

American Dreamer
US 1984 105m Technicolor
Warner/Rank/CBS (Doug Chapin)
V*

An Ohio housewife writes a novel, wins a trip to Paris, and finds her romantic dreams coming true.

A kind of lower-case reprise of *Romancing the Stone*, this modest comedy works only in fits and starts.

w Jim Kouf, David Greenwalt story Ann Biderman d Rick Rosenthal ph Giuseppe Rotunno m Lewis Furey pd Brian Eatwell ed Anne Goursaud

JoBeth Williams, Tom Conti, Giancarlo Giannini, Coral Browne, James Staley

'A pleasant throwback to earlier forms of Hollywood farce.' – *Variety*

'The nation-blazing epic of America's westward march!'
American Empire
US 1942 82m bw
Harry Sherman/UA
V*
GB title: *My Son Alone*

Brothers fall out over management of their Texas ranch.

Reasonable but forgettable semi-Western.

w Ben Grauman Kohn, Gladys Atwater, Robert Bren d William McGann

Richard Dix, Preston Foster, Frances Gifford, Leo Carrillo

American Flyers
US 1985 114m/Panavision Technicolor
Warner/Gareth Wigan, Paula Weinstein
V, V*, L

Two brothers compete in a gruelling bicycle race.

Ambitious but ineffective drama with too much effort to explore personal dramas instead of getting on with the action.

w Steve Tesich d John Badham ph Don Peterman m Lee Ritenour, Greg Mathieson pd Lawrence G. Paull ed Frank Morriss

Kevin Costner, David Grant, Rae Dawn Chong, Alexandra Paull, Janice Rule

'Overblown production just pumps hot air in too many directions and comes up limp.' – *Variety*

The American Friend *
West Germany 1977 127m colour
Road Movies/WDR/Wim Wenders
V, V*, L
original title: *Der amerikanische Freund*

A Hamburg picture-framer thinks he is dying and is persuaded to become a Mafia hitman.

Strange melodrama which got the ear of the cognoscenti.

w Wim Wenders, Fritz Müller-Scherz novel *Ripley's Game* by Patricia Highsmith d Wim Wenders ph Robby Müller m Jürgen Knieper

Dennis Hopper, Bruno Ganz, Lisa Kreuzer, Gerard Blain, Nicholas Ray, Samuel Fuller

American Friends *
GB 1991 95m Eastmancolor
Virgin/British Screen/Millennium/Mayday/Prominent Features (Patrick Cassavetti, Steve Abbott)
V, V*, L

In Victorian England, a middle-aged Oxford academic, who is about to be elected president of his college, a post for a bachelor, falls in love with an American woman.

Gentle, quirky tale of romantic and academic intrigue that yields small pleasures.

w Michael Palin, Tristram Powell d Tristram Powell ph Philip Bonham-Carter m Georges Delerue pd Andrew McAlpine ed Dennis McTaggart

Michael Palin, Trini Alvarado, Connie Booth, Bryan Pringle, Fred Pearson, Alfred Molina, Susan Denaker, Robert Eddison

'Not really the stuff of the big screen, but rather a perfectly acceptable, reasonably touching TV drama.' – *Empire*

'He's the highest paid lover in Beverly Hills!'
American Gigolo
US 1980 117m Metrocolor
Paramount/Pierre Associates (Freddie Fields)
V, V*, L

A male prostitute finds that a client won't clear him when he is falsely charged with murder.

Thoroughly unattractive wallow on the seamy side of Los Angeles, with none of *Midnight Cowboy*'s compassion.

wd Paul Schrader ph John Bailey m Giorgio Moroder

Richard Gere, Lauren Hutton, Hector Elizondo, Nina Van Pallandt

'A hot subject, cool style and overly contrived plotting don't all mesh.' – *Variety*

'A perverse film devoted to perversity, typical of Schrader's apparently sadistic intent to pillory his audience with every kind of degenerate act he can manufacture.' – *Motion Picture Guide*

† Christopher Reeve allegedly refused one million dollars to play the lead.

American Gothic
GB/Canada 1988 90m colour
Manor Ground/Vidmark (John Quested/Christopher Harrop)
V*, L

A murderous family, living in an old house on an otherwise deserted island, invites some stranded travellers to stay.

Ludicrous, hammily acted horror.

w Burt Wetanson, Michael Vines   d John Hough
ph Harvey Harrison   m Alan Parker   pd David
Hiscox   sp Allen Benjamin   ed John Victor Smith

Rod Steiger, Yvonne de Carlo, Sarah Torgov, Michael
J. Pollard, Fiona Hutchinson, William Hootkins

'Where were you in '62?'
American Graffiti **
US 1973 110m Techniscope
Universal/Lucasfilm/Coppola Company (Francis Ford Coppola, Gary Kurtz)
V, V*, L, S

In 1962 California, four young men about to leave for college gather for a night's girl-chasing and police-baiting.

Nostalgic comedy recalling many sights and sounds of the previous generation and carefully crystallizing a particular time and place. Successful in itself, it led to many imitations.

wd George Lucas   ph Ron Eveslage, Jan D'Alquen
m popular songs

Richard Dreyfuss, Ronny Howard, Paul le Mat, Charlie
Martin Smith, Cindy Williams, Candy Clark,
Mackenzie Philips

† The film cost 750,000 dollars, and grossed 55 million.

AAN: best picture; George Lucas (as writer); George Lucas (as director); Candy Clark

An American Guerrilla in the Philippines *
US 1950 105m Technicolor
TCF (Lamar Trotti)
GB title: I Shall Return

World War II, Pacific Zone: two American sailors try to make their way to Australia after MacArthur's surrender at Bataan.

Rather dull adventure story shot in the actual locations.

w Lamar Trotti   novel Ira Wolfert   d Fritz Lang
ph Harry Jackson   m Cyril Mockridge

Tyrone Power, Micheline Presle, Tom Ewell, Bob
Patten, Tommy Cook, Robert Barrat (as MacArthur),
Jack Elam

'Cannot be regarded as a serious war film.' – Penelope
Houston

'Jack Kelson is going straight. And his son's breaking the law to help him.'
American Heart *
US 1992 114m colour
Entertainment/Avenue/World Films (Rosilyn Heller, Jeff Bridges)

Out on parole, a former prisoner tries to go straight and also look after his teenage son.

An interesting attempt to deal with the lower reaches of American life in a realistic manner, but one that is only partly successful.

w Peter Silverman   story Martin Bell, Mary Ellen
Mark, Peter Silverman   d Martin Bell   ph James
R. Bagdonas   m James Newton Howard   pd Joel
Schiller   ed Nancy Baker

Jeff Bridges, Edward Furlong, Lucinda Jenney, Don
Harvey, Tracey Tyla Kapisky, John Boylan

'Has plenty of passion and commitment but is rather too straightforward and disappointingly resolved to qualify as a total success.' – Variety

'The film tries now and then to be upbeat in the familiar American manner but doesn't press it and is rarely sentimental. Bell goes for the jugular when he can.' – Derek Malcolm, Guardian

American Hot Wax
US 1978 91m Metrocolor
Paramount (Art Linson)
V*

The early days of rock and roll as seen by a prominent disc jockey of the time.

Mildly entertaining ragbag of semi-historical facts and authentic music, strictly for the youth market.

w John Kaye   d Floyd Mutrux   ph William A.
Fraker   md Kenny Vance

Tim McIntire (as Alan Freed), Fran Drescher, Jay
Leno, Laraine Newman, Chuck Berry, Jerry Lee
Lewis, Screamin' Jay Hawkins

An American in Paris ****
US 1951 113m Technicolor
MGM (Arthur Freed)
V, V*, L, S

A carefree young artist scorns a rich woman's patronage and wins the love of a gamine.

Altogether delightful musical holiday, one of the highspots of the Hollywood genre, with infectious enthusiasm and an unexpected sense of the Paris that was.

w Alan Jay Lerner   d Vincente Minnelli   ph Al Gilks,
John Alton   m George Gershwin   ly Ira Gershwin
ch Gene Kelly   ad Cedric Gibbons, Preston Ames
ed Adrienne Fazan

Gene Kelly, Oscar Levant, Nina Foch, Leslie Caron, Georges
Guetary

songs: 'I Got Rhythm'; 'Embraceable You'; 'By
Strauss'; 'Swonderful'; 'Tra La La'; 'Our Love Is Here
to Stay'; 'Stairway to Paradise'; 'Concerto in F'
(instrumental); 'An American in Paris' (ballet)

'Too fancy and overblown, but the principal performers are in fine form and the Gershwin music keeps everything good-spirited.' – New Yorker, 1977

† Chevalier was originally paged for the Georges Guetary role, but turned it down because he lost the girl. The production cost $2,723,903, of which $542,000 went on the final ballet.

AA: best picture; Alan Jay Lerner; Al Gilks, John Alton; musical arrangements (Saul Chaplin, Johnny Green); art direction; costumes (Walter Plunkett, Irene Sharaff)

AAN: Vincente Minnelli; editing

American Madness **
US 1932 80m bw
Columbia

When a bank failure threatens, hundreds of small savers increase their deposits to save the situation.

Vivid, overstressed topical melodrama with crowd scenes typical of its director's later output.

w Robert Riskin   d Frank Capra   ph Joseph
Walker

Walter Huston, Pat O'Brien, Kay Johnson, Constance
Cummings, Gavin Gordon, Berton Churchill

'It's a money picture. That goes both ways. It's about money and banks and spells dough for the box office. It's timely, topical, human, dramatic, punchy and good entertainment at one and the same time.' – Variety

'The sequence of the mounting panic and the storming of the bank are effectively staged, but the resolution is the usual Capra/Riskin populist hokum.' – New Yorker, 1977

American Me **
US 1992 125m DeLuxe
Y.O.Y. (Sean Daniel, Robert M. Young, Edward James Olmos)
V, V*, L, S

A young Hispanic hoodlum serves an 18-year jail sentence and tries to make sense of his life on his release.

Grim, forceful and engrossing depiction of a savage world, inside and outside prison, where violence, crime and drugs are the shaping influences.

w Floyd Mutrux, Desmond Nakano   d Edward James
Olmos   ph Reynaldo Villalobos   m Dennis Lambert,
Claude Gaudette   pd Joe Aubel   ed Arthur
R. Coburn, Richard Candib

Edward James Olmos, William Forsythe, Pepe Serna,
Danny de La Paz, Evelina Fernandez, Cary Hiroyuki
Tagawa, Daniel Villareal, Sal Lopez

'Represents a massive downer by any conventional audience standards, and also runs the risk of attracting the type of crowd that will groove on the violence and ignore the message.' – Variety

'True tragedy; there are moments of Shakespearean power as well as graphic violence.' – John Anderson, Newsday

American Ninja
US 1986 95m TVC Color
Cannon/Menahem Golan/Yoram Globus
V, V*, S
GB title: American Warrior

Two GIs use extreme violence to thwart gun-runners and other enemies in the Philippines.

Flaccid martial arts movie.

w Paul de Mielche   story Avi Kleinberger, Gideon
Amir   d Sam Firstenberg   ph Hanania Baer
m Michael Linn   pd Adrian H. Gorton   ed Andrew
Horvitch

Michael Dudikoff, Steve James, Judie Aronson,
Guich Koock

American Ninja 2: The Confrontation
US 1987 100m TVC Color
Cannon/Menahem Golan/Yoram Globus
V, V*, L, S

Two US Army Rangers are sent to a small Caribbean island to investigate a mystery of disappearing marines.

Non-stop action, leavened with a touch of humour.

w Gary Conway, James Booth   d Sam Firstenberg
ph Gideon Porath   m George S. Clinton   pd Holger
Gross   ed Michael J. Duthie

Michael Dudikoff, Steve James, Larry Poindexter,
Gary Conway, Jeff Weston

American Ninja 3: Blood Hunt
US 1989 93m Rank Color
Cannon/Breton (Harry Alan Towers)
V, V*, L, S

The toughest man in the world takes his revenge after he is infected with a deadly disease by the men who murdered his father.

Dreary action movie, full of ineptly-staged fights.

wd Cedric Sundstrom   story Gary Conway
ph George Bartels   m George S. Clinton   pd Ruth
Strimling   ed Michael J. Duthie

David Bradley, Steve James, Marjoe Gortner, Michele
Chan, Yehuda Efroni, Calvin Jung

American Ninja 4: The Annihilation
US 1991 95m colour
Cannon (Christopher Pearce)
V, V*, L

A teacher reverts to his martial arts training to rescue friends taken prisoner by an evil sheikh.

Dim and unexciting sequel, with little sign of life or interest from the participants.

w David Geeves   d Cedric Sundstrom   ph Joseph
Wein   m Nicolaas Tenbroek   pd Ruth Stripling
ed Claudio Yrtuc

Michael Dudikoff, David Bradley, James Booth, Dwayne Alexandre, Robin Stille, Ken Gampu

'Low-budget, no-talent programmer . . . Even the genre's most devoted fans will be disappointed by the lack of imagination and energy in the fight scenes.' – *Variety*

An American Romance *
US   1944   151m   Technicolor
MGM (King Vidor)

The life of a European immigrant who becomes a master of industry.

Mind-boggling pageant of the American dream, coldly presented and totally humourless. Its saving grace is its smooth physical presentation.

w Herbert Dalmas, William Ludwig   *d* King Vidor
ph Harold Rosson   *m* Louis Gruenberg

Brian Donlevy, Ann Richards, John Qualen, Walter Abel, Stephen McNally

'A thousand chances to inform, excite or even interest have been flung away.' – *Richard Winnington*

'The whole aim of it is to boost The American Way.' – *Richard Mallett, Punch*

American Samurai
US   1992   87m   colour
Cannon/Global (Allan Greenblatt)
V, V*

An American journalist investigating a murder using a samurai sword is forced to enter a fight to the death.

Mundane action film, offering little that cannot be found in a dozen similar movies of equal banality.

w John Corcoran   *d* Sam Firstenberg   *ph* David Gurfinkel   *m* Robbie Patton   *pd* Kuly Sander
ed Sebastian Serrell-Watts, Shlomo Chazan

David Bradley, Mark Dacascos, Valarie Trapp, Rex Ryon, Melissa Hellman, John Fujioka

'Cheap and trite, this is yet another hymn to the ability of a handsome white guy to beat up ethnic opponents.' – *Empire*

The American Success Company *
US   1980   94m   colour
Columbia (Edgar J. Scherick and Daniel H. Blatt)

The inexperienced son of a credit card tycoon becomes a tough guy.

Tilts at the American myth: not a notable success.

w William Richert, Larry Cohen   *d* William Richert

Jeff Bridges, Belinda Bauer, Ned Beatty, Steven Keats, Bianca Jagger

An American Tail *
US   1986   80m   DeLuxe
Universal/Steven Spielberg (Don Bluth, John Pomeroy, Gary Goldman)
V, V*, L, S

Russian mice encounter all kinds of trouble when in the 1880s they emigrate to the United States.

Expensive cartoon feature with old-fashioned full animation but not much in the way of narrative interest or indeed humour.

w Judy Freudberg, Tony Geiss   *d* Don Bluth (also designer)

voices: Cathianne Blore, Christopher Plummer, Dom de Luise, Madeline Kahn

'Every character and every situation have been presented a thousand times before . . . anyone over the age of 12 will likely experience more boredom than pleasure.' – *Variety*

AAN: song, 'Somewhere Out There' (James Horner, Barry Mann, Cynthia Weil)

'Look Out Pardeners, There's A New Mouse In Town!'

An American Tail: Fievel Goes West **
US   1991   75m   colour
UIP/Universal/Amblin (Steven Spielberg, Robert Watts)
V, V*, L, S

A confidence trickster of a cat persuades a family of mice to move to the West.

Enjoyable and high-spirited animated film that borrows plot and attitudes from classic Westerns.

w Flint Dille   *story* Charles Swenson   *d* Phil Nibbelink, Simon Wells   *m* James Horner

voices of Phillip Glasser, James Stewart, Erica Yohn, Cathy Cavadini, Nehemiah Persoff, Dom de Luise, Amy Irving, John Cleese, Jon Lovitz

'Drama that happens around you every day – when the wild life of impetuous youth burns away age-old barriers!'

An American Tragedy **
US   1931   95m   bw
Paramount

An ambitious young man murders his pregnant fiancée when he has a chance to marry a rich girl.

Dated but solidly satisfying adaptation of a weighty novel, more compelling than the 1951 remake *A Place in the Sun*.

wd Josef von Sternberg   *novel* Theodore Dreiser
ph Lee Garmes   *ad* Hans Dreier

Phillips Holmes, *Sylvia Sidney*, Frances Dee, Irving Pichel, Frederick Burton, Claire McDowell

'It unreels as an ordinary programme effort with an unhappy ending . . . as Sternberg has seen fit to present it the celluloid structure is slow, heavy and not always interesting drama. Its box office success is very doubtful.' – *Variety*

'It is the first time, I believe, that the subjects of sex, birth control and murder have been put into a picture with sense, taste and reality.' – *Pare Lorentz*

'An aimless, lugubrious mess. The fireworks may dazzle to schoolboys of criticism, but they will add no permanent color to the motion picture.' – *Harry Alan Potamkin*

American Warrior: see *American Ninja*

An American Werewolf in London *
GB   1981   97m   Technicolor
Polygram/Lycanthrope (Peter Guber, Jon Peters)
V, V*, L, S

Two American tourists are bitten by a werewolf.

Curious but oddly endearing mixture of horror film and spoof, of comedy and shock, with everything grist to its mill including tourist Britain and the wedding of Prince Charles. The special effects are notable, and signalled new developments in this field.

wd John Landis   *ph* Robert Paynter   *m* Elmer Bernstein   *sp Effects Associates*, Rick Baker

David Naughton, Jenny Agutter, Griffin Dunne, John Woodvine

'The gear changes of tone and pace make for a very jerkily driven vehicle.' – *Sunday Times*

'Seems curiously unfinished, as though Landis spent all his energy on spectacular set-pieces and then didn't want to bother with things like transitions, character development, or an ending.' – *Roger Ebert*

The Americanization of Emily *
US   1964   115m   bw
MGM/Filmways (John Calley)
V*, L

World War II: just before the Normandy landings, a war widow driver falls for an American commander who is a self-confessed coward.

Bizarre comedy full of eccentric characters, an uneasy choice for its female star but otherwise successful in patches in its random distillation of black comedy, sex and the tumbling of old-fashioned virtues.

w Paddy Chayevsky   *novel* William Bradford Huie
d Arthur Hiller   *ph* Philip Lathrop, Chris Challis
m Johnny Mandel

Julie Andrews, James Garner, *Melvyn Douglas*, James Coburn, Liz Fraser, Joyce Grenfell, Edward Binns, Keenan Wynn, William Windom

'Out of it all there comes the definite feeling that Hitler's war is incidental to Paddy Chayevsky's war of ideas . . . no plot synopsis could begin to suggest how much the characters talk.' – *MFB*

AAN: Philip Lathrop

The Americano
US   1916   60m approx (24 fps)   bw   silent
Triangle (D. W. Griffith)

A young American engineer becomes involved in a revolution in Patagonia.

Early star adventure vehicle, an immense popular success; the last film Fairbanks made for Griffith.

w Anita Loos, John Emerson   *novel Blaze Derringer* by Eugene P. Lyle Jnr   *d* John Emerson   *ph* Victor Fleming

Douglas Fairbanks, Alma Rubens, Spottiswoode Aitken, Lillian Langdon

The Americano
US   1955   85m   Technicolor
RKO (Robert Stillman)

A Westerner takes three prize bulls to Brazil, but finds the buyer has been murdered.

A Western with a twist, but otherwise extremely dull, with poor pace, colour and use of settings.

w Guy Trosper   *d* William Castle   *ph* William Snyder   *m* Roy Webb

Glenn Ford, Frank Lovejoy, Abbe Lane, Cesar Romero, Ursula Thiess

L'Ami de Mon Amie: see *My Girlfriend's Boyfriend*

L'Ami Retrouvé: see *Reunion*

Un Ami Viendra ce Soir
France   1946   111m   bw
CGC (R. Artus)

During World War II a French patriot uses a lunatic asylum as a resistance headquarters.

Rather glum wartime melodrama, lacking in tension.

w Jacques Companeez, Raymond Bernard
d Raymond Bernard   *ph* Robert Le Fèbvre
m Arthur Honegger

Michel Simon, Louis Salou, Saturnin Fabre, Paul Bernard, Madeleine Sologne, Marcel André

Le Amiche *
Italy   1955   90m   bw
Trionfalcine (Giovanni Addessi)
aka: *The Girl Friends*

The interaction of five girls living together in Turin.

Highbrow lending library stuff, quite watchable but equally forgettable.

w Suso Cecchi d'Amico, Alba de Cespedes   *story* Tra Donne Sole by Cesare Pavese   *d* Michelangelo Antonioni   *ph* Gianni di Venanzo   *m* Giovanni Fusco

Eleanora Rossi Drago, Valentina Cortese, Yvonne Furneaux, Gabriele Ferzetti, Franco Fabrizi, Madeleine Fischer

La Amiga
Argentina/West Germany   1988   108m   colour
Journal/Alma/Jorge Estrada Mora (Jorge Estrada, Klaus Volkenberg)
aka: *The Girlfriend*

Stages in the life of two women in Buenos Aires: one a Jewish actress, the other a mother who becomes politically involved after her son is taken away by security officers and never seen alive again.

Involved and somewhat sentimental drama of survival in a hostile world.

w Jeanine Meerapfel, Alcides Chiesa   *d* Jeanine Meerapfel   *ph* Axel Block   *pd* Jorge Marchegiano, Rainer Schaper   *ed* Juliane Lorenz

Liv Ullmann, Cipe Lincovsky, Federico Luppi, Victor Laplace, Harry Baer, Lito Cruz, Greger Hansen, Nicolas Frei

The Amityville Horror

US   1979   118m   Movielab
AIP/Cinema 77 (Ronald Saland, Elliot Geisinger)
V, V*, L

Newlyweds move into a house where a murder was committed, and experience strange manifestations which drive them away.

Sub-*Exorcist* goings on, a shameless exaggeration of some of the alleged facts retailed in the best-selling book. A shocker for the uncritical.

w Sandor Stern,   *book* Jay Anson   *d* Stuart Rosenberg   *ph* Fred J. Koenekamp   *m* Lalo Schifrin

James Brolin, Margot Kidder, Rod Steiger, Don Stroud, Murray Hamilton

AAN: Lalo Schifrin

Amityville II: The Possession

US   1982   104m   DeLuxe
Dino de Laurentiis/Orion (Ira N. Smith, Stephen R. Greenwald)
V, V*, L

The sequel turns out to be a prequel, dealing with the events that led to the house at Amityville becoming haunted.

Everything but the kitchen sink is thrown into this ghoulish brew, and most of it is red; but the script is hopeless from the start.

w Tommy Lee Wallace,   *book* Murder in Amityville by Hans Holzer   *d* Damiano Damiani   *ph* Franco Di Giacomo   *m* Lalo Schifrin   *pd* Pierluigi Basile   *ed* Sam O'Steen

Burt Young, Rutanya Alda, James Olson, Jack Magner, Andrew Prine

'There probably isn't a more unsympathetic bunch on screen this year. They're sure to make audiences root for the house.' – *Variety*

Amityville 3-D

US   1984   93m   colour   ArriVision 3-D
EMI/Universal/Dino de Laurentiis/Orion (Stephen F. Kesten)
V*, L

A sceptical journalist moves into the haunted house but is jolted out of his complacency.

Ragbag of supernatural incident with neither cohesion nor plausibility, but good 3-D.

w William Wales   *d* Richard Fleischer   *ph* Fred Schuler   *m* Howard Blake   *ad* Giorgio Postiglione, Justin Scoppa   *ed* Frank J. Urioste

Tony Roberts, Tess Harper, Robert Joy, Candy Clark, John Beal, Leora Dana

'An assortment of unrelated happenings precedes the final appearance of a crude bug-eyed monster.' – *MFB*

Amok: see *Schizo*

Among the Living *

US   1941   68m   bw
Paramount (Sol C. Siegel)

In a small town live twin brothers, one of whom is a murderer.

Offbeat suspenser with effective performances.

w Lester Cole, Garrett Fort   *d* Stuart Heisler   *ph* Theodor Sparkuhl

Albert Dekker, Susan Hayward, Frances Farmer, Harry Carey, Gordon Jones

'Head and shoulders above all the filler shows ground out by Hollywood to perpetuate the double feature system.' – *Howard Barnes, New York Herald Tribune*

'Born With Everything They Had To Have More.'
Amongst Friends

US   1993   87m   Technicolor
Rank/Last Outlaw/Island World (Matthew Blumberg)
V, V*, L, S

Three boyhood friends from the wealthy middle class fall out when they try to become gangsters.

Heavily influenced by Martin Scorsese's *Mean Streets*, this lacks any sense of observable reality, relying instead on fast talking and undistinguished songs to carry the action, which disintegrates into violence to compensate for its lack of anything better to show.

wd Rob Weiss   *ph* Michael Bonvillain   *m* Mick Jones   *pd* Terrence Foster   *ed* Leo Trombetta

Steve Parlavecchio, Joseph Lindsey, Patrick McGaw, Mira Sorvino, Chris Santos, Brett Lambson, Michael Artura, Frank Medrano, Louis Lombardi

'A truly numbskulled use of violence.' – *Nigel Andrews, Financial Times*

'The whole structure is a mess and there's a strong sense of been-here-before about the project.' – *Derek Malcolm, Guardian*

El Amor Brujo: see *A Love Bewitched*

L'Amore *

Italy   1948   79m   bw
Tevere Film (Roberto Rossellini)

Two short films. *The Human Voice:* a woman talks on the phone to the man who has forsaken her. *The Miracle:* a peasant woman is seduced and is convinced she will give birth to a new Messiah.

A *tour de force* by an actress to be reckoned with; but hardly compulsive as cinema.

w Tullio Pinelli, Roberto Rossellini, Federico Fellini   *play* Jean Cocteau   *d* Roberto Rossellini   *ph* Robert Juillard, Aldo Tonti   *m* Renzo Rossellini

Anna Magnani, Federico Fellini

† *The Miracle* was separately released in some countries.

'The rollicking story of a ribald century that should have been ashamed of itself!'
The Amorous Adventures of Moll Flanders

GB   1965   125m   Technicolor   Panavision
Paramount/Winchester (Marcel Hellman)
V*

An ambitious servant girl loses her virtue to a succession of rich gentlemen but finally settles for a highwayman.

The aim was to make a female *Tom Jones*, but this bawdy romp never achieves the freewheeling fluency of that surprise success, and a vacuous central performance makes the constant couplings more boring than exciting.

w Dennis Cannan, Roland Kibbee   *novel* Daniel Defoe   *d* Terence Young   *ph* Ted Moore   *m* John Addison   *pd* Syd Cain

Kim Novak, Richard Johnson, George Sanders, Lilli Palmer, Angela Lansbury, Leo McKern, Vittorio de Sica, Cecil Parker, Daniel Massey

'Further from Defoe than *Tom Jones* was from Fielding, but with much the same combination of crude table manners and clean sets to stand in for period flavour.' – *MFB*

The Amorous Prawn *

GB   1962   89m   bw
BL/Covent Garden (Leslie Gilliat)
US title: *The Playgirl and the War Minister* (an attempt to cash in on the Profumo case)

A hard-up general's wife invites American paying guests to their official highland home.

This film version of a stage success seems very mild, but the cast is eager to please: the result is a frantic high-class farce.

w Anthony Kimmins, Nicholas Phipps   *play* Anthony Kimmins   *d* Anthony Kimmins   *ph* Wilkie Cooper   *m* John Barry

Joan Greenwood, Ian Carmichael, Cecil Parker, Dennis Price, Robert Beatty, Finlay Currie, Liz Fraser, Derek Nimmo

L'Amour à Mort *

France   1984   90m   colour
Dussart/Ariane/A2 (Philippe Dussart)

An archaeologist and his mistress come to the conclusion that their love will reach its fullest expression in death.

Chilly symbolic drama, a continuation of the same team's preoccupations with the meaning of life which were previously explored (via the same four actors) in *Mon Oncle d'Amérique* and *La Vie est un Roman*. Interesting but not especially rewarding.

w Jean Gruault   *d* Alain Resnais   *ph* Sacha Vierny   *m* Hans Werner Henze

Sabine Azema, Fanny Ardant, Pierre Arditi, André Dussolier

Un Amour de Pluie: see *Loving in the Rain*

Un Amour de Swann: see *Swann in Love*

L'Amour, L'Après-midi *

France   1972   97m   colour
Les Films du Losange/Barbet Schroeder (Pierre Cottrell)
V
US title: *Chloë In The Afternoon;* aka: *Love In The Afternoon*

A married man's flirtation with an old flame leads him to a greater appreciation of his wife.

The last of Rohmer's six moral tales and the least interesting.

wd Eric Rohmer   *ph* Nestor Almendros   *m* Arié Dzierlatka   *ad* Nicole Rachline   *ed* Cécile Decugis, Martine Kalfon

Bernard Verley, Zouzou, Françoise Verley, Daniel Ceccaldi, Malvina Penne, Babette Ferrier

'The director shows life going on realistically enough. But the elegance with which he presents it, the wit – and the film doesn't merely sound witty, it looks witty – remove it from the tedium of the realistic.' – *Dilys Powell*

Les Amours de la Reine Elisabeth: see *Queen Elizabeth*

Amsterdam Affair

GB   1968   91m   Eastmancolor
LIP/Trio/Group W (Gerry Willoughby)

Inspector Van der Valk investigates when a writer is accused of murdering his mistress.

Tolerable *roman policier*.

w Edmund Ward   *novel* Love in Amsterdam by Nicholas Freeling   *d* Gerry O'Hara   *ph* Gerry Fisher   *m* Patrick John Scott

Wolfgang Kieling, William Marlowe, Caterina von Schell

The Amsterdam Kill

Hong Kong 1977 93m Technicolor Panasonic
Golden Harvest/Fantastic Films/Raymond Chow
V*, L

An American ex-Drug Enforcement Agency officer
tries to protect an old friend caught in the Hong Kong
drug wars.

Roughly made and uninventive thriller in which the
Hong Kong film makers fail to consolidate the
international ground they gained with kung fu films.

w Robert Clouse, Gregory Teifer   *d* Robert Clouse
ph Alan Hume   *m* Hal Schaffer

Robert Mitchum, Bradford Dillman, Richard Egan,
Leslie Nielsen, Keye Luke

'Be glad you're afraid. It means you're still alive'

Amsterdamned *

Netherlands 1988 113m colour
Vestron/First Floor Features (Laurens Geels, Dick Maas)
V, V*, L

A cop is assigned to discover the murderer of a
prostitute found floating in a canal.

Deft action picture that makes the most of its
waterfront setting.

wd Dick Maas   *ph* Marc Felperlaan   *m* Dick Maas
pd Dick Schillemans   *ed* Hans Van Dongen

Huub Stapel, Monique Van de Ven, Serge-Henri
Valcke, Tanneke Hartsuiker, Wim Zomer, Hidde Maas

Amy

US 1981 100m Technicolor
Walt Disney
V*

A spinster is taught a little about life and love.

Unmemorable family comedy drama.

w Noreen Stone   *d* Vincent McEveety

Jenny Agutter, Barry Newman, Kathleen Nolan, Chris
Robinson, Margaret O'Brien, Nanette Fabray

'The most amazing conspiracy the world has ever known,
     and love as it never happened to a man and woman
     before!'

Anastasia **

GB 1956 105m Eastmancolor Cinemascope
TCF (Buddy Adler)
V*, L, S

In 1928 Paris, a group of exiled White Russians claim
to have found the living daughter of the Tsar,
presumed executed in 1918; but the claimant is a fake
schooled by a general, with whom she falls in love.

Slick, highly theatrical entertainment for the upper
classes; it dazzles and satisfies without throwing any
light on history.

w Arthur Laurents   *play* Marcelle Maurette, Guy
Bolton   *d* Anatole Litvak   *ph* Jack Hildyard
m Alfred Newman   *ad* Andrei Andreiev, Bill
Andrews

Ingrid Bergman (her Hollywood comeback after some
years in Europe under a cloud for her 'immoral'
behaviour), Yul Brynner, *Helen Hayes*, Martita Hunt,
Akim Tamiroff, Felix Aylmer, Ivan Desny

'Little weight but considerable and urbane charm.' –
John Cutts

AA: Ingrid Bergman

AAN: Alfred Newman

Anatahan

Japan 1953 92m bw
Daiwa (K. Takimura)
aka: *The Saga of Anatahan*

During World War II, Japanese seamen are
shipwrecked on the same deserted island as a man
and a woman; the latter causes jealousy and murder.

Downright peculiar studio-set melodrama, based on
true events and its creator through interpreters, with
results far from happy.

wd/ph Josef von Sternberg   *m* A. Ifukube

Akemi Negishi, T. Sugunuma, K. Onoe, T. Bandoh

'The main impression is of tedium relieved by
moments of far from intentional humour.' – *Penelope
Houston*

The Anatolian Smile: see *America, America*

'Last year's number one best seller. This year's (we hope)
     number one motion picture!'

Anatomy of a Murder **

US 1959 161m bw
Columbia/Carlyle/Otto Preminger
V*, L, S

A small-town lawyer successfully defends an army
officer accused of murdering a bartender who had
assaulted his wife.

Overlong and over-faithful version of a highly
detailed courtroom bestseller. The plot is necessarily
equivocal, the characterizations overblown, but the
trial commands some interest, and the use of 'daring'
words in evidence caused controversy at the time.

w Wendell Mayes   *novel* Robert Traver   *d* Otto
Preminger   *ph* Sam Leavitt   *m* Duke Ellington
pd Boris Leven   *ed* Louis R. Loeffler

James Stewart, Ben Gazzara, Lee Remick, Eve Arden,
Arthur O'Connell, George C. Scott (his first notable
role, as the prosecutor), Kathryn Grant, Orson Bean,
Murray Hamilton

† The trial judge was played by Joseph N. Welch, a
real-life judge who had gained fame in 1954 by
representing the army against Senator McCarthy.

AAN: best picture; Wendell Mayes; Sam Leavitt;
James Stewart; Arthur O'Connell; George C. Scott;
editing

Anchoress

GB/Belgium 1993 108m bw
BFI/Corsan (Paul Breuls, Ben Gibson)

In 14th-century England, a young woman obsessed
by the Virgin Mary is walled up in a small cell in the
village church and then decides she wants to leave.

Grimly downbeat account of medieval life, hovering
on the edge of parody and lacking narrative drive.

w Judith Stanley-Smith, Catherine Vandeleene
d Chris Newby   *ph* Michel Baudour   *pd* Niek
Kortekaas   *ed* Brand Thumin

Natalie Morse, Eugene Bervoets, Toyah Wilcox, Peter
Postlethwaite, Christopher Eccleston, Michael Pas,
Brenda Bertin

'Evocatively designed period pic creates a long ago
world yet remains relevant on such issues as what
recourse women have in a man's world and how faith
grounded in nature fares against faith dictated by the
clergy.' – *Variety*

Anchors Aweigh **

US 1945 139m Technicolor
MGM (Joe Pasternak)
V, V*, L

Two sailors on leave in Los Angeles get involved with
a small boy who wants to join the navy.

Rather droopy musical most notable as a forerunner of
On the Town, though on much more conventional lines.
Amiable performances, and a brilliant dance with a
cartoon mouse, save the day.

w Isobel Lennart   *d* George Sidney   *ph* Robert
Planck, Charles Boyle   *m* George Stoll   *pd* Cedric
Gibbons   *m/ly* Jule Styne, Sammy Cahn

Frank Sinatra, Gene Kelly, Kathryn Grayson, Jose
Iturbi, Sharon McManus, Carlos Ramirez, Dean
Stockwell, Pamela Britton

songs: 'We Hate to Leave'; 'What Makes the Sun Set?';
'The Charm of You'; 'I Begged Her'; 'I Fall in Love Too
Easily'; 'The Worry Song'

AA: George Stoll

AAN: best picture; Robert Planck; Gene Kelly; song 'I
Fall in Love Too Easily' (*m* Jule Styne, *ly* Sammy
Cahn)

And Baby Makes Three

US 1950 83m bw
Columbia (Robert Lord)

A wife divorces her compromised husband before
discovering that she is pregnant.

Thin marital comedy with minor compensations.

w Lou Breslow, Joseph Hoffman   *d* Henry Levin
ph Burnett Guffey   *m* George Duning

Robert Young, Barbara Hale, Billie Burke, Robert
Hutton, Janis Carter, Nicholas Joy, Lloyd Corrigan

'It has everything but a story that hangs together.' –
New York Herald Tribune

'And God created woman. But the Devil created Brigitte
     Bardot'

And God Created Woman

France 1957 90m Eastmancolor Cinemascope
Iéna-Hodu/UCIL/Cocinor (Raoul Lévy)
V, V*, L
original title: *Et Dieu Créa la Femme*; aka: *And Woman
     ... Was Created*

An 18-year-old finds herself fatally attracted towards
men.

Rather a feeble excuse for its star to strip on the St
Tropez beach, but one that made her an international
star.

w Roger Vadim, Raoul Lévy   *d* Roger Vadim
ph Armand Thirard   *m* Paul Misraki   *ad* Jean
André

Brigitte Bardot, Curt Jurgens, Jean-Louis Trintignant,
Christian Marquand, Georges Poujouly, Jane Marken,
Paul Faivre

'An open violation of conventional morality.' – *Catholic
Legion of Decency*

'I'm prepared to bet an overcoat to a bikini that this
film will make its star Miss Sex of the Universe.' –
Sketch

'One of the most genuine, youthful and original
works produced in France since 1945.' – *Louis
Marcorelles, Sight and Sound*

† Vadim made a second film with this title (US 1987),
see below.

And God Created Woman

US 1987 100m DeLuxe Color
Crow/Vestron (George P. Braunstein/Ron Hamady)
V, L

A woman marries so that she can get parole from
prison and pursue her ambition to become a rock star.

Silly raucous remake that has nothing in common
with Vadim's original but the title. This time the
stripping is done by Rebecca de Mornay.

w R. J. Stewart   *d* Roger Vadim   *ph* Stephen M.
Katz   *m* Tom Chase, Steve Rucker   *pd* Victor
Kempster   *ed* Suzanne Pettit

Rebecca de Mornay, Vincent Spano, Frank Langella,
Donovan Leitch

And Hope To Die

US/Fr/Canada 1972 104m bw
Serge Silberman/TCF
V*
original title: *La Course du lièvre à travers les champs*

A fugitive Frenchman in Canada runs foul of
criminals and gypsies and causes several deaths.

Muddled melodrama of the worst 'international' kind.

w Sebastien Japrisot   d René Clément

Jean-Louis Trintignant, Robert Ryan, Aldo Ray, Tisa Farrow, Lea Massari

And Justice For All
US   1979   119m   Metrocolor
Columbia/Malton (Joe Wizan)
V, V*, L

An American lawyer gets into all kinds of trouble, including the defence of a judge on a rape charge.

Not so much a satire as a series of random pot-shots at the legal system, sometimes funny but cumulatively stultifying.

w Valerie Curtin, Barry Levinson   d Norman Jewison   ph Frank Holgate   m Dave Grusin

Al Pacino, Jack Warden, John Forsythe, Lee Strasberg, Christine Lahti, Sam Levene, Jeffrey Taybor

'Most incriminating is its own hysterical imprecision and sentimental pleading.' – Sight and Sound

AAN: Al Pacino; screenplay

And Now for Something Completely Different **
GB   1971   88m   colour
Columbia/Kettledrum/Python (Patricia Casey)
V*, L

Monty Python's Flying Circus perform again a selection of sketches from the BBC television series.

The first Monty Python film, intended to introduce the team's humour to an American audience. It lacks any overall coherence, but many of the individual sketches are a joy.

w Graham Chapman, John Cleese, Terry Gilliam, Eric Idle, Terry Jones, Michael Palin   d Ian Macnaughton   ph David Muir   ad Colin Grimes   ed Thom Noble

Graham Chapman, John Cleese, Terry Gilliam, Eric Idle, Terry Jones, Michael Palin, Carol Cleveland

'Very funny.' – MFB

And Now Miguel *
US   1965   95m   Technicolor
Universal/Robert B. Radnitz

A 10-year-old Mexican boy proves himself worthy to work on the mountain with the sheep.

A children's film typical of its producer: good to look at, documentarily convincing, but too slight and too slow.

w Ted Sherdeman, Jane Klove   novel Joseph Krumgold   d James B. Clark   ph Clifford Stine   m Phillip Lambro

Pat Cardi, Guy Stockwell, Clu Gulager, Michael Ansara, Joe de Santis

And Now My Love **
France/Italy   1974   121m   Technicolor
Avco Embassy/Films 13/Rizzoli (Pierre Pardon)
original title: Toute une Vie

The love stories of three generations, from 1900 to 1974: a son is born to the wife of a soldier who dies in the First World War; he marries a woman who dies in childbirth; their daughter finds happiness with a film director.

An enjoyably romantic, if somewhat bland, panorama of the 20th century, taking in on the way most of the major events, seen as a background to individual relationships; the passage of time is paralleled by the development of cinema, the story beginning with grainy black and white photography and moving through the silent period to colour.

w Claude Lelouch, Pierre Uytterhoeven   d Claude Lelouch   ph Jean Collomb   m Francis Lai   ad François de Lamothe   ed George Klotz

Marthe Keller, André Dussolier, Charles Denner, Carla Gravina, Charles Gerard, Gilbert Bécaud, Alain Basnir, Daniel Boulanger

'No amount of technical wizardry can fully disguise the naivety of Lelouch's basic concept.' – Geoff Brown, MFB

† The version released in France ran for 150m and included a sequence set in the future.

And Now The Screaming Starts
GB   1973   91m   colour
Amicus (Max J. Rosenberg, Milton Subotsky)
V*

A new bride in a country house is haunted by hallucinations of the past.

Grisly ghost story which overplays its hand and outstays its welcome.

w Roger Marshall   novel Fengriffen by David Case   d Roy Ward Baker   ph Denys Coop   m Douglas Gamley

Peter Cushing, Stephanie Beacham, Herbert Lom, Patrick Magee, Ian Ogilvy, Geoffrey Whitehead, Guy Rolfe, Rosalie Crutchley

'Who are you that a man can't make love to you?'
And Now Tomorrow *
US   1944   86m   bw
Paramount (Fred Kohlmar)

A rich girl goes deaf, loses her fiancé, but wins the poor doctor who cares for her.

Bestselling slush turned into a routine star romance.

w Frank Partos, Raymond Chandler (!)   novel Rachel Field   d Irving Pichel   ph Daniel L. Fapp   m Victor Young

Loretta Young, Alan Ladd (his first film in confirmed top-star status after a meteoric rise interrupted by war service), Susan Hayward, Beulah Bondi, Cecil Kellaway, Barry Sullivan

'A vernal sign of the boys getting back to one of their favourite legends after the wintry days of war.' – Richard Winnington

And One Was Beautiful
US   1940   68m   bw
MGM (Frederick Stephani)

A girl sets a trap for a playboy, who falls for her sister.

Cinderella-style second feature, quite unremarkable.

w Harry Clork   story Alice Duer Miller   d Robert Sinclair

Robert Cummings, Laraine Day, Jean Muir, Billie Burke, Esther Dale

And So They Were Married
US   1935   74m   bw
Columbia (B. P. Schulberg)

A widow and a widower try to get married despite the ill-feeling of their children.

Predictable romantic farce.

w Doris Anderson, Joseph Anthony   d Elliott Nugent   ph Henry Freulich   m Howard Jackson

Melvyn Douglas, Mary Astor, Edith Fellows, Jackie Moran, Donald Meek, Dorothy Stickney

And Soon the Darkness *
GB   1970   99m   Technicolor
Associated British (Albert Fennell, Brian Clemens)

Of two young nurses on a cycling holiday in France, one is murdered by a local sex maniac and the other almost shares her fate.

Slow, overstretched, often risible suspenser on vanishing lady lines; long on red herrings and short on humour, but with some pretension to style. The action all takes place along a mile or two of sunlit country road.

w Brian Clemens, Terry Nation   d Robert Fuest   ph Ian Wilson   m Laurie Johnson

Pamela Franklin, Michele Dotrice, Sandor Eles, John Nettleton

And Sudden Death
US   1936   60m   bw
Paramount

A young man denies a hit and run charge but confesses on his death bed.

Preachy melodrama with little entertainment value.

w Joseph Moncure March   d Charles Barton

Randolph Scott (as the cop in the case), Tom Brown, Frances Drake, Billy Lee, Fuzzy Knight, Porter Hall

'There's nothing but trouble in Paradise when the bandleader tries to make love to a whole sister act – simultaneously!'
And the Angels Sing *
US   1943   95m   bw
Paramount (E. D. Leshin)

Four singing sisters have hectic adventures with a bandleader.

Mildly disarming romantic comedy with music, more firmly set in a recognizable social milieu than the usual fan product from this studio.

w Melvin Frank, Norman Panama, Claude Binyon   d George Marshall   ph Karl Struss   m Victor Young   m/y Johnny Burke, Jimmy Van Heusen

Dorothy Lamour, Diana Lynn, Betty Hutton, Mimi Chandler, Fred MacMurray, Raymond Walburn, Eddie Foy Jnr, Frank Albertson, Mikhail Rasumny

'Slapstick sophistication in a sub-Sturges manner.' – MFB

'Cruel, soggily professional, over-elaborate, and inclined towards snobbish whimsy.' – James Agee

And the Band Played On *
US   1993   141m   colour
ITC/Odyssey/HBO (Midge Sanford, Sarah Pillsbury)

Doctors investigating a disease affecting homosexual men in America discover that it is sexually transmitted and first name it GRID (Gay Related Immune Deficiency) and then, when it is discovered that the virus is no respecter of sexuality, call it AIDS.

A confusing dramatization of Shilts's angry book on the first years of AIDS and the inactivity of the government and other organizations in dealing with it; it leaves one little wiser, though sadder, than before.

w Arnold Schulman   book Randy Shilts   d Roger Spottiswoode   ph Paul Elliott, Paul Ryan   m Carter Burwell   pd Victoria Paul   ed Lois Freeman-Fox

Matthew Modine, Alan Alda, Richard Gere, Patrick Bauchau, Nathalie Baye, Christopher Clemenson, Phil Collins, Bud Cort, Alex Courtney, David Dukes, David Clennon, Anjelica Huston, Steve Martin, Ian McKellen, Lily Tomlin

'Spottiswoode's engrossing, powerful work still accomplishes its mission: Shilts' book, with all its shock, sorrow and anger, has been transferred decisively to the screen.' – Variety

'The result is sometimes both informative and moving but also in places a little dull and unfocused, as if those who made the film were too conscientious to leave anything out and too scared to make a proper fiction out of history.' – Derek Malcolm, Guardian

† The film, made for American television, was given a cinema release in Britain. The book was originally optioned in 1989 but twice plans to film it fell through. This version had a troubled production, with two directors quitting and Spottiswoode leaving during the post-production process, and it was criticized by Shilts himself shortly before his death in February 1994.

And the Same To You
GB   1960   70m   bw
Monarch

A clergyman's nephew decides to become a boxer.

Uninventive and unfunny comedy.

w John Paddy Carstairs, John Junkin   play A. P.
Dearsley   d George Pollock

Brian Rix, Leo Franklyn, William Hartnell, Vera Day,
Tommy Cooper, Dick Bentley, Sid James

And the Ship Sails On *
Italy/France   1983   132m   Technicolor   Panavision
RAI/Vides/Gaumont (Franco Cristaldi)
V*, S
original title: *E la Nave Va*

From Naples in 1914 a luxurious liner sets forth to
scatter the ashes of an opera singer.

Less a Ship of Fools than a theatre of the absurd, with
familiar Fellini caricatures going through their paces
against studio sets. Fascination alternates with
boredom.

w Federico Fellini, Tonino Guerra   d Federico
Fellini   ph Giuseppe Rotunno   m Gianfranco
Plenizio   ad Dante Ferretti   ed Ruggero
Mastroianni

Freddie Jones, Barbara Jefford, Victor Poletti, Peter
Cellier, Elisa Mainardi, Norma West

'A genial movie, although a bit discontinuous.' –
Alberto Moravia

'A vessel that is chock-full of his best gags, visual fun
and love of cinema as artful technique.' – *Variety*

'Too much a work of the pure imagination with the
result that the audience is cast adrift on a styrofoam
sea without a lifeline to any kind of recognizable
reality.' – *Andrew Sarris, Village Voice*

And Then There Were None ****
US   1945   97m   bw
Popular Pictures/Harry M. Popkin (René Clair)
V, V*
GB title: *Ten Little Niggers*

Ten people are invited to a house party on a lonely
island, and murdered one by one.

A classic mystery novel is here adapted and directed
with the utmost care to provide playful black comedy,
stylish puzzlement, and some splendid acting cameos.

w *Dudley Nichols   novel* Agatha Christie (*aka: Ten Little
Niggers*)   d René Clair   ph Lucien Andriot   m Mario
Castelnuovo-Tedesco

Walter Huston, Barry Fitzgerald, Louis Hayward, June
Duprez, *Roland Young, Richard Haydn,* C. Aubrey Smith,
Judith Anderson, Queenie Leonard, Mischa Auer

  MISS BRENT: 'Very stupid to kill the only servant
in the house. Now we don't even know where to find
the marmalade.'
  JUDGE QUINCANNON: 'Mr Owen could only
come to the island in one way. It's perfectly clear. Mr
Owen is one of us.'
  ROGERS: 'Never in my life have I been accused of
any crime, sir – and if that's what you think of me, I
shan't serve any dinner.'

'Rich in the elements which have made mystery
melodramas popular, yet not in the precise form of
any previously made.' – *Hollywood Reporter*

'The efforts at sprightly, stylish comedy don't gain
much momentum.' – *Pauline Kael, New Yorker, 70s*

And Then There Were None
GB   1974   98m   Technicolor
EMI/Filibuster (Harry Alan Towers)
US title: *Ten Little Indians*

Ten people are lured to an isolated Persian hotel and
murdered one by one.

Listless remake, often so inept you could scream.

w Peter Welbeck (Harry Alan Towers)   d Peter
Collinson   ph Fernando Arribas   m Bruno Nicolai

Oliver Reed, Richard Attenborough, Elke Sommer,
Herbert Lom, Gert Frobe, Stéphane Audran, Charles
Aznavour, Adolfo Celi, Alberto de Mendoza, Maria
Rohm

And There Was Jazz *
Poland   1981   90m   bw
Zespoly Filmowe (Andrzej Soltysik)
aka: *Byl Jazz*

In Poland of the 1950s, a group of students playing
classic jazz become a symbol of opposition in a
conformist society.

Like its subject matter, a small but engaging gesture of
revolt. It was banned by the Polish authorities.

wd Feliks Falk   ph Witold Sobocinski   m Jerzy
Matula   ad Teresa Smus-Barska   ed Miroslawa
Garlicka

Bozena Adamkowna, Michal Bajor, Andrzej
Grabarczyk, Kazimierz Wysota, Jerzy Gudejko,
Adrezej Chichlowski, Jacek Strzemzalski, Jacek Sass-
Uhrynowski

And Woman . . . Was Created: see *And God
Created Woman*

The Anderson Tapes *
US   1971   98m   Technicolor   Panavision
Columbia/Robert M. Weitman
V*, L

An ex-con forms a gang to rob a building, not
knowing that police and others, for various purposes,
are making tape recordings of his conversations.

Superficially slick and fashionable crime thriller,
marred by unnecessarily flashy direction, a failure to
explain enough about the tapes, and a climax which
oddly mixes bloodshed and farce.

w Frank R. Pierson   novel Lawrence Sanders
d Sidney Lumet   ph Arthur J. Ornitz   m Quincy
Jones

Sean Connery, *Martin Balsam*, Dyan Cannon, Alan
King, Ralph Meeker

Andrei Rublev ****
USSR   1966   181m   colour (part)   Cinemascope
Mosfilm
V (W), V*

Imaginary episodes from the life of a 15th-century
icon painter.

A superb recreation of medieval life dramatizes the
eternal problem of the artist, whether to take part in
the life around him or merely comment on it.

w Andrei Mikhalkov-Konchalovsky, Andrei
Tarkovsky   d *Andrei Tarkovsky   ph Vadim Yusov
m Vyacheslav Tcherniaiev*

Anatoly Solonitsin, Ivan Lapikov, Nikolai Grinko, Nikolai
Sergeyev

'The one indisputable Russian masterpiece of the last
decade.' – *Nigel Andrews, MFB, 1973*

'With the exception of the great Eisenstein, I can't
think of any film which has conveyed a feeling of the
remote past with such utter conviction . . . a durable
and unmistakable masterpiece.' – *Michael Billington,
Illustrated London News*

Androcles and the Lion **
US   1952   96m   bw
RKO (Gabriel Pascal)
V*

A slave takes a thorn from the paw of a lion which
later, in the arena, refuses to eat him.

Shavian drollery, with interpolated discussions on
faith, is scarcely ideal cinema material, but gusto in
the performances keeps it going despite stolid
direction.

w Chester Erskine   play Bernard Shaw   d Chester
Erskine   ph Harry Stradling   m Frederick
Hollander   ad Harry Horner

*Alan Young, Jean Simmons, Robert Newton, Victor Mature,
Maurice Evans* (as Caesar), Reginald Gardiner, Elsa
Lanchester, Alan Mowbray, Gene Lockhart

† Production had previously begun with Harpo Marx
as Androcles and Rex Harrison as Caesar.

Android *
US   1982   80m   DeLuxe
New World/Android (Mary Ann Fisher)
V*, L

In 2036, a police transport vehicle is hijacked in
space, and the scientists on board, some of them
androids, react in unexpected ways.

Cheaply made, but a bobby dazzler for science fiction
addicts.

w James Reigle, Don Opper   d Aaron Lipstadt
ph Tim Suhrstedt   m Don Preston

Klaus Kinski, Brie Howard, Norbert Weisser, Crofton
Hardester, Kendra Kirchner, Don Opper

'The best first feature since *Dark Star*.' – *Tom Milne, MFB*

The Andromeda Strain **
US   1970   131m   Technicolor   Panavision
Universal/Robert Wise
V*, L

Scientists work frantically to neutralize an infected
village, knowing that the least infection will cause
their laboratory to self-destruct.

Solemn and over-detailed but generally suspenseful
thriller, with a sense of allegory about man's
inhumanity to man.

w Nelson Gidding   novel Michael Crichton
d Robert Wise   ph Richard H. Kline   m Gil Melle
ad Boris Leven

Arthur Hill, David Wayne, James Olson, Kate Reid,
Paula Kelly

Andy Hardy Comes Home *
US   1958   81m   bw
MGM (Red Doff)

Fortyish Andy returns to Carvel, his home town, to
negotiate a land deal.

Rather dismal sequel to the celebrated series of Hardy
family comedies which were enormously popular in
the early forties: a thirteen-year gap is too long, and
although most of the family is reunited the old Judge
is sadly missed.

w Edward Everett Hutshing, Robert Morris Donley
d Howard W. Koch   ph William W. Spencer, Harold
E. Wellman   m Van Alexander

Mickey Rooney, Fay Holden, Cecilia Parker, Patricia
Breslin, Sara Haden, Jerry Colonna

† See also under *Hardy Family*.

Andy Warhol's Bad
US   1976   109m   Technicolor
EMI/Andy Warhol (Jeff Tomberg)
V*, L

A housewife, who runs an assassination bureau using
young female killers, employs a man – with fatal
results.

A tedious, sloppily made horror movie.

w Pat Hackett, George Abagnalo   d Jed Johnson
ph Alan Metzger   m Mike Bloomfield   ad Eugene
Rudolf   ed David McKenna

Carroll Baker, Perry King, Gordon Oas-Heim, Cyrinda
Fox, Matthew Anton, Cathy Roskam, Susan Tyrell,
Brigid Polk, Lawrence Tierney

† The film was cut to 104m on its British release.

Andy Warhol's Dracula: see *Dracula*

Andy Warhol's Flesh: see *Flesh*

Andy Warhol's Heat: see *Heat*

Andy Warhol's Lonesome Cowboys: see
Lonesome Cowboys

Andy Warhol's Trash: see *Trash*

'I want love – and I'm going to get it!'
Angel *
US   1937   98m   bw
Paramount (Ernst Lubitsch)

The wife of an English diplomat finds herself
neglected and almost has an affair with his old friend.

A curious romantic comedy in many ways typical of
its time, yet with very few laughs, showing none of its
director's usual cinematic sense, and compromised by
the censor's refusal to let a spade be called a spade.
Underplaying, and a sense that we watch a way of life
about to be swept away, just about save it.

w Samson Raphaelson   play Melchior Lengyel
d Ernst Lubitsch   ph Charles Lang   m Frederick
Hollander

Marlene Dietrich, Herbert Marshall, Melvyn Douglas,
Edward Everett Horton, Laura Hope Crews, Ernest
Cossart

    MARIA: 'What's the matter, darling? Is it France?'
    SIR FREDERICK: 'No, no. Jugoslavia.'
    MARIA: 'Oh, I see.'

'A rich Hollywood dish that copies foreign recipes.
It's a good picture and in the keys, especially for the
carriage trade, it can't miss.' – *Variety*

'Very sophisticated, very subtle, very chic, vastly
polished and entertaining.' – *Literary Digest*

'The production is performed with studied
deliberation.' – *New York Times*

'This movie isn't essentially different from the best of
Lubitsch, but it's attenuated. It's the sort of cultivated
triangular love affair in which each of the three has a
turn at the piano.' – *Pauline Kael, 70s*

Angel *
Eire   1982   92m   Technicolor
Motion Picture Company of Ireland/Irish Film Board/Channel 4
    (John Boorman)
V
US title: *Danny Boy*

Against a background of the Irish troubles, a
saxophonist is drawn into a maze of violence when he
attempts to avenge the murder of a mute girl.

Glumly Irish thriller with metaphysical overtones as
well as references to the state of Ireland. Keen
narrative style is dissipated by overkill.

wd Neil Jordan   ph Chris Menges   m Verdi

Stephen Rea, Veronica Quilligan, Alan Devlin, Peter
Caffrey

'The film's style might be called flamboyant or
baroque – or damned as pretentious – but it's a
genuine style, a way of speaking. No one else speaks
quite this way.' – *Michael Wilmington, Los Angeles Times*

'Honor student by day – hooker by night!'
'You're young, attractive and healthy – and swimming in a
    toilet bowl!'
Angel
US   1983   93m   CFI colour
New World/Adam's Apple/Angel (Sandy Howard)
V*, L, S

A 15-year-old student doubles as a Hollywood hooker
and takes on a psychopathic killer.

Yucky melodrama with no holds barred, not even
moments of humour.

w Robert Vincent O'Neil, Joseph M. Cala   d Robert
Vincent O'Neil   ph Andrew Davis   m Craig Safan

Cliff Gorman, Donna Wilkes, Rory Calhoun, Susan
Tyrrell, Dick Shawn, John Diehl, Elaine Giftos

'A tasteless blend of realism and farce.' – *Sunday Times*

† A sequel appeared in 1985 under the title *Avenging
Angel.* Betsy Russell was the girl, now hunting down
her mentor.

Angel and the Badman *
US   1947   100m   bw
Republic (John Wayne)
V, V*, L

The love of a Quaker girl converts a wounded
gunslinger to an honourable life.

Thoughtful Western with good background detail and
a fair measure of action.

wd James Edward Grant   ph Archie Stout
m Richard Hageman   pd Ernst Fegte

John Wayne, Gail Russell, Harry Carey, Bruce Cabot,
Irene Rich, Tom Powers

'Unpretentious, sweet-tempered and quite likeable.' –
James Agee

Angel, Angel, Down We Go
US   1969   93m   colour
AIP (Jerome F. Katzman)

Decadence in Hollywood: rock and rollers invade the
lives of a rich family.

Unpleasant blather with a star well past her prime.

wd Robert Thom

Jennifer Jones, Jordan Christopher, Roddy
McDowall, Lou Rawls, Holly Near, Charles Aidman

An Angel at My Table **
New Zealand/Australia   1990   160m   colour
Hibiscus Films/N.Z. Film Commission/TV New Zealand/ABC
    (Bridget Ikin)
V, V*, S

A shy and introverted writer is wrongly diagnosed as
a schizophrenic.

The biography of a notable poet, edited from a three-
hour television miniseries.

w Laura Jones   book Janet Frame's autobiographies
d Jane Campion   ph Stuart Dryburgh   m Don
McGlashan   pd Grant Major   ed Veronica Haussler

Kerry Fox, Alexia Keogh, Karen Fergusson, Iris
Churn, K. J. Wilson, Melina Bernecker, Glynis
Angell, Sarah Smuts-Kennedy, Colin McColl

'A potentially painful and harrowing film is imbued
with gentle humor and great compassion, which
makes every character (even the unappealing ones)
come vividly to life.' – *Variety*

Angel Baby *
US   1960   97m   bw
Madera (Thomas F. Woods)
V*

A mute girl is cured by an evangelist, and renounces
her sins.

Strident, vigorous low-budget melodrama.

w Oris Borstem, Samuel Roeca, Paul Mason
novel *Jenny Angel* by Elsie Oaks Barbour   d Paul
Wendkos   ph Haskell Wexler, Jack Marta   m Wayne
Shanklin

Salome Jens, George Hamilton, Joan Blondell,
Mercedes McCambridge, Henry Jones, Burt Reynolds

Angel Dust *
France   1987   95m   colour
UGC/President Films/Top No 1/FR3/Films de La Saga/La Sofica
    (Jacques-Eric Strauss)
V
aka: *Poussière d'Ange*

A detective, whose life begins to fall to pieces after his
wife leaves him, becomes involved with a young girl
and a series of strange murders.

Acerbic thriller about the corrupting influence of
sexual desire.

w Edouard Niermans, Jacques Audiard, Alain le
Henry   d Edouard Niermans   ph Bernard Lutic
m Leon Senza, Vincent-Marie Bouvot
pd Dominique Maleret   ed Yves Deschamps,
Jacques Witta

Bernard Giraudeau, Fanny Bastien, Fanny Cottencon,
Michel Aumont, Jean-Pierre Sentier, Gérard Blain,
Luc Lavandier

El Angel Exterminador: see *The Exterminating
Angel*

Angel Face *
US   1952   91m   bw
RKO (Otto Preminger)

A demented girl murders her father and stepmother,
involving her chauffeur, whom she finally kills, and
commits suicide.

Outrageous melodrama, so absurd as to be almost
endearing.

w Frank Nugent, Oscar Millard   d Otto Preminger
ph Harry Stradling   m Dimitri Tiomkin

Jean Simmons, Robert Mitchum, Herbert Marshall,
Barbara O'Neil, Leon Ames, Mona Freeman, Kenneth
Tobey, Raymond Greenleaf

'The one lyrical nightmare in the cinema.' – *Ian
Cameron*

An Angel from Texas *
US   1940   69m   bw
Warner (Robert Fellows)

Misadventures of a country boy in New York.

Modest revamping of a much filmed farce, also made
as *The Tenderfoot* (1928) and *Dance Charlie Dance* (1937).

w Fred Niblo Jnr, Bertram Millhauser   play *The
Butter and Egg Man* by George F. Kaufman   d Ray
Enright   ph Arthur L. Todd   m Howard Jackson

Eddie Albert, Rosemary Lane, Wayne Morris, Ronald
Reagan, Milburn Stone

Angel Heart *
US   1987   113m   Technicolor
Tri-Star/Kassar-Vajna/Carolco/Winkast-Union (Alan Marshall,
    Elliott Kastner)
V, V*, L, S

In 1955, a New York private eye descends into Hell.

He does, literally, in pursuit of a missing person
who's opted out of a pact with the devil. Thoroughly
unpleasant in detail, this wallow in the private eye
cult constantly takes the eye with its pictorial
qualities, even at its most nauseating.

wd Alan Parker   novel *Falling Angel* by William
Hjortsberg   ph Michael Seresin   m Trevor Jones
pd Brian Morris

Mickey Rourke, Robert de Niro, Lisa Bonet, Charlotte
Rampling, Stocker Fontelieu, Brownie McGhee

'Faustian theme, heavy bloodletting and pervasive
grimness may represent barriers too great for general
audiences to surmount.' – *Daily Variety*

Angel in Exile
US   1948   90m   bw
Republic

An ex-con heads for an abandoned Arizona mine to
recover stolen gold.

Modest, effective Western about a baddie who
reforms.

w Charles Larson   d Allan Dwan, Philip Ford
ph Reggie Lanning   m Nathan Scott

John Carroll, Adele Mara, Thomas Gomez

Angel in My Pocket
US   1969   105m   Technicolor
Universal (Ed Montagne)

A minister and his family arrive in a small town.

Simplistic comedy-drama with nothing to distinguish it from a dozen others in similar vein.

w Jim Fritzell, Everett Greenbaum   d Alan Rafkin

Andy Griffith, Jerry Van Dyke, Kay Medford, Edgar Buchanan, Margaret Hamilton, Gary Collins, Lee Meriwether, Henry Jones

The Angel Levine *
US   1970   105m   DeLuxe
UA/Belafonte Enterprises (Chiz Schultz)

An elderly Jewish tailor complains to God of his bad luck; a black angel appears and seems to help him for a while.

Muddled and seemingly pointless parable with occasional felicities.

w Bill Gunn, Ronald Ribman   story Bernard Malamud   d Jan Kadar   ph Richard Kratina   m Zdenek Linka   pd George Jenkins

Zero Mostel, Harry Belafonte, Ida Kaminska, Milo O'Shea, Eli Wallach, Anne Jackson, Gloria Foster

'A prolonged variation on the theme that faith can produce miracles, but only if there is enough of it.' – *John Gillett*

The Angel of Broadway *
US   1927   82m approx   bw   silent
DeMille/Pathé

A night-club entertainer haunts Salvation Army missions in search of material, but ultimately joins the cause.

Fairly impressive propaganda piece of its time.

w Lenore J. Coffee   d Lois Weber

Leatrice Joy, Victor Varconi, May Robson, Alice Lake

Angel on My Shoulder **
US   1946   101m   bw
UA/Charles R. Rogers
V*

The devil promises leniency to a dead gangster if he will return to Earth and take over the body of a judge who is stamping out evil.

Crude but lively fantasy on the tail-end of the *Here Comes Mr Jordan* cycle, and by the same author.

w Harry Segall, Roland Kibbee   d Archie Mayo   ph James Van Trees   m Dimitri Tiomkin

Paul Muni, Claude Rains, Anne Baxter, Erskine Sanford, Hardie Albright

'The story is so imitative that it's hard to feel any more towards it than a mildly nostalgic regard.' – *Bosley Crowther*

'Witty, caustic and exciting.' – *Motion Picture Guide*

Angel on the Amazon
US   1948   86m   bw
Republic (John H. Auer)
GB title: *Drums Along the Amazon*

An elderly white lady resident of the Amazon jungle looks only 25 after being scared by a panther . . .

Ludicrous melodrama which the actors take seriously.

w Lawrence Kimble   d John H. Auer   ph Reggie Lanning   m Nathan Scott

George Brent, Constance Bennett, Vera Hruba Ralston, Brian Aherne, Fortunio Bonanova, Alfonso Bedoya, Gus Schilling

Angel Square *
Canada   1990   106m   colour
Rendez-Vous/Wheeler-Hendren/Western International/Arvi Liimatainen
V*

During Christmas in the late 1940s, a dreamy youth solves the mystery of who attacked the father of his Jewish friend.

Genial account of boyhood fantasies, complete with excursions into cartoon-like parodies of comic-strip adventures.

w James Defelice, Anne Wheeler   novel Brian Doyle   d Anne Wheeler   ph Tobias Schliesller   m George Blondheim   pd John Blackie   ed Peter Svab, Lenka Svab

Ned Beatty, Jeremy Radick, Guillaume Lemay Thivierge, Marie Stefane Gaudry, Sarah Meyette, Nicola Cavendish, Brian Dooley, Michel Barrette

Angel Street: see *Gaslight* (1939)

The Angel Who Pawned Her Harp *
GB   1954   76m   bw
Group Three (Sidney Cole)

A real angel arrives on a goodwill visit to seamy Islington, and manages to right a few wrongs.

Simple-minded whimsy, spottily effective, with good performances.

w Charles Terrot, Sidney Cole   d Alan Bromly   ph Arthur Grant   m Antony Hopkins

Diane Cilento, Felix Aylmer, Robert Eddison, Jerry Desmonde, Sheila Sweet, Alfie Bass

The Angel with the Trumpet
GB   1949   98m   bw
British Lion/London Films (Karl Hartl)

An Austrian lady has an affair with a crown prince but marries for security and dies in defiance of the Nazis.

Curious European cavalcade, dully directed to keep the budget down and accommodate long stretches of an Austrian original. An eccentricity.

w Karl Hartl, Franz Tassie   novel Ernst Lothar   d Anthony Bushell   ph Robert Krasker   m Willy Schmidt-Gentner

Eileen Herlie, Basil Sydney, Norman Wooland, Anthony Bushell, Maria Schell, John Justin, Oskar Werner, Andrew Cruickshank

The Angel Wore Red
US   1960   105m   bw
MGM/Titanus/Spectator (Gottfredo Lombardo)

The love story of a priest and a prostitute in the Spanish Civil War.

Turgid farrago, unsatisfactory both romantically and politically.

wd Nunnally Johnson   ph Giuseppe Rotunno   m Bronislau Kaper

Ava Gardner, Dirk Bogarde, Joseph Cotten, Vittorio de Sica, Aldo Fabrizi, Finlay Currie

'The stars show no apparent surprise that a film so empty of reward should take itself so seriously.' – *Peter John Dyer*

Angela
US   1955   81m   bw
TCF/Patricia/Telecinema (Steven Pallos)

A former American racing driver working as a salesman in Italy finds himself involved in murder when he falls in love with a secretary.

Moody, unoriginal thriller in the *film noir* tradition, given a slight twist by being set in Rome.

w Jonathan Rix, Eduardo Anton   story Steve Carruters   d Dennis O'Keefe   ph Leonida Barboni   m Mario Nascimbene   ad Alfredo Montori   ed Giancarlo Cappelli

Dennis O'Keefe, Mara Lane, Rossano Brazzi, Arnoldo Foa, Galeazzo Benti, Nino Crisman, Enzo Fiermonte, John Fostini, Aldo Pini, Maria Teresa Paliani

The Angelic Conversation
GB   1985   80m   colour
BFI/Derek Jarman (James Mackay)
V

Readings from Shakespeare's sonnets by Judi Dench are accompanied by a film of young men striking Christ-like poses or caressing each other.

Moody, grainy photography, much of it in jerky slow-motion, fails to illuminate the text.   d Derek Jarman   ph Derek Jarman   m Coil   ed Cerith Wyn Evans, Peter Cartwright

Paul Reynolds, Philip Williamson

Angelina *
Italy   1947   98m   bw
Lux-Ora (Paulo Frasca)

An impoverished housewife becomes the spokeswoman for her community on flooding, housing and other slum problems.

Reasonably rewarding star vehicle in the neo-realist tradition, this time angled for comedy.

w Suso Cecchi d'Amico, Piero Tellini, Luigi Zampa   d Luigi Zampa   ph Mario Craveri   m Enzio Masetti

Anna Magnani, Nando Bruno, Gianni Glori, Franco Zeffirelli

'At once kindly and fierce, witty and humorous, sad and richly gay. It warms your heart and breaks it, and has you laughing almost continuously.' – *Fred Majdalany*

'Behind the bubble and the chatter, the shouting and the running, the crowd and cortiledges that the Italians have always adored in their cinema, there is a genuine spring of fun that can only rise from a hopeful attitude towards God, and the right sort of optimism about one's neighbour.' – *C. A. Lejeune*

Angélique
France/West Germany/Italy   1964   116m
    Eastmancolor   Dyaliscope
Francos/CICC/Gloria/Fona Roma (Francis Cosne)
original title: *Angélique Marquise des Anges*

Adventures of a nobleman's daughter at the court of Louis XIV.

Watchable swashbuckling nonsense, a kind of French *Forever Amber*. Several sequels were made.

w Claude Brûlé, Bernard Borderie, Francis Cosne   novel Serge and Anne Golon   d Bernard Borderie   ph Henri Pérsin   m Michel Magne

Michèle Mercier, Robert Hossein, Giuliano Gemma, Jean Rochefort, François Maistre, Jacques Toja

Angelo My Love
US   1982   116m   colour
Lorton
V*, L

Adventures of an eight-year-old gypsy boy in Manhattan.

Angelo is a precocious little rogue, but two hours is a long haul for this kind of ethnic medley.

wd Robert Duvall

Angelo Evans, Michael Evans, Ruthie Evans, Steve Tsigonoff

'Duvall has done wonders with his actors and then robbed them of their glory by mishandling the tempo of the piece.' – *Sunday Times*

Angelos
Greece   1982   119m   colour
Cannon/Greek Film Centre (Yorgos Katakouzinos)

A youth falls in love with a sailor and becomes a transvestite prostitute.

Doom-ridden tale unlikely to interest an audience of any sexual orientation.

wd Yorgos Katakouzinos *ph* Tasos Alexakis *m* Stamatis Spanoudakis *ed* Aristide Karydis-Maniatis

Michalis Maniatis, Dionisis Xanthos, Katerina Chelmi, Maria Alkaiou

Angels and the Pirates: see *Angels in the Outfield*

Angels Hard as They Come
US   1971   90m   Metrocolor
New Realm/New World (Jonathan Demme)
V*

Three bikers run into trouble in a ghost town inhabited by hippies but controlled by another gang of bikers.

Ponderous action movie, with a plot that seems to have been wrenched from some spaghetti Western, in which violence is seen as a force for good.

w Jonathan Demme, Joe Viola *d* Joe Viola *ph* Steve Katz *m* Richard Hieronymus, Carp *ad* Jack Fisk *ed* Joe Ravetz

Scott Glenn, Charles Dierkop, Gilda Texter, James Inglehart, Garry Littlejohn, Gary Busey, Janet Wood, Don Carerra, Brendan Kelly, Larry Tucker

'The film's strivings for social and political significance are effectively smothered by the obligatory overlay of sex and violence.' – *John Raisbeck, MFB*

† The film was cut to 82m on its British release.

Angel's Holiday
US   1937   74m   bw
John Stone/TCF

The niece of a newspaper editor rounds up a gang of racketeers.

Smart comedy vehicle for Shirley Temple's only rival.

w Frank Fenton, Lynn Root *d* James Tinling

Jane Withers, Robert Kent, Joan Davis, Sally Blane, Harold Huber, Frank Jenks, John Qualen, Lon Chaney Jnr

Angels in the Outfield
US   1952   99m   bw
MGM (Clarence Brown)
GB title: *Angels and the Pirates*

The profane and bad-tempered manager of an unsuccessful baseball team gets help from an angel.

Unamusing, saccharine whimsy which does not deserve its excellent production values.

w Dorothy Kingsley, George Wells *d* Clarence Brown *ph* Paul C. Vogel *m* Daniele Amfitheatrof

Paul Douglas, Janet Leigh, Keenan Wynn, Lewis Stone, Donna Corcoran, Spring Byington, Bruce Bennett

Angels One Five *
GB   1952   98m   bw
Templar (John W. Gossage)
V

A slice of life in an RAF fighter station during the Battle of Britain.

Underplayed semi-documentary drama with stiff upper lips all round and the emphasis on characterization rather than action. A huge commercial success in Britain.

w Derek Twist *d* George More O'Ferrall *ph* Christopher Challis, Stanley Grant (air scenes) *m* John Wooldridge

Jack Hawkins, John Gregson, Michael Denison, Andrew Osborn, Cyril Raymond, Humphrey Lestocq, Dulcie Gray, Veronica Hurst

Angels Over Broadway
US   1940   80m   bw
Columbia/Ben Hecht
V*, L

During one rainy New York night, three of life's failures have one last stab at success.

Would-be poetic, moralizing melodrama very typical of its author; interesting but not a success.

w Ben Hecht *d* Ben Hecht, Lee Garmes *ph* Lee Garmes *m* George Antheil

Douglas Fairbanks Jnr, Rita Hayworth, Thomas Mitchell, John Qualen, George Watts, Ralph Theodore

'There's a genial, original spirit to it.' – *New Yorker, 1978*

'It has excitement, fast talk, some knowable people, cynicism and sentiment.' – *Otis Ferguson*

† Sample dialogue: 'This town's a giant dice game . . . come on, seven!'

AAN: Ben Hecht (as writer)

Angels Wash Their Faces *
US   1939   86m   bw
Warner (Max Siegel)
original title: *The Battle of City Hall*

A bad boy joins the Dead End Kids, but they all reform in the end.

Routine programmer, hastily concocted after the success of *Angels with Dirty Faces*.

w Michael Fessier, Niven Busch, Robert Buckner *d* Ray Enright *ph* Arthur Todd *m* Adolph Deutsch

Ann Sheridan, Ronald Reagan, the Dead End Kids, Bonita Granville, Frankie Thomas, Henry O'Neill, Berton Churchill, Eduardo Ciannelli

'Ray Enright's terrific meller pace makes it the sort of fare the average audience will eat up . . . he has an eye for the spectacular, including a thrilling fire sequence and a dramatic courtroom scene.' – *Variety*

Angels with Dirty Faces ****
US   1938   97m   bw
Warner (Sam Bischoff)
V, V*, L

A Brooklyn gangster is admired by slum boys, but for their sake pretends to be a coward when he goes to the electric chair.

A shrewd, slick entertainment package and a seminal movie for all kinds of reasons. It combined gangster action with fashionable social conscience; it confirmed the Dead End Kids as stars; it provided archetypal roles for its three leading players and catapulted the female lead into stardom. It also showed the Warner style of film-making, all cheap sets and shadows, at its most effective.

w John Wexley, Warren Duff *story* Rowland Brown *d* Michael Curtiz *ph* Sol Polito *m* Max Steiner

James Cagney (gangster with redeeming features), *Pat O'Brien* (priest), *Humphrey Bogart* (gangster with no redeeming features), *The Dead End Kids, Ann Sheridan*, George Bancroft, Edward Pawley

'Should do fair business, but the picture itself is no bonfire.' – *Variety*

'A rousing, bloody, brutal melodrama.' – *New York Mirror*

AAN: Rowland Brown; Michael Curtiz; James Cagney

Les Anges du Péché *
France   1943   73m   bw
Synops/Robert Paul

A novice nun has trouble with the mother superior because of her obsessive interest in a rebellious delinquent girl, and dies before taking her vows.

Interesting study of an enclosed society, notable as its director's first film.

w R. P. Bruckberger, Jean Giraudoux, *Robert Bresson* *d* Robert Bresson *ph* Philippe Agostini *m* Jean-Jacques Grunenwald

Renée Faure, Jany Holt, Sylvie, Mila Parély, Marie-Hélène Dasté

Anglagard: see *House of Angels*

Angora Love **
US   1929   20m   bw   silent
Hal Roach
V

Laurel and Hardy keep a goat in their lodgings.

Lively comedy, even funnier when remade two years later as *Laughing Gravy*.

w Leo McCarey and H. M. Walker *d* Lewis R. Foster

Laurel and Hardy, Edgar Kennedy, Charlie Hall

The Angry Dragon
Hong Kong   1974   80m   Eastmancolor   Scope
Mark Associates/Oriental Film (Mah Jam Sheng)

A police inspector defeats a local gangster with the aid of martial arts students.

The usual high-kicking kung-fu mayhem, with an uninteresting narrative and unattractive leads.

wd Chiang Hung

Cheng Lei, Christine Hui, Lee Wan Chung

'Possibly the least prepossessing of all independent Hong Kong features.' – *Tony Rayns, MFB*

Angry Harvest: see *Bittere Ernte*

The Angry Hills
GB   1959   105m   bw
MGM/Raymond Stross

In 1940, an American war correspondent is helped by Greek freedom fighters.

Laboured war melodrama with pretentious dialogue but little characterization.

w A. I. Bezzerides *novel* Leon Uris *d* Robert Aldrich *ph* Stephen Dade *m* Richard Rodney Bennett *ad* Ken Adam

Robert Mitchum, Gia Scala, Elisabeth Mueller, Stanley Baker, Donald Wolfit, Kieron Moore, Theodore Bikel, Sebastian Cabot, Peter Illing, Marius Goring, Leslie Phillips

The Angry Red Planet *
US   1959   83m   colour   Cinemagic
Sino (Sid Pink, Norman Maurer)
V, V*, L

Four astronauts who land on Mars fight for their lives against a variety of monsters and giant Martians.

Enjoyably quaint science fiction, filmed in a process that gives a pink tinge to the action.

w Ib Melchior, Sid Pink *d* Ib Melchior *ph* Stanley Cortez *ad* Herman Townsley, Michael Sternlight, Art Wasson

Gerald Mohr, Nora Hayden, Les Tremayne, Jack Kruschen

The Angry Silence **
GB   1960   94m   bw
British Lion/Beaver (Richard Attenborough, Bryan Forbes)
V

A worker who refuses to join an unofficial strike is 'sent to Coventry' by his mates; the matter hits national headlines, and the communists use it to their own advantage.

Irresistibly reminding one of a po-faced *I'm All Right Jack*, this remains a fresh and urgent film which unfortunately lost excitement in its domestic scenes.

w Bryan Forbes   *story* Michael Craig, Richard Gregson   *d* Guy Green   *ph* Arthur Ibbetson   *m* Malcolm Arnold

Richard Attenborough, Michael Craig, Pier Angeli, Bernard Lee, Alfred Burke, Laurence Naismith, Geoffrey Keen

'Vastly entertaining as well as thought-provoking. Matter and manner are for once wholly in harmony.' – *Daily Mail*

'A film made by people who care about the screen and care what they are saying on it.' – *Dilys Powell*

AAN: Bryan Forbes, Richard Gregson, Michael Craig

Die Angst des Tormanns beim Elfmeter: see
The Goalkeeper's Fear of the Penalty Kick

Animal Crackers ***
US   1930   98m   bw
Paramount
V, V*, L

Thieves covet a valuable oil painting unveiled at a swank party.

An excuse for the Marx Brothers, and a lively one in patches, though sedate and stage bound in treatment. The boys are all in top form, and many of the dialogue exchanges are classics.

w Morrie Ryskind   *musical play* Morrie Ryskind, George F. Kaufman   *d* Victor Heerman   *ph* George Folsey   *m/ly* Bert Kalmar, Harry Ruby

Groucho, Chico, Harpo, Zeppo, Margaret Dumont, Lillian Roth, Louis Sorin, Robert Greig, Hal Thompson

GROUCHO: 'You're the most beautiful woman I've ever seen, which doesn't say much for you.'
GROUCHO: 'One morning I shot an elephant in my pajamas. How he got into my pajamas I'll never know.'
GUESTS: 'Hooray for Captain Spaulding, the African explorer!'
GROUCHO: 'Did someone call me schnorrer?'
GUESTS: 'Hooray, hooray, hooray!'
ZEPPO: 'He went into the jungle, where all the monkeys *throw* nuts.'
GROUCHO: 'If I stay here, I'll *go* nuts.'
GUESTS:
'Hooray, hooray, hooray!
He put all his reliance
In courage and defiance
And risked his life for science.'
GROUCHO: 'Hey, hey!'
MRS RITTENHOUSE: 'He is the only white man who covered every acre . . .'
GROUCHO: 'I think I'll try and make her . . .'
GUESTS: 'Hooray, hooray, hooray!'

'A hit on the screen before it opened, and in the money plenty.' – *Variety*

Animal Farm **
GB   1955   75m   Technicolor
Louis de Rochemont/Halas and Batchelor
V, V*, L

Oppressed by the cruelty and inefficiency of their master, the animals take over a farm but find fresh tyrants among themselves.

George Orwell's political fable – 'all animals are equal but some animals are more equal than others' – is faithfully followed in this ambitious but rather disappointingly flat cartoon version.

w/p/d John Halas, Joy Batchelor   *m* Matyas Seiber

voices: Maurice Denham

'A melodramatic fantasy that is mordant, tender and quixotic, shot with ironic humour.' – *New York Times*

The Animal Kingdom *
US   1932   95m   bw
RKO (David O. Selznick)
V*
GB title: *The Woman in His House*

An intellectual publisher tries to justify keeping both a wife and a mistress.

Smart comedy-drama from a Broadway success, later bowdlerized as *One More Tomorrow* (qv).

w Horace Jackson   *play* Philip Barry   *d* Edward H. Griffith   *ph* Lucien Andriot   *m* Max Steiner

Leslie Howard, Ann Harding, Myrna Loy, Neil Hamilton, William Gargan, Henry Stephenson, Ilka Chase

'A wise and engaging picture addressed to the upper levels of fandom.' – *Variety*

'Two billion years in the making!'
The Animal World *
US   1956   80m   Technicolor
Warner/Windsor (Irwin Allen)

The evolution of animals from their primitive beginnings.

Ambitious documentary with a popular science approach; very variable, with poorish model work.

wd Irwin Allen   *ph* Harold Wellman   *m* Paul Sawtell   *sp* Willis O'Brien, Ray Harryhausen

The Animals
US   1970   86m   Technicolor   Techniscope
MGM-EMI/XYZ (Richard Bakalyan)
aka: *Five Savage Men*

A schoolteacher, raped by a sadistic killer and his gang, takes her revenge with the aid of an Indian who saves her life.

Notably grim and violent Western, made with no sense of style or period and overweighted by the heavy irony of its climax.

w Richard Bakalyan   *d* Ron Joy   *ph* Keith Smith   *m* Rupert Holmes   *ed* Pier Laskey

Henry Silva, Keenan Wynn, Michele Carey, John Anderson, Joseph Turkel, Pepper Martin, Bobby Hall, Peter Hellmann

'As with other forms of pornography, the possibilities of originality within the pornography of violence are distinctly finite.' – *James D. White, MFB*

The Animals Film *
GB/US   1981   136m   colour/bw
Slick Pix

A hard-hitting documentary recording human ill-treatment of animals, with obvious hints that humans themselves will be next. Narrated by Julie Christie.

Not for the squeamish.

wd Victor Schonfeld

Animated Genesis *
GB   1952   22m   Technicolor (blown up from 16mm)
Korda/British Lion

Greed and the machine enslave mankind.

Ambitious and decorative cartoon conceived and drawn by *Joan and Peter Foldes*, from whom little was subsequently heard.   *m* Thomas Henderson

Anne and Muriel **
France   1971   108m   Eastmancolor
Gala/Les Films du Carrosse/Cinetel (Marcel Berbert)
original title: *Les Deux Anglaises et le Continent*

A French writer falls in love with two English sisters.

Elegant variation on the eternal triangle.

w François Truffaut, Jean Gruault   *novel* Henri-Pierre Roche   *d* François Truffaut   *ph* Nestor Almendros   *m* Georges Delerue   *ad* Michel de Broin   *ed* Yann Dedet

Jean-Pierre Léaud, Kika Markham, Stacey Tendeter, Sylvia Marriott, Marie Mansart, Philippe Leotard, Irene Tunch

Ann Vickers *
US   1933   72m   bw
RKO (Pandro S. Berman)
V*

A feminist social worker is taught a thing or two by life and settles down with a corrupt judge.

Reasonably effective version of a popular though heavy-going novel of the time.

w Jane Murfin   *novel* Sinclair Lewis   *d* John Cromwell   *ph* David Abel, Edward Cronjager   *m* Max Steiner

Irene Dunne, Walter Huston, Conrad Nagel, Bruce Cabot, Edna May Oliver, Mitchell Lewis, Murray Kinnell

'Her sufferings are bearable and her ultimate happiness is assured, so this is vicarious enjoyment for any woman. Lovely romance, moderate penance, final respectability. All of which suggests that Ann Vickers should do moderately good biz.' – *Variety*

Anna
Italy   1951   100m   bw
Lux (Ponti/de Laurentiis)

A novice nun recalls her former life and almost gives up her vocation.

Soupy woman's picture of no particular merit.

w Giuseppe Berto, Dino Risi, Ivo Perilli, Franco Brusati, Rodolfo Sonego   *d* Alberto Lattuada   *ph* Otello Martelli   *m* Nino Rota

Silvana Mangano, Raf Vallone, Vittorio Gassman, Gaby Morlay, Jacques Dumesnil

Anna
US   1987   100m   TVC colour
Magnus (Zanne Devine, Yurek Bogayevicz)
V*, L

A Czech-born actress in the New York fringe theatre is betrayed by a young female admirer.

Echoes of *All About Eve* seem less important than the political asides, and the whole thing is a bit of a muddle.

w Agnieszka Holland   *d* Yurek Bogayevicz   *ph* Bobby Bukowski   *m* Greg Hawkes

Sally Kirkland, Robert Fields, Paulina Porizkova

AAN: Sally Kirkland

Anna and the King of Siam **
US   1946   128m   bw
TCF (Louis D. Lighton)
V*

In 1862 an English governess arrives in Bangkok to teach the 67 children of the king.

Unusual and lavish drama, tastefully handled and generally absorbing despite miscasting and several slow passages.

w Talbot Jennings, Sally Benson   *book* Margaret Landon   *d* John Cromwell   *ph* Arthur Miller   *m* Bernard Herrmann   *ad* Lyle Wheeler, William Darling

Irene Dunne, Rex Harrison, Linda Darnell, Gale Sondergaard, Lee J. Cobb, Mikhail Rasumny

'A film that never touches the imagination, a film that leaves the mind uninformed and the memory unburdened.' – *Richard Winnington*

'It's pitifully unauthentic, and not a very good movie either, but the story itself holds considerable interest.' – *Pauline Kael, 70s*

AA: Arthur Miller

AAN: Talbot Jennings, Sally Benson; Bernard Herrmann; Gale Sondergaard

'Garbo talks!'

Anna Christie **
US 1930 86m bw
MGM
V*

A waterfront prostitute falls in love with a young seaman.

Primitive sound version of an earthy theatrical warhorse: it has a niche in history as the film in which Garbo first talked.

w Frances Marion play Eugene O'Neill
d Clarence Brown ph William Daniels

Greta Garbo, Charles Bickford, Marie Dressler, James T. Mack, Lee Phelps

'Great artistically and tremendous commercially . . . in all respects a wow picture.' – Variety

'A very talkie, uncinematic affair, more old-fashioned than the silent movies. If it were not so well acted it would be pretty tiresome.' – National Board of Review

† A 1923 silent version starred Blanche Sweet and was directed by John Wray.

AAN: Clarence Brown; William Daniels; Greta Garbo

Anna Karenina **
US 1935 95m bw
MGM (David O. Selznick)
V, V*

The wife of a Russian aristocrat falls for a dashing cavalry officer.

Well-staged but finally exasperating romantic tragedy, sparked by good performances and production.

w Clemence Dane, Salka Viertel novel Leo Tolstoy
d Clarence Brown ph William Daniels m Herbert Stothart

Greta Garbo (Anna), Fredric March (Vronsky), Basil Rathbone (Karenin), Freddie Bartholomew (Sergei), Maureen O'Sullivan (Kitty), May Robson (Countess), Reginald Owen (Silva), Reginald Denny (Yashvin)

'Cinch b.o. anywhere. In the foreign markets it should come close to establishing modern-day highs.' – Variety

'A dignified and effective drama which becomes significant because of that tragic, lonely and glamorous blend which is the Garbo personality.' – André Sennwald

'It reaches no great heights of tragedy or drama but rather moves forward relentlessly and a little coldly.' – The Times

† Previously filmed as a 1928 silent called Love, with Garbo and John Gilbert.

Anna Karenina *
GB 1948 139m bw
London Films (Alexander Korda)
V, V*

Tiresomely overlong but very handsomely staged remake marred by central miscasting.

w Jean Anouilh, Guy Morgan, Julien Duvivier
d Julien Duvivier ph Henri Alekan m Constant Lambert ad André Andrejew ed Russell Lloyd

Vivien Leigh, Kieron Moore, Ralph Richardson, Marie Lohr, Sally Ann Howes, Niall MacGinnis, Michael Gough, Helen Haye, Mary Kerridge

'Vivien Leigh is lashed about by the tremendous role of Anna like a pussy cat with a tigress by the tail. She is not helped by a script which insists on sentimentally ennobling one of fiction's most vehemently average women.' – James Agee

Anna Lucasta *
US 1949 86m bw
Columbia/Security (Philip Yordan)

The bad girl of a farming family comes home to marry, but her past catches up with her.

Polish immigrant melodrama, a touring company staple, adequately transferred to the screen.

w Philip Yordan, Arthur Laurents play Philip Yordan d Irving Rapper ph Sol Polito m David Diamond

Paulette Goddard, Oscar Homolka, Broderick Crawford, William Bishop, Gale Page, Mary Wickes

Anna Lucasta *
US 1958 97m bw
(UA) Longridge Enterprises (Sidney Harmon)

Black version of the long-running play; performances standard.

w Philip Yordan d Arnold Laven ph Lucien Ballard m Elmer Bernstein

Eartha Kitt, Frederick O'Neal, Sammy Davis Jnr, Henry Scott, Rex Ingram, James Edwards

Anna of Brooklyn
Italy/France/US 1958 106m colour Technirama
Circeo Cinematografica/France Cinema/RKO (Milko Skofic)

An attractive widow returns from New York to her native Italian village in search of a husband.

Footling romantic drama which wastes its cast and budget.

w Ettore Margadonna, Dino Risi d Reginald Denham, Carlo Lasticati ph Giuseppe Rotunno m Alessandro Cicognini, Vittorio de Sica

Gina Lollobrigida, Dale Robertson, Vittorio de Sica, Amedeo Nazzari, Peppino de Felippo, Gabriella Palotta

Annabelle Partagée
France 1990 80m colour
Gala/ça Films (Sophie Delochée, Anne Fieschl)
V

A student dancer ditches her middle-aged boyfriend for someone younger.

Dull film, in which little happens and nothing of any consequence.

wd Francesca Comencini ph Michel Abramowicz m Les Valentins, Etienne Daho ad Valérie Grall ed Yves Deschamps

Delphine Zingg, François Marthouret, Jean-Claude Adelin

'A French film about l'amour in which l'ennui takes over early on.' – Nigel Andrews, Financial Times

'The one notable moment of Francesca Comencini's mildly feminist debut is an erect penis, slightly out of focus and looking rather like a toadstool, seen in the foreground of the opening shot. This might be a small milestone, so to speak, in popular French cinema.' – Philip French, Observer

Annabelle's Affairs
US 1931 74m bw
Fox
V*

When her husband disappears, a young bride becomes head cook at his rival's home. Then the husband turns up.

Standard farce which worked pretty well in its day.

w Leon Gordon play Good Gracious Annabelle by Clare Kummer d Alfred Werker

Jeanette MacDonald, Victor McLaglen, Roland Young, Sam Hardy, William Collier Snr

Annabel Takes a Tour
US 1939 69m bw
RKO
V*

A star on a publicity tour balks at the stunts she is expected to perform.

Thinnish sequel to The Affairs of Annabel.

w Bert Granet and Oliver Cooper d Lew Landers

Lucille Ball, Jack Oakie, Ruth Donnelly, Bradley Page, Ralph Forbes

Annapolis Farewell
US 1935 75m bw
Paramount (Louis D. Lighton)
GB title: Gentlemen of the Navy

An old officer so loves the service that he continues to live near the Naval Academy.

Tolerable sentimentality of a familiar kind.

w Dale Van Every, Frank Craven, Grover Jones, William Slavens McNutt d Alexander Hall

Sir Guy Standing, Tom Brown, Richard Cromwell, Rosalind Keith, John Howard, Benny Baker, Louise Beavers, Samuel S. Hinds, Minor Watson

An Annapolis Story
US 1953 81m colour
Allied Artists/Walter Mirisch
V*
GB title: The Blue and the Gold

Two cadets at the naval academy love the same girl.

Artless recruiting poster heroics.

w Dan Ullman d Don Siegel ph Sam Leavitt m Marlin Skiles

Diana Lynn, John Derek, Kevin McCarthy, Pat Dooley, L. Q. Jones

'Seldom have so many scrubbed, wholesome-looking young people thronged any picture.' – New York Times

Anne of Green Gables *
US 1934 79m bw
RKO (Kenneth MacGowan)
V*

An orphan girl goes to the country to live with her aunt.

Standard version of the classic for young girls.

w Sam Mintz novel L. M. Montgomery d George Nicholls Jnr ph Lucien Andriot m Max Steiner

Anne Shirley (who had been known as Dawn O'Day and legally adopted the name of her character in this, her first starring role), Tom Brown, O. P. Heggie, Helen Westley, Sara Haden, Charley Grapewin

'Made up and monotonous – tragedy having its breakfast in bed.' – Otis Ferguson

† Anne of Windy Willows, with the same stars and production team, followed in 1940.

Anne of the Indies *
US 1951 87m Technicolor
TCF (George Jessel)

Lady pirate Anne Bonney, the terror of the Caribbean, is at odds with her former master Blackbeard.

Routine swashbuckler, generally well handled.

w Philip Dunne, Arthur Caesar d Jacques Tourneur ph Harry Jackson m Franz Waxman

Jean Peters, Louis Jourdan, Debra Paget, Herbert Marshall, Thomas Gomez, James Robertson Justice, Sean McClory, Francis Pierlot

Anne of the Thousand Days *
GB 1969 146m Technicolor Panavision
Universal/Hal B. Wallis
V*

Henry VIII divorces his wife to marry Anne Boleyn, but soon finds evidence of adultery.

A somewhat unlikely view of history, rather boringly presented on a woman's magazine level, but with occasional good moments from a cast of British notables.

w John Hale, Bridget Boland *play* Maxwell Anderson *d* Charles Jarrott *ph* Arthur Ibbetson *m* Georges Delerue *pd* Maurice Carter

Richard Burton, Geneviève Bujold, John Colicos (as Cromwell), Irene Papas, Anthony Quayle, Michael Hordern, Katharine Blake, Peter Jeffrey, William Squire, Esmond Knight, Nora Swinburne

'The costumes, beautiful in themselves, have that unconvincing air of having come straight off the rack at Nathan's.' – *Brenda Davies*

'A decent dullness is, alas, the keynote.' – *Michael Billington, Illustrated London News*

'The quintessential work of art for people who haven't the foggiest notion of what art is.' – *John Simon*

'Intelligent from line to line, but the emotions supplied seem hypocritical, and the conception lacks authority . . . Burton's performance is colourless. It's as though he *remembered* how to act but couldn't work up much enthusiasm or involvement.' – *Pauline Kael*

AA: costumes (Margaret Furse)

AAN: best picture; John Hale, Bridget Boland; Arthur Ibbetson; Georges Delerue; Richard Burton; Geneviève Bujold; Anthony Quayle

L'Année Dernière à Marienbad: see *Last Year at Marienbad*

Annie
US   1982   128m   Metrocolor   Panavision
Columbia/Ray Stark (Joe Layton)
V, V*, L, S

In 1933 an orphan waif charms a munitions millionaire and is adopted by him.

Misguided opening-out of a charming stage musical based on the comic strip which is basically a reversal of *Oliver Twist*. Some of the best numbers have been discarded, the dancing is ponderous, the acting distinctly uneasy, and the choice of director stupefying. None of it works at all.

w Carol Sobieski, from the stage play *book* Thomas Meehan *ly* Martin Charnin *m* Charles Strouse *comic strip* Harold Gray *d* John Huston *ph* Richard Moore *m* Ralph Burns *pd* Dale Hennesy

Albert Finney, Carol Burnett, Aileen Quinn, Ann Reinking, Bernadette Peters, Tim Curry, Geoffrey Holder, Edward Herrmann (as Franklin D. Roosevelt)

'Whatever indefinable charm the stage show had is completely lost in this lumbering and largely uninteresting and uninvolving exercise, where the obvious waste reaches almost Pentagonian proportions.' – *Variety*

'The whole thing has the air of a vast, hollow Christmas tree bauble intended not so much for children as for the infantile-minded middle-aged.' – *Sunday Times*

'This is the film I want on my tombstone.' – *Ray Stark*

'Funeral services may be held starting this week at a theatre near you.' – *Time*

† The cost of *Annie*, starting with $9,000,000 for the rights, rose to $42,000,000. It was not recovered.

AAN: art direction; original song score

Annie Get Your Gun *
US   1950   107m   Technicolor
MGM (Arthur Freed)
S

A young female hillbilly joins Frank Butler's sharpshooting act, and is sophisticated by her love for him.

Gaudy, stagey, generally uninspired screen version of the famous musical show based remotely on a historical character of post-wild-west days. There is a lack of dancing, the direction is stodgy, and in general

flair the production falls disappointingly below MGM's usual standard.

w Sidney Sheldon *musical play* Herbert and Dorothy Fields *d* George Sidney *ph* Charles Rosher *md* Adolph Deutsch, Roger Edens *m/ly* Irving Berlin *ad* Cedric Gibbons, Paul Groesse *ch* Robert Alton

Betty Hutton, *Howard Keel*, Edward Arnold, J. Carrol Naish, Louis Calhern

songs: 'Colonel Buffalo Bill'; 'Doing What Comes Naturally'; 'The Girl That I Marry'; 'You Can't Get a Man with a Gun'; 'There's No Business Like Show Business'; 'My Defenses Are Down'; 'I'm an Indian Too'; 'I Got the Sun in the Morning'; 'Anything You Can Do'; 'They Say It's Wonderful'

† The real Annie Oakley was born Phoebe Ann Oakley Mozie in 1860, and died in 1926. The role was to have been played by Judy Garland, who was fired after displays of temperament; also considered were Doris Day, Judy Canova and Betty Garrett.
†† Louis Calhern replaced Frank Morgan, who died during production.

AA: music direction

AAN: Charles Rosher

Annie Hall ****
US   1977   93m   DeLuxe
UA/Jack Rollins-Charles H. Joffe (Fred T. Gallo)
V, V*, L
Sub-title: *A Nervous Romance*

Against the neuroses of New York and Los Angeles, a Jewish comedian has an affair with a midwestern girl.

Semi-serious collage of jokes and bits of technique, some of the former very funny and some of the latter very successful. For no very good reason it hit the box-office spot and turned its creator, of whom it is very typical, from a minority performer to a superstar.

w Woody Allen, Marshall Brickman *d* Woody Allen *ph* Gordon Willis *m* various

Woody Allen, Diane Keaton, Tony Roberts, Carol Kane, Paul Simon, Shelly Duvall

ALLEN: 'Hey, don't knock masturbation. It's sex with someone I love.'

'The film's priceless vignettes about the difficulties in chitchatting with strangers, the awkward moments in family visits, and the frequent breakdowns in communication and failures in intimacy, its reminiscences about the palpable horrors of growing up in Brooklyn, and its comic encounters with lobsters in the kitchen or spiders in the bathroom, all seem like snapshots from Allen and Keaton's own romance.' – *Les Keyser, Hollywood in the Seventies*

† The narrative supposedly mirrors the real-life affair of the stars, who separated before the film came out. (Diane Keaton's family name is Hall.)

AA: best picture; script; direction; Diane Keaton

AAN: Woody Allen (as actor)

Annie Oakley *
US   1935   90m   bw
RKO (Cliff Reid)
V*

The historical story, more or less, of the lady later immortalized in *Annie Get Your Gun*.

Lively semi-Western with good dialogue but gluey plot development.

w Joel Sayre, John Twist *d* George Stevens *ph* J. Roy Hunt *md* Alberto Colombo *ad* Van Nest Polglase

Barbara Stanwyck, Preston Foster, Melvyn Douglas, Moroni Olsen, Pert Kelton, Andy Clyde, Chief Thunderbird

'A swell idea that doesn't quite come through.' – *Variety*

Annie's Coming Out *
Australia   1984   93m   Eastmancolor
Film Australia (Don Murray)

A physically handicapped child, wrongly characterized as mentally retarded also, is brought out by a devoted teacher.

Fictionalized version of a true story: predictably well intentioned, shocking, and consistently watchable.

w John Patterson, Chris Borthwick *book* Rosemary Crossley *d* Gil Brealey *ph* Mick Van Borneman *m* Simon Walker

Angela Punch-McGregor, Drew Forsythe, Tina Arhondis, Liddy Clark, Monica Maughan

The Annihilators
US   1985   84m   colour
New World (Allan C. Pedersen, Tom Chapman)
V, V*

Vietnam veterans are hired as small-town vigilantes.

Violent action film of no visible merit.

w Brian Russell *d* Charles E. Sellier Jnr *ph* Henning Schellerup *m* Bob Summers *ad* Simon Gittins *ed* Dan Gross

Christopher Stone, Andy Wood, Lawrence Hilton-Jacobs, Gerrit Graham, Dennis Redfield, Paul Koslo

The Anniversary *
GB   1968   95m   Technicolor
Warner/Hammer (Jimmy Sangster)

A malevolent one-eyed widow will stop at nothing to prevent her grown sons from leaving the family orbit, and they meet each year to mourn the death of the husband she really hated.

Agreeable but over-talkative black comedy with a splendid role for its star and some good scattered moments, marred by a general lack of style.

w Jimmy Sangster *play* Bill MacIlwraith *d* Roy Ward Baker *ph* Harry Waxman *m* Philip Martell *ad* Reece Pemberton *ed* James Needs, Peter Weatherley

Bette Davis, Jack Hedley, *James Cossins*, Sheila Hancock, Elaine Taylor, Christian Roberts, Timothy Bateson

'It all reminds one of a love scene in a funeral parlour.' – *Variety*

'Magisterially grotesque in elegantly tailored eye-patch and exotic gown, she snaps out her bitchy insults with all 57 varieties of relish.' – *MFB*

† Alvin Rakoff was replaced as director during filming.

El Anonimo
Spain   1990   87m   Eastmancolor
Sagutxo (Alfonso Arandia)

Four students try to recover an incriminating letter addressed to one of their professors.

Amiable, lackadaisical comedy.

w Alfonso Arandia, Jose Antonio Gomez *d* Alfonso Arandia *ph* Gonzalo F. Berridi *m* Mikel Erentxum *ed* Juan I. Sanmateo

Miguel Molina, Jorge de Juan, Martxelo Rudio, Carlos Zabala, Nacho Martinez, Rosa Maria Sarda, Alejandra Greppi

The Anonymous Letter: see *El Anonimo*

'Convention outraged . . . a class abandoned . . . a country betrayed!'

Another Country *
GB   1984   90m   colour
TCF/Virgin/Goldcrest (Alan Marshall)
V, V*, L

A homosexual defector to Russia reflects on the public school pressures which influenced him.

Upper-crust militarism, arrogance, sadism and homosexuality rolled up in a package which pleased the West End theatre crowds but seems faintly absurd on film. Not much of a recruiting poster for Eton.

w Julian Mitchell play Julian Mitchell d Marek Kanievska ph Peter Biziou m Michael Storey pd Brian Morris

Rupert Everett, Colin Firth, Michael Jenn, Robert Addie, Anna Massey, Rupert Wainwright, Betsy Brantley

'Inevitably it went down well at the Cannes Film Festival, where movies critical of their own country's shortcomings are always favoured.' – *Margaret Hinxman, Daily Mail*

Another Dawn

US   1937   73m   bw
Warner (Harry Joe Brown)

In a British army post in Africa, a wife is torn between duty and romance.

Absurdly sudsy melodrama, a potboiler for stars between more important assignments.

w Laird Doyle d William Dieterle ph Tony Gaudio m Erich Wolfgang Korngold

Errol Flynn, Kay Francis, Ian Hunter, Frieda Inescort, Herbert Mundin

† In every Warner film where a cinema canopy was shown, the title advertised was *Another Dawn*, so its use here as an actual title is presumably a piece of cynicism.

Another Face

US   1935   72m   bw
RKO
GB title: *It Happened in Hollywood*

A gangster has his face lifted and becomes a film star.

Rather heavy comedy with some good laughs.

w Garrett Graham, John Twist, Ray Mayer, Thomas Dugan d Christy Cabanne

Brian Donlevy, Wallace Ford, Phyllis Brooks, Erik Rhodes, Molly Lamont, Alan Hale

Another Fine Mess **

US   1930   30m   bw
Hal Roach

On the run from a cop, Stan and Ollie masquerade as master and maid.

Elaborate star comedy with spoken introduction instead of titles; very satisfying but not quite vintage.

w H. M. Walker, from a sketch by Stan Laurel's father d James Parrott

Laurel and Hardy, James Finlayson, Thelma Todd, Charles Gerrard

Another 48 Hrs

US   1990   95m   Technicolor
Paramount/Eddie Murphy Productions (Lawrence Gordon, Robert D. Wachs)
V, V*, L, S

A cop enters into a partnership with a criminal to catch a drug dealer.

A virtual remake of *48 Hours* (qv), but lacking in energy or interest.

w John Fasano, Jeb Stuart, Larry Gross story Fred Braughton d Walter Hill ph Matthew F. Leonetti m James Horner pd Joseph C. Nemec III ad Gary Wissner ed Freeman Davies, Carmel Davies, Donn Aron

Eddie Murphy, Nick Nolte, Brion James, Kevin Tighe, Ed O'Ross, David Anthony Marshall, Andrew Divoff, Bernie Casey, Brent Jennings, Ted Markland, Tisha Campbell

'Disappoints in its failure, after eight years, to introduce even the faintest wrinkle of something new.' – *Variety*

Another Girl, Another Planet

US   1992   56m   bw   Pixelvision
ICA/Michael Almereyda, Robin O'Hara, Bob Gosse

A man attempts to seduce women passing through his apartment by showing them old cartoon films, while his married neighbour looks on or discusses the meaning of life.

Depression as an art form: a minimalist film shot with a toy camera that renders everything slightly out of focus and provides at best a murky image of shadows and fog, turning human life into a grey smear on the wall.

wd Michael Almereyda ph Jim Denault ed David Leonard

Nic Ratner, Barry Sherman, Mary Ward, Lisa Perisot, Maggie Rush

'An elegantly-crafted chamber piece that effortlessly belies its no-budget origins.' – *Steve Bode, London Film Festival*

'We're so often up to the director's pretensions in angst that despair starts to creep almost palpably off the screen and into the auditorium. Joyful it ain't.' – *Tom Hutchinson, Film Review*

† The film was shot using a Fisher-Price PXL 2000 child's camcorder, made of moulded plastic, with a fixed lens, and recording on standard audio cassettes. The images it produces fade rapidly and are composed of easily visible pixels, like an over-enlarged computer image. The camera, which was made as a toy for Christmas 1987 and discontinued soon after, has become a favourite of a group of experimental film-makers because of its technical limitations.

Another Language

US   1933   75m   bw
MGM (Walter Wanger)

A young wife does not fit in with her husband's snobby family and falls in love with his nephew.

Flat treatment of a dated play.

w Herman J. Mankiewicz, Gertrude Purcell, Donald Ogden Stewart play Rose Franken d Edward H. Griffith ph Ray June

Helen Hayes, Robert Montgomery, John Beal, Louise Closser Hale, Henry Travers, Margaret Hamilton

'A very good picture that will get more than average box office attention . . . everything is handled with intellect and due restraint.' – *Variety*

Another Man, Another Chance

France/US   1977   132m   Eastmancolor
UA/Films 13/Ariane (Alexandre Mnouchkine, George Dancigers)
V*
French title: *Un Autre Homme, une Autre Chance*; aka: *Another Man, Another Woman*

A Yank vet and a French widow meet and fall in love in the old west.

Pretty, overlong, rather enervating romance with an unusual and not entirely convincing setting.

wd Claude Lelouch ph Jacques Lefrançois m Francis Lai

James Caan, Geneviève Bujold, Francis Huster, Susan Tyrrell

Another Man's Poison *

GB   1951   89m   bw
Douglas Fairbanks Jnr/Daniel M. Angel

A lady novelist poisons her husband and lover, then unwittingly takes a fatal dose herself.

Hysterical vehicle for a fading Hollywood star reduced to repeating her tantrums in an English studio on a low budget; she should have stayed home, as should her director.

w Val Guest play *Deadlock* by Leslie Sands d Irving Rapper ph Robert Krasker m John Greenwood

Bette Davis, Anthony Steel, Gary Merrill, Emlyn Williams, Barbara Murray, Reginald Beckwith, Edna Morris

'Barnstormers as rich and improbable as this are rare . . . the general atmosphere takes one back to 1935.' – *Gavin Lambert*

'Like reading Ethel M. Dell by flashes of lightning.' – *Frank Hauser*

'The melodramatic gamut has seldom experienced such a workout.' – *Hollywood Reporter*

Another Part of the Forest *

US   1948   108m   bw
U-I (Jerry Bresler)

In the post-Civil War years, Marcus Hubbard leads his family to worldly success by cheating and the misuse of power: he lives to regret it, as the children learn their lessons all too well.

This backwards sequel to *The Little Foxes*, showing how the characters of that play got to be their nasty selves, is quite absorbingly acted but stagily presented, with plenty of care but no style.

w Vladimir Pozner play Lillian Hellman d Michael Gordon ph Hal Mohr m Daniele Amfitheatrof

Fredric March, Florence Eldridge, Ann Blyth, Dan Duryea, Edmond O'Brien, John Dall

'The Hubbards are the greatest collection of ghouls since *The Old Dark House*.' – *Pauline Kael, 70s*

Another Shore *

GB   1948   77m   bw
Ealing (Ivor Montagu)

A young Irishman dreams of life in the South Seas but gives up his fancies for love.

Curiously whimsical, artificial and unconvincing comedy drama from a famous studio, but not without its moments of interest.

w Walter Meade novel Kenneth Reddin d Charles Crichton ph Douglas Slocombe m Georges Auric

Robert Beatty, Stanley Holloway, Moira Lister, Michael Medwin, Dermot Kelly, Wilfred Brambell, Irene Worth

'The Perfect Family Has Just Moved Into The Neighbourhood.'
Another Stakeout

US   1993   108m   Technicolor   Scope
Buena Vista/Touchstone (Jim Kouf, Cathleen Summers, Lynn Bigelow)
V, V*

Two cops and a lawyer pretend to be a family when they stake out a house for the witness to a murder.

Slight and ineffectual flop that substitutes poor gags for thrills.

w Jim Kouf d John Badham ph Roy H. Wagner m Arthur B. Rubinstein pd Lawrence G. Paull ed Frank Morris, Kevin Stitt

Richard Dreyfuss, Emilio Estevez, Rosie O'Donnell, Dennis Farina, Marcia Strassman, Cathy Moriarty, Madeleine Stowe, John Rubinstein, Miguel Ferrer

'The "another" . . . is a declaration by the makers of *Stakeout*, a successful 1987 comedy-thriller, that this follow-up is a reprise rather than a sequel, and an indication that they suspect the targeted audience might have trouble reading roman numerals.' – *Philip French, Observer*

'It's one of those sequels that, though reasonably entertaining, go in one eye and out the other.' – *Derek Malcolm, Guardian*

'It's a blessed event!'

Another Thin Man
US   1939   102m   bw
MGM (Hunt Stromberg)
V*, L

Nick Charles solves a murder on a Long Island weekend.

Overwritten and distinctly tedious star sequel to *The Thin Man* and *After the Thin Man*. The title refers (erroneously) to Nick and Nora's baby.

w Frances Goodrich, Albert Hackett   *d* W. S. Van Dyke II   *ph* Oliver T. Marsh, William Daniels   *m* Edward Ward

William Powell, Myrna Loy, Otto Kruger, C. Aubrey Smith, Virginia Grey, Nat Pendleton, Tom Neal, Ruth Hussey, Sheldon Leonard

'The screenplay tosses shootings and skulduggery and repartee at us before we're ready, and then Nick Charles takes an unconscionable amount of time sorting things out.' – *Pauline Kael, 70s*

Another Time, Another Place
GB   1958   98m   bw   Vistavision
Paramount/Kaydor (Lewis Allen, Smedley Aston)
V*, L

During World War II an American newspaperwoman has an affair with a British war correspondent; when he is killed in action, she consoles his widow.

Drippy romance, unsympathetically played and artificially set in a Cornish village.

w Stanley Mann   *novel* Lenore Coffee   *d* Lewis Allen   *ph* Jack Hildyard   *m* Douglas Gamley

Lana Turner, Barry Sullivan, Glynis Johns, Sean Connery, Sidney James

Another Woman *
US   1988   84m   colour
Rank/Orion/Jack Rollins, Charles H. Joffe (Robert Greenhut)
V, V*, L

An unemotional academic discovers her inner self.

Woody Allen at his most gloomy and introspective.

wd Woody Allen   *ph* Sven Nykvist   *pd* Santo Loquasto   *ed* Susan E. Morse

Gena Rowlands, Mia Farrow, Ian Holm, Blythe Danner, Gene Hackman, Betty Buckley, Martha Plimpton, John Houseman

'Not only Allen's most wholly personal movie since *Stardust Memories* but arguably the most substantial achievement of his career.' – *Tim Pulleine, MFB*

Ansiktet: see *The Face*

Antefatto: see *A Bay of Blood*

Anthony Adverse *
US   1936   141m   bw
Warner (Henry Blanke)
S

Adventures of an ambitious young man in early 19th-century America.

A rousing spectacle of its day, from a bestselling novel, this award-winning movie quickly dated and now seems very thin and shadowy despite the interesting talents involved.

w Sheridan Gibney   *novel* Hervey Allen   *d* Mervyn Le Roy   *ph* Tony Gaudio   *m* Erich Wolfgang Korngold   *ad* Anton Grot   *ed* Ralph Dawson

Fredric March, Olivia de Havilland, Gale Sondergaard, Edmund Gwenn, Claude Rains, Anita Louise, Louis Hayward, Steffi Duna, Donald Woods, Akim Tamiroff, Ralph Morgan, Henry O'Neill

'A bulky, rambling and indecisive photoplay which has not merely taken liberties with the letter of the original but with its spirit.' – *Frank S. Nugent, New York Times*

'In the dramatizing there is shown no relish or conviction, only a retentive memory for all the old clothes of show business.' – *Otis Ferguson*

'A lavish gold-leaf from Hervey Allen's book, an earnest cinema endeavour, taxing alike its studio's purse and artistry.' – *Douglas Gilbert, New York World Telegraph*

'The show is fairly glutted with plot and counter-plot and is apt to make one feel that one is witnessing a serial run off continuously at a single performance.' – *Howard Barnes, New York Herald Tribune*

'It goes on too long, otherwise it might have been the funniest film since *The Crusades*.' – *Graham Greene*

AA: Tony Gaudio; Erich Wolfgang Korngold; Gale Sondergaard; Ralph Dawson

AAN: best picture; Anton Grot

Antoine et Antoinette *
France   1947   87m   bw
SNEG/Gaumont

A young married couple find they have won a lottery but lost the ticket.

A bubbly soufflé, most expertly served but leaving one still a little hungry; not quite in the Clair class.

w Françoise Giroud, M. Griffe, Jacques Becker   *d* Jacques Becker   *ph* Pierre Montazel   *m* Jean-Jacques Grunenwald

Roger Pigaut, Clair Maffei

Antonio (dubbed)
Chile   1973   82m   colour
Saga/Claudio Guzmán

A poor village potter, given an expensive car by an indulgent American millionaire, drives to Santiago so that he can return the gift.

A confused and innocuous little fable about the corruption of urban life, aimed at a family audience.

w Mervin Walkenstein, Claudio Guzmán   *d* Claudio Guzmán   *ph* Andres Martorell   *m* Ralph Ferraro   *pd* Pato Guzmán

Trini Lopez, Larry Hagman, Naomi Guerrero, Mervin Walkenstein

Antonio das Mortes **
Brazil   1969   95m   Eastmancolor
Connoisseur/Produções Cinematograficas Mapa/Glauber Rocha (Claude-Antoine Mapa, Glauber Rocha)
original title: *O Dragao da Maldade contra o Santo Guerreiro*

A mercenary, hired by a rich landowner to kill an outlaw and his poor followers, realises that he is supporting the wrong side.

Vivid, exotic South American Western with political overtones, a sequel of sorts to *Black God, White Devil* (qv).

wd Glauber Rocha   *ph* Alfonso Beato   *m* Marlos Nobre, Walter Queiroz, Sergio Ricardo   *ad* Glauber Rocha   *ed* Eduardo Escorel

Mauricio Do Valle, Odete Lara, Hugo Carvana, Othon Bastos, Joffre Soares, Lorival Pariz

'Rocha's magnificent film is in fact firmly tied to the present-day political and social reality of his underdeveloped homeland.' – *Konstantin Bazarov, MFB*

Antony and Cleopatra *
GB/Spain/Switzerland   1972   170m   Technicolor   Todd-AO 35
Transac/Izaro/Folio Films (Peter Snell)
V, V*, S

Well-meaning, well-mounted, but quite uninspired rendering.

wd Charlton Heston   *play* William Shakespeare   *ph* Rafael Pacheco   *m* John Scott   *pd* Maurice Pelling

Charlton Heston, Hildegarde Neil, Eric Porter, *John Castle* (as Octavius), Fernando Rey, Freddie Jones, Peter Arne, Roger Delgado

† Olivier and Orson Welles were both sought for the lead.

Any Number Can Play *
US   1949   103m   bw
MGM (Arthur Freed)

A gambling casino owner has health problems, is reconciled with his son and retires from the game.

Rather boring drama redeemed by slightly offbeat dialogue and excellent star acting, albeit in routine roles.

w Richard Brooks   *novel* E. H. Heth   *d* Mervyn Le Roy   *ph* Harold Rosson   *m* Lennie Hayton

Clark Gable, Alexis Smith, Mary Astor, Wendell Corey, Audrey Totter, Lewis Stone, Frank Morgan, *Marjorie Rambeau*, Barry Sullivan

Any Old Port *
US   1932   20m   bw
Hal Roach
V

Stan and Ollie are sailors on leave, and Ollie enters Stan for a boxing match.

Minor star comedy with good moments but a weak finish.

w H. M. Walker   *d* James W. Horne

Laurel and Hardy, Walter Long

Any Wednesday *
US   1966   109m   Technicolor
Warner (Julius J. Epstein)
V*
GB title: *Bachelor Girl Apartment*

A millionaire businessman spends every Wednesday with his mistress, but complications arise when his young associate is accidentally sent to use the company flat.

Overlong screen version of a thinly scripted Broadway success in which yawns gradually overtake laughs.

w Julius J. Epstein   *play* Muriel Resnik   *d* Robert Ellis Miller   *ph* Harold Lipstein   *m* George Duning

Jane Fonda, Dean Jones, Jason Robards Jnr, Rosemary Murphy (a breath of air as the deceived wife who doesn't mind), Ann Prentiss, King Moody

Any Which Way You Can
US   1980   116m   DeLuxe
Malpaso/Warner (Fritz Manes)
V, V*, L

The hero of *Every Which Way But Loose* becomes involved in further brawls and car crashes, with the help of his friendly orang-utan.

A sequel designed entirely for the box-office, its tone set by the scene in which the villains on motorcycles are covered in tar.

w Stanford Sherman   *d* Buddy Van Horn   *ph* David Worth   *md* Steve Dorf   *pd* William J. Creber   *ed* Ferris Webster, Ron Spang

Clint Eastwood, Ruth Gordon, Sondra Locke, Geoffrey Lewis, William Smith, Harry Guardino

'This kind of thing is clearly beyond or beneath criticism.' – *Variety*

'Where the previous comedy set up a zany situation, this one ploughs it into the ground.' – *Daily Mail*

Anybody's Woman
US   1930   80m   bw
Paramount

A drunken lawyer marries a chorus girl and regrets it, but she reforms him.

Tedious matrimonial drama.

w Zoe Akins, Doris Anderson, Gouverneur Morris
d Dorothy Arzner

Ruth Chatterton, Clive Brook, Paul Lukas, Huntley Gordon, Virginia Hammond

'It can't lose through that title and the stars.' – *Variety*

Anything Can Happen *
US   1952   93m   bw
Paramount/William Perlberg, George Seaton

Adventures of a Russian immigrant family in New York.

A standard Hollywood product based on a sentimental best-seller.

w George Seaton, George Oppenheimer
book George and Helen Papashvily   d George Seaton   ph Daniel L. Fapp   m Victor Young

José Ferrer, Kim Hunter, Kurt Kasznar, Alex Danaroff, Oscar Beregi

'Exploits to the hilt the somewhat limited possibilities of quaintness and whimsicality with a broken accent.' – *Penelope Houston*

Anything Goes **
US   1936   92m   bw
Paramount (Benjamin Glazer)
TV title: *Tops is the Limit*

Romantic adventures on board a transatlantic liner.

Amiably batty musical comedy, zestfully directed and blithely performed.

w Guy Bolton, P. G. Wodehouse, Howard Lindsay, Russel Crouse, from their Broadway show   d Lewis Milestone   ph Karl Struss   md Victor Young
m/y Cole Porter   ad Hans Dreier

Bing Crosby, Ethel Merman, Charles Ruggles, Grace Bradley, Ida Lupino, Chill Wills, the Avalon Boys, Arthur Treacher

† Only three of Cole Porter's songs were retained from the Broadway show: 'Anything Goes', 'You're the Top' and 'I Get a Kick out of You'. Others by various hands include 'Moonburn', 'Sailor Beware', 'My Heart and I', 'Am I Awake?', 'Hopelessly in Love'.

Anything Goes *
US   1956   106m   Technicolor   Vistavision
Paramount (Robert Emmett Dolan)

The male stars of a musical comedy each sign a girl to play the female lead; resulting complications are ironed out during a transatlantic voyage.

Below-par reworking of the 1936 film in which technical gloss and dull sets virtually reduce the characters to puppets. A few good moments transcend the general lack of imagination.

w Sidney Sheldon, from show as credited in 1936 version   d Robert Lewis   ph John F. Warren
md Joseph J. Lilley   ch: Nick Castle, Roland Petit
m/y Cole Porter   ad Hal Pereira, Joseph M. Johnson

Bing Crosby, Donald O'Connor, Zizi Jeanmaire, Mitzi Gaynor, Phil Harris, Kurt Kasznar

Anzio
Italy   1968   117m   Technicolor   Panavision
Columbia/Dino de Laurentiis (Marcel Bebert)
V, V*
GB title: *The Battle for Anzio*

A war correspondent joins American and British troops preparing for the 1944 landing in Italy.

Threadbare war film which wastes an all-star American cast.

w H. A. L. Craig   book Wynford Vaughan Thomas
d Edward Dmytryk   ph Giuseppe Rotunno   m Riz Ortolani

Robert Mitchum, Peter Falk, Arthur Kennedy, Robert Ryan, Earl Holliman, Mark Damon, Reni Santoni, Anthony Steel, Patrick Magee

'It must be a long time since a script managed to pack in so many crassly portentous statements about why men fight wars.' – *MFB*

Apache *
US   1954   91m   Technicolor
UA/Hecht-Lancaster (Harold Hecht)
V*

After the surrender of Geronimo, one Apache leader is unconquered; after creating much havoc, he settles for domesticity, and the white men let him go unharmed.

Sober Western in the wake of *Broken Arrow*, with a predictably sympathetic star performance and a surprising happy ending. More decency than excitement along the way.

w James R. Webb   novel *Bronco Apache* by Paul I. Wellman   d Robert Aldrich   ph Ernest Laszlo
m David Raksin

Burt Lancaster, Jean Peters, John McIntire, Charles Bronson, John Dehner, Paul Guilfoyle, Walter Sande, Monte Blue

'The picture was seriously compromised. You make a picture about one thing, the inevitability of Massai's death. His courage is measured against the inevitable. The whole previous two hours becomes reduced if at the end he can just walk away.' – *Robert Aldrich*

Apache Drums
US   1951   75m   Technicolor
U-I (Val Lewton)

A gambler helps a town under Indian attack.

Standard co-feature Western, perfectly adequate but showing no sign of its producer's former tastes and skills.

w David Chandler   d Hugo Fregonese   ph Charles Boyle   m Hans Salter

Stephen McNally, Willard Parker, Coleen Gray, Arthur Shields, James Griffith

Apache Rifles
US   1964   92m   DeLuxe
Admiral Pictures/TCF

In 1879 Arizona, an Indian-hating officer falls for a half-caste.

Tolerable mid-budget Western.

w Charles B. Smith   d William H. Witney

Audie Murphy, Michael Dante, Linda Lawson, L. Q. Jones

Apache Trail
US   1942   66m   bw
MGM (Sam Marx)

A highwayman's brother guards the stagecoach mail box.

Routine Western support, quite watchable.

w Maurice Geraghty   story Ernest Haycox
d Richard Thorpe

Lloyd Nolan, Donna Reed, William Lundigan, Ann Ayars, Connie Gilchrist, Chill Wills, Miles Mander, Gloria Holden

Apache Uprising
US   1965   90m   Techniscope
Paramount/A. C. Lyles
V*

Assorted passengers in a stagecoach survive an Indian attack at a way station.

It sounds like a remake, and almost is, but the handling is lively enough and the producer's usual cast of nostalgic stars is in evidence.

w Harry Sanford, Max Lamb   d R. G. Springsteen
ph W. Wallace Kelley   m Jimmie Haskell

Rory Calhoun, Corinne Calvet, John Russell, Lon Chaney Jnr, Gene Evans, DeForest Kelley, Arthur Hunnicutt, Richard Arlen, Johnny Mack Brown, Jean Parker

Apache War Smoke
US   1952   67m   bw
MGM

An Indian killer is among those sheltering in a desert outpost before an Apache raid.

Talkative but tense lower-berth Western.

w Jerry Davis   story Ernest Haycox   d Harold Kress

Gilbert Roland, Robert Horton, Glenda Farrell, Barbara Ruick, Henry Morgan

Aparajito ****
India   1956   113m   bw
Epic Films Private Ltd (Satyajit Ray)
V, V*
aka: *The Unvanquished*

After his father's death, a poor country boy is helped by his mother to study for the university.

A detailed and moving study of two characters who are universally familiar despite an unusual background.

wd Satyajit Ray   ph Subrata Mitra   m Ravi Shankar

Pinaki Sen Gupta, Karuna Banerjee, Kanu Banerjee

† This was the sequel to *Pather Panchali,* and was itself followed by *The World of Apu.*

'Movie-wise, there has never been anything like it – laugh-wise, love-wise, or otherwise-wise!'

The Apartment **
US   1960   125m   bw   Panavision
UA/Mirisch (Billy Wilder)
V, V*, L

A lonely, ambitious clerk rents out his apartment to philandering executives and finds that one of them is after his own girl.

Overlong and patchy but agreeably mordant and cynical comedy with a sparkling view of city office life and some deftly handled individual sequences.

w Billy Wilder, I. A. L. Diamond   d Billy Wilder
ph Joseph LaShelle   m Adolph Deutsch
ad Alexander Trauner   ed Daniel Mandell

Jack Lemmon (C. C. Baxter), *Shirley Maclaine* (Miss Kubelik), *Fred MacMurray* (Jeff D. Sheldrake), Ray Walston (Joe Dobisch), Jack Kruschen (Dr Dreyfuss), Joan Shawlee (Sylvia), Edie Adams (Miss Olsen), David Lewis (Al Kirkeby)

Baxter's opening narration: 'On November 1st, 1959, the population of New York City was 8,042,753. If you laid all these people end to end, figuring an average height of five feet six and a half inches, they would reach from Times Square to the outskirts of Karachi, Pakistan. I know facts like this because I work for an insurance company – Consolidated Life of New York. We are one of the top five companies in the country. Last year we wrote nine point three billion dollars worth of policies. Our home office has 31,259 employees, which is more than the entire population of Natchez, Mississippi, or Gallup, New Mexico. I work on the 19th floor – Ordinary Policy department – Premium Accounting division – Section W – desk number 861.'

BAXTER: 'Miss Kubelik, one doesn't get to be a second administrative assistant around here unless he's a pretty good judge of character, and as far as I'm concerned you're tops. I mean, decency-wise and otherwise-wise.'

BAXTER: 'You know, I used to live like Robinson Crusoe – shipwrecked among eight million people. Then one day I saw a footprint in the sand and there you were. It's a wonderful thing, dinner for two.'

MISS KUBELIK: 'Shut up and deal.' (Last line of film.)

'Without either style or taste, shifting gears between pathos and slapstick without any transition.' – *Dwight MacDonald*

'Billy Wilder directed this acrid story as if it were a comedy, which is a cheat, considering that it involves pimping and a suicide attempt and many shades of craven ethics.' – *New Yorker, 1980*

AA: best picture; Billy Wilder, I. A. L. Diamond (as writers); Billy Wilder (as director)

AAN: Joseph LaShelle; Jack Lemmon; Shirley Maclaine; Jack Kruschen; art direction; editing

Apartment for Peggy *
US   1948   98m   Technicolor
TCF (William Perlberg)

A retired professor finds a new lease of life through caring for the homeless family of an ex-GI.

Sentimental comedy with serious undertones (the professor twice attempts suicide). Signs of enterprise are smothered by regulation charm.

wd George Seaton   *story* Faith Baldwin   *ph* Harry Jackson   *m* David Raksin

Edmund Gwenn, Jeanne Crain, William Holden, Gene Lockhart, Henri Letondal, Charles Lane, Houseley Stevenson

'A first rate experience for observers with comprehending minds.' – *Bosley Crowther, New York Times*

The Apartment on the Thirteenth Floor: see *Cannibal Man*

Apartment Zero
UK   1988   125m   colour
Mainline/The Summit Company (Martin Donovan, David Koepp)
V*, L, S

In Buenos Aires, a repressed crypto-Englishman takes as a lodger a mysterious American.

Unpleasant psychological thriller about unlovely people.

w Martin Donovan, David Koepp   *d* Martin Donovan   *ph* Miguel Rodriguez   *m* Elia Cmiral   *pd* Miguel Angel Lumaldo   *ed* Conrad M. Gonzalez

Colin Firth, Hart Bochner, Dora Bryan, Liz Smith, Cipe Lincovsky

The Ape
US   1940   61m   bw
Monogram (Scott R. Dunlap)
V*

Dr Adrian seeks to cure polio by means of a serum which can only be obtained from the spinal fluid of a human being. He kills an escaped ape and dresses in its skin to seek victims.

Silly and rather boring addition to the mad doctor cycle.

w Curt Siodmak, Richard Carroll   *play* Adam Shirk   *d* William Nigh   *ph* Harry Neumann   *m* Edward Kay

Boris Karloff, Maris Wrixon, Gertrude Hoffman, Henry Hall

Ape and Super Ape
Netherlands/USA   1972   103m   Technicolor
Unicorn (Bert Haanstra Films)
original title: *Bij de Beesten Af*

An alleged documentary comparing human and animal behaviour seems regrettably to turn into a series of episodes depicting animal savagery in close-up.

wd Bert Haanstra   *ph* Anton Van Munstered Bert Haanstra

'It lacks even associational interest for the wild-life enthusiast, and is best written off as an inconclusive,

unoriginal and often repellent exercise unworthy of its maker.' – *John Baxter, MFB*

AAN: documentary

The Ape Man
US   1943   64m   bw
Monogram (Sam Katzman, Jack Dietz)
V*
GB title: *Lock Your Doors*

A scientist injects himself with spinal fluid which turns him into an ape creature.

Cheap rubbish shot in a couple of corners and offering no thrill whatever.

w Barney A. Sarecky   *story* They Creep in the Dark by Karl Brown   *d* William Beaudine   *ph* Mack Stengler   *m* Edward Kay

Bela Lugosi, Wallace Ford, Louise Currie, Minerva Urecal

'Bela Lugosi, rigged out in a shaggy beard and formal morning attire, ambling like an ape and sharing a cage with a gorilla, scares nobody. It's strictly a dual support.' – *Variety*

† A supposed sequel the following year, *Return of the Ape Man*, had in fact no plot connection. In this Lugosi thawed out a neanderthal man, inserted John Carradine's brain, and the composite turned into George Zucco!

Der Apfel ist ab **
West Germany   1949   105m   bw
Camera Film/Helmut Beck-Herzog
Translated title: The Apple Fell

Adam and Eve have marital problems in Paradise, and consult a psychiatrist.

Lively sophisticated fantasy, perhaps a bit arch for general consumption, but about as interesting in post-war Nazi Germany as *Caligari* was in 1919.

w Kurd E. Heyne, Helmut Kautner, Bobby Todd, from their musical comedy   *d* Helmut Kautner   *ph* Igor Oberberg   *m* Bernhard Eichhorn

Bobby Todd, Bettina Moissi, Joana Maria Gorvin

'Hollywood should look over this Kautner. He has a Lubitsch touch that runs all over this picture.' – *Variety*

Aphrodite, Goddess of Love
Italy   1958   90m   Ferrania colour
Schermi (Adriano Merkel)
original title: *Afrodite Dea Dell'Amore*; aka: *Slave Women of Corinth*

The governor of Corinth has to cope with the Emperor Nero, his infatuation with a prostitute, plague, Christians and revolting locals.

Better-than-average example of its genre, mixing power politics and romance to some effect.

w Ugo Moretti, Mario Bonnard, Sergio Leone, Marco Di Nardo   *d* Mario Bonnard   *ph* Tino Santoni   *m* Giovanni Fusco   *pd* Saverio D'Eugenio   *ed* Nella Nannuzzi

Isabelle Corey, Antonio de Teffe, Irene Tunc, Ivo Garrani, Giulio Donnini, Carlo Tamberlani

Apocalypse Now **
US   1979   153m   Technicolor   Technovision
Omni Zoetrope (Francis Coppola)
V, V (W), V*, L, S

A Vietnam captain is instructed to eliminate a colonel who has retired to the hills and is fighting his own war.

Pretentious war movie, made even more hollow-sounding by the incomprehensible performance of Brando as the mad martinet. Some vivid scenes along the way, and some interesting parallels with Conrad's *Heart of Darkness*, but these hardly atone for the director's delusion that prodigal expenditure of time and money will result in great art. (The movie took so long to complete that it was dubbed *Apocalypse Later*.)

w John Milius, Francis Coppola   *d* Francis Coppola   *ph* Vittorio Storaro   *m* Carmine Coppola, Francis Coppola   *pd* Dean Tavoularis

Martin Sheen, Robert Duvall, Frederic Forrest, Marlon Brando, Sam Bottoms, Dennis Hopper

'The characters are living through Vietnam as pulp adventure fantasy, as movie, as stoned humour.' – *New Yorker*

'Emotionally obtuse and intellectually empty.' – *Time*

† Coppola admitted the following at the Cannes Film Festival: 'It's more of an experience than a movie. At the beginning there's a story. Along the river the story becomes less important and the experience more important.'

AA: Vittorio Storaro

AAN: best picture; best writing; best direction; Robert Duvall

The Appaloosa *
US   1966   99m   Techniscope
Universal (Alan Miller)
V, V*, L
GB title: *Southwest to Sonora*

A cowboy's plan to start a stud farm with his magnificent horse is interrupted by badmen who think he has molested their girl.

Mannered, slow Western set on the Mexican border, with star and director apparently striving to upstage each other.

w James Bridges, Roland Kibbee   *novel* Robert MacLeod   *d* Sidney J. Furie   *ph* Russell Metty   *m* Frank Skinner

Marlon Brando, Anjanette Comer, John Saxon, Rafael Campos, Frank Silvera

'Seems intent less on telling a story than in carving out the incidental details.' – *MFB*

'The camerawork concentrates on beady eyes, sweaty foreheads, spurred boots and anonymous midriffs being studied through a variety of frames, ranging from tequila bottles to cook fires to grillwork to fingers to feet.' – *Judith Crist*

'A dog of a movie about a horse.' – *Pauline Kael*

'Is Kitty a mother?'
Applause **
US   1929   78m   bw
Paramount (Jesse L. Lasky, Walter Wanger)
V*

A vaudeville star gradually loses the love of her daughter.

Absorbing treatment of a has-been tearjerking theme, full of cinematic touches and with unusual use of New York locations.

w Garrett Fort   *novel* Beth Brown   *d* Rouben Mamoulian   *ph* George Folsey

Helen Morgan, Joan Peers, Henry Wadsworth, Fuller Mellish Jnr

'An oasis of filmic sophistication in a desert of stage-bound early talkies.' – *William Everson, 1966*

'A cohesive, well integrated series of pictures. Its intensity, its sharp projection of tragedy, emerge from the eye of the camera; an omniscient, omnipresent eye that slides easily over the links of the story and emphasizes only the true and the relevant.' – *Thornton Delehanty, The Arts*

The Apple Dumpling Gang
US   1974   100m   Technicolor
Walt Disney (Bill Anderson)
V*, L

Three orphan children strike gold in 1878 California.

Better-than-average Disney romp.

w Don Tait   *novel* Jack M. Bickham   *d* Norman Tokar   *ph* Frank Phillips   *m* Buddy Baker

Bill Bixby, Susan Clark, David Wayne, Don Knotts, Tim Conway, Slim Pickens, Harry Morgan, John McGiver, Marie Windsor, Iris Adrian

The Apple Dumpling Gang Rides Again
US   1979   88m   Technicolor
Walt Disney (Ron Miller)
V*

Two incompetent bank robbers trying to go straight find themselves in trouble with a sheriff, the cavalry, Indians and a rival gang.

Limp, slow-paced comedy Western that is a dull sequel to an ordinary original.

w Don Tait   d Vincent McEveety   ph Frank Phillips   m Buddy Baker   ad John B. Mansbridge, Frank T. Smith   ed Gordon D. Brenner

Tim Conway, Don Knotts, Tim Matheson, Kenneth Mars, Elyssa Davalos, Jack Elam, Robert Pine, Harry Morgan, Ruth Buzzi

The Apple Fell: see Der Apfel ist ab

The Appointment *
US   1969   100m   colour
MGM (Martin Poll)

A businessman suspects his wife of spare time prostitution.

Unusual sophisticated fable, dressed to kill but rather stretched out for its substance. Shades of El and The Chinese Room.

w James Salter   d Sidney Lumet   m John Barry, Don Walker

Omar Sharif, Anouk Aimée, Lotte Lenya

Appointment for Love *
US   1941   89m   bw
Universal (Bruce Manning)

A doctor and a playwright agree to marry 'without love'.

A familiar theme quite amusingly explored by a practised cast.

w Bruce Manning, Felix Jackson   d William A. Seiter   ph Joseph Valentine   m Frank Skinner, Charles Previn

Charles Boyer, Margaret Sullavan, Eugene Pallette, Rita Johnson, Gus Schilling, Reginald Denny, Ruth Terry

Appointment in Berlin
US   1943   77m   bw
Columbia (Sam Bischoff)

An RAF wing commander expresses unpopular views and is recruited by the Nazis as a 'voice of truth' broadcaster.

World War II potboiler.

w Horace McCoy, Michael Hogan   d Alfred E. Green   ph Franz Planer   m Werner Heymann

George Sanders, Marguerite Chapman, Gale Sondergaard, Onslow Stevens, Alan Napier, H. P. Sanders (the star's father)

Appointment in Honduras
US   1953   79m   Technicolor print
RKO/Benedict Bogeaus
V*

Three assorted types and four criminals escape through the jungle from a revolution.

Predictable adventure drama sabotaged by poor colour.

w Karen de Wolf   d Jacques Tourneur   ph Joseph Biroc   m Louis Forbes

Glenn Ford, Ann Sheridan, Zachary Scott, Rodolfo Acosta, Jack Elam

Appointment in London *
GB   1952   96m   bw
Mayflower (Aubrey Baring, Maxwell Setton)

The exploits of a squadron of Bomber Command during one month in 1943.

Dullish war film with standard credits.

w John Wooldridge, Robert Westerby   d Philip Leacock   ph Stephen Dade   m John Wooldridge

Dirk Bogarde, Ian Hunter, Dinah Sheridan, Bill Kerr, Bryan Forbes, William Sylvester, Charles Victor

Appointment with a Shadow
US   1957   72m   bw   Cinemascope
Universal-International
GB title: The Big Story

An alcoholic reporter redeems himself by capturing a criminal single-handed.

Maudlin melodrama which takes itself too seriously.

w Alec Coppel, Norman Jolley   d Richard Carlson

George Nader, Joanna Moore, Brian Keith, Virginia Field

Appointment with Crime
GB   1945   97m   bw
British National

Ex-convict revenges himself on the former friends who shopped him.

Stodgy melodrama which seemed about to make a big star of William Hartnell.

wd John Harlow

William Hartnell, Robert Beatty, Joyce Howard, Raymond Lovell, Herbert Lom

Appointment with Danger *
US   1949   89m   bw
Paramount (Robert Fellows)

A nun becomes the government's chief witness in identifying the murderers of a US postal inspector.

Routine but entertaining star thick ear.

w Richard Breen, Warren Duff   d Lewis Allen   ph John Seitz   m Victor Young

Alan Ladd, Phyllis Calvert, Paul Stewart, Jan Sterling, Jack Webb, Henry Morgan

Appointment with Death
GB   1988   108m   colour
Cannon (Michael Winner)
V*, L

Another starry Hercule Poirot tale, this time in 30s Palestine.

w Anthony Shaffer, Peter Buckman, Michael Winner   novel Agatha Christie   d Michael Winner   ph David Gurfinkel   m Pino Donaggio   pd John Blezard

Peter Ustinov, Lauren Bacall, Carrie Fisher, John Gielgud, Piper Laurie

'They came home with the milk!'
Appointment with Venus **
GB   1951   89m   bw
GFD/British Film Makers (Betty E. Box)
US title: Island Rescue

During World War II, a pedigree cow is rescued from the German-occupied Channel Islands.

Curious but generally agreeable mixture of comedy and war adventure, pleasantly shot on Sark.

w Nicholas Phipps   novel Jerrard Tickell   d Ralph Thomas   ph Ernest Steward   m Benjamin Frankel

David Niven, Glynis Johns, George Coulouris, Barry Jones, Kenneth More, Noel Purcell, Bernard Lee, Jeremy Spenser

Apprentice to Murder
Norway   1988   94m   colour
New World (Howard K. Grossman)
V*, L

In Pennsylvania in the 1920s, a teenaged boy comes under the influence of a faith healer who is cursed by the devil.

Odd little thriller that relies too heavily on special effects to hold an audience's attention.

w Alan Scott, Wesley Moore   d R. L. Thomas   ph Kelvin Pike   m Charles Gross   pd Gregory Bolton   sp Derek Meddings, Mar Meddings, Roy Spencer   ed Patrick McMahon

Donald Sutherland, Chad Lowe, Mia Sara, Knut Husebo, Rutanya Alda, Eddie Jones, Mark Burton, Adrian Sparks

The Apprenticeship of Duddy Kravitz *
Canada   1974   121m   Bellevue-Pathé   Panavision
Duddy Kravitz Syndicate (Gerald Schneider)
V*

An ambitious young Jew finds that it is best to be liked.

Amusing adventures of an anti-hero; good scenes but rather patchy technique.

w Mordecai Richler   novel Mordecai Richler   d Ted Kotcheff   ph Miklos Lente   m Stanley Myers

Richard Dreyfuss, Micheline Lanctot, Jack Warden, Randy Quaid, Denholm Elliott, Joseph Wiseman

AAN: Mordecai Richler

Après l'Amour *
France   1992   105m   colour
Mayfair/Alexandre/TF1/Prodeve (Jean-Bernard Fetoux)
V

Love and desire among the thirty-somethings of Parisian glitterati.

A complex story of sexual relationships over a period of a year, enjoyable enough if you can keep track of all the shifting couplings, but not particularly insightful.

w Diane Kurys, Antoine Lacomblez   d Diane Kurys   ph Fabio Conversi   m Yves Simon, Serge Parathoner, Jannick Top   ad Tony Egry   ed Hervé Schneid

Isabelle Huppert, Bernard Giraudeau, Hippolyte Girardot, Lio, Yvan Attal, Judith Reval, Ingrid Held, Laure Killing, Mehdi Ioossen, Florian Billon

'It copes with agony, bluster, lies and voyeurism in a cynically relaxed spirit that places it firmly in the French "relationship movie" genre; though with the difference, outdated as it may seem anywhere except France, that it is a woman through whose eyes we look.' – Amanda Lipman, Sight and Sound

The April Fools *
US   1969   95m   Technicolor   Panavision
Cinema Center/Jalem (Gordon Carroll)
V*

An unhappy New York husband elopes to Paris with an unhappy wife.

Whimsical romantic comedy which rather strains its resources without giving full value for money in romance, humour or simple charm. Good moments, though.

w Hal Dresner   d Stuart Rosenberg   ph Michel Hugo   m Marvin Hamlisch   pd Richard Sylbert

Jack Lemmon, Catherine Deneuve, Myrna Loy, Charles Boyer, Peter Lawford, Jack Weston, Harvey Korman, Sally Kellerman

'Painfully modish, from the opening party in an apartment filled with fashionable objets d'art to the final mad dash to the airport in an expensive sports car.' – MFB

April Fool's Day
US   1986   88m   Metrocolor   Panavision
Paramount/Hometown (Frank Mancuso Jnr)
V, V*, L

College friends go to spend a weekend in an isolated house with a wealthy practical joker, who has a taste for murderous pranks.

A teenage slasher movie with an original twist, but one that does not alter the usual tedium of the genre.

w Danilo Bach   d Fred Walton   ph Charles Minsky   m Charles Bernstein   ad Stewart Campbell   ed Bruce Green

Jay Baker, Deborah Foreman, Deborah Goodrich, Ken Olandt, Griffin O'Neal, Leah King Pinsent, Clayton Rohner

April in Paris *
US   1952   100m   Technicolor
Warner (William Jacobs)
V, V*, L

A chorus girl is mistakenly invited to a US Arts Festival in Paris, and bewitches the bureaucrat in charge.

Poorly produced star musical with a thin plot and a few redeeming wisps of wit.

w Jack Rose, Melville Shavelson   d David Butler   ph Wilfrid Cline   md Ray Heindorf   ch Le Roy Prinz   m/ly Sammy Cahn, Vernon Duke, E. Y. Harburg

Doris Day, *Ray Bolger*, Claude Dauphin, Eve Miller, George Givot

April Love
US   1957   99m   Eastmancolor   Cinemascope
TCF (David Weisbart)

For stealing a car, a teenager is sent on probation to his uncle's stud farm, where circumstances seem once again to put him in trouble with the law.

Easygoing star vehicle with little to recommend it to adults.

w Winston Miller   novel George Agnew Chamberlain   d Henry Levin   ph Wilfrid Cline   m/ly Sammy Fain, Paul Francis Webster

Pat Boone, Shirley Jones, Dolores Michaels, Arthur O'Connell, Jeanette Nolan

† A remake of *Home in Indiana*.

AAN: title song (m Sammy Fain, ly Paul Francis Webster)

April Romance: see *Blossom Time*

April Showers *
US   1948   94m   bw
Warner (William Jacobs)

In a family vaudeville act, Dad takes to drink.

Hoary musical melodrama enlivened by occasional acts.

w Peter Milne   d James V. Kern   ph Carl Guthrie   md Ray Heindorf   musical adaptation Max Steiner   songs various

Jack Carson, Robert Alda, Ann Sothern, Robert Ellis, S. Z. Sakall

The Arab: see *The Barbarian*

Arabella
US/Italy   1969   91m   Technicolor
Cram Film/Universal

A female confidence trickster needs the money to pay her grandmother's back taxes.

Floppy, tedious comedy adventure with an international cast all at sea.

w Adriano Barocco   d Mauro Bolognini

Virna Lisi, James Fox, Terry-Thomas, Margaret Rutherford

Arabesque **
US   1966   118m   Technicolor   Panavision
Universal (Stanley Donen)
V*

An Oxford professor is asked by Middle Eastern oil magnates to decipher a hieroglyphic, and finds afterwards that he is marked for assassination.

The ultimate in sixties spy kaleidoscopes, in which the working out of the plot matters much less than the stars, the jokes and the lavish backgrounds. Fast moving, amusing and utterly forgettable.

w Julian Mitchell, Stanley Price, Pierre Marton   novel The Cipher by Gordon Cotler   d Stanley Donen   ph Christopher Challis   m Henry Mancini   ad Reece Pemberton

Gregory Peck, Sophia Loren, *Alan Badel*, Kieron Moore, Carl Duering

'Nothing could look more "with it", or somehow matter less.' – *MFB*

'A strikingly visual chase and intrigue yarn.' – *Robert Windeler*

'All rather too flashy for comfort.' – *Sight and Sound*

† Pierre Marton was a pen name for Peter Stone.

Arabian Adventure
GB   1979   98m   colour
Badger Films/John Dark

The dictator of Jadur promises his daughter's hand in marriage if a young prince will seek and find a magic rose.

Artless juggling of elements from *The Thief of Baghdad*, including magic carpets, monsters and a bottle djinn.

w Brian Hayles   d Kevin Connor   ph Alan Hume   m Ken Thorne   pd Elliot Scott

Christopher Lee, Oliver Tobias, Mickey Rooney, Milo O'Shea, Elizabeth Welch, Peter Cushing, Capucine

'Resolutely well mounted, but somehow lacking that necessary fillip of Hollywood vulgarity or exuberance.' – *John Pym, MFB*

Arabian Nights *
US   1942   86m   Technicolor
Universal (Walter Wanger)

The Caliph of Baghdad is deposed by his half-brother but wins back his throne with the help of a dancer and an acrobat.

Well presented oriental adventure which has nothing to do with its source material but entertained multitudes in search of relief from total war and was followed by several vaguely similar slices of hokum with the same stars.

w Michael Hogan   d John Rawlins   ph Milton Krasner, William V. Skall, W. Howard Greene   m Frank Skinner   ad Alexander Golitzen, Jack Otterson

Jon Hall, Maria Montez, Sabu, Leif Erickson, Thomas Gomez, Turhan Bey, John Qualen, Billy Gilbert, Shemp Howard

AAN: Milton Krasner, William V. Skall, W. Howard Greene; Frank Skinner; art direction

Arabian Nights
Italy   1974   155m   Technicolor
UA/PEA/Artistes Associés (Alberto Grimaldi)
V*, L
original title: *Il Fiore delle Mille e una Notte*

A travelling prince listens to three erotic stories.

Unappealing, too realistic trilogy which the director saw as a companion to his *Canterbury Tales* and *The Decameron*. The public saw it as a lengthy bore.

wd Pier Paolo Pasolini   ph Giuseppe Ruzzolini   m Ennio Morricone   ad Dante Ferretti   ed Enzo Ocone

Ninetto Davoli, Franco Merli, Ines Pellegrini, Luiginia Rocci

'Even without its extraordinary visual beauties, and the innovative aesthetic position it represents, *Arabian Nights* would go down in film history as the first movie whose scenes of carnality were smothered in the sounds of laughter.' – *Tony Rayns, MFB*

† After its initial screenings, Pasolini cut the film to 130m by dropping two of the stories. The British release ran for 128m.

'Eight legs. Two fangs. And an attitude.'
Arachnophobia **
US   1990   109m   DeLuxe
Hollywood Pictures/Amblin/Tangled Web (Kathleen Kennedy, Richard Vane)
V, V*, L, S

A doctor moves with his family from the town to the country to find himself confronting local hostility and a plague of killer spiders.

Executive producer Steven Spielberg's influence is evident in this effectively scary movie set in a small town threatened by a menace it doesn't understand.

w Don Jacoby, Wesley Strick   story Don Jacoby, Al Williams   d Frank Marshall   ph Mikael Salomon   m Trevor Jones   pd James Bissell   ad Christopher Burian-Mohr   sp Chris Walas (creatures effects)   ed Michael Kahn

Jeff Daniels, Harley Jane Kozak, John Goodman, Julian Sands, Stuart Pankin, Brian McNamara, Mark L. Taylor, Henry Jones

'Not since *Jaws* has a film come along to make audiences jump in their seats so regularly and enjoyably.' – *Variety*

Aranyer Din Ratri: see *Days and Nights in the Forest*

The Arc
US   1991   95m   colour
Cinema Parallel/Film Four (J. K. Eareckson)

A welder, who loses his job, his house, his friends and his wife, decides to take the first bus out of Baltimore.

An episodic, eccentric, low-budget road movie of occasional sharp humour, but more often given over to windy philosophizing.

wd Rob Tregenza   ph Rob Tregenza   pd Dolores Deluxe

Jason Adams, Kathryn Kelley, Catherine Fogarty, Jennifer Mendenhall

'The story of an outcast and a killer!'
Arch of Triumph *
US   1948   120m   bw
Enterprise (Lewis Milestone)
V, V*

In postwar Paris, an embittered refugee seeks his former Nazi tormentor and has a tragic romance with a would-be suicide.

Doleful, set-bound melodrama knee-deep in misery and artificial melodramatics. An expensive, ambitious failure, both commercially and artistically, but an interesting one.

w Lewis Milestone, Harry Brown   novel Erich Maria Remarque   d Lewis Milestone   ph Russell Metty   md Morris Stoloff   m Leonard Gruenberg

Ingrid Bergman, Charles Boyer, Charles Laughton, Louis Calhern

† The film cost 5 million dollars and grossed 1.5 million.

†† The story was remade for TV in 1984.

Are Husbands Necessary?
US   1942   79m   bw   Paramount

A bickering couple decide to adopt a baby.

Mild marital comedy in a familiar mould.

w Tess Slesinger, Frank Davis   novel Mr and Mrs Cugat by Isabel Scott Rorick   d Norman Taurog   ph Charles Lang   m Robert Emmett Dolan

Ray Milland, Betty Field, Patricia Morison, Eugene Pallette, Charles Dingle, Cecil Kellaway, Leif Erickson, Richard Haydn, Elizabeth Risdon

'A chaos of farcical situations, conceived without gusto and played without conviction.' – Richard Mallett, Punch

Are These Our Children?
US   1931   75m   bw
RKO

A teenager gets into bad company and ends up facing the electric chair.

Shapeless and uncompelling moralistic farrago of no entertainment value.

w Howard Estabrook   d Wesley Ruggles

Eric Linden, Rochelle Hudson, Arline Judge, Ben Alexander, Robert Quirk, Beryl Mercer

Are These Our Parents?
US   1944   74m   bw
Monogram (Jeffrey Bernerd)
GB title: They Are Guilty

Parents neglect their children, who become suspects in a murder case.

Cheap yellow press sensationalism without much production expertise to back it up.

w Michel Jacoby, Hilary Lynn   d William Nigh

Helen Vinson, Lyle Talbot, Ivan Lebedeff, Addison Richards

'Juvenile delinquency yarn is a dualer, twenty years too late; must rely on exploitation for biz.' – Variety

Are We All Murderers?: see Nous Sommes Tous Les Assassins

Are You a Mason?
GB   1934   70m   bw
Twickenham

A stockbroker has been pretending to be a Masonic grand master so that he can get out nights.

Fairly simple-minded farce which could have done with slicker production.

w H. Fowler Mear   play Leo Dietrichstein, Emmanuel Lederer   d Henry Edwards

Sonnie Hale, Robertson Hare, Davy Burnaby, Gwyneth Lloyd, Bertha Belmore

Are You Being Served?
GB   1977   95m   Technicolor
EMI (Andrew Mitchell)
V

The staff of the clothing section of a department store go on holiday to the Costa Plonka.

Feeble enlargement of an old-fashioned but very popular TV series relying heavily on sexual badinage and ancient jokes.

w Jeremy Lloyd, David Croft   d Bob Kellett   ph Jack Atcheler   m various

John Inman, Frank Thornton, Mollie Sugden, Trevor Bannister, Wendy Richard, Arthur Brough, Nicholas Smith, Arthur English, Harold Bennett, Glyn Houston

'A withering selection of patent British puns.' – John Pym, MFB

Are You Listening?
US   1932   73m   bw
MGM

A radio continuity announcer accidentally kills his wife.

Curious disjointed melodrama, the sidelights on the new radio business being its main interest.

w Dwight Taylor   story J. P. McEvoy   d Harry Beaumont

William Haines, Karen Morley, Madge Evans, Anita Page, Neil Hamilton, Wallace Ford, Jean Hersholt

Are You With It? *
US   1948   90m   bw
Universal-International (Robert Arthur)

An insurance executive with doubts joins a fun fair and has a whale of a time.

Pleasantly lively low-budget musical.

w Oscar Brodney   musical comedy Sam Perrin, George Balzer   d Jack Hively   ph Maury Gertsman   md Walter Scharf   m/ly Sidney Miller, Inez James

Donald O'Connor, Olga San Juan, Martha Stewart, Lew Parker

Arena
US   1953   83m   Anscocolor   3-D
MGM (Arthur M. Loew Jnr)

A rodeo rider regains his wife and his sense when his best friend is killed.

Routine actioner, distinguished by 3-D camerawork.

w Harold Jack Bloom   d Richard Fleischer   ph Paul C. Vogel   m Rudolph G. Kopp

Gig Young, Jean Hagen, Polly Bergen, Henry Morgan, Barbara Lawrence, Robert Horton, Lee Van Cleef

The Arena
US   1973   83m   Technicolor   Techniscope
EMI/New World (Mark Damon)
V*
aka: Naked Warriors

Female slaves, who have been forced to fight one another as gladiators, rebel against their small-town owner.

Standard exploitation picture, ringing a slight change on the genre's usual women's prison dramas but employing many of the same clichés.

w John William Corrington, Joyce Hooper Corrington   d Steve Carver   ph Aristide Massacessi   m Francesco de Masi   ad Mimmo Scavia   ed Joe Dante, Piera Bruni

Pam Grier, Margaret Markov, Lucretia Love, Paul Muller, Daniel Vargas, Marie Louise, Mary Count

Aren't Men Beasts! *
GB   1937   66m   bw
BIP (Walter Mycroft)

A dentist poses as his aunt to stop a plot to prevent his son's marriage.

Archetypal British star farce.

w Marjorie Deans, William Freshman   play Vernon Sylvaine   d Graham Cutts   ph Roy Kellino

Robertson Hare, Alfred Drayton, June Clyde, Billy Milton, Judy Kelly

Aren't We All?
GB   1932   67m   bw
Paramount British

A society wife commits a momentary indiscretion.

A pale shadow of the theatrical success of the twenties.

w Basil Mason, Gilbert Wakefield   play Frederick Lonsdale   d Harry Lachman, Rudolf Maté   ph Jack Whitehead

Gertrude Lawrence, Hugh Wakefield, Owen Nares, Harold Huth, Marie Lohr, Renée Gadd, Aubrey Mather

L'Argent *
Switzerland/France   1983   84m   colour
EOS/Marion's Films/FR3 (Jean-Marc Henchoz)
V, V*

A tragic chain of events is started when a forged note is passed in a photographer's shop.

A bleak Bressonian study of conscience, fate and atonement.

wd Robert Bresson   story The False Note by Leo Tolstoy   ph Emmanuel Machuel, Pasqualino de Santis   m Bach

Christian Patey, Sylvie Van Den Elsen, Michel Briguet, Caroline Lang

L'Argent de Poche: see Small Change

Argentine Nights
US   1940   75m   bw
Universal

The Ritz Brothers and the Andrews Sisters head for Argentina to avoid their creditors.

Fair low-budget musical.

w Arthur Horman, Ray Golden, Sid Kuller   d Albert S. Rogell

The Ritz Brothers, the Andrews Sisters, Constance Moore, George Reeves, Peggy Moran, Anne Nagel

Aria *
GB/US   1988   98m   colour
Virgin Vision/Warner (Don Boyd)
V*, L, S

A man wanders through Italian streets and buildings, a journey interrupted as operatic arias are combined with glossy visuals.

Ten directors, given freedom to illustrate the music in any manner they wanted, display a paucity of imagination.

w Nicolas Roeg, Charles Sturridge, Jean-Luc Godard, Julien Temple, Bruce Beresford, Robert Altman, Franc Roddam, Ken Russell, Derek Jarman, Bill Bryden, Don Boyd   d Nicolas Roeg, Charles Sturridge, Jean-Luc Godard, Julien Temple, Bruce Beresford, Robert Altman, Franc Roddam, Ken Russell, Derek Jarman, Bill Bryden   ph Harvey Harrison, Gale Tattersall, Carolyn Champetier, Oliver Stapleton, Dante Spinotti, Pierre Mignot, Frederick Elmes, Gabriel Beristain, Mike Southon, Christopher Hughes   md Ralph Mace   m Verdi, Lully, Korngold, Rameau, Wagner, Puccini, Charpentier, Leoncavallo   pd Diana Johnstone, Andrew McAlpine, Stephen Altman, Piers Plowden, Scott Bushnell, John Hay, Matthew Jacobs, Paul Dufficey, Christopher Hobbs   ed Marie Therese Boiche, Mike Cragg, Tony Lawson, Matthew Longfellow, Neil Abrahamson, Jennifer Auge, Rich Elgood, Michael Bradsell, Peter Cartwright, Angus Cook

Theresa Russell, Nicola Swain, Jack Kyle, Marion Peters, Valerie Allain, Buck Henry, Anita Morris, Beverley D'Angelo, Elizabeth Hurley, Peter Birch, Bertrand Bonvoison, Julie Hagerty, Bridget Fonda, James Mathers, Linzi Drew, Andreas Wisniewski, Tilda Swinton, Spencer Leigh, John Hurt, Sophie Ward

Ariane
Germany   1931   78m   bw
Nerofilm

An innocent young girl falls for a man of the world and makes him think she is a cocotte.

Sophisticated comedy later remade as Love in the Afternoon; this version is interesting chiefly for its presentation of a new star.

w Paul Czinner, Carl Mayer   novel Claude Anet   d Paul Czinner

Elisabeth Bergner, Rudolf Forster, Annemarie Steinsieck, Hertha Guthmar

Ariel *
Finland   1988   72m   colour
Electric/Villealfa (Aki Kaurismäki)
V*

A redundant miner is forced by circumstances to take
to a life of crime.

Episodic movie with not much sense of reality.

wd Aki Kaurismäki   *ph* Timo Salminen   *pd* Risto
Karhula   *ed* Raija Talvio

Turo Pajala, Susanna Haavisto, Matti Pellonpää, Eetu
Hilkamo, Erkki Pajala, Matti Jaaranen, Hannu
Viholainen

'It's a documentation of the destruction of Finland.' –
Aki Kaurismäki

'Here's the gay, glorious story of a war correspondent and
    a war ace . . . a romance that could happen only in 1940!'

Arise My Love ***
US   1940   113m   bw
Paramount (Arthur Hornblow Jnr)

American reporters in Europe and in love survive the
Spanish Civil War, a wrathful editor in Paris and the
sinking of the *Athenia*.

Unique sophisticated entertainment gleaned from the
century's grimmest headlines, ending with a plea
against American isolationism. A significant and
stylish comedy melodrama.

w Charles Brackett, Billy Wilder   *d* Mitchell Leisen
ph Charles Lang   *m* Victor Young   *ad* Hans Dreier,
Robert Usher

Claudette Colbert, Ray Milland, Walter Abel (who as the
harassed editor inaugurated his celebrated line 'I'm
not happy. I'm not happy at all . . .'), Dennis O'Keefe,
George Zucco, Dick Purcell

'Against the background of European fisticuffs,
Paramount brings forth a film of absorbing romantic
interest, proving that love will find a way through the
hazards of air raids, torpedo attacks and enemy
invasions.' – *Variety*

† Joel McCrea was originally cast for the Milland role.

AA: original story (Benjamin Glazer, John S. Toldy)

AAN: Charles Lang; Victor Young; art direction

The Aristocats **
US   1970   78m   Technicolor
Walt Disney (Wolfgang Reiterman, Winston Hibler)

Two cats are deliberately lost by a butler who fears
they will inherit his mistress's wealth; but a variety of
animal friends restore them to their rightful place.

Cartoon feature, a moderate example of the studio's
work after Disney's death, with rather too few
felicitous moments.

w Larry Clemmons and others   *d* Wolfgang
Reitherman

voices of Phil Harris, Eva Gabor, Sterling Holloway,
Scatman Crothers, Paul Winchell, Hermione
Baddeley, Roddy Maude-Roxby

Arizona
US   1940   125m   bw
Columbia (Wesley Ruggles)

A Tucson wildcat meets her match in a travelling
Missourian who helps her outwit villains who are
sabotaging her wagon trains.

Loosely built, deliberately paced Western which for
all its pretensions makes very little impact.

w Claude Binyon   *d* Wesley Ruggles   *ph* Joseph
Walker, Harry Hollenberger, Fayte Brown   *m* Victor
Young   *ad* Lionel Banks, Robert Peterson

Jean Arthur, William Holden, Warren William, Porter
Hall, Paul Harvey, George Chandler, Byron Foulger,
Regis Toomey, Edgar Buchanan

'Lacks the sweep and dramatic impulse that would
have made it a great picture.' – *Variety*

AAN: Victor Young; art direction

Arizona Bushwhackers
US   1968   86m   Techniscope
Paramount (A. C. Lyles)

A Confederate prisoner is given a chance as a Western
sheriff.

Stolid Western, notable only, as is usual with this
producer, for its gallery of ageing but still reliable
familiar faces.

w Steve Fisher   *d* Lesley Selander   *ph* Lester Shorr
m Jimmie Haskell

Howard Keel, Yvonne de Carlo, Brian Donlevy, John
Ireland, Marilyn Maxwell, Scott Brady, Barton
MacLane, James Craig

The Arizona Kid
US   1930   84m   bw
Fox

A wanted bandit finds a secret gold mine in Utah.

Disappointing semi-sequel to *In Old Arizona:* same
star, much less talent to back him up.

w Ralph Block   *d* Alfred Santell

Warner Baxter, Mona Maris, Carole Lombard,
Theodore von Eltz

Arizona Raiders
US   1965   88m   Techniscope
Admiral/Columbia
V*

Two of Quantrell's Raiders are offered a pardon if
they will round up renegades.

Stereotyped Western, poorly processed.

w Alex Gottleib, Mary and Willard Willingham
d William Witney

Audie Murphy, Michael Dante, Ben Cooper, Buster
Crabbe, Gloria Talbott

Arizona to Broadway
US   1933   66m   bw
Fox

A small-town girl in the big city is changed by a con
man.

Fast-moving support which has its moments.

w William Conselman, Henry Johnson   *d* James
Tinling

James Dunn, Joan Bennett, Herbert Mundin, Sammy
Cohen, Theodore von Eltz, J. Carrol Naish, Walter
Catlett

The Arizonian
US   1935   72m   bw
RKO

Lawless Silver City gets a reform marshal.

Adequate first-feature Western, but not a spectacular.

w Dudley Nichols   *d* Charles Vidor

Richard Dix, Margot Grahame, Preston Foster, Louis
Calhern

'Through the names it can slip into the keys where
westerns rarely treat, and where, therefore, horse
operas are regarded as refreshing novelties.' – *Variety*

The Arkansas Traveller
US   1938   85m   bw
Paramount

A small-town widow is helped to keep her
newspaper going by a stranger who happens to be
passing through.

Archetypal mid-American fantasy.

w Viola Brothers Shore, George Sessions Perry
story Jack Cunningham   *d* Alfred Santell

Bob Burns, Fay Bainter, Jean Parker, Irvin S. Cobb

'It will get over nicely in the key spots, but its biggest
b.o. will be in the nabes and smaller communities.' –
Variety

Armed and Dangerous
US   1985   85m   DeLuxe
Columbia (Brian Grazer, James Keach)
V*, L

An ex-cop and a former lawyer uncover criminal
activities at a private security company.

Comedy in which most of the humour depends on
high-speed car crashes.

w Harold Ramis, Peter Torokvei   *story* Brian Grazer,
Harold Ramis, James Keach   *d* Mark L. Lester
ph Fred Schuler   *pd* David L.Snyder   *ed* Michael
Hill, Daniel Hanley, Gregory Prange

John Candy, Eugene Levy, Robert Loggia, Kenneth
McMillan, Meg Ryan, Brion James, Jonathan Banks,
Don Stroud, Larry Hankin

'In a way, this is a highly immoral film. It is made for
the very young and will undoubtedly give them the
idea that they can drive as recklessly and the like
without doing anyone serious damage. Not a pint of
blood is spilled. Victims climb unscathed out of cars
that have been reduced to so much abstract sculpture.
This is bad propaganda, but, like so much that is
immoral, it is highly entertaining.' – *Quentin Crisp*

Armed Response
US   1986   85m   United Color
Cinetel (Paul Hertzberg)
V*, L

A private eye retrieves a jade antique for a Japanese
gangster.

Violent low budgeter with allusions for film buffs.

w T. L. Lankford   *d* Fred Olen Ray

David Carradine, Lee Van Cleef, Mako, Lois
Hamilton, Ross Hagen

L'Armée Des Ombres: see *The Army In The
Shadows*

Armored Attack: see *North Star*

Armored Car Robbery *
US   1950   67m   bw
RKO (Herman Schlom)
V*

A police lieutenant leads the recovery of half a million
dollars stolen by gangsters.

Good competent second feature with Los Angeles
locations and detailed observation of police methods.

w Earl Felton, Gerald Drayson Adams   *d* Richard
Fleischer   *ph* Guy Roe   *m* Constantin
Bakaleinikoff

Charles McGraw, Adele Jergens, William Talman,
Douglas Fowley, Steve Brodie

Armored Command
US   1961   105m   bw
Allied Artists (Ron W. Alcorn)
V*

During the Battle of the Bulge, a ravishing Nazi spy is
infiltrated into an American army outpost.

Incredible Mata Hari melodrama posing as a war film,
nicely shot in bleak snowscapes. Not exactly
rewarding, but unusual.

w Ron W. Alcorn   *d* Byron Haskin   *ph* Ernest
Haller   *m* Bert Grund

Howard Keel, Tina Louise, Burt Reynolds, Earl
Holliman, Warner Anderson, Carleton Young, Marty
Ingels

The Armour of God
Hong Kong   1987   90m   colour
Golden Harvest (L. K. C. Ho, Chua Lam)
V
original title: *Long Xiong Hu Di*

A martial arts expert goes in search of a valuable suit of armour.

Standard kung-fu adventure.

w Edward Tang   *story* Barry Wong   *d* Jackie Chan
ph Bob Thompson   *m* Michael Rai   *ad* William
Cheung   *ed* Cheung Yiu Chung

Jackie Chan, Alan Tam, Rosamund Kwan, Lola
Forner

Armour of God II: see *Operation Condor*

Arms and the Girl: see *Red Salute*

Arms and the Man
GB   1932   85m   bw
BIP/Wardour

A soldier who finds discretion the better part of valour hides in a girl's bedroom.

Faithful but uninspired version of Bernard Shaw's play.   *wd* Cecil Lewis

play George Bernard Shaw   *ad* John Mead
ed Walter Stokvis

Barry Jones, Anne Grey, Angela Baddeley

Arms and the Woman: see *Mr Winkle Goes to War*

Army Girl
US   1938   90m   bw
Republic
GB title: *The Last of the Cavalry*

Old loyalties flare at an army post when tanks replace cavalry troops.

Modest flagwaver which got by at the time.

w Barry Trivers, Sam Ornitz   *d* George Nichols Jnr
ph Ernest Miller, Harry Wild   *m* Victor Young

Madge Evans, Preston Foster, James Gleason, H. B.
Warner, Ruth Donnelly, Neil Hamilton, Billy Gilbert,
Heather Angel, Ralph Morgan

'Thoroughly entertaining . . . suitable as single in smaller spots, or action half of double bill in keys.' – *Variety*

AAN: Ernest Miller, Harry Wild; Victor Young

The Army in the Shadows ***
France/Italy   1969   143m   colour
Films Corona/Fono Roma (Jacques Dorfman)
original title: *L'Armée Des Ombres*

A group of Resistance fighters in Lyon try to discover the traitors in their midst.

Moving, harrowing and, in its depiction of a bungled execution, horrific account of the French Resistance at work, notable for the excellence of the direction and acting.

wd Jean-Pierre Melville   *novel* Joseph Kessel
ph Pierre L'homme   *m* Eric de Marsan
ad Théobald Meurisse   *ed* Françoise Bonnot

Lino Ventura, Simone Signoret, Jean-Pierre Cassel,
Paul Meurisse, Claude Mann, Paul Crauchet,
Christian Barbier

Army of Darkness
US   1992   109m   DeLuxe
Guild/Renaissance/Introvision (Robert Tapert)
V, V*
aka: *Evil Dead III; Army of Darkness: The Medieval Dead*

Thrust back in time to medieval England, a supermarket assistant searches for a spell to return him to his own time and instead causes the dead to rise from their graves.

Comic horror of uncertain tone, which occasionally raises a smile, but is much influenced for the worse by the work of the Three Stooges.

w Sam Raimi, Ivan Raimi   *d* Sam Raimi   *ph* Bill
Pope   *m* Joseph LoDuca   *pd* Tony Tremblay
ed Bob Murawski, R. O. C. Sandstorm

Bruce Campbell, Embeth Davidtz, Marcus Gilbert, Ian
Abercrombie, Richard Grove, Michael Earl Reid,
Bridget Fonda

'Preoccupied with repetitive and clumsy battle scenes and mild, bloodless effects, *Army of Darkness* falls off the knife-edge between humour and horror.' – *Kim Newman*

'Neither fantastic nor funny enough, despite its plethora of special effects and artful jokiness, to pass muster as anything much.' – *Derek Malcolm, Guardian*

† It was the third film in Raimi's sequence, following *The Evil Dead* and *The Evil Dead II*.

The Arnelo Affair
US   1946   86m   bw
MGM

Lawyer's wife gets involved with night-club owner.

Yawnworthy murder melodrama.

wd Arch Oboler

George Murphy, Frances Gifford, John Hodiak, Eve
Arden

Arnold
US   1973   95m   DeLuxe
Avco/Fenady (Charles A. Pratt, Andrew Fenady)
V*

Via cassette recordings, a dead man toys with his would-be heirs, and several are murdered.

Unpleasant and very laboured black comedy on the lines of *And Then There Were None* and a hundred others, all better than this.

w Jameson Brewer, John Fenton Murray   *d* Georg
Fenady   *ph* William Jurgenson   *m* George Duning

Stella Stevens, Roddy McDowall, Elsa Lanchester,
Shani Wallis, Farley Granger, Victor Buono, John
McGiver, Bernard Fox, Patric Knowles

† Apparently made back to back with *Terror in the Wax Museum*, which has very similar credits.

Around the World
US   1943   81m   bw
RKO (Allan Dwan)
V*, L

Kay Kyser's band goes on a world tour to entertain troops overseas.

Typical wartime patriotic musical, now of sociological interest.

w Ralph Spence   *d* Allan Dwan   *ph* Russell Metty
md Constantin Bakaleinikoff   *m* George Duning
m/ly Jimmy McHugh, Harold Adamson

Kay Kyser, Ish Kabibble, Ginny Simms, Joan Davis,
Mischa Auer

'It's a wonderful world, if you'll only take the time to go around it!'

Around the World in Eighty Days ***
US   1956   178m   Technicolor   Todd-AO
UA/Michael Todd
V, V*, L S

A Victorian gentleman and his valet win a bet that they can go round the world in eighty days.

Amiable large-scale pageant resolving itself into a number of sketches, which could have been much sharper, separated by wide screen spectacle. What was breathtaking at the time seems generally slow and blunted in retrospect, but the fascination of recognizing 44 cameo stars remains. The film is less an exercise in traditional skills than a tribute to its producer's energy.

w James Poe, John Farrow, S. J. Perelman
novel Jules Verne   *d* Michael Anderson, Kevin
McClory   *ph* Lionel Lindon   *m* Victor Young
titles Saul Bass   *ad* James W. Sullivan, Ken Adams
ed Gene Ruggiero, Paul Weatherwax

David Niven, Cantinflas, Robert Newton, Shirley Maclaine,
Charles Boyer, Joe E. Brown, Martine Carol, John
Carradine, Charles Coburn, *Ronald Colman,* Melville
Cooper, *Noël Coward,* Finlay Currie, Reginald Denny,
Andy Devine, Marlene Dietrich, Luis Dominguin,
Fernandel, *John Gielgud,* Hermione Gingold, Jose
Greco, Cedric Hardwicke, Trevor Howard, Glynis
Johns, *Buster Keaton,* Evelyn Keyes, Beatrice Lillie,
Peter Lorre, Edmund Lowe, A. E. Matthews, Mike
Mazurki, Tim McCoy, Victor McLaglen, John Mills,
Alan Mowbray, Robert Morley, Jack Oakie, George
Raft, Gilbert Roland, Cesar Romero, Frank Sinatra,
Red Skelton, Ronald Squire, Basil Sidney, *Harcourt
Williams,* Ed Murrow

'Michael Todd's "show", shorn of the ballyhoo and to critics not mollified by parties and sweetmeats, is a film like any other, only twice as long as most . . . the shots of trains and boats seem endless.' – *David Robinson*

AA: best picture; James Poe, John Farrow, S. J.
Perelman; Lionel Lindon; Victor Young

AAN: Michael Anderson; art direction; editing

Around the World in Eighty Minutes
US   1931   80m   bw
United Artists

An account of Douglas Fairbanks's travels, mainly in the Far East.

Awfully padded travelogue which seems to have been a bore even at the time, despite a few magic-carpet tricks.

w Robert E. Sherwood   *d* Douglas Fairbanks, Victor
Fleming

'Fairbanks enlivens much of the drab footage with his acrobatics.' – *Variety*

Around the World under the Sea
US   1966   110m   Metrocolor   Panavision
MGM/Ivan Tors (Andrew Marton)

An ultra-modern underwater craft travels around the seabed fixing sensors to give early warning of volcanoes.

Earnest, dullish, elementary sci-fi with cardboard characters providing routine five men-one woman skirmishes.

w Arthur Weiss, Art Arthur   *d* Andrew Marton,
Ricou Browning   *ph* Clifford Poland, Lamar Boren
m Harry Sukman

Lloyd Bridges, Shirley Eaton, Brian Kelly, David
McCallum, Keenan Wynn, Marshall Thompson, Gary
Merrill

Arouse and Beware: see *The Man from Dakota*

The Arrangement **
US   1969   127m   Technicolor   Panavision
Warner/Athena (Elia Kazan)
V (W), V*, L

A wealthy advertising man fails in a suicide attempt and spends his convalescence reflecting on his unsatisfactory emotional life.

A lush, all-American melodrama, rich in technique but peopled by characters who have nothing to say; the film makes no discernible point except as a well-acted tirade against the compromises of modern urban living.

wd Elia Kazan   *novel* Elia Kazan   *ph* Robert Surtees
m David Amram   *pd* Malcolm C. Bert

Kirk Douglas, Faye Dunaway, Deborah Kerr, Richard
Boone, Hume Cronyn

'The sort of collage that won't fit together, no matter where you stand.' – *PS*

'As dead as a flower arrangement in an undertaker's parlour . . . all possible cinematic clevernesses – usually yesterday's – are dragged out in an endless parade, to illustrate a senseless and banal story that reels from platitude to platitude.' – *John Simon*

Arrest Bulldog Drummond: see *Bulldog Drummond*

Arrivederci Baby: see *Drop Dead Darling*

Arrowhead
US   1953   105m   Technicolor   3D
Paramount (Nat Holt)
V*, L

Enmity between an army scout and an Indian chief is resolved by single combat.

Standard Western, good-looking but rather lifeless.

wd Charles Marquis Warren   *novel* W. R. Burnett
ph Ray Rennahan   *m* Paul Sawtell

Charlton Heston, Jack Palance, Katy Jurado, Brian Keith, Milburn Stone

Arrowsmith *
US   1931   108m   bw
Samuel Goldwyn
V*

The self-sacrificing career of a doctor.

Emotionally satisfactory, dramatically slow and unsurprising variation on a theme which has since been treated far too often.

w Sidney Howard   *novel* Sinclair Lewis   *d* John Ford   *ph* Ray June   *m* Alfred Newman
ad Richard Day

Ronald Colman, Helen Hayes, Richard Bennett, Myrna Loy, Charlotte Henry, Beulah Bondi, A. E. Anson

'Pictures would do better to stay clear of these elaborately biographical novels with their wealth of actionless detail. . . . That portion of the citizenry which read the Sinclair Lewis novel will probably be in sympathy with the film, those who didn't will not be prone to deem this macabre tale entertainment.' – *Variety*

† The negative was later cut to about 89m for reissue, and this version, virtually eliminating Myrna Loy, is the only one now available.

AAN: best picture; Sidney Howard; Ray June; Richard Day

Arsenal *
USSR   1929   99m(16 fps)   bw   silent
VUFKU
V

The 1914 war is made worse by strikes at home.

Patchy propagandist drama with brilliant sequences.

wd Alexander Dovzhenko   *ph* Danylo Demutsky

S. Svashenko, A. Buchma, M. Nademsky

'A romantic and lyrical masterpiece.' – *Georges Sadoul*

The Arsenal Stadium Mystery
GB   1939   85m   bw
G&S/GFD
V

A footballer is poisoned during a match.

Brisk little mystery, with an amiable star performance.

w Thorold Dickinson, Donald Bull   *novel* Leonard Gribble   *d* Thorold Dickinson

Leslie Banks, Greta Gynt, Esmond Knight, Brian Worth

'This picture is as good to watch as either of the *Thin Man* films, and Dickinson gives us wit instead of

facetiousness – wit of cutting and wit of angle.' – *Graham Greene*

Arsène Lupin *
US   1932   75m   bw
MGM

The Parisian gentleman thief accomplishes some daring robberies and is almost caught stealing the Mona Lisa.

Amusing crook comedy with a few flat passages but much sparkle in between, and a lively finale.

w Carey Wilson, Lenore Coffee, Bayard Veiller
d Jack Conway   *ph* Oliver Marsh

John Barrymore, Lionel Barrymore, Karen Morley, Tully Marshall, John Miljan

'First screen appearance of John and Lionel together and their acting of this old standard detective story ensures its box office in spite of the absence of other qualities that make for notable screen successes. . .. At least it addresses itself to a higher class of fans than the lurid type of dime novel subject.' – *Variety*

Arsène Lupin Returns
US   1938   81m   bw
MGM (John W. Considine Jnr)

The reformed jewel thief helps an American detective to track down a French criminal.

Smooth but disappointingly scripted sequel which never quite rises to a climax despite sympathetic casting.

w James Kevin McGuinness, Howard Emmett Rogers, George Harmon Coxe   *d* George Fitzmaurice
ph George Folsey   *m* Franz Waxman

Melvyn Douglas, Warren William, Virginia Bruce, John Halliday, Nat Pendleton, Monty Woolley, George Zucco, E. E. Clive

'A first-class mystery jewel theft combo . . . for the top side of the marquee pairing, missing A classification quite a little, but still being okay.' – *Variety*

Arsenic and Old Lace **
US   1942 (released 1944)   118m   bw
Warner (Frank Capra)
V, V*, L

Two dear, well-meaning old ladies invite lonely old men to their Brooklyn home, poison them with elderberry wine, and have their mad brother, who believes the corpses are yellow fever victims, bury them in the cellar. A homicidal nephew then turns up with bodies of his own.

A model for stage play adaptations, this famous black farce provided a frenzy of hilarious activity, and its flippant attitude to death was better received in wartime than would have been the case earlier or later. The director coaxes some perfect if overstated performances from his star cast, and added his own flair for perpetuating a hubbub.

w Julius J. and Philip G. Epstein, with help from Howard Lindsay, Russel Crouse   *play* Joseph Kesselring   *d* Frank Capra   *ph* Sol Polito
m Max Steiner

Cary Grant (Mortimer Brewster), *Josephine Hull* (Abby Brewster), *Jean Adair* (Martha Brewster), Priscilla Lane (Elaine Harper), Raymond Massey (Jonathan Brewster), *John Alexander* (Teddy Brewster), Peter Lorre (Dr Einstein), James Gleason (Lt Rooney), Jack Carson (officer O'Hara), Edward Everett Horton (Mr Witherspoon), Grant Mitchell (Reverend Harper)

   MORTIMER: 'Insanity runs in my family. It practically gallops.'
   MARTHA: 'One of our gentlemen found time to say "How delicious!" before he died. . ..'

The Art of Dying
US   1991   93m   Foto-Kem colour
PM (Richard Pepin, Joseph Merhi)
V, V*

A maverick cop tracks down a pornographer who films and kills his victims while re-enacting famous murders from the movies.

Slow, unpleasant homophobic thriller about a cut-rate Dirty Harry; the emphasis is on atmosphere and the hero's uninteresting love-life rather than on action.

w Joseph Merhi   *d* Wings Hauser   *ph* Richard Pepin   *m* John Gonzalez   *pd* Greg Martin
ed Geraint Bell, Paul Volk

Wings Hauser, Kathleen Kinmont, Michael J. Pollard, Gary Werntz, Mitch Hara, Sarah Douglas, Sydney Lassick

The Art of Love
US   1965   99m   Technicolor
Universal/Cherokee/Ross Hunter

To stimulate interest in his work, a penniless artist fakes suicide, subsequently becoming so famous that he finds it difficult to reappear.

A pleasant black comedy idea is buried under lush production, dull direction and a host of unattractive Parisian sets.

w Carl Reiner   *d* Norman Jewison   *ph* Russell Metty   *m* Cy Coleman

James Garner, Dick Van Dyke, Angie Dickinson, Elke Sommer, Ethel Merman, Pierre Olaf

'I race cars, I play tennis, I fondle women, but I have weekends off and I am my own boss!'
Arthur *
US   1981   97m   Technicolor
Warner/Orion (Robert Greenhut)
V, V*, L, S

A rich New York layabout is forced to moderate his life style in order to qualify for his inheritance.

An unattractive excuse for the star to do his drunk act. In effect his thunder was stolen by Gielgud as the valet who is not above a few choice four-letter words; but over the whole enterprise hung a pall of desperation. It is a sign of its times that it made a lot of money.

wd Steve Gordon   *ph* Fred Schuler   *m* Burt Bacharach   *pd* Stephen Hendrikson

Dudley Moore, *John Gielgud*, Liza Minnelli, Geraldine Fitzgerald, Jill Eikenberry, Stephen Elliott

'It comes as no surprise to find the funniest sequences packed into the first half-hour.' – *Martyn Auty, MFB*

'Gielgud may be the most poised and confident funnyman you'll ever see.' – *New Yorker*

'Arthur may be the surprise hit of 1981, but to me he's a pain in the neck.' – *Margaret Hinxman, Daily Mail*

AA: John Gielgud (supporting actor); song 'Best That You Can Do'(Burt Bacharach, Carole Bayer Sager, Christopher Cross, Peter Allen)

AAN: screenplay; Dudley Moore

Arthur 2: On the Rocks
US   1988   113m   colour
Warner (Robert Shapiro)
V, V*

Arthur's fortune is threatened by his former fiancée's father, bent on revenge, while his wife wants to adopt a baby.

Moore and friends are much less funny the second time around, and much more sentimental; it's just a sloppy would-be comedy.

w Andy Breckman   *d* Bud Yorkin   *ph* Stephen H. Burum   *m* Burt Bacharach   *ed* Michael Kahn

Dudley Moore, Liza Minelli, Geraldine Fitzgerald, Paul Benedict, John Gielgud

'Still manages to be an amusing romp.' – *Variety*

'When the heroes are forgotten. When the stakes are life and death. There's one stand you've got to take. There's one rule you've got to break.'

Article 99
US   1992   100m   DeLuxe
Orion/Gruskoff/Levy (Michael Gruskoff, Michael I. Levy)
V, V*, L, S

Doctors and surgeons at a Veterans' Administration hospital ignore red tape in order to treat their patients.

A frenetic movie with more than a touch of hysteria in its treatment of an emotive subject.

w Ron Cutler   *d* Howard Deutch   *ph* Richard Bowen   *m* Danny Elfman   *pd* Virginia L. Randolph   *ed* Richard Halsey

Ray Liotta, Kiefer Sutherland, Forest Whitaker, Lea Thompson, John Mahoney, John C. McGinley, Keith David, Kathy Baker, Eli Wallach

'Is ultimately more successful in awakening the viewer to a desperate situation than in providing a good time.' – *Variety*

An Artist with Ladies: see *Coiffeur pour Dames*

Artistes at the Top of the Big Top: Disorientated **
West Germany   1968   103m   bw/colour
Kairos Film

The daughter of a dead trapezist dreams of creating the ideal circus with a moral for mankind but step by step gives up her ambition.

A melancholy satire, told in fragmented fashion with some brilliant tricks and memorable sequences.

wd Alexander Kluge   *ph* Gunther Hörmann, Thomas Mauch

Hannelore Hoger, Siegfried Graue, Alfred Edel, Bernd Höltz

'Those who interpret it simply as an allegory of German politics or of the present crisis in film-making narrow it unnecessarily.' – *Jan Dawson, MFB*

Artists and Models *
US   1937   97m   bw
Paramount (Lewis E. Gensler)

An advertising man has to find the right girl as symbol for a silverware company.

Fairly stylish comedy musical with many elements typical of its studio.

w Walter de Leon, Francis Martin   *d* Raoul Walsh   *ph* Victor Milner   *m* Victor Young   *songs* various

Jack Benny, Ida Lupino, Richard Arlen, Gail Patrick, Ben Blue, Judy Canova, Martha Raye, Donald Meek, Hedda Hopper, André Kostelanetz and his Orchestra, Louis Armstrong and his Orchestra

'Should be a box-office bonanza for exhibitors. It holds enough variety, comedy, colour, spectacle, flash, dash and novelty for a couple of pictures.' – *Variety*

AAN: song 'Whispers in the Dark' (*m* Frederick Hollander, *ly* Leo Robin)

Artists and Models *
US   1955   109m   Technicolor   Vistavision
Paramount/Hal B. Wallis
V*

A goonish young man receives telepathic top secret information in his nightmares, which are used by his artist friend in comic strips; foreign agents and the CIA get interested.

A good zany idea is worked into an overlong dyspeptic comedy which neither the stars nor frantic treatment can hope to save.

w Frank Tashlin, Don McGuire   *d* Frank Tashlin   *ph* Daniel Fapp   *m* Walter Scharf

Dean Martin, Jerry Lewis, Shirley Maclaine, Dorothy Malone, Eddie Mayehoff, Eva Gabor, Anita Ekberg, George 'Foghorn' Winslow, Jack Elam

'It's an ooh-la-lalapalooza!'
Artists and Models Abroad *
US   1938   90m   bw   Paramount (Arthur Hornblow Jnr)

V, V*, L
GB title: *Stranded in Paris*

Stranded in Paris, a troupe of girls and their manager are helped by a Texas oil millionaire.

Generally agreeable comedy musical with emphasis on fashion.

w Howard Lindsay, Russel Crouse, Ken Englund   *d* Mitchell Leisen   *ph* Ted Tetzlaff   *md* Boris Morros   *songs* various   *ad* Hans Dreier, Ernst Fegte

Jack Benny, Joan Bennett, Mary Boland, Charley Grapewin, Joyce Compton, the Yacht Club Boys, Fritz Feld, G. P. Huntley, Monty Woolley

'Straight farce comedy. The models are in a fashion show and the artists are missing entirely.' – *Variety*

The Aryan *
US   1916   75m (16 fps)   bw   silent
Triangle (Thomas Ince)

A gold prospector is cheated by a woman and becomes an outlaw.

Striking early star Western.

w C. Gardner Sullivan   *d* William S. Hart, Clifford Smith   *ph* Joseph August, Clyde de Vinna

William S. Hart, Bessie Love, Louise Glaum, Hershall Mayall

As Husbands Go
US   1934   65m   bw
Fox/Jesse Lasky

Lover and husband become friends, making infidelity impossible.

Minor smart-set comedy from a then popular play.

w Sam Behrman, Sonya Levien   *play* Rachel Crothers   *d* Hamilton McFadden

Warner Baxter, Helen Vinson, Warner Oland, G. P. Huntley Jnr, Catherine Doucet

'Pleasant entertainment all the way, but a lack of action will bore children and annoy that not inconsiderable body of Americans who violently resent too much suavity of speech and manner.' – *Variety*

As Long as They're Happy *
GB   1955   91m   Eastmancolor
Rank/Regroup (Raymond Stross)

The suburban home of a London stockbroker is invaded by an American sob singer.

Frantic farce expanded from a stage satire of the Johnnie Ray cult; a patchy but sometimes funny star vehicle.

w Alan Melville   *play* Vernon Sylvaine   *d* J. Lee-Thompson   *ph* Gilbert Taylor   *m* Stanley Black

Jack Buchanan, Brenda de Banzie, Diana Dors, Jean Carson, Janette Scott, Susan Stephen, Jerry Wayne, Hugh McDermott

As Long as You're Near Me
West Germany   1954   94m   colour
Warner/NDF
original title: *Solange Du da bist*

A film director almost ruins a small-part actress's life by insisting on making her a star.

Reasonably absorbing drama chiefly remarkable for being a great hit in the US when dubbed.

w Jochen Huth   *d* Harold Braun

O. W. Fischer, Hardy Kruger, Maria Schell

As the Earth Turns
US   1934   73m   bw
Warner

The problems of three farming families in Maine.

Reliable rustic soap opera, pretty well presented.

w Ernest Pascal   *book* Gladys Hasty Carroll   *d* Alfred E. Green

Jean Muir, Donald Woods, Emily Lowry, William Janney, David Landau, Dorothy Peterson

'What it may lack in box office, it makes up in entertainment . . . the sort of story that commands attention and favour.' – *Variety*

'You don't need us to tell you not to miss this film. You couldn't be kept away!'
As You Desire Me *
US   1931   71m   bw
MGM (George Fitzmaurice)
V*

The amnesiac mistress of a novelist rediscovers her real husband and falls in love with him again.

Interesting star vehicle with good cast and production.

w Gene Markey   *play* Luigi Pirandello   *d* George Fitzmaurice   *ph* William Daniels

Greta Garbo, Melvyn Douglas, Erich von Stroheim, Owen Moore, Hedda Hopper, Rafaela Ottiano

'Pretty subtle for the generality of fans. It was more of a courageous gesture towards production ideals than good business judgement that dictated its choice for filming in the first place.' – *Variety*

As You Like It *
GB   1936   96m   bw
TCF/Inter-Allied (Joseph M. Schenck, Paul Czinner)
V*, L

The fortunes of an exiled king take a turn in the Forest of Arden.

Stylized, rather effete but often amusing version of Shakespeare's pastoral comedy.

w J. M. Barrie, Robert Cullen   *play* William Shakespeare   *d* Paul Czinner   *ph* Harold Rosson   *m* William Walton

Elisabeth Bergner, Laurence Olivier, Sophie Stewart, Leon Quartermaine, Henry Ainley, Richard Ainley, Felix Aylmer, Mackenzie Ward, Aubrey Mather, John Laurie, Peter Bull

'Rather too respectably lighthearted, but by no means a contemptible production.' – *New Yorker, 1978*

'There are far too many dull middle-length shots from a fixed camera, so that we might just as well be seated in the circle above the deep wide stage at Drury Lane.' – *Graham Greene*

As You Like It
GB   1992   117m   colour
Squirrel/Sands Films (Richard Goodwin)
V

Banished from City of London splendour to a grimy slum where locals live in cardboard boxes, Orlando falls in love with the banished and disguised Rosalind.

Modern-dress version of the play, with the Forest of Arden becoming an urban wasteland inhabited by the homeless. It sounds as ugly as it looks, with some wretched speaking of the verse.   *play* William Shakespeare   *d* Christine Edzard   *ph* Robin Vidgeon   *m* Michel Sanvoisin   *ed* Christine Edzard

James Fox, Emma Croft, Cyril Cusack, Griff Rhys Jones, Andrew Tiernan, Miriam Margolyes, Don Henderson, Celia Bannerman, Murray Melvin

'We feel like victims of a mobile theatre experiment, moving our camp stools from one daft venue to the next as we follow a bunch of under-rehearsed actors belting it out into the void.' – *Nigel Andrews, Financial Times*

'In this misguided and also perversely endearing version, Christine Edzard ultimately proves the Bard's resilience, but she proves it the hard way.' – *Adam Mars-Jones, Independent*

'Edzard restores to filmed Shakespeare the means and immediacy of cinema, daring to present, as the theatre has been doing since the nineteenth century, Shakespearean text in a modern context.' – *Ilona Halberstadt, Sight and Sound*

As Young as You Feel *
US   1951   77m   bw
TCF (Lamar Trotti)
V*

An elderly employee, forced to retire, impersonates the company president, saves the firm from bankruptcy, and proves his continued worth.

Good-natured comedy, ably presented.

w Lamar Trotti   *story* Paddy Chayevsky   *d* Harmon Jones   *ph* Joe MacDonald   *m* Cyril Mockridge

Monty Woolley, Constance Bennett, Thelma Ritter, David Wayne, Jean Peters, Marilyn Monroe, Allyn Joslyn, Albert Dekker

Ascendancy *
GB   1982   85m   colour
British Film Institute Production Board (Penny Clark, Ian Elsey)

In 1920 Belfast a shipyard owner's daughter, shocked by the death of her brother in the war, cannot come to terms with the sectarian slaughter around her.

Unilluminatingly argumentative character study which fails to make its purpose very clear despite a stunning central performance.

w Edward Bennett, Nigel Gearing   *d* Edward Bennett   *ph* Clive Tickner   *m* Ronnie Leahy

Julie Covington, Ian Charleson, John Phillips, Susan Engel, Philip Locke

Ascenseur pour l'Echafaud: see *Lift to the Scaffold*

Ash Wednesday
US   1973   99m   Technicolor
Sagittarius (Dominick Dunne)
V*

An ageing American beauty rejuvenates herself via plastic surgery, leads a vivid sex life, and leaves her stolid husband.

The bloodthirsty operation scenes are revolting, yet this joyless saga seems meant as a celebration of the wonders of cosmetic surgery and Sex for the Aged. Hypnotic but hardly rewarding.

w Jean Claude Tramont   *d* Larry Peerce   *ph* Ennio Guarnieri   *m* Maurice Jarre

Elizabeth Taylor, Henry Fonda, Helmut Berger, Keith Baxter, Maurice Teynac

'Endless shots of Elizabeth Taylor expensively attired against the plush background of Cortina.' – *Michael Billington, Illustrated London News*

'A long-drawn-out ghoulish commercial for cosmetic surgery – made apparently for people who can't think of anything to do with their lives but go backwards.' – *Pauline Kael*

Ashanti
Switzerland   1979   117m   Technicolor   Panavision
Columbia/Beverly (Luciano Sacripanti)
V, V*

In West Africa, the wife of a member of the World Health Organization is seized by slave traders.

Absurd and rather unattractively brutal adventure story, decked out with appearances by guest stars.

w Stephen Geller   *novel* Ebano by Alberto Vasquez-Figueroa   *d* Richard Fleischer   *ph* Aldo Tonti   *m* Michael Melvoin

Michael Caine, Omar Sharif, Peter Ustinov, Rex Harrison, Kabir Bedi, William Holden, Zia Mohyeddin, Beverly Johnson

Ashes and Diamonds ****
Poland   1958   104m   bw
Film Polski
V*
original title: *Popiol y Diament*

A Polish partisan is confused by the apparent need to continue killing after the war is over.

A chilling account of the intellectual contradictions to which war leads, and a moving and sensitive film in its own right.

wd Andrzej Wajda,   *novel* Jerzy Andrzejewski   *ph* Jerzy Wojcik

Zbigniew Cybulski, Ewa Krzyzanowska, Adam Pawlikowski

Ashik Kerib **
USSR   1988   78m   colour
Georgia Film Studio
V*
aka: *The Lovelorn Minstrel*

A poor minstrel goes to seek his fortune so that he can marry the daughter of a rich Turkish merchant.

Richly coloured, episodic fable, told in the artful and artless manner of silent cinema.

w Giya Badridze   *story* Mikhail Lermontov   *d* Sergei Paradjanov, David Abashidze   *ph* Albert Yavuryan   *m* Zhavanshir Kuliev   *pd* G. Meskhishvili, Shota Gogolashvili, Nikolai Zandukeli, K. Davidov

Yuri Mgoyan, Veromique Matonidze, Levan Natroshvili, Solico Chaureli

'The film chronicles a spiritual journey in profane, worldly terms, and it is the earthy vulgarity of the detail that gives the spirituality its edge.' – *Tony Rayns, MFB*

Ask a Policeman **
GB   1938   82m   bw
Gainsborough (Edward Black)

In a small coastal village, incompetent policemen accidentally expose smugglers who are scaring the locals with a headless horseman legend.

One of the best comedies of an incomparable team, with smart dialogue, good situations and a measure of suspense.

w Marriott Edgar, Val Guest, J. O. C. Orton   *d* Marcel Varnel   *ph* Derek Williams   *md* Louis Levy

Will Hay, Moore Marriott, Graham Moffatt, Glennis Lorimer, *Peter Gawthorne, Herbert Lomas*, Charles Oliver

'A good laugh getter and safe second feature on any programme.' – *Variety*

Ask Any Girl *
US   1959   98m   Metrocolor   Cinemascope
MGM/Euterpe (Joe Pasternak)
V*

A husband-hunting receptionist in New York catches the eye of a wealthy playboy but finally settles for his elder brother.

Predictable Cinderella story with a lively but forgettable script and actors going through familiar paces.

w George Wells   *novel* Winifred Wolfe   *d* Charles Walters   *ph* Robert Bronner   *m* Jeff Alexander

David Niven, Shirley Maclaine, Gig Young, Rod Taylor, Jim Backus, Claire Kelly

'Like a comic strip transposed to the glossy pages of *Vogue*.' – *MFB*

Asking for Trouble *
GB   1941   81m   bw
British National

A bookie poses as a big game hunter.

The last opportunity to see a great music hall comic on film, his style admittedly bowdlerized.

w Oswald Mitchell, Con West   *d* Oswald Mitchell

Max Miller, Carole Lynne, Wilfrid Hyde-White, Mark Lester

Aspern *
Portugal   1981   96m   colour
VO/Oxala (Paulo Branco)

The French biographer of a deceased poet goes to Venice to get unpublished papers from his aged mistress.

This very well-known story (see also *The Lost Moment* and various theatrical versions) is styled with exceeding solemnity in this well-acted but boring version.

w Michael Graham   *story* Henry James   *d* Eduardo de Grigorio   *ph* Acacio de Almeida   *m* mainly from Mozart

Alida Valli, Jean Sorel, Bulle Ogier, Ana Marta

Asphalt *
Germany   1929   101m   bw
UFA

A young policeman accidentally kills his rival for a worthless girl.

Heavily expressionist melodrama, overlong but good to watch.

w Rolf Vanloo, Fred Majo, Hans Szekely   *d* Joe May   *ph* Günther Rittau

Gustav Fröhlich, Betty Amann, Else Heller, Louise Brooks

'So well produced that it is good entertainment in spite of itself.' – *Variety*

The Asphalt Jungle ***
US   1950   112m   bw
MGM (Arthur Hornblow Jnr)
V, V*, L

An elderly crook comes out of prison and assembles a gang for one last robbery.

Probably the very first film to show a 'caper' from the criminals' viewpoint (a genre which has since been done to death several times over), this is a clever character study rather than a thriller, extremely well executed and indeed generally irreproachable yet somehow not a film likely to appear on many top ten lists; perhaps the writer-director stands too far back from everybody, or perhaps he just needed Humphrey Bogart.

w Ben Maddow, John Huston   *novel* W. R. Burnett   *d* John Huston   *ph* Harold Rosson   *m* Miklos Rozsa

Sterling Hayden (Dix Handley), Louis Calhern (Alonzo D Emmerich), *Sam Jaffe* (Doc Erwin Riedenschneider), Jean Hagen (Doll Conovan), James Whitmore (Gus Minissi), John McIntire (Police Commissioner Hardy), Marc Lawrence (Cobby), Marilyn Monroe (Angela Phinlay), Barry Kelley (Lt Ditrich)

RIEDENSCHNEIDER: 'Crime is a left-handed form of human endeavour.'

'Where this film excels is in the fluency of its narration, the sharpness of its observation of character and the excitement of its human groupings.' – *Dilys Powell*

'That Asphalt Pavement thing is full of nasty, ugly people doing nasty things. I wouldn't walk across the room to see a thing like that.' – *Louis B. Mayer* (who was head of the studio which made it)

† Apart from imitations, the film has been directly remade as *The Badlanders, Cairo* and *A Cool Breeze.*

AAN: Ben Maddow, John Huston (writers); John Huston (as director); Harold Rosson; Sam Jaffe

The Asphyx

GB 1973 99m Eastmancolor Todd-AO 35
Glendale (John Brittany)
V*

A Victorian aims to become immortal by separating the spirit of death from his body.

Interminable hocus pocus with a plethora of talk, seldom exciting but watchable because of its remarkable cast and other credits.

w Brian Comport *d* Peter Newbrook *ph* Freddie Young *m* Bill McGuffie *sp* Ted Samuels

Robert Stephens, Robert Powell, Jane Lapotaire

The Assam Garden

GB 1985 90m colour
Contemporary/Moving Picture Company (Nigel Stafford-Clark)

A widow returns from Assam to the English house where many years previously her husband had created a garden full of eastern plants, and where events now help her to free herself of the past.

Muted and somewhat ineffective treatment of a familiar television theme. Not unpleasant to watch despite obvious economies, but instantly forgettable.

w Elisabeth Bond *d* Mary McMurray *ph* Bryan Loftus *m* Richard Harvey

Deborah Kerr, Madhur Jaffrey, Alec McCowen, Zia Mohyeddin, Iain Cuthbertson

The Assassin (1947): see
Gunfighters

The Assassin (1952): see
Venetian Bird

The Assassin **

Italy/France 1961 105m bw
Titanus-Vides-SGC (Franco Cristaldi)

A prosperous antique dealer is accused of murder and his unsavoury past is revealed; but when he is freed, he prides himself on his new personality.

A careful, detailed and wholly enjoyable character study, somewhere between comedy and drama.

w Elio Petri and others *d* Elio Petri *ph* Carlo di Palma *m* Piero Piccioni

Marcello Mastroianni, Salvo Randone, Micheline Presle, Andrea Checci

Assassin

GB 1973 83m Technicolor
Pemini (David M. Jackson)

MI5 arranges the liquidation of an Air Ministry spy.

Old hat espionage melodrama, top heavy with artiness which makes it look like an endless TV commercial.

w Michael Sloan *d* Peter Crane *ph* Brian Jonson *m* Zack Lawrence

Ian Hendry, Edward Judd, Frank Windsor, Ray Brooks, John Hart Dyke

Assassin (1993): see
Point of No Return

Assassin for Hire *

GB 1951 67m bw
Merton Park (Julian Wintle/Anglo Amalgamated)

A professional killer is trapped into admitting a murder he didn't do.

Taut little suspenser, quite watchable.

w Rex Rienits *d* Michael McCarthy

Sydney Tafler, Ronald Howard, John Hewer, Martin Benson

L'Assassin habite au 21 **

France 1947 83m bw
Mage/Liote
aka: *The Murderer Lives at 21*

A police detective assumes the guise of a clergyman to investigate mass killings which seem to centre on a boarding house.

Agreeable, straight-faced but tongue-in-cheek comedy thriller which was probably even funnier in French.

wd Henri-Georges Clouzot, *novel* S. A. Steerman *ph* Armand Thirard

Pierre Fresnay, Suzy Delair, Pierre Larquey, Noel Roquevert

Assassin of the Tsar (dubbed)

Russia/GB 1991 104m Eastmancolor
Blue Dolphin/Mosfilm/Spectator/Courier (Christopher Gawor, Erik Vaisberg, Anthony Sloman)
Russian title: *Tsareubiitsa*

A doctor decides on a dangerous plan to cure a patient in a Russian psychiatric ward who believes he is both the killer of Tsar Alexander II in 1881 and one of the murderers of Tsar Nicholas and his family in 1918.

An odd movie that is unsuccessful in its attempt to frame the demise of the Russian royal family within a modern-day story; the result is confusing and unconvincing.

w Aleksandr Borodianski, Karen Shakhnazarov *d* Karen Shakhnazarov *ph* Nikolai Nemoliaev *m* John Altman, Vladislav Shut *ad* Liudmila Kusakova *ed* Lidiia Miliotti

Malcolm McDowell, Oleg Yankovsky, Armen Dzhigarkhanyan, Iurii Sherstnev, Angela Ptashuk, Viktor Seferov

'Both a compelling modern pyschodrama and a powerful recreation of one of the pivotal events of modern history, addressing Russian history and the current turbulent state of the country in an effective and compelling manner.' – *Kim Newman, Empire*

'Unsatisfactory psychology and unsatisfactory historiography.' – *Sight and Sound*

Assassination

US 1986 88m TVC Color
Cannon (Pancho Kohner)
V, V*, L

A White House secret service man finds himself on the run with the first lady.

Mildly diverting but over-mysterious chase movie, less violent than the Bronson norm.

w Richard Sale *d* Peter Hunt

Charles Bronson, Jill Ireland, Stephen Elliott, Joe Gan Boyd, Randy Brooks, Michael Ansara

The Assassination Bureau *

GB 1968 110m Technicolor
Paramount/Heathfield (Michael Relph)
V*

In 1906 a lady journalist breaks up an international gang of professional killers by falling in love with their leader.

Black comedy period pastiche which resolves itself into a series of sketches leading up to a spectacular zeppelin climax. Plenty going on, but the level of wit is not high.

w Michael Relph, Wolf Mankowitz *d* Basil Dearden *ph* Geoffrey Unsworth *m* Ron Grainer

Oliver Reed, Diana Rigg, Telly Savalas, Curt Jurgens, Philippe Noiret, Warren Mitchell, Clive Revill, Beryl Reid, Kenneth Griffith

The Assassination of the Duc de Guise *

France 1908 15m (16 fps) bw silent
Film d'Art

Henry III arranges the killing of the Duc de Guise when he comes to court.

Influential early story film.

w Henri Lavedan *d* Charles le Bargy *m* Saint-Saëns

Charles le Bargy, Albert Lambert, Gabrielle Lavinne

'For one moment, they hold history in their hands. With one terrible blow, they make it'

The Assassination of Trotsky

Italy/GB/France 1972 103m Technicolor
Dino de Laurentiis/Josef Shaftel/Cinetel (Norman Priggen, Joseph Losey)
V*, L, S

In 1940, Trotsky is hiding out in Mexico; a Stalinist infiltrates his presence and kills him with an ice pick.

Glum historical reconstruction with much fictitious padding; basically undramatic.

w Nicholas Mosley, Masolino d'Amico *d* Joseph Losey *ph* Pasquale de Santis *m* Egisto Macchi

Richard Burton, Alain Delon, Romy Schneider, Valentina Cortese, Jean Desailly

'Not for anyone who knows, or cares, anything about Leon Trotsky.' – *New Yorker, 1977*

Assassino . . . è al telefono: see *The Killer Is on the Phone*

Les Assassins du Dimanche

France 1956 94m bw Cinepanoramic
EDIC
aka: *Every Second Counts*

Dozens of people help to track down a holiday car which has been driven away from a garage in a dangerous condition.

Watchable but artificial suspenser.

w Alex Joffe, Gabriel Arout *d* Alex Joffe *ph* Jean Bourgoin

Barbara Laage, Jean-Marc Thibault, Dominique Wilms, Paul Frankeur

Assault

GB 1970 91m Eastmancolor
Rank/Peter Rogers (George H. Brown)

An art mistress helps police to solve a case of multiple rape in an English village.

Old-fashioned police mystery with new-fangled shock treatment. Routine excitements.

w John Kruse *novel* Kendal Young *d* Sidney Hayers *ph* Ken Hodges *m* Eric Rogers

Frank Finlay, Suzy Kendall, James Laurenson, Lesley-Anne Down, Freddie Jones, Tony Beckley, Anthony Ainley, Dilys Hamlett

'All right for that wet afternoon.' – *Michael Billington, Illustrated London News*

The Assault ***

Netherlands 1986 148m colour
Cannon (Fons Rademakers)
V*
original title: *De Aanslag*

An adult is forced to recall the traumatic events of his childhood, when he saw his family murdered by the Nazis.

Part gripping thriller, part indictment of those who would forget the past, and wholly watchable.

w Gerard Soeteman *novel* Harry Mulisch *d* Fons Rademakers *ph* Their Van Der Sande *m* Jurriaan Andriessen *ed* Kees Linthorst

Derek de Lint, Marc Van Uchelen, Monique Van de Ven, John Kraaykamp, Huub Van Der Lubbe, Elly Weller, Ina Van Der Molen

AA: best foreign film

Assault on a Queen

US   1966   106m   Technicolor   Panavision
Paramount/Seven Arts/Sinatra Enterprises (William Goetz)
V*

Crooks dredge up a submarine and use it to hi-jack the *Queen Mary*.

Strained caper film which remains uncertain whether to play for drama or thrills, and achieves neither. Special effects unconvincing.

w Rod Serling   *novel* Jack Finney   *d* Jack Donohue   *ph* William Daniels   *m* Duke Ellington

Frank Sinatra, Virna Lisi, Tony Franciosa, Alf Kjellin, Errol John, Richard Conte, Murray Matheson, Reginald Denny

'Just about as enthralling as plastic boats in the bath.' – *MFB*

Assault on Precinct 13 ***

US   1976   91m   Metrocolor   Panavision
CKK (Joseph Kaufman)
V, V*

Gang members on a vendetta attack a police station.

Violent but basically efficient and old-fashioned programmer which shows that not all the expertise of the forties in this then-familiar field has been lost.

wd/m John Carpenter   *ph* Douglas Knapp

Austin Stoker, Darwin Joston, Laurie Zimmer, Martin West

'One of the most effective exploitation movies of the last ten years . . . Carpenter scrupulously avoids any overt socio-political pretensions, playing instead for laughs and suspense in perfectly balanced proportions.' – *Time Out*

Assignment in Brittany

US   1943   96m   bw
MGM (J. Walter Ruben)

A Free French soldier stays in occupied France to fight the Nazis.

Routine propagandist actioner, totally unbelievable.

w Anthony Veiller, William Wright, Howard Emmett Rogers   *novel* Helen MacInnes   *d* Jack Conway   *ph* Charles Rosher   *m* Lennie Hayton

Jean Pierre Aumont, Signe Hasso, Susan Peters, Reginald Owen, Richard Whorf, Margaret Wycherly, John Emery, Miles Mander, George Coulouris

'Any moment the world might blow up in their double faces!'

Assignment K

GB   1968   97m   Techniscope
Columbia/Mazurka (Ben Arbeid, Maurice Foster)

The European head of a toy firm is also head of a special spy unit.

Dreary espionage thriller, instantly forgettable, and only watchable at odd moments while it's on.

w Val Guest, Bill Strutton, Maurice Foster   *novel* Hartley Howard   *d* Val Guest   *ph* Ken Hodges   *m* Basil Kirchin

Stephen Boyd, Michael Redgrave, Camilla Sparv, Leo McKern, Jeremy Kemp

Assignment Paris

US   1952   85m   bw
Columbia (Sam Marx, Jerry Bresler)

A reporter on the Paris staff of the *New York Herald-Tribune* goes to Yugoslavia, is arrested as a spy, and has to be exchanged.

Dim cold war melodrama with occasional entertaining moments.

w William Bowers   *novel* *Trial by Terror* by Paul Gallico   *d* Robert Parrish   *ph* Burnett Guffey, Ray Cory   *m* George Duning

George Sanders, Dana Andrews, Sandro Giglio, Marta Toren, Audrey Totter, Herbert Berghof

Assignment Redhead

GB   1956   79m   bw
W. G. Chalmers/Butcher's
US title: *Million Dollar Manhunt*

An international criminal gang arrives in London looking for counterfeit dollars printed by the Nazis during the war.

Initially sharp but eventually yawnworthy thick ear on the smallest scale.

wd Maclean Rogers   *story* Lindsay Hardy

Richard Denning, Ronald Adam, Carole Mathews, Danny Green, Brian Worth, Jan Holden

Assignment to Kill

US   1967   99m   Technicolor   Panavision
Warner Seven Arts (William Conrad)

A New York insurance company hires a private eye to investigate a dubious European financier.

Routine international intrigue with muddled plot and unusual cast. A nice production wasted.

wd Sheldon Reynolds   *ph* Harold Lipstein   *m* William Lava

Patrick O'Neal, John Gielgud, Peter Van Eyck, Joan Hackett, Herbert Lom, Eric Portman, Oscar Homolka, Leon Greene

The Assisi Underground

Italy/US   1985   178m   colour
Cannon (Menahem Golan, Yoram Globus)
V*, S

During World War II, Assisi monasteries hide Jewish refugees.

Expansive but generally abysmal war adventure which was released in various forms, including a television miniseries. No amount of re-editing can disguise an empty script and incompetent direction.

wd Giuseppe Ramati   *novel* Giuseppe Ramati   *ph* Giuseppe Rotunno   *m* Dov Seltzer   *pd* Luciano Spadoni

Ben Cross, James Mason, Irene Papas, Maximilian Schell

'There is simply not enough story to fill three hours, so the scenery upstages the actors.' – *Variety*

Asterix and the Big Fight

France/West Germany   1989   81m   Eastmancolor
Palace/Gaumont/Extrafilm (Nicolas Pesques)
V
original title: *Le Coup de Menhir*

Asterix attempts to restore the village soothsayer's memory in order to make a potion to defeat the invading Romans.

Dull adaptation of a far wittier comic-book original.

w George Roubicek   *novel* *Asterix and the Big Fight* and *Asterix and the Soothsayer* by Rene Goscinny and Alberto Uderzo   *d* Philippe Grimond   *ph* Craig Simpson   *m* Michel Colombier   *pd* Nicolas Pesques   *ed* Jean Goudier

voices of Bill Oddie, Bernard Bresslaw, Ron Moody, Sheila Hancock, Peter Hawkins, Brian Blessed, Michael Elphick, Andrew Sachs, Tim Brooke-Taylor, Douglas Blackwell

Asterix in Britain

Denmark/France   1986   74m   Eastmancolor
Gaumont Dargaud (Yannik Piel)
V

Asterix and friends go to Britain to help the locals repel the Roman invasion.

Amiable animated version of the comic-book characters, poking good-natured fun at national stereotypes.

w Pierre Tchernia   *comic* Goscinny and Uderzo   *d* Pino Van Lamsweerde   *m* Vladimir Cosma

voices of Jack Beaver, Bill Kearns, Graham Bushnell, Herbert Baskind, Ed Marcus

The Astonished Heart *

GB   1949   89m   bw
Gainsborough/Sydney Box (Antony Darnborough)

A psychiatrist is permitted by his wife to fall in love with another woman but finds the situation intolerable and kills himself.

The star, looking like a Chinese mandarin, reached his nadir in this unwise screen adaptation, inelegantly directed, of one of his slightest short plays about boring and effete people. It sank without trace.

w Noël Coward   *play* Noël Coward   *d* Terence Fisher, Antony Darnborough   *ph* Jack Asher   *m* Noël Coward

Noël Coward, Margaret Leighton, Celia Johnson, Graham Payn, Joyce Carey, Ralph Michael, Michael Hordern

The Astounding She-Monster

US   1957   59m   bw
Hollywood International (Ronnie Ashcroft)
V*
GB title: *Mysterious Invader*

In a remote spot, some crooks and a scientist combat a female space visitor with remarkable powers.

An early sub-Corman pot-boiler with only its camp qualities to recommend it.

w Frank Hall   *d* Ronnie Ashcroft

Robert Clarke, Kenne Duncan, Marilyn Harvey

Asya's Happiness **

USSR   1967   94m   bw
Artificial Eye/Mosfilm (M. Zarzhitskaya)
original title: *Istoria Asi Klyachinoi, kotoraya lyubila, da nie vshla zamuzh*

The film's epigraph is 'The story of a woman who loved but did not marry', but it is more a loving account of a rural community at work and play.

A candid portrait of Soviet life, using amateur actors, that was banned for more than 20 years for reasons only the Russians will understand.

w Yuri Klepikov   *d* Andrei Mikhalkov-Konchalovsky   *ph* Georgy Rerberg   *pd* Mikhail Romadin   *ed* L. Pokrovskoi

Ilya Savvina, Lyubov Sokolova, Alexander Surin, Gennady Yegorychev, Ivan Petrov

'A major film in its own right, a worthy addition to that great agrarian cinema of Vidor and Ford.' – *Ian Christie, MFB*

'You have nothing to lose but your mind!'

Asylum *

GB   1972   88m   Eastmancolor
Amicus (Max J. Rosenberg, Milton Subotsky)
V*, L
aka: *House of Crazies*

A doctor applies for a job at an asylum, hears weird stories from four patients, and finds himself in the middle of a weirder one.

Lively horror compilation with echoes of *Caligari* and *Dead of Night*. Gruesomeness sometimes overdone.

w Robert Bloch   *d* Roy Ward Baker   *ph* Denys Coop   *m* Douglas Gamley

Patrick Magee, Robert Powell, Geoffrey Bayldon, Barbara Parkins, Sylvia Syms, Richard Todd, Peter Cushing, Barry Morse, Britt Ekland, Charlotte Rampling, James Villiers, Megs Jenkins, Herbert Lom

At Close Range

US 1986 111m CFI color Panavision
Orion/Hemdale (Elliott Lewitt, Don Guest)
V*, L

In Pennsylvania, a gang of young robbers is picked off one by one by the father of one of them, who feels they know too much about his own criminal activities.

Relentlessly brutal, dispiriting and quite pointless melodrama, even with the saving grace of a factual basis.

w Nicholas Kazan d James Foley ph Juan Ruiz-Anchia m Patrick Leonard

Sean Penn, Christopher Walken, Mary Stuart Masterson, Christopher Penn, Millie Perkins, Eileen Ryan, Candy Clark

'A very tough picture . . . runs the risk of being an audience turnoff.' – Variety

At Dawn We Die: see Tomorrow We Live

At Gunpoint

US 1955 80m Technicolor Cinemascope
Allied Artists
V*
GB title: Gunpoint

A Western storekeeper accidentally kills a bank robber, whose brothers seek revenge; will the townsfolk come to his aid?

Fair Western on the lines of High Noon.

w Dan Ullman d Alfred Werker

Fred MacMurray, Dorothy Malone, Walter Brennan, John Qualen, Skip Homeier

'A new kind of musical!'
At Long Last Love

US 1975 114m Technicolor
TCF/Copa de Oro (Peter Bogdanovich)

The 1935 romance of a New York millionaire and a musical star.

An attempt to recapture the simple pleasures of an Astaire-Rogers musical; unfortunately true professionalism is lacking and the wrong kind of talent is used. The result is awful to contemplate.

wd Peter Bogdanovich ph Laszlo Kovacs m Cole Porter pd Gene Allen

Burt Reynolds, Cybill Shepherd, Eileen Brennan, Madeline Kahn, Duilio del Prete, John Hillerman, Mildred Natwick

'He works hard at reducing all his sets and costumes to variations of black against silver or white on white, and uncovers in his most oft-repeated visual motif – the elegant mirrors before which his cast seem at all times to be posed – the perfect metaphor for this endlessly narcissistic, thoroughly calcified enterprise.' – Richard Combs

'It just lies there, and it dies there.' – Variety

'Studios bury more films than the public or the critics. Fox gave up on At Long Last Love instantly. A six million dollar film was written off while it was doing well because their lawyers told them they could make more money that way.' – Peter Bogdanovich

'It is justly included on most lists of the ten worst films ever made.' – Les Keyser, Hollywood in the Seventies

'Stillborn . . . a relentlessly vapid pastiche.' – Pauline Kael

At Play in the Fields of the Lord *

US 1991 186m Technicolor
Entertainment/Saul Zaentz
V, V*, L, S

American mercenaries become embroiled in a battle for the land and souls of an Indian tribe in the Amazon.

Over-long and over-earnest treatment of a fashionable theme, though it does have its moments.

w Jean-Claude Carrière, Hector Babenco
novel Peter Mathiessen d Hector Babenco
ph Lauro Escorel m Zbigniew Preisner pd Clovis Bueno ed William Anderson, Aremn Minasian, Louise Innes

Tom Berenger, John Lithgow, Daryl Hannah, Aidan Quinn, Tom Waits, Kathy Bates, Stenio Garcia, Nelson Xavier

'The Amazonian tragedy is surely not best served by three hours of tedium.' – Empire

At Sword's Point *

US 1951 81m Technicolor
RKO (Jerrold T. Brandt)
V*, L
GB title: Sons of the Musketeers

The sons of the three musketeers rally around their ageing queen to prevent her daughter's marriage to a villain.

Adequate swashbuckler with plenty of pace and a sound cast.

w Walter Ferris, Joseph Hoffman d Lewis Allen
ph Ray Rennahan m Roy Webb

Cornel Wilde, Maureen O'Hara, Gladys Cooper, Robert Douglas, Dan O'Herlihy, Alan Hale Jnr, Blanche Yurka, Nancy Gates

At the Circus **

US 1939 87m bw
MGM (Mervyn Le Roy)
V*, L
aka: The Marx Brothers at the Circus

A shyster lawyer and two incompetents save a circus from bankruptcy.

This film began the decline of the Marx Brothers; in it nothing is ill done but nothing is very fresh either apart from the rousing finale which shows just what professionalism meant in the old Hollywood. Highlights include Groucho singing about Lydia the tattooed lady, his seduction of Mrs Dukesbury, and the big society party.

w Irving Brecher d Edward Buzzell ph Leonard M. Smith m Franz Waxman m/ly Harold Arlen, E. Y. Harburg

Groucho, Chico, Harpo, Margaret Dumont, Florence Rice, Kenny Baker, Eve Arden, Nat Pendleton, Fritz Feld

songs: 'Lydia', 'Two Blind Loves', 'Step up and Take a Bow'

GROUCHO: 'I don't know what I'm doing here when I could be at home in bed with a hot toddy. That's a drink.'

'Rousing physical comedy and staccato gag dialogue . . . geared for fine b.o. and general audience appeal.' – Variety

'We must regretfully accept the fact that, thanks to the Metro millions, the Marx Brothers are finally imprisoned in the Hollywood world.' – Graham Greene

At the Earth's Core

GB 1976 90m Technicolor
Amicus (John Dark)
V*

Scientists testing a geological excavator are carried by it to the centre of the Earth, and find a prehistoric land inhabited by feuding tribes.

Mainly feeble science fiction for kids, with occasional amusing moments.

w Milton Subotsky novel Edgar Rice Burroughs
d Kevin Connor ph Alan Hume m Mike Vickers
pd Maurice Carter sp Ian Wingrove

Doug McClure, Peter Cushing, Caroline Munro, Cy Grant, Godfrey James, Keith Barron

'Papier mâché people-eaters, idiotic situations, and a frequent sense of confusion as to what is going on.' – David Stewart, Christian Science Monitor

At the Stroke of Nine

GB 1957 72m bw
Tower/Grand National

A mad concert pianist plots to murder a young girl reporter.

Absurd and rather endearing melodrama of the very old school.

w Tony O'Grady, Harry Booth, Jon Pennington, Michael Deeley d Lance Comfort

Stephen Murray, Patricia Dainton, Patrick Barr, Dermot Walsh

At the Villa Rose

This murder mystery by A. E. W. Mason has had three British filmings: in 1920 with Teddy Arundell as Inspector Hanaud; in 1930 with Austin Trevor; in 1939 with Keneth Kent. All were adequate to their time. The story concerns a medium framed for the murder of a rich widow.

At War with the Army

US 1951 93m bw
Paramount/Fred K. Finklehoffe
V

A couple of song and dance men have trouble as army recruits.

American service farce, based on a play and confined largely to one set; rather untypical of Martin and Lewis, yet oddly enough the film which sealed their success.

w Fred K. Finklehoffe play James Allardice
d Hal Walker ph Stuart Thompson m Joseph Lilley

Dean Martin, Jerry Lewis, Mike Kellin, Polly Bergen, Jimmie Dundee

L'Atalante *

France 1934 89m bw
J. L. Nounez-Gaumont
V

A barge captain takes his new wife down river.

One of those classics which no longer provide the authentic thrill; its lack of incident and plot leads quickly to boredom.

w Jean Guinée, Jean Vigo, Albert Riera d Jean Vigo ph Boris Kaufman, Louis Berger m Maurice Jaubert

Jean Dasté, Dita Parlo, Michel Simon, Giles Margarites

'The singular talent – for once I think I may say genius – of the film lies in its translation into visual images of the mysterious and terrible and piteous undertones of even the simplest human life.' – Dilys Powell

¡Atame!: see Tie Me Up! Tie Me Down!

El Ataque de los Muertos sin Ojo: see The Return of the Evil Dead

Athena

US 1954 96m Eastmancolor
MGM (Joe Pasternak)
V*, L

A young lawyer falls in love with the eldest of seven sisters brought up to high standards of moral conduct and physical fitness.

Promising but unfulfilling light musical which smothers a good idea in routine treatment.

w William Ludwig, Leonard Spigelgass   *d* Richard Thorpe   *ph* Robert Planck   *md* George Stoll *m/ly* Hugh Martin, Ralph Blane

Edmund Purdom, Jane Powell, Debbie Reynolds, Louis Calhern, Evelyn Varden, Vic Damone, Linda Christian, Ray Collins

'The Leviathan of Talkies'
'A thunderbolt of drama impossible to describe'

Atlantic
GB 1929 90m bw
BIP

A passenger liner sinks in mid-Atlantic.

Veiled retelling of the *Titanic* story, here in a clumsy Anglo-German version with extremely primitive sound and a plethora of pregnant silences.

w Victor Kendall   *play The Berg* by Ernest Raymond *d* E. A. Dupont

Franklin Dyall, Madeleine Carroll, Monty Banks, John Stuart, John Longden, Ellaline Terriss

'If you want to be mentally shipwrecked or lost at sea, see *Atlantic*. . . . It's something unnecessary to see; something no one wants to see; something horrible to even think of.

'. . . It will draw to and drive away from the box office. Draw to because it holds horror, thrills and suspense; drive away through children not being permitted to see it and the suggested gruesomeness too strong for many, not only women.

'. . . A faint try at comedy with a valet was like a ghoul in a cemetery . . . but Franklin Dyall excelled as an aged invalid with John Longden as a ship's officer, making a splendid appearance.' – *Variety*

Atlantic Adventure *
US 1935 68m bw
Columbia

A reporter captures a murderer on an ocean liner.

Lively double-biller, better than average in all departments.

w John T. Neville, Nat Dorfman   *d* Albert Rogell

Nancy Carroll, Lloyd Nolan, Harry Langdon, Arthur Hohl, Robert Middlemass, John Wray, E. E. Clive

'Only lack of cast names keeps this in dual pix classification.' – *Variety*

Atlantic City *
US 1944 87m bw
Republic (Albert J. Cohen)

Before World War I, a young showman aims to make Atlantic City the entertainment centre of the world.

Simple-minded romantic musical, quite pacy and effectively staged for a Republic product.

w Doris Gilbert, Frank Gill Jnr, George Carlton Brown   *d* Ray McCarey   *ph* John Alton *m/ly* various

Constance Moore, Brad Taylor, Jerry Colonna, Charley Grapewin

Atlantic City ***
Canada/France 1981 105m colour
Cine-Neighbour/Selta Films (Denis Heroux)
V, V*, L S

Small-time crooks congregate round Atlantic City's new casinos.

Elegiac character drama which often achieves the mood it seeks but on the whole remains too understated for its own good.

w John Guare   *d* Louis Malle   *ph* Richard Ciupka *m* Michel Legrand   *pd* Anne Pritchard

Burt Lancaster, Susan Sarandon, Kate Reid, Michel Piccoli, Hollis McLaren

AAN: best picture; John Guare; Burt Lancaster; Susan Sarandon; Louis Malle

BFA: best direction; Burt Lancaster

Atlantic Episode: see *Catch As Catch Can*

Atlantic Ferry *
GB 1941 108m bw
Warner (Max Milder)
US title: *Sons of the Sea*

In 1837 Liverpool, two brothers build the first steamship to cross the Atlantic.

Ponderous historical romance with points of interest.

w Gordon Wellesley, Edward Dryhurst, Emeric Pressburger   *d* Walter Forde   *ph* Basil Emmott *m* Jack Beaver

Michael Redgrave, Valerie Hobson, Griffith Jones, Margaretta Scott, Hartley Power, Bessie Love, Milton Rosmer

'Probably the finest collection of model shots in captivity.' – *C. A. Lejeune*

L'Atlantide *
France 1921 125m approx (16 fps) bw silent
Thalman

Two explorers find the lost continent of Atlantis and fall in love with its queen.

Highly commercial adventure fantasy of its day; it cost two million francs and ran in Paris for a year. Some scenes still sustain, and the desert scenes are impressive.

wd Jacques Feyder   *novel* Pierre Benoît *ph* Georges Specht, Victor Morin

Jean Angelo, Stacia Napierkowska, Georges Melchior

† Other versions include *Queen of Atlantis* (Germany 1932, *d* G. W. Pabst, with Brigitte Helm); *Siren of Atlantis* (US 1948, *d* Gregg Tallas, with Maria Montez); *L'Atlantide* (France/Italy 1961, *d* Edgar G. Ulmer).

The version released on video in 1994 is the 1931 European version, which runs for 115m.

Atlantis **
France 1991 75m colour
Warner/Gaumont/Cecchi Gori

An episodic documentary, with musical accompaniment, on life under the sea.

A fascinating attempt at what its director defined as an 'underwater opera', full of quirky detail and showing various species that may soon die out.
d Luc Besson   *ph* Christian Petron   *m* Eric Serra *ed* Luc Besson

Atlantis, the Lost Continent *
US 1961 91m Metrocolor
MGM/Galaxy/George Pal

A Greek fisherman is imprisoned when he returns a maiden he has rescued to her island home of Atlantis, but escapes just before volcanic eruption overtakes the decadent nation.

Penny-pinching fantasy spectacle with very little entertainment value.

w Daniel Mainwaring   *play* Sir Gerald Hargreaves *d* George Pal   *ph* Harold E. Wellman   *m* Russell Garcia

Anthony Hall, Joyce Taylor, John Dall, Edward Platt, Frank de Kova, Jay Novello

Atoll K: see *Robinson Crusoeland*

Atom Man vs Superman
US 1950 bw serial: 15 eps
Columbia

The evil Luthor threatens Metropolis with mad and dangerous devices.

Absurd but still quite watchable adventures for those experiencing second childhood.   *d* Spencer Bennet

Kirk Alyn, Noel Neill, Lyle Talbot, Tommy Bond, Pierre Watkin

The Atomic City *
US 1952 85m bw
Paramount (Joseph Sistrom)
V*

The young son of a leading atomic scientist is kidnapped but his father and the FBI rescue him.

Routine but well-paced thriller with a documentary background of research at Los Alamos.

w Sidney Boehm   *d* Jerry Hopper   *ph* Charles B. Lang Jnr   *m* Leith Stevens

Gene Barry, Lydia Clarke, Lee Aaker, Nancy Gates, Milburn Stone

AAN: Sidney Boehm

The Atomic Kid
US 1954 86m bw
Republic/Mickey Rooney (Maurice Duke)
V*

After an atomic blast, a prospector accidentally left in the area proves immune to uranium, and after various adventures rounds up some communist spies.

Inane romp which raises a few laughs.

w Benedict Freeman, John Fenton Murray *story* Blake Edwards   *d* Leslie H. Martinson *ph* John L. Russell Jnr   *m* Van Alexander

Mickey Rooney, Robert Strauss, Elaine Davis, Bill Goodwin, Whit Bissell

The Atonement of Gösta Berling **
Sweden 1924 200m approx (16 fps) bw silent
Svensk Filmindustri
V*
original title: *Gösta Berlings Saga*

A pastor is defrocked for drinking, becomes a tutor, and has various love affairs.

Lumpy but often engrossing picturization of a famous novel, veering mostly into melodrama but finding its way to a happy ending.

w Mauritz Stiller, Ragnar Hylten-Cavallius *novel* Selma Lagerlof   *d* Mauritz Stiller   *ph* Julius Jaenzon

Lars Hanson, Gerda Lundeqvist, Ellen Cederstrom, Mona Martensson, Jenny Hasselqvist, Otto Elg-Lundberg, Greta Garbo

'Stiller was a master at unifying visual beauty and emotional effect; the complicated narrative is blurry, but there are sequences as lovely and expressive as any on film.' – *New Yorker, 1980*

† It was her small role in this film which led directly to Greta Garbo's American stardom.

Attack **
US 1956 104m bw
UA/Associates and Aldrich

In 1944 Belgium, an American infantry command is led by a coward.

High-pitched, slick, violent and very effective war melodrama, even though by the end we seem to be in the company of raving lunatics rather than soldiers.

w James Poe,   *play Fragile Fox* by Norman Brooks *d* Robert Aldrich   *ph* Joseph Biroc   *m* Frank de Vol

Jack Palance, Eddie Albert, Lee Marvin, Buddy Ebsen, Robert Strauss, Richard Jaeckel, William Smithers, Peter Van Eyck

'The film does not so much tackle a subject as hammer it down.' – *Penelope Houston*

Attack Force Z
Australia 1982 110m colour
John McCallum/Central Motion Picture Corp (Lee Robinson)
V, V*

A secret commando group attempts to rescue survivors of a plane crash in Japanese-held territory during the Second World War.

Downbeat adventure, which was intended as a tribute to Australasian special operations, but conveys instead the waste of humanity that war entails.

w Roger Marshall   d Tim Burstall   ph Lin Hun-Chung   m Eric Jupp   ed David Stiven

John Phillip Law, Mel Gibson, Sam Neill, Chris Haywood, John Waters, Koo Chuan-Hsiung, Sylvia Chang, O Ti

'From the depths of the sea . . . A Tidal Wave of Terror!'
Attack of the Crab Monsters
US   1956   62m   bw
Allied Artists (Roger Corman)
V*

25-foot mutant crabs cause landslides on a Pacific island.

Bottom-of-the-barrel monster mayhem from this tongue-in-cheek producer; now a cult.

w Charles B. Griffith   d Roger Corman   ph Floyd Crosby   m Ronald Stein   ed Charles Gross Jnr

Richard Garland, Pamela Duncan, Russell Johnson

The Attack of the 50-Foot Woman
US   1958   72m   bw
Allied Artists
V*, L

A neurotic woman is lured inside a space ship, becomes radio-active, and grows to alarming proportions.

Hilarious tailpiece to the fifties monster cycle, a dismal movie worth remembering only for its title.

w Mark Hanna   d Nathan Hertz (Nathan Juran)   ph Jacques Marquette   m Ronald Stein

Allison Hayes, William Hudson, Roy Gordon

Attack of the Giant Leeches
US   1959   62m   bw
Corman/AIP
V*
aka: Demons of the Swamp

A bar owner forces his wife and her lover into a swamp to be eaten by monsters.

The bottom of the Corman/AIP barrel, good only for a few unintentional laughs.

w Leo Gordon   d Bernard Kowalski   ph John M. Nickolaus Jnr

Ken Clark, Michael Emmet, Yvette Vickers, Bruno Ve Sota

Attack of the Killer Tomatoes
US   1978   87m   colour
Four Square/NAI
V*

Vegetables go berserk in the big city.

Apparently a cult film made deliberately as such, which is a contradiction in terms. Nothing for the ordinary audience, anyway.

w Costa Dillon, Steve Peace, John de Bello   d John de Bello

David Miller, George Wilson, Sharon Taylor, Jack Riley

'Though the idea sounds funny, actually sitting through nearly 90 minutes of it is enough to make anyone long for Attack of the Fifty Foot Woman.' – Motion Picture Guide

Attack of the Puppet People
US   1957   79m   bw
Alta Vista (Bert I. Gordon)
GB title: Six Inches Tall

A doll-maker has also learned to shrink people.

Inferior entry in the Dr Cyclops mould; mildly amusing moments are sandwiched between chunks of tedium.

w George Worthing Yates   d Bert I. Gordon

John Hoyt, John Agar, June Kenny

Attack on the Iron Coast
GB   1967   90m   DeLuxe
UA/Mirisch (John Champion)

In World War II, a Canadian commando unit destroys a German installation on the French coast.

Stagey low-budgeter with modest action sequences.

w Herman Hoffman   d Paul Wendkos   ph Paul Beeson   m Gerard Schurmann

Lloyd Bridges, Andrew Keir, Mark Eden, Sue Lloyd

Attila the Hun
Italy/France   1954   79m   Technicolor
Lux Ponti de Laurentiis/LCCF (Georgio Andriani)
V*
original title: Attilo Flagello di Dio

The barbarian chief attacks the forces of the Emperor Valentinian and marches on Rome.

Predictably violent adventures after de Mille; a bit slow to start.

w Ennio de Concini, Primo Zeglio   d Pietro Francisci   ph Aldo Tonti   m Enzo Masetti

Anthony Quinn, Sophia Loren, Henri Vidal, Irene Papas, Ettore Manni, Claude Laydu

Attilo Flagello di Dio: see Attila the Hun

Attorney for the Defense
US   1932   70m   bw
Columbia

A prosecutor's wiles result in an innocent man being executed, so he turns crusader and takes on defence cases.

Punchy if unconvincing courtroom melodrama which would certainly satisfy at the time.

w Jo Swerling, J. K. McGuinness   d Irving Cummings

Edmund Lowe, Evelyn Brent, Constance Cummings, Donald Dillaway, Dorothy Peterson, Dwight Frye, Nat Pendleton, Clarence Muse

Au delà des Grilles
Italy/France   1949   90m   bw
Italia Produzione/Francinex (Alfredo Guarini)
aka: Beyond the Gates; The Walls of Malapaga; Italian title: La mura de Malapaga

A murderer on the run in Genoa falls in love with a waitress and loses his chance of escape.

Quai des Brumes reworked against an Italian neo-realist setting; dramatic values less interesting now than historical ones.

w Jean Aurenche, Pierre Bost, Cesare Zavattini, Suso Cecchi d'Amico   d René Clément   ph Louis Page   m Roman Vlad

Jean Gabin, Isa Miranda, Vera Talchi, Andrea Checci

AA: best foreign film

Au Hasard, Balthazar: see Balthazar

Au Revoir Les Enfants ****
France   1988   107m   Eastmancolor
Nouvelles Éditions de Films/MK2/Stella Films (Louis Malle)
V, V*, L, S

During the German occupation of France, a boy at a Catholic school inadvertently betrays his Jewish schoolfriend to the Nazis.

A coolly-understated, intensely personal, semi-autobiographical movie much admired by the French and winner of the Golden Lion at the Venice Film Festival.

wd Louis Malle   ph Renato Berta   ad Willy Holt   ed Emmanuelle Castro

Gaspard Manesse, Raphaël Fejtö, Francine Racette, Stanlislas Carre de Malberg, Philippe Morier-Genoud, François Berleand

'Malle has said of Au Revoir, "I reinvented the past in the pursuit of a haunting and timeless truth." Maybe that's why I felt as if I were watching a faded French classic, something I dimly recalled.' – Pauline Kael, New Yorker

AAN: best foreign film

Au Royaume des Cieux
France   1949   108m   bw
Regina (Julien Duvivier)
aka: Woman Hunt

An 18-year-old girl suffers at a reform school.

Shoddy melodrama, more sensational than Hollywood ever dared to be.

wd Julien Duvivier   ph Victor Armenise

Suzanne Cloutier, Serge Reggiani, Monique Mélinand, Suzy Prim, Jean Davy, Juliette Greco

'A depressing exhibit from a director who once had a serious reputation.' – Gavin Lambert

L'Auberge Rouge: see The Red Inn

Auch Zwerge Haben Klein Angefangen: see Even Dwarfs Started Small

Audrey Rose *
US   1977   113m   DeLuxe   Panavision
United Artists/Robert Wise
V, V*

A man believes that a 12-year-old girl is the reincarnation of his dead daughter.

Rather painful and not very persuasive spiritualist thriller in the wake of The Exorcist; only moments of dramaturgy survive.

w Frank de Felitta   novel Frank de Felitta   d Robert Wise   ph Victor J. Kemper   m Michael Small   ed Harry Horner

Anthony Hopkins, Marsha Mason, John Beck, Susan Swift, Norman Lloyd, John Hillerman, Robert Walden

Aunt Clara
GB   1954   84m   bw
London Films (Colin Lesslie, Anthony Kimmins)

A pious old person inherits from a reprobate uncle five greyhounds, a pub and a brothel.

Extremely mild star vehicle with a gallery of comedy character cameos.

w Kenneth Horne   novel Noel Streatfeild   d Anthony Kimmins   ph C. Pennington-Richards   m Benjamin Frankel

Margaret Rutherford, Ronald Shiner, A. E. Matthews, Fay Compton, Nigel Stock, Jill Bennett, Reginald Beckwith, Raymond Huntley

Aunt Julia and The Scriptwriter: see Tune In Tomorrow

Aunt Sally
GB   1933   84m   bw
Gainsborough (Michael Balcon)
US title: Along Came Sally

A fake French star saves a night-club owner from gangsters.

Predictable star vehicle.

w Austin Melford, Guy Bolton, A. R. Rawlinson   d Tim Whelan   ph Charles Van Enger   ad Vetchinsky

Cicely Courtneidge, Sam Hardy, Billy Milton, Phyllis Clare, Hartley Power

Auntie Mame *
US   1958   144m   Technirama
Warner (Morton da Costa)
V*, L

An orphan boy is adopted by his volatile extravagant aunt, whose giddy escapades fill his memory of the twenties and thirties.

A rather unsatisfactory star revue from a book and play later turned into a musical, *Mame*. A few splendid moments, otherwise rather dull and irritating.

w Betty Comden, Adolph Green   *play* Jerome Lawrence, Robert E. Lee   *novel* Patrick Dennis   d Morton da Costa   ph Harry Stradling   m Bronislau Kaper   ad Malcolm Bert   ed William Ziegler

Rosalind Russell, Forrest Tucker, *Coral Browne*, Fred Clark, Roger Smith, Patric Knowles, Peggy Cass, Lee Patrick, Joanna Barnes

AAN: best picture; Harry Stradling; Rosalind Russell; Peggy Cass; art direction; editing

Aus Einem Deutschen Leben: see *Death Is My Trade*

Une Aussi Longue Absence *
France/Italy   1961   96m   bw
Procinex/Lyre/Galatea (Jacques Nahum)
aka: *The Long Absence*

A widow who owns a Paris café meets an amnesiac tramp who may be her long-lost husband.

Romantic character study which just about comes off thanks to good acting.

w Marguerite Duras, Gérald Jarlot   d Henri Colpi   ph Marcel Weiss   m Georges Delerue

Alida Valli, Georges Wilson, Jacques Harden

Austerlitz
France/Italy/Liechtenstein/Yugoslavia   1959   166m   Eastmancolor   Dyaliscope
CFPI/SCLF/Galatea/Michael Arthur/Dubrava (Alexander and Michael Salkind)
aka: *The Battle of Austerlitz*

Napoleon defeats the Austro-Russian army.

Elaborate pageant with a hopelessly cluttered narrative line arranged to take in a roster of guest stars who merely distract from the central theme.

wd Abel Gance   ph Henri Alekan, Robert Juillard   m Jean Ledrut

Pierre Mondy, Jean Mercure, Jack Palance, Orson Welles, Michel Simon, Jean-Louis Trintignant, Martine Carol, Leslie Caron, Claudia Cardinale, Rossano Brazzi, Ettore Manni, Jean Marais, Vittorio de Sica

'Strictly for connoisseurs of Gance's brand of hyperbolic history.' – *Peter John Dyer, MFB*

Australia
France/Belgium/Switzerland   1989   124m   colour
Christian Bourgois/AO/Les Films de La Dreve/CAB/RTBF/Cine 5 (Marie Pascale Osterrieth)

A Belgium wool merchant, returning home from Australia to sort out a family problem, falls in love with a married woman.

Superior soap opera.

w Jean Gruault, Jacques Audiard, Jean-Jacques Andrien   d Jean-Jacques Andrien   ph Yorgos Arvanitis   m Nicola Piovani   pd Herbert Westbrook   ed Ludo Troch

Jeremy Irons, Fanny Ardant, Tcheky Karyo, Agnes Soral, Danielle Lyttleton, Helene Surgere

Austria 1700: see *Mark of the Devil*

Author, Author! *
US   1982   109m   TVC Color
TCF (Irwin Winkler)
V*

A Broadway playwright has worries about his wife's fidelity.

Like a sixties update of *All About Eve*, this thin but sometimes witty sex-behind-the-footlights comedy had nothing to offer the general audience of the eighties, and one can only speculate as to why it was made. The acting does help, but it's a long haul.

w Israel Horovitz   d Arthur Hiller   ph Victor J. Kemper   m Dave Grusin   pd Gene Rudolf   ed William Reynolds

Al Pacino, Dyan Cannon, Tuesday Weld, Bob Dishy, Bob Elliott

'In trying to dig a little deeper than the average Neil Simon comedy, it only prepares its own grave.' – *Observer*

Autobus ***
France   1991   98m   colour
Artificial Eye/Les Productions Lazennec/FR3/SGGC/La Générale d'Images/Canal+ (Alain Rocca)
V, S
French title: *Aux yeux du monde*

A frustrated and unemployed youth hijacks a bus full of schoolchildren so that he can go to visit his girlfriend.

An unexpected and uplifting exploration of a familiar theme which manages to avoid all the conventional routes.

wd Eric Rochant   ph Pierre Novion   m Gérard Torikian   pd Pascale Fenouillet   ed Catherine Quesemand

Yvan Attal, Kristin Scott-Thomas, Marc Berman, Charlotte Gainsbourg, Renan Mazeas

'Slight and well-meaning, and less incisive than it could be. But it is also much more appealing than its rather whimsical premise would suggest.' – *Verina Glaessner, Sight and Sound*

Automania 2000 **
GB   1963   10m   Eastmancolor
Halas and Batchelor

New cars have the ability to reproduce themselves: city dwellers of the future consequently live in stationary vehicles piled on top of each other.

Amusing cartoon fantasy, neatly executed.

w Joy Batchelor   d John Halas

Un Autre Homme, une Autre Chance: see *Another Man, Another Chance*

An Autumn Afternoon ***
Japan   1962   113m   Agfa-Shochikucolor
Shochiku
V*
original title: *Samma no Aji*

A widower, horrified by the thought of his daughter becoming an old maid by looking after him, is encouraged by his friends to find her a husband.

Ozu's last film, in which form matters as much as content, is an elegiac account of the disintegration of family life and the prospect of lonely old age.

w Kogo Noda, Yasujiro Ozu   d Yasujiro Ozu   ph Yuharu Atsuta   m Kojun Saito   ad Tatsuo Hamada   ed Yoshiyasu Hamamura

Shima Iwashita, Chishu Ryu, Keji Sata, Mariko Okada, Shinichiro Mikami, Teruo Yoshida, Noriko Maki, Nobuo Nakamura, Eijiro Tono

Autumn Crocus
GB   1934   86m   bw
ATP

A British schoolmistress on holiday falls for her Tyrolean innkeeper.

Difficult now to conceive the popularity in its day of this novelettish romance, which seems frozen in amber.

wd Basil Dean   play C. L. Anthony

Ivor Novello, Fay Compton, Jack Hawkins, Diana Beaumont, Muriel Aked, George Zucco

'In the dark, when I feel his heart pounding against mine – is it love? or frenzy? or terror?'

Autumn Leaves *
US   1956   108m   bw
Columbia/William Goetz
V*

A middle-aged spinster marries a young man who turns out to be a pathological liar and tries to murder her.

Skilfully tailored star vehicle for female audiences.

w Jack Jevne, Lewis Meltzer, Robert Blees   d Robert Aldrich   ph Charles Lang   m Hans Salter

Joan Crawford, Cliff Robertson, Lorne Greene, Vera Miles, Ruth Donnelly, Shepperd Strudwick

Autumn Sonata *
Sweden/West Germany/GB   1978   97m   colour
ITC/Personafilm (Ingmar Bergman)
V*, L

When her lover dies, a concert pianist visits the daughter she has not seen for many years.

Typically Bergmanesque, understated conversation piece with no obvious happy ending for anybody.

wd Ingmar Bergman   ph Sven Nykvist   m Chopin, Handel, Bach

Ingrid Bergman, Liv Ullmann, Halvar Bjork

'Professional gloom.' – *Time*

'It fills these middle-class rooms with the deep music of conflict and reconciliation that must strike home to any audiences in any culture or society.' – *Jack Kroll, Newsweek*

AAN: script; Ingrid Bergman

Aux yeux du monde: see *Autobus*

'Six million tons of icy terror!'
Avalanche
US   1978   91m   Metrocolor
New World (Roger Corman)
V*

Snow threatens holidaymakers at a ski lodge.

A disaster movie which, while quite competent in most ways, is no better than TV movies of this kind, especially as it resorts for its climaxes to scratched old stock film.

w Claude Pola, Corey Allen   d Corey Allen   ph Pierre-William Glenn   m William Kraft

Rock Hudson, Mia Farrow, Robert Forster, Jeanette Nolan, Rick Moses, Steve Franken, Barry Primus

Avalanche Express
Eire   1979   88m   DeLuxe   Panavision
TCF/Lorimar (Mark Robson)
V*

Spies of all nations converge on a train from Milan to Rotterdam.

Fitfully amusing hodgepodge which had to be finished off in a hurry following the death of its star and director in mid-production.

w Abraham Polonsky   novel Colin Forbes   d Mark Robson   ph Jack Cardiff   m Allyn Ferguson

Robert Shaw, Lee Marvin, Linda Evans, Maximilian Schell, Mike Connors, Joe Namath, Horst Buchholz

'The most impressive work of montage to emerge from a big-budget adventure movie.' – *Richard Combs, MFB*

'Pell-mell direction and editing perform a precarious, oddly suspenseful balancing act.' – *Sight and Sound*

Avalon **

US   1990   128m   Technicolor
Columbia TriStar/Baltimore Pictures (Mark Johnson, Barry Levinson)
V, V*, L, S

The lives and good times over half-a-century of an immigrant family in Baltimore.

Sprawling, episodic and too stolid for its ambitions, but with enjoyable moments from the ensemble cast.

wd Barry Levinson   ph Allen Daviau   m Randy Newman   pd Norman Reynolds   ed Stu Linder

Armin Mueller-Stahl, Elizabeth Perkins, Joan Plowright, Kevin Pollak, Aidan Quinn, Leo Fuchs, Eve Gordon, Lou Jacobi

'A lifeless experience devoid of a central conflict or purpose . . . The film is mostly a celebration of the mundane, and, while watching grandma and grandpa bicker at the dinner table may spur a fond glimmer of recognition, it's a wispy premise on which to hang this sort of lavish undertaking.' – *Variety*

'This movie is an elegy to a mythical past. That's probably why people emerge from the theatre sniffling.' – *Pauline Kael, New Yorker*

'When someone knocks at your door and says "Permesso?", be careful before you say . . .'
Avanti! **

US   1972   144m   DeLuxe
UA/Mirisch/Phalanx/Jalem (Billy Wilder)

A young American goes to Ischia to collect the body of his father who has died on holiday. He finds that the fatal accident had also killed his father's mistress, and amid overwhelming bureaucratic problems proceeds to fall in love with her daughter.

Absurdly overlong black comedy, with compensations in the shape of a generally witty script and some fine breakneck sequences of culminating confusion.

w Billy Wilder, I. A. L. Diamond,   play Samuel Taylor
d Billy Wilder   ph Luigi Kuveiller   m Carlo Rustichelli

Jack Lemmon, Juliet Mills, Clive Revill, Edward Andrews, Gianfranco Barra

Avanti-Popolo

Israel   1986   88m   colour
TTG/Kastel Communications (Rafi Bukaee)

In the final hours of the Six Day War between Israel and Egypt in 1967, two Egyptian conscripts flee towards the safety of the Suez Canal.

Drama on the futility of war that lacks the performances to compensate for its snail-like pace, or the style to accommodate its mix of comedy and death.

wd Rafi Bukaee   ph Yoav Kosh   m Uri Ofir
ad Ariel Glazer   ed Zohar Sela

Salim Daw, Suhel Hadad, Dani Roth, Dani Segev, Tuvya Gelber

The Avengers: see *The Day Will Dawn*

'May God Have Mercy On His Enemies!'
The Avenging Boxer (dubbed)

Hong Kong   1973   90m   colour
Alpha Motion Picture Co. (Jimmy Shaw)
US title: *Fearless Young Boxer*

A son learns kung fu so that he can avenge his father's death at the hands of a hired killer.

Standard martial-arts mayhem consisting of acrobatic fights interspersed with broad comedy, although it does manage a spectacular finale.

wd Jimmy Shaw   m Chang Fang Gi   ad David Wong   ed W. C. Leung

Peter Chang, Ca Sa Fa, Lee Lo Ling, Lee Kwun, Chan Wai Lau, Lung Fee

The Avenging Conscience *

US   1914   58m (24 fps)   bw   silent
Mutual

An elaboration of Poe's *The Tell Tale Heart* in which Griffith first shows his ability to control a feature-length movie, with many cinematic devices.

wd D. W. Griffith   ph Billy Bitzer

Henry B. Walthall, Blanche Sweet, Spottiswoode Aitken, Mae Marsh

The Avenging Hand

GB   1936   64m   bw
Motion Pictures (John Stafford)

A Chicago gangster holidaying in London turns detective to track down a murderer.

Tepid thriller built around Beery's brash and breezy performance.

w Reginald Long   d Frank Richardson   ph James Wilson   md Jack Beaver   ad MacDonald Sutherland   ed Sidney Cole

Noah Beery, Kathleen Kelly, Louis Borell, Charles Oliver, Reginald Long, Penelope Parkes, Tarver Penna, Joan Kemp-Welch

L'Avenir d'Emilie: see *The Future of Emily*

Les Aventures de Rabbi Jacob

France/Italy   1973   94m   Eastmancolor
Fox-Rank/Films Pomereu/Horse Film (Bernard Javal)
GB title: *The Mad Adventures of 'Rabbi' Jacob*

A French businessman with anti-Semitic views is forced by an Arab agitator on the run to impersonate a rabbi presiding at a Bar Mitzvah in Paris.

Broad comedy that raises a few laughs at the expense of xenophobia.

w Gérard Oury, Danielle Thompson, Josy Eisenberg
d Gérard Oury   ph Henri Decae   m Vladimir Cosma   ad Théo Meurisse   ed Albert Jurgenson

Louis de Funès, Suzy Delair, Marcel Dalio, Claude Giraud, Claude Piéplu, Renzo Montagnani

'Much loved in France, this comedy of errors has not travelled well and turns up in Britain looking painfully unfunny.' – *David McGillivray*

L'Aveu: see *The Confession*

The Aviator

US   1930   73m   bw
Warner

A timid clerk lends his name to a technical book on aviation, and finds himself having to back up the pretence by flying.

Predictable star comedy.   play James Montgomery
d Roy del Ruth

Edward Everett Horton, Patsy Ruth Miller, Johnny Arthur, Lee Moran

'Peg this as a good one.' – *Variety*

The Aviator

US   1985   96m   Metrocolor
MGM-UA/Mace Neufeld
V*

In 1928, a spoiled rich girl is cared for by a sullen pilot when they crashland in the Sierras.

Drawn-out, actionless adventure concerning unattractive characters; it has been seen before in at least two TV movies.

w Marc Norman   novel Ernest Gann   d George Miller   ph David Connell   m Dominic Frontiere   pd Brenton Swift   ed Duane Hartzell

Christopher Reeve, Rosanna Arquette, Jack Warden, Sam Wanamaker, Scott Wilson, Tyne Daly

'Doesn't fly.' – *Variety*

The Aviator's Wife *

France   1980   106m   Eastmancolor (blown up from 16mm)
Les Films du Losange (Margaret Menegoz)
V
original title: *La Femme de L'Aviateur*

Anne and François are having an affair, but each has other entanglements.

Meticulously arranged conversations in this director's best style, but this time not seeming to amount to very much.

wd Eric Rohmer   ph Bernard Lutic   m Jean-Louis Valero

Philippe Marlaud, Marie Rivière, Anne-Laure Maeury, Matthieu Carrière

'Does the aviator Christian's wife exist? It really does not matter: she is a formal device in a play of formalist devices.' – *Jill Forbes, MFB*

De Avonden: see *Evenings*

L'Avventura **

Italy/France   1960   145m   bw
Cino del Duca/PCE/Lyre (Amato Pennasilico)
S

Young people on a yachting holiday go ashore on a volcanic island. One of them disappears; this affects the lives of the others, but she is never found.

Aimless, overlong parable with lots of vague significance; rather less entertaining than the later *Picnic at Hanging Rock* (qv), it made its director a hero of the highbrows.

w Michelangelo Antonioni, Elio Bartolini, Tonino Guerra   d Michelangelo Antonioni   ph Aldo Scavarda   m Giovanni Fusco

Monica Vitti, Lea Massari, Gabriele Ferzetti, Dominique Blanchar, James Addams, Lelio Luttazi

'A film of complete maturity, sincerity and creative intuition.' – *Peter John Dyer, MFB*

The Awakening

GB   1980   105m   Technicolor
EMI/Orion (Robert Solo)
V*, L

An obsessed archaeologist believes that the spirit of a long-dead Egyptian queen has entered into the soul of his daughter.

Unpersuasive and humourless mumbo jumbo from the same intractably complex novel that provided the basis for *Blood from the Mummy's Tomb*.

w Allan Scott, Chris Bryant, Clive Exton   novel *Jewel of the Seven Stars* by Bram Stoker   d Mike Newell   ph Jack Cardiff   m Claude Bolling   pd Michael Stringer

Charlton Heston, Susannah York, Jill Townsend, Stephanie Zimbalist, Patrick Drury, Bruce Myers

'An almost total waste of the talents involved.' – *Sunday Times*

'It is difficult to imagine a film more likely to put you to sleep.' – *Guardian*

Awakenings *

US   1990   121m   Technicolor   Panavision
Columbia TriStar (Walter F. Parkes, Lawrence Lasker)
V, V*, L, S

A young doctor discovers a treatment that temporarily revives sufferers from encephalitis who have been in a state of suspended animation for 30 years or more.

Over-sentimentalized treatment of a fascinating subject, too insistent on leaving its audience feeling good.

w Steven Zaillian   *book* Oliver Sacks   *d* Penny Marshall   *ph* Miroslav Ondricek   *m* Randy Newman   *pd* Anton Furst   *ed* Jerry Greenberg, Battle Davis

Robert de Niro, Robin Williams, Julie Kavner, Ruth Nelson, John Heard, Penelope Ann Miller, Alice Drummond, Judith Malina, Barton Heyman, Max von Sydow

'The movie douses everything fiery. Everything is shaped for you to root for the resurrections, and then nothing much happens . . . the humanism is so pallid that the awakened patients don't seem very different from the way they were in their comatose states.' – *Pauline Kael, New Yorker*

Away All Boats!

US   1956   114m   Technicolor   Vistavision
U-I (Howard Christie)
V*

Adventures of a small transport boat during the Pacific War.

Competent drum-beating war heroics with expensive action sequences.

w Ted Sherdeman   *novel* Kenneth M. Dodson   *d* Joseph Pevney   *ph* William Daniels, Clifford Stine   *m* Frank Skinner

Jeff Chandler, George Nader, Julie Adams, Lex Barker, Keith Andes, Richard Boone, Frank Faylen

The Awful Dr Orloff

Spain   1962   88m   bw
Hispamer (Serge Newman, Leo Lax)
V, V*
original title: *Gritos en la Noche*

A mad doctor tries to restore his disfigured daughter to beauty by kidnapping and skinning young women.

Sleazy ill-made horror, notable only for being the first of a sequence of films featuring the awful doctor.

wd Jesús Franco   *novel* David Kuhne   *ph* Godofredo Pacheco

Howard Vernon, Conrado Sanmartin, Perla Cristal, Diana Lorys, Ricardo Valle

'An utterly dreadful movie.' – *The Dark Side*

The Awful Truth ***

US   1937   90m   bw
Columbia (Leo McCarey)
V, V*, L

A divorcing couple endure various adventures which lead to reconciliation.

Classic crazy comedy of the thirties, marked by a mixture of sophistication and farce and an irreverent approach to plot.

w Vina Delmar   *play* Arthur Richman   *d* Leo McCarey   *ph* Joseph Walker   *md* Morris Stoloff   *ed* Al Clark

Irene Dunne, Cary Grant, Ralph Bellamy, Alexander D'Arcy, Cecil Cunningham, Molly Lamont, Esther Dale, Joyce Compton

IRENE DUNNE: 'You've come back and caught me in the truth, and there's nothing less logical than the truth.'
CARY GRANT: 'In the spring a young man's fancy lightly turns to what he's been thinking about all winter.'

'Fast, smart comedy that will please everywhere and do strong general biz.' – *Variety*

'The funniest picture of the season.' – *Otis Ferguson*

'Among the ingredients the raising powder is the important thing and out of the oven comes a frothy bit of stuff that leaves no taste in the mouth and is easy on the stomach.' – *Marion Fraser, World Film News*

'Delightfully effective entertainment.' – *Time Out, 1985*

† Remade 1953 as *Let's Do It Again* (qv).

AA: Leo McCarey

AAN: best picture; script; Irene Dunne; Ralph Bellamy; Al Clark

AWOL

US   1990   108m   colour
Guild/Wrong Bet Productions/Imperial Entertainment (Ash R. Shah, Eric Karson)
V*, L, S
US title: *Lionheart*; aka: *The Wrong Bet*

A deserter from the Foreign Legion becomes a bare-knuckle fighter in America.

Musclebound action movie, sentimental when it is not violent.

w Sheldon Lettich, Jean-Claude Van Damme   *ph* Robert C. New   *m* John Scott   *pd* Gregory Pickrell   *ed* Mark Conte

Jean-Claude Van Damme, Harrison Page, Deborah Rennard, Lisa Pelikan, Ashley Johnson, Brian Thompson

Ay, Carmela! **

Spain/Italy   1990   103m   colour
Iberoamericana/Ellepi/Television Espanola (Andres Vicente Gomez)
V, V*, S

During the Spanish Civil War a trio of vaudeville performers entertaining the Republican troops are taken prisoner by the Nationalist army.

Very watchable but flawed political film with a bungled ending.

w Rafael Azcona, Carlos Saura   *play* José Sanchis Sinistierra   *d* Carlos Saura   *ph* José Luis Alcaine   *m* Alejandro Masso   *ad* Rafael Palmero   *ed* Pablo G. Del Amo

Carmen Maura, Andres Pajares, Gabino Diego, Maurizio de Razza, José Sancho, Mario de Candia

B

B.F.'s Daughter *
US 1948 106m bw
MGM (Edwin A. Knopf)
GB title: *Polly Fulton*

The wife of a penniless lecturer secures her husband's
rise to fame without his knowing that she is the
daughter of a millionaire.

Solid upper class romantic drama with a touch of
Peg's Paper.

w Luther Davis *novel* John P. Marquand
d Robert Z. Leonard *ph* Joseph Ruttenberg
m Bronislau Kaper

Barbara Stanwyck, Van Heflin, Charles Coburn,
Richard Hart, Keenan Wynn, Margaret Lindsay,
Spring Byington, Marshall Thompson

B.S. I Love You
US 1971 98m DeLuxe
Motion Pictures International/Fox (A. M. Broidy)

A director of TV commercials is beset by passionate
women.

Tiresomely trendy sex comedy with a visual style that
never lets up.

wd Steven Hilliard Stern *ph* David Dans
m Jimmy Dale, Mark Shekter

Peter Kastner, Joanna Cameron, Louise Sorel, Gary
Burghoff, Joanna Barnes, Richard B. Shull

† The initials in the title are short for bullshit.

Ba Wang Bie Ji: see *Farewell My Concubine*

Baara
Mali 1979 93m colour
Souleymanne Cissé Productions

A factory owner orders the killing of his manager for
calling a meeting of workers to improve their
conditions.

A slice of African industrial life, contrasting the lives
of the rich and corrupt with the poor and exploited.

wd Souleymanne Cissé *ph* Etienne Carton de
Grammont *m* Lamine Konté

Ball Moussa Keita, Baba Niaré, Bubakar Keita, Umu
Diarra, Ismalia Sarr, Umir Kone

Bab El Hadid: see *Cairo Station*

Babar: The Movie
Canada/France 1989 76m colour
Winstone/Nelvana/Ellipse (Patrick Loubert, Michael Hirsch,
Clive A. Smith)
V, V*, L

King Babar tells his children of his adventures as a
young elephant.

Lacklustre story, with simple animation.

w Peter Sauder, J. D. Smith, John de Klein, Raymond
Jaffelice, Alan Bunce *story* Peter Sauder, Patrick
Loubert, Michael Hirsch, based on characters created
by Jean de Brunhoff, Laurent de Brunhoff *d* Alan
Bunce *m* Milan Kymlicka *pd* Ted Bastien
m/ly Maribeth Solomon *ad* Clive Powsey, Carol
Bradbury *ed* Evan Landis

voices of Gordon Pinsent, Elizabeth Hanna, Lisa
Yamanaka, Marsha Moreau, Bobby Beckon, Amos
Crawley, Gavin Magrath, Sarah Polley

Babbitt *
US 1934 74m bw
Warner (Sam Bischoff)

Problems of a middle-aged man in a small American
town.

A minor attempt to film a major novel: quite tolerable
but lacking density.

w Mary McCall Jnr *novel* Sinclair Lewis
d William Keighley *ph* Arthur Todd

Guy Kibbee, Aline MacMahon, Claire Dodd, Maxine
Doyle, Minor Watson, Minna Gombell, Alan Hale,
Berton Churchill, Russell Hicks, Nan Grey

'Smooth, pleasant but trite.' – *Variety*

† Previously filmed in 1924 with Willard Louis.

The Babe
US 1992 115m DeLuxe
Universal (John Fusco)
V, V*, S

Biopic of the life of the baseball player Babe Ruth.

An undistinguished film with little appeal outside
America, although Goodman brings some
individuality to his portrayal of the flawed hero.

w John Fusco *d* Arthur Hiller *ph* Haskell Wexler
m Elmer Bernstein *pd* James D. Vance *ed* Robert
C. Jones

John Goodman, Kelly McGillis, Trini Alvarado, Bruce
Boxleitner, James Cromwell, Peter Donat, Bernard
Kates, Michael McGrady

'The thinly dramatised, overly episodic Babe Ruth
biopic resembles a telepic that has lost its way to the
big screen.' – *Variety*

† The film was released direct to video in Britain.

The Babe Ruth Story
US 1948 107m bw
Allied Artists (Roy del Ruth)
V*

The biography of a baseball player who was thought
of as something of a saint.

Dim, sentimental and faintly mystical biopic,
throughout which the star presents his familiar image.

w Bob Considine, George Callahan *d* Roy del Ruth
ph Philip Tannura, James Van Trees *m* Edward
Ward

William Bendix, Claire Trevor, Charles Bickford

Babes in Arms **
US 1939 96m bw
MGM (Arthur Freed)
V*, L

The teenage sons and daughters of retired
vaudevillians put on a big show.

Simple-minded backstage musical which marked the
first enormously successful teaming of its two young
stars.

w Jack McGowan, Kay Van Riper *Broadway
show* Rodgers and Hart *d/ch* Busby Berkeley
ph Ray June *m* Roger Edens, George Stoll
m/ly Rodgers and Hart and others

Judy Garland, Mickey Rooney, Charles Winninger,
Douglas Macphail, Leni Lynn, June Preisser

songs: 'Where or When'; 'Babes in Arms'; 'I Cried for
You'; 'God's Country'; 'Good Morning'; 'You Are My
Lucky Star'

'A topflight filmusical entertainment. It will click
mightily in the key deluxers, and roll up hefty profits
for exhibits in the subsequent runs and smaller
situations.' – *Variety*

AAN: Roger Edens, George Stoll; Mickey Rooney

Babes in Baghdad
US 1952 77m Exotic Color
UA (Danziger Brothers)

Harem ladies go on strike.

Embarrassing attempt at satire by stars who are over
the hill and not helped by abysmal technique.

w Felix E. Feist, Joe Anson *d* Edgar G. Ulmer

Paulette Goddard, Gypsy Rose Lee, Richard Ney,
John Boles, Sebastian Cabot

Babes in Toyland **
US 1934 77m bw
Hal Roach
V, V*, L
aka: *Wooden Soldiers; March of the Wooden Soldiers;
Laurel and Hardy in Toyland*

Santa Claus's incompetent assistants accidentally
make some giant wooden soldiers, which come in
useful when a villain tries to take over Toyland.

Comedy operetta in which the stars have pleasant but
not outstanding material; the style and decor are
however sufficient to preserve the film as an eccentric
minor classic.

w Nick Grinde, Frank Butler *original book* Glen
MacDonough *d* Gus Meins, Charles Rogers
ph Art Lloyd, Francis Corby *m* Victor Herbert

Stan Laurel, Oliver Hardy, Charlotte Henry, Henry
Brandon, Felix Knight, Florence Roberts, Johnny
Downs, Marie Wilson

'It is amusing enough to entertain older persons who
remember when they were young.' – *Variety*

Babes in Toyland
US 1961 105m Technicolor
Walt Disney
V*, L

A misfiring remake, all charm and no talent apart
from some excellent special effects at the climax.

w Ward Kimball, Joe Rinaldi, Lowell S. Hawley
d Jack Donohue *ph* Edward Colman *md* George
Bruns *sp* Eustace Lycett, Robert A. Mattey, Bill
Justice, Xavier Atencio, Yale Gracey

Ray Bolger (miscast as the villain), Tommy Sands,
Annette Funicello, Tommy Kirk, Gene Sheldon
(imitating Stan Laurel), Henry Calvin (imitating
Oliver Hardy), Ed Wynn, Kevin Corcoran

AAN: George Bruns

Babes on Broadway **
US 1941 118m bw
MGM (Arthur Freed)
V*, L

A sequel to *Babes in Arms,* in which the kids get to
Broadway and share some disillusion.

Inflated and less effective than the original, but with good numbers.

w Fred Finklehoffe, Elaine Ryan   *d/ch* Busby Berkeley   *ph* Lester White   *m/ly* Burton Lane, Ralph Freed

Judy Garland, Mickey Rooney, Virginia Weidler, Ray Macdonald, Richard Quine, Fay Bainter

'Enough energy and enthusiasm to make older people wish they were young, and young people glad that they are.' – *MFB*

† The Virginia Weidler role was originally intended for Shirley Temple, but TCF wouldn't loan her.

AAN: song 'How About You' (*m* Burton Lane, *ly* Ralph Freed)

Babette Goes to War
France   1959   103m   Eastmancolor   Cinemascope
Iéna (Raoul Lévy)
original title: *Babette S'en Va-t-en Guerre*

In 1940 a French refugee girl is sent by British intelligence from London to Paris as bait in a plot to kidnap a German general and delay the Nazi invasion of England.

Witless war farce which goes on for ever.

w Raoul Lévy, Gérard Oury   *d* Christian-Jaque   *ph* Armand Thirard   *m* Gilbert Bécaud

Brigitte Bardot, Jacques Charrier, Hannes Messemer, Yves Vincent, Ronald Howard, Francis Blanche

'A kind of *Private's Progress* without comedians.' – *MFB*

Babette S'en Va-t-en Guerre: see *Babette Goes to War*

Babette's Feast **
Denmark   1987   103m   Eastmancolor
Panorama/Nordisk/Danish Film Institute
V, V*, L, S

A French refugee in 19th-century Norway wins 10,000 francs in a lottery and spends it all on preparing a sumptuous banquet for her Lutheran employers and their friends.

Ironic and elegant fable juxtaposing bacchanalian extravagance with narrow piety.

wd Gabriel Axel   *story* Isak Dinesen   *ph* Henning Kristiansen   *m* Per Norgard   *ad* Sven Wichman

Stéphane Audran, Jean-Philippe Lafont, Jarl Kulle, Bibi Andersson, Bodil Kjer, Birgitte Federspiel

AA: best foreign-language film

Baboona
US   1935   78m   bw
Fox

Africa photographed from the air as well as the jungle.

One of the better documentary features of the mid-thirties.

d/ph Martin Johnson

The Baby and the Battleship
GB   1956   96m   Eastmancolor
British Lion/Jay Lewis
V*

Two sailors hide an Italian baby on their battleship.

Simple-minded lower decks farce, with lots of confusion and cooing over the baby, but not much to laugh at.

w Jay Lewis, Gilbert Hackforth-Jones, Bryan Forbes   *d* Jay Lewis   *ph* Harry Waxman   *m* James Stevens

John Mills, Richard Attenborough, André Morell, Bryan Forbes, Michael Howard, Lisa Gastoni, Ernest Clark, Lionel Jeffries, Thorley Walters

'In this British film the predicament is made splendidly funny.' – *Dilys Powell*

Baby Be Good: see *Brother Rat and a Baby*

Baby Blue Marine *
US   1976   90m   Metrocolor
Columbia/Spelling-Goldberg (Robert LaVigne)

In 1943, a failed marine returns home and pretends to be a war hero.

Careful small-town drama with good period feel but not much dramatic punch: *Hail the Conquering Hero* did it better.

w Stanford Whitmore   *d* John Hancock   *ph* Laszlo Kovacs   *m* Fred Karlin

Jan-Michael Vincent, Glynnis O'Connor, Katherine Helmond, Dana Elcar, Bert Remsen, Richard Gere

'A rickety structure of strange events.' – *New York Post*

Baby Boom
US   1987   110m   colour
UIP/MGM
V, V*, L

The life of a busy executive changes when she acquires a small baby.

Moderately enjoyable comedy, though it lacks any particular distinction.

w Nancy Meyers, Charles Shyer   *d* Charles Shyer   *ph* William A. Fraker   *m* Bill Conti   *pd* Jeffrey Howard   *ed* Lynzee Klingman

Diane Keaton, Harold Ramis, Sam Wanamaker, Sam Shepard, James Spader, Pat Hingle, Britt Leach

'If there were justice in the world of entertainment, *Baby Boom* would be unwatchable. But Diane Keaton gives a smashing, glamorous performance that rides over many of the inanities.' – *Pauline Kael, New Yorker*

'19 years old and married ... but not really!'
Baby Doll **
US   1956   116m   bw
Warner/Elia Kazan
V, V*

In the deep South, the child wife of a broken-down cotton miller is seduced by her husband's revenge-seeking rival.

An incisive, cleverly-worked-out study of moral and physical decay; whether it was worth doing is another question, for it's a film difficult to remember with affection.

w Tennessee Williams   *play* 27 Wagonloads of Cotton by Tennessee Williams   *d* Elia Kazan   *ph* Boris Kaufman   *m* Kenyon Hopkins   *ad* Richard Sylbert

Karl Malden, Eli Wallach, Carroll Baker, Mildred Dunnock, Lonny Chapman

'Just possibly the dirtiest American-made motion picture that has ever been legally exhibited, with Priapean detail that might well have embarrassed Boccaccio.' – *Time*

'He views southern pretensions with sardonic humor, and builds an essentially minor story into a magnificently humorous study of the grotesque and the decadent.' – *Hollis Alpert*

'A droll and engrossing carnal comedy.' – *Pauline Kael, 1968*

'A film in which everything works: narration, casting, tempo, rhythm, dramatic tension.' – *Basil Wright, 1972*

† Another publicity tag read: 'Condemned by Cardinal Spellman!'

AAN: script; Boris Kaufman; Carroll Baker; Mildred Dunnock

'She climbed the ladder of success – wrong by wrong!'
Baby Face **
US   1933   70m   bw
Warner (Ray Griffith)
V*, L

Amorous adventures of an ambitious working girl.

Sharp melodrama very typical of its time, with fast pace and good performances.

w Gene Markey, Kathryn Scola, Mark Canfield (Darryl F. Zanuck)   *d* Alfred E. Green   *ph* James Van Trees

Barbara Stanwyck, George Brent, Donald Cook, Margaret Lindsay, Arthur Hohl, John Wayne, Henry Kolker, Douglass Dumbrille

'Blue and nothing else. It possesses no merit for general or popular appeal, is liable to offend the family trade and can't count on any juve attendance.'

'. . . This is reputed to be a remake on the first print, which was considered too hot. Anything hotter than this for public showing would call for an asbestos audience blanket.' – *Variety*

Baby Face Harrington
US   1935   63m   bw
MGM

A timid man is mistakenly identified as a public enemy, and chased by both cops and rival gangsters.

Thin but appealing comedy.

w Nunnally Johnson, Edwin Knopf   *d* Raoul Walsh

Charles Butterworth, Una Merkel, Nat Pendleton, Eugene Pallette, Donald Meek

'Weak satire, grievously overacted.' – *Variety*

Baby Face Morgan
US   1942   60m   bw
Jack Schwartz/PRC

The son of a racketeer is made a figurehead by his father's old mob.

Curious comedy of non-violent crime; also non-entertaining.

w Edward Dein, Jack Rubin, Oscar Brodney   *d* Arthur Dreifuss

Richard Cromwell, Mary Carlisle, Robert Armstrong, Chick Chandler, Warren Hymer, Vince Barnett

'Don't see it unless your nerves are bullet proof!'
Baby Face Nelson *
US   1957   85m   bw
UA/Fryman-ZS (Al Zimbalist)

Fragmentary account of the life of a thirties public enemy, with the star over the top and the technicians doing what they can on an obviously low budget.

w Irving Shulman, Daniel Mainwaring   *d* Don Siegel   *ph* Hal Mohr   *m* Van Alexander

Mickey Rooney, Cedric Hardwicke, Carolyn Jones, Chris Dark, Ted de Corsia, Leo Gordon, John Hoyt, Anthony Caruso, Jack Elam

Baby It's You *
US   1982   104m   colour
Paramount/Double Play (Griffin Dunne, Andy Robinson)
V*, L

In the sixties, a well-heeled high school girl is wooed and won by a greasy street sheik with ambitions.

Curious sweet-and-sour romance with a determination to be modern; agreeable in parts but basically empty, and rather undermined by a torrent of rock music on the sound track.

wd John Sayles   *story* Amy Robinson   *ph* Michael Ballhaus   *md* Joel Dorn   *pd* Jeffrey Townsend

Rosanna Arquette, Vincent Spano, Joanna Merlin, Jack Davidson, Nick Ferrari, Leora Dana

Baby Love

GB 1968 93m Eastmancolor
Avco/Avton/Michael Klinger (Guido Coen)

An orphaned nymphet causes trouble among the men in her foster home.

Ludicrous sexploiter which embarrasses a good cast and descends into bathos.

w Alastair Reid, Guido Coen, Michael Klinger
novel Tina Chad Christian d Alastair Reid
ph Desmond Dickinson m Max Harris

Linda Hayden, Ann Lynn, Keith Barron, Derek Lamden, Diana Dors, Patience Collier, Dick Emery

The Baby Maker

US 1970 109m Technicolor
Robert Wise/National General (Richard Goldstone)
V*

A freewheeling girl agrees to have a baby for a childless couple.

Stretched-out fable for our time which refrains from pointing a moral and is generally tastefully done but nevertheless outstays its welcome.

wd James Bridges m Fred Karlin, Tylwyth Kymry

Barbara Hershey, Collin Wilcox-Horne, Sam Groom, Scott Glenn, Jeannie Berlin

AAN: Fred Karlin, Tylwyth Kymry

The Baby of Macon **

GB/Netherlands/France/Germany 1993 122m
colour
Allarts/UGC/La Sept/Cine Electra II/Channel 4/Filmstiftung/
Canal+ (Kees Kasander)
V (W), S

In the 1650s, encouraged by a naïve and sadistic prince, a play about a miraculous child, exploited by his sister and the church, becomes all too real, and rape, death and dismemberment follow.

A puzzling and audacious work, visually sumptuous and frequently confusing in its mix of artifice and actuality, but original and intriguing as it explores the themes of art and its influence, the translation of experience into consumerism, alienation and voyeurism. Audiences are likely to love or hate the film, though at Cannes and elsewhere it mostly met with a hostile reception.

wd Peter Greenaway ph Sacha Vierny m Henry Purcell, Matthew Locke and others pd Jan Roelfs, Ben van Os ed Chris Wyatt

Julia Ormond, Ralph Fiennes, Philip Stone, Jonathan Lacey, Don Henderson, Celia Gregory, Jeff Nuttall, Kathryn Hunter, Gabrielle Reidy, Jessica Stevenson, Frank Egerton

'An uneven film which, for all its formal excellence, is a major let-down.' – Geoffrey Macnab, Sight and Sound

'All fluff and no filling.' – Variety

Baby – Secret of the Lost Legend

US 1985 95m Technicolor Supertechnirama
Touchstone (Jonathan T. Taplin)
V*, L

Palaeontologists in the African jungle discover a family of living dinosaurs.

Technically and dramatically less than effective, this latter-day King Kong demonstrates yet again the Disney company's difficulties in hitting the right note for the modern family audience.

w Clifford and Ellen Green d B. W. L. Norton
ph John Alcott m Jerry Goldsmith sp Philip Meador, Peter Anderson

William Katt, Sean Young, Patrick McGoohan, Julian Fellowes

Baby Take a Bow *

US 1934 76m bw
Fox
V*

An ex-convict is accused of theft, but his small daughter unmasks the real culprit.

Shirley Temple's first star vehicle was a solid enough commercial property to take her right to the top.

w Philip Klein, E. E. Paramore Jnr d Harry Lachman

Shirley Temple, James Dunn, Claire Trevor, Alan Dinehart

'A pretty obvious and silly melodrama, but it has Shirley Temple, so it can go down in the books as a neat and sure b.o. hit.' – Variety

'The more he gets into trouble, the more he gets under her skin!'

Baby, the Rain Must Fall

US 1964 100m bw
Columbia/Pakula-Mulligan (Alan Pakula)
V*, L

A parolee rejoins his wife and daughter in a Southern town, but his outbursts of violence separate them again.

Hard work by all concerned scarcely produces absorbing interest in this filmed play of the Tennessee Williams school.

w Horton Foote play The Travelling Lady by Horton Foote d Robert Mulligan ph Ernest Laszlo
m Elmer Bernstein

Steve McQueen, Lee Remick, Don Murray, Paul Fix, Josephine Hutchinson, Ruth White, Charles Watts

The Baby Vanishes: see Broadway Limited

The Bacchantes

Italy/France 1961 96m colour
Cino Del Duca/Vic Film/Lyre Film (Gian Paolo Bigazzi)
original title: Le Baccanti

Dionysius takes his revenge after King Pentheus bans his worship in his home city of Thebes.

Enjoyably silly mythological romp, with bacchantes looking as if they had stepped out of the pages of pin-up magazines.

w Giorgio Stegani, Giorgio Ferroni play The Bacchae by Euripides d Giorgio Ferroni ph Pier Ludovico Pavoni m Mario Nascimbene ch Herbert Ross
ad Arrigo Equini

Taina Elg, Pierre Brice, Alberto Lupo, Alessandro Panaro, Raf Mattioli, Akym Tamiroff

The Bachelor and the Bobbysoxer ***

US 1947 95m bw
RKO (Dore Schary)
V*, L
GB title: Bachelor Knight

A lady judge allows her impressionable young sister to get over her crush on an errant playboy by forcing them together.

Simple but unexpectedly delightful vehicle for top comedy talents, entirely pleasant and with several memorable moments.

w Sidney Sheldon d Irving Reis ph Robert de Grasse, Nicholas Musuraca m Leigh Harline

Cary Grant, Myrna Loy, Shirley Temple, Ray Collins, Rudy Vallee, Harry Davenport, Johnny Sands, Don Beddoe

'Sure-fire stuff guaranteed to do no conceivable harm . . . the audience laughed so loud I missed some of the lines.' – Shirley O'Hara, New Republic

AA: Sidney Sheldon

Bachelor Apartment

US 1931 77m bw
RKO (William Le Baron)
V*

A virtuous working girl in New York falls for a rich woman-chasing bachelor.

Mildly agreeable early talking romantic comedy.

w J. Walter Ruben, John Howard Lawson d Lowell Sherman ph Leo Tover

Irene Dunne, Lowell Sherman, Mae Murray, Norman Kerry, Claudia Dell, Ivan Lebedeff

'It oversteps the reasonable limits of sophisticated art . . . thus the film is doubtful for small towns.' – Variety

Bachelor Bait: see Adventure in Baltimore

Bachelor Daddy *

US 1941 61m bw
Universal

Three bachelors find themselves in charge of a baby.

Best of the comedies starring Baby Sandy.

w Robert Lees, Fred Rinaldo d Harold Young

Baby Sandy, Edward Everett Horton, Franklin Pangborn, Raymond Walburn, Donald Woods, Evelyn Ankers

Bachelor Father

US 1931 90m bw
MGM (B. P. Fineman)

A much-married elderly man visits his grown children.

Unremarkable star comedy of its day.

w Laurence E. Johnson play Edward Childs Carpenter d Robert Z. Leonard ph Oliver T. Marsh

Marion Davies, C. Aubrey Smith, Ray Milland, Ralph Forbes, Halliwell Hobbes, Guinn Williams, David Torrence

'Where they have used the old hoke they have masked it with commendable skill.' – Variety

Bachelor Flat

US 1961 91m DeLuxe Cinemascope
TCF/Jack Cummings

An English professor at an American university is unrelentingly pursued by girls.

Flat one-joke comedy which simply hasn't the style to sustain itself.

w Frank Tashlin, Budd Grossman play Budd Grossman d Frank Tashlin ph Daniel L. Fapp
m Johnny Williams

Terry-Thomas, Richard Beymer, Tuesday Weld, Celeste Holm, Francesca Bellini, Howard McNear

Bachelor Girl Apartment: see Any Wednesday

Bachelor Girls: see The Bachelor's Daughter

Bachelor in Paradise

US 1961 109m Metrocolor Cinemascope
MGM/Ted Richmond

A famous writer of advice to the lovelorn settles incognito in a well-heeled Californian community to observe its social habits.

Mildly amusing satire is too frequently interrupted by unsuitable romantic interludes in this rather ill-considered star comedy.

w Valentine Davies, Hal Kanter d Jack Arnold
ph Joseph Ruttenberg m Henry Mancini

Bob Hope, Lana Turner, Janis Paige, Don Porter, Paula Prentiss, Jim Hutton, Virginia Grey, Reta Shaw, John McGiver, Agnes Moorehead

AAN: title song (m Henry Mancini, ly Mack David)

Bachelor Knight: see *The Bachelor and the Bobbysoxer*

'Just ten tiny fingers and ten tiny toes ... Trouble? Scandal? Gosh, nobody knows!'
Bachelor Mother ***
US   1939   82m   bw
RKO (B. G. de Sylva)
V*, L

A shopgirl finds an abandoned baby and is thought to be its mother; the department store owner's son is then thought to be the father.

Blithely-scripted comedy which stands the test of time and provided several excellent roles.

w Norman Krasna   *story* Felix Jackson   *d* Garson Kanin   *ph* Robert de Grasse   *m* Roy Webb

Ginger Rogers, David Niven, Charles Coburn, Frank Albertson, E. E. Clive, Ernest Truex

'Carries some rather spicy lines aimed at the adult trade, but broad enough in implication to catch the fancy of general audiences . . . a surprise laugh hit that will do biz generally and overcome hot weather box office lethargy.' – *Variety*

'An excellent comedy, beautifully done.' – *Richard Mallett, Punch*

'This is the way farce should be handled, with just enough conviction to season its extravagances.' – *New York Times*

† Remade as *Bundle of Joy* (qv).

AAN: Felix Jackson

Bachelor of Hearts
GB   1958   94m   Technicolor
Rank/Independent Artists (Vivian A. Cox)

Adventures of a German student at Cambridge University.

Sometimes agreeable, sometimes annoying, especially when romance gets in the way of the possibilities for fun.

w Leslie Bricusse, Frederic Raphael   *d* Wolf Rilla   *ph* Geoffrey Unsworth   *m* Hubert Clifford

Hardy Kruger, Sylvia Syms, Ronald Lewis, Eric Barker, Newton Blick

The Bachelor Party ***
US   1957   93m   bw
UA/Norma (Harold Hecht)

New York book-keepers throw a wedding eve party for one of their fellows, but drink only brings to the fore their own private despairs.

Though the last half-hour lets it down, most of this is a brilliantly observed social study of New York life at its less attractive, and the acting matches the incisiveness of the script.

w Paddy Chayevsky   *TV play* Paddy Chayevsky   *d* Delbert Mann   *ph* Joseph LaShelle   *m* Alex North

Don Murray, E. G. Marshall, Jack Warden, Philip Abbott, Larry Blyden, Patricia Smith, Carolyn Jones

AAN: Carolyn Jones

Bachelor Party
US   1984   105m   DeLuxe
Fox/Aspect Ratio/Twin Continental (Ron Moler, Bob Israel)
V*, L

A bachelor party is beset by a series of disasters.

Crude, exploitative farce full of physical mess and tending to get most of its humour from the destruction of order and some teetering on the brink of pornography.

w Neal Israel, Pat Proft   *story* Bob Israel   *d* Neal Israel   *ph* Hal Trussell   *m* Robert Folk   *ad* Kevin Conlin, Martin Price   *ed* Tom Walls

Tom Hanks, Tawny Kitaen, Adrian Zmed, George Grizzard, Barbara Stuart, Robert Prescott

Bachelor's Affairs
US   1931   64m   bw
Fox

A middle-aged bachelor thinks he needs a young wife, but can't keep up with the one he gets.

Strained star comedy of no surviving interest.

w Barry Conners, Philip Klein   *play* Precious by James Forbes   *d* Alfred Werker

Adolphe Menjou, Minna Gombell, Arthur Pierson, Joan Marsh, Alan Dinehart

'Neither farce nor a social problem development, it misses throughout.' – *Variety*

The Bachelor's Daughters *
US   1946   90m   bw
UA/Andrew Stone
GB title: *Bachelor Girls*

Four shopgirls and a floorwalker rent a Long Island house and pass themselves off as a wealthy family in order to lure suitable husbands for the girls.

Mildly amusing comedy with good performances.

wd Andrew Stone   *ph* Theodor Sparkuhl   *m* Heinz Roemheld

Adolphe Menjou, Gail Russell, Claire Trevor, Billie Burke

Back Door to Heaven
US   1939   81m   bw
Odessco/Paramount (William K. Howard)
V*

A boy born on the wrong side of the tracks is prevented from going straight, and, having escaped execution for murder, is bumped off by gangsters.

Heavy-going indictment of society; too glum to work, it seems to have finished off the career of its talented director.

w John Bright, Robert Tasker   *story* William K. Howard   *d* William K. Howard

Wallace Ford, Aline MacMahon, Stuart Erwin, Jimmy Lydon, William Harrigan, Bert Frohman

'Artistic drama, too heavy and slow-tempoed for general b.o.' – *Variety*

† William K. Howard also appears as the prosecuting attorney.

Back from Eternity
US   1956   97m   bw
RKO (John Farrow)
V*, L

An airliner is forced to crashland in headhunter country, and when repairs are made only five of the eight survivors can be saved.

Remake by the same producer-director of his own 1939 'B', *Five Came Back*, this time to considerably less effect despite superior production.

w Jonathan Latimer   *d* John Farrow   *ph* William Mellor   *m* Franz Waxman

Robert Ryan, Anita Ekberg, Rod Steiger, Phyllis Kirk, Gene Barry, Keith Andes, Beulah Bondi, Fred Clark, Cameron Prud'homme, Jesse White

Back from the Dead
US   1957   78m   bw   Regalscope
TCF/Regal (Robert Stabler)

A girl on honeymoon becomes possessed by the spirit of her husband's first wife.

Blithe Spirit played for real but getting just as many laughs, unintentional this time.

w Catherine Turney   *novel The Other One* by Catherine Turney   *d* Charles Marquis Warren   *ph* Ernest Haller   *m* Raoul Kraushaar

Peggie Castle, Arthur Franz, Marsha Hunt, Don Haggerty

Back in Circulation
US   1937   80m   bw
Warner

Girl news reporter wins her editor's attention by solving a murder.

Sub-*Front Page* melodrama, of no intrinsic interest.

w Warren Duff   *d* Ray Enright

Pat O'Brien, Joan Blondell, Margaret Lindsay

'The newspaper boys, the goofy photographers and the hysterical city are on the murder trail, relentlessly pursuing the accused, telling coroners, district attorneys and defence counsel how to conduct their business.' – *Variety*

Back Roads
US   1981   95m   DeLuxe   Panavision
CBS Theatrical/Meta Films (Ronald Shedlo)
V*

A hooker and an ex-boxer hitch-hike to California.

Tiresomely with-it update of *It Happened One Night*; the humour and romance of the original are preferable to this dollop of bad language, boring people and bed-hopping.

w Gary Devore   *d* Martin Ritt   *ph* John A. Alonzo   *m* Henry Mancini

Sally Field, Tommy Lee Jones, David Keith, Miriam Colon, Michael Gazzo

'Decidedly sticky, and instantly forgettable.' – *Guardian*

Back Room Boy *
GB   1942   82m   bw
GFD/Gainsborough (Edward Black)
V

A timid meteorologist is sent to an Orkney lighthouse and unmasks a bunch of spies.

Fairly spirited star comedy of interest as a shameless rip-off of *The Ghost Train* and *Oh Mr Porter*, whose plotlines are milked but not improved: note also that Askey took over Will Hay's discarded stooges.

w Val Guest, Marriott Edgar   *d* Herbert Mason   *ph* Jack Cox

Arthur Askey, Moore Marriott, Graham Moffatt, Googie Withers, Vera Frances, John Salew

Back Street *
US   1932   93m   bw
Universal (Carl Laemmle Jnr)

A married man has a sweet-tempered mistress who effaces herself for twenty years.

Popular version of a sudsy bestselling novel.

w Gladys Lehman, Lynn Starling   *novel* Fannie Hurst   *d* John M. Stahl   *ph* Karl Freund

Irene Dunne, John Boles, June Clyde, George Meeker, ZaSu Pitts, Doris Lloyd

'Swell romance, a little tear-jerking, and a woman's picture – which means a money production.' – *Variety*

Back Street *
US   1941   89m   bw
Universal (Bruce Manning)

Competent remake.

w Bruce Manning, Felix Jackson   *d* Robert Stevenson   *ph* William Daniels   *m* Frank Skinner

Margaret Sullavan, Charles Boyer, Richard Carlson, Frank McHugh, Tim Holt, Frank Jenks, Esther Dale, Samuel S. Hinds

AAN: Frank Skinner

Back Street *

US   1961   107m   Technicolor
U-I/Ross Hunter/Carrollton
V*

Glossy remake typical of its producer: unfortunately it fails to work because the heroine suffers too luxuriously.

w Eleanore Griffin, William Ludwig   d David Miller   ph Stanley Cortez   m Frank Skinner

Susan Hayward, John Gavin, Vera Miles, Virginia Grey, Charles Drake, Reginald Gardiner

'Though there is a lot to be said for this new version's thesis that one can be just as lonely in a series of apartments and lovers' nests apparently never less than a hundred yards wide, the illusion is quickly shattered the moment one gets the impression that the lovers prefer to keep much the same distance during their moments of passion.' – Peter John Dyer

'Ross Hunter has updated this old faithful and given it a contemporary lack of significance.' – Hollis Alpert, Saturday Review

'The bathrooms look like the lobby of the Beverly Hilton . . . the fallen woman falls, not into the pit of shame, but into the lap of luxury.' – Time

Back to Bataan

US   1945   97m   bw
RKO (Robert Fellows)
V, V*, L

When Bataan is cut off, a Marine colonel organizes guerrilla resistance.

Modestly made and rather dislikeable flagwaver.

w Ben Barzman, Richard Landau   d Edward Dmytryk   ph Nicholas Musuraca   m Roy Webb

John Wayne, Anthony Quinn, Beulah Bondi, Fely Franquelli, Leonard Strong, Richard Loo, Philip Ahn, Lawrence Tierney, Paul Fix

Back to God's Country

US   1953   78m   Technicolor
U-I (Howard Christie)

A sea captain battles the Canadian winter and a villain who wants his wife and his cargo of furs.

Old-fashioned adventure story, moderately well presented.

w Tom Reed   novel James Oliver Curwood   d Joseph Pevney   ph Maury Gertsman   m Frank Skinner

Rock Hudson, Steve Cochran, Marcia Henderson, Hugh O'Brian

Back to School

US   1986   94m   DeLuxe
Orion/Paper Clip (Chuck Russell)
V, V*, L

A millionaire enrols in university as a freshman so as to teach his son the ropes.

Crass and ineptly made comedy vehicle for a star with distinct limitations.

w Steven Kampmann, Harold Ramis, Will Porter, Peter Torokvei   d Alan Metter   ph Thomas E. Ackerman   m Danny Elfman   pd David Snyder   ed David Rawlins

Rodney Dangerfield, Sally Kellerman, Burt Young, Keith Gordon, Paxton Whitehead

Back to the Beach

US   1987   92m   colour
Paramount (Frank Mancuso Jnr)
V*, L

Former teenage surfers return to the beach in middle age and help kids with problems.

Not so bad as it sounds, but for cultists only.

w Peter Krikes, Steve Meerson, Christopher Thompson, Lyndall Hobbs   ph Bruce Surtees   m Steve Dorff   pd Michael Helmy   ed David Finfer

Annette Funicello, Frankie Avalon, Connie Stevens, Lori Loughlin, Tommy Hinkley. Plus Don Adams, Bob Denver, Jerry Mathers, Pee-wee Herman

'A wonderfully campy trip down pop culture's trash-filled memory lane.' – Daily Variety

Back to the Future ***

US   1985   116m   Technicolor
Universal/Steven Spielberg (Bob Gale, Neil Canton)
V (W), V*, L, S

With the help of a not-so-crazy scientist, a teenager goes back thirty years to make a man out of his dimwit father.

Lighthearted Twilight Zone fantasy which certainly pleased the international multitudes.

w Robert Zemeckis, Bob Gale   d Robert Zemeckis   ph Dean Cundey   m Alan Silvestri   pd Lawrence G. Paull   ed Arthur Schmidt, Harry Keramidas

Michael J. Fox, Christopher Lloyd, Crispin Glover, Lea Thompson, Claudia Wells

'Accelerates with wit, ideas, and infectious, wide-eyed wonder.' – Variety

AAN: original screenplay

Back to the Future II

US   1989   108m   DeLuxe
UIP/Amblin Entertainment (Bob Gale, Neil Canton)
V, V (W), V*, L, S

A scientist and his young friend discover, on their return from a trip to the future, that the present has been altered for the worse.

Extraordinarily raucous, confusingly plotted, poorly performed (rarely have actors aged so unconvincingly) sequel that amounts to little more than a trailer for the third part of the series.

w Bob Gale   story Bob Gale, Robert Zemeckis   d Robert Zemeckis   ph Dean Cundey   m Alan Silvestri   pd Rick Carter   ad Margie Stone McShirley   ed Arthur Schimdt, Harry Keramidas

Michael J. Fox, Christopher Lloyd, Lea Thompson, Thomas F. Wilson, Harry Waters Jnr, Charles Fleischer, Joe Flaherty

'They've saved the best trip to the last. But this time they may have gone too far.'

Back to the Future III **

US   1990   118m   DeLuxe
UIP/Amblin (Bob Gale, Neil Canton)
V, V (W), V*, L, S

A teenager travels back in time to rescue his friend, a scientist stranded in the Wild West.

Good-natured fun at the expense of classic Western movies.

w Bob Gale   story Robert Zemeckis   d Robert Zemeckis   ph Dean Cundey   m Alan Silvestri   pd Rick Carter   ed Arthur Schmidt, Harry Keramidas

Michael J. Fox, Christopher Lloyd, Mary Steenburgen, Thomas F. Wilson, Lea Thompson, Elisabeth Shue, Matt Clark, Richard Dysart, James Tolkan

'Has a joyousness seldom seen on the screen these days, a sense of exuberance in the breaking of boundaries of time, space and genre.' – Variety

Backbeat *

GB   1993   100m   Eastmancolor   Panavision
Rank/Polygram/Scala/Channel 4 Films/Royal (Finola Dwyer, Stephen Woolley)
S

Stuart Sutcliffe, a promising young painter, plays with the Beatles in Hamburg, where he falls for a German photographer and decides his future is with art not rock.

A deft and enjoyable movie about the birth of the 60s and the Beatles, concentrating on the tragically short life of Sutcliffe, who died of a brain tumour in 1962.

w Ian Softley, Michael Thomas, Stephen Ward   d Ian Softley   ph Ian Wilson   m Don Was   pd Joseph Bennett   ed Martin Walsh

Sheryl Lee, Stephen Dorff, Ian Hart, Gary Bakewell, Chris O'Neill, Scot Williams, Kai Wiesinger, Jennifer Ehle

'Shrewd rather than clever, lively rather than memorable and possessed of just enough wit and heart to convince that it is essentially more than a nostalgia-stirring package.' – Derek Malcolm, Guardian

'Has quite a bit going for it in the way of cultural and musical history but lacks a crucial, heightened artistic quality and point of view that would have given it real distinction.' – Variety

Backdraft *

US   1991   136m   DeLuxe
UIP/Trilogy/Imagine (Richard B. Lewis, Pen Densham, John Watson)
V, V*, L, S

Two brothers track down an arsonist and expose corruption in the fire department.

Overheated, muddled melodrama saved from tedium by its fiery special effects.

w Gregory Widen   d Ron Howard   ph Mikael Salomon   m Hans Zimmer   pd Albert Brenner   sp Visual effects: Industrial Light and Magic. Pyrotechnics: Allen Hall   ed Daniel Hanley, Michael Hill

Kurt Russell, William Baldwin, Robert de Niro, Donald Sutherland, Jennifer Jason Leigh, Scott Glenn, Rebecca DeMornay, Jason Gedrick, J. T. Walsh

'Visually, pic is often exhilarating, but it's shapeless and dragged down by corny, melodramatic characters and situations.' —Variety

Backfire

US   1949   90m   bw
Warner (Anthony Veiller)

A war veteran solves the murder of which his best friend is accused.

Confusing murder mystery of a very familiar kind, adequately made but with no particular style. Flashbacks don't help.

w Larry Marcus, Ivan Goff, Ben Roberts   d Vincent Sherman   ph Carl Guthrie   m Ray Heindorf   ad Anton Grot

Gordon Macrae, Virginia Mayo, Edmond O'Brien, Dane Clark, Viveca Lindfors, Ed Begley

Backfire

US   1987   91m   colour
Virgin/ITC (Danton Rissner)
V*, L

A Vietnam veteran with nightmares seems to be in the middle of a murder plot.

Too-murky thriller which takes an awful long time to come clean.

w Larry Brand, Rebecca Reynolds   d Gilbert Cates   ph Tak Fujimoto   m David Shire   pd Daniel Lomino   ed Melvin Shapiro

Karen Allen, Keith Carradine, Jeff Fahey, Bernie Casey, Dean Paul Martin

Background *

GB   1953   82m   bw
Group Three (Herbert Mason)
US title: Edge of Divorce

Two people decide on divorce, but thoughts of their children bring them together again.

Low-budget, stiff-upper-lip marriage guidance tract, well acted but more well-intentioned than memorable.

w Warren Chetham Strode, Don Sharp *play* Warren Chetham Strode *d* Daniel Birt *ph* Arthur Grant

Valerie Hobson, Philip Friend, Norman Wooland, Janette Scott, Mandy Miller, Jeremy Spenser, Richard Wattis

Background to Danger
US 1943 80m bw
Warner (Jerry Wald)
V*

An adventurer thwarts Nazi intrigue in Turkey.

Flat, studio-bound wartime potboiler with a good cast all at sea.

w W. R. Burnett *novel Uncommon Danger* by Eric Ambler *d* Raoul Walsh *ph* Tony Gaudio *m* Frederick Hollander

George Raft, Brenda Marshall, Sydney Greenstreet, Peter Lorre, Osa Massen, Turhan Bey, Kurt Katch

'You could use this film for one kind of measurement of the unconquerable difference between a good job by Hitchcock and a good job of the Hitchcock type.' – *James Agee*

'There's nothing for the cast to do other than concentrate on the display of melodramatics.' – *Variety*

Backlash *
US 1956 84m Technicolor
U-I (Aaron Rosenberg)

A gunman seeks the father he has never met, who turns out to be a villain who sold his partners for gold to attacking Indians.

Rather unusual suspense Western, very watchable for its mystery elements.

w Borden Chase *d* John Sturges *ph* Irving Glassberg *m* Herman Stein

Richard Widmark, Donna Reed, John McIntire, William Campbell, Barton MacLane

Backlash
Australia 1986 110m colour
Mermaid Beach/Multifilms (Bill Bennett)
V*

An antagonistic pair of cops – one male, one female – are stranded in the outback with an Aborigine woman accused of the castration and murder of her employer.

Glum melodrama: its heart may be in the right place, but its mind is elsewhere.

wd Bill Bennett *ph* Tony Wilson *m* Michael Atkinson, Michael Spicer *ed* Denise Hunter

David Argue, Gia Carides, Lydia Miller, Brian Syron

The Bacon Grabbers *
US 1929 20m bw silent
Hal Roach

Bailiffs fail to recover a radio on which the instalments are overdue.

Modestly pleasing star comedy on the lines of *Big Business*.

w Leo McCarey, H. M. Walker *d* Lewis R. Foster

Laurel and Hardy, Edgar Kennedy, Jean Harlow, Charlie Hall

'The story of a blonde who wanted to go places, and a brute who got her there – the hard way.'
The Bad and the Beautiful **
US 1952 118m bw
MGM (John Houseman)
V, V*, L, S

A director, a star, a screenwriter and an executive recall their experiences at the hands of a go-getting Hollywood producer.

Very much a Hollywood 'in' picture, this rather obvious flashback melodrama offers good acting chances and a couple of intriguing situations; never quite finding the style it seeks, it offers good bitchy entertainment along the way, and there are references back to it in *Two Weeks in Another Town*, made ten years later.

w Charles Schnee *d* Vincente Minnelli *ph* Robert Surtees *m* David Raksin *ad* Cedric Gibbons, Edward Carfagno

Kirk Douglas (Jonathan Shields), Lana Turner (Georgia Lorrison), Walter Pidgeon (Harry Pebbel), Dick Powell (James Lee Bartlow), Barry Sullivan (Fred Amiel), Gloria Grahame (Rosemary Bartlow), Gilbert Roland (Victor Ribera), Leo G. Carroll (Henry Whitfield), Vanessa Brown (Kay Amiel), Paul Stewart (Syd Murphy)

'For all the cleverness of the apparatus, it lacks a central point of focus.' – *Penelope Houston*

'Clever, sharply observed little scenes reflect the Hollywood surface: the egotistic babble at a party, the affectations of European directors, the sneak preview, the trying on of suits for catmen in a B picture.' – *MFB*

'It is a crowded and colourful picture, but it is choppy, episodic and vague. There does not emerge a clear picture of exactly how movies are made.' – *Bosley Crowther*

AA: Charles Schnee; Robert Surtees; art direction; Gloria Grahame

AAN: Kirk Douglas

Bad Bascomb *
US 1946 110m bw
MGM (Orville Dull)

A sentimental bank robber becomes the hero of a group of travelling Mormons.

Pleasing though overlong star Western, with good production values.

w William Lipman, Grant Garrett *d* S. Sylvan Simon *ph* Charles Schoenbaum *m* David Snell

Wallace Beery, Margaret O'Brien, Marjorie Main, J. Carrol Naish, Russell Simpson, Sara Haden

'The Mother, The Planner And The Gobshite.'
Bad Behaviour
GB 1993 104m colour
First Independent/Channel 4/British Screen/Parallax (Sarah Curtis)
V, V*, L

An Irish couple living in North London with their two young sons muddle through life, not helped by the attentions of a neighbour, an unscrupulous landlord and his slapdash friends in the building trade.

A small-scale improvised comedy that concerns itself with the details of everyday existence to the detriment of drama; it may be realistic, but it is often uninteresting, despite the best efforts of its cast.

d Les Blair *ph* Witold Stok *m* John Altman *pd* Jim Grant *ed* Martin Walsh

Stephen Rea, Sinead Cusack, Philip Jackson, Clare Higgins, Phil Daniels, Saira Todd, Mary Jo Randle

'A delightful comedy of manners . . . The pic is character, not knockabout, comedy, but this is a group of mild eccentrics you want to follow to the end.' – *Variety*

Bad Blood (1986): see *The Night Is Young*

Bad Blood *
New Zealand/GB 1981 105m colour
Southern (Andrew Brown)
V*

A paranoid farmer kills seven people and goes on the run.

Based on a true story, a grim, tense thriller that maintains its excitement.

w Andrew Brown *book* Manhunt: The Story of Stanley Graham by Howard Willis *d* Mike Newell *ph* Gary Hansen *m* Richard Hartley *ad* Kai Hawkins *ed* Peter Hollywood

Jack Thompson, Carol Burns, Dennis Lill, Donna Akersten, Martyn Sanderson, Marshall Napier

Bad Boys
US 1983 123m Astro Color
EMI/Robert Solo
V*, L

Delinquents get out of control in a Juvenile Correctional Facility.

Ugly but yawnworthy saga of up-to-date Dead End Kids.

w Richard di Lello *d* Rick Rosenthal *ph* Bruce Surtees, Don Thorin *m* Bill Conti

Sean Penn, Reni Santoni, Jim Moody, Eric Gurry, Esai Morales, Ally Sheedy

Bad Company **
US 1972 92m Technicolor
Paramount (Stanley R. Jaffe)
V*

During the Civil War, two youths on the run team up and become outlaws.

A successful attempt to recreate the feeling of past time, by the writers of another criminal myth, *Bonnie and Clyde*.

w David Newman, Robert Benton *d* Robert Benton *ph* Gordon Willis *m* Harvey Schmidt

Jeff Bridges, Barry Brown, Jim Davis, David Huddleston, John Savage

Bad Day at Black Rock ****
US 1955 81m Eastmancolor Cinemascope
MGM (Dore Schary)
V, V*, L

A one-armed stranger gets off the train at a sleepy desert hamlet and is greeted with hostility by the townsfolk, who have something to hide.

Seminal suspense thriller – the guilty town motif became a cliché – with a terse script and professional presentation. The moments of violence, long awaited, are electrifying.

w Millard Kaufman, *story Bad Time at Hondo* by Howard Briskin *d* John Sturges *ph* William C. Mellor *m* André Previn

*Spencer Tracy, Robert Ryan, Dean Jagger, Walter Brennan, Ernest Borgnine, Lee Marvin, Anne Francis, John Ericson, Russell Collins

'A very superior example of motion picture craftsmanship.' – *Pauline Kael*

'The movie takes place within twenty-four hours. It has a dramatic unity, an economy of word and action, that is admirable in an age of flabby Hollywood epics that maunder on forever.' – *William K. Zinsser, New York Herald Tribune*

'The skill of some sequences, the mood and symbiosis between man and nature makes this film sometimes superior to High Noon.' – *G. N. Fenin*

AAN: Millard Kaufman; John Sturges; Spencer Tracy

Bad for Each Other
US 1954 83m bw
Columbia (William Fadiman)

A doctor back from the army scorns his home town for high society, but a mine disaster reverses his decision.

Misleadingly titled cliché drama, patterned after *The Citadel*. Actors ill at ease, handling competent but routine.

w Irving Wallace, Horace McCoy   *novel* Horace McCoy   *d* Irving Rapper   *ph* Franz Planer   *md* Mischa Bakaleinikoff

Charlton Heston, Lizabeth Scott, Dianne Foster, Mildred Dunnock, Arthur Franz, Ray Collins, Marjorie Rambeau

Bad Girl *
US   1931   90m   bw
Fox

Two New York youngsters have to get married and find life bewildering.

Typical Borzage sentiment which was well received at the time.

w Edwin Burke   *novel* Vina Delmar   *d* Frank Borzage   *ph* Chester Lyons

Sally Eilers, James Dunn, Minna Gombell, William Pawley, Frank Darien

AA: Frank Borzage; Edwin Burke

AAN: best picture

Bad Influence *
US   1990   99m   DeLuxe
Entertainment/Epic/Sarlui/Diamant (Steve Tisch)
V, V*, L

A mysterious stranger manipulates the life of a disgruntled office worker.

Thriller requiring a more-than-usual suspension of disbelief.

w David Koepp   *d* Curtis Hanson   *ph* Robert Elswit   *m* Trevor Jones   *ed* Bonnie Koehler

Rob Lowe, James Spader, Lisa Zane, Christian Clemenson, Kathleen Wilhoite, Tony Maggio, Marcia Cross

'A reasonably taut, suspenseful thriller that provides its share of twists before straying into silliness during its final third.' – *Variety*

Bad Lieutenant
US   1992   96m   colour
Guild/Pressman (Edward R. Pressman, Mary Kane)
V*, L

A corrupt cop goes from bad to worse.

A lurid and exploitative melange of drugs, sex, masturbation, rape and religiosity, hardly justified by the suggestion of redemption tacked on to its end. What does save it, even if it doesn't justify it, is the force of Harvey Keitel's performance.

w Zoe Lund, Abel Ferrera   *d* Abel Ferrera   *ph* Ken Kelsch   *m* Joe Delia   *pd* Charles Logola   *ed* Anthony Redman

Harvey Keitel, Frankie Thorn, Zoe Lund, Anthony Ruggiero, Eddie Daniels, Bianca Bakija

'Film's frank treatment of drug addiction, obsessive sexuality and loss of religious faith spells instant controversy.' – *Variety*

'Not exactly comfortable viewing, of course, but this is disturbing, raw filmmaking and award-winning acting.' – *Kim Newman, Empire*

Bad Little Angel
US   1939   72m   bw
MGM

A sad little girl flees an orphanage and brightens up several lives in a small town.

Pollyanna-type period drama, definitely for small-town audiences but well enough done.

w Dorothy Yost   *novel Looking after Sandy* by Margaret Turnbull   *d* William Thiele

Virginia Weidler, Gene Reynolds, Guy Kibbee, Ian Hunter, Elizabeth Patterson, Reginald Owen, Henry Hull, Lois Wilson

'Homespunner for the nabes.' – *Variety*

The Bad Lord Byron *
GB   1948   85m   bw
Triton (Aubrey Baring)

Byron lies dying, and imagines his life and loves under review in a heavenly court.

Thought risible at the time, this historical romance in flashback now seems no worse and even a little more stylish than most, though the script suffers from too many cooks.

w Terence Young, Anthony Thorne, Peter Quennell, Laurence Kitchin, Paul Holt   *d* David MacDonald   *ph* Stephen Dade   *m* Cedric Thorpe Davie

Dennis Price, Mai Zetterling, Linden Travers, *Joan Greenwood,* Sonia Holm, Raymond Lovell, Leslie Dwyer

† The end of the British costume cycle which began with *The Man in Grey.*

The Bad Man
US   1940   70m   sepia
MGM (J. Walter Ruben)
GB title: *Two Gun Cupid*

A Mexican outlaw helps a former friend and unites two lovers.

Forgettable Western comedy drama with a sterling cast.

w Wells Root   *play* Porter Emerson Brown   *d* Richard Thorpe   *ph* Clyde de Vinna   *m* Franz Waxman

Wallace Beery, Lionel Barrymore, Laraine Day, Ronald Reagan, Henry Travers

Bad Man of Brimstone
US   1937   89m   bw
MGM

An old bandit discovers his long-lost son and sees the light.

Hilariously predictable but enjoyable star vehicle, quite palatable when it isn't too lachrymose.

w Richard Maibaum, Cyril Hume   *d* J. Walter Ruben

Wallace Beery, Virginia Bruce, Noah Beery, Dennis O'Keefe, Lewis Stone, Guy Kibbee, Joseph Calleia

Bad Man of Wyoming: see *Wyoming* (1940)

Bad Man's River
Spain/Italy/France   1972   90m   Eastmancolor
Franscope
Zurbano/Apollo/Roitfeld (Bernard Gordon)
V*

Four outlaws accept the job of blowing up a government arsenal in Mexico.

Lurid Western with comedy leanings and a somewhat eccentric cast.

w Philip Yordan, Eugenio Martin   *d* Eugenio Martin   *ph* Alexander Ulloa   *m* Waldo de Los Rios

Lee Van Cleef, James Mason, Gina Lollobrigida, Simon Andreu, Diana Lorys

'When shooting a western in Spain one should not say to oneself, "Never mind, no one is going to see it," because that will be just the film which the Rank Organization will choose to release in England.' – *James Mason*

Bad Medicine
US   1985   96m   DeLuxe
TCF/Lantana (Alex Winitsky, Arlene Sellers)
V

A student goes to medical school in Mexico.

Condescending farce which the Mexicans certainly won't like. Nothing much in it for general audiences either.

wd Harvey Miller   *novel* Steven Horowitz   *ph* Kelvin Pike   *m* Lalo Schifrin   *pd* Les Dilley

Steve Guttenberg, Alan Arkin, Julie Hagerty, Bill Macy

'With the tone shifting constantly from realistic to slapstick, the film has no center and just sprawls on.' – *Variety*

Bad Men of Missouri
US   1941   72m   bw
Warner

The Younger brothers become outlaws when they fight the influence of carpetbaggers.

Whitewashing of a family of Western criminals; good double-bill entertainment.

w Charles Grayson   *d* Ray Enright

Dennis Morgan, Arthur Kennedy, Wayne Morris, Jane Wyman, Victor Jory, Walter Catlett

Bad Men of Tombstone
US   1949   75m   bw
King Brothers/Allied Artists

Adventurers clash during gold rush days.

Workaday Western with some vigour.

w Philip Yordan and Arthur Strawn   *d* Kurt Neumann

Broderick Crawford, Barry Sullivan, Marjorie Reynolds, Julie Gibson

The Bad News Bears
US   1976   103m   Movielab
Paramount (Stanley Jaffe)
V*, L

An ex-baseball professional coaches a team of tough kids.

Rough-tongued, sentimental star comedy.

w Bill Lancaster   *d* Michael Ritchie   *ph* John A. Alonzo   *m* Jerry Fielding (after Bizet)

Walter Matthau, Tatum O'Neal, Vic Morrow, Joyce Van Patten

The Bad News Bears in Breaking Training
US   1977   100m   Movielab
Paramount/Leonard Goldberg (Fred T. Gallo)
V*, L

The Bears are invited to play in the Houston Astrodome but have trouble finding a coach.

Dimwitted and alarmingly sentimental sequel to a raucously vulgar oncer which should have been left alone.

w Paul Brickman   *d* Michael Pressman   *ph* Fred J. Koenekamp   *m* Craig Safan from Tchaikovsky's 1812 Overture   *ed* John W. Wheeler

William Devane, Clifton James, Jackie Earle Haley, Jimmy Baio, Chris Barnes

The Bad News Bears Go to Japan
US   1978   91m   Movielab
Paramount (Michael Ritchie)
V*, L

Yet another unnecessary sequel with a self-explanatory title.

w Bill Lancaster   *d* John Berry   *ph* Gene Polito   *m* Paul Chihara

Tony Curtis, Jackie Earle Haley, Tomisaburo Wayakama, George Wyner

The Bad One
US   1930   70m   bw
UA/Art Cinema Corporation

A prostitute falls for a client and saves him from prison.

Artificial to the point of risibility, this incredible melodrama demeans all concerned with it.

w Carey Wilson, Howard E. Rogers, John Farrow   *d* George Fitzmaurice

Dolores del Rio, Edmund Lowe, Don Alvarado, Blanche Friderici

The Bad Seed *
US   1956   129m   bw
Warner (Mervyn Le Roy)
V*, L

A sweet-looking 8-year-old girl is a liar and a murderess; her mother finds out and attempts to kill her and commit suicide.

A real curiosity from an unexpected stage hit: absurd melodrama treated with astonishing high literary style and some censor-induced levity; at the end, after the little villainess has been struck by lightning, a curtain call shows her being soundly spanked.

w John Lee Mahin   *play* Maxwell Anderson
novel William March   *d* Mervyn Le Roy   *ph* Harold Rosson   *m* Alex North

Nancy Kelly (rather uneasily recreating her stage role as the mother), *Patty McCormack*, Henry Jones, Eileen Heckart, Evelyn Varden, William Hopper, Paul Fix, Jesse White

AAN: Harold Rosson; Nancy Kelly; Patty McCormack; Eileen Heckart

Bad Sister
US   1931   71m   bw
Universal (Carl Laemmle Jnr)

A small-town coquette falls for a city slicker, and her quiet sister gets her steady boyfriend.

A teenager potboiler of its day, remarkable only for its cast.

w Raymond L. Schrock, Tom Reed   *story* The Flirt by Booth Tarkington   *d* Hobart Henley   *ph* Karl Freund

Conrad Nagel, Sidney Fox, Bette Davis, Humphrey Bogart, ZaSu Pitts, Slim Summerville, Emma Dunn, Bert Roach

Bad Sister (1947): see
The White Unicorn

The Bad Sleep Well **
Japan   1960   151m   bw
Toho (Tomoyuki Tanaka, Akira Kurosawa)
V, V*
original title: *Warui Yatsu Yoku Nemuru*

As part of his plan for revenge, a man marries the daughter of the businessman responsible for his father's death.

Moody thriller, in the style of American gangster movies of the 40s, but with an ending that Hollywood would have rejected as too downbeat.

w Akira Kurosawa, Hideo Oguni, Eijiro Kusaka, Ryuzo Kikushima, Shinobu Hashimoto   *novel* Ed McBain   *d* Akira Kurosawa   *ph* Yazuru Aizawa   *m* Sasuru Sato

Toshiro Mifune, Masayuki Mori, Kyoko Kagawa, Tatsuya Mihashi, Takashi Shimura, Akira Nishimura, Takeshi Kato

'It's a strangely mixed movie – an attempt at social significance but with several borrowings from Hamlet that take bizarre forms.' – *Pauline Kael*

Bad Taste
New Zealand   1987   92m   colour
Blue Dolphin/Wing Nut Films/Peter Jackson
V, V*, L, S

Alien fast-food restaurateurs add humans to their menu.

A deliberately gross low-budget movie, mixing gore and comedy, that gained a cult following among those with strong stomachs. *Chacun à son goût.*

w Peter Jackson, Tony Hiles, Ken Hammon   *d/ ph* Peter Jackson   *m* Michelle Scullion   *sp* Peter Jackson   *ed* Peter Jackson, Jamie Selkirk

Terry Potter, Pete O'Herne, Craig Smith, Mike Minett, Peter Jackson, Doug Wren

'Some kind of triumph in its horror-comic verve.' – *MFB*

Bad Timing
GB   1980   123m   colour   Technovision
Rank/Recorded Picture Company (Jeremy Thomas)

In Vienna, an American divorcee has a strange and unhappy affair with a psychoanalyst.

Weird and unsympathetic sex melodrama, presented with the disconnected style expected from this director as a series of flashbacks from the heroine's near-deathbed.

w Yale Udoff   *d* Nicolas Roeg   *ph* Anthony Richmond   *m* Richard Hartley

Art Garfunkel, Theresa Russell, Harvey Keitel, Denholm Elliott, Daniel Massey

'An enervating experience. Technically flashy, and teeming with degenerate chic, the downbeat tale is unrelieved by its tacked-on thriller ending, and deals purely in despair.' – *Variety*

The Badge of Marshal Brennan
US   1957   75m   bw
Allied Artists

A man on the run takes on the identity of a dying marshal, and cleans up a corrupt town.

Satisfying lower-case Western.

w Thomas G. Hubbard   *d* Albert C. Gannoway

Jim Davis, Arleen Whelan, Louis Jean Heydt, Lee Van Cleef

Badge 373
US   1973   116m   Technicolor
Paramount (Howard W. Koch)

A police detective is enraged by the murder of his partner and his own suspension after the death of a suspect.

'Realistic' (i.e. violent and foul-mouthed) cop thriller in the wake of *The French Connection,* tolerable only for action highlights.

w Pete Hamill, from the exploits of Eddie Egan   *d* Howard W. Koch   *ph* Arthur J. Ornitz   *m* J. J. Johnson

Robert Duvall, Verna Bloom, Henry Darrow, Eddie Egan, Felipe Luciano, Tina Christiana, Marina Durell

'A deeply divided and scarcely reassuring addition to the movies' composite portrait of the American police force.' – *John Gillett*

'Nasty, violent and humourless.' – *Sight and Sound*

'A movie well worth protesting about.' – *Michael Billington, Illustrated London News*

The Badlanders *
US   1958   83m   Metrocolor   Cinemascope
MGM/Arcola (Aaron Rosenberg)
V*

Crooked Westerners plan to rob a goldmine.

Rather sloppy Western remake of *The Asphalt Jungle.*

w Richard Collins   *d* Delmer Daves   *ph* John Seitz

Alan Ladd, Ernest Borgnine, Katy Jurado, Claire Kelly, Kent Smith, *Nehemiah Persoff*, Robert Emhardt

Badlands ****
US   1973   94m   Consolidated Color
Warner/Pressman/Williams/Badlands (Terrence Malick)
V (W), V*, L

A teenage girl and a young garbage collector wander across America leaving a trail of murder behind them.

A violent folk tale for moderns; very well put together, it quickly became a cult film. It has proved to be a seminal film in its depiction of aimless anger as a means of attempting to connect with the world.

wd Terrence Malick   *ph* Brian Probyn, Tak Fujimoto, Stevan Larner   *m* George Tipton

Martin Sheen, Sissy Spacek, Warren Oates, Ramon Bieri

'One of the finest literate examples of narrated cinema since the early days of Welles and Polonsky.' – *Jonathan Rosenbaum*

'So preconceived that there's nothing left to respond to.' – *New Yorker*

Badlands of Dakota
US   1941   75m   bw
Universal

A young man steals his elder brother's girl and becomes sheriff of a corrupt Western town.

Standard family fare.

w Gerald Geraghty   *d* Alfred E. Green

Robert Stack, Richard Dix, Broderick Crawford, Ann Rutherford, Frances Farmer, Hugh Herbert, Andy Devine, Lon Chaney Jnr

Badman's Country
US   1958   72m   bw
Warner

Pat Garrett, Wyatt Earp, Buffalo Bill Cody and Bat Masterson have a showdown with Butch Cassidy.

Wildly unhistorical Western.

w Orville H. Hampton   *d* Fred F. Sears

George Montgomery, Buster Crabbe, Malcolm Atterbury, Gregory Walcott, Neville Brand

'The west's worst killers strike again!'
Badman's Territory
US   1946   97m   bw
RKO
V*

The brutality of the Texas state police forces a sheriff to seek help from outlaws.

Unconvincing Western with good moments.

w Jack Natteford and Luci Ward   *d* Tim Whelan

Randolph Scott, Steve Brodie, Gabby Hayes, Ann Richards

Bagdad
US   1949   81m   Technicolor
U-I (Robert Arthur)

A chieftain's daughter seeks revenge for her father's death.

Thinly-conceived Arabian Nights modernization, unsure whether to take itself seriously.

w Robert Hardy Andrews   *d* Charles Lamont   *ph* Russell Metty   *m* Frank Skinner, Jack Brooks

Maureen O'Hara, Vincent Price, Paul Christian, John Sutton, Jeff Corey, Frank Puglia

'Silly, but not in the least muddle-headed. The producers are fully aware that all the customers want to see of Bagdad is Maureen O'Hara, with a touch of leopard-skin at the throat to warm up a generous décolletage.' – *C. A. Lejeune*

Bagdad Café ***
West Germany   1988   91m   Eastmancolor
Mainline/Pelemele/Pro-Ject (Percy and Eleonore Adlon)
V, V*, S
aka: *Out of Rosenheim*

A middle-aged Bavarian woman, left stranded in the Mojave desert by her husband, transforms a seedy motel she stumbles across.

High-spirited comedy, full of gentle wit and charm.

w Percy and Eleonore Adlon, Christopher Doherty   *d* Percy Adlon   *ph* Bernd Heinl   *m* Bob Telson   *ad* Bernt Amadeus Capra   *ed* Norbert Herzner

Marianne Sägebrecht, Jack Palance, C. C. H. Pounder, Christine Kaufmann, Monica Calhoun, Darron Flagg

† The success of the film resulted in an American TV series starring Whoopi Goldberg.

'The two most gorgeous humans you've ever beheld – caressed by soft tropic winds – tossed by the tides of love!'

Bahama Passage
US 1941 82m Technicolor
Paramount (Edward H. Griffith)

A sophisticated girl is determined to live on a salt-mining island in the West Indies.

Forgettable tropical romance in very pleasing early colour.

w Virginia Van Upp novel Nelson Hayes
d Edward H. Griffith ph Leo Tover m David Buttolph

Madeleine Carroll, Sterling Hayden, Flora Robson, Leo G. Carroll, Cecil Kellaway, Dorothy Dandridge

La Baie des Anges **
France 1962 85m bw
Sud-Pacifique (Paul-Edmond Decharme)
GB title: Bay of Angels

A bank clerk who has had unexpected winnings at the Nice Casino falls in love with a compulsive gambler.

Good-looking romantic drama utilizing many of the cinema's most dazzling resources.

wd Jacques Demy ph Jean Rabier m Michel Legrand

Jeanne Moreau, Claude Mann, Paul Guers, Henri Nassiet

'Immense lightness, speed and gaiety . . . stunning visual texture.' – Tom Milne, MFB

'It's like a French attempt to purify, to get to the essence of, a Warner's movie of the 30s.' – Pauline Kael

Bail Out at 43,000
US 1957 82m bw
Pine-Thomas-Shane/UA

Airmen test ejection seats for jet bombers.

Humdrum flagwaver.

w Paul Monash d Francis D. Lyon

John Payne, Paul Kelly, Karen Steele, Richard Eyer

Baisers Volés: see Stolen Kisses

Bait
US 1954 79m bw
Columbia (Hugo Haas)

Gold prospectors fall out over a mine and a woman.

Antediluvian melodrama typical of this director, made more risible than usual by Cedric Hardwicke's introduction in the shape of Satan.

w Samuel W. Taylor d Hugo Haas ph Edward P. Fitzgerald m Vaclav Divina

Hugo Haas, Cleo Moore, John Agar, Emmett Lynn

The Baited Trap: see The Trap

Baker's Hawk *
US 1976 96m colour
Doty-Dayton
V*

A reclusive Westerner becomes the victim of hoodlum vigilantes and is helped by a boy and his father.

Refreshingly simple-minded Western for the family audience.

w Dan Greer, Hal Harrison Jnr novel Jack Bickham
d Lyman D. Dayton

Clint Walker, Burl Ives, Diane Baker, Lee H. Montgomery, Alan Young

The Baker's Wife: see La Femme du Boulanger

Bakushu: see Early Summer

Le Bal **
France/Italy/Algeria 1982 112m Fujicolor
S.A./A2/Massfil/Oncic (Giorgio Silvagni)

Scenes from the history of a small Paris ballroom between 1936 and 1983.

Striking if overlong attempt at a totally speechless drama, with handling very nearly good enough to meet the challenge, though the result will not be to everyone's taste, and one's reaction in any case will depend very much on mood.

w Jean-Claude Penchenat, Ruggero Maccari, Furio Scarpelli, Ettore Scola, from an idea by the first-named and the stage production by the Théâtre du Campagnol d Ettore Scola ph Ricardo Aranovich m Vladimir Cosma

Jean-Claude Penchenat, Chantal Capron, Etienne Guichard and large company each playing several roles

Balalaika *
US 1939 102m bw
MGM (Lawrence Weingarten)

Russian exiles gather in Paris.

Mildly pleasing star musical.

w Jacques Deval, Leon Gordon play Eric Maschwitz d Reinhold Schunzel ph Joseph Ruttenberg, Karl Freund m Herbert Stothart

Nelson Eddy, Ilona Massey, Charles Ruggles, Frank Morgan, C. Aubrey Smith, Lionel Atwill, Walter Woolf King, Joyce Compton

songs: 'At the Balalaika'; 'Tanya'; 'Ride, Cossack, Ride'; 'Shadows on the Sand'; 'Tale of the Tailors'; 'Beneath the Winter's Snows'; 'In a Heart as Brave as Your Own'; 'Soldiers of the Czar'; 'How Many Miles to Go'; 'The Magic of Your Love'; 'My Heart Is a Gypsy'

'A sumptuously produced operetta in the opulent MGM tradition.' – Variety

† Only the title song was retained from the original score.

La Balance **
France 1982 102m colour
Les Films Ariane/Films A2 (Georges Dancigers, Alexandre Mnouchkine)

A pimp and his girlfriend are pressured by the police into becoming informers.

Tough thriller in which the only difference between the cops and the crooks is that the police are the more violent. A box-office success in France, where it was voted the best film of the year.

w M. Fabiani, Bob Swaim d Bob Swaim ph Bernard Ziztermann m Roland Bocquet pd Eric Moulard ed Françoise Javet

Nathalie Baye, Phillipe Léotard, Richard Berry, Maurice Ronet

The Balcony *
US 1963 86m bw
Walter Reade/Sterling/Allen Hodgdon/City Film (Joseph Strick, Ben Maddow)
V*, L

In a war-torn world, a brothel continues to attract customers of every variety.

Low-budget adaptation of a rather confused allegorical play: vivid moments hardly atone for reels of surrealist groping.

w Ben Maddow play Jean Genet d Joseph Strick ph George Folsey m Igor Stravinsky

Shelley Winters, Peter Falk, Lee Grant, Peter Brocco, Kent Smith, Ruby Dee, Jeff Corey, Leonard Nimoy

'Relentlessly funny, shaggy, shocking.' – Times

'Unfit for exhibition to man, woman or child.' – The People

AAN: George Folsey

Ball of Fire *
US 1941 111m bw
Samuel Goldwyn
V*, L
working title: The Professor and the Burlesque Queen

Seven professors compiling a dictionary give shelter to a stripteaser on the run from gangsters.

Rather overstretched but fitfully amusing romp inspired by Snow White and the Seven Dwarfs.

w Charles Brackett, Billy Wilder d Howard Hawks ph Gregg Toland m Alfred Newman

Barbara Stanwyck, Gary Cooper, Oscar Homolka, Henry Travers, S. Z. Sakall, Tully Marshall, Leonid Kinskey, Richard Haydn, Aubrey Mather, Allen Jenkins, Dana Andrews, Dan Duryea

'It's played as if it were terribly bright, but it's rather shrill and tiresome.' – New Yorker, 1982

† Ginger Rogers was first choice for the Stanwyck role.

AAN: original story (Thomas Monroe, Billy Wilder); Alfred Newman; Barbara Stanwyck

Ballad in Blue
GB 1964 88m bw
(Warner) Alexander and Miguel Salkind (Herman Blaser)
V*
US title: Blues for Lovers

A famous pianist becomes friendly with a blind boy and helps reconcile his parents.

Curious sentimental drama with the star playing himself; competent but hardly rousing.

w Burton Wohl d Paul Henreid ph Ron Taylor m Ray Charles, Stanley Black

Ray Charles, Mary Peach, Dawn Addams, Tom Bell, Piers Bishop, Betty McDowell

Ballad of a Soldier **
USSR 1959 89m bw
Mosfilm
original title: Ballada o Soldate

A soldier is granted four days' home leave before returning to be killed at the front.

Lyrical tear-jerker most notable for its impeccably photographed detail of Russian domestic and everyday life.

w Valentin Yoshov, Grigori Chukrai d Grigori Chukrai ph Vladimir Nikolayev, Era Saveleva m Mikhail Ziv

Vladimir Ivashev, Sharma Prokhorenko, Antonina Maximova

'In an epoch when the entertainment in most entertainment films is little more than offensive, its persuasive charm is particularly welcome.' – MFB

AAN: Valentin Yoshov, Grigori Chukrai

The Ballad of Berlin: see Berliner Ballade

The Ballad of Cable Hogue *
US 1970 121m Technicolor
Warner/Phil Feldman (Sam Peckinpah)
V*, L

A gold prospector takes a lengthy and ineffectual revenge on men who robbed him, and dies trying to be a hero.

Curious peripatetic Western with the director in uncharacteristically experimental and comparatively non-violent mood. All concerned seem to be enjoying themselves, but the fun is not always communicated.

w John Crawford, Edward Penney   *d Sam Peckinpah*
ph Lucien Ballard   m Jerry Goldsmith

Jason Robards, David Warner, Strother Martin, Slim Pickens, L. Q. Jones, Peter Whitney, R. G. Armstrong, Gene Evans, Stella Stevens

'A curiously compelling film. Like a child's playhouse, we come to love it not for its perfect symmetry but for the open way it expressed the feelings of its creator.' – *Richard Schickel*

The Ballad of Joe Hill **
Sweden   1971   115m   Eastmancolor
Bo Widerberg Film (Waldemar Bergendahl)
aka: *Joe Hill*

In 1902, a Swedish immigrant in New York becomes a revolutionary and is executed for the murder of a grocer.

Romantic propaganda which incidentally gives a delightfully detailed outsider's view of period America.

wd Bo Widerberg   *ph* Peter Davidson, Jorgen Persson   *m* Stefan Grossman   *ad* Ulf Axen

Thommy Berggren, Anja Schmidt, Evert Anderson, Cathy Smith

The Ballad of Josie
US   1967   102m   Techniscope
Universal (Marty Melcher)

Cleared of the manslaughter of her husband, a Western widow renovates a derelict ranch and sets up as a sheep farmer.

Tediously whimsical, unsuitably cast women's lib comedy with so few laughs that it may require to be taken seriously.

w Harold Swanton   *d* Andrew V. McLaglen
ph Milton Krasner   *m* Frank de Vol

Doris Day, Peter Graves, George Kennedy, William Talman, Andy Devine, Audrey Christie

'In 1866, A Woman Had Two Choices … She Could Be A Wife Or She Could Be A Whore. Josephine Monaghan Made The Boldest Choice Of All. She Chose To Be A Man.'

The Ballad of Little Joe
US   1993   121m   Technicolor   Panavision
Rank/Fine Line/Polygram/Joco (Fred Berner, Brenda Goodman)
S

A New York woman disguises herself as a man and becomes a cowboy and rancher.

Based on a true story, this becomes a feminist tract about the impossibility of being free and female in the West, which may also be true but here makes for a dull movie.

wd Maggie Greenwald   *ph* Declan Quinn
m David Mansfield   *pd* Mark Friedberg   *ed* Keith Reamer

Suzy Amis, Bo Hopkins, Ian McKellen, David Chung, Carrie Snodgress, Rene Auberjonois, Heather Graham, Sam Robards, Tom Bower

'This well-intentioned, revisionist frontier saga is too solemn and dramatically unexciting to generate wild appeal beyond a core of female viewers and ardent followers of indie pics.' – *Variety*

'It has a nice feeling for the smallness of man and his or her tenuous presence on the Western landscape.' – *Philip French, Observer*

The Ballad of Narayama *
Japan   1983   130m   colour
Cannon/Toei
original title: *Narayama Bushi-Ko*

An old woman prepares to die in a community where the elderly are exposed on a mountainside when they reach the age of 70.

Often ponderous, though gripping, remake of Keisuke Kinoshita's more restrained movie, made in

1958. It won the prize for the best film at the Cannes Film Festival in 1983.

wd Shohei Imamura   *novel Narayama Bushi-Ko* by Shichiro Fukazawa   *ph* Masao Tochizawa
m Shinichiro Ikebe   *pd* Toshio Inagaki   *ed* Hajime Okayasu

Ken Ogata, Sumiko Sakamoto, Tonpei Hidari, Takejo Aki, Shoichi Ozawa, Mitsuaki Fukamizu

'One of the most intense portraits of personal fulfilment in all cinema.' – *Tony Rayns, MFB*

The Ballad of Tam-Lin: see *Tam-Lin*

The Ballad of the Sad Café
US/GB   1990   101m   Technicolor
Hobo/Merchant Ivory (Ismail Merchant)
V, V*, S

On his release from prison, a rejected husband takes his revenge on his wife, a small-town store-owner.

A Southern Gothic fairy-tale transferred poorly to the screen.

w Michael Hirst   *play* Edward Albee   *novel* Carson McCullers   *d* Simon Callow   *ph* Walter Lassally
m Richard Robbins   *pd* Bruno Santini   *ed* Andrew Marcus

Vanessa Redgrave, Keith Carradine, Cork Hubbert, Rod Steiger, Austin Pendleton, Beth Dixon, Lanny Flaherty, Mert Hatfield, Earl Hindman, Anne Pitoniak

'A film of quite exceptional gracelessness.' – *Tom Milne, Sight and Sound*

'Difficult to respond to and probably will not engage mainstream audiences.' – *Variety*

Ballada o Soldate: see *Ballad of a Soldier*

Ballet Mécanique *
France   1924   10m   bw   silent
Fernand Léger, Dudley Murphy

Famous experimental short in which everyday images form abstract patterns.

A key to all subsequent surrealist experiments in the cinema.

wd Fernand Léger, Dudley Murphy   m Georges Antheil

Balthazar *
France/Sweden   1966   95m   bw
Parc/Ardos/Athos/Svenska Filminstitutet (Philippe Dussart)
original title: *Au Hasard, Balthazar*

The life of a talented donkey, born in the Swiss alps and eventually killed during a smuggling escapade.

Something between *Black Beauty* and a Christian parable, this quiet, episodic film is counted by some as its director's best work.

wd Robert Bresson   ph Ghislain Cloquet   *m* Jean Wiener (and Schubert)   *ad* Pierre Charbonnier
ed Raymond Lamy

Anne Wiazemsky, François Lafarge, Walter Green (amateur cast)

Baltic Deputy *
USSR   1937   100m   bw   Lenfilm

An old professor is finally reconciled to the 1917 revolution.

Propagandist biography (of scientist K. A. Timiriazev) with interesting scenes and a strong central performance.

w the directors and others   *d* Alexander Zharki, Josef Heifits   *ph* M. Kaplan   *m* M. Timofeyev

Nikolai Cherkassov, M. Damasheva, A. Melnikov

The Baltimore Bullet
US   1980   103m   Eastmancolor
Avco Embassy/Filmfair (John F. Brescia)
V*

Adventures of a pair of pool sharks.

Flabby comedy attempting a lighthearted version of *The Hustler*. The rewards are meagre.

w John F. Brescia, Robert Vincent O'Neill   *d* Robert Ellis Miller   *ph* James A. Crabe   *m* Johnny Mandel

James Coburn, Omar Sharif, Bruce Boxleitner, Ronee Blakley, Calvin Lockhart

'It manages to be stupidly macho and hopelessly incompetent at one and the same time.' – *Guardian*

La Bamba *
US   1987   108m   colour
New Visions/Columbia (Taylor Hackford, Bill Borden)
V, V*, L, S

The brief life of 1950s rock-and-roller Ritchie Valens, who at 17 was killed in the Buddy Holly plane crash.

Palatable biopic, for those who can stand the kind of music.

wd Luis Valdez   *ph* Adam Greenberg   *m* Carlos Santana, Miles Goodman   *pd* Vince Cresciman
ed Sheldon Kahn, Don Brochu

Lou Diamond Philips (as Valens), Esai Morales, Rosana de Soto, Elizabeth Pena, Danielle von Zerneck, Marshall Crenshaw (as Buddy Holly)

Bambi ****
US   1942   72m   Technicolor
Walt Disney
V, V*, L

The story of a forest deer, from the book by Felix Salten.

Anthropomorphic cartoon feature, one of Disney's most memorable and brilliant achievements, with a great comic character in Thumper the rabbit and a climactic forest fire sequence which is genuinely thrilling. A triumph of the animator's art.
supervisor David Hand   *m* Frank Churchill, Edward Plumb

voices of Peter Behn, Paula Winslowe

'The ultimate stag movie.' – *anon*

'The film, charming and touching as it can be, belongs more to the Disney of whimsy and sentiment than it does to the creative artist; and those who remember the Schubert in *Fantasia* will know what I mean when I say that a good deal of this tale of a forest deer is in Disney's Ave Maria manner.' – *Dilys Powell*

'Sheer enchantment.' – *C. A. Lejeune*

AAN: Frank Churchill, Edward Plumb; song 'Love Is a Song' (*m* Frank Churchill, *ly* Larry Morey)

The Bamboo Blonde
US   1946   68m   bw
Herman Schlom/RKO

A night-club singer falls for a B29 pilot who christens her – and his plane – The Bamboo Blonde.

Mediocre filler with the star ill at ease except when singing.

w Olive Cooper, Lawrence Kimble, Wayne Williams
d Anthony Mann

Frances Langford, Ralph Edwards, Russell Wade, Iris Adrian, Jane Greer

The Bamboo Prison
US   1955   80m   bw
Columbia

An American prisoner-of-war in Korea poses as a collaborator in order to get secret information.

Forlorn war drama which makes little impact.

w Edwin Blum and Jack de Witt   *d* Lewis Seiler

Robert Francis, Brian Keith, E. G. Marshall, Dianne Foster, Jerome Courtland

Banana Ridge

GB 1941 87m bw
ABPC

A business man's old flame presents him with an alleged son.

Stagey farce salvaged by star performances.

w Walter C. Mycroft, Lesley Storm, Ben Travers play Ben Travers d Walter C. Mycroft

Robertson Hare, Alfred Drayton, Isabel Jeans, Nova Pilbeam, Adele Dixon, Stewart Rome

Bananas *

US 1971 81m DeLuxe
UA/Rollins and Joffe (Jack Grossberg)
V, V*, L

A meek and mild product tester for a New York corporation accidentally becomes a South American rebel hero.

Disjointed anarchic comedy with a few good jokes typical of their author.

w Woody Allen, Mickey Rose d Woody Allen ph Andrew M. Costikyan m Marvin Hamlisch

Woody Allen, Louise Lasser, Carlos Montalban, Jacobo Morales

'Full of hilarious comic ideas and lines, supplied by Allen and his collaborator; then Allen, the director and actor, murders them.' – Stanley Kauffmann

† Asked why his film was called Bananas, Allen replied: 'Because there are no bananas in it.'

Band of Angels

US 1957 127m Warnercolor
Warner (no producer credited)
S

In 1865, a Kentucky girl learns that her mother was black and is sold as a slave, but quickly becomes her owner's mistress.

Long-winded romantic adventure, rather lamely scripted and developed. The star's presence reinforces the impression of sitting through the ghost of Gone with the Wind.

w John Twist, Ivan Goff, Ben Roberts novel Robert Penn Warren d Raoul Walsh ph Lucien Ballard m Max Steiner

Clark Gable, Yvonne de Carlo, Sidney Poitier, Efrem Zimbalist Jnr, Patric Knowles, Rex Reason, Torin Thatcher, Andrea King

'Too absurd to be dislikeable.' – MFB

The Band Plays On

US 1934 87m bw
MGM

Four street kids are saved by football and eventually become national stars.

Ho-hum sentimental melodrama with plot trouble.

w Bernard Schubert, Ralph Spence, Harvey Gates d Russell Mack

Robert Young, Stuart Erwin, Leo Carrillo, Betty Furness, Ted Healy, Preston Foster, Russell Hardie, William Tannen

'Slow, long, and weak on cast names.' – Variety

Band Waggon *

GB 1939 85m bw
GFD/Gainsborough (Edward Black)

Comedians running a pirate TV station in a ghostly castle round up a gang of spies.

Film version of a long-running radio comedy series; quite a serviceable record of a phenomenon.

w Marriott Edgar, Val Guest d Marcel Varnel ph Henry Harris

Arthur Askey, Richard Murdoch, Jack Hylton and his band, Pat Kirkwood, Moore Marriott, Peter Gawthorne, Wally Patch, Donald Calthrop

The Band Wagon ****

US 1953 112m Technicolor
MGM (Arthur Freed)
V, V*, L, S

A has-been Hollywood dancer joins forces with a temperamental stage producer to put on a Broadway musical.

Simple but sophisticated musical with the bare minimum of plot, told mostly in jokes, and the maximum of music and song. Numbers include those listed below, as well as a spoof Mickey Spillane ballet finale. Level of technical accomplishment very high.

w Adolph Green, Betty Comden d Vincente Minnelli ph Harry Jackson m Adolph Deutsch m/y Howard Dietz, Arthur Schwartz ad Cedric Gibbons, Preston Ames

Fred Astaire, Jack Buchanan, Oscar Levant, Cyd Charisse, Nanette Fabray

'The best musical of the month, the year, the decade, or for all I know of all time.' – Archer Winsten

† The Jack Buchanan character, Jeffrey Cordova, was first offered to Clifton Webb. It was loosely based on José Ferrer, who in the early fifties produced four Broadway shows all running at the same time, and acted in a fifth.

songs: 'A Shine on Your Shoes', 'By Myself', 'That's Entertainment', 'Dancing in the Dark', 'Triplets', 'New Sun in the Sky', 'I Guess I'll Have to Change My Plan', 'Louisiana Hayride', 'I Love Louisa', 'Girl Hunt' ballet.

AAN: Adolph Green, Betty Comden; Adolph Deutsch

Bande à Part

France 1964 95m bw
Anouchka/Orsay (Philippe Dussart)
aka: The Outsiders

Aimless young people plan a robbery which ends in murder.

Despite the plot, the emphasis is on fragments of lyricism, and the film is not among its director's greatest successes.

wd Jean-Luc Godard novel Fool's Gold by Dolores and B. Hitchens ph Raoul Coutard m Michel Legrand

Anna Karina, Claude Brasseur, Sami Frey, Louisa Colpeyn

'In a sense, the whole film is a metaphor illustrating this glancing collision, when fantasy and reality merge but one may still remain unsure which is which.' – Tom Milne, MFB

Bandido

US 1956 92m DeLuxe Cinemascope
UA/Robert L. Jacks

Mexico 1916: an American adventurer helps a rebel leader to defeat a gun runner.

Standard action fare, rather slackly handled.

w Earl Felton d Richard Fleischer ph Ernest Laszlo m Max Steiner

Robert Mitchum, Gilbert Roland, Zachary Scott, Ursula Thiess

The Bandit *

Brazil 1953 119m bw
Companhia Cinematographica (Cid Leite da Silva)
original title: O'Cangaceiro

The leader of a gang of outlaws comes to grief after falling out with his second in command over a woman.

One of the few Brazilian films to achieve international popularity, mainly because of its memorable theme

tune. The film itself looks attractive but becomes a bit of a bore.

wd Lima Barreto ph Chick Fowle m Gabriel Migliori

Alberto Ruschel, Milton Ribeiro, Marisa Prado

The Bandit of Sherwood Forest *

US 1946 87m Technicolor
Columbia (Leonard S. Picker, Clifford Sanforth)

Robin Hood frustrates the Regent who plans to usurp the throne from the boy king.

A lively romp through Sherwood Forest with a capable cast.

w Wilfrid H. Pettit, Melvin Levy novel Son of Robin Hood by Paul A. Castleton d George Sherman, Henry Levin ph Tony Gaudio, William Snyder, George Meehan m Hugo Friedhofer

Cornel Wilde, Anita Louise, Edgar Buchanan, Jill Esmond, Henry Daniell, George Macready, Russell Hicks, John Abbott, Lloyd Corrigan

The Bandit of Zhobe

GB 1959 81m Technicolor Cinemascope
Warwick/Columbia

An Indian chieftain kidnaps a British major's daughter in retaliation for the death of his wife.

Tinpot action melodrama in the wake of the rather better Zarak.

wd John Gilling

Victor Mature, Anthony Newley, Anne Aubrey, Norman Wooland

The Bandit Queen

US 1950 69m bw
Lippert (William Berke)

The daughter of murdered Spaniards in California takes revenge against violent settlers from the east.

Predictable Western adventure on a low budget.

w Victor West and Budd Lesser d William Berke

Barbara Britton, Willard Parker, Barton MacLane, Philip Reed, Victor Kilian, Thurston Hall

Banditi a Orgoloso: see Bandits of Orgoloso

Bandits of Corsica *

US 1951 83m bw
Global/UA
GB title: The Return of the Corsican Brothers

Mario and his gypsy twin get together to unseat a tyrant.

Rather muffled actioner with adequate highlights.

w Richard Schayer d Ray Nazarro

Richard Greene, Paula Raymond, Raymond Burr, Dona Drake, Raymond Greenleaf, Lee Van Cleef

† See also: The Corsican Brothers.

Bandits of Orgosolo

Italy 1961 98m bw
Vittorio de Seta
Titanus

A Sardinian shepherd shelters some bandits and becomes one of them.

Rather slow character adventure which achieved some international reputation in its first release.

w Vittorio de Seta, Vera Gherarducci d/ph Vittorio de Seta m Valentino Bucci

Michele Cossu, Peppeddu Cuccu, and amateur cast

Bandolero! *

US 1968 108m DeLuxe Panavision
Fox (Robert L. Jacks)
V*, S

In Texas, fugitive outlaw brothers run into trouble with their Mexican counterparts.

Dour and downbeat but well-staged Western with emphasis on hanging and rape; an unusual mixture but smoothly assembled.

w James Lee Barrett d Andrew V. McLaglen
ph William H. Clothier m Jerry Goldsmith

James Stewart, Dean Martin, Raquel Welch, George Kennedy, Will Geer, Andrew Prine

Bang the Drum Slowly
US 1973 96m Movielab
Paramount (Maurice and Lois Rosenfeld)
V*, L

A baseball star finds that he is dying of leukemia.

Cliché-ridden tearjerker in the modern style.

w Mark Harris novel Mark Harris d John Hancock ph Richard Shore m Stephen Lawrence

Michael Moriarty, Robert de Niro, Vincent Gardenia, Phil Foster

AAN: Vincent Gardenia

Bang, You're Dead
GB 1954 88m bw
British Lion/Wellington (Lance Comfort)
US title: Game of Danger

A small boy accidentally shoots a local villain, and another man is arrested.

Singularly pointless and unattractive melodrama, a long way behind The Window and The Yellow Balloon.

w Guy Elmes, Ernest Borneman d Lance Comfort
ph Brendan J. Stafford m Eric Spear

Jack Warner, Derek Farr, Veronica Hurst, Gordon Harker, Michael Medwin, Anthony Richmond, Philip Saville

Banjo on my Knee **
US 1936 95m bw
TCF (Nunnally Johnson)

In a Mississippi riverboat shanty town, a wedding night is interrupted when the groom is arrested during a brawl.

Unusual, easy-going comedy in which the stars sing and dance as well as fool around.

w Nunnally Johnson novel Harry Hamilton d John Cromwell ph Ernest Palmer m Arthur Lange
m/ly Jimmy McHugh, Harold Adamson

Barbara Stanwyck, Joel McCrea, Buddy Ebsen, Walter Brennan, Helen Westley, Walter Catlett, Tony Martin, Katherine de Mille

'Too complicated for any better than moderate reception.' – Variety

The Bank Breaker: see Kaleidoscope

The Bank Detective: see The Bank Dick

The Bank Dick ***
US 1940 73m bw
Universal
V*, L
GB title: The Bank Detective

In Lompoc, California, a ne'er-do-well accidentally stops a hold-up, is made a bank detective, acquires deeds to a worthless mine and interferes in the production of a film.

Imperfect, but probably the best Fields vehicle there is: the jokes sometimes end in mid-air, but there are delicious moments and very little padding. The character names are sometimes funnier than the script: they include Egbert Sousè (accent grave over the 'e'), J. Pinkerton Snoopington, Ogg Oggilbie and Filthy McNasty.

w Mahatma Kane Jeeves (W. C. Fields) d Eddie Cline ph Milton Krasner md Charles Previn

W. C. Fields, Franklin Pangborn, Shemp Howard, Jack Norton, Grady Sutton, Cora Witherspoon

'One of the great classics of American comedy.' – Robert Lewis Taylor

'When the man is funny he is terrific . . . but the story is makeshift, the other characters are stock types, the only pace discernible is the distance between drinks or the rhythm of the fleeting seconds it takes Fields to size up trouble coming and duck the hell out.' – Otis Ferguson

'Individualistic display of broad comedy . . . adequate program supporter.' – Variety

† Fields's writing nom-de-plume was allegedly borrowed from noble characters in old English plays he squirmed through as a youth. They kept saying: 'M'hat, m'cane, Jeeves.'

Bank Holiday *
GB 1938 86m bw
GFD/Gainsborough (Edward Black)
US title: Three on a Weekend

The lives of various people intertwine during a day out in Brighton.

Simple but effective slice-of-life comedy-drama, establishing several actors and a director. Still quite refreshing.

w Hans Wilhelm, Rodney Ackland, Roger Burford
d Carol Reed ph Arthur Crabtree md Louis Levy
ad Vetchinsky ed R. E. Dearing, Alfred Roome

Margaret Lockwood, Hugh Williams, John Lodge, Kathleen Harrison, Wally Patch, Rene Ray, Linden Travers, Garry Marsh, Wilfrid Lawson

'Ranges from pathos to farce with a nice avoidance of overstatement.' – Daily Telegraph

The Bank Shot *
US 1974 83m DeLuxe
UA/Hal Landers, Bobby Roberts
V*

Using house-moving equipment, an escaped convict steals a whole bank.

Extended chase comedy with scenes of gleeful destruction. Acceptable for those in the mood, but a shade overdone.

w Wendell Mayes novel Donald E. Westlake
d Gower Champion ph Harry Stradling Jnr
m John Morris

George C. Scott, Joanna Cassidy, Sorrell Booke, G. Wood, Clifton James

Bannerline *
US 1951 87m bw
MGM (Henry Berman)

To comfort a dying old man, a young reporter prints a fake newspaper showing the indictment of the old man's gangster enemy. By an odd chain of events, the story becomes true.

Worthy but rather dull MGM 'B', typical of the regime of Dore Schary, boasting a pleasing small-town atmosphere and a remarkable cast of old actors.

w Charles Schnee story Samson Raphaelson
d Don Weis ph Harold Lipstein m Rudolph Kopp

Lionel Barrymore, Keefe Brasselle, Sally Forrest, Lewis Stone, Elizabeth Risdon, J. Carrol Naish, Spring Byington, Larry Keating

Banning
US 1967 102m Techniscope
Universal (Dick Berg)

A golf pro has sporting and amorous adventures at a country club.

Tedious, complexly plotted melodrama of life among the idle rich; handling generally laboured. A showcase for the studio's young contract talent.

w James Lee d Ron Winston ph Loyal Griggs
m Quincy Jones

Robert Wagner, Anjanette Comer, Jill St John, Guy Stockwell, James Farentino, Susan Clark, Howard St John, Mike Kellin, Sean Garrison, Gene Hackman

AAN: song 'The Eyes of Love' (m Quincy Jones, ly Bob Russell)

The Bar Sinister
US 1955 87m Eastmancolor Cinemascope
MGM (Henry Berman)
V*
GB title: It's a Dog's Life

The rise in lifestyle of a Bowery bull terrier, as told by himself.

Tolerable whimsy, in MGM's best family manner; ten years earlier it might have been a hit.

w John Michael Hayes story Richard Harding Davis
d Herman Hoffman ph Paul Vogel m Elmer Bernstein

Edmund Gwenn, Jeff Richards, Jarma Lewis, Dean Jagger

Barabbas *
Italy/US 1962 144m Technirama
Columbia/Dino de Laurentiis
V, V*

Pardoned instead of Christ, Barabbas is sentenced to the silver mines, turns Christian, and becomes a gladiator.

Overblown epic which starts with a genuine eclipse of the sun and has nowhere to go but down. The cast sparks a few moments, but it is generally a gaudy display of carnage.

w Christopher Fry, Nigel Balchin, Diego Fabbri, Ivo Perilli novel Pär Lagerkvist d Richard Fleischer
ph Aldo Tonti m Mario Nascimbene ad Mario Chiari

Anthony Quinn, Silvana Mangano, Vittorio Gassman, Ernest Borgnine, Jack Palance, Arthur Kennedy, Norman Wooland, Valentina Cortese, Harry Andrews, Katy Jurado, Michael Gwynn

'Unacceptable in its pain-preoccupation and its religiosity.' – Peter John Dyer

† The eclipse of the sun at the beginning is a real one, photographed at Nice.

'A world beyond words.'
Baraka *
US 1992 97m colour 70mm
Mayfair/Magidson (Mark Magidson)
S

Scenes of nature are followed by those of religious celebrations around the world, of human life and work, of death in war and funeral rituals.

A film made by the cinematographer of Koyaanisqatsi (qv), and similar in style, though less coherent in its selection of images, stunning though they often are.

w Ron Fricke, Mark Magidson, Bob Green d Ron Fricke ph Ron Fricke m Michael Stearns
ed Ron Fricke, Mark Magidson, David E. Aubrey, Alton Walpole

'Comes over as an animated National Geographic.' – Sight and Sound

'Perhaps one needs to see it on a psychedelic substance to discern a pattern or coherent structure.' – Empire

'See her do her thing!'
Barbarella *
France/Italy 1967 98m Technicolor Panavision
Marianne/Dino de Laurentiis
V, V*, L

A beautiful young 40th-century astronaut prevents the positronic ray from getting into the wrong hands.

Campy and slightly sick adventures with angels and other space people, from a highly censorable comic strip; some ingenious gadgetry and design, but not much of interest in the foreground.

w Terry Southern   *book* Jean-Claude Forest *d* Roger Vadim   *ph* Claude Renoir   *m* Bob Crewe, Charles Fox   *pd* Mario Garbuglia

Jane Fonda, John Phillip Law, Anita Pallenberg, Milo O'Shea, David Hemmings, Marcel Marceau, Ugo Tognazzi, Claude Dauphin

'A leading science fiction authority has claimed that if Lewis Carroll were alive today he would inevitably have written not *Alice's Adventures in Wonderland* but *Lolita*. He might perhaps equally well have written *Barbarella*.' – *Jack Ibberson*

'A flaccid, jaded appeal to our baser appetites, always liberally doused with essence of cop-out, resulting in elucubrated, anaemic pornography.' – *John Simon*

The Barbarian

US   1933   82m approx   bw
MGM
GB title: *A Night in Cairo*

An American lady travelling in the Middle East falls for a local potentate.

Shades of *The Sheik*. Actually this version was first filmed in 1915 by Edgar Selwyn from his own play, then again in 1924. Any version would seem fairly hysterical now.

w Anita Loos, Elmer Harris   *play* Edgar Selwyn *d* Sam Wood   *ph* Harold Rosson

Ramon Novarro, Myrna Loy, Reginald Denny, C. Aubrey Smith, Louise Closser Hale, Edward Arnold

'An abrupt switch to melodrama at the halfway mark makes this a maudlin, doubtful desert melodrama.' – *Variety*

The Barbarian and the Geisha *

US   1958   105m   Eastmancolor   Cinemascope
TCF (Eugene Frenke)
V, V*

In 1856 the first US diplomat to visit Japan meets local opposition but is helped by a geisha.

Episodic semi-historical romance which scarcely suits the talents of those involved.

w Charles Grayson   *d* John Huston   *ph* Charles G. Clarke   *m* Hugo Friedhofer

John Wayne, Eiko Ando, Sam Jaffe, So Yamamura

'It is saddening to think that the director of *The Asphalt Jungle* has gained professional freedom and international celebrity to become, at 51, yet another taskmaster who goes out in the midday sun.' – *Arlene Croce*

Barbarian Queen

US   1985   82m   colour
Concorde/Rodeo (Frank Isaac, Alex Sessa)
V, V*

When their men are kidnapped, women warriors go on the warpath.

One of the reasons that the fad for films of the sword and sorcery genre was so short-lived – muscle-bound men and scantily clad women of minimal acting ability are not enough to attract an audience.

d Hector Olivera   *ph* Rudy Donovan   *m* Chris Young, Jamie Horner   *pd* Julia Bertram   *sp* Willy Smith, Arny Alfieri   *ed* Sylvia Roberts, Leslie Rosenthal

Lana Clarkson, Katt Shea, Frank Zagarino, Dawn Dunlap, Susana Traverso, Victor Bo, Arman Chapman, Andrea Barbizon

† A sequel of even less interest, *Barbarian Queen 2*, directed by Joe Finley, followed in 1988.

The Barbarians

US/Italy   1987   88m   colour
Cannon (John Thompson)
V, V*, L

In a primitive world, twin musclemen take on warring tribes and wizards to rescue their queen.

Dim-witted sword and sorcery movie that never rises above the risible.

w James R. Silke   *d* Ruggero Deodata   *ph* Lorenzo Battaglia   *m* Pino Donaggio   *pd* Giuseppe Mangano   *ed* Eugene Alabiso

David Paul, Peter Paul, Richard Lynch, Eva La Rue, Virginia Bryant, Sheeba Alahani, Michael Berryman, Nanni Bernini

Barbarosa *

US   1981   90m   Eastmancolor
ITC/Wittliff-Nelson-Busey (Paul N. Lazarus III)
V*, L

An outlaw's legend grows along with his enemies.

Undercast but interestingly directed Western, with more than enough elegiac qualities mixed with some nods to the old enjoyable style.

w William D. Wittliff   *d* Fred Schepisi   *ph* Ian Baker *m* Bruce Smeaton

Willie Nelson, Gary Busey, Isela Vega, Gilbert Roland, George Voskovec

'The most spirited and satisfying new western epic in several years.' – *New Yorker*

'More than its share of artistic merit.' – *Variety*

Barbary Coast **

US   1935   91m   bw
Samuel Goldwyn
V, V*

During San Francisco's gold rush days a ruthless club owner builds a lonely girl into a star attraction but cannot win her love.

Juicy melodrama tailored for its stars, but with excellent background detail, sets and lighting.

w Ben Hecht, Charles MacArthur   *d* Howard Hawks *ph* Ray June   *m* Alfred Newman

Edward G. Robinson, Miriam Hopkins, Joel McCrea, Walter Brennan, Frank Craven, Brian Donlevy, Donald Meek

'More than a year ago Sam Goldwyn picked Barbary Coast as a title and called in Hecht and MacArthur to write a story to fit. Result is a picture that has all it takes to get along in thoroughbred company.' – *Variety*

† David Niven made his first screen appearance as an extra.

AAN: Ray June

Barbary Coast Gent

US   1944   87m   bw
MGM (Orville Dull)

A bandit from the Californian goldfields tries to go straight in San Francisco.

Star comedy drama, somewhat below par despite attractive settings and good production.

w William Lipman, Grant Garrett, Harry Ruskin *d* Roy del Ruth   *ph* Charles Salerno Jnr   *m* David Snell

Wallace Beery, Binnie Barnes, Frances Rafferty, Chill Wills, Ray Collins, John Carradine, Noah Beery, Morris Ankrum, Henry O'Neill, Donald Meek, Paul Hurst, Louise Beavers

Barbed Wire *

US   1927   85m approx   bw   silent
Paramount

A French girl falls for a German prisoner of war.

Almost forgotten war film which seems at least worthy of comparison with *All Quiet on the Western Front*, which was made three years later.

w Jules Furthman and Rowland V. Lee   *novel The Woman of Knockaloe* by Hall Caine   *d* Rowland V. Lee *ph* Bert Glennon

Pola Negri, Clive Brook, Einar Hanson, Claude Gillingwater, Gustav von Seyffertitz

Bardelys the Magnificent

US   1926   88m at 24 fps   bw   silent
MGM

A 16th-century French adventurer finally wins his fair lady.

Laboured swashbuckler.

w Dorothy Farnum   *novel* Rafael Sabatini   *d* King Vidor

John Gilbert, Eleanor Boardman, George K. Arthur

Barefaced Flatfoot ***

US   1952   7m   Technicolor
UPA (Stephen Bosustow)

Mr Magoo battles shortsightedly to save his nephew from the underworld.

Archetypal Magoo cartoon. ('Didn't we meet in Heidelberg?' he murmurs to the dummy he is duelling with his umbrella.) The title is a spoof on a contemporary Columbia movie, *The Barefoot Mailman*.

pd John Hubley

Barefoot Battalion

Greece   1954   89m   bw
Peter Boudoures

War orphans inhabit a derelict barge and band together to harass the Germans.

Unlikely true story, roughly dramatized and poorly produced.

w Nico Katsiotes   *d* Gregg Tallas   *ph* Mixalis Gaziadis   *m* Mikis Theodorakis

Maria Costi, Nico Fermas, Stavros Krozos

'The world's most beautiful animal!'
The Barefoot Contessa *

US   1954   128m   Technicolor
UA/Figaro (Forrest E. Johnston)
V, V*

A glamorous barefoot dancer in a Spanish cabaret is turned into a Hollywood star, but her sexual frustrations lead to a tragic end.

A fascinating farrago of addled philosophy and lame wisecracks, very typical of a writer-director here not at his best, decorated by a splendid gallery of actors and some attractive settings.

wd Joseph L. Mankiewicz   *ph* Jack Cardiff   *m* Mario Nascimbene

Humphrey Bogart (Harry Dawes), Ava Gardner (Maria Vargas), Edmond O'Brien (Oscar Muldoon), Marius Goring (Alberto Bravano), Valentina Cortesa (Eleonora Torlato-Favrini), Rossano Brazzi (Vincenzo Torlato-Favrini), Elizabeth Sellars (Jerry), Warren Stevens (Kirk Edwards), Franco Interlenghi (Pedro), Mari Aldon (Myrna)

HARRY: 'Life, every now and then, behaves as though it had seen too many bad movies, when everything fits too well – the beginning, the middle, the end – from fade-in to fade-out.'

'This example of the Higher Lunacy must vie with *Johnny Guitar* for the silliest film of the year.' – *Gavin Lambert*

'A trash masterpiece: a Cinderella story in which the prince turns out to be impotent.' – *Pauline Kael, 1968*

AA: Edmond O'Brien

AAN: Joseph L. Mankiewicz (as writer)

The Barefoot Executive *
US   1970   96m   Technicolor
Walt Disney (Bill Anderson)
V*

A TV network discovers that its most infallible
average viewer is a chimpanzee.

Quite a beguiling little farcical comedy with mild
doses of satire.

w Joseph L. McEveety   d Robert Butler
ph Charles F. Wheeler   m Robert F. Brunner

Kurt Russell, Harry Morgan, Joe Flynn, Wally Cox,
Heather North, Alan Hewitt, Hayden Rorke

'Break the rules! Make love! Fall over laughing!'
Barefoot in the Park **
US   1967   109m   Technicolor
Paramount/Hal B. Wallis
V*, L

A pair of New York newlyweds rent a cold water flat
at the top of a liftless building, and manage to marry
the bride's mother to an eccentric neighbour.

Breezy but overlong adaptation of a stage play which
succeeded through audience response to its one-
liners, which on the screen sometimes fall flat. The
people are nice, though.

w Neil Simon   play Neil Simon   d Gene Saks
ph Joseph LaShelle   m Neal Hefti

Robert Redford (Paul Bratter), Jane Fonda (Corie
Bratter), Mildred Natwick (Ethel Banks), Charles Boyer
(Victor Velasco), Herb Edelman (Harry Pepper),
Mabel Albertson (Aunt Harriet), Fritz Feld (restaurant
owner)

ETHEL: 'Make him feel important. If you do that,
you'll have a happy and wonderful marriage – like
two out of every ten couples.'
ETHEL: 'I feel like we've died and gone to heaven –
only we had to climb up.'

AAN: Mildred Natwick

The Barefoot Mailman
US   1951   82m   Supercinecolor
Columbia (Robert Cohn)

In 19th-century Florida, the mailman is joined by a
confidence trickster who later has a change of heart.

Inept comedy adventure which never really gets
started.

w James Gunn, Francis Swann   novel Theodore
Pratt   d Earl McEvoy   ph Ellis W. Carter
m George Duning

Robert Cummings, Jerome Courtland, Terry Moore,
John Russell, Will Geer, Arthur Shields, Trevor
Bardette

† This is the title parodied by the Mr Magoo cartoon
Barefaced Flatfoot.

Barfly *
US   1987   99m   TVC Color
Cannon/Barbet Schroeder, Fred Roos, Tom Luddy
V*, L

A self-styled poet of the bottle lords it over a Los
Angeles bar.

Unrelieved serio-comic wallow in the underside of
American life. For connoisseurs and idiots as well as
star fans.

w Charles Bukowski   d Barbet Schroeder
ph Robby Muller   m none   pd Bob Ziembicki

Mickey Rourke, Faye Dunaway, Alice Krige, Jack
Nance

The Bargee *
GB   1964   106m   Techniscope
AB/Galton-Simpson (W. A. Whitaker)
V

A canal barge Casanova is trapped into marriage.

The long-awaited comedy which was supposed to
make a film star out of TV's Young Steptoe turned out
to be rough and vulgar but not very funny.

w Ray Galton, Alan Simpson   d Duncan Wood
ph Harry Waxman   m Frank Cordell

Harry H. Corbett, Ronnie Barker, Hugh Griffith, Eric
Sykes, Julia Foster, Miriam Karlin, Eric Barker, Derek
Nimmo, Norman Bird, Richard Briers

Baritone **
Poland   1984   96m   colour
PRF Zespoly Filmowe/Zespol Perspektywa (Barbara Pec-
Slesicka)
original title: Baryton

In the early 1930s a famous Polish opera singer
returns home after 25 years, only to lose his voice
before a celebratory concert.

Zestful satiric portrayal of egomania and doublecross,
set against the rise of Nazism.

w Feliks Falk   d Janusz Zaorski   ph Witold
Adamek   m Jerzy Satanowski   ad Allan Starski
ed Halina Pruga-Ketling

Zbigniew Zapasiewicz, Piotr Fronczewski, Janusz
Blyczyński, Marcin Troński, Malgorzata Pieczyńska,
Zofia Saretok

The Barkleys of Broadway *
US   1949   109m   Technicolor
MGM (Arthur Freed)
V, V*, L

A quarrelling couple of musical comedy stars split up,
and she becomes a serious actress.

A rather flat and unattractive reunion for a famous
pair, with a witless script, poorish numbers and very
little style. The compensations are minor.

w Adolph Green, Betty Comden   d Charles Walters
ph Harry Stradling   md Lennie Hayton   m/ly Harry
Warren, Ira Gershwin

Fred Astaire, Ginger Rogers, Oscar Levant, Jacques
François, Billie Burke

† Ginger Rogers was in fact second choice; Judy
Garland was cast but withdrew through illness.

songs: 'They Can't Take That Away from Me', 'Shoes
with Wings On', 'My One and Only Highland Fling',
'Swing Trot', 'Manhattan Downbeat', 'You'd be So
Hard to Replace', 'A Weekend in the Country', 'Sabre
Dance'.

AAN: Harry Stradling

Barnacle Bill
US   1941   90m   bw
MGM (Milton Bren)

A fishing boat skipper gets romantic in the hope of
financing his enterprises.

Adequate waterfront comedy on Min and Bill lines,
consolidating a popular star teaming.

w Jack Jevne, Hugo Butler   d Richard Thorpe
ph Clyde de Vinna   m Bronislau Kaper

Wallace Beery, Marjorie Main, Leo Carrillo, Virginia
Weidler, Donald Meek, Barton MacLane, Connie
Gilchrist, Sara Haden

Barnacle Bill *
GB   1957   87m   bw
Ealing (Michael Balcon)
US title: All at Sea

The last of a long line of sailors suffers from
seasickness, and takes command of a decaying
Victorian pier at an English seaside resort.

Quite an amusing comedy which had the misfortune
to come at the tag-end of the Ealing classics and so
seemed too mild and predictable. Perhaps it was a
little staid.

w T. E. B. Clarke   d Charles Frend   ph Douglas
Slocombe   m John Addison

Alec Guinness, Irene Browne, Percy Herbert, Harold
Goodwin, Maurice Denham, George Rose, Lionel
Jeffries, Victor Maddern

Baron Blood (dubbed)
Italy/West Germany   1972   92m   Technicolor
Leone International/Cinevision (Alfred Leone)
V, V*, S
original title: Gli Orrori del Castello di Norimberga; aka:
Chamber of Tortures; The Thirst of Baron Blood; The
Torture Chamber of Baron Blood

In Austria, an American student brings back to life his
sadistic 300-year-old ancestor, who resumes his old
pastime of torturing the locals.

Dull, unimaginative and lurid horror, in which the
director's penchant for pointless zooms detracts from
his attempts at atmosphere; an occasional chase
sequence reveals what might have been, if those
involved had been more committed or if its stars had
bothered to act.

w Vincent Fotre, William A. Bairn   d Mario Bava
ph Antonio Rinaldi   m Stelvio Cipriani   ad Enzo
Bulgarelli   sp Franco Tocci   ed Carlo Reali

Joseph Cotten, Elke Sommer, Massimo Girotti, Rada
Rassimov, Antonio Cantafora, Humi Raho, Alan
Collins, Dieter Tressler

Le Baron Fantôme *
France   1943   100m   bw
Consortium de Productions de Films (Robert Florat)
GB title: The Phantom Baron

In the early 19th century, the disappearance of a
nobleman causes problems for his heirs.

Macabre fairy tale with effective scenes which seem to
relate to Cocteau's later fantasies; the film as a whole
is less effective.

wd Serge de Poligny   narrator Jean Cocteau
ph Roger Hubert   m Louis Beydts

Jany Holt, Odette Joyeux, Alain Cuny, Gabrielle
Dorziat

Baron Münchhausen *
Czechoslovakia   1962   81m   Agfacolor
Ceskoslovensky Film
V*
original title: Baron Prasil

An astronaut finds on the moon the famous liar Baron
Münchhausen, who takes him back to Earth and a
variety of exaggerated adventures.

Amusing variation on the old stories, using live action
against deliberately artificial backgrounds.

wd Karel Zeman   novel Gottfried Burger (illustrations
by Gustave Doré)   ph Jiri Tarantik   m Zdenek
Liska

Milos Kopecky, Rudolf Jelinek, Jana Becjchova

The Baron of Arizona
US   1950   85m   bw
Lippert (Carl Hittleman)
V*

In the 19th century a clerk tries to claim the whole of
Arizona by false land grants.

Initially appealing but basically rather feeble tall tale,
ineffectively worked out and decidedly
undernourished as a production.

wd Samuel Fuller   ph James Wong Howe   m Paul
Dunlap

Vincent Price, Ellen Drew, Beulah Bondi, Vladimir
Sokoloff, Reed Hadley, Robert Barrat

Baron Prasil: see Baron Münchhausen

The Baroness and the Butler
US   1938   75m   bw
TCF (Raymond Griffith)

The Hungarian prime minister's butler is loved by a princess.

Thin mittel-European romantic star whimsy.

w Sam Hellman, Lamar Trotti, Kathryn Scola play *The Lady Has a Heart* by Ladislaus Bus-Fekete d Walter Lang ph Arthur Miller md Louis Silvers

William Powell, Annabella, Henry Stephenson, Nigel Bruce, Helen Westley, Joseph Schildkraut, J. Edward Bromberg, Lynn Bari

Barquero!

US 1970 114m DeLuxe
Aubrey Schenck (Hal Klein)

A Western ferryman is taken prisoner by bandits but turns the tables.

Long, violent, rather uninteresting Western in the Spanish manner.

w George Schenck, William Marks d Gordon Douglas ph Jerry Finnermann m Dominic Frontiere

Lee Van Cleef, Forrest Tucker, Warren Oates, Kerwin Mathews, Mariette Hartley, Brad Weston, John Davis Chandler

'When poets love, heaven and earth fall back to watch!'
The Barretts of Wimpole Street **

US 1934 109m bw
MGM (Irving Thalberg)
V*, L
TV title: *Forbidden Alliance*

Invalid Elizabeth Barrett plans to marry poet Robert Browning, against her tyrannical father's wishes.

Claustrophobic but well-acted adaptation of a stage play which has become more forceful than history. Stilted now, but still better than the remake.

w Ernst Vajda, Claudine West, Donald Ogden Stewart play Rudolf Besier d Sidney Franklin ph William Daniels m Herbert Stothart

Norma Shearer (Elizabeth Barrett), Fredric March (Robert Browning), *Charles Laughton* (Edward Moulton-Barrett), Maureen O'Sullivan (Henrietta), Katherine Alexander (Arabel), Una O'Connor (Wilson), Ralph Forbes (Captain Surtees-Cook), Ian Wolfe (Harry Bevan)

'Box office for all its celluloid lethargy . . . truly an actor's picture, with long speeches and verbose philosophical observations.' – *Variety*

AAN: best picture; Norma Shearer

The Barretts of Wimpole Street

GB 1956 105m Metrocolor Cinemascope
MGM (Sam Zimbalist)
V*, L

Dreadful, miscast remake of the above, with emphasis on the Freudian father-daughter relationship.

An unattractive and boring film.

w John Dighton d Sidney Franklin ph Frederick A. Young m Bronislau Kaper

Jennifer Jones, Bill Travers, John Gielgud, Virginia McKenna

Barricade

US 1939 71m bw
TCF (Edward Kaufman)

A newsman and a girl with a past fight Mongolian bandits in North China.

A bagful of clichés which does not quite add up to entertainment.

w Granville Walker d Gregory Ratoff ph Karl Freund m David Buttolph

Warner Baxter, Alice Faye, Charles Winninger, Arthur Treacher, Keye Luke, Willie Fung, Doris Lloyd

'Inadequate and confusing . . . it was launched as an A, but winds up as a B that will have to groove generally in the supporting spots.' – *Variety*

Barricade

US 1949 75m Technicolor
Warner (Saul Elkins)

A tough mine-owner who runs a camp miles from civilization meets his come-uppance when three strangers are forced to accept his hospitality.

Rough Western only notable as an (almost) scene-for-scene steal from *The Sea Wolf*: a text-book adaptation.

w William Sackheim d Peter Godfrey ph Carl Guthrie m William Lava

Raymond Massey, Dane Clark, Ruth Roman, Robert Douglas, Morgan Farley

The Barrier

US 1926 79m at 24 fps bw silent
MGM

A brutal sea captain tries to prevent his protégé's marriage.

Brooding melodrama climaxing in an Alaskan storm.

w Rex Beach d George Hill

Lionel Barrymore (in his first film for the studio where he spent the rest of his career), Henry B. Walthall, Marceline Day, Norman Kerry

The Barrier

US 1937 90m bw
Paramount/Harry Sherman

A gold rush prospector kidnaps a child and brings her up in the belief that she is a half-breed.

Lyceum-like melodrama against spectacular natural settings; somehow not of interest.

w Bernard Schubert, Mordaunt Shairp, Harrison Jacobs novel Rex Beach d Lesley Selander

Leo Carrillo, Jean Parker, Robert Barrat, James Ellison, Otto Kruger, Andy Clyde, Addison Richards, Sara Haden

Barry Lyndon **

GB 1975 187m Eastmancolor
Warner/Hawk/Peregrine (Stanley Kubrick)
V*, L

Adventures of an 18th-century Irish gentleman of fortune.

A curiously cold-hearted enterprise, like an art gallery in which the backgrounds are sketched in loving detail and the human figures totally neglected; there is much to enjoy, but script and acting are variable to say the least, and the point of it all is obscure, as it certainly does not tell a rattling good story.

wd Stanley Kubrick novel W. M. Thackeray ph John Alcott md Leonard Rosenman pd Ken Adam

Ryan O'Neal, Marisa Berenson, Patrick Magee, Hardy Kruger, Steven Berkoff, Gay Hamilton, Marie Kean, Murray Melvin, André Morell, Leonard Rossiter, Philip Stone narrator Michael Hordern

'The motion picture equivalent of one of these very large, very expensive, very elegant and very dull books that exist solely to be seen on coffee tables.' – *Charles Champlin*

'Watching the movie is like looking at illustrations for a work that has not been supplied.' – *John Simon*

'All art and no matter: a series of still pictures which will please the retina while denying our hunger for drama. And far from re-creating another century, it more accurately embalms it.' – *Michael Billington, Illustrated London News*

AA: John Alcott; Leonard Rosenman; Ken Adam; costumes (Britt Soderlund, Milena Canonero)

AAN: best picture; Stanley Kubrick (as writer); Stanley Kubrick (as director)

Bartleby *

GB 1970 79m Eastmancolor
Pantheon (Rodney Carr-Smith)
V*, L

A young clerk gradually refuses to take part in life.

A non-action film from an independent source, praiseworthy but overlong and fairly lacking in any kind of appeal except to literary connoisseurs.

w Anthony Friedmann, Rodney Carr-Smith story Herman Melville d Anthony Friedmann ph Ian Wilson m Roger Webb

Paul Scofield, John McEnery, Thorley Walters, Colin Jeavons

'There's Only One Thing Stranger Than What's Going On Inside His Head. What's Going On Outside.'
'Between Heaven and Hell there's always Hollywood.'
Barton Fink ***

US 1991 116m colour
Rank/Circle (Ethan Coen)
V, V*, L

In the 1940s an intellectual left-wing playwright goes to work in Hollywood, where he is told to write a wrestling picture for Wallace Beery.

What begins as a satire on the film industry, with a central character owing much to Clifford Odets, turns halfway through into something darker and more disturbing, a dizzying trip inside two disturbed minds.

w Ethan and Joel Coen d Joel Coen m Carter Burwell pd Dennis Gassner ed Roderick Jaynes

John Turturro, John Goodman, Judy Davis, Michael Lerner, John Mahoney, Tony Shalhoub, Jon Polito, Steve Buscemi

'Scene after scene is filled with a ferocious strength and humour.' – *Variety*

† The film took an unprecedented three prizes at the 1991 Cannes Film Festival: Palme d'Or for best film, best actor (John Turturro) and best director.

AAN: Michael Lerner; Dennis Gassner

Baryton: see *Baritone*

Bas Ya Bahar: see *La Mer Cruelle*

Les Bas-fonds *

France 1936 92m bw
Albatros (Alexander Kamenka)
aka: *The Lower Depths*

A clash of temperaments flares up between derelicts in a dosshouse.

Uneven transposition of a famous work, with patches of good acting.

w Jean Renoir, Charles Spaak and others play Maxim Gorky d Jean Renoir ph Jean Bachelet m Jean Wiener

Jean Gabin, Louis Jouvet, Vladimir Sokoloff, Robert Le Vigan, Suzy Prim

'Flesh seduces. Passion kills.'
Basic Instinct *

US 1991 128m (127m US) Technicolor Panavision
Guild/Carolco/Canal+ (Alan Marshall)
V, V*, L, S

A violent, suspended detective falls in love with the chief suspect in a murder investigation, a bisexual millionairess whose latest novel contains a detailed description of a similar killing.

Overheated, overlong melodramatic thriller with an implausible plot that requires its audience to accept that Michael Douglas is irresistibly attractive to bisexual women. But the skill and pace of the direction makes one regret that they were not exercised on better material.

w Joe Eszterhas   d Paul Verhoeven   ph Jan de Bont   m Jerry Goldsmith   pd Terence Marsh   sp Rob Bottin   ed Frank J. Urioste

Michael Douglas, Sharon Stone, George Dzunda, Jeanne Tripplehorn, Denis Arndt, Leilani Sarelle, Dorothy Malone

'Saddled with extremely unattractive characters, vile dialogue and sex that appeals only to your baser instincts.' – *Jami Bernard, New York Post*

'The film falls down simply because its three-million-dollar script is just a gimmick, an unfeeling house of cards which falls apart when the loopholes and logical flaws that sustain the ambiguous resolution come to light.' – *Kim Newman, Sight and Sound*

'An outrageous film, a great big rubbishy sort of popcorn Saturday night movie with bags of sex and violence, blokes being blokes and ice-cool blondes being just that, and even a couple of quite stupendous car chases thrown in just for old times' sake.' – *Empire*

AAN: Jerry Goldsmith; editing

Basil, The Great Mouse Detective: see *The Great Mouse Detective*

'The Tenant In Room Seven Is Very Small, Very Twisted And Very Mad.'
Basket Case
US   1982   93m   TVC Color
Alpha (Edgar Ievins)
V, V*

Siamese twins, one a tiny, deformed creature, take revenge on the doctors who separated them.

Grisly, jokey, low-budget horror that gained a cult following.

wd Frank Henenlotter   ph Bruce Torbet   m Gus Russo   ad Frederick Loren   ed Frank Henenlotter

Kevin Van Hentenryck, Terri Susan Smith, Beverly Bonner, Robert Vogel, Diana Browne, Lloyd Pace

Basket Case 2
US   1990   90m   TVC Color
Medusa/Shapiro, Glickenhaus Entertainment/Ievins-Henenlotter (Edgar Ievins)
V, V*, L, S

Twins, one of them a deformed creature in a basket, take refuge in a community of freaks.

Tediously grotesque comedy.

wd Frank Henenlotter   ph Robert M. Baldwin   m Joe Renzetti   pd Michael P. Moran   ad Daniel Ouellette   ed Kevin Tent

Kevin Van Hentenryck, Judy Grafe, Annie Ross, Heather Rattray, Chad Brown, Beverley Bonner, Leonard Jackson, Alexandra Auder

'Henenlotter seems unsure whether to play his outré offerings for laughs, shocks or sympathy, and this remains an uncertain (and somewhat unnecessary) sequel to a sure-footed original.' – *MFB*

'It's Time To Build A Bigger Basket!'
Basket Case 3: The Progeny
US   1992   90m   TVC colour
Shapiro Glickenhaus (Edgar Ievins)
V*, L

A deformed twin becomes a father of monsters, but has to battle to protect them from the forces of law and order.

The mixture much as before, only of interest to fans of cheap horror.

w Frank Henenlotter, Robert Martin   d Frank Henenlotter   ph Bob Paone   m Joe Renzetti   pd William Barclay   sp creature effects: Gabe Bartalos, David Kindlon   ed Greg Sheldon

Annie Ross, Kevin Van Hentenryck, Dan Biggers, Gil Roper, Tina Louise Hilbert, James O'Doherty

'The flick's fast pace, perverse tone, clever dialog and suitably grotesque cartoon-styled gore make it a legit treat for frightcom fans.' – *New York Daily News*

'Henenlotter's mix of wild over-acting, cartoon color scheme and heavy-handed message regarding tolerance is tough to take for the uninitiated.' – *Variety*

'When it flies, someone dies!'
The Bat
US   1959   78m   bw
AA/Liberty (C. J. Tevlin)
V*

A lady mystery writer rents a spooky old house and finds herself and her guests at the mercy of a maniac in search of hidden loot.

Poor remake of a standard twenties stage thriller; everyone chews the scenery.

wd Crane Wilbur   play Mary Roberts Rinehart   ph Joseph Biroc   m Louis Forbes

Vincent Price, Agnes Moorehead, Gavin Gordon, John Sutton, Lenita Lane, Darla Hood

Bat 21 **
US   1988   105m   DeLuxe
Tri-Star/Vision/Eagle (David Fisher, Gary A. Neill, Michael Balson)
V, V*, L

In Vietnam an American pilot attempts to rescue a 53-year-old Air Force missile intelligence expert when he is shot down behind enemy lines.

Effective and suspenseful drama of the muddle and moral expediencies of war, based on a true story.

w William C. Anderson, George Gordon   book William C. Anderson   d Peter Markle   ph Mark Irwin   m Christopher Young   pd Vincent Cresciman   ed Stephen E. Rivkin

Gene Hackman, Danny Glover, Jerry Reed, David Marshall Grant, Clayton Rohner, Erich Anderson, Joe Dorsey

'Greatest all talking thriller!'
The Bat Whispers **
US   1930   82m   bw
UA (Roland West)
V*, L

Classic early sound version of *The Bat* (qv) by the director of the 1926 silent version.

Excellent use of camera, sets, and unusual models.

wd Roland West   ph Ray June, Robert Planck

Chester Morris, Una Merkel, Chance Ward, Grayce Hampton, Maude Eburne, Spencer Charters, Gustav von Seyffertitz

Originally released in a 'wide screen' process.

† West had also made a silent version in 1926.

'The story America will never forget!'
Bataan *
US   1943   114m   bw
MGM (Irving Starr)
V*

Thirteen soldiers holding a bridge against the Japanese die one by one.

Uncredited remake of *The Lost Patrol* (qv) transposed to the Pacific war, with stereotyped characters and much flagwaving. Very dated, but a big box-office film of its time, despite its studio jungles.

w Robert D. Andrews   d Tay Garnett   ph Sidney Wagner   m Bronislau Kaper

Robert Taylor, George Murphy, Thomas Mitchell, Lloyd Nolan, Lee Bowman, Robert Walker, Desi Arnaz, Barry Nelson, Philip Terry

'Naïve, coarse-grained, primitive, honest, accomplished and true.' – *James Agee*

'One of the most convincing attempts I have ever seen to show a bit of hell on the screen.' – *Observer*

La Bataille du Rail **
France   1945   87m   bw
CGCF

Reconstructions of heroic resistance work by the French railwaymen during World War II.

Reasonably compulsive documentary fiction which was plainly more inspiring at the time than it seems now.

wd René Clément   ph Henri Alekan   m Yves Baudrier

Salina, Daurand, Lozach, Tony Laurent

Bathing Beauty
US   1944   101m   Technicolor
MGM (Jack Cummings)
V*, L

A songwriter plans to retire and settle down, but his publisher schemes to set his fiancée against him.

Witless, artificial aqua-musical, with plenty of unpersuasive high jinks but no real style despite a capable cast.

w Dorothy Kingsley, Allen Boretz, Frank Waldman   d George Sidney   ph Harry Stradling   m Johnny Green   ch John Murray Anderson

Esther Williams, Red Skelton, Basil Rathbone, Keenan Wynn, Ethel Smith, Xavier Cugat, Bill Goodwin

songs: 'Faculty Row'; 'Tico Tico'; 'Echo of a Serenade'; 'I Cried for You'; 'Bim Bam Boom'; 'By the Waters of Minnetonka'; 'I've Got a Problem'; 'I'll Take the High Note'

'I could not resist the wish that MGM had topped its aquatic climax – a huge pool full of girls, fountains and spouts of flame – by suddenly draining the tank and ending the show with the entire company writhing like goldfish on a rug.' – *James Agee*

Batman
US   1943   bw   serial: 15 eps
Columbia

With the help of the Boy Wonder, the Caped Crusader battles an enemy underground ring led by Dr Daka.

Reasonably spirited romp marred by the usual tinpot sets.   d Lambert Hillyer

Lewis Wilson, Douglas Croft, J. Carrol Naish, William Austin

† *Batman and Robin* (15 eps) followed in 1948, directed by Spencer Bennet. The leads were played by Robert Lowery and John Duncan: they combated The Wizard with the help of Lyle Talbot as the police commissioner.

Batman *
US   1966   105m   DeLuxe
TCF/Greenlawn/National Periodical Publications (William Dozier)
V*, L

The cloaked avenger saves an important executive from the clutches of four of the world's most notorious criminals.

Glossy feature version of the old and new serials about the comic strip hero who scurries around in his Batmobile making sure that justice is done. The scriptwriter's invention unfortunately flags halfway, so that despite a fairly sharp production the result is more childish than camp.

w Lorenzo Semple Jnr   d Leslie Martinson   ph Howard Schwartz   m Nelson Riddle

Adam West, Burt Ward, Cesar Romero, Frank Gorshin, Burgess Meredith, Lee Meriwether, Alan Napier, Neil Hamilton

Batman **
US   1989   126m   Technicolor
Warner (Jon Peters, Peter Guber)
V, V (W), V*, L, S

A young boy who witnesses his parents' murder grows up to become Batman, a masked and emotionally disturbed vigilante who battles against an arch-criminal known as The Joker.

The campness of earlier versions of the comic-book hero gives way to a gloomier psychological interpretation that loses much of the fun of the original, while the brilliant production design, of a grim, grey metropolis, overshadows all. Narrative is reduced to a succession of set-pieces.

w Sam Hamm, Warren Skaaren d Tim Burton
ph Roger Pratt m Danny Elfman pd Anton Furst
m/ly Prince, John L. Nelson sp John Evans ed Ray Lovejoy

Michael Keaton, Jack Nicholson, Kim Basinger, Robert Wuhl, Pat Hingle, Billy Dee Williams, Michael Gough, Jack Palance, Jerry Hall

'A moderately entertaining fantasy, with good design, some strong performances and a desperate need of a script doctor.' – *Adam Mars-Jones, Independent*

AA: best art direction

Batman Returns **
US 1992 126m Technicolor
Warner (Denise Di Novi, Tim Burton)
V, V*, L, S

Batman does battle with Catwoman and The Penguin.

More comic-strip story-telling, done as a succession of set pieces, with the towering design of the city and its sewers overshadowing the performances.

w Daniel Waters Daniel Waters, Sam Hamm
d Tim Burton ph Stefan Czapsky m Danny Elfman pd Bo Welch ed Chris Lebenzon, Bob Badami

Michael Keaton, Danny DeVito, Michelle Pfeiffer, Christopher Walken, Michael Gough, Michael Murphy, Cristi Conaway, Pat Hingle

'Resembles nothing so much as a blacker, spikier but less focused version of a Disney animation feature made flesh.' – *Derek Malcolm, Guardian*

'A blend of playful novelty and reassuring familiarity – a difficult mixture to get right.' – *New Yorker*

AAN: Visual effects; make-up

La Battaglia di Algeri: see *The Battle of Algiers*

La Battaglia di El Alamein: see *The Battle of El Alamein*

Battement de Coeur **
France 1940 100m bw
Ciné Alliance/Osso

A poor Parisienne joins a school for pickpockets but falls for the ambassador she robs.

Amusing romance later remade in the US as *Heartbeat* (qv).

w Jean Villeme, Max Colpet, Michel Duran
d Henri Decoin

Danielle Darrieux, André Luguet, Claude Dauphin, Julien Carette, Saturnin Fabre

'Dauphin fails to rate in hero roles . . . he lacks personality, is short of stature, and dresses like a bank clerk.' – *Variety*

Batteries Not Included
US 1987 106m DeLuxe
UIP/Universal (Ronald L. Schwarz)
V, V*, L, S

A Manhattan neighbourhood where everyone has problems is helped out by miniature flying saucers with angelic intentions.

Frank Capra would have done it much better.

w Matthew Robbins, Brad Bird, Brent Maddock, S. S. Wilson story Mick Garris d Matthew Robbins

ph John McPherson m James Horner pd Ted Haworth ed Cynthia Scheider

Hume Cronyn, Jessica Tandy, Frank McRae, Elizabeth Pena, Michael Carmine

'Forced by her husband to love another man . . . to exchange her kisses for naval secrets!'
The Battle *
France 1934 85m bw
Lionofilm (Leon Garganoff)
English language version aka: Thunder in the East, Hara Kiri

A Japanese aristocrat urges his wife to befriend an English naval attaché and steal secrets from him; she does, and falls in love.

Stagey but discreet melodrama of the old school, quite well made and acted.

w Nicolas Farkas, Bernard Zimmer, Robert Stevenson novel Claude Farrère d Nicolas Farkas ph Roger Hubert

Charles Boyer, Merle Oberon, John Loder, Betty Stockfield, Miles Mander

The Battle at Apache Pass
US 1952 85m Technicolor
U-I

Cochise negotiates peace with the whites, but Geronimo won't agree.

Standard cavalry-versus-Indians Western, with Jeff Chandler repeating his famous Cochise impersonation.

w Gerald Drayson Adams d George Sherman

John Lund, Susan Cabot, Bruce Cowling, Richard Egan

The Battle at Bloody Beach
US 1961 80m Cinemascope
TCF/API (Richard Maibaum)
GB title: *Battle on the Beach*

Guerrillas fight Japs in the Philippines.

Tedious war melodrama with interludes for an eternal triangle.

w Richard Maibaum, Willard Willingham
d Herbert Coleman ph Kenneth Peach m Henry Vars

Audie Murphy, Gary Crosby, Dolores Michaels, Alejandro Rey

Battle Beneath the Earth *
GB 1967 92m Technicolor
MGM/Reynolds/Vetter (Charles Reynolds)
V*
US title: *Battle Beneath the Sea*

Enemy agents burrow under the US by means of a giant laser.

Agreeable schoolboy science fiction with fair special effects.

w L. Z. Hargreaves d Montgomery Tully
ph Kenneth Talbot m Ken Jones sp Tom Howard

Kerwin Mathews, Vivienne Ventura, Robert Ayres, Peter Arne, Martin Benson

Battle Beneath the Sea: see *Battle Beneath the Earth*

Battle Beyond the Stars *
US 1980 104m Metrocolor
New World/Roger Corman (Ed Carlin)
V*, L

A small planet hires help to repel invaders.

Impertinent and sometimes amusing space fiction rip-off of *Seven Samurai*, with plenty of in-jokes and quite pleasant special effects.

w John Sayles d Jimmy T. Murakami ph Daniel Lacambre m James Horner ad Jim Cameron, Charles Breen

Richard Thomas, Robert Vaughn, John Saxon, George Peppard, Sam Jaffe, Morgan Woodward, Darlanne Fluegel, Sybil Danning

Battle Circus
US 1952 90m bw
MGM (Pandro S. Berman)
V*

A patriotic nurse and a disillusioned major fall in love at a mobile army hospital in Korea.

A flat, studio-bound potboiler with miscast stars, bound to provoke hilarity now as a serious version of *M*A*S*H*.

wd Richard Brooks ph John Alton m Lennie Hayton

Humphrey Bogart, June Allyson, Keenan Wynn, Robert Keith, William Campbell

'It is disappointing that Brooks, whose early work . . . suggested considerable promise, should have descended to such a glib, uninteresting piece of film-making.' – *MFB*

Battle Cry
US 1955 148m Warnercolor Cinemascope
Warner (producer not credited)
V*, L

During World War II, marines endure tough training before combat in Saipan; their sex lives come a close second to the war.

Interminable cheapie epic with both eyes on the box-office: the cast salvages an odd moment or two, but violence of all kinds is the key to the entertainment.

w Leon Uris novel Leon Uris d Raoul Walsh
ph Sid Hickox m Max Steiner

Van Heflin, Aldo Ray, Mona Freeman, Dorothy Malone, Raymond Massey, Nancy Olson, James Whitmore, Tab Hunter, Anne Francis, William Campbell

AAN: Max Steiner

The Battle Cry of Peace *
US 1915 120m approx bw silent
Blackton/VIT

Lost film in which New York was invaded by forces of apparently German origin.

It caused great political unrest and was followed by Thomas Ince's *Civilisation* which took the pacifist point of view.

w J. Stuart Blackton book *Defenceless America* by Hudson Maxim d Wilfred North

Charles Richman, L. Rogers Lytton, Charles Kent, James Morrison

The Battle for Anzio: see *Anzio*

Battle for Music *
GB 1943 87m bw
Strand Films (Donald Taylor)

The story of the wartime ups and downs of the London Philharmonic Orchestra.

Not many films feature a classical orchestra, and this simple tribute, a mediocre production at best, has considerable historical interest.

w St John L. Clowes d Donald Taylor

Hay Petrie, Joss Ambler, Charles Carson, Jack Hylton, J. B. Priestley, Eileen Joyce, Moiseiwitch, Sir Adrian Boult, Sir Malcolm Sargent

Battle for Russia ***
US 1943 80m bw
US Army Signal Corps (Anatole Litvak)

Fifth of Frank Capra's Why We Fight documentaries,

and like the others a brilliant compilation of carefully selected footage.

commentary Anthony Veiller   *m* Dimitri Tiomkin

Battle for the Planet of the Apes
US   1973   86m   DeLuxe   Panavision
TCF/APJAC (Frank Capra Jnr)
V, V*

Following a nuclear war, apes are the only surviving leaders of society, but begin to fight among themselves.

Fifth and last in an increasingly confusing chronology, this is at least more thoughtful than violent.

w John William Corrington, Joyce Hooper Corrington   *d* J. Lee-Thompson   *ph* Richard H. Kline   *m* Leonard Rosenman   *make-up* John Chambers

Roddy McDowall, Claude Akins, John Huston, Natalie Trundy, Severn Darden, Lew Ayres, Paul Williams

† See *Planet of the Apes.*

Battle Hell: see *Yangtse Incident*

Battle Hymn
US   1957   108m   Technicolor   Cinemascope
U-I (Ross Hunter)

An American preacher with a guilt complex volunteers to help the South Koreans and after many adventures founds an orphanage.

Earnest, somnolent biopic of one Dean Hess; its mixture of drama, comedy, religion and war heroics is indigestible despite professional handling.

w Charles Grayson, Vincent B. Evans   *d* Douglas Sirk   *ph* Russell Metty   *m* Frank Skinner

Rock Hudson, Anna Kashfi, Dan Duryea, Don Defore, Martha Hyer, Jock Mahoney, James Edwards, Carl Benton Reid

'The film seems to infer that heroic self-sacrifice, a little homely Eastern philosophy and a capacity for combining battle experience with an awareness of spiritual values are enough to overcome all emergencies.' – *John Gillett*

'The Revolt That Stirred The World!'
The Battle of Algiers ****
Algeria/Italy   1965   135m   bw
Casbah/Igor (Antonio Musi, Yacef Saadi)
V, V*, L, S
original title: *La Battaglia di Algeri*

In 1954 Algiers, an ex-convict joins the terrorists in rebellion against the French government.

Politically oriented reconstruction of a bitter period of French colonial history, made better propaganda by its wealth of effective detail.

w Franco Solinas   *d* Gillo Pontecorvo   *ph* Marcello Gatti   *m* Ennio Morricone, Gillo Pontecorvo

Brahim Haggiag, Jean Martin, Yacef Saadi, Tommaso Neri

'An astonishing piece of work in directorial technique processing to achieve not merely a newsreel tempo but a grainy realism unmatched by the average news film and all too rarely approached by even the better ventures into cinema verité. What is equally noteworthy is Pontecorvo's objectivity in showing both the exhilaration and the heart-break of a fight for liberation, with neither the oppressed nor the oppressor able to survive at ease with his conscience.' – *Judith Crist*

AAN: best foreign film; Franco Solinas; Gillo Pontecorvo (as director)

The Battle of Austerlitz: see *Austerlitz*

Battle of Britain ***
US   1943   52m   bw

Fourth of the Why We Fight series. (See *Battle for Russia.*)

'It will emerge as one of the vital documents depicting a people's courage when the torch of freedom flickered at its lowest.' – *Variety*

Battle of Britain *
GB   1969   131m   Technicolor   Panavision
UA/Spitfire (Harry Saltzman, Ben Fisz)
V, V*, L, S

Summer 1940: England defends itself against aerial onslaught.

Plodding attempt to cover an historic event from too many angles and with too many guest stars, all indistinguishable from each other when masked in the cockpit during the repetitive and interminable dogfight sequences. On the ground, things are even duller.

w James Kennaway, Wilfrid Greatorex   *d* Guy Hamilton   *ph* Frederick A. Young   *m* William Walton, Ron Goodwin

Laurence Olivier (as Dowding), Robert Shaw, Michael Caine, Christopher Plummer, Kenneth More, Susannah York, Trevor Howard, Ralph Richardson, Patrick Wymark, Curt Jurgens, Michael Redgrave, Nigel Patrick, Robert Flemyng, Edward Fox

† The film lost ten million dollars worldwide.

Battle of Broadway
US   1938   84m   bw
TCF

Two American legionnaires at a New York convention try to break up the infatuation of their boss's son with a showgirl.

Amiably rowdy Flagg-and-Quirt imitation.

w Lou Breslow, John Patrick   *d* George Marshall

Victor McLaglen, Brian Donlevy, Gypsy Rose Lee, Raymond Walburn, Lynn Bari, Jane Darwell, Hattie McDaniel

'Flagg and Quirt shenanigans . . . rowdy, good-natured fun.' – *Variety*

The Battle of City Hall: see *Angels Wash Their Faces*

The Battle of El Alamein
Italy/France   1968   105m   Eastmancolor   Cromoscope
Zenith Cinematografica/Les Films Corona (Mino Loy, Luciano Martino)
V*
original title: *La Battaglia di El Alamein*; aka: *Desert Tanks*

In June 1942 Italian troops, who have been ordered to beat their German allies to Alexandria, run into British resistance.

The North African campaign as seen from an Italian viewpoint: the Italian troops are gallant and courageous, the British foolish and treacherous, and the Germans coldly inhumane and equally treacherous.

w Ernesto Gastaldi, Remigio Del Grosso   *d* Calvin Jackson Padget (Giorgio Ferroni)   *ph* Sergio D'Offizi   *m* Carlo Rustichelli   *ed* Eugenio Alabiso

Frederick Stafford, George Hilton, Michael Rennie (as Field Marshal Montgomery), Robert Hossein (as Rommel), Marco Guglielmi, Ettore Manni, Gérard Herter, Ira Furstenberg, Enrico Maria Salerno

'An ingenious attempt to whitewash Italy's military record in the last war and to justify her alliance with Germany as part of that lovable Mediterranean characteristic of being "too trusting".' – *Jan Dawson, MFB*

The Battle of Gallipoli: see *Tell England*

The Battle of Midway: see *Midway*

The Battle of Neretva
Yugoslavia/US/Italy/W. Germany   1969   106m in dubbed version   colour   Cinemascope
Jadran-Bosna
V*, S

In 1943, Yugoslav partisans resist German and Italian invaders.

War spectacular with international cast; despite brilliant handling of the climaxes it didn't travel.

w Ugo Pirro and others   *d* Veljko Bulajic

Yul Brynner, Curt Jurgens, Sylva Koscina, Orson Welles, Hardy Kruger, Franco Nero

AAN: best foreign film

The Battle of Paris
US   1929   71m   bw   Paramount

A lady music seller teams up with a pickpocket and falls for an American artist.

Primitive sound musical notable chiefly for its cast.

w Gene Markey   *d* Robert Florey   *ph* Bill Steiner   *m/ly* Cole Porter

Gertrude Lawrence, Charles Ruggles, Walter Petrie, Arthur Treacher, Gladys du Bois

Battle of Powder River: see *Tomahawk*

The Battle of Rogue River
US   1954   71m   Technicolor
Columbia

A disciplinarian major at a Western fort discovers that his friend is fanning hatred between Indians and whites, for personal reasons.

Tatty Western with little action, and that very lame.

w Douglas Heyes   *d* William Castle

George Montgomery, Richard Denning, Martha Hyer, John Crawford

Battle of the Bulge **
US   1965   167m   Technicolor   Ultra Panavision
Warner/United States Pictures (Sidney Harmon, Milton Sperling, Philip Yordan)
V*, L, S

In December 1944, the Allies take longer than expected to win a land battle in the Ardennes because of a crack Nazi Panzer commander.

Bloody and unbowed war spectacle, quite literate and handsome but deafeningly noisy and with emphasis on strategy rather than character.

w Philip Yordan, Milton Sperling, John Melson   *d* Ken Annakin   *ph* Jack Hildyard   *m* Benjamin Frankel

Henry Fonda, Robert Shaw, Robert Ryan, Telly Savalas, Dana Andrews, George Montgomery, Ty Hardin, Pier Angeli, Barbara Werle, Charles Bronson, James MacArthur, Werner Peters

The Battle of the Century **
US   1927   20m   bw   silent
Hal Roach
V

The manager of an unsuccessful boxer accidentally starts a marathon pie fight.

The first reel is lost, but the pie sequence is what matters, being one of the most celebrated pieces of slapstick in cinema history.

w Hal Roach, H. M. Walker   *d* Clyde Bruckman

Laurel and Hardy, Eugene Pallette

Battle of the Coral Sea
US   1959   85m   bw
Columbia (Charles H. Schneer)
V

During World War II a submarine commander, sent to photograph the Japanese fleet, is captured but escapes. Routine, unconvincing war heroics.

w Dan Ullman, Stephen Kandel   d Paul Wendkos

Cliff Robertson, Gia Scala, Patricia Cutts

The Battle of the River Plate *
GB   1956   119m   Technicolor   Vistavision
Rank/Powell and Pressburger
V, V*
US title: Pursuit of the Graf Spee

Semi-documentary account of the 1939 trapping of the German pocket battleship *Graf Spee* in Montevideo Harbour, and of her subsequent scuttling.

A sympathetic view of a German hero, Commander Langsdorff (not unexpected from these producers) is the most notable feature of this disappointingly patchy and studio-bound war epic, with too many actors in ill-defined bit parts, too undisciplined a storyline, and too confusing scenes of battle.

wd Michael Powell, Emeric Pressburger
ph Christopher Challis   m Brian Easdale

John Gregson, Anthony Quayle, Peter Finch, Bernard Lee, Ian Hunter, Jack Gwillim, Lionel Murton, Anthony Bushell, Peter Illing

'It is difficult to understand how English film-makers can have done thus badly with material so apt to their gifts.' – Stanley Kauffmann

The Battle of the Sexes
US   1914   60m approx   bw   silent
Mutual/Reliance-Majestic

A wealthy middle-aged man is taken in by a fortune-hunting couple.

A commercial potboiler, made on the cheap but enormously successful.

wd D. W. Griffith   play The Single Standard by Daniel Carson Goodman   ph G. W. Bitzer

Lillian Gish, Owen Moore, Mary Alden, Fay Tincher, Robert Harron

† In 1928 Griffith remade the property with Phyllis Haver, Jean Hersholt, Belle Bennett, Sally O'Neil and Don Alvarado.

The Battle of the Sexes *
GB   1960   83m   bw
Prometheus (Monja Danischewsky)
V, V*

A lady efficiency expert upsets the even tenor of life at an Edinburgh tweed manufactory, and the chief accountant plans to eliminate her.

Sub-Ealing black comedy which tends to misfire despite effort all round.

w Monja Danischewsky   story The Catbird Seat by James Thurber   d Charles Crichton   ph Freddie Francis   m Stanley Black

Peter Sellers, Constance Cummings, Robert Morley, Jameson Clark, Moultrie Kelsall, Alex Mackenzie, Roddy McMillan, Donald Pleasence, Ernest Thesiger

The Battle of the V I
GB   1958   109m   bw
Criterion (George Maynard)
US titles: Unseen Heroes; Missiles from Hell

Polish patriots sabotage the German rocket installation at Peenemunde.

Effective though schoolboyish war adventure shot on a low budget: story development reasonably brisk though predictable.

w Jack Hanley, Eryk Wlodek   book Bernard Newman   d Vernon Sewell   ph Basil Emmott   m Robert Sharples

Michael Rennie, Patricia Medina, Milly Vitale, David Knight, Esmond Knight, Christopher Lee

The Battle of the Villa Fiorita
GB   1964   111m   Technicolor   Panavision
Warner (Delmer Daves)
US title: Affair at the Villa Fiorita

Two children aim to break up their mother's romance with an Italian concert pianist.

Quite lively, old-fashioned romantic comedy-drama largely set in a splendid Mediterranean villa; happy ending never in doubt.

wd Delmer Daves   novel Rumer Godden   ph Oswald Morris   m Mischa Spoliansky

Maureen O'Hara, Rossano Brazzi, Richard Todd, Phyllis Calvert, Olivia Hussey, Martin Stephens, Elizabeth Dear

Battle on the Beach: see The Battle at Bloody Beach

Battle Stations
US   1956   81m   bw
Columbia

Life on an aircraft carrier as seen by the padre.

Cliché-strewn, mini-budgeted war thriller.

w Crane Wilbur   d Lewis Seiler

John Lund, William Bendix, Keefe Brasselle, Richard Boone

Battle Stripe: see The Men

Battle Taxi
US   1954   82m   bw
UA (Ivan Tors)

A newcomer to the helicopter rescue service in Korea resents his non-combatant status, but becomes a hero.

The story takes second place to one damned rescue after another in this lively but overlong second feature.

w Malvin Wald   d Herbert L. Strock

Sterling Hayden, Arthur Franz, Marshall Thompson

Battle Zone
US   1952   81m   bw
Walter Wanger/Allied Artists

Two official war photographers in Korea fall out over a girl.

Very conventional war programmer.

w Steve Fisher   d Lesley Selander

John Hodiak, Stephen McNally, Linda Christian, Martin Milner, Dave Willock

'The guts! The girls! The glory! of a lot of wonderful guys!'
Battleground *
US   1949   118m   bw
MGM (Dore Schary)

How a group of American soldiers in 1944 endured the Battle of the Bulge.

Enormously successful at the box-office, this studio-bound production now seems stilted and unpersuasive, despite some good writing and direction.

w Robert Pirosh   d William Wellman   ph Paul C. Vogel   m Lennie Hayton   ed John Dunning

Van Johnson, John Hodiak, Ricardo Montalban, George Murphy, Marshall Thompson, Jerome Courtland, Don Taylor, Bruce Cowling, James Whitmore, Douglas Fowley, Leon Ames

'Engrossingly well done.' – Richard Mallett, Punch

AA: Robert Pirosh; Paul C. Vogel

AAN: best picture; William Wellman; James Whitmore; editing

Battles of Chief Pontiac
US   1953   75m   bw
Jack Broder

In the mid-18th century, peace talks with the Detroit Indians are sabotaged.

Slightly unusual but undistinguished slice of Western history.

w Jack de Witt   d Felix E. Feist

Lon Chaney Jnr, Lex Barker, Helen Westcott, Berry Kroeger, Roy Roberts

The Battleship Potemkin ****
USSR   1925   75m approx (16 fps)   bw   silent;
   sound version 65m
Goskino
V, V*, L
original title: Bronenosets Potemkin

A partly fictitious account of the mutiny at Odessa, an episode in the 1905 revolution. (The film was made as part of the 20th anniversary celebrations.)

A textbook cinema classic, and masterpiece of creative editing, especially in the famous Odessa Steps sequence in which innocent civilians are mown down in the bloodshed; the happenings of a minute are drawn into five by frenzied cross-cutting. The film contains 1,300 separate shots, and was judged the best film ever made in 1948 and 1958 by a panel of international judges.

wd Sergei Eisenstein   ph Edouard Tissé, V. Popov

A. Antonov, Grigori Alexandrov, Vladimir Barsky, Levshin

Battlestar Galactica
US   1979   125m   colour
Universal (John Dykstra)
V*, L

A spaceship crew battles its way back towards Earth.

Cobbled together from episodes of an unsuccessful TV series, the movie resembles a space version of another TV series, *Bonanza*, and borrows heavily from *Star Wars* to little effect.

w Glen A. Larson   d Richard A. Colla   ph Ben Coleman   m Stu Phillips   John E. Chilberg II   sp Apogee   ed Robert L. Kimble, Leon Ortiz-Gil, Larry Strong

Richard Hatch, Dirk Benedict, Lorne Greene, Ray Milland, Lew Ayres, Jane Seymour, Wilfred Hyde-White, John Colicos, Patrick Macnee

Battletruck
New Zealand   1981   94m   colour
Battletruck Films (Lloyd Phillips, Rob Whitehouse)
V*
aka: Warlords of the 21st Century

In the future, when civilization has been reduced to a few isolated communities, a lone hero on a motorbike battles a ruthless gang leader and his armoured truck.

A latter-day Western, full of gratuitous sadism, and no more than a pale shadow of *Mad Max*.

w Irving Austin, Harley Cokliss, John Beech   d Harley Cokliss   ph Chris Menges   m Kevin Peek   pd Gary Hansen   ed Michael Horton

Michael Beck, Annie McEnroe, James Wainwright, Bruno Lawrence, John Bach, John Ratzenberger, Randolph Powell

Battling Bellhop: see Kid Galahad (1937)

Battling Butler *
US   1926   68m approx (24 fps)   bw   silent
MGM (Joseph M. Schenck)

A young millionaire pretends to be a boxer in order to win a sweetheart.

Middling star comedy.

w Al Boasberg, Charles Smith, Paul Gerard Smith, Lex Neal   d Buster Keaton   ph J. Devereux Jennings, Bert Haines

Buster Keaton, Sally O'Neil

Battling with Buffalo Bill
US   1931   bw   serial: 12 eps
Universal

Buffalo Bill rids a town of a murderous gambler and also calms down hostile Indians.

Elementary serial stuff.   d Ray Taylor

Tom Tyler, Rex Bell, Francis Ford, Lucile Browne, William Desmond, Jim Thorpe, Yakima Canutt

The Bawdy Adventures of Tom Jones
GB   1976   94m   Technicolor
Universal/Robert Sadoff
V*

See *Tom Jones*, of which this is a musical version.

Not quite as bad as one would expect, but not up to the original.

w Jeremy Lloyd   play Don McPherson   d Cliff Owen   ph Douglas Slocombe   m Ron Grainer m/ly Paul Holden

Nicky Henson, Trevor Howard, Terry-Thomas, Arthur Lowe, Georgia Brown, Joan Collins, William Mervyn, Murray Melvin, Geraldine McEwan, Michael Bates, James Hayter, Isabel Dean, Gladys Henson

'A cheap, crude, sexed-up rehash with only three actual musical numbers . . . more boring than bawdy.' – Kevin Thomas, *Los Angeles Times*

Baxter *
GB   1972   100m   Technicolor
EMI/Performing Arts (Arthur Lewis)

An American son of divorced parents comes to London with his mother, meets tragedy in the shape of a friend's death, and responds to treatment for a speech defect.

Slight, appealing case history of a maladjusted 12-year-old; a rather unnecessarily uncommercial slice of life with no easy solution offered.

w Reginald Rose   d Lionel Jeffries   ph Geoffrey Unsworth   m Michael J. Lewis

Patricia Neal (as the therapist), Scott Jacoby, Britt Ekland, Jean-Pierre Cassel, Lynn Carlin, Paul Eddington

The Bay Boy
Canada/France   1984   101m   colour
Rank/Hachette Fox/Antenne 2/A2/CTV/HBO/Orion (John Kemeny, Denis Héroux)
V*, L

In 1937 Nova Scotia, a 16-year-old boy is distracted by real-life problems from his supposed vocation as a priest.

Doleful, weatherbeaten slice of autobiography which remains of interest only to those who know the country and the people.

wd Daniel Petrie   ph Claude Agostini   m Claude Bolling   pd Wolf Kroeger   ed Susan Shanks

Liv Ullmann, Kiefer Sutherland, Peter Donat, Allan Scarfe, Chris Wiggins

Bay of Angels: see *La Baie des Anges*

'The first motion picture to require a face-to-face warning. May be the last shock film you will ever want to see!'
A Bay of Blood (dubbed)
Italy   1971   90m   colour
Nuovo Linea (Giuseppe Zaccariello)
V (W), V*
original title: *Ecologia del Delitto*; aka: *Antefatto*; *Bloodbath Bay of Blood*; *Carnage*; *Last House on the Left Part II*; *Twitch of the Death Nerve*

In a struggle to gain control of a beautiful bay ripe for development, thirteen people are murdered.

There's not much narrative in this movie, which is more an exercise in thinking up inventive ways for people to die, with each victim killed by a different means. It is original, in that there are multiple killers at work, as each murderer becomes a victim in turn, and it is done with some style and a heavy irony.

w Mario Bava, Joseph McLee (Giuseppe Zaccariello), Filippo Ottoni   story Dardano Sacchetti, Franco Barberi   d Mario Bava   ph Mario Bava   m Stelvio Cipriani   ad Sergio Canevari   ed Carlo Realy

Claudine Auger, Luigi Pistilli, Claudio Volonte, Anna M. Rosati, Chris Avram, Leopoldo Trieste, Laura Betti, Brigitte Skay, Isa Miranda

† The British video release runs for 81m. When it was first shown in America, as a gimmick ticket-holders had to pass through a 'final warning station' before being allowed to see the film.

The Bay of St Michel
GB   1963   73m   bw
Rank/Trionyx

Commandos return to Normandy to seek hidden Nazi loot.

Uninspired hokum programmer.

w Christopher David   d John Ainsworth

Keenan Wynn, Mai Zetterling, Ronald Howard, Rona Anderson, Trader Faulkner, Edward Underdown

Be Big *
US   1931   20m   bw
Hal Roach
V

Ollie feigns illness to avoid a trip with his wife, but Stan's help proves disastrous.

Comedy warm-up for *Sons of the Desert*; Ollie spends most of the second reel trying to rid himself of a tight boot.

w H. M. Walker   d James Parrott

Laurel and Hardy, Anita Garvin, Isabelle Keith

The Beach Girls and the Monster
US   1966   70m   bw
Edward Janis/Films

An oceanographer finds something very strange emerging from the waters of Waikiki Beach.

Elementary horror flick which fails to scare and is only notable for the re-emergence of its star.

w Joan Gardner   d Jon Hall

Jon Hall, Sue Casey, Walker Edmiston, Arnold Lessing

The Beach of Lost Children
Mali   1991   88m   colour
Paris Plage/Herakles (Mohamed Abderrahman Tazi)
aka: *La Plage des Enfants Perdus*

A father hides away his simple-minded daughter when he discovers that she is pregnant by a local taxi driver.

Leaden and curiously inert treatment of a dramatic story.

wd Jillali Ferhati   ph Gilberto Azevedo, Jacques Besse   m Djamel Allam   ad Abdelkrim Akkelach ed Natalie Perrey

Souad Ferhati, Mohamed Timod, Fatima Loukili, Larbi El Yacoubi, Nezha Zakaria, Mohamed Larbi Khazzan, Safia Ziani

Beach Party *
US   1963   104m   Pathecolor   Panavision
AIP/Alta Vista (James H. Nicholson)
V*

An anthropologist sets up house on a California beach to study the mating habits of young people but

becomes personally involved when one of them falls for him.

Vaguely satirical pop musical with relaxed performances; quite tolerable in itself, it started an excruciating trend.

w Lou Rusoff   d William Asher   ph Kay Norton m Les Baxter

Robert Cummings, Dorothy Malone, Annette Funicello, Frankie Avalon, Vincent Price, Harvey Lembeck, Morey Amsterdam, Jody McCrea

Beach Red *
US   1967   105m   Technicolor
UA/Theodora (Cornel Wilde)

In 1943, American assault craft take a Japanese-held Pacific island.

Brutal, pacifist war film, simply and clearly portrayed but not exactly entertaining.

w Clint Johnston, Donald A. Peters, Jefferson Pascal d Cornel Wilde   ph Cecil R. Cooney   m Antonio Buenaventura

Cornel Wilde, Rip Torn, Burr de Benning, Jean Wallace

The Beachcomber (1938): see
Vessel of Wrath

The Beachcomber *
GB   1954   90m   Technicolor
GFD/London Independent (William MacQuitty)
V*

An alcoholic ne'er-do-well in the Dutch East Indies reforms after an unexpected adventure with a lady missionary.

Styleless remake of *Vessel of Wrath* (qv); the acting just about holds the interest, but all other contributions are flat.

w Sydney Box   story Somerset Maugham d Muriel Box   ph Reg Wyer   m Francis Chagrin

Robert Newton, Glynis Johns, Donald Sinden, Paul Rogers, Donald Pleasence, Walter Crisham, Michael Hordern, Ronald Lewis

Beaches *
US   1988   123m   Metrocolor
Warner/Touchstone/An All Girl Production (Bonnie Bruckheimer-Martell, Bette Midler, Margaret Jennings South)
V, V*, L, S

A singer visits her dying friend, a lawyer, and recalls their long and volatile friendship.

In another age, this sentimental feminist weepie would have been classified as a woman's picture, though Midler's singing gives it a wider appeal.

w Mary Agnes Donoghue   novel Iris Rainer Dart d Garry Marshall   ph Dante Spinotti   m Georges Delerue   pd Albert Brenner   ad Garrett Lewis ed Richard Halsey

Bette Midler, Barbara Hershey, John Heard, Spalding Gray, Lainie Kazan, James Read, Grace Johnston, Mayim Bialik, Marcie Leeds

AAN: best art direction

Beachhead
US   1953   90m   Technicolor
UA (Aubrey Schenck)

American marines land on a Pacific island to bring back a planter who has supplied information.

World War II jungle thriller, not too badly done.

w Richard Alan Simmons   d Stuart Heisler

Tony Curtis, Frank Lovejoy, Mary Murphy, Eduard Franz

The Beads of One Rosary *
Poland   1979   116m   colour
Cinegate/PRF-Zespol Filmowy
original title: *Paciorki Jednego Różańca*

A retired miner and his wife defy attempts by
property developers to demolish their cottage.

There is something of the charm of an Ealing comedy
in this tale of a little man standing up to bureaucratic
pressures.

wd Kazimierz Kutz   *ph* Wieslaw Zdort
m Wojciech Kilar   *ad* Andrzej Plocki, Miroslaw
Krelik   *ed* Jozef Bartczak

Augustyn Halotta, Marta Straszna, Ewa Wiśniewska,
Franciszek Pieczka

The Bear **
France   1989   98m   Eastmancolor   Panavision
Tri-Star/Renn/Price Entertainment (Claude Berri)
V, V*, L, S

An orphaned bear cub tries to cope with life in the
wild.

Charming film, told from the bear's point of view,
with natural sounds substituting for dialogue.

w Gérard Brach   *novel* *The Grizzly King* by James
Oliver Curwood   *d* Jean-Jacques Annaud
ph Philippe Rousselot   *m* Philippe Sarde   *pd* Toni
Ludi   *ed* Noelle Boisson

Bart, Youk, Jack Wallace, Tcheky Karyo, André
Lacombe

AAN: best film editing

Bear Country: see *The Living Desert*

'Below freezing and beyond fear . . . will anyone survive its
terror?'
Bear Island
GB/Canada   1979   118m   colour   Panavision
Columbia/Bear Island/Selkirk (Peter Snell)
V, V*

Meteorological experts on an Arctic island are
menaced by neo-Nazis.

Highly implausible adventure yarn, indifferently
presented.

w David Butler, Don Sharp   *novel* Alistair MacLean
d Don Sharp   *ph* Alan Hume   *m* Robert Farnon

Vanessa Redgrave, Donald Sutherland, Richard
Widmark, Christopher Lee, Barbara Parkins,
Lloyd Bridges

The Bears and I
US   1974   89m   Technicolor
Walt Disney (Winston Hibler)
V*

An army veteran goes to live near an Indian
settlement and adopts three bear cubs, later becoming
a Park Ranger.

Simple, pleasing outdoor family film.

w John Whedon   *novel* Robert Franklin Leslie
d Bernard McEveety   *ph* Ted D. Landon   *m* Buddy
Baker

Patrick Wayne, Chief Dan George, Andrew Duggan,
Michael Ansara

'A Thrill-Story Beyond All Imagining!'
'King of Prehistoric Sea Giants . . . Raging Up From The
Bottom of Time!'
The Beast from Twenty Thousand Fathoms
US   1953   80m   bw
Warner (Hal Chester, Jack Dietz)
V*, L

Heat generated by an atomic bomb test in the Arctic
thaws out a prehistoric rhedosaurus which travels
down the American coast to cause havoc in New York
until cornered and destroyed on Coney Island.

Flat-footed addition to the monster cycle, with an
interminable wait for the beast's appearance and
inferior trick work when he goes on the rampage.

w Lou Morheim, Fred Freiburger   *d* Eugène Lourié
ph Jack Russell   *m* David Buttolph   *sp* Ray
Harryhausen

Paul Christian, Paula Raymond, Cecil Kellaway (as a
professor gobbled up in a bathysphere), Kenneth
Tobey, Donald Woods, Lee Van Cleef

The Beast in the Cellar
GB   1970   87m   Eastmancolor
Tigon-Leander (Tony Tenser, Graham Harris)

A rampaging killer in the Lancashire woods turns out
to be the deranged ex-soldier brother of two elderly
spinsters who have kept him locked up for thirty
years.

Idiotically boring farrago, totally lacking in suspense
and wasting good talent.

wd James Kelly   *ph* Harry Waxman, Desmond
Dickinson   *m* Tony Macaulay

Flora Robson, Beryl Reid, Tessa Wyatt, John Hamill,
T. P. McKenna

The Beast Must Die *
GB   1974   93m   Technicolor
BL/Amicus (Milton Subotsky)
V, V*, L
aka: *Black Werewolf*

A millionaire big game hunter holds a weekend party
to track down a werewolf, but his guest list rapidly
gets smaller . . .

A savage variation on *Ten Little Indians*, not badly
done, with such gimmicks as a 'guess who' break near
the end.

w Michael Winner   *story* James Blish   *d* Paul
Annett   *ph* Jack Hildyard   *m* Douglas Gamley

Calvin Lockhart, Peter Cushing, Charles Gray, Anton
Diffring, Marlene Clark, Ciaran Madden, Michael
Gambon

The Beast of Hollow Mountain
US/Mexico   1956   78m   DeLuxe   Cinemascope/
Regiscope
UA/Peliculas Rodriguez (William and Edward Nassour)

An American rancher in Mexico has to deal with a
jealous rival and a rampaging tyrannosaurus rex.

Uneasy mix of routine cowboy movie and
substandard science fiction.

w Robert Hill, Jack DeWitt   *story* Willis O'Brien
d Edward Nassour, Ismael Rodriguez   *ph* Jorge
Stahl Jnr   *m* Raul Lavista   *ed* Holbrook Todd,
Maury Wright

Guy Madison, Patricia Medina, Carlos Rivas, Edward
Noriega, Julio Villaneal, Mario Novarro

'It should rack up handsome returns for its producers
and provide moppet audiences particularly with
edge-of-the-seat entertainment during its fantasy
sequences.' – *Variety*

† The Regiscope system promised 'animation in
depth', but its stop motion effects with fuzzy back
projection are comic rather than horrific. The central
notion of this first science-fiction Western turned up
again in *Valley of Gwangi* (qv).

Beast of Morocco: see *The Hand of Night*

Beast of the City
US   1932   80m   bw
MGM

A police captain is determined to get a ruthless
racketeer by fair means or foul.

Curiously dour little crime melodrama with a high
death rate; the cast does not quite save it.

w John Lee Mahin   *story* W. R. Burnett   *d* Charles
Brabin   *ph* Barney McGill

Walter Huston, Jean Harlow, Wallace Ford, Jean
Hersholt, Dorothy Petersen, Tully Marshall, John
Miljan

'A gang story for rural and home circle consumption,
preaching the gospel of civic righteousness and the
glory of steadfast purpose. Aiming at domestic
patronage, they even make Miss Harlow keep her
skirts down.' – *Variety*

'Endowed with vitality and realism.' – *New York Times*

The Beast with a Million Eyes
US   1955   84m   bw
San Matteo/AIP

A malicious space creature lands in the desert but is
defeated by human love.

Semi-professional would-be horror story, on a level
with the Corman horrors of the period.

w Tom Filer   *d* David Karmansky

Paul Birch, Lorna Thayer, Dick Sargent

The Beast with Five Fingers *
US   1946   88m   bw
Warner (William Jacobs)
V*

A famous pianist dies and his severed hand returns to
commit murder.

Slow-moving, Italian-set horror thriller which wastes
an excellent original; a superb central performance
and clever trick effects can hardly redeem the stodgy
script or the ending which reveals the hauntings as an
hallucination.

w Curt Siodmak   *story* W. F. Harvey   *d* Robert
Florey   *ph* Wesley Anderson   *m* Max Steiner

Peter Lorre, Andrea King, Robert Alda, J. Carrol Naish,
Victor Francen, Charles Dingle

The Beastmaster
US   1982   118m   colour
EMI/Ecta/Leisure Investments (Paul Pepperman, Sylvio Tabet)
V, V*, L

A royal child, stolen at birth by a witch, is rescued by
a peasant who brings him up skilled in the martial
arts.

Comic strip sword and sorcery: fairly high budget but
very low intelligence.

w Don Coscarelli, Paul Pepperman   *d* Don
Coscarelli   *ph* John Alcott   *m* Lee Holdridge
pd Conrad E. Angone   *ed* Roy Watts

Marc Singer, Tanya Roberts, Rip Torn, John Amos,
Rod Loomis

Beastmaster 2: Through the Portals of Time
US   1991   107m   CFI colour
Republic/Films 21 (Sylvio Tabet)
V, V*, L, S

A mythical warrior and his animal friends are
transported through time to present-day Los Angeles
to battle against his evil brother.

More comic-strip sword and sorcery: very low budget,
even lower intelligence.

w R. J. Robertson, Jim Wynorski, Sylvio Tabet, Ken
Hauser, Doug Miles   *novel* *The Beastmaster* by André
Norton   *d* Sylvio Tabet   *m* Ronn Schmid
m Robert Folk   *pd* Allen Jones   *ed* Adam Bernardi

Marc Singer, Kari Wuhrer, Wings Hauser, Sarah
Douglas, Charles Young

'Despite this low-budget sequel's silly dialogue and
cheesy special effects . . . a mildly engaging tongue-
in-cheek fantasy.' —*Variety*

The Beat Generation
US   1959   95m   bw   Cinemascope
Albert Zugsmith
L
aka: *This Rebel Age*

A vicious rapist joins the beatniks.

Bankrupt exploitation melodrama, not easy to sit through.

w Richard Matheson, Lewis Meltzer   d Charles Haas   ph Walter H. Castle   m Albert Glasser

Ray Danton, Steve Cochran, Fay Spain, Mamie Van Doren, Jackie Coogan, Louis Armstrong, Maggie Hayes, Jim Mitchum, Irish McCalla, Maxie Rosenbloom

'An enervating mixture of slapstick, religiosity, psychological hokum and grubby sensationalism.' – *MFB*

Beat Girl
GB   1960   85m   bw
Renown
US title: *Wild for Kicks*

An architect's teenage daughter goes to the dogs.

Risible exposé-style melodrama.

w Dail Ambler   d Edmond T. Greville

David Farrar, Noelle Adam, Christopher Lee, Gillian Hills, Adam Faith

Beat Street
US   1984   106m   DeLuxe   Movielab
Orion (David V. Picker, Harry Belafonte)

An aspiring DJ from South Bronx has trouble getting into showbiz.

For teenagers only; a rehash of *Saturday Night Fever* applied to the new fad of break-dancing.

w Andy Davis, David Gilbert, Paul Golding   d Stan Lathan   ph Tom Priestley   m Harry Belafonte   pd Patrizia von Brandenstein   ed Dov Hoenig

Rae Dawn Chong, Guy Davis, Jon Chardiet, Leon W. Grant, Saundra Santiago

'Adventure at its boldest! Bogart at his best!'
Beat the Devil *
GB   1953   100m   bw
Romulus/Santana (Jack Clayton)
V*, L

In a small Mediterranean port, and subsequently on a boat bound for the African coast, oddly assorted travellers plan to acquire land known to contain uranium deposits. Unsatisfactory, over-talkative and inconsequential burlesque of the director's own *The Maltese Falcon* and *Across the Pacific*.

Good fun was obviously had by the cast, but audiences were mostly baffled by the in-jokes, the extra-strange characters, and the lack of attention to pace, suspense and plot development.

w Truman Capote, John Huston   novel James Helvick   d John Huston   ph Oswald Morris   m Franco Mannino

Humphrey Bogart (Billy Dannreuther), *Jennifer Jones* (Gwendolen Chelm), Gina Lollobrigida (Maria Dannreuther), *Edward Underdown* (Harry Chelm), Peter Lorre (O'Hara), Robert Morley (Petersen), *Ivor Barnard* (Major Ross), Bernard Lee (Inspector), Marco Tulli (Ravello)

GWENDOLEN: 'Harry, we must beware of these men. They're desperate characters. Not one of them looked at my legs.'

DANNREUTHER: 'Trouble with England, it's all pomp and no circumstance. You're very wise to get out of it, escape while you can.'

O'HARA: 'Time! Time! What is time? The Swiss manufacture it. The French hoard it. Italians want it. Americans say it is money. Hindus say it does not exist. Do you know what I say? I say time is a crook.'

'A potential treat emerged as a wet firecracker . . . the incidents remain on a naggingly arch and lagging verbal keel.' – *New York Times*

'Each of its cinematic clichés appears to be placed in the very faintest of mocking quotation marks.' – *Time*

'Only the phonies liked it. It's a mess!' – *Humphrey Bogart*

'The formula of *Beat the Devil* is that everyone is slightly absurd.' – *John Huston*

† James Helvick was the pseudonym of Claud Cockburn.

Beau Brummell *
US   1924   104m approx at 24 fps   bw   silent
Warner

A Regency dandy becomes the right-hand man of the Prince of Wales, but falters through his own arrogance.

Elegant period romance which marked the beginning of its star's great movie decade.

w Dorothy Farnum   d Harry Beaumont

John Barrymore, Mary Astor, Carmel Myers, Willard Louis

Beau Brummell *
GB   1954   111m   Eastmancolor
MGM (Sam Zimbalist)
V*

A Regency dandy enjoys a close relationship with the Prince of Wales, and when this is eventually withdrawn he dies in penury.

Stodgy historical romance with entertaining patches; the main story is too graceful and conventional to be believed.

w Karl Tunberg   play Clyde Fitch   d Curtis Bernhardt   ph Oswald Morris   m Richard Addinsell   ad Alfred Junge

Stewart Granger, Elizabeth Taylor, *Peter Ustinov* (as the Prince), *Robert Morley* (as George III), James Donald, James Hayter, Rosemary Harris, Paul Rogers, Noel Willman, Peter Bull, Peter Dyneley

Beau Chumps: see *Beau Hunks*

'Hard lives, quick deaths, undying love!'
Beau Geste **
US   1926   120m approx (24 fps)   bw (colour sequences)   silent
Paramount (Herbert Brenon)

Three English brothers join the Foreign Legion, suffer under a brutal sergeant, and die fighting the Arabs.

Although outmoded even when first filmed, this tale of derring-do and self sacrifice usually works, and in this case it gave its star a fresh image. One of the best remembered silents of the twenties.

w Paul Schofield   novel P. C. Wren   d Herbert Brenon   ph Roy Hunt   ad Julian Boone Fleming

Ronald Colman, Neil Hamilton, Ralph Forbes, Alice Joyce, Mary Brian, *Noah Beery*, William Powell, Victor McLaglen

† Remade 1939 and 1966; sequel, *Beau Ideal*, 1931.

'Three against the world! Brothers and soldiers all!'
Beau Geste **
US   1939   120m   bw
Paramount (William Wellman)
V*, L

Spirited remake, with the famous flashback opening of the desert fort defended by corpses.

Style and acting generally satisfactory.

w Robert Carson   d William Wellman   ph Theodor Sparkuhl, Archie Stout   m Alfred Newman   ad Hans Dreier, Robert Odell

Gary Cooper, Ray Milland, Robert Preston, *Brian Donlevy*, J. Carrol Naish, Susan Hayward, Heather

Thatcher, James Stephenson, Donald O'Connor, G. P. Huntley Jnr, Albert Dekker, Broderick Crawford

FOREWORD: 'The love of a man for a woman waxes and wanes like the moon, but the love of brother for brother is steadfast as the stars and endures like the word of the prophet . . .' Arabian proverb

MARKOFF: 'Keep shooting, you scum! You'll get a chance yet to die with your boots on!'

'Its melodrama is sometimes grim but never harrowing, its pace is close to hectic and its suspense is constant.' – *Herbert Cohn, Brooklyn Daily Eagle*

'A morbid picture, but I doubt whether any morality council will take action, the whole story being so wrapped up in the school colours – in comradeship and loyalty and breeding, and the pure girl left behind; morbid because the brutality has no relation whatever to the real world; it is uncriticized daydreaming.' – *Graham Greene*

'A handsome treatment of a well-loved adventure tale.' – *New York Daily Mirror*

'Will do nominal biz, but lacks punch for smash proportions.' – *Variety*

Shot in Buttercup Valley, west of Yuma.

† The nasty sergeant, originally Lejeune, became Markoff to avoid offending the French.

AAN: Brian Donlevy; Hans Dreier, Robert Odell

Beau Geste
US   1966   105m   Techniscope
Universal (Walter Seltzer)

The central desert section of the story is here augmented, with violence stressed, and Beau allowed to survive at the end.

A cheap leery melodrama is what results from the jettisoning of all the romantic portions of the original.

wd Douglas Heyes   ph Bud Thackery   m Hans Salter

Telly Savalas (rampant as the sadistic sergeant), Guy Stockwell, Doug McClure, Leslie Nielsen, Leo Gordon, Michael Constantine

Beau Hunks **
US   1931   40m   bw
Hal Roach
V
GB title: *Beau Chumps*

A fool and his friend join the Foreign Legion to forget.

Patchy but amiable star comedy with memorable high spots. In-joke: the woman the whole legion wants to forget is Jean Harlow.

w H. M. Walker   d James W. Horne

Laurel and Hardy, Charles Middleton

Beau Ideal
US   1931   75m   bw
RKO (William Le Baron)

John Geste and a new legionnaire friend become involved in a religious war started by a rascally emir.

Lame sequel to *Beau Geste*, fettered by primitive dialogue.

w Paul Schofield   novel P. C. Wren   d Herbert Brenon   ph J. Roy Hunt   m Max Steiner

Lester Vail, Ralph Forbes, Don Alvarado, Loretta Young, Irene Rich

'Ordinary programme picture with slight romance. Doubtful draw for women.' – *Variety*

'He took New York for its wildest joy ride!'
Beau James *
US   1957   107m   Technicolor   Vistavision
Paramount/Hope Enterprises (Jack Rose)

The vaguely crooked career of Jimmy Walker, mayor of New York in the twenties.

Romanticized biopic with few funny moments: Hope cannot cope with the drama, and the result is a creaking vehicle apart from a well-recreated twenties atmosphere and excellent production values.

w Jack Rose, Melville Shavelson   *book* Gene Fowler
d Melville Shavelson   *ph* John F. Warren
m Joseph J. Lilley

Bob Hope, Paul Douglas, Vera Miles, Alexis Smith, Darren McGavin, Joe Mantell, Walter Catlett   *guest stars* Jack Benny, George Jessel, Jimmy Durante   *narrator* Walter Winchell (Alistair Cooke in GB)

Le Beau Mariage *
France   1981   97m   colour
Les Films du Losange/Les Films du Carrosse (Margaret Menegoz)
V
GB title: *A Good Marriage*

An art student abandons her many affairs and announces her intention of getting married, but her intended proves reluctant . . .

Quietly amusing conversation piece in the style expected of this director; an after-dinner entertainment for the *Sunday Times* set.

wd Eric Rohmer   *ph* Bernard Lutic   *m* Ronan Girre, Simon des Innocents

Beatrice Ronand, André Dussollier, Feodor Atkine, Arielle Dombasle

Beau Sabreur
US   1928   85m (24 fps)   bw   silent
Paramount

A French officer is sent to the Sahara to negotiate a treaty with a powerful sheik.

Romantic adventure concocted to use up bits and pieces left over from *Beau Geste*. Not a hit.

w Tom Geraghty   *d* John Waters

Gary Cooper, Evelyn Brent, Noah Beery, William Powell, Roscoe Karns

Le Beau Serge *
France   1958   97m   bw
AYJM (Jean Cotet)

A student returns to his home town and tries to redeem his old friend who has become a drunkard.

Enjoyable character drama with well observed village backgrounds. Credited with being the spearhead of the 'new wave'.

wd Claude Chabrol   *ph* Henri Decaë   *m* Emile Delpierre

Gérard Blain, Jean-Claude Brialy, Michèle Meritz, Bernadette Lafont

La Beauté du Diable ***
Italy/France   1949   96m   bw
AYJM

The Faust story with the protagonists agreeing to change places.

Dazzling plot twists and cinematic virtuosity make this a richly enjoyable fantasy, though perhaps not among Clair's greatest works.

w René Clair, Armand Salacrou   *d* René Clair
ph Michel Kelber   *m* Roman Vlad   *ad* Léon Barsacq

Michel Simon, Gérard Philipe, Raymond Cordy, Nicole Besnard, Gaston Modot, Paolo Stoppa

'She's got the biggest six-shooters in the west!'
The Beautiful Blonde from Bashful Bend *
US   1949   77m   Technicolor
TCF (Preston Sturges)
V*, L

A temperamental saloon entertainer accidentally shoots the sheriff and takes refuge as a schoolmistress.

A dishevelled Western farce unworthy of its creator, but with the advantage of appearances by many of his usual repertory of players.

wd Preston Sturges   *ph* Harry Jackson   *m* Cyril Mockridge

Betty Grable, Cesar Romero, El Brendel, Hugh Herbert, Rudy Vallee, Olga San Juan, Sterling Holloway, Porter Hall, Esther Howard, Margaret Hamilton

'It erects a fabric of roaring slapstick on a conventional western foundation, and from time to time it succeeds in being very funny.' – *Richard Mallett, Punch*

'Somehow the ramshackle air of Bashful Bend itself seems to have permeated the whole film.' – *MFB*

Beautiful but Broke
US   1944   74m   bw
Columbia (Irving Briskin)

An agent and a girls' band get romantically marooned on the way to a date in Cleveland.

Haphazard comedy with music; just an occasional smile amid the tedium.

w Manny Seff, Arthur Housman   *d* Charles Barton

Joan Davis, Jane Frazee, John Hubbard, Judy Clark, Willie West and McGinty

'Commonplace B entry.' – *Variety*

Beautiful But Dangerous: see *She Couldn't Say No*

The Beautiful Cheat: see *What a Woman*

Beautiful Dreamers
Canada   1990   105m   colour
Blue Dolphin/Starway/National Film Board of Canada (Michael MacLear, Martin Walters, Sally Bochner)
V, V*, L

The poet Walt Whitman forms a friendship with the liberal superintendent of a Canadian mental asylum.

Hokum, disguised as a life-enhancing drama.

wd John Kent Harrison   *ph* François Protat
m Lawrence Shragge   *pd* Seamus Flannery
ed Ron Wisman

Colm Feore, Rip Torn, Wendel Meldrum, Sheila McCarthy, Colin Fox, David Gardner, Barbara Gordon, Marsha Moreau, Albert Schultz

The Beautiful End of this World
West Germany   1983   95m   colour
Pentagramma (Rainer Erler)

Sent to Australia to establish a pesticide factory, a German chemical engineer is persuaded that the project would be an ecological disaster.

Dull, if well-meaning, demonstrating that, in movies, good intentions are never enough.

wd Rainer Erler   *ph* Wolfgang Grasshoff   *m* Eugen Thomass   *ad* Chris Harrison, Michael Pilz
ed Ulrike Pahl

Robert Atzorn, Claire Oberman, Judy Winter, Gotz George

The Beautiful Rebel: see *Janice Meredith*

Beautiful Stranger
GB   1954   89m   bw
Marksman (Maxwell Setton, John R. Sloan)
V*
US title: *Twist of Fate*

On the Riviera, an actress discovers that her fiancé is a criminal.

Tawdry star melodrama of virtually no interest.

w Robert Westerby, Carl Nystrom   *d* David Miller
ph Robert Day, Ted Scaife   *m* Malcolm Arnold

Ginger Rogers, Jacques Bergerac, Herbert Lom, Stanley Baker, Margaret Rawlings, Eddie Byrne, Coral Browne

Beauty and the Beast (1946): see
La Belle et la Bête

'The most beautiful love story ever told.'
Beauty and the Beast *
US   1991   85m   Technicolor
Buena Vista/Walt Disney/Silver Screen Partners IV (Don Hahn)
V, V*, L, S

A prince, turned into a beast by enchantment, is rescued by the love of a beautiful girl.

A return to top form by Disney, with excellent animation and a singable score. The picture has been credited with starting a new Hollywood fashion for animated musicals.

w Linda Woolverton   *d* Gary Trousdale, Kirk Wise
m/ly Alan Menken, Howard Ashman   *ad* Brian McEntee   *ed* John Carnochan

voices of Paige O'Hara, Robby Benson, Jerry Orbach, Angela Lansbury, Richard White, David Ogden Stiers, Jesse Corti, Rex Everhart, Bradley Michael Pierce, Jo Anne Worley, Kimmy Robertson

'A lovely film that ranks with the best of Disney's animated classics.' – *Variety*

'It's got storytelling vigour and clarity, bright eclectic animation, and a frisky musical wit.' – *New Yorker*

AA: Alan Menken; song 'Beauty and the Beast' (*m* Alan Menken, *ly* Howard Ashman)

AAN: film; song 'Belle'; song 'Be Our Guest'; sound

Beauty and the Boss
US   1932   75m   bw
Warner

A girl down on her luck becomes secretary to an amorous banker and eventually becomes his wife.

Artless Cinderella story in an uneasy Viennese setting.

w Joseph Jackson   *play The Church Mouse* by Ladislas Fodor, Paul Frank   *d* Roy del Ruth

Warren William, Marian Marsh, Charles Butterworth, Frederick Kerr, Lillian Bond

'Elementary stuff for the B houses, titularly phrased for flap appeal.' – *Variety*

Beauty for Sale
US   1933   85m   bw
MGM
aka: *Beauty!*

An innocent girl snares a rich man while working in a beauty parlour.

Well-mounted romantic comedy-drama with most of the elements the 1933 public wanted.

w Zelda Sears and Eve Greene   *novel Beauty* by Faith Baldwin   *d* Richard Boleslawski

Madge Evans, Alice Brady, Una Merkel, Otto Kruger, May Robson, Phillips Holmes, Eddie Nugent, Hedda Hopper

'Pulp magazine fiction made for subway-riding stenographers . . . romantic hoke skilfully dressed up.' – *Variety*

Beauty for the Asking
US   1939   68m   bw
RKO
V*

Jealousies flourish among the women in a cosmetics showroom.

Average supporting drama for female audiences.

w Doris Anderson, Paul Jarrico   *d* Glenn Tryon

Lucille Ball, Frieda Inescort, Patric Knowles, Donald Woods, Inez Courtney

The Beauty Jungle *
GB   1964   114m   Eastmancolor   Cinemascope
Rank/Val Guest
US title: *Contest Girl*

A typist enters a beauty contest and step by step becomes Miss Globe; but her descent is equally rapid.

Wicked show biz and the road to ruin in one glossy package, predictable, but not badly done; always something going on, and performed with gusto.

w Robert Muller, Val Guest   *d* Val Guest   *ph* Arthur Grant   *m* Laurie Johnson

Janette Scott, Ian Hendry, Ronald Fraser, Edmund Purdom, Kay Walsh, Norman Bird, Janina Faye, Tommy Trinder, Francis Matthews

Because of Him *
US   1945   88m   bw
Universal (Felix Jackson)

A waitress pesters a Broadway author and actor for a leading role in their new show.

Moderately sprightly star vehicle with bonuses in the leading men; handling disappointingly routine.

w Edmund Beloin   *d* Richard Wallace   *ph* Hal Mohr   *m* Miklos Rozsa

Deanna Durbin, Charles Laughton, Franchot Tone, Helen Broderick, Stanley Ridges, Donald Meek

'Even in the first wild joy of his arms, she realized that she would be ... an unfit mother!'
Because of You
US   1952   95m   bw
U-I (Albert J. Cohen)

A female ex-convict marries on parole but does not tell her husband of her past. Her old associates involve her innocently in another crime, and her husband divorces her; but years later she gets him and their child back.

Soap opera of the stickiest kind, made quite tolerable by good production.

w Ketti Frings   *d* Joseph Pevney   *ph* Russell Metty   *m* Frank Skinner

Loretta Young, Jeff Chandler, Alex Nicol, Frances Dee, Lynne Roberts, Alexander Scourby, Mae Clarke

'Shows the most whole-hearted devotion to woman's magazine conventions.' – *MFB*

'Whoever you are, you're in this picture! Because this tells of youth's challenge to grown-ups who can't understand!'
Because They're Young
US   1960   98m   bw
Columbia/Drexel (Jerry Bresler)

A high school teacher helps one of his tougher pupils not to slip into crime.

Routine sentimental melodrama, slightly redeemed by directorial expertise.

w James Gunn   *novel* Harrison High by John Farris   *d* Paul Wendkos   *ph* Wilfrid Cline   *m* Johnny Williams

Dick Clark, Michael Callan, Tuesday Weld, Victoria Shaw, Warren Berlinger, Doug McClure

Because You're Mine
US   1952   103m   Technicolor
MGM (Joe Pasternak)
V*

An opera singer becomes a GI and wins the sergeant's sister.

Lumbering inept star vehicle, giving the impression of nothing at all happening between the songs.

w Leonard Spigelgass, Karl Tunberg   *d* Alexander Hall   *ph* Joseph Ruttenberg   *md* Johnny Green

Mario Lanza, Doretta Morrow, James Whitmore, Dean Miller, Paula Corday, Jeff Donnell, Spring Byington

'On a dull day in Manchester it will bring colour to the greyness of life.' – *Sunday Express*

AAN: title song (*m* Nicholas Brodszky, *ly* Sammy Cahn)

'The screen explodes with rage and passion and greatness!'
Becket **
GB   1964   149m   Technicolor   Panavision
Paramount/Hal B. Wallis
V*, L

Henry II leans on his boisterous Saxon friend Thomas à Becket, but when the latter is made first chancellor and then archbishop a rift between them widens and ends in Becket's assassination by Henry's over-eager knights.

Jean Anouilh's bitter stage comedy is filmed literally and soberly as a rather anaemic epic, so that the point is lost and the edge blunted. The paucity of physical action causes good scenes to alternate with long stretches of tedium.

w Edward Anhalt   *d* Peter Glenville   *ph* Geoffrey Unsworth   *m* Laurence Rosenthal

Richard Burton, Peter O'Toole, Donald Wolfit, *John Gielgud*, Martita Hunt, Pamela Brown, Sian Phillips, Paolo Stoppa

'Handsome, respectable and boring.' – *John Simon*

'The power of the film is in the close-up, the concentration on the two protagonists. And what is so fascinating is that Burton and O'Toole provide no ultimate answers for each other or for us.' – *Judith Crist*

AA: Edward Anhalt

AAN: best picture; Peter Glenville; Geoffrey Unsworth; Laurence Rosenthal; Richard Burton; Peter O'Toole; John Gielgud

Becky Sharp **
US   1935   83m   Technicolor
RKO (Kenneth MacGowan)
V*

An ambitious girl makes her way into Regency society.

Chiefly notable as the first feature in three-colour Technicolor, this rather theatrical piece has its civilized enjoyments and the director made a few predictable cinematic experiments; the overall effect, however, is patchy.

w Francis Edwards Faragoh   *play* Landon Mitchell   *novel* Vanity Fair by W. M. Thackeray   *d* Rouben Mamoulian   *ph* Ray Rennahan   *m* Roy Webb   *pd* Robert Edmond Jones

Miriam Hopkins, *Cedric Hardwicke*, Frances Dee, Billie Burke, Alison Skipworth, Nigel Bruce, Alan Mowbray, Colin Tapley, G. P. Huntley Jnr

'Beautiful cinematographically but weak on story. No cinch, and should be sold on colour angle.' – *Variety*

'As pleasing to the eye as a fresh fruit sundae, but not much more.' – *Otis Ferguson*

'If colour is to be of permanent importance a way must be found to use it realistically, not only as a beautiful decoration. It must be made to contribute to our sense of truth. The machine gun, the cheap striped tie, the battered Buick and the shabby bar will need a subtler colour sense than the Duchess of Richmond's ball, the girls of Miss Pinkerton's Academy, the Marquess of Steyne's dinner for two. Can Technicolor reproduce with the necessary accuracy the suit that has been worn too long, the oily hat?' – *Graham Greene*

AAN: Miriam Hopkins

Bed and Board **
France/Italy   1970   97m   Eastmancolor
Columbia/Les Films du Carrosse/Valoria/Fida Cinematografica (Marcel Berbert)
original title: *Domicile Conjugal*

Antoine Doinel, the hero of three previous films, becomes a husband, father, writer and adulterer.

The fourth, and least rewarding, of the series of five films, although it has some amusing moments.

w François Truffaut, Claude de Givray, Bernard Revon   *d* François Truffaut   *ph* Nestor Almendros   *m* Antoine Duhamel   *ad* Jean Mandaroux   *ed* Agnes Guillemot

Jean-Pierre Léaud, Claude Jade, Hiroko Berghauer, Daniel Ceccaldi, Claire Duhamel, Barbara Laage

'It's nice to have a man around the house.'
Bed and Breakfast
US   1992   98m   DuArt Color
Hemdale (Jack Schwartzman)
V, V*, S

A widow running a seaside boarding house falls for an affable con man.

Mundane romantic drama that trundles along on familiar lines.

w Cindy Myers   *d* Robert Ellis Miller   *ph* Peter Sova   *m* David Shire   *pd* Suzanne Cavedon   *ed* John F. Burnett

Roger Moore, Talia Shire, Colleen Dewhurst, Nina Siemaszk, Ford Rainey, Stephen Root, Jamie Walters, Cameron Arnett

'Pic is so predictable and sentimental that it will be quickly forgotten at the box office.' – *Variety*

† The film was released direct to video in Britain.

'The girl who took a short cut down the primrose path!'
Bed of Roses
US   1933   67m   bw
RKO

A reform-school graduate determines to be a scarlet woman but falls for an upright riverboat captain.

Adequate vehicle for a fading star who had played too many such roles.

w Wanda Tuchock, Eugene Thackrey   *d* Gregory La Cava

Constance Bennett, Joel McCrea, Pert Kelton, Samuel S. Hinds, John Halliday

The Bed Sitting Room *
GB   1969   91m   DeLuxe
UA/Oscar Lewenstein (Richard Lester)

Surrealist romance; after a nuclear war, motley survivors in the waste lands turn into bed sitting rooms, cupboards and parakeets.

Arrogantly obscure fantasy, a commercial flop which kept its director in the wilderness for four years. Fans of Monty Python may salvage a joke or two.

w John Antrobus   *play* John Antrobus, Spike Milligan   *d* Richard Lester   *ph* David Watkin   *m* Ken Thorne   *pd* Assheton Gorton

Ralph Richardson, Rita Tushingham, Michael Hordern, Arthur Lowe, Mona Washbourne, Peter Cook, Dudley Moore, Spike Milligan, Harry Secombe, Marty Feldman, Jimmy Edwards

Bedazzled *
GB   1967   96m   DeLuxe   Panavision
TCF/Stanley Donen
V, V*, S

A short order cook is saved from suicide by Mr Spiggott, who offers him seven wishes in exchange for his soul.

A camped-up version of *Faust* which resolves itself into a series of threadbare sketches for the stars. All rather desperate apart from the leaping nuns.

w Peter Cook   *d* Stanley Donen   *ph* Austin Dempster   *m* Dudley Moore

Peter Cook, Dudley Moore, Michael Bates, Raquel Welch, Eleanor Bron

Bedelia

GB 1946 90m bw
John Corfield (Isadore Goldsmith)

A psychotic woman is discovered to have poisoned three husbands.

Dreary upper-class British murder drama, totally devoid of style or suspense but a big star hit of the time.

w Vera Caspary, Moie Charles, Herbert Victor, Roy Ridley, Isadore Goldsmith novel Vera Caspary
d Lance Comfort ph F. A. Young

Margaret Lockwood, Ian Hunter, Barry K. Barnes, Anne Crawford, Jill Esmond, Ellen Pollock

Bedevilled

US 1955 86m Eastmancolor Cinemascope
MGM (Henry Berman)

In Paris, a novice priest befriends a girl on the run from gangsters. She turns out to be a murderess and is shot by her victim's brother.

Absurd high-flown bosh, unsuitably cinemascoped in ugly colour, and surprisingly badly handled by old professionals.

w Jo Eisinger d Mitchell Leisen ph Frederick A. Young m William Alwyn

Anne Baxter, Steve Forrest, Simone Renant, Victor Francen, Maurice Teynac, Joseph Tomelty

'This mixture of melodrama and religion provides a most unedifying entertainment.' – MFB

The Bedford Incident ***

GB 1965 102m bw
Columbia/Bedford Productions (James B. Harris)
V*

A ruthlessly efficient US destroyer captain in the Arctic chases a Russian submarine and accidentally fires an atomic weapon.

Gripping mixture of themes from Dr Strangelove and The Caine Mutiny, very tense and forceful, with excellent acting.

w James Poe novel Mark Rascovitch d James B. Harris ph Gilbert Taylor m Gerald Schurrmann

Richard Widmark, Sidney Poitier (his first role with no reference to his colour), James MacArthur, Eric Portman, Wally Cox, Martin Balsam, Phil Brown, Michael Kane, Garry Cockrell, Donald Sutherland

'Strong on virtues of a rather negative kind.' – Penelope Houston

Bedknobs and Broomsticks

US 1971 117m Technicolor
Walt Disney (Bill Walsh)
V, V*, L

In 1940 three evacuee children and a kindly witch ride on a magic bedstead and defeat the invasion of England.

Extraordinarily dishevelled and incompetent Disney follow-up to Mary Poppins, a very muddled narrative with few high points and evidence of much cutting. Redeemed occasionally by camera trickery.

w Bill Walsh, Don DaGradi d Robert Stevenson ph Frank Phillips m/ly Richard M. Sherman, Robert B. Sherman sp Eustace Lycett, Alan Maley, Danny Lee

Angela Lansbury, David Tomlinson, Roy Smart, Cindy O'Callaghan, Sam Jaffe, Roddy McDowall, Bruce Forsyth, Tessie O'Shea, Reginald Owen

AA: special visual effects (Alan Maley, Eustace Lycett, Danny Lee)

AAN: Richard M. Sherman, Robert B. Sherman; song 'The Age of Not Believing' by the Shermans

Bedlam **

US 1946 80m bw
RKO (Val Lewton)
V*, L

In 18th-century London, a sane girl is confined by the malevolent asylum master.

Interesting but rather flatly handled addition to the Val Lewton gallery of horrors, perhaps too carefully and discreetly done for pace or suspense.

w Mark Robson, Carlos Keith d Mark Robson ph Nicholas Musuraca m Roy Webb

Boris Karloff, Anna Lee, Billy House, Richard Fraser, Glenn Vernon

† Carlos Keith was Val Lewton's pseudonym.

† Bedlam was never granted a certificate in Britain.

The Bedroom Window

US 1986 115m colour JDC Widescreen
De Laurentiis (Robert Towne, Martha Schumacher)
V*, L

From her boyfriend's apartment window, an adulterous wife witnesses an assault, and sends her boyfriend to the police in her place.

Sub-Hitchcock thriller, almost as creaky as it sounds.

wd Curtis Hanson ph Gil Taylor m Michael Shrieve, Patrick Gleeson ed Scott Conrad

Steve Guttenberg, Elizabeth McGovern, Isabelle Huppert, Paul Shenar, Frederick Coffin, Wallace Shawn

'Less than riveting entertainment.' – Daily Variety

Bedside Manner

US 1945 79m bw
UA (Andrew Stone)
V*

A lady doctor falls for a war worker.

Flat and contrived comedy which just about manages to keep going.

w Frederick Jackson, Malcolm Stuart Boylan story Robert Carson d Andrew Stone

Ruth Hussey, John Carroll, Charles Ruggles, Ann Rutherford, Claudia Drake, Grant Mitchell, Frank Jenks, Charles Drake

Bedtime for Bonzo

US 1951 83m bw
U-I (Michel Kraike)
V*

To prove that environment determines character, a chimpanzee is brought up as a human baby.

Very moderate fun and games which proved successful enough for a sequel, Bonzo Goes to College.

w Val Burton, Lou Breslow d Frederick de Cordova ph Carl Guthrie m Frank Skinner

Ronald Reagan, Diana Lynn, Walter Slezak, Lucille Barkley, Herbert Heyes

A Bedtime Story *

US 1933 89m bw
Paramount (Emanuel Cohen)

A breezy Frenchman has to interrupt his romances to look after an abandoned baby.

Mild star vehicle in which the agreeable comedy is largely supplanted by sentimental cooing.

w Benjamin Glazer novel Bellamy the Magnificent by Roy Horniman d Norman Taurog ph Charles Lang m/ly Ralph Rainger, Leo Robin

Maurice Chevalier, Helen Twelvetrees, Baby LeRoy, Edward Everett Horton, Adrienne Ames

Bedtime Story *

US 1941 85m bw
Columbia (B. P. Schulberg)

A playwright's wife wants to retire instead of acting in his next play.

Pleasantly sparkling comedy with good performances.

w Horace Jackson, Grant Garrett, Richard Flournoy d Alexander Hall ph Joseph Walker m Werner Heymann

Fredric March, Loretta Young, Robert Benchley, Allyn Joslyn, Eve Arden, Helen Westley, Joyce Compton, Tim Ryan

Bedtime Story *

US 1964 99m Eastmancolor
U-I/Lankershim/Pennebaker (Stanley Shapiro)
V*

Two Riviera confidence tricksters outwit each other.

A fairly lively script is defeated by dull handling, but performances and backgrounds are attractive.

w Stanley Shapiro, Paul Henning d Ralph Levy ph Clifford Stine m Hans Salter

David Niven, Marlon Brando, Shirley Jones, Dody Goodman, Aram Stephan, Marie Windsor

'The most vulgar and embarrassing film of the year.' – Daily Express

† It was remade as Dirty Rotten Scoundrels (qv).

A Bee in the Rain

Portugal 1968 74m bw
Media (Fernando Matos Silva)
original title: Uma Abelha na Chuva

A farmer's unhappy marriage to an aristocratic wife brings tragedy in its wake.

Slow-moving, doom-laden tale of marital discord, not helped by the self-consciously arty direction, with freeze frames and lingering, inconsequential close-ups.

wd Fernando Lopes novel Carlos de Oliveira ph Manuel Costa e Silva m Manuel Jorge Veloso ed Fernando Lopes

Laura Soveral, João Guedes, Zita Duarte, Ruy Furtado, Carlos Ferreiro, Adriano Reys

The Beekeeper **

Greece/France 1986 122m colour
Greek Film Centre/ERTI/MK2/Theodorus Angelopoulos
S
original title: O Melissokomos

A retired schoolmaster, visiting the sites of beehives around Greece, picks up a teenage hitchhiker, an act which is to drive him to desperation.

Melancholy but moving film, with a finely judged performance from Mastroianni.

w Theodorus Angelopoulos, Dimitris Nollas d Theodorus Angelopoulos ph Giorgos Arvantis m Helen Karaindrou ad Mikes Karapiperis ed Takis Yannopoulos

Marcello Mastroianni, Nadia Mourouzi, Serge Reggiani, Jenny Roussea, Dinos Iliopoulos, Vassia Panagopolou, Dimitris Poulikakos

Beer

US 1985 82m DeLuxe
Orion (Robert Chartoff)
V*
original title: The Selling of America

A lady executive on Madison Avenue promotes a brand of beer by promoting three honest Joes from the street and turning them into macho media figures.

Another shred of proof that satire is what closes Saturday night. A few smiles, but no release.

w Allan Weissbecker d Patrick Kelly ph Bill Butler m Bill Conti pd Bill Bordie ed Alan Heim

Loretta Swit, Rip Torn, Kenneth Mars, David Alan Grier, William Russ, Dick Shawn

Bees in Paradise

GB   1943   75m   bw
Gainsborough

Four airmen find themselves on a South Sea island ruled by women who kill their spouses after the honeymoon.

Saucy farce, too talkative to be very interesting even in the dark days of war.

w Val Guest, Marriott Edgar   d Val Guest

Arthur Askey, Peter Graves, Max Bacon, Anne Shelton, Jean Kent

'The head of the family is the one with the tail.'

Beethoven

US   1992   87m   DeLuxe
UIP/Universal (Joe Medjuck, Michael C. Gross)
V, V*, L, S

A St Bernard dog causes havoc in a family household to the delight of the children and the annoyance of their father.

Predictable comedy of the dreariest kind.

w Edmond Dantes, Amy Holden Jones   d Brian Levant   ph Victor J. Kemper   m Randy Edelman   pd Alex Tavoularis   ed Sheldon Kahn, William D. Gordean

Charles Grodin, Bonnie Hunt, Dean Jones, Oliver Platt, Stanley Tucci, David Duchovny, Patricia Heaton, Laurel Cronin, O-Lan Jones

'Could be called harmless if it wasn't so badly made and blandly characterised.' – *Derek Malcolm, Guardian*

'Laugh? We wait like locked-in dogs whose noses are pressed to the window for the first sign of life or human interest coming up the driveway. Wit we have already despaired of in reel one.' – *Nigel Andrews, Financial Times*

Beethoven's 2nd

US   1993   89m   DeLuxe
Universal (Michael C. Gross, Joe Medjuck)
S

Beethoven becomes the father of pups, which are promptly kidnapped.

A sentimental sequel that will be enjoyed by fans of large, slobbering dogs and obvious jokes.

w Len Blum   d Rod Daniel   ph Bill Butler   m Randy Edelman   pd Lawrence Miller   ed Sheldon Kahn, William D. Gordean

Charles Grodin, Bonnie Hunt, Nicholle Tom, Christopher Castille, Sarah Rose Karr, Debi Mazar, Chris Penn, Ashley Hamilton, Maury Chaykin

'Universal unleashes what should be a big, slobbering hit with this reasonably entertaining sequel, certainly a more pleasing tale than the one that sired it.' – *Variety*

'It's so insubstantial that it flies from the mind's eye almost as soon as the lights go up.' – *Derek Malcolm, Guardian*

'All the wit and spontaneity of a suet pudding.' – *Sight and Sound*

AAN: song 'The Day I Fall In Love' (m/y Carole Bayer Sager, James Ingram, Cliff Magness)

Beetlejuice *

US   1988   92m   Technicolor
Warner Bros/Geffen (Michael Bender)
V, V*, L, S

The newly dead at a New England barn try to scare off objectionable new buyers.

Mainly unpleasant and seldom funny fantasy.

w Michael McDowell, Warren Skaaren   d Tim Burton   ph Thomas Ackerman   m Danny Elfman   pd Bo Welch

Alec Baldwin, Geena Davis, Michael Keaton, Catherine O'Hara, Glenn Shadix

Before Dawn *

US   1933   60m   bw
RKO

Three murders take place in a mysterious mansion.

Lively comedy-thriller which won't bore anybody: good in its class.

w Garrett Fort, Marian Dix, Ralph Block   story Edgar Wallace   d Irving Pichel   m Max Steiner

Warner Oland, Stuart Erwin, Dorothy Wilson, Dudley Digges, Oscar Apfel

Before Hindsight **

GB   1977   78m   Eastmancolor
Elizabeth Taylor-Mead

Interviews and clips show how inadequately cinema newsreels covered world events in the 1930s.

Hard tack for entertainment seekers, but a clear exposition of a proven case of importance to film-makers and politicians.

w Elizabeth Taylor-Mead   d Jonathan Lewis

'Certainly not the kind of picture people will pay money to see.' – *Variety*

'Beware! When Karloff Stops The Clock . . . Your Hour Has Come!'

Before I Hang *

US   1940   71m   bw
Columbia (Wallace MacDonald)
V*, L

A research scientist experiments with a new serum which turns him into a murderer.

Archetypal Karloff mad doctor flick, Jekyll and Hyde model: still quite tolerable.

w Robert D. Andrews   d Nick Grinde   ph Benjamin Kline   md Morris Stoloff

Boris Karloff, Evelyn Keyes, Bruce Bennett, Pedro de Cordoba, Edward Van Sloan, Don Beddoe

'Karloff is so good he makes you believe this nonsense.' – *The Dark Side*

Before the Nickelodeon **

US   1982   60m   bw/colour
Film for Thought

The life, times and films of the pioneer Edwin S. Porter.

Valuable documentary on a little-known figure, with films ranging from 1896 to 1907.

w Warren D. Leight, Charles Musser   d Charles Musser

Before the Revolution *

Italy   1964   115m   bw
Cineriz/Iride
V, V*
original title: *Prima della Rivoluzione*

The suicide of a friend leads a middle-class youth living in Parma to consider his own life and attitudes before opting for safe conformity.

A talented but confused debate on politics, which upset Catholic authorities at the time, but leaves an audience only a little wiser.

wd Bernardo Bertolucci   md Aldo Scavarda   m Gino Paoli, Ennio Morricone   ad Romano Pampaloni   ed Roberto Perpignani

Francesco Barilli, Adriana Asti, Alain Midgette, Morando Morandini

'He captures what has rarely been seen on the screen – the extravagance and poetry of youthful ardour.' – *Pauline Kael, New Yorker*

Before Winter Comes *

GB   1968   107m   Technicolor
Columbia/Windward (Robert Emmett Ginna)

Austria 1945: a British major in charge of

displaced persons is helped and hindered by a cheerful Yugoslav refugee who turns out to be a Russian deserter.

Likeable, well-produced drama hampered by a plot which becomes unnecessarily schematic, coincidental and downbeat in its attempts to tug at the heartstrings.

w Andrew Sinclair   novel The Interpreter by Frederick L. Keefe   d J. Lee-Thompson   ph Gilbert Taylor   m Ron Grainer

David Niven, Topol, Ori Levi, Anna Karina, John Hurt, Anthony Quayle

'One of those films with a message on every page of its script.' – *MFB*

Beg, Borrow or Steal

US   1937   70m   bw
MGM

An American expatriate lives by his wits in Paris.

Flabby comedy which misses on all cylinders.

w Leonard Lee, Harry Ruskin, Marion Parsonnet   d William Thiele

Frank Morgan, Florence Rice, John Beal, Janet Beecher, Herman Bing, Erik Rhodes, E. E. Clive, Reginald Denny, George Givot

'Nothing quite so incredible as this story has been tossed to the double bills since the major studios started competing among themselves to turn out low-grade entertainment for the filler-in spots.' – *Variety*

Beggars in Ermine

US   1934   70m   bw
Monogram

A steelworker who loses his legs and his livelihood organizes beggars into a wealthy union.

Curious semi-fantasy, probably worth a mark for trying.

w Tristam Tupper   novel Esther Lynd Daly   d Phil Rosen

Lionel Atwill, Henry B. Walthall, Betty Furness, Jameson Thomas, Astrid Allwyn

Beggars of Life *

US   1928   80m   bw   part-talkie
Paramount

Adventures of a hobo.

Curious melodramatic farrago notable chiefly for technical advances but far from boring to watch for its own sake.

w Benjamin Glazer, Jim Tully   d William Wellman

Richard Arlen, Wallace Beery, Louise Brooks, Edgar Blue Washington, H. A. Morgan, Roscoe Karns

The Beggar's Opera *

GB   1952   94m   Technicolor
British Lion/Imperadio (Herbert Wilcox, Laurence Olivier)

A highwayman in Newgate jail devises an opera based on his own exploits.

Exuberant potted version of the 1728 low opera, generally likeable but lacking a strong coherent approach and marred by violent colour and raggedly theatrical presentation. It nearly but not quite comes off.

w Dennis Cannan, Christopher Fry   opera John Gay   d Peter Brook   ph Guy Green   ad George Wakhevitch, William C. Andrews   musical arrangement and additions Arthur Bliss

Laurence Olivier, Stanley Holloway, Dorothy Tutin, Daphne Anderson, Mary Clare, George Devine, Athene Seyler, Hugh Griffith, Margot Grahame, Sandra Dorne, Laurence Naismith

'The failure is equalled only by the ambition.' – *Gavin Lambert*

'New Thrills! New Shocks! New Terror!'
The Beginning of the End
US   1957   73m   bw
ABPT/Republic (Bert I. Gordon)
V*

Radiation breeds giant grasshoppers which are only stopped when they can't withstand the waters of Lake Michigan.

Bottom-of-the-sci-fi-barrel rubbish, very boring to watch.

w Fred Freiberger, Lester Corn   d Bert I. Gordon

Peggie Castle, Peter Graves, Morris Ankrum, James Seay, Richard Benedict, Pierre Watkin

The Beginning or the End
US   1947   112m   bw
MGM (Samuel Marx)

During World War II American scientists continue to perfect the atom bomb despite their own misgivings, and one dies in an explosion.

Semi-documentary marred by sentimental personal asides and of very little continuing interest.

w Robert Considine   d Norman Taurog   ph Ray June   m Daniele Amfitheatrof

Brian Donlevy, Robert Walker, Tom Drake, Beverly Tyler, Hume Cronyn, Audrey Totter, *Godfrey Tearle* (as Roosevelt)

'The documentary value is so offset by sickly sentiment that it is practically just another love story.' – W. A. Wilcox, Sunday Dispatch

Begone Dull Care ****
Canada   1953   9m   colour
National Film Board (Norman McLaren)

Abstract images drawn directly onto the film are accompanied by three pieces of jazz performed by the Oscar Peterson Trio.

The central movement is a little too slow, but the first piece is witty and the climax is an irresistible frenzy of sound and image. Undeniably a classic short, and probably McLaren's best.

conceived and made by Norman McLaren

'One man … seven women … in a strange house!'
The Beguiled *
US   1971   109m   Technicolor
Universal/Malpaso (Don Siegel)
V*, L

A wounded Unionist soldier hides out in a Confederate ladies' school; the teachers fend for him until he causes trouble among the sexually frustrated women, who eventually kill him.

Eccentric melodrama which does not really work despite its credentials and patient work all round.

w John B. Sherry, Grimes Grice   *novel* Thomas Cullinan   d Don Siegel   ph Bruce Surtees   m Lalo Schifrin   pd Ted Haworth

Clint Eastwood, Geraldine Page, Elizabeth Hartman, Jo Ann Harris, Darleen Carr, Mae Mercer

'A must for sadists and woman-haters.' – *Judith Crist*

Behave Yourself *
US   1951   81m   bw
RKO (Jerry Wald, Norman Krasna)
V*

A young married couple and their dog get mixed up in a chain of murders.

Zany black comedy in the wake of *A Slight Case of Murder* and *The Thin Man*. The humour is spread too thin for success.

wd George Beck   ph James Wong Howe   m Leigh Harline

Farley Granger, Shelley Winters, William Demarest, Francis L. Sullivan, Margalo Gillmore, Lon Chaney, Hans Conried, Elisha Cook Jnr

Behemoth the Sea Monster: see *The Giant Behemoth*

Behind Green Lights
US   1945   64m   bw
TCF

A murderer is spotted during one night in the press room of a police station.

A pale shadow of *The Front Page,* with inferior work all round.

w W. Scott Darling, Charles G. Booth   d Otto Brower

Carole Landis, William Gargan, Richard Crane, Mary Anderson, John Ireland, Roy Roberts, Mabel Paige

Behind Prison Gates
US   1939   63m   bw
Columbia

A secret agent follows bank robbers into prison.

Standard undercover crime support.

w Arthur T. Horman, Leslie T. White   d Charles Barton

Brian Donlevy, Jacqueline Wells, Joseph Crehan, Paul Fix

Behind Prison Walls
US   1943   64m   bw
PRC (Arthur Ripley)
GB title: *Youth Takes a Hand*

Too-honest son gets his tycoon father sent to prison, but ends up there himself.

Curious moral comedy drama which can't work on a low budget.

w Van Norcross, W. A. Ulman Jnr   d Steve Sekely

Alan Baxter, Tully Marshall, Gertrude Michael, Edwin Maxwell, Matt Willis

Behind That Curtain
US   1929   91m   bw
Fox
V*

Murder follows when a ne'er-do-well aspires to marry an heiress.

Nominally the third Charlie Chan film, but Chan, played by E. L. Park, is whittled down to a tiny role. As it stands, a clumsy effort, but could be worth remaking.

w Sonya Levien, Clarke Silvernail   *novel* Earl Derr Biggers   d Irving Cummings

Warner Baxter, Lois Moran, Gilbert Emery, Claude King, Philip Strange, Boris Karloff

Behind the Door: see *The Man with Nine Lives*

Behind the Eight Ball
US   1942   60m   bw
Universal
GB title: *Off the Beaten Track*

Actors are mistaken for spies.

Very patchy but commendably brief star comedy.

w Stanley Roberts, Mel Ronson   d Edward F. Cline

The Ritz Brothers, Carol Bruce, Dick Foran, William Demarest

Behind the High Wall
US   1956   85m   bw
U-I (Stanley Rubin)

A prison warder, taken as hostage by escaping convicts, steals some of the money they have taken.

Glum melodrama, capably presented.

w Harold Jack Bloom   d Abner Biberman   ph Maury Gertsman   m Joseph Gershenson

Tom Tully, Sylvia Sidney, John Gavin, Betty Lynn, John Larch, Barney Phillips, Don Beddoe

Behind the Iron Mask: see *The Fifth Musketeer*

Behind the Make-up
US   1930   65m   bw
Paramount

A talented clown is constantly frustrated by the ill-advised schemes of his partner.

Seamy melodrama from another age; barely playable now.

w George Manker Watters, Howard Estabrook   *story* Mildred Cram   d Robert Milton

Hal Skelly, William Powell, Fay Wray, Kay Francis, E. H. Calvert, Paul Lukas

'Who is the murdering monster?'
Behind the Mask
US   1932   68m   bw
Columbia

A crazy doctor operates fatally on those who know too much.

Semi-horror mystery using two members of the Frankenstein cast.

w Jo Swerling   d John Francis Dillon

Jack Holt, Constance Cummings, Edward Van Sloan, Boris Karloff

Behind the Mask *
GB   1958   99m   Eastmancolor
BL/GW Films (Sergei Nolbandov, Josef Somlo)

Political infighting causes tension on the board of a local hospital.

Oddly titled social drama with interesting detail but not much tension or conclusion.

w John Hunter   *novel* The Pack by John Rowan Wilson   d Brian Desmond Hurst   ph Robert Krasker   m Geoffrey Wright

Michael Redgrave, Tony Britton, Carl Mohner, Niall MacGinnis, Vanessa Redgrave, Ian Bannen, Brenda Bruce, Lionel Jeffries, Miles Malleson, John Welsh, Ann Firbank

Behind the Rising Sun *
US   1943   88m   bw
RKO
V*

An American-educated Japanese goes home in the thirties, comes under the influence of war-mongers, and causes his father to commit hara-kiri.

Outrageous wartime flagwaver designed to vilify 'Uncle Tojo's dogs', from the writer and director of the similar *Hitler's Children* (qv).

w Emmet Lavery   *novel* James R. Young   d Edward Dmytryk   ph Russell Metty   m Roy Webb

J. Carrol Naish, Tom Neal, Margo, Robert Ryan, Gloria Holden, Don Douglas, Adeline de Walt Reynolds

Behold a Pale Horse *
US   1964   121m   bw
Columbia/Highland/Brentwood (Fred Zinnemann, Alexander Trauner)
V*

A Spanish guerrilla goes into exile at the end of the Civil War. Twenty years later he is persuaded to return and kill a brutal police chief.

An action film which unfortunately insists on saying something significant about morality, destiny and death. Impeccably made, but somehow not very interesting apart from the action sequences.

w J. P. Miller   *novel Killing a Mouse on Sunday* by Emeric Pressburger   *d* Fred Zinnemann   *ph* Jean Badal   *m* Maurice Jarre   *ad* Alexander Trauner

Gregory Peck, Omar Sharif, Anthony Quinn, Raymond Pellegrin, Paolo Stoppa, Mildred Dunnock, Daniela Rocca, Christian Marquand

'A fine example of a high class failure.' – *Judith Crist*

'Her savage heart pounded with revenge when her love went unwanted!'
Behold My Wife
US   1934   79m   bw
Paramount (B. P. Schulberg)

A wealthy young man brings back and marries a New Mexico Indian girl to show up his snobbish family.

Dated melodrama, of interest solely for its racial theme.

w William R. Lipman, Oliver LaFarge   *novel The Translation of a Savage* by Sir Gilbert Parker   *d* Mitchell Leisen   *ph* Leon Shamroy

Sylvia Sidney, Gene Raymond, Juliette Compton, Laura Hope Crews, H. B. Warner, Monroe Owsley, Ann Sheridan

'Frank melodrama of the hokiest sort.' – *Variety*

'Suddenly One Summer...'
Being at Home with Claude
Canada   1993   85m   colour/bw
Out on a Limb/Les Productions du Cerf (Louise Gendron)
V, V*

A young hustler explains to a policeman why he murdered his lover, a shy intellectual.

This small-scale play transferred to the screen retains its theatrical air, being all talk and no action; the talk, though, and the interaction between the two protagonists retain one's interest for the most part.

wd Jean Beaudin   *play* René-Daniel Dubois   *ph* Thomas Vamos   *m* Richard Grégoire   *ed* André Corriveau

Roy Dupuis, Jacques Godin, Jean-François Pichette, Gaston Lepage

'It's hard not to respect something so extreme in its stylisation, emotional intensity and naked romanticism, but it's also hard to cosy up to a film which combines such posiness with hidebound theatre conventions. Beautifully crafted but entirely resistible.' – *Kim Newman, Empire*

'Getting there is half the fun; being there is all of it!'
Being There **
US   1979   130m   Metrocolor
Lorimar/North Star/CIP (Andrew Braunsberg)
V*, L

An illiterate gardener is taken for a homespun philosopher and becomes a national celebrity.

Overlong serio-comic parable hinging on a somewhat dubious star performance. Chance made it a popular urban success, but few who saw it were enthused.

w Jerzy Kosinski   *novel* Jerzy Kosinski   *d* Hal Ashby   *ph* Dianne Schroeder   *m* John Mandel   *pd* Michael Haller

Peter Sellers, Shirley Maclaine, *Melvyn Douglas*, Jack Warden, Richard Dysart, Richard Basehart

'It pulls off its long shot and is a confoundingly provocative movie.' – *Roger Ebert*

AA: Melvyn Douglas

AAN: Peter Sellers

screenplay

Beiqing Chengshi *
Taiwan   1989   160m   colour
Artificial Eye/3-H/Era International (Qui Fusheng)
aka: *A City of Sadness*

During the 1940s, from the end of the Japanese occupation of Taiwan to the communist takeover of the Chinese mainland, a family, headed by a local gangster, undergoes domestic upheavals.

Winner of the Golden Lion at the Venice Film Festival in 1989, it nevertheless remains fairly impenetrable to Western audiences not familiar with the political intricacies of the period.

w Wu Nianzhen, Zhu Tianwen   *d* Hou Hsiao-Hsien   *ph* Chen Huai'en   *m* Tachikawa Naoki, Zhang Hongyi   *pd* Liu Zhihua, Lin Chongwen   *ed* Liao Qingsong

Li Tianlu, Chen Songyong, Gao Jie, Tony Leung, Wu Yifang, Xin Shufen, Chen Shufang, Ke Suyun, Lin Liqing, He Aiyun

'Its balance between the personal and the political is spectacular and exemplary, as if a brilliant miniaturist had miraculously filled a huge canvas.' – *Tony Rayns, MFB*

Bela Lugosi Meets a Brooklyn Gorilla
US   1952   74m   bw
Jack Broder
GB title: *The Monster Meets the Gorilla*

A tropical island scientist turns one half of a stranded comedy team into a gorilla.

Stupid farce which never rises to the occasion.

w Tim Ryan   *d* William Beaudine

Bela Lugosi, Duke Mitchell, Sammy Petrillo, Ray 'Crash' Corrigan, Muriel Landers

'Neighbourhood and small-town audiences will get some laughs.' – *Box Office*

Believe in Me
US   1971   90m   colour
MGM (Irwin Winkler, Robert Chartoff)

Two young marrieds take to drugs.

Tedious and unenlightening modern drama which seems to think it's saying something new.

w Israel Horovitz   *d* Stuart Hagmann   *ph* Dick Kratina, Richard C. Brooks   *m* Fred Karlin

Michael Sarrazin, Jacqueline Bisset, Jon Cypher, Allen Garfield

The Believers *
US   1987   114m   DeLuxe
Orion/John Schlesinger, Michael Childers, Beverly Camhe
V*, L

New York's occult underworld is permeated by a sinister Catholic ritual.

Most of the time it's hard to say what's going on in this intensely melodramatic thriller, but there are the odd rewards along the way. Not too many, actually.

w Mark Frost   *book The Religion* by Nicholas Conde   *d* John Schlesinger   *ph* Robby Müller   *m* J. Peter Robinson   *pd* Simon Holland   *ed* Peter Honess

Martin Sheen, Helen Shaver, Harley Cross, Robert Loggia, Elizabeth Wilson, Harris Yulin

'If nothing else, Schlesinger knows how to produce a film where pain and horror are beautiful to watch.' – *Daily Variety*

'A bewitching comedy about an enchanting subject!'
Bell, Book and Candle *
US   1958   103m   Technicolor
Columbia/Phoenix (Julian Blaustein)
V*, L

A publisher slowly becomes aware that his new girlfriend is a witch.

A gossamer stage comedy has been fatally flattened in translation; most of the actors are miscast, and sentiment soaks the script. But it remains a civilized entertainment.

w Daniel Taradash   *play* John Van Druten   *d* Richard Quine   *ph* James Wong Howe   *m* George Duning   *ad* Cary Odell

James Stewart, Kim Novak, Jack Lemmon, Ernie Kovacs, *Hermione Gingold*, Elsa Lanchester, Janice Rule

AAN: art direction

Bell Bottom George
GB   1943   97m   bw
Columbia

A medically exempt waiter dons uniform and catches a ring of spies.

Formula star comedy, too long and too familiar.

w Peter Fraser, Edward Dryhurst   *d* Marcel Varnel

George Formby, Anne Firth, Reginald Purdell, Peter Murray Hill

A Bell for Adano *
US   1945   104m   bw
TCF (Louis D. Lighton, Lamar Trotti)

An American major takes over an Italian town and wins affection by replacing the local bell.

Slight end-of-war mood piece, still quite pleasant but without the undercurrents of feeling it had at the time.

w Lamar Trotti, Norman Reilly Raine   *novel* John Hersey   *d* Henry King   *ph* Joseph LaShelle   *m* Alfred Newman

John Hodiak, Gene Tierney, William Bendix, Glenn Langan, Richard Conte, Stanley Prager, Henry Morgan

The Bell Jar
US   1979   107m   colour
Peerce-Goldston/Avco
V*

A teenage girl becomes mentally ill when her father dies.

Numbingly tedious case history without much apparent point.

w Marjorie Kellogg   *novel* Sylvia Plath   *d* Larry Peerce

Marilyn Hassett, Julie Harris, Anne Jackson, Barbara Barrie

Belladonna
GB   1934   91m   bw
Twickenham (Julius Hagen)

A selfish woman tries to poison her husband for love of an Egyptian.

Intriguingly-cast version of a story that was later filmed in Hollywood as *Temptation* (qv).

w H. Fowler Mear   *play* J. B. Fagan   *novel* Robert Hichens   *d* Robert Milton   *ph* Sydney Blythe, William Luff   *ad* James Carter

Mary Ellis, Conrad Veidt, Cedric Hardwicke, John Stuart, Michael Shepley

Il Bell'Antonio *
Italy/France   1960   105m   bw
Cina Del Duca-Arco/Lyre Cinématographique (Alfredo Bini)
GB title: *Handsome Antonio*

A youngish man returns to his native town with the reputation of a lady-killer, but when married turns out to be impotent.

Amusing but finally exhausting Sicilian comedy with all the expected exaggeration of speech and gesture.

w Pier Paolo Pasolini, Gino Visentini   *novel* Vitaliano Brancati   *d* Piero Piccioni

Marcello Mastroianni, Claudia Cardinale, Pierre Brasseur, Rina Morelli, Tomas Milian

The Bellboy *
US   1960   72m   bw
Paramount/Jerry Lewis Productions (Jerry Lewis)
V, V*, L

An incompetent bellboy causes havoc in a Miami hotel.

Plotless essence of a comedian who divides opinion and will never be better than variable. This ragbag of old gags at least prevents his usual sentimental excesses, and is mercifully short.

wd Jerry Lewis *ph* Haskell Boggs *m* Walter Scharf

Jerry Lewis, Alex Gerry, Bob Clayton, Herkie Styles, Milton Berle

La Belle Américaine *

France 1961 101m bw (colour finale)
CCFC/Film d'Art/Panorama/Corflor (Henri Diamant-Berger, Arthur Lesser)

GB/US titles: What a Chassis; The American Beauty

A Parisian factory worker gets into all kinds of trouble when he buys an American supercar for a ridiculously low price.

Some brilliant gags are separated by long dull spots of unnecessary storytelling.

w Robert Dhéry, Pierre Tchernia, Alfred Adam *d* Robert Dhéry *ph* Ghislain Cloquet *m* Gérard Calvi

Robert Dhéry, Louis de Funes, Colette Brosset, Alfred Adam, Bernard Lavalette, Annie Ducaux

Belle de Jour ****

France/Italy 1967 100m Eastmancolor
Paris Film/Five Film (Robert and Raymond Hakim)
V

A surgeon's wife finds herself drawn to afternoon work in a brothel.

Fascinating Buñuel mixture of fact and fantasy, impeccably woven into a rich fabric.

w Luis Buñuel, Jean-Claude Carrière, *novel* Joseph Kessel *d* Luis Buñuel *ph* Sacha Vierny *m* none *ad* Robert Clavel *ed* Louisette Hautecoeur, Walter Spohr

Catherine Deneuve, Jean Sorel, Michel Piccoli, Genevieve Page, Pierre Clémenti

'Oppressively powerful. Like being buried alive in Sarah Bernhardt's dressing room.' – *Wilfred Sheed*

'The rhythm of the writing, the color changes, acting tempos, camera angles, the whole editing – all this is perfect. There is not one extraneous shot, nor one that is missing. Disparate elements are embraced in a self-possessed, lucidly enchanting flow.' – *John Simon*

Belle Epoque *

Spain 1992 109m Eastmancolor Cinemascope
Mayfair/Lola/Animatografo/French Production/Fernando Trueba

In Spain in the early 30s, a deserter from the army hides in the house of a widower with four attractive daughters, who teach him the pleasures of life.

A leisurely, enjoyable film of the past, as seen through rose-coloured spectacles; it is inoffensive and amusing without being particularly memorable.

w Rafael Azcona *story* Rafael Azcona, José Luis Garcia Sanchez, Fernando Trueba *d* Fernando Trueba *ph* José Luis Alcaine *m* Antoine Duhamel *ad* Juan Botella *ed* Carmen Frias

Fernando Fernán Gómez, Jorge Sanz, Maribel Verdú, Ariadna Gil, Miriam Diaz-Aroca, Penélope Cruz, Gabino Diego, Michel Galbru

'The tone is merry as well as erotic, but generally takes the easy way out, suggesting there is more than one country in Europe that sees the benefit of making warmly pleasurable period films that will attract nostalgic audiences.' – *Derek Malcolm, Guardian*

AA: best foreign film

La Belle Equipe *

France 1936 74m bw
Ciné Arts

Five unemployed Parisians win the lottery and open a restaurant, but things do not go smoothly.

Interesting but rather lumpy star drama which finally descends into melodrama; alternative tragic and happy endings were originally offered.

w Charles Spaak, Julien Duvivier *d* Julien Duvivier *ph* Jules Kruger, Marc Fessard *m* Maurice Yvain

Jean Gabin, Charles Vanel, Viviane Romance, Raymond Aimes, Robert Lynen, Raymond Cordy, Raphael Medina

La Belle et la Bête **

France 1946 96m (87m US) bw
Discina (André Paulvé)
V, V*, L
aka: Beauty and the Beast

Beauty gives herself to the Beast who has kidnapped her father; through love the monster turns into a handsome prince.

Slightly heavy-handed though usually stunning-looking adaptation of the fairy tale.

wd Jean Cocteau *story* Madame LePrince de Beaumont *ph* Henri Alekan *m* Georges Auric *ad* Christian Bérard *ed* Claude Ibéria

Jean Marais, Josette Day, Mila Parély, Marcel André, Nane Germon, Michel Auclair

'Perhaps the most sumptuously elegant of all filmed fairy tales.' – *New Yorker, 1980*

'Absolute magic: diamond cold and lunar bright.' – *CBS*

'A sensuously fascinating film, a fanciful poem in movement given full articulation on the screen.' – *Bosley Crowther, New York Times*

Une Belle Fille Comme Moi

France 1972 98m colour
Columbia/Les Films du Carrosse (Marcel Berbert, Claude Ganz)
US title: Such a Gorgeous Kid Like Me

A gullible sociologist hears the confession of a promiscuous murderess.

Moderately interesting black comedy.

w Jean-Louis Dabadie, François Truffaut *novel* Henry Farrell *d* François Truffaut *ph* Pierre-William Glenn *m* Georges Delerue *ad* Jean-Pierre Kohut *ed* Yann Dedet, Martine Barraque

Bernadette Lafont, Claude Brasseur, Charles Denner, Guy Marchand, André Dussoller, Anne Kreis, Philippe Léotard

Belle le Grand

US 1951 89m bw
Republic

The proprietress of a Barbary Coast gambling house is plagued by an ex-husband on whose account she served a prison term.

Confused and incompetent period melodrama.

w D. D. Beauchamp *d* Allan Dwan *ph* Reggie Lanning *m* Victor Young

Vera Ralston, John Carroll, William Ching, Hope Emerson, Stephen Chase, Grant Withers, John Qualen

La Belle Noiseuse ***

France 1991 240m colour
Artificial Eye/Pierre Grise
V, V*

The beautiful young mistress of a friend inspires a famous artist to finish a painting, for which his wife modelled, that he put aside ten years before.

A gripping and penetrating movie on the themes of obsession, art and love, although it offers little in the way of conventional narrative.

w Pascal Bonitzar, Christine Laurent, Jacques Rivette *story* Le Chef d'oeuvre Inconnu (The Unknown Masterpiece) by Honoré de Balzac *d* Jacques Rivette *ph* William Lubtchansky *m* Stravinsky *ad* Emmanuel de Chauvigny *ed* Nicole Lubtchansky

Michel Piccoli, Jane Birkin, *Emmanuelle Béart*, Marianne Denicourt, David Burstein, Gilles Arbona

'Perhaps the most meticulous and seductive depiction in movies of the hard work of making art.' – *Richard Corliss, Time*

† Artist Bernard Dufour, whose hand is the only part of him to be seen, did the painting.

†† *La Belle Noiseuse: Divertimento*, a two-hour version of the film using different takes, was produced for French TV and also given a cinema and video release.

The Belle of New York *

US 1952 82m Technicolor
MGM (Arthur Freed)
V*, L, S

An 1890s playboy falls for a Salvation Army girl.

A rather dreary version of the old musical, with undistinguished additions.

w Robert O'Brien, Irving Elinson *d* Charles Walters *ph* Robert Planck *md* Adolph Deutsch *m/ly* Johnny Mercer, Harry Warren *ad* Jack Martin Smith

Fred Astaire, Vera-Ellen, Marjorie Main, Keenan Wynn, Alice Pearce, Clinton Sundberg, Gale Robbins

songs: 'When I'm Out with the Belle of New York'; 'Oops'; 'Baby Doll'; 'Naughty but Nice'; 'Seeing's Believing'; 'Thank You Mr Currier, Thank You Mr Ives'; 'I Love to Beat a Big Bass Drum'; 'I Wanna Be a Dancing Man'; 'Let a Little Love Come In'

Belle of the Nineties *

US 1934 75m bw
Paramount (William Le Baron)

A saloon entertainer loves two men, one of whom is a crook.

Much-laundered star vehicle which despite superior production seems a pale shadow of the star's better pieces.

w Mae West *d* Leo McCarey *ph* Karl Struss *m/ly* Arthur Johnston, Sam Coslow

Mae West, Roger Pryor, John Miljan, John Mack Brown, Katherine de Mille, Duke Ellington and his Orchestra

'It's been sufficiently denatured from within, yet not completely emasculated.' – *Variety*

Belle of the Yukon *

US 1945 84m Technicolor
International

A troupe of saloon entertainers in the Yukon become involved with a bank robbery.

Threads of plot support comedy, dancing and songs in this thin but reasonably fresh musical imitation of *The Spoilers.*

w James Edward Grant *d* William A. Seiter *ph* Ray Rennahan *md* Arthur Lange

Gypsy Rose Lee, Randolph Scott, Dinah Shore, Charles Winninger, Bob Burns

AAN: Arthur Lange; song 'Sleigh Ride in July' (*m* Jimmy Van Heusen, *ly* Johnny Burke)

Belle Starr

US 1941 87m Technicolor
TCF (Kenneth MacGowan)

Absurdly laundered version of the life of the west's

most notorious female outlaw, with the star laughably miscast.

w Lamar Trotti d Irving Cummings ph Ernest Palmer, Ray Rennahan m Alfred Newman

Gene Tierney, Randolph Scott, Dana Andrews, Shepperd Strudwick, Elizabeth Patterson, Chill Wills, Louise Beavers

Les Belles de Nuit **
France/Italy   1952   89m   bw
Franco London/Rizzoli

A discontented music teacher dreams of beautiful women through the ages.

Charming but very slight dream fantasy with many of the master's touches. (He claims to have intended a comic *Intolerance*.)

wd *René Clair* ph Armand Thirard, Robert Juilliard, Louise Née m *Georges Van Parys* ad *Léon Barsacq*

Gérard Philipe, Gina Lollobrigida, Martine Carol, Magali Vendeuil, Paolo Stoppa, Raymond Bussières, Raymond Cordy

The Belles of St Trinian's *
GB   1954   91m   bw
BL/London Films/Launder and Gilliat
V, V*

At an unruly and bankrupt school for girls, more time is spent backing horses than studying subjects, and the headmistress's bookmaker brother has a scheme or two of his own.

Fairly successful film version of Ronald Searle's awful schoolgirl cartoons, the emphasis shifted to a grotesque older generation with the star in drag. An enormous commercial success, but the three sequels *Blue Murder at St Trinian's, The Pure Hell of St Trinian's, The Great St Trinian's Train Robbery* went from bad to awful.

w Frank Launder, Sidney Gilliat, Val Valentine d Frank Launder ph Stan Pavey m Malcolm Arnold

Alastair Sim, George Cole, Joyce Grenfell, Hermione Baddeley, Betty Ann Davies, Renée Houston, Beryl Reid, Irene Handl, Mary Merrall

'Not so much a film as an entertainment on celluloid, a huge charade, a rich pile of idiotic and splendidly senseless images.' – *David Robinson*

Belles on Their Toes
US   1952   89m   Technicolor
TCF (Samuel G. Engel)

Further adventures in the growing up of the twelve Gilbreth children.

Flat sequel to *Cheaper by the Dozen* (qv) with sentimentality instead of Clifton Webb. Period atmosphere attractive.

w Phoebe and Henry Ephron book Frank B. Gilbreth Jnr and Ernestine Gilbreth Carey d Henry Levin ph Arthur E. Arling m Cyril Mockridge

Myrna Loy, Jeanne Crain, Debra Paget, Jeffrey Hunter, Edward Arnold, Hoagy Carmichael, Barbara Bates, Robert Arthur

Bellissima *
Italy   1951   100m   bw
Bellissima Films (Salvo d'Angelo)
V*

A mother struggles to get a part in a film for her 7-year-old daughter.

Highly detailed, very noisy star vehicle with neo-realist working-class backgrounds. Exhausting.

w Suso Cecchi d'Amico, Francesco Rosi, Luchino Visconti, Cesare Zavattini d Luchino Visconti ph Piero Portalupi m Franco Mannino

Anna Magnani, Walter Chiari, Tina Apicella, Gastone Renzelli, Alessandro Blasetti

Bellman and True *
GB   1987   122m   Technicolor
Handmade/Euston (Michael Wearing, Christopher Neame)
V, V*

A young burglar in a heist is protected by an older crook's computer skills.

Good crime drama with television derivation.

w Desmond Lowder, Richard Loncraine, Michael Wearing novel Desmond Lowder d Richard Loncraine ph Ken Westbury m Colin Towns pd Jon Bunker ed Paul Green

Bernard Hill, Derek Newark, Kieran O'Brien, Richard Hope, Frances Tomelty

The Bells
GB   1931   75m   bw
PDC/BSFP (Sergei Nolbandov)

An Alsatian burgomaster is forced by conscience to confess to the killing of a Jew.

Only sound version of a famous melodrama first played on stage by Henry Irving in 1871.

w C. H. Dand play Leopold Lewis, from *Le Juif Polonais* by Erckmann and Chatrian d Oscar M. Werndorff, Harcourt Templeman (in three language versions) ph Gunther Krampf, Eric Cross m Gustav Holst ad Oscar Werndorff ed Lars Moen, Michael Hankinson

Donald Calthrop, Jane Welsh, Edward Sinclair

† In a 1926 silent version Lionel Barrymore played the murderer and Boris Karloff the mesmerist.

Bells Are Ringing *
US   1960   126m   Metrocolor   Cinemascope
MGM (Arthur Freed)
V*, L, S

A telephone answering service operator becomes passionately involved in the lives of her clients.

Dull, rather ugly and boring transcription of a Broadway musical, with all talents below par, not enough dancing and too much plot.

w Betty Comden, Adolph Green play Betty Comden, Adolph Green d Vincente Minnelli ph Milton Krasner md André Previn m Jule Styne ly Betty Comden, Adolph Green ad George W. Davis, Preston Ames ch Charles O'Curran

Judy Holliday, Dean Martin, Fred Clark, Eddie Foy Jnr, Jean Stapleton, Ruth Storey, Frank Gorshin

AAN: André Previn

The Bells Go Down *
GB   1943   89m   bw
Ealing (S. C. Balcon)

The exploits of a London firefighting unit during World War II.

Tragi-comedy with lively scenes, a good record of the historical background of the blitz.

w Roger Macdougall, Stephen Black d Basil Dearden ph Ernest Palmer m Roy Douglas

Tommy Trinder, James Mason, Mervyn Johns, Philippa Hyatt, Finlay Currie, Philip Friend, Meriel Forbes, Beatrice Varley, Billy Hartnell

The Bells of St Angelo
US   1947   78m   Trucolor
Republic (Edward J. White)

In between songs, Roy Rogers foils smugglers who are taking silver across the Mexican border.

A tougher movie than usual for Rogers, but still a curious mixture of comedy, songs, fist-fights and death.

w Sloan Nibley story Paul Gangelin d William Witney ph Jack Marter md Morton Scott ad Gano Chittenden ed Les Orlebeck

Roy Rogers, Dale Evans, Andy Devine, Bob Nolan and the Sons of the Pioneers

'Your heart will be wearing a smile!'
The Bells of St Mary's **
US   1945   126m   bw
RKO/Rainbow (Leo McCarey)
V, V*, L

At a big city Catholic school, Father O'Malley and Sister Benedict indulge in friendly rivalry, and succeed in extending the school through the gift of a building.

Sentimental and very commercial sequel to *Going My Way*, with the stars at their peak and the handling as cosy and well-paced as might be expected.

w Dudley Nichols d Leo McCarey ph George Barnes m Robert Emmett Dolan ed Harry Marker

Bing Crosby, Ingrid Bergman, Henry Travers, William Gargan, Ruth Donnelly, Rhys Williams, Una O'Connor, Eva Novak

'The picture is full of shrewd and pleasant flashes. It is also fascinating to watch as a talented, desperate effort to repeat the unrepeatable. But on the whole it is an unhappy film.' – *James Agee*

AAN: best picture; Leo McCarey; Robert Emmett Dolan; Bing Crosby; Ingrid Bergman; song 'Aren't You Glad You're You' (m Jimmy Van Heusen, ly Johnny Burke); Harry Marker

The Belly of an Architect
GB/Italy   1987   118m   Technicolor
Recorded Releasing/Mondial/Tangram/Film Four International/British Screen (Colin Callender, Walter Donohue)
V, V*, L, S

An American architect in Rome discovers he is terminally ill, is deserted by his wife, and commits suicide.

Ravishing evocation of 18th-century Roman architecture is no compensation for the multi-layered psychological complexity.

wd Peter Greenaway ph Sacha Vierny m Wim Mertens ad Luciana Vedovelli ed John Wilson

Brian Dennehy, Chloe Webb, Lambert Wilson

Beloved
US   1933   80m   bw
Universal (Bennie F. Zeidman)

A composer ages from 10 to 90 while trying to place his symphony; he dies happy.

Curious fictional biopic with plenty of incident but no plot.

w Paul Gangelin, George O'Neil d Victor Schertzinger

John Boles, Gloria Stuart, Albert Conti, Dorothy Peterson, Morgan Farley

'Too hopelessly muddled in conception to reach the important money class.' – *Variety*

The Beloved Bachelor
US   1931   72m   bw
Paramount

A man falls in love with his adopted daughter.

Innocuous tearjerker made with some style.

w Sidney Buchman, Raymond Griffith, Agnes Brand Leahy, Edward H. Peple d Lloyd Corrigan

Paul Lukas, Dorothy Jordan, Betty Van Allen, Charles Ruggles, Vivienne Osborne

'A particularly femme appealing yarn with apt dialogue and natural continuity.' – *Variety*

Beloved Enemy *

US   1936   90m   bw
Samuel Goldwyn (George Haight)
V*

During the 1921 Irish rebellion, the fiancée of a British army officer falls in love with the leading revolutionary.

Dreamy-eyed romance with little relevance to the real situation; not badly done of its kind.

w John Balderston, Rose Franken, William Brown Meloney, David Hart   d H. C. Potter   ph Gregg Toland   m Alfred Newman

Brian Aherne, Merle Oberon, David Niven, Karen Morley, Jerome Cowan, Henry Stephenson, Donald Crisp

'One of the most incredible screen yarns which has been shown in many a day. . .. If when the film is shown in Dublin a tidal wave engulfs Hollywood, it will be caused by the Emerald Isle turning somersaults.' – Variety

Beloved Infidel *

US   1959   123m   DeLuxe   Cinemascope
TCF/Company of Artists (Jerry Wald)

Sheilah Graham, a British chorus girl turned Hollywood columnist, lives with Scott Fitzgerald but fails to cure him of alcoholism.

A bitter and even sordid true story becomes a slice of Hollywood romance, with stars unsuitably cast. On all levels it falls between two stools, satisfying nobody.

w Sy Bartlett   book Sheilah Graham, Gerold Frank   d Henry King   ph Leon Shamroy   m Franz Waxman

Gregory Peck, Deborah Kerr, Eddie Albert, Philip Ober, Herbert Rudley, Karin Booth, Ken Scott

'Catastrophically misguided.' – Penelope Houston

The Beloved Rogue *

US   1927   99m at 24 fps   bw   silent
Art Cinema Corporation
V*, L

15th-century poet and thief François Villon becomes a friend of the king, but is banished when he falls for a lady of the court.

Stylish star vehicle remade as If I Were King (qv).

w Paul Bern   d Alan Crosland   pd William Cameron Menzies

John Barrymore, Conrad Veidt, Marceline Day, Mack Swain, Slim Summerville

'He kissed many but loved one!'

The Beloved Vagabond *

GB   1936   78m   bw
ABFD/Ludovico Toeplitz

At the turn of the century, a jilted French artist becomes a vagabond and falls in love with an orphan girl.

Mildly amusing bi-lingual production from a bestselling picaresque novel; production quite lively.

w Wells Root, Arthur Wimperis, Hugh Mills, Walter Creighton   novel W. J. Locke   d Curtis Bernhardt   ph Franz Planer   md Leslie Bridgewater   m Darius Milhaud   ad Andrei Andreiev   ed Dug Myers

Maurice Chevalier, Margaret Lockwood, Betty Stockfield, Desmond Tester, Austin Trevor, Peter Haddon, Cathleen Nesbitt

'A weak sister, mostly for the duals.' – Variety

Below Zero **

US   1930   20m   bw
Hal Roach

Street musicians treat a policeman to lunch on the contents of a found wallet which turns out to be his.

Slow-paced but likeable star comedy from their best period.

w H. M. Walker   d James Parrott

Laurel and Hardy, Frank Holliday, Tiny Sandford

The Belstone Fox *

GB   1973   103m   Eastmancolor   Todd-AO 35
Rank/Independent Artists (Sally Shuter)
V

A fox and a hound grow up together but the fox leads to tragedy for its masters.

Good animal and countryside photography barely compensate for a fragmentary story with unpleasant moments or for a muddled attitude towards humans and animals; one is not clear what audience the result is supposed to appeal to.

wd James Hill   novel The Ballad of The Belstone Fox by David Rook   ph John Wilcox, James Allen   m Laurie Johnson

Eric Porter, Rachel Roberts, Jeremy Kemp, Bill Travers, Dennis Waterman

Ben

US   1972   92m   DeLuxe
Cinerama/Bing Crosby (Mort Briskin)
V*

A sickly boy inherits an army of trained rats.

Boring reprise of Willard in which the audience knows only too well what to expect. Production and development quite routine.

w Gilbert A. Ralston   d Phil Karlson   ph Russell Metty   m Walter Scharf

Lee Harcourt Montgomery, Arthur O'Connell, Rosemary Murphy, Meredith Baxter, Kaz Garas, Paul Carr, Kenneth Tobey, Joseph Campanella

AAN: title song (m Walter Scharf, ly Don Black)

'The great decade (1915—25) of the progress of motion picture art reaches its summit! A cast of 125,000!'
'The inspired love of the prince of Hur for the gentle lovely Esther!'

Ben-Hur ***

US   1925   170m approx (16 fps)   bw (colour sequence)   silent
MGM
V*, L

In the time of Christ, a Jew suffers mightily under the Romans.

The American silent screen's biggest epic; the sea battle and the chariot race are its most famous sequences.

w Bess Meredyth, Carey Wilson   novel Lew Wallace   d Fred Niblo   ph Karl Struss, Clyde de Vinna, and others   ad Horace Jackson, Ferdinand Pinney Earle

Ramon Novarro, Francis X. Bushman, Carmel Myers, May McAvoy, Betty Bronson

'Masterpiece of study and patience, a photodrama filled with artistry.' – New York Times

† To begin with, the film was directed by Charles Brabin and starred George Walsh. Both were replaced after Louis Mayer saw the first rushes. Previously filmed in 1907.

Ben-Hur **

US   1959   217m   Technicolor   Camera 65
MGM (Sam Zimbalist)
V, V (W), V*, L, S

Solid, expensive, surprisingly unimaginative remake; generally less sprightly than the silent version.

w Karl Tunberg   d William Wyler, Andrew Marton   ph Robert L. Surtees   m Miklos Rozsa   ad William A. Horning, Edward Carfagno   ed Ralph E. Winters, John D. Dunning

Charlton Heston, Haya Harareet, Jack Hawkins, Stephen Boyd, Hugh Griffith, Martha Scott, Sam Jaffe,

Cathy O'Donnell, Finlay Currie, Frank Thring, Terence Longdon, André Morell, George Relph

'Watching it is like waiting at a railroad crossing while an interminable freight train lumbers by, sometimes stopping altogether.' – Dwight MacDonald

'A Griffith can make a hundred into a crowd while a Wyler can reduce a thousand to a confused cocktail party.' – Ibid.

'The most tasteful and visually exciting film spectacle yet produced by an American company.' – Albert Johnson, Film Quarterly

'Spectacular without being a spectacle . . . not only is it not simple-minded, it is downright literate.' – Saturday Review

'A major motion picture phenomenon.' – Films in Review

† The production cost four million dollars, twice the maximum at the time. Rock Hudson, Marlon Brando and Burt Lancaster were all sought in vain for the lead before Heston was selected.
†† This version was subtitled 'A Tale of the Christ'.

AA: best picture; William Wyler; Robert L. Surtees; Miklos Rozsa; Charlton Heston; Hugh Griffith; art direction; editing; special effects (Arnold Gillespie, Robert MacDonald, Milo Lory)

AAN: Karl Tunberg

Benchley

The one-reel shorts in which Robert Benchley, sitting behind a desk, delivered nonsensical lectures on aspects of modern life were very popular with better-class audiences, and launched Benchley onto his movie career as a light actor. Here is a list of them:

1928: THE TREASURER'S REPORT; THE SEX LIFE OF THE POLYP; THE SPELLBINDER.
1929: LESSON NUMBER ONE (2 reels); FURNACE TROUBLE (2 reels); STEWED, FRIED AND BOILED (2 reels).
1933: YOUR TECHNOCRACY AND MINE (2 reels).
1935: HOW TO BREAK 90 AT CROQUET; HOW TO SLEEP (AA for best short).
1936: HOW TO BEHAVE; HOW TO TRAIN A DOG; HOW TO VOTE; HOW TO BE A DETECTIVE.
1937: THE ROMANCE OF DIGESTION; HOW TO START THE DAY; A NIGHT AT THE MOVIES (AAN for best short).
1938: HOW TO FIGURE INCOME TAX; MUSIC MADE SIMPLE; AN EVENING ALONE; HOW TO RAISE A BABY; THE COURTSHIP OF THE NEWT; HOW TO READ; HOW TO WATCH FOOTBALL; OPENING DAY; MENTAL POISE; HOW TO SUBLET.
1939: AN HOUR FOR LUNCH; DARK MAGIC; HOME EARLY; HOW TO EAT; THE DAY OF REST; SEE YOUR DOCTOR.
1940: THAT INFERIOR FEELING; HOME MOVIES; THE TROUBLE WITH HUSBANDS.
1941: WAITING FOR BABY; CRIME CONTROL; THE FORGOTTEN MAN; HOW TO TAKE A VACATION.
1942: NOTHING BUT NERVES; THE WITNESS; KEEPING IN SHAPE; THE MAN'S ANGLE.
1943: MY TOMATO; NO NEWS IS GOOD NEWS.
1944: IMPORTANT BUSINESS; WHY, DADDY?
1945: BOOGIE WOOGIE (2 reels); I'M A CIVILIAN HERE MYSELF.

† In the late seventies a feature compilation was made under the title Those Wonderful Benchley Shorts.

Bend of the River *

US   1952   91m   Technicolor
U-I (Aaron Rosenberg)
V*
GB title: Where the River Bends

1880 wagon trains arrive in Oregon, and the pioneers have trouble with the local bad man.

Good standard Western with pace and period feeling but not much plot sense.

w Borden Chase   novel *Bend of the Snake* by William Gulick   d Anthony Mann   ph Irving Glassberg   m Hans Salter

James Stewart, Arthur Kennedy, Rock Hudson, Julia Adams, Lori Nelson, Jay C. Flippen, Henry Morgan, Royal Dano, Stepin Fetchit

Beneath the Planet of the Apes *
US   1969   94m   DeLuxe   Panavision
TCF/APJAC (Mort Abrahams)
V, V*, L

Astronauts on the ape planet discover that it is really Earth and that subterranean human mutants are nursing a live atom bomb.

Violence replaces the thoughtfulness of the original, but this is not at all a bad sequel as sequels go.

w Paul Dehn, Mort Abrahams   d Ted Post   ph Milton Krasner   m Leonard Rosenman

James Franciscus, Charlton Heston, Linda Harrison, Kim Hunter, Maurice Evans, Paul Richards, Victor Buono, Jeff Corey, James Gregory, Thomas Gomez

† See *Planet of the Apes.*

Beneath the Twelve Mile Reef
US   1953   102m   Technicolor   Cinemascope
TCF (Robert Bassler)
V*, L

Jealousy, tragedy and romance among the Florida sponge fishers.

Fox's early Cinemascope production involved much underwater shooting, a trick octopus, and predictable plot devices.

w A. I. Bezzerides   d Robert D. Webb   ph Edward Cronjager   m Bernard Herrmann

Robert Wagner, Terry Moore, Gilbert Roland, Peter Graves, J. Carrol Naish, Richard Boone, Angela Clarke, Jay Novello

'The dead weight of a melodramatic script overtaxes the gallant attempts at conviction.' – *MFB*

AAN: Edward Cronjager

Benefit of the Doubt
US/Germany   1993   91m   DeLuxe
Warner/Benefit/Cine Vox/Monument (Michael Spielberg, Brad M. Gilbert)

Out on parole after more than 20 years in prison for the murder of his wife, a man goes to live near his daughter, persuading her that he is innocent of the crime.

A dull thriller that warms over familar plot devices to little purpose.

w Jeffrey Polman, Christopher Keyser   story Michael Lieber   d Jonathan Heap   ph Johnny E. Jensen   m Hummie Mann   pd Marina Kieser   ed Sharyn L. Ross

Donald Sutherland, Amy Irving, Rider Strong, Christopher McDonald, Graham Greene, Theodore Bikel, Gisela Kovach, Ferdinand Mayne

'The result is pretty silly and demeaning.' – *Derek Malcolm, Guardian*

Bengal Brigade
US   1954   87m   Technicolor
U-I (Ted Richmond)
GB title: *Bengal Rifles*

In 19th-century India, an officer is cashiered through false evidence, and becomes an undercover man with the wicked local rajah.

Routine Hollywood heroics with a few unintended laughs.

w Richard Alan Simmons   novel *Bengal Tiger* by Hall Hunter   d Laslo Benedek   ph Maury Gertsman   m Hans Salter

Rock Hudson, Arlene Dahl, Dan O'Herlihy, Ursula Thiess, Torin Thatcher, Michael Ansara, Arnold Moss

Bengal Rifles: see *Bengal Brigade*

Bengazi
US   1955   79m   bw   Superscope
RKO/Panamint (Sam Wiesenthal, Eugene Tevlin)

Various unsavoury characters set out into the African desert to look for gold hidden by the Nazis.

Poor potboiler on predictable lines.

w Endre Bohem, Louis Vittes   d John Brahm   ph Joseph Biroc   m Roy Webb

Richard Conte, Victor McLaglen, Richard Carlson, Mala Powers, Richard Erdman, Gonzales Gonzales, Hillary Brooke

Benjamin, or The Diary of an Innocent Young Man
France   1966   104m   Eastmancolor
Paramount/Parc/Marianne (Mag Bodard)

In the 18th century, a 17-year-old orphan is taken in hand by his wealthy aunt and initiated into the mysteries of sex.

Imitation *Tom Jones,* quite good to look at but rather boring.

w Nina Companeez   d Michel Déville   ph Ghislain Cloquet

Pierre Clémenti, Michèle Morgan, Catherine Deneuve, Michel Piccoli, Francine Bergé, Anna Gaël, Odile Versois

'Heavy with Gallic naughtiness rather than airy charm . . . a plethora of colourful costumes, foliage and fireworks.' – *MFB*

'A marathon tease . . . an unending series of interrupted coitions . . . a gorgeously wrapped and beribboned Christmas package containing an empty box.' – *John Simon*

Benji *
US   1974   86m   CFI color
Mulberry Square (Joe Camp)
V*

A stray mongrel dog saves two kidnapped children.

Family film *par excellence* which rang the box-office bell in a big way in the US. Its modest merits are rather beside the point.

wd Joe Camp   ph Don Reddy   m Euel Box

Peter Breck, Edgar Buchanan, Terry Carter, Christopher Connelly

† A sequel, *For the Love of Benji,* followed in 1977. In 1980 came the curious *Oh Heavenly Dog* (qv). Then in 1987 the same team presented a quirky movie of a different kind: *Benji the Hunted* (qv).

AAN: song 'I Feel Love' (m Euel Box, ly Betty Box)

Benji the Hunted
US   1987   88m   CFI Color
Mulberry Square/Embark/Buena Vista (Ben Vaughn)
V*, L

A mongrel dog is shipwrecked and fosters a pack of cougar cubs.

Freaky fable about a dog with a high IQ; but the training is remarkable.

wd Joe Camp   ph Don Reddy   m Euel Box, Betty Box   sp Bryan L. Renfro, Frank and Juanita Inn (Benji's trainers)

Benji, Frank Inn (trainer), Red Steagall

'Benny's breaking up his sister Joon's romance. Isn't that what big brothers are for?'
'A romance on the brink of reality.'

Benny and Joon
US   1993   99m   DeLuxe
MGM (Susan Arnold, Donna Roth)
V, V*, S

A mentally disturbed painter falls for a fey mime, to the displeasure of her uptight brother.

A romantic comedy about mental illness, by turns whimsical and sentimental and never less than saccharine.

w Barry Berman, Leslie McNeil   d Jeremiah Chechik   ph John Schwartzman   m Rachel Portman   pd Neil Spisak   ed Carol Littleton

Johnny Depp, Mart Stuart Masterson, Aidan Quinn, Julianne Moore, Oliver Platt, C. C. H. Pounder, Dan Hedaya, Joe Grifasi

'Embarrassingly, relentlessly cute.' – *Observer*

The Benny Goodman Story *
US   1955   117m   Technicolor
U-I (Aaron Rosenberg)
V*

A clarinettist from the Jewish section of Chicago becomes internationally famous.

Sentimental biopic of a familiar figure which comes to life when the sound track is given its head (and the real Goodman's clarinet).

wd Valentine Davies   ph William Daniels   md Joseph Gershenson

Steve Allen, Donna Reed, *Berta Gersten,* Herbert Anderson, Robert F. Simon, Sammy Davis Snr, Harry James, Martha Tilton, Gene Krupa

'The customary fictional liberties appear to have been taken.' – *MFB*

Benny's Video *
Austria/Switzerland   1992   105m   colour
ICA/Wega/Bernard Lang

A bored, middle-class, video-obsessed teenager picks up a girl at a video-rental store, takes her home and kills her on camera.

A low-budget movie of alienation that creates unease and questions the role of video violence in society.

wd Michael Haneke   ph Christian Berger   pd Christoph Kanter   ed Marie Homolkova

Arno Frisch, Angela Winkler, Ulrich Mühe, Ingrid Stassner

'Neatly states its case against the anesthetizing properties of too much violent imagery too soon. Urban terror story plays like an icy thriller, but the message runs deeper, lending an intellectual edge.' – *Variety*

† The director has said that the film is a statement 'about the American sensational cinema and its power to rob viewers of their ability to form their own opinions'.

Benvenuta *
Belgium   1983   106m   Eastmancolor
Artificial Eye/La Nouvelle Imageries/UGC/Europe I/FR3/Opera Film (Jean-Claude Batz)

A screenwriter meets a reclusive novelist to write a treatment of her once-famous semi-autobiographical book.

Constantly shifting between fiction and reality, between appearance and fantasy, it soon wears out its welcome.

wd André Delvaux   novel *La Confession Anonyme* by Suzanne Lilar   ph Charlie Van Damme   m Frédérick Devreese   ad Claude Pignot   ed Jean Goudier

Fanny Ardant, Vittorio Gassman, Françoise Fabian, Mathieu Carrière, Claire Wauthion, Philippe Geluck

Bequest to the Nation *

GB   1973   116m   Technicolor
Universal/Hal B. Wallis
US title: The Nelson Affair

The story of Nelson's long affair with the tempestuous Lady Hamilton.

Undistinguished historical drama from a thin play which despite hard work all round makes very ordinary screen entertainment.

w Terence Rattigan   play Terence Rattigan
d James Cellan Jones   ph Gerry Fisher   m Michel Legrand   pd Carmen Dillon

Peter Finch, Glenda Jackson (way over the top), Michael Jayston, Anthony Quayle, Margaret Leighton, Dominic Guard, Nigel Stock, Roland Culver

'As empty as an out-of-town matinee.' – MFB

Berkeley Square **

US   1933   87m   bw
Fox (Jesse L. Lasky)

A London house reincarnates its owner as his 18th-century ancestor.

Romantic fantasy on a time lapse theme, the first of many and perhaps the most stylish and self-assured.

w Sonya Levien, John Balderston   play John Balderston   d Frank Lloyd   ph Ernest Palmer   m Louis de Francesco   ad William Darling

Leslie Howard, Heather Angel, Valerie Taylor, Irene Browne, Beryl Mercer, Colin Keith-Johnston, Alan Mowbray

'Too far above the heads of ordinary theatregoers and too British in tempo and execution to break any box office records.' – Variety

† Remade as The House on the Square (qv).

AAN: Leslie Howard

Berlin Correspondent

US   1942   70m   bw
TCF (Bryan Foy)

In pre-war Germany an American reporter is kidnapped by the Nazis and replaced by a double . . .

Preposterous melodrama, so silly as to be often quite funny.

w Steve Fisher, Jack Andrews   d Eugene Forde   ph Virgil Miller   md Emil Newman

Dana Andrews, Virginia Gilmore, Mona Maris, Martin Kosleck, Sig Rumann, Kurt Katch, Torben Meyer

Berlin, die Symphonie einer Grosstadt: see Berlin, Symphony of a Great City

Berlin Express *

US   1948   87m   bw
RKO (Bert Granet)
V*, L

Police of four nations guard a German VIP on a crack train to Berlin.

Rather muddled suspenser with attempts at political moralizing; the cast provides some good moments.

w Harold Medford   d Jacques Tourneur   ph Lucien Ballard   m Frederick Hollander

Merle Oberon, Robert Ryan, Charles Korvin, Paul Lukas, Robert Coote

Berlin, Symphony of a Great City ***

Germany   1927   78m   bw   silent
Fox-Europa
original title: Berlin, die Symphonie einer Grosstadt

An impression of the life of a city from dawn to midnight, expressed by cinematic montages, angles, sequences, etc, and set to music.

A leader in the field of 'impressionistic' documentaries which are now so familiar (Rien que les

---

Heures did a similar job for Paris at around the same time), this still has moments of poetry which have seldom been equalled.

w Walter Ruttman, Karl Freund, Carl Mayer   d Walter Ruttman   ph Reimar Kuntze, Robert Baberske, Laszlo Schäffer   m Edmund Meisel   ed Walter Ruttman

Berliner Ballade *

Germany   1948   77m   bw
Comedia Film (Alf Teichs)
aka: The Ballad of Berlin

Otto Nobody, an unwilling soldier, returns home to find himself at the mercy of bureaucrats and black marketeers.

Melancholy satire presented as a series of sketches, almost a forerunner of That Was the Week That Was.

w Gunter Neumann   d Robert Stemmle   ph Georg Krause   m/y Gunter Neumann, Werner Eisbrenner

Gert Fröbe, Anton Zeithammer, Tatjana Sais, O. E. Hasse

'Very much the film of a defeated people.' – Penelope Houston

Bermuda Affair

GB   1956   77m   bw
Bermuda Studio Productions

The pilot of a West Indian airline falls for his partner's wife but dies in an air accident.

Tedious and unconvincing marital drama with back-projected local colour.

w Robert J. Shaw, Edward Sutherland   d Edward Sutherland

Kim Hunter, Gary Merrill, Ron Randell, Zena Marshall

The Bermuda Mystery

US   1944   65m   bw
TCF

Friends who have invested in a joint insurance policy are murdered one by one.

Competent lower-berth murder mystery.

w W. Scott Darling   story John Larkin   d Ben Stoloff

Preston Foster, Ann Rutherford, Charles Butterworth, Helene Reynolds, Richard Lane

Bernadette

France   1988   105m   colour
Cannon/Films de L'Etoile D'Or/Bernadette Association International (Jacques Quintard)

A peasant girl sees visions of the Virgin Mary at Lourdes and invokes the hostility of the authorities.

Ponderously reverent treatment of a saintly girl, providing no more than moments of piety.

w Jean Delannoy, Robert Arnaut   d Jean Delannoy   ph Jean-Bertrand Penzer   m Francis Lai   ad Alain Paroutaud   ed Annick Charvein

Sydney Penney, Jean-Marc Bory, Michèle Simonnet, Roland Lesaffre, Bernard Dhéran, François Dalout, Stephan Garcin

Bernardine *

US   1957   95m   Eastmancolor   Cinemascope
TCF (Samuel G. Engel)

A college student forced to swot for exams asks a friend's elder brother to look after his girl.

Henry Aldrich-style high school comedy, showing the lighter side of Rebel without a Cause. Notable for the clean-living hero played by a clean-living singing star, and the reappearance of Janet Gaynor for the only time since 1939, in a routine mother role.

w Theodore Reeves   play Mary Chase   d Henry Levin   ph Paul Vogel   m Lionel Newman

---

Pat Boone, Richard Sargent, Terry Moore, Janet Gaynor, Walter Abel, Dean Jagger, Natalie Schafer, James Drury

Berserk!

GB   1967   96m   Technicolor
Columbia (Herman Cohen)
V*

A lady circus owner revels in the publicity brought about by a series of murders.

Grisly and unattractive thriller with an ageing star in a series of unsuitably abbreviated costumes; the script is beyond redemption.

w Herman Cohen, Aben Kandel   d Jim O'Connolly   ph Desmond Dickinson   m Patrick John Scott

Joan Crawford, Diana Dors, Ty Hardin, Judy Geeson, Michael Gough, Robert Hardy, Geoffrey Keen, Sidney Tafler, Philip Madoc

Bert Rigby, You're a Fool

USA   1989   94m   Metrocolor
Warner/Lorimar/A Clear Production (George Shapiro)
V*, L

A former miner becomes a mostly unsuccessful song-and-dance man in Hollywood.

Dim comedy, intended as a showcase for the slight charm of Robert Lindsay.

wd Carl Reiner   ph Jan de Bont   m Ralph Burns   pd Terence Marsh   ad Dianne Wager, Michael Seirton   ed Bud Molin, Stephen Myers

Robert Lindsay, Anne Bancroft, Corbin Bernsen, Robbie Coltrane, Cathryn Bradshaw, Jackie Gayle, Bruno Kirby, Liz Smith, Lila Kaye

'Mixes sentimentality with vulgarity with reckless abandon.' – John Pym, MFB

Berth Marks

US   1929   20m   bw   silent
Hal Roach
V, V (C)

Stan and Ollie, on a train, have to share an upper berth.

Overstretched single-situation comedy, one of the team's poorest.

w Leo McCarey, H. M. Walker   d Lewis R. Foster

Laurel and Hardy

Die Berührte: see No Mercy No Future

The Bespoke Overcoat **

GB   1956   33m   bw
Romulus (Jack Clayton)

A clerk in a clothing warehouse is refused a coat and asks a tailor friend to make him one. But he dies of cold and his ghost persuades the tailor to steal the coat he deserved.

The story seems stiff, but the production has a rich Dickensian feel and may be the best short drama filmed in Britain.

w Wolf Mankowitz   story Gogol   d Jack Clayton   ph Wolfgang Suschitzky   m Georges Auric

Alfie Bass, David Kossoff

'A triumph of talent, small means and originality.' – New Statesman

AA: best short

Best Boy ***

US   1979   111m   colour   16mm
Ira Wohl
V*, L

A documentary, shot by his cousin, of the problems of a mentally retarded 53-year-old man whose elderly parents are ailing.

A film with very moving elements, though they would have been even sharper at half the length.

wd Ira Wohl

AA: best documentary

Best Defense
US   1984   94m   Movielab
Paramount (Gloria Katz)
V*, L

A US tank goes hopelessly out of control in Kuwait; intercut with this are some of the problems which confronted its designer two years earlier.

Weird, unappetizing and disjointed farce, composed mainly of irrelevancies.

w Gloria Katz, Willard Huyck   *novel Easy and Hard Ways Out* by Robert Grossbach   *d* Willard Huyck *ph* Don Peterman   *m* Patrick Williams   *pd* Peter Jamison

Dudley Moore, Eddie Murphy, Kate Capshaw, George Dzundza, Helen Shaver

'As bereft of charm and spontaneity as it is overburdened with tedious gesticulation.' – *Tim Pulleine, MFB*

'About as funny as getting hi-jacked by a group of kamikaze terrorists.' – *Derek Malcolm, Guardian*

'How did I get involved? The door opened, and four men came in carrying a cheque.' – *Eddie Murphy*

Best Foot Forward
US   1943   94m   Technicolor
MGM (Arthur Freed)
V*, L

A glamorous publicity-seeking film star accepts an invitation to a military college ball.

Old-fashioned formula musical based on a lightweight Broadway success.

w Irving Brecher, Fred Finklehoffe   *play* John Cecil Holmes   *d* Edward Buzzell   *ph* Leonard Smith *md* Lennie Hayton   *ch* Charles Walters   *m/ly* Hugh Martin, Ralph Blane

Lucille Ball, William Gaxton, Virginia Weidler, Harry James and his Orchestra, June Allyson, Gloria de Haven

Best Friends *
US   1982   116m   Technicolor
Warner/Joe Wizan/Norman Jewison
V*, L

Two writers who have enjoyed a peaceful professional relationship find problems when they get married and visit their respective families.

Rather a heavy comedy which seems to have no real point, this gets by on enjoyable sequences and star performances.

w Valerie Curtin, Barry Levinson   *d* Norman Jewison   *ph* Jordan Cronenweth   *m* Michel Legrand   *ad* Joe Russo   *ed* Don Zimmerman

Burt Reynolds, Goldie Hawn, Jessica Tandy, Barnard Hughes, Audra Lindley, Keenan Wynn

'A print-out of a script conference at which everyone collapsed at everyone else's contributory sally.' – *Sunday Times*

AAN: song 'How Do You Keep the Music Playing?' (Michel Legrand, Alan and Marilyn Bergman)

The Best House in London *
GB   1968   96m   Eastmancolor
MGM/Bridge/Carlo Ponti (Philip Breen, Kurt Unger)

A Victorian publicity agent tries to organize a government-sponsored brothel.

Cheerful slam-bang historical send-up with as many dull thuds of banality as pleasant witticisms.

w Denis Norden   *d* Philip Saville   *ph* Alex Thompson   *m* Mischa Spoliansky   *pd* Wilfrid Shingleton

David Hemmings, George Sanders, Joanna Pettet, Warren Mitchell, Dany Robin, William Rushton

The Best Intentions ***
Sweden   1992   181m   colour
Artificial Eye/STV1/ZDF/Channel 4/RAIDU/La Sept/DR/YLE 2/ NRK/RUV (Lars Bjälkeskog)
V, V*

original title: *Den Goda Viljan*

In Sweden in the early 1900s, a priest overcomes parental objections to marry a nurse, but their union is a troubled one.

A sharply observed, fascinating semi-biographical account by a son of the early years of his parents' marriage, ending just before his birth.

w Ingmar Bergman   *d* Bille August   *ph* Jörgen Persson   *m* Stefan Nilsson   *pd* Anna Asp *ed* Janus Billeskov Jansen

Samuel Fröler, *Pernilla August*, Max von Sydow, Ghita Norby, Lennart Hjulström, Mona Malm, Lena Endre, Keve Hjelm

'The picture is uniformly well acted, has a wonderful feeling for the distinct Scandinavian seasons, and re-creates social occasions with an acute moral edge.' – *Philip French, Observer*

'Ingmar Bergman may have officially retired from film direction, but his genius marches on.' – *Geoff Brown, The Times*

† At the 1992 Cannes Film Festival, the film won the Palme D'Or for best film and Pernilla August the award for best actress.

The Best Little Whorehouse in Texas
US   1982   114m   Technicolor   Panavision
Universal/RKO (Thomas L. Miller, Edward K. Milkis, Robert L. Boyett)
V, V*, L, S

A long-established Texas whorehouse becomes the object of a clean-up campaign.

Flat and feeble screen version of a limp and tuneless musical which astonishingly was a Broadway hit, perhaps because people thought it was naughty. Onscreen the acting is too easy-going and the script too coy for anybody to have a good time.

w Larry L. King, Peter Masterson   *play* Larry L. King, Peter Masterson   *d* Colin Higgins *ph* William A. Fraker   *m* Patrick Williams *pd* Robert F. Boyle   *m/ly* Carol Hall

Burt Reynolds, Dolly Parton, Charles Durning, Dom DeLuise, Jim Nabors, Robert Mandan, Lois Nettleton, Noah Beery Jnr

'Rancid, self-deceiving, hypocritical stuff.' – *Observer*

'A sanitized, coyly predictable piece of brothel creeping, set to musak by a poorly programmed computer.' – *Guardian*

'Almost everything about it is misjudged.' – *Daily Mail*

'High on jollity, low on country and western, and very uncertainly directed.' – *Sight and Sound*

'Never gets beyond the concept stage.' – *Roger Ebert*

AAN: Charles Durning

The Best Man ***
US   1964   104m   bw
UA/Stuart Millar, Lawrence Turman
V*

Two contenders for a presidential nomination seek the support of the dying ex-president.

Brilliant political melodrama, ingeniously adapted on a low budget from an incisive play, with splendid dramatic scenes, memorable performances and good convention detail.

w Gore Vidal   *play* Gore Vidal   *d* Franklin Schaffner *ph* Haskell Wexler   *m* Mort Lindsey

Henry Fonda, Cliff Robertson, Lee Tracy, Margaret Leighton, Edie Adams, Kevin McCarthy, *Shelley Berman, Ann Sothern, Gene Raymond, Mahalia Jackson*

'A fine opportunity to watch pros at work in a hard-hitting and cogent drama that seems to become more topical and have more relevance with each showing.' – *Judith Crist*

'Some of the wittiest lines since *Strangelove* . . . the acting fairly crackled with authenticity.' – *Isabel Quigly*

'You are left gasping at its sheer professionalism.' – *Evening News*

AAN: Lee Tracy

The Best Man Wins
US   1934   75m   bw
Columbia

A harbour cop finds himself tracking down the friend who had saved his life.

Predictable tough-guy programmer.

w Ethel Hill, Bruce Manning   *d* Erle C. Kenton

Edmund Lowe, Jack Holt, Bela Lugosi, Florence Rice, Forrester Harvey

The Best of Enemies
US/Italy   1961   104m   colour   Technirama
Columbia/Dino de Laurentiis

During the Abyssinian campaign of 1941, an Italian and a British officer learn mutual respect.

Mild satirical comedy drama with a few points to make about war; the elements blend rather obviously and dispiritingly.

w Jack Pulman   *d* Guy Hamilton   *ph* Giuseppe Rotunno   *m* Nino Rota

David Niven, Alberto Sordi, Michael Wilding, Amedeo Nazzari, Harry Andrews, David Opatoshu, Kenneth Fortescue, Duncan Macrae

The Best of Everything *
US   1959   121m   DeLuxe   Cinemascope
TCF (Jerry Wald)

Personal problems of a New York publisher's female staff.

Slick novelette on the lines of a naughty *Peg's Paper*; pure Hollywood gossamer.

w Edith Sommer, Mann Rubin   *novel* Rona Jaffe *d* Jean Negulesco   *ph* William C. Mellor   *m* Alfred Newman

Hope Lange, Stephen Boyd, Joan Crawford, Louis Jourdan, Suzy Parker, Martha Hyer, Diane Baker, Brian Aherne, Robert Evans, Brett Halsey, Donald Harron

'A cautionary tale sensationally told.' – *Alexander Walker*

AAN: title song (*m* Alfred Newman, *ly* Sammy Cahn)

Best of the Badmen *
US   1951   84m   Technicolor
RKO (Herman Schlom)

At the end of the Civil War Jeff Clanton organizes the break-up of Quantrell's Raiders, but is himself arrested on a trumped-up charge and needs the Raiders' help.

Standard Western notable for a good cast and for bringing in a remarkable number of historical outlaws, doing rather unhistorical things.

w Robert Hardy Andrews, John Twist   *d* William D. Russell   *ph* Edward Cronjager   *m* Paul Sawtell

Robert Ryan, Claire Trevor, Jack Buetel, Robert Preston, Walter Brennan, Bruce Cabot, John Archer, Lawrence Tierney

'Apart, They're Tough. Together, They're Awesome.'
Best of the Best
US   1989   97m   CFI
Entertainment/Best of the Best/Kuys (Phillip Rhee, Peter E. Strauss)
V, V*, L

An American Taekwondo team prepares to compete against the Korean champions.

Plodding, sentimental and over-familiar variation on *The Karate Kid* and *Rocky*.

w Paul Levine   story Phillip Rhee, Paul Levine   d Bob Radler   ph Doug Ryna   pd Kim Rees   ed William Hoy

Eric Roberts, James Earl Jones, Sally Kirkland, John P. Ryan, John Dye, David Agresta, Tom Everett, Louise Fletcher, Simon Rhee

Best of the Best II
US   1992   100m   DeLuxe
Entertainment/Picture Securities (Peter E. Strauss, Phillip Rhee)
V, V*, S

Members of the US karate team avenge a friend's death at the hands of a ruthless champion who wants them killed.

The stock plot of virtually every martial arts movie is wheeled out yet again, together with the obligatory violence and the chest-thumping moral that might is right; it is no more convincing this time around.

w Max Strom, John Allen Nelson   d Robert Radler   ph Fred Tammes   m David Michael Frank   pd Gary Frutkoff   ed Bert Lovitt

Eric Roberts, Phillip Rhee, Edan Gross, Ralph Moeller, Christopher Penn, Sonny Landham, Wayne Newton, Meg Foster

'Film looks and plays like a drive-in picture of 20 years ago, only less fun.' – *Variety*

The Best of Times
US   1985   104m   Technicolor
Universal/Kings Road (Gordon Carroll)
V, V*, L

A small-town loser determines to have one more shot at the big time.

Curious, almost plotless comedy drama with nothing to draw the punters.

w Ron Shelton   d Roger Spottiswoode   ph Charles F. Wheeler   m Arthur B. Rubinstein

Robin Williams, Kurt Russell, Pamela Reed, Holly Palance, Donald Moffat, M. Emmet Walsh

'Required magic is in too short supply and box office returns should be also.' – *Variety*

Best Seller *
US   1987   110m   CFI Color
Orion/Hemdale (Carter de Haven)
V*, L

A former hit-man helps an ex-cop write a book based on an old unsolved case.

Tortuous but generally lively and interesting melodrama which at least tries to be different.

w Larry Cohen   d John Flynn   ph Fred Murphy   m Jay Ferguson   pd Gene Rudolf   ed David Rosenbloom

James Woods, Brian Dennehy, Victoria Tennant, Allison Balson, Paul Shenar, George Coe

Best Shot: see *Hoosiers*

The Best Things in Life Are Free *
US   1956   103m   Eastmancolor   Cinemascope
TCF (Henry Ephron)

From Broadway to Hollywood in the twenties, the story of songwriting team de Sylva, Brown and Henderson.

Gangsters, movie studios and the writing of 'Sonny Boy' for Al Jolson all figure in this amiable musical which spends more time on jokes than romance; the numbers are disappointing despite good tunes.

w William Bowers, Phoebe Ephron   d Michael Curtiz   ph Leon Shamroy   md Lionel Newman

Ernest Borgnine, Gordon Macrae, Dan Dailey, Sheree North, Jacques d'Amboise, Norman Brooks, Murvyn Vye

AAN: Lionel Newman

'Three wonderful loves in the best picture of the year!'
The Best Years of Our Lives ****
US   1946   182m   bw
Samuel Goldwyn
V, V*, L, S

Three men come home from war to a small middle-American community, and find it variously difficult to pick up where they left off.

The situations and even some of the characters now seem a little obvious, but this was a superb example of high-quality film-making in the forties, with smiles and tears cunningly spaced, and a film which said what was needed on a vital subject.

w *Robert Sherwood*   novel *Glory for Me* by Mackinlay Kantor   d *William Wyler*   ph *Gregg Toland*   m Hugo Friedhofer   ed Daniel Mandell

Fredric March, Myrna Loy, Teresa Wright, Dana Andrews, Virginia Mayo, Cathy O'Donnell, *Hoagy Carmichael, Harold Russell* (a non-actor-trained handless veteran whose only film this was until *Inside Moves* in 1980), Gladys George, Roman Bohnen, Ray Collins

'One of the best pictures of our lives!' – *Variety*

'The result is a work of provocative and moving insistence and beauty.' – *Howard Barnes*

'One recognizes everything and in the end this recognition is all the excitement, for what is on the screen becomes finally as accustomed and undramatic as the shabby decor of the theatre itself.' – *Robert Warshow, The Immediate Experience*

'One of the very few American studio-made movies in years that seem to me profoundly pleasing, moving and encouraging.' – *James Agee*

'Easily the best film from Hollywood on the warrior's return.' – *Sunday Graphic*

† In 1977 came a TV remake *Returning Home* but it did not lead to the expected series.

AA: best picture; Robert Sherwood; William Wyler; Hugo Friedhofer; Fredric March; Harold Russell; Daniel Mandell

La Bête Humaine **
France   1938   99m   bw
Paris Films (Robert Hakim)
V
aka: *The Human Beast; Judas Was a Woman*

A psychopathic train driver falls for a married woman, plans with her to kill her husband, but finally strangles her instead.

Curious melodrama with strong visual sequences, flawed by its ambivalent attitude to its hero-villain.

wd *Jean Renoir*,   novel Emile Zola   ph Curt Courant   m Joseph Kosma

Jean Gabin, Simone Simon, Julien Carette, Fernand Ledoux, Jean Renoir

'French production at its best.' – *Variety*

'Marvellous atmosphere and a fine cast, but the material turns oppressive.' – *New Yorker, 1978*

'What is most deft is the way Renoir works the depot and the man's job into every scene – conversations on platforms, in washrooms and canteens, views from the station master's window over the steaming metal waste: the short sharp lust worked out in a wooden

platelayer's shed among shunted trucks under the steaming rain.' – *Graham Greene*

† Remade in Hollywood as *Human Desire*.

Betrayal *
GB   1982   95m   colour
Horizon/Sam Spiegel (Eric Rattray)
V, V*

The story of a publisher, his wife and her lover is told in scenes that go backwards in time.

Sharply acted stuff very typical of its author, for audiences with wideawake minds; but more theatrical than cinematic.

w Harold Pinter   play Harold Pinter   d David Jones   ph Mike Fash   m Dominic Muldowney

Jeremy Irons, Ben Kingsley, Patricia Hodge, Avril Elgar

'Occasionally I pined for a little zest – perhaps a nude lesbian chariot race on ice.' – *Quentin Crisp*

AAN: screenplay adaptation

Betrayal from the East
US   1945   83m   bw
RKO (Herman Schlom)
V*

Japanese out to sabotage the Panama Canal are thwarted by a carnival showman.

Extravagant but penny-pinching flagwaver.

w Kenneth Gamet, Aubrey Wisberg   novel Alan Hynd   d William Berke   ph Russell Metty   m Roy Webb

Lee Tracy, Nancy Kelly, Richard Loo, Abner Biberman, Regis Toomey, Philip Ahn, Addison Richards, Sen Yung, Drew Pearson

Betrayed
US   1954   108m   Eastmancolor
MGM (Gottfried Reinhardt)
V*, L

In 1943 a Dutch intelligence officer works with a resistance leader who turns out to be a traitor.

Slow-moving, studio-set romantic melodrama of the old school; not very lively.

w Ronald Millar, George Froeschel   d Gottfried Reinhardt   ph Frederick A. Young   m Walter Goehr

Clark Gable, Victor Mature, Lana Turner, Louis Calhern, O. E. Hasse, Wilfrid Hyde-White, Ian Carmichael, Niall MacGinnis, Nora Swinburne

Betrayed (1944): see
When Strangers Marry

Betrayed *
US   1988   128m   Alpha/Astro
MGM/UA/Irwin Winkler (Joe Eszterhas)
V, V*, L, S

Following the murder of a radio talk show hostess, a couple on the run find themselves in a web of political intrigue.

Heavygoing piece with Something to Say, but not much to watch.

w Joe Eszterhas   d Costa-Gavras   ph Patrick Blossier   m Bill Conti   pd Patrizia von Brandenstein

Debra Winger, Tom Berenger, John Heard, Betsy Blair, John Mahoney

Betrogen bis zum Jungsten Tag: see *Duped Till Doomsday*

'The Harold Robbins people: what you dream, they do!'

The Betsy

US   1977   125m   Technicolor
Allied Artists/Harold Robbins International (Robert R. Weston)
V*

Jockeying for power in the boardroom and the family life of an aged car manufacturer.

Rather tame and obvious melodrama enlivened by its star performance.

w William Bast, Walter Bernstein   novel Harold Robbins   d Daniel Petrie   ph Mario Tosi   m John Barry

Laurence Olivier, Robert Duvall, Tommy Lee Jones, Katharine Ross, Jane Alexander, Lesley-Anne Down, Joseph Wiseman, Edward Herrmann

'Almost compulsively dreadful.' – Derek Malcolm, Guardian

Betsy's Wedding *

US   1990   94m   Technicolor
Warner/Touchstone/Silver Screen Partners IV (Martin Bregman, Louis A. Stroller)
V, V*, L

A father gives his daughter a no-expense-spared wedding.

Intermittently amusing comedy of domestic mishaps.

wd Alan Alda   ph Kelvin Pike   m Bruce Broughton   pd John Jay Moore   ed Michael Polakow

Alan Alda, Joey Bishop, Madeline Kahn, Anthony LaPaglia, Catherine O'Hara, Joe Pesci, Molly Ringwald, Ally Sheedy, Burt Young

'Surges ahead with tart one-liners, absurd spectacle, and ebullient side turns.' – MFB

Better Late Than Never

US   1983   87m   colour
Warner (Jack Haley Jnr, David Niven Jnr)
V*

From two possibilities, an heiress selects her true grandfather. (Her grandmother wasn't sure.)

Would-be risqué comedy which fails to spark despite the talents involved.

wd Bryan Forbes   m Henry Mancini

David Niven, Art Carney, Maggie Smith, Kimberley Partridge, Catherine Hicks, Lionel Jeffries

'As predictable as a rumbling stomach after a bowl of chilli.' – Motion Picture Guide

Better Off Dead

US   1985   98m   Technicolor
Warner/A&M (Michael Jaffe)
V, V*, L

When his fickle girlfriend leaves him, a lonely teenager becomes despondent, but the sun shines when another girl shows interest.

Plotless, almost legless comedy drama with no direction whatever.

wd Savage Steve Holland   ph Isidore Mankovsky   m Rupert Hine   pd Herman Zimmerman

John Cusack, David Ogden Stiers, Kim Darby, Demian Slade, Scooter Stevens, Diane Franklin

'Kids deserve better than this.' – Variety

The Better 'Ole

US   1926   97m (24 fps)   bw   silent

A British sergeant in Flanders proves that his major is actually a German spy.

Comedy-drama based on the cartoons of Old Bill by Bruce Bairnsfather. (The title comes from one in which Old Bill, in the trenches, is saying to a disgruntled soldier: 'If yer knows of a better 'ole, go to it.'). Criticism is irrelevant now, but the piece has historical interest.

w Charles Reisner, Darryl F. Zanuck   d Charles Reisner   ph Ed Du Par, Walter Robinson

Syd Chaplin, Doris Hill, Harold Goodwin, Edgar Kennedy

Betty Blue *

France   1986   120m   Fujicolor
Gaumont/Constellation/Cargofilms (Claudie Ossard)
V, V*, L, S
original title: 37.2° au matin

A waitress indulges her animal attraction for an odd job man but discovers him to be a literary genius.

What virtues this film has are more in style than content, but most people will find it over the top anyway.

wd Jean-Jacques Beineix   novel Philippe Djian   ph Jean-François Robin   m Gabriel Yared   ed Monique Prim

Béatrice Dalle, Jean-Hugues Anglade, Consuelo de Haviland

Between Heaven and Hell

US   1956   94m   Eastmancolor   Cinemascope
TCF (David Weisbart)
V*

After Pearl Harbor a young Southern landowner is called up and finds himself on active service with mixed racial types.

Vaguely anti-war, pro-understanding action thriller which ends up going through predictable heroics in a professional but not too sympathetic manner.

w Harry Brown   novel The Day the Century Ended by Francis Gwaltney   d Richard Fleischer   ph Leo Tover   m Hugo Friedhofer

Robert Wagner, Buddy Ebsen, Broderick Crawford, Brad Dexter, Mark Damon, Robert Keith, Ken Clark, Skip Homeier, Harvey Lembeck

AAN: Hugo Friedhofer

Between Midnight and Dawn

US   1950   89m   bw
Columbia (Hunt Stromberg)

Radio policemen track down a racketeer.

Competent, undistinguished programmer.

w Eugene Ling   d Gordon Douglas   ph George E. Diskant   m George Duning

Mark Stevens, Edmond O'Brien, Gale Storm, Donald Buka, Gale Robbins, Roland Winters

Between the Lines *

US   1977   101m   TVC colour
Essential/Midwest Film Productions (Raphael Silver)
V*

Workers on a Boston underground newspaper are worried by rumours of an impending sale.

Sharply observed but slackly structured slice of provincial life.

w Fred Barron   d Joan Micklin Silver   ph K. V. Sickle   pd Stuart Wurtzel   ed John Carter

John Heard, Lindsay Crouse, Jeff Goldblum, Jill Eikenberry, Bruno Kirby, Stephen Collins, Michael J. Pollard

Between Two Women

US   1937   88m   bw
MGM

Romance between doctor and nurse is interrupted by her alcoholic husband and his infatuation with a patient.

Incident-packed men-in-white melodrama.

w Carey Wilson   story Erich von Stroheim   d George B. Seitz

Franchot Tone, Maureen O'Sullivan, Virginia Bruce, Edward Norris, Cliff Edwards, Janet Beecher

'Class B that almost grew up. Eternal triangle in a hospital; okay dualler for nabes.' – Variety

† Title later changed to Surrounded by Women to avoid confusion with a Dr Kildare episode.

Between Two Worlds *

US   1944   112m   bw
Warner (Mark Hellinger)

A number of air-raid victims, and two lovers who have committed suicide, find themselves on a luxury ship en route to the next world.

Nice-looking but slow and turgid remake of Outward Bound (qv), largely sunk in its own misery but redeemed by two performances.

w Daniel Fuchs   play Sutton Vane   d Edward A. Blatt   ph Carl Guthrie   m Erich Wolfgang Korngold

John Garfield, Edmund Gwenn, Eleanor Parker, Paul Henreid, Sydney Greenstreet, Sara Allgood, George Tobias, Faye Emerson, George Coulouris, Dennis King, Isobel Elsom

'For ferry service from a world so saturated with death, the ship seems strangely empty – a fact that was not obtrusive in a day when death was not intrusive.' – James Agee

Between Us Girls

US   1942   89m   bw
Universal (Henry Koster, Phil Karlson)

A mother and daughter are both involved in romances which tend to cross.

Mild comedy, a disappointing bid for stardom for a disappointing young star.

w Myles Connolly, True Boardman   play Le Fruit Vert by Regis Gignoux, Jacques Thery   d Henry Koster   ph Joseph Valentine   m Frank Skinner

Diana Barrymore, Kay Francis, Robert Cummings, John Boles, Scotty Beckett, Ethel Griffies

The Beverly Hillbillies

US   1993   93m   DeLuxe
TCF (Ian Bryce, Penelope Spheeris)
S

A hillbilly family strike oil and move to live in a Beverly Hills mansion.

Based on the mouldering television sit-com, this is a wearisome concoction of old jokes about country folk trying to cope with city ways; its unsophisticated appeal is limited.

w Lawrence Konner, Mark Rosenthal, Jim Fisher, Jim Staahl   d Penelope Spheeris   ph Robert Brinkmann   m Lalo Schifrin   pd Peter Jamison   ed Ross Albert

Diedrich Bader, Dabney Coleman, Erika Eleniak, Cloris Leachman, Rob Schneider, Lea Thompson, Lily Tomlin, Jim Varney, Buddy Ebsen, Zsa Zsa Gabor, Dolly Parton

'Just as corny and stupid as the long-running series, pic version has been cleverly cast and shrewdly skewed to appeal jointly to original fans of the show and younger viewers only vaguely familiar with it.' – Variety

† The TV series ran from 1962 to 1971 and starred Buddy Ebsen in Jim Varney's role as Jed Clampett, Irene Ryan in Cloris Leachman's role as Granny, Donna Douglas in Erika Eleniak's role as the nubile Elly May, and Max Baer Jnr in Diedrich Bader's role of the dim Jethro. Created by Paul Henning, in its early years it was the most popular programme on American television, with a weekly audience of around 60 million.

Beverly Hills Cop **

US   1984   105m   Technicolor
Paramount/Don Simpson/Jerry Bruckheimer
V, V*, L, S

A Detroit cop races to Los Angeles to track down the killers of his best friend.

Filled with foul language and frenetic action, this rough-edged action comedy became one of the top box-office grossers of its year. So much for its year.

w Daniel Petrie Jnr   d Martin Brest   ph Bruce Surtees   m Harold Faltermeyer   pd Angelo Graham   ed Billy Weber, Arthur O. Coburn

Eddie Murphy, Judge Reinhold, Lisa Eilbacher, John Ashton, Ronny Cox, Steven Berkoff

'The film's only function is to provide Murphy with the opportunity to work a dozen or so variations on his familiar and oddly endearing routine.' – *Time*

† The role was originally tailored for Sylvester Stallone.

AAN: original screenplay

'Axel Foley Is Back. Back Where He Doesn't Belong.'
Beverly Hills Cop 2
US   1987   102m   Technicolor   Panavision
UIP/Paramount/Don Simpson-Jerry Bruckheimer/Eddie Murphy
V, V*, L, S

A cop returns to Beverly Hills to solve a series of crimes.

Further helpings from the same bowl. In no respect is the second film an improvement on the first.

w Larry Ferguson, Warren Skaaren, David Giler, Dennis Klein   story Eddie Murphy, Robert D. Wachs   d Tony Scott   ph Jeffrey L. Kimball   m Harold Faltermeyer   pd Ken Davis   ed Billy Weber, Chris Lebenzon, Michael Tronick

Eddie Murphy, Judge Reinhold, Jurgen Prochnow, Ronnie Cox, Allen Garfield, Brigitte Nielsen, Dean Stockwell, Paul Guilfoyle

'A noisy, numbing, unimaginative, heartless remake . . . all has gone sour and cold.' – *Daily Variety*

Beverly of Graustark
US   1926   85m approx at 24 fps   bw   silent
MGM

When a prince falls ill, his girl cousin impersonates him at an important ceremony.

Cheerful Ruritanian comedy.

w Agnes Christine Johnston   d Sidney Franklin

Marion Davies, Antonio Moreno, Roy D'Arcy, Creighton Hale

Beware My Lovely
US   1952   77m   bw
RKO/Filmmakers (Collier Young)
V*, L

A handyman employed by a widow turns out to be a mental defective who imprisons and threatens to rape and murder her.

Dismal suspenser with a lot of screaming and running around but very little flair.

w Mel Dinelli   play The Man by Mel Dinelli   d Harry Horner   ph George E. Diskant   m Leith Stevens

Ida Lupino, Robert Ryan, Taylor Holmes, Barbara Whiting

'Inept characterization and ludicrously repetitive situations will surely rank this among the silliest films of the year.' – *MFB*

Beware of Children: see *No Kidding*

Beware of Pity *
GB   1946   106m   bw
Two Cities (W. P. Lipscomb)

An officer courts a crippled girl out of pity. She finds out and kills herself.

Ambitious but rather artificial and dreary drama, a shade too pleased with its own literariness; performances straitjacketed by production.

w W. P. Lipscomb, Elizabeth Baron, Marguerite Steen   novel Stefan Zweig   d Maurice Elvey   ph Derick Williams

Lilli Palmer, Albert Lieven, Cedric Hardwicke, Gladys Cooper, Linden Travers, Ernest Thesiger, Emrys Jones

Beware Spooks!
US   1939   65m   bw
Columbia (Robert Sparks)

A nervous policeman routs crooks operating from a fairground.

Standard star comedy with some funny moments.

w Richard Flournoy, Albert Duffy, Brian Marlow   d Edward Sedgwick

Joe E. Brown, Mary Carlisle, Clarence Kolb, Marc Lawrence, Don Beddoe

Beware! The Blob
US   1971   88m   DeLuxe
Jack H. Harris
V, V*
GB title: *Son of Blob*

A mysterious jelly from outer space consumes most of the population of a small town.

Spoofy sequel to one of the original space monster movies of the fifties. It's all too laboured to raise a thrill or a smile.

w Jack Woods, Anthony Harris   d Larry Hagman   ph Al Hamm   m Mort Garson   sp Tim Baar

Robert Walker, Gwynne Gilford, Godfrey Cambridge, Richard Webb, Shelley Berman, Carol Lynley, Burgess Meredith, Gerrit Graham, Larry Hagman

Bewitched
US   1945   65m   bw
MGM (Jerry Bresler)

A girl with twin personalities has her murderous element exorcized by a spiritualist.

Hilarious nonsense, ancestor of the Eve and Lizzie schizos of the fifties.

wd Arch Oboler   story Alter Ego by Arch Oboler   ph Charles Salerno Jnr   m Bronislau Kaper

Phyllis Thaxter, Edmund Gwenn, Addison Richards, Kathleen Lockhart

'Oboler manages the first persuasive imitations of stream of consciousness I know of in a movie. Much more often, he bores to desperation with the vulgarity and mere violence of his effects.' – *James Agee*

Beyond a Reasonable Doubt *
US   1956   80m   bw
RKO (Bert Friedlob)
V, V*

A novelist is persuaded by a crusading newspaper proprietor to fake circumstantial evidence incriminating himself in a murder, thus proving the uselessness of such evidence. He does it so well that he is convicted . . . but that doesn't matter as he was guilty all the time.

Ingenious but rather cheerless and mechanical thriller. The actors extract what they can from a script intent on sleight of hand, but the distinguished director is at his most flatulent.

w Douglas Morrow   d Fritz Lang   ph William Snyder   m Herschel Burke Gilbert

Dana Andrews, Joan Fontaine, Sidney Blackmer, Philip Bourneuf, Shepperd Strudwick, Arthur Franz, Edward Binns

'An adventure which cowards quit early and weaklings never finish at all!'
Beyond Glory
US   1948   82m   bw
Paramount (Robert Fellows)

The honour of a West Point cadet is vindicated.

Proficient but dramatically turgid vehicle for an absurdly over-age star.

w Jonathan Latimer, Charles Marquis Warren, William Wister Haines   d John Farrow   ph John F. Seitz   m Victor Young

Alan Ladd, Donna Reed, George Coulouris, George Macready, Audie Murphy

Beyond Mombasa
GB   1955   90m   Technicolor
Columbia/Hemisphere (Adrian Worker)

In East Africa, an American avenges his brother's death at the hands of the Mau Mau (here called the Leopard Men and revealed to be run by a mad English missionary).

Tasteless and rather humdrum jungle adventure using real-life problems purely as a backdrop.

w Richard English, Gene Levitt   novel Mark of the Leopard by James Eastwood   d George Marshall   ph Frederick A. Young   m Humphrey Searle

Cornel Wilde, Donna Reed, Leo Genn, Ron Randell, Christopher Lee

Beyond Reasonable Doubt
New Zealand   1980   108m   colour
Endeavour/New Zealand Film Commission (John Barnett)
V*

A vengeful inspector convicts a farmer who may or may not be guilty of a triple murder.

Sometimes striking but generally muddled crime story, which is based rather remotely on a real case but keeps shifting its angle.

w David Yallop   book David Yallop   d John Laing   ph Alun Bollinger   m Dave Fraser

David Hemmings, John Hargreaves, Tony Barry, Martyn Sanderson

'The queen of the tropics finds a new jungle man!'
Beyond the Blue Horizon *
US   1942   76m   Technicolor
Paramount (Monta Bell)

An orphan white girl grows up on a tropical island with a chimpanzee and a swimming tiger; when rescued and her story doubted, she leads an expedition back to prove it.

The most tongue-in-cheek of the Lamour jungle extravaganzas, with plenty of simple fun.

w Frank Butler   d Alfred Santell   ph Charles Boyle   m Victor Young

Dorothy Lamour, Richard Denning, Jack Haley, Patricia Morison, Walter Abel, Helen Gilbert, Elizabeth Patterson

Beyond the Curtain
GB   1960   88m   bw
Rank/Welbeck (John Martin)

A flying officer rescues a stewardess whose plane has been forced down in East Germany.

Inept, penny-pinching cold war melodrama in which very little happens.

w John Cresswell, Compton Bennett   novel Thunder Above by Charles F. Blair   d Compton Bennett   ph Eric Cross   m Kenneth Pakeman

Richard Greene, Eva Bartok, Marius Goring, Lucie Mannheim, Andree Melly, George Mikell, John Welsh

Beyond the Door: see *Devil within Her*

'A twelve o'clock girl in a nine o'clock town!'
'Nobody's as good as Bette when she's bad!'

Beyond the Forest
US   1949   96m   bw
Warner (Henry Blanke)
V*

The discontented wife of a small-town doctor has an affair with a wealthy Chicagoan, murders a witness, attempts suicide, and dies of fever.

The star caricatures herself in this overblown melodrama which marked the unhappy end of her association with the studio. The rest of the cast suffer more dumbly from the script's unintentional hilarities.

w Lenore Coffee   novel Stuart Engstrand   d King Vidor   ph Robert Burks   m Max Steiner

Bette Davis (Rosa Moline), Joseph Cotten (Dr Lewis Moline), David Brian (Neil Latimer); and Ruth Roman, Minor Watson, Dona Drake, Regis Toomey

  ROSA: 'What a dump!'
  ROSA: 'If I don't get out of here, I'll just die! Living here is like waiting for the funeral to begin.'

'This peerless piece of camp.' – New Yorker, 1978

'Miss Davis makes a regrettably melodramatic mess of what is undoubtedly one of the most unfortunate stories she has ever tackled.' – Newsweek

AAN: Max Steiner

Beyond the Gates: see Au delà des Grilles

Beyond the Limit: see The Honorary Consul

Beyond the Poseidon Adventure
US   1979   114m   Technicolor   Panavision
Warner/Irwin Allen
V*

When rescuers reach the topsy-turvy passenger liner, one of them is intent on plunder.

Dreary alternative ending to The Poseidon Adventure, with cardboard character studies, cut-price action, and tenth-rate technicalities.

w Nelson Gidding   d Irwin Allen   ph Joseph Biroc   m Jerry Fielding   pd Preston Ames

Michael Caine, Telly Savalas, Karl Malden, Sally Field, Peter Boyle, Jack Warden, Shirley Knight, Shirley Jones, Slim Pickens

Beyond the River: see The Bottom of the Bottle

Beyond the Stars
US   1989   94m   TVC colour
Five Star Entertainment (Joseph Perez)
V, V*, L
aka: Personal Choice

A mixed-up adolescent, determined to walk on the moon, strikes up a friendship with a former astronaut who has become a reclusive alcoholic after a strange incident on his last mission.

Meandering and sentimental account of a youth's coming of age, overweighted with messages about the environment.

wd David Saperstein   ph John Bartley   m Geoff Levin, Chris Many   pd John J. Moore   ed Frank Irvine, Stanley Warnow, Judith Blume

Martin Sheen, Christian Slater, Robert Foxworth, Sharon Stone, Olivia d'Abo, F. Murray Abraham

'Trapped! . . . in the incredible cosmic world that moves 100 years beyond time!'
'Adam and Eve of the year 2024! Only they could repopulate the world!'
Beyond the Time Barrier
US   1959   75m   bw
AIP/Pacific International/Miller-Consolidated (Robert Clarke)
V*

A test pilot crosses the fifth dimension and finds

himself in 2024 when civilization has gone underground to avoid nuclear contamination.

Crude science fiction, roughly on the level of Flash Gordon but less entertaining.

w Arthur G. Pierce   d Edgar G. Ulmer   ph Meredith Nicholson   m Darrell Calker

Robert Clarke, Darlene Tompkins, Arianne Arden, Vladimir Sokoloff, Stephen Bekassy

Beyond the Universe
US   1978   90m   colour/bw
Gold Key

A hundred years after a nuclear holocaust, a scientist trying to save a dying Earth uncovers a plot to exterminate all the sick and elderly.

Earnest, deadly dull ecological fable. Fortunately the entire cast is sucked into a black hole; unfortunately, they survive.

w uncredited   d Robert Emenegger   ph José Luis Mignone   ad Michael Scheffe   ed Brian Varaday

David Ladd, Jacqueline Ray, Christopher Cary, John Dewey-Carter, Frank A. Miller, Stephanie Faulkner, Henry Darrow

Beyond the Valley of the Dolls
US   1970   109m   DeLuxe   Panavision
TCF (Russ Meyer)
V, V*

Three girls in Hollywood enjoy the wilder reaches of show biz high life.

The skinflick director's first film for a major studio, with positively no connection with Valley of the Dolls, is not explicitly pornographic but pussyfoots around with as many general excesses as can be crammed into two hours. If taken as high camp it provides a laugh or two, but is chiefly notable as marking a major studio's deepest dip into muddy waters.

w Roger Ebert   d Russ Meyer   ph Fred J. Koenekamp   m Stu Phillips, William Loose

Dolly Read, Cynthia Myers, Marcia McBroom, John La Zar, Michael Blodgett, Edy Williams

'If one can resist walking out, the last half hour is quite manic.' – MFB

'A film whose total, idiotic, monstrous badness raises it to the pitch of near-irresistible entertainment.' – Alexander Walker

'Awful, stupid and preposterous . . . also weirdly funny and a real curio, rather like a Grandma Moses illustration for a work by the Marquis de Sade.' – John Simon

Beyond Therapy
US   1986   93m   colour
Entertainment/Sandcastle 5/New World (Steven M. Haft)

Psychiatrists become personally involved in the hang-ups of young New Yorkers.

Unfunny film version of a play which may have had something.

w Robert Altman, Christopher Durang   play Christopher Durang   d Robert Altman   ph Pierre Mignot   m Gabriel Yared   pd Stephen Altman   ed Jennifer Augé

Glenda Jackson, Tom Conti, Julie Hagerty, Jeff Goldblum, Christopher Guest, Genevieve Page

Beyond This Place *
GB   1959   90m   bw
Renown/Georgefield (Maxwell Setton, John R. Sloan)
US title: Web of Evidence

An American visiting London finds his supposedly dead father in prison serving a life sentence for murder; he delves into history and finds the real culprit.

Spiritless murder mystery with less serious intent than the original novel; tolerable entertainment.

w Kenneth Taylor   novel A. J. Cronin   d Jack Cardiff   ph Wilkie Cooper   m Douglas Gamley   ad Ken Adam

Van Johnson, Vera Miles, Bernard Lee, Emlyn Williams, Jean Kent, Moultrie Kelsall, Leo McKern, Ralph Truman

Beyond Tomorrow
US   1940   84m   bw
RKO
V*

Two elderly ghosts return at Christmas to help young lovers.

An amiably modest example of the kind they don't do any more.

w Adele Commandini   story Mildred Cram   d Edward Sutherland

Richard Carlson, Jean Parker, C. Aubrey Smith, Charles Winninger

Bez Konca: see No End

Bez Svidetelei: see A Private Conversation

Bezhin Lug: see Bezhin Meadow

Bezhin Meadow **
USSR   1937   31m   bw
Mosfilm
V
original title: Bezhin Lug

Fragments from an incomplete Eisenstein film are held together by freeze frames.

Even this collection of bits and pieces shows the power of the master.

w Alexander Rozhdestvenski   story Ivan Turgenev   d Sergei Eisenstein   ph Edouard Tissé

Vitya Kartashov, Boris Zakhava, Igor Pavlenko

† The film was reconstructed in 1966.

Bezness **
Tunis/France   1992   100m   colour
CTF/Flach/TMP/Canal+ (Ahmed Baha Eddine Attia, Jean-François Lepetit)

A young Tunisian offering sexual and other services to tourists is torn between Islamic and Western ways of life and confused by his own double standards.

Absorbing account of cultural conflict, of exploitation and corruption told through the interlocking lives of a gigolo, the girl he wishes to marry, and a French photographer.

wd Nouri Bouzid   ph Alain Levent   m Anouar Braham   ad Khaled Joulak   ed Kahena Attia

Abdel Kechiche, Jacques Penot, Ghalia Lacroix, Ahmed Ragoubi

'A Day To Set Yourself Free!'
Bhaji on the Beach *
GB   1993   101m   colour
First Independent/Umbi/Channel 4 (Nadine Marsh-Edwards)
S

A group of Asian women living in Birmingham go on a day trip to the seaside at Blackpool.

An enjoyable slice of life, covering not only racism and culture clashes, but the generational differences between the young and the old women as well as problems of gender.

w Meera Syal   d Gurinda Chadha   ph John Kenway   m Craig Pruess, John Altman, Kuljit Bhamra   pd Derek Brown   ed Oral Norrie Otley

Kim Vithana, Jimmi Harkishin, Sarita Khajuria, Mo Sesay, Lalita Ahmed, Shaheen Khan, Zohra Segal, Amer Chadha-Patel, Nisha Nayar

'As a look at the Afro-Asian community in Britain, it's everything one could ask for: funny and serious at the same time, good-tempered but not afraid of giving offence.' – *Alexander Walker*

Bhowani Junction *
GB 1956 110m Eastmancolor Cinemascope
MGM (Pandro S. Berman)
V*, L

Adventures of an Anglo-Indian girl during the last years of British India.

Disappointingly anaemic semi-epic from a gutsy novel, variably handled by all concerned.

w Sonya Levien, Ivan Moffat *novel* John Masters *d* George Cukor *ph* Frederick A. Young *m* Miklos Rozsa

Ava Gardner, Stewart Granger, *Francis Matthews*, Bill Travers, Abraham Sofaer, Marne Maitland, Peter Illing, Freda Jackson, Edward Chapman

'An unwieldy, flatly-conceived charade.' – *MFB*

'One may believe with Henry Ford that history is bunk; if so, be assured that the labour pains of India are not half as much bunk as the romance of Victoria Jones, daughter of a Hindu lady, and a Welsh engine driver.' – *Alexander Walker*

Bian Zhou Bian Chang: see *Life on a String*

The Bible *
US/Italy 1966 174m DeLuxe Dimension 150
(70mm)
TCF/Dino de Laurentiis (Luigi Luraschi)
V*, L, S

Through the Old Testament from Adam to Isaac.

A portentous creation with whispered commentary gives way to a dull misty Eden with decorous nudes, a sprightly Noah's Ark, a spectacular Babel, a brooding Sodom and a turgid Abraham. The pace is killingly slow and the script has little religious sense, but the pictures are often pretty.

w Christopher Fry and others *d* John Huston *ph* Giuseppe Rotunno *m* Toshiro Mayuzumi *ad* Mario Chiari

Michael Parks (Adam), Ulla Bergryd (Eve), Richard Harris (Cain), *John Huston* (Noah), Stephen Boyd (Nimrod), George C. Scott (Abraham), Ava Gardner (Sarah), Peter O'Toole (the three angels)

'An Old Testament spectacular like any other.' – *David Robinson*

'At a time when religion needs all the help it can get, John Huston may have set its cause back a couple of thousand years.' – *Rex Reed*

AAN: Toshiro Mayuzumi

Les Biches **
France/Italy 1968 99m Eastmancolor
La Boétie/Alexandra (André Génovès)
aka: *The Does*

Two lesbians form an uneasy *ménage à trois* with a young architect, who loves both of them.

Fascinating and well-detailed character study with more depth than at first appears.

w Paul Gégauff, Claude Chabrol *d* Claude Chabrol *ph* Jean Rabier *m* Pierre Jansen

Stéphane Audran, Jacqueline Sassard, Jean-Louis Trintignant

'You can almost see tubes attached to the heels of all the characters, through which the meaning has been sucked out of them and Chabrol pumped in.' – *John Simon*

Bicycle Thieves ***
Italy 1948 90m bw
PDS-ENIC (Umberto Scarparelli)
V*, L
original title: *Ladri di Biciclette*; US title: *Bicycle Thief*

An Italian workman, long unemployed, is robbed of

the bicycle he needs for his new job, and he and his small son search Rome for it.

The epitome of Italian neo-realism, the slight human drama is developed so that it has all the force of King Lear, and both the acting and the backgrounds are vividly compelling.

w Cesare Zavattini *d* Vittorio de Sica *ph* Carlo Montuori *m* Alessandro Cicognini

Lamberto Maggiorani, Enzo Staiola

'A film of rare humanity and sensibility.' – *Gavin Lambert*

'A memorable work of art with the true flavour of reality. To see it is an experience worth having.' – *Richard Mallett, Punch*

'My idea is to de-romanticize the cinema.' – *Vittorio de Sica*

AA: best foreign film

AAN: Cesare Zavattini

Les Bicyclettes de Belsize *
GB 1969 29m Eastmancolor
Delmore/Ullustria (Jacques de Lane Lea)

The way to true love for a Hampstead shop owner is found through his bicycle.

Mildly attractive whimsy, obviously patterned after *Les Parapluies de Cherbourg* but not quite hitting the spot.

w Michael Newling *d* Douglas Hickox *ph* Wolfgang Suschitzky *m/ly* Les Reed, Barry Mason

Anthony May, Judy Huxtable

Il Bidone **
Italy/France 1955 109m bw
Titanus/SGC
aka: *The Swindlers*

A group of petty swindlers fails to move into the higher criminal bracket.

Sharply observed but rather sentimental melodrama with tragic pretensions.

w Federico Fellini, Ennio Flaiano, Tullio Pinelli *d* Federico Fellini *ph* Otello Martelli *m* Nino Rota

Broderick Crawford, Richard Basehart, Franco Fabrizi, Giulietta Masina

Big **
US 1988 102m DuArt/DeLuxe
TCF (James L. Brooks, Robert Greenhut, Anne Spielberg, Gary Ross)
V, V*, L

A 13-year-old boy has his wish to grow 'big' granted by a carnival wishing machine.

Magic fun, better done than it has been since *Turnabout* in 1940.

w Gary Ross, Anne Spielberg *d* Penny Marshall *ph* Barry Sonnenfeld *m* Howard Shore *pd* Santo Loquasto

Tom Hanks, Elizabeth Perkins, John Heard, Jared Rushton, Robert Loggia, David Moscow

AAN: Tom Hanks; best original screenplay

The Big and the Bad (dubbed)
Italy/France/Spain 1971 84m Technicolor
MGM-EMI/Sancrosiap-Terzafilm/Jaques Roitfeld/Atlantida
(Alfonso Sansone, Enrico Chroscicki)
original title: *Si Può Fare … Amigo*

A gunfighter hunts for the man who seduced his sister so that he can force him to marry her before he kills him.

Comic, slapstick spaghetti Western, with heavy-handed jokes.

w Rafael Azcona *story* Ernesto Gastaldi *d* Maurizio Lucidi *ph* Aldo Tonti *m* Luis

Enriquez Bacalov *ad* Eduardo Torre della Fuentes *ed* Renzo Lucidi

Jack Palance, Bud Spencer (Carlo Pedersoli), Francisco Rabal, Renato Cestiè, Dany Saval

'Men, money and moonshine … when it comes to vice, Mama knows best!'
Big Bad Mama
US 1974 85m Metrocolor
Santa Cruz (Roger Corman)
V*

In 1932 Texas, a desirable widow becomes a bank robber.

Fast moving, violent nonsense, like a caricature of *Bonnie and Clyde*, which was itself a caricature.

w William Norton, Frances Doel *d* Steve Carver *ph* Bruce Logan *m* David Grisman

Angie Dickinson, William Shatner, Tom Skerritt, Susan Sennett, Robbie Lee

Big Bad Mama II
US 1987 83m colour
Concorde (Roger Corman)
V, V*

A mother and her daughters rob banks as a revenge for her husband's death.

A sequel that is more like a re-run of the original movie, and it is less interesting and stylish the second time around.

w R. J. Robertson, Jim Wynorski *d* Jim Wynorski *ad* Billie Breenbaum

Angie Dickinson, Robert Culp, Danielle Brisebois, Julie McCullough, Jeff Yagher, Bruce Glover, Ebbe Roe Smith, Charles Cyphers

The Big Bang *
US 1989 81m colour
Kanter/Toback (Joseph H. Kanter)
V*

A documentary in which people, from a nun to a gangster, a restaurant owner to a basketball player, are asked about the meaning of life.

Engaging conversational piece, cutting quickly from one person to another, that holds one's interest.
d James Toback *ad* Nicole C. Nicola *ed* Stephanie Kempf, Keith Robinson

Emma Astner, Missy Boyd, Max Brockman, Darryl Dawkins, Eugene Fodor, Polly Frost, Veronica Geng, Julius Hemphill, Fred Hess, Elaine Kaufman, Sheila Kennedy, Anne Marie Keyes, Charles Lassiter, Marcia Oakley, Jack Richardson, Don Simpson, Tony Sirico, José Torres, Barbara Traub

The Big Bankroll: see *King of the Roaring Twenties*

The Big Blockade *
GB 1941 73m bw
Ealing (Alberto Cavalcanti)

A semi-documentary showing the importance of blockading Germany in winning the war.

A curious all-star propaganda revue with some sketches more effective than others.

w Charles Frend, Angus Macphail *d* Charles Frend *ph* Wilkie Cooper *m* Richard Addinsell

Leslie Banks, Michael Redgrave, John Mills, Will Hay (his only serious role), Frank Cellier, Robert Morley, Alfred Drayton, Michael Rennie, Marius Goring, Bernard Miles

'Topical subject matter, graphic descriptive work, pungent commentary, thrilling spectacle, clever characterisation.' – *Kine Weekly*

The Big Blue

US   1988   119m   Eastmancolor   Cinemascope
TCF (Patrice Ledoux)
V, V*, L, S

Two competitive deep-sea divers combine to rescue a dolphin.

Bizarre, over-long fantasy, much of it filmed murkily underwater.

w Luc Besson, Robert Garland, Marilyn Goldin, Jacques Mayol, Marc Perrier   *d* Luc Besson   *ph* Carlo Varini, Luc Besson, Christian Petron   *m* Eric Serra, Bill Conti   *pd* Dan Weil   *ed* Olivier Mauffroy

Rosanna Arquette, Jean-Marc Barr, Jean Reno

'The director's future as a significant cinematic navigator looks, on this evidence, rather less than watertight.' – *Philip Strick, MFB*

† The film was cut by nine minutes for its US release. It was released on video in two versions, one running for the same length of time as the cinema release, and the other, a special edition, running for 168m.

The Big Boodle

US   1957   83m   bw
UA/Montelfor (Lewis F. Blumberg)
GB title: *Night in Havana*

A croupier in an Havana gambling casino is suspected of knowing where counterfeited plates are hidden . . .

An undistinguished chase film with the star very tired and a long way from home.

w Jo Eisinger   *novel* Robert Sylvester   *d* Richard Wilson   *ph* Lee Garmes   *m* Raul Lavista

Errol Flynn, Pedro Armendariz, Gia Scala, Rossana Rory

The Big Boss (dubbed) **

Hong Kong   1971   98m   Eastmancolor   Dyaliscope
Cathay/Golden Harvest (Raymond Chow)
V, V*
aka: *Fists of Fury*

A worker in an ice factory takes revenge on a gang of heroin smugglers led by his crooked and murderous boss.

Possibly Bruce Lee's best film; certainly it is the one that shows his skills to best advantage.

wd Lo Wei   *ph* Chen Ching Cheh   *m* Wang Fu Ling   *ed* Fan Chia Kun

Bruce Lee, Maria Yi Yi, James Tien, Nora Miao

The Big Bounce

US   1969   102m   Technicolor   Panavision
Warner/Greenway (William Dozier)

An ex-GI with a criminal record gets into sexual and criminal trouble while working at a Californian motel.

Unattractive melodrama with no discernible point, certainly not to entertain.

w Robert Dozier   *novel* Elmore Leonard   *d* Alex March   *ph* Howard R. Schwartz   *m* Michael Curb

Ryan O'Neal, Leigh Taylor Young, Van Heflin, James Daly, Robert Webber, Lee Grant

Big Boy

US   1930   68m approx   bw
Warner
L

A negro jockey wins a big race.

Star musical from a Broadway original; routine except that Jolson plays in blackface, then comes on as himself for the finale.

w William K. Wells, Perry Vekroff   *d* Alan Crosland

Al Jolson, Louise Closser Hale, Noah Beery

'Comedy entertaining in hoke way, but production inferior to previous Jolson pictures.' – *Variety*

The Big Brawl

US   1980   95m   Technicolor   Panavision
Warner Brothers/Golden Harvest (Raymond Chow)
V*

The son of a Chinese restaurateur in Chicago outwits gangsters.

Silly but quite entertaining chopsocky melodrama laced with comedy.

wd Robert Clouse   *ph* Robert Jessup   *m* Lalo Schifrin

Jackie Chan, José Ferrer, Kristine de Bell, Mako, David Sheiner

The Big Broadcast **

US   1932   78m   bw
Paramount

A failing radio station is saved by an all-star show.

Revue-style show with a minimum of plot, valuable as archive material covering many stars of the time.

w George Marion Jnr   *novel Wild Waves* by William Ford Manley   *d* Frank Tuttle   *ph* George Folsey

Bing Crosby, Kate Smith, George Burns, Gracie Allen, Stuart Erwin, Leila Hyams, Cab Calloway, the Mills Brothers, the Boswell Sisters

songs: 'Please'; 'Here Lies Love'; 'Hot Toddy'; 'Where the Blue of the Night Meets the Gold of the Day'; 'Tiger Rag'; 'Crazy People'; 'It Was So Beautiful'; 'Kicking the Gong Around'

'Flock of radio names ensures b.o. interest, especially in hinterland.' – *Variety*

'A musical meteor of songs, comedy and romance!'

The Big Broadcast of 1936 *

US   1935   97m   bw
Paramount (Ben Glazer)

The 'radio lover' of a small radio station is kidnapped by a man-hungry countess.

Zany comedy with interpolated variety acts and a totally Marxian climax.

w Walter de Leon, Francis Martin, Ralph Spence   *d* Norman Taurog   *ph* Leo Tover   *ch* LeRoy Prinz

songs: 'Miss Brown to You'; 'Through the Doorway of Dreams'; 'Double Trouble'; 'Why Dream?'; 'Amargura'; 'I Wished on the Moon'; 'Crooner's Lullaby'; 'Why Stars Come Out at Night'

Jack Oakie, George Burns, Gracie Allen, Henry Wadsworth, Wendy Barrie, Lyda Roberti, C. Henry Gordon, Benny Baker, Bing Crosby, Ethel Merman, Richard Tauber, Amos 'n Andy, Mary Boland, Charles Ruggles, Virginia Weidler, Guy Standing, Gail Patrick, Bill Robinson, the Nicholas Brothers, the Vienna Boys Choir, Akim Tamiroff

'Names are in and out as fast and as often as a firefly's tail light.' – *Variety*

'It hasn't much story, but the lack won't bother.' – *Variety*

AAN: Leroy Prince

The Big Broadcast of 1937 **

US   1936   100m   bw
Paramount (Lewis Gensler)

A radio station manager has trouble with his sponsors.

More recorded acts separated by a measure of plot.

w Erwin Gelsey, Arthur Kober, Barry Travers, Walter de Leon, Francis Martin   *d* Mitchell Leisen   *ph* Theodor Sparkuhl   *songs* various

Jack Benny, George Burns, Gracie Allen, Bob Burns, Martha Raye, Shirley Ross, Ray Milland, Benny Fields, Benny Goodman and his Orchestra, Leopold Stokowski and the Philadelphia Orchestra, Eleanore Whitney, Larry Adler, Louis da Pron

'It isn't a comedy and it isn't a musical, but it has a lot of laughs, the best in several types of music, and I

don't know where in the world you will see anything like it.' – *Otis Ferguson*

The Big Broadcast of 1938 **

US   1937   90m   bw
Paramount (Harlan Thompson)

A steamship owner engaged in a transatlantic race is hampered by his practical joking twin brother.

Glamorous, empty-headed all-star nonsense with the expected bevy of interpolated acts.

w Walter de Leon, Francis Martin, Ken Englund, Frederick Hazlitt Brennan   *d* Mitchell Leisen   *ph* Harry Fischbeck   *m/ly* Ralph Rainger, Leo Robin

songs: 'Thanks for the Memory'; 'Don't Tell a Secret to a Rose'; 'You Took the Words Right Out of My Heart'; 'Mama That Moon Is Here Again'; 'This Little Ripple Has Rhythm'; 'The Waltz Lives On'; 'Zuni Zuni'; 'Sawing a Woman in Half'

W. C. Fields, Bob Hope (debut), Martha Raye, Dorothy Lamour, Shirley Ross, Lynne Overman, Ben Blue, Leif Erickson, Kirsten Flagstad, Tito Guizar, Shep Fields and his Rippling Rhythm Orchestra

'Pictorially original and alluring, with the rejuvenated W. C. Fields at his inimitable best.' – *Variety*

AA: song 'Thanks for the Memory' (*m* Ralph Rainger, *ly* Leo Robin)

Big Brown Eyes

US   1936   76m   bw
Paramount (Walter Wanger)

A private detective and his wisecracking girlfriend catch a jewel thief.

Minor league *Thin Man* stuff, quite acceptably done.

w Raoul Walsh, Bert Hanlon   *d* Raoul Walsh   *ph* George Clemens   *md* Morris Stoloff   *m* Gerald Carbonara

Cary Grant, Joan Bennett, Walter Pidgeon, Lloyd Nolan, Alan Baxter, Marjorie Gateson, Isabel Jewell, Douglas Fowley

The Big Bus

US   1976   88m   Movielab   Panavision
Paramount (Fred Freeman, Lawrence J. Cohen)
V*

Misadventures of a giant atomic-powered bus on its first cross-country trip.

Rather feeble spoof on disaster pictures, with some good moments.

w Fred Freeman, Lawrence J. Cohen   *d* James Frawley   *ph* Harry Stradling Jnr   *m* David Shire   *pd* Joel Schiller

Joseph Bologna, Stockard Channing, John Beck, René Auberjonois, Ned Beatty, Bob Dishy, José Ferrer, Ruth Gordon, Harold Gould, Larry Hagman, Sally Kellerman, Richard Mulligan, Lynn Redgrave

'It's all fast, bright, surface stuff, almost obsessively intent on never letting a laugh get away, misfiring, backfiring, skidding and crashing gears gaily all the way, often quite as thrilling, if not always as ludicrous, as some of the films it mocks.' – *Alan Brien, Sunday Times*

'It has been produced with such consummate bad taste, schlock acting and feeble attempts at verbal and visual humour that whatever laughs are engendered are at it rather than with it.' – *Dave Pomeroy, Film Information*

Big Business ****

US   1929   20m   bw   silent
Hal Roach
V

Stan and Ollie fail to sell a Christmas tree to a belligerent householder.

Classic silent comedy consisting largely of a brilliant tit-for-tat routine of reciprocal destruction, to which scripting, acting and editing equally combine.

w Leo McCarey, H. M. Walker   *d* James W. Horne*ed* Richard Currier

Laurel and Hardy, James Finlayson

Big Business
US   1988   97m   Metrocolor
Buena Vista/Touchstone/Silver Screen Partners III (Steve Tisch, Michael Peyser)
V, V*, L

Big business complexities are made more so by the fact that the principals are discovered to have been exchanged at birth.

Loud-shouting farce which just about gets by on star value.

w Dori Pierson, Marc Rubel   *d* Jim Abrahams *ph* Dean Cundey   *m* Lee Holdridge

Bette Midler, Lily Tomlin, Fred Ward, Edward Herrmann

The Big Cage
US   1933   71m   bw
Universal

A lion tamer is worshipped by an orphan boy.

Pretty awful programme filler capitalizing on the animal act from the Ringling Brothers circus.

w Edward Anthony, Ferdinand Reyher   *d* Kurt Neumann

Clyde Beatty, Andy Devine, Mickey Rooney, Anita Page, Vince Barnett, Wallace Ford, Raymond Hatton

The Big Carnival: see Ace in the Hole

The Big Cat
US   1949   75m   Technicolor
Eagle-Lion

Feuding mountain families combine to track a marauding lion.

Standard outdoor melodrama, almost a straight version of *Track of the Cat.*

w Morton Grant, Dorothy Yost   *d* Phil Karlson

Peggy Ann Garner, Lon McCallister, Preston Foster, Forrest Tucker, Skip Homeier, Sara Haden

'How much love, sex, fun and friendship can a person take?'
'In a cold world, you need your friends to keep you warm!'
The Big Chill **
US   1983   105m   Metrocolor
Columbia/Carson Productions (Michael Shamberg)
V, V*, L, S

University contemporaries try to comfort each other after the death of a friend.

Wry satirical comedy which seems to be nostalgic for the sixties, but is funny anyway.

w Lawrence Kasdan, Barbara Benedek   *d* Lawrence Kasdan   *ph* John Bailey   *m* various   *pd* Ida Random   *ed* Carol Littleton

Tom Berenger, Glenn Close, Jeff Goldblum, William Hurt, Kevin Kline, Mary Kay Place, Meg Tilly, JoBeth Williams, Don Galloway

'The final impression left is of a collage of small relishable moments.' – *Kim Newman, MFB*

'An entertainment in which humour and sentiment are finely balanced and profundities are artfully skirted.' – *Sight and Sound*

'A splendid technical exercise . . . but there's no pay-off and it doesn't lead anywhere.' – *Roger Ebert*

AAN: best picture; Glenn Close; screenplay

The Big Circus *
US   1959   109m   Technicolor   Cinemascope
AA (Irwin Allen)
V, V*

A bankrupt circus owner tries to get his show back on the road despite the murderous schemes of his ex-partners.

Fast-paced melodrama which makes little sense but generally provides the expected thrills.

w Irwin Allen, Charles Bennett, Irving Wallace *d* Joseph Newman   *ph* Winton C. Hoch   *m* Paul Sawtell, Bert Shefter

Victor Mature, Red Buttons, Rhonda Fleming, Kathryn Grant, Vincent Price, Peter Lorre, *Gilbert Roland,* David Nelson, Adele Mara, Steve Allen

The Big City
US   1927   80m approx (24 fps)   bw   silent
MGM

A cabaret owner has a jewel robbery gang as a sideline.

Minor star melodrama.

w Waldemar Young, Tod Browning   *d* Tod Browning

Lon Chaney, Betty Compson, James Murray, Marceline Day

The Big City *
US   1937   80m   bw
MGM (Norman Krasna)

An honest cab driver and his wife hold out against corruption.

Sentimental realism of the type expected of its director. Smooth and syrupy.

w Dore Schary, Hugo Butler   *d* Frank Borzage *ph* Joseph Ruttenberg   *m* William Axt

Spencer Tracy, Luise Rainer, Charley Grapewin, Janet Beecher, Irving Bacon, William Demarest, Eddie Quillan

Big City
US   1948   103m   bw
MGM (Joe Pasternak)

In New York's East Side, a little girl is the adopted daughter of three bachelors, but trouble looms when they all get ideas of romance.

Latter-day star vehicle for which the young star is really too old and all else is excessively sentimental and sprawling.

w Whitfield Cook, Ann Chapin   *d* Norman Taurog *ph* Robert Surtees

Margaret O'Brien, Robert Preston, Danny Thomas, George Murphy, Karin Booth, Jackie Butch Jenkins, Betty Garrett, Lotte Lehmann, Edward Arnold

The Big City **
India   1963   131m   bw
R. D. Bansal
original title: *Mahanagar*

A poverty-stricken Calcutta bank accountant sends his wife out to work; then the bank crashes, and she becomes the sole breadwinner.

Immensely detailed, overlong, but mainly fascinating account of modern urban India and its attitudes.

wd Satyajit Ray   *novel* Narendra Nath Mitra *ph* Subrata Mitra   *m* Satyajit Ray

Madhabi Mukherjee, Anil Chatterjee, Haren Chatterjee, Haradhan Banerjee

Big City Blues
US   1932   65m   bw
Warner

A country boy gets into trouble on his first trip to New York.

Predictable comedy drama which seems to have no point other than the obvious one.

w Ward Morehouse, Lillie Hayward   *d* Mervyn Le Roy

Joan Blondell, Eric Linden, Inez Courtney, Evalyn Knapp, Guy Kibbee, Walter Catlett, Humphrey Bogart, Ned Sparks

'The strangest and most savage manhunt in history!'
The Big Clock *
US   1947   95m   bw
Paramount (John Farrow)

A publishing magnate murders his mistress and assigns one of his editors to solve the crime.

Slick but rather empty thriller with judicious use of adequate talent.

w Jonathan Latimer   *novel* Kenneth Fearing *d* John Farrow   *ph* John Seitz   *m* Victor Young

Charles Laughton, Ray Milland, Maureen O'Sullivan, Rita Johnson, Elsa Lanchester

The Big Combo *
US   1955   80m   bw
Allied Artists/Security-Theodora (Sidney Harmon)
V, V*

The police crush a crime syndicate.

An otherwise uninspired thriller memorable for starting the new violence, with some ugly scenes of torture which suffered at the time from the censor.

w Philip Yordan   *d* Joseph H. Lewis   *ph* John Alton   *m* David Raksin

Cornel Wilde, Richard Conte, Jean Wallace, Brian Donlevy, Robert Middleton, Lee Van Cleef, Ted de Corsia, Helen Walker, John Hoyt

The Big Country ***
US   1958   165m   Technirama
UA/Anthony/Worldwide (William Wyler, Gregory Peck)
V, V*, S

The Terills and the Hannesseys feud over water rights, and peace is brought about only with the deaths of the family heads.

Big-scale Western with a few pretensions to say something about the Cold War. All very fluent, star-laden and easy to watch.

w James R. Webb, Sy Bartlett, Robert Wilder *novel* Donald Hamilton   *d* William Wyler   *ph* Franz Planer   *m* Jerome Moross

Gregory Peck, Jean Simmons, Charlton Heston, Carroll Baker, *Burl Ives, Charles Bickford,* Alfonso Bedoya, Chuck Connors

'Has, in fact, most of the elements one asks for in the Western. Especially it has a feeling of size and space . . . Yet something, I think, is missing: the romantic heart.' – *Dilys Powell*

AA: Burl Ives

AAN: Jerome Moross

The Big Cube
US   1969   98m   Technicolor
Warner (Francisco Diez Barroso)

Girl tries to murder her actress stepmother by feeding her overdoses of LSD.

Stultifyingly boring melodrama.

w William Douglas Lansford   *d* Tito Davison

Lana Turner, George Chakiris, Dan O'Herlihy, Karin Mossberg, Richard Egan

Big Deal at Dodge City: see A Big Hand for the Little Lady

Big Deal on Madonna Street: see Persons Unknown

The Big Easy *

US   1986   108m   DeLuxe
Kings Road (Stephen Friedman)
V, V*, L, S

A New Orleans homicide detective is persuaded by a lady investigator from the DA's office to look into irregularities in the department.

Sassy, easy-going melodrama with comedy asides.

w Dan Petrie Jnr   d Jim McBride   ph Afonso Beato   m Brad Fiedel   pd Jeannine Claudia Oppewall

Dennis Quaid, Ellen Barkin, Ned Beatty, John Goodman, Ebbe Roe Smith

'The cooks did the best they could with ingredients that tasted good but were a little tough to chew.' – *Daily Variety*

Big Executive

US   1933   70m   bw
Paramount

A go-getting market operator finds himself competing with the grandfather of the girl he loves.

Ho-hum melodrama with no compelling angles.

w Laurence Stallings   story Alice Duer Miller   d Erle C. Kenton

Ricardo Cortez, Richard Bennett, Elizabeth Young, Sharon Lynn, Dorothy Peterson, Barton MacLane

'It will be anything but big at the box office.' – *Variety*

Big Fella *

GB   1937   73m   bw
British Lion/Fortune (H. Fraser Passmore)

In Marseilles, a black man returns a lost child to his English parents.

Pleasant light vehicle with the star in typical easy form.

w Fenn Sherie, Ingram d'Abbes   novel Banjo by Claude McKay   d J. Elder Wills   ph Cyril Bristow   m Eric Ansell

Paul Robeson, Elizabeth Welch, Roy Emerton, Marcelle Rogez

'A very unpretentious vehicle.' – *Variety*

The Big Fisherman

US   1959   166m   Technicolor   Panavision
Centurion (Rowland V. Lee)

An Arab princess meets disciple Simon Peter, who dissuades her from her plan to assassinate her stepfather Herod.

Well-meaning but leaden adaptation of a bestselling novel which followed on from *The Robe*. Too reverent by half, and in many respects surprisingly incompetent.

w Howard Estabrook, Rowland V. Lee   novel Lloyd C. Douglas   d Frank Borzage   ph Lee Garmes   m Albert Hay Malotte   pd John DeCuir

Howard Keel, Alexander Scourby, Susan Kohner, John Saxon, Martha Hyer, Herbert Lom, Ray Stricklyn, Beulah Bondi

'Its overall flatness of conception and execution is a stiff price to pay for the lack of spectacular sensationalism characterizing its fellow-epics.' – *MFB*

'The picture is three hours long, and, except for those who can be dazzled by big gatherings of props, horses and camels, it is hard to find three minutes of entertainment in it.' – *Hollywood Reporter*

AAN: Lee Garmes; John DeCuir

The Big Fix

US   1978   108m   Technicolor
Universal (Carl Borack, Richard Dreyfuss)
V*

An industrial investigator fancies himself as a private eye and gets involved in a political corruption case.

Hard to follow and harder still to care about, this rather sloppy, with-it movie is a little too pleased with itself from the word go.

w Roger L. Simon   novel Roger L. Simon   d Jeremy Paul Kagan   ph Frank Stanley   m Bill Conti   pd Robert F. Boyle

Richard Dreyfuss, Susan Anspach, Bonnie Bedelia, John Lithgow

'The strength of this film lies in the cool, meandering discretion with which its central theme is fleshed out: regret for lost illusions as the protest generation of the sixties finds its arteries hardening.' – *Tom Milne, MFB*

The Big Gamble *

US   1960   100m   DeLuxe   Cinemascope
TCF/Darryl F. Zanuck

Three people drive an ailing truck to a remote African township where they hope to start a haulage business.

Curious comedy-drama-adventure which starts off with family matters in Dublin and gradually develops into a lighter-hearted *Wages of Fear*. It has its moments.

w Irwin Shaw   d Richard Fleischer, Elmo Williams   ph William Mellor, Henri Persin   m Maurice Jarre

Stephen Boyd, Juliette Greco, David Wayne, *Gregory Ratoff*, Sybil Thorndike, Fernand Ledoux

Big Girls Don't Cry . . . They Get Even

US   1992   104m   CFI colour
Rank/New Line/Perlman/MG Entertainment (Laurie Perlman, Gerald T. Olson)
V*, L
GB title: *Stepkids*

A 13-year-old girl runs away from home, unhappy at the lack of attention she is getting from her mother and her new family, and from her father who has started another family of his own.

Sentimental domestic drama that is no more than a soap opera screened large.

w Frank Mugavero   story Mark Goddard, Melissa Goddard   d Joan Micklin Silver   ph Theo Van de Sande   m Patrick Williams   pd Victoria Paul   ed Janice Hampton

Griffin Dunne, Dan Futterman, Patricia Kalember, Jenny Lewis, Ben Savage, Adrienne Shelly, David Strathairn, Trenton Teigen, Margaret Whitton, Hilary Wolf

'Promises much, delivers little.' – *Kim Newman, Empire*

The Big Gundown

Italy/Spain   1966   105m   Techniscope
PEA/PC (Alberto Grimaldi)
Italian title: *La Resa dei Conti*

A Texas lawman is hired to catch a Mexican outlaw, who repeatedly escapes and finally proves his innocence.

Violent but moderately enjoyable spaghetti Western.

w Sergio Donati, Sergio Sollima   d Sergio Sollima   ph Carlo Carlini   m Ennio Morricone

Lee Van Cleef, Tomas Milian, Walter Barnes, Luisa Rivelli

The Big Guy

US   1939   78m   bw
Universal

A young convict becomes involved in a prison break which leads to murder.

Suspenseful routine melodrama with adequate production values.

w Lester Cole   d Arthur Lubin

Victor McLaglen, Jackie Cooper, Edward Brophy, Peggy Moran, Ona Munson, Russell Hicks, Jonathan Hale, Edward Pawley

'All the action you can take . . . all the adventure you can wish for!'

A Big Hand for the Little Lady **

US   1966   96m   Technicolor
Warner/Eden (Fielder Cook)
GB title: *Big Deal at Dodge City (though the action clearly takes place in Laredo)*

Five rich poker players are outwitted by a family of confidence tricksters.

Diverting but thinly stretched acting-piece from a much shorter TV original; still, suspense builds nicely until the disappointingly handled revelation.

w Sidney Carroll   TV play Sidney Carroll   d Fielder Cook   ph Lee Garmes   m David Raksin

Henry Fonda, *Joanne Woodward*, Jason Robards, Paul Ford, Kevin McCarthy, *Charles Bickford*, Robert Middleton, *Burgess Meredith*, John Qualen

The Big Hangover

US   1950   82m   bw
MGM (Norman Krasna)
V*

A lawyer struggling to mingle with the mighty finds he is allergic to strong drink.

Woefully unfunny comedy with virtually no plot.

wd Norman Krasna   ph George Folsey   m Adolph Deutsch

Van Johnson, Elizabeth Taylor, Percy Waram, Fay Holden, Leon Ames, Edgar Buchanan, Rosemary de Camp, Gene Lockhart, Selena Royle

The Big Heart: see *Miracle on 34th Street*

Big Hearted Herbert

US   1934   60m   bw
Warner

A prosperous plumber becomes more concerned with money than with his family's happiness.

Pleasing moral comedy, well cast.

w Lillie Hayward, Ben Markson   play Sophie Kerr, Anna Steese Richardson   d William Keighley

Guy Kibbee, Aline MacMahon, Patricia Ellis, Philip Reed, George Chandler

† 1940 brought a remake under the title *Father Is a Prince*, with Grant Mitchell.

'A hard cop and a soft dame!'

The Big Heat **

US   1953   90m   bw
Columbia (Robert Arthur)
V*, L

A police detective's wife is killed by a bomb meant for himself; he goes undercover to track down the gangsters responsible.

Considered at the time to reach a new low in violence (boiling coffee in the face), this dour little thriller also struck a new note of realism in crime films and produced one of Glenn Ford's most typical performances.

w Sydney Boehm   novel William P. McGivern   d Fritz Lang   ph Charles Lang   md Mischa Bakaleinikoff   m Arthur Morton

Glenn Ford, Gloria Grahame, Alexander Scourby, Jocelyn Brando, Lee Marvin, Jeanette Nolan, Peter Whitney

'The main impression is of violence employed arbitrarily, mechanically and in the long run pointlessly.' – *Penelope Houston*

The Big House **

US   1930   88m   bw
MGM (Irving Thalberg)

Tensions in prison lead to an attempted breakout and a massacre.

Archetypal prison melodrama and a significant advance in form for early talkies.

w *Frances Marion* *d* *George Hill* *ph* Harold Wenstrom

Chester Morris, Wallace Beery, Robert Montgomery, Lewis Stone, Leila Hyams, George F. Marion, J. C. Nugent, Karl Dane

'Not a two-dollar talker, but virile, realistic melodrama, a cinch for any week-stand and hold-overable generally.' – *Variety*

'We all gave our roles the best that was in us, and the virility and truthfulness of the picture were more satisfying than anything else I've done.' – *Chester Morris, 1953*

† The role played by Wallace Beery had been intended for Lon Chaney, who died during preparation.

AA: Frances Marion

AAN: best picture; Wallace Beery

Big House USA
US 1954 82m bw
UA/Bel Air (Aubrey Schenck)

Convicts stage a break-out to get at hidden loot.

Though less explicit in its violence than many later films, this is a singularly unpleasant melodrama with not one attractive character.

w John C. Higgins *d* Howard W. Koch
ph Gordon Avil *m* Paul Dunlap

Broderick Crawford, Ralph Meeker, Lon Chaney, Charles Bronson, William Talman, Reed Hadley

Big Jack
US 1949 85m bw
MGM (Gottfried Reinhardt)

Adventures of a couple of amiable scoundrels in 1890 Virginia.

The elements don't jell in this outdoor comedy-drama, which was its star's last film.

w Gene Fowler, Marvin Borowsky, Otto Van Eyss *d* Richard Thorpe *ph* Robert Surtees *m* Herbert Stothart

Wallace Beery, Marjorie Main, Richard Conte, Edward Arnold, Vanessa Brown, Clinton Sundberg, Charles Dingle, Clem Bevans

Big Jake *
US 1971 110m Technicolor Panavision
Batjac/Cinema Center (Michael A. Wayne)
V, V*, L

An elderly Texas cattleman swings into action when his grandson is kidnapped.

Satisfactory example of the star's later vehicles, with efficient production and familiar cast and brawling.

w Harry Julian Fink, R. M. Fink *d* George Sherman *ph* William Clothier *m* Elmer Bernstein

John Wayne, Richard Boone, Maureen O'Hara, Patrick Wayne, Chris Mitchum, Bobby Vinton, Bruce Cabot, Glenn Corbett, Harry Carey Jnr, John Agar

'Another genial celebration of Big John's ability to carry a film practically single-handed.' – *MFB*

Big Jim McLain
US 1952 90m bw
Wayne/Fellows (Robert Fellows)

A special agent for the House of UnAmerican Activities Committee routs communists in Hawaii.

Curious and rather offensive star vehicle in which the right-wing political shading interferes seriously with the entertainment value.

w James Edward Grant *d* Edward Ludwig
ph Archie Stout *md* Emil Newman *m* Paul Dunlap

John Wayne, Nancy Olson, James Arness, Alan Napier, Veda Ann Borg, Hans Conried, Gayne Whitman

'Brings to the screen all the unattractively hysterical mentality of the witch hunt.' – *Penelope Houston*

The Big Knife *
US 1955 111m bw
UA/Aldrich and Associates
V*, L

A depressed Hollywood star who wants better things for himself is blackmailed into signing a new contract.

Overheated argument between Art and Mammon, with rather disagreeable people shouting at each other, for too long a time. Limited interest is provided by the acting.

w James Poe *play* Clifford Odets *d* Robert Aldrich *ph* Ernest Laszlo *m* Frank de Vol

Jack Palance, Ida Lupino, *Rod Steiger*, Everett Sloane, Jean Hagen, Shelley Winters, Wendell Corey, Ilka Chase, Wesley Addy

'Everything in it is garish and overdone: it's paced too fast and pitched too high, immorality is attacked with almost obscene relish, the knife turns into a buzz saw.' – *Pauline Kael, 1968*

The Big Land
US 1957 92m Warnercolor
Warner/Jaguar (George C. Bertholon)
GB title: *Stampeded*

Cattlemen encourage the building of a rail link for Texas.

Undistinguished star Western.

w David Dortort, Martin Rackin *novel* *Buffalo Grass* by Frank Gruber *d* Gordon Douglas *ph* John F. Seitz *m* David Buttolph

Alan Ladd, Virginia Mayo, Edmond O'Brien, Anthony Caruso, Julie Bishop, John Qualen

'Hackneyed, humdrum western.' – *Howard Thompson*

Big Leaguer
US 1953 73m bw
MGM (Matthew Rapf)

An ageing baseball player is given the job of running a youth training camp.

Even the synopsis is boring. A routine job from the doldrums of the star's career.

w Herbert Baker *d* Robert Aldrich *ph* William Mellor *md* Alberto Colombo

Edward G. Robinson, Vera-Ellen, Jeff Richards, William Campbell, Richard Jaeckel

'The film treats its subject with an almost hushed reverence and its appeal is restricted almost entirely to baseball enthusiasts.' – *MFB*

The Big Lift *
US 1950 119m bw
TCF (William Perlberg)
V*

When the Russians blockade Berlin, British and American airmen get supplies there via a massive airlift; two men on one plane hold opposite views of the matter, and both have chastening experiences.

Rather heavy-going fiction based on fact, with earnest performances and good production.

wd George Seaton *ph* Charles G. Clarke *m* Alfred Newman

Montgomery Clift, Paul Douglas, Cornell Borchers, O. E. Hasse, Bruni Lobel

'There are some acute touches . . . just enough to make the slick evasions of the rest all the more regrettable.' – *Gavin Lambert*

The Big Man
GB 1990 116m colour
Palace/Miramax/BSB/British STV Film Enterprises (Stephen Woolley)
V, L

An unemployed miner becomes a bare-knuckle fighter.

What begins as social realism, at its most powerful in a brutal fight sequence, ends as a mess of sentimental cinematic clichés.

w Don MacPherson *novel* William McIlvanney *d* David Leland *ph* Ian Wilson *m* Ennio Morricone *pd* Carol Amies *ed* George Akers

Liam Neeson, Joanne Whalley-Kilmer, Billy Connolly, Ian Bannen, Maurice Roeves, Kenny Ireland, John Beattie, Amanda Walker

'Rarely plausible, frequently risible, occasionally embarrassing, this morally confused melodrama falls with a dull thud between social realism and mythic fable.' – *Philip French, Observer*

The Big Money
GB 1956 86m Technicolor Vistavision
Rank (Joseph Janni)

A family of petty crooks is ashamed of its eldest son, who is an incompetent thief.

A would-be high-spirited lark in which none of the jokes comes off, and a note of forced artificiality hangs over the whole production.

w John Baines *d* John Paddy Carstairs *ph* Jack Cox *m* Van Phillips

Ian Carmichael, Belinda Lee, Kathleen Harrison, Robert Helpmann, James Hayter, George Coulouris, Jill Ireland, Renée Houston, Leslie Phillips

The Big Mouth
US 1967 107m Pathecolor
Columbia (Jerry Lewis)
V*

A meek bank auditor finds he is the double of a dying gangster and is put on the trail of stolen diamonds.

The comedian at his worst, most repetitive and long drawn out.

w Jerry Lewis, Bill Richmond *d* Jerry Lewis
ph W. Wallace Kelley, Ernest Laszlo *m* Harry Betts

Jerry Lewis, Harold J. Stone, Susan Day, Buddy Lester, Del Moore

The Big Night
US 1951 75m bw
UA/Philip A. Waxman

A 17-year-old youth goes on the rampage in the underworld to avenge the beating up of his father by gangsters.

Hysterical melodrama presenting a rather false and dismal view of the world. Amazingly typical of its director's later output.

w Stanley Ellin, Joseph Losey *novel* *Dreadful Summit* by Stanley Ellin *d* Joseph Losey *ph* Hal Mohr
m Lyn Murray

John Barrymore Jnr, Preston Foster, Howard St John, Philip Bourneuf, Howland Chamberlin, Emile Meyer, Dorothy Comingore, Joan Lorring

'We are in that familiar underworld of the American cinema: dark streets gleaming with rain, sleazy apartments, garish night clubs, with Negro singers, drunks who spout philosophy, discontented blondes and fierce pock-marked thugs.' – *Gavin Lambert*

The Big Noise
US 1944 74m bw
TCF (Sol M. Wurtzel)

Two incompetent detectives accidentally round up a spy gang.

Very thin star vehicle consisting largely of poorly staged and warmed up versions of a few old routines.

w Scott Darling   *d* Mal St Clair   *ph* Joe MacDonald   *m* Cyril Mockridge

Stan Laurel, Oliver Hardy, Doris Merrick, Arthur Space, Jack Norton

The Big Operator
US   1959   91m   bw   Cinemascope
MGM/Albert Zugsmith-Fryman (Red Doff)

The racketeer head of a labour union goes berserk when the government has him investigated.

Unpleasant gangster exploitation melodrama from the bottom of the barrel.

w Robert Smith, Allen Rivkin   *d* Charles Haas   *ph* Walter H. Castle   *m* Van Alexander

Mickey Rooney, Steve Cochran, Mamie Van Doren, Mel Tormé, Ray Danton, Jim Backus, Jackie Coogan, Ray Anthony, Charles Chaplin Jnr

'The epic of the American doughboy!'
The Big Parade ***
US   1925   115m approx (24 fps)   bw   silent
MGM
V*, L

A young American enlists in 1917, learns the realities of war, is wounded but survives.

Enormously successful commercially, this 'anti-war' film survives best as a thrilling spectacle and a well-considered piece of film-making.

w Laurence Stallings, Harry Behn   *d* King Vidor   *ph* John Arnold   *m* William Axt, David Mendoza

John Gilbert, Renee Adoree, Hobart Bosworth, Karl Dane, George K. Arthur

'The human comedy emerges from a terrifying tragedy.' – *King Vidor*

'A cinegraphically visualized result of a cinegraphically imagined thing . . . something conceived in terms of a medium and expressed by that medium as only that medium could properly express it.' – *National Board of Review*

'The extraordinary impression of the rush of lorries, the queer terror of the woods . . . it was amazing how much fear could be felt in the mere continuous pace of movement.' – *Bryher, Close Up*

† The biggest grossing silent film of all.

The Big Parade **
China   1986   103m   colour   Scope
ICA/Guangxi Film Studio (Chen Liguo)
original title: *Da Yuebing*

Four hundred volunteers from the Airborne Division of the People's Liberation Army train for the National Day Parade in Beijing's Tiananmen Square.

Well-made film that concentrates on the relationship between individuals and the institution they serve. Changes to the movie were forced on the director by the People's Army, including the final scenes of the parade itself.

w Gao Lili   *d* Chen Kaige   *ph* Zhang Yimou   *m* Qu Xiasong, Zhao Jiping   *ad* He Qun   *ed* Zhou Xinxia

Wang Xueqi, Sun Chun, Lu Lei, Wu Ruofu, Guan Qiang, Kang Hua

The Big Parade of Comedy **
US   1964   90m approx   bw
MGM (Robert Youngson)
aka: *MGM's Big Parade of Comedy*

A compilation by Robert Youngson, including material as diverse as *Ninotchka*, Laurel and Hardy and the Marx Brothers.

One is grateful for the excerpts but the assembly of them is somewhat graceless.

The Big Picture **
US   1988   101m   DeLuxe
Hobo/Columbia (Michael Varhol)
V, V*, L

A student film maker goes to Hollywood.

Amusing satire of the movie business.

w Michael Varhol, Christopher Guest, Michael McKean   *d* Christopher Guest   *ph* Jeff Jur   *m* David Nichtern   *pd* Joseph T. Garrity   *ad* Patrick Tagliaferro   *ed* Martin Nicholson

Kevin Bacon, Emily Longstreth, J. T. Walsh, Jennifer Jason Leigh, Martin Short, Michael McKean, Kim Miyori, Teri Hatcher

The Big Pond *
US   1930   79m   bw
Paramount (Monta Bell)

The son of an important French family acts as a tourist guide in Venice.

Reasonably lively, semi-satirical early musical with Americans the butt of the jokes.

w Robert Presnell, Garrett Fort, Preston Sturges   *play* George Middleton, A. E. Thomas   *d* Hobart Henley   *ph* George Folsey   *songs* various   *m* arranged by John Green

Maurice Chevalier, Claudette Colbert, George Barbier, Nat Pendleton, Marion Ballou

'An amiable and ingratiating comedy that will give the Chevalier momentum another good shove.' – *Variety*

AAN: Maurice Chevalier

The Big Punch
US   1948   80m   bw
Warner

A boxer refuses to throw a fight and is framed for murder.

Routine time-passer with a second team before and behind the camera.

w Bernard Girard   *d* Sherry Shourds

Gordon MacRae, Wayne Morris, Lois Maxwell, Mary Stewart

Big Red
US   1962   89m   Technicolor
Walt Disney (Winston Hibler)
V*

An orphan boy protects a dog which later saves him from a mountain lion.

Simple boy-and-dog yarn with impressive Canadian settings.

w Louis Pelletier   *d* Norman Tokar   *ph* Edward Colman   *m* Oliver Wallace

Walter Pidgeon, Gilles Payant, Emile Genest

The Big Red One **
US   1980   111m   colour
UA/Lorimar (Gene Corman)
V*, L

Five foot-soldiers survive action in several theatres of war between 1940 and 1945.

Symbolic action drama, very well made but finally lacking a cumulative impact.

wd Samuel Fuller   *ph* Adam Greenberg   *m* Dana Kaproff

Lee Marvin, Mark Hamill, Robert Carradine, Bobby DiCicco, Kelly Ward, Stéphane Audran, Serge Marquand

'A picture of palpable raw power which manages both intense intimacy and great scope at the same time.' – *Variety*

'Like all Fuller movies, about an inch from cliché all the way.' – *Guardian*

The Big Shakedown
US   1934   64m   bw
Warner (Sam Bischoff)

A racketeer finds a new gimmick: cut-price medicine.

Action programmer with emphasis on the young couple forced into helping the racket.

w Niven Busch, Rian James   *d* John Francis Dillon   *ph* Sid Hickox

Bette Davis, Ricardo Cortez, Charles Farrell, Glenda Farrell, Allen Jenkins, Henry O'Neill, Samuel S. Hinds

'A routine assortment of gang-film impedimenta.' – *New York Times*

The Big Shave **
US   1967   6m   colour   16mm
Contemporary/McGraw-Hill
V

To the soundtrack accompaniment of Bunny Berigan's 'I Can't Get Started', a man shaves in a white bathroom, imperturbably cutting himself almost with every stroke until his face runs with blood.

A short, gruesome, macabre joke, intended by Scorsese as an angry comment on the process of self-mutilation that was the war in Vietnam.

wd Martin Scorsese   *ph* Ares Demertzis

Peter Bernuth

† The film carries the credit 'Whiteness Herman Melville' as well as the line 'Viet '67'. It was released on video with three other shorts under the title *Scorsese x 4*.

The Big Shot *
US   1942   82m   bw
Warner (Walter MacEwen)

An ill-fated criminal has trouble with women and his former companions.

Dullish star vehicle.

w Bertram Millhauser, Abem Finkel, Daniel Fuchs   *d* Lewis Seiler   *ph* Sid Hickox   *m* Adolph Deutsch

Humphrey Bogart, Irene Manning, Richard Travis, Donald Crisp, Stanley Ridges, Henry Hull, Susan Peters, Howard da Silva

The Big Show
US   1961   113m   DeLuxe   Cinemascope
TCF/API (Ted Sherdeman)

A circus proprietor dominates his sons; after his death they fight for supremacy.

Another remake of *House of Strangers*, which was also remodelled as *Broken Lance*. Not too bad as circus melodramas go.

w Ted Sherdeman   *d* James B. Clark   *ph* Otto Heller   *m* Paul Sawtell, Bert Shefter

Esther Williams, Cliff Robertson, *Nehemiah Persoff*, Robert Vaughn, Carol Christensen, Margia Dean, David Nelson

The Big Silence
France/Italy   1969   115m   Eastmancolor
Adelphia/Corona
original title: *Il Grande Silencio*

A mute gunfighter comes to a small lawless town to kill a ruthless bounty hunter.

Brutal Western in which the bad guys win, but one with a genuine feeling for the genre and the snowbound landscape.

wd Sergio Corbucci   *m* Ennio Morricone

Jean-Louis Trintignant, Klaus Kinski, Vonetta McGee

The Big Sky *

US   1952   122m   bw
RKO/Winchester (Howard Hawks)
V*

In 1830 two Kentucky mountain men join an exploration up the Missouri and become preoccupied with Indian trouble.

A large-scale adventure, loaded with talent, which becomes oddly tedious.

w Dudley Nichols   novel A. B. Guthrie Jnr
d Howard Hawks   ph Russell Harlan   m Dimitri Tiomkin

Kirk Douglas, Arthur Hunnicutt, Elizabeth Threatt, Dewey Martin, Buddy Baer, Steve Geray, Jim Davis

'It has the timeless, relentless quality of the long American historical novel.' – Penelope Houston

AAN: Russell Harlan; Arthur Hunnicutt

The Big Sleep ***

US   1946   114m   bw
Warner (Howard Hawks)
V, V*, L

Private eye Philip Marlowe is hired to protect General Sternwood's wild young daughter from her own indiscretions, and finds several murders later that he has fallen in love with her elder sister.

Inextricably complicated, moody thriller from a novel whose author claimed that even he did not know 'who done it'. The film is nevertheless vastly enjoyable along the way for its slangy script, star performances and outbursts of violence, suspense and sheer fun.

w William Faulkner, Leigh Brackett, Jules Furthman   novel Raymond Chandler   d Howard Hawks   ph Sid Hickox   m Max Steiner

Humphrey Bogart (Philip Marlowe), Lauren Bacall (Vivian Sherwood Rutledge), John Ridgely (Eddie Mars), Martha Vickers (Carmen Sternwood), Dorothy Malone (Proprietress), Regis Toomey (Bernie Ohls), Charles Waldron (General Sternwood), Charles D. Brown (Norris), Elisha Cook Jnr (Harry Jones), Louis Jean Heydt (Joe Brody), Bob Steele (Canino), Peggy Knudsen (Mona Mars), Sonia Darrin (Agnes)

MARLOWE: 'My, my, my. Such a lot of guns around town and so few brains.'
GENERAL: 'You may smoke, too. I can still enjoy the smell of it. Nice thing when a man has to indulge his vices by proxy.'
VIVIAN: 'So you're a private detective. I didn't know they existed, except in books – or else they were greasy little men snooping around hotel corridors. My, you're a mess, aren't you?'
MARLOWE: 'I don't mind if you don't like my manners. I don't like 'em myself. They're pretty bad. I grieve over 'em on long winter evenings.'
GENERAL: 'If I seem a bit sinister as a parent, Mr Marlowe, it's because my hold on life is too slight to include any Victorian hypocrisy. I need hardly add that any man who has lived as I have and indulges for the first time in parenthood at the age of 55 deserves all he gets.'
MARLOWE: 'Speaking of horses . . . you've got a touch of class, but I don't know how far you can go.'
VIVIAN: 'A lot depends on who's in the saddle. Go ahead Marlowe. I like the way you work. In case you don't know it, you're doing all right.'

'A sullen atmosphere of sex saturates the film, which is so fast and complicated you can hardly catch it.' – Richard Winnington

'A violent, smoky cocktail shaken together from most of the printable misdemeanours and some that aren't.' – James Agee

'Harder, faster, tougher, funnier and more laconic than any thriller since.' – NFT, 1974

'Wit, excitement and glamour in generous doses.' – Francis Wyndham

'Some days business is good – and some days it's murder!'

The Big Sleep

GB   1977   99m   DeLuxe
Winkast (Elliott Kastner, Michael Winner)
V*

Straight remake of the 1946 film, curiously and ineffectively set in London.

wd Michael Winner   ph Robert Paynter   m Jerry Fielding

Robert Mitchum, Sarah Miles, Richard Boone, Candy Clark, Edward Fox, Joan Collins, John Mills, James Stewart, Oliver Reed, Harry Andrews, Richard Todd, James Donald, Colin Blakely

'The 1946 film takes on even more stature in light of this. For a Winner film, however, it's quite good.' – Variety

The Big Steal **

US   1949   72m   bw
RKO (Jack J. Gross)
V*, L

An army officer is framed for the theft of a payroll, and sets off across Mexico in hectic pursuit of the real culprit.

Unexpectedly enjoyable comedy melodrama with a plethora of twists and a pace that never lets up. Routine Hollywood at a level seldom achieved, and short enough to leave one asking for more.

w Gerald Drayson Adams, Geoffrey Homes   story The Road to Carmichael's by Richard Wormser   d Don Siegel   ph Harry J. Wild   m Leigh Harline

Robert Mitchum, Jane Greer, William Bendix, Ramon Novarro, Patric Knowles, Don Alvarado, John Qualen

'Vigour and excellent craftsmanship.' – Gavin Lambert

'He Wants The Key To Her Heart. They Want The Key To His Car.'

The Big Steal *

Australia   1990   100m   colour
Hobo/Cascade/Film Victoria/Australia Film Finance Corp. (David Parker, Nadia Tass)
V

An 18-year-old boy plots revenge against the car salesman who sold him a faulty Jaguar with which he had hoped to impress his new girl-friend.

Mildly amusing comedy of the eccentricity underlying suburban life.

w David Parker, Max Dunn   d Nadia Tass   ph David Parker   m Philip Judd   pd Paddy Reardon   ed Peter Carrodus

Ben Mendelsohn, Claudia Karvan, Steve Bisley, Marshall Napier, Damon Herriman, Angelo D'Angelo, Tim Robertson, Maggie King

'Has a low-key charm that's appealing, and a couple of riotously funny scenes.' – Variety

The Big Store *

US   1941   83m   bw
MGM (Louis K. Sidney)
V, V*, L

An eccentric private eye saves a department store from the hands of crooks.

Reckoned to be the Marx Brothers' weakest MGM vehicle, but it has its moments, especially the first reel and the bedding department scene, also Groucho's rendering of 'Sing While You Sell'.

w Sid Kuller, Hal Fimberg, Ray Golden   d Charles Reisner   ph Charles Lawton   m George Stoll

Groucho, Chico, Harpo, Margaret Dumont, Douglass Dumbrille, Tony Martin, Virginia Grey, Virginia O'Brien, Henry Armetta

The Big Story: see Appointment with a Shadow

The Big Street *

US   1942   88m   bw
RKO (Damon Runyon)
V*, L

A Broadway night-club waiter falls in love with a crippled singer who selfishly accepts his help without loving him in return.

Unusual but mawkish material from an author who never really suited the screen; a mixture of laughs, tears and sentimentality, with a comic gangster background.

w Leonard Spigelgass   story Little Pinks by Damon Runyon   d Irving Reis   ph Russell Metty   m Roy Webb

Henry Fonda, Lucille Ball, Eugene Pallette, Virginia Weidler, Agnes Moorehead, Barton MacLane, Ozzie Nelson and his Orchestra, Sam Levene, Ray Collins, Marion Martin

Big Time Operators: see The Smallest Show on Earth

Big Town

US   1947   59m   bw
Paramount/Pine-Thomas
V, V*, L

Adventures of the crusading editor of a city newspaper.

Anaemic support which surprisingly started a series.

w Geoffrey Homes from radio scripts   d William Thomas

Philip Reed, Hillary Brooke, Robert Lowery, Byron Barr, Veda Ann Borg

The Big Town

US   1987   110m   colour
Rank/Columbia (Martin Ransohoff, Don Carmody)
V*, L

A crapshooter on a winning streak goes to the big city to make good.

Ineffectual drama of a youth learning about life from his elders, drably directed.

w Robert Roy Pool   novel The Arm by Clark Howard   d Ben Bolt   ph Ralf D. Bode   m Michael Melvoin   pd Bill Kenney   ed Stuart Pappe

Matt Dillon, Diane Lane, Tommy Lee Jones, Bruce Dern, Tom Skerritt, Lee Grant, David Marshall Grant, Don Francks

Big Town Girl

US   1937   66m   bw
TCF (Milton H. Feld)

A night-club singer adopts a disguise to elude her escaped convict husband.

Satisfactory supporting comedy-melodrama.

w Lou Breslow, John Patrick, Robert Ellis, Helen Logan   d Alfred Werker

Claire Trevor, Donald Woods, Alan Dinehart, Alan Baxter, Murray Alper, Spencer Charters

'First-class dualler which should please everywhere.' – Variety

The Big Trail *

US   1930   125m   bw
Fox
V, V*

A wagon train struggles along the Oregon trail.

Simple-minded early talkie Western spectacular with a new young star who took another nine years to make it big. Originally shown on a giant 70mm gauge and intended for big screens.

w Jack Peabody, Marie Boyle, Florence Postal   d Raoul Walsh   ph Lucien Andriot, Arthur Edeson

John Wayne, Marguerite Churchill, El Brendel, Tully Marshall, Tyrone Power Snr, David Rollins, Ward Bond, Helen Parrish

'Failing to own a kick or a punch, other than scenically, and with no outstanding cast names, it remains only a western of the pioneering sort, so thoroughly made familiar by those pioneering epics preceding it.' – *Variety*

'Printed upon the new wide film and projected upon the vastly large Grandeur screen, the landscapes, wagon trains, vistas and camp scenes achieve an incredibly greater sweep [than *The Covered Wagon*]. *The Big Trail* is often stagey, melodramatic, ranty.' – *Theatre Magazine*

The Big Trees **
US 1952 89m Technicolor
Warner (Louis F. Edelman)
V*, L

An unscrupulous lumberman tries to exploit California's giant redwood forests but is won over by the local Quakers who hold the trees in awe.

Pleasing, old-fashioned outdoor drama with a plot which allows the star much opportunity for derring-do.

w John Twist, James R. Webb   d Felix Feist
ph Bert Glennon   m Heinz Roemheld

Kirk Douglas, Eve Miller, Patrice Wymore, Edgar Buchanan, John Archer, Alan Hale Jnr

† A remake of *Valley of the Giants* (qv).

Big Trouble
US 1984/86 93m Metrocolor
Columbia/Delphi III (Michael Lobell)
V*, L

Two incompetent con men try to swindle an insurance company.

Witless comic farrago apparently designed to cash in on the success of *The In-Laws* by utilizing the plot of *Double Indemnity*. Not a goer.

w Warren Bogle (Andrew Bergman)   d John Cassavetes   ph Bill Butler   m Bill Conti

Peter Falk, Alan Arkin, Beverly D'Angelo, Charles Durning, Paul Dooley, Robert Stack, Valerie Curtin

Big Trouble in Little China
US 1986 99m DeLuxe Panavision
TCF/Paul Monash, Keith Barish (Larry J. Franco)
V, V*, L, S

A philosophizing truck driver in San Francisco finds himself combating an ancient, evil Chinese magician.

Misfiring attempt to equal the nonsense of the Indiana Jones sagas; occasional effective action moments don't stop the whole from being tiresome.

w W. D. Richter, Gary Goldman, David Z. Weinstein   d John Carpenter   ph Dean Cundey   m John Carpenter   pd John J. Lloyd

Kurt Russell, Kim Cattrall, Dennis Dun, James Hong, Victor Wong, Kate Burton

'Glitzy sets, vacuous characters, limping fantasy.' – *Sight and Sound*

Big Wednesday *
US 1978 119m Metrocolor Panavision
Warner/A-Team (Alex Rose, Tamara Asseyev)
V (W), V*, L

Three California surfing friends of the early sixties get back together after the Vietnam war.

It isn't clear whether the intent is to extol or deride the mystical camaraderie of surfing, but for those who can stand rumbustious beach behaviour this curious movie may have at least as much to say as *The Deer Hunter*.

w John Milius, Dennis Aaberg   d John Milius
ph Bruce Surtees   surfing photography Greg MacGillivray   m Basil Poledouris

Jan-Michael Vincent, William Katt, Gary Busey, Darrell Fetty

The Big Wheel
US 1949 92m bw
UA/Popkin/Stiefel/Dempsey (Samuel H. Stiefel)
V*

The son of a racing driver is determined to follow in father's footsteps.

Grubby star actioner.

w Robert Smith   d Edward Ludwig   ph Ernest Laszlo   m Nat W. Finston

Mickey Rooney, Spring Byington, Thomas Mitchell, Mary Hatcher, Allen Jenkins

Big Zapper
GB 1973 90m Technicolor Techniscope
Miracle/Lindsay Shonteff
V*
aka: *The Sex Life of a Female Private Eye*

A tough female detective with a masochistic boyfriend, Rock Hard, is hired to discover the fate of a brother and sister, who have been murdered by a pimp.

Dreary and sniggering would-be erotic thriller, concerned solely and ineptly with sex and violence.

w Hugh Brody   d Lindsay Shonteff   ph John C. Taylor   m Colin Pearson   ed Spencer Reeve

Linda Marlowe, Richard Monette, Gary Hope, Sean Hewitt, Michael O'Malley

'A paltry and nasty sexual fantasy which looks as though it has been dreamed up for the entertainment of impotent sadists.' – *Sylvia Miller, MFB*

'Wanted by two women!'
The Bigamist *
US 1953 80m bw
Filmmakers (Collier Young)
V*

A travelling salesman has two wives.

Minor melodrama which took its subject seriously but failed to make absorbing drama of it. Very much a family affair, starring the producer's present and past wives, the latter also directing.

w Collier Young   d Ida Lupino   ph George Diskant   m Leith Stevens

Edmond O'Brien, Joan Fontaine, Ida Lupino, Edmund Gwenn, Jane Darwell

'The film seems to have summoned all its energy to shout defiantly that bigamous marriages exist and, finding no one to defy, retires deflated.' – *MFB*

The Bigamist *
Italy/France 1956 97m bw
Royal/Filmel/Alba

An innocent young salesman is accused of bigamy and dragged into court.

Noisy comedy of mistaken identity; some laughs, but the talents are not at their best.

w Sergio Amidei, Age Scarpelli, Franco Rosi, Elio Talarico   d Luciano Emmer   ph Mario Montuori   m Alessandro Cicognini

Marcello Mastroianni, Vittorio de Sica, Franca Valeri, Giovanna Ralli

Bigfoot and the Hendersons: see *Harry and the Hendersons*

Bigger than Life *
US 1956 95m Eastmancolor Cinemascope
TCF/James Mason

A small-town schoolteacher is prescribed cortisone for arthritis; it gradually turns him into a bullying megalomaniac full of grandiose schemes.

Exaggerated and sensationalized but still not very dramatic expansion of a genuine case history. A curious choice for all concerned.

w Cyril Hume, Richard Maibaum   d Nicholas Ray   ph Joe MacDonald   m David Raksin

James Mason, Barbara Rush, Walter Matthau, Robert Simon, Roland Winters

'This is the world's sexiest robbery!'
The Biggest Bundle of Them All
US 1967 110m Metrocolor Panavision
MGM/Shaftel-Stewart

A retired gangster is kidnapped by other gangsters and shows them how to steal five million dollars worth of platinum.

Very moderately amusing international comedy caper.

w Josef Shaftel, Sy Salkowitz   d Ken Annakin   ph Piero Portalupi   m Riz Ortolani

Raquel Welch, Robert Wagner, Vittorio de Sica, Edward G. Robinson, Godfrey Cambridge, Davy Kaye

'It begins like one of these really bad movies that are unintentionally funny. Then it becomes clear that it intends to be funny, and it isn't.' – *Renata Adler*

Biggles
GB 1986 92m Technicolor
UIP/Compact Yellowbill/Tambarle (Kent Walwin, Pom Oliver)
V, V*, L

A young New York businessman is transported back in time to 1917, and his help solicited by a daredevil airman.

The bookends set a spoofy tone, but most of the movie is the same old teenage gunge.

w John Groves, Kent Walwin, characters created by Captain W. E. Johns   d John Hough   ph Ernest Vincze   m Stanislas   pd Terry Pritchard

Neil Dickson, Alex Hyde-White, Peter Cushing, Fiona Hutchison, Marcus Gilbert, William Hootkins

'If you're in the right undemanding mood it's just daft enough to be enjoyable.' – *The Dark Side*

Bij de Beesten Af: see *Ape and Super Ape*

Les Bijoutiers du Clair de Lune: see *Heaven Fell That Night*

Bike Boy *
US 1967 96m Eastmancolor
Vaughan/Factory Films (Andy Warhol)

A motorcyclist from the West Coast visiting New York has encounters with various women, one of whom seduces him.

Leisurely and occasionally witty exploration of low life, enlivened by the casually commanding presence of Viva.

w Andy Warhol and cast   d Andy Warhol   ph Paul Morrissey

Joe Spencer, Viva, Bridgit Polk, Ingrid Superstar, Ed Hood

'A strikingly pure exposition of Warhol's belief that the actor is the most important element in a film, and that the film-maker's job is simply to situate the actor to his best advantage.' – *Tony Rayns, MFB*

Bikini Beach
US 1964 100m Pathecolor
American International
V*

A California beach is disputed by surfers, motor bikers, and a businessman who wants to build a retirement community.

Mindless youth nonsense with flashes of satire.

w William Asher, Leo Townsend, Robert Diller
d William Asher

Frankie Avalon, Annette Funicello, Martha Hyer, Don
Rickles, Harvey Lembeck, Keenan Wynn, John
Ashley, Boris Karloff (guest appearance)

Bill and Coo
US   1947   61m   colour
Republic
V*

Trials and tribulations of the inhabitants of
Chirpendale are enacted entirely by birds, mostly
wearing hats and neckties.

An eccentricity which won its creator, Ken Murray, a
special Academy Award.

'By conservative estimate, the goddamnedest thing
ever seen.' – *James Agee*

Bill & Ted's Bogus Journey
'Once ... they made history. Now ... they are history.'
US   1991   93m   DeLuxe
Columbia TriStar/Orion/Nelson Entertainment (Scott Kroopf)
V, V*, L, S

Killed by robots designed to resemble them, two
inept college boys trick Death, enlist the help of God
and become heavy-metal heroes.

A sequel that, like the original, has attracted a cult
following, though the joke, depending on the slang
spoken by its dim heroes, remains a thin one.

w Ed Solomon, Chris Matheson   *d* Pete Hewitt
ph Cliver Wood   *m* David Newman   *ed* David
Finfer

Alex Winter, Keanu Reeves, Jeff Miller, David
Carrera, George Carlin, Joss Ackland, William Sadler

'A sequel that contrives another elaborate but non-
excellent adventure.' – *Variety*

Bill and Ted's Excellent Adventure
US   1988   89m   Technicolor   Panavision
Castle Premier/Interscope Communications/Soisson-Murphey
Productions/De Laurentiis Film Partners (Scott Kroopf,
Michael S. Murphey, Joel Soisson)
V, V*, L, S

In order to improve their essays, two high-school
students, with the aid of a time machine, abduct
famous historical figures and take them to modern-
day America.

Mild comedy depending for its effect on an
understanding of teenage Californian mores.

w Chris Matheson, Ed Solomon   *d* Stephen Herek
ph Timothy Suhrstedt   *m* David Newman   *pd* Roy
Forge Smith, Lynda Paradise   *ad* Gordon White,
Pierluigi Basile   *ed* Larry Bock, Patrick Rand

Keanu Reeves, Alex Winter, Robert V. Barron, Terry
Camilleri, Clifford David, Al Leong, Ron Loomis, Dan
Shor, Tony Steedman, Jane Wiedlin

A Bill of Divorcement **
US   1932   76m   bw
RKO/David O. Selznick
V, V*

A middle-aged man, released from a mental
institution, comes home and meets his strong-willed
daughter.

Pattern play which became a celebrated star vehicle;
now very dated but the performances survive.

w Howard Estabrook, Harry Wagstaff Gribble
play Clemence Dane   *d* George Cukor   *ph* Sid
Hickox   *m* Max Steiner, W. Franke Harling

John Barrymore, Katharine Hepburn (her debut), Billie
Burke, David Manners, Paul Cavanagh, Henry
Stephenson, Elizabeth Patterson

'A money picture for all classes of houses ... the most
potent tear jerker in many a moon.' – *Variety*

'A very good picture, tender, emotional and intensely
gripping.' – *Picturegoer*

A Bill of Divorcement *
US   1940   69m   bw
RKO
GB title: *Never To Love*

Virtually a scene-for-scene remake of the above.

Again the acting holds the material together.

w Dalton Trumbo   *d* John Farrow   *ph* Nicholas
Musuraca   *m* Roy Webb

Adolphe Menjou, Maureen O'Hara, Patric Knowles,
Herbert Marshall, C. Aubrey Smith, Dame May
Whitty

Billie
US   1965   87m   Techniscope
UA/Peter Lawford (Don Weis)
V*, L

A teenage tomboy runs into trouble because she is
better at sport than her boyfriends.

Routine American college/domestic comedy with a
young star and good comedy support.

w Ronald Alexander   *play* *Time Out for Ginger* by
Ronald Alexander   *d* Don Weis   *ph* John Russell
m Dominic Frontière

Patty Duke, Jim Backus, Jane Greer, Warren Berlinger,
Billy de Wolfe, Charles Lane, Dick Sargent, Richard
Deacon

Billion Dollar Brain
GB   1967   111m   Technicolor   Panavision
UA/Lowndes (Harry Saltzman)

Ex-secret agent Harry Palmer agrees to take a
mysterious canister to Finland and becomes involved
in an American megalomaniac's bid to take over the
world.

Incomprehensible spy story smothered in the kind of
top dressing now expected from this director, but
which almost killed his career at the time. Occasional
pictorial pleasures, but the total kaleidoscopic effect is
enough to drive most audiences to the exit.

w John McGrath   *novel* Len Deighton   *d* Ken
Russell   *ph* Billy Williams   *m* Richard Rodney
Bennett   *pd* Syd Cain

Michael Caine, *Oscar Homolka,* Françoise Dorléac, Karl
Malden, Ed Begley

Billion Dollar Scandal
US   1932   81m   bw
Paramount

Ex-convicts are involved by a millionaire in a shady
oil deal.

Competent but complex and talky melodrama 'from
the headlines'.   *story* Gene Towne, Graham Baker
d Harry Joe Brown

Robert Armstrong, Constance Cummings, Frank
Morgan, Olga Baclanova, James Gleason, Irving
Pichel

A Billion for Boris
US   1990   89m   TVC colour
Comworld Pictures (Sandy Russell Gartin, Ned Kandel)
V*

An adolescent boy, who has problems with his
mother, tries to get rich quick after he discovers that
his old TV set shows the next day's programmes.

Predictable, soft-centred, slow-moving, lacklustre
comedy.

w Sandy Russell Gartin   *novel* Mary Rodgers
d Alex Grasshoff   *ph* Peter Stein   *m* Robert
Christianson   *pd* Dan Leigh   *ed* Sheila Bakerman

Scott Tiler, Mary Tanner, Seth Green, Tim
Kazurinsky, Lee Grant

Billy Bathgate
US   1991   106m   DuArt
Warner/Touchstone (Arlene Donovan, Robert F. Colesbury)
V, V*, L, S

A teenager becomes an assistant to gangster Dutch
Schultz.

Curiously uninvolving and tepid thriller, with a
lacklustre central performance.

w Tom Stoppard   *novel* E. L. Doctorow   *d* Robert
Benton   *ph* Nestor Almendros   *m* Mark Isham
pd Patrizia von Brandenstein   *ed* Alan Heim, Robert
Reitano

Dustin Hoffman, Nicole Kidman, Loren Dean, Bruce
Willis, Steven Hill, Steve Buscemi, Billy Jaye

'This refined, intelligent drama about thugs appeals
considerably to the head but has little impact in the
gut, which is not exactly how it should be with
gangster films.' – *Variety*

'A film of minor virtues and major faults.' – *Sight and
Sound*

'It has a grace and gravity rare just now in American
films.' – *Richard Corliss, Time*

Billy Budd *
GB   1962   125m   bw   Cinemascope
Anglo-Allied (A. Ronald Lubin, Peter Ustinov)
V*

In 1797 the sadistic master at arms of a British
warship terrorizes the crew and is killed by young
Billy Budd, who must hang for his unpremeditated
crime.

Handsomely photographed but obtusely scripted and
variously acted attempt at the impossible, an allegory
of good and evil more suited to opera or the printed
page than film: in any case, a hopelessly and defiantly
uncommercial enterprise. Some actors bore, others
chew the scenery.

w Peter Ustinov, Robert Rossen   *novel* Herman
Melville   *d* Peter Ustinov   *ph* Robert Krasker
m Antony Hopkins

Peter Ustinov, Robert Ryan, Terence Stamp, Melvyn
Douglas, Paul Rogers, John Neville, Ronald Lewis,
David McCallum, Lee Montague, John Meillon,
Thomas Heathcote, Niall MacGinnis, Cyril Luckham

'A beautiful, terrifying and heartbreaking film.' – *Time*

AAN: Terence Stamp

Billy Galvin *
US   1986   94m   bw
American Playhouse/Vestron (Sue Jett, Tony Mark)
V*

Frictions develop between father and son in blue
collar Boston.

Old-fashioned family drama, quite rewarding for old-
fashioned audiences.

wd John Gray   *ph* Eugene Shlugleit   *pd* Shay
Austin   *ed* Lou Kleinman

Karl Malden, Lenny von Dohlen, Joyce Van Patten,
Toni Kalem, Paul Guilfoyle

Billy Jack *
US   1971   113m   Technicolor
Warner/National Student Film Corporation (Mary Rose Solti)
V*, L

A half-breed Vietnam veteran roams the Arizona
desert protecting wild mustangs and a runaway
teenager.

A trendy radical drama, virtually a one-man show
which had an enormous success in the US and led to a
sequel, *The Trial of Billy Jack.*

w Tom Laughlin, Delores Taylor   *d* Tom Laughlin
(T. C. Frank)   *ph* Fred Koenekamp, John Stephens
m Mundell Lowe

Tom Laughlin, Delores Taylor, Bert Freed, Clark
Howat, Julie Webb, Ken Tobey, Victor Izay

'A plea for the alternative society with a format of the crudest melodrama.' – *MFB*

Billy Liar ***
GB 1963 98m bw Cinemascope
Vic Films (Joe Janni)
V, V*

In a drab North Country town, an undertaker's clerk lives in a world of fantasy.

Flawed only by its unsuitable Cinemascope ratio, this is a brilliant urban comedy of its time, seminal in acting, theme, direction and permissiveness.

w Keith Waterhouse, Willis Hall play Keith Waterhouse, Willis Hall *novel* Keith Waterhouse inspired by Thurber's Walter Mitty *d John Schlesinger ph* Denys Coop *m* Richard Rodney Bennett

Tom Courtenay, Julie Christie, Wilfred Pickles, Mona Washbourne, *Ethel Griffies,* Finlay Currie, Rodney Bewes, Leonard Rossiter

'John Schlesinger's direction, I am delighted to say, is rich in wit.' – *Dilys Powell*

† It was later turned into a TV series and a successful stage musical, making Billy a universal figure of the period.

Billy Rose's Diamond Horseshoe: see *Diamond Horseshoe*

Billy Rose's Jumbo: see *Jumbo*

Billy the Kid *
US 1930 90m bw
MGM

A young Western outlaw is relentlessly pursued by Sheriff Pat Garrett.

Mildly interesting early talkie Western with the usual romanticized view of Billy. Originally made and shown in 70mm.

w Wanda Tuchock, Laurence Stallings, Charles MacArthur *d* King Vidor *ph* Gordon Avil

Johnny Mack Brown, Wallace Beery, Kay Johnson, Karl Dane, Roscoe Ates

'Should stand up for slightly better than average business where shown on Realife. Otherwise just an ordinary western.' – *Variety*

Billy the Kid *
US 1941 95m Technicolor
MGM (Irving Asher)

Remake of the above, equally false and rather less well acted, but a striking outdoor colour film of its period.

w Gene Fowler *d* David Miller *ph* Leonard Smith, William V. Skall *m* David Snell

Robert Taylor, Brian Donlevy, Ian Hunter, Mary Howard, Gene Lockhart, Henry O'Neill, Frank Puglia, Cy Kendall, Ethel Griffies

AAN: Leonard Smith, William V. Skall

Billy the Kid and the Green Baize Vampire
GB 1985 93m colour
ITC/Zenith (Simon Mallin)

A hustling young snooker player takes on a formidable opponent.

Predictable sporting melodrama with curious supernatural overtones; not a coherent whole.

w Trevor Preston *d* Alan Clarke *ph* Clive Tickner *m* George Fenton *pd* Jamie Leonard

Phil Daniels, Alun Armstrong, Bruce Payne, Louise Gold, Eve Ferret

'Weird, not to say downright perverse.' – *Sight and Sound*

Billy the Kid vs Dracula
US 1965 89m (GB 73m) Pathé Color
Avco Embassy/Circle/Embassy (Carroll Case)
V*

Billy the Kid rescues his fiancée from the clutches of Dracula.

Comic treatment of horror and Westerns, with Billy as a clean-cut hero, that may appeal to fans of bad movies.

w Carl K. Hittleman *d* William Beaudine *ph* Lothrop Worth *m* Raoul Kraushaar *ad* Paul Sylos, Harry Reif *ed* Roy Livingston

Chuck Courtney, John Carradine, Melinda Plowman, Virginia Christine, Walter Janovitz, Olive Carey, Harry Carey Jnr

'Great fun, pleasingly economical, and by no means an unworthy conclusion to Beaudine's career' – *David McGillivray, MFB*

Billy Two Hats
US 1973 99m Technicolor
UA/Algonquin (Norman Jewison, Patrick Palmer, Mitchell Lifton)
aka: *The Lady and the Outlaw*

The friendship of an old Scottish outlaw and a young half-breed is broken only by the old man's death.

Curiously miscast Western shot in Israel; it makes no discernible point and is not very entertaining.

w Alan Sharp *d* Ted Kotcheff *ph* Brian West *m* John Scott

Gregory Peck, Desi Arnaz Jnr, Jack Warden, Sian Barbara Allen, David Huddleston

Biloxi Blues *
US 1988 106m colour Panavision
Universal/Rastar (Ray Stark)
V, V*, L

Standard, quite pleasing version of a Broadway comedy about a conscript called up in 1945 when World War Two was ending.

w Neil Simon *play* Neil Simon *d* Mike Nichols *ph* Bill Butler *m* Georges Delerue *pd* Paul Sylbert *ed* Sam O'Steen

Matthew Broderick, Christopher Walken, Matt Mulhern, Corey Parker

The Bingo Long Traveling All-Stars and Motor Kings
US 1976 111m Technicolor
Universal (Rob Cohen)
V*

Adventures of a black baseball team in the 1940s.

High-spirited japes and exhibitions of athleticism which dramatically do not add up to very much.

w Hal Barwood, Matthew Robbins *novel* William Brashler *d* John Badham *ph* Bill Butler *m* William Goldstein

Billy Dee Williams, James Earl Jones, Richard Pryor, Rico Dawson

'Modest pleasures and dull stretches co-exist in equal abundance.' – *Frank Rich, New York Times*

Biography (of a Bachelor Girl) *
US 1935 84m bw
MGM (Irving Thalberg)

The biography of a sophisticated lady portrait painter reveals surprising details of her love life.

Leaden, bowdlerized screen version of a sparkling Broadway play, fragments of which do however survive.

w Anita Loos *play* S. N. Behrman *d* Edward H. Griffith *ph* James Wong Howe *m* Herbert Stothart

Ann Harding (miscast), Robert Montgomery, Edward Everett Horton, Edward Arnold, Una Merkel, Charles Richman, Donald Meek

'Smart entertainment for top houses. Possibly too smart for the other end.' – *Variety*

Birch Interval
US 1976 105m colour
Gamma III (Robert B. Radnitz)
V*

A twelve-year-old girl goes to live with her Amish relations in the country.

Simple-minded moral tale which needed some old-fashioned style to bring it off.

w Joanna Crawford *novel* Joanna Crawford *d* Delbert Mann

Eddie Albert, Rip Torn, Susan McClung, Ann Wedgeworth, Bill Lucking

Bird *
US 1988 161m Technicolor
Warner/Malpaso (Clint Eastwood)
V, V*, L, S

The life of Charlie Parker.

Long, downbeat, heavygoing treatment of America's greatest black alto saxophonist; but not a popular choice.

w Joel Oliansky *d* Clint Eastwood *ph* Jack N. Green *m* Lennie Niehaus

Forest Whitaker, Diane Venora, Michael Zelniker

Bird of Paradise
US 1932 80m bw
RKO (David O. Selznick)
V*

An adventurer on a South Sea island marries a native girl and causes trouble.

Never-never romance which remains stilted despite care obviously taken.

w Wells Root *d* King Vidor *ph* Clyde de Vinna *m* Max Steiner

Joel McCrea, John Halliday, *Dolores del Rio,* Skeets Gallagher

'The old tropical romance nicely done. OK for the main stem stands.' – *Variety*

Bird of Paradise
US 1951 100m Technicolor
TCF (Harmon Jones)

Opulent remake of the above; the trappings make it even more absurd, and the ritual sacrifice of the heroine seems misplaced in what is otherwise a pantomime.

wd Delmer Daves *ph* Winton Hoch *m* Daniele Amfitheatrof

Louis Jourdan, Jeff Chandler, Debra Paget, Maurice Schwartz, Everett Sloane, Jack Elam

'The Kahuna is a naively grotesque figure, with a Central European accent and carrying what appears to be an outsize radish: he personifies the film's dubious approach to Polynesian myth and culture.' – *Gavin Lambert*

Bird on a Wire
US 1990 111m DeLuxe
UIP/Universal/Badham-Cohen-Interscope Communications (Ron Cohen)
V, V*, L

A lawyer and her former lover run from their would-be assassins.

Chase comedy, too frenetic to be funny.

w David Seltzer, Louis Venosta, Eric Lerner *d* John Badham *ph* Robert Primes *m* Hans Zimmer *pd* Philip Harrison *ad* Richard Hudolin *ed* Frank Morriss, Dallas Puett

Mel Gibson, Goldie Hawn, David Carradine, Bill Duke, Stephen Tobolowsky, Joan Severance, Harry Caesar, Jeff Corey

'One of those star vehicles from deepest Hollywood for which there seems no adequate reason other than to pay someone's mortgage.' – *Derek Malcolm, Guardian*

The Bird with the Crystal Plumage
Italy   1969   98m   colour
Salvatore Argento
V*, L
GB title: *The Gallery Murders*

A supposed murderer is vindicated when his alleged next victim turns out to be a psychopath.

Tolerable shocker which was popular in dubbed version.

wd Dario Argento

Suzy Kendall, Tony Musante

Birdman of Alcatraz *
US   1962   148m   bw
UA/Hecht-Lancaster (Stuart Millar, Guy Trosper)
V, V*, L

An imprisoned murderer makes a name for himself as an ornithologist.

Overlong and rather weary biopic of Robert Stroud, who spent nearly sixty years in prison and became a *cause célèbre*. One cannot deny many effective moments, notably of direction, but it's a long haul.

w Guy Trosper   *book* Thomas E. Gaddis   *d* John Frankenheimer   *ph* Burnett Guffey   *m* Elmer Bernstein

Burt Lancaster, Karl Malden, Thelma Ritter, Edmond O'Brien, Betty Field, Neville Brand, Hugh Marlowe, Telly Savalas, James Westerfield

AAN: Burnett Guffey; Burt Lancaster; Thelma Ritter; Telly Savalas

'Suspense and shock beyond anything you have ever seen or imagined!'
The Birds ***
US   1963   119m   Technicolor
Universal/Alfred Hitchcock
V, V*, L

In a Californian coastal area, flocks of birds unaccountably make deadly attacks on human beings.

A curiously absorbing work which begins as light comedy and ends as apocalyptic allegory, this piece of Hitchockery has no visible point except to tease the audience and provide plenty of opportunity for shock, offbeat humour and special effects (which despite the drumbeating are not quite as good as might be expected). The actors are pawns in the master's hand.

w Evan Hunter   *story* Daphne du Maurier   *d* Alfred Hitchcock   *ph* Robert Burks   *sound consultant* Bernard Herrmann   *sp* Lawrence A. Hampton

Rod Taylor, Tippi Hedren, Jessica Tandy, Suzanne Pleshette, Ethel Griffies

'Enough to make you kick the next pigeon you come across.' – *Judith Crist*

'The dialogue is stupid, the characters insufficiently developed to rank as clichés, the story incohesive.' – *Stanley Kauffmann*

'We must sit through half an hour of pachydermous flirtation between Rod and Tippi before the seagull attacks, and another fifteen minutes of tedium . . . before the birds attack again. If one adds later interrelations between mother, girlfriend and a particularly repulsive child actress, about two-thirds of the film is devoted to extraneous matters. Poe would have been appalled.' – *Dwight MacDonald*

The Birds and the Bees (1948): see
Three Daring Daughters

The Birds and the Bees
US   1956   94m   Technicolor   Vistavision
Paramount (Paul Jones)
V*

On a transatlantic voyage a wealthy simpleton is fleeced by a card sharp and his daughter; but the latter falls in love with her victim.

Competent but uninspired reworking of *The Lady Eve* as a vehicle for a rather charmless comic. Lacking Preston Sturges at the helm, the mixture of slapstick and sentiment fails to jell.

w Sidney Sheldon after Preston Sturges   *d* Norman Taurog   *ph* Daniel Fapp   *m* Walter Scharf

George Gobel, David Niven, Mitzi Gaynor, Fred Clark, Reginald Gardiner, Harry Bellaver, Hans Conried

'Beneath her icy composure lay a deep desire to love!'
Birds Come to Die in Peru
France   1968   98m   Technicolor   Franscope
Universal France (Jacques Natteau)

On a Peruvian beach a tormented nymphomaniac makes love to several men and attempts suicide, but is rescued by her true love.

Elaborate high-flown bosh, quite fun to watch.

wd Romain Gary   *ph* Christian Matras   *m* Kenton Coe

Jean Seberg, Maurice Ronet, Danielle Darrieux, Pierre Brasseur

Birds Do It
US   1966   88m   colour
Columbia (Ivan Tors, Stanley Colbert)

A janitor at an atomic plant is accidentally ionized and finds he can fly, which enables him to catch a spy or two.

Childish stunt comedy.

w Arnie Kogen   *d* Andrew Marton   *ph* Howard Winner   *m* Samuel Maltovsky

Soupy Sales, Tab Hunter, Arthur O'Connell, Edward Andrews, Doris Dowling, Beverly Adams, Louis Quinn

Birds of a Feather: see *La Cage aux Folles*

The Birds, the Bees and the Italians
Italy/France   1965   98m   colour
Dear Film/Films du Siècle (Robert Haggiag, Pietro Germi)
original title: *Signore e Signori*

Stories of adultery in an Italian provincial town.

Mainly tedious sex comedy full of gesticulating actors.

w Furio Scarpelli, Luciano Vincenzoni, Pietro Germi   *d* Pietro Germi   *ph* Aiace Parolin   *m* Carlo Rustichelli

Gastone Moschin, Virna Lisi, Alberto Lionello, Gigi Ballista, Beba Loncar, Franco Fabrizi

The Birdwatcher *
Estonia   1987   84m   colour

A young man studying seagulls on a remote island nature reserve has a stormy relationship with a grouchy middle-aged widow.

Enjoyable account of a clash of temperaments – town against country, idealism versus pragmatism, masculine and feminine – with an unexpectedly harsh ending.

w Marina Sheptunova   *d* Arvo Ikho   *ph* Tatyana Loginova   *m* Lepo Sumera

Svetlana Tormakhova, Eric Ruus

Birdy
US   1984   120m   Metrocolor
Tri-Star (Alan Marshall)
V, V*, L, S

A psychologically disturbed war veteran thinks he can fly like a bird.

A case history which somewhat lacks plot advancement. Too self-indulgent even to earn marks for trying.

w Sandy Kroopf, Jack Behr   *novel* William Wharton   *d* Alan Parker   *ph* Michael Seresin   *m* Peter Gabriel   *pd* Geoffrey Kirkland

Matthew Modine, Nicolas Cage, John Harkins, Sandy Baron

'Likely will fall short of taking full flight at the box office.' – *Variety*

Birth of a Legend *
US   1966   26m   bw
Mary Pickford Corporation

Sprightly compilation of clips from the films of Mary Pickford and Douglas Fairbanks; the treatment is cursory but sympathetic.

wd Matty Kemp

'The dawn of a new art!'
The Birth of a Nation ****
US   1915   approx 185m (16 fps)   bw   silent
Epoch (D. W. Griffith, Harry E. Aitken)
V*, L, S

Northern and Southern families are caught up in the Civil War.

The cinema's first and still most famous epic, many sequences of which retain their mastery despite negro villains, Ku Klux Klan heroes, and white actors in blackface. Originally shown as *The Clansman*; a shorter version with orchestral track was released in 1931.

w D. W. Griffith, Frank E. Woods   *novel The Klansman* by Thomas Dixon Jnr   *d* D. W. Griffith   *ph* G. W. Bitzer

Henry B. Walthall, Mae Marsh, Miriam Cooper, Lillian Gish, Robert Harron, Wallace Reid, Donald Crisp, Joseph Henabery, Raoul Walsh, Eugene Pallette, Walter Long

'A film version of some of the melodramatic and inflammatory material contained in *The Clansman* . . . a great deal might be said concerning the sorry service rendered by its plucking at old wounds. But of the film as a film, it may be reported simply that it is an impressive new illustration of the scope of the motion picture camera.' – *New York Times*

'Griffith was, in his prime, a nineteenth-century humanist working in a twentieth-century medium. And, speaking for myself, I should welcome today some infusion of that unashamed humane sentiment into the smart machine-made films I see every week.' – *Dilys Powell, 1945*

† The soundtrack album features a recording of the score written by Joseph Carl Breil to accompany the film in 1915.
†† Joseph Briel's original score for the film has been released on CD.

The Birth of the Blues *
US   1941   85m   bw
Paramount (B. G. de Sylva, Monta Bell)

Trials and tribulations of a jazz band in New Orleans.

Thin fiction on which is strung a multitude of dark brown musical entertainment. Not bad, even now.

w Harry Tugend, Walter de Leon   *d* Victor Schertzinger   *ph* William C. Mellor   *md* Robert Emmett Dolan

Bing Crosby, Mary Martin, Brian Donlevy, Jack Teagarden, Eddie Rochester Anderson, Carolyn Lee

AAN: Robert Emmett Dolan

The Birthday Party *
GB   1968   126m   Technicolor
Palomar (Max Rosenberg, Milton Subotsky)

The down-at-heel lodger in a seaside boarding house is menaced by two mysterious strangers, who eventually take him away.

Overlong but otherwise satisfactory film record of an entertaining if infuriating play, first of the black absurdities which proliferated in the sixties to general disadvantage, presenting structure without plot and intelligence without meaning.

w Harold Pinter play Harold Pinter d William Friedkin ph Denys Coop m none pd Edward Marshall

Sidney Tafler, Patrick Magee, Robert Shaw, *Dandy Nichols*, Moultrie Kelsall

The Birthday Present *
GB   1957   100m   bw
BL/Jack Whittingham

A toy salesman's life is changed when he is charged with smuggling a watch through the customs.

Downcast, prolonged and rather uninteresting domestic drama; attention is held by generally good acting.

w Jack Whittingham d Pat Jackson ph Ted Scaife m Clifton Parker

Tony Britton, Sylvia Syms, Jack Watling, Walter Fitzgerald, Geoffrey Keen, Howard Marion Crawford, John Welsh

Biruma no Tategoto: see *The Burmese Harp*

Bis ans Ende der Welt: see *Until the End of the World*

The Biscuit Eater
GB title, 1940 version: God Gave Him a Dog

Two versions exist of this story by James Street about a white and a black boy who turn a stray into a crack hunting dog. The first was by Stuart Heisler for Paramount in 1940; it starred Billy Lee and made quite a box-office impact. The second was by Vincent McEveety for Disney in 1972, with Johnny Whittaker; despite the presence of Earl Holliman and Lew Ayres it made no impact at all.

The Bishop Misbehaves *
US   1935   87m   bw
MGM
GB title: *The Bishop's Misadventures*

A bishop gets on the wrong side of the law when he helps a young girl to see justice done.

Amusing trifle with strong cast.

w Leon Gordon, George Auerbach play Frederick Jackson d E. A. Dupont

Edmund Gwenn, Maureen O'Sullivan, Lucile Watson, Reginald Owen, Robert Greig, Dudley Digges, Melville Cooper, Lillian Bond

'Reaches a grade above the average programmer, but points mainly to sophisticated patronage.' – *Variety*

The Bishop Murder Case
US   1930   91m   bw
MGM

Philo Vance unmasks a killer who sends warning notes in rhyme.

Mildly interesting early talkie detection which moves at too stately a pace.

w Lenore Coffee novel S. S. Van Dine d Nick Grinde, David Burton

Basil Rathbone, Leila Hyams, Alec B. Francis, Roland Young, George Marion

The Bishop's Wife **
US   1947   108m   bw
Samuel Goldwyn
V, V*, L

An angel is sent down to mend the ways of a bishop

whose absorption with cathedral buildings has put him out of touch with his wife and parishioners.

Whimsical, stolid and protracted light comedy saved by its actors and its old-fashioned Hollywood style.

w Robert E. Sherwood, Leonardo Bercovici novel Robert Nathan d Henry Koster ph Gregg Toland m Hugo Friedhofer ed Monica Collingwood

Cary Grant, Loretta Young, David Niven, Monty Woolley, James Gleason, Gladys Cooper, Elsa Lanchester, Sara Haden, Regis Toomey

'It is the Protestant comeback to the deadly successful RC propaganda of *Going My Way* and *The Bells of St Mary's*. It surpasses in tastelessness, equals in whimsy and in technique falls well below those crooning parables. It is really quite a monstrous film.' – *Richard Winnington, News Chronicle*

'When a film undertakes to bring audiences a spiritual message, we wonder whether the director doesn't owe it to us to clothe such messages in less muddled characterizations and to dispense with caricature.' – *Scholastic Magazine*

'A sophisticated *Christmas Carol*.' – *Philip Hartung*

'As cheerful an invasion of the realm of conscience as we have seen.' – *New York Times*

† Director William A. Seiter was replaced when the film was half complete; this caused nearly one million dollars to be wasted.

AAN: best picture; Henry Koster; Hugo Friedhofer; editing

The Bishop's Misadventures: see *The Bishop Misbehaves*

The Bit Player: see *Salut l'Artiste*

The Bitch
GB   1979   94m   colour
Brent Walker (John Quested)

A woman of much influence in London's underworld has a temporary liaison with a young gangster wanted by the Mafia.

Intolerable sexed-up sequel to *The Stud,* hard on both eyes and ears.

wd Gerry O'Hara story Jackie Collins ph Denis Lewiston m Biddu ad Malcolm Middleton ed Ed Joseph

Joan Collins, Kenneth Haigh, Michael Coby, Ian Hendry, Carolyn Seymour, Sue Lloyd, Mark Burns

'Appropriately enough for a film whose sole rationale seems to be its chic consumerist decoration (and of course its disco soundtrack), *The Bitch* ruthlessly pares away any other elements of interest.' – *Richard Combs, MFB.*

The Bitch
France   1984   100m   colour
Sara Films/FR3 (Alain Sarde)
French title: *La Garce*

After serving a six-year sentence for rape, a former cop finds work as a private detective and finds himself investigating the girl he assaulted.

Routine thriller of double-crossed lovers.

w Pierre Fabre, Laurent Heynemann, Christine Pascal, A. M. Delocque Fourcaud d Christine Pascal ph Raoul Coutard m Philippe Sarde ed Jacques Comets

Isabelle Huppert, Richard Berry, Vittorio Mezzogiomo, Jean Benguigui, Jean-Claude Legay, Jean-Pierre Moulin, Clement Harrari

Bite the Bullet *
US   1975   131m   Metrocolor   Panavision
Columbia/Persky-Bright/Vista (Richard Brooks)
V*, L

Several cowboys compete in a 700-mile endurance horse race.

Episodic adventure story with too much muddled chat and a very thin connecting story line; good to look at, though.

wd Richard Brooks ph Harry Stradling Jnr m Alex North

Gene Hackman, Candice Bergen, James Coburn, Ben Johnson, Ian Bannen, Jan-Michael Vincent, Paul Stewart

AAN: Alex North

Bittere Ernte **
West Germany   1985   102m   colour
Filmkunst (Artur Brauner)
GB title: *Angry Harvest*

An inhibited farmer shelters a Jewish woman from the authorities, with tragic results.

Intermittently moving, though heavy going at times.

w Paul Hengge, Agnieszka Holland d Agnieszka Holland ph Josef Ort-Snep m Jorg Strass Burger ed Barbara Kunze

Armin Muller-Stahl, Elisabeth Trissenaar, Kathe Jaenicke, Hans Beerhenke, Isla Haller, Margit Carstensen

AAN: best foreign film

'I want something good to happen to me before I die!'
Bitter Harvest
GB   1963   96m   Eastmancolor
Rank/Independent Artists (Albert Fennell)

An innocent Welsh girl comes to London, is deflowered, and sets off in search of wealth and luxury at any price.

Naïve 60s version of the road to ruin, quite well done if you like that kind of thing.

w Ted Willis d Peter Graham Scott ph Ernest Steward m Laurie Johnson

Janet Munro, John Stride, Anne Cunningham, Alan Badel, Thora Hird, Vanda Godsell, Terence Alexander

'Some lovers never know when to stop …'
Bitter Moon
GB/France   1992   139m   colour
Columbia Tristar/Les Films Alain Sarde/Canal+/R.P.
    Productions/Timothy Burrill Productions (Roman Polanski)
V, V*, L, S
original title: *Lunes de Fiel*

On board a liner an English couple are drawn into the sadistic sexual fantasies of a crippled American writer and his French wife.

Incoherent melodrama of the corruption of innocence; but we've all been here too many times before for this treatment to carry any appeal.

w Roman Polanski, Gérard Brach, John Brownjohn novel Pascal Bruckner d Roman Polanski ph Tonino Delli Colli m Vangelis pd Willy Holt, Gérard Viard ed Hervé de Luze

Peter Coyote, Emmanuelle Seigner, Hugh Grant, Kristin Scott-Thomas, Victor Banerjee, Sophie Patel, Stockard Channing

'A slick psycho-drama . . . the work of a perverse, exhausted talent narrated by a perverse, exhausted, talentless writer to trap a dim-witted listener.' – *Philip French, Observer*

Bitter Rice *
Italy   1949   108m   bw
Lux Films
V*
original title: *Riso Amaro*

In the rice fields of the Po valley, a thief on the run meets a girl who tries to steal his loot.

Well-made exploitation melodrama which made a star of the well-endowed Mangano but is not otherwise more memorable than its innumerable American counterparts.

w Carlo Lizzani, Carlo Musso, Gianni Puccini, Corrado Alvaro, Ivo Perillo, Giuseppe de Santis d Giuseppe de Santis ph Otello Martelli m Goffredo Petrassi

Silvana Mangano, Raf Vallone, Doris Dowling, Vittorio Gassman

AAN: original story

Bitter Springs *
GB 1950 89m bw
Ealing (Leslie Norman)

A pioneer family in Australia buys a patch of ground but has trouble with aborigines.

Thinnest of the Ealing attempts to make movies down under, suffering from a lack of pace and sharpness as well as obvious studio settings.

w Monja Danischewsky, W. P. Lipscomb d Ralph Smart ph George Heath m Vaughan Williams

Chips Rafferty, Tommy Trinder, Gordon Jackson, Jean Blue, Charles Tingwell

Bitter Sweet
GB 1933 93m bw
UA/British and Dominion (Herbert Wilcox)
V*

In 1875 Vienna, a violinist marries a girl dancer and is later killed by a gambler.

Rather feeble filming of Noël Coward's operetta: it pleased a lot of people at the time.

w Lydia Hayward, Herbert Wilcox, Monckton Hoffe d Herbert Wilcox ph Freddie Young md Lew Stone m Noël Coward ad L. P. Williams

Anna Neagle, Fernand Gravet, Ivy St Helier, Miles Mander, Esmé Percy, Hugh Williams, Pat Paterson, Kay Hammond

Bitter Sweet
US 1940 94m Technicolor
MGM (Victor Saville)
V*

Remake of the above, retailored for unsuitable leads and with the story and music unattractively rearranged.

w Lesser Samuels d W. S. Van Dyke II ph Oliver T. Marsh, Allen Davey m Noël Coward ad Cedric Gibbons, John S. Detlie

Jeanette Macdonald, Nelson Eddy, George Sanders, Felix Bressart, Ian Hunter, Fay Holden, Sig Rumann, Herman Bing, Curt Bois

'It's now chiefly eye-and-ear entertainment, with the original sentimental charm and romance missing.' – *Variety*

AAN: Oliver T. Marsh, Allen Davey; art direction

The Bitter Tea of General Yen **
US 1932 89m bw
Columbia (Walter Wanger)
V

An American lady missionary in Shanghai is captured by a Chinese warlord and falls in love with him.

Arty miscegenation story which bids fair to become a cult film and certainly has a number of interesting sequences.

w Edward Paramore story Grace Zaring Stone d Frank Capra ph Joseph Walker m W. Franke Harling

Barbara Stanwyck, Nils Asther, Toshia Mori, Walter Connolly, Gavin Gordon, Lucien Littlefield

'It is doubtful whether this picture can make the grade without support . . . photographic advantages cannot overcome the queer story.' – *Variety*

† The film chosen to open Radio City Music Hall.

The Bitter Tears of Petra von Kant
West Germany 1972 124m colour
Tango/Rainer Werner Fassbinder, Michael Fengler
V*
original title: *Die bitteren Tränen der Petra von Kant*

Lesbian jealousies in the fashion world.

Interesting but exhausting hothouse confection, no more likeable than the Hollywood kind for being more intelligent about its perversions.

wd Rainer Werner Fassbinder ph Michael Ballhaus m The Platters and others ed Thea Eymèsz

Margit Carstensen, Irm Hermann, Hanna Schygulla, Eva Mattes

'Dazzling in the brittle brilliance of its execution, the precision of its structure and movement, the total hermetic self-containment of the little world it creates.' – *David Robinson, The Times*

Bitter Victory
US/France 1957 100m bw Cinemascope
Columbia/Transcontinental/Robert Laffont

Two officers sent on a document raid in Libya during World War II become poor soldiers because one suspects the other of an affair with his wife.

Glum desert melodrama, turgidly scripted and boringly made.

w René Hardy, Nicholas Ray, Gavin Lambert novel Bitter Victory by René Hardy d Nicholas Ray ph Michel Kelber m Maurice Le Roux

Richard Burton, Curt Jurgens, Ruth Roman, Raymond Pellegrin, Anthony Bushell, Andrew Crawford, Nigel Green, Christopher Lee

Bittersweet Love
US 1976 92m colour
Zappala-Slott
V*

Newlyweds discover that they both had the same father.

Old-fashioned family shocker which needed a lot more zip if it was going to shock anybody.

w Adrian Morrall, D. A. Kellogg d David Miller

Lana Turner, Robert Alda, Celeste Holm, Robert Lansing, Scott Hylands, Denise DeMirjian

'Performances and settings are all very high class. I mean, when you have all that money and those great surroundings you can still suffer, but you do have multiple choices.' – *Archer Winsten, New York Post*

Bizarre, Bizarre: see *Drôle de Drame*

Black and White in Colour *
France/Switzerland/Ivory Coast 1976 100m
  Eastmancolor
Reggance/SFP/Artco/Société Ivorienne de Production (Arthur Cohn, Jacques Perrin, Giorgio Silvagni)
V*, L
original title: *La Victoire en Chantant*

In French West Africa in 1915, easy-going colonials learn of the outbreak of war and prepare to attack a neighbouring German garrison.

Curious mixture of Ealing-style comedy and mordant satire; interesting without being wholly engaging.

w Georges Conchon, Jean-Jacques Annaud d Jean-Jacques Annaud ph Claude Agostini, Eduardo Serra, Nanamoudou Magassouda m Pierre Bachelet, Mat Camison

Jean Carmet, Jacques Dufilho, Catherine Rouvel, Jacques Spiesser, Dora Doll

AA: best foreign film

Black Angel *
US 1946 80m bw
U-I (Roy William Neill, Tom McKnight)

A drunk sets out to find the murderer of his wife, and finds it was himself.

Stylish but empty version of a tired theme, interesting for performances and atmosphere.

w Roy Chanslor novel William Irish d Roy William Neill ph Paul Ivano m Frank Skinner

Dan Duryea, Peter Lorre, Broderick Crawford, June Vincent, Wallace Ford, Hobart Cavanaugh, Constance Dowling

The Black Abbot
GB 1934 56m bw
Ambassador/Real Art (Julius Hagen)

Crooks take advantage of a legend of a ghost to kidnap a wealthy man.

Dire upper-class thriller with stilted acting and excruciating comic relief supplied by the servants.

w Terence Egan novel The Grange Mystery by Philip Godfrey d George A. Cooper ph Ernest Palmer ad James A. Carter ed Lister Laurance

John Stuart, Judy Kelly, Richard Cooper, Edgar Norfolk, Ben Welden

Black Arrow
US 1944 bw serial: 15 eps
Columbia

A young Indian chief turns out to be the son of a white man.

Rather tedious chapter play with few of the regular Western excitements. d B. Reeves Eason

Robert Scott, Adele Jergens, Robert Williams, Charles Middleton

The Black Arrow
US 1948 76m bw
Columbia
V*
GB title: *The Black Arrow Strikes*

During the Wars of the Roses, an English knight seeks the murderer of his father.

Pennypinching swashbuckler which contrives to entertain despite total disregard of probability.

w Richard Schayer, David P. Sheppard, Thomas Seller novel R. L. Stevenson d Gordon Douglas ph Charles Lawton Jnr

Louis Hayward, Janet Blair, George Macready, Edgar Buchanan, Paul Cavanagh

The Black Arrow Strikes: see *The Black Arrow*

Black Bart
US 1948 80m Technicolor
U-I (Leonard Goldstein)
GB title: *Black Bart, Highwayman*

Lola Montez, on an American tour, falls for an American bandit.

Acceptable Western programmer with historical trimmings and some evidence of tongue-in-cheek attitudes.

w Luci Ward, Jack Natteford, William Bowers d George Sherman ph Irving Glassberg m Frank Skinner

Yvonne de Carlo, Dan Duryea, Jeffrey Lynn, Percy Kilbride, Lloyd Gough, Frank Lovejoy, John McIntire, Don Beddoe

Black Bart, Highwayman: see *Black Bart*

Black Beauty
US 1946 74m bw
TCF (Edward L. Alperson)
V*

In Victorian England, a girl searches for her lost colt.

Stilted children's film with little relation to the book.

w Lillie Hayward, Agnes Christine Johnston *novel* Anna Sewell   *d* Max Nosseck   *ph* J. Roy Hunt   *m* Dimitri Tiomkin

Mona Freeman, Richard Denning, Evelyn Ankers, J. M. Kerrigan, Terry Kilburn

Black Beauty *
GB   1971   106m   colour
Tigon/Chilton (Tony Tenser)
V*, L

A luckless horse passes from hand to hand but is finally restored to its original young master and has a happy retirement.

Pleasant, episodic animal story which stays pretty close to the book. A shade yawn-inducing for adults, but fine for children.

w Wolf Mankowitz   *novel* Anna Sewell   *d* James Hill   *ph* Chris Menges   *m* Lionel Bart, John Cameron

Mark Lester, Walter Slezak, Peter Lee Lawrence, Patrick Mower, John Nettleton, Maria Rohm

The Black Bird
US   1975   98m   colour
Columbia/Rastar (Michael Levee, Lou Lombardo)
V*

Sam Spade's son finds himself beset by crooks still after the Maltese falcon.

Dismal, witless, boring parody of a classic crime film, with none of the humour of the original.

wd David Giler   *ph* Philip Lathrop   *m* Jerry Fielding

George Segal, Stéphane Audran, *Lee Patrick,* Elisha Cook Jnr, Lionel Stander, John Abbott, Signe Hasso, Felix Silla

'A dumb comedy with an insecure tone and some good ideas mixed up with some terrible ones.' – *Variety*

'It doesn't work because it has nothing to say.' – *Michael Billington, Illustrated London News*

The Black Book *
US   1949   88m   bw
Eagle-Lion
GB title: *Reign of Terror*

A member of a secret organization which plans to replace Robespierre with a moderate goes undercover with the French Revolutionaries.

Moderate period melodrama with an attractive though artificial look.

w Philip Yordan, Aeneas Mackenzie   *d* Anthony Mann   *ph* John Alton   *m* Sol Kaplan

Robert Cummings, Arlene Dahl, Richard Basehart, Richard Hart, Arnold Moss

Black Caesar
US   1973   87m   DeLuxe
Gala/Larco (Larry Cohen)
V*, L, S
GB title: *The Godfather of Harlem*

A black hoodlum takes over Mafia territory to become a Harlem big-shot.

Slapdash movie that attempts to update the style of Warner's 30s gangster movies.

wd Larry Cohen   *ph* Fenton Hamilton, James Signorelli   *m* James Brown   *pd* Larry Lurin   *ed* George Folsey Jnr

Fred Williamson, D'Urville Martin, Julius W. Harris, Gloria Hendry, Art Lund, Val Avery, Minnie Gentry

'A welcome attempt to move black films off the beaten track.' – *David McGillivray, MFB*

† The film was cut to 84m on its British release. It was followed by a sequel, *Hell up in Harlem.*

The Black Camel
US   1931   67m   bw
Fox

Charlie Chan solves the murder of a film starlet in Honolulu.

Second in the Oland series (see under Charlie Chan), not easy to see these days.

w Barry Conners, Philip Klein   *d* Hamilton McFadden

Warner Oland, Dorothy Revier, Bela Lugosi, Sally Eilers, Victor Varconi, Robert Young

The Black Cannon Incident *
China   1985   99m
ICA/Xi'an Film Studio (Wu Tiangming, Manfred Durniok)

An engineer and interpreter involved in a project with the Germans is replaced by an incompetent after Party members suspect him of spying.

A satire on bureaucratic bungling, one of the few to have emerged from China.

w Li Wei   *story Langman de Heipao* by Zhang Xianliang   *d* Huang Jianxin   *ph* Wang Xinsheng, Feng Wei   *m* Zhu Shirui   *ad* Liu Yichuan   *ed* Chen Dali

Liu Zifeng, Gerhard Olschewski, Gao Ming, Wang Yi, Yang Yazhou, Ge Hui

The Black Castle
US   1952   80m   bw
Universal-International (William Alland)
V*

An 18th-century knight avenges the deaths of two friends who have attended a hunting party at the castle of a sadistic Viennese count.

A variation on *The Most Dangerous Game,* and not a good one: the pace is far too plodding and the atmosphere unpleasant.

w Jerry Sackheim   *d* Nathan Juran   *ph* Irving Glassberg   *md* Joseph Gershenson   *m* Hans Salter

Richard Greene, Stephen McNally, Boris Karloff, Lon Chaney Jnr, Paula Corday, John Hoyt, Michael Pate

'It's tremonstrous! The absolute apex of the super-shivery!'
The Black Cat *
US   1934   65m   bw
Universal (Carl Laemmle Jnr)
V*, L
GB title: *House of Doom*

A revengeful doctor seeks out the Austrian architect and devil-worshipper who betrayed his country in World War I.

Absurd and dense farrago set in a modernistic but crumbling castle which is eventually blown to bits just as its owner is skinned alive. Mostly rather dull despite the extraordinary plot, but the thing has moments of style, a delightful cod devil worship sequence (especially for audiences with a rudimentary knowledge of Latin) and nothing at all to do with the title or Edgar Allan Poe.

w Peter Ruric   *d* Edgar G. Ulmer   *ph* John Mescall   *md* Heinz Roemheld   *ad* Charles D. Hall

Boris Karloff, *Bela Lugosi,* David Manners, Jacqueline Wells, Egon Brecher

'On the counts of story, novelty, thrills and distinction, the picture is sub-normal.' – *Variety*

'A truly bizarre concoction of mayhem, necrophilia, sadism and satanism.' – *Clive Hirschhorn, 1980s*

The Black Cat *
US   1941   70m   bw
Universal (Burt Kelly)

Murder follows the summoning of the family to the spooky house of a cat-loving recluse.

Disappointing mystery which squanders a splendid cast on a script full of non-sequiturs and makes heavy weather of its light relief.

w Robert Lees, Fred Rinaldo, Eric Taylor, Robert Neville   *d* Albert S. Rogell   *ph* Stanley Cortez

Basil Rathbone, Gladys Cooper, Broderick Crawford, Hugh Herbert, Gale Sondergaard, Anne Gwynne, Alan Ladd, Cecilia Loftus, Bela Lugosi

HUGH HERBERT (reading inscription): 'That house is doubly blest, Which to our feline friends gives rest.'
BRODERICK CRAWFORD (not impressed): 'Her hats are full of bats, For spending all her dough on cats.'

The Black Cauldron *
US   1985   80m   Technicolor
Walt Disney Productions (Joe Hale)
S

A medieval hero combats magic swords, wicked witches and skeletal tyrants.

Assured but somehow quite forgettable Disney cartoon feature.

w David Jonas, Vance Gerry, Ted Berman, Richard Rich, Al Wilson, Roy Morita, Peter Young, Art Stevens, Joe Hale, from *The Chronicles of Prydain* by Lloyd Alexander   *d* Ted Berman, Richard Rich   *key animator* Walt Stanchfield   *m* Elmer Bernstein

voices of Freddie Jones, Nigel Hawthorne, John Hurt, John Huston, John Byner, Arthur Malet

† Production allegedly took ten years and cost 25 million dollars.

'If this doesn't make your skin crawl . . . it's on too tight!'
Black Christmas
Canada   1974   97m   Technicolor
EMI/Film Funding/Vision IV (Robert Clark)
V*
aka: *Silent Night, Evil Night*

Girls in a college sorority house are attacked by a lurking psychopath.

Moderate suspense chiller.

w Roy Moore   *d* Robert Clark

Olivia Hussey, Keir Dullea, Margot Kidder, Andre Martin, John Saxon, Marian Waldman, Art Hindle

The Black Coin
US   1936   bw   serial: 15 eps
Weiss-Mintz

American secret agents try to intercept papers which hold the key to a smuggling ring.

Archetypal serial hokum during which the 'McGuffin' is quickly forgotten.   *d* Albert Herman

Dave O'Brien, Ralph Graves, Ruth Mix, Matthew Betz, Snub Pollard, Bryant Washburn

Black Diamond Rush
US   1993   100m   colour
Black Diamond (Kurt Miller, Peter Speek)

A documentary on the pleasures of skiing.

A celebration of skiers as exemplars of personal freedom, filmed to a rock soundtrack; it is likely to appeal only to the initiated.

w Warren Miller   *d* Kurt Miller, Peter Speek   *ph* Don Brolin   *m* Middleman   *ed* Paul Burack, Kim Schneider

Narrator: Warren Miller

Black Eyes
GB   1939   72m   bw
Associated British (Walter Mycroft)

A Moscow head waiter has raised his daughter to believe he's a big wheel in the business world.

Well-made comedy drama from a French original, *Les Yeux Noirs.*

w Dudley Leslie d Herbert Brenon ph Gunther Krampf m Walford Hyden, Bela Bizoni ad Ian White

Otto Kruger, Mary Maguire, Walter Rilla, John Wood

Black Eyes **
Italy 1987 117m colour
Excelsior/RAI (Silvia D'Amico Bendico)
V, S
original title: Oci Ciornie; GB title: Dark Eyes

At the turn of the century, an aged Italian recounts his lapses.

Highly amusing star vehicle based on stories by Chekhov.

w Nikita Mikhalkov, Alexander Adabachian, Suso Cecchi d'Amico d Nikita Mikhalkov ph Franco di Giacomo m Francis Lai pd Mario Garbuglia, Alexander Adabachian

Marcello Mastroianni, Silvana Mangano, Marthe Keller, Elena Sofonova

'The film effortlessly swings from farce to tenderness, love to betrayal, exuberance to poignancy without missing a beat.' – Daily Variety

AAN: Marcello Mastroianni

Black Flowers for the Bride: see Something for Everyone

Black Fox
US 1962 89m bw
Jack Le Vien
V*

Slick documentary on the rise of Hitler, using the expected newsreels reinforced not too artfully by references to art and to the medieval folk tale of Reynard the Fox.

wd Louis Clyde Stoumen

Narrator: Marlene Dietrich

AA: best documentary

Black Friday *
US 1940 70m bw
Universal (Burt Kelly)

After an accident, a college professor is given a gangster's brain, and the surgeon encourages him to believe that he is the gangster so as to find hidden loot.

Plot-packed melodrama which fails to provide the chills suggested by the cast, but passes the time agreeably enough.

w Curt Siodmak, Eric Taylor d Arthur Lubin ph Woody Bredell m Hans Salter

Boris Karloff, Bela Lugosi, Stanley Ridges, Anne Nagel, Anne Gwynne, Virginia Brissac, Paul Fix

† Lugosi was originally cast as the professor, but proved wrong for the part; Stanley Ridges replaced him and walked off with the movie.

Black Fury *
US 1935 95m bw
Warner (Robert Lord)
V*

A coal miner comes up against union problems, unsafe conditions and corruption.

Typical Warner social drama, good for its time but now very obvious.

w Abem Finkel, Carl Erickson play Bohunk by Harry R. Irving d Michael Curtiz ph Byron Haskin md Leo Forbstein

Paul Muni, Karen Morley, William Gargan, Barton MacLane, John Qualen, J. Carrol Naish, Vince Barnett, Tully Marshall, Henry O'Neill

'Basic box office, packed with promotional potentialities.' – Variety

'The most powerful strike picture that has yet been made, and I am aware of the better-known Soviet jobs in the field.' – Otis Ferguson

Black God, White Devil **
Brazil 1964 110m bw
New Cinema/Luiz Augosto Mendes/Copacabana (Glauber Rocha)
original title: Deus e o Diabo na Terra do Sol

A peasant follows the teachings of a fanatical prophet who preaches a gospel of suffering and death and becomes an outlaw.

Grim and violent tale of striving humanity at the mercy of a desolate landscape which established the reputation of its director as a new and disquieting voice in international cinema.

wd Glauber Rocha ph Waldemar Lima m Villa-Lobos ad Glauber Rocha ed L. Ririra

Yona Magalhaes, Geraldo Del Rey, Othon Bastos, Mauricio Do Valle, Lidio Silva

'One is left wondering what a film so locked in its own oppressive landscape can really communicate to a European audience – other than the seduction of alien violence and alien despair.' – Penelope Houston, Sight and Sound

† The hired killer Antonio das Mortes became the eponymous hero of a film Rocha made in 1969 (qv).

Black Gold
US 1947 90m Cinecolor
Allied Artists
V*

An Indian couple on the reservation adopt a Chinese boy who becomes a famous jockey.

Tears all round in this enterprising if rather muddled B picture with a social conscience.

w Agnes Christine Johnston story Caryl Coleman d Phil Karlson

Anthony Quinn, Katherine de Mille, Elyse Knox, Kane Richmond, Ducky Louie, Raymond Hatton, Thurston Hall, Alan Bridge

Black Gold
US 1963 98m bw
Warner

Novice wildcatter makes it rich in Oklahoma despite villains on every side.

Absolutely predictable actioner which unspools like a remake even if it isn't.

w Bob and Wanda Duncan d Leslie H. Martinson

Philip Carey, Diane McBain, Claude Akins, Iron Eyes Cody, James Best

Black Gunn
US 1972 95m Eastmancolor
Columbia-Warner/Champion (John Heyman, Norman Priggen)
V*

With the aid of a group of black militants, an LA club owner takes revenge on gangsters who killed his brother.

Mundane action film, with nothing to distinguish it from a hundred others.

w Franklin Coen, Robert Shearer d Robert Hartford-Davis ph Richard H. Kline m Tony Osborne ad Jack DeShields ed Pat Somerset

Jim Brown, Martin Landau, Brenda Sykes, Luciana Paluzzi, Vida Blue, Stephen McNally, Keefe Brasselle

Black Hand *
US 1949 92m bw
MGM (William H. Wright)
V*

In New York at the turn of the century, an Italian boy avenges his father's death at the hands of the Mafia.

Neatly produced, studio-set melodrama, unusual in subject but very stereotyped and artificial in treatment.

w Luther Davis d Richard Thorpe ph Paul C. Vogel m Alberto Colombo

Gene Kelly, J. Carrol Naish, Teresa Celli, Marc Lawrence, Frank Puglia, Barry Kelley

'A journey that begins where everything ends!'
The Black Hole *
US 1979 98m Technicolor Technovision
Walt Disney (Ron Miller)
V, V*, L

A research team in space is welcomed aboard a mysterious survey ship poised on the edge of a black hole.

The special effects are superb, though achieved through a general gloom which is barely acceptable. But the story is an ill-worked-out remake of Twenty Thousand Leagues under the Sea, the characterization is ridiculously inept, and the final disclosure that black holes are doorways to hell sends one home rather bemused.

w Jeb Rosebrook, Gerry Day d Gary Nelson ph Frank Phillips m John Barry pd Peter Ellenshaw

Maximilian Schell, Robert Forster, Anthony Perkins, Joseph Bottoms, Yvette Mimieux, Ernest Borgnine

'As pastiche, it sounds promising; as drama, encumbered with references to Cicero and Goethe, it is merely tedious.' – John Halford, MFB

'Rated PG, but the only danger to children is that it may make them think that outer space is not much fun any more.' – New Yorker

AAN: Frank Phillips

Black Horse Canyon
US 1954 81m Technicolor
Universal-International

Two cowpunchers help a lady rancher to capture and train a wild black stallion.

Slight but agreeable outdoor programmer.

w Geoffrey Homes d Jesse Hibbs

Joel McCrea, Mari Blanchard, Race Gentry, Murvyn Vye, Irving Bacon

Black Jack
GB 1979 110m colour
Enterprise/Kestrel (Tony Garnett)

In 1750 Yorkshire, a rascally French sailor recovers from a hanging and has adventures on the road with a young apprentice.

The purpose of this costume adventure, from these creators, is obscure, but the execution of it is muddled and amateurish.

w none credited novel Leon Garfield d Kenneth Loach ph Chris Menges m Bob Pegg ad Martin Johnson ed Bill Shapter

Jean Franval, Stephen Hirst, Louise Cooper

'Ploddingly unpersuasive. Not only narrative clarity but simple credibility is lacking.' – Tim Pulleine, MFB

Black Joy *
GB 1977 109m Eastmancolor
Winkast/West One (Elliott Kastner, Martin Campbell)

A Guyanan immigrant in Brixton is tricked by a Jamaican good-for-nothing but later goes into partnership with him and learns to stand up for his rights.

Vivid but eventually wearying ethnic comedy-melodrama.

w Anthony Simmons, Jamal Ali play Dark Days and Light Nights by Jamal Ali d Anthony Simmons ph Philip Meheux md Lou Reizner from reggae songs

Norman Beaton, Trevor Thomas, Floella Benjamin, Dawn Hope

'I wanted to show the reality of life in an immigrant area, angry and frustrated like so many parts of Britain – but full of hope and humour.' – *Anthony Simmons*

The Black Knight

GB 1954 85m Technicolor
Warwick (Irving Allen, Albert R. Broccoli)

A humble swordmaker reveals a traitor to King Arthur.

Hilarious travesty of English historical legend, meant seriously for Anglo-American consumption. Shades of *Zorro*, *Babes in the Wood* and *1066 and All That*.

w Alec Coppel   d Tay Garnett   ph John Wilcox   m John Addison

Alan Ladd, Peter Cushing, Patricia Medina, Harry Andrews, André Morell, Anthony Bushell, Patrick Troughton, Laurence Naismith, John Laurie

'Alan Ladd galahads with wild west *gentillesse* in this Technicolored rampage through British history.' – *MFB*

'Unmasking America's brotherhood of butchery!'

Black Legion **

US 1937 83m bw
Warner (Robert Lord)

A factory worker becomes involved with the Ku Klux Klan.

Social melodrama typical of its studio, and good of its kind.

w Robert Lord, Abem Finkel, William Wister Haines   d Archie Mayo   ph George Barnes

Humphrey Bogart, Erin O'Brien Moore, Dick Foran, Ann Sheridan, Robert Barrat, John Litel, Charles Halton

'Powerful story of the horror spread by the hooded order; Surefire man's picture.' – *Variety*

'An honest job of film work, and one of the most direct social pieces released from Hollywood.' – *Otis Ferguson*

AAN: Robert Lord (original story)

Black Limelight *

GB 1938 70m bw
ABPC (Walter C. Mycroft)

The wife of a man convicted of killing his mistress proves that a 'moon murderer' did it.

Naïve but effective little chiller.

w Dudley Leslie, Walter Summers   play Gordon Sherry   d Paul Stein   ph Claude Friese-Greene   ad Cedric Dawe

Raymond Massey, Joan Marion, Walter Hudd, Henry Oscar, Coral Browne

'The biggest picture in ten years! The greatest cavalcade of intrigue, spectacle, adventure and excitement you'll ever see on the screen'

Black Magic *

US 1949 105m bw
Edward Small (Gregory Ratoff)
V*, L

Cagliostro the magician becomes involved in a plot to supply a double for Marie Antoinette.

Deliriously complicated historical romp which unfortunately suffers from a stolid script and production which kill all the flights of fancy.

w Charles Bennett   d Gregory Ratoff   ph Ubaldo Arata, Anchise Brizzi   m Paul Sawtell

Orson Welles, Nancy Guild, Akim Tamiroff, Valentina Cortese, Margot Grahame, Charles Goldner, Frank Latimore, Stephen Bekassy

'At times a grotesque, and at others a melancholy spectacle; including one scene of humiliating burlesque at the expense of physical disability that is as vile as anything I have witnessed in a cinema. But on the whole, absurdity predominates, and one must grin if one is to bear it. Whether Mr Welles deliberately enhanced the joke by adding bad acting to bad material is between him and his own soul.' – *C. A. Lejeune*

The Black Marble

US 1980 113m DeLuxe
Avco/Frank Capra Jnr
V*

A drunken cop redeems himself when teamed with a policewoman who is less cynical about the work.

Curious cop show with emphasis on child murders and dog torturing. An unhappy film with a garbled message.

w Joseph Wambaugh   novel Joseph Wambaugh   d Harold Becker   ph Owen Roizman   m Maurice Jarre

Robert Foxworth, Paula Prentiss, Harry Dean Stanton, Barbara Babcock, John Hancock

Black Market Babies

US 1946 71m bw
Monogram (Jeffrey Bernerd)

An ex-medico runs a baby farm for illegitimate offspring.

Routine exploitationer with no surprises.

w George Morris, George W. Sayre   d William Beaudine

Ralph Morgan, Kane Richmond, Teala Loring, George Meeker

'Should bring fair returns on double bills.' – *Variety*

Black Moon Rising

US 1985 100m CFI colour
Thorn EMI/New World (Joel B. Michaels, Douglas Curtiss)
V*, L

An adventurer in the pay of the US government hides much-wanted evidence in the back of a super-high-powered car.

Absurd, almost impenetrable action shenanigans with more than enough violent action.

w John Carpenter, Desmond Nakano, William Gray   d Harley Cokliss   ph Mischa Suslov   m Lalo Schifrin   pd Bryan Ryman   ed Todd Ramsay

Tommy Lee Jones, Linda Hamilton, Robert Vaughn, Richard Jaeckel, Keenan Wynn

Black Narcissus ***

GB 1946 100m Technicolor
GFD/The Archers (Michael Powell, Emeric Pressburger)
V*, L

Anglo-Catholic nuns in the Himalayas have trouble with climate, morale, and one of their number who goes mad of sex frustration.

An unlikely theme produces one of the cinema's most beautiful films, a visual and emotional stunner despite some narrative uncertainty.

wd Michael Powell, Emeric Pressburger   novel Rumer Godden   ph Jack Cardiff   m Brian Easdale

Deborah Kerr, David Farrar, Sabu, Jean Simmons, Kathleen Byron, Flora Robson, Esmond Knight, Jenny Laird, May Hallatt, Judith Furse

AA: Jack Cardiff

Black on White *

Finland 1967 95m Eastmancolor
Jorn Donner/FJ Film
original title: *Mustaa Valkoisella*

A successful young executive falls in love with a girl

hitch-hiker, but when his wife leaves him the girl is no longer interested.

Showy romantic melodrama which tries to make rather too much of a slender theme.

wd Jorn Donner   ph Esko Nevaleinen   m George Riedel

Jorn Donner, Kristina Halkola, Liisamaija Laaksonen

The Black Orchid *

US 1958 95m bw Vistavision
Paramount (Carlo Ponti, Marcello Girosi)
V*

A widower incurs hostility from his daughter when he plans to marry a gangster's widow.

Rather solemn New York/Italian romantic melodrama, with much gesticulation all round.

w Joseph Stefano   d Martin Ritt   ph Robert Burks   m Alessandro Cicognini

Sophia Loren, Anthony Quinn, Ina Balin, Jimmy Baird, Mark Richman

Black Orpheus *

France/Italy/Brazil 1958 106m Eastmancolor
Cinemascope
Dispatfilm/Gemma/Tupan (Sacha Gordine)
V*, L, S
original title: *Orfeu Negro*

Against a background of the Rio carnival, a black tram driver accidentally kills his girlfriend, and after seeking her in the nether regions kills himself to be with her.

Rather irritating and noisy attempt to update a legend, without showing very much reason for doing so.

w Vinitius de Moraes   d Marcel Camus   ph Jean Bourgoin   m Luis Bonfa, Antonio Carlos Jobim

Breno Mello, Marpessa Dawn, Ademar da Silva, Lourdes de Oliviera

AA: best foreign film

The Black Panther

GB 1977 98m Technicolor
Impics

A small-time post office robber becomes a kidnapper and murderer.

Tasteless re-enactment of a case which made headlines in 1975.

w Michael Armstrong   d Ian Merrick

Donald Sumpter, Debbie Farrington, Marjorie Yates, David Swift

The Black Parachute

US 1944 65m bw
Jack Fier/Columbia

An American soldier parachutes into a mythical European kingdom to free its king from the Nazis.

Thick-ear propaganda fare; it has its moments.

w Clarence Upson Young   d Lew Landers

Larry Parks, John Carradine, Osa Massen, Jeanne Bates, Jonathan Hale

Black Patch

US 1957 84m bw
Warner/Montgomery

A marshal is wrongly suspected of murder.

Dour, dark Western, occasionally worth looking at.

wd Allen H. Miner

George Montgomery, Diane Brewster, Tom Pittman, Leo Gordon

The Black Pirate ***
US   1926   76m approx (24 fps)   Technicolor
silent
Douglas Fairbanks
V*, L

A shipwrecked mariner swears revenge on the pirates who blew up his father's ship.

Cheerful swashbuckler with the star in top form.

w Douglas Fairbanks, Jack Cunningham   d Albert Parker   ph Henry Sharp   ad Oscar Borg, Dwight Franklin

Douglas Fairbanks, Billie Dove, Donald Crisp, Sam de Grasse

Black Rain *
Japan   1988   123m   bw
Artificial Eye/Imamura Productions/ Hayashibara/Tohokushinsha (Hisa Iino)
V*, L
Kuroi Ame

Caught in the destruction of Hiroshima, a Japanese family cope with the onset of radiation sickness in the ensuing years.

Intermittently moving, despite its uncertainties of tone.

w Toshiro Ishido, Shohei Imamura   *novel* Masuji Ibuse   d Shohei Imamura   ph Takashi Kawamata   m Toru Takemitsu   ad Hiasao Inagaki   ed Hajime Okayasu

Yoshiko Tanaka, Kazuo Kitamura, Etsuko Ichihara, Shoichi Ozawa, Norihei Miki

'When Imamura conjures a string of imagery out of next to nothing, he achieves results as disquieting and resonant as anything he has ever done.' – *Tony Rayns, MFB*

Black Rain
US   1989   125m   Technicolor
UIP/Paramount/Stanley R. Jaffe, Sherry Lansing
V, V*, L, CD, S

A rebellious and corrupt New York cop tracks down an escaped killer in Tokyo.

Effective thriller, though many may find unappetising its theme of redemption through revenge and violence.

w Craig Bolotin, Warren Lewis   d Ridley Scott   ph Jan de Bont   m Hans Zimmer   pd Norris Spencer   ad John J. Moore, Herman F. Zimmerman, Kazuo Takenaka   ed Tom Rolf

Michael Douglas, Andy Garcia, Ken Takakura, Kate Capshaw, Yusaku Matsuda, Shigeru Koyama, John Spencer

Black Rainbow
GB   1989   103m   colour
Palace/Goldcrest (John Quested, Geoffrey Helman)
V

A medium foretells the violent death of members of her audience, including her father.

Unconvincing story of the supernatural.

wd Mike Hodges   ph Gerry Fisher   m John Scott   pd Voytek   ad Patty Klawonn   ed Malcolm Cooke

Rosanna Arquette, Jason Robards, Tom Hulce, Mark Joy, Ron Rosenthal, John Bennes, Linda Pierce

Black Robe ***
Canada/Australia   1991   100m   Eastmancolor
Samuel Goldwyn/Alliance/Samson/Telefilm Canada (Robert Lantos, Stephane Reichel, Sue Milliken)
V, V*, L, S

In the 17th century, a Jesuit priest travels through Quebec to convert the Indians.

Tough-minded, compassionate, excellently acted account of inadvertent tragedy.

w Brian Moore   *novel* Brian Moore   d Bruce Beresford   ph Peter James   m Georges Delerue   pd Herbert Pinter   ed Tim Wellburn

Lothaire Bluteau, Aden Young, Sandrine Holt, August Schellenberg, Tantoo Cardinal, Frank Wilson

'A magnificently staged combination of top talents delivering a gripping and tragic story.' – *Variety*

'An adventure story in the truest sense: the filmmakers lead us into unknown territory, and keep pushing us farther and farther on, until, by the end, we find ourselves deep in the wilderness of the seventeenth-century consciousness.' – *Terrence Rafferty, New Yorker*

The Black Room *
US   1935   70m   bw
Columbia
V*, L

A nobleman's power is claimed by his evil twin brother.

Rather splendid old barnstormer with touches of horror, a neatly produced star vehicle.

w Henry Myers, from the writings of Arthur Strawn   d Roy William Neill   ph Al Siegler

Boris Karloff, Marian Marsh, Katherine de Mille, Thurston Hall

'Eerie affair, dull and destined for negative results. Its best qualities are scenic investiture and photography, which do not excite dollars to elope from people's pokes.' – *Variety*

'Mrs Radcliffe would not have been ashamed of this wild and exciting film, of the bones in the oubliette, the scene at the altar when the dog leaps and the paralysed arm comes to life in self-defence, of the Count's wild drive back to the castle, of the rearing horses, the rocketing coach, the strange valley of rocks with its leaning cross and neglected Christ, the graveyard with its owls and ivy.' – *Graham Greene*

The Black Rose *
GB   1950   120m   Technicolor
TCF (Louis D. Lighton)

A 13th-century English scholar journeys to the land of the Mongols, and after many adventures returns to a knighthood for his scientific discoveries.

Portentous and slow-moving adventure with good things along the way.

w Talbot Jennings   *novel* Thomas B. Costain   d Henry Hathaway   ph Jack Cardiff   m Richard Addinsell   ad Paul Sheriff

Tyrone Power, Orson Welles, Cecile Aubry, Jack Hawkins, Finlay Currie, Henry Oscar, Michael Rennie

'This is the night of the nightmare … when a headless corpse rides the cold night wind, when a woman's soul inhabits the body of a buzzing fly.'

Black Sabbath
Italy   1963   99m   Pathecolor
American International
V*, L

Three supernatural stories introduced by Boris Karloff. *The Drop of Water* (Jacqueline Pierreux); *The Telephone* (Michele Mercier); *The Wurdelak* (Boris Karloff, Mark Damon).

Tolerable horror portmanteau.   *stories* Anton Chekhov, Howard Snyder, Leo Tolstoy   d Mario Bava

'The management reserves the right to put up the lights any time the audience becomes too emotionally disturbed. We urge you not to panic or bolt from your seats.'

The Black Scorpion
US   1957   88m   bw
Warner (Frank Melford, Jack Dietz)
V*

Volcanic explosions uncover a nest of prehistoric giant scorpions near a Mexican village.

Apart from a genuinely terrifying sequence in the scorpion's lair, this is a poor monster movie in which excessively dark photography seems intended to cover up very variable trick work.

w David Duncan, Robert Blees   d Edward Ludwig   ph Lionel Lindon   m Paul Sawtell   sp Willis O'Brien

Richard Denning, Mara Corday, Carlos Rivas, Mario Navarro

Black Shack Alley: see *Rue Cases Nègres*

Black Shampoo
US   1975   83m   Movielab
Transit/World Amusement (Alvin L. Fast)
V*

A hairdresser fights back when a rival sends thugs to wreck his salon.

Presumably intended as an attempt to cash in on the success of *Shampoo*, it develops instead into a dull gangster movie; or maybe it was always a dull gangster movie, and was given a catch-penny title.

w Alvin L. Fast, Greydon Clark   d Greydon Clark   ph Dean Cundey, Michael J. Mileham   m Gerald Lee   ed Earl Watson Jnr

John Daniels, Tanya Boyd, Joe Ortiz, Skip Lowe, Gary Allen, Bruce Kerley, Jack Mehoff

'Script and performances are strictly make-and-mend; the direction, which contrives several flashily irrelevant optical effects, and finally sacrifices all for a blood bath involving a fashionable chain-saw, is audacious.' – *David McGillivray, MFB*

Black Sheep
US   1935   70m   bw
Fox

A high-class gambler finds his forgotten son on a transatlantic liner.

Mouldy compromise of sophistication and soul-searching.

wd Allan Dwan

Edmund Lowe, Claire Trevor, Tom Brown, Eugene Pallette, Herbert Mundin, Adrienne Ames

'It doesn't rate as a solo performer.' – *Variety*

The Black Sheep of Whitehall *
GB   1941   80m   bw
Ealing (S. C. Balcon)

An incompetent teacher is mistaken for an economics expert and saves the real expert from spies who run a nursing home.

Pretty good wartime star comedy, with a succession of briskly timed gags.

w Angus Macphail, John Dighton   d Basil Dearden, Will Hay   ph Gunther Krampf

Will Hay, John Mills, Basil Sydney, Frank Cellier, Felix Aylmer

The Black Shield of Falworth *
US   1954   99m   Technicolor   Cinemascope
U-I (Robert Arthur, Melville Tucker)

The film in which Tony Curtis says 'Yonda lies the castle of my fodda' (or something like it) is an amiable romp which alternates between comic strip dialogue and a surprisingly convincing sense of medieval custom. The training scenes are as sharp as the romantic asides are pallid.

w Oscar Brodney   *novel* Men of Iron by Howard Pyle   d Rudolph Maté   ph Irving Glassberg   m Herman Stein, Hans Salter

Tony Curtis, Janet Leigh, David Farrar, Barbara Rush, Herbert Marshall, Rhys Williams, Dan O'Herlihy, Torin Thatcher

'A straightforward piece of hokum with no pretensions, and spoken in a variety of accents that only Hollywood could muster.' – *John Gillett*

'A horror horde of monster mutants walk the earth!'

The Black Sleep
US   1956   81m   bw
UA/Bel Air (Howard W. Koch)
V*

A Victorian brain surgeon experiments on human beings and produces freaks who eventually turn on him.

Gruesome and humourless horror film notable only for its gallery of wasted talent.

w John C. Higgins   d Reginald Le Borg
ph Gordon Avil   m Les Baxter

Basil Rathbone, Bela Lugosi, Lon Chaney Jnr, John Carradine, Akim Tamiroff, Tor Johnson, Herbert Rudley, Patricia Blake

The Black Stallion *
US   1980   117m   Technicolor
UA/Omni Zoetrope (Francis Coppola)
V*, L

After a 1946 shipwreck, a boy and a stallion are cast up on the African shore; many years later, he rides the horse to victory at Santa Anita.

1980 seems a bit late for boy-and-horse pictures, but this one is so beautifully directed and photographed, if drastically overlong, that most adults thought their children should see it.

w Melissa Mathison, Jeanne Rosenberg, William D. Witliff   novel Walter Farley   d Carroll Ballard
ph Caleb Deschanel   m Carmine Coppola

Kelly Reno, Mickey Rooney, Teri Garr, Clarence Muse, Hoyt Axton

'A perfect gem – the beautiful craftsmanship alone makes it a joy to behold.' – *Variety*

AAN: Mickey Rooney

The Black Stallion Returns
US   1983   93m   Technicolor
MGM-UA/Coppola/Zoetrope (Tom Sternberg)
V*, L

Rather desperate sequel in which a teenager loses his horse in Morocco and gets him back after various daredevil adventures.

Tame, predictable and boring.

w Richard Kletter, Jerome Kass   novel Walter Farley
d Robert Dalva   ph Carlo DiPalma   m Georges Delerue   ad Aurelio Crugnolo   ed Paul Hirsch

Kelly Reno, Ferdy Mayne, Woody Strode, Vincent Spano, Allen Goorwitz

'Well-intentioned, but overall it doesn't look like a winner.' – *Variety*

'The undead demons of hell terrorize the world!'

Black Sunday *
Italy   1960   83m   bw
Galatra/Jolly
V*, L
aka: *Mask of the Demon*

A beautiful witch is put to death in an iron maiden but rises from the dead to wreak vengeance.

Stylish horror comic which started the Italian cult for such things.

wd Mario Bava   story Gogol

Barbara Steele, John Richardson, Ivo Garrani

Black Sunday *
US   1977   143m   Movielab   Panavision
Paramount (Robert Evans)
V*, L

The Black September movement threatens a football game to be held in Miami's Superbowl.

Spectacular, heavily detailed, but somehow unexciting disaster melodrama.

w Ernest Lehman, Kenneth Ross, Ivan Moffat
novel Thomas Harris   d John Frankenheimer
ph John A. Alonzo   m John Williams

Robert Shaw, Marthe Keller, Bruce Dern, Fritz Weaver, Steven Keats, Bekim Fehmiu, Michael V. Gazzo, William Daniels, Walter Gotell

'There's only one real motivation for this movie, and that's the desire to make money. Why else would anyone make an ostensibly anti-terrorist film that in actuality could end up promoting terrorism?' – *Frank Rich, New York Post*

Black Sunday: see *Mask of Satan*

The Black Swan ***
US   1942   85m   Technicolor
TCF (Robert Bassler)

Morgan the pirate is made governor of Jamaica and enlists the help of his old friends to rid the Caribbean of buccaneers.

Rousing adventure story with comic asides: just what action hokum always aimed to be, with a spirited gallery of heroes and villains and an entertaining narrative taken at a spanking pace.

w Ben Hecht, Seton I. Miller   novel Rafael Sabatini
d Henry King   ph Leon Shamroy   m Alfred Newman

Tyrone Power, Maureen O'Hara, *Laird Cregar, Thomas Mitchell, George Sanders,* Anthony Quinn, George Zucco, Edward Ashley

'Performed by actors as though to the hokum born.' – *Time*

'Battles between sailing ships, realistic sword fights, assaults, abductions, tortures and love making.' – *CEA Report*

AA: *Leon Shamroy*

AAN: Alfred Newman

The Black Tent
GB   1956   93m   Technicolor   Vistavision
Rank/William MacQuitty
V*

During a Libyan battle a wounded army captain is cared for by Arabs and marries the sheik's daughter. Ten years later, after his death, his son elects to live with the tribe.

Pleasantly shot but otherwise dull, formless and interminable romantic drama, all very stiff upper lip.

w Robin Maugham, Bryan Forbes   d Brian Desmond Hurst   ph Desmond Dickinson   m William Alwyn

Anthony Steel, Donald Sinden, *André Morell,* Anna Maria Sandri, Ralph Truman, Donald Pleasence, Anthony Bushell, Michael Craig

'What was the deadly power that desired and devoured the women of Fordyke?'

The Black Torment *
GB   1964   85m   Eastmancolor
Compton-Tekli (Robert Hartford-Davis)

The second wife of an 18th-century baronet investigates the hauntings which have followed the apparent suicide of his first.

Agreeably unpretentious period ghost story (with a rational explanation). Not exactly good, but better than one might expect.

w Donald and Derek Ford   d Robert Hartford-Davis
ph Peter Newbrook   m Robert Richards

John Turner, Heather Sears, Ann Lynn, Joseph Tomelty, Peter Arne, Raymond Huntley

Black Tuesday *
US   1954   80m   bw
UA/Leonard Goldstein (Robert Goldstein)

A killer escapes from Death Row and hides out with hostages in a disused warehouse.

Starkly melodramatic gangster vehicle with the star up to his oldest tricks. Good tension, but generally rather unpleasant.

w Sydney Boehm   d Hugo Fregonese   ph Stanley Cortez   m Paul Dunlap

Edward G. Robinson, Jean Parker, Peter Graves, Milburn Stone, Warren Stevens, Jack Kelly, James Bell

The Black Widow
US   1947   bw   serial: 13 eps
Republic

An Asian king sends his daughter to America to steal an atomic rocket engine.

Lively hokum with a lady villain for a change.
d Spencer Bennet, Fred C. Brannon

Bruce Edwards, Virginia Lindley, Carol Forman, Anthony Warde, I. Stanford Jolley

The Black Widow
GB   1951   62m   bw
Exclusive/Hammer (Anthony Hinds)

A man succeeds in killing his would-be murderer; his wife schemes to bury the body as her real husband so that she can marry again.

A whole lot less interesting than it sounds, acting and direction being alike laborious.

w Alan MacKinnon   serial Return from Darkness by Lester Powell   d Vernon Sewell   ph Walter Harveyed James Needs

Christine Norden, Robert Ayres, Anthony Forwood, John Longden

'An electrifying drama about a predatory female! All the suspense your system can take!'

Black Widow *
US   1954   95m   DeLuxe   Cinemascope
TCF (Nunnally Johnson)

A Broadway producer is suspected of the murder of an ambitious young girl.

Reasonably classy whodunnit with glamorous settings and an able cast, but a little lacking in wit and pace.

wd Nunnally Johnson   novel Fatal Woman by Patrick Quentin   ph Charles G. Clarke   m Leigh Harline

Ginger Rogers, Van Heflin, George Raft, Gene Tierney, Peggy Ann Garner, Reginald Gardiner, Virginia Leith, Otto Kruger, Hilda Simms, Cathleen Nesbitt

Black Widow *
US   1987   103m   colour
TCF/Laurence Mark (Harold Schneider)
V, V*, L

A lady cop tracks down a lady murderer in Hawaii.

Watchable but overlong cop show with nothing very surprising about it once the plot is clear: TV movies have done just as well.

w Ronald Bass   d Bob Rafelson   ph Conrad Hall
m Michael Small   pd Gene Callahan

Debra Winger, Theresa Russell, Sami Frey, Dennis Hopper, Nicol Williamson, Lois Smith

'A moderately interesting tale of one woman's obsession for another's glamorous and criminal lifestyle.' – *Daily Variety*

The Black Windmill *
GB   1974   106m   Technicolor   Panavision
Universal/Zanuck-Brown (Don Siegel)
V*

A secret service agent has to fight a lone battle when his young son is kidnapped by spies.

Unconvincing variant on *The Man Who Knew Too Much*, with an unwieldy and incoherent plot and more borrowings from Hitchcock than you can count. It ends up as fair predictable fun despite its jaded air.

w Leigh Vance novel *Seven Days to a Killing* by Clive Egleton d Don Siegel ph Ousama Rawi m Roy Budd

Michael Caine, Janet Suzman, Joseph O'Conor, Donald Pleasence, Delphine Seyrig, John Vernon, Joss Ackland

'A flaccid spy thriller, vaguely reminiscent of Hitchcock and *Foreign Correspondent*, with direction as blank as the expression on Michael Caine's face throughout.' – *Sight and Sound*

'Fang And Claw Killers Stalk The City Streets!'
Black Zoo
US   1962   88m   Eastmancolor   Panavision
Allied Artists/Herman Cohen

The owner of a private Los Angeles zoo trains his animals to kill his enemies.

Stultifyingly inept and uninteresting horror film.

w Herman Cohen d Robert Gordon ph Floyd Crosby m Paul Dunlap

Michael Gough, Jeanne Cooper, Rod Lauren, Virginia Grey, Jerome Cowan, Elisha Cook Jnr, Marianna Hill

Blackbeard the Pirate *
US   1952   99m   Technicolor
RKO (Edmund Grainger)
V*, L

In the 17th century, reformed pirate Sir Henry Morgan is commissioned to rid the Caribbean of the rascally Blackbeard.

A farrago of action clichés with the star giving his eye-rolling all. The romantic element is dreary and the whole a shade bloodthirsty for family fare.

w Alan le May d Raoul Walsh ph William E. Snyder m Victor Young

Robert Newton, Linda Darnell, Keith Andes, William Bendix, Torin Thatcher, Irene Ryan, Alan Mowbray, Richard Egan

Blackbeard's Ghost
US   1967   107m   Technicolor
Walt Disney (Bill Walsh)
V, V*, L

The famous pirate returns as a ghost to help the old ladies who own a hotel he loved.

Ponderous and lengthy comedy, partially salvaged by performances.

w Bill Walsh, Don Da Gradi d Robert Stevenson ph Edward Colman m Robert F. Brunner

Peter Ustinov, Dean Jones, Suzanne Pleshette, Elsa Lanchester, Richard Deacon

The Blackbird
US   1925   70m at 24 fps   bw   silent
MGM

A Limehouse thief pretends to be a cripple, and after committing a murder finds that he is.

Standard star vehicle with recollections of several others.

wd Tod Browning

Lon Chaney, Renee Adoree, Owen Moore, Doris Lloyd

'I'm a teacher. My pupils are the kind you don't turn your back on, even in class!'
The Blackboard Jungle *
US   1955   101m   bw
MGM (Pandro S. Berman)
V*, L

In a slum school, a teacher finally gains the respect of his class of young hooligans.

Seminal fifties melodrama more notable for its introduction of 'Rock Around the Clock' behind the credits than for any intrinsic interest.

wd Richard Brooks novel Evan Hunter ph Russell Harlan m Bill Haley and the Comets ad Cedric Gibbons, Randall Duell ed Ferris Webster

Glenn Ford, Anne Francis, Louis Calhern, Margaret Hayes, John Hoyt, Richard Kiley, Emile Meyer, Warner Anderson, Basil Ruysdael, *Sidney Poitier*, Vic Morrow, Rafael Campos

'It could just as well have been the first good film of this kind. Actually, it will be remembered chiefly for its timely production and release.' – *G. N. Fenin, Film Culture*

AAN: Richard Brooks (as writer); Russell Harlan; art direction; editing

Blackhawk
US   1952   bw   serial: 15 eps
Columbia

An organization dedicated to the freedom of mankind uncovers a saboteur.

Fast-moving chapter play.

d Spencer Bennet

Kirk Alyn, Carol Forman, John Crawford, Michael Fox

Blackjack Ketchum, Desperado
US   1956   76m   bw
Columbia (Sam Katzman)

A former gunslinger turns sheriff and defeats the local badman.

Standard lower-case Western with predictable excitements.

w Luci Ward, Jack Natteford novel Louis L'Amour d Earl Bellamy

Howard Duff, Victor Jory, Maggie Mahoney, Angela Stevens

Blackmail ***
GB   1929   78m   bw
BIP (John Maxwell)
V, V*, L

A Scotland Yard inspector finds that his girl is involved in a murder; he conceals the fact and is blackmailed.

Hitchcock's first talkie is now a very hesitant entertainment but fully bears the director's stamp and will reward patient audiences in several excitingly staged sequences.

w Alfred Hitchcock, Benn W. Levy, Charles Bennett play Charles Bennett d Alfred Hitchcock ph Jack Cox md John Reynders m Campbell and Connelly, arranged Hubert Bath, Henry Stafford ad Wilfred and Norman Arnold ed Emile de Ruelle

Anny Ondra, Sara Allgood, John Longden, Charles Paton, Donald Calthrop, Cyril Ritchard

'Hitchcock's ending was to have been ironic, the detective seeing the cell door shut on the arrested girl, going home and then being asked if he was going out with his girlfriend that evening. His answer: "Not tonight." This was unacceptable commercially and a happy ending was substituted.' – *George Perry*

Blackmail
US   1939   81m   bw
MGM (John Considine Jnr)

A man is released from prison after serving a sentence for a crime he did not commit. Immediately a blackmailer pounces . . .

Co-feature drama for a star marking time; not bad in its way.

w David Hertz, William Ludwig d H. C. Potter ph Clyde de Vinna m David Snell, Edward Ward

Edward G. Robinson, Ruth Hussey, Gene Lockhart, Guinn Williams, Esther Dale

'The family circuit will accept it as sufficient entertainment for a suspenseful evening.' – *Variety*

Blackmailed
GB   1950   85m   bw
GFD/Harold Huth

Several victims of a blackmailer are involved in his murder.

Interestingly plotted and well cast melodrama which suffers from a flat script and production.

w Hugh Mills, Roger Vadim novel *Mrs Christopher* by Elizabeth Myers d Marc Allégret ph George Stretton m John Wooldridge

Dirk Bogarde, Mai Zetterling, Fay Compton, Robert Flemyng, Michael Gough, James Robertson Justice, Joan Rice, Wilfrid Hyde-White, Harold Huth

Blackout (1940): see *Contraband*

Blackout
GB   1950   73m   bw
Tempean/Eros

A man supposedly killed in an air crash turns out to be the head of a counterfeiting ring.

Fairly entertaining British support of its time.

w John Gilling d Robert S. Baker, Monty Berman

Dinah Sheridan, Maxwell Reed, Patrick Doonan, Eric Pohlmann

Blackwell's Island
US   1939   71m   bw
Warner (Bryan Foy)

A reporter goes to jail to get the goods on a smart gangster.

Forgettable exposé of the lighter kind.

w Crane Wilbur d William McGann ph Sid Hickox

John Garfield, Rosemary Lane, Dick Purcell, Victor Jory, Stanley Fields

'An exploitation natural . . . a portrayal of incredible events taken from real life.' – *Variety*

Blacula
US   1972   93m   Movielab
AIP (Joseph T. Naar)
V*, L

In 1815 in Transylvania, an African prince falls victim to Dracula. A hundred and fifty years later, his body is shipped to Los Angeles and accidentally revivified.

Jaded semi-spoof notable chiefly as the first black horror film. The star's performance is as stately as could be wished in the circumstances.

w Joan Torres, Raymond Koenig d William Crain ph John Stevens m Gene Page

William Marshall, Vonetta McGee, Denise Nicholas, Gordon Pinsent, Charles Macaulay

'A chilling, bold, mesmerizing, futuristic detective thriller.'
Blade Runner **
US   1982   117m   Technicolor   Panavision
Warner/Ladd/Blade Runner Partnership (Michael Deeley, Ridley Scott)
V, V*, L, S

Los Angeles, AD 2019; a licensed-to-kill policeman tracks down and destroys a group of intelligent robots who have hijacked a space shuttle and returned to Earth.

Gloomy futuristic thriller, looking like a firework display seen through thick fog, and for all the tiring tricks and expense adding up to little more than an updated Philip Marlowe case.

w Hampton Fancher, David People novel *Do Androids Dream of Electric Sheep?* by Philip K. Dick

d Ridley Scott   *ph* Jordan Cronenweth
m Vangelis   *pd* Lawrence G. Paull

Harrison Ford, Rutger Hauer, Sean Young, Edward James Olmos, M. Emmet Walsh, Daryl Hannah

'The sets are indeed impressive, but they are no compensation for a narrative so lame that it seems in need of a wheelchair.' – *Tom Milne, MFB*

'A richly detailed and visually overwhelming trip to 2019 which sticks with you like a recurrent nightmare.' – *Sunday Times*

'A massive assault on the senses which seems to have been launched from a madhouse equipped with all computerized mod cons.' – *Daily Mail*

'Glitteringly and atmospherically designed; but ultimately mechanics win out over philosophizing.' – *Sight and Sound*

† Ridley Scott's original cut of the film, which dispenses for the most part with the voice-over narration and has a different ending, was shown to general critical approval in 1991 and also released on video.

AAN: art direction; visual effects (Douglas Trumbull, Richard Yuricich, David Dryer)

Blake of Scotland Yard
US   1937   bw   serial: 15 eps
Victory

A munitions millionaire offers The Scorpion a fabulous sum to steal a death ray.

Just what you expect from an old-time serial.

d Bob Hill

Ralph Byrd, Joan Barclay, Dickie Jones, Herbert Rawlinson

'She's the hottest thing on the beach. She's also his best friend's daughter!'
Blame It on Rio
US   1983   100m   Metrocolor
Sherwood (Stanley Donen)
V, V*, L

A businessman is enlisted by his best friend to find his daughter's seducer, who is in fact himself.

Totally joyless and witless comedy with a South American background which is supposedly presumed to take away the bad taste.

w Charlie Peters, Larry Gelbart, from Claude Berri's 1977 film *Un Moment d'Egarement*   *d* Stanley Donen   *ph* Reynaldo Villalobos   *md* Ken Wannberg

Michael Caine, Joseph Bologna, Valerie Harper, Michelle Johnson

'Murder, mistresses, madness and mayhem ... It's all part of the service.'
Blame It on the Bellboy
GB   1992   78m   Technicolor
Warner/Bellboy/Hollywood Pictures (Jennifer Howarth)
V, V*, L

At a hotel in Venice, a bellboy confuses the identities of a hitman, a timid estate agent and a mayor who has arranged a romantic assignation.

Tired and tepid farce, given the performances it deserves.

wd Mark Herman   *ph* Andrew Dunn   *md* Guy Dagel   *pd* Gemma Jackson   *ed* Mike Ellis

Dudley Moore, Bryan Brown, Richard Griffiths, Andreas Katsulas, Patsy Kensit, Alison Steadman, Penelope Wilton, Bronson Pinchot, Lindsay Anderson

'A lightweight ensemble comedy that should check out fast from most hospices. Ingenious plotting is let down by weak dialog and stop-go direction that largely squanders the talent involved.' – *Variety*

Blame It on the Night
US   1984   85m   Technicolor
Tri-Star (Gene Taft)
V*

A rock star tries to make friends with the 13-year-old son he's only just met.

Resolutely uninteresting pattern play which slouches its way to a predictable ending.

w Len Jenkin   *d* Gene Taft   *ph* Alex Phillips *m* Ted Whitfield   *pd* Ted Haworth   *ed* Tony Lombardo

Nick Mancuso, Byron Thames, Leslie Ackerman, Dick Bakalyan

Blanche *
France   1971   92m   Eastmancolor
Telepresse/Abel et Charton (Dominique Duvergé, Philippe d'Argila)

In 13th-century France, a baron's beautiful young wife excites dark passions in her stepson and in the king.

An adult fairy tale full of symbols for those who seek them; but its main virtue is its highly decorative pictorialism.

wd Walerian Borowczyk   *novel* Mazepa by Juliusz Slowacki   *ph* Guy Durban   *m* 13th-century music

Ligia Branice, Michel Simon, Lawrence Trimble, Jacques Perrin

'Live-action *Jeux des Anges*, a brilliant, terrifying ballad of imprisonment.' – *Philip Strick, MFB*

Blanche Fury
GB   1948   95m   Technicolor
GFD/Cineguild (Anthony Havelock-Allan)
V

A governess marries a wealthy heir, then with a steward connives at his murder.

Chilly Victorian melodrama without much interest outside the decor: the actors have unplayable roles and the handling is very flat.

w Audrey Erskine Lindop, Hugh Mills, Cecil McGivern   *novel* Joseph Shearing   *d* Marc Allégret *ph* Guy Green, Geoffrey Unsworth   *m* Clifton Parker

Valerie Hobson, Stewart Granger, Walter Fitzgerald, Michael Gough, Maurice Denham, Sybilla Binder

Blaze *
US   1989   117m   DuArt
Warner/Touchstone/Silver Screen Partners IV/A & M (Gil Friesen, Dale Pollock)
V, V*, L

Earl Long, the governor of Louisiana, enjoys an affair with a stripper.

Warmed-over political scandal from the 1950s.

w Ron Shelton   *book* Blaze Starr by Blaze Starr, Huey Perry   *d* Ron Shelton   *ph* Haskell Wexler *m* Bennie Wallace   *pd* Armin Ganz   *ad* Edward Richardson   *ed* Robert Leighton, Adam Weiss

Paul Newman, Lolita Davidovich, Jerry Hardin, Gailard Sartain, Jeffrey DeMunn, Garland Bunting

'The combination of sex and political intrigue would probably be enough to make *Blaze* a winner, but Shelton's characteristically quirky perspective and surreal ear for dialogue propels the film into a higher league.' – *MFB*

AAN: best cinematography

'She kept her love for one – by sharing it with all!'
Blaze of Noon
US   1947   91m   bw
Paramount (John Farrow)

Three stunt-flyer brothers in the 20s leave their circus to start a commercial airline.

Predictable romantic drama with little flying: tragic pretensions, routine performances.

w Frank Wead, Arthur Sheekman   *d* John Farrow *ph* William C. Mellor   *m* Adolph Deutsch

William Holden, Anne Baxter, Sonny Tufts, Sterling Hayden, William Bendix, Howard da Silva

'So long as it sticks to stunt flying and mild comedy it is pleasant enough, but the last half, during which the obsessed brothers come one by one to grief and the little woman waits it out, gets pretty monotonous.' – *James Agee*

The Blazing Forest
US   1952   90m   Technicolor
Paramount/Pine—Thomas (William H. Pine, William C. Thomas)

A lady landowner has trouble with her rival timber bosses.

Fair period programmer.

w Lewis R. Foster, Winston Miller   *d* Edward Ludwig   *ph* Lionel Lindon   *m* Lucien Cailliet

John Payne, Agnes Moorehead, William Demarest, Richard Arlen, Susan Morrow, Roscoe Ates, Lynne Roberts

Blazing Magnum
Canada   1976   99m   colour   Panavision
Security Investment Trust Inc

A tough cop solves his sister's murder.

Tired rehash of the *Dirty Harry* formula, with plenty of violent action.

w Vincent Mann, Frank Clark   *d* Martin Herbert

Stuart Whitman, John Saxon, Martin Landau, Tisa Farrow, Gayle Hunnicutt, Carole Laure

'The stunts are well-managed and staged; the script, performances and direction make it unlikely that any viewer will care who survives them.' – *Scott Meek, MFB*

Blazing Saddles *
US   1974   93m   Technicolor   Panavision
Warner/Crossbow (Michael Herzberg)
V, V*, L

A black railroad worker and an alcoholic ex-gunfighter foil a crooked attorney and his henchmen.

Wild Western parody in which the action eventually shifts to the Warner backlot, after which the actors repair to Grauman's Chinese Theatre to find out what happened at the end of the story. At least as many misses as hits, and all aimed squarely at film buffs.

w Norman Steinberg, Mel Brooks, Andrew Bergman, Richard Pryor, Alan Unger   *d* Mel Brooks *ph* Joseph Biroc   *m* John Morris

Cleavon Little, Gene Wilder, Slim Pickens, Harvey Korman, Madeline Kahn, Mel Brooks, Burton Gilliam, Alex Karras

'One suspects that the film's gradual disintegration derives not from the makers' inability to end it, so much as from their inability to stop laughing at their own jokes.' – *Jan Dawson*

'A surfeit of chaos and a scarcity of comedy.' – *Judith Crist*

'"I just about got everything out of me," said Brooks, "all my furor, my frenzy, my insanity, my love of life and hatred of death." Audiences flocked to this insane affirmation of dancing girls, Hollywood production numbers, stomach gas around the campfire, and gallows humor. Brooks had found the perfect vehicle for the age.' – *Les Keyser, Hollywood in the Seventies*

AAN: Madeline Kahn; title song (*m* John Morris, *ly* Mel Brooks)

Blazing the Overland Trail
US   1952   bw   serial: 15 eps
Columbia

An unscrupulous outlaw raids wagon trains and blames the Indians.

One of the last of all serials, but by no means the best.
d Spencer Bennet

Lee Roberts, Dennis Moore, Norma Brooks, Gregg
Barton

Bleak Moments *
GB 1971 110m Eastmancolor
Autumn/Memorial/BFI (Leslie Blair)
V

Scenes from drab lives in a south London suburb.

Clearly not likely to appeal to the entertainment-
seeking masses, and undeniably overlong, this small
movie nevertheless has plenty of telling and even
amusing detail about life as most of us recognize it.

wd Mike Leigh *ph* Bahram Manoochehri
songs: Mike Bradwell

Anne Raitt, Sarah Stephenson, Eric Allan, Mike
Bradwell

'A prolonged poem to inhibitions, speechlessness,
and social unease.' – *John Coleman, New Statesman*

Die Blechtrommel: see *The Tin Drum*

Die Bleierne Zeit: see *The German Sisters*

Bless the Beasts and Children *
US 1971 110m colour
Columbia/Stanley Kramer
V*

Six boys on an adventure holiday try to free a herd of
buffalo earmarked for destruction.

Rather obviously pointed melodrama, well enough
done but not very interesting.

w Mac Benoff *novel* Glendon Swarthout
d Stanley Kramer

Bill Mumy, Barry Robins, Miles Chapin, Jesse White,
Ken Swofford

AAN: title song (*m/ly* Barry de Vorzon, Perry Botkin
Jnr)

Bless This House
GB 1972 89m Eastmancolor
Rank/Peter Rogers

A suburbanite's multifarious frustrations culminate in
preparations for his son's wedding.

This tedious spin-off from a TV sitcom virtually
abandons plot in favour of an endless series of
slapstick gags which could have been better
presented.

w Dave Freeman *d* Gerald Thomas

Sid James, Diana Coupland, Terry Scott, June
Whitfield, Peter Butterworth, Sally Geeson, Robin
Askwith, Bill Maynard

Blessed Event **
US 1932 84m bw
Warner (Ray Griffith)
V*

A gossip columnist gets himself into hot water.

Amusing vehicle for a fast-talking star, and quite an
interesting historical document.

w Howard Green *play* Manuel Seff, Forest Wilson
d Roy del Ruth *ph* Sol Polito

Lee Tracy, Ned Sparks, Mary Brian, Dick Powell, Ruth
Donnelly, Frank McHugh, Allen Jenkins

'A potential clean-up . . . a sustained hour and a half
or so of smart entertainment.' – *Variety*

'Quick and pacy and very likeable.' – *Pauline Kael, 70s*

† A historically interesting note was small-part actress
Emma Dunn's use of the expression 'Well I'll be
damned', which was technically forbidden at the
time.

Blighty *
GB 1926 93m (24 fps) bw silent
Gainsborough—Piccadilly (Michael Balcon, Carlyle Blackwell)

A chauffeur becomes an officer and after the war finds
himself looking after the master's family.

Fairly unwatchable in a normal sense, but of
historical interest as one of the key British films of the
twenties to make a comment about the war.

w Elliot Stannard, Charles McEvoy, Ivor Montagu
d Adrian Brunel

Jameson Thomas, Ellaline Terriss, Lilian Hall Davis,
Godfrey Winn, Wally Patch, Seymour Hicks

'It was, quietly, an anti-war picture rather than a pro-
war picture.' – *Adrian Brunel*

Blind Adventure
US 1933 65m bw
RKO

An American in London gets mixed up with
blackmailers and kidnappers.

Light-hearted but ill-explained second feature.

w Ruth Rose *d* Ernest B. Schoedsack *m* Max
Steiner

Robert Armstrong, Helen Mack, Roland Young, Ralph
Bellamy, John Miljan, Laura Hope Crews, Henry
Stephenson, Phyllis Barry

'Has some fine things but won't mean much more
than a programmer in the split spots.' – *Variety*

† The film seems to have been undertaken as a
diversion by the makers of *King Kong*.

Blind Alley **
US 1939 68m bw
Columbia

An escaped killer takes refuge in the home of a
psychiatrist, who explores his subconscious and
tames him.

Unusual lowercase thriller with effective dream
sequences; it was much imitated.

w Michael Blankfort, Albert Duffy *play* James
Warwick *d* Charles Vidor *ph* Lucien Ballard
m Morris Stoloff

Chester Morris, Ralph Bellamy, Ann Dvorak, Melville
Cooper, Rose Stradner, Marc Lawrence

'Psychoanalysis of a criminal provides a new twist to
what would otherwise be another crime picture of
general trend.' – *Variety*

'As un-Hollywood as anything that has come from
France this year.' – *New York Daily News*

'Survive a sticky ten minutes and you have a thriller
of quite unusual merit.' – *Graham Greene*

† Remake: *The Dark Past* (qv).

Blind Alley
US 1984 91m colour
Hemdale (Paul Kurta)
V*
aka: *Perfect Strangers*

A three-year-old witnesses a murder, and the hitman
responsible begins a relationship with the boy's
mother.

Lacklustre thriller, lacking in any tension or suspense.

wd Larry Cohen *ph* Paul Glickman *m* Dwight
Dixon *ed* Armond Lebowitz

Anne Carlisle, Brad Rijn, John Woehrle, Matthew
Stockley, Stephen Lack

'Abandon everything – even sex – to watch it . . . its
real power lies not in what we are shown but in what
we fear may happen. Interest never flags from the
grim beginning of this tale to its appalling climax.' –
Quentin Crisp

A Blind Bargain *
US 1922 60m approx bw silent
Goldwyn

A demented scientist creates an ape monster.

Interesting star vehicle, a precursor of many hokum
thrillers.

w J. G. Hawks *novel* The Octave of Claudius by Barry
Pain *d* Wallace Worsley

Lon Chaney, Jacqueline Logan, Raymond McKee,
Virginia True Boardman

Blind Date
US 1934 71m bw
Columbia

A working girl jilts a man because he is not the
marrying kind, then regrets it.

Tedious homespun drama.

w Ethel Hill *d* Roy Willian Neill

Ann Sothern, Neil Hamilton, Paul Kelly, Mickey
Rooney, Jane Darwell, Spencer Charters

'Vida Hurst is credited with the basic story, but a lot
of others used it before her. Used to be a favourite
with Corinne Griffith.' – *Variety*

Blind Date *
GB 1959 95m bw
Rank/Sydney Box/Independent Artists (David Deutsch)
US title: *Chance Meeting*

A young Dutch painter in London discovers his
mistress's body and finds himself in a web of deceit.

Tolerable, comparatively sophisticated murder puzzle;
rather glum looking, but the plot holds the interest.

w Ben Barzman, Millard Lampell *novel* Leigh
Howard *d* Joseph Losey *ph* Christopher Challis
m Richard Rodney Bennett

Hardy Kruger, Stanley Baker, Micheline Presle,
Robert Flemyng, Gordon Jackson, John Van Eyssen

Blind Date *
US 1987 93m Metrocolor
Tri-Star/Blake Edwards (Tony Adams)
V*, L, S

A company executive needs a date for a company
function, and takes a remote relative who turns out to
be an easy drunk.

One-note gag movie which spurs some laughs but
wears out its welcome.

w Dale Launer *d* Blake Edwards *ph* Harry
Stradling *m* Henry Mancini

Kim Basinger, Bruce Willis, John Larroquette,
William Daniels, Phil Hartman, Alice Hirson

'In short, hokey and hip – which in this case is a
foolproof formula.' – *Daily Variety*

The Blind Dead: see *Tombs of the Blind Dead*

Blind Fury
US 1989 86m Technicolor
Columbia TriStar (Daniel Grodnik, Tim Matheson)
V, V*, L

A blind martial arts expert takes on a drug dealer and
his gang.

Violent American variation on a Japanese samurai
series of the 1960s featuring Zatoichi the blind
swordsman, which gains nothing from being
transferred from the 1800s to present-day Los
Angeles.

w Charles Robert Carner *screenplay* Ryozo Kasahara
d Phillip Noyce *ph* Don Burgess *m* J. Peter
Robinson *pd* Peter Murton *ad* John Myhre
ed David Simmons

Rutger Hauer, Terrance O'Quinn, Brandon Call,
Noble Willingham, Lisa Blount, Nick Cassavetes, Rick
Overton, Randall 'Tex' Cobb

The Blind Goddess
GB   1947   88m   bw
Gainsborough (Betty Box)

The private secretary to a public figure finds that his idol has feet of clay, and suffers in court for his discovery.

Courtroom drama from an old-fashioned stage play: surefire for addicts, but routine as a film.

w Muriel and Sydney Box   play Patrick Hastings
d Harold French   ph Ray Elton

Eric Portman, Anne Crawford, Hugh Williams, Michael Denison, Nora Swinburne, Claire Bloom, Raymond Lovell, Frank Cellier

Blind Husbands **
US   1919   90m approx (24 fps)   bw   silent
Universal (Erich von Stroheim)

An Austrian officer, on holiday in the Alps, seduces the wife of a rich American.

Stroheim's first comedy of sexual manners, now of mainly archival interest.

wd Erich von Stroheim   ph Ben Reynolds   ad Erich von Stroheim

Erich von Stroheim, Sam de Grasse, Gibson Gowland, Francella Billington

Blind Man's Buff
GB   1936   72m   bw
Present Day/Fox British

A doctor jealous of his wife does not reveal the fact that he has been cured of blindness.

Yawnworthy melodrama.

w Cecil Maiden   play Smoked Glasses by William Foster, B. Scott-Elder   d Albert Parker   ph Roy Kellino

Basil Sydney, James Mason, Enid Stamp-Taylor, Barbara Greene, Iris Ashley

Blind Man's Bluff (1968): see
Cauldron of Blood

'No Witness, No Evidence, No Way Out.'
Blind Side
US   1993   CFI colour
HBO (Jay Roewe)
V, V*

Returning from Mexico, a couple run over a cop and leave his apparently dead body by the roadside; later, a stranger who claims to have witnessed the accident turns up to blackmail them.

A non-too-serious variation on the familiar theme of the psychopath who comes to call, with over-the-top performances and a parody of a spaghetti Western to add a little novelty.

w Stewart Lindh, Solomon Weingarten, John Carlen
d Geoff Murphy   ph Paul Elliott   m Brian May
pd Nina Ruscio   ed Rick Shaine

Rutger Hauer, Rebecca DeMornay, Ron Silver, Jonathan Banks, Mariska Hargitay, Tamara Clatterbuck

'A cracking thriller combining an ingenious script, effective direction and good acting.' – Sight and Sound

Blind Terror
GB   1971   89m   colour
Columbia/Filmways/Genesis (Basil Appleby)
V
US title: See No Evil

A blind girl is the sole, hunted survivor of a maniac's rampage on a lonely estate.

Shocks, screams and starts fill a cliché-ridden but still effective script which is faithfully turned into a competent but routine heart-stopper.

w Brian Clemens   d Richard Fleischer   ph Gerry Fisher   m Elmer Bernstein

Mia Farrow, Robin Bailey, Dorothy Alison, Diane Grayson, Norman Eshley, Brian Rawlinson

'For those who like to watch folks pull the wings off flies.' – Judith Crist

Blindfold **
US   1965   102m   Technicolor   Panavision
Universal (Marvin Schwartz)

A society psychiatrist is enlisted by the CIA to make regular blindfold journeys to a secret destination where he treats a neurotic physicist. Discovering that his contacts are really enemy agents, he tracks down the destination by sound and guesswork, and routs the villains.

Lively spy spoof with rather too much knockabout between the Hitchcockian suspense sequences; it has indeed the air of a script which Hitchcock rejected, but provides reliable entertainment.

w Philip Dunne, W. H. Menger   novel Lucille Fletcher   d Philip Dunne   ph Joseph MacDonald
m Lalo Schifrin

Rock Hudson, Claudia Cardinale, Jack Warden, Guy Stockwell, Brad Dexter

Blindman (dubbed)
US/Italy   1971   96m   Technicolor   Techniscope
Fox-Rank/ABKCO/Primex (Tony Anthony, Saul Swimmer)

A blind man goes in search of 50 mail-order brides who have been stolen by a bandit and his gang.

Comic spaghetti Western in which the only point of interest, apart from its bizarre hero, lies in seeing a former Beatle in the role of a Mexican outlaw.

w Tony Anthony, Piero Anchisi, Vincenzo Cerami
story Tony Anthony   d Ferdinando Baldi
ph Riccardo Pallottino   m Stelvio Cipriani
ad Gastone Garsetti   ed Roberto Perpignani

Tony Anthony, Ringo Starr, Agneta Eckemyr, Lloyd Batista, Magda Konopka, Raf Baldassare

'Indistinguishable from the ruck in its crude direction, garbled plot, obsessive violence, variable technical achievements, and pot-pourri cast and acting styles.' – Tom Milne, MFB

† The original version of the film ran for 105m.

Bliss *
Australia   1985   111m   colour
Entertainment (Anthony Buckley)
V, V*, L

After a heart attack, an advertising executive realises the rottenness of his wife and children and seeks happiness elsewhere.

Energetic black comedy, intermittently entertaining, that won awards in its home country.

w Ray Lawrence, Peter Carey   novel Peter Carey
d Ray Lawrence   ph Paul Murphy   m Peter Best
ad Owen Paterson   ed Wayne Leclos

Barry Otto, Lynette Curran, Helen Jones, Miles Buchanan, Gia Carides, Tim Robertson, Jeff Truman, Bryan Marshall

The Bliss of Mrs Blossom
GB   1968   93m   Technicolor
Paramount (Josef Shaftel)
V*

The wife of a bra manufacturer keeps her lover in the attic.

Silly, wild-eyed sex comedy decorated with the flashy tinsel of swinging London's dying fall.

w Alec Coppel, Denis Norden   d Joe McGrath
ph Geoffrey Unsworth   m Riz Ortolani
pd Assheton Gorton

Richard Attenborough, Shirley Maclaine, James Booth, Freddie Jones, William Rushton, Bob Monkhouse, Patricia Routledge

Blithe Spirit ***
GB   1945   96m   Technicolor
Two Cities/Cineguild (Anthony Havelock-Allan)
V, V*

A cynical novelist's second marriage is disturbed when the playful ghost of his first wife materializes during a séance.

Direction and acting carefully preserve a comedy which on its first West End appearance in 1941 achieved instant classic status. The repartee scarcely dates, and altogether this is a most polished job of film-making.

w Noël Coward   play Noël Coward   scenario David Lean, Anthony Havelock-Allan, Ronald Neame
d David Lean   ph Ronald Neame   m Richard Addinsell

Rex Harrison, Kay Hammond, Constance Cummings, Margaret Rutherford, Hugh Wakefield, Joyce Carey, Jacqueline Clark

'Ninety minutes of concentrated, cultivated fun.' – C. A. Lejeune

† After seeing this, Noël Coward reputedly told Rex Harrison: 'After me you're the best light comedian in the world.'

Blitz on Britain *
GB   1960   71m   bw
Anglo-Continental/British Lion

A very acceptable record of the Battle of Britain as it affected the home front, narrated by Alistair Cooke.

w Patrick Brawn   d/ed Harry Booth

'Indescribable . . . Indestructible! Nothing Can Stop It!'
The Blob
US   1958   83m   DeLuxe
Tonylyn/Jack H. Harris
V, V*, L

A small town combats a slimy space invader.

Padded hokum for drive-ins, with a few effective moments.

w Theodore Simonson, Kate Phillips   d Irwin S. Yeaworth Jnr   ph Thomas Spalding   m Ralph Carmichael

Steve McQueen, Aneta Corseaut, Olin Howlin, Earl Rowe

'Classic teen horror which really sums up the spirit of 50s drive-in movies.' – The Dark Side

† Sequel 1971: Beware! The Blob (aka Son of Blob).

The Blob
US   1988   92m   Technicolor
Tri-Star (Jack H. Harris/Elliott Kastner)
V, V*, L

Fifties sci-fi horror dressed up for the 80s.

w Chuck Russell, Frank Darabout   d Chuck Russell
ph Mark Irwin   m Michael Hoenig   pd Craig Stearns   ed Terry Stokes, Tod Feuerman

Shawnee Smith, Kevin Dillon, Donovan Leitch, Jeffrey de Munn, Candy Clark, Joe Seneca

'A great B-movie with an A-pic budget.' – Variety

Blockade *
US   1938   84m   bw
Walter Wanger

During the Spanish Civil War, a peace-loving young farmer has to take up arms to defend his land.

Much touted as Hollywood's first serious contribution to international affairs, this dogged drama was in fact so bland that audiences had difficulty ascertaining which side it was on, especially as neither Franco nor the Fascists were mentioned. As a romantic action drama, however, it passed muster.

w John Howard Lawson   d William Dieterle
ph Rudolph Maté   m Werner Janssen

Henry Fonda, Madeleine Carroll, Leo Carrillo, John Halliday, Vladimir Sokoloff, Robert Warwick, Reginald Denny

'It misses any claim to greatness because it pulls its punches . . . and it's going to be tough to sell.' – *Variety*

'The film has a curious unreality considering the grim reality behind it.' – *Frank S. Nugent*

'There is achieved a deadly numb level of shameless hokum out of which anything true or decent rises only for a second to confound itself.' – *Otis Ferguson*

† Original publicity carried this disclaimer:NOTE: Care has been taken to prevent any costume of the production from being accurately that of either side in the Spanish Civil War. The story does not attempt to favour any cause in the present conflict.

AAN: John Howard Lawson; Werner Janssen

Blockheads ***
US   1938   60m   bw
Hal Roach/Stan Laurel
V, V (C), V*

Twenty years after World War I, Stan is still guarding a trench because nobody told him to stop. Olly takes him home to meet the wife, with disastrous consequences.

The last first-class Laurel and Hardy comedy is shapeless but hilarious, a fragmented reworking of earlier ideas, all of which work beautifully. Gags include encounters with a tip-up truck and an automatic garage, and a brilliantly worked out sequence up and down several flights of stairs.

w James Parrott, Harry Langdon, Felix Adler, Charles Rogers, Arnold Belgard   d John G. Blystone   ph Art Lloyd   m Marvin Hatley

Stan Laurel, Oliver Hardy, Billy Gilbert, Patricia Ellis, Minna Gombell, James Finlayson

'Hodge-podge of old-fashioned slapstick and hoke.' – *Variety*

AAN: Marvin Hatley

Den Blodiga Tiden: see *Mein Kampf*

Blonde Bombshell: see *Bombshell*

Blonde Crazy *
US   1931   74m   bw
Warner
V*, L
GB title: *Larceny Lane*

A bellhop and a chambermaid set out to fleece all-comers.

Smart con man comedy with the star in excellent form.

w Kubec Glasmon, John Bright   d Roy del Ruth   ph Sid Hickox

James Cagney, Joan Blondell, Ray Milland, Louis Calhern, Guy Kibbee, Polly Walters, Charles Lane, Maude Eburne

'Naughty cracks galore, and one says "Nuts". But he doesn't push a grapefruit in the girlfriend's face, though they expect it any time.' – *Variety*

'A chipper, hard-boiled, amusing essay in petty thieving.' – *Time*

Blonde Fever
US   1944   69m   bw
MGM

A middle-aged husband falls for a blonde waitress.

Very ho-hum comedy on familiar lines.

w Patricia Coleman   play Ferenc Molnar   d Richard Whorf

Philip Dorn, Mary Astor, Gloria Grahame, Felix Bressart, Marshall Thompson, Curt Bois

Blonde Fist
GB   1991   102m   colour
Blue Dolphin/Film Four (Christopher Figg, Joseph D'Morais)

The fighting daughter of a bare-knuckle boxer goes in search of her father and of a new life.

Brain-damaged knockabout comedy.

wd Frank Clarke   ph Bruce McGowan   m Alan Gill   pd Colin Pocock   ed Brian Peachey

Margi Clarke, Carroll Baker, Ken Hutchinson, Sharon Power, Angela Clarke, Lewis Bester

The Blonde from Peking
US/France   1968   80m   colour
Paramount

The CIA thinks that a girl with amnesia may know Chinese nuclear secrets.

Witless international spy stuff, neither funny nor thrilling.

w Nicolas Gessner and Marc Behm   story James Hadley Chase   d Nicolas Gessner

Mireille Darc, Claudio Brook, Edward G. Robinson, Pascale Roberts

A Blonde in Love: see *Loves of a Blonde*

Blonde Sinner: see *Yield to the Night*

'What could she do but flee from love? She loved two men at once!'

Blonde Venus *
US   1932   97m   bw
Paramount
V*

A German café singer marries an English research chemist, but their marriage doesn't run smoothly.

Rather dreary, fragmented star vehicle with good moments, notably the star's opening appearance as a gorilla.

w Jules Furthman, S. K. Lauren   d Josef von Sternberg   ph Bert Glennon   m Oscar Potoker

Marlene Dietrich, Herbert Marshall, Cary Grant, Dickie Moore

'Weak story, inept direction and generally sluggish total count heavily against it . . . it'll require plenty of bally.' – *Variety*

'The story has all the dramatic integrity of a sashweight murderer's tabloid autobiography.' – *Pare Lorentz*

'There is more pleasure for the eye in *Blonde Venus* than in a hundred of its fellows. But what does beauty ornament? The story of a wife who becomes a kept woman for the sake of her husband, and a prostitute for the sake of her child.' – *Forsyth Hardy, Cinema Quarterly*

Blondes for Danger
GB   1938   68m   bw
British Lion/Herbert Wilcox

A cockney taxi driver takes an unwanted fare and becomes involved in a deep dark plot.

Modest but effective star vehicle.

w Gerald Elliott   novel *Red for Danger* by Evadne Price   d Jack Raymond

Gordon Harker, Enid Stamp-Taylor, Ivan Brandt

Blondie *
US   1938   68m   bw
Columbia
V*

Misadventures of a harassed suburban family man.

Dagwood Bumstead and his wife Blondie were Mr and Mrs Small Town America throughout the thirties and forties, and received their perfect screen incarnations in this unambitious but quite watchable

series, which provided familiar and often quite observant fun.

w Richard Flournoy   comic strip Chic Young   d Frank R. Strayer   ph Henry Freulich

Arthur Lake, Penny Singleton, Larry Simms, Daisy the Dog, Jonathan Hale (as the boss, Mr Dithers), Gene Lockhart, Ann Doran, Irving Bacon (as the mailman)

'Light fare, but universal in appeal . . . could be clicko series.' – *Variety*Other episodes were as follows:

1939: BLONDIE MEETS THE BOSS, BLONDIE TAKES A VACATION, BLONDIE BRINGS UP BABY
1940: BLONDIE ON A BUDGET, BLONDIE HAS SERVANT TROUBLE, BLONDIE PLAYS CUPID
1941: BLONDIE GOES LATIN, BLONDIE IN SOCIETY
1942: BLONDIE GOES TO COLLEGE, BLONDIE'S BLESSED EVENT, BLONDIE FOR VICTORY
1943: IT'S A GREAT LIFE, FOOTLIGHT GLAMOUR
1945: LEAVE IT TO BLONDIE
1946: BLONDIE KNOWS BEST, LIFE WITH BLONDIE, BLONDIE'S LUCKY DAY
1947: BLONDIE'S BIG MOMENT, BLONDIE'S HOLIDAY, BLONDIE IN THE DOUGH, BLONDIE'S ANNIVERSARY
1948: BLONDIE'S REWARD
1949: BLONDIE'S SECRET, BLONDIE'S BIG DEAL, BLONDIE HITS THE JACKPOT
1950: BLONDIE'S HERO, BEWARE OF BLONDIE

† TV series were started in the fifties and sixties, but both failed.

Blondie Johnson
US   1933   67m   bw
Warner

The career of a female larcenist who eventually takes her medicine.

Competent programmer very typical of its studio and year.

w Earl Baldwin   d Ray Enright

Joan Blondell, Chester Morris, Allen Jenkins, Claire Dodd

'After she departs for the pen, she lets the public in on the fact that crime doesn't pay. Neither will the picture.' – *Variety*

Blondie of the Follies *
US   1932   97m   bw
MGM (Marion Davies)

Two New York showgirls graduate from tenements to luxury.

Adequate comedy-melodrama with an interesting cast and good dialogue.

w Frances Marion, Anita Loos   d Edmund Goulding   ph George Barnes   m William Axt

Marion Davies, Jimmy Durante, Robert Montgomery, Billie Dove, James Gleason, ZaSu Pitts, Sidney Toler, Douglass Dumbrille

'Not bad, but not very good, with chances that it will just get by. Length and slow pace the drawbacks. . .. It isn't padded out, it's just flatfooted.' – *Variety*

'An unjustly forgotten film.' – *New Yorker, 1979*

Blood Alley
US   1955   115m   Warnercolor   Cinemascope
Warner/Batjac (no producer credited)
V*, L

An American sailor is helped by local people to escape from a Chinese jail; he then escorts them to Hong Kong.

Rudimentary anti-Red heroics with expensive spectacle punctuating a tacky script.

w A. S. Fleischmann   *novel* A. S. Fleischmann
d William Wellman   *ph* William H. Clothier
m Roy Webb   *pd* Alfred Ybarra

John Wayne, Lauren Bacall, Paul Fix, Joy Kim, Berry Kroeger, Mike Mazurki, Anita Ekberg

'Becomes A Terror House Of Blood!'
'Guaranteed! The 8 Greatest Shocks Ever Filmed!'

Blood and Black Lace

Italy   1964   90m   Eastmancolor
Emmepi
V*

original title: *Sei Donne per l'Assassino*

Six women are nastily murdered in a fashion house.

Vaguely necrophiliac but trendy suspense-horror flick in the wake of *Psycho*.

w Marcel Fondato, Giuseppe Barilla, Mario Bava
d Mario Bava

Cameron Mitchell, Thomas Reiner, Mary Arden

'The wooden nature of the script and performances makes it hard to get into the complicated narrative. Don't bother. Just settle back and enjoy the sex and violence.' – *The Dark Side*

Blood and Roses

France/Italy   1960   87m   colour   Technirama
Eger/Documento (Raymond Eger)
V*

original title: *Et Mourir de Plaisir*

Carmilla takes on the vampiric personality of her ancestress Millarca, whom she closely resembles.

A rather half-hearted attempt to make an elegant horror story; boring rather than charming or frightening.

w Claude Brûlé, Claude Martin, Roger Vadim
d Roger Vadim   *ph* Claude Renoir   *m* Jean Prodromidès

Mel Ferrer, Elsa Martinelli, Annette Vadim, Marc Allégret

Blood and Sand *

US   1922   80m (24 fps)   bw   silent
Paramount
V*, L

A matador falls under the spell of an aristocratic woman.

Elegant star vehicle which established his image.

w June Mathis   *novel* Vicente Blasco Ibanez
d Fred Niblo

Rudolph Valentino, Nita Naldi, Lila Lee, Walter Long

'Love flamed in the shadow of death!'

Blood and Sand *

US   1941   123m   Technicolor
TCF (Darryl F. Zanuck, Robert T. Kane)
V, V*, S

Rather boring remake, fine to look at but dramatically deadly.

w Jo Swerling   *novel* Vicente Blasco Ibanez
d Rouben Mamoulian   *ph* Ernest Palmer, Ray Rennahan   *m* Alfred Newman   *ad* Richard Day, Joseph C. Wright

Tyrone Power, Rita Hayworth, Linda Darnell, Nazimova, Anthony Quinn, J. Carrol Naish, John Carradine, Lynn Bari, Laird Cregar, Monty Banks

AA: Ernest Palmer, Ray Rennahan

AAN: Richard Day, Joseph C. Wright

Blood Beach

US   1980   90m   colour
Miracle/Empress (Steven Nalevansky)
V*

A monster, lurking beneath the sand of a beach, swallows passers-by.

Dull, lethargic, low-budget variation on *Jaws*; not only could they not afford much of a monster, they also skimped on the script and actors.

w Jeffrey Bloom   *story* Jeffrey Bloom, Steven Nalevansky   *d* Jeffrey Bloom   *ph* Steve Poster
m Gil Mellé   *ad* William Sandell   *ed* Gary Griffen

David Huffman, Mariana Hill, John Saxon, Otis Young, Stefan Gierasch, Burt Young

'It's so slow and boring, just like a bad television movie.' – *The Dark Side*

Blood Beast from Outer Space: see *The Night Caller*

The Blood Beast Terror

GB   1967   88m   Eastmancolor
Tigon (Arnold L. Miller, Tony Tenser)

A Victorian entomologist creates human beings who can change themselves into monster death's-head moths.

Unpersuasive and totally idiotic cheapjack horror fare.

w Peter Bryan   *d* Vernon Sewell   *ph* Stanley A. Long   *m* Paul Ferris

Robert Flemyng, Peter Cushing, Wanda Ventham, Vanessa Howard, David Griffin, John Paul, Kevin Stoney, Roy Hudd

The Blood Demon

West Germany   1967   76m   colour
New Realm/Constantin (Wolfgang Kuehnlenz)
V*

original title: *Die Schlangengrube und das Pendel*; aka: *The Torture Chamber of Dr Sadism*

An aristocrat dismembered after killing 12 virgins returns from the dead to kill a 13th and achieve immortality.

An extremely free adaptation of Poe, given over to narrative incoherence and startling images.

w Manfred R. Koehler   *story* The Pit and the Pendulum by Edgar Allan Poe   *d* Harald Reinl
ph Ernst W. Kalinke

Christopher Lee, Lex Barker, Karin Dor, Carl Lange, Vladimir Medar, Christiane Rucker, Dieter Eppler

Blood Feud

Italy   1979   112m   Technospes
ITC/Liberty Films (Harry Columbo)
V*

aka: *Revenge*

In Sicily, as the fascists come to power, a rich socialist lawyer and a small-time crook court the same vengeful woman.

Unsatisfactory, melodramatic mix of romance and politics.

wd Lina Wertmuller   *ph* Tonino Delli Colli
m Dangio-Nando de Luca   *ad* Enrico Job
ed Franco Fraticelli

Sophia Loren, Marcello Mastroianni, Giancarlo Giannini, Mario Scarpetta

Blood from the Mummy's Tomb *

GB   1971   94m   Technicolor
MGM-EMI/Hammer (Howard Brandy)

Twenty years after a female mummy is brought back to England, members of the expedition are killed one by one, and their leader's daughter is possessed by the spirit of the dead princess.

Interesting but over-complicated and hard-to-enjoy attempt to maintain the mummy saga without an actual marauding mummy. Intelligently handled but sadly lacking in a sense of humour.

w Christopher Wicking   *novel* Jewel of the Seven Stars by Bram Stoker   *d* Seth Holt, Michael Carreras
ph Arthur Grant   *m* Tristam Cary   *ad* Scott MacGregor   *ed* Peter Weatherley

Andrew Keir, Valerie Leon, James Villiers, Hugh Burden, George Coulouris, Mark Edwards, Rosalie Crutchley, Aubrey Morris, David Markham

'Makes the genre seem like new.' – *Tony Rayns*

† Seth Holt died while the shooting was still incomplete, and Michael Carreras took over for the last few days.

Blood In, Blood Out **

US   1992   180m   Technicolor
Buena Vista/Hollywood Pictures/Touchstone Pacific Partners I (Taylor Hackford, Jerry Gershwin)
V, V*, L, S

A decade in the life of three Chicanos, two half-brothers and their half-white cousin, caught up in gang warfare on the streets and in prison.

Tough, violent, gripping drama of oppression and redemption in the East Los Angeles barrio, depicting an aspect of America not often seen on-screen; its length is justified not only by its narrative drive but by the fleshing out of individual lives caught in a destructive system.

w Jimmy Santiago Baca, Jeremy Iacone, Floyd Mutrux   *story* Ross Thomas   *d* Taylor Hackford
ph Gabriel Beristain   *m* Bill Conti   *pd* Bruno Rubeo   *ed* Fredric Steinkamp, Karl F. Steinkamp

Jesse Borrego, Benjamin Bratt, Enrique Castillo, Damian Chapa, Delroy Lindo, Tom Wilson, Karmin Murcelo, Ving Rames, Jenny Gago

'Triumphs over cliché to sustain its vast length and space. The key to this success lies in its epic size, a mood and a scale more akin to a mini-series than grandiose cinema.' – *Olly Blackburn, Sight and Sound*

'Seems compelled to say something profound but too often stands on a soapbox to do it.' – *Variety*

Blood Is My Heritage: see *Blood of Dracula*

Blood Money *

US   1933   66m   bw
Fox/Darryl F. Zanuck

The decline of a bail-bond racketeer.

Smartly made melodrama with good work all round.

wd Rowland Brown

George Bancroft, Judith Anderson, Chick Chandler, Frances Dee, Blossom Seeley

Blood Money (1962): see Requiem for a Heavyweight

Blood Oath

Australia   1990   108m   Eastmancolor
Rank/Sovereign/Village Roadshow/Siege (Graham Burke, Greg Coote, John Tarnoff)
V

In 1946, an Australian Army captain prosecutes the Japanese commandant of a camp where the bodies of more than 300 prisoners were discovered in a mass grave.

A routine courtroom drama of no particular interest, despite its factual basis.

w Denis Whitburn, Brian A. Williams   *d* Stephen Wallace   *ph* Russell Boyd   *m* David McHugh
ad Virginia Bieneman   *ed* Nicholas Beauman, Bernard Hides

Bryan Brown, George Takei, Terry O'Quinn, John Bach, Toshi Shioya, John Clarke, Deborah Unger, Jason Donovan

'Reduces the moral complexities of war to the simplest *Boy's Own* level.' – *Sight and Sound*

The Blood of a Poet **

France   1931   58m   bw
Vicomte de Noailles
V, V*

original title: *Le Sang d'un Poète*

Aspects of a poet's vision, taking place while a chimney is falling down.

An indescribable film full of striking imagery which may, or may not, be meaningful. Its author claims that it is not surrealist, but that label for most people will do as well as any other.

wd Jean Cocteau *ph* Georges Périnal *m* Georges Auric *ad* Jean Gabriel d'Aubonne

Lee Miller, Enrique Rivero, Pauline Carton, Feral Benga, Jean Desbordes, Barbette, Odette Talazac

'It must be placed among the classic masterpieces of the seventh art.' – *Revue du Cinéma*

'In her eyes Desire! In her veins the blood of a ... Monster!'
Blood of Dracula
US   1957   68m   bw
Anglo Amalgamated/Carmel/AIP (Herman Cohen)
V
GB title: *Blood Is My Heritage*; aka: *Blood of the Demon*

A feminist high-school chemistry teacher hypnotizes an unhappy student into becoming a vampire to prove that men control, and will destroy, the world.

Risible mix of horror and teenage rebellion movies that does not miss a cliché of either genre.

w Ralph Thornton   *d* Herbert L. Strock
ph Monroe Askins   *m* Paul Dunlap   *ad* Leslie Thomas   *sp* Philip Scheer   *ed* Robert Moore

Sandra Harrison, Louise Lewis, Gail Ganley, Jerry Blaine, Heather Ames, Malcolm Atterbury, Mary Adams

† With a change in gender for the leading characters and a different monster, the script was recycled by Thornton as *I Was a Teenage Werewolf*.

Blood of the Demon: see Blood of Dracula

Blood of the Dragon
Japan   1974   88m   Eastmancolor
Eural/Toei-Kyoto Eiga/Titan (Norimichi Matsudaira)
V
original title: *Satsujinken 2*

Double-crossed by his employers, who front for the Mafia, an assassin goes on the rampage.

Convoluted martial arts mayhem that makes little narrative sense; but then all that matters is its fights.

w Hajime Takaiwa, Shigehiro Ozawa   *story* Koji Yakada   *d* Sonny Chiba, Gerald Yamada, Doris Nakajima, Tony Cetera, Tatsuro Endo, Masashi Ishibashi   *m* Tony Tsushima   *ad* Tokumichi Igawa   *ed* Kozo Horiike

Sonny Chiba, Yoko Ichiji, Masafumi Suzuki, Kaoru Nakajima, Naoki Shima, Masashi Ishibashi

Blood of the Undead: see Schizo

Blood of the Vampire
GB   1958   85m   Eastmancolor
Baker-Berman/Artistes Alliance
V*

A doctor, raised from the dead, takes over an asylum and experiments on the inmates.

Heavy-handed, crudely made horror comic.

w Jimmy Sangster   *d* Henry Cass   *ph* Geoffrey Seaholm

Donald Wolfit, Barbara Shelley, Vincent Ball, Victor Maddern, Andrew Faulds

Blood on His Lips: see The Hideous Sun Demon

Blood on My Hands: see Kiss the Blood Off My Hands

Blood on Satan's Claw
GB   1970   93m   Eastmancolor
Tigon-Chilton (Tony Tenser, Malcolm B. Heyworth, Peter L. Andrews)
V*
aka: *Satan's Skin*

A devil's claw wreaks havoc among children in a 17th-century English village.

Moderately frightening, rather silly but at least original period horror comic.

w Robert Wynne-Simmons   *d* Piers Haggard
ph Dick Bush   *m* Marc Wilkinson

Patrick Wymark, Linda Hayden, Barry Andrews, Avice Landon, Simon Williams, Tamara Ustinov, Anthony Ainley

Blood on the Arrow
US   1964   91m   DeLuxe
Leon Fromkess/Allied Artists

An outlaw is the only survivor of an Indian raid, and later becomes a hero when the Indians attack again.

Unremarkable Western, with every turn of plot to order.

w Robert E. Kent   *d* Sidney Salkow

Dale Robertson, Martha Hyer, Wendell Corey, Paul Mantee, Ted de Corsia

Blood on the Moon *
US   1948   88m   bw
RKO (Sid Rogell, Theron Warth)
V*

A homesteader finds that his best friend is the villainous leader of a group of cattlemen.

Good-looking but rather pedestrian Western, generally well handled.

w Lillie Hayward   *novel Gunman's Choice* by Luke Short   *d* Robert Wise   *ph* Nicholas Musuraca   *m* Roy Webb

Robert Mitchum, Barbara Bel Geddes, Robert Preston, Walter Brennan

Blood on the Streets: see Borsalino & Co

Blood on the Sun *
US   1945   94m   bw
Cagney Productions (William Cagney)
V*, L

In the twenties, the American editor of a Tokyo newspaper reveals a Japanese militarist plan for world conquest.

Satisfactory star actioner with good production and exciting highlights.

w Lester Cole   *d* Frank Lloyd   *ph* Theodor Sparkuhl   *m* Miklos Rozsa   *ad* Wiard Ihnen

James Cagney, Sylvia Sidney, Wallace Ford, Rosemary de Camp, Robert Armstrong, John Emery, Leonard Strong, Frank Puglia

'It ought to be fine for those who enjoy a good ninety-minute massacre.' – *New Yorker*

'Tough, hard-hitting and explosive, with just enough rudimentary suspense.' – *Bosley Crowther*

'Pure unadulterated melodrama has a safe niche in cinematic offerings, but this folderol is more pretentious than persuasive.' – *Howard Barnes*

AA: Wiard Ihnen

Blood Relatives
Canada/France   1977   100m   colour   Panavision
Classic/Cinevideo/Filmel (Denis Heroux, Eugene Lepecier)
V*
aka: *Les Liens du Sang*

A 15-year-old girl accuses her brother of murdering their 17-year-old cousin.

Dull psychological thriller, with stock characters and showing none of the flair that Chabrol has exhibited when examining the French middle classes under pressure.

w Claude Chabrol, Sydney Banks   *novel* Ed McBain   *d* Claude Chabrol   *ph* Jean Rabier   *m* Howard Blake   *pd* Anne Pritchard   *ed* Yves Langlois

Donald Sutherland, Stephane Audran, Micheline Lanctot, Aude Landry, Lisa Langlois, Laurent Malet, Donald Pleasence, David Hemmings

Blood Simple *
US   1983   99m   DuArt
Palace/River Road (Ethan Coen)
V, V*, L

A saloon owner hires a hit man to kill his unfaithful wife and her lover, but the plot rebounds on him.

Yet another variation on *The Postman Always Rings Twice*, and one with strong moments.

w Joel and Ethan Coen   *d* Joel Coen   *ph* Barry Sonnenfeld   *m* Carter Burwell   *pd* Jane Musky   *ed* Roderick Jaynes, Don Wiegmann, Peggy Connolly

John Getz, Frances McDormand, Dan Hedaya, M. Emmet Walsh

Blood Sisters: see Sisters

Bloodbath at the House of Death
GB   1983   92m   colour
EMI/Wildwood (Ray Cameron)

Scientists investigate a haunted house.

Spoof tailored to the requirements of a zany television comedian who never knows when enough is enough. Too much gore and far too much smut.

w Ray Cameron, Barry Cryer   *d* Ray Cameron   *ph* Brian West, Dusty Miller   *m* Mike Moran, Mark London

Kenny Everett, Pamela Stephenson, Vincent Price, Gareth Hunt, Don Warrington, John Fortune, Sheila Steafel, Graham Stark

'Presumably intended as high camp; looks like low-grade *Carry On*.' – *Martyn Auty, MFB*

Bloodbath Bay of Death: see A Bay of Blood

Bloodbrothers
US   1978   116m   Technicolor
Warner/Stephen Friedman/Kings Road
V*

The disintegration through failure and inadequacy of a noisy Italian-American family.

The kind of self-indulgence that has one seeking the exit before it's half over.

w Walter Newman   *novel* Richard Price   *d* Robert Mulligan   *ph* Robert Surtees   *m* Elmer Bernstein   *pd* Gene Callahan

Paul Sorvino, Tony Lo Bianco, Richard Gere, Lelia Goldoni

'The director is trying for something crude, powerful, volatile ... but it goes terribly wrong. People laugh with hysterical heartiness, or say things like: "Life can hurt. It's made me feel close to all those doing the hurting dance."' – *Pauline Kael, New Yorker*

AAN: Walter Newman

Bloodfist
US   1989   85m   colour
Concorde (Roger Corman)
V*

A kick-boxer seeks to avenge his brother's death.

Unexciting and turgid action movie.

w Robert King   *d* Terence H. Winkless
ph Ricardo Jacques Gale   *m* Sasha Matson
ed Karen Horn

Don 'The Dragon' Wilson, Joe Marie Avellana,
Michael Shaner, Riley Bowman, Rob Kamen, Billy
Blanks, Kris Aguilar

Bloodfist II

US   1990   88m   colour
Concorde (Roger Corman)
V*

A kick-boxer attempts to infiltrate an island fortress.

A cheap re-run of *Enter the Dragon* with a far less
charismatic hero.

w Catherine Cyran d Andy Blumenthal ph Bruce
Dorfman m Nigel Holton ed Karen Joseph

Don 'The Dragon' Wilson, Rina Reyes, Joe Marie
Avellana, Robert Marius, Maurice Smith, Tim Baker,
James Warring

Bloodfist III

US   1992   88m   Foto-Kem colour
Concorde (Roger Corman)
V*

A wrongly imprisoned kick-boxer goes to the aid of a
friend attacked by fellow convicts.

Fast action movie, with some fierce fights, which
should satisfy fans of the genre.

w Allison Burnett, Charles Mattera d Oley Sassone
ph Rick Bota m Nigel Holton pd James
Shumaker ed Eric L. Beason

Don 'The Dragon' Wilson, Richard Roundtree,
Gregory McKinney, Rick Dean, Richard Paul, Charles
Boswell, John Cardone

Bloodhounds of Broadway *

US   1952   90m   Technicolor
TCF (George Jessel)

With the help of a gangster, an orphan girl and her pet
bloodhounds make a big hit in cabaret.

Absurd but sporadically amusing gangster burlesque,
typical of its author. Lively production values.

w Sy Gomberg story Damon Runyon d Harmon
Jones ph Edward Cronjager md Lionel Newman
m David Raksin

Mitzi Gaynor, Scott Brady, Mitzi Green, Marguerite
Chapman, Michael O'Shea, Wally Vernon, George E.
Stone

Bloodhounds of Broadway

US   1989   90m   DeLuxe
Columbia (Howard Brookner)
V, V*, L

Interwoven stories of the escapades of gangsters, guys
and dolls on New Year's Eve, 1928.

Bland and forgettable and lacking the particular
flavour of the original tales.

wd Howard Brookner story short stories by Damon
Runyon ph Elliot Davis m Jonathan Sheffer
pd Linda Conway-Parsole ed Camilla Toniolo

Josef Sommer, Madonna, Tony Azito, Jennifer Grey,
Tony Longo, Rutger Hauer, Matt Dillon, Julie
Hagerty, Randy Quaid, William Burroughs

Bloodline

US   1979   117m   Movielab
Paramount/Geria (David V. Picker, Sidney Beckerman)
V*

A pharmaceutical tycoon is murdered and his
daughter seems likely to be the next victim.

Involved all-star suspense shocker which seems
constantly about to be better than it ever is.

w Laird Koenig novel Sidney Sheldon d Terence
Young ph Freddie Young m Ennio Morricone
pd Ted Haworth

Audrey Hepburn, Ben Gazzara, James Mason, Claudia
Mori, Omar Sharif, Irene Papas, Maurice Ronet, Romy

Schneider, Beatrice Straight, Gert Frobe, Micheline
Phillips

'Unutterably chic, inexpressibly absurd, and saved
from being painfully tedious only by a personable
cast doing their damnedest.' – *Tom Milne, MFB*

Bloodsport

US   1988   92m   TVC colour
Cannon (Mark DiSalle)
V*, L, S

An American commando goes to Hong Kong to take
part in the Kumite, a clandestine martial arts
competition.

Despite being based on the true story of Frank Dux
(who supervised the fight sequences), the movie
emerges as pulp fiction that will be of interest only to
martial arts enthusiasts, who may not wonder why an
American should speak with a heavy Belgian accent.

w Sheldon Lettich, Christopher Crosby, Mel
Friedman d Newt Arnold ph David Worth
m Paul Hertzog pd David Searl ed Carl Kress

Jean Claude Van Damme, Donald Gibb, Leah Ayres,
Norman Burton, Forest Whitaker, Roy Chiao, Philip
Chan, Pierre Rafini, Bolo Yeung

Bloodsuckers: see *Incense of the Damned*

The Bloody Bushido Blade: see *The Bushido Blade*

'The family that stays together slays together!'
Bloody Mama *

US   1969   90m   Movielab
AIP (Roger Corman)
V*, L

In the thirties, outlaw Kate Barker and her four sons
conduct a reign of terror until what's left of the gang is
riddled with machine gun bullets.

Violent gangster story with a star on the rampage; the
attempt to philosophize is more than the facts will
bear, but the production moves smartly enough.

w Robert Thom d Roger Corman ph John Alonzo
m Don Randi

Shelley Winters, Pat Hingle, Don Stroud, Diane Varsi,
Bruce Dern, Clint Kimbrough, Robert de Niro, Robert
Walden, Alex Nicol

Bloomfield

GB   1969   95m   Technicolor
World Film Services/Limbridge (John Heyman, Wolf
Mankowitz)
US title: *The Hero*

A 10-year-old Israeli boy hitchhikes to Jaffa to see his
football idol play his last game.

Sentimental whimsy, unattractively interpreted.

w Wolf Mankowitz d Richard Harris ph Otto
Heller m Johnny Harris

Richard Harris, Romy Schneider, Kim Burfield,
Maurice Kaufmann, Yossi Yadin

Blossom Time

GB   1934   90m   bw
BIP (Walter Mycroft)
US title: *April Romance*

In old Vienna, a composer stands by while the girl he
loves weds a dragoon.

Stilted musical romance redeemed by its star's singing
presence.

w John Drinkwater, Walter Burford, Paul Perez, G. H.
Clutsam story Franz Schulz d Paul Stein
ph Otto Kanturek, Bryan Langley md Idris Lewis
m Schubert ad David Rawnsley, Clarence Elder
ed Leslie Norman

Richard Tauber, Jane Baxter, Carl Esmond, Athene
Seyler

Blossoms in the Dust **

US   1941   99m   Technicolor
MGM (Irving Asher)
V*

A woman who loses her husband and child founds a
state orphanage.

Archetypal tearjerker of the forties, a glossy 'woman's
picture' which distorts the facts into a star vehicle.
Excellent colour helped to make it an enormous
success.

w Anita Loos, based on the life of Edna Gladney
d Mervyn Le Roy ph Karl Freund, W. Howard
Greene m Herbert Stothart ad Cedric Gibbons,
Urie McCleary

Greer Garson, Walter Pidgeon, Felix Bressart, Marsha
Hunt, Fay Holden, Samuel S. Hinds

AA: art direction

AAN: best picture; Karl Freund, W. Howard Greene;
Greer Garson

'Heading for the laff round-up!'
Blossoms on Broadway

US   1937   88m   bw
Paramount (B. P. Schulberg)

A girl who owns a Death Valley gold mine comes to
New York and is hounded by confidence men.

Tolerably fast-moving comedy.

w Theodore Reeves d Richard Wallace

Edward Arnold, Shirley Ross, John Trent, Weber and
Fields, Frank Craven, Rufe Davis, William Frawley

'Won't do much b.o. blossoming. Good songs, but
story stumbles badly.' – *Variety*

Blotto *

US   1930   20m   bw
Hal Roach
V, V (C)

Ollie helps Stan escape his wife for a night on the
town, but the lady takes revenge.

Palatable star comedy with a strained second half
following a splendidly typical opening.

w Leo McCarey, H. M. Walker d James Parrott

Laurel and Hardy, Anita Garvin

Blow-Out **

France/Italy   1973   133m   Eastmancolor
Panavision
Gala/Mara/Les Films 66/Capitolina (Jean-Pierre Rassam)
V (W)
original title: *La Grande Bouffe*

A master chef, a television personality, a pilot
and a judge get together for a prolonged orgy of
gourmandizing and sex that ends with their
deaths.

Grotesque celebration of, or satire on, the consumer
society in which amusement gradually turns to
disgust.

w Marco Ferreri, Rafael Azcona, Francis Blanche
d Marco Ferreri ph Mario Vulpiani m Philippe
Sarde ad Michel de Broin ed Claudine Merlin,
Gina Pignier

Marcello Mastroianni, Ugo Tognazzi, Michel Piccoli,
Philippe Noiret, Andréa Ferreol, Solange Florence,
Blondeau Giorgetti, Michele Alexandre, Monique
Chaumette

'The film is never negligible thanks to Ferreri's
consistently inventive use of detail; and whatever
else, it stands as an overdue riposte to the
contemporary cinema's ubiquitous hymns to male
camaraderie.' – *Tony Rayns, MFB*

'Murder has a sound all of its own!'

Blow Out

US 1981 108m Technicolor Panavision
Filmways/Cinema 77/Geria (George Litto)
V, V*, L

A sound effects man accidentally captures on film what turns out to be a murder.

Showily unpleasant thriller concocted of equal parts of *The Conversation*, *Blow Up*, and Kennedy at Chappaquiddick; the work of a copycat talent operating below par.

wd Brian de Palma *ph* Vilmos Zsigmond *m* Pino Donaggio *pd* Paul Sylbert

John Travolta, Nancy Allen, John Lithgow, Dennis Franz, John McMartin, John Aquino

'The camera is better deployed than the script.' – *Guardian*

Blow to the Heart

Italy 1982 105m colour
Other Cinema/RAI/Antea Cinematografica (Enzo Porcelli)
original title: *Colpire Al Cuore*

A conformist son suspects his radical father of terrorist sympathies.

Moderately gripping, though it suffers from indecision over whether its subject matter is politics or family relationships.

w Gianni Amelio, Vincenzo Cerami *d* Gianni Amelio *ph* Tonino Nardi *m* Franco Piersanti *ad* Marco Dentici *ed* Anna Napoli

Jean-Louis Trintignant, Laura Morante, Fausto Rossi, Sonia Gessner, Vanni Corbellini

Blow-Up **

GB 1966 110m Eastmancolor
MGM/Carlo Ponti
V, V*, L

A London fashion photographer thinks he sees a murder, but the evidence disappears.

Not a mystery but a fashionable think-in on the difference (if any) between fantasy and reality. Agreeable to look at for those who can stifle their irritation at the non-plot and non-characters; a huge audience was lured by flashes of nudity and the trendy 'swinging London' setting.

wd Michelangelo Antonioni *ph* Carlo di Palma *m* Herbert Hancock *ad* Assheton Gorton

David Hemmings, Sarah Miles, Vanessa Redgrave

'A beautiful and startling film, startling because if the credits didn't say it was coauthored and directed by Michelangelo Antonioni you'd never believe it on the basis of the movie itself, and beautiful because in his first made-in-England English-language film the Italian director proves himself a master of the use of color, both literally and figuratively.' – *Judith Crist*

AAN: Michelangelo Antonioni (as writer and director)

Blowing Wild *

US 1953 88m bw
Warner/United States (Milton Sperling)
V*, L

A Mexican oil driller becomes involved with the psychotic wife of an old friend; the triangle leads to murder and retribution.

Pot-boiling star vehicle with adequate melodramatic interest, full of reminiscences of other movies, with a wicked lady to end them all.

w Philip Yordan *d* Hugo Fregonese *ph* Sid Hickox *m* Dimitri Tiomkin

Gary Cooper, Barbara Stanwyck, Anthony Quinn, Ruth Roman, Ward Bond

'Trusting Someone Can Be Deadly.'

Blown Away

Canada 1992 92m colour
Norstar (Peter R. Simpson)
V, V*

A young resort worker becomes involved with the spoilt, self-destructive 17-year-old daughter of his violent boss.

Tawdry tale of thwarted teenage sex that is both trivial and tedious, shot in the style of an unimaginative promotional video for a pop song.

w Robert Cooper *d* Brenton Spencer *ph* Perci Young *m* Paul J. Zaza *ad* Ian Brock *ed* Bill Towgood

Corey Haim, Corey Feldman, Nicole Eggert, Gary Farmer, Kathleen Robertson, Jean LeClerc

'Daft "erotic" thriller.' – *Sight and Sound*

Blue

US 1968 113m Technicolor Panavision
Paramount/Kettledrum (Judd Bernard, Irwin Winkler)
V*

The white adopted son of a Mexican bandit prevents his cohorts from raping a white girl, and falls in love with her.

Pretentious, self-conscious, literary Western without much zest.

w Meade Roberts, Ronald M. Cohen *d* Silvio Narizzano *ph* *Stanley Cortez* *m* Manos Hadjidakis

Terence Stamp, Joanna Pettet, Karl Malden, Ricardo Montalban

'I don't know which is worse – bad cowboy movies or bad arty cowboy movies. *Blue* is both.' – *Rex Reed*

Blue **

GB 1993 76m Technicolor
Basilisk/Uplink (James Mackay, Takashi Asai)
V, S

A meditation on AIDS and the colour blue; the screen is suffused with a blue light as the director muses on the death of friends and his own illness and deteriorating sight.

Jarman's valediction to the cinema is more a radio play than a film, but is nevertheless a superior piece of radio.

wd Derek Jarman *m* Simon Fisher Turner

voices of John Quentin, Derek Jarman, Nigel Terry, Tilda Swinton

'Given the choice between art and socially oriented moviemaking, he has opted for art.' – *Robert Horton, Film Comment*

† *Blue* was given a simultaneous first broadcast on British television and stereo radio. Jarman himself said of it, 'I think it's quite nice to have that visual silence in the cinema.'

The Blue and the Gold: see *An Annapolis Story*

The Blue Angel ****

Germany 1930 98m bw
UFA (Erich Pommer)
V, V*, L

A fuddy-duddy professor is infatuated with a tawdry night-club singer. She marries him but is soon bored and contemptuous; humiliated, he leaves her and dies in his old classroom.

A masterwork of late twenties German grotesquerie, and after a slowish beginning an emotional powerhouse, set in a dark nightmare world which could be created only in the studio. Shot also in English, it was highly popular and influential in Britain and America.

w Robert Liebmann, Karl Zuckmayer, Karl Vollmoeller *novel* *Professor Unrath* by Heinrich Mann *d* Josef von Sternberg *ph* Günther Rittau, Hans

Schneeberger *m* Frederick Hollander (inc 'Falling in Love Again', 'They Call Me Wicked Lola') *ad* Otto Hunte, Emil Hasler

Emil Jannings, Marlene Dietrich (who was instantly catapulted to international stardom), Kurt Gerron, Hans Albers

'It will undoubtedly do splendidly in the whole of Europe and should also appeal strongly in the States . . . only fault is a certain ponderousness of tempo which tends to tire.' – *Variety*

'At the time I thought the film was awful and vulgar and I was shocked by the whole thing. Remember, I was a well brought up German girl.' – *Marlene Dietrich*

The Blue Angel

US 1959 107m DeLuxe Cinemascope
TCF (Jack Cummings)

Ill-advised attempt at a 'realistic', updated remake of the above; the result is a total travesty, with the actors aware that stylized melodrama is turning before their eyes into unintentional farce.

w Nigel Balchin *d* Edward Dmytryk *ph* Leon Shamroy *m* Hugo Friedhofer

Curt Jurgens, May Britt, Theodore Bikel, John Banner

'It totally lacks the stifling atmosphere of sordid and oppressive sexuality which is essential to give conviction to the German sadism of the story.' – *Brenda Davies*

The Blue Bird ***

US 1940 98m Technicolor (bw prologue)
TCF (Gene Markey)
V*

In a Grimm's Fairy Tale setting, the two children of a poor woodcutter seek the bluebird of happiness in the past, the future and the Land of Luxury, but eventually discover it in their own back yard.

An imaginative and often chilling script clarifies Maurice Maeterlinck's fairy play, and the art direction is outstanding, but the children are necessarily unsympathetic and the expensive production paled beside the success of the more upbeat *Wizard of Oz*, which was released almost simultaneously. Slashed for re-release, the only existing prints now open with confusing abruptness and no scene-setting before the adventures begin.

w Ernest Pascal *d* Walter Lang *ph* Arthur Miller, Ray Rennahan *m* Alfred Newman *ad* Richard Day, Wiard B. Ihnen

Shirley Temple, Johnny Russell, *Gale Sondergaard* (as the cat), *Eddie Collins* (as the dog), Nigel Bruce, Jessie Ralph, Spring Byington, Sybil Jason, Helen Ericson, Russell Hicks, Al Shean, Cecilia Loftus

'One of the most deliciously lovely productions to be brought to the screen.' – *MFB*

AAN: Arthur Miller, Ray Rennahan

The Blue Bird

US/USSR 1976 83m Technicolor Panavision
TCF/Edward Lewis/Lenfilm

Abortive remake of the above, widely touted as the first Russian—American co-production, but sabotaged by a flabby script, unsuitable casting and unresolved production problems.

w Hugh Whitemore, Alfred Hayes *d* George Cukor *ph* Freddie Young, Ionas Gritzus *m* Irwin Kostal, Andrei Petrov

Elizabeth Taylor (as Mother, Maternal Love, Light and the Witch), Ava Gardner, Cicely Tyson, Jane Fonda, Harry Andrews, Will Geer, Mona Washbourne, George Cole

'It works so hard at making history that it forgets to make sense.' – *David Sterritt, Christian Science Monitor*

'If you have any naughty children you want to punish, take them to *The Blue Bird* and make them sit all the way through it.' – *William Wolf, Cue*

'It turns a work for adults that children can enjoy into a charade for children that must sicken adults.' – *John Simon, New Yorker*

'Senile and interminable.' – *Stephen Farber, New West*

'Lavishly done; limited box office.' – *Variety*

Blue Black Permanent
GB   1992   86m   colour
BFI/Channel 4/Viz Permanent (Barbara Grigor)

An Edinburgh photographer remembers her childhood in the Orkneys and returns there with her lover to sort out the problems that plague her.

A shifting and complex narrative explores feminine identity across two generations

wd Margaret Tait   *ph* Alex Scott   *m* John Gray   *pd* Andrew Semple   *ed* John MacDonnell

Celia Imrie, Jack Shepherd, Gerda Stevenson, James Fleet, Sean Scanlan, Hilary Maclean, Walter Leask, Sheena Mar

'Tait's achievement is to suggest the processes that lie behind our ways of seeing, our declarations, and to find a style that enacts, or at least simulates, those very processes.' – *Robert Yates, Sight and Sound*

Blue Blood
GB   1973   86m   Technicolor
Mallard-Impact Quadrant (Kent Walwin, John Trent)

A German governess arrives at an English stately home and finds the malevolent butler plotting to show his supremacy over his effete master.

An extremely unattractive, would-be satirical melodrama which plays like a Grand Guignol version of *The Servant*.

wd Andrew Sinclair   *novel* The Carry-Cot by Alexander Thynne   *ph* Harry Waxman   *m* Brian Gascoigne

Oliver Reed, Derek Jacobi, Fiona Lewis, Anna Gael, Meg Wynn Owen

Blue Collar *
US   1978   114m   Technicolor
Universal/TAT (Don Guest)
V*, L

Three car factory workers try to improve their lot by unionization and robbery.

Salty, rough, downbeat but impressively realistic modern drama, a belated American equivalent of *Saturday Night and Sunday Morning*.

w Paul Schrader, Leonard Schrader   *d* Paul Schrader   *ph* Bobby Byrne   *m* Jack Nitzsche

Richard Pryor, Harvey Keitel, Yaphet Kotto, Ed Begley Jnr, Harry Bellaver

'This is Schrader's first directing job and the best elements in the script fit his ability like a role tailored for an actor. His work is easy and quick, imaginative but not ostentatious.' – *Stanley Kauffmann*

'Tamed by a brunette – framed by a blonde – blamed by the cops!'
The Blue Dahlia **
US   1946   99m   bw
Paramount (John Houseman)

A returning war veteran finds his faithless wife murdered and himself suspected.

Hailed on its first release as sharper than average, this mystery suspenser is now only moderately compelling despite the screenplay credit; direction and editing lack urgency and the acting lacks bounce.

w Raymond Chandler   *d* George Marshall   *ph* Lionel Lindon   *m* Victor Young

Alan Ladd, Veronica Lake, William Bendix, Howard da Silva, Doris Dowling, Tom Powers, Hugh Beaumont, Howard Freeman, Will Wright

'It threatens to turn into something, but it never does.' – *New Yorker, 1978*

'The picture is as neatly stylized and synchronized, and as uninterested in moral excitement, as a good ballet; it knows its own weight and size perfectly and carries them gracefully and without self-importance; it is, barring occasional victories and noble accidents, about as good a movie as can be expected from the big factories.' – *James Agee*

AAN: Raymond Chandler

Blue Denim *
US   1959   89m   bw   Cinemascope
TCF (Charles Brackett)
GB title: *Blue Jeans*

Teenagers confronted with the prospect of illegitimate parenthood consult an abortionist, but all ends with wedding bells.

First of its rather dreary kind but better than most, this only slightly mawkish domestic drama has its heart in the right place and steers surprisingly towards a nick-of-time chase climax.

w Edith Sommer, Philip Dunne   *play* James Leo Herlihy, William Noble   *d* Philip Dunne   *ph* Leo Tover   *m* Bernard Herrmann

Carol Lynley, Brandon de Wilde, Macdonald Carey, Marsha Hunt, Nina Shipman, Warren Berlinger

The Blue Gardenia
US   1953   90m   bw
Warner/Gloria/Blue Gardenia (Alex Gottlieb)

A girl gets drunk and wakes up in a strange apartment with a dead man by her side.

Totally undistinguished mystery which leaves egg on the actors' faces.

w Charles Hoffman   *d* Fritz Lang   *ph* Nicholas Musuraca   *m* Raoul Kraushaar

Anne Baxter, Richard Conte, Ann Sothern, Raymond Burr, Jeff Donnell, Richard Erdman, Nat King Cole

Blue Hawaii
US   1961   101m   Technicolor   Panavision
Hal B. Wallis
V, V*, L, S

A GI comes home to Honolulu and becomes a beachcomber.

Lifeless star vehicle shot on glamorous locations.

w Hal Kanter   *d* Norman Taurog   *ph* Charles Lang Jnr   *m* Joseph J. Lilley

Elvis Presley, Joan Blackman, Nancy Walters, Roland Winters, Angela Lansbury, John Archer, Howard McNear

Blue Heat
US   1990   106m   colour
Rank/Orion/Davis (John A. Davis)
V, V*, L
US title: *The Last of the Finest*

An ex-cop goes after the drugs and arms dealer who caused his resignation from the force.

Standard cops 'n' robbers mayhem.

w Jere Cunningham, Thomas Lee Wright, George Armitage   *d* John MacKenzie   *ph* Juan Ruiz-Anchia   *m* Jack Nitzsche, Michael Hoenig   *pd* Laurence G. Paull   *ed* Graham Walker, Gregory Mark Gerlich, Albert Coleman, Karen Dale Greene

Brian Dennehy, Joe Pantoliano, Jeff Fahey, Bill Paxton, Michael C. Gwynne

'If Harry's past ever catches up with him, he won't live long enough to regret it.'
Blue Ice
US   1992   105m   colour
Guild/M&M (Martin Bregman, Michael Caine)
V

A jazz-club owner, a former secret agent, is asked by his mistress to find an old boyfriend and becomes embroiled in murder and arms smuggling.

Dreary thriller, lacking in surprise and suspense, with a cast that gives the impression that its attention is understandably elsewhere.

w Ron Hutchinson   *novel* Ted Allbeury   *d* Russell Mulcahy   *ph* Denis Crossan   *m* Michael Kamen   *pd* Grant Hicks   *ed* Seth Flaum

Michael Caine, Sean Young, Ian Holm, Bobby Short, Alun Armstrong, Sam Kelly, Jack Shepherd, Philip Davis, Patricia Hayes, Alan MacNaughton, Bob Hoskins

'Belongs to that familiar genre, the bad British thriller, with Michael Caine playing a version of Harry Palmer depoliticised for the Nineties and Sean Young giving the non-performance of her career.' – *Sheila Johnston, Independent*

'A resolutely old-fashioned thriller which, in its quaint view of London (all Tower Bridge and Soho dives), seems like an inflated 50s quota quickie.' – *Kim Newman, Sight and Sound*

Blue Jean Cop
US   1988   105m   colour
Universal/Shapiro Glickenhaus Entertainment (J. Boyce Harman Jnr)
V, V*, L
US title: *Shakedown*

A lawyer defending a drug dealer uncovers corruption in the police force.

Over-the-top car chases and gun battles mar what might have been a good action thriller.

wd James Glickenhaus   *ph* John Lindley   *m* Jonathan Ellis   *pd* Charles Bennett   *ed* Paul Fried

Peter Weller, Sam Elliott, Patricia Charbonneau, Antonio Fargas, William Prince, Blanche Baker

Blue Jeans: see *Blue Denim*

The Blue Kite **
China/Japan   1993   138m   colour
Longwick/Beijing Film Studio
original title: *Lan Fengzheng*

A boy recalls his mother's three marriages and the troubles that beset his family life during the 1950s and 60s, a time of political upheaval during China's Great Leap Forward and the Cultural Revolution inspired by the Red Guards.

A gripping, though often depressing, domestic drama seen against the ideological upheavals that made a hero of one period a villain of the next; there is warmth and humour in the telling, but the story is one of personal tragedy.

w Xiao Mao   *d* Tian Zhuangzhuang   *ph* Hou Yong   *m* Yoshihide Otomo   *ad* Zhang Xiande   *ed* Qian Lengleng

Zhang Wenyao, Chen Xiaoman, Lu Piping, Pu Quanxin, Li Xuejian, Guo Baochang, Zhong Ping, Chu Qhuangzhong, Song Xiaoying, Zhang Hong

'Major surprise of the movie is that, despite a story and multi-character cast that looks more fitted to a miniseries, it works on a simple emotional level as a feature film. Characters emerge as real people rather than political stereotypes.' – *Variety*

'Vividly and touchingly conveys the insecurity, fear and confusion of the family.' – *Sheila Johnston, Independent*

† The film had a troubled production with interference from Chinese officials, who forbade a print to leave the country for post-production work. The film was finished from the director's script and notes after a print was smuggled out of the country. In a statement made at the 1993 Cannes Film Festival the director said, 'The stories in the film are real, and they are related with total sincerity. What worries me is that it is precisely a fear of reality that has led to the ban on such stories being told.' It has not been shown in China, and in April 1994 Tian Zhuangzhuang was

one of seven film directors banned from making films in mainland China.

The Blue Lagoon *
GB   1949   103m   Technicolor
GFD/Individual (Frank Launder, Sidney Gilliat)

A shipwrecked boy and girl grow up on a desert island, ward off smugglers, have a baby, and eventually sail away in search of civilization.

Rather lifeless, though pretty, treatment of a famous novel: the story never becomes vivid despite splendid Fijian locations.

w Frank Launder, John Baines, Michael Hogan
novel H. de Vere Stacpoole   d Frank Launder
ph Geoffrey Unsworth   m Clifton Parker

Jean Simmons, Donald Houston, Noel Purcell, Cyril Cusack, James Hayter

The Blue Lagoon
US   1980   102m   Colorfilm
Columbia/Randal Kleiser
V, V*, L, S

Remake of the above with poor narrative balance and a great deal of nudity and adolescent frankness about sex.

Adolescents are probably its only audience.

w Douglas Day Stewart   d Randal Kleiser
ph Nestor Almendros   m Basil Poledouris

Brooke Shields, Christopher Atkins, Leo McKern, William Daniels

'At best a damp dream, a Sunday school fairy tale which makes the story of Adam and Eve seem like hard porn, as hygienically sanitized as a Hilton Hotel lavatory seat.' – Sunday Times

'A total fraud from beginning to end.' – Guardian

'The film has an inevitable, built-in prurience. All we have to look forward to is: when are these two going to discover fornication?' – Pauline Kael, New Yorker

'This movie made me itch.' – Roger Ebert

AAN: Nestor Almendros

The Blue Lamp ***
GB   1949   84m   bw
Ealing (Michael Relph)
V, V*

A young man joins London's police force. The elderly copper who trains him is killed in a shootout, but the killer is apprehended.

Seminal British police film which spawned not only a long line of semi-documentary imitations but also the twenty-year TV series Dixon of Dock Green for which the shot PC was happily revived. As an entertainment, pacy but dated; more important, it burnished the image of the British copper for generations.

w T. E. B. Clarke   d Basil Dearden   ph Gordon Dines
md Ernest Irving

Jack Warner, Jimmy Hanley, Dirk Bogarde, Meredith Edwards, Robert Flemyng, Bernard Lee, Patric Doonan, Peggy Evans, Gladys Henson, Dora Bryan

'The mixture of coyness, patronage and naive theatricality which has vitiated British films for the last ten years.' – Gavin Lambert

'A soundly made crime thriller which would not be creating much of a stir if it were American.' – Richard Mallett, Punch

'It is not only foreigners who find the English policeman wonderful, and, in composing this tribute to him, the Ealing Studios are giving conscious expression to a general sentiment.' – The Times Film Correspondent

The Blue Light *
Germany   1932   68m   bw
H. R. Sokal/Leni Riefenstahl
V*

In the early 19th century, a painter defies a local legend to climb a Dolomite mountain.

Romantic fairy tale with a story more suited to a ballet. It still takes the eye, and is recognizable as the work of its director.

wd Leni Riefenstahl   ph Hans Schneeberger, Henry Jaworsky   m Giuseppe Becce

Leni Riefenstahl, Matthias Wieman, Max Holsboer

† This version was put together in 1950 after the original negative had been lost; among other things, a flashback frame was removed.

'There was no quiet on the western front for the heroes and cowards who flew to their rendezvous with hell!'

The Blue Max *
US   1966   156m   DeLuxe   Cinemascope
TCF (Christian Ferry)
V, V*, L, S

In Germany after World War I an ambitious and skilful pilot causes the death of his comrades and steals the wife of his High Command superior, who eventually finds a means of revenge.

For once, an action spectacular not too badly let down by its connecting threads of plot, apart from some hilarious and unnecessary bedroom scenes in which the female star's bath towel seems to become conveniently adhesive.

w David Pursall, Jack Seddon, Gerald Hanley
novel Jack Hunter   d John Guillermin   ph Douglas Slocombe   m Jerry Goldsmith

George Peppard, James Mason, Ursula Andress, Jeremy Kemp, Karl Michael Vogler, Anton Diffring, Derren Nesbitt

'Addicts of flying movies swear by this one, but for others, the monoplanes and biplanes can't smash or burn fast enough' – Pauline Kael

Blue Murder at St Trinians *
GB   1957   86m   bw
British Lion/John Marvel (Launder and Gilliat)
V, V*

The awful schoolgirls win a UNESCO prize trip which takes them to Rome where they become involved with a jewel thief.

Possibly the best of this series, which isn't saying much. See The Belles of St Trinians.

w Frank Launder, Val Valentine, Sidney Gilliat
d Frank Launder   ph Gerald Gibbs   m Malcolm Arnold

Terry-Thomas, George Cole, Joyce Grenfell, Alastair Sim, Judith Furse, Sabrina, Lionel Jeffries, Lloyd Lamble, Thorley Walters, Kenneth Griffith, Eric Barker, Richard Wattis

The Blue Peter
GB   1955   93m   Eastmancolor
British Lion/Beaconsfield (Herbert Mason)
US title: Navy Heroes

A confused war hero becomes a trainer at an Outward Bound school for boys.

Pleasant but uninspired open air adventure for young people.

w Don Sharp, John Pudney   d Wolf Rilla
ph Arthur Grant   m Antony Hopkins

Kieron Moore, Greta Gynt, Sarah Lawson, Mervyn Johns, Ram Gopal, Edwind Richfield, Harry Fowler, John Charlesworth

'It's the nearest thing to heaven!'

Blue Skies *
US   1946   104m   Technicolor
Paramount (Sol C. Siegel)
S

A dancing star and a night-club owner fight for years over the same girl.

Thin musical with splendid Irving Berlin tunes and lively individual numbers.

w Arthur Sheekman   d Stuart Heisler   ph Charles Lang Jnr, William Snyder   md Robert Emmett Dolan
ad Hans Dreier, Hal Pereira   ed LeRoy Stone

Fred Astaire (dancing 'Putting On the Ritz'), Bing Crosby, Joan Caulfield, Billy de Wolfe, Olga San Juan, Robert Benchley, Frank Faylen, Victoria Horne, Jack Norton

AAN: Robert Emmett Dolan; song 'You Keep Coming Back Like a Song' (m/y Irving Berlin)

Blue Steel
US   1934   54m   bw
Lone Star (Paul Malvern)
V*, L

A sheriff goes undercover to expose a gang of crooks attempting to swindle a town out of its riches.

Lacklustre Western enlivened by a few stunts.

wd Robert N. Bradbury   ph Archie Stout   ed Carl Pierson

John Wayne, Eleanor Hunt, George Hayes, Edward Peil, Yakima Canutt, George Cleveland

'For a rookie cop, there's one thing more dangerous than uncovering a killer's fantasy. Becoming it.'

Blue Steel
US   1990   102m   Technicolor
Vestron/Lightning Pictures/Precision Films/Mack-Taylor Productions (Edward R. Pressman, Oliver Stone)
V, V*, L

A new cop, hunting a serial killer, falls for the chief suspect.

Lurid and ludicrous melodrama.

w Kathryn Bigelow, Eric Red   d Kathryn Bigelow
ph Amir Mokri   m Brad Fiedel   pd Tony Corbett
ed Hal Levinsohn

Jamie Lee Curtis, Ron Silver, Clancy Brown, Elizabeth Pena, Louise Fletcher, Philip Bosco

Blue Thunder *
US   1983   110m   Technicolor   Panavision
Columbia/Rastar/Gordon Carroll
V, V*, L

A policeman in Los Angeles' Astro Division is haunted by memories of Vietnam and goes berserk when using his new ultra-sophisticated helicopter to wage war against crime.

Slick but hollow thriller most remarkable for its helicopter stunting between city skyscrapers. Otherwise, it is too often fashionably inaudible and almost invisible.

w Dan O'Bannon, Don Jakoby   d John Badham
ph John A. Alonzo   aerial photography Frank Holgate
m Arthur B. Rubinstein   ed Frank Morriss, Edward Abroms

Roy Scheider, Warren Oates, Candy Clark, Daniel Stern, Malcolm McDowell

† A watered-down TV version was quickly assembled, but its comic-strip dialogue grounded it after 13 episodes.

AAN: film editing

The Blue Veil *
US   1951   114m   bw
RKO/Wald-Krasna (Raymond Hakim)

The vocational career of a children's nurse who descends into poverty but is rescued by one of her own charges, now grown up.

Sober American remake of a French tearjerker (Le Voile bleu) with the star suffering nobly but being upstaged by the cameo players.

w Norman Corwin, from the original by François Campaux   d Curtis Bernhardt   ph Franz Planer
m Franz Waxman

Jane Wyman, Charles Laughton, Richard Carlson, Joan Blondell, Agnes Moorehead, Don Taylor, Audrey Totter, Everett Sloane, Cyril Cusack, Natalie Wood, Warner Anderson

AAN: Jane Wyman; Joan Blondell

Blue Velvet
US   1986   120m   colour
De Laurentiis (Richard Roth)
V, V (W), V*, L, S

Murder, mutilation and sexual perversion in Middle America.

Bizarrely stylish exercise by the director of *The Elephant Man*, popular at the box-office.

wd David Lynch   *ph* Frederick Elmes   *m* Angelo Badalamenti   *pd* Patricia Norris

Kyle MacLachlan, Isabella Rossellini, Dennis Hopper, Laura Dern, Hope Lange, Dean Stockwell

AAN: David Lynch

Blue Water, White Death *
US   1971   99m   Techniscope
Blue Water Films/Cinema Center

A skilful and quite frightening documentary about the habits of the Great White Shark, with a lead-up showing events on the expedition which set out in search of it.

wd Peter Gimbel   *ph* James Lipscomb

Bluebeard *
US   1944   73m   bw
PRC
V*

A strangler of young girls is at large in Paris.

Poverty Row chiller with effective moments; possibly the most interesting film ever to come from PRC (which isn't saying *very* much).

w Pierre Gendron   *d* Edgar G. Ulmer   *ph* Jockey Feindel

John Carradine, Jean Parker, Ludwig Stossel, Nils Asther, Iris Adrian

Bluebeard (1962): see
Landru

Bluebeard
France/Italy/Germany   1972   124m   Technicolor
Barnabé/Gloria/Geiselgasteig (Alexander Salkind)
V*

The lady-killer in this case is an Austrian aristocrat who has been driven to desperation and murder by a long line of mistresses whose bodies he keeps frozen in his cellar.

Would-be macabre comedy which becomes totally off-putting by its emphasis on close-up death agonies.

w Ennio di Concini, Edward Dmytryk, Maria Pia Fusco   *d* Edward Dmytryk   *ph* Gabor Pogany   *m* Ennio Morricone

Richard Burton, Raquel Welch, Joey Heatherton, Virna Lisi, Nathalie Delon, Marilu Tolo

'Somewhere between (and a long way behind) *Kind Hearts and Coronets* and *The Abominable Dr Phibes*.' – *Clyde Jeavons, MFB*

Bluebeard's Eighth Wife *
US   1938   85m   bw
Paramount (Ernst Lubitsch)

The daughter of an impoverished French aristocrat marries for money a millionaire who has had seven previous wives, and determines to teach him a lesson.

Very thin sophisticated comedy with unsympathetic characters and little wit after the first scene; a disappointment from the talent involved.

w Charles Brackett, Billy Wilder   *play* Alfred Savoir   *d* Ernst Lubitsch   *ph* Leo Tover   *m* Werner Heymann, Frederick Hollander

Claudette Colbert, Gary Cooper, David Niven, Edward Everett Horton, Elizabeth Patterson, Herman Bing, Warren Hymer, Franklin Pangborn

'Light and sometimes bright, but it gets a bit tiresome.' – *Variety*

'In these days it is bad enough to have to admire millionaires in any circumstances; but a millionaire with a harem complex simply can't help starting the bristles on the back of a sensitive neck.' – *New York Times*

† A previous version, released by Paramount in 1923 and directed by Sam Wood, starred Gloria Swanson and Huntley Gordon.

Bluebeard's Seven Wives *
US   1926   94m approx   bw   silent
First National

A bank teller becomes a film star and is transformed, notably by seven imaginary marriages.

Amusing spoof on the film industry that was.

w Blanche Merrill, Paul Scofield   *d* Alfred Santell

Ben Lyon, Lois Wilson, Blanche Sweet, Dorothy Sebastian, Sam Hardy

Bluebeard's Ten Honeymoons
GB   1960   93m   bw
Anglo-Allied (Roy Parkinson)

Another version of the story of Landru, alternating wildly between fantasy, farce and melodrama.

Not a success in any of its moods.

w Myles Wilder   *d* W. Lee Wilder   *ph* Stephen Dade   *m* Albert Elms

George Sanders, Corinne Calvet, Patricia Roc, Ingrid Hafner, Jean Kent, Greta Gynt, Maxine Audley, Selma Vaz Diaz, George Coulouris

'The unedifying narrative is developed along the most obvious lines imaginable.' – *MFB*

The Bluebird: see *The Blue Bird*

A Blueprint for Murder *
US   1953   77m   bw
TCF (Michael Abel)

After the death of his brother and niece, a man proves that his sister-in-law is a murderess.

Unpleasant but efficient murder story with enough twists to keep one watching.

wd Andrew Stone   *ph* Leo Tover   *md* Lionel Newman   *m* David Raksin

Jean Peters, Joseph Cotten, Gary Merrill, Catherine McLeod, Jack Kruschen

Blueprint for Robbery *
US   1960   87m   bw
Paramount (Bryan Foy)

Crooks plan and execute a robbery, agreeing not to touch the proceeds for two and a half years. But some get tired of waiting . . .

Minor but effective crime melodrama in semi-documentary vein.

w Irwin Winehouse, A. Sanford Wolf   *d* Jerry Hopper   *ph* Loyal Griggs   *m* Van Cleave

J. Pat O'Malley, Robert Gist, Romo Vincent, Marion Ross, Tom Duggan

'A not uninteresting entry in the screen log-book on crime.' – *MFB*

The Blues Brothers *
US   1980   133m   Technicolor
Universal (Robert K. Weiss)
V, V*, L, S

A massive car chase develops when two brothers collect money for their old orphanage without too much regard for law and order.

Fashionable chase comedy with so many stunts that its cost ran up to 33,000,000 dollars. The public stayed away, though it has gained a cult following since.

w Dan Aykroyd, John Landis   *d* John Landis   *ph* Stephen M. Katz   *md* Ira Newborn   *pd* John Lloyd

John Belushi, Dan Aykroyd, Kathleen Freeman, James Brown, Henry Gibson, Cab Calloway, Carrie Fisher

'It meanders expensively like some pedigreed shaggy dog through 70s/80s American cinema and 50s/60s American rock, cocking its leg happily at every popular landmark on the way.' – *Paul Taylor, MFB*

'There's not a *soupçon* of wit or ingenuity in this brainless exercise in overspending.' – *Daily Mail*

'There's even room, in the midst of the carnage and mayhem, for a surprising amount of grace, humor and whimsy.' – *Roger Ebert*

Blues for Lovers: see *Ballad in Blue*

Blues in the Night *
US   1941   88m   bw
Warner (Henry Blanke)

Career and romantic problems for the members of a travelling jazz band.

Atmospheric little melodrama with good score and smart dialogue.

w Robert Rossen   *play* Hot Nocturne by Edwin Gilbert   *d* Anatole Litvak   *ph* Ernest Haller   *m/ly* Harold Arlen, Johnny Mercer

Priscilla Lane, Richard Whorf, Lloyd Nolan, Betty Field, Jack Carson, Elia Kazan, Wallace Ford, Billy Halop, Peter Whitney

AAN: title song (*m* Harold Arlen, *ly* Johnny Mercer)

Blume in Love *
US   1973   116m   Technicolor
Warner (Paul Mazursky)
V*

A divorced American lawyer in Venice reminisces about his love life.

Shapeless but enjoyable 'serious comedy' with star and director in good form.

wd Paul Mazursky   *ph* Bruce Surtees   *m* various

George Segal, Susan Anspach, Kris Kristofferson, Marsha Mason, Shelley Winters

BMX Bandits
Australia   1984   90m   colour   Panavision
Rank/BMX/Nilsen (Tom Broadbridge, Paul Davies)

Bike enthusiasts become unpopular when they cause havoc in the streets, but become heroes when they capture bank robbers.

Lively action piece with unacceptable behaviour followed by reformation and an old-fashioned moral for early teenagers.

w Patrick Edgeworth   *story* Russell Hagg   *d* Brian Trenchard-Smith   *ph* John Seale   *m* Colin Stead, Frank Strangio   *pd* Ross Major   *ed* Alan Lake

David Argue, John Ley, Nicole Kidman, Bryan Marshall, Angelo d'Angelo

Boardwalk
US   1979   100m   Eastmancolor
ITC/Stratford (Gerald T. Herrod)

An old couple in Coney Island are affected by escalating violence.

Well-meaning but somewhat absurd moral tale for our times, in which the harassed septuagenarian finally chokes the young punk leader to death.

w Stephen Verona, Leigh Chapman *d* Stephen Verona *ph* Billy Williams *m* various

Ruth Gordon, Lee Strasberg, Janet Leigh, Joe Silver, Eddie Barth

'One would probably have to reach as far back as *The Birth of a Nation* to find a more direct incitement to racial hatred.' – *Richard Combs, MFB*

The Boat **
West Germany 1981 149m Fujicolor
Columbia/Bavaria Atelier/Radiant Film (Gunter Röhrbach)
V, V*, L, S
original and US title: *Das Boot*

Adventures of a German U-boat during World War II.

Well-crafted but totally unsurprising saga of heroism and self-sacrifice; a decent view of war from the German side, designed to impress world markets. It did so only moderately.

wd Wolfgang Petersen *ph* Jost Vacano *m* Klaus Doldinger *pd* Rolf Zehetbauer

Jürgen Prochnow, Herbert Grönemeyer, Klaus Wennemann, Hubertus Bengsch, Martin Semmelrogge

AAN: direction; screenplay (adaptation); cinematography; editing; sound; sound editing

The Boatniks *
US 1970 100m Technicolor
Walt Disney (Ron Miller)

An accident-prone coastguard officer creates havoc at a yachting marina but is acclaimed a hero after catching three jewel thieves.

Simple fresh-air farce for the family, pleasantly set but flatly directed.

w Arthur Julian *d* Norman Tokar *ph* William Snyder *m* Robert F. Brunner

Phil Silvers, Robert Morse, Stefanie Powers, Norman Fell, Mickey Shaughnessy, Wally Cox, Don Ameche, Joey Forman

Bob & Carol & Ted & Alice **
US 1969 105m Technicolor
Columbia/M. J. Frankovich (Larry Tucker)
V*, L

Two California couples, influenced by a group therapy session advocating natural spontaneous behaviour, decide to admit their extra-marital affairs and narrowly avoid a wife-swapping party.

Fashionable comedy without the courage of its convictions: it starts and finishes very bashfully, but there are bright scenes in the middle. An attempt to extend it into a TV series was a failure.

w Paul Mazursky, Larry Tucker *d* Paul Mazursky *ph* Charles E. Lang *m* Quincy Jones

Natalie Wood, Robert Culp, Elliott Gould, Dyan Cannon, Horst Ebersberg

'An old-fashioned romantic comedy disguised as a blue picture.' – *Arthur Schlesinger Jnr*

AAN: Paul Mazursky, Larry Tucker; Charles E. Lang; Elliot Gould; Dyan Cannon

The Bob Mathias Story
US 1954 80m bw
Allied Artists
GB title: *The Flaming Torch*

The biography of an American athlete who won the Decathlon in the 1952 Olympics.

Predictable low-budgeter of no abiding interest.

w Richard Collins *d* Francis D. Lyon

Bob Mathias, Ward Bond, Melba Mathias, Ann Doran, Howard Petrie

Bob Roberts **
US 1992 104m Technicolor
Rank/Polygram/Working Title/Live Entertainment (Forrest Murray)
V, V*, L

An American folk singer and right-wing politician makes a record that goes to the top of the hit parade and wins a seat in the Senate.

Clever satire on politics, done as a documentary film, that has the message that it is appearance and the manipulation of the media that counts, not reality.

wd Tim Robbins *ph* Jean Lépine *m* David Robbins *pd* Richard Hoover *ed* Lisa Churgin

Tim Robbins, Giancarlo Esposito, Alan Rickman, Ray Wise, Brian Murray, Gore Vidal, Rebecca Jenkins, Harry J. Lennix, Susan Sarandon, John Cusack, Bob Balaban

'Both a stimulating social satire and a depressing commentary on the devolution of the US political system.' – *Variety*

Bobbikins
GB 1959 90m bw Cinemascope
TCF (Oscar Brodney, Bob McNaught)

A downtrodden variety artist finds that his baby can not only talk but also give him tips on the stock exchange.

Not at all a good idea, and feebly executed.

w Oscar Brodney *d* Robert Day *ph* Geoffrey Faithfull *m* Philip Green

Max Bygraves, Shirley Jones, Billie Whitelaw, Barbara Shelley, Colin Gordon, Charles Tingwell, Lionel Jeffries, Rupert Davies

'He had to meet her – to find himself!'
Bobby Deerfield
US 1977 123m Metrocolor Panavision
Warner/First Artists (Sydney Pollack)
V*

A depressive motor racing driver falls for a girl with an incurable illness.

A kind of understated *Love Story* for intellectuals; nicely made, but nothing that anybody will be wildly concerned about.

w Alvin Sargent *novel* Heaven Has No Favourites by Erich Maria Remarque *d* Sydney Pollack *ph* Henri Decaë *m* Dave Grusin *pd* Stephen Grimes

Al Pacino, Marthe Keller, Anny Duperey, Walter McGinn, Romolo Valli, Jaime Sanchez

The Bobo
US 1967 105m Technicolor
Warner/Gina (Elliott Kastner, Jerry Gershwin) (David R. Schwarz)
V*, L

An unsuccessful and timid bullfighter is offered a contract if within three days he can seduce the local belle.

Stylized, silly and boring comedy from an obviously dated play; Chaplinesque pathos was not this star's strong suit.

w David R. Schwarz *play* David R. Schwarz *novel* Olimpia by Burt Cole *d* Robert Parrish *ph* Gerry Turpin *m* Francis Lai

Peter Sellers, Britt Ekland, Rossano Brazzi, Adolfo Celi, Hattie Jacques, Ferdy Mayne, Kenneth Griffith, John Wells

La Boca del Lobo **
Peru/Spain 1988 116m Agfacolor
New People's Cinema/Twinray/Inca Films/Tornasol Films (Gerardo Herrero, Francisco J. Lombardi)
English title: *The Lion's Den*

A tough and embittered lieutenant orders his troops to massacre villagers sympathetic to the Communists.

Gripping investigation of the morality of war, based on a true incident.

w Augusto Cabada, Giovanni Pollarolo, Gerardo Herrero *d* Francisco J. Lombardi *ph* Jose Luis Lopez Linares *m* Bernardo Bonezzi *pd* Marta Mendez *ed* Juan San Mateo

Gustavo Bueno, Tono Vega, Joe Tejada, Gilberto Torres, Antero Sanchez, Aristoteles Picho, Fernando Vasquez, Luis Saavedra, Bertha Pagaza

Boccaccio '70 *
Italy/France 1962 210m Eastmancolor
TCF/CCC/Cineriz/Francinex/Gray Films (Antonio Cervi, Carlo Ponti)
V*, S

Four modern stories which Boccaccio might have written (on an off day).

Overlong portmanteau with inevitable bright moments but many more longueurs. The fourth episode was dropped when the film was released in the States and elsewhere.

'The Temptation of Dr Antonio': (*w*) Federico Fellini, Tullio Pinelli, Ennio Flaiano (*d*) Federico Fellini (*ph*) Otello Martelli; with Anita Ekberg 'The Job': (*w*) Suso Cecchi d'Amico, Luchino Visconti (*d*) Luchino Visconti (*ph*) Giuseppe Rotunno; with Romy Schneider, Tomas Milian 'The Raffle': (*w*) Cesare Zavattini (*d*) Vittorio de Sica (*ph*) Otello Martelli; with Sophia Loren 'Renzo and Luciana': (*d*) Mario Monichelli

Boda Secreta: see *Secret Wedding*

Bodies, Rest and Motion
US 1993 94m DeLuxe
Electric/Fine Line/August (Allan Mindel, Denise Shaw, Eric Stoltz)
S

A couple split up: he goes in search of his parents with a stolen television set, she begins a casual affair with a decorator.

An aimless movie about feckless people, the sort of film you'd continue watching on television if the remote control was not to hand.

w Roger Hedden *d* Michael Steinberg *ph* Bernd Heinl *m* Michael Convertino *pd* Stephen McCabe *ed* Jay Cassidy

Phoebe Cates, Bridget Fonda, Tim Roth, Eric Stoltz, Alicia Witt, Sandra Lafferty, Peter Fonda

'Uncompelling but moderately engaging throughout.' – *Variety*

'Billed as a comedy, it's mighty short on laughs.' – *Sheila Johnston, Independent*

Body and Soul
US 1931 82m bw
Fox

In the 1914–1918 war, a flyer falls for the wife of his dead buddy.

Tedious and often risible romantic melodrama.
play Squadrons by E. W. Springs, A. E. Thomas *d* Alfred Santell

Charles Farrell, Elissa Landi, Humphrey Bogart, Myrna Loy, Donald Dillaway

'Kidding is almost bound to creep in.' – *Variety*

Body and Soul *
US 1947 104m bw
Enterprise (Bob Roberts)
V*, L

A young boxer fights his way unscrupulously to the top.

Melodramatic but absorbing study of prizefighting's seamy side. (Is there any other?) Inventively studio-bound and almost impressionist in treatment.

w *Abraham Polonsky* *d* *Robert Rossen* *ph* *James Wong Howe* *md* Rudolph Polk *m* Hugo Friedhofer *ed* Francis Lyon, Robert Parrish

John Garfield, Lilli Palmer, Hazel Brooks, Anne Revere, William Conrad, Joseph Pevney, Canada Lee

'Here are the gin and tinsel, squalor and sables of the depression era, less daring than when first revealed in *Dead End* or *Golden Boy* but more valid and mature because shown without sentiment or blur.' – *National Board of Review*

AA: Francis Lyon, Robert Parrish

AAN: Abraham Polonsky; John Garfield

Body and Soul
US   1981   122m   colour
Cannon/Golan-Globus (Cliff Roquemore)
V*

An amateur boxer turns professional to earn money for medical treatment for his kid sister.

Blood in the ring, sentimentality on the sidelines. Despite the credit, this repellent movie has virtually no connection with the previous 'version'.

w Leon Isaac Kennedy *screenplay* Abraham Polonsky *d* George Bowers *ph* James Forrest *m* Webster Lewis

Leon Isaac Kennedy, Jayne Kennedy, Muhammed Ali, Michael Gazzo, Perry Lang, Kim Hamilton, Peter Lawford

The Body Disappears
US   1941   72m   bw
Warner (Ben Stoloff)

A professor invents an invisibility formula.

Uninspired comedy switch on a familiar theme.

w Scott Darling, Erna Lazarus *d* D. Ross Lederman *ph* Allen G. Seigler *m* Howard Jackson

Edward Everett Horton, Jeffrey Lynn, Jane Wyman, Herbert Anderson, Marguerite Chapman, Craig Stevens, David Bruce, Willie Best

Body Double
US   1984   114m   Metrocolor
Columbia/Delphi II (Brian de Palma)
V, V*, L

An out-of-work actor finds himself drawn into a nightmare when he spies on a lady stripteaser across the street.

Semi-porno melodrama with many echoes of Hitchcock overlaid with fashionable extremes of violence.

w Robert J. Avrech, Brian de Palma *d* Brian de Palma *ph* Stephen H. Burum *m* Pino Donaggio *pd* Ida Random *ed* Jerry Greenberg, Bill Pankow

Craig Wasson, Gregg Henry, Melanie Griffith

'De Palma lets all his obsessions hang out.' – *Variety*

Body Melt
Australia   1993   84m   colour
Dumb Films/Australian Film Commission/Film Victoria (Rod Bishop, Daniel Scharf)
V

A mad scientist invents a vitamin supplement that has an appalling side-effect: it causes people to explode or disintegrate.

A gruesomely visceral horror with stomach-turning effects; beneath all the gore there are signs of a certain wit and intelligence at work.

w Philip Brophy, Rod Bishop *d* Philip Brophy *ph* Ray Argall *m* Philip Brophy *pd* Maria Kozic *sp* Bob McCarron *ed* Bill Murphy

Gerard Kennedy, Andrew Daddo, Ian Smith, Vince Gil, Regina Gaigalas, Maurie Annese, Nick Polites, William McInnes

'A schlocky, tongue-in-cheek gore pic . . . cheerfully sick humor.' – *Variety*

† The film's credits include the unusual lines: 'Testicles Philip Brophy, Buttocks Maria Kozic'.

Body of Evidence
US   1992   99m   DeLuxe
UIP/Dino de Laurentiis
V, V*, L, S

A woman, who is accused of killing by too much sexual activity the elderly man who left her a fortune in his will, begins an affair with her defence counsel.

Almost silly enough to be enjoyable, in its calculated mix of kinky sex and courtroom scenes, but finally it is just too silly for words.

w Brad Mirman *d* Uli Edel *ph* Doug Milsome *m* Graeme Revell *pd* Victoria Paul *ed* Thom Noble

Madonna, Willem Dafoe, Joe Mantegna, Anne Archer, Julianne Moore, Jurgen Prochnow, Frank Langella, Stan Shaw

'This showcase for the singer-thesp as femme fatale is titillating enough to lure an initially curious public and follow up as a good video title, but its theatrical endurance would seem closer to that of her victim than to Madonna's.' – *Variety*

'She taught him everything he knew – about passion and murder!'
Body Heat **
US   1981   113m   Technicolor
Warner/Ladd (Fred T. Gallo)
V, V*, L

A Florida lawyer becomes involved with a married woman and they plot to kill her businessman husband.

Oversexed and superfluous, not to mention uncredited, revamp of *Double Indemnity*. Some evidence of flair does not relieve that 'I have been here before' feeling.

wd *Lawrence Kasdan* *ph* Richard H. Kline *m* John Barry *pd* Bill Kenney *ed* Carol Littleton

William Hurt, *Kathleen Turner*, Richard Crenna, Ted Danson

'Film noir, if it is to be successfully reworked, needs to be approached with a sense of analysis, rather than simple excess.' – *Steve Jenkins, MFB*

Body Slam
US   1987   89m   CFI color
Musifilm/Hemdale (Shel Lytton, Mike Curb)
V*

A promoter on the skids accidentally creates the rock'n wrestling craze.

Easy-going comedy which would have benefited from more confident production.

w Shel Lytton, Steve Burkow *d* Hal Needham *ph* Mike Shea *m* Michael Lloyd, John D'Andrea *ad* Pamela Warner *ed* Randy Thornton

Dirk Benedict, Tanya Roberts, Roddy Piper, Lou Albano, Charles Nelson Reilly, Billy Barty, Barry Gordon, John Astin

'Shriek And Shudder.'
'Graves Raided! Coffins Robbed! Corpses Carved! Midnight Murder! Body Blackmail! Stalking Ghouls! Mad Thrills Of Terror And Macabre Mystery!
The Body Snatcher ***
US   1945   77m   bw
RKO (Val Lewton)
V*, L

In 19th-century Edinburgh a doctor obtains 'specimens' from grave-robbers, and murder results when supplies run short.

A familiar theme very imaginatively handled, and well acted, though the beginning is slow. The best of the Lewton thrillers.

w *Philip MacDonald, Carlos Keith* (Val Lewton) *story* R. L. Stevenson *d* Robert Wise *ph* Robert de Grasse *m* Roy Webb

Henry Daniell, Boris Karloff, Bela Lugosi, Edith Atwater, Russell Wade

'A humane sincerity and a devotion to good cinema . . . However, most of the picture is more literary than lively.' – *Time*

'Imagine . . . You're Gone And Someone Else Is Living Inside Your Body.'
Body Snatchers **
US   1993   90m   Technicolor
Warner (Robert H. Solo)
V, V*

Aliens replicate and replace the inhabitants of military camps.

An effective and suspenseful retelling of the classic of conformity and paranoia, given a modern gloss with its teenage heroine and its concerns about toxic waste and environmental damage.

w Stuart Gordon, Dennis Paoli, Nicholas St John *novel* Jack Finney *story* Raymond Cistheri, Larry Cohen *d* Abel Ferrara *ph* Bojan Bazelli *m* Joe Delia *pd* Peter Jamison *ed* Anthony Redman

Gabrielle Anwar, Terry Kinney, Billy Wirth, Meg Tilley, Christine Elise, R. Lee Ermey, G. Elvis Phillips, Reilly Murphy, Kathleen Doyle, Forest Whitaker

'A tremendously exciting thriller that compares favourably with Don Siegel's classic.' – *Variety*

'A gem which seduces the eye, captures the imagination and makes the adrenalin race.' – *Sight and Sound*

† The film was released direct to video in Britain. Jack Finney's novel was filmed in 1956 by Don Siegel and remade in 1978 by Philip Kaufman under the title *Invasion of the Body Snatchers* (qqv), the later version also being produced by Robert H. Solo.

Body Stealers
GB   1969   91m   colour
Tigon (Tony Tenser)
US title: *Thin Air*

A NATO general calls for an investigation when parachutists training for space disappear in mid-air.

Conventional low-budget science fiction, predictable from the first moment to the last.

w Mike St Clair, Peter Marcus *d* Gerry Levy *ph* Johnny Coquillon *m* Reg Tilsey *ad* Wilfred Arnold *ed* Howard Lanning

George Sanders, Maurice Evans, Patrick Allen, Hilary Dwyer, Lorna Wilde, Neil Connery, Robert Flemyng, Allan Cuthbertson

The Bodyguard (1961): see
Yojimbo

'Never let her out of your sight. Never let your guard down. Never fall in love.'
The Bodyguard
US   1992   129m   Technicolor
Warner/Tig/Kasdan Pictures (Lawrence Kasdan, Jim Wilson, Kevin Costner)
V, V*, L, S

A former CIA agent is hired as a bodyguard by a singer who has received threats on her life.

Predictable mix of song, romance and action that found surprising favour at the box-office.

w Lawrence Kasdan *d* Mick Jackson *ph* Andrew Dunn *m* Alan Silvestri *pd* Jeffrey Beecroft *ed* Richard A. Harris

Kevin Costner, Whitney Houston, Gary Kemp, Bill Cobbs, Ralph Waite, Tomas Arana, Michele Lamar Richards, Mike Starr

'A jumbled mess with a few enjoyable moments but little continuity or flow.' – *Variety*

'The film is highly professional and perfectly watchable. But there's nothing memorable in it at all.' – *Derek Malcolm, Guardian*

AAN: Song: 'I Have Nothing' (*m* Jud Friedmann, *ly* Allan Rich); song: 'Run to You'

'The big comedy of nineteen sexty-sex!'
Boeing-Boeing
US 1965 102m Technicolor
Paramount/Hal B. Wallis
V*

By successfully juggling with plane schedules, a Paris journalist manages to live with three air hostesses at the same time.

Frenetic, paper-thin sex comedy from a one-joke play; film style generally undistinguished.

w Edward Anhalt *play* Marc Camoletti *d* John Rich *ph* Lucien Ballard *m* Neal Hefti

Tony Curtis, Jerry Lewis (his only 'straight' part), Dany Saval, Christiane Schmidtner, Suzanna Leigh, *Thelma Ritter*

'A sort of jet-age French farce.' – *Judith Crist*

The Bofors Gun *
GB 1968 105m Technicolor
Rank/Everglades (Robert A. Goldston, Otto Plaschkes)

In 1954 Germany a British army unit runs into trouble when a violent and unstable Irish private picks on a weakly National Service corporal.

Keen, fascinating, but often crude and eventually rather silly expansion of a TV play chiefly notable for the excellent acting opportunities provided by its unattractive but recognizable characters.

w John McGrath *play* Events While Guarding the Bofors Gun by John McGrath *d* Jack Gold *ph* Alan Hume *m* Carl Davis

Nicol Williamson, John Thaw, *David Warner*, Ian Holm

La Bohème
US 1926 75m approx at 24 fps bw silent
MGM

Mimi starves to death in a Paris garret.

Overacted straight version of the opera, with two passionate star performances.

w Harry Behn, Ray Doyle, after Murger *d* King Vidor

Lillian Gish, John Gilbert, Renee Adoree, Edward Everett Horton

La Bohème *
France/Italy 1988 107m Eastmancolor
Electric Pictures/Erato Films/La Sept/SFPC/Generale d'Images, Travelling Productions/Video-Schermo (Jean-Claude Borlat)

Uncinematic treatment of Puccini's opera, though well-enough sung.

w Giuseppe Giacosa, Luigi Illica *novel* Scènes de la vie de Bohème by Henri Murger *d* Luigi Comencini *ph* Armando Nannuzzi *md* James Conlon *m* Giacomo Puccini *ad* Paolo Comencini *ed* Sergio Buzi, Reine Wekstein

Barbara Hendricks, Luca Canonici, Jose Carreras (voice only), Angela Maria Blasi, Gino Quilico

The Bohemian Girl *
US 1936 74m bw
Hal Roach
V, V (C), V*, L

Gypsies kidnap a nobleman's daughter and bring her up as their own.

One of several operettas reworked for Laurel and Hardy, this is an inoffensive entertainment which devotes too little care to their need for slowly built-up gag structure; their sequences tend to fizzle out and the singing is a bore.

operetta Michael W. Balfe *d* James Horne, Charles Rogers *ph* Art Lloyd, Francis Corby *md* Nathaniel Shilkret *ed* Bert Jordan, Louis McManus

Stan Laurel, Oliver Hardy, Mae Busch, Antonio Moreno, Jacqueline Wells, Darla Hood, Zeffie Tilbury, James Finlayson, Thelma Todd (for one song, apparently dubbed: presumably before her sudden death she had been cast as the heroine)

'A comedy with little or no comedy'. – *Variety*

† There was in 1922 a British silent version with a splendid cast including Ivor Novello, Gladys Cooper, C. Aubrey Smith, Ellen Terry and Constance Collier.

Il Boia di Venezia: see *Executioner of Venice*

Boiling Point *
US/France 1993 92m Technicolor
Guild/Warner/Hexagon (Marc Frydman, Leonardo de la Fuente)
V, V*

Two men have a week to solve their problems: a Treasury agent, obsessed with revenging the murder of his partner, and the con man whose partner is responsible for the killing.

Although promoted as an action film, this is more an engaging character study that hovers on the edge of cliché but manages to maintain its balance.

wd James B. Harris *novel* Money Men by Gerald Petievich *ph* King Baggot *m* Cory Lerois, John D'Andrea *pd* Ron Foreman *ed* Jerry Brady

Wesley Snipes, Dennis Weaver, Lolita Davidovich, Viggo Mortensen, Dan Hedaya, Seymour Cassel, Jonathan Banks, Christine Elise, Tony Lo Biano, Valerie Perrine

'Low-key and bland in the extreme, it's strictly for film buffs.' – *Variety*

'Hardly substantial, but it's also consistently entertaining.' – *Sight and Sound*

The Bold and the Brave
US 1956 87m bw Superscope
RKO/Hal E. Chester

An assortment of American types come together in the Italian campaign of 1944.

Routine war heroics chiefly remembered (if at all) for a crap game sequence.

w Robert Lewin *d* Lewis Foster *ph* Sam Leavitt *m* Herschel Burke Gilbert

Wendell Corey, *Mickey Rooney*, Nicole Maurey, Don Taylor

AAN: Robert Lewin; Mickey Rooney

'He rose to fame on a ladder of dancing ladies!'
Bolero *
US 1934 85m bw Paramount

A New York dancer neglects his personal life to become king of the European night-club circuit.

Lively romantic drama which performed remarkably at the box-office and led to a kind of sequel, *Rumba*.

w Carey Wilson, Kubec Glasmon, Ruth Ridenour, Horace Jackson *d* Wesley Ruggles *ph* Leo Tover

George Raft, Carole Lombard, Sally Rand (doing her fan dance), Frances Drake, William Frawley, Ray Milland, Gertrude Michael

'A studio conference product: lots of surefire elements. On screen it's a little enervating . . . depends on Raft's popularity with the women.' – *Variety*

Bolero
US 1984 104m colour
Cannon/City (Bo Derek)
V*, L

In 1926, a wealthy romantic girl travels the world in search of a man worthy of the sacrifice of her virginity.

Ludicrous sexual charade with unpleasant overtones resulting from the fact that the star's husband wrote and photographed this embarrassing piece of near-pornography.

wd John Derek *ph* John Derek *m* Peter Bernstein *pd* Alan Roderick-Jones

Bo Derek, George Kennedy, Andrea Occhipinti, Greg Bensen, Ana Obregon

'The only ecstatic moment a filmgoer might derive will be at the discovery that it's over.' – *Philip Strick, MFB*

Bomba the Jungle Boy
US 1949 71m bw or sepia
Monogram (Walter Mirisch)

Photographers in Africa meet a junior Tarzan who rescues their girlfriend.

Cut-rate hokum starring the lad who had played Johnny Weissmuller's 'son' in earlier Tarzan movies; it led to several tedious sequels.

w Jack de Witt, from the comic strip by Roy Rockwell *d* Ford Beebe *ph* William Sickner *m* Edward Kay

Johnny Sheffield, Peggy Ann Garner, Onslow Stevens, Charles Irwin

† Sequels were as follows:

1948: BOMBA ON PANTHER ISLAND (76m) with Allene Roberts
1949: BOMBA AND THE LOST VOLCANO (76m) with Donald Woods; BOMBA AND THE HIDDEN CITY (71m) with Paul Guilfoyle
1950: BOMBA AND THE ELEPHANT STAMPEDE (71m) with Myron Sealey
1951: BOMBA AND THE AFRICAN TREASURE (70m) with Lyle Talbot; BOMBA AND THE JUNGLE GIRL (70m) with Karen Sharpe; BOMBA AND THE LION HUNTERS (75m) with Morris Ankrum
1953: SAFARI DRUMS (71m) with Douglas Kennedy
1954: THE GOLDEN IDOL (71m) with Paul Guilfoyle; KILLER LEOPARD (70m) with Beverly Garland
1955: D OF THE JUNGLE (69m) with Wayne Morris

Bombardier
US 1943 99m bw
RKO (Robert Fellows)
V*

Cadet bombardiers learn the realities of war on raids over Japan.

Totally routine recruiting poster heroics.

w John Twist *d* Richard Wallace *ph* Nicholas Musuraca *m* Roy Webb

Pat O'Brien, Randolph Scott, Anne Shirley, Eddie Albert, Walter Reed, Robert Ryan, Barton MacLane

Bombay Clipper
US 1941 54m bw
Universal

On a clipper bound for Bombay, a reporter becomes involved in mystery and romance.

Capsule actioner with stock studio talent.

w Roy Chanslor, Stanley Rubin *d* John Rawlins

William Gargan, Irene Hervey, Maria Montez, Charles Lang, Turhan Bey, Lloyd Corrigan, Mary Gordon

Bombay Mail
US 1933 66m bw
Universal

On a train between Calcutta and Bombay a Scotland

Yard detective solves the murder of the Governor of Bengal.

Very tolerable mystery filler.

w Tom Reed, L. G. Blochman   d Edwin L. Marin

Edmund Lowe, Shirley Grey, Onslow Stevens, Ralph Forbes, Hedda Hopper

'It mixes a colourful set of characters and maintains a moderately absorbing pace.' – *Variety*

Bombay Talkie *
India   1970   105m   Eastmancolor
Merchant-Ivory (Ismail Merchant)
V*

A sophisticated American woman comes to Bombay and falls for two men involved in film-making.

Interesting but unsatisfactory romantic drama, rather pointlessly set against film studio backgrounds.

w Ruth Prawer Jhabvala, James Ivory   d James Ivory   ph Subrata Mitra   m Shankar Jaikishan

Jennifer Kendal, Shashi Kapoor, Zia Mohyeddin

Bombers B-52
US   1957   106m   Warnercolor   Cinemascope
Warner (Richard Whorf)
GB title: *No Sleep till Dawn*

A USAF sergeant considers applying for a discharge so that he can earn more money in civilian life.

Glossy domestic melodrama punctuated by aircraft shots.

w Irving Wallace   d Gordon Douglas   ph William Clothier   m Leonard Rosenman

Karl Malden, Marsha Hunt, Natalie Wood, Efrem Zimbalist Jnr, Don Kelly

'No one questions the basic assumption – that the good life consists of servicing bigger and better bombers.' – *MFB*

Bomber's Moon
US   1943   70m   bw
TCF

An American pilot crashlands into Germany and makes for the coast.

Modestly budgeted war adventure with conventional thrills.

w Kenneth Gamet   d 'Charles Fuhr' (Edward Ludwig and Harold Schuster)

George Montgomery, Annabella, Kent Taylor, Walter Kingsford, Martin Kosleck

Bombs Over Burma
US   1942   67m   bw
PRC/Alfred Stern-Arthur Alexander

Chinese carry out intelligence work on the Burma road.

Cheapjack heroics, almost unwatchable even at the time.

w Milton Raison, Joseph H. Lewis   d Joseph H. Lewis

Anna May Wong, Noel Madison, Leslie Denison, Nedrick Young

Bombshell ***
US   1933   91m   bw
MGM (Hunt Stromberg)
V*
GB title and aka: *Blonde Bombshell*

A glamorous film star yearns for a new image.

Crackpot farce which even by today's standards moves at a fair clip and enabled the star to give her best comedy performance.

w Jules Furthman, John Lee Mahin, play Caroline Francke, Mack Crane   d Victor Fleming   ph Chester Lyons, Hal Rosson

Jean Harlow, Lee Tracy, Frank Morgan, Franchot Tone, Pat O'Brien, Ivan Lebedeff, Una Merkel, Ted Healy, Isabel Jewell, C. Aubrey Smith, Louise Beavers, Leonard Carey, Mary Forbes

'Bound to click and the best legitimate comedy in a long time.' – *Variety*

Bombsight Stolen: see *Cottage to Let*

Bon Voyage *
US   1962   133m   Technicolor
Walt Disney (Bill Walsh, Ron Miller)
V*

An American family spends a holiday in Paris.

Simple-minded, overlong comedy of mishaps, with daddy finally trapped in the sewer. Smoothly done of its kind.

w Bill Walsh   novel Marrijane and Joseph Hayes   d James Neilson   ph William Snyder   m Paul Smith

Fred MacMurray, Jane Wyman, Michael Callan, Deborah Walley, Jessie Royce Landis, Tommy Kirk, Ivan Desny

Bonaventure: see *Thunder on the Hill*

Bond Street
GB   1948   107m   bw
ABP/World Screenplays (Anatole de Grunwald)

Four stories, each concerning an item of an expensive wedding trousseau.

Mild and laboured short story compendium.

w Anatole de Grunwald   d Gordon Parry   ph Otto Heller   m Benjamin Frankel

Roland Young, Jean Kent, Paula Valenska, Kathleen Harrison, Derek Farr, *Kenneth Griffith*, Hazel Court, Ronald Howard

'Even a glimpse of actual Bond Street makes little contact with reality.' – *MFB*

'Take one Wall Street tycoon, his Fifth Avenue mistress, a reporter hungry for fame, and make the wrong turn in The Bronx … then sit back and watch the sparks fly'

The Bonfire of the Vanities
US   1990   125m   Technicolor
Warner (Brian de Palma)
V, V*, L

The successful life of a New York bond dealer crumbles when he is arrested for injuring a black youth in a street accident.

Strained attempt at social satire, miscast and missing all its targets.

w Michael Cristofer   novel Tom Wolfe   d Brian de Palma   ph Vilmos Zsigmond   m Dave Grusin   pd Richard Sylbert   ad Peter Lansdown Smith   ed David Ray, Bill Pankow

Tom Hanks, Bruce Willis, Melanie Griffith, Kim Cattrall, Saul Rubinek, Morgan Freeman, F. Murray Abraham, John Hancock, Kevin Dunn, Clifton James

'A misfire of inanities.' – *Variety*

† Julie Salamon's book *The Devil's Candy: The Bonfire of the Vanities Goes to Hollywood* follows the production from its inception to its release.

Le Bonheur *
France   1965   79m   Eastmancolor
Parc/Mag Bodard

A young carpenter is happy with his wife and family, happier still when he finds a mistress, whom he marries when his wife is found drowned.

Slight, good looking, ambivalent little fable which finally expires in a surfeit of style.

wd Agnès Varda   ph Jean Rabier, Claude Beausoleil   m Mozart

Jean-Claude Drouot, Claire Drouot, Marie-France Boyer

Bonjour Tristesse *
GB   1957   93m   Technicolor   Cinemascope
Columbia/Wheel Films (Otto Preminger)
V*

A teenage girl becomes involved with her sophisticated father's amours and causes the death of his would-be mistress.

The novel's rather repellent characters are here played like royal personages against a background of Riviera opulence. The result is very odd but often entertaining, especially when it slips into self-parody.

w Arthur Laurents   novel Françoise Sagan   d Otto Preminger   ph Georges Périnal   m Georges Auric   pd Roger Furse

David Niven, Deborah Kerr, Jean Seberg, Mylene Demongeot, Geoffrey Horne, Juliette Greco, Martita Hunt, Walter Chiari, Jean Kent, Roland Culver

'An elegant, ice-cold charade of emotions.' – *Judith Crist*

'Sagan not so much translated as traduced – opened out, smartened up, the sickness overlaid with Riviera suntan.' – *Alexander Walker*

'Long, untidy, muddled and mushy.' – *Financial Times*

† Shot in monochrome for Paris, colour for the Riviera.

La Bonne Année: see *Happy New Year*

Bonne Chance
France   1935   75m   bw
Sacha Guitry

An artist who wins a lottery takes on holiday with him, on a purely platonic basis, the girl who gave him half her ticket.

Modest star comedy which pleased at the time.

wd Sacha Guitry

Sacha Guitry, Jacqueline Delubac, Robert Darthez

La Bonne Soupe
France/Italy   1963   97m   bw
Belstar/Du Siècle/Dear Film (André Hakim)

A high-class prostitute tells her life story.

A saucy frolic complete with three-in-a-bed and rapidly closing doors; quite enjoyable of its kind.

wd Robert Thomas   play Félicien Marceau   ph Roger Hubert   m Raymond le Sénéchal

Annie Girardot, Marie Bell, Gérard Blain, Bernard Blier, Jean-Claude Brialy, Claude Dauphin, Sacha Distel, Daniel Gélin, Blanchette Brunoy, Jane Marken, Raymond Péllégrin, Franchot Tone

Les Bonnes Femmes **
France   1960   102m   bw
Paris/Panitalia (Robert and Raymond Hakim)
aka: *The Girls*

Four shop assistants dream of getting away from the boredom and mediocrity of their lives.

Tough and compassionate study of women trapped in a second-rate world, from which death offers the only real escape.

w Paul Gégauff, Claude Chabrol   d Claude Chabrol   ph Henri Decae   m Paul Misraki, Pierre Jansen   ed Jacques Gaillard

Bernadette Lafont, Clotilde Joano, Stéphane Audran, Lucile Saint-Simon, Pierre Bertin, Jean-Louis Maury, Claude Berri, Mario David

'Uneven and, in parts, somewhat tedious and tawdry, yet it has more tenderness and is more emotionally compelling than much of Chabrol's more refined work.' – *Pauline Kael*

'They're young … they're in love … and they kill people!'
Bonnie and Clyde ****
US   1967   111m   Technicolor
Warner/Seven Arts/Tatira/Hiller (*Warren Beatty*)
V, V*, L

In the early thirties, a car thief and the daughter of his
intended victim team up to become America's most
feared and ruthless bank robbers.

Technically brilliant evocation of sleepy mid-America
at the time of the public enemies, using every kind of
cinematic trick including fake snapshots, farcical
interludes, dreamy soft-focus and a jazzy score. For all
kinds of reasons a very influential film which even
made extreme violence quite fashionable (and very
bloody it is).

w *David Newman, Robert Benton*   d *Arthur Penn*
ph *Burnett Guffey*   m *Charles Strouse*, using 'Foggy
Mountain Breakdown' by Flatt and Scruggs

*Warren Beatty, Faye Dunaway, Gene Hackman, Estelle
Parsons, Michael J. Pollard, Dub Taylor, Denver Pyle,
Gene Wilder*

'It is a long time since we have seen an American film
so perfectly judged.' – *MFB*

'. . . all to the rickety twang of a banjo and a saturation
in time and place.' – *Judith Crist*

'The formula is hayseed comedy bursting sporadically
into pyrotechnical bloodshed and laced with
sentimental pop-Freudianism.' – *John Simon*

'A film from which we shall date reputations and
innovations in the American cinema.' – *Alexander
Walker*

'It works as comedy, as tragedy, as entertainment, as a
meditation on the place of guns and violence in
American society.' – *Roger Ebert*

AA: Burnett Guffey; Estelle Parsons

AAN: best picture; David Newman, Robert Benton;
Arthur Penn; Warren Beatty; Faye Dunaway; Gene
Hackman; Michael J. Pollard

The Bonnie Parker Story
US   1958   80m   bw
James H. Nicholson, Sam Arkoff

A waitress joins up with a cheap crook in a series of
bank raids.

Tinpot 'B' gangster film chiefly notable for comparison
with the later *Bonnie and Clyde*. All it really has is a
certain exuberance in the action sequences.

w *Stan Shpetner*   d *William Witney*

Dorothy Provine, Jack Hogan, Richard Bakalyan,
Joseph Turkel

Bonnie Prince Charlie
GB   1948   140m approx (later cut to 118m)
    Technicolor
British Lion/London Films (Edward Black)
V, V*

The hope of the Stuarts returns from exile but is
eventually forced to flee again.

Good highland photography combines with appalling
studio sets, an initially confused narrative, a draggy
script and uneasy performances to produce an ill-fated
attempt at a British historical epic. Alexander Korda,
who masterminded it, sulked in public at the critical
roasting, but on this occasion the critics were right.

w *Clemence Dane*   d *Anthony Kimmins*
ph *Robert Krasker*   m *Ian Whyte*

David Niven, Margaret Leighton, Jack Hawkins, Judy
Campbell, Morland Graham, Finlay Currie, John
Laurie

'I have a sense of wonder about this film, beside
which *The Swordsman* seems like a dazzling work of
veracity and art. It is that London Films, having
surveyed the finished thing, should not have quietly
scrapped it.' – *Richard Winnington*

'The picture is not lacking in moments of unconscious
levity, what with David Niven rallying his hardy
Highlanders to his standard in a voice hardly large
enough to summon a waiter.' – *New Yorker*

'Time has made it the film industry's biggest joke. But
the joke turns a little sour when one reflects how
extravagance, recklessness and sheer bungling
administration during the fat and prosperous years
left the British film industry so poor and vulnerable
when the hard times came along.' – *Gerald Garret, 1975*

Bonnie Scotland *
US   1935   80m   bw
MGM/Hal Roach
V, V*, L

Two Americans journey to Scotland to collect a non-
existent inheritance, then follow their friend in the
army and wind up in India.

Generally disappointing star comedy which still
contains excellent sequences when it is not vainly
trying to preserve interest in a boring plot. An
obvious parody on *Lives of a Bengal Lancer*, released
earlier that year; Scotland has almost nothing to do
with it.

w *Frank Butler, Jeff Moffitt*   d *James Horne*
ph *Art Lloyd, Walter Lundin* ed *Bert Jordan*

Stan Laurel, Oliver Hardy, James Finlayson, Daphne
Pollard, William Janney, June Lang

'Packed with Laurel and Hardy hokum and good for
plenty of laughs' – *Boxoffice*

Bonnie's Kids
US   1972   105m   Eastmancolor
Variety/Tommy J. Productions (Charles Stroud)
V*

After killing their lecherous stepfather, two young
women take to a life of sex and crime.

Cut-rate exploitation picture, celebrating amorality,
that attempts to cash in on the success of *Bonnie
and Clyde*.

wd *Arthur Marks*   ph *Robert Charles Wilson*
m *Carson Whitsett*   ed *Richard Greer*

Tiffany Bolling, Robin Mattson, Leo Gordon, Steve
Sandor, Scott Brady, Leonore Stevens, Alex Rocco,
Timothy Brown

'You'll be tickled to death over this gay chiller diller!'
The Boogie Man Will Get You
US   1944   66m   bw
Columbia (Colbert Clark)

Bodies accumulate when mad doctors get to work
creating supermen in a small village.

Desperately unfunny spoof notable only for the fact
that it was attempted with these players and at that
time.

w *Edwin Blum*   d *Lew Landers*   ph *Henry
Freulich*   md *Morris Stoloff*

Boris Karloff, Peter Lorre, Maxie Rosenbloom, Jeff
Donnell, Larry Parks, Maude Eburne, Don Beddoe

Book of Love *
US   1990   87m   CFI colour
Entertainment/New Line
V, V*, L

A successful writer remembers when he was 16 and
was too shy to ask the girl he loved to go to the prom.

Pleasantly done, nostalgic rites-of-passage movie. It
travels over familiar ground, but with a light tread.

w *William Kotzwinkle*   novel *Jack in the Box* by
William Kotzwinkle   d *Robert Shaye*   ph *Peter
Deming*   m *Stanley Clarke*   pd *C. J. Strawn*
ed *Terry Stokes*

Chris Young, Keith Coogan, Aeryk Egan, Josie
Bissett, Tricia Leigh Fisher, Danny Nucci, John
Cameron Mitchell, Beau Dremann

'She outlived six rich men!'
Boom!
GB   1968   113m   Technicolor   Panavision
Universal/World Film Services/Moon Lake Productions (John
    Heyman, Norman Priggen)

On the volcanic Mediterranean island which she
owns, a dying millionairess plans to take as her last
lover a wandering poet who is the angel of death.

Pretentious, boring nonsense, showing that when
talent goes awry it certainly goes boom.

w *Tennessee Williams*,   play *The Milk Train Doesn't
Stop Here Any More* by Tennessee Williams   d *Joseph
Losey*   ph *Douglas Slocombe*   m *John Barry*

Elizabeth Taylor, Richard Burton, *Noël Coward*,
Michael Dunn, Joanna Shimkus

'It's a beautiful picture, the best ever made of one of
my plays.' – *Tennessee Williams*

'A pointless, pompous nightmare.' – *Paul D.
Zimmermann, Newsweek*

'An ordeal in tedium,' – *Hollywood Reporter*

'Outright junk.' – *Saturday Review*

'The title could not be more apt: it is precisely the
sound of a bomb exploding.' – *Richard Schickel, Life*

'*Boom!* isn't doing little business; it's doing no
business at all.' – *Universal executive*

Boom in the Moon (dubbed)
Mexico   1946   90m   bw
Alsa (Alexander Salkind)
V*

original title: *El Moderno Barba Azul*

A shipwrecked sailor is mistaken for a mass murderer
and sent on the first expedition to the moon.

Embarrassingly bad, feebly scripted and cheaply
made comedy in which Keaton displays none of his
skill or invention, but sleepwalks through his role.

w *Victor Trivas, Jaime Salvador*   d *Jaime Salvador*
m *George Tzipine*

Buster Keaton, Angel Garasa, Virginia Seret, Luis
Bareiro, Fernando Sotto

† The film was never released in American cinemas
and was hardly seen outside Mexico until its video
release; it surfaces occasionally on television in a
version that runs for 70m.

Boom Town **
US   1940   120m   bw
MGM (Sam Zimbalist)
V*, L

Two friendly oil drillers strike it rich.

Enjoyable four-star, big-studio product of its time:
world-wide entertainment of assured success, with a
proven mix of romance, action, drama and comedy.

w *John Lee Mahin*   story James Edward Grant
d *Jack Conway*   ph *Harold Rosson*   m *Franz
Waxman*   ad *Cedric Gibbons*

Clark Gable, Spencer Tracy, Claudette Colbert, Hedy
Lamarr, *Frank Morgan*, Lionel Atwill, Chill Wills

'Western high jinks, a wee child, and courtroom
speeches about individual enterprise constitute the
various come-ons in a scrambled and inept picture.' –
New York Herald Tribune

'More colourful action in the oil fields and less
agitation indoors might have made it a great picture.'
– *Bosley Crowther*

AAN: Harold Rosson

Boomerang ***
US   1947   88m   bw
TCF (Louis de Rochemont)

In a New England town, a clergyman is shot dead on
the street. The DA prevents an innocent man from
being convicted, but cannot track down the guilty
party.

Incisive real life thriller: based on a true case, it was shot in an innovative documentary style which was much copied, and justice is not seen to be done, though the murderer is known to the audience. A milestone movie of its kind.

w Richard Murphy   *d* Elia Kazan   *ph* Norbert Brodine   *m* David Buttolph

Dana Andrews, Jane Wyatt, Lee J. Cobb, Cara Williams, Arthur Kennedy, Sam Levene, Taylor Holmes, Robert Keith, Ed Begley

'A study of integrity, beautifully developed by Dana Andrews against a background of political corruption and chicanery that is doubly shocking because of its documentary understatement.' – *Richard Winnington*

'For the first time in many a moon we are treated to a picture that gives a good example of a typical small American city – the people, their way of living, their mode of government, the petty politics practised, the power of the press.' – *Frank Ward, National Board of Review*

AAN: Richard Murphy

'A Player Who's About To Be Played.'
Boomerang
US   1992   117m   Technicolor
UIP/Paramount (Brian Grazer, Warrington Hudlin)
V, V*, L, S

An executive in a cosmetics firm has an unsuccessful affair with his boss before finding true love.

Dim comedy that substitutes gloss for wit and deprives its star of everything except uncritical adulation.

w Barry W. Blaustein, David Sheffield   *d* Reginald Hudlin   *ph* Woody Omens   *m* Marcus Miller   *pd* Jane Musky   *ed* Earl Watson, John Carter, Michael Jablow

Eddie Murphy, Robin Givens, Halle Berry, David Alan Grier, Martin Lawrence, Grace Jones, Geoffrey Holder, Eartha Kitt, Melvin Van Peebles

'This Eddie Murphy vehicle tries hard to be positive. It's a pity that the movie isn't any good.' – *Michael Sragow, New Yorker*

'An ill-fitting comedy vehicle that's desperately in need of a reality check.' – *Variety*

The Boost *
US   1988   95m   colour
Hemdale/Becker-Blatt-Ponicsan (Daniel H. Blatt)
V, V*, L

A fast-talking salesman and his wife are ruined by their addiction to cocaine.

Cautionary tale of an acquisitive society, coolly told.

w Darryl Ponicsan   *novel* Ludes by Benjamin Stein   *d* Harold Becker   *ph* Howard Atherton   *m* Stanley Myers   *ad* Ken Hardy   *ed* Maury Winetrobe

James Woods, Sean Young, John Kapelos, Steven Hill, Kelle Kerr, John Rothman, Amanda Blake, Grace Zabriskie

Das Boot: see *The Boat*

Boots Malone
US   1952   103m   bw
Columbia (Milton Holmes)
V*

A would-be jockey tags along with a down-at-heel agent who gets him work and finally persuades him not to throw a crooked race.

Dullish racetrack melodrama bogged down by repetitive and unsympathetic plot twists.

w Milton Holmes   *d* William Dieterle   *ph* Charles Lawton   *m* Elmer Bernstein

William Holden, Johnny Stewart, Stanley Clements, Basil Ruysdael, Carl Benton Reid, Ed Begley, Henry Morgan

The Border
US   1981   108m   Technicolor   Panavision
Universal/RKO (Neil Hartley)
V*, L

A Los Angeles cop joins the border patrol in El Paso and becomes involved in the squalor, violence and double-dealing.

A rather solemn elaboration on a well-worn theme, with nothing very memorable except its excesses.

w Deric Washburn, Walon Green, David Freeman   *d* Tony Richardson   *ph* Ric Waite   *m* Ry Cooder   *pd* Toby Rafelson   *ed* Robert K. Lambert

Jack Nicholson, Harvey Keitel, Valerie Perrine, Warren Oates, Elpidia Carrillo

Border Incident
US   1949   93m   bw
MGM (Nicholas Nayfack)

Police stop the illegal immigration of labourers from Mexico.

Routine semi-documentary cops and robbers, well enough made.

w John C. Higgins   *d* Anthony Mann   *ph* John Alton   *m* André Previn

Ricardo Montalban, George Murphy, Howard da Silva, James Mitchell, Alfonso Bedoya

Border River
US   1953   80m   Technicolor
Universal-International

At the end of the Civil War, an ex-Confederate officer gets involved with a gold war in the Mexican free zone.

Slightly unusual Western programmer.

w William Sackheim, Louis Stevens   *d* George Sherman

Joel McCrea, Yvonne de Carlo, Pedro Armendariz, Ivan Triesault, Alfonso Bedoya, Howard Petrie

Borderline
US   1980   97m   colour
ITC (Martin Starger)
V*

A Mexican border patrolman chases illegal immigrants and the big time crooks making money out of them.

Routine, quite effective action programmer.

w Steve Kline, Jerrold Freedman   *d* Jerrold Freedman   *ph* Tak Fujimoto   *m* Gil Melle

Charles Bronson, Bruno Kirby, Karmin Murcelo, Michael Learner, Ed Harris

Borderlines: see *The Caretakers*

Bordertown *
US   1934   80m   bw
Warner (Robert Lord)

In a North Mexican town, a shabby lawyer becomes infatuated with the neurotic wife of a businessman.

Satisfying melodrama whose plot climax was later borrowed for *They Drive by Night.*

w Laird Doyle, Wallace Smith   *novel* Carroll Graham   *d* Archie Mayo   *ph* Tony Gaudio   *md* Leo Forbstein

Paul Muni, Bette Davis, Margaret Lindsay, Eugene Pallette, Robert Barrat, Henry O'Neill, Hobart Cavanaugh

'A strictly box office film, well written and paced.' – *Variety*

† *Blowing Wild* (qv) was also a partial uncredited remake.

Born Again
US   1978   110m   Technicolor
Robert L. Munger/Frank Capra Jnr
V*

Charles Colson, sent to prison after Watergate, becomes a devout Christian.

Part evangelism, part reconstruction through rose-tinted spectacles; not particularly entertaining or instructive as either.

w Walter Block   *d* Irving Rapper   *ph* Harry Stradling Jnr   *m* Les Baxter

Dean Jones, Anne Francis, Jay Robinson, Dana Andrews, Raymond St Jacques, George Brent, Harry Spillman (as Nixon)

Born for Glory: see *Brown on Resolution*

Born for Trouble: see *Murder in the Big House*

Born Free **
GB   1966   95m   Technicolor   Panavision
Columbia/Open Road (Carl Foreman)/High Road/Atlas (Sam Jaffe, Paul Radin)
V, V*, L

A Kenyan game warden and his wife rear three lion cubs, one of which eventually presents them with a family.

Irresistible animal shots salvage this rather flabbily put together version of a bestselling book. An enormous commercial success, it was followed by the even thinner *Living Free,* by a TV series, and by several semi-professional documentaries.

w Gerald L. C. Copley   *book* Joy Adamson   *d* James Hill   *ph* Kenneth Talbot   *m* John Barry

Virginia McKenna, Bill Travers, Geoffrey Keen

AA: John Barry; title song (*m* John Barry, *ly* Don Black)

Born in East L.A.
US   1987   87m   colour
Universal (Peter Macgregor-Scott)
V*, L

An American Mexican is mistaken for an illegal immigrant and deported to Tijuana.

Mercifully short brain-dead comedy.

wd Cheech Marin   *ph* Alex Phillips   *m* Lee Holdridge   *ed* Don Brochu

Cheech Marin, Daniel Stern, Paul Rodriguez, Jan Michael Vincent, Kamala Lopez, Tony Plana

Born Losers
US   1967   112m   colour
AIP (Delores Taylor)
V*

California teeny-boppers claim to have been gang-raped by wandering motorcyclists.

Teenage shocker, only notable for its credits, and for being the first Billy Jack film.

wd Tom Laughlin   *ph* Gregory Sandor   *m* Mike Curb

Tom Laughlin, Jane Russell, Elizabeth James, Jeremy Slate, William Wellman Jnr

'It's so pokey and crudely obvious that it seems almost guileless – helplessly inept.' – *Pauline Kael*

'A true story of innocence lost and courage found'
Born on the Fourth of July **
US   1989   144m   DeLuxe   Panavision
UIP/Ixtlan (A Kitman Ho, Oliver Stone)
V, V (W), V*, L, S

A crippled Vietnam veteran joins the anti-war movement.

Rousing drama, based on fact.

w Oliver Stone, Ron Kovic   *book* Ron Kovic   *d* Oliver Stone   *ph* Robert Richardson   *m* John

Williams   *pd* Bruno Rubeo   *ad* Victor Kempster, Richard L. Johnson   *ed* David Brenner

Tom Cruise, Bryan Larkin, Raymond J. Barry, Caroline Kava, Josh Evans, Seth Allan, Jamie Talisman, Sean Stone, Anne Bobby, Jenna von Oy

AA: Oliver Stone; best film editing

AAN: Tom Cruise; John Williams; best picture; best adapted screenplay; best cinematography

Born Reckless
US   1930   73m   bw
Fox

Doings of an Italian gangster bootlegger.

A generally poorly regarded early work of its director.

w Donald Henderson Clarke   *novel Louis Beretti* by Donald Henderson Clarke   *d* John Ford

Edmund Lowe, Catherine Dale Owen, Lee Tracy, Marguerite Churchill, Warren Hymer, Frank Albertson

'A singularly full and sprawling scenario . . . Fox originally intended the yarn for Paul Muni. It's possible the script got kicked around the lot and came out as beef stew.' – *Variety*

Born Reckless
US   1937   60m   bw
TCF

Big-town taxi drivers start a war among themselves.

Second-feature actioner, well enough done.

w John Patrick, Helen Logan, Robert Ellis   *d* Malcolm St Clair

Brian Donlevy, Rochelle Hudson, Barton MacLane, Robert Kent, Harry Carey, Pauline Moore, Chick Chandler

'Houses in the knuckle districts will give it its best play.' – *Variety*

Born to be Bad
US   1934   70m   bw
Twentieth Century (William Goetz, Raymond Griffith)

A girl schemes to seduce the man who has adopted her illegitimate son.

Batty mother-love melodrama.

w Ralph Graves   *d* Lowell Sherman   *ph* Barney McGill   *m* Alfred Newman

Loretta Young, Cary Grant, Jackie Kelk, Henry Travers, Russell Hopton, Andrew Tombes, Harry Green

Born to be Bad
US   1950   70m   bw
RKO (Robert Sparks)
V*

An ambitious girl marries a millionaire but continues her affair with a novelist; finally both men discover her true character.

Tentative bad girl novelette, just about passable.

w Edith Sommer   *novel All Kneeling* by Anne Parrish   *d* Nicholas Ray   *ph* Nicholas Musuraca   *m* Frederick Hollander

Joan Fontaine, Robert Ryan, Zachary Scott, Joan Leslie, Mel Ferrer

'Trash story too much for cast and director to live down.' – *Variety*

Born to Dance *
US   1936   108m   bw
MGM (Jack Cummings)
V*, L

A sailor meets a girl in New York.

Well remembered musical with good numbers but a rather lame look.

w Jack McGowan, Sid Silvers, B. G. de Sylva   *d* Roy del Ruth   *ph* Ray June   *md* Alfred Newman   *m/y* Cole Porter   *ad* Cedric Gibbons   *ch* Dave Gould   *ed* Blanche Sewell

Eleanor Powell, James Stewart, Virginia Bruce, Una Merkel, Sid Silvers, Frances Langford, Raymond Walburn, *Reginald Gardiner,* Buddy Ebsen

songs: 'I've Got You Under My Skin'; 'Easy to Love'; 'Rap Tap on Wood'; 'Swinging the Jinx Away'; 'Rolling Home'; 'Hey Babe Hey'; 'Love Me Love My Pekinese'

'Corking entertainment . . . Cast is youthful, sight stuff is lavish, the specialities are meritorious, and as for songs, the picture is positively filthy with them.' – *Variety*

'The plot is a half-hearted reprise of *42nd Street* . . . this time Eleanor Powell is the understudy who replaces the star . . . and by the time she finishes the finale, you're overpowered and feel you should cheer.' – *Pauline Kael, 70s*

AAN: song 'I've Got You Under My Skin'; Dave Gould

Born to Kill *
US   1947   92m   bw
RKO
V*
GB title: *Lady of Deceit*

A psychotic involves his new wife in his criminal pursuits.

Unusual, heavy-going, well acted melodrama.

w Eve Greene, Richard Macaulay   *d* Robert Wise   *ph* Robert de Grasse   *m* Paul Sawtell

Lawrence Tierney, Claire Trevor, Walter Slezak, Phillip Terry, Elisha Cook Jnr

Born to Kill (1974): see
Cockfighter

Born to Love
US   1931   84m   bw
RKO

During World War I a nurse bears the child of an army pilot who is reported missing; but he turns up after she has married an English milord.

A useful compendium of thirties romantic clichés, quite attractively packaged.

w Ernest Pascal   *d* Paul Stein   *ph* John Mescall

Constance Bennett, Joel McCrea, Paul Cavanagh, Frederick Kerr, Anthony Bushell, Louise Closser Hale, Edmond Breon, Mary Forbes

Born to Sing
US   1941   82m   bw
Frederick Stephani/MGM

Kids put together a patriotic show.

Curiously undernourished family musical in the wake of *Babes in Arms:* lots of talent but no star.

w Franz Spencer, Harry Clork   *d* Edward Ludwig

Virginia Weidler, Douglas McPhail, Leo Gorcey, Ray McDonald, Rags Ragland, Sheldon Leonard, Margaret Dumont, Larry Nunn, Henry O'Neill

Born to Win
US   1971   89m   colour
UA/Tokafsky-Philip Langer
V*

A Times Square junkie with delusions of grandeur runs out of luck.

Dim low-life drama unworthy of its talent.

w David Scott Milton   *d* Ivan Passer

George Segal, Paula Prentiss, Karen Black, Hector Elizondo

'A perfectly swell motion picture!'

Born Yesterday **
US   1950   103m   bw
Columbia (S. Sylvan Simon)
V, V*, L

The ignorant ex-chorus girl mistress of a scrap iron tycoon takes English lessons, falls for her tutor, and politically outmanoeuvres her bewildered lover.

Pleasant film version of a cast-iron box-office play, subtle and intelligent in all departments yet with a regrettable tendency to wave the flag.

w Albert Mannheimer   *play Garson Kanin*   *d* George Cukor   *ph* Joseph Walker   *m* Frederick Hollander

Judy Holliday, Broderick Crawford, William Holden, Howard St John

† The original choices for the Judy Holliday role were Rita Hayworth and Jean Parker (who had played it on tour).

AA: Judy Holliday

AAN: best picture; Albert Mannheimer; George Cukor

Born Yesterday
US   1993   100m   Technicolor
Warner/Hollywood/Touchwood Pacific Partners I (D. Constantine Conte)
V, V*

A journalist turns a millionaire's seemingly dumb chorus-girl mistress into a bright and intelligent woman, falling in love with her in the process.

A remake that does nothing but point up the superiority of the original and, in particular, Judy Holliday's priceless gift for comedy; the jokes are mistimed here and the romance is hardly in evidence.

w Douglas McGrath   *play Garson Kanin*   *d* Luis Mandoki   *ph* Lajos Koltai   *m* George Fenton   *pd* Lawrence G. Paull   *ed* Lesley Walker

Melanie Griffith, John Goodman, Don Johnson, Edward Herrmann, Max Perlich, Benjamin C. Bradlee, Sally Quinn, William Frankfather, Fred Dalton Thompson

'This version has great casting, canny scripting and only fair direction, but still jollies along nicely.' – *Kim Newman, Empire*

The Borrower
US   1989   88m   colour
Cannon/Vision (R. P. Sekon, Steven A. Jones)
V, V*

An alien murderer is 'genetically devolved' and marooned on Earth; but his head keeps exploding so he replaces it by ripping off fresh human ones.

Hysterical gore-filled horror – so ineptly made that the body of the alien also changes whenever he gains a new head (since he is played by a different actor each time).

w Mason Nage, Richard Fire   *d* John McNaughton   *ph* Julio Macat, Robert New   *m* Robert McNaughton, Ken Hale, Steven A. Jones   *pd* Robert Henderson   *ed* Elena Maganini

Rae Dawn Chong, Don Gordon, Antonio Fargas, Tom Towles

Borsalino *
France/Italy   1970   126m   Eastmancolor
Adel-Marianne-Mars (Alain Delon)

In the thirties two Marseilles gangsters become firm friends and join forces.

Semi-spoof, but with 'real' blood, and period atmosphere laid on thick. The stars just about keep it ticking over.

w Jean-Claude Carrière, Claude Sautet, Jacques Deray, Jean Cau   *d* Jacques Deray   *ph* Jean-Jacques Tarbès   *m* Claude Bolling

Jean-Paul Belmondo, Alain Delon, Michel Bouquet, Catherine Rouvel, Corinne Marchand

'Rather like a Hollywood musical where someone has forgotten to insert the production numbers.' – *MFB*

Borsalino & Co (dubbed)
France/Italy/West Germany   1974   91m
Eastmancolor
Adel/Comacico/Medusa/TIT (Maurice Jacquin, Alain Delon)
aka: *Blood on the Streets*

A fascist gangleader runs into trouble when he tries to take over Marseilles.

A violent thriller, a sequel to *Borsalino* but lacking wit and substance. It was among the top ten box-office successes of the year in France.

w Pascal Jardin   d Jacques Deray   ph Jean-Jacques Tarbes   m Claude Bolling   ad François de Lamothe   ed Henru Lanoë

Alain Delon, Catherine Rouvel, Riccardo Cucciolla, Daniel Ivernel, Catherine Rouvel

Bosambo: see *Sanders of the River*

The Boss *
US   1956   89m   bw
UA/Frank N. Seltzer
V*

After World War I, a ne'er-do-well becomes a corrupt small town political boss.

Low budgeted, complexly plotted, occasionally quite powerful and efficient crime melodrama.

w Ben L. Parry   d Byron Haskin   ph Hal Mohr   m Albert Glasser

John Payne, William Bishop, Gloria McGhee, Doe Avedon, Joe Flynn

Boston Blackie
An American second feature series made by Columbia between 1941 and 1949. There had been silent films about the character, a reformed crook and con man who has to solve crimes because he is suspected by the law.

Cheap but sometimes vigorous productions, they had a loyal following and starred Chester Morris with George E. Stone as his assistant the Runt.

The titles were:

1941: MEET BOSTON BLACKIE, CONFESSIONS OF BOSTON BLACKIE
1942: ALIAS BOSTON BLACKIE, BOSTON BLACKIE GOES TO HOLLYWOOD
1943: AFTER MIDNIGHT WITH BOSTON BLACKIE
1944: ONE MYSTERIOUS NIGHT
1945: BOSTON BLACKIE BOOKED ON SUSPICION, BOSTON BLACKIE'S RENDEZVOUS
1946: A CLOSE CALL FOR BOSTON BLACKIE, THE PHANTOM THIEF
1947: BOSTON BLACKIE AND THE LAW
1948: TRAPPED BY BOSTON BLACKIE
1949: BOSTON BLACKIE'S CHINESE VENTURE

† A television series starring Kent Taylor followed in 1951.

The Boston Strangler **
US   1968   118m   DeLuxe   Panavision
TCF (Robert Fryer)
V, V*

A semi-factual account of the sex maniac who terrified Boston in the mid-sixties.

Ambitious *policier* rendered less effective by pretentious writing and flashy treatment, including multi-image sequences; the investigation is more interesting than the psychoanalysis.

w Edward Anhalt   book Gerold Frank   d Richard Fleischer   ph Richard Kline   m Lionel Newman

Henry Fonda, *Tony Curtis* (as the murderer), George Kennedy, Mike Kellin, Hurd Hatfield, Murray Hamilton, Sally Kellerman, Jeff Corey, George Voskovec

The Bostonians
GB   1984   122m   colour
Merchant Ivory/WGBH/Rediffusion/Almi (Ismail Merchant)
V*, L

In 1876 Boston, the cause of female emancipation wrecks Verena Tarrant's relationship with the determined Basil Ransome.

Another sluggish literary adaptation from the heavily meaningful Merchant Ivory team: the material, one feels, would have worked better as a TV bestseller.

w Ruth Prawer Jhabvala   novel Henry James   d James Ivory   ph Walter Lassally   m Richard Robbins   pd Leo Austin

Christopher Reeve, Vanessa Redgrave, Madeleine Potter, Jessica Tandy, Nancy Marchand, Linda Hunt, Wesley Addy

'Although it's not so limp as some of their other collaborations, they don't dramatize the material, and Ivory doesn't shape the performances.' – *Pauline Kael, New Yorker*

AAN: Vanessa Redgrave

Botany Bay
US   1952   94m   Technicolor
Paramount (Joseph Sistrom)
V*

On a convict ship in 1787 an American student unjustly accused of robbery clashes with the brutal captain for the favours of the only woman aboard.

Cramped and brutal action melodrama, a let-down considering the talent involved.

w Jonathan Latimer   novel Charles Nordhoff and James Hall   d John Farrow   ph John Seitz   m Franz Waxman

James Mason, Alan Ladd, Patricia Medina, Cedric Hardwicke, Murray Matheson, Jonathan Harris

Both Ends of the Candle: see *The Helen Morgan Story*

Both Sides of the Law: see *Street Corner*

The Bottom of the Bottle
US   1956   86m   Eastmancolor   Cinemascope
TCF (Buddy Adler)
GB title: *Beyond the River*

A wealthy attorney is visited by his drunken brother, on the run from the police and needing help to escape into Mexico.

Dreary drama in muddy colour, a clearly misguided enterprise.

w Sydney Boehm   novel Georges Simenon   d Henry Hathaway   ph Lee Garmes   m Leigh Harline

Joseph Cotten, Van Johnson, Ruth Roman, Jack Carson

'For those who like to laugh and sing when tears get in their eyes!'

Bottoms Up
US   1934   85m   bw
Fox (B. G. de Sylva)

A slick promoter in Hollywood disguises his pals as British nobility and gets them lucrative jobs.

Mild musical with a rather interesting cast.

w B. G. de Sylva, David Butler, Sid Silvers   d David Butler   ph Arthur Miller   md Constantin Bakaleinikoff

Spencer Tracy, Pat Paterson, John Boles, Harry Green, Herbert Mundin, Sid Silvers, Thelma Todd, Robert Emmett O'Connor

'In the best 1934 filmusical manner and contributes handily toward the perpetuation of the cycle.' – *Variety*

Bottoms Up
GB   1960   89m   bw
ABPC (Mario Zampi)

A seedy schoolmaster passes off his bookie's son as an eastern prince.

Rambling film version of a successful TV series *Whacko!*, written by Frank Muir and Denis Norden.

w Michael Pertwee   d Mario Zampi   ph Gilbert Taylor   m Stanley Black   ad Ivan King   ed Richard Best

Jimmy Edwards, Arthur Howard, Martita Hunt, Sidney Tafler, Raymond Huntley, Reginald Beckwith, Vanda Hudson

Le Boucher **
France/Italy   1969   94m   Eastmancolor
La Boétie/Euro International (André Génoves)
aka: *The Butcher*

Murders in a small French town are traced to the inoffensive-seeming young butcher who is courting the local schoolmistress.

Curious, mainly charming film which can't make up its mind whether to be an eccentric character study or a Hitchcock thriller, but has its moments as each.

wd *Claude Chabrol*   ph Jean Rabier   m Pierre Jansen

Stéphane Audran, Jean Yanne, Antonio Passalia, Mario Beccaria

'A thriller, but a superlative example of the genre.' – *Times*

Boudu Sauvé des Eaux ***
France   1932   87m   bw
Michel Simon/Jean Gehret
V*
aka: *Boudu Saved from Drowning*

A scruffy tramp is not grateful for being rescued from suicide, and plagues the family who invite him to stay.

A minor classic of black comedy, interesting equally for its characterizations, its acting, and its film technique.

wd *Jean Renoir*,   play René Fauchois   ph Marcel Lucien   m from Raphael and Johann Strauss

Michel Simon, Charles Grandval, Marcelle Hainia, Séverine Lerczinska, Jean Dasté, Jacques Becker

'A beautifully rhythmed film that makes one nostalgic for the period when it was made.' – *New Yorker, 1977*

† Remade 1985, more or less, as *Down and Out in Beverly Hills*.

Boudu Saved from Drowning: see *Boudu Sauvé des Eaux*

Bought
US   1931   70m   bw
Warner

An ambitious working girl rebels against her slum existence and seeks a rich man.

Typical star vehicle of its time, with a predictable and unlikely change of heart for a finale.

w Charles Kenyon, Raymond Griffith   novel *Jackdaw's Strut* by Harriet Henry   d Archie Mayo   ph Ray June

Constance Bennett, Ben Lyon, Richard Bennett, Dorothy Peterson, Ray Milland, Doris Lloyd, Maude Eburne

'It's an entertainment in itself to be seated among women auditors during a Constance Bennett picture. They love that girl and she mustn't be worsted by men.' – *Variety*

Boulder Dam

US   1936   70m   bw
Sam Bischoff/Warner

A mechanic accidentally kills a man and seeks anonymity among the crews building Boulder Dam.

Routine melo with an unusual setting.

w Sy Barlett, Ralph Block   d Frank McDonald

Ross Alexander, Patricia Ellis, Lyle Talbot, Eddie Acuff, Henry O'Neill

Boulevard Nights

US   1979   102m   colour
Warner (Bill Benenson)
V*

Two Mexican-American brothers become involved with a street gang.

Well-meaning but uninvolving account of life lived at an inescapably violent level.

w Desmond Nakano   d Michael Pressman
ph John Bailey   m Lalo Schifrin   pd Jackson DeGovia   ed Richard Halsey

Richard Yniguez, Danny de La Paz, Marta Du Bois, James Victor, Betty Carvalho

'Earnest, uninspired.' – Pauline Kael

Bound and Gagged – A Love Story

US   1992   94m   colour
Metro Tartan/Cinescope (Dennis J. Mahoney)

A woman, married to a violent husband, is abducted by her female lover and her friend, a suicidal, unhappily married man who has lost the ability to speak.

A doggedly well-meaning movie about abusive and dependent behaviour that is also virtually unwatchable.

wd Daniel B. Appleby   ph Dean Lent   m William Murphy   pd Dane Pizzuti Krogman   ed Kaye Davis

Ginger Lynn Allen, Karen Black, Chris Denton, Elizabeth Saltarrelli, Mary Ella Ross, Chris Mulkey

'This is not a good film. In fact, it is a pretty bad one – unevenly acted, scripted without much real wit and directed with the kind of careless abandon that sometimes passes for imagination when one's had too much of Hollywood's professional vacuity.' – Derek Malcolm, Guardian

'Resolutely unengaging, almost repugnant. It is muddily photographed and poorly scripted.' – Caren Myers, Sight and Sound

† The film has been described by its director, who is noted for his documentaries on similar subject-matter, as a labour of love, taking two and a half years to make.

Bound for Glory *

US   1976   148m   DeLuxe   Panavision
UA/Robert F. Blumhofe, Harold Leventhal
V*, L

In 1936 Woody Guthrie leaves the Texas dust bowl for California, and after various hardships his musical talent is recognized.

Care and occasional beauty in the photography do not obscure memories of The Grapes of Wrath, which told much the same story more dramatically and succinctly, and with less earnestness and self-pity.

w Robert Getchell   autobiography Woody Guthrie
d Hal Ashby   ph Haskell Wexler   m Leonard Rosenman   songs Woody Guthrie   pd Michael Haller

David Carradine, Ronny Cox, Melinda Dillon, Gail Strickland, John Lehne

'The movie spends two-and-a-half hours and seven million dollars gazing wistfully at a little man and a big country, and it ends up prettily embalming them both.' – Janet Maslin, Newsweek

AA: Haskell Wexler; Leonard Rosenman

AAN: best picture; Robert Getchell

The Bounty *

GB   1984   133m   Technicolor   Panavision
Dino de Laurentiis (Bernard Williams)
V*, L

William Bligh is summoned before a court martial to explain the events leading up to the famous mutiny.

Rather independent version of the twice-told movie tale, and the least compelling of all. Despite the emphasis on character, only occasionally interesting.

w Robert Bolt   d Roger Donaldson   ph Arthur Ibbetson   m Vangelis   pd John Graysmark

Anthony Hopkins (Bligh), Mel Gibson (Fletcher Christian), Laurence Olivier (Admiral Hood), Edward Fox (Captain Greetham), Daniel Day-Lewis (John Fryer), Bernard Hill (Cole)

'A long voyage to nowhere.' – Nick Roddick, MFB

'This misshapen movie doesn't work as an epic – it doesn't have the scope or the emotional surge.' – Pauline Kael, New Yorker

'A great adventure, a lush romance, and a good movie.' – Roger Ebert

The Bounty Hunter

US   1954   79m   WarnerColor
Warner

Three respectable citizens are unmasked as masterminds behind a series of train robberies.

Predictable but enjoyable star action fare.

w Winston Miller   d André de Toth

Randolph Scott, Dolores Dorn, Marie Windsor, Ernest Borgnine

The Bounty Hunters (dubbed) *

Italy   1970   106m   Technicolor   Techniscope
UA/PEA (Alberto Grimaldi)
original title: Indio Black, Sai che ti Dico: Sei un Gran Figlio di . . . ; aka: Adios, Sabata

In Mexico in the 1860s, a time of revolution, a bounty hunter leads an expedition to steal a shipment of Austrian gold.

Dubbing turned the central character from Indio Black into Sabata, a role played by Lee Van Cleef in a successful movie made by the same director a year earlier; this time around, the result was more conventional and less enjoyable.

w Renato Izzo, Gianfranco Parolini   d Frank Kramer (Gianfranco Parolini)   ph Sandro Mancori
m Bruno Nicolai   ad Pierluigi Basile
ed Gianfranco Parolini, Salvatore Avantario

Yul Brynner, Dean Reed, Pedro Sanchez (Ignazio Spalla), Gerard Herter, Sal Borgese, Franco Fantasia, Gianni Rizzo

'Since the characterisations are quite lively and the message agreeably cynical . . . it is a pity that so much of the action is clogged up by that old stand-by of the Italian Western – extras falling off roofs in graceful death-falls.' – Tom Milne, MFB

† Return of Sabata (qv), a sequel to the original Sabata, appeared in 1972.

The Bowery ***

US   1933   92m   bw
Twentieth Century (Darryl F. Zanuck) (Raymond Griffith, William Goetz)

In 1890s New York, two boisterous rivals settle their differences after one has jumped off the Brooklyn Bridge for a bet.

Roistering saga of cross and double cross on the seamy side, splendidly vigorous in acting and treatment.

w Howard Estabrook, James Gleason   d Raoul Walsh
ph Barney McGill   m Alfred Newman   ad Richard Day

Wallace Beery, George Raft, Pert Kelton, Jackie Cooper, Fay Wray, Herman Bing

'It delivers as entertainment. It should draw by itself, while the cast will be a considerable help.' – Variety

'A model of skilful reconstruction and ingenious research.' – Times

'Fairly reeking with authentic, rowdy, hurdy-gurdy atmosphere . . . a grand evening of fun for everybody.' – Photoplay

† The Bowery was the first production of Twentieth Century.
†† Gable was sought for the Raft role, but proved unavailable.

Bowery at Midnight

US   1942   61m   bw
Monogram
V*

A criminal by night doubles as a mission proprietor by day.

Star horror cheapie with echoes of his previous Dark Eyes of London.

w Gerald Schnitzer   d Wallace Fox

Bela Lugosi, John Archer, Wanda McKay, Tom Neal, Dave O'Brien, Vince Barnett

The Bowery Boys

A cheap and cheerful series of American second features, immensely popular between 1946 and 1958, these adventures of a group of ageing Brooklyn layabouts had their origin in the 1937 film Dead End, from which the Dead End Kids graduated to other features at Warner: Crime School, They Made Me a Criminal, Angels with Dirty Faces, Angels Wash their Faces, etc. A couple of the 'boys' then defected to Universal and made Little Tough Guy and a series of half a dozen subsequent pictures; while in 1940 Monogram took a couple more and built up another group called the East Side Kids. In 1946 a formal merger of talent at Monogram consolidated the remaining members into the Bowery Boys. The members were Leo Gorcey, Huntz Hall, Bobby Jordan, Gabriel Dell (all from the Dead End Kids), Bernard Gorcey, David Gorcey, Billy Benedict, and Bennie Bartlett. The films are:

1946: IN FAST COMPANY, BOWERY BOMBSHELL, LIVE WIRES, SPOOK BUSTERS, MR HEX
1947: BOWERY BUCKAROOS, HARD BOILED MAHONEY, NEWS HOUNDS, ANGELS' ALLEY
1948: JINX MONEY, SMUGGLER'S COVE, TROUBLE MAKERS
1949: ANGELS IN DISGUISE, FIGHTING FOOLS, HOLD THAT BABY, MASTER MINDS
1950: BLONDE DYNAMITE, BLUES BUSTERS, LUCKY LOSERS, TRIPLE TROUBLE
1951: BOWERY BATTALION, CRAZY OVER HORSES, GHOST CHASERS, LET'S GO NAVY
1952: FEUDIN' FOOLS, HERE COME THE MARINES, HOLD THAT LINE, NO HOLDS BARRED
1953: CLIPPED WINGS, JALOPY, LOOSE IN LONDON, PRIVATE EYES
1954: THE BOWERY BOYS MEET THE MONSTERS, JUNGLE GENTS, PARIS PLAYBOYS
1955: BOWERY TO BAGDAD, HIGH SOCIETY, JAIL BUSTERS, SPY CHASERS
1956: DIG THAT URANIUM, CRASHING LAS VEGAS, FIGHTING TROUBLE, HOT SHOTS
1957: SPOOK CHASERS, HOLD THAT HYPNOTIST, LOOKING FOR DANGER
1958: UP IN SMOKE, IN THE MONEY

Bowery to Broadway

US   1944   94m   bw
Universal (John Grant)

In the 1890s, a Bowery songstress makes it to the big time.

Simple-minded musical in which the drama has no drive and the guest stars are given inferior material.

w Joseph Lytton, Arthur T. Horman   d Charles Lamont   ph Charles Van Enger   md Edward Ward

Maria Montez, Turhan Bey, Susanna Foster, Jack Oakie, Donald Cook, Louise Allbritton, Andy Devine, Rosemary de Camp, Ann Blyth, Donald O'Connor, Peggy Ryan, Frank McHugh, Leo Carrillo, Evelyn Ankers, Mantan Moreland

songs: 'The Love Waltz'; 'There'll Always Be a Moon'; 'My Song of Romance'; 'Montevideo'; 'Coney Island Waltz' (plus standards)

Boxcar Bertha *
US   1972   88m   DeLuxe
AIP (Roger Corman)
V, V*, L

In early thirties Arkansas, an unhappy girl falls in with gangsters and train robbers.

Competent imitation of *Bonnie and Clyde*.

w Joyce H. and John W. Corrington   d *Martin Scorsese*
ph John Stephens   m Gib Guilbeau, Thad Maxwell

Barbara Hershey, David Carradine, Barry Primus, Bernie Casey, John Carradine

'A Deep Dark Obsession That Bares A Woman's Body And A Man's Soul.'
Boxing Helena
US   1993   105m   Technicolor   Panavision
Entertainment/Main Line (Carl Mazzocone)
V, V*, L

A surgeon seemingly takes advantage of an accident to amputate the legs and arms of the woman who rejected his love.

A tedious, neurotic tale that would have benefitted from hefty cuts; it is unable to sustain interest in either its minimal plot or its unsympathetic characters.

wd Jennifer Chambers Lynch   story Philippe Caland
ph Frank Byers   m Graeme Revell   ad Paul Huggins   ed David Finfer

Julian Sands, Sherilyn Fenn, Bill Paxton, Art Garfunkel, Betsy Clark, Kurtwood Smith

'Not only is the script unbelievably bad – packed with clumsy, forced and often banal dialogue – but some of the acting has to be seen to be believed.' – *Amanda Lipman, Sight and Sound*

'Just might have passed muster as a 15-minute film school gag. With performances as inept as the script, the self-parody cannot be passed off as intentional.' – *David Robinson, The Times*

'Simply cannot be taken seriously, in a large part because it takes itself so seriously that we can only respond to it with gales of derisive crowing.' – *Michael Atkinson, Movieline*

† The film was most memorable for what happened off-screen, when Kim Basinger was sued for changing her mind over her agreement to star in it, and ordered to pay some $8 million in damages.

A Boy a Girl and a Bike
GB   1947   92m   bw
Gainsborough (Ralph Keene)

Romantic jealousies arise between members of a Yorkshire cycling club.

Mild comedy drama with the advantage of fresh air locations.

w Ted Willis   d Ralph Smart   ph Ray Elton
m Kenneth Pakeman

John McCallum, Honor Blackman, Patrick Holt, Diana Dors, Leslie Dwyer, Thora Hird, Anthony Newley, Megs Jenkins, Maurice Denham

'A rather kinky tale of survival.'
A Boy and His Dog *
colour   1975   89m   colour
LG Jaf (Alvy Moore)
V*, L

While searching for food in an apocalyptic future, a young man and his more intelligent telepathic dog find an apparently Utopian community that needs masculine input.

Quirky science fiction, not to be taken too seriously, and managing a surprise ending.

wd L. Q. Jones   novel Harlan Ellison   ph John Arthur Morrill   m Tim McIntire   pd Ray Boyle
ed Scott Conrad

Don Johnson, Susanne Benton, Jason Robards, Ron Feinberg, Tim McIntire, Charles McGraw

The Boy and the Bridge
GB   1959   91m   bw
Xanadu (Kevin McClory)

A boy who believes he has committed a murder hides in the ramparts of Tower Bridge.

This tiny fable adds up to very weak entertainment, despite inventive photography, because it has virtually no plot development.

w Geoffrey Orme, Kevin McClory, Desmond O'Donovan   d Kevin McClory   ph Ted Scaife
m Malcolm Arnold

Ian MacLaine, Liam Redmond, James Hayter, Norman Macowan, Geoffrey Keen, Jack MacGowran, Royal Dano, Rita Webb

The Boy and the Pirates
US   1960   84m   Eastmancolor   Perceptovision
United Artists

A small boy finds an old bottle on the seashore, wishes he could live in pirate days, and hey presto.

Modest juvenile fantasy on the lines of *The Wizard of Oz* but without the talent.

w Lillie Hayward, Jerry Sackheim   d Bert I. Gordon

Charles Herbert, Susan Gordon, Murvyn Vye, Paul Guilfoyle

The Boy Cried Murder
GB/West Germany/Yugoslavia   1965   86m
    Eastmancolor
CCC/Carlos/Avala

A small boy has such a vivid imagination that nobody except the criminal believes him when he says he has witnessed a murder.

Flat and unnecessary remake of *The Window* (which was later done again as *Eye Witness*).

w Robin Estridge   story Cornell Woolrich
d George Breakston

Frazer MacIntosh, Veronica Hurst, Phil Brown, Tim Barrett

'No more bubble bath, she screamed!'
Boy, Did I Get a Wrong Number
US   1966   99m   DeLuxe
UA/Edward Small (George Beck)
V*

Trying to phone his wife, an estate agent gets involved with a runaway actress.

Lifeless and generally resistible star comedy, the first of several hard and unfunny vehicles for an ageing Bob Hope seeming to hark back to the least attractive aspects of burlesque rather than the sympathetic wisecracking which suits him best.

w Burt Styler, Albert E. Lewin, George Kennett
d George Marshall   ph Lionel Lindon   m Richard Lasalle   ly By Dunham

Bob Hope, Elke Sommer, Phyllis Diller, Marjorie Lord, Cesare Danova, Benny Baker

The Boy Friend *
GB   1971   125m   Metrocolor   Panavision
MGM/Russflix (Ken Russell)
V, V*, L, S

On a wet Wednesday afternoon in the late twenties, a tatty company with backstage problems puts on an empty-headed musical.

Russell the mastermind effectively destroys Sandy Wilson's charming period pastiche, sending up all the numbers (via badly staged dream sequences on the wrong shape screen) in a Busby Berkeley manner which had not yet been invented. Moments do work, but a non-star doesn't help, and the whole thing is an artistic disaster of some significance both to Russell's career and to the cinema of the early seventies.

wd Ken Russell   musical play Sandy Wilson
ph David Watkin   md Ian Whittaker, Peter Greenwell, Peter Maxwell Davies   pd Tony Walton

Twiggy, Christopher Gable, *Max Adrian*, Tommy Tune, Barbara Windsor, Moyra Fraser, Bryan Pringle, Vladek Sheybal, *Antonia Ellis, Glenda Jackson*

'The glittering, joyless numbers keep coming at you: you never get any relief from Russell's supposed virtuosity.' – *New Yorker, 1977*

AAN: Ian Whittaker, Peter Greenwell, Peter Maxwell Davies

The Boy from Oklahoma *
US   1953   88m   Warnercolor
Warner (David Weisbart)

A genial plainsman studying law becomes sheriff of a small town and uncovers its mayor as a killer.

Modest, pleasing Western with the star imitating his father.

w Frank Davis, Winston Miller   d Michael Curtiz
ph Robert Burks   m Max Steiner

Will Rogers Jnr, Nancy Olson, Lon Chaney Jnr, Anthony Caruso, Wallace Ford, Clem Bevans, Merv Griffin

The Boy from Barnardo's: see *Lord Jeff*

Boy Meets Girl *
US   1938   86m   bw
Warner (George Abbott)
V*

Two crazy Hollywood scenario writers make a star of an infant yet unborn.

Freewheeling film version of a hilarious play: fine crazy comedy and excellent Hollywood satire.

w *Bella and Sam Spewack*,   play Bella and Sam Spewack   d Lloyd Bacon   ph Sol Polito   m Leo Forbstein

James Cagney, Pat O'Brien, Marie Wilson, Ralph Bellamy, Frank McHugh, Dick Foran, Bruce Lester, Ronald Reagan, James Stephenson

'Satisfactory, but not socko.' – *Variety*

'It bounces from one hilarious absurdity to another with all the resilience of a rubber ball.' – *MFB*

Boy Meets Girl *
France   1984   100m   bw
Other Cinema/Abilene (Patricia Moraz)

An aimless youth ends his romance with one girl and starts a new one with another.

A low-budget movie, made by its writer-director at the age of 22, of interest mainly for its photography of Paris by night.

wd Leos Carax   ph Jean-Yves Escoffier   m Jacques Pinault   ad Serge Marzolff, Jean Bauer   ed Nelly Meunier, Francine Sandberg

Denis Lavant, Mireille Pérrier, Carroll Brooks, Elie Poicard, Anna Baldaccini

Boy of the Streets
US   1937   75m   bw
Monogram

A city youngster falls in with racketeers.

Ho-hum Dead End melodrama.

w Scott Darling, Gilson Brown   d William Nigh

Jackie Cooper, Maureen O'Connor, Kathleen Burke, Marjorie Main, Robert Emmett O'Connor

'Will do biz for independents . . . easily Monogram's most ambitious production effort to date.' – *Variety*

Boy on a Dolphin *
US   1957   111m   Eastmancolor   Cinemascope
TCF (Samuel G. Engel)
V, V*, S

A Greek girl diver discovers a sunken artifact of great value and the news spreads to an American archaeologist and an unscrupulous collector.

Likeable, sunswept Mediterranean adventure romance marred by the miscasting of the male lead.

w Ivan Moffat, Dwight Taylor   novel David Divine   d Jean Negulesco   ph Milton Krasner   md Lionel Newman   m Hugo Friedhofer

Alan Ladd, Sophia Loren, *Clifton Webb*, Laurence Naismith, Alexis Minotis, Jorge Mistral

AAN: Hugo Friedhofer

Boy Slaves
US   1938   70m   bw
RKO

A boy leaves home and ends up in a forced labour camp. Topical preachment drama which kicked up a bit of dust at the time.

w Albert Bein, Ben Orkow   d P. J. Wolfson

Anne Shirley, Roger Daniel, James McCallion, Alan Baxter.

'Devoid of essential entertainment factors for general theatre showings.' – *Variety*

A Boy Ten Feet Tall: see *Sammy Going South*

Boy Trouble
US   1939   75m   bw
Paramount

A small-towner finds his life upset when his wife adopts two orphans.

Sentimental comedy which caused a few tears to trickle.

w Laura and S. J. Perelman   story Lloyd Corrigan, Monte Brice   d George Archainbaud

Charles Ruggles, Mary Boland, Donald O'Connor, Joyce Matthews, Billy Lee, Andrew Tombes

'Good old hokum with an emotional wallop . . . Exhibitors can use more pictures of this type.' – *Variety*

'Those who don't believe – are dead!'
The Boy Who Cried Werewolf
US   1973   93m   Technicolor
Universal

On a camping trip, a boy and his father are attacked by a werewolf, and later on dad starts acting mighty strange . . .

Disappointingly straight rewrite of the old hokum.

w Bob Homel   d Nathan Juran

Kerwin Matthews, Elaine Devry, Scott Sealey

The Boy Who Had Everything
Australia   1984   94m   colour
Multi Films Alfred Roads (Richard Mason, Julia Overton)

In 1965, as Australian troops are about to be sent to Vietnam a university freshman submits to initiation rites but renounces his mother and his future.

Angry, rather muddled character study which seems to be drawn from life but doesn't know what moral to point.

wd Stephen Wallace   ph Geoff Burton   m Ralph Schneider

Jason Connery, Diane Cilento, Laura Williams, Lewis Fitzgerald

The Boy Who Stole a Million
GB   1960   81m   bw
Fanfare/George H. Brown/British Lion

A young page in a Spanish bank 'borrows' some money to help his father but finds Dad, police and crooks all after him.

Half-hearted attempt at a British *Bicycle Thieves*, oddly set in Spain and never quite managing to convince or interest us.

w John Eldridge, Charles Crichton   d Charles Crichton

Maurice Reyna, Virgilia Texera, Harold Kasket, George Coulouris, Edwin Richfield

The Boy with Green Hair
US   1948   82m   Technicolor
RKO (Stephen Ames)
V*, L

When he hears that his parents were killed in an air raid, a boy's hair turns green; other war orphans encourage him to parade himself publicly as an image of the horror and futility of war.

Muddled, pretentious and unpersuasive fantasy, typical of this producer's do-goodery. One of those oddities which make Hollywood endearing, but not very entertaining apart from Pat O'Brien's garrulous grandpa.

w Ben Barzman, Alfred Lewis Levitt   story Betsy Beaton   d Joseph Losey   ph George Barnes   m Leigh Harline

Dean Stockwell, Pat O'Brien, Robert Ryan, Barbara Hale

The Boyars' Plot: see *Ivan the Terrible*

The Boys
GB   1962   123m   bw   Cinemascope
Gala/Columbia (Sidney J. Furie)

Four boys are on trial for killing a garage attendant.

Elaborate courtroom drama with flashbacks, stars for counsel, a tricksy director, and about forty minutes too much footage.

w Stuart Douglass   d Sidney J. Furie   ph Gerald Gibbs   m The Shadows

Richard Todd, Robert Morley, Felix Aylmer, Dudley Sutton, Ronald Lacey, Tony Garnett, Jess Conrad, Wilfrid Brambell, Allan Cuthbertson, Colin Gordon

'94 men must die to keep alive a dream – or a nightmare!'
The Boys from Brazil *
US/GB   1978   124m   DeLuxe
ITC/Producer Circle (Martin Richards, Stanley O'Toole)
V, V*, L, S

A renegade Nazi in hiding has a sinister plot to reconquer the world.

Suspense fantasy firmly based on a gripping book; excellent performances, but a shade too long.

w Heywood Gould   novel Ira Levin   d Franklin Schaffner   ph Henri Decaë   m Jerry Goldsmith   pd Gil Parrando

Gregory Peck, Laurence Olivier, James Mason, Lilli Palmer, Uta Hagen, Steven Guttenberg, Denholm Elliott, Rosemary Harris, John Dehner, John Rubinstein, Anne Meara, David Hurst, Michael Gough

AAN: Jerry Goldsmith; Laurence Olivier

The Boys from Fengkuei **
Taiwan   1983   104m   colour
Evergreen
original title: *Feng-Kuei-Lai-Te Jen*; aka: *All the Youthful Days*

In search of excitement, three youths move to the city from the fishing village where they were born.

Absorbingly detailed drama of the young coming to terms with the pleasures and problems of adult life.

w Chu T'ien-wen   d Hou Hsiao-hsien   ph Ch'en K'un'hou

Niu Cheng-tse, Lin Xiuling, To Tsung-hua, Chang Shih

The Boys from Syracuse *
US   1940   74m   bw
Universal (Jules Levey)

The Comedy of Errors with modern wisecracks, and a few songs.

Predictable well-drilled confusion arises from master and slave having identical twins, but the general tone is a bit flat for an adaptation from a hilarious Broadway success. Still, the songs are lively and the chariot race finale shows spirit.

w Leonard Spigelgass, Charles Grayson, Paul Gerard Smith   play George Abbott, William Shakespeare   d Edward A. Sutherland   ph Joseph Valentine   md Charles Previn   m Frank Skinner   m/ly Richard Rodgers, Lorenz Hart   ad John Otterson

Allan Jones, Joe Penner, Charles Butterworth, Rosemary Lane, Irene Hervey, Martha Raye, Alan Mowbray

songs: 'Who Are You?'; 'This Can't be Love'; 'Falling in Love with Love'; 'The Greeks Have no Word for It'; 'Sing for Your Supper'; 'He and She'

† The writing credit on screen ends: 'After a play by William Shakespeare . . . long, long after!'

AAN: John Otterson

The Boys in Blue
GB   1983   91m   colour
Elstree/Rank

Village policemen catch art thieves.

Horribly incompetent remake of *Ask a Policeman*, with a totally untalented star team.

wd Val Guest

Tommy Cannon, Bobby Ball, Suzanne Danielle, Roy Kinnear, Eric Sykes, Jack Douglas, Edward Judd, Jon Pertwee, Arthur English

'The perfect antidote to sweeping claims about the British renaissance.' – *Geoff Brown, MFB*

Boys in Brown
GB   1949   84m   bw
Gainsborough (Anthony Darnborough)

Life in a Borstal institution.

The stars make elderly boys, but Jack Warner is a cuddly governor. Boring and unpersuasive non-documentary fiction in Britain's most tiresome style.

wd Montgomery Tully   play Reginald Beckwith   ph Gordon Lang, Cyril Bristow   m Doreen Carwithen

Jack Warner, Dirk Bogarde, Michael Medwin, Jimmy Hanley, Richard Attenborough, Alfie Bass, Barbara Murray, Thora Hird

† Made by the Independent Frame method, which blended real backgrounds with studio sets.

The Boys in Company C
Hong Kong   1977   125m   Technicolor   Panavision
Golden Harvest (Andre Morgan)
V*, L

Five marines find their lives changed by the Vietnam war.

Crude action melodrama.

w Rick Natkin, Sidney J. Furie   *d* Sidney J. Furie
ph Godfrey Godar   *m* Jaime Mendoza-Nava

Stan Shaw, Andrew Stevens, James Canning,
Michael Lembeck, Craig Wasson, James
Whitmore Jnr

'Laden with barrack room dialogue and played at the
enlisted man's level.' – *Variety*

'An exploitation war movie, like dirty TV.' – *New
Yorker*

The Boys in the Band *
US   1970   120m   Technicolor
Cinema Center/Leo (Mart Crowley, Kenneth Utt)
V, V*, L

Tempers fray and true selves are revealed when a
heterosexual is accidentally invited to a homosexual
party.

Careful but claustrophobic filming of a Broadway
play, which at the screen's closer quarters becomes
overpowering well before the end.

w Mart Crowley   *play* Mart Crowley   *d* William
Friedkin   *ph* Arthur J. Ornitz   *m* none

Leonard Frey, Kenneth Nelson, Cliff Gorman,
Frederick Combs, Reuben Greene, Robert La
Tourneaux, Laurence Luckinbill, Keith Prentice,
Peter White

'They crack jokes while their hearts are breaking.' –
New Yorker

Boys' Night Out
US   1962   115m   Metrocolor   Cinemascope
MGM/Filmways (Martin Ransohoff)

Three married men and their bachelor friend share a
flat and a 'mistress'.

Would-be saucy comedy in which nothing sexy ever
happens and the helpless players are as witless as the
script.

w Ira Wallach   *d* Michael Gordon   *ph* Arthur E.
Arling   *m* Frank de Vol

James Garner, Kim Novak, Tony Randall, Howard
Duff, Howard Morris, Oscar Homolka, Janet Blair,
Patti Page, Jessie Royce Landis

Boys' Ranch
US   1946   97m   bw
MGM (Robert Sisk)

A baseball player persuades Texas millionaires to
finance a ranch where deprived city youngsters can
learn life's true values.

Predictable sentimental hogwash without much pace
or star value.

w William Ludwig   *d* Roy Rowland

James Craig, Jackie 'Butch' Jenkins, Skip Homeier,
Dorothy Patrick, Ray Collins, Darryl Hickman

'More laughs than Laurel and Hardy! More thrills than *Test
Pilot!* More tears than *Captains Courageous!*

Boys Town *
US   1938   93m   bw
MGM (John W. Considine Jnr)
V*, L

The story of Father Flanagan and his school for
juvenile delinquents.

Well-made, highly successful, but sentimental crowd
pleaser.

w John Meehan, Dore Schary   *story* Eleanore
Griffin, Dore Schary   *d* Norman Taurog   *ph* Sidney
Wagner   *m* Edward Ward

Spencer Tracy, Mickey Rooney, Henry Hull, Gene
Reynolds, Sidney Miller, Frankie Thomas, Bobs
Watson, Tommy Noonan

'A production that should build goodwill for the
whole industry.' – *Variety*

AA: Eleanore Griffin, Dore Schary; Spencer Tracy

AAN: best picture; John Meehan, Dore Schary;
Norman Taurog

Boys Will be Boys **
GB   1935   75m   bw
Gaumont/Gainsborough (Michael Balcon)
V

An incompetent headmaster thwarts a jewel robber.

The first recognizable Will Hay vehicle, based in part
on J. B. Morton's Narkover sketches.

w Will Hay, Robert Edmunds   *d* William Beaudine
ph Charles Van Enger   *m* Louis Levy

Will Hay, Gordon Harker, Jimmy Hanley, Davy
Burnaby, Norma Varden, Claude Dampier, Charles
Farrell, Percy Walsh

'It is hard to see how his distinctive sketch writing
could have found a satisfactory screen equivalent.
Nevertheless, a good augury of the films to come.' –
Ray Seaton and Roy Martin, 1978

'Increase The Peace.'

Boyz N The Hood **
US   1991   112m   DeLuxe
Columbia TriStar (Steve Nicolaides)
V, V*, L, S

Young blacks try to survive in the hostile urban world
of Los Angeles gangs.

Episodic in form and over-schematic in its depiction
of social difficulties, particularly those caused by
absentee fathers, but it holds one's interest
throughout.

wd John Singleton   *ph* Charles Mills   *m* Stanley
Clarke   *ad* Bruce Bellamy   *ed* Bruce Cannon

Ice Cube, Cuba Gooding Jnr, Morris Chestnut, Larry
Fishburne, Nia Long, Tyra Ferrell

'An absorbing, smartly made dramatic encyclopedia
of problems and ethics in the black community, 1991.'
– *Variety*

'Conveys a vivid sense of the dangers, both physical
and emotional, of day-to-day existence in this ravaged
urban environment.' – *New Yorker*

AAN: John Singleton (as director); John Singleton
(screenplay)

The Brain (1962): see
Vengeance

The Brain
France/US   1969   115m   colour
Paramount (Alain Poire)
original title: *Le Cerveau*

A British colonel leads an international crew in an
attempt to rob NATO.

Exhausting and generally misfiring international
crook comedy.

w Gérard Oury, Marcel Julian, Daniele Thompson
d Gérard Oury   *ph* Vladimir Ivanov, Armand
Thirard   *m* Georges Delerue

David Niven, Jean-Paul Belmondo, Bourvil, Eli
Wallach, Silvia Monti

Brain Damage
US   1988   90m   colour
Palace/Frank Henenlotter (Edgar Levins)
V, V*

A man is provided with hallucinatory pleasures in
return for helping a brain-eating parasite.

Low-budget nastiness intended to amuse rather than
shock.

wd Frank Henenlotter   *ph* Bruce Torbet   *m* Gus
Russo, Clutch Reiser   *ad* Ivy Rosovsky   *ed* James
Y. Kwei, Frank Henenlotter

Rick Herbst, Jennifer Lowry, Gordon Macdonald,
Theo Barnes, Lucille Saint-Peter, Vicki Darnell

Brain Donors
US   1992   79m   colour
Paramount/Zucker (Gil Netter, James D. Brubaker)
V, V*

A trio of idiots attempt to part a widow from her
wealth by running a ballet company for her.

A misfiring farce and a leaden attempt to revive the
Marx Brothers' style of comedy. Inspired by *A Night at
the Opera*, it doesn't even approach the low level of
Love Happy.

w Pat Proft   *d* Dennis Dugan   *ph* David M. Walsh
m Ira Newborn   *pd* William J. Cassidy
ed Malcolm Campbell

John Turturro, Bob Nelson, Mel Smith, Nancy
Marchand, John Savident, George de La Pena

'Sounds like a horror film and for those expecting a
comedy, it is.' – *Variety*

'Crawling, Slimy Things Terror-Bent On Destroying The
World!'

The Brain Eaters
US   1958   60m   bw
AIP/Corinthian (Edwin Nelson)
V, V*

Parasites from the Earth's core isolate a small town
and begin to take over its citizens.

Low-budget imitation of *Invasion of The Body Snatchers*,
but with little evidence of intelligence in its making.

w Gordon Urquhart   *d* Bruno Vesota   *ph* Larry
Raimond   *m* Tom Jonson   *ad* Burt Shonberg
ed Carlo Lodato

Edwin Nelson, Alan Frost, Jack Hill, Joanna Lee,
Jody Fair, David Hughes, Leonard Nimoy (credited as
Nemoy and playing a bearded ancient)

'Science-fiction's most astounding story!'

The Brain from Planet Arous
US   1958   70m   bw
Howco International (Jacques Marquett)
V*, L

A criminal alien, consisting of a disembodied brain,
takes possession of the body of a nuclear scientist.

Laughably inept science fiction that leaves few clichés
unspoken.

w Ray Buffum   *d* Nathan Hertz (Nathan Juran)
ph Jacques Marquette   *m* Walter Greene   *ed* Irving
Schoenberg

John Agar, Joyce Meadows, Robert Fuller, Thomas B.
Henry

The Brain Machine *
GB   1954   83m   bw
Alec Snowden/Merton Park

Through an electroencephalograph, a hospital
psychiatrist recognizes a patient as a dangerous
psychopath.

Very tolerable crime thriller with a fresh angle.

wd Ken Hughes

Elizabeth Allan, Patrick Barr, Maxwell Reed, Russell
Napier, Vanda Godsell, Gibb McLaughlin

Brain Waves
US   1982   80m   colour
CinAmerica Pictures (Ulli Lommel)
V*

A brain-dead accident victim is brought back to life
through the electronic transfer of the brain patterns of
a murder victim, with disastrous results.

Ponderous and sentimental fantasy, a high-tech
variation on Frankenstein.

wd Uli Lommel   *ph* Jon Kranhouse   *m* Robert O.
Ragland   *ed* Richard Brummer

Tony Curtis, Keir Dullea, Suzanne Love, Vera Miles,
Percy Rodrigues, Paul Willson

'A romantic comedy about a boy, a girl and their power tools.'

Braindead
New Zealand 1992 104m colour
Polygram/Wingnut Films (Jim Booth)
V

A bite from a rat monkey turns a woman into a zombie; soon her cellar is full of other zombies.

Grossly gory horror, played for sick laughs, with a climactic massacre of the zombies by lawnmower that must rank as one of the bloodiest twenty minutes on film. It is difficult to understand why the British censors are happy to let us watch such jejune and tiresome stuff uncut while refusing a video release for such films as *Straw Dogs* and *Reservoir Dogs*.

w Stephen Sinclair, Frances Walsh, Peter Jackson d Peter Jackson ph Murray Milne pd Kenneth Leonard-Jones ed Jamie Selkirk

Timothy Balme, Diana Penalver, Elizabeth Moody, Ian Watkin, Brenda Kendal, Stuart Devenie, Jed Brophy

'Soon jettisons characterisations and story development in favour of an orgy of tasteless effects.' – *Kim Newman*

'It's impossible to imagine anyone out-grossing the New Zealander's effort, or wanting to.' – *Sight and Sound*

Brainstorm
US 1965 110m bw Panavision
Warner/Kodima (William Conrad)

A passer-by saves a married woman from suicide, has an affair with her, and conspires to murder her husband. This accomplished, she leaves him and he goes insane.

Overlong thriller which starts off agreeably in the *Double Indemnity* vein; but goes slow and solemn around the half way mark.

w Mann Rubin d William Conrad ph Sam Leavitt m George Duning

Jeffrey Hunter, Anne Francis, Dana Andrews, Viveca Lindfors, Stacy Harris

'A sub-B potboiler for those who find comic books too intellectual.' – *Judith Crist*

Brainstorm
US 1983 106m Metrocolor Super Panavision
MGM/UA/JF (Douglas Trumbull)
V*, L, S

A technological device records emotions so faithfully as to make other people feel them through each of the five senses. The enemy is discovered to be using it for brainwashing purposes; but it has recorded the experience of death . . .

Scientific mumbo jumbo which went far too far as an attack on the audience's senses, and was jinxed by the death of its star during production.

w Robert Stitzel, Philip Frank Messina, Bruce Joel Rubin d Douglas Trumbull ph Richard Yuricich m James Horner pd John Vallone

Natalie Wood, Christopher Walken, Louise Fletcher, Cliff Robertson, Jordan Christopher, Alan Fudge

'A monstrous bore, with uninteresting characters buried beneath a mass of even less interesting technology.' – *Tom Milne, MFB*

Brainwashed
France/Italy 1972 Eastmancolor
Lira/Fox Europa/Pegaso (Roland Girard, Jean Bolvary)
original title: *Le Droit d'Aimer*; aka: *The Right to Love*

After a two-year wait, a woman visits her lover, a political prisoner held on a grim island jail, and discovers that their relationship has changed.

A glum fable of requited love.

w Jean-Claude Carrière, Françoise Xenakis, Jean Bolvary, Éric Le Hung novel *Elle Lui Dirait dans l'Île* by Françoise Xenakis d Éric Le Hung ph Henri Decae m Philippe Sarde ed Jacqueline Thiédot

Omar Sharif, Florinda Bolkan, Pierre Michael, Gilles Ségal

Bram Stoker's Count Dracula
Spain/Italy/West Germany/Liechtenstein 1970 98m Eastmancolor Panavision
Hemdale/Fénix/Corona/Filmar/Towers of London (Harry Alan Towers)
original title: *El Conde Dracula*; aka: *Count Dracula*, *Dracula 71*

An English solicitor, Jonathan Harker, tracks Dracula to his castle after the Count kills his wife's friend, and destroys him by burning his coffin.

A feeble effort, in which a good cast is wasted by directorial incompetence. It was claimed, wrongly, that it was the first film to stick closely to the original story.

w Peter Welbeck (Harry Alan Towers), Carlo Fadda, Milo C. Cuccia, Dietmar Behnke novel *Dracula* by Bram Stoker d Jess (Jesús) Franco ph Manuel Merino m Bruno Nicolai sp Sergio Pagoni

Christopher Lee, Herbert Lom, Klaus Kinski, Frederick Williams, Maria Rohm, Soledad Miranda, Jack Taylor

'Disappointingly unimaginative in treatment . . . the evidently low budget reveals day-for-night shots for what they are, also permitting a cardboard rock clearly to be seen bouncing off a horse's head before "crushing" a peasant.' – *John Raisbeck, MFB*

'Love Never Dies.'

Bram Stoker's Dracula
US 1992 128m Technicolor
Columbia TriStar/American Zoetrope/Osiris (Francis Ford Coppola, Fred Fuchs, Charles Mulvehill)
V, V*, L, S

In the 1480s Dracula curses God and becomes a vampire after his wife, thinking that he has died in battle, commits suicide; 400 or so years later in London he falls in love with a woman who seems to be her reincarnation.

A lush, over-dressed Gothic romance that plays down the menace and dread of the original, with performances that range from the inadequate to the over-ripe.

w James V. Hart d Francis Ford Coppola ph Michael Ballhaus m Wojciech Kilar pd Thomas Sanders sp Roman Coppola ed Nicholas C. Smith, Glen Scantlebury, Anne Goursaud

Gary Oldman, Winona Ryder, Anthony Hopkins, Keanu Reeves

'Remains in essentials a fairly comprehensive and often vulgar mess . . . The whole somehow seems to sum up what people want from cinema nowadays: style hinting at content but gradually drowning it out with pyrotechnics.' – *Derek Malcolm, Guardian*

'You emerge from the vampire's feast hungry and disappointed.' – *Geoff Brown, The Times*

'Everybody knows that Dracula has a heart; Coppola knows that it is more than an organ to drive a stake into. To the director, the count is a restless spirit who has been condemned for too many years to interment in cruddy movies. This luscious film restores the creature's nobility and gives him peace.' – *Richard Corliss, Time*

AA: Eiko Ishioka (costumes); make-up; sound effects editing

AAN: Thomas Sanders

The Bramble Bush
US 1960 105m Technicolor
Warner/United States (Milton Sperling)

A doctor returns to his home town and finds himself involved in old tragedies including the mercy killing of his friend.

Sordid small-town melodrama in the *Peyton Place* vein, with adequate production values but dispiriting treatment.

w Milton Sperling, Philip Yordan novel Charles Mergendahl d Daniel Petrie ph Lucien Ballard m Leonard Rosenman

Richard Burton, Barbara Rush, Jack Carson, Angie Dickinson, James Dunn, Tom Drake, Henry Jones, Frank Conroy, Carl Benton Reid, William Hansen

The Branches of the Tree **
India 1990 120m colour
Erato/DD/Soproffilms

When their famous father is taken ill, his three successful sons and their wives and children return home to visit him.

A rigorous examination of family relationships and values.

wd Satyajit Ray ph Sandip Ray m Satyajit Ray

Ajit Banerjee, Soumitra Chatterjee, Maradan Banerjee, Lily Charraborty, Deepankar De, Mamata Shankar, Ranjit Malik

'An honest, thoughtful, compassionate film.' – *Philip French, Observer*

Branded
US 1950 104m Technicolor
Paramount (Mel Epstein)
V*, L

A gunman poses as a rancher's lost heir, but redeems himself by finding the real one.

Competent, brisk Western.

w Sydney Boehm, Cyril Hume d Rudolph Maté ph Charles Lang Jnr m Roy Webb

Alan Ladd, Charles Bickford, Mona Freeman, Robert Keith, Joseph Calleia, Peter Hansen, Selena Royle, Tom Tully

Branded to Kill **
Japan 1967 91m colour Nikkatsu-scope
Nikkatsu (Iwai Kaneo)
original title: *Koroshi No Rakuin*

The number three hitman in Tokyo, whose fetish is smelling boiled rice, finds himself the target of the top killer.

A strange but enjoyable thriller, with its quirky originality, odd angles and odder hero as well as some effective suspense.

w Guryu Hachiro d Suzuki Seijun ph Nagatsuka Kazue m Yamamoto Naozumi ad Kawahara Sukezo ed Tanji Mutsuo

Shishido Jo, Ogawa Mariko, Mari Annu, Nanbara Koji, Tamagawa Isao, Minami Hiroshi

'His film-making remains a wonderful subversion of commercial genres, wildly over-the-top, stylistically imaginative and totally watchable for its sheer (possibly ironic) audacity.' – *Derek Malcolm, Guardian*

'One of Suzuki's greatest, and it stands as his last word to date on the yakuza genre.' – *Tony Rayne*

† The film caused Suzuki's sacking from the Nikkatsu studios, when he became a scapegoat for a change in policy.

Brandy for the Parson *
GB 1951 79m bw
Group Three (Alfred O'Shaughnessy)

A couple on a yachting holiday find themselves unwittingly smuggling brandy into Britain.

Pleasant little sub-Ealing comedy with agreeable locations but not much drive.

w John Dighton, Walter Meade   *story* Geoffrey Household   *d* John Eldridge   *ph* Martin Curtis   *m* John Addison

James Donald, Kenneth More, Jean Lodge, Frederick Piper, Charles Hawtrey, Michael Trubshawe, Alfie Bass, Reginald Beckwith

'Detective-Lieutenant Brannigan is in London . . . God Save the Queen!'

Brannigan *
GB   1975   111m   DeLuxe   Panavision
UA/Wellborn (Jules Levy, Arthur Gardner)
V, V*

A Chicago policeman is sent to London to pick up a gangster.

Cheerful crime pastiche and tour of London, quite an agreeable entertainment despite its obviously over-age star.

w Christopher Trumbo, Michael Butler, William P. McGivern, William Norton   *d* Douglas Hickox   *ph* Gerry Fisher   *m* Dominic Frontière

John Wayne, Richard Attenborough, Judy Geeson, Mel Ferrer, John Vernon, Daniel Pilon, John Stride, James Booth, Barry Dennen

The Brasher Doubloon *
US   1946   72m   bw
TCF
GB title: *The High Window*

Philip Marlowe investigates the theft of a rare coin and finds himself involved in a series of murders.

The poorest of the Chandler adaptations, previously filmed as *Time to Kill*, still contains good moments, though the star is lightweight and the production low-budget.

w Dorothy Bennett   *novel The High Window* by Raymond Chandler   *d* John Brahm   *ph* Lloyd Ahern   *m* David Buttolph

George Montgomery, Nancy Guild, Florence Bates, Conrad Janis, Fritz Kortner

The Brass Bottle
US   1964   89m   Eastmancolor
U-I/Scarus (Robert Arthur)

A young architect finds an old brass bottle which contains a troublesome genie.

Simple-minded farce with little invention and poor trickwork.

w Oscar Brodney   *novel* F. Anstey   *d* Harry Keller   *ph* Clifford Stine   *m* Bernard Green   *sp* Roswell Hoffman

Tony Randall, Burl Ives, Barbara Eden, Edward Andrews, Ann Doran

The Brass Legend
US   1956   79m   bw
UA (Herman Cohen/Bob Goldstein)

A sheriff finds himself in trouble when he tries to protect his fiancée's young brother.

Stolid programmer of the *High Noon* school, but without the flair.

w Don Martin   *d* Gerd Oswald

Hugh O'Brian, Nancy Gates, Raymond Burr, Reba Tassell

The Brass Monkey
GB   1948   84m   bw
Diadem/Alliance/UA
aka: *Lucky Mascot*

A radio singer thwarts the theft of a Buddhist idol.

Flat thriller based round a radio 'discovery' programme.

w Alec Coppel, Thornton Freeland   *d* Thornton Freeland

Carole Landis, Carroll Levis, Herbert Lom, Avril Angers, Ernest Thesiger

Brass Target
US   1978   111m   Metrocolor
MGM (Berle Adams)
V*, L

The alleged story behind the death of General Patton, who according to these sources was eliminated because he had discovered a bullion robbery attempt.

Good-looking but interminably complex and talkative, with nothing much for its star cast to do.

w Alvin Boretz   *novel The Algonquin Project* by Frederick Nolan   *d* John Hough   *ph* Tony Imi   *m* Laurence Rosenthal

Sophia Loren, George Kennedy, Max von Sydow, John Cassavetes, Patrick McGoohan, Robert Vaughn, Bruce Davison, Edward Herrmann, Ed Bishop

Brats *
US   1930   20m   bw
Hal Roach

Stan and Ollie have trouble baby-sitting their own mischievous kids.

Fairly ambitious star comedy with trick sets and photography enabling Laurel and Hardy to play their own sons. About half the gags come off.

w Leo McCarey, H. M. Walker, Hal Roach   *d* James Parrott   *ph* George Stevens   *ed* Richard Currier

Stan Laurel, Oliver Hardy

The Bravados *
US   1958   98m   Eastmancolor   Cinemascope
TCF (Herbert B. Swope)
V, V*

A widower chases four killers who, he believes, raped and murdered his wife.

Dour Western with a downbeat ending; production good, but entertainment uneasy.

w Philip Yordan   *novel* Frank O'Rourke   *d* Henry King   *ph* Leon Shamroy   *md* Emil Newman   *m* Hugo Friedhofer

Gregory Peck, Stephen Boyd, Joan Collins, Albert Salmi, Henry Silva, George Voskovec, Barry Coe, Lee Van Cleef

The Brave and the Beautiful: see *The Magnificent Matador*

The Brave Bulls
US   1951   108m   bw
Columbia (Robert Rossen)

A Mexican matador regains his courage but loses his girl in a car crash.

Muddled narrative with dollops of bull-fighting mystique; a rather miserable movie despite effort all round.

w John Bright   *novel* Tom Lea   *d* Robert Rossen   *ph* James Wong Howe, Floyd Crosby

Mel Ferrer, Miroslava, Anthony Quinn, Eugene Iglesias

The Brave Don't Cry *
GB   1952   90m   bw
Group Three (John Baxter)

Over a hundred men are rescued in a Scottish mine disaster.

Semi-documentary based on a real incident well done on a small budget, but hardly memorable.

w Montagu Slater   *d* Philip Leacock   *ph* Arthur Grant   *m* none

John Gregson, Meg Buchanan, John Rae, Fulton Mackay, Andrew Keir, Russell Waters, Jameson Clark, Jean Anderson, Eric Woodburn

The Brave Little Toaster
US   1987   90m   DeLuxe
Castle Premier/Hyperion/Kushner-Locke/WangFilm/Global Communications (Donald Kushner, Thomas L. Wilhite)
V*, L

Domestic appliances go in search of their owner.

Odd fantasy of pots and pans with no more than adequate animation.

w Jerry Rees, Joe Ranft   *novel* Thomas M. Disch   *d* Jerry Rees   *m* David Newman

voices of Jon Levitz, Tim Stack, Timothy E. Day, Thurl Ravenscroft, Deanna Oliver, Phil Hartman, Joe Ranft

The Brave One *
US   1956   100m   Technicolor   Cinemascope
King Brothers
V*

A small boy saves the life of his pet bull when it is sent into the ring.

Mildly beguiling minor drama for those who adore small boys and bulls.

w Harry Franklin, Merrill G. White   *story* Robert Rich   *d* Irving Rapper   *ph* Jack Cardiff   *m* Victor Young   *ed* Merrill G. White

Michel Ray, Rodolfo Hoyos, Elsa Cardenas, Joi Lansing, Carlos Navarro

AA: Robert Rich. (There was much confusion when the mysterious Rich turned out to be Dalton Trumbo, who was blacklisted at the time.)

AAN: editing

Brazil
US   1944   91m   bw
Republic (Robert North)

A lady novelist goes to Brazil for material; a local composer poses as her guide in order to pay her back for her previous remarks about his country.

Acceptable lower case musical with pleasant tunes and humour.

w Frank Gill Jnr, Laura Kerr   *d* Joseph Santley   *ph* Jack Marta

songs Bob Russell and others   *m* Walter Scharf

Virginia Bruce, Tito Guizar, Edward Everett Horton, Roy Rogers

AAN: song 'Rio de Janeiro' (*m* Ary Barrosa, *ly* Ned Washington); Walter Scharf

Brazil *
GB   1985   142m   colour
Embassy (Arnon Milchan)
V, V*, L, S

A comically pessimistic view of the future, seen through the eyes of a dutiful civil servant who is eventually crushed by the system.

An expensive, wild, overlong, hit-or-miss Orwellian satire: enough good jabs to please the intelligentsia, but a turnoff for patrons at the local Odeon.

w Terry Gilliam, Tom Stoppard, Charles McKeown   *d* Terry Gilliam   *ph* Roger Pratt   *m* Michael Kamen   *pd* Norman Garwood   *ed* Julian Doyle

Jonathan Pryce, Robert de Niro, Michael Palin, Kim Greist, Katherine Helmond, Ian Holm, Ian Richardson, Peter Vaughan, Bob Hoskins

'It will not be everybody's cup of poisoned tea.' – *Variety*

'Exuberantly violent, cruelly funny and sometimes sickeningly scatological . . . the whole is wrapped up in a melancholy wistfulness.' – *Sight and Sound*

AAN: original screenplay, art direction

Breach of Promise
GB   1941   79m   bw
British Mercury/MGM
US title: *Adventure in Blackmail*

A girl chases the man she wants by filing a breach of promise suit against him.

Dated but lively comedy with agreeable playing.

w Roland Pertwee   *d* Harold Huth, Roland Pertwee

Clive Brook, Judy Campbell, C. V. France, Margaret Allan, Percy Walsh

Bread and Chocolate *
Italy   1973   112m   Eastmancolor
Verona Cinematografica (Maurizio Lodo-Fe)

An Italian waiter in Switzerland is accused of murder and indecent exposure.

Amusing and often pathetic account of an inveterate loser, its flavour impossible to define.

w Franco Brusati, Iaia Fiastri, Nino Manfredi   *d* Franco Brusati   *ph* Luciano Tovoli   *md* Daniele Patrucchi

Nino Manfredi, Anna Karina, Johnny Dorelli, Paolo Turco

Bread, Love and Dreams *
Italy   1953   90m   bw
Titanus (Marcello Girosi)

The new sergeant of police in a small rural village comes looking for a wife.

Pleasant rather than exciting rural comedy which spun off a number of vaguely related sequels (*Bread, Love and Jealousy*, etc.).

w Luigi Comencini   *story* Ettore Margadonna   *d* Luigi Comencini   *ph* Arturo Gallea   *m* Alessandro Cicognini

Vittorio de Sica, Gina Lollobrigida, Marisa Merlini, Roberto Risso

AAN: Ettore Margadonna

Break in the Circle
GB   1955   91m (69m US)   Eastmancolor (bw in US)
Exclusive/Hammer (Michael Carreras)
V*

The owner of a cabin cruiser is hired to smuggle a scientist out of Germany.

Routine action yarn of cross and double-cross, tolerably staged.

wd Val Guest   *novel* Philip Loraine   *ph* Walter Harvey   *m* Doreen Carwithen   *ad* J. Elder Wills   *ed* Bill Lenny

Forrest Tucker, Eva Bartok, Marius Goring, Eric Pohlmann, Guy Middleton, Arnold Marlé

Break of Hearts
US   1935   80m   bw
RKO (Pandro S. Berman)

A girl composer falls in love with a distinguished conductor who becomes a dipsomaniac.

Well acted soap opera, not really worthy of its stars.

w Sarah Y. Mason, Victor Heerman, Anthony Veiller   *d* Philip Moeller   *ph* Robert de Grasse   *m* Max Steiner

Katharine Hepburn, Charles Boyer, Jean Hersholt, John Beal, Sam Hardy

'A stale turnip story that relies entirely upon characterization to hide the basic dullness.' – *Variety*

'In spite of some capable acting, it lacks a certain compelling warmth. The audience's heart never breaks.' – *Eileen Creelman, New York Sun*

Break the News *
GB   1938   78m   bw
GFD/Jack Buchanan

A dancer arranges his partner's 'death' for publicity reasons but is sent to jail when the partner disappears.

Thin but lively comedy with a remarkable couple of song and dance men. Negative apparently lost.

w Geoffrey Kerr   *novel La Mort en Fuite* by Loic de Gouriadec   *d* René Clair   *ph* Phil Tannura   *md* Van Phillips   *m* Theo Mackeben   *m/ly* Cole Porter   *ad* Lazare Meerson   *ed* Francis Lyon, Fred Wilson

Jack Buchanan, Maurice Chevalier, June Knight, Marta Labarr, Garry Marsh, Felix Aylmer, Robb Wilton

† Various remakes include *The Art of Love* (qv).

Break to Freedom: see *Albert RN*

Breakdance: see *Breakin'*

Breakdance 2: Electric Boogaloo: see *Breakin' 2: Electric Boogaloo*

Breaker Morant *
Australia   1980   107m   Eastmancolor   Panavision
South Australian Film Corporation (Matthew Carroll)
V, V*, L

During the Boer War three Australian officers are courtmartialled for murdering prisoners.

Careful, moving military drama which gives a more sympathetic view of the facts than history does.

w Jonathan Hardy, Bruce Beresford, David Stevens   *play* Kenneth Ross   *d* Bruce Beresford   *ph* Donald McAlpine   *md* Phil Cuneen

Edward Woodward, Jack Thompson, John Waters, Charles Tingwell, Terence Donovan, Vincent Ball

'It is impossible to suppress a feeling that the spirit of Stanley Kramer is abroad on the veldt.' – *Tim Pulleine, MFB*

AAN: screenplay

Breakfast at Tiffany's *
US   1961   115m   Technicolor
Paramount (Martin Jurow, Richard Shepherd)
V, V*, L, S

A young New York writer has as neighbour the volatile Holly Golightly, a slightly crazy call girl with an exotic social and emotional life.

Impossibly cleaned up and asexual version of a light novel which tried to be the American *I Am a Camera*. Wild parties, amusing scenes and good cameos, but the pace is slow, the atmosphere is unconvincingly clean and luxurious, and the sentimentality kills it.

w George Axelrod   *novel* Truman Capote   *d* Blake Edwards   *ph* Franz Planer   *m Henry Mancini*

Audrey Hepburn, George Peppard, Patricia Neal, Buddy Ebsen, Martin Balsam, *John McGiver* (as the Tiffany salesman), Mickey Rooney

AA: Henry Mancini; song 'Moon River' (*m* Henry Mancini, *ly* Johnny Mercer)

AAN: George Axelrod; Audrey Hepburn

The Breakfast Club
US   1985   97m   Technicolor
A&M/Universal (Ned Tanen, John Hughes)
V, V*, L, S

Five rebellious students at Shermer High blame their parents for their misfortunes.

Abysmal apologia for loutish teenage behaviour.

wd John Hughes   *ph* Thomas Del Ruth, George Bouillet   *m* Keith Forsey   *ed* Dede Allen

Emilio Estevez, Judd Nelson, Molly Ringwald, Anthony Michael Hall, Ally Sheedy

Breakfast for Two *
US   1937   65m   bw
RKO (Edward Kaufman)

A Texas heiress turns a playboy into a businessman.

Star crazy comedy with some wildly funny scenes.

w Charles Kaufman, Paul Yawitz, Viola Brothers Shore   *d* Alfred Santell   *ph* J. Roy Hunt

Barbara Stanwyck, Herbert Marshall, Donald Meek, Glenda Farrell, Eric Blore, Etienne Girardot

'Heaps of laughs in a breezily-paced farce.' – *Variety*

Breakfast in Hollywood
US   1945   90m   bw
Golden Pictures/United Artists
V*
GB title: *The Mad Hatter*

A day in the life of a radio breakfast show host.

Topical programme filler, more interesting historically than entertaining.

w Earl W. Baldwin   *d* Harold Schuster

Tom Breneman, Bonita Granville, Beulah Bondi, Eddie Ryan, Raymond Walburn, Billie Burke, ZaSu Pitts, Spike Jones and his City Slickers, Andy Russell, Hedda Hopper

Breakheart Pass *
US   1975   94m   DeLuxe
UA/Elliott Kastner (Jerry Gershwin)
V*, L

Various mysterious passengers on an 1873 train across the frozen west to Fort Humboldt turn out to have smuggling and murder in mind.

Botched murder mystery on wheels: there are some exciting scenes, but the plot makes little sense and the 'action finale' is muddled.

w Alistair MacLean   *novel* Alistair MacLean   *d* Tom Gries   *ph* Lucien Ballard   *m* Jerry Goldsmith

Charles Bronson, Ben Johnson, Richard Crenna, Jill Ireland, Charles Durning, Archie Moore, Ed Lauter

Breakin'
US   1984   87m   Metrocolor
MGM-UA/Cannon (Allen DeBevoise, David Zito)
V*, L, S
GB title: *Breakdance*

Youngsters promote a new form of dancing.

Minor exploitation item, the form little improved on *Rock around the Clock* thirty years earlier.

w Charles Parker, Allen DeBevoise, Gerald Scaife   *d* Joel Silberg   *ph* Hanania Baer   *m* Gary Remal, Michael Boyd   *pd* Ivo Cristante   *ed* Mark Helfrich

Lucinda Dickey, Adolfo 'Shabba-Doo' Quinones, Michael 'Boogaloo-Shrimp' Chambers, Ben Lokey, Phineas Newborn III, Tracey 'Ice T' Marrow

Breakin' 2: Electric Boogaloo
US   1984   94m   TVC
Cannon
V*, L, S
GB title: *Breakdance 2: Electric Boogaloo*

Youngsters raise 200,000 dollars to save their local community centre; a dance show does it.

Hurried sequel of no interest apart from the briefly popular musical gyrations.

w Jan Ventura, Julie Reichert   *d* Sam Firstenberg

Lucinda Dickey, Adolfo Quinones, Michael Chambers, Susie Bono

Breaking Away *
US   1979   101m   DeLuxe
TCF (Peter Yates)
V*, L

An imaginative teenager has trouble adjusting to adult life after high school.

Andy Hardy would have felt at home in this fragmented comedy of the American hinterland; 1979 audiences found it a welcome relief from the stronger brews to which they had become accustomed.

w Steve Tesich   *d* Peter Yates   *ph* Matthew F. Leonetti   *md* Lionel Newman   *m* Patrick Williams

Dennis Christopher, Dennis Quaid, Daniel Stern, Jackie Earle Haley, Barbara Barrie, Paul Dooley

'Affection for the middle classes, the landscapes of Indiana, and bicycle racing.' – *New Yorker*

'It is not devoid of pleasures . . . but it fatally lacks a clear purpose and identity.' – *Geoff Brown, MFB*

'Here's a sunny, goofy, intelligent little film about coming of age in Bloomington, Indiana.' – *Roger Ebert*

† An unsuccessful TV series followed in 1980.

AA: Steve Tesich

AAN: best picture; Peter Yates; Patrick Williams; Barbara Barrie

'The experience is shattering!'
Breaking Glass
GB   1980   104m   Technicolor   Panavision
GTO/Film and General (Dodi Fayed)
V, S

Vicissitudes of a pop band and of its singer who can't stand the pace.

Garish, freakish musical with unattractive characters strung along an oft-told tale. Some commendable vigour in the presentation, but it won't appeal to anybody over 21.

wd Brian Gibson   *ph* Stephen Goldblatt   *md* Tony Visconti

Hazel O'Connor, Phil Daniels, Jon Finch, Jonathan Pryce

Breaking In *
US   1989   94m   colour
Castle Premier/Breaking In Productions/Sam Goldwyn
    Company (Harry Gittes)
V, V*, L

A veteran safe-breaker teaches a teenager the tricks of the trade.

Mildly rewarding comedy of crooked manners.

w John Sayles   *d* Bill Forsyth   *ph* Michael Coulter *pd* Adrienne Atkinson, John Willett   *ed* Michael Ellis

Burt Reynolds, Casey Siemaszko, Sheila Kelley, Lorraine Toussaint, Albert Salmi, Harry Carey, Maury Chaykin

'Less a barrel of laughs than elliptically funny in its observation of the unconscious discrepancy between word and deed.' – *Tom Milne, MFB*

The Breaking of Bumbo
GB   1970   90m   colour
Associated British (Jeffrey Selznick)

A misfit of a Guards officer goes to pieces thanks to his own, and his fellow officers', shortcomings.

A misfiring comedy which, like its hero, falls flat on its face.

wd Andrew Sinclair   *novel* Andrew Sinclair

Richard Warwick, Joanna Lumley, Natasha Pyne, Jeremy Child, John Bird, Donald Pickering

† The film was never given a general release and was shown briefly in one London cinema, although it is occasionally seen on television.

'There's nothing more deadly than a gentle man pushed too far!'
The Breaking Point *
US   1950   97m   bw
Warner (Jerry Wald)

A charterboat owner becomes involved with crooks but turns them in when they have killed his friend.

Adequate if slightly humdrum attempt by Warner to atone for what they had done to a Hemingway novel, the infidelity of *To Have and Have Not* and the

unauthorized variation of *Key Largo.* (See also: *The Gun Runners.*)

w Ranald MacDougall   *novel To Have and Have Not* by Ernest Hemingway   *d* Michael Curtiz   *ph* Ted McCord   *m* (uncredited) William Lava, Max Steiner

John Garfield, Patricia Neal, Phyllis Thaxter, Juano Hernandez, Wallace Ford, Edmon Ryan, William Campbell

'Innocence and fury don't mix – they explode!'
Breaking Point
Canada   1976   92m   colour   Panavision
TCF/Astral Belle Vue (Harold Greenberg, Harold Pariser)
V*

An innocent witness against the Mafia takes off against them vigilante style when his partner is murdered and his own life threatened.

Comic strip thuggery with performances to match; plenty of excitement for toughies.

w Roger E. Swaybill, Stanley Mann   *d* Bob Clark *ph* Marc Champion   *m* David McLey

Bo Svenson, Robert Culp, John Colicos, Belinda J. Montgomery, Stephen Young

Breaking the Ice
US   1938   80m   bw
RKO/Sol Lesser

A Pennsylvania Dutch boy runs away to the city so that his mother can afford her own farm.

Slim star musical which had its pleasing moments.

w Mary McCall Jnr, Manuel Seff, Bernard Schubert *d* Edward F. Cline   *ph* Jack MacKenzie   *m* Victor Young

Bobby Breen, Charles Ruggles, Dolores Costello, Robert Barrat, Dorothy Peterson, John King, Billy Gilbert, Margaret Hamilton

'Moderately engrossing, combination folk drama and musical.' – *Variety*

AAN: Victor Young

Breaking the Sound Barrier: see The Sound
    Barrier

Breakout (1958): see
Danger Within

Breakout
US   1975   96m   colour   Panavision
Columbia/Persky-Bright (Robert Chartoff, Irwin Winkler)
V*, L

A professional rescuer gets an innocent man out of a Mexican jail.

Rough and ready adventure thriller which starts slowly and confusingly but later works up a fair head of steam.

w Howard B. Kreitsek, Frank Kowalski   *novel Ten Second Jailbreak* by Howard B. Kreitsek, Frank Kowalski   *d* Tom Gries   *ph* Lucien Ballard *m* Jerry Goldsmith

Charles Bronson, Robert Duvall, John Huston, Jill Ireland, Randy Quaid, Sheree North

Breakthrough
US   1950   91m   bw
Warner (Bryan Foy)
V, V*

Adventures of a US army unit in Normandy after D-Day.

Routine low-budgeter which improves after a slow start.

w Bernard Girard, Ted Sherdeman, Joseph I. Breen Jnr   *d* Lewis Seiler   *ph* Edwin DuPar *m* William Lava

David Brian, John Agar, Frank Lovejoy, William Campbell, Paul Picerni, Greg McClure, Edward Norris, Matt Willis, Dick Wesson

The Breakup: see La Rupture

Breath of Scandal (1929): see His Glorious Night

A Breath of Scandal
US   1960   98m   Technicolor
Paramount/Titanus/Ponti-Girosi (Carlo Ponti, Marcello Girosi)
V*

A spirited Ruritanian princess falls for an American industrialist.

Exceedingly flat-footed and boring international co-production of an old Molnar play; if anyone concerned had bright ideas, they don't show.

w Walter Bernstein   *play Olimpia* by Ferenc Molnar *d* Michael Curtiz, Mario Russo   *ph* Mario Montuori *m* Alessandro Cicognini

Sophia Loren, Maurice Chevalier, John Gavin, Isabel Jeans, Angela Lansbury, Roberto Risso, Frederick Ledebur, Tullio Carminati, Milly Vitale

† A remake of *His Glorious Night* (qv), filmed by MGM in 1929.

Breathless (1959): see A Bout de Souffle

Breathless
US   1983   101m   DeLuxe
Miko/Breathless Associates/Greenberg Brothers (Martin Erlichman)
V*, L

A street-smart hustler steals a car in Las Vegas and heads for the coast.

Fashionable amalgam of sex and violence, borrowed from *A Bout de Souffle* but far too long after the event.

w L. M. Kit Carson, James McBride   *d* James McBride   *ph* Richard H. Kline   *m* Jack Nitzsche *pd* Richard Sylbert

Richard Gere, Valerie Kaprisky, William Tepper, John P. Ryan, Art Metrano

'Not much more than an ego trip for a bankable star.' – *Daily Mail*

A Breed Apart
US   1984   101m   colour   Panavision
Hemdale/Sagittarius (John Daly, Derek Gibson)
V, V*

A rich collector hires a mountaineer to rob the almost inaccessible nest of a rare bald eagle, guarded by a militant conservationist.

Ecological propaganda given the sugar coating of a sentimental love story with a little action thrown in.

w Paul Wheeler   *d* Philippe Mora   *ph* Geoffrey Stephenson   *m* Maurice Gibb   *pd* William Barclay *ed* Christopher Lebenzon

Rutger Hauer, Powers Boothe, Kathleen Turner, Brion James, Donald Pleasence

Breezy
US   1973   107m   Technicolor
Universal/Malpaso (Robert Daley)

A divorced 50-year-old real estate agent is rejuvenated by an affair with a young girl hippy.

An abrasive veneer covers the most stereotyped of January/May love stories. Technically an attractive piece of work.

w Jo Heims   *d* Clint Eastwood   *ph* Frank Stanley *m* Michel Legrand

William Holden, Kay Lenz, Roger C. Carmel, Marj Dusay, Joan Hotchkis

Brenda Starr, Reporter

US   1945   bw   serial: 15 eps
Columbia

A girl reporter traces a dead gangster's loot.

Adequate who's-following-who melodramatics.
d Wallace W. Fox

Joan Woodbury, Kane Richmond, Syd Saylor, Joe Devlin, George Meeker, Wheeler Oakman

Brewster McCloud

US   1970   105m   Metrocolor   Panavision
MGM/Adler-Phillips/Lion's Gate (Lou Adler)
V*

A man hides out under the roof of the Houston Astrodrome, prepares to learn to fly with man-made wings, and refuses all offers of help; when he launches himself, he falls to his death.

Anarchic, allegorical fantasy, a delight no doubt for connoisseurs of way-out humour. Everyone else, forget it.

w Doran William Cannon   *d* Robert Altman
ph Lamar Boren, Jordan Cronenweth   *m* Gene Page

Bud Cort, Sally Kellerman, Michael Murphy, William Windom, Shelley Duvall, René Auberjonois, Stacy Keach, John Schuck, Margaret Hamilton

'Amorphous and rather silly . . . the idea seems to be left over from a Victorian fable, but the style is like a Road Runner cartoon.' – *New Yorker, 1974*

Brewster's Millions *

GB   1935   84m   bw
British and Dominion (Herbert Wilcox)

If he can spend a million pounds within two months, a playboy will inherit many millions more.

Artless but lively version of a famous comedy which provided a good role for its star.

w Arthur Wimperis, Paul Gangelin, Douglas Furber, Clifford Grey, Donovan Pedelty, Wolfgang Wilhelm *play* George Barr McCutcheon, Winchell Smith *novel* George Barr McCutcheon   *d* Thornton Freeland   *ph* Henry Harris, Barney McGill   *m* Ray Noble   *ad* L. P. Williams   *ed* Merrill White

Jack Buchanan, Lili Damita, Nancy O'Neil, Amy Veness, Sydney Fairbrother, Fred Emney, Sebastian Shaw

'As near 100% film entertainment as can be expected.' – *Variety*

† There had been silent versions in 1916 (with Edward Abeles) and 1921 (with Roscoe Arbuckle).

Brewster's Millions *

US   1945   79m   bw
Edward Small
V*

Competent American remake of the above.

w Sig Herzig, Charles Rogers   *d* Allan Dwan
ph Charles Lawton Jnr   *m* Hugo Friedhofer

Dennis O'Keefe, Eddie 'Rochester' Anderson, Helen Walker, Gail Patrick, Mischa Auer, June Havoc, Joe Sawyer, Nana Bryant, John Litel, Thurston Hall, Byron Foulger

† Remade as *Three on a Spree* (GB 1961).

AAN: Lou Forbes (music scoring)

Brewster's Millions

US   1985   97m   Technicolor
Universal (Lawrence Gordon, Joel Silver)
V*, L

A baseball player learns that in order to inherit 30 million dollars he must spend one million a day for 30 days.

Frantically noisy remake of an old chestnut.

w Herschel Weingrod, Timothy Harris   *d* Walter Hill   *ph* Ric Waite   *m* Ry Cooder   *pd* John Vallone   *ed* Freeman Davis, Michel Ripps

Richard Pryor, John Candy, Lonette McKee, Stephen Collins, Jerry Orbach, Pat Hingle, Tovah Feldshuh

The Bribe *

US   1949   98m   bw
MGM (Pandro S. Berman)

A US agent tracks down a group of criminals in Central America.

Steamy melodrama with pretensions but only moderate entertainment value despite high gloss. The rogues' gallery, however, is impressive.

w Marguerite Roberts   *d* Robert Z. Leonard
ph Joseph Ruttenberg   *m* Miklos Rozsa

Robert Taylor, Ava Gardner, Charles Laughton, Vincent Price, John Hodiak

Brick Bradford

US   1947   bw   serial: 15 eps
Columbia

A tough crusader is asked by the United Nations to protect the Interceptor Ray.

No holds are barred for typical serial action.
d Spencer Bennet

Kane Richmond, Rick Vallin, Linda Johnson, Pierre Watkin

The Bridal Path *

GB   1959   95m   Technicolor
Vale (Sidney Gilliat, Frank Launder)

A stalwart Hebridean islander journeys to the mainland in search of a wife.

Mild, episodic, very pleasant open-air comedy set amid splendid locations.

w Frank Launder, Geoffrey Willans   *novel* Nigel Tranter   *d* Frank Launder   *ph* Arthur Ibbetson
m Cedric Thorpe Davie

Bill Travers, Fiona Clyne, George Cole, Duncan Macrae, Gordon Jackson, Dilys Laye, Bernadette O'Farrell

Bridal Suite

US   1939   70m   bw
MGM

A playboy seldom turns up for his own weddings, but his new intended takes him and his mother in hand.

Frothy comedy with dependable cast.

w Samuel Hoffenstein   *d* William Thiele

Robert Young, Annabella, Walter Connolly, Billie Burke, Reginald Owen, Arthur Treacher

'Dull and uninteresting, with static direction, commonplace story and situations, and inability to catch audience attention except for brief moments.' – *Variety*

† First known as *Maiden Voyage*.

'A woman born of electricity . . . a man driven by passion!'
The Bride

US   1985   118m   Rank colour
Columbia/Victor Drai
V, V*, L, S

Frankenstein creates a bride for his monster, but she falls for him instead, and the monster goes off with a garrulous dwarf.

Insane romantic-feminist remake of *The Bride of Frankenstein*, extremely dull and aimless after an arresting start.

w Lloyd Fonvielle   *d* Franc Roddam   *ph* Stephen H. Burum   *m* Maurice Jarre   *pd* Michael Seymour   *ed* Michael Ellis

Sting, Jennifer Beals, Clancy Brown, David Rappaport, Geraldine Page, Anthony Higgins, Quentin Crisp

'A misbegotten exercise.' – *Sight and Sound*

Bride by Mistake

US   1944   84m   bw
RKO

An heiress tests her suitors by posing as her own secretary.

Pleasant little comedy with hard-working cast.

w Phoebe and Henry Ephron   *d* Richard Wallace

Laraine Day, Alan Marshal, Allyn Joslyn, Marsha Hunt

The Bride Came C.O.D. *

US   1941   92m   bw
Warner (Hal B. Wallis)
V*

A charter pilot agrees to kidnap a temperamental heiress, but is stuck with her when they crashland in the desert.

Feeble comedy with a script totally unworthy of its stars. The mass of talent does however provide a smile or two towards the end.

w Julius J. and Philip G. Epstein   *d* William Keighley   *ph* Ernest Haller   *m* Max Steiner

Bette Davis, James Cagney, Harry Davenport, Stuart Erwin, Eugene Pallette, Jack Carson, George Tobias, William Frawley, Edward Brophy, Chick Chandler

'Neither the funniest comedy ever made, nor the shortest distance between two points, but for the most part a serviceable romp.' – *Theodore Strauss*

'Both of them mug good-naturedly, and it's pleasantly fast.' – *New Yorker, 1977*

The Bride Comes Home *

US   1935   82m   bw
Paramount (Wesley Ruggles)

A penniless socialite helps a wealthy man and his roughneck bodyguard in a magazine venture.

Slight but freshly handled romantic comedy, still worth a look.

w Elizabeth Sanxay Holding, Claude Binyon
d Wesley Ruggles   *ph* Leo Tover

Claudette Colbert, Robert Young, Fred MacMurray, William Collier Snr, Donald Meek, Edgar Kennedy, Richard Carle, Jimmy Conlin

'Another galloping lithograph off the boy-and-girl-always-fighting woodblock.' – *Variety*

Bride for Sale

US   1949   87m   bw
RKO (Jack H. Skirball)

A practical-minded businesswoman has two admirers.

Skittish romantic comedy for ageing stars.

w Bruce Manning, Islin Auster   *d* William D. Russell   *ph* Joseph Valentine   *m* Frederick Hollander

Claudette Colbert, George Brent, Robert Young, Max Baer, Gus Schilling, Charles Arnt, Thurston Hall

The Bride Goes Wild

US   1948   98m   bw
MGM (William H. Wright)

As his lady illustrator finds out, a writer of children's books is not quite the sober uncle she expected, especially when he has to pretend to adopt an unruly orphan.

Scatty comedy with farcical interludes, quite pleasantly played but lacking style.

w Albert Beich   *d* Norman Taurog   *ph* Ray June   *m* Rudolf Kopp

June Allyson, Van Johnson, Jackie 'Butch' Jenkins, Hume Cronyn, Richard Derr

'The monster demands a mate!'
The Bride of Frankenstein ****
US   1935   85—90m   bw
Universal (Carl Laemmle Jnr)
V, V*, L

Baron Frankenstein is blackmailed by Dr Praetorius into reviving his monster and building a mate for it.

Frankenstein was startlingly good in a primitive way; this sequel is the screen's sophisticated masterpiece of black comedy, with all the talents working deftly to one end. Every scene has its own delights, and they are woven together into a superb if wilful cinematic narrative which, of its gentle mocking kind, has never been surpassed.

w John L. Balderston, William Hurlbut d James Whale ph John Mescall m Franz Waxman

Boris Karloff, Colin Clive, Ernest Thesiger, Valerie Hobson, E. E. Clive, Dwight Frye, O. P. Heggie, Una O'Connor, Elsa Lanchester (as Mary Shelley and the monster's mate), Gavin Gordon (as Byron), Douglas Walton (as Shelley)

    FRANKENSTEIN: 'I've been cursed for delving into the mysteries of life!'

'It is perhaps because Whale was by now master of the horror film that this production is the best of them all.' – *John Baxter, 1968*

'An extraordinary film, with sharp humour, macabre extravagance, and a narrative that proceeds at a fast, efficient pace.' – *Gavin Lambert, 1948*

'A great deal of art has gone into it, but it is the kind of art that gives the healthy feeling of men with their sleeves rolled up and working, worrying only about how to put the thing over in the best manner of the medium – no time for nonsense and attitudes and long hair.' – *Otis Ferguson*

† The regular release version runs 75m, having dropped part of the Mary Shelley prologue and a sequence in which the monster becomes unsympathetic by murdering the burgomaster.
†† The title was originally to have been *The Return of Frankenstein*.

Bride of the Gorilla
US   1951   65m   bw
Jack Broder Productions
V*

The manager of a rubber plantation is poisoned by a native woman and turns into a gorilla.

Incredibly inane two-bit shocker, a strong contender for any list of the worst films of all time.

wd Curt Siodmak

Barbara Payton, Lon Chaney Jnr, Raymond Burr, Tom Conway, Paul Cavanagh (a rare cast of non-actors)

'The screen's master of the weird … In his newest and most daring shocker!'
Bride of the Monster
US   1953   69m   bw
Rolling M (Edward D. Wood)
V*

Dr Vornoff has an atomic machine which will convert people into beings of superhuman strength; it is turned on himself, but a giant octopus, also with superoctopus strength, gets him.

A perfectly terrible movie, on a par with this director's other works.

w Edward D. Wood Jnr, Alex Gordon d Edward D. Wood Jnr

Bela Lugosi, Tor Johnson, Tony McCoy, Loretta King, Harvey Dunne

Bride of the Re-Animator: see Re-Animator 2

Bride of the Regiment
US   1930   79m   Technicolor
First National
GB title: *Lady of the Rose*

In northern Italy a band of aristocrats rises against the invading Austrians.

Early talkie operetta, well received at the time. No colour material survives.

w Ray Harris operetta *The Lady in Ermine* by Rudolph Schanzer, Ernest Wellsch d John Francis Dillon ph Dev Jennings, Charles Schoenbaum ch Jack Haskell m/ly Al Bryan, Ed Ward

Vivienne Segal, Allan Prior, Walter Pidgeon, Louise Fazenda, Ford Sterling, Myrna Loy, Lupino Lane

'Entertaining all the way, deserves returns above the average.' – *Variety*

Bride of Vengeance *
US   1948   91m   bw
Paramount (Richard Maibaum)

The story of the Borgias (whitewashing Lucretia) and the Duke of Ferrara.

Superb looking but appallingly acted and rather stodgily directed piece of historical melodrama. Totally studio-bound, but one of these days it could find a sympathetic audience.

w Cyril Hume, Michael Hogan d Mitchell Leisen ph Daniel L. Fapp m Hugo Friedhofer ad Hans Dreier, Roland Anderson, Albert Nozaki

Paulette Goddard, John Lund, Macdonald Carey, Albert Dekker, Raymond Burr

'A dud … it just couldn't be that bad by accident.' – *Los Angeles Times*

The Bride Walks Out
US   1936   81m   bw
RKO (Edward Small)
V*

A successful mannequin tries to manage on her engineer husband's lowly salary.

Thin, pleasant marital comedy with no surprises.

w P. J. Wolfson, Philip G. Epstein d Leigh Jason ph J. Roy Hunt m Roy Webb

Barbara Stanwyck, Gene Raymond, Robert Young, Ned Sparks, Helen Broderick, Willie Best, Robert Warwick, Billy Gilbert, Hattie McDaniel, Irving Bacon

The Bride Wasn't Willing: see Frontier Gal

The Bride Wore Black *
France/Italy   1968   107m   Eastmancolor
UA/Films du Carrosse/Artistes Associés/Dino de Laurentiis (Marcel Bébert)
V*, L
original title: *La Mariée Était en Noir*

A melancholy lady traces and kills the five men responsible for her fiancé's death.

Uncertain and not very entertaining attempt to turn a Hitchcock situation into a character study.

w François Truffaut, Jean-Louis Richard novel William Irish d François Truffaut ph Raoul Coutard m Bernard Herrmann ad Pierre Guffroy ed Claudine Bouché

Jeanne Moreau, Jean-Claude Brialy, Michel Bouquet, Charles Denner, Claude Rich, Michel Lonsdale

'Truffaut has called the film a love story; others have taken it as a tribute to his master, a Hitchcockian thriller. In fact it is neither; it is a piece of junk.' – *John Simon*

The Bride Wore Boots
US   1946   86m   bw
Paramount (Seton I. Miller)

A woman who loves horses is married to a man who does not.

Flimsy, silly, but mainly quite tolerable light comedy sustained by its stars.

w Dwight Mitchell Wiley d Irving Pichel ph Stuart Thompson m Frederick Hollander

Barbara Stanwyck, Robert Cummings, Diana Lynn, Patric Knowles, Peggy Wood, Robert Benchley, Willie Best, Natalie Wood

The Bride Wore Crutches
US   1941   55m   bw
TCF

A young reporter witnesses a bank robbery and tracks down the criminals.

Lightweight support.

w Ed Verdier d Shepherd Traube

Ted North, Lynne Roberts, Edgar Kennedy, Lionel Stander, Richard Lane, Grant Mitchell, Horace MacMahon

The Bride Wore Red *
US   1937   103m   bw
MGM (Joseph L. Mankiewicz)
V*

A whimsical count arranges for a chorus girl to spend two weeks at an aristocratic Tyrol resort, where she is pursued by two rich men.

Cinderella retold in fancy dress; a typically unreal but quite entertaining star confection of its day.

w Tess Slesinger, Bradbury Foote play *The Girl from Trieste* by Ferenc Molnar d Dorothy Arzner ph George Folsey m Franz Waxman

Joan Crawford, Robert Young, Franchot Tone, Billie Burke, Reginald Owen, George Zucco, Lynne Carver, Mary Phillips, Paul Porcasi

'Marquee values will have to bolster this one.' – *Variety*

'In the privacy of a girls' school he sought his prey – turning innocent beauty into a thing of unspeakable horror!'
Brides of Dracula **
GB   1960   85m   Technicolor
U-I/Hammer/Hotspur (Anthony Hinds)
V*, L

Baron Meinster, a disciple of Dracula, is locked up by his mother; but a servant lets him out and he goes on the rampage in a girls' school.

The best of the Hammer *Draculas,* with plenty of inventive action, some classy acting and a good sense of place and period.

w Jimmy Sangster, Peter Bryan, Edward Percy d Terence Fisher ph Jack Asher m Malcolm Williamson ed James Needs, Alfred Cox

David Peel (as Meinster), Peter Cushing, Freda Jackson, Martita Hunt, Yvonne Monlaur, Andrée Melly, Mona Washbourne, Henry Oscar, Miles Malleson

The Brides of Fu Manchu *
GB   1966   94m   Eastmancolor
Anglo Amalgamated
V

The yellow peril kidnaps twelve young women in order to blackmail their influential boyfriends.

Very adequate sequel to *The Face of Fu Manchu* (qv for details of series), after which Fu Manchu went rapidly downhill.

w Harry Alan Towers (Peter Welbeck) d Don Sharp

Christopher Lee, Douglas Wilmer, Howard Marion Crawford, Marie Versini, Tsai Chin, Rupert Davies

The Bridge *
West Germany   1959   106m   bw
Fono/Jochen Severin (Hermann Schwerin)

In 1945, only a handful of 16-year-old schoolboys is left to defend the bridge of a small German town.

Painful but memorable war vignette, almost an updating of *All Quiet on the Western Front*.

w Michael Mansfield, Karl-Wilhelm Vivier *novel* Manfred Gregor d Bernhard Wicki ph Gerd von Bonen m Hans-Martin Majewski

Vokler Bohnet, Fritz Wepper, Michael Hinz, Frank Glaubrecht, Karl Michael Balzer, Gunther Hoffman

AAN: foreign film

The Bridge

GB 1991 99m Fujicolor
Moonlight/British Screen/Film Four (Lyn Goleby)
V, S

A young artist and a bored wife, who is on holiday with her young daughters, fall in love.

Genteel period drama, lacking in any dramatic impetus.

w Adrian Hodges d Sydney MacCartney ph David Tattersall m Richard G. Mitchell pd Terry Pritchard ed Michael Ellis

Saskia Reeves, David O'Hara, Joss Ackland, Anthony Higgins, Rosemary Harris, Geraldine James

'Beautiful but inert. . . firmly belongs to the Laura Ashley school of genteel British cinema.' – *Variety*

'Frozen with timidity. This British costume drama sits on the screen like little Miss Muffet, spinning the trite tale of a summer's dalliance.' – *Geoff Brown, The Times*

The Bridge at Remagen *

US 1968 116m DeLuxe Panavision
UA/Wolper (David L. Wolper)
V*

February 1945: Germans and Americans fight over a Rhine bridge.

Disenchanted, violent war film in which incessant bang-bang, adroitly staged, is all that matters.

w Richard Yates, William Roberts d John Guillermin ph Stanley Cortez m Elmer Bernstein

George Segal, Robert Vaughn, Ben Gazzara, Bradford Dillman, E. G. Marshall, Peter Van Eyck

'Viable viewing if explosions and clichés are your shtick and exciting if you're not sure who won that war.' – *Judith Crist*

The Bridge of San Luis Rey *

US 1944 85m bw
UA/Benedict Bogeaus
V*, L

Five people die when a Peruvian rope bridge collapses; the film investigates why they were each on the bridge at the time.

An intriguing novel is turned into tedious film drama, with actors, director, scenarist and production designer all making heavy weather.

w Howard Estabrook *novel* Thornton Wilder d Rowland V. Lee ph John Boyle m Dimitri Tiomkin

Lynn Bari, Francis Lederer, Nazimova, Louis Calhern, Akim Tamiroff, Blanche Yurka, Donald Woods

'As a remake for present-day audiences, up to their ears in war news, this picture will be a welcome divertissement.' – *Variety*

† A silent version, with a few minutes of hasty talk, was made in 1929 by Charles Brabin for MGM, from a script by Alice Duer Miller, Ruth Cummings and Marian Ainslee. The cast included Lili Damita, Ernest Torrence, Don Alvarado, Raquel Torres, and Henry B. Walthall.

AAN: Dimitri Tiomkin

'It spans a whole new world of entertainment!'

The Bridge on the River Kwai ****

GB 1957 161m Technicolor Cinemascope
Columbia/Sam Spiegel
V, V (W), V*, L, S

British POWs in Burma are employed by the Japs to build a bridge; meanwhile British agents seek to destroy it.

Ironic adventure epic with many fine moments but too many centres of interest and an unforgivably confusing climax. It is distinguished by Guinness's portrait of the English CO who is heroic in his initial stand against the Japs but finally cannot bear to see his bridge blown up: and the physical detail of the production is beyond criticism.

w Carl Foreman *novel* Pierre Boulle d David Lean ph Jack Hildyard m Malcolm Arnold ed Peter Taylor

Alec Guinness (Colonel Nicholson), William Holden (Shears), Jack Hawkins (Major Warden), Sessue Hayakawa (Colonel Saito), James Donald (Major Clipton), Geoffrey Horne (Lieut. Joyce), Andre Morell (Col. Green), Percy Herbert (Grogan)

'It may rank as the most rousing adventure film inspired by the last World War.' – *Alton Cook, New York World Telegram*

† Cary Grant was originally sought for the William Holden role.
†† The script was actually written by Michael Wilson, who was blacklisted by the anti-communists.

AA: best picture; best adaptation (now credited to Carl Foreman, Michael Wilson and Pierre Boulle); David Lean; Jack Hildyard; Malcolm Arnold; Alec Guinness; editing

AAN: Sessue Hayakawa

Bridge to the Sun *

France/US 1961 112m bw
MGM/Cité Films (Jacques Bar)

Just before Pearl Harbor, an American girl marries a Japanese diplomat and goes to live in Tokyo.

Romantic drama which oddly sides with the Japanese and shows America in a poor light. Interesting if not very compelling, with some unfamiliar views of Japan.

w Charles Kaufman *autobiography* Gwendolen Terasaki d Etienne Périer ph Marcel Weiss, Seiichi Kizuka, Bill Kelly m Georges Auric

Carroll Baker, James Shigeta, James Yagi, Tetsuro Tamba

'In yet another burst of national flagellation, Hollywood turns on itself and unthinking Americans for being so beastly about the wartime Japanese.' – *MFB*

A Bridge Too Far **

US/GB 1977 175m Technicolor Panavision
UA/Joseph E. Levine (John Palmer)
V, L

The story of the Allied defeat at Arnhem in 1944.

Like all large-scale military films, this one fails to make its tactics clear, and its sober intent conflicts with its roster of guest stars. For all that, there are impressive moments of acting and production.

w William Goldman *book* Cornelius Ryan d Richard Attenborough (and Sidney Hayers) ph Geoffrey Unsworth, Harry Waxman, Robin Browne m John Addison pd Terence Marsh

Dirk Bogarde, James Caan, Michael Caine, Sean Connery, Edward Fox, Elliott Gould, Gene Hackman, Anthony Hopkins, Hardy Kruger, *Laurence Olivier*, Ryan O'Neal, Robert Redford, Maximilian Schell, Liv Ullmann, Arthur Hill, Wolfgang Preiss

'A film too long.' – *Anon*

'So wearily, expensively predictable that by the end the viewer will in all likelihood be too enervated to notice Attenborough's prosaic moral epilogue.' – *John Pym, MFB*

The Bridges at Toko-Ri *

US 1954 104m Technicolor
Paramount/Perlberg-Seaton
L

The comradeship and death of two jet pilots during the Korean War.

Ambitiously staged action thriller with points to make about war, death and politics: a well-worn American formula pitched very hard.

w Valentine Davies *novel* James A. Michener d Mark Robson ph Loyal Griggs m Lyn Murray ed Alma Macrorie

William Holden, Mickey Rooney, Grace Kelly, Fredric March, Robert Strauss, Charles McGraw, Earl Holliman, Willis Bouchey

'A taut, thrilling, top flight documentary drama of men, war, ships and planes.' – *Cue*

AAN: editing

Brief Encounter ****

GB 1945 86m bw
Eagle-Lion/Cineguild (Anthony Havelock-Allan, Ronald Neame)
V

A suburban housewife on her weekly shopping visits develops a love affair with a local doctor; but he gets a job abroad and they agree not to see each other again.

An outstanding example of good middle-class cinema turned by sheer professional craft into a masterpiece; even those bored by the theme must be riveted by the treatment, especially the use of a dismal railway station and its trains.

w Noël Coward, David Lean, Ronald Neame, Anthony Havelock-Allan, *play Still Life* by Noël Coward d David Lean ph Robert Krasker md Muir Matheson m Rachmaninov ad L. P. Williams ed Jack Harris

Celia Johnson, Trevor Howard, Stanley Holloway, Joyce Carey, Cyril Raymond

'Both a pleasure to watch as a well-controlled piece of work, and deeply touching.' – *James Agee*

'Polished as is this film, its strength does not lie in movie technique, of which there is plenty, so much as in the tight realism of its detail.' – *Richard Winnington*

'A celebrated, craftsmanlike tearjerker, and incredibly neat. There's not a breath of air in it.' – *Pauline Kael, 70s*

† A TV film version was made in 1975 by ITC, starring Richard Burton and Sophia Loren and directed by Alan Bridges. It was an unqualified disaster.

AAN: script; David Lean; Celia Johnson

A Brief History of Time **

GB/US 1992 84m Technicolor
(David Hickman)
V, V*

A documentary on the theories of Stephen Hawking concerning the origins and likely fate of the universe.

A more accessible but less complex approach to Hawking's views than his bestselling, if seldom finished, book. It includes interviews with Hawking himself.

wd Errol Morris *book* Stephen Hawking ph John Bailey m Philip Glass pd Ted Bafaloukos ed Brad Fuller

Brigadoon *

US 1954 108m Anscocolor Cinemascope
MGM (Arthur Freed)
V, V*, L

Two Americans in Scotland find a ghost village which awakens only once every hundred years.

Likeable but disappointing adaptation of a Lost Horizonish Broadway musical, marred by artificial sets and jaded direction.

w Alan Jay Lerner play Alan Jay Lerner
d Vincente Minnelli ph Joseph Ruttenberg
md Johnny Green m/ly Frederick Loewe, Alan Jay Lerner ad Cedric Gibbons, Preston Ames

Gene Kelly, Cyd Charisse, Van Johnson, Jimmy Thompson, Elaine Stewart, Barry Jones, Eddie Quillan

'The whimsical dream world it creates holds no compelling attractions.' – Penelope Houston

AAN: art direction

The Brigand *
US 1952 93m Technicolor
Columbia

A Moroccan adventurer looks like the king and is reprieved from execution if he will impersonate the latter and root out his enemies.

Cheeky revamp of The Prisoner of Zenda, quite acceptably done.

w Jesse Lasky Jnr d Phil Karlson ph W. Howard Greene m Mario Castelnuovo-Tedesco

Anthony Dexter, Jody Lawrance, Gale Robbins, Anthony Quinn, Carl Benton Reid, Ron Randell

The Brigand of Kandahar
GB 1965 81m Technicolor Scope
EMI/Hammer (Anthony Nelson-Keys)

A cashiered Bengal Lancer officer throws in his lot with a troublesome bandit.

Feeble frontier adventure with nothing ringing true.

wd John Gilling ph Reg Wyer m Don Banks
pd Bernard Robinson ed James Needs

Oliver Reed, Ronald Lewis, Duncan Lamont, Yvonne Romain, Catherine Woodville, Glyn Houston

Brigham Young *
US 1940 112m bw
TCF (Kenneth MacGowan)

The story of the Mormon trek to Utah.

Ambitious but rather dull interpretation of history, seen as a Western with romantic fictional trimmings.

w Lamar Trotti story Louis Bromfield d Henry Hathaway ph Arthur Miller m Alfred Newman

Dean Jagger, Tyrone Power, Linda Darnell, Brian Donlevy, Jane Darwell, John Carradine, Mary Astor, Vincent Price, Moroni Olsen

'A big picture in every respect.' – Variety

'One of the year's outstanding films.' – Newsweek

† The production had a 133-day schedule, and cost 2,700,000 dollars.

Bright Eyes *
US 1934 84m bw
Fox (Sol M. Wurtzell)

An orphan finds herself torn between foster-parents.

The first of Shirley Temple's genuine star vehicles has a liveliness and cheerfulness hard to find today. As a production, however, it is decidedly economical.

w William Conselman d David Butler ph Arthur Miller m Samuel Kaylin

Shirley Temple, James Dunn, Lois Wilson, Jane Withers, Judith Allen

'It seems a cinch to please generally, the family and sentimental strata particularly.' – Variety

Bright Leaf
US 1950 110m bw
Warner (Henry Blanke)

A 19th-century tobacco farmer builds a cigarette empire.

Quite agreeable but disjointed fictional biopic, more about love than tobacco.

w Ranald MacDougall novel Robert Wilder
d Michael Curtiz ph Karl Freund m Victor Young

Gary Cooper, Lauren Bacall, Patricia Neal, Jack Carson, Donald Crisp, Gladys George, Elizabeth Patterson, Jeff Corey, Taylor Holmes

Bright Lights *
US 1935 86m bw
Warner
GB title: Funny Face

A vaudevillian lets success go to his head.

The plot served for a score or more of thirties musicals, but this had Busby Berkeley routines and an unusual star role for Joe E. Brown.

w Bert Kalmar, Harry Ruby d Busby Berkeley

Joe E. Brown, Ann Dvorak, Patricia Ellis, William Gargan

'Practically an 86-minute monologue, with the star doing everything but taking tickets.' – Variety

† The same title covered a 1925 MGM silent with Charles Ray as a country boy in love with a Broadway star, also a 1930 Warner film with Frank Fay.

Bright Lights, Big City
US 1988 107m colour
UIP/United Artists (Mark Rosenberg, Sydney Pollack)
V, V*, L, S

A cocaine-snorting magazine researcher goes to pieces in New York.

Some good performances compensate for the unsympathetic central character of a lightweight drama.

w Jay McInerney novel Jay McInerney d James Bridges ph Gordon Willis m Donald Fagen
pd Santo Loquasto ed John Bloom

Michael J. Fox, Kiefer Sutherland, Phoebe Cates, Frances Sternhagen, Dianne Wiest, Swoosie Kurtz, John Houseman, Jason Robards, Tracy Pollan

'The banality comes down on you like drizzle.' – Pauline Kael, New Yorker

Bright Road *
US 1953 69m bw
MGM (Sol Baer Fielding)

In an all-black school, a problem child finds himself when he helps to rid the school of a swarm of bees.

Slight but attractive second feature, unostentatiously set in a black community.

w Emmett Lavery d Gerald Mayer ph Alfred Gilks m David Rose

Dorothy Dandridge, Harry Belafonte, Robert Horton, Philip Hepburn, Barbara Ann Sanders

Bright Victory *
US 1951 97m bw
Universal (Robert Buckner)
GB title: Lights Out

A blinded soldier adjusts to civilian life.

Well-meaning if rather slow and sticky, this drama is more sentimental than realistic but has good performances.

w Robert Buckner novel Baynard Kendrick
d Mark Robson ph William Daniels m Frank Skinner

Arthur Kennedy, Peggy Dow, Julie Adams, James Edwards, Will Geer, Minor Watson, Jim Backus

AAN: Arthur Kennedy

A Brighter Summer Day ***
Taiwan 1991 237m colour
ICA/Yang and His Gang (Yu Welyan)
original title: Guling Jie Shaonian Sha Ren Shijan

In the early 1960s, a 14-year-old boy falls in love with the girlfriend of a young gang leader.

A long but engrossing film, set against troubled times and the fear of Communist China, which provides a detailed examination of the society of the time.

w Edward Yang, Yan Hongya, Yang Shunqing, Lai Mingtang d Edward Yang ph Zhang Hulgong, Li Longyu pd Yu Welyan, Edward Yang ed Chen Bowen

Lisa Yang, Zhang Zhen, Zhang Guozhu, Elaine Jin, Wang Juan, Zhang Han

'One of the major feats of non-American cinema of its time . . . Gathers an extraordinary momentum, showing that you really can delineate the lives of ordinary people in an extraordinary way without either flashiness or pretension.' – Derek Malcolm, Guardian

† The film also exists in a version that is 50m shorter. The longer version is the director's preferred cut.

Brightness: see Yeelen

Brighton Beach Memoirs *
US 1986 108m colour
Universal/Rastar (David Chasman)
V, V*, L

In 1937 Brooklyn, a lower middle class Jewish family has assorted crises.

Standard picturization of a Neil Simon play, somewhat flattened out in the process but with funny moments.

w Neil Simon play Neil Simon d Gene Saks
ph John Bailey m Michael Small

Blythe Danner, Bob Dishy, Brian Drillinger, Stacey Glick, Judith Ivey, Lisa Waltz

Brighton Rock ***
GB 1947 92m bw
Associated British/Charter Films (Roy Boulting)
V, V*
US title: Young Scarface

The teenage leader of a racetrack gang uses a waitress as alibi to cover a murder, and marries her. He later decides to be rid of her, but fate takes a hand in his murder plot.

A properly 'seedy' version of Graham Greene's 'entertainment', very flashily done for the most part but with a trick ending which allows the heroine to keep her illusions.

w Graham Greene, Terence Rattigan novel Graham Greene d John Boulting ph Harry Waxman m Hans May

Richard Attenborough, Hermione Baddeley, Harcourt Williams, William Hartnell, Alan Wheatley, Carol Marsh, Nigel Stock

'The film is slower, much less compelling, and, if you get me, less cinematic than the book, as a child's guide to which I hereby offer it.' – Richard Winnington

'It proceeds with the efficiency, the precision and the anxiety to please of a circular saw.' – Dilys Powell

The Brighton Strangler
US 1945 67m bw
RKO
V*

An actor takes over in real life the part he is playing – of a murderer.

This hoary plot had seen better days even in 1945, and was not helped by an establishing shot which put Parliament on the wrong side of the Thames.

w Arnold Philips, Max Nosseck   *d* Max Nosseck

John Loder, June Duprez

Brimstone

US   1949   90m   Trucolor
Republic
V*

A US Marshal tracks down Public Outlaw Number One.

High-spirited Western co-feature.

w Thames Williamson   *d* Joseph Kane

Rod Cameron, Walter Brennan, Adrian Booth, Forrest Tucker, Jack Holt, Jim Davis, James Brown, Guinn Williams

Brimstone and Treacle *

GB   1982   87m   Technicolor
Namara/Alan E. Salke/Herbert Solow
V*

A strange young man has a sinister effect on the family of a middle-aged writer of doggerel, whose crippled daughter he finally rapes.

Similar in mood to *Pennies from Heaven*, this is basically a television play very typical of its author. (Some years ago it was taped and then banned by the BBC.) In substance no more than a reversal of *The Passing of the Third Floor Back*, its points of interest are mainly technical.

w Dennis Potter   *play* Dennis Potter   *d* Richard Loncraine   *ph* Peter Hannan   *m* Sting   *pd* Milly Burns

Sting, Denholm Elliott, Joan Plowright, Suzanna Hamilton, Benjamin Whitrow, Dudley Sutton

Bring 'Em Back Alive

US   1932   65m   bw
RKO/Van Beuren
V*

A documentary showing how an animal hunter scoured Malayan jungles for specimens to stock the world's zoos.

Very dated now, but quite an attraction in its day. The title was used again in 1982 for a TV series in which Bruce Boxleitner played Buck; the emphasis now, however, was on serial-like intrigue.   *d* Clyde Elliott

Frank Buck

'Will get money but needs alert exploitation.' – *Variety*

'It's got guts!'
Bring Me the Head of Alfredo Garcia

US   1974   112m   DeLuxe
UA/Optimus/Churubusco (Martin Baum)

A wealthy Mexican offers a million dollars for the head of a man who seduced his daughter, and claimants find that grave robbing is involved.

Gruesome, sickly action melodrama with revolting detail; the nadir of a director obsessed by violence.

w Gordon Dawson, Sam Peckinpah   *d* Sam Peckinpah   *ph* Alex Phillips Jnr   *m* Jerry Fielding

Warren Oates, Gig Young, Isela Vega, Robert Webber, Helmut Dantine, Emilio Fernandez, Kris Kristofferson

'Few movies are as tedious. Bring me the head of the studio that released this one.' – *Gene Shalit*

'The only kind of analysis it really invites is psychoanalysis.' – *Wall Street Journal*

'Peckinpah clearly doesn't lack talent – what he lacks is brains.' – *John Simon*

Bring On the Girls

US   1945   92m   Technicolor
Paramount (Fred Kohlmar)

A millionaire joins the navy in the hope that a girl will love him for himself.

A good example of the gaily-coloured but witless drivel which occasionally came out of the big studios towards the end of the war.

w Karl Tunberg, Darrell Ware   *d* Sidney Lanfield   *ph* Karl Struss   *md* Robert Emmett Dolan

Veronica Lake, Eddie Bracken, Sonny Tufts, Marjorie Reynolds, Grant Mitchell, Alan Mowbray, Porter Hall

Bring Your Smile Along

US   1955   83m   Technicolor
Columbia

A lady schoolteacher goes to New York to write songs.

Amiable musical filler with rather flat jokes.

wd Blake Edwards

Frankie Laine, Keefe Brasselle, Constance Towers, Lucy Marlow

Bringing Up Baby ***

US   1938   102m   bw
RKO (Howard Hawks)
L

A zany girl causes a zoology professor to lose a dinosaur bone and a pet leopard in the same evening.

Outstanding crazy comedy which barely pauses for romance and ends up with the whole splendid cast in jail.

w Dudley Nichols, Hagar Wilde   *d* Howard Hawks   *ph* Russell Metty   *m* Roy Webb

Katharine Hepburn, Cary Grant, May Robson, Charles Ruggles, Walter Catlett, Fritz Feld, Jonathan Hale, Barry Fitzgerald

'Harum-scarum farce comedy . . . definite box-office.' – *Variety*

'I am happy to report that it is funny from the word go, that it has no other meaning to recommend it . . . and that I wouldn't swap it for practically any three things of the current season.' – *Otis Ferguson*

'It may be the American movies' closest equivalent to Restoration comedy.' – *Pauline Kael*

'Crazy comedies continue to become crazier, and there will soon be few actors and actresses left who have no straw in their hair.' – *Basil Wright*

† The dog George was played by Asta from *The Thin Man* movies.

Bringing Up Father

US   1928   approx 70m at 24 fps   bw   silent
MGM

Mild domestic comedy about a henpecked husband, from the famous comic strip.

It marked the successful comeback of Marie Dressler (as the maid).

w Frances Marion   *d* Jack Conway

J. Farrell MacDonald, Marie Dressler, Polly Moran, Gertrude Olmsted, Grant Withers

† Two or three second features about Jiggs and Maggie, featuring Renie Riano and Joe Yule, appeared in the late forties.

Brink of Hell: see *Toward the Unknown*

The Brinks Job

US   1978   103m   Technicolor
Universal/Dino de Laurentiis (Ralph Serpe)
V

In 1944, amateur criminals bring off a raid on the vaults of a Boston security company.

Farcical variation of a much-told true tale. Despite much mugging by the stars and a frantic narrative style, it does not come off.

w Walon Green   *book* Big Stick-Up at Brinks by Noel Behn   *d* William Friedkin   *ph* Norman Leigh   *m* Richard Rodney Bennett   *pd* Dean Tavoularis

Peter Falk, Warren Oates, Peter Boyle, Allen Goorwitz, Gena Rowlands, Paul Sorvino, Sheldon Leonard

Britannia Hospital

GB   1982   116m   colour
EMI/Film and General/NFFC (Davina Belling, Clive Parsons)
V

Problems besetting a British hospital celebrating its 500th anniversary include strikes, demonstrators, and a mad doctor who transplants heads.

Looking as crummy as a Carry On at the end of its tether, this intended lampoon of the state of the nation never warms up and can only fire off state jokes in all directions while repelling the eye with its Frankenstein scenes.

w David Sherwin   *d* Lindsay Anderson   *ph* Mike Fash   *m* Alan Price   *pd* Norris Spencer

Malcolm McDowell, Leonard Rossiter, Graham Crowden, Fulton Mackay, Vivian Pickles, Joan Plowright, Peter Jeffrey, Robin Askwith, Dandy Nichols, Valentine Dyall, Roland Culver, Alan Bates, Arthur Lowe, Marsha Hunt

'It has all the intensity, along with the flailing incoherence, of a soapbox jeremiah.' – *Richard Combs, MFB*

'Having once created a general shambles, the film is at a loss to clean it up.' – *Margaret Hinxman, Daily Mail*

'Inexplicably muddled and inconclusive.' – *Guardian*

'It mentholates the tubes and oxygenates the brain.' – *Sunday Telegraph*

Britannia Mews

GB   1948   91m   bw
TCF (William Perlberg)
US title: The Forbidden Street

In Victorian times, the widow of a puppetmaster eventually marries his lookalike who rebuilds their puppet theatre.

Curious and uncertain comedy drama set among yesterday's high society, with poorly played leads but an interesting supporting cast and technical assurance.

w Ring Lardner Jnr   *novel* Margery Sharp   *d* Jean Negulesco   *ph* Georges Périnal   *m* Malcolm Arnold   *ad* Andrei Andreiev

Dana Andrews, Maureen O'Hara, Sybil Thorndike, Wilfrid Hyde-White, Fay Compton, A. E. Matthews

British Agent *

US   1934   75m   bw
Warner (Henry Blanke)

In 1910 Russia, a Britisher falls in love with a lady spy.

Sluggish and dated romantic melodrama, notable only for Howard's performance and some directional felicities.

w Laird Doyle   *novel* H. Bruce Lockhart   *d* Michael Curtiz   *ph* Ernest Haller   *ad* Anton Grot

Leslie Howard, Kay Francis, William Gargan, *Irving Pichel*, Philip Reed, Walter Byron, J. Carrol Naish, Halliwell Hobbes

'One of those rare cases of a film both artistically and cinematically good entertainment . . . an exciting story well told, excellent acting, draw names and production value.' – *Variety*

British Intelligence

US   1940   63m   bw
Warner (Bryan Foy)
GB title: Enemy Agent

During World War I a German lady spy becomes a guest in the house of a British war official, the butler of which is the leader of a German spy ring.

Second feature remake of *Three Faces East* (qv); still quite an entertaining melodrama.

w Lee Katz   *play* Anthony Paul Kelly   *d* Terry Morse   *ph* Sid Hickox   *m* Heinz Roemheld

Boris Karloff, Margaret Lindsay, Maris Wrixon, Bruce Lester, Leonard Mudie, Holmes Herbert

Broadcast News *
US   1987   31m   DeLuxe
UKFD/Fox/Gracie Films (James L. Brooks)
V, V*, L

An ambitious TV news reader with personality but little talent gets to the top.

Mildly satirical look at the world of television journalism that slips into romantic comedy.

wd James L. Brooks   *ph* Michael Ballhaus   *m* Bill Conti   *pd* Charles Rosen   *ed* Richard Marks

William Hurt, Albert Brooks, *Holly Hunter*, Robert Prosky, Lois Chiles, Joan Cusack, Jack Nicholson (uncredited cameo)

AAN: best picture; William Hurt; Holly Hunter; Albert Brooks; best original screenplay; best cinematography; best film editing

Broadminded *
US   1931   65m   bw
First National

A bashful swain leaves town after a misunderstanding and becomes involved in an intercontinental chase.

Modest star farce with some hilarious moments.

w Bert Kalmar, Harry Ruby   *d* Mervyn Le Roy

Joe E. Brown, Ona Munson, William Collier Jnr, Marjorie White, Holmes Herbert, Bela Lugosi

'Best he has ever done . . . any audience will enjoy it.' – *Variety*

Broadway
US   1942   90m   bw
Universal (Bruce Manning)

George Raft recalls his days as a hoofer in a New York speakeasy, and in particular a murder involving gangsters and chorus girls.

Minor crime melodrama which after interminable scene-setting paints an effective picture of the twenties but has too slack a grip on narrative.

w Felix Jackson, John Bright   *play* Philip Dunning, George Abbott   *d* William A. Seiter   *ph* George Barnes   *md* Charles Previn

George Raft, Pat O'Brien, S. Z. Sakall, Janet Blair, Broderick Crawford, Marjorie Rambeau

Broadway Bad
US   1933   59m   bw
Fox

A scheming chorus girl makes a rich marriage.

Paper-thin melodrama, one of a hundred on similar lines.

w Arthur Kober, Maud Fulton   *d* Sidney Lanfield

Joan Blondell, Ginger Rogers, Ricardo Cortez, Adrienne Ames, Spencer Charters, Donald Crisp

Broadway Bill *
US   1934   104m   bw
Columbia (Frank Capra)
V, V*
GB title: *Strictly Confidential*

A cheerful horse trainer finds he has a winner.

Easygoing romantic comedy with the energetic Capra style in fairly full bloom.

w Robert Riskin   *story* Mark Hellinger   *d* Frank Capra   *ph* Joseph Walker

Warner Baxter, Myrna Loy, Walter Connolly, Helen Vinson, Douglass Dumbrille, Raymond Walburn, Lynne Overman, Clarence Muse, Margaret Hamilton, Paul Harvey, Claude Gillingwater, Charles Lane, Ward Bond

'The effect of capable direction is discernible in every foot.' – *Variety*

'It will be a long day before we see so little made into so much: it is gay and charming and will make you happy, and I am sorry to say I do not know recommendations much higher.' – *Otis Ferguson*

† Remade as *Riding High* (qv).

Broadway Bound *
US   1991   94m   colour
Blue Dolphin/ABC Productions (Terry Nelson)
V, V*

In the 40s, two brothers struggle to become writers and move away from home, where their father and mother quarrel and their grandfather grumbles.

An autobiographical slice of life, delivered with a gently effective humour.

w Neil Simon   *play* Neil Simon   *d* Paul Bogart   *ph* Isidore Mankofsky   *m* David Shire   *pd* Ben Edwards   *ed* Andy Zall

Anne Bancroft, Hume Cronyn, Corey Parker, Jonathan Silverman, Jerry Orbach, Michele Lee

'Certain to delight those with a taste for the theatrical.' – *Empire*

Broadway Danny Rose *
US   1984   84m   DeLuxe
Orion (Robert Greenhut)
V, V*, L, S

An artists' agent and former comic falls foul of the Mafia while promoting a client.

Generally appealing comedy-melodrama with rather less self-examination than has latterly been typical of its star.

wd Woody Allen   *ph* Gordon Willis   *md* Nick Hyman   *pd* Mel Bourne   *ed* Susan E. Morse

Woody Allen, Mia Farrow, Nick Apollo Forte, Craig Vandenbergh, Herb Reynolds

AAN: direction, original screenplay

BFA: original screenplay

Broadway Gondolier
US   1935   98m   bw
Warner

A taxi driver wants to become a radio singer.

Rather tedious musical with second-rate elements.

w Warren Duff, Sig Herzig   *d* Lloyd Bacon   *m/y* Al Dubin, Harry Warren

Dick Powell, Adolphe Menjou, Joan Blondell, Louise Fazenda, the Mills Brothers, Judy Canova, Ted Fiorito and his band

'Loose on story and even lethargic, it holds enough for gate values.' – *Variety*

Broadway Hostess
US   1935   69m   bw
Warner

A small-town girl becomes a night-club singer.

Modest musical which failed to create a new star.

w George Bricker   *d* Frank McDonald   *ch* Bobby Connolly

Wini Shaw, Genevieve Tobin, Lyle Talbot, Allen Jenkins, Phil Regan, Marie Wilson, Spring Byington

'Adequate for family audience consumption.' – *Variety*

AAN: Bobby Connolly

Broadway Limited *
US   1941   75m   bw
Hal Roach
V*
GB title: *The Baby Vanishes*

On an express train, a Hollywood publicity stunt backfires.

Wild farce which is not very funny as a whole but has entertaining comic performances.

w Rian James   *d* Gordon Douglas   *ph* Henry Sharp   *m* Charles Previn

Victor McLaglen, Patsy Kelly, *Leonid Kinskey*, Marjorie Woodworth, Dennis O'Keefe, ZaSu Pitts, George E. Stone

'The pulsating drama of Broadway's bared heart speaks and sings with a voice to stir your soul!'
'The new wonder of the screen!'

Broadway Melody *
US   1929   110m   bw (Technicolor scenes)
MGM (Lawrence Weingarten)
V*, L

Chorus girls try to make it big on Broadway.

The screen's very first musical, exceedingly primitive by the standards of even a year later, but rather endearing and with a splendid score.

w James Gleason, Norman Houston, Edmund Goulding   *d* Harry Beaumont   *ph* John Arnold   *m/y* Nacio Herb Brown, Arthur Freed   *ad* Cedric Gibbons

Charles King, Anita Page, Bessie Love, Jed Prouty, Kenneth Thomson, Mary Doran, Eddie Kane

'A basic story with some sense to it, action, excellent direction, laughs, a tear, a couple of great performances and plenty of sex.' – *Variety*

† The plot resurfaced in *Two Girls On Broadway* (qv), made by MGM in 1940.

AA: best picture

AAN: Harry Beaumont, Bessie Love

'You have waited seven years for this!'
**Broadway Melody of 1936 ** **
US   1935   103m   bw
MGM (John W. Considine Jnr)
V*, L

A Broadway producer is at loggerheads with a columnist.

Fairly lively musical with lavish numbers.

w Jack McGowan, Sid Silvers, Harry Conn   *story* Moss Hart   *d* Roy del Ruth   *ph* Charles Rosher   *m* Alfred Newman   *m/y* Nacio Herb Brown, Arthur Freed   *ch* Dave Gould   *ed* Blanche Sewell

Jack Benny, Robert Taylor, Una Merkel, *Eleanor Powell*, June Knight, Vilma and Buddy Ebsen, Nick Long Jnr

songs: 'You Are My Lucky Star'; 'I've Gotta Feelin' You're Foolin' '; 'Broadway Rhythm'; 'On a Sunday Afternoon'; 'Sing Before Breakfast'; 'All I Do Is Dream Of You'

'Smash musical with strong dancing and comedy framework.' – *Variety*

AA: Dave Gould

AAN: best picture; Moss Hart

Broadway Melody of 1938 *
US   1937   110m   bw
MGM (Jack Cummings)
V*, L, S

Backstage problems threaten the opening of a musical show.

Lavish but fairly forgettable musical with top talent.

w Jack McGowan, Sid Silvers   *d* Roy del Ruth   *ph* William Daniels   *md* George Stoll   *m/y* Nacio Herb Brown, Arthur Freed   *ed* Blanche Sewell

Eleanor Powell, George Murphy, *Sophie Tucker*, Judy Garland, Robert Taylor, Buddy Ebsen, Sid Silvers, Billy Gilbert, Raymond Walburn

songs: 'Some Of These Days'; 'Your Broadway and My Broadway'; 'Yours and Mine'; 'I'm Feelin' Like a Million'; 'Dear Mr Gable'

'Explosion in the cash drawers . . . will do smash business everywhere.' – *Variety*

Broadway Melody of 1940 *

US 1939 102m bw
MGM (Jack Cummings)
V*, L

A dance team gets to the top.

Splendidly produced but thinly plotted extravaganza with good numbers.

w Leon Gordon, George Oppenheimer *story* Jack McGowan, Dore Schary *d* Norman Taurog *ph* Oliver T. Marsh, Joseph Ruttenberg *md* Alfred Newman *m/y* Cole Porter *ad* Cedric Gibbons *ed* Blanche Sewell

Fred Astaire, Eleanor Powell, George Murphy, Douglas Macphail, Florence Rice, Frank Morgan, Ian Hunter

songs: 'I Concentrate On You'; 'Begin the Beguine'; 'Between You and Me'

Broadway Musketeers

US 1938 62m bw
Warner (Bryan Foy)

Three girls from the same orphanage meet again in New York.

Uninspired remake of *Three on a Match*.

w Don Ryan, Ken Gamet *d* John Farrow

Ann Sheridan, Marie Wilson, Margaret Lindsay, John Litel, Dick Purcell

'A programmer of average distinction . . . ought to get by satisfactorily.' – *Variety*

Broadway Rhythm *

US 1943 113m Technicolor
MGM (Jack Cummings)
V*

Originally intended as *Broadway Melody of 1944*, this putting-on-a-show extravaganza had only the numbers to commend it.

w Dorothy Kingsley, Harry Clork *operetta Very Warm for May* by Jerome Kern and Oscar Hammerstein *d* Roy del Ruth *ph* Leonard Smith *md* John Green *m/y* various

George Murphy, Ginny Simms, Charles Winninger, Gloria de Haven, Lena Horne, Nancy Walker, Hazel Scott, Eddie Anderson, Ben Blue, Tommy Dorsey and his Orchestra

'It contains perhaps three minutes of good acrobatic dancing and lasts nearly two hours.' – *James Agee*

Broadway Serenade

US 1939 114m bw
MGM (Robert Z. Leonard)
V*
GB title: *Serenade*

Career problems split the marriage of a songwriter and his singing wife.

Lavish but rather dull romantic drama with music.

w Charles Lederer, Lew Lipton, John T. Foote, Hans Kraly *d* Robert Z. Leonard *ph* Oliver T. Marsh *md* Herbert Stothart

Jeanette Macdonald, Lew Ayres, Frank Morgan, Ian Hunter, Rita Johnson, Virginia Grey, William Gargan, Katherine Alexander *songs*: 'No Time to Argue'; 'Time Changes Everything but Love'; 'For Every Lonely Heart'; 'Broadway Serenade'; 'High Flyin' '; 'One Look at You'

'With all its lavishness, it impresses as only mild box office material.' – *Variety*

Broadway Singer: see *Torch Singer*

Broadway thru a Keyhole *

US 1933 90m bw
UA/Twentieth Century (William Goetz, Raymond Griffith)

A tough New York gangster falls for a singer in his night-club.

Reputed acid observation of the New York scene distinguishes this low-budget gangster drama.

w Gene Towne, Graham Baker *story* Walter Winchell *d* Lowell Sherman *ph* Barney McGill *m/y* Mack Gordon, Harry Revel

Constance Cummings, Russ Columbo, Paul Kelly, *Blossom Seeley*, Gregory Ratoff, *Texas Guinan*, Hobart Cavanaugh, C. Henry Gordon

'Not a big picture, but good entertainment.' – *Variety*

Broadway to Hollywood

US 1933 90m bw
MGM
GB title: *Ring Up the Curtain*

A vaudeville family makes it in movies.

Cliché-strewn rags-to-riches saga with songs; good moments. *wd* Willard Mack

Frank Morgan, Alice Brady, Jackie Cooper, Madge Evans, Jimmy Durante, Nelson Eddy, May Robson, Una Merkel, Mickey Rooney

'A saga of the theatre that will please.' – *Variety*

† Some material was salvaged from an abandoned MGM musical of 1929, *The March of Time*.

Broken Arrow *

US 1950 92m Technicolor
TCF (Julian Blaustein)
V*

A US army scout brings about peace between white man and Apache.

Solemn Western which at the time was acclaimed for giving the Indian's point of view (something which had scarcely happened since silent days). As entertainment it was not exciting, but it set Jeff Chandler off on a career playing Cochise with variations, and a TV series of the same name surfaced in 1956.

w Michael Blankfort *novel Blood Brother* by Elliott Arnold *d* Delmer Daves *ph* Ernest Palmer *md* Alfred Newman *m* Hugo Friedhofer

James Stewart, Jeff Chandler, Debra Paget, Basil Ruysdael, Will Geer, Arthur Hunnicutt, Jay Siverheels

'It has probably done more to soften racial hostilities than most movies designed to instruct, indict and inspire.' – *Pauline Kael*

AAN: Michael Blankfort; Ernest Palmer; Jeff Chandler

Broken Blossoms **

US 1919 105m (16 fps) bw silent
UA/D. W. Griffith
V, V*, L

In slummy Limehouse, a young Chinaman loves the daughter of a brute, who kills her; the Chinaman then kills him and commits suicide.

Victorian-style melodrama presented by Griffith with all the stops out; sometimes striking, but very dated even on its first appearance. *wd* D. W. Griffith *story* 'The Chink and the Child' in Thomas Burke's *Limehouse Nights ph* G. W. Bitzer, Hendrik Sartov, Karl Brown

Lillian Gish, Donald Crisp, Richard Barthelmess

'This is a Limehouse which neither Mr Burke nor anybody else who knows his East End of London will

be able to recognize . . . but *Broken Blossoms* is a genuine attempt to bring real tragedy onto the screen as opposed to machine-made drama, and for that Mr Griffith deserves the thanks of all who are convinced of the potentialities of the film.' – *The Times*

'I know of no other picture in which so much screen beauty is obtained . . . attributable to the Whistlerian fogs and shadows, with that dock in Limehouse recurring like some pedal point.' – *James Agate, 1928*

† The film was made for $88,000, but Adolph Zukor regarded it as uncommercial and sold it to United Artists for $250,000. It went on to make a profit of $700,000. Leslie Henson appeared in a parody, *Broken Bottles*, in 1920.

Broken Blossoms *

GB 1936 84m bw
Twickenham (Julius Hagen)

A remake originally intended to be directed by Griffith.

Quite stylish, and in some ways more interesting than its predecessor.

w Emlyn Williams *d* John Brahm *ph* Curt Courant

Dolly Haas, Arthur Margetson, Emlyn Williams, Donald Calthrop, Ernest Sefton, Kathleen Harrison, Basil Radford

'There isn't much reason for this one.' – *Variety*

Broken Journey

GB 1948 89m bw
Gainsborough (Sydney Box)

A plane crashes in the Alps, and the survivors take different attitudes to their situation.

Unpersuasive and stagey melodrama which wastes some good talent.

w Robert Westerby *d* Ken Annakin *ph* Jack Cox *m* John Greenwood

Phyllis Calvert, James Donald, Margot Grahame, Francis L. Sullivan, Raymond Huntley, Derek Bond, Guy Rolfe, David Tomlinson

Broken Lance *

US 1954 96m DeLuxe Cinemascope
TCF (Sol C. Siegel)
V, V*, L

An autocratic cattle baron causes dissension among his sons.

Western remake of *House of Strangers*, quite well done.

w Richard Murphy *story* Philip Yordan *d* Edward Dmytryk *ph* Joe MacDonald *m* Leigh Harline

Spencer Tracy, Richard Widmark, Robert Wagner, Jean Peters, Katy Jurado, Earl Holliman, Hugh O'Brian, Eduard Franz, E. G. Marshall

AA: Philip Yordan

AAN: Katy Jurado

Broken Lullaby *

US 1931 77m bw Paramount

GB and original title: The Man I Killed

A young Frenchman goes to Germany to seek out the family of the man he killed in the war, and is accepted by them as a friend.

This most untypical Lubitsch film now seems very dated but was deeply felt at the time and has plenty of cinematic grip.

w Ernest Vajda, Samson Raphaelson *play L'Homme que J'ai Tué* by Maurice Rostand *d* Ernst Lubitsch *ph* Victor Milner *m* W. Franke Harling *ad* Hans Dreier

Lionel Barrymore, Phillips Holmes, Nancy Carroll, Tom Douglas, ZaSu Pitts, Lucien Littlefield, Louise Carter, Emma Dunn

'Well made, but heavy themes and actionless . . . hardly attuned to film patronage as a whole.' – *Variety*

'The best talking picture that has yet been seen and heard.' – *Robert E. Sherwood*

'I cannot remember a film so beautifully made, so completely fine in its execution.' – *John Grierson*

'Lubitsch can't entirely escape his own talent, and the film is beautifully crafted, but he mistook drab, sentimental hokum for ironic, poetic tragedy.' – *Pauline Kael, 70s*

Broken Mirrors
Holland   1984   116m   Eastmancolor
Sigma (Matthijs van Heijningen)

Brothel girls consider the worthlessness of their lives.

Would-be symbolic melodrama with feminist overtones. Hard to take from beginning to end.
wd Marleen Gorris   ph Frans Bromet   m Lodewijk de Boer

Lineke Rijxman, Henriette Tol, Edda Barends, Coby Stunnenberg

Broken Noses *
US   1987   77m   bw/colour
Mainline/Kira Films (Emie Amemiya)

Documentary of a young boxer training younger boys.

Ambivalent account of a violent sport, chicly photographed.   d Bruce Weber   ph Julio Macat   md Cherry Vanilla   ed Phyllis Famiglietti, Howie Weisbrot

Andy Minsker, The Mount Scott Boxing Club

'This is not so much a sporting profile as a poetic essay on American masculinity using boxing as a metaphor for the transformations involved in acquiring male identity.' – *MFB*

The Broken Wing
US   1932   71m   bw   Paramount

A Mexican girl jilts a bandit for an American pilot.

Hokey romantic melodrama.

w Grover Jones, William Slavens McNutt   play Paul Dickey, Charles Goddard   d Lloyd Corrigan   ph Henry Sharp

Lupe Velez, Leo Carrillo, Melvyn Douglas, George Barbier, Willard Robertson

'Too much of a monologue to get far as a talker. Entire first half is just a stage-setter for what follows, and what follows isn't important.' – *Variety*

Bronco Billy **
US   1980   116m   DeLuxe   Panavision
Warner/Second Street (Neal Dobrofsky, Dennis Hackin)
V, V*, L

A New Jersey shoe salesman takes over a rundown wild west show.

Enjoyable, sentimental, satirical comedy which unaccountably let down its star's box-office record.

w Dennis Hackin   d Clint Eastwood   ph David Worth   md Snuff Garrett, Steve Dorff   ad Eugene Lourie

Clint Eastwood, Sondra Locke, Geoffrey Lewis, Scatman Crothers, Bill McKinney, Sam Bottoms

'Eastwood seems to have most enjoyed toying with some distinctly old-fashioned materials: a runaway heiress, a murder plot that isn't, some consequent punning on points of identity, and the most mischievously brittle set of greedy Eastern sophisticates since Frank Capra.' – *Richard Combs, MFB*

Bronco Buster
US   1952   80m   Technicolor
U-I (Ted Richmond)

A champion rodeo rider meets a challenge from a younger man.

Totally routine programmer.

w Horace McCoy, Lillie Hayward   d Budd Boetticher

John Lund, Scott Brady, Joyce Holden, Chill Wills, Don Haggerty

Bronenosets Potemkin: see *The Battleship Potemkin*

A Bronx Tale *
US   1993   121m   Technicolor
Rank/Price/Tribeca (Jane Rosenthal, Jon Kilik, Robert de Niro)
V*, L, S

In the 1960s, in the Italian neighbourhood of the Bronx, a boy grows up, torn between affection for his father, a bus driver, and admiration for the local gang boss, and caught in the growing struggle for control between blacks and whites.

An enjoyable stroll through familiar territory, which at least shows the ordinary life of the time, even if it, too, is seduced by the glamour of the gangsters.

w Chazz Palminteri   play Chazz Palminteri   d Robert de Niro   ph Reynaldo Villalobos   m Butch Barbella   pd Wynn Thomas   ed David Ray, R. Q. Lovett

Robert de Niro, Chazz Palminteri, Lillo Brancato, Francis Capra, Taral Hicks, Katherine Narducci, Clem Caserta, Joe Pesci, Alfred Sauchelli Jnr

'A wonderfully vivid snapshot of a colorful place and time, as well as a very satisfactory directorial debut.' – *Variety*

The Brood
Canada   1979   91m   colour
Mutual/Elgin (Claude Heroux)
V*, L, S

The rage of a mentally disturbed woman produces homicidal 'babies'.

Idiotic and repellent shocker.   wd David Cronenberg   ph Mark Irwin   m Howard Shore   ad Carol Spier   ed Allan Collins

Oliver Reed, Samantha Eggar, Art Hindle, Cindy Hinds

'In Cronenberg's hands, horror is no longer a disreputable bastard genre but a new avenue of expression, glistening with possibility . . . Horror is his native language. He dreams in it.' – *Stephen Schiff*

Broth of a Boy
Eire   1958   77m   bw
Emmet Dalton (Alec Snowden)

TV covers the village festivities celebrating an old poacher's 110th birthday.

Mildly amusing regional comedy.

w Patrick Kirwan, Blanaid Irvine   play *The Big Birthday* by Hugh Leonard   d George Pollock   ph Walter J. Harvey   m Stanley Black

Barry Fitzgerald, June Thorburn, Tony Wright, Harry Brogan, Eddie Golden, Maire Kean, Godfrey Quigley, Dermot Kelly

Brother Can You Spare a Dime?
GB   1975   109m   bw
VPS/Goodtimes
V*

A 'documentary' picture of America in the thirties, attempted by an apparently random collage of newsreel and feature film extracts, sometimes difficult to tell one from the other.

Sometimes entertaining but mainly unpardonable.
wd Philippe Mora

The Brother from Another Planet
US   1984   108m   Movielab
A-Train Films
V*

An alien lands in Harlem and is protected by locals from the horrors he finds there.

Moderately amusing combination of science fiction, farce and satire, which outstays its welcome by at least half an hour.   wd John Sayles

Joe Morton, Tom Wright, Caroline Aaron, Randy Sue Carter

Brother John *
US   1970   94m   Eastmancolor
Columbia/E and R (Joel Glickman)
V*

A mysterious black man comes to town for a family funeral and is suspected by the townsfolk of various sinister motives, but when they imprison him he is freed by a sympathizer.

The humans are all mean-minded, the saintly visitor is either Christ or an emissary from another planet. Either way, we have been here before, but although this little fantasy has nothing clear to say it is quite enjoyable on the surface.

w Ernest Kinoy   d James Goldstone   ph Gerald Perry Finnerman   m Quincy Jones

Sidney Poitier, Bradford Dillman, Will Geer, Beverly Todd, Ramon Bieri, Warren J. Kemmerling, Paul Winfield, Lincoln Kilpatrick

'It starts out as an engaging mystery with sociological overtones but ends up as a muddle-headed doomsday parable.' – *Judith Crist, 1977*

Brother Orchid *
US   1940   91m   bw
Warner (Hal B. Wallis)
V*, L

A gangster, 'taken for a ride' by his former friends, escapes and becomes a monk.

Rather uneasy blend of comedy, drama and religion, with some good scenes.

w Earl Baldwin   story Richard Connell   d Lloyd Bacon   ph Tony Gaudio   m Heinz Roemheld

Edward G. Robinson, Humphrey Bogart, Donald Crisp, Ann Sothern, Ralph Bellamy, Allen Jenkins, Cecil Kellaway

Brother Rat *
US   1938   89m   bw
Warner (Robert Lord)

Fun and games with the cadets at a military academy.

Brisk but dated farce from a highly successful Broadway original; remade as *About Face*.

w Richard Macaulay, Jerry Wald   play Fred Finklehoffe, John Monks Jnr   d William Keighley   ph Ernest Haller

Wayne Morris, Eddie Albert, Ronald Reagan, Priscilla Lane, Jane Bryan, Jane Wyman, Johnnie Davis, Henry O'Neill

'Exhibs who dig into exploitation fields will hit paydirt.' – *Variety*

Brother Rat and a Baby
US   1939   87m   bw
Warner (Robert Lord)
GB title: *Baby Be Good*

Scatty follow-up to the above, with the cadets graduating.

w Jerry Wald, Richard Macaulay   d Ray Enright   ph Charles Rosher   m Heinz Roemheld

Wayne Morris, Eddie Albert, Ronald Reagan, Priscilla Lane, Jane Wyman, Jane Bryan, Arthur Treacher, Moroni Olsen

Brother Sun, Sister Moon
GB/Italy   1972   122m   Technicolor   Panavision
Paramount/Vic Films/Euro International (Luciano Perugia)
V, V*, S

The life of Francis of Assisi.

Good-looking but relentlessly boring view of a medieval saint as a kind of early flower person.

w Suso Cecchi d'Amico, Kenneth Ross, Lina Wertmuller, Franco Zeffirelli   *d* Franco Zeffirelli   *ph* Ennio Guarnieri   *m* Riz Ortolani

Graham Faulkner, Judi Bowker, Alec Guinness (as Pope Innocent III), Leigh Lawson, Kenneth Cranham, Lee Montague, Valentina Cortese

'If I were Pope, I would burn it.' – *Stanley Kauffmann*

The Brotherhood *

US   1968   96m   Technicolor
Paramount/Brotherhood Company (Kirk Douglas)
V*, L

A Mafia executive welcomes his younger brother into the syndicate, but is finally executed by him.

Dour melodrama with tragic pretensions: well made but rather tedious and violent.

w Lewis John Carlino   *d* Martin Ritt   *ph* Boris Kaufman   *m* Lalo Schifrin

Kirk Douglas, Alex Cord, *Luther Adler*, Irene Papas, Susan Strasberg, Murray Hamilton, Eduardo Ciannelli

The Brotherhood of Satan *

US   1970   93m   Techniscope
Columbia/LQJAF/Four Star Excelsior (L. Q. Jones, Alvy Moore)
V*

A village is isolated by an outbreak of diabolism.

Fresh and intriguing minor horror film with imaginative touches.

w William Welch   *d* Bernard McEveety   *ph* John Arthur Morril   *m* Jaime Mendoza-Nava

Strother Martin, L. Q. Jones, Charles Bateman, Ahna Capri, Charles Robinson, Alvy Moore, Geri Reischl

Brotherly Love: see *Country Dance*

The Brothers **

GB   1947   98m   bw
Triton (Sydney Box)

An orphan girl comes to a Skye fishing family at the turn of the century, and causes superstition, sexual jealousy and tragedy.

Wildly melodramatic but good-looking open-air melodrama, a surprising and striking British film of its time.

w Muriel and Sydney Box   *novel* L. A. G. Strong   *d* David Macdonald   *ph* Stephen Dade   *m* Cedric Thorpe Davie

Patricia Roc, Maxwell Reed, *Duncan Macrae* (a splendidly malevolent performance), Will Fyffe, Andrew Crawford, Finlay Currie

'Heavy breathing, heavier dialect, and any number of quaint folk customs . . . the island and its actual inhabitants are all right; the rest is Mary Webb with hair on her chest.' – *James Agee*

Brothers in Law *

GB   1957   97m   bw
British Lion/The Boultings (John Boulting)
V*

A young barrister has comic misdemeanours in and out of court.

The lighter side of the law, from a bestseller by a judge; mechanically amusing and not in the same street as its predecessor *Private's Progress*, though it seemed hilarious at the time.

w Roy Boulting, Frank Harvey, Jeffrey Dell   *novel* Henry Cecil   *d* Roy Boulting   *ph* Max Greene   *m* Benjamin Frankel

Ian Carmichael, Terry-Thomas, Richard Attenborough, *Miles Malleson*, *Eric Barker*, Irene Handl, John Le Mesurier, Olive Sloane, Kynaston Reeves

FOREWORD: If all the characters in this film were not fictitious – it would be alarming!

CLERK: 'You start with a blue robing bag, sir. Then if you do good work for counsel, he'll give you a red one. If at the end of seven years you haven't been given a red bag – use a suitcase.'

The Brothers Karamazov *

US   1958   146m   Metrocolor
MGM/Avon (Pandro S. Berman)
V*

In 19th-century Russia, the father of three sons is murdered and the wrong brother is found guilty.

Decent but decidedly unenthralling Hollywood compression of a classic, faithful to the letter but not the spirit of the book, and with few memorable moments or performances.

w Richard Brooks   *novel* Fyodor Dostoyevsky   *d* Richard Brooks   *ph* John Alton   *m* Bronislau Kaper   *ad* William A. Horning, Paul Groesse

Yul Brynner, Maria Schell, Richard Basehart, Claire Bloom, Lee J. Cobb, Albert Salmi, William Shatner, Judith Evelyn

'A picture full of ferocity and passion, with streaks of genius in the lighting, mounting and music.' – *News of the World*

† In 1968 came Ivan Pyryev's massive 220m Russian version, little seen in the west.

AAN: Lee J. Cobb

The Brothers Rico

US   1957   91m   bw
Columbia/William Goetz (Lewis J. Rachmil)

An accountant fails to retrieve his brothers from a life of crime.

Moderate gangster fare with good credentials but more talk than action.

w Lewis Meltzer, Ben Perry   *novel* Georges Simenon   *d* Phil Karlson   *ph* Burnett Guffey   *m* George Duning

Richard Conte, James Darren, Dianne Foster, Kathryn Grant, Larry Gates, Lamont Johnson, Harry Bellaver

Brown of Harvard

US   1926   approx 70m at 24 fps   bw   silent
MGM

Two college students, one academic and one sporty, love the same girl.

Best-known version of a 1909 play first filmed in 1917: archetypal campus drama.

w Donald Ogden Stewart, A. P. Younger   *play* Rida Johnson Young   *d* Jack Conway

William Haines, Jack Pickford, Mary Brian

Brown on Resolution *

GB   1935   80m   bw
Gaumont (Michael Balcon)
Later retitled: Forever England
US title: *Born for Glory*

In the 1914 war in the Mediterranean, a seaman holds a German warship at bay with a rifle.

Uneasy amalgam of adventure heroics and character study, interesting for its effort.

w Michael Hogan, Gerard Fairlie, J. O. C. Orton   *novel* C. S. Forester   *d* Walter Forde   *ph* Bernard Knowles

John Mills, Betty Balfour, Barry Mackay, Jimmy Hanley, Howard Marion Crawford, H. G. Stoker

'A milestone in British pictures . . . an attractive and interesting feature anywhere.' – *Variety*

The Browning Version *

GB   1951   90m   bw
GFD/Javelin (Teddy Baird)
V*

Retiring through ill health, a classics master finds that he is hated by his unfaithful wife, his headmaster and his pupils. An unexpected act of kindness gives him courage to face the future.

A rather thin extension of a one-act play, capped by a thank-you speech which is wildly out of character. Dialogue and settings are smooth, but the actors are not really happy with their roles.

w Terence Rattigan   *play* Terence Rattigan   *d* Anthony Asquith   *ph* Desmond Dickinson

Michael Redgrave, Jean Kent, Nigel Patrick, Wilfrid Hyde-White, Bill Travers, Ronald Howard

'If the sustained anguish of the role does not allow Redgrave a great deal of room to move around in, it does give him a chance to show what he can do in tight quarters, and that, it turns out, is considerable.' – *Pauline Kael, 70s*

Brubaker *

US   1980   130m   DeLuxe
TCF (Ron Silverman)
V, V*, L

A new governor fails to make much headway with his reform plan at Wakefield Prison Farm.

Fairly brutal but unsurprising prison drama which takes itself somewhat too seriously.

w W. D. Richter   *d* Stuart Rosenberg   *ph* Bruno Nuytten   *m* Lalo Schifrin

Robert Redford, Yaphet Kotto, Jane Alexander, Murray Hamilton, David Keith, Morgan Freeman

'It's hard to imagine a broad audience wanting to share the two hours of agony.' – *Variety*

AAN: screenplay

Bruce Gentry – Daredevil of the Skies

US   1949   bw   serial: 15 eps
Columbia

A scientist's assistant sets out to unmask a villain called The Recorder, who controls an electronic flying disc.

Routine serial exploits.

d Spencer Bennet, Thomas Carr

Tom Neal, Judy Clark, Ralph Hodges, Forrest Taylor

Brushfire!

US   1961   80m   bw
Obelisk/Paramount

Planters in south-east Asia are attacked by rebel forces.

Exploitation melodrama with a flat-footed script.

w Irwin R. Blacker   *d* Jack Warner Jnr

John Ireland, Jo Morrow, Everett Sloane, Al Avalon, Carl Esmond

The Brute *

Mexico   1952   83m   bw
International Cinematografica
V*
original title: *El Bruto*

Victimized slum tenants call for help to a slow-witted giant, who kills the landlord and falls in love with his daughter.

Eccentric melodrama which doesn't quite seem to make its point.   *wd* Luis Buñuel   *ph* Augustin Jiminez   *m* Raul Lavista

Pedro Armendariz, *Katy Jurado*, Rosita Arenas, Andres Soler

The Brute

GB   1975   90m   Technicolor
Rank/Trigon (John Quested)

A model is married to a man who beats her and threatens to take away her son if she complains.

Glumly fashionable domestic drama that is more interested in displaying violence than explaining it.

wd Gerry O'Hara   *ph* Dennis Lewiston
m Kenneth V. Jones   *ad* Terence Pritchard
ed Gerry Hambling

Sarah Douglas, Julian Glover, Bruce Robinson, Jenny Twigge, Suzanne Stone, Peter Bull, Charlotte Cornwell

'A glossy piece of pornography pretentiously packaged and sold under the guise of a social document.' – *MFB*

Brute Force **
US   1947   96m   bw
U-I (Mark Hellinger)

Six violent convicts revolt against a sadistic warden and try to escape.

Vivid and rather repellent prison melodrama leading up to an explosive climax; its savagery seemed at the time to break fresh ground.

w Richard Brooks   *d* Jules Dassin   *ph* William Daniels   *m* Miklos Rozsa

Burt Lancaster, Charles Bickford, Hume Cronyn, Ella Raines, Yvonne de Carlo

The Brute Man
US   1946   60m   bw
Universal
V*, L

A disfigured paranoic is helped by a blind pianist and kills again to help her.

Schlock horror programmer.

w George Bricker, M. Coates Webster   *d* Jean Yarbrough

Rondo Hatton, Tom Neal, Jane Adams

† Universal were so ashamed of it that they farmed it out to PRC

El Bruto: see *The Brute*

The Bubble *
US   1966   112m   Eastmancolor   Spacevision (aka Stereovision 3D)
Arch Obler
V*
aka: *Fantastic Invasion of Planet Earth*

Three people find themselves trapped in a small town that is surrounded by an invisible bubble of energy.

Originally made in 3D, the film was a good advertisement for that process but not, with its indifferent acting and talky, slow-moving narrative, for any other reason.

wd Midwestern Magic-Vuers (Arch Obler)
ph Charles F. Wheeler   *m* Paul Sawtell, Bert Shefter   *ad* Marvin Chomsky   *ed* Igo Kanter

Michael Cole, Deborah Walley, Johnny Desmond, Virgina Gregg, Chester Jones

† The film was cut to 94m and re-released in 1972 as *Fantastic Invasion of Planet Earth,* though no invasion occurs during the film. It has been released on video in its 3D version.

The Buccaneer *
US   1938   125m   bw
Paramount (Cecil B. de Mille)

During the 1812 war, pirate Jean Lafitte helps president Andrew Jackson to repel the British.

Sprightly adventure romance with generally good production and acting.

w Jeanie Macpherson, Edwin Justus Mayer, Harold Lamb, C. Gardner Sullivan   *d* Cecil B. de Mille   *ph* Victor Milner   *md* Boris Morros   *m* Georges Antheil

Fredric March, Franciska Gaal, *Akim Tamiroff,* Margot Grahame, Walter Brennan, Ian Keith, Spring Byington, Douglass Dumbrille, Robert Barrat, Hugh Sothern, Beulah Bondi, Anthony Quinn, Montagu Love

'A cinch for big box-office returns around the world.' – *Variety*

'From de Mille's skilled craftsmanship have come other pictures quite as ambitious, none more adroitly fabricated, skilfully adjusted to the norm of appeal to the world audience that such imposing and costly productions must command.' – *Terry Ramsaye*

AAN: Victor Milner

The Buccaneer
US   1958   121m   Technicolor   Vistavision
Paramount/Cecil B. de Mille (Henry Wilcoxon)
V*, L

Slow, slack and stolid remake of the 1938 film, with practically no excitement or interest and very obvious studio sets.

w Jesse L. Lasky Jnr, Bernice Mosk, from the earlier screenplay   *d* Anthony Quinn   *ph* Loyal Griggs   *m* Elmer Bernstein

Yul Brynner, Claire Bloom, Charles Boyer, Inger Stevens, Henry Hull, Charlton Heston, E. G. Marshall, Douglass Dumbrille, Lorne Greene, Ted de Corsia, Robert F. Simon

Buccaneer's Girl
US   1949   77m   Technicolor
Universal-International

A New Orleans entertainer helps to free a pirate who was her friend.

Cheerful action programmer.

w Harold Shumate, Joseph Hoffman   *d* Frederick de Cordova

Yvonne de Carlo, Philip Friend, Robert Douglas, Elsa Lanchester

Buchanan Rides Alone
US   1958   78m   colour
Columbia

A wandering Texan helps a young Mexican accused of murder.

Very moderate star Western.

w Charles Lang   *d* Budd Boetticher

Randolph Scott, Craig Stevens, Barry Kelley, Peter Whitney

Die Büchse der Pandora: see *Pandora's Box*

Buck and the Preacher
US   1971   103m   colour
Columbia/E and R/Belafonte (Joel Glickman)

Nightriders chasing escaped slaves are outwitted by a wagon train guide and a con man.

Lively, easygoing Western with a largely black cast, and a message of militancy sugar-coated by Hollywood hokum.

w Ernest Kinoy   *d* Sidney Poitier   *ph* Alex Phillips   *m* Benny Carter

Sidney Poitier, Harry Belafonte, Ruby Dee, Cameron Mitchell, Denny Miller, Nita Talbot, John Kelly

Buck Benny Rides Again *
US   1940   82m   bw
Paramount (Mark Sandrich)

A radio comedian goes west but finds he's no cowboy.

Moderate filming of episodes and characters from the star's weekly radio show.

w William Morrow, Edmund Beloin   *d* Mark Sandrich

Jack Benny, Ellen Drew, Eddie Anderson, Andy Devine, Phil Harris, Dennis Day

'Swell mass entertainment.' – *Variety*

Buck Privates *
US   1941   84m   bw
Universal (Alex Gottlieb)
GB title: *Rookies*

Two incompetents accidentally enlist in the army.

Abbott and Costello's first starring vehicle is a tired bundle of army jokes and old routines separated by plot and romance, but it sent the comedians right to the top, where they stayed for ten years.

w Arthur T. Horman   *d* Arthur Lubin   *ph* Milton Krasner   *md* Charles Previn

Bud Abbott, Lou Costello, Lee Bowman, Alan Curtis, Jane Frazee, *The Andrews Sisters, Nat Pendleton,* Samuel S. Hinds, Shemp Howard

AAN: Charles Previn; song 'The Boogie Woogie Bugle Boy of Company B' (*m* Hugh Prince, *ly* Don Raye)

Buck Privates Come Home
US   1946   77m   bw
U-I (Robert Arthur)
GB title: *Rookies Come Home*

Incompetent war veterans are demobilized and find civilian life tough.

Thin star comedy with a good final chase.

w John Grant, Frederic I. Rinaldo, Robert Lees   *d* Charles T. Barton   *ph* Charles Van Enger

Bud Abbott, Lou Costello, Beverly Simmons, Tom Brown, Nat Pendleton

Buck Rogers *
US   1939   bw   serial: 12 eps
Universal

After crashing in the Arctic and being preserved by gas for five hundred years, Buck discovers that the world has been conquered by gangsters led by Killer Kane.

Acceptable science fiction hokum with moments of ingenuity.

d Ford Beebe, Saul Goodkind

Buster Crabbe, Constance Moore, Jackie Moran, Jack Mulhall, Anthony Warde

Buck Rogers in the 25th Century
US   1979   89m   colour
Universal (Richard Coffey)

Launched 500 years into the future, an astronaut helps save civilization.

Dull and bland version of comic strip heroics, originally made for television, which lacks even the low-budget charm of the 30s serial.

w Glen A. Larson, Leslie Stevens   *d* Daniel Haller   *ph* Frank Beascoechea   *m* Stu Phillips   *ad* Paul Peters   *ed* John J. Dumas

Gil Gerard, Pamela Hensley, Erin Gray, Henry Silva, Tim O'Connor, Joseph Wiseman, Duke Butler, Felix Silla, Mel Blanc (voice)

'You'll be sick – from laughing!'
A Bucket of Blood
US   1959   65m   bw
Alta Vista (Roger Corman)

A waiter becomes a renowned sculptor when he hits on the idea of moulding clay round corpses.

Heavy-handed spoof with a few choice if bloody moments.

w Charles B. Griffith   *d* Roger Corman   *ph* Jack Marquette   *m* Fred Katz   *ad* Daniel Haller   *ed* Anthony Carras

Dick Miller, Barboura Morris, Antony Carbone, Ed Nelson

Buckskin

US 1968 97m Pathecolor
Paramount/A. C. Lyles

In the frontier town of Gloryhole a gambler is routed by the new marshal.

Routine old-fashioned Western with this producer's predictable gallery of weatherbeaten familiar faces.

w Michael Fisher d Michael Moore ph W. Wallace Kelley m Jimmie Haskell

Barry Sullivan, Joan Caulfield, Lon Chaney Jnr, John Russell, Richard Arlen, Barbara Hale, Bill Williams, Barton MacLane

Buckskin Frontier

US 1943 75m bw
United Artists/George Sherman
GB title: The Iron Road

In the 1860s, cattle empires are born as the railroad stretches west.

Ambitious mini-Western; a bit stodgy.

w Norman Houston novel Buckskin Empire by Harry Sinclair Drago d Lesley Selander

Richard Dix, Jane Wyatt, Lee J. Cobb, Albert Dekker, Victor Jory

Buddies

Australia 1983 95m colour Panavision
J. D. Productions/John Dingwall

Two sapphire miners outwit an attempt by an unscrupulous rival to grab their claim.

Comic celebration of what an Australian premier once described as 'mateship'.

w John Dingwall d Arch Nicholson ph David Eggby m Chris Neal pd Philip Warner ad Ron Highfield ed Martyn Down

Colin Friels, Harold Hopkins, Kris McQuade, Norman Kaye, Dennis Miller, Bruce Spence

Buddy Buddy

US 1981 96m Metrocolor Panavision
MGM (Jay Weston)
V

A hit man on a job is hampered by a woebegone fellow intent on committing suicide.

Painful remake of the French L'Emmerdeur (A Pain in the A . . .). Lugubriously funny at times, but generally much less attractive than the original.

w Billy Wilder, I. A. L. Diamond play Francis Veber d Billy Wilder ph Harry Stradling Jnr m Lalo Schifrin pd Daniel A. Lomino

Walter Matthau, Jack Lemmon, Paula Prentiss, Klaus Kinski, Dana Elcar

'The saddest episode in Wilder's career.' – Richard Combs, MFB

The Buddy Holly Story

US 1978 113m colour
Columbia/Innovisions/ECA (Fred Bauer)
L

The life of a fifties rock-and-roller who died young in an accident.

Solidly carpentered showbiz biopic for the youth market.

w Robert Gittler d Steve Rash ph Stevan Larner md Joe Renzetti

Gary Busey, Don Stroud, Charles Martin Smith, William Jordan, Maria Richwine

'A B movie leavened by grade-A talent.' – Les Keyser, Hollywood in the Seventies

AA: Joe Renzetti
AAN: Gary Busey

Buddy's Song

GB 1990 106m Eastmancolor
Castle Premier/Buddy/Bill Curbishley, Roy Baird, Roger Daltrey
V, L, S

A rock 'n' roll father becomes manager of his son's more modern band, with mixed results.

Dreary attempt at a generation gap musical, unlikely to appeal to any age-group.

w Nigel Hinton novel Nigel Hinton d Claude Whatham ph John Hooper m Roger Daltrey pd Grant Hicks ed John Grover

Roger Daltrey, Chesney Hawkes, Sharon Duce, Michael Elphick, Douglas Hodge, Paul McKenzie

'Breezy, anodyne fare better suited to the tube.' – Variety

Buffalo Bill *

US 1944 89m Technicolor
TCF (Harry Sherman)

A moderately fictitious account of the life of William Cody, from buffalo hunter to wild west showman.

Easygoing entertainment which turns from Western excitements to domestic drama. Generally watchable.

w Aeneas Mackenzie, Clements Ripley, Cecile Kramer d William Wellman ph Leon Shamroy m David Buttolph

Joel McCrea, Maureen O'Hara, Linda Darnell, Thomas Mitchell, Edgar Buchanan, Anthony Quinn, Moroni Olsen

Buffalo Bill and the Indians, or Sitting Bull's History Lesson

US 1976 118m colour Panavision
EMI/Dino de Laurentiis (Robert Altman)
V, V*

During winter camp for his wild west show, Buffalo Bill Cody and his friends discuss life and his own myth.

Anti-action, alienation-effect talk piece which has some points of interest for sophisticates but is likely to set Western addicts asking for their money back.

w Alan Rudolph, Robert Altman play Indians by Arthur Kopit d Robert Altman ph Paul Lohmann m Richard Baskin

Paul Newman, Burt Lancaster, Joel Grey, Kevin McCarthy, Geraldine Chaplin, Harvey Keitel, John Considine, Denver Pyle

'The western is an enormously resilient form, but never has that resilience been tested quite so much as in this movie . . . it isn't really a movie, it's a happening.' – Arthur Knight

'Whereas Kopit's play offered a hallucinatory mosaic, Altman's script has the one-dimensional clarity of a cartoon.' – Michael Billington, Illustrated London News

'That American history is the creation of flamboyant lies and showmanship strikes us at first as an amusing trifle and then quickly becomes an epigram shaggy-dogging its way across two hours of eccentric Altmanship.' – Will Aitken, Take One

Buffalo Bill – Hero of the Far West

France/Italy/West Germany 1964 90m Technicolor Techniscope

Buffalo Bill thwarts a gang of gun-runners selling rifles to renegade Indians.

Standard Western, slavishly imitating its Hollywood models.

w Nino Stresa, Luciano Martino d J. W. Fordson (Mario Costa) ph Jack Dalmas

Gordon Scott, Jan Hendricks, Mirko Ellis, Mario Brega, Roldano Lupi, Hans von Borsody, Peter Lull

Buffet Froid **

France 1979 93m Eastmancolor Sara Films/Antenna 2 (Alain Sarde)

V*, L
US title: Cold Cuts

A police inspector joins up with two new acquaintances: they discover that they all like killing people.

Satirical black comedy which goes on a little too long for its own good; invention gives way to glumness.

wd Bertrand Blier ph Jean Penzer m classical extracts

Gérard Depardieu, Bernard Blier, Jean Carmet, Geneviève Page

Buffy the Vampire Slayer

US 1992 94m DeLuxe
TCF/Sandollar/Kuzui (Kaz Kazui, Howard Rosenman)
V, V*, L, S

A Californian bimbo learns that her destiny is to be a killer of vampires.

Curiously ineffectual teen comedy.

w Joss Whedon d Fran Rubel Kuzui ph James Hayman m Carter Burwell pd Lawrence Miller ed Camilla Toniolo, Jill Savitt, Richard Candib

Kristy Swanson, Donald Sutherland, Paul Reubens, Rutger Hauer, Luke Perry, Michele Abrams, Hilary Swank, Paris Vaughan, David Arquette

'A bloodless comic resurrection of the undead that goes serious just when it should get wild and woolly.' – Variety

'To enjoy this moronic rubbish, you need to put your IQ into total unconsciousness.' – Alexander Walker, Evening Standard

The Bug

US 1975 101m Movielab
Paramount/William Castle
V*

Large rocklike insects appear after an earthquake and set fire to themselves and their victims.

Absurd, overlong and rather nasty horror film with no visible redeeming features.

w William Castle, Thomas Page novel The Hephaestus Plague by Thomas Page d Jeannot Szwarc ph Michel Hugo, Ken Middleham m Charles Fox

Bradford Dillman, Joanna Miles, Richard Gilliland, Jamie Smith Jackson, Alan Fudge, Patty McCormack

'The finer scientific points are to say the least elusive.' – David Robinson

The Bugle Sounds

US 1941 101m bw
MGM (J. Walter Ruben)

An old cavalry sergeant, discharged for insubordination, rounds up fifth columnists and is reinstated.

Ho-hum star vehicle on familiar lines but at undue length.

w Cyril Hume d S. Sylvan Simon ph Clyde de Vinna m Lennie Hayton

Wallace Beery, Marjorie Main, Lewis Stone, George Bancroft, William Lundigan, Henry O'Neill, Donna Reed, Chill Wills, Roman Bohnen, Jerome Cowan, Tom Dugan, Guinn Williams, Jonathan Hale

Bugles in the Afternoon

US 1952 85m Technicolor
Warner/Cagney Productions (William Cagney)
V*

In the US army at the time of Custer's last stand, a young officer is victimized by a jealous rival.

Modest, adequate Western with nice scenery but no surprises.

w Geoffrey Homes, Harry Brown   *novel* Ernest
Haycox   *d* Roy Rowland   *ph* Wilfrid Cline
m Dimitri Tiomkin

Ray Milland, Hugh Marlowe, Helena Carter, Forrest
Tucker, Barton MacLane, George Reeves, James
Millican, Gertrude Michael

Bugsy **
US 1991 135m Technicolor
Columbia TriStar/Mulholland/Baltimore (Mark Johnson, Barry
   Levinson, Warren Beatty)
V, V*, L, S

A starstruck gangster goes to Las Vegas and
transforms the place into a gambler's paradise.

Romanticized account of the life and violent death of
Bugsy Siegel, done with charm and style.

w James Toback   *d* Barry Levinson   *ph* Allen
Daviau   *m* Ennio Morricone   *pd* Dennis Gassner
ed Stu Linder

Warren Beatty, Annette Bening, Harvey Keitel, Ben
Kingsley, Elliott Gould, Joe Mantegna, Bebe
Neuwirth, Wendy Phillips, Richard Sarafian, Bill
Graham

'Elegantly made, wickedly perverse and very smart.' –
Richard Schickel, Time

'An absorbing narrative flow and a parade of colourful
underworld characters vie for screen time with an
unsatisfactory central romance.' – *Variety*

AA: Dennis Gassner; costume (Albert Wolsky)

AAN: film; Barry Levinson; Warren Beatty; Harvey
Keitel; Ben Kingsley; James Toback; Allen Daviau;
Ennio Morricone

Bugsy Malone **
GB 1976 93m Eastmancolor
Rank/Bugsy Malone Productions (David Puttnam, Allan
   Marshall)
V, V*, L

New York 1929: gangster Fat Sam fights it out with
Dandy Dan, and the best man wins the girl.

Extremely curious musical gangster spoof with all the
parts played by children and the guns shooting ice
cream. Very professionally done, but one wonders to
whom it is supposed to appeal.

wd Alan Parker   *ph* Michael Seresin, Peter Biziou
m/songs Paul Williams   *pd* Geoffrey Kirkland

Scott Baio, Jodie Foster, Florrie Dugger, John Cassisi

'If for nothing else, you would have to admire it for
the sheer doggedness of its eccentricity.' – *David
Robinson, The Times*

'All the pizazz in the world couldn't lift it above the
level of empty camp.' – *Frank Rich, New York Post*

'I only wish the British could make adult movies as
intelligent as this one.' – *Michael Billington, Illustrated
London News*

'In an uncanny way the movie works as a gangster
movie and we remember that the old Bogart and
Cagney classics had a childlike innocence too. The
world was simpler then. Now it's so complicated
maybe only a kid can understand the Bogart role.' –
Roger Ebert

AAN: Paul Williams

Build My Gallows High: see *Out of the Past*

Bull Durham *
US 1988 108m colour
Rank/Orion/Mount Company (Tom Mount, Mark Burg)
V, V*, L, S

An English teacher prevaricates between choosing a
rookie or an experienced baseball player as her latest
lover.

Odd-ball movie, more in love with the game than its
characters.   *wd* Ron Sheldon   *ph* Bobby Byrne

m Michael Convertino   *pd* Armin Ganz   *ad* David
Lubin   *ed* Robert Leighton, Adam Weiss

Kevin Costner, Susan Sarandon, Tim Robbins, Trey
Wilson, Robert Wuhl, William O'Leary, David
Neidorf, Danny Gans

AAN: best original screenplay

The Bulldog Breed
GB 1960 97m bw
Rank (Hugh Stewart)
V

A grocer joins the navy.

Elementary raw recruit comedy with many familiar
ruses.

w Jack Davies, Henry Blyth, Norman Wisdom
d Robert Asher

Norman Wisdom, Edward Chapman, Ian Hunter,
David Lodge, Robert Urquhart, Eddie Byrne, Peter
Jones

'A farce which ought never to have put to sea.' – *MFB*

Bulldog Drummond *
US 1929 90m bw
Samuel Goldwyn
V*

After advertising for adventure, ex-war hero
Drummond is approached by an American girl whose
uncle is being held prisoner in a fake nursing home
by villainous Carl Petersen.

This is the closest the screen ever came to the original
Drummond character, debonair yet taking personal
and unnecessary vengeance on the chief villain. A
fairly primitive talkie with little movement, yet
consistently interesting.

w Sidney Howard   *play* Sapper by H. C. McNeile
d F. Richard Jones   *ph* George Barnes, Gregg
Toland   *ad* William Cameron Menzies

Ronald Colman, Joan Bennett, *Claud Allister* (as Algy),
Lilyan Tashman, Montagu Love, Lawrence Grant

AAN: Ronald Colman; William Cameron Menzies

Bulldog Drummond at Bay
GB 1937 78m bw
BIP/ABPC (Walter Mycroft)
V*

Foreign spies use a peace club as a front, but are
routed by Drummond the adventurer.

A very poor entry in this occasional series:
production, directing and acting are as bad as the
dialogue.

w Patrick Kirwan, James Parrish   *novel* Sapper by H.
C. McNeile   *d* Norman Lee   *ph* Walter Harvey
ad John Mead   *ed* J. Corbett

John Lodge, Dorothy Mackaill, Victor Jory, Claude
Allister, Richard Bird

Bulldog Drummond Strikes Back *
US 1934 83m bw
UA/Twentieth Century (Darryl F. Zanuck)

Drummond gets married, but delays his honeymoon
to investigate a mysterious London house with a
disappearing body.

Slow-starting, then intriguing light mystery which
becomes repetitive and silly. Performances and
production enjoyable.

w Nunnally Johnson   *d* Roy del Ruth   *ph* Peverell
Marley   *m* Alfred Newman

Ronald Colman, Loretta Young, C. Aubrey Smith,
Charles Butterworth (Algy), Warner Oland, Mischa
Auer, Una Merkel

'Zippy, snappy comedy melodrama with a
swashbuckling flavour. Packed with what it takes.' –
Variety

† The full complement of Drummond films is as
follows:
BULLDOG DRUMMOND (GB 1922); silent with
   Carlyle Blackwell.
THE THIRD ROUND (GB 1925); silent with Jack
   Buchanan.
BULLDOG DRUMMOND (US 1929); see above.
TEMPLE TOWER (US 1930); lost Fox film with
   Kenneth MacKenna.
THE RETURN OF BULLDOG DRUMMOND (GB
   1934); perhaps the most Fascist of the series, with
   Ralph Richardson.
BULLDOG JACK (GB 1934); amiable spoof with Jack
   Hulbert (and Richardson as the Moriarty-like
   villain). Finale in an Underground tunnel.
BULLDOG DRUMMOND STRIKES BACK (US
   1934); see above.
BULLDOG DRUMMOND AT BAY (GB 1937, V*); see
   above.
BULLDOG DRUMMOND ESCAPES (US 1937, V);
   start of minor series with Ray Milland, later
   replaced by John Howard (and Guy Standing as
   Colonel Neilson).
BULLDOG DRUMMOND COMES BACK (US 1937,
   V*); John Howard takes over from Milland, John
   Barrymore from Standing.
BULLDOG DRUMMOND'S REVENGE (US 1938,
   V*); Howard and Barrymore.
BULLDOG DRUMMOND'S PERIL (US 1938); ditto.
BULLDOG DRUMMOND IN AFRICA (US 1938, V*);
   Howard and H. B. Warner.
ARREST BULLDOG DRUMMOND (US 1938); ditto.
BULLDOG DRUMMOND'S SECRET POLICE (US
   1939); ditto.
BULLDOG DRUMMOND'S BRIDE (US 1939, V*);
   ditto.
BULLDOG SEES IT THROUGH (GB 1939); imitation
   with Jack Buchanan.
BULLDOG DRUMMOND AT BAY (US 1947); second
   feature with Ron Randell.
BULLDOG DRUMMOND STRIKES BACK (US
   1947); see above.
THE CHALLENGE (US 1948); with Tom Conway.
THIRTEEN LEAD SOLDIERS (US 1948); ditto.
CALLING BULLDOG DRUMMOND (GB 1951); with
   Walter Pidgeon.
DEADLIER THAN THE MALE (GB 1967); Richard
   Johnson as a Bond-like Drummond.
SOME GIRLS DO (GB 1970); Johnson again in a
   feeble sequel.

Bulldog Jack *
GB 1934 72m bw
Gaumont (Michael Balcon)
V*
US title: *Alias Bulldog Drummond*

A playboy poses as Bulldog Drummond when the real
man is injured, and manages to foil the thieves and
save the girl.

After a slowish start, this comedy thriller works up
into a fine frenzy with exciting scenes on the London
Underground and in the British Museum.

w Gerard Fairlie, J. O. C. Orton, Sidney Gilliat, Jack
Hulbert   *novel* Sapper *d* Walter Forde   *ph* Mutz
Greenbaum (Max Greene)   *md* Louis Levy
ad Alfred Junge   *ed* Otto Ludwig

Jack Hulbert, Ralph Richardson, *Claude Hulbert*, Fay Wray,
Athole Fleming, Paul Graetz

'There is . . . a mad train ride towards the terminus
and destruction, as good as anything in screen
melodrama.' – *Peter John Dyer, 1965*

'A sense of showmanship that is rewarded in a full
quota of thrills and laughs.' – *Kine Weekly*

Bullet for a Badman
US 1964 80m Technicolor
Universal-International

An ex-Texas Ranger escapes from prison to prove his
innocence of murder.

Lively Western programmer.

w Mary and Willard Winningham   *d* R. G. Springsteen

Audie Murphy, Darren McGavin, Ruta Lee, Skip Homeier, George Tobias

A Bullet for Joey

US   1955   85m   bw
UA/Sam Bischoff, David Diamond

A Canadian policeman prevents the murder of an atomic scientist.

Listless low-budgeter with familiar stars below par.

w Geoffrey Homes, A. I. Bezzerides   *d* Lewis Allen
ph Harry Neumann   *m* Harry Sukman

Edward G. Robinson, George Raft, Audrey Totter, George Dolenz, Peter Hanson, Peter Van Eyck

A Bullet for the General (dubbed) *

Italy   1966   126m   colour   Scope
MCM (Bianco Manini)
V, V*, S
original title: *El Chucho, Quién Sabe?*

An American mercenary joins a gang of bandits in order to assassinate a Mexican revolutionary leader.

Slow-paced, interesting spaghetti Western concerned with matters of life and death and the making of moral choices.

w Salvatore Laurani, Franco Solinas   *d* Damiano Damiani   *ph* Tony Secchi   *md* Ennio Morricone
m Luis Bacalov   *ad* Sergio Canevari   *ed* Renato Cinquini

Gian-Maria Volontè, Klaus Kinski, Martine Beswick, Lou Castel, Jaime Fernandez

† The film exists in several versions, ranging in length from 77 to 135 minutes, with the shorter concentrating on its moments of violence.

Bullet in the Head

Hong Kong   1990   100m   colour
Milestone/John Woo

Three young tough Chinese gangsters continue their criminal activities in Saigon during the Vietnamese war.

Blood soaked adventure with an individual, frenetic style.

w John Woo, Patrick Leung, Janet Chun   *d* John Woo   *ph* Ardy Lam, Wilson Chan, Somchai Kittikun, Wong Wing-Hang   *m* James Wong, Romeo Diaz   *ad* James Leung   *ed* John Woo

'Graphically violent, vile and thoroughly disturbing depiction of war.' – *Variety*

A Bullet Is Waiting

US   1954   82m   Technicolor
Columbia/Welsch (Howard Welsch)
V*

A plane accident brings a policeman and his prisoner to a lonely farm, where a girl and her father bring a fresh twist to the situation.

Disappointing melodrama full of pretentious moralizing and fey characterization.

w Thames Williamson, Casey Robinson   *d* John Farrow   *ph* Franz Planer   *m* Dimitri Tiomkin

Jean Simmons, Rory Calhoun, Stephen McNally, Brian Aherne

Bullet Scars

US   1942   59m   bw
Warner

A doctor is kidnapped to patch up a bullet-scarred gunman.

Just another second feature.

w Robert E. Kent   *d* D. Ross Lederman

Regis Toomey, Adele Longmire, Howard da Silva, John Ridgley

Bulletproof

US   1987   94m   colour
Virgin/Bulletproof Productions (Paul Hertzberg, N. C. Lundell)
V*, L

A Los Angeles cop undertakes a dangerous mission against terrorists in Mexico.

Absurd action picture.

w T. L. Lankford, Steve Carver   *d* Steve Carver
ph Francis Grumman   *m* Tom Chase, Steve Rucker
pd Adrian H. Gorton   *ed* Jeff Freeman

Gary Busey, Darlanne Fluegel, Henry Silva, Thalmus Rasulala, L. Q. Jones, Rene Enriquez, Mills Watson, James Andronica

Bullets for O'Hara

US   1941   50m   bw
Warner

A gangster's wife helps an FBI man to trap her husband.

Fast-moving filler with action scenes lifted from its original, *Public Enemy's Wife* (qv).

w Raymond L. Schrock   *d* William K. Howard

Roger Pryor, Anthony Quinn, Joan Perry, Maris Wrixon, Dick Purcell

'Every real citizen should see it!'

Bullets or Ballots *

US   1936   81m   bw
Warner (Lou Edelman)
V, V*, L

A city cop goes undercover to break the mob.

Vivid routine gangster thriller, not quite of the top flight, but nearly.

w Seton I. Miller   *d* William Keighley   *ph* Hal Mohr   *m* Heinz Roemheld

Edward G. Robinson, Joan Blondell, Humphrey Bogart, Barton MacLane, Frank McHugh, Dick Purcell, George E. Stone

'A good gangster film of the second class . . . all the old chivalrous situations of *Chums* and the *Boy's Own Paper* are agreeably translated into sub-machine gun terms.' – *Graham Greene*

The Bullfighter and the Lady

US   1951   87m   bw
Republic/John Wayne (Budd Boetticher)
V*, L

A young American in Mexico is fascinated by bullfighting but during training accidentally causes the death of a great matador.

Predictable, rather boring plot given routine treatment: for aficionados only.

w James Edward Grant   *d* Budd Boetticher
ph Jack Draper   *m* Victor Young

Robert Stack, Gilbert Roland, Joy Page, Katy Jurado, Virginia Grey, John Hubbard

AAN: original story (Budd Boetticher, Ray Nazarro)

The Bullfighters *

US   1945   60m   bw
TCF (William Girard)
V, V*

Two detectives in Mexico find that one of them resembles a famous matador.

Laurel and Hardy's last American feature is poor enough as a whole, but at least has a few sequences in their earlier style.

w Scott Darling   *d* Mal St Clair   *ph* Norbert Brodine   *m* David Buttolph   *ad* Lyle Wheeler, Chester Gore   *ed* Stanley Rabjohn

Stan Laurel, Oliver Hardy, Richard Lane, Margo Woode, Carol Andrews

Bullitt **

US   1968   113m   Technicolor
Warner/Solar (Philip D'Antoni)
V, V*, L

A San Francisco police detective conceals the death of an underground witness in his charge, and goes after the killers himself.

Routine cop thriller with undoubted charisma, distinguished by a splendid car chase which takes one's mind off the tedious plot. Technical credits first class.

w Harry Kleiner, Alan R. Trustman   *novel Mute Witness* by Robert L. Pike   *d* Peter Yates   *ph* William A. Fraker   *m* Lalo Schifrin   *ed* Frank P. Keller

Steve McQueen, Jacqueline Bisset, Robert Vaughn, Don Gordon, Robert Duvall, Simon Oakland

'It has energy, drive, impact, and above all, style.' – *Hollis Alpert*

AA: Frank P. Keller

Bullseye!

US   1990   92m   colour
Castle Premier/21st Century (Michael Winner)
V, V*, L

Two con-men impersonate crooked nuclear scientists.

Tedious comedy with few laughs.

w Leslie Bricusse, Laurence Marks, Maurice Gran
story Leslie Bricusse, Michael Winner, Nick Mead
d Michael Winner   *ph* Alan Jones   *pd* John Blezard   *ad* Alan Cassie   *ed* Arnold Crust

Michael Caine, Roger Moore, Sally Kirkland, Deborah Barrymore, Lee Patterson, Mark Burns, Derren Nesbitt

'Wallowing in its excremental humour, *Bullseye!* is content to reinforce the crudest of racial and sexual stereotypes.' – *MFB*

Bullshot

GB   1983   88m   Technicolor
HandMade (Ian La Frenais)
V*

In the twenties, Bullshot Crummond is pitted against his arch enemy Count Otto von Bruno.

Very flat-footed spoof which belies the talents involved.

w Ron House, Diz White, Alan Shearman   *d* Dick Clement   *ph* Alex Thomson   *m* John Du Prez
pd Norman Garwood

Alan Shearman, Diz White, Ron House, Frances Tomelty, Michael Aldridge, Ron Pember, Mel Smith, Billy Connolly, Geoffrey Bayldon, Bryan Pringle

'Unrelievedly ghastly . . . even canned laughter would be hard pressed to raise a titter.' – *Gilbert Adair, MFB*

'Behind every mannered line you can hear technicians laughing the fun to death on the studio floor.' – *Sunday Times*

Bun Ngo Tsong Tinngai: see *Wild Search*

Bunco Squad

US   1950   67m   bw
RKO

The police expose a fake medium.

Slightly unusual cop caper.

w George E. Callahan   *d* Herbert Leeds

Robert Sterling, Ricardo Cortez, Joan Dixon

Bundle of Joy

US   1956   98m   Technicolor   RKOscope
RKO/Edmund Grainger
V*

A shopgirl finds an abandoned baby and everyone thinks it is hers.

Tame musical remake of *Bachelor Mother;* some laughs, but poor numbers.

w Norman Krasna, Arthur Sheekman, Robert Carson *d* Norman Taurog *ph* William Snyder *m* Josef Myrow

Debbie Reynolds, Eddie Fisher, Adolphe Menjou, Melville Cooper, Tommy Noonan, Nita Talbot, Una Merkel, Robert H. Harris

Bunker Bean
US 1936 67m bw
RKO
aka: *His Majesty Bunker Bean*

A meek office clerk rises to power after a personality course.

Old-fashioned comedy previously filmed in 1917 and 1924.

w Edmund North, James Gow and Dorothy Yost *novel* Harry Leon Wilson *d* William Hamilton, Edward Killy

Owen Davis Jnr, Lucille Ball, Berton Churchill, Louise Latimer, Jessie Ralph, Hedda Hopper

Bunny Lake is Missing **
GB 1965 107m bw Panavision
Columbia/Wheel (Otto Preminger)

The 4-year-old illegitimate daughter of an American girl in London disappears, and no one can be found to admit that she ever existed.

A nightmarish gimmick story, with more gimmicks superimposed along the way to say nothing of a *Psycho*ish ending; some of the decoration works and makes even the unconvincing story compelling, while the cast is alone worth the price of admission.

w John and Penelope Mortimer *novel* Evelyn Piper *d* Otto Preminger *ph* Denys Coop *m* Paul Glass *pd* Don Ashton *titles* Saul Bass

Laurence Olivier, Carol Lynley, Keir Dullea, Noël Coward, Martita Hunt, Finlay Currie, Clive Revill, Anna Massey, Lucie Mannheim

'It has the enjoyable hallmarks of really high calibre professionalism.' – *Penelope Houston*

Bunny O'Hare
US 1971 92m Movielab
AIP (Gerd Oswald, Norman T. Herman)

A middle-aged widow and an ex-con plumber become bank robbers, dressed as hippies and escaping on a motor cycle.

Unappealing, ill-thought-out comedy with pretensions to satire, an unhappy venture for both stars.

w Stanley Z. Cherry, Coslough Johnson *d* Gerd Oswald *ph* Loyal Griggs, John Stephens *m* Billy Strange

Bette Davis, Ernest Borgnine, Jack Cassidy, Joan Delaney, Jay Robinson, John Astin

Buona Sera Mrs Campbell *
US 1968 113m Technicolor
UA/Connaught (Melvin Frank)
V*, L

Wartime USAF comrades reassemble twenty years later in an Italian village, and three find that they have been paying paternity money to the same local glamour girl.

Agreeably cast, pleasantly set and photographed, quite funny in parts, this comedy of middle age unfortunately outstays its welcome and lets its invention peter out.

w Melvin Frank, Denis Norden, Sheldon Keller *d* Melvin Frank *ph* Gabor Pogany *m* Riz Ortolani

Gina Lollobrigida, Telly Savalas, Phil Silvers, Peter Lawford, Lee Grant, Marian Moses, Shelley Winters

Il Buono, il Brutto, il Cattivo: see *The Good, the Bad and the Ugly*

The 'burbs **
US 1988 102m DeLuxe
UIP/Imagine (Michael Finnell, Larry Brezner)
V, V*, L

Neighbours decide that there is something sinister about a new family on the block.

One-joke black comedy that has its moments.

w Dana Olsen *d* Joe Dante *ph* Robert Stevens *m* Jerry Goldsmith *pd* James Spencer *ed* Marshall Harvey

Tom Hanks, Bruce Dern, Carrie Fisher, Rick Ducommun, Corey Feldman, Wendy Schaal, Henry Gibson, Brother Theodore, Courtney Gains, Gale Gordon

'For the most part, this is one of the most extraordinary major studio films of the late 80s.' – *Kim Newman, MFB*

Bureau of Missing Persons *
US 1933 73m bw
Warner
V*

Police chief helps a girl find her husband, who turns out to have been murdered.

Fast-moving potboiler typical of its studio.

w Robert Presnell *story Missing Men* by John H. Ayres, Carol Biro *d* Roy del Ruth

Pat O'Brien, Bette Davis, Lewis Stone, Glenda Farrell, Allen Jenkins, Hugh Herbert

'Pretty fair entertainment. Nothing socko, but it will please.' – *Variety*

The Burglar *
US 1957 80m bw
Columbia (Louis W. Kellerman)

A burglar is shadowed by a policeman who is also after the loot.

Slightly pretentious but watchable low-budgeter.

w David Goodis *novel* David Goodis *d/ed* Paul Wendkos *ph* Don Malkames *m* Sol Kaplan

Dan Duryea, Jayne Mansfield, Martha Vickers, Peter Capell

Burglar
US 1987 102m Technicolor
Warner/Nelvana (Kevin McCormick, Michael Hirsch)
V, V*, L, S

An ex-con turns tec to avoid arrest as a cat burglar.

Strained comedy which is too goofy to sustain its mystery elements.

w Joseph Loeb III, Matthew Weisman, Hugh Wilson *books* Lawrence Block *d* Hugh Wilson *ph* William A. Fraker *m* Sylvester Levay

Whoopi Goldberg, Bob Goldthwait, G. W. Bailey, Lesley Ann Warren, James Handy, Anne de Salvo

The Burglar
Russia 1987 89m colour
First Film Group/Lenfilm
original title: *Vzlomshchik*

A youth steals a synthesiser in order to prevent his elder brother, a rock musician, from committing the crime.

Teenage alienation among Soviet punk rockers.

w Valery Priyomkhov *d* Valery Ogorodnikov *ph* Valery Mironov *m* Viktor Kisin *ad* Irakli Kvirikadze

Oleg Elykomov, Konstantin Kirchev, Yuri Tsapnik, Svetlana Gaitan, Polina Petrenko, Mikhail Parfonov, Pyotr Semak, Oleg Garkusha, Valdimir Dyatlov

The Burglars
France/Italy 1971 120m Eastmancolor
Panavision
Columbia/Vides (Henri Verneuil)
original title: *La Casse*

A determined policeman chases three burglars and their girl accomplice.

Expensive, camped-up version of *The Burglar,* with plenty going on, most of it borrowed from other films.

w Vahe Katcha, Henri Verneuil *novel The Burglar* by David Goodis *d* Henri Verneuil *ph* Claude Renoir *m* Ennio Morricone

Omar Sharif, Jean-Paul Belmondo, Dyan Cannon, Robert Hossein, Nicole Calfan, Renato Salvatori

'Electronic equipment, wild action, exotic locales and bland villainy.' – *Tom Milne, MFB*

Buried Alive
US 1991 91m colour
21st Century/Breton (Harry Alan Towers)
V*, L

A psychiatrist, made mad by his father's experiments, turns a former asylum into a school for disturbed girls.

Dim and gory exploitation movie that borrows ideas from several of Poe's stories but has little notion of what to do with them.

w Jake Clesi, Stuart Lee *story* Edgar Allan Poe *d* Gérard Kikoine *ph* Gérard Loubeau *m* Frederic Targorn *pd* Leonardo Coen Calgi *ed* Gilbert Kikoine

Robert Vaughn, Donald Pleasence, Karen Witter, John Carradine, Nia Long, Ginger Lynn Allen, Bill Butler

† It was John Carradine's last film.

Burke and Hare
GB 1971 91m DeLuxe
UA/Kenneth Shipman/Armitage (Guido Coen)

The story of anatomist Dr Knox and his body snatchers, retold with emphasis on the local brothel.

Depressing in its childish attempts to be gruesome and perverted.

w Ernie Bradford *d* Vernon Sewell *ph* Desmond Dickinson *m* Roger Webb

Harry Andrews, Derren Nesbitt, Glynn Edwards, Yootha Joyce, Dee Sjendery, Alan Tucker

Burke and Wills *
Australia 1985 140m Eastmancolor Panavision
Hoyts Edgley (Graeme Clifford, John Sexton)
V*, L

An account of the 1860 expedition across Australia.

Downbeat epic with interesting highlights; but the length is against it.

w Michael Thomas *d* Graeme Clifford *ph* Russell Boyd *m* Peter Sculthorpe *pd* Ross Major

Jack Thompson, Nigel Havers, Greta Scacchi, Matthew Fargher

† A parody film, *Wills and Burke,* appeared simultaneously.

Burma Convoy
US 1941 72m bw
Universal

A trucking convoy on the Burma Road is terrorized by enemy smugglers.

Adequately two-fisted second feature.

w Stanley Rubin, Roy Chanslor *d* Noel M. Smith

Charles Bickford, Evelyn Ankers, Cecil Kellaway, Frank Albertson, Keye Luke, Turhan Bey, Willie Fung

The Burmese Harp ***

Japan 1956 116m bw
Nikkatsu (Masayuki Takagi)
V*, L
original title: *Biruma no tategoto*

A shell-shocked Japanese soldier stays in the
Burmese jungle to bury the unknown dead.

Deeply impressive and horrifying war film with an
epic, folk-tale quality, emphasized by superbly
controlled direction.

w Natto Wada *novel* Michio Takeyama *d* Kon
Ichikawa *ph* Minoru Yokoyama *m* Akira Ifukube

Shoji Yasui, Rentaro Mikuni, Tatsuya Mihashi

AAN: best foreign film

Burn!: see *Queimada!*

Burn 'Em Up Barnes

US 1934 bw serial: 12 eps
Mascot

A racing driver and his adopted son combat
racketeers.

Routine serial hokum. *d* Colbert Clark, Armand
Schaefer

Jack Mulhall, Frankie Darro, Lola Lane, Julian
Rivero, Edwin Maxwell

Burn 'Em Up O'Connor

US 1938 70m bw
MGM

The life and loves of a speedway ace.

Modestly effective second from the time when the
studios were trying to make a star of Dennis O'Keefe.

w Milton Merlin, Byron Morgan *novel Salute to the
Gods* by Sir Malcolm Campbell *d* Edward Sedgwick

Dennis O'Keefe, Harry Carey, Cecilia Parker, Nat
Pendleton, Charley Grapewin

'Will fill better half of duals for good b.o.' – *Variety*

Burn, Witch, Burn: see *Night of the Eagle*

'Don't look he'll see you. Don't breathe he'll hear you.
  Don't move you're dead.'

The Burning

US 1981 91m colour
HandMade/Miramax (Harvey Weinstein)
V*

An incinerated caretaker takes his revenge on
teenagers at a summer camp.

Dire, totally predictable, uninventive low-budget
horror.

w Peter Lawrence, Bob Weinstein *story* Harvey
Weinstein, Tony Maylam, Brad Grey *d* Tony
Maylam *ph* Harvey Harrison *m* Rick Wakeman
ad Peter Politanoff *ed* Jack Sholder

Brian Matthews, Leah Ayres, Brian Backer, Larry
Joshua, Jason Alexander, Ned Eisenberg, Holly
Hunter

Burning an Illusion

GB 1981 111m Eastmancolor
BFI (Vivien Pottersman)

A black secretary in London, reluctantly intrigued by
the activities of her political boyfriend, becomes a
political militant.

Most people would sigh at the thought of sitting
through this decently made but rather earnest
document which preaches only to the converted.
wd Menelik Shabazz *ph* Roy Cornwall
songs various

Cassie McFarlane, Victor Romero, Beverley Martin,
Angela Wynter

The Burning Cross

US 1947 79m bw
Screen Guild

A frustrated war veteran succumbs temporarily to the
wiles of the Ku Klux Klan.

Cheap semi-documentary with a clear exploitation
purpose.

w Aubrey Wisberg *d* Walter Colmes

Hank Daniels, Virginia Patton, Raymond Bond

The Burning Hills

US 1956 92m Warnercolor Cinemascope
Warner (Richard Whorf)

A young rancher gets even with a cattle baron who
had his brother killed.

Reasonable but unexciting star vehicle.

w Irving Wallace *novel* Louis L'Amour *d* Stuart
Heisler

Natalie Wood, Tab Hunter, Skip Homeier, Eduard
Franz, Earl Holliman

Burning Rubber

West Germany 1980 84m colour
Ocean Films/Safe Productions (Stefan Abendroth, Barrie Saint
  Clair)

A car mechanic becomes a drag-racer with the aid of a
rich girlfriend.

An attempt to combine the appeals of pop music and
motor-racing, to the detriment of both.

w Dale Cutts, Bill Flynn *d* Norman Cohen
ph Keith Jones *m* Bay City Rollers *ed* Wayne
Lines

Olivia Pascal, Alan Longmuir, Sascha Hehn, Stuart
'Woody' Wood, Derek Longmuir, Duncan Faure

Burning Secret *

UK/US 1988 105m colour
Vestron/NFH/CLG Films (Norma Heyman, Eberhard
  Junkersdoft, Carol Lynn Greene)
V, V*, L, S

An asthmatic boy on the edge of adolescence
interferes in a holiday romance between his mother
and a stranger.

Constantly promising more than it delivers, though
with some interesting stops on an unsatisfying
journey. *wd* Andrew Birkin *story Brennendes
Geheimnis* by Stefan Zweig *ph* Ernest Day *m* Hans
Zimmer *pd* Bernd Lepel *ed* Paul Green

Faye Dunaway, David Eberts, Klaus Maria
Brandauer, Ian Richardson

'Stately, elegant, and stiflingly old-fashioned,
producing many exquisite coils of smoke but nothing
resembling a real fire.' – *Philip Strick, MFB*

Burnt Offerings

US 1976 115m DeLuxe
UA/PEA-Dan Curtis (Robert Singer)
V*

An evil house restores itself by feeding on its tenants.

An agreeably macabre idea for a five-page story is
dragged out to interminable length, and seizes the
attention only by a few shock moments. The title is
mysteriously irrelevant.

w William F. Nolan, Dan Curtis *novel* Robert
Marasco *d* Dan Curtis *ph* Jacques Marquette
m Robert Colbert *pd* Eugene Lourie

Oliver Reed, Karen Black, Bette Davis, Lee
Montgomery, Burgess Meredith, Eileen Heckart, Dub
Taylor

'Before the ludicrous dénouement, the movie merely
piles on one special effect after another – none of them
too special – and stalls for time.' – *Janet Maslin,
Newsweek*

Bury Me Dead *

US 1947 68m bw
Charles F. Reisner/Eagle Lion

A girl reappears on the day of her 'funeral', and
determines to discover who is being buried in her
name.

Complex mystery which might have been worthy of a
Grade A production.

w Karen de Wolf, Dwight V. Babcock *story* Irene
Winston *d* Bernard Vorhaus

Cathy O'Donnell, June Lockhart, Hugh Beaumont,
Mark Daniels, Greg McClure

Bus Riley's Back in Town *

US 1965 93m Eastmancolor
U-I (Elliott Kastner)

An ex-sailor wants to settle back into small-town life
but finds that his girlfriend has married.

Watchable, middling, routine small-town drama in
the style of *Picnic*.

w Walter Gage (William Inge) *d Harvey Hart*
ph Russell Metty *m* Richard Markowitz

Michael Parks, Ann-Margret, Jocelyn Brando, Janet
Margolin, Kim Darby, Brad Dexter, Larry Storch,
Crahan Denton, Mimsy Farmer, David Carradine

Bus Stop **

US 1956 96m Eastmancolor Cinemascope
TCF (Buddy Adler)
V, V*, L
TV title: *The Wrong Kind of Girl*

In a rodeo town, a simple-thinking cowboy meets a
café singer and asks her to marry him.

Sex comedy-drama, a modest entertainment in
familiar American vein, very well done but rather
over-inflated by its star.

w George Axelrod *play* William Inge *d* Joshua
Logan *ph* Milton Krasner *m* Alfred Newman,
Cyril Mockridge

Marilyn Monroe, Don Murray, Betty Field, Arthur
O'Connell, Eileen Heckart, Robert Bray, Hope Lange,
Hans Conried, Casey Adams

'The film demands of its principal performers a purely
physical display of their bodies viewed as sexual
machinery.' – *David Robinson*

AAN: Don Murray

Bush Christmas

GB 1947 77m bw
ABFD/Children's Entertainment Films (Ralph Smart)

Australian children on holiday help catch horse
thieves.

Rather stolid family feature which got a reputation it
hardly deserved. *wd* Ralph Smart

Chips Rafferty, John Fernside, Stan Tolshurst, Pat
Penny, Thelma Grigg, John McCallum

The Bushido Blade

GB/US 1978 92m colour
Trident/Rankin-Bass (Arthur Rankin Jnr)
V*
aka: *The Bloody Bushido Blade*

Yokohama 1854; a US-Japanese treaty is in jeopardy
because the Shogun's gift of a ceremonial sword has
been stolen.

Unappealing hybrid with much beheading and other
random action, but little sense.

w William Overgard *d* Tom Kotani *ph* Shoji
Uedo *m* Maury Laws

Richard Boone, Frank Converse, Laura Gemser,
Toshiro Mifune, Sonny Chiba, James Earl Jones,
Mako

Business and Pleasure
US   1931   76m   bw
Fox

A down-to-earth husband is tempted by a *femme fatale*.

Mild star comedy for his regular fans.

w Gene Towne, William Conselman   *novel The Plutocrat* by Booth Tarkington   *d* David Butler

Will Rogers, Jetta Goudal, Joel McCrea, Dorothy Peterson, Jed Prouty

'West of Albany, perhaps, it will see some good business.' – *Variety*

Business As Usual
GB   1987   90m   colour
Cannon (Sara Geater)
V*

The manageress of a shop, sacked for objecting to her boss's sexual harassment of his staff, fights back.

Agit-prop drama with some forceful performances.
wd Lezli-An Barrett   *ph* Ernie Vincze
ad Hildegarde Betchler   *ed* Henry Richardson

Glenda Jackson, John Thaw, Cathy Tyson, Mark McGann, Buki Armstrong, Stephen McGann, Philip Foster, Natalie Duffy, James Hazeldine, Mel Martin

Busman's Honeymoon *
GB   1940   99m   bw
MGM (Harold Huth)
US title: *Haunted Honeymoon*

Lord Peter Wimsey finds a murder to be solved in his honeymoon cottage.

Pleasant, slightly flat film version of a favourite old-fashioned detective novel.

w Monckton Hoffe, Angus Macphail, Harold Goldman   *novel* Dorothy L. Sayers   *d* Arthur Woods   *ph* F. A. Young   *m* Louis Levy   *ad* Alfred Junge   *ed* Al Barnes

Robert Montgomery, Constance Cummings, Leslie Banks, *Seymour Hicks,* Robert Newton, Googie Withers, Frank Pettingell, Joan Kemp-Welch

Busses Roar
US   1942   61m   bw
Warner

A saboteur fixes a bomb to explode on a bus as it passes through an oilfield.

Passable time-filler.

w Anthony Coldeway, George Bilson   *d* D. Ross Lederman

Richard Travis, Eleanor Parker, Julie Bishop, Charles Drake

Buster
GB   1988   102m   colour
Vestron/The Movie Group (Norma Heyman)
V, V*, L, S

True story of Great Train Robber, actually a small-time thief, on the run.

Uneasy combination of romantic comedy and chase thriller.

w Colin Schindler   *d* David Green   *ph* Tony Imi   *m* Anne Dudley   *pd* Simon Holland   *ed* Lesley Walker

Phil Collins, Julie Walters, Larry Lamb, Stephanie Lawrence, Martin Jarvis, Sheila Hancock, Anthony Quayle

AAN: best song 'Two Hearts' (*m/ly* Lamont Dozier, Phil Collins)

Buster and Billie
US   1973   99m   CFI colour
Black Creek Billie/Columbia
V*

A sensitive high school senior elects to marry the school's derided 'easy lay', with tragic results.

Unattractive reminiscences of rural Georgia with a rather desperate appeal to oversexed teenagers.

w Ron Turbeville   *d* Daniel Petrie   *ph* Mario Tosi

Jan-Michael Vincent, Pamela Sue Martin, Joan Goodfellow, Clifton James

Buster Keaton: A Hard Act to Follow ***
GB   1987   156m   colour/bw
Thames TV (Kevin Brownlow, David Gill)
V

A three-part investigation of the art and life of Keaton, including many clips from his films as well as interviews with him and those who worked with him.

An exemplary and fascinating documentary on one of the greatest of cinematic clowns.

w Kevin Brownlow, David Gill   *m* Carl Davis

Lindsay Anderson (narrator)

The Buster Keaton Story *
US   1957   91m   bw   Vistavision
Paramount (Sidney Sheldon, Robert Smith)

A biopic of the great silent comedian, with the emphasis on his years of downfall through drink.

An interesting recreation of Hollywood in the twenties and thirties is the main asset of this otherwise dismal tribute to a man whose greatness the star is unable to suggest apart from a few acrobatic moments.

w Robert Smith, Sidney Sheldon   *d* Sidney Sheldon   *ph* Loyal Griggs   *m* Victor Young

Donald O'Connor, Rhonda Fleming, Ann Blyth, Peter Lorre, Larry Keating, Richard Anderson, Dave Willock

Busting
US   1973   92m   DeLuxe
UA/Chartoff-Winkler (Henry Gellis)
V*

Two Los Angeles vice squad officers fight corruption inside and outside the force.

Violent, exhausting, but totally routine police caper of the seventies.   *wd* Peter Hyams   *ph* Earl Rath   *m* Billy Goldenberg

Elliott Gould, Robert Blake, Allen Garfield, Antonio Fargas

'The farcical version of Serpico.' – *Michael Billington, Illustrated London News*

Bustin' Loose
US   1981   94m   Technicolor
Universal/Richard Pryor (William Greaves)
V*, L

A thief on parole learns to look after a school for maladjusted children en route to a mountain retreat.

A fairly nauseous compendium of pratfalls and sentiment, not too bad while it keeps on the move.

w Roger L. Simon   *d* Oz Scott   *ph* Dennis Dalzell   *m* Mark Davis, Roberta Flack

Richard Pryor, Cicely Tyson, Angel Ramirez, Jimmy Hughes

'The sort of forties-style warm experience I could well do without.' – *Derek Malcolm, Guardian*

Busy Bodies **
US   1933   20m   bw
MGM/Hal Roach
V

Stan and Ollie are involved in various disasters in a sawmill.

Though not among their most sympathetic comedies, this is a sustained and brilliantly contrived slapstick sequence.

w Anon (and Stan Laurel)   *d* Lloyd French   *ph* Art Lloyd   *ed* Bert Jordan

Laurel and Hardy, Tiny Sandford, Charlie Hall

The Busy Body
US   1966   102m   Techniscope
Paramount/William Castle

A gangster is buried in a suit with a million dollar lining which various people are out to get.

Unfunny black comedy; laboured handling makes it a joke in poor taste.

w Ben Starr   *novel* Donald E. Westlake   *d* William Castle   *ph* Hal Stine   *m* Vic Mizzy

Robert Ryan, Sid Caesar, Arlene Golonka, Anne Baxter, Kay Medford, Charles McGraw

But Not for Me
US   1959   105m   bw
Paramount (William Perlberg, George Seaton)
V*

An ageing, washed-up Broadway producer is loved by his young drama student secretary.

Rather heavy-going remake of *Accent on Youth*, efficiently performed but lacking the original gaiety.

w John Michael Hayes   *d* Walter Lang   *ph* Robert Burks   *m* Leith Stevens

Clark Gable, Carroll Baker, Lilli Palmer, Lee J. Cobb, Barry Coe, Thomas Gomez

But the Flesh Is Weak
US   1932   82m   bw
MGM

A widower and his son both decide to marry wealthy widows.

Amusing high society comedy from Ivor Novello's *The Truth Game*.

w Ivor Novello   *d* Jack Conway

Robert Montgomery, C. Aubrey Smith, Heather Thatcher, Edward Everett Horton, Nils Asther

Butch and Sundance: The Early Days *
US   1979   112m   DeLuxe
TCF (Gabriel Katzka, Stephen Bach)
V*

Early episodes in the careers of the famous outlaws, culminating in a train robbery.

'Prequel' to a more celebrated but not a fresher or more lyrical Western.

w Allan Burns   *d* Richard Lester   *ph* Laszlo Kovacs   *m* Patrick Williams   *pd* Brian Eatwell

Tom Berenger, William Katt, Jeff Corey, John Schuck, Michael C. Gwynne, Brian Dennehy, Peter Weller

'Not that it matters, but most of it is true!'
Butch Cassidy and the Sundance Kid ****
US   1969   110m   DeLuxe   Panavision
TCF/Campanile (John Foreman)
V, V*, L, S

A hundred years ago, two Western train robbers keep one step ahead of the law until finally tracked down to Bolivia.

Humorous, cheerful, poetic, cinematic account of two semi-legendary outlaws, winningly acted and directed. One of the decade's great commercial successes, not least because of the song 'Raindrops Keep Fallin' on My Head'.

w William Goldman   *d* George Roy Hill   *ph* Conrad Hall   *m* Burt Bacharach

Paul Newman, Robert Redford, Katharine Ross, Strother Martin, Henry Jones, Jeff Corey, Cloris Leachman, Ted Cassidy, Kenneth Mars

'A mere exercise in smart-alecky device-mongering, chock-full of out of place and out of period one-upmanship, a battle of wits at a freshman smoker.' – *John Simon*

'The film does wonderful things with mood and atmosphere. The touches are fleeting, but they are there.' – *Hollis Alpert, Saturday Review*

AA: William Goldman; Conrad Hall; Burt Bacharach; song 'Raindrops Keep Fallin' on My Head' (*m* Burt Bacharach, *ly* Hal David)

AAN: best picture; George Roy Hill

The Butcher: see *Le Boucher*

'It's not about meat, it's about magic.'
The Butcher's Wife
US 1991 105m Technicolor
Blue Dolphin/Paramount (Wallis Nicita, Lauren Lloyd)
V, V*, L

A clairvoyant marries a butcher and tells customers of her premonitions concerning them.

Whimsical romantic comedy that sank without a trace.

w Ezra Litwak, Marjorie Schwartz *d* Terry Hughes *ph* Frank Tidy *m* Michael Gore *pd* Charles Rosen *ed* Donn Cambern

Demi Moore, Jeff Daniels, George Dzundza, Mary Steenburgen, Frances McDormand, Margaret Colin, Max Perlich, Miriam Margolyes

'The jokes and folksy apophthegms are the sort that fill out the pages of *Reader's Digest*, the over-acting is the kind of thing good performers resort to in long-running Broadway plays.' – *Philip French, Observer*

The Butler's Dilemma
GB 1943 83m bw
British National/Shaftesbury (Elizabeth Hiscott)

A jewel thief has to pose as his fiancée's butler.

Predictable comedy of pretence and mistaken identity; a tolerable co-feature of its day.

w Michael Barringer *d* Leslie Hiscott *ph* James Wilson *m* John Blore

Richard Hearne, Francis L. Sullivan, Judy Kelly, Hermione Gingold, Henry Kendall, Wally Patch

Butley *
US/GB 1973 130m Eastmancolor
American Express/Ely Landau/Cinevision
V*

Personal problems assail an English lecturer at a university college.

Adequate but not outstanding transcription (for the American Film Theatre) of a successful and percipient play.

w Simon Gray *play* Simon Gray *d* Harold Pinter *ph* Gerry Fisher *m* none

Alan Bates, Jessica Tandy, Richard O'Callaghan, Susan Engel, Michael Byrne

The Butter and Egg Man
US
Warner

This pleasant George S. Kaufman comedy about a cowboy in New York was filmed as a silent in 1928, with Jack Mulhall; in 1932 as *The Tenderfoot* (qv) with Joe E. Brown; in 1937 as *Dance Charlie Dance* with Stuart Erwin; and in 1940 as *An Angel from Texas* (qv) with Eddie Albert.

The Buttercup Chain *
GB 1970 95m Technicolor Panavision
Columbia (Leslie Gilliat, John Whitney, Philip Waddilove)

A hothouse sex quartet changes partners with bewildering rapidity against a background of European splendour.

Chi-chi romance with a fashionably disillusioned and tragic ending. As watchable as the best TV commercials, but totally empty.

w Peter Draper *novel* Janice Elliott *d* Robert Ellis Miller *ph* Douglas Slocombe *m* Richard Rodney Bennett

Hywel Bennett, Leigh Taylor-Young, Jane Asher, Sven-Bertil Taube, Clive Revill, Roy Dotrice

'British bathos about the unhappy overprivileged.' – *Variety*

'The most desirable woman in town, and the easiest to find!'
Butterfield Eight
US 1960 108m Metrocolor Cinemascope
MGM/Afton/Linebrook (Pandro S. Berman)
V*, L

A society call girl has a complex love life.

This coy sex drama seemed mildly daring in 1960, but has since been well outclassed in that field and certainly has nothing else going for it except good production values.

w Charles Schnee, John Michael Hayes *novel* John O'Hara *d* Daniel Mann *ph* Joseph Ruttenberg, Charles Harten *m* Bronislau Kaper

Elizabeth Taylor, Laurence Harvey, Eddie Fisher, Dina Merrill, Mildred Dunnock, Betty Field, Jeffrey Lynn, Kay Medford, Susan Oliver

'The mixture resolutely refuses to come to the boil.' – *John Gillett*

AA: Elizabeth Taylor

AAN: Joseph Ruttenberg, Charles Harten

Butterflies Are Free
US 1972 109m Eastmancolor
Columbia/M. J. Frankovich
V*

An aspiring actress falls for a blind neighbour but is handicapped by his possessive mother.

Three-character comedy-drama from a slight, sentimental but successful Broadway play.

w Leonard Gershe *play* Leonard Gershe *d* Milton Katselas *ph* Charles B. Lang *m* Bob Alcivar

Goldie Hawn, Edward Albert, Eileen Heckart

AA: Eileen Heckart

AAN: Charles B. Lang

Butterfly
US 1981 108m Metrocolor
Par Par (Matt Cimber)
V, V*. L, S

A 17-year-old sexpot reappears in her father's life, commits incest with him, and sets in train a grotesque series of plot developments.

Risible concatenation of murders, repentances, illegitimate sex and various kinds of lust, all revolving round butterfly marks and set in 1937 backwoods Arizona. *Tobacco Road* it ain't, though.

w John Goff, Matt Cimber *novel* The Butterfly by James M. Cain *d* Matt Cimber *ph* Eddy Van Der Enden *m* Ennio Morricone

Stacy Keach, Pia Zadora, Orson Welles, Lois Nettleton, Edward Albert, Stuart Whitman, Ed MacMahon, June Lockhart, James Franciscus

The Butterfly Murders ***
Hong Kong 1979 colour
Ng See Yuen (Ng See Kin)

A wandering scholar, at a time of warring factions, solves the mystery of an aristocratic family apparently plagued by killer butterflies.

A visually splendid martial arts fantasy with elaborately choreographed fight sequences, done with immense melodramatic style.

w Lam Fan *d* Tsui Hark *ph* Fun Chin Yu

Lau Siu Ming, Wong Shee Tong, Michelle, Chan Chi Chi, Cheong Kwok Chu, Kuo Hung, Wong Cheong, Kiu Fung

Buy Me That Town *
US 1941 70m bw
Paramount (Sol C. Siegel)

Gangsters take over a small town and pull the community out of bankruptcy.

Unusual comedy-drama, quite well done for a second feature.

w Gordon Kahn *d* Eugene Forde *ph* Theodor Sparkuhl

Lloyd Nolan, Albert Dekker, Constance Moore, Sheldon Leonard, Vera Vague, Edward Brophy, Horace MacMahon, Warren Hymer

Bwana Devil
US 1952 79m Anscocolor 3D
(UA) Arch Oboler

At the turn of the century, two man-eating lions threaten an African railroad.

Inept actioner notable only as the first film in 3-D ('Natural Vision'), advertised with the famous slogan 'A lion in your lap'. *wd* Arch Oboler *ph* Joseph Biroc *m* Gordon Jenkins

Robert Stack, Barbara Britton, Nigel Bruce, Ramsay Hill

By Candlelight *
US 1933 70m bw
Universal (Carl Laemmle Jnr)

On a transcontinental train a woman meets a butler and takes him for a prince; he does not disillusion her.

Moderately pleasing romantic comedy of the old school.

w Hans Kraly, F. Hugh Herbert, Karen de Wolf, Ruth Cummings *play* Siegfried Geyer *d* James Whale

Elissa Landi, *Paul Lukas*, Nils Asther

'A nice little class picture that should make money all round.' – *Variety*

'A dazzling display of romantic confidence trickery which takes on Lubitsch in his own territory.' – *Tom Milne, 1978*

By Hook or by Crook: see *I Dood It*

By Love Possessed *
US 1961 116m DeLuxe Panavision
UA/Mirisch/Seven Arts (Walter Mirisch)
V*, L

A Massachusetts lawyer reflects on the outlandish sexual mores of himself, his family and friends.

Peyton Place moved up in the social scale; a reasonably absorbing melodrama but hardly memorable.

w John Dennis *novel* James Gould Cozzens *d* John Sturges *ph* Russell Metty *m* Elmer Bernstein

Lana Turner, Efrem Zimbalist Jnr, Jason Robards Jnr, Barbara Bel Geddes, George Hamilton, Susan Kohner, Thomas Mitchell, Yvonne Craig, Everett Sloane

'A talky succession of soap opera situations.' – *Robert Windeler*

By the Light of the Silvery Moon *
US 1953 101m Technicolor
Warner (William Jacobs)
V*, L

In a small American town in 1918, the Winfield family has several problems arising from the return of daughter Marjorie's soldier boyfriend.

A sequel to *On Moonlight Bay* (qv), presenting further situations from the Penrod stories retailored for Doris

Day. Inoffensive, well-made, old-fashioned entertainment with nostalgic songs and an archetypal family.

w Robert O'Brien, Irving Elinson   *stories* Booth Tarkington   *d* David Butler   *ph* Wilfrid M. Cline   *m* Max Steiner

Doris Day, Gordon Macrae, *Leon Ames, Rosemary de Camp, Mary Wickes*

AA: William Goldman

By Whose Hand?

US   1932   63m   bw
Columbia

Murder on a train between Los Angeles and San Francisco.

Brisk little 'B' thriller.

w Isadore Bernstein, Stephen Roe, Harry Adler   *d* Ben Stoloff

Ben Lyon, Barbara Weeks, Ethel Kenyon, Kenneth Thomson, Tom Dugan, Dwight Frye

'The answer to a grind house exhib's prayer.' – *Variety*

By Your Leave

US   1934   81m   bw
RKO

A restless husband tries to be a Don Juan.

Very mild domestic comedy.

w Allan Scott   *play* Gladys Hurlbut, Emma B. C. Wells   *d* Lloyd Corrigan

Frank Morgan, Genevieve Tobin, Neil Hamilton, Marian Nixon, Glenn Anders, Gene Lockhart, Margaret Hamilton, Betty Grable, Charles Ray

'Once the customers are in they'll get some laughs, but they're not going to be easy to entice.' – *Variety*

Bye Bye Birdie

US   1963   112m   Eastmancolor   Panavision
Columbia/Fred Kohlmar/George Sidney
V*, L, S

Havoc suffuses the last TV show of a pop star before he goes into the army.

Noisy, frenetic musical, hard to follow and even harder to like, with all the satire of the stage original subtracted. For young audiences who enjoy incoherence.

w Irving Brecher   *musical* Michael Stewart   *d* George Sidney   *ph* Joseph Biroc   *md* Johnny Green   *m/y* Charles Strouse, Lee Adams

Janet Leigh, Dick Van Dyke, Maureen Stapleton, Ann-Margret, Bobby Rydell, Jesse Pearson, Ed Sullivan, Paul Lynde, Robert Paige

AAN: Johnny Green

Bye Bye Blues

Canada   1989   117m   colour
Artificial Eye/True Blue Films/Allarcom/Telefilm Canada/CFCN TV/CITV (Anne Wheeler, Arvi Liimatainen, Jerry Krepakevich)
V*

A mother with two young children awaits the return of her soldier husband.

Uninteresting throwback to women's movies of the 1940s.

wd Anne Wheeler   *ph* Vic Sarin   *m* George Blondheim   *pd* John Blackie   *ad* Scott Dobbie, Jayoo Patwarchan, Chinu Patwarchan   *ed* Christopher Tate

Michael Ontkean, Rebecca Jenkins, Luke Reilly, Stuart Margolin, Wayne Robson, Robyn Stevan

'A film which, without exactly bowling one over, will probably remain in the memory longer than most.' – *Derek Malcolm, Guardian*

Bye Bye Braverman *

US   1968   92m   Technicolor
Warner/Sidney Lumet

New Yorkers get drunk and disillusioned on their way home from the funeral of a friend.

Witty, downbeat Jewish comedy which does not quite come off and would in any case be caviare to the general.

w Herbert Sargent   *novel* To an Early Grave by Wallace Markfield   *d* Sidney Lumet   *ph* Boris Kaufman   *m* Peter Matz

George Segal, Jack Warden, Joseph Wiseman, Sorrell Booke, Jessica Walter, Phyllis Newman, Zohra Lampert, Alan King, Godfrey Cambridge

'You don't have to be Jewish to love it, but it helps a lot to be a New Yorker.' – *Robert Hatch, The Nation*

Bye Bye Monkey

Italy/France   1977   114m   Eastmancolor
18 Dicembre/Prospectacle/Action Film (Giorgio Nocella, Maurice Bernart)
V
original title: *Ciao Maschio*

A Frenchman, dividing his time between a wax museum and a theatre group run by women, finds a chimpanzee and adopts it as his son.

Desultory drama of misfits drifting through New York that is never sharp or observant enough to be either amusing or interesting; and the deaths at the end do not make it tragic.

w Marco Ferreri, Gérard Brach, Rafael Azcona   *d* Marco Ferreri   *ph* Luciano Tovoli   *m* Philippe Sarde   *ad* Dante Ferretti   *ed* Ruggero Mastroianni

Gérard Depardieu, James Coco, Marcello Mastroianni, Geraldine Fitzgerald, Gail Lawrence, Stefania Casini, Francesca de Sapio, Mimsy Farmer

C

CB4
US 1993 88m DeLuxe
Universal (Nelson George)
V, V*, S

Clean-living middle-class youths form a gangsta rap group called Cell Block 4 and pretend to be tough.

Brief appearances from Ice T, Ice Cube, Flavour Flav and others add a little authenticity to a slight but amusing satire at the expense of the macho posturing of rappers. It will be most enjoyed by those attuned to the phenomenon of hip hop.

w Chris Rock, Nelson George, Robert LoCash
d Tamra Davis ph Karl Walter Lindenlaub
m John Barnes pd Nelson Coates ed Earl Watson

Chris Rock, Allen Payne, Deezer D, Phil Hartman, Arthur Evans, Theresa Randle, Willard E. Pugh, Richard Gant, Charlie Murphy, Chris Elliott

'Lively is the word for its better parts. Terminally disorganised would be the best one for the rest.' – *Derek Malcolm, Guardian*

'The satire is feeble, the pastiche documentary botched. Stereotypes are peeled away to reveal stereotypes beneath.' – *Philip French, Observer*

C.C. and Company
US 1971 84m colour
Allan Carr-Roger Smith/Avco Embassy

Adventures of a motorcycle gang.

Bottom of the barrel programme-filler.

w William Smith d Seymour Robbie

Joe Namath, Ann-Margret, William Smith, Jennifer Billingsley, Don Chastain

C.H.O.M.P.S.: see *Chomps*

C Man
US 1949 75m bw
Film Classics

Customs agents track down a murderer.

Lively little independent co-feature of its day.

w Berne Giler d Irving Lerner

Dean Jagger, John Carradine, Lotte Elwen, Harry Landers

Ça Peut Pas Être L'Hiver, On N'a Même Pas Eu Été: see *It Can't Be Winter, We Haven't Had Summer Yet*

'A divinely decadent experience!'
Cabaret ****
US 1972 123m Technicolor
ABC Pictures/Allied Artists (Cy Feuer)
V, V*, L, S

In the early thirties, Berlin is a hot-bed of vice and anti-semitism. In the Kit Kat Klub, singer Sally Bowles shares her English lover with a homosexual German baron, and her Jewish friend Natasha has troubles of her own.

This version of Isherwood's Berlin stories regrettably follows the plot line of the play *I Am a Camera* rather than the Broadway musical on which it is allegedly based, and it lacks the incisive remarks of the MC, but the very smart direction creates a near-masterpiece of its own, and most of the songs are intact.

w Jay Presson Allen, novel *Goodbye to Berlin* by Christopher Isherwood d/ch Bob Fosse
ph Geoffrey Unsworth md Ralph Burns pd Rolf Zehetbauer m/ly John Kander, Fred Ebb

Liza Minnelli, Joel Grey, Michael York, Helmut Griem, Fritz Wepper, Marisa Berenson

'A stylish, sophisticated entertainment for grown-up people.' – *John Russell Taylor*

'Film journals will feast for years on shots from this picture; as it rolled along, I saw page after illustrated page from a not-too-distant book called *The Cinema of Bob Fosse*.' – *Stanley Kauffmann*

AA: Bob Fosse (as director); Geoffrey Unsworth; Ralph Burns; Liza Minnelli; Joel Grey

AAN: best picture; Jay Presson Allen

Cabeza de Vaca *
Mexico/Spain 1990 111m Eastmancolor
Iguana Productions (Rafael Cruz, Jorge Sánchez, Julio Solórzano Foppa, Bertha Navarro)

In the 1520s, the leader of a group of Spanish conquistadores, shipwrecked off the coast of Florida, survives ambush, torture and privation by learning to live with the natives.

An ambitious, overlong, often mystic and sometimes violent epic, taken from a contemporary account, which is on the side of the native Americans.

w Guillermo Sheridan, Nicolás Echevarria
book *Naufragios* by Alvar Nunez Cabeza de Vaca
d Nicolás Echevarria ph Guillermo Navarro
m Mario Lavista ad José Luis Aguilar Gil
ed Rafael Castanedo

Juan Diego, Daniel Gimenez Cacho, Roberto Sosa, Carlos Castañón, Gerardo Villarreal, Roberto Cobo, José Flores

'It's a demanding pic for audiences, but they will be well rewarded with a film that's exotic, mysterious, bizarre (shades of Alexandro Jodorowsky) and dramatic.' – *Variety*

The Cabin in the Cotton *
US 1932 79m bw
Warner (Hal B. Wallis)
V*

A sharecropper is almost ruined by a Southern belle.

Dated melodrama with interesting style and performances.

w Paul Green novel Harry Harrison Kroll
d Michael Curtiz ph Barney McGill

Richard Barthelmess, Dorothy Jordan, Bette Davis, David Landau, Tully Marshall, Henry B. Walthall, Hardie Albright

'Not well done . . . less than a moderate grosser all round.' – *Variety*

† The film in which Bette Davis drawled: 'Ah'd love to kiss yuh, but Ah just washed mah hair.'

'Broadway's big, fun-jammed music show is on the screen at last – crowded with stars and songs and spectacle in the famed MGM manner!'
Cabin in the Sky **
US 1943 99m bw
MGM (Arthur Freed)
V*, L

An idle, gambling husband is reformed by a dream of his own death, with God and Satan battling for his soul.

Consistently interesting, often lively, but generally rather stilted all-black musical which must have seemed a whole lot fresher on the stage. Still, a good try.

w Joseph Schrank musical play Lynn Root
d Vincente Minnelli ph Sidney Wagner
md George Stoll m/ly Harold Arlen, E. Y. Harburg, Vernon Duke, John Latouche, Ted Fetter ad Cedric Gibbons, Leonid Vasian

Eddie 'Rochester' Anderson, Ethel Waters, Lena Horne, Louis Armstrong, Rex Ingram, Kenneth Spencer, John W. Sublett ('Bubbles'), Ford L. Washington ('Buck')

'Whatever its box office fate, a worthwhile picture for Metro to have made, if only as a step toward Hollywood recognition of the place of the colored man in American life.' – *Variety*

songs: 'Li'l Black Sheep'; 'Ain't It De Truth'; 'Life's Full Of Consequence'; 'Honey in the Honeycomb'; 'Taking a Chance on Love'; 'Going Up'; 'I Got A Song'; 'Shine'

AAN: song 'Happiness Is Just a Thing Called Joe'

(m Harold Arlen, ly E. Y. Harburg)

'No one permitted out or in during the last thirteen nerve-shattering minutes!'
The Cabinet of Caligari
US 1962 105m bw Cinemascope
TCF/Lippert (Roger Kay)

A young woman whose car breaks down near a country house is held prisoner by the sinister Caligari. Eventually it transpires that the mystery is all in her imagination: he is a psychiatrist and she an old lady whose sexual fantasies he has been curing.

Interminably talkative and frequently (unintentionally) funny trick film with the odd moment of effective suspense. The original ending, which cast some doubt on who was mad and who sane, is no longer available. The actors do not entirely escape absurdity.

w Robert Bloch d Roger Kay ph John Russell
m Gerald Fried

Glynis Johns, Dan O'Herlihy, Constance Ford, Dick Davalos, Lawrence Dobkin

'It is impossible to be grateful for the film on any of its levels.' – *MFB*

'The most complete essay in the décor of delirium.' – *New Yorker, 1979*

† The fact that the story is told through the eyes of a mad person is the only link with the 1919 classic.

'See the sleepwalker, floating down the street, ripped from some nightmare! A street of misshapen houses with brooding windows, streaked by dagger strokes of light and darkened by blots of shadow! You will immediately feel the terror in the movements of that floating grotesque!' (American advertising)
The Cabinet of Dr Caligari ****
Germany 1919 90m approx (16 fps) bw silent
Decla-Bioscop (Erich Pommer)
V, V*, L

A fairground showman uses a somnambulist for

purposes of murder and is finally revealed to be the director of a lunatic asylum; but the whole story is only the dream of a madman.

Faded now, but a film of immense influence on the dramatic art of cinema, with its odd angles, stylized sets and hypnotic acting, not to mention the sting in the tail of its story (added by the producer).

w Carl Mayer, Hans Janowitz d Robert Wiene ph Willy Hameister ad Hermann Warm, Walter Röhrig, Walter Reiman

Werner Krauss, Conrad Veidt, Lil Dagover, Friedrich Feher, Hans von Twardowski

'The first hundred shocks are the hardest.' – *New York Evening Post, 1924*

† The film cost 18,000 dollars to make.

Cabiria ***
Italy/France 1957 110m bw
Dino de Laurentiis/Les Films Marceau
V*, S
original title: *Le Notti di Cabiria*; aka: *Nights of Cabiria*

A Roman prostitute has dreams of romance and respectability.

A bitter Cinderella story which was later turned into the Broadway musical *Sweet Charity*. Much of interest, but the leading lady is too Chaplinesque.

w Federico Fellini, Ennio Flaiano, Tullio Pinelli d Federico Fellini ph Aldo Tonti m Nino Rota

Giulietta Masina, François Périer, Amedeo Nazzari, Franca Marzi, Dorian Gray

'Any nobility in the original conception slowly suffocates in an atmosphere of subjective indulgence bordering dangerously on self-pity.' – *Peter John Dyer*

'Stylistically the whole film with its dejected setting and its riotously fluent movement is brilliant. And the acting is superb.' – *Dilys Powell*

AA: best foreign film

Caboblanco
US 1981 87m colour Panavision
Avco/Martin V. Smith
V*, S

A café proprietor in the Caribbean dodges various groups of criminals.

Witless spoof of *Casablanca* which seems to have been cobbled together from a half-finished negative.

w Mort Fine, Milton Gelman d J. Lee Thompson ph Alex Phillips Jnr m Jerry Goldsmith

Charles Bronson, Jason Robards Jnr, Dominique Sanda, Fernando Rey, Simon MacCorkindale, Camilla Sparv, Denny Miller, Gilbert Roland

Caccia Tragica *
Italy 1947 89m bw
Lux/ANPI
aka: *The Tragic Pursuit*

A bandit is hunted through the Po valley but finally allowed to escape.

Minor peripatetic melodrama, well-handled and exciting but uncertain in mood.

w Giuseppe de Santis, Michelangelo Antonioni, Cesare Zavattini, Carlo Lizzani, Umberto Barbaro d Giuseppe de Santis ph Otello Martelli m Giuseppe Rosati

Massimo Girotti, Andrea Checci, Vivi Gioi

Cactus *
Australia 1986 96m colour
Dofine/Film Victoria/AFC (Jane Ballantyne, Paul Cox)
V*

A Frenchwoman, whose eyesight begins to deteriorate after a car crash, falls in love with a blind man.

Austere and sensitive drama about a woman finding herself, but too underplayed to be entirely effective.

w Paul Cox, Bob Ellis, Norman Kaye, Morris Lurie d Paul Cox ph Yuri Sokol pd Asher Bilu ed Tim Lewis

Isabelle Huppert, Robert Menzies, Norman Kaye, Monica Maughan, Banduk Marika, Sheila Florance

Cactus Flower *
US 1969 103m Technicolor
Columbia/M. J. Frankovich
V, V*, L

To deceive his mistress, a dentist employs his starchy secretary to pose as his wife, and falls for her when she loosens up.

Amusing sophisticated comedy, generally well handled.

w I. A. L. Diamond play Abe Burrows, French original by Pierre Barillet, Jean Pierre Gredy d Gene Saks ph Charles E. Lang m Quincy Jones pd Robert Clatworthy

Ingrid Bergman, Walter Matthau, Goldie Hawn, Jack Weston, Rick Lenz, Vito Scotti, Irene Hervey

AA: Goldie Hawn

Cactus in the Snow: see *You Can't Have Everything*

Cactus Jack: see *The Villain*

Cadaveri Eccellenti: see *Illustrious Corpses*

Caddie *
Australia 1976 106m Eastmancolor
Roadshow/Anthony Buckley
V*

A deceived wife takes off with her two children and becomes a barmaid.

Desultory account of aimless low life to which Caddie brings a spark of sunshine. Watchable but forgettable.

w Joan Long, from the autobiography by 'Caddie' d Donald Crombie ph Peter James m Peter Flynn

Helen Morse, Takis Emmanuel, Kirrily Nolan, Jacki Weaver, Jack Thompson

The Caddy
US 1953 95m bw
Paramount (Paul Jones)
V*

A music hall comedy act recall how they got together.

Less a feature than a series of short sketches, this ragbag has its choice moments, but they are few.

w Edmund Hartmann, Danny Arnold d Norman Taurog ph Daniel L. Fapp m Joseph L. Lilley

Dean Martin, Jerry Lewis, Donna Reed, Barbara Bates, Joseph Calleia, Fred Clark, Clinton Sundberg, Marshall Thompson

AAN: song 'That's Amore' (*m* Harry Warren, *ly* Jack Brooks)

Caddyshack
US 1980 98m Technicolor
Warner/Orion (Douglas Kenney)
V, V*, L, S

Misadventures at a golf club.

A relentlessly crude and lumbering series of farcical incidents which mainly fail to raise laughs.

w Brian Doyle-Murray, Harold Ramis, Douglas Kenney d Harold Ramis ph Stevan Larner m Johnny Mandel pd Stan Jolley ed William Carruth

Chevy Chase, Rodney Dangerfield, Ted Knight, Michael O'Keefe

'There are jests about vomiting and nose-picking, while the most elaborate gag sequence involves a chocolate bar falling into a swimming pool and being mistaken for a turd . . . a sustained exercise in tiresomeness.' – *Tim Pulleine, MFB*

Caddyshack II
US 1988 99m colour
Warner (Neil Canton, Jon Peters, Peter Guber)
V*, L, S

A self-made millionaire is persuaded by his upwardly mobile daughter to apply for membership of an exclusive golf club.

Dim sequel that reprises the central situation of the original without even managing its crude humour; this one is just crude.

w Harold Ramis, Peter Torokvei d Allan Arkush ph Harry Stradling Jnr m Ira Newborn pd Bill Matthews ed Bernard Gribble

Jackie Mason, Robert Stack, Dina Merrill, Dyan Cannon, Jonathan Silverman, Randy Quaid, Chevy Chase, Dan Aykroyd

Cadillac Man
US 1990 97m colour
Rank/Orion (Charles Roven, Roger Donaldson)
V, V*, L

A car salesman is held hostage by a jealous husband.

Frenetic farce that is rarely funny.

w Ken Friedman d Roger Donaldson ph David Gribble m J. Peter Robinson pd Gene Rudolf ed Richard Francis-Bruce

Robin Williams, Tim Robbins, Pamela Reed, Fran Drescher, Zack Norman, Annabella Sciorra, Lori Petty, Paul Guilfoyle, Bill Nelson, Eddie Jones

'A rarity among recent films – a comedy that is in touch with a recognizable reality.' – *Richard Schickel, Time*

'Days of magnificent adventure . . . nights of maddest revelry . . . a temptation in Technicolor!'

Caesar and Cleopatra **
GB 1945 135m Technicolor
Rank/Gabriel Pascal
V*

An elaborate screen treatment of Bernard Shaw's comedy about Caesar's years in Alexandria.

Britain's most expensive film is an absurd extravaganza for which the producer actually took sand to Egypt to get the right colour. It has compensations however in the sets, the colour, the performances and the witty lines, though all its virtues are theatrical rather than cinematic and the play is certainly not a major work.

w Bernard Shaw d Gabriel Pascal ph F. A. Young, Robert Krasker, Jack Hildyard, Jack Cardiff m Georges Auric decor/costumes Oliver Messel sets John Bryan

Claude Rains, Vivien Leigh, Cecil Parker, Stewart Granger, Flora Robson, Francis L. Sullivan, Raymond Lovell, Anthony Harvey, Anthony Eustrel, Basil Sydney, Ernest Thesiger, Stanley Holloway, Leo Genn, Jean Simmons, Esmé Percy, Michael Rennie

'It cost over a million and a quarter pounds, took two and a half years to make, and well and truly bored one spectator for two and a quarter hours.' – *Richard Winnington*

'It is so wonderful as to make my other films look naive.' – *Bernard Shaw*

'When Rains played a small part he sometimes gave the impression that he was carrying the movie, but here his impish grin and his equanimity aren't enough.' – *Pauline Kael, 70s*

AAN: John Bryan

Café Colette
GB 1936 73m bw
Garrick (W. Devenport Hackney)
US title: *Danger in Paris*

A diplomat in charge of a secret formula falls for a Russian princess.

Old-hat spy melodrama, quite neatly staged.

w Eric Maschwitz, Val Gielgud, Walford Hyden
d Paul L. Stein ph Ronald Neame m George
Posford, Walford Hyden

Paul Cavanagh, Greta Nissen, Sally Gray, Bruce
Seton, Donald Calthrop, Dino Galvani

Café Metropole
US 1937 83m bw
TCF (Nunnally Johnson)

An heiress in Paris romances a Russian nobleman
who is actually a penniless American.

Lighter-than-air romance which passed the time at the
time.

w Jacques Duval d Edward H. Griffith ph Lucien
Andriot md Louis Silvers

Loretta Young, Adolphe Menjou, Tyrone Power,
Charles Winninger, Gregory Ratoff, Christian Rub,
Helen Westley

'It's smart, sophisticated (not too much so), has the
proper romantic ingredients, and will pull 'em in
almost anywhere.' – Variety

'Here is a very amusing script, admirable acting . . . all
thrown away by inferior direction. The camera is
planked down four-square before the characters like a
plain, honest, inexpressibly dull guest at a light and
loony party.' – Graham Greene

Café of Seven Sinners: see Seven Sinners

Café Society
US 1939 84m bw
Paramount

A publicity-seeking socialite impulsively marries a
reporter who has annoyed her, but instead of making
a fool of him she falls in love.

Faded light comedy which was never outstanding.

w Virginia Van Upp d Edward H. Griffith ph Ted
Tetzlaff

Madeleine Carroll, Fred MacMurray, Shirley Ross,
Claude Gillingwater

'Good cast will carry it nicely into okay if not wow
business.' – Variety

La Cage aux Folles *
France/Italy 1978 91m Eastmancolor
UA/PAA/Da Ma (Marcello Danon)
V, V*, L
aka: Birds of a Feather

A homosexual night-club owner is persuaded by his
straight son to behave properly in front of his
girlfriend's parents, but chaos comes on the night of
the party.

Internationally popular near-the-knuckle farce with
excellent moments and some longueurs.

w Francis Veber, Edouard Molinaro, Marcello Danon,
Jean Poiret play Jean Poiret d Edouard Molinaro
ph Armando Nannuzzi m Ennio Morricone

Ugo Tognazzi, Michel Serrault, Michel Galabru, Claire
Maurier, Remi Laurent

AAN: Edouard Molinaro (as director); script

La Cage aux Folles II
France/Italy 1980 99m Technicolor
UA/PAA/Da Ma (Marcello Danon)
V*, L

An ageing homosexual tells his partner he is too old
to be an effective female impersonator. Trying to
prove the opposite, the partner becomes involved in a
spy search for hidden microfilm.

Rather dimwitted sequel to a comedy which though
deliberately 'naughty' showed some restraint; here,
all is noise and excess.

w Jean Poiret, Francis Veber, Marcello Danon
d Edouard Molinaro ph Armando Nannuzzi
m Ennio Morricone

Ugo Tognazzi, Michel Serrault, Marcel Bozzuffi, Paola
Borboni

'The juxtaposition of campy histrionics with the
dreariest kind of espionage comedy offers quickly
diminishing returns.' – Gilbert Adair, MFB

La Cage aux Folles III
France/Italy 1985 87m Eastmancolor
Da Ma/Columbia (Marcello Danon)
V*, L

In order to inherit a fortune, Albin must marry and
produce an heir.

Yawnworthy attempt to milk more gags out of a
formula which exhausted itself with number one.

w Philippe Nicaud, Christine Carere, Marcello
Danon, Jacques Audiard, Michel Audiard, Georges
Lautner, Gerald Lamballe d Georges Lautner
ph Luciano Tavoli m Ennio Morricone pd Mario
Garbuglia ed Michelle David, Elisabeth Guido,
Lidia Pascolini

Ugo Tognazzi, Michel Serrault, Michel Galabru,
Antonella Interlenghi

'Lots of cooks but not much broth.' – Variety

La Cage aux Rossignols *
France 1947 88m bw
Gaumont
GB title: A Cage of Nightingales

A reform school teacher fires difficult pupils with new
hope.

Low-key star vehicle with moderately pleasing
results.

w Noel-Noel, René Wheeler d Jean Dreville

Noel-Noel, Micheline Francey, Georges Biscot, René
Blancard

AAN: Georges Chaperot, René Wheeler (original
story)

Cage of Doom: see Terror from the Year 5000

Cage of Gold *
GB 1950 83m bw
Ealing (Michael Relph)

A girl's philandering ex-husband comes back into her
life and is murdered.

Mild mystery melodrama in which the puzzle comes
too late.

w Jack Whittingham d Basil Dearden
ph Douglas Slocombe m Georges Auric

Jean Simmons, David Farrar, James Donald,
Madeleine Lebeau, Maria Mauban, Herbert Lom,
Bernard Lee, Gladys Henson, Harcourt Williams,
Grégoire Aslan

A Cage of Nightingales: see La Cage aux
Rossignols

'Will she come out woman or wildcat?'
Caged *
US 1950 96m bw
Warner (Jerry Wald)

After being involved in a robbery a 19-year-old girl is
sent to prison, and finds the staff more terrifying than
the inmates.

Slick, superficial, hysterically harrowing women-in-
prison melodrama; predictably overblown but also
effective and powerful.

w Virginia Kellogg, Bernard Schoenfeld d John
Cromwell ph Carl Guthrie m Max Steiner

Eleanor Parker, Agnes Moorehead, Ellen Corby, Hope
Emerson, Betty Garde, Jan Sterling, Lee Patrick, Olive
Deering, Jane Darwell, Gertrude Michael, Joan Miller

† Remade in 1962 as House of Women, directed by
Walter Doniger, with Shirley Knight.

AAN: Virginia Kellogg, Bernard Schoenfeld; Eleanor
Parker; Hope Emerson

Caged Heat *
US 1974 83m DeLuxe
Target/Artists Entertainment Complex/Renegade Women
   (Samuel Gelfman)
V*

A new convict is horrified by the way a crippled
governess runs a women's prison.

Quirky, individual, anti-authoritarian take on the
standard ingredients of an exploitation picture set
among female prisoners.

wd Jonathan Demme ph Tak Fujimoto m John
Cale ad Eric Thierman ed Johanna Demetrakis,
Carolyn Hicks

Juanita Brown, Roberta Collina, Erica Gavin, Ella
Reid, Lynda Gold, Warren Miller, Barbara Steele,
Toby Carr

'A distinctly exceptional exploitation movie.' – Tony
Rayns, MFB

† The British release was cut to 79m.

'Break the law and he's the last man you'll want to see.
   And the last man you ever will!'
Cahill, US Marshal
US 1973 103m Technicolor Panavision
Warner/Batjac (Michael A. Wayne)
V, V*, L

A stalwart Western marshal finds that his own young
sons are involved in a robbery he is investigating.

Satisfactory but sentimental John Wayne vehicle with
the star too often yielding place to the rather boring
young folk.

w Harry Julian Fink, Rita M. Fink d Andrew V.
McLaglen ph Joseph Biroc m Elmer Bernstein

John Wayne, George Kennedy, Gary Grimes, Neville
Brand, Clay O'Brien, Marie Windsor, Royal Dano,
Denver Pyle, Jackie Coogan

La Caida: see The Fall

'It's unlike any musical you've ever seen before – Timed to
   the Tantalizing Tempo of Today!'
Cain and Mabel *
US 1936 90m bw
Warner (Sam Bischoff)

Tribulations of a prizefighter in love with a showgirl.

Generously produced but weakly written comedy
drama with rather unexpected musical numbers; not a
successful whole, but interesting.

w Laird Doyle, H. C. Witwer d Lloyd Bacon
ph George Barnes m/ly Harry Warren, Al Dubin
ch Bobby Connolly

Clark Gable, Marion Davies, Allen Jenkins, Roscoe
Karns, Walter Catlett, Hobart Cavanaugh, Pert Kelton,
Ruth Donnelly, E. E. Clive

AAN: Bobby Connolly

'As big as the ocean!'
The Caine Mutiny **
US 1954 125m Technicolor
Columbia/Stanley Kramer
V, V*, L

Jealousies and frustrations among the officers of a
peacetime destroyer come to a head when the neurotic
captain panics during a typhoon and is relieved of his
post. At the resulting trial the officers learn about
themselves.

Decent if lamely paced version of a bestseller which
also made a successful play; the film skates too lightly
over the characterizations and even skimps the
courtroom scene, but there are effective scenes and
performances.

w Stanley Roberts   *novel* Herman Wouk
d Edward Dmytryk   *ph* Franz Planer   *m* Max
Steiner   *ed* William A. Lyon, Henry Batista

Humphrey Bogart (Captain Queeg), José Ferrer (Lt
Barney Greenwald), Van Johnson (Lt Steve Maryk),
Fred MacMurray (Lt Tom Keefer), Robert Francis
(Ensign Willie Keith), May Wynn (May), Tom Tully
(Captain DeVriess), E. G. Marshall (Lt Cdr Challee),
Lee Marvin (Meatball), Claude Akins (Horrible)

QUEEG: 'There are four ways of doing things on
board my ship. The right way, the wrong way, the
navy way, and my way. If they do things my way,
we'll get along.'
QUEEG: 'Ah, but the strawberries! That's where I
had them. They laughed and made jokes, but I proved
beyond the shadow of a doubt, and with geometric
logic, that a duplicate key to the wardroom icebox did
exist. And I'd have produced that key if they hadn't
pulled the *Caine* out of action. I know now they were
out to protect some fellow officer.'
KEEFER: 'There is no escape from the *Caine*, save
death. We're all doing penance, sentenced to an
outcast ship, manned by outcasts, and named after the
greatest outcast of them all.'

AAN: best picture; Stanley Roberts; Max Steiner;
Humphrey Bogart; Tom Tully; editing

Cairo *
US   1942   100m   bw
MGM (Joseph L. Mankiewicz)

An American war reporter in Egypt meets a screen
star and thinks she is a spy.

Mildly pleasing light comedy-drama with self-
spoofing elements.

w John McClain   *d* W. S. Van Dyke II   *ph* Ray
June   *md* Herbert Stothart

Jeanette MacDonald, Robert Young, Ethel Waters,
Reginald Owen, Lionel Atwill, Mona Barrie, Eduardo
Ciannelli, Dennis Hoey, Dooley Wilson

'Confusing if not amusing.' – *Variety*

Cairo
GB   1963   91m   bw
MGM (Ronald Kinnoch)
V*

Crooks plan to steal Tutankhamun's jewels from the
Cairo Museum.

Spiritless remake of *The Asphalt Jungle* (qv).

w Joanne Court   *d* Wolf Rilla   *ph* Desmond
Dickinson   *m* Kenneth V. Jones

George Sanders, Richard Johnson, Faten Hamama,
John Meillon, Eric Pohlmann, Walter Rilla

Cairo Road
GB   1950   95m   bw
ABP (Aubrey Baring)

An Egyptian police chief lays traps for drug
smugglers.

Oddly cast, reasonably lively but routine police
adventure in an unfamiliar setting.

w Robert Westerby   *d* David MacDonald
ph Oswald Morris   *m* Robert Gill

Eric Portman, Laurence Harvey, Maria Mauban, Karel
Stepanek, Harold Lang, Camelia, Grégoire Aslan,
Oscar Quitak

Cairo Station
Egypt   1958   95m   bw
Gabriel Talhami
original title: *Bab El Hadid*

A crippled newspaper seller goes mad through
thwarted love.

Popular melodrama, acted with verve.

d Youssef Chahine   *ph* Alvise   *m* Fouad El Zahiry
ad Gabriel Karraze   *ed* Kamal Abul Ela

Farid Chawki, Hind Rostom, Youssef Chahine, Safia
Sarwat, Assaad Kellam, Sherine

Cal *
GB   1984   102m   colour
Warner/Goldcrest/Enigma (Stuart Craig, David Puttnam)
V, V*, S

A young Catholic in Ulster falls for the widow of the
policeman in whose murder he has been an
accomplice.

More clichés about the troubles: the film belies its
publicity as 'a love story which happens to take place
in Northern Ireland'. But it has style.

w Bernard MacLaverty   *novel* Bernard MacLaverty
d Pat O'Connor   *ph* Jerzy Zielinski   *m* Mark
Knopfler   *pd* Stuart Craig

Helen Mirren, John Lynch, Donal McCann, John
Kavanagh, Ray McAnally

Calabuch *
Spain/Italy   1956   93m   bw
Aguila/Constellaxione (José Luis Jerez)

An atomic scientist settles delightedly in a peaceful
Spanish village, but sacrifices his own privacy when
he invents a sky rocket.

Semi-satirical Ealing-type comedy which starts
engagingly but runs out of steam.

w Leonardo Martin, Ennio Flaiano, Florentino Soria,
Luis Berlanga   *d* Luis Berlanga   *ph* Francisco
Sempere   *m* Francesco Lavagnino

Edmund Gwenn, Valentina Cortese, Franco Fabrizi

Calamity Jane **
US   1953   101m   Technicolor
Warner (William Jacobs)
V, V*, L

Calamity helps a saloon owner friend find a star
attraction, and wins the heart of Wild Bill Hickok.

Agreeable, cleaned-up, studio-set Western musical
patterned after *Annie Get Your Gun*, but a much
friendlier film, helped by an excellent score.

w James O'Hanlon   *d* David Butler   *ph* Wilfrid
Cline   *md* Ray Heindorf   *ch* Jack Donohue
m/ly Sammy Fain, Paul Francis Webster

Doris Day, Howard Keel, Allyn McLerie, Phil Carey,
Dick Wesson, Paul Harvey

AA: song 'Secret Love'

AAN: Ray Heindorf

Calamity Jane and Sam Bass
US   1949   85m   Technicolor
Universal-International

Sam Bass murders the man who poisoned his horse,
becomes an outlaw, and tangles with Jane Carraway.

Routine Western programmer from this stable.

w Maurice Geraghty, Melvin Levy   *d* George
Sherman

Yvonne de Carlo, Howard Duff, Dorothy Hart, Willard
Parker, Houseley Stevenson, Ann Doran, Norman
Lloyd

Calcutta
US   1946   83m   bw
Paramount (Seton I. Miller)

Two flyers seek the murderer of their friend in the
hotels and bazaars of Calcutta.

Studio-bound action potboiler, simple-minded but
quite good fun.

w Seton I. Miller   *d* John Farrow   *ph* John F. Seitz
m Victor Young

Alan Ladd, Gail Russell, William Bendix, June
Duprez, Lowell Gilmore

The Calendar
GB   1948   80m   bw
Gainsborough

A girl trainer helps an owner to prove he didn't
nobble his horse.

Very average racecourse melodrama.

w Geoffrey Kerr   *novel* Edgar Wallace   *d* Arthur
Crabtree

Greta Gynt, John McCallum, Leslie Dwyer, Raymond
Lovell, Charles Victor, Barry Jones

† It was previously filmed in 1932 with Herbert
Marshall and Edna Best.

Calendar Girl
US   1947   88m   bw
Republic

In New York at the turn of the century, young
boarding-house residents hope for fame and fortune.

Dim, uncertain musical with fair talents.

w Mary Loos, Richard Sale, Lee Loeb   *d* Allan
Dwan

Jane Frazee, William Marshall, Gail Patrick, Kenny
Baker, Victor McLaglen, Irene Rich, James Ellison,
Franklin Pangborn, Gus Schilling

'No town would have her! No man could tame her!'
California
US   1946   97m   Technicolor
Paramount (Seton I. Miller)

An army deserter joins the 1848 California gold rush.

Standard glamorized star Western; not bad if you
accept the conventions.

w Frank Butler, Theodore Strauss   *d* John Farrow
ph Ray Rennahan   *m* Victor Young

Ray Milland, Barbara Stanwyck, Barry Fitzgerald,
Albert Dekker, George Coulouris, Anthony Quinn

'It quickly loses its stirrups and ends up caught by the
chaps in a bed of cactus.' – *Newsweek*

California Conquest
US   1952   79m   Technicolor
Columbia (Sam Katzman)

Spanish Californians band together against Russian
would-be invaders.

Tedious and unsympathetic historical Western on a
'B' budget.

w Robert E. Kent   *d* Lew Landers

Cornel Wilde, Teresa Wright, Alfonso Bedoya, Lisa
Ferraday, Ivan Lebedeff, John Dehner

The California Dolls: see *All the Marbles*

California Holiday: see *Spinout*

California Split *
US   1974   109m   Metrocolor   Panavision
Columbia/Persky-Bright/Reno (Robert Altman, Joseph Walsh)

Two cheerful gamblers get drunk, laid, cheated and
happy.

Sporadically entertaining character comedy sunk in a
sea of chatter.

w Joseph Walsh   *d* Robert Altman   *ph* Paul
Lohmann   *m* Phyllis Shotwell

Elliott Gould, George Segal, Gwen Welles, Ann
Prentiss, Joseph Walsh

'The film seems to be being improvised . . . we catch
at events and personalities by the ends of threads.' –
New Yorker

† An end title reads: FOR BARBARA, 1933–1973.
This was Barbara Ruick, who played the barmaid and
died on location.

California Straight Ahead *

US   1937   57m   bw
Universal (Trem Carr)

A nationwide race is held between a special train and a convoy of high-powered trucks.

Unusual and quite lively second feature shot on location.

w Scott Darling   story Herman Boxer   d Arthur Lubin   ph Harry Neumann   m Charles Previn

John Wayne, Louise Latimer, Robert McWade, Tully Marshall

'Everything happens as the audience expects and wishes, so in its field it will do okay.' – *Variety*

California Suite *

US   1978   103m   colour
Columbia/Ray Stark
V, V*, L

Misadventures of four groups of guests at the Beverly Hills Hotel.

Two hits, two misses; closer intercutting might have helped. No doubt that Maggie Smith and Michael Caine come off best, with bitcheries about the Academy Awards.

w Neil Simon   play Neil Simon   d Herbert Ross   ph David M. Walsh   m Claude Bolling   pd Albert Brenner

Michael Caine, Maggie Smith, Walter Matthau, Elaine May, Alan Alda, Jane Fonda, Richard Pryor, Bill Cosby

'By turns silly and thoughtful, tedious and charming, broad and delicate.' – *Frank Rich*

AA: Maggie Smith

AAN: Neil Simon; art direction

'What would you have done if you had been given absolute power of life and death over everyone else in the whole wide world?'

Caligula

Italy/US   1979   150m   Eastmancolor
GTO/Felix/Penthouse Films (Bob Guccione, Franco Rossellini)
V, V*, L

The violent life and times of a decadent Roman emperor.

What would have been a dull and worthless pseudo-epic has been perked up by violence and hardcore sex. The result is a vile curiosity of interest chiefly to sado-masochists.

w Bob Guccione   screenplay Gore Vidal   d Tinto Brass, Giancarlo Lui, Bob Guccione   ph Silvano Ippoliti   ph Danilo Donati   m Paul Clemente   ed Nino Bragli

Malcolm McDowell, John Gielgud, Peter O'Toole, Helen Mirren, Teresa Ann Savoy, John Steiner

'An anthology of sexual aberrations in which incest is the only face-saving relationship . . . far more Gore than Vidal.' – *Variety*

'It just keeps rolling along at inordinate length, suggesting de Mille grinding slowly to a frequent stoppage for a display of bums, breasts and pubic hair.' – *Time Out*

Call a Messenger

US   1939   65m   bw
Universal

Working as telegraph messengers, the Little Tough Guys prevent a hold-up.

Second-feature offshoot of the Dead End Kids, some of whom had now departed to become the East Side Kids (who later blossomed forth as the Bowery Boys).

w Arthur T. Horman   d Arthur Lubin

Billy Halop, Huntz Hall, Billy Benedict, David Gorcey, Robert Armstrong, Mary Carlisle, Anne Nagel, Victor Jory, El Brendel, Larry 'Buster' Crabbe

'A rowdy, gripping production patterned as heavy bolstering in dual set-ups.' – *Variety*

Call Harry Crown: see *99 and 44 á100 Per Cent Dead*

Call Her Savage

US   1932   88m   bw
Paramount (Sam E. Rork)

Trials and tribulations of a half-breed Indian girl who marries a cad and later takes to the streets.

Rough and ready melodrama for female audiences; the penultimate appearance of a star who did not take to talkies.

w Edwin Burke   novel Tiffany Thayer   d John Francis Dillon   ph Lee Garmes

Clara Bow, Gilbert Roland, Monroe Owsley, Thelma Todd, Estelle Taylor

'The return of Clara Bow in a madcap role makes a natural . . . the result is bound to be money.' – *Variety*

Call Him Mr Shatter: see *Shatter*

Call Him Savage

France/Italy   1975   103m   colour
Lira/Produzioni Artistiche Internazionali (Raymond Danon)
aka: *Lovers Like Us*

A French parfumier, trying to escape from his business, meets a woman on the run from her Venezuelan fiancé.

Dim attempt at a romantic comedy.

w Jean-Paul Rappeneau, Elisabeth Rappeneau, Jean-Loup Dabadie   d Jean-Paul Rappeneau   ph Pierre Lhomme   m Michel Legrand   ed Marie-Joseph Yoyotte

Yves Montand, Catherine Deneuve, Tony Roberts, Luigi Vannucchi, Dana Wynter

Call It a Day *

US   1937   89m   bw
Warner (Henry Blanke)

An upper-class British family has problems during a single day.

Surprising, and not very effective, Hollywood treatment of a very British comedy.

w Casey Robinson   play Dodie Smith   d Archie Mayo   ph Ernest Haller

Olivia de Havilland, Ian Hunter, Anita Louise, Alice Brady, Roland Young, Frieda Inescort, Bonita Granville, Peggy Wood, Walter Woolf King, Una O'Connor, Beryl Mercer

'A fine cast rowing a very thin boat . . . charm, many a giggle but nary a sock laugh.' – *Variety*

Call It Murder: see *Midnight*

Call Me Bwana *

GB   1962   93m   Eastmancolor
Rank/Eon (Harry Saltzman, Albert R. Broccoli)

A fake African explorer is sent to the jungle to recover a space capsule.

Moderate star farce with occasional bright moments.

w Nate Monaster, Johanna Harwood   d Gordon Douglas   ph Ted Moore   m Monty Norman

Bob Hope, Anita Ekberg, Edie Adams, Lionel Jeffries, Percy Herbert, Paul Carpenter, Orlando Martins

Call Me Genius: see *The Rebel*

Call Me Madam ***

US   1953   114m   Technicolor
TCF (Sol C. Siegel)

A Washington hostess is appointed Ambassador to Lichtenberg and marries the foreign minister.

Studio-bound but thoroughly lively transcription of Irving Berlin's last big success, with most of the performers at their peak and some topical gags which may now be mystifying.

w Arthur Sheekman   play Howard Lindsay, Russel Crouse   d Walter Lang   ch Robert Alton   ph Leon Shamroy   md Alfred Newman   m/y Irving Berlin

Ethel Merman, Donald O'Connor, George Sanders, Vera-Ellen, Billy de Wolfe, Humint Dantine, Walter Slezak, Steve Geray, Ludwig Stossel

'Good-tempered, warm, generous and about as quiet as a massed brass band festival.' – *Dilys Powell*

AA: Alfred Newman

Call Me Mister

US   1951   95m   Technicolor
TCF (Fred Kohlmar)

A husband-and-wife dance team entertain the troops in Japan and after the war.

Passable musical of a very predictable kind.

w Albert E. Lewin, Burt Styler   d Lloyd Bacon   ph Arthur E. Arling   m Leigh Harline   ch Busby Berkeley   original show credits: m Harold Rome   book Arnold Auerbach, Arnold B. Horwitt   m/y various

Betty Grable, Dan Dailey, Danny Thomas, Dale Robertson, Richard Boone

Call Northside 777 **

US   1948   111m   bw
TCF (Otto Lang)

A Chicago reporter helps a washerwoman prove her son not guilty of murdering a policeman.

Overlong semi-documentary crime thriller based on a real case. Acting and detail excellent, but the sharp edge of *Boomerang* is missing.

w Jerome Cady, Jay Dratler   d Henry Hathaway   ph Joe MacDonald   m Alfred Newman

James Stewart, Lee J. Cobb, Helen Walker, *Kasia Orzazewski*, Betty Garde, Richard Conte

'A most satisfying thriller, generously streaked with class.' – *Daily Mail*

'Absorbing, exciting, realistic.' – *Star*

Call of the Blood

GB   1947   88m   bw
Pendennis

A Sicilian fisherman takes revenge on his daughter's seducer.

Antediluvian melodrama with stiff-upper-lip English looking on.

w John Clements, Akos Tolnay, Basil Mason   novel Robert Hichens   d John Clements, Ladislas Vajda

John Clements, Kay Hammond, John Justin, Lea Padovani, Robert Rietti

Call of the Flesh

US   1930   100m   bw/colour sequence
MGM

A convent girl falls for a man of the world.

Would-be tempestuous melodrama which fails through lack of pace.

w Dorothy Farnum, John Colton   d Charles Brabin

Ramon Novarro, Dorothy Jordan, Ernest Torrence, Nance O'Neil, Renee Adoree

'Money picture, but can stand a lot of cutting.' – *Variety*

The Call of the Savage

US   1935   bw   serial: 13 eps
Universal

A scientist's baby son survives a disaster in Africa and

grows up with chimpanzees. Or, how to play Tarzan without paying royalties.

Fair serial hokum about the wiles of a wicked prince.

d Louis Friedlander

Noah Beery Jnr, Dorothy Short, H. L. Woods, Bryant Washburn

Call of the Wild *
US   1935   81m   bw
Twentieth Century (Darryl F. Zanuck)

A young widow falls in love with a wild Yukon prospector.

Inaccurate but pleasing adaptation of an adventure novel with dog interest.

w Gene Fowler, Leonard Praskins   *novel* Jack London   *d* William Wellman   *ph* Charles Rosher   *m* Alfred Newman

Clark Gable, Loretta Young, Jack Oakie, Reginald Owen, Frank Conroy

'The lion-hearted dog emerges as a stooge for a rather conventional pair of human lovebirds . . . looks like box office.' – *Variety*

Call of the Wild
GB/W. Germany/Spain/Italy/France   1972   105m
Eastmancolor
Massfilms/CCC/Izaro/Oceania/UPF (Harry Alan Towers)
V*

During the Klondike gold rush, a stolen dog becomes a miner's best friend before joining the wolf-pack.

Closer to the book than the previous version, but curiously scrappy and unsatisfactory.

w Harry Alan Towers, Wyn Wells, Peter Yeldhan   *d* Ken Annakin   *ph* John Cabrera, Dudley Lovell   *m* Carlo Rustichelli

Charlton Heston, Michèle Mercier, Raimund Harmstorf, George Eastman

Call Out the Marines *
US   1942   67m   bw
RKO
V*

Two adventurers re-enlist in the Marines and foil a spy plot.

The last of many action comedies featuring the original Flagg and Quirt from *What Price Glory?*
wd Frank Ryan, William Hamilton

Victor McLaglen, Edmund Lowe, Binnie Barnes, Paul Kelly, Franklin Pangborn

Callan *
GB   1974   106m   Eastmancolor
EMI/Magnum (Derek Horne)
V*
aka: *The Neutralizer*

A former secret agent is seconded to a government section devoted to the elimination of undesirables.

Expanded rewrite of the first episode of a long-running TV series, quite fresh and vivid in the circumstances, especially as it comes at the tail end of ten years of similar bouts of blood and thunder.

w James Mitchell   *novel A Magnum for Schneider* by James Mitchell   *d* Don Sharp   *ph* Ernest Steward   *m* Wilfred Josephs

Edward Woodward, Eric Porter, Carl Mohner, Catherine Schell, Peter Egan, Russell Hunter, Kenneth Griffith

Callaway Went Thataway *
US   1951   81m   bw
MGM (Melvin Frank, Norman Panama)
GB title: *The Star Said No*

The old movies of a Hollywood cowboy become popular on TV, but the star has become a hopeless drunk and an actor is hired to pose as him for public appearances.

Reasonably engaging comedy using charm rather than acid.

wd Melvin Frank, Norman Panama   *ph* Ray June   *m* Marlin Skiles

Dorothy McGuire, Fred MacMurray, Howard Keel, Jesse White, Natalie Schafer

Calle Mayor *
Spain/France   1956   95m   bw
Play Art Iberia/Cesareo Gonzales
aka: *Grande Rue*

In a small Spanish town, a young stud pretends for a bet to be in love with a plain spinster.

Interesting but rather unattractive and certainly unconvincing little comedy-drama, rather too obviously styled for its American star after her success in *Marty*.

wd Juan Antonio Bardem   *ph* Michel Kelber   *m* Joseph Kosma

Betsy Blair, Yves Massard, René Blancard, Lila Kedrova

Calling Bulldog Drummond
GB   1951   80m   bw
MGM (Hayes Goetz)

Drummond goes undercover to catch a gang of thieves.

Minor-league quota quickie addition to the exploits of a long-running character (see *Bulldog Drummond*).

w Howard Emmett Rogers, Gerard Fairlie, Arthur Wimperis   *d* Victor Saville   *ph* F. A. Young   *m* Rudolph Kopp

Walter Pidgeon, Margaret Leighton, Robert Beatty, David Tomlinson, Peggy Evans, Charles Victor, Bernard Lee, James Hayter

'Terror strikes as a madman rules!'
Calling Doctor Death
US   1943   63m   bw
Universal

A doctor's wife is murdered; her lover is arrested; but did the doctor himself do it?

Probably not, as the tendency of the tinpot *Inner Sanctum* series, of which this was the first, was to make its star look anguished for six reels and then show him to be as innocent as the film was (mercifully) short.

w Edward Dein   *d* Reginald Le Borg

Lon Chaney, Patricia Morison, Fay Helm, David Bruce, Ramsay Ames, J. Carrol Naish

Calling Dr Gillespie *
US   1942   84m   bw
MGM

A deranged ex-patient breaks into Blair Hospital for the purpose of killing Dr Gillespie.

The point at which cranky old wheelchair-bound Dr Gillespie took over the Kildare series, its star (Lew Ayres) having effectually abdicated from acting by declaring himself a conscientious objector. Production values up to par.

w Kubec Glasmon, Willis Goldbeck, Harry Ruskin   *d* Harold S. Bucquet

Lionel Barrymore, Philip Dorn, Phil Brown, Donna Reed, Nat Pendleton, Mary Nash, Alma Kruger, Walter Kingsford

† See *Dr Kildare* for titles in series.

Calling Dr Kildare *
US   1939   86m   bw
MGM

Kildare becomes innocently involved in murder and needs Dr Gillespie's help.

The second in the Kildare series had the confidence that comes of box-office approval.

w Harry Ruskin, Willis Goldbeck   *d* Harold S. Bucquet

Lew Ayres, Lionel Barrymore, Lana Turner, Nat Pendleton, Samuel S. Hinds, Laraine Day, Alma Kruger

Calling Philo Vance
US   1939   62m   bw
Warner

A manufacturer is murdered and foreign agents are discovered among his servants.

Essentially a remake of *The Kennel Murder Case;* inferior as a whole, but with an excellent new Vance.

w Tom Reed   *d* William Clemens

James Stephenson, Margot Stevenson, Henry O'Neill, Ed Brophy, Ralph Forbes, Martin Kosleck

Calm Yourself
US   1935   70m   bw
MGM

An advertising man helps solve a kidnapping.

Spoofy comedy-drama which simply doesn't work.

w Edward Hope, Arthur Kober   *d* George B. Seitz

Robert Young, Madge Evans, Betty Furness, Nat Pendleton, Hardie Albright, Ralph Morgan

'Strictly for the not too particular nabe clientele.' – *Variety*

Caluga o Menta
Chile   1991   90m   colour
Arca/TVE/Filmocentro (Patricia Navarrete)
aka: *Candy or Mint*

In Santiago, a gang of disaffected youngsters turn to crime and drug-running to relieve the everyday monotony of their lives.

A downbeat study of no-hopers, filmed with a partly non-professional cast, which is mainly of sociological interest.

w Gonzalo Justiniano, Gustavo Frias, Jose Andres Peña   *d* Gonzalo Justiniano   *ph* Gaston Roca   *m* Jaime de Aguirre   *ed* Claudio Martinez

Mauricio Vega, Patricia Rivadeneira, Aldo Parodi, Myriam Palacios

Camelot **
US   1967   181m   Technicolor   Panavision 70
Warner (Jack L. Warner)
V, V*, L, S

King Arthur marries Guinevere, loses her to Lancelot, and is forced into war.

A film version of a long-running Broadway show with many excellent moments. Unfortunately the director cannot make up his mind whether to go for style or realism, and has chosen actors who cannot sing. The result is cluttered and overlong, with no real sense of period or sustained imagination, but the photography and the music linger in the mind.

w Alan Jay Lerner,   *novel The Once And Future King* by T. H. White   *d* Joshua Logan   *ph* Richard H. Kline   *pd/costumes* John Truscott   *md* Ken Darby, Alfred Newman   *m/ly* Frederick Loewe, Alan Jay Lerner   *ad* Edward Carrere

Richard Harris, Vanessa Redgrave, David Hemmings, Lionel Jeffries, Laurence Naismith, Franco Nero

'One wonders whether the fashion for musicals in which only the chorus can actually sing may be reaching its final stage.' – *MFB*

'Three hours of unrelieved glossiness, meticulous inanity, desperate and charmless striving for charm.' – *John Simon*

'The sets and costumes and people seem to be sitting there on the screen, waiting for the unifying magic that never happens.' – *New Yorker, 1977*

songs: 'The Merry Month of May'; 'Camelot'; 'If Ever I Would Leave You'; 'Take Me to the Fair'; 'C'est Moi'

AA: art direction; costumes; music direction

AAN: cinematography

The Camels are Coming
GB   1934   80m   bw
Gainsborough (Michael Balcon)

An officer in the camel corps catches Egyptian drug smugglers.

Light, bouncy star vehicle.

w Jack Hulbert, Guy Bolton, W. P. Lipscomb   d Tim Whelan   ph Glen MacWilliams, Bernard Knowles   md Louis Levy   m Ray Noble, Max Kester, Noel Gay   ad Oscar Werndorff   ed Frederick Y. Smith

Jack Hulbert, Anna Lee, Hartley Power, Harold Huth, Allan Jeayes

Camera Buff *
Poland   1979   112m   colour
Cinegate/Zespoly Filmowe/Film Polski
original title: Amator

A factory worker finds himself in conflict with his bosses when he becomes obsessed with making films at work.

Lively political allegory.

wd Krzysztof Kieslowski   ph Jacek Petrycki   m Krzysztof Knittel   ad Rafal Waltenberger   ed Halina Nawrocka

Jerzy Stuhr, Malgorzata Zabkowska, Ewa Pokas, Stefan Czyzewski, Jerzy Nowak, Tadeusz Bradecki, Krzysztof Zanussi

The Cameraman ***
US   1928   78m approx (24 fps)   bw   silent
MGM (Lawrence Weingarten)
V*, L

In order to woo a film star, a street photographer becomes a newsreel cameraman.

Highly regarded chapter of farcical errors, among the star's top features.

w Clyde Bruckman, Lex Lipton, Richard Schayer   d Edward Sedgwick   ph Elgin Lessley, Reggie Manning

Buster Keaton, Marceline Day, Harry Gribbon, Harold Goodwin

† The film was remade in 1948 for Red Skelton as Watch the Birdie, with Keaton sadly supervising the gags but getting no credit.

Cameron's Closet
US   1987   87m   colour
Medusa/Smart Egg (Luigi Cingolani)
V, V*, L

Subjected by his father to experiments in psychokinesis, a boy summons up a demon.

Ineffectual horror, with a boring monster.

w Gary Brandner   novel Gary Brandner   d Armand Mastroianni   ph Russell Carpenter   m Harry Manfredini   pd Michael Bingham   ed Frank de Palma

Cotter Smith, Mel Harris, Scott Curtis, Chuck McCann, Leigh McCloskey, Kim Lankford

'The contents of this particular closet are decidedly shop-worn and second-hand.' – MFB

Camila **
Argentina/Spain   1984   97m   colour
GEA Cinematografica/Impala (Lila Stanic)

In Argentina in the 1840s the strong-willed daughter of an upper-class family scandalizes Church and government by eloping with a priest.

A powerful drama that manages to say much about present-day repression despite its period setting.

w Maria Luisa Bemberg, Beda Docampo Feijoo, Juan Bautista Stagnaro   d Maria Luisa Bemberg

ph Fernando Arribas   m Luis Maria Serra   ad Miguel Rodriguez   ed Luis Cesar D'Angiolillo

Susu Pecoraro, Imanol Arias, Hector Alterio, Carlos Muñoz, Hector Pelligrini, Juan Levrado, Cecilio Madanes, Mona Maris, Elena Tasisto

'You who are so young – where can you have learned all you know about women like me?'
'Their lips meet for the first time . . . a superb thrill seared in your memory forever!'

Camille **
US   1937   108m   bw
MGM (Irving Thalberg, Bernard Hyman)
V*

A dying courtesan falls for an innocent young man who loves her, and dies in his arms.

This old warhorse is an unsuitable vehicle for Garbo but magically she carries it off, and the production is elegant and pleasing.

w Frances Marion, James Hilton, Zoe Akins   novel Alexandre Dumas   d George Cukor   ph William Daniels   m Herbert Stothart

Greta Garbo, Robert Taylor, Lionel Barrymore, Henry Daniell, Elizabeth Allan, Lenore Ulric, Laura Hope Crews, Rex O'Malley, Jessie Ralph, E. E. Clive

'Pretty close to the top mark in showmanship, direction, photography and box office names.' – Variety

'The slow, solemn production is luxuriant in its vulgarity: it achieves that glamor which MGM traditionally mistook for style.' – Pauline Kael, 1968

'The surprise is to find a story that should by rights be old hat coming to such insistent life on the screen.' – Otis Ferguson

'It steadily builds up an impression of being a spectacle of manners and fashions, a socially true background for its characters to move against.' – National Board of Review

'This is not death as mortals know it. This is but the conclusion of a romantic ritual.' – Bosley Crowther

† A 1927 silent version starred Norma Talmadge with Gilbert Roland.

AAN: Greta Garbo

Camille Claudel **
France   1988   174m   colour   Panavision
Cannon/Films Christian Fechner/Lilith Films/Gaumont/A2 TV France/Films A2/DD Productions (Bernard Artigues)
V, V*, L, S

A talented sculptress becomes Rodin's pupil and mistress with tragic results.

Overlong, and lacking a visual flair to match its subject, but nevertheless engrossing for the most part.

w Bruno Nuytten, Marilyn Goldin   book Reine-Marie Paris   d Bruno Nuytten   ph Pierre Lhomme   m Gabriel Yared   ad Bernard Vezat   ed Joëlle Hache, Jeanne Kef

Isabelle Adjani, Gérard Depardieu, Laurent Grevill, Alain Cuny, Philippe Clevenot, Katrine Boorman, Danielle Lebrun, Maxime Leroux

'As a cultural coffee-table artefact, it has everything.' – Tom Milne, MFB

AAN: Isabelle Adjani; best foreign film

El Camino del Sur: see Journey to the South

Il Cammino della Speranza *
Italy   1950   105m   bw
Lux (Luigi Rovere)
aka: The Road to Hope

Unemployed Sicilian miners travel to France in search of work.

Episodic location melodrama with a social conscience, a kind of Italian Grapes of Wrath. Very watchable, but not moving.

w Federico Fellini, Tullio Pinelli   d Pietro Germi   ph Leonido Barboni   m Carlo Rustichelli

Raf Vallone, Elena Varzi, Saro Urzi, Franco Navarra

Camorra: the Naples Connection
Italy   1985   106m   colour
Cannon/Italian International (Menahem Golan, Yoram Globus)
original title: Un complicato intrigo di donne, vicoli e delitto

Mothers take revenge on the drug dealers who have killed their children.

Highly charged, full of sound and fury and signifying very little.

w Lina Wertmuller, Elvio Porta   d Lina Wertmuller   ph Giuseppe Lanci   m Tony Esposito   ad Enrico Job   ed Luigi Zita

Angela Molina, Francisco Rabal, Harvey Keitel, Daniel Ezralow

Camp de Thiaroye **
Senegal/Algeria/Tunisia   1988   152m   colour
Metro/SNPC/ENAPROC/SATPEC (Mamadou Mbengue)

African soldiers, returning home after fighting in the Second World War, are massacred in a dispute over pay.

Powerful indictment of colonialism.

wd Ousmane Sembène, Thierno Faty Sow   ph Ismail Lakhdar Hamina   m Ismaila Lo   ad El hadj Abdoulaye Diouf   ed Kahena Attia-Riveill

Ibrahima Sane, Sigiri Bakara, Hamed Camara, Ismaila Cissé, Ababacar Sy Cissé

The Camp on Blood Island
GB   1958   81m   bw   MegaScope
Columbia/Hammer (Anthony Hinds)

The sadistic commandant of a Japanese POW camp swears to kill all the inmates. Japan surrenders, and a great effort is made to prevent the news from reaching him.

Dubious melodrama parading sadism and brutality as entertainment.

w Jon Manchip White, Val Guest   d Val Guest   ph Jack Asher   m Gerard Schurmann   ad John Stoll   ed James Needs, Bill Lenny

André Morell, Carl Mohner, Edward Underdown, Michael Goodliffe, Ronald Radd, Walter Fitzgerald, Phil Brown, Barbara Shelley, Michael Gwynn, Richard Wordsworth, Marne Maitland, Mary Merrall

Campbell's Kingdom *
GB   1957   102m   Eastmancolor
Rank (Betty E. Box)

A young man who thinks he is dying arrives in the Canadian Rockies to take over his father's oil valley, but a scheming contractor opposes him.

Competent and entertaining romantic thick ear.

w Robin Estridge   novel Hammond Innes   d Ralph Thomas   ph Ernest Steward   m Clifton Parker

Dirk Bogarde, Michael Craig, Stanley Baker, Barbara Murray, Athene Seyler, Mary Merrall, James Robertson Justice

'Yet another large budget British film doggedly maintaining a B-picture standard' – John Osborne, London Evening Standard

Can Can
US   1960   131m   DeLuxe   Todd-AO
TCF/Suffolk-Cummings (Jack Cummings)
V*, L, S

A Parisian night-club dancer in the 90s is sued for performing the Can Can.

Flat film of a dull musical, with just a few plums in the pudding.

w Dorothy Kingsley, Charles Lederer   play Abe Burrows   d Walter Lang   ph William Daniels ch Hermes Pan md Nelson Riddle m/y Cole Porter

Frank Sinatra, Shirley Maclaine, Maurice Chevalier, Louis Jourdan, Juliet Prowse, Marcel Dalio, Leon Belasco

AAN: Nelson Riddle

Can Hieronymus Merkin Ever Forget Mercy Humppe and Find True Happiness?
GB 1969 117m Technicolor
Universal/Taralex (Anthony Newley)

A performer on a beach assembles a huge pile of personal bric-à-brac and reminisces about his life in the style of a variety show.

Obscure and pointless personal fantasy, financed at great expense by a major film company as a rather seedy monument to Anthony Newley's totally uninteresting sex life, and to the talent which he obviously thinks he possesses. The few mildly amusing moments are not provided by him.

w Herman Raucher, Anthony Newley d Anthony Newley ph Otto Heller m Anthony Newley

Anthony Newley, Joan Collins, George Jessel, Milton Berle, Bruce Forsyth, Stubby Kaye, Patricia Hayes, Victor Spinetti

'If I'd been Anthony Newley I would have opened it in Siberia during Christmas week and called it a day.' – Rex Reed

'The kindest thing for all concerned would be that every available copy should be quietly and decently buried.' – Michael Billington, Illustrated London News

Can She Bake a Cherry Pie?
US 1983 90m DuArt
Jagfilm/International Rainbow
V*

An abandoned wife has an experimental affair with a hypochondriac divorcé.

What the writer-director calls 'a bitter-sweet comedy about loneliness and love' has more to say to him than to an audience; but there are wryly amusing moments.

wd Henry Jaglom

Karen Black, Michael Emil Jaglom, Michael Margotta, Frances Fisher

Can This Be Dixie?
US 1936 68m bw
TCF (Sol M. Wurtzel)

In the old South, a medicine showman and his daughter help a bankrupt Kentucky colonel.

Agreeable supporting material, with elements of satire, spoof and musical comedy.

w Lamar Trotti d George Marshall

Jane Withers, Slim Summerville, Claude Gillingwater, Helen Wood, Thomas Beck, Sara Haden, Donald Cook, Hattie McDaniel

'Plenty of ingredients were thrown into the soup . . . it will hold its own in the duals.' – Variety

Canadian Mounties vs Atomic Invaders
US 1953 bw serial: 12 eps
Republic

Foreign agents build rocket-launching platforms in the Arctic.

The title suggests that serials were near the end of their tether by now; this was about ten from the end.

d Franklin Adreon

Bill Henry, Susan Morrow, Arthur Space, Dale Van Sickel, Pierre Watkin

'The blazing saga of untamed men and a savage wilderness!'

Canadian Pacific
US 1949 95m Cinecolor
TCF (Nat Holt)

A surveyor discovers the vital pass through the Rockies, and chooses between a lady doctor and a wilful half-breed.

Fairly unhistorical Western; watchable, though.

w Jack de Witt, Kenneth Gamet d Edwin L. Marin

Randolph Scott, Jane Wyatt, Nancy Olson, J. Carrol Naish, Victor Jory, Robert Barrat

The Canadians
GB/Canada 1961 85m DeLuxe Cinemascope
TCF (Herman E. Webber)

After Custer's defeat at Little Big Horn, 6,000 Sioux flee north and are victimized by villainous Canadians; but the Mounties come to the rescue.

Dreary, stumbling semi-Western which set back Canadian production by a year or two. The blame seems to be equally shared by all concerned.

wd Burt Kennedy ph Arthur Ibbetson m none

Robert Ryan, John Dehner, Torin Thatcher, Burt Metcalfe, Teresa Stratas, Michael Pate, John Sutton

Canaries Sometimes Sing
GB 1930 90m bw
British and Dominions (Herbert Wilcox)

Two unhappily married couples change partners.

Mild sophisticated comedy, a shade daring for its time, but only in concept.

w W. P. Lipscomb play Frederick Lonsdale d Tom Walls ph Bernard Knowles ad L. P. Williams ed Duncan Mansfield

Tom Walls, Yvonne Arnaud, Athole Stewart, Cathleen Nesbitt

Cancel My Reservation
US 1972 99m Technicolor
Naho Enterprises
V*

A TV talk show host retreats to his ranch and finds himself mixed up with murder.

Bob Hope's last film, though it reverted to farce and his bumbling coward persona, proved a sorry affair with egg on the face of everybody concerned.

w Arthur Marx, Robert Fisher novel The Broken Gun by Louis L'Amour d Paul Bogart

Bob Hope, Eva Marie Saint, Ralph Bellamy, Forrest Tucker, Anne Archer, Keenan Wynn, Doodles Weaver

The Candidate **
US 1972 110m Technicolor
Warner/Redford-Ritchie (Walter Coblenz)
V, V*, L

A young Californian lawyer is persuaded to run for senator; in succeeding, he alienates his wife and obscures his real opinions.

Put together in a slightly scrappy but finally persuasive style, this joins a select band of rousing, doubting American political films.

w Jeremy Larner d Michael Ritchie ph Victor J. Kemper m John Rubinstein

Robert Redford, Peter Boyle, Don Porter, Allen Garfield, Karen Carlson, Quinn Redeker, Morgan Upton, Melvyn Douglas

'Decent entertainment . . . it is never boring, but it is never enlarging, informationally or emotionally or thematically.' – Stanley Kauffmann

AA: Jeremy Larner

Candide
France 1960 90m bw
CLM/SN Pathé (Clément Duhour)

Ever optimistic, a 20th-century Candide tours Nazi prison camps, communist countries and various South American revolutions.

Scrappily-made satire which soon overstays its welcome.

wd Norbert Carbonneaux novel Voltaire ph Robert Le Fèbvre m Hubert Rostaing

Jean-Pierre Cassel, Daliah Lavi, Pierre Brasseur, Nadia Gray, Michel Simon, Louis de Funès

Candlelight in Algeria
GB 1943 85m bw
British Aviation

Spies seek whereabouts of Allied rendezvous.

Elementary spy thriller using modest talents.

w Katherine Strueby, Brock Williams d George King

Carla Lehmann, James Mason, Walter Rilla, Raymond Lovell, Enid Stamp Taylor

Candles at Nine
GB 1944 86m bw
British National

A young heiress in her benefactor's old mansion is menaced by his housekeeper.

Elementary Cat and the Canary reprise; cast understandably uneasy.

w John Harlow, Basil Mason novel Anthony Gilbert d John Harlow

Jessie Matthews, John Stuart, Beatrix Lehmann, Winifred Shotter, Reginald Purdell

Candleshoe
GB 1977 101m Technicolor
Walt Disney Productions (Hugh Attwooll)
V*, L

An attempt to pass off a fake heiress to an English stately home is prevented by the resourceful butler.

Slackly handled comedy adventure full of easy targets and predictable incidents.

w David Swift, Rosemary Anne Sisson novel Christmas at Candleshoe by Michael Innes d Norman Tokar ph Paul Beeson m Ron Goodwin

David Niven, Helen Hayes, Jodie Foster, Leo McKern, Veronica Quilligan, Ian Sharrock, Vivian Pickles

'It might have been conceived by a computer called upon to produce the definitive pastiche of a Disney film of the 1970s.' – Financial Times

Candy
US/France/Italy 1968 124m Technicolor
Selmur/Dear/Corona (Robert Haggiag)

An innocent girl defends herself from a fate worse than death in a variety of international situations.

Witless and charmless perversion of a sex satire in which the point (if any) was that the nymphet gladly surrendered herself to all the gentlemen for their own good. A star cast flounders helplessly in a morass of bad taste, bad film-making, and boredom.

w Buck Henry novel Terry Southern d Christian Marquand ph Giuseppe Rotunno m Dave Grusin

Ewa Aulin, Richard Burton, Marlon Brando, James Coburn, Walter Matthau, Charles Aznavour, John Huston, Elsa Martinelli, Ringo Starr, John Astin

'Hippy psychedelics are laid on with the self-destroying effect of an overdose of garlic.' – MFB

'As an emetic, liquor is dandy, but Candy is quicker.' – John Simon

The Candy Man
US 1968 98m Eastmancolor
Sagittarius
V*

A British drug pusher in Mexico City plots the kidnap of an American film star's child.

Abysmal independent thriller with a star at the end of
his tether.

wd Herbert J. Leder

George Sanders, Leslie Parrish, Gina Roman, Manolo
Fabregas

Candy Mountain *

Switzerland/France/Canada 1987 92m
Eastmancolor
Oasis/Xanadu/Films Plant Chant/Films Vision 4 (Ruth
Waldburger)
V*

An enterprising musician goes in search of a reclusive
guitar-maker.

An occasionally engaging road movie, accompanied
by many songs, of an innocent being taken for a ride,
literally and metaphorically.

w Rudy Wurlitzer *d* Robert Frank, Rudy Wurlitzer
ph Pio Corradi *m* Dr John, David Johansen, Leon
Redbone and others *ed* Jennifer Auge

Kevin J. O'Connor, Harris Yulin, Tom Waits, Bulle
Ogier, Roberts Blossom, Leon Redbone, Dr John, Rita
McNeil, Joe Strummer, Laurie Metcalf

Candy or Mint: see *Caluga o Menta*

Candyman *

US 1992 93m DeLuxe
Columbia TriStar/Polygram/Propaganda (Steve Golin, Sigurjon
Sighvatsson, Alan Poul)
V, V*, L

An anthropology student becomes convinced of the
reality of a mythical hook-handed serial killer, the son
of a murdered slave.

Effective horror that manages not only to be scary but
also delivers a parable on contemporary attitudes to
race and sex.

wd Bernard Rose *story* The Forbidden by Clive Barker
ph Anthony B. Richmond *m* Philip Glass *pd* Jane
Ann Stewart *sp* Image Animation *ed* Dan Rae

Virginia Madsen, Tony Todd, Xander Berkeley, Kasi
Lemmons, Vanessa Williams, DeJuan Guy, Michael
Culkin, Stanley DeSantis, Gilbert Lewis

'An upper-register horror item that delivers the
requisite shocks and gore but doesn't cheat or cop
out.' – *Variety*

O'Cangaceiro: see *The Bandit*

Cannery Row

US 1982 120m Metrocolor
MGM/Michael Philips
V*

Incidents in the life of a 1940s marine biologist who
lives on the waterfront with bums and floozies.

Badly out of its time, this curious attempt at
sentimental realism was long in the works but
emerged as a bloodless, stultifying entertainment.

wd David S. Ward *novel* John Steinbeck *ph* Sven
Nykvist *m* Jack Nitzsche *pd* Richard MacDonald
ed David Bretherton

Nick Nolte, Debra Winger, Audra Lindley, Frank
McRae, M. Emmet Walsh, John Huston (narrator)

'Another MGM item in which the entertainment
values are difficult to locate.' – *Variety*

† Raquel Welch, originally cast for the Winger role,
was fired in mid-production.

Cannibal Girls

Canada 1972 84m Eastmancolor
Target/Scary Pictures (Daniel Goldberg)

A couple whose car breaks down check into a motel
in a small town where the inhabitants are cannibals.

Standard undistinguished and improvised horror fare,
influenced by George Romero's *Night of the Living Dead*
and itself an influence on *The Texas Chainsaw Massacre.*

The film is not helped by the gimmick of a buzzer that
sounds just before shock scenes and a bell that signals
when the horror is over.

w Robert Sandler *d* Ivan Reitman *ph* Robert
Saad *m* Doug Riley *sp* Richard Whyte, Michael
Lotosky *ed* Daniel Goldberg

Eugene Levy, Andrea Martin, Ronald Ulrich, Randall
Carpenter, Bonnie Neilson, Mira Pawluk

'Aggravatingly hammy and corny.' – *MFB*

Cannibal Man (dubbed)

Spain 1972 120m colour
Atlas (Joe Truchado)
V
original title: *La Semana del Asesino*; aka: *The Apartment
on the Thirteenth Floor*

A slaughterhouse worker embarks on a killing spree
to cover up his murder of a taxi driver during an
argument over the fare.

An unconvincing psychological thriller. Cannibalism
plays no part in the movie, other than indirectly,
when human remains are fed with other meat into a
machine for making soup.

w Eloy de la Iglesia, Anthony Fos, Robert H. Oliver
d Eloy de la Iglesia *ph* Raul Artigot *m* Fernando
G. Morcillo *sp* Baquero *ed* Joe Louis Martinez

Vincent Parra, Emma Cohen, Eusebio Poncela, Vicky
Lagos, Lola Herrera

† The English video release was cut to 92m.

The Cannibals

Italy 1969 87m Technicolor Techniscope
Cinegate/Doria/San Marco (Enzo Doria, Bino Cicogna)
S
original title: *I Cannibali*

In Milan, where a harsh military ruler brutally puts
down a revolution, a woman searches for the dead
body of her brother so that she can bury him.

An unsuccessful updating of Sophocles, with the
emphasis on sensationalism rather than tragedy.

w Italo Moscati, Liliana Cavani, Fabrizio Onofri
play Antigone by Sophocles *d* Liliana Cavani
ph Giulio Albonico *m* Ennio Morricone *ad* Ezio
Frigerio *ed* Nino Baragli

Britt Ekland, Pierre Clémenti, Tomas Milian,
Francesco Leonetti, Delia Boccardo

Cannon for Cordoba

US 1970 104m DeLuxe Panavision
UA/Mirisch (Stephen Kandel, Vincent Fennelly)

In 1912, the Mexican bandit Cordoba is outgunned
and outwitted by a US army captain.

Fast-moving but rather uninteresting action
adventure.

w Stephen Kandel *d* Paul Wendkos *ph* Antonio
Macasoli *m* Elmer Bernstein

George Peppard, Raf Vallone, Giovanna Ralli, Pete
Duel, Don Gordon, Nico Minardos, John Russell

'A free-wheeling, stunt-studded, dented and demented
story of a road racer without rules.'

Cannonball

US/Hong Kong 1976 93m Metrocolor
Harbor/Shaw Brothers (Samuel W. Gelfman)
V*
GB title: *Carquake*

Aggressive drivers compete in the Trans-American
Grand Prix.

The plot is a thin excuse for multiple pile-ups and
other road disasters. Moments amuse, but the
violence quickly palls.

w Paul Bartel, Donald C. Simpson *d* Paul Bartel
ph Tak Fujimoto *m* David A. Axelrod

David Carradine, Bill McKinney, Veronica Hamel,
Gerrit Graham, Judy Canova

The Cannonball Run

US 1980 95m Technicolor
Golden Harvest (Albert S. Ruddy)
V, V*, L

The adventures of ill-assorted contestants in the
illegal Cannonball coast-to-coast race.

Well-known stars are all at sea in this comedy/
disaster extravaganza, which seems to have begun as
a joke rather than a script.

w Brock Yates *d* Hal Needham *ph* Michael Butler
md Al Capps

Burt Reynolds, Roger Moore, Farrah Fawcett, Dom
DeLuise, Dean Martin, Sammy Davis Jnr, Adrienne
Barbeau, Jack Elam, Bert Convy, Jamie Farr, Peter
Fonda, Molly Picon, Bianca Jagger

'Lacking any recognizable plot or characterization, or
indeed incidental invention, it merely offers a parade
of inept whimsy and lame intra-mural reference.' –
Tim Pulleine, MFB

'Moviegoers who relish the screech of tyres taking a
fast turn on a narrow bend should have a whale of a
time.' – *Daily Mail*

Cannonball Run II

US 1983 108m Technicolor
Golden Harvest/Warner (Albert S. Ruddy)
V*, L

An Arab sheik puts up a million-dollar prize for the
Cannonball Run.

Dispirited rehash of number one, with poor technique
and non-performances by stars who should have
known better than to get involved.

w Hal Needham, Albert S. Ruddy, Harvey Miller
d Hal Needham *ph* Nick McLean *m* Al Capps
ad Thomas E. Azzari *ed* William Gordean, Carl
Kress

Burt Reynolds, Dom DeLuise, Sammy Davis Jnr,
Dean Martin, Jamie Farr, Telly Savalas, Shirley
Maclaine, Frank Sinatra, Susan Anton, Catherine
Bach, Richard Kiel, Tim Conway, Sid Caesar, Don
Knotts, Ricardo Montalban, Jim Nabors, Henry Silva

Canon City *

US 1948 82m bw
Eagle Lion/Bryan Foy (Robert T. Kane)

Convicts break out of the Colorado State Prison.

Minor semi-documentary melodrama, quite
effectively presented.

wd Crane Wilbur *ph* John Alton

Scott Brady, Jeff Corey, Whit Bissell, Stanley
Clements, De Forrest Kelley

Can't Buy Me Love

US 1987 94m colour
Warner/Touchstone (Thom Mount)
V*, L

A wimp hires a popular cheerleader to be his
girlfriend for a month to improve his social standing.

Predictable comedy aimed at a teenage audience, and
they are welcome to it.

w Michael Swerdlick *d* James Foley *ph* Peter
Lyons Collister *m* Robert Folk *pd* Donald Light-
Harris *ed* Jeff Gourson

Patrick Dempsey, Amanda Peterson, Courtney Gains,
Seth Green, Tina Caspary, Devin Devasquez, Darcy de
Moss, Eric Bruskotter

Can't Help Singing *

US 1944 90m Technicolor
Universal (Frank Ross)

A Washington heiress chases her army lieutenant
lover across the Wild West to California.

Lively star musical which could have used a little
more wit in its lighthearted script.

w Lewis Foster, Frank Ryan   d Frank Ryan
ph Woody Bredell, W. Howard Greene   md Jerome Kern, Hans Salter   m/ly Jerome Kern, E. Y. Harburg

Deanna Durbin, David Bruce, Robert Paige, *Akim Tamiroff*, Leonid Kinskey, Ray Collins, Thomas Gomez

'This could have been a beautiful and gay picture, but it is made without much feeling for beauty or gaiety.' – James Agee

'She can carry a simple part charmingly; she looks very well; her manners are impeccable; and she can sing a role just short of grand opera better than any actress on the screen.' – Observer

songs: 'Elbow Room'; 'Any Moment Now'; 'Californ-i-ay'; 'Swing Your Sweetheart round the Fire'; 'Finale Ultimo'

AAN: Jerome Kern, Hans Salter; song 'More and More'

Can't Stop the Music
US   1980   124m   Metrocolor   Panavision
EMI/Allan Carr
V*

A Greenwich Village pop group hits the bigtime.

Curiously old-fashioned youth musical, unwisely touted as something special, which it isn't.

w Bronte Woodward, Allan Carr   d Nancy Walker
ph Bill Butler   m Jacques Morali

The Village People, Valerie Perrine, Paul Sand, Bruce Jenner, Tammy Grimes, June Havoc, Barbara Rush, Jack Weston

'The hype disaster of the 80s, a grisly rehash of the let's-start-a-group-of-our-own plot, peopled with butch gay stereotypes of both sexes pretending to be straight. The pervasive tackiness is unrelieved.' – Time Out

'Desperately knowing about the eighties but fixed remorselessly in a time warp of fifties hokum.' – Guardian

'All noise, lights, slogans, movement and dazzle, like a 124m commercial devoted to selling you a product you can't use.' – Sunday Times

'One doesn't watch it, one is attacked by it.' – New England Entertainment Digest

'Considering the low level of wit, perhaps the Village People should consider renaming themselves the Village Idiots.' – Los Angeles Magazine

'This shamefully tacky musical extravaganza fails on every aesthetic level.' – Los Angeles Herald Examiner

'A forced marriage between the worst of sitcom plotting and the highest of high camp production numbers.' – New West

Cantata de Chile *
Cuba   1976   119m   colour
ICAIC (Orlando de La Huerta, Camilo Vives)

Revolutionary history of Cuba, told from a Marxist viewpoint.

An ambitious, epic mix of realism, symbolic action, songs and poems, intermixed with scenes of appalling violence, and filmed with exuberance and panache. But two hours in the company of excessively noble peasants is too much.   wd Humberto Solas
ph Jorge Herrera   m Leo Brouwer   pd Fedora Robles   ed Nelson L. Rodriguez

Nelson Villagra, Shenda Roman, Eric Heresmann

A Canterbury Tale **
GB   1944   124m   bw
Rank/Archers (Michael Powell, Emeric Pressburger)
V, V*

A batty magistrate is unmasked by a land girl, an army sergeant and a GI.

Curious would-be propaganda piece with Old England bathed in a roseate wartime glow, but the plot seems to have little to do with Chaucer. Indeed,

quite what Powell and Pressburger thought they were up to is hard to fathom, but the detail is interesting.

wd Michael Powell, Emeric Pressburger   ph Erwin Hillier

Eric Portman, Sheila Sim, John Sweet, Dennis Price, Esmond Knight, Charles Hawtrey, Hay Petrie, George Merritt, Edward Rigby

'To most people the intentions of the filmmakers remained highly mysterious; nor did this picture of the British administration of justice commend itself to the authorities, who showed some reluctance to encourage its export to our allies.' – Basil Wright, 1972

The Canterbury Tales
Italy/France   1971   109m (English version)
   Technicolor
UA/PEA/PAA (Alberto Grimaldi)
V*, L

Medieval pilgrims amuse each other by telling stories on the way to Canterbury.

A sweaty selection of the tales in their more prurient aspects, with relentless emphasis on excrement and sex perversions.

wd Pier Paolo Pasolini, after Chaucer   ph Tonino Delli Colli   m Ennio Morricone

Pier Paolo Pasolini (as Chaucer), Hugh Griffith, Laura Betti, Tom Baker, Ninetto Davoli, Franco Citti

'Caricature Chaucer, with pilgrims losing the way to Canterbury amid a forest of male genitalia.' – Sight and Sound

'The vivid depiction of taboo subjects emerges less as an affirmation of the Chaucerian belief that all human activity lies within the artist's scope, than as a bludgeoning over-emphasis on physical appetite as man's primal motive for action.' – Nigel Andrews, MFB

The Canterville Ghost *
US   1944   95m   bw
MGM (Arthur Field)
V, V*

The young girl heiress of an English castle introduces GIs to the resident ghost.

Leaden comedy a long way after Oscar Wilde, sunk by slow script and direction, but partly salvaged by the respective roguishness and infant charm of its stars.

w Edwin Blum   d Jules Dassin   ph Robert Planck
m George Bassman

Charles Laughton, Margaret O'Brien, Robert Young, William Gargan, Rags Ragland, Peter Lawford, Una O'Connor, Mike Mazurki

† In the mid 1970s, a television version starring David Niven was made by HTV.

Canyon Crossroads
US   1954   84m   bw
MPT/UA

A uranium prospector is trailed by thieves.

Acceptable modern Western.

w Emmett Murphy, Leonard Heideman   d Alfred Werker

Richard Basehart, Phyllis Kirk, Stephen Elliott, Russell Collins, Charles Wagenheim

Canyon Pass: see Raton Pass

Canyon Passage *
US   1946   99m   Technicolor
Universal (Walter Wanger)

In the 1850s along the pioneering tracks the west's first towns were being built . . .

Simple, scrappy but generally pleasing film which gives a vivid picture of pioneering life while minimizing its hardships.

w Ernest Pascal, William Fosche   d Jacques Tourneur   ph Edward Cronjager   m Frank Skinner

Dana Andrews, Patricia Roc, Hoagy Carmichael, Brian Donlevy, Susan Hayward, Ward Bond, Andy Devine, Lloyd Bridges

'Miles of beautiful scenery, lavishly punctuated with rough-and-tumble episodes, moments of tender romance and a smattering of folk customs.' – New York Times

AAN: song 'Ole Buttermilk Sky' (m/ly Hoagy Carmichael, Jack Brooks)

Cape Fear
US   1962   106m   bw
U-I/Melville-Talbot (Sy Bartlett)
V, V*, L, S

An ex-convict blames a lawyer for his sentence and threatens to rape the lawyer's wife.

Unpleasant and drawn out suspenser with characters of cardboard and situations from stock.

w James R. Webb   novel The Executioners by John D. MacDonald   d J. Lee-Thompson   ph Sam Leavitt
m Bernard Herrmann

Gregory Peck, Robert Mitchum, Polly Bergen, Martin Balsam, Lori Martin, Jack Kruschen, Telly Savalas

'There is nothing in the dark that isn't there in the light. Except fear.'

Cape Fear ***
US   1991   128m   Technicolor   Panavision
Universal/Amblin/Cappa/Tribeca (Barbara de Fina)
V, V*, L

A psychopathic ex-convict returns to threaten the family of the lawyer who unsuccessfully defended him on a charge of rape.

A remake superior to the original, a grimly effective thriller, filled with a sense of brooding menace.

w Wesley Strick   screenplay James R. Webb
novel The Executioners by John D. MacDonald
d Martin Scorsese   ph Freddie Francis   md Elmer Bernstein   m Bernard Herrmann   pd Henry Bumstead   ed Thelma Schoonmaker

Robert de Niro, Nick Nolte, Jessica Lange, Juliette Lewis, Joe Don Baker, Robert Mitchum, Gregory Peck, Martin Balsam, Illeana Douglas

'A highly potent thriller that will strike fear into the hearts of a sizable public.' – Variety

'The film begins as it goes on; undeviatingly and unrelievedly brutal. This said, I must admit I mistrust myself for admiring it so much. For more than two hours it puts one's moral conscience under assault, not just one's nerves.' – Alexander Walker, London Evening Standard

'A picture whose sole aim is to give its audience huge, bowel-loosening shocks; the veneer of moral seriousness and psychological complexity that Scorsese brings to the enterprise feels like an attempt to convince himself that he's not doing what he's doing . . . This is Scorsese's worst picture – an ugly, incoherent piece of work.' – New Yorker

'Have our lives truly become so hollow that this kind of unapologetic bludgeoning of our sensibilities passes for jolly weekend entertainment?' – Kenneth Turan, Los Angeles Times

'I'm glad I saw the film. I found it as gripping and offensive as Scorsese intended. But, apart from de Niro's transcendent performance, I'm not sure I'd want to see it again.' – Ian Johnstone, Sunday Times

† Gregory Peck, Robert Mitchum and Martin Balsam all featured in the 1962 version, as did Bernard Herrmann's score.

AAN: Robert de Niro, Juliette Lewis

The Caper of the Golden Bulls
US   1966   104m   Pathecolor
Embassy (Clarence Greene)
V*
GB title: Carnival of Thieves

Ex-air-aces rob banks in order to pay for the restoration of a French cathedral they had to bomb; to avoid incrimination they are blackmailed into doing one last job in Pamplona.

Ingeniously plotted, flatly executed suspenser set in Pamplona during the bull run.

w Ed Waters, William Moessinger   novel William P. McGivern   d Russel Rouse   ph Hal Stine   m Vic Mizzy

Stephen Boyd, Giovanna Ralli, Yvette Mimieux, Walter Slezak, Vito Scotti

Capetown Affair
US/SA   1967   100m   DeLuxe
TCF/Killarney (Robert D. Webb)

A pickpocket on a South African bus steals a purse containing secret microfilm.

Flatulent remake of *Pickup on South Street* with nothing but the unfamiliar locale to recommend it.

w Harold Medford, Samuel Fuller   d Robert D. Webb   ph David Millin   m Bob Adams

James Brolin, Jacqueline Bisset, Claire Trevor, Bob Courtney, Jon Whiteley

'The man who made the twenties roar! Now, after 45 years, his true story can be told!'

Capone
US   1975   101m   DeLuxe
TCF/Santa Fe (Roger Corman)

Exploitation version of the Capone story, with the emphasis on unpleasant violence.

w Howard Browne   d Steve Carver   ph Vilis Lapenieks   m David Grisman

Ben Gazzara, Sylvester Stallone, Susan Blakely, Harry Guardino, John Cassavetes, John Davis Chandler, Peter Maloney, Royal Dano

† See also: *Al Capone.*

Le Caporal Epinglé: see *The Vanishing Corporal*

Caprice *
US   1967   98m   DeLuxe   Cinemascope
TCF/Aaron Rosenberg, Marty Melcher
V

A career girl investigating the death of her boss discovers that a cosmetics empire is the front for international drug smuggling.

Incoherent kaleidoscope which switches from farce to suspense and Bond-style action, scattering in-jokes along the way. Bits of it however are funny, and it looks good.

w Jay Jayson, Frank Tashlin   d Frank Tashlin   ph Leon Shamroy (who also appears)   m Frank de Vol

Doris Day, Richard Harris, Edward Mulhare, Ray Walston, Jack Kruschen, Lilia Skala, Irene Tsu, Michael Romanoff, Michael J. Pollard

Capricious Summer *
Czechoslovakia   1968   75m   Eastmancolor
Ceskoslovensky Film (Jan Libora)

The beautiful assistant of a wandering tightrope walker sets up sexual tensions when they stop at a sleepy riverside town.

Amusing little period comedy in a period setting.

wd Jiri Menzel   ph Jaromir Sofr   m Jiri Sust

Rudolf Hrusinsky, Vlastimil Brodsky, Frantisek Rehak, Jana Drchalova, Jiri Menzel

Capricorn One
US   1978   128m   CFI colour   Panavision
Associated General/Lew Grade (Paul N. Lazarus III)
V*, L, S

A reporter discovers that the first manned space flight to Mars was a hoax.

Smartly packaged topical adventure thriller rather marred by its all star cast.

wd Peter Hyams   ph Bill Butler   m Jerry Goldsmith   pd Albert Brenner

Elliott Gould, James Brolin, Brenda Vaccaro, Sam Waterston, O. J. Simpson, Hal Holbrook, Telly Savalas, Karen Black, David Huddleston

'After weighing in with some Watergate/Bernstein pretensions, the makers then opt for boring, Bondish derring-do.' – *Sight and Sound*

Captain America *
US   1944   bw   serial: 15 eps
Republic

A masked avenger who is really a district attorney combats a museum curator who is really The Scarab.

Serial elements in fairly fine fettle: one for sociologists of the future to work over.

d John English, Elmer Clifton

Dick Purcell, Lionel Atwill, Lorna Gray, Charles Trowbridge, Russell Hicks, Frank Reicher

Captain America
US   1989   97m   Eastmancolor
Castle/21st Century/Marvel/Jadran Film (Menahem Golan)
V

Frozen in the ice for decades, Captain America is freed to battle against an arch-criminal The Red Skull.

Comic-book nonsense, half-heartedly presented.

w Stephen Tolkin   d Albert Pyun   ph Philip Alan Waters   m Barry Goldberg   ed David Reale

Matt Salinger, Ronny Cox, Ned Beatty, Darren McGavin, Michael Nouri, Melinda Dillon, Francesca Neri, Bill Mumy, Kim Gillingham

'It comprises reams of tedious exposition interlarded with out-dated heroics.' – *MFB*

Captain Apache
US/Spain   1971   94m   Technicolor   'Scope
Benmar (Milton Sperling, Philip Yordan, Irving Lerner)
V*

An Indian serving with US army intelligence tracks down a gun runner.

An old formula tarted up with the new violence. Very ho-hum.

w Philip Yordan, Milton Sperling   novel S. E. Whitman   d Alexander Singer   ph John Cabrera   m Dolores Claman

Lee Van Cleef, Carroll Baker, Stuart Whitman, Percy Herbert, Tony Vogel

Captain Applejack
US   1931   70m   bw
Warner

A timid man turns the tables on crooks who plan to find treasure beneath his ancestral home.

Early talkie version of a well-worn play previously filmed in 1923.

w Maude Fulton   novel *Ambrose Applejohn's Adventure* by Walter Hackett   d Hobart Henley

John Halliday, Kay Strozzi, Arthur Edmund Carewe, Mary Brian, Louise Closser Hale

Captain Bill
GB   1935   81m   bw
Leslie Fuller (Joe Rock)

A bargee saves a schoolmistress from trouble with crooks.

By reputation the best of its star's modest comedies, which have not yet been rediscovered.

w Val Valentine, Syd Courtenay and George Harris   d Ralph Ceder

Leslie Fuller, Georgie Harris, Judy Kelly, Hal Gordon, O. B. Clarence

Captain Blackjack
US/France   1952   90m   bw
Walter Gould

A Riviera socialite pretends to be an undercover agent but is really a smuggler; she is unmasked by a doctor who is really a detective.

Trashy hodgepodge with a remarkable cast of ageing stars.

w Julien Duvivier, Charles Spaak   d Julien Duvivier

George Sanders, Agnes Moorehead, Herbert Marshall, Patricia Roc, Marcel Dalio

'A million dollars worth of adventure! To do justice in words to its fascination is impossible!'
'His sword carved his name across the continents – and his glory across the seas!'

Captain Blood **
US   1935   119m   bw
Warner (Harry Joe Brown)
V, V*, L

A young British surgeon, wrongly condemned by Judge Jeffreys for helping rebels, escapes and becomes a Caribbean pirate.

Modestly produced but quite exhilarating pirate adventure notable for making a star of Errol Flynn. Direction makes the most of very limited production values.

w Casey Robinson   novel Rafael Sabatini   d Michael Curtiz   ph Hal Mohr   m Erich Wolfgang Korngold   ad Anton Grot

Errol Flynn, Olivia de Havilland, *Basil Rathbone*, Lionel Atwill, Guy Kibbee, Ross Alexander, Henry Stephenson, Forrester Harvey, Hobart Cavanaugh, Donald Meek

'A lavish, swashbuckling saga of the Spanish Main . . . it can't fail at the wickets.' – *Variety*

'Here is a fine spirited mix-up with clothes and wigs which sometimes hark back to the sixteenth century and sometimes forward to the period of Wolfe . . . one is quite prepared for the culminating moment when the Union Jack breaks proudly, anachronistically forth at Peter Blood's masthead.' – *Graham Greene*

'Magnificently photographed, lavishly produced, and directed with consummate skill.' – *Picturegoer*

AAN: best picture

Captain Blood, Fugitive: see *Captain Pirate*

Captain Boycott *
GB   1947   93m   bw
GFD/Individual (Frank Launder, Sidney Gilliat)

In 1880, poor Irish farmers rebel against their tyrannical English landlords.

Modest historical drama in which a splendid cast is rather subdued.

w Wolfgang Wilhelm, Frank Launder, Paul Vincent Carroll, Patrick Campbell   novel Philip Rooney   d Frank Launder   ph Wilkie Cooper   m William Alwyn   ad Ted Carrick

Stewart Granger, Kathleen Ryan, Alastair Sim, Robert Donat (a cameo as Parnell), Cecil Parker, Mervyn Johns, Noel Purcell, Niall MacGinnis

'It is said that no actor can survive playing opposite a child or a dog. Let me add here that it is just as lethal playing with the Abbey Players. Apart from being able to act you off the stage, they can also drink you under the table.' – *Sidney Gilliat, 1982*

Captain Carey USA
US   1950   83m   bw
Paramount (Richard Maibaum)
GB title: *After Midnight*

After the war, a military officer returns to an Italian village to expose the informer who betrayed his comrades.

Muddled and rather boring melodrama with a labyrinthine plot which seems to have stultified all concerned. It did produce a hit song, 'Mona Lisa'.

w Robert Thoeren novel Dishonoured by Martha Albrand d Mitchell Leisen ph John F. Seitz m Hugo Friedhofer

Alan Ladd, Francis Lederer, Wanda Hendrix, Joseph Calleia, Celia Lovsky, Angela Clarke, Jane Nigh, Frank Puglia, Luis Alberni

AA: song 'Mona Lisa' (m/y Ray Evans, Jay Livingston)

Captain Caution
US 1940 84m bw
Hal Roach
V*

In 1812, a girl takes over her dead father's ship and fights the British.

Lively though unconvincing adventure with emphasis on comedy.

w Grover Jones novel Kenneth Roberts d Richard Wallace ph Norbert Brodine m Phil Ohman

Victor Mature, Louise Platt, Bruce Cabot, Leo Carrillo, Robert Barrat, Vivienne Osborne, Alan Ladd

Captain China
US 1949 97m bw
Paramount/Pine-Thomas (William H. Pine, William C. Thomas)

A wandering seafarer seeks the mate who betrayed him.

Action melodrama with a second team look; all rather listless.

w Lewis R. Foster, Gwen Bagni d Lewis R. Foster ph John Alton m Lucien Cailliet

John Payne, Gail Russell, Jeffrey Lynn, Lon Chaney Jnr, Michael O'Shea, Ellen Corby

Captain Clegg *
GB 1962 82m Technicolor
Universal/Hammer (John Temple-Smith)
US title: Night Creatures

The vicar of an 18th-century village in Romney Marsh is really a retired pirate, now doing a little smuggling on the side.

Mild remake of Dr Syn with a few moments of violence added; watchable for those who like totally predictable plot development.

w John Elder (Anthony Hinds) d Peter Graham Scott ph Arthur Grant m Don Banks ad Bernard Robinson, Don Mingaye ed James Needs, Eric Boyd-Perkins

Peter Cushing, Patrick Allen, Michael Ripper, Oliver Reed, Derek Francis, Milton Reid, Martin Benson, David Lodge, Yvonne Romain

Captain Eddie
US 1945 107m bw
TCF/Eureka

Eddie Rickenbacker, adrift on a life raft after a plane crash in the Pacific, thinks back on his adventurous life in aviation.

Flat and surprisingly poorly made biopic with little to hold the attention.

w John Tucker Battle d Lloyd Bacon ph Joe MacDonald m Cyril Mockridge

Fred MacMurray, Lynn Bari, Thomas Mitchell, Lloyd Nolan, Charles Bickford

Captain from Castile
US 1947 140m Technicolor
TCF (Lamar Trotti)

A young 15th-century Spaniard hopes for fame and fortune in the New World.

Rather empty and boring adventure epic from a bestseller; high production values produce moments of interest.

w Lamar Trotti novel Samuel Shellabarger d Henry King ph Charles Clarke, Arthur E. Arling m Alfred Newman ad Richard Day, James Basevi

Tyrone Power, Jean Peters, Lee J. Cobb, Cesar Romero, John Sutton, Antonio Moreno, Thomas Gomez, Alan Mowbray, Barbara Lawrence, George Zucco, Roy Roberts, Marc Lawrence

'The first few reels have flow and a kind of boy's-book splendour; the rest is locomotor ataxia.' – James Agee

AAN: Alfred Newman

Captain Fury *
US 1939 91m bw
Hal Roach

In 19th-century Australia, an adventurer fights the evil head of a penal colony.

Shades of Zorro and Robin Hood in a brawling, comic actioner typical of this producer.

w Grover Jones, Jack Jevne, William de Mille d Hal Roach ph Norbert Brodine m Marvin Hatley ad Charles D. Hall

Brian Aherne, Victor McLaglen, Paul Lukas, June Lang, John Carradine

'Action, fast riding, gunplay, surprise attacks, some broad comedy and a few dashes of romance . . . will do pretty good biz in the keys, but will hit a more profitable stride in the subsequents.' – Variety

AAN: Charles D. Hall

The Captain Hates the Sea *
US 1934 92m bw
Columbia

Crime and comedy on an ocean voyage.

Zany, rather endearing comedy which gave the star his last role.

w Wallace Smith d Lewis Milestone ph Joseph August

John Gilbert, Victor McLaglen, Walter Connolly, Alison Skipworth, Wynne Gibson, Helen Vinson, Leon Errol, Walter Catlett, Donald Meek, Arthur Treacher, Akim Tamiroff

'A fine cast, excellent comedy relief and expert direction.'—Variety

'The best neglected picture in two years.' – Otis Ferguson, 1936

Captain Horatio Hornblower RN
GB 1951 117m Technicolor
Warner (Raoul Walsh)
V*, L

Events from the adventure novels about a 19th-century sailor who outwits the Spaniards and the French and marries his admiral's widow.

Sprawling, plotless sea saga with the cast ill at ease in highly unconvincing sets: no air seems to blow across the decks of the Lydia.

w Ivan Goff, Ben Roberts, Aeneas Mackenzie novels C. S. Forester d Raoul Walsh ph Guy Green m Robert Farnon ad Tom Morahan

Gregory Peck, Virginia Mayo, Robert Beatty, James Robertson Justice, Terence Morgan, Moultrie Kelsall, Richard Hearne, Denis O'Dea

'No point makes a strong enough impression to suggest a main line of criticism.' – Richard Mallett, Punch

The Captain Is a Lady *
US 1940 63m bw
MGM

A sea captain is forced by ill-fortune to send his wife

to an old ladies' home, but he dresses as a woman to be with her.

Absurd-sounding comedy not without a certain lunatic charm.

w Harry Clork play Rachel Crothers d Robert Sinclair

Charles Coburn, Billie Burke, Beulah Bondi, Dan Dailey, Virginia Grey, Helen Broderick, Helen Westley

Captain January *
US 1936 74m bw
TCF (Darryl F. Zanuck)
V*

A little girl is rescued from a shipwreck by a lighthouse keeper.

Standard Shirley Temple vehicle with pleasing dialogue and numbers.

w Sam Hellman, Gladys Lehman, Harry Tugend novel Laura E. Richards d David Butler ph John F. Seitz m Louis Silvers m/y Lew Pollack, Sidney Mitchell, Jack Yellen

Shirley Temple, Guy Kibbee, Buddy Ebsen, Slim Summerville, June Lang, Sara Haden, Jane Darwell

Captain Kidd
US 1945 90m bw
Benedict Bogeaus

A pirate tricks King William III into giving him royal orders, but enemies he believes dead return to see him hanged.

Rather poorly produced vehicle for a star who however rants and raves to some effect.

w Norman Reilly Raine d Rowland V. Lee ph Archie Stout m Werner Janssen

Charles Laughton, Randolph Scott, Barbara Britton, Reginald Owen, John Carradine, Gilbert Roland, Sheldon Leonard

AAN: Werner Janssen

Captain Kidd and the Slave Girl
US 1954 82m CFI color
Reliance/UA

A scheming earl reprieves Captain Kidd so that he can steal his treasure.

Cut-price swashbuckler with more vigour than some.

w Aubrey Wisberg, Jack Pollexfen d Lew Landers

Anthony Dexter, Eva Gabor, Alan Hale Jnr, James Seay

Captain Kronos, Vampire Hunter *
GB 1973 91m colour
Hammer (Albert Fennell, Brian Clemens)
V*

The title explains almost all; in this case he tackles an old vampire crone who becomes young when she sucks blood.

Lively horror yarn with amusing asides.

wd Brian Clemens ph Ian Wilson pd Robert Jones ed James Needs

Horst Janson, John Carson, Shane Briant, Caroline Munro, John Cater, Wanda Ventham

Captain Lash *
US 1929 72m approx bw silent
Fox

Late silent adventure: a stoker gets involved with smuggling for a society girl.

Mildly amusing goings-on with a star in good form.

w John Stone, Daniel G. Tomlinson d John Blystone

Victor McLaglen, Claire Windsor, Arthur Stone, Albert Conti, Clyde Cook

Captain Lightfoot
US 1955 92m Technicolor print Cinemascope
U-I (Ross Hunter)

Adventures of a 19th-century Irish rebel.

Dullish adventure story with the star ill at ease.

w W. R. Burnett, Oscar Brodney   d Douglas Sirk
ph Irving Glassberg   m Hans Salter

Rock Hudson, Barbara Rush, Jeff Morrow, Kathleen
Ryan, Finlay Currie, Denis O'Dea, Geoffrey Toone

Captain Midnight
US 1942 bw serial: 15 eps
Columbia

Ivan Shark terrifies the nation with night bombing
planes, but an intrepid aviator comes to the rescue.

Serial elements topically adapted to wartime
sabotage. Fair fun.

d James W. Horne

Dave O'Brien, Dorothy Short, James Craven, Bryant
Washburn

Captain Nemo and the Underwater City
GB 1969 106m Metrocolor Panavision
MGM/Omnia (Steven Pallos, Bertram Ostrer)

Six survivors from an Atlantic shipwreck are picked
up by a mysterious submarine and have adventures in
a spectacular underwater city.

Further adventures of Jules Verne's engaging
Victorian character from *Twenty Thousand Leagues under
the Sea.* Here however the general production values
are stolid rather than solid, and the script makes
heavy weather.

w Pip Baker, Jane Baker, R. Wright Campbell
d James Hill   ph Alan Hume, Egil Woxholt
m Walter Stott   ad Bill Andrews

Robert Ryan, Chuck Connors, Bill Fraser, Kenneth
Connor, Nanette Newman, John Turner, Luciana
Paluzzi, Allan Cuthbertson

Captain Newman MD *
US 1963 126m Eastmancolor
Universal-Brentwood-Reynard (Robert Arthur)
V*

At an army air base during World War II, a
psychiatrist has varied success with his patients.

A decidedly curious comedy drama on the fringe of
bad taste; it should have turned out better than it
does, but will entertain those who like hospital
heroics drenched in bitter-sweet sentimentality.

w Richard L. Breen, Phoebe and Henry Ephron
novel Leo Rosten   d David Miller   ph Russell
Metty   m Joseph Gershenson

Gregory Peck, Tony Curtis, Angie Dickinson, Eddie
Albert, Bobby Darin, James Gregory, Jane Withers,
Bethel Leslie, Robert Duvall, Larry Storch, Robert F.
Simon, Dick Sargent

AAN: script; Bobby Darin

Captain of the Guard
US 1930 83m bw
Carl Laemmle/Universal

During the French Revolution, a guards captain
changes sides.

Unexciting historical melodrama which failed to make
the intended impression.

w Arthur Ripley   story Houston Branch   d Paul
Fejos and John S. Robertson   m Charles Wakefield
Cadman

John Boles, Laura La Plante, Lionel Belmore, Sam de
Grasse, James Marcus, Otis Harlan

'Universal's most pretentious release of the season . . .
liberal expenditure shows on the screen.' – *Variety*

'Passions run hot and blood runs cold!'
Captain Pirate
US 1952 85m Technicolor
Columbia (Harry Joe Brown)
GB title: *Captain Blood, Fugitive*

A reformed pirate, accused of sacking Cartagena,
returns to piracy to discover the perpetrators.

Lively buccaneering programmer with an adequate
budget and plenty of high spirits.

w Robert Libbott, Frank Burt, John Meredyth Lucas
novel *Captain Blood Returns* by Rafael Sabatini
d Ralph Murphy   ph Charles Lawton Jnr
m George Duning

Louis Hayward, Patricia Medina, John Sutton, George
Givot, Rex Evans, Ted de Corsia, Charles Irwin

'The only thing Martin wanted was a nice, quiet family
vacation. Instead, he got . . . Captain Ron.'
Captain Ron
US 1992 100m Technicolor
Touchstone/Touchwood Pacific Partners I (David Permut, Paige
Simpson)
V, V*, L

An American family inherit an ancient yacht in the
Caribbean and hire a dubious one-eyed captain to
help them sail it back to the States.

Tedious and indifferently acted comedy, in which the
jokes consist of people either falling over or falling
into the water.

w John Dwyer, Thom Eberhardt   d Thom Eberhardt
ph Daryn Okada   m Nicholas Pike   pd William F.
Matthews   ed Tina Hirsch

Kurt Russell, Martin Short, Mary Kay Place, Benjamin
Salisbury, Meadow Sisto, Paul Anka

'Inoffensive but unexciting.' – *Variety*

† The film was released direct to video in Britain.

Captain Scarlett
US 1952 75m Technicolor
UA/Craftsman (Howard Dimsdale)

After the Napoleonic wars, southern France is in need
of a protector against the villainous Duke of Corlaine.
Captain Scarlett rides into action . . .

Robin Hood in all but name, an old tale retold
without much flair.

w Howard Dimsdale   d Thomas Carr   ph Charles
Carbajal   m Elias Breeskin

Richard Greene, Leonora Amar, Nedrick Young,
Eduardo Noriega

Captain Sinbad *
US/Germany 1963 88m Eastmancolor
Wonderscope
King Brothers
V*

Sinbad returns to Baristan and by means of magic
deposes a sultan.

Rather splendid adventure fantasy with a European
flavour, good trick effects and full-blooded
performances.

w Samuel B. West, Harry Relis   d Byron Haskin
ph Gunther Senftleben, Eugen Shuftan   m Michel
Michelet   ad Werner and Isabell Schlicting
sp Tom Howard

Guy Williams, Pedro Armendariz, Heidi Bruhl,
Abraham Sofaer

Captain Tugboat Annie
US 1945 70m bw
Republic

Annie wants to adopt a small boy but by clerical error
gets a young man instead.

A silly story which prevented this reworking of the
old Dressler-Beery vehicle from becoming a series.

w George Callahan   d Phil Rosen

Jane Darwell, Edgar Kennedy, Charles Gordon

Captains Courageous **
US 1937 116m bw
MGM (Louis D. Lighton)
V, V*, L

A spoiled rich boy falls off a cruise liner and lives for
a while among fisherfolk who teach him how to live.

Semi-classic Hollywood family film which is not all
that enjoyable while it's on but is certainly a good
example of the prestige picture of the thirties. (It also
happened to be good box-office.)

w John Lee Mahin, Marc Connelly, Dale Van Every
novel Rudyard Kipling   d Victor Fleming
ph Harold Rosson   m Franz Waxman   ed Elmo
Veron

Spencer Tracy, Lionel Barrymore, Freddie
Bartholomew, Mickey Rooney, Melvyn Douglas,
Charley Grapewin, Christian Rub, John Carradine,
Walter Kingsford, Leo G. Carroll, Charles Trowbridge

'Will not have to go begging for patronage . . . one of
the best pictures of the sea ever made.' – *Variety*

'Another of those grand jobs of movie-making we
have come to expect from Hollywood's most profligate
studio.' – *Frank S. Nugent, New York Times*

† 1977 brought a TV movie remake.

AA: Spencer Tracy

AAN: best picture; script; editing

The Captain's Kid
US 1936 72m bw
Warner

In New England, a retired sea captain's blood-chilling
tales thrill a little girl and involve him in a real-life
court case.

Slightly unusual tale which deserved better handling
than this routine second feature allows.

w Tom Reed   d Nick Grinde

Guy Kibbee, May Robson, Sybil Jason, Jane Bryan,
Dick Purcell

Captains of the Clouds
US 1942 113m Technicolor
Warner (Hal B. Wallis, William Cagney)

A flippant Canadian Air Force pilot proves his worth
under fire.

Recruiting poster heroics, reasonably well done but
lacking the vital spark.

w Arthur T. Horman, Richard Macaulay, Norman
Reilly Raine   d Michael Curtiz   ph Sol Polito,
Wilfrid M. Cline   m Max Steiner   ad Ted Smith

James Cagney, Dennis Morgan, Brenda Marshall,
George Tobias, Alan Hale, Reginald Gardiner,
Reginald Denny, Paul Cavanagh, Clem Bevans, J. M.
Kerrigan

'Pure tribute to the unchanging forcefulness of James
Cagney.' – *New York Post*

AAN: Sol Polito, Wilfrid M. Cline; Ted Smith

The Captain's Paradise *
GB 1953 89m bw
BL/London (Anthony Kimmins)
V, V*, L

The captain of a steamer plying between Gibraltar and
Tangier has a wife in each port, one to suit each of his
personalities.

Over-dry comedy in which the idea is much funnier
than the script. One is left with the memory of a
pleasant star performance.

w Alec Coppel, Nicholas Phipps   d Anthony
Kimmins   ph Ted Scaife   m Malcolm Arnold

Alec Guinness, Celia Johnson, Yvonne de Carlo, Charles Goldner, Miles Malleson, Bill Fraser, Nicholas Phipps, Ferdy Mayne, George Benson

AAN: original story (Alec Coppel)

The Captain's Table *
GB   1958   89m   Eastmancolor
Rank (Joseph Janni)
V*

A cargo skipper is given command of a luxury liner and has to watch his manners.

Lively adaptation of a frivolous book of obvious jokes, most of which come up quite funny amid the luxurious surroundings.

w John Whiting, Bryan Forbes, Nicholas Phipps *novel* Richard Gordon d Jack Lee ph Christopher Challis m Frank Cordell

John Gregson, Peggy Cummins, Donald Sinden, Reginald Beckwith, Nadia Gray, Richard Wattis, Maurice Denham, Nicholas Phipps, Joan Sims, Miles Malleson

The Captive City **
US   1951   91m   bw
UA/Aspen (Theron Warth)

Small-town corruption imposed by the Mafia is revealed by a crusading editor who defies threats to his wife and family and tells all to the Kefauver Commission.

Excellent documentary melodrama made in a style then original, also notable for use of the Hoge deep focus lens.

w *Karl Lamb, Alvin Josephy Jnr* d *Robert Wise* ph *Lee Garmes* m Jerome Moross

John Forsythe, Joan Camden, Harold J. Kennedy, Marjorie Crossland, Victor Sutherland, Ray Teal, Martin Milner, Hal K. Dawson

The Captive City
Italy   1963   110m   bw
Paramount
Italian title: La Città Prigionera

Rebels keep an assorted group of people captive in an Athens hotel.

Dim would-be thriller which rambles on far too long.

w Guy Elmes, Eric Bercovici, Marc Brandel *novel* John Appleby d Joseph Anthony

David Niven, Lea Massari, Ben Gazzara, Daniela Rocca, Martin Balsam, Michael Craig, Percy Herbert

La Captive du Desert
France   1990   101m   colour
Artificial Eye/La Sept/Roger Diamantis/St-André-des-Arts/Jean-Bernard Fetoux/SGGC/Jean-Luc Larguier/Titane (Pascale Dauman, Jean-Luc Ormires)

A Frenchwoman is held captive in the desert by nomadic tribesmen.

A minimalist movie, based on a true story, with little dialogue or action but a great deal of sand.

d Raymond Depardon ph Raymond Depardon m Jean-Jacques Lemtre ed Roger Ikhief, Camille Cotte, Pascale Charolais

Sandrine Bonnaire, Dobi Kor, Fadi Taha, Dobi Wachink, Badei Barka

'Half the audience with whom I watched the film left before the end while the other half remained, fascinated by the vividness of the photography and the highly personal nature of the film. It is one of those in which nothing, and everything, happens.' – *Derek Malcolm, Guardian*

The Captive Heart **
GB   1946   108m   bw
Ealing (Michael Relph)
V, V*

Stories of life among British officers in a German

POW camp, especially of a Czech who has stolen the papers of a dead Britisher.

Archetypal POW drama lacing an almost poetic treatment with humour and melodrama.

w Angus Macphail, Guy Morgan d Basil Dearden ph Lionel Banes, Douglas Slocombe m Alan Rawsthorne

Michael Redgrave, *Jack Warner*, Basil Radford, Mervyn Johns, Jimmy Hanley, Gordon Jackson, Ralph Michael, Derek Bond, Karel Stepanek, Guy Middleton, Jack Lambert, Gladys Henson, Rachel Kempson, Meriel Forbes

'A warm, emotional, intensely human document, entitled to rate among the best twenty films of the last ten years.' – *News of the World*

'A human form with animal instincts!'
Captive Wild Woman
US   1943   60m   bw
Universal

A doctor finds a way of developing the glands of an ape and turning it into a beautiful girl.

Lamebrain horror item which amazingly spawned two sequels, *Jungle Woman* (1944) and *Jungle Captive* (1945).

w Griffin Jay, Henry Sucher d Edward Dmytryk

Evelyn Ankers, Aquanetta, John Carradine, Martha Vickers, Milburn Stone

Captured
US   1933   72m   bw
Warner

A prisoner-of-war discovers that his best friend was his wife's lover.

Turgid and heavy-going early variation on a theme which would become very familiar indeed; the stars couldn't save it.

w Edward Chodorov *novel* Sir Philip Gibbs d Roy Del Ruth

Leslie Howard, Paul Lukas, Douglas Fairbanks Jnr, Margaret Lindsay, J. Carrol Naish, Arthur Hohl

'Too many obviously adverse ingredients, chiefly story, to chalk this one up as a winner . . . at best its earnings shape up as spotty.' – *Variety*

'Is it a phantom, a demon, or the devil himself?'
The Car
US   1977   98m   Technicolor   Panavision
Universal (Peter Saphier)
V*

A small south-western town is terrorized by a driverless car which may be a creation of the devil.

Silly suspenser with a draggy midsection.

w Dennis Shryack, Michael Butler, Lane Slate d Elliot Silverstein ph Gerald Hirschfeld m Leonard Rosenman

James Brolin, Kathleen Lloyd, John Marley. R. G. Armstrong, John Rubinstein

Car 99
US   1935   70m   bw
Paramount

A novice state trooper redeems early failure by capturing bank robbers.

Competent routine programmer which helped to establish its star.

w Karl Detzer, C. Gardner Sullivan d Charles Barton

Fred MacMurray, Ann Sheridan, Sir Guy Standing

'Heaps of excitement and comedy make a swell hour of entertainment for the nabe element.' – *Variety*

Car of Dreams
GB   1935   72m   bw
Gaumont British (Michael Balcon)

A rich man's son buys a car for one of his father's factory girls.

Silly comedy with sillier music, remade from a German original.

w Austin Melford d Austin Melford, Graham Cutts ph Mutz Greenbaum m Mischa Spoliansky ad Alfred Junge

John Mills, Grete Mosheim, Mark Lester, Robertson Hare, Norah Howard

Car Trouble
GB   1986   93m   colour
Thorn EMI/GTO/Goldfarb (Howard Malin, Gregory J. DeSantis)
V, V*

A woman having an affair with a car salesman finds herself sexually locked to him in her husband's new vehicle.

This weird premise for a comedy rings up remarkably few laughs.

w James Whaley, A. J. Tipping d David Green ph Michael Garfath

Julie Walters, Ian Charleson, Stratford Johns, Vincenzo Ricotta

Car Wash
US   1976   96m   Technicolor
Universal
V, V*

Various eccentrics congregate around the Dee Luxe Car Wash.

Zany ethnic (black) comedy with little rhyme or reason in its development but a certain vigour in some of its sketches. A subsequent TV series didn't last.

w Joel Schumacher d Michael Schultz

Franklyn Ajaye, Sully Boyar, Richard Pryor, Ivan Dixon, Antonio Fargas, Tracy Reed

'Its specialty is yanking laughs by having blacks do dirtier versions of the standard pranks that naughty kids used to do in comedies.' – *Pauline Kael*

Caravaggio *
GB   1986   89m   Technicolor
BFI/Channel 4/Nicholas Ward-Jackson (Sarah Radclyffe)
V

An imaginary biopic of the Italian painter who died in 1610, with emphasis on homosexual models, a variety of scandals, and jokey anachronisms.

A classic for the gay crowd; something of a mystery for everyone else.

wd Derek Jarman ph Gabriel Beristain m Simon Fisher Turner pd Christopher Hobbs

Nigel Terry, Sean Bean, Garry Cooper, Spencer Leigh

'It rises above its financial restrictions to prove that less can be a lot more.' – *Variety*

Caravan
US   1934   101m   bw
Fox

A countess marries a gypsy.

Odd romantic drama with music: too whimsical to succeed.

w Samson Raphaelson d Erik Charell ph Ernest Palmer, Theodor Sparkuhl m/ly Werner B. Heymann, Gus Kahn

Loretta Young, Charles Boyer, Jean Parker, Phillips Holmes, Louise Fazenda, Eugene Pallette, C. Aubrey Smith, Charley Grapewin, Noah Beery, Dudley Digges

'Big, beautiful and boring . . . peasants come popping out of nowhere, in pairs, tens, hundreds, thousands, and burst into song.' – *Variety*

Caravan
GB   1946   122m   bw
Gainsborough (Harold Huth)

A young man on a mission in Spain is left for dead by emissaries of his rival in love; he is nursed back to health by a gypsy girl who falls in love with him.

Artificial, romantic, high-flown period tosh without the courage of its lack of convictions. At the time, an exhibitor's dream.

w Roland Pertwee novel Lady Eleanor Smith
d Arthur Crabtree ph Stephen Dade

Stewart Granger, Jean Kent, Anne Crawford, *Robert Helpmann*, Dennis Price, Gerard Heinz, Enid Stamp-Taylor, David Horne, John Salew

Caravan to Vaccares
GB/France 1974 98m Eastmancolor Panavision
Crowndale (Geoffrey Reeve)

An American drifter on the Riviera is employed to escort a mysterious Hungarian to New York.

Lumpy Alistair MacLean action thriller, all a bit *déjà vu.*

w Paul Wheeler d Geoffrey Reeve ph Frederic Tammes m Stanley Myers

David Birney, Charlotte Rampling, Michel Lonsdale, Marcel Bozzuff, Michael Bryant

'An undernourished plot advanced only by a series of venerable clichés.' – *MFB*

'The biggest load of schoolboy hokum since Boy's Own Paper ceased circulation.' – *Michael Billington, Illustrated London News*

Caravans
US/Iran 1978 123m Technicolor Panavision
Ibex/FIDCI (Elmo Williams)
S

In the Middle East in 1948, a junior diplomat is sent to bring back the daughter of a US politician, who has married an Arab, left him, and joined a Bedouin caravan.

Curiously halting succession of pretty pictures and not much plot; what there is tends to take second place to philosophy and eastern promise.

w Nancy Voyles Crawford, Thomas A. MacMahon, Lorraine Williams novel James Michener d James Fargo ph Douglas Slocombe m Mike Batt

Anthony Quinn, Michael Sarrazin, Jennifer O'Neill, Christopher Lee, Joseph Cotten, Barry Sullivan, Jeremy Kemp

'A tiresome exercise in anti-climax.' – *Tim Pulleine, MFB*

† The film cost 14 million dollars and is said to have been financed by the Shah of Iran.

Carbine Williams
US 1952 93m bw
MGM (Armand Deutsch)

An imprisoned bootlegger perfects a new gun and is pardoned.

Flat fictionalization of a true story, with the star miscast.

w Art Cohn d Richard Thorpe ph William Mellor m Conrad Salinger

James Stewart, Jean Hagen, Wendell Corey, Carl Benton Reid, Paul Stewart, Otto Hulett, James Arness

Carbon Copy
US 1981 91m Metrocolor
Hemdale/RKO (Stanley Shapiro, Carter de Haven)
V*, L

An executive is shocked when his long-lost son turns out to be black.

Stale comedy. The producers clearly think the basic idea worth ramming home a score of times; the characterization is thin and the production undernourished.

w Stanley Shapiro d Michael Schultz ph Fred J. Koenekamp m Bill Conti

George Segal, Susan Saint James, Jack Warden, Dick Martin, Denzel Washington, Paul Winfield

'It makes *Guess Who's Coming to Dinner?* look like a tract for the nineties.' – *Derek Malcolm, Guardian*

'He's the cheekiest man in town!'
The Card **
GB 1952 91m bw
Rank/British Film Makers (John Bryan)
V*
US title: *The Promoter*

A bright young clerk from the potteries finds many ingenious ways of improving his bank account and his place in society.

Pleasing period comedy with the star in a made-to-measure role and excellent production values.

w Eric Ambler novel Arnold Bennett d Ronald Neame ph Oswald Morris m William Alwyn ad T. Hopwell Ash

Alec Guinness, Glynis Johns, Petula Clark, *Valerie Hobson*, Edward Chapman, Veronica Turleigh, Gibb McLaughlin, Frank Pettingell

Card of Fate: see *Le Grand Jeu*

Cardboard Cavalier *
GB 1949 96m bw
Rank/Two Cities (Walter Forde)

In Cromwellian England, royalists commission a barrow boy to carry a secret letter. Helped by Nell Gwynn, he succeeds after encounters with a castle ghost and custard pies.

A pantomime crossed with an Aldwych farce in a period setting. It failed at the time but now seems a brave try, with nice judgment all round.

w Noel Langley d Walter Forde ph Jack Hildyard m Lambert Williamson

Sid Field, Margaret Lockwood, Mary Clare, Jerry Desmonde, Claude Hulbert, Irene Handl, Brian Worth, Edmund Willard (as Cromwell)

Cardigan's Last Case: see *State's Attorney*

The Cardinal *
US 1963 175m Technicolor Panavision 70
Gamma/Otto Preminger
V*, L, S

A 1917 ordinand becomes a Boston curate, a fighter of the Ku Klux Klan, a Rome diplomat, and finally gets a cardinal's hat.

Heavy-going documentary melodrama with many interesting sequences marred by lack of cohesion, too much grabbing at world problems, and over-sensational personal asides.

w Robert Dozier novel Henry Morton Robinson d Otto Preminger ph Leon Shamroy m Jerome Moross pd Lyle Wheeler titles Saul Bass

Tom Tryon, *Carol Lynley*, Dorothy Gish, Maggie Macnamara, Cecil Kellaway, John Saxon, *John Huston*, Robert Morse, Burgess Meredith, Jill Haworth, Raf Vallone, Tullio Carminati, Ossie Davis, Chill Wills, Arthur Hunnicutt, Murray Hamilton, Patrick O'Neal, Romy Schneider

'Very probably the last word in glossy dishonesty posturing as serious art.' – *John Simon*

'Mere and sheer wide screen Technicolor movie.' – *Stanley Kauffmann*

AAN: Otto Preminger; Leon Shamroy; John Huston

'To thwart a king's passion, he gambled the fate of a nation!'
Cardinal Richelieu *
US 1935 83m bw
Twentieth Century (Darryl F. Zanuck)

Fictionalized biography of the unscrupulous cardinal who was the grey eminence behind Louis XIII.

One of George Arliss's better star vehicles, with not much conviction but excellent production values.

w Maude Howell, Cameron Rogers, W. P. Lipscomb d Rowland V. Lee ph Peverell Marley m Alfred Newman

George Arliss, Maureen O'Sullivan, Edward Arnold, Cesar Romero

'In selecting the churchly cardinal of Bulwer-Lytton rather than the cavalier-cardinal beloved of Dumas, they have lost romance and dash but gained compensating dignity . . . a fine technical production.' – *Variety*

The Care Bears' Adventure In Wonderland!
Canada 1987 75m colour
Fox/Nelvana Productions (Michael Hirsch, Patrick Loubert, Clive A. Smith)
V, V*, L

The Care Bears go through the looking glass with Alice.

Undemanding and uninteresting whimsy for the under-sixes.

w Susi Snooks, John DeKlein story Peter Sauder d Raymond Jafelice m Trish Cullen, John Sebastian

voices of Colin Fox, Bob Dermer, Eva Almos, Dan Hennessy, Jim Henshaw

The Care Bears Movie
US 1985 75m colour
Nelvana (Michael Hirsch, Patrick Loubert, Clive Smith)
V, V*

Magical bears combat an evil spirit who aims to make everybody miserable.

Cartoon feature, sluggishly animated and narrated, with appeal to nobody over five years old. Produced as a back-up to a range of toys.

w Peter Sauder d Arna Selznick m John Sebastian

voices of Mickey Rooney, Georgia Engel, Harry Dean Stanton

Career
US 1939 80m bw
RKO (Robert Sisk)

A respected small-town storekeeper has old scores to settle against the local banker.

Modest, pleasing, rather faded 'B' picture.

w Dalton Trumbo, Bert Granet novel Phil Stong d Leigh Jason ph Frank Redman

Edward Ellis, Samuel S. Hinds, Anne Shirley, Janet Beecher, Leon Errol, Raymond Hatton, Hobart Cavanaugh

'Small-town story will sell better outside major playdates.' – *Variety*

† The film featured the winners of the Gateway to Hollywood talent contest, John Archer and Alice Eden.

Career *
US 1959 105m bw
Paramount/Hal B. Wallis (Paul Nathan)
V*

An actor from the midwest finally gets his chance in New York.

A location melodrama with the feel of a documentary, well played but slow and rather indeterminate.

w James Lee play James Lee d Joseph Anthony ph Joseph LaShelle m Franz Waxman

Anthony Franciosa, Dean Martin, Shirley Maclaine, Carolyn Jones, Joan Blackman, Robert Middleton, Frank McHugh, Donna Douglas

AAN: Joseph LaShelle

Career Opportunities
US 1991 85m DeLuxe
Universal/Hughes Entertainment (John Hughes, A. Hunt Lowry)
V, V*, L

A young nightwatchman outwits thieves trying to rob a department store.

Tired teen comedy that runs out of jokes long before the end.

w John Hughes d Bryan Gordon ph Don McAlpine m Thomas Newman pd Paul Sylbert ed Glenn Farr, Peck Prior

Frank Whaley, Jennifer Connelly, Dermot Mulroney, Kieran Mulroney, John M. Jackson, Jenny O'Hara, Noble Willingham, Barry Corbin, John Candy (uncredited)

'Plenty of absorbing characters, smart, snappy dialog and delightful stretches of comic foolery.' – Variety

Career Woman
US 1936 75m bw
TCF

A shyster lawyer helps a girl student to win a murder case.

Passable programme material which didn't bore.

w Lamar Trotti story Gene Fowler d Lewis Seiler

Michael Whalen, Claire Trevor, Isabel Jewell, Eric Linden, Virginia Field, Gene Lockhart, Ed Brophy, El Brendel

'Teeters between farce and stark realism . . . not exactly for the family trade.' – Variety

Carefree *
US 1938 85m bw
RKO (Pandro S. Berman)
V*, L

A humourless lawyer sends his undecided girlfriend to an alienist, with whom she falls in love.

Slight, frothy comedy musical; quite palatable, but it signalled the end of the Astaire-Rogers series.

w Allan Scott, Ernest Pagano d Mark Sandrich ph Robert de Grasse md Victor Baravalle m/ly Irving Berlin ch Hermes Pan ad Van Nest Polglase

Fred Astaire, Ginger Rogers, Ralph Bellamy, Luella Gear, Clarence Kolb, Jack Carson, Franklin Pangborn, Walter Kingsford, Hattie McDaniel

songs: 'I Used to Be Colour Blind'; 'The Yam'; 'The Night Is Filled with Music'

'Perhaps their poorest musical . . . a disappointing story and the stars alone may save it.' – Variety

AAN: Victor Baravalle; Van Nest Polglase; song 'Change Partners'

Careful
Canada 1992 100m colour
ICA/Greg and Tracy Film Ministry (Greg Klymkiw, Tracy Traeger)

Sex and death engulf two families living in constant danger of being killed by Alpine avalanches.

A deliberately over-the-top melodramatic concoction, a heady stew of rape, incest, requited and unrequited love, a deformed child kept hidden in an attic and ghosts bringing warnings of doom. It's a low-budget camp extravaganza that can amuse, but can as easily infuriate by its knowing air.

w George Toles, Guy Maddin d Guy Maddin ph Guy Maddin m John McCulloch pd Guy Maddin ed Guy Maddin

Kyle McCulloch, Gosia Dobrowolska, Sarah Neville, Brent Neale, Paul Cox, Victor Cowie, Jackie Burroughs

'In a film which can afford real animals but not real mountains, a couple of goats running up a slope – swathed in dry ice, shot in purple or blue

monochrome and captioned to tell us the altitude – stand in for the Alps.' – Claire Monk, Sight and Sound

Careful, Soft Shoulders *
US 1942 69m bw
TCF (Walter Morosco)

A Washington socialite becomes a spy for both sides.

Modest, slightly unusual second feature which over the years has gathered for itself more reputation than it really deserves.

wd Oliver H. P. Garrett ph Charles Clarke m Leigh Harline

Virginia Bruce, James Ellison, Aubrey Mather, Sheila Ryan, Ralph Byrd

Careless Lady
US 1932 76m bw
Fox

A young girl from the country pretends to be a married society woman and finds herself with a husband she doesn't want.

It was the scriptwriter who was careless: the story doesn't make much sense.

w Guy Bolton story Reita Lambert d Kenneth MacKenna

Joan Bennett, John Boles, Minna Gombell, Weldon Heyburn, Raul Roulien, Fortunio Bonanova, Josephine Hull

'Reaching house averages will be beyond expectations regardless of campaign.' – Variety

The Caretaker *
GB 1964 105m bw
Caretaker Films (Michael Birkett)
US title: The Guest

Two brothers invite a revolting tramp to share their attic.

Rather doleful filming of the fashionable play with its non-plot, irregular conceits and interesting interplay of character. It remains a theatrical experience.

w Harold Pinter d Clive Donner ph Nicolas Roeg m Ron Grainer

Alan Bates, Robert Shaw, Donald Pleasence

'Now the screen tells what makes a woman – and what breaks her!'

The Caretakers *
US 1963 97m bw
UA/Hall Bartlett
GB title: Borderlines

The interrelationship of several cases in a state mental hospital.

Rather hysterical melodrama, lacking in the stature required for its subject, but sometimes perversely entertaining.

w Henry F. Greenberg novel Daniel Telfer d Hall Bartlett ph Lucien Ballard m Elmer Bernstein

Polly Bergen, Robert Stack, Joan Crawford, Diane McBain, Janis Paige, Van Williams, Robert Vaughn, Herbert Marshall, Constance Ford

AAN: Lucien Ballard

The Carey Treatment *
US 1972 101m Metrocolor Panavision
MGM (William Belasco)

A Boston pathologist investigating the death of an abortion victim becomes the potential murder victim of a father turned killer.

Pretentious thriller with a tendency to make moral points among the bloodshed; vigorously but variably made.

w James P. Bonner novel A Case of Need by Jeffrey Hudson d Blake Edwards ph Frank Stanley m Roy Budd

James Coburn, Jennifer O'Neill, Skye Aubrey, Pat Hingle, Dan O'Herlihy, Elizabeth Allen, Alex Dreier, Regis Toomey

Cargo of Innocents: see Stand By for Action

Cargo to Capetown
US 1950 84m bw
Columbia

A merchant ship captain Shanghais his friend on a long voyage.

Routine, competently staged thick ear.

w Lionel Houser d Earl McEvoy

Broderick Crawford, John Ireland, Ellen Drew, Edgar Buchanan, Ted de Corsia

Caribbean
US 1952 94m Technicolor
Paramount/Pine-Thomas (William H. Pine, William C. Thomas)
GB title: Caribbean Gold

An 18th-century pirate captures the nephew of his old enemy.

Adequate but not very exciting swashbuckler with fair production values.

w Frank L. Moss, Edward Ludwig d Edward Ludwig ph Lionel Lindon m Lucien Cailliet

John Payne, Arlene Dahl, Cedric Hardwicke (incredibly cast as the pirate), Francis L. Sullivan, Dennis Hoey

Caribbean Gold: see Caribbean

The Caribbean Mystery
US 1945 65m bw
William Girard/TCF

A retired cop investigates the disappearance of several geologists on an oil company payroll.

Modest mystery, previously filmed as Murder in Trinidad.

w W. Scott Darling novel John W. Vandercook d Robert Webb

James Dunn, Sheila Ryan, Edward Ryan, Jackie Paley, Reed Hadley

The Cariboo Trail
US 1949 80m Cinecolor
Nat Holt (TCF)
V*, L

Prospectors get involved in a cattle war.

Standard Western full of predictable elements.

w Frank Gruber d Edwin L. Marin

Randolph Scott, Gabby Hayes, Bill Williams, Karin Booth, Victor Jory

Carlito's Way *
US 1993 145m DeLuxe
Universal (Martin Bregman, Willi Baer, Michael S. Bregman)
S

A drug dealer finds it tough when he tries to go straight.

A good, if unoriginal, gangster movie with some action sequences that add a little distinction; it would benefit, though, from being shorter.

w David Koepp novel Carlito's Way and After Hours by Edwin Torres d Brian de Palma ph Stephen H. Burum m Patrick Doyle pd Richard Sylbert ed Bill Pankow, Kristina Boden

Al Pacino, Sean Penn, Penelope Ann Miller, John Leguizamo, Ingrid Rogers, Luis Guzman, James Rebhorn, Viggo Mortensen

'Handsomely made, expertly directed and colorfully acted, it should satisfy action buffs and slightly more sophisticated audiences.' – Variety

'An old-style gangster movie with some neat contemporary knobs on.' – Derek Malcolm

Carlton-Browne of the FO

GB 1958 88m bw
British Lion/Charter Films (John Boulting)
V
US title: *Man in a Cocked Hat*

When valuable mineral deposits are found in a small British colony, the diplomat sent to cement good relations does quite the reverse.

Hit-or-miss farcical comedy several rungs below the Ealing style, with all concerned in poor form.

wd Jeffrey Dell, Roy Boulting *ph* Max Greene
m John Addison

Terry-Thomas, Peter Sellers, Ian Bannen, Thorley Walters, Raymond Huntley, John Le Mesurier, Luciana Paluzzi, Miles Malleson, Kynaston Reeves, Marie Lohr

Carmen **

Spain 1983 101m Eastmancolor
Emiliano Piedra Productions/Television Española (Emiliano Piedra)
V*, L

A rehearsal for the ballet *Carmen* finds dancers playing out in reality the parts of the drama.

Enjoyable but exhausting melodrama with elements of *The Red Shoes;* meticulous choreography and direction are its chief assets.

w Carlos Saura, Antonio Gades *novel* Prosper Mérimée *d* Carlos Saura *ph* Teo Escamilla *m* Paco de Lucia *ad* Felix Murcia *ed* Pedro del Rey

Antonio Gades, Laura del Sol, Paco de Lucia, Cristina Hoyos

'Extremely enjoyable, but lacks the edge that would make it in any way compelling.' – *Jill Forbes, MFB*

AAN: best foreign film

Carmen **

Italy/France 1984 152m Eastmancolor
Panavision
Opera/Gaumont (Patrice Ledoux)
V, V*, L, S

A luxuriantly filmed version of Bizet's opera, generally received with critical rapture.

d Francesco Rosi *ph* Pasqualino de Santis *pd* Enrico Job

Julia Migenes-Johnson, Placido Domingo, Ruggiero Raimondi

† Silent versions stretch back to 1915 – that one starred Geraldine Farrar the opera singer (in a silent movie, by producer Cecil B. de Mille's whim).

Carmen Jones *

US 1954 105m DeLuxe Cinemascope
TCF (Otto Preminger)
V*, L, S

A factory girl marries a soldier, and is strangled by him for infidelity.

Black American updating of Bizet's opera, not really satisfactory but given full marks for trying, though the main singing is dubbed and the effect remains doggedly theatrical.

w Harry Kleiner *d* Otto Preminger *ph* Sam Leavitt *ly* Oscar Hammerstein II *titles* Saul Bass *md* Herschel Burke Gilbert

Dorothy Dandridge, Harry Belafonte, *Pearl Bailey,* Olga James, Joe Adams, Roy Glenn, Nick Stewart, Diahann Carroll, Brock Peters

'All one regrets is that the director has been unable to impose a unifying style on this promising material.' – *Gavin Lambert*

AAN: Herschel Burke Gilbert; Dorothy Dandridge

Carnage: see *A Bay of Blood*

Carnal Knowledge *

US 1971 97m Technicolor Panavision
Avco Embassy/Icarus (Mike Nichols)
V, V*, L

A college student embarks on an enthusiastic and varied sex life but by middle age is bored and empty.

Hampered by an unsuitable wide screen, this pretentious but fragmented comedy drama is embarrassingly conscious of its own daring in subject and language, and good performances are weighed down by an unsubtle script and tricksy direction.

w Jules Feiffer *d* Mike Nichols *ph* Giuseppe Rotunno *m* various songs *pd* Richard Sylbert

Jack Nicholson, *Arthur Garfunkel,* Candice Bergen, *Ann-Margret,* Rita Moreno

AAN: Ann-Margret

Carnegie Hall

US 1947 134m bw
Federal Films (Boris Morros, William Le Baron)

The story of New York's music centre, based on a fiction about a cleaner who finally becomes a concert organizer when her son is a famous pianist.

Slim and risible excuse for a classical concert, featuring among others Bruno Walter, Leopold Stokowski, Artur Rubinstein, Jascha Heifitz, Lily Pons, Rise Stevens, Ezio Pinza, Jan Peerce, Harry James, Vaughn Monroe and the New York Philharmonic Symphony Orchestra.

w Karl Kamb *d* Edgar G. Ulmer *ph* William Miller

Marsha Hunt, William Prince, Frank McHugh, Martha O'Driscoll

'The thickest and sourest mess of musical mulligatawny I have yet had to sit down to.' – *James Agee*

Un Carnet de Bal **

France 1937 135m bw
Lévy/Strauss/Sigma
aka: *Life Dances On*

A rich widow seeks her partners at a ball she remembers from her youth, finding that they are all failures and the ball a village hop.

Considering its fame, this is a lumpy porridge of a picture, good in parts but often slow, pretentious and banal. Its gallery of actors is, however, unique.

w Jean Sarment, Pierre Wolff, Bernard Zimmer, Henri Jeanson, Julien Duvivier *d* Julien Duvivier *ph* Michel Kelber, Philippe Agostini *m* Maurice Jaubert

Marie Bell, Françoise Rosay, *Louis Jouvet, Raimu,* Harry Baur, *Fernandel, Pierre Blanchar*

'Recent winner of the Mussolini Cup is loaded with top names, but it is not the film of the year . . . it tries to take in too much and takes too long to put across.' – *Variety*

† The film's international success took Duvivier to Hollywood, where he half-remade it as *Lydia* and went on to other multi-story films such as *Tales of Manhattan* and *Flesh and Fantasy.*

Les Carnets de Major Thompson: see *The Diary of Major Thompson*

Carnival

US 1934 77m bw
Columbia

A widowed puppeteer takes custody of his child, which is sought by the maternal grandfather, and seeks anonymity in a circus.

Curious sentimental melodrama with the stars shown in an unusual light.

w Robert Riskin *d* Walter Lang

Lee Tracy, Jimmy Durante, Sally Eilers, Dickie Walters, Thomas Jackson, Florence Rice, Lucille Ball

'This should hold its own, though it probably will not climb to big grosses.' – *Variety*

Carnival

GB 1946 93m bw
Rank/Two Cities (John Sutro, William Sassoon)

In the 1890s, a ballet dancer marries a dour Cornish farmer, who shoots her when her erstwhile lover comes after her.

Flimsy screen version of a solidly old-fashioned romantic drama.

w Eric Maschwitz *novel* Compton Mackenzie *d* Stanley Haynes *ph* Guy Green

Sally Gray, Michael Wilding, Bernard Miles, Cathleen Nesbitt, Stanley Holloway, Jean Kent, Nancy Price, Hazel Court, Brenda Bruce, Catherine Lacey

† The story was previously filmed in 1931, as *Dance Pretty Lady,* with Ann Casson and Carl Harbord. The 1931 film *Carnival,* with Matheson Lang, is based on a story identical to *Men Are Not Gods* and *A Double Life:* an actor becomes obsessed with the part of Othello and strangles his wife.

Carnival in Costa Rica

US 1947 97m Technicolor
TCF (William A. Bacher)

A young Costa Rican, engaged to an American singer, returns home to find that his parents expect him to marry his childhood sweetheart.

Decidedly rundown musical in which incessant carnival largely supplants the wispy plot.

w John Larkin, Samuel Hoffenstein, Elizabeth Reinhardt *d* Gregory Ratoff *ph* Harry Jackson *ch* Leonid Massine *m/y* Harry Ruby, Ernesto Lecuona

Dick Haymes, Vera-Ellen, Celeste Holm, J. Carrol Naish, Cesar Romero

Carnival in Flanders: see *La Kermesse Héroïque*

Carnival of Souls

US 1962 80m bw
Herts-Lion (Herk Harvey)
V, V*, L

After an accident, a lady ghost emerges to become the new church organist.

Absurd but occasionally compelling independently made horror film which would have been better in half-hour form.

w John Clifford *d* Herk Harvey *ph* Maurice Prather *m* Gene Moore *ed* Dan Palmquist, Bill de Jarnette

Candace Hilligoss, Herk Harvey, Francis Feist, Sidney Berger

'Has the power to detach you from your surroundings and put you in the middle of its own distinctive nowhere.' – *Terrence Rafferty, New Yorker*

† Made in Kansas, allegedly for less than 100,000 dollars.

Carnival of Terror: see *The Funhouse*

Carnival of Thieves: see *The Caper of the Golden Bulls*

Carnival Story

US/Germany 1954 95m Technicolor
The King Brothers
V*

A starving girl becomes a trapezist at a German circus and stirs up jealousy among her partners.

Bleak reworking of *The Three Maxims* (qv), reworked again with more expertise in *Trapeze* (qv); this version is a cheap and unattractive co-production.

w Kurt Neumann, Hans Jacoby d Kurt Neumann
ph Ernest Haller m Willy Schmidt-Gentner

Anne Baxter, Steve Cochran, Lyle Bettger, George
Nader, Jay C. Flippen

'63 million years ago they ruled the Earth. They're back,
    and it's no theme park!'
Carnosaur
US   1993   83m   Foto Kem colour
New Horizons (Mike Elliott)
V, V*, S

A scientist breeds giant meat-eating mutant chickens
in an attempt to recreate dinosaurs and replace
humans by a kinder species.

Cheap attempt to cash in on the *Jurassic Park* craze
from Roger Corman's outfit, recast as a conventional,
gory, monster-on-the-loose, mad-scientist horror pic:
nasty, brutish and, fortunately, short.

wd Adam Simon novel Harry Adam Knight (John
Brosnan) ph Keith Holland m Nigel Holton
pd Aaron Osborne sp John Buechler, Magical
Media Industries, Alan Lasky ed Richard Genter

Diane Ladd, Raphael Sbarge, Jennifer Runyon,
Harrison Page, Ned Bellamy, Clint Howard

'This breezy outing is a not-very-filling popcorn treat.
Predictably plotted with bargain-basement effects, it's
a serviceable programmer.' – *Variety*

Carny
US   1980   105m   Technicolor
Lorimar/Jonathan Taplin (Robbie Robertson)
V*

Three wacky characters join a travelling carnival.

Sordid, sexy melodrama which seems to be doing a
Jules and Jim with no holds barred. Not badly made,
but full of people one would cross the road to avoid.

w Thomas Baum d Robert Kaylor ph Harry
Stradling Jnr m Alex North

Gary Busey, Jodie Foster, Robbie Robertson, Kenneth
McMillan, Meg Foster, Elisha Cook Jnr

'Too dark and turbulent a vision to be palatable to a
large public.' – *Variety*

Carolina
US   1934   85m   bw
Fox (Darryl F. Zanuck)
GB title: *House of Connelly*

A Yankee farmer's daughter falls in love with a
Southern plantation owner.

Mildly pleasing period piece.

w Reginald Berkeley play The House of Connelly by
Paul Green d Henry King ph Hal Mohr
m Louis de Francesco

Janet Gaynor, Lionel Barrymore, Robert Young,
Henrietta Crosman, Mona Barrie, Richard Cromwell,
Stepin Fetchit

'An arresting saga of a proud old southern family that
starts out threateningly strong but peters to the point
where it misses being another *State Fair*.' – *Variety*

Carolina Blues
US   1944   81m   bw
Columbia

A bandleader needs a new singer.

Wispy comedy musical towards the end of Kyser's
unlikely popularity.

w M. M. Musselman, Kenneth Earl, Joseph Hoffman,
Al Martin d Leigh Jason

Kay Kyser and his band, Ann Miller, Victor Moore

Caroline Chérie
France   1951   115m approx   bw
SNEG/Cinéphonie

Adventures of an attractive and willing young French
girl in the days of the revolution.

A cheerful French imitation of *Forever Amber;* witless
and not very entertaining despite good period sense
and a certain amount of self-mockery.

w Jean Anouilh novel Cécil Saint-Laurent
d Richard Poitier ph Maurice Barry m Georges
Auric

Martine Carol, Jacques Dacqmine, Marie Déa, Paul
Bernard, Pierre Cressoy

† After several sequels, a colour remake appeared in
1967.

Carousel *
US   1956   128m   Eastmancolor   Cinemascope 55
TCF (Henry Ephron)
V, V (W), V*, L, S

A ne'er-do-well dies while committing a holdup.
Fifteen years later he returns from heaven to set his
family's affairs in order.

Based on a fantasy play with an honourable history,
this super-wide-screen version of an effective stage
musical is hollow and boring, a humourless whimsy
in which even the songs seem an intrusion.

w Phoebe and Henry Ephron, from the musical based
on Ferenc Molnar's play *Liliom* d Henry King
ph Charles G. Clarke m/ly Rodgers and
Hammerstein ch Rod Alexander, Agnes de Mille

Gordon Macrae, Shirley Jones, Cameron Mitchell,
Gene Lockhart, Barbara Ruick, Robert Rounseville

'This is adult entertainment!'
The Carpetbaggers **
US   1964   150m   Technicolor   Panavision
Paramount/Embassy (Joseph E. Levine)
V*

A young playboy inherits an aircraft business,
becomes a megalomaniac tycoon, and moves to
Hollywood in his search for power.

Enjoyable pulp fiction clearly suggested by the career
of Howard Hughes. Lashings of old-fashioned
melodrama, quite well pointed by all concerned.

w John Michael Hayes novel Harold Robbins
d Edward Dmytryk ph Joseph MacDonald
m Elmer Bernstein ad Hal Pereira, Walter Tyler

George Peppard, Carroll Baker, *Alan Ladd* (his last film),
Martin Balsam, Bob Cummings, Martha Hyer,
Elizabeth Ashley, Lew Ayres, Ralph Taeger, Archie
Moore, Leif Erickson, Audrey Totter

'One of those elaborate conjuring tricks in which
yards and yards of coloured ribbon are spread all over
the stage merely to prove that the conjuror has
nothing up his sleeve.' – *Tom Milne*

Carquake: see *Cannonball*

Carrefour *
France   1938   75m   bw
BUP Tuscherer

A French manufacturer, wounded during the war,
finds himself the centre of blackmail plots.

Intriguing melodrama which was later rather flatly
remade in Hollywood as *Crossroads.*

w Hans Kofka d Kurt Bernhardt

Charles Vanel, Jules Berry, Suzy Prim, Tania Fedor

'One of the best French films of the late season, and
worthy of American attention.' – *Variety*

Carrie **
US   1952   122m   bw
Paramount (William Wyler)
V*, L

In the early 1900s a country girl comes to Chicago,
loses her innocence and goes on the stage, meanwhile
reducing a wealthy restaurant manager to penury
through love for her.

A famous satirical novel is softened into an unwieldy
narrative with scarcely enough dramatic power to

sustain interest despite splendid production values.
Heavy pre-release cuts remain obvious, and the
general effect is depressing; but it is very good to look
at.

w Ruth and Augustus Goetz novel Sister Carrie by
Theodore Dreiser d William Wyler ph Victor Milner
m David Raksin ad Hal Pereira, Roland Anderson

Laurence Olivier, Jennifer Jones, Miriam Hopkins,
Eddie Albert, Basil Ruysdael, Ray Teal, Barry Kelley,
Mary Murphy

'Olivier is so impassioned and so painfully touching
that everything else in the movie, including the girl
whose story it's meant to be, fades into
insignificance.' – *Variety*

'They shot the later episodes for the strongest
dramatic effect only, despite the fact that the story had
stopped following a melodramatic line and become a
sociological study . . . each additional episode exploits
the audience's hope that things will be brought to a
satisfactory conclusion, but they never are.' – *Films in
Review*

AAN: art direction

Carrie *
US   1976   98m   MGM-DeLuxe
UA/Red Bank (Paul Monash)
V, V*, L

A repressed teenager with remarkable mental powers
takes a macabre revenge on classmates who taunt and
persecute her.

Stylish but unattractive shocker which works its way
up to a fine climax of gore and frenzy, and takes care
to provide a final *frisson* just when the audience thinks
it can safely go home.

w Lawrence D. Cohen novel Stephen King
d Brian de Palma ph Mario Tosi m Pino Donaggio

Sissy Spacek, *Piper Laurie*, Amy Irving, William Katt,
John Travolta

'Combining Gothic horror, offhand misogyny and an
air of studied triviality, *Carrie* is de Palma's most
enjoyable movie in a long while, and also his silliest.'
– *Janet Maslin, Newsweek*

'The horror is effective only once, and the attempts at
humour are never very successful and come almost
when one is inclined to be moved by somebody's
plight, so that the non-jokes yield authentic bad taste.'
– *John Simon, New York*

AAN: Sissy Spacek; Piper Laurie

Carrington VC *
GB   1954   106m   bw
British Lion/Romulus (Teddy Baird)
V*
US title: *Court Martial*

An army major is courtmartialled for embezzling mess
funds.

Good courtroom drama with a few plot surprises,
convincing characters, and very serviceable acting and
direction.

w John Hunter play Dorothy and Campbell
Christie d Anthony Asquith ph Desmond
Dickinson

David Niven, Margaret Leighton, Noelle Middleton,
Laurence Naismith, Clive Morton, Mark Dignam,
Allan Cuthbertson, Victor Maddern, John Glyn-
Jones, Raymond Francis, Newton Blick, John
Chandos

Le Carrosse d'Or: see *The Golden Coach*

Carry Me Back
New Zealand   1982   90m   colour
Kiwi Films/New Zealand Film Commission (Graeme Crowley)

Two sons attempt to smuggle their father's corpse
from the city to their farm in order to benefit from his
will.

Blackish comedy of mishaps and misfits that occasionally amuses.

w Derek Morton, Keith Aberdeen, John Reid *story* Joy Cowley *d* John Reid *ph* Graeme Cowley *m* Tim Bridgewater, James Hall *ad* Jim Barr *ed* Simon Reece, Michael Horton

Grant Tilley, Kelly Johnson, Dorothy McKegg, Derek Hardwick, Joanne Mildenhall

Carry On Abroad *
GB 1972 88m Eastmancolor
Fox-Rank/Peter Rogers
V

A couple who go on a package holiday to Spain find that their hotel is still being built and there is a staff of no more than three.

Every opportunity for bathroom jokes is relished in what is otherwise an average effort.

w Talbot Rothwell *d* Gerald Thomas *ph* Alan Hume *m* Eric Rogers *ad* Lionel Couch *ed* Alfred Roome

Sidney James, Kenneth Williams, Charles Hawtrey, Joan Sims, Bernard Bresslaw, Barbara Windsor, Kenneth Connor, Peter Butterworth, Jimmy Logan, June Whitfield, Hattie Jacques

'Travelling well-trodden paths of slapstick, *double entendre* and nudging innuendo.' – *Nigel Andrews*

Carry On Again Doctor
GB 1969 89m Eastmancolor
Rank/Adder (Peter Rogers)
V

A doctor, exiled to a tropical island, returns to Britain with a special slimming cure.

A slight air of desperation hangs over the often-used setting of a hospital, and most of the jokes remain in intensive care.

w Talbot Rothwell *d* Gerald Thomas *ph* Ernest Steward *m* Eric Rogers *pd* Jack Blezard *ed* Alfred Roome

Sidney James, Kenneth Williams, Jim Dale, Charles Hawtrey, Joan Sims, Barbara Windsor, Hattie Jacques, Patsy Rowlands, Peter Butterworth, Pat Coombs

'Perhaps the team go that much further than ever before. Their fans will be delighted; those who aren't won't care.' – *Richard Davis, Films and Filming*

Carry On at Your Convenience
GB 1971 90m Eastmancolor
Rank/Peter Rogers
V

A union leader at the firm of W. C. Boggs, makers of fine toiletware, keeps ordering the workers to come out on strike.

No toilet joke is left unplumbed here, and the result is dire.

w Talbot Rothwell *d* Gerald Thomas *ph* Ernest Steward *m* Eric Rogers *ed* Alfred Roome

Sidney James, Kenneth Williams, Charles Hawtrey, Joan Sims, Bernard Bresslaw, Hattie Jacques, Kenneth Cope, Patsy Rowlands, Jacki Piper, Richard O'Callaghan

'One of the least funny of this staggeringly successful series.' – *Eric Braun*

'Even more scrappily assembled than usual and, with the exception of a fairly amusing parody of sex education films, the level of humour, though noticeably cleaner than of late, is still rock bottom.' – *David McGillivray*

Carry On Behind **
GB 1975 90m Eastmancolor
Fox-Rank/Peter Rogers
V

Archaeologists arrive to search for Roman remains at a caravan site full of holiday-makers.

One of the best of the series and certainly the last watchable film the team produced.

w Dave Freeman *d* Gerald Thomas *ph* Ernest Steward *m* Eric Rogers *ed* Alfred Roome

Elke Sommer, Kenneth Williams, Joan Sims, Bernard Bresslaw, Kenneth Connor, Peter Butterworth, Jack Douglas, Windsor Davies, Liz Fraser, Patsy Rowlands

'Emerges as the most consistently funny *Carry On* in many years . . . a strong vein of comedy is mined from the simple situation of campsite overcrowding, with some of the best sight gags involving a lugubrious Irish wolf-hound and a foul-mouthed mynah bird.' – *Verina Glaessner, MFB*

Carry On Cabby *
GB 1963 91m bw
Anglo Amalgamated/Peter Rogers
V

The neglected wife of the owner of a taxi firm sets up a rival firm with women drivers.

A deft farcical battle of the sexes.

w Talbot Rothwell *d* Gerald Thomas *ph* Alan Hume *m* Eric Rogers *ed* Archie Ludski

Sidney James, Charles Hawtrey, Kenneth Connor, Hattie Jacques, Esma Cannon, Liz Fraser, Bill Owen, Milo O'Shea, Jim Dale

'The golden formula of the *Carry On* series is back with a bang.' – *Variety*

Carry On Camping *
GB 1969 88m Eastmancolor
Rank/Peter Rogers
V

Two men take their girlfriends on holiday to a nudist camp in the hope that it will make them less inhibited.

A partly successful attempt to provide the characters with fewer sexual repressions than usual.

w Talbot Rothwell *d* Gerald Thomas *ph* Ernest Steward *m* Eric Rogers *ad* Lionel Couch *ed* Alfred Roome

Sidney James, Kenneth Williams, Joan Sims, Charles Hawtrey, Terry Scott, Barbara Windsor

'Suffers somewhat in comparison to some of its predecessors in that it lacks a storyline, however slim.' – *Variety*

Carry On Cleo *
GB 1964 92m Eastmancolor
Anglo Amalgamated/Peter Rogers
V, V*

Ancient Britons are captured by the Romans while Mark Antony carries on with Cleopatra.

Sporadically amusing parody of the Elizabeth Taylor epic, though it should have been much funnier.

w Talbot Rothwell *d* Gerald Thomas *ph* Alan Hume *m* Eric Rogers *ad* Bert Davey *ed* Archie Ludski

Sidney James, Kenneth Williams, Charles Hawtrey, Joan Sims, Kenneth Connor, Jim Dale, Amanda Barrie, E. V. H. Emmett, Sheila Hancock, Jon Pertwee

'Gags, both verbal and visual, suffer from repetition.' – *Variety*

† As a result of a court case for breach of copyright brought by Twentieth Century-Fox, the film's poster, which parodied the advertising for *Cleopatra*, had to be withdrawn.

'Up your anchor for a well crewed voyage!!'
Carry On Columbus
GB 1992 91m colour
Island World/Comedy House/Peter Rogers (John Goldstone)
V

Columbus's voyage to find a route to the East is sabotaged by spies in the pay of the Sultan of Turkey.

Ill-starred attempt, with a succession of single entendres and some inept performances, to revive a tired old formula.

w Dave Freeman *d* Gerald Thomas *ph* Alan Hume *m* John Du Prez *pd* Harry Pottle *ed* Chris Blunden

Jim Dale, Bernard Cribbins, Maureen Lipman, Peter Richardson, Rik Mayall, Alexei Sayle, Charles Fleischer, Larry Miller, Leslie Phillips, Julian Clary, Sara Crowe, Rebecca Lacey, Nigel Planer, June Whitfield, Richard Wilson

'Painfully unfunny, lacking imagination and energy.' – *Philip French, Observer*

Carry On Constable *
GB 1960 86m bw
Anglo Amalgamated/Peter Rogers
V

Four new and inept constables report for duty at their local police station.

In part a parody of the popular TV series *Dixon of Dock Green* and moderately amusing despite the absence of a plot.

w Norman Hudis *story* Brock Williams *d* Gerald Thomas *ph* Ted Scaife *m* Bruce Montgomery *ad* Carmen Dillon *ed* John Shirley

Sidney James, Kenneth Williams, Charles Hawtrey, Joan Sims, Kenneth Connor, Eric Barker, Leslie Phillips, Hattie Jacques, Shirley Eaton, Cyril Chamberlain, Irene Handl, Esma Cannon, Freddie Mills

'Simply an anthology of police gags and situations.' – *Variety*

'How The West Was Lost!!'
Carry On Cowboy **
GB 1965 95m Eastmancolor
Anglo Amalgamated/Peter Rogers
V

A sanitary engineer is given the task of cleaning up a town being terrorized by outlaws.

Amusing parody of *High Noon* and other classic Westerns.

w Talbot Rothwell *d* Gerald Thomas *ph* Alan Hume *m* Eric Rogers *ad* Bert Davey *ed* Rod Keys

Sidney James, Kenneth Williams, Charles Hawtrey, Joan Sims, Jim Dale, Percy Herbert, Angela Douglas, Bernard Bresslaw, Peter Butterworth, Jon Pertwee

'Less a string of irrelevant situations than usual, giving the team more opportunity for comedy thesping.' – *Variety*

Carry On Cruising
GB 1962 89m Eastmancolor
Anglo Amalgamated/Peter Rogers
V

The captain of a cruise liner finds his peace of mind threatened by new crew members and tourists.

Weak comedy that doesn't seem to know where it's going.

w Norman Hudis *story* Eric Barker *d* Gerald Thomas *ph* Alan Hume *m* Bruce Montgomery, Douglas Gamley *ad* Carmen Dillon *ed* John Shirley

Sidney James, Kenneth Williams, Kenneth Connor, Liz Fraser, Dilys Laye, Esma Cannon, Lance Perceval, Ronnie Stevens, Cyril Chamberlain, Anton Rodgers

'Direction by Gerald Thomas is boisterously effective.' – *Variety*

Carry On Dick

GB 1974 91m Eastmancolor
Rank/Peter Rogers
V

Bow Street Runners ask a village clergyman to help them catch the highwayman Dick Turpin, better known as Big Dick.

Inspiration flags in a comedy where both cast and director seem hardly interested in what they were doing, probably because they had been doing it for too long.

w Talbot Rothwell story Lawrie Wyman, George Evans d Gerald Thomas ph Ernest Steward m Eric Rogers ed Alfred Roome

Sidney James, Kenneth Williams, Kenneth Connor, Barbara Windsor, Hattie Jacques, Bernard Bresslaw, Joan Sims, Peter Butterworth, Jack Douglas, Patsy Rowlands, Bill Maynard

'These tireless upholders of the "saucy" postcard tradition soldier on with their perennial rib-poking, elbow-nudging, albeit scarcely jaw-breaking esprit . . . Maybe their continuing appeal is beyond criticism – or according to taste, beneath it.' – Nigel Gearing, MFB

'The script is utterly banal. It is incredible that human minds can put such muck on to paper.' – Kenneth Williams

Carry On Doctor *

GB 1968 94m Eastmancolor
Rank/Peter Rogers
V, V*

Hospital patients revolt against a tyrannical matron when their favourite doctor is sacked.

Occasionally amusing farce.

w Talbot Rothwell d Gerald Thomas ph Alan Hume m Eric Rogers ed Alfred Roome

Frankie Howerd, Sidney James, Kenneth Williams, Jim Dale, Charles Hawtrey, Joan Sims, Barbara Windsor, Hattie Jacques, Anita Harris, Bernard Bresslaw, Peter Butterworth

'Usual unabashed mixture of double-meanings, down-to-earth vulgarity, blue jokes.' – Variety

Carry On – Don't Lose Your Head

GB 1966 90m Eastmancolor
Rank/Peter Rogers
V
aka: Don't Lose Your Head

A foppish Briton, the Black Fingernail, rescues French aristocrats from the guillotine during the French Revolution.

A limp parody of The Scarlet Pimpernel causes no more than a few chuckles.

w Talbot Rothwell d Gerald Thomas ph Alan Hume m Eric Rogers ed Rod Keys

Sidney James, Kenneth Williams, Jim Dale, Charles Hawtrey, Joan Sims, Peter Butterworth, Dany Robin, Peter Gilmore

'A crazy debauch of duelling, doublecrossing and disaster. The troupers jump through their well-known hoops with agility.' – Variety

Carry On Emmannuelle

GB 1978 88m Technicolor
Hemdale/Peter Rogers
V

The wife of an impotent French ambassador to England seduces every man she meets.

A doomed attempt to update the formula for more sexually permissive times that resulted in the worst of the series, and the last for fourteen years, until it was revived in 1992.

w Lance Peters d Gerald Thomas ph Alan Hume m Eric Rogers ad Jack Shampan ed Peter Boita

Suzanne Danielle, Kenneth Williams, Kenneth Connor, Jack Douglas, Joan Sims, Peter Butterworth, Larry Dann, Beryl Reid, Eric Barker

'This one is rude, certainly, but the relentless phallic innuendo is as labored as makers' determination to show nothing to worry the censor. Leaden comic timing . . .' – Variety

'It's rather like watching endearing elderly relatives disgracing themselves at a party.' – Andy Medhurst, Sight and Sound

Carry On England

GB 1976 89m colour
Rank/Peter Rogers
V

In 1940 the men and women who form an experimental anti-aircraft battery prefer to make love rather than war, to the annoyance of their new commanding officer.

One of the weakest of the series and a sign that the series was running out of energy, unable to find suitable replacements for its usual team and handicapped more than usual by a weak script.

w Jack Seddon, David Pursall d Gerald Thomas ph Ernest Steward m Max Harris ad Lionel Couch ed Richard Marden

Kenneth Connor, Windsor Davies, Patrick Mower, Judy Geeson, Jack Douglas, Diane Langton, Melvyn Hayes, Joan Sims, Peter Jones, Peter Butterworth, David Lodge

'Suffers from a particularly unfortunate hangup. It's not funny.' – Variety

'The laboured puns and overacting are as tiresome as ever.' – MFB

Carry On – Follow That Camel

GB 1966 90m Eastmancolor
Rank/Peter Rogers
V
aka: Follow That Camel

An English gentleman, accused of behaving badly at cricket, joins the Foreign Legion to regain his honour.

An ill-match between American and English styles of vaudeville and music-hall humour results in a direly unamusing movie.

w Talbot Rothwell d Gerald Thomas ph Alan Hume m Eric Rogers ed Alfred Roome

Phil Silvers, Kenneth Williams, Jim Dale, Charles Hawtrey, Joan Sims, Peter Butterworth, Anita Harris, Bernard Bresslaw, Angela Douglas, Peter Gilmore

'It all works with considerable bounce, with elements of parody of Beau Geste-style movies for those alert to them. All the regular comics are on first-rate form.' – Variety

Carry On Girls

GB 1973 88m Eastmancolor
Fox-Rank/Peter Rogers
V

The organizer of a seaside beauty contest annoys the local members of the Women's Liberation movement.

Below average romp.

w Talbot Rothwell d Gerald Thomas ph Alan Hume m Eric Rogers ed Alfred Roome

Sidney James, Kenneth Connor, Joan Sims, Barbara Windsor, Bernard Bresslaw, Peter Butterworth, June Whitfield, Jack Douglas, Patsy Rowlands, Jimmy Logan, Joan Hickson, David Lodge

'Herculean efforts on the part of the entire cast do eventually pull off (in the context, I must insist this is not meant as a double entendre) some fairly effective slapstick.' – Eric Braun

'Thriving as ever on the sexual repression of its audience, Talbot Rothwell's windy, radio-style script . . . turns out the routine quota of puns on such words as bang, boob, bed, bust, bristol and bash, and makes

such weary labour of it that every joke can be heard creaking into place long before the arrival of the punch-line.' – Gareth Jones, MFB

'A Great Guy With His Chopper!'
Carry On Henry **

GB 1971 89m Eastmancolor
Rank/Adder (Peter Rogers)
V

King Henry tries to get rid of his wife when he discovers she smells of garlic.

A coarsely successful parody of Anne of the Thousand Days and other period films.

w Talbot Rothwell d Gerald Thomas ph Alan Hume m Eric Rogers ed Alfred Roome

Sidney James, Kenneth Williams, Charles Hawtrey, Joan Sims, Terry Scott, Barbara Windsor, Kenneth Connor, Peter Butterworth, Peter Gilmore, Patsy Rowlands

'They have managed to come up with a bit of a winner . . . there is a delicious send up of that most boring and perennial line of cinematic yawns, the historical romance.' – Peter Buckley

'The cast is the familiar stock company at full force; the script is from Talbot Rothwell at his most characteristic; and the film is at any rate better looking than most of its shoe-string predecessors.' – John Pidgeon, MFB

'I read the script of Carry On Henry and I think it's abysmal.' – Kenneth Williams, 1970

'We saw the TV and it was Carry On Henry . . . amazing how well this was made! Everyone in it was competent and the sheer look of the thing was very professional.' – Kenneth Williams, 1979

'ITV showed Carry On Henry. Oh dear! It was so bad in places . . . truly chronic dialogue . . . dreadful acting. Sid James had never been quite as bad as this. A collection of such rubbish you're amazed it could ever have been stuck together. Only an audience of illiterates could ever have found this tripe amusing.' – Kenneth Williams, 1988

Carry On Jack

GB 1964 91m Eastmancolor
Anglo Amalgamated/Peter Rogers
V
US title: Carry On Venus

A midshipman finds himself at the mercy of a bullying captain and they are both put overboard after a mutiny.

Salty but unamusing parody of Mutiny on The Bounty and other sea-faring sagas.

w Talbot Rothwell d Gerald Thomas ph Alan Hume m Eric Rogers ad Jack Shampan ed Archie Ludski

Bernard Cribbins, Kenneth Williams, Charles Hawtrey, Juliet Mills, Donald Houston, Percy Herbert, Peter Gilmore, Jim Dale, Anton Rogers, Cecil Parker, Patrick Cargill

'Gerald Thomas steers his cast through a maze of mixups and misadventures.' – Variety

Carry On Loving

GB 1970 88m Eastmancolor
Rank/Adder (Peter Rogers)
V

Assorted misfits try their luck at a computer dating agency.

Limp comedy for which the regulars show little enthusiasm.

w Talbot Rothwell d Gerald Thomas ph Ernest Steward m Eric Rogers ad Lionel Couch ed Alfred Roome

Sidney James, Kenneth Williams, Charles Hawtrey, Joan Sims, Terry Scott, Hattie Jacques, Richard

O'Callaghan, Bernard Bresslaw, Jacki Piper, Imogen Hassall, Patsy Rowlands, Bill Maynard

'Full of tired jokes, obvious situations and ludicrous performances, we have all been here at least three times before, but the crew have a way of working over the old material.' – *Peter Buckley, Films and Filming*

'Scrapings from the bottom of Talbot Rothwell's barrel of well-worn double entendre, delivered with mechanical efficiency by an equally well-worn cast.' – *MFB*

Carry On Matron *
GB 1972 87m Eastmancolor
Rank/Peter Rogers
V

A con man persuades his son to dress as a nurse in order to infiltrate a maternity hospital to steal contraceptive pills.

Intermittently amusing comedy.

w Talbot Rothwell d Gerald Thomas ph Ernest Steward m Eric Rogers ad Lionel Couch ed Alfred Roome

Sidney James, Kenneth Williams, Charles Hawtrey, Joan Sims, Hattie Jacques, Bernard Bresslaw, Terry Scott, Kenneth Cope, Barbara Windsor, Kenneth Connor, Jacki Piper, Patsy Rowlands, Jack Douglas

'A largely successful if slightly patchy addition to the series; its comic highlight involves Sid James, required to assume a medical alias, introducing himself as "Dr Zhivago".' – *Kenneth Thompson, MFB*

Carry On Nurse **
GB 1959 86m bw
Anglo Amalgamated/Peter Rogers
V, V*

Male patients in a hospital rebel against the dictatorial matron.

The first true *Carry On*, done when the whole notion was still fresh and the cast responded with glee to its crudities.

w Norman Hudis story Patrick Cargill, Jack Searle d Gerald Thomas ph Reg Wyer m Bruce Montgomery ad Alex Vetchinsky ed John Shirley

Shirley Eaton, Kenneth Williams, Charles Hawtrey, Hattie Jacques, Joan Sims, Kenneth Connor, Terence Longden, Bill Owen, Leslie Phillips, Wilfrid Hyde-White, Irene Handl

'The yocks come thick and fast.' – *Variety*

'A seaside postcard come to life, a shameless procession of vulgarities. Utterly irresistible.' – *Andy Medhurst, Sight and Sound*

† The film topped the box-office in Britain and was surprisingly successful in the US where it ran for two-and-a-half years.

Carry On Regardless
GB 1960 90m bw
Anglo Amalgamated/Peter Rogers
V

A group of incompetent unemployed join an odd-job agency.

Less a film than a series of sketches, which are very variable in quality.

w Norman Hudis d Ralph Thomas ph Alan Hume m Bruce Montgomery ed John Shirley

Sidney James, Kenneth Williams, Charles Hawtrey, Joan Sims, Kenneth Connor, Bill Owen, Liz Fraser, Terence Longden, Esma Cannon, Hattie Jacques, Fenella Fielding

'Ingenuity of scriptwriter Norman Hudis is sometimes a bit strained, but he has come up with some sound comedy situations.' – *Variety*

Carry On Screaming *
GB 1966 97m Eastmancolor
Anglo Amalgamated/Peter Rogers
V

Police investigate a mad doctor and his sister, who are turning young women into mannequins.

A send-up of Hammer horrors that manages to emulate the garishness of the originals.

w Talbot Rothwell d Gerald Thomas ph Alan Hume m Eric Rogers ed Rod Keys

Harry H. Corbett, Kenneth Williams, Jim Dale, Charles Hawtrey, Fenella Fielding, Joan Sims, Angela Douglas, Bernard Bresslaw, Peter Butterworth, Jon Pertwee

'Puts the skids under horror pix. Snag is that most horror films themselves teeter on the edge of parody and it is rather tough trying to burlesque a parody.' – *Variety*

Carry On Sergeant
GB 1958 83m bw
Anglo Amalgamated/Insignia (Peter Rogers)

An army training sergeant accepts a bet that his last platoon of raw recruits will win the Star Squad award.

Shabby farce with humdrum script and slack direction, saved by energetic performances.

w Norman Hudis play The Bull Boys by R. F. Delderfield d Gerald Thomas ph Peter Hennessy m Bruce Montgomery

Bob Monkhouse, William Hartnell, Kenneth Williams, Charles Hawtrey, Shirley Eaton, Eric Barker, Dora Bryan, Bill Owen, Kenneth Connor

'They're At It Again – O.O.O.H!'
Carry On Spying
GB 1964 87m bw
Anglo Amalgamated/Peter Rogers
V

British spies are sent to recapture a secret formula stolen by the Society for the Total Extinction of Non-Conforming Humans, otherwise known as Stench.

A feeble parody of the Bond films.

w Talbot Rothwell, Sid Colin d Gerald Thomas ph Alan Hume m Eric Rogers ed Archie Ludski

Kenneth Williams, Bernard Cribbins, Charles Hawtrey, Barbara Windsor, Eric Pohlmann, Eric Barker, Dilys Laye, Jim Dale, Richard Wattis

'A dazzling return to form, milking every last drop from the ripe targets of espionage in general and Bond in particular.' – *Andy Medhurst, Sight and Sound*

Carry On Teacher *
GB 1959 86m bw
Anglo Amalgamated/Peter Rogers
V

Pupils at a school sabotage the headmaster's attempts to get another job because they don't want to lose him.

Amiable comedy that is less frenetic than many in the series, and all the better for it.

w Norman Hudis d Gerald Thomas ph Reginald Wyer m Bruce Montgomery ed John Shirley

Ted Ray, Kenneth Williams, Charles Hawtrey, Leslie Phillips, Joan Sims, Kenneth Connor, Hattie Jacques, Rosalind Knight, Cyril Chamberlain

'The laughs come readily.' – *Variety*

Carry On up the Jungle
GB 1970 89m Eastmancolor
Rank/Peter Rogers
V

An ornithologist journeys to Africa in search of the rare Oozulum bird.

A tired parody of Tarzan and jungle films; the jokes get lost in the undergrowth.

w Talbot Rothwell d Gerald Thomas ph Ernest Steward m Eric Rogers ad Alex Vetchinsky ed Alfred Roome

Frankie Howerd, Sidney James, Charles Hawtrey, Joan Sims, Terry Scott, Kenneth Connor, Bernard Bresslaw, Jacki Piper

'The film is an assured success.' – *Films and Filming*

Carry On up the Khyber ***
GB 1968 88m Eastmancolor
Rank/Adder (Peter Rogers)
V

A Scots regiment, the Third Foot and Mouth, fails to defend British interests in India.

The best of the series, a wonderfully vulgar and ripe low comedy on an imperial theme.

w Talbot Rothwell d Gerald Thomas ph Alan Hume m Eric Rogers ed Alfred Roome

Sidney James, Kenneth Williams, Charles Hawtrey, Joan Sims, Roy Castle, Bernard Bresslaw, Peter Butterworth, Terry Scott, Angela Douglas, Cardew Robinson, Julian Holloway, Peter Gilmore

'Continues to rely primarily on low-comedy visual and verbal gag situations for its yocks.' – *Variety*

† The movie was filmed in Wales.

Carry On Venus: see *Carry On Jack*

The Cars that Ate Paris *
Australia 1974 88m Eastmancolor Panavision
Saltpan/AFDC/Royce Smeal (Jim and Howard McElroy)
V, V*

Car travellers become victims of a small town whose youthful inhabitants live on the pickings of engineered road accidents.

Another small town with a guilty secret, in this case more suitable to a half-hour than a feature, but with rewarding attention to detail.

wd Peter Weir ph John McLean m Bruce Smeaton

Terry Camillieri, John Meillon, Melissa Jaffa, Kevin Miles

Carson City *
US 1952 87m Warnercolor
Warner (David Weisbart)

A stagecoach service suffers from bandit raids, so a local banker finances a railroad.

Agreeably conventional Western with plenty of reliable plot and a satisfactory outcome for the goodies.

w Sloan Nibley, Winston Miller d André de Toth ph John Boyle m David Buttolph

Randolph Scott, Raymond Massey, Lucille Norman, Richard Webb, James Millican, Larry Keating, George Cleveland

Cartouche
Italy/US 1954 85m approx bw
Venturini/RKO (John Nasht)

A French prince clears himself of a murder charge and brings the villain to book.

Flat costume drama.

w Louis Stevens, Tullio Pinelli d Steve Sekely, Gianni Vernuccio ph Massimo Dallamano m Bruce Montgomery

Richard Basehart, Patricia Roc, Massimo Serato, Akim Tamiroff

Cartouche **

France/Italy 1961 114m Eastmancolor
Dyaliscope
Ariane/Filmsonor/Vides (Georges Danciger)
V, V*
aka: *Swords of Blood*

An 18th-century cooper's son becomes a quick-witted
and gallant thief.

Slightly bitter fairy tale based on a French legend,
vigorously encompassing tragedy, farce, violence and
high-flown adventure.

w Daniel Boulanger, Philippe de Broca   *d Philippe de
Broca*   ph Christian Matras   m Georges Delerue

Jean-Paul Belmondo, Claudia Cardinale, Odile Versois,
Marcel Dalio, Philippe Lemaire, Jean Rochefort

'A tour de force of virtuosity.' – *Peter John Dyer, MFB*

Carve Her Name with Pride *

GB 1958 119m bw
Rank/Keyboard (Daniel M. Angel)
V

In 1940, the young British widow of a French officer
is enlisted as a spy, and after various adventures dies
before a German firing squad.

Slightly muddled if ultimately moving biopic in
which initial light comedy gives way to romance,
documentary, character study, blazing war action and
finally tragedy. Generally well made.

w Vernon Harris, Lewis Gilbert   *book* R. J. Minney
d Lewis Gilbert   ph John Wilcox   m William Alwyn

Virginia McKenna (as Violette Szabo), *Paul Scofield,* Jack
Warner, Sidney Tafler, Denise Grey, Alain Saury,
Maurice Ronet, Nicole Stéphane, Noel Willman, Bill
Owen, William Mervyn, Anne Leon

'What is missing is the deeply charged passion which
would have gone beyond the quietly decent statement
intermittently achieved.' – *John Gillett*

La Casa del Angel: see *The House of the Angel*

'As big and timely a picture as ever you've seen! You can
tell by the cast it's important! gripping! big!'

Casablanca ****

US 1942 102m bw
Warner (Hal B. Wallis)
V, V (C), V*, L

Rick's Café in Casablanca is a centre for war refugees
awaiting visas for America. Rick abandons his
cynicism to help an old love escape the Nazis with her
underground leader husband.

Cinema *par excellence*: a studio-bound Hollywood
melodrama which after various chances just fell
together impeccably into one of the outstanding
entertainment experiences of cinema history, with
romance, intrigue, excitement, suspense and humour
cunningly deployed by master technicians and a
perfect cast.

w *Julius J. Epstein, Philip G. Epstein, Howard Koch
play Everybody Comes to Rick's* by Murray Burnett and
Joan Alison   *d Michael Curtiz*   ph Arthur Edeson
m *Max Steiner*   ed Owen Marks

Humphrey Bogart (Rick Blaine), *Ingrid Bergman* (Ilse
Lund), *Paul Henreid* (Victor Laszlo), *Claude Rains*
(Captain Louis Renault), Sydney Greenstreet
(Ferrari), Peter Lorre (Ugarte), S. Z. Sakall (Carl),
Conrad Veidt (Major Strasser), *Dooley Wilson* (Sam),
Marcel Dalio (Croupier) and Madeleine LeBeau, Joy
Page, John Qualen, Ludwig Stossel, Leonid Kinskey,
Helmut Dantine, Ilka Gruning

songs: 'As Time Goes By', 'Knock on Wood'

RICK: 'I stick out my neck for nobody. I'm the only
cause I'm interested in.'
  LOUIS: 'How extravagant you are, throwing away
women like that. Someday they may be scarce.'
  RICK: 'Ilse, I'm no good at being noble, but it
doesn't take much to see that the problems of three
little people don't amount to a hill of beans in this

crazy world. Someday you'll understand that. Not
now. Here's looking at you, kid.'
  RICK: 'I came to Casablanca for the waters.'
  LOUIS: 'What waters? We're in the desert.'
  RICK: 'I was misinformed.'
  RICK: 'Louis, I think this is the beginning of a
beautiful friendship.'

'A picture which makes the spine tingle and the heart
take a leap . . . they have so combined sentiment,
humour and pathos with taut melodrama and
bristling intrigue that the result is a highly
entertaining and even inspiring film.' – *New York Times*

'Its humour is what really saves it, being a mixture of
Central European irony of attack and racy Broadway-
Hollywood Boulevard cynicism.' – *Herman G. Weinberg*

'The happiest of happy accidents, and the most
decisive exception to the *auteur* theory.' – *Andrew
Sarris, 1968*

'A film which seems to have been frozen in time . . .
the sum of its many marvellous parts far exceeds the
whole.' – *NFT, 1974*

'It's far from a great film, but it has an appealingly
schlocky romanticism, and you're never really pressed
to take its melodramatic twists and turns seriously.' –
Pauline Kael, 70s

† Originally named for the leads were Ronald
Reagan, Ann Sheridan and Dennis Morgan.

AA: best picture; Julius J. and Philip G. Epstein,
Howard Koch; Michael Curtiz

AAN: Arthur Edeson; Max Steiner; Humphrey
Bogart; Claude Rains; Owen Marks

Casanova

Italy 1976 163m (English version) Technicolor
Scope
TCF/PEA (Alberto Grimaldi)
V*, S
aka: *Fellini's Casanova*

Episodes from the life of the 18th-century libertine, in
the course of which he seduces, among others, a nun,
a mechanical doll, and a hunchbacked
nymphomaniac.

A curiously rarefied spectacle which seldom comes to
anything like life and despite its vast expense seems
more likely to provoke yawns than lust.

w Federico Fellini, Barnardino Zapponi   *d Federico
Fellini*   ph Giuseppe Rotunno   m Nino Rota
pd Danilo Donati, Federico Fellini

Donald Sutherland, Tina Aumont, Cicely Browne,
Carmen Scarpitta

'It may well be the most ponderous specimen of
imaginative vacuity ever devised.' – *John Simon, New
York*

AAN: script

Casanova Brown

US 1944 99m bw
International/Christie (Nunnally Johnson)

Just as his divorce comes through, a man discovers
that his wife is pregnant.

Very mild star comedy which tiptoes round its
subject.

w Nunnally Johnson   *play Bachelor Father* by Floyd
Dell, Thomas Mitchell   *d Sam Wood*   ph John F.
Seitz   m Arthur Lange   ad Perry Ferguson

Gary Cooper, Teresa Wright, Frank Morgan, Anita
Louise, Patricia Collinge, Edmond Breon, Jill
Esmond, Isobel Elsom, Mary Treen, Halliwell Hobbes

'There is so much clowning with so little subject that
one is exposed to the impression that anything went
for a laugh.' – *Bosley Crowther, New York Times*

† A remake of *Little Accident* (qv).

AAN: Arthur Lange; Perry Ferguson

Casanova in Burlesque

US 1944 74m bw
Republic

A professor has a secret summer life as a burlesque
performer.

Unusual, amiable comedy.

w Frank Gill   *d Leslie Goodwins*

Joe E. Brown, June Havoc

Casanova's Big Night

US 1954 86m Technicolor
Paramount (Paul Jones)
V, V*, L

In old Italy, the great lover is fleeing from his creditors
and changes places with a tailor's apprentice.

The last of Bob Hope's big-budget, big-studio
burlesques is a lumbering vehicle which wastes its
star cast and mistimes its laughs.

w Hal Kanter, Edmund Hartmann   *d Norman Z.
McLeod*   ph Lionel Lindon   m Lyn Murray

Bob Hope, Joan Fontaine (an unhappy comedy foil),
Basil Rathbone, Vincent Price, Audrey Dalton, Hugh
Marlowe, John Carradine, Primo Carnera, Arnold
Moss, Lon Chaney Jnr

Casbah

US 1948 94m bw
Universal (Erik Charell)

Remake of *Algiers* (qv) with songs added.

Not too bad in the circumstances, but a wholly
artificial exercise, and another version was really not
needed. The sets seem overlit and claustrophobic.

w Ladislaus Bus-Fekete, Arnold Manoff
novel Detective Ashelbe   *musical* Erik Charell
d John Berry   ph Irving Glassberg   m/y Harold
Arlen, Leo Robin

Tony Martin, Yvonne de Carlo, Marta Toren, *Peter Lorre,*
Hugo Haas

AAN: song 'For Every Man There's a Woman'

The Case against Brooklyn

US 1958 81m bw
Charles H. Schneer/Columbia

An undercover cop smashes a gambling syndicate.

Competent second feature treatment of a story we
have heard somewhere before.

w Raymond T. Marcus   *d Paul Wendkos*

Darren McGavin, Maggie Hayes, Warren Stevens,
Emile Meyer, Nestor Paiva

'Is she an unfit mother?'
The Case against Mrs Ames

US 1936 85m bw
Paramount (Walter Wanger)

The prosecutor in a murder case is convinced of the
defendant's innocence.

Tired rehash of a familiar theme.

w Gene Towne, Graham Baker   *d William A. Seiter*
ph Lucien Andriot   md Boris Morros

Madeleine Carroll, George Brent, Arthur Treacher,
Alan Baxter, Beulah Bondi, Alan Mowbray, Esther
Dale, Ed Brophy

A Case for P.C. 49

GB 1950 80m bw
Hammer

A police constable solves a millionaire's murder.

Incompetent and virtually unwatchable transcription
of a juvenile TV series.

w Alan Stranks, Vernon Harris from their series
d Francis Searle

Brian Reece, Joy Shelton, Christine Norden, Leslie
Bradley, Gordon McLeod

The Case of Charles Peace

GB 1949 88m bw
John Argyle

The story of a burglar and murderer of the 1870s whose career caught the public fancy.

Antediluvian and largely fictitious treatment of a Victorian *cause célèbre*.

w Doris Davison, Norman Lee   d Norman Lee

Michael Martin Harvey, Chili Bouchier, Valentine Dyall, Bruce Belfrage, Ronald Adam

The Case of Mrs Pembroke: see *Two Against the World*

The Case of Sergeant Grischa

US 1930 82m bw
RKO

A Russian no-good escapes from a German prison camp and after many adventures is shot as a spy.

Oddball entertainment to come from Hollywood at any time, this seems to have no intent to please.

story Arnold Zweig   d Herbert Brenon

Chester Morris, Betty Compson, Alec B. Francis, Gustav von Seyffertitz, Jean Hersholt, Leyland Hodgson

'No sympathy, no fan appeal and no entertainment. Can only be exploited as "a fine production" or "a new era in pictures".' – *Variety*

The Case of the Black Cat

US 1936 66m bw
Warner

An old man is murdered after changing his will: Perry Mason investigates.

One of the better tales of the lawyer sleuth.

w F. Hugh Herbert   d William McGann

Ricardo Cortez, Harry Davenport, June Travis, Jane Bryan

The Case of the Black Parrot

US 1941 60m bw
Warner

Was it the butler who murdered to steal a case of diamonds?

This sounds like a Perry Mason but is not; a reporter solves the puzzle.

w Robert E. Kent   play Eleanor Robeson Belmont, Harriet Ford   d Noel Smith

William Lundigan, Maris Wrixon, Eddie Foy Jnr, Paul Cavanagh

The Case of the Curious Bride

US 1935 80m bw
Warner

Perry Mason helps a woman who is being blackmailed by her 'dead' husband.

Smoothish mystery.

w Tom Reed   story Erle Stanley Gardner
d Michael Curtiz

Warren William, Margaret Lindsay, Donald Woods, Claire Dodd, Allen Jenkins, Errol Flynn

The Case of the Frightened Lady

GB 1940 81m bw
Pennant

A dowager knows that her son is mad and tries to prevent him from strangling his cousin.

Quite a lively suspenser of its time.

w Edward Dryhurst   novel Edgar Wallace
d George King

Marius Goring, Penelope Dudley Ward, Helen Haye, Patrick Barr, Felix Aylmer

† A previous version was released in 1932 as *The Frightened Lady* (qv).

The Case of the Howling Dog

US 1934 75m bw
Warner

Two men claim the same woman as their wife.

Adequate Perry Mason mystery.

w Ben Markson   story Erle Stanley Gardner
d Alan Crosland

Warren William, Mary Astor, Allen Jenkins, Grant Mitchell, Helen Trenholme, Dorothy Tree

The Case of the Lucky Legs

US 1935 77m bw
Warner
V*

Perry Mason chases a beauty contest promoter who skips town with the winnings.

Fair lighthearted mystery, with a somewhat dissipated sleuth.

w Ben Markson, Brown Holmes   story Erle Stanley Gardner   d Archie Mayo

Warren William, Genevieve Tobin, Allen Jenkins, Patricia Ellis, Lyle Talbot, Barton MacLane

The Case of the Missing Blonde: see *Lady in the Morgue*

The Case of the Stuttering Bishop

US 1937 70m bw
Warner

Perry Mason investigates an heiress who may be an impostor.

Thin mystery with another different star in the lead.

w Don Ryan, Kenneth Gamet   story Erle Stanley Gardner   d William Clemens

Donald Woods, Ann Dvorak, Anne Nagel, Linda Perry

The Case of the Velvet Claws

US 1936 63m bw
Warner

Perry Mason's honeymoon is postponed when he finds himself on a murder charge.

Moderate light-hearted mystery, but they should have awarded prizes to anyone who could explain the title.

w Tom Reed   story Erle Stanley Gardner
d William Clemens

Warren William, Claire Dodd, Wini Shaw, Gordon Elliott, Addison Richards

Casey's Shadow

US 1978 116m Metrocolor Panavision
Columbia/Ray Stark (Michael Levee)
V*

A Cajun family in New Mexico breeds a champion horse which wins the annual race.

Shades of *Maryland*: an old-fashioned movie of the kind which absolutely nobody should want to revive, at least not so ineptly or at such length.

w Carol Sobieski   story Ruidoso by John McPhee
d Martin Ritt   ph John A. Alonzo   m Patrick Williams

Walter Matthau, Alexis Smith, Robert Webber, Murray Hamilton, Andrew A. Rubin, Stephan Burns, Michael Hershewe

C.A.S.H.: see *W.H.I.F.F.S.*

Cash

GB 1933 73m bw
Paramount/London Films (Alexander Korda)
V*
US title: For Love Or Money; aka: If I Were Rich

A bank clerk embezzles money.

Quota quickie that never rises above the totally mundane.

w Arthur Wimperis   story Anthony Gibbs, Dorothy Greenhill   d Zoltan Korda   ph Robert Martin
ed Stephen Harrison

Edmund Gwenn, Wendy Barrie, Robert Donat, Morris Harvey, Lawrence Grossmith

Cash and Carry: see *Maisie (Ringside Maisie)*

Cash McCall

US 1960 102m Technicolor
Warner (Henry Blanke)

A Napoleon of the stock market gets into trouble for the first time when love interferes with business.

Slightly unusual comedy drama, quite sharply made and played, but not adding up to much.

w Lenore Coffee, Marion Hargrove   novel Cameron Hawley   d Joseph Pevney   ph George Folsey
m Max Steiner

James Garner, Natalie Wood, Nina Foch, Dean Jagger, E. G. Marshall, Henry Jones, Otto Kruger, Roland Winters

Cash on Demand *

GB 1963 86m bw
Columbia/Woodpecker/Hammer (Michael Carreras)

A fussy bank manager outwits a classy robber.

Quietly effective suspenser with an admirable middle-aged cast and no love interest.

w Lewis Greifer, David T. Chantler   TV play Jacques Gillies   d Quentin Lawrence   ph Arthur Grant
m Wilfred Josephs

Peter Cushing, André Morell, Richard Vernon, Norman Bird, Edith Sharpe

Casino de Paree: see *Go Into Your Dance*

The Casino Murder Case

US 1935 85m bw
MGM

Philo Vance solves a murder in a family of neurotics.

Rather heavy-going detection.

w Florence Ryerson, Edgar Allen Woolf   story S. S. Van Dine   d Edwin Marin

Paul Lukas, Rosalind Russell, Eric Blore, Donald Cook, Louise Fazenda, Ted Healy, Isabel Jewell, Leo G. Carroll

Casino Royale

GB 1967 130m Technicolor Panavision
Columbia/Famous Artists (Charles K. Feldman, Jerry Bresler)
V, V*, L, S

The heads of the allied spy forces call Sir James Bond out of retirement to fight the power of *SMERSH*.

Woeful all-star kaleidoscope, a way-out spoof which generates far fewer laughs than the original. One of the most shameless wastes of time and talent in screen history.

w Wolf Mankowitz, John Law, Michael Sayers
novel Ian Fleming   d John Huston, Ken Hughes, Val Guest, Robert Parrish, Joe McGrath, Richard Talmadge   ph Jack Hildyard   m Burt Bacharach
pd Michael Stringer

David Niven, Deborah Kerr, Orson Welles, Peter Sellers, Ursula Andress, Woody Allen, William Holden, Charles Boyer, John Huston, Joanna Pettet, Daliah Lavi, Kurt Kasznar, Jacqueline Bisset, Derek Nimmo, George Raft, Ronnie Corbett, Peter O'Toole, Jean-Paul Belmondo, Geoffrey Bayldon, Duncan Macrae

'One of those wild wacky extravaganzas in which the audience is expected to have a great time because everybody making the film did. It seldom works out that way, and certainly doesn't here.' – *John Russell Taylor*

'The dialogue is witless and unhampered by taste, and the interminable finale is a collection of clichés in a brawl involving the cavalry, parachuted Indians, split-second appearances by George Raft and Jean-Paul Belmondo, every variety of mayhem, and Woody Allen burping radiation as a walking atom bomb.' – *Judith Crist*

'The worst film I ever enjoyed.' – *Donald Zec*

AAN: song 'The Look of Love' (*m* Burt Bacharach, *ly* Hal David)

Casque d'Or ***
France   1952   96m   bw
Speva/Paris (Robert Hakim)
aka: *Golden Marie*

1898. In the Paris slums, an Apache finds passionate love but is executed for murder.

A tragic romance which on its first release seemed bathed in a golden glow and is certainly an impeccable piece of film-making.

w Jacques Becker, Jacques Companeez *d* *Jacques Becker* *ph* Robert Le Fèbvre *m* Georges Van Parys

Simone Signoret, Serge Reggiani, Claude Dauphin, Raymond Bussières, Gaston Modot

'Takes its place alongside *Le Jour Se Lève* among the masterpieces of the French cinema.' – *Karel Reisz*
'A screen alive with sensuousness and luminous figures.' – *Dilys Powell*

Cass Timberlane *
US   1947   119m   bw
MGM (Arthur Hornblow Jnr)
V*

A judge marries a working-class girl, who is unsettled at first but finally comes to realize her good fortune.

Solid drama with an understanding star performance and good production values.

w Donald Ogden Stewart *novel* Sinclair Lewis
d George Sidney *ph* Robert Planck *m* Roy Webb

Spencer Tracy, Lana Turner, Zachary Scott, Tom Drake, Mary Astor, Albert Dekker, Selena Royle, Josephine Hutchinson, Margaret Lindsay

The Cassandra Crossing
GB/Italy/West Germany   1976   129m   Technicolor Panavision
AGF/CCC/International Cine (Lew Grade, Carlo Ponti)
V*, S

A terrorist carrying a deadly plague virus boards a transcontinental train.

Disaster spectacular with a number of fashionable interests but no observable filmmaking technique.

w Tom Mankiewicz, Robert Katz, George Pan Cosmatos *d* George Pan Cosmatos *ph* Ennio Guarnieri *m* Jerry Goldsmith *pd* Aurelio Crugnola

Sophia Loren, Richard Harris, Ava Gardner, Burt Lancaster, Richard Harris, Ava Gardner, Burt Lancaster, Martin Sheen, Ingrid Thulin, Lee Strasberg, John Phillip Law, Lionel Stander, Ann Turkel, O. J. Simpson, Alida Valli

La Casse: see *The Burglars*

Cast a Dark Shadow *
GB   1955   82m   bw
Frobisher/Daniel M. Angel (Herbert Mason)
V*

A wife-murderer marries an ex-barmaid and tries again.

Unambitious but enjoyable melodrama, well acted though with directorial opportunities missed.

w John Cresswell *play* *Murder Mistaken* by Janet Green *d* Lewis Gilbert *ph* Jack Asher
m Antony Hopkins

Dirk Bogarde, *Margaret Lockwood,* Kay Walsh, Kathleen Harrison, Robert Flemyng, Mona Washbourne, Walter Hudd

'Outnumbered – unarmed – unprepared – they hurled back their answer in flesh and flame!'
Cast a Giant Shadow *
US   1966   141m   DeLuxe   Panavision
UA/Mirisch/Llenroc/Batjac (Melville Shavelson)
V*

An American military lawyer and ex-colonel goes to Israel in 1947 to help in the fight against the Arabs.

Spectacular war biopic with all concerned in good form but lacking the clarity and narrative control of a real smash.

w Melville Shavelson, from Ted Berkman's biography of Col. David Marcus *d* Melville Shavelson *ph* Aldo Tonti *m* Elmer Bernstein
pd Michael Stringer

Kirk Douglas, Angie Dickinson, Senta Berger, Luther Adler, Stathis Giallelis, Chaim Topol, John Wayne, Frank Sinatra, Yul Brynner, James Donald, Gordon Jackson, Michael Hordern, Gary Merrill, Allan Cuthbertson, Jeremy Kemp

Cast a Long Shadow
US   1959   82m   bw
Mirisch/UA
V*

A hard-drinking drifter thinks he may be the illegitimate son of a dead cattle baron.

Would-be psychological Western with not enough going for it.

w Martin H. Goldsmith, John McGreevey
novel Wayne D. Overholser *d* Thomas Carr

Audie Murphy, John Dehner, Terry Moore, James Best, Denver Pyle

Cast Iron: see *The Virtuous Sin*

Castaway
GB   1986   118m   Fujicolor
Cannon/United British Artists (Rick McCallum)
V, V*

A bored London girl answers an ad placed by a man who wants a wife to take to a tropical island for a year; but he expects sex and she doesn't.

Extended absurdity uncharacteristic of its director.

w Allan Scott *book* Lucy Irvine *d* Nicolas Roeg
ph Harvey Harrison *m* Stanley Myers *pd* Andrew Sanders *ed* Tony Lawson

Oliver Reed, Amanda Donohoe, Georgina Hale

'Prospects are good for those interested in beautiful scenery and naked bodies.' – *Daily Variety*

The Castaway Cowboy *
US   1974   91m   Technicolor
Walt Disney (Ron Miller, Winston Hibler)
V*

In 1850, a Shanghaied sailor on Hawaii helps a lady potato farmer to turn her land into a cattle ranch.

Unexciting and unexceptional family fare.

w Don Tait *d* Vincent McEveety *ph* Andrew Jackson *m* Robert F. Brunner

James Garner, Vera Miles, Robert Culp, Eric Shea, Elizabeth Smith

The Castle
West Germany   1969   93m   colour
Maximilian Schell/Alfa/Glarus/Rudolf Noelte
V*

A surveyor is summoned to a remote castle but prevented by the villagers from getting there.

Attempt, partly successful, to film an unfinished Kafka obscurity. Marks all round for trying.

wd Rudolf Noelte

Maximilian Schell, Cordula Trantow, Trudik Daniel, Franz Misar

Castle in the Air
GB   1952   90m   bw
Hallmark/ABP

A nobleman fails to turn his castle into a hotel but hopes to sell it to the Coal Board.

Topical comedy which sparkled rather more on the stage.

w Alan Melville, Edward Dryhurst *play* Alan Melville *d* Henry Cass

David Tomlinson, Helen Cherry, Margaret Rutherford, Barbara Kelly, A. E. Matthews, Pat Dainton, Brian Oulton, Ewan Roberts

Castle in the Desert *
US   1942   62m   bw
TCF
V*

Murders take place at the remote castle of an eccentric millionaire.

One of the sharpest Charlie Chan mysteries, with a lively plot and some good lines.

w John Larkin *d* Harry Lachman

Sidney Toler, Arleen Whelan, Richard Derr, Douglass Dumbrille, Henry Daniell, Steve Geray, Sen Yung, Ethel Griffies, Milton Parsons

'A one-eyed major and his oddball heroes fight a twentieth-century war in a tenth-century castle!'
Castle Keep *
US   1969   107m   Technicolor   Panavision
Columbia/Filmways (Martin Ransohoff, John Calley)

During World War II seven battle-weary American soldiers occupy a 10th-century castle filled with art treasures, then die defending it. Or are they dead all the time?

The film version of this fantastic novel never seems quite sure, and the uncertainty finally deadens it despite careful work all round.

w Daniel Taradash, David Rayfiel *novel* William Eastlake *d* Sydney Pollack *ph* Henri Decaë
m Michel Legrand

Burt Lancaster, Peter Falk, Jean Pierre Aumont, Patrick O'Neal, Al Freeman Jnr, Scott Wilson, Tony Bill, Bruce Dern, Astrid Heeren

Castle of Evil
US   1966   81m   Eastmancolor
NTA
V*

A disfigured industrialist summons six people to a remote Caribbean island for the reading of his will.

Tedious variation on *Ten Little Niggers* and *The Cat and the Canary,* with horror asides and the lowest of budgets.

w Charles A. Wallace *d* Francis D. Lyon

Virginia Mayo, Scott Brady, David Brian, Lisa Gaye, Hugh Marlowe

Castle of Fu Manchu
West Germany/Spain/Italy/GB   1968   92m   Eastmancolor
Terra Filmkunst/Balcazar/Italian International/Towers of London
V, V*

The yellow peril wrecks an ocean-going liner by turning water into ice, and keeps the inventor a prisoner.

Extraordinarily tatty entry in a series which started off well. (See *Fu Manchu* for list.)

w Harry Alan Towers (Peter Welbeck) *d* Jesus Franco

Christopher Lee, Richard Greene, Howard Marion Crawford, Gunther Stoll, Maria Perschy

Castle on the Hudson *
US 1940 77m bw
Warner (Sam Bischoff)
GB title: *Years without Days*

A hardened criminal is not helped by his years in prison.

Adequate, gloomy remake of *Twenty Thousand Years in Sing Sing.*

w Seton I. Miller, Brown Holmes, Courtney Terrett
d Anatole Litvak ph Arthur Edeson m Adolph Deutsch

John Garfield, Pat O'Brien, Ann Sheridan, Burgess Meredith, Jerome Cowan, Henry O'Neill, Guinn Williams, John Litel

Casual Sex?
US 1988 97m colour
Universal/Jascat (Ilona Herzberg, Sheldon Kahn)
V, V*, L

Two women, one promiscuous, the other prim, who are both scared of being single, find true love at a health resort.

Based on a stage musical and transferred to the screen without songs, it is an inconsequential jejune look at sexual relationships, full of direct-to-camera monologues that are at best coy and often embarrassing.

w Wendy Goldman, Judy Toll play book and lyrics Wendy Goldman, Judy Toll, music Alan Alexrod d Genevieve Robert ph Rolf Kestermann m Van Dyke Parks pd Randy Ser ed Sheldon Kahn, Donn Cambern

Lea Thompson, Victoria Jackson, Stephen Shellen, Jerry Levine, Mary Gross, Peter Dvorsky, Andrew Dice Clay

Casualties of War *
US 1989 113m DeLuxe Panavision
Columbia TriStar (Art Linson)
V, V*, L, S

In Vietnam, a soldier is horrified when others kidnap and rape a village girl.

Simple minded, melodramatic account of a true incident.

w David Rabe book Daniel Lang d Brian de Palma ph Stephen H. Burum m Ennio Morricone pd Wolf Kroeger ed Bill Pankow

Michael J. Fox, Sean Penn, Don Harvey, John C. Reilly, John Leguizamo, Thuy Thu Le, Erik King, Jack Gwaltney

'This new film is the kind that makes you feel protective. When you leave the theatre, you'll probably find that you're not ready to talk about it. You may also find it hard to talk lightly about anything.' – *Pauline Kael*

The Cat *
France 1973 88m colour
Raymond Danon

After twenty-five years of marriage an embittered trapeze star and her husband simply don't talk to each other.

Absorbing drama for two characters, brilliantly acted, but with a somewhat unsatisfactory conclusion.

w Pascal Jardin d Pierre Granier-Deferre

Jean Gabin, Simone Signoret

Cat and Mouse *
GB 1958 79m bw
Eros/Anvil (Paul Rotha)

The daughter of a man executed for murder is threatened by criminals seeking hidden loot.

Interesting rather than exciting second feature thriller directed by a documentary maker.

wd Paul Rotha novel Michael Halliday
ph Wolfgang Suschitzky

Lee Patterson, Ann Sears, Hilton Edwards, Victor Maddern, George Rose, Roddy McMillan

The Cat and the Canary ***
US 1927 84m (24 fps) bw silent
Universal
V*

Greedy relatives assemble in an old house to hear an eccentric's will, and a young girl's sanity is threatened.

Archetypal spooky house comedy horror, here given an immensely stylish production which influenced Hollywood through the thirties and was spoofed in *The Old Dark House.*

w Alfred Cohn, Robert F. Hill play John Willard d Paul Leni ph Gilbert Warrenton ad Charles D. Hall

Creighton Hale, Laura La Plante, Forrest Stanley, Tully Marshall, Flora Finch, Gertrude Astor, Arthur Carewe

The Cat and the Canary ***
US 1939 72m bw
Paramount (Arthur Hornblow Jnr)

A superbly staged remake, briskly paced, perfectly cast and lusciously photographed.

The comedy-thriller *par excellence,* with Bob Hope fresh and sympathetic in his first big star part.

w Walter de Leon, Lynn Starling d Elliott Nugent ph Charles Lang m Dr Ernst Toch ad Hans Dreier, Robert Usher

Bob Hope (Wally Campbell), *Paulette Goddard* (Joyce Norman), *Gale Sondergaard* (Miss Lu), Douglass Montgomery (Charlie Wilder), John Beal (Fred Blythe), George Zucco (Lawyer Crosby), *Nydia Westman* (Cicily), *Elizabeth Patterson* (Aunt Susan), John Wray (Hendricks)

   CICILY: 'Do you believe people come back from the dead?'
   WALLY: 'You mean like republicans?'
   CICILY: 'Don't these big empty houses scare you?'
   WALLY: 'Not me, I was in vaudeville.'
   WALLY: 'I get goose pimples. Even my goose pimples have goose pimples.'

'The objective is carried out briskly and to our complete satisfaction.' – *New York Times*

'A top programmer for upper-bracket bookings in the keys, and will hit a consistent stride down the line in the subsequents.' – *Variety*

'Beautifully shot, intelligently constructed.' – *Peter John Dyer, 1966*

The Cat and the Canary
GB 1979 98m Technicolor
Gala/Grenadier (Richard Gordon)
V*

An overpoweringly cast but half-heartedly scripted remake of the above, which after a spirited beginning bores more than it thrills.

wd Radley Metzger ph Alex Thomson m Steven Cagan

Honor Blackman, Michael Callan, Edward Fox, Wendy Hiller, Beatrix Lehmann, Olivia Hussey, Daniel Massey, Carol Lynley, Peter McEnery, Wilfrid Hyde-White

'So mechanically are characters shunted through the indistinguishable rooms and corridors that one is surprised not to see the parquet marked off in neat little squares, as on a Cluedo board.' – *Gilbert Adair, MFB*

The Cat and the Fiddle
US 1933 90m bw/colour sequence
MGM
V*

In a taxi in Brussels, a leading lady of Broadway musicals meets a European composer.

Very lightweight musical comedy.

w Sam and Bella Spewack stageshow Jerome Kern, Otto Harbach d William K. Howard

Jeanette MacDonald, Ramon Novarro, Charles Butterworth, Frank Morgan, Jean Hersholt, Vivienne Segal, Henry Armetta

'The only thing remaining of merit is the music.' – *Variety*

Cat Ballou **
US 1965 96m Technicolor
Columbia (Harold Hecht)
V, V*

Young Catherine Ballou hires a drunken gunfighter to protect her father from a vicious gunman, but despite her efforts he is shot, so she turns outlaw.

Sometimes lively, sometimes somnolent Western spoof which considering the talent involved should have been funnier than it is. The linking ballad helps.

w Walter Newman, Frank R. Pierson novel Roy Chanslor d Eliot Silverstein ph Jack Marta m Frank de Vol

Jane Fonda, *Lee Marvin*, Michael Callan, Dwayne Hickman, Nat King Cole, Stubby Kaye, Tom Nardini, John Marley, Reginald Denny

'Uneven, lumpy, coy and obvious.' – *Pauline Kael*

'The ultimate American spoof of the American Western, done with a judicious restraint and sly satire and, above all, a consistency all too rarely found in Hollywood.' – *Judith Crist*

AA: Lee Marvin

AAN: Walter Newman, Frank R. Pierson; Frank de Vol; song 'The Ballad of Cat Ballou' (m Jerry Livingston, ly Mack David)

Cat Chaser
US 1988 98m Technicolor
Whiskers Productions (Peter S. Davis, William Panzer)
V, V*

A motel owner becomes involved with an old girlfriend, who is now married to an exiled Dominican thug who keeps a fortune in banknotes in a secret hiding place.

Another botched attempt to find the cinematic equivalent to Leonard's tense, witty novels, not helped by an obtrusive voice-over.

w James Borelli, Elmore Leonard novel Elmore Leonard d Abel Ferrara ph Anthony B. Richmond m Chick Corea pd Dan Leigh ed Anthony Redman

Peter Weller, Kelly McGillis, Charles Durning, Frederic Forrest, Tomas Milian, Juan Fernandez, Phil Leeds, Kelly Jo Minton, Tony Bolano

The Cat Creeps *
US 1930 71m bw
Universal

A sound remake of the 1927 *Cat and the Canary.* Not too bad on its own account.

w Gladys Lehman, William Hurlbut d Rupert Julian

Helen Twelvetrees, Raymond Hackett, Neil Hamilton, Jean Hersholt, Montagu Love, Blanche Friderici, Elisabeth Patterson, Theodore von Eltz, Lilyan Tashman, Lawrence Grant

The Cat Creeps
US 1946 58m bw
Universal

A reporter and photographer solve a murder and uncover missing millions.

Terrible programme filler, nothing to do with *The Cat and the Canary.*

w Edward Dein, Jerry Warner   d Erle C. Kenton

Noah Beery Jnr, Lois Collier, Paul Kelly, Douglass Dumbrille, Rose Hobart, Jonathan Hale

The Cat from Outer Space
US   1978   103m   Technicolor
Walt Disney Productions (Ron Miller)
V*

A superintelligent extraterrestrial cat is forced to land on Earth for running repairs.

Fairly modest studio offering which pleased its intended market but could have been sharper.

w Ted Key   d Norman Tokar   ph Charles F. Wheeler   m Lalo Schifrin   sp Eustace Lycett, Art Cruickshank, Danny Dee

Ken Berry, Roddy McDowall, Sandy Duncan, Harry Morgan, McLean Stevenson, Jesse White, Alan Young, Hans Conried

Cat o'Nine Tails
Italy/France/Germany   1971   112m   Technicolor
    Techniscope
Spettacoli/Mondial/Terra/Labrador (Salvatore Argento)

A blind reporter overhears an industrial espionage plot that turns into murder.

Smart surface mechanics camouflage poor storytelling.
wd Dario Argento   story Dario Argento, Luigi Collo, Dardano Sacchetti   ph Enrico Menczer   m Ennio Morricone   ad Carlo Leva   ed Franco Fraticelli

Karl Malden, James Franciscus, Catherine Spaak

'The sort of thriller where professional expertise amd a certain visual elegance struggle to give "tone" and "style" to blandly undistinguished material.' – *Richard Combs, MFB*

Cat on a Hot Tin Roof **
US   1958   108m   Metrocolor
MGM/Avon (Lawrence Weingarten)
V, V*, L

A rich plantation owner, dying of cancer, finds his two sons unsatisfactory: one is a conniver, the other a neurotic who refuses to sleep with his wife.

Slightly bowdlerized version of Tennessee Williams's most straightforward melodrama, watchable for the acting but still basically a theatrical experience.

w Richard Brooks, James Poe   play Tennessee Williams   d Richard Brooks   ph William Daniels   m uncredited

Paul Newman, Burl Ives, Elizabeth Taylor, Jack Carson, Judith Anderson, Madeleine Sherwood, Larry Gates

BIG DADDY: 'Truth is pain and sweat and paying bills and making love to a woman that you don't love any more. Truth is dreams that don't come true and nobody prints your name in the paper until you die.'
MAGGIE: 'Win what? What is the victory of a cat on a hot tin roof?'
BRICK: 'Just staying on it, I guess.'

AAN: best picture; Richard Brooks, James Poe; Richard Brooks (as director); William Daniels; Paul Newman; Elizabeth Taylor

'Kiss me and I'll claw you to death!'
Cat People **
US   1942   73m   bw
RKO (Val Lewton)
V*, L

A beautiful Yugoslavian girl believes she can turn into a panther; before she is found mysteriously dead, several of her acquaintances are attacked by such a beast.

The first of Lewton's famous horror series for RKO is a slow starter but has some notable suspense

sequences. It was also the first monster film to refrain from showing its monster.

w De Witt Bodeen   d Jacques Tourneur   ph Nicholas Musuraca   m Roy Webb

Simone Simon, Kent Smith, Tom Conway, Jane Randolph, Jack Holt

'(Lewton) revolutionized scare movies with suggestion, imaginative sound effects and camera angles, leaving everything to the fear-filled imagination.' – *Pauline Kael, 1968*

† *Curse of the Cat People* (qv) was a very unrelated sequel.

Cat People
US   1982   118m   Technicolor
Universal (Charles Fries)
V, V*, L, S

A kinky version of the 1942 horrorpic. The feline lady now has an incestuous relationship with her brother, only changes after sex, and then must kill to become human again. (It is therefore safe to mate only with relatives.)

One presumes that among the eroticism and bloodlust a statement is being made, but it is never evident.

w Alan Ormsby   d Paul Schrader   ph John Bailey   m Giorgio Moroder   sp Tom Burman, Albert Whitlock   visual consultant Ferdinando Scarfiotti   ed Jacqueline Cambas

Nastassja Kinski, Malcolm McDowell, John Heard, Annette O'Toole, Ruby Dee, Ed Begley Jnr

'The final impression is of a phantasmagoric indulgence in sound and vision by a filmmaker who fears sex and is excited by violence.' – *Sunday Times*

'The hobgoblins of an actual horror movie aren't easily translatable into the demons that haunt a Schrader hero on his way to a religious transcendence that is also a renunciation.' – *Richard Combs, MFB*

The Cat that Hated People **
US   1948   7m   Technicolor
MGM

A weary Manhattan cat rockets to the moon but finds it even noisier and is glad to come home.

Violent but dazzlingly inventive cartoon from this madcap director; a little classic of its kind.

w Heck Allen   d Tex Avery

Cat Women of the Moon
US   1953   63m   bw   3D
Three Dimensional Pictures
V*
aka: *Rocket to the Moon*

Five American astronauts find the moon inhabited solely by ravenous cat women.

One of the top claimants to film history's booby prize, along with such other space fiction entrants as *Fire Maidens from Outer Space, Plan 9 from Outer Space* and *Santa Claus Conquers the Martians*. It has more than a chance.

w Roy Hamilton   d Arthur Hilton

Sonny Tufts, Victor Jory, Marie Windsor, William Phipps, Douglas Fowley

Catacombs
GB   1964   90m   bw
Parroch/McCallum

A rich woman is murdered by her husband and her male secretary.

Involved melodrama with rather too many twists.

w Dan Mainwaring   d Gordon Hessler

Gary Merrill, Neil McCallum, Georgina Cookson, Jane Merrow, Rachel Thomas, Jack Train

Catch As Catch Can
GB   1937   71m   bw
Fox British
aka: *Atlantic Episode*

Crooks after a valuable diamond converge on a transatlantic liner.

Modest comedy-thriller.

w Richard Llewellyn   d Roy Kellino

James Mason, Viki Dobson, Eddie Pola, Finlay Currie

Catch Me a Spy
GB   1971   94m   Technicolor
Rank/Ludgate/Capitol/Films de la Pleiade (Steven Pallos)
V*

A British agent smuggling Russian manuscripts into England falls for the wife of a Russian spy and finally gets his money as well.

Complex, patchy comedy thriller with dispirited action scenes in Bucharest and Scotland. Technical credits rather dim.

w Dick Clement, Ian La Frenais   novel George Marton, Tibor Meray   d Dick Clement   ph Christopher Challis   m Claude Bolling

Kirk Douglas, Trevor Howard, Tom Courtenay, Marlene Jobert, Patrick Mower, Bernadette Lafont, Bernard Blier

Catch Me If You Can
US   1989   105m   Foto Kem
Medusa/Management Company Entertainment Group/Sterling Entertainment (Jonathan D. Krane)

A high-school student becomes a champion drag-racer to prevent his school from closing through lack of funds.

A drive-in movie for undemanding adolescents.

wd Stephen Sommers   ph Ronn Schmidt   m Tangerine Dream   ad Stuart Blatt   ed Bob Ducsay

Matt Lattanzi, Loryn Locklin, Grant Heslov, Billy Morrissette, M. Emmet Walsh

Catch My Soul
US   1973   95m   DeLuxe
Fox-Rank/Metromedia (Richard Rosenbloom, Jack Good)

A black evangelist, led astray by a member of his congregation possessed by a demon, becomes jealous of his wife and murders her.

A rock and country musical version of *Othello*, in which the tragic original is trivialized to the point of boredom.

w Jack Good   musical play Jack Good from Shakespeare's *Othello*   d Patrick McGoohan   ph Conrad Hall   md Delaney Bramlett   m Paul Glass   pd Tex Reed   m/y Tony Joe White, Jack Good   ed Sid Levin

Richie Havens, Lance LeGault, Season Hubley, Tony Joe White, Susan Tyrrell

'A sort of comic strip travesty of the play.' – *Tom Milne, MFB*

Catch 22 *
US   1970   122m   Technicolor   Panavision
Paramount/Filmways (John Calley, Martin Ransohoff)
V, V*, L

At a US Air Force base in the Mediterranean during World War II, one by one the officers are distressingly killed; a survivor paddles towards neutral Sweden.

Intensely black comedy, more so than *M*A*S*H* and less funny, effectively mordant in places but too grisly and missing several tricks.

w Buck Henry   novel Joseph Heller   d Mike Nichols   ph David Watkin   m none   pd Richard Sylbert

Alan Arkin, Martin Balsam, Richard Benjamin, Art Garfunkel, Jack Gilford, Buck Henry, Bob Newhart,

Anthony Perkins, Paula Prentiss, Jon Voight, Martin Sheen, Orson Welles

'There are startling effects and good revue touches here and there, but the picture keeps going on and on, as if it were determined to impress us.' – *New Yorker*, 1977

'As hot and heavy as the original was cool and light.' – *Richard Schickel*

'It goes on so long that it cancels itself out, even out of people's memories; it was long awaited and then forgotten almost instantly.' – *Pauline Kael*

'Dr Strangelove out of Alice in Wonderland.' – *Daily Mail*

Catch Us If You Can
GB   1965   91m   bw
Anglo Amalgamated/Bruton (David Deutsch)
V
US title: *Having a Wild Weekend*

Freelance stuntmen have various adventures in the west of England.

The first film of a pretentious director is a bright but wearisomely high-spirited imitation of *A Hard Day's Night*.

w Peter Nichols   d John Boorman   *ph Manny Wynn*
m Dave Clark

The Dave Clark Five, Barbara Ferris, David Lodge, Robin Bailey, Yootha Joyce

'An uneven script, rather uncertainly making its point about disillusionment and capitulation to the sham; but – like Mr Boorman's direction – at its best well worth your attention.' – *Dilys Powell*

Catchfire
US   1989   99m   CFI colour
Vestron/Precision Films/Mack-Taylor Productions (Dick Clark, Dan Paulson)
V, V*

A female artist who witnessed a Mafia killing falls in love with the man sent to murder her.

Unbelievable, though occasionally enjoyable, thriller.

w Rachel Kronstadt Mann, Ann Louise Bardach
d Alan Smithee (Dennis Hopper)   *ph* Ed Lachman
m Curt Sobel   *pd* Ron Foreman   *ed* David Rawlins

Dennis Hopper, Jodie Foster, Dean Stockwell, Vincent Price, John Turturro, Joe Pesci, Fred Ward, Julie Adams, G. Anthony Sirico

The Catered Affair *
US   1956   93m   bw
MGM (Sam Zimbalist)
V*
GB title: *Wedding Breakfast*

When the daughter of a New York taxi driver gets married, her mother insists on a bigger function than they can afford.

Rather heavy-going comedy with amusing dialogue, from the period when Hollywood was seizing on TV plays like *Marty* and *Twelve Angry Men*.

w *Gore Vidal*   TV play *Paddy Chayevsky*   d Richard Brooks   *ph* John Alton   *m* André Previn

Bette Davis, Ernest Borgnine, Debbie Reynolds, Barry Fitzgerald, Rod Taylor, Robert Simon, Madge Kennedy, Dorothy Stickney

Catherine the Great *
GB   1934   93m   bw
London Films/Alexander Korda
V*, L

How Catherine married the mad prince and slowly conquered the Russian court.

Dated but well acted and written account, sober by comparison with *The Scarlet Empress* which came out at the same time.

w Lajos Biro, Arthur Wimperis, Marjorie Deans
play The Czarina by Melchior Lengyel, Lajos Biro
d Paul Czinner   *ph* Georges Périnal, Robert Lapresle
md Muir Mathieson   *m* Ernest Toch   *ad* Vincent Korda   *ed* Harold Young

Elisabeth Bergner, Douglas Fairbanks Jnr, Flora Robson, Gerald du Maurier, Irene Vanbrugh, Griffith Jones, Joan Gardner, Diana Napier

'It rates no raves but is a good piece of merchandise.' – *Variety*

† The style is typified by a speech given to Grand Duke Peter: 'If she wasn't on the throne she'd be on the street.'

Catlow *
GB   1971   101m   Metrocolor
MGM/Euan Lloyd
V*

A likeable outlaw tries to avoid problems while recovering his hidden gold.

Light-hearted, cheerfully cast, fast-moving, Spanish-located Western.

w Scot Finch, J. J. Griffith   *novel* Louis L'Amour
d Sam Wanamaker   *ph* Ted Scaife   *m* Roy Budd

Yul Brynner, Leonard Nimoy, Richard Crenna, Daliah Lavi, Jo Ann Pflug, Jeff Corey, Bessie Love, David Ladd

Catman of Paris
US   1946   63m   bw
Republic (Marek M. Libkov)

An amnesia victim may be the mad killer who prowls the boulevards.

Poverty Row thriller with a few sharp moments.

w Sherman L. Lowe   d Lesley Selander

Carl Esmond, Lenore Aubert, Adele Mara, Douglass Dumbrille, Gerald Mohr, Fritz Feld

'Settings have solid mahogany look but the script has only a literate veneer.' – *Variety*

Cat's Eye
US   1985   93m   Technicolor
Famous Films/Dino de Laurentiis (Martha J. Schumacher)
V, V*, L

Three semi-horror stories linked by a cat.

This omnibus is weak in every department.

w Stephen King   d Lewis Teague   *ph* Jack Cardiff
m Alan Silvestri   *pd* Giorgio Postiglione

Drew Barrymore, James Woods, Alan King, Kenneth McMillan, Robert Hays, Candy Clark, James Naughton

'It creeps in on foggy feet.' – *Variety*

The Cat's Paw *
US   1936   101m   bw
Harold Lloyd

The son of a Chinese missionary returns home and finds himself in the middle of a Tong war.

Very moderate star comedy from the time when he was considering himself a character comedian rather than a slapstick ace.

w Harold Lloyd, Sam Taylor   *story* Clarence Budington Kelland   d Sam Taylor

Harold Lloyd, George Barbier, Una Merkel, Nat Pendleton, Grant Mitchell, Vince Barnett

'The picture gets its laughs all right, but it approaches them at a crawl.' – *Variety*

Cattle Annie and Little Britches
US   1980   98m   CFI colour
Hemdale/UATC (David Korda)

In 1893, two girls head west in search of adventure.

Rather winsome family Western, with too little real action and too much romping about.

w Robert Ward   *novel* Robert Ward   d Lamont Johnson   *ph* Larry Pizer   *m* Sanh Berti, Tom Slocum

Burt Lancaster, John Savage, Rod Steiger, Diane Lane, Amanda Plummer, Scott Glenn, Steven Ford

'Its storyline meanders and it never clinches any central conflict. But it has qualities of feeling that grab-'em movies can't approach.' – *Peter Rainer, Los Angeles Herald Examiner*

Cattle Drive
US   1951   78m   Technicolor
Universal-International (Aaron Rosenberg)

The spoiled teenage son of a magnate finds humanity and friendship with a cowhand during a cattle drive.

Captains Courageous out west, not badly done.

w Jack Natteford, Lillie Hayward   d Kurt Neumann

Joel McCrea, Dean Stockwell, Chill Wills, Leon Ames, Bob Steele

Cattle Empire
US   1958   82m   DeLuxe   Cinemascope
TCF (Robert Stabler)

A trail boss out of prison gets a new assignment and signs up helpers who had previously made life difficult for him.

Fair general Western, entirely dependent on its star.

w Endre Bohem, Eric Norden   d Charles Marquis Warren   *ph* Brydon Baker   *m* Paul Sawtell, Bert Shefter

Joel McCrea, Gloria Talbott, Don Haggerty, Phyllis Coates, Paul Brinegar

Cattle King
US   1963   90m   Metrocolor
MGM/Missouri (Nat Holt)
GB title: *Guns of Wyoming*

A big rancher opposes a cattle trail and starts a range war.

Moderately expert but very familiar star Western.

w Thomas Thompson   d Tay Garnett   *ph* William E. Snyder   *m* Paul Sawtell

Robert Taylor, Joan Caulfield, Robert Middleton, Robert Loggia, Larry Gates, Malcolm Atterbury

Cattle Queen of Montana
US   1954   88m   Technicolor
RKO/Benedict Bogeaus
V*, L

A tough woman inherits her father's rangeland and resists cattle rustlers.

A Western which runs in predictable grooves, and could have done with more vigour.

w Robert Blees, Howard Estabrook   d Allan Dwan

Barbara Stanwyck, Ronald Reagan, Gene Evans, Lance Fuller, Anthony Caruso, Jack Elam

Cattle Town
US   1952   71m   bw
Warner

After the Civil War, returning ranch owners find their land appropriated by squatters.

Reach-me-down Western programmer.

w Tom Blackburn   d Noel Smith

Dennis Morgan, Amanda Blake, Rita Moreno, Ray Teal, Philip Carey

Caught!
US   1931   71m   bw
Paramount

A US cavalry officer discovers that Calamity Jane is his mother.

Curious mother-love Western.

w Agnes Brand Leahy, Keane Thompson, Sam and Bella Spewack   *d* Edward Sloman

Richard Arlen, Louise Dresser, Frances Dee

Caught *
US   1948   88m   bw
Enterprise (Wolfgang Reinhardt)
V*

The ill-treated wife of a vicious millionaire leaves him for a doctor, but finds she is to have the millionaire's baby.

Pretentious *film noir*, rather typical of its time, with much talent squandered on a very boring plot.

w Arthur Laurents   *novel* Wild Calendar by Libbie Block   *d* Max Ophuls   *ph* Lee Garmes   *m* Frederick Hollander

James Mason (the doctor), Robert Ryan (the millionaire), Barbara Bel Geddes, Natalie Schafer, Curt Bois

'Ophuls had suffered at Hughes' hands . . . had wasted time on worthless projects . . . and had been referred to as "the oaf". Laurents built the script on stories which Ophuls told him about Hughes, and on the accounts given by one of Hughes' girls.' – *Pauline Kael*

Caught in the Draft **
US   1941   82m   bw
Paramount (B. G. de Sylva)

A nervous film star cannot avoid being drafted into the army.

Sprightly comedy from the star's best period, with gags and supporting cast well up to form.

w Harry Tugend   *d* David Butler   *ph* Karl Struss   *m* Victor Young

Bob Hope, Lynne Overman, Dorothy Lamour, Clarence Kolb, Eddie Bracken, Paul Hurst, Irving Bacon

Caught Plastered
US   1931   68m   bw
RKO

In helping an old lady save her drug store, two hams get mixed up with bootleggers.

Tedious star farce.

w Ralph Spence, Douglas MacLean   *d* William Seiter

Bert Wheeler, Robert Woolsey, Dorothy Lee, Lucy Beaumont, Jason Robards

'Best for combo and three-dayers.' – *Variety*

Caught Short
US   1930   approx 75m   bw
Cosmopolitan/MGM

Feuding boarding house landladies play the stock market – and win.

Lumbering comedy which marked the first big success for the team of Dressler and Moran.

w Willard Mack, Robert Hopkins   *d* Charles Reisner

Marie Dressler, Polly Moran, Charles Morton, Anita Page

'A gold mine . . . the apex of the career of this pair of sublimated film-makers . . . a box office smash for all classes anywhere.' – *Variety*

† A credit reads: Story suggested by Eddie Cantor's gag book.

Cauldron of Blood
Spain/US   1968   97m   Eastmancolor
Tigon/Hispamer/Robert D. Weinbach
V*
aka: *Blind Man's Bluff*

A sculptor, blinded in a car crash, is unaware that his wife has turned killer to keep him supplied with the skeletons he uses in his work.

Dreary horror movie that is interesting only for the presence of Karloff, and even he seems to wish himself elsewhere.

w John Melson, Edward Mann, José Luis Bayonas   *d* Edward Mann (Santos Alcocer)   *ph* Francisco Sempere   *m* Ray Ellis   *ad* Gil Parrondo   *sp* Thierre Pathé   *ed* J. Antonio Rojo

Boris Karloff, Viveca Lindfors, Jean-Pierre Aumont, Jacqui Speed

'Its heavy Freudian symbolism becomes almost laughable in conjunction with the wooden dialogue and ludicrous situations.' – *David Pirie, MFB*

† The film was cut to 87m for its British release.

Cause for Alarm *
US   1951   74m   bw
MGM (Tom Lewis)
V*

A housewife tries frantically to retrieve a posted letter containing manufactured evidence which may put her on a murder charge.

Minor-league suspenser, watchable but disappointingly handled.

w Mel Dinelli, Tom Lewis   *d* Tay Garnett   *ph* Joe Ruttenberg   *m* André Previn

Loretta Young, Barry Sullivan, Bruce Cowling, Margalo Gillmore, Irving Bacon

'A love that suffered and rose triumphant above the crushing events of this modern age! The march of time measured by a mother's heart!'

Cavalcade **
US   1932   109m   bw
Fox (Winfield Sheehan)
V*

The story of an upper-class English family between the Boer War and World War I.

Rather static version of the famous stage spectacular, very similar in setting and style to TV's later *Upstairs Downstairs*. Good performances, flat handling.

w Reginald Berkeley   *play* Noël Coward   *d* Frank Lloyd   *ph* Ernest Palmer   *war scenes* William Cameron Menzies   *m* Louis de Francesco   *ad* William Darling

Clive Brook, Diana Wynyard, Ursula Jeans, Herbert Mundin, Una O'Connor, Irene Browne, Merle Tottenham, Beryl Mercer, Frank Lawton, Billy Bevan

'Dignified and beautiful spectacle that will demand respect.' – *Variety*

'If there is anything that moves the ordinary American to uncontrollable tears, it is the plight – the constant plight – of dear old England . . . a superlative newsreel, forcibly strengthened by factual scenes, good music, and wonderful photography.' – *Pare Lorentz*

'Greater even than *Birth of a Nation*!' – *Louella Parsons*

'An orgy of British self-congratulation.' – *Pauline Kael, 70s*

AA: best picture; Frank Lloyd; William Darling

AAN: Diana Wynyard

The Cave Dwellers: see One Million BC

The Cave Man
US   1926   approx 78m at 24 fps   bw   silent
Warner

A bored socialite cuts a high denomination note in half, throws one half away, and offers riches to the first man to find it.

Typical twenties comedy which seemed very modern at the time.

w Darryl F. Zanuck   *d* Lewis Milestone

Marie Prevost, Matt Moore, Phyllis Haver, Myrna Loy

Cave of Outlaws
US   1951   76m   Technicolor
Universal-International

After surviving a long prison term, a bandit returns to the caves where his partners hid their booty.

Modest Western with scenes shot in the Carlsbad Caverns.

w Elizabeth Wilson   *d* William Castle

Macdonald Carey, Alexis Smith, Edgar Buchanan, Victor Jory, Hugh O'Brian, Houseley Stevenson

Caveman
US   1981   91m   Technicolor
UA (Lawrence Turman, David Foster)
V*

Adventures of a prehistoric man.

Witless farrago of puns and farts on a lower level than Mel Brooks, if such a thing were possible.

w Rudy de Luca, Carl Gottlieb   *d* Carl Gottlieb   *ph* Alan Hume   *m* Lalo Schifrin   *pd* Philip M. Jeffries   *ed* Gene Fowler

Ringo Starr, Dennis Quaid, Jack Gilford, Barbara Bach, Avery Schreiber

'Too gross and leery for children and not nearly sprightly or sly enough for adults.' – *Daily Mail*

'Worth about half an hour of anybody's time. Unfortunately it runs 97 minutes.' – *Guardian*

The Cavern
US/Italy   1966   96m   bw
Ulmer/TCF

In the last days of World War II, six soldiers and a girl are trapped by aerial bombardment in a cave in the Italian mountains.

Enervating psychological drama, glum to look at and listen to.

w Michael Pertwee, Jack Davis   *d* Edgar G. Ulmer

John Saxon, Rosanna Schiaffino, Larry Hagman, Brian Aherne, Nino Castelnuovo

Cease Fire
US   1985   97m   Continental Color
Double Helix/Cineworld (William Grefe)
V*

Ex-Vietnam vets in Miami have trouble getting work and forgetting the past.

Honest but predictable drama from behind the headlines.

w George Fernandez   *play* Vietnam Trilogy by George Fernandez   *d* David Nutter   *ph* Henning Schellerup   *m* Gary Fry   *ad* Alan Avchen   *ed* Julio Chaves

Don Johnson, Lisa Blount, Robert F. Lyons, Richard Chaves, Rick Richards

Ceiling Zero *
US   1935   95m   bw
Warner/Cosmopolitan (Harry Joe Brown)
V*

Amorous and airborne adventures of an irresponsible but brilliant civil airlines pilot.

Splendid star vehicle which turns maudlin in the last reel but until then provides crackling entertainment.

w Frank 'Spig' Wead   *play* Frank Wead   *d* Howard Hawks   *ph* Arthur Edeson

James Cagney, Pat O'Brien, June Travis, Stuart Erwin, Henry Wadsworth, Isabel Jewell, Barton MacLane

'An entertainment wallop of extraordinary power.' – *Variety*

'The best of all airplane pictures.' – *Otis Ferguson, 1939*

'Directed at a breakneck pace which emphasizes its lean fibre and its concentration on the essentials of its theme.' – *Andrew Sarris, 1963*

† Remade in 1939 as *International Squadron*.

Cela s'appelle l'Aurore *
France/Italy   1955   108m   bw
Marceau/Laetitia

A Corsican company doctor falls for a young widow while his wife is on holiday, and events lead to tragedy.

Efficient melodrama, given an extra dimension by its *auteur*.

w Luis Buñuel, Jean Ferry   *novel* Emmanuel Robles   d Luis Buñuel   ph Robert Le Fèbvre   m Joseph Kosma

Georges Marchal, Lucia Bose, Gianni Esposito, Julien Bertheau, *Henri Nassiet*

Céleste
West Germany   1981   106m   Eastmancolor
Artificial Eye/Pelemele/Bayerische Rundfunk (Eleonore Adlon)
V*

Proust's housekeeper recalls their life together.

Stifling, slow-moving account, likely to interest only admirers of the author.

wd Percy Adlon   *book Monsieur Proust* by Céleste Albaret   ph Jürgen Martin, Horst Becker, Helmo Sahliger, Hermann Ramelow   m Cesar Franck   ad Hans Gailling   ed Clara Fabry

Eva Mattes, Jürgen Arndt, Norbert Wartha, Wolf Euba, Joseph Manoth, Leo Bardischewski

Celia *
Australia   1988   103m   colour
BCB/Seon (Timothy White, Gordon Glenn)

Grieving over the death of her grandmother and caught up in political and sexual acrimony that she doesn't understand, a nine-year-old girl retreats into a fantasy world of childish violence.

Unconvincing tale of a child's development, warped by the red-baiting, rabbit-hating suburban Australian society of the 1950s.

wd Ann Turner   ph Geoffrey Simpson   m Chris Neal   pd Peta Lawson   ed Ken Sallows

Rebecca Smart, Nicholas Eadie, Victoria Longley, Mary-Anne Fahey

Celine and Julie Go Boating *
France   1974   192m   Eastmancolor
Les Films du Losange (Barbet Schroeder)
V

Two girls change the outcome of a drama played daily in a haunted house.

Odd, dreamlike, absurdly long and semi-improvisational mood piece, with reverberations from *Alice in Wonderland* and *Orphée*. Not an unpleasant experience, but sometimes a tiresome one.

w Eduardo de Gregorio, Juliet Berto, Dominique Labourier, Bulle Ogier, Marie-France Pisier, Jacques Rivette, partly suggested by two stories by Henry James   d Jacques Rivette   ph Jacques Renard   m Jean-Marie Senia

Juliet Berto, Dominique Labourier, Bulle Ogier, Marie-France Pisier, Barbet Schroeder

'Rivette uncannily combines slapstick, suspense and tears in his most watchable assault on the narrative form.' – *Jan Dawson*

† Shot in 16mm.

Cell 2455 Death Row
US   1955   77m   bw
Columbia (Wallace MacDonald)

A convicted murderer staves off execution with appeal after appeal.

Cheap run-off of the case of Caryl Chessman, who was executed ten years after his trial for rape and murder. Retold in a 1977 TV movie, *Kill Me If You Can*.

w Jack de Witt   *book* Caryl Chessman   d Fred F. Sears   ph Fred Jackman Jnr   md Mischa Bakaleinikoff

William Campbell, Kathryn Grant, Harvey Stephens, Marian Carr, Vince Edwards

Celui Qui Doit Mourir: see *He Who Must Die*

'Love Knows No Limits.'
The Cement Garden *
GB/Germany/France   1993   105m   colour
Metro Tartan/Constantin/Torii/Sylvia Montalti/Laurentic (Bee Gilbert, Ene Vanaveski)
V

After their parents die, a teenage boy and girl, while trying to look after their younger brothers and sisters, begin an incestuous affair.

A cool, distanced and unsettling account of adolescent angst and sexuality, notable for some excellent acting.

wd Andrew Birkin   *novel* Ian McEwan   ph Stephen Blackman   m Edward Shearmur   pd Bernd Lepel   ed Toby Tremlett

Andrew Robertson, Charlotte Gainsbourg, Alice Coulthard, Ned Birkin, Sinead Cusack, Hanns Zischler, Jochen Horst, Gareth Brown, William Hootkins

'Neither a black comedy nor a horror story, but a delicate and beautifully filmed and performed account of the innocence and confusions of youth, within an adult world, unlikely to be mature enough to comprehend it.' – *Derek Malcolm, Guardian*

† Birkin won the award for best director at the Berlin Film Festival.

Centennial Summer **
US   1946   102m   Technicolor
TCF (Otto Preminger)

A Philadelphia family responds to the Great Exposition of 1876.

Pleasing family comedy with music, the kind of harmless competence Hollywood used to throw off with ease but can no longer manage.

w Michael Kanin   *novel* Albert E. Idell   d Otto Preminger   ph Ernest Palmer   m Alfred Newman   m/ly Jerome Kern, Oscar Hammerstein II, E. Y. Harburg, Leo Robin

Jeanne Crain, Cornel Wilde, Linda Darnell, William Eythe, Walter Brennan, *Constance Bennett*, Dorothy Gish

AAN: Alfred Newman; song 'All Through the Day' (*m* Jerome Kern, *ly* Oscar Hammerstein II)

Central Airport
US   1933   75m   bw
Warner

After the war the only job an ace pilot can get is as 'chauffeur' to a lady parachutist.

Rather stiff romantic drama with aeronautics thrown in.

w Rian James, James Seymour   *story Hawk's Mate* by Jack Moffitt   d William A. Wellman   ph Sid Hickox   m Leo F. Forbstein   ad Jack Okey   ed James Morley

Richard Barthelmess, Sally Eilers, Tom Brown, Glenda Farrell, Harold Huber

'The aerial excitement should bring sufficient response to bring it over to the right side of the box office.' – *Variety*

Central Park
US   1932   57m   bw
Warner

Stories of life in New York's park.

Nifty portmanteau which moves fast and does not bore.

w Ward Morehouse, Earl Baldwin   d John Adolfi

Joan Blondell, Guy Kibbee, Wallace Ford, Henry B. Walthall, Patricia Ellis, Spencer Charters

Century *
GB   1994   112m   colour
Electric/BBC/Beambright (Therese Pickard)
S

At the end of the 19th century, a Jewish doctor goes to work at a research institute where the doctor in charge is sterilizing poor women to prevent them breeding.

An interesting drama of the beginning of the 20th century, but one that often seems too diagrammatic in its concerns to be convincing.

wd Stephen Poliakoff   ph Witold Stok   m Michael Gibbs   pd Michael Pickwoad   ed Michael Parkinson

Charles Dance, Clive Owen, Miranda Richardson, Robert Stephens, Joan Hickson, Lena Headey, Neil Stuke, Liza Walker

'Deserves to be celebrated for its effortless integration of contemporary issues – immigration, genetic engineering in the broadest sense of that phrase – with a convincing historical story.' – *Adam Mars-Jones, Independent*

'While rarely less than intelligent and provocative, *Century* is frequently implausible – dramatically, psychologically and historically.' – *Philip French, Observer*

Le Cercle Rouge: see *The Red Circle*

The Ceremony
US/Spain   1963   107m   bw
UA/Magla (Laurence Harvey)

In a Tangier jail, a bank robber awaits the firing squad, but he and his brother have an escape plan.

Murky and pretentious melodrama with aspirations to high style and symbolism. A bore.

w Ben Barzman   *novel* Frederic Grendel   d Laurence Harvey   ph Oswald Morris   m Gerard Schurmann

Laurence Harvey, Sarah Miles, Robert Walker, John Ireland, Ross Martin, Lee Patterson, Jack McGowran, Murray Melvin, Fernando Rey

A Certain Smile *
US   1958   105m   Eastmancolor   Cinemascope
TCF (Henry Ephron)

A girl student falls in love with her philandering uncle.

Another sordid novella by Françoise Sagan (see *Bonjour Tristesse*), transformed by Hollywood into a glowing romantic saga of life among the Riviera rich. On this level, very competent.

w Frances Goodrich, Albert Hackett   d Jean Negulesco   ph Milton Krasner   m Alfred Newman   ad Lyle R. Wheeler, John DeCuir

Christine Carere, Rossano Brazzi, Joan Fontaine, Bradford Dillman, Eduard Franz, Kathryn Givney, Steve Geray

AAN: title song (*m* Sammy Fain, *ly* Paul Francis Webster); art direction

Cervantes
Spain/Italy/France   1968   119m   Eastmancolor   Supertotalvision
Prisma/Protor/Procinex (Alexander Salkind)

Cervantes, an assistant papal envoy, helps persuade Philip of Spain to join the Holy League, then turns soldier and has various adventures.

Rather boring spectacular with conventional set-pieces.

w Enrique Llovet, Enrico Bomba   *novel* Bruno Frank   *d* Vincent Sherman   *ph* Edmond Richard   *m* Jean Ledrut

Horst Buchholz, Gina Lollobrigida, Louis Jourdan, José Ferrer, Fernando Rey, Francisco Rabal

César (1931): see *Marius*

César ***
France   1936   117m   bw
La Société des Films Marcel Pagnol

A son sets out to find his real father, who returns home after 20 years of unhappy exile.

The triumphant climax of Pagnol's trilogy, marked with the same wit, warmth and humanity as the previous episodes.

wd Marcel Pagnol   *ph* Willy   *m* Vincent Scotto   *ed* Suzanne de Troeye, Jeanette Ginestet

Raimu, Orane Demazis, Pierre Fresnay, Fernand Charpin, André Fouché, Alida Rouffe, Robert Vattier, Auguste Mouriès, Milly Mathis, Maupi, Edouard Delmont, Paul Dulac

† This was the third film in Pagnol's Marseilles trilogy, following *Marius* and *Fanny* (qqv).

César and Rosalie *
France/Italy/West Germany   1972   105m   Eastmancolor
Fildebroc/UPS/Mega Paramount/Orion (Michèle de Broca)
V*, L, S

A divorcee living with a rich merchant becomes attracted to a young artist. Unexpectedly, the two become friends . . .

Wryly amusing comedy for adults.

w Jean-Loup Dabadie, Claude Sautet   *d* Claude Sautet   *ph* Jean Boffety   *m* Philippe Sarde

Yves Montand, Romy Schneider, Sami Frey, Umberto Orsini

C'est arrivé près de chez vous: see *Man Bites Dog*

C'est la Vie *
France   1990   96m   colour
Electric/Contemporary/Alexandre/SGGC/A2/CNC (Alexandre Arcady)
original title: *La Baule-les pins*

During a summer holiday, two sisters are onlookers at the end of their parents' marriage as their mother begins a romance with a younger man.

A slight domestic tale, but filmed with some charm and humour.

w Diane Kurys, Alain Le Henry   *d* Diane Kurys   *ph* Giuseppe Lanci   *m* Philippe Sarde   *ad* Tony Egry   *ed* Raymonde Guyot

Nathalie Baye, Richard Berry, Zabou, Jean-Pierre Bacri, Vincent Lindon, Valéria Bruni-Tedeschi, Didier Benureau, Julie Bataille, Candice Lefranc

Chad Hanna *
US   1940   86m   Technicolor
TCF (Darryl F. Zanuck, Nunnally Johnson)

Life in a New York state circus in the 1840s.

Mild romantic drama from a bestseller; local colour excellent, dramatic interest thin.

w Nunnally Johnson   *novel* *Red Wheels Rolling* by Walter D. Edmonds   *d* Henry King   *ph* Ernest Palmer   *m* David Buttolph

Henry Fonda, Dorothy Lamour, Linda Darnell, Guy Kibbee, Jane Darwell, John Carradine, Ted North, Roscoe Ates

The Chain *
GB   1984   100m   Eastmancolor
Quintet/County Bank/Channel 4 (Victor Glynn)

Seven groups of people, corresponding to the seven deadly sins, are involved in a house-moving chain.

Rather tedious and predictable 'all star' comedy with effective moments but no narrative command.

w Jack Rosenthal   *d* Jack Gold   *ph* Wolfgang Suschitzky   *m* Stanley Myers

Denis Lawson, Maurice Denham, Nigel Hawthorne, Billie Whitelaw, Judy Parfitt, Leo McKern, Warren Mitchell, Gary Waldhorn, Anna Massey

Chain Lightning
US   1950   94m   bw
Warner (Anthony Veiller)
V*

After World War II a bomber pilot learns how to control the new jets.

Absolutely routine romance and heroics.

w Liam O'Brien, Vincent Evans   *d* Stuart Heisler   *ph* Ernest Haller   *m* David Buttolph

Humphrey Bogart, Eleanor Parker, Raymond Massey, Richard Whorf, James Brown, Roy Roberts, Morris Ankrum

Chain of Desire
US   1992   107m   Technicolor
Distant Horizon/Anant Singh (Brian Cox)

Sexual permutations link a group of 14 people.

A bisexual updating of *La Ronde* for the AIDS generation, among people given over to the kinkier forms of sex; for all that its treatment tends to the unsophisticated and lacks any sense of irony.

wd Temistocles Lopez   *ph* Nancy Schreiber   *m* Nathan Birnbaum   *pd* Scott Chambliss   *ed* Suzanne Fenn

Linda Fiorentino, Elias Koteas, Tim Guinee, Grace Zabriskie, Assumpta Serna, Patrick Bauchau, Seymour Cassel, Malcolm McDowell

'An uneven but alluringly sexy melodrama that gets better as it goes along.' – *Variety*

'Avoid.' – *Empire*

'When she's in his arms, it's the grandest thrill the screen can give!'
Chained *
US   1934   77m   bw
MGM (Hunt Stromberg)
V*

A devoted wife has a shipboard romance with another man.

Moderate star romantic drama.

w John Lee Mahin   *d* Clarence Brown   *ph* George Folsey   *m* Herbert Stothart

Joan Crawford, Clark Gable, Otto Kruger, Stuart Erwin, Una O'Connor, Akim Tamiroff

'Simple in story and unoriginal in idea, its weight is in words rather than action and dramatic potency.' – *Variety*

Chained for Life
US   1950   70m   bw
Classic films

One of two girl Siamese twins is accused of murder.

Real life freak show starring the English Hilton twins (1908–64) who were joined at the hip. Hard to watch because of the subject but otherwise a routine lower-case effort.

w Nat Tanchuck   *d* Harry L. Fraser

Violet and Daisy Hilton, Allen Jenkins

Chained to Yesterday: see *Limbo*

The Chairman: see *The Most Dangerous Man in the World*

A Chairy Tale **
Canada   1957   10m   bw
National Film Board of Canada

A young man finds that a kitchen chair is unwilling for him to sit on it, but they arrive at a compromise.

The simplest and most effective of fantasies is told at somewhat excessive length but remains among its director's more memorable creations.

wd Norman McLaren

Claude Jutra

The Chalk Garden *
GB   1964   106m   Technicolor
U-I/Quota Rentals (Ross Hunter)
V*

The governess in a melancholy household has an effect on the lives of her aged employer and the young granddaughter.

Sub-Chekhovian drama in a house by the sea, flattened by routine handling into something much less interesting than it was on the stage.

w John Michael Hayes   *novel* Enid Bagnold   *d* Ronald Neame   *ph* Arthur Ibbetson   *m* Malcolm Arnold

Edith Evans, Deborah Kerr, Hayley Mills, John Mills, Felix Aylmer, Elizabeth Sellars, Lally Bowers, Toke Townley

'Crashing symbolism, cracker-motto sententiousness.' – *MFB*

AAN: Edith Evans

The Challenge
GB   1938   75m   bw
London Films (Alexander Korda, Gunther Stapenhorst)

On the Matterhorn in 1865, a guide proves that an English climber did not sacrifice his friends.

Fictionalized mountain climbing history, a little dull.

w Emeric Pressburger, Milton Rosmer, Patrick Kirwan   *d* Milton Rosmer, Luis Trenker   *ph* George Périnal, Albert Benitz   *m* Allan Gray   *ad* Vincent Korda, Frederick Pusey   *ed* E. B. Jarvis

Luis Trenker, Robert Douglas, Joan Gardner, Mary Clare, Ralph Truman

'A rather simple story, yet seldom dull.' – *Variety*

The Challenge
US   1948   69m   bw
Reliance (TCF)

Bulldog Drummond solves the mystery of a yacht which is stolen after its owner is murdered.

Modest addition to a long-running series.

w Frank Gruber, Irving Elman   *d* Jean Yarbrough

Tom Conway, June Vincent, Richard Stapley

The Challenge
GB   1960   89m   bw
John Temple-Smith/Alexandra
US title: *It Takes a Thief*

In search of buried loot, a lady gangster kidnaps a convict's son.

Murky and unsympathetic melodrama.

wd John Gilling

Jayne Mansfield, Anthony Quayle, Carl Mohner, Barbara Mullen, Peter Reynolds, Dermot Walsh

The Challenge
US   1982   112m   Eastmancolor
CBS Theatrical Film Group (Lyle Poncher, Robert L. Rosen, Ron Beckman)
V*

An American boxer in Japan becomes involved in a feud between two brothers.

Belated martial arts saga with a good deal of head-lopping and plenty of pretensions but no apparent message to spike its dismal entertainment values.

w Richard Maxwell, John Sayles   d John Frankenheimer   ph Kozo Okazaki   m Jerry Goldsmith   pd Yoshiyuki Ishida   ed Jack Wheeler

Scott Glenn, Toshiro Mifune, Donna Kei Benz, Atsuo Nakamura, Calvin Young, Clyde Kusatsu

'Ridiculous, demeaning stuff.' – Guardian

A Challenge for Robin Hood *
GB   1967   96m   Technicolor
Hammer (Clifford Parkes)

A retelling of the original Robin Hood legend.

Unassuming, lively, predictable adventure hokum.

w Peter Bryan   d C. Pennington-Richards   ph Arthur Grant   m Gary Hughes

Barrie Ingham, James Hayter, Leon Greene, John Arnatt, Peter Blythe, Gay Hamilton, William Squire

Chamber of Horrors (1940): see The Door with Seven Locks

'The unspeakable vengeance of the crazed Baltimore strangler!'
Chamber of Horrors
US   1966   99m   Warnercolor
Warner (Hy Averback)

A maniacal murderer is finally trapped by two amateur criminologists who run a wax museum in Baltimore.

Zany horror thriller originally meant for TV; it turned out a shade too harrowing. Advertised as 'the picture with the Fear Flasher and the Horror Horn', shock gimmicks which proved much more startling than the crude events they heralded.

w Stephen Kandel   d Hy Averback   ph Richard Kline   m William Lava

Patrick O'Neal, Cesare Danova, Wilfrid Hyde-White, Laura Devon, Patrice Wymore, Suzy Parker, Jeanette Nolan, Tony Curtis (guest)

Chamber of Tortures: see Baron Blood

'Don't fail to get a ringside seat!'
'The knockout picture of the year!'
The Champ *
US   1931   87m   bw
MGM (Harry Rapf)
V*, L

A young boy has faith in a washed-up prizefighter.

Maudlin drama, highly commercial in its day and a box-office tonic for its two stars. Remade as The Clown (qv).

w Leonard Praskins, Frances Marion   d King Vidor   ph Gordon Avil

Wallace Beery, Jackie Cooper, Irene Rich, Roscoe Ates, Edward Brophy

'This picture will hit 'em all, large or small, and that means lots of money.' – Variety

AA: original story (Frances Marion); Wallace Beery

AAN: best picture; King Vidor

The Champ *
US   1979   122m   Metrocolor
MGM (Dyson Lovell)
V, V*, L

A remake of the above, with Florida racetrack asides.

A lush version, so little updated in mood that its tearfulness seems to have strayed from another age.

w Walter Newman   d Franco Zeffirelli   ph Fred J. Koenekamp   m Dave Grusin   pd Herman A. Blumenthal

Jon Voight, Faye Dunaway, Ricky Schroder, Jack Warden, Arthur Hill, Strother Martin, Joan Blondell, Elisha Cook

AAN: Dave Grusin

Champagne
GB   1928   90m (24 fps)   bw   silent
BIP (John Maxwell)
V*

A millionaire pretends to be bankrupt so that his daughter won't marry.

Tedious comedy drama with very few of the master's touches.

w Eliot Stannard, Walter C. Mycroft, Alfred Hitchcock   d Alfred Hitchcock   ph Jack Cox

Betty Balfour, Jean Bradin, Gordon Harker, Theodore von Alten

'Dreadful.' – Alfred Hitchcock

Champagne Charlie *
GB   1944   107m   bw
Ealing (John Croydon)

The life of Victorian music hall singer George Leybourne and his rivalry with the Great Vance.

Careful period reconstruction and good songs and acting are somehow nullified by unsympathetic handling and photography.

w Austin Melford, Angus Macphail, John Dighton   d Alberto Cavalcanti   ph Wilkie Cooper   md Ernest Irving

Tommy Trinder, Stanley Holloway, Betty Warren, Austin Trevor, Jean Kent, Guy Middleton, Frederick Piper, Harry Fowler

'Cavalcanti's taste for the bizarre and the vigour of the performances make it something more than a museum piece.' – Time Out, 1984

Champagne for Caesar *
US   1950   99m   bw
Cardinal (George Moskov)
V*, L

A self-confessed genius with a grudge against a soap company determines to win astronomical sums on its weekly radio quiz.

Agreeable, mildly satirical star comedy which tends to peter out halfway.

w Hans Jacoby, Fred Brady   d Richard Whorf   ph Paul Ivano   m Dimitri Tiomkin

Ronald Colman, Vincent Price, Celeste Holm, Barbara Britton, Art Linkletter

Champagne for Everybody: see Here Come the Girls

The Champagne Murders
France   1967   107m   Techniscope
Universal (France) (Jacques Natteau)
original title: Le Scandale

A disturbed champagne millionaire thinks he may be a murderer.

Complex but uninvolving mystery story in which the director's eye seems to be more on satire than on narrative.

w Claude Brûlé, Derek Prouse, Paul Gégauff   d Claude Chabrol   ph Jean Rabier   m Pierre Jansen

Anthony Perkins, Maurice Ronet, Stéphane Audran, Yvonne Furneaux, Suzanne Lloyd

'As gay and sparkling as a champagne cocktail!'
Champagne Waltz
US   1937   90m   bw
Paramount

A press agent takes a swing band to Vienna.

Rather tedious romantic comedy with music.

w Don Hartman, Frank Butler   story Billy Wilder, H. S. Kraft, Vienna Hall   d Edward Sutherland

Fred MacMurray, Gladys Swarthout, Jack Oakie

'On the slow side, but should do fairly.' – Variety

'This is the only sport in the world where two guys get paid for doing something they'd be arrested for if they got drunk and did it for nothing.'
Champion **
US   1949   99m   bw
Stanley Kramer
V*, L

An ambitious prizefighter alienates his friends and family, and dies of injuries received in the ring.

Interesting exposé of the fight racket, presented in good cinematic style and acted with great bravura.

w Carl Foreman   story Ring Lardner   d Mark Robson   ph Franz Planer   m Dimitri Tiomkin   ed Harry Gerstad

Kirk Douglas, Arthur Kennedy, Marilyn Maxwell, Paul Stewart, Ruth Roman, Lola Albright, Luis Van Rooten

AA: Harry Gerstad

AAN: Carl Foreman; Franz Planer; Dimitri Tiomkin; Kirk Douglas; Arthur Kennedy

Champions *
GB   1983   115m   colour
Embassy/Archerwest/Ladbroke/United British Artists (Peter Shaw, Eva Monley)
V, V*, L

A leading jockey develops cancer and his horse receives a leg injury, but both survive to win the Grand National.

Gruelling factual story which could have done with a little more drama, not to mention a more sympathetic hero.

w Evan Jones   book Bob Champion, Jonathan Powell   d John Irvin   ph Ronnie Taylor   m Carl Davis

John Hurt, Edward Woodward, Ben Johnson, Jan Francis, Peter Barkworth, Ann Bell, Judy Parfitt

'It ignores any inner aspect, the better to concentrate on tearjerking externals.' – Tom Milne, MFB

'Told as an indecent tearjerker, directed with the discretion of a rampaging steamroller.' – Sight and Sound

Champions (1992): see The Mighty Ducks

Chan Is Missing *
US   1981   80m   bw
Wayne Wang Productions/Wayne Wang
V*

In San Francisco, two Chinese-American cab drivers search for a friend who has disappeared with $4,000 of their money.

Rambling but engaging in its different perspective on America.

w Isaac Cronin, Wayne Wang, Terrel Seltzer   d Wayne Wang   ph Michael Chin   m Robert Kikuchi-Yngojo

Wood Moy, Marc Hayashi, Lauren Chew, Peter Wang, George Woo

Chance Meeting (1954): see The Young Lovers

Chance Meeting (1959): see Blind Date

Chance of a Lifetime *
GB   1950   93m   bw
Pilgrim Pictures (Bernard Miles)

The owner of a small engineering works, impatient with the unionism of his men, gives them a chance to run the factory themselves.

Quiet comedy-drama on sub-Ealing lines; always interesting, it never quite catches fire despite a reliable cast.

w Walter Greenwood, Bernard Miles d Bernard Miles ph Eric Cross

Bernard Miles, Basil Radford, Niall MacGinnis, Geoffrey Keen, Julien Mitchell, Josephine Wilson, Kenneth More, Hattie Jacques

'The film's triumph lies in the integrity with which it draws its picture of factory life and it is flawlessly acted.' – The Times

'It held me from beginning to end. I found it amusing, exciting and at times moving enough to raise some embarrassing and surreptitious tears.' – Milton Shulman

'British workmen are shown for the first time as characters, not comic caricatures. They are authentic, breezy and warm, sympathetically played by comparatively fresh actors.' – Richard Winnington

† The major circuits in Britain refused to give a showing to this independent movie, which was made at a cost of £150,000, on the grounds that it wasn't entertaining. They were forced to do so after its director appealed to the Film Selection Committee.

Chances *
US 1931 72m bw
Warner

In wartime London, two soldiers on leave fall for the same girl.

Unexpectedly sensitive and pleasing romance, generally well handled.

w Waldemar Young novel Hamilton Gibbs d Allan Dwan

Douglas Fairbanks Jnr, Anthony Bushell, Rose Hobart

'Enough contributing sidelights to keep the emphasis away from the combat . . . should be pleasant b.o.' – Variety

Chances Are
US 1989 108m Metrocolor
Tri-Star (Mike Lobell)
V, V*, L

A widow realizes that her daughter's boyfriend is the reincarnation of her dead husband.

Excessively contrived romantic comedy; we have all been here before and there is nothing noteworthy about this particular variation on a familiar theme.

w Perry Howze, Randy Howze d Emile Ardolino ph William A. Fraker m Maurice Jarre pd Dennis Washington ed Harry Keramidas

Cybill Shepherd, Robert Downey Jnr, Ryan O'Neal, Mary Stewart Masterson, Christopher McDonald, Josef Sommer, Joe Grifasi, Henderson Forsythe

Chandler
US 1971 88m Metrocolor Panavision
MGM

An ex-private eye becomes a security guard and an alcoholic but even worse befalls when he agrees to keep an eye on a government witness.

Downbeat, generally unamusing and little seen piece of thick ear which harks back unsuccessfully to the forties.

w John Sacret Young d Paul Magwood

Warren Oates, Leslie Caron, Alex Dreier, Mitchell Ryan, Gordon Pinsent, Charles McGraw, Richard Loo, Walter Burke, Gloria Grahame, Royal Dano, Scatman Crothers

Chandu the Magician *
US 1932 74m bw
Fox

A spiritualist battles against a madman with a death ray which could destroy the world.

Rather dim serial-like thriller, with interesting talent not at its best.

w Philip Klein, Barry Conners d Marcel Varnel, William Cameron Menzies ph James Wong Howe m Louis de Francesco

Edmund Lowe, Bela Lugosi, Irene Ware, Herbert Mundin, Henry B. Walthall

† Sequels (whittled down from serials) include The Return of Chandu and Chandu and the Magic Isle.

Chanel Solitaire
France/GB 1981 124m colour
Gardenia/Todrest (Larry G. Spangler)
V, V*, L

Fashion designer Coco Chanel thinks back on her long career.

Moderately elegant but frigid autobiopic with very little entertainment value.

w Julian More novel Claude Dulay d George Kaczender ph Ricardo Aronovich m Jean Musy

Marie-France Pisier, Timothy Dalton, Rutger Hauer, Karen Black, Brigitte Fossey

'The producer says the film is devoted to providing what every woman wants – men, money, jewellery, castles, caviare, champagne and love, love, love. I never realized they could be so boring.' – Sunday Times

Chang **
US 1927 71m (24 fps) bw silent
Paramount
V*, L

The life of a rice-grower in Thailand.

Influential but now rather boring documentary with animal interest.

wd/ph/ed Merian C. Cooper, Ernest B. Schoedsack

'I can remember no more terrible adventure in the kinema than the moment in the middle of Chang when suddenly the curtains divide, and the screen seems to swell and tremble and burst its bounds, and the great herd of elephants comes trampling out of the picture and bears down upon us in a multitude of tossing trunks and angry feet.' – C. A. Lejeune

AAN: Unique and Artistic Picture

Change of Habit
US 1969 97m colour
Universal
V, V*

A young doctor working in a ghetto has his opinions changed by three nuns.

A notably unsuccessful attempt by a star to change his image.

w James Lee, S. S. Schweltzer, Eric Bercovici d William Graham

Elvis Presley, Mary Tyler Moore, Barbara McNair, Ed Asner, Leora Dana, Jane Elliot, Robert Emhardt

Change of Heart
US 1934 74m bw
Fox

Four young Californian students make good in New York.

Minor fairy tale which marked the last of twelve teamings for Gaynor and Farrell.

w Sonya Levien, James Gleason, Samuel Hoffenstein novel Kathleen Norris d John G. Blystone ph Hal Mohr m Louis de Francesco

Janet Gaynor, Charles Farrell, Ginger Rogers, James Dunn, Beryl Mercer, Gustav von Seyffertitz, Shirley Temple

'They are on the back of a nag that never quite gets started . . . most of the time it causes that tired feeling.' – Variety

Change of Heart
US 1937 65m bw
TCF (Sol M. Wurtzel)

A bored man and wife go their separate ways but are eventually reconciled.

Bright little comedy on a tired old theme.

w Frances Hyland, Albert Ray d James Tinling

Michael Whalen, Gloria Stuart, Lyle Talbot, Jane Darwell

'More originality, freshness of treatment and solid entertainment than in half the more expensive efforts from the Hollywood studios.' – Variety

Change of Heart
US 1943 87m bw
Republic
original title: Hit Parade of 1943

A country girl writes songs and a publisher steals them.

Slim basis for a so-so musical.

w Frank Gill Jnr d Albert S. Rogell

Susan Hayward, John Carroll, Eve Arden, Gail Patrick, Walter Catlett, Melville Cooper, Count Basie and his Orchestra

Change of Mind
US 1969 98m Eastmancolor
Sagittarius (Seeleg Lester, Richard Wesson)

The life of a liberal white DA can only be 'saved' by transplanting his brain into the body of a dead black man.

Fantasy melodrama with a social conscience, about a half-and-half which is acceptable to neither whites nor blacks. Very obvious and rather boring.

w Seeleg Lester, Richard Wesson d Robert Stevens ph Arthur J. Ornitz m Duke Ellington

Raymond St Jacques, Susan Oliver, Janet McLachlan, Leslie Nielsen

A Change of Seasons
US 1980 102m DeLuxe
TCF/Martin Ransohoff/Film Finance Group Ltd
V*

A college professor takes a mistress and his wife retaliates.

Zestless and unhumorous rehash of Who's Afraid of Virginia Woolf? and Bob and Carol and Ted and Alice. Not a new thought anywhere.

w Erich Segal, Ronni Kern, Fred Segal d Richard Lang ph Philip Lathrop m Henry Mancini pd Bill Kenney

Shirley Maclaine, Anthony Hopkins, Bo Derek, Michael Brandon, Mary Beth Hurt, Ed Winter

'A tired rehash of themes that might have been provocative a decade ago . . . it would take a Lubitsch to do justice to the incredibly tangled relationships.' – Variety

'The situation soon melts into a gooey mess, like a Mars bar left too long in a trouser pocket.' – Sunday Times

The Changeling
Canada 1979 107m colour Panavision
Chessman Palk Productions (Joel B. Michaels, Garth H. Drabinsky)

A widowed academic takes on an old house haunted by the spirit of a murdered child.

Tedious and not very brief, this uninspired ghost story comes very late in the horror stakes and contains very little to make one care about its outcome.

w William Gray, Diana Maddox *d* Peter Medak *ph* John Coquillon *m* Rick Wilkins

George C. Scott, Melvyn Douglas, Trish Van Devere, John Colicos, Jean Marsh, Barry Morse

'None of its most eerily untoward occurrences proceed from any spectral intervention, but from the worst abuses of Peter Medak's infuriatingly fidgety camera.' – *Gilbert Adair, MFB*

Channel Crossing *
GB 1933 70m bw
Gaumont (Angus MacPhail, Ian Dalrymple)

Various characters converge on a ferry boat to France.

Somewhat stilted potboiler with interesting cast.

w W. P. Lipscomb, Cyril Campion *d* Milton Rosmer *ph* Phil Tannura *ad* Alfred Junge *ed* Dan Birt

Matheson Lang, Max Miller, Constance Cummings, Edmund Gwenn, Anthony Bushell, Dorothy Dickson, Nigel Bruce

The Chant of Jimmie Blacksmith ****
Australia 1978 122m Eastmancolor Panavision
Film House (Fred Schepisi)

In 1900, a half-caste mingles with high-class whites, goes berserk, and slaughters several of them with an axe.

A powerful film on the tragedy of an outcast at home in no society, torn between the world he has lost and the one he cannot gain. The violence is shocking, as it is meant to be. It is one of the great achievements of Australian cinema.

wd Fred Schepisi *novel* Thomas Keneally *ph* Ian Baker *m* Bruce Smeaton *pd* Wendy Dickson *ed* Brian Cavanagh

Tommy Lewis, Ray Barrett, Jack Thompson, Freddy Reynolds

'One of the greatest pieces of political film making I know, because it doesn't impose rhetorical nobility on its characters or twist their lives into social statement.' – *Stephen Schiff*

'This is a large scale film – a visually, impassioned epic.' – *Pauline Kael*

'A big film intended for a big audience. On its own terms, it is a powerful indictment of the insidious, pervasive canker of white racism.' – *David Wilson, Sight and Sound*

Chapayev *
USSR 1934 94m bw
Lenfilm
V

Exploits of a Red Army commander during the 1919 battles.

Moderately striking propaganda piece.

wd Sergei and Georgy Vasiliev *ph* Alexander Sigayev *m* Gavril Popov

Boris Babochkin, B. Blinov, Leonid Kmit

'Easily the best film turned out in Russia since sound.' – *Variety*

Un Chapeau de Paille d'Italie: see *An Italian Straw Hat*

'He made the whole world laugh and cry. He will again.'
'Everyone has a wild side. Even a legend.'
Chaplin **
GB 1992 145m Technicolor
Guild/Lambeth/Carolco/Studio Canal+ (Richard Attenborough, Mario Kassar)
V, V*, L, S

In old age, Charlie Chaplin tells the story of his life to a biographer – from his early childhood to his Hollywood triumphs, his exile from America and his honorary Oscar in 1972.

Somewhat stolid biopic that tries to cram in too much of a long life, but which has a fascinating story to tell and often tells it well; it might have been better had it been longer.

w William Boyd, Bryan Forbes, William Goldman *book* My Autobiography by Charles Chaplin; *Chaplin – His Life and Art* by David Robinson *story* Diana Hawkins *d* Richard Attenborough *ph* Sven Nykvist *m* John Barry *pd* Stuart Craig *ed* Anne V. Coates

Robert Downey Jnr, Dan Aykroyd, Geraldine Chaplin, Kevin Dunn, Anthony Hopkins, Milla Jovovich, Kevin Kline, Diane Lane, Penelope Ann Miller, Paul Rhys, John Thaw, Marisa Tomei, Nancy Travis, James Woods

'Old-fashioned bio-pic does an inadequate job of getting beneath the skin of one of the most famous Englishmen of the century.' – *Iain Johnstone, Sunday Times*

AAN: Robert Downey Jnr; Stuart Craig; John Barry

The Chapman Report
US 1962 125m Technicolor
Warner/Darryl F. Zanuck (Richard D. Zanuck)

Dr Chapman conducts a study of female sex behaviour in an American suburb.

Influenced by the Kinsey report, this melodramatic compendium takes itself far too seriously, and the director's smooth style is barely in evidence.

w Wyatt Cooper, Don M. Mankiewicz *novel* Irving Wallace *d* George Cukor *ph* Harold Lipstein *m* Leonard Rosenman

Shelley Winters, Claire Bloom, *Glynis Johns,* Efrem Zimbalist Jnr, Jane Fonda, Ray Danton, Ty Hardin, Andrew Duggan, John Dehner, Henry Daniell, Corey Allen, Harold J. Stone

'We had a preview which went very well, and then it was sent over to Mr Zanuck, who did what I thought was a most horrendous job of cutting it up.' – *George Cukor*

Chapter Two
US 1979 127m Metrocolor
Columbia/Rastar (Margaret Booth)
V*, L

A widowed novelist reluctantly embarks on an affair with a divorcee.

Simon in sad mood means that the wisecracks are still there but the pauses between them are longer. The thin but heavy-going plot finally militates against enthusiasm.

w Neil Simon *d* Robert Moore *ph* David M. Walsh, Richard Kratina *m* Marvin Hamlisch *pd* Gene Callahan

James Caan, Marsha Mason, Joseph Bologna, Valerie Harper, Alan Fudge

'The regular Neil Simon Broadway takeaway for people who watch movies with their ears. Over two hours of theatrical smart talk and unfailing wit-under-pressure as Simon-surrogate Caan and the real Mrs Simon swap marital repartee in front of a reverent camera.' – *Time Out*

'All the couple have to do is swap wisecracks and nurse their rather pretty emotional bruises.' – *Observer*

'More than two hours of discussions, arguments, debates, reconciliations and accusations that quickly become tedious.' – *Roger Ebert*

AAN: Marsha Mason

Charade
US 1952 83m bw
Portland (James Mason)

Three stories conceived and produced by the stars.

Everything about this triptych is on the dull side, and Mason himself later regretted embarking on it.

w James and Pamela Mason *d* Roy Kellino

James Mason, Pamela Mason, Scott Forbes, Paul Cavanagh, Bruce Lester

† Roy Kellino was Pamela Mason's first husband.

Charade **
US 1963 113m Technicolor
Universal/Stanley Donen
V, V*

A Parisienne finds her husband murdered. Four strange men are after her, and she is helped by a handsome stranger . . . but is he hero, spy or murderer?

Smoothly satisfying sub-Hitchcock nonsense, effective both as black romantic comedy and macabre farce.

w Peter Stone *d* Stanley Donen *ph* Charles Lang Jnr *m* Henry Mancini

Cary Grant (sixty but concealing the fact by taking a shower fully clothed), *Audrey Hepburn, Walter Matthau,* James Coburn, George Kennedy, Ned Glass, Jacques Marin

'One hesitates to be uncharitable to a film like *Charade,* which seeks only to provide a little innocent merriment and make a pot of money. . . . Of itself, it is a stylish and amusing melodrama, but in the context of the bloodlust that seems unloosed in our land it is as sinister as the villains who stalk Miss Hepburn through the cobbled streets of Paris.' – *Arthur Knight*

AAN: song 'Charade' (*m* Henry Mancini, *ly* Johnny Mercer)

The Charge at Feather River *
US 1953 96m Warnercolor
Warner (David Weisbart)

An army platoon composed of men from the guardhouse tries to rescue two women kidnapped by Indians.

Formula Western distinguished by 3-D photography, probably the best to be achieved in the brief life of the medium. Warnerphonic sound was less successfully added; the sum total would be trying for nervous people.

w James R. Webb *d* Gordon Douglas *ph* Peverell Marley *m* Max Steiner

Guy Madison, Frank Lovejoy, Vera Miles, Helen Westcott, Dick Wesson, Onslow Stevens, Steve Brodie

'From the start we are involved in a whirl of frenzied activity: a cavalry charge, knife throwing, sabre practice, flaming arrows – not a trick missed.' – *MFB*

The Charge Is Murder: see *Twilight of Honor*

Charge of the Lancers
US 1953 74m Technicolor
Columbia (Sam Katzman)

During the Crimean War, the Russians capture an English major who knows the details of a new cannon.

Action cheapie which seems to be largely shot in the producer's back garden but provides a laugh or two.

w Robert E. Kent *d* William Castle

Paulette Goddard, Jean-Pierre Aumont, Richard Stapley, Karin Booth, Lester Matthews

'The reckless lancers sweep on and on – so that a woman's heart might not be broken! You're not fighting a single legion – you're fighting the entire British army, Surat Khan!'
The Charge of the Light Brigade ***
US 1936 115m bw
Warner (Hal B. Wallis, Sam Bischoff)
V*, L

An army officer deliberately starts the Balaclava charge to even an old score with Surat Khan, who's on the other side.

Though allegedly 'based on the poem by Alfred Lord Tennyson', this is no more than a travesty of history, most of it taking place in India. As pure entertainment however it is a most superior slice of Hollywood hokum and the film which set the seal on Errol Flynn's superstardom.

w Michel Jacoby, Rowland Leigh   d Michael Curtiz   ph Sol Polito, Fred Jackman   m Max Steiner

Errol Flynn, Olivia de Havilland, Patric Knowles, Donald Crisp, C. Aubrey Smith, David Niven, Henry Stephenson, Nigel Bruce, C. Henry Gordon, Spring Byington, E. E. Clive, Lumsden Hare, Robert Barrat, J. Carrol Naish

'When the noble six hundred, lances level and stirrups touching, pace, canter and, finally, charge down the mile-long valley, with the enemy guns tearing great holes in their ranks, you are a dead stock if your pulses don't thunder and your heart quicken perceptibly. This scene may be villainous history, but it is magnificent cinema, timed, shot, and cut with brilliance. It only cramps the patriotic effect a trifle that the Union Jack, nine times out of ten in the picture, is shown resolutely flying upside down.' – C. A. Lejeune

AAN: Max Steiner

The Charge of the Light Brigade *
GB   1968   141m   DeLuxe   Panavision
UA/Woodfall (Neil Hartley)
V (W)

An historical fantasia with comic, sociological and cartoon embellishments.

This version for the swinging sixties has a few splendid moments but apes Tom Jones all too obviously and leaves audiences with an even dimmer view of history than they started with.

w Charles Wood   d Tony Richardson   ph David Watkin, Peter Suschitzky   m John Addison   animation Richard Williams   ad Edward Marshall

Trevor Howard, John Gielgud, David Hemmings, Vanessa Redgrave, Jill Bennett, Harry Andrews, Peter Bowles, Mark Burns

'Considering the lucid book on which it is largely based, it is almost as inexcusably muddled as the British commanders at Balaclava.' – John Simon

'The point of the film is to recreate mid-Victorian England in spirit and detail.' – Stanley Kauffmann

'Notions for at least three interesting films are on view ... what seems signally lacking is a guiding hand, an overriding purpose.' – John Coleman

'This epic has so little feeling for the courage that went with the idiocies of the past that it diminishes itself along with its targets.' – Pauline Kael

Charing Cross Road
GB   1935   72m   bw
British Lion (Herbert Smith)

Struggling boy and girl singers try to move into high society.

Dated and artificial filler.

w Con West, Clifford Grey   play Gladys and Clay Keys   d Albert de Courville   ph Phil Tannura   m Percival Mackey, Arthur Young   ad Norman Arnold

John Mills, June Clyde, Derek Oldham, Jean Colin, Judy Kelly

'Two men chasing dreams of glory!'
Chariots of Fire ***
GB   1981   121m   colour
TCF/Allied Stars/Enigma (David Puttnam)
V, V*, L, S

In the 1924 Paris Olympics, a Jew and a Scotsman run for Britain.

A film of subtle qualities, rather like those of a BBC classic serial. Probably not quite worth the adulation

it received, but full of pleasant romantic touches and sharp glimpses of the wider issues involved.

w Colin Welland   d Hugh Hudson   ph David Watkin   m Vangelis

Ben Cross, Ian Charleson, Nigel Havers, Nicholas Farrell, Daniel Gerroll, Cheryl Campbell, Alice Krige, John Gielgud, Lindsay Anderson, Nigel Davenport, Ian Holm, Patrick Magee

'The whole contradictory bundle is unexpectedly watchable.' – Jo Imeson, MFB

'A piece of technological lyricism held together by the glue of simple-minded heroic sentiment.' – Pauline Kael

'A hymn to the human spirit as if scored by Barry Manilow.' – Richard Corliss, Film Comment

AA: best picture; Colin Welland; Vangelis; costume design (Milera Canonero)

AAN: Hugh Hudson; editing (Terry Rawlings); Ian Holm (supporting actor)

BFA: best picture; costume design; Ian Holm

Charles and Lucie *
France   1979   97m   colour
Avon/Cythere Films/Films de La Chouette/Antenne 2 (Claude Makovski)
original title: Charles et Lucie

An antique dealer and a singer, both down on their luck, are the victims of a confidence trick.

An enjoyable divertissement.

w Jean Chapot   d Nelly Kaplan   ph Gilbert Sandoz   m Pierre Perret   ed Nelly Kaplan, Jean Chapot

Daniel Ceccaldi, Ginette Garcin, Jean-Marie Proslier, Samson Fainsilber, Georges Claisse, Guy Grosso

Charley and the Angel *
US   1974   93m   Technicolor
Walt Disney (Bill Anderson)
V*

A small-town sporting goods storekeeper in the thirties escapes death three times and finds an impatient angel waiting for him.

Mild sentimental whimsy on the lines of On Borrowed Time, but with a happy ending and attractive period trappings.

w Roswell Rogers   novel The Golden Evenings of Summer by Will Stanton   d Vincent McEveety   ph Charles F. Wheeler   m Buddy Baker

Fred MacMurray, Cloris Leachman, Harry Morgan, Kurt Russell, Kathleen Cody, Edward Andrews, Barbara Nichols

Charley Moon *
GB   1956   92m   Eastmancolor
Colin Lesslie, Aubrey Baring

A music hall comic becomes swollen-headed but returns to his home village and marries his childhood sweetheart.

Faltering musical lacking the gusto of its background, but providing a generally believable impression of life on the halls.

w/songs Leslie Bricusse   novel Reginald Arkell   d Guy Hamilton   ph Jack Hildyard   m Francis Chagrin

Max Bygraves, Dennis Price, Michael Medwin, Florence Desmond, Shirley Eaton, Patricia Driscoll, Reginald Beckwith

'When he runs out of dumb luck he always has genius to fall back on!'
Charley Varrick **
US   1973   111m   Technicolor   Panavision
Universal (Don Siegel)
V*

A bank robber discovers he has stolen Mafia money,

and devises a clever scheme to get himself off the hook.

Sharp, smart, well-observed but implausible thriller, astringently handled and agreeably set in Californian backlands. Accomplished, forgettable entertainment.

w Howard Rodman, Dean Riesner   novel The Looters by John Reese   d Don Siegel   ph Michael Butler   m Lalo Schifrin

Walter Matthau, Joe Don Baker, Felicia Farr, Andy Robinson, John Vernon, Sheree North, Norman Fell

'It proves there is nothing wrong with an auteur director that a good script can't cure.' – Stanley Kauffmann

'The narrative line is clean and direct, the characterizations economical and functional, and the triumph of intelligence gloriously satisfying.' – Andrew Sarris

Charley's American Aunt: see Charley's Aunt

Charley's Aunt **
US   1941   81m   bw
TCF (William Perlberg)
GB title: Charley's American Aunt

For complicated reasons, an Oxford undergraduate has to impersonate his friend's rich aunt from Brazil (where the nuts come from).

Very adequate version of the Victorian farce, with all concerned in excellent form.

w George Seaton   play Brandon Thomas   d Archie Mayo   ph Peverell Marley   m Alfred Newman   ad Richard Day, Nathan Juran

Jack Benny, Kay Francis, James Ellison, Anne Baxter, Laird Cregar, Edmund Gwenn, Reginald Owen, Richard Haydn, Arleen Whelan, Ernest Cossart

† See also: Where's Charley?

Charley's Big-Hearted Aunt
GB   1940   76m   bw
Gainsborough (Edward Black)

Rather disappointing British version of the famous farce, dully assembled and rather unsuitably cast.

w Marriott Edgar, Val Guest   d Walter Forde   ph Jack Cox

Arthur Askey, Phyllis Calvert, Moore Marriott, Graham Moffatt, Richard Murdoch, Jeanne de Casalis, J. H. Roberts, Felix Aylmer, Wally Patch

Charlie Bubbles ***
GB   1968   91m   Technicolor
Universal/ Memorial (Michael Medwin, George Pitcher)

A successful novelist loathes the pointlessness of the good life and tries unsuccessfully to return to his northern working class background.

A little arid and slow in its early stages, and with a rather lame end (our hero escapes by air balloon), this is nevertheless a fascinating, fragmentary character study with a host of wry comedy touches and nimbly sketched characters; in its unassuming way it indicts many of the symbols people lived by in the sixties.

w Shelagh Delaney   d Albert Finney   ph Peter Suschitzky   m Mischa Donat

Albert Finney, Billie Whitelaw, Liza Minnelli, Colin Blakely, Timothy Garland, Diana Coupland, Alan Lake, Yootha Joyce, Joe Gladwin

'A modest thing, but like all good work in minor keys it has a way of haunting the memory.' – Richard Schickel

'The supreme deadweight is Liza Minnelli, whose screen debut proves easily the most inauspicious since Turhan Bey's.' – John Simon

Charlie Chan
The Oriental detective created by Earl Derr Biggers began his film career as a minor character (played by

George Kuwa) in a 1926 serial called HOUSE WITHOUT A KEY. In 1928 Kamiyama Sojin had a bigger role in THE CHINESE PARROT, but in 1929 E. L. Park did almost nothing in BEHIND THAT CURTAIN. In 1931 however began the fully-fledged Chan movies, which entertained a generation. Chan, based on a real-life Chinese detective named Chang Apana, became a citizen of Honolulu and was developed as a polite family man, aided by his impulsive number one or number two son (out of a family of fourteen), in solving murder puzzles. He had a treasury of aphorisms (a whole book of which has been published), and his technique was to gather all the suspects into one room before unmasking one as the murderer. The films built to a peak around 1936—9, but tailed off disastrously in the mid-forties. They were never noted for production values, but many retain interest for their scripts, their puzzles, and their casts of budding stars, as well as the central character. This is a complete list:

For Fox (later Twentieth Century Fox), with *Warner Oland* as Chan:

1931: CHARLIE CHAN CARRIES ON*, THE BLACK CAMEL
1932: CHARLIE CHAN'S CHANCE
1933: CHARLIE CHAN'S GREATEST CASE
1934: CHARLIE CHAN'S COURAGE, CHARLIE CHAN IN LONDON
1935: CHARLIE CHAN IN PARIS* (V*, L), CHARLIE CHAN IN EGYPT, CHARLIE CHAN IN SHANGHAI
1936: CHARLIE CHAN'S SECRET* (V*), CHARLIE CHAN AT THE CIRCUS*, CHARLIE CHAN AT THE RACE TRACK, CHARLIE CHAN AT THE OPERA** (V*, L)
1937: CHARLIE CHAN AT THE OLYMPICS, CHARLIE CHAN ON BROADWAY*, CHARLIE CHAN AT MONTE CARLO

For Twentieth Century Fox, with *Sidney Toler:*

1938: CHARLIE CHAN IN HONOLULU
1939: CHARLIE CHAN IN RENO, CHARLIE CHAN ON TREASURE ISLAND**, CITY OF DARKNESS
1940: CHARLIE CHAN IN PANAMA, CHARLIE CHAN'S MURDER CRUISE, CHARLIE CHAN AT THE WAX MUSEUM* (V*, L), MURDER OVER NEW YORK
1941: DEAD MEN TELL, CHARLIE CHAN IN RIO (L), CASTLE IN THE DESERT*

For Monogram, with Sidney Toler:

1944: CHARLIE CHAN IN THE SECRET SERVICE (V*), THE CHINESE CAT, BLACK MAGIC (V*)
1945: THE SCARLET CLUE, THE JADE MASK, SHANGHAI COBRA, RED DRAGON
1946: SHADOWS OVER CHINATOWN, DANGEROUS MONEY
1947: THE TRAP

For Monogram, with Roland Winters:

1947: THE CHINESE RING
1948: DOCKS OF NEW ORLEANS, SHANGHAI CHEST, THE GOLDEN EYE, THE FEATHERED SERPENT
1949: SKY DRAGON

In the late fifties J. Carrol Naish appeared in a half-hour TV series as Chan, but the episodes were dull. In 1971 Universal tried to revive the character in a 96-minute pilot film *Happiness is a Warm Clue*, but Ross Martin was woefully miscast. See also below.

Charlie Chan and the Curse of the Dragon Queen

US 1980 95m CFI color
UA/American Cinema/Jerry Sherlock
V*

The villainous Dragon Queen puts a curse on Chan and his descendants, and works it out some years later in San Francisco.

The targets in this spoof are somewhat elementary (the sinister housekeeper is Mrs Danvers, the

wheelchair-bound butler Gillespie) and almost all the jokes fall flat on their faces.

w Stan Burns, David Axelrod d Clive Donner ph Paul Lohmann m Patrick Williams

Peter Ustinov, Angie Dickinson, Richard Hatch, Brian Keith, Roddy McDowall, Rachel Roberts, Johnny Sekka

Charlie McCarthy, Detective

US 1939 65m bw
Universal

Ventriloquist Edgar Bergen helps to solve a murder.

Slightly tiresome mystery comedy with no real place for the wisecracking dummy.

w Edward Eliscu d Frank Tuttle

Edgar Bergen, Robert Cummings, Constance Moore, John Sutton, Louis Calhern, Edgar Kennedy, Samuel S. Hinds, Warren Hymer, Harold Huber

'Looks like a corner-cutter . . . will have to struggle as top half of the duallers.' – *Variety*

Charlie the Lonesome Cougar *

US 1967 75m colour
Disney

The growing-up of a cougar.

Amiable true-life adventure.

w Jack Speirs d Winston Hibler

Charlotte

France/Italy/West Germany 1974 103m Eastmancolor
New Realm/Claude Capra/Sedimo/Gerico/TIT (Roger Vadim)
original title: *La Jeune Fille Assassinée*

An author investigates the unsolved murder of a former lover, a police chief's promiscuous daughter, at the invitation of a rich German who claims to have killed her.

A glossy, essentially trivial mix of sex and murder.

wd Roger Vadim ph William Glenn m Mike Oldfield ed Victoria Mercanton

Sirpa Lane, Michel Duchaussoy, Mathieu Carrière, Roger Vadim, Alexander Astruc

† The film was cut to 99m on its British release.

Charlotte's Web

US 1972 96m Technicolor
Sagittarius/Hanna-Barbera
V, V*, L

Farmyard animals who sense their fate are stimulated and encouraged by a resourceful spider.

Interesting but overlong and rather plodding version of a stylish book for children; the animation has no style at all.

w Earl Hanmer Jnr novel E. B. White d Charles A. Nichols, Iwao Takamoto md Irwin Kostal m/ly Richard and Robert Sherman

voices of Debbie Reynolds, Henry Gibson, Paul Lynde, Martha Scott, Agnes Moorehead

Charly *

US 1968 106m Techniscope
Selmur/Robertson Associates (Ralph Nelson)
V, V*, L

New methods of surgery cure a mentally retarded young man, who becomes a genius, but the effects wear off.

Smooth, unconvincing, rather pointless fantasy which ultimately leaves a bad taste in the mouth.

w Sterling Silliphant novel Flowers for Algernon by Daniel Keyes d Ralph Nelson ph Arthur J. Ornitz m Ravi Shankar

Cliff Robertson, Claire Bloom, Leon Janney, Lilia Skala

'The most distressing thing about *Charly* is not its ticklish subject, nor yet its clumsily modish surface,

but its insistent, persistent sentimentality.' – *Tom Milne*

AA: Cliff Robertson

Charmant Garçons: see *Too Many Lovers*

Le Charme Discret de la Bourgeoisie: see *The Discreet Charm of the Bourgeoisie*

Charming Sinners

US 1929 66m bw
Paramount

A society wife schemes to regain the attention of her wayward husband.

Early talkie version of Somerset Maugham's *The Constant Wife;* of historical interest only.

w Doris Anderson d Robert Milton

Ruth Chatterton, Clive Brook, William Powell, Mary Nolan, Florence Eldridge

Charro

US 1969 98m Technicolor Panavision
National General (Charles Marquis Warren)
V*

A reformed outlaw is framed for the theft of a cannon.

Dismal Western with a singing star playing straight. A bad experience. wd Charles Marquis Warren ph Ellsworth Fredericks m Hugo Montenegro

Elvis Presley, Ina Balin, Barbara Werle, Lynn Kellogg, Victor French, Solomon Sturges

Chartroose Caboose

US 1960 76m Eastmancolor Panavision
Red-Bill/U-I

A runaway couple take refuge with a retired train conductor in his converted rolling stock home.

Old-fashioned to the point of seeming half-witted, this comedy has little to offer but geniality.

w Rod Peterson d William Reynolds

Molly Bee, Ben Cooper, Edgar Buchanan, O. Z. Whitehead, Slim Pickens

The Chase *

US 1947 84m bw
Nero Pictures (Seymour Nebenzal)

A shell-shocked ex-serviceman foils a criminal and falls for his wife.

Weird Cuban-set *film noir* with a strange cast and stranger atmosphere. A genuine bomb, but worth a look for its pretensions, its cast, and its trick ending.

w Philip Yordan novel The Black Path of Fear by Cornell Woolrich d Arthur Ripley ph Franz Planer m Michel Michelet

Robert Cummings, Michèle Morgan, Peter Lorre, Steve Cochran, Lloyd Corrigan, Jack Holt

The Chase *

US 1966 135m Technicolor Panavision
Columbia/Sam Spiegel
V*, L

When a convict escapes and heads for his small Texas home town, almost all the inhabitants are affected in one way or another.

Expensive but shoddy essay in sex and violence, with Brando as a masochistic sheriff lording it over Peyton-Place-in-all-but-name. Literate moments do not atone for the general pretentiousness, and we have all been here once too often.

w Lillian Hellman novel Horton Foote d Arthur Penn ph Joseph LaShelle m John Barry pd Richard Day

Marlon Brando, Jane Fonda, Robert Redford, Angie Dickinson, Janice Rule, James Fox, Robert Duvall, E. G. Marshall, Miriam Hopkins, Henry Hull

'The worst thing that has happened to movies since Lassie played a war veteran with amnesia.' – *Rex Reed*

'Considering all the talent connected with it, it is hard to imagine how *The Chase* went so haywire.' – *Philip T. Hartung*

Chase a Crooked Shadow **
GB   1957   87m   bw
ABP/Associated Dragon Films (Douglas Fairbanks Jnr)

An heiress finds her home invaded by a stranger posing as her dead brother.

Tricksy, lightly controlled suspense melodrama with a perfectly fair surprise ending. Handling equivocal but competent.

w David D. Osborn, Charles Sinclair   d Michael Anderson   ph Erwin Hillier   m Matyas Seiber

Richard Todd, Anne Baxter, Faith Brook, Herbert Lom, Alexander Knox, Alan Tilvern

'It'll lead the wisest guessers up the garden and give them the surprise of their life!' – *Kine Weekly*

† The plot was borrowed from an episode in *The Whistler* TV series, and later reversed for a 1975 TV film, *One of my Wives is Missing*.

The Chaser
US   1938   73m   bw
MGM

An ambulance-chasing lawyer falls for the girl whose intent is to show him up.

Tolerable second feature.

w Everett Freeman, Bella and Sam Spewack, Harry Ruskin   d Edwin L. Marin

Dennis O'Keefe, Ann Morriss, Lewis Stone, Nat Pendleton, Henry O'Neill, John Qualen

Chasing Rainbows
US   1929   100m   bw/colour sequence
MGM

True love finds a way while a big musical is rehearsing.

Naïve attempt to repeat the success of *Broadway Melody*.

w Bess Meredyth   d Charles Riesner

Bessie Love, Charles King, Marie Dressler, Polly Moran, Jack Benny

'Numerous exploitable names and a snappy set of tunes.' – *Variety*

songs: 'Happy Days Are Here Again'; 'Everybody Tap'; 'Lucky Me, Loveable You'; 'Poor but Honest'; 'Dynamic Personality'; 'Love Ain't Nothing but the Blues'; 'Gotta Feeling for You'

Chasing Yesterday
US   1935   78m   bw
RKO

An elderly archaeologist seeks to renew his lost youth through the daughter of the woman he once loved but lost.

Slow and old-fashioned melodrama.

w Francis E. Faragoh   novel The Crime of Sylvestre Bonnard by Anatole France   d George Nicholls Jnr

O. P. Heggie, Anne Shirley, Elizabeth Patterson, Helen Westley, John Qualen, Etienne Girardot

'Prospects not bright.' – *Variety*

The Chastity Belt
Italy   1967   110m   Eastmancolor
Warner/Julia (Francesco Mazzei)
aka: On My Way to the Crusades I Met a Girl Who …

A 12th-century knight is called to the Crusades just as he is consummating his marriage, and when he locks his wife in a chastity belt she follows him.

Abysmal international romp which looks nice but is killed stone dead by writing, dubbing and direction.

w Luigi Magni, Larry Gelbart   d Pasquale Festa Campanile   ph Carlo di Palma   m Riz Ortolani

Tony Curtis, Monica Vitti, Hugh Griffith, John Richardson, Nino Castelnuovo

Chastnaya Zhizn: see *Private Life*

Le Château de Ma Mère *
France   1990   98m   Eastmancolor
Gaumont/Gueville/TF1 (Marc Goldstaub, Guy Azzi)
V, V*, L
aka: My Mother's Castle

A novelist and film-maker remembers his childhood holidays spent among the hills of Provence.

Slow-paced, soft-centred account of a blissful past; nostalgia is laid on with a trowel.

w Jérôme Tonnere, Yves Robert autobiography Marcel Pagnol   d Yves Robert ph Robert Alazraki   m Vladimir Cosma ad Jacques Dugied   ed Pierre Gillette

Philippe Caubère, Nathalie Roussel, Didier Pain, Thérèse Liotard, Julien Ciamaca, Victorien Delamare, Joris Molinas, Julie Timmerman, Jean Carmet, Jean Rochefort, Georges Wilson, Jean-Pierre Darras (as narrator).

† A sequel to *La Gloire de Mon Papa* (qv).

Chato's Land
GB   1971   100m   Technicolor
UA/Scimitar (Michael Winner)
V*

An Apache half-breed kills a man in self-defence, subsequently eluding and destroying the sheriff's posse.

Exhaustingly violent Western in which the audience is spared no gory detail; efficiently put together for those who like this kind of fracas.

w Gerald Wilson   d Michael Winner   ph Robert Paynter   m Jerry Fielding

Charles Bronson, Jack Palance, Richard Basehart, James Whitmore, Simon Oakland, Richard Jordan, Ralph Waite, Victor French, Lee Patterson

Chattahoochee
US   1989   97m   TVC colour
Hemdale (Aaron and Faye Schwab)
V, V*, L

In the mid-1950s a veteran of the Korean War suffers a breakdown and is sent to a decaying, violent mental hospital.

Downbeat and depressing.

w James Hicks   d Mick Jackson   ph Andrew Dunn   m John Keane   pd Joseph T. Garrity ed Don Fairservice

Gary Oldman, Dennis Hopper, Frances McDormand, Pamela Reed, Ned Beatty, M. Emmet Walsh

Chatterbox
US   1935   68m   bw
RKO

A country maiden aspires to the stage.

Mildly likeable comedy for family audiences.

w Sam Mintz   play David Carb   d George Nicholls Jnr

Anne Shirley, Phillips Holmes, Edward Ellis, Erik Rhodes, Margaret Hamilton, Granville Bates

'Discounting the nice job all around, the picture isn't there.' – *Variety*

Chatterbox
US   1943   77m   bw
Republic (Albert J. Cohen)

A radio cowboy gets a film contract but can't stand horses.

Flat star comedy which borrows some well-worn situations but handles them badly.

w George Carleton Brown, Frank Gill Jnr   d Joseph Santley   ph Ernest Miller   md Walter Scharf

Joe E. Brown, Judy Canova, Rosemary Lane, John Hubbard, Chester Clute

'With a dream of justice, he created a nightmare of violence!'

Che!
US   1969   94m   DeLuxe   Panavision
TCF (Sy Bartlett)
V*

Fidel Castro is helped in his subversion of Batista's Cuban regime by an Argentinian doctor named Che Guevara.

Fictionalized biography, and a dull one, of a man who became a myth.

w Michael Wilson, Sy Bartlett   d Richard Fleischer ph Charles Wheeler   m Lalo Schifrin

Omar Sharif, Jack Palance (as Castro), Cesare Danova, Robert Loggia, Woody Strode, Barbara Luna

'It goes at the pace of a drugged ox, and hasn't an ounce of political or historical sense in its nut.' – *New Yorker*

Che?: see *What?*

The Cheap Detective
US   1978   92m   Metrocolor   Panavision
Columbia/Ray Stark
V*

Forties private eye Lou Peckinpaugh is involved in a complex case with echoes of *Casablanca*, *The Big Sleep*, *The Maltese Falcon* and *Farewell My Lovely*.

Lame spoof which might have seemed funnier on a small screen in black and white; as it is, the strain is evident and desperate.

w Neil Simon   d Robert Moore   ph John A. Alonzo   m Patrick Williams

Peter Falk (Bogart), John Houseman (Greenstreet), Nicol Williamson (Veidt), *Louise Fletcher* (Bergman), Fernando Lamas (Henreid), Madeline Kahn (Astor), Dom de Luise (Lorre), Paul Williams (Cook), Marsha Mason (Gladys George), Ann-Margret (Claire Trevor), Eileen Brennan (Bacall), Stockard Channing (Lee Patrick), Sid Caesar (Miles Mander), Scatman Crothers (Dooley Wilson); and James Coco, Phil Silvers, Abe Vigoda, Vic Tayback

'Frankly they did this sort of thing just as well, and a lot more quickly, on *The Carol Burnett Show*.' – *Richard Shickel, Time*

'There is about enough talent around for a twenty-minute sketch at the Edinburgh fringe.' – *Derek Malcolm, Guardian*

† The film was a follow-up to the not much more effective but at least more controlled *Murder by Death*.

Cheaper by the Dozen **
US   1950   86m   Technicolor
TCF (Lamar Trotti)

Efficiency expert Frank Gilbreth and his wife Lillian have twelve children, a fact which requires mathematical conduct of all their lives.

Amusing family comedy set in the twenties, unconvincing in detail though based on a book by two of the children. A great commercial success and a Hollywood myth-maker. Sequel: *Belles on their Toes* (qv).

w Lamar Trotti   book Frank B. Gilbreth Jnr, Ernestine Gilbreth Carey   d Walter Lang   ph Leon Shamroy   md Lionel Newman   m Cyril Mockridge ad Lyle Wheeler, Leland Fuller

Clifton Webb, *Myrna Loy*, Jeanne Crain, Edgar Buchanan, Barbara Bates, Betty Lynn, Mildred Natwick, Sara Allgood

The Cheat *

US   1915   95m (16 fps)   bw   silent
Famous Players Lasky/Paramount

A society lady borrows from a rich Japanese, and he brands her when she refuses to become his mistress.

Hoary melodrama which caused a sensation in its day.

w Hector Turnbull   d Cecil B. de Mille   ph Alvin Wyckoff

Fanny Ward, Jack Dean, Sessue Hayakawa, James Neill

† Remade in 1923 by George Fitzmaurice, in 1931 by George Abbott, and in 1937 (in France, as *Forfaiture*) by Marcel L'Herbier.

The Cheaters *

US   1945   86m   bw
Republic

A selfish and ostentatious family is reformed by the ministrations of a down-and-out actor.

Fairly engaging variation on *The Passing of the Third Floor Back*, with sweetness and light brought into people's lives by a fireside recital of *A Christmas Carol*.

w Frances Hyland   d Joseph Kane   ph Reggie Lanning   m Walter Scharf

Joseph Schildkraut, Billie Burke, Eugene Pallette, Ona Munson, Raymond Walburn

Cheating Cheaters

US   1934   67m   bw
Universal

Two groups of jewel thieves clash when posing as society swells.

Tolerable programmer from an old stage hit.

w Gladys Unger, Allen Rivkin   play Max Marcin   d Richard Thorpe

Fay Wray, Cesar Romero, Minna Gombell, Hugh O'Connell, Henry Armetta, Francis L. Sullivan, Ann Shoemaker

'Rather creaky entertainment, but it will about get by.' – *Variety*

Check and Double Check

US   1930   71m   bw
RKO
V*, L

Comic adventures of a couple of black handymen.

Feeble comedy notable only for the film appearance of radio's immensely popular Amos 'n' Andy, played by white actors in blackface.

w Bert Kalmar, Harry Ruby, J. Walter Ruben   d Melville Brown   ph William Marshall   m Max Steiner

Freeman F. Gosden, Charles V. Correll, Sue Carol, Charles Morton, Irene Rich, Ralf Harolde, Duke Ellington and his Orchestra

'The best picture for children ever put on the screen . . . as a freak talking picture it's in the money immediately.' – *Variety*

The Checkered Coat

US   1948   66m   bw
TCF (Sam Baerwitz)

A psychopathic killer is captured during one of his cataleptic seizures.

Fairly routine programme filler which manages to keep the attention.

w John C. Higgins   d Edward L. Cahn

Tom Conway, Hurd Hatfield, Noreen Nash, James Seay

Checkers

US   1937   79m   bw
TCF

The niece of a ne'er-do-well horse owner brings him success.

One of the most successful vehicles of Shirley Temple's arch rival.

w Lynn Root, Frank Fenton, Karen de Wolf   play Rida Johnson Young   d H. Bruce Humberstone

Jane Withers, Stuart Erwin, Una Merkel, Marvin Stephens, Andrew Tombes, Minor Watson

'Will delight the moppet's following . . . due for heavy dual booking.' – *Variety*

Checking Out

GB   1988   95m   Technicolor
Virgin/Handmade (Ben Myron)
V, V*, L

A successful advertising man becomes a hypochondriac after the sudden death of a friend.

Mildly amusing comedy.

w Joe Esterhas   d David Leland   ph Ian Wilson   m Carter Burwell   pd Barbara Ling   ed Lee Percy

Jeff Daniels, Melanie Mayron, Michael Tucker, Kathleen York, Ann Magnuson, Allan Harvey, Jo Harvey Allen, Ian Wolfe

Checkpoint *

GB   1956   84m   Eastmancolor
Rank (Betty Box)

A tycoon sends an industrial spy to Italy in search of new motor racing car designs.

Acceptable hokum, cleanly assembled, with motor race highlights.

w Robin Estridge   d Ralph Thomas   ph Ernest Steward   m Bruce Montgomery

Anthony Steel, Stanley Baker, James Robertson Justice, Odile Versois, Maurice Denham, Michael Medwin, Lee Patterson

Cheech and Chong: Still Smokin'

US   1983   92m   colour
Paramount/Cheech & Chong's Comedy Film Festival Number One Inc (Peter MacGregor-Scott)

Two slobbish comedians attend a Burt Reynolds-Dolly Parton film festival in Amsterdam.

Dreary, plotless exercise in futility that reaches its nadir in excerpts from the duo's concert performance.

w Thomas Chong, Cheech Marin   d Thomas Chong   ph Harvey Harrison   m George S. Clinton   ad Ruud Van Dijk   ed David Ramirez, James Coblenz

Cheech Marin, Thomas Chong, Hans Man In't Veld, Carol Van Herwijnen, Shireen Strocker, Susan Hahn

Cheech and Chong's Next Movie

US   1980   95m   Technicolor
Howard Brown/Universal
V, V*, L
GB title: *High Encounters of the Ultimate Kind*

Two dopers have various rude adventures.

Totally repulsive comedy which gives a bad name to self-indulgence.

w Cheech Marin, Thomas Chong   d Thomas Chong

Cheech Marin, Thomas Chong, Evelyn Guerrero, Betty Kennedy, Sy Kramer

Cheech and Chong's The Corsican Brothers

US   1984   90m   colour
Orion (Peter MacGregor-Scott)
V*, L

Twin brothers run amuck during the French Revolution.

Coarse and unfunny parody of a swashbuckling adventure.

w Cheech Marin, Thomas Chong   d Thomas Chong   ph Harvey Harrison   m GEO   ad Daniel Budin   ed Tom Avildsen

Cheech Marin, Thomas Chong, Roy Dotrice, Shelby Fiddis, Rikki Marin, Edie McClurg, Rae Dawn Chong, Robbi Chong

Cheer Boys Cheer

GB   1939   84m   bw
ATP (Michael Balcon)

Brewery owners hate each other but their children fall in love.

A highly predictable plot provides some incidental pleasures in this modest precursor of the Ealing comedies.

w Roger MacDougall, Allan MacKinnon   story Ian Dalrymple, Donald Bull   d Walter Forde   ph Ronald Neame, Gordon Dines   md Ernest Irving   ad Wilfred Shingleton   ed Ray Pitt

Nova Pilbeam, Edmund Gwenn, Jimmy O'Dea, Moore Marriott, Graham Moffatt, C. V. France, Alexander Knox

Cheers for Miss Bishop *

US   1941   94m   bw
UA (Richard A. Rowland)
V*

The life of a schoolmistress in a small mid-western town.

Acceptable sentimental hokum, quite pleasantly done.

w Adelaide Heilbron   novel Bess Streeter Aldrich   d Tay Garnett   ph Hal Mohr   m Edward Ward

Martha Scott, William Gargan, Edmund Gwenn, Sterling Holloway, Sidney Blackmer, Mary Anderson, Dorothy Peterson

AAN: Edward Ward

Chelovek s Kinoapparatom: see *The Man with the Movie Camera*

The Chelsea Girls **

US   1966   255m   bw/colour
Andy Warhol

Episodic look at life in a series of hotel rooms, consisting of unedited conversations between spaced-out individuals – the Pope of Greenwich Village hearing confessions and losing his temper, a drug dealer talking to a customer as she injects them both, a woman being reduced to tears by aggressive questioning, a mother chastising her son, a dancer stripping as he talks about his desires, and so on.

Shown on a double screen, with two different rooms visible at a time, but only one conversation audible, this was the film which, more than any other, brought the underground to public attention. It has worn less well than some of Morrissey and Warhol's other work but survives as a monument of sorts, exactly capturing the sights and sounds of a particular era despite its technical shortcomings.

d Paul Morrissey   ph Andy Warhol   m The Velvet Underground

Marie Mencken, Mary Woronow, Gerard Malanga, International Velvet, Ingrid Superstar, Ondine, Mario Montez, Eric Emerson, Nico, Brigid Polk

'An epic movie-novel.' – *Jonas Mekas*

'Warhol's people are more real than real because the camera encourages their exhibitionism. They are all "performing" because their lives are one long performance and their party is never over.' – *Andrew Sarris, Village Voice*

'It has come time to wag a warning finger at Andy Warhol and his underground friends and tell them politely but firmly that they are pushing a reckless thing too far.' – *Bosley Crowther, New York Times*

'A three and a half hour cesspool of vulgarity and talentless confusion which is about as interesting as the inside of a toilet bowl.' – *Rex Reed*

† The film, which cost less than $3,000 to make, took more than $300,000 in its first six months.

Chère Inconnue: see *I Sent a Letter To My Love*

'America's favourite two-gun star battles for love and glory!'

Cherokee Strip
US   1940   86m   bw
Harry Sherman/Paramount

A marshal brings law and order to a frontier town.

Competent Western programmer.

w Norman Houston, Bernard McConville   *d* Lesley Selander

Richard Dix, Florence Rice, William Henry, Victor Jory, Andy Clyde

The Cherry Picker
GB   1972   92m   Eastmancolor
Fox-Rank/Elsinore (Peter Curran, Derek Kavanagh)

The rich, hippy son of an American tycoon loses his appetite for the sybaritic life.

Typical British product of its time, a failed attempt to mix sex and satire; what we get instead is a cheap-looking movie with a confused narrative and an uncertain tone.

wd Peter Curran   *novel* Pick Up Sticks by Mickey Phillips   *ph* Billy Jordan   *m* Bill McGuffie   *pd* Frank White   *ed* Jack Knight

Lulu, Bob Sherman, Wilfrid Hyde-White, Spike Milligan, Patrick Cargill, Robert Hutton, Priscilla Morgan, Jack Hulbert, Terry-Thomas

'The film dithers over an inadequately scripted and crudely shot narrative that might be charitably described as "rambling" or "picaresque".' – *MFB*

Chess Fever *
USSR   1925   20m (24 fps)   bw   silent
Mezhrabpom-Russ
V

A chess fanatic is so absorbed that he misses his wedding.

Spirited visual comedy which still raises the intended laughs.

w Nikolai Shpikovsky   *d* Nikolai Shpikovsky, Vsevolod Pudovkin

Vladimir Fogel, Anna Zemtsova

The Chess Players *
India   1977   129m   Eastmancolor
Devki Chitra (Suresh Jindal)
V
original title: Shatranj Ke Khilari

In 1856 Lucknow, two noblemen are more interested in playing chess than in their state's imminent annexation by the British.

Patchy but frequently charming historical piece with more specifically Indian elements than are usual from its director.

wd Satyajit Ray   *story* Prem Chand   *m* Satyajit Ray   *ad* Bansi Chandragupta   *ed* Dulal Dutta

Sanjeev Kumar, Saeed Jaffrey, Richard Attenborough, Amjad Khan

Chetniks – The Fighting Guerrillas
US   1942   73m   bw
Sol M. Wurtzel/TCF

Yugoslav freedom fighters oppose the Nazi occupation.

Standard co-feature wartime heroics.

w Jack Andrews, Ed Paramore   *d* Louis King

Philip Dorn, Anna Sten, John Shepperd, Frank Lackteen, Virginia Gilmore, Martin Kosleck

Le Cheval d'Orgueil: see *The Proud Ones*

Cheyenne
US   1947   100m   bw
Warner
later retitled: The Wyoming Kid

A gambler turns lawman, catches a robber and marries his wife.

Rather sluggish Western which later inspired a long-running TV series.

w Alan Le May, Thames Williamson   *d* Raoul Walsh

Dennis Morgan, Bruce Bennett, Jane Wyman, Arthur Kennedy, Janis Paige, Alan Hale

Cheyenne Autumn *
US   1964   170m   Technicolor   Panavision 70
Warner/Ford-Smith (Bernard Smith)
V, V*, L, S

In the 1860s, Cheyenne Indians are moved to a new reservation 1500 miles away; wanting aid, they begin a trek back home, and various battles follow.

Dispirited, shapeless John Ford Western with little of the master's touch; good to look at, however, with effective cameos, notably an irrelevant and out-of-key comic one featuring James Stewart as Wyatt Earp.

w James R. Webb   *novel* Mari Sandoz   *d* John Ford   *ph* William H. Clothier   *m* Alex North   *ad* Richard Day   *ed* Otho Lovering

Richard Widmark, Carroll Baker, Karl Malden, *Dolores del Rio*, Sal Mineo, Edward G. Robinson, *James Stewart*, Ricardo Montalban, Gilbert Roland, Arthur Kennedy, Patrick Wayne, Elizabeth Allen, Victor Jory, John Carradine, Mike Mazurki, John Qualen, George O'Brien

'Although one would like to praise the film for its high-minded aims, it is hard to forget how ponderous and disjointed it is.' – *Moira Walsh*

'The acting is bad, the dialogue trite and predictable, the pace funereal, the structure fragmented and the climaxes puny.' – *Stanley Kauffmann*

AAN: William H. Clothier

The Cheyenne Social Club *
US   1970   102m   Technicolor   Panavision
National General (James Lee Barrett, Gene Kelly)
V*

Two itinerant cowboys inherit a high-class brothel.

Disappointing star comedy Western with pleasing moments and a lively climactic shootout. Perhaps the girls are just a shade too winsome.

w James Lee Barrett   *d* Gene Kelly   *ph* William H. Clothier   *m* Walter Scharf

James Stewart, Henry Fonda, Shirley Jones, Sue Ane Langdon, Robert Middleton, Arch Johnson

'Co-starring Shirley Jones and Rigor Mortis, who enters early and stays through the very last scene.' – *Rex Reed*

Chi sei?: see *Devil within Her*

Chicago Calling *
US   1951   75m   bw
UA/Arrowhead/Joseph Justman (Peter Berneis)

A drunk cannot pay his phone bill and is waiting for a vital call about his daughter's involvement in a car crash.

Moderate, location-shot minor melodrama with a few good ideas.

w John Reinhardt, Peter Berneis   *d* John Reinhardt   *ph* Robert de Grasse   *m* Heinz Roemheld

Dan Duryea, Mary Anderson, Gordon Gebert, Ross Elliott

Chicago, Chicago: see *Gaily, Gaily*

Chicago Confidential
US   1957   74m   bw
Peerless/UA

A gambling syndicate takes over a labour union and frames its incorruptible president for murder.

Very routine gangster potboiler.

w Raymond T. Marcus   *d* Sidney Salkow

Brian Keith, Beverly Garland, Dick Foran, Elisha Cook Jnr

Chicago Deadline
US   1949   87m   bw
Paramount (Robert Fellows)

A reporter researches the life of a lonely girl who died of tuberculosis.

Flat star vehicle consisting mainly of overplayed cameos.

w Warren Duff, Tiffany Thayer   *d* Lewis Allen   *ph* John F. Seitz   *m* Victor Young

Alan Ladd, Donna Reed, *June Havoc*, Berry Kroeger, Arthur Kennedy, Gavin Muir, Shepperd Strudwick

† Remade as the TV pilot of *The Name of the Game*.

'Where desire has no limits … Fantasies become dangerous realities!'

Chicago Joe and the Showgirl
GB   1989   103m   colour
Palace/New Line/Polygram/Working Title/BSB (Tim Bevan)
V, V*, L

During the Second World War, an American deserter and his English girlfriend, a stripper, enhance their affair by committing a series of crimes.

Based on actual events, but a movie that rarely seems more than a laboured fantasy and one that the public ignored.

w David Yallop   *d* Bernard Rose   *ph* Mike Southon   *m* Hans Zimmer, Shirley Walker   *pd* Gemma Jackson   *ed* Dan Rae

Kiefer Sutherland, Emily Lloyd, Patsy Kensit

Chicago Masquerade: see *Little Egypt*

Chicago Syndicate
US   1955   86m   bw
Clover/Columbia
V*

A young accountant breaks up an outwardly respectable crime syndicate.

Formula racket-busting melodrama.

w Joseph Hoffman   *d* Fred F. Sears

Dennis O'Keefe, Abbe Lane, Paul Stewart, Xavier Cugat, Alison Haynes

Chick Carter, Detective
US   1946   bw   serial: 15 eps
Columbia

A private eye finds himself in deep water when he investigates a jewel robbery at a night-club.

Unsuitable serial material, thinly stretched and with not enough action highpoints.

d Derwin Abrahams

Lyle Talbot, Douglas Fowley, Julie Gibson, Pamela Blake, Eddie Acuff

The Chicken Chronicles
US   1977   94m   CFI color
Chicken Enterprises/Avco Embassy
V*

Problems of a teenager in an American small town.

Extremely boring comedy drama, obsessed with sex and lacking background detail.

w Paul Diamond d Francis Simon

Phil Silvers, Ed Lauter, Steven Guttenberg, Meredith Baer, Lisa Reeves

Chicken Every Sunday *
US   1949   94m   bw
TCF

The Hefferans have run a boarding house for twenty years, but dad's wild schemes run away with any possible profit.

Archetypal, folksy, American small-town chronicle, reasonably well made, for an audience that later watched The Waltons.

w George Seaton, Valentine Davies d George Seaton ph Harry Jackson m Alfred Newman

Dan Dailey, Celeste Holm, Colleen Townsend, Alan Young, Natalie Wood

The Chicken Wagon Family
US   1939   81m   bw
TCF

Louisiana backwooders make a trip to New York.

Feeble country cousin comedy.

w Viola Brothers Shore d Herbert I. Leeds

Jane Withers, Leo Carrillo, Marjorie Weaver, Spring Byington, Kane Richmond, Hobart Cavanaugh

'Nabes and second runs will write best ledger marks.' – Variety

Chickens Come Home *
US   1931   30m   bw
Hal Roach
V (C)

Stan helps his boss Ollie to evade the attentions of an old flame.

Rather heavy and untypical, but mainly very enjoyable star comedy, a remake of Love 'Em and Weep in which all three leading players had appeared four years earlier in different roles.

w H. M. Walker story Hal Roach d James W. Horne ph Art Lloyd, Jack Stevens ed Richard Currier

Laurel and Hardy, James Finlayson, Mae Busch, Thelma Todd

The Chief
US   1933   80m   bw
MGM
GB title: My Old Man's a Fireman

A fireman's son becomes a Bowery candidate for alderman.

Feeble comedy with the star ill at ease.

w Arthur Caesar, R. E. Hopkins d Charles F. Riesner

Ed Wynn, Dorothy Mackaill, Charles 'Chic' Sale, William Boyd, George Givot, C. Henry Gordon

'With the radio draw angle discarded it is weak entertainment.' – Variety

Chief Crazy Horse
US   1954   86m   Technicolor   Cinemascope
U-I (William Alland)
GB title: Valley of Fury

The tribal problems of the Indian chief who defeated Custer at Little Big Horn.

Competent pro-Indian Western.

w Franklin Coen, Gerald Drayson Adams d George Sherman ph Harold Lipstein m Frank Skinner

Victor Mature, Suzan Ball, John Lund, Ray Danton, Keith Larsen, Paul Guilfoyle, David Janssen

Un Chien Andalou *
France   1928   17m   bw   silent
Luis Buñuel
V

Famous surrealist short which includes dead donkeys on pianos and starts with a woman's eyeball being cut by a razor blade.

It had meaning for its makers, but very few other people saw anything in it but sensationalism.

w Luis Buñuel, Salvador Dali d Luis Buñuel ph Albert Dubergen ed Luis Buñuel

Simone Mareuil, Pierre Batcheff, Jaime Miravilles, Salvador Dali, Luis Buñuel

La Chienne *
France   1931   85m   bw
Braunberger-Richebé

A bank clerk falls for a prostitute and later kills her; her pimp is executed for the crime and the bank clerk becomes a tramp.

Heavy-going, old-fashioned melodrama with some interesting detail.

wd Jean Renoir novel Georges de la Fouchardière ph Theodor Sparkuhl, Roger Hubert

Michel Simon, Janie Marèze, Georges Flament, Jean Gehret

'If the English translation of the title is unfit to print, the film's dialogue cannot be translated into English. Okay for sophisticated audiences that look for a taste of spice in a ritzy spot.' – Variety

† Remade as Scarlet Street (qv).

Child in the House
GB   1956   88m   bw
Eros/Golden Era (Ben Fisz)

When her mother is ill and her father in hiding from the police, a 12-year-old girl goes to stay with her fussy uncle and aunt.

Modest family drama of the novelette type in which adult problems are put right by the wisdom of a child.

wd C. Raker Endfield novel Janet McNeill ph Otto Heller m Mario Nascimbene ad Ken Adam

Eric Portman, Phyllis Calvert, Stanley Baker, Mandy Miller, Dora Bryan, Joan Hickson, Victor Maddern, Percy Herbert

A Child Is Born
US   1939   79m   bw
Warner (Sam Bischoff)

A slice of life in the maternity ward.

Adequately dramatic sequence of cameos, with mothers-to-be including a gangster's moll: a remake of Life Begins (qv).

w Robert Rossen play Mary M. Axelson d Lloyd Bacon ph Charles Rosher m Heinz Roemheld

Geraldine Fitzgerald, Jeffrey Lynn, Gladys George, Gale Page, Spring Byington, Henry O'Neill, John Litel, Gloria Holden, Eve Arden, Nanette Fabares, Hobart Cavanaugh, Johnny Downs, Johnnie Davis

A Child Is Waiting **
US   1963   104m   bw
UA/Stanley Kramer
V*, L

A mixed-up spinster joins the staff of a school for mentally handicapped children.

Worthy semi-documentary marred by having a normal boy play the central character (albeit very well). A little over-dramatized but cogent and unsentimental.

w Abby Mann d John Cassavetes ph Joseph LaShelle m Ernest Gold

Burt Lancaster, Judy Garland, Bruce Ritchey, Steven Hill, Gena Rowlands, Paul Stewart, Lawrence Tierney

Child of Manhattan
US   1933   70m   bw
Columbia

A night-club hostess has an affair with a millionaire, but her baby dies.

Hokey melodrama on familiar lines (at the time).

w Gertrude Purcell play Preston Sturges d Edward Buzzell

John Boles, Nancy Carroll, Warburton Gamble, Clara Blandick, Jane Darwell, Betty Grable

'Programme fodder, with more simplicity than purity.' – Variety

The Childhood of Maxim Gorky ***
USSR   1938—40   bw
Soyuzdetfilm
V

Orphan Gorky is raised by his grandparents, and becomes a ship's cook and a painter before going on to university.

This simple and direct story is told in three beautifully detailed if rather overlong films:

'The Childhood of Maxim Gorky': 101m
'Out in the World': 98m
'My Universities': 104m

w Mark Donskoi, I. Grudzev d Mark Donskoi ph Pyotr Yermolov m Lev Schwartz ad I. Stepanov

Alexei Lyarsky, Y. Valbert, M. Troyanovski, Valeria Massalitinova

The Children *
GB/West Germany   1990   115m   colour
Isolde/Arbo Film & Maran/Channel 4 (Andrew Montgomery)
V*

Returning from Brazil to marry a rich widow, an engineer finds his plans disrupted when he becomes guardian to the boisterous children of an old friend.

A leisurely account of thwarted love, held together by Kingsley's strong central performance of repressed emotion.

w Timberlake Wertenbaker novel Edith Wharton d Tony Palmer ph Nic Knowland m Benjamin Britten, Samuel Barber, Vaughan Williams, Evelyn Glennie pd Chris Bradley, Paul Templeman

Ben Kingsley, Kim Novak, Siri Neal, Geraldine Chaplin, Joe Don Baker, Britt Ekland, Karen Black, Donald Sinden, Robert Stephens, Rupert Graves, Rosemary Leach

Children of a Lesser God *
US   1986   110m   Film Lab Color
Paramount (Burt Sugarman, Patrick Palmer)
V, V*, L, S

A deaf woman falls in love with her speech therapist.

Sluggish adaptation of a play which meant more on the stage.

w Hesper Anderson, Mark Medoff play Mark Medoff d Randa Haines ph John Seale m Michael Convertino pd Gene Callahan ed Lisa Fruchtman

William Hurt, Marlee Matlin, Piper Laurie, Philip Bosco

AA: Marlee Matlin

AAN: best picture; William Hurt; Piper Laurie

Children of Hiroshima **
Japan   1952   97m   bw
Kendai Eiga Lyokai/Gekidan Mingei

A young teacher returns to Hiroshima seven years after the bomb.

Restrained yet harrowing social documentary in fiction form, with the most effective use of flashbacks to show the horror of the bomb and its aftermath.

wd *Kaneto Shindo*   novel *Arata Osada*   ph *Takeo Itoh*
m *Akira Ifukube*

Nobuko Otowa, Chikako Hoshawa, Niwa Saito

Children of Paradise: see *Les Enfants du Paradis*

The Children of Sanchez
US/Mexico   1978   126m   colour
Hall Bartlett
V*

A macho Mexican and one of his daughters have ideas
above the semi-slum in which they live.

The star is still looking for another *Zorba the Greek*, but
this isn't it. Glum, glum, glum.

w Cesare Zavattini, Hall Bartlett   novel Oscar Lewis
d Hall Bartlett   ph Gabriel Figueroa   m Chuck
Mangione

Anthony Quinn, Dolores del Rio, Lupita Ferrer, Katy
Jurado, Stathis Giallelis

Children of the Corn
US   1984   92m   CFI colour
New World/Angeles/Cinema Group (Donald P. Borchers,
Terence Kirby)
V, V*, L

A doctor and his girlfriend run down a child, discover
that his throat has been cut, and find themselves in a
community of murderous adolescents.

Nightmarish modern fantasy with style but very little
to like.

w George Goldsmith   story Stephen King   d Fritz
Kiersch   ph Raoul Lomas   m Jonathan Elias

Peter Horton, Linda Hamilton, R. G. Armstrong, John
Franklin

'The aim seems to be to reassure rather than to
disturb.' – *Robert Murphy, MFB*

Children of the Corn II: The Final Sacrifice
US   1992   Foto-Kem colour
Fifth Avenue Entertainment (Scott A. Stone, David G. Stanley)
V, V*, S

Teenagers who have killed all the adults in a small
town in the Bible Belt are moved to another small
town, where they proceed to do the same.

Inept sequel, so predictable as to be almost
unwatchable.

w A. L. Katz, Gilbert Adler   story *Children of the Corn*
by Stephen King   d David F. Price   ph Levie
Isaacks   m Daniel Licht   pd Greg Melton   sp Bob
Keen   ed Barry Zetlin

Terence Knox, Paul Scherrer, Ryan Bollman, Christie
Clark, Rosalind Allen, Ned Romero

'More effective on a shock and shriek level than the
original but not a major contribution to anything.' –
Empire

'So young, so innocent, so deadly – they came to conquer
the world!'
Children of the Damned *
GB   1964   90m   bw
MGM (Ben Arbeid)
V*, L

Six super-intelligent children of various nations are
brought to London by UNESCO, and turn out to be
invaders from another planet.

Moderate sequel to *Village of the Damned*, well made
but with no new twists.

w John Briley   d Anton M. Leader   ph David
Boulton   m Ron Goodwin

Ian Hendry, Alan Badel, Barbara Ferris, Alfred Burke,
Sheila Allen, Ralph Michael, Martin Miller, Harold
Goldblatt

The Children's Hour *
US   1961   108m   bw
UA/Mirisch (William Wyler)
V*, L
GB title: *The Loudest Whisper*

A spoilt schoolgirl spreads a rumour that her
schoolmistresses are lesbians.

Frank sixties version of a play originally filmed in a
much bowdlerized version as *These Three*.
Unfortunately frankness in this case leads to dullness,
as nothing is done with the theme once it is stated,
and the treatment is heavy-handed.

w Lillian Hellman   play Lillian Hellman
d William Wyler   ph Franz Planer   m Alex North

Audrey Hepburn, Shirley Maclaine, James Garner,
Miriam Hopkins, Fay Bainter, Karen Balkin

'All very exquisite, and dead as mutton.' – *Tom Milne*

AAN: Franz Planer; Fay Bainter

Child's Play *
GB   1952   68m   bw
British Lion/Group 3 (Herbert Mason)

Village children find a way to create atomic energy
and use the power to set up a flourishing popcorn
business.

A lively children's feature that has now acquired a
quaint charm in its attitude to nuclear energy.

w Peter Blackmore   story Don Sharp, Margaret
Thomson   d Margaret Thomson   ph Denny
Densham   m Anthony Hopkins   ad Michael
Stringer   ed John Legard

Mona Washbourne, Peter Martyn, Dorothy Alison,
John Sharp, Peter Sallis, Christopher Beeny, Wendy
Westcott

'A child's chief glories are its energy and its noise; and
this picture very properly bombinates with both.' –
Paul Dehn

Child's Play *
US   1972   100m   colour   Movielab
Paramount (David Merrick)

In a Catholic boarding school for boys, an unpopular
master is hounded and discredited by another whose
motives may be diabolic.

Enjoyable overblown melodrama with hints of many
nasty goings on, rather spoiled by too much talk and
too little local colour.

w Leon Prochnik   play Robert Marasco   d Sidney
Lumet   ph Gerald Hirschfeld   m Michael Small

James Mason, *Robert Preston*, Beau Bridges, Ronald
Weyand

Child's Play
US   1988   87m   Astro Color
UIP/United Artists (David Kirschner)
V, V*, L, S

The personality of a serial killer is transferred to a
young boy's doll.

Unexciting horror, too predictable to be frightening.

w Don Mancini, John Lafia, Tom Holland   d Tom
Holland   ph Bill Butler   m Joe Renzetti
pd Daniel A. Lomino   ed Edward Warschilka, Roy
E. Peterson

Catherine Hicks, Chris Sarandon, Alex Vincent, Brad
Dourif, Dinah Manoff, Tommy Swerdlow

Child's Play 2
US   1990   85m   DeLuxe
Universal (David Kirschner)
V, V*, L

A doll possessed by the spirit of a mass murderer
attempts to kill a small boy.

Tiresome and unpleasant.

w Don Mancini   d John Lafia   ph Stefan Czapsky
m Graeme Revell   pd Ivo Cristsante   ad Donald
Maskovich   ed Edward Warschilka

Alex Vincent, Jenny Agutter, Gerrit Graham,
Christine Elise, Brad Dourif, Grace Zabriskie

'Another case of rehashing the few novel elements of
the original to the point of utter numbness.' – *Variety*

Child's Play 3
US   1991   89m   DeLuxe
Universal/David Kirschner (Robert Latham Brown)
V, V*, L

A killer doll infiltrates a military school in order to
kill the students.

Mindless and unpleasant sequel, ever straining for
effect.

w Don Mancini   d Jack Bender   ph John
R. Leonetti   m Cory Lerios, John D'Andrea
pd Richard Sawyer   ed Edward Warschilka

Justin Whalin, Perrey Reeves, Jeremy Sylvers, Travis
Fine, Dean Jacobson, Brad Dourif, Andrew Robinson

Chilly Scenes of Winter: see *Head Over Heels*
(1980)

The Chiltern Hundreds *
GB   1949   84m   bw
Rank/Two Cities (George H. Brown)
US title: *The Amazing Mr Beecham*

An aged earl is bewildered when his son fails to be
elected to parliament as a socialist but his butler gets
in as a Tory.

Satisfactory filming of an amusing stage comedy, with
the aged A. E. Matthews repeating his delightful if
irrelevant act as the dotty earl.

w William Douglas Home, Patrick Kirwan
play *William Douglas Home*   d John Paddy Carstairs
ph Jack Hildyard   m Benjamin Frankel

*A. E. Matthews, Cecil Parker, David Tomlinson, Marjorie
Fielding*, Joyce Carey

Chimes at Midnight **
Spain/Switz   1966   119m   bw
Internacional Films Española/Alpine (Alessandro Tasca)
V*, S
aka: *Falstaff*

Prince Hal becomes King Henry V and rejects his old
friend Falstaff.

Clumsy adaptation of Shakespeare with brilliant
flashes and the usual Welles vices of hasty production,
poor synchronization and recording, etc. One wonders
why, if he wanted to make a telescoped version of the
plays, he did not spare the time and patience to make
it better.

wd Orson Welles   ph Edmond Richard   m Angelo
Francesco Lavagnino   ed Fritz Mueller

Orson Welles, Keith Baxter, John Gielgud (Henry IV),
Margaret Rutherford (Mistress Quickly), Jeanne
Moreau (Doll Tearsheet), Norman Rodway, Alan
Webb, Marina Vlady, Tony Beckley, Fernando Rey

'One of Orson Welles' best and least-seen movies . . .
The film is a near-masterpiece.' – *New Yorker*

'Ridiculous is the word for the whole enterprise – not
funny and certainly not moving.' – *John Simon*

'A testament to the enduring genius of Orson Welles
as screenwriter, director and actor . . . does justice to
Shakespeare, to cinema and to his own great talents.'
– *Judith Crist*

The Chimp *
US   1932   30m   bw
Hal Roach
V

Stan and Ollie try to get lodgings without revealing
that their friend is a chimp, their share of a bankrupt
circus.

The circus scenes are better than the rather tired farce which follows, especially as it is so similar to *Laughing Gravy*.

w H. M. Walker *d* James Parrott *ph* Walter Lundin*ed* Richard Currier

Laurel and Hardy, James Finlayson, Billy Gilbert, Tiny Sandford

'Alan Ladd and twenty girls – trapped by the rapacious Japs!'

China

US   1943   79m   bw
Paramount (Richard Blumenthal)

An oil salesman joins a Chinese guerrilla force and sacrifices himself.

Solemnly hilarious propaganda piece tailored to its star, showing the immense superiority of one lone American to the entire Japanese army.

w Frank Butler *novel* The Fourth Brother by Reginald Forbes *d* John Farrow *ph* Leo Tover *m* Victor Young

Alan Ladd, Loretta Young, William Bendix, Philip Ahn, Iris Wong, Sen Yung, Richard Loo, Tala Birell

China Caravan: see *A Yank on the Burma Road*

China Clipper *

US   1936   89m   bw
Warner (Sam Bischoff)

An aviator neglects his wife while building up a trans-Pacific civil aviation link.

Solid entertainment feature of its day, with adequate production and performance.

w Frank 'Spig' Wead *d* Ray Enright *ph* Arthur Edeson *m* Bernhard Kaun, W. Franke Harling

Pat O'Brien, Beverly Roberts, Ross Alexander, Humphrey Bogart, Marie Wilson, Henry B. Walthall, Joseph Crehan, Addison Richards

China Corsair

US   1951   76m   bw
Columbia

An American ship's engineer is stranded on an island off the China coast.

Routine escapist hokum.

w Harold R. Greene *d* Ray Nazarro

Jon Hall, Lisa Ferraday, Ron Randell, Douglas Kennedy, Ernest Borgnine

China Doll

US   1958   99m   bw
Romina/Batjac (Frank Borzage)

In 1943 an American air force officer accidentally buys the services of a young Chinese housekeeper. He marries her but they are both killed in action; years later their daughter is welcomed to America by members of his old air crew.

Incurably sentimental and icky romantic drama in the style of the director's silent films; something of a curiosity for historians.

w Kitty Buhler *d* Frank Borzage *ph* William H. Clothier *m* Henry Vars

Victor Mature, Li Li Hua, Bob Mathias, Ward Bond, Stuart Whitman

'An American dynamiter love-locked in war-locked China!'
China Gate

US   1957   90m   bw   Cinemascope
TCF (Samuel Fuller)
V*

A Eurasian girl guides her American husband to a communist arms dump.

Anti-Red thick ear, slick but undistinguished.

wd Samuel Fuller *ph* Joseph Biroc *m* Victor Young, Max Steiner

Gene Barry, Angie Dickinson, Nat King Cole, Paul Dubov, Lee Van Cleef, George Givot

China Girl

US   1943   95m   bw
TCF (Ben Hecht)

A newsreel cameraman in China falls in love with a Eurasian schoolteacher.

Routine adventure romance with splodges of love and self-sacrifice.

w Ben Hecht *d* Henry Hathaway *ph* Lee Garmes *m* Hugo Friedhofer

Gene Tierney, George Montgomery, *Lynn Bari*, Victor McLaglen, Alan Baxter, Sig Rumann, Myron McCormick, Philip Ahn

China Girl

US   1987   90m   colour
Vestron (Michael Nozik)

In New York an Italian youth with Mafia connections falls in love with a Chinese girl from a family involved with the Triads.

Romeo and Juliet updated to Little Italy and Chinatown and used as an occasion for blood-letting and much gang violence.

w Nicholas St John *d* Abel Ferrara *ph* Bojan Bazelli *m* Joe Delia *ed* Anthony Redman

James Russo, Richard Panebianco, Sari Chang, David Caruso, Russell Wong, Joey Chin, Judith Malina, James Hong

'A masterfully directed, uncompromising drama and romance.' – *Variety*

'Even die-hard fans of New York urban violence movies will find this tough going.' – *Stefan Jaworzyn, Shock Xpress*

China, My Sorrow: see *Niu-Peng*

China 9, Liberty 37 *

Spain/Italy   1978   109m   Technicolor
    Technovision
Lorimar/Compagnia Europe Cinematografica/Aspa (Gianni Bozzacchi, Valerio de Paolis, Monte Hellman)
V*, S
aka: *Gunfire*

Hired to shoot a retired killer, a gunfighter runs off with his wife instead and is pursued by the irate husband and his brothers.

Intriguing spaghetti Western, slow-paced, with a brooding atmosphere and some sharp dialogue.

w Jerry Harvey, Douglas Venturelli *d* Monte Hellman *ph* Giuseppe Rotunno *m* Pino Donaggio *ad* Luciano Spadoni *ed* Cesare D'Amico

Warren Oates, Fabio Testi, Jenny Agutter, Sam Peckinpah, Isabel Mestres, Gianrico Tondivelli, Franco Interlenghi, Carlos Bravo

† The title refers to a signpost which a travelling hangman passes at the beginning of the film. He takes the road to China.

China O'Brien

US   1988   90m   Image Transform colour
Golden Harvest/Fred Weintraub
V, V*

A former cop replaces her murdered father as sheriff of a small town.

The usual martial arts mayhem with the novelty of a high-kicking female hero.

wd Robert Clouse *story* Sandra Weintraub *ph* Kent Wakeford *m* David Wheatley, Paul Antonelli *ed* Mark Harrah

Cynthia Rothrock, Richard Norton, Keith Cooke, Patrick Adamson, David Blackwell

China O'Brien II

US   1989   86m   colour
Imperial/Golden Harvest (Fred Weintraub)
V, V*

A female sheriff is threatened by an escaped drug pusher.

Routine high-kicking martial arts, with the usual rudimentary acting.

w James Hennessy, Craig Clyde *story* Sandra Weintraub *d* Kent Wakeford *m* David Wheatley, Paul F. Antonelli *ed* Mark Harrah

Cynthia Rothrock, Richard Norton, Keith Cooke, Frank Magner, Harlow Marks, Tiffany Soter

'A haphazard affair, generating little interest.' – *Variety*

China Seas **

US   1935   89m   bw
MGM (Albert Lewin)
V*

Luxury cruise passengers find themselves involved with piracy.

Omnibus shipboard melodrama, tersely scripted and featuring a splendid cast all somewhere near their best; slightly dated but very entertaining.

w Jules Furthman, James Kevin McGuinness *novel* Crosbie Garstin *d* Tay Garnett *ph* Ray June *m* Herbert Stothart

Clark Gable, Jean Harlow, Wallace Beery, Rosalind Russell, Lewis Stone, C. Aubrey Smith, Dudley Digges, Robert Benchley

'It will do double-barrelled duty, drawing business and providing ace entertainment.' – *Variety*

'The hell with art this time. I'm going to produce a picture that will make money.' – *Irving Thalberg*

China Sky

US   1945   78m   bw
RKO (Maurice Geraghty)
V*, L

Two American doctors live with Chinese guerrillas; the jealousy of the wife of one of them causes problems.

Routine adventure romance with generally unconvincing production and performance.

w Brenda Weisberg, Joseph Hoffman *novel* Pearl Buck *d* Ray Enright *ph* Nicholas Musuraca *m* Roy Webb

Randolph Scott, Ellen Drew, Ruth Warrick, Anthony Quinn, Carol Thurston, Richard Loo, Philip Ahn

The China Syndrome **

US   1979   122m   Metrocolor
Columbia/IPC (Michael Douglas)
V, V*, L

The controller of a nuclear power plant discovers an operational flaw which could lead to disaster, but the unscrupulous authorities want to cover it up.

Topical thriller-with-a-moral, absorbingly done in the old style but perhaps in the end a shade too hysterical and self-congratulatory.

w Mike Gray, T. S. Cook, James Bridges *d* James Bridges *ph* James Crabe *m* various *pd* George Jenkins *ed* David Rawlins

Jane Fonda, *Jack Lemmon*, Michael Douglas, Scott Brady, Peter Donat, James Hampton

'The performances are so good, and the screen so bombarded with both action and informative images . . . that it's only with considerable hindsight that one recovers sufficient breath to reproach the script with the occasional glib symmetry.' – *Jan Dawson, MFB*

AAN: Jack Lemmon, Jane Fonda; script

China Venture

US   1953   83m   bw
Columbia (Anson Bond)

In 1945, American marines are sent into the Chinese jungle to recover a Japanese admiral held captive there.

Topical thick ear, played and presented without conviction.

w George Worthing Yates, Richard Collins   d Don Siegel

Edmond O'Brien, Barry Sullivan, Jocelyn Brando, Richard Loo

Chinatown ****
US   1974   131m   Technicolor   Panavision
Paramount/Long Road (Robert Evans)
V, V*, L

In 1937, a Los Angeles private eye takes on a simple case and burrows into it until it leads to murder and a public scandal.

Teasing, complex mystery that uses the conventions of detective stories to explore civic and personal corruption, in the style of Raymond Chandler, but adding a more modern perspective. It is eminently watchable, with effective individual scenes and performances and photography which is lovingly composed though tending to suggest period by use of an orange filter.

w Robert Towne   d Roman Polanski   ph John A. Alonso   m Jerry Goldsmith   pd Richard Sylbert

Jack Nicholson, Faye Dunaway, John Huston, Perry Lopez, John Hillerman, Roman Polanski, Darrell Zwerling, Diane Ladd

'You are swept along as helpless as any of the corpses so unaccountably drowned in empty lake-beds.' – Dilys Powell

'The success of Chinatown – with its beautifully structured script and draggy, overdeliberate direction – represents something dialectically new: nostalgia (for the thirties) openly turned to rot, the celebration of rot.' – Pauline Kael

AA: Robert Towne

AAN: best picture; Roman Polanski; John A. Alonso; Jerry Goldsmith; Jack Nicholson; Faye Dunaway

Chinatown at Midnight
US   1949   67m   bw
Columbia

Police seek a killer in Chinatown.

Efficient lower-case police thriller.

w Robert Libott, Frank Burt   d Seymour Friedman

Hurd Hatfield, Jean Willes, Tom Powers, Ray Walker

Chinese Boxes
GB   1984   87m   colour
Palace/Road Movies (Chris Sievernich)

An American in Berlin discovers a dead 15-year-old girl in his apartment.

A thriller that resembles a jigsaw with some of the pieces missing. It is told in such an elliptical fashion as to leave the viewer not only confused but indifferent.

w L. M. Kit Carson, Christopher Petit
d Christopher Petit   ph Peter Harvey   m Günter Fischer   ad Edgar Hinz, Klaus Beiger   ed Fred Srp

Will Patton, Gottfried John, Adelheid Arndt, Robbie Coltrane, Beate Jensen, L. M. Kit Carson, Chris Sievernich, Christopher Petit

The Chinese Bungalow
GB   1939   72m   bw
George King
US title: Chinese Den

A Chinese merchant plots to kill the lover of his English wife.

Stolid version of an old melodrama which can hardly fail; previously filmed in 1926 with Matheson Lang and Genevieve Townsend (directed by Sinclair Hill)

and in 1930 with Matheson Lang and Anna Neagle (directed by J. B. Williams).

w A. R. Rawlinson, George Wellesley
play Matheson Lang, Marian Osmond   d George King   ph Hone Glendinning

Paul Lukas, Jane Baxter, Robert Douglas, Kay Walsh, Jerry Verno

The Chinese Connection: see Fist of Fury

Chinese Den: see The Chinese Bungalow

Chinese Roulette *
West Germany/France   1976   86m   Eastmancolor
Albatros/Losange (Rainer Werner Fassbinder)
V*, L

Various related people, mainly adulterous, meet in a country château and play a truth game which ends in violence.

Interestingly enigmatic character melodrama reminiscent of Bergman at his prime, but concerning people who barely seem to matter.

wd Rainer Werner Fassbinder   ph Michael Ballhaus   m Peer Raben

Margit Carstensen, Andrea Schober, Ulli Lommel, Anna Karina, Macha Meril

'Locked into their private hell . . . this vicious octet form their own coherent and compelling universe.' – Jan Dawson, MFB

Chino
US/Italy   1973   98m   colour
Dino de Laurentiis
V*

A runaway boy helps a half-breed run a ranch in New Mexico.

Undistinguished Western.

w Clair Huffaker   novel Lee Hoffman   d John Sturges

Charles Bronson, Jill Ireland, Vincent Van Patten

La Chinoise ***
France   1967   95m   Eastmancolor
Fair Enterprises/Productions de la Guéville/Parc/Simar/ Anouchka/Athos

In 1967, five Parisian Maoist revolutionaries debate the best ways of achieving the end of the capitalist system, from closing the universities to acting Brecht, and decide that terrorism is the way forward.

With hindsight, a prophetic movie of the student politics that shook Paris a year later, which is still a troubling and wittily intriguing film in its search for new means of cinematic expression.

wd Jean-Luc Godard   ph Raoul Coutard   m Karl-Heinz Stockhausen   ed Agnès Guillemot, Delphine Desfons

Anne Wiazemsky, Jean-Pierre Léaud, Michel Sémeniako, Lex de Brujin, Juliet Berto, Omar Diop, Francis Jeanson

'The movie is like a speed-freak's anticipatory vision of the political horrors to come; it's amazing.' – Pauline Kael

'A piece of mitigated trash . . . Godard, his material, his pretentiousness and undisciplined garrulity, are boring when not exasperating.' – John Simon

Chip off the Old Block
US   1944   76m   bw
Universal (Bernard W. Burton)

The son of a seafaring family gets into expected romantic trouble.

Lightweight comedy-musical which performed adequately at the time.

w Eugene Conrad, Leo Townsend   d Charles Lamont

Donald O'Connor, Peggy Ryan, Ann Blyth, Patric Knowles, Helen Broderick, Helen Vinson, Arthur Treacher, J. Edward Bromberg, Ernest Truex

'Effervescing juvenile comedy-drama for wide audience appeal.' – Variety

Chisum *
US   1970   110m   Technicolor   Panavision
Warner/Batjac (Michael Wayne, Andrew J. Fenady)
V, V*

A corrupt businessman plots against the head of a vast cattle empire, who is saved by the intervention of numerous friends including Pat Garrett and Billy the Kid.

Desultory, overlong, friendly Western in the Ford manner. Easy to watch and easier to forget.

w Andrew J. Fenady   d Andrew V. McLaglen
ph William H. Clothier   m Dominic Frontière

John Wayne, Forrest Tucker, Christopher George, Ben Johnson, Glenn Corbett, Bruce Cabot, Andrew Prine, Patric Knowles, Richard Jaeckel, Linda Day George, John Agar, Ray Teal, Glenn Langan, Alan Baxter, Abraham Sofaer, Pete Duel

'A curious mixture of styles and myths.' – John Gillett

Chitty Chitty Bang Bang
GB   1968   145m   Technicolor   Super Panavision 70
UA/Warfield/DFI (Albert R. Broccoli)
V, V*, L

An unsuccessful inventor rescues a derelict car and gives it magical properties, then helps the children who own it to overthrow the government of a country which hates children.

A bumpy ride. Sentiment, slapstick, whimsy and mild scares do not combine but are given equal shares of the limelight, while poor trickwork prevents the audience from being transported.

w Roald Dahl, Ken Hughes   d Ken Hughes
ph Christopher Challis   m Irwin Kostal   ad Ken Adam   m/ly The Sherman Brothers   ad Rowland Emmett

Dick Van Dyke, Sally Ann Howes (as Truly Scrumptious), Lionel Jeffries, Robert Helpmann, Gert Frobe, Benny Hill, James Robertson Justice

AAN: title song

Chloë in the Afternoon: see L'Amour, L'Après-midi

Le Choc: see The Shock

Chocolat **
France/Germany/Cameroon   1988   105m   colour
Electric/Cinemanuel/MK2/Cerio/Wim Wenders Produktion/ TF1/SEPT/Caroline/FODIC (Alain Belmondo, Gerard Crosnier)
V, V*, L

A French woman recalls her colonial childhood in French West Africa and her relationship with the family servant.

Cool, distanced, semi-autobiographical account of racism and its effects.

w Claire Denis, Jean-Pol Fargeau   d Claire Denis
ph Robert Alazraki   m Abdullah Ibrahim
pd Thierry Flamand   ed Claudine Merlin

Isaach de Bankole, Giula Boschi, François Cluzet, Jean-Claude Adelin

'Undoubtedly over-generous, fictionalised and nostalgic, but it is also well paced, well observed and shot through with a dry sense of humour.' – Jill Forbes, MFB

The Chocolate Soldier *
US   1941   102m   bw
MGM (Victor Saville)
V*

Married opera singers fall out backstage.

Talky musical remake of *The Guardsman:* nearly comes off but not quite.

w Keith Winter, Leonard Lee   d Roy del Ruth
ph Karl Freund   m Herbert Stothart, Bronislau Kaper   m/y Oscar Straus

Nelson Eddy, Rise Stevens, Nigel Bruce, Florence Bates, Nydia Westman

AAN: Karl Freund; Herbert Stothart, Bronislau Kaper

The Choice
Burkina Faso   1987   88m   colour
Les Films de L'Avenir
original title: *Yam Daabo*

The pleasures and tribulations of African village life.

Rudimentary and episodic first feature, lacking the resonance of the director's later films such as *Yaaba* and *Tilai* (qv).

wd Idrissa Ouedraogo   ph Jean Monsigny, Sekou Ouedraogo, Issaka Thiombiano   m Francis Bebey
ed Arnaud Blin

Aoua Guiraud, Moussa Bologo, Ousmana Sawadogo, Fatima Ouedraogo

Choice of Arms *
France   1981   130m   Fuji colour
Sara/Parafrance/Antenne 2/RMC (Daniel Deschamps)
original title: *Le Choix des Armes*

A successful, retired gangster is drawn back into a world of violence when, after a jail break, a seriously wounded friend seeks refuge at his stud farm together with a young, violent, reckless hoodlum.

Interesting but too-leisurely account of people unable to escape their past.

w Michel Grisolia, Alain Corneau   d Alain Corneau
ph Pierre William Glenn   m Philippe Sarde
ad Jean-Pierre Kohut Svelko   ed Thierry Derocles

Yves Montand, Gérard Depardieu, Catherine Deneuve, Michel Galabru, Gérard Lanvin, Jean-Claude Dauphin, Jean Rougerie, Christian Marquand, Richard Anconina

Choice of Weapons: see *Trial by Combat*

The Choirboys
US   1978   119m   Technicolor
Lorimar/Airone (Lee Rich, Merv Adelson)
V*

Members of a police department are if anything more delinquent, vicious and mentally retarded than their quarries.

A vulgar and repellent anti-establishment display, apparently intended as black comedy. Just the thing to put an end to the art of the movie once and for all.

w Christopher Knopf   novel Joseph Wambaugh
d Robert Aldrich   ph Joseph Biroc   m Frank de Vol

Charles Durning, Lou Gossett Jnr, Perry King, Stephen Macht, Tim McIntyre, Clyde Kusatsu, Randy Quaid, Don Stroud, Robert Webber, Blair Brown

Le Choix des Armes: see *Choice of Arms*

Chomps
US   1979   89m   Movielab
American International (Joseph Barbera)
V*

A young inventor is successful with a robot dog (Canine Home Protection System).

Rather feeble family-oriented comedy.

w Dick Robbins, Duane Poole   story Joseph Barbera
d Don Chaffey   ph Charles F. Wheeler   m Hoyt Curtin   pd Ted Shell   ed Warner Leighton, Dick Darling

Wesley Eure, Jim Backus, Valerie Bertinelli, Chuck McCann, Regis Toomey, Red Buttons, Hermione Baddeley

Choose Me
US   1984   106m   Movielab
Island Alive/Tartan (Carolyn Pfeiffer, David Blocker)
V*, L

Two lonely people in LA become a couple.

Even for those not irritated by the director's style and interests, this is an entertainment which goes around in circles and gets nowhere, except Las Vegas.

wd Alan Rudolph   ph Jan Kiesser   m Luther Vandross   pd Steve Legler   ed Mia Goldman

Geneviève Bujold, Keith Carradine, Lesley Ann Warren, Patrick Bachau, Rae Dawn Chong

'An L.A. flower, a neon orchid – hip, outrageous, beautiful. It's a romance – music at its heart and farce around its edges – for those afraid to be in love.' – *Sheila Benson, Los Angeles Times*

Choose Your Partner: see *Two Girls on Broadway*

A Chorus Line
US   1985   111m   Technicolor   Panavision
Embassy/Polygram (Cy Feuer, Ernest Martin)
V, V*, L, S

A Broadway musical chorus is selected.

Overpraised musical drama which took nine years to reach the screen because nobody could figure out how to 'open it up', despite Universal's payment of 5.5 million dollars for the rights. The present team has not solved the problem.

w Arnold Schulman   play Nicholas Dante, James Kirkwood   d Richard Attenborough   ph Ronnie Taylor   pd Patrizia von Brandenstein   m/y Marvin Hamlisch, Edward Kleban   ed John Bloom

Michael Douglas, Terence Mann, Alyson Reed, Cameron English, Vicki Frederick

'Static and confined, rarely venturing beyond the immediate.' – *Variety*

'He makes his camera fly like a bird around the near-deserted theatre.' – *Shaun Usher, Daily Mail*

AAN: editing

A Chorus of Disapproval *
GB   1988   99m   colour
Hobo/Curzon/Palisades Entertainment (André Blay, Elliott Kastner)
V, V*

A new tenor joins an amateur choir to find the sopranos lusting after him.

Ponderous direction almost ruins a witty comedy of suburban life.

w Michael Winner, Alan Ayckbourn   play Alan Ayckbourn   d Michael Winner   ph Alan Jones
pd John Du Prez   ed Arnold Crust

Anthony Hopkins, Jeremy Irons, Richard Briers, Gareth Hunt, Patsy Kensit, Alexandra Pigg, Prunella Scales, Jenny Seagrove, Peter Lee-Wilson, Barbara Ferris, Lionel Jeffries, Sylvia Sims, David King

The Chosen
US   1981   108m   Movielab
The Chosen Film Company (Edie and Ely Landau)
V*

In New York in the early forties, a family feud between Zionist and Hassidic Jews interferes with a friendship between two boys.

A sentimental minority piece which does what it has to do quite effectively.

w Edwin Gordon   novel Chaim Potok   d Jeremy Paul Kagan   ph Arthur Ornitz   m Elmer Bernstein
pd Stuart Wurtzel

Maximilian Schell, Rod Steiger, Robby Benson, Barry Miller, Hildy Brooks, Kaethe Fine

The Chosen (1977): see *Holocaust 2000*

Chosen Survivors
US   1974   98m   colour
Alpine/Metromedia (Charles Fries)

Ten people with special skills are chosen to test human reaction to thermo-nuclear war, but find themselves at the mercy of vampire bats.

Another misfit group united by disaster; more shocks than suspense, and not much characterization, but for adventure/horror addicts it will pass the time.

w H. B. Cross, Joe Reb Moffly   d Sutton Roley
ph Gabriel Torres   m Fred Karlin

Jackie Cooper, Alex Cord, Richard Jaeckel, Diana Muldaur, Lincoln Kilpatrick, Bradford Dillman, Pedro Armendariz Jnr, Gwen Mitchell, Barbara Babcock, Christina Moreno

Les Choses de la Vie
France/Italy   1969   89m   Eastmancolor
Lira/Fida (Raymond Danon)
V, S
aka: *These Things Happen; The Things of Life*

An architect has his wife and mistress neatly balanced when an accident upsets his scheme of things.

Nicely observed tragi-comedy in the best French manner; since it starts with the car crash, a mini-*Bridge of San Luis Rey.*

w Paul Guimard, Claude Sautet, Jean-Loup Dabadie
novel Paul Guimard   d Claude Sautet   ph Jean Boffety   m Philippe Sarde

Michel Piccoli, Romy Schneider, Lea Massari, Gérard Lartigau, Jean Bouise

Christ Stopped at Eboli *
Italy/France   1979   155m   Technospes colour
Vides Cinematografica/RAI/Action Film/Gaumont (Franco Cristaldi, Nicola Carraro)
V, V*

In 1935 an Italian doctor is exiled because of his political views to a remote southern part of the country.

An attractively faithful account of a book which was part personal statement, part symbolism, part political opinion and part local colour. Non-Italians will be unable to extract the full flavour.

w Francesco Rosi, Tonino Guerra, Raffaele La Capria
book Carlo Levi   d Francesco Rosi   ph Pasqualino de Santis   m Piero Piccioni

Gian Maria Volonte, Alain Cuny, Paolo Bonacelli, Lea Massari, Irene Papas, François Simon

BFA: best foreign film

The Christian Licorice Store
US   1971   90m   colour
National General

A Hollywood tennis player succumbs to corrupting influences.

Odd item with interesting credits but not much flesh on the bones.

w Floyd Mutrux   d James Frawley

Beau Bridges, Maud Adams, Gilbert Roland, Alan Arbus, Monte Hellman

Christiane F *
West Germany   1981   131m   colour
Maran Film/Popular Film/Hans H. Kaden/TCF (Bernd Eichinger, Hans Weth)

A teenage girl becomes a drug addict.

Slick melodrama hoked up from 'true' confessions with excellent background detail.

w Herman Weigel   d Ulrich Edel   ph Justus Pankau, Jürgen Jürges   m David Bowie   ed Jane Seitz

Natja Brunckhorst, Thomas Haustein, Jens Kuphal

'How do you kill something that can't possibly be alive?'

Christine

US   1983   110m   Technicolor   Panavision
Columbia/Delphi (Richard Kobritz)
V*, L, S

A diabolical car maims and kills its owner's girlfriends.

Thin and gruesomely extended horror flick which never begins to be convincing. For teenagers only.

w Bill Phillips   *novel* Stephen King   d John Carpenter   ph Donald M. Morgan   m John Carpenter   pd Daniel Lomino

Keith Gordon, John Stockwell, Alexandra Paul, Robert Prosky, Harry Dean Stanton, Christine Belford

'The kind of movie where you walk out with a silly grin, get in your car, and lay rubber halfway down the freeway.' — *Roger Ebert*

A Christmas Carol *

US   1938   69m   bw
MGM (Joseph L. Mankiewicz)
V, V*, L

Scrooge the miser is reformed when four ghosts visit him on Christmas Eve.

Standard Dickensian frolic, quite well mounted.

w Hugo Butler   d Edwin L. Marin   ph Sidney Wagner   m Franz Waxman

Reginald Owen, Gene Lockhart, Kathleen Lockhart, Terry Kilburn, Leo G. Carroll, Lynne Carver

'Top production, inspired direction, superb acting.' – *Variety*

† See also *Scrooge*.

Christmas Eve *

US   1947   92m   bw
Benedict Bogeaus
aka: *Sinners' Holiday*

An old lady needs the help of her three adopted sons to prevent herself from being swindled.

Basically three short stories sealed by a Christmas Eve reunion, this is old-fashioned sentimental stuff, but it works on its level and the cast is interesting.

w Laurence Stallings   d Edwin L. Marin   ph Gordon Avil   m Heinz Roemheld

Ann Harding, George Raft, Randolph Scott, George Brent, Joan Blondell, Virginia Field, Reginald Denny

Christmas Holiday

US   1944   93m   bw
Universal (Felix Jackson)

A young girl marries a murderer, and later, as a shady songstress in a night-club, is forced to help him escape.

A weird change of pace for Deanna Durbin, whose forte had been sweetness and light, this relentlessly grim and boring melodrama was also a travesty of the novel on which it was based.

w Herman J. Mankiewicz   *novel* Somerset Maugham   d Robert Siodmak   ph Elwood Bredell   m Hans Salter

Deanna Durbin, Gene Kelly, Dean Harens, Gladys George, Richard Whorf, Gale Sondergaard

'A jolly title for a Deanna Durbin film, but it's the only jolly thing about it. Miss Durbin is an accomplished singer; so they cut her songs to two and make them blues numbers. She has a naturally modest and ingenuous manner, so they cast her as a hostess in a seedy night club.' – *C. A. Lejeune*

AAN: Hans Salter

Christmas in Connecticut *

US   1945   101m   bw
Warner (William Jacobs)
V*, L
GB title: *Indiscretion*

The spinster writer of a successful column about love and marriage has to conjure up a family for herself in the cause of publicity.

Predictable but fairly brisk comedy with excellent talent well deployed.

w Lionel Houser, Adele Commandini   d Peter Godfrey   ph Carl Guthrie   m Frederick Hollander

Barbara Stanwyck, Dennis Morgan, Sydney Greenstreet, Reginald Gardiner, S. Z. Sakall, Robert Shayne, Una O'Connor, Frank Jenks

† Arnold Schwarzenegger directed a remake for cable television in 1992 starring Dyan Cannon, Kris Kristofferson and Tony Curtis.

'If you can't sleep at night, it isn't the coffee – it's the bunk!'

Christmas in July **

US   1940   67m   bw
Paramount
V*, L

A young clerk and his girl win first prize in a big competition.

Slightly unsatisfactory as a whole, this Preston Sturges comedy has echoes of Clair and a dully predictable plot line, but is kept alive by inventive touches and a gallery of splendid character comedians.

wd Preston Sturges   ph Victor Milner   m Sigmund Krumgold

Dick Powell, Ellen Drew, Ernest Truex, *Al Bridge*, Raymond Walburn, William Demarest

'The perfect restorative for battered humors and jangled nerves.' – *Bosley Crowther*

'Agreeable enough, but it lacks the full-fledged Sturges lunacy.' – *New Yorker, 1977*

A Christmas Story *

US   1983   93m   colour
MGM/UA (René Dupont, Bob Clark)
V, V*, L

In an Indiana suburb during the 1940s, a schoolboy hopes to get a rifle for Christmas.

Curious, almost plotless family comedy of the old school, with the difference that some grotesquerie and tastelessness is added. On the whole, however, an amusing entertainment for adults who don't mind their mood of sentimental nostalgia being tilted at by the director of *Porky's*.

w Jean Shepherd, Leigh Brown, Bob Clark   *novel In God We Trust, All Others Pay Cash* by Jean Shepherd   d Bob Clark   ph Reginald H. Morris   m Carl Zittrer, Paul Zaza   pd Gavin Mitchell   ed Stan Cole

Peter Billingsley, Melinda Dillon, Darren McGavin, Ian Petrella

The Christmas Tree

France/Italy   1969   110m   Eastmancolor
Corona/Jupiter (Robert Dorfmann)
V*

The small son of a millionaire widower is fatally infected by radioactivity.

Painfully sentimental and overdrawn weepie, the most lachrymose film of the sixties.

wd Terence Young   *novel* Michel Bataille   ph Henri Alekan   m Georges Auric

William Holden, Virna Lisi, Brook Fuller, Bourvil

'Depending on your taste threshold, there may not be a dry eye – nor a full stomach – in the house.' – *Judith Crist*

Christopher Bean *

US   1933   80m   bw
MGM
aka: *Her Sweetheart*

A dying artist appoints his housekeeper as his executor.

Solid family entertainment very typical of its studio.

w Laurence Johnson, Sylvia Thalberg   *play The Late Christopher Bean* by Sidney Howard   d Sam Wood

Marie Dressler (her last film), Lionel Barrymore, Beulah Bondi, Helen Mack, George Coulouris, H. B. Warner, Jean Hersholt

Christopher Columbus

US   1949   104m   Technicolor
Rank/Gainsborough/Sydney Box (Betty E. Box)
V, V*, S

Columbus seeks and receives the patronage of the Spanish court for his voyage to the west.

An extraordinarily tediously paced historical account of basically undramatic events; interesting without being stimulating.

w Muriel and Sydney Box, Cyril Roberts   d David MacDonald   ph Stephen Dade   m Arthur Bliss

Fredric March, Florence Eldridge, Francis L. Sullivan, Linden Travers

'Even ten-year-olds will find it about as thrilling as an afternoon spent looking at Christmas cards.' – *Time*

Christopher Columbus: The Discovery

US   1992   121m   Technicolor   Panavision
Rank/Peel Enterprises (Alexander Salkind, Ilya Salkind)
V, V*, L, S

Backed by Spain, Columbus sets sail to discover the New World on a disastrous voyage, but returns in triumph to be created Viceroy of the Indies.

Risible pageant with some notably poor performances and little to maintain one's interest.

w John Briley, Cary Bates, Mario Puzo   d John Glen   ph Alec Mills, Arthur Wooster   m Cliff Eidelman   pd Gil Parrondo   ed Matthew Glen

Marlon Brando, Tom Selleck, George Corraface, Rachel Ward, Robert Davi, Catherine Zeta Jones, Oliver Cotton, Benicio Del Toro, Matthieu Carrière, Nigel Terry

'Dead meat. It's the sort of film that makes you worry not about its characters but about the actors playing them . . . The basic trouble is that the whole film is devised in cliché terms.' – *Derek Malcolm, Guardian*

'She gave herself to the great God speed, and tried to run away from the fires within her!'
'The personal story of a million daughters!'

Christopher Strong *

US   1933   72m   bw
RKO (Pandro S. Berman)
V*, L

A daring lady aviator has an affair with a married businessman and commits suicide when she finds herself pregnant.

A curious and unsatisfactory yarn for Hepburn's second film; well enough made, it died at the box-office.

w Zoe Akins   *novel* Gilbert Frankau   d Dorothy Arzner   ph Bert Glennon   m Max Steiner

Katharine Hepburn, Colin Clive, Billie Burke, Helen Chandler, Ralph Forbes, Irene Browne, Jack La Rue

'Draggy society play with circusy aeroplane stunt incidentals . . . interest in the star will outweigh other elements.' – *Variety*

Chronicle of a Death Foretold **

Italy/France   1987   110m   Eastmancolor
Panavision
Virgin/Italmedia/Soprafilms/Ariane/FR3/RAI (Frances von Buren, Yves Gasset)
S
original title: *Cronica di una Morte Annunciata*

After 27 years a doctor returns to his home-town to discover the truth about the death of his best friend.

Despite its stately rhythm, a powerful examination of the codes of masculine honour and female virtue.

w Francesco Rosi, Tonino Guerra   novel Gabriel García Marquez   d Francesco Rosi   ph Pasqualino de Santis   m Piero Piccioni   pd Andrea Crisanti   ed Ruggero Mastroianni

Rupert Everett, Ornella Muti, Gian Maria Volonte, Irene Papas, Lucia Bose, Anthony Delon, Alain Cuny

Chronique d'un Eté *
France   1961   90m   bw
Argos

Parisians talk about their lives.

Curious but rather stimulating acted documentary, with two interviewers pontificating; saved by shrewd editing to keep interest at its maximum.

wd Jean Rouch, Edgar Morin   ph various

Chu Chin Chow *
GB   1934   102m   bw
Gaumont British/Gainsborough (Michael Balcon)

In old Arabia, a slave girl foils a robber posing as a dead mandarin.

Second screen version (the first was silent) of the old Arabian Nights stage musical. A curiosity.

w Edward Knoblock, L. DuGarde Peach, Sidney Gilliat   play Oscar Asche, Frederick Norton   d Walter Forde   ph Max Greene   ch Anton Dolin   md Louis Levy   m/ly Frederick Norton   ad Ernö Metzner   ed Derek Twist

George Robey, Fritz Kortner, Anna May Wong, John Garrick, Pearl Argyle, Malcolm MacEachern, Dennis Hoey, Francis L. Sullivan, Sydney Fairbrother

'A colourful, extravagant costume film that makes its bid for attention purely on an extravaganza platform, and makes the grade.' – Variety

'Gaumont British have broken away for the first time from their careful refinement, and produced something that has guts as well as grace.' – C. A. Lejeune

Chu Chu and the Philly Flash
US   1981   100m   colour
TCF (Jay Weston)
V*

A one-woman band performer and a drunken ex-baseball player lay claim to the same lost briefcase.

Weird comedy which doesn't come off except at odd moments.

w Barbara Dana   d David Lowell Rich

Carol Burnett, Alan Arkin, Jack Warden, Danny Aiello, Adam Arkin, Ruth Buzzi

Chubasco
US   1967   100m   Technicolor   Panavision
Warner Seven Arts (William Conrad)

A wild beach boy takes a job on a tuna fishing boat.

Old-fashioned boy-makes-good melodrama à la Captains Courageous. Excellent action sequences at sea.

wd Allen H. Miner   ph Louis Jennings, Paul Ivano   m William Lava

Chris Jones, Richard Egan, Susan Strasberg, Ann Sothern, Simon Oakland, Preston Foster, Audrey Totter, Peter Whitney

Chuka
US   1967   105m   Technicolor
Paramount/Rod Taylor
V*

A wandering gunfighter defends the inhabitants of a fort against Indian attack.

Ill-assorted characters under stress is the theme of this rather pedestrian and slightly pretentious Western.

w Richard Jessup   d Gordon Douglas   ph Harold Stine   m Leith Stevens

Rod Taylor, Ernest Borgnine, John Mills, Luciana Paluzzi, James Whitmore, Louis Hayward, Angela Dorian

A Chump at Oxford **
US   1940   63m   bw
Hal Roach
V, V*, L

Two street cleaners foil a bank hold-up and are presented with an Oxford education.

Patchy but endearing Laurel and Hardy romp, starting with an irrelevant two reels about their playing butler and maid, but later including Stan's burlesque impersonation of Lord Paddington.

w Charles Rogers, Harry Langdon, Felix Adler   d Alfred Goulding   ph Art Lloyd   m Marvin Hatley   ed Bert Jordan

Stan Laurel, Oliver Hardy, James Finlayson, Forrester Harvey, Wilfrid Lucas, Peter Cushing

'Ranks with their best pictures – which, to one heretic, are more agreeable than Chaplin's. Their clowning is purer; they aren't out to better an unbetterable world; they've never wanted to play Hamlet.' – Graham Greene

'It Will Make You Squirm.'
The Church (dubbed)
Italy   1991   98m   colour
ADC/Cecchi Gori/Tiger/Reteitalia (Dario Argento)
V

A group of worshippers are trapped in a cathedral where the new librarian has been possessed by the spirits of devil worshippers, massacred in medieval times and buried beneath the building.

Stylishly gruesome horror with a confused narrative, much influenced by the work of its producer and co-writer Dario Argento and likely to appeal to admirers of his work.

w Dario Argento, Franco Ferrini, Michele Soavi   d Michele Soavi   ph Renato Tafuri   m Keith Emerson, The Goblins   ad Antonello Geleng   ed Franco Fraticelli

Hugh Quarshie, Tomas Arana, Feodor Chaliapin, Barbara Cupisti, Antonella Vitale, Giovanni Lombardo Radice, Asia Argento

'Inventively gory deaths, lavish surreal set-pieces and lashings of religious hokum make this a treat which yields greater rewards on subsequent viewings.' – Sight and Sound

'Visually it's great, but don't bother trying to strain your brain figuring out the plot.' – Dark Side

Ciao Maschio: see Bye Bye Monkey

'Earth-shaking in its grandeur! A titanic canvas sprung to life!'
Cimarron *
US   1930   130m   bw
RKO (Louis Sarecky)
V*

The life of an Oklahoma homesteader from 1890 to 1915.

Sprawling Western family saga; a big early talkie, it dates badly.

w Howard Estabrook   novel Edna Ferber   d Wesley Ruggles   ph Edward Cronjager   m Max Steiner   ad Max Ree

Richard Dix, Irene Dunne, Estelle Taylor, Nance O'Neil, William Collier Jnr, Roscoe Ates, George E. Stone, Stanley Fields, Edna May Oliver

'An elegant example of super film-making . . . big money feature for all classes.' – Variety

AA: best picture; Howard Estabrook

AAN: Wesley Ruggles; Edward Cronjager; Richard Dix; Irene Dunne; Max Ree

Cimarron *
US   1960   147m   Metrocolor   Cinemascope
MGM (Edmund Grainger)

Flabby, relentlessly boring remake of the above.

w Arnold Schulman   d Anthony Mann   ph Robert L. Surtees   m Franz Waxman   ad George W. Davis, Addison Hehr

Glenn Ford, Maria Schell, Anne Baxter, Lili Darvas, Russ Tamblyn, Henry Morgan, David Opatoshu, Charles McGraw, Aline MacMahon, Edgar Buchanan, Arthur O'Connell, Mercedes McCambridge, Vic Morrow, Robert Keith, Mary Wickes, Royal Dano, Vladimir Sokoloff

AAN: art direction

The Cincinnati Kid **
US   1965   113m   Metrocolor
MGM/Filmways (Martin Ransohoff, John Calley)
V, V*, L

In New Orleans in the late thirties, stud poker experts compete for supremacy.

This is to poker what The Hustler was to pool, a fascinating suspense study of experts at work; as before, the romantic asides let down the effectiveness of the others.

w Ring Lardner Jnr, Terry Southern   novel Richard Jessup   d Norman Jewison   ph Philip Lathrop   m Lalo Schifrin

Steve McQueen, Edward G. Robinson, Karl Malden, Ann-Margret, Tuesday Weld, Joan Blondell, Rip Torn, Jack Weston, Cab Calloway, Jeff Corey

'I took out all the primaries. There are no reds, greens, whites or blues in the film outside of the red cards and the cockfight.' – Norman Jewison

Cinderella **
US   1950   75m   Technicolor
Walt Disney
V, V*, L

The Perrault fairy tale embroidered with animal characters.

A feature cartoon rather short on inspiration, though with all Disney's solid virtues. The mice are lively and the villainous cat the best character.

supervisor Ben Sharpsteen   d Wilfred Jackson, Hamilton Luske, Clyde Geronimi   m Oliver Wallace, Paul J. Smith

voices of Ilene Woods, William Phipps, Eleanor Audley, Rhoda Williams, Lucille Bliss, Verna Felton

AAN: Oliver Wallace, Paul J. Smith; song 'Bibbidy Bobbidy Boo' (m/ly Mack David, Al Hoffman, Jerry Livingston)

Cinderella Jones
US   1946   89m   bw
Warner (Alex Gottlieb)

To collect an inheritance, a girl must marry a brainy man.

Witless comedy for the easily pleased.

w Charles Hoffman   story Philip Wylie   d Busby Berkeley   ph Sol Polito   m Frederick Hollander

Joan Leslie, Robert Alda, S. Z. Sakall, Edward Everett Horton, Julie Bishop, William Prince, Charles Dingle, Ruth Donnelly, Elisha Cook Jnr, Hobart Cavanaugh, Chester Clute

'A movie for every woman who thinks she can never fall in love again!'
Cinderella Liberty
US   1974   117m   DeLuxe   Panavision
TCF/Sanford (Mark Rydell)
V, V*

A sailor on shore leave picks up a prostitute and falls in love with her.

Assertively 'modern' yet glutinously sentimental love story in squalid settings. It presumably has an audience.

w Darryl Ponicsan novel Darryl Ponicsan d Mark Rydell ph Vilmos Zsigmond m John Williams

James Caan, Marsha Mason, Eli Wallach, Kirk Calloway, Allyn Ann McLerie

'A sordid, messy affair which wants to jerk tears but just doesn't have the knack.' – New Yorker

AAN: John Williams; Marsha Mason; song 'You're So Nice To Be Around' (m John Williams, ly Paul Williams)

Cinderfella
US   1960   91m   Technicolor
Paramount/Jerry Lewis
V, V*

Luxury pantomime featuring a male Cinderella.

Annoyingly lavish and empty star vehicle with precious little to laugh at: Lewis's own jokes are strung out to snapping point and no one else gets a look in.

wd Frank Tashlin ph Haskell Boggs m Walter Scharf

Jerry Lewis, Ed Wynn, Judith Anderson, Anna Maria Alberghetti, Henry Silva, Robert Hutton, Count Basie

'A drought of comic inspiration, followed by a flood of mawkish whimsy, gradually increases one's early misgivings to a degree which finally verges on revulsion.' – Peter John Dyer

Cinema Paradiso ****
Italy/France   1989   122m   colour
Palace/Films Ariana/RAI TRE/Forum/Franco Cristaldi
V, V*, L, S
original title: Nuovo Cinema Paradiso

A film director remembers his early life and his boyhood friendship with the projectionist at his local cinema.

Nostalgic in its celebration of the cinema, beautifully detailed in its enjoyment of the rituals of small-town life with, underneath it all, a toughness in its depiction of a child's growth to maturity.

wd Giuseppe Tornatore ph Blasco Giurato m Ennio Morricone, Andrea Morricone pd Andrea Crisanti ed Mario Morra

Antonelli Attli, Enzo Cannavale, Isa Danieli, Leo Gullotta, Marco Leonardi, Pupella Maggio, Agnese Nano, Leopoldo Trieste, Salvatore Cascio, Jacques Perrin, Philippe Noiret

† A director's cut lasting 175m was released in 1994.

AA: best foreign film

Cinque Bambole per la Luna d'Agosto: see Five Dolls for an August Moon

La Ciociara: see Two Women

The Circle
US

Somerset Maugham's brittle play contrasting noble breeding with vulgar riches was filmed by Frank Borzage as a Hollywood silent, in 1925 for MGM, with Eleanor Boardman, Creighton Hale and Alec B. Francis. In 1930 the same studio made it as a talkie under the title Strictly Unconventional, with Catherine Dale Owen, Tyrrell Davis and Lewis Stone; directed by David Burton.

Neither version really worked.

The Circle (1957): see The Vicious Circle

Circle of Danger *
GB   1951   89m   bw
Coronado/David Rose (Joan Harrison)

An American in England investigates the strange

death some years earlier of his brother during a commando raid.

Individual scenes are well milked for suspense and dramatic emphasis, but the plot line has virtually no mystery and absolutely no danger. It all seems mildly reminiscent of several Hitchcock films.

w Philip MacDonald d Jacques Tourneur ph Oswald Morris m Robert Farnon

Ray Milland, Patricia Roc, Marius Goring, Hugh Sinclair, Naunton Wayne, Marjorie Fielding, Edward Rigby, Colin Gordon, Dora Bryan

Circle of Deceit *
West Germany/France   1981   109m   Eastmancolor
Bioskop/Artemis/Hessischer Rundfunk/Argos (Eberhard Junkersdorf)
original title: Die Fälschung

A German journalist has a crisis of conscience while covering the war in Beirut.

Fashionable self-scrutiny based on a published 'faction'. As a film, quite engrossing and occasionally hair-raising.

w Volker Schlöndorff, Jean Claude Carrière, Margarethe von Trotta, Kai Hermann novel Nicolas Born d Volker Schlöndorff ph Igor Luther m Maurice Jarre

Bruno Ganz, Hanna Schygulla, Jerzy Skolimowski, Gila von Weitershausen

'Rarely can a fiction film about war have had such a vividly authentic background, with real corpses and real destruction lending a bleak chill never captured by staged reconstructions.' – Tom Milne, MFB

Circle of Deception
GB   1960   100m   bw   Cinemascope
TCF (T. H. Morahan)

An officer is parachuted into Germany with the intention that he should crack under interrogation and reveal false information.

Depressing World War II tall tale, with suspense sacrificed by flashback structure.

w Nigel Balchin, Robert Musel novel Alec Waugh d Jack Lee ph Gordon Dines m Clifton Parker

Bradford Dillman, Harry Andrews, Suzy Parker, Robert Stephens, John Welsh, Paul Rogers, Duncan Lamont, Michael Ripper

Circle of Two
Canada   1980   105m   colour
Film Consortium of Canada (Henk Van der Kolk)
V*

A 60-year-old artist falls for a teenage student.

Dreary and uninteresting star drama which never really gets going.

w Thomas Hedley novel A Lesson in Love by Marie Terese Baird d Jules Dassin ph Lazlo George m Paul Hoffert

Richard Burton, Tatum O'Neal, Nuala Fitzgerald, Kate Reid, Robin Gammell, Patricia Collins

Circonstances Atténuantes *
France   1939   85m   bw
CCFC

A retired magistrate becomes innocently involved with a gang of crooks.

Nimble farce, most skilfully acted.

w Jean-Pierre Feydeau novel Marcel Arnac d Jean Boyer

Michel Simon, Arletty, Suzanne Dantes, Arnoux, Mila Parely

The Circus *
US   1928   72m (24 fps)   bw   silent
(UA) Charles Chaplin
V, V*, L

A tramp on the run from the police takes refuge in a circus and falls for an equestrienne.

Pathos often descends to bathos in this self-constructed star vehicle which has far too few laughs.

wd Charles Chaplin ph Rollie Totheroh, Jack Wilson, Mark Marlott

Charles Chaplin, Merna Kennedy, Allan Garcia, Harry Crocker

AA: Special Award to Chaplin for acting, writing, directing and producing the film

Circus Boys *
Japan   1989   106m   bw
ICA/Eizo Tanteisha/CBS Sony (Mituhisa Hida, Yoichi Sakurai)
original title: Ni ju-seiki Shonen Dokuhon

A boy grows up to become a circus clown before leaving to work as an itinerant pedlar and falling in love with a gangster's concubine.

Strange and wayward film with a powerful poetic quality.

wd Kaizo Hayashi ph Yuichi Nagata ad Takeo Kimura, Hidemitsu Yamazaki ed Osamu Tanaka

Hiroshi Mikami, Moe Kamura, Xia Jian, Michiru Akiyoshi, Yuki Asayama, Sanshi Katsura, Haruko Wanibuchi

'It isn't very often you see a film that understands so well that the cinema should be a place with some magic in it as well as simple story-telling ability.' – Derek Malcolm, Guardian

'One man's lust turns men into beasts, strips women of their souls!'
Circus of Horrors
GB   1960   91m   Eastmancolor
Anglo Amalgamated/Lynx/Independent Artists (Norman Priggen)
V*, L

A plastic surgeon staffs a semi-derelict circus with criminals whose faces he has altered, and murders any who try to flee.

Stark horror comic; quite professionally made, but content-wise a crude concoction of sex and sadism.

w George Baxt d Sidney Hayers ph Douglas Slocombe m Franz Reizenstein, Muir Mathieson

Anton Diffring, Erika Remberg, Yvonne Monlaur, Donald Pleasence, Jane Hylton, Kenneth Griffith, Conrad Phillips, Jack Gwillim

The Circus Queen Murder *
US   1933   63m   bw
Columbia

Thatcher Colt solves murders in a travelling circus.

Reasonably slick second feature of its period.

w Jo Swerling novel Anthony Abbot d Roy William Neill

Adolphe Menjou, Greta Nissen, Ruthelma Stevens, Dwight Frye, Donald Cook

Circus World
US   1964   138m   Super Technirama
Bronston/Midway (Samuel Bronston)
V*, L
GB title: The Magnificent Showman

An American circus owner tours Europe in search of his alcoholic ex-wife who left him when her lover fell to death from the trapeze.

Lethargic big-screen epic which exhausts its spectacle in the first hour and then settles down to a dreary will-daughter-guess-who-the-strange-lady-isplot, without even the plus of an exciting finale.

w Ben Hecht, Julian Halevy, James Edward Grant d Henry Hathaway ph Jack Hildyard m Dimitri Tiomkin pd John DeCuir

John Wayne, *Rita Hayworth*, Claudia Cardinale, John Smith, Lloyd Nolan, Richard Conte, Wanda Rotha, Kay Walsh

'To sit through this film is something like holding an elephant on your lap for two hours and fifteen minutes.' – *Time*

The Cisco Kid

The Cisco Kid, a ruthless Mexican bandit originally created by O. Henry in a short story, was turned by Hollywood into a dashing wild Western Robin Hood in twenty-three sound features (following a few silent ones) and a long-running TV series. In most of them he was accompanied by his fat side-kick Pancho.

For Fox:

1929: IN OLD ARIZONA (Warner Baxter)
1931: THE CISCO KID (Baxter)

For Twentieth Century Fox:

1939: THE RETURN OF THE CISCO KID (Baxter), THE CISCO KID AND THE LADY (Cesar Romero: who played the role in all the remaining TCF movies).
1940: VIVA CISCO KID, LUCKY CISCO KID, THE GAY CABALLERO
1941: ROMANCE OF THE RIO GRANDE, RIDE ON, VAQUERO

For Monogram:

1945: THE CISCO KID RETURNS (Duncan Renaldo), THE CISCO KID IN OLD NEW MEXICO (Renaldo), SOUTH OF THE RIO GRANDE (Renaldo)
1946: THE GAY CAVALIER (Gilbert Roland), SOUTH OF MONTEREY (Roland), BEAUTY AND THE BANDIT (Roland)
1947: RIDING THE CALIFORNIA TRAIL (Roland), ROBIN HOOD OF MONTEREY (Roland), KING OF THE BANDITS (Roland)

For United Artists (all with Renaldo):

1949: THE VALIANT HOMBRE, THE GAY AMIGO, THE DARING CABALLERO, SATAN'S CRADLE
1950: THE GIRL FROM SAN LORENZO

† The 50s TV series starred Renaldo with Leo Carrillo.

Cisco Pike

US   1971   94m   Eastmancolor
Columbia/Acrobat (Gerald Ayres)

A former pop group leader and drug pusher is blackmailed by a cop into selling heroin. Low-key, would-be realistic study of a section of life in 70s LA. Flashy, boring and almost plotless.

wd Bill L. Norton   *ph* Vilis Lapenieks   *m* various

Kris Kristofferson, Gene Hackman, Karen Black, Harry Dean Stanton

'A moody, melancholy little film whose strength lies in its evocation of the rootless, aimless, irresponsible life-style of the pop/drug culture.' – *Brenda Davies*

'Secrets of a doctor as told by a doctor!'
The Citadel **
GB   1938   113m   bw
MGM (Victor Saville)
V*

A young doctor has a hard time in the mining villages but is later swayed by the easy rewards of a Mayfair practice.

Solidly produced adaptation of a bestseller; the more recent deluge of doctors on television make it appear rather elementary, but many scenes work in a classical way. One of the first fruits of MGM's British studios which were closed by World War II.

w Elizabeth Hill, Ian Dalrymple, Emlyn Williams, Frank Wead   *novel* A. J. Cronin   *d* King Vidor   *ph* Harry Stradling   *m* Louis Levy   *ad* Lazare Meerson, Alfred Junge   *ed* Charles Frend

Robert Donat, Rosalind Russell, Ralph Richardson, Emlyn Williams, Penelope Dudley Ward, Francis L. Sullivan, Rex Harrison

'General audience limited . . . strong for the Anglo market.' – *Variety*

'I think any doctor will agree that here is a medical picture with no Men in White hokum, no hysterical, incredible melodrama, but with an honest story, honestly told. And that's a rare picture.' – *Pare Lorentz*

'We are grateful that a worthy idea has been handled with intelligence and imagination, that Vidor has shown respect both for his talent and for the sensibilities of the audience.' – *Robert Stebbins*

'Numerous passages shine brilliantly with those deft touches that first brought Vidor to prominence.' – *Variety*

'The pace of Hollywood, the honest characterization of England's best.' – *New York Times*

† The parts played by Russell and Richardson were originally intended for Elizabeth Allan and Spencer Tracy.

AAN: best picture; script; King Vidor; Robert Donat

The Citadel: see *El Kalaa*

Citizen Kane ****
US   1941   119m   bw
RKO (Orson Welles)
V, V*, L, S

A newspaper tycoon dies, and a magazine reporter interviews his friends in an effort to discover the meaning of his last words.

A brilliant piece of Hollywood cinema using all the resources of the studio; despite lapses of characterization and gaps in the narrative, almost every shot and every line is utterly absorbing both as entertainment and as craft. See *The Citizen Kane Book* by Pauline Kael, and innumerable other writings.

w Herman J. Mankiewicz, Orson Welles   *d* Orson Welles   *ph* Gregg Toland   *m* Bernard Herrmann   *ad* Van Nest Polglase   *sp* Vernon L. Walker   *ed* Robert Wise

Orson Welles (Kane), *Joseph Cotten* (Jedediah Leland), *Dorothy Comingore* (Susan Alexander), *Everett Sloane* (Bernstein), *Ray Collins* (Boss Jim Geddes), *Paul Stewart* (Raymond), *Ruth Warrick* (Emily Norton), *Erskine Sanford* (Herbert Carter), *Agnes Moorehead* (Kane's mother), *Harry Shannon* (Kane's father), *George Coulouris* (Walter Parks Thatcher), *William Alland* (Thompson), *Fortunio Bonanova* (music teacher)

'What is his name? It's Charlie Kane! I'll bet you five you're not alive if you don't know his name!'
NEWSREEL: 'Then, last week, as it must to all men, death came to Charles Foster Kane.'
BERNSTEIN: 'Old age . . . it's the only disease you don't look forward to being cured of.'
THOMPSON: 'Mr Kane was a man who got everything he wanted, and then lost it. Maybe Rosebud was something he couldn't get, or something he lost. Anyway, I don't think it would have explained everything. I don't think any word can explain a man's life. No, I guess Rosebud is just a piece in a jigsaw puzzle . . . a missing piece.'
SUSAN: 'Forty-nine acres of nothing but scenery and statues. I'm lonesome.'
KANE: 'You're right, Mr Thatcher, I did lose a million dollars last year. I expect to lose a million dollars this year. I expect to lose a million dollars next year. You know, Mr Thatcher, at the rate of a million dollars a year, I'll have to close this place – in sixty years.'
KANE: 'I run a couple of newspapers. What do you do?'
BERNSTEIN: 'One day back in 1896 I was crossing over to Jersey on the ferry, and as we pulled out, there was another ferry pulling in, and on it there was a girl waiting to get off. A white dress she had on. She was carrying a white parasol. I only saw her for one second. She didn't see me at all, but I'll bet a month

hasn't gone by since that I haven't thought of that girl.'

'On seeing it for the first time, one got a conviction that if the cinema could do that, it could do anything.' – *Penelope Houston*

'What may distinguish *Citizen Kane* most of all is its extracting the mythic from under the humdrum surface of the American experience.' – *John Simon, 1968*

'Probably the most exciting film that has come out of Hollywood for twenty-five years. I am not sure it isn't the most exciting film that has ever come out of anywhere.' – *C. A. Lejeune*

'At any rate Orson Welles has landed in the movies, with a splash and a loud yell.' – *James Shelley Hamilton*

'More fun than any great movie I can think of.' – *Pauline Kael, 1968*

'It is a fascinating picture, but because of its congestion of technical stunts, it fails to move us.' – *Egon Larsen*

'A quite good film which tries to run the psychological essay in harness with the detective thriller, and doesn't quite succeed.' – *James Agate*

AA: Herman J. Mankiewicz, Orson Welles (script)

AAN: best picture; Orson Welles (as director); Gregg Toland; Bernard Herrmann; Orson Welles (as actor); art direction; Robert Wise

Citizens' Band: see *FM*

Citizens Band (1977): see *Handle with Care*

La Città delle Donne: see *City of Women*

La Città Si Difende
Italy   1951   90m   bw
Cines (Carlo Civallero)

A gang is recruited to rob a football stadium.

Moderate forerunner of *The Good Die Young*, *The Killing*, and a hundred other caper films.

w Federico Fellini, Tullio Pinelli, Luigi Comencini   *d* Pietro Germi   *ph* Carlo Montuori   *m* Carlo Rustichelli

Fausto Tozzi, Gina Lollobrigida, Patrizia Manca, Enzo Maggio

'As anonymous as the average B picture.' – *Gavin Lambert*

The City *
US   1939   32m   bw
American Institute of Planners

A historical, social and psychoanalytical study of urban living.

Slightly guarded but convention-breaking documentary which though of its time still fascinates mildly by its style.

w Henwar Rodakiewicz   *book* *The Culture of Cities* by Lewis Mumford   *d* Ralph Steiner, Willard Van Dyke   *ph* Ralph Steiner, Willard Van Dyke

City across the River
US   1949   91m   bw
U-I (Howard Christie)

Brooklyn delinquents get involved in murder.

Semi-documentary throwback to the Dead End Kids, with location shooting influenced by *The Naked City*. Dull.

w Maxwell Shane, Dennis Cooper novel The Amboy Dukes by Irving Shulman d Maxwell Shane ph Maury Gertsman m Walter Scharf

Stephen McNally, Barbara Whiting, Peter Fernandez, Al Ramsen, Joshua Shelley, Anthony Curtis (Tony Curtis in his first film role)

City After Midnight: see That Woman Opposite

The City and the Dogs **
Peru 1985 135m colour
Inca Films (Francisco J. Lombardi)
original title: La Ciudad Y Los Perros

With the aid of an incorruptible officer, a cadet tries to expose the organized brutality at a military academy.

A passionate allegory of military dictatorship.

w José Watanbe novel Mario Vargas Llosa d Francisco J. Lombardi ph Pili Flores Guerra m Enrique Iturriaga ad Lloyd Moore ed Gianfranco Annichini, Augusto Tamayo San Roman

Pablo Serra, Gustavo Bueno, Luis Alvarez, Jan Manuel Ochva, Eduardo Adrianzen

City Beneath the Sea
US 1953 87m Technicolor
U-I (Albert J. Cohen)

Deep sea divers fall out over a sunken treasure.

Adequate double-biller with little to stir the interest.

w Jack Harvey, Ramon Romero d Budd Boetticher ph Charles P. Boyle md Joseph Gershenson

Robert Ryan, Anthony Quinn, Mala Powers, Suzan Ball, George Mathews, Karel Stepanek, Lalo Rios

City Beneath the Sea
US 1970 98m DeLuxe
Warner/Kent/Motion Pictures International (Irwin Allen)
GB theatrical release title: One Hour to Doomsday

An undersea city is threatened by an errant planetoid.

Futuristic adventure from a familiar stable; it will satisfy followers of Voyage to the Bottom of the Sea. Originally made for TV.

w John Meredyth Lucas d Irwin Allen ph Kenneth Peach m Richard La Salle ad Rodger E. Maus, Stan Jolley

Stuart Whitman, Robert Wagner, Rosemary Forsyth, Robert Colbert, Burr de Benning, Richard Basehart, Joseph Cotten, James Darren, Sugar Ray Robinson, Paul Stewart

City for Conquest **
US 1940 106m bw
Warner (Anatole Litvak)
V*, L

An East Side truck driver becomes a boxer but is blinded in a fight; meanwhile his composer brother gives up pop music for symphonies.

Phony but oddly persuasive melodrama set in a studio in New York and heavily influenced by the pretensions of the Group theatre.

w John Wexley novel Aben Kandel d Anatole Litvak ph Sol Polito, James Wong Howe m Max Steiner

James Cagney, Ann Sheridan, Frank Craven, Donald Crisp, Arthur Kennedy, Frank McHugh, George Tobias, Anthony Quinn, Jerome Cowan, Lee Patrick, Blanche Yurka, Thurston Hall

'Sometimes we wonder whether it wasn't really the Warner brothers who got New York from the Indians, so diligent and devoted have they been in feeling the great city's pulse, picturing its myriad facets and recording with deep compassion the passing life of its seething population.' – Bosley Crowther

City Girl *
US 1930 77m bw
Fox

A city girl finds rural life has its own drama.

Rural drama distinguished by directorial touches.

w Berthold Viertel, Marion Orth play The Mud Turtle by Elliot Lester d F. W. Murnau ph Ernest Palmer m Arthur Kay

Charles Farrell, Mary Duncan, David Torrence, Edith Yorke, Dawn O'Day

City Girl
US 1937 60m bw
TCF

A slightly dumb waitress becomes a gangster's moll.

Fast-moving B picture which undoubtedly gave satisfaction.

w Frances Hyland, Robin Harris, Lester Ziffren d Alfred Werker

Phyllis Brooks, Ricardo Cortez, Robert Wilcox, Douglas Fowley, Chick Chandler, Esther Muir

City Heat
US 1984 97m Technicolor
Warner/Malpaso/Deliverance (Fritz Manes)
V, V*, L

In the early thirties, a private eye's partner is bumped off, and he teams against the baddies with an old cop friend.

A tedious teaming for two tired stars who seem to imagine that all they have to do is show up.

w Sam O. Brown (Blake Edwards), Joseph C. Stinson d Richard Benjamin ph Nick McLean m Lennie Niehaus pd Edward Carfagno

Clint Eastwood, Burt Reynolds, Jane Alexander, Madeline Kahn, Rip Torn, Irene Cara, Richard Roundtree, Tony Lo Bianco

'It evaporates from the mind instantly upon its conclusion.' – Variety

The City Is Dark: see Crime Wave

The City Jungle: see The Young Philadelphians

City Lights ***
US 1931 87m bw silent (with music and effects)
UA/Charles Chaplin
V, V*, L

A tramp befriends a millionaire and falls in love with a blind girl.

Sentimental comedy with several delightful sequences in Chaplin's best manner.

wd/m Charles Chaplin ph Rollie Totheroh md Alfred Newman

Charles Chaplin, Virginia Cherrill, Florence Lee, Harry Myers

'Chaplin has another good picture, but it gives indications of being short-winded, and may tire fast after a bombastic initial seven days . . . he has sacrificed speed to pathos, and plenty of it.' – Variety

'Even while laughing, one is aware of a faint and uneasy feeling that Chaplin has been pondering with more than a bit of solemnity on conventional story values, and it has led him further than ever into the realms of what is often called pathetic.' – National Board of Review

City of Bad Men *
US 1953 82m Technicolor
TCF (Leonard Goldstein)

In Carson City during the Corbett/Fitzsimmons boxing match, outlaws plan to rob the arena of its receipts.

Slightly unusual Western suspenser with generally accomplished handling.

w George W. George, George Slavin d Harmon Jones ph Charles G. Clarke md Lionel Newman

Dale Robertson, Jeanne Crain, Richard Boone, Lloyd Bridges, Carl Betz, Carole Mathews, Whitfield Connor

The City of Beautiful Nonsense
GB 1935 88m bw
Butcher's (Wilfred Noy)

A poor composer wins the girl he loves from a rich man.

Thin and dated version of a fashionable novel.

w Donovan Pedelty novel E. Temple Thurston d Adrian Brunel ph Desmond Dickinson

Emlyn Williams, Sophie Stewart, Eve Lister, George Carney

City of Chance *
US 1939 57m bw
Sol M. Wurtzel/TCF

A girl reporter crusades against gangster gamblers.

Smart little second feature with no time to be boring.

w John Larkin, Barry Trivers d Ricardo Cortez

Lynn Bari, C. Aubrey Smith, Donald Woods, Amanda Duff, June Gale, Richard Lane

'A half crazed man in a terror crazed town!'
City of Fear
US 1958 81m bw
Columbia/Orbit (Leon Chooluck)

A convict escapes with a canister of radioactive cobalt, which he believes to be heroin. After terrifying the city, he finally dies of exposure to it.

Rough-edged but occasionally gripping minor thriller from an independent company.

w Steven Ritch, Robert Dillon d Irving Lerner ph Lucien Ballard m Jerry Goldsmith

Vince Edwards, John Archer, Patricia Blair, Steven Ritch, Lyle Talbot

City of Gold **
Canada 1957 23m bw
National Film Board of Canada

The story of Dawson City, capital of the Klondike in 1897–8, is told by an accumulation of details from still photographs.

A film with much to answer for, being the first documentary exclusively using the rostrum camera, a technique later adopted extensively by television. The subject matter is fascinating.

w and narrated by Pierre Berton d/ph Colin Low, Wolf Koenig

City of Hope ***
US 1991 130m DuArt Panavision
Mainline/Esperanza
V, V*, L

Corruption and crime in Hudson City, New Jersey touches the lives of locals, from building contractors and petty thieves to the mayor.

Complex and engrossing, with a narrative style that brings to busy life a whole community.

wd John Sayles ph Robert Richardson m Mason Daring pd Dan Bishop, Dianna Freas ed John Sayles

Vincent Spano, Joe Morton, Tony Lo Bianco, Barbara Williams, Stephen Mendillo, Chris Cooper, Charlie Yanko, Jace Alexander, Todd Graff, Scott Tiler, John Sayles, Frankie Faison, Gloria Foster, Tom Wright

'A major film, suggesting that Sayles might become as significant a film-maker for the 90s as Altman was for the 70s.' – Kim Newman, Sight and Sound

'Epic, masterly, urgent, adult and unforgettable. Put simply – which is grossly unfair to its complexity – it is Bonfire of the Vanities without the vanities.' – Alexander Walker, London Evening Standard

'It plays as if it were still on the drawing board.' – *Michael Sragow, New Yorker*

'He was a man who couldn't care less . . . until he met a man who couldn't care more.'

City of Joy *
GB/France   1992   135m   Eastmancolor
Warner/Lightmotive/Pricel (Jake Eberts, Roland Joffé)
V, V*, L, S

In Calcutta an American doctor becomes involved in a clinic for the poor and helps them in their struggle against local gangsters.

Well-meaning movie that tends to talk about, rather than dramatize, its theme of the need for commitment.

w Mark Medoff   *book* Dominic LaPierre   *d* Roland Joffé   *ph* Peter Biziou   *m* Ennio Morricone   *pd* Roy Walker   *ed* Gerry Hambling

Patrick Swayze, Pauline Collins, Om Puri, Shabana Azmi, Art Malik, Ayesha Dharker, Santu Chowdhury, Imran Badsah Khan

'Joffé's noble attempt to portray the tenacity and strength of the human spirit under the most trying conditions comes off as curiously ineffectual due to predictable plotting and character evolution.' – *Variety*

'Hopelessly fraudulent, with an uplifting finale that could make a strong man heave.' – *Stephen Farber, Movieline*

A City of Sadness: see *Beiqing Chengshi*

City of Silent Men
US   1942   64m   bw
PRC (Dixon R. Harwin)

Two ex-convicts finally get work but are hounded by a newspaper publisher.

Decent second feature, a cut above the average for its source.

w Joseph Hoffman, Robert E. Kent   *d* William Nigh

Frank Albertson, June Lang, Jan Wiley, Richard Clarke

City of the Dead *
GB   1960   78m   bw
Vulcan (Donald Taylor)
US title: *Horror Hotel*

In Massachusetts, a woman burned as a witch 250 years ago is still 'alive', running a local hotel and luring unwary strangers into becoming sacrificial victims.

A deadly first half gives way to splendid cinematic terror when the scene shifts to the village by night, all dry ice and limpid fog, and the heroine becomes a human sacrifice. A superior horror comic.

w George Baxt   *d* John Moxey   *ph* Desmond Dickinson   *m* Douglas Gamley, Ken Jones

Patricia Jessel, Betta St John, Christopher Lee, Dennis Lotis, Valentine Dyall, Venetia Stevenson, Norman Macowan, Fred Johnson

'From The Bowels Of The Dead They Came To Collect The Living . . .'
City of The Living Dead (dubbed)
Italy   1980   93m   colour
Dania/Medusa/National Cinematografia (Giovanni Masini)
V
original title: *Paura nella Città dei Morti Viventi*; aka: *Gates of Hell; Twilight of The Dead; The Fear*

In the Massachusetts town of Dunwich a priest hangs himself and opens a gateway to hell, through which stagger the living dead.

A slow-moving horror with little narrative and a great deal of gore. It was supposedly inspired by H. P. Lovecraft, although it bears little resemblance to his stories.

w Lucio Fulci, Dardano Sacchetti   *d* Lucio Fulci   *ph* Sergio Salvati   *m* Fabio Frizzi   *pd* Massimo Antonello Geleng   *ed* Vincenzo Tomassi

Christopher George, Katriona MacColl, Carlo de Mejo, Antonella Interlenghi, Giovanni Lombardo Radice, Daniela Doria, Janet Agren

'The ending is somewhat incomprehensible and acting and dialogue as usual leave a good deal to be desired. However, one doesn't really look to the "fantastique" for that kind of thing' – *Julian Petley, Films and Filming*

† The film was cut to 92m on its British cinema release in 1982 and to 86m for its video release, removing the goriest episodes, including a youth having an electric drill pushed through his head, and making the narrative, like a few of its characters, somewhat disjointed.

City of Women *
Italy–France   1980   140m   Eastmancolor
Opera Film-Gaumont (Renzo Rossellini)
V*
original title: *La Città delle Donne*

A businessman finds himself trapped and threatened by women en masse.

Often leaden but sometimes spectacular fantasy in which the director spews out his views of the war between men and women. Fascinating in patches, but generally indigestible.

w Federico Fellini, Bernardino Zapponi   *d* Federico Fellini   *ph* Giuseppe Rotunno   *m* Luis Bacalov

Marcello Mastroianni, Anna Prucnal, Bernice Stegers, Ettore Manni, Donatella Damiani

'Another visual tour de force in an elaborate dream framework; narrative thin, overlong, and finally overweight.' – *Variety*

City on Fire
Canada/US   1979   106m   colour
Rank/Astral Bellevue/Pathé/Sandy Howard/Harold Greenberg (Claude Héroux)
V*

A slum fire threatens an entire city.

Shoddy disaster movie which does its cast no favour.

w Jack Hill, David P. Lewis, Celine La Frenière   *d* Alvin Rakoff   *ph* René Verzier   *m* William and Matthew Macauley   *pd* William McCrow   *sp* Cliff Wenger, Carol Lynn   *ed* Jean-Pol Passer, Jacques Clairoux

Barry Newman, Susan Clark, Shelley Winters, Henry Fonda, Leslie Nielsen, James Franciscus, Ava Gardner

'Three urban hombres heading west, seeking adventure, craving excitement . . . and longing for room service.'
City Slickers ***
US   1991   114m   CFI
First Independent/Castle Rock/Nelson/Face (Irby Smith)
V, V*, L, S

Three friends, all facing midlife crises, decide to spend their vacation on a cattle drive.

A witty and engaging comedy for the most part, with some affectionate parodies of moments from classic Westerns.

w Lowell Ganz, Babaloo Mandel   *d* Ron Underwood   *ph* Dean Semler   *m* Marc Shaiman, Hummie Mann   *pd* Lawrence G. Paull   *ed* O. Nicholas Brown

Billy Crystal, Daniel Stern, Bruno Kirby, Patricia Wettig, Helen Slater, Jack Palance, Josh Mostel, David Paymer, Noble Willingham

'A deft blend of wry humour and warmth (albeit with a little too much *thirty-something*-esque angst for its own good).' – *Variety*

AA: Jack Palance

'Love and courage pitted against a ruthless hate!'
City Streets **
US   1931   86m   bw
Paramount (Rouben Mamoulian)

A gangster's daughter is sent to jail for a murder she did not commit, and on release narrowly escapes being 'taken for a ride'.

Tense, dated gangland melodrama of primary interest because of its director's very cinematic treatment.

w Max Marcin, Oliver H. P. Garrett, Dashiell Hammett   *story Ladies of the Mob* by Ernest Booth   *d* Rouben Mamoulian   *ph* Lee Garmes

Sylvia Sidney, Gary Cooper, Paul Lukas, Guy Kibbee, William (Stage) Boyd, Stanley Fields, Wynne Gibson

TYPICAL GANGSTER DIALOGUE OF THE TIME: Who's running this show, anyhow?
– I am.
Who says so?
– I say so, for one. And when you talk to me, take that toothpick outa your mouth!

'So many brilliant touches that anyone who sees it will have to predict for Mamoulian a brilliant career.' – *Film Spectator*

'Too much attempt to artify hurts though the sophisticated treatment and elegant settings will help.' – *Variety*

'A love story in a gangster setting which got carried away into so much fancy expressionism and symbolism that it seems stylized out of all relationship to the actual world.' – *Pauline Kael, 70s*

City that Never Sleeps
US   1953   90m   bw
Republic (John H. Auer)
V*

The work of the Chicago police force during one night.

Adequate minor semi-documentary police yarn.

w Steve Fisher   *d* John H. Auer   *ph* John I. Russell   *m* R. Dale Butts

Gig Young, Mala Powers, William Talman, Edward Arnold, Chill Wills, Paula Raymond, Marie Windsor

'They dared the most romantic journey that has ever challenged the imagination!'
City under the Sea
GB   1965   84m   Eastmancolor   Colorscope
Bruton/AIP (Daniel Haller)
V, V*
US title: *War Gods of the Deep*

An American heiress in Cornwall meets Victorian smugglers who have lived a hundred years under the sea in Lyonesse.

Childlike, unpersuasive nonsense which wastes some good talent.

w Charles Bennett, Louis M. Heyward   *d* Jacques Tourneur   *ph* Stephen Dade   *m* Stanley Black

Vincent Price, David Tomlinson, Susan Hart, Tab Hunter, Henry Oscar, John Le Mesurier

City without Men
US   1943   75m   bw
Columbia

A boarding house near a prison is filled with women awaiting the parole of their menfolk.

Stereotyped programmer.

w W. L. River, George Skier, Donald Davis   *d* Sidney Salkow

Linda Darnell, Michael Duane, Sara Allgood, Edgar Buchanan, Glenda Farrell, Leslie Brooks, Margaret Hamilton, Sheldon Leonard

A City's Child
Australia   1971   80m   Eastmancolor
Pleasant Pastures/Brian Kavanagh

A reclusive woman, who becomes obsessed with dolls after her mother's death, takes as a lover a young man who may not exist.

A daft excursion into experimental cinema which fails to hold the attention.

w Don Battye story Brian Kavanagh d Brian Kavanagh ph Bruce McNaughton m Peter Pinne ad Trevor Ling ed Brian Kavanagh

Monica Maughan, Sean Scully, Moira Carelton, Vivean Gray, Marguerite Lofthouse

The City's Edge
Australia 1985 86m colour
Eastcaps (Pom Oliver, Errol Sullivan)

A troubled man takes a room in a Bondi boarding house and finds others worse off than himself.

Dreary mini-dramas, somewhat arbitrarily linked and without a shred of hope in sight for anybody.

w Robert J. Merritt, Ken Quinnell novel W. A. Harbinson d Ken Quinnell

Hugo Weaving, Tommy Lewis, Shirley Cameron, Mark Lee, Ralph Cotterill

La Ciudad Y Los Perros: see *The City And The Dogs*

Civilization ***
US 1916 68m (1931 'sound' version) bw silent
Triangle

A mythical country starts war, but one of the principals has a vision of Christ on the battlefields and the king is persuaded to sign a peace treaty.

Surprisingly impressive parable showing this early director at his best; intended as a pacifist tract in the middle of World War I.

w C. Gardner Sullivan d Thomas Ince ph Irwin Willat

Enid Markey, Howard Hickman, J. Barney Sherry

Claire's Knee ***
France 1970 106m Eastmancolor
Gala/Les Films du Losange (Pierre Cottrell)
V, V*, L
original title: *Genou de Claire*

A 35-year-old diplomat who is about to be married confides to a female friend that he is attracted to a 16-year-old girl and her 17-year-old half-sister.

Witty and perceptive conversation piece, probably the best of Rohmer's explorations of the ambiguities of love and desire.

wd Eric Rohmer ph Nestor Almendros ed Cécile Decugis

Jean-Claude Brialy, Aurora Cornu, Béatrice Romand, Laurence de Monaghan, Michèle Montel, Gérard Falconetti, Fabrice Luchini

'Rohmer's quiet, complacent movie-novel game is pleasing.' – *Pauline Kael, New Yorker*

The Clairvoyant *
GB 1934 80m bw
Gainsborough (Michael Balcon)
V*

A fraudulent mindreader predicts a disaster which comes true.

Effective minor suspenser on predictable but enjoyable lines.

w Charles Bennett, Bryan Edgar Wallace, Robert Edmunds novel Ernst Lothar d Maurice Elvey ph Glen MacWilliams ad Alfred Junge

Claude Rains, Fay Wray, Jane Baxter, Mary Clare, Athole Stewart, Ben Field, Felix Aylmer, Donald Calthrop

Clambake
US 1967 98m Techniscope
UA/Rhodes (Laven-Gardner-Levy)
V, V*

The son of an oil millionaire sets out to see life.

Painless, forgettable star vehicle.

w Arthur Browne Jnr d Arthur H. Nadel ph William Margulies m Jeff Alexander

Elvis Presley, Shelley Fabares, Bill Bixby, James Gregory, Will Hutchins, Gary Merrill

Clan of the Cave Bear
US 1985 98m Technicolor Technovision
Warner/PSO/Guber-Peters/Jozak-Decade/Jonesfilm (Gerald I. Isenberg)
V*, L, S

In Neanderthal days, a blonde outcast girl is adopted by a swarthy tribe who think her ugly.

Comic-strip prehistory: better revive *One Million BC* or even the 1912 Griffith epic *Man's Genesis*.

w John Sayles novel Jean M. Auel d Michael Chapman ph Jan de Bont m Alan Silvestri pd Anthony Masters

Daryl Hannah, Pamela Reed, James Remar, Thomas G. Waites

AAN: make-up (Michael G. Westmore, Michele Burke)

Clancy of the Mounted
US 1933 bw serial: 12 eps
Universal

Clancy saves his brother, who has been framed for murder.

Tolerable Western serial.

d Ray Taylor

Tom Tyler, Jacqueline Wells, Earl McCarthy, William Desmond

Clarence the Cross-Eyed Lion
US 1965 98m Metrocolor
MGM (Leonard Kaufman)
V*

Adventures of animal farmers in Africa.

Amiable theatrical 'pilot' for the *Daktari* TV series.

w Alan Caillou, Marshall Thompson, Art Arthur d Andrew Marton ph Lamar Boren

Marshall Thompson, Betsy Drake, Richard Haydn, Cheryl Miller

'Livin' in my house! Lovin' another man! Is that what you call honest? That's just givin' it a nice name!'
Clash by Night *
US 1952 105m bw
RKO (Harriet Parsons) (A Wald-Krasna Production)
V*, L

In a northern fishing village, jealousy and near-tragedy are occasioned by the return home of a hardened girl from the big city.

Absurdly overblown melodrama of the *Anna Christie* school, burdened with significance and doggedly acted by a remarkable cast.

w Alfred Hayes play Clifford Odets d Fritz Lang ph Nicholas Musuraca m Roy Webb

Barbara Stanwyck, Paul Douglas, Robert Ryan, Marilyn Monroe, J. Carrol Naish, Keith Andes

'When Stanwyck snarls into a pub and belts down a straight shot, we think we're watching a remake of *Anna Christie*; when she is shyly and ineptly courted by Douglas we think it's a remake of *Min and Bill*; a sub-plot involving Monroe and Andes plays like *Gidget Faces an Identity Crisis*.' – *Kit Parker catalogue*

Clash of the Titans
GB 1981 118m Metrocolor Dynarama
MGM/Charles H. Schneer, Ray Harryhausen
V*, L

Perseus sets out to win Andromeda despite the impossible obstacles set for him by Thetis, which include a number of mythical monsters.

Star-packed but feebly imagined mythological spectacular, further hampered by gloomy photography which is presumably required to offset the jerkiness of the monsters. A very few moments provide the right kind of elation.

w Beverley Cross d Desmond Davis ph Ted Moore m Laurence Rosenthal pd Frank White sp Ray Harryhausen

Laurence Olivier, Claire Bloom, Maggie Smith, Ursula Andress, Jack Gwillim, Harry Hamlin, Judi Bowker, Burgess Meredith, Siân Phillips, Flora Robson, Freda Jackson, Donald Houston

'There's a real possibility some audiences will be turned to stone before Medusa even appears.' – *Geoff Brown, MFB*

'Unspeakable dialogue, muddy photography and a motley, lacklustre cast.' – *Sight and Sound*

'The good news is, Jonathan's having his first affair. The bad news is, she's his roommate's mother!'
Class
US 1983 98m Astro Color
Orion/Martin Ransohoff
V, V*, L

A shy student has an affair with an older woman who turns out to be his best friend's mother.

Ghastly travesty of *The Graduate* which aspires to every kind of sophistication it can think of but ends nowhere.

w Jim Kouf, David Greenwalt d Lewis John Carlino ph Ric Waite m Elmer Bernstein ad Jack Poplin

Jacqueline Bisset, Cliff Robertson, Rob Lowe, Andrew McCarthy, Stuart Margolin, John Cusack

'It is not often that one comes across a film of such muddled aspirations and widely divergent achievements.' – *Nick Roddick, MFB*

Class Act
US 1992 98m Technicolor
Warner/Wizan Black/Gordy de Passe (Todd Black, Maynell Thomas)
V, V*, L, S

Two high-school students – one an intellectual, the other a delinquent – swop identities.

Dim-witted teen comedy.

w John Semper, Cynthia Friedlob story Michael Swerdlick, Wayne Rice, Richard Brenne d Randall Miller ph Francis Kenny m Vassal Benford pd David L. Snyder ed John F. Burnett

Christopher Reid, Christopher Martin, Karyn Parsons, Alysia Rogers, Meshach Taylor, Doug E. Doug, Lamont Johnson

'Nothing Personal. It's Just Father vs Daughter In The Fight Of Their Lives.'
Class Action
US 1990 109m colour
TCF/Interscope (Ted Field, Scott Kroopf, Robert W. Cort)
V, V*, L, S

A father and a daughter, both lawyers, find themselves on opposing sides in the courtroom.

Moderately engrossing, though predictable, drama.

w Carolyn Shelby, Christopher Ames, Samantha Shad d Michael Apted ph Conrad L. Hall m James Horner pd Todd Hallowell ed Ian Crafford

Gene Hackman, Mary Elizabeth Mastrantonio, Colin Friels, Joanna Merlin, Larry Fishburne, Donald Moffat, Jan Rubes, Matt Clark

'A remarkably well-made and well-mannered film.' – *Sight and Sound*

'Pic's parameters may be worn, but Apted's keen focus on its emotional core helps it transcend the everyday.' – *Variety*

Class of 84
Canada 1981 98m colour
Columbia/Guerrilla (Arthur Kent)
V*, L

A new teacher finds his students involved in drug and vice rackets.

The Blackboard Jungle goes several steps further, to general indifference.

w Mark Lester, John Saxton, Tom Holland *d* Mark Lester *ph* Albert Dunk *m* Lalo Schifrin *ad* no credit

Perry King, Merrie Lynn Ross, Timothy Van Patten, Roddy McDowall

Class of '44
US 1973 95m Technicolor Panavision
Warner (Paul Bogart)
V*

Sex problems of college students during World War II.

Thin sequel to *Summer of '42*, nostalgic to Americans over forty but not much of a trip for anyone else.

w Herman Raucher *d* Paul Bogart *ph* Andrew Laszlo *m* David Shire

Gary Grimes, Jerry Houser, Oliver Conant, William Atherton, Sam Bottoms, Deborah Winters

The Class of Miss McMichael
GB 1978 90m colour
Brut/Kettledrum (Judd Bernard)
V*

A dedicated schoolmistress has no chance against her slum surroundings.

The Blackboard Jungle lives on, very boringly.

w Judd Bernard *novel* Sandy Hutson *d* Silvio Narizzano *ph* Alex Thomson *m* Stanley Myers

Glenda Jackson, Oliver Reed, John Standing, Michael Murphy, Rosalind Cash

'Poorly mannered, simple minded, badly disciplined . . . gives social science a bad name.' – *Variety*

Class of 1999
US 1989 93m colour
Original Pictures (Mark L. Lester)
V, V*

Three android teachers, hired to bring discipline to a lawless high school, go haywire.

A sort of robot *Blackboard Jungle*, aimed at teenage audiences in love with violence.

w C. Courtney Joyner *story* Mark L. Lester *d* Mark L. Lester *ph* Mark Irwin *m* Michael Hoenig *pd* Steven Legler *ed* Scott Conrad

Bradley Gregg, Traci Lin, John P. Ryan, Pam Grier, Patrick Kilpatrick, Joshua Miller, Stacy Keach, Malcolm McDowell

Claudelle Inglish
US 1961 99m bw
Warner (Leonard Freeman)
GB title: *Young and Eager*

A poor farmer's daughter scorns a wealthy man for a succession of young studs.

Would-be sensational novelette from the author of *Tobacco Road*; it does not begin to be interesting.

w Leonard Freeman *novel* Erskine Caldwell *d* Gordon Douglas *ph* Ralph Woolsey *m* Howard Jackson

Diane McBain, Arthur Kennedy, Constance Ford, Chad Everett, Claude Akins, Will Hutchins, Robert Colbert, Ford Rainey, James Bell

Claudia **
US 1943 92m bw
TCF (William Perlberg)

A middle-class husband helps his child-wife to mature.

Typical of the best of Hollywood's 'woman's pictures' of the period, this is a pleasant domestic comedy-drama featuring recognizably human characters in an agreeable setting.

w Morrie Ryskind *novel and play* Rose Franken *d* Edmund Goulding *ph* Leon Shamroy *m* Alfred Newman

Dorothy McGuire (her film debut), *Robert Young, Ina Claire*, Reginald Gardiner, Olga Baclanova, Jean Howard, Elsa Janssen

'It won't leave a dry eye in the house.' – *Variety*

† Cary Grant was sought for the Robert Young part.

Claudia and David *
US 1946 78m bw
TCF (William Perlberg)

Claudia and her husband survive assorted crises including their son's illness and David's involvement in a car crash.

Patchwork sequel to *Claudia*, quite pleasant but obviously contrived quickly from scraps.

w Rose Franken, William Brown Meloney *d* Walter Lang *ph* Joseph LaShelle *m* Cyril Mockridge

Dorothy McGuire, Robert Young, Mary Astor, John Sutton, Gail Patrick, Florence Bates

Claudine
US 1974 92m DeLuxe
Fox-Rank/Third World Cinema/Joyce Selznick, Tina Pine (Hannah Weinstein)

A garbage collector falls for a poor woman with six kids.

Sugar-coated account, with romantic overtones, of life at the bottom in New York.

w Tina and Lester Pine *d* John Berry *ph* Gayne Rescher *m* Curtis Mayfield *pd* Ted Haworth *ed* Luis San Andres

Diahann Carroll, James Earl Jones, Lawrence Hilton-Jacobs, Tamu, David Kruger, Yvette Curtis, Eric Jones

'Substitute white actors for the black cast, tone down the fashionably outspoken situations a little, and it would be just like one of those perennial Disney movies about happy families and the difficulty of living and loving in this problematic world.' – *Tom Milne, MFB*

AAN: Diahann Carroll

The Clay Pigeon **
US 1949 63m bw
RKO (Herman Schlom)
V*

An amnesiac sailor finds himself courtmartialled for treason, but discovers the real culprit.

Tidily efficient second feature thriller; good enjoyable stuff of its kind.

w Carl Foreman *d* Richard Fleischer *ph* Robert de Grasse *m* Paul Sawtell

Bill Williams, Barbara Hale, Richard Quine, Richard Loo, Frank Fenton

Clean and Sober **
US 1988 124m Technicolor
Warner/Imagine Entertainment (Tony Ganz, Deborah Blum)
V, V*, L

An embezzler hides out in a rehabilitation clinic, refusing to admit to himself that he is an alcoholic and cocaine addict.

Unrelenting and powerful drama.

w Tod Carroll *d* Glenn Gordon Caron *ph* Jan Kiesser *m* Gabriel Yared *pd* Joel Schiller *ed* Richard Chew

Michael Keaton, Kathy Baker, Morgan Freeman, Tate Donovan, Henry Judd Baker, Claudia Christian, M. Emmet Walsh, Luca Bercovici

'I only wish there were some honest way of describing this movie that would make everyone go and see it.' – *Philip French, Observer*

Clean Slate: see *Coup de Torchon*

Cleo from Five to Seven *
France/Italy 1961 90m part colour
Rome/Paris (Bruno Drigo)

A girl waiting for the result of a medical examination wanders around Paris thinking she has cancer.

Impressively handled character sketch with gratifying attention to detail.

wd Agnès Varda *ph* Jean Rabier *m* Michel Legrand

Corinne Marchand, Antoine Bourseiller, Dorothée Blanck, Michel Legrand

'The love affair that shook the world!'
Cleopatra **
US 1934 101m bw
Paramount/Cecil B. de Mille
V*, L

After Julius Caesar's death, Cleopatra turns her attention to Mark Antony.

More of the vices than the virtues of its producer are notable in this fustian epic, which is almost but not quite unwatchable because of its stolid pace and miscasting. Some of the action montages and the barge scene, however, are superb cinema.

w Waldemar Young, Vincent Lawrence *d* Cecil B. de Mille *ph* Victor Milner *m* Rudolph Kopp *ed* Anne Bauchens

Claudette Colbert, Henry Wilcoxon (Antony), Warren William (Caesar), Gertrude Michael, Joseph Schildkraut, Ian Keith, C. Aubrey Smith, Leonard Mudie, Irving Pichel, Arthur Hohl

'He has certainly made the most sumptuous of Roman circuses out of Roman history . . . a constant succession of banquets, dancers, triumphs, and a fleet set on fire.' – *The Times*

'Gorgeous optically but mentally weak . . . a handpicked audience was polite but not over-enthusiastic.' – *Variety*

'A great cinematic achievement, a spectacle of breathtaking brilliance.' – *Daily Express*

'It is remarkable how Cecil B. de Mille can photograph so much on such a vast scale and still say nothing . . . it reeks of so much pseudo-artistry, vulgarity, philistinism, sadism, that it can only be compared with the lowest form of contemporary culture: Hitlerism. This is the type of "culture" that will be fed to the audience of Fascist America.' – *Irving Lerner, 1968*

AA: Victor Milner

AAN: best picture; Anne Bauchens

'The motion picture the world has been waiting for!'
Cleopatra
US 1963 243m DeLuxe Todd-AO
TCF (Walter Wanger)
V, V*, L

The unsurprising story is told at inordinate length and dullness in this ill-starred epic, one of the most heralded and mismanaged, in film history. (Its story is best told in the producer's *My Life with Cleopatra*.)

The most expensive film ever made, for various reasons which do not appear on the screen.

w Joseph L. Mankiewicz, Ranald MacDougall, Sidney Buchman, and others *d* Joseph L. Mankiewicz (and others) *ph* Leon Shamroy *m* Alex North *ad* John DeCuir, Jack Martin Smith, and others

Elizabeth Taylor, Richard Burton, Rex Harrison, Pamela Brown, George Cole, Hume Cronyn, Cesare Danova, Kenneth Haigh, Andrew Keir, Martin Landau, Roddy McDowall, Robert Stephens, Francesca Annis, Martin Benson, Herbert Berghof, Grégoire Aslan, Richard O'Sullivan

'Whatever was interesting about it clearly ended up somewhere else: on the cutting room floor, in various hotel rooms, in the newspaper columns . . . it lacks not only the intelligent spectacle of *Lawrence of Arabia* but the spectacular unintelligence of a Cecil B. de Mille product . . .' – *John Simon*

'The small screen does more than justice to this monumental mouse.' – *Judith Crist*

'I only came to see the asp.' – *Charles Addams*

'Surely the most bizarre piece of entertainment ever to be perpetrated.' – *Elizabeth Taylor*

AA: Leon Shamroy; John DeCuir and others; costumes (Irene Sharaff, Vittorio Nino Novarese, Renie); special visual effects (Emil Kosa Jnr)

AAN: best picture; Alex North; Rex Harrison

Cleopatra Jones
US   1973   89m   Technicolor   Panavision
Warner
V*

A black female CIA agent eliminates a ring of dope peddlers.

Grotesque comic strip fantasy with a high mortality rate.

w Max Julien, Sheldon Keller   d Jack Starrett

Tamara Dobson, Shelley Winters, Bernie Casey, Brenda Sykes

'It hampers the cause of racial entente more effectively than any work since *Uncle Tom's Cabin*.' – *John Baxter, MFB*

Cleopatra Jones and the Casino of Gold
US/Hong Kong   1975   96m   Technicolor
    Panavision
Warner/Shaw Bros (William Tennant, Run Run Shaw)
V*

A tough female government agent goes to Hong Kong to smash a drugs ring.

Feeble sequel lacking the brashness of the original, but equally tasteless.

w William Tennant   d Chuck Bail   ph Alan Hume   m Dominic Frontiere   ad Johnson Tsao   ed Willy Kemplen

Tamara Dobson, Stella Stevens, Tanny, Norman Fell, Albert Popwell

'The film is cut together quite incoherently, and Chuck Bail's barely competent direction seizes up completely when called upon now and then for some large-scale action set-piece.' – *Verina Glaessner, MFB*

'Hang On.'
Cliffhanger *
US   1993   112m   Technicolor
Carolco/Canal+/Pioneer/RCS Video (Alan Marshall, Renny Harlin)
V, V*, S

A mountain rescue expert turns the tables on violent gangsters who crash in the Rocky Mountains with suitcases stuffed with money.

Enjoyably silly action adventure, with some spectacular, edgy stunts, although it never touches reality at any point and has one of the more ludicrous lip-smacking villains this side of melodrama.

w Michael France, Sylvester Stallone   story Michael France, based on a premise by John Long   d Renny Harlin   ph Alex Thomson   m Trevor Jones   pd John Vallone   sp Neil Krepela, John Richardson, John Bruno, Pamela Easley   ed Frank J. Urioste

Sylvester Stallone, John Lithgow, Michael Rooker, Janine Turner, Rex Linn, Caroline Goodall, Leon, Craig Fairbrass, Gregory Scott Cummins, Paul Winfield, Ralph Waite

'Harlin displays perfect pitch, not just with the individual scenes of jaw-dropping stunt work, but in the way these episodes flow into each other with varying degrees of intensity.' – *Henry Sheehan, Sight and Sound*

'A two-hour roller-coaster ride that never stops from first minute to last. A high-octane action suspenser with thrilling vertiginous footage unlike anything seen before in a feature.' – *Variety*

AAN: sound; sound effects editing; visual effects

The Climax *
US   1944   86m   Technicolor
Universal (George Waggner)

A young opera singer is hypnotized by a mad doctor, who has kept his murdered mistress embalmed for ten years.

Gothic romantic melodrama invented to capitalize on the success – and the sets – of *Phantom of the Opera*. Curiously endearing, with a good eye-rolling part for Karloff.

w Curt Siodmak, Lynn Starling   play Edward Cochran   d George Waggner   ph Hal Mohr, W. Howard Greene   m Edward Ward   ad John B. Goodman, Alexander Golitzen

Boris Karloff, Susanna Foster, Gale Sondergaard, Turhan Bey, Thomas Gomez, Scotty Beckett

'All quite unalarming, which is a bit of a handicap.' – *New Yorker, 1978*

AAN: art direction

Climbing High *
GB   1938   78m   bw
Gaumont (Michael Balcon)

A rich man pretends to be a male model in order to win a girl.

Light-hearted romantic musical with interesting credits.

w Stephen Clarkson   story Lesser Samuels, Marian Dix   d Carol Reed   ph Mutz Greenbaum (Max Greene)   ad Alfred Junge   ed Michael Gordon

Jessie Matthews, Michael Redgrave, Noel Madison, Alastair Sim, Margaret Vyner, Mary Clare, Francis L. Sullivan

The Clinging Vine *
US   1926   71m (24 fps)   bw   silent
Cecil B. de Mille

The president's secretary is the real driving force of a paint company, but finds that love is more important than business.

Interesting silent predecessor of many career girl comedies of the thirties and forties.

w Jeannie McPherson   d Paul Sloane

Leatrice Joy, Tom Moore, Toby Claude, Robert Edeson

'People are going to **** whether you like it or not – and this place is here to see that they enjoy it!'
The Clinic *
Australia   1982   92m   colour
Film House/Generation Films (Bob Weis, Robert le Tet)
V*

One day in the life of a clinic for venereal diseases.

Slightly dishevelled comedy-drama which will be generally remembered as a very naughty carry-on.

w Greg Millen   d David Stevens

Chris Haywood, Simon Burke, Gerda Nicolson, Rona McLeod, Suzanne Roylance

'Six words from a woman changed the map of Asia!'
Clive of India *
US   1934   90m   bw
Twentieth Century (Darryl F. Zanuck, William Goetz, Raymond Griffith)

The life of the 18th-century empire builder, with special emphasis on his marriage.

A very tame and now faded epic, with more romance than adventure. The production relies more on stars than technique, but it works.

w W. P. Lipscomb, R. J. Minney   play W. P. Lipscomb, R. J. Minney   d Richard Boleslawski   ph Peverell Marley   m Alfred Newman

Ronald Colman, Loretta Young, Colin Clive, Francis Lister, Montagu Love, Robert Greig, Leo G. Carroll, C. Aubrey Smith, Mischa Auer

'It may be spoken of as another of the best British pictures made in Hollywood . . . Should be strong b.o.' – *Variety*

'Patriotic pageantry, undistorted by facts.' – *J. R. Parish*

AAN: art direction

'The moment he fell in love was his moment of greatest danger!'
Cloak and Dagger *
US   1946   106m   bw
United States Pictures (Milton Sperling)
V*, L

A physics professor joins the secret service and is parachuted into Germany to interview a kidnapped scientist.

Supposedly authoritative espionage adventure which turned out dull and humourless; plot routine, direction absent-minded.

w Albert Maltz, Ring Lardner Jnr   d Fritz Lang   ph Sol Polito   m Max Steiner

Gary Cooper, Lilli Palmer, Robert Alda, Vladimir Sokoloff, J. Edward Bromberg, Ludwig Stossel, Helene Thimig, Marc Lawrence

'Just a B plot dressed up in A trimmings.' – *Newsweek*

Clochemerle
France   1948   93m   bw
Cinéma Productions (Ralph Baum)

The progressive mayor of a French village erects a gentlemen's convenience in the main street and shocks the local reactionaries.

Most of the book's political satire was ironed out in this cheap and opportunist production which got a few easy laughs but failed to sustain itself.

w Gabriel Chevalier   novel Gabriel Chevalier   d Pierre Chénal   ph Robert Le Fèbvre   m Henri Sauguet

Brochard, Maximilienne, Simone Michels, Jane Marken, Paul Demange, Felix Oudart, Saturnin Fabre

The Clock **
US   1945   90m   bw
MGM (Arthur Freed)
V*, L
GB title: *Under the Clock*

A girl meets a soldier at New York's Grand Central Station and marries him during his 24-hour leave.

Everyone now seems far too nice in this winsome romance full of comedy cameos and convincing New York locations, but if you can relive the wartime mood it still works as a corrective to the Betty Grable glamour pieces.

w Robert Nathan, Joseph Schrank   story Paul and Pauline Gallico   d Vincente Minnelli   ph George Folsey   m George Bassman

Judy Garland, Robert Walker, James Gleason, Lucille Gleason, Keenan Wynn, Marshall Thompson, Chester Clute

'Sweetly charming, if maybe too irresistible . . . fortunately the director fills the edges with comic characters.' – *New Yorker, 1978*

'The emotion may have been honest, but the method was too rich for my eyes, and the writing as used on the screen too weak for my mind.' – *Stephen Longstreet*

'Strictly a romance . . . safely told, disappointing and angering in the thought of the great film it might have been.' – *James Agee*

'Amazingly, it was all shot in the studio, using street sets and back projection; even the old Penn Station, where so much of the action takes place, is a set.' – *Pauline Kael, 70s*

Clockwise *
GB 1986 97m Technicolor
EMI/Moment (Michael Codron)
V, V*, L

A headmaster on his way to a conference is delayed by circumstance.

What was intended as an escalating climax of comic chaos falls away as the script runs out of steam, but the nation's need for comedy ensured box-office success.

w Michael Frayn d Christopher Morahan
ph John Coquillon m George Fenton pd Roger
Murray-Leach ed Peter Boyle

John Cleese, Alison Steadman, Penelope Wilton, Stephen Moore, Joan Hickson, Charon Maiden

'Being the adventures of a young man whose principal interests are rape, ultra-violence, and Beethoven!'

A Clockwork Orange *
GB 1971 136m colour
Warner/Polaris (Bernard Williams)
V*, L, S

In a future Britain of desolation and violence, a young gangster guilty of rape and murder obtains a release from prison after being experimentally brainwashed; he finds society more violent than it was in his time.

A repulsive film in which intellectuals have found acres of social and political meaning; the average judgement is likely to remain that it is pretentious and nasty rubbish for sick minds who do not mind jazzed-up images and incoherent sound.

wd Stanley Kubrick novel Anthony Burgess
ph John Alcott m Walter Carlos pd John Barry

Malcolm McDowell, Michael Bates, Adrienne Corri, Patrick Magee, Warren Clarke

'Very early there are hints of triteness and insecurity, and before half an hour is over it begins to slip into tedium . . . Inexplicably the script leaves out Burgess' reference to the title.' – *Stanley Kauffmann*

'It might be the work of a strict and exacting German professor who set out to make a porno violent sci-fi comedy.' – *New Yorker, 1980*

'Kubrick handles his medium with a confidence almost insolent. For the rest – the flashes of farce, the variations on distance and distortion and dream-imagery – he has given us the most audacious of horror-films. And the most inhuman.' – *Dilys Powell*

AAN: best picture; Stanley Kubrick (as writer and director)

'We are not alone . . .'

Close Encounters of the Third Kind *
US 1977 135m Metrocolor Panavision
Columbia/EMI (Julia and Michael Phillips)
V, V (W), V*, L, S

A series of UFOs takes Indiana by surprise, and a workman is led by intuition and detection to the landing site which has been concealed from the public.

There's a lot of padding in this slender fantasy, which has less plot and much less suspense than *It Came from Outer Space* which was made on a tiny budget in 1955; but the technical effects are masterly though their

exposure is over-prolonged, and the benevolent mysticism filled a current requirement of popular taste, accounting for the enormous box-office success of a basically flawed film. Much of the dialogue is inaudible.

wd Steven Spielberg ph Vilmos Zsigmond
m John Williams sp Douglas Trumbull pd Joe
Alves

Richard Dreyfuss, François Truffaut, Teri Garr, Melinda Dillon, Cary Guffey

'It somehow combines Disney and 1950s SF and junk food into the most persuasive (if arrested) version of the American dream yet.' – *Time Out*

'It has visionary magic and a childlike comic spirit, along with a love of surprises and a skeptical, let's-try-it-on spirit.' – *New Yorker*

† The cost of this film was estimated at 20,000,000 dollars.

† In 1980 a 'special edition' (V, L) was released with some success: this pared down the idiotic middle section and extended the final scenes of the space ship, including some new interiors.
†† This film used the largest set in film history: the inside of an old dirigible hangar. Of the special edition, Derek Malcolm in the *Guardian* wrote: 'One is inclined to feel that with all the money at his disposal, Spielberg might have got it right the first time.'

AA: Vilmos Zsigmond

AAN: direction; John Williams; Melinda Dillon; visual effects (Douglas Trumbull and others)

Close My Eyes
GB 1991 108m colour
Artificial Eye/Beambright/Film Four (Thérèse Pickard)
V, V (W), V*

A long-separated brother and sister meet and fall in love.

Hysterical and dull, peopled by fashionable but inert characters given to boring introspection.

wd Stephen Poliakoff ph Witold Stok m Michael
Gibbs pd Luciana Arrighi ed Michael Parkinson

Alan Rickman, Saskia Reeves, Clive Owen, Karl Johnson, Lesley Sharp, Kate Gartside, Karen Knight, Niall Buggy

'Should have a solid career ahead of it and is a major plus for all concerned.' – *Variety*

'Drags itself across the screen. After much huffing and puffing, the script refuses to become the sum of its many, many scholarly observations about life, love, the universe. The lack of feeling is fatal.' – *John Lyttle, Independent*

Close to Eden (1991): see *Urga*

Close to Eden
US 1992 111m colour
Rank/Propaganda/Sandollar/Isis (Steve Golin, Sigurjon
Sighvatsson, Howard Rosenman)

A female cop infiltrates the Hasidic community in New York to track down a murderer.

An odd and unconvincing thriller, ignoring the narrative for much of the time as it becomes almost a promotional film on behalf of the Hasidim.

w Robert J. Avrech d Sidney Lumet ph Andrzej
Bartowiak m Jerry Bock pd Philip Rosenberg
ed Andrew Mondshein

Melanie Griffith, Eric Thal, John Pankow, Tracy Pollan, Lee Richardson, Mia Sara, Jamey Sheridan, Jake Weber

'With its *Fiddler on the Roof* score and some sneakily hypocritical espousing of deeply conservative religious values, this is little more than a 111-minute love letter to Sidney Lumet's rabbi.' – *Kim Newman, Empire*

Close to My Heart
US 1951 90m bw
Warner (William Jacobs)

An adopted baby is discovered to have a murderer for a father; but environment is proved to be more important than heredity.

Routine sentimental drama.

wd William Keighley story *A Baby for Midge* by
James R. Webb ph Robert Burks m Max Steiner

Ray Milland, Gene Tierney, Fay Bainter, Howard St John, Mary Beth Hughes

Closely Observed Trains **
Czechoslovakia 1966 92m bw
Ceskoslovensky Film (Zdenek Oves)
V

During World War II, an apprentice railway guard at a country station falls in love and becomes a saboteur.

Warm, amusingly detailed comedy with a disconcerting downbeat ending.

wd Jiri Menzel novel Bohumil Hrabal ph Jaromir
Sofr m Jiri Pavlik

Vaclav Neckar, Jitka Bendova, Vladimir Valenta, Josef Somr

'Like Forman, Menzel seems incapable of being unkind to anybody.' – *Tom Milne*

'The director has made extraordinarily effective use of the solitude which the characters share.' – *Dilys Powell*

AA: best foreign film

Cloud Dancer
US 1977 108m colour
Melvin Simon
V*

Episodes in the life of a stunt flyer.

Technically proficient, loosely assembled amble through the problems of a man with an obsession for danger; not a great crowd-puller.

w William Goodhart d Barry Brown

David Carradine, Jennifer O'Neill, Joseph Bottoms, Albert Salmi, Salome Jens, Colleen Camp

Cloudburst
GB 1951 92m bw
Hammer

A vengeful code expert goes after the criminals who ran down his wife in making a getaway.

Watchable potboiler.

w Leo Marks d Francis Searle

Robert Preston, Elizabeth Sellars, Colin Tapley, Sheila Burrell, Harold Lang

The Clouded Yellow *
GB 1950 96m bw
Sydney Box/Carillon (Betty Box)

A sacked secret service agent gets work tending a butterfly collection and finds that this involves him in a murder plot.

Implausible but quite engaging thriller in the Hitchcock style, involving a chase across the Lake District.

w Janet Green, Eric Ambler d Ralph Thomas
ph Geoffrey Unsworth

Trevor Howard, Jean Simmons, Barry Jones, Sonia Dresdel, Maxwell Reed, Kenneth More, André Morell

Clouds Over Europe: see *Q Planes*

The Clown
US 1952 91m bw
MGM (William H. Wright)

A drunken clown, once a great star, is idolized by his son who believes in a comeback.

Maudlin reworking of *The Champ* (qv), with not a surprise in the plot and a star way over the top.

w Martin Rackin   *d* Robert Z. Leonard   *ph* Paul C. Vogel   *m* David Rose

Red Skelton, Jane Greer, Tim Considine, Loring Smith, Philip Ober

A Clown Must Laugh: see *Pagliacci*

The Club **
Australia   1980   90m   colour   Panavision
South Australia Film Corp/New South Wales Film Corp (Matt Carroll)
V*
aka: *Players*

The arrival of an expensive, university-educated player precipitates a crisis among management and players at a football club.

Incisive, excellently acted drama of boardroom manoeuvres and conflicting loyalties.

w David Williamson   *play* David Williamson   *d* Bruce Beresford   *ph* Don McAlpine   *pd* David Copping   *ed* William Anderson

Jack Thompson, Harold Hopkins, Graham Kennedy, John Howard, Frank Wilson, Alan Cassell

Club Havana
US   1946   62m   bw
PRC

Several stories come to a head in a night-club.

Slight musical multi-drama with moments of interest.

w Raymond L. Schrock, Fred Jackson   *d* Edgar G. Ulmer

Tom Neal, Margaret Lindsay, Don Douglas, Isabelita, Ernest Truex, Renee Riano, Paul Cavanagh, Marc Lawrence

Club Paradise
US   1986   104m   Technicolor
Warner (Michael Shamberg)
V, V*, L

A Chicago fireman retires to a Caribbean island to manage a rundown club.

Dismal waste of talent.

w Harold Ramis, Brian Doyle-Murray   *story* Ed Roboto, Tom Leopold, Chris Miller, David Standish   *d* Harold Ramis   *ph* Peter Hannan   *m* David Mansfield, Van Dyke Parks   *pd* John Graysmark   *ed* Marion Rothman

Robin Williams, Peter O'Toole, Rick Moranis, Jimmy Cliff, Twiggy, Adolph Caesar, Eugene Levy, Joanna Cassidy

'Like one of those giddy, casual farces that Paramount turned out in the thirties . . . Those pictures often got terrible reviews but kept audiences giggling cheerfully.' – *Pauline Kael, New Yorker*

Clue
US   1985   87m   Metrocolor
Paramount/Guber-Peters/Debra Hill/Polygram
V*, L

A murder game becomes reality.

A rather arch attempt to film an internationally popular board game; those not in on the joke may tend to restlessness.

wd Jonathan Lynn   *ph* Victor J. Kemper   *m* John Morris   *pd* John Lloyd

Eileen Brennan, Tim Curry, Madeline Kahn, Christopher Lloyd, Michael McKean, Lesley Ann Warren

'Enough wit, neuroses and motive to intrigue even the most inept whodunnit solver.' – *Variety*

† Three alternative solutions were originally provided.

Cluny Brown **
US   1946   100m   bw
TCF (Ernst Lubitsch)

A plumber's niece goes into service and falls for a Czech refugee guest.

Romantic comedy in a never-never pre-war England; it does no more than poke casual fun at upper-class conventions, but the smooth direction and some excellent character comedy keep it well afloat.

w Samuel Hoffenstein, Elizabeth Reinhardt   *novel* Margery Sharp   *d* Ernst Lubitsch   *ph* Joseph LaShelle   *m* Cyril Mockridge, Emil Newman

Jennifer Jones, Charles Boyer, *Richard Haydn, Una O'Connor*, Peter Lawford, Helen Walker, Reginald Gardiner, Reginald Owen, C. Aubrey Smith, Sara Allgood, Ernest Cossart, Florence Bates, Billy Bevan

'A lovely, easygoing comedy, full of small surprising touches.' – *Pauline Kael, 70s*

The Clutching Hand *
US   1936   bw   serial: 15 eps
Stage and Screen

A scientist with a formula for synthetic gold is kidnapped, and rescue attempts are hampered by a sinister shadowy figure.

Archetypal spooky house serial.

d Albert Herman

Jack Mulhall, Marion Shilling, Yakima Canutt, Reed Howes, William Farnum

Coal Miner's Daughter *
US   1980   124m   Technicolor
Universal (Bob Larson)
V*, L

The wife of a Kentucky hillbilly becomes a pop star.

'With-it' version of the old show business story: gradual success, stardom, nervous breakdown, reconciliation. Based on the life of Loretta Lynn, but mainly notable for its depiction of backwoods Kentucky.

w Tom Rickman   *d* Michael Apted   *ph* Ralf D. Bode   *md* Owen Bradley   *pd* John W. Corso

Sissy Spacek, Tommy Lee Jones, Levon Helm, Jennifer Beasley, Phyllis Boyens

AA: Sissy Spacek

AAN: best film; Tom Rickman; Ralf D. Bode; editing (Arthur Schmidt); art direction (John W. Corso, John M. Dwyer)

Coast to Coast
US   1980   94m   Movielab
Paramount (Terry Carr)

A Los Angeles wife flees her husband and hitches a lift from a truck driver with problems.

Comedy for easy watching: pleasant characters are given very little of interest to do.

w Stanley Weiser   *d* Joseph Sargent   *ph* Joel King   *m* Charles Bernstein

Dyan Cannon, Robert Blake, Quinn Redeker, Michael Lerner, Bill Lucking, Maxine Stuart

Cobra
US   1925   85m approx   bw   silent
Ritz-Carlton

An impoverished Italian nobleman collects women as a hobby.

The star's first independent production won no plaudits and was thought to be a mistake conceived by his wife Natacha Rambova, who appeared in a dance act with him.

w Anthony Coldeway   *d* Joseph Henabery

Rudolph Valentino, Nita Naldi, Casson Ferguson, Gertrude Olmstead, Hector V. Sarno

Cobra
US   1986   87m   Technicolor
Warner/Cannon (James D. Brubaker)
V, V*, L, S

A tough LA cop tracks down a serial killer.

Relentless but unsurprising carbon of *Dirty Harry*, a bit too tough for its own good.

w Sylvester Stallone   *novel* Fair Game by Paula Gosling   *d* George Pan Cosmatos   *ph* Ric Waite   *m* Sylvester Levay   *pd* Bill Kenney   *ed* Don Zimmerman, James Symons

Sylvester Stallone, Brigitte Nielsen, Reni Santoni, Andrew Robinson

† 2,131 prints were made for the launch.

Cobra Verde
West Germany   1988   111m   colour
Palace/Concorde/Werner Herzog Film Production/ZDF/Ghana Film Industry Corp (Luigi Stipetic)
V, S

A Brazilian peasant-turned-bandit goes to West Africa to revive the slave trade.

Disjointed, episodic and uninteresting.

w Werner Herzog   *novel* The Viceroy of Ouidah by Bruce Chatwin   *d* Werner Herzog   *ph* Viktor Ruzicka   *m* Popol Vuh   *pd* Ulrich Bergfelder   *ed* Maximiliane Mainka

Klaus Kinski, King Ampaw, Jose Lewgoy, Salvatore Basile

Cobra Woman
US   1944   71m   Technicolor
U-I (George Waggner)

A South Seas girl is abducted by snake worshippers ruled by her evil twin.

A monument of undiluted hokum with some amusing sets and performances but not enough self-mockery in the script.

w Richard Brooks, Gene Lewis   *d* Robert Siodmak   *ph* George Robinson, W. Howard Greene   *m* Edward Ward

Maria Montez, Jon Hall, Sabu, Lon Chaney Jnr, Mary Nash, Edgar Barrier, Lois Collier, Samuel S. Hinds, Moroni Olsen

'Among the exotic treats: a rumbling volcano, a pet chimp, ominous gong sounds, forest glade love scenes, human sacrifices, handmaidens in high-heeled pumps, Tollea's imperious writhing during a demonic dance, and the good Nadja's plea for the symbol of the power that is rightly hers: "Gif me the cobra jool."' – *Pauline Kael, 70s*

The Cobweb
US   1955   124m   Eastmancolor   Cinemascope
MGM (John Houseman)
L

Tensions among the staff of a private mental clinic reach a new high over the purchase of curtains.

The patients seem saner than the doctors in this strained and verbose character drama which despite its cast and big studio look never begins to engage the interest.

w John Paxton   *novel* William Gibson   *d* Vincente Minnelli   *ph* George Folsey   *m* Leonard Rosenman

Richard Widmark, Lauren Bacall, Charles Boyer, *Lillian Gish*, Gloria Grahame, John Kerr, Susan Strasberg, *Oscar Levant*, Tommy Rettig, Paul Stewart, Adèle Jergens

'An overwrought and elaborately artificial exercise, made scarcely more plausible by reliance on the basic jargon of psychiatry.' – *Penelope Houston*

'By the mid-50s, nobody was surprised that the new variant on *Grand Hotel* was an expensive, exclusive loony bin.' – *Pauline Kael, 70s*

The Coca Cola Kid

Australia 1985 94m Eastmancolor
Palace/Cinema Enterprises/Film Gallery/Columbia (David Roe)
V*, L

A Coca Cola rep is sent to Australia to combat a
remote land baron who brews and distributes his
own brand.

Flaccid drama with an eventually mystifying
superabundance of style.

w Frank Moorhouse d Dusan Makavejev
ph Dean Semler m William Motzing pd Graham
(Grace) Walker ed John Scott

Eric Roberts, Greta Scacchi, Bill Kerr, Max Gillies,
Kris McQuade

Cockeyed Cavaliers

US 1934 72m bw
RKO
V*

Two idiots have various adventures in medieval
England.

Fairly tolerable slapstick from a team which never
seemed quite at its best.

w Edward Kaufman, Ben Holmes d Mark Sandrich

Bert Wheeler, Robert Woolsey, Thelma Todd, Noah
Beery, Dorothy Lee, Franklin Pangborn, Robert Greig

'With a fair quota of laughs, it eclipses their previous
releases.' – Variety

The Cockeyed Cowboys of Calico County

US 1969 99m Technicolor
Universal

A Western blacksmith stops working when his mail
order bride doesn't arrive.

Styleless American rehash of La Femme du Boulanger,
with all concerned trying too hard.

w Ranald MacDougall d Tony Leader

Dan Blocker, Nanette Fabray, Mickey Rooney

The Cockeyed Miracle

US 1946 92m bw
MGM
GB title: Mr Griggs Returns

Family ghosts return to sort out domestic chaos.

Moderate 'Topper'-style comedy with amiable cast.

w Karen de Wolf play George Seaton d S. Sylvan
Simon

Frank Morgan, Cecil Kellaway, Gladys Cooper,
Audrey Totter, Marshall Thompson, Leon Ames

The Cockeyed World *

US 1929 115m bw
Fox

Further adventures of Sergeants Flagg and Quirt, the
boisterous heroes of What Price Glory.

Lively early talkie; the adventure comedy remains
interesting, though the technique is badly faded.

w William K. Wells, Laurence Stallings, Maxwell
Anderson, Wilson Mizner, Tom Barry d Raoul
Walsh ph Arthur Edeson

Victor McLaglen, Edmund Lowe, Lili Damita, Lelia
Karnelly, El Brendel, Bobby Burns, Stuart Erwin

Cockfighter

US 1974 83m Metrocolor
Rio Pinto/New World/Artists Entertainment Complex (Roger
Corman)
V*
aka: Born to Kill

A professional cockfighter ends a run of bad luck but
loses his girl.

Not badly made but rather seedy film about appalling
people.

w Charles Willeford novel Charles Willeford
d Monte Hellman ph Nestor Almendros
m Michael Franks

Warren Oates, Richard B. Shull, Harry Dean Stanton,
Ed Begley Jnr, Laurie Bird, Troy Donahue

Cockleshell Heroes

GB 1955 97m Technicolor Cinemascope
Columbia/Warwick (Phil C. Samuel)
V

During World War II, ten marines are trained to travel
by canoe into Bordeaux harbour and attach limpet
mines to German ships.

Absolutely predictable semi-documentary war
heroics, with barrack-room humour turning
eventually into tragedy. The familiar elements,
including a display of stiff upper lips, ensured box-
office success.

w Bryan Forbes, Richard Maibaum d José Ferrer
ph John Wilcox, Ted Moore m John Addison

José Ferrer, Trevor Howard, Dora Bryan, Victor
Maddern, Anthony Newley, Peter Arne, David Lodge,
Walter Fitzgerald, Beatrice Campbell

Cocktail

US 1988 103m Metrocolor
Warner/Touchstone/Silver Screen Partners III/Interscope
Communications (Ted Field, Robert W. Cort)
V, V*, L, S

A young man becomes a bartender in the belief he
will meet rich and beautiful women.

Glossy nonsense.

w Heywood Gould novel Heywood Gould
d Roger Donaldson ph Dean Semler m Peter
Robinson pd Mel Bourne ad Dan Davis ed Neil
Travis, Barbara Dunning

Tom Cruise, Bryan Brown, Elisabeth Shue, Lisa
Banes, Laurence Luckinbill, Kelly Lynch, Gina
Gershon, Ron Dean

Cocoanut Grove

US 1938 85m bw
Paramount (George Arthur)

A band is fired from an excursion boat but makes it
big in a Los Angeles night-club.

Vacuous comedy musical with a watchable number or
two.

w Sy Bartlett, Olive Cooper d Alfred Santell
ph Leo Tover m/y various

Fred MacMurray, Harriet Hilliard, The Yacht Club
Boys, Ben Blue, Eve Arden, Billy Lee, Rufe Davis

'No mind-wearier as to plot, it shapes up as nice
summer film fare.' – Variety

The Cocoanuts **

US 1929 96m bw
Paramount (Walter Wanger, James R. Cowan)
V*, L

A chiselling hotel manager tries to get in on the
Florida land boom.

Considering its age and the dismal prints which
remain, this is a remarkably lively if primitive first
film by the Marxes, with some good routines among
the excess footage.

w George S. Kaufman, Morrie Ryskind d Robert Florey,
Joseph Santley ph George Folsey m/y Irving
Berlin

The Four Marx Brothers, Margaret Dumont, Oscar Shaw,
Mary Eaton, Kay Francis, Basil Ruysdael

'The camerawork showed all the mobility of a
concrete fire hydrant caught in a winter freeze.' – Paul
D. Zimmermann

Cocoon **

US 1985 117m DeLuxe
TCF/Zanuck-Brown (Lili Zanuck)
V, V*, L, S

Aliens from another galaxy leave pods in the pool of a
Florida retirement home, whose bathers are
rejuvenated.

Unusual, amusing and sentimentally effective movie
of the kind which gets hearty word-of-mouth
recommendation.

w Tom Benedek novel David Saperstein d Ron
Howard ph Don Peterman m James Horner
pd Jack T. Collis ed Daniel Hanley, Michael J. Hill

Don Ameche, Wilford Brimley, Hume Cronyn, Brian
Dennehy, Jack Gilford, Steve Guttenberg, Maureen
Stapleton, Jessica Tandy, Gwen Verdon

'A mesmerizing tale that's a certified audience
pleaser.' – Variety

AA: best supporting actor, Don Ameche

Cocoon: The Return

US 1988 116m DeLuxe
Fox/Richard D. Zanuck, David Brown, Lili Fini Zanuck
V, V*, L, S

After a visit to another planet, three rejuvenated
elderly couples return to Earth to rescue alien pods.

Lacklustre sequel, a concept in search of a script.

w Stephen McPherson story Stephen McPherson,
Elizabeth Bradley d Daniel Petrie ph Tak
Fujimoto m James Horner pd Lawrence Paull
ed Mark Warner

Don Ameche, Wilford Brimley, Courtenay Cox, Hume
Cronyn, Jack Gilford, Steve Guttenberg, Barret
Oliver, Maureen Stapleton, Elaine Stritch, Jessica
Tandy, Gwen Verdon, Tahnee Welch

'Extraordinarily scrappy.' – MFB

Code Name: Emerald

US 1985 93m Metrocolor
NBC/MGM-UA
V*, L

A double agent is sent to Paris in 1944 to make sure
that a captured American officer doesn't talk about the
D-Day plans.

Plodding, old hat war melodrama with no specific
virtues.

w Ronald Bass novel The Emerald Illusion by Ronald
Bass d Jonathan Sanger

Ed Harris, Max von Sydow, Horst Buchholz, Helmut
Berger, Graham Crowden

Code of Scotland Yard: see The Shop at Sly Corner

Code of Silence

US 1985 101m AstroColor
Rank/Orion (Raymond Wagner)
V, V*, L

A Chicago cop raids a drug den and sets off a gang
war.

Routine tough stuff which just about avoids self-
parody.

w Michael Butler, Dennis Shryack, Mike Gray
d Andy Davis ph Frank Tidy m David Frank
pd Maher Ahmed ed Peter Parasheles, Christopher
Holmes

Chuck Norris, Henry Silva, Bert Remsen, Molly
Hagan

Code of the Secret Service

US 1939 58m bw
Warner

Agents track a gang who stole treasury banknote
plates.

Serial-like adventures, one of several from the same
stable, all featuring the future president of the US.

w Lee Katz, Dean Franklin d Noel Smith

Ronald Reagan, Eddie Foy Jnr, Rosella Towne, Moroni Olsen, Edgar Edwards

'Filler fodder; a wild actioner for lower dual bookings.' – *Variety*

Code Two
US 1953 69m bw
MGM

Three young men join the police academy.

Predictable second biller.

w Marcel Klauber d Fred M. Wilcox
Ralph Meeker, Sally Forrest, Keenan Wynn, James Craig, Robert Horton, Elaine Stewart, Jeff Richards

Codename Wild Geese
Italy 1984 101m colour
Entertainment/Ascot/Gico Cinematografica (Erwin C. Dietrich)
V, V*

Mercenaries are sent to destroy heavily guarded opium depots in Thailand.

Brisk but undistinguished action movie, with a large cast of expendable Orientals.

w Michael Lester d Anthony M. Dawson (Antonio Margheriti) ph Peter Baumgartner m Jan Nemec

Lewis Collins, Lee Van Cleef, Ernest Borgnine, Klaus Kinski, Manfred Lehmann, Mimsy Farmer, Thomas Dannenberg, Wolfgang Pampel, Harmut Neugubauer

Cody of the Pony Express
US 1950 bw serial: 15 eps
Columbia

An express rider exposes an apparently respectable attorney as an outlaw leader.

Pretty fair Western serial. d Spencer Bennet

Jock O'Mahoney, Dickie Moore, Peggy Stewart, William Fawcett, George J. Lewis

Un Coeur en Hiver *
France 1991 104m colour
Artificial Eye/Film Par Film/Cinea/Orly/Sedif/Paravision/DA Films/FR 3 (Jean-Louis Livi, Philippe Carcassonne)
V
aka: *A Heart in Winter*

A young violinist, about to leave the home of her female manager to live with a violin maker, falls in love with his friend and partner.

A familiar story, impeccably acted but failing to touch the emotions, possibly because of its distanced direction and the rigid, symphonic structure which restricts its humanity.

w Claude Sautet, Jacques Fieschi, Jérôme Tonnerre d Claude Sautet ph Yves Angelo m Philippe Sarde ad Christian Marti ed Jacqueline Thiedot

Daniel Auteuil, Emmanuelle Béart, André Dussollier, Elisabeth Bourgine, Brigitte Catillon, Maurice Garrel

'Extremely subtle and intensely enjoyable, impressive pic deserves international art house attention.' – *Variety*

Cohen and Tate
US 1988 86m DeLuxe
Guild/Nelson Films (Antony Rufus Isaacs, Jeff Young)
V, V*, L

Two hit men kidnap a boy who witnessed a gangland murder.

A thriller lacking suspense.

wd Eric Red ph Victor J. Kemper pd David M. Haber ed Edward Abroms

Roy Scheider, Adam Baldwin, Harley Cross, Cooper Huckabee, Suzanne Savoy, Marco Perella, Tom Campitelli, Andrew R. Gill

The Cohens and the Kellys
Seven comedies were made, all for Universal, about the friendly rivalry of Jewish and Irish neighbours. They were:

1926: THE COHENS AND KELLYS
1928: THE COHENS AND KELLYS IN PARIS
1929: THE COHENS AND KELLYS IN ATLANTIC CITY
1930: THE COHENS AND KELLYS IN SCOTLAND
1931: THE COHENS AND KELLYS IN AFRICA
1932: THE COHENS AND KELLYS IN HOLLYWOOD
1933: THE COHENS AND KELLYS IN TROUBLE

George Sidney played Cohen in all of the series and Charlie Murray played Kelly in five films. He was replaced by J. Farrell MacDonald in *Paris* and by Mack Swain in *Atlantic City*.

Coiffeur pour Dames
France 1952 87m approx bw
Hoche (Jean Boyer)
GB title: *An Artist with Ladies*

A Provençal sheep shearer becomes a fashionable ladies' hairdresser with a Champs-Élysées salon, and finds that his clients are all susceptible to his charms.

Obvious star comedy with a fair measure of laughs; more in fact than the much later *Shampoo*.

w Serge Véber, Jean Boyer play P. Armont, M. Gerbidon d Jean Boyer ph Charles Suin m Paul Misraki

Fernandel, Blanchette Crunoy, Renée Devillers, Arlette Poirier

Cold Comfort
Canada 1989 88m colour
Norstar/Telefilm (Lana Frank, Ray Sager)

A snowbound motorist is kidnapped by an unbalanced truck driver as a birthday present for his 18-year-old daughter.

Claustrophobic thriller that lacks suspense.

w Richard Beattie, Elliot L. Sims play James Garrard d Vic Sarin ph Vic Sarin m Jeff Dana ad Jo-Ann Chorney ed Nick Rotundo

Maury Chaykin, Margaret Langrick, Paul Gross

Cold Cuts: see *Buffet Froid*

Cold Dog Soup
US 1989 88m Technicolor
Palace/HandMade/Aspen (Richard G. Abramson, William E. McEuen)
V

Given a dead dog to bury by his new girlfriend, a man attempts to sell it to a furrier and a Chinese restaurateur.

Dismal attempt at a black comedy.

w Thomas Pope book Stephen Dobyns d Alan Metter ph Frederick Elmes m Michael Kamen, Mark Snow pd David L. Snyder ed Kaja Fehr

Randy Quaid, Frank Whaley, Christine Harnos, Sheree North, Nancy Kwan

'Miserably unwatchable.' – *MFB*

Cold Feet *
US 1989 94m colour
Virgin/Avenue Pictures (Cassian Elwes)
V*, L, S

Three petty crooks fall out after smuggling emeralds into America inside a horse.

Amusingly ramshackle semi-Western.

w Thomas McGuane, Jim Harrison d Robert Dornheim ph Brian Duggan m Tom Bahler pd Bernt Capra

Keith Carradine, Sally Kirkland, Tom Waits, Bill Pullman, Rip Torn, Kathleen York, Macon McCalman

Cold Sweat
Italy/France 1974 94m colour
Emerson
V*
aka: *The Man With Two Shadows*

An American living peaceably on the Riviera is forced into drug smuggling.

Reliable tough stuff for those who like that sort of thing.

w Shimon Wincelberg, Albert Simonin novel *Ride the Nightmare* by Richard Matheson d Terence Young

Charles Bronson, James Mason, Liv Ullmann, Jill Ireland, Jean Topart

Cold Turkey *
US 1970 102m DeLuxe
UA/Tandem/DFI (Bud Yorkin, Norman Lear)
V*

A tobacco company offers 25 million dollars to any town which can give up smoking for thirty days.

Rather wild and strained but sporadically amusing satirical comedy, aggressively littered with unpleasant detail.

w Norman Lear novel *I'm Giving Them Up for Good* by Margaret and Neil Rau d Norman Lear ph Charles F. Wheeler m Randy Newman

Dick Van Dyke, Pippa Scott, Tom Poston, Edward Everett Horton, Bob Newhart, Vincent Gardenia, Jean Stapleton

'An eager desire to debunk and shock at the same time.' – *David McGillivray*

A Cold Wind in August *
US 1960 77m bw
UA/Troy Films (Robert L. Ross, Philip Hazleton)

An ageing stripper seduces a 17-year-old janitor but the affair ends when he sees her do her act.

Roughly-made, well-acted sex drama which at the time seemed mildly shocking but can only survive for its central acting performance.

w Burton Wohl novel Burton Wohl d Alexander Singer ph Floyd Crosby m Gerald Fried

Lola Albright, Scott Marlowe, Joe de Santis, Herschel Bernardi

The Colditz Story **
GB 1954 97m bw
British Lion/Ivan Foxwell
V

Adventures of British POWs in the German maximum security prison in Saxony's Colditz Castle during World War II.

Probably the most convincing of the British accounts of POW life, with a careful balance of tragedy and comedy against a background of humdrum, boring daily existence. A TV series followed in 1972.

w Guy Hamilton, Ivan Foxwell book P. R. Reid d Guy Hamilton ph Gordon Dines m Francis Chagrin

John Mills, Eric Portman, Christopher Rhodes, Lionel Jeffries, Bryan Forbes, Ian Carmichael, Richard Wattis, Frederick Valk, Anton Diffring, Eugene Deckers, Theodore Bikel

'It has all the realism, dignity and courage of the men it commemorates.' – *News of the World*

'You won't dare open your mouth, but you'll be screaming for her to escape!'

The Collector *
US 1965 119m Technicolor
Columbia (Jud Kinberg, John Kohn)
V, V*, L, S

An inhibited young butterfly specialist kidnaps a girl to add to his collection.

Talkative and unrewarding suspenser with pretensions, sluggishly handled and not very interestingly acted.

w Stanley Mann, John Kohn *novel* John Fowles *d* William Wyler *ph* Robert L. Surtees, Robert Krasker *m* Maurice Jarre

Terence Stamp, Samantha Eggar, Mona Washbourne

AAN: Stanley Mann, John Kohn; William Wyler; Samantha Eggar

Colleen *
US 1936 89m bw
Warner (Robert Lord)

Boy meets Irish girl in New York.

Typical light musical of the period with standard studio talent.

w Peter Milne, F. Hugh Herbert, Sig Herzig *d* Alfred E. Green *ph* Byron Haskin, Sol Polito *m/y* Harry Warren, Al Dubin *ch* Bobby Connolly *gown* Orry-Kelly

Dick Powell, Ruby Keeler, Jack Oakie, Joan Blondell, Hugh Herbert, Louise Fazenda, Paul Draper, Marie Wilson, Luis Alberni, Hobart Cavanaugh, Berton Churchill

'You'll graduate with a perpetual smile!'

College *
US 1927 65m (24 fps) bw silent
Buster Keaton Productions (Joseph M. Schenck)
V*, L

A brainy high school student becomes a college football star.

Disappointing comedy from this great stone-faced clown: the plums are there, but few and far between.

w Carl Harbaugh, Bryan Foy *d* James W. Horne *ph* J. Devereux Jennings, Bert Haines

Buster Keaton, Ann Cornwall, Harold Goodwin, Snitz Edwards, Florence Turner

College Coach *
US 1933 75m bw
Warner

A tough football coach finds that his best star is a timid chemistry student.

Unremarkable studio programmer despite a strong cast.

w Niven Busch, Manuel Seff *d* William A. Wellman

Dick Powell, Pat O'Brien, Ann Dvorak, Arthur Byron, Lyle Talbot, Hugh Herbert, Guinn Williams, Donald Meek

'Hasn't enough punch for real sock grosses.' – *Variety*

College Confidential
US 1960 91m bw
Universal (Albert Zugsmith)

A professor surveys the sexual habits of his students.

Tinpot exposé of a highly dubious kind.

w Irvin Shulman *d* Albert Zugsmith

Steve Allen, Jayne Meadows, Mamie Van Doren, Rocky Marciano, Mickey Shaughnessy, Herbert Marshall, Conway Twitty

College Holiday
US 1936 87m bw
Paramount (Harlan Thompson)

Bright young specimens are invited to spend a summer with a lady hotelier interested in eugenics.

Boisterous fun and games which may have seemed funny at the time.

w J. P. McEvoy, Harlan Ware, Jay Gorney, Henry Myers *d* Frank Tuttle *ph* Theodor Sparkuhl *m/y* various

Jack Benny, George Burns, Gracie Allen, Mary Boland, Martha Raye, Etienne Girardot, Marsha Hunt, Leif Erickson, Eleanore Whitney, Johnny Downs, Olympe Bradna, Ben Blue, Jed Prouty

'For a picture that permits the cast to run around practically on the loose, it gets along remarkably well.' – *Variety*

College Humor
US 1933 84m bw
Paramount

A freshman discovers that football and necking are at least as important as studies.

Easy-going comedy-musical which helped to establish its star.

w Claude Binyon, Frank Butler *story* Dean Fales *d* Wesley Ruggles *ph* Leo Tover *m/y* Arthur Johnston, Sam Coslow

Bing Crosby, Jack Oakie, George Burns, Gracie Allen, Richard Arlen, Mary Carlisle

'A light frothy musical that doesn't give the customers much of a mental workout.' – *Variety*

College Rhythm
US 1934 75m bw
Paramount

A college football team fights to help an old-fashioned department store to modernize itself.

Of its time, a pleasant 'youth' movie, but with nothing for posterity.

w Walter de Leon, John McDermott, Francis Martin, George Marion Jnr *d* Norman Taurog *m/y* Mack Gordon, Harry Revel

Jack Oakie, Joe Penner, Mary Brian, Lanny Ross, Helen Mack, Lyda Roberti, George Barbier, Franklin Pangborn, Dean Jagger

songs: 'Stay as Sweet as You Are'; 'Goo Goo'; 'Let's Give Three Cheers for Love'; 'Take a Number from One to Ten'

'Entertaining semi-musical with bright box-office possibilities.' – *Variety*

College Scandal
US 1935 75m bw
Paramount

A killer attacks three male students.

After *College Humor* and *College Rhythm*, this amounts to College Murder. With stars, it could have been memorable.

w Frank Partos, Charles Brackett, Marguerite Roberts *d* Elliott Nugent

Arline Judge, Kent Taylor, Wendy Barrie, Mary Nash, William Stack, William Frawley, Benny Baker, Johnny Downs

'Worthwhile summer fare for high-grade dual houses.' – *Variety*

College Swing
US 1938 86m bw
Paramount (Lewis Gensler)
GB title: *Swing, Teacher, Swing*

A dumb girl must graduate if a college is to inherit a fortune.

Mild comedy more notable for its cast than its script.

w Walter de Leon, Francis Martin *d* Raoul Walsh *ph* Victor Milner *m/y* various

George Burns, Gracie Allen, Martha Raye, Bob Hope, Edward Everett Horton, Florence George, Ben Blue, Betty Grable, Jackie Coogan, John Payne, Cecil Cunningham, Robert Cummings

'A medley of vaude specialties, bits and numbers strung together in not too happy a manner.' – *Variety*

Collegiate
US 1935 80m bw
Paramount

A girls' college is kept going by the whim of an amnesiac.

Mild comedy in the vein of *College Rhythm*.

w Walter de Leon, Francis Martin *play* The Charm School by Alice Duer Miller *d* Ralph Murphy

Jack Oakie, Joe Penner, Frances Langford, Ned Sparks, Betty Grable, Lynne Overman, Mack Gordon, Harry Revel, Julius Tannen

'Light, diverting, no sock, but no bore.' – *Variety*

Colonel Blimp: see *The Life and Death of Colonel Blimp*

Colonel Effingham's Raid
US 1946 70m bw
TCF (Lamar Trotti)
V*
GB title: *Man of the Hour*

A retired Southern colonel tries to straighten out a corrupt Georgia town.

Competent, unsurprising programmer.

w Kathryn Scola *novel* Berry Fleming *d* Irving Pichel *ph* Edward Cronjager *m* Cyril Mockridge

Charles Coburn, Joan Bennett, William Eythe, Allyn Joslyn, Elizabeth Patterson, Donald Meek, Frank Craven, Thurston Hall, Cora Witherspoon, Emory Parnell, Henry Armetta, Roy Roberts, Charles Trowbridge

Colonel Redl **
Hungary/West Germany/Austria 1984 149m Eastmancolor
Mafilm/Mokep/Manfred Durniok/ZDF/ORF
V*, L
original title: *Oberst Redl*

The career of a railwayman's son who in the early years of the century rises high in the military but is condemned by his own insecurities and forced to commit suicide as a spy.

Whether or not one cares for the ironic parable (also treated by John Osborne in his play *A Patriot for Me*) this is a handsome film full of brilliant visuals.

w Istvan Szabo, Peter Dobai *d* Istvan Szabo *ph* Lajos Koltai *m* Zdenko Tamassy

Klaus Maria Brandauer, Hans-Christian Blech, Armin Müller-Stahl, Gudrun Landgrebe, Jan Niklas

AAN: best picture

BFA: best foreign film

The Color of Money **
US 1986 119m DuArt
Touchstone (Irving Axelrod, Barbara de Fina)
V*, L, S

Twenty-five years later, the hero of *The Hustler* teaches a young man his skills.

Slackly told but consistently enjoyable adventures of Fast Eddie Felson in his older age.

w Richard Price, based on characters created by Walter Tevis *d* Martin Scorsese *ph* Michael Ballhaus *m* Robbie Robertson

Paul Newman, Tom Cruise, Mary Elizabeth Mastrantonio, Helen Shaver, Bill Cobbs, John Turturro

AA: Paul Newman

AAN: Michael Balhaus; Boris Leven (art direction);
Kevin J. O'Hara (sound); Mary Elizabeth
Mastrantonio

The Color Purple **
US   1985   152m   DeLuxe
Warner/Amblin (Steven Spielberg, Kathleen Kennedy, Frank
    Marshall, Quincy Jones)
V, V*, L, S

The growth of a Southern black family during the first
half of the century.

Well-intentioned and gracious but not always
dramatically cohesive generation saga from a director
trying to prove he has depth.

w Menno Meyjes novel Alice Walker d Steven
Spielberg ph Allen Daviau m Quincy Jones pd J.
Michael Riva ed Michael Kahn

Whoopi Goldberg, Danny Glover, Margaret Avery,
Oprah Winfrey, Willard Pugh, Adolph Caesar

AAN: best picture; Whoopi Goldberg; Margaret
Avery (supporting actress); Oprah Winfrey
(supporting actress); adapted screenplay;
photography; music; editing; costumes (Aggie
Guerard Rodgers)

Colorado Territory *
US   1949   93m   bw
Warner (Anthony Veiller)

An outlaw escapes from prison planning one last
robbery but is shot in the attempt.

Moderate Western remake of High Sierra.

w John Twist, Edmund H. North d Raoul Walsh
ph Sid Hickox m David Buttolph

Joel McCrea, Virginia Mayo, Dorothy Malone, Henry
Hull, John Archer, James Mitchell, Morris Ankrum,
Basil Ruysdael, Frank Puglia

Colors *
US   1988   120m   Metrocolor
Rank/Orion (Robert H. Solo)
V, V*, L, S

A veteran cop and his young and cocky partner try to
keep the peace between rival Los Angeles street
gangs.

A documentary-style look at street violence and its
relationship to poverty and drugs. It works well for
the first half-hour, but soon loses coherence as a
narrative and goes on too long before the effective
climax.

w Michael Schiffer d Dennis Hopper ph Haskell
Wexler m Herbie Hancock pd Ron Foreman
ed Robert Estrin

Sean Penn, Robert Duvall, Maria Conchita Alonso,
Randy Brooks, Grand Bush, Don Cheadle, Damon
Wayans

'A solidly crafted depiction of some current big-city
horrors.' – Variety

The Colossus of New York
US   1958   70m   bw
Paramount (William Alland)

An international scientist is killed in an accident; his
father puts his brain into a robot, which goes on the
rampage.

Absurd horror comic for kids, with hilariously
unexplained detail and poor technical effects.

w Thelma Schnee d Eugene Lourie

Otto Kruger, Ross Martin, Robert Hutton, John
Baragrey, Mala Powers

The Colossus of Rhodes
Italy   1960   129m   Technicolor   SuperTotalScope
MGM (Michele Scaglione)

In 300 BC, a huge statue doubles as a fortress to
prevent the Phoenicians from invading.

Good-looking spectacle with the usual muddled
script.

w Sergio Leone and seven others d Sergio Leone

Rory Calhoun, Lea Massari, Georges Marchal

Colossus, the Forbin Project: see The Forbin
Project

Colour Me Dead
Australia   1970   97m   colour
Goldsworthy (Eddie Davis)
V*

An accountant discovers that he has been given a
slow-acting poison.

Poor remake of the 1949 semi-classic D.O.A.: no reason
to see it.

w Russel Rouse, Clarence Greene d/p Eddie Davis

Tom Tryon, Carolyn Jones, Rick Jason, Patricia
Connolly

The Colour of Pomegranates ***
USSR   1969   73m   colour
Armenfilm
V, V*
original title: Tsvet Granata

Biopic of the 18th-century Armenian poet Sayat Nova,
as he rises from a child working as a wool dyer to
courtier and monk, told in the manner of his poems.

Extraordinary lyrical film, full of richly coloured
emblematic images, like a succession of animated
icons.

wd Sergei Paradjanov ph Suren Shakhbazian
m Tieran Mansurian ad Stepan Andranikan

Sofiko Chiaureli, M. Alekian, V. Glastian, G.
Gegechkori, O. Minasian

Colpire Al Cuore: see Blow to the Heart

Colt 45
US   1950   74m   Technicolor
Warner
American TV title: Thundercloud

A new kind of gun, intended to bring law and order
to the west, gets into the wrong hands.

Routine, watchable Western which achieved a
surprising popularity.

w Thomas Blackburn d Edwin L. Marin

Randolph Scott, Zachary Scott, Ruth Roman, Lloyd
Bridges

'Has all the artistry of a picture-strip.' – C. A. Lejeune

Column South
US   1953   84m   colour
Universal

A cavalry officer shows how to live peaceably with
Indians.

Tolerable co-feature Western.

w William Sackheim d Frederick de Cordova

Audie Murphy, Joan Evans, Robert Sterling, Ray
Collins, Dennis Weaver

Coma *
US   1978   113m   Metrocolor
MGM (Martin Erlichman)
V, V*, L, S

A lady doctor suspects that patients are being put
deliberately into coma so that their organs can be sold,
and finds herself in deadly peril.

Hitchcockian suspense thriller with nobody but the
audience believing the heroine; the fact that there are
more dead than living characters makes it slightly too
ghoulish at times.

wd Michael Crichton novel Robin Cook ph Victor
J. Kemper, Gerald Hirschfeld m Jerry Goldsmith
pd Albert Brenner

Geneviève Bujold, Michael Douglas, Richard
Widmark, Elizabeth Ashley, Rip Torn, Lois Chiles,
Harry Rhodes

'A stupid, silly mad-scientist thriller, with a plucky
Girl-Surgeon out to solve the mysteries of some
strange deaths.' – Stanley Kauffmann

Comanche
US   1955   87m   DeLuxe   Cinemascope
UA (Carl Krueger)

In 1875 New Mexico, a renegade Indian prevents
peace between white and red man.

Cheerful action Western, satisfying to the easily
pleased.

w Carl Krueger d George Sherman

Dana Andrews, Kent Smith, Nestor Paiva, Henry
Brandon, John Litel, Lowell Gilmore, Mike Mazurki

Comanche Station
US   1960   74m   Technicolor   Cinemascope
Columbia (Harry Joe Brown)

A man seeks his wife, taken prisoner by Indians.

Below-par star Western, indifferently plotted.

w Burt Kennedy d Budd Boetticher

Randolph Scott, Nancy Gates, Claude Akins, Skip
Homeier

Comanche Territory
US   1950   76m   Technicolor
Universal-International

Jim Bowie assists the Comanches against treacherous
whites.

Double-bill Western, adequate for its purpose.

w Oscar Brodney and Louis Meltzer d George
Sherman

Maureen O'Hara, Macdonald Carey, Will Geer,
Charles Drake

The Comancheros **
US   1961   107m   DeLuxe   Cinemascope
TCF (George Sherman)
S

A Texas Ranger and his gambler prisoner join forces
to clean up renegade gunmen operating from a remote
armed compound.

Easy-going, cheerfully violent Western with lively
roughhouse sequences.

w James Edward Grant, Clair Huffaker d Michael
Curtiz ph William H. Clothier m Elmer Bernstein

John Wayne, Stuart Whitman, Nehemiah Persoff, Lee
Marvin, Ina Balin, Bruce Cabot

Come and Get It *
US   1936   99m   bw
Samuel Goldwyn (Merritt Hulburd)
V*

The life and loves of a lumber tycoon in 19th-century
Wisconsin.

Disappointingly conventional, mainly studio-bound
action drama using top talent of the period.

w Jules Furthman, Jane Murfin novel Edna Ferber
d Howard Hawks, William Wyler ph Gregg
Toland, Rudolph Maté m Alfred Newman
ed Edward Curtiss

Edward Arnold, Joel McCrea, Frances Farmer, Walter
Brennan, Andrea Leeds

AA: Walter Brennan

AAN: Edward Curtiss

Come Back Charleston Blue *
US   1972   101m   Technicolor
Warner/Formosa (Samuel Goldwyn Jnr)

Harlem detectives Coffin Ed Johnson and

Gravedigger Jones investigate the case of a long-dead gangster who seems to be still taking vengeance.

Occasionally funny but disturbingly violent crime kaleidoscope with a black ambience, more sophisticated and therefore more generally acceptable than its predecessor *Cotton Comes to Harlem* (qv).

w Bontche Schweig, Peggy Elliott *novel* *The Heat's On* by Chester Himes d Mark Warren ph Dick Kratina m Donny Hathaway

Godfrey Cambridge, Raymond St Jacques, Peter de Anda, Jonelle Allen, Percy Rodrigues, Minny Gentry

'That girl in their house spelled trouble!'

Come Back Little Sheba *
US 1952 99m bw
Paramount (Hal B. Wallis)
V*, L

An ex-alcoholic is let down not only by his slovenly wife but by the young girl he idolizes.

Stagey but theatrically effective transcription of a popular domestic drama, with one outstanding performance.

w Ketti Frings *play* *William Inge* d Daniel Mann ph James Wong Howe m Franz Waxman ed Warren Low

Shirley Booth, Burt Lancaster, Terry Moore, Richard Jaeckel

AA: Shirley Booth

AAN: Terry Moore; editing

Come Back to Me: see *Doll Face*

Come Back to the Five and Dime, Jimmy Dean, Jimmy Dean
US 1983 110m DuArt Color
Sandcastle 5/Mark Goodman/Viacom
V, V*, L

Misfits meet to celebrate the twentieth anniversary of the death of James Dean.

Filmed play which descends from cynicism through gloom to hysteria and is never very revealing.

w Ed Graczyk *play* *Ed Graczyk* d Robert Altman ph Pierre Mignot m various

Sandy Dennis, Karen Black, Cher, Sudie Bond, Kathy Bates

'It may seem perverse to describe as Altman's masterpiece so self-contained and "alien" a work, with an existence pre-dating his own involvement and a thrusting (if perverse) biological life that owes nothing to the audience's willingness to participate. But the irony depends solely on which side of Altman's own two-way world one stands.' – Richard Combs, MFB

Come Blow Your Horn *
US 1963 112m Technicolor Panavision
Paramount/Lear and Yorkin
V*

A country boy in New York is envious of his older brother's sophisticated life.

Amusing characters and funny lines permeate this stolid transcription of an early Neil Simon success; the big screen is not the place for them.

w Norman Lear *play* *Neil Simon* d Bud Yorkin ph William Daniels m Nelson Riddle

Frank Sinatra, Tony Bill, Lee J. Cobb, Molly Picon, Jill St John, Barbara Rush, Dan Blocker

Come Clean **
US 1931 20m bw
Hal Roach

Two much-married men go out for ice-cream and bring back a woman of the streets they have saved from suicide.

Splendid star comedy with the famous characterizations fully rounded.

w H. M. Walker d James W. Horne ph Art Lloyd*ed* Richard Currier

Laurel and Hardy, Mae Busch, Charlie Hall, Gertrude Astor, Linda Loredo

† Remade in 1942 as *Brooklyn Orchid*, with William Bendix and Joe Sawyer.

Come Fill the Cup *
US 1951 113m bw
Warner (Henry Blanke)

An alcoholic newspaperman cures himself, then his boss's alcoholic son who is involved with gangsters.

Unlikely but solidly entertaining melodrama, powerfully cast.

w Ivan Goff, Ben Roberts *novel* *Harlan Ware* d Gordon Douglas ph Robert Burks m Ray Heindorf

James Cagney, Gig Young, Raymond Massey, Phyllis Thaxter, James Gleason, Selena Royle, Larry Keating

AAN: Gig Young

Come Fly with Me *
US 1962 109m Metrocolor Panavision
MGM/Anatole de Grunwald

The romantic adventures of three air hostesses.

Good-looking girls and airplanes but little else make thin entertainment.

w William Roberts d Henry Levin ph Oswald Morris m Lyn Murray

Hugh O'Brian, Dolores Hart, Karl Malden, Pamela Tiffin, Lois Nettleton, Karl Boehm

Come Live with Me *
US 1941 86m bw
MGM (Clarence Brown)

In order to stay in America, a girl refugee from Vienna arranges a strictly platonic marriage with a struggling author.

Hypnotically predictable comedy, quite well presented and performed.

w Patterson McNutt, Virginia Van Upp d Clarence Brown ph George Folsey m Herbert Stothart

James Stewart, Hedy Lamarr, Ian Hunter, Verree Teasdale, Donald Meek, Barton MacLane, *Adeline de Walt Reynolds*

Come Next Spring *
US 1955 92m Trucolor Republic

A drunkard returns to his Arkansas farm family and wins the respect of them and the community.

D. W. Griffith-type pastoral melodrama which surprisingly works pretty well and leaves one with the intended warm glow.

w Montgomery Pittman d R. G. Springsteen ph Jack Marta m Max Steiner

Ann Sheridan, Steve Cochran, Walter Brennan, Sherry Jackson, Richard Eyer, Edgar Buchanan, Sonny Tufts, Mae Clarke

'An unpretentious film with a good deal of charm.' – MFB

The Come On *
US 1956 83m bw Superscope
AA (Lindley Parsons)

Husband and wife confidence tricksters get homicidal when she falls in love.

In trade parlance, strictly a lower berth item; but with points of mild interest.

w Warren Douglas *novel* *Whitman Chambers* d Russell Birdwell ph Ernest Haller m Paul Dunlap

Anne Baxter, Sterling Hayden, John Hoyt, Jesse White, Paul Picerni

Come on George *
GB 1939 88m bw
ATP/Ealing (Jack Kitchin)
V

A stableboy calms a nervous racehorse and rides him to victory.

Standard comedy vehicle, well mounted, with the star at his box-office peak.

w Anthony Kimmins, Leslie Arliss, Val Valentine d Anthony Kimmins ph Ronald Neame, Gordon Dines m Ernest Irving ad Wilfred Shingleton ed Ray Pitt

George Formby, Pat Kirkwood, Joss Ambler, Meriel Forbes, Cyril Raymond, George Carney, Ronald Shiner

Come Out of the Pantry *
GB 1935 73m bw
British and Dominions (Herbert Wilcox)

An English milord is forced by circumstance to take a job as his boss's footman.

Pleasing if obvious comedy, later remodelled as *Spring in Park Lane*.

w Austin Parker, Douglas Furber *story* *Alice Duer Miller* d Jack Raymond ph Freddie Young, Henry Harris ad L. P. Williams ed Frederick Wilson

Jack Buchanan, Fay Wray, James Carew, Ronald Squire, Olive Blakeney, Fred Emney

Come See the Paradise *
US 1990 133m DeLuxe
Fox (Robert F. Colesberry)
V, V*, L, S

After Pearl Harbor, a Japanese-American woman, married to an Irish-American soldier, is interned with her family.

A fascinating subject, of racism and culture clash, is submerged by a concentration on an ordinary romance.

wd Alan Parker ph Michael Seresin m Randy Edelman pd Geoffrey Kirkland ed Gerry Hambling

Dennis Quaid, Tamlyn Tomita, Sab Shimono, Shizuko Hoshi, Stan Egi, Ronald Yamamoto, Akemi Nishino, Naomi Nakano, Brady Tsurutani, Elizabeth Gilliam

Come September
US 1961 112m Technicolor CinemaScope
Universal/7 Pictures Corporation/Raoul Walsh Enterprises (Robert Arthur)

A wealthy American discovers that his Italian villa is being used as a hotel by his once-a-year mistress, who is about to marry.

Clumsy sex farce with lush trimmings and generation gap asides; effort more noticeable than achievement.

w Stanley Shapiro, Maurice Richlin d Robert Mulligan ph William Daniels m Hans J. Salter

Rock Hudson, Gina Lollobrigida, Sandra Dee, Bobby Darin, Walter Slezak, Brenda de Banzie, Joel Grey, Rosanna Rory, Ronald Howard

Come to the Stable *
US 1949 94m bw
TCF (Samuel G. Engel)

Two French nuns arrive in New England to build a local hospital, and melt the hearts of the local grumps.

This old-time charmer simply brims with sweetness and light and is produced with high-class studio efficiency.

w Oscar Millard, Sally Benson *story* *Clare Boothe Luce* d Henry Koster ph Joseph LaShelle *md* Lionel Newman *m* Cyril Mockridge *ad* Lyle Wheeler, Joseph C. Wright

Loretta Young, Celeste Holm, Hugh Marlowe, Elsa Lanchester, Thomas Gomez, Dorothy Patrick, Basil Ruysdael, Dooley Wilson, Regis Toomey, Henri Letondal

AAN: Clare Boothe Luce; Joseph LaShelle; Loretta Young; Celeste Holm; Elsa Lanchester; song 'Through a Long and Sleepless Night' (*m* Alfred Newman, *ly* Mack Gordon); art direction

'Millions loved him, could someone hate him enough to kill and kill again?'

The Comeback

GB 1978 100m colour
Enterprise (Peter Walker)
aka: *The Day the Screaming Stopped*

An American singer in London deals with the murder of his wife – and with her ghost.

Dim mixture of mystery and horror, not at all persuasive.

w Murray Smith *d* Peter Walker *m* Stanley Myers

Jack Jones, Sheila Keith, Pamela Stephenson, David Doyle, Bill Owen, Richard Johnson

The Comedians *

US/Bermuda/France 1967 160m Metrocolor
Panavision
MGM/Maximilian/Trianon (Peter Glenville)
V*

A variety of English-speaking eccentrics are caught up in the violent events of Haiti under Papa Doc Duvalier.

Clumsy and heavy-going compression of a too-topical novel, with most of the plot left in at the expense of character. Neither entertaining nor instructive, but bits of acting please.

w Graham Greene *novel* Graham Greene *d* Peter Glenville *ph* Henri Decaë *m* Laurence Rosenthal

Richard Burton, Elizabeth Taylor, *Alec Guinness*, Peter Ustinov, Lillian Gish, Paul Ford, Roscoe Lee Browne, James Earl Jones, Raymond St Jacques, Cicely Tyson

'So thick and fast do the clichés come that one feels the script can only have been salvaged from some *New Statesman* competition.' – *Tom Milne*

'It's pleasant to spend two hours again in Greeneland, still well-stocked with bilious minor crucifixions, furtive fornication, cynical politics, and reluctant hope.' – *Stanley Kauffmann*

The Comedy Man *

GB 1964 92m bw
British Lion-Gray-Consort (Jon Pennington)
V

A middle-aged actor on the skids desperately rounds up his contacts and becomes the star of a TV commercial.

Determinedly depressing satirical melodrama with engaging moments; comedy emphasis would have better suited the talents.

w Peter Yeldham *novel* Douglas Hayes *d* Alvin Rakoff *ph* Ken Hodges *m* Bill McGuffie

Kenneth More, Cecil Parker, Dennis Price, Billie Whitelaw, Norman Rossington, Angela Douglas, Edmund Purdom, Frank Finlay, Alan Dobie

'Humour and intelligent irony.' – *Sunday Express*

'A merciless and accurate picture of the brave band of actors who live from hand to mouth and commute between the Salisbury Arms pub and the Poland Street Labour exchange.' – *Evening News*

The Comedy of Terrors *

US 1963 88m Pathecolor Panavision
Alta Vista/AIP (Anthony Carras, Richard Matheson)
V*, L

Two impecunious funeral directors decide to speed up the demise of their prospective clients.

Disappointingly slackly-handled and rather tiresome macabre frolic, notable for a few splendid moments and an imperishable cast.

w Richard Matheson *d* Jacques Tourneur *ph* Floyd Crosby *m* Les Baxter

Vincent Price, Peter Lorre, Boris Karloff, Basil Rathbone, Joe E. Brown, Joyce Jameson

Comes a Horseman

US 1978 118m Technicolor Panavision
UA/Chartoff-Winkler (Robert Caan)
V, V*

In the forties, Montana ranchers have a hard time holding onto their land against the pressures of progress and a villainous cattle baron.

Portentous and wholly unexciting modern Western, not helped by a loftily unexplained title and show-off photography.

w Dennis Lynton Clark *d* Alan J. Pakula *ph* Gordon Willis *m* Michael Small *pd* George Jenkins

Jane Fonda, Jason Robards Jnr, James Caan, George Grizzard, Richard Farnsworth, Jim Davis

'It's a film of few words (and about a quarter of them mangled by the sound recording). The melodrama is smothered under sullen, overcast skies. How can you get involved in the conflict between the good guys and the bad guys if you can't even see them?' – *Pauline Kael*

AAN: Richard Farnsworth

Comet over Broadway

US 1938 65m bw
Warner

An actress, having been involved in a murder, is torn between burning ambition and mother love.

Arrant melodrama which overtaxes its star.

w Mark Hellinger, Robert Buckner *story* Faith Baldwin *d* Busby Berkeley

Kay Francis, Ian Hunter, John Litel, Donald Crisp, Minna Gombell, Sybil Jason, Melville Cooper

'A backstage yarn that goes overboard on assorted heartbreaks.' – *Variety*

Comfort and Joy *

GB 1984 106m colour
Lake/EMI/STV (Davina Belling, Clive Parsons)
V, V*

A Scottish radio disc jockey becomes involved in a war between two ice-cream firms.

Heavy comedy, short of laughs and sympathy; a distinct descent from *Local Hero*, which was a comedown after *Gregory's Girl*.

wd Bill Forsyth *ph* Chris Menges *m* Mark Knopfler

Bill Paterson, Eleanor David, C. P. Grogan, Alex Norton

The Comfort of Strangers

Italy/GB 1990 104m Technicolor
Rank/Erre/Sovereign/Reteitalia (Angelo Rizzoli)
V, V*, S
original title: *Cortesie per gli ospiti*

On holiday in Venice, a conventional husband and wife become involved with a sadomasochistic couple.

Bleak and icy tale that will induce a shiver, although the mannered performances aren't an attraction.

w Harold Pinter *novel* Ian McEwan *d* Paul Schrader *ph* Dante Spinotti *m* Angelo Badalamenti *pd* Gianni Quaranta *ed* Bill Pankow

Christopher Walken, Rupert Everett, Natasha Richardson, Helen Mirren, Manfredi Aliquo

The Comic *

US 1969 95m Technicolor
Columbia (Carl Reiner)
V*, L

The success, downfall and old age of a silent film comedian in Hollywood.

Remarkably bright and cinematic tragicomedy obviously based on Buster Keaton, with a *Citizen Kane*-type framework. Not a commercial success, but a must for professionals.

w Carl Reiner, Aaron Rubin *d* Carl Reiner *ph* W. Wallace Kelley *m* Jack Elliott

Dick Van Dyke, Mickey Rooney (more or less playing Ben Turpin), Cornel Wilde, Carl Reiner, Michele Lee, Pert Kelton

'Offers a variety of delights.' – *Judith Crist*

'A furious editorial about a business that treats its veterans like over-exposed celluloid.' – *Variety*

Comic Strip Hero: see *Jeu de Massacre*

Comin' at Ya!

US 1981 101m Technicolor Dimensionscope 3-D
GTO Films (Marshall Lupo, Stan Torchia)

An ex-outlaw goes in search of three outlaws who kidnapped his wife-to-be.

Determined three-dimensional attack on the sensibilities, with nothing to interest in story or acting.

w Wolf Lowenthal, Lloyd Battista, Gene Quintano *story* Tony Petitto *d* Ferdinando Baldi *ph* Fernando Arribas *m* Carlo Savina *ad* Luciano Spadoni *ed* Franco Fraticelli

Tony Anthony, Gene Quintano, Victoria Abril, Ricardo Palacios

Comin' thro' the Rye

GB 1923 approx 85m (24 fps) bw silent
Hepworth Picture Plays

In Victorian England, lovers meet periodically in a rye field, but events move against them.

Statuesque romantic drama whose reputation may be largely due to its accidental survival. (There was a previous version from the same producer in 1916, with the same leading actress.)

w Blanche McIntosh *novel* Helen Mathers *d* Cecil M. Hepworth *ph* Geoffrey Faithfull

Alma Taylor, Shayle Gardner, Eileen Dennes, Ralph Forbes, Francis Lister

'My best and most important film.' – *Cecil M. Hepworth*

'Hepworth's directorial style matches his material in simplicity.' – *Geoff Brown, MFB, 1976*

'A man who believed in war! A man who believed in nothing! And a woman who believed in both of them!'

Coming Home *

US 1978 128m DeLuxe
UA/Jerome Hellman
V*, L

An embittered Vietnam veteran falls for the wife of a serving soldier.

Self-pitying romantic wallow which must mean more to American audiences than to others. Goodish acting.

w Waldo Salt, Robert C. Jones *story* Nancy Dowd *d* Hal Ashby *ph* Haskell Wexler *m* various *pd* Mike Haller *ed* Don Zimmerman

Jane Fonda, Jon Voight, Bruce Dern, Robert Carradine, Penelope Milford

'Just one more story about a wife who gets entangled with another man while her husband is away. Everything in the script that is contemporary is mere updating of that perennial story.' – *Stanley Kauffmann*

AA: Jon Voight; Jane Fonda; best screenplay

AAN: best picture; Hal Ashby; Bruce Dern; Penelope Milford; editing

Coming to America

US   1988   116m   Technicolor
UIP/Paramount (George Folsey Jnr, Robert D. Wachs)
V, V*, L, S, CD

A wealthy African prince poses as a poor student in New York so he can find a bride who will love him for himself.

Tired comedy that fails to exploit Murphy's strengths, despite his popping up heavily disguised in several minor roles.

w David Sheffield, Barry W. Blaustein   story Eddie Murphy   d John Landis   ph Woody Omens   m Nile Rodgers   sp make-up: Rick Baker   ed Malcolm Campbell, George Folsey Jnr

Eddie Murphy, Arsenio Hall, John Amos, James Earl Jones, Shari Headley, Madge Sinclair

'A true test for loyal fans.' – Variety

Coming Up Roses *

GB   1986   93m   Eastmancolor
Red Rooster/S4C
Welsh Title: Rhosyn a Rhith

When the local cinema closes down the local community take it over for mushroom-growing.

Charming curiosity in Welsh with English subtitles, reminiscent of Ealing in its heyday.

w Ruth Carter   d Stephen Bayley   ph Dick Pope   m Michael Story   pd Hildegard Bechtler

Dafydd Hywel, Iola Gregory, Olive Michael, Mari Emlyn

A Coming-Out Party: see Very Important Person

The Command

US   1954   94m   Warnercolor   Cinemascope
Warner (David Weisbart)

A cavalry troop escorts a wagon train through Indian country.

Competent but unsurprising 'second team' Western.

w Russell Hughes   novel James Warner Bellah   d David Butler   ph Wilfrid M. Cline   m Dimitri Tiomkin

Guy Madison, Joan Weldon, James Whitmore, Carl Benton Reid, Harvey Lembeck, Ray Teal, Bob Nichols

'Heroes, cowards, fighters, braggarts, liars . . . and what goes on in their hearts!'

Command Decision *

US   1949   111m   bw
MGM (Sidney Franklin)
V*, L

War among the back-room boys; a general, his staff and his peers debate the aerial bombardment of Germany.

Plainly reproduced version of a determinedly serious play, with a remarkable cast partly at sea.

w William R. Laidlaw, George Froeschel   play William Wister Haines   d Sam Wood   ph Harold Rosson   m Miklos Rozsa

Clark Gable, Walter Pidgeon, Van Johnson, Brian Donlevy, John Hodiak, Charles Bickford, Edward Arnold, Marshall Thompson, Richard Quine, Cameron Mitchell, Clinton Sundberg, Ray Collins, Warner Anderson, John McIntire, Moroni Olsen

Command Performance

GB   1937   84m   bw
Grosvenor (Harcourt Templeman)

Fearing a breakdown through overwork a singer takes to the open road and falls in love with a gypsy.

Innocuous musical, which is mainly a vehicle for Tracy to sing sentimental ballads and attempt an operatic aria.

w Stafford Dickens, George Pearson, Michael Hankinson   story Sinclair Hill   d Sinclair Hill   ph Cyril Bristow   md Louis Levy   m/ly Tolchard Evans, Stanley Damerell, Irwin Dash   ad C. Wilfred Arnold   ed Michael Hankinson

The Street Singer (Arthur Tracy), Lilli Palmer, Mark Daly, Finlay Currie, Jack Milford, Stafford Hilliard

Commando

US   1985   88m   DeLuxe
TCF (Joel Silver)
V, V*, L

Unlikely mates are thrown together in pursuit of a deadly Latin dictator.

Hard action nonsense with the saving grace of humour.

w Steven de Souza   d Mark L. Lester   m James Horner   pd John Vallone   ed Mark Goldblatt, John F. Link, Glenn Farr

Arnold Schwarzenegger, Rae Dawn Chong, Dan Hedaya, Vernon Wells, David Patrick Kelly

'Palatable actioner, inoffensively silly.' – Variety

The Commandos Strike at Dawn *

US   1942   98m   bw
Columbia (Lester Cowan)
V*

Norwegian commandos outwit the Nazis with the help of the British navy.

Standard war adventure shot on Vancouver Island.

w Irwin Shaw   story C. S. Forester   d John Farrow   ph William C. Mellor   m Louis Gruenberg

Paul Muni, Anna Lee, Lillian Gish, Cedric Hardwicke, Robert Coote, Ray Collins, Rosemary de Camp, Richard Derr, Alexander Knox, Rod Cameron

AAN: Louis Gruenberg

The Commissar: see Komissar

'They Had Absolutely Nothing. But They Were Willing To Risk It All.'

The Commitments **

US   1991   118m   Technicolor
TCF/Beacon/First Film/Dirty Hands (Roger Randall-Cutler, Lynda Myles)
V, V*, L, S

Dublin youths, believing that the Irish are the blacks of Europe, form a soul band.

Lively and energetic account of backstage traumas, troubles and triumphs.

w Dick Clement, Ian La Frenais, Marc Abraham   novel Roddy Doyle   d Alan Parker   ph Gale Tattersall   pd Brian Morris   ed Gerry Hambling

Robert Arkins, Michael Aherne, Angeline Ball, Maria Doyle, Dave Finnegan, Bronagh Gallagher, Félim Gormley, Glen Hansard, Dick Massey, Johnny Murphy, Kenneth McCluskey, Andrew Strong

'Isn't likely to overwhelm at the box-office, any more than a band like this one devoted to covering classics would get much mileage in the music industry. Still, the pic is so fresh, well-executed and original that, properly handled, it should enjoy a long if modest run and inspire much hardcore devotion among music fans.' – Variety

'A hilariously funny, richly humane, consistently truthful story . . . the movie pulsates with vitality, high spirits and the exhilarating feeling of people growing as they work together to transcend the seeming hopelessness of their surroundings.' – Philip French, Observer

AAN: editing

Common Clay

US   1930   68m   bw
Fox

A speakeasy hostess becomes a maid in a wealthy household and falls in love with her betters.

Archetypal soap opera which caused a mild sensation and sent its star into half a dozen imitations.

w Jules Furthman   novel Cleves Kincaid   d Victor Fleming   ph Glen MacWilliams

Constance Bennett, Lew Ayres, Tully Marshall, Matty Kemp, Purnell Pratt, Beryl Mercer

'Emotional play of 1916 bearing the marks of that artificial school . . . heavy for fan diet.' – Variety

The Common Touch *

GB   1941   104m   bw
British National (John Baxter)

A rich young man poses as a tramp to save a dosshouse from destruction.

Naïve drama with a social conscience, remade from the 1932 talkie Dosshouse. A brave try.

w Barbara K. Emery, Geoffrey Orme   novel Herbert Ayres   d John Baxter   ph James Wilson

Geoffrey Hibbert, Greta Gynt, Joyce Howard, Harry Welchman, Edward Rigby, George Carney, Bransby Williams, Wally Patch, Eliot Makeham, Bernard Miles, Bill Fraser, John Longden   guests Sandy Macpherson, Scott Sanders, Mark Hambourg, Carrol Gibbons

Communion

US   1978   108m   colour
Allied Artists (Richard K. Rosenberg)
V*
aka: Alice, Sweet Alice; Holy Terror

A young girl is suspected of killing several of her relatives.

Moderate low-budget thriller, mainly of interest for the brief appearances of Brooke Shields, in her first film, and of Roth as a pathologist.

w Rosemary Ritvo, Alfred Sole   d Alfred Sole   ph John Friberg, Chuck Hall, Edward Salier   m Stephen Lawrence

Paula Sheppard, Brooke Shields, Linda Miller, Jane Lowry, Alphonso DeNoble, Rudolph Willrich, Lillian Roth

'On December 25 1985 Whitley Strieber had a dream. Weeks later he discovered his family had the same dream. Months later he made the most shocking discovery of his life. Now, you will discover it.'

Communion

US   1990   101m   DeLuxe
Vestron/Pheasantry Films/Allied Vision/The Picture Property Co. (Philippe Mora, Whitley Strieber, Dan Allingham)
V, V*, L

A writer recalls his meeting with extra-terrestrials and resolves to write a book about it.

Supposedly based on fact, the film has the style of an ill-conceived fantasy more rewarding to its author than to any audience.

w Whitley Strieber   book Whitley Strieber   d Philippe Mora   ph Louis Irving   m Eric Clapton   pd Linda Pearl   ed Lee Smith

Christopher Walken, Lindsay Crouse, Joel Carlson, Frances Sternhagen, Andreas Katsulas, Terri Hanauer, Basil Hoffman

Como agua para chocolate: see Like Water for Chocolate

Company Limited **

India   1971   112m   bw
Chitranjali (Bharat Shamsher Rana)
original title: Seemabaddha

A sales manager uses underhand methods to gain promotion.

Long-winded drama of Calcutta life among westernized young executives where ambition stifles morality.

wd Satyajit Ray   *novel Seemabaddha* by Shankar *ph* Soumendu Roy   *m* Satyajit Ray   *ad* Ashoke Bose   *ed* Dulal Dutta

Sharmila Tagore, Barun Chanda, Parumita Chowdhury

Company of Cowards: see *Advance to the Rear*

The Company of Strangers **
Canada   1990   101m   colour
Electric/Contemporary/National Film Board of Canada (David Wilson)
aka: *Strangers In Good Company*

Seven old women are forced to camp out for several days in a derelict farmhouse after their bus breaks down.

A small gem of a movie, using a cast of non-actors to great effect.

w Gloria Demers, Cynthia Scott, David Wilson, Sally Bochner   *d* Cynthia Scott   *ph* David de Volpi *m* Marie Bernard   *ed* David Wilson

Alice Diabo, Constance Garneau, Winifred Holden, Cissy Meddings, Mary Meigs, Catherine Roche, Michelle Sweeney, Beth Webber

'In its quiet way this truthful, affecting, unsentimental movie tells us as much as any film I know about the female experience in this century.' – *Philip French, Observer*

The Company of Wolves **
GB   1984   95m   colour
ITC/Palace (Chris Brown, Stephen Woolley)
V, V*, S

A young girl dreams of wolves and werewolves.

Fragmentary adult fantasy which had an unexpected box-office success, chiefly because of its sexual allusiveness, its clever make-up and its pictorial qualities.

w Angela Carter, Neil Jordan   *stories* Angela Carter *d* Neil Jordan   *ph* Bryan Loftus   *m* George Fenton *special make-up effects* Christopher Tucker   *pd* Anton Furst

Angela Lansbury, David Warner, Graham Crowden, Brian Glover, Sarah Patterson, Micha Bergese, Stephen Rea

'A horror film as literate as it is visionary, it's great fun – and that's not a cheap thrill.' – *J. Hoberman, Village Voice*

The Company She Keeps
US   1950   83m   bw
RKO (John Houseman)

A self-sacrificing parole officer allows a parolee to steal her fiancé.

Considering the credits, a dismally novelettish drama of almost no interest.

w Ketti Frings   *d* John Cromwell   *ph* Nicholas Musuraca   *m* Leigh Harline

Lizabeth Scott, *Jane Greer,* Dennis O'Keefe, Fay Baker, John Hoyt, James Bell, Don Beddoe, Bert Freed

Compartment Tueurs: see *The Sleeping Car Murders*

The Competition *
US   1980   129m   Metrocolor
Columbia/Rastar/William Sackheim
V*, L

An ageing piano prodigy has one last shot at fame in a San Francisco piano competition.

Slightly curious, old-fashioned but heavy-handed romance which aims to do for the piano what *The*

Turning Point did for ballet. It doesn't sustain its length but at least the milieu is interesting.

wd Joel Oliansky   *ph* Richard H. Kline   *m/md* Lalo Schifrin   *pd* Dale Hennesy   *ed* David Blewitt

Richard Dreyfuss, Lee Remick, Amy Irving, Sam Wanamaker, Joseph Cali

AAN: film editing; best song 'People Alone' (*m* Lalo Schifrin, *ly* Wilbur Jennings)

Un Complicato Intrigo di Donne, Vicoli e Delitto: see *Camorra: The Naples Connection*

Compromising Positions
US   1985   98m   colour
Paramount (Frank Perry)
V*, L

The murder of a philandering dentist has repercussions among his many mistresses.

Combination sex comedy and whodunnit which never seems to hit the right groove.

w Susan Isaacs   *novel* Susan Isaacs   *d* Frank Perry *ph* Barry Sonnenfeld   *m* Brad Fiedel   *pd* Peter Larkin   *ed* Peter Frank

Susan Sarandon, Raul Julia, Edward Herrmann, Judith Ivey, Mary Beth Hurt, Joe Mantegna

Compulsion *
US   1959   103m   bw   Cinemascope
TCF/Darryl F. Zanuck Productions (Richard F. Zanuck)

In the twenties, two Chicago students kidnap and murder a young boy for kicks.

Rather dogged but earnest fictionalization of the Leopold-Loeb case with solid performances and production.

w Richard Murphy   *play* Meyer Levin   *d* Richard Fleischer   *ph* William C. Mellor   *m* Lionel Newman

Dean Stockwell, Bradford Dillman, Orson Welles (in a cameo court appearance as a lawyer based on Clarence Darrow), Diane Varsi, E. G. Marshall, Martin Milner, Richard Anderson, Robert Simon

The Computer Wore Tennis Shoes
US   1970   90m   Technicolor
Disney
V*

While mending a computer a college student gets an electric shock and becomes omniscient.

Ho-hum Disney comedy, eager to please but instantly forgotten.

w Joseph L. McEveety   *d* Robert Butler

Kurt Russell, Cesar Romero, Joe Flynn, William Schallert, Alan Hewitt

Comrade X *
US   1940   89m   bw
MGM (Gottfried Reinhardt)

An American correspondent in Russia is blackmailed into smuggling a girl out of the country.

Lame satirical comedy in the wake of *Ninotchka;* a few good moments, but generally heavy-handed.

w Ben Hecht, Charles Lederer   *story* Walter Reisch *d* King Vidor   *ph* Joseph L. Ruttenberg *m* Bronislau Kaper

Clark Gable, Hedy Lamarr, Felix Bressart, Oscar Homolka, Eve Arden, Sig Rumann

'Broadest comedic strokes and not-too-subtle satire . . . a smacko entry for topflight biz.' – *Variety*

AAN: Walter Reisch

Comrades ***
GB   1987   180m   colour
Curzon/Skreba/National Film Finance (Simon Relph)

In the 1830s six Dorset farm labourers who form a

union to campaign against low wages are tried and transported to Australia as criminals.

Subtitled 'a lanternist's account', and based on the true story of the Tolpuddle Martyrs, it is a flawed masterpiece: too long and too preachy, yet its qualities outweigh these defects.

wd Bill Douglas   *ph* Gale Tattersall   *m* Hans Werner Henze, David Graham   *pd* Michael Pickwoad   *ed* Mick Audsley

Robin Soans, William Gammara, Stephen Bateman, Philip Davis, Jeremy Flynn, Keith Allen, Alex Norton, Michael Clark, Arthur Dignam, James Fox, John Hargreaves, Michael Hordern, Freddie Jones, Vanessa Redgrave, Robert Stephens, Murray Melvin, Barbara Windsor, Imelda Staunton

Comradeship *
GB   1919   67m (24 fps)   bw   silent
Stoll

Two friends endure varying fortunes during World War I.

An early British 'A' feature which was highly popular in its day.

w Jeffrey Bernerd   *d* Maurice Elvey

Lily Elsie, Gerald Ames, Guy Newall, Peggy Carlisle

Comradeship (1931): see *Kameradschaft*

'Thief. Warrior. Gladiator. King.'
Conan the Barbarian
US   1981   129m   Technicolor   Todd-AO
Dino de Laurentiis/Edward R. Pressman (Buzz Feitshans, Raffaella de Laurentiis)
V*, L, S

In the Dark Ages, a young stalwart seeks out the barbarian tribe which murdered his parents.

Intolerably doomladen, slow-moving and mainly unintelligible rubbish which failed to put a lift into the long-announced sword-and-sorcery cycle.

w John Milius, Oliver Stone, from a character created by Robert E. Howard   *d* John Milius   *ph* Duke Callaghan   *m* Basil Poledouris   *pd* Ron Cobb *ed* C. Timothy O'Meara

Arnold Schwarzenegger, James Earl Jones, Max von Sydow, Sandahl Bergman, Ben Davidson, Mako, Gerry Lopez

'A ragbag of half-witted kitsch, where even locations resemble a set, actors look like extras, violence like a stunt and life a bad dream.' – *Sunday Times*

'An indigestible blend of anti-liberal braggadocio, post-60s mysticism and echt-60s blockbusting.' – *Sight and Sound*

Conan the Destroyer
US   1984   101m   Technicolor   Scope
Dino de Laurentiis
V, V*, L, S

An evil queen offers to bring Conan's last love back to life, if he will undertake a magical quest for her.

More heavy-handed and unpleasant nonsense, with a slightly better pace than before.

w Stanley Mann   *d* Richard Fleischer   *ph* Jack Cardiff

Arnold Schwarzenegger, Grace Jones, Wilt Chamberlain, Mako, Tracey Walter, Sarah Douglas

Concealment: see *The Secret Bride*

Concerto: see *I've Always Loved You*

The Concierge: see *For Love or Money*

The Concorde: Airport '79
US   1979   113m   Technicolor
Universal (Jennings Lang)
V*
GB title: *Airport '80: The Concorde*

Various disasters befall the Concorde on its way from Washington to Paris.

Stultified final (one presumes) effort in the *Airport* series; it could hardly be funnier if it were intended as a comedy, but somehow it entertains.

w Eric Roth   *d* David Lowell Rich   *ph* Philip Lathrop   *m* Lalo Schifrin

Alain Delon, Susan Blakely, Robert Wagner, Sylvia Kristel, George Kennedy, Eddie Albert, Bibi Andersson, John Davidson, Martha Raye, Cicely Tyson, Mercedes McCambridge

'Larger-than-life characters are thrown together on a storyboard and must fend for themselves against attacks, chases and assorted escapades . . . this would be soporific even as a transatlantic inflight movie.' – *Martyn Auty, MFB*

The Concrete Jungle: see *The Criminal*

El Conde Dracula: see *Bram Stoker's Count Dracula*

'A kiss that cannot be forgotten!'
Condemned *
US   1930   86m   bw
Samuel Goldwyn
aka: *Condemned to Devil's Island*

A bank robber is sent to Devil's Island and falls in love with the wife of the brutal warden.

Slow-moving but pictorially attractive melodrama with old-style performances.

w Sidney Howard   *novel Condemned to Devil's Island* by Blair Niles   *d* Wesley Ruggles   *ph* George Barnes, Gregg Toland   *pd* William Cameron Menzies

Ronald Colman, Ann Harding, Louis Wolheim, Dudley Digges, William Elmer

'A piece of nonsense from which it would appear that French convicts on Devil's Island live a life consisting entirely of hot-towel shaves and flirtations with the governor's wife.' – *James Agate*

AAN: Ronald Colman

The Condemned of Altona *
Italy/France   1962   113m   bw
(TCF) Titanus/SGC (Carlo Ponti)

The head of a German shipping empire discovers he has only a few months to live and tries to bring his family to order.

Strident intellectual melodrama whose credits tell all. Watchable for the acting, but very glum.

w Abby Mann, Cesare Zavattini   *play* Jean-Paul Sartre   *d* Vittorio de Sica   *ph* Roberto Gerardi   *m* Dmitri Shostakovich

Fredric March, Sophia Loren, Robert Wagner, Maximilian Schell, Françoise Prévost, Alfredo Franchi

'This film is such a hopeless mess that it is difficult to know where to begin criticizing it.' – *Tom Milne*

Condemned to Death *
GB   1932   75m   bw
Twickenham (Julius Hagen)

A condemned killer hypnotizes a judge into murdering those who turned him in.

Irresistible nonsense of the old school, with spirited direction and a good cast.

w Bernard Merivale, Harry Fowler Mear, Brock Williams   *play Jack O'Lantern* by George Goodchild, James Dawson   *d* Walter Forde   *ph* Sidney Blythe, William Luff

Arthur Wontner, Gillian Lind, Edmund Gwenn, Gordon Harker, Jane Welsh, Cyril Raymond

'A weak daily changer with double-headed programming its merited rating.' – *Variety*

'It would be difficult to find a dull moment.' – *The Bioscope*

Condemned to Devil's Island: see *Condemned*

Condemned to Life: see *Life for Ruth*

Condemned Women *
US   1938   77m   bw
RKO

Murder in a prison for women.

Rough-and-tumble melodrama with predictable elements.

w Lionel Houser   *d* Lew Landers

Sally Eilers, Anne Shirley, Louis Hayward, Esther Dale, Lee Patrick

'Indelicate stuff and doubtful b.o.' – *Variety*

Condorman
US   1981   90m   Technicolor   Panavision
Walt Disney (Jan Williams)
V*

The author of a 'superman' comic tries to act like his hero in real life.

Very mildly amusing spy spoof with inadequate special effects.

w Marc Sturdivant, Glen Caron, Mickey Rose   *novel The Game of X* by Robert Sheckley   *d* Charles Jarrott   *ph* Charles F. Wheeler   *m* Henry Mancini   *pd* Albert Witherick   *sp* Art Cruickshank

Michael Crawford, Oliver Reed, Barbara Carrera, James Hampton, Jean-Pierre Kalfon

Conduct Unbecoming
GB   1975   107m   Technicolor
British Lion/Crown (Michael Deeley, Barry Spikings)
V, V*

In an officers' mess in India in the 1890s, a cadet is accused of assault on a lady but the real culprit is a paranoiac who has taken to pigsticking in quite the wrong way.

Disappointingly flatly-handled and quite unatmospheric picturization of an absorbing West End melodrama. The cast is largely wasted, but stretches of dialogue maintain their interest.

w Robert Enders   *play* Barry England   *d* Michael Anderson   *ph* Bob Huke   *m* Stanley Myers

Michael York, Stacy Keach, Trevor Howard, Christopher Plummer, Richard Attenborough, Susannah York, James Faulkner, James Donald

The Conductor *
Poland   1979   102m   Orwocolor
PRF/X Films of Poland
original title: *Dyrygent*

A Polish girl violinist finds her life affected when an elderly international conductor returns to her town.

Initially interesting but finally tedious and muddled allegory, further handicapped by stilted post-synching of the English version.

w Andrzej Kijowski   *d* Andrzej Wajda   *ph* Slawomir Idziak   *m* from Beethoven

John Gielgud, Krystyna Janda, Andrzej Seweryn

Cone of Silence *
GB   1960   92m   bw
British Lion/Bryanston (Aubrey Baring)
US title: *Trouble in the Sky*

A seasoned pilot is condemned for an error which caused a crash and later dies in similar circumstances. A flying examiner discovers scientific reasons for exonerating him.

Tolerable suspense drama let down by thin dialogue and confused characterization.

w Robert Westerby   *novel* David Beaty   *d* Charles Frend   *ph* Arthur Grant   *m* Gerhard Schurmann

Michael Craig, Bernard Lee, Peter Cushing, George Sanders, Elizabeth Seal, André Morell, Gordon

Jackson, Delphi Lawrence, Noel Willman, Charles Tingwell

'Young ones! Parental units! We summon you!'
Coneheads
US   1993   83m   DeLuxe
Paramount (Lorne Michaels)
V, V*, L, S

An illegal pointy-headed alien crash-lands in the United States.

Dim one-joke comedy at the expense of suburbia.

w Tom Davis, Dan Aykroyd, Bonnie Turner, Terry Turner   *d* Steve Barron   *ph* Francis Kenny   *m* David Newman   *pd* Gregg Fonseca   *ed* Paul Trejo

Dan Aykroyd, Jane Curtin, Michael McKean, Laraine Newman, Jason Alexander, Lisa Jane Persky, Chris Farley, David Spade, Michelle Burke

'A sweet, funny, anarchic pastiche that should find broad-based popularity.' – *Variety*

'Quite extraordinarily bad . . . worth renting only if you take a perverse pleasure in watching a very large amount of someone else's money going down the drain.' – *Jonathan Ross, Empire*

† The film was released direct to video in Britain.

Coney Island *
US   1943   96m   Technicolor
TCF (William Perlberg)

Two fairground showmen vie for the affections of a songstress.

Brassy, simple-minded, entertaining musical. Very typical of its time; later remade as *Wabash Avenue* (qv).

w George Seaton   *d* Walter Lang   *ph* Ernest Palmer   *m* Alfred Newman   *ch* Hermes Pan   *m/ly* Leo Robin, Ralph Rainger   *ad* Richard Day, Joseph C. Wright

Betty Grable, George Montgomery, Cesar Romero, Charles Winninger, Phil Silvers, Matt Briggs, Paul Hurst, Frank Orth, Andrew Tombes, Alec Craig, Hal K. Dawson

AAN: Alfred Newman

Confession
US   1937   90m   bw
Warner (Henry Blanke)

An errant mother shoots her former lover to protect her daughter.

Stilted romantic melodrama copied scene for scene from a 1936 German film *Mazurka*.

w Julius J. Epstein, Margaret Le Vino   *original screenplay* Hans Rameau   *d* Joe May   *ph* Sid Hickox   *md* Leo F. Forbstein   *m* Peter Kreuder   *ad* Anton Grot

Kay Francis, Ian Hunter, Basil Rathbone, Jane Bryan, Donald Crisp, Dorothy Peterson, Laura Hope Crews, Robert Barrat

'Distinctly in the upper bracket and made to order for important first runs.' – *Variety*

Confession
GB   1955   90m   bw
Anglo Guild
US title: *The Deadliest Sin*

A murderer stalks the priest who knows his guilt through the confessional but may not reveal it.

So-so reworking of the theme that daunted Hitchcock in *I Confess;* some pleasant touches are nullified by slow pacing.

wd Ken Hughes

Sydney Chaplin, Audrey Dalton, John Welsh, John Bentley, Peter Hammond

The Confession (1965): see *Quick Let's Get Married*

The Confession *

France/Italy   1970   160m   Eastmancolor
Films Corona/Films Pomereu/Selena Cinematografica (Robert Dorfmann)
original title: L'Aveu

In Prague in 1951, a minister is secretly imprisoned and interrogated, and finally confesses under duress to anti-communist activities.

Brutally long but frequently impressive anti-Soviet tract, extremely well acted but less exciting than Z. Based on a true account.

w Jorge Semprun   book Lise and Artur London
d Costa-Gavras   ph Raoul Coutard   m not credited

Yves Montand, Simone Signoret, Gabriele Ferzetti, Michel Vitold

Confessions of a Counterspy: see Man on a String

Confessions of a Driving Instructor

GB   1976   90m   colour
Columbia-Warner/Swiftdown (Greg Smith)
V

A newly qualified driving instructor seduces his female pupils and all the other women he meets.

A tired farce that cannot even rise to the level of the Carry On series' double entendres.

w Christopher Wood   novel Timothy Lea
d Norman Cohen   ph Ken Hodges   m Ed Welch
ad Albert Witherick   ed Geoffrey Foot

Robin Askwith, Anthony Booth, Sheila White, Doris Hare, Bill Maynard, Windsor Davies, Liz Fraser, Irene Handl, Lynda Bellingham, Avril Angers

'A fifth-rate potboiler of proven commercial value.' – John Pym, MFB

Confessions of a Nazi Spy ***

US   1939   110m   bw
Warner (Robert Lord)

How G-men ferreted out Nazis in the United States.

Topical exposé with all concerned in top form; a semi-documentary very typical of Warner product throughout the thirties and forties, from G-Men to Mission to Moscow and I Was a Communist for the FBI: well made, punchy, and smartly edited, with a loud moral at the end.

w Milton Krims, John Wexley, from materials gathered by former FBI agent Leon G. Turrou
d Anatole Litvak   ph Sol Polito   m Max Steiner

Edward G. Robinson, Paul Lukas, George Sanders, Francis Lederer, Henry O'Neill, Lya Lys, James Stephenson, Sig Rumann, Dorothy Tree, Joe Sawyer

'Its social implications are far more important than the immediate question of how much money the release makes for Warner Brothers.' – Variety

'The Warner brothers have declared war on Germany with this one . . . with this precedent there is no way any producer could argue about dramatizing any social or political theme on the grounds that he's afraid of domestic or foreign censorship. Everybody duck.' – Pare Lorentz

'Has a remarkable resemblance to a full-length Crime Does Not Pay.' – David Wolff

'One of the most sensational movie jobs on record, workmanlike in every respect and sprang across the headlines.' – Otis Ferguson

Confessions of a Pop Performer

GB   1975   91m   colour
Columbia-Warner/Swiftdown
V

A window cleaner joins a rock group and enjoys the groupies.

A broad and unsubtle slapstick comedy.

w Christopher Wood   novel Confessions from the Pop Scene by Timothy Lea   d Norman Cohen   ph Alan

Hume   m Bugatti Musker   pd Robert Jones
ed Geoffrey Foot

Robin Askwith, Anthony Booth, Sheila White, Doris Hare, Bill Maynard, Bob Todd, Jill Gascoine, Peter Jones, Diane Langton, Ian Lavender

'Creaky gags, overly familiar slapstick routines, sniggering innuendo, grimly leaden mugging and a nervously regular injection of titillating sequences on the lines of the average German sex comedy.' – Verina Glaessner, MFB

Confessions of a Sex Maniac

GB   1974   81m   Eastmancolor
Oppidan/Rothermorth (Alan Birkinshaw)
aka: Design for Lust; The Man Who Couldn't Get Enough

An architect searches for the perfect breast so that he can use it as the design for a new building.

Tired farce, intended to titillate, but more likely to act as a soporific.

w Alan Paz   d Alan Birkinshaw   ph Arthur Lavis
m Derek Warne, John Shakespeare   ad Tessa Davis
ed David White

Roger Lloyd Pack, Vicki Hodge, Derek Royle, Stephanie Marrian, Louise Rush, Candy Baker

'A perilously weak plot premise is just about kept alive by the two appealing lead performances, before being smothered by a platitudinous ton of groping and grappling.' – Richard Combs

Confessions of a Window Cleaner

GB   1974   90m   Eastmancolor
Columbia-Warner/Swiftdown (Greg Smith)
V

A window cleaner discovers many amorous housewives on his round.

A broad, but not bawdy, comedy for the sexually repressed. Despite its low level, it did well enough at the box-office to spawn several sequels.

w Christopher Wood, Val Guest   d Val Guest
ph Norman Warwick   m Sam Sklair   pd Robert Jones   ed Bill Lenny

Robin Askwith, Anthony Booth, Sheila White, Dandy Nicholls, Bill Maynard, Linda Hayden, John Le Mesurier, Joan Hickson, Richard Wattis, Katya Wyeth, Sam Kydd

'The humour is of the sniggering, innuendo-squeezing variety and is aimed with unnerving mediocrity at a particular kind of embarrassed – and distinctly British – audience reaction.' – Gareth Jones, MFB

Confessions of an Opium Eater

US   1962   85m   bw
Albert Zugsmith
V*
GB title: Evils of Chinatown

In San Francisco in the 1890s, a seaman falls into the clutches of a tong.

The hero is called de Quincey, but that is the only association with the famous book of the same title. This absurd melodrama is just about bad enough to be funny, but not very.

w Robert Hill   d Albert Zugsmith   ph Joseph Biroc   m Albert Glasser   ad Eugene Lourié

Vincent Price, Linda Ho, Richard Loo, Philip Ahn, June Kim

'Has to be seen to be believed . . . starved girls captive in cages, secret panels, sliding doors, sewer escape routes, opium dens and nightmares . . .' – MFB

Confidential Agent **

US   1945   122m   bw
Warner (Robert Buckner)

An emissary of Franco's Spain comes to England in the late thirties to make a munitions deal, and falls in love with the tycoon's daughter.

Heavy-going simplification of Graham Greene's lowering novel, with cast and (especially) set designers all at sea but nevertheless providing striking moments.

w Robert Buckner   d Herman Shumlin   ph James Wong Howe   m Franz Waxman

Charles Boyer, Lauren Bacall, Katina Paxinou, Peter Lorre, Victor Francen, George Coulouris, Wanda Hendrix, George Zucco, Miles Mander

'In some ways an exciting and good picture, the best attempt yet, though still inadequate, to make the best of a Greene novel.' – James Agee

Confidential Report

Spain   1955   99m   bw
Sevilla Studios (Louis Dolivet, Orson Welles)
V, V*, L
aka: Mr Arkadin

A wealthy and powerful financier employs a young American to seek out figures from his own past, who are soon found dead . . .

Silly melodrama which might have been suspenseful if done by Hitchcock, or even by Welles at his peak; as it is, weak writing and sloppy production remove most of the interest and reveal it as a very obvious bag of tricks.

wd Orson Welles   novel Mr Arkadin by Orson Welles
ph Jean Bourgoin   m Paul Misraki   pd Orson Welles   ed Renzo Lucidi

Orson Welles, Michael Redgrave, Katina Paxinou, Akim Tamiroff, Mischa Auer, Patricia Medina, Jack Watling, Peter Van Eyck, Paola Mori, Robert Arden, Grégoire Aslan, Suzanne Flon

'Tilted camera angles, heavy atmospheric shots, overlapping dialogue – all the trademarks are here, sometimes over-used to an almost hysterical degree, but they have little significance . . . (the film) springs not from life but from the earlier cinematic world of Welles himself and from the kind of thriller written about thirty years ago by E. Philips Oppenheim.' – Gavin Lambert

'The quality of the soundtrack is quite disastrous, but there is a certain grandeur about the carelessness of the film's construction which makes one forget everything except the immediacy of the moment.' – Basil Wright, 1972

Confidentially Connie

US   1953   71m   bw
MGM

A Texas rancher starts a price war when he strikes a deal with a local butcher so that the rancher's impecunious son can get half-price meat for his family.

Modest comedy which adequately filled the lower half of a bill.

w Max Shulman   story Max Shulman, Herman Wouk   d Edward Buzzell

Louis Calhern, Janet Leigh, Van Johnson, Walter Slezak, Gene Lockhart, Hayden Rorke

Confirm or Deny *

US   1941   78m   bw
TCF (Len Hammond)

An American reporter falls for a wireless operator in wartime London.

Artificial but watchable minor romantic melodrama.

w Jo Swerling, Henry Wales, Samuel Fuller
d Archie Mayo   ph Leon Shamroy

Don Ameche, Joan Bennett, Roddy McDowall, Arthur Shields, Raymond Walburn, John Loder

† Fritz Lang directed some scenes.

Conflict *
US   1945   86m   bw
Warner (William Jacobs)
V, V*

A man murders his wife and is apparently haunted by her; but the odd happenings have been arranged by a suspicious psychiatrist.

Leaden and artificial melodrama with both stars miscast; a few effective moments.

w Arthur T. Horman, Dwight Taylor   d Curtis Bernhardt   ph Merritt Gerstad   m Frederick Hollander

Humphrey Bogart, Sydney Greenstreet, Alexis Smith, Rose Hobart, Charles Drake, Grant Mitchell

† The film was completed in August 1943.

Conflict of Wings *
GB   1953   84m   Eastmancolor
Group Three (Herbert Mason)
US title: Fuss over Feathers

East Anglian villagers fight to save a bird sanctuary from being taken over by the RAF as a rocket range.

Sub-Ealing comedy-drama with a highly predictable outcome; generally pleasant but without much bite.

w Don Sharp, John Pudney   d John Eldridge   ph Arthur Grant   m Philip Green

John Gregson, Muriel Pavlow, Kieron Moore, Niall MacGinnis, Sheila Sweet, Harry Fowler, Barbara Hicks, Charles Lloyd Pack

The Conformist **
Italy/France/West Germany   1969   108m   Technicolor
Mars/Marianne/Maran (Giovanni Bertolucci)
V*, L
original title: Il Conformista

In 1938 an inhibited young man tries to conform to the prevailing mood of Fascism, but gets out of his depth when he turns informer.

Psychologically confusing but brilliantly realized recreation of an age.

wd Bernardo Bertolucci   novel Alberto Moravia   ph Vittorio Storaro   m Georges Delerue

Jean-Louis Trintignant, Stefania Sandrelli, Gastone Moschin, Enzo Taroscio, Dominique Sanda, Pierre Clementi

'It's a triumph of feeling and of style – lyrical, flowing, velvety style, so operatic that you come away with sequences in your head like arias.' – New Yorker

AAN: Bernardo Bertolucci (as writer)

Il Conformista: see The Conformist

Congo Bill
US   1948   bw   serial: 15 eps
Columbia

A wild animal trainer and jungle expert agrees to deliver a letter to an heiress missing in Africa.

Standard serial hokum with witch doctors for villains.
d Spencer Bennet, Thomas Carr

Don McGuire, Cleo Moore, Jack Ingram, I. Stanford Jolley

Congo Crossing
US   1956   85m   Technicolor
U-I (Howard Christie)

Assorted fugitives from justice gather at Congotanga, which has no extradition laws.

The poor man's Casablanca, quite good looking but dully written and presented.

w Richard Alan Simmons   d Joseph Pevney   ph Russell Metty   m Joseph Gershenson

George Nader, Virginia Mayo, Peter Lorre, Michael Pate, Rex Ingram

Congorilla *
US   1932   74m   bw
Fox

A record of two years spent in the Belgian Congo by Mr and Mrs Martin Johnson.

Excellent exploration documentary of its time.

wd The Johnsons

'Replete with thrills, adventure and laughs, making withal for an excellent entertainment.' – Variety

Congress Dances *
Germany   1931   92m   bw
UFA (Erich Pommer)
original title: Der Kongress Tanzt

At the Congress of Vienna, Metternich attempts to decoy the Tsar with a countess; but the Tsar has a double.

Lubitsch-like treatment of sexual dalliance in high places; no doubt a stunner in its time, but rather faded now.

w Norbert Falk, Robert Liebmann   d Erik Charrell   ph Carl Hoffmann   m Werner Heymann

Conrad Veidt, Henri Garat/Willy Fritsch, Lilian Harvey

'A revue more than a story . . . grace, taste and a light hand.' – Variety

A Connecticut Yankee *
US   1931   96m   bw
Fox
V*

A man dreams himself back to the court of King Arthur, and teaches the Middle Ages a thing or two about modern living.

First sound version of Mark Twain's classic fantasy, also filmed in 1921 and 1949. Creaky now, but amiable.

w William Conselman   d David Butler   ph Ernest Palmer

Will Rogers, Maureen O'Sullivan, Myrna Loy, Frank Albertson, William Farnum

'Good deluxe comedy . . . should draw substantial grosses.' – Variety

'Its laughter will ring through the centuries!'
A Connecticut Yankee in King Arthur's Court *
US   1949   106m   Technicolor
Paramount (Robert Fellows)
V*, L
GB title: A Yankee in King Arthur's Court

Gossamer musical version of the above with the emphasis on song and knockabout.

Palatable, with the 'Busy Doin' Nothin'' sequence the most memorable.

w Edmund Beloin   d Tay Garnett   ph Ray Rennahan   md Victor Young   m/ly Johnny Burke, Jimmy Van Heusen

Bing Crosby, Rhonda Fleming, William Bendix, Cedric Hardwicke, Murvyn Vye

'The tacky pageantry is more suited to the opening of a West Coast supermarket than to an English court in the 6th century.' – Pauline Kael, 70s

Connecting Rooms
GB   1969   103m   Technicolor
Telstar/Franklin Gollings (Harry Field)

In a seedy Bayswater boarding house, a dismissed schoolmaster befriends a failed cellist whose protégé is a sponging songwriter.

Aggressively dismal melodrama which would be hilarious if it were not so sadly slow and naïve.

wd Franklin Gollings   play The Cellist by Marion Hart   ph John Wilcox   m John Shakespeare

Bette Davis, Michael Redgrave, Alexis Kanner, Kay Walsh, Gabrielle Drake, Leo Genn, Olga Georges-Picot, Richard Wyler, Brian Wilde

The Connection
US   1961   110m   bw
Shirley Clarke/Lewis Allen
V*

Junkies hang around waiting for a fix and are filmed by a documentary unit.

Unattractive low-budgeter with occasional impressive moments.

w Jack Gelber   play Jack Gelber   d Shirley Clarke   ph Arthur J. Ornitz   m Freddie Redd   ad Richard Sylbert

Warren Finnerty, Jerome Raphael, Jim Anderson, Carl Lee, Roscoe Browne

The Conquering Horde
US   1931   73m   bw
Paramount

In Texas after the Civil War, resistance to railroads hampers the movement of cattle.

Strongish Western of its period, but of no continuing interest.

w Grover Jones, William Slavens McNutt   d Edward Sloman

Richard Arlen, Fay Wray, Claude Gillingwater, Ian MacLaren

'Good story, plenty of love interest, action and comedy . . . will do above average.' – Variety

'Spectacular as its barbaric passions and savage conquests!'
The Conqueror
US   1955   112m   Technicolor   Cinemascope
Howard Hughes (Dick Powell)
V*

A romance of the early life of Genghis Khan, who captures and is enamoured by the daughter of an enemy.

Solemn pantomime with a measure of bloodthirsty action and dancing girls, but featuring too many dull spots between, especially as the star is the most unlikely of eastern warriors and the production values careful but not too steady.

w Oscar Millard   d Dick Powell   ph Joseph LaShelle, Leo Tover, Harry J. Wild   m Victor Young

John Wayne, Susan Hayward, Pedro Armendariz, Agnes Moorehead, Thomas Gomez, John Hoyt, William Conrad, Ted de Corsia, Lee Van Cleef

GENGHIS KHAN: 'This tartar woman is for me, and my blood says, take her!'

'Simply an oriental western.' – New York Times

'History has not been well served and nor has the popcorn public.' – Richard Hatch, Nation

'It's all that its makers wanted it to be.' – Manchester Guardian

'John Wayne as Genghis Khan – history's most improbable piece of casting unless Mickey Rooney were to play Jesus in King of Kings.' – Jack Smith, L.A. Times

† The location was Utah's Escalante Desert, and three local mountains were renamed Mount Wayne, Mount Hughes and Mount Powell. The desert had been used for atom bomb tests, and twenty-five years after the production, questions were asked when several members of the cast died of cancer.
†† Wayne asked for his role. 'The way the screenplay reads, this is a cowboy picture, and that's how I am going to play Genghis Khan. I see him as a gunfighter.'

The Conqueror Worm: see Witchfinder General

The Conquerors

US   1932   88m   bw
RKO (David O. Selznick)
TV title: *Pioneer Builders*

Nebraska settlers in the 1870s set the seeds of a banking empire.

Routine family epic with the star playing himself and his own grandson.

w Robert Lord   *story* Howard Estabrook
d William Wellman   *ph* Edward Cronjager
m Max Steiner

Richard Dix, Ann Harding, Edna May Oliver, Guy Kibbee, Donald Cook, Julie Haydon, Jed Prouty

'As good as a depression story can be, which isn't much box office.' – *Variety*

Conquest **

US   1937   115m   bw
MGM (Bernard Hyman)
V*
GB title: *Marie Walewska*

The life of Napoleon's most enduring mistress.

Measured, dignified, and often rather dull historical fiction, lightened by excellent performances and production.

w Samuel Hoffenstein, Salka Viertel, S. N. Behrman, from a Polish play dramatized by Helen Jerome
d Clarence Brown   *ph* Karl Freund   *m* Herbert Stothart   *ad* Cedric Gibbons

Greta Garbo, *Charles Boyer*, Reginald Owen, Alan Marshal, Henry Stephenson, Dame May Whitty, Leif Erickson

'For special first-run openings – and then the clean up.' – *Variety*

'Ornate, unexpectedly tasteful, carefully detailed – and lifeless.' – *Pauline Kael, 70s*

AAN: Charles Boyer; Cedric Gibbons

Conquest of Cochise

US   1953   78m   Technicolor
Columbia (Sam Katzman)
V*

An army major is sent to make peace with Cochise, the Apache.

Feeble Western cheapie.

w Arthur Lewis, De Vallon Scott   d William Castle

Robert Stack, John Hodiak, Joy Page

'See how it will happen – in your lifetime!'
Conquest of Space

US   1955   80m   Technicolor
Paramount (George Pal)
V*

In 1980, the Americans have built a space station in the atmosphere, and plan a voyage to the moon but are sent to Mars instead.

So history catches up with science fiction. This sober prophecy looks good but very little happens and the result is as dull as it is bright and shiny.

w James O'Hanlon   d Byron Haskin   *ph* Lionel Lindon   *m* Van Cleeve   *ad* Hal Pereira, James McMillan Johnson   *sp* John P. Fulton, Irmin Roberts, Paul Lerpae, Ivyl Burks, Jan Domella

Eric Fleming, Walter Brooke, Mickey Shaughnessy, William Hopper, Ross Martin

Conquest of the Air

GB   1940   71m   bw
London Films/Alexander Korda

A history of man's discovery of the power of flight.

Curious schoolbook documentary, of historical interest.

w Hugh Gray, Peter Bezencenet   d Zoltan Korda and others

Laurence Olivier (as Lunardi), Franklin Dyall, Henry Victor, Hay Petrie, John Turnbull

† Work began on the film in 1935, when it was planned as part of a series on land, sea and air transport through the ages. It was completed in 1937 but not released for another three years.

Conquest of the Planet of the Apes

US   1972   85m   DeLuxe   Todd-AO 35
TCF/APJAC (Arthur P. Jacobs)
V*

In the 1990s, apes used as slaves revolt against their human masters.

Ragged science fiction in a series that was going rapidly downhill.

w Paul Dehn   d J. Lee Thompson   *ph* Bruce Surtees   *m* Tom Scott   *ad* Philip Jefferies   *ed* Marjorie Fowler, Allan Jaggs

Roddy McDowall, Don Murray, Ricardo Montalban, Natalie Trundy, Hari Rhodes, Severn Darden

'In spite of some crude allegorical pretensions, it can't really be considered seriously as more than another excuse for APJAC to get maximum wear out of an expensive set of costumes. Even on that score, the film falls down rather badly.' – *Clyde Jeavons, MFB*

† The film was fourth in the series that began with *The Planet of the Apes*, and continued with *Beneath the Planet of the Apes* and *Escape from the Planet of the Apes*. It was followed by *Battle for the Planet of the Apes* (qqv).

Conquest of the South Pole

GB   1989   95m   colour
Jam Jar Films/Channel 4 (Gareth Wardell)

Five unemployed Glaswegian youths recreate Amussen's expedition to Antarctica in a decaying urban landscape.

Awkward transfer to the screen of an impressionistic play.

w Gareth Wardell   *play* Manfred Karge   d Gillies Mackinnon   *ph* Sean Van Hales   *m* Guy Woolfenden   *ad* Andy Harris   *ed* Stephen Singleton

Stefan Rimkus, Ewen Bremner, Leonard O'Malley, Laura Girling, Gordon Cameron, Alastair Galbraith, John Michie, Julie-Kate Olivier

Conrack *

US   1974   106m   DeLuxe   Panavision
TCF (Martin Ritt, Irving Ravetch)
V*

A young white teacher is assigned to an all-black school in South Carolina, and after some difficulty makes friends with children and parents.

Nostalgically mellow happy-film, lit by bright smiles all around.

w Irving Ravetch, Harriet Frank Jnr   *novel The Water Is Wide* by Pat Conroy   d Martin Ritt   *ph* John Alonzo   *m* John Williams

Jon Voight, Paul Winfield, Hume Cronyn, Madge Sinclair, Tina Andrews

'For all its craftsman-like virtues, it seems a conscious turning aside from the complexities of modern cinema to the simpler alternatives of yesteryear. Indeed, with underprivileged white children instead of black and Greer Garson substituting for Jon Voight, the film might have been made all of thirty years ago.' – *John Raisbeck*

'Thou Shalt Not Covet Thy Neighbor's Wife.'
Consenting Adults

US   1992   99m   Technicolor
Buena Vista/Hollywood Pictures (Alan J. Pakula, David Permut)
V, V*, S

A money-obsessed financial adviser accuses his friend of murdering his wife after a night in which they swopped partners.

A thriller that owes much to Hitchcock but is unable to maintain either interest or suspense.

w Matthew Chapman   d Alan J. Pakula
ph Stephen Goldblatt   *m* Michael Small   *pd* Carol Spier   *ed* Sam O'Steen

Kevin Kline, Mary Elizabeth Mastrantonio, Kevin Spacey, Rebecca Miller, E. G. Marshall, Forest Whitaker

'Initially seems a little brainier than its brethren but soon gives way to the same cavernous lapses in logic and formula ending.' – *Variety*

'Nobody can do anything much to enliven this ponderous telling of a barely credible story and the result is curiously flat and unholding.' – *Derek Malcolm, Guardian*

Consider Your Verdict

GB   1938   40m   bw
Charter (John Boulting)

A juror proves an accused man not guilty by falsely confessing to the crime himself.

Fairly smart little entry into the feature film scene for the Boulting Brothers, from a popular radio play of the time.

w Francis Miller   *play* Laurence Housman   d Roy Boulting   *ph* D. P. Cooper

Marius Goring, Manning Whiley, Olive Sloane, Hay Petrie, George Carney

Consolation Marriage

US   1931   62m   bw
RKO
V*

A wife keeps a stiff upper lip when her husband strays.

Ho-hum domestic drama with attempts at comedy relief.

w Humphrey Pearson   d Paul Sloane

Irene Dunne, Pat O'Brien, John Halliday, Matt Moore, Myrna Loy

'Fair entertainment; will satisfy with good stage support.' – *Variety*

'What conflict in the heart of a nun would make her break her vows?'
Conspiracy of Hearts *

GB   1960   113m   bw
Rank (Betty E. Box)

During World War II, Italian nuns smuggle Jewish children across the border from a nearby prison camp.

Highly commercial combination of exploitable sentimental elements: Germans, Jews, nuns, children, war, suspense. Remarkably, it gets by without causing nausea.

w Robert Presnell Jnr   d Ralph Thomas   *ph* Ernest Steward   *m* Angelo Lavagnino

Lilli Palmer, Sylvia Syms, Yvonne Mitchell, Albert Lieven, Ronald Lewis, Peter Arne, Nora Swinburne, Michael Goodliffe, Megs Jenkins, David Kossoff, Jenny Laird, George Coulouris, Phyllis Neilson-Terry

Conspirator

GB   1949   87m   bw
MGM (Arthur Hornblow Jnr)

A guards officer, unknown to his young wife, is a communist spy.

Singularly awful romantic melodrama which never convinces or entertains for a moment.

w Sally Benson, Gerard Fairlie   *novel* Humphrey Slater   d Victor Saville   *ph* F. A. Young   *m* John Wooldridge

Robert Taylor, Elizabeth Taylor, Harold Warrender, Robert Flemyng, Marie Ney

The Conspirators *
US   1944   101m   bw
Warner (Jack Chertok)

A Dutch underground leader escapes to Lisbon and clears up international intrigue.

Interestingly cast but often listless wartime melodrama, a doomed attempt to reprise *Casablanca* without Humphrey Bogart.

w Vladimir Pozner, Leo Rosten   novel *City of Shadows* by Frederick Prokosch   d Jean Negulesco   ph Arthur Edeson   m Max Steiner

Hedy Lamarr, Paul Henreid, Sydney Greenstreet, Peter Lorre, *Victor Francen*, Carol Thurston, Vladimir Sokoloff, Joseph Calleia, Edward Ciannelli, Steve Geray, Kurt Katch, George Macready

SYDNEY GREENSTREET (as Quintanilla): 'This may seem to you melodramatic, but indulge me, please, I like melodrama.'

'As exciting as baseball and almost as gentlemanly as cricket.' – *New Statesman*

'I enjoyed it as much as any Warner melodrama since *Casablanca*.' – *Observer*

Constans: see *The Constant Factor*

The Constant Factor *
Poland   1980   91m   Eastmancolor
Cinegate/PRF/Zespol Filmowy
original title: *Constans*

A precise idealist refuses to adjust to the petty corruptions of life.

Cool dissection of human fallibility.

wd Krzysztof Zanussi   ph Slawomir Idziak   m Wojciech Kilar   ad Tadeusz Wybult, Maciej Putowski   ed Urszula Sliwinska, Ewa Smal

Tadeusz Bradecki, Zofia Mrozowska, Malgorzata Zajaczkowska, Cezary Morawski, Witold Pyrkosz

The Constant Husband *
GB   1955   88m   Technicolor print
British Lion/London Films (Frank Launder, Sidney Gilliat)

An amnesiac discovers that he is a multiple bigamist, still wanted by each of his five wives.

Flimsy comedy which never really gets going despite an attractive cast.

w Sidney Gilliat, Val Valentine   d Sidney Gilliat   ph Ted Scaife   m Malcolm Arnold

Rex Harrison, Kay Kendall, Margaret Leighton, Cecil Parker, Nicole Maurey, George Cole, Raymond Huntley, Michael Hordern, Eric Pohlmann, Robert Coote

The Constant Nymph *
GB   1933   98m   bw
Gaumont (Michael Balcon)

In the Tyrol, a composer leaves his rich wife for a schoolgirl suffering from a heart condition.

Archetypal romantic drama from Margaret Kennedy's book, first filmed in 1928 by the same producer (and then directed by Adrian Brunel, starring Ivor Novello and Mabel Poulton). A standard production of its time, which seems to have vanished with the literary copyright.

w Margaret Kennedy, Basil Dean, from their play based on her novel   d Basil Dean   ph Max Greene   m John Greenwood

Brian Aherne, Victoria Hopper, Leonora Corbett, Lyn Harding, Mary Clare, Jane Baxter

'Beautifully done artistic success from England, of doubtful box office for America.' – *Variety*

'One can say that it has a beginning, a middle and an end, but it lacks something vital.' – *E. V. Lucas, Punch*

The Constant Nymph *
US   1943   112m   bw
Warner (Henry Blanke)

Artificially well-produced, overlong Hollywood version of the above.

w Kathryn Scola   d Edmund Goulding   ph Tony Gaudio   m Erich Wolfgang Korngold

Charles Boyer, *Joan Fontaine*, Alexis Smith, Brenda Marshall, Charles Coburn, Dame May Whitty, Peter Lorre, Joyce Reynolds, Jean Muir, Edward Ciannelli, Montagu Love, André Charlot

AAN: Joan Fontaine

Consuming Passions
GB/US   1988   100m   colour
Samuel Goldwyn/Euston Films (William Cartlidge)
V, V*

By adding a new ingredient to chocolate – human flesh – a young man rises to the top of his profession.

Dire attempt to revive the tradition of Ealing comedy.

w Paul D. Zimmerman, Andrew Davies   play *Secrets* by Michael Palin, Terry Jones   d Giles Foster   ph Roger Pratt   m Richard Hartley   pd Peter Lamont   ed John Grover

Vanessa Redgrave, Freddie Jones, Jonathan Pryce, Tyler Butterworth, Sammi Davis, Thora Hird, Prunella Scales

The Contact Man: see *Alias Nick Beal*

Conte de Printemps **
France   1990   110m   colour
Roissy Films/Films du Losange (Margaret Menegoz)
V, V*, L

A teenage daughter, whose parents are separated, attempts to persuade her father to change girlfriends.

Witty, sophisticated comedy of manners.

wd Eric Rohmer   ph Luc Pages   m Beethoven, Schumann   ed Lisa Garcia

Anne Teyssedre, Hugues Quester, Florence Durrell, Eloise Bennett, Sophie Robin

Conte d'hiver **
France   1992   114m   bw
Artificial Eye/Films du Losange (Margaret Menegoz)
V
aka: *A Winter's Tale*

A French hairdresser, waiting in hope for the man who fathered her child to return to her, has unsatisfactory relationships with two other men.

An enjoyable variation on the themes of Shakespeare's play, complete with happy ending and as little concerned with reality.

wd Eric Rohmer   ph Luc Pages, Maurice Giraud   m Sebastian Erms   ed Mary Stephen

Charlotte Very, Frederic Van Den Driessche, Michel Voletti, Hervé Furic, Ava Loraschi, Christiane Desbois, Rosette, Jean-Luc Revol

'Fittingly, Rohmer's winter story has an affirmative inner glow.' – *Philip Strick, Sight and Sound*

Contest Girl: see *The Beauty Jungle*

Continental Divide
US   1981   103m   Technicolor
Universal/Amblin (Bob Larson)
V*, L

A national columnist finds himself banished to the wilds with a lady ornithologist studying the bald eagle.

Old-fashioned comedy, a cross between *Bringing Up Baby* and *Woman of the Year*. Not actually bad, but somewhat lacking in personality.

w Lawrence Kasdan   d Michael Apted   ph John Bailey   m Michael Small

John Belushi, Blair Brown, Allen Goorwitz, Carlin Glynn

Continuavamo a Chiamarlo Trinity: see *Trinity Is Still My Name*

Contraband **
GB   1940   92m   bw
British National (John Corfield)
V*
US title: *Blackout*

A Danish merchant captain and a girl in wartime London expose a gang of spies using a cinema as headquarters.

Enjoyable lightweight comedy melodrama on Hitchcock lines, reuniting the unlikely star team from *The Spy in Black*.

w Emeric Pressburger, Michael Powell, Brock Williams   d Michael Powell   ph F. A. Young

Conrad Veidt, Valerie Hobson, Esmond Knight, Hay Petrie, Raymond Lovell, Harold Warrender, Charles Victor, Manning Whiley

Contraband Spain
GB   1955   82m   Eastmancolor
Diadem/ABP

An American agent in Barcelona investigates the death there of a compatriot involved in drug smuggling.

Pretty awful formula thick ear with bland stars and a boring look.

wd Lawrence Huntingdon

Richard Greene, Anouk Aimée, Michael Denison, John Warwick

The Contract **
Poland   1980   111m   colour
Cinegate/PRF/Zespol Filmowy
original title: *Kontrakt*

Despite the reluctance of a couple to marry, the groom's father celebrates with a lavish reception.

Comic and satirical look at Polish high life.

wd Krzysztof Zanussi   ph Slawomir Idziak   m Wojciech Kilar   ad Tadeusz Wybult   ed Urszula Sliwinska, Ewa Smal

Maja Komorowska, Tadeusz Lomnicki, Magda Jaroszowna, Krzysztof Kilberger, Leslie Caron

Convention City *
US   1933   78m   bw
Warner (Henry Blanke)

Extra-marital fun and games at a Chicago convention.

Amusing and rather risqué comedy which helped to bring down on Hollywood the wrath of the Legion of Decency.

w Robert Lord   d Archie Mayo   ph William Reese

Joan Blondell, Guy Kibbee, Adolphe Menjou, Dick Powell, Mary Astor, Frank McHugh, Ruth Donnelly, Hugh Herbert, Hobart Cavanaugh

'Not a dull foot . . . probably the fastest complex comedy of the year and a certain money picture.' – *Variety*

The Conversation **
US   1974   113m   Technicolor
Paramount/Francis Ford Coppola
V*, L

A bugging device expert lives only for his work, but finally develops a conscience.

Absorbing but extremely difficult to follow in detail, this personal, timely (in view of Watergate), Kafkaesque suspense story centres almost entirely on director and leading actor, who have a field day.

wd *Francis Ford Coppola*   ph Bill Butler   m David Shire

Gene Hackman, John Cazale, Allen Garfield, Frederic Forrest

'A private, hallucinatory study in technical expertise and lonely guilt.' – *Sight and Sound*

'A terrifying depiction of a ransacked spirit.' – *New Yorker, 1977*

'Alert, truthful, unarty and absolutely essential viewing.' – *Michael Billington, Illustrated London News*

AAN: best picture; Francis Ford Coppola (as writer)

Conversation Piece

Italy/France   1974   121m   Technicolor
Todd-AO 35
Rusconi/Gaumont (Giovanni Bertolucci)
V*
original title: *Gruppo di Famiglia in un Interno*

When a reclusive professor is persuaded to let his top floor to a young couple he is brought face to face with his latent homosexuality and his approaching death.

Death in Venice revisited, but with much less style and even more obscurity.

w Luchino Visconti, Suso Cecchi d'Amico, Enrico Medioli   *d* Luchino Visconti   *ph* Pasqualino de Santis   *m* Franco Mannino

Burt Lancaster, Helmut Berger, Claudia Marsani, Silvana Mangano

Convict 99 *

GB   1938   91m   bw
Gainsborough (Edward Black)

A seedy schoolmaster accidentally becomes a prison governor and lets the convicts run the place.

Patchily funny if overlong and in some ways rather serious Will Hay comedy, not quite typical of him.

w Marriott Edgar, Val Guest, Ralph Smart, Jack Davies   *d* Marcel Varnel   *ph* Arthur Crabtree   *md* Louis Levy   *ad* Vetchinsky   *ed* R. E. Dearing

Will Hay, Graham Moffatt, Moore Marriott, Googie Withers, Garry Marsh, Peter Gawthorne, Basil Radford, Kathleen Harrison

Convicted *

US   1950   91m   bw
Columbia (Jerry Bresler)

When a prison informer is killed, one convict knows who did it.

Routine, over-plotted, strongly cast prison melodrama.

w William Bowers, Fred Niblo Jnr, Seton I. Miller   *play* Martin Flavin   *d* Henry Levin   *ph* Burnett Guffey   *m* George Duning

Glenn Ford, Broderick Crawford, Millard Mitchell, Dorothy Malone, Frank Faylen, Carl Benton Reid, Will Geer

Convicts Four *

US   1962   106m   bw
Allied Artists-Lubin-Kaufman (A. Ronald Lubin)
V*
original and GB title: *Reprieve*

A convict reprieved from the electric chair spends eighteen years in prison, becomes a painter, and is rehabilitated.

Odd and unsatisfactory mixture of documentary, melodrama, sentimentality and character study, with stars unexpectedly popping in for cameo appearances. Something worthier was obviously intended.

wd Millard Kaufman   *autobiography* John Resko   *ph* Joseph Biroc   *m* Leonard Rosenman

Ben Gazzara, Vincent Price, Rod Steiger, Broderick Crawford, Stuart Whitman, Ray Walston, Jack Kruschen, Sammy Davis Jnr

Convoy *

GB   1940   90m   bw
Ealing (Sergei Nolbandov)

A German pocket battleship menaces a British convoy, and a merchant ship sacrifices itself to prevent disaster.

Fluent British war film of the early days, the only substantial work of a much vaunted director who was subsequently killed.

w Pen Tennyson, Patrick Kirwan   *d* Pen Tennyson   *ph* Gunther Krampf, Roy Kellino   *m* Ernest Irving

Clive Brook, John Clements, Edward Chapman, Judy Campbell, Penelope Dudley Ward, Edward Rigby, Allan Jeayes, Albert Lieven

Convoy *

US   1978   110m   DeLuxe   Panavision
UA/EMI (Robert M. Sherman)
V*

A folk hero truck driver survives several crashes and his policeman nemesis.

A virtually plotless anthology of wanton destruction. Too noisy to sleep through.

w B. W. L. Norton, based on the song by C. W. McCall   *d* Sam Peckinpah   *ph* Harry Stradling Jnr   *m* Chip Davis

Kris Kristofferson, Ali MacGraw, Ernest Borgnine, Burt Young, Madge Sinclair

'There's a whole lot of nothing going on here . . . strictly a summer popcorn picture for the nondiscriminating.' – *Variety*

'Roughly as much fun as a ride on the New Jersey turnpike with the window open. It not only numbs the brain but pollutes the senses.' – *Richard Schickel, Time*

Coogan's Bluff **

US   1968   94m   Technicolor
Universal (Don Siegel)
V*, L

An Arizona sheriff takes an escaped killer back to New York, and when the man escapes uses Western methods to recapture him.

Violent, well-done police story which inspired the TV series *McCloud*.

w Herman Miller, Dean Riesner, Howard Rodman   *d* Don Siegel   *ph* Bud Thackery   *m* Lalo Schifrin

Clint Eastwood, Lee J. Cobb, Susan Clark, Don Stroud, Tisha Sterling, Betty Field, Tom Tully

The Cook, the Thief, His Wife & Her Lover **

GB/France   1989   124m   colour   Cinemascope
Palace/Allarts Cook/Erato Films (Kees Kasander)
V, V*, L, S

A coarse gangster holds court in a fashionable restaurant while his wife conducts a passionate affair in the kitchens with a fellow diner.

Elegant, stylized, painterly and extremely brutal variation on a Jacobean revenge tragedy, though some have seen it as a political satire on our materialistic times.

wd Peter Greenaway   *ph* Sacha Vierny   *m* Michael Nyman   *pd* Ben Van Os, Jan Roelfs   *ed* John Wilson

Richard Bohringer, Michael Gambon, Helen Mirren, Alan Howard, Tim Roth, Ciaran Hinds, Gary Olsen, Ewan Stewart, Roger Ashton Griffiths, Ron Cook, Liz Smith

Cookie

US   1989   93m   DuArt
Warner/Lorimar (Laurence Mark)
V, V*, L, S

A gangster's daughter shows that she has her father's dubious skills.

Lame drama of family relationships in gangland setting.

w Nora Ephron, Alice Arlen   *d* Susan Seidelman   *ph* Oliver Stapleton   *m* Thomas Newman   *pd* Michael Haller   *ad* Bill Groom   *ed* Andrew Mondshein

Peter Falk, Dianne Wiest, Emily Lloyd, Michael V. Gazzo, Brenda Vaccaro, Adrian Pasdar, Lionel Stander, Jerry Lewis, Bob Gunton, Ben Rayson, Ricki Lake

'Cookie has the feel of a worn-out vehicle grinding to a halt.' – *Pam Cook, MFB*

'Seven savage punks on a binge of violence.'
The Cool and the Crazy

US   1958   78m   bw
AIP/Imperial Productions (E. C. Rhoden Jnr)

A rebellious high-school student causes havoc after he persuades his fellow students to smoke marijuana.

Typical teen drive-in drama of its time, never less than hysterical and acted by a cast who look as if they've left puberty far behind.

w Richard C. Sarafian   *d* William Witney   *ph* Harry Birch   *m* Raoul Kraushaar   *ed* Helene Turner

Scott Marlowe, Gigi Perreau, Dick Bakalyan, Dick Jones

Cool Breeze

US   1972   102m   Metrocolor
MGM/Penelope (Gene Corman)

A miscellaneous gang of crooks is rounded up to commit a robbery, which ultimately fails.

Third, all-black remake of *The Asphalt Jungle* (the others being *The Badlanders* and *Cairo*). Fashionable violence against a Los Angeles backdrop, but not at all memorable.

wd Barry Pollack   *ph* Andy Davis   *m* Solomon Burke

Thalmus Rasulala, Judy Pace, Jim Watkins, Raymond St Jacques, Lincoln Kilpatrick

'What we've got here is a failure to communicate.'
Cool Hand Luke **

US   1967   126m   Technicolor   Panavision
Warner/Jalem (Gordon Carroll)
V, V*, L

Sentenced to two years' hard labour with the chain gang, a convict becomes a legend of invulnerability but is eventually shot during an escape.

Allegedly a Christ-allegory, this well-made and good-looking film is only partially successful as an entertainment; slow stretches of soul-searching alternate with brutality, and not much acting is possible.

w Donn Pearce, Frank R. Pierson   *novel* Donn Pearce   *d* Stuart Rosenberg   *ph* Conrad Hall   *m* Lalo Schifrin

Paul Newman, George Kennedy, Jo Van Fleet, J. D. Cannon, Lou Antonio, Robert Drivas, Strother Martin, Clifton James

'May be the best American film of 1967.' – *John Simon*

AA: George Kennedy

AAN: Donn Pearce, Frank R. Pierson; Lalo Schifrin; Paul Newman

The Cool Ones

US   1967   96m   Technicolor   Panavision
Warner (William Conrad)

Former pop singer makes a comeback.

Zazzy showbiz saga with ear-splitting track, quite professionally assembled.

w Joyce Geller   *d* Gene Nelson   *ph* Floyd Crosby   *m* Ernie Freeman

Roddy McDowall, Debbie Watson, Robert Coote, Phil Harris, Nita Talbot

Cool Runnings *
US   1993   97m   Technicolor
Buena Vista/Walt Disney (Dawn Steel)
S

A Jamaican athlete who fails to qualify for the Olympics decides to compete by forming a bobsled team with the aid of a white coach living on the island.

Based on the true story of the Jamaican bobsled team in the 1988 Olympics, an amiable, good-natured comedy of some charm.

w Lynn Siefert, Tommy Swerdlow, Michael Goldberg story Lynn Siefert, Michael Ritchie   d Jon Turteltaub ph Phedon Papamichael   m Hans Zimmer pd Stephen Marsh   ed Bruce Green

John Candy, Leon, Doug E. Doug, Malik Yoba, Rawle D. Lewis, Raymond Barry, Larry Gilman, Peter Outerbridge, Paul Coeur

'The offbeat, fact-based saga is enlivened by the perfect balance of humor, emotion and insight.' – Variety

Cool World
US   1992   102m   Technicolor
Blue Dolphin/Paramount (Frank Mancuso Jnr)
V, V*, L, S

A cartoonist and his creations flit in and out of the real world and the Cool World of his imagination.

Dreary attempt to marry live action and cartoon characters, with a plot obsessed by the possibility of sex between the two, which seems nothing to get excited about.

w Michael Grais, Mark Victor   d Ralph Bakshi ph John A. Alonzo   m Mark Isham, John Dixon pd Michael Corenblith   ed Steve Mirkovich, Annamaria Szanto

Kim Basinger, Gabriel Byrne, Brad Pitt, Michele Abrams, Deirdre O'Connell, Janni Brenn-Lowen

'A combination funhouse ride/acid trip that will prove an ordeal for most visitors in the form of trial by animation. Visually dazzling but utterly soulless.' – Variety

Cooley High
US   1975   107m   Movielab
Brent Walker/AIP (Steve Krantz)
V*, L

The adventures of high-school students in Chicago of the mid-60s.

A lively first feature, full of energy but lacking in focus.

w Eric Monte   d Michael Schultz   ph Paul von Brack   m Freddie Perren   ad William B. Fosser ed Christopher Holmes

Glynn Turman, Lawrence-Hilton Jacobs, Garrett Morris, Cynthia Davis, Corin Rogers, Maurice Leon Havis

'The promising debut of a very talented director, intermittently doing what he can with an uneven and somewhat routine script.' – Jonathan Rosenbaum, MFB

† The film was the basis of a US TV sitcom, What's Happening (1976–79).

The Co-Optimists *
GB   1929   83m   bw
New Era (Edwin Greenwood)

A revue by a popular pierrot troupe of the time.

Famous as Britain's first musical, this is a dated but valuable record of a stage performance of the kind long vanished.

w Melville Gideon, Laddie Cliff   d Edwin Greenwood, Laddie Cliff   ph Basil Emmott, Sydney Blythe

Davy Burnaby, Stanley Holloway, Laddie Cliff, Phyllis Monkman, Melville Gideon, Gilbert Childs, Betty Chester, Elsa MacFarlane, Peggy Petronella, Harry S. Pepper

Le Cop *
France   1985   107m   Eastmancolor   Panavision
Cannon/Films 7/Editions 23

A corrupt veteran cop is teamed with an incorruptible recruit.

Enjoyably comic exposé, much admired by the French.

w Claude Zidi   story Simon Mickael   d Claude Zidi   ph Jean-Jacques Tarbes   m Francis Lai ad Françoise de Leu   ed Nicole Saunier

Philippe Noiret, Thierry Lhermitte, Regine, Grace de Capitani, Claude Brosset, Albert Simono

Le Cop 2
France   1989   108m   Eastmancolor
Gala/Films 7/Orly/Sedif/TF1 (Pierre Gauchet)
V, S
original title: Ripoux contre ripoux

Two corrupt policemen, suspended from duty, turn the tables on the crooks and cops who try to put them out of the force.

Weak sequel, with a complicated but uninteresting plot and nowhere to go for its central characters.

w Simon Michael, Claude Zidi, Didier Kaminka d Claude Zidi   ph Jean-Jacques Tarbes   m Francis Lai   ad Françoise Deleu   ed Nicole Saunier

Phillippe Noiret, Thierry Lhermitte, Guy Marchand, Line Renaud, Grace de Capitani, Michel Aumont, Jean-Pierre Castaldi, Jean-Claude Brialy

Cop
US   1987   110m   colour
Entertainment/Atlantic (James B. Harris)
V*, L

A cop tracks down a serial killer to the detriment of his marriage and his relationship with his colleagues.

Tough, violent but not particularly memorable thriller.

wd James B. Harris   novel Blood on the Moon by James Ellroy   ph Steve Dubin   m Michael Colombier pd Gene Rudolf   ed Anthony Spano

James Woods, Lesley Ann Warren, Charles Durning, Charles Haid, Raymond J. Barry, Randi Brooks, Steven Lambert, Christopher Wynne, Jan McGill

Cop and a Half
US   1993   97m   DeLuxe
Universal/Imagine (Paul Maslansky)

An eight-year-old boy, witness to a murder, gets to be a cop for a day.

Ghastly, sentimental comedy aimed at the lowest common demoninator.

w Arne Olsen   d Henry Winkler   ph Bill Butler m Alan Silvestri   pd Maria Caso   ed Daniel Hanley, Roger Tweten, C. Timothy O'Mara

Burt Reynolds, Norman D. Golden II, Ruby Dee, Holland Taylor, Ray Sharkey, Sammy Hernandez, Frank Sivero

'Unashamedly caters to children's crudest fantasies and leaves the rest of the world at a loss. There are few adult pleasures to be had.' – Sight and Sound

Cop au Vin *
France   1984   110m   Eastmancolor   Panavision
Virgin/MK2/Marin Karmitz
original title: Poulet au Vinaigre

An unorthodox police inspector investigates two deaths in a small provincial town.

Glossy thriller exposing the pettiness of the bourgoisie.

w Dominique Roulet, Claude Chabrol   novel Un Mort En Trop by Dominique Roulet   d Claude Chabrol ph Jean Rabier   m Matthieu Chabrol ad Françoise Benoît-Fresco   ed Monique Fardoulis

Jean Poiret, Stéphane Audran, Michel Bouquet, Jean Topart, Lucas Blevaux, Pauline Lafont, Caroline Cellier, Josephine Chaplin

Copacabana
US   1947   91m   bw
UA/Sam Coslow
V*, L

A quick-thinking agent forms two acts out of one client, which makes things awkward when both are needed at once.

Thinly produced comedy with both stars doing what is expected of them in surroundings less glamorous than those to which they were previously accustomed.

w Laslo Vadnay, Allen Boretz, Howard Harris d Alfred E. Green   ph Bert Glennon   m Edward Ward

Groucho Marx, Carmen Miranda, Steve Cochran, Gloria Jean, Andy Russell

Copper Canyon
US   1949   84m   Technicolor
Paramount

After the Civil War, Southern veterans trying to rebuild their homes are helped by a gunslinger.

Shiny unpersuasive Western with stars ill at ease.

w Jonathan Latimer   d John Farrow

Ray Milland, Hedy Lamarr, Macdonald Carey, Mona Freeman, Harry Carey Jnr

Cops ***
US   1922   20m (24 fps)   bw   silent
First National/Comique Film (Joseph M. Schenck)
V

An innocent disrupts a parade and is pursued by a horde of policemen.

The perfect Keaton short, a careful assembly of perfectly timed gags.

wd Buster Keaton   ph Elgin Lessley

Buster Keaton, Virginia Fox

Cops and Robbers *
US   1973   89m   DeLuxe
UA/EK Corp (Elliott Kastner)
V*

Two New York cops turn crook and pull off a job for the Mafia.

Trendily anti-establishment comedy, quite snappy and smart when you can follow it.

w Donald E. Westlake   d Aram Avakian ph David L. Quaid   m Michel Legrand

Cliff Gorman, Joe Bologna, Dick Ward, Shepperd Strudwick, Ellen Holly, John P. Ryan

Coquette
US   1929   75m   bw
Mary Pickford
V*

A Southern belle has a flirtatious nature.

Disappointing talkie start for a first lady of the silents; she did not recover from it, despite her Oscar.

w John Grey, Allen McNeil, Sam Taylor play George Abbott, Anne Preston   d Sam Taylor

Mary Pickford, Johnny Mack Brown, Matt Moore, William Janney

AA: Mary Pickford

Le Corbeau **
France   1943   92m   bw
L'Atelier Français
US title: The Raven

Poison pen letters disturb a small provincial town.

Impressively characterized whodunnit with the usual French qualities of detail and discretion. Remade in Hollywood to less effect as *The Thirteenth Letter* (qv).

w Louis Chavance *d* Henri-Georges Clouzot
ph Nicholas Hayer *m* Tony Aubain

Pierre Fresnay, Pierre Larquey, Ginette Leclerc, Hélène Manson

'By no means as malign or as brilliant as it's cracked up to be, but a sour, clever, amusing job.' – *James Agee*

Coriolanus – Hero without a Country (dubbed)
Italy/France 1965 100m Eastmancolor
Euroscope
Dorica/Explorer/CFFP (Diego Alchimede)
original title: *Coriolano, Eroe senza Patria*; aka: *Thunder of Battle*

In a Rome riven by class conflict, its greatest general, Coriolanus, is exiled by the popular leaders.

Above-average Italian historical epic.

w Remigio Del Grosso *d* Giorgio Ferroni
ph Augusto Tiezzi *m* Carlo Rustichelli *ad* Arrigo Equini *ed* Antonietta Zita

Gordon Scott, Alberto Lupo, Lilla Brignone, Philippe Hersent, Rosalba Neri

Corky
US 1971 88m colour
MGM (Bruce Geller)

An arrogant auto mechanic becomes a stock car racer.

Noisy and unattractive movie about an anti-hero.

w Eugene Price *d* Leonard Horn

Robert Blake, Patrick O'Neal, Charlotte Rampling, Christopher Connolly, Laurence Luckinbill, Ben Johnson

The Corn Is Green *
US 1945 118m bw
Warner (Jack Chertok)
V*

In 1895 Miss Moffat starts a village school for Welsh miners, and after some tribulations sees one of them off to Oxford.

A very theatrical production with unconvincing sets and mannered acting, but the original play has its felicities.

w Casey Robinson, Frank Cavett *play* Emlyn Williams *d* Irving Rapper *ph* Sol Polito *m* Max Steiner *ad* Carl Jules Weyl

Bette Davis, John Dall, Nigel Bruce, Joan Lorring, Rhys Williams, Rosalind Ivan, Mildred Dunnock, Arthur Shields

'It's very apparent that Hollywood isn't Wales . . . but the film lingers in the memory anyway.' – *New Yorker, 1978*

† Remade as a TV movie in 1978, with Katharine Hepburn.

AAN: John Dall; Joan Lorring

Cornered *
US 1945 102m bw
RKO

After demobilization, a French-Canadian pilot tracks down the collaborationist responsible for the death of his wife.

Well-made but humourless revenge thriller.

w John Paxton *story* John Wexley *d* Edward Dmytryk *ph* Harry J. Wild *m* Roy Webb

Dick Powell, Micheline Cheirel, Walter Slezak, Morris Carnovsky

Coronado
US 1935 77m bw
Paramount

Marital misunderstandings abound at a swanky beach hotel.

Thinly plotted but star-spotted comedy musical, notable now for the talent.

w Don Hartman, Frank Butler *d* Norman McLeod

Jack Haley, Leon Errol, Eddy Duchin and his Orchestra, Johnny Downs, Betty Burgess, Andy Devine, Alice White, Jameson Thomas

Coroner Creek
US 1948 89m Cinecolor
Columbia (Harry Joe Brown)
V*

A Western crusader tracks down the man behind a stagecoach raid.

Solid action Western between the A and B categories.

w Kenneth Gamet *novel* Luke Short *d* Ray Enright

Randolph Scott, Marguerite Chapman, George Macready, Sally Eilers, Edgar Buchanan, Barbara Reed, Wallace Ford, Forrest Tucker, Douglas Fowley

Corps Profond *
France 1963 21m Technicolor
Delpire

A tour inside the human body by courtesy of micro-photography.

Spellbinding and educative documentary of a new kind, and just the right length; the later British imitation, *The Body*, outstayed its welcome.

wd Igor Barrière, Etienne Lalou

The Corpse Came COD
US 1947 87m bw
Columbia (Sam Bischoff)

Rival reporters try to solve the mystery of a wandering body.

Routine crime comedy with too few smart lines.

w George Bricker, Dwight Babcock *novel* Jimmy Starr *d* Henry Levin *ph* Lucien Andriot *m* George Duning

George Brent, Joan Blondell, Adele Jergens, Jim Bannon, Leslie Brooks, Grant Mitchell, Una O'Connor

'Horror to make your hair stand on end!'
The Corpse Vanishes
US 1942 70m bw
Monogram (Sam Katzman)
V*

A botanist kidnaps young brides for their body fluids, in the hope of reviving his dead wife.

An especially dreary example of Poverty Row horror.

w Harvey Gates *d* Wallace Fox

Bela Lugosi, Frank Moran, Minerva Urecal, Luana Walters

Corregidor
US 1943 74m bw
PRC/Dixon R. Harwin-Edward Finney
V*

Doctors on Corregidor sort out an eternal triangle while US forces fight the Japs.

Feeble wartime quickie, inept in almost every respect.

w Doris Malloy, Edgar G. Ulmer *d* William Nigh

Elissa Landi, Otto Kruger, Donald Woods, Frank Jenks, Rick Vallin, Ian Keith

Corridor of Mirrors
GB 1948 105m bw
Cartier-Romney-Apollo (Rudolph Cartier)

An eccentric art collector believes that he and his

mistress are reincarnations of 400-year-old lovers in a painting; but they are separated by murder.

Pretentious melodrama of no urgent narrative interest, with all concerned sadly at sea.

w Rudolph Cartier, Edana Romney *novel* Chris Massie *d* Terence Young *ph* André Thomas *m* Georges Auric

Eric Portman, Edana Romney, Barbara Mullen, Hugh Sinclair

'It has aimed at Art. It is, in fact, Effect. Some members of the cast wander in and out of the scenes as if they are not quite sure what has happened to them. Their confusion is not beyond comprehension.' – *MFB*

Corridors of Blood *
GB 1958 86m bw
Producers' Associates (John Croydon)
V*
original title: *Doctor from Seven Dials*

Seeking to discover anaesthetics, a Victorian doctor falls a prey to resurrection men.

Unpleasant but well-mounted semi-horror backed by strong cast and art direction.

w Jean Scott Rogers *d* Robert Day *ph* Geoffrey Faithfull *m* Buxton Orr *ad* Anthony Masters

Boris Karloff, Christopher Lee, Finlay Currie, Frank Pettingell, Betta St John, Francis Matthews, Adrienne Corri, Marian Spencer

† Not released until 1964.

The Corrupt Ones
West Germany 1967 92m colour
Warner (Arthur Brauner)
V*
aka: *The Peking Medallion; Hell to Macao*

An American photographer in the Far East is pursued by a tong.

Rubbishy adventure which just about passes the time.

w Brian Clemens *story* Ladislas Fodor *d* James Hill

Robert Stack, Elke Sommer, Nancy Kwan, Christian Marquand, Werner Peters

Corruption
GB 1967 91m Technicolor
Columbia/Titan (Peter Newbrook)

A surgeon kills for pituitary gland fluid to restore his fiancée's beauty.

Highly derivative shocker with no inspiration of its own except an accumulation of gory detail.

w Donald and Derek Ford *d* Robert Hartford Davis *ph* Peter Newbrook *m* Bill McGuffie

Peter Cushing, Sue Lloyd, Noel Trevarthen, Kate O'Mara, David Lodge

Corsa dell'Innocente: see *Flight of the Innocent*

Corsair *
US 1931 75m bw
Roland West

A college football hero turns hi-jacker.

Modest gangster saga with signs of style smothered by the script.

w Josephine Lovett *novel* Walon Green *d* Roland West

Chester Morris, Alison Loyd, William Austin, Frank McHugh, Ned Sparks

'A bit out-dated . . . will take a lot of nursing to reach average grosses.' – *Variety*

† Alison Loyd was a name momentarily adopted by Thelma Todd.

The Corsican Brothers *
US 1942 111m bw
UA/Edward Small
V*

Siamese twins are separated but remain spiritually tied through various adventures.

Adequately exciting picturization of the Dumas swashbuckler.

w George Bruce, Howard Estabrook d Gregory Ratoff ph Harry Stradling m Dimitri Tiomkin

Douglas Fairbanks Jnr, Akim Tamiroff, Ruth Warrick, J. Carrol Naish, H. B. Warner, Henry Wilcoxon

† In 1953 came an undistinguished sequel, *Bandits of Corsica* (GB: *The Return of the Corsican Brothers*), with Richard Greene, Paula Raymond, Raymond Burr and Dona Drake. Written by Richard Schayer; directed by Ray Nazarro; for Global/UA.

AAN: Dimitri Tiomkin

Cortesie per gli ospiti: see *The Comfort of Strangers*

Corvette K 225 *
US 1943 97m bw
Universal (Howard Hawks)
GB title: *The Nelson Touch*

A Canadian corvette commander encounters submarines and bombers in mid-Atlantic.

Good war film of its period, marred by romantic interest.

w Lt John Sturdy d Richard Rosson ph Tony Gaudio m David Buttolph

Randolph Scott, James Brown, Ella Raines, Barry Fitzgerald, Andy Devine, Richard Lane

AAN: Tony Gaudio

Corvette Summer
US 1979 104m Metrocolor
MGM/Plotto (Hal Barwood)
V*
GB title: *The Hot One*

A Los Angeles student spends the summer looking for his stolen customized car, and has various adventures around Las Vegas.

There are a few choice moments in this disconnected comedy drama, but the appeal is almost entirely to moonstruck teenagers.

w Hal Barwood, Matthew Robbins d Matthew Robbins ph Frank Stanley m Craig Safan

Mark Hamill, Annie Potts, Eugene Roche, Kim Milford, Richard McKenzie

The Cosmic Man
US 1959 72m bw
Futura (Robert A. Terry)

An alien is met with hostility when he visits Earth preaching peace.

Typical low-budget sci-fi movie of its time that offers nothing out of the ordinary.

w Arthur C. Pierce d Herbert Greene ph John F. Warren m Paul Sawtell, Bert Shefter ed Helene Turner

Bruce Bennett, John Carradine, Angela Greene, Paul Langton, Scotty Morrow, Lyn Osborn, Walter Maslow

Cosmic Monsters: see *Strange World of Planet X*

Cottage on Dartmoor
GB 1929 75m bw
BIP (Bruce Woolfe)
US title: *Escaped from Dartmoor*

A farmer's wife shelters her ex-lover when he breaks jail.

Crude early talkie notable only as an immature work of its director.

wd Anthony Asquith story Herbert Price ph Stanley Rodwell md William Hodgson ad Ian Campbell-Gray

Norah Baring, Uno Hemming, Hans Schlettow, Judd Green

Cottage to Let *
GB 1941 90m bw
Gainsborough (Edward Black)
US title: *Bombsight Stolen*

Evacuated to Scotland, a Cockney helps prevent spies from kidnapping his inventor foster-father.

Stagey but often amusing comedy-thriller which after a shaky start becomes agreeably Hitchcockian.

w Anatole de Grunwald, J. O. C. Orton play Geoffrey Kerr d Anthony Asquith ph Jack Cox md Louis Levy

Leslie Banks, *Alastair Sim, John Mills,* Jeanne de Casalis, George Cole, Carla Lehmann, Michael Wilding, Frank Cellier, Wally Patch, Muriel Aked, Muriel George, Catherine Lacey, Hay Petrie

'Where crime lords rub elbows with the rich and famous!'
The Cotton Club
US 1984 127m Technicolor Panavision
Zoetrope (Robert Evans)
V, V*, L, S

The story of Harlem's famous night-club and the gangsters who frequented it.

A lumpy vehicle, eventually costing fifty million dollars, for some of the talents who made *The Godfather* ten years earlier. Despite a few effective moments, a prime example of the careless extravagance which all but killed the film business.

w William Kennedy, Francis Coppola d Francis Coppola ph Stephen Goldblatt m John Barry pd Richard Sylbert ed Barry Malkin, Robert Lovett

Richard Gere, Gregory Hines, Diane Lane, Lonette McKee, Bob Hoskins, James Remar, Nicolas Cage, Allen Garfield, Fred Gwynne, Gwen Verdon

'The narrative is a mess, and keeps interrupting the heartstopping hoofing.' – *Time Out*

AAN: editing, art direction

Cotton Comes to Harlem
US 1970 97m DeLuxe
Formosa/UA
V*

Two black detectives try to beat the police to a bale of cotton containing a fortune in stolen dollars.

Rickety vehicle for two amiable black characters presented rather more surely in *Come Back Charleston Blue* (qv).

w Arnold Perl, Ossie Davis, Chester Himes novel Chester Himes d Ossie Davis

Godfrey Cambridge, Raymond St Jacques, Calvin Lockhart, Judy Pace, Redd Foxx

Cotton Queen
GB 1937 bw
British Independent Exhibitors/Joe Rock

Two fiercely competitive Manchester mill-owners agree, after many misunderstandings, to co-operate.

Drear provincial comedy, in which a talented cast is given no opportunity to shine.

w Syd Courtenay, Barry Peak, Scott Pembroke, Louis Golding d Bernard Vorhaus ph Eric Cross md Cyril Ray ad George Provis ed Sam Simmonds, Dr Max Brenner

Will Fyffe, Stanley Holloway, Mary Lawson, Jimmy Hanley, Helen Haye, Marcelle Rogez, Syd Courtenay

The Couch
US 1962 100m bw
Warner (Owen Crump)

A psychiatrist's patient goes on the rampage with an ice pick.

Overstretched suspenser which never really holds the interest.

w Robert Bloch d Owen Crump

Grant Williams, Shirley Knight, Onslow Stevens

The Couch Trip *
US 1988 98m colour
Rank/Orion (Lawrence Gordon)
V*, L

A mental patient escapes to Los Angeles where he becomes a success as a radio doctor.

Sporadically amusing comedy that mocks obvious targets.

w Stephen Kampmann, Will Port, Sean Stein novel Ken Kolb d Michael Ritchie ph Donald E. Thorin m Michel Colombier pd Jimmy Bly ed Richard A. Harris

Dan Aykroyd, Walter Matthau, Charles Grodin, Donna Dixon, Richard Romanus, Mary Gross, David Clennon

Council of the Gods *
Germany 1950 106m bw
DEFA (Adolf Fischer)

A research chemist working for a big chemical company denounces them after the war when he finds they have been producing poison gas for the concentration camps.

Self-flagellatory expiation of war crimes encased in an absorbing drama.

w Friedrich Wolff, Philipp Gebb d Kurt Maetzig ph Friedl Behn-Grund m Hanns Eisler, Erwin Lehn

Paul Bildt, Agnes Windeck, Yvonne Merin, Fritz Tillman

Counsel for Crime
US 1937 61m bw
Columbia

A crooked lawyer fixes alibis for his clients before they commit a crime, until he finds his own son on the other side of one of his cases.

Adequate programmer.

w Fred Niblo Jnr, Grace Neville, Lee Loeb, Harold Buchman d John Brahm

Otto Kruger, Douglass Montgomery, Jacqueline Wells, Thurston Hall, Nana Bryant

'Won't disappoint those who get caught with it on a dual.' – *Variety*

Counsellor at Law *
US 1933 78m bw
Universal (Henry Henigson)

Life in the New York office of a successful Jewish lawyer.

Practised film-making from a Broadway hit.

w Elmer Rice play Elmer Rice d William Wyler ph Norbert Brodine

John Barrymore, Bebe Daniels, Melvyn Douglas, Doris Kenyon, Onslow Stevens, Isabel Jewell, Thelma Todd, Mayo Methot

'Good drama, well produced and with strong b.o. potentialities.' – *Variety*

† Paul Muni was the first choice for the lead, but refused to play a Jewish role.

Counsel's Opinion
GB 1933 76m bw
London Films (Alexander Korda)

A widow wins a barrister by pretending to be a flighty socialite.

Semi-sophisticated comedy; this rather thin quickie version was done over four years later and became *The Divorce of Lady X* (qv).

w Dorothy Greenhill, Arthur Wimperis *play* Gilbert Wakefield *d* Allan Dwan *ph* Bernard Browne *ad* Holmes Paul *ed* Harold Young

Henry Kendall, Binnie Barnes, Cyril Maude, Laurence Grossmith

'There is perhaps more naivety than usual about this comedy of a divorce counsel who imagines himself mixed up in his own case. The director is an American, Allan Dwan, who must either have come or gone away with odd ideas of British humour.' – *Observer*

Count A Lonely Cadence: see *Stockade*

Count Dracula: see *Bram Stoker's Count Dracula*

Count Five and Die *
GB 1957 92m bw Cinemascope
TCF/Zonic (Ernest Gartside)

British intelligence seeks to give the Nazis false information about the 1944 invasion, but conviction grows that a double agent is among them.

Terse, downbeat war suspenser, gripping in parts but quite forgettable.

w Jack Seddon, David Pursall *d* Victor Vicas *ph* Arthur Grant *m* John Wooldridge

Nigel Patrick, Jeffrey Hunter, Anne-Marie Duringer, David Kossoff

The Count of Monte Cristo ***
US 1934 114m bw
Reliance (Edward Small)
V*

After spending years in prison, Edmond Dantes escapes and avenges himself on those who framed him.

Classic swashbuckler, extremely well done with due attention to dialogue as well as action; a model of its kind and period.

w Philip Dunne, Dan Totheroh, Rowland V. Lee *novel* Alexandre Dumas *d* Rowland V. Lee *ph* Peverell Marley *m* Alfred Newman

Robert Donat, Elissa Landi, Louis Calhern, Sidney Blackmer, Raymond Walburn, O. P. Heggie, William Farnum

'A near-perfect blend of thrilling action and grand dialogue.' – *Variety*

Count the Hours
US 1952 74m bw
Benedict Bogeaus/RKO
GB title: *Every Minute Counts*

A man's wife and lawyer fight to save him from the gallows.

Stiff and unconvincing suspenser.

w Doane R. Hoag, Karen DeWolf *d* Don Siegel

Teresa Wright, Macdonald Carey, Dolores Moran, Adele Mara, Edgar Barrier, John Craven, Jack Elam

Count Three and Pray
US 1955 92m Technicolor Cinemascope
Columbia/Copa (Ted Richmond)

After the Civil War a roistering Southerner comes home to rebuild his town and become its parson.

Moderate semi-Western, fresh and pleasing but not memorable.

w Herb Meadow *d* George Sherman *ph* Burnett Guffey *m* George Duning

Van Heflin, Joanne Woodward (debut), Phil Carey, Raymond Burr, Allison Hayes, Myron Healey, Nancy Kulp, James Griffiths

'Don't dare come alone!'
Count Yorga Vampire
US 1970 90m Movielab
Erica/AIP (Michael Macready)
V*, L

Inquisitive Los Angeles teenagers are vampirized by a suave foreign visitor.

A semi-professional film that looks it but amid the longueurs provides one or two nasty *frissons*.

wd Bob Kelljan *ph* Arch Archambault *m* William Marx

Robert Quarry, Roger Perry, Michael Murphy, Michael Macready, Donna Anders, Judith Lang

† *The Return of Count Yorga* followed a year later.

Count Your Blessings
US 1959 102m Metrocolor Cinemascope
MGM (Karl Tunberg)

An English girl marries an aristocratic Frenchman, but the war and other considerations make them virtual strangers until their son is nine years old, when it becomes clear that daddy is a philanderer.

Slight upper-crust comedy, basically rather tedious but kept buoyant by Chevalier as commentator.

w Karl Tunberg *novel* The Blessing by Nancy Mitford *d* Jean Negulesco *ph* Milton Krasner, George Folsey *m* Franz Waxman

Deborah Kerr, *Maurice Chevalier*, Rossano Brazzi, Martin Stephens, Tom Helmore, Ronald Squire, Patricia Medina, Mona Washbourne

'Negulesco's aspirations to elegance are now familiar . . . this is far too absurd an example of Hollywood's infatuation with Old Europe to arouse much interest.' – *MFB*

Countdown *
US 1967 101m Technicolor Panavision
Warner (William Conrad)

Russian and American spaceships race for the moon.

Earnest, simply-plotted science-fiction in which technology is the centre of interest.

w Loring Mandel *d* Robert Altman *ph* William W. Spencer *m* Leonard Rosenman *ad* Jack Poplin

James Caan, Robert Duvall, Barbara Baxley, Joanna Moore, Charles Aidman, Steve Ihnat

Counterattack
US 1945 89m bw
Columbia
GB title: *One against Seven*

Resistance fighters go behind enemy lines for purposes of sabotage.

Standard World War II actioner, the star appearing above his surroundings.

w John Howard Lawson *play* Janet and Philip Stevenson *d* Zoltan Korda *ph* James Wong Howe *m* Louis Gruenberg

Paul Muni, Marguerite Chapman, Larry Parks, George Macready, Roman Bohnen

Counterblast
GB 1948 99m bw
British National

An escaped Nazi poses as a British scientist in a research laboratory.

Overlong espionage thick ear with some compensations.

w Jack Whittingham *story* Guy Morgan *d* Paul Stein

Robert Beatty, Mervyn Johns, Nova Pilbeam, Margaretta Scott, Marie Lohr, Karel Stepanek, Alan Wheatley

The Counterfeit Traitor *
US 1962 140m Technicolor
Paramount/Perlberg-Seaton
V*

An oil importer, a naturalized Swede born in America, is blackmailed by the Allies into becoming a spy.

Heavy-going espionage drama which divides its time between action and moralizing. Excellent production does not quite make it exciting.

wd George Seaton *book* Alexander Klein *ph* Jean Bourgoin *m* Alfred Newman

William Holden, Lilli Palmer, Hugh Griffith, Werner Peters, Eva Dahlbeck

'The picture is too long, it is also incessantly exciting, occasionally witty . . . and in its expression of organized sadism comparatively subtle.' – *Time*

Counterpoint *
US 1967 107m Techniscope
Universal (Dick Berg)

In 1944, an American symphony orchestra is captured by the Germans and threatened with execution.

Bizarre war suspenser, quite unconvincing but with effectively suspenseful moments and an old-fashioned portrayal of the Nazis as sadistic music-loving Huns.

w James Lee, Joel Oliansky *novel* The General by Alan Sillitoe *d* Ralph Nelson *ph* Russell Metty *m* Bronislau Kaper

Charlton Heston, Maximilian Schell, Anton Diffring, Kathryn Hays, Leslie Nielsen

Countess Dracula
GB 1971 93m Eastmancolor
Rank/Hammer (Alexander Paal)
V, V*

A Hungarian noblewoman restores her youth by bathing in the blood of young virgins.

Risibly sub-Freudian addition to a grotesque Hammer gallery of monsters, indistinguishable from the others once it gets going.

w Jeremy Paul, Alexander Paal, Peter Sasdy, Gabriel Ronay *d* Peter Sasdy *ph* Ken Talbot *m* Harry Robinson *ad* Philip Harrison *ed* Henry Richardson

Ingrid Pitt, Nigel Green, Sandor Eles, Maurice Denham, Patience Collier, Peter Jeffrey, Lesley-Anne Down

'At its best the film employs the kind of romantic imagery one associates with Keats; and if it doesn't quite live up to that comparison, it is at least a worthy companion to Corman's *Bloody Mama*.' – *David Pirie, MFB*

A Countess from Hong Kong
GB 1967 120m Technicolor
Universal (Jerome Epstein)

An American millionaire diplomat is followed from Hong Kong by his Russian émigrée girlfriend, and complications mount when his wife boards the ship at Hawaii.

Flatulent comedy with neither the sparkle of champagne nor even the fizz of lemonade: Chaplin's writing, direction and music are alike soporific, and commiserations are due to the cast.

wd/m Charles Chaplin *ph* Arthur Ibbetson *pd* Don Ashton

Marlon Brando, Sophia Loren, *Patrick Cargill*, Margaret Rutherford, Charles Chaplin, Sydney Chaplin, Oliver Johnston, John Paul

'An unfunny, mindless mess.' – *Robert Windeler*

'So old-fashioned and dull that one can hardly believe it was made now.' – *Philip T. Hartung*

The Countess of Monte Cristo
US   1933   74m   bw
Universal

A bit player in a musical convinces her friends she is a
countess.

Mild comedy.

w Karen de Wolf, Gene Lewis   d Karl Freund

Fay Wray, Paul Lukas, Patsy Kelly, Reginald Owen

† It was remade in 1948 as an even milder vehicle for
Sonja Henie.

Country *
US   1984   109m   Technicolor   Panavision
Touchstone/Far West/Pangaea (William D. Wittliff, Jessica
Lange)
V*, L, S

Iowa farmers, on the breadline after a tornado, face
foreclosure.

Deeply felt modern variation on *The Grapes of Wrath*,
not particularly dramatic for those who have not felt
the pressure.

w William D. Wittliff   d Richard Pearce   ph David
M. Walsh   m Charles Gross   pd Ron Hobbs
ed Bill Yahraus

Jessica Lange, Sam Shepard, Wilford Brimley, Matt
Clark, Therese Graham

AAN: Jessica Lange

Country Dance
GB   1969   112m   Metrocolor
MGM/Keep-Windward (Robert Emmett Ginna)
aka: *Brotherly Love*

An eccentric baronet's incestuous love for his sister
finally breaks up her marriage.

Rambling melodrama with O'Toole going mad in
squire's tweeds; tediously fashionable but too pallid
for general success, it was barely released.

w James Kennaway   novel *Household Ghosts* by James
Kennaway   d J. Lee-Thompson   ph Ted Moore
m John Addison

Peter O'Toole, Susannah York, Michael Craig, Harry
Andrews, Cyril Cusack, Judy Cornwell, Brian Blessed

The Country Doctor *
US   1936   94m   bw
TCF (Darryl F. Zanuck)

A rural physician becomes famous when quintuplets
are born to one of his patients.

Fictionalization of the birth of the Dionne
Quintuplets; pleasantly nostalgic even forty years
after its *raison d'être*.

w Sonya Levien   d Henry King   ph John F. Seitz,
Daniel B. Clark

Jean Hersholt, the Dionne Quins, Dorothy Peterson,
June Lang, Slim Summerville, Michael Whalen,
Robert Barrat

† Sequels: *Reunion* (1936), *Five of a Kind* (1938).

Country Gentlemen
US   1936   66m   bw
Republic

A couple of con men help a widow who runs a small-
town hotel.

Strained comedy in which the gag men misguidedly
try to play straight.

w Milton Raison, Jack Harvey, Jo Graham   d Ralph
Staub

Ole Olsen, Chic Johnson, Joyce Compton, Lila Lee,
Pierre Watkin

'Missing is the rapidfire buffoonery with which they
have been identified in vaudeville.' – *Variety*

'How far should a woman go to redeem the man she
loves?'

The Country Girl *
US   1954   104m   bw
Paramount (William Perlberg)
V*

The wife of an alcoholic singer blossoms when he is
stimulated into a comeback.

Theatrically effective but highly unconvincing, this
rather glum stage success made a cold film, miscast
with an eye on the box-office.

w Stanley Roberts   play Clifford Odets   d George
Seaton   ph John F. Warren   m Victor Young
m/ly Ira Gershwin, Harold Arlen   ad Hal Pereira,
Roland Anderson

Bing Crosby, Grace Kelly, William Holden, Anthony
Ross, Gene Reynolds

'The dramatic development is not really interesting
enough to sustain a film of the intensity for which it
strives.' – *Karel Reisz*

'Rather inexplicably, this sado-masochist morass was
one of the biggest box office hits of its year.' – *Pauline
Kael, 70s*

AA: Grace Kelly

AAN: best picture; John F. Warren; Bing Crosby;
George Seaton; Stanley Roberts; art direction

The County Chairman
US   1934   85m   bw
Fox

A small-town attorney competes with his prospective
son-in-law for the post of public prosecutor.

Small-town period comedy drama, not among its
star's best.

w Sam Hellman, Gladys Lehman   novel George Ade
d John Blystone

Will Rogers, Evelyn Venable, Kent Taylor, Louise
Dresser, Mickey Rooney, Stepin Fetchit, Berton
Churchill

County Hospital **
US   1932   20m   bw
Hal Roach
V, V (C)

Ollie is in hospital; Stan brings him some hardboiled
eggs and some nuts, and nearly wrecks the place.

Archetypal star comedy with brilliant character and
slapstick sequences, let down by a badly processed
car ride home.

w H. M. Walker   d James Parrott   ph Art
Lloyd   ed Bert Jordan, Richard Currier

Laurel and Hardy, Billy Gilbert, William Austin, May
Wallace

Coup de Foudre *
France   1983   111m   colour   Cinemascope
Gala/Partners Productions/Alexandre Films/Hachette Première/
A2/SFPC (Ariel Zeitoun)
V*
US title: *Entre Nous*

Two women leave their husbands to live and work
together.

Charm predominates in this nostalgic piece, based on
the life of the director's mother.

w Olivier Cohen, Diane Kurys   book Diane Kurys
d Diane Kurys   ph Bernard Lutic   m Luis Bacalov
pd Jacques Bufnoir   ed Joele Van Effenterre

Miou-Miou, Isabelle Huppert, Guy Marchand, Jean-
Pierre Bacri, Robin Renucci, Patrick Bauchau, Jacques
Alric

AAN: best foreign-language film

Coup de Torchon
France   1981   128m   colour
Les Films de la Tour/Les Films A2/Little Bear (Adolphe Viezzi)
V*
GB title: *Clean Slate*

In French West Africa in 1938, an apparently easy-
going police officer is inspired to commit a series of
murders.

Well-made, heavy-going study of mania.

w Jean Aurenche, Bertrand Tavernier   novel POP.
1280 by Jim Thompson   d Bertrand Tavernier
ph Pierre William Glenn   m Philippe Sarde

Philippe Noiret, Isabelle Huppert, Jean-Pierre
Marielle, Stéphane Audran, Eddy Mitchell

AAN: best foreign film

'A movie for everyone who's ever struggled to love a
brother … Or strangle one.'

Coup de Ville **
US   1990   97m   DeLuxe
Warner/Morgan Creek (Larry Brezner, Paul Schiff)
V, V*, L

In the early 1960s, a father asks his three sons to drive
a 1950s Cadillac Coupe de Ville from Michigan to
Miami for their mother's birthday.

Engaging and amusing low-key road movie centring
on family relationships.

w Mike Binder   d Joe Roth   ph Reynaldo
Villalobos   m James Newton Howard   pd Angelo
Graham   ed Paul Hirsch

Patrick Dempsey, Arye Gross, Daniel Stern, Annabeth
Gish, Rita Taggart, Joseph Bologna, Alan Arkin

'A road movie with a difference, this one has heart
and quality.' – *Shaun Usher, Daily Mail*

'For the most part a very shrewd, well-made and
well-acted film.' – *Derek Malcolm, Guardian*

Courage
US   1930   65m   bw
Warner
V*

A widow has a large family of which the one sweet-
natured son is left a fortune by the old lady next door.

Glutinous mother-love saga from a popular play.

w Walter Anthony   d Archie Mayo

Belle Bennett, Marian Nixon, Rex Bell, Leon Janney,
Blanche Friderici

'Should be certain in neighbourhood houses. For
abroad, a perfect picture for a glimpse of a real
American boy of breeding and the sort of mother who
lives in every nation.' – *Variety*

Courage (1985): see Raw Courage

Courage Fuyons *
France   1979   98m   Eastmancolor
Gaumont/Gueville (Yves Robert)

A middle-aged man embarks on a series of surprising
romantic adventures.

A mainly enjoyable exercise in wish-fulfilment,
sharply written and acted.

w Jean-Loup Dabadie, Yves Robert   d Yves Robert
ph Yves Lafaye   m Vladimir Cosma

Jean Rochefort, Catherine Deneuve, Robert Webber,
Philippe Leroy-Beaulieu

Courage Mountain
US   1989   98m   CFI colour
Entertainment/Epic/Stone Group (Stephen Ujlaki)
V, V*, L

A Swiss schoolgirl, stranded in Italy with some
friends, makes her way back home.

A new adventure, told in an old-fashioned way, of
that one-time children's favourite Heidi.

w Weaver Webb   *story* Fred Brogger, Mark Brogger
d Christopher Leitch   *ph* Jacques Steyn
m Sylvester Levay   *pd* Robb Wilson King
ed Martin Walsh

Juliette Caton, Charlie Sheen, Leslie Caron, Yorgo Voyagis, Laura Betti, Jan Rubes, Joanna Clarke

The Courageous Mr Penn: see *Penn of Pennsylvania*

The Courier
Ireland   1987   85m
Palace/City Vision (Hilary McLoughlin)
S

A motorcycle messenger becomes an unknowing carrier of drugs.

Violent, low-budget thriller with no redeeming qualities.

w Frank Deasy   *d* Joe Lee, Frank Deasy
ph Gabriel Beristain   *m* Declan MacManus
pd David Wilson   *ed* Derek Trigg, Annette D'Alton

Gabriel Byrne, Ian Bannen, Cait O'Riordan, Padraig O'Loingsigh, Patrick Bergen, Andrew Connolly

Cours du Soir
France   1967   25m   colour
Telecip/Specta (Bernard Maurice)
V

An evening-class lecturer demonstrates the various ways people smoke, walk and play sport.

Tati goes through some of his familiar routines, but the setting is not a sympathetic one and he looks tired and unenthusiastic about what he is doing.

w Jacques Tati   *d* Nicolas Rybowski   *ph* Jean Badal   *m* Léo Petit   *ed* Nicole Cauduchon

Jacques Tati

It was released on video together with *Soigne Ton Gauche* and *L'Ecole des Facteurs* as *Tati Shorts*.

The Court Jester ***
US   1955   101m   Technicolor   Vistavision
Paramount/Dena (Melvin Frank, Norman Panama)
V, V*, L

Opposition to a tyrannical king is provided by the Fox, but it is one of the rebel's meekest men who, posing as a jester, defeats the usurper.

One of the star's most delightful vehicles, this medieval romp has good tunes and lively action, not to mention an exceptional cast and the memorable 'chalice from the palace' routine.

wd Norman Panama, Melvin Frank   *ph* Ray June
m/ly Sylvia Fine, Sammy Cahn   *ad* Hal Pereira, Roland Anderson

Danny Kaye, Glynis Johns, *Basil Rathbone*, Cecil Parker, *Mildred Natwick*, Angela Lansbury, Edward Ashley, Robert Middleton, Michael Pate, Alan Napier

Court Martial: see *Carrington VC*

The Court Martial of Billy Mitchell *
US   1955   100m   Warnercolor   Cinemascope
United States Pictures (Milton Sperling)
V*, L
GB title: *One Man Mutiny*

In the early twenties, an American general of the Army Air Service is court-martialled for accusing the war department of criminal negligence.

Adequate recreation of a historical incident, with a cast of excellent actors converging for a courtroom scene of some effectiveness.

w Milton Sperling, Emmet Lavery   *d* Otto Preminger   *ph* Sam Leavitt   *m* Dimitri Tiomkin

Gary Cooper, *Rod Steiger*, Ralph Bellamy, Charles Bickford, Elizabeth Montgomery, Fred Clark, Darren McGavin, James Daly

AAN: Milton Sperling, Emmet Lavery

The Courtney Affair: see *The Courtneys of Curzon Street*

The Courtneys of Curzon Street *
GB   1947   120m   bw
Imperadio (Herbert Wilcox)
V*
US title: *The Courtney Affair*

In Victorian times, a baronet's son marries a lady's maid . . . and many years later, their grandson marries a factory worker.

Unbelievable upstairs-downstairs romantic drama spanning three generations; all to be taken with a gigantic pinch of salt, but a huge success when released.

w Nicholas Phipps   *novel* Florence Tranter
d Herbert Wilcox   *ph* Max Greene   *m* Anthony Collins   *ad* William C. Andrews   *ed* Flora Newton, Vera Campbell

Anna Neagle, Michael Wilding, Gladys Young, Coral Browne, Michael Medwin, Daphne Slater, Jack Watling, Helen Cherry, Bernard Lee

'The dignity of Curzon Street is Hollywoodized, and it is rare in 1945 that people in their sixties look as though they have one foot in the grave.' – *MFB*

'If my livelihood depended on booking the right film into the average cinema, this is one I would not dare to miss.' – *Observer*

The Courtship of Eddie's Father *
US   1962   117m   Metrocolor   Panavision
MGM/Joe Pasternak
V*

The small son of a widower tries to interest Dad in another woman.

Fairly icky American-style sentimental comedy with most of the stops pulled out; way over-length and too self-indulgently solemn in the last part, but with professional touches.

w John Gay   *novel* Muriel Toby   *d* Vincente Minnelli   *ph* Milton Krasner   *m* George Stoll

Glenn Ford, Ronny Howard, Shirley Jones, Stella Stevens, Dina Merrill

† A TV series starring Bill Bixby followed in 1971.

Cousin Bobby *
US   1992   69m   colour
Electric/Tesauro
V*

A documentary on the life and work of the Rev. Robert Castle, an outspoken Episcopalian priest working in Harlem, made by his film director cousin.

Well-made and interesting account of a dedicated priest that cuts from the public life to the private man.

d Jonathan Demme   *ph* Ernest Dickerson, Craig Haagensen, Tony Jannelli, Jacek Laskus, Declan Quinn   *m* Anton Sanko   *ed* David Greenwald

'A low-key, occasionally touching documentary . . . essentially a home movie, but one with broad appeal.' – *Variety*

Cousin, Cousine **
France   1975   95m   Eastmancolor
Pomereu/Gaumont (Bertrand Javal)
V*, L

Various furtive love affairs centre on a family wedding.

Sprightly satirical comedy full of pleasing touches, mostly jibes at French bourgeois standards.

wd Jean-Charles Tacchella   *ph* Georges Lendi
m Gerard Anfosso

Marie-France Pisier, Marie-Christine Barrault, Victor Lanoux, Guy Marchand, Ginette Garcin

'One of those rare delights you want to see again and again just to share the sheer joy of living, zest for love,

genuine affection, all-too-human absurdity, and pure happiness of all those delicious people on screen.' – *Judith Crist, Saturday Review*

AAN: best foreign film; script; Marie-Christine Barrault

Les Cousins *
France   1959   110m   bw
AJYM (Claude Chabrol)

A law student stays with his sophisticated cousin in Paris, and his life is altered.

The country cousin fable filled with undramatic detail and given a rather perverse ending without any apparent point.

wd Claude Chabrol   *ph* Henri Decaë   *m* Paul Misraki
ad Jacques Saulnier, Bernard Evein   *ed* Jacques Gaillard

Jean-Claude Brialy, Gérard Blain, Juliette Mayniel, Claude Cerval

Cousins
US   1989   113m   Technicolor
UIP/Paramount (William Allyn)
V, V*, L, S

Two couples, who meet at a relative's wedding, swop partners.

An adaptation of the French film *Cousin, Cousine* without the exuberant charm of the original.

w Stephen Metcalfe   *d* Joel Schumacher   *ph* Ralf Bode   *m* Angelo Badalamenti   *pd* Mark S. Freeborn   *ed* Robert Brown

Ted Danson, Isabella Rossellini, Sean Young, William Petersen, Lloyd Bridges, Norma Aleandro, Keith Coogan, Gina DeAngelis, George Coe

'Combines satire, near-farce, and incipient fantasy with great dexterity.' – *Tim Pulleine, MFB*

A Covenant with Death
US   1966   97m   Technicolor
Warner (William Conrad)

A half-Mexican judge in a border town convicts a man who accidentally kills the hangman just as the real murderer confesses.

Dreary moral melodrama with accents, nicely photographed but cold, remote and drawn out.

w Larry Marcus, Saul Levitt   *novel* Stephen Becker
d Lamont Johnson   *ph* Robert Burks   *m* Leonard Rosenman

George Maharis, Katy Jurado, Earl Holliman, Sidney Blackmer, Laura Devon, Gene Hackman

'Too thrilling for words, so they set it to music!'
Cover Girl **
US   1944   107m   Technicolor
Columbia (Arthur Schwartz)
V, V*, L

The road to success for magazine cover models.

Wartime glamour musical with a stronger reputation than it really deserves apart from Kelly's solos; it does however manage a certain *joie de vivre* which should not be despised.

w Virginia Van Upp   *d* Charles Vidor   *ph* Rudolph Maté   *md* Morris Stoloff, Carmen Dragon
m/ly Jerome Kern, Ira Gershwin   *ad* Lionel Banks, Cary Odell

Rita Hayworth, Gene Kelly, Phil Silvers, Lee Bowman, Jinx Falkenberg, Otto Kruger, Eve Arden, Ed Brophy

'Kelly and Silvers are better than Kelly and Hayworth, though she does look sumptuous, and her big smile could be the emblem of the period.' – *New Yorker, 1977*

'Much of it is not as fresh as it may seem; but its second-handedness and its occasional failures cannot obliterate the pleasure of seeing the work of a production company which obviously knows, cares about and enjoys what it is doing.' – *James Agee*

AA: Morris Stoloff, Carmen Dragon

AAN: Rudolph Maté; song 'Long Ago and Far Away'; art direction

Cover Girl Killer
GB 1959 61m bw
Parroch/Eros

A trap is set for the mad murderer of cover models.

Good unpretentious second feature with plenty of suspense.

wd Terry Bishop

Harry H. Corbett, Felicity Young, Spencer Teakle, Victor Brooks

Cover Up
US 1948 82m bw
Strand/UA

An insurance investigator finds senior officials conspiring to obscure the facts of a small-town murder.

Modest mystery, initially intriguing but finally unsatisfying.

w Jerome Odlum, Jonathan Ritz *d* Alfred E. Green

Dennis O'Keefe, William Bendix, Barbara Britton, Art Smith

The Covered Wagon *
US 1923 103m (24 fps) bw silent
Paramount/Famous Players-Lasky
V*, L

Pioneer settlers travel west by wagon train.

A classic Western which now seems painfully undernourished in terms of plot and character but still retains moments of epic sweep.

w Jack Cunningham *novel* Emerson Hough *d* James Cruze *ph* Karl Brown

Ernest Torrence, Tully Marshall, J. Warren Kerrigan, Lois Wilson, Alan Hale

'There wasn't a false whisker in the film.' – *James Cruze*

'Forthright, impressive and vigorous, it brought a breath of fresh air into the jazz-ridden film world.' – *Lewis Jacobs*

The Cow and I
France 1959 119m bw
Cyclope/Omnia (Walter Rupp)
original title: *La Vache et le Prisonnier*

A French soldier escapes from a prison camp and takes a farm cow as cover.

Curiously overlong war adventure which hovers uncertainly between comedy and suspense.

w Henri Verneuil, Henri Jeanson, Jean Manse *d* Henri Verneuil *ph* Roger Hubert *m* Paul Durand

Fernandel, René Havard, Albert Remy, Bernard Musson

Cowboy *
US 1958 92m Technicolor
Columbia/Phoenix (Julian Blaustein)

Frank Harris becomes a cattle herder for love of a lady but is quickly disillusioned with the outdoor life.

Fashioned from a lively autobiography, this has interesting moments but is never as fascinating as one would expect.

w Edmund H. North *book* On the Trail by Frank Harris *d* Delmer Daves *ph* Charles Lawton Jnr *m* George Duning *ed* William A. Lyon, Al Clark

Jack Lemmon, Glenn Ford, Brian Donlevy, Anna Kashfi, Dick York, Richard Jaeckel, King Donovan

AAN: editing

The Cowboy and the Girl: see *A Lady Takes a Chance*

The Cowboy and the Lady
US 1938 91m bw
Samuel Goldwyn
V, V*

The daughter of a presidential candidate becomes infatuated with a rodeo cowboy.

Insubstantial and witless romantic comedy which suffered many sea changes from script to screen.

w Leo McCarey, S. N. Behrman, Sonya Levien *d* H. C. Potter *ph* Gregg Toland *m* Alfred Newman

Gary Cooper, Merle Oberon, Patsy Kelly, Walter Brennan, Fuzzy Knight, Henry Kolker, Harry Davenport

'By and large only mildly diverting . . . the interest and promise of the early reels is not sustained in the latter half.' – *Variety*

'Just a lot of chestnuts pulled out of other people's dead fires.' – *Otis Ferguson*

AAN: Alfred Newman; title song (*m* Lionel Newman, *ly* Arthur Quenzer)

Cowboy from Brooklyn
US 1938 80m bw
Warner

A supposed cowboy crooner is taken out west and proves to be terrified of animals.

Genial but witless spoof of a trend of the times.

w Earl Baldwin, *play* Howdy Stranger by Robert Sloane, Louis Pelletier Jnr *d* Lloyd Bacon

Pat O'Brien, Dick Powell, Priscilla Lane, Dick Foran, Ann Sheridan, Ronald Reagan, Johnnie Davis, James Stephenson

† Remade as *Two Guys from Texas*.

The Cowboys *
US 1972 128m Technicolor Panavision 70
Sanford/Warner (Mark Rydell)
V, V*

Deserted by his ranch hands, a cattle drover on a long trail enlists the help of eleven schoolboys, who later avenge his death.

Ambling, climactically violent, extremely unlikely Western with good scenes along the way.

w Irving Ravetch, Harriet Frank Jnr *novel* William Dale Jennings *d* Mark Rydell *ph* Robert Surtees *m* John Williams

John Wayne, Roscoe Lee Browne, Bruce Dern, Colleen Dewhurst, Slim Pickens, Sarah Cunningham

† A TV series followed in 1974 but was shortlived.

Crack in the Mirror
US 1960 97m bw Cinemascope
TCF/Darryl F. Zanuck

A young lawyer and his ageing mentor are at opposite sides of a murder case.

Pointless Paris-set melodrama in which for no obvious reason each of the three stars plays two roles. Relentlessly boring.

w Mark Canfield (Darryl F. Zanuck) *d* Richard Fleischer *ph* William C. Mellor *m* Maurice Jarre

Orson Welles, Bradford Dillman, Juliette Greco, William Lucas, Alexander Knox, Catherine Lacey

Crack in the Mirror
US 1988 94m colour
Blue Dolphin/Jubran Group (Fred Berner, Jubran Jubran)
V, V*

A drug-dealer, on the run from a rival gangster, asks a friend to look after his business.

Convoluted tale of killers and addicts, full of heavy-handed anti-drugs polemic.

w Robert Madero *d* Robby Benson *ph* Neil Smith *m* Nile Rodgers *ed* Alan Miller, Craig McKay

Robby Benson, Tawny Kitaen, Danny Aiello, Kevin Gray, Cliff Bemis, Tony Gillan, Paul Herman, Tony Sirico, Mark Ornstein

'Thank God it's only a motion picture!'

Crack in the World
US 1965 96m Technicolor
Paramount/Security (Philip Yordan, Bernard Glasser, Lester A. Sansom)

A dying scientist fires a missile into the Earth's centre, and nearly blows the planet apart.

Jaded science-fiction melodrama, overburdened with initial chat but waking up when the special effects take over.

w Jon Manchip White, Julian Halevy *d* Andrew Marton *ph* Manuel Berenguer *m* John Douglas *ad* Eugene Lourié *sp* John Douglas

Dana Andrews, Janette Scott, Kieron Moore, Alexander Knox, Peter Damon, Gary Lasdun

Crack Up
US 1936 65m bw
TCF

Espionage agents try to corrupt a test pilot.

Modestly efficient thriller.

w Charles Kenyon, Sam Mintz *d* Mal St Clair

Peter Lorre, Brian Donlevy, Helen Wood, Ralph Morgan, Thomas Beck

Crack Up *
US 1946 93m bw
RKO
V*, L

A museum curator with an eye for forgery is discredited by crooks who make him appear drunk or half-crazed when he recounts a set of strange events which have happened to him . . .

The intriguing mystery of the opening reels, when solved, is replaced by rather dull detection, but this remains a thriller with a difference, generally well presented.

w John Paxton *d* Irving Reis *ph* Robert de Grasse *m* Leigh Harline

Pat O'Brien, Claire Trevor, Herbert Marshall, Ray Collins

Cracked Nuts
US 1931 65m bw
RKO

Two Americans get mixed up in a revolution in a mythical country.

Padded farce vehicle for a comedy team.

w Al Boasberg, Ralph Spence *d* Edward Cline

Bert Wheeler, Robert Woolsey, Ben Turpin, Edna May Oliver, Dorothy Lee

'As a two-reeler it would be fair entertainment.' – *Variety*

Crackerjack *
GB 1938 79m bw
Gainsborough (Edward Black)
US title: *The Man with a Hundred Faces*

A gentleman thief poses as butler at a stately home.

Fairly smart sardonic star vehicle.

w A. R. Rawlinson, Michael Pertwee, Basil Mason *novel* W. B. Ferguson *d* Albert de Courville *ph* J. J. Cox

Tom Walls, Lilli Palmer, Noel Madison, Leon M. Lion, Edmund Breon, Charles Heslop

'Carelessly made but fairly engrossing.' – *Variety*

Crackers
US 1984 92m Technicolor
Universal/Edward Lewis
V*, L

Incompetent crooks run a pawnshop.

Insufficiently rethought, San Francisco set, updating of Monicelli's 1956 comedy *Big Deal on Madonna Street* (*I Soliti Ignoti*). No longer at all funny.

w Jeffrey Fiskin d Louis Malle ph Laszlo Kovacs m Paul Chihara pd John L. Lloyd

Donald Sutherland, Jack Warden, Sean Penn, Wallace Shawn, Larry Riley, Trinidad Silva, Charlaine Woodard, Irwin Corey

'One can sense that it would all sound much funnier in Italian.' – *Variety*

The Cracksman
GB 1963 112m Technicolor Cinemascope
ABPC
V

A master locksmith becomes the unwitting dupe of a gang of safecrackers.

The most elaborate vehicle devised for this diminutive star; despite bright moments, conventional mounting and over-generous length finally defeat it.

w Lew Schwartz, Charlie Drake d Peter Graham Scott

Charlie Drake, George Sanders, Dennis Price, Nyree Dawn Porter, Eddie Byrne, Finlay Currie, Percy Herbert

Cradle Song *
US 1933 78m bw
Paramount (E. Lloyd Sheldon)

A nun adopts a foundling.

Stately transcription of a once-fashionable play, too concerned with its own artistic background and handicapped by a star who didn't travel well, except to those partial to Jewish nuns.

w Marc Connelly play G. M. Martinez Sierra d Mitchell Leisen ph Charles Lang m W. Franke Harling

Dorothea Wieck, Evelyn Venable, Sir Guy Standing, Louise Dresser, Kent Taylor, Gertrude Michael, Nydia Westman, Eleanor Wesselhoeft

'It moves slowly, laboriously . . . as a commercial entry decidedly dubious.' – *Variety*

Craig's Wife *
US 1936 77m bw
Columbia
V*

A middle-class wife lets her house take precedence over her husband.

Capable picturization of a Broadway success, later remade as *Harriet Craig* (qv).

w Mary McCall Jnr, George Kelly play George Kelly d Dorothy Arzner ph Lucien Ballard md Morris Stoloff

Rosalind Russell, John Boles, Billie Burke, Jane Darwell, Dorothy Wilson, Alma Kruger, Thomas Mitchell, Elizabeth Risdon, Raymond Walburn

Crainquebille *
France 1922 70m approx (16 fps) bw silent
Trarieux Films

A street trader is unjustly accused and imprisoned, afterwards finding happiness as a tramp.

Somewhere between Chaplin and Kafka, this fable was long admired for its style.

wd Jacques Feyder story Anatole France ph Léonce Burel

Maurice de Féraudy, Françoise Rosay, Felix Oudart

† Remade 1933 by Jacques de Baroncelli with Maurice Tramel; 1954 by Ralph Habib with Yves Deniaud.

The Cranes Are Flying **
USSR 1957 94m bw
Mosfilm
V*, L
original title: *Letyat Zhuravli*

When her lover goes to war, a girl refuses to believe later reports of his death even though she has suffered much, including marriage to a bully, in the interim.

Sleek, moving love story with most of the Hollywood production virtues plus an attention to detail and a realism which are wholly Russian.

w Victor Rosov d Mikhail Kalatozov ph Sergei Urusevski

Tatiana Samoilova, Alexei Batalov, Vasili Merkuriev

The Crash
US 1932 59m bw
Warner

An unfaithful wife finds her life changed by the stock market crash.

Dim high-society goings-on make a poor star vehicle.

w Earl Baldwin novel Children of Pleasure by Larry Barratto d William Dieterle

Ruth Chatterton, George Brent, Paul Cavanagh, Henry Kolker, Barbara Leonard

'A weak sister . . . nothing happens to pique interest or capture sympathy or even provoke hostility.' – *Variety*

Crash!
US 1977 85m DeLuxe Panavision
Group One/Charles Band

A crippled husband sets out to murder his wife, but she is protected by a good-luck charm with magic powers.

Ineffably silly occult thriller, consisting mainly of unspectacular car crashes which are all reprised towards the end of the film to ensure total tedium.

w Marc Marais d Charles Band ph Andrew Davis, Bill Williams m Andrew Belling ad Patrick McFadden ed Harry Keramidas

José Ferrer, Sue Lyon, John Ericson, Leslie Parrish, John Carradine, Jerome Guardino, Reggie Nalder

Crash Dive *
US 1943 105m Technicolor
TCF (Milton Sperling)

A submarine lieutenant and his commander love the same girl.

Well-staged war thrills in the final reels are prefaced by a long romantic comedy build-up, which probably seemed good propaganda at the time.

w Jo Swerling story W. R. Burnett d Archie Mayo ph Leon Shamroy md Emil Newman m David Buttolph sp Fred Sersen

Tyrone Power, Anne Baxter, Dana Andrews, James Gleason, Dame May Whitty, Henry Morgan, Frank Conroy, Minor Watson

'One of those films which have no more sense of reality about this war than a popular song.' – *Bosley Crowther*

The Crash of Silence: see *Mandy*

Crashing Hollywood *
US 1937 60m bw
RKO

A studio screenwriter selects a criminal as collaborator, and gets into all kinds of trouble.

Lively melodramatic star vehicle with a reasonably vivid background.

w Paul Yawitz, Gladys Atwater play Paul Dickey, Mann Page d Lew Landers

Lee Tracy, Joan Woodbury, Paul Guilfoyle, Lee Patrick, Richard Lane, Jack Carson, Tom Kennedy

'Completely satisfactory programme picture.' – *Variety*

Crashout
US 1955 83m bw
Hal E. Chester/Standard
V*

Six convicts escape from prison, but most of them die en route.

Watchable melodrama, fairly savage for its day.

w Hal E. Chester, Lewis R. Foster d Lewis R. Foster

William Bendix, Arthur Kennedy, Luther Adler, William Talman, Gene Evans, Marshall Thompson, Beverly Michaels

The Crawling Eye: see *The Trollenberg Terror*

Craze
GB 1973 95m Technicolor
EMI/Harbour (Herman Cohen)
V*

An African idol accidentally causes a death which brings money to its owner, who kills again and again in the hope of more loot.

Crude shocker from the bottom of even this producer's barrel, notable for the star cast which was surprisingly roped in.

w Aben Kandel, Herman Cohen novel Infernal Idol by Henry Seymour d Freddie Francis ph John Wilcox m John Scott

Jack Palance, Diana Dors, Julie Ege, Edith Evans, Hugh Griffith, Trevor Howard, Michael Jayston, Suzy Kendall, Martin Potter, Percy Herbert, Kathleen Byron

Crazy House
US 1943 80m bw
Universal (Erle C. Kenton)

Olsen and Johnson go to Hollywood to make a film.

Lame sequel to *Hellzapoppin*; after an explosively well edited first reel of panic in the studio, it degenerates into a slew of below-par variety turns.

w Robert Lees, Frederic I. Rinaldo d Edward Cline ph Charles Van Enger md George Hale, Milt Rosen

Ole Olsen, Chic Johnson, Martha O'Driscoll, Patric Knowles, Percy Kilbride, Cass Daley, Thomas Gomez, Edgar Kennedy

† Sherlock Holmes fans may or may not wish to record a two-line comic bit by Basil Rathbone and Nigel Bruce in character.

Crazy Joe
US/Italy 1973 99m Technicolor
Bright-Persky/De Laurentiis
V*

The rise and fall of a Mafia hood in New York.

Noisy, violent, reasonably proficient gangster movie which seems to have some pretensions to play against stereotype.

w Lewis John Carlino d Carlo Lizzani

Peter Boyle, Paula Prentiss, Fred Williamson, Charles Cioffi, Rip Torn, Luther Adler, Eli Wallach, Henry Winkler

Crazy Love *
Belgium   1987   87m   Eastmancolor
Mainline/Multimedia (Erwin Provoost, Alain Keytsman)
V
US title: Love Is a Dog from Hell

A frustrated boy, full of romantic longings, grows up to be a necrophiliac.

Episodic and squalid story of a journey from innocence to drug-addicted desperation, told with style.

w Marc Didden, Dominique Deruddere   story The Copulating Mermaid of Venice, California and other works by Charles Bukowski   d Dominique Deruddere   ph Willy Stassen   m Raymond Van Het Groenewoud   pd Hubert Pouille, Erik Van Belleghem   ed Ludo Troch, Guido Henderickx

Josse de Pauw, Geert Hunaerts, Michael Pas, Gene Bervoets, Amid Chakir, François Beukelaers, Florence Beliard, Carmela Locantore

'A movie for people with a perverse sense of humor or a persistent sexual acne – a low-keyed sexual reverie.' – Pauline Kael, New Yorker

Crazy Mama **
US   1975   80m   colour
New World (Julie Corman)
V*

In 1958 Arkansas, mother and daughter set off on a series of robberies and kidnaps which end in violence.

Exploitation crime movie with no apparent basis in fact; as such, occasionally exciting for those who can tolerate this kind of thing.

w Robert Thom   d Jonathan Demme   ph Tak Fujimoto   m Snotty Scotty and the Hankies

Cloris Leachman, Ann Sothern, Stuart Whitman, Jim Backus, Linda Purl, Brian Englund

Crazy People
US   1990   92m   Technicolor
UIP/Paramount (Thomas Barad)
V, V*, L

An ad-man runs his business from a rest home for mental patients.

Unsatisfactory would-be satire.

w Mitch Markowitz   d Tony Bill   ph Victor J. Kemper   m Cliff Eidelman   ad Steven Schwartz   ed Mia Goldman

Dudley Moore, Daryl Hannah, Paul Reiser, J. T. Walsh, Bill Smitrovich, Alan North, David Paymer

'Damp, indulgent squib of a film.' – Geoff Brown, MFB

The Crazy Ray: see Paris Qui Dort

Crazy to Kill: see Dr Gillespie's Criminal Case

The Crazy World of Julius Vrooder
US   1974   98m   colour
TCF

A Vietnam veteran withdraws from the world.

Well-meaning but tiresome problem pic which gets nowhere.

w Daryl Henry   d Arthur Hiller

Timothy Bottoms, Barbara Seagull, Lawrence Pressman, Albert Salmi

The Crazy World of Laurel and Hardy **
US   1964   83m   bw
Hal Roach/Jay Ward

A compilation of Laurel and Hardy extracts from their classic period.

Although the material is in itself excellent and some of the build-up sequences well done, the clips are all too short to achieve maximum impact, and virtually none is identified.

w Bill Scott   m Jerry Fielding   narrator Garry Moore

Creator
US   1985   107m   Technicolor
Entertainment/Universal/Kings Road (Stephen Friedman)
V, V*, L

A research scientist tries to clone his dead wife.

Sentimental and eccentric comedy of little interest.

w Jeremy Leven   novel Jeremy Leven   d Ivan Passer   ph Robbie Greenberg   m Sylvester Levay   ad Josan F. Russo   ed Richard Chew

Peter O'Toole, Mariel Hemingway, Vincent Spano, Virginia Madsen, David Ogden Stiers, John Dehner

'Not since the beginning of time has the world beheld terror like this!'
The Creature from the Black Lagoon
US   1954   79m   bw   3-D
U-I (William Alland)
V*, L

Up the Amazon, scientists encounter a fearful fanged creature who is half man, half fish.

Unpersuasive and unsuspenseful horror hokum from the bottom drawer of imagination: it did, however, coin enough pennies to generate two even worse sequels, Revenge of the Creature (1955) and The Creature Walks Among Us (1956). And the underwater photography is super.

w Harry Essex, Arthur Ross   d Jack Arnold   ph William E. Snyder   md Joseph Gershenson   m Herman Stein, Hans Salter

Richard Carlson, Julie Adams, Richard Denning, Antonio Moreno, Nestor Paiva, Ricou Browning (in the rubber suit)

The Creature with the Atom Brain
US   1955   80m   bw
Columbia (Sam Katzman)

A scientist creates super-strong robot men, who go on the rampage.

Comic strip style chiller, not too bad to sit through.

w Curt Siodmak   d Edward L. Cahn

Richard Denning, Angela Stevens, Gregory Gaye, Tristram Coffin

Creatures the World Forgot
GB   1971   95m   Technicolor
Columbia/Hammer (Michael Carreras)
V*

Quarrels break out between rival tribes of Stone Age men.

Feeble follow-up to One Million Years BC and When Dinosaurs Ruled the Earth: someone forgot to order any monsters.

w Michael Carreras   d Don Chaffey   ph Vincent Cox   m Mario Nascimbene   pd John Stoll   ed Chris Barnes

Julie Ege, Brian O'Shaughnessy, Robert John, Marcia Fox, Rosalie Crutchley

The Creeper
US   1948   63m   bw
TCF
V*

Scientists disagree over a serum which changes humans into cats.

Nonsense horror item with stalwart cast.

w Maurice Tombragel   d Jean Yarbrough

Ralph Morgan, Eduardo Ciannelli, Onslow Stevens, June Vincent, Richard Lane

The Creeping Flesh *
GB   1972   91m   Eastmancolor
Tigon/World Film Services (Michael Redbourn)
V*, L

A Victorian scientist discovers that water causes the recomposing of tissue on the skeleton of a Neanderthal man.

Absurd but persuasive horror film, quite well done in all departments.

w Peter Spenceley, Jonathan Rumbold   d Freddie Francis   ph Norman Warwick   m Paul Ferris

Peter Cushing, Christopher Lee, Lorna Heilbron, George Benson, Kenneth J. Warren, Duncan Lamont, Michael Ripper

The Creeping Unknown: see The Quatermass Experiment

'The most fun you'll ever have being scared!'
Creepshow
US   1982   120m   colour
United Film Distribution/Laurel Show (Richard P. Rubenstein)
V, V*, S

A boy reads five gruesome stories from a horror comic.

Supposedly funny but mainly rather nasty recreation of a famous 'comic' style; far too extended for its own good.

w Stephen King   d George A. Romero   ph Michael Gornick   m John Harrison   pd Tom Savini

Carrie Nye, Viveca Lindfors, Stephen King, Leslie Nielsen, Hal Holbrook, Adrienne Barbeau, E. G. Marshall

'Robert Bloch and Freddie Francis did it all so much better in Torture Garden.' – Tom Milne, MFB

Creepshow 2
US   1987   89m   colour
Laurel/New World (David Ball)
V, V*, L

Cheapjack sequel, of no interest whatsoever.

w George A. Romero   stories Stephen King   d Michael Gornick   ph Dick Hart, Tom Hurwitz   m Les Reed   ed Peter Weatherly

Lois Chiles, George Kennedy, Dorothy Lamour, Tom Savini, Page Hannah

'An omnibus snoozefest, utterly lacking in chills or thrills.' Daily Variety

'The night the loving ended and the killing began!'
Crescendo *
GB   1970   95m   Technicolor
Warner/Hammer (Michael Carreras)

A girl researcher goes to stay with the widow of a famous composer, and finds herself in mortal danger . . .

Lunatic Hammer horror with the courage of its shameless borrowings from Taste of Fear, Fanatic, Nightmare, Maniac and all the films about mad twin brothers, to which this chaotic brew adds dollops of sex and heroin addiction.

w Jimmy Sangster, Alfred Shaughnessy   d Alan Gibson   ph Paul Beeson   m Malcolm Williamson   ad Scott MacGregor   ed Chris Barnes

Stefanie Powers, James Olson, Margaretta Scott, Jane Lapotaire, Joss Ackland

Crest of the Wave: see Seagulls over Sorrento

Cries and Whispers ****
Sweden   1972   91m   Eastmancolor
Cinematograph (Ingmar Bergman)
V*
original title: Viskningar och Rop

A young woman dying of cancer in her family home is tended by her two sisters.

Quiet, chilling, classical chapter of doom which variously reminds one of Chekhov, Tolstoy and Dostoievsky but is also essential Bergman. Tough but important viewing, it lingers afterwards in the mind like a picture vividly painted in shades of red.

wd Ingmar Bergman *ph* Sven Nykvist *m* Chopin and Bach

Harriet Andersson, Kari Sylwan, Ingrid Thulin, Liv Ullmann

'Harrowing, spare and perceptive, but lacking the humour that helps to put life and death into perspective.' – *Michael Billington, Illustrated London News*

AA: Sven Nykvist

AAN: best picture; Ingmar Bergman (as writer); Ingmar Bergman (as director)

Crime and Punishment *
US 1935 88m bw
Columbia

A student kills a pawnbroker and is tortured by remorse.

Heavy-going rendering of Dostoievsky with some pictorial interest.

w S. K. Lauren, Joseph Anthony *d* Josef von Sternberg *ph* Lucien Ballard *md* Louis Silvers *m* Arthur Honegger

Peter Lorre, Edward Arnold, Tala Birell, Marian Marsh, Elizabeth Risdon, Mrs Patrick Campbell

'Will have to be sold, but should average fair takings.' – *Variety*

Crime and Punishment *
France 1935 110m bw

Incisive, well-acted French version.

w Marcel Aymé *d* Pierre Chenal *m* Arthur Honegger

Pierre Blanchar, Harry Baur, Marcelle Geniat, Madeleine Ozeray

'There's a real picture in this Dostoievsky book, and the French have proved it.' – *Variety*

Crime and Punishment USA
US 1958 96m bw
Allied Artists/Sanders Associates (Terry Sanders)

A student murders an old pawnbroker and is driven mad by guilt.

Pointless updating of Dostoievsky by two young film-makers who seemed for years to be on the brink of a masterpiece but never actually produced it. Some points of interest, but the low budget is cramping.

w Walter Newman *d* Denis Sanders *ph* Floyd Crosby *m* Herschel Burke Gilbert

George Hamilton, Frank Silvera, Mary Murphy, John Harding, Marian Seldes

'There is about it a strange quality of aimlessness which nullifies much of its effect.' – *MFB*

Crime by Night *
US 1944 72m bw
Warner (William Jacobs)

A private detective reluctantly solves a small-town murder, and finds a spy.

Second feature which was thought at the time to have established a new pair of married detectives in the tradition of *The Thin Man*. However, one poor sequel, *Find the Blackmailer*, put paid to the idea.

w Richard Weil, Joel Malone *novel Forty Whacks* by Geoffrey Homes *d* William Clemens *ph* Henry Sharpe

Jerome Cowan, Jane Wyman, Faye Emerson, Charles Lang, Eleanor Parker, Cy Kendall, Creighton Hale

Crime Doctor
US 1934 75m bw
RKO

A criminologist uses his special knowledge to wreak vengeance on his wife's lover.

Smart co-feature which doubtless pleased a good many audiences.

w Jane Murfin *story* Israel Zangwill *d* John Robertson

Otto Kruger, Karen Morley, Nils Asther, Judith Wood, William Frawley, Donald Crisp

'Good in every department, with mounting suspense.' – *Variety*

Crime Doctor *
US 1943 66m bw
Columbia

An amnesiac becomes a successful psychiatrist, then discovers that he was once a wanted gangster.

Time-passing second feature from a popular radio series. Ten *Crime Doctor* films were made between 1943 and 1949, all starring Warner Baxter, all except the first being locked room mysteries which seldom played fair with the audience.

w Graham Baker, Louise Lantz *d* Michael Gordon *m* Louis Silvers

Warner Baxter, Margaret Lindsay, John Litel, Ray Collins, Harold Huber, Leon Ames, Don CostelloThe sequels:

1943: CRIME DOCTOR'S STRANGEST CASE
1944: SHADOWS IN THE NIGHT, CRIME DOCTOR'S COURAGE
1945: CRIME DOCTOR'S WARNING
1946: CRIME DOCTOR'S MANHUNT, JUST BEFORE DAWN
1947: THE MILLERSON CASE
1948: CRIME DOCTOR'S GAMBLE
1949: CRIME DOCTOR'S DIARY

Crime Does Not Pay

A celebrated series of two-reel shorts made by MGM between 1935 and 1947.

In a hard-driving, tensely commentated manner more reminiscent of Warner filmmaking, they gave ample scope to trainee actors and directors in allegedly truthful re-enactments of contemporary crimes, often introduced by the state governor or police commissioner. The titles were as follows:

BURIED LOOT (1935); *d* George B. Seitz; with Robert Taylor, Robert Livingston.
ALIBI RACKET (1935); *d* George B. Seitz.
DESERT DEATH (1935); *d* George B. Seitz; with Raymond Hatton, Harvey Stephens.
A THRILL FOR THELMA (1935); *d* Edward Cahn; with Irene Hervey, Robert Warwick.
HIT AND RUN DRIVER (1935); *d* Edward Cahn; with Morgan Wallace, Jonathan Hale.
PERFECT SET-UP (1936); *d* Edward Cahn.
FOOLPROOF (1936); *d* Edward Cahn; with Niles Welch, Alonzo Price.
THE PUBLIC PAYS (1936); *d* Errol Taggart; with Paul Stanton, Cy Kendall; AA.
TORTURE MONEY (1936); *d* Harold S. Bucquet; AA.
IT MAY HAPPEN TO YOU (1937); *d* Harold S. Bucquet.
SOAK THE POOR (1937); *d* Harold S. Bucquet.
GIVE TILL IT HURTS (1937); *d* Felix Feist; with Janet Beecher, Howard Hickman.
BEHIND THE CRIMINAL (1937); *d* Harold S. Bucquet; with Edward Emerson, Walter Kingsford.
WHAT PRICE SAFETY (1938); *d* Harold S. Bucquet; with John Wray, George Houston.
MIRACLE MONEY (1938); *d* Leslie Fenton; with John Miljan, Claire DuBrey.
COME ACROSS (1938); *d* Harold S. Bucquet; with Bernard Nedell, Donald Douglas.
A CRIMINAL IS BORN (1938); *d* Leslie Fenton; with George Breakston, David Durand.
THEY'RE ALWAYS CAUGHT (1938); *d* Harold S. Bucquet; with Stanley Ridges, John Eldredge; AAN.

THINK IT OVER (1938); *d* Jacques Tourneur; with Lester Matthews, Dwight Frye.
THE WRONG WAY OUT (1938); *d* Gustav Machaty; with Linda Terry, Kenneth Howell.
MONEY TO LOAN (1939); *d* Joe Newman; with Alan Dinehart, Paul Guilfoyle.
WHILE AMERICA SLEEPS (1939); *d* Fred Zinnemann; with Dick Purcell, Roland Varno.
HELP WANTED (1939); *d* Fred Zinnemann; with Tom Neal, Jo Ann Sayers.
THINK FIRST (1939); *d* Roy Rowland; with Laraine Day, Marc Lawrence, Sara Haden.
DRUNK DRIVING (1939); *d* David Miller; with Dick Purcell, Jo Ann Sayers; AAN.
POUND FOOLISH (1940); *d* Felix Feist; with Neil Hamilton, Lynne Carver.
KNOW YOUR MONEY (1940); *d* Joe Newman; with Dennis Moore, Noel Madison.
JACKPOT (1940); *d* Roy Rowland; with Tom Neal, Ann Morriss.
WOMEN IN HIDING (1940); *d* Joe Newman; with Marsha Hunt, C. Henry Gordon.
BUYER BEWARE (1940); *d* Joe Newman; with Charles Arnt.
SOAK THE OLD (1940); *d* Sammy Lee; with Ralph Morgan, Kenneth Christy.
YOU THE PEOPLE (1940); *d* Roy Rowland; with C. Henry Gordon, Paul Everton.
RESPECT THE LAW (1941); *d* Joe Newman.
FORBIDDEN PASSAGE (1941); *d* Fred Zinnemann; with Harry Woods; AAN.
COFFINS ON WHEELS (1941); *d* Joe Newman; with Cy Kendall, Darryl Hickman.
SUCKER LIST (1941); *d* Roy Rowland; with Lynne Carver, John Archer.
FOR THE COMMON DEFENSE (1942); *d* Allen Kenward; with Van Johnson, Douglas Fowley.
KEEP 'EM SAILING (1942); *d* Basil Wrangell; with Jim David, Lou Smith.
PLAN FOR DESTRUCTION (1943); *d* Edward Cahn; with Lewis Stone.
PATROLLING THE ETHER (1944); *d* Paul Burnford.
EASY LIFE (1944); *d* Walter Hart; with Bernard Thomas, Steve Geray.
DARK SHADOWS (1944); *d* Paul Burnford; with Arthur Space, Henry O'Neill.
FALL GUY (1945); *d* Paul Burnford; with Leon Ames.
THE LAST INSTALLMENT (1945); *d* Walter Hart; with Cameron Mitchell, Walter Sande.
PHANTOMS INC. (1945); *d* Harold Young; with Frank Reicher, Ann Shoemaker.
A GUN IN HIS HAND (1945); *d* Joseph Losey; with Anthony Caruso, Richard Gaines; AAN.
PURITY SQUAD (1945); *d* Harold Kress; with Byron Foulger, Dick Elliott.
LUCKIEST GUY IN THE WORLD (1947); *d* Joe Newman; with Barry Nelson, Eloise Hardt.

Crime in the Streets *
US 1956 91m bw
Allied Artists (Vincent M. Fennelly)
V*

Rival knife gangs bring havoc to tenement dwellers.

Lively semi-documentary low-life melodrama; routine subject, excellent credits.

w Reginald Rose *TV play* Reginald Rose *d* Don Siegel *ph* Sam Leavitt *m* Franz Waxman

John Cassavetes, James Whitmore, Sal Mineo, Mark Rydell

The Crime of Dr Crespi
US 1935 64m bw
Republic
V*

A surgeon induces suspended animation in a hated rival, and has him buried.

Crude and tasteless variation on Poe's 'The Premature Burial'.

w Lewis Graham, Edward Olmstead   *d* John H. Auer

Erich von Stroheim, Dwight Frye, Paul Guilfoyle, Harriet Russell

'As a baby scarer it's a weak entry.' – *Variety*

The Crime of Dr Forbes
US   1936   75m   bw
TCF

A gravely injured scientist asks to be put out of his misery, and a colleague is accused of murder.

Competently handled minor item, more a mystery story than a consideration of euthanasia.

w Frances Hyland, Saul Elkins   *d* George Marshall

Robert Kent, J. Edward Bromberg, Gloria Stuart, Henry Armetta, Sara Haden, Alan Dinehart

The Crime of Dr Hallet
US   1938   68m   bw
Universal

A doctor working on jungle fever finds it convenient to disappear and take over a dead colleague's identity.

Implausible time-passer.

w Lester Cole, Brown Holmes   *d* S. Sylvan Simon

Ralph Bellamy, Josephine Hutchinson, William Gargan, Barbara Read

† Remade in 1946 as *Strange Conquest,* with Lowell Gilmore and Jane Wyatt.

The Crime of Monsieur Lange **
France   1936   85m   bw
Obéron (André Halley des Fontaines)
V*

When the hated boss of a publishing house is believed killed, the workers turn it into a successful co-operative. When he reappears, they kill him.

The political elements of this fable now seem unimportant, but it still shows its original charm and cinematic skill.

w Jacques Prévert   *d* Jean Renoir   *ph* Jean Bachelet   *m* Jean Wiener

René Lefèbvre, Jules Berry, Florelle, Sylvie Bataille, Henri Guisol

Crime of Passion
US   1956   86m   bw
UA/Bob Goldstein (Herman Cohen)

An executive's wife sleeps her way to the top, but when the boss does not come through with promotion she shoots him.

Old-fashioned star melodrama on a low budget.

w Jo Eisinger   *d* Gerd Oswald   *ph* Joseph LaShelle   *m* Paul Dunlap

Barbara Stanwyck, Sterling Hayden, Raymond Burr, Fay Wray, Royal Dano, Virginia Grey

Crime of the Century
US   1933   74m   bw
Paramount (B. P. Schulberg)

A doctor commits a robbery by hypnotism, but is himself assaulted and the money disappears.

Smart exploitation mystery with an intermission for the audience to check the clues, and a revelation that the police investigator is the guilty man.

w Florence Ryerson, Brian Marlow   *play The Grootman Case* by Walter Maria Espe   *d* William Beaudine

Jean Hersholt, Robert Elliott, Wynne Gibson, Stuart Erwin, Frances Dee, David Landau

'Can be built up into a better than average below the de luxe theatres.' – *Variety*

The Crime of the Century (1952): see *Walk East on Beacon*

Crime over London
GB   1936   84m   bw
UA/Criterion (Marcel Hellman, Douglas Fairbanks Jnr)

A department store becomes a hide-out for gangsters.

Stolid attempt at a British gangster picture; doesn't come off.

w Norman Alexander, Harold French   *novel House of a Thousand Windows* by Louis de Wohl   *d* Alfred Zeisler   *ph* Victor Armenise, Claude Friese-Greene   *ad* Edward Carrick   *ed* Conrad von Molo

Margot Grahame, Paul Cavanagh, Joseph Cawthorn, Basil Sydney, Rene Ray

Crime School *
US   1938   86m   bw
Warner (Bryan Foy)

Problems of the warden of a reform school.

Predictable vehicle for the Dead End Kids; watchable at the time.

w Crane Wilbur, Vincent Sherman   *d* Lewis Seiler   *ph* Arthur Todd   *m* Max Steiner

Humphrey Bogart, Gale Page, Billy Halop, Huntz Hall, Leo Gorcey, Bobby Jordan, Gabriel Dell, Bernard Punsley, Paul Porcasi, Al Bridge

'A rough entertainment, sometimes brutal . . . should do well where audiences like 'em tough.' – *Variety*

Crime Wave
US   1954   74m   bw
Warner
GB title: *The City Is Dark*

An ex-con is prevented from going straight.

Basically humdrum programmer with lively detail.

w Crane Wilbur   *d* André de Toth

Sterling Hayden, Gene Nelson, Phyllis Kirk, Ted de Corsia, Charles Bronson

'He had tired of her – and for that he was sorry! He was tied to her – and for that he hated her!'

Crime without Passion **
US   1934   82m   bw
Paramount (Ben Hecht, Charles MacArthur)

A lawyer is driven to commit murder.

Effective melodrama notable for then-new techniques which were blended into the mainstream of movie-making, and for the first appearance in Hollywood of a smart new writer-producer-director team.

wd Ben Hecht, Charles MacArthur   *story Caballero of the Law* by Ben Hecht, Charles MacArthur   *ph* Lee Garmes   *m* Oscar Levant   *sp* Slavko Vorkapich

Claude Rains, Margo, Whitney Bourne, Stanley Ridges

'It turns a lot of established motion picture conventions topsy-turvy . . . shouldn't have much trouble at the box office, and inside the theatre it is safe.' – *Variety*

'The whole venture seems to take a long stride forward for the movies.' – *Otis Ferguson*

'A flamboyant, undisciplined, but compulsively fascinating film classic.' – *Peter John Dyer, 1966*

Crimes and Misdemeanors ***
US   1989   104m   DeLuxe
Rank/Orion (Robert Greenhut)
V*, L

Brothers-in-law deal with marital crises.

Two interlinked stories, one comic, the other tragic, form a winning combination.

wd Woody Allen   *ph* Sven Nykvist   *md* Joe Malin   *pd* Santo Loquasto   *ed* Susan E. Morse

Caroline Aaron, Alan Alda, Woody Allen, Claire Bloom, Mia Farrow, Joanna Gleason, Anjelica Huston, Martin Landau, Jenny Nichols, Jerry Orbach

AAN: best director; best original screenplay; Martin Landau

Crimes at the Dark House
GB   1939   69m   bw
Pennant (George King)

A Victorian landowner kills his wife and conceals the fact by using a lunatic as her double.

Cheeky adaptation of a classic to make one of the star's most lip-smacking barnstormers.

w Edward Dryhurst, Frederick Hayward, H. F. Maltby   *novel The Woman in White* by Wilkie Collins   *d* George King   *ph* Hone Glendinning

Tod Slaughter, Hilary Eaves, Sylvia Marriott, Hay Petrie, David Horne

Crimes of Passion
US   1984   104m   colour
New World (Barry Sandler)
V, S

A prostitute tells her story at a group therapy session.

Predictably from this director, a hysterically overheated stew of sex and murder; one to walk away from.

w Barry Sandler   *d* Ken Russell   *ph* Dick Bush   *m* Rick Wakeman

Kathleen Turner, Anthony Perkins, John Laughlin, Annie Potts

'Film walks an uneasy line at times between comedy and drama, but is entertaining in the manner of a great B picture all about sex.' – *Variety*

'One of the silliest movies in a long time.' – *Roger Ebert*

The Crimes of Stephen Hawke
GB   1936   69m   bw
MGM (George King)

A 19th-century moneylender is exposed as the mysterious murderer who had terrorized London.

Amusing barnstormer.

w H. F. Maltby   *story* Jack Celestin   *d* George King   *ph* Ronald Neame

Tod Slaughter, Eric Portman, Marjorie Taylor, Gerald Barry

Crimes of the Heart *
US   1986   105m   Technicolor
De Laurentiis/Freddie Fields-Burt Sugarman
V, V*, L, S

Three sisters try to reconcile themselves with their family past.

Somewhat overwrought but generally compelling Southern comedy-drama.

w Beth Henley   *play* Beth Henley   *d* Bruce Beresford   *ph* Dante Spinotti   *m* Georges Delerue   *pd* Ken Adam

Diane Keaton, Jessica Lange, Sissy Spacek, Sam Shepard, Tess Harper, David Carpenter, Hurd Hatfield

AAN: Sissy Spacek, Tess Harper

Crimewave
US   1986   83m   Technicolor
Embassy/Pressman/Renaissance (Robert Tapert)
V, V*

Two psychopaths are hired by a timid security man to murder his double-crossing partner.

Broad black farcical horror that is very noisy, but never funny.

w Ethan Coen, Joel Coen, Sam Raimi   *d* Sam Raimi   *ph* Robert Primes   *m* Arlon Ober   *ad* Gary Papierski   *ed* Michael Kelly, Kathie Weaver

Louise Lasser, Paul L. Smith, Brion James, Sheree J. Wilson, Edward R. Pressman, Bruce Campbell, Reed Birney

The Criminal *
GB 1960 97m bw
Merton Park (Jack Greenwood)
V
US title: *The Concrete Jungle*

Sent to jail for a racecourse snatch, a gangster comes out fifteen years later to regain the loot and is followed by other criminals who kill him.

Relentlessly grim saga of prison life, with a few sensational trimmings.

w Alun Owen, Jimmy Sangster   d Joseph Losey
ph Robert Krasker   m Johnny Dankworth

Stanley Baker, Sam Wanamaker, Margit Saad, *Patrick Magee*, Noel Willman, Grégoire Aslan, Jill Bennett, Kenneth J. Warren, Nigel Green, Patrick Wymark, Murray Melvin

'A savage, almost expressionistic picture of English underworld life.' – *NFT, 1973*

The Criminal Code *
US 1930 97m bw
Columbia (Harry Cohn)
V*

A young man kills in self-defence, is railroaded into jail and becomes involved in another murder.

Impressive melodrama with good performances and sharp handling.

w Seton I. Miller, Fred Niblo Jnr   play Martin Flavin   d Howard Hawks   ph James Wong Howe, William O'Connell

Walter Huston, Phillips Holmes, Constance Cummings, Mary Doran, De Witt Jennings, John Sheehan, Boris Karloff

'It can play to any type of audience: they'll understand it and talk about it. A corking picture.' – *Variety*

† Remade as *Penitentiary* (1938) with Walter Connolly and *Convicted* (1950) with Broderick Crawford.

AAN: Seton I. Miller, Fred Niblo Jnr

Criminal Court
US 1946 63m bw
RKO
V*

A lawyer is blackmailed by a crooked club owner.

Stock crime and lawcourt yarn, rather stodgily put together but with interesting moments.

w Lawrence Kimble   d Robert Wise

Tom Conway, Martha O'Driscoll, Robert Armstrong, Addison Richards

'Whoever fights monsters should see to it that in the process he does not become a monster.' Nietzsche

Criminal Law
US 1989 118m colour Panavision
Hemdale/Northwood (Robert MacClean, Hilary Heath)
V, V*, L, S

A successful lawyer decides that his client is a murderer.

Hysterical thriller that never convinces on any level.

w Mark Kasdan   d Martin Campbell   ph Philip Meheux   m Jerry Goldsmith   ed Chris Wimble

Gary Oldman, Kevin Bacon, Karen Young, Joe Don Baker, Tess Harper, Ron Lea, Karen Woolridge, Terence Labrosse, Jennie Walker

'It dares to elaborate on its unbelievable central relationship between a driven yuppie lawyer and a charming old-money psychopath with hokey devices more redolent of some 40s old-dark-house movie than of a supposedly "serious" modern thriller.' – *Kim Newman, MFB*

Criminal Lawyer
US 1936 72m bw
RKO

A smart lawyer who has devoted his career to getting criminals off the hook has a change of heart when appointed district attorney.

Standard programmer with a first-rate star performance.

w G. V. Atwater, Thomas Lennon   story Louis Stevenson   d Christy Cabanne

Lee Tracy, Margot Grahame, Eduardo Ciannelli, Erik Rhodes

'Strong fronter for a dual, but can go solo where Tracy's name will draw.' – *Variety*

The Criminal Life of Archibaldo de la Cruz *
Mexico 1955 91m bw
Alianza Cinematografica (Roberto Figueroa)
V*
original title: *Ensayo de un Crimen*

A fantasist determines to kill all women who cross his path, but fate intervenes.

Cheaply made macabre joke, one of its director's throwaway oddities: not too smooth, but often amusing.

w Luis Buñuel, E. Ugarte   d Luis Buñuel
ph Augusto Jimenez   md Jorge Perez

Ernesto Alonso, Ariadna Welter, Miroslava Stern, Rita Macedo

'Buñuel has not only given a frightful reality to melodramatic obsessions; he has created, in place of the grimaces, by now laughable, of the conventional madman of the screen, a whole repertory of erotic and deathly gestures which chill the flesh.' – *Dilys Powell*

The Crimson Blade: see *The Scarlet Blade*

The Crimson Canary
US 1945 64m bw
Universal (Bob Faber)

A jazz band vocalist is murdered.

Routine murder mystery with appearances by Coleman Hawkins, Oscar Pettiford and Josh White.

w Henry Blankfort, Peggy Phillips   d John Hoffman

Noah Beery Jnr, Lois Collier, Danny Morton, John Litel, Steve Geray

The Crimson Circle
GB 1936 76m bw
Wainwright/Richard Wainwright

Scotland Yard rounds up a blackmail gang.

Lively Edgar Wallace adaptation.

w Howard Irving Young   story Edgar Wallace
d Reginald Denham   ph Phil Tannura

Hugh Wakefield, Alfred Drayton, Noah Beery, June Duprez, Niall MacGinnis

'Considerably superior to pictures of its kind coming out of the tight little isle.' – *Variety*

† An earlier version in 1929 (part-talkie) with Stewart Rome was directed by Fred Zelnick for British Talking Pictures.

The Crimson Cult: see *Curse of the Crimson Altar*

The Crimson Curtain *
France 1952 43m bw
Argos
original title: *Le Rideau Cramoisi*

An officer billeted with a bourgeois family is visited at night by the beautiful daughter, who finally dies in his arms.

A curious polished fragment with narration replacing spoken dialogue. For those in the mood, it works.

wd Alexandre Astruc   story Barbey d'Aurevilly
ph Eugene Schufftan   m Jean-Jacques Grunenwald

Jean-Claude Pascal, Anouk Aimée, Madeleine Garcia, Jim Gerald

'In its limited time, with the greatest economy of means, it evokes an authentic sense of the past, as well as telling a story movingly and dramatically.' – *Richard Roud*

The Crimson Ghost
US 1946 bw serial: 12 eps
Republic

Professor Chambers invents a counteratomic device called the Cyclotrode; a criminologist prevents The Crimson Ghost from getting his hands on it.

Typical serial of its time, with a deathshead-style villain.

d William Witney, Fred Brannon

Charles Quigley, Linda Stirling, Clayton Moore (later the Lone Ranger, here as a villain), I. Stanford Jolley

The Crimson Kimono *
US 1959 82m bw
Columbia/Globe (Samuel Fuller)

Detectives seeking the murderer of a stripper in Los Angeles' Little Tokyo both fall in love with a witness.

Self-conscious local colour, though quite freshly observed and well photographed, finally overwhelms an ordinary little murder mystery.

wd Samuel Fuller   ph Sam Leavitt   m Harry Sukman

Glenn Corbett, James Shigeta, Victoria Shaw, Anna Lee, Paul Dubov

'Ask me no questions: believe only what you see!'
The Crimson Pirate *
GB 1952 104m Technicolor
Warner/Norma (Harold Hecht)
V*, L

An 18th-century pirate and an eccentric inventor lead an island's people in rebellion against a tyrant.

One suspects that this started off as a straight adventure and was turned halfway through production into a spoof; at any rate, the effect is patchy but with spirited highlights, and the star's acrobatic training is put to good use.

w Roland Kibbee   d Robert Siodmak   ph Otto Heller   m William Alwyn

Burt Lancaster, Nick Cravat, Eva Bartok, Torin Thatcher, James Hayter, Margot Grahame, Noel Purcell, Frank Pettingell

Crimson Romance
US 1934 70m bw
Mascot

Two Americans join the German Air Force and one is killed fighting Americans.

Very curious action drama which does not make its actual sympathies very clear.

w Al Martin, Sherman Lowe   d David Howard

Ben Lyon, James Bush, Erich von Stroheim, Sari Maritza, Bodil Rosing, Herman Bing

'By indie standards a pretentious production . . . but not very promising for localities where resentment is rife.' – *Variety*

Crin Blanc **
France 1953 47m bw
Albert Lamorisse
aka: *Wild Stallion*

A small boy befriends and rides a wild horse in the Camargue.

A favourite short film of great beauty, but a shade overlong for its content.

wd Albert Lamorisse   ph Edmond Séchan
m Maurice Le Roux

Alain Emery, Pascal Lamorisse

'For every man who struck gold – a hundred tried to take it away from him!'

Cripple Creek

US 1952 78m colour
Columbia (Edward Small)

A federal agent uncovers smugglers during a gold rush.

Adequate co-feature Western in murky colour.

w Richard Schayer d Ray Nazarro

George Montgomery, Karin Booth, Jerome Courtland, William Bishop, Richard Egan, Don Porter

La Crise *

France 1992 95m colour
Electric/TFI/Leader/Raidue/Canal+/Alain Sarde

A man loses his wife and his job on the same day and cannot find anyone, apart from a drunk, to sympathize with his predicament.

An amusing, if slightly mechanical comedy, of a workaholic discovering that life has more to offer than work.

wd Coline Serreau ph Robert Alazraki m Sonia Wieder-Atherton pd Guy-Claude François ed Catherine Renault

Vincent Lindon, Patrick Timsit, Annik Alane, Valerie Alane, Gilles Privat, Nanou Garcia, Christian Benedetti, Didier Flamand

'Amiable, crowd-pleasing entertainment with more than its fair share of good jokes.' – Sight and Sound

Crisis *

US 1950 96m bw
MGM (Arthur Freed)
S

A brain surgeon is forced to operate secretly on a South American dictator, and his wife is kidnapped by revolutionaries.

Dour intellectual suspense piece, in key with the genteel enlightenment of the Dore Schary regime at MGM. Well made but cold.

wd Richard Brooks story George Tabori ph Ray June m Miklos Rozsa

Cary Grant, José Ferrer, Signe Hasso, Paula Raymond, Ramon Navarro, Antonio Moreno, Leon Ames, Gilbert Roland

'Original, arresting and considered . . . so far the most striking example of Dore Schary's policy of encouraging the development of new talents.' – Gavin Lambert

'A bold piece of movie adventuring.' – L.A. Mirror

Criss Cross *

US 1948 87m bw
U-I (Michael Kraike)
V*

An armoured car guard and his double-crossing ex-wife get mixed up with vicious gangsters.

Sordid film noir with a poor plot but suspenseful sequences.

w Daniel Fuchs novel Don Tracy d Robert Siodmak ph Franz Planer m Miklos Rozsa

Burt Lancaster, Yvonne de Carlo, Dan Duryea, Stephen McNally, Richard Long, Tom Pedi, Alan Napier

'Siodmak's talent for brooding violence and the sombre urban setting gives the film a relentlessly mounting tension.' – Peter John Dyer

CrissCross

US 1992 100m colour
MGM/Hawn-Sylbert (Anthea Sylbert)
V, V*, L, S

A 12-year-old boy turns to crime to help his mother who works as a waitress and a stripper in order to support them.

Slow-moving domestic drama that fails to sustain one's interest.

w Scott Sommer novel Scott Sommer d Chris Menges ph Ivan Strasburg m Trevor Jones pd Crispian Sallis ed Tony Lawson

Goldie Hawn, Arliss Howard, James Gammon, David Arnott, Keith Carradine, J. C. Quinn, Steve Buscemi

Critical Condition

US 1986 100m Technicolor
Paramount (Ted Field, Robert Cort)
V, V*, L

Pretending to be mad in order to escape the Mafia, our hero is instead mistaken for a doctor.

Zany, hepped-up comedy which fails on all counts.

w Denis and John Hamill d Michael Apted ph Ralf D. Bode m Alan Silvestri pd John Lloyd ed Robert K. Lambert

Richard Pryor, Rachel Ticotin, Ruben Blades, Joe Mantegna, Bob Dishy

'Fans will find little to cheer about.' – Daily Variety

Critic's Choice

US 1963 100m Technicolor Panavision
Warner/Frank P. Rosenberg
V*

A ruthless Broadway critic is forced by his scruples to write a bad review of his wife's play.

Unsuitable vehicle for stars who have shorn a good comedy of wit and strive vainly for sentiment, wisecracks and pratfalls.

w Jack Sher play Ira Levin d Don Weis ph Charles Lang m George Duning

Bob Hope, Lucille Ball, Marilyn Maxwell, Rip Torn, Jessie Royce Landis, John Dehner, Jim Backus, Marie Windsor

'For instant stultification.' – Judith Crist

Critters

US 1986 86m DeLuxe
Sho Films/Smart Egg/New Line (Rupert Harvey)
V, V*, L, S

Hair-ball-like creatures arrive from an asteroid and devastate Kansas.

Childish horror spoof which makes Gremlins look like War and Peace.

w Stephen Herek, Dominic Muir d Stephen Herek ph Tim Suhrstedt, Chris Tufty m David Newman pd Gregg Fonseca ed Larry Bock

Dee Wallace Stone, M. Emmet Walsh, Billy Green Bush, Scott Grimes

'Irritatingly insipid and lightweight.' – Variety

Critters 2

US 1988 86m colour
Palace/New Line/Sho films (Barry Opper)
V, V*, L, S
original title: Critters 2: The Main Course

Killer aliens terrorise a town.

Even judged by the standards of the original, a dull and boring movie.

w D. T. Twohy, Mick Garris d Mick Garris ph Russell Carpenter m Nicholas Pike pd Philip Dean Foreman ed Charles Bornstein

Terence Mann, Don Opper, Cynthia Garris, Scott Grimes, Al Stevenson, Tom Hodges, Douglas Rowe, Liane Curtis

'A soft-centred remake of its amiable but unremarkable original.' – MFB

Critters 3

US 1992 86m colour
Newline/OH Films (Barry Opper, Rupert Harvey)
V, V*

Furry man-eating aliens invade an apartment block in Los Angeles.

A mixture of gore and comedy that borrows from Die Hard.

w David J. Schow story Barry Opper, Rupert Harvey d Kristine Peterson ph Tom Callaway m David C. Williams pd Philip Dean Foreman ed Terry Stokes

Aimee Brooks, John Calvin, Katherine Cortez, Leonard DiCaprio, Geoffrey Blake, Don Opper, Diana Bellamy, Terence Mann

Critters 4

US 1992 90m colour
New Line/OH Films (Barry Opper, Rupert Harvey)
V, V*

A space salvage crew is trapped on a space station between the last surviving Krites and ruthless killers who want the creatures for biological warfare.

Almost a standard low-budget space parody of Alien, with a couple of jokes and the Critters reduced to occasional roll-on, roll-off roles.

w Joseph Lyle, David J. Schow story Barry Opper, Rupert Harvey d Rupert Harvey ph Tom Callaway m Peter Manning Robinson pd Philip Dean Foreman ed Terry Stokes

Don Keith Opper, Paul Whitthorne, Angela Bassett, Anders Hove, Eric DaRe, Brad Dourif

Crocodile Dundee *

Australia 1986 102m Kodacolour Panavision
Paramount/Hoyts/Rimfire (John Cornell)
V, V*, L, S

An outback hero goes to Manhattan and puts New Yorkers in their place.

Easygoing comedy with no real style, which astounded the industry by becoming one of America's most popular films in 1986.

w Paul Hogan, Ken Shadie d Peter Faiman ph Russell Boyd m Peter Best

Paul Hogan, Linda Koslowski, John Meillon, Mark Blum

'Romancing the Stone combined with Tarzan's New York Adventure.' – Sight and Sound

'A movie doggedly designed to make you feel good.' – Vincent Canby, New York Times

† Crocodile Dundee II (V), which followed in 1988, offered very much the mixture as before.

AAN: best original screenplay

Cromwell *

GB 1970 141m Technicolor Panavision
Columbia/Irving Allen (Andrew Donally)
V, V*, L

An account of the rise of Cromwell to power, the execution of Charles I, and the Civil War.

Disappointingly dull schoolbook history, with good production values but glum handling.

wd Ken Hughes ph Geoffrey Unsworth m Frank Cordell pd John Stoll

Richard Harris, Alec Guinness, Robert Morley, Dorothy Tutin, Frank Finlay, Timothy Dalton, Patrick Wymark, Patrick Magee, Nigel Stock, Charles Gray, Michael Jayston, Anna Cropper, Michael Goodliffe

'It tries to combine serious intentions with the widest kind of popular appeal and falls unhappily between the two. It will offend the purists and bore the kiddies.' – Brenda Davies

'Shakespeare spoiled us for this sort of thing. We wait for great speeches and witty remarks, for rage and poetry, and we get dedicated stodginess.' – Pauline Kael

AA: costumes (Nino Novarese)

AAN: Frank Cordell

Cronica di una Morte Annunciata: see *Chronicle of a Death Foretold*

The Crook: see *Le Voyou*

The Crooked Billet
GB   1929   82m   bw
Gainsborough (Michael Balcon)

Spies and detectives converge on an old inn where documents are hidden.

Fairly unwatchable now, this once-entertaining melodrama was shot as a silent and had sound clumsily added.

w Angus Macphail   play Dion Titherage   d Adrian Brunel   ph Claude McDonnell   md Louis Levy   ed Ian Dalrymple

Carlyle Blackwell, Madeleine Carroll, Miles Mander, Gordon Harker

'The subject never appealed to me – it was a conventional crook melodrama – and I had raging toothache during most of the shooting.' – *Adrian Brunel*

The Crooked Road
GB/Yugoslavia   1964   92m   bw
Agro/Triglav

An American journalist plans to expose as a crook the dictator of a small Balkan state, but finds himself framed for murder.

Lugubrious and too-talkative melodrama of political intrigue.

w J. Garrison, Don Chaffey   novel The Big Story by Morris West   d Don Chaffey

Robert Ryan, Stewart Granger, Marius Goring, Nadia Gray, Catherine Woodville, George Coulouris

The Crooked Way
US   1949   87m   bw
Benedict Bogeaus

An amnesiac ex-veteran finds that he was once a minor gangster.

Predictable thick ear with *film noir* aspirations.

w Richard Landau   play No Blade Too Sharp by Robert Monroe   d Robert Florey   ph John Alton

John Payne, Sonny Tufts, Ellen Drew, Rhys Williams

The Crooked Web
US   1955   77m   bw
Columbia (Sam Katzman)

A restaurant owner is lured into a scheme to recover buried Nazi gold from Germany, but finds it is a means of arresting him on an old murder charge.

Ingenious but somehow uninteresting puzzle melodrama.

w Lou Breslow   d Nathan Juran

Frank Lovejoy, Richard Denning, Mari Blanchard

Crooks and Coronets
GB   1969   106m   Technicolor
Warner Seven Arts/Herman Cohen
V*
US title: *Sophie's Place*

American gangsters plan to rob a stately home but are taken over by the dowager in charge.

Overlong and mainly flatulent comedy, with a good climax involving a vintage plane.

wd Jim O'Connelly   ph Desmond Dickinson   m Patrick John Scott

Telly Savalas, Edith Evans, Warren Oates, Nicky Henson, Cesar Romero, Harry H. Corbett

Crooks Anonymous *
GB   1962   87m   bw
Anglo Amalgamated (Nat Cohen)

A pretty thief joins an organization for reforming criminals, but is tempted again . . . and so are they.

Amusingly devised and plotted minor comedy with an exceptional cast.

w Jack Davies, Henry Blyth   d Ken Annakin   ph Ernest Steward   m Muir Mathieson, Henry Martin

Leslie Phillips, Stanley Baxter, Wilfrid Hyde-White, Julie Christie, James Robertson Justice, Robertson Hare, Charles Lloyd Pack

Crooks in Cloisters
GB   1963   97m   Technicolor   Scope
ABPC

Forgers pose as monks but are reformed by the country life.

Busy comedy full of familiar faces; perhaps a small cut above the *Carry Ons*.

w Mike Watts   d Jeremy Summers

Ronald Fraser, Barbara Windsor, Grégoire Aslan, Bernard Cribbins, Davy Kaye, Wilfred Brambell

Crooks in Clover: see *Penthouse*

Crooks' Tour *
GB   1940   84m   bw
British National (John Corfield)

English tourists are mistaken for spies by Nazis in Baghdad.

Amusing vehicle for two comic actors who excelled at portraying the English abroad.

w John Watt, Max Kester   radio serial Sidney Gilliat, Frank Launder   d John Baxter   ph James Wilson   m Kennedy Russell

Basil Radford, Naunton Wayne, Greta Gynt, Abraham Sofaer, Gordon McLeod

'Their bland imperturbability in the face of extraordinary circumstances provides no little fun.' – *Picture Show*

Crooner
US   1932   64m   bw
Warner

A radio singer who is more than something of a prig gets his come-uppance.

Would-be satire with more bore than bite.

w Charles Kenyon   story Rian James   d Lloyd Bacon

David Manners, Ann Dvorak, Ken Murray, William Janney, Eddie Nugent, J. Carrol Naish

'A general slap at that ether pest who for a time held popular sway . . . but there is no sympathy for anybody in the cast.' – *Variety*

The Cross and the Switchblade
US   1970   106m   colour
Fox/Dick Ross Associates
V*

A minister sets out to rid his New York streets of delinquents.

Arrant but alas unconvincing do-goodery.

w Don Murray, James Bonnet   d Don Murray

Pat Boone, Erik Estrada, Jackie Giroux, Jo-Ann Robinson

Cross Country
Canada   1983   104m   colour
Filmline/Yellowbill

The boyfriend of a murdered girl finds himself being driven west at gunpoint by a mad nymphomaniac and her protector.

No-holds-barred 'adult' thriller whose excesses become risible.

w Logan N. Danforth (John Hunter)   d Paul Lynch

Richard Beymer, Nina Axelrod, Michael Ironside, Brent Carver

'The true story about the woman who wrote *The Yearling*'
Cross Creek *
US   1983   122m   Technicolor
EMI/Radnitz/Ritt (Robert B. Radnitz)
V*

In 1928 Marjorie Kinnan Rawlings leaves her journalist husband and goes to live in the Florida backwoods, where she hopes to write a Gothic romance.

Elongated study of writer's block (though the subject did eventually write *The Yearling*). Altogether too typical of its producer and director – and too slow – to hold much surprise or interest.

w Dalene Young   memoir Marjorie Kinnan Rawlings   d Martin Ritt   ph John A. Alonzo   m Leonard Rosenman   pd Walter Scott Herndon

Mary Steenburgen, Rip Torn, Peter Coyote, Dana Hill, Ike Eisenmann, Alfre Woodard

'The landscapes are attractive, but much too lushly filmed with lyrical inserts in which the wonders of the bayou are contemplated. Good performances fail to mask the fact that the characters are stereotypes from start to finish.' – *Tom Milne, MFB*

'Everything is lighted to look holy, and when the score isn't shimmering and burnishing, nature is twittering.' – *New Yorker*

AAN: Rip Torn, Alfre Woodard, Leonard Rosenman

Cross My Heart *
US   1945   83m   bw
Paramount (Harry Tugend)

A romantic girl confesses to murder, is acquitted, and finds the real murderer.

Modest remake of *True Confession* (qv), with frenetic pace but not much style.

w Claude Binyon, Harry Tugend, Charles Schnee   d John Berry   ph Charles Lang Jnr   m Robert Emmett Dolan

Betty Hutton, Sonny Tufts, Michael Chekhov, Rhys Williams, Ruth Donnelly, Al Bridge, Howard Freeman, Iris Adrian

Cross My Heart *
Canada   1990   105m   colour
Belbo (Ludi Boeken, Jacques Fansten)
V*, S
original title: *La Fracture du Myocarde*

Frightened of being sent to an orphanage, a 12-year-old boy tries to conceal the death of his mother.

Enjoyable comedy that stretches credulity at times but at least presents believable children living in a recognizable world.

wd Jacques Fansten   ph Jean-Claude Saillier   m Jean Marie Senia   pd Gilbert Gagneux

Sylvain Copans, Nicolas Parodi, Cecilia Rouaud, Lucie Blossier, Delphine Gouttman

'Delightfully offbeat first feature . . . Few will remain unmoved.' – *Variety*

Cross of Iron *
GB/West Germany   1977   133m   Technicolor
EMI-Rapid Film/Terra Filmkunst (Wolf. C. Hartwig)
V, V*

Militarily and emotionally at the end of its tether, a German battalion is decimated while fighting the Russians in 1943.

Painful to follow, occasionally beautiful to watch, this quite horrid film offers too much opportunity for its director to wallow in unpleasant physical details, and its main plot of bitter rivalry offers no relief.

w Julius J. Epstein, Herbert Asmodi   d Sam Peckinpah   ph John Coquillon   m Ernest Gold

James Coburn, James Mason, Maximilian Schell, David Warner, Klaus Löwitsch, Senta Berger

'Morally dubious but technically brilliant.' – *Michael Billington, Illustrated London News*

The Cross of Lorraine *
US   1944   91m   bw
MGM (Edwin Knopf)

In a German camp for French prisoners, an escape leads to a rising by local villagers.

Standard war propaganda piece, made with enthusiasm on unconvincing sets.

w Michael Kanin, Ring Lardner Jnr, Alexander Esway, Robert Andrews   *d* Tay Garnett   *ph* Sidney Wagner   *m* Bronislau Kaper

Gene Kelly, Jean-Pierre Aumont, Cedric Hardwicke, Peter Lorre, Joseph Calleia, Richard Whorf, Hume Cronyn

'Half a football team worked on the story, yet except for a foolish coda it is one of the most edged, well-characterized, and naturally cinematic scripts of the year.' – *James Agee*

Cross Shot
Italy   1976   95m   colour
P.A.C. (Teodoro Agrimi)

A quick-tempered police inspector, a sensational journalist and a gangster attempt to track down a young cop-killer.

Portentous, studiedly slow thriller with nothing to recommend it, not even Lee J. Cobb (in a minor role, despite his star billing) as a blind Mafioso.

w Lucio de Caro, Piero Poggio, Maurizio Mengoni, Dardano Saccheti, Ted Rusoff   *story* Lucio de Caro   *d* Stelvo Massi   *ph* Mario Vulpiani   *m* Piero Pintucci   *pd* Carlo Leva   *ed* Mauro Bonanni

John Saxon, Lee J. Cobb, Renzo Palmer, Rosanna Fratello, Antonella Lualdi, Lino Capolicchio

Crossed Swords
Italy/USA   1954   83m   Pathecolor
Viva Films (J. Barrett Mahon, Vittorio Vassarotti)
original title: *Il Maestro di Don Giovanni*

The son of an Italian duke prevents an uprising.

A thin swashbuckler showing the perils of early co-production.

wd Milton Krims   *ph* Jack Cardiff

Errol Flynn, Gina Lollobrigida, Cesare Danova, Nadia Gray, Paola Mori

Crossed Swords: see *The Prince and the Pauper*
(1977)

'Sensational? No, it's dynamite!'
Crossfire ****
US   1947   86m   bw
RKO (Adrian Scott)
V*, L

A Jew is murdered in a New York hotel, and three soldiers are suspected.

Tense, talky thriller shot entirely at night with pretty full expressionist use of camera technique; notable for style, acting, experimentation, and for being the first Hollywood film to hit out at racial bigotry.

w *John Paxton*   novel *The Brick Foxhole* by Richard Brooks   *d* Edward Dmytryk   *ph* J. Roy Hunt   *m* Roy Webb

Robert Young, Robert Mitchum, *Robert Ryan*, Gloria Grahame, *Paul Kelly*, Sam Levene, Jacqueline White, Steve Brodie

AAN: best picture; John Paxton; Edward Dmytryk; Robert Ryan; Gloria Grahame

Crossing Delancey *
US   1988   97m   DuArt
Warner (Michael Nozik)
V, V*, L, S

A bookshop manager vacillates between an author and a pickle manufacturer as a suitable lover.

Small but enjoyable celebration of the simple life.

w Susan Sandler   *play* Susan Sandler   *d* Joan Micklin Silver   *ph* Theo Van de Sande   *m* Paul Chihara, The Roches   *pd* Dan Leigh   *ed* Rick Shaine

Amy Irving, Peter Riegert, Reizl Bozyk, Jeroen Krabbe, Sylvia Miles, George Martin, John Bedford Lloyd

The Crossing of the Rhine *
France/Italy/West Germany   1960   125m   bw
Franco-London-Gibe-Jonia-UFA (Ralph Baum)
original title: *Le Passage du Rhin*

Two French soldiers escape from the Germans in 1940 and after various adventures meet up again in Paris in 1945.

Two crowded plots and not a great deal of point emerge from this watchable war film full of conventional set-pieces.

w André Cayatte, Armand Jammot   *d* André Cayatte   *ph* Roger Fellous   *m* Louiguy

Charles Aznavour, Nicole Courcel, Georges Rivière, Cordula Trantow

Crossplot
GB   1969   97m   Eastmancolor
UA/Tribune (Robert S. Baker)

An advertising executive gets involved in a spy ring.

Old-fashioned, London-set amalgam of secret codes, disappearing bodies, helicopter attacks, and a finale frustrating the assassination of a statesman in Hyde Park.

w Leigh Vance   *d* Alvin Rakoff   *ph* Brendan J. Stafford   *m* Stanley Black

Roger Moore, Martha Hyer, Alexis Kanner, Francis Matthews, Bernard Lee

Crossroads **
Japan   1928   80m approx   bw   silent
Shochiku
original title: *Jujiro*

A woman kills her seducer. Her brother thinks he has killed a man and takes refuge with her, only to die of shock when he sees the man alive.

The only widely distributed Japanese silent film, this curious piece is fragmentarily told and will remind many of *Rashomon* with its mixture of flashbacks and dreams.

wd Teinosuke Kinugasa   *ph* Kohei Sugiyama

J. Bandoha, A. Tschihaya, Yujiko Ogawa, I. Sohma

Crossroads *
US   1942   84m   bw
MGM (Edwin Knopf)

A French diplomat who once lost his memory is blackmailed by crooks who claim he was once a criminal.

Smooth mystery melodrama adapted from the French film *Carrefour*.

w Guy Trosper   *story* Howard Emmett Rogers, John Kafka   *d* Jack Conway   *ph* Joseph Ruttenberg   *m* Bronislau Kaper

William Powell, Hedy Lamarr, Basil Rathbone, Claire Trevor, Margaret Wycherly, Felix Bressart, Sig Rumann

'Well directed and acted with polish, delightful romantic moments breaking up the general atmosphere of excitement and suspense.' – *Picturegoer*

Crossroads
US   1986   96m   Technicolor
Delphi IV/Columbia (Mark Carliner)
V*, L

Urged by a young musician, an old blues singer travels the South in search of his legendary companion's lost music.

Rather specialized and unsatisfactory road pic which loses its way well before the end.

w John Fusco   *d* Walter Hill   *ph* John Bailey   *m* Ry Cooder   *ad* Albert Heschong   *ed* Freeman Davies

Ralph Macchio, Joe Seneca, Jamie Gertz, Joe Morton

'You can tell what's wrong with *Crossroads* when you try to describe it to friends. Half-way through the plot description, their eyes glaze over.' – *People*

Crosswinds
US   1951   93m   Technicolor
Paramount/Pine/Thomas

Treasure-hunting boatmen fall out in New Guinea.

Adequate outdoor thick ear; good value for money as the lower half of a double bill.

wd Lewis R. Foster

John Payne, Rhonda Fleming, Forrest Tucker, Robert Lowery, Alan Mowbray, John Abbott

The Crouching Beast
GB   1935   80m   bw
RKO (John Stafford)

In Turkey during World War I an American newspaperwoman is menaced by a Turkish agent.

Slow and muddled espionage melodrama.

w Valentine Williams   *novel* Clubfoot by Valentine Williams   *d* W. Victor Hanbury

Fritz Kortner, Wynne Gibson, Richard Bird, Isabel Jeans, Peter Gawthorne

The Crowd ***
US   1928   98m   bw   silent
MGM (King Vidor)
V*, L

Episodes in the life of a city clerk.

A deliberately humdrum story, chosen to show that drama can exist in the lowliest surroundings, retains much of its original power, though some of the director's innovations have become clichés.

w King Vidor, John V. A. Weaver, Harry Behn   *d* King Vidor   *ph* Henry Sharp   *ad* Cedric Gibbons, Arnold Gillespie   *ed* Hugh Wynn

James Murray, Eleanor Boardman, Bert Roach, Estelle Clark

'No picture is perfect, but this comes as near to reproducing reality as anything you have ever witnessed.' – *Photoplay*

AAN: King Vidor; Unique and Artistic Picture

The Crowd Roars *
US   1932   85m   bw
Warner

A star motor-racing driver tries to prevent his young brother from following in his footsteps.

Typical early Cagney vehicle, still spectacularly pacy but dated in its dialogue scenes.

w Kubec Glasmon, John Bright, Niven Busch   *d* Howard Hawks   *ph* Sid Hickox, John Stumar   *md* Leo Forbstein

James Cagney, Joan Blondell, Ann Dvorak, Eric Linden, Guy Kibbee, Frank McHugh, Regis Toomey

'A thin and uneventful story, but a majority of the footage is devoted to three stirring contests.' – *Variety*

'As so often Hawks seems bitter at the world men have created but respects those who have to attempt to live it to the full.' – *NFT, 1963*

'The story is not precisely exciting . . . the closing episode is the best, for it reveals a certain originality in having the injured automobile racers eager to continue the race in ambulances on the way to hospital.' – *Mordaunt Hall, New York Times*

† Remade in 1939 as *Indianapolis Speedway.*

The Crowd Roars *
US   1938   90m   bw
MGM (Sam Zimbalist)

A young boxer becomes involved with the underworld.

Standard star vehicle with efficient trimmings.

w Thomas Lennon, George Bruce, George Oppenheimer   *d* Richard Thorpe   *ph* John Seitz   *m* Edward Ward

Robert Taylor, Frank Morgan, Edward Arnold, Maureen O'Sullivan, William Gargan, Frank Craven, Jane Wyman, Lionel Stander, Nat Pendleton

'Exciting melodrama with plenty of ring action, some plausible romance and several corking good characterizations.' – *Variety*

† Remade as *Killer McCoy.*

The Crowded Day
GB   1954   82m   bw
Advance

Problems of five assistants in a department store during the Christmas rush.

Naïve little portmanteau which suited its purpose.

w Talbot Rothwell   *d* John Guillermin

Joan Rice, John Gregson, Freda Jackson, Patricia Marmont, Josephine Griffin, Sonia Holm, Rachel Roberts, Thora Hird, Dora Bryan, Edward Chapman, Sid James, Richard Wattis

The Crowded Sky
US   1960   104m   Technicolor
Warner (Michael Garrison)

As two planes fly unwittingly towards each other, the passengers muse on their personal problems. An emergency landing averts total disaster.

The format goes back as far as *Friday the Thirteenth,* and forward to *Airport 75,* but this was in fact a cut-rate rehash of *The High and the Mighty,* with dull characters and insufficiently tense handling, not to mention a second team cast.

w Charles Schnee   *d* Joseph Pevney   *ph* Harry Stradling   *m* Leonard Rosenman

Dana Andrews, Rhonda Fleming, Efrem Zimbalist Jnr, John Kerr, Anne Francis, Keenan Wynn, Troy Donahue, Joe Mantell, Patsy Kelly

Crows And Sparrows *
China   1949   113m   bw
Peak Film Industries (Xia Yunhu, Ren Zongde)
original title: *Wuya Yu Maque*

Preparing to flee from the victorious Red Army, a landlord decides to sell his house and evict the tenants.

Lively slice-of-Chinese-life, made just before the Communist revolution.

w Shen Fu, Xu Tao, Zhao Dan, Lin Gu, Chen Baichen, Zheng Junli   *d* Zheng Junli   *ph* Miao Zhenhua, Hu Zhenhua   *md* Wang Yunjie

Zhao Dan, Wu Yin, Sun Daoling, Shanggluan Yunzhu, Wei Heling, Li Tianji, Huang Zongying, Wang Pei

The Cruel Sea **
GB   1953   126m   bw
Ealing (Leslie Norman)
V, V*

Life and death on an Atlantic corvette during World War II.

Competent transcription of a bestselling book, cleanly produced and acted; a huge box-office success.

w Eric Ambler   *novel* Nicholas Monsarrat   *d* Charles Frend   *ph* Gordon Dines, Jo Jago, Paul Beeson   *m* Alan Rawsthorne

Jack Hawkins, Donald Sinden, Stanley Baker, John Stratton, Denholm Elliott, John Warner, Bruce Seton, Virginia McKenna, Moira Lister, June Thorburn

'This is a story of the battle of the Atlantic, a story of an ocean, two ships and a handful of men. The men are the heroes. The heroines are the ships. The only villain is the sea – the cruel sea – that man has made even more cruel.' – *opening narration*

'One is grateful nowadays for a film which does not depict war as anything but a tragic and bloody experience, and it is this quality which gives the production its final power to move.' – *John Gillett*

'Sensitivity, faithfulness, and almost inevitable tedium.' – *Time Out, 1984*

AAN: Eric Ambler

Cruise Missile
Germany/Italy/Spain   1978   90m   colour
Noble Productions/Echberg Film (Ika Panajotovic)

An American and Russian agent team up with the local police to prevent a terrorist blowing up a peace conference in Iran.

Substandard thriller, in which the Iranian police are portrayed as wonderful.

w Clark Reynolds, Elio Romano   *d* Leslie H. Martinson   *ph* Claudio Catozzo   *m* Alberto Baldan   *ed* Enzio Monachesi

Peter Graves, Curt Jurgens, Michael Dante, John Carradine

Cruisin' Down the River
US   1953   79m   colour
Columbia

A night-club singer inherits a riverboat.

Slim excuse for a musical variety bill.

w Blake Edwards, Richard Quine   *d* Richard Quine

Dick Haymes, Audrey Totter, Billy Daniels, Cecil Kellaway, the Bell Sisters, Erze Ivan

Cruising
US   1980   106m   Technicolor
Lorimar (Jerry Weintraub)
V*

A New York cop becomes degraded in his search among homosexuals for a sadistic killer.

Alleged thriller with phoney pretensions and repellent detail.

wd William Friedkin   *ph* James Contner   *m* Jack Nitzsche

Al Pacino, Paul Sorvino, Karen Allen, Richard Cox, Don Scardino, Joe Spinell

'Like any approach to the bizarre, it's fascinating for about fifteen minutes. After that, it suffers from the same boring repetition that makes porno so uninteresting generally.' – *Variety*

'Wonders to dazzle the human imagination – in a flaming love story set in titanic world conflict!'

The Crusades **
US   1935   127m   bw
Paramount/Cecil B. de Mille

Spurred by his wife Berengaria, Richard the Lionheart sets off on his holy wars.

Heavily tapestried medieval epic, spectacular sequences being punctuated by wodges of uninspired dialogue. A true de Mille pageant.

w Harold Lamb, Waldemar Young, Dudley Nichols   *d* Cecil B. de Mille   *ph* Victor Milner   *m* Rudolph Kopp   *sp* Gordon Jennings

Henry Wilcoxon, Loretta Young, C. Aubrey Smith, Ian Keith, Katherine de Mille, Joseph Schildkraut, Alan Hale, C. Henry Gordon, George Barbier, Montagu Love, Lumsden Hare, William Farnum, Hobart Bosworth, Pedro de Cordoba, Mischa Auer

'Mr de Mille's evangelical films are the nearest equivalent today to the glossy German colour prints which decorated mid-Victorian bibles. There is the same lack of a period sense, the same stuffy horsehair atmosphere of beards and whiskers, and, their best quality, a childlike eye for detail.' – *Otis Ferguson*

'Cinema addicts by now have some idea what to expect in a de Mille version of the Holy Wars. *The Crusades* should fulfil all expectations. As a picture it is historically worthless, didactically treacherous, artistically absurd. None of these defects impairs its entertainment value. It is a hundred-million-dollar sideshow which has at least three features to distinguish it from the long line of previous de Mille extravaganzas. It is the noisiest; it is the biggest; it contains no baths.' – *Time*

'Probably only de Mille could make a picture like this and get away with it. It's long, and slow, and the story is not up to some of his previous films, but the production has sweep and spectacle.' – *Variety*

AAN: Victor Milner

Crush
New Zealand   1992   96m   colour
Metro/Hibiscus/NZFC/NFU/NZ On Air/Movie Partners
   (Bridget Ikin)

While she is in hospital recovering from a car crash, a female journalist is angered to discover that her best friend has begun an affair with a novelist she planned to interview.

A bisexual revenge thriller that attempts to expose bourgeois values, but fails to convince.

w Alison Maclean, Anne Kennedy   *d* Alison Maclean   *ph* Dion Beebe   *m* JPS Experience, Antony Partos   *pd* Meryl Cronin   *ed* John Gilbert

Marcia Gay Harden, William Zappa, Donogh Rees, Caitlin Bossley, Pete Smith, Jon Brazier

'Often as murky as the bubbling New Zealand mud springs Maclean cuts to in order to underscore the otherworldly ambience.' – *Empire*

The Crush
US   1993   89m   Technicolor
Warner/Morgan Creek (James G. Robinson)
V, V*

A teenage girl develops a crush on her new neighbour, a writer, and becomes violent when he ignores her advances.

Predictable and unintelligent thriller, recycling familiar themes in an uninspired fashion.

wd Alan Shapiro   *ph* Bruce Surtees   *m* Graeme Revell   *pd* Michael Bolton   *ed* Ian Crafford

Cary Elwes, Alicia Silverstone, Jennifer Rubin, Amber Benson, Kurtwood Smith, Gwynyth Walsh, Matthew Walker

'Another by-the-numbers thriller longer on suspense than brains. Silly and predictable.' – *Variety*

Crusoe *
US   1988   94m   Technicolor
Virgin/Island Pictures (Andrew Braunsberg)
V*

A slave-owner, shipwrecked on a desert island, makes friends with a cannibal.

Deft variation on the original familiar story.

w Walon Green, Christopher Logue   *novel Robinson Crusoe* by Daniel Defoe   *d* Caleb Deschanel   *ph* Tom Pinter   *m* Michael Kamen   *pd* Velco Despotovic   *ed* Humphrey Dixon

Aidan Quinn, Elvis Payne, Richard Sharp, Colin Bruce, William Hootkins, Shane Rimmer, Jimmy Nail, Patrick Monkton, Chris Pitt, Ade Sapara

The Cry: see *Il Grido*

Cry Baby Killer
US   1958   62m   bw
Roger Corman/AA

A gunman on the run barricades himself and hostages in a storeroom.

Modest second feature which served its purpose.

w Leo Gordon, Melvin Levy   d Jus Addiss

Jack Nicholson, Harry Lauter, Carolyn Mitchell, Brett Halsey

Cry Danger *
US   1951   79m   bw
RKO/Olympic (Sam Wiesenthal, W. R. Frank)
V*

After serving five years for robbery, a man gets out on parole and clears his name.

Slick little slice of thick ear, very lively all round.

w William Bowers   story Jerome Cady   d Robert Parrish   ph Joseph F. Biroc   m Emil Newman, Paul Dunlap   ad Richard Day

Dick Powell, Rhonda Fleming, Richard Erdman, William Conrad, Regis Toomey, Jay Adler

Cry for Happy
US   1961   110m   Eastmancolor   Cinemascope
Columbia (William Goetz)

Four navy cameramen in Japan help geishas to found an orphanage.

As bad as it sounds, a repellent mixture of sentiment and knockabout.

w Irving Brecher   d George Marshall   ph Burnett Guffey   m George Duning

Glenn Ford, Donald O'Connor, Miiko Taka, James Shigeta, Mikoshi Umeki, Joe Flynn, Howard St John

'Any film which expends most of its energies on a protracted joke about how far you can go with a geisha could hardly fail to be as charmless and witless as this.' – MFB

Cry Freedom **
GB   1987   158m   colour   Panavision
Marble Arch/Universal (Richard Attenborough)
V, V*, L, S

South African journalist Donald Woods is forced to flee the country after attempting to investigate the death in custody of his friend the black activist Steve Biko.

Part thriller, part social conscience tract, the film has magnificent set-pieces typical of the director's work. However, it failed to satisfy either opponents or supporters of apartheid.

w John Briley   d Richard Attenborough   ph Ronnie Taylor   m George Fenton, Jonas Gwangwa   pd Stuart Craig

Kevin Kline, Penelope Wilton, Denzel Washington, Alec McCowen, Kevin McNally, Zakes Mokae

AAN: Denzel Washington

A Cry from the Streets
GB   1958   100m   bw
Film Traders (Ian Dalrymple)
V*

Episodes from the work of child welfare officers.

Mildly pleasing but unconvincing semi-documentary, with children competing with the star at scene-stealing.

w Vernon Harris   novel The Friend in Need by Elizabeth Coxhead   d Lewis Gilbert   ph Harry Gilliam   m Larry Adler

Max Bygraves, Barbara Murray, Colin Petersen, Dana Wilson, Kathleen Harrison, Eleanor Summerfield, Mona Washbourne

Cry Havoc
US   1943   97m   bw
MGM (Edwin Knopf)

War nurses are caught up in the Bataan retreat.

An all-woman cast adequately handles a stagey melodrama about a tragic situation.

w Paul Osborn   play Proof thro' the Night by Allen R. Kenward   d Richard Thorpe   ph Karl Freund   m Daniele Amfitheatrof

Margaret Sullavan, Joan Blondell, Ann Sothern, Fay Bainter, Marsha Hunt, Ella Raines, Frances Gifford, Diana Lewis, Heather Angel, Connie Gilchrist

'A sincere fourth-rate film made from a sincere fifth-rate play.' – James Agee

'Its popularity will stem less from its probably factual record of nurses starving, sweating and dying in the beleaguered Philippine jungle than from the impressive all-woman cast which MGM has rounded up for the occasion.' – Newsweek

A Cry in the Dark *
Australia   1988   121m   colour
Pathé/Evil Angels/Cannon International (Verity Lambert)
V, V*, L, S

A woman is tried for the murder of her baby daughter, who was carried off by a wild dog during a family camping expedition.

Skilful reconstruction of a sensational true-life court case.

w Robert Caswell, Fred Schepisi   book Evil Angels by John Bryson   d Fred Schepisi   ph Ian Baker   m Bruce Smeaton   pd Wendy Dickson, George Liddle   ed Jill Bilcock

Meryl Streep, Sam Neill, Dale Reeves, David Hoflin, Jason Reason, Michael Wetter, Kane Barton, Trent Roberts, Brian Jones, Dorothy Alison

'May be the most quietly uncondescending film ever made about religious fundamentalists.' – Peter Rainer, Los Angeles Herald Examiner

AAN: Meryl Streep

A Cry in the Night
US   1956   75m   bw
Warner/Jaguar (George C. Bertholon)

A peeping Tom, caught by a teenage couple, abducts the girl and threatens rape.

Odd little domestic thriller, with parents and police working together. Watchable, but a bit over the top.

w David Dortort   novel Whit Masterson   d Frank Tuttle   ph John Seitz   m David Buttolph

Edmond O'Brien, Brian Donlevy, Natalie Wood, Raymond Burr, Richard Anderson, Irene Hervey, Anthony Caruso

Cry of the Banshee
GB   1970   87m   Movielab
AIP (Gordon Hessler)
V*, L

A 16th-century magistrate is cursed by a witch, who sends a devil in the form of a young man to destroy him.

Modest horror film which fails to do justice to its interesting plot.

w Tim Kelly, Christopher Wicking   d Gordon Hessler   ph John Coquillon   m Les Baxter

Vincent Price, Elisabeth Bergner, Patrick Mower, Essy Persson, Hugh Griffith, Hilary Dwyer, Sally Geeson

The Cry of the Black Wolves
West Germany   1972   90m   colour
Hillenbrand (Gunter Eulan)

In Alaska, a fur-trapper is accused of killing the man who stole his dog-team.

Standard Western in an icy setting, complete with the bad guys in black hats.

w Kurt Nachmann, Rolf Olsen   story Jack London   d Harald Reinl   ph Franz X. Lederle   m Gerhard Heinz   ad Rolf Zehetbauer, Herbert Strabel   ed Eva Zeyn

Ron Ely, Raimund Harmstorf, Gila von Weitershausen, Heinrich Schweiger

Cry of the City **
US   1948   96m   bw
TCF (Sol C. Siegel)

A ruthless gangster on the run is pursued by a policeman who was once his boyhood friend.

Very well produced but relentlessly miserable New York thriller on the lines of Manhattan Melodrama and Angels with Dirty Faces.

w Richard Murphy   novel The Chair for Martin Rome by Henry Helseth   d Robert Siodmak   ph Lloyd Ahern   m Alfred Newman

Victor Mature, Richard Conte, Mimi Aguglia, Shelley Winters, Tommy Cook, Fred Clark, Debra Paget

'When the city cries in a movie, it's with the desolate wail of police sirens and with rain-streaked sidewalks; but most of all with poetic justification.' – Paul Taylor, Time Out, 1980

Cry Terror **
US   1958   96m   bw
MGM/Andrew Stone

As security against ransom money being delivered, an airline bomber kidnaps a family.

Unabashed suspenser which screws panic situations as far as they will go and farther.

wd Andrew Stone   ph Walter Strenge   m Howard Jackson

James Mason, Rod Steiger, Inger Stevens, Neville Brand, Angie Dickinson, Kenneth Tobey, Jack Klugman, Jack Kruschen

Cry the Beloved Country *
GB   1951   96m   bw
London Films (Alan Paton)
V, V*
US title: African Fury

In South Africa, a white farmer and a black preacher find friendship through linked family tragedies.

Well-intentioned, earnest, rather high-flown racial drama.

w Alan Paton   novel Alan Paton   d Zoltan Korda   ph Robert Krasker   m Raymond Gallois-Montbrun

Canada Lee, Sidney Poitier, Charles Carson, Charles McRae, Joyce Carey, Geoffrey Keen, Michael Goodliffe, Edric Connor

Cry Vengeance
US   1954   81m   bw
Allied Artists (Lindsley Parsons)
V*

An innocent man is released from jail and seeks vengeance against the man who framed him and killed his wife and child.

Adequate toughie with no particular flair.

w Warren Douglas, George Bricker   d Mark Stevens   ph William Sickner   m Paul Dunlap

Mark Stevens, Martha Hyer, Skip Homeier, Joan Vohs, Douglas Kennedy

Cry Wolf
US   1947   83m   bw
Warner (Henry Blanke)

A widow claims her husband's estate and finds his mysterious uncle very difficult to deal with . . .

Rather obvious old dark house mystery with a not very interesting solution, all relying too heavily on star performances.

w Catherine Turney   *novel* Marjorie Carleton
d Peter Godfrey   *ph* Carl Guthrie   *m* Franz
Waxman

Barbara Stanwyck, Errol Flynn (as the apparent
heavy), Geraldine Brooks, Richard Basehart, Helene
Thimig

Cry Wolf
GB   1980   31m   bw
Picture Partnership/Paramount

A scientist accidentally imbibes a canine serum and
turns into a werewolf.

Flattish comedy which is mainly indistinguishable
from the low-budget British shockers it satirizes, but
manages a few good moments.

w Stan Hey   *d* Leszek Burzynski   *ph* Robert
Krasker

Paul Maxwell, Rosalind Ayres, Stephen Greif

Cry-Baby
US   1990   85m   DeLuxe
UIP/Imagine Entertainment (Rachel Talalay)
V, V*, L, S

A delinquent rock 'n' roll singer falls in love with an
upper-class girl.

Kitsch celebration of the early 60s that soon grows
tedious.

wd John Waters   *ph* David Insley   *m* Patrick
Williams   *pd* Vincent Peranio   *ad* Delores Deluxe
ed Janice Hampton

Johnny Depp, Amy Locane, Susan Tyrrell, Polly
Bergen, Iggy Pop, Ricki Lake, Traci Lords, Kim
McGuire, Darren E. Burrows

Crying Freeman, Chapter One: Portrait of a Killer (dubbed)
Japan   1992   50m   colour
Toei (Shoko Takahashi, Akira Sasaki, Tomirou Kuriyama)
V

A 29-year-old Japanese artist who witnessed a
Japanese assassin, working for the Chinese Mafia, kill
three people awaits her own death at his hands.

A gore-filled cartoon for an adult audience that enjoys
indifferent animation, sex and violence.

w Higashi Shimizu   *d* Daisuke Nishio   *ph* Hisao
Shirai   *m* Hiroaki Yoshino   *ad* Mitsutaka
Nakamura   *ed* Shigeru Nishiyama

Voices of Stephen Tremblay, Edita Brychta, Vincent
Marzello, Bob Sherman, Burt Kwouk

Crying Freeman, Chapter Two: The Enemy Within (dubbed)
Japan   1992   50m   colour
Toei (Shoko Takahashi, Akira Sasaki, Tomirou Kuriyama)
V

A Japanese hitman, who cries whenever he kills,
suspects that the élite corps of killers he commands
for the Chinese Mafia contains a traitor.

Another gore-filled cartoon for an adult audience that
enjoys indifferent animation, sex and violence.

w Kazuo Kioke, Toichi Ikegami   *d* Nishizawa
Nobukata   *ph* Yoshijuki Tamagawa   *m* Hiroaki
Yoshino   *ed* Shigeru Nishiyama

Voices of Stephen Tremblay, Edita Brychta, Vincent
Marzello, John Baddeley

Crying Freeman, Chapter Three: Retribution (dubbed)
Japan   1992   50m   colour
Toei (Akira Sasaki, Tomirou Kuriyama)
V

Crying Freeman finds himself confronting a group of
African terrorists, while his wife gains a mystical
sword.

The mixture as before: rudimentary animation and
comic strip heroics, featuring much sudden and
bloody death.

w Kazuo Koike, Toichi Ikegami   *d* Johei Matsuura
ph Yoichi Takanashi   *m* Hiroaki Yoshino
ad Tomoshi Urushibana   *ed* Shigeru Nishiyama

Voices of Stephen Tremblay, Edita Brychta, John
Baddeley, Rosemary Miller, Deborah Weston

'Desire Is A Danger Zone.'
The Crying Game ***
GB   1992   112m   Metrocolor   Panavision
Palace/Channel 4/Eurotrustees/NDF/British Screen (Stephen
Woolley)
V, V*, L, CD, S

An IRA gunman makes friends with a black British
soldier who is taken hostage and, after the soldier's
death, goes to London where he falls for the man's
lover.

Complex and brilliantly successful examination of
matters of identity and gender.

wd Neil Jordan   *ph* Ian Wilson   *m* Anne Dudley
pd Jim Clay   *ed* Kant Pan

*Stephen Rea, Miranda Richardson, Forest Whitaker, Jim
Broadbent, Ralph Brown, Adrian Dunbar, Jaye
Davidson, Tony Slattery*

'An astonishingly good and daring film.' – *Variety*

'Every so often, a "little" film hits the collective heart.
The Crying Game is one of these, because it shows that a
man is never so naked as when he reveals his secret
self.' – *Richard Corliss, Time*

AA: Neil Jordan (as writer)

AAN: best picture; Neil Jordan (as director); Kant
Pan; Stephen Rea; Jaye Davidson

Crypt of the Living Dead
US   1972   83m   Metrocolor   Scope
Golden Era/Coast Industries (Lou Shaw)
GB title: *Vampire Woman*

A female vampire comes back to life after her tomb is
opened.

Uninteresting low-budget horror that fails to raise a
shiver.

w Lou Shaw   *d* Ray Danton   *ph* Juan Gelpi
m Phillip Lambro   *ad* Juan Alberto   *ed* David
Rawlins

Andrew Prine, Mark Damon, Patty Sheppard, Teresa
Gimpera, Ihsan Genik, Mariano Rey, Frank Brana

'A dismal sortie into sanguineous legend.' – *Sight and
Sound*

The Crystal Ball *
US   1943   82m   bw
UA/Richard Blumenthal

A failed beauty contestant becomes a fortune teller
and is involved in a land swindle.

Pleasant comedy with fanciful moments, ending with
a pie-throwing contest.

w Virginia Van Upp   *d* Elliott Nugent   *ph* Leo
Tover   *m* Victor Young

Paulette Goddard, Ray Milland, Gladys George,
Virginia Field, Cecil Kellaway, William Bendix,
Ernest Truex

Cuba
US   1979   122m   Technicolor
UA/Alex Winitsky, Arlene Sellers
V*

Upper-crust characters are caught in Havana when the
Castro revolution starts.

Aimless romantic melodrama which gets absolutely
nowhere and might have been better played in the
Casablanca vein.

w Charles Wood   *d* Richard Lester   *ph* David
Watkin   *m* Patrick Williams   *pd* Gil Parrando

Sean Connery, Brooke Adams, Jack Weston, Hector
Elizondo, Denholm Elliott, Martin Balsam, Chris
Sarandon

Cuba Si! *
France   1961   58m   bw
Films de la Pléïade

A documentary on the Cuban revolution and Castro's
rise to power.

Remarkable and influential at the time for its use of
techniques which are now the commonplaces of
television, this documentary still has its flashes of
interest.

wd/ph Chris Marker   *m* E. G. Mantici, J. Calzada
ed Eva Zora

'An eloquent, personal record of history in the
making.' – *Georges Sadoul*

Cuban Love Song
US   1931   86m   bw
MGM (Albert Lewin)

A marine on leave in Cuba falls in love; years later he
returns to retrieve his illegitimate child, whose
mother has died.

Pathetic musical melodrama which did not advance
its singing star's film career.

w John Lynch   *d* W. S. Van Dyke   *ph* Harold
Rosson   *m* Charles Maxwell   *m/ly* various

Lawrence Tibbett, Lupe Velez, Jimmy Durante, Ernest
Torrence, Karen Morley, Louise Fazenda

'Tibbett may be a sensation on the concert stage, but
it's not the same in pictures.' – *Variety*

Cuban Pete
US   1946   61m   bw
Universal (Will Cowan)

A Cuban orchestra leader comes to New York.

Flatfooted second feature introducing the gentleman
who later married Lucille Ball.

w Robert Presnell Snr, M. Coates Webster   *d* Jean
Yarbrough

Desi Arnaz, Joan Fulton, Beverly Simmons, Don
Porter

'Dull pace and few chuckles.' – *Variety*

A Cuckoo in the Nest *
GB   1933   85m   bw
Gaumont (Ian Dalrymple, Angus MacPhail)

A newlywed husband is forced to spend a night at an
inn with an old flame pretending to be his wife.

Classic Aldwych farce with the stage company in
excellent form; directorial style on the stagey side.

w Ben Travers, A. R. Rawlinson   *play* Ben Travers
d Tom Walls   *ph* Glen MacWilliams   *ad* Alfred
Junge   *ed* Helen Lewis

*Ralph Lynn, Tom Walls, Yvonne Arnaud, Mary Brough,
Veronica Rose, Gordon James, Cecil Parker, Roger
Livesey, Robertson Hare*

† Remade 1955 as *Fast and Loose.*

The Cuckoos
US   1930   90m   bw/Technicolor sequences
RKO

Two tramps become fortune tellers.

The most ambitiously staged, and probably the most
popular of this team's gag marathons.

w Cy Woods   *musical comedy* The Ramblers by Philip
H. Goodman   *d* Paul Sloane

Bert Wheeler, Robert Woolsey, Jobyna Howland,
June Clyde, Hugh Trevor, Dorothy Lee

'It holds little between the laughs and doesn't need
anything else.' – *Variety*

Cujo

US 1983 91m CFI colour
ITC/Sunn Classic/Taft (Daniel H. Blatt)
V*, L

A St Bernard dog is bitten by a rabies-infected bat, and becomes a vicious killer.

Not much of a basis for a horror film, and this is not much of a horror film.

w Don Carlos Dunaway, Lauren Currier
novel Stephen King d Lewis Teague ph Jan de Bont m Charles Bernstein pd Guy Comtois ed Neil Travis

Dee Wallace, Daniel-Hugh Kelly, Danny Pintauro, Ed Lauter, Christopher Stone

Cul de Sac

GB 1966 111m bw
Compton-Tekli (Gene Gutowski)
V, V*

Two gangsters on the run take refuge in an old castle on a desolate Northumbrian island, but find their nemesis in the effeminate owner and his voluptuous wife.

Overlong, eccentric black comedy, more perplexing than entertaining.

w Roman Polanski, Gerard Brach d Roman Polanski ph Gilbert Taylor m Komeda

Lionel Stander, Donald Pleasence, Jack MacGowran, Françoise Dorléac, William Franklyn, Robert Dorning, Renée Houston

'A voyeur's wallow in schizophrenia and murder to no point beyond sensation – but one could not deny the creative talent at work.' – Judith Crist

The Culpeper Cattle Company *

US 1972 92m DeLuxe
TCF (Paul A. Helmick)
V*

A 16-year-old would-be cowboy joins a cattle trail but is shocked at the harsh realities of Western life.

Excellent moody photography helps to convince us that the old west was really like this, but the story is more brutal than interesting.

w Eric Bercovici, Gregory Prentiss d Dick Richards ph Lawrence Edward Williams, Ralph Woolsey m Tom Scott, Jerry Goldsmith

Gary Grimes, Billy 'Green' Bush, Luke Askew, Bo Hopkins, Geoffrey Lewis, Wayne Sutherlin

Cult of the Cobra

US 1955 79m bw
Universal-International

Six GIs are cursed by the high priest of an Indian cobra cult. Back in New York, a mysterious woman brings about their deaths, and when the survivor kills a cobra, it turns into her.

Glossy but wholly unconvincing and unexciting non-horror potboiler.

w Jerry Davis, Cecil Maiden, Richard Collins d Francis D. Lyon

Faith Domergue, Richard Long, Marshall Thompson, Kathleen Hughes, Jack Kelly

'No Winners In This Game.'
'A soldier from Israel, captured in the Lebanon, but his goal was to be at the ...'

Cup Final

Israel 1992 110m colour
(Michael Sharfshstein)
original title: G'mar Giviya

An Israeli soldier finds common ground with his PLO captors in talk of football.

A story of coexistence that may mean more to Israeli audiences than others. It points out the similarities that exist between enemies, but does little else to advance one's understanding.

w Eyal Halfon d Eran Riklis ph Amnon Salomon m Raviv Gazit ed Anat Lubarsky

Moshe Ivgi, Muhammed Bakri, Suheil Haddad

'Exciting, touching and politically even-handed.' – Empire

A Cup of Kindness

GB 1934 81m bw
Gaumont (Michael Balcon)

Young lovers marry despite parental disapproval on both sides.

Farcical updating of Romeo and Juliet; it hasn't worn too well, but the stars are at their peak.

w Ben Travers play Ben Travers d Tom Walls ph Phil Tannura ad Alfred Junge ed A. W. Roome

Tom Walls, Ralph Lynn, Robertson Hare, Claude Hulbert, Dorothy Hyson, Eva Moore

The Cure ****

US 1917 20m approx bw silent
Mutual/Charles Chaplin

A dipsomaniac sent to a spa gets his booze mixed up with the spa water.

One of the funniest of the Chaplin shorts, with no pathos intervening (nor come to that much plot); it is simply a succession of balletic slapstick scenes of the highest order.

wd Charles Chaplin ph William C. Foster, Rollie Totheroh

Charles Chaplin, Edna Purviance, Eric Campbell, Henry Bergman

The Cure *

GB 1950 18m bw
Richard and Betty Massingham

A health nut tries every possible remedy for lumbago.

Richard Massingham huffs and puffs in his endearing way through a short which is too long by far to be effective in his particular vein; but it does identify his particular persona.

wd Richard and Betty Massingham

The Cure for Love

GB 1949 98m bw
London Films (Robert Donat)

An ex-soldier goes home and tries to get married.

Thin Lancashire comedy which seemed an astonishing choice for Robert Donat, whose acting and direction are equally ill at ease.

w Robert Donat, Alexander Shaw, Albert Fennell play Walter Greenwood d Robert Donat ph Jack Cox m William Alwyn

Robert Donat, Renée Asherson, Dora Bryan, Marjorie Rhodes, Charles Victor, Thora Hird, Gladys Henson

'Antediluvian regional farce.' – MFB

The Cure Show

GB 1993 96m bw/colour
Rank/Fiction/Polygram Video (Steve Swartz)

Documentary on the British rock group The Cure performing at two concerts in Detroit in July 1992.

A concert recording strictly for fans of the group, with the cameras staying at a distance from the on-stage action, revealing nothing more than could be seen from the auditorium.

d Aubrey Powell, Leroy Bennett ph Jeff Zimmerman ed Ian Mallett, Liam Hall

'So depressingly ordinary – it could fill a late night TV slot and attract no reaction – that it is hard to see why it was made at all.' – Sight and Sound

'Big laughs come in small packages.'
Curly Sue

US 1991 101m Technicolor
Warner (John Hughes)
V, V*, L, S

A con man and a nine-year-old orphan win the heart of a successful woman lawyer.

Gruesomely sentimental and manipulative comedy.

wd John Hughes ph Jeffrey Kimball m Georges Delerue pd Doug Kraner ed Peck Prior, Harvey Rosenstock

James Belushi, Kelly Lynch, Alisan Porter, John Getz

'With its mix of childish gags and shameless melodrama, Curly Sue could make off with a tidy box-office take.' – Variety

'John Hughes here graduates from the most successful comedy in film history to scripting and directing a large piece of non-biodegradable tosh.' – Nigel Andrews, Financial Times

'Lacks the charm, good jokes or vigour to hide its contrivances.' – Geoff Brown, The Times

Curly Top *

US 1935 78m bw
Fox (Darryl F. Zanuck, Winfield Sheehan)
V*

An orphan waif is adopted by a playboy, and not only sets his business right but fixes his romantic interest in her sister.

Archetypal Temple vehicle, a loose remake of Daddy Longlegs.

w Patterson McNutt, Arthur Beckhard d Irving Cummings ph John Seitz m/ly Ray Henderson, Ted Koehler, Edward Heyman, Irving Caesar

Shirley Temple, John Boles, Rochelle Hudson, Jane Darwell, Rafaela Ottiano, Esther Dale, Arthur Treacher, Etienne Girardot

'Cinch b.o. for almost any house.' – Variety

The Curse: see Xala

Curse of Dark Shadows: see House of Dark Shadows

'The creature created by man is forgotten by nature!'
The Curse of Frankenstein **

GB 1957 83m Eastmancolor
Warner/Hammer (Anthony Hinds)
V*

A lurid revamping of the 1931 Frankenstein, this time with severed eyeballs and a peculiarly unpleasant and uncharacterized creature, all in gory colour.

It set the trend in nasty horrors from which we have all suffered since, and launched Hammer Studios on a long and profitable career of charnelry. But it did have a gruesome sense of style.

w Jimmy Sangster d Terence Fisher ph Jack Asher m James Bernard ad Ted Marshall ed James Needs

Peter Cushing, Christopher Lee, Hazel Court, Robert Urquhart, Valerie Gaunt, Noel Hood

'Among the half-dozen most repulsive films I have encountered in the course of some 10,000 miles of film reviewing. Indeed, at the moment, I can only think of two which sickened me more.' – C. A. Lejeune

'A tender tale of terror!'
The Curse of the Cat People *

US 1944 70m bw
RKO (Val Lewton)
V*, L

A child is haunted by the spirit of the cat people.

A gentle film ordered by the studio as a sequel to Cat People but turned by Lewton into a fantasy of childhood. Slow to start but finally compelling, it's a pleasing and unusual film in a minor key.

w De Witt Bodeen   *d* Robert Wise, Gunther von Fritsch   *ph* Nicholas Musuraca   *m* Roy Webb

Kent Smith, Simone Simon, Jane Randolph, Julia Dean, Ann Carter, Elizabeth Russell

'Full of the poetry and danger of childhood.' – *James Agee*

'A clumsy coming together of unrealized ideas, gothic effects, and stiff, dull acting.' – *New Yorker, 1979*

Curse of the Crimson Altar

GB   1968   89m   Eastmancolor
Tigon/AIP (Tony Tenser)
V*, L
aka: *The Crimson Cult*

Witchcraft, diabolism and mystery in an English country house.

A derivative, muddled scribble of a horror film, making no sense and wasting much talent.

w Mervyn Haisman, Henry Lincoln   *d* Vernon Sewell   *ph* John Coquillon   *m* Peter Knight

Boris Karloff, Christopher Lee, Rupert Davies, Mark Eden, Barbara Steele, Michael Gough

Curse of the Demon: see *Night of the Demon*

The Curse of the Ellanbys: see *She Wolf of London*

'Entombed for eons – turned to stone – seeking women, women, women!'
Curse of the Faceless Man

US   1958   67m   bw
Vogue/United Artists

An encrusted man, found in the earth near Pompeii, is revived and goes on the rampage, but is eventually dissolved by water.

Absurd chiller with the saving grace of not taking itself seriously.

w Jerome Bixby   *d* Edward L. Cahn

Richard Anderson, Elaine Edwards, Adele Mara, Gar Moore, Felix Locher

Curse of the Living Corpse

US   1963   78m   bw
TCF (Del Tenney)
V*

A millionaire vows to return and kill all his relatives if he is buried alive, which he is . . .

Gothic cheapie made in Stamford, Connecticut, where they have little experience of such things.

wd Del Tenney

Roy Scheider, Candace Hilligoss

'Half bone, half bandage . . . all bloodcurdling terror!'
Curse of the Mummy's Tomb

GB   1964   80m   Technicolor   Techniscope
Columbia/Swallow/Hammer (Michael Carreras)
V

An Egyptian mummy taken to London goes on the rampage, and meets its own wicked brother who has been cursed to eternal life.

Absurd farrago which takes too long to set up its plot and then finds little to do with its monster.

w Henry Younger (Michael Carreras)   *d* Michael Carreras   *ph* Otto Heller   *m* Carlo Martelli   *ad* Bernard Robinson   *ed* James Needs, Eric Boyd-Perkins

Ronald Howard, Terence Morgan, *Fred Clark*, Jeanne Roland, George Pastell, Jack Gwillim, John Paul

Curse of the Pink Panther

GB   1983   110m   Technicolor   Panavision
MGM-UA/Titan/Jewel (Blake Edwards, Gerald T. Nutting)
V, V*

Inspector Clouseau has disappeared, and Dreyfus selects the world's worst detective to replace him.

Unspeakably awful attempt at prolonging a series whose star died two episodes ago. Crude, tasteless and unfunny throughout.

w Blake Edwards, Geoffrey Edwards   *d* Blake Edwards   *ph* Dick Bush   *m* Henry Mancini   *pd* Peter Mullins

Ted Wass, Joanna Lumley, Herbert Lom, David Niven, Robert Wagner, Capucine, Harvey Korman, Burt Kwouk

'Another bout of film-making as grave robbing.' – *Sight and Sound*

'The ultimate version of deadpan humour . . . the most tedious of the whole series.' – *Richard Combs, MFB*

Curse of the Undead

US   1959   79m   bw
Universal-International

A black-clad stranger in a Western town turns out to be a vampire of Spanish origin.

Abysmal attempt to substitute Wyoming for Transylvania; more skill and sensitivity were required.

wd Edward Dein

Michael Pate, Eric Fleming, Kathleen Crowley, John Hoyt

'He had but one body – yet lived with two souls!'
Curse of the Werewolf

GB   1960   92m   Technicolor
U-I/Hotspur/Hammer (Anthony Hinds)
V*

A beggar rapes a servant girl and their offspring grows up to be a werewolf.

Doleful Hammer horror in a Spanish setting, with an absurd but predictable plot and a lack of sympathy for its fancy, hairy hero.

w John Elder (Anthony Hinds)   *novel* The Werewolf of Paris *by* Guy Endore   *d* Terence Fisher   *ph* Arthur Grant   *m* Benjamin Frankel   *ad* Bernard Robinson   *ed* James Needs, Alfred Cox

Oliver Reed, Clifford Evans, Catherine Feller, Yvonne Romain, Anthony Dawson, Richard Wordsworth, Warren Mitchell

The Curse of the Wraydons

GB   1946   94m   bw
Bushey

The Victorian story of Spring-heeled Jack, here depicted as a mad inventor out for revenge.

Too long and stagey to be one of its star's better barnstormers, especially as by this time his girth made the notion of his springing about somewhat hilarious.

w Michael Barringer   *d* Victor M. Gover

Tod Slaughter, Bruce Seton, Gabriel Toyne

Curtain Call *

US   1940 . 63m   bw
RKO

Two Broadway producers buy an awful play in order to get even with a temperamental star, but she likes it.

Amusing second feature, a kind of flashforward to *The Producers*. A reprise the following year, *Footlight Fever*, did not work.

w Dalton Trumbo   *d* Frank Woodruff   *ph* Russell Metty   *m* Roy Webb

Alan Mowbray, Donald MacBride, Helen Vinson, Barbara Read, John Archer

Curtain Call at Cactus Creek *

US   1949   83m   Technicolor
U-I (Robert Arthur)
GB title: *Take the Stage*

A travelling repertory company in the old west exposes a gang of bank robbers.

Cheerful minor comedy with good pace and amusing burlesques of old melodramas.

w Oscar Brodney   *d* Charles Lamont   *ph* Russell Metty   *m* Walter Scharf

Donald O'Connor, Gale Storm, Eve Arden, Vincent Price, Walter Brennan, Chick Chandler

Curtain Up *

GB   1952   85m   bw
Rank/Constellation (Robert Garrett)

A seaside repertory company runs into trouble when the producer is at loggerheads with the author of next week's play.

Fairly amusing farce which has now acquired historical value for the light it throws on the old weekly reps.

w Michael Pertwee, Jack Davies   *play* On Monday Next *by* Philip King   *d* Ralph Smart   *ph* Stanley Pavey   *m* Malcolm Arnold

Margaret Rutherford, Robert Morley, Olive Sloane, Joan Rice, Charlotte Mitchell, Kay Kendall, Liam Gaffney, Michael Medwin

Curucu, Beast of the Amazon

US   1956   76m   colour
Universal

Amazon explorers set out to find a man masquerading as a monster.

Rubbishy hokum, for tolerant kids.

wd Curt Siodmak

John Bromfield, Beverly Garland, Tom Payne

Custer of the West

US   1967   146m   Super Technirama 70
Cinerama/Security (Louis Dolivet, Philip Yordan, Irving Lerner)

After the Civil War, Custer is offered a cavalry command, becomes disillusioned, and is massacred with his troops at Little Big Horn.

Gloomily inaccurate spectacular with pauses for Cinerama carnival thrills and dour bits of melodrama.

w Bernard Gordon, Julian Halevy   *d* Robert Siodmak   *ph* Cecilio Paniagua   *m* Bernardo Segall

Robert Shaw, Mary Ure, Robert Ryan, Jeffrey Hunter, Ty Hardin, Lawrence Tierney, Kieron Moore

Custer's Last Stand

US   1936   bw   serial: 15 eps
Stage and Screen

An Indian brave is involved in a search for gold while trying to warn Custer of the danger at Little Big Horn.

Fanciful Western serial without much excitement. Custer does not appear.

d Elmer Clifton

Rex Lease, William Farnum, Reed Howes, Jack Mulhall

Cutter and Bone

US   1981   109m   Technicolor
United Artists/Gurian
V*
GB title: *Cutter's Way*

A California failure witnesses the aftermath of murder, and with a crippled ex-Vietnam veteran turns detective.

Heavy-going melodrama which tries very hard to be something more than a thriller, and manages only to imply that the world stinks; so it might as well have stuck to Philip Marlowe.

w Jeffrey Alan Fiskin   *novel* Newton Thornburg   *d* Ivan Passer   *ph* Jordan Cronenweth   *m* Jack Nitzsche   *ed* Caroline Ferriol

Jeff Bridges, John Heard, Lisa Eichhorn, Ann Dusenberry, Stephen Elliott, Nina Van Pallandt

Cutter's Way: see *Cutter and Bone*

'The King Of The Rink Is About To Meet America's Ice Queen.'

The Cutting Edge

US 1992 110m DeLuxe
UIP/MGM/Interscope (Ted Field, Karen Murphy, Robert W. Cort)
V, V*

A tough former ice-hockey player becomes the partner of a spoiled and wealthy figure-skater.

Predictable romantic teen movie of winning against the odds.

w Tony Gilroy d Paul M. Glaser ph Elliot Davis m Patrick Williams pd David Gropman ed Michael E. Polakow

D. B. Sweeney, Moira Kelly, Roy Dotrice, Terry O'Quinn, Dwier Brown, Chris Benson, Kevin Peeks, Barry Flatman

Cybèle ou les Dimanches de Ville d'Avry: see Sundays and Cybèle

Cyborg

US 1989 85m colour
Cannon/Golan-Globus
V, V*

A martial arts expert accompanies a female cyborg, holding information to save mankind, across post-apocalyptic America.

Charmless, cliché-packed action movie, carrying the explicit message that violence is good for you.

w Kitty Chalmers d Albert Pyun ph Philip Alan Waters m Kevin Bassinson pd Douglas Leonard ed Rozanne Zingale, Scott Stevenson

Jean-Claude Van Damme, Deborah Richter, Vincent Klyn, Alex Daniels, Rolf Muller, Jackson Pinckney, Dayle Haddon

'He was programmed to kill ... Nobody can stop him.'

Cyborg Cop

US 1993 93m colour
Nu Image/Nu World (Danny Lerner)
V, V*

An ex-cop goes to the rescue of his brother, who has been captured and turned into a killer cyborg by a mad millionaire drug dealer on a Caribbean island.

Dim standard robot action fodder, remarkable only for its violent, cliché-ridden plot and dialogue.

w Gregg Latter d Sam Firstenberg ph Joseph Wein m Paul Fishman pd John Rosewarne ed Alan Patillo

David Bradley, Todd Jensen, Alonna Shaw, Rufus Swart, John Rhys-Davies

'Some effective special effects make this watchable trash' – Sight and Sound

The Cyclops

US 1956 65m bw
B and H (Bert I. Gordon)

Explorers in Mexico find animals turned by radiation into monsters, plus a one-eyed 25-foot-tall human.

Modest monster movie, quite palatable of its kind.

wd Bert I. Gordon ph Ira Morgan m Albert Glasser

James Craig, Lon Chaney Jnr, Gloria Talbott, Tom Drake

Cynara **

US 1933 78m bw
Samuel Goldwyn

A London barrister has an affair with a young girl who commits suicide when he goes back to his wife.

Solidly carpentered, effective star vehicle of the old school, now dated but preserving its dignity.

w Frances Marion, Lynn Starling novel An Imperfect Lover by Robert Gore Brown d King Vidor ph Ray June m Alfred Newman

Ronald Colman, Kay Francis, Phyllis Barry, Henry Stephenson, Paul Porcasi

'The values it involves are wholly unlike those which US audiences are usually called upon to comprehend.' – Time

Cynthia

US 1947 98m bw
MGM (Edwin H. Knopf)
GB title: The Rich Full Life

An over-protected girl finds an outlet in music and her parents finally allow her to lead her own life.

An overlong domestic drama in which thin writing and acting are backed by unsound psychology.

w Harold Buchman, Charles Kaufman play Vina Delmar d Robert Z. Leonard ph Charles Schoenbaum m Bronislau Kaper

Elizabeth Taylor, George Murphy, Mary Astor, S. Z. Sakall, James Lydon, Gene Lockhart, Spring Byington

Cynthia's Secret: see Dark Delusion

Cyrano de Bergerac *

US 1950 112m bw
Stanley Kramer
V, V*, L

In the 17th century a long-nosed poet, philosopher and buffoon writes letters enabling a friend to win the lady he loves himself.

The classic romantic verse play does not take kindly to a hole-in-corner black-and-white production, but at the time it was lapped up as a daring cultural breakthrough.

w Brian Hooker play Edmond Rostand d Michael Gordon ph Franz Planer m Dimitri Tiomkin

José Ferrer, Mala Powers, William Prince, Morris Carnovsky, Ralph Clanton, Virginia Farmer, Edgar Barrier, Elena Verdugo

'Vigorous, respectful, full of lively movement, and pictorially well-composed.' – C. A. Lejeune

AA: José Ferrer

Cyrano de Bergerac ***

France 1990 138m colour
Hachette Première/Camera One/Films A2/D.D. Productions/ UGC (Rene Cleitman, Michael Seydoux)
V, V*, L, S

A dashing soldier and noted duellist, handicapped by his long nose, helps a handsome friend make love to the woman he adores from afar.

Exuberant version of the romantic French classic, using the rhymed couplets of the original. The English subtitles, in a rhyming translation by Anthony Burgess, are a distraction, though.

w Jean-Paul Rappeneau, Jean-Claude Carrière play Edmond Rostand d Jean-Paul Rappeneau ph Pierre Lhomme m Jean-Claude Petit ad Ezio Frigerio ed Noëlle Boisson

Gérard Depardieu, Anne Brochet, Vincent Perez, Jacques Weber, Roland Bertin, Philippe Morier-Genoud, Philippe Volter, Pierre Maguelon

'A near-perfect balance of verbal and visual flamboyance.' – Variety

'Cyrano? Bravo!' – Le Monde

AAN: Gérard Depardieu; best foreign language film; best art direction; best costume design; best make-up

Czar of the Slot Machines: see King of Gamblers

Czarina: see A Royal Scandal

Czlowiek Z Marmur: see Man of Marble

Czlowiek Z Zelaza: see Man of Iron

D. C. Cab

US   1983   99m   Technicolor
RKO-Universal (Topper Carew)
GB title: *Street Fleet*

Cab drivers for a run-down Washington company capture kidnappers.

Brainless extravaganza with aspirations somewhere between *Taxi* and *Carry On*.

wd Joel Schumacher   *ph* Dean Cundey, Ron Van Nostrand   *m* Giorgio Moroder   *pd* John Lloyd   *ed* David Blewitt

Mr T, Max Gail, Adam Baldwin, Charlie Barnett, Gary Busey, Gloria Gifford

'Artificial energy used to bolster wretched material.' – *Steve Jenkins, MFB*

The DI

US   1957   106m   bw
Warner/Mark VII (Jack Webb)

A tough marine drill instructor takes a special interest in a backward member of his platoon.

Noisy recruiting poster heroics in which the producer gives himself a loud but boring part. The drill sequences are well done, but the film is overlong and repetitive.

w James Lee Barrett   *d* Jack Webb   *ph* Edward Colman   *m* David Buttolph

Jack Webb, Don Dubbins, Jackie Loughery, Lin McCarthy, Monica Lewis

D.O.A. **

US   1950   83m   bw
UA/Leo C. Popkin
V*, L

The victim of a slow poison tracks down his own killer.

Semi-classic suspense drama, sufficiently original to be remembered though the plot details become hazy.

w Russel Rouse, Clarence Greene (partly from a 1931 German film *Der Mann der seinen Mörder Sucht*)   *d* Rudolph Maté   *ph* Ernest Laszlo   *m* Dimitri Tiomkin

Edmond O'Brien, Pamela Britton, Luther Adler, Neville Brand, Beverly Campbell

† The title is a police abbreviation for 'dead on arrival'.
†† Remade as *Colour Me Dead* (qv) and see below.

D.O.A.

US   1988   97m   CFI
Warner/Touchstone/Silver Screen Partners III (Ian Sander, Laura Ziskin)
V*, L, S

A college professor, discovering that he has been poisoned, and with less than 48 hours to live, solves the mystery of his murder.

Ambitious but inept remake, lacking in suspense.

w Charles Edward Pogue   *story* Charles Edward Pogue, Russel Rouse, Clarence Greene   *d* Rocky Morton, Annabel Jankel   *ph* Yuri Neyman   *m* Chaz Jankel   *pd* Richard Amend   *ed* Michael R. Miller, Raja Gosnell

Dennis Quaid, Meg Ryan, Charlotte Rampling, Daniel Stern, Jane Kaczmarek, Christopher Neame, Robin Johnson, Rob Knepper, Jay Patterson

Da **

US   1988   102m   colour
Premier/Film Dallas/A. J. Corman-Sheen/Greenblatt/Auerbach (Julie Corman)
V, V*, L, S

A playwright, returning to Ireland for his father's funeral, finds himself discussing life with his father's ghost.

An autobiographical work which runs deep with emotion.

w Hugh Leonard   *play* Hugh Leonard   *d* Matt Clark   *ph* Alar Kivilo   *m* Elmer Bernstein   *pd* Frank Conway   *ed* Nancy Nuttal Beyda

Barnard Hughes, Martin Sheen, William Hickey, Doreen Hepburn, Karl Hayden, Hugh O'Conor, Ingrid Craigie, Joan O'Hara, Jill Doyle

Da Yuebing: see *The Big Parade* (1986)

Dad

US   1989   118m   DeLuxe
UIP/Universal/Amblin Entertainment (Joseph Stern, Gary David Goldberg)
V, V*, L, S

A son helps his father face up to death.

Excessively sentimental family drama.

wd Gary David Goldberg   *novel* William Wharton   *ph* Jan Kiesser   *m* James Horner   *pd* Jack DeGovia   *ed* Eric Sears

Jack Lemmon, Ted Danson, Olympia Dukakis, Kathy Baker, Kevin Spacey, Ethan Hawke, Zakes Mokae, J. T. Walsh, Peter Michael Goetz

'Emotional exploitation at its most objectionable.' – *MFB*

Dad Rudd films: see *On Our Selection*

Daddy Longlegs *

US   1931   80m   bw
Fox

An orphan girl grows up to fall in love with her mysterious benefactor.

Cinderella-like romance, adequately adapted from a novel which became the classic American version of the January–May romance.

w Sonya Levien   *novel* Jean Webster   *d* Alfred Santell   *ph* Lucien Andriot

Janet Gaynor, Warner Baxter, Una Merkel, John Arledge, Claude Gillingwater, Louise Closser Hale

'A smash . . . one of those rare talkers with universal appeal.' – *Variety*

† Other versions were made in 1919 with Mary Pickford and Mahlon Hamilton, directed by Marshal Neilan; in 1935 disguised as *Curly Top* (qv) and in 1955 (see below).

Daddy Longlegs *

US   1955   126m   Technicolor   Cinemascope
TCF (Samuel G. Engel)
V*, L

Overlong and unsuitably wide-screened musical version of a popular story (see above).

Generally clumsy and dispirited, but Astaire is always worth watching and a couple of the dances are well staged.

w Phoebe and Henry Ephron   *d* Jean Negulesco   *ph* Leon Shamroy   *m* Alfred Newman   *m/y* Johnny Mercer

Fred Astaire, Leslie Caron, Fred Clark, Thelma Ritter, Terry Moore, Charlotte Austin, Larry Keating

AAN: Alfred Newman; song 'Something's Gotta Give'

Daddy Nostalgie **

France   1990   106m   Eastmancolor
Clea/Little Bear/Solyfic Eurisma (Adolphe Viezzi)
V, S
aka: *These Foolish Things*

A screenwriter returns home to be close to her invalid father.

Gently understated domestic drama.

w Colo Tavernier O'Hagan   *d* Bertrand Tavernier   *ph* Denis Lenoir   *m* Antoine Duhamel   *pd* Jean-Louis Poveda   *ed* Ariane Boeglin

Dirk Bogarde, Jane Birkin, Emmanuelle Bataille, Charlotte Kady, Michele Minns

'A miniature jewel of a film . . . acted and directed with great subtlety.' – *Variety*

Daddy's Dyin', Who's Got the Will?

US   1990   95m   DeLuxe
Palace/Propaganda Films/Artist Circle Entertainment (Sigurjon Sighvatsson, Steve Golin, Monty Montgomery)
V, V*, L

Children gather at home after their father has a stroke.

Raucous comedy of family relationships that ends in sentimentality.

w Del Shores   *play* Del Shores   *d* Jack Fisk   *ph* Paul Elliot   *m* David McHugh   *pd* Michelle Minch   *ed* Edward A. Warschilka Jnr

Beau Bridges, Beverly D'Angelo, Tess Harper, Judge Reinhold, Amy Wright, Patrika Darbo, Bert Remsen, Molly McClure, Keith Carradine, Newell Alexander

Daddy's Gone A-Hunting

US   1969   108m   Technicolor
Warner/Red Lion (Mark Robson)
V*

A child and its mother are threatened by her deranged ex-husband.

Unpleasant and protracted suspenser with the emphasis on sex rather than thrills.

w Larry Cohen, Lorenzo Semple Jnr   *d* Mark Robson   *ph* Ernest Laszlo   *m* John Williams

Carol White, Paul Burke, Scott Hylands, Mala Powers, Andrea King

Dad's Army **

GB   1971   95m   Technicolor
Columbia/Norcon (John R. Sloan)
V

Misadventures of a number of elderly gents in Britain's wartime Home Guard.

Expanded big-screen version of the long-running TV series, a pleasant souvenir but rather less effective than was expected because everything is shown – the town, the Nazis, the wives – and thus the air of gentle fantasy disappears, especially in the face of much coarsened humour.

w Jimmy Perry, David Croft   d Norman Cohen
ph Terry Maher   m Wilfred Burns

Arthur Lowe, John Le Mesurier, John Laurie, James Beck, Ian Lavender, Arnold Ridley, Liz Fraser, Clive Dunn, Bill Pertwee, Frank Williams, Edward Sinclair

Daens *
Belgium/France/Netherlands   1992   138m   colour
Mayfair/Favourite/Investco/Kredietbank Luxembourg/Films Dérive/Titane/Shooting Star/BRTN/KRO (Dick Impens)
S

At the turn of the century, a Catholic priest champions the half-starved, underpaid workers in the city of Aalst.

Dogged biopic celebrating a remarkable man, but without much flair in its telling.

w François Chevallier, Stijn Coninx   *novel* Pieter Daens by Louis Paul Boon   d Stijn Coninx
ph Wather Vanden Ende   m Dirk Brossé   pd Allan Starski   ed Ludo Troch

Jan Decleir, Gérard Desarthe, Antje de Boeck, Michael Pas, Johan Leysen, Idwig Stéphane, Wim Meuwissen

'A bit of a pudding, and long with it. It says all the right things . . . But it says them so slowly and deliberately that your patience is at times sorely tested.' – *Derek Malcolm, Guardian*

'A bit of a plod. But it does have dramatic force, a passionate central performance and the great virtue of clarity.' – *Adam Mars-Jones, Independent*

AAN: best foreign film

Dahong Denglong Gaogao Gua: see Raise The Red Lantern

Daisies **
Czechoslovakia   1966   80m   colour
Bohumil Smida (Lasislav Fikar)
V
original title: *Sedmikrasky*

Bored by their lives, two girls go in search of decadence.

Witty, playful, visually exuberant attack on conformity and a materialistic society that the Czech authorities banned for a time.

w Ester Krumbachova, Vera Chytilova   d Vera Chytilova   ph Jaroslav Kucera   pd Ester Krumbachova

Jitka Cerhova, Ivana Karbanova, Julius Albert

'What makes this film particularly distasteful is its idiot yearning for Western beatnikdom, its slobbering (and, I suspect, lesbian) adulation of its ghastly heroines.' – *John Simon*

Daisy Kenyon
US   1947   99m   bw
TCF (Otto Preminger)

A fashion designer has two men in her life.

Adequate woman's picture which hardly justifies its cast.

w David Hertz   *novel* Elizabeth Janeway   d Otto Preminger   ph Leon Shamroy   m David Raksin

Joan Crawford, Henry Fonda, Dana Andrews, Ruth Warrick, Martha Stewart, Peggy Ann Garner

Daisy Miller *
US   1974   92m   Technicolor
Paramount/Copa de Oro (Peter Bogdanovich)
V*

In the 19th century, an American girl tourist in Europe falls in love but dies of the Roman fever.

Curious attempt to film a very mild and uneventful Henry James story, with careful production but inadequate leads. The first sign that Bogdanovich was getting too big for his boots.

w Frederic Raphael   *story* Henry James   d Peter Bogdanovich   ph Alberto Spagnoli   m classical themes   ad Ferdinando Scarfiotti

Cybill Shepherd, Barry Brown, Cloris Leachman, Mildred Natwick, Eileen Brennan, James MacMurtry

'A historical film bereft of any feeling for history, and a literary adaptation which reveals a fine contempt for literary subtlety.' – *Jan Dawson*

'Appallingly crass . . . directed with all the subtlety of a sledgehammer.' – *Michael Billington, Illustrated London News*

'Trying to make that little thing he's with into Daisy Miller was hilarious. God almighty couldn't do that. She's so coy.' – *Henry Hathaway*

Dakota
US   1945   82m   bw
Republic (Joseph Kane)

The daughter of a railroad tycoon elopes with a cowboy and becomes involved in a land war.

Adequate star Western.

w Lawrence Hazard   *story* Carl Foreman   d Joseph Kane   ph Jack Marta   m Walter Scharf

John Wayne, Vera Hruba Ralston, Walter Brennan, Ward Bond, Ona Munson, Hugo Haas, Mike Mazurki, Paul Fix, Grant Withers, Jack La Rue

Dakota Incident
US   1956   88m   bw
Republic
V*

Strangers take cover when they are attacked by Indians.

A formula older than *Stagecoach* is played out to humdrum results.

w Frederic Louis Fox   d Lewis R. Foster

Linda Darnell, Dale Robertson, Regis Toomey, John Lund, Ward Bond, Skip Homeier, Irving Bacon, John Doucette, Whit Bissell

Dakota Road
GB   1990   89m   colour
Mayfair/Dakota Road/Working Title/Film Four/British Screen (Donna Grey)

In East Anglia a 15-year-old girl suffers from her father's suicide, her family's eviction from their home and an unsatisfactory love affair with a local youth.

Rural melodrama so unrelievedly tragic that it hovers on the edge of parody.

wd Nick Ward   ph Ian Wilson   m Paul Stacey   pd Careen Hertzog   ed William Diver

Charlotte Chatton, Jason Carter, Rachel Scott, Amelda Brown, Matthew Scurfield, Alan Howard, David Warrilow

'A melodrama with the *angst* button set to full volume, all the way through.' – *Sheila Johnston, Independent*

'Though the film is splendidly shot by Ian Wilson, making the most of the exposed landscape and its patches of unexpected lushness, it founders on a relentless rural miserabilism.' – *Hugo Davenport, Daily Telegraph*

Daleks: Invasion Earth 2150 AD: see Dr Who and the Daleks

Dallas *
US   1950   94m   Technicolor
Warner (Anthony Veiller)

A renegade ex-Confederate colonel is pardoned for bringing law and order to Dallas.

Routinely competent top-of-the-bill Western.

w John Twist   d Stuart Heisler   ph Ernest Haller   m Max Steiner

Gary Cooper, Ruth Roman, Raymond Massey, Steve Cochran, Barbara Payton, Leif Erickson, Antonio Moreno, Jerome Cowan

The Daltons Ride Again
US   1945   72m   bw
Universal (Howard Welsch)

An outlaw gang's last raid is complicated when one of them falls in love.

Unhistorical action Western with B-feature appeal.

w Roy Chanslor, Paul Gangelin   d Ray Taylor

Alan Curtis, Kent Taylor, Lon Chaney Jnr, Noah Beery Jnr, Martha O'Driscoll, Thomas Gomez, Milburn Stone, John Litel

The Dam Busters **
GB   1954   125m   bw
ABPC (Robert Clark)
V, V*

In 1943 the Ruhr dams are destroyed by Dr Barnes Wallis's bouncing bombs.

Understated British war epic with additional scientific interest and good acting and model work, not to mention a welcome lack of love interest.

w R. C. Sherriff   *books* Guy Gibson and Paul Brickhill   d Michael Anderson   ph Erwin Hillier   m Leighton Lucas, Eric Coates   sp George Blackwell

Michael Redgrave, Richard Todd, Basil Sydney, Derek Farr, Patrick Barr, Ernest Clark, Raymond Huntley, Ursula Jeans

A dama do cine Shanghai: see The Lady from the Shanghai Cinema

Dama s Sobachkoi: see The Lady with the Little Dog

'Desire. Deceit.'
Damage
GB/France   1992   111m   Technicolor
Entertainment/Skreba/NEF/Canal+ (Louis Malle)
V, V*, L, S

A Conservative minister is destroyed by his obsessive love for his son's girlfriend.

Disappointingly thin tale that carries very little conviction.

w David Hare   *novel* Josephine Hart   d Louis Malle   ph Peter Biziou   m Zbigniew Preisner   pd Brian Morris   ed John Bloom

Jeremy Irons, Juliette Binoche, *Miranda Richardson*, Rupert Graves, Leslie Caron, Ian Bannen, Gemma Clarke, Julian Fellowes, Tony Doyle, Benjamin Whitrow

'A cold, brittle film about raging, traumatic emotions.' – *Variety*

'A carefully controlled picture about uncontrollable passion, in which precise camera movements and unobtrusive editing subtly complement the immaculate acting.' – *Philip French, Observer*

AAN: Miranda Richardson

Damaged Goods
US   1937   56m   bw
Grand National

A young man infects his wife and child with syphilis.

An 'awful warning' which seemed naïve even at the time; there had been a silent version in 1914.

w Upton Sinclair   *play* Eugene Brieux   d Phil Stone

Pedro de Cordoba, Douglas Walton, Arletta Duncan, Esther Dale, Phyllis Barry

Damaged Lives
US   1937   61m (plus a 29m lecture)   bw
Weldon

A young man infects his wife with syphilis.

One of a rival pair of moral tales (see above); both had trouble with the censors on subject matter alone. Not otherwise notable.

w Donald Davis, Edgar G. Ulmer   d Edgar G. Ulmer

Diane Sinclair, Lyman Williams, Cecilia Parker, George Irving, Jason Robards

Dames **
US   1934   90m   bw
Warner (Robert Lord)
V*, L

A millionaire purity fanatic tries to stop the opening of a Broadway show.

Typical Warner musical of the period: its real *raison d'être* is to be found in the splendidly imaginative numbers at the finale, but it also gives very full rein to the roster of comic actors under contract at the time.

w Delmer Daves   d Ray Enright   ch Busby Berkeley   ph Sid Hickox, George Barnes   m various

Joan Blondell, Hugh Herbert, Guy Kibbee, ZaSu Pitts, Dick Powell, Ruby Keeler

'That Warners was able to fashion so zestful an entertainment under post-Haysian restrictions is a credit to the collective ingenuities of the studio artificers. . .. Swell entertainment, no matter how you slice it.' – *Variety*

† Originally intended as *Gold Diggers of 1934.*

Les Dames du Bois de Boulogne *
France   1946   90m   bw
Consortium du Film (Raoul Ploquin)
US title: *Ladies of the Park*

A woman revenges herself on her faithless lover by inveigling him into a marriage with a nightclub dancer-cum-prostitute.

An austerely directed romantic melodrama that fails to satisfy.

w Jean Cocteau, Robert Bresson   story Diderot   d Robert Bresson   ph Philippe Agostini   m Jean-Jacques Grunenwald   pd Max Douy

Paul Bernard, Maria Casarès, Elina Labourdette, Lucienne Bogaert, Jean Marchat

'The first time was only a warning!'
Damien: Omen Two
US   1978   109m   DeLuxe   Panavision
TCF (Harvey Bernhard)
V, V*, L, S

The antichrist who got rid of the entire cast of *The Omen* now, as a teenager, starts in on his foster parents.

Once was enough.

w Stanley Mann, Michael Hodges   d Don Taylor   ph Bill Butler   m Jerry Goldsmith

William Holden, Lee Grant, Jonathan Scott-Taylor, Robert Foxworth, Lucas Donat, Lew Ayres, Sylvia Sidney, Elizabeth Shepherd

Damn the Defiant: see *HMS Defiant*

Damn Yankees **
US   1958   110m   Technicolor
Warner (George Abbott, Stanley Donen)
V, V*, L, S
GB title: *What Lola Wants*

The devil interferes in the fortunes of a failing baseball team.

Smartly-styled but very American musical based on *Faust;* brilliant moments but some tedium.

w George Abbott   novel Douglas Wallop   d George Abbott, Stanley Donen   ph Harold Lipstein   md Ray Heindorf   m/ly Richard Adler, Jerry Ross

Gwen Verdon, Tab Hunter, Ray Walston, Russ Brown, Shannon Bolin

AAN: Ray Heindorf

Damnation Alley
US   1977   95m   DeLuxe
TCF/Hal Landers, Bobby Roberts, Jerome M. Zeitman

Four survivors from World War Three try to reach a colony of fellow-survivors in New York.

Feeble attempt at a low-budget blockbuster.

w Alan Sharp, Lukas Heller   novel Roger Zelazny   d Jack Smight   ph Harry Stradling Jnr   m Jerry Goldsmith   pd Preston Ames

Jan-Michael Vincent, George Peppard, Dominique Sanda, Paul Winfield

The Damned *
France   1947   105m   bw
Speva Film
original title: *Les Maudits*

In 1945 fanatical Nazis escape in a submarine but make the mistake of stopping to sink a freighter.

Unusual melodrama with a brilliant sense of claustrophobia, good characterization and much suspense.

w Jacques Remy, René Clément, Henri Jeanson   d René Clément   ph Henri Alekan   m Yves Baudrier

Paul Bernard, Henri Vidal, Marcel Dalio, Michel Auclair, Florence Marly

The Damned *
GB   1963   87m (77m US)   bw   HammerScope
Columbia/Hammer-Swallow (Anthony Hinds)
US title: *These Are the Damned*

A scientist keeps radioactive children in a cliff cave, sealed off from the world's corruption.

Absurdly pompous, downcast and confused sci-fi melodrama set in Weymouth, with a secondary plot about motor-cycling thugs.

w Evan Jones   novel *The Children of Light* by H. L. Lawrence   d Joseph Losey   ph Arthur Grant   m James Bernard   pd Bernard Robinson

Macdonald Carey, Shirley Ann Field, Alexander Knox, Viveca Lindfors, Oliver Reed, Walter Gotell, James Villiers

'A *folie de grandeur.*' – *Tom Milne*

'Out of this wild mishmash some really magnificent images loom.' – *John Coleman*

The Damned **
West Germany/Italy   1969   164m   Eastmancolor
Praesidens/Pegaso
V (W), V*, L, S
original title: *Götterdämmerung*

A family of German industrialists divides and destroys itself under Nazi influence.

A film which has been called baroque, Wagnerian, and just plain unpleasant; it is also rather a strain to watch, with exaggerated colour and make-up to match the rotting theme.

w Nicola Badalucco, Enrico Medioli, Luchino Visconti   d Luchino Visconti   ph Armando Nannuzzi, Pasquale de Santis   m Maurice Jarre   ad Enzo del Prato, Pasquale Romano

Dirk Bogarde, Ingrid Thulin, Helmut Berger, Renaud Verley, Helmut Griem, René Kolldehof, Albrecht Schönhals, Umberto Orsini

'One is left lamenting that such a quondam master of realism as Visconti is making his films look like

operas from which the score has been inexplicably removed.' – *MFB*

'The ludicrous flailings of puny puppets in inscrutable wooden frenzies.' – *John Simon*

AAN: script

'The private lady of a public enemy!'
The Damned Don't Cry
US   1950   103m   bw
Warner (Jerry Wald)

A middle-class housewife leaves her husband for a gambler, and becomes involved with gangsters, but eventually reforms.

Rather dreary stimulation for female audiences who like safe dreams of danger.

w Harold Medford, Jerome Weidman   novel *Case History* by Gertrude Walker   d Vincent Sherman   ph Ted McCord   m Daniele Amfitheatrof

Joan Crawford, Kent Smith, David Brian, Steve Cochran, Hugh Sanders, Selena Royle, Morris Ankrum, Richard Egan

'Mad adventure! Daring deeds! White hot love with music!'
A Damsel in Distress *
US   1937   101m   bw
RKO (Pandro S. Berman)
V*, L

An American dancing star falls for an aristocratic young Englishwoman.

Astaire without Rogers, but the style is the same and there are some very good numbers.

w P. G. Wodehouse, S. K. Lauren, Ernest Pagano   d George Stevens   ph Joseph H. August   m/ly George and Ira Gershwin   ch Hermes Pan   ad Carroll Clark

Fred Astaire, George Burns, Gracie Allen, Joan Fontaine, Reginald Gardiner, Constance Collier, Ray Noble, Montagu Love

'Plenty for the b.o. – dancing, comedy, marquee values, the usual sumptuous investiture accorded by Pandro Berman, and those Gershwin songs.' – *Variety*

† Rogers had demanded a break from musicals, so she was replaced by the demure Miss Fontaine, who was generally thought disappointing.

AA: Hermes Pan

AAN: Carroll Clark

Dance Band
GB   1935   75m   bw
BIP (Walter Mycroft)

A band leader who croons falls for the boss of an all-ladies orchestra.

Fairly slick light musical fare of its period.

w Roger Burford, Jack Davies, Denis Waldock   d Marcel Varnel   ph Bryan Langley   md Harry Acres   ad David Rawnsley   ed Sidney Cole

Buddy Rogers, June Clyde, Fred Duprez, Richard Hearne, Steve Geray, Magda Kun

'Popular entertainment from start to finish, cut to a point where there is hardly a draggy moment.' – *Variety*

Dance Fools Dance
US   1931   82m   bw
MGM
V*

A lady reporter in Chicago proves her worth.

Bizarrely-titled gangster thriller based on the Jake Lingle killing. Very moderate of its kind.

w Richard Schayer, Aurania Rouverol   d Harry Beaumont   ph Charles Rosher

Joan Crawford, Lester Vail, Cliff Edwards, William Bakewell, William Holden (the other one), Clark Gable, Earle Foxe, Joan Marsh

'It will rock the b.o. . .. sex, romance, punch, suspense, and everything a deluxer can sell.' – *Variety*

Dance Girl Dance *
US 1940 88m bw
RKO (Erich Pommer)
V*, L

Private problems of the members of a night-club dance troupe.

Competent and sometimes interesting formula drama with a harder edge than usual.

w Tess Slesinger, Frank Davis *story* Vicki Baum
d *Dorothy Arzner* ph Russell Metty m Edward Ward

Maureen O'Hara, Louis Hayward, Lucille Ball, Maria Ouspenskaya, Ralph Bellamy, Virginia Field, Mary Carlisle, Walter Abel, Edward Brophy, Harold Huber

Dance Hall
US 1941 73m bw
Sol M. Wurtzel/TCF

A ballroom singer is chased by the manager.

Slim romantic drama.

w Stanley Rauh, Ethel Hill *novel* W. R. Burnett
d Irving Pichel

Carole Landis, Cesar Romero, J. Edward Bromberg, William Henry, June Storey, Charles Halton

Dance Hall *
GB 1950 80m bw
Ealing (Michael Balcon, E. V. H. Emmett)
V*

Four factory girls seek relaxation and various kinds of romance at the local palais.

Untypically flat Ealing slice of life, now watchable only with a smile as musical nostalgia.

w E. V. H. Emmett, Diana Morgan, Alexander Mackendrick d Charles Crichton ph Douglas Slocombe md Ernest Irving m Joyce Cochran ed Seth Holt

Natasha Parry, Donald Houston, Diana Dors, Bonar Colleano, Jane Hylton, Petula Clark, Gladys Henson, Sydney Tafler; the bands of Geraldo and Ted Heath

'Not a film that will please everyone. Its story is tiresome and not varied enough for the length of the picture.' – A. Jympson Harman

Dance Little Lady
GB 1954 87m Eastmancolor
George Minter/Renown

An ambitious man tries to turn his balletomane daughter into a film star.

Artless melodrama in poor colour.

w Val Guest, Doreen Montgomery d Val Guest

Terence Morgan, Mai Zetterling, Mandy Miller, Guy Rolfe, Eunice Gayson

The Dance of Death *
GB 1968 149m Technicolor
BHE/National Theatre (John Brabourne)

Edgar and Alice live alone on an island, their marriage having become a constant war.

Too-literal film transcription of an applauded theatrical production, with the camera anchored firmly in the middle of the stalls.

w August Strindberg (*translation* C. D. Locock)
d David Giles ph Geoffrey Unsworth

Laurence Olivier, Geraldine McEwan, Robert Lang, Carolyn Jones

Dance of the Vampires: see *The Fearless Vampire Killers*

Dance Pretty Lady
GB 1932 64m bw
British Instructional (H. Bruce Woolfe)

Ballerina loves artist but settles unwisely for respectability.

Stilted early talkie from Compton Mackenzie's *Carnival*, qv under its own title.

wd Anthony Asquith ph Jack Parker m John Reynders ad Ian Campbell-Gray

Ann Casson, Carl Harbord, Michael Hogan

Dance Team
US 1931 80m bw
Fox

Struggles of a couple to become top ballroom dancers.

Easy-going star fare which needed tightening.

w Edwin Burke *novel* Sarah Addington d Sidney Lanfield

James Dunn, Sally Eilers, Minna Gombell, Ralph Morgan

'Its comedy overcomes drawn-out sequences laden with sentimentality.' – *Variety*

Dance with a Stranger *
GB 1985 101m Technicolor
Goldcrest/NFFC/First Picture Co (Roger Randall-Cutler)
V, V*, L

Ex-prostitute Ruth Ellis, infatuated with a worthless sponger, shoots him dead rather than lose him.

Muddled account of the last woman to hang in Great Britain; no sympathies are aroused and no clear viewpoint taken.

w Shelagh Delaney d Mike Newell ph Peter Hannan m Richard Hartley pd Andrew Mollo ed Mick Audsley

Miranda Richardson, Rupert Everett, Ian Holm, Matthew Carroll, Stratford Johns

Dancers
US 1987 99m colour
Cannon/Hera/Baryshnikov/Golan/Globus
V*, L, S

On tour in Italy, a leading dancer recovers his inspiration when a young ballerina joins the company.

Trite script, dull romance and moments of exciting dance.

w Sara Kernochan d Herbert Ross ph Ennio Guarieri m Pino Donnagio pd Gianni Quaranta ed William Reynolds

Mikhail Baryshnikov, Alessandra Ferri, Leslie Browne, Thomas Rall, Lynn Seymour, Victor Barbee, Julie Kent

Dancers in the Dark
US 1932 76m bw
Paramount

A nightclub dancer with a shady past tries to prove that she's really in love.

Banal show business melodrama with authentic-seeming night-club background.

w Herman J. Mankiewicz d David Burton

Miriam Hopkins, Jack Oakie, George Raft, William Collier Jnr, Lyda Roberti, Eugene Pallette

'Only fair for Times Square, looks surefire in the hinterland.' – *Variety*

Dances with Wolves **
US 1990 180m DeLuxe Panavision
Guild/Tig Productions/Jim Wilson, Kevin Costner
V, V (W), V*, L, S

A cavalry officer is adopted by the Sioux Indians.

A liberal Western – the Indians (or Native Americans) are the good guys – sentimental and over-long, but nonetheless affecting. A version of 'the director's cut' was promised for videocassette, with a running time of 240 minutes.

w Michael Blake *novel* Michael Blake d Kevin Costner ph Dean Semler m John Barry pd Jeffrey Beecroft ad William Ladd Skinner ed Neil Travis

Kevin Costner, Mary McDonnell, Graham Greene, Rodney A. Grant, Floyd Red Crow Westerman, Tantoo Cardinal, Robert Pastorelli, Charles Rocket, Maury Chaykin, Jimmy Herman, Nathan Lee Chasing His Horse

'*Dances with Wolves* would be easier to love if screenwriter Blake had resisted the temptation to plug every positive stereotype about Native Americans. The characters, alternately stoic, are ecologically aware and brave. Even Hollywood Indians don't have to be like this.' – Michael Dorris, Premiere

'Long, simplistic and lacking in irony, though not in pawky humour. The action set-pieces (two ambushes, two pitched battles, a grand buffalo hunt) are dynamically handled. But the picture lacks the visual and dramatic authority of the best Westerns.' – Philip French, Observer

'Costner has feathers in his hair and feathers in his head.' – Pauline Kael

† A special edition of the film with an extra 53 minutes added was given a London cinema release in 1991.

AA: best film; Kevin Costner (as director); Michael Blake; John Barry; Dean Semler; Neil Travis; best sound

AAN: Kevin Costner (as actor); Mary McDonnell; Graham Greene; best costume design; best art direction

Dancin' Thru the Dark **
GB 1990 95m colour
Palace/BBC Films/Formost Films (Andre Molyneux)
V, S

On the night before her wedding, a woman goes out with her girl-friends for a celebration at a night-club, only to meet there her former lover, now a successful rock singer, and her fiancé, drunk from his stag-night party.

High-spirited and witty domestic drama.

w Willy Russell *play Stags and Hens* by Willy Russell d Mike Ockrent ph Philip Bonham-Carter m Willy Russell pd Paul Joel

Claire Hackett, Con O'Neill, Angela Clarke, Mark Womack, Julia Deakin, Simon O'Brien, Louise Duprey, Andrew Naylor, Sandy Hendrickse, Peter Watts

'A satisfying and enjoyable work.' – *Variety*

Dancing Co-ed
US 1939 90m bw
MGM (Edgar Selwyn)
GB title: *Every Other Inch a Lady*

A college girl makes it in show business as well as the groves of academe.

Mindless vehicle for a 19-year-old star.

w Albert Mannheimer *story* Albert Treynor d S. Sylvan Simon ph Alfred Gilks m David Snell, Edward Ward

Lana Turner, Richard Carlson, Artie Shaw, *Leon Errol*, Ann Rutherford, Lee Bowman, Monty Woolley, Roscoe Karns, June Preisser, Walter Kingsford

'Better than average programme entertainment.' – *Variety*

Dancing Fool: see *Harold Teen*

Dancing in the Dark *

US   1949   92m   Technicolor
TCF (George Jessel)

A silent movie idol makes a comeback as a talent scout, and spots his own daughter.

Thin but unusual Hollywood drama with music; in the long run too sentimental.

w Mary C. McCall Jnr   play The Band Wagon by George S. Kaufman, Howard Dietz, Arthur Schwartz   d Irving Reis   ph Harry Jackson   m Alfred Newman

William Powell, Adolphe Menjou, Mark Stevens, Betsy Drake, Hope Emerson, Lloyd Corrigan, Walter Catlett, Jean Hersholt

Dancing Lady *

US   1933   94m   bw
MGM (David O. Selznick)
V*, L

A successful dancer chooses between a playboy and her stage manager.

Routine backstage semi-musical with interesting talent applied rather haphazardly.

w Allen Rivkin, P. J. Wolfson   novel James Warner Bellah   d Robert Z. Leonard   ph Oliver T. Marsh   md Louis Silvers   m various

Joan Crawford, Clark Gable, Fred Astaire, Franchot Tone, May Robson, Ted Healy and his Stooges (the Three Stooges), Winnie Lightner, Robert Benchley, Nelson Eddy

'Very potent b.o. in the screen musical cycle.' – Variety

The Dancing Masters

US   1943   63m   bw
TCF (Lee Marcus)
V

Laurel and Hardy run a ballet school, and get involved with gangsters and inventors.

Insubstantial star comedy featuring reworkings of old routines, and a back-projected runaway bus climax.

w Scott Darling, George Bricker   d Mal St Clair   ph Norbert Brodine   m Arthur Lange   ad James Basevi, Chester Gore   ed Norman Colbert

Stan Laurel, Oliver Hardy, Trudy Marshall, Bob Bailey, Margaret Dumont, Matt Briggs, Robert Mitchum

Dancing with Crime

GB   1947   83m   bw
Coronet-Alliance (James Carter)

A dance hall is the front for black marketeers, who are exposed by a resourceful taxi driver.

Tolerable post-war melodrama aping Hollywood.

w Brock Williams   story Peter Fraser   d John Paddy Carstairs

Richard Attenborough, Barry K. Barnes, Sheila Sim, Garry Marsh, John Warwick, Barry Jones

The Dancing Years

GB   1949   97m   Technicolor
ABPC (Warwick Ward)

A composer loves a singer who leaves him after a misunderstanding but later bears his son . . . all in the Alps pre-1914.

Lamentable transcription of an operetta; precisely the ingredients which worked so well on stage seem embarrassing on film, and the performances and direction do not help.

w Warwick Ward, Jack Whittingham   operetta Ivor Novello   d Harold French   ph Stephen Dade   m Ivor Novello

Dennis Price. Gisèle Préville, Patricia Dainton, Anthony Nicholls, Grey Blake, Muriel George, Olive Gilbert

Dandy Dick

GB   1935   72m   bw
BIP (Walter Mycroft)

A country vicar becomes innocently involved with racehorse doping.

Flatly-handled farce which helped to introduce Will Hay to the screen, though not in his accustomed role.

w William Beaudine, Frank Miller, Clifford Grey, Will Hay   play Sir Arthur Wing Pinero   d William Beaudine   ph Jack Parker   ad Duncan Sutherland   ed A. C. Hammond

Will Hay, Nancy Burne, Esmond Knight, Davy Burnaby

'His mission is murder! His victim – himself!'

A Dandy in Aspic

GB   1968   107m   Technicolor   Panavision
Columbia (Anthony Mann)
V*, L

A double agent in Berlin is given orders to kill himself.

Muddled, pretentious spy thriller; flat, nebulous and boring.

w Derek Marlowe   novel Derek Marlowe   d Anthony Mann   ph Christopher Challis   m Quincy Jones

Laurence Harvey, Tom Courtenay, Lionel Stander, Mia Farrow, Harry Andrews, Peter Cook, Per Oscarsson

† Anthony Mann died during shooting, and Laurence Harvey completed the direction.

Dandy the All-American Girl

US   1976   90m   Metrocolor   Panavision
MGM
GB title: Sweet Revenge

A much convicted woman car thief determines to become the legitimate owner of a Dino Ferrari.

The American dream gone sour again, this time offering in its wake a curious stream of moral values.

w B. J. Perla, Marilyn Goldin   d Jerry Schatzberg

Stockard Channing, Sam Waterston, Richard Doughty, Franklin Ajaye

Danger: Diabolik

Italy/France   1967   105m   Technicolor
Dino de Laurentiis/Marianne (Bruno Todini)
V*

International police bait a golden trap for a master criminal.

Superior Batman-type adventures with a comic strip hero-villain.

w Dino Maiuri, Adriano Baracco, Mario Bava   d Mario Bava   ph Antonio Rinaldi   m Ennio Morricone

John Phillip Law, Marisa Mell, Michel Piccoli, Adolfo Celi, Terry-Thomas

Danger Island

US   1931   bw   serial: 12 eps
Universal

A radium deposit on an African island attracts adventurers of all kinds.

Modest serial excitements.

d Ray Taylor

Kenneth Harlan, Lucile Browne, Tom Ricketts

Danger Lights *

US   1930   87m   bw
RKO
V*

Railroad owners face various problems.

Routine would-be thriller intended to show off a wide screen system called Spoor-Bergen Natural

Vision; it failed owing to cost and the thin quality of the film.

w James Ashmore Creelman   d George B. Seitz

Louis Wolheim, Robert Armstrong, Jean Arthur, Hugh Herbert

Danger, Love at Work *

US   1937   84m   bw
TCF (Harold Wilson)

A young lawyer needs the signature of a rich crazy family to conclude a land sale.

The title doesn't suggest it, but this is a not inconsiderable comedy in the tradition of My Man Godfrey and You Can't Take It With You. A highly competent cast does its best.

w James Edward Grant, Ben Markson   d Otto Preminger   ph Virgil Miller   md David Buttolph

Ann Sothern, Jack Haley, Edward Everett Horton, Mary Boland, Walter Catlett, John Carradine, Maurice Cass, Alan Dinehart, E. E. Clive

'Not important enough to be a main feature but a very good dualler.' – Variety

Danger Route

GB   1967   92m   DeLuxe
UA/Amicus (Max J. Rosenberg, Milton Subotsky)

An 'eliminator' for the British secret service finds after a series of adventures that he must dispose of his own girlfriend.

Dour sub-Bondian thriller with little to commend it.

w Meade Roberts   novel The Eliminator by Andrew York   d Seth Holt   ph Harry Waxman   m John Mayer

Richard Johnson, Diana Dors, Sylvia Syms, Carol Lynley, Barbara Bouchet, Gordon Jackson, Sam Wanamaker, Maurice Denham, Harry Andrews

Danger Signal

US   1945   77m   bw
Warner (William Jacobs)

A smooth heel implicated in murder charms a modest stenographer and her mother.

Tedious and less than competent melodrama.

w Adele Comandini, Graham Baker   novel Phyllis Bottome   d Robert Florey

Faye Emerson, Zachary Scott, Dick Erdman, Rosemary de Camp, Bruce Bennett, Mona Freeman

'Four hundred plan to escape – one plans to betray!'

Danger Within **

GB   1958   101m   bw
British Lion/Colin Lesslie
US title: Breakout

Escape plans of officers in a prisoner-of-war camp are threatened by an informer.

Familiar comedy and melodrama with an added whodunnit element, smartly handled and very entertaining.

w Bryan Forbes, Frank Harvey   novel Michael Gilbert   d Don Chaffey   ph Arthur Grant   m Francis Chagrin

Richard Todd, Bernard Lee, Michael Wilding, Richard Attenborough, Dennis Price, Donald Houston, William Franklyn, Vincent Ball, Peter Arne

Dangerous *

US   1935   78m   bw
Warner (Harry Joe Brown)
V*, L

An alcoholic actress is rehabilitated.

Unconvincing and only adequately handled melodrama which won the star her first Oscar, presumably from sympathy at her losing it the previous year for Of Human Bondage.

w Laird Doyle   *d* Alfred E. Green   *ph* Ernest Haller

Bette Davis, Franchot Tone, Margaret Lindsay, Alison Skipworth, John Eldredge, Dick Foran

'Well-acted and directed drama with *femme* appeal.' – *Variety*

† Remade 1941 as *Singapore Woman.*

AA: Bette Davis

Dangerous Blondes

US   1943   81m   bw
Columbia (Samuel Bischoff)

A detective story writer and his wife solve a real life murder.

More *Thin Man* imitations, rather tepid this time.

w Richard Flournoy and Jack Henley   *d* Leigh Jason

Allyn Joslyn, Evelyn Keyes, John Hubbard, Edmund Lowe, Anita Louise, Frank Craven, William Demarest

Dangerous Corner *

US   1934   67m   bw
RKO
V*

After dinner conversation reveals what might have been if friends had spoken the truth about a long-ago suicide.

A fascinating trick play makes interesting but scarcely sparkling cinema.

w Anne Morrison Chapin, Madeleine Ruthven
play J. B. Priestley   *d* Phil Rosen   *ph* J. Roy Hunt
m Max Steiner

Melvyn Douglas, Conrad Nagel, Virginia Bruce, Erin O'Brien Moore, Ian Keith, Betty Furness, Henry Wadsworth

'Confusing mixture of a mystery and problem play . . . doubtful as to general fan appeal.' – *Variety*

Dangerous Crossing *

US   1953   75m   bw
TCF (Robert Bassler)

At the start of an Atlantic sea voyage a woman's husband disappears, and she is assured that he never existed. He does, and is trying to murder her.

Adequately handled twist on the vanishing lady story: grade A production covers lapses of grade B imagination.

w Leo Townsend   *story* John Dickson Carr
d Joseph M. Newman   *ph* Joseph LaShelle
md Lionel Newman

Jeanne Crain, Michael Rennie, Carl Betz, Casey Adams, Mary Anderson, Willis Bouchey

Dangerous Curves

US   1929   75m   bw
Paramount
V

A bareback rider loves a high wire artist.

Obvious circus melodrama, a modest star vehicle.

w Donald Davis, Florence Ryerson   *d* Lothar Mendes   *ph* Harry Fischbeck

Clara Bow, Richard Arlen, Kay Francis, David Newell, Anders Randolf

Dangerous Days: see *Wild Boys of the Road*

Dangerous Exile

GB   1957   90m   Eastmancolor   Vistavision
Rank (George H. Brown)

After the French Revolution, the young would-be Louis XVII is brought across the Channel and hidden in Pembrokeshire, where enemies attack him.

Historical romance, ineptly plotted but quite well produced.

w Robin Estridge   *novel* Vaughan Wilkins   *d* Brian Desmond Hurst   *ph* Geoffrey Unsworth   *m* Georges Auric

Louis Jourdan, Belinda Lee, Keith Michell, Richard O'Sullivan, Martita Hunt, Finlay Currie, Anne Heywood, Jacques Brunius

Dangerous Female: see *The Maltese Falcon* (1931)

A Dangerous Game

US   1941   61m   bw
Universal

Various weird characters converge on a lunatic asylum where a fortune is hidden.

Failed attempt at black farce: the actors are game, but the material doesn't hold water.

w Larry Rhine, Ben Chapman, Maxwell Shane
d John Rawlins

Richard Arlen, Andy Devine, Jeanne Kelly, Edward Brophy, Marc Lawrence, Andrew Tombes, Tom Dugan

'For all its frantic, deafening slapstick it remains stubbornly humourless . . . if there's such a thing as a Class D picture, this is it.' – *Variety*

Dangerous Liaisons **

US   1988   120m   Eastmancolor
Warner/Lorimar/NFH (Norma Heyman, Hank Moonjean)
V, V*, L, S

Two jaded French aristocrats play games of sexual politics.

A cool dissection of sexual feeling.

w Christopher Hampton   *play* Christopher Hampton
novel Choderlos de Laclos   *d* Stephen Frears
ph Philippe Rousselot   *m* George Fenton
pd Stuart Craig   *ed* Mick Audsley

Glenn Close, John Malkovich, Michelle Pfeiffer, Swoosie Kurtz, Keanu Reeves, Mildred Natwick, Uma Thurman

'Beautifully acted (by Glenn Close in particular), elegantly phrased, carefully shot on location in an appropriate selection of chateaux, directed with a limpidly formalised serenity, it's a handsome and intelligent piece of work.' – *Tom Milne, MFB*

AA: Christopher Hampton; Stuart Craig

AAN: best picture; Glenn Close; Michelle Pfeiffer; George Fenton

Dangerous Millions

US   1946   69m   bw
TCF
GB title: *The House of Tao Ling*

Eight would-be inheritors of a millionaire's estate find themselves at the mercy of a warlord in the Chinese mountains.

Odd little second feature confusion of *The Cat and the Canary* and *Shanghai Express;* quite watchable.

w Irving Cummings Jnr, Robert G. North   *d* James Tinling

Kent Taylor, Dona Drake, Tala Birell, Leonard Strong, Konstantin Shayne

Dangerous Mission

US   1954   75m   Technicolor   3-D
RKO (Irwin Allen)

In Montana's Glacier National Park, a policeman tries to protect an innocent girl witness from big city gangsters.

Tolerable routine double-bill thriller with a predictable cable car climax.

w Horace McCoy, W. R. Burnett, Charles Bennett, James Edmiston   *d* Louis King   *ph* William Snyder   *m* Roy Webb

Victor Mature, Piper Laurie, Vincent Price, William Bendix, Betta St John, Dennis Weaver

'The scenery received the best notices.' – *James Robert Parish, 1976*

'This is your melody – you gave it to me. I'll never play it again without thinking of you!'

Dangerous Moonlight *

GB   1941   98m   bw
RKO (William Sistrom)
V*
US title: *Suicide Squadron*

A Polish pianist escapes from the Nazis and loses his memory after flying in the Battle of Britain.

Immensely popular wartime romance which introduced Richard Addinsell's *Warsaw Concerto.* Production values and script somewhat below par.

w Shaun Terence Young, Brian Desmond Hurst, Rodney Ackland   *d* Brian Desmond Hurst
ph Georges Périnal, Ronald Neame   *m* Richard Addinsell

Anton Walbrook, Sally Gray, Derrick de Marney, Cecil Parker, Percy Parsons, Kenneth Kent, Guy Middleton, John Laurie, Frederick Valk

Dangerous Moves

Switzerland   1985   100m   colour
Enterprise/Spectrafilm (Arthur Cohn)
V*

The world championship chess showdown is between the Soviet title holder and an exiled dissident challenger.

Interesting, rather specialized actor's piece with political overtones.

wd Richard Dembo   *ph* Raoul Coutard   *m* Gabriel Yared   *ad* Ivan Maussion   *ed* Agnès Guillemot

Michel Piccoli, Leslie Caron, Liv Ullmann, Alexandre Arbatt

AA: best foreign film

Dangerous Number *

US   1937   71m   bw
MGM

A showgirl is confused by her husband's rich relations.

Rather tedious comedy drama which never really gets anywhere.

w Carey Wilson   *story* Leona Dalrymple   *d* Richard Thorpe

Robert Young, Ann Sothern, Reginald Owen, Cora Witherspoon, Dean Jagger, Barnett Parker

'A compact piece of entertainment, though pretty shallow on the drama end.' – *Variety*

Dangerous Partners

US   1945   74m   bw
Arthur J. Field/MGM

Nazi agents trying to get out of America are converted to democracy.

Bewildering mixture of propaganda and melodrama: nothing seems to mesh.

w Marion Parsonnet, Edmund L. Hartmann
story Oliver Weld Bayer   *d* Edward L. Cahn

James Craig, Signe Hasso, Edmund Gwenn, Audrey Totter, Mabel Paige

A Dangerous Profession

US   1949   79m   bw
RKO

An ex-detective tries to help a beautiful woman and becomes involved in murder and the bail bond racket.

Undistinguished crime melodrama providing a satisfactory vehicle for its stars.

w Martin Rackin, Warren Duff   *d* Ted Tetzlaff

Pat O'Brien, George Raft, Ella Raines, Jim Backus, Bill Williams

A Dangerous Summer
Australia 1982 94m colour Panavision
McElroy and McElroy
V*

In a Blue Mountain resort, a partner decides to burn
down the buildings for the insurance.

Modest melodrama with spectacular fire sequences.

w David Ambrose, Quentin Masters novel Kit
Denton d Quentin Masters

James Mason, Tom Skerritt, Ian Gilmour, Wendy
Hughes, Kim Deacon

Dangerous to Know *
US 1938 70m bw
Paramount

A ruthless Chicago gangster comes a cropper when
his Chinese mistress discovers he has fallen for a
socialite.

Flatly handled but mildly interesting adaptation of a
highly successful play, the potential of which seems
to have been thrown away.

w William R. Lippmann, Horace McCoy play On the
Spot by Edgar Wallace d Robert Florey
ph Theodor Sparkuhl

Akim Tamiroff, Anna May Wong, Gail Patrick, Lloyd
Nolan, Harvey Stephens, Anthony Quinn, Porter Hall

Dangerous When Wet **
US 1953 95m Technicolor
MGM (George Wells)
V*, L

An entire Arkansas family is sponsored to swim the
English Channel.

A bright and lively vehicle for an aquatic star, who in
one sequence swims with Tom and Jerry. Amusing
sequences give opportunities to a strong cast.

w Dorothy Kingsley d Charles Walters ph Harold
Rosson md George Stoll m/ly Johnny Mercer,
Arthur Schwartz

Esther Williams, Charlotte Greenwood, William Demarest,
Fernando Lamas, Jack Carson, Denise Darcel, Barbara
Whiting

Dangerous Youth: see These Dangerous Years

Dangerously They Live
US 1941 77m bw
Warner (Ben Stoloff)

American Nazi agents try to get a secret memorized by
a British girl agent injured in a car crash.

Watchable, routine spy propaganda fare.

w Marion Parsonnet d Robert Florey ph William
O'Connell

John Garfield, Raymond Massey, Nancy Coleman,
Moroni Olsen, Lee Patrick, Christian Rub, Frank
Reicher

Dangerously Yours
US 1933 74m bw
Fox

A gentleman crook falls for a lady detective.

Ho-hum society crook drama.

w Horace Jackson story Paul Hervey Fox d Frank
Tuttle

Warner Baxter, Miriam Jordan, Herbert Mundin,
Florence Eldridge, Florence Roberts, Mischa Auer

'None too potent.' – Variety

Dangerously Yours
US 1937 60m bw
TCF (Sol M. Wurtzel)

On board ship a detective captures a lady jewel thief
but reforms her.

Very tolerable programme filler with watchable
performances.

w Lou Breslow, John Patrick d Mal St Clair
ph Harry Davis md Samuel Kaylin

Cesar Romero, Phyllis Brooks, Jane Darwell, Alan
Dinehart, Douglas Wood, Leon Ames

'Fox is turning out a pretty good quality of B product.'
– Variety

Dangers of the Canadian Mounted
US 1948 bw serial: 12 eps
Republic

Mounties and outlaws clash over the discovery of
ancient Chinese treasure.

Standard serial heroics with a high proportion of
action highlights.

d Fred Brannon, Yakima Canutt

Jim Bannon, Virginia Belmont, Anthony Warde,
Dorothy Granger

Daniel
US 1983 129m Technicolor
World Film Services (John Van Eyssen)
V*

The children of executed spies are traumatized by the
past.

Patchwork vision of thirties America, with
Jewishness thrown in for added weight. Not easy to
watch.

w E. L. Doctorow novel The Book of Daniel by E. L.
Doctorow d Sidney Lumet ph Andrzej
Bartkowiak m Bob James pd Philip Rosenberg

Timothy Hutton, Mandy Patinkin, Lindsay Crouse, Ed
Asner, Ellen Barkin, Tovah Feldshuh

'Only with the last scene does one realize that it has
collapsed into an empty liberal squeak.' – Tom Milne,
MFB

Daniel and the Devil: see All That Money Can Buy

Danny Boy
GB 1941 80m bw
Butcher's

A singer searches for her estranged husband and
small son who have become street entertainers.

Sentimental drama with music; not for the critical.

w Oswald Mitchell, A. Barr-Carson d Oswald
Mitchell

Ann Todd, Wilfrid Lawson, Grant Tyler, John
Warwick, David Farrar

Danny Boy: see Angel (1982)

Danny the Champion of the World *
GB 1989 99m colour
Portobello Productions (Eric Abraham)
V

A poacher's son devises a plan to discomfit the
obnoxious squire.

Pleasant film aimed at a family audience, if it still
exists.

w John Goldsmith novel Roald Dahl d Gavin
Millar ph Oliver Stapleton m Stanley Myers
pd Don Homfray ed Peter Tanner, Angus Newton

Jeremy Irons, Robbie Coltrane, Samuel Irons, Cyril
Cusack, Michael Hordern, Lionel Jeffries, Ronald
Pickup, Jean Marsh, Jimmy Nail, William Armstrong,
John Woodvine

Dans la Poussière du Soleil: see Lust in the Sun

Dans la Ville Blanche: see In the White City

Dante's Inferno **
US 1935 89m bw
Fox (Sol M. Wurtzel)

A ruthless carnival owner gets too big for his boots,
and has a vision of hell induced by one of his own
attractions.

Curiously unpersuasive melodrama with a moral, but
the inferno sequence is one of the most unexpected,
imaginative and striking pieces of cinema in
Hollywood's history.

w Philip Klein, Robert Yost d Harry Lachmann
ph Rudolph Maté m Hugo Friedhofer, Samuel
Kaylin, R. H. Bassett, Peter Brunelli sp Fred F. Sersen,
Ralph Hammeras, sets Willy Pogany, from drawings by
Gustav Doré

Spencer Tracy, Claire Trevor, Henry B. Walthall, Alan
Dinehart, Scotty Beckett, Rita Hayworth (her first
appearance, as a dancer)

'A pushover for vigorous exploitation . . . accentuate
the inferno sequence and forget the rest, including the
story.' – Variety

'We depart gratefully, having seen papier mâché
photographed in more ways than we had thought
possible.' – Robert Herring

'One of the most unusual and effectively presented
films of the thirties.' – John Baxter, 1968

'The spectacle is shattering.' – Sunday Times

'Immediately following the 10-minute picturization of
Hell, the story reverts to its native dullness.' – Variety

Danton *
France/Poland 1982 136m colour
Losange/Group X (for Gaumont/TFI)
V, V*, L

Robespierre quarrels with his colleague Danton, who
hopes for a new spirit of tolerance.

Vivid historical re-creation which finally exhausts the
spectator and is a little too concerned to make political
points.

w Jean-Claude Carrière play The Danton Affair by
Stanislawa Przybyszewska d Andrzej Wajda
ph Igor Luther m Jean Prodromides

Gérard Depardieu, Wojciech Pszoniak, Anne Alvaro,
Roland Blanche

'The temptation to see it in terms of Solidarity is
unavoidable.' – Philip Strick, MFB

'By any reasonable standard, terrible.' – New Yorker

BFA: best foreign-language film

Danzón *
Spain 1991 96m colour
Metro/Instituto Mexicano Cinematografia/Macondo Cine
  Video/Fondo de Fomento a la Calidad Cinematografia/
  Televisión Española/Tabasco/Gobierno del Estado de
  Veracruz (Jorge Sanchez)
V, S

A telephone operator goes in search of her ballroom
dancing partner, who has fled Mexico City after being
accused of a crime, and finds new friends and
excitement before returning home.

Slight but charming film of a woman finding herself.

w Beatriz Navaro, Maria Novaro d Maria Novaro
ph Rodrigo Garcia ad Marisa Pecarlins, Noberto
Sanchez-Mejorada ed Nelson Rodriguez, Maria
Novaro

Maria Rojo, Carmen Salinas, Bianca Guerra, Tito
Vasconcelos, Victor Carpinteiro, Margarita Isabel

'Despite its lack of pace, and sometimes because of it,
this is a lovely film which will remain in the memory
longer than most.' – Derek Malcolm, Guardian

Darby O'Gill and the Little People *
US 1959 90m Technicolor
Walt Disney
V*, L

An Irish caretaker falls down a well and is captured by leprechauns, who allow him three wishes to rearrange his life.

Pleasantly barmy Irish fantasy with brilliant trick work but some tedium in between.

w Lawrence Edward Watkin   stories H. T. Kavanagh   d Robert Stevenson   ph Winton C. Hoch   m Oliver Wallace   sp Peter Ellenshaw, Eustace Lycett, Joshua Meador

Albert Sharpe, Jimmy O'Dea, Sean Connery, Janet Munro, Kieron Moore, Estelle Winwood, Walter Fitzgerald, Denis O'Dea, J. G. Devlin, Jack MacGowran

'One of the best fantasies ever put on film.' – Leonard Maltin

Darby's Rangers
US   1957   121m   bw
Warner (Martin Rackin)
V*
GB title: The Young Invaders

A tough American commando unit is trained in Britain before seeing action in Africa and Sicily.

Standard World War II actioner, adequately executed.

w Guy Trosper   book Major James Altieri   d William Wellman   ph William H. Clothier   m Max Steiner

James Garner, Etchika Choureau, Jack Warden, Edward Byrnes, Venetia Stevenson, Torin Thatcher, Stuart Whitman, Andrea King, Frieda Inescort, Reginald Owen, Adam Williams

Daredevils of the Red Circle
US   1939   bw   serial: 12 eps
Republic

Three college athletes foil the dastardly plans of an ex-convict impersonating a powerful businessman.

No-holds-barred serial adventures with an unusual array of familiar faces.

d William Witney, John English

Charles Quigley, Carole Landis, Herman Brix, David Sharpe, Miles Mander, Charles Middleton, Raymond Bailey

Daredevils of the West
US   1943   bw   serial: 12 eps
Republic

Duke Cameron foils a plot to ruin the Foster Stage Line.

Unremarkable serial exploits.

d John English

Allan Lane, Kay Aldridge, Eddie Acuff, William Haade, Robert Frazer

The Daring Game
US   1967   101m   Eastmancolor
Paramount/Tors (Gene Levitt)
V*

A commercial group experiments with airborne and underwater inventions, and rescues a scientist from a police state.

Well photographed but haphazardly assembled adventures, aimed at TV.

w Andy White   d Laslo Benedek   ph Edmund Gibson   m George Bruns

Lloyd Bridges, Nico Minardos, Joan Blackman, Michael Ansara

The Dark
US   1979   92m   DeLuxe   Panavision
Film Ventures International (Dick Clark, Edward L. Montoro)
V*

A homicidal alien stalks Los Angeles, ripping off people's heads.

Unconsidered shocker with nothing to it but the shocks.

w Stanford Whitmore   d John Cardos   ph John Morrill   m Roger Kellaway   ad Rusty Rosene   ed Martin Dreffke

William Devane, Cathy Lee Crosby, Richard Jaeckel, Keenan Wynn, Vivian Blaine

The Dark: see The Haunted House of Horror

The Dark Angel *
US   1925   83m (24 fps)   bw   silent
First National (Samuel Goldwyn)

During World War I, a blinded officer tries to persuade his fiancée to marry another man, without her knowing of his own infirmity.

Vilma Banky's first American film, her first teaming with Colman and a mid-twenties hit of colossal proportions.

w Frances Marion   play Guy Bolton   d George Fitzmaurice   ph George Barnes

Ronald Colman, Vilma Banky, Wyndham Standing, Frank Elliott, Charles Lane, Florence Turner, Helen Jerome Eddy

The Dark Angel *
US   1935   105m   bw
Samuel Goldwyn

Tearstained melodrama from another age (see above), neatly packaged for the romantic 1935 public.

w Lillian Hellman, Mordaunt Shairp   d Sidney Franklin   ph Gregg Toland   m Alfred Newman   ad Richard Day

Merle Oberon, Fredric March, Herbert Marshall, Janet Beecher, John Halliday, Henrietta Crosman, Frieda Inescort, George Breakston, Claud Allister

'A sockaroo woman's picture.' – Variety

'A highly literate screen adaptation, telling the story with feeling and good taste.' – New York Times

'It makes a systematic and skilful appeal to those untrustworthy emotions which may suddenly cause the most hardened intellects to dissolve before the most obvious sentimentality.' – The Times

AA: Richard Day

AAN: Merle Oberon

'Good Cop. Bad Alien. Big Trouble.'
Dark Angel *
US   1990   93m   DeLuxe
Vision/Damon/Saunders (Jeff Young)
V, V*, L
US title: I Come in Peace

A maverick cop and the FBI chase after a killer from another planet.

A cut above the usual aliens-on-the-rampage action, thanks to occasional wit and a narrative with unexpected twists.

w Jonathan Tydor, Leonard Maas Jnr   d Craig R. Baxley   ph Mark Irwin   m Jan Hammer   pd Philip M. Leonard   ad Nino Candido   ed Mark Helfrich

Dolph Lundgren, Brain Benben, Betsy Brantley, Matthias Hues, Jay Bilas, Jim Haynie, David Ackroyd, Sherman Howard, Sam Anderson

'This undemanding cinematic comic book may come in peace but doesn't seem likely to go all that quietly.' – Variety

'Every time a woman turns her face away because she's tired or unwilling, there's someone waiting like me ...'
The Dark at the Top of the Stairs **
US   1960   124m   Technicolor
Warner (Michael Garrison)

Twenties small town drama about a young boy's awakening to the sexual tensions around him.

Archetypal family drama set in that highly familiar American street. The perfect essence of this playwright's work, with high and low spots, several irrelevancies, and a real feeling for the people and the place.

w Harriet Frank Jnr, Irving Ravetch   play William Inge   d Delbert Mann   ph Harry Stradling   m Max Steiner

Robert Preston, Dorothy McGuire, Angela Lansbury, Eve Arden, Shirley Knight, Frank Overton, Lee Kinsolving, Robert Eyer

† The curious title turns out to be a synonym for life, which one should never be afraid of.

AAN: Shirley Knight

The Dark Avenger *
GB   1955   85m   Eastmancolor   Cinemascope
Allied Artists (Vaughan N. Dean)
V*
US title: The Warriors

The Black Prince quells some French rebels.

Good-humoured historical romp with the ageing star in his last swashbuckling role, helped by a good cast and brisk pace.

w Daniel B. Ullman   d Henry Levin   ph Guy Green   m Cedric Thorpe Davie

Errol Flynn, Peter Finch, Joanne Dru, Yvonne Furneaux, Patrick Holt, Michael Hordern, Moultrie Kelsall, Robert Urquhart, Noel Willman

Dark City
US   1950   97m   bw
Paramount/Hal B. Wallis

A bookmaker finds himself on the run from a revenge-seeking psychopath.

Unattractive and heavily-handled underworld melodrama, a disappointment from the talents involved.

w John Meredyth Lucas, Larry Marcus   d William Dieterle   ph Victor Milner   m Franz Waxman

Charlton Heston (his first Hollywood appearance), Lizabeth Scott, Viveca Lindfors, Dean Jagger, Don Defore, Jack Webb, Ed Begley, Henry Morgan, Mike Mazurki

'A jaded addition to a type of thriller which has become increasingly tedious and unreal.' – MFB

Dark Command *
US   1940   92m   bw
Republic (Sol C. Siegel)
V*

In pre-Civil War Kansas, an ambitious ex-schoolteacher named Cantrill organizes guerrilla bands to pillage the countryside.

Semi-historical hokum, quite well done with a good cast.

w Grover Jones, Lionel Houser, F. Hugh Herbert   novel W. R. Burnett   d Raoul Walsh   ph Jack Marta   m Victor Young   ad John Victor Mackay

John Wayne, Claire Trevor, Walter Pidgeon, Roy Rogers, George 'Gabby' Hayes, Porter Hall, Marjorie Main

'It's the highest budgeter for Republic to date, running in neighbourhood of 700,000 dollars in negative cost. In the family and action houses, it's a natural to roll up good grosses.' – Variety

AAN: Victor Young; art direction

The Dark Corner *
US   1946   98m   bw
TCF (Fred Kohlmar)
V*

A private eye with a criminal record thinks he is being menaced by an old adversary, but the latter is found murdered.

Moody, brutish, well-made thriller with a plot put together from bits and pieces of older, better movies, notably Clifton Webb's reprise of his *Laura* performance and William Bendix ditto *The Glass Key*.

w Jay Dratler, Bernard Schoenfeld   *story* Leo Rosten   d Henry Hathaway   *ph* Joe MacDonald   *m* Cyril Mockridge

Mark Stevens, Clifton Webb, Lucille Ball, William Bendix, Kurt Kreuger, Cathy Downs, Reed Hadley, Constance Collier

JARDINE (Clifton Webb): 'I hate the dawn. The grass always looks as though it's been left out all night.'
BRAD (Mark Stevens): 'There goes my last lead. I feel all dead inside. I'm backed up in a dark corner, and I don't know who's hitting me.'

'Not so much a whodunnit as a whodunnwhat . . . all seem bent on "getting" each other and their internecine plottings add up to an alpha thriller.' – *Daily Mail*

The Dark Crystal **
GB   1982   94m   Technicolor   Panavision
Universal/AFD/ITC (David Lazer)
V, V*, L

Two young people defeat the evil creatures who have taken over the world by replacing a shard which has been taken from the Dark Crystal.

Surprisingly effective piece of mysticism performed entirely by puppets from the Muppet stable.

w David Odell   d Jim Henson, Frank Oz   *conceptual designer* Brian Froud   *ph* Oswald Morris   *pd* Harry Lange   *ed* Ralph Kemplen

'A dazzling technological and artistic achievement . . . could teach a lesson in morality to youngsters at the same time as it is entertaining their parents.' – *Variety*

Dark Delusion
US   1947   90m   bw
MGM
GB title: *Cynthia's Secret*

A neurotic girl may have to be committed to an asylum.

Last episode of the Dr Gillespie series; not a sensation on its own account.

w Jack Andrews, Harry Ruskin   d Willis Goldbeck

Lionel Barrymore, James Craig, Lucille Bremer, Edward Arnold, Keye Luke

Dark Eyes: see *Black Eyes*

Dark Eyes of London *
GB   1939   75m   bw
Pathé/Argyle (John Argyle)
V, V*
US title: *The Human Monster*

The proprietor of a home for the blind uses a mute giant to drown insured victims.

Reasonably effective British horror, a rarity at the time.

w John Argyle, Walter Summers, Patrick Kirwan   *novel* Edgar Wallace   d Walter Summers   *ph* Bryan Langley   *m* Guy Jones   *ad* Duncan Sutherland   *ed* E. G. Richards

Bela Lugosi, Hugh Williams, Greta Gynt, Wilfrid Walter, Edmon Ryan

'Though it creaks a bit and some of the performances are stilted, this is actually one of Lugosi's better vehicles.' – *The Dark Side*

† It was the first British film to be given an H (for Horror) certificate.

Dark Habits
Spain   1983   100m   colour
Metro/Tesauro (Luis Calvo)
V*, L
original title: *Entre Tinieblas*

A drug-addicted singer takes refuge from the police in a convent full of decadent nuns.

High spirited, but for the easily amused only.

wd Pedro Almodovar   *ph* Angel L. Fernandez   m Cam España   *pd* Pin Morales, Roman Arango   *ed* Jose Salcedo

Cristina S. Pascual, Marisa Paredes, Mari Carrillo, Lina Canalejas, Manuel Zarzo, Carmen Maura, Chus Lampreave

'A rather labored series of jokes.' – *Pauline Kael, New Yorker*

The Dark Half
US   1991   122m   DeLuxe
Orion/Dark Half (Declan Baldwin)
V, V*, S

A writer has two personalities – one an unsuccessful novelist, the other a disreputable bestselling author who is also a killer.

A literary twist on Dr Jekyll and Mr Hyde, but only of minor interest; it neither shocks nor thrills.

wd George A. Romero   *novel* Stephen King   ph Tony Pierce-Roberts   *m* Christopher Young   pd Cletus Anderson   *sp* make-up: John Vulich, Everett Burrell; visual effects: VCE/Peter Kuran; Video Image   *ed* Pasquale Buba

Timothy Hutton, Amy Madigan, Michael Rooker, Julie Harris, Robert Joy, Kent Broadhurst, Beth Grant, Chelsea Field, Royal Dano

'Features enough gruesome killings and special effects to satisfy hardcore horror fans, but also has sufficient narrative and thematic substance to keep more mainstream viewers interested.' – *Variety*

'A classy psychological horror movie, this delivers its share of visual shock moments, but relies for the most part on a controlled build-up of cumulative tension.' – *Nigel Floyd, The Dark Side*

† The film was released direct to video in Britain.

Dark Hazard
US   1934   72m   bw
Warner (Robert Lord)

A compulsive gambler loses his wife as well as his money.

Modest star drama, remade in 1937 as *Wine, Women and Horses*.

w Ralph Block, Brown Holmes   *novel* W. R. Burnett   d Alfred E. Green

Edward G. Robinson, Glenda Farrell, Robert Barrat, Hobart Cavanaugh

The Dark Horse
US   1932   75m   bw
Warner
V*

A nitwit runs for governor and nearly makes it.

Mild political satire; closer to farce, really.

w Joseph Jackson, Wilson Mizner   d Alfred E. Green

Guy Kibbee, Bette Davis, Warren William, Frank McHugh

Dark Journey *
GB   1937   82m   bw
London Films/Victor Saville
V*

In 1915 Stockholm, a French woman spy masquerading as a traitor falls in love with her German spy contact.

Unconvincing but entertaining romantic adventure with good star performances.

w Lajos Biro, Arthur Wimperis   *play* Lajos Biro   d Victor Saville   *ph* Georges Périnal, Harry Stradling   *m* Richard Addinsell   *ad* Andrei Andreiev   *ed* William Hornbeck, Hugh Stewart

Conrad Veidt, Vivien Leigh, Joan Gardner, Anthony Bushell, Ursula Jeans, Eliot Makeham, Austin Trevor, Edmund Willard

'An exceptional quantity of carefully thought out direction . . . the financial success will depend on whether the general public will understand and keep pace with the plot.' – *Variety*

The Dark Man
GB   1950   91m   bw
Rank/Independent Artists (Julian Wintle)

A mysterious murderer haunts a seaside resort.

Limp, disappointing location police thriller, with too much chat and generally mishandled moments of suspense.

wd Jeffrey Dell   *ph* Eric Cross   *m* Hubert Clifford

Maxwell Reed, Edward Underdown, Natasha Parry, Barbara Murray, William Hartnell, Cyril Smith, Geoffrey Summer

'The contrivances of the script are not helped by stilted dialogue.' – *MFB*

'One twin loves – and one twin loves to kill!'
The Dark Mirror **
US   1946   85m   bw
International
V*

A police detective works out which of identical twin girls is a murderer.

Unconvincing but highly absorbing thriller with all credits plus; the best brand of Hollywood moonshine.

w Nunnally Johnson   *story* Vladimir Pozner   d Robert Siodmak   *ph* Milton Krasner   *m* Dimitri Tiomkin

Olivia de Havilland, Lew Ayres, Thomas Mitchell, Gary Owen

'Smooth and agreeable melodrama . . . the detective work involves inkblot and word association tests and an amusingly sinister tandem of oscillating pens which register concealed emotions as one of the sisters talks.' – *James Agee*

AAN: Vladimir Pozner

Dark Obsession: see *Diamond Skulls*

Dark of the Sun: see *The Mercenaries*

The Dark Page: see *Scandal Sheet*

Dark Passage **
US   1947   106m   bw
Warner (Jerry Wald)
V, V*, L

A convicted murderer escapes from jail and proves his innocence.

Loosely assembled, totally unconvincing star thriller which succeeds because of its professionalism, some good cameos, and a number of narrative tricks including subjective camera for the first half hour.

w Delmer Daves   *novel* David Goodis   d Delmer Daves   *ph* Sid Hickox   *m* Franz Waxman

Humphrey Bogart, Lauren Bacall, Agnes Moorehead, Bruce Bennett, Tom D'Andrea, Houseley Stevenson

'An almost total drag.' – *New Yorker, 1977*

The Dark Past **
US   1948   75m   bw
Columbia (Buddy Adler)
V*

A psychiatrist turns the tables on convicts who break into his home.

Tense, economical remake of *Blind Alley* (qv); a fresh look at a familiar situation (*The Small Voice, The Desperate Hours*, etc.) helped by excellent performances.

w Philip Macdonald, Malvin Wald, Oscar Saul *d* Rudolph Maté *ph* Joseph Walker *m* George Duning

William Holden, Lee J. Cobb, Nina Foch, Adele Jergens, Stephen Dunne

'A picture so packed with skill and imagination that every minute is absorbing.' – *Richard Mallett, Punch*

The Dark Road
GB   1948   70m   bw
Exclusive/Marylebone-Hammer (Henry Halsted)

An American hack writer spins to his editor the story of the rise and fall of an English petty thief.

Mundane thriller that unabashedly revels in its own mediocrity.

d Alfred Goulding *ph* Stanley Clinton

Charles Stuart, Joyce Linden, Farnaham Baxter, Cyril Chamberlain, Sydney Bromley, Gale Douglas, Veronica Rose, Michael Ripper

Dark Sands: see *Jericho*

The Dark Side of the Moon
Denmark   1986   94m   colour
Cannon/Film-Cooperative Denmark (Per Arman)
original title: *Manden I Manen*

A wife murderer, released from prison, tries to effect a reconciliation with his daughter.

Ponderously slow and introverted, with darkly expressionistic camerawork.

wd Eric Clausen *ph* Morten Bruus *m* John Hoybe *pd* Leif Sylvester *ed* Ghita Beckendorff

Peter Thiel, Catherine Poul Dupont, Christina Bengtsson, Kim Jansson, Yavuzer Cetinkaya, Royt Richards, Berthe Qvistgaard, Erik Truxa

'The mission of the Strangelove generation!'
Dark Star *
US   1974   83m   Metrocolor
Jack H. Harris (John Carpenter)
V, V*, L, S

In the 22nd century, the bored crew of a starship on an intergalactic mission become prey to their own phobias and to the alien mascot they are taking back to Earth.

A semi-professional film which turned out to be one of the screen's neatest low-budget entries in the pulp science fiction genre. That doesn't make it wholly entertaining, but its credentials are impeccable.

w John Carpenter, Dan O'Bannon *d* John Carpenter *pd/ed* Dan O'Bannon *ph* Douglas Knapp *m* John Carpenter

Brian Narelle, Dre Pahich, Cal Kuniholm, Dan O'Bannon

The Dark Tower
GB   1943   93m   bw
Warner (Max Milder)

A circus hypnotist possessively controls a girl trapezist.

Heavy-handed but quite effective melodrama.

w Brock Williams, Reginald Purdell *play* Alexander Woollcott, George S. Kaufman *d* John Harlow *ph* Otto Heller

Ben Lyon, Anne Crawford, David Farrar, Herbert Lom, William Hartnell, Frederick Burtwell, Josephine Wilson

'Never a love so exquisite! She smiled at the cost, and bravely paid the reckoning when her heart's happy dancing was ended!'
Dark Victory **
US   1939   106m   bw
Warner (David Lewis)
V, V*, L

A good-time society girl discovers she is dying of a brain tumour.

A highly commercial tearjerker of its day, this glutinous star vehicle now works only fitfully.

w Casey Robinson *play* George Brewer Jnr, Bertram Bloch *d* Edmund Goulding *ph* Ernest Haller *m* Max Steiner

Bette Davis, George Brent, Humphrey Bogart, Ronald Reagan, Geraldine Fitzgerald, Henry Travers, Cora Witherspoon, Dorothy Peterson

JUDITH (Bette Davis): 'Nothing can hurt us now. What we have can't be destroyed. That's our victory – our victory over the dark. It is a victory because we're not afraid.'

'If it were an automobile, it would be a Rolls-Royce with the very best trimmings.' – *Time*

'Will turn in a good account of itself at the box office, though not rating socko proportions.' – *Variety*

'A completely cynical appraisal would dismiss it all as emotional flim-flam . . . but it is impossible to be that cynical about it.' – *Frank S. Nugent*

'A gooey collection of clichés, but Davis slams through them in her nerviest style.' – *New Yorker, 1976*

† Remade 1963 as *Stolen Hours*, with Susan Hayward; 1975 as *Dark Victory* (TV movie) with Elizabeth Montgomery.

AAN: best picture; Bette Davis; Max Steiner

Dark Water *
GB   1980   28m   colour
Dragonfly/ITC

A girl locked in a swimming pool is terrorized by a mad killer.

Agreeably watchable thriller full of shadows and shocks.

w Andrew Bogle, Tony Grisoni *d* Andrew Bogle

Phil Davis, Gwyneth Strong, David Beames

Dark Waters **
US   1944   90m   bw
Benedict Bogeaus
V*, L

Recovering from being torpedoed, an orphan girl visits her aunt and uncle in Louisiana and has some terrifying experiences.

Competent frightened-lady melodrama helped by its bayou surroundings. Possibly discarded by Hitchcock, but with sequences well in his manner.

w Joan Harrison, Marian Cockrell *d* André de Toth *ph* John Mescall *m* Miklos Rozsa

Merle Oberon, Franchot Tone, *Thomas Mitchell, Fay Bainter, John Qualen*, Elisha Cook Jnr, Rex Ingram

Dark Wind
US   1991   111m   Technicolor
Guild/Carolco/North Face Motion Picture Company (Patrick Markey)
V, V*

Hassled by corrupt FBI agents, a Navajo cop investigates drugs-related murders.

Despite its unusual hero, a disappointingly mundane thriller.

w Neil Jiminez, Eric Bergren, Mark Horowitz *novel* Tony Hillerman *d* Errol Morris *ph* Stefan Czapsky *m* Michel Colombier *pd* Ted Bafaloukos *ed* Susan Crutcher, Freeman Davies

Lou Diamond Phillips, Gary Farmer, Fred Ward, Guy Boyd, John Karlen, Jane Loranger, Gary Basaraba, Blake Clark

'A smooth genre piece, well acted, slickly written and benefiting from the natural beauty of the setting.' – *Kim Newman, Empire*

Darker than Amber
US   1970   96m   Technicolor
Cinema Center/Major Films (Walter Seltzer)
V*

A Florida private eye rescues a girl who is subsequently murdered and turns out to be part of a confidence racket.

Routine suspenser from the Travis McGee books; not very stimulating.

w Ed Waters *novel* John D. MacDonald *d* Robert Clouse *ph* Frank Phillips *m* John Parker

Rod Taylor, Suzy Kendall, Theodore Bikel, James Booth, Jane Russell, Janet McLachlan, William Smith

Darkest Africa
US   1936   bw   serial: 15 eps
Republic
V*

A lion trapper meets a jungle boy and rescues a fair heroine from a lost city.

Great stuff, but the budget is a lot less than Steven Spielberg had to play with 45 years later.

d B. Reeves Eason, Joseph Kane

Clyde Beatty, Manuel King, Elaine Shepherd, Lucien Prival

Darkman
US   1990   91m   DeLuxe
UIP/Universal (Robert Tapert)
V, V*, L, S

A hideously deformed scientist invents a synthetic skin that makes him a master of disguise.

Relentlessly silly horror movie full of extravagantly pointless camera movements.

w Chuck Pfarrer, Sam Raimi, Ivan Raimi, Daniel Goldin, Joshua Goldin *d* Sam Raimi *ph* Bill Pope *m* Danny Elfman *pd* Randy Ser *ed* David Stiven

Liam Neeson, Frances McDormand, Colin Friels, Larry Drake, Nelson Mashita, Jesse Lawrence Ferguson, Rafael H. Robledo, Danny Hicks, Theodore Raimi

'When she was good she was very very good. When she was bad, she was . . .'
Darling **
GB   1965   127m   bw
Anglo-Amalgamated/Vic/Appia (Joseph Janni, Victor Lyndon)
V, V*, L

An ambitious young woman deserts her journalist mentor for a company director, an effeminate photographer and an Italian prince.

Fashionable mid-sixties concoction of smart swinging people and their amoral doings. Influential, put over with high style, and totally tiresome in retrospect.

w Frederic Raphael *d* John Schlesinger *ph* Ken Higgins *m* John Dankworth

Julie Christie, Dirk Bogarde, Laurence Harvey, Roland Curram, Alex Scott, Basil Henson, Pauline Yates

BOGARDE to Christie: 'Your idea of being fulfilled is having more than one man in bed at the same time.'

'As empty of meaning and mind as the empty life it's exposing.' – *Pauline Kael*

'A cool, clear and devastating look at the glossy success set.' – *Judith Crist*

AA: Frederic Raphael; Julie Christie

AAN: best picture; John Schlesinger

Darling How Could You
US 1951 96m bw
Paramount (Harry Tugend)
GB title: Rendezvous

Children long separated from their parents have fantasies about them.

Faded-looking Edwardian comedy which does not quite have the style or the cast for success. (Or the title, come to that.)

w Dodie Smith, Lesser Samuels *play Alice Sit by the Fire* by J. M. Barrie d Mitchell Leisen ph Daniel L. Fapp m Frederick Hollander

Joan Fontaine, John Lund, Mona Freeman, Peter Hanson, David Stollery, Lowell Gilmore, Robert Barrat, Gertrude Michael

Darling I am Growing Younger: see Monkey Business

Darling Lili *
US 1970 136m Technicolor Panavision
Paramount/Geoffrey (Owen Crump)
V*

During World War I, an American air ace falls for a German lady spy, and waits till the war is over to marry her.

Farce and romance mix oddly with aerial acrobatics in this expensive and dull extravaganza which bore the sub-title *Where Were You the Night I Shot Down Baron von Richthofen?* (which probably sums up its aims and its failure). A coffee table film, good to look at and with occasional striking moments.

w Blake Edwards, William Peter Blatty d Blake Edwards ph Russell Harlan, Harold E. Wellman m Henry Mancini pd Fernando Carrere

Julie Andrews, Rock Hudson, Jeremy Kemp, Lance Percival, Michael Witney, Jacques Marin, André Maranne

AAN: Henry Mancini; song 'Whistling Away the Dark' (m Henry Mancini, ly Johnny Mercer)

The Darwin Adventure *
GB 1971 91m Eastmancolor
TCF/Palomar (Joseph Strick, Irving Lerner)

In 1831, Charles Darwin becomes ship's naturalist on the *Beagle* and studies wildlife in South America.

Rather naïve biopic of Darwin which tries to cover too much with too slender resources but makes a pleasant introduction to the subject.

w William Fairchild d Jack Couffer ph Denys Coop, Jack Couffer m Marc Wilkinson

Nicholas Clay, Susan Macready, Ian Richardson, Christopher Martin, Robert Flemyng, Aubrey Woods, Hugh Morton

'The biopic plague, which has ravaged the screen lives of Pasteur, Juarez, Cole Porter and countless others, has now struck down the memory of famed naturalist Charles Darwin. The filmgoing public's own version of Darwin's natural selection theory will immediately weed out this inferior species.' – Variety

D.A.R.Y.L.
US 1985 99m TVC colour Panavision
Columbia (Burt Harris, Gabrielle Kelly)
V, V*, L

A mysterious young man is really a robot, 'data analysing robot youth lifeform'; but he begins to have feelings . . .

Muddled sentimental fantasy which doesn't seem to know where it's going.

w David Ambrose, Allan Scott, Jeffrey Ellis d Simon Wincer ph Frank Watts m Marvin Hamlisch pd Alan Cassie ed Adrian Carr

Mary Beth Hurt, Michael McKean, Kathryn Walker, Colleen Camp

'The kind of project that must have looked great on paper.' – Variety

A Date with a Lonely Girl: see T.R. Baskin

A Date with Destiny (1941): see The Mad Doctor

A Date with Destiny (1948): see The Return of October

A Date with Judy
US 1948 113m Technicolor
MGM (Joe Pasternak)
V*, L

A teenager wrongly suspects her friend of an illicit affair.

Ambitious but flat comedy musical which neatly wraps up all kinds of forties people and institutions: teenagers, small towns, families, Carmen Miranda and Miss Taylor, not to mention the producer.

w Dorothy Cooper, Dorothy Kingsley d Richard Thorpe ph Robert Surtees md George Stoll m/ly various

Wallace Beery, Elizabeth Taylor, Jane Powell, Carmen Miranda, Xavier Cugat, Robert Stack, Selena Royle, Scotty Beckett, Leon Ames

Daughter of Darkness
GB 1947 91m bw
Kenilworth-Alliance (Victor Hanbury)

A murderous Irish servant girl has a fatal flair for men.

Absurd melodrama, almost Grand Guignol, louringly set on the Yorkshire moors but lethargically handled all round.

w Max Catto play They Walk Alone by Max Catto d Lance Comfort ph Stanley Pavey

Siobhan McKenna, Anne Crawford, Maxwell Reed, George Thorpe, Barry Morse, Honor Blackman, Liam Redmond, David Greene

Daughter of Dr Jekyll
US 1957 74m bw
Allied Artists
V*

An evil doctor tells his ward that she is the daughter of the unfortunate Dr Jekyll and therefore responsible for a series of werewolf killings.

Bathetic cheapie with risible views of England and a tendency to mix up several myths in one package.

w Jack Pollexfen d Edgar G. Ulmer

Arthur Shields, John Agar, Gloria Talbott, John Dierkes

Daughter of Luxury: see Five and Ten

The Daughter of Rosie O'Grady *
US 1950 104m Technicolor
Warner (William Jacobs)

A girl determines to follow in her dead mother's musical comedy footsteps against the wishes of her still-grieving father.

Absolutely standard period musical, quite pleasantly handled but with below-par musical numbers.

w Jack Rose, Mel Shavelson, Peter Milne d David Butler ph Wilfred M. Cline md David Buttolph

June Haver, Gordon Macrae, James Barton, S. Z. Sakall, Gene Nelson, Debbie Reynolds, Sean McClory, Jane Darwell

Daughter of Shanghai *
US 1937 63m bw
Paramount

The daughter of a wealthy merchant revenges herself on smugglers who kill him.

Pacy lower-berth melodrama packed with good talent.

w Gladys Unger, Garnett Weston d Robert Florey

Anna May Wong, Charles Bickford, Philip Ahn, Larry Crabbe, Cecil Cunningham, Anthony Quinn, J. Carrol Naish, Evelyn Brent

'Meaningless title to a routine crime meller . . . downstairs dualler, but not half bad.' – Variety

Daughter of the Dragon
US 1931 70m bw
Paramount
V*

Fu Manchu continues to seek revenge on Dr Petrie for the loss of his wife in the Boxer rebellion.

Muddled thriller with too much plot and too little action.

w Lloyd Corrigan, Monte Katterjohn d Lloyd Corrigan

Warner Oland, Anna May Wong, Sessue Hayakawa, Bramwell Fletcher, Holmes Herbert

'Chinese blunderings, murders, and silly acting. Best for the combos where the kids may get a kick out of it.' – Variety

Daughter of the Nile *
Taiwan 1988 91m colour
Artificial Eye/Fu Film Productions (Li Xianchang)
original title: Nilouhe, Nuer

A lovesick schoolgirl on the fringes of gangster society escapes from her workaday chores by reading a comic, *Daughter of the Nile*.

Impressively controlled direction and well observed characters flesh out a minimal story.

w Zhu Tianwen d Hou Hsiao-Hsien ph Chen Huai'en m Chen Zhiyuan, Zhang Hongyi pd Liu Zhihua, Lin Ju ed Liao Qingsong, Chen Liyu

Yang Lin, Gao Jie, Yang Fan, Xin Shufen, Li Tianlu, Cui Fusheng

'By far the most achieved and mature of the cycle of "young criminal" films in recent Taiwanese cinema.' – Tony Rayns, MFB

Daughters Courageous *
US 1939 107m bw
Warner (Hal B. Wallis)

A prodigal father returns to his family and sorts out their problems.

Following the success of *Four Daughters* (qv) the cast was reassembled to make this amiable rehash about a different family.

w Julius and Philip Epstein play Fly Away Home by Dorothy Bennett, Irving White d Michael Curtiz ph James Wong Howe m Max Steiner

Claude Rains, John Garfield, Jeffrey Lynn, Fay Bainter, Priscilla Lane, Rosemary Lane, Lola Lane, Gale Page, Donald Crisp, May Robson, Frank McHugh, Dick Foran, Berton Churchill

'Suited to the family trade anywhere . . . but there's something to be said against a running time of an hour and 47 minutes.' – Variety

'For its intelligent use of small town locations, its skilled acting, fine camerawork and evenly paced, sympathetic direction, it surpasses everything of its type.' – John Baxter, 1968

'Attractive people, good dialogue and camerawork, and skilful direction can work wonders.' – Richard Mallett, Punch

Daughters of Destiny: see Love, Soldiers and Women

Daughters of the Dust *
US 1991 112m colour
BFI/American Playhouse/WMG/Geechee Girls (Julie Dash)
V (W), V*

At the turn of the century, a family of Gullahs,

descendants of African slaves living on islands off South Carolina, prepare to make a journey to the mainland to travel to the North.

A commemoration and celebration of black experience in America and its African roots, told in overlapping voices of the old and the unborn, and shot with an eye for beauty.

wd Julie Dash   *ph* A. Jaffa Fielder   *m* John Barnes
pd Kerry Marshall   *ed* Amy Carey, Joseph Burton

Adisa Anderson, Barbara-O, Cheryl Lynn Bruce, Cora Lee Day, Geraldine Dunston, Vertamae Grosvenor, Tommy Hicks, Trula Hoosier, Kaycee Moore, Eartha D. Robinson, Alva Rodgers, Cornell Royal, Catherine Tarver, Bahni Turpin

'This is balletic, operatic cinema, and a celebration of cinema itself.' – *Lizzie Francke, Sight and Sound*

'In a country where anybody can become President, anybody just did.'
'Dave Kovic was an ordinary guy who was asked to impersonate the president. When they gave him a chance to make the country better…he did.'

Dave *
US   1993   110m   colour
Warner (Lauren Schuler-Donner, Ivan Reitman)
V, V*, L, S

After the President of the United States has a stroke, a Baltimore businessman is recruited by the White House to impersonate him.

A slight but amusing comedy of political life that nevertheless manages to evade most of the issues it raises.

w Gary Ross   *d* Ivan Reitman   *ph* Adam Greenberg   *m* James Newton Howard
pd J. Michael Riva   *ed* Sheldon Kahn

Kevin Kline, Sigourney Weaver, Frank Langella, Kevin Dunn, Ben Kingsley, Charles Grodin, Ving Rhames, Faith Prince, Laura Linney

'A dear and funny movie.' – *Richard Corliss, Time*

'A delightful, buoyant new take on an old theme that will win at the polls because it never strikes a false note.' – *Variety*

AAN: Gary Ross

'For this woman – he broke God's own commandments! The fire and tempest of their love still flames across 3000 years!'
David and Bathsheba *
US   1951   116m   Technicolor
TCF (Darryl F. Zanuck)
V*, L

King David loves the wife of one of his captains, and ensures that the latter is killed in battle.

Deliberately sober bible-in-pictures, probably intended as a riposte to Cecil B. de Mille. Somewhat lacking in excitement, but you can't call it gaudy.

w Philip Dunne   *d* Henry King   *ph* Leon Shamroy
m Alfred Newman   *ad* Lyle Wheeler, George Davis

Gregory Peck, Susan Hayward, James Robertson Justice, Raymond Massey, Kieron Moore, Jayne Meadows, John Sutton, Dennis Hoey, Francis X. Bushman, George Zucco

'Hardly a single unintentional laugh.' – *Richard Mallett, Punch*

AAN: Philip Dunne; Leon Shamroy; Alfred Newman; art direction

David and Lisa *
US   1962   94m   bw
Continental (Paul M. Heller)
V*, L

Two disturbed adolescents at a special school fall in love.

Case history drama, earnest and well meaning rather than exciting.

w Eleanor Perry   *book* Theodore Isaac Rubin
d Frank Perry   *ph* Leonard Hirschfield   *m* Mark Lawrence

Keir Dullea, Janet Margolin, Howard da Silva, Neva Patterson, Clifton James, Richard McMurray

'It recognises and probes the wounds of the mind and the heart and the power of love to penetrate even the most private of worlds.' – *Judith Crist*

† Made for 180,000 dollars, it took more than one million dollars in its first run in the States.

AAN: Eleanor Perry; Frank Perry

'One of the greatest stories of love and adventure ever told is brought to the screen as Dickens himself would wish it!'
David Copperfield ****
US   1934   132m   bw
MGM (David O. Selznick)
V, V*, L

Disliked by his cruel stepfather and helped by his eccentric aunt, orphan David grows up to become an author and eventually to marry his childhood sweetheart.

Only slightly faded after sixty years, this small miracle of compression not only conveys the spirit of Dickens better than the screen has normally managed but is a particularly pleasing example of Hollywood's handling of literature and of the deployment of a great studio's resources. It also overflows with memorable character cameos, and it was a box-office giant.

w Hugh Walpole, Howard Estabrook   *novel* Charles Dickens   *d* George Cukor   *ph* Oliver T. Marsh
montage Slavko Vorkapich   *m* Herbert Stothart
ad Cedric Gibbons   *ed* Robert J. Kern

Freddie Bartholomew (young David), *Frank Lawton* (David as a man), *W. C. Fields* (Micawber), *Roland Young* (Uriah Heep), *Edna May Oliver* (Aunt Betsy), *Lennox Pawle* (Mr Dick), *Basil Rathbone* (Mr Murdstone), *Violet Kemble Cooper* (Miss Murdstone), Maureen O'Sullivan (Dora), Madge Evans (Agnes), Elizabeth Allan (Mrs Copperfield), *Jessie Ralph* (Peggotty), Lionel Barrymore (Dan Peggotty), Hugh Williams (Steerforth), Lewis Stone (Mr Wickfield), *Herbert Mundin* (Barkis), Elsa Lanchester (Clickett), Jean Cadell (Mrs Micawber), Una O'Connor (Mrs Gummidge), John Buckler (Ham), Hugh Walpole (the Vicar), Arthur Treacher (donkey man)

'One of the best ensembles ever…unusually good production which will win general approval.' – *Variety*

'Though half the characters are absent, the whole spectacle of the book, Micawber always excepted, is conveyed.' – *James Agee*

'The most profoundly satisfying screen manipulation of a great novel that the camera has ever given us.' – *André Sennwald*

'Perhaps the finest casting of all time.' – *Basil Wright, 1972*

† Charles Laughton was originally cast as Micawber, but resigned from the role after two days of shooting. It was said at the time that he 'looked as though he were about to molest the child'.

AAN: best picture; editing

David Harum *
US   1934   83m   bw
Fox

A wily old rancher plays matchmaker.

Simple, pleasing small-town comedy-drama, ably fashioned for its star.

w Walter Woods   *play* Edward Westcott   *d* James Cruze   *ph* Hal Mohr   *m* Louis de Francesco

Will Rogers, Evelyn Venable, Kent Taylor, Louise Dresser, Stepin Fetchit, Charles Middleton, Noah Beery

'Looks like a sugar picture.' – *Variety*

Davy *
GB   1957   84m   Technirama
Ealing (Basil Dearden)

A member of a family music hall act auditions at Covent Garden.

Curiously unsuccessful vehicle for a popular singing comic; the script and continuity are simply poor, and swamped by the wide screen.

w William Rose   *d* Michael Relph   *ph* Douglas Slocombe   *m* various classics

Harry Secombe, Ron Randell, George Relph, Alexander Knox, Susan Shaw, Bill Owen

Davy Crockett *
US   1955   93m   Technicolor
Walt Disney
V*

Episodes in the career of the famous Tennessee hunter and Indian scout who died at the Alamo.

Disjointed and naïve but somehow very fresh and appealing adventures; made for American television (as 3 × 50m episodes) but elsewhere an enormous hit in cinemas.

w Tom Blackburn   *d* Norman Foster   *ph* Charles Boyle   *m* George Bruns

Fess Parker, Buddy Ebsen, Basil Ruysdael, William Bakewell, Hans Conried, Kenneth Tobey, Nick Cravat

† 1956 sequel on similar lines: *Davy Crockett and the River Pirates* (V*, L).

Dawandeh: see *The Runner*

Dawn *
GB   1928   90m approx   bw   silent
British and Dominions (Herbert Wilcox)

In 1914 Brussels, Nurse Edith Cavell helps 210 English soldiers to escape before the Germans catch and execute her.

Inspirational piece, totally dated now; remade by the same producer in 1939 as *Nurse Edith Cavell,* with Anna Neagle.

w Herbert Wilcox, Robert J. Cullen   *play* Reginald Berkeley   *d* Herbert Wilcox

Sybil Thorndike, Marie Ault, Mary Brough, Haddon Mason

Dawn at Socorro
US   1954   80m   Technicolor
Universal-International

A gunfighter is trapped into one last duel.

Moderate Western programmer.

w George Zuckerman   *d* George Sherman

Rory Calhoun, David Brian, Alex Nicol, Piper Laurie, Edgar Buchanan

'When there's no more room in Hell, the dead will walk the earth…'
Dawn of the Dead
US   1979   127m   Technicolor
Target International/Laurel Group/Dawn Associates (Richard P. Rubinstein)
V, V*, L, S
GB title: *Zombies*

America is filled by legions of carnivorous zombies.

Seemingly endless horror comic with absurd pretensions to be an allegory of something or other; occasionally laughable, otherwise sickening or boring.

wd George A. Romero   *ph* Michael Gornick
m The Goblins, Dario Argento   *ad* Josie Caruso, Barbara Lifsher   *ed* George A. Romero

David Emge, Ken Foree, Scott H. Reininger, Gaylen Ross

'Roaring into the blood-red dawn – fighting for women they had never seen – for love they might never know!'
'Forty youngsters sporting with fate!'

The Dawn Patrol **
US   1930   90m   bw
Warner

In France during World War I, flying officers wait their turn to leave on missions which may mean death.

The second version (see below) is more watchable today, but this early talkie was highly effective in its time, and much of its aerial footage was re-used.

w John Monk Saunders   d Howard Hawks
ph Ernest Haller

Richard Barthelmess, Douglas Fairbanks Jnr, Neil Hamilton, William Janney, James Finlayson, Clyde Cook, Edmund Breon, Frank McHugh

'No women and few laughs, so needs good surrounding comedy shorts.' – *Variety*

'Bare, cleancut, uncluttered technique, a stark story line, terse dialogue . . . and a pervasive atmosphere of hopelessness captured with economy and incisiveness.' – *Andrew Sarris, 1963*

† TV title is *Flight Commander*, which was the title of Saunders's original story.

AA: John Monk Saunders

'There's no chance for a flight to get through, but one man – flying low, hedgehopping – might make it!'

The Dawn Patrol **
US   1938   103m   bw
Warner (Hal B. Wallis)
V*

A remarkably early but trim and competent remake of the above, using much of the same aerial footage.

w Seton I. Miller, Dan Totheroh   d Edmund Goulding
ph Tony Gaudio   m Max Steiner

Errol Flynn, Basil Rathbone, David Niven, Melville Cooper, Donald Crisp, Barry Fitzgerald, Carl Esmond

'A powerful, red-corpuscled drama . . . geared for top grosses.' – *Variety*

'A great deal of self-pity and romanticism have gone into the making of this excellent ham sandwich.' – *Graham Greene*

The Dawn Rider
US   1935   56m   bw
Lone Star (Paul Malvern)
V*

A cowboy revenges the murder of his father.

Standard quickie Western with little to recommend it.

wd Robert N. Bradbury   ph Archie Stout

John Wayne, Marion Burns, Yakima Canutt, Reed Howes, Denny Meadows, Bert Dillard

The Dawning *
GB   1988   97m   colour
Enterprise/TVS (Sarah Lawson)
V*

In the 1920s in Southern Ireland, at the beginning of the Troubles between the Irish and the English, a teenage girl becomes involved with a mysterious stranger, to the annoyance of her English fiancé.

A small-scale but affecting film of the end of innocence.

w Moira Williams   novel The Old Jest by Jennifer Johnson   d Robert Knights   ph Adrian Biddle
m Simon May   pd Mike Porter   ed Max Lemon

Trevor Howard, Hugh Grant, Anthony Hopkins, Rebecca Pidgeon, Jean Simmons, Adrian Dunbar, Tara MacGowran

The Day
GB   1960   26m   bw
Peter Finch

A young Ibizan travels a long way to collect his relatives for the celebration of the birth of a baby.

Vivid and yet rather boring short which could have done with a twist in the tail.

wd Peter Finch

A Day at the Races ****
US   1937   109m   bw/blue-tinted ballet sequence
MGM (Lawrence Weingarten)
V, V*, L

The Marxes help a girl who owns a sanatorium and a racehorse.

Fashions in Marxism change, but this top quality production, though lacking their zaniest inspirations, does contain several of their funniest routines and a spectacularly well integrated racecourse climax. The musical and romantic asides are a matter of taste but delightfully typical of their time.

w Robert Pirosh, George Seaton, George Oppenheimer
d Sam Wood   ph Joseph Ruttenberg   m Franz Waxman
ch Dave Gould

Groucho, Chico, Harpo, Margaret Dumont, Maureen O'Sullivan, Allan Jones, Douglass Dumbrille, Esther Muir, Sig Rumann

'The money is fairly splashed about; the capitalists have recognized the Marx Brothers; ballet sequences, sentimental songs, amber fountains, young lovers. Easily the best film to be seen in London, but all the same I feel a nostalgia for the old cheap rickety sets.' – *Graham Greene*

AAN: Dave Gould

Day for Night ****
France/Italy   1973   116m   Eastmancolor
Films du Carrosse/PECF/PIC (Marcel Bébert)
V, V*
original title: *La Nuit Américaine*

Frictions and personality clashes beset the making of a romantic film in Nice.

Immensely enjoyable, richly detailed, insider's-eye-view of the goings-on in a film studio. A fun film with melodramatic asides.

w François Truffaut, Jean-Louis Richard, Suzanne Schiffman   d François Truffaut   ph Pierre-William Glenn   m Georges Delerue

Jacqueline Bisset, Valentina Cortese, Jean-Pierre Aumont, Jean-Pierre Léaud, Dani, Alexandra Stewart, Jean Champion, François Truffaut, David Markham

'I thought I'd had my last dram of enjoyment out of the Pagliacci theme and studio magic, and Truffaut shows there's life in the old whirl yet.' – *Stanley Kauffmann*

'Made with such dazzling craftsmanship and confidence that you can never quite believe Truffaut's point that directing a movie is a danger-fraught experience.' – *Michael Billington, Illustrated London News*

† Graham Greene, as Henry Graham, played an insurance representative.

AA: best foreign film

AAN: script; François Truffaut (as director); Valentina Cortese

A Day in the Death of Joe Egg **
GB   1971   106m   Eastmancolor
Columbia/Domino (David Deutsch)
V*

A teacher and his wife are frustrated by their own inability to cope with the problem of their spastic daughter.

A well-filmed version of a sincerely human play, with humour and fantasy sequences leavening the gloom.

w Peter Nichols   play Peter Nichols   d Peter Medak
ph Ken Hodges   m Elgar

Alan Bates, Janet Suzman, Peter Bowles, Sheila Gish, Joan Hickson

'It's unsatisfying, and it's not to be missed.' – *Stanley Kauffmann*

A Day in the Country: see Une Partie de Campagne

A Day of Fury
US   1956   78m   Technicolor
Universal (Robert Arthur)

A marshal is reluctant to shoot a wandering gunman who once saved his life.

Fair little Western with more tension than usual.

w James Edmiston, Oscar Brodney   d Harmon Jones

Dale Robertson, Jock Mahoney, Mara Corday, Carl Benton Reid

The Day of the Animals
US   1976   98m   DeLuxe   Todd-AO 35
Film Ventures International (Edward L. Montero)
V*

In the Californian High Sierras, animals of all kinds suddenly turn on human beings, but a day later are all found dead.

Irritatingly pointless horror fable borrowing heavily from *The Birds;* basically an exploitation shocker, most efficient when most unpleasant.

w William and Eleanor Norton   d William Girdler
ph Tom McHugh   m Lalo Schifrin

Christopher George, Lynda Day George, Leslie Nielsen, Robert Sorrentino, Richard Jaeckel, Michael Ansara, Ruth Roman, Paul Mantee, Gil Lamb

Day of the Badman
US   1957   82m   Eastmancolor   Cinemascope
Universal-International

A circuit judge stands up against threatening outlaws.

Uninvolving Western which can't fill the wide screen.

w Irving Glassberg   d Harry Keller

Fred MacMurray, Joan Weldon, John Ericson, Robert Middleton, Edgar Buchanan

Day of the Dead
US   1985   102m   colour
Laurel/United (Richard P. Rubinstein)
V*, L

Zombies outnumber normal humans by 400,000 to one, but a doctor is trying to domesticate them.

Gory but very talkative successor to *Dawn of the Dead;* not for regular audience consumption.

wd George A. Romero   ph Michael Gornick
m John Harrison   pd Cletus Anderson
ed Pasquale Buba

Lori Cardille, Terry Alexander, Jarlath Conroy, Joseph Pilato

The Day of the Dolphin *
US   1973   104m   Technicolor   Panavision
Avco-Embassy/Icarus (Robert E. Relyea)
V, V*, L, S

A marine biologist researching dolphins off the Florida coast discovers they are being used in a plot to blow up the President's yacht.

A strangely unexpected and unsuccessful offering from the talent involved: thin and repetitive as scientific instruction (the dolphins' language in any case topples it into fantasy), and oddly childlike as spy adventure.

w Buck Henry   novel Robert Merle   d Mike Nichols   ph William A. Fraker   m Georges Delerue
pd Richard Sylbert

George C. Scott, Trish Van Devere, Paul Sorvino, Fritz Weaver

'The whole thing seems to have been shoved through the cameras as glibly as possible, so that everyone concerned could grab the money and run.' – *Stanley Kauffmann*

'An eight and a half million dollar Saturday afternoon special for sheltered nine-year-olds.' – *Judith Crist*

'Dolphins may live in a state of ecstasy, but the cast of this film seems lost in a state of confusion, wondering whether they are in an enlightened documentary, juvenile fantasy, or lurid soap opera.' – *Les Keyser, Hollywood in the Seventies*

'The most expensive Rin Tin Tin movie ever made.' – *Judith Crist*

AAN: Georges Delerue

The Day of the Evil Gun *
US   1968   93m   Metrocolor   Panavision
MGM (Jerry Thorpe)

Returning home after three years, a rancher finds that his wife and child have been carried off by Indians.

Competent standard Western which resolves itself into a duel of wits between the hero and his rival.

w Charles Marquis Warren, Eric Bercovici   *d* Jerry Thorpe   *ph* W. Wallace Kelley   *m* Jeff Alexander

Glenn Ford, Arthur Kennedy, Dean Jagger, Paul Fix, John Anderson, Nico Minardos

The Day of the Jackal **
GB/France   1973   142m   Technicolor
Universal/Warwick/Universal France (John Woolf, David Deutsch)
V, V*, L

British and French police combine to prevent an OAS assassination attempt on de Gaulle by use of a professional killer.

An incisive, observant and professional piece of work based on a rather clinical bestseller. Lack of a channel for sympathy, plus language confusions, are its main drawbacks.

w Kenneth Ross   *novel* Frederick Forsyth   *d* Fred Zinnemann   *ph* Jean Tournier   *m* Georges Delerue   *ed* Ralph Kemplen

Edward Fox, Michel Lonsdale, Alan Badel, Eric Porter, Cyril Cusack, Delphine Seyrig, Donald Sinden, Tony Britton, Timothy West, Olga Georges-Picot, Barrie Ingham, Maurice Denham, Anton Rodgers

'Before *Jackal* is five minutes old, you know it's just going to be told professionally, with no flavour and no zest.' – *Stanley Kauffmann*

'All plot, with scarcely a character in sight.' – *Michael Billington, Illustrated London News*

'A better than average thriller for those who haven't read the book.' – *Judith Crist*

'A rare lesson in film-making in the good old grand manner.' – *Basil Wright, 1972*

AAN: Ralph Kemplen

'It happened in Hollywood – but it could have happened in Hell!'
The Day of the Locust **
US   1975   143m   Technicolor
Paramount/Long Road (Jerome Hellman, Sheldon Shrager)
V*, L

In Hollywood in the 1930s, a novice is bewildered by the eccentricities of life and an innocent man is martyred by the crowd.

A curious and interesting work from a savagely satirical novel; full of stimulating scenes and characters, it barely succeeds as a whole and was a disaster at the box-office.

w Waldo Salt   *novel* Nathanael West   *d* John Schlesinger   *ph* Conrad Hall   *m* John Barry   *pd* Richard MacDonald

Donald Sutherland, William Atherton, Karen Black, Burgess Meredith, Geraldine Page, Richard A. Dysart, Bo Hopkins, Lelia Goldoni

'The sense of horror which the film excites is all the sharper because the monstrosities of action are man-produced. In this brilliantly devised film it is the human heart, not some freak of an indifferent nature, which kills.' – *Dilys Powell*

AAN: Conrad Hall; Burgess Meredith

The Day of the Outlaw **
US   1958   96m   bw
UA/Security Pictures (Sidney Harmon)

Two rival cattlemen forget their differences to fight six outlaws who ride into town.

Bleak and wintry Western, well done and sufficiently unusual to stick in the mind.

w Philip Yordan   *novel* Lee Wells   *d* André de Toth   *ph* Russell Harlan   *m* Alexander Courage

Robert Ryan, Burl Ives, Tina Louise, Nehemiah Persoff, David Nelson, Venetia Stevenson, Jack Lambert, Lance Fuller

'In the best William S. Hart tradition.' – *MFB*

The Day of the Triffids *
GB   1962   95m   Eastmancolor   Cinemascope
Philip Yordan (George Pitcher)
V*, L

Almost everyone in the world is blinded by meteorites prior to being taken over by intelligent plants.

Rough and ready adaptation of a famous sci-fi novel, sometimes blunderingly effective and with moments of good trick work.

w Philip Yordan   *novel* John Wyndham   *d* Steve Sekely   *ph* Ted Moore   *m* Ron Goodwin

Howard Keel, Nicole Maurey, Kieron Moore, Janette Scott, Alexander Knox

Day of Wrath ***
Denmark   1943   105m   bw
Palladium
V*
original title: *Vredens Dag*

In a 17th-century village an old woman is burned as a witch and curses the pastor who judged her. He dies and his mother accuses her daughter-in-law, in love with another man, of using witchcraft to kill him.

Harrowing, spellbinding melodrama with a message, moving in a series of Rembrandtesque compositions from one horrifying sequence to another. Depressing, but marvellous.

w Carl Dreyer, Poul Knudsen, Mogens Skot-Hansen   *play Anne Pedersdotter* by Hans Wiers Jenssen   *d* Carl Dreyer   *ph* Carl Andersson   *m* Poul Schierbeck   *ad* Erik Ases, Lis Fribert

Thorkild Roose, Lisbeth Movin, Sigrid Neiiendam, Preben Lerdoff Rye, Anna Svierkier

'An exceptional piece of cinema . . . the film will, I think, be remembered for its realistic treatment of the incredible; for its vicious terror; for the unrivalled horror of its picture of human callousness.' – *Dilys Powell*

The Day the Earth Caught Fire **
GB   1961   99m   bw with filters   Dyaliscope
British Lion/Pax (Val Guest)
V*

Nuclear tests knock the world off its axis and send it careering towards the sun.

A smart piece of science fiction told through the eyes of Fleet Street journalists and showing a sharp eye for the London scene. Rather exhaustingly talkative, but genuinely frightening at the time.

w Wolf Mankowitz, Val Guest   *d* Val Guest   *ph* Harry Waxman   *m* Monty Norman

Edward Judd, Janet Munro, Leo McKern, *Arthur Christiansen* (ex-editor of the *Daily Express*), Michael

Goodliffe, Bernard Braden, Reginald Beckwith, Austin Trevor, Renée Asherson, Edward Underdown

'From out of space – a warning and an ultimatum!'
The Day the Earth Stood Still **
US   1951   92m   bw
TCF (Julian Blaustein)
V, V*, L, S

A flying saucer arrives in Washington and its alien occupant, aided by a robot, demonstrates his intellectual and physical power, warns the world what will happen if wars continue, and departs.

Cold-war wish-fulfilment fantasy, impressive rather than exciting but very capably put over with the minimum of trick work and the maximum of sober conviction. 'Klaatu barada nikto', the command given to the robot, has achieved cult status.

w Edmund H. North   *d* Robert Wise   *ph* Leo Tover   *m* Bernard Herrmann

Michael Rennie, Patricia Neal, Hugh Marlowe, Sam Jaffe, Billy Gray

'Quite wry and alarmingly smooth.' – *New Yorker, 1977*

The Day the Fish Came Out
GB/Greece   1967   109m   DeLuxe
TCF/Michael Cacoyannis

Atomic material contaminates a Mediterranean island.

Addle-pated, would-be satirical mod fantasy with establishment figures cast as world villains.

wd Michael Cacoyannis   *ph* Walter Lassally   *m* Mikis Theodorakis

Tom Courtenay, Colin Blakely, Sam Wanamaker, Candice Bergen, Ian Ogilvy, Patricia Burke

The Day the Hot Line Got Hot
US   1968   92m   Eastmancolor
Commonwealth United
V*

Russian and American agents are outwitted by their go-between.

Feeble espionage comedy teaming two big stars at the end of their careers.

w Paul Jarrico, Dominique Fabre, M. Trueblood   *d* Etienne Périer

Charles Boyer, Robert Taylor, George Chakiris, Marie Dubois

'A new high in naked shrieking terror.'
The Day the World Ended
US   1955   82m   bw   Superscope
AIP/Golden State (Roger Corman)
V*

Survivors of the nuclear war take refuge in a mountain hideout where they are attacked by three-eyed, cannibalistic mutants.

Small-scale, paranoid science-fiction thriller from what the film calls 'the age of anxiety'.

w Lou Rusoff   *d* Roger Corman   *ph* Jock Feindel   *m* Ronald Stein   *ed* Ronald Sinclair

Richard Denning, Lori Nelson, Adele Jurgens, Touch Connors, Paul Birch, Raymond Hatton

The Day They Gave Babies Away: see *All Mine to Give*

The Day They Robbed the Bank of England *
GB   1960   85m   bw
MGM/Summit (Jules Buck)

In 1901 Irish patriots plan a coup against the British government . . .

Small-scale, well-detailed period caper story, marred by a slow-starting script and unsympathetic acting.

w Howard Clewes, Richard Maibaum   *novel* John Brophy   *d* John Guillermin   *ph* Georges Périnal   *m* Edwin Astley

Peter O'Toole, Aldo Ray, Elizabeth Sellars, Kieron Moore, Albert Sharpe, Hugh Griffith, John Le Mesurier, Joseph Tomelty, Miles Malleson, Colin Gordon

A Day to Remember
GB   1953   92m   bw
Rank/Box-Thomas/GFD

A darts team takes a day trip to France.

Pleasant compendium of mini-stories with an agreeable cast.

w Robin Estridge   novel The Hand and Flower by Jerrard Tickell   d Ralph Thomas

Stanley Holloway, Donald Sinden, Joan Rice, Odile Versois, James Hayter, Edward Chapman, Harry Fowler, Peter Jones, Bill Owen

The Day Will Dawn *
GB   1942   98m   bw
Niksos (Paul Soskin)
V*
US title: The Avengers

Norwegian freedom fighters destroy a U-boat base and are saved by commandos.

Dated propaganda piece with an interesting cast.

w Terence Rattigan, Anatole de Grunwald, Patrick Kirwan   d Harold French   ph Bernard Knowles m Richard Addinsell

Ralph Richardson, Deborah Kerr, Hugh Williams, Griffith Jones, Francis L. Sullivan, Roland Culver, Niall MacGinnis, Finlay Currie, Bernard Miles, Patricia Medina

Daybreak *
US   1931   85m approx   bw
MGM

An Austrian guardsman falls in love out of his class.

Elegant romantic fable comparable with Letter From an Unknown Woman; equally unpopular and quite forgotten.

w Ruth Cummings, Zelda Sears, Cyril Hume play Arthur Schnitzler   d Jacques Feyder   ph J. Merrit Gerstad

Ramon Novarro, Helen Chandler, C. Aubrey Smith, Karen Morley, Kent Douglass, Jean Hersholt, Glenn Tryon

'One of those pictures that won't draw after opening . . . pretty flat all the way . . . good only insofar as Novarro will draw anywhere.' – Variety

Daybreak (1939): see Le Jour Se Lève

Daybreak
GB   1948   81m   bw
GFD/Triton (Sydney Box)

A barber and part-time hangman marries a destitute girl, loses her to a Swedish seaman, and kills himself in such a way as to implicate the other man.

Dockside melodrama of extraordinary pretentious gloominess; laughable in most respects. A curious follow-up from the Seventh Veil team.

w Muriel and Sydney Box   play Monckton Hoffe d Compton Bennett   ph Reg Wyer

Ann Todd, Eric Portman, Maxwell Reed, Edward Rigby, Bill Owen, Jane Hylton, Maurice Denham

† The film was made in 1946 but its release was delayed by censorship problems. When it was released, Sydney Box complained that the censor had ruined it by insisting on numerous cuts.

Daydream Believer
Australia   1991   86m   colour
Feature/View Films/Australian Film Finance Corp (Ben Gannon)

A would-be actress, who imagined as a child that she was a horse, proves to a stud-farm owner that she understands the needs of his unhappy mares.

Ludicrous comedy, which ranks among the silliest movies of the decade.

w Saturday Rosenberg   d Kathy Mueller ph Andrew Lesnie, Ian Jones, Roger Lanser m Todd Hunter, Johanna Pigott   pd Roger Ford ed Robert Gibson

Miranda Otto, Martin Kemp, Anne Looby, Alister Smart, Gia Carides, Bruce Venables

'This insipid Australian comedy again prompts the question: what happened to their emerging film industry.' – Ian Johnstone, Sunday Times

'Truly abysmal.' – Alexander Walker, London Evening Standard

Days and Nights in the Forest ***
India   1969   115m   bw
Contemporary/Priya (Nepal Dutta, Ashim Dutta)
original title: Aranyer Din Ratri

A group of friends leave Calcutta to spend a few days in the country.

Episodic drama of four middle-class idlers forced to re-examine their lives in an unfamiliar environment, comic in tone, with an underlying seriousness.

wd Satyajit Ray   novel Sunil Ganguli   ph Soumendu Roy, Purnendu Bose   m Satyajit Ray   ad Bansi Chandragupta   ed Dulal Dutta

Soumitra Chatterjee, Subhendu Chatterjee, Samit Bhanja, Rabi Ghose, Pahari Sanyal, Sarmila Tagore, Kaveri Bose, Simi Garewal, Aparna Sen

'One would rate this lucid, ironic and superlatively graceful film among the very best of his work.' – Penelope Huston, MFB

'A major film by one of the great film artists.' – Pauline Kael

'Pretentious, short on plot but striving to be long on character, stylistically awkward as a sign of sincere emotions, and all of it held together by a title that is more poetic than anything in the movie itself.' – William Paul, Village Voice

Days of Glory
US   1944   86m   bw
RKO (Casey Robinson)
V*

Russian peasants fight the invading Nazis.

Lower-berth wartime propaganda piece chiefly notable for introducing Gregory Peck to the screen.

w Casey Robinson   story Melchior Lengyel d Jacques Tourneur   ph Tony Gaudio   m Daniele Amfitheatrof

Tamara Toumanova, Gregory Peck, Alan Reed, Maria Palmer, Lowell Gilmore, Hugo Haas

'Your eyes – your ears – your senses will be overwhelmed!'

Days of Heaven ****
US   1978   95m   Metrocolor
Paramount/OP (Bert and Harold Schneider)
V*, L

In the early 20th century, three young immigrants leave Chicago for the wheatfields.

Visually a superb slice of period life, it has an emotional force that emerges slowly from the conjunction of the vast landscape and its reticent intruders, who have fled from the dark of the city to find no peace in the country.

wd Terrence Malick   ph Nestor Almendros   m Ennio Morricone

Richard Gere, Brooke Adams, Sam Shepard, Linda Manz

'It's serious, yes, very solemn, but not depressing.' – Roger Ebert

'Superbly directed and acted; see it for a second time and its hold is still more relentless.' – Dilys Powell, Punch

'One of the great cinematic achievements of the 1970s.' – Variety

'Terrence Malick's innocently convoluted parable of love lost and found, and reconciliation achieved and then fatally broken, is superbly counterpointed, thanks to Nestor Almendros' photography, by the burgeoning expansiveness of Texas during the First War.' – Sight and Sound

AA: Nestor Almendros

AAN: Ennio Morricone

Days of Hope: see Espoir

Days of Thrills and Laughter ***
US   1961   93m   bw
TCF (Robert Youngson)
V*

Appealing if rather miscellaneous silent film compilation with the accent on action and thrills as well as comedy.

Like the other Youngson histories, a boon to film archivists despite a facetious commentary.

m Jack Shaindlin   narrator Jay Jackson

Stan Laurel, Oliver Hardy, Snub Pollard, Douglas Fairbanks, Charles Chaplin, Pearl White, Houdini, Harry Langdon, Ben Turpin, Charlie Chase, Boris Karloff, Warner Oland, Fatty Arbuckle, Keystone Kops

Days of Thunder
US   1990   107m   Technicolor   Panavision
Paramount (Don Simpson, Jerry Bruckheimer)
V, V*, L, S

An eager young stock car driver challenges the champion. Guess who wins?

An over-familiar story rendered no more interestingly than usual. Despite its star, it flopped at the box-office.

w Robert Towne   story Robert Towne, Tom Cruise d Tony Scott   ph Ward Russell   m Hans Zimmer ad Benjamin Fernandez, Thomas E. Sanders ed Billy Weber, Chris Lebenzon

Tom Cruise, Robert Duvall, Nicole Kidman, Randy Quaid, Michael Rooker, Cary Elwes, Fred Dalton Thompson, John C. Reilly, J. C. Quinn, Don Simpson

'Simply a flashy, noisy star vehicle for Tom Cruise, one which – like the stock cars he drives – goes around in circles getting nowhere.' – MFB

Days of Wine and Roses **
US   1962   117m   bw
Warner (Martin Manulis)
V*, L

A PR man becomes an alcoholic; his wife gradually reaches the same state, but he recovers and she does not.

Smart satirical comedy confusingly gives way to melodrama, then sentimentality; quality is evident throughout, but all concerned are happiest with the first hour.

w J. P. Miller   d Blake Edwards   ph Philip Lathrop m Henry Mancini

Jack Lemmon, Lee Remick, Charles Bickford, Jack Klugman, Alan Hewitt, Debbie Megowan, Jack Albertson

AA: title song (m Henry Mancini, ly Johnny Mercer)

AAN: Jack Lemmon; Lee Remick

A Day's Pleasure *
US   1919   20m   bw   silent
First National/Charles Chaplin
V

Mishaps of a family picnic.

Very mild Chaplin, reaching for but not achieving a kind of lyric quality. Amusing bits rather than scenes.

wd Charles Chaplin   ph Rollie Totheroh

Charles Chaplin, Edna Purviance, Jackie Coogan, Henry Bergman, Babe London

Daytime Wife

US 1939 71m bw
TCF

A young wife finds that her husband is still dating his secretary, and retaliates by dating his colleague.

Hollywood version of a French farce; not terrific, but watchable.

w Art Arthur, Robert Harari d Gregory Ratoff

Tyrone Power, Linda Darnell, Warren William, Binnie Barnes, Wendy Barrie, Joan Davis, Leonid Kinskey

'Will give a good account of itself in the key runs.' – *Variety*

Dayton's Devils

US 1968 103m Eastmancolor
Madison/Harold Goldman (Robert W. Stabler)
V*

A former USAF colonel assembles a group of misfits and adventurers to steal an army payroll.

Overlong, routine caper film with a surprisingly crisp climax (when it comes).

w Fred de Gorter d Jack Shea ph Brick Marquard
m Marlin Skiles

Leslie Nielsen, Rory Calhoun, Lainie Kazan, Hans Gudegast

D-Day the Sixth of June

US 1956 106m Eastmancolor Cinemascope
TCF (Charles Brackett)
V*

On the way to invade France in 1944, a British colonel and an American captain reminisce about their love for the same woman.

Turgid war romance with some good action scenes and the usual hilarious Hollywood view of London. General effect very wooden.

w Ivan Moffat, Harry Brown novel Lionel Shapiro
d Henry Koster ph Lee Garmes m Lyn Murray

Robert Taylor, Richard Todd, Dana Wynter, Edmond O'Brien, John Williams, Jerry Paris, Richard Stapley

'Reminiscent of *Mrs Miniver* in style and feeling.' – *MFB*

'He made evil an art, vice a virtue and pain a pleasure!'

De Sade *

US/Germany 1969 113m Movielab
AIP/CCC/Transcontinental (Louis M. Heyward, Artur Brauner)

The unbalanced Marquis de Sade is tormented by his wicked uncle with thoughts of his past.

Mildly interesting attempt by AIP at European debauchery, with a good theatrical framework for the fantasies but too much flailing about by all concerned, especially in the slow motion orgy sequences, which are relentlessly boring, as is the film.

w Richard Matheson d Cy Endfield ph Heinz Pehlke m Billy Strange ad Jurgen Kiebach

Keir Dullea, *John Huston*, Lilli Palmer, Senta Berger, Anna Massey, Uta Levka

The Dead ****

GB 1987 83m FotoKem colour
Vestron/Zenith/Liffey Films (Wieland Schulz-Keil, Chris Sievernich)
V, V*, L, S

Two Irish spinster sisters throw a winter dinner for their relatives and friends.

Its director's last film is a warm and somehow invigorating reminiscence of things past.

w Tony Huston novel Dubliners by James Joyce
d John Huston ph Fred Murphy m Alex North
pd Stephen Grimes, Dennis Washington
costumes Dorothy Jeakins

Anjelica Huston, Donal McCann, Rachel Dowling, Cathleen Delany, Dan O'Herlihy, Helena Carroll, Donal Donnelly

'A delicate coda in a minor key to an illustrious 46-year career.' – *Daily Variety*

'A small masterpiece, perfectly achieved.' – *Time Out*

AAN: best adapted screenplay; Dorothy Jeakins

'How many times can you die for love?'

Dead Again *

US 1991 108m Technicolor/bw
UIP/Paramount/Mirage (Lindsay Doran, Charles H. Maguire)
V, V*, L, S

A private detective is hired to investigate an amnesiac who can only remember a past life as a concert pianist murdered by her husband.

Tricksy thriller, switching between past and present, which is frequently too clever for its own good.

w Scott Frank d Kenneth Branagh ph Matthew F. Leonetti m Patrick Doyle pd Tim Hervey
ed Peter E. Berger

Kenneth Branagh, Emma Thompson, Andy Garcia, Derek Jacobi, Robin Williams, Wayne Knight, Hanna Schygulla

'Briskly entertaining enough to generate mostly positive word of mouth among mature audiences.' – *Variety*

'A monstrous cinematic folly.' – *Geoff Brown, Sight and Sound*

Dead Bang

US 1989 102m Metrocolor
Warner/Lorimar (Steve Roth)
V, V*, L

A detective, hunting a killer, uncovers a white racist organization.

Loud and undistinguished thriller.

w Robert Foster d John Frankenheimer ph Gerry Fisher m Gary Chang, Michael Kamen pd Ken Adam ed Robert F. Shugrue

Don Johnson, Penelope Ann Miller, William Forsythe, Bob Balaban, Frank Military, Tate Donovan, Antoni Stutz, Mickey Jones, Ron Campbell

'John Frankenheimer's boldest, most enjoyable, and at least partially successful attempt both to recreate the halcyon days of his early 60s reputation, and to adapt them to changing times.' – *Richard Coombs, MFB*

Dead Calm *

Australia 1988 96m colour
Warner/Kennedy Miller Productions (Terry Hayes, Doug Mitchell, George Miller)
V, V*, L

A couple bring a dangerous stranger aboard their yacht.

Effectively suspenseful.

w Terry Hayes novel Charles Williams d Phillip Noyce ph Dean Semler m Graeme Revell
pd Graham 'Grace' Walker ed Richard Francis-Bruce

Nicole Kidman, Sam Neill, Billy Zane, Rod Mulloiner, Joshua Tilden, George Shevtsov, Michael Long

The Dead Can't Lie

US 1988 97m colour
Cannon/Showtime (David Latt)

A private eye is hired to prevent a millionaire being harassed by his dead wife.

Silly supernatural thriller, dead from the neck up.

wd Lloyd Fonvielle ph Michael Chapman
m George Clinton pd Carol Spier ed Evan Lottman

Tommy Lee Jones, Virginia Madsen, Colin Bruce, Kevin Jarre, Frederic Forrest

'You may not like these people, nor pity them, but you'll never forget this picture!'

Dead End ***

US 1937 92m bw
Samuel Goldwyn
V*, L

A slice of life in New York's east side, where slum kids and gangsters live in a river street next to a luxury apartment block.

Highly theatrical film of a highly theatrical play, more or less preserving the single set and overcoming the limitations of the script and setting by sheer cinematic expertise. It is chiefly remembered, however, for introducing the Dead End Kids to a delighted world.

w Lillian Hellman play Sidney Kingsley d William Wyler ph Gregg Toland m Alfred Newman
ad Richard Day

Joel McCrea, Sylvia Sidney, *Humphrey Bogart*, Wendy Barrie, Claire Trevor, Allen Jenkins, *Marjorie Main*, James Burke, Ward Bond, *The Dead End Kids* (Billy Halop, Leo Gorcey, Bernard Punsley, Huntz Hall, Bobby Jordan, Gabriel Dell)

'Tense and accurate transcription, but sordid and depressing . . . in for a disappointing career.' – *Variety*

AAN: best picture; Gregg Toland; Claire Trevor; Richard Day

The Dead End Kids

The films in which the original gang of young 'hooligans' (see above) appeared were as follows:

1937: DEAD END
1938: CRIME SCHOOL, ANGELS WITH DIRTY FACES
1939: THEY MADE ME A CRIMINAL, HELL'S KITCHEN, ANGELS WASH THEIR FACES, ON DRESS PARADE.

Subsequently they broke up into the LITTLE TOUGH GUYS, the EAST SIDE KIDS, and the BOWERY BOYS (all qv).

Dead Heat

US 1988 83m Technicolor
Entertainment/New World Pictures (Michael Meltzer, David Helpern)
V*, L

Two zombie cops track down their killer.

Asinine comic combination of *DOA* and *The Night of the Living Dead*.

w Terry Black d Mark Goldblatt ph Robert D. Yeoman m Ernest Troost pd Craig Stearns
ed Harvey Rosenstock

Treat Williams, Joe Piscopo, Lindsay Frost, Darren McGavin, Vincent Price, Clare Kirkconnell, Keye Luke, Ben Mittleman

Dead Heat on a Merry Go Round

US 1967 108m Technicolor
Columbia (Carter de Haven)
V*

An ex-con breaks parole and plans to rob Los Angeles Airport.

Boringly arty caper comedy-melodrama, concentrating less on the robbery than on its hero's sexual prowess. All very superficially flashy, and what the title means is anybody's guess.

wd Bernard Girard ph Lionel Lindon m Stu Phillips

James Coburn, Camilla Sparv, Aldo Ray, Nina Wayne, Robert Webber, Rose Marie, Todd Armstrong, Marian Moses, Severn Darden

'Just fills the space between a frisky title and a tricky TV-comedy ending, but doesn't fill it with any revels that require a viewer's complete attention.' – *Time*

Dead Image: see *Dead Ringer*

Dead Man's Eyes

US   1944   64m   bw
Universal

In order to trap a murderer, a blind artist pretends to have recovered his sight.

Cheerless lower-case thriller from the disappointing *Inner Sanctum* series.

w Dwight V. Babcock   d Reginald LeBorg

Lon Chaney Jnr, Jean Parker, Paul Kelly

Dead Man's Shoes

GB   1939   67m   bw
Associated British (Walter Mycroft)

A wealthy Paris manufacturer is accused of being a criminal who once disappeared.

Sufficiently absorbing courtroom/amnesia melodrama, with British actors in a French setting.

w Hans Kafka, Nina Jarvis   d Thomas Bentley
ph Gunther Krampf   ad Ian White   ed Monica Kimmick

Leslie Banks, Joan Marion, Geoffrey Atkins, Wilfred Lawson, Judy Kelly, Nancy Price, Peter Walter Hudd, Ludwig Stossel

'Goes straight into tense situations, and there are unexpected twists . . . should do well.' – *Variety*

Dead Men Are Dangerous

GB   1938   69m   bw
Pathé/Welwyn (Warwick Ward)

A down-and-out changes clothes with a corpse and is accused of murder.

Lethargic thriller, unconvincing in detail.

w Victor Kendall, Harry Hughes, Vernon Clancy
novel Hidden by H. C. Armstrong   d Harold French

Robert Newton, Betty Lynne, John Warwick, Peter Gawthorne

Dead Men Don't Wear Plaid *

US   1982   88m   bw
Universal/Aspen Film Society (David V. Picker, William E. McEuen)
V, V*, L, S

A private eye is hired by a beautiful girl to find her father's murderer.

Ingenious but overstretched prank in which the hero apparently (by intercutting) gets involved with famous crime stars of the forties: Bogart, Ladd, Bacall, Stanwyck, etc. The basic script is simply not funny enough to support the superstructure, though the selection of lines from the oldies is often ingenious.

w Carl Reiner, George Gipe, Steve Martin   d Carl Reiner   ph Michael Chapman   m Miklos Rozsa
pd John DeCuir   ed Bud Molin

Steve Martin, Rachel Ward, Carl Reiner, Reni Santoni

'The content is undergraduate facetiousness at its worst, but at least the excerpts themselves provide a pleasant *noir* anthology.' – *Sight and Sound*

Dead Men Tell No Tales

GB   1938   80m   bw
British National (John Corfield)

The matron of a school for boys is murdered after winning a lottery.

Reasonably intriguing mystery.

w Walter Summers, Stafford Dickens, Emlyn Williams   *novel* The Norwich Victims by Francis Beeding   d David MacDonald   ph Bryan Langley
md W. L. Trytel   ed James Corbett

Emlyn Williams, Hugh Williams, Marius Goring, Lesley Brook, Sara Seegar

Dead Men Walk

US   1943   64m   bw
PRC
V*

A vampire returns from death to destroy his twin brother.

Incompetent chiller partly sustained by its star performance.

w Fred Myton   d Sam Newfeld

George Zucco, Mary Carlisle

Dead of Night ****

GB   1945   104m   bw
Ealing (Sidney Cole, John Croydon)
V*, L

An architect is caught up in an endless series of recurring dreams, during which he is told other people's supernatural experiences and finally murders the psychiatrist who is trying to help him.

Chillingly successful and influential compendium of the macabre, especially effective in its low-key handling of the linking sequence with its circular ending.

w *John Baines, Angus Macphail,* based on stories by themselves, H. G. Wells, E. F. Benson   d *Cavalcanti, Charles Crichton, Robert Hamer, Basil Dearden*
ph Douglas Slocombe, Stan Pavey   m *Georges Auric*
ad Michael Relph

Mervyn Johns, Roland Culver, Mary Merrall, Judy Kelly, Anthony Baird, Sally Ann Howes, Frederick Valk, Googie Withers, Ralph Michael, Esmé Percy, Basil Radford, Naunton Wayne, Miles Malleson, *Michael Redgrave,* Hartley Power, Elizabeth Welch

'In a nightmare within a nightmare are contained five separate ghost stories . . . they have atmosphere and polish, they are eerie, they are well acted.' – *Richard Winnington*

'One of the most successful blends of laughter, terror and outrage that I can remember.' – *James Agee*

'The five ghost stories accumulate in intensity until the trap closes in the surrealist climax.' – *Pauline Kael, 1968*

Dead of Winter

US   1986   100m   Metrocolor
UIP/MGM-UA (John Bloomgarden, Marc Shmuger)
V*, L

An actress finds herself cast for a role which involves her being trapped in a country house with two villains.

Oddball suspenser with talent which seems to have expected something better.

w Marc Shmuger, Mark Malone   d Arthur Penn
ph Jan Weincke   m Richard Einhorn   pd Bill Brodie   ed Rick Shaine

Mary Steenburgen, Roddy McDowall, Jan Rubes, William Russ

Dead or Alive

Italy/US   1967   89m   Eastmancolor
Documento/Selmur (Albert Band)
V
US title: *A Minute to Pray, a Second to Die*

A gunman with a paralysed right arm helps a state governor rid a town of bandits.

Semi-spaghetti Western with a strong cast and violent action scenes.

w Ugo Liberatore, Louis Garfinkle   d Franco Giraldi
ph Aiace Parolin   m Carlo Rustichelli

Robert Ryan, Arthur Kennedy, Alex Cord, Nicoletta Machiavelli

Dead Pigeon on Beethoven Street

West Germany   1972   103m   DeLuxe
Bavaria Atelier

An American private eye is shot dead in Germany by an international extortion gang, and his partner arrives to seek revenge.

Cheapskate thriller of interest only to addicts of the director.   wd Samuel Fuller

Glenn Corbett, Christa Lang, Anton Diffring

Dead Poets Society **

US   1989   129m   Metrocolor
Warner/Touchstone/Silver Screen Partners IV/Witt-Thomas Productions (Steven Haft, Paul Junger Witt, Tony Thomas)
V, V*, L, S

A new English teacher subverts tradition by encouraging his students to enjoy life.

Heartfelt, but a little too manipulative to be totally successful.

w Tom Schulman   d Peter Weir   ph John Seale
m Maurice Jarre   pd Wendy Stites   ed William Anderson, Lee Smith, Priscilla Nedd

Robin Williams, Robert Sean Leonard, Ethan Hawke, Josh Charles, Gale Hansen, Dylan Kussman, Allelon Ruggiero, James Waterston, Norman Lloyd

AA: Tom Schulman

AAN: best picture; Robin Williams; Peter Weir

The Dead Pool

US   1988   91m   Technicolor
Warner/Malpaso (David Valdes)
V, V*, L

Inspector Callahan investigates a murder and the game of Dead Pool, in which people bet on certain celebrities dying within a specified time.

Fifth and worst in the series involving a tough cop that began with *Dirty Harry.*

w Steve Sharon   *story* Steve Sharon, Durk Pearson, Sandy Shaw   d Buddy Van Horn   ph Jack N. Green   m Lalo Schifrin   pd Edward C. Carfagno
ed Ron Spang

Clint Eastwood, Patricia Clarkson, Liam Neeson, Evan C. Kim, David Hunt, Michael Currie, Michael Goodwin, Darwin Gillett, Anthony Charnota

Dead Reckoning *

US   1947   100m   bw
Columbia (Sidney Biddell)
V*, L

Two war veterans are on their way to be decorated in Washington when one disappears.

Dour, complexly plotted thriller, a typical Hollywood *film noir* of the post-war years but a long way behind *Gilda* in likeability. The hero confesses the plot to a priest, and all the way it is more glum than fun.

w Oliver H. P. Garrett, Steve Fisher   d John Cromwell
ph Leo Tover   md Morris Stoloff   m Marlin Skiles

Humphrey Bogart, Lizabeth Scott, *Morris Carnovsky,* Charles Cane, William Prince, Marvin Miller, Wallace Ford, James Bell

'The atmosphere is fraught with sinister suggestion.' – *Sunday Express*

Dead Ringer *

US   1964   116m   bw
Warner (William H. Wright)
V, V*, L
GB title: *Dead Image*

A woman shoots her rich twin sister and assumes her identity.

High camp star vehicle, full of memories of long ago but rather drearily assembled and far too long, though Miss Davis as ever is in fighting form.

w Albert Beich, Oscar Millard   d Paul Henreid
ph Ernest Haller   m André Previn

Bette Davis, Karl Malden, Peter Lawford, Philip Carey, Jean Hagen, Estelle Winwood, George Chandler, Cyril Delevanti

Dead Ringers *

Canada 1988 115m colour

Rank/The Mantle Clinic II/Morgan Creek Productions (David Cronenberg, Marc Boyman)

V, V*, L, S

Identical twins, top gynaecologists, indulge in confusing their identities.

Downbeat and grisly, though possessing a certain elegance of style.

w David Cronenberg, Norman Snider book Twins by Barry Wood d David Cronenberg ph Peter Suschitsky m Howard Shore pd Carol Spier ed Ronald Sanders

Jeremy Irons, Geneviève Bujold, Heidi von Palleske, Barbara Gordon, Shirley Douglas, Stephen Lack, Nick Nicholas, Lynne Cormack

'Its disturbing impact derives from a laying bare of male fantasies in such a way that masculinity itself is revealed as fragile, unstable, even impossible.' – Pam Cook, MFB

Dead Run

France 1967 100m colour

SNC (René Picneres)

original title: Deux Billets pour Mexico

A pickpocket steals top-secret papers and is chased across Europe by the CIA and a ruthless freelance espionage outfit.

Lightweight thriller, with performances to match, and of little interest, even on the level of a travelogue.

w Christian-Jaque, Michael Levine, Pascal Jardin novel Dead Run by Robert Sheckley d Christian-Jaque ph Pierre Petit m Gerard Calvi ad Jurgen Kiebach ed Jacques Desagneaux

Peter Lawford, Ira von Furstenberg, Georges Geret, Maria Bucella, Werner Peters, Wolfgang Kieling, Horst Frank

The Dead that Walk: see The Zombies of Mora Tau

The Dead Zone *

US 1983 103m Technicolor

Lorimar/Dino de Laurentiis (Debra Hill)

V, V*, L

The survivor of a road accident discovers that he has psychic powers.

Glum thriller with a fairly predictable outcome but some well-staged episodes.

w Jeffrey Boam novel Stephen King d David Cronenberg ph Mark Irwin m Michael Kamen pd Carol Spier

Christopher Walken, Brooke Adams, Tom Skerritt, Herbert Lom, Anthony Zerbe, Colleen Dewhurst

Deadfall

GB 1968 120m DeLuxe

TCF/Salamanda (Paul Monash, Jack Rix)

Robbery turns sour when a cat burglar falls in love with the wife of his homosexual partner.

Drearily fashionable romantic melodrama with far too few high spots and generally dull performances.

wd Bryan Forbes novel Desmond Cory ph Gerry Turpin m John Barry

Michael Caine, Eric Portman, Giovanna Ralli, Nanette Newman, David Buck

'Exhausted no doubt by their past passions and childhood traumas, the principal protagonists move like so many somnambulists through the turgid labyrinth . . . whatever the intention, Deadfall merely falls flat on its somewhat ludicrous face.' – MFB

Deadlier Than the Male

GB 1966 101m Techniscope

Rank/Sydney Box (Betty E. Box)

Bulldog Drummond traces the death of oil company executives to a master criminal using glamorous female assassins.

Just about tolerable recreation of Drummond in the modern world, with too little style, too much violence and sex, and an almost total lack of self-mockery. A sequel Some Girls Do (qv) was an unmitigated disaster.

w Jimmy Sangster, David Osborn, Liz Charles-Williams d Ralph Thomas ph Ernest Steward m Malcolm Lockyer ad Alex Vetchinsky

Richard Johnson, Nigel Green, Elke Sommer, Sylva Koscina, Suzanna Leigh, Zia Mohyeddin, Steve Carlson

'The original Drummond would have found the whole thing rather distasteful.' – MFB

Deadline: see Deadline USA

Deadline at Dawn

US 1946 82m bw

RKO

A sailor on leave passes out, finds the girl he was with has been murdered, and is helped by a philosophical taxi driver and a girl.

This could have been another Crossfire, but is smothered by pretentious writing and uncertain direction. The credits are interesting, though.

w Clifford Odets d Harold Clurman ph Nicholas Musuraca m Hanns Eisler

Paul Lukas, Bill Williams, Susan Hayward, Osa Massen, Lola Lane

Deadline for Murder

US 1946 64m bw

TCF (Sol M. Wurtzel)

A gambler gets mixed up in the theft of a government document.

Reliable supporting fare.

w Irving Cummings Jnr d James Tinling

Paul Kelly, Kent Taylor, Sheila Ryan, Jerome Cowan, Renee Carson

Deadline Midnight: see —30—

Deadline USA *

US 1952 87m bw

TCF (Sol C. Siegel)

GB title: Deadline

Despite threats and the killing of a witness, a crusading newspaper goes ahead with a story about the crimes of a powerful gangster.

Watchable newspaper melodrama with nothing much to say except that America must wake up to the enemy within. Smooth production, but too much semi-pretentious talk.

wd Richard Brooks ph Milton Krasner m Cyril Mockridge

Humphrey Bogart, Kim Hunter, Ethel Barrymore, Ed Begley, Paul Stewart, Warren Stevens, Martin Gabel, Joe de Santis, Audrey Christie, Jim Backus

Deadlock: see Wedlock

The Deadly Affair **

GB 1966 106m Technicolor

Columbia/Sidney Lumet

A Foreign Office man apparently commits suicide; his colleague is unconvinced and finally uncovers a spy ring.

Compulsive if heavy-going thriller from the sour-about-spies era, deliberately glum, photographed against the shabbiest possible London backgrounds in muddy colour. Solidly entertaining for sophisticated grown-ups.

w Paul Dehn novel Call for the Dead by John Le Carré d Sidney Lumet ph Frederick A. Young m Quincy Jones

James Mason, Simone Signoret, Harry Andrews, Maximilian Schell, Harriet Andersson, Kenneth Haigh, Max Adrian, Robert Flemyng, Roy Kinnear, Lynn Redgrave

'The whole film is a most skilful organisation of action, motive and character.' – Dilys Powell

The Deadly Bees

GB 1966 83m Technicolor

Amicus

A pop singer goes on holiday to a remote farm and finds herself menaced by killer bees.

Flat little thriller with one very obvious twist and no monster: just those bees.

w Robert Bloch, Anthony Marriott d Freddie Francis

Frank Finlay, Guy Doleman, Suzanna Leigh, Catherine Finn

'To the valley of mystery came the shadow of death!'

Deadly Blessing

US 1981 102m Metrocolor

Polygram/Interplanetary (William Gilmore)

V*

A strict Hittite sect in Pennsylvania is disrupted by the murderous activities of an incubus.

Further developments from the school of Alien, Omen and The Exorcist; basically a succession of well-engineered shocks punctuated by long periods of boredom.

w Glenn M. Benest, Matthew Barr, Wes Craven d Wes Craven ph Robert Jessup m James Horner sp Jack Bennett

Maren Jensen, Susan Buckner, Jeff East, Ernest Borgnine, Lisa Hartman, Lois Nettleton

The Deadly Companions *

US 1961 90m Pathecolor Panavision

Warner/Pathé America (Charles B. Fitzsimmons)

V*, L

An army sergeant, a deserter, a trigger-happy gunman and a saloon hostess join forces to rob a bank.

Disjointed but rather attractive little Western let down by corny moments in the script.

w A. S. Fleishman d Sam Peckinpah ph William H. Clothier m Martin Skiles, Raoul Kraushaar

Brian Keith, Maureen O'Hara, Chill Wills, Steve Cochran

Deadly Force

US 1983 95m Consolidated Film Industries colour

Hemdale/Sandy Howard

V*

An ex-cop returns to Los Angeles to hunt a serial killer, to the annoyance of local police, gangsters and his estranged wife.

Tacky, dim-witted thriller, never less than implausible and hardly watchable.

w Ken Barnett, Barry Schneider, Robert Vincent O'Neil d Paul Aaron ph Norman Leigh, David Myers m Gary Scott pd Alan Roderick-Jones ed Roy Watts

Wings Hauser, Joyce Ingalls, Paul Shenar, Al Ruscio, Arlen Dean Snyder, Lincoln Kilpatrick

Deadly Friend

US 1986 99m Technicolor

Warner/Pan Arts Layton (Robert M. Sherman)

V, V*, L

A bright kid robotizes a victimized girl and helps her get her revenge.

Silly but nasty horror flick of the Elm Street genre.

w Bruce Joel Rubin novel Friend by Diana Henstell d Wes Craven ph Philip Lathrop m Charles Bernstein pd Daniel Lomino ed Michael Eliot

Matthew Laborteaux, Kristy Swanson, Michael Sharrett, Anne Twomey

Deadly is the Female: see *Gun Crazy*

'See a 1000-ton insect monster hungering for human prey!'
The Deadly Mantis
US 1957 78m bw
Universal-International

A 'prehistoric' mantis escapes from Arctic ice and travels rapidly towards New York.

Absurd and poorly crafted monster movie.

w Martin Berkeley   d Nathan Juran

Craig Stevens, Alix Talton, William Hopper

Deadly Peacemaker: see *Man with the Gun*

Deadly Strangers
GB 1974 93m Eastmancolor
Rank/Silhouette (Peter Miller)
V*

A girl accepts a lift from a motorist at a time when a mad strangler is on the loose.

Sub-Hitchcock melo-thriller with enough red herrings to sink a ship. Smartly enough done, but the grisliness needed balancing by humour.

w Philip Levene   d Sidney Hayers   ph Graham Edgar   m Ron Goodwin

Hayley Mills, Simon Ward, Sterling Hayden, Ken Hutchison, Peter Jeffrey

The Deadly Trackers
US 1973 104m Technicolor
Warner/Cine Film (Ed Rosen, Fouad Said)
V*, L

A sheriff stalks the bandits who killed his wife and son.

Lurid and ludicrous Western started, and abandoned, by Samuel Fuller; the challenge need not have been taken up.

w Lukas Heller   d Barry Shear   ph Gabriel Torres   m various

Rod Taylor, Richard Harris, Al Lettieri, Neville Brand, William Smith

'It is no more than the outline of a shadow.' – *Tony Rayns*

'An incoherent, blood-soaked chase story.' – *New Yorker, 1977*

The Deadly Trap
France/Italy 1971 100m Eastmancolor
Corona/Pomereu/Oceania
V*

The children of an American couple in Paris are kidnapped.

Smoothly made thriller which spends rather too much time being chic.

w Sidney Buchman, Eleanor Perry   novel *The Children are Gone* by Arthur Cavanaugh   d René Clément

Faye Dunaway, Frank Langella, Barbara Parkins

Deadwood Dick
US 1940 bw serial: 15 eps
Columbia

A crusading editor in disguise takes on a gang of renegades led by The Skull.

Mildly hilarious Western serial, under the gun of Laurel and Hardy's old director.

d James W. Horne

Don Douglas, Lane Chandler, Harry Harvey

Deadwood '76
US 1965 97m Technicolor Techniscope
Ember/Fairway (Nicholas Meriwether)

In Deadwood, a young man who is mistaken for Billy the Kid finds himself at odds with the townspeople.

Poor acting and production values do nothing to aid an incoherent and convoluted narrative.

w Arch Hall Jnr   d James Landis   ph William Zsigmond, Lewis Guinn   m Manuel Francisco ad D. Reed III   ed Anthony M. Lanza

Arch Hall Jnr, Jack Lester, Melissa Morgan, William Watters, Robert Dix, La Donna Cottier

'It looks like a carbon copy of the worst of the Italian Westerns.' – *David McGillivray, MFB*

† Unshown in its home country, the film received a British release six years after it was made.

Deal of the Century
US 1983 98m Technicolor
Warner (Bud Yorkin)
V*, L

An arms dealer is urged not to sell a new weapon to a warmongering dictator.

Complex comedy, descending into farce when the visiting general is bribed by the availability of American women. Not a success.

w Paul Brickman   d William Friedkin   ph Richard H. Kline   m Arthur B. Rubinstein   pd Bill Malley ed Bud Smith

Chevy Chase, Sigourney Weaver, Gregory Hines, Vince Edwards, William Jarvis, William Marquez

Dealers
GB 1989 91m colour
Rank/Euston Films (William P. Cartlidge)
V, V*, L

An ambitious young dealer in the City makes good.

An admiring look at the unacceptable face of capitalism.

w Andrew MacLear   d Colin Bucksey   ph Peter Sinclair   m Richard Hartley   pd Peter J. Hampton ed Jon Costelloe

Paul McGann, Rebecca de Mornay, Derrick O'Connor, John Castle, Paul Guilfoyle, Rosalind Bennett, Adrian Dunbar, Nicholas Hewetson

Dear Brigitte
US 1965 100m DeLuxe Cinemascope
TCF (Henry Koster)
V*

The small son of an American professor writes a love letter to Brigitte Bardot, and when they finally go to Paris she is charming to them.

Mild family comedy quaintly set around a decaying Mississippi riverboat home; despite assured performances, it all gets a bit icky at times.

w Hal Kanter   novel *Erasmus with Freckles* by John Haase   d Henry Koster   ph Lucien Ballard m George Duning

James Stewart, Glynis Johns, Fabian, Cindy Carol, Billy Mumy, John Williams, Jack Kruschen, Brigitte Bardot, Ed Wynn, Alice Pearce

Dear Heart *
US 1964 114m bw
Warner (Martin Manulis)

At a postmasters' convention in New York, two middle-aged delegates fall in love.

Charming, understated, overlong romantic drama in the *Marty* tradition; all quite professional and satisfying.

w Tad Mosel   d Delbert Mann   ph Russell Harlan m Henry Mancini

Glenn Ford, Geraldine Page, Angela Lansbury, Michael Anderson Jnr, Barbara Nichols, Patricia Barry, Charles Drake, Ruth McDevitt, Neva Patterson, Alice Pearce, Richard Deacon

AAN: title song (m Henry Mancini, ly Jay Livingston, Ray Evans)

Dear Inspector *
France 1977 105m Eastmancolor
Ariane/Mondex (Alexander Mnouchkine)
V*
original title: *Tendre Poulet*

A female detective chases a murderer, helped by her professor boyfriend.

Very likeable comedy-thriller with neat performances. Popular in America, it was translated into a series for television, but didn't run.

w Michel Audiard, Philippe de Broca   novel Jean-Paul Rouland, Claude Olivier   d Philippe de Broca ph Jean-Paul Schwartz   m Georges Delerue

Annie Girardot, Philippe Noiret, Catherine Alric, Hubert Deschamps

Dear John *
Sweden 1964 111m bw
Sandrew (Bo Jonsson)
original title: *Kare John*

An unmarried mother in a seaside village falls for a seaman.

A slight story effectively tricked out with all manner of cinematic devices including a multitude of flashbacks. Very watchable if a little self-conscious.

wd Lars Magnus Lindgren   novel Olle Lansburg ph Rune Ericson   m Bengt-Arne Wallin

Jarl Kulle, Christina Schollin, Helena Nilsson, Morgan Anderson

'It shines with the cool clear light of the Swedish summer, and despite its glossy surface manages also to convey strong sensual pleasure.' – *Brenda Davies*

AAN: best foreign film

Dear Mr Prohack
GB 1949 91m bw
GFD/Wessex (Ian Dalrymple, Dennis Van Thal)

A treasury official copes admirably with public money but is helpless when he comes into a private fortune.

Flat little comedy in which the minor amusements are incidental to the story.

w Ian Dalrymple, Donald Bull   novel Arnold Bennett   d Thornton Freeland   ph H. E. Fowle m Temple Abady

Cecil Parker, Hermione Baddeley, Dirk Bogarde, Sheila Sim, Glynis Johns, Heather Thatcher, Henry Edwards, Judith Furse

Dear Murderer
GB 1947 94m bw
GFD/Gainsborough (Betty E. Box)
V*

Plot and counterplot among an adulterous triangle.

Thoroughly artificial pattern play set among the unreal rich, from one of those unaccountable West End successes, here boringly filmed.

w Muriel and Sydney Box, Peter Rogers   play St John L. Clowes   d Arthur Crabtree   ph Stephen Dade

Eric Portman, Greta Gynt, Dennis Price, Maxwell Reed, Jack Warner, Hazel Court, Andrew Crawford, Jane Hylton

'A quite alarming little picture.' – *Alan Dent, News Chronicle*

Dear Octopus **

GB 1943 86m bw
GFD/Gainsborough (Edward Black)
US title: *The Randolph Family*

Members of a well-to-do British family reunite for Golden Wedding celebrations.

Traditional upper-class British comedy drama, and very well done too, with opportunities for excellent character acting.

w R. J. Minney, Patrick Kirwan *play* Dodie Smith *d* Harold French *ph* Arthur Crabtree

Margaret Lockwood, Michael Wilding, *Helen Haye, Frederick Leister, Celia Johnson, Roland Culver, Athene Seyler,* Basil Radford, Nora Swinburne, Jean Cadell, Kathleen Harrison, Ann Stephens, Muriel George, Antoinette Cellier, Graham Moffatt

'The screen's gayest love story!'

Dear Ruth *

US 1947 95m bw
Paramount (Paul Jones)

A schoolgirl causes confusion when she writes love letters to a soldier using her elder sister's photograph.

Smoothly amusing family comedy from a Broadway success.

w Arthur Sheekman *play* Norman Krasna *d* William D. Russell *ph* Ernest Laszlo *m* Robert Emmett Dolan

Joan Caulfield, William Holden, Mona Freeman, Billy de Wolfe, Edward Arnold, Mary Philips, Virginia Welles

'It is unlikely that 1947 will bring a more satisfying comedy . . . so many surprising and funny twists.' – *John Thompson, New York Mirror*

† Two less amusing sequels were made using virtually the same cast: *Dear Wife* (1949, 88m, *d* Richard Haydn); *Dear Brat* (1951, 82m, *d* William A. Seiter).

Dearest Love: see *Le Souffle au Coeur*

Death at Broadcasting House *

GB 1934 71m bw
ABFD/Phoenix (Hugh Perceval)

A radio actor is murdered during a broadcast.

Intriguing little murder mystery with an unusual background.

w Basil Mason *novel* Val Gielgud *d* Reginald Denham *ph* Gunther Krampf *md* Geoffrey Goodhardt *ad* R. Holmes Paul

Ian Hunter, Austin Trevor, Mary Newland, Henry Kendall, Val Gielgud, Peter Haddon, Betty Ann Davies, Jack Hawkins, Donald Wolfit

'Your basic black comedy.'

Death Becomes Her

US 1992 104m colour
UIP/Universal (Robert Zemeckis, Steve Starkey)
V, V*, L, S

An ageing Broadway star and a novelist, both rivals for the same man, take an elixir that gives eternal life.

A small comedy overwhelmed by its impressive special effects and suffering from its director's belief that louder and faster is funnier.

w Martin Donovan, David Koepp *d* Robert Zemeckis *ph* Dean Cundey *m* Alan Silvestri *pd* Rick Carter *sp* Industrial Light and Magic *ed* Arthur Schmidt

Meryl Streep, Goldie Hawn, Bruce Willis, Isabella Rossellini, Ian Ogilvy, Adam Storke, Nancy Fish, Alaina Reed Hall, Michelle Johnson, Mary Ellen Trainor

'A black comedy that is so pleased with its own blackness that it frequently forgets to be funny.' – *Kenneth Turan, Los Angeles Times*

AAN: Visual effects

Death before Dishonor

US 1986 95m DeLuxe
Kubik/MPI/BIMA/New World
S

The Marines fight terrorists in an Arab country.

Violent exploitation actioner which will satisfy its audience.

w Frank Capra Jnr, Lawrence Kubik, John Gatliff *d* Terry J. Leonard *m* Brian May

Fred Dryer, Brian Keith, Paul Winfield, Joanna Pacula

Death Drums along the River

GB 1963 83m Technicolor Techniscope
Big Ben Films/Hallam
US title: *Sanders*

In Africa, a police commissioner foils a murderous diamond smuggler.

Stilted, often facetious cut-price version of the old warhorse, and one that should have been put out to grass.

novel Sanders of the River by Edgar Wallace *d* Lawrence Huntington *ph* Bob Huke *ed* Allan Morrison

Richard Todd, Marianne Cook, Albert Lieven, Walter Rilla, Jeremy Lloyd, Robert Arden, Vivi Bach, Bill Brewer, Simon Sabela

Death by Hanging ***

Japan 1968 117m bw VistaVision
Academy/Connoisseur/Sozosha (Masayuki Nakajima, Takuji Yamaguchi, Nagisa Oshima)
original title: *Koshikei*

A Korean student survives being hanged for the rape and killing of two Japanese girls but loses his memory and refuses to accept responsibility for his past actions.

A complex, challenging and blackly comic examination of racism, guilt and justice, filmed as a succession of re-enacted episodes, complete with chapter headings, in the life of the central character.

w Tsutomu Tamura, Mamoru Sasaki, Michinori Faukao, Nagisa Oshima *d* Nagisa Oshima *ph* Yasuhiro Yoshioka *m* Hikaru Hayashi *ad* Jusho Toda *ed* Sueko Shiraishi

Nagisa Oshima (narrator), Yun-Do Yun, Kei Sato, Fumio Watanabe, Toshiro Ishido, Masao Adachi, Mutsuhiro Toura

'For three-quarters of its length, the film can be read as a brilliantly, insolently witty Brechtian parable; an alienation effect taking one away from the appalling realities of death by hanging, the better to make one understand the implications of those realities.' – *Tom Milne*

Death from a Distance

US 1936 73m bw
Chesterfield (Maury M. Cohen)

A murderer is trapped in a planetarium.

Modest second feature which benefits from its unusual setting.

w John Krafft *d* Frank Strayer

Russell Hopton, Lola Lane, George Marion Snr, Lee Kohlmar

Death Hunt

US 1981 97m Technicolor
Golden Harvest (Murray Shostak)
V*, L

In 1931 Yukon, a reclusive trapper turns to violence when goaded by other wanderers and drunken mounties.

An arctic cross between *Straw Dogs* and *Death Wish*, and not even so good as either.

w Michael Grais, Mark Victor *d* Peter Hunt *ph* James Devis *m* Jerrold Immel

Charles Bronson, Lee Marvin, Angie Dickinson, Andrew Stevens, Ed Lauter, Carl Weathers, Henry Beckman

Death in a French Garden *

France 1985 101m Eastmancolor
Artificial Eye/Gaumont (Emmanuel Schlumberger)
V
original title: *Péril en la Demeure*; aka: *Péril*

A music teacher, seduced by the mother of his pupil, finds himself embroiled in other sexual entanglements and murder.

Elegantly stylish thriller.

w Michel Deville, Rosalinde Damamme *novel Sur la Terre Comme au Ciel* by Rene Belletto *d* Michel Deville *ph* Martial Thury *ad* Philippe Combastel *ed* Raymonde Guyot

Michel Piccoli, Nicole Garcia, Anemone, Christophe Malavoy, Richard Bohringer, Anaïs Jeanneret, Jean-Claude Jay

Death in Brunswick **

Australia 1990 109m Eastmancolor
Meridian/Film Victoria/Australian Film Finance Corp (Timothy White)
V, S

The new cook in a sleazy night-club accidentally kills his drunken assistant and asks an old friend to help him get rid of the body.

Witty black comedy of losers adrift in a world they cannot control.

w John Ruane, Boyd Oxlade *novel* Boyd Oxlade *d* John Ruane *ph* Ellery Ryan *m* Philip Judd *pd* Chris Kennedy *ed* Neil Thumpston

Sam Neill, Zoe Carides, John Clarke, Yvonne Lawley, Deborah Kennedy

'An unusual, intelligent black comedy. Some will find the film outrageous, but word-of-mouth should give the pic legs on the international art-house circuit.' – *Variety*

Death in Venice **

Italy 1971 128m Technicolor Panavision
Warner/Alfa (Mario Gallo)
V, V*, S
original title: *Morte a Venezia*

In a lush Venetian hotel one summer in the early years of the century, a middle-aged German composer on holiday falls for the charms of a silent young boy, and stays in the city too long to escape the approaching plague.

Incredibly extended and rather pointless fable enriched by moments of great beauty and directorial style; these do not quite atone for the slow pace or the muddled storyline.

w Luchino Visconti, Nicola Badalucco *novel* Thomas Mann *d* Luchino Visconti *ph* Pasquale de Santis *md* Franco Mannino *m* Gustav Mahler *ad* Ferdinando Scarfiotti

Dirk Bogarde, Bjorn Andresen, Silvana Mangano, Marisa Berenson, Mark Burns

'Maybe a story as elusive as *Death in Venice* simply can't be filmed. Visconti has made a brave attempt, always sensitive to the original; but it's finally not quite the same thing.' – *David Wilson, MFB*

'Camp and miscalculated from start to finish . . . a prime contender for the title Most Overrated Film of All Time.' – *Time Out, 1985*

AAN: costumes (Piero Tosi)

Death is My Trade **
West Germany 1977 145m colour
Contemporary/WDR/Iduna (Fred Ilgner)
original title: *Aus Einem Deutschen Leben*

A working class man rises through the Nazi hierarchy to become commandant at Auschwitz.

Dispassionate and chilling account of the banality of evil.

wd Theodor Kotulla *novel* Robert Merle *ph* Dieter Naujeck *m* Eberhard Weber *ad* Wolfgang Schunke *ed* Wolfgang Richter

Gotz George, Kai Taschner, Elisabeth Schwartz, Kurt Hubner, Hans Korte, Sigurd Fitzek, Peter Franke, Wilfried Elste, Matthias Fuchs

Death Japanese Style **
Japan 1984 124m colour/bw
Yashushi Tamaoki, Yutaka Okada
original title: *Ososhiki*; aka: *The Funeral*

An actress arranges the three-day wake and funeral of her father.

Witty and well-observed account of domestic dramas.

wd Juzo Itami *ph* Yonezo Yuasa *ad* Hiroshi Tokuda *ed* Akira Suzuki

Nobuko Miyamoto, Tsutomu Yamazaki, Kin Sugai, Shuji Otaki, Ichiro Zaitsu

The Death Kiss
US 1932 74m bw
KBS/World Wide
V*

During the making of a film an actor is murdered.

Promising murder mystery which becomes more and more muddled as it progresses; it wasn't helped by advertising suggesting that Lugosi was again playing a vampire instead of a red herring.

w Barry Barringer, Gordon Kahn *novel* Madelon St Dennis *d* Edwin L. Marin

David Manners, Adrienne Ames, Bela Lugosi, John Wray, Vince Barnett, Edward Van Sloan

Death Line
GB 1972 87m Technicolor
Rank/Jay Kanter-Alan Ladd Jnr (Paul Maslansky)
aka: *Raw Meat*

Police investigating missing persons at a London underground station discover the existence of cannibals living in abandoned tunnels.

Tightly constructed thriller, unpleasant but effective, and revelling in violence and decaying flesh.

w Ceri Jones *story* Gary Sherman *d* Gary Sherman *ph* Alex Thomson *m* Jeremy Rose *ad* Denis Gordon-Orr *sp* John Horton *ed* Geoffrey Foot

Donald Pleasence, Christopher Lee, Norman Rossington, David Ladd, Sharon Gurney, Hugh Armstrong, Clive Swift, James Cossins

'The film, a coherent whole in which the parts inter-relate suggestively rather than schematically, and rich in mythological overtones, represents one of the most remarkable debuts of recent years.' – *Robin Wood, MFB*

Death of a Champion
US 1939 67m bw
Paramount

A champion show dog is murdered, and a memory expert and a small boy solve the mystery.

Medium support with few opportunities for its star.

w Stuart Palmer, Cortland Fitzsimmons *story* Frank Gruber *d* Robert Florey

Lynne Overman, Donald O'Connor, Virginia Dale, Joseph Allen Jnr, Harry Davenport, Robert Paige

'Skimpy on plot; fair dualler.' – *Variety*

Death of a Cyclist *
Spain/Italy 1955 85m bw
Guion-Suevia/Trionfalcine
original title: *Muerte de un Ciclista*

An accident – a cyclist is knocked down and killed by an adulterous couple – tragically affects the lives of many people.

Rather like a politically conscious version of *An Inspector Calls*, this mannered and unemotional film was most interesting because of its almost Hollywoodian self-assurance.

wd Juan Antonio Bardem, *story* Luis de Igoa *ph* Alfredo Fraile *m* Isrido Maiztegui

Lucia Bose, Alberto Closas, Otello Toso, Carlos Casaravilla

'I can remember no other film which succeeds without either jealousy or absurdity in presenting a serious convincing picture of sophisticated European society.' – *Dilys Powell*

'Is it love or guilt that's making you marry me after all these years?'

Death of a Gunfighter *
US 1969 100m Technicolor
Universal (Richard E. Lyons)
V*

An unpopular marshal refuses to resign, and the situation leads to gunplay.

Downcast character Western set in the early years of the century.

w Joseph Calvelli *d* Robert Totten, Don Siegel *ph* Andrew Jackson *m* Oliver Nelson

Richard Widmark, Lena Horne, John Saxon, Carroll O'Connor, Larry Gates, Kent Smith

'A salesman's got to dream – it comes with the territory!'
'One mistake – seen by his son – unleashes with overwhelming power the great drama of our day!'

Death of a Salesman ***
US 1951 112m bw
Columbia (Stanley Kramer)

An ageing travelling salesman recognizes the emptiness of his life and commits suicide.

A very acceptable screen version of a milestone play which has become an American classic; stage conventions and tricks are cleverly adapted to cinematic use, especially when the hero walks from the present into the past and back again.

w Stanley Roberts *play* Arthur Miller *d* Laslo Benedek *ph* Franz Planer *md* Morris Stoloff *m* Alex North

Fredric March, Kevin McCarthy, Cameron Mitchell, Mildred Dunnock, Howard Smith, Royal Beal, Jesse White

　MRS LOMAN: 'Attention must finally be paid to such a man. He's not to be allowed to fall into his grave like an old dog.'
　WILLY LOMAN: 'A salesman is somebody way up there in the blue, riding on a smile and a shoeshine . . .'

'Its time shifts with light, which were poetic in the theatre, seemed shabby in a medium that can dissolve time and space so easily.' – *Stanley Kauffmann*

AAN: Franz Planer; Alex North; Fredric March; Kevin McCarthy; Mildred Dunnock

Death of a Scoundrel *
US 1956 119m bw
RKO/Charles Martin
V*, L

A Czech in New York becomes rich by fraud.

Unconvincing but intermittently entertaining melodrama, a vehicle for a male Bette Davis.

wd Charles Martin *ph* James Wong Howe *m* Max Steiner

George Sanders, Yvonne de Carlo, Coleen Gray, Victor Jory, Zsa Zsa Gabor, Nancy Gates, John Hoyt, Tom Conway

'Vague moralizing and some attempts at social comment scarcely enliven this protracted study in megalomania.' – *MFB*

Death of a Soldier
Australia 1986 93m colour Panavision
Suatu/Scotti
V*

The story of Edward J. Leonski, a psychopathic GI hanged in 1942 for the murders of three women.

Case history, most interesting for its re-creation of a period.

w William Nagle *d* Philippe Mora

James Coburn, Reb Brown, Bill Hunter, Maurie Fields, Michael Pate

The Death of Mario Ricci *
Switzerland/France/West Germany 1983 101m
　Eastmancolor
Pegase/TSR/Swanie/FR3/Tele München

A Swiss TV journalist arrives in a remote village to record an interview with a malnutrition expert, and finds himself in the middle of a mystery about the death of an Italian immigrant worker.

A rather uncontrolled drama which begins by suggesting *Bad Day at Black Rock* but becomes less interesting as it proceeds.

w Claude Goretta, Georges Haldas *d* Claude Goretta *ph* Hans Liechti *m* Arie Dzierlatka

Gian-Maria Volonte, Magali Noel, Mimsy Farmer, Heinz Bennent, Jean-Michael Dupuis

Death on the Diamond
US 1934 69m bw
MGM

Murder during a baseball game.

The story isn't much, so the picture's appeal depends on one's addiction to baseball.

w Harvey Thew, Joseph Sherman, Ralph Spence, Courtland Fitzsimmons *d* Edward Sedgwick

Robert Young, Madge Evans, Nat Pendleton, Ted Healy, C. Henry Gordon, Paul Kelly, Edward Brophy, Mickey Rooney, David Landau

'Due to plot, miscasting and some minor league technical preparation, it was two strikes to the bad before the cameras started to grind.' – *Variety*

Death on the Nile *
GB 1978 140m Technicolor
EMI (John Brabourne, Richard Goodwin)
V, V*, L, S

Hercule Poirot solves the mystery of who killed the spoilt heiress on a steamer cruising down the Nile.

A pleasant thirties atmosphere and the travel poster backgrounds are the chief assets of this rather hesitant whodunnit which plays fair enough with the audience but gives its popular cast too little to do, while its constant repetitions of the crime become rather ghoulish. On the whole, though, a very passable representation of an old-fashioned genre, and a few points up on *Murder on the Orient Express*.

w Anthony Shaffer *novel* Agatha Christie *d* John Guillermin *ph* Jack Cardiff *m* Nino Rota *pd* Peter Murton

Peter Ustinov, Bette Davis, Mia Farrow, Angela Lansbury, Jane Birkin, David Niven, George Kennedy, Jack Warden, Simon MacCorkindale, Lois Chiles, Jon Finch, Maggie Smith, Olivia Hussey, Harry Andrews, I. S. Johar

AA: costumes (Anthony Powell)

Death Race 2000 *
US   1975   79m   colour
New World (Roger Corman)
V, V*

In the year 2000, the world's most popular sport involves motor racers who compete for the highest total of human casualties.

Cheaply made macabre satire, quite well enough made to please addicts of the blackest of black comedy.

w Robert Thom, Charles Griffith, Ib Melchior
d Paul Bartel   ph Tak Fujimoto   m Paul Chihara

David Carradine, Simone Griffeth, Sylvester Stallone, Mary Woronov

'The script is hardly Swiftian and therefore treads a thin delicate line between mockery and exploitation.' – Michael Billington, Illustrated London News

Death Ship
Canada   1980   91m   CFI color
Astral Bellevue Pathé/Bloodstar

Survivors of a shipwreck take refuge on a mysterious empty ship which sets about killing them one by one.

Yes, that's the synopsis, in the wake of Killdozer and The Car, and this film is stupider than either.

w John Robins   d Alvin Rakoff

George Kennedy, Richard Crenna, Nick Mancuso, Sally Ann Howes, Kate Reid

'No woman ever loved such a man! The whole world waited while he made love!'
Death Takes a Holiday *
US   1934   78m   bw
Paramount (E. Lloyd Sheldon)

In the form of a mysterious prince, Death visits an Italian noble family to see why men fear him so.

A somewhat pretentious classic from a popular play of the twenties; interesting handling and performances, but a slow pace by modern standards.

w Maxwell Anderson, Gladys Lehman, Walter Ferris plays Maxwell Anderson and Alberto Casella
d Mitchell Leisen   ph Charles Lang   m Bernhard Kaun, Sigmund Krumgold   ad Ernst Fegte

Fredric March, Evelyn Venable, Sir Guy Standing, Katherine Alexander, Gail Patrick, Helen Westley, Kathleen Howard, Henry Travers, Kent Taylor

'Highly fantastic, but well done . . . likely to have greater appeal among the intelligentsia.' – Variety

Death Trap
US   1976   89m   colour
Mars (Mohammed Rustam)
V*

The proprietor of a motel on the edge of a swamp is a maniac who murders his guests and feeds them to his pet crocodile.

Pretty sick rip-off of Psycho, with no holds barred; a typical and regrettable example of the so-called Gothic horrors of the independent American cinema in the late seventies.

w Alvin L. Fast, Mardi Rustam   d Tobe Hooper
ph Jack Beckett   m Tobe Hooper, Wayne Bell

Neville Brand, Mel Ferrer, Carolyn Jones, Marilyn Burns, William Finley, Stuart Whitman

Death Trap (1982): see Deathtrap

'Not even a scream escapes!'
Death Valley
US   1981   88m   Technicolor
Universal (Elliott Kastner)
V*

A boy on vacation in Arizona finds himself being chased by a murderer.

Tedious shocker with little in the way of scenic background to relieve the unpleasant monotony.

w Richard Rothstein   d Dick Richards   ph Stephen H. Burum   m Dana Kaproff   ed Joel Cox

Paul Le Mat, Catherine Hicks, Stephen McHattie, A. Wilford Brimley, Edward Herrmann

Death Vengeance: see Fighting Back

Death Warrant
US   1990   89m   DeLuxe
UIP/MGM/Pathé (Mark DiSalle)
V, V*, L

A Canadian Mounted Policeman goes undercover to discover who is responsible for a series of prison murders.

An implausible thriller, given little sense of reality but affording opportunities, readily taken, for violence.

w David S. Goyer   d Deran Sarafian   ph Russell Carpenter   m Gary Chang   pd Curtis Schnell   ed G. Gregg McLaughlin, John A. Barton

Jean-Claude Van Damme, Robert Guillaume, Cynthia Gibb, George Dickerson, Art Laffeur, Patrick Kilpatrick, Joshua Miller

'Unusually sadistic even by genre standards, this well-made exploitation yarn unravels under the weight of its dim-witted carnage.' – Variety

'It began with a rape. It ended with a massacre'
Death Weekend
Canada   1976   94m   Eastmancolor   Panavision
Reitman/Dunning/Link (Ivan Reitman)
V*

Four louts take revenge on a lady driver by following her to a secluded country house.

Hoary shocker chiefly concerned with rape, the threat of rape, and various unpleasant methods of murder.

wd William Fruet   ph Robert Saad   ad Roy Forge Smith   ed Jean Lafleur, Debbie Karjala

Brenda Vaccaro, Don Stroud, Chuck Shamata

'Exploitation of the emptiest and most blatant kind.' – MFB

'Vigilante, city style . . . judge, jury and executioner!'
Death Wish *
US   1974   94m   Technicolor
Paramount/Dino de Laurentiis (Hal Landers, Bobby Roberts, Michael Winner)
V*, L

When his wife dies and his daughter becomes a vegetable after an assault by muggers, a New York businessman takes the law into his own hands.

After a highly unpleasant and sensational opening, this curious and controversial film settles down into what amounts to black comedy, with the audience well on the vigilante's side. It's not very good, but it keeps one watching.

w Wendell Mayes   novel Brian Garfield   d Michael Winner   ph Arthur J. Ornitz   m Herbie Hancock

Charles Bronson, Hope Lange, Vincent Gardenia, Stuart Margolin, Stephen Keats, William Redfield

'This urban version of Walking Tall transcends its violence to satisfy every base instinct that "we liberals" are heir to.' – Judith Crist

Death Wish 2
US   1981   95m   colour
Golan-Globus/Landers-Roberts
V, V*, L

His maid gang-raped and killed, his handicapped daughter driven to her death, Paul Kersey resumes his stalking of urban thugs.

A badly made exercise in the exploitation of the most repellent aspects of violence, without the first film's saving grace of slickness and humour.

w David Engelbach   d Michael Winner
ph Richard L. Kline, Tom Del Ruth   m Jimmy Page

Charles Bronson, Jill Ireland, Vincent Gardenia, J. D. Cannon, Anthony Franciosa

'Bad art is one thing, but Death Wish II is ludicrous.' – Variety

'The sort of sequel which makes you realize that the original wasn't half so bad as you thought.' – Margaret Hinxman, Daily Mail

'It doesn't contain an ounce of life. It slinks onto the screen and squirms for a while, and is over.' – Roger Ebert

Death Wish 3
US   1985   90m   colour
Cannon (Menahem Golan, Yoram Globus)
V, V*, L

Paul Kersey, the urban vigilante, eliminates a gang of thugs terrorizing an apartment block.

The killing sprees have become routine, and there's nothing else of interest in this boring sequel to a sequel.

w Michael Edmonds   d Michael Winner   ph John Stanier   m Jimmy Page   pd Peter Mullins   ed Arnold Crust

Charles Bronson, Deborah Raffin, Ed Lauter, Martin Balsam, Gavan O'Herlihy

Death Wish 4: The Crackdown
US   1987   99m   colour
Cannon (Pancho Kohner)
V, V*, L

The ageing vigilante attacks drug dealers in Los Angeles.

Repetitious violence, with little narrative, other than villains being set up so that they can be mown down.

w Gail Morgan Hickman   d J. Lee-Thompson   ph Gideon Porath   m Paul McCallum, Valentine McCallum, John Bisharat   ad Whitney Brooke Wheeler   ed Peter Lee Thompson

Charles Bronson, Kay Lenz, John P. Ryan, Perry Lopez, Soon-Tek Oh, George Dickerson, Dana Barron, Jesse Dabson

'The Vigilante Is Back . . .'
Death Wish 5: The Face of Death
US   1993   90m   colour
21st Century (Damian Lee)
V, V*

A university professor seeks revenge after his girlfriend is first disfigured and then killed by her former lover, a gangster.

A rerun of the original movie, adding little that is new and nothing that is interesting.

wd Allan A. Goldstein   ph Curtis Petersen   m Terry Plumeri   pd Csaba A. Kertesz   ed Patrick Rand

Charles Bronson, Lesley-Anne Down, Michael Parks, Saul Rubinek, Kenneth Welsh

'Comes off as a flat-footed, by-the-numbers programmer that, judging from what's on-screen, failed to spark much enthusiasm among the people who made it.' – Variety

† The film was released direct to video in Britain.

Deathcheaters
Australia   1976   96m   colour
Australian Film Commission/Roadshow/D. L. Taffner/Trenchard Productions (Brian Trenchard Smith)

Two Vietnam veterans turned stuntmen are hired to infiltrate a Filipino fortress guarded by 150 men.

Jocular romp that provides an excuse for a succession of low-cost stunts, from car crashes to hang gliding.

w Michael Cove   *story* Brian Trenchard Smith
d Brian Trenchard Smith   *ph* John Seale   *m* Peter
Martin   *ad* Darrell Lass   *ed* Ron Williams

John Hargreaves, Grant Page, Margaret Gerard, Noel
Ferrier, Judith Woodroffe

The Deathmaster
US   1973   88m   DeLuxe
RF World Entertainment/AIP

California surfers cheerfully adopt a local mystic, not
knowing that he is a vampire.

Modestly budgeted teenage screamer, competently
made but of interest only to avid bibliographers of
Count Dracula.

w R. L. Grove   *d* Ray Danton

Robert Quarry, Brenda Dickson, Bill Ewing, John
Fiedler

Deathsport
US   1978   83m   Metrocolor
New World (Roger Corman)
V*

A popular game of the future involves gladiators
willing to lose their lives against lethal motorcyclists.

Low-budget shocker for teenagers, by *Rollerball* out of
Death Race. Of no possible interest except as
exploitation.

w Henry Suso, Donald Stewart   *d* Henry Suso,
Allan Arkush   *ph* Gary Graver   *m* Andrew Stein

David Carradine, Claudia Jennings, Richard Lynch,
William Smithers

Deathtrap *
US   1982   116m   Technicolor
Warner/LAH (Burtt Harris)
V, V*

A playwright past his best conceives a plan to murder
an upcoming rival and steal his script.

This thriller on the lines of *Sleuth* was enjoyable
enough on stage, but on the screen, despite
pretensions to style, it takes far too long to unravel its
very few twists, the last of which is badly fumbled.

w Jay Presson Allen   *play* Ira Levin   *d* Sidney
Lumet   *ph* Andrzej Bartkowiak   *m* Johnny Mandel
pd Tony Walton

Michael Caine, Christopher Reeve, Dyan Cannon,
Irene Worth, Henry Jones

'It plays absolutely fair, more or less, and yet fools us
every time, more or less.' – *Roger Ebert*

Deathwatch **
France/West Germany   1980   128m   Fuji colour
   Panavision
Contemporary/Quartet (Gabriel Boustiani, Janine Rubeiz)
V*, L

In the future, a TV documentary producer has a
cameraman, who has the apparatus implanted in his
brain, follow every moment in the life of a dying
woman.

Grim fable of media manipulation and sensationalist
pressures on popular entertainment that retains its
resonance.

w Bertrand Tavernier, David Rayfiel   *novel The
Continuous Katherine Mortenhoe* by David Compton
d Bertrand Tavernier   *ph* Pierre-William Glenn
m Antoine Duhamel   *ad* Tony Pratt   *ed* Armand
Psenay, Michael Ellis

Romy Schneider, Harvey Keitel, Harry Dean Stanton,
Max von Sydow, Therese Liotard

'Degenerate, disgusting, and ... deliciously funny!'
Decadence
GB/Germany   1993   108m   colour
Mayfair/Vendetta (Lance W. Reynolds, Christoph Meyer-Weil)

A newly rich, upwardly mobile couple indulge in
affairs: the husband with an upper-class woman, the
wife with an investigator she has hired to spy on her
husband.

An intensely theatrical work transfers unsuccessfully
to film, with Berkoff playing a philandering husband
and a private eye who mixes sex and business, and
Collins as both a wealthy and a nouveau-riche
woman; its stylized, over-the-top acting seems merely
grotesque on the big screen and its satire on the get-
rich-quick decade of the 80s is without bite.

wd Steven Berkoff   *ph* Denis Lenoir   *m* Stewart
Copeland   *pd* Yolanda Sonnabend, Simon Holland
ed John Wilson

Steven Berkoff, Joan Collins, Christopher Biggins,
Michael Winner, Marc Sinden

'A ripe, belching, heaving, power-drill satire of 1980s
Thatcherite Britain that's as full of excesses as the
passé targets it parodies.' – *Variety*

'This offers very little to keep you glued to your seat
for what is, in reality, two rather uncomfortable
hours.' – *Kim Newman, Empire*

Decameron Nights
GB   1952   94m   Technicolor
Film Locations (M. J. Frankovich)

Young Boccaccio entertains a glamorous widow and
her three guests with stories.

Feeble costume charade with all the cuckolding off-
screen: insipid and artificial.

w George Oppenheimer   *d* Hugo Fregonese
ph Guy Green   *m* Antony Hopkins

Louis Jourdan, Joan Fontaine, Binnie Barnes, Joan
Collins, Godfrey Tearle, Eliot Makeham, Noel Purcell

'The sort of hybrid international production of which
experience has made one mistrustful.' – *Gavin Lambert*

Deceived
US   1991   108m   Eastmancolor
Warner/Touchstone/Silver Screen Partners IV (Michael Finnell,
   Wendy Dozoretz, Ellen Collett)
V, V*, L

A happily married New York art dealer discovers that
her husband is not the person he claims to be.

An interesting premise is ignored in preference to an
increasingly predictable narrative.

w Mary Agnes Donoghue, Derek Saunders
d Damian Harris   *ph* Jack N. Green   *m* Thomas
Newman   *pd* Andrew McAlpine   *ed* Neil Travis,
Lisa M. Citron

Goldie Hawn, John Heard, Ashley Peldon, Robin
Bartlett, Tom Irwin, Amy Wright, Jan Rubes, Kate
Reid

'A visually interesting but essentially made-to-order
thriller.' – *Sight and Sound*

The Deceivers
GB/India   1988   112m   colour
Merchant-Ivory/Michael White/Cinecom/Film Four (Ismail
   Merchant, Tim Van Rellim)
V*, L, S

An English army officer serving in India in the 1820s
infiltrates the cult of Thuggee, a secret society of
murderers.

Muddled melodrama that fails to carry any conviction.

w Michael Hirst   *novel* John Masters   *d* Nicholas
Meyer   *ph* Walter Lassally   *m* John Scott   *pd* Ken
Adam   *ed* Richard Trevor

Pierce Brosnan, Saeed Jaffrey, Shashi Kapoor, Helena
Michell, Keith Michell, David Robb

'Two men loved her ... she loved them both'
December Bride *
GB   1990   90m   colour
BFI/Film Four/CTE/British Screen/Little Bird (Jonathan
   Cavendish)
V

A servant girl with an illegitimate daughter defies
local and religious feeling when she refuses to marry
either of the two brothers who might be the father.

Engaging drama of individual struggle.

w David Rudkin   *novel* Sam Hanna Bell
d Thaddeus O'Sullivan   *ph* Bruno de Keyzer
m Jurgen Kneiper   *pd* Adrian Smith   *ed* Rodney
Holland

Donal McCann, Saskia Reeves, Ciaran Hinds, Patrick
Malahide, Brenda Bruce, Michael McKnight, Geoffrey
Golden, Dervia Kirwan

Deception **
US   1946   112m   bw
Warner (Henry Blanke)
V*

A European cellist returning to America after the war
finds that his former girlfriend has a rich and jealous
lover.

Downcast melodrama made when its star was
beginning to slide; today it seems irresistible bosh
with a background of classical music, done with
intermittent style especially by Claude Rains as the
egomaniac lover.

w John Collier   *play Monsieur Lamberthier* by Louis
Verneuil   *d* Irving Rapper   *ph* Ernest Haller
m Erich Wolfgang Korngold

Bette Davis, *Claude Rains*, Paul Henreid, John Abbott,
Benson Fong

'It's like grand opera, only the people are thinner ... I
wouldn't have missed it for the world.' – *Cecelia Ager*

'Exquisitely foolish: a camp classic.' – *New Yorker, 1977*

† Previously filmed in 1929 as *Jealousy*, with Fredric
March and Jeanne Eagels.

Decision Against Time: see *The Man in the Sky*

Decision at Sundown
US   1957   77m   Technicolor
Columbia (Harry Joe Brown)
V*

A cowboy tracks down the badman who has seduced
his wife.

Routine small-town Western, efficiently done.

w Charles Lang Jnr   *d* Budd Boetticher

Randolph Scott, John Carroll, Karen Steele, Valerie
French, Noah Beery Jnr, Andrew Duggan

Decision before Dawn *
US   1951   119m   bw
TCF (Anatole Litvak, Frank McCarthy)

In 1944, anti-Nazi German POWs are parachuted into
Germany to obtain information.

Meticulous, well made but unexciting spy story
which seldom comes vividly to life.

w Peter Viertel   *novel Call It Treason* by George Howe
d Anatole Litvak   *ph* Franz Planer   *m* Franz
Waxman   *ed* Dorothy Spencer

Oskar Werner, Richard Basehart, Gary Merrill,
Hildegarde Neff, Dominique Blanchar, Helene
Thimig, O. E. Hasse, Hans Christian Blech

AAN: best picture; editing

The Decision of Christopher Blake
US   1948   75m   bw
Warner (Ranald MacDougall)

A 12-year-old boy reunites his divorcing parents.

Sentimental slop, surprisingly ill done, but with a few
good lines.

w Ranald MacDougall   *play* Moss Hart   *d* Peter
Godfrey   *ph* Karl Freund   *m* Max Steiner

Alexis Smith, Robert Douglas, *Cecil Kellaway*, Ted
Donaldson, *Harry Davenport*, John Hoyt, Mary Wickes,
Art Baker, Lois Maxwell

The Decks Ran Red
US 1958 84m bw
MGM/Andrew and Virginia Stone

Unscrupulous sailors plan to murder the entire crew of a freighter and claim the salvage money.

Solidly crafted but basically uninteresting melodrama.

w Andrew and Virginia Stone d Andrew Stone
ph Meredith M. Nicholson

James Mason, Broderick Crawford, Dorothy Dandridge, Stuart Whitman

Decline and Fall
GB 1968 113m DeLuxe
TCF/Ivan Foxwell
aka: Decline and Fall of a Birdwatcher

An innocent, accident-prone Oxford undergraduate is expelled and after various adventures in high and low society is convicted as a white slaver.

Flabby, doomed attempt to film a satirical classic which lives only on the printed page. Odd moments amuse.

w Ivan Foxwell novel Evelyn Waugh d John Krish ph Desmond Dickinson m Ron Goodwin

Robin Phillips, Donald Wolfit, Genevieve Page, Robert Harris, Leo McKern, Colin Blakely, Felix Aylmer, Donald Sinden, Griffith Jones

'The British Graduate.' – New Yorker

'Literate, lavishly furnished, tastefully faithful.' – Observer

Decline and Fall of a Birdwatcher: see Decline and Fall

Decline of the American Empire ***
Canada 1986 101m colour
Malofilm/National Film Board Of Canada (Rene Malo, Roger Frappier)
V, V*
original title: Le Déclin de l'Empire Américain

A group of intellectuals discuss their attitudes to gender, sex and love.

Witty, perceptive conversation piece that won the Film Critics' award at the Cannes Film Festival in 1986.

wd Denys Arcand ph Guy Dufaux md François Dompierre, based on themes by Handel
ad Gaudeline Sauriol ed Monique Forcier

Dorothée Berryman, Louise Portal, Pierre Curzi, Rémy Girard, Yves Jacques, Genevieve Rioux, Daniel Briere, Gabriel Arcand

AAN: foreign film

The Decline of Western Civilization *
US 1981 100m colour
Nu-Image (Penelope Spheeris)
V, V*

A documentary of punk rock in Los Angeles in the late 70s, with disenchanted and alienated teenagers both as performers and audience.

Quirky and fascinating study of some of the unlovelier aspects of youthful rebellion; it makes an interesting companion piece to the director's first feature film, Suburbia.

d Penelope Spheeris ph Steve Conant, Bill Muerer, Penelope Spheeris m Fear, Black Flag, Germs, X, Alice Bag Band, The Circle Jerks, Catholic Discipline
ed Charles Mullin, Peter Wiehl, David Colburn

The Decline of Western Civilization Part II: The Metal Years *
US 1988 90m colour
New Line (Jonathan Dayton, Valerie Faris)
V, V*, S

Documentary on the bands and personalities of heavy metal rock.

Lively documentary of one of the noisier forms of popular entertainment, including interviews with some of its wilder practitioners.

d Penelope Spheeris ph Jeff Zimmerman, Julio Macat ed Earl Ghaffari

Aerosmith, Alice Cooper, Kiss, Ozzy Osborne, Megadeath

Decoy
US 1947 76m bw
Monogram

The girlfriend of an executed gangster tries to get her hands on his buried loot.

Surprisingly tough little co-feature of its day; even more surprisingly, the leading lady is British.

w Nedrick Young d Jack Bernhard

Jean Gillie, Edward Norris, Herbert Rudley, Robert Armstrong

Decoy (1962): see Mystery Submarine

Dédée: see Dédée d'Anvers

Dédée d'Anvers *
France 1948 95m bw
Sacha Gordine (André Paulvé)
aka: Woman of Antwerp; Dédée

A dockside prostitute falls for a sailor and arouses the jealousy of her protector.

Seamy low life melodrama, presented con brio, but rather like a tenth copy of Quai des Brumes.

w Yves Allégret, Jacques Sigurd d Yves Allégret
ph Jean Bourgoin m Jacques Besse

Simone Signoret, Marcel Pagliero, Bernard Blier, Marcel Dalio, Jane Marken

The Deep
US 1977 124m Metrocolor Panavision
Columbia/EMI/Casablanca (Peter Guber)
V*, L

Underwater treasure seekers off Bermuda clash with black villains seeking a lost consignment of morphine.

An expensive action picture which is singularly lacking in action and even in plot, but oozes with brutality and overdoes the splendours of submarine life, forty per cent of it taking place under water.

w Peter Benchley, Tracy Keenan Wynn novel Peter Benchley d Peter Yates ph Christopher Challis, Al Giddings, Stan Waterman m John Barry
pd Tony Masters

Jacqueline Bisset, Robert Shaw, Nick Nolte, Lou Gossett, Eli Wallach

'The ultimate disco experience . . . it dances on the spot for two hours, taking voodoo, buried treasure, morphine, violence and sea monsters in its stride.' – Time Out

'Peter Yates has knocked himself out doing masterly underwater action sequences in the service of a woefully crummy book.' – Russell Davies, Observer

The Deep Blue Sea *
GB 1955 99m Eastmancolor Cinemascope
TCF/London Films (Anatole Litvak)

A judge's wife attempts suicide when jilted by her ex-RAF lover.

Undistinguished adaptation of a very good play, hampered by wide screen and muddy colour, helped by thoughtful performances.

w Terence Rattigan play Terence Rattigan
d Anatole Litvak ph Jack Hildyard m Malcolm Arnold

Vivien Leigh, Kenneth More, Eric Portman, Emlyn Williams, Moira Lister, Arthur Hill, Dandy Nichols, Jimmy Hanley, Miriam Karlin

'He'd be the perfect criminal if he wasn't the perfect cop.'
Deep Cover **
US 1992 112m DeLuxe
First Independent/Image Organisation (Pierre David)
V, V*, S

A cop finds himself in trouble when he is recruited to infiltrate the operation of a Los Angeles drug dealer with powerful South American connections.

Vigorous, intelligent thriller that offers more complexity than most of its type.

w Michael Tolkin, Henry Bean d Bill Duke
ph Bojan Bazelli m Michel Colombier pd Pam Warner ed John Carter

Larry Fishburne, Jeff Goldblum, Victoria Dillard, Charles Martin Smith, Gregory Sierra, Clarence Williams III, Sydney Lassick

'Deeply cynical, almost despairing second feature from Bill Duke features enough promotable hard action, rough violence and bad attitude to make a small spring stash.' – Variety

'A formulaic police thriller with a hip-hop musical tail that constantly wags the cinematic dog.' – Philip French, Observer

Deep End *
West Germany/USA 1970 88m Eastmancolor
Maran/Kettledrum/Bavaria Atelier (Judd Bernard)

Sexual problems of two young people on the staff of a London municipal bathhouse.

Interestingly made but rather dreary and vaguely symbolic modern fable.

w Jerzy Skolimowski, Jerzy Gruza, Boleslaw Sulik
d Jerzy Skolimowski ph Charly Steinberger
m Cat Stevens

Jane Asher, John Moulder-Brown, Diana Dors, Karl Michael Vogler, Christopher Sandford

'A study in the growth of obsession that is both funny and frighteningly exact.' – Nigel Andrews, MFB

Deep in My Heart *
US 1954 132m Eastmancolor
MGM (Roger Edens)
V, V*, L, S

Sigmund Romberg, a composer-waiter in New York, is helped by writer Dorothy Donnelly and showman Florenz Ziegfeld to become a famous writer of musicals.

Standard fictionalized biopic with plenty of good turns and a sharper script than usual.

w Leonard Spigelgass d Stanley Donen
ph George Folsey m Sigmund Romberg
ad Cedric Gibbons, Edward Carfagno ch Eugene Loring

José Ferrer, Merle Oberon, Paul Henreid (as Ziegfeld), Walter Pidgeon, Helen Traubel, Doe Avedon, Tamara Toumanova, Paul Stewart, Isobel Elsom, David Burns, Jim Backus . . . and Gene Kelly, Fred Kelly, Rosemary Clooney, Jane Powell, Ann Miller, Cyd Charisse, James Mitchell, Howard Keel, Tony Martin, Joan Weldon

'When was the last time you were really scared!!!?'
'You will never forget it!!!'
Deep Red **
Italy 1975 120m Eastmancolor
Rizzoli Film/SEDA Spettacoli/Salvatore Argento
V, V*, S
original title: Profondo Rosso; aka: The Hatchet Murders

A jazz pianist who witnesses a horrific murder obsessively and ineffectually tracks down the killer.

Slick, stylish, decadent, suspenseful thriller, with a disquieting atmosphere that continually puts its audience, like its victims, off-balance. Hemmings's character owes much to his role in Antonioni's *Blow Up.*

w Dario Argento, Bernardino Zapponi d Dario Argento ph Luigi Kuveiller m Giorgio Gaslini, Goblin ad Giuseppe Bassan sp Germano Nobile, Carlo Rambaldi ed Franco Fraticelli

David Hemmings, Daria Nicolodi, Gabriele Lavia, Macha Meril, Eros Pagni, Giuliana Calandra, Glauco Mauri, Clara Calamai

'An Argento movie to treasure.' – *The Dark Side*

'A director of incomparable incompetence.' – *Vincent Canby, New York Times*

† The current British video release is of the subtitled original version. The film has also been released in an inferior dubbed version cut to 98m, which robs it of much of its narrative structure. The shorter version has been available on video.

The Deep Six
US   1958   110m   Warnercolor
Jaguar (Martin Rackin)
V*

A Quaker is unhappy at being drafted into the navy, but after initial unpopularity becomes a hero.

An ageing star contends with many hazards: slipshod production, poor colour, a dull script, and an unplayable part.

w John Twist, Martin Rackin, Harry Brown d Rudolph Maté ph John Seitz m David Buttolph

Alan Ladd, William Bendix, Efrem Zimbalist Jnr, Dianne Foster, Keenan Wynn, James Whitmore, Joey Bishop, Jeanette Nolan

Deep Valley
US   1947   104m   bw
Warner (Henry Blanke)

The daughter of a poor California farmer falls for a convict on a work gang.

Downright peculiar melodrama, a cross between *Tobacco Road* and *Cold Comfort Farm*, with touches of *High Sierra.* For collectors.

w Salka Viertel, Stephen Morehouse Avery novel Dan Totheroh d Jean Negulesco ph Ted McCord m Max Steiner

Ida Lupino, Dane Clark, Wayne Morris, Henry Hull, Fay Bainter, Willard Robertson

Deep Waters
US   1948   85m   bw
TCF

A problem orphan boy is content when adopted by a lobster fisherman.

Forgettable family film, smoothly directed and photographed.

w Richard Murphy d Henry King ph Joseph LaShelle m Cyril Mockridge

Jean Peters, Dana Andrews, Dean Stockwell, Cesar Romero, Anne Revere

Deepstar Six *
US   1989   100m   Technicolor
Tri-Star (Sean S. Cunningham, Patrick Markey)
V, V*, L, S

Underwater workers blow a hole in the sea-floor that releases a monster from the depths.

Modest, moderately suspenseful thriller with an excess of gore.

w Lewis Abernathy, Geoff Miller d Sean S. Cunningham ph Mac Ahlberg m Harry Manfredini pd John Reinhart ed David Handman

Taurean Blacque, Nancy Everhard, Greg Evigan, Miguel Ferrer, Matt McCoy, Nia Peeples, Cindy Pickett, Marius Weyers

The Deer Hunter *
US   1978   182m   Technicolor   Panavision
Universal/EMI (Barry Spikings, Michael Deeley, Michael Cimino, John Peverall)
V, V*, L, S

Three friends from a small Pennsylvania town go to fight in Vietnam.

The three-hour running time is taken up with crosscutting of a wedding, a deer hunt and a game of Russian roulette. Presumably the audience has to guess the point, if any; meanwhile it may be repelled by this long and savage if frequently engrossing film.

w Deric Washburn story Michael Cimino, Louis Garfinkle, Quinn K. Redeker and Deric Washburn d Michael Cimino ph Vilmos Zsigmond m Stanley Myers

Robert de Niro, John Cazale, John Savage, Christopher Walken, Meryl Streep

'A hollow spectacle, less about war than its effect on a community, full of specious analogies, incoherent sentimentality and belief in its own self-importance.' – *Time Out*

AA: best picture; direction; Christopher Walken

AAN: Deric Washburn; Vilmos Zsigmond; Robert de Niro; Meryl Streep

Def by Temptation
US   1990   95m   Technicolor
BFI/Troma/Orpheus/Bonded Filmworks (James Bond III)
V, V*, L

A young black man, intent on becoming a preacher, meets a woman possessed by a demon.

Slow-moving, low-budget occult thriller, more concerned with male/female relationships than horror, and showing promise of better movies to come from its first-time writer-director.

wd James Bond III ph Ernest Dickerson m Paul Laurence pd David Carrington sp Rob Benevides ed Li-Shin Yu

James Bond III, Kadeem Hardison, Bill Nunn, Samuel L. Jackson, Minnie Gentry, Rony Clanton, Melba Moore, Stephen Van Cleef

'An instant addition to the canon of so-bad-it's-good classics and, inadvertently, a fascinating glimpse into the contradictions of contemporary American black culture.' – *John Lyttle, Independent*

'Sharp, funny and borderline creepy socio-sexual horror story.' – *Kim Newman, Sight and Sound*

The Defector
France/West Germany   1966   101m   Eastmancolor
PECF/Rhein Main (Raoul Lévy)
original title: *L'Espion*

An American physicist in East Germany gets involved in the spy game.

Disenchanted espionage 'realism', not very well styled and hampered by a star at the end of his tether.

w Robert Guenette, Raoul Lévy novel *The Spy* by Paul Thomas d Raoul Lévy ph Raoul Coutard m Serge Gainsbourg

Montgomery Clift, Hardy Kruger, Macha Meril, Roddy McDowall, David Opatoshu, Christine Delaroche, Jean-Luc Godard

'All that we're finally left with is the cliché, a relatively new one, along with the triple-viced hero, that spying is not a nice profession but the good guys have to go in and win for our team. Well, East, West, or Western, what this country needs, moviewise, is a good cliché-breaker – and hang the expense.' – *Judith Crist*

Defence of the Realm **
GB   1985   96m   colour
(Rank) Enigma/NFFC (David Puttnam) (Linda Miles)
V, V*, L

A journalist tries to check the relationship between an MP and a Russian agent.

Efficient political melodrama, basically too old-fashioned to start a cult.

w Martin Stellman d David Drury ph Roger Deakins m Richard Hartley pd Roger Murray-Leach ed Michael Bradsall

Gabriel Byrne, Greta Scacchi, Denholm Elliott, Ian Bannen, Fulton Mackay, Bill Paterson

BFA: best supporting actor, Denholm Elliott

Defenceless
US   1991   104m   colour
New Visions (Renee Missel, David Bombyk)
V, V*, L

A female attorney is hired to defend the wife of her lover, who is accused of his murder.

Moderately engaging thriller, in which the acting is better than the plot.

w James Hicks story James Hicks, Jeff Burkhart d Martin Campbell ph Phil Meheux m Curt Sobel pd Curtis A. Schnell ed Lou Lombardo, Chris Wimble

Barbara Hershey, Sam Shepard, Mary Beth Hurt, J. T. Walsh, Kellie Overbey, Sheree North, Randy Brooks

'Effective (if somewhat predictable) thriller . . . Tense and engrossing.' – *Sight and Sound*

'A trite whodunnit dressed up with some good performances and an unusually emotional finale.' – *Empire*

† The film was released direct to video in Britain.

Defending Your Life **
US   1991   111m   Technicolor
Warner/Geffen (Michael Grillo)
V, V*, L

Killed in a car crash, an advertising executive finds himself in Judgement City where he must defend what he did with his life in a trial to decide his ultimate fate.

Enjoyable comedy of modern manners, less concerned with the afterlife than with the here-and-now.

wd Albert Brooks ph Allen Daviau m Michael Gore pd Ida Random ed David Finfer, Spencer Gross

Albert Brooks, Meryl Streep, Rip Torn, Lee Grant, Buck Henry, Michael Durrell, James Eckhouse, Gary Beach, Julie Cobb

'Original in concept, funny in spasms and pretty good about the American propensity to examine themselves in such minute detail that Judgement Day is likely to seem like just another spell on the analyst's couch.' – *Derek Malcolm, Guardian*

Defiance
US   1980   102m   Movielab
AIP

A young seaman staying in New York fights back against the power of an urban gang.

Belated and unnecessary addition to the gang cycle; violent nonsense.

w Thomas Michael Donnelly d John Flynn

Jan Michael Vincent, Theresa Saldana, Danny Lopez

The Defiant Ones **
US   1958   96m   bw
UA/Stanley Kramer
V, V*, L

A black and a white convict escape from a chain gang, still linked together but hating each other.

Schematic melodrama with a moral, impeccably done and with good performances.

w Nathan E. Douglas, Harold Jacob Smith   d Stanley
Kramer   ph Sam Leavitt   m Ernest Gold
ed Frederic Knudtson

Tony Curtis, Sidney Poitier, Theodore Bikel, Charles
McGraw, Lon Chaney Jnr, King Donovan, Claude
Akins, Lawrence Dobkin, Whit Bissell, Carl 'Alfalfa'
Switzer, Cara Williams

'Probably Kramer's best picture. The subject matter is
relatively simple, though "powerful"; the action is
exciting; the acting is good. But the singleness of
purpose behind it all is a little offensive.' – Pauline
Kael

† Nathan E. Douglas was a pseudonym for the
blacklisted writer Ned Young.

AA: Nathan E. Douglas, Harold Jacob Smith; Sam
Leavitt

AAN: best picture; Stanley Kramer; Tony Curtis;
Sidney Poitier; Theodore Bikel; Cara Williams;
editing

Le Défroqué *
France   1953   111m   bw
SFC/SNEG

A defrocked priest performs a gallant action which
persuades an acquaintance to become a priest himself
and try to draw his friend back into the fold.

Curious but holding moral melodrama embellished
by good acting.

w Leo Joannon, Denys de la Patellière   d Leo
Joannon   ph Nicolas Torporkoff   m Jean-Jacques
Grunenwald

Pierre Fresnay, Pierre Trabaud, Nicole Stéphane,
Marcelle Geniat, Guy Decomble, Leo Joannon, René
Blancard

Déjà Vu
GB   1985   90m   colour
Cannon (Michael Kagan)

Lovers discover that they are reincarnations of a
couple who perished 50 years ago in a fire.

Muddling, over-talkative supernatural thriller with
dollops of sex.

w Ezra D. Rappaport, Anthony Richmond
book Trevor Meldal-Johnsen   d Anthony Richmond

Jaclyn Smith, Nigel Terry, Claire Bloom, Shelley
Winters

Déjeuner sur l'Herbe: see Lunch on the Grass

The Delavine Affair
GB   1954   64m   bw
John Croydon/Monarch
US title: Murder Is News

A reporter is framed for killing an informer.

Routine British second feature.

w George Fisher   story Winter Wears a Shroud by
Robert Chapman   d Douglas Pierce

Honor Blackman, Peter Reynolds, Gordon Jackson,
Michael Balfour

A Delicate Balance *
US   1975   134m   colour
American Express/Ely Landau/Cinevision
V*

A quarrelsome Connecticut family is dominated by an
ageing matriarch, and tensions mount to a climax of
fear and threats.

Honourable but slightly boring film version of an
essentially theatrical play: the acting is the thing.

w Edward Albee   play Edward Albee   d Tony
Richardson   ph David Watkin   m none

Katharine Hepburn, Paul Scofield, Joseph Cotten, Lee
Remick, Kate Reid, Betsy Blair

The Delicate Delinquent
US   1956   101m   bw   Vistavision
Paramount/Jerry Lewis
V*, L

A New York policeman tries to make friends with an
eccentric youth who mixes with thugs; the boy
decides to train as a policeman.

Jerry Lewis's first film without Dean Martin: a
sobering experience combining zany comedy,
sentiment, pathos and social comment. The mixture
fails to rise.

wd Don McGuire   ph Haskell Boggs   m Buddy
Bregman

Jerry Lewis, Darren McGavin, Martha Hyer, Robert
Ivers, Horace McMahon

Delicatessen ***
France   1990   99m   colour
Electric/Constellation/UGC/Hachette Première (Claudie
Ossard)
V, V*, L, S

In a decaying city of the future, a butcher, who
flourishes by killing his workers and selling their
flesh, is attacked by underground vegetarian
terrorists.

A gruesome theme given exuberant, witty, cartoon-
like treatment.

wd Jean-Pierre Jeunet, Marc Caro   ph Darius
Khondji   m Carlos D'Alessio   ad Marc Caro
ed Hervé Schneid

Dominique Pinon, Marie-Laure Dougnac, Jean-
Claude Dreyfus, Karin Viard, Ticky Holgado, Anne-
Marie Pisani, Jacques Mathou

'Beautifully textured, cleverly scripted and eerily shot
. . . a zany little film that should get terrific word of
mouth.' – Variety

'An impressive achievement and extremely funny.' –
Philip French, Observer

Delicious
US   1931   106m   bw
Fox

An Irish girl in New York falls for a rich man.

Early musical, very thin, but an agreeable museum
piece for collectors.

w Guy Bolton, Sonya Levien   d David Butler
ph Ernest Palmer   m/ly George and Ira Gershwin

Janet Gaynor, Charles Farrell, El Brendel, Lawrence
O'Sullivan, Virginia Cherrill, Mischa Auer

'Cream puffs, applesauce, and plenty of nuts . . .
should do the team's business on its name strength.' –
Variety

Delightfully Dangerous
US   1945   93m   bw
UA (Charles R. Rogers)

A straitlaced girl discovers that her eldest sister is a
burlesque dancer.

Mild family comedy with music.

w Walter de Leon, Arthur Phillips   d Arthur Lubin

Jane Powell, Constance Moore, Ralph Bellamy,
Arthur Treacher

The Delinquents
Australia   1989   101m   colour
Warner/Village Roadshow (Alex Cutler, Michael Wilcox)
V, S

Two teenagers ignore adult disapproval and fall in
love.

Tiresome account of adolescent angst.

w Mac Gudgeon, Clayton Frohman   novel Criena
Rohan   d Chris Thomson   ph Andrew Lesnie
m Miles Goodman   pd Laurence Eastwood
ed John Scott

Kylie Minogue, Charlie Schlatter, Angela Punch
McGregor, Bruno Lawrence, Todd Boyce, Desiree
Smith, Melissa Jaffer

Deliverance ****
US   1972   109m   Technicolor   Panavision
Warner/Elmer Enterprises (John Boorman)
V, V(W), V*, L, S

Four men spend a holiday weekend canoeing down a
dangerous river, but find that the real danger to their
lives comes from themselves and other humans.

Vigorous, meaningful, almost apocalyptic vision of
man's inhumanity, disguised as a thrilling adult
adventure.

w James Dickey   novel James Dickey   d John Boorman
ph Vilmos Zsigmond   m Eric Weissberg

Burt Reynolds, Jon Voight, Ned Beatty, Ronny Cox,
James Dickey

'There is fundamentally no view of the material, just a
lot of painful grasping and groping.' – Stanley
Kauffmann

AAN: best picture; John Boorman

Delta Force
US   1986   129m   colour
Cannon (Menahem Golan)
V, V*, L

A TWA plane is hijacked in Athens and rescued by an
elite force.

What starts more or less as a recapitulation of fact
turns at the half-way point into macho fantasy. Oddly
enough, the paying customers rejected the mix.

w James Bruner, Menahem Golan   d Menahem
Golan   ph David Gurfinkel   m Alan Silvestri

Chuck Norris, Lee Marvin, Martin Balsam, Joey
Bishop, Shelley Winters, Robert Forster, Lainie
Kazan, George Kennedy, Hanna Schygulla, Susan
Strasberg, Bo Svenson, Robert Vaughn

'An exercise in wish fulfilment . . . it's easy to get off
on all this, as millions surely will, so long as you are
willing to put your brain in hibernation for more than
two hours.' – Variety

Delta Force 2
US   1990   111m   colour
UIP/Cannon (Yoram Globus, Christopher Pearce)
V, V*, L, S

US commandos go into action against a South
American drug baron.

Ridiculous action film with a superhuman hero and a
high body-count.

w Lee Reynolds   d Aaron Norris   ph Joâ
Fernandes   m Frederic Talgorn   pd Ladislav
Wilheim   ed Michael J. Duthie, Daniel Candib

Chuck Norris, Billy Drago, John P. Ryan, Richard
Jaeckel, Begonia Plaza, Paul Perri

'When A Hollywood Cop Teams Up With A Detective
From The Swamps Of New Orleans . . . All Hell Is
About To Break Loose.'

Delta Heat
US   1992   91m   colour
Harkham/Karen/Sawmill Entertainment (Richard L. Albert, Rudy
Cohen)
V, V*

A Los Angeles detective goes to New Orleans to track
down the killer of his partner with the help of a one-
armed renegade ex-cop.

Energetic and occasionally amusing thriller providing
some engaging, if mindless, entertainment.

w Sam A. Scribner   d Michael Fischa   ph Avi
Karpik   m Christopher Tyng, Rockin' Dopsie
pd Don Day   ed Robert Edwards, Robert Gordon

Anthony Edwards, Lance Henriksen, Betsy Russell,
Linda Doná, Rod Masterson, John 'Spud' McConnell,
Clyde R. Jones

'Nothing special, but not an ordeal.' – *Empire*

Demasiado Miedo a la Vida, O Plaff: see *Plaff! Or Too Afraid Of Life*

Dementia 13 *
US/Eire   1963   81m   bw
Filmgroup/AIP (Roger Corman)
V*
GB title: *The Haunted and the Hunted*

An axe murderer attacks members of a noble Irish family at their lonely castle.

Nastily effective macabre piece with interesting credits.

wd Francis Ford Coppola   *ph* Charles Hannawalt
m Ronald Stein

Luana Anders, William Campbell, Bart Patton, Mary Mitchell, Patrick Magee, Eithne Dunn

Demetrius and the Gladiators **
US   1954   101m   Technicolor   Cinemascope
TCF (Frank Ross)
V, V (W), V*, L

A Greek slave who keeps Christ's robe after the crucifixion is sentenced to be one of Caligula's gladiators and becomes involved in Messalina's wiles.

Lively, efficient sequel to *The Robe,* with emphasis less on religiosity than on the brutality of the arena and our hero's sexual temptations and near-escapes. Good Hollywood hokum.

w Philip Dunne   *d* Delmer Daves   *ph* Milton Krasner
m Franz Waxman

Victor Mature, Susan Hayward, Michael Rennie (as Peter), Debra Paget, Anne Bancroft, Jay Robinson, Barry Jones, William Marshall, Richard Egan, Ernest Borgnine

'An energetic attempt to fling the mantle of sanctity over several more millions of the entertainment dollar.' – *The Times*

The Demi-Paradise *
GB   1943   114m   bw
Two Cities (Anatole de Grunwald)
V*
US title: *Adventure for Two*

In 1939, a Russian inventor is sent to observe the British way of life.

Pleasant, aimless little satirical comedy in which this blessed plot seems to be peopled entirely by eccentrics.

w Anatole de Grunwald   *d* Anthony Asquith
ph Bernard Knowles   *m* Nicholas Brodszky

Laurence Olivier, Penelope Dudley Ward, *Margaret Rutherford,* Leslie Henson, Marjorie Fielding, Felix Aylmer, Guy Middleton, Michael Shepley, George Thorpe, Edie Martin, Muriel Aked, Joyce Grenfell

'A backhanded way of showing us poor juvenile-minded cinemagoers that the England of Mr Punch and Mrs Malaprop lives forever.' – *Richard Winnington*

Demobbed
GB   1944   96m   bw
Butcher/Mancunian (F. W. Baker, John E. Blakeley)

Four incompetent ex-servicemen prevent a crooked manager from robbing a factory.

A rudimentary comedy from one of Britain's regional film companies that retains a slight interest by showcasing the performances of once popular variety theatre and radio performers.

w Roney Parsons, Anthony Toner   *d* John E. Blakeley   *ph* Geoffrey Faithfull, G. Gibbs
md Percival Mackey   *ad* Jim Carter   *ed* Ted Richards

Norman Evans, Nat Jackley, Dan Young, Betty Jumel, Webster Booth, Anne Ziegler, Tony Dalton, James Plant

Les Demoiselles de Rochefort: see *The Young Girls of Rochefort*

Demolition Man **
US   1993   115m   Technicolor
Warner/Silver Pictures (Joel Silver, Michael Levy, Howard Kazanjian)
S

In the non-violent, politically correct world of the 21st century, a violent criminal from the 1990s escapes after being thawed out from his cryo-prison – and his arch-enemy, a cop framed on a murder charge, is brought back to life to catch him.

An exciting adventure, clever and violent, that has fun at the expense of a sanitized future, complete with the President Scwarzenegger Memorial Library, and also indulges in self-parody without compromising the action.

w Daniel Waters, Robert Reneau, Peter M. Lenkov
d Marco Brambilla   *ph* Alex Thomson   *m* Elliot Goldenthal   *pd* David L. Snyder   *ed* Stuart Baird

Sylvester Stallone, Wesley Snipes, Sandra Bullock, Nigel Hawthorne, Benjamin Bratt, Bob Gunton, Denis Leary

'A noisy, soulless, self-conscious pastiche that mixes elements of sci-fi, action-adventure and romance, then pours on a layer of comedy replete with Hollywood in-jokes.' – *Variety*

'Decently constructed, almost witty at times and a genuine attempt to make an action thriller that's halfway intelligent.' – *Derek Malcolm, Guardian*

Demon: see *God Told Me To*

Demon Seed
US   1977   95m   Metrocolor   Panavision
MGM (Herb Jaffe)
V*, L

A scientist invents too perfect a computer: it locks up his wife, rapes her, and incubates a child . . .

Science fiction at the end of its tether, all very smart and self-conscious, but at this length very tasteless. Hitchcock would have got it into a television half-hour.

w Robert Jaffe, Roger O. Hirson   *novel* Dean R. Koontz   *d* Donald Cammell   *ph* Bill Butler
m Jerry Fielding   *pd* Edward Carfagno

Julie Christie, Fritz Weaver, Gerrit Graham, Berry Kroeger, Lisa Lu

The Demons (dubbed)
Portugal/France   1972   116m   Eastmancolor
Interfilme/Comptoir (Victor de Costa)
V, V*
original title: *Os Demonios*

Two nuns, the daughters of a witch burned at the stake, revenge their mother's death.

Bizarre and low-budget horror, exploiting sex and violence.

w Jesús Franco   *novel* David Kuhne (Jesús Franco)
d Clifford Brown (Jesús Franco)   *ph* Raoul Artigot
m Jean-Bernard Raiteux

Anne Libert, Britt Nichols, Doris Thomas, John Foster, Howard Vernon, Karin Field, Albert Dalbes

† The film was cut to 97m for its British release.

Demons
Italy   1985   89m   colour
Dacfilm (Dario Argento)
V, V*, L
original title: *Demoni*

Members of an audience watching a horror movie

about demons ravaging the world are themselves transformed into murderous monsters.

Gore-filled horror, derivative of modern American zombie movies.

w Lamberto Bava, Dario Argento, Dardano Sacchetti, Franco Ferrini   *d* Lamberto Bava

Urbano Barberini, Natasha Harvey, Karl Zinny, Fiore Argento, Paolo Cozzo, Fabiola Toledo

Demons 2
Italy   1987   91m   colour
Avatar (Dario Argento)
V, V*, S
original title: *Demoni 2*

The occupants of an apartment block, watching a TV documentary about demons, are turned into rampaging monsters.

A sequel that repeats, with a slight twist, the events of the original and also its gore-filled content with less effect.

w Lamberto Bava, Dario Argento, Franco Ferrini, Dardano Sacchetti   *d* Lamberto Bava
ph Gianlorenzo Battaglia   *pd* Davide Bassan
ed Franco Fraticelli, Pietro Bozza

David Knight, Nancy Brilli, Coralina Cataldi Tassoni, Bobby Rhodes, Asia Argento, Virginia Bryant

Demons of the Swamp: see *Attack of the Giant Leeches*

Den Goda Viljan: see *The Best Intentions*

Den Sedmy – Osma Noc: see *Seventh Day, Eighth Night*

Dennis the Menace
US   1993   96m   Technicolor
Warner (John Hughes, Richard Vane)
V, V*, L, S
GB title: *Dennis*

A mischievous six year-old boy makes his neighbours' life a misery.

Dull and saccharine comedy, indulging in the broadest slapstick and with Matthau going through his grumpiest grimaces.

w John Hughes, based on characters created by Hank Ketchum   *d* Nick Castle   *ph* Thomas Ackerman
m Jerry Goldsmith   *pd* James Bissell   *ed* Alan Heim

Walter Matthau, Mason Gamble, Joan Plowright, Christopher Lloyd, Lea Thompson, Robert Stanton, Amy Sakasitz, Kellen Hathaway, Paul Winfield

'Very young children may find the numbskull, by-the-numbers gags here amusing, but teens will consider this kids' stuff and adults will be pained.' – *Variety*

La Dentellière: see *The Lacemaker*

The Dentist **
US   1932   19m   bw
Paramount/Sennett

Classic star short with W. C. Fields working up briskly to a dentist sketch in which he deals summarily with a variety of patients.

d Leslie Pearce

Dentist in the Chair
GB   1960   88m   bw
Briand (Bertram Ostrer)
V

Students at a dental college discover that the instruments they have sold to their colleagues were stolen and try to recover them with the aid of a burglar.

Routine and dispiriting farce, much in the manner of the *Carry On* and *Doctor* series.

w Val Guest, Bob Monkhouse, George Wadmore novel Matthew Finch d Don Chaffey ph Reginald Wyer m Ken Jones ad Bill Andrews ed Bill Lenny

Bob Monkhouse, Peggy Cummins, Kenneth Connor, Eric Barker, Ronnie Stevens, Vincent Ball, Eleanor Summerfield, Reginald Beckwith, Stuart Saunders

† It was followed by a less amusing sequel, *Dentist on the Job*, directed by C. M. Pennington-Richards in 1961.

Denver and Rio Grande

US 1952 89m Technicolor
Nat Holt/Paramount
V*

Railroad companies compete to lay track through a narrow gorge.

Adequate Western thick ear.

w Frank Gruber d Byron Haskin

Edmond O'Brien, Sterling Hayden, Dean Jagger, Laura Elliot, ZaSu Pitts, Lyle Bettger, J. Carrol Naish

Deported

US 1950 88m bw
Universal-International

A gangster is sent back to his native Italy and tries to smuggle in his stolen money, but is finally redeemed.

Slightly unusual from this studio at this time, but not very interesting.

w Robert Buckner d Robert Siodmak

Jeff Chandler, Marta Toren, Claude Dauphin, Marina Berti, Richard Rober

The Depraved

GB 1957 63m bw
The Danzigers

An American officer helps his beloved kill her unattractive husband.

Shades of *Double Indemnity*, but only shades.

w Brian Clemens d Paul Dickson

Anne Heywood, Robert Arden, Carroll Levis, Basil Dignam

Derby Day

GB 1952 84m bw
British Lion/Wilcox-Neagle (Maurice Cowan)
US title: *Four Against Fate*

Intercut comic and melodramatic stories of four people who go to the Derby.

Quietly efficient, class-conscious entertainment on the lines of *Friday the 13th* and *The Bridge of San Luis Rey*. No surprises, but plenty of familiar faces.

w John Baines, Monckton Hoffe, Alan Melville d Herbert Wilcox ph Max Greene m Anthony Collins

Anna Neagle, Michael Wilding, Googie Withers, Gordon Harker, John McCallum, Peter Graves, Suzanne Cloutier, Gladys Henson, Ralph Reader, Alfie Bass, Edwin Styles, Nigel Stock

'Excessive loyalty to a formula has produced far from happy results.' – *Penelope Houston, MFB*

Derelict

US 1930 73m bw
Paramount

Two sea dogs battle over a ship and a girl.

Well-filmed melodrama, with plenty of location work.

w Max Marcin, William Slavens McNutt, Grover Jones d Rowland V. Lee

George Bancroft, William Boyd, Jessie Royce Landis, Donald Stuart

'One of the best sea pictures filmed . . . a cinch for the deluxers.' – *Variety*

Le Dernier Combat: see *The Last Battle*

Le Dernier Milliardaire *

France 1934 100m bw
Pathé-Natan

The queen of a small principality invites a financial wizard to pay court to her daughter. The girl elopes with a bandleader, the financier is engaged to the queen, and is then revealed as a sham.

Rather too determined to be satirical, this comedy sadly lacks the pace and flair of the director's best work but there are several sequences of interest.

wd René Clair ph Rudolph Maté, Louis Née m Maurice Jaubert

Max Dearly, Renée Saint-Cyr, Marthe Mellot, Raymond Cordy

'This film is so unpopular here that the crowd is rioting against it nightly – partly because they think it's rotten and partly because they don't like the way it kids the State . . . despite flop here, American specialized houses should do well with it.' – *Variety, Paris*

Le Dernier Tournant *

France 1939 90m bw
Lux

A French version of *The Postman Always Rings Twice*, qv for plot.

Interesting but not remarkable.

w Charles Spaak, Henry Torres novel James M. Cain d Pierre Chenal

Fernand Gravet, Corinne Luchaire, Michel Simon, Marcel Vallée, Florence Marly

'Class B at best.' – *Variety*

Les Dernières Vacances *

France 1947 95m bw
Pathé

During a country house holiday in the twenties, the last before the house is sold, old friends conduct amorous intrigues and so do their teenage progeny.

A moderately charming little fable making a rather obscure social point.

w R. Breuil, Roger Leenhardt d Roger Leenhardt ph Philippe Agostini

Berthe Bovy, Renée Devillers, Pierre Dux, Jean d'Yd, Odile Versois, Michel François

Derrière la Façade *

France 1939 90m bw
Filmsonor

A judge, his son, a soldier and a prostitute are involved in a night of attempted and actual murders.

Complex puzzle drama which made its mark.

d Yves Mirade, Georges Lacombe

Lucien Baroux, Jacques Baumer, Jules Berry, Gaby Morlay, Michel Simon, Betty Stockfield, Erich von Stroheim, Carette, André Lafaur

Dersu Uzala *

USSR/Japan 1975 140m colour
Mosfilm/Toho
V*

A Russian surveyor mapping Siberian wastes becomes friendly with a wily Mongolian hunter.

Magnificent vistas punctuate an essentially plodding propaganda piece which does not rank with its director's best work.

w Yuri Nagibin, Akira Kurosawa d Akira Kurosawa

Maxim Munzuk, Juri Solomine

AA: best foreign film

Desert Attack: see *Ice Cold in Alex*

Desert Bloom

US 1985 104m Metrocolor
Columbia/Carson/Delphi IV (Michael Hausman)
V, V*, L

In 1950 Las Vegas, an ex-GI runs a gas station, illtreats his stepdaughters and falls for his sister-in-law.

Why do paying customers need to know all this? A downbeat enterprise which never got released.

wd Eugene Corr story Linda Remy ph Reynaldo Villalobos m Brad Fiedel

Jon Voight, JoBeth Williams, Ellen Barkin, Allen Garfield, Annabeth Gish

'Viewers looking for sensitive, discreetly handled fare will be amply rewarded.' – *Variety*

The Desert Fox **

US 1951 88m bw
TCF (Nunnally Johnson)
V, V*, L
GB title: *Rommel, Desert Fox*

Rommel returns, disillusioned, to Hitler's Germany after his North African defeat, and is involved in the July plot.

Vivid but scrappy account of the last years of a contemporary hero. At the time it seemed to show a new immediacy in film-making, and was probably the first film to use an action sequence to arrest attention before the credit titles.

w Nunnally Johnson book *Rommel* by Desmond Young d Henry Hathaway ph Norbert Brodine m Daniele Amfitheatrof

James Mason, Jessica Tandy, Cedric Hardwicke, Luther Adler (as Hitler), Everett Sloane, *Leo G. Carroll, George Macready*, Richard Boone, Eduard Franz, Desmond Young

'Two men wanted her love – the third wanted her life!'
Desert Fury

US 1947 96m Technicolor
Paramount (Hal B. Wallis)

Against advice, a girl is attracted to a neurotic gambler who may have murdered his first wife.

Muddled melodrama slightly helped by Arizona colour settings; unconvincing characters mouth unspeakable lines in an airless tedium.

w Robert Rossen novel *Desert Town* by Ramona Stewart d Lewis Allen ph Charles Lang, Edward Cronjager m Miklos Rozsa

Lizabeth Scott, Wendell Corey, Burt Lancaster, John Hodiak, Mary Astor, Kristine Miller

'The only fury I could sense was in my corner of the balcony.' – *C. A. Lejeune*

The Desert Hawk

US 1944 bw serial: 15 eps
Columbia

Evil Hassan slips back into his native land and plots to overthrow his twin brother.

Standard serial heroics with a dual role for the star.

d B. Reeves Eason

Gilbert Roland, Mona Maris, Ben Welden, Kenneth MacDonald, Frank Lackteen, I. Stanford Jolley

The Desert Hawk

US 1950 77m Technicolor
Universal-International

Against an Arabian Nights background, a cheerful outlaw abducts a princess.

Tolerable cloak-and-sandal action comedy.

w Aubrey Wisberg, Jack Pollexfen, Gerald Drayson Adams   *d* Frederick de Cordova

Richard Greene, Yvonne de Carlo, Jackie Gleason, George Macready, Rock Hudson, Carl Esmond

Desert Hearts
US   1985   91m   colour
Desert Heart Productions (Donna Deitch)
V, V*, L

A would-be divorcée in Reno becomes a lesbian.

A fairly accessible piece of special pleading, nicely made and good to look at.

w Natalie Cooper   *novel* Desert of the Heart by Jane Rule   *d* Donna Deitch   *ph* Robert Elswit
m various   *pd* Jeannine Oppewall   *ed* Robert Estrin

Helen Shaver, Patricia Charbonneau, Audra Lindley, Andra Akers

Desert Law
Italy   1990   155m   Eastmancolor
Titanus/Reteitalia/International Dean Film (Rossella Angeletti, David Pash)
V

A New York businesswoman hires an ex-CIA agent to rescue her son, who has been kidnapped by his Arab grandfather to become the future leader of a tribe of desert warriors.

Glossy and competent thriller, most likely to appeal to 10-year-olds who can identify with the central character of a young boy.

w Adriano Bolzoni, Sergio Donati, Luigi Montefiori   *d* Duccio Tessari   *ph* Giorgio Di Battista   *m* Ennio Morricone   *pd* Luciano Sagoni   *ed* Maria Morra

Rutger Hauer, Carol Alt, Omar Sharif, Elliott Gould, Kabir Bedi, Brett Halsey, Peter Sands

'The Legion's my life. A girl doesn't fit into it. Especially a girl like you!'
Desert Legion
US   1953   86m   Technicolor
Universal (Ted Richmond)

A Foreign Legion captain rids a lost city of menacing bandits.

Schoolboy stuff, impudent in its silly story and its unconvincing Shangri-La, but quite entertaining for those prepared to let their hair down.

w Irving Wallace, Lewis Meltzer   *d* Joseph Pevney   *ph* John Seitz   *m* Frank Skinner

Alan Ladd, Richard Conte, Arlene Dahl, Akim Tamiroff, Leon Askin

Desert Mice
GB   1959   83m   bw
Artna/Welbeck/Sydney Box (Michael Relph, Basil Dearden)

Adventures of a concert party sent to entertain the troops in North Africa during World War II.

A most promising idea is wasted on a singularly unfunny script which leaves its actors all at sea.

w David Climie   *d* Michael Relph   *ph* Ken Hodges   *m* Philip Green

Alfred Marks, Sid James, Patricia Bredin, Dick Bentley, Dora Bryan, Irene Handl, Kenneth Fortescue, Reginald Beckwith, Joan Benham, Marius Goring

Desert Patrol: see *Sea of Sand*

The Desert Rats *
US   1953   88m   bw
TCF (Robert L. Jacks)
V, V*

An English captain commands an Australian detachment in the siege of Tobruk, and survives an encounter with Rommel.

Actioner made to cash in on the success of *The Desert Fox* (qv). Stars and battle scenes survive a studio look.

w Richard Murphy   *d* Robert Wise   *ph* Lucien Ballard   *md* Nathaniel Finston   *m* Leigh Harline

James Mason (as Rommel), Richard Burton, Robert Newton, Robert Douglas, Torin Thatcher, Chips Rafferty

AAN: Richard Murphy

The Desert Song
US   1929   106m   bw/Technicolor sequences
Warner

A romantic and mysterious figure leads North African natives against evil Arabs.

Primitive sound version of the highly successful 1926 operetta.

w Harvey Gates   *play* Otto Harbach, Lawrence Schwab, Frank Mandel   *d* Roy del Ruth
ph Barney McGill   *m/ly* Sigmund Romberg, Oscar Hammerstein II

John Boles, Carlotta King, Louise Fazenda, Johnny Arthur, Edward Martindel, Jack Pratt

The Desert Song
US   1943   96m   Technicolor
Warner (Robert Florey)

Updated version with Nazis as the real villains.

w Robert Buckner   *d* Robert Florey   *ph* Bert Glennon   *m* Heinz Roemheld

Dennis Morgan, Irene Manning, Bruce Cabot, Lynne Overman, Gene Lockhart, Victor Francen, Faye Emerson, Curt Bois, Jack La Rue, Marcel Dalio, Nestor Paiva, Gerald Mohr

The Desert Song
US   1953   110m   Technicolor
Warner (Rudi Fehr)
V

Well staged straight version of the musical, with full score.

w Roland Kibbee   *d* Bruce Humberstone
ph Robert Burks   *md* Max Steiner

Gordon Macrae, Kathryn Grayson, Steve Cochran, Raymond Massey, Dick Wesson, Allyn McLerie, Ray Collins, Paul Picerni, William Conrad

Desert Tanks: see *The Battle of El Alamein*

The Desert Trail
US   1935   54m   bw
Lone Star (Paul Malvern)
V*

A cowboy and a womanizing gambler hunt down the man who framed them for the murder of a rodeo owner in Rattlesnake Gulch.

Sub-standard semi-comic Western.

w Lindsley Parsons   *d* Cullen Lewis   *ph* Archie Stout   *ed* Carl Pierson

John Wayne, Mary Kornman, Paul Fix, Eddy Chandler, Carmen LaRoux, Lafe McKee, Al Ferguson, Henry Hall

Desert Victory ***
GB   1943   60m   bw
Ministry of Information/British Army Film Unit
V

Montgomery's army chases the Nazis through Tripoli.

Classic war documentary.

w anonymous   *d* David MacDonald   *m* William Alwyn   *ed* A. Best, F. Clarke   *narrator* James Langdale Hodson

'The greatest battle film of the war . . . it puts the audience right in the middle . . . Americans who see this film will be anxiously waiting for the next – and a US equivalent.' – *Variety*

'A first rate work of art.' – *Time*

'The finest factual film ever made.' – *Daily Telegraph*

'Profoundly moving, and fierce in its impact upon imagination, eye and ear.' – *Scotsman*

† A few shots were reconstructed in the studio.

AA: documentary feature

The Deserter
Italy/Yugoslavia/USA   1970   99m   Technicolor   Panavision
Dino de Laurentiis/Jadran/Heritage (Norman Baer, Ralph Serpe)
original title: *La Spina Dorsale del Diavolo*

In the South-west in 1886, a cavalry captain tracks down the Apaches who tortured his wife to death.

Brutal revenge Western, as muddled as its international credits would suggest.

w Clair Huffaker   *d* Burt Kennedy   *ph* Aldo Tonti   *m* Piero Piccione   *pd* Mario Chiari

Bekim Fehmiu, John Huston, Richard Crenna, Chuck Connors, Ricardo Montalban, Ian Bannen, Brandon de Wilde, Slim Pickens, Albert Salmi, Woody Strode, Patrick Wayne, Fausto Tozzi

Il Deserto Rosso: see *The Red Desert*

'Three people who loved each other very much!'
Design for Living **
US   1933   88m   bw
Paramount (Ernst Lubitsch)

Two friends love and are loved by the same worldly woman, and they set up house together.

Elegant but miscast version of a scintillating play, with all the sex and the sting removed (at the insistence of the Legion of Decency, then coming into power). Ben Hecht claimed to have removed all but one line of Coward's dialogue: 'For the good of our immortal souls!'

w Ben Hecht   *play* Noël Coward   *d* Ernst Lubitsch   *ph* Victor Milner   *m* Nathaniel Finston   *ad* Hans Dreier

Gary Cooper, Fredric March, Miriam Hopkins, Edward Everett Horton, Franklin Pangborn, Isabel Jewell

'Can't miss because it holds plenty . . . an improvement on the original.' – *Variety*

'A delightfully smart, crisp piece of entertainment, cleverly conceived and delightfully executed.' – *New York American*

'A partial cleansing for the screen of a stage story notorious for its wealth and variety of moral code infractions.' – *Martin Quigley*

Design for Lust: see *Confessions of a Sex Maniac*

Design for Scandal
US   1941   85m   bw
MGM

A reporter is assigned by his boss to get a lady judge disbarred.

Mechanical star comedy.

w Lionel Houser   *d* Norman Taurog

Rosalind Russell, Walter Pidgeon, Edward Arnold, Guy Kibbee, Lee Bowman

Designing Woman *
US   1957   118m   Metrocolor   Cinemascope
MGM (Dore Schary)
V*, L

A sports reporter marries a dress designer and finds that their common interests are few.

Lumbering comedy which aims for sophistication but settles for farce: tolerable for star watchers who have dined well.

w George Wells   *d* Vincente Minnelli   *ph* John Alton   *m* André Previn

Gregory Peck, Lauren Bacall, Dolores Gray, Sam Levene, Tom Helmore, Mickey Shaughnessy, Jesse White, Chuck Connors, Jack Cole

AA: George Wells

Desirable

US 1934 68m bw
Warner (Edward Chodorov)

An actress keeps her daughter at school rather than admit she is 19.

Mildly amusing comedy-drama of its day.

w Mary McCall Jnr d Archie Mayo

Verree Teasdale, Jean Muir, George Brent, John Halliday

'The purity seal is remembered throughout.' – Variety

Desire **

US 1936 89m bw
Paramount (Ernst Lubitsch)

In Spain, an American car designer falls for a glamorous jewel thief.

Romantic comedy which the producer should have worked on longer: it begins brilliantly and keeps its style, but the pace and wit ebb away.

w Edwin Justus Mayer, Waldemar Young, Samuel Hoffenstein, from a German film Die schönen Tage von Aranjuez play Hans Szekely, R. A. Stemmle d Frank Borzage ph Charles Lang, Victor Milner m Frederick Hollander ad Hans Dreier, Robert Usher

Marlene Dietrich, Gary Cooper, John Halliday, William Frawley, Ernest Cossart, Akim Tamiroff, Alan Mowbray, Zeffie Tilbury

'It sparkles and twinkles . . . one of the most engaging pictures of the season.' – Frank S. Nugent, New York Times

'A sure, beautifully written piece about the usual Lubitsch trifles, about crooks and fake countesses breathless before the dawn of romance.' – Alistair Cooke

'Brilliant treatment, superb staging and inspiring acting. Irresistible entertainment.' – CEA Film Report

Desire in the Dust

US 1960 102m bw Cinemascope
TCF/Associated Producers (William F. Claxton)

A wealthy Southern aristocrat is involved in a fatal car crash and persuades a young farmhand to take the blame.

Derivative hothouse drama, a little better than its title, with a cast breathing heavily in imitation of refugees from Tennessee Williams or William Faulkner.

w Charles Lang novel Harry Whittington d William F. Claxton ph Lucien Ballard m Paul Dunlap

Raymond Burr, Martha Hyer, Joan Bennett, Ken Scott, Brett Halsey, Anne Helm, Jack Ging, Edward Binns

Desire Me

US 1947 91m bw
MGM (Arthur Hornblow Jnr)

The wife of a Normandy villager hears that he has died in a concentration camp. She marries the bearer of the news, who turns out to be a psychotic who has left her husband for dead . . . but he is not.

Dreary drama, troubled during production and offering little for the actors to chew on.

w Marguerite Roberts, Zoë Akins, Casey Robinson novel Leonhard Frank d not credited, but mostly by George Cukor, Mervyn Le Roy, Jack Conway ph Joseph Ruttenberg m Herbert Stothart

Greer Garson, Robert Mitchum, Richard Hart, George Zucco, Morris Ankrum

'The supporting cast includes a number of characters who give the appearance of having come out of a

dusty cupboard marked "French Types – Assorted".' – MFB

† Robert Montgomery shot a few scenes before bowing out to be replaced by Richard Hart.

Desire under the Elms

US 1958 111m bw Vistavision
Paramount (Don Hartman)
V*, L

A New England farmer brings home a young bride and causes friction with his son.

This bid for culture turns out like a hoary and very slow melodrama, not exactly risible but annoying because it teeters between several styles.

w Irwin Shaw play Eugene O'Neill d Delbert Mann ph Daniel L. Fapp m Elmer Bernstein

Sophia Loren, Burl Ives, Anthony Perkins, Frank Overton, Pernell Roberts, Anne Seymour

'The film is consistently and unhappily out of its depth.' – Penelope Houston

'A challenging and inspiring picture.' – News of the World

AAN: Daniel L. Fapp

'Their story is not in the history books. It has never been seen on the screen – until now!'

Desirée

US 1954 110m DeLuxe Cinemascope
TCF (Julian Blaustein)
V, V*, L

Fictionalized biopic of one of Napoleon's mistresses.

Heavy-going costume piece, with all contributors distinctly uncomfortable.

w Daniel Taradash novel Annemarie Selinko d Henry Koster ph Milton Krasner m Alex North ad Lyle Wheeler, Leland Fuller

Jean Simmons, Marlon Brando, Merle Oberon, Michael Rennie, Cameron Mitchell, Elizabeth Sellars, Cathleen Nesbitt, Isobel Elsom

AAN: art direction

The Desk Set **

US 1957 103m Eastmancolor Cinemascope
TCF (Henry Ephron)
V*, L
GB title: His Other Woman

Ladies in a broadcasting company's reference section are appalled when an electronics expert is sent to improve their performance.

Thin comedy, altered from a Broadway success; patchy as a whole, but with several splendid dialogue scenes for the principals.

w Phoebe and Henry Ephron play William Marchant d Walter Lang ph Leon Shamroy m Cyril Mockridge

Spencer Tracy, Katharine Hepburn, Joan Blondell, Gig Young, Dina Merrill, Neva Patterson

'They lope through this trifling charade like a couple of oldtimers who enjoy reminiscing with simple routines.' – Bosley Crowther, New York Times

Despair *

West Germany/France 1978 119m Eastmancolor
NF Geria/Bavaria/SFP (Peter Märthesheimer)
V*
West German title: Eine Reise ins Licht

In 1930 Berlin, a Russian immigrant businessman leads a fantasy life which drives him to murder and insanity.

Filmed in English, this curious cross between Lolita and Repulsion found surprisingly little critical favour, considering its participants.

w Tom Stoppard novel Vladimir Nabokov d Rainer Werner Fassbinder ph Michael Ballhaus m Peer Raben pd Rolf Zehetbauer

Dirk Bogarde, Andrea Ferreol, Volker Spengler, Klaus Löwitsch, Bernhard Wicki

'It begins magnificently, remains sporadically brilliant throughout, but grows heavier and heavier until it finally sinks into inertia.' – Tom Milne, MFB

Desperadoes

US 1943 85m Technicolor
Columbia (Harry Joe Brown)

A gunman rides into town to cause trouble, but finds romance and renews an old friendship.

Lively star Western of its day.

w Max Brand, Robert Carson d Charles Vidor

Randolph Scott, Glenn Ford, Evelyn Keyes, Edgar Buchanan, Claire Trevor, Guinn Williams

† This was Columbia's first film in colour.

Desperadoes of the West

US 1950 bw serial: 12 eps
Republic

Ranchers drilling for oil are hampered by marauding gangs.

Routine serial exploits.

d Fred C. Brannon

Richard Powers, Judy Clark, Roy Barcroft, I. Stanford Jolley

'Hang on to your money, your woman, and your life!'

The Desperados

US 1968 90m Technicolor
Columbia/Meadway (Irving Allen)
V*

After the Civil War, a fanatic 'parson' leads a tribe of violent outlaws including his three sons.

Rough-and-tumble Western in the modern savage manner; made in Spain.

w Walter Brough d Henry Levin ph Sam Leavitt m David Whitaker

Vince Edwards, Jack Palance, George Maharis, Neville Brand, Sylvia Syms, Christian Roberts, Kate O'Mara, Kenneth Cope, John Paul

Desperate *

US 1947 73m bw
RKO (Michel Kraike)
V*

A trucker becomes innocently involved in a robbery and goes on the run.

Lively second feature from the studio's best period, with plenty of burgeoning talent.

w Harry Essex d Anthony Mann ph George E. Diskant m Paul Sawtell

Steve Brodie, Audrey Long, Raymond Burr, Jason Robards Snr, Douglas Fowley, William Challee, Ilka Gruning

'Amazingly watchable within its formulary limits.' – Tom Milne, MFB, 1982

Desperate Characters *

US 1971 106m colour
ITC/TDJ (Frank D. Gilroy)
V*

Residents of New York's east side find the rigours of life hard to take.

Curious but interesting suburban drama, a kind of deglamorized and updated City for Conquest.

wd Frank D. Gilroy novel Paula Fox ph Urs Furrer m Lee Konitz, Ron Carter, Jim Hall

Shirley Maclaine, Gerald S. O'Loughlin, Kenneth Mars, Sada Thompson, Jack Somack

'The most blistering indictment of New York City since Midnight Cowboy.' – Rex Reed

'A film of authenticity, of delicately realized intangibles.' – *Stanley Kauffmann*

The Desperate Hours *
US   1955   112m   bw   Vistavision
Paramount (William Wyler)
V*, L

Three escaped convicts take over a suburban house but are finally outwitted by the family.

Ponderous treatment of an over-familiar situation with only the acting and an 'A' picture look to save it.

w Joseph Hayes   *play* Joseph Hayes   *novel* Joseph Hayes   d William Wyler   ph Lee Garmes   m Gail Kubik

Fredric March, Humphrey Bogart, Martha Scott, Arthur Kennedy, Gig Young, Dewey Martin, Mary Murphy, Robert Middleton, Richard Eyer

'A solid, deliberate and long-drawn-out exercise in the mechanics of suspense.' – *Penelope Houston*

† Bogart's role had been played on stage by Paul Newman. March's role had been offered to Spencer Tracy, but he wouldn't take second billing.

Desperate Hours
US   1990   105m   Technicolor
TCF/Dino de Laurentiis (Michael Cimino)
V, V*, L, S

An armed robber on the run with two friends takes a family hostage.

A failure, even by the standards of the 1955 version.

w Lawrence Konner, Mark Rosenthal, Joseph Hayes   *novel* Joseph Hayes   d Michael Cimino   ph Doug Milsome   m David Mansfield   pd Victoria Paul   ed Peter Hunt

Mickey Rourke, Anthony Hopkins, Mimi Rogers, Lindsay Crouse, Kelly Lynch, Elias Koteas, David Morse, Shawnee Smith

'A coldly mechanical and uninvolving remake.' – *Variety*

Desperate Journey **
US   1942   109m   bw
Warner (Hal B. Wallis)
V, V*

Three POWs in Nazi Germany fight their way back to freedom.

When you pit Errol Flynn against the Nazis, there's no doubt who wins; and the last line is 'Now for Australia and a crack at those Japs!' Exhilarating adventure for the totally uncritical; professional standards high.

w Arthur Horman   d Raoul Walsh   ph Bert Glennon   m Max Steiner

Errol Flynn, Alan Hale, Ronald Reagan, Nancy Coleman, Raymond Massey, Arthur Kennedy, Ronald Sinclair, Albert Basserman, Sig Rumann, Ilka Gruning, Pat O'Moore

'Yarn is an extreme strain on anyone's credulity, and yet it's so exciting that the preposterousness of it all is only something to be thought about on the way home from the theatre.' – *Variety*

'A 1942 treatment of *The Three Musketeers,* packed with action, shorn of romance, and utilizing the Third Reich for terrain. Folks who sacrifice reason for fast action and the joy of seeing Nazis foiled, will find it entirely gratifying.' – *New York Times*

Desperate Living
US   1977   95m   colour
New Line/Charm City (John Waters)

A paranoid housewife kills her husband with the aid of her maid and flees to a community of murderers and degenerates.

A typical Waters work, concerned with obesity, transvestism, transsexuality and nudity. It also features bad acting, uninspired direction,

unimaginative camera-work and adolescent notions of what is shocking.

wd John Waters   ph Thomas Loizeaux   m Chris Lobinger   ad Vincent Peranio   ed Charles Roggero

Mink Stole, Susan Lowe, Edith Massey, Mary Vivian Pearce, Jean Hill

Desperate Moment
GB   1953   88m   bw
GFD/Fanfare (George H. Brown)

In Poland, a man imprisoned for murder finds he didn't do it, escapes, and tracks down the real criminal, his best friend.

Cliché-ridden melodrama climaxing in a car chase; poor in all departments.

w Patrick Kirwan, George H. Brown   *novel* Martha Albrand   d Compton Bennett   ph C. Pennington-Richards   m Ronald Binge

Dirk Bogarde, Mai Zetterling, Philip Friend, Albert Lieven, Carl Jaffe, Gerard Heinz

Desperate Remedies *
New Zealand   1993   93m   colour
Electric/NFU Studios/NZ on Air/New Zealnd Film
   Commission/James Wallace

In the 19th century, a bisexual wealthy woman finds herself involved in deceit and murder when she attempts to buy a husband for her sex- and drug-addicted sister.

A swooning parody of period romances, deliberately larger than life (more, in fact, similar to an *Imitation of Life*) and over-elaborate in its approach to costume and plot, enjoyable if you're in the mood for tongue-in-cheek melodrama.

wd Stewart Main, Peter Wells   ph Leon Narbey   m Peter Scholes   pd Michael Kane   ed David Coulson

Jennifer Ward-Lealand, Kevin Smith, Lisa Chappell, Cliff Curtis, Michael Hurst, Kiri Mills, Bridget Armstrong, Timothy Raby

'An extravagant, opulent and mostly enjoyable exercise in high camp (or low kitsch).' – *Variety*

'The cumulative effect is to make costume melodrama's classic preoccupations with strict social hierarchy and sexual propriety seem hilariously gratuitous, irrational and redundant.' – *Claire Monk, Sight and Sound*

Desperate Siege: see *Rawhide*

Desperately Seeking Susan *
US   1985   104m   DeLuxe
Orion/Sarah Pillsbury, Midge Sanford
V, V*, L, S

A bored housewife causes confusion and mayhem when out of curiosity she tracks down what's behind some intriguing ads in the personal column.

Mildly diverting romantic mystery which could have been both funnier and more thrilling.

w Leona Barish   d Susan Seidelman   ph Edward Lachman   m Thomas Newman   pd Santo Loquasto   ed Andrew Mondsheim

Rosanna Arquette, Madonna, Aidan Quinn, Mark Blum, Robert Joy

'Simply easy entertainment, with a lively cast caught up in a silly situation.' – *Variety*

BFA: Rosanna Arquette

'Roaring across the land of Marco Polo and Genghis Khan come Uncle Sam's sailors on camels!'
Destination Gobi *
US   1953   90m   Technicolor
TCF (Stanley Rubin)

American soldiers get Mongol help against the Japanese in the Gobi desert.

A curious war adventure, a kind of camel opera, apparently based on fact; mildly enjoyable, though the outlandish is gradually replaced by the predictable.

w Everett Freeman   d Robert Wise   ph Charles G. Clarke   m Sol Kaplan

Richard Widmark, Don Taylor, Casey Adams, Murvyn Vye, Darryl Hickman, Martin Milner, Ross Bagdasarian, Rodolfo Acosta

Destination Moon *
US   1950   91m   Technicolor
Universal/George Pal
V*, L

An American inventor gets private backing to build a rocket so that the US can reach the moon before the Russians.

Semi-documentary prophecy with impressive gadgetry encased in a tedious and totally unsurprising script.

w Rip Van Ronkel, Robert Heinlein, James O'Hanlon   d Irving Pichel   ph Lionel Lindon   m Leith Stevens

Warner Anderson, John Archer, Tom Powers, Dick Wesson

'Heavy-handed, unimaginative and very badly acted.' – *MFB*

Destination Murder
US   1950   70m   bw
RKO (Edward L. Cahn, Maurie M. Suess)

A college girl investigates the murder of her father by dating the man she thinks is responsible.

An unimaginative second feature, of no lasting interest.

w Don Martin   d Edward L. Cahn   ph Jackson J. Rose   m Irving Gertz   ad Boris Leven   ed Philip Cahn

Joyce MacKenzie, Stanley Clements, Hurd Hatfield, Albert Dekker, Myrna Dell, James Flavin, John Dehner

Destination Tokyo *
US   1943   135m   bw
Warner (Jerry Wald)
V, V*

A US submarine is sent into Tokyo harbour.

Solid, well acted war suspenser, but overlong.

w Delmer Daves, Albert Maltz   *story* Steve Fisher   d Delmer Daves   ph Bert Glennon   m Franz Waxman

Cary Grant, John Garfield, Alan Hale, John Ridgely, Dane Clark, Warner Anderson, William Prince, Robert Hutton, Tom Tully, Peter Whitney, Faye Emerson, John Forsythe

'We don't say it is credible; we don't even suggest that it makes sense. But it does make a pippin of a picture from a purely melodramatic point of view.' – *Bosley Crowther*

'Even moviegoers who have developed a serious allergy for service pictures should find it high among the superior films of the war.' – *Newsweek*

AAN: Steve Fisher

Destination Unknown
US   1933   69m   bw
Universal

Bootleggers, in a crippled ship with a mutinous crew, are saved by a mysterious stranger.

Curious melodrama which turns halfway through into *The Passing of the Third Floor Back*.

w Tom Buckingham   d Tay Garnett

Pat O'Brien, Ralph Bellamy, Alan Hale, Russell Hopton, Tom Brown, Betty Compson, Noel Madison

'Good sea melodrama ruined by change of intent.' – *Variety*

Destinées: see *Love, Soldiers and Women*

Destiny *
Germany   1921   100m approx   bw   silent
Decla-Bioscop
original title: *Der Müde Tod*

In the 19th century a young woman tries to save her lover from the presence of Death, who shows her that whatever she does it is inevitable.

A solemn fantasy on the lines of *Appointment in Samarra*, the framing story being more effective than the 'illustrations'.

w Thea von Harbou, Fritz Lang   d Fritz Lang
ph Fritz Arno Wagner, Erich Nitschmann, Hermann Saalfrank

Lil Dagover, Rudolph Klein-Rogge, Bernhard Götzke, Walter Janssen

Destiny *
US   1944   65m   bw
Universal (Roy William Neill)

An escaped convict on the run finds refuge with a blind girl on a lonely farm.

Curious second feature, interesting because it began as a story eliminated from *Flesh and Fantasy* (qv); extra footage was added to bring it up to the required length. The original footage is mainly the nightmare suffered by the girl.

w Roy Chanslor (*F and F* Ernest Pascal)   d Reginald Le Borg (*F and F* Julien Duvivier)   ph George Robinson (*F and F* Paul Ivano)   m Frank Skinner

Gloria Jean, Alan Curtis (who died in the original but here survives), Frank Craven, Grace McDonald

Destiny of a Man **
USSR   1959   98m   bw
Sovexportfilm/Mosfilm (G. Kuznetsov)
original title: *Sudba Cheloveka*

During World War II a Russian is captured by Nazis but escapes and returns home only to find his family dead.

Strikingly styled sob story whose very glumness prevented it from being hailed as a masterpiece; in technique however it is in the best Russian tradition.

w Y. Lukin, F. Shakhmagonov   story Mikhail Sholokhov   d Sergei Bondarchuk   ph Vladimir Monakhov   m V. Basnov

Sergei Bondarchuk, Zinaida Kirienko, Pavlik Boriskin

'Of all Soviet post-war films, this will be looked on as the greatest and most original work of the period.' – *MFB*

'What nation will survive?'
Destroy all Monsters
Japan   1969   89m   colour
Toho/AIP

Moon invaders gain control of Godzilla and his friends.

Typically inept Japanese monster rally full of men in rubber suits.

w Kaoru Mabuchi   d Ishiro Honda

Akira Kubo, Jun Tazaki, Kyoko Ai

'Her only rival is his ship!'
Destroyer
US   1943   99m   bw
Columbia (Louis F. Edelmann)
V*

An old sea dog talks himself into a job on a World War II destroyer but works his men too hard.

Flat propaganda piece, not too well made.

w Frank Wead, Lewis Meltzer, Borden Chase
d William A. Seiter   ph Franz Planer   m Anthony Collins

Edward G. Robinson, Glenn Ford, Marguerite Chapman, Edgar Buchanan, Leo Gorcey, Regis Toomey, Ed Brophy

The Destructors: see *The Marseilles Contract*

Destry *
US   1954   95m   Technicolor
U-I (Stanley Rubin)

Almost scene-for-scene remake of *Destry Rides Again* (qv).

Well enough made and tolerably acted, but it doesn't have the sparkle, despite employing the same director.

w Edmund H. North, D. D. Beauchamp   d George Marshall   ph George Robinson   m Joseph Gershenson

Audie Murphy, Mari Blanchard, Lyle Bettger, Thomas Mitchell, Edgar Buchanan, Wallace Ford, Lori Nelson, Alan Hale Jnr, Mary Wickes

'The impression is of a school revival of the original production.' – *MFB*

'They make the fighting sinful west blaze into action before your eyes!'
Destry Rides Again ****
US   1939   94m   bw
Universal (Joe Pasternak)
V*, L

A mild-mannered sheriff finally gets mad at local corruption and straps on his guns.

Classic Western which manages to encompass suspense, comedy, romance, tenderness, vivid characterization, horseplay, songs and standard Western excitements, without moving for more than a moment from a studio main street set. It starts with a sign reading 'Welcome to Bottleneck' and an outburst of gunfire; it ends with tragedy followed by a running joke. Hollywood expertise at its very best.

w Felix Jackson, Gertrude Purcell, Henry Myers   novel Max Brand   d George Marshall   ph Hal Mohr   m Frank Skinner   m/ly Frederick Hollander, Frank Loesser

James Stewart, Marlene Dietrich, Brian Donlevy, Charles Winninger, Samuel S. Hinds, Mischa Auer, Irene Hervey, Jack Carson, *Una Merkel*, Allen Jenkins, Warren Hymer, *Billy Gilbert*

'Makes the b.o. grade in a big way . . . just plain, good entertainment.' – *Variety*

'I think it was Lord Beaverbrook who said that Marlene Dietrich standing on a bar in black net stockings, belting out *See What the Boys in the Back Room Will Have*, was a greater work of art than the Venus de Milo.' – *Richard Roud*

† An early sound version in 1932 starred Tom Mix; *Frenchie* (1950) was a slight variation. See also *Destry*.

The Detective (1954): see *Father Brown*

The Detective **
US   1968   114m   DeLuxe   Panavision
TCF/Arcola/Millfield (Aaron Rosenberg)
V*

A New York police detective fights crime and corruption.

Determinedly sleazy and 'frank' cop stuff, quite arrestingly narrated and with something to say about police methods. Good violent entertainment, with just a shade too many homosexuals and nymphomaniacs for balance.

w Abby Mann   novel Roderick Thorp   d Gordon Douglas   ph Joseph Biroc   m Jerry Goldsmith

Frank Sinatra, Lee Remick, Jacqueline Bisset, Ralph Meeker, Jack Klugman, Horace MacMahon, Lloyd

Bochner, William Windom, Tony Musante, Al Freeman Jnr, Robert Duvall

'It vacillates uncertainly between murder mystery, political allegory, and a psychological study of the hero.' – *Jan Dawson*

Detective *
France   1985   98m   colour
Sara/JLG
V

Four groups of people find their paths intersecting in a Paris hotel while the hotel detective tries to solve a murder.

Eccentric *Grand Hotel*-style compendium with many baffling asides presumably attributable to the director. One suspects that the audience is expected to be a detective too.

w Alain Sarde, Philippe Setbon, Anne-Marie Mieville, Jean-Luc Godard   d Jean-Luc Godard

Claude Brasseur, Nathalie Baye, Johnny Hallyday, Laurent Terzieff, Jean-Pierre Léaud, Alain Cuny

Detective Kitty O'Day: see *The Adventures of Kitty O'Day*

Detective Lloyd *
GB   1932   bw   serial: 12 eps
Universal

Lloyd of the Yard combats The Panther for a valuable amulet also coveted by priests of the temple of Amenhotep II.

A remarkable novelty: the only serial filmed in England, and not bad of its naïve kind.

d Henry McRae

Jack Lloyd, Wallace Geoffrey, Muriel Angelus, Lewis Dayton, Janice Adair

'A man whose wife was more woman than angel!'
Detective Story **
US   1951   103m   bw
Paramount (William Wyler)

A day in a New York precinct police station, during which a detective of almost pathological righteousness discovers a stain on his family and himself becomes a victim of violence.

Clever, fluent transcription of a Broadway play with some of the pretensions of Greek tragedy; it could have been the negation of cinema, but professional handling makes it the essence of it.

w Philip Yordan, Robert Wyler   play Sidney Kingsley   d William Wyler   ph Lee Garmes

Kirk Douglas, Eleanor Parker, William Bendix, Cathy O'Donnell, George Macready, Horace MacMahon, Gladys George, *Joseph Wiseman, Lee Grant*, Gerald Mohr, Frank Faylen, Luis Van Rooten

'The admirably directed interaction of movement and talk all over the big room is what gives the thing its satisfying texture.' – *Richard Mallett, Punch*

† No music was used.

AAN: Philip Yordan, Robert Wyler; William Wyler; Eleanor Parker; Lee Grant

Detour *
US   1945   68m   bw
PRC (Leon Fromkess)
V, V*, L

On his way to Hollywood to meet a girlfriend, a night-club pianist assumes the identity of a dead man.

A minor cult movie with as much doomladen dialogue and *film noir* angles as could be shovelled into a Poverty Row 'B' at the time. On the whole, less than meets the eye.

w Martin Goldsmith   d Edgar G. Ulmer
ph Benjamin H. Kline   m Leo Erdody

Tom Neal, Ann Savage, Claudia Drake, Edmund MacDonald, Tim Ryan

Deus e o Diabo na Terra do Sol: see *Black God, White Devil*

Les Deux Anglaises et le Continent: see *Anne and Muriel*

Deux ou trois choses que je sais d'elle: see *Two or Three Things I Know about Her*

Devi *
India   1960   93m   bw
Satyajit Ray Productions
aka: *The Goddess*

While his son is away at university, a farmer persuades his daughter-in-law that she is a goddess, and the events which follow, including the death of her son, are too much for her reason.

A curious, 'foreign' story which does not have the usual Ray tempo or feeling for character, but wins one's attention by its very strangeness.

wd Satyajit Ray   *story* Prabhat Kumar Mukherjee
ph Subrata Mitra   *m* Ali Akbar Khan   *ad* Bansi Chandragupta   *ed* Dulal Dutta

Chhabi Biswas, Sharmila Tagore, Soumitra Chatterjee, Karuna Banerjee

The Devil and Daniel Webster: see *All That Money Can Buy*

The Devil and Max Devlin
US   1981   95m   Technicolor
Walt Disney (Jerome Courtland)
V*

An unscrupulous apartment manager is knocked down by a bus. Finding himself in hell, he is offered freedom if he can buy three young souls within two months.

Frowsty Freudian comedy, a very unhappy indication of the depths to which Disney productions have sunk since Walt's death. To carry this kind of thing off requires a hundred times more style than is evidenced here.

w Mary Rodgers   *d* Steven Hilliard Stern
ph Howard Schwartz   *m* Buddy Baker

Elliott Gould, Bill Cosby, Susan Anspach, Adam Rich, Charles Shamata, Ronnie Schell

The Devil and Miss Jones **
US   1941   97m   bw
RKO/Frank Ross, Norman Krasna
V*

A millionaire masquerades as a clerk in his own department store to investigate worker complaints.

Attractive comedy with elements of the crazy thirties and the more socially conscious forties.

w *Norman Krasna*   *d* Sam Wood   *ph* Harry Stradling   *m* Roy Webb

Jean Arthur, *Charles Coburn*, Robert Cummings, Spring Byington, S. Z. Sakall, William Demarest

AAN: Norman Krasna; Charles Coburn

'Her sin – their death?'
Devil and the Deep *
US   1932   73m   bw
Paramount (Emmanuel Cohen)

A submarine commander goes mad with jealousy of his faithless wife.

A turgid melodrama notable for its stars.

w Benn Levy   *d* Marion Gering   *ph* Charles Lang

Tallulah Bankhead, Charles Laughton, Gary Cooper, Cary Grant, Paul Porcasi

'Of femme interest despite lukewarm performance of Tallulah Bankhead . . . a fair commercial release.' – *Variety*

The Devil and the Nun *
Poland   1960   108m   bw
Kadr
original title: *Matka Joanna od Aniolow*; aka: *Mother Joan of the Angels*

In a 17th-century convent nuns are possessed by devils. A priest who tries to help is burned at the stake; another becomes possessed himself.

Reasonably dispassionate and fairly stylized version of the same facts that were treated so hysterically by Ken Russell in *The Devils*.

w Tadeusz Konwicki, Jerzy Kawalerowicz
novel Jaroslav Iwaszkiewicz   *d* Jerzy Kawalerowicz
ph Jerzy Wojcik   *m* Adam Walacinski

Lucyna Winnicka, Mieczyslaw Voit, Anna Ciepielewska

The Devil at Four o'Clock
US   1961   126m   Eastmancolor
Columbia/Leroy/Kohlmar (Fred Kohlmar)

A drunken missionary and three convicts save a colony of leper children from a South Seas volcano.

Muddled adventure melodrama with a downbeat ending long delayed.

w Liam O'Brien   *novel* Max Catto   *d* Mervyn Le Roy   *ph* Joseph Biroc   *m* George Duning

Spencer Tracy, Frank Sinatra, Kerwin Mathews, Jean-Pierre Aumont, Grégoire Aslan, Alexander Scourby, Barbara Luna

The Devil Bat
US   1941   70m   bw
PRC
V*

A crazed scientist trains bats to kill at the scent of a certain perfume.

Horror comic hokum from the bottom of the barrel.

w John Neville   *d* Jean Yarbrough

Bela Lugosi, Suzanne Kaaren, Dave O'Brien

Devil Bat's Daughter
US   1946   67m   bw
PRC
V*

A girl who thinks she is the daughter of a vampire consults a psychiatrist, who encourages her to murder his wife.

Tolerable, potboiling shocker.

w Griffin Jay   *story* Frank Wisbar, Erns Jaeger
d Frank Wisbar

Rosemary La Planche, John James, Michael Hale, Nolan Leary

The Devil Came from Arkansas
West Germany   1970   85m   colour
CCC Films/Fenix Films (Karl-Heinz Mannchen)

Rival groups attempt to control a stone with mystic powers.

Nonsensical adventure, barely competent in all departments.

w Paul Andre, Lladislas Fedor   *d* Jess Frank (Jesús Franco)   *ph* Manuel Merino   *m* Manfred Hubler, Siegfried Schwab

Fred Williams, Susann Korda, Horst Tappert, Ewa Stroemberg, Siefried Schurenberg, Walter Rilla, Paul Muller

The Devil Commands *
US   1941   65m   bw
Columbia (Wallace MacDonald)

An electrical scientist tries to communicate with his dead wife through a medium.

Modestly effective horror thriller, though rather too deliberately paced.

w Robert D. Andrews, Milton Gunzberg   *story* *The Edge of Running Water* by William Sloane   *d* Edward Dmytryk   *ph* Allan G. Siegler   *md* Morris Stoloff

Boris Karloff, Richard Fiske, Amanda Duff, Anne Revere, Ralph Penney

Devil Dogs of the Air *
US   1935   86m   bw
Warner (Lou Edelman)
V*

Rivalry and romance in the Marine Flying Corps.

Standard, lively vehicle for Cagney and O'Brien, with excellent stunt flying sequences.

w Malcolm Stuart Boylan, Earl Baldwin   *novel* John Monk Saunders   *d* Lloyd Bacon   *ph* Arthur Edeson
md Leo F. Forbstein

James Cagney, *Pat O'Brien*, Margaret Lindsay, Frank McHugh, Helen Lowell, John Arledge, Robert Barrat, Russell Hicks, Ward Bond

'Exhibs should have no squawks and may even cheer if they put a little steam behind their selling.' – *Variety*

'A loud and roughneck screen comedy, both amusing and exciting.' – *André Sennwald*

The Devil Doll **
US   1936   79m   bw
MGM (E. J. Mannix)
V*

A refugee from Devil's Island disguises himself as an old lady who sells human dolls which murder those responsible for his imprisonment.

Interesting rather than exciting tall tale with a Paris backdrop; despite impressive moments it does not quite have the right *frisson*.

w Tod Browning, Garrett Fort, Erich von Stroheim, Guy Endore   *novel* *Burn Witch Burn* by A. A. Merritt
d Tod Browning   *ph* Leonard Smith   *m* Franz Waxman   *ad* Cedric Gibbons

Lionel Barrymore, Maureen O'Sullivan, Frank Lawton, Henry B. Walthall, Rafaela Ottiano, Grace Ford, Arthur Hohl

'Grotesque, slightly horrible and consistently interesting.' – *Frank Nugent, New York Times*

'Earth menaced by fantastic powers!'
Devil Girl from Mars
GB   1954   76m   bw
Edward J. and Harry Lee Danziger
V, V*

A female Martian is sent to Earth to bring back a stock of men for breeding purposes.

Absurd attempt to cash in on the then new space fiction craze. The budget matches the imagination.

w John C. Maher, James Eastwood   *d* David MacDonald   *ph* Jack Cox   *m* Edwin Astley

Patricia Laffan, Hugh McDermott, Joseph Tomelty, Adrienne Corri, Peter Reynolds, Hazel Court, John Laurie, Sophie Stewart

'There is really no fault in this film that one would like to see eliminated. Everything, in its way, is quite perfect.' – *Gavin Lambert, Sight and Sound*

Devil Horse
US   1932   bw   serial: 12 eps
Mascot

A wild boy defends wild horses from poachers.

Earnest stuff for a serial, and not enough violent incident.

d Otto Brower

Harry Carey, Noah Beery, Frankie Darro

Devil in the Flesh: see *Le Diable au Corps*

The Devil Is a Sissy
US   1936   92m   bw
MGM (Frank Davis)
aka: *The Devil Takes the Count*

The young son of divorcing parents gets into bad
company.

Adequate juvenile melodrama.

w John Lee Mahin, Richard Schayer, Roland Brown
d W. S. Van Dyke   *ph* Harold Rosson, George
Schneiderman   *m* Herbert Stothart

Freddie Bartholomew, Jackie Cooper, Mickey
Rooney, Ian Hunter, Peggy Conklin, Katherine
Alexander, Gene Lockhart, Dorothy Peterson

'Men are my slaves – and glad to be!'
The Devil Is a Woman *
US   1935   82m   bw
Paramount

In Seville in the 1890s a *femme fatale* has several
admirers.

The last Dietrich vehicle to be directed by von
Sternberg, and rather splendid in its highly decorative
and uncommercial way; a treat for addicts.

w John Dos Passos, S. K. Winston   *novel La Femme et
le Pantin* by Pierre Louÿs   *d* Josef von Sternberg
ph Josef von Sternberg, Lucien Ballard   *m* from Rimsky-
Korsakov   *ad* Hans Dreier

Marlene Dietrich, Lionel Atwill, Cesar Romero,
Edward Everett Horton, Alison Skipworth, Don
Alvarado, Morgan Wallace, Tempe Pigott

'A somewhat monotonous picture . . . sophisticated
audiences are its best bet.' – *Variety*

'One of the most sophisticated films ever produced in
America.' – *André Sennwald, New York Times*

'Light and shadow are splashed liberally around over
the white-painted sets; cafés, tobacco factories, stairs
and balconies are decorated with every conceivable
device and camera-level.' – *Peter John Dyer, 1964*

'A clever, perversely dehumanized picture said to be
one of von Sternberg's favourites.' – *New Yorker, 1977*

The Devil Is Driving
US   1937   69m   bw
Columbia

An attorney protects a friend's son from a drunk
driving charge, but finally indicts himself for perjury.

Standard moral melodrama with the star in good
form.

w Jo Milward, Richard Blake   *d* Harry Lachman

Richard Dix, Joan Perry, Nana Bryant, Frank
C. Wilson, Ian Wolfe, Elisha Cook Jnr, Henry Kolker,
Ann Rutherford, Walter Kingsford

'Carries a good deal of punch, but not enough to lug it
above the moderate biz bracket.' – *Variety*

The Devil Makes Three
US   1952   90m   bw
MGM (Richard Goldstone)

An American intelligence officer in post-war Germany
becomes involved with neo-Nazis.

A curious break from dancing for Gene Kelly, this
obscurely titled thriller has little to commend it but
authentic locations.

w Jerry Davis   *story* Lawrence Bachmann
d Andrew Marton   *ph* Vaclav Vich   *m* Rudolph G.
Kopp

Gene Kelly, Pier Angeli, Richard Rober, Richard
Egan, Claus Clausen

The Devil Never Sleeps: see *Satan Never Sleeps*

Devil on Horseback
GB   1954   89m   bw
Group 3 (John Grierson, Isobel Pargiter)
V*

A teenage jockey gets to the top the hard way.

Highly resistible compendium of racetrack clichés and
sentiment, not at all what one expected from Group 3.

w Neil Paterson, Montagu Slater   *d* Cyril Frankel
ph Denny Densham   *m* Malcolm Arnold

Googie Withers, John McCallum, Jeremy Spenser,
Meredith Edwards, Liam Redmond, Sam Kydd

The Devil, Probably *
France   1977   95m   Eastmancolor
Sunchold/GMF (Stéphane Tchalgadchieff)
original title: *Le Diable, Probablement*

A young Parisian goes to the devil and arranges to
have himself shot.

A despairing vision of an arid world, seen through
unpleasant details of city life. A fascinating but
enervated film very typical of its director.

wd Robert Bresson   *ph* Pasqualino de Santis
m Philippe Sarde   *pd* Eric Simon

Antoine Monnier, Tina Irissari, Henri de Maublanc

The Devil Rides Out *
GB   1968   95m   Technicolor
Warner/Hammer (Anthony Nelson-Keys)
V
US title: *The Devil's Bride*

The Duc de Richleau rescues a friend from a group of
Satanists.

Rather stodgy adaptation of a frightening novel;
moments of suspense.

w Richard Matheson   *novel* Dennis Wheatley
d Terence Fisher   *ph* Arthur Grant   *m* James
Bernard   *ad* Bernard Robinson   *ed* James Needs,
Spencer Reeve

Christopher Lee, *Charles Gray*, Leon Greene, Patrick
Mower, Gwen Ffrangcon Davies

Devil Ship Pirates
GB   1964   96m   Technicolor   Hammerscope
ABP/Hammer (Anthony Nelson-Keys)

At the time of the Armada, Spanish privateers
terrorize a Cornish seaside village.

Lacklustre pirate yarn with not much action and some
elements of Hammer horror.

w Jimmy Sangster   *d* Don Sharp   *ph* Michael
Reed   *m* Gary Hughes   *ad* Bernard Robinson, Don
Mingaye   *ed* James Needs

Christopher Lee, John Cairney, Barry Warren, Ernest
Clark, Andrew Keir, Duncan Lamont

The Devil Takes the Count: see *The Devil Is a
Sissy*

The Devil Thumbs a Ride
US   1947   63m   bw
RKO

A commercial traveller gives a lift to a man who turns
out to be wanted for murder.

Predictable suspenser without much entertainment
value.

wd Felix Feist

Ted North, Lawrence Tierney, Nan Leslie

The Devil to Pay *
US   1930   72m   bw
Samuel Goldwyn

The prodigal son of a snooty English family returns to
cheer them all up.

Agreeably lighthearted star comedy in the drawing-
room tradition.

w Frederick Lonsdale   *d* George Fitzmaurice
ph Gregg Toland, George Barnes   *m* Alfred
Newman

Ronald Colman, Loretta Young, Myrna Loy, Frederick
Kerr

'Snappy British comedy that should please
everywhere . . . a set-up for femmes.' – *Variety*

'Six reels of Mr Colman being charming . . . a
polished, tasteful and entirely likeable screen
comedy.' – *New York Herald Tribune*

The Devil with Hitler
US   1942   44m   bw
Hal Roach

Hell's board of directors want to sack Satan and bring
in Hitler.

Somewhat infantile war farce, one of this producer's
very few successful medium-length 'screenliners'.

w Cortland FitzSimmons, Al Martin   *d* Gordon
Douglas

Alan Mowbray, Bobby Watson, George E. Stone, Joe
Devlin

† The Hays Office gave special permission, in a just
cause, for the use of the word 'Hell'.

A Devil with Women
US   1930   76m   bw
Fox (George Middleton)

Soldiers of fortune in a banana republic end the
regime of a notorious bandit and compete for a fair
señorita.

Primitive Flagg-and-Quirt style knockabout.

w Dudley Nichols, Henry M. Johnson   *novel Dust
and Sun* by Clements Ripley   *d* Irving Cummings
ph Arthur Todd   *m* Peter Brunelli

Victor McLaglen, Humphrey Bogart, Mona Maris,
Michael Vavitch

'No real plot or continuity, but has some laughs. Best
for neighbourhood grinds.' – *Variety*

Devil within Her (dubbed)
Italy   1974   109m   Technicolor
UA/AR Cinematografica (Ovisio Assonitis, Giorgio C. Rossi)
V, V*
original title: *Chi Sei?*; US title: *Beyond the Door*

The Devil gives a black magician ten days to obtain
the unborn child of his former mistress.

An unoriginal and unexciting variation on *The Exorcist*,
repeating to lesser effect that film's tricks.

w Sonia Molteni, Antonio Troisio, Giorgio Marini,
Aldo Crudo, Robert D'Ettore Piazzoli   *d* Oliver
Hellman   *ph* Robert D'Ettore Piazzoli   *m* Franco
Micalizzi   *ad* Piero Filippone, Franco Pellecchia
Velchi   *ed* Angelo Curi

Juliet Mills, Richard Johnson, Gabriele Lavia,
Barbara Fiorini, David Colin Jnr, Joan Acti

'A disastrous foray into the fashionable area of
demonic possession, unencumbered with any trace of
subtlety or conviction.' – *Verina Glaessner*

The Devil within Her (1975): see *I Don't Want to
Be Born*

'Hell holds no surprises . . . for them!'
The Devils **
GB   1970   111m   Technicolor   Panavision
Warner/Russo (Robert H. Solo, Ken Russell)
V, V*, S

An account of the apparent demoniacal possession of
the 17th-century nuns of Loudun, climaxing in the
burning of their priest as a sorcerer.

Despite undeniable technical proficiency this is its
writer-director's most outrageously sick film to date,
campy, idiosyncratic and in howling bad taste from
beginning to end, full of worm-eaten skulls,

masturbating nuns, gibbering courtiers, plague sores, rats and a burning to death before our very eyes . . . plus a sacrilegious dream of Jesus.

wd Ken Russell   *play* John Whiting   *book The Devils of Loudun* by Aldous Huxley   *ph David Watkin*
m Peter Maxwell Davies   *ad* Robert Cartwright

Vanessa Redgrave, Oliver Reed, Dudley Sutton, Max Adrian, Gemma Jones, Murray Melvin, Michael Gothard, Graham Armitage

'Ken Russell doesn't report hysteria, he markets it.' – *New Yorker, 1976*

'Russell's swirling multi-colored puddle . . . made me glad that both Huxley and Whiting are dead, so that they are spared this farrago of witless exhibitionism.' – *Stanley Kauffmann*

'A garish glossary of sado-masochism . . . a taste for visual sensation that makes scene after scene look like the masturbatory fantasies of a Roman Catholic boyhood.' – *Alexander Walker*

The Devil's Advocate
West Germany   1977   109m   colour
Geria (Lutz Hengst)

A dying priest is summoned to Rome to investigate the cult of a dead partisan nominated for sainthood.

Well-meaning but rather tepid and inconclusive adaptation of a bestseller which presumably made its points more firmly.

w Morris West   *novel* Morris West   *d* Guy Green   *ph* Billy Williams   *m* Bert Grund

John Mills, Stéphane Audran, Jason Miller, Timothy West, Patrick Mower, Paola Pitagora, Daniel Massey, Leigh Lawson, Raf Vallone, Jack Hedley

The Devil's Agent
GB   1962   77m   bw
British Lion/Emmet Dalton

A wine salesman in Germany is duped by Soviet agents.

Scrappy cold war adventures which look as though they were originally intended as episodes in a TV series.

w Robert Westerby   *d* John Paddy Carstairs   *ph* Gerald Gibbs   *m* Philip Green

Peter Van Eyck, Marianne Koch, Macdonald Carey, Christopher Lee, Billie Whitelaw, David Knight, Marius Goring, Helen Cherry, Colin Gordon, Niall MacGinnis, Eric Pohlmann, Peter Vaughan

Devil's Bait
GB   1959   58m   bw
Rank/Independent Artists

A baker accidentally bakes a loaf containing poison.

B-feature thriller of minimal interest.

w Peter Johnson, Diana K. Watson   *d* Peter Graham Scott   *ph* Michael Reed   *md* Muir Mathieson   *m* William Alwyn   *ad* Eric Saw   *ed* John Trumper

Geoffrey Keen, Jane Hylton, Gordon Jackson, Rupert Davies, Dermot Kelly

The Devil's Bride: see *The Devil Rides Out*

The Devil's Brigade
US   1968   132m   DeLuxe   Panavision
UA/David L. Wolper
V*

For combat in Norway and Italy during World War II a US officer assembles a platoon of thugs and misfits to work with crack Canadian commandos.

Flagrant but routine imitation of *The Dirty Dozen*, quite undistinguished.

w William Roberts   *d* Andrew V. McLaglen   *ph* William Clothier   *m* Alex North

William Holden, Cliff Robertson, Vince Edwards, Andrew Prine, Claude Akins, Carroll O'Connor, Richard Jaeckel

'After nearly three decades of World War II films, it is hardly surprising that Hollywood is beginning to suffer from combat fatigue.' – *Time*

The Devil's Brother: see *Fra Diavolo*

Devil's Canyon
US   1953   92m   Technicolor   3-D
RKO/Edmund Grainger
V*

Life in a notorious Arizona prison in the 1880s; a marshal is unjustly convicted but wins his pardon.

Fairly brutal Western, quite unmemorable.

w Frederick Hazlitt Brennan   *d* Alfred Werker   *ph* Nicholas Musuraca   *m* Daniele Amfitheatrof

Dale Robertson, Virginia Mayo, Stephen McNally, Arthur Hunnicutt, Robert Keith, Jay C. Flippen, Whit Bissell

The Devil's Disciple *
GB   1959   82m   bw
UA/Hecht-Hill-Lancaster/Brynaprod (Harold Hecht)
V*

In 1777 an American ne'er-do-well almost allows himself to be hanged by the British in mistake for a rebel pastor.

Star-studded but indifferently staged adaptation of a minor Shavian frolic. Patchy, with good moments.

w John Dighton, Roland Kibbee   *play* Bernard Shaw   *d* Guy Hamilton   *ph* Jack Hildyard   *m* Richard Rodney Bennett   *ad* Terence Verity, Edward Carere

Burt Lancaster, Kirk Douglas, Laurence Olivier (as General Burgoyne), Eva Le Gallienne, Janette Scott, Harry Andrews, Basil Sidney, George Rose, Neil McCallum, David Horne, Mervyn Johns

Devil's Doorway
US   1950   84m   bw
MGM (Nicholas Nayfack)

A Shoshone Indian fights valiantly in the Civil War but on his return to Wyoming finds himself hated and threatened by his former colleagues.

Dull pro-Indian Western with a most unsuitable star.

w Guy Trosper   *d* Anthony Mann   *ph* John Alton   *m* Daniele Amfitheatrof

Robert Taylor, Louis Calhern, Paula Raymond, Marshall Thompson, James Mitchell, Edgar Buchanan, Rhys Williams, Spring Byington

The Devil's Eight
US   1968   98m   Pathecolor
AIP/Burt Topper

A federal agent on the trail of a moonshine gang recruits a gang of hardened convicts and arranges for them to escape.

The Dirty Dozen all over again, and not good.

w James Gordon White, Willard Huyck, John Milius   *d* Burt Topper   *ph* Richard C. Glouner   *m* Mike Curb

Christopher George, Ralph Meeker, Fabian, Tom Nardini, Leslie Parrish, Ross Hagen

The Devil's Envoys: see *Les Visiteurs du Soir*

The Devil's Eye *
Sweden   1960   90m   bw
Svensk Filmindustri
V*

An old proverb says that a woman's chastity is a stye in the devil's eye. So when Satan has a sore eye he comes down to earth to put things right.

Surprisingly shoddily-made comedy with just a few of the sharpnesses of technique and mystifications of plot which one had come to expect from this maestro.

wd Ingmar Bergman   *ph* Gunnar Fischer   *m* Domenico Scarlatti

Jarl Kulle, Bibi Andersson, Nils Poppe, Stig Järrel, Gunnar Björnstrand

The Devil's General
West Germany   1955   121m   bw
Ryal (Gyula Trebitsch)

In 1941 a German air ace becomes estranged from the high command and is tortured by the Gestapo. On release he helps a Jewish couple . . .

Heavy-going melodrama which nevertheless paints a convincing picture of Berlin during the war.

w George Hurdalek, Helmut Kautner   *play* Carl Zuckmayer   *d* Helmut Kautner   *ph* Albert Benitz

Curt Jurgens, Victor de Kowa, Karl John, Eva-Ingeborg Scholz

The Devil's Hairpin
US   1957   83m   Technicolor   Vistavision
Paramount/Cornel Wilde

A former motor racing champion makes a comeback, and redeems his past boorish behaviour.

Efficient routine melodramatics with good action sequences.

w James Edmiston, Cornel Wilde   *d* Cornel Wilde   *ph* Daniel Fapp   *m* Van Cleave

Cornel Wilde, Jean Wallace, Arthur Franz, *Mary Astor*, Paul Fix

Devil's Holiday *
US   1930   80m   bw
Paramount

A mercenary lady repents her life on the make.

Very dated moral story which at the time was showered with praise.

wd Edmund Goulding

Nancy Carroll, Phillips Holmes, James Kirkwood, Hobart Bosworth, Ned Sparks, Jed Prouty, Paul Lukas, ZaSu Pitts

'It is pictures such as this which revive the drooping confidence in the screen as a mirror of things as they really are.' – *Variety*

AAN: Nancy Carroll

The Devil's Impostor: see *Pope Joan*

The Devil's in Love
US   1933   70m   bw
Fox

At a French Foreign Legion post, an outcast doctor falls in love with the niece of a mission father.

Old-fashioned and predictable romantic drama.

w Howard Estabrook   *story* Harry Hervey   *d* William Dieterle

Victor Jory, Loretta Young, Vivienne Osborne, David Manners, C. Henry Gordon, Herbert Mundin, J. Carrol Naish

'Given any kind of a break returns should be fair.' – *Variety*

Devil's Island *
US   1939   63m   bw
Warner (Bryan Foy)

A surgeon is sent to Devil's Island for aiding an escaped convict.

Sharply-made exposé of the notorious French penal colony; commendable pace and vigour all round.

w Kenneth Gamet, Don Ryan   *d* William Clemens

Boris Karloff, James Stephenson, Nedda Harrigan, Adia Kuznetzoff, Robert Warwick, Pedro de Cordoba

The Devil's Mask
US   1946   66m   bw
Columbia

An unclaimed parcel containing a shrunken head is found after a plane crash; murder follows.

Involved but amusing entry in the *I Love a Mystery* series.

w Charles O'Neal   d Henry Levin

Jim Bannon, Anita Louise, Michael Duane, Mona Barrie, Byron Foulger

Devils of Darkness
GB   1964   90m   Eastmancolor
Planet (Tom Blakeley)

A vampire disguises himself as a French count and preys on young girls.

Mainly tatty shocker with a few lively scenes.

w Lyn Fairhurst   d Lance Comfort

William Sylvester, Hubert Noel, Tracy Reed, Diana Decker, Rona Anderson

The Devil's Own: see *The Witches*

The Devil's Playground *
Australia   1976   107m   Eastmancolor
The Feature Film House (Fred Schepisi)

Tensions between masters and boys in a Catholic seminary in the fifties.

Well made but rather dislikeable intrusion into *Mr Perrin and Mr Traill* country with the addition of modern frankness.

wd Fred Schepisi   ph Ian Baker   m Bruce Smeaton

Arthur Dignam, Nick Tate, Simon Burke, Charles McCallum, John Frawley

The Devil's Rain
US   1975   86m   colour   Todd-AO 35
Rank/Sandy Howard (James V. Cullen, Michael S. Glick)
V*, L

Witchcraft in the modern west causes victims to melt; the son of one of them takes arms against the leading Satanist.

Interestingly cast example of the low-budget seventies exploitation picture, with more nastiness than logic.

w Gabe Essoe, James Ashton, Gerald Hopman
d Robert Fuest   ph Alex Phillips Jnr   m Al de Lory

Ernest Borgnine, Ida Lupino, Eddie Albert, William Shatner, Keenan Wynn, Tom Skerritt

The Devil's Wanton *
Sweden   1949   80m   bw
Terrafilm
V*
original title: *Fängelse;* aka: *Prison*

Film-makers discuss some rather unpleasant projects but put them aside as unsatisfactory.

A bit of a Scandinavian wallow, with heavy expressionism and low-life themes.

wd Ingmar Bergman   ph Göran Strindberg
m Erland von Koch

Doris Svedlund, Birger Malmsten, Eva Henning, Hasse Ekman

'It employs all the paraphernalia associated with Scandinavian angst.' – *John Gillett, MFB*

The Devil's Widow: see *Tam-Lin*

Devlin
US   1992   106m   colour
Viacom (Paula de Oliviera, Craig Roessler)
V, V*

A cop fights back when he discovers he is being framed for the murder of his brother-in-law, a leading politician.

An unoriginal movie that is acted and directed with enough pace and energy to make it enjoyable.

w David Taylor   *novel* Roderick Thorp   d Rick Rosenthal   ph Neil Roach   m John Altman
pd Barbara Dunphy   ed Tony Gibbs

Bryan Brown, Roma Downey, Lloyd Bridges, Whip Hubley, Lawrence Dane, Lisa Eichhorn, Carole Shelley, Jan Rubes, Frances Fisher

'A slick thriller that really does thrill.' – *Alan Frank, Movies*

Devotion
US   1931   84m   bw
RKO-Pathé

A woman falls in love with a barrister and takes a job as governess to his son.

Rather winsome tear-jerker entirely dependent on its stars.

w Graham John, Horace Jackson   *novel A Little Flat in the Temple* by Pamela Wynne   d Robert Milton

Ann Harding, Leslie Howard, Robert Williams, O. P. Heggie, Louise Closser Hale, Dudley Digges

'Much talk and little action. Star's name its best chance of rating more than mild financially.' – *Variety*

'It tells ALL about those Brontë sisters! … They didn't dare call it love – they tried to call it devotion!'

Devotion **
US   1943 (released 1946)   107m   bw
Warner (Robert Buckner)

A highly romanticized account of the lives of the Brontë sisters and their brother Branwell.

An enjoyable bad example of a big-budget Hollywood production which tampers with things it cannot understand, in this case life in a Yorkshire parsonage in Victorian times. An excuse is found to give the curate an Austrian accent to fit the available actor, but this and other *faux pas* are atoned for by the vividness of Emily's recurrent dream of death as a silhouetted man on horseback. In general, an interesting period piece in more senses than one.

w Keith Winter   d Curtis Bernhardt   ph Ernest Haller
m Erich Wolfgang Korngold

Ida Lupino (Emily), Olivia de Havilland (Charlotte), Nancy Coleman (Anne), Arthur Kennedy (Branwell), Montagu Love (Revd Brontë), Paul Henreid (Revd Nicholls), Ethel Griffies (Aunt Branwell), Sidney Greenstreet (Thackeray), Eily Malyon, Forrester Harvey, Victor Francen

'I found it painless. It never got nearer to the subject than names and consequently didn't hurt. But I would like to know who was devoted to whom and why.' – *Richard Winnington*

† More items from the extraordinary publicity campaign devised by Warner for this placid Victorian romance:

Emily: she ruled in that strange quiet house! None could resist the force of her will!
The man in black (i.e. the Revd Nicholls): he fled from her demands into her sister's arms!
Charlotte: the sweetness of love and the meaning of torment – she learned them both together!
The 'friend' – the furious fat man (i.e. William Makepeace Thackeray): they couldn't fool him – they couldn't trust him!
†† Dialogue includes the celebrated exchange between two celebrated London literary figures:

THACKERAY: 'Morning, Dickens.'
DICKENS: 'Morning, Thackeray.'

Dharmaga Tongjoguro Kan Kkadalgun?: see *Why Did Bodhi-Dharma Leave for the East?*

Le Diable au Corps *
France   1947   110m   bw
Transcontinental
US title: *Devil in the Flesh*

When her husband is away at war, a young married woman falls for a college student and dies bearing his child.

A love story of World War I; a great commercial success, but tending to be slow and dreary.

w Jean Aurenche, Pierre Bost   *novel* Raymond Radiguet   d Claude Autant-Lara   ph Michel Kelber   m René Cloërc

Micheline Presle, Gérard Philipe, Jean Debucourt, Denise Grey, Jacques Tati

Le Diable, Probablement: see *The Devil, Probably*

Diabolique: see *Les Diaboliques*

Les Diaboliques ***
France   1954   114m   bw
Filmsonor (Henri-Georges Clouzot)
V, V*, L
aka: *Diabolique; The Fiends*

A sadistic headmaster's wife and mistress conspire to murder him; but his body disappears and evidence of his presence haunts them.

Highly influential, suspenseful and scary thriller with a much-copied twist typical of its authors. Slow to start and shabby-looking as befits its grubby school setting, it gathers momentum with the murder and turns the screw with fine professionalism.

w Henri-Georges Clouzot, G. Geronimi   *novel The Woman Who Was* by Pierre Boileau and Thomas Narcejac   *d Henri-Georges Clouzot   ph* Armand Thirard   m Georges Van Parys

Simone Signoret, Vera Clouzot, Charles Vanel, Paul Meurisse

'Scary, but so calculatedly sensational that it's rather revolting.' – *New Yorker, 1978*

'It depends very much on the intimate details of the seedy fourth-rate school, with its inadequate education and uneatable food, its general smell of unwashed children, hatred and petty perversions.' – *Basil Wright, 1972*

† Remade in 1976 as a TV movie, *Reflections of Murder.*

Diagnosis: Murder
GB   1974   90m   Eastmancolor
Silhouette (Patrick Dromgoole, Peter Miller)

A psychiatrist's wife disappears, and the police suspect her husband.

Well-upholstered but sadly old-fashioned domestic crime thriller; one is vaguely surprised to see it in colour, having seen it so often in black-and-white.

w Philip Levene   d Sidney Hayers   ph Bob Edwards   m Laurie Johnson

Jon Finch, Judy Geeson, Christopher Lee, Tony Beckley, Dilys Hamlett, Jane Merrow, Colin Jeavons

'If a woman answers – hang on for dear life!'

Dial M For Murder **
US   1954   105m   Warnercolor   3-D
Warner (Alfred Hitchcock)
V, V*, L

An ageing tennis champion tries to arrange the death of his wife so that he will inherit, but his complex plan goes wrong.

Hitchcock did not try very hard to adapt this highly commercial play for the cinema, nor did he exploit the possibilities of 3-D. But for a one-room film with a not very exciting cast the film holds its grip pretty well.

w Frederick Knott   *play* Frederick Knott   d Alfred Hitchcock   ph Robert Burks   m Dimitri Tiomkin
ed Rudi Fehr

Ray Milland, John Williams, Grace Kelly, Robert
Cummings, Anthony Dawson

'All this is related with Hitchcock's ghoulish chic but
everyone in it seems to be walking around with tired
blood.' – *Pauline Kael, 1968*

† Although shot in 3-D, it was never released in that
form.

Dial 1119 *
US   1950   75m   bw
MGM (Richard Goldstone)
GB title: *The Violent Hour*

An assortment of people are held up in a bar by a
maniac.

Suspenseful thriller when it sticks to its central
theme; dullish when it tries characterization. A good
second feature.

w John Monks Jnr   *d Gerald Mayer   ph* Paul Vogel
m André Previn

Marshall Thompson, Virginia Field, Andrea King, Leon
Ames, Keefe Brasselle, Richard Rober, James Bell,
William Conrad

The Diamond
GB   1954   83m   bw   3D
Gibraltar Films (Stephen Pallos)
US title: *The Diamond Wizard*

An American agent in London investigates a million-
dollar treasury robbery involving a process for
making synthetic diamonds.

Leaden cops-and-robbers which went out on the
bottom of a bill instead of being shown in three
dimensions.

w John C. Higgins   *story The Bowstring Murders* by
Maurice Procter   *d* Montgomery Tully   *m* Matyas
Seiber

Dennis O'Keefe, Margaret Sheridan, Philip Friend,
Alan Wheatley, Francis de Wolff

Diamond City
GB   1949   90m   bw
GFD/Gainsborough (A. Frank Bundy)

Law and order is maintained during the working of a
South African diamond field.

British imitation of a Wyatt Earp Western; very milk-
and-water.

w Roger Bray, Roland Pertwee   *d* David MacDonald
ph Reginald Wyer   *m* Clifton Parker

David Farrar, Honor Blackman, Diana Dors, Niall
MacGinnis, Andrew Crawford, Mervyn Johns, Bill
Owen, Phyllis Monkman

Diamond Frontier
US   1940   72m   bw
Universal

An honest diamond dealer is framed and sent to
prison.

Co-feature action stuff, with South Africa standing in
for the west.

w Edmund L. Hartmann, Stanley Rubin   *d* Harold
Schuster

Victor McLaglen, Anne Nagel, John Loder, Philip
Dorn, Cecil Kellaway

Diamond Head
US   1962   107m   Eastmancolor   Panavision
Columbia (Jerry Bresler)
V*, L

A domineering Hawaiian landowner almost ruins the
lives of his family.

Predictable, heavy-going transcription of a bestseller.

w Marguerite Roberts   *novel* Peter Gilman   *d* Guy
Green   *ph* Sam Leavitt   *m* Johnny Williams

Charlton Heston, Yvette Mimieux, George Chakiris,
France Nuyen, James Darren, Aline MacMahon,
Elizabeth Allen, Richard Loo

Diamond Horseshoe
US   1945   104m   Technicolor
TCF (William Perlberg)
V
aka: *Billy Rose's Diamond Horseshoe*

A night-club singer gives up her career for a medical
student.

Lavish but humourless star vehicle with standard
numbers.

wd George Seaton   *play The Barker* by Kenyon
Nicholson   *ph* Ernest Palmer   *m/y* Mack Gordon,
Harry Warren

Betty Grable, Dick Haymes, *William Gaxton*, Phil
Silvers, Beatrice Kay, Carmen Cavallero, Margaret
Dumont

Diamond Jim *
US   1935   93m   bw
Universal (Edmund Grainger)

A fantasia on the life of the 1890s millionaire who
sailed pretty close to the wind in business, adored
Lillian Russell, and developed a gargantuan appetite.

Cheerful period comedy drama with plenty of gusto.

w Preston Sturges   *d* A. Edward Sutherland
ph George Robinson   *m* Ferde Grofe, Franz
Waxman

Edward Arnold, Jean Arthur, Binnie Barnes, Cesar
Romero, Eric Blore

'Good picture and title. Lacks real pull names.' –
Variety

The Diamond Queen
US   1953   80m   Supercinecolor
Warner/Melson (Frank Melford, Edward L. Alperson Jnr)

Frenchmen journey to India to bring back a diamond
for the crown of Louis XIV.

The adventures are basically lively enough to warrant
a better production.

w Otto Englander   *d* John Brahm   *ph* Stanley
Cortez   *m* Paul Sawtell

Fernando Lamas, Arlene Dahl, Gilbert Roland,
Sheldon Leonard, Michael Ansara

Diamond Skulls
GB   1989   87m   Technicolor
Virgin Vision/Working Title/British Screen/Channel 4 (Tim
Bevan)
V
US title: *Dark Obsession*

An aristocrat kills a woman in a hit-and-run accident
and lets his friend take the blame.

Confused melodrama of sex and the old boy network
that seems uncertain of what kind of film it wants to
be.

w Tim Rose Price   *d* Nick Broomfield   *ph* Michael
Coulter   *m* Hans Zimmer   *pd* Jocelyn James
ed Rodney Holland

Gabriel Byrne, Amanda Donohue, Michael Hordern,
Judy Parfitt, Douglas Hodge, Sadie Frost, Matthew
Marsh, Ian Carmichael

'All in all, a promising portrait of aristocratic thuggery
in changing times, yet ultimately too diffuse to deliver
its punch with the force it needs.' – *Julian Petley, MFB*

The Diamond Wizard: see *The Diamond*

Diamonds
US   1975   108m   Eastmancolor
Avco Embassy/AmeriEuro (Menahem Golan)

A London diamond merchant sets himself up to be
robbed so that he can blackmail the culprits into a
raid on the Tel Aviv diamond repository.

Cheerful but unremarkable caper movie with an
upbeat ending.

w David Paulsen, Menahem Golan   *d* Menahem
Golan   *ph* Adam Greenberg   *m* Roy Budd

Robert Shaw, Richard Roundtree, Barbara Seagull,
Shelley Winters

Diamonds Are Forever *
GB   1971   120m   Technicolor   Panavision
UA/Eon/Danjaq (Harry Saltzman, Albert R. Broccoli)
V, V (W), V*, L, S

Seeking a diamond smuggler, James Bond has
adventures in Amsterdam, a Los Angeles
crematorium, various Las Vegas gambling parlours,
and a secret installation in the desert.

Campy, rather vicious addition to a well-worn cycle,
with an element of nastiness which big-budget stunts
cannot conceal. Panavision does not help, and
Connery's return to the role for a final throw is
disappointing.

w Richard Maibaum, Tom Mankiewicz   *novel* Ian
Fleming   *d* Guy Hamilton   *ph* Ted Moore
m John Barry   *pd* Ken Adam

Sean Connery, Jill St John, Charles Gray, Lana Wood,
Jimmy Dean, Bruce Cabot, Bernard Lee, Lois Maxwell

'It has been claimed that the plot is impossible to
describe, but I think I could if I wanted to. I can't
think why anyone would want to, though.' – *Roger
Ebert*

Diamonds for Breakfast
GB   1968   102m   Eastmancolor
Paramount/Bridge Films (Carlo Ponti, Pierre Rouve)

An impoverished Russian aristocrat decides to
retrieve from a museum the crown jewels of his
ancestors, and seduces seven female accomplices.

Yawning caper yarn embellished with sex and
slapstick.

w N. F. Simpson, Pierre Rouve, Ronald Harwood
d Christopher Morahan   *ph* Gerry Turpin
m Norman Kay

Marcello Mastroianni, Rita Tushingham, Elaine
Taylor, Warren Mitchell, Nora Nicholson, Bill Fraser,
Leonard Rossiter

Diane
US   1956   110m   Eastmancolor   Cinemascope
MGM (Edwin H. Knopf)
V*

Diane de Poitier becomes a consultant to the king and
falls in love with his son.

Solidly boring slice of Hollywood history, with all
concerned out of their depth.

w Christopher Isherwood   *d* David Miller
ph Robert Planck   *m* Miklos Rozsa

Lana Turner, Roger Moore, Cedric Hardwicke, Pedro
Armendariz, Marisa Pavan

Diary for My Children ***
Hungary   1982   107m   bw
Artificial Eye/Mafilm/Hungarofilm
original title: *Napló Gyermekeimnek*

An orphan, returning to Budapest in 1947, recalls her
happy childhood while dealing with a less enjoyable
present.

Three generations of a family encapsulate the modern
history of Hungary in a gripping film. Withheld from
the West for two years, it won a special jury prize at
the Cannes Film Festival in 1984.

w Márta Mészáros, Balàzs Fakan, András Szeredás
d Márta Mészáros   ph Miklós Jancsó Jnr   *m* Zsolt
Döme

Zsuzsa Czinkóczi, Anna Polony, Jan Nowicki, Mari
Szémes, Pàl Zolnay

Diary for My Loves **
Hungary 1987 130m bw
Artificial Eye/Mafilm/Hungarofilm/Magyar Film/Zespoly Filmowe
original title: *Napló Szerelmeimnek*

An eighteen-year-old Hungarian girl goes to Moscow to become a film-maker and to search for her father.

Absorbing sequel to *Diary for my Children*, tracing the end of Stalinism.

w Márta Mészáros *d* Márta Mészáros
ph Nyika Jancsó *pd* Éva Martin *ed* Éva Kármentö

Zsuzsa Czinkóczi, Anna Polony, Jan Nowicki, Irina Kouberskaya, László Szabó, Pál Zolnay, Adél Kováts, Erzsébet Kútvölgyi

A Diary for Timothy ***
GB 1945 40m bw
Basil Wright/Crown Film Unit

A baby is born as the war ends, and the narrator ponders its future.

Brilliant sentimental documentary, a summing up of the aims and feelings of Britain at the time.

w E. M. Forster *d* Humphrey Jennings
narrator Michael Redgrave

Diary of a Bride: see *I, Jane Doe*

The Diary of a Chambermaid *
US 1946 86m bw
Benedict Bogeaus (Burgess Meredith, Paulette Goddard)
V*

A 19th-century serving girl causes sexual frustration and other troubles in two households.

Hollywood notables were all at sea in this wholly artificial and unpersuasive adaptation of a minor classic.

w Burgess Meredith *novel* Octave Mirbeau *d* Jean Renoir *ph* Lucien Andriot *m* Michel Michelet
pd Eugene Lourié

Paulette Goddard, Burgess Meredith, Hurd Hatfield, Francis Lederer, Judith Anderson, Florence Bates, Irene Ryan, Reginald Owen, Almira Sessions

'I do not mean to disparage Renoir's direction of the piece; erratic and with a curious element of flippancy and even vulgarity at the start, it advances with the melodramatic development of the plot to a fine climax of excitement, movement, terror. But the theme is incurably novelettish.' – *Dilys Powell*

The Diary of a Chambermaid *
France/Italy 1964 98m bw Franscope
Speva/Ciné Alliance/Filmsonor/Dear (Serge Silberman, Michel Sabra)
V, V*, L
original title: *Le Journal d'une Femme de Chambre*

Interesting but not especially successful Buñuel version: the subject is certainly up his street, but the novel seems to restrict him and the visual quality is unattractive.

w Luis Buñuel, Jean-Claude Carrière *d* Luis Buñuel *ph* Roger Fellous *m* none

Jeanne Moreau, Georges Géret, Michel Piccoli, Françoise Lugagne

'The film remains notable but inconclusive: a half-Buñuel.' – *Dilys Powell*

The Diary of a Country Priest ***
France 1950 120m bw
Union Générale Cinématographique (Léon Carré)
V*
original title: *Journal d'un Curé de Campagne*

A lonely young priest fails to make much impression in his first parish; and, falling ill, he dies alone.

Striking, depressing, slow and austere, with little dialogue but considerable visual beauty; a very typical work of its director.

wd Robert Bresson *novel* Georges Bernanos *ph* L. Burel *m* Jean-Jacques Grunenwald

Claude Laydu, Jean Riveyre, Armand Guibert, Nicole Ladmiral

'Nothing personal, purely business.'

Diary of a Hitman
US 1992 91m Technicolor
Vision International/Continental (Amin Q. Chaudhri)
V, V*

A hired killer begins to have doubts when a husband pays him to murder his wife and baby.

A wordy, claustrophobic thriller that betrays its stage origins and strains credulity.

w Kenneth Pressman *play* Insider's Price by Kenneth Pressman *d* Roy London *ph* Yuri Sokol
m Michel Colombier *pd* Stephen Hendrickson
ed Brian Smedley-Aston

Forest Whitaker, John Bedford-Lloyd, James Belushi, Seymour Cassel, Lois Chiles, Lewis Smith, Sharon Stone, Sherilyn Fenn

Diary of a Lost Girl **
Germany 1929 110m approx bw silent
G. W. Pabst Film
V, V*, L
original title: *Tagebuch einer Verlorenen*

A rich man's daughter is seduced, has an illegitimate child, is placed in a house of correction and finds herself later in a brothel.

Heavily Germanic Road to Ruin, superbly mounted in best cinematic style, with several memorable sequences. Heavily mutilated by censors; according to the screenwriter the film ends just after the middle of his script.

w Rudolf Leonhardt *novel* Margaret Böhme *d* G. W. Pabst *ph* Sepp Allgeier

Louise Brooks, Fritz Rasp, Josef Ravensky

† A previous version had been made in 1918, written and directed by Richard Oswald.

Diary of a Mad Housewife **
US 1970 95m Technicolor
Universal/Frank Perry
V*

The bored and repressed wife of a lawyer tries an affair, walks out on her husband, and opts for group therapy.

An agreeably mordant view of the contemporary American scene, with good dialogue and performances, but the little bits of satire do not really add up to a satisfactory film.

w Eleanor Perry *novel* Sue Kaufman *d* Frank Perry *ph* Gerald Hirschfeld

Carrie Snodgress, Richard Benjamin, Frank Langella, Lorraine Cullen, Frannie Michel

'A prototypical contemporary American artifact . . . all its assorted talents and technological smartness are turned to the varnishing of mediocrity.' – *Stanley Kauffmann*

AAN: Carrie Snodgress

The Diary of a Madman
US 1962 96m Technicolor
UA/Admiral (Robert E. Kent)
V*

A murderer explains to a magistrate that he was possessed by an evil spirit.

Ponderous transcription of a Maupassant story with a few moments of horror.

w Robert E. Kent *d* Reginald Le Borg *ph* Ellis W. Carter *m* Richard La Salle

Vincent Price, Nancy Kovack, Chris Warfield, Stephen Roberts

The Diary of a Married Woman
Germany 1953 83m bw
Magna
original title: *Tagebuch einer Verliebten*

A wife divorces her adulterous husband, but their small son brings them together again.

One long Hollywood cliché, assembled with some spirit; notable only as one of the rare post-war German films to get distribution in English-speaking countries.

w Emil Burri, Johann Mario Simmel *d* Josef von Baky *ph* Oskar Snirch *m* Alois Melichar

Maria Schell, O. W. Fischer, Franco Andrei

Diary of a Shinjuku Thief *
Japan 1969 94m bw/Eastmancolor
Sozosha (Masayuki Nakajima)
original title: *Shinjuku Dorobo Nikki*

A minor theft in a bookstore brings a young man in contact with a mysterious girl who leads him into various sexual experiments.

Inexplicable but quite fascinating piece of oriental mystification in which sex equates to some extent with revolution.

w Tsutomu Tamura and others *d* Nagisa Oshima *ph* Yasuhiro Yamaguchi *m* none

Tadanori Yokoo, Rie Yokoyama, Moichi Tanabe

The Diary of Anne Frank **
US 1959 170m bw Cinemascope
TCF/George Stevens
V*, L

In 1942, a family of Dutch Jews hides in an attic from the Nazis; just before the war ends they are found and sent to concentration camps.

Based on the famous diaries of a girl who died at Auschwitz, this solemn adaptation is elephantine in its length, its ponderousness and its use of Cinemascope when the atmosphere is supposed to be claustrophobic.

w Frances Goodrich, Albert Hackett from their play based on Anne Frank's diaries *d* George Stevens
ph William C. Mellor *m* Alfred Newman *ad* Lyle R. Wheeler, George W. Davis

Millie Perkins, *Joseph Schildkraut, Shelley Winters, Ed Wynn*, Richard Beymer, Gusti Huber, Lou Jacobi, Diane Baker

AA: William C. Mellor; Shelley Winters; art direction

AAN: best picture; George Stevens; Alfred Newman; Ed Wynn

The Diary of Lady M
Switzerland/Belgium/Spain/France 1993 112m colour
Filmograph/Nomad/Messidor/Lazennec (Alain Tanner, Jacques de Clercq, Dimitri de Clercq, Gerardo Herrero, Marta Esteban, Christophe Rossignon)
original title: *Le Journal de Lady M*

A Parisian singer begins a passionate affair with a Spanish painter and, discovering that he is married, invites his wife and family to join them.

Supposedly based on the star's diaries, this is a throwback to the sad sex films of the 60s, a drearily egocentric, uninteresting drama.

w Myriam Mézières *d* Alain Tanner *ph* Denis Jutzeler *m* Arie Dzierlatka *ad* Jordi Canora, Alain Chennaux *ed* Monica Goux

Myriam Mézières, Juanjo Puligcorbé, Félicité Wouassi, Antoine Basler, Makeda, Marie Peyrucq-Yamou, Gladys Gambie

'A preposterously clichéd, would-be (but not-at-all) titillating film that charts the sad decline of Alain Tanner . . . I started noting down the worst lines but soon gave up; I was transcribing the script.' – *Sheila Johnston, Independent*

'Pic's extremely frank sex scenes have a shocking realism and seem a natural outgrowth of Mézières' honesty in recounting her feelings. A scene in which Lady M shaves her pubic hair and dances for her lover clothed only in a long, dangling earring must set some kind of art-film precedent.' – *Variety*

The Diary of Major Thompson
France   1955   83m   bw
SNE Gaumont/Paul Wagner
original title: *Les Carnets de Major Thompson*; US title: *The French They Are a Funny Race*

An Englishman married to a Frenchwoman keeps notes on the French way of life.

Tatty filming of a mildly amusing book; it falls away into a number of badly-timed and presented gags, and one can't believe that its creator was once the top comedy genius of Hollywood.

wd Preston Sturges   *ph* Maurice Barry, Christian Matras   *m* Georges Van Parys

Jack Buchanan, Martine Carol, Noel-Noel, Genevieve Brunet

'Even allowing for the appalling editing and the frequently incomprehensible dubbed soundtrack, there is little evidence to suggest that this film could ever have been anything but a shambles.' – *Peter John Dyer, MFB*

Il Diavolo e il Morto: see *Lisa and The Devil*

Dice Rules
US   1991   83m   Foto-Kem
Seven Arts/Fleebin Dabble (Fred Silverstein)
V*

A 20-minute short on the emergence of the comedian is followed by footage of a concert performance in Madison Square Gardens.

Like strychnine, an acquired and less than enjoyable taste.

w Lenny Shulman, Andrew Dice Clay   *d* Jay Dubin   *ph* Michael Negrin   *ed* Mitchell Sinoway

Andrew Dice Clay, Eddie Griffin, Sylvia Harman, Lee Lawrence, Noodles Levenstein, Maria Parkinson

'A pretty accurate snapshot of the comedian's standup act – crude, sexist, racist, homophobic and designed to shock.' – *Variety*

'A humorous look at man's greatest asset . . . and liability.'
Dick *
US   1990   13m   bw
Island (Jo Menell)
V

Documentary in which photographs of multifarious flaccid male organs are flashed on screen to the accompaniment of women's voices answering such questions as 'Would you want one?'

Amusing novelty, although one that was denied a television showing in Britain.

d Jo Menell, B. Moel   *ph* Paul Latoures   *m* John Cale

'Menell's liberating, wholly unprurient film should put an end to Freud's theory of penis envy.' – *Philip French, Observer*

Dick Barton

The radio detective was created by Edward J. Mason in the mid-forties, and three rough-and-ready film versions were subsequently made by Hammer/Exclusive. They were *Dick Barton Special Agent* (1948); *Dick Barton Strikes Back* (1949); and *Dick Barton at Bay* (1950); all with Don Stannard.

Critical comment would be irrelevant.

Dick Deadeye, or Duty Done
GB   1975   81m   Technicolor
Bill Melendez Productions (Leo Rost)

A naval officer is commissioned by Queen Victoria to retrieve the Ultimate Secret from the Wicked Sorcerer.

Fairly joyless animated amalgam of several Gilbert and Sullivan operas, fussily designed by Ronald Searle and with modernized lyrics. Sure to infuriate G and S devotees and to bewilder everyone else.

w Robin Miller, Leo Rost   *d* Bill Melendez   *animation d* Dick Horn

Dick Tracy
US   1937   bw   serial: 15 eps
Republic

The fearless detective combats an arch-criminal known as The Spider.

Hearty serialized thick ear.

d Ray Taylor, Alan James

Ralph Byrd, Kay Hughes, Smiley Burnette, Francis X. Bushman

Dick Tracy
US   1945   61m   bw
RKO (Herman Schlom)
V*, L
GB title: *Splitface*

The jut-jawed detective routs a disfigured criminal named Splitface.

Vigorous second feature from the comic strip.

w Eric Taylor   *comic strip* Chester Gould   *d* William Berke   *ph* Frank Redman   *m* Roy Webb

Morgan Conway, Jane Greer, Mike Mazurki, Anne Jeffreys, Lyle Latell, Joseph Crehan, Trevor Bardette

† Sequels: *Dick Tracy vs Cueball* (1946) with Morgan Conway, *d* John Rawlins; *Dick Tracy Meets Gruesome* (1947) with Ralph Byrd, Boris Karloff, *d* John Rawlins; *Dick Tracy's Dilemma* (1947), with Ralph Byrd, *d* John Rawlins. There had been several Republic serials featuring Tracy, and in the fifties a cartoon series appeared.

Dick Tracy *
US   1990   103m   Technicolor
Touchstone/Silver Screen Partners IV (Warren Beatty)
V, V*, L, S

Detective Dick Tracy tangles with a master criminal.

A limp narrative is bolstered by a lavish and stylized production design, using comic-book primary colours, and by the careful re-creation of the bizarre appearance of the gangsters from the original newspaper strip-cartoon.

w Jim Cash, Jack Epps Jnr   *comic strip* Chester Gould   *d* Warren Beatty   *ph* Vittorio Storaro   *m* Danny Elfman   *pd* Richard Sylbert   *m/ly* Stephen Sondheim   *ad* Harold Michelson   *sp* character make-up by John Caglione Jnr, Doug Drexler   *ed* Richard Marks

Warren Beatty, Charlie Korsmo, Glenne Headly, Madonna, Al Pacino, Dustin Hoffman, William Forsythe, Charles Durning, Mandy Patinkin, Paul Sorvino, R. G. Armstrong, Dick Van Dyke

'This is no ready-to-wear movie; it's the work of a cinematic couturier. Take it for what it is: a simple gift, consummately wrapped.' – *David Ansen, Newsweek*

'A charming and beautifully designed work of American popular art.' – *David Denby, New York Magazine*

'A grand exercise in cinema imagination and wit for their own sake.' – *Vincent Canby, New York Times*

'A major disappointment.' – *Variety*

AA: best art direction; best song 'Sooner or Later'; best make-up

AAN: Al Pacino; Vittorio Storaro; best costume design; best sound

Dick Tracy Returns
US   1938   bw   serial: 15 eps
Republic

Dick Tracy combats a criminal family, the Starks.

More hectic and hilarious exploits of the jut-jawed hero, now a G-man.

d William Witney, John English

Ralph Byrd, Lynne Roberts, Charles Middleton, Jerry Tucker, David Sharpe

Dick Tracy's G-Men
US   1939   bw   serial: 15 eps
Republic

Dick Tracy combats Zarnoff, an international spy who has been executed but revived by powerful drugs.

Serial cliffhangers *par excellence*.

d William Witney, John English

Ralph Byrd, Irving Pichel, Ted Pearson, Phyllis Isley (Jennifer Jones)

Dick Tracy vs Crime Inc
US   1941   bw   serial: 15 eps
Republic

Dick Tracy combats a master criminal known as The Ghost.

Repetition is now beginning to set in.

d William Witney, John English

Ralph Byrd, Michael Owen, Jan Wiley, Ralph Morgan

Dick Turpin
GB   1933   79m   bw
Stoll-Stafford (Clyde Cook)

In this version the highwayman's ride to York is to prevent an enforced marriage.

Mild British costume piece which sent its star to Hollywood.

w Victor Kendall   *novel Rookwood* by Harrison Ainsworth   *d* Victor Hanbury, John Stafford   *ph* Desmond Dickinson   *ad* Wilfred Arnold

Victor McLaglen, Jane Carr, Frank Vosper, James Finlayson, Gillian Lind

Dick Turpin's Ride: see *The Lady and the Bandit*

The Dictator *
GB   1935   86m   bw
Toeplitz
aka: *For Love of a Queen; The Loves of a Dictator*

In 18th-century Denmark, a country doctor falls in love with his queen and overthrows the mad king.

Stiff-backed middle-class romance, an interesting example of English-German co-production at the time.

w Benn Levy, Hans Wilhelm, H. G. Lustig, Michael Hogan   *d* Victor Saville, Alfred Santell   *ph* Franz Planer   *m* Karol Rathaus   *ad* Andrei Andreiev   *ed* Paul Weatherwax

Clive Brook, Madeleine Carroll, Helen Haye, Emlyn Williams, Isabel Jeans, Alfred Drayton, Frank Cellier

'One of the most lavish costume pictures that has yet come out of England: supposed to have cost 500,000 dollars. It's great pictorially, but not moving enough.' – *Variety*

Did You Hear the One about the Traveling Saleslady?
US   1967   96m   Techniscope
Universal (Si Rose)

In a Kansas town in 1910 an eccentric saleslady offers pianolas which tend to go berserk.

Cornbelt comedy vehicle for an unappealing star.

w John Fenton Murray   *d* Don Weis   *ph* Bud Thackery   *m* Vic Mizzy

Phyllis Diller, Bob Denver, Joe Flynn, Jeanette Nolan

Die! Die! My Darling: see *Fanatic*

Die Hard **
US   1988   132m   DeLuxe   Panavision
Fox/Gordon Company/Silver Pictures (Lawrence Gordon, Joel Silver)
V, V (W), V*, L

A cop battles with terrorists who have taken over the building where his wife and children are.

Powerful, suspenseful action movie, with splendid special effects, although it goes on rather too long.

w Jeb Stuart, Steven E. de Souza   *novel Nothing Lasts Forever* by Roderick Thorp   *d* John McTiernan   *ph* Jan de Bont   *m* Michael Kamen   *pd* Jackson DeGovia   *ed* Frank J. Urioste, John F. Link

Bruce Willis, Bonnie Bedelia, Reginald VelJohnson, Paul Gleason, De'Voreaux White, William Atherton, Hart Bochner, James Shigeta, Alan Rickman, Alexander Godunov

Die Hard 2 *
US   1990   124m   DeLuxe   Panavision
Fox/Gordon Co./Silver Pictures (Lawrence Gordon, Joel Silver, Charles Gordon)
V, V (W), V*, L, S

A cop, going to meet his wife at an airport, discovers that terrorists have taken it over.

Frenetically unsubtle, and very bloody, action movie.

w Steven E. de Souza, Doug Richardson   *novel 58 Minutes* by Walter Wager   *d* Renny Harlin   *ph* Oliver Wood   *m* Michael Kamen   *pd* John Vallone   *ad* Christiaan Wagener   *ed* Stuart Baird, Robert A. Ferretti

Bruce Willis, Bonnie Bedelia, William Atherton, Reginald VelJohnson, Franco Nero, William Sadler, John Amos, Dennis Franz, Art Evans, Fred Dalton Thompson

† The film was advertised with the title *Die Hard 2: Die Harder*.

Die Laughing
US   1980   108m   Technicolor
Orion/Warner (Jon Peters)
V*

After the murder of a nuclear scientist, a young musician who knows too much is chased by the murderers and the FBI.

Witless black comedy rehash of *The 39 Steps*.

w Jerry Segal, Robby Benson, Scott Parker   *d* Jeff Werner

Robby Benson, Linda Grovenor, Charles Durning, Elsa Lanchester, Bud Cort

Dieu A Besoin des Hommes *
France   1950   100m   bw
Transcontinental (Paul Graetz)
aka: *Isle of Sinners; God Needs Men*

The priest of a Breton island leaves in horror at the sinfulness of his flock, and the fisherfolk appoint one of their number as priest.

Cold, gloomy, rather pointless fable, often a pleasure to look at.

w Jean Aurenche, Pierre Bost   *novel Un Recteur de l'Ile de Sein* by H. Quefflec   *d* Jean Delannoy   *ph* Robert Le Fèbvre   *m* René Cloërc

Pierre Fresnay, Madeleine Robinson, Daniel Gélin, Andrée Clément, Sylvie, Jean Brochard

Diexue Shuang Xiong: see *The Killer*

A Different Story
US   1978   106m   CFI color
Avco/Alan Belkin

A homosexual falls in love with a lesbian.

One supposes it had to come, but one doesn't really have to watch it.

w Henry Olek   *d* Paul Aaron   *ph* Philip Lathrop   *m* David Frank

Perry King, Meg Foster, Valerie Curtin, Peter Donat

'There's something in *A Different Story* to turn off audiences of every sexual persuasion – and movie lovers most of all.' – *Richard Schickel, Time*

La Diga sul Pacifico: see *This Angry Age*

Digby: the Biggest Dog in the World
GB   1973   88m   Technicolor
TCF/Walter Shenson
V*

An old English sheepdog accidentally eats a chemical intended to increase the size of vegetables . . .

Nice to see this kind of gimmick used for comedy instead of horror, but the result is rather tame and old-fashioned, though for several years it made a pleasant television offering for Christmas.

w Michael Pertwee   *d* Joseph McGrath   *ph* Harry Waxman   *m* Edwin T. Astley   *sp* Tom Howard

Jim Dale, Spike Milligan, Angela Douglas, Milo O'Shea, Dinsdale Landen, Garfield Morgan, Victor Spinetti, Bob Todd

Diggstown *
US   1992   98m   DeLuxe
UIP/MGM/Electric (Robert Schaffel)
V, V*, S
GB title: *Midnight Sting*

Two con men journey to a town noted for unofficial prize fights and take a $1 million bet that their boxer can beat 10 local fighters in a period of 24 hours.

Enjoyable enough caper, though it risks monotony with its repeated fights; it flopped at the box-office.

w Steven McKay   *novel The Diggstown Ringers* by Leonard Wise   *d* Michael Ritchie   *ph* Gerry Fisher   *m* James Newton Howard   *pd* Steve Hendrickson   *ed* Don Zimmerman

James Woods, Louis Gossett Jnr, Bruce Dern, Oliver Platt, Heather Graham, Randall 'Tex' Cobb, Thomas Wilson Brown, Duane Davis, Willie Green

'This crowd-pleaser mixes it up with boxing, revenge and salty one-liners that should satisfy audiences.' – *Variety*

Dillinger *
US   1945   70m   bw
Monogram (Frank and Maurice King)
V*

The life of American public enemy number one who was shot by the police in 1934.

Slick, speedy gangster thriller, possibly the most tolerable movie to come from this low-budget studio.

w Philip Yordan   *d* Max Nosseck   *ph* Jackson Rose   *m* Dimitri Tiomkin

Lawrence Tierney, Edmund Lowe, Anne Jeffreys

AAN: Philip Yordan

Dillinger *
US   1973   107m   Movielab
AIP (Buzz Feitshans)
V, V*, L

Violence-soaked version, with black comedy touches, of the last year of Dillinger's life.

Not badly done, with a style reminiscent of *Bonnie and Clyde*.

wd John Milius   *ph* Jules Brenner   *m* Barry Devorzon

Warren Oates, Ben Johnson (as Melvin Purvis), Michelle Philips, Cloris Leachman, Harry Dean Stanton, Richard Dreyfuss

Dim Sum: a Little Bit of Heart *
US   1985   89m   colour
CIM (Tom Sternberg, Wayne Wang, Danny Yung)
V, V*, L

Convinced that she will soon die, a Chinese widow living in San Francisco tries to persuade her daughter to marry.

Domestic drama full of a gentle, rambling charm.

w Terrel Seltzer   *d* Wayne Wang   *ph* Michael Chin   *m* Todd Boekelheide   *ad* Danny Yung   *ed* Ralph Wikke

Lauren Chew, Kim Chew, Victor Wong, Ida F. O. Chung, Cora Miao, John Nishio

Un Dimanche à la Campagne: see *Sunday in the Country*

Dimension 5
US   1966   88m   colour
United Pictures Corporation

CIA agents use a time converter to jump ahead three weeks and prevent the Chinese from bombing Los Angeles.

Silly spy fantasy with inadequate effects.

w Arthur C. Pierce   *d* Franklin Adreon

Jeffrey Hunter, France Nuyen, Harold Sakata, Donald Woods

Dimples **
US   1936   82m   bw
TCF (Darryl F. Zanuck, Nunnally Johnson)
V*

In the New York Bowery in pre-Civil War days, a child and her reprobate grandfather win the hearts of high society.

Excellent Temple vehicle with good period flavour.

w Arthur Sheekman, Nat Perrin   *d* William A. Seiter   *ph* Bert Glennon   *m* Louis Silvers   *m/ly* Jimmy McHugh, Ted Koehler

Shirley Temple, Frank Morgan, Helen Westley, Berton Churchill, Robert Kent, Delma Byron, Astrid Allwyn

'What they wanted most wasn't on the menu'
Diner **
US   1982   110m   Technicolor
MGM/SLM (Jerry Weintraub)
V, V*, L, S

In 1959 Baltimore, college students congregate at their old meeting place and find themselves more occupied by adult problems than of yore.

Generally amusing group character study, an awkward attempt to divine the meaning of life through the accumulation of detail. A little masterpiece of observation, for those with ears to hear; but not necessarily a great film.

wd Barry Levinson   *ph* Peter Sova   *m* Bruce Brody, Ivan Kral   *pd* Leon Harris   *ed* Stu Linder

Steve Guttenberg, Daniel Stern, Mickey Rourke, Kevin Bacon, Timothy Daly, Ellen Barkin, Paul Reiser, Kathryn Dowling, Michael Tucker, Jessica James

'A terrific movie – a gentle, lyrical, magically funny portrait of the games young men play to keep from growing up, and of the oddly childish society that encourages them.' – *Stephen Schiff*

AAN: original screenplay

Dingaka
South Africa   1965   97m   Technicolor
Cinemascope
Embassy (Jamie Uys)

Tribal antagonisms cause a simple native to seek revenge in the city.

Unconvincing and now very dated melodrama with rather too much local colour.

wd Jamie Uys   *ph* Manie Botha   *m* Bertha Egnos, Eddie Domingo, Basil Gray

Ken Gampu, Stanley Baker, Juliet Prowse, Siegfried Mynhardt, Paul Makgoba

Dinky
US   1935   65m   bw
Warner

The mother of a military school cadet is framed into a prison term.

Sentimental drama of little interest.

w Harry Sauber   *d* D. Ross Lederman, Howard Bretherton

Jackie Cooper, Mary Astor, Roger Pryor, Henry Armetta, Henry O'Neill, Edith Fellowes

'A rapidly maturing Jackie Cooper is revealed here as lacking the strength to stand alone.' – *Variety*

Dinner at Eight ***
US   1933   113m   bw
MGM (David O. Selznick)
V, V*, L

Guests at a society dinner party all find themselves in dramatic circumstances.

Artificial but compelling pattern play from a Broadway success.

w Frances Marion, Herman J. Mankiewicz *play* George S. Kaufman, Edna Ferber   *d George Cukor*   *ph* William Daniels   *m* William Axt

Marie Dressler, John Barrymore, Lionel Barrymore, Billie Burke, Wallace Beery, *Jean Harlow*, Lee Tracy, Edmund Lowe, Madge Evans, Jean Hersholt, Karen Morley, Louise Closser Hale, Phillips Holmes, May Robson, Grant Mitchell, Elizabeth Patterson

   KITTY (Jean Harlow): 'You know, I read a book the other day. It's all about civilization or something – a nutty kind of a book. Do you know that the guy said machinery is going to take the place of every profession?'
   CARLOTTA (Marie Dressler): 'Oh, my dear. That's something you need never worry about!'

'Marquee speaks for itself. It spells money, and couldn't very well be otherwise.' – *Variety*

Dinner at the Ritz
GB   1937   77m   bw
New World (Robert T. Kane)

A French girl exposes swindlers who faked her father's suicide.

Once-diverting comedy melodrama with an international cast.

w Roland Pertwee, Romney Brent   *d* Harold Schuster   *ph* Philip Tannura   *m* Lee Sims *ed* James B. Clark

Annabella, Paul Lukas, David Niven, Romney Brent, Stewart Rome, Francis L. Sullivan, Nora Swinburne, Frederick Leister

'Slow and shoddily made British product.' – *Variety*

'It moves with old world decorum and occasional touches of gout.' – *New York Times*

Dino
US   1957   93m   bw
AA/Bernice Block
V*

A juvenile delinquent released from prison has trouble reforming.

Adequately made social drama with good credentials.

w Reginald Rose   *play* Reginald Rose   *d* Thomas Carr

Sal Mineo, Brian Keith, Susan Kohner, Frank Faylen, Joe DeSantis

Dinosaurus!
US   1960   85m   DeLuxe   Cinemascope
Jack H. Harris, Irvin S. Yeaworth Jnr

Workers on a tropical island bring up from the seabed a frozen Neanderthal man and two dinosaurs, who promptly thaw out.

Risible monster movie with effects that are more comic than horrific.

w Dan E. Weisburd, Jean Yeaworth   *d* Irvin S. Yeaworth Jnr   *ph* Stanley Cortez   *m* Ronald Stein   *ad* Jack Senter   *sp* Tim Baar, Wah Chang, Gene Warren   *ed* John A. Bushelman

Ward Ramsey, Paul Lukather, Kristina Hanson, Alan Roberts, Gregg Martell

The Dion Brothers: see *The Gravy Train*

Diplomaniacs
US   1933   59m   bw
RKO
V*

Two halfwits are offered a fortune to go to Geneva and make the peace delegates stop fighting.

Fatuous comedy which never gets going.

w Joseph Mankiewicz, Henry Meyers   *d* William Seiter

Bert Wheeler, Robert Woolsey, Hugh Herbert, Marjorie White, Phyllis Barry, Louis Calhern

'A baddie; rhymed dialogue no help for inane plot.' – *Variety*

The Diplomatic Corpse
GB   1958   65m   bw
Rank/ACT Films (Francis Searle)

A crime reporter, investigating the identity of a corpse found in the Thames, uncovers a drug-smuggling ring.

Programme filler of a thriller, involving a great deal of talk and not much action.

w Sidney Nelson, Maurice Harrison   *d* Montgomery Tully   *ph* Philip Grindrod   *ad* Joseph Bato *ed* James Connock

Robin Bailey, Susan Shaw, Liam Redmond, Harry Fowler, André Mikhelson, Bill Shine, Charles Farrell

Diplomatic Courier *
US   1952   98m   bw
TCF (Casey Robinson)
V*

American and Russian agents clash on a train between Salzburg and Trieste; an unexpected master spy is revealed after several chases.

Lively cold war intrigue, well produced and played with relish.

w Casey Robinson, Liam O'Brien   *novel Sinister Errand* by Peter Cheyney   *d* Henry Hathaway *ph* Lucien Ballard   *md* Lionel Newman   *m* Sol Kaplan

Tyrone Power, Patricia Neal, Stephen McNally, Hildegarde Neff, Karl Malden, James Millican, Herbert Berghof

'A reversion to the oldest tradition of spy fiction.' – *Penelope Houston*

Dirigible *
US   1931   102m   bw
Columbia

The story of an airship disaster.

Economical epic with a few Capra touches.

w Jo Swerling, Dorothy Howell   *story* Frank 'Spig' Wead   *d* Frank Capra   *ph* Joe Wilbur, Elmer Dyer, Joseph Walker

Jack Holt, Fay Wray, Ralph Graves, Hobart Bosworth, Roscoe Karns

'Plenty of everything expected in a flying film spectacle.' – *Variety*

Dirty Dancing *
US   1987   97m   colour
Vestron (Linda Gottlieb)
V, V*, L, S

In 1963, kids go dance crazy at a borscht belt resort.

Mildly agreeable variant on *Saturday Night Fever*, almost equally successful at the box-office.

w Eleanor Bergstein   *d* Emile Ardolino   *ph* Jeff Jur   *m* John Morris   *pd* David Chapman   *ed* Peter C. Frank

Jennifer Grey, Patrick Swayze, Jerry Orbach, Cynthia Rhodes, Jack Weston

AA: song 'I've Had the Time of My Life' (Franke Previte, John DeNicola, Donald Markowitz)

Dirty Dingus Magee
US   1970   91m   Metrocolor   Panavision
MGM (Burt Kennedy)

A likeable Western outlaw crosses swords with an old enemy.

Fair burlesque Western often stooping to vulgarity.

w Tom Waldman, Frank Waldman, Joseph Heller *novel* David Markson   *d* Burt Kennedy   *ph* Harry Stradling   *m* Jeff Alexander

Frank Sinatra, George Kennedy, Anne Jackson, Lois Nettleton, Jack Elam, John Dehner, Henry Jones, Harry Carey Jnr, Paul Fix

'Skittish burlesque, scripted in the brash and undisciplined style of a TV show . . . heavily reliant on the *Carry On* brand of humour.' – *David McGillivray*

'Damn them or praise them – you'll never forget them!'
The Dirty Dozen **
US/Spain   1967   150m   Metrocolor   70mm
MGM/Kenneth Hyman (Raymond Anzarut)
V, V*, L

In 1944, twelve convicts serving life sentences are recruited for a commando suicide mission.

Professional, commercial but unlikeable slice of wartime thick ear; pretensions about capital punishment are jettisoned early on in favour of frequent and violent bloodshed. Much imitated, e.g. by *The Devil's Brigade, A Reason to Live, a Reason to Die*, etc.

w Nunnally Johnson, Lukas Heller   *novel* E. M. Nathanson   *d Robert Aldrich*   *ph* Edward Scaife *m* Frank de Vol

Lee Marvin, Ernest Borgnine, Robert Ryan, Charles Bronson, Jim Brown, John Cassavetes, George Kennedy, Richard Jaeckel, Trini Lopez, Telly Savalas, Ralph Meeker, Clint Walker, Robert Webber, Donald Sutherland

AAN: John Cassavetes

Dirty Hands: see *Les Mains Sales*

'You don't assign him to murder cases – you just turn him loose!'
Dirty Harry **
US   1971   103m   Technicolor   Panavision
Warner/Malpaso (Don Siegel)
V, V*, L

A violently inclined San Francisco police inspector is the only cop who can bring to book a mad sniper.

When the man is released through lack of evidence, he takes private revenge.

A savage cop show which became a cult and led to a spate of dirty cop movies, including four sequels, *Magnum Force, The Enforcer, Sudden Impact* and *The Dead Pool* (qqv). Well done for those who can take it.

w Harry Julian Fink, Rita M. Fink, Dean Riesner *d* Don Siegel *ph* Bruce Surtees *m* Lalo Schifrin

Clint Eastwood, Harry Guardino, Reni Santoni, John Vernon, Andy Robinson, John Larch, John Mitchum

Dirty Little Billy

US 1972 92m Eastmancolor
Columbia/WRG/Dragoti (Jack L. Warner)

The violent young life of Billy the Kid.

Squalid little Western with few attractive aspects except that it presents its hero as the mentally retarded delinquent which history says he was.

w Charles Moss, Stan Dragoti *d* Stan Dragoti *ph* Ralph Woolsey *m* Sascha Burland

Michael J. Pollard, Lee Purcell, Richard Evans, Charles Aidman

'The gap between its ostensible aims and its manner of realizing them continually leaves the film bogged down in its own scrupulously realistic mud.' – *Tony Rayns*

Dirty Mary, Crazy Larry

US 1974 92m DeLuxe
Academy Pictures Corporation (Norman T. Herman)
V*

Two racing drivers and a kooky groupie rob a supermarket and almost elude their police pursuers.

Elaborately stunted chase film, agreeable enough to watch if the characters were not so disagreeable.

w Leigh Chapman, Antonio Santean *novel The Chase* by Richard Unekis *d* John Hough *ph* Mike Margulies *m* Jimmie Haskell

Peter Fonda, Susan George, Adam Roarke, Vic Morrow, Kenneth Tobey, Roddy McDowall, Eugene Daniels

'The film's general delight in destruction and despoilation makes one wonder if it is the cinema that reflects the ugliness of modern society or the ugliness of modern society that reflects trends in the cinema.' – *Michael Billington, Illustrated London News*

Dirty Money (dubbed) *

France/Italy 1972 98m Eastmancolor
Columbia-Warner/Corona/Oceania/Euro (Robert Dorfmann)
original title: *Un Flic*

While investigating a drug-running operation, a police inspector solves a robbery and discovers that his mistress is double-crossing him.

Glum investigation of betrayal in which atmosphere is all, but not enough to sustain interest.

wd Jean-Pierre Melville *ph* Walter Wottitz *m* Michel Colombier *pd* Théo Muerisse *ed* Patricia Renaut

Alain Delon, Catherine Deneuve, Richard Crenna, Ricardo Cucciolla, Michael Conrad, André Pousse

'It is curiously fitting that Melville's last feature should reaffirm the genre's hardiest conventions in a context of disenchantment and failure; and happy that this final, equivocal embrace of the genre should be distinguished by the director's most adventurous experiments with form.' – *Tony Rayns, MFB*

Dirty Rotten Scoundrels

US 1988 110m DeLuxe
Rank/Orion (Bernard Williams)
V, V*, L

Two con men compete in a contest of skills.

Heavy-handed remake of Ralph Levy's *Bedtime Story*, made in 1964.

w Dale Launer, Stanley Shapiro, Paul Henning *d* Frank Oz *ph* Michael Ballhaus *m* Miles Goodman *pd* Roy Walker *ed* Stephen A. Rotter, William Scharf

Steve Martin, Michael Caine, Glenne Headly, Anton Rodgers, Barbara Harris, Ian McDiarmid, Dana Ivey, Meagen Fay, Frances Conroy, Nicole Calfan

Dirty Weekend

GB 1993 103m colour
UIP/Scimitar (Michael Winner, Robert Earl)
V, S

A woman, harassed by a succession of lecherous males, decides to kill them.

A sleazy little tale of a female vigilante, directed and acted in a perfunctory, over-emphatic manner.

w Michael Winner, Helen Zahavi *novel* Helen Zahavi *d* Michael Winner *ph* Alan Jones *m* David Fanshawe *pd* Crispian Sallis *ed* Arnold Crust

Lia Williams, Rufus Sewell, Michael Cule, David McCallum, Christopher Ryan, Sean Pertwee, Ian Richardson

'Michael Winner aims low and half misses.' – *Variety*

'The film is uniquely awful . . . sheer murder to watch.' – *Nick James, Sight and Sound*

Dirty Work ***

US 1933 20m bw
Hal Roach

Chimney sweeps cause havoc in the house of an eccentric scientist.

Hilarious star comedy with splendid timing and comedy touches.

w H. M. Walker *d* Lloyd French *ph* Kenneth Peached *Bert Jordan*

Laurel and Hardy, Lucien Littlefield, Sam Adams

Dirty Work

GB 1934 78m bw
Gaumont (Michael Balcon)

Shop assistants pose as crooks in order to catch thieves.

Rather thin Ben Travers farce with some authentic moments.

w Ben Travers *play* Ben Travers *d* Tom Walls *ph* Phil Tannura *md* Louis Levy *ad* Alfred Junge *ed* Alfred Roome

Ralph Lynn, Gordon Harker, Robertson Hare, Lillian Bond, Basil Sydney, Cecil Parker, Margaretta Scott, Gordon James, Peter Gawthorne

The Disappearance

GB/Canada 1977 102m Eastmancolor
Trofar/Tiberius (David Hemmings)
V*

An international hit man finds that his wife has disappeared.

Confusing and pretentious thriller which spends more time on introspection than action and ends up not satisfying anybody.

w Paul Mayersberg *novel Echoes of Celandine* by Derek Marlowe *d* Stuart Cooper *ph* John Alcott *m* Robert Farnon

Donald Sutherland, Francine Racette, David Hemmings, John Hurt, David Warner, Peter Bowles, Virginia McKenna, Christopher Plummer

Disbarred

US 1938 58m bw
Paramount

A lady lawyer is paid by a crime czar to defend a gangster.

Slick mini-melo of the kind at which this studio excelled at the time.

w Lillie Hayward, Robert Presnell *d* Robert Florey

Otto Kruger, Gail Patrick, Robert Preston, Sidney Toler, Charles D. Brown

'Moderately entertaining drama; nicely fills the lower brackets.' – *Variety*

The Discreet Charm of the Bourgeoisie ****

France/Spain/Italy 1972 105m Eastmancolor
Greenwich (Serge Silberman)
V, V*, L
original title: *Le Charme Discret de la Bourgeoisie*

The efforts of a group of friends to dine together are continually frustrated.

A frequently hilarious, sometimes savage surrealist fable which makes all its points beautifully and then goes on twenty minutes too long. The performances are a joy.

w Luis Buñuel, Jean-Claude Carrière *d* Luis Buñuel *ph* Edmond Richard

Fernando Rey, Delphine Seyrig, Stéphane Audran, Bulle Ogier, Jean-Pierre Cassel, Paul Frankeur, Julien Bertheau

'A perfect synthesis of surreal wit and blistering social assault.' – *Jan Dawson, MFB*

AA: best foreign film

AAN: Luis Buñuel, Jean-Claude Carrière (script)

The Disembodied

US 1957 73m bw
Allied Artists

In the tropics, a doctor's wife is really a voodoo queen who is trying to kill him by supernatural means.

Verbose rubbish with more yawns than thrills.

w Jack Townley *d* Walter Grauman

Allison Hayes, Paul Burke, John Wengraf

Dishonored **

US 1931 91m bw
Paramount

An officer's widow turned streetwalker is hired by the German government as a spy.

Rather gloomy melodrama which helped to establish its star as a top American attraction; but the heavy hand of her Svengali, von Sternberg, was already evident.

w Daniel H. Rubin *d* Josef von Sternberg *ph* Lee Garmes *m* Karl Hajos

Marlene Dietrich, Victor McLaglen, Lew Cody, Gustav von Seyffertitz, Warner Oland, Barry Norton, Wilfred Lucas

'Miss Dietrich rises above her director . . . should make the money grade of an A1 draw talker.' – *Variety*

'The most exciting movie I have seen in several months . . . yet I hope I may die young if I ever again have to listen to a manuscript so full of recusant, stilted, outmoded theatrical mouthings.' – *Pare Lorentz*

'The whole film has a kind of magnificent grandeur embellished, of course, by its shining central performance.' – *John Gillett, 1964*

'She insulted her soul!'
Dishonored Lady

US 1947 85m bw
Mars Film (Hedy Lamarr)
V*

A girl with a past is cleared of a murder charge by her psychiatrist.

Melodramatic showpiece designed for herself by a glamorous star; OK for the silly season.

w Edmund H. North *play* Edward Sheldon, Margaret Ayer Barnes *d* Robert Stevenson *ph* Lucien Andriot *m* Carmen Dragon

Hedy Lamarr, John Loder, Dennis O'Keefe, Paul Cavanagh, William Lundigan, Natalie Schafer, Morris Carnovsky

Dishonour Bright *
GB   1936   82m   bw
GFD/Cecil (Herman Fellner, Max Schach)

An ageing playboy is blackmailed about a past affair.

Interesting semi-smart comedy of the period, tailored for its star.

w Ben Travers   d Tom Walls   ph Phil Tannura

Tom Walls, Eugene Pallette, Betty Stockfield, Diana Churchill, Arthur Wontner, Cecil Parker, George Sanders, Henry Oscar, Basil Radford

The Disorderly Orderly
US   1964   89m   Technicolor
Paramount/York (Paul Jones)
V*

A hospital orderly creates havoc by his inefficiency and his sympathy for other people's predicaments.

Spasmodic farce with far too much pathos between its highlights.

wd Frank Tashlin   ph W. Wallace Kelley
m Joseph Lilley

Jerry Lewis, Glenda Farrell, Everett Sloane, Kathleen Freeman, Karen Sharpe, Susan Oliver, Alice Pearce

Disorderly Conduct
US   1932   82m   bw
Fox

A cop turns crook after being demoted.

Heavy-going melodrama apparently intended as a tribute to the New York police.

w William Anthony McGuire   d John W. Considine Jnr

Spencer Tracy, Sally Eilers, El Brendel, Dickie Moore, Ralph Bellamy, Ralph Morgan, Alan Dinehart

'Good entertainment . . . mother-love sentiment with some kid atmosphere.' – Variety

Disorganized Crime
US   1989   98m   Metrocolor
Touchstone/Silver Screen Partners IV (Lynn Bigelow)
L

A gang of incompetent crooks await the arrival of their leader, who has escaped from prison, so that they can attempt the perfect bank robbery.

Dull and uninteresting crime caper with stereotyped characters that flopped at the box-office.

wd Jim Kouf   ph Ron Garcia   m David Newman
pd Waldemar Kalinowski   ed Frank Morriss, Dallas Puett

Hoyt Axton, Corbin Bernsen, Ruben Blades, Fred Gwynne, Ed O'Neill, Lou Diamond Phillips, Daniel Roebuck, William Russ

Les Disparus de St Agil *
France   1938   95m   bw
Vog Films

Students disappear in a school whose headmaster is a forger and murderer.

Curious black comedy: a half-success.

w J. H. Blanchon   novel Pierre Véry   d Christian-Jaque

Michel Simon, Erich von Stroheim, Aimé Clariond, Armand Bernard

A Dispatch from Reuters **
US   1940   90m   bw
Warner (Henry Blanke)
GB title: This Man Reuter

The story of the man who provided Europe's first news service.

Acceptable if slightly dull addition to Warner's prestige biopics; well made and acted.

w Milton Krims   d William Dieterle   ph James Wong Howe   m Max Steiner

Edward G. Robinson, Edna Best, Eddie Albert, Albert Basserman, Gene Lockhart, Otto Kruger, Montagu Love, Nigel Bruce, James Stephenson

Disputed Passage *
US   1939   90m   bw
Paramount (Harlan Thompson)

A young scientist who wants to marry meets resistance from his mentor.

Adequate screen version of a bestseller.

w Anthony Veiller, Sheridan Gibney   novel Lloyd C. Douglas   d Frank Borzage   ph William C. Mellor   m Frederick Hollander, James Leopold

Dorothy Lamour, John Howard, Akim Tamiroff, Judith Barrett, William Collier Snr, Victor Varconi, Keye Luke, Elizabeth Risdon

'Fine drama of medical science: a top-of-the-bill attraction.' – Variety

'I should describe the flavour as a rather nauseating blend of iodine and glucose.' – Graham Greene

'It dwarfs the stage!'
Disraeli *
US   1929   89m   bw
Warner
V*

Fictionalized episodes in the life of the Victorian statesman, including his activities as a matchmaker.

Very early star talkie, of primarily archival interest; Arliss had appeared in a silent version in 1921.

w Julian Josephson   play Louis N. Parker
d Alfred E. Green   ph Lee Garmes   md Louis Silvers

George Arliss, Joan Bennett, Florence Arliss, Anthony Bushell, David Torrence, Ivan Simpson, Doris Lloyd

'Those seeking a fuller assessment of the man and his work would have been better off in a library.' – Clive Hirschhorn, 1982

AA: George Arliss

AAN: best picture; Julian Josephson

'The rescue . . . the throbbing jungle drums . . . the man-devouring marsh wilderness aflame with unseen menace!'
Distant Drums
US   1951   101m   Technicolor
United States Pictures (Milton Sperling)
V*, L

In 1840 Florida, an army officer rescues prisoners from an Indian fort and decimates the Seminoles who threaten their return journey.

Overlong action saga, with dull stretches compensated by a dominating star and some lively incident.

w Niven Busch, Martin Rackin   d Raoul Walsh
ph Sid Hickox   m Max Steiner

Gary Cooper, Mari Aldon, Richard Webb, Ray Teal, Arthur Hunnicutt, Robert Barrat

'Don't look for surprises. Mr Cooper is kept steady and laconic throughout, the action is serio-comic, and the pace is conventionally maintained.' – Bosley Crowther, New York Times

Distant Thunder **
India   1973   100m   colour
Balaka (Sarbani Bhattacharya)
V*
original title: Asani Sanket

In 1943 a Brahmin teacher-priest and his wife experience in their small village the beginnings of a famine in Bengal.

A potent account of the breakdown of traditional values under the pressure of terrible events.

wd Satyajit Ray   novel Bibhutibhusan Banerjee
ph Soumendu Ray   m Satyajit Ray   ad Asok Bose
ed Dulal Dutta

Soumitra Chatterjee, Babita, Ramesh Mukherjee, Chitra Banerjee, Gobinda Chakravarti, Sandhya Roy

'I don't know when I've been so moved by a picture that I knew was riddled with flaws. It must be that Ray's vision comes out of so much hurt and guilt and love that the feeling pours over all the cracks in Distant Thunder and fills them up.' – Pauline Kael, New Yorker

† It won the Golden Bear award for Best Film at the Berlin Film Festival in 1973.

A Distant Trumpet
US   1964   116m   Technicolor   Panavision
Warner (William H. Wright)

The new commander of a cavalry outpost tightens up discipline, which serves him well when Indian trouble erupts.

Moderate Western, quite well staged but with a second team cast.

w John Twist   novel Paul Horgan   d Raoul Walsh
ph William Clothier   m Max Steiner

Troy Donahue, Suzanne Pleshette, James Gregory, Diane McBain, William Reynolds, Claude Akins, Kent Smith, Judson Pratt

Distant Voices, Still Lives *
GB   1988   84m   colour
BFI/Film Four International (Colin MacCabe)
V, V*, L

Working-class family life in Liverpool in the 40s and 50s.

Low-budget labour of love filmed at intervals over two years, succeeding through close, unsentimental observation and excellent performances by a cast of unknowns.

wd Terence Davies   ph William Diver, Patrick Duval
pd Miki van Zwanenberg

Freda Dowie, Pete Postlethwaite, Angela Walsh

'While its pacing and structure may exasperate some, should envelop receptive audiences with its special magic.' – Variety

The Distinguished Gentleman *
US   1992   112m   Technicolor
Buena Vista/Hollywood Pictures (Leonard Goldberg, Michael Peyser)
V, V*, L, S

A con man decides that the best place for his talents is in government.

Enjoyable, broad comedy, which gives Murphy a good opportunity to display his fast-talking talents.

w Marty Kaplan   d Jonathan Lynn   ph Gabriel Beristain   m Randy Edelman   pd Leslie Dilley
ed Tony Lombardo, Barry B. Leirer

Eddie Murphy, Lane Smith, Sheryl Lee Ralph, Joe Don Baker, Victoria Rowell, Grant Shaud, Kevin McCarthy

'A lazily slung together collection of clichés, mixing diet politics with laughter-free comedy.' – Kim Newman, Empire

Ditte, Child of Man *
Denmark   1946   106m   bw
Nordisk
original title: Ditte Menneskebarn

An unmarried mother abandons her daughter, who grows up to be a servant and to be seduced in her turn.

Impressive, doom-laden Scandinavian saga, highly thought of on its release.

wd Astrid and Bjarne Henning-Jensen **novel** Martin Andersen **ph** Werner Jenssen **m** Herman Koppel

Tove Maes, Rasmus Ottesen, Karen Poulsen

Ditte Menneskebarn: see *Ditte, Child of Man*

Diva *
France 1981 117m Eastmancolor
Galaxie/Greenwich/Antenne 2 (Irene Silberman)
V*, L, S

A black prima donna in Paris becomes accidentally involved in drug smuggling and murder.

A curious hybrid of violence and surrealism which doesn't seem to know what effect it's aiming at, or at least doesn't let the viewer in on the secret, being content to entertain in a flashy and sometimes shocking way.

w Jean-Jacques Beineix, Jean Van Hamme **novel** Delacorta **d** Jean-Jacques Beineix **ph** Philippe Rousselot **m** Vladimir Cosma **pd** Hilton McConnico

Frederic Andrei, Roland Bertin, Richard Bohringer, Wilhelmenia Wiggins Fernandez, Jean-Jacques Moreau, Chantal Deruaz

The Dive
GB/Norway 1989 95m colour
Filmeffekt/Millennium/British Screen (Dag Alveberg, Patrick Cassavetti)

Deep-sea divers are trapped underwater while attempting to repair a pipeline.

Standard rescue melodrama, more lethargically directed than most.

w Leidulv Risan, Carlos Wiggen **d** Tristan de Vere Cole **ph** Harald Paalgard **m** Geir Bøhren, Bent Aserud **pd** Jarle Blesvik **ed** Russell Lloyd

Bjørn Sundquist, Frank Grimes, Eindride Eidsvold, Marika Lagercrantz, Nils Ole Oftebro, Michael Kitchen, Sverre Anker Ousdal

Dive Bomber *
US 1941 133m Technicolor
Warner (Hal B. Wallis)
V*

Aviation scientists work to eliminate pilot blackout.

Somewhat rarefied propaganda piece with too many reels of romantic banter but tense climactic scenes and good star performances.

w Frank 'Spig' Wead, Robert Buckner **d** Michael Curtiz **ph** Bert Glennon, Winton C. Hoch **md** Leo F. Forbstein **m** Max Steiner

Errol Flynn, Fred MacMurray, Ralph Bellamy, Alexis Smith, Regis Toomey, Robert Armstrong, Allen Jenkins, Craig Stevens, Moroni Olsen, Gig Young, William Hopper, Charles Drake, Russell Hicks, Addison Richards, Ann Doran, Herbert Anderson

AAN: Bert Glennon, Winton C. Hoch

The Divided Heart **
GB 1954 89m bw
Ealing (Michael Truman)

A boy believed to be a war orphan is lovingly brought up by foster parents; then his real mother turns up and wants him back.

Effective 'woman's picture' set in Europe and giving a genuine sense of post-war feelings and problems.

w Jack Whittingham **d** Charles Crichton **ph** Otto Heller **m** Georges Auric

Cornell Borchers, Yvonne Mitchell, Armin Dahlen, Alexander Knox, Geoffrey Keen, Michel Ray, Liam Redmond, Eddie Byrne

The Dividing Line: see *The Lawless*

The Divine Lady *
US 1929 100m bw
Warner

The adventures of Emma, Lady Hamilton.

Historical charade which titillated at the time.

w Agnes Christine Johnston, Forrest Halsey **d** Frank Lloyd **ph** John Seitz

Corinne Griffith, Victor Varconi, H. B. Warner, Montagu Love, Marie Dressler

AA: Frank Lloyd

AAN: John Seitz; Corinne Griffith

Divine Madness
US 1980 93m Technicolor Panavision
Ladd Company/Warner
V*, L

A record of a Bette Midler concert performance. 'Since this is the time capsule version of my show, I may as well do everything I know.'

It certainly isn't a movie.

d Michael Ritchie **ph** William A. Fraker

The Divine Woman *
US 1927 95m approx (24 fps) bw silent
MGM

The loves of Sarah Bernhardt.

Garbo's first star role; a typical Hollywood melodramatization of facts.

w Dorothy Farnum **play** *Starlight* by Gladys Unger **d** Victor Sjostrom

Greta Garbo, Lars Hanson, Lowell Sherman, John Mack Brown, Polly Moran

Divorce
US 1945 71m bw
Monogram/Jeffrey Bernerd/Kay Francis

A much-married woman tries to break up another happy family.

This somewhat elementary tract was the star's first independent production, and not a success.

w Sidney Sutherland, Harvey Gates **d** William Nigh

Kay Francis, Bruce Cabot, Helen Mack, Jonathan Hale, Jerome Cowan

'A lacklustre script grooves it for the duals.' – *Variety*

'In America the ring costs two dollars to put on – and a fortune to take off!'
Divorce American Style **
US 1967 109m Technicolor
Columbia/Tandem (Norman Lear)

Well-heeled Los Angeles suburbanites toy with divorce but eventually resume their domestic bickering.

Rather arid and patchy but often sharply sardonic comedy about a society in which people can't afford to divorce.

w Norman Lear **d** Bud Yorkin **ph** Conrad Hall **m** David Grusin **pd** Edward Stephenson

Dick Van Dyke, Debbie Reynolds, Jean Simmons, Jason Robards Jnr, Van Johnson, Joe Flynn, Shelley Berman, Martin Gabel, Lee Grant, Tom Bosley, Dick Gautier

AAN: Norman Lear

A Divorce in the Family
US 1932 78m bw
MGM

A boy is affected by his parents' divorce.

Dated drama, an odd choice of vehicle for a boy star fresh from *The Champ*.

w Delmer Daves, Maurice Rapf **d** Charles Reisner

Jackie Cooper, Conrad Nagel, Lois Wilson, Lewis Stone, Jean Parker, Lawrence Grant

'Not more than medium box office; Cooper fans will not be attracted by the title.' – *Variety*

'A delightfully daring plan to give marriage a surprise ending!'
Divorce Italian Style **
Italy 1961 108m bw
Lux/Vides/Galatea (Franco Cristaldi)
V*
original title: *Divorzio all'Italiana*

A Sicilian nobleman explains how, wishing to be rid of his wife, he arranged for her to be seduced and later shot by a jealous lover.

Sardonic, stylized comedy which, rather in the manner of *Kind Hearts and Coronets*, manages while retailing a black comedy plot to satirize Italian manners and institutions.

w Ennio de Concini, Pietro Germi, Alfredo Gianetti **d** Pietro Germi **ph** Leonida Barboni **m** Carlo Rustichelli

Marcello Mastroianni, Daniela Rocca, Stefania Sandrelli, Leopoldo Trieste

AA: script

AAN: Pietro Germi; Marcello Mastroianni

The Divorce of Lady X **
GB 1938 92m Technicolor
London Films (Alexander Korda)
V*

A nobleman's daughter wins a barrister by posing as a divorce client.

Pleasing comedy with high production standards of its time, deftly performed by a distinguished cast.

w Lajos Biro, Arthur Wimperis, Ian Dalrymple **play** *Counsel's Opinion* by Gilbert Wakefield **d** Tim Whelan **ph** Harry Stradling **m** Miklos Rozsa **ad** Lazare Meerson, Paul Sheriff **ed** William Hornbeck

Laurence Olivier, Merle Oberon, Binnie Barnes, Ralph Richardson, Morton Selten, J. H. Roberts

'Her sin was no greater than his, but she was a woman! If the world permits the husband to philander – why not the wife?'
The Divorcee *
US 1930 83m bw
MGM (Robert Z. Leonard)
V*

Would-be liberal young marrieds divorce when she puts up with his affairs but he can't tolerate hers. She falls in love with another married man but sends him back to his wife.

Rather wan illustration of the double standard which was being much discussed in society at the time.

w John Meehan, Nick Grinde, Zelda Sears **novel** *Ex-Wife* by Ursula Parrott **d** Robert Z. Leonard **ph** Norbert Brodine **ad** Cedric Gibbons

Norma Shearer, Chester Morris, Conrad Nagel, Robert Montgomery, Florence Eldridge

'Shearer's specialty was sexy suffering in satin gowns by Adrian; here, she almost seems to want to abandon herself to naughtiness, but one line after another stops her.' – *Pauline Kael, 70s*

AA: Norma Shearer

AAN: best picture; Robert Z. Leonard; John Meehan, Nick Grinde, Zelda Sears

Divorzio all'Italiana: see *Divorce Italian Style*

Dixiana
US 1930 100m bw/Technicolor sequences
RKO
V*

A Dutchman from Pennsylvania tries to run a plantation in Louisiana.

Lavish but utterly witless musical comedy which just lies there and dies there.

wd Luther Reed *play* Ann Caldwell

Bebe Daniels, Bert Wheeler, Robert Woolsey, Everett Marshall, Joseph Cawthorn, Jobyna Howland, Dorothy Lee, Bill Robinson

'Not much but bigness for exploiting.' – *Variety*

Dixie *
US   1943   90m   Technicolor
Paramount (Paul Jones)

The life of old-time minstrel man Dan Emmett.

Lighter-than-air fictionalized biography with pleasing mid-19th-century settings.

w Karl Tunberg, Darrell Ware *d* A. Edward Sutherland *ph* William C. Mellor *m* Robert Emmett Dolan *m/ly* Johnny Burke, Jimmy Van Heusen

Bing Crosby, Dorothy Lamour, Marjorie Reynolds, *Lynne Overman, Eddie Foy Jnr, Billy de Wolfe, Raymond Walburn*, Grant Mitchell

Dixie Dugan
US   1943   63m   bw
TCF (Walter Morosco)

A secretary with a screwball family gets a government job in Washington.

Fairly feeble adaptation from a popular comic strip.

w Lee Loeb, Harold Bruckman *d* Otto Brower

Lois Andrews, James Ellison, Charlie Ruggles, Charlotte Greenwood, Raymond Walburn, Eddie Foy Jnr

Django **
Italy/Spain   1966   95m   colour
BRC/Tecisa (Manolo Bolognini)
V, S

A gunfighter who carries a machine-gun in a coffin rids a town of its gangs of Mexican bandits and the Ku Klux Klan.

One of the earliest, most notorious and influential of spaghetti Westerns, marked by a high level of violence but nevertheless watchable for its operatic style.

w Sergio Corbucci, Bruno Corbucci, Franco Rosetti, José G. Naesso, Piero Vivarelli *d* Sergio Corbucci *ph* Enzo Barboni *m* Luis Enrique Bacalov

Franco Nero, Eduardo Fajardo, Loredana Nusciak, José Bodalo, Angel Alvarez

'After Leone, Corbucci was the genius of the spaghettis.' – *Empire*

Django against Sartana (dubbed)
Italy   1970   90m   Telecolor
P.A.C./B.C.R. (Roberto Bessi)
original title: *Django Sfida Sartana*

Django avenges the death of his brother, hanged for a crime he did not commit.

Mundane spaghetti Western, a sequel lacking the excesses of the original and content to provide the minimum in interest or excitement.

wd William Redford (Pasquale Squitteri) *ph* Eugenio Bentivoglio *m* Piero Umiliani

George Ardisson, Tony Kendall, José Torres, Bernard Faber, Adler Gray, John Alvar

Django Sfida Sartana: see *Django against Sartana*

Django Spara per Primo
Italy   1966   95m   Technicolor   Techniscope
Gala/Fida (Edmondo Amati)
aka: *He Who Shoots First*

Django is framed for a bank robbery by the man who murdered his father.

Tedious re-run of the usual theme of vengeance, done without style or originality.

w Sandro Continenza, Massimiliano Capriccoli, Florenzo Carpi, Vincenzo Flamini, Alberto de Martino *d* Alberto de Martino *ph* Ricardo Pallottini *m* Bruno Nicolai *ad* Pier Vittorio Marchi *ed* Otello Colangeli

Glenn Saxon, Fernando Sancho, Evelyn Stewart (Ida Galli), Nando Gazzolo, Lee Burton (Guido Lollobrigida)

'A lifeless Italian Western . . . plods wearily through the required rituals.' – *MFB*

En Djunselsaga: see *The Flute and the Arrow*

The Do It Yourself Cartoon Kit **
GB   1961   6m   Eastmancolor
Biographic

A commercial for the kit in question, poking fun at all comers in a Monty Pythonish way.

Great stuff for those who like zany humour well controlled.

w Colin Pearson *d* Bob Godfrey

'What should a girl do when opportunity knocks . . . twice?'
Do Not Disturb
US   1965   102m   DeLuxe   Cinemascope
TCF/Melcher/Arcola (Aaron Rosenberg, Martin Melcher)

An American wool executive is posted to London; his dizzy wife makes him jealous by flirting with a French antique dealer.

Silly farce which paints a lunatic picture of English and French life but occasionally raises a wild laugh or two. Thin script and production.

w Milt Rosen, Richard Breen *play* William Fairchild *d* Ralph Levy *ph* Leon Shamroy *m* Lionel Newman

Doris Day, Rod Taylor, *Sergio Fantoni*, Reginald Gardiner, Hermione Baddeley, Leon Askin

Do the Right Thing ***
US   1989   120m   colour
UIP/Forty Acres And A Mule Filmworks/Spike Lee
V, V*, L, S

A white pizza parlour owner in a black neighbourhood sparks off a riot.

Complex, witty, street-wise and passionate film about racism.

w Spike Lee *d* Spike Lee *ph* Ernest Dickerson *m* Bill Lee *pd* Wynn Thomas *ed* Barry Alexander Brown

Danny Aiello, Ossie Davis, Ruby Dee, Richard Edson, Giancarlo Esposito, Spike Lee, Bill Nunn, John Turturro, John Savage, Rosie Perez

AAN: best original screenplay; Danny Aiello

Do You Like Women?
France/Italy   1964   100m   bw
Francoriz/Number One/Federiz (Pierre Kalfon)
original title: *Aimez-Vous Les Femmes?*

Secret rival sects of woman-eaters cause an outbreak of murders in Paris.

Bizarre black comedy that doesn't quite work but provides ghoulish fun along the way.

w Roman Polanski, Gérard Brach *novel* Georges Bardawil *d* Jean Léon *ph* Sacha Vierny *m* Ward Swingle

Sophie Daumier, Guy Bédos, Edwige Feuillère, Grégoire Aslan, Roger Blin

'It has the provoking quality of a carefully-prepared firework display which, due to faulty timing or bad connections, is never actually ignited.' – *MFB*

Do You Love Me?
US   1946   91m   Technicolor
TCF (George Jessel)

The lady dean of a music school gets herself glamorized.

Thin, mildly agreeable but forgettable musical.

w Robert Ellis, Helen Logan *d* Gregory Ratoff *ph* Edward Cronjager *m/ly* various

Maureen O'Hara, Dick Haymes, Harry James and his Orchestra, Reginald Gardiner, Richard Gaines, Stanley Prager

The Doberman Gang
US   1972   87m   Eastmancolor
Fox-Rank/Rosamond (David Chudnow)
V*

After his accomplices bungle a robbery, a crook trains six Dobermans to rob a bank.

The dogs run away with the picture, but invention and budget are both on too tight a leash to offer much more than the equivalent of an over-long pet-food commercial.

w Louis Garfinkle, Frank Ray Perilli *d* Byron Ross Chudnow *ph* Robert Caramigo *m* Bradford Craig, Alan Silvestri *ad* Budd Costello *ed* Herman Freedman

Byron Mabe, Hal Reed, Julie Parrish, Simmy Bow, Jojo D'Amore

'The film hovers uncertainly between straight thriller and comedy.' – *MFB*

† It was followed by two sequels with similar plots, *The Daring Dobermans*, 1973, and the bigger-budget *The Amazing Dobermans*, 1976 (qv), in which the dogs were on the side of the law.

Doc *
US   1971   96m   DeLuxe
UA/Frank Perry

Doc Holliday goes to Tombstone to die of TB, but is drawn into the feud between the Clantons and his friend Wyatt Earp, whose motives are not of the highest.

A somewhat glum debunking of the west's most heroic myth, backing dour character study with grubby pictures. The result lacks excitement but maintains interest.

w Pete Hamill *d* Frank Perry *ph* Gerald Hirschfeld *m* Jimmy Webb

Stacy Keach (Doc), Harris Yulin (Earp), Faye Dunaway (Kate Elder), Mike Witney, Denver John Collins, Dan Greenberg

'The physical realism that *Doc* is at pains to establish becomes simply a convention of its own.' – *Richard Combs*

Doc Hollywood *
US   1991   103m   Warner (Susan Solt, Deborah D. Johnson)
Technicolor
V, V*, L, S

On the way to a new job as a plastic surgeon in Hollywood, a young doctor crashes his car in a small town and is sentenced to work at the local hospital.

Amiable, inoffensive comedy in a familiar vein.

w Jeffrey Price, Peter S. Seaman, Daniel Pyne *novel What? . . . Dead Again* by Neil B. Shulman *d* Michael Caton-Jones *ph* Michael Chapman *m* Carter Burwell *pd* Lawrence Miller *ed* Gregg London

Michael J. Fox, Julie Warner, Barnard Hughes, Woody Harrelson, David Ogden Stiers, Frances Sternhagen, George Hamilton, Bridget Fonda, Mel Winkler, Helen Martin, Roberts Blossom

'This serving of recycled Capracorn has no real taste of its own, but, in its mildness and predictability, offers the reassurance of a fast-food or motel chain.' – *Variety*

'Have no fear, Doc Savage is here!'
Doc Savage, Man of Bronze
US   1975   100m   Technicolor
Warner (George Pal)
V*

A thirties superman and his assistants the Amazing Five fly to South America to avenge the death of Doc's father.

Stolid, humourless adaptation from a comic strip, totally lacking in the necessary panache.

w George Pal, Joe Morhaim   *stories* Kenneth Robeson   d Michael Anderson   ph Fred Koenekamp   m John Philip Sousa

Ron Ely, Paul Gleason, Bill Lucking, Michael Miller, Eldon Quick

'A slick, ultra-self-conscious camp that denies the material its self-respect.' – *Colin Pahlow*

'Nothing in this unfortunate enterprise is likely to please anyone: former Savage fans will be enraged, newcomers bored, and children will probably feel superior to the whole mess . . .' – *New Yorker*

The Dock Brief
GB   1962   88m   bw
MGM/Dimitri de Grunwald
US title: *Trial and Error*

An incompetent barrister defends his client on a murder charge. The client is found guilty but the sentence is quashed on the grounds of inadequate defence.

Flat filming of a TV play which was a minor milestone; the film is twice the length and half as funny, and both stars quickly become tiresome.

w John Mortimer, Pierre Rouve   *play* John Mortimer   d James Hill   ph Ted Scaife   m Ron Grainer

Peter Sellers, Richard Attenborough, Beryl Reid, David Lodge, Frank Pettingell

Docks of New York **
US   1928   80m (24 fps)   bw   silent
Paramount

A stoker marries a girl he has saved from suicide. Further unfortunate incidents result in his going to prison, but she waits for him.

Glum melodrama chiefly remarkable for its sets and lighting, reminiscent of the later *Quai des Brumes*.

w Jules Furthman   *story* The Dock Walloper *by* John Monk Saunders   d Josef von Sternberg   ph Harold Rosson   ad Hans Dreier

George Bancroft, Betty Compson, Olga Baclanova, Clyde Cook, Gustav von Seyffertitz

'One comes away with the memory of a film impregnated with a life whose essential is in its energy and force.' – *Louis Chavance*

The Doctor **
US   1991   125m   Technicolor
Buena Vista/Touchstone/Silver Screen Partners IV (Laura Ziskin)
V, V*, L

A repressed surgeon alters his attitudes after he becomes a cancer patient at his own hospital.

Well-made drama of personal redemption.

w Robert Caswell   *book* A Taste of My Own Medicine *by* Ed Rosenbaum   d Randa Haines   ph John Seale   m Michael Convertino   pd Ken Adam   ed Bruce Green, Lisa Fruchtman

William Hurt, Christine Lahti, Elizabeth Perkins, Mandy Patinkin, Adam Arkin, Charlie Korsmo, Wendy Crewson, Bill Macy

'Grapples powerfully with themes seldom faced in today's escapist marketplace: mortality, compassion, social responsibility.' – *Variety*

The Doctor and the Debutante: see *Dr Kildare's Victory*

The Doctor and the Devils
GB   1985   93m   Rank Colour   Panavision
Brooksfilm (Jonathan Sanger)
V, V*

In the late 18th century an Edinburgh surgeon starts to pay for bodies as specimens, and doesn't ask their provenance.

Yet another version (see *The Body Snatcher, The Flesh and the Fiends, Burke and Hare*) of the tale of Dr Knox, and this time a pretty poor one, justified by the use of Dylan Thomas's script.

w Ronald Harwood, from Dylan Thomas   d Freddie Francis   ph Gerry Turpin, Norman Warwick   m John Morris   pd Robert Laing

Timothy Dalton, Jonathan Pryce, Twiggy, Julian Sands, Lewis Fiander, Stephen Rea

'Unrelentingly serious treatment of a gruesome subject is unlikely to attract many warm bodies to the box office.' – *Variety*

The Doctor and the Girl
US   1949   98m   bw
MGM (Pandro S. Berman)

A young doctor renounces specialization to help the poor.

Antediluvian medical romance full of the nicest people. Technically very competent.

w Theodore Reeves, from 'a literary work' by Maxene Van Der Meersch   d Curtis Bernhardt   ph Robert Planck   m R. G. Kopp

Glenn Ford, Charles Coburn, Gloria de Haven, Janet Leigh, Bruce Bennett, Warner Anderson

Doctor at Large
GB   1957   104m   Eastmancolor
Rank (Betty E. Box)
V*

Simon Sparrow tries two country practices, but returns at last to St Swithin's.

Hit-or-miss medical comedy with honours about even.

w Nicholas Phipps   *novel* Richard Gordon   d Ralph Thomas   ph Ernest Steward   m Bruce Montgomery

Dirk Bogarde, Muriel Pavlow, James Robertson Justice, Donald Sinden, Shirley Eaton, Derek Farr, Michael Medwin, Edward Chapman, Barbara Murray, Gladys Henson, Lionel Jeffries, A. E. Matthews, Athene Seyler, George Coulouris

Doctor at Sea *
GB   1955   93m   Technicolor   VistaVision
Rank/Group Films (Betty E. Box)
V*

Simon Sparrow becomes medical officer on a cargo steamer.

Reasonably lively comedy of errors with nice seascapes and predictable jokes.

w Nicholas Phipps, Jack Davies   d Ralph Thomas   ph Ernest Steward   m Bruce Montgomery

Dirk Bogarde, Brigitte Bardot, Brenda de Banzie, James Robertson Justice, Maurice Denham, Michael Medwin, Hubert Gregg, Raymond Huntley, Geoffrey Keen, George Coulouris, Jill Adams, James Kenney

'Brisk professional humour has given way to the more elementary business of traditional British farce.' – *Penelope Houston, MFB*

Doctor Blood's Coffin
GB   1960   92m   Eastmancolor
UA/Caralan (George Fowler)
V*

A disbarred doctor sets up in a Cornish tin mine and begins to emulate Dr Frankenstein.

Lurid horror piece which makes no sort of sense.

w Jerry Juran   d Sidney J. Furie   ph Stephen Dade   m Buxton Orr

Kieron Moore, Hazel Court, Ian Hunter, Gerald C. Lawson, Kenneth J. Warren, Fred Johnson

'It lacks style, suspense and imagination and will scarcely satisfy even the most naive necrophiliac.' – *MFB*

'He's the main stem's specialist in heart trouble – and lead poisoning!'
Dr Broadway
US   1942   75m   bw
Paramount

A young medico gets involved with guns, girls and gangsters.

Adequate filler which failed to spawn the intended series.

w Art Arthur   *story* Borden Chase   d Anthony Mann

Macdonald Carey, Jean Phillips, J. Carrol Naish, Richard Lane, Eduardo Ciannelli

Dr Bull
US   1933   75m   bw
Fox

A genial country doctor triumphs over his own lack of medical knowledge.

Rather lumpy star vehicle which paid its way.

w Paul Green   *novel* The Last Adam *by* James Gould Cozzens   d John Ford

Will Rogers, Vera Allen, Marian Nixon, Berton Churchill, Louise Dresser, Andy Devine, Ralph Morgan

'Drips with human interest and can scarcely miss.' – *Variety*

Dr Christian

Following the success of THE COUNTRY DOCTOR (qv), a rival studio (RKO) made a series of second features about a fictional country doctor, the rights to Dr Dafoe's life story being unavailable. Jean Hersholt again played the leading role and the films were immensely popular in small towns. A TV series followed in the fifties, starring Macdonald Carey.

1939: MEET DR CHRISTIAN
1940: THE COURAGEOUS DR CHRISTIAN, DR CHRISTIAN MEETS THE WOMEN, REMEDY FOR RICHES
1941: MELODY FOR THREE, THEY MEET AGAIN

Dr Crippen *
GB   1962   98m   bw
ABP/John Clein
V

A quiet doctor murders his wife and elopes with a typist.

Straightforward account of a famous and rather unsurprising Edwardian murder case; well enough made but with no special *raison d'être*.

w Leigh Vance   d Robert Lynn   ph Nicolas Roeg   m Kenneth Jones

Donald Pleasence, Coral Browne, Samantha Eggar, Donald Wolfit

'Diabolical dictator ... devastating discoverer of the most
frightening invention in the history of civilized man!'
'The picture made behind locked doors!'

Dr Cyclops *
US   1940   76m   Technicolor
Paramount (Merian C. Cooper)

Jungle travellers are captured and miniaturized by a
mad scientist.

Splendid special effects and an appropriately sombre
atmosphere are hampered by a slow-paced narrative
in this minor horror classic.

w Tom Kilpatrick   *d* Ernest Schoedsack   *ph* Henry
Sharp, Winton Hoch   *m* Ernst Toch, Gerard Carbonera,
Albert Hay Malotte

Albert Dekker, Janice Logan, Victor Kilian, Thomas
Coley, Charles Halton

Doctor Death: Seeker of Souls
US   1973   89m   Movielab
Fox-Rank/Freedom Arts (Eddie Saeta)
V*

Doctor Death, who has the power to pass his and
others' souls into the bodies of those he kills, attempts
to re-animate a woman at the request of her grieving
husband.

Bizarre low-budget horror which, judging from a brief
turn by one of the Three Stooges, is presumably
meant to amuse, though, seeing its general ineptitude,
it is hard to be sure.

w Sal Ponti   *d* Eddie Saeta   *ph* Kent Wakeford,
Emil Oster   *m* Richard LaSalle   *ad* Ed Graves
ed Tony DiMarco

John Considine, Barry Coe, Cheryl Miller, Stewart
Moss, Leon Askin, Joe Morrow, Moe Howard

'The spectator who brings a properly black frame of
mind to it may well be entertained.' – *Jonathan
Rosenbaum, MFB*

Dr Dolittle
US   1967   152m   DeLuxe   Todd-AO
TCF/APJAC (Arthur P. Jacobs)
V, V*

In a Victorian English village, Dr Dolittle is a
veterinary surgeon who talks to his patients; escaping
from a lunatic asylum, he travels with friends to the
South Seas in search of the Great Pink Sea Snail.

Lumpish family spectacular with no imagination
whatever, further handicapped by charmless
performances and unsingable songs.

w/songs Leslie Bricusse   *novels* Hugh Lofting
d Richard Fleischer   *ph* Robert Surtees   *md* Lionel
Newman, Alex Courage   *pd* Mario Chiari

Rex Harrison, Anthony Newley, Samantha Eggar,
Richard Attenborough, William Dix, Peter Bull

AA: song 'Talk to the Animals'; special effects (L. B.
Abbott)

AAN: best picture; Robert Surtees; Lionel Newman,
Alex Courage; Leslie Bricusse (*m*)

Dr Ehrlich's Magic Bullet ***
US   1940   103m   bw
Warner (Wolfgang Reinhardt)
aka: *The Story of Dr Ehrlich's Magic Bullet*

A German scientist develops a cure for venereal
disease.

Excellent period biopic: absorbing, convincing and
extremely well put together.

w John Huston, Heinz Herald, Norman Burnside
d William Dieterle   *ph* James Wong Howe   *m* Max
Steiner

Edward G. Robinson, Ruth Gordon, Otto Kruger,
Donald Crisp, Maria Ouspenskaya, Montagu Love,
Sig Rumann, Donald Meek, Henry O'Neill, Albert
Basserman, Edward Norris, Harry Davenport, Louis
Calhern, Louis Jean Heydt

'A superb motion picture.' – *Pare Lorentz*

AAN: John Huston, Heinz Herald, Norman Burnside

Dr Faustus
GB   1967   93m   Technicolor
Columbia/Oxford University Screen Productions/Nassau Films/
Venfilms (Richard Burton, Richard McWhorter)
V*

A medieval scholar conjures up Mephistopheles and
offers his soul in exchange for a life of
voluptuousness.

Marlowe's play has been adapted and 'improved',
and there is some good handling of the poetry, but the
production is flat, dingy and uninspired, as well as
ludicrous when Miss Taylor makes her silent
appearances.

w Nevill Coghill   *play* Christopher Marlowe
d Richard Burton, Nevill Coghill   *ph* Gabor Pogany
m Mario Nascimbene   *pd* John DeCuir

Richard Burton, Andreas Teuber, Ian Marter, Elizabeth
Donovan, Elizabeth Taylor (as Helen of Troy)

'It is of an awfulness that bends the mind. The whole
enterprise has the immense vulgarity of a
collaboration in which academe would sell its soul for
a taste of the glamour of Hollywood, and the stars are
only too happy to appear a while in academe.' – *John
Simon*

'It turns out to be the story of a man who sold his soul
for Elizabeth Taylor.' – *Judith Crist*

Doctor from Seven Dials: see *Corridors of Blood*

'A new prescription for terror.'
Dr Giggles
US   1992   95m   DeLuxe
Universal (Stuart M. Besser)
V, V*, S

A mad doctor takes his revenge on those who lynched
his equally murderous father.

Predictably grisly horror played for laughs.

w Manny Coto, Graeme Whifler   *d* Manny Coto
ph Robert Draper   *m* Brian May   *pd* Bill Malley
sp Phil Cory Special EFX, Digital Fantasy   *ed* Debra
Neil

Larry Drake, Holly Marie Combs, Cliff de Young,
Glenn Quinn, Keith Diamond, Richard Bradford,
Michelle Johnson

'Picture is aimed at the low end of the shock
audience.' – *Variety*

'A piece of excrement.' – *Nigel Floyd*

'What this project really needs is major script surgery.'
– *The Dark Side*

Dr Gillespie's Criminal Case
US   1943   89m   bw
MGM
GB title: *Crazy to Kill*

The elderly doctor solves a murder for which an
innocent man is in prison.

Skilled programme filler with beloved characters.

w Martin Berkeley, Harry Ruskin, Lawrence
Bachmann   *d* Willis Goldbeck

Lionel Barrymore, Margaret O'Brien, Donna Reed,
Van Johnson, Keye Luke, Marilyn Maxwell

† See also *Dr Kildare*.

Dr Gillespie's New Assistant
US   1942   88m   bw
MGM

Shorn of young Dr Kildare, Gillespie chooses a new
support from three interns, and meanwhile
concentrates on an amnesia case.

Slick series entry which played widely as top of the
bill.

w Willis Goldbeck, Harry Ruskin, Lawrence
Bachmann   *d* Willis Goldbeck

Lionel Barrymore, Van Johnson, Keye Luke, Richard
Quine, Susan Peters

† See also *Dr Kildare*.

Dr Goldfoot and the Bikini Machine
US   1965   90m   Pathecolor   Panavision
AIP (Anthony Carras)

Dr G. makes girl robots programmed to lure wealthy
men into their clutches.

Way-out farce for the jaded end of the teenage market;
a few lively touches and a climactic chase partly atone
for the general tastelessness.

w Elwood Ullman, Robert Kaufman   *d* Norman
Taurog   *ph* Sam Leavitt   *m* Les Baxter   *ad* Daniel
Haller

Vincent Price, Fred Clark, Frankie Avalon, Dwayne
Hickman, Susan Hart, Jack Mullaney

'Meet the girls with the thermo-nuclear navels! The most
titillating time bombs you've ever been tempted to
trigger!'
Dr Goldfoot and the Girl Bombs
US/Italy   1966   86m   colour
AIP

The evil mastermind teams up with Red China to
cause trouble between Russia and the USA.

Inane teenage nonsense, almost enough to make one
swear off movies.

w Louis M. Heyward, Robert Kaufmann   *d* Mario
Bava

Vincent Price, Fabian Forte, Franco Franchi, Laura
Antonelli

Dr Heckyl and Mr Hype
US   1980   99m   Metrocolor
Golan-Globus
V*

An ugly scientist is transformed into a handsome
young sadist.

Would-be comic variation on a well-worn theme; the
level of comedy is indicated by the title.

wd Charles B. Griffith

Oliver Reed, Sunny Johnson, Mel Wells, Maia
Danziger

Doctor in Clover
GB   1966   101m   Eastmancolor
Rank/Betty E. Box-Ralph Thomas

Grimsdyke goes back to his old hospital for a
refresher course and finds a rejuvenating drug useful
in his philandering.

Depressing mixture of smut and slapstick.

w Jack Davies   *novel* Richard Gordon   *d* Ralph
Thomas   *ph* Ernest Steward   *m* John Scott

Leslie Phillips, James Robertson Justice, Shirley
Anne Field, Joan Sims, John Fraser, Arthur Haynes,
Fenella Fielding, Noel Purcell, Jeremy Lloyd, Eric
Barker, Terry Scott, Alfie Bass

Doctor in Distress
GB   1963   102m   Eastmancolor
Rank/Betty E. Box-Ralph Thomas
V*

Simon Sparrow goes back to work for Sir Lancelot
Spratt and finds his old mentor in love.

Tedious flummery whose characters fail to perform
with the old pizazz.

w Nicholas Phipps, Ronald Scott Thorn   *d* Ralph
Thomas   *ph* Ernest Steward   *m* Norrie Paramour

Dirk Bogarde, James Robertson Justice, Mylene
Demongeot, Samantha Eggar, Barbara Murray,

Donald Houston, Jessie Evans, Ann Lynn, Leo McKern, Dennis Price

Doctor in Love

GB 1960 97m Eastmancolor
Rank/Betty E. Box-Ralph Thomas

Dr Burke and Dr Hare have various adventures, mostly amorous, in city and country practices.

Virtually plotless collection of weak sketches based on schoolboy smut.

w Nicholas Phipps novel Richard Gordon d Ralph Thomas ph Ernest Steward m Bruce Montgomery

Michael Craig, Leslie Phillips, James Robertson Justice, Virginia Maskell, Nicholas Phipps, Reginald Beckwith, Joan Sims, Liz Fraser, Ambrosine Philpotts, Irene Handl

Doctor in the House **

GB 1954 91m Eastmancolor
Rank (Betty E. Box)
V, V*

Amorous and other misadventures of medical students at St Swithin's Hospital.

A comedy with much to answer for: several sequels and an apparently endless TV series. The original is not bad, as the students, though plainly over age, constitute a formidable mass of British talent at its peak.

w Nicholas Phipps novel Richard Gordon d Ralph Thomas ph Ernest Steward m Bruce Montgomery

Dirk Bogarde, Kenneth More, Donald Sinden, Donald Houston, Kay Kendall, Muriel Pavlow, James Robertson Justice, Geoffrey Keen

'Works its way with determined high spirits through the repertoire of medical student jokes.' – MFB

'An uproarious, devil-may-care, almost wholly ruthless picture.' – Dilys Powell

† Sequels, of increasing inanity and decreasing connection with the original characters, were: Doctor at Sea, Doctor at Large, Doctor in Love, Doctor in Distress, Doctor in Clover and Doctor in Trouble. Carry on Doctor and Carry on Again Doctor were horses of a different colour.

Doctor in the Village *

Holland 1958 92m bw
Nationale Filmproductie Maatschappij (Bobby Roosenboom)
original title: Dorp aan de Rivier

Stories are recalled of an eccentric but respected country doctor at the turn of the century.

Tragi-comic incidents in the vein of Pagnol, a little too rich in farce and melodrama to be convincingly human.

w Hugo Claus novel Antoon Coolen d Fons Rademakers ph Eduard J. R. van der Enden m Jurriaan Andriessen

Max Croiset, Mary Dresselhuys, Bernhard Droog, Jan Teulings

'Scenes which should have had disturbing power crowd one upon another with an almost repellent relish which falls over into parody.' – Peter John Dyer, MFB

Doctor in Trouble

GB 1970 90m Technicolor
Rank/Betty E. Box
V*

Dr Burke inadvertently becomes a stowaway on an Atlantic cruise.

Witless tailpiece to the Doctor saga, like a half-hearted wrapping-up of discarded jokes from the other episodes.

w Jack Davies novel Doctor on Toast by Richard Gordon d Ralph Thomas ph Ernest Steward m Eric Rogers

Leslie Phillips, Harry Secombe, Angela Scoular, Irene Handl, Robert Morley, Simon Dee, Freddie Jones, James Robertson Justice, Joan Sims, John Le Mesurier, Fred Emney

'The cinematic equivalent of an end-of-the-pier summer show.' – Films and Filming

Doctor Jack *

US 1922 72m approx (24 fps) bw silent
Pathé/Rolin

A quack country doctor does more good than the licensed medicos.

Pleasing but not hilariously funny star vehicle.

w Sam Taylor, Jean Havez d Fred Newmeyer

Harold Lloyd, Mildred Davis, John Prince, Eric Mayne

'The greatest drama of dual identity ever written!'

Dr Jekyll and Mr Hyde **

US 1921 63m (24 fps) bw silent
Paramount Artcraft
V*, L

A respected London physician experiments with a drug which separates out the evil part of his soul.

A lively star vehicle which renewed John Barrymore's popularity with film audiences. Some scenes still grip, and Barrymore accomplished some transformations in full view of the camera, by facial contortions.

w Clara S. Beranger novel Robert Louis Stevenson d John S. Robertson

John Barrymore, Nita Naldi, Martha Mansfield, Louis Wolheim

'Strange desires! Loves and hates and secret yearnings … hidden in the shadows of a man's mind!'

Doctor Jekyll and Mr Hyde ****

US 1931 98m bw
Paramount (Rouben Mamoulian)
V*, L

A Victorian research chemist finds a formula which separates the good and evil in his soul; when the latter predominates, he becomes a rampaging monster.

The most exciting and cinematic version by far of the famous horror story; the make-up is slightly over the top, but the gas-lit London settings, the pace, the performances and clever camera and sound tricks make it a film to enjoy over and over again. Subjective camera is used at the beginning, and for the first transformation the actor wore various layers of make up which were sensitive to different colour filters and thus produced instant change.

w Samuel Hoffenstein, Percy Heath novel Robert Louis Stevenson d Rouben Mamoulian ph Karl Struss ad Hans Dreier

Fredric March, Miriam Hopkins, Rose Hobart, Holmes Herbert, Halliwell Hobbes, Edgar Norton

'Promises abundant shocks and returns now that the fan public is horror conscious. Probably loses something on popular appeal by highbrow treatment.' – Variety

'As a work of cinematic imagination this film is difficult to fault.' – John Baxter, 1968

† The screenplay with 1,400 frame blow-ups was published in 1976 in the Film Classics Library (editor Richard J. Anobile).
†† The film was subsequently edited down to 80m, and this is the only version remaining.

AA: Fredric March

AAN: Samuel Hoffenstein, Percy Heath; Karl Struss

'A romantic gentleman by day – a love-mad beast at night!'

Dr Jekyll and Mr Hyde **

US 1941 122m bw
MGM (Victor Saville, Victor Fleming)
V*, L

Curiously misconceived, stately, badly cast version with elaborate production including Freudian dream sequences.

Always worth watching, but not a success.

w John Lee Mahin d Victor Fleming ph Joseph Ruttenberg m Franz Waxman ed Harold F. Kress

Spencer Tracy, Ingrid Bergman, Lana Turner, Ian Hunter, C. Aubrey Smith, Donald Crisp, Sara Allgood

'Not so much evil incarnate as ham rampant . . . more ludicrous than dreadful.' – New York Times

† Other versions: The Two Faces of Dr Jekyll (1960), I Monster (1970). Variations: Daughter of Dr Jekyll (1957), Abbott and Costello Meet Dr Jekyll and Mr Hyde (1954), Son of Dr Jekyll (1951), The Ugly Duckling (1960), House of Dracula (1945), The Nutty Professor (1963), Dr Jekyll and Sister Hyde (1971).

AAN: Joseph Ruttenberg; Franz Waxman; Harold F. Kress

Dr Jekyll and Sister Hyde *

GB 1971 97m Technicolor
MGM-EMI/Hammer (Albert Fennell, Brian Clemens)
V, V*, L

A twist: Jekyll now turns into a young and beautiful woman, and kills prostitutes so that he can continue his research.

Half-successful attempt to link the legend with Jack the Ripper, killed by gore and overlength.

w Brian Clemens d Roy Ward Baker ph Norman Warwick m David Whitaker pd Robert Jones ed James Needs

Ralph Bates, Martine Beswick, Gerald Sim, Lewis Fiander, Dorothy Alison

Dr Kildare

This long-running screen hero was a young intern at Blair Hospital, under the cranky tutelage of old Dr Gillespie. Created by Max Brand in a series of novels, he first appeared on the screen in a 1937 Paramount double-biller called INTERNS CAN'T TAKE MONEY, played by Joel McCrea with Barbara Stanwyck, no less, providing the love interest. Kildare came up against gangsters; Gillespie did not appear. MGM then took over the property and went to town with it, making fifteen films in ten years. They were as follows:

1938: YOUNG DR KILDARE
1939: CALLING DR KILDARE, THE SECRET OF DR KILDARE
1940: DR KILDARE'S STRANGE CASE (qv), DR KILDARE GOES HOME (qv), DR KILDARE'S CRISIS (qv)
1941: THE PEOPLE vs DR KILDARE
1942: DR KILDARE'S WEDDING DAY (qv)
1942: DR KILDARE'S VICTORY (qv), CALLING DR GILLESPIE, DR GILLESPIE'S NEW ASSISTANT (qv)
1943: DR GILLESPIE'S CRIMINAL CASE (qv)
1944: THREE MEN IN WHITE, BETWEEN TWO WOMEN
1947: DARK DELUSION (qv)

Lew Ayres played Kildare, but in 1942 declared himself a conscientious objector and was dropped. The emphasis shifted to Gillespie, played by Lionel Barrymore from a wheelchair, and he proceeded to deal with a whole series of interns. The films were well enough made on medium budgets; nine were directed by Harold S. Bucquet and the last five by Willis Goldbeck, one by W. S. Van Dyke. In 1961 a TV series began with Richard Chamberlain and Raymond Massey, and ran for seven years.

Dr Kildare Goes Home

US 1940 79m bw
MGM

Young Dr Kildare temporarily deserts Blair Hospital to help his father establish a small-town clinic.

Rather below par episode with obvious outcome.

w Willis Goldbeck, Harry Ruskin d Harold
S. Bucquet

Lew Ayres, Lionel Barrymore, Laraine Day, Samuel
S. Hinds, Gene Lockhart

Dr Kildare's Crisis
US   1940   75m   bw
MGM

Dr Kildare's fiancée may have epilepsy in the family.

The series at its peak.

w Willis Goldbeck, Harry Ruskin d Harold
S. Bucquet

Lew Ayres, Lionel Barrymore, Robert Young, Laraine
Day, Nat Pendleton, Marie Blake

Dr Kildare's Strange Case
US   1940   77m   bw
MGM
V*

The young doctor cures a mental patient by the
newest methods.

Crisp series episode.

w Willis Goldbeck, Harry Ruskin d Harold
S. Bucquet

Lew Ayres, Lionel Barrymore, Laraine Day, Shepperd
Strudwick, Samuel S. Hinds

Dr Kildare's Victory
US   1942   92m   bw
MGM
GB title: The Doctor and the Débutante

Back at Blair, Dr Kildare fights ambulance zoning
regulations.

Rather heavy-going episode, its star's last before
becoming a conscientious objector and leaving
Hollywood for the duration.

w Harry Ruskin, Willis Goldbeck d W. S. Van
Dyke

Lew Ayres, Lionel Barrymore, Ann Ayars, Robert
Sterling

Dr Kildare's Wedding Day
US   1941   83m   bw
MGM
GB title: Mary Names the Day

Dr Kildare's fiancée is killed in a road accident.

Rather deliberately downbeat episode, well enough
assembled.

w Lawrence Bachmann, Ormond Ruthven
d Harold S. Bucquet

Lew Ayres, Lionel Barrymore, Laraine Day, Red
Skelton, Nils Asther

Dr Knock *
France   1936   74m   bw
Pathé-Natan

A sly young doctor takes over a country practice and
turns the townsfolk into hypochondriacs.

Amusing version of a modern French comedy classic.

w Jules Romains play Jules Romains d Louis
Jouvet, Roger Goupillières

Louis Jouvet, Palau, Le Vigan, Moor, Alexandre
Rignault

'Once under way it scoots along like a Bermuda sloop,
and holds right till the surprise fadeout.' – Variety

'Death is the ultimate vacation.'
Dr M
West Germany/France/Italy   1989   116m   colour
Hobo/NEF/Ellepi Film/Clea Productions (Ingrid Windisch)
V, V*

A doctor indoctrinates holidaymakers with the desire
to commit suicide.

Limp thriller.

w Sollace Mitchell story Thomas Bauermeister
d Claude Chabrol ph Jean Rabier m Paul
Hindemith pd Wolfgang Hundhammer, Dante
Ferretti ed Monique Fardoulis

Alan Bates, Jennifer Beals, Jan Niklas, Hanns
Zischler, Benoit Regent, William Berger, Alexander
Radszun, Peter Fitz, Daniela Poggi

Doctor Mabuse the Gambler ***
Germany   1922   101m (24 fps)   bw   silent
UFA (Erich Pommer)
V, V*
original title: Doktor Mabuse, der Spieler

A criminal mastermind uses hypnotism and blackmail
in his efforts to obtain world domination, but when
finally cornered is discovered to be a raving maniac.

A real wallow in German post-war depression and
melodrama, in the form of a Fu Manchu/Moriarty type
thriller. Fascinating scene by scene, but by now a
slightly tiresome whole.

w Thea von Harbou, Fritz Lang novel Norbert
Jacques d Fritz Lang ph Carl Hoffman ad Otto
Hunte, Stahl-Urach, Erich Kettelhut, Karl Vollbrecht

Rudolph Klein-Rogge, Alfred Abel, Gertrude
Welcker, Lil Dagover, Paul Richter

† Originally issued in Germany in two parts, Der
Grosse Spieler and Inferno, adding up to a much longer
running time.
†† See sequels, The Testament of Dr Mabuse and The
Thousand Eyes of Dr Mabuse.

Dr Monica
US   1934   80m   bw
Warner (Henry Blanke)

A lady doctor allows her husband to fall for another
woman.

Heavy-handed 'woman's picture' which did well at
the time.

w Charles Kenyon play Marja Morozowicz
d William Keighley

Kay Francis, Warren William, Jean Muir, Verree
Teasdale, Philip Reed, Emma Dunn

Doctor No ***
GB   1962   111m   Technicolor
UA/Eon (Harry Saltzman, Albert R. Broccoli)
V, V*, L, S

A British secret service agent foils a master criminal
operating in the West Indies.

First of the phenomenally successful James Bond
movies, mixing sex, violence and campy humour
against expensive sets and exotic locales. Toned down
from the original novels, they expressed a number of
sixties attitudes, and proved unstoppable box-office
attractions for nearly twenty-five years. The first was,
if not quite the best, reasonably representative of the
series.

w Richard Maibaum, Johanna Harwood, Berkely
Mather novel Ian Fleming d Terence Young
ph Ted Moore m Monty Norman

Sean Connery, Ursula Andress, Jack Lord, Joseph
Wiseman, John Kitzmiller, Bernard Lee, Lois
Maxwell, Zena Marshall, Eunice Gayson, Anthony
Dawson

† The subsequent titles, all qv, were From Russia with
Love (1963), Goldfinger (1964), Thunderball (1965), You
Only Live Twice (1967), On Her Majesty's Secret Service
(1969), Diamonds Are Forever (1971), Live and Let Die
(1973), The Man with the Golden Gun (1974), The Spy
Who Loved Me (1977), Moonraker (1979), For Your Eyes
Only (1981), Octopussy (1983), A View To A Kill (1985),
The Living Daylights (1987), Licence To Kill (1989). Never
Say Never Again (1984) was not part of the series,

though it brought back Sean Connery as Bond. Casino
Royale (1967) was a Bond spoof made by other hands.

Dr O'Dowd
GB   1940   70m   bw
Warner

A drunken doctor redeems himself.

Somewhat woebegone tearjerker with an interesting
cast.

w Derek Twist, Austin Melford story L. A. G.
Strong d Herbert Mason

Shaun Glenville, Peggy Cummins, Mary Merrall,
Liam Gaffney, Patricia Roc, Walter Hudd, Irene Handl

Dr Petiot
France   1990   102m   colour/bw
Electric/MS/Sara/Cine 5 (Alain Sarde, Philippe Chapelier-
  Dehesdin)
V

In wartime Paris, a doctor who claims to help Jews to
escape the Nazis kills them instead.

An unflinching examination of a serial killer, filmed
in the style of an old-fashioned horror movie.

w Dominique Garnier, Christian de Chalonge
d Christian de Chalonge ph Patrick Blossier
m Michel Portal ad Yves Brover ed Anita
Fernandez

Michel Serrault, Pierre Romans, Zbigniew Horoks,
Berange Bonvoisin, Aurore Prieto, André Chaumeau,
Axel Bogousslavski

'The sting's in the tale!'
Dr Phibes Rises Again *
GB   1972   89m   DeLuxe
AIP (Richard Dalton)
V*, L

The immortal Phibes and his wife rise from the dead
to seek an Egyptian elixir of life, and cross swords
with a satanic Egyptologist.

Uncertainly paced but generally zippy comic strip for
adults, with all concerned entering gleefully into the
evil spirit of the thing. See prequel, The Abominable Dr
Phibes.

w Robert Fuest, Robert Blees d Robert Fuest
ph Alex Thomson m John Gale ad Brian Eatwell

Vincent Price, Robert Quarry, Valli Kemp, Fiona Lewis,
Peter Cushing, Beryl Reid, Terry-Thomas, Hugh
Griffith, Peter Jeffrey, Gerald Sim, John Thaw, John
Cater, Lewis Fiander

'It's refreshing to find a sequel which is better than its
prototype.' – Philip Strick, MFB

Dr Renault's Secret
US   1942   58m   bw
TCF

A scientist turns an ape into a semi-human, which
runs amok.

Fairly well done horror support.

w William Bruckner, Robert F. Metzler d Harry
Lachman

George Zucco, J. Carrol Naish, John Shepperd, Lynne
Roberts

Dr Rhythm *
US   1938   80m   bw
Paramount

A veterinary surgeon goes into show business.

Easy-going star musical with pleasant songs.

w Jo Swerling, Richard Connell story O. Henry
d Frank Tuttle

Bing Crosby, Beatrice Lillie, Mary Carlisle, Andy
Devine, Laura Hope Crews, Rufe Davis

'Armed with a doctor's kit, he fought a thousand killers!'
Dr Socrates *
US 1935 70m bw
Warner (Robert Lord)

A small-town doctor is forced to help wounded gangsters, and becomes involved.

Good star melodrama.

w Robert Lord novel W. R. Burnett d William Dieterle ph Tony Gaudio md Leo F. Forbstein

Paul Muni, Ann Dvorak, Barton MacLane, Robert Barrat, John Eldridge, Hobart Cavanaugh, Mayo Methot, Samuel S. Hinds, Henry O'Neill

'Arriving at the tail end of the G-man and gangster cycle, *Dr Socrates* is a graceful valedictory.' – *Variety*

'Rapid, strong and exciting.' – *Sunday Times*

† Remade as *King of the Underworld* and *Bullet Scars*.

'The hot line suspense comedy!'
Dr Strangelove; or, How I Learned to Stop Worrying and Love the Bomb ****
GB 1963 93m bw
Columbia/Stanley Kubrick (Victor Lyndon)
V, V*, L

A mad USAF general launches a nuclear attack on Russia, and when recall attempts fail, and retaliation is inevitable, all concerned sit back to await the destruction of the world.

Black comedy resolving itself into a series of sketches, with the star playing three parts (for no good reason): the US president, an RAF captain, and a mad German-American scientist. Historically an important film in its timing, its nightmares being those of the early sixties, artistically it clogs its imperishable moments by untidy narrative.

w Stanley Kubrick, Terry Southern, Peter George novel *Red Alert* by Peter George d Stanley Kubrick ph Gilbert Taylor m Laurie Johnson ad Ken Adam

Peter Sellers, George C. Scott, Peter Bull, Sterling Hayden, Keenan Wynn, Slim Pickens, James Earl Jones, Tracy Reed

GENERAL (George C. Scott): 'I don't say we wouldn't get our hair mussed, but I do say no more than ten to twenty million people killed.'

'Scarcely a picture of relentless originality; seldom have we seen so much made over so little.' – *Joan Didion*

'The double-face of the story – serious events broken up into farcical incidents – is expressed in double-face acting of a high order.' – *Dilys Powell*

'Irreverent to the point of savagery; it is funny and it is engrossing. And it's heady stuff for moviegoers, for Kubrick, boy genius that he is, assumes that we're grown-up enough to share his bitter laughter.' – *Judith Crist*

† *Fail Safe* (qv), which took the same theme more seriously, was released almost simultaneously.

AAN: best picture; script; Stanley Kubrick (as director); Peter Sellers

Dr Syn *
GB 1937 80m bw
Gaumont (Michael Balcon)

The vicar of Dymchurch in 1780 is really a pirate believed dead.

This now obscure, lively pirate yarn was its star's last film.

w Michael Hogan, Roger Burford novel Russell Thorndike d Roy William Neill ph Jack Cox md Louis Levy ad Vetchinsky ed R. E. Dearing, Alfred Roome

George Arliss, Margaret Lockwood, John Loder, Roy Emerton, Graham Moffatt, Frederick Burtwell, Meinhart Maur, George Merritt

'With Arliss in the name part it doesn't ring true.' – *Variety*

Dr Syn Alias the Scarecrow
GB 1962 98m Technicolor
Walt Disney (Bill Anderson)
V*

The vicar of Dymchurch is really a smuggler who manages to outwit a rascally general and save a prisoner from Dover Castle.

Oddly released the same year as another version of the story, *Captain Clegg*, this rather set-bound adventure yarn turns its hero into a Robin Hood figure. It was originally made to be shown in three parts on American TV.

w Robert Westerby novel *Christopher Syn* by Russell Thorndike, William Buchanan d James Neilson ph Paul Beeson m Gerard Schurmann

Patrick McGoohan, George Cole, Tony Britton, Geoffrey Keen, Kay Walsh, Patrick Wymark, Alan Dobie, Eric Pohlmann

The Doctor Takes a Wife *
US 1940 89m bw
Columbia (William Perlberg)

A young doctor has to pretend to be the husband of a socialite.

Typical high life comedy of its period, quite brisk and diverting.

w George Seaton, Ken Englund d Alexander Hall ph Sid Hickox md Morris Stoloff m Frederick Hollander

Loretta Young, Ray Milland, Edmund Gwenn, Reginald Gardiner, Gail Patrick, Frank Sully, George Metaxa, Charles Halton, Chester Clute

Dr Terror's House of Horrors
GB 1965 98m Techniscope
Amicus (Milton Subotsky)
V*

An eccentric, who turns out to be Death himself, tells the fortunes of five men in a railway carriage.

One of the first Amicus horror compendiums and a weak one, not helped by wide screen, a couple of naïve scripts and ho-hum acting. The book-ends are quite pleasant, though.

w Milton Subotsky d Freddie Francis ph Alan Hume m Elisabeth Lutyens

Peter Cushing, Ursula Howells, Max Adrian, Roy Castle, Alan Freeman, Bernard Lee, Jeremy Kemp, Kenny Lynch, Christopher Lee, Michael Gough, Donald Sutherland

† Later collections from the same stable include *Torture Garden, Tales from the Crypt, Vault of Horror* and *Asylum.*

Dr Who and the Daleks
GB 1965 83m Techniscope
British Lion/Regal/Aaru (Milton Subotsky, Max J. Rosenberg)
V

Three children and their grandfather accidentally start his time machine and are whisked away to a planet where villainous robots rule.

Junior science fiction from the BBC series. Limply put together, and only for indulgent children.

w Milton Subotsky d Gordon Flemyng ph John Wilcox m Malcolm Lockyer

Peter Cushing, Roy Castle, Jennie Linden, Roberta Tovey, Barrie Ingham

† A sequel, no better, emerged in 1966: *Daleks: Invasion Earth 2150 AD,* with similar credits except that Bernard Cribbins instead of Roy Castle provided comic relief.

'A full moon was his signal to kill!'
Dr X **
US 1932 82m Technicolor
Warner (Hal Wallis)

A reporter investigates a series of moon murders and narrows his search to one of several doctors at a medical college.

Fascinating, German-inspired, overblown and generally enjoyable horror mystery whose armless villain commits murders by growing limbs from 'synthetic flesh'.

w Earl Baldwin, Robert Tasker play Howard W. Comstock, Allen C. Miller d Michael Curtiz ph Richard Tower, md Leo Forbstein

Lee Tracy, Lionel Atwill, Preston Foster, Fay Wray, George Rosener, Mae Busch, Arthur Edmund Carewe, John Wray

'The settings, lighting and final battle with the man-monster are quite stunning.' – *NFT, 1974*

'It almost makes Frankenstein seem tame and friendly.' – *New York Times*

Doctor You've Got to be Kidding
US 1967 93m Metrocolor Panavision
MGM/Trident (Douglas Laurence)

A girl arrives at a maternity hospital chased by three prospective husbands.

Wild and wacky farce which leaves little impression.

w Phillip Shuken novel Patte Wheat Mahan d Peter Tewkesbury ph Fred Koenekamp m Kenyon Hopkins

Sandra Dee, George Hamilton, Celeste Holm, Bill Bixby, *Dwayne Hickman,* Dick Kallman, Mort Sahl, Allen Jenkins

'A love caught in the fire of revolution!'
Doctor Zhivago ***
US 1965 192m Metrocolor Panavision 70
MGM/David Lean/Carlo Ponti
V, V (W), V*, L, S

A Moscow doctor is caught up in World War I, exiled for writing poetry, forced into partisan service and separated from his only love.

Beautifully photographed and meticulously directed, this complex epic has been so reduced from the original novel that many parts of the script simply do not make any kind of sense. What remains is a collection of expensive set-pieces, great for looking if not listening.

w Robert Bolt novel Boris Pasternak d David Lean ph Frederick A. Young m Maurice Jarre pd John Box ed Norman Savage

Omar Sharif, Julie Christie, Rod Steiger, Alec Guinness, Rita Tushingham, Ralph Richardson, Tom Courtenay, Geraldine Chaplin, Siobhan McKenna, Noel Willman, Geoffrey Keen, Adrienne Corri

'A long haul along the road of synthetic lyricism.' – *MFB*

'David Lean's *Doctor Zhivago* does for snow what his *Lawrence of Arabia* did for sand.' – *John Simon*

'It isn't shoddy (except for the music); it isn't soap opera; it's stately, respectable, and dead. Neither the contemplative Zhivago nor the flow of events is intelligible, and what is worse, they seem unrelated to each other.' – *Pauline Kael*

AA: Robert Bolt; Frederick A. Young; Maurice Jarre

AAN: best picture; David Lean; Tom Courtenay

A Doctor's Diary
US 1937 77m bw
Paramount

The resident physician of a privately-endowed hospital is impatient with the niceties of procedure.

Unsurprising medical drama which adequately filled half a bill.

w Sam Ornitz, Joseph Anthony   *d* Charles Vidor

George Bancroft, John Trent, Helen Burgess, Ruth Coleman, Charles Waldron, Ra Hould, Sidney Blackmer

'Packs enough drama to hold attention.' – *Variety*

The Doctor's Dilemma *
GB   1958   99m   Metrocolor
MGM/Anatole de Grunwald

Eminent Harley Street surgeons debate the case of a devoted wife and her tubercular artist husband.

Well acted but curiously muffled filming of Shaw's Edwardian play about ethics and human values.

w Anatole de Grunwald   *play* Bernard Shaw
d Anthony Asquith   *ph* Robert Krasker   *m* Joseph Kosma   *ad* Paul Sheriff

Leslie Caron, Dirk Bogarde, *John Robinson*, Alastair Sim, Felix Aylmer, Robert Morley, Michael Gwynn, Maureen Delany, Alec McCowen

Doctors' Wives
US   1970   102m   Eastmancolor
Columbia/M. J. Frankovich
V*

When Dr Dellman shoots his unfaithful wife, his colleagues reconsider their sex lives.

Adult soap opera from talents who at other times have found better things to do. In the sensational circumstances, two sanguinary operation sequences are tastelessly irrelevant.

w Daniel Taradash   *novel* Frank G. Slaughter
d George Schaefer   *ph* Charles B. Lang   *m* Elmer Bernstein

Richard Crenna, Janice Rule, Gene Hackman, John Colicos, Dyan Cannon, Diana Sands, Rachel Roberts, Carroll O'Connor, Cara Williams, Ralph Bellamy, Richard Anderson

'Crisis follows hard on crisis to breathlessly ludicrous effect.' – *Tom Milne*

Dodes'ka-den **
Japan   1970   140m   Eastmancolor
Essential Cinema/Yonki-No-Kai/Toho (Akira Kurosawa, Keisuke Kinoshita, Kon Ichikawa, Masaki Kobayashi)
V*

In a shanty town on the outskirts of Tokyo, a group of down-and-outs go about the daily business of surviving.

Fascinating, detailed portrait of ordinary and eccentric lives in the lower depths.

w Akira Kurosawa, Hideo Orguni, Shinobu Hashimoto   *novel* *Kisetsu No Nai Machi* by Shugoro Yamamoto   *d* Akira Kurosawa   *ph* Takao Saito, Yasumichi Fukusawa   *m* Toru Takemitsu
ad Yoshiro Muraki, Shinobu Muraki   *ed* Reiko Keneko

Yoshitaka Zushi, Kin Sugai, Kaou Kato, Junzaburo Ban, Kiyoko Tange, Michiko Hino, Tatsuhei Shimokawa

AAN: Foreign language film

'West of Chicago there was no law! West of Dodge City there was no God!'
Dodge City ***
US   1939   104m   Technicolor
Warner (Robert Lord)
V, V*, L

An ex-soldier and trail boss helps clean up the west's great railroad terminus.

Standard, satisfying big-scale Western with all clichés intact and very enjoyable, as is the soft, rich early colour. The story is plainly inspired by the exploits of Wyatt Earp.

w Robert Buckner   *d Michael Curtiz*   *ph Sol Polito, Ray Rennahan*   *m* Max Steiner

Errol Flynn, Olivia de Havilland, Ann Sheridan, Bruce Cabot, Alan Hale, Frank McHugh, John Litel, Victor Jory, William Lundigan, Henry Travers, Henry O'Neill, Guinn Williams, Gloria Holden

'A lusty Western, packed with action, including some of the dandiest mêlée stuff screened.' – *Variety*

'It looks programmed and underpopulated, though in an elegantly stylized way.' – *New Yorker, 1980*

Dodsworth ***
US   1936   101m   bw
Samuel Goldwyn
V*, L

An American businessman takes his wife on a tour of Europe, and their lives are changed.

Satisfying, well-acted drama from a bestselling novel; production values high.

w Sidney Howard   *novel Sinclair Lewis*   *d William Wyler*   *ph* Rudolph Maté   *m* Alfred Newman
ad Richard Day

Walter Huston, Mary Astor, Ruth Chatterton, David Niven, Paul Lukas, Gregory Gaye, *Maria Ouspenskaya,* Odette Myrtil, Spring Byington, John Payne

'No one, I think, will fail to enjoy it, in spite of its too limited and personal plot, the sense it leaves behind of a very expensive, very contemporary, Bond Street vacuum flask.' – *Graham Greene*

'William Wyler has had the skill to execute it in cinematic terms, and a gifted cast has been able to bring the whole alive to our complete satisfaction.' – *New York Times*

'A smoothly flowing narrative of substantial interest, well-defined performances and good talk.' – *New York Times*

'An offering of dignity and compelling power to provide you with a treat you can rarely experience in a picture house.' – *Hollywood Spectator*

AA: Richard Day

AAN: best picture; Sidney Howard; William Wyler; Walter Huston; Maria Ouspenskaya

The Does: see *Les Biches*

Dog Day Afternoon **
US   1975   130m   Technicolor
Warner/AEC (Martin Bregman, Martin Elfland)
V, V*, L

Two incompetent robbers are cornered in a Brooklyn bank.

Recreation of a tragi-comic episode from the newspaper headlines; for half its length a fascinating and acutely observed film which then bogs itself down in a surplus of talk and excessive sentiment about homosexuality.

w Frank Pierson   *book* Patrick Mann   *d Sidney Lumet*   *ph* Victor J. Kemper   *m* none

Al Pacino, John Cazale, *Charles Durning,* Sully Boyar, James Broderick, *Chris Sarandon*

'There is plenty of Lumet's vital best here in a film that at least glancingly captures the increasingly garish pathology of our urban life.' – *Jack Kroll*

'Scattered moments of wry humour, sudden pathos and correct observation.' – *John Simon*

'The mask of frenetic cliché doesn't spoil moments of pure reporting on people in extremity.' – *New Yorker*

'A long and wearying case history of the beaten, sobbing, despairing and ultimately powerless anti-hero.' – *Karyn Kay, Jump Cut*

'Full of galvanic mirth rooted in human desperation.' – *Michael Billington, Illustrated London News*

'Brisk, humorous and alive with urban energies and angers fretting through the 92 degree heat.' – *Sight and Sound*

AA: Frank Pierson

AAN: best picture; Sidney Lumet; Al Pacino; Chris Sarandon

A Dog of Flanders
US   1959   97m   DeLuxe   Cinemascope
TCF/Associated Producers (Robert B. Radnitz)
V*

A small boy wants to be an artist; when he runs away in frustration, his shaggy dog, formerly a stray, leads his family to him.

Old-fashioned tear-jerker for well-brought-up children, previously filmed as a silent; quite accomplished in presentation.

w Ted Sherdeman   *novel* Ouida   *d* James B. Clark   *ph* Otto Heller   *m* Paul Sawtell, Bert Shefter

David Ladd, Donald Crisp, Theodore Bikel, Max Croiset, Monique Ahrens

Dog Soldiers: see *Who'll Stop the Rain?*

Dogpound Shuffle
Canada   1974   97m   Eastmancolor
Elliott Kastner/Bulldog
V*
aka: *Spot*

An old Irish hobo lives on the earnings of his dancing dog.

Dog-eared 'family film' which didn't seem to entertain many families.

wd Jeffrey Bloom

Ron Moody, David Soul, Ray Stricklyn

Dogs In Space *
Australia   1986   108m   colour
Recorded Releasing/Skouras/Atlantic (Glenys Rowe)
V*

Punks and hippies gather in a squat in Melbourne in the late 1970s.

Episodic, rambling film with a raucous rock soundtrack, but with an engaging affection for its lost tribe of teenagers.

wd Richard Lowenstein   *ph* Andrew de Groot
m Iggy Pop, Dogs In Space and others   *ad* Jody Borland   *ed* Jill Bilcock

Michael Hutchence, Saskia Post, Nique Needles, Deanna Bond, Tony Helou, Chris Haywood, Peter Walsh, Laura Swanson

A Dog's Life *
US   1918   30m approx   bw   silent
First National/Charles Chaplin

A tramp and a stray mongrel help each other towards a happy ending.

Threatening sentiment is kept at bay by amusing sight gags in this pleasing star featurette.

wd Charles Chaplin   *ph* Rollie Totheroh

Charles Chaplin, Edna Purviance, Chuck Riesner, Henry Bergman, Albert Austin, Scraps

A Dog's Life (1961): see *Mondo Cane*

The Dogs of War
GB   1980   118m   Technicolor
UA/Silverwold (Norman Jewison, Patrick Palmer)
V, V*, L

A disenchanted mercenary becomes involved in a plot to take over an impoverished West African state.

Tough but seemingly dated modern irony, somewhat lacking in action and surprise.

w Gary DeVore, George Malko   *novel* Frederick Forsyth   *d* John Irvin   *ph* Jack Cardiff
m Geoffrey Burgon

Christopher Walken, Tom Berenger, *Colin Blakely*, Hugh Millais, Paul Freeman, Robert Urquhart

Doktor Mabuse, der Spieler: see *Doctor Mabuse*

La Dolce Vita ****
Italy/France 1960 173m bw Totalscope
Riama/Pathé Consortium (Giuseppe Amato)
V, S
aka: *The Sweet Life*

A journalist mixes in modern Roman high society and is alternately bewitched and sickened by what he sees.

Episodic satirical melodrama, a marathon self-indulgent wallow with a wagging finger never far away. Full of choice moments such as a statue of Christ being flown by helicopter over the city.

w Federico Fellini, Tullio Pinelli, Ennio Flaiano, Brunello Rondi d Federico Fellini ph Otello Martelli m Nino Rota ad Piero Gherardi

Marcello Mastroianni, Anita Ekberg, Anouk Aimée, Alain Cuny, Yvonne Furneaux, Magali Noel, Nadia Gray, Lex Barker

'Its personification of various familiar symbols – love, death, purity, sin, reason and so on – never succeeds in reflecting human values or creating intellectual excitement . . . Its actual significance rests in the way its (albeit specious) social attack has stirred the imagination of other Italian film-makers, as well as public interest in their work.' – *Robert Vas, MFB*

'An awesome picture, licentious in content but moral and vastly sophisticated in its attitude and what it says.' – *Bosley Crowther, New York Times*

'One of the few films that one feels can be seen with increasing enjoyment a second or third time.' – *Paul V. Backley, New York Herald Tribune*

AAN: script; Federico Fellini

Doll Face
US 1945 80m bw
TCF (Bryan Foy)
GB title: *Come Back to Me*

A burlesque queen goes to Broadway.

Lower case musical of minimal interest.

w Leonard Praskins d Lewis Seiler ph Joseph LaShelle m/ly Harold Adamson, Jimmy McHugh

Vivian Blaine, Dennis O'Keefe, Carmen Miranda, Perry Como, Martha Stewart, Michael Dunne, Reed Hadley, George E. Stone, Donald McBride, Edgar Norton

The Doll Squad
US 1973 101m Eastmancolor
Nationwide/Feature-Faire (Ted V. Mikels)

A female team of CIA agents track down the man who sabotaged an American space project.

Badly made, poorly scripted and acted comedy thriller.

w Jack Richesin, Pam Eddy, Ted V. Mikels d Ted V. Mikels ph Anthony Salinas m Nicholas Carras pd Mike McCloskey ed Ted V. Mikels

Michael Ansara, Francine York, Anthony Eisley, John Carter, Rafael Campos, William Bagdad, Lillian Garrett

'The endless running, jumping and kicks-to-the-groin stunts of this bevy of Emma Peels are conceived and executed with about as much conviction as knockabout comedy.' – *David Pirie, MFB*

The Dollar Bottom
GB 1981 33m Eastmancolor
Rocking Horse Films/Paramount

A sharp-witted public schoolboy sells his friends insurance against being beaten.

Ingenious but thinly acted short, with the added hazard of impenetrable accents.

w Shane Connaughton story James Kennaway d Roger Christian

Rikki Fulton, Robert Urquhart, Jonathan McNeil

Dollars *
US 1971 120m Technicolor
Columbia/M. J. Frankovich
V*, L
GB title: *The Heist*

An American security expert installs an electronic system in a Hamburg bank which he plans to rob himself.

Overlong caper comedy-drama which is quite good to watch when it starts moving, though the quick cutting, short takes and deliberately obscure narrative leave one breathless.

wd Richard Brooks ph Petrus Schloemp m Quincy Jones

Warren Beatty, Goldie Hawn, Gert Frobe, Robert Webber, Scott Brady, Arthur Brauss

'An essay in virtuoso film construction . . . rather as if one were watching a perfect machine in full throttle but with nowhere to go.' – *John Gillet*

Dolls
US 1986 77m colour
Empire Pictures/Taryn Productions (Brian Yuzna)
V*, L

On a dark and stormy night, stranded travellers take refuge in an old house inhabited by an elderly couple and their killer dolls.

Risible, low-budget horror with more clichés than corpses.

w Ed Naha d Stuart Gordon ph Mac Ahlberg m Fuzzbee Morse, Victor Spiegel pd Giovanni Natalucci ed Lee Percy

Stephen Lee, Guy Rolfe, Hilary Mason, Ian Patrick Williams, Carolyn Purdy-Gordon, Cassie Stuart, Bunty Bailey, Carrie Lorraine

A Doll's House *
GB 1973 95m Eastmancolor
Elkins/Freeward (Hillard Elkins)
V*

A wife begins to resist her husband's will. Ibsen's feminist play was always good value; set in Norway in the 1890s, it was taken up eighty years later as a precursor of women's lib, which accounts for two film versions in one year.

This one is simply staged and well performed, but suffers from a bad translation.

w Christopher Hampton play Henrik Ibsen d Patrick Garland ph Arthur Ibbetson m John Barry

Claire Bloom, Anthony Hopkins, Ralph Richardson, Denholm Elliott, Anna Massey, Edith Evans

A Doll's House
GB/France 1973 106m Eastmancolor
World Film Services/Les Films de la Boétie (Joseph Losey)
V*

Opened out but less effective version of the above, with too much solemnity and the central part miscast.

w David Mercer play Henrik Ibsen d Joseph Losey ph Gerry Fisher m Michel Legrand

Jane Fonda, David Warner, Trevor Howard, Edward Fox, Delphine Seyrig, Anna Wing

The Dolly Sisters **
US 1945 114m Technicolor
TCF (George Jessel)

The lives of a Hungarian sister act in American vaudeville.

Fictionalized biographical musical, only fair in the script department but glittering to look at in superb

colour, and enriched by splendid production values. Undoubtedly among the best of its kind.

w John Larkin, Marian Spitzer d Irving Cummings ph Ernest Palmer md Alfred Newman, Charles Henderson ch Seymour Felix m/ly various ad Lyle Wheeler, Leland Fuller

Betty Grable, June Haver, John Payne, S. Z. Sakall, Reginald Gardiner, Frank Latimore, Gene Sheldon, Sig Rumann, Trudy Marshall

AAN: song 'I Can't Begin to Tell You' (m James Monaco, ly Mack Gordon)

Dom Za Vesanje: see *Time Of the Gypsies*

Domani è Troppo Tardi
Italy 1950 101m bw
Rizzoli (Giuseppe Amato)
GB title: *Tomorrow Is Too Late*

Inquisitive pupils and repressive teachers at a co-educational school almost cause a tragedy.

Possibly well intentioned, but in effect an old-fashioned melodrama which works well enough on its level.

w Alfred Machard, Leonide Moguy d Leonide Moguy ph Mario Craveri, Renato del Frate m Alessandro Cicognini

Vittorio de Sica, Lois Maxwell, Gabrielle Dorziat, Anna Maria Pierangeli, Gino Leurini

Domenica d'Agosto **
Italy 1950 75m bw
Colonna (Sergio Amidei)
GB title: *Sunday in August*

Various Romans enjoy Sunday by the sea at Ostia.

Fragmented comedy-drama which succeeds in being charming throughout, every detail being freshly observed through an inquisitive eye.

w Franco Brusati, Luciano Emmer, Giulio Macchi, Cesare Zavattini d Luciano Emmer ph Domenico Scala, Leonida Barboni, Ubaldo Marelli m Roman Vlad ed Jolanda Benvenuti

Anna Baldini, Franco Interlenghi, Elvy Lissiak, Massimo Serato, Marcello Mastroianni, Corrado Verga

Domicile Conjugal: see *Bed and Board*

The Dominant Sex
GB 1937 71m bw
BIP (Walter Mycroft)

A woman demands the right to her own individuality after marriage.

Tepid comedy drama from a popular stage play.

w Vina de Vesci, John Fernald play Michael Egan d Herbert Brenon ph J. J. Cox, Roy Clark ad Cedric Dawe

Phillips Holmes, Diana Churchill, Carol Goodner, Romney Brent, Hugh Miller, Billy Milton

Dominick and Eugene: see *Nicky and Gino*

Dominion Tank Police Acts I & II (dubbed)
Japan 1989 80m colour
Masamune Shirow/Hakusensha/Agent 21/Toshiba Video
  (Ritsuko Kakita, Kazuhiko Inomata, Tomaki Harada)
V

A girl who joins the Tank Police in its fight against crime accidentally destroys a large tank and builds a smaller, cute one.

Japanese animated comic-book fare, revealing a debt to American strip cartoons, done with less violence and more humour than usual. The story, such as it is, is continued in *Dominion Tank Police Acts III & IV*.

w Kouichi Mashimo story Masamune Shirow d Kouichi Mashimo ad Matsuharu Miyamae voices of Toni Barry, Stephen Graf, Sean Barrett, Jesse Vogel, Bill Armstrong, John Bull, Marc Smith

† The film was released direct to video.

Dominion Tank Police Acts III & IV (dubbed)
Japan   1989   70m   colour
Masamune Shirow/Hakusensha/Agent 21/Toshiba Video
   (Kazuhiko Inomata, Tomaki Harada)
V

An android criminal and his two cat-like female accomplices who steal a priceless painting and kidnap a policewoman are hunted down by the Tank Police and a private security organization.

Bizarre animated movie, mixing comedy, violence, science fiction and mysticism in a manner that is unlikely to engage the interest of occidental audiences, despite its slick, cartoon-like style.

w Dai Kohno   story Masamune Shirow   d Takaaki Ishiyama   ph Kazushi Torigoe   m Brown Eyes   ad Osamu Honda

voices of Toni Barry, Stephen Graf, Sean Barrett, Jesse Vogel, Bill Armstrong, John Bull, Marc Smith, Alison Dowling, Garrick Hagon

† The film was released direct to video.

'Dominique will make you shriek!'
Dominique
GB   1978   100m   colour
Grand Prize/Melvin Simon (Milton Subotsky, Andrew Donally)
V*

A woman who was convinced that her husband was deliberately driving her mad is found dead, and buried, but seemingly returns . . .

The old *Diabolique* syndrome revamped in a very parsimonious production with little to hold the interest.

w Edward and Valerie Abraham   novel What Beckoning Ghost by Harold Lawlor   d Michael Anderson   ph Ted Moore   m David Whitaker

Cliff Robertson, Jean Simmons, Jenny Agutter, Simon Ward, Ron Moody, Judy Geeson, Michael Jayston, Flora Robson, David Tomlinson, Jack Warner

The Domino Killings: see *The Domino Principle*

'Trust no one. No one!'
The Domino Principle
US   1977   100m   CFI color
Associated General Films (Lew Grade, Martin Starger)/Stanley
   Kramer
V, V*
GB title: *The Domino Killings*

A murderer is offered his freedom if he will assassinate a national figure.

Fashionable, complex and rather boring political thriller.

w Adam Kennedy   novel Adam Kennedy   d Stanley Kramer   ph Fred Koenekamp, Ernest Laszlo   m Billy Goldenberg

Gene Hackman, Richard Widmark, Candice Bergen, Mickey Rooney, Edward Albert, Eli Wallach, Ken Swofford, Neva Patterson

'Terrible movies tend to start with a preposterous premise and then laboriously work their way to an impossible conclusion. This one however starts with an arrant impossibility and works its way to whatever lies beyond and below that.' – *John Simon*

Don Camillo e l'Onorevole Peppone: see *Don Camillo's Last Round*

Don Camillo's Last Round *
Italy   1955   98m   bw
Rizzoli
original title: *Don Camillo e l'Onorevole Peppone*

The village Catholic priest tries to stop the re-election of the communist mayor.

Pleasant third collection of encounters with familiar characters.

w Giovanni Guareschi and others   books Giovanni Guareschi   d Carmine Gallone   ph Anchise Brizzi   m Alessandro Cicognini

Fernandel, Gino Cervi, Claude Silvain, Leda Gloria

'The episodic narrative is full of mildly amusing incident.' – *MFB*

Don Daredevil Rides Again
US   1951   bw   serial: 12 eps
Republic

A young rancher assumes the character of Don Daredevil to fight off marauding badmen.

Or, *Zorro Rides Again* in this adequate Western serial.

d Fred C. Brannon

Ken Curtis, Aline Towne, Roy Barcroft, Lane Bradford

Don Giovanni
France-Italy-Germany   1979   184m   colour
Gaumont-Opera-Camera One (Michel Seydoux)
V

Grandiose but artistically somewhat hesitant version of Mozart's opera; little here for film buffs.

cinematic conception Rolf Lieberman   d Joseph Losey   ph Gerry Fisher   ad Alexander Trauner

Ruggero Raimondi, John Macurdy, Edda Moser, Kiri Te Kanawa

The Don Is Dead
US   1973   117m   Technicolor
Universal/Hal B. Wallis (Paul Nathan)
V*

Cross and double cross among Mafia families.

A failed attempt to cash in on *The Godfather*, this endless melodrama is boringly violent and totally predictable.

w Marvin H. Albert   novel Marvin H. Albert   d Richard Fleischer   ph Richard H. Kline   m Jerry Goldsmith

Anthony Quinn, Frederic Forrest, Robert Forster, Al Lettieri, Angel Tompkins, Charles Cioffi

Don Juan **
US   1926   126m (synchronized)   bw
Warner
V*, L

Exploits of the famous lover and adventurer at Lucretia Borgia's court.

Lithe swashbuckler in the best silent tradition, but with a synchronized score (by William Axt) which made it a sensation and led directly to the talkie revolution.

w Bess Meredyth   d Alan Crosland   ph Byron Haskin

John Barrymore, Mary Astor, Warner Oland, Estelle Taylor, Myrna Loy, Phyllis Haver, Willard Louis, Montagu Love

Don Juan Quilligan
US   1945   76m   bw
TCF

A would-be romantic bargee becomes engaged to two girls simultaneously, one on each side of the Hudson.

Thin comedy of bigamy, similar to *The Captain's Paradise*, which came later.

w Arthur Kober, Frank Gabrielson   d Frank Tuttle

William Bendix, Phil Silvers, Joan Blondell, Mary Treen, Anne Revere, George Macready

'The finest adventure tale ever screened!'
Don Q Son of Zorro *
US   1925   170m (16 fps)   bw   silent
United Artists

Further adventures in the manner of the star's 1920 hit (see *The Mark of Zorro*).

w Jack Cunningham   novel K. and H. Pritchard   d Donald Crisp   ph Henry Sharp

Douglas Fairbanks, Mary Astor, Donald Crisp, Jack McDonald, Jean Hersholt

Don Quixote *
France   1933   82m   bw
Vandor/Nelson/Wester
S

An adequate potted version starring Fedor Chaliapin and in the English version George Robey (French version: Dorville).

w Paul Morand, Alexandre Arnoux, from Cervantes   d G. W. Pabst   ph Nikolas Farkas, Paul Portier   m Jacques Ibert   ad Andrei Andreiev

'Strictly for the arty clientele . . . for general consumption tedious and dull. Americans in general may feel that the story scarcely rates retelling.' – *Variety*

Don Quixote **
USSR   1957   105m   Agfacolor   Sovscope
Lenfilm

An extremely handsome version with a commanding star performance.

w E. Schwarz   d Grigori Kozintsev   ph Andrei Moskvin, Apollinari Dudko   m Kara-Karayev   ad Yevgeny Yenei

Nikolai Cherkassov, Yuri Tolubyev

† Other versions came from France in 1902 and 1908, Italy in 1910, France in 1911, USA in 1915, Britain in 1923, Denmark in 1926, Spain in 1947, Britain in 1972, and Britain (ballet version with Nureyev) in 1975.

Don Winslow of the Navy
US   1942   bw   serial: 15 eps
Universal

A hero of Naval Intelligence combats The Scorpion.

Plenty of serial action with a maritime background.

d Ford Beebe, Ray Taylor

Don Terry, Walter Sande, Wade Boteler, John Litel

Dona Flor and Her Two Husbands
Brazil   1976   110m   Eastmancolor
Carnaval (Luis Carlos Barreto)

A young widow remarries, and has to share her bed with her late husband's ghost.

Semi-pornographic comedy which achieved some fashionable success.

wd Bruno Barreto   novel Jorge Amado   ph Maurito Salles   m Chico Buarque de Holanda

Sonia Braga, Jose Wilker, Mauro Mendonca

Dona Herlinda and Her Son *
Mexico   1986   90m   colour
Clasa Films Mondiales (Manuel Barbachano Ponce)
original title: *Doña Herlinda y Su Hijo*

A mother insists that her homosexual son, a doctor, get married, whereupon he sets up home with his wife and boyfriend.

An amusing comedy of manners, on how to remain gay in a masculine society.

wd Jaime Humberto Hermosillo   ph Miguel Erhenberg   ed Luis Kelly

Arturo Meza, Marco Antonio Treviño, Leticia Lupercio, Guadalupe Del Toro, Angelica Guerrero, Donato Casteñeda, Guillermina Alba

Dondi
US   1960   80m   bw
Allied Artists

GIs in Italy adopt an orphan boy, who stows away to be with them in America.

Glutinous, sentimental comedy-drama.

w Albert Zugsmith, Gus Edson, from a comic strip d Albert Zugsmith

David Janssen, Patti Page, Walter Winchell, Mickey Shaughnessy, Robert Strauss, Arnold Stang, Gale Gordon

Donna Donna
Holland   1987   90m   colour
Movies Film (Chris Brouwer, Haig Balian)

Distressed by his inability to attract a girlfriend, a bright but inept student falls in love with a girl on a poster.

A small-scale, lackadaisical comedy, amiable enough in its casual way.

w Luc Van Beek   d Hans Van Beek, Luc Van Beek ph Peter de Bont   m Bert Hermelink   ad Harry Ammerlaan   ed Wim Louwrier

René Van 'Thof, Simone Walraven, Glenn Durfort, Guusje Van Tilborgh, Bridget George, Joke Tjalsma, Lou Landré, Heleen Van Meurs

Donovan's Brain *
US   1953   81m   bw
UA/Dowling (Tom Gries)

An unscrupulous tycoon is fatally injured, but his brain is kept alive by a surgeon who finds himself dominated by it.

Modest competence marks this version of a much filmed novel, with quiet suspense and a firm central performance.

wd Felix Feist   novel Curt Siodmak   ph Joseph Biroc   m Eddie Dunstedter

Lew Ayres, Gene Evans, Nancy Davis, Steve Brodie, Lisa K. Howard

Donovan's Reef
US   1963   108m   Technicolor
Paramount (John Ford)

War veterans settle down on a South Sea island; when the daughter of one of them comes to visit, his reputation must be protected.

Good-humoured but finally enervating mixture of rough-house and slapstick, with the appearance of an old friends' benefit and the director in familiar sub-standard form.

w Frank Nugent, James Edward Grant   d John Ford ph William H. Clothier   m Cyril Mockridge

John Wayne, Lee Marvin, Jack Warden, Elizabeth Allen, Dorothy Lamour, Cesar Romero, Mike Mazurki

Don's Party *
Australia   1976   90m   Eastmancolor
Miracle/Double Head/AFC (Philip Adams)
V, V*

In suburban Sydney, a political celebration party turns into a pretence of wife-swapping.

Fairly acute observation of middle-class antipodean mores, interrupted with predictable bouts of antipodean crudeness.

w David Williamson   play David Williamson d Bruce Beresford

Ray Barrett, Clare Binney, Pat Bishop, Graeme Blundell, John Hargreaves

Don't Bother to Knock *
US   1952   76m   bw
TCF (Julian Blaustein)
V*

A deranged girl gets a baby-sitting job in a hotel and terrifies all concerned by threatening to kill her charge.

Curious vehicle for the emergent Monroe, who is not up to it, as who would be? Technical credits par, but entertainment value small.

w Daniel Taradash   novel Charlotte Armstrong d Roy Baker   ph Lucien Ballard   m Lionel Newman

Marilyn Monroe, Richard Widmark, Anne Bancroft, Donna Corcoran, Jeanne Cagney, Lurene Tuttle, Jim Backus, Elisha Cook Jnr

Don't Bother to Knock
GB   1961   89m   Technicolor   Cinemascope
ABP/Haileywood (Frank Godwin)
V
US title: Why Bother to Knock

A Casanova travel agent gives each of his girlfriends a key to his Edinburgh flat.

Poorly developed and self-conscious sex farce.

w Dennis Cannan, Frederick Gotfurt, Frederic Raphael   novel Clifford Hanley   d Cyril Frankel ph Geoffrey Unsworth   m Elisabeth Lutyens

Richard Todd, Judith Anderson, Elke Sommer, June Thorburn, Nicole Maurey, Rik Battaglia, Eleanor Summerfield, John Le Mesurier

Don't Drink the Water
US   1969   100m   Berkeley Pathé
Avco Embassy (Jack Rollins, Charles H. Joffe)
V*

Americans, visiting Europe for the first time, are stranded in Bulgaria, where they are mistaken for spies and forced to take refuge in the American embassy staffed by incompetents.

Frenetic and stagey version of the play, with broad acting that diminishes what is left of the comedy.

w R. S. Allen, Harvey Bullock   play Woody Allen d Howard Morris   ph Harvey Genkins   m Pat Williams   ad Robert Gundlach   ed Ralph Rosenblum

Jackie Gleason, Estelle Parsons, Ted Bessell, Joan Delaney, Michael Constantine, Howard St John, Danny Meehan

Don't Ever Leave Me
GB   1949   85m   bw
Triton/Rank

A kidnapped teenager falls for her abductor.

No Orchids for Miss Blandish played as a family comedy; quite unmemorable.

w Robert Westerby   novel The Wide Guy by Anthony Armstrong   d Arthur Crabtree

Jimmy Hanley, Petula Clark, Edward Rigby, Hugh Sinclair, Linden Travers, Anthony Newley

Don't Give Up the Ship
US   1959   89m   bw
Hal Wallis (Paramount)
V*

A dim-witted naval lieutenant is accused of stealing a destroyer.

Feeble American service farce.

w Herbert Baker, Edmund Beloin, Henry Garson d Norman Taurog

Jerry Lewis, Dina Merrill, Diana Spencer, Mickey Shaughnessy, Robert Middleton, Gale Gordon

Don't Go Near the Water *
US   1957   107m   Metrocolor   Cinemascope
MGM/Avon (Lawrence Weingarten)

The US Navy sets up a public relations unit on a South Pacific island.

Loosely cemented service farce full of fumbling lieutenants and bumbling commanders, a more light-hearted M*A*S*H. Boring romantic interludes separate some very funny farcical sequences.

w Dorothy Kingsley, George Wells   novel William Brinkley   d Charles Walters   ph Robert Bronner m Bronislau Kaper

Glenn Ford, Fred Clark, Gia Scala, Romney Brent, Mickey Shaughnessy, Earl Holliman, Anne Francis, Keenan Wynn, Eva Gabor, Russ Tamblyn, Jeff Richards, Mary Wickes

'Drop everything! And see the cheekiest comedy of the year!'
Don't Just Lie There, Say Something!
GB   1973   91m   Eastmancolor
Comocroft/Rank

By a strange chapter of accidents, a politician finds himself in bed with his under-secretary and a lady not his wife.

Stupefying from-the-stalls rendering of a successful stage farce; in this form it simply doesn't work.

w Michael Pertwee   play Michael Pertwee   d Bob Kellett

Brian Rix, Leslie Phillips, Joan Sims, Joanna Lumley, Derek Royle, Peter Bland

Don't Just Stand There
US   1967   99m   Techniscope
Universal (Stan Margulies)

A mild-mannered watch smuggler gets himself involved with kidnapping, murder, and finishing a sex novel.

Frantic but ineffective farce which keeps on the move but does not arrive anywhere.

w Charles Williams   novel The Wrong Venus by Charles Williams   d Ron Winston   ph Milton Krasner   m Nick Perito

Mary Tyler Moore, Robert Wagner, Barbara Rhoades, Glynis Johns, Harvey Korman

'Paris locations might have helped, but we're stuck with the San Fernando Valley.' – Robert Windeler

'The Kings of Rock are rollin' back to the screen in their biggest!'
Don't Knock the Rock *
US   1956   84m   bw
Columbia/Clover (Sam Katzman)

A singer returns to his home town to show adults that rock is harmless fun.

Cheap exploitation movie, most notable for Little Richard's performances of 'Long Tall Sally', 'Rip It Up' and 'Tutti Frutti'.

w Robert E. Kent, James B. Gordon   d Fred F. Sears

Alan Dale, Alan Freed, Bill Haley and the Comets, Jimmy Ballard, Little Richard, the Treniers, Dave Appell and his Applejacks

Don't Look Now ****
GB   1973   110m   Technicolor
BL/Casey/Eldorado (Peter Katz)
V, V*, L, S

After the death of their small daughter, the Baxters meet in Venice two old sisters who claim mediumistic connection with the dead girl. The husband scorns the idea, but repeatedly sees a little red-coated figure in shadowy passages by the canals. Then he confronts it . . .

A macabre short story has become a pretentious and puzzling piece of high cinema art full of vague suggestions and unexplored avenues. Whatever its overall deficiencies, it is too brilliant in surface detail to be dismissed. Depressingly but fascinatingly set in wintry Venice, it has to be seen to be appreciated.

w Allan Scott, Chris Bryant   story Daphne du Maurier   d Nicolas Roeg   ph Anthony Richmond m Pino D'Onnagio   ad Giovanni Soccol

Donald Sutherland, Julie Christie, Hilary Mason, Clelia Matania, Massimo Serrato

'The fanciest, most carefully assembled enigma yet seen on the screen.' – *New Yorker*

'A powerful and dazzling visual texture.' – *Penelope Houston*

Don't Look Now . . . We're Being Shot At! *
France 1966 130m Eastmancolor Panavision
Les Films Corona (Robert Dorfmann)
original title: *La Grande Vadrouille*

During World War II three members of a British bomber crew bale out over Paris and make a frantic escape to the free zone by means of various wild disguises.

Freewheeling star farce, a shade lacking in control, but with some funny sequences.

wd Gérard Oury   *ph* Claude Renoir   *m* Georges Auric

Terry-Thomas, Bourvil, Louis de Funès, Claudio Brook, Mike Marshall

'Both the sight gags and the characters evoke pale echoes of Laurel and Hardy, but it is not familiarity that breeds contempt here so much as the debasement of the familiar.' – *MFB*

Don't Lose Your Head: see *Carry On – Don't Lose Your Head*

Don't Make Waves
US 1967 97m Metrocolor Panavision
MGM/Filmways (Julian Bercovici)

A swimming-pool salesman attempts to get his own back on an impulsive young woman who has wrecked his car.

Malibu beach farce for immature adults, made by professionals helpless in the face of a weak script, but boasting a funny climax with a house teetering on the edge of a cliff.

w Ira Wallach, George Kirgo   *novel Muscle Beach* by Ira Wallach   *d* Alexander Mackendrick   *ph* Philip Lathrop   *m* Vic Mizzy

Tony Curtis, Claudia Cardinale, Robert Webber, Joanna Barnes, Sharon Tate, Jim Backus, Mort Sahl

Don't Move, Die and Rise Again!: see *Zamri, Umri, Voskresni!*

Don't Open the Window: see *The Living Dead at the Manchester Morgue*

Dracula versus Frankenstein (dubbed)
Spain/West Germany/Italy 1971 87m Eastmancolor
Totalvision
Monarch/Eichberg/International Jaguar/Jaime Prades
aka: *El Hombre que Vino de Ummo*

Aliens attempt to conquer Earth by reviving Dracula, Frankenstein's monster, the Mummy and a werewolf.

Dire mix of horror and science fiction, cheaply and unimaginatively made.

w Jacinto Molina Alvarez   *d* Tulio Demichelli   *ph* Godofredo Pachecho   *m* Franco Salina   *ad* Adolfo Cofiño   *sp* Antonio Molna   *ed* Emilio Rodriguez

Michael Rennie, Karin Dor, Craig Hill, Patty Sheppard, Paul Naschi

'The film's sole claim on anyone's attention is the unabashed sadism of several sequences . . . As for the English title, Dracula and Frankenstein are never in the same shot together, let alone in conflict.' – *Tony Rayns*

Don't Open till Christmas
GB 1983 86m colour
21st Century

A maniac goes about killing Father Christmases.

Tawdry horror film of marginal interest because of subject and cast.

w Derek Ford, Al McGoohan   *d* Edmund Purdom

Edmund Purdom, Alan Lake, Gerry Sundquist, Belinda Mayne, Mark Jones

Don't Panic, Chaps!
GB 1959 85m bw
Columbia/Hammer/ACT (Teddy Baird)

British and German units are sent to set up observation posts on the same Adriatic island, and agree to sit out the war in comfort.

An ingenious idea is ill-served by a poorly written script and a rather bored cast.

w Jack Davies   *story* Michael Corston, Ronald Holroyd   *d* George Pollock   *ph* Arthur Graham   *m* Philip Green   *ad* Scott MacGregor   *ed* Harry Aldous

Dennis Price, George Cole, Thorley Walters, Harry Fowler, Nicholas Phipps, Percy Herbert, Nadja Regin

'The fun never sets on the British Empire!'
Don't Raise the Bridge, Lower the River
GB 1967 100m Technicolor
Columbia/Walter Shenson
V*

An American turns his English wife's home into a discotheque.

Dreary comedy apparently intent on proving that its star can be just as unfunny abroad as at home.

w Max Wilk   *d* Jerry Paris   *ph* Otto Heller   *m* David Whitaker

Jerry Lewis, Terry-Thomas, Jacqueline Pearce, Bernard Cribbins, Patricia Routledge, Nicholas Parsons, Michael Bates

Don't Take it to Heart *
GB 1944 90m bw
GFD/Two Cities (Sydney Box)

A genial castle ghost is unleashed by a bomb and affects the love affair of a researcher with the daughter of the house.

Amiably lunatic British-upper-class extravaganza with eccentric characters and some felicitous moments.

wd Jeffrey Dell   *ph* Eric Cross   *m* Mischa Spoliansky

Richard Greene, *Edward Rigby*, Patricia Medina, Alfred Drayton, Richard Bird, Wylie Watson, Moore Marriott, Brefni O'Rourke, Amy Veness, Claude Dampier, Joan Hickson, Joyce Barbour, Ronald Squire, Ernest Thesiger

'A cheerful and rewarding entertainment.' – *Richard Mallett, Punch*

'Not funny accidental but funny deliberate, and nine times out of ten the joke comes off.' – *Observer*

Don't Tell Her It's Me
US 1990 102m CFI
Rank/Sovereign (George Braunstein, Ron Hamady)
V, V*, L

A romantic novelist persuades her wimpish brother, who is recovering from radiation treatment, to pretend to be a biker in order to get a girlfriend.

Trivial, depressingly unsubtle comedy with matching performances.

w Sarah Bird   *novel The Boyfriend School* by Sarah Bird   *d* Malcolm Mowbray   *ph* Reed Smoot   *m* Michael Gore   *pd* Linda Pearl, Daryl Kerrigan   *ed* Marshall Harvey

Shelley Long, Steve Guttenberg, Jami Gertz, Kyle MacLachlan, Madchen Amick, Kevin Scannell

'Takes the germ of an amusing notion about the division between realistic and fantastic romantic hero and hammers it painfully into the ground.' – *Kim Newman, Sight and Sound*

'Grotesquely unfunny comedy.' – *Variety*

Don't Tell Mom the Babysitter's Dead
US 1991 105m DeLuxe
Warner/HBO/Cinema Plus/Outlaw/Mercury/Douglas (Robert Newmyer, Brian Reilly, Jeffrey Silver)
V, V*, L

A young girl supports her siblings while their mother is away on holiday.

Lamentably silly comedy.

w Neil Landau, Tara Ison   *d* Stephen Herek   *ph* Tim Suhrstedt   *m* David Newman, Brian Nazarian   *pd* Stephen Marsh   *ed* Larry Bock

Christina Applegate, Joanna Cassidy, John Getz, Josh Charles, Keith Coogan, Concetta Tomei, David Duchovny, Kimmy Robertson

'Starts with the enjoyable, if crude, black comedy situation promised by the title, but then it turns into an incredibly dumb teenage girl's fantasy of making it in the business world. Even backward teenagers won't fall for this knuckle-headed release.' —*Variety*

Don't Trust Your Husband
US 1948 90m bw
James Nasser/United Artists

An executive conceals from his wife the sex of the client with whom he has to spend a lot of time.

Ho-hum comedy with a laborious plotline and a flagging cast.

w Lou Breslow, Joseph Hoffman   *d* Lloyd Bacon

Fred MacMurray, Madeleine Carroll, Charles Rogers

The Doolins of Oklahoma
US 1949 90m bw
Harry Joe Brown/Columbia
V*
GB title: *The Great Manhunt*

When his old gang claims his return to lawlessness, Bill Doolin walks into the sheriff's guns rather than cause his wife unhappiness.

Moderate Western with an unusually less-than-sympathetic role for its star.

w Kenneth Gamet   *d* Gordon Douglas

Randolph Scott, George Macready, Louise Allbritton, John Ireland, Noah Beery Jnr, Dona Drake

Doomed: see *Ikiru*

The Doomed Battalion *
US/Germany 1932 74m bw
Universal

Austrians fight Italians high in the Alps.

Interesting but not very effective attempt to internationalize a German 'bergfilm'.

w Luis Trenker, Carl Hartl   *d* Cyril Gardner

Luis Trenker, Tala Birell, Victor Varconi, Albert Conti, C. Henry Gordon, Gibson Gowland, Henry Armetta, Gustav von Seyffertitz

'Beaucoup snow and ice stuff for hot weather appeal . . . capable of sustaining bally.' – *Variety*

Doomed Cargo: see *Seven Sinners*

Doomed to Die: see *Mr Wong*

Doomwatch
GB 1972 92m colour
Tigon (Tony Tenser)

An investigator of coastal pollution discovers a village in which dumped chemicals have given all the inhabitants a distorting disease called acromegaly.

An unsatisfactory horror film is drawn from a moderately serious TV series about ecology.

w Clive Exton   *d* Peter Sasdy   *ph* Kenneth Talbot   *m* John Scott

Ian Bannen, Judy Geeson, John Paul, Simon Oates,
George Sanders, Percy Herbert, Geoffrey Keen,
Joseph O'Conor

The Door in the Wall *
GB   1956   29m   Technicolor   Vistavision
AB Pathé/BFI/Lawrie (Howard Thomas)

A man is obsessed by a childhood dream of a green
door which leads into a beautiful garden.

The story is chosen to experiment with Dynamic
Frame, a system in which the picture changes shape
and size according to the subject matter. In this case
the results are entertaining enough.

wd Glenn H. Alvey Jnr   *ph* Jo Jago   *m* James
Bernard

Stephen Murray, Ian Hunter

The Door with Seven Locks
GB   1940   89m   bw
Rialto (John Argyle)
V*
US title: *Chamber of Horrors*

A mad doctor abducts an heiress in the hope of
gaining her wealth.

Old-fashioned barnstormer, ineptly made.

w Norman Lee, John Argyle, Gilbert Gunn
novel Edgar Wallace   *d* Norman Lee   *ph* Desmond
Dickinson

Leslie Banks, Lilli Palmer, Romilly Lunge, Gina Malo,
Richard Bird, David Horne, Cathleen Nesbitt

'The Ceremony Is About To Begin.'
The Doors **
US   1991   134m   DeLuxe   Panavision
Guild/Carolco/Imagine (Bill Graham, Sasha Harari, A. Kitman
Ho)
V, V*, L, S

A film school drop-out and poet becomes a drug-
abusing, self-destructive rock star.

Despite the title, the focus of this grandiose biopic is
The Door's singer Jim Morrison. Fans will enjoy it
most; others are likely to find it noisy, overlong and
over-busy.

w J. Randal Johnson, Oliver Stone   *d* Oliver Stone
ph Robert Richardson   *m* The Doors   *pd* Barbara
Ling   *ed* David Brenner, Joe Hutching

Val Kilmer, Frank Whaley, Kevin Dillon, Meg Ryan,
Kyle MacLachlan, Billy Idol, Dennis Burkley, Josh
Evans, Michael Madsen, Michael Wincott, Kathleen
Quinlan

'It is folly to lavish $40 million (that's $10 million a
Door!) and 2hr 15 min. of your time on a proposition –
some guys can't handle fame – that was evident two
decades ago. Maybe it was fun to bathe in decadence
back then. But this is no time to wallow in that mire.'
– Richard Corliss, Time

Doorway to Hell
US   1930   79m (approx)   bw
Warner
GB title: *A Handful of Clouds*

A young gangster tries to go straight but is driven
back into crime.

Vividly written but dramatically evasive crime-does-
not-pay story, trying to eat its cake and have it.

w George Rosener   *story* A Handful of Clouds by
Rowland Brown   *d* Archie Mayo   *ph* Barney
McGill   *md* Leo Forbstein

Lew Ayres, Charles Judels, James Cagney, Dorothy
Matthews, Leon Janney, Robert Elliott

'Swell gang picture, handled so as to just slip by the
censors.' – Variety

AAN: original story

Dop Bey Kuan Wan: see *One Armed Boxer*

Doppelganger: see *Journey to the Far Side of the Sun*

Doro No Kawa: see *Muddy River*

Dorp aan de Rivier: see *Doctor in the Village*

Dosshouse *
GB   1933   53m   bw
MGM/Sound City (John Baxter)

An escaped convict is captured by a reporter and
detective posing as tramps.

Low-budget featurette which deserves a footnote in
film history for its social consciousness, rare at the
time, especially in the dosshouse scenes.

w Herbert Ayres   *d* John Baxter   *ph* George Stretton
md Colin Wark   *ad* D. W. L. Daniels
ed R. Gardener, R. Swan

Frank Cellier, Arnold Bell, Herbert Franklyn, J.
Hubert Leslie

The Double: see *Kagemusha*

Double Bunk
GB   1961   92m   bw
British Lion/Bryanston (George H. Brown)

Newlyweds live in an old houseboat.

Thin comedy which turns out not to be leakproof.

wd C. M. Pennington-Richards

Ian Carmichael, Janette Scott, Liz Frazer, Sid James,
Dennis Price, Reginald Beckwith, Irene Handl, Noel
Purcell, Naunton Wayne

Double Confession
GB   1950   85m   bw
ABP/Harry Reynolds

At a seaside resort, a man finds his wife dead and tries
to frame her lover, but becomes confused with two
real murderers with a different purpose.

Confused and unlikely melodrama which signally
lacks the ancient mariner's eye.

w William Templeton   *novel* All on a Summer's Day by
John Garden   *d* Ken Annakin   *ph* Geoffrey
Unsworth   *m* Benjamin Frankel

Derek Farr, Peter Lorre, William Hartnell, Joan
Hopkins, Naunton Wayne, Ronald Howard, Kathleen
Harrison, Leslie Dwyer, Edward Rigby

Double Crime in the Maginot Line
France   1939   83m   bw
Felix Gandera

A spy is discovered in the French system of
international fortifications.

A topical melodrama which quickly became very
dated indeed.

w Felix Gandera, Robert Bibal   *novel* Pierre Nord
d Felix Gandera

Victor Francen, Jacques Baumer, Vera Korene,
Fernand Fabre

Double Crossbones
US   1950   75m   Technicolor
Universal-International

Circumstances force our hero to assume the identity of
a pirate, in which disguise he rescues a fair lady.

Lamebrained burlesque unworthy of its star.

w Oscar Brodney   *d* Charles T. Barton

Donald O'Connor, Helena Carter, Will Geer, John
Emery, Hope Emerson, Charles McGraw, Alan Napier

Double Deal
Australia   1981   90m   colour   Panavision
Rychemond Film Productions (Brian Kavanagh, Lynn Barker)
V*

A wealthy businessman plans an elaborate scheme to
rid himself of his disenchanted wife.

Silly thriller in the style of *Sleuth*.

wd Brian Kavanagh   *ph* Ross Berryman   *m* Bruce
Smeaton   *ad* Jill Eden   *ed* Tim Lewis

Louis Jourdan, Angela Punch McGregor, Diane Craig,
Warwick Comber, Peter Cummins, Bruce Spence,
June Jago, Kerry Walker

'Frankenstein, Dracula and other screen monsters pale by
comparison with this fiendish, decadent woman!'
Double Door
US   1934   75m   bw
Paramount

A selfish, wealthy Fifth Avenue spinster takes a
dislike to her brother's girlfriend and locks her up in a
vault.

Silly, rather boring melodrama which may have
worked on the stage but did not take to the screen.

w Gladys Lehman, Jack Cunningham
play Elizabeth McFadden   *d* Charles Vidor

Mary Morris (the American one), Evelyn Venable,
Kent Taylor, Sir Guy Standing, Anne Revere, Colin
Tapley, Halliwell Hobbes

'Not likely to get anywhere at the b.o. . .. dull, drab
and incredible.' – Variety

Double Dynamite
US   1951 (produced 1948)   80m   bw
RKO (Irving Cummings Jnr)
V*
aka: *It's Only Money*

A bank teller wins a fortune at the race track but is
afraid his winnings will be thought the proceeds of a
bank robbery.

Insultingly mild comedy, nearly saved by a few quips
from Groucho.

w Melville Shavelson, Harry Crane, Leo Rosten
d Irving Cummings   *ph* Robert de Grasse
m Leigh Harline

Frank Sinatra, Jane Russell, Groucho Marx, Don
McGuire, Howard Freeman

Double Harness
US   1933   70m   bw
RKO

A girl sets out to trick a rich man into marriage.

Mildly amusing comedy which in its time was
considered risqué.

w Jane Murfin   *play* Edward Montgomery   *d* John
Cromwell

Ann Harding, William Powell, Henry Stephenson,
Lillian Bond, Reginald Owen, George Meeker, Kay
Hammond

'Managed with such reticence that at no time is there a
note of offence . . . this class actress again triumphs
over her surroundings, and the picture will please her
large following.' – Variety

'Twin brothers torn apart by violence. On a mission of
revenge. One packs a punch. One packs a piece.
Together they deliver . . .'
Double Impact
US   1991   109m   DeLuxe
Columbia TriStar/Stone Group (Ashok Amritaj, Jean-Claude
Van Damme)
V, V*, L, S

Twin brothers, separated when young, get together
when grown up to avenge their parents' murder by
gangsters.

Two Van Dammes for the price of one merely doubles
the incoherence of this otherwise ordinary martial arts
movie.

w Sheldon Lettich, Jean-Claude Van Damme
story Sheldon Lettich, Jean-Claude Van Damme,
Steve Meerson, Peter Krikes   *d* Sheldon Lettich
ph Richard Kline   *m* Arthur Kempel   *pd* John Jay
Moore   *ed* Mark Conte, Brent White

Jean-Claude Van Damme, Geoffrey Lewis, Alan Scarfe, Alonna Shaw, Cory Everson, Philip Can Yan Kin, Bolo Yeung, Sarah-Jane Varley

'Turns on a typically lame revenge plot while dragging out unimaginatively shot action sequences until no one will give a good Van Damme. Tedious story-telling should mute the pic's b.o. impact.' – *Variety*

'You can't kiss away a murder!'
Double Indemnity ****
US   1944   107m   bw
Paramount (Joseph Sistrom)
V*, L

An insurance agent connives with the glamorous wife of a client to kill her husband and collect.

Archetypal *film noir* of the forties, brilliantly filmed and incisively written, perfectly capturing the decayed Los Angeles atmosphere of a Chandler novel but using a simpler story and more substantial characters. The hero/villain was almost a new concept.

w Billy Wilder, Raymond Chandler   *novel* James M. Cain   *d* Billy Wilder   *ph* John Seitz   *m* Miklos Rozsa

Fred MacMurray, Barbara Stanwyck, Edward G. Robinson, Tom Powers, Porter Hall, Jean Heather, Byron Barr, Richard Gaines

opening narration: Office memorandum. Walter Neff to Barton T. Keyes, Claims Manager, Los Angeles, July 16, 1938. Dear Keyes: I suppose you'll call this a confession when you hear it. Well, I don't like the word confession. I just want to set you right about something you couldn't see because it was smack up against your nose . . . I killed Dietrichson. Me, Walter Neff, insurance salesman, 35 years old, unmarried, no visible scars. Until a while ago, that is . . .

'The sort of film which revives a critic from the depressive effects of bright epics about the big soul of America or the suffering soul of Europe and gives him a new lease of faith.' – *Richard Winnington*

'The most pared-down and purposeful film ever made by Billy Wilder.' – *John Coleman, 1966*

'Profoundly, intensely entertaining.' – *Richard Mallett, Punch*

'One of the highest summits of *film noir* . . . without a single trace of pity or love.' – *Charles Higham, 1971*

AAN: best picture; script, direction; John Seitz; Miklos Rozsa; Barbara Stanwyck

Double Indemnity (1956): see *The River's Edge*

'This woman inspired him – this woman feared him!'
A Double Life **
US   1947   103m   bw
Universal/Kanin Productions (Michael Kanin)
V*

An actor playing Othello is obsessed by the role and murders a woman he imagines to be Desdemona.

An old theatrical chestnut (cf *Men Are Not Gods*) is decked out with smartish backstage dialogue but despite a pleasant star performance remains unrewarding if taxing, and the entertainment value of the piece is on the thin side considering the mighty talents involved.

w Ruth Gordon, Garson Kanin   *d* George Cukor   *ph* Milton Krasner   *m* Miklos Rozsa

Ronald Colman, Shelley Winters, Signe Hasso, Edmond O'Brien, Millard Mitchell

'As a piece of film story-telling it is generally skilled. Yet the central situation is artificial.' – *Dilys Powell*

AA: Miklos Rozsa; Ronald Colman

AAN: Ruth Gordon, Garson Kanin; George Cukor

The Double Life of Véronique **
France/Poland   1991   98m   colour
Gala/Sidéral/Canal Plus/TOR/Norsk Film (Leonardo de la Fuente)
V, S
original title: *La Double Vie de Véronique*

Two young women, one Polish, the other French, seem to share a single existence.

A complex, finely acted and directed puzzle of a film, but one that grips the attention throughout.

w Krzysztof Kieślowski, Krzysztof Piesiewicz   *d* Krzysztof Kieślowski   *ph* Slawomir Idziak   *m* Zbigniew Preisner   *pd* Patrice Mercier, Halina Dobrowolska   *ed* Jacques Witta

Irène Jacob, Halina Gryglaszewska, Kalina Jedrusik, Aleksander Bardini, Wladyslaw Kowalski, Jerzy Gudejko

'Despite pic's many-splendoured outbursts of filmic creativity and intense emotion, final result remains a head-scratching cipher with blurred edges.' – *Variety*

The Double McGuffin *
US   1979   100m   colour
Mulberry Square/Joe Camp
V*

Kids turn into amateur detectives when they find that a visiting foreign leader is to be assassinated.

Barely tolerable lightweight mystery for an audience which probably doesn't exist.

wd Joe Camp   *ph* Don Reddy   *m* Euel Box   *pd* Harland Wright

Ernest Borgnine, George Kennedy, Elke Sommer, Rod Browning

The Double Man *
GB   1967   105m   Technicolor
Warner/Hal E. Chester

A CIA agent investigates the death of his son on a Swiss skiing holiday and finds the murder was a lure to get him there so that an enemy lookalike can substitute for him.

Rather ruthless but good-looking and generally watchable spy melodrama.

w Frank Tarloff, Alfred Hayes   *novel* Henry S. Maxfield   *d* Franklin Schaffner   *ph* Denys Coop   *m* Ernie Freeman

Yul Brynner, Clive Revill, Anton Diffring, Britt Ekland, Moira Lister

Double Negative
Canada   1980   96m   colour
Quadrant
V*

A photo journalist tries to find the murderer of his wife, and discovers he's an amnesiac and did it himself.

Ho-hum mystery thriller centring on an ancient wheeze; treatment resolutely plodding.

w Thomas Hedley Jnr, Janis Allen, Charles Dennis   *novel* The Three Roads by Ross Macdonald   *d* George Bloomfield

Michael Sarrazin, Susan Clark, Anthony Perkins, Howard Duff, Kate Reid

Double or Nothing
US   1937   90m   bw
Paramount

Inheritors under a trick will must double their bequests or lose them.

Flat comedy with music; none of the elements are really up to scratch.

w Charles Lederer and others   *d* Theodore Reed

Bing Crosby, Martha Raye, Andy Devine, William Frawley, Mary Carlisle, Benny Baker

'Due for big openings and tapering-off business. Will squeeze through.' – *Variety*

Double Wedding
US   1937   87m   bw
MGM (Joseph L. Mankiewicz)

A bohemian artist makes a play for the lady of his choice by romancing her sister.

Zany star comedy which doesn't quite come off.

w Jo Swerling   *play* Great Love by Ferenc Folnar   *d* Richard Thorpe   *ph* William Daniels   *m* Edward Ward

William Powell, Myrna Loy, John Beal, Florence Rice, Jessie Ralph, Edgar Kennedy, Sidney Toler, Barnett Parker, Katherine Alexander, Donald Meek

'OK for topflight business . . . would be funnier if it were shorter.' – *Variety*

Double Whoopee **
US   1928   20m   bw   silent
Hal Roach

Incompetent doormen at a swank hotel cause havoc.

Simple-minded but pleasing star farce.

w Leo McCarey, H. M. Walker   *d* Lewis R. Foster   *ph* George Stevens, Jack Roach *ed* Richard Currier

Laurel and Hardy, Jean Harlow, Charlie Hall

Double X
GB   1991   97m   Technicolor
Feature/String of Pearls (Shani S. Grewal)
V

A reformed safebreaker asks a former Chicago cop-turned-hitman to help him rescue his kidnapped daughter from a vicious gangleader.

Dismal thriller, with a dreary plot and uninspired direction and acting, which suggests that the British film industry is bent on committing ritual suicide.

wd Shani S. Grewal   *story* Vengeance by David Fleming   *ph* Dominique Grosz   *m* Raf Ravenscroft   *pd* Colin Pocock   *ed* Michael Johns

Simon Ward, William Katt, Norman Wisdom, Bernard Hill, Gemma Craven, Leon Herbert, Derren Nesbit, Vladek Sheybal, Chloe Annett

'An inept low-budget suspenser. Reliable cast is double-crossed by a laughable script and clumsy heiming. Result, which hardly cuts it even as a TV pic, should expire fast.' – *Variety*

Doubting Thomas
US   1935   78m   bw
Fox
V*

Small-town 'society' puts on an amateur show.

Slight but attractive star vehicle.

w William Conselman, Bartlett Cormack   *novel* The Torch Bearers by George Kelly   *d* David Butler

Will Rogers, Billie Burke, Alison Skipworth, Sterling Holloway, Andrew Tombes, Gail Patrick

'There is one thing that Rogers knows, and that is how to get laughs with any sort of a situation, and he didn't learn that just from reading the papers.' – *Variety*

Douce *
France   1943   106m   bw
Société Parisienne de l'Industrie Cinématographique

In 1887 Paris a sheltered young rich girl falls for a steward and encounters family opposition.

A charming old-fashioned story which provides a well-taken opportunity for a portrait of the old bourgeoisie.

w Jean Aurenche, Pierre Bost   *d* Claude Autant-Lara   *ph* Gaston Thonnart   *m* René Cloërc

Odette Joyeux, Jean Debucourt, Marguerite Moreno, Roger Pigaut, Madeleine Robinson

'Direction and camerawork constantly reveal touches of felicity.' – MFB

Doucement Les Basses: see *Take It Easy*

Doughboys *
US 1930 80m approx bw
MGM/Buster Keaton (Lawrence Weingarten)
V*
GB title: *Forward March*

A young eccentric joins the army.

Simple-minded farce with a few good routines for the star.

w Richard Schayer d Edward Sedgwick
ph Leonard Smith

Buster Keaton, Sally Eilers, Cliff Edwards, Edward Brophy

'Keaton's first talker is comedy with a kick.' – *Variety*

The Doughgirls *
US 1944 102m bw
Warner (Mark Hellinger)

In a crowded wartime Washington hotel, a honeymoon is frustrated by constant interruption, not to mention the discovery that the wedding was not legal.

Frantic farce, generally well adapted, and certainly played with gusto.

w James V. Kern, Sam Hellman play Joseph Fields
d James V. Kern ph Ernest Haller m Adolph Deutsch

Alexis Smith, Jane Wyman, Jack Carson, Ann Sheridan, Irene Manning, *Eve Arden*, Charlie Ruggles, John Alexander, John Ridgely, Craig Stevens, Alan Mowbray, Donald MacBride

'There's nothing so good in it that you must attend, just as there is nothing bad enough to keep you away.' – *Archer Winsten*

The Dove *
US 1968 15m bw
Coe/Davis Ltd

Back in the countryside of his childhood, a Nobel prize winner recalls the events of a summer . . .

Elaborate Ingmar Bergman spoof complete with subtitles and pidgin Swedish. Hilarious at the time for those who had just seen *Wild Strawberries*.

w Sidney Davis d George Coé, Anthony Lover

David Zirlin, George Coe, Pamela Burrell

The Dove *
US 1974 104m Technicolor Panavision
St George Productions (Gregory Peck)
V*

Yachtsman Robin Lee Graham makes a five-year voyage around the world.

Bland, rather stolid adventure story for boat-niks, based on real incidents; good to look at.

w Peter Beagle, Adam Kennedy book Robin Lee Graham, Derek Gill d Charles Jarrott ph Sven Nykvist m John Barry

Joseph Bottoms, Deborah Raffin, John McLiam, Dabney Coleman

'Postcard views flick by to the strains of a saccharine score.' – *David McGillivray*

The Dover Road: see *Where Sinners Meet*

Down Among the Sheltering Palms
US 1952 86m Technicolor
TCF (Fred Kohlmar)

An American army unit takes over a South Sea island, but fraternization is forbidden.

Tolerable comedy-musical with familiar jokes and situations.

w Claude Binyon, Albert Lewin, Burt Styler
d Edmund Goulding ph Leon Shamroy m Leigh Harline m/y Harold Arlen, Ralph Blane

William Lundigan, Jane Greer, Mitzi Gaynor, David Wayne, Gloria de Haven, Gene Lockhart, Jack Paar, Billy Gilbert

Down and Out in Beverly Hills *
US 1985 97m Technicolor
Touchstone (Paul Mazursky)
V, V*, L

A wandering con artist is taken in by an insecure Beverly Hills family.

Somewhat bumbling but sporadically effective rehash of Renoir's *Boudu Sauvé des Eaux* (qv), with a few modern jabs and effectively eccentric performances.

w Paul Mazursky, Leon Capetanos play René Fauchois d Paul Mazursky ph Donald McAlpine m Andy Summers pd Pato Guzman

Nick Nolte, Richard Dreyfuss, Bette Midler, Little Richard, Tracy Nelson, Elizabeth Pena

'What makes this picture so enjoyable is not the exaggerations of its narrative but the richness of its texture. Every inch of every frame is utilized. While, in the foreground, the actors are doing or saying one thing, behind them a television screen is telling us something else. The audience is completely embroiled in every incident.' – *Quentin Crisp*

Down Argentine Way *
US 1940 94m Technicolor
TCF (Harry Joe Brown)
V*, L

A wealthy American girl falls in love with an Argentinian horse-breeder.

A very moderate musical which happened to bring both Grable and Miranda to star stature and set Fox off on their successful run of forties extravaganzas, reasonably pleasant to look at but empty-headed.

w Karl Tunberg, Darrell Ware d Irving Cummings
ph Ray Rennahan, Leon Shamroy m/y Harry Warren, Mack Gordon ad Richard Day, Joseph C. Wright

Betty Grable, Carmen Miranda, Don Ameche, Charlotte Greenwood, J. Carrol Naish, Henry Stephenson, Leonid Kinskey, The Nicholas Brothers

'I dislike Technicolor in which all pinks resemble raspberry sauce, reds turn to sealing wax, blues shriek of the washtub, and yellows become suet pudding.' – *James Agate*

'So outrageous – that it's hard to believe it isn't at least partly intentional – but why would anybody make this picture on purpose.' – *New Yorker, 1976*

AAN: Ray Rennahan, Leon Shamroy; title song (*m* Harry Warren, *ly* Mack Gordon); art direction

Down by Law *
US 1986 107m bw
Island Pictures/Black Snake/Grokenburger Films (Alan Kleinberg)
V, V*

A disc jockey and a pimp, framed for crimes they did not commit, escape from jail with an Italian who has a minimal grasp of English.

Engaging lowlife comedy.

wd Jim Jarmusch ph Robby Müller m John Lurie, Tom Waits ed Melody London

Tom Waits, John Lurie, Roberto Benigni, Ellen Barkin, Billie Neal, Rockets Redgrave, Vernel Bagneris, Nicoletta Braschi

Down Memory Lane *
US 1949 70m bw
Aubrey Schenck

A kaleidoscope of Mack Sennett comedy shorts,

linked by Steve Allen as a disc jockey. Much Bing Crosby; Fields in *The Dentist;* an appearance by Sennett himself.

d Phil Karlson

Down Three Dark Streets *
US 1954 85m bw
UA/Edward Small (Arthur Gardner, Jules V. Levy)

An FBI agent is shot on duty, and his friend avenges him in the course of clearing up three cases in which he was involved.

Competent, enjoyable police film with three cases for the price of one.

w The Gordons, Bernard C. Schoenfeld book Case File FBI by the Gordons d Arnold Laven ph Joseph Biroc m Paul Sawtell

Broderick Crawford, Ruth Roman, Martha Hyer, Marisa Pavan, Casey Adams, Kenneth Tobey

† One of the first collaborations of the prolific production company Laven-Gardner-Levy.

Down to Earth
US 1932 79m bw

Nouveau riche Americans return from Europe and find themselves misfits at home.

Thin sequel to *They Had to See Paris*.

w Edwin Burke story Homer Croy d David Butler

Will Rogers, Dorothy Jordan, Irene Rich, Matty Kemp, Mary Carlisle

'Will need support . . . the least powerful in draw of all Rogers' pictures.' – *Variety*

Down to Earth *
US 1947 101m Technicolor
Columbia (Don Hartman)
V*, L

The muse Terpsichore comes down to help a Broadway producer fix a new show in which she is featured.

Pleasant but undistinguished musical fantasy, a sequel to *Here Comes Mr Jordan*. The heavenly sequences promise more amusement than they produce.

w Edwin Blum, Don Hartman d Alexander Hall
ph Rudolph Maté m Heinz Roemheld

Rita Hayworth, Larry Parks, Roland Culver (as Mr Jordan), *Edward Everett Horton* (repeating as Messenger 7013), Marc Platt, James Gleason

'Just the film to make the spectator forget the troubles of life.' – *MFB*

'Celestial whimsy musical, with arch acting and a dull score.' – *New Yorker, 1977*

Down to the Sea in Ships *
US 1948 120m bw
TCF (Elmer Clifton)
V*

An old whaling skipper wants his grandson to follow in his footsteps.

Seagoing spectacle with strong characters; all concerned show Hollywood in its most professional form, but the film somehow fails to catch the imagination or live in the memory.

w John Lee Mahin, Sy Bartlett d Henry Hathaway
ph Joe MacDonald m Alfred Newman

Lionel Barrymore, Dean Stockwell, Richard Widmark, *Cecil Kellaway*, Gene Lockhart

Down Went McGinty: see *The Great McGinty*

Downhill
GB 1927 80m approx (24 fps) bw silent
Gainsborough (Michael Balcon)
US title: *When Boys Leave Home*

A sixth-form schoolboy, accused of theft, is expelled and goes to the bad in Marseilles before being found innocent.

Absurd novelette with only marginal glimpses of the director's emerging talent.

w Eliot Stannard play David Lestrange (Ivor Novello, Constance Collier) d Alfred Hitchcock ph Claude McDonnelled Ivor Montagu

Ivor Novello, Ben Webster, Robin Irvine, Sybil Rhoda, Lillian Braithwaite, Isabel Jeans, Ian Hunter

Famous line: 'Does this mean, sir, that I shall not be able to play for the Old Boys?'

Downhill Racer *
US   1969   101m   Technicolor
Paramount/Wildwood (Richard Gregson)
V*, L

An ambitious American skier gains a place on the team competing in Europe.

Virtually plotless, casually assembled study of a man and a sport, good to look at, often exciting, but just as frequently irritating in its throwaway style.

w James Salter novel Oakley Hall d Michael Ritchie ph Brian Probyn m Kenyon Hopkins

Robert Redford, Gene Hackman, Camilla Sparv, Joe Jay Jalbert, Timothy Kirk, Dabney Coleman

Downstairs
US   1932   77m   bw
MGM

A villainous chauffeur blackmails the other servants.

Failed attempt by a falling star to do something different.

w Melville Baker, Lenore Coffee story John Gilbert d Monta Bell

John Gilbert, Virginia Bruce, Paul Lukas, Hedda Hopper, Reginald Owen, Olga Baclanova

Drachenfutter: see Dragon's Food

'The strangest love a woman has ever known ... a livid face bent over her in the ghostly mist!'
Dracula ***
US   1931   84m   bw
Universal (Carl Laemmle Jnr)
V*, L

A Transylvanian vampire count gets his come-uppance in Yorkshire.

A film which has much to answer for. It started its star and its studio off on horror careers, and it launched innumerable sequels (see below). In itself, after two eerie reels, it becomes a pedantic and slow transcription of a stage adaptation, and its climax takes place offscreen; but for all kinds of reasons it remains full of interest.

w Garrett Fort play Hamilton Deane, John Balderston novel Bram Stoker d Tod Browning ph Karl Freund m Tchaikovsky

Bela Lugosi, Helen Chandler, David Manners, Dwight Frye, Edward Van Sloan

'Must have caused much uncertainty as to the femme fan reaction . . . as it turns out the signs are that the woman's angle is all right and that sets the picture for better than average money . . . it comes out as a sublimated ghost story related with all surface seriousness and above all with a remarkably effective background of creepy atmosphere.' – Variety

'A too literal adaptation of the play (not the book) results in a plodding, talkative development, with much of the vital action taking place off-screen.' – William K. Everson

'The mistiest parts are the best; when the lights go up the interest goes down.' – Ivan Butler

'It'll chill you and fill you with fears. You'll find it creepy and cruel and crazed.' – New York Daily News

† Later advertising variations concentrated on the horror element: 'In all the annals of living horror one name stands out as the epitome of evil! So evil, so fantastic, so degrading you'll wonder if it isn't all a nightmare! Innocent girls lured to a fate truly worse than death!'

† Lugosi was not the first choice for the role of the Count. Ian Keith and William Powell were strongly favoured.

†† Sequels include Dracula's Daughter (qv), Son of Dracula (qv); the later Hammer sequence consists of Dracula (see below), Brides of Dracula (qv), Dracula Prince of Darkness (qv), Dracula Has Risen From the Grave (qv), Taste the Blood of Dracula (qv), Scars of Dracula (qv), Dracula AD 1972 (qv), The Satanic Rites of Dracula (qv). Other associated films in which the Count or a disciple appears include (all qv) Return of the Vampire (1944), House of Frankenstein (1945), House of Dracula (1945), Abbott and Costello Meet Frankenstein (1948), The Return of Dracula (1958), Kiss of the Vampire (1963), The Fearless Vampire Killers (1967), Count Yorga Vampire (1969), Countess Dracula (1970), Vampire Circus (1970), The House of Dark Shadows (1970), Vampire Lovers (1971), Blacula (1972), Dracula (1974), Martin (1978), Dracula (1979), Salem's Lot (1979), Nosferatu The Vampyre (1979), The Hunger (1983), The Lost Boys (1987). Minor potboilers are legion.

'Who will be his bride tonight?'
Dracula ***
GB   1958   82m   Technicolor
Rank/Hammer (Anthony Hinds)
V*, L
US title: Horror of Dracula

A remake of the 1930 film.

Commendably brief in comparison with the later Hammer films, this was perhaps the best horror piece they turned out as well as the most faithful to its original. Decor and colour were well used, and the leading performances are striking.

w Jimmy Sangster, novel Bram Stoker d Terence Fisher ph Jack Asher m James Bernard ad Bernard Robinson ed James Needs, Bill Lenny

Peter Cushing (as Van Helsing), Christopher Lee (as Dracula), Melissa Stribling, Carol Marsh, Michael Gough, John Van Eyssen, Valerie Gaunt, Miles Malleson

Dracula
Italy   1974   93m   colour
V*
aka: Andy Warhol's Dracula
Andrew Braunsberg

In this sick and gory version, Dracula becomes ill if he feasts on anything but pure virgin's blood. The hero saves the heroine in the predictable way.

Not for the squeamish.

wd Paul Morrissey

Udo Kier, Arno Juerging, Vittorio de Sica, Maxime McEmory, Joe Dalessandro

Dracula *
GB   1979   112m   Technicolor   Panavision
Universal/Mirisch (Marvin Mirisch/Tom Pevsner)
V*, L

A lush, expensive and romantic version which presents the count as a matinee idol and spends too much time on the romantic scenes to distract attention from an old old story.

w W. D. Richter d John Badham ph Gilbert Taylor m John Williams pd Peter Murton

Frank Langella, Laurence Olivier, Donald Pleasence, Kate Nelligan, Trevor Eve

'A triumphantly lurid creation that seems bound to be either under-valued for its circus effects or over-valued for the stylishness with which it steers

between the reefs of camp and theatrical indulgence.' – Richard Combs, MFB

Dracula (1992): see Bram Stoker's Dracula

'The Count is back, with an eye for London's hot pants, and a taste for everything!'
Dracula AD 1972
GB   1972   95m   Eastmancolor
Warner/Hammer (Josephine Douglas)
V

Dracula reappears among Chelsea teenagers practising black magic.

Depressed attempt to update a myth; the link with modern sin makes it seem not only tarnished but tasteless, and the film itself is lamentably short on excitement.

w Don Houghton d Alan Gibson ph Richard Bush m Michael Vickers pd Don Mingaye ed James Needs

Peter Cushing, Christopher Lee, Stephanie Beacham, Michael Coles, Christopher Neame, William Ellis

Dracula contra Frankenstein: see Dracula – Prisoner of Frankenstein

'You just can't keep a good man down!'
Dracula Has Risen from the Grave
GB   1968   92m   Technicolor
Hammer (Aida Young)
V, V*, L

Dracula again terrorizes the village in the shadow of his castle, and is routed by a bishop.

Tedious, confined and repetitive shocker with little conventional action and an unusual emphasis on sex.

w John Elder (Anthony Hinds) d Freddie Francis ph Arthur Grant m James Bernard ad Bernard Robinson ed James Needs, Spencer Reeve

Christopher Lee, Rupert Davies, Veronica Carlson, Barbara Ewing, Barry Andrews, Ewan Hooper

'A bloody bore.' – Judith Crist

Dracula is Alive and Well and Living in London: see The Satanic Rites of Dracula

Dracula Prince of Darkness
GB   1966   90m   Techniscope
Warner/Hammer/Seven Arts (Anthony Nelson-Keys)
V

Stranded travellers are made welcome at the late count's castle by his sinister butler, who proceeds to use the blood of one of them to revivify his master.

Ingenious rehash of incidents from the original story, largely dissipated by poor colour and unsuitable wide screen.

w John Sansom story John Elder d Terence Fisher ph Michael Reed m James Bernard pd Bernard Robinson ed James Needs, Chris Barnes

Christopher Lee, Philip Latham, Barbara Shelley, Thorley Walters, Andrew Keir, Francis Matthews, Suzan Farmer, Charles Tingwell

'Run-of-the-coffin stuff . . . only for ardent fang-and-cross fans.' – Judith Crist

Dracula – Prisoner of Frankenstein (dubbed)
Spain/France   1972   90m   Telecolor
Interfilme/Fenix/Prodif ETS
original title: Dracula contra Frankenstein; aka: The Screaming Dead

Frankenstein revives Dracula in order to create an army of vampires to take over the world.

Horrendous not for its subject matter but for its total incompetence, including an incoherent narrative and a directorial style that consists of meaningless zooms and out-of-focus close-ups. An ailing Price plays

Frankenstein as a somnambulistic zombie and the acting honours go to a rubber bat.

w Jess Franco, Paul D'Ales d Jess Franco (Jesús Franco) ph José Climent m Bruno Nicolai ed R. Aventer

Howard Vernon (Mario Lippert), Dennis Price, Genevieve Deloir, Josiane Gilbert, Albert D'Albes, Mary Francis

Dracula 71: see Bram Stoker's Count Dracula

'More sensational than her unforgettable father!'
Dracula's Daughter **
US   1936   70m   bw
Universal (E. M. Asher)
V*

The daughter of the old count follows his remains to London.

Lively sequel which develops in the manner of a Sherlock Holmes story.

w Garrett Fort d Lambert Hillyer ph George Robinson m Heinz Roemheld

Otto Kruger, Marguerite Churchill, Edward Van Sloan, Gloria Holden, Irving Pichel, Nan Grey, Hedda Hopper, Gilbert Emery, Claud Allister, E. E. Clive, Halliwell Hobbes, Billy Bevan

'There's more to the legend than meets the throat!'
Dracula's Dog
US   1977   88m   DeLuxe
Vic (Albert Band, Frank Ray Perelli)
V, V*
GB title: Zoltan, Hound of Dracula

The resurrected servant of Dracula tries to use his vampire dog to create a new master.

Ingenious but unattractive addition to the saga, with dogs as chief villains; the style varies between spoof and rather nasty horror.

w Frank Ray Perelli d Albert Band ph Bruce Logan m Andrew Belling

José Ferrer, Reggie Nalder, Michael Pataki, Jan Shutan

Dracula versus Frankenstein (dubbed)
Spain/West Germany/Italy   1971   87m   Eastmancolor Totalvision
Monarch/Eichberg/International Jaguar/Jaime Prades
aka: El Hombre que Vino de Ummo

Aliens attempt to conquer Earth by reviving Dracula, Frankenstein's monster, the Mummy and a werewolf.

Dire mix of horror and science fiction, cheaply and unimaginatively made.

w Jacinto Molina Alvarez d Tulio Demichelli ph Godofredo Pachecho m Franco Salina ad Adolfo Cofiño sp Antonio Molna ed Emilio Rodriguez

Michael Rennie, Karin Dor, Craig Hill, Patty Sheppard, Paul Naschi

'The film's sole claim on anyone's attention is the unabashed sadism of several sequences . . . As for the English title, Dracula and Frankenstein are never in the same shot together, let alone in conflict.' – Tony Rayns

Draegerman Courage
US   1937   59m   bw
Warner

Problems of a Nova Scotian gold mine cave-in.

Adequate action fare inspired by a real event. (Draegermen are burrowers.)

w Anthony Coldeway d Louis King

Jean Muir, Barton MacLane, Henry O'Neill, Robert Barrat. Addison Richards, Gordon Oliver

'Vivid and often thrilling.' – Variety

Dragao da Maldade contra o Santo Guerreiro: see Antonio das Mortes

The Dragnet *
US   1928   77m approx (24 fps)   bw   silent
Paramount
V

When his buddy is killed, a detective resigns from the force and takes to the bottle.

Obviously interesting sequel to Underworld. It can't be evaluated because no print is known to exist.

w Jules and Charles Furthman story Night Stick by Oliver H. P. Garrett d Josef von Sternberg ph Harold Rosson ad Hans Dreier

George Bancroft, Evelyn Brent, William Powell, Fred Kohler, Francis MacDonald, Leslie Fenton

Dragnet *
US   1954   93m   Warnercolor
Mark VII (Jack Webb)
V*

Sgt Joe Friday solves the murder of an ex-convict.

Moderately interesting but overlong attempt to transfer television techniques to the big screen; laconic dialogue, question and answer, cheap sets, close-ups and convenient Los Angeles locations.

w Richard Breen d Jack Webb ph Edward Colman m Walter Schumann

Jack Webb, Ben Alexander, Richard Boone, Stacy Harris, Ann Robinson, Virginia Gregg

Dragnet
US   1987   106m   DeLuxe
Universal/Applied Action/Bernie Brillstein
V*, L

The nephew of Sgt Joe Friday gets involved in a murder case.

Overlong parody with some obvious amusements before the whole thing becomes tiresome.

w Dan Aykroyd, Alan Zweibel, Tom Mankiewicz d Tom Mankiewicz ph Matthew F. Leonetti m Ira Newborn pd Robert F. Boyle

Dan Aykroyd, Tom Hanks, Christopher Plummer, Harry Morgan, Alexander Paul, Elizabeth Ashley, Dabney Coleman

Dragon Seed *
US   1944   144m   bw
MGM (Pandro S. Berman)
V*

Chinese peasants fight the Japanese.

Ill-advised attempt to follow the success of The Good Earth; badly cast actors mouth propaganda lines in a mechanical script which provokes more boredom and unintentional laughter than sympathy.

w Marguerite Roberts, Jane Murfin novel Pearl S. Buck d Jack Conway, Harold S. Bucquet ph Sidney Wagner m Herbert Stothart

Katharine Hepburn, Walter Huston, Turhan Bey, Aline MacMahon, Akim Tamiroff, Hurd Hatfield, Frances Rafferty, Agnes Moorehead, Henry Travers, J. Carrol Naish

'A kind of slant-eyed North Star. Often awkward and pretentious, it nevertheless has moments of moral and dramatic grandeur.' – Time

'A fine film in anybody's sweepstakes. It'll wow 'em at the box office.' – Variety (It didn't.)

AAN: Sidney Wagner; Aline MacMahon

'The Mystery. The Life. The Love. The Legend.'
Dragon: The Bruce Lee Story *
US   1993   120m   DeLuxe   Panavision
Universal (Raffaella de Laurentiis)
V, V*, L, S

A boy who trains in martial arts grows up to become a

star of kung-fu movies, haunted by a vision of a dragon representing his inner fears, and dies young.

Enjoyable, if unenlightening, biopic of Bruce Lee that does little to explain why he became the genre's most famous performer, but notable for starring an interesting actor, the unrelated Jason Scott Lee.

w Edward Khmara, John Raffo, Rob Cohen book Bruce Lee: The Man Only I Knew by Linda Lee Cadwell d Rob Cohen ph David Eggby m Randy Edelman pd Robert Ziembicki ed Peter Amundson

Jason Scott Lee, Lauren Holly, Robert Wagner, Michael Learned, Nancy Kwan, Kay Tong Lim, Ric Young, John Cheung

'Seemingly contrary elements and styles nonetheless mesh into an entertaining whole and the result provides extremely touching and haunting material.' – Variety

'It's less about daring deeds than about Lee's triumph over adversity.' – Vincent Canby, New York Times

'Cheerful, downmarket hagiography.' – Derek Malcolm, Guardian

Dragonfly: see One Summer Love

Dragon's Food **
West Germany   1987   75m   bw
Novoskop Film Jan Schutte/Probst Film (Eric Nellessen)
original title: Drachenfutter, aka: Spicy Rice

A Pakistani and a Chinese immigrant struggle to open their own restaurant in Hamburg.

The dialogue mixes half-a-dozen languages, but succeeds in communicating its message of lives wasted by prejudice and intolerance.

w Jan Schutte, Thomas Strittmatter d Jan Schutte ph Lutz Konermann m Claus Bantzer ed Andreas Schreitmiller

Bhaskar, Ric Young, Buddy Uzzaman, Wolf-Dieter Springer, Ulrich Wildgruber

Dragons Forever (dubbed)
Japan   1988   90m   colour
Golden Harvest (Leonard K. C. Ho)
V

A lawyer discovers, when he falls in love, that he is on the wrong side in a case involving pollution and drug-dealing.

Comic martial arts adventure with romantic overtones and spectacular combat, for the undemanding.

w Szeto Cheuk-Hon story Gordon Chan, Leung Yiu Ming d Samo Hung ph Jimmy Leung, Cheung Yiu Tso m James Wong pd Oliver Wong ed Peter Cheung, Josephy Chiang

Jackie Chan, Samo Hung, Yuen Biao, Deannie Yip, Pauline Yeung, Crystal Kwok

'Only sorcery can destroy it!'
Dragonslayer
US   1981   110m   Metrocolor   Panavision
Walt Disney/Paramount (Howard W. Koch, Hal Barwood)
V*, L

A sorcerer's apprentice uses his master's magic amulet to ward off various dangers.

Heavy-going sword-and-sorcery fable, not helped at all by slow plotting and dark photography. The dragons, however, are genuinely fierce.

w Hal Barwood, Matthew Robbins d Matthew Robbins ph Derek Vanlint m Alex North pd Elliot Scott sp Thomas Smith

Peter MacNichol, Caitlin Clarke, Ralph Richardson, John Hallam, Peter Eyre, Albert Salmi

'Verges on the nasty for the nippers; sails too close to déjà vu for fantasy fans.' – Time Out

AAN: Alex North; visual effects (Dennis Muren and others)

Dragonwyck *

US 1946 103m bw
TCF (Darryl F. Zanuck)

In the 1840s a farmer's daughter marries her rich cousin, not knowing that he has poisoned his first wife.

Good-looking but rather tedious romance of the Jane Eyre/Rebecca school: tyrannical recluse, mystery upstairs, spooky house, etc. Heavy going.

wd Joseph L. Mankiewicz novel Anya Seton ph Arthur Miller m Alfred Newman

Gene Tierney, Vincent Price, Glenn Langan, Walter Huston, Anne Revere, Spring Byington, Henry Morgan, Jessica Tandy

Dragoon Wells Massacre *

US 1957 88m DeLuxe CinemaScope
Allied Artists (Lindsley Parsons)

A group of travellers are stranded in hostile Indian territory.

Moderately suspenseful Western on a familiar theme.

w Warren Douglas story Oliver Drake d Harold Schuster ph William Clothier m Paul Dunlap ed Maurice Wright

Barry Sullivan, Dennis O'Keefe, Mona Freeman, Katy Jurado, Sebastian Cabot, Jack Elam

'Car crazy, speed crazy, boy crazy!'

Dragstrip Girl

US 1957 69m bw
AIP/Golden State (Alex Gordon)

Two young hot-rodders are rivals for a new girl in town.

Stalled low-budget drive-in movie, requiring minimal attention from its audience.

w Lou Rusoff d Edward L. Cahn ph Frederick E. West m Ronald Stein ad Don Ament ed Ronald Sinclair

Fay Spain, Steve Terrell, John Ashley, Frank Gorshin, Russ Bender, Tommy Ivo

Drake of England

GB 1935 104m bw
BIP (Walter C. Mycroft)
US titles: Drake the Pirate; Elizabeth of England

Sir Francis Drake is knighted by Queen Elizabeth for his seafaring exploits, and defeats the Spanish Armada.

Stiffly moving historical pageant; you can smell the mothballs.

w Clifford Grey, Akos Tolney, Marjorie Deans, Norman Watson play Drake by Louis N. Parker d Arthur Woods ph Claude Friese-Greene, Ronald Neame, Jack Parker m G. H. Clutsam ad Duncan Sutherland, Clarence Elder ed E. B. Jarvis

Matheson Lang, Athene Seyler, Jane Baxter, Donald Wolfit, Henry Mollison, George Merritt, Amy Veness, Sam Livesey, Ben Webster

Drake the Pirate: see Drake of England

A Drama of Jealousy: see Jealousy Italian Style

Dramatic School *

US 1938 80m bw
MGM (Mervyn Le Roy)

Young actresses compete for success.

Another, less lively, Stage Door; tolerable but not exciting.

w Ernst Vajda, Mary McCall Jnr play School of Drama by Hans Szekely, Zoltan Egyed d Robert B. Sinclair Jnr ph William Daniels m Franz Waxman

Luise Rainer, Paulette Goddard, Alan Marshal, Lana Turner, Anthony Allan (later John Hubbard), Henry Stephenson, Genevieve Tobin, Gale Sondergaard, Melville Cooper, Erik Rhodes, Ann Rutherford, Margaret Dumont, Virginia Grey, Hans Conried

'A disappointing effort which arouses little interest in its unfolding.' – Variety

Dramma della Gelosia – Tutti i Particolari in Cronaca: see Jealousy Italian Style

Drango

US 1957 92m bw
UA/Hall Bartlett

After the Civil War, a Union Army officer is assigned to bring law and order to a Georgia community.

Eccentric, downbeat semi-Western with aspirations to be some kind of film noir; does not come off.

wd Hall Bartlett ph James Wong Howe m Elmer Bernstein

Jeff Chandler, Ronald Howard, Joanne Dru, Julie London, Donald Crisp, John Lupton, Morris Ankrum

The Draughtsman's Contract **

GB 1982 108m colour
BFI/Channel 4 (David Payne)
V*, S

In 1694 a young draughtsman receives a curious commission from a country gentlewoman, his rewards to include bed and bawd.

Pleasantly unusual, stylized puzzle film which involves both sex and murder while maintaining a detached attitude to both. The period costumes help to give it an air of fantasy which was presumably intended.

wd Peter Greenaway ph Curtis Clark m Michael Nyman ed John Wilson

Anthony Higgins, Janet Suzman, Anne Louise Lambert, Neil Cunningham, Hugh Fraser, Dave Hill

'Mannered and idiosyncratic, the speeches are so arch and twitty that they seem to be pitched higher than a dog whistle.' – Pauline Kael, New Yorker

'Perhaps the four-hour version which may one day become available is clearer if not more concise.' – Guardian

'Best enjoyed as a sly piece of double bluff, a puzzle without a solution, an avant garde hoax in the spirit of Dada and the surrealists.' – Observer

Dream Demon

GB 1988 89m colour
Palace (Paul Webster)

A woman begins to have horrific nightmares before her marriage to a hero of the Falklands War.

A moderately effective psychological thriller, though over-reliant on shock effects.

w Harley Cokliss, Christopher Wicking d Harley Cokliss ph Ian Wilson m Bill Nelson pd Hugo Luczyc-Wyhowski ed Ian Crafford, David Martin

Jemma Redgrave, Jimmy Nail, Timothy Spall, Kathleen Wilhoite, Annabelle Lanyon, Susan Fleetwood, Nickolas Grace

'One of this, or any year's, worst . . . proof of the low levels the genre can sink to.' – Stefan Jaworzyn, Shock Xpress

Dream Girl

US 1947 86m bw
Paramount (P. J. Wolfson)

A girl revels in her own romantic dreams, one of which nearly comes true.

Potentially pleasant comedy about a female Walter Mitty does not work because the director has run out of ideas, the star is miscast and Hollywood has insisted on making the girl rich to begin with, which robs the dreams of any point.

w Arthur Sheekman play Elmer Rice d Mitchell Leisen ph Daniel L. Fapp m Victor Young

Betty Hutton, Macdonald Carey, Walter Abel, Patric Knowles, Virginia Field, Peggy Wood, Lowell Gilmore

Dream Lover

US 1986 104m Technicolor
MGM-UA/Alan J. Pakula, Jon Boorstin
V*

A dream researcher is assigned to the case of a girl who has fatally stabbed an intruder.

Flabby and overlong case history with no very interesting conclusion.

w Jon Boorstin d Alan J. Pakula ph Sven Nykvist m Michael Small

Kristy McNichol, Ben Masters, Paul Shenar, John McMartin, Gayle Hunnicutt, Justin Deas

The Dream of a Rarebit Fiend *

US 1906 4m (24 fps) bw silent

Early trick film depicting a nightmare resulting from overeating.

w Winsor McKay d Edwin S. Porter

A Dream of Kings

US 1969 110m Technicolor
National General (Jules Schermer)
V*

Episodes in the life of an improvident, lusty, poetical Chicago Greek with a dying son.

The part screamed for Anthony Quinn and got him, with the result that it has all been seen before, too frequently. Well made, with strong appeal to Chicago Greeks.

w Harry Mark Patrakis, Ian Hunter novel Harry Mark Patrakis d Daniel Mann ph Richard H. Kline m Alex North

Anthony Quinn, Irene Papas, Inger Stevens, Sam Levene, Val Avery, Tamara Daykarhanova

A Dream of Life: see Life Begins

The Dream of Olwen: see While I Live

A Dream of Passion

Greece 1978 110m Eastmancolor
Branfilm/Melinafilm (Jules Dassin)
V*

A woman who, Medea-like, has killed her children is drawn into an eccentric relationship with an actress playing Medea on the stage.

Weird and ineffective character drama which badly needs discipline.

wd Jules Dassin ph George Arvanitis m Ionnis Markopoulos

Melina Mercouri, Ellen Burstyn, Andreas Voutsinas, Despo Diamantidou

Dream Street *

US 1921 89m (at 24 fps) bw silent
D. W. Griffith Inc
V*

Three Limehouse folk, torn between good and evil, act out their dreams.

Trilogy of moral tales, fancifully and often charmingly assembled by the master director who often reminds one of a Victorian lace maker.

wd D. W. Griffith stories Thomas Burke ph Henrik Sartov

Carol Dempster, Ralph Graves, Charles Emmett Mack, Edward Peil, Tyrone Power Snr, W. J. Ferguson

The Dream Team *

US   1989   113m   DeLuxe   Panavision
UIP/Imagine Entertainment (Christopher W. Knight)
V, V*, L

On a day trip to New York, four inmates of a
psychiatric hospital foil a murder plot.

Enjoyable sentimental comedy that avoids most of the
pitfalls of its subject matter.

w Jon Connolly, David Loucka   d Howard Zieff
ph Adam Holender   m David McHugh   pd Todd
Hallowell   ad Christopher Nowak   ed C. Timothy
O'Meara

Michael Keaton, Christopher Lloyd, Peter Boyle,
Stephen Furst, Dennis Boutsikaris, Lorraine Bracco,
Milo O'Shea, Philip Bosco, James Remar

'Sharp and punchily acted.' – John Pym, MFB

Dream Wife

US   1953   99m   bw
MGM (Dore Schary)

An executive leaves his ambitious wife for a sheik's
daughter schooled in the art of pleasing men, but
naturally finds drawbacks.

Very moderate comedy with strained situations and
few laughs. The stars work hard.

w Sidney Sheldon, Herbert Baker, Alfred L. Levitt
d Sidney Sheldon   ph Milton Krasner   m Conrad
Salinger

Cary Grant, Deborah Kerr, Walter Pidgeon, Betta St
John, Eduard Franz, Buddy Baer, Les Tremayne

Dreamboat *

US   1952   83m   bw
TCF (Sol C. Siegel)

A romantic star of the silent film era is embarrassed
when his old movies turn up on television.

Hollywood rather blunderingly makes fun of its arch
enemy in this sometimes sprightly but often
disappointing comedy which should have been a
bull's-eye.

wd Claude Binyon   ph Milton Krasner   m Cyril
Mockridge

Clifton Webb, Ginger Rogers, Anne Francis, Jeffrey
Hunter, Elsa Lanchester, Fred Clark, Ray Collins, Paul
Harvey

'A merry comedy filled with uproarious laughter from
beginning to end.' – Hollywood Reporter

Dreamchild **

GB   1985   94m   Technicolor
Thorn EMI/PFH (Rick McCallum, Kenith Trodd)
V*

Travelling to New York for the centenary of Lewis
Carroll's birth, Alice Hargreaves, the original of his
Alice, remembers her relationship with him.

Complex and intriguing drama of a woman coming to
terms with her past and present.

w Dennis Potter   d Gavin Miller   ph Billy
Williams   m Stanley Myers   pd Roger Hall
sp Jim Henson's Creature Shop   ed Angus Newton

Coral Browne, Peter Gallagher, Ian Holm, Jane Asher,
Nicola Cowper, Caris Corfman, Amelia Shankley

'Not a movie for a wide audience: it simply isn't
conceived in the broad narrative patterns that please
most moviegoers. Yet it's very enjoyable; it has a
twinkling subtext, and in some scenes it achieves
levels of feeling that the new mainstream films don't
get near.' – Pauline Kael, New Yorker

'Ambitious but unsatisfying and gimmicky.' – Variety

Dreaming

GB   1944   78m   bw
Ealing

A soldier on leave gets a bump on the head, and
dreams . . .

Rather elementary series of sketches with a few good
laughs and interesting guest appearances.

w Bud Flanagan, Reginald Purdell   d John Baxter

Flanagan and Allen, Hazel Court, Dick Francis, Philip
Wade, Teddy Brown, Reginald Foort, Gordon
Richards, Alfredo Campoli

Dreaming Lips *

GB   1936   94m   bw
Trafalgar (Max Schach, Paul Czinner)

The wife of an invalid musician has an affair with
another man and commits suicide.

Standard star fare, possibly Miss Bergner's most
notable film, also available in a German version.

w Margaret Kennedy, Lady Cynthia Asquith, Carl
Mayer   play Melo by Henry Bernstein   d Paul
Czinner, Lee Garmes   ph Roy Clark   m William
Walton   ad Andrei Andreiev, Tom Morahan
ed David Lean

Elisabeth Bergner, Romney Brent, Raymond Massey,
Joyce Bland, Sydney Fairbrother, Felix Aylmer,
Donald Calthrop

'In many respects one of the finest productions ever
made in England . . . made in Hollywood, the story
would be whitewashed and much of its strength
weakened.' – Variety

Dreams That Money Can Buy *

US   1946   81m   Technicolor
Art of the Century (Hans Richter, Peggy Guggenheim, Kenneth
   MacPherson)

A young itinerant sells dreams to people who need
them.

Semi-underground surrealist film, momentarily of
interest, but disjointed and with no real apparent
purpose.

wd Hans Richter   ph Arnold Eagle   md Louis
Applebaum

'Arch, snobbish and sycophantic, about as genuinely
experimental as a Chemcraft set.' – James Agee

† The individual dreams are Max Ernst, Man Ray,
Fernand Leger, Marcel Duchamp and Alexander
Calder as well as Richter.

Dreamscape

US   1984   99m   CFI color
Thorn-EMI/Zuplein-Curtis/Bella (Bruce Cohn Curtis)
V, V*, L, S

Experiments prove that it is possible for a dreamer to
enter the dreams of others, and a subject finds himself
being used for a plot against the president of the US.

Complex fantasy melodrama with a cold war basis;
neither exciting nor praiseworthy.

w David Loughery, Joseph Ruben, Chuck Russell
d Joseph Ruben   ph Brian Tufano, Kevin Kutchaver
m Maurice Jarre   ad Jeff Stags   ed Richard Halsey

Dennis Quaid, Max von Sydow, Christopher
Plummer, Eddie Albert, Kate Capshaw

Drei von der Tankstelle *

Germany   1930   80m   bw
UFA

Three penniless young men find happiness as petrol
station attendants.

Light-hearted operetta of the Depression era, well
received at the time.

w Franz Schultz, Paul Frank   d William Thiele
ph Franz Planer   m Werner Heymann

Willy Fritsch, Lilian Harvey, Oskar Karlweis, Heinz
Ruhmann, Olga Tchekhova

'When leaving this charming talker operetta, one feels
in good humour, humming the catchy hits of its
talented composer . . . constant laughter and
enthusiasm.' – Variety

† Remade 1955 by Hans Wolff, with a cast still led by
Willy Fritsch.

Die Dreigroschenoper **

Germany   1931   114m   bw
Warner/Tobis/Nero
US title: The Threepenny Opera

In turn-of-the-century London, Mack the Knife
marries the daughter of the beggar king and runs into
trouble.

Heavy-footed but interesting updating of The Beggar's
Opera, with splendid sets.

w Bela Balazs, Leo Lania, Ladislas Vajda
play Bertolt Brecht   d G. W. Pabst   ph Fritz Arno
Wagner   m Kurt Weill   ad Andrei Andreiev

Lotte Lenya, Rudolf Forster, Fritz Rasp, Caroline Neher,
Reinhold Schunzel, Valeska Gert, Vladimir Sokoloff

† Brecht disliked the film and sued the makers, but
lost.
†† A French version was also released under the title
L'Opéra de Quat'sous, with Albert Préjean.

Dressed to Kill (1946): see Sherlock Holmes

'Every nightmare has a beginning. This one never ends!'
Dressed to Kill **

US   1980   105m   Technicolor
Filmways/Samuel Z. Arkoff/Cinema 77 (George Litto)
V, V*, L, S

A sexually disturbed matron under analysis is
murdered by a transvestite slasher, who then goes
after a witness.

Occasionally brilliant, generally nasty suspenser
clearly derived from many viewings of Psycho.
Certainly not for the squeamish.

wd Brian de Palma   ph Ralf Bode   m Pino Donaggio
pd Gary Weist

Michael Caine, Angie Dickinson, Nancy Allen, Keith
Gordon, Dennis Franz

'De Palma goes right for the audience jugular . . . it
fully milks the boundaries of its "R" rating.' – Variety

'By casting a halo of excitement around killing, a glow
of degradation around living, and linking the two in a
queasy, guilty partnership, de Palma is asking us to
celebrate the joys of barbarism in a world already
drunk on rape, torture, murder and war.' – Sunday
Times

'De Palma earns the title of master, all right . . . but
Hitch remains the grand master.' – Roger Ebert

The Dresser ***

GB   1983   118m   colour
Columbia/Goldcrest/World Film Services (Peter Yates)
V*, L

An exhausted Shakespearean actor-manager has a
wild last day on tour, comforted and restrained by his
homosexual dresser.

A strained film, but a valuable record of a play based
on the touring career of Donald Wolfit, whose dresser
the author was.

w Ronald Harwood   play Ronald Harwood
d Peter Yates   ph Kelvin Pike   m James Horner
pd Stephen Grimes

Albert Finney, Tom Courtenay, Edward Fox, Zena
Walker, Eileen Atkins, Michael Gough, Betty
Marsden, Lockwood West

'The best sort of drama, fascinating us on the surface
with colour and humour and esoteric detail, and then
revealing the truth underneath.' – Roger Ebert

'It is not an American picture; it is not like 42nd Street.
It is British and therefore tells a tale not of effortless
overnight success but of day by day humiliation and
defeat . . . It is utterly joyless. I can only claim that it
tells its grim tale with sparks of humor and in
merciless detail.' – Quentin Crisp

AAN: best picture; Tom Courtenay; Albert Finney; Peter Yates as director; Ronald Harwood (adaptation)

The Dressmaker *
GB 1988 91m colour
Rank/Film Four International/British Screen (Ronald Shedlo)
V, V*, L

Tensions arise in wartime within a puritanical working-class family with the arrival of American GIs.

Well acted, but depressing.

w John McGrath *novel* Beryl Bainbridge *d* Jim O'Brien *ph* Michael Coulter *m* George Fenton *pd* Caroline Amies *ed* William Diver

Joan Plowright, Billie Whitelaw, Jane Horrocks, Tim Ransom, Peter Postlethwaite, Pippa Hinchley, Rosemary Martin, Tony Haygarth

'A masterpiece of minimalist compression.' – *Hal Hinson, Washington Post*

Dreyfus *
GB 1931 80m bw
BIP (F. W. Kraemer)
US title: *The Dreyfus Case*

In 1894 France, a Jewish officer is accused of spying.

Primitive version of a much-filmed story (cf *The Life of Emile Zola, I Accuse*).

w Reginald Berkeley, Walter C. Mycroft *play The Dreyfus Case* by Hans Rehfisch, Wilhelm Herzog *d* F. W. Kraemer, Milton Rosmer *ph* Willy Minterstein

Cedric Hardwicke, George Merritt (as Zola), Charles Carson, Sam Livesey, Garry Marsh (as Esterhazy), Randle Ayrton, George Zucco

'A picture of the documentary class, well out of the ordinary.' – *Variety*

Drifters *
GB 1929 40m approx bw
Empire Marketing Board (John Grierson)

A documentary of the North Sea fishing fleet.

A highly influential documentary, made at a time when British films were totally unrealistic and studio-bound. Unfortunately it now seems extremely dull.

wd John Grierson *ph* Basil Emmott *ed* John Grierson

Driftwood
US 1947 90m bw
Republic

An orphan is adopted by a kindly doctor.

Lavender-scented family yarn with pleasant backgrounds and expert performances.

w Mary Loos, Richard Sale *d* Allan Dwan

Natalie Wood, Ruth Warrick, Walter Brennan, Dean Jagger, Charlotte Greenwood

'She needed the money – and I needed her!'
Drive a Crooked Road
US 1954 82m bw
Columbia (Jonie Taps)

A garage mechanic falls in with bank robbers.

Terse crime melodrama, quite watchable.

w Blake Edwards *d* Richard Quine *ph* Charles Lawton Jnr *md* Ross di Maggio

Mickey Rooney, Kevin McCarthy, Dianne Foster

Drive He Said
US 1970 90m colour
Columbia/Drive Productions/BBS (Steve Blauner)

An easygoing college basketball star is helped by an eccentric rebel to ensure his own unfitness for military service. Both run into trouble.

Flabby celebration of against-the-government attitudes, expressed partly through sex and bad language. Defiantly hard to like.

w Jeremy Larner, Jack Nicholson *d* Jack Nicholson *ph* Bill Butler *m* David Shire

Michael Margotta, William Tepper, Bruce Dern, Karen Black, Robert Towne, Henry Jaglom

Drive-in
US 1976 96m Technicolor
Columbia (George Litto)
V*

In Texas, various illicit activities find their climax at a drive-in movie.

Mild sex-and-destruction comedy which raises few laughs and makes little sense.

w Bob Peete *d* Rod Amateau *ph* Robert Jessup *m* various

Lisa Lemole, Glen Morshower, Gary Cavagnaro, Billy Milliken, Lee Newsome, Regan Kee

The Driver ****
US 1978 91m DeLuxe
TCF/EMI/Lawrence Gordon
V, V*

A detective determines to catch an old enemy, a getaway driver.

Deft and clever thriller that has been stripped of all redundancies and reduced to its core, of two obsessional men on different sides of the law locked in deadly conflict. It is a simple, spare story of bleak lives, brilliantly told.

wd Walter Hill *ph* Philip Lathrop *m* Michael Small

Ryan O'Neal, Bruce Dern, Isabelle Adjani, Ronee Blakley

'Comic book cops and robbers existentialism.' – *Pauline Kael*

'Because of the quiet and mysterious mood of this picture, it has a pretentious quality to it.' – *Variety*

Driving Me Crazy: see *Dutch*

Driving Miss Daisy *
US 1989 99m Technicolor Panavision
Warner/Zanuck Company/Richard Zanuck, Lili Fini Zanuck
V, V*, S

A elderly rich Jewish widow at first resists, and then succumbs to, the obsequious attentions of her black chauffeur.

Old-fashioned and charming, but slight to the point of inconsequentiality.

w Alfred Uhry *play* Alfred Uhry *d* Bruce Beresford *ph* Peter James *m* Hans Zimmer *pd* Bruno Rubeo *ed* Mark Warner

Morgan Freeman, Jessica Tandy, Dan Aykroyd, Patti LuPone

AA: best picture; best makeup; Alfred Uhry; Jessica Tandy

AAN: Morgan Freeman; Dan Aykroyd; best art direction; best costume design

Le Droit d'Aimer: see *Brainwashed*

Drôle de Drame *
France 1936 100m approx bw
aka: *Bizarre, Bizarre* (84m American version)

A complicated chain of bizarre events is set in motion when a botanist pretends not to be a detective story writer, a bishop tries to be a detective, and a murderer seeks revenge for libel.

A curious satirical comedy which is never quite as funny as it seems about to be, but should be seen for its downright peculiar London sets and its array of actors in top form.

w Jacques Prévert *novel The Lunatic at Large* by J. Storer Clouston *d* Marcel Carné *ph* Eugene Schufftan *m* Maurice Jaubert *pd* Alexandre Trauner

Françoise Rosay, Michel Simon, Louis Jouvet, Jean-Louis Barrault, Jean-Pierre Aumont

'Art theatres and foreign-language houses will do fair business.' – *Variety*

'No one with any taste for nonsense should miss it.' – *Richard Mallett, Punch*

Drôle d'endroit pour une Rencontre *
France 1988 98m colour
Artificial Eye/Hachette/A2/DD/Deneuve/Orly/Editions Sidonie (Patrick Bordier)
V
GB title: *A Strange Place to Meet*

A doctor falls in love with an abandoned wife, who is waiting for her husband to return.

An unconvincing romance, full of longueurs.

w François Dupreyron, Dominique Faysse *d* François Dupreyron *ph* Charlie Van Damme *ad* Carlos Conti *ed* Françoise Collin

Catherine Deneuve, Gérard Depardieu, André Wilms, Nathalie Cardone, Jean-Pierre Sentier, Alain Rimoux, Vincent Martin

Drop Dead Darling
GB 1966 100m Technicolor Panavision
Seven Arts (Ken Hughes)
US title: *Arrivederci Baby*

A con man who marries and murders rich women meets a con lady with similar intentions.

Loud, restless black comedy which squanders its moments of genuine inventiveness among scenes of shouting, confusion and action for action's sake.

wd Ken Hughes *story The Careful Man* by Richard Deming *ph* Denys Coop *m* Dennis Farnon

Tony Curtis, Rosanna Schiaffino, Lionel Jeffries, Zsa Zsa Gabor, Nancy Kwan, Fenella Fielding, Anna Quayle, Warren Mitchell, Mischa Auer

'He creates the havoc. She takes the blame.'
Drop Dead Fred
US 1991 99m colour
Rank/Working Title/Polygram (Paul Webster)
V, V*, L

A young woman in difficulties is revisited by her imaginary, destructive childhood friend.

Singularly tasteless comedy, lacking any vestige of wit or even humour.

w Carlos Davis, Anthony Fingleton *story* Elizabeth Livingston *d* Ate de Jong *ph* Peter Deming *m* Randy Edelman *pd* Joseph T. Garrity *ed* Marshall Harvey

Phoebe Cates, Rik Mayall, Marsha Mason, Tim Matheson, Bridget Fonda, Carrie Fisher, Keith Charles, Ashley Peldon, Daniel Gerroll

'Harvey reimagined for the Beetlejuice generation, with strident gags standing in for magic and relentless obviousness overriding the disturbing ambiguity that might have made the film work.' – *Kim Newman, Sight and Sound*

'This celebration of mental retardation is where the nadirs of two current Hollywood cycles – the regression to childhood/life swap movie and the ghost/revenant picture – intersect.' – *Philip French, Observer*

Drowning by Numbers **
GB 1988 119m Kodacolour
Film Four International/Elsevier Vendex
V, V*, L, S

Three women (all with the same name) murder their respective husbands with the collusion of the local coroner.

Cynical black comedy, beautifully played and more accessible than this director's earlier work, although with some obscure formalism.

wd Peter Greenaway *ph* Sacha Vierny *m* Michael Nyman *pd* Ben Van Os, Jan Roelfs

Bernard Hill, Joan Plowright, Juliet Stevenson, Joely Richardson, Jason Edwards

The Drowning Pool

US 1975 108m Technicolor Panavision
Warner/Coleytown (Lawrence Turman, David Foster)
V*

Private eye Lew Harper goes to New Orleans to investigate an anonymous letter which ends in murder.

Dreary sequel to *Harper* (qv), full of boring characters uninventively deployed.

w Tracy Keenan Wynn, Lorenzo Semple Jnr, Walter Hill *novel* John Ross MacDonald *d* Stuart Rosenberg *ph* Gordon Willis *m* Michael Small

Paul Newman, Joanne Woodward, Coral Browne, Tony Franciosa, Murray Hamilton, Gail Strickland, Linda Hayes, Richard Jaeckel

'The impenetrable mystery is not particularly gripping; and the general air of pointlessness is only intensified by the sudden rush of clarifications at the end.' – *Tom Milne*

'It recycles every private eye cliché known to civilized man as it crawls through Louisiana talking all the way.' – *Paul D. Zimmermann*

'All the clichés of cheapjack TV private eye capers have been added to MacDonald's book; whatever separates him from the paperback hacks has been deleted.' – *Judith Crist*

Drugstore Cowboy **

US 1989 100m colour
Avenue Pictures (Nick Wechsler, Karen Murphy)
V, V*, L, S

A drug-addict, his wife and two friends travel across America, robbing drug-stores to support their habit.

Low-key, effective melodrama with an unconvincing ending.

w Gus Van Sant, Daniel Yost *novel* James Fogle *d* Gus Van Sant *ph* Robert Yeoman *m* Elliot Goldenthal *pd* David Brisbin *ed* Curtiss Clayton

Matt Dillon, Kelly Lynch, James Remar, James Le Gros, Heather Graham, William S. Burroughs

'A rather thoughtless and unenlightening film about drug addiction.' – *MFB*

The Drum *

GB 1938 96m Technicolor
UA/London Films (Alexander Korda)
V*
US title: *Drums*

The British army helps an Indian prince to resist his usurping uncle.

Reasonably entertaining story of the Raj, with adequate excitement after a meandering start.

w Lajos Biro, Arthur Wimperis, Patrick Kirwan, Hugh Gray *novel* A. E. W. Mason *d* Zoltan Korda *ph* Georges Périnal, Osmond Borradaile *m* John Greenwood, Miklos Rozsa *ad* Vincent Korda *ed* William Hornbeck, Henry Cornelius

Sabu, Roger Livesey, Raymond Massey, Valerie Hobson, Desmond Tester, David Tree, Francis L. Sullivan, Roy Emerton, Edward Lexy

'Looks like a 100% commercial bet.' – *Variety*

Drum

US 1976 100m Metrocolor Panavision
Dino de Laurentiis (Ralph Serpe)
V*

In 1860 New Orleans, a bordello house slave faces all manner of sexual predators.

Tediously single-minded sequel to the appalling *Mandingo*.

w Norman Wexler *novel* Kyle Onstott *d* Steve Carver *ph* Lucien Ballard *m* Charles Smalls

Warren Oates, Ken Norton, Isela Vega, Yaphet Kotto, John Colicos

'Shamelessly it exploits the factors which explain the success of the prototype: a feeble pretence at outraged historical exposé of the abuses of the slave trade provides the excuse for an orgy of wish dreams, of sadism, flagellation, domination, sexuality of all tastes, popular fantasies of negro potency.' – *David Robinson, The Times*

Drum Beat

US 1954 111m Warnercolor CinemaScope
Jaguar (no producer credited)
V*

An Indian fighter sets out to make peace with a renegade.

Long, dull Western, stolid all round.

wd Delmer Daves *ph* J. Peverell Marley *m* Victor Young

Alan Ladd, Audrey Dalton, Marisa Pavan, Robert Keith, Rodolfo Acosta, Charles Bronson, Warner Anderson, Elisha Cook Jnr, Anthony Caruso

Drum Crazy: see *The Gene Krupa Story*

Drums: see *The Drum*

Drums Across the River

US 1954 78m Technicolor
Universal-International (Melville Tucker)

A young Westerner who hates Indians finally helps them to overthrow a white crook.

Slick little Western with almost every familiar ingredient.

w John K. Butler, Lawrence Roman *d* Nathan Juran *ph* Harold Lipstein *m* Joseph Gershenson

Audie Murphy, Walter Brennan, Lyle Bettger, Lisa Gaye, Hugh O'Brian, Jay Silverheels, Emile Meyer

Drums Along the Amazon: see *Angel on the Amazon*

Drums Along the Mohawk **

US 1939 103m Technicolor
TCF (Raymond Griffith)
V*, L

Colonists survive Indian attacks in upstate New York during the Revolutionary War.

Patchy, likeable period adventure story with domestic and farming interludes; in its way a key film in the director's canon.

w Lamar Trotti, Sonya Levien *novel* Walter Edmonds *d* John Ford *ph* Bert Glennon, Ray Rennahan *m* Alfred Newman

Claudette Colbert, Henry Fonda, *Edna May Oliver*, Eddie Collins, John Carradine, Dorris Bowdon, Jessie Ralph, Arthur Shields, Robert Lowery, Roger Imhof, Ward Bond

'Outdoor spec, a top-bracketer, though not in the smash division.' – *Variety*

'No one appears to know why the picture is being made, or what its point is, exactly.' – *Pauline Kael, 70s*

AAN: Edna May Oliver

Drums in the Deep South

US 1951 87m Supercinecolor
RKO/King Brothers
V*

A Confederate officer finds himself fighting a lonely battle with his best friend from West Point.

Barely stimulating semi-Western in appalling colour.

w Philip Yordan, Sidney Harmon *d* William Cameron Menzies *pd* William Cameron Menzies

James Craig, Barbara Payton, Guy Madison, Barton MacLane, Craig Stevens, Tom Fadden, Taylor Holmes

Drums of Fu Manchu *

US 1940 bw serial: 15 eps
Republic

The Yellow Peril seeks the long-lost sceptre of Genghis Khan, which will allow him to rule the eastern hordes.

Spirited rendering of an ideal serial theme.

d William Witney, John English

Henry Brandon, William Royle, Robert Kellard, Gloria Franklin, Olaf Hytten, Luana Walters, Dwight Frye

'A volcano erupts! A hurricane strikes! A man … a woman … discover passion in each other's arms!'

Drums of Tahiti

US 1953 73m Technicolor 3D
Columbia (Sam Katzman)

In 1877 an American helps the queen of Tahiti, who doesn't want to become a French possession.

Cheapskate potboiler with an extended volcanic climax (courtesy of older, better movies).

w Douglas Heyes, Robert E. Kent *d* William Castle

Dennis O'Keefe, Patricia Medina, Francis L. Sullivan, Sylvia Lewis

Drunken Angel **

Japan 1948 102m bw
Toho
V
original title: *Yoidore Tenshi*

A gruff, hot-tempered, alcoholic doctor befriends a young gangster who is dying of tuberculosis.

Moving drama of sacrifice and redemption, filmed in an understated, realistic style.

w Keinosuke Ueksa, Akira Kurosawa *d* Akira Kurosawa *ph* Takeo Ito *m* Fumio Hayasaka

Takashi Shimura, *Toshiro Mifune*, Reizaburo Yamamoto, Chieko Nakakita, Michiyo Kogure

Dry Rot

GB 1956 87m bw
Romulus (Jack Clayton)

Three bookmakers plot to make a fortune by substituting a doped horse for the favourite.

Flat filming of a long-running theatrical farce.

w John Chapman *play* John Chapman *d* Maurice Elvey *ph* Arthur Grant *m* Peter Akister

Ronald Shiner, Brian Rix, Sid James, Michael Shepley, Joan Haythorne, Joan Sims, Heather Sears, Lee Patterson, Peggy Mount

A Dry White Season *

US 1989 107m DeLuxe
UIP/MGM/Star Partners II (Paula Weinstein)
V*, L

A white South African is transformed into a radical after investigating the death of his gardener at the hands of the police.

Filmed with a passion that does not always communicate to the audience.

w Colin Welland, Euzhan Palcy *novel* André Brink *d* Euzhan Palcy *ph* Kevin Pike, Pierre William Glenn *pd* John Fenner *ed* Sam O'Steen, Glenn Cunningham

Donald Sutherland, Janet Suzman, Zakes Mokae, Jurgen Prochnow, Susan Sarandon, Marlon Brando, Winston Ntshona, Thoko Ntshinga, Leonard Maguire

AAN: Marlon Brando

Dual Alibi

GB   1947   81m   bw
British National (Louis H. Jackson)

Twin trapezists fall out over a lottery ticket and a worthless woman, but later extract a unique revenge.

Sprightly circus melodrama, shot on a shoestring.

w Alfred Travers, Stephen Clarkson   *d* Alfred Travers   *ph* James Wilson

Herbert Lom, Phyllis Dixey, Ronald Frankau, Terence de Marney, Abraham Sofaer, Eugene Deckers

Du Barry, Woman of Passion

US   1930   88m   bw
United Artists (Talmadge)

Incidents in the life of the mistress of Louis XV.

Tedious early talkie which marked the virtual end of its star's career.

play David Belasco   *d* Sam Taylor

Norma Talmadge, William Farnum, Hobart Bosworth, Conrad Nagel, Alison Skipworth

'Wholly unimpressive . . . nix for kids and the sticks.' – *Variety*

Du Rififi chez les Hommes: see *Rififi*

Dubarry Was a Lady

US   1943   101m   Technicolor
MGM (Arthur Freed)
V*

A New Yorker imagines himself back at the court of Louis XIV.

Dull, stiff adaptation of a Broadway musical comedy, with changed songs.

w Irving Brecher   *book* B. G. de Sylva, Herbert Fields   *d* Roy del Ruth   *ph* Karl Freund   *md* George Stoll   *m/y* Cole Porter

Gene Kelly, Lucille Ball, Red Skelton, Virginia O'Brien, Zero Mostel, Rags Ragland, Tommy Dorsey and his Orchestra

'If the rustlers didn't get you . . . the hustlers did!'
The Duchess and the Dirtwater Fox

US   1976   104m   DeLuxe   Panavision
TCF (Melvin Frank)
V*

A Barbary Coast con man and a saloon singer have various hectic adventures.

Wild and woolly spoof Western which fires off aimlessly in a variety of styles and becomes merely tiresome despite good scenes.

w Melvin Frank, Barry Sandler   *d* Melvin Frank   *ph* Joseph Biroc   *m* Charles Fox

George Segal, Goldie Hawn, Conrad Janis, Thayer David, Roy Jenson, Bob Hoy, Bennie Dobbins

'The classic Western has now been shot to death by Sam Peckinpah, laughed to death by Mel Brooks and pondered to death by Arthur Penn, and Frank is like a scavenger picking up stray relics from its body.' – *Newsweek*

'The relentless vulgarity of the enterprise suggests that Mr Frank, having been so long constrained by the Hollywood Production Code when churning out vehicles for Bob Hope and Danny Kaye, is still making up for lost time.' – *Philip French*

The Duchess of Idaho

US   1950   98m   Technicolor
MGM (Joe Pasternak)

Romantic misunderstandings among candidates for Miss Idaho Potato.

Lightweight musical, quite pleasant if routine, with guest spots.

w Dorothy Cooper, Jerry Davis   *d* Robert Z. Leonard   *ph* Charles Schoenbaum   *md* Georgie Stoll

Esther Williams, Van Johnson, John Lund, Paula Raymond, Clinton Sundberg; guests: Red Skelton, Eleanor Powell, Lena Horne

Duck Soup ****

US   1933   68m   bw
Paramount
V*, L

An incompetent becomes President of Fredonia and wages war on its scheming neighbour.

The satirical aspects of this film are fascinating but appear to have been unintentional. Never mind, it's also the most satisfying and undiluted Marx Brothers romp, albeit the one without instrumental interludes. It does include the lemonade stall, the mirror sequence, and an endless array of one-liners and comedy choruses.

w Bert Kalmar, Harry Ruby, Arthur Sheekman, Nat Perrin   *d* Leo McCarey   *ph* Henry Sharp   *m/y* Bert Kalmar, Harry Ruby   *ad* Hans Dreier, Wiard Ihnen

The Four Marx Brothers, Margaret Dumont, Louis Calhern, Edgar Kennedy, Raquel Torres

'Practically everybody wants a good laugh right now, and this should make practically everybody laugh.' – *Variety*

'So much preliminary dialogue is necessary that it seems years before Groucho comes on at all; and waiting for Groucho is agony.' – *E. V. Lucas, Punch*

'The most perfect of all Marxist masterpieces.' – *Time Out, 1984*

Duck, You Sucker: see *A Fistful of Dynamite*

Dudes

US   1987   90m   colour
Recorded Releasing/New Century/Vista (Herbert Jaffe, Miguel Tejada Flores)
V, V*, L

Three punk rockers, on their way to California, fall foul of a gang of murderous rednecks.

Haphazard, absurdist account of a violent culture clash.

w John Randall Johnson   *d* Penelope Spheeris   *ph* Robert Richardson   *m* Charles Bernstein   *pd* Robert Ziembicki   *ed* Andy Horvitch

Jon Cryer, Daniel Robecuk, Flea, Catherine Mary Stewart, Lee Ving

Due Soldi di Speranza *

Italy   1952   98m   bw
Universalcine (Sandro Ghenzi)
GB title: *Two Pennyworth of Hope*

Demobilized after World War II, Antonio finds life in his native village hard to take.

Neo-realist comedy-melodrama full of gesticulating rustics; good for those who like this sort of thing.

w Renato Castellani, Titina de Filippo   *d* Renato Castellani   *ph* Arturo Gallea   *m* Alessandro Cicognini

Vincenzo Musolino, Maria Fiore, Filumena Russo, Luigi Astarita

Le Due Vite di Mattia Pascal: see *The Two Lives of Mattia Pascal*

Duel **

US   1971   90m   colour
Universal (George Eckstein)
V, V*

A travelling salesman discovers that the driver of the petrol tanker following him is determined to kill him.

Tense, suspenseful drama that made Spielberg's name as a bright young director.

w Richard Matheson   *story* Richard Matheson   *d* Steven Spielberg

Dennis Weaver, Jacqueline Scott, Eddie Firestone, Lou Frizzell

† Made for television, the film received a UK release in 1972, but was not seen in American cinemas until 1983.

Duel at Diablo *

US   1966   103m   DeLuxe
UA/Nelson/Engel/Cherokee/Rainbow/Brien
V*

White and black man fight together as Apaches attack.

Well-paced, old-fashioned, shoot-'em-up star Western.

w Marvin H. Albert, Michel M. Grilikhes   *d* Ralph Nelson   *ph* Charles F. Wheeler   *m* Neal Hefti

Sidney Poitier, James Garner, Bibi Andersson, Bill Travers, William Redfield, John Hoyt, John Hubbard

Duel at Silver Creek

US   1952   77m   Technicolor
U-I (Leonard Goldstein)

An honest man is murdered by claim jumpers, and the Silver Kid is suspected.

Modest, efficient Western.

w Gerald Drayson Adams, Joseph Hoffman   *d* Don Siegel   *ph* Irving Glassberg   *m* Hans Salter

Audie Murphy, Stephen McNally, Faith Domergue, Susan Cabot, Gerald Mohr, Eugene Iglesias, Lee Marvin, Walter Sande

Duel in the Jungle

GB   1954   101m   Technicolor
ABP/Marcel Hellman

An African explorer intends to defraud an insurance company and sets traps for the investigator who pursues him.

Lackadaisical romp in the studio jungle, none of it with much style or film sense.

w Sam Marx, T. J. Morrison   *d* George Marshall   *ph* Erwin Hillier   *m* Mischa Spoliansky

Dana Andrews, Jeanne Crain, David Farrar, Patrick Barr

Duel in the Sun **

US   1946   135 or 138m   Technicolor
David O. Selznick
V, V*

A half-breed girl causes trouble between two brothers.

Massive Western, dominated and fragmented by its producer, who bought the best talent and proceeded to interfere with it, so that while individual scenes are marvellous, the narrative has little flow. The final gory shoot-up between two lovers was much discussed at the time.

w David O. Selznick, Oliver H. P. Garrett   *novel* Niven Busch   *d* King Vidor (and others)   *second unit* B. Reeves Eason, Otto Brower   *ph* Lee Armes, Harold Rosson, Ray Rennahan   *m* Dimitri Tiomkin   *pd* J. McMillan Johnson   *ad* James Basevi

Jennifer Jones, Joseph Cotten, Gregory Peck, Lionel Barrymore, Lillian Gish, Walter Huston, Herbert Marshall, Charles Bickford, Tilly Losch, Joan Tetzel, Harry Carey, Otto Kruger, Sidney Blackmer

'A knowing blend of oats and aphrodisiac.' – *Time*

'Cornographic is a word that might have been coined for it.' – *Daily Mail*

'As sexual melodrama with a spectacular background it is in its way remarkable.' – *New Statesman*

'A razzmatazz of thunderous naïvety simmering into a kind of majestic dottiness.' – *Basil Wright, 1972*

'A lavish, sensual spectacle, so heightened it becomes a cartoon of passion.' – *Pauline Kael, 70s*

† The uncredited directors included Josef von Sternberg, William Dieterle, B. Reeves Eason, and Selznick himself.

AAN: Jennifer Jones; Lillian Gish

Duel on the Mississippi

US   1955   72m   Technicolor
Columbia (Sam Katzman)

A river planter owes money to pirates.

Standard second feature excitements with romantic interludes.

w Gerald Drayson Adams   *d* William Castle

Patricia Medina, Lex Barker, Craig Stevens, Warren Stevens

The Duellists *

GB   1977   101m   colour
Scott Free/NFFC/David Puttnam
V*, L

In the early 1800s, two Hussar Officers challenge each other to a series of duels; after sixteen years an ironic truce is called.

A singularly pointless anecdote; its main virtue is that it is coldly attractive to look at.

w Gerald Vaughan-Hughes   *story* The Point of Honour by Joseph Conrad   *d* Ridley Scott   *ph* Frank Tidy   *m* Howard Blake   *pd* Peter J. Hampton

Keith Carradine, Harvey Keitel, Albert Finney, Edward Fox, Cristina Raines, Tom Conti, Robert Stephens, John McEnery

Duet for One

GB   1987   107m   Rank colour
Cannon (Menaham Golan, Yoram Globus)
V, V*

A leading lady violinist contracts multiple sclerosis.

Lamentable opening out of a two-character play, all gloom and doom and overstatement.

w Tom Kempinski, Jeremy Lipp, Andrei Konchalovsky   *play* Tom Kempinski   *d* Andrei Konchalovsky   *ph* Alex Thomson   *pd* John Graysmark   *ed* Henry Richardson

Julie Andrews, Alan Bates, Max von Sydow, Rupert Everett, Margaret Courtenay

'Some helpful hints for those who are very rich, very beautiful, very hip, elaborately oversexed, tuned in, turned on and bored to death!'
Duffy

GB   1968   101m   Technicolor
Columbia/Martin Manulis

Two half-brothers plan to rob their millionaire father.

Would-be with-it caper film, all flashy fragments and pop art, like sitting through a feature-length commercial. Exasperating.

w Donald Cammell, Harry Joe Brown Jnr   *d* Robert Parrish   *ph* Otto Heller   *m* Ernie Freeman

James Coburn, James Mason, James Fox, Susannah York, John Alderton, Guy Deghy, Tutte Lemkow, Carl Duering, Marne Maitland

Duffy of San Quentin

US   1953   78m   bw
Allied Artists (Berman Swartz, Walter Doniger)
GB title: *Men Behind Bars*

An elderly warden institutes prison reforms which cause him problems.

Semi-true melodrama with standard excitements and too much talk.

wd Walter Doniger   *ph* John Alton   *m* Paul Dunlap

Paul Kelly, Louis Hayward, Maureen O'Sullivan, Joanne Dru, George Macready, Horace MacMahon

Duffy's Tavern

US   1945   97m   bw
Paramount (Danny Dare)

The owner of a bar is helped by Hollywood stars.

Flat comedy based on a radio show and not helped by dismal guest star appearances.

w Melvin Frank, Norman Panama   *d* Hal Walker   *ph* Lionel Lindon   *m* Robert Emmett Dolan

Ed Gardner, Victor Moore, Marjorie Reynolds, Barry Sullivan and guests including Bing Crosby, Bob Hope, Betty Hutton, Alan Ladd, Dorothy Lamour, Veronica Lake, William Bendix, Joan Caulfield

'Two thousand men and a girl!'
The Duke of West Point *

US   1938   112m   bw
Edward Small

An extrovert army cadet finds the going tough.

Dated romantic flagwaver which pleased at the time.

w George Bruce   *d* Alfred E. Green   *ph* Robert Planck

Louis Hayward, Joan Fontaine, Tom Brown, Richard Carlson, Alan Curtis, Donald Barry, Gaylord Pendleton, Jed Prouty, Marjorie Gateson

'Fairly good entertainment. Much human interest, but the comedy relief is rather light.' – *Variety*

The Duke Wore Jeans

GB   1958   89m   bw
Insignia (Peter Rogers)

An aristocrat persuades his cockney double to woo a princess on his behalf.

Moderately lively comedy with songs, tailored for Britain's new musical star.

w Norman Hudis   *d* Gerald Thomas

Tommy Steele, June Laverick, Michael Medwin, Alan Wheatley, Eric Pohlmann

Dulcima

GB   1971   98m   Technicolor
EMI (Basil Rayburn)

A farmer's daughter reluctantly moves in with a persistent, lecherous old miser.

Weird sex melodrama from *Cold Comfort Farm* country, more risible than interesting.

wd Frank Nesbitt   *story* H. E. Bates   *ph* Tony Imi   *m* Johnny Douglas

John Mills, Carol White, Stuart Wilson, Bernard Lee, Dudley Foster

Dulcimer Street: see *London Belongs to Me*

Dumb Dicks

US   1986   90m   Telecolor
Cannon (Menahem Golan, Yoram Globus)

Incompetent private eyes become involved with feuding Italian families.

Uninteresting location comedy with a title that suits its style.

w David Landsberg, Lorin Dreyfuss   *d* Filippo Ottoni

David Landsberg, Lorin Dreyfuss, Christian De Sica, Valeria Golino

Dumbo ****

US   1941   64m   Technicolor
Walt Disney
V, V*, L

A baby circus elephant finds that his big ears have a use after all.

Delightful cartoon feature notable for set-pieces such as the drunken nightmare and the crows' song.

w various   *d* Ben Sharpsteen   *m* Frank Churchill, Oliver Wallace

voices of Sterling Holloway, Edward Brophy, Verna Felton, Herman Bing, Cliff Edwards

AA: music

AAN: song, 'Baby Mine' (*m* Frank Churchill, *ly* Ned Washington)

The Dummy Talks

GB   1943   85m   bw
British National

A ventriloquist turns to blackmail and is murdered backstage.

Curious, oddly cast murder mystery, not unentertaining at the time.

w Michael Barringer   *d* Oswald Mitchell

Jack Warner, Claude Hulbert, Beryl Orde, G. H. Mulcaster, Ivy Benson, Manning Whiley

Dune

US   1984   140m   Technicolor   Todd-AO
Dino de Laurentiis (Raffaella de Laurentiis)
V, V*, L, S

Armies from several planets descend on another which has valuable spice guarded by monster worms.

A basically simple space fiction plot is immensely complicated by a welter of characters who are not properly introduced and who indeed are mostly irrelevant. The result, which cost nearly 50 million dollars, is inaudible, invisible (because of dim lighting) and unentertaining: a disaster of the very first order.

wd David Lynch   *novel* Frank Herbert   *ph* Freddie Francis   *m* Toto   *pd* Anthony Masters   *ed* Antony Gibbs

Francesca Annis, Jose Ferrer, Sian Phillips, Brad Dourif, Dean Stockwell, Freddie Jones, Linda Hunt, Kenneth McMillan, Richard Jordan, Kyle MacLachlan, Silvana Mangano, Jurgen Prochnow, Max Von Sydow, Sting

'Huge, hollow, imaginative and cold.' – *Variety*

'This movie is a real mess, an incomprehensible, ugly, unstructured, pointless excursion into the murkier realms of one of the most confusing screenplays of all time.' – *Roger Ebert*

Dunkirk **

GB   1958   135m   bw
MGM/Ealing (Michael Balcon)

In 1940 on the Normandy beaches, a small group gets detached from the main force.

Sober, small-scale approach to an epic subject; interesting but not inspiring, with performances to match.

w W. P. Lipscomb, David Divine   *d* Leslie Norman   *ph* Paul Beeson   *m* Malcolm Arnold

John Mills, Richard Attenborough, Bernard Lee, Robert Urquhart, Ray Jackson

'Men invoke its horror! Women invite its shame!'
The Dunwich Horror *

US   1970   90m   Movielab
AIP (Roger Corman, Jack Bohrer)
V*

A young warlock plans to use his girlfriend in a fertility rite.

Bookish horror story, quite well done against a village background.

w Curtis Lee Hanson, Henry Rosenbaum, Ronald Silkosky   *story* H. P. Lovecraft   *d Daniel Haller*
ph Richard C. Glouner   *m* Les Baxter

Dean Stockwell, Sandra Dee, Ed Begley, Sam Jaffe, Lloyd Bochner

'A bit psychedelic in places, but with a real feeling for sinister rites and strange manifestations.' – *Sight and Sound*

Duped Till Doomsday *

East Germany   1957   97m   bw
DEFA (Adolf Fischer)
original title: *Betrogen bis zum Jüngsten Tag*

Three Nazi NCOs go to the bad.

Propagandist anti-Nazi war melodrama, very well made in parts.

w Kurt Bortfeldt   *novel Kameraden* by Franz Fuhmann   *d* Kurt Jung-Alsen   *ph* Walter Fehdmer

Wolfgang Kieling, Rudolph Ulrich, Hans-Joachim Martens

During One Night

GB   1961   80m   bw
Galaworldfilm

During World War II, a country girl helps a USAAF deserter dispel his fear of impotence.

Glum sex drama, a curious and unsuccessful attempt.

wd Sidney J. Furie

Don Borisenko, Susan Hampshire, Sean Sullivan, Joy Webster

Dust

Belgium/France   1985   87m   Fujicolor
Mans/Daska/Flach/FR3
V*

On an isolated South African farm, a girl murders her adulterous father.

Doomladen saga redeemed by strong pictorial style.

wd Marion Hansel   *novel In the Heart of the Country* by J. M. Coetzee

Jane Birkin, Trevor Howard, John Matshikiza

Dust Be My Destiny *

US   1939   88m   bw
Warner (Lou Edelman)

A young misfit tries to find himself in the country.

Dated but well made social melodrama.

w Robert Rossen   *story* Jerome Odlum   *d* Lewis Seiler   *ph* James Wong Howe   *m* Max Steiner

John Garfield, Priscilla Lane, Alan Hale, Frank McHugh, John Litel, Charles Grapewin, Billy Halop, Bobby Jordan, Stanley Ridges

'Strong programmer, though overlong and episodic.' – *Variety*

'You can tell from the title that John Garfield has his usual part – the angry, bitter, tough poor young man with slight persecution mania.' – *Richard Mallett, Punch*

† Remade 1942 as *I Was Framed*, with Michael Ames.

Dust Devil: The Final Cut

GB   1992   103m   Technicolor
Polygram/Palace/Film Four/Richard Stanley
V, S

An alien, which has to kill in order to return to its own world, journeys to a ghost town, where he is attracted by two people with a death-wish: a battered wife fleeing her husband and a black cop who has lost his wife and son.

Confused science-fiction thriller that never quite comes to life; whatever message the director is striving to impart, it remains obscure.

wd Richard Stanley   *ph* Steven Chivers   *m* Simon Boswell   *pd* Joseph Bennett   *sp* The Dream Machine, Rick Cresswell   *ed* Derek Trigg, Paul Carlin

Robert Burke, Chelsea Field, Zakes Mokae, John Matshikiza, Marianne Sagebrecht, William Hootkins, Rufus Swart

'Overflowing with ideas, visual invention and genre references but saddled by a weak, unfocused script.' – *Variety*

'In any of its several versions, this is a considerable and remarkable film.' – *Kim Newman*

† The film exists in several versions. The above is the director's preferred version, which he restored with his own money. A shorter version, cut by its American distributor, was released in Europe under the title *Demonica*. The US version of the film was re-dubbed and had a new voice-over added.

Dust in the Wind *

Taiwan   1987   100m   colour
ICA/Central Motion Picture (Ling Deng Fei, Xu Guo Liang)
original title: *Lien-lien feng-ch'en*

Instead of going to high school, a youth leaves his mining village to seek work in the big city, where his girlfriend joins him.

A leisurely, intermittently insightful examination of the tensions and pleasures of family life and the problems of surviving without much education in an unsympathetic urban environment.

w Wu Nien-jen, Chu Tien-wen   *d* Hou Hsiao-hsien
ph Li Ping-pin   *pd* Zhao Qi Bin

Wang Ching-Wen, Hsing Shu-fen, Ch'en Shu-fang, Li Tien-lu

Dusty

Australia   1982   85m   colour   Panavision
Kestrel Films/Dusty Productions (Gil Brealey)
V*

An old shepherd takes to the bush to save his half-wild dog from being shot by sheep farmers.

Sentimental tale with pleasant landscape photography.

w Sonia Berg   *novel* Frank Dalby Davison   *d* John Richardson   *ph* Alex McPhee   *m* Frank Strangio
pd Robbie Perkins   *ad* Ivana Perkins   *ed* David Greig

Bill Kerr, Noel Trevarthen, Carol Burns, John Stanton, Nicholas Holland

Dusty Ermine

GB   1938   74m   bw
Julius Hagen/Twickenham
US title: *Hideout in the Alps*

Scotland Yard chases counterfeiters to Switzerland, and the hunt ends in a ski chase.

Modestly effective melodrama with dated romantic leads.

w Paul Hervey Fox   *play* Neil Grant   *d* Bernard Vorhaus

Jane Baxter, Anthony Bushell, Ronald Squire, Margaret Rutherford, Athole Stewart, Katie Johnson, Austin Trevor, Felix Aylmer

'The humour is of the British kind – not too hilarious but still tickling.' – *Variety*

Dutch

US   1991   107m   DeLuxe
TCF (John Hughes, Richard Vane)
V, V*, L
GB title: *Driving Me Crazy*

An arrogant and snobbish twelve-year-old boy is reformed by his divorced mother's working-class boyfriend.

Inert comedy of class warfare, part of the cycle of buddy-buddy movies in which antagonists at the beginning become friends by the end.

w John Hughes   *d* Peter Faiman   *ph* Charles Minsky   *m* Alan Silvestri   *pd* Stan Jolley   *ed* Paul Hirsch, Adam Bernardi

Ed O'Neill, Ethan Randall, Christopher McDonald, Ari Meyers, E. G. Daily, L. Scott Caldwell, Kathleen Freeman

Dutchman *

GB   1966   56m   bw
Gene Persson

On a New York subway train a woman humiliates a black man and finally knifes him.

An allegory for addicts who can ferret out the meaning; on the surface, vaguely Pinterish and mainly boring.

w LeRoi Jones   *play* LeRoi Jones   *d* Anthony Harvey   *ph* Gerry Turpin   *m* John Barry

Shirley Knight, Al Freeman Jnr

'Just when she'd given up on love, she fell for a guy who'd given up on life.'

Dying Young

US   1991   111m
TCF/Fogwood (Sally Field, Kevin McCormick)
V, V*, L, S

A man suffering from leukaemia falls in love with the nurse he hires to look after him.

Inane romance, meandering and glossily sentimental, and coming to the conclusion that death is nothing to worry about if you've Julia Roberts by your side.

w Richard Friedenberg   *novel* Marti Leimbach
d Joel Schumacher   *ph* Juan Ruiz Anchia
m James Newton Howard   *ad* Guy J. Comtois, Richard Johnson   *ed* Robert Brown, Jim Prior

Julia Roberts, Campbell Scott, Vincent D'Onofrio, Colleen Dewhurst, David Selby, Ellen Burstyn, Dion Anderson, George Martin

'Starpower should carry this rather thin and maudlin weeper through some heated weeks, but the only real legs likely to be shown are those amply exposed by the femme lead.' – *Variety*

Dynamite **

US   1929   129m   bw
MGM (Cecil B. de Mille)

In order to gain an inheritance, a socialite marries a man about to be executed . . . but he is reprieved.

Dated but still dynamic social melodrama of the early talkie period.

w Jeanie Macpherson   *d* Cecil B. de Mille
ph Peverell Marley   *m* Herbert Stothart
ad Mitchell Leisen

Kay Johnson, Charles Bickford, Conrad Nagel, Julia Faye, Joel McCrea

'A pot-pourri of all previous de Mille efforts crammed into one picture.' – *Variety*

'Exuberant, wonderfully vigorous, the film skilfully evokes the look and character of the Jazz Age.' – *Charles Higham*

'An astonishing mixture, with artificiality vying with realism and comedy hanging on the heels of grim melodrama.' – *Mordaunt Hall, New York Times*

AAN: Mitchell Leisen

Dynamite Man from Glory Jail: see *Fools Parade*

Dyrygent: see *The Conductor*

E

E la Nave Va: see *And the Ship Sails On*

. . . E Poi Lo Chiamarono Il Magnifico: see *Man of the East*

E Tornato Sabata . . . Hai Chiuso un'Altra Volta: see *Return of Sabata*

E.T. ****
US 1982 115m DeLuxe
Universal (Steven Spielberg, Kathleen Kennedy)
V, V (W), V*, L, S

When an alien spacecraft is disturbed in a Los Angeles suburb, one of its crew members is left behind and befriended by a small boy.

Stupefyingly successful box-office fairy tale by the current wonder kid Spielberg, taken to the world's heart because he dares to make films without sex, violence or bad language. This one could hardly be simpler, but it works; and the ailing cinema would love to know how to repeat the trick several times a year.

w *Melissa Mathison* d *Steven Spielberg* ph Allen Daviau m *John Williams* pd James D. Bissell, sp Creator of E.T.: *Carlo Rimbaldi*

Dee Wallace, Henry Thomas, Peter Coyote, Robert MacNaughton, Drew Barrymore, K. C. Martel

'The most moving science-fiction movie ever made on earth.' – *Pauline Kael, New Yorker*

'E.T. is the closest film to my own sensibilities, my own fantasies, my own heart.' – *Steven Spielberg*

† E.T. extra-terrestrial.

AA: visual effects; music; sound

AAN: best picture; direction; original screenplay; cinematography; editing

BFA: best score

Each Dawn I Die *
US 1939 84m bw
Warner (David Lewis)
V, V*, L
original title: *Killer Meets Killer*

A crusading reporter is framed for manslaughter and becomes a hardened prisoner.

Efficient, vigorous yet slightly disappointing star vehicle; the talents are in the right background, but the script is wobbly.

w Norman Reilly Raine, Warren Duff, Charles Perry novel Jerome Odlum d William Keighley ph Arthur Edeson m Max Steiner ad William Cameron Menzies

James Cagney, George Raft, Jane Bryan, George Bancroft, Maxie Rosenbloom, Stanley Ridges, Alan Baxter, Victor Jory

'Rich in horror and brutality.' – *New York Sunday Mirror*

'In addition to its crackling screenplay, it is made memorable by the easy mastery of its two principals.' – *Time*

'Towards the end of the thirties Warners' underworld pictures began to get hazy and high-minded, and in this one the pre-Second World War spiritual irradiation blurs the conventions of the prison genre.' – *Pauline Kael, 70s*

Eadie was a Lady
US 1945 80m bw
Columbia (Michel Kraike)

An upper-crust co-ed leads a double night life as a burlesque dancer.

Modestly effective minor musical.

w Monte Brice d Arthur Dreifuss

Ann Miller, Joe Besser, William Wright, Jeff Donnell

The Eagle **
US 1925 80m approx (24 fps) bw silent
United Artists/Joseph M. Schenck
V, V*, L

A Cossack lieutenant turns masked outlaw when his father's lands are annexed.

Enjoyable romp in the wake of Robin Hood, the Scarlet Pimpernel and Zorro; the eye-flashing star is somewhere near his best.

w Hans Kraly story *Dubrowsky* by Alexander Pushkin d Clarence Brown ph George Barnes

Rudolph Valentino, Vilma Banky, Louise Dresser

The Eagle and the Hawk **
US 1933 72m bw
Paramount

In 1918 France, two American army flyers dislike each other but come together before the death of one of them.

Dawn Patrol melodrama, well done with unusually vivid dialogue and acting.

w Bogart Rogers, Seton I. Miller story John Monk Saunders d Stuart Walker ph Harry Fischbeck

Fredric March, Cary Grant, Carole Lombard, Sir Guy Standing, Jack Oakie, Forrester Harvey

'Will make good with those it attracts, but is handicapped by the mass of earlier flight pictures.' – *Variety*

The Eagle and the Hawk
US 1949 86m bw
(Paramount) Pine-Thomas

During the Mexican wars, a US government agent tracks down a traitor who is supplying arms to the rebel Juarez.

Stolid adventure yarn, energetically played.

w Geoffrey Homes, Lewis R. Foster d Lewis R. Foster ph James Wong Howe m David Chudnow

John Payne, Dennis O'Keefe, Rhonda Fleming, Thomas Gomez, Fred Clark, Frank Faylen, Eduardo Noriega

The Eagle Has Landed *
GB 1976 135m Eastmancolor Panavision
ITC/Associated General (Jack Wiener, David Niven Jnr)
V, V*, S

During World War II, enemy aliens infiltrate an English village in the hope of killing Churchill.

Elaborately plotted but uninvolving spy melodrama, lethargically directed, muddily coloured and too concerned to create some good Germans.

w Tom Mankiewicz novel Jack Higgins d John Sturges ph Anthony Richmond m Lalo Schifrin

Michael Caine, Donald Sutherland, Robert Duvall, Jenny Agutter, Donald Pleasence, Anthony Quayle, Jean Marsh, Sven-Bertil Taube, John Standing, Judy Geeson, Larry Hagman, Maurice Roeves

Eagle in a Cage *
GB 1970 103m Eastmancolor
Group W/Ramona (Millard Lampell, Albert Schwarz)

In 1815, a professional soldier becomes governor of St Helena and jailer to Napoleon.

Talkative, anecdotal, heavily serious historical reconstruction with good acting but little control.

w Millard Lampell d Fielder Cook ph Frano Vodopivec m Marc Wilkinson

John Gielgud, Ralph Richardson, Kenneth Haigh, Billie Whitelaw, Moses Gunn, Ferdy Mayne, Lee Montague

Eagle Squadron
US 1942 102m bw
Universal (Walter Wanger)

During World War II, American flyers join the RAF.

Studio-bound air epic, leavened with conventional romance but little humour or sympathy.

w Norman Reilly Raine story C. S. Forester d Arthur Lubin ph Stanley Cortez m Frank Skinner

Robert Stack, Diana Barrymore, John Loder, Eddie Albert, Nigel Bruce, Leif Erickson, Edgar Barrier, Jon Hall, Evelyn Ankers, Isobel Elsom, Alan Hale Jnr, Don Porter, Frederick Worlock, Gladys Cooper

Eagle's Wing
GB 1979 111m Eastmancolor Panavision
Rank/Peter Shaw (Ben Arbeid)
V, V*

A Comanche chief pursues a white man who has stolen a prize Indian horse.

Would-be poetic Western which emerges as very pretty but stultifyingly dull; an odd thing indeed to come from a moribund British studio.

w John Briley d Anthony Harvey ph Billy Williams m Marc Wilkinson pd Herbert Westbrook

Martin Sheen, Sam Waterston, Harvey Keitel, Stephane Audran, John Castle

Earl Carroll Sketchbook
US 1946 90m bw
Republic
GB title: *Hats Off to Rhythm*

A songwriter gives up and sells radio jingles.

Modest follow-up to *Earl Carroll Vanities*, a background for half-a-dozen songs.

w Frank Gill Jnr, Parke Levy d Albert S. Rogell

Constance Moore, William Marshall, Bill Goodwin, Edward Everett Horton, Vera Vague, Johnny Coy, Hillary Brooke

Earl Carroll Vanities
US 1945 91m bw
Republic (Albert J. Cohen)

A Ruritanian princess in need of a loan becomes the singing star of a New York night-club.

Nit-witted musical with no style but an engaging cast.

w Frank Gill Jnr   d Joseph Santley   ph Jack Marta
md Walter Scharf   m/ly Walter Kent, Kim Gannon

Constance Moore, Dennis O'Keefe, Alan Mowbray,
Eve Arden, Otto Kruger (as Earl Carroll), Pinky Lee,
Mary Forbes, Stephanie Bachelor, Parkyakarkus,
Leon Belasco, Robert Greig

AAN: song 'Endlessly'

The Earl of Chicago *
US   1939   87m   bw
MGM (Victor Saville)

An American gangster accedes to an English earldom
but is tried for murder.

Unusual but unsatisfactory comedy-drama which
rambles to a dismal conclusion but has entertaining
passages.

w Lesser Samuels   novel Brock Williams
d Richard Thorpe   ph Ray June   m Werner
Heymann

Robert Montgomery, Edward Arnold, Reginald
Owen, Edmund Gwenn

† This had been planned as a British production, but
the war intervened.

The Early Bird
GB   1965   98m   Eastmancolor
Rank/Hugh Stewart
V

A milkman gets involved in an inter-company war.

Star farcical comedy; not the worst of Wisdom, but
overlong and mainly uninventive.

w Jack Davies, Norman Wisdom, Eddie Leslie, Henry
Blyth   d Robert Asher   ph Jack Asher   m Ron
Goodwin

Norman Wisdom, Edward Chapman, Jerry
Desmonde, Paddie O'Neil, Bryan Pringle, Richard
Vernon, John Le Mesurier, Peter Jeffrey

Early Spring *
Japan   1956   108m   bw
Shochiku
original title: Soshun

The marriage of an office worker breaks down when
he begins an affair with a typist.

A slight, unengaging tale of the dreariness of domestic
and office life.

w Kogo Noda, Yasujiro Ozu   d Yasujiro Ozu
ph Yuharu Atsuta   m Kojun Saito   ad Tatsuo
Hamada   ed Yoshiyasu Hamamura

Chikage Awajima, Ryo Ikebe, Keiko Kishi, Teiji
Takahashi, Chishu Ryu, So Yamamura, Haruko
Sugimura, Takako Fujino

Early Summer ***
Japan   1951   125m   bw
Shochiku
V*
original title: Bakushu

A family breaks up when the daughter rejects the man
chosen as her husband and marries someone else.

A complex, compassionate, beautifully observed
study of family tensions, traced over three generations
living together.

w Kogo Noda, Yasujiro Ozu   d Yasujiro Ozu
ph Yuharu Atsuta   m Senji Ito   ad Toshio Hamada
ed Yoshiyasu Hamamura

Setsuko Hara, Chishu Ryu, Chikage Awajima, Kuniko
Miyake, Ichiro Sugai, Chieko Higashiyama, Haruko
Sugimura

Early to Bed
US   1928   20m   bw   silent
Hal Roach

Stan becomes Ollie's butler but rebels when his
friend's fortune goes to his head.

One of the most untypical and seldom seen of the
stars' comedies, with both prankishly out of character.
On its own account however it is mainly very funny.

w H. M. Walker   d Emmett Flynn   ph George
Stevens ed Richard Currier

Laurel and Hardy

The Earrings of Madame de: see Madame De

Earth ***
USSR   1930   63m approx (24 fps)   bw   silent
VUFKU
V, V*
original title: Zemlya

Trouble results in a Ukrainian village when a
landowner refuses to hand over his land for a
collective farm.

The melodramatic little plot takes second place to
lyrical sequences of rustic beauty, illustrating life,
love and death in the countryside.

wd Alexander Dovzhenko   ph Danylo Demutsky
ed Alexander Dovzhenko

Semyon Svashenko, Stephan Shkurat, Mikola
Nademsky, Yelena Maximova

'Stories in themselves do not interest me. I choose
them in order to get the greatest expression of
essential social forms.' – Dovzhenko

'A picture for filmgoers who are prepared to take their
cinema as seriously as Tolstoy took the novel.' – James
Agate

Earth Girls Are Easy
US   1988   100m   colour   Panavision
Fox/De Laurentiis/Kestrel Films (Tony Garnett)
V, V*, L

Three aliens crashland on Earth and learn to enjoy
disco dancing.

Ineffectual teenage musical.

w Julie Brown, Charlie Coffey, Terrence E. McNally
d Julien Temple   ph Oliver Stapleton   md Nile
Rodgers   pd Dennis Gassner   ed Richard Halsey

Geena Davis, Jeff Goldblum, Jim Carrey, Damon
Wayans, Julie Brown, Michael McKean, Charles
Rocket, Larry Linville, Rick Overton

Earth Versus the Flying Saucers
US   1956   83m   bw
Columbia (Charles H. Schneer)
V, V*, L

Saucermen from another planet try to disintegrate the
Earth.

Elementary science fiction with special effects in a
similar if enthusiastic vein.

w George Worthing Yates, Raymond T. Marcus
story Curt Siodmak   d Fred F. Sears   sp Ray
Harryhausen

Hugh Marlowe, Joan Taylor, Donald Curtis, Morris
Ankrum

Earth vs The Spider
US   1958   72m   bw
AIP (Bert I. Gordon)
V, V*

A seemingly dead giant spider is brought back to life
by the playing of a high-school rock 'n' roll group.

Ineffably silly horror movie with poor special effects.

w Lazlo Gorog, George Worthing Yates   story Bert I.
Gordon   d Bert I. Gordon   ph Jack Marta
m Albert Glasser   ad Walter Keller   sp Bert I.
Gordon   ed Ronald Sinclair

Ed Kemmer, June Kenney, Gene Persson

Earthbound *
US   1940   67m   bw
TCF (Sol M. Wurtzel)

The ghost of a murdered man helps his widow to
bring the murderer to justice.

Curious attempt at Topper without laughs, nicely done
once you get used to the idea.

w John Howard Lawson, Samuel Engel   story Basil
King   d Irving Pichel

Warner Baxter, Lynn Bari, Andrea Leeds, Charles
Grapewin, Henry Wilcoxon, Elizabeth Patterson

Earthquake *
US   1974   123m   Technicolor   Panavision
Universal/Jennings Lang/Mark Robson
V*, L, S

Various personal stories intertwine in a Los Angeles
earthquake.

Dreary drama with very variable special effects,
gimmicked up by Sensurround. A box-office bonanza.

w George Fox, Mario Puzo   d Mark Robson
ph Philip Lathrop   m John Williams
pd Alexander Golitzen   sp Albert Whitlock

Charlton Heston, Ava Gardner, Lorne Greene, Marjoe
Gortner, Barry Sullivan, George Kennedy, Richard
Roundtree, Geneviève Bujold, Walter Matthau (under
the alias of his real name)

'The picture is swell, but it isn't a cheat. It's an
entertaining marathon of Grade A destruction effects,
with B-picture stock characters spinning through it.' –
Pauline Kael

AAN: Philip Lathrop

Earthworm Tractors
US   1936   69m   bw
Warner
GB title: A Natural Born Salesman

A salesman whose fiancée wants him to think big
turns to tractors.

One of the star's livelier comedies.

w Richard Macauley, Joe Traub, Hugh Cummings
d Ray Enright

Joe E. Brown, June Travis, Guy Kibbee, Dick Foran

'The frank fearless drama of a woman who sinned!'
The Easiest Way
US   1931   86m   bw
MGM

A hard-working slum girl falls into the lap of luxury
but her easy virtue finally causes her to be rejected.

Familiar moral melodrama which got past the Hays
Office only after some heavy deletions.

w Edith Ellis   play Eugene Walter   d Jack Conway
ph John Mescall

Constance Bennett, Robert Montgomery, Adolphe
Menjou, Anita Page, Marjorie Rambeau, J. Farrell
MacDonald, Clark Gable, Clara Blandick

'Gilded wickedness played by flawless cast: will
entice.' – Variety

East End Chant: see Limehouse Blues

East Is West
US   1930   72m   bw
Universal

Half-caste Big Time Charlie Young lords it over San
Francisco's Chinatown.

Muddled melodrama reminiscent of many silent
films.

w Tom Reed   play Sam Shipman, John Hymer
d Monta Bell

Edward G. Robinson, Lupe Velez, Lew Ayres, Henry Kolker, Mary Forbes, Edgar Norton

'Good daily change grind meller.' – *Variety*

East Lynne

US   1931   102m   bw
Fox

A Victorian lady is unjustly divorced by her husband, and later loses both her lover and her sight.

Much caricatured melodrama, here presented in stolidly acceptable form.

w Bradley King, Tom Barry   novel Mrs Henry Wood   d Frank Lloyd   ph John Seitz   m Richard Fall

Ann Harding, Clive Brook, O. P. Heggie, Conrad Nagel, Cecilia Loftus, Beryl Mercer, Flora Sheffield

'A lavish production, some corking direction, and the elemental appeal of all dramatic hokum.' – *Variety*

† Previous versions had been made by Fox, in 1916 with Theda Bara and in 1925 with Alma Rubens.

AAN: best picture

East Lynne on the Western Front

GB   1931   85m   bw
Gaumont-Welsh-Pearson (T. A. Welsh)

War rookies produce *East Lynne* to relieve boredom.

Slapstick army farce which tickled a few fancies at the time.

w Donovan Parsons, Mary Parsons   story George Pearson   d George Pearson   ph Percy Strong

Herbert Mundin, Wilfred Lawson, Mark Daly, Harold French

'Recording is not good and the production shoddy, but it's crammed with hoke and will do good business for juvenile matinées and in the neighbourhoods.' – *Variety*

East Meets West

GB   1936   74m   bw
Gaumont

A proud sultan learns that his son is having an affair with the wife of a crook.

Derivative star vehicle, very stagey even then.

w Maude Howell   play *The Lake of Life* by Edwin Greenwood   d Herbert Mason   ph Bernard Knowles   m John Greenwood   ad Oscar Werndorff

George Arliss, Godfrey Tearle, Lucie Mannheim, Romney Brent, Ballard Berkeley, John Laurie

'Of what a boy did … what a girl did … of ecstasy and revenge!'
'The most shocking revenge a girl ever let one brother take on another!'

East of Eden **

US   1955   115m   Warnercolor   Cinemascope
Warner (Elia Kazan)
V, V*, L, S

In a California farming valley in 1917 a wild adolescent rebels against his stern father and discovers that his mother, believed dead, runs a nearby brothel.

Turgid elaboration of Genesis with strong character but nowhere to go. Heavily over-directed and rousingly acted.

w Paul Osborn   novel John Steinbeck   d Elia Kazan   ph Ted McCord   m Leonard Rosenman   ad James Basevi, Malcolm Bert

Raymond Massey, James Dean (his first star role), *Julie Harris, Dick Davalos, Jo Van Fleet, Burl Ives, Albert Dekker*

'The first distinguished production in Cinemascope.' – *Eugene Archer*

AA: Jo Van Fleet

AAN: Paul Osborn; Elia Kazan; James Dean

East of Elephant Rock

GB   1976   92m   colour
Boyd's Company/Kendon (Don Boyd)
V*

In 1948 Malaya a womanizing civil servant is shot by his jealous mistress.

Style-less and quite uncredited re-hash of *The Letter*, striving vainly to recreate the spirit of Somerset Maugham.

wd Don Boyd   ph Keith Goddard   m Peter Skellern

Judi Bowker, Jeremy Kemp, John Hurt, Christopher Cazenove, Anton Rodgers, Vajira, Tariq Yunus

'Punishingly inept in every department.' – *David Badder, MFB*

East of Java

US   1935   72m   bw
Universal

After a shipwreck, menagerie animals take refuge along with the passengers on a tropic island.

The synopsis says it all; the production is sub-standard.

w James Ashmore Creelman, Paul Perez   story *Tiger Island* by Gouverneur Morris   d George Melford

Charles Bickford, Elizabeth Young, Frank Albertson, Sig Rumann

'Highly thrilling, weak on names.' – *Variety*

East of Java (1949): see South Sea Sinner

East of Piccadilly

GB   1940   79m   bw
ABPC (Walter C. Mycroft)
US title: *The Strangler*

A novelist and a girl reporter catch a silk stocking murderer.

Adequate lower case mystery with good atmosphere.

w Lesley Storm, J. Lee-Thompson   novel Gordon Beckles   d Harold Huth   ph Claude Friese-Greene

Sebastian Shaw, Judy Campbell, Henry Edwards, Niall MacGinnis, George Pughe, Martita Hunt, George Hayes, Cameron Hall, Edana Romney

East of Shanghai: see Rich and Strange

East of Sudan

GB   1964   94m   Techniscope
Columbia/Ameran (Charles H. Schneer)

A trooper, a governess and others escape downriver from one of General Gordon's outposts.

Shameless borrowing of plot from *The African Queen* and footage from *The Four Feathers*. The purest hokum.

w Jud Kinberg   d Nathan Juran   ph Wilkie Cooper   m Laurie Johnson

Anthony Quayle, Sylvia Syms, Jenny Agutter

'Nathan Juran could direct this kind of thing blindfold, and for once would appear to have done so.' – *MFB*

East of Sumatra *

US   1953   82m   Technicolor
U-I (Albert J. Cohen)

A mining engineer has trouble with the ruthless chief of a Pacific island.

A good example of routine Hollywood hokum, efficiently staged and acted.

w Frank Gill Jnr   novel Louis L'Amour   d Budd Boetticher   ph Clifford Stine   md Joseph Gershenson

Jeff Chandler, Anthony Quinn, Marilyn Maxwell, John Sutton

East of the Rising Sun: see Malaya

East of the River

US   1940   73m   bw
Warner

A young gangster and his respectable brother both love the same girl.

Tedious formula melodrama in a studio New York.

w Fred Niblo Jnr   d Alfred E. Green

John Garfield, William Lundigan, Brenda Marshall, Marjorie Rambeau, George Tobias

East Side of Heaven

US   1939   85m   bw
Universal

A singing taxi driver looks after an abandoned baby.

Modestly pleasing comedy with music and sentiment; Baby Sandy subsequently starred in her own series.

w William Conselman   d David Butler

Bing Crosby, Joan Blondell, Mischa Auer, C. Aubrey Smith, Irene Hervey, Baby Sandy

'A grand package of entertainment that will play a merry tune at the b.o.' – *Variety*

The East Side Kids

US   1940   62m   bw
Monogram (Sam Katzman)
V*

Street kids reform after helping to catch counterfeiters.

See entry for *The Dead End Kids*; this is the first attempt at a splinter group, and one that did not suggest longevity.

w Robert Lively   d Bob Hill

Leon Ames, Dave O'Brien, Joyce Bryant; and Hally Chester (later Hal E. Chester, producer), Harris Burger, Frankie Burke, Donald Haines, David Durand

'An absurdly poor picture that will command little interest even from the vast army of Dead End Kids devotees.' – *Variety*

East Side West Side *

US   1949   108m   bw
MGM (Voldemar Veltuguin)
V*

A New York businessman is torn between his wife and another woman.

High-class soap opera with all the production stops pulled out; generally well acted and reasonably entertaining.

w Isobel Lennart   novel Marcia Davenport   d Mervyn Le Roy   ph Charles Rosher   m Miklos Rozsa

James Mason, Barbara Stanwyck, Van Heflin, Ava Gardner, Gale Sondergaard, Cyd Charisse, Nancy Davis, William Conrad

'No company is quite so adept as MGM at presenting basically uninteresting material with such style, and such a strong cast, that it cannot fail to entertain.' – *Penelope Houston*

Easter Parade **

US   1948   109m   Technicolor
MGM (Arthur Freed)
V, V*, L

A song and dance man quarrels with one partner but finds another.

A musical which exists only in its numbers, which are many but variable. All in all, an agreeable lightweight entertainment without the style to put it in the top class.

w Sidney Sheldon, Frances Goodrich, Albert Hackett
d Charles Walters   *ph* Harry Stradling   *md* Roger
Edens, Johnny Green   *m/y* Irving Berlin

Fred Astaire, Judy Garland, Ann Miller, Peter Lawford,
Clinton Sundberg, Jules Munshin

'The important thing is that Fred Astaire is back, with
Irving Berlin calling the tunes.' – *Newsweek*

† Fred Astaire was actually second choice, replacing
Gene Kelly who damaged an ankle.

AA: Roger Edens, Johnny Green

Easy Come, Easy Go
US   1947   78m   bw
Paramount (Kenneth MacGowan)

An old Irishman gambles away the money his
daughter earns.

Whimsical sentimental comedy with an unattractive
central character.

w Francis Edward Faragoh, John McNulty, Anne
Froelich   *d* John Farrow   *ph* Daniel L. Fapp
m Roy Webb

Barry Fitzgerald, Diana Lynn, Sonny Tufts, Dick
Foran, Frank McHugh, Allen Jenkins, John Litel,
Arthur Shields

Easy Come, Easy Go
US   1966   97m   Technicolor
Paramount/Wallis-Hazen
V, V*

A frogman tries to salvage a treasure from a wreck off
the California coast.

Empty-headed star vehicle, almost indistinguishable
from many of the others.

w Allan Weiss, Anthony Lawrence   *d* John Rich
ph William Margulies   *m* Joseph J. Lilley

Elvis Presley, Dodie Marshall, Pat Priest, Pat
Harrington, Skip Ward, Frank McHugh, Elsa
Lanchester

'Where there's smoke, there must be somebody smoking!'
Easy Living **
US   1937   91m   bw
Paramount (Arthur Hornblow Jnr)
V*, L

A fur coat is thrown out of a window and lands on a
typist . . .

Amusing romantic comedy with farcical trimmings; it
now stands among the semi-classic crazy comedies of
the thirties.

w Preston Sturges   *d* Mitchell Leisen   *ph* Ted Tetzlaff
md Boris Morros

Jean Arthur, Ray Milland, *Edward Arnold,* Luis Alberni,
Mary Nash, Franklin Pangborn, William Demarest,
Andrew Tombes

'Slapstick farce which does not fulfil the box office
possibilities of its stars.' – *Variety*

'Secretaries, millionaires, jokes, sight gags, furies,
attacks of cool sense – there are always three things
going on at once.' – *New Yorker, 1977*

Easy Living
US   1949   77m   bw
RKO (Robert Sparks)
V*, L

An ageing football star wants to retire but has to
satisfy the living standards of his ambitious wife.

Dim drama.

w Charles Schnee   *story* Irwin Shaw   *d* Jacques
Tourneur   *ph* Harry J. Wild   *m* Roy Webb

Victor Mature, Lucille Ball, Lizabeth Scott, Sonny
Tufts, Lloyd Nolan, Paul Stewart, Jack Paar, Jeff
Donnell

Easy Money
GB   1948   93m   bw
GFD/Gainsborough (A. Frank Bundy)

Four people win big prizes on the football pools.

Short story compendium; very average.

w Muriel and Sydney Box   *play* Arnold Ridley
d Bernard Knowles   *ph* Jack Asher   *m* Temple
Abady

Edward Rigby, Greta Gynt, Dennis Price, Jack Warner,
Mervyn Johns, Petula Clark, Marjorie Fielding, Bill
Owen, Raymond Lovell

Easy Money
US   1983   100m   bw
Orion
V*, L

A baby photographer is left a fortune provided that he
totally reforms.

Overlong and increasingly feeble comedy with a star
who quickly outstays his welcome.

w Rodney Dangerfield, Michael Endler, P. J.
O'Rourke, Dennis Blair   *d* James Signorelli

Rodney Dangerfield, Joe Pesci, Geraldine Fitzgerald,
Candy Azzara, Val Avery

'A man went looking for America and couldn't find it
anywhere!'
Easy Rider ****
US   1969   94m   Technicolor
Columbia/Pando/Raybert (Peter Fonda)
V, V*, L, S

Two drop-outs ride across America on motorcycles.

Happening to please hippies and motor-cycle
enthusiasts as well as amateur politicians, this
oddball melodrama drew freakishly large audiences
throughout the world and was much imitated though
never equalled in its casual effectiveness.

w Peter Fonda, Dennis Hopper, Terry Southern
d Dennis Hopper   *ph* Laszlo Kovacs   *m* various
recordings

Peter Fonda, Dennis Hopper, *Jack Nicholson*

'Cinéma-vérité in allegory terms.' – *Peter Fonda*

'Ninety-four minutes of what it is like to swing, to
watch, to be fond, to hold opinions and to get killed
in America at this moment.' – *Penelope Gilliatt*

AAN: script; Jack Nicholson

Easy Street ****
US   1917   22m approx   bw   silent
Mutual/Charles Chaplin

In a slum street, a tramp is reformed by a dewy-eyed
missionary, becomes a policeman, and tames the local
bully.

Quintessential Chaplin, combining sentimentality
and social comment with hilarious slapstick.

wd Charles Chaplin   *ph* William C. Foster, Rollie
Totheroh

Charles Chaplin, Edna Purviance, Albert Austin, Eric
Campbell

Easy to Love *
US   1933   62m   bw
Warner

A pair of couples get into a romantic mix-up.

Innocent predecessor of *Bob and Carol and Ted and Alice;*
come to think of it, quite sophisticated for its year.

w Carl Erickson, Manuel Seff   *play* Thompson
Buchanan   *d* William Keighley

Adolphe Menjou, Genevieve Tobin, Mary Astor,
Edward Everett Horton, Guy Kibbee, Patricia Ellis,
Hugh Herbert

'Adaptation, direction and able performances make an
old story amusing entertainment.' – *Variety*

Easy to Love
US   1953   96m   Technicolor
MGM (Joe Pasternak)
V*

The romances of an aqua-queen in Florida's Cypress
Gardens.

Thin, humourless and forgettable musical vehicle
sustained by spectacular water ballets.

w Laslo Vadnay, William Roberts   *d* Charles
Walters   *ph* Ray June   *md* Lennie Hayton, George
Stoll   *ch* Busby Berkeley

Esther Williams, Tony Martin, Van Johnson, John
Bromfield, Carroll Baker

Easy to Wed *
US   1946   110m   Technicolor
MGM (Jack Cummings)

A socialite threatens a newspaper with libel; he
postpones his own wedding and sets a friend to
compromise her.

Bright but tasteless remake of *Libelled Lady,* with a
second team cast trying hard.

w Dorothy Kingsley, Maurine Watkins, Howard
Emmett Rogers, George Oppenheimer   *d* Edward
Buzzell   *ph* Harry Stradling   *m* Johnny Green

Van Johnson, Esther Williams, *Lucille Ball,* Keenan
Wynn, Cecil Kellaway, Carlos Ramirez, Ben Blue,
Ethel Smith

Easy Virtue
GB   1927   73m (24 fps)   bw   silent
Gainsborough (Michael Balcon)

A drunkard's wife falls for a young man who kills
himself. Her past then prevents her attempts to lead a
respectable life.

Vapid social melodrama with minimal points of
interest despite its credits.

w Eliot Stannard   *play* Noël Coward   *d* Alfred
Hitchcock   *ph* Claude McDonnelled Ivor Montagu

Isabel Jeans, Franklyn Dyall, Eric Bransby Williams,
Ian Hunter, Violet Farebrother, Robin Irvine

Eat a Bowl of Tea **
US   1989   104m   DeLuxe   Panavision
Artificial Eye/American Playhouse Theatre (Tom Sternberg)
V, V*, L

A young Chinese-American brings back to New York
a Chinese-born bride, but finds that family pressures
to produce children make him impotent.

Sharply observed, witty domestic drama, set in the
1940s when Chinese immigrants were first allowed to
bring their wives to America.

w Judith Rascoe   *novel* Louis Chu   *d* Wayne Wang
ph Amir Mokri   *m* Mark Adler   *pd* Bob Ziembicki
ed Richard Candib

Cora Miao, Russell Wong, Victor Wong, Lau Sui
Ming, Eric Tsang Chi Wai

'An engaging and welcome picture. Good-humoured,
sincere, it is nothing more than it modestly aspires to
be.' – *MFB*

Eat the Peach *
Eire   1986   95m   Technicolor
Strongbow/Film Four International (David Collins)
V, V*

Out-of-work Irish devise a mad scheme to construct a
motorcycle Wall of Death.

Fairly amusing comedy, like an Irish version of an
Ealing movie.

w Peter Ormrod, John Kelleher   *d* Peter Ormrod
ph Arthur Wooster   *m* Donal Lummy

Stephen Brennan, Eamon Morrissey, Catherine Byrne,
Niall Toibin, Joe Lynch, Tony Doyle

Eating Raoul *

US   1982   83m   Pacific Color
Bartel Film (Anne Kimmel)
V*

A restaurateur kills a drunken swinger, and finds that
he has a profitable sideline on his hands . . .

Black comedy with insufficient humour to offset
tastelessness.

w Richard Blackburn, Paul Bartel   d Paul Bartel
ph Gary Thieltges   m Arlon Ober

Paul Bartel, Mary Woronov, Robert Beltran, Susan
Saiger, Richard Blackburn

'I wanted to make a film about two greedy, uptight
people who are at the same time not so unlike you
and me and Nancy and Ronnie, to keep it funny and
yet communicate something about the psychology and
perversity of these values . . . My movie touches on
many things: the perversion of middle class values,
the resurgence of Nixonism, machismo versus WASP
fastidiousness, film noir . . .' – Paul Bartel

Ebb Tide **

US   1937   92m   Technicolor
Paramount (Lucien Hubbard)

Sailors are stranded with a dangerous fanatic on a
South Sea island.

Interesting adaptation of Stevenson, notable both for
its early colour and its genuinely sour, anti-romantic
mood, almost unique for Hollywood in this period.

w Bertram Millhauser   novel R. L. Stevenson, Lloyd
Osbourne   d James Hogan   ph Leo Tover
m Victor Young

Ray Milland, Frances Farmer, Oscar Homolka, Barry
Fitzgerald, Lloyd Nolan

'More pretentious as to production than dramatically.
Does not suggest big b.o.' – Variety

† Remade 1946 as Adventure Island.

Ebirah, Horror of the Deep

Japan   1966   85m   Eastmancolor   Tohoscope
Toho (Tomoyuki Tanaka)

Scientists creating nuclear weapons on an island
guarded by a giant lobster are foiled with the aid of
Godzilla.

The usual hokum, enlivened by fight sequences that
have Godzilla heading rocks with the aplomb of a
football striker, and a giant moth that looks as if it has
been made from an old carpet.

w Shinichi Sekizawa   d Jun Fukuda   ph Kazuo
Yamada   ad Takeo Kita   sp Eiji Tsuburaya

Akira Takarada, Kuni Mizuno, Akihiko Hirata, Jun
Tazaki, Hideo Sunazuka, Chotaro Togin, Toru
Watanabe

The Echo Murders

GB   1945   80m   bw
British National

Sexton Blake conquers Nazi spies.

Feebly made addition to the short Blake cycle.

wd John Harlow

David Farrar, Dennis Price, Pamela Stirling, Julien
Mitchell

'About as modern as a reissue of The Perils of Pauline.' –
Variety

Echo of Barbara

GB   1958   58m   bw
Independent Artists

A stripper poses as the daughter of an ex-con in a plot
to retrieve hidden loot.

Taut little crime support, not bad at all.

w John Kruse   novel Jonathan Burke   d Sidney
Hayers

Mervyn Johns, Maureen Connell, Paul Stassino,
Ronald Hines, Tom Bell

Echo Park *

Austria   1985   92m   colour
Sasha Wein/Walter Shenson
V*, L

In a rundown area of Los Angeles, three unsuccessful
youngsters await the big break.

Vaguely entertaining slice-of-life drama with good
observational touches.

w Michael Ventura   d Robert Dornhelm   ph Karl
Kofler   m David Rickets

Susan Dey, Thomas Hulce, Michael Bowen,
Christopher Walker

Echoes of a Summer

US/Canada   1975   98m   Eastmancolor
Beata/Castle/Astral/Bryanston (Robert L. Joseph)

An 11-year-old girl dying of heart disease spends her
last summer with her parents on holiday in a Nova
Scotian village.

Excruciating.

w Robert L. Joseph   d Don Taylor   ph John
Coquillon   m Terry James

Jodie Foster, Richard Harris, Lois Nettleton,
Geraldine Fitzgerald, William Windom, Brad Savage

'The only honest thing about this movie is its desire to
make a buck.' – Frank Rich, New York Post

The Eclipse **

Italy/France   1962   125m   bw
Interopa-Cineriz/Paris Film (Robert and Raymond Hakim)
V*
original title: L'Eclisse

A young Roman woman breaks off one affair and
begins another.

A portrait in depth, rather tiresomely long and with at
least one totally irrelevant stock-market sequence; but
superbly done for connoisseurs.

wd Michelangelo Antonioni, Tonino Guerra, Elio
Bartolini, Ottiero Ottieri   ph Gianni di Venanzo
m Giovanni Fusco

Monica Vitti, Alain Delon, Francisco Rabal

'The first time I saw the film I thought it magnificent
but chill, played glitteringly . . . At a second visit the
passion breaks through.' – Dilys Powell

L'Eclisse: see The Eclipse

L'École Buissonière *

France   1948   89m   bw
UGC/CGCF
US title: I Have a New Master

At a provincial village school, a new teacher
introduces new methods and takes a while to win
over the locals.

Rustic comedy-drama of a kind the French do well.

w Jean-Paul Le Chanois, Elise Freinet   d Jean-Paul
Le Chanois   ph Marc Fossard, Maurice Pecqueux,
André Dumaître   m Joseph Kosma

Bernard Blier, Juliette Fabre, Edouard Delmont

L'École des Facteurs **

France   1947   14m   bw
Cady (Fred Orain)
V

A village postman puts into practice what he has
learned at training school.

Amusing short, full of a humane humour, which was
to blossom a year later into the wonderful Jour de Fête.

wd Jacques Tati   m Jean Yatove   ed Marcel
Moreau

Jacques Tati, Paul Demange

† It was released on video together with Cours du Soir
and Soigne Ton Gauche as Tati Shorts.

Ecologia del Delitto: see A Bay of Blood

Ecstasy: see Extase

'It's big and bright as those banjo eyes!'
The Eddie Cantor Story

US   1953   116m   Technicolor
Warner (Sidney Skolsky)

After a tough childhood on New York's east side,
Israel Iskowitz becomes a famous entertainer.

Deliberately patterned after the success of The Jolson
Story, this is an unhappy example of how close are
success and failure; the elements are the same, but
this film suffers from unsure timing, lack of humour,
rather apologetic numbers, a really dismal script and a
caricature performance in the lead.

w Jerome Weidman, Ted Sherdeman, Sidney Skolsky
d Alfred E. Green   ph Edwin DuPar   md Ray
Heindorf   ch: Le Roy Prinz   m/y various

Keefe Brasselle, Marilyn Erskine, Aline MacMahon,
Arthur Franz, Alex Gerry, Gerald Mohr, William
Forrest (as Ziegfeld), Will Rogers Jnr (as Will Rogers),
and Eddie Cantor (who also sings the songs off
screen)

Eddie Holm's Second Life **

Denmark   1985   95m   colour
Scenograf (Poul Amt Thomsen)
original title: Eddie Holms Andet Liv

A suicidal musician is taken back through his life to
discover what drove him to end it.

Witty, black comedy of love, death and family life.

w Bjarne Henriksen, Gert Henriksen   d Esben
Hùilund Carlsen   ph Ole Schultz   m Bo Lykke
Jùrgensen   ed Jette Allarp

Kristian Halken, Pernille Hansen, Lisbet Lundquist,
Claus Nissen, Holger Boland, Karen Marie Lowert,
Frederik Esbensen

Eddie Macon's Run

US   1983   95m   Technicolor
Universal/Martin Bregman (Louis A. Stroller)
V*, L

A man innocently convicted escapes and hotfoots it
back home.

Old-style chase film marred by passages of sex and
crude backwoods violence.

wd Jeff Kanew   novel James McLendon   ph James
A. Contner   m Norton Buffalo   ed Jeff Kanew

John Schneider, Kirk Douglas, Lee Purcell, Leah
Ayres

The Eddy Duchin Story

US   1956   123m   Technicolor   Cinemascope
Columbia (Jonie Taps, Jerry Wald)
V*, L, S

The success story of a pianist who died of leukemia.

Predictable, glossy, sentimental musical biopic.

w Samuel Taylor   story Leo Katcher   d George
Sidney   ph Harry Stradling   md George Duning
piano Carmen Cavallero

Tyrone Power, Kim Novak, Victoria Shaw, James
Whitmore, Shepperd Strudwick, Frieda Inescort,
Gloria Holden, Larry Keating

AAN: Leo Katcher; Harry Stradling; George Duning

Edes Emma, Draga Böbe – Vazlatok, Aktok:
see Dear Emma, Sweet Böbe

Edgar Wallace

Between 1960 and 1966 no fewer than 46 second
features emerged from Jack Greenwood's production

unit at the London suburban studios of Merton Park, under the Edgar Wallace banner and prefaced by a sinister revolving bust of the author (though few had very much to do with his original stories).

All maintained a better standard than any other crime second features of the period, and a few were seized on with delight by the critics. They were subsequently popular on television, though the Independent Broadcasting Authority banned repeats on the grounds that they were without merit. In this complete list, details are given for the more interesting items:

THE CLUE OF THE TWISTED CANDLE
A MARRIAGE OF CONVENIENCETHE MAN WHO WAS NOBODY
THE CLUE OF THE NEW PIN*
(w Philip Mackie, d Allan Davis, with Paul Daneman, Bernard Archard)
PARTNERS IN CRIME
THE FOURTH SQUARE
THE MAN AT THE CARLTON TOWER
THE CLUE OF THE SILVER KEY
ATTEMPT TO KILL
THE SINISTER MAN*
(w Philip Mackie, d Clive Donner, with Patrick Allen, John Bentley)
NEVER BACK LOSERS
MAN DETAINED
RICOCHET
THE DOUBLE
THE RIVALS
TO HAVE AND TO HOLD
THE PARTNER
FIVE TO ONE
ACCIDENTAL DEATH
WE SHALL SEE
DOWNFALL
THE VERDICT
WHO WAS MADDOX?*
(w Roger Marshall, d Geoffrey Nethercott, with Bernard Lee, Finlay Currie)
ACT OF MURDER*
(w Lewis Davidson, d Alan Bridges, with John Carson, Anthony Bate)
FACE OF A STRANGER
NEVER MENTION MURDER
(w Robert Banks Stewart, d John Nelson Burton, with Maxine Audley, Dudley Foster)
THE MAIN CHANCE
GAME FOR THREE LOSERS
DEAD MAN'S CHEST
CHANGE PARTNERS
STRANGLER'S WEB*
(w George Baxt, d John Moxey, with Griffith Jones, Gerald Harper)
BACKFIRE
CANDIDATE FOR MURDER*
(w Lukas Heller, d David Villers, with Michael Gough, John Justin)
FLAT TWO
THE SHARE-OUT
NUMBER SIX
TIME TO REMEMBER
PLAYBACK*
(w Robert Banks Stewart, d John Nelson Burton, with Maxine Audley, Dudley Foster)
SOLO FOR SPARROW
LOCKER 69
DEATH TRAP
THE SET-UP
ON THE RUN
THE £20,000 KISS
INCIDENT AT MIDNIGHT
RETURN TO SENDER

Edge of Darkness *
US   1943   124m   bw
Warner (Henry Blanke)
V*

Norwegian village patriots resist the Nazis.

High-intentioned, ambitiously cast but ultimately bathetic resistance melodrama, high principled down to its tragic finale but compromised by backlot shooting and the presence of Errol Flynn.

w Robert Rossen   d Lewis Milestone   ph Sid Hickox   m Franz Waxman

Errol Flynn, Ann Sheridan, Walter Huston, Judith Anderson, Ruth Gordon, Nancy Coleman, Helmut Dantine, Morris Carnovsky, Charles Dingle, John Beal, Richard Fraser, Helene Thimig

'It is not a tea party. It is an icy shower turned loose on audiences in the hope of driving home what this war is about.' – *Motion Picture Herald*

Edge of Divorce: see *Background*

Edge of Doom
US   1950   97m   bw
Samuel Goldwyn
GB title: *Stronger than Fear*

A desperate youth kills a priest and struggles with his conscience.

A sanctimonious weirdie, extremely odd coming from this producer, and unhappily re-edited before release. Someone was interested enough to want to make it, but it seems to have been killed by the cast and the front office.

w Philip Yordan   novel Leo Brady   d Mark Robson   ph Harry Stradling   m Hugo Friedhofer

Dana Andrews, Farley Granger, Joan Evans, Robert Keith, Paul Stewart, Mala Powers, Adele Jergens, Harold Vermilyea, Mabel Paige

Edge of Eternity *
US   1959   80m   Technicolor   Cinemascope
Columbia/Thunderbird (Kendrick Sweet)

A Grand Canyon sheriff traces three murders to an ownership struggle over a disused mine.

Routine but suspenseful thriller with splendid locations.

w Knut Swenson, Richard Collins   d Don Siegel   ph Burnett Guffey   m Daniele Amfitheatrof

Cornel Wilde, Victoria Shaw, Edgar Buchanan, Mickey Shaughnessy, Jack Elam

Edge of Hell
US   1956   76m   bw
Universal-International (Hugo Haas)

In a slummy rooming house, a beggar who lives by his dog's talents falls for the new lodger.

Self-parodying sub-Jannings melodrama with an unlikely star.

wd Hugo Haas

Hugo Haas, Francesca de Scaffa, Ken Carlton, June Hammerstein

Edge of Honor *
US   1991   92m   Western Cine colour
Merit Badge/Guerilla Film Unit (Jay B. Davis, Peter Garrity, David O'Malley)
V, V*, L

Scouts are attacked by a gang of ruthless arms smugglers after they discover a cache of weapons hidden in a forest.

A violent but effective action adventure intended for a teenage audience.

w Mark Rosenbaum, Michael Spence, David O'Malley   d Michael Spence   ph Billy Dickson   m William Stromberg   pd Charles Armstrong   ed Ellen Keneshea

Corey Feldman, Meredith Salenger, Scott Reeves, Ken Jenkins, Don Swayze, Christopher Neame

'A great action movie with a gung-ho performance by Don Swayze.' – *Sight and Sound*

Edge of Sanity
GB   1988   90m   Eastmancolor
Palace/Allied Vision (Edward Simons, Harry Alan Towers)
V*, L

Dr Jekyll, under the influence of drugs, becomes Jack the Ripper.

Dire variation on Robert Louis Stevenson's classic.

w J. P. Felix, Ron Raley   d Gerard Kikoine   ph Tony Spratling   m Frederic Talgorn   pd Jean Charles Dedieu   ed Malcolm Cooke

Anthony Perkins, Glynis Barber, Sarah Maur-Thorp, David Lodge, Ben Cole, Ray Jewers, Jill Melford

Edge of the City **
US   1957   85m   bw
MGM/Jonathan (David Susskind, Jim di Ganci)
GB title: *A Man is Ten Feet Tall*

Racial tensions lead to tragedy in the railroad yards of New York's waterfront.

Tense, brutal melodrama, which has historical interest as an effective opening-up in cinematic terms of a TV play, in its imitation of *On the Waterfront*, and in its rebel hero and relaxed black friend.

w Robert Alan Aurthur, play Robert Alan Aurthur   d Martin Ritt   ph Joseph Brun   m Leonard Rosenman

Sidney Poitier, John Cassavetes, Jack Warden, Kathleen Maguire, Ruby Dee, Robert Simon, Ruth White

Edge of the World **
GB   1937   80m   bw
GFD/Rock (Joe Rock)
V

Life, love and death on Foula, a remote Shetland island.

Rare for its time, a vigorous location drama in the Flaherty tradition; sometimes naïve, usually exhilarating.

wd Michael Powell   ph Ernest Palmer, Monty Berman, Skeets Kelly   m Lambert Williamson   ed Derek Twist

Niall MacGinnis, Belle Chrystall, John Laurie, Finlay Currie, Eric Berry

'Scant of plot and unlikely to be hailed by the public at large.' – *Variety*

'The love of a woman … the courage of a fighting America … lifted him from obscurity to thrilling fame!'
Edison the Man **
US   1940   107m   bw
MGM (John W. Considine Jnr)
V*, L

Edison struggles for years in poverty before becoming famous as the inventor of the electric light bulb.

Standard, well-made biopic following on from *Young Tom Edison*; reasonably absorbing, but slightly suspect in its facts.

w Dore Schary, Talbot Jennings, Bradbury Foote, Hugo Butler   d Clarence Brown   ph Harold Rosson   m Herbert Stothart

Spencer Tracy, Rita Johnson, Lynne Overman, Charles Coburn, Gene Lockhart, Henry Travers, Felix Bressart

AAN: Dore Schary, Hugo Butler (original story)

Edith and Marcel *
France   1984   140m   Eastmancolor
Gala/Cannon/Film 13/Parafrance/Miramax (Tania Zazulinsky)
V*

Two French idols indulge in a tragic love affair.

Effective biopic based on the affair between singer Edith Piaf and boxer Marcel Cerdan.

wd Claude Lelouch   ph Jean Boffety   m Francis Lai   ed Hugues Darmois

Evelyne Bouix, Jacques Villeret, Francis Hustler, Jean-Claude Brialy, Jean Bouise, Charles Gérard, Marcel Cerdan Jnr

Edouard et Caroline **

France 1951 99m bw
UGC/CICC

A young pianist and his wife quarrel while preparing for an important recital.

Gay, slight, charming comedy, a two-hander taking place within the course of a few hours.

w *Annette Wademant, Jacques Becker* d *Jacques Becker* ph Robert Le Fèbvre m Jean-Jacques Grunenwald

Daniel Gélin, Anne Vernon, Jacques François, William Tubbs, Jean Galland, Elina Labourdette, Betty Stockfield

'It lifts its weighty trivialities into a world of enchantment.' – *Sunday Times*

Educated Evans

GB 1936 86m bw
Warner (Irving Asher)

A racetrack bookie becomes a trainer.

Rather unyielding vehicle for a fast-talking star.

w Frank Launder and Robert Edmunds story Edgar Wallace d William Beaudine ph Basil Emmott ad Peter Proud

Max Miller, Nancy O'Neil, Clarice Mayne, Albert Whelan, Hal Walters

† A sequel followed in 1938: *Thank Evans.*

Educating Rita *

GB 1983 110m Technicolor
Rank/Acorn (Lewis Gilbert)
V, V*, L, S

A cheerful young hairdresser improves her knowledge of English Literature by enrolling on an Open University course.

Rather dismal, thinly characterized and ill-lit variation on *Pygmalion*, with endless talk leading nowhere (it was originally a two-character play). Due to its Liverpudlian modishness it achieved surprising box-office success.

w Willy Russell play Willy Russell d Lewis Gilbert ph Frank Watts m David Hentschel

Michael Caine, Julie Walters, Michael Williams, Maureen Lipman

'If only I'd been able to believe they were actually reading the books, everything else would have fallen into place.' – *Roger Ebert*

AAN: Michael Caine; Julie Walters; Willy Russell

Edvard Munch *

Norway/Sweden 1976 215m colour
New Yorker/SR

The life of the 19th-century Norwegian expressionist painter.

A yawn for the majority but a delight for connoisseurs of a certain kind; with a wholly non-professional cast.

wd Peter Watkins

Geir Westby, Gro Fraas, Johan Halsborg, Lotte Teig

Edward My Son

GB 1949 112m bw
MGM (Edwin H. Knopf)

A rich, unscrupulous man remembers the people he has made unhappy, and the son to whom he never behaved as a father should.

Unsatisfactory, rather ugly-looking adaptation of a gripping piece of theatre, with casting and direction remarkably uncertain from such professionals.

w Donald Ogden Stewart play Robert Morley d George Cukor ph F. A. Young m John Wooldridge, Malcolm Sargent

Spencer Tracy, Deborah Kerr, Ian Hunter, James Donald, Leueen McGrath, Mervyn Johns

AAN: Deborah Kerr

Edward Scissorhands **

US 1990 98m colour
Fox (Denise de Novi)
V, V*, L, S

A boy with artificial hands upsets the community in which he lives.

Bizarre fairy-tale with a good deal of charm.

w Caroline Thompson story Tim Burton d Tim Burton ph Stefan Czapsky m Danny Elfman pd Bo Welsh ad Tom Duffield ed Richard Halsey

Johnny Depp, Winona Ryder, Dianne Wiest, Anthony Michael Hall, Alan Arkin, Kathy Baker, Robert Oliver, Conchata Ferrell, Vincent Price

'A delightful and delicate comic fable.' – *Variety*

AAN: best makeup

Edward II **

GB 1991 90m colour
Palace/Edward II/Working Title/British Screen/BBC (Steve Clark-Hall, Antony Root)
V, V*, S

Edward II's love for Piers Gaveston leads to his downfall.

An explicitly homosexual reworking of Marlowe's play, done in modern dress and given a contemporary twist.

w Derek Jarman, Stephen McBride, Ken Butler play Christopher Marlowe d *Derek Jarman* ph Ian Wilson m Simon Fisher Turner pd Christopher Hobbs ed George Akers

Steven Waddington, Kevin Collins, Andrew Tiernan, John Lynch, Dudley Sutton, Tilda Swinton, Jerome Flynn, Jody Graber, Nigel Terry, Annie Lennox

'Provocative and challenging . . . likely will be the director's most commercial production to date.' – *Variety*

'Through the miracle of cinema, two sensibilities and centuries become wondrously fused. Bold, passionate and savagely beautiful.' – *Geoff Brown, The Times*

The Effect of Gamma Rays on Man-in-the-Moon Marigolds

US 1972 101m DeLuxe
Newman-Foreman (Paul Newman)

A slatternly middle-aged woman dreams of better times for herself and her children.

Well-written but essentially banal and pretentious domestic drama, the kind of film that only gets made when powerful stars see in it a juicy role.

w Alvin Sargent play Paul Zendel d Paul Newman ph Adam Holender m Maurice Jarre

Joanne Woodward, Nell Potts, Roberta Wallach, Judith Lowry

Effi Briest *

West Germany 1974 140m bw
Tango Film (Rainer Werner Fassbinder)
V, V*
original title: *Fontane Effi Briest*

A teenage girl is married to a rich baron, but fails to understand what is expected of her.

Overlong but often fascinating picture of a vanished society in which not the slightest weakening of structure is permitted.

wd Rainer Werner Fassbinder novel Theodor Fontane ph Jürgen Jürges, Dietrich Lohmann m from Saint-Saëns

Hanna Schygulla, Wolfgang Schenck, Ulli Lommel, Karl-Heinz Böhm, Ursula Strätz

'Beautiful. It renders the book as fully and texturally as could be possible in 140 minutes, and it's a work, in and of itself, intrinsically cinematic.' – *Stanley Kauffmann*

The Efficiency Expert: see *Spotswood*

L'Effrontée: see *The Impudent Girl*

The Egg and I *

US 1947 104m bw
U-I (Chester Erskine)
V*,

A city couple try to become gentleman farmers.

Mild, pleasant comedy notable chiefly for introducing a hillbilly couple, Ma and Pa Kettle, who went on, in the personae of Main and Kilbride, to make several later features. (See under *Kettles.*)

w Chester Erskine, Fred Finklehoffe novel Betty Macdonald d Chester Erskine ph Milton Krasner m Frank Skinner

Claudette Colbert, Fred MacMurray, *Marjorie Main, Percy Kilbride,* Louise Allbritton, Richard Long, Billy House, Ida Moore, Donald MacBride

'Marjorie Main, in an occasional fit of fine, wild comedy, picks the show up and brandishes it as if she were wringing its neck. I wish to God she had.' – *James Agee*

AAN: Marjorie Main

'10,965 pyramids! 5,337 dancing girls! One million swaying bulrushes! 802 sacred bulls!'

The Egyptian *

US 1954 140m DeLuxe Cinemascope
TCF (Darryl F. Zanuck)
V*, L, S

In ancient Egypt an abandoned baby grows up to be physician to the pharaoh.

More risible than reasonable, sounding more like a parody than the real thing, this pretentious epic from a bestseller flounders helplessly between its highlights but has moments of good humour and makes an excellent example of the pictures they don't make 'em like any more.

w Philip Dunne, Casey Robinson novel Mika Waltari d Michael Curtiz ph Leon Shamroy m Bernard Herrmann, Alfred Newman ad Lyle Wheeler, George W. Davis

Edmund Purdom, Victor Mature, *Peter Ustinov,* Bella Darvi, Gene Tierney, Michael Wilding, Jean Simmons, Judith Evelyn, Henry Daniell, John Carradine, Carl Benton Reid

'The novel . . . supplied the reader with enough occurrences and customs of Akhnaton's time . . . to hide some of the more obvious contrivances of the story. The film does not do this.' – *Carolyn Harrow, Films in Review*

AAN: Leon Shamroy

Ehi, Amico . . . C'è Sabata, Hai Chiuso: see *Sabata*

The Eiger Sanction *

US 1975 125m Technicolor Panavision
Universal/Malpaso (Jennings Lang)
V, V*, L, S

An art teacher returns to the CIA as an exterminator, and finds himself in a party climbing the Eiger.

Silly spy melodrama with some breathtaking mountain sequences.

w Warren B. Murphy, Hal Dresner, Rod Whitaker novel Trevanian d Clint Eastwood ph Frank Stanley, John Cleare, Jeff Schoolfield, Peter Pilafian, Pete White m John Williams

Clint Eastwood, George Kennedy, Vonetta McGee, Jack Cassidy, Heidi Bruhl, Thayer David

'All the villains have been constructed from prefabricated Bond models.' – *Richard Combs*

Eight and a Half ****
Italy   1963   138m   bw
Cineriz (Angelo Rizzoli)
V, V*, L
original title: *Otto e Mezzo*

A successful film director on the verge of a nervous breakdown has conflicting fantasies about his life.

A Fellini self-portrait in which anything goes.

w Federico Fellini, Ennio Flaiano, Tullio Pinelli, Brunello Rondi   *d* Federico Fellini   *ph* Gianni di Venanzo   *m* Nino Rota   *ad* Piero Gherardi

Marcello Mastroianni, Claudia Cardinale, Anouk Aimée, Sandra Milo, Rossella Falk, Barbara Steele, Madeleine Lebeau

'The whole may add up to a magnificent folly, but it is too singular, too candid, too vividly and insistently alive to be judged as being in any way diminishing.' – *Peter John Dyer, MFB*

'Fellini's intellectualizing is not even like dogs dancing; it is not done well, nor does it surprise us that it is done at all. It merely palls on us, and finally appals us.' – *John Simon*

'A de luxe glorification of creative crisis, visually arresting but in some essential way conventional-minded.' – *Pauline Kael, 70s*

AA: best foreign film

AAN: script; direction

Eight Iron Men
US   1952   80m   bw
Columbia/Stanley Kramer

In the ruins of an Italian village, eight American infantrymen wait for relief.

Quickie war film in which everyone talks a lot and they all survive; from the time when Kramer was discovering how fast he could turn 'em out.

w Harry Brown   *play* *A Sound of Hunting* by Harry Brown   *d* Edward Dmytryk   *ph* Roy Hunt   *m* Leith Stevens   *pd* Rudolph Sternad

Bonar Colleano, Lee Marvin, Arthur Franz, Richard Kiley, Nick Dennis, James Griffith, Dick Moore, George Cooper

Eight Men Out ***
US   1988   119m   colour
Rank/Orion (Sarah Pilsbury, Midge Sandford)
V, V*, L, S

In 1919 members of the great Chicago White Sox baseball team take bribes to lose the World Series.

Absorbing drama, excellently filmed, with good ensemble acting.

w John Sayles   *book* Eliot Asinof   *d* John Sayles   *ph* Robert Richardson   *m* Mason Daring   *pd* Nora Chavooshian   *ed* John Tintori

John Cusack, Clifton James, Michael Lerner, Christopher Lloyd, John Mahoney, Charlie Sheen, David Strathairn, D. B. Sweeney

Eight O'Clock Walk
GB   1953   87m   bw
British Lion/George King

A young barrister proves a taxi driver innocent of murder.

Minor-league courtroom stuff, an adequate time-passer.

w Katherine Strueby, Guy Morgan   *story* Jack Roffey, Gordon Harbord   *d* Lance Comfort   *ph* Brendan Stafford   *m* George Melachrino

Richard Attenborough, Derek Farr, Cathy O'Donnell, Ian Hunter, Maurice Denham, Bruce Seton, Harry Welchman

Eight on the Lam
US   1966   107m   DeLuxe
United Artists/Hope Enterprises (Bill Lawrence)
GB title: *Eight on the Run*

A bank teller is suspected of embezzlement and goes on the run with his seven children.

Feeble comedy punctuated by even feebler chases; the star had lost his comic character.

w Albert E. Lewin, Burt Styler, Bob Fisher, Arthur Marx   *d* George Marshall   *ph* Alan Stensvold   *m* George Romanis

Bob Hope, Phyllis Diller, Jonathan Winters, Shirley Eaton, Jill St John

Eight on the Run: see *Eight on the Lam*

18 Again!
US   1988   100m   DeLuxe
Entertainment/New World (Walter Coblenz)
V*, L

After a car crash, the mind of an 81-year-old grandfather is switched into the body of his 18-year-old grandson.

Feeblest of the body-swap cycle of films, with little to entertain.

w Josh Goldstein, Jonathan Prince   *d* Paul Flaherty   *ph* Stephen M. Katz   *m* Billy Goldenberg   *pd* Dena Roth   *ed* Danford B. Greene

George Burns, Charlie Schlatter, Tony Roberts, Anita Morris, Miriam Flynn, Jennifer Runyon, Red Buttons

1871
GB   1989   100m   Metrocolor
ICA/Looseyard/Film Four/La Sept/Palawood/Animatografo (Stewart Richards)

An Irish rebel, in love with an actress-cum-prostitute whom he is forced to share with an English aristocrat and spy, takes part in the doomed Paris Commune of 1871.

Blinkered and fussy look at a failed revolution.

w Terry James, James Leahy, Ken McMullen   *d* Ken McMullen   *ph* Elso Roque   *m* Barrie Guard   *pd* Paul Cheetham   *ed* William Diver

Roshan Seth, John Lynch, Timothy Spall, Alexandre de Sousa, Ian McNeice, Alan Braine, Maria João Toscano, Maria de Medeiros, Ana Padrao, Jacqueline Dankworth

'Another melancholy example of rigid radicalism lacking mainstream and popular sophistication.' – *Raymond Durgnat, Sight and Sound*

'Has all the elements of terrific television: romance, revolution, murder, a good cast and top-notch production values.' – *Variety*

Eighty Thousand Suspects *
GB   1963   113m   bw   Cinemascope
Rank/Val Guest

A smallpox epidemic terrorizes the city of Bath.

Predictable melodrama which adequately passes the time.

wd Val Guest   *novel* *Pillars of Midnight* by Elleston Trevor   *ph* Arthur Grant   *m* Stanley Black

Claire Bloom, Richard Johnson, Yolande Donlan, Cyril Cusack, Michael Goodliffe, Mervyn Johns, Kay Walsh, Basil Dignam, Ray Barrett

84 Charing Cross Road **
GB   1986   97m   Rank colour
Columbia/Brooksfilm (Geoffrey Helman)
V, V*, L

A New York woman conducts a long correspondence with an antiquarian bookseller in London.

Pleasant picturization of a now famous book which had already been seen on TV and stage.

w Hugh Whitemore   *book* Helene Hanff   *d* David Jones   *ph* Brian West   *m* George Fenton   *pd* Eileen Diss, Edward Pisoni

Anne Bancroft, Anthony Hopkins, Judi Dench, Maurice Denham, Jean de Baer, Eleanor David

84 Charlie Mopic *
US   1989   95m   colour
Charlie Mopic Company (Michael Nolin)
V, V*, L

An army cameraman and an inexperienced officer accompany a reconnaissance patrol in Vietnam.

A documentary-style account of war as it affects the individual, as seen from the subjective viewpoint of the cameraman.

wd Patrick Duncan   *ph* Alan Casco   *m* Donovan   *ad* Douglas Dick   *ed* Stephen Purvis

Jonathan Emerson, Nicholas Cascone, Jason Tomlins, Christopher Burgard, Glenn Morshower, Richard Brooks, Byron Thames

Einmal Ku'damm und Zurück: see *Girl In a Boot*

El **
Mexico   1952   91m   bw
Nacional Film (Oscar Dancigers)
aka: *This Strange Passion; Torments*

A middle-aged aristocrat marries a beautiful young girl and falls victim to insane jealousy.

A tragi-comic case history with chilling and memorable details; not one of its director's great works, but an engaging minor one.

w Luis Buñuel, Luis Alcoriza   *novel* *Pensamientos* by Mercedes Pinto   *d* Luis Buñuel   *ph* Gabriel Figueroa   *m* Luis Hernandez Breton

Arturo de Cordova, Delia Garces, Luis Beristain, Aurora Walker

El Chucho, Quién Sabe?: see *A Bullet for the General*

El Cid *
US/Spain   1961   184m   Super Technirama
Samuel Bronston
V, V*, L

A legendary 11th-century hero drives the Moors from Spain.

Endless glum epic with splendid action sequences as befits the high budget.

w Frederic M. Frank, Philip Yordan   *d* Anthony Mann   *ph* Robert Krasker   *m* Miklos Rozsa

Charlton Heston, Sophia Loren, Raf Vallone, Genevieve Page, John Fraser, Gary Raymond, Herbert Lom, Hurd Hatfield, Massimo Serato, Andrew Cruickshank, Michael Hordern, Douglas Wilmer, Frank Thring

'A Lone Ranger liberation tale.' – *Judith Crist*

AAN: Miklos Rozsa; song 'The Falcon and the Dove' (*m* Miklos Rozsa, *ly* Paul Francis Webster)

El Condor
US   1970   102m   Technicolor
National General/Carthay Continental (André de Toth)
V*

An escaped convict and a con man seek a fortune in gold believed to be hidden in a fortress in the Mexican desert.

Blood and guts Western with few moments of interest.

w Larry Cohen, Steven Carabatsos   *d* John Guillermin   *ph* Henri Persin   *m* Maurice Jarre

Jim Brown, Lee Van Cleef, Patrick O'Neal, Marianna Hill, Iron Eyes Cody, Elisha Cook Jnr

'The kind of fun you can find at your friendly neighbourhood abattoir.' – *Judith Crist, 1977*

'The big one with the big two!'
El Dorado *
US   1966   126m   Technicolor
Paramount/Laurel (Howard Hawks)
V*, L

A gunfighter and a drunken sheriff tackle a villainous cattle baron.

Easy-going, semi-somnolent, generally likeable but disappointing Western . . . an old man's movie all round.

w Leigh Brackett   *novel The Stars in their Courses* by Harry Joe Brown   *d* Howard Hawks   *ph* Harold Rosson   *m* Nelson Riddle

John Wayne, Robert Mitchum, James Caan, Charlene Holt, Michele Carey, Ed Asner, Arthur Hunnicutt, R. G. Armstrong, Paul Fix, Christopher George

'A rumbustious lament for the good days of the bad old west.' – *Tom Milne*

'A claustrophobic, careless and cliché-ridden thing, wavering constantly between campy self-deprecation and pretentious pomposity.' – *Richard Schickel*

'Wayne and Mitchum, parodying themselves while looking exhausted.' – *Pauline Kael, 70s*

El Dorado *
France/Spain   1988   123m   colour
Palace/Iberoamericana/Chrysalide/UGC-Top1/FR3/CanalPlus (Victor Albarran)
S

Conquistadores set out from Peru to find El Dorado, the fabled land of gold.

Ambitious but flawed epic, handicapped by its ponderous approach.

d Carlos Saura   *ph* Teo Escamilla   *md* Alejandro Masso   *ad* Terry Pritchard   *ed* Pedro del Rey

Omero Antonutti, Eusebio Poncela, Lambert Wilson, Gabriela Roel, Jose Sancho, Feodor Atkine, Patxi Bisquert, Francisco Algora, Francisco Merino

El Greco
Italy/France   1964   94m   Eastmancolor
Cinemascope
(TCF) Artistiche Internazionale/Arco-Films du Siècle (Alfredo Bini, Mel Ferrer)
S

In the 16th century, a Greek-Italian painter finds favour in Spain and falls in love with an aristocratic girl.

Heavily embellished history with a few good scenes.

w Guy Elmes, Massimo Franciosa, Luigi Magni, Luciano Salce   *d* Luciano Salce   *ph* Leonida Barboni   *m* Ennio Morricone

Mel Ferrer, Rosanna Schiaffino, Adolfo Celi, Angel Aranda

El Mariachi **
US   1992   81m   Technicolor
Columbia/Los Hooligans (Robert Rodriguez, Carlos Gallardo)
V, V*

In a small Mexican town a wandering musician with his guitar-case is mistaken for a hitman.

Witty, visually inventive low-budget thriller, cleverly taking apart the conventions of Westerns and reassembling them in a quirky and individual way.

wd Robert Rodriguez   *ph* Robert Rodriguez   *m* Marc Trujillo, Alvaro Rodriguez, Chris Knudson, Cecilio Rodriguez, Eric Guthrie   *ed* Robert Rodriguez

Carlos Gallardo, Consuelo Gómez, Reinol Martinez, Peter Marquardt, Jaime de Hoyos, Ramiro Gómez, Jesus Lopez, Luis Baro

'Uses a broad genre to make subtle points: about change and tradition, about Mexicans and Chicanos with separate values and voices. Despite its superficial sense of low-budget genre-as-usual, this

project offers something truly new for American film.' – *Sight and Sound*

'Has an exhilarating rawness that works for, rather than against it, its kinetic pacing, visceral editing and bravura camerawork revealing the presence of a director with unbridled visual panache. A minor masterpiece.' – *Empire*

† The film, by a 24-year-old director born in Texas, is said to have cost $7,000 (coming in $2,000 under budget) to shoot in 14 days and became the cheapest movie to be given international distribution by Columbia. He was signed to remake the film with a budget of $6m.

El Paso
US   1949   92m   Cinecolor
Paramount/Pine-Thomas

After the civil war, a young lawyer brings a corrupt township to its senses by learning to outshoot the badmen.

Lively, fairly tough Western with all the familiar ingredients.

wd Lewis R. Foster   *ph* Ellis Carter   *m* Darrell Calker

John Payne, Gail Russell, Dick Foran, Sterling Hayden, George 'Gabby' Hayes

El Topo *
Mexico   1971   124m   Eastmancolor   Producciones Panic

An evil gunfighter rides through the old west and has various encounters, after which he sets himself on fire.

Curious, perverse, powerful surrealist allegory which takes in the life of Christ and the fate of man among some exceedingly unpleasant violence. A treat for connoisseurs of the unpleasantly absurd.

wd/m/ad Alexandro Jodorowsky   *ph* Raphael Corkidi

Alexandro Jodorowsky, Brontis Jodorowsky, Mara Lorenzio, David Silva

'He's a good cop on a big bike on a bad road!'
Electra Glide in Blue *
US   1973   113m   DeLuxe   Panavision
UA/James William Guercio/Rupert Hitzig
V, V*, L

A small-town motor-cycle cop becomes disillusioned.

Agreeable desert melodrama in the wake of *Easy Rider*, freshly observed with mordant humour, marred by a fashionable downbeat ending.

w Robert Boris   *d/m* James William Guercio   *ph* Conrad Hall

Robert Blake, Billy Green Bush, Mitch Ryan, Jeannine Riley, Elisha Cook Jnr, Royal Dano

Electric Dreams
GB   1984   112m   Metrocolor
Virgin/MGM-UA (Rusty Lemorande, Larry de Waay)
V, V*, L, S

A computer becomes jealous of its owner's love affair.

Gruesomely extended revue sketch which totally fails to develop its characters and offers instead a very sparing amount of cleverness.

w Rusty Lemorande   *d* Steve Barron   *ph* Alex Thomson   *m* Giorgio Moroder   *pd* Richard MacDonald

Lenny von Dohlen, Virginia Madsen, Maxwell Caulfield, Bud Cort, Don Fellows

The Electric Horseman *
US   1979   120m   Technicolor   Panavision
Columbia/Universal (Ray Stark/Wildwood)
V, V*, L, S

A horseman advertising breakfast cereal in Las Vegas suddenly tires of it all and heads for the wilderness.

Pretty but slightly sheepish moral saga with too much technique for its own good.

w Robert Garland   *d* Sydney Pollack   *ph* Owen Roizman   *m* Dave Grusin   *pd* Stephen Grimes

Robert Redford, Jane Fonda, Valerie Perrine, Willie Nelson, John Saxon, Nicolas Coster

'Overlong, talky and diffused.' – *Variety*

The Electric Man: see *Man Made Monster*

Electric Moon
GB   1991   103m   Technicolor
Winstone/Grapevine Media/Channel 4/Times Television (Sundeep Singh Bedi)

Rivalry between an Indian hotelier, a former Maharajah, and the director of the national park in which the hotel is situated causes problems for a group of Western tourists.

Uncertain comedy that mocks the expectations and preconceptions of tourists in India.

w Arundhati Roy   *d* Pradip Krishen   *ph* Giles Nuttgens   *m* Basaya Khan, Zakab Khan, Deepak Castelino, Sanjee Saith   *pd* Arundhati Roy   *ed* Pradip Krishen

Roshan Seth, Naseruddin Shah, Leela Naidu, Gerson Da Cunha, Raghubir Yadav, Alice Spivak, Frances Helm, James Fleet, Francesca Brill

'Loses its shine early on. This amiable, good-humored satire on cultural stereotypes on both sides of the Indian tourist fence is too low-voltage to create much of a theatrical buzz.' – *Variety*

Eleni
US   1985   117m   colour
CBS/Vanoff/Pick/Gage
V*, L

A journalist back in Greece investigates his mother's death in the civil war of the late 1940s.

Deadeningly boring true life drama with flashbacks which fail to communicate the author's sense of revenge.

w Steve Tesich   *book* Nicholas Gage   *d* Peter Yates   *ph* Billy Williams   *m* Bruce Smeaton   *pd* Roy Walker   *ed* Ray Lovejoy

Kate Nelligan, John Malkovich, Linda Hunt, Oliver Cotton, Ronald Pickup, Rosalie Crutchley

'As lofty in ambition as it is deficient in accomplishment.' – *Variety*

Elenya *
GB   1992   82m   colour
Frankfurter Film/S4C/BFI/Ffilmian/ZDF (Heidi Ulmke)
V

An elderly woman remembers how, as a young girl living in Wales in 1940, she tried to hide and care for a German pilot she discovered wounded in a wood.

Pleasant low-budget feature, but lacking in any particular individuality or originality.

wd Steve Gough   *ph* Patrick Duval   *m* Simon Fisher Turner   *pd* Hayden Pearce   *ed* Alan Smithee

Margaret John, Pascale Delafouge Jones, Seirol Tomos, Sue Jones Davies, Iago Wynn Jones, Lilo Milward, Catrin Llwyd, Edward Elwyn Jones, Ioan Meredith, Klaus Behrendt

'Very quiet, acutely sensitive in some areas and a debut from which much could spring.' – *Derek Malcolm, Guardian*

Elephant Boy **
GB   1937   91m   bw
London Films (Alexander Korda)
V*

In India, a boy elephant keeper helps government conservationists.

Documentary drama which seemed fresh and extraordinary at the time, has dated badly since, but did make an international star of Sabu.

w John Collier, Akos Tolnay, Marcia de Sylva *novel* *Toomai of the Elephants* by Rudyard Kipling *d* Robert Flaherty, Zoltan Korda *ph* Osmond Borradaile *m* John Greenwood *ed* William Hornbeck, Charles Crichton

Sabu, Walter Hudd, Allan Jeayes, W. E. Holloway, Wilfrid Hyde-White

'Should draw anywhere in the world.' – *Variety*

'This is a fractured film, its skeleton is awry, its bones stick out through the skin.' – *Richard Griffith, 1941*

'It has gone the way of *Man of Aran*: enormous advance publicity, director out of touch with the press for months, rumours of great epics sealed in tins, and then the disappointing diminutive achievement.' – *Graham Greene*

Un Eléphant Ça Trompe Enormément: see *Pardon Mon Affaire*

Elephant Gun: see *Nor the Moon By Night*

The Elephant Man **
US   1980   124m   bw   Panavision
EMI/Brooksfilms (Stuart Cornfield)
V, V*, L

In 1884 London, a penniless man deformed by a rare illness is rescued by a doctor from a fairground freak show, and becomes a member of fashionable society.

A curious story which happens to be true; the film sets its scene superbly, has splendid performances and a fascinating make-up. Yet it fails to move quite as it should, perhaps because the central figure is treated as a horrific come-on, like the hunchback of Notre Dame.

w Christopher de Vore, Eric Bergren, David Lynch, from various memoirs   *d* David Lynch   *ph* Freddie Francis   *m* John Morris   *pd* Stuart Craig

Anthony Hopkins, John Hurt, John Gielgud, Anne Bancroft, Freddie Jones, Wendy Hiller, Michael Elphick, Hannah Gordon

'If there's a wrong note in this unique movie – in performance, production design, cinematography or anywhere else – I must have missed it.' – *Paul Taylor, Time Out*

'In an age of horror movies this is a film which takes the material of horror and translates it into loving kindness.' – *Dilys Powell, Punch*

AAN: best film; screenplay; David Lynch; editing (Anne V. Coates); art direction (Stuart Craig, Bob Cartwright, Hugh Scaife); John Morris; costume design (Patricia Norris); John Hurt

BFA: best film; production design; John Hurt

Elephant Walk *
US   1954   103m   Technicolor
Paramount (Irving Asher)
V*

The owner of a Ceylon tea plantation takes back an English wife who finds the atmosphere strange and turns to a friendly overseer for comfort.

Echoes of *Jane Eyre* and *Rebecca,* with stampeding elephants instead of a mad or dead wife.

w John Lee Mahin   *novel* Robert Standish *d* William Dieterle   *ph* Loyal Griggs   *m* Franz Waxman

Elizabeth Taylor, Peter Finch, Dana Andrews, Abraham Sofaer

'The climactic elephant stampede's a rouser – if you're still awake.' – *Judith Crist*

Elephants Never Forget: see *Zenobia*

Eleven Harrowhouse *
GB   1974   108m   DeLuxe   Panavision
TCF/Harrowhouse (Elliott Kastner)
V*

An American diamond merchant is robbed of a valuable jewel, and finds himself in the middle of an ingenious plot.

Amusing caper story marred by sudden changes of mood.

w Jeffrey Bloom   *novel* Gerald A. Browne   *d* Aram Avakian   *ph* Arthur Ibbetson   *m* Michael J. Lewis

Charles Grodin, *James Mason,* Trevor Howard, John Gielgud, Candice Bergen, Peter Vaughan, Helen Cherry, Jack Watson, Jack Watling

'This lackadaisical caper comedy is inoffensive, but the comic ideas don't build or erupt, and since the director fails to get any suspense going, it becomes a bumbling and stupid romp.' – *Pauline Kael*

Elinor Norton *
US   1935   71m   bw
Fox

A wife has a jealous husband and a South American lover.

Underwritten triangle drama which never comes to boiling point.

w Rose Franken, Philip Klein   *novel* *The State versus Elinor Norton* by Mary Roberts Rinehart   *d* Hamilton McFadden

Claire Trevor, Gilbert Roland, Hugh Williams, Henrietta Crosman, Norman Foster

'No cast for b.o. and results look mild.' – *Variety*

Eliza Fraser *
Australia   1976   127m   colour
Hexagon (Tim Burstall)

A shipwrecked couple have to live with Aborigines; later she becomes a fairground attraction.

Would-be bawdy historical romp on the lines of *Tom Jones;* it seldom works.

w David Williamson   *d* Tim Burstall

Susannah York, Trevor Howard, Noel Ferrier, John Waters, Charles Tingwell

Elizabeth and Essex: see *The Private Lives of Elizabeth and Essex*

Elizabeth of England: see *Drake of England*

Elizabeth of Ladymead *
GB   1948   97m   Technicolor
BL/Imperadio (Herbert Wilcox)

Four husbands of different generations come home from war (1854, 1903, 1919, 1946) to find their wives altered.

Thin star vehicle turns into an amateur-night compendium with a few funny moments.

w Frank Harvey   *play* Frank Harvey   *d* Herbert Wilcox   *ph* Max Greene

Anna Neagle, Hugh Williams, Bernard Lee, Michael Laurence, Nicholas Phipps, Isobel Jeans, Michael Shepley, Jack Allen

Elizabeth the Queen: see *The Private Lives of Elizabeth and Essex*

Ella Cinders **
US   1926   83m approx   bw   silent
First National
V*

A servant girl wins a trip to Hollywood.

Famous and still pleasing comedy from the comic strip *Cinderella in the Movies.*

w Frank Griffin, Mervyn Le Roy   *d* Alfred E. Green

Colleen Moore, Lloyd Hughes, Vera Lewis, Doria Baker

Ellen: see *The Second Woman*

Ellery Queen

The debonair detective created by Manfred B. Lee and Frederic Dannay was seen in several unremarkable second features, usually with his secretary Nikki and his police inspector father. The first two were made for Republic, the rest for Columbia.

1935: THE SPANISH CAPE MYSTERY with Donald Cook
1936: THE MANDARIN MYSTERY (Eddie Quillan)
1940: ELLERY QUEEN MASTER DETECTIVE (Ralph Bellamy)
1941: ELLERY QUEEN'S PENTHOUSE MYSTERY, ELLERY QUEEN AND THE PERFECT CRIME, ELLERY QUEEN AND THE MURDER RING (all Bellamy)
1942: A CLOSE CALL FOR ELLERY QUEEN, A DESPERATE CHANCE FOR ELLERY QUEEN, ENEMY AGENTS MEET ELLERY QUEEN (all William Gargan)

In 1971 Peter Lawford starred in a TV pilot, *Don't Look Behind You,* and in 1975 a one-season series starred Jim Hutton. The books, pseudonymously authored by Ellery Queen, were far more popular than any of the movies.

Elmer and Elsie
US   1934   65m   bw
Paramount

A wife harbours big ideas for her meek-and-mild husband.

Unsuccessful attempt to find a change of pace for a fading star.

w Humphrey Pearson   *play* *To the Ladies* by George S. Kaufman, Marc Connelly   *d* Gilbert Pratt

George Bancroft, Frances Fuller, Roscoe Karns, George Barbier, Nella Walker

'Screen version has not only removed most of the verve, pace and bite but has loaded itself down with a couple of maladroit cases of miscasting.' – *Variety*

'From a book that shook a nation with its sledgehammer theme ... From a Nobel Prize-winning author ... comes the raging story of the man who used the Holy Bible and broke every rule in it!'
Elmer Gantry **
US   1960   146m   Eastmancolor
UA/Bernard Smith
V*, L

The exploits of an American evangelist in the twenties.

Mainly gripping but overlong exposé of commercialized small-town religion.

wd Richard Brooks   *novel* Sinclair Lewis   *ph* John Alton   *m* André Previn   *ad* Edward Carrere

Burt Lancaster, Jean Simmons, Arthur Kennedy, *Shirley Jones,* Dean Jagger, Edward Andrews, Patti Page, John McIntire

AA: Richard Brooks (as writer); Burt Lancaster; Shirley Jones

AAN: best picture; André Previn

Elmer the Great *
US   1933   74m   bw
Warner (Ray Griffith)

A country hick turns out to be a great baseball hitter.

Best and most farcical version of a play also filmed in 1929 as *Fast Company* and in 1939 as *The Cowboy Quarterback.*

w Tom Geraghty   *play* Ring Lardner, George M. Cohan   *d* Mervyn Le Roy

Joe E. Brown, Patricia Ellis, Frank McHugh, Claire Dodd, Sterling Holloway, Emma Dunn, Douglass Dumbrille, Jessie Ralph, J. Carrol Naish

'A picture that goes beyond what men think about . . . because no man ever thought about it in quite this way!'

Elopement
US   1951   82m   bw
TCF (Fred Kohlmar)

A girl student eloping with her professor is chased by her father.

Unconvincing domestic comedy with some lively chase sequences.

w Bess Taffell   d Henry Koster   ph Joseph LaShelle   m Cyril Mockridge

Clifton Webb, Charles Bickford, Anne Francis, William Lundigan, Margalo Gillmore, Evelyn Varden, Reginald Gardiner

Elstree Calling *
GB   1930   95m   bw/Pathécolour
Wardour/BIP (John Maxwell)

A film studio mounts a television show.

Slender excuse for an all-star revue which luckily preserves much light entertainment talent of the time.

w Adrian Brunel, Walter C. Mycroft, Val Valentine   d Adrian Brunel, Alfred Hitchcock, Jack Hulbert, André Charlot, Paul Murray   ph Claude Friese-Greene   m Reg Casson, Vivian Ellis, Chick Endor, Ivor Novello, Jack Strachey   ed Émile de Ruelle, A. C. Hammond

Tommy Handley, Jack Hulbert, Cicely Courtneidge, Will Fyffe, Lily Morris, Teddy Brown, Anna May Wong, Gordon Harker, Donald Calthrop, John Longden, Jameson Thomas, Bobbie Comber

The Elstree Story *
GB   1952   61m   bw
ABPC (Gilbert Gunn)

A compilation drawn from 25 years of filmmaking at Elstree Studios.

Highlights include Hitchcock's Number Seventeen; The White Sheik; Piccadilly; Bulldog Drummond; Arms and the Man; The Informer; Blossom Time; and Poison Pen. Commentary and presentation are adequate.

d Gilbert Gunn   m Philip Green

The Elusive Pimpernel *
GB   1950   109m   Technicolor
BL/London Films (Michael Powell, Emeric Pressburger)
V, V*
US title: The Fighting Pimpernel

A foppish 18th-century London dandy is actually the hero who rescues French aristocrats from the guillotine.

Expensive remake of The Scarlet Pimpernel which fails to please, apparently because the talents were not congenial to the subject. Interesting detail, though.

wd Michael Powell, Emeric Pressburger   novel Baroness Orczy   ph Christopher Challis   ph Hein Heckroth   m Brian Easdale

David Niven, Margaret Leighton, Cyril Cusack, Jack Hawkins, David Hutcheson, Robert Coote

'The quality of excitement which should carry the film is quite lost. The Elusive Pimpernel is highly – often too highly – coloured, and has an artificiality quite different in character from that of the original.' – Penelope Houston

'I never thought I should feel inclined to leave a Powell and Pressburger film before the end; but I did here.' – Richard Mallett, Punch

'Niven plays the Scarlet Pimpernel with the sheepish lack of enthusiasm of a tone deaf man called upon to sing solo in church. His companions lumber through their parts like schoolboys about to go down with mumps.' – Daily Express

Elvira Madigan *
Sweden   1967   95m   Eastmancolor
Europa Film (Waldemar Bergendahl)
V, V*, L

A married army officer runs off with a tightrope dancer; when they run out of money they live in the woods and finally commit suicide rather than part.

A simple Victorian romantic idyll, based on a true incident; a director's and photographer's piece which entrances the eyes and ears while starving the mind.

wd Bo Widerberg   ph Jörgen Persson   m Mozart

Thommy Berggren, Pia Degermark

Elvira, Mistress of the Dark
US   1988   96m   CFI color
Entertainment/New World/NBC/Queen B (Eric Gardner, Mark Pierson)
V, V*, L

The hostess of a TV horror show discovers that she has magic powers.

Camp nonsense, limply performed.

w Sam Egan, John Paragon, Cassandra Peterson   d James Signorelli   ph Hanania Baer   m James Campbell   pd John DeCuir Jnr   ed Battle Davis

Cassandra Peterson, W. Morgan Shepherd, Daniel Greene, Susan Kellermann, Jeff Conaway, Edie McClurg, Kurt Fuller, Pat Crawford Brown

Elvis! Elvis!
Sweden   1977   100m   colour
Moviemakers/SF1/SR-TV2 (Bert Sundberg)

A sensitive seven-year-old boy tries to cope with a mother obsessed by Elvis Presley.

Unimaginative family drama.

w Maria Gripe, Kay Pollak   novel Maria Gripe   d Kay Pollak   ph Mikael Salomon   m Ralph Lundsten   ed Lasse Lundberg

Lele Dorazio, Lena-Pia Bernhardsson, Fred Gunnarsson, Elisaveta, Allan Adwall

Embassy *
US   1972   90m   colour
Hemdale/Triad/Weaver (Mel Ferrer)

At the US Embassy in Beirut, a Soviet official seeking asylum is in danger from a KGB killer.

Goodish suspenser with reasonably literate dialogue and several Hitchcockian sequences.

w William Fairchild   d Gordon Hessler   ph Raoul Coutard   m Jonathan Hodge

Richard Roundtree, Chuck Connors, Max von Sydow, Broderick Crawford, Ray Milland

Embraceable You
US   1948   80m   bw
Warner

A gangster on the run fatally injures a young girl, and stays to nurse her during her last weeks.

Incredible heavy-handed romantic melodrama.

w Edna Anhalt   d Felix Jacoves

Dane Clark, Geraldine Brooks, Wallace Ford, S. Z. Sakall, Richard Rober

Embryo
US   1976   104m   colour
Cine Artists (Arnold H. Orgolini, Anita Doohan)

A researcher experiments on foetuses with growth hormones, and lives to regret it.

Rather unpleasant mixture of science fiction and old-fashioned horror; slickness can't conceal a total lack of taste.

w Anita Doohan, Jack W. Thomas   d Ralph Nelson   ph Fred Koenekamp   m Gil Melle

Rock Hudson, Diane Ladd, Barbara Carrera, Roddy McDowall

The Emerald Forest **
GB   1985   113m   Technicolor   Panavision
Embassy/John Boorman
V, V*, L

An American engineer sets off to find his lost son in the jungles of Brazil.

Heavy-going, dazzling to look at, finally uncomforting dalliance with themes originally explored in Tarzan the Ape Man, e.g. would man do better to return to nature?

w Rospo Pallenberg   d John Boorman   ph Philippe Rousselot   m Junior Homrich, Brian Gascoyne   pd Simon Holland

Powers Boothe, Meg Foster, Charley Boorman

'Begins as a breathtaking fable and ends as a routine action movie. Somewhere along the way, there was a failure of the imagination.' – Roger Ebert

Emergency!: see Emergency Call

Emergency Call *
GB   1952   90m   bw
Butcher's/Nettlefold (Ernest G. Roy)
US title: Emergency!

Inspector Lane tracks down several people who share a rare blood group needed to save a life.

Now a boringly predictable collection of mild anecdotes, but then a rather smart idea, much better executed than one would normally expect of Britain's Poverty Row.

w Vernon Harris, Lewis Gilbert   d Lewis Gilbert   ph Wilkie Cooper   m Wilfred Burns

Jack Warner, Joy Shelton, Anthony Steel, Sidney James, Freddie Mills, Earl Cameron, John Robinson, Thora Hird

The Emigrants *
Sweden   1970   191m   Technicolor
Svensk Filmindustri (Bengt Forslund)
original title: Utvandrarna

A family of farmers leaves famine-stricken 19th-century Sweden for America, and builds a homestead in Minnesota.

Solemn, forceful, overlong epic which while full of trial and tribulation is sufficiently well made to cast a hypnotic spell and was a major hit among Swedish-Americans.

w Jan Troell, Bengt Forslund, from four novels by Vilhelm Moberg   d/ph/ed Jan Troell   m Erik Nordgren   ed Jan Troell

Max von Sydow, Liv Ullmann, Eddie Axberg, Svenolof Bern

'A Fordian canvas without the Fordian warmth.' – Sight and Sound

† A sequel, The New Land, shortly appeared, and this was also the title of a short-lived TV series on the subject.

AAN: best picture; best foreign film; Jan Troell (direction and script); Liv Ullmann

Emil and the Detectives *
Germany   1931   80m   bw
UFA

City children discover and chase a crook, who is finally arrested.

A pleasing fable for children which has survived several subsequent versions; the original is probably the best.

w Billy Wilder   novel Erich Kästner   d Gerhard Lamprecht   ph Werner Brandes   m Allan Grey

Fritz Rasp, Kathe Haack

† Other versions: Britain 1935, directed by Milton Rosmer, with George Hayes; West Germany 1954, directed by R. A. Stemmle, with Kurt Meisel; US 1964 (Walt Disney), directed by Peter Tewkesbury, with Walter Slezak.

Emma *
US   1932   73m   bw
MGM

A servant marries into the family.

Predictably cosy family drama tailored for its star.

w Frances Marion, Leonard Praskins, Zelda Sears   d Clarence Brown   ph Oliver T. Marsh

Marie Dressler, Richard Cromwell, Jean Hersholt, Myrna Loy, John Miljan, Purnell E. Pratt

'A hoke story saved by the star.' – *Variety*

AAN: Marie Dressler

Emmanuelle *
France   1974   94m   Eastmancolor
Trinacra/Orphée (Yves Rousset-Rouard)
V, S

The bored bride of a French Embassy official in Siam is initiated by well-meaning friends into various forms of sexual activity.

Not much sexier than a Sunday colour supplement, this fashionable piece of suberoticism took off like a bomb and spawned half-a-dozen so-called sequels. Future students may well wonder why.

w Jean-Louis Richard   *novel* Emmanuelle Arsan   d Just Jaeckin   ph Richard Suzuki, Marie Saunier   m Pierre Bachelet

Sylvia Kristel, Marika Green, Daniel Sarky, Alain Cuny

'Much hazy, soft-focus coupling in downtown Bangkok.' – *Michael Billington, Illustrated London News*

L'Emmerdeur **
France/Italy   1973   84m   Eastmancolor
Miracle/Les Films Ariane/Mondex/OPIC (George Dancigers)
aka: *A Pain in the A—*

A hit-man, waiting in a Paris hotel to kill a witness, befriends a suicidal husband and is unable to get rid of him.

Amusing character comedy of a strong, silent man and a chattering weakling.

w Edouard Molinaro, Francis Veber   *play* Le Contrat by Francis Veber   d Edouard Molinaro   ph Raoul Coutard   m Jacques Brel, François Gabuber   ad Jacques Brizzio   ed Robert Isnardon, Monique Isnardon

Lino Ventura, Jacques Brel, Caroline Cellier, Nino Castelnuovo, Jean-Pierre Darras, André Vallardy

'A black comedy par excellence. All that really need be said about it is that it begins well, sustains its chosen mood efficiently, builds to a satisfying climax and is in other words a delight from start to finish.' – *David McGillivray, Films and Filming*

† The film was remade by Billy Wilder as *Buddy Buddy*.

The Emperor Jones *
US   1933   72m   bw
UA
V*

A train porter becomes king of the Haitian jungle.

Stagey transcript of a stagey play, with acting of some interest at the time.

w DuBose Heyward   *play* Eugene O'Neill   d Dudley Murphy

Paul Robeson, Dudley Digges, Frank Wilson

'For the classes rather than the masses, and questionable commercially.' – *Variety*

Emperor of the North: see *Emperor of the North Pole*

Emperor of the North Pole *
US   1973   119m   DeLuxe
TCF/Inter Hemisphere (Robert Aldrich)
V
GB title: *Emperor of the North*

In 1933 Oregon, freeloading hobos are brutally attacked by a sadistic train guard.

Unlikely melodrama with vicious but exhilarating high spots separating acres of verbiage.

w Christopher Knopf   d Robert Aldrich   ph Joseph Biroc   m Frank de Vol

Lee Marvin, Ernest Borgnine, Keith Carradine, Charles Tyner, Malcolm Atterbury, Elisha Cook Jnr

'It's hard, contrived, pointless in its thesis, repulsive in its people, and it's singularly joyless and contemptible in its glorification of the bum and freeloader.' – *Judith Crist*

'The biggest thing that ever happened to Bing – or to you!'
The Emperor Waltz
US   1948   106m   Technicolor
Paramount (Charles Brackett)

In 1901 Austria, a countess falls for an American phonograph salesman.

Thin to the point of emaciation, this witless comedy with music, dully set-bound, proved its director's strangest and most unsatisfactory choice.

w Charles Brackett, Billy Wilder   d Billy Wilder   ph George Barnes   m Victor Young   m/y Johnny Burke, Jimmy Van Heusen   ad Hans Dreier, Franz Bachelin

Bing Crosby, Joan Fontaine, Roland Culver, Lucile Watson, Richard Haydn, Harold Vermilyea, Sig Rumann, Julia Dean

AAN: Victor Young

The Emperor's Candlesticks *
US   1937   89m   bw
MGM (John Considine Jnr)

In old Russia, spies on opposite sides fall in love.

Lavish romantic comedy drama, generally well handled; superior Hollywood moonshine.

w Monckton Hoffe, Herman J. Mankiewicz, Harold Goldman   *novel* Baroness Orczy   d George Fitzmaurice   ph Harold Rosson   m Franz Waxman

William Powell, Luise Rainer, Maureen O'Sullivan, Robert Young, Frank Morgan, Douglass Dumbrille

'It's about international spies in evening dress during that long ago period when Russia had a Czar, Vienna was the scene of brilliant *valasques*, and the favour of royalty was something to get excited over . . . it's acted with unusual seriousness midst settings of unusual extravagance.' – *Variety*

L'Empire des Sens: see *Ai No Corrida*

Empire of the Ants
US   1977   89m   Movielab
AIP/Cinema 77 (Bert I. Gordon)

Giant ants menace a stretch of the Florida coast.

A long way behind *Them,* but as exploitation it could be worse.

w Jack Turley   *story* H. G. Wells   d Bert I. Gordon   ph Reginald Morris   m Dana Kaproff

Joan Collins, Robert Lansing, John David Carson, Albert Salmi, Jacqueline Scott

Empire of the Passions: see *Ai No Corrida*

Empire of the Sun ***
US   1987   152m   Technicolor
Robert Shapiro/Amblin (Steven Spielberg, Kathleen Kennedy, Frank Marshall)
V, V*, L, S

Semi-autobiographical story of an 11-year-old English boy learning to grow up in a Japanese internment camp during World War II.

w Tom Stoppard   *novel* J. G. Ballard   d Steven Spielberg   ph Allen Daviau   m John Williams   pd Norman Reynolds   ed Michael Kahn

Christian Bale, John Malkovich, Miranda Richardson, Nigel Havers, Joe Pantoliano

'A masterpiece of popular cinema.' – *MFB*

AAN: Allen Daviau; editing

Empire State
GB   1987   104m   colour
Miracle/Virgin (Norma Heyman)

An American gangster tries to infiltrate London's East End.

Over-the-top melodrama with an irritating pictorial style.

w Ron Peck, Mark Ayres   d Ron Peck   ph Tony Imi   m Steve Parsons   pd Adrian Smith   ed Chris Kelly

Cathryn Harrison, Jason Hoganson, Elizabeth Hickling, Jamie Foreman, Martin Landau, Ray McAnally

The Empire Strikes Back **
US   1980   124m   Eastmancolor   Panavision
TCF/Lucasfilm (Gary Kurtz)
V, V (W), V*, L, S

The Rebel Alliance takes refuge from Darth Vader on a frozen planet.

More exhilarating interplanetary adventures, as mindless as *Star Wars* but just as enjoyable for aficionados.

w Leigh Brackett, Lawrence Kasdan   *story* George Lucas   d Irvin Kershner   ph Peter Suschitzky   m John Williams   pd Norman Reynolds

Mark Hamill, Harrison Ford, Carrie Fisher, Billy Dee Williams

'Slightly encumbered by some mythic and neo-Sophoclean overtones, but its inventiveness, humour and special effects are scarcely less inspired than those of its phenomenally successful predecessor.' – *New Yorker*

AAN: John Williams; art direction

BFA: music

Employees' Entrance *
US   1933   75m   bw
Warner

A ruthless department store manager gets his come-uppance.

Smart comedy-melodrama with solidly familiar cast.

w Robert Presnell   *play* David Boehm   d Roy del Ruth

Warren William, Loretta Young, Alice White, Wallace Ford, Allen Jenkins, Marjorie Gateson

'Here's one that calls for preferred dating . . . plenty to sell for the mobs.' – *Variety*

The Empty Canvas
Italy/France   1964   118m   bw
CC Champion/Concordia (Joseph E. Levine, Carlo Ponti)
V*
original title: *La Noia*

A young painter, obsessed by his own spiritual emptiness, becomes paranoically jealous of his promiscuous young mistress.

An extraordinarily boring film version of a novel which needed Buñuel, if anybody, to handle it.

w Tonino Guerra, Ugo Liberatore, Damiano Damiani *novel* Alberto Moravia *d* Damiano Damiani *ph* Roberto Gerardi *m* Luis Enriquez Bacalov

Horst Buchholz, Catherine Spaak, Bette Davis, Isa Miranda, Lea Padovani

The Empty Table

Japan 1985 142m colour
Electric Pictures/Marugen Building Group/Haiyu-za Film/Herald Ace (Ginichi Kishimoto, Kyoto Oshima)
original title: *Shokutaku No Nai Ie*

A family disintegrates when the eldest son is arrested for terrorism.

Slow and ponderous, without much to interest a Western audience.

wd Masaki Kobayashi *story* Fumiko Enji *ph* Kozo Okazaki *md* Toru Takemitsu *pd* Shigemasha Toda *ed* Nobuo Ogawa

Tatsuya Nakadai, Mayumi Ogawa, Kie Nakaj, Kiichi Nakai, Takeyuki Takemoto, Shima Iwashita

En Cas de Malheur *

France/Italy 1958 120m bw
Iena/UCIL/Incom
aka: *Love Is My Profession*

A wealthy, middle-aged lawyer leaves his wife for a worthless young wanton whom he is defending on a robbery charge.

Good solid melodrama with excellent credits: it caught all concerned on top form and had international success, but the theme is not in itself very interesting.

w Jean Aurenche, Pierre Bost *novel* Georges Simenon *d* Claude Autant-Lara *ph* Jacques Natteau *m* René Cloërc

Jean Gabin, Edwige Feuillère, Brigitte Bardot, Franco Interlenghi

En Compagnie de Max Linder: see Laugh with Max Linder

En Rade *

France 1927 60m approx bw silent
Neofilm

A Marseilles docker dreams of escaping his pent-in existence and fleeing with his mistress to the South Seas.

More realistic than Pagnol's *Marius* trilogy, which used the same setting, this remains an interesting slice of romantic realism, with good attention to detail.

w Alberto Cavalcanti, Claude Heymann *d* Alberto Cavalcanti *ph* Jimmy Rogers, A. Fairli, P. Enberg

Catherine Hessling, Philippe Heriat, Georges Charlia

Enchanted April

US 1935 66m bw
RKO

A woman becomes lonely when her husband turns into a successful novelist.

Thin marital comedy-drama for fans of the star.

w Samuel Hoffenstein, Ray Harris *novel* Elizabeth von Arnim *d* Harry Beaumont

Ann Harding, Frank Morgan, Katharine Alexander, Reginald Owen, Jane Baxter, Jessie Ralph

'Very British in background and proceeding at all times with a lifted eyebrow.' – *Variety*

'Escaping From Winter In London, They Planned A Holiday In Paradise ... Everything Was Going Perfectly, Until The Men Arrived.'

Enchanted April

GB 1991 99m colour
Curzon/Miramax/BBC/Greenpoint (Ann Scott)
V*, S

In the 1920s four Englishwomen, bored with their lives, take a holiday in Italy.

Stilted period movie that is pretty to look at but has little to engage the mind.

w Peter Barnes *novel* Elizabeth von Arnim *d* Mike Newell *ph* Rex Maidment *m* Richard Rodney Bennett *pd* Malcolm Thornton *ed* Dick Allen

Miranda Richardson, Josie Lawrence, Polly Walker, Joan Plowright, Alfred Molina, Michael Kitchen, Jim Broadbent

'A slim comedy of manners about Brits discovering their emotions in Italy . . . Strong cast's reliable playing is undercut by a script that dawdles over well-trod territory.' – *Variety*

'Crude, fussy, bland stuff gauged to please American anglophiles who watch Masterpiece Theatre.' – *Philip French, Observer*

AAN: Joan Plowright; Peter Barnes

The Enchanted Cottage *

US 1945 92m bw
RKO
V*, L

A plain girl and a disfigured man are beautiful to each other.

Wartime updating of a sentimental old play; insufficiently well considered to be more than tolerable.

w De Witt Bodeen, Herman J. Mankiewicz *play* Sir Arthur Wing Pinero *d* John Cromwell *ph* Ted Tetzlaff *m* Roy Webb

Dorothy McGuire, Robert Young, Herbert Marshall, Mildred Natwick

'A silly film with considerable charm. It will be liked by millions, who are fully aware of its silliness while being captivated by its charm. It will be liked for the best of reasons; because it is based on a solid and humane truth.' – *C. A. Lejeune*

† A silent version in 1924 starred Richard Barthelmess and May McAvoy.

AAN: Roy Webb

The Enchanted Forest *

US 1945 77m Cinecolor
PRC
V*

Old John the Hermit talks to trees and animals, and rescues a lost child.

Surprising piece of Victorian whimsy, remarkably effective in its unambitious way, especially as a product of this studio. The best known example of Cinecolor.

w Robert Lee Johnson, John Le Bar, Lou Brock *d* Lew Landers *ph* Marcel Le Picard *m* Alfred Hay Malotte

Harry Davenport, Edmund Lowe, Brenda Joyce, Billy Severn

Enchanted Island

US 1958 94m Technicolor
Waverly (Benedict Bogeaus)
V*

In the 1840s two sailors jump ship and settle on what they later discover to be a cannibal island.

Tame adaptation of a minor classic, with the actors all at sea.

w James Leicester, Harold Jacob Smith *novel* Typee by Herman Melville *d* Allan Dwan *ph* George Stahl *m* Raul Lavista

Jane Powell (an unconvincing Polynesian), Dana Andrews, Don Dubbins, Arthur Shields, Ted de Corsia, Friedrich Ledebur

Enchantment *

US 1948 101m bw
Samuel Goldwyn
V

A London house tells the story of three generations.

Yes, a house tells the story, and the leading characters are called Rollo and Lark, but this is a very appealing piece of period romantic nonsense, with the highest possible gloss upon it.

w John Patrick *novel* A Fugue in Time by Rumer Godden *d* Irving Reis *ph* Gregg Toland *m* Hugo Friedhofer *ed* Daniel Mandell

David Niven, Teresa Wright, Evelyn Keyes, Farley Granger, Jayne Meadows, Leo G. Carroll

'Deliberate in pace, and artfully contrived as an emotional holiday, yet genuinely moving on its own terms.' – *Newsweek*

'Genuinely moving on its own terms, produced with a careful good taste that should disarm the critics of lachryma and old lace.' – *Newsweek*

Encino Man

US 1992 88m Technicolor
Warner/Hollywood Pictures/Touchwood Pacific Partners 1 (George Zaloom)
V, V*, S
GB title: *California Man*

Two high-school students revive a frozen prehistoric youth who quickly adapts to the prevailing life-style.

A depressing youth comedy, though those with a Neanderthal sense of humour may be amused.

w Shawn Schepps *story* George Zaloom, Shawn Schepps *d* Les Mayfield *ph* Robert Brickmann *m* J. Peter Robinson *pd* James Allen *ed* Eric Sears, Jonathan Siegel

Sean Astin, Brendan Fraser, Pauly Shore, Megan Ward, Robin Tunney, Michael DeLuise, Patrick Van Horn, Dalton James, Rick Ducommun

'Mindless would-be comedy . . . insulting even within its own no-effort parameters.' – *Variety*

'Less funny than your own funeral.' – *Washington Post*

Encore *

GB 1951 88m bw
GFD/Two Cities (Antony Damborough)
V*

Three more Somerset Maugham short stories introduced by the author.

The final follow-up to the success of *Quartet* and *Trio;* television playlets quickly made this kind of short story seem old-fashioned, but the standard here was high.

w T. E. B. Clarke, Arthur Macrae, Eric Ambler *stories* The Ant and the Grasshopper, Winter Cruise, Gigolo and Gigolette by Somerset Maugham *d* Pat Jackson, Anthony Pelissier, Harold French *ph* Desmond Dickinson *m* Richard Addinsell

Nigel Patrick, Roland Culver, *Kay Walsh,* Noel Purcell, Ronald Squire, John Laurie, Glynis Johns, Terence Morgan, David Hutcheson

Encounter: see Stranger On the Prowl

Encounter at Raven's Gate

Australia 1989 93m colour
Castle Premier/Hemdale/FGH/International Film Management (Rolf de Heer, Marc Rosenberg)
V, L

A strange scientist appears to orchestrate a series of bizarre happenings at an isolated farming community.

Low budget science fiction non-thriller that rarely explains what is happening but staggers from one spooky event to the next.

w Rolf de Heer, Marc Rosenberg *screenplay* James Michael Vernon   d Rolf de Heer   ph Richard Michalak   m Graham Tardif, Roman Kronen   pd Judith Russell   ed Suresh Ayyar

Stephen Vidler, Celine Griffin, Ritchie Singer, Vince Gil, Saturday Rosenberg, Max Cullen, Terry Camilleri

'A comedy for you and your next of kin!'
The End
US   1978   100m   DeLuxe
UA/Lawrence Gordon (Hank Moonjean)
V*, L

A selfish man finds he is dying and unsuccessfully tries to change what remains of his life.

Presumably intended as an ironic black comedy, this comes over as tasteless ham; nobody involved, least of all the director-star, has any idea how to handle it.

w Jerry Belson   d Burt Reynolds   ph Bobby Byrne   m Paul Williams   pd Jan Scott

Burt Reynolds, Dom de Luise, Sally Field, Strother Martin, David Steinberg, Joanne Woodward, Norman Fell, Myrna Loy, Pat O'Brien, Robby Benson, Carl Reiner

End as a Man: see *The Strange One*

The End of August *
US   1981   107m   Metrocolor
Sewanee (Martin Jurow)

In 1900, a bored young wife takes a lover beneath her station.

Unexpectedly nostalgic wallow in days gone by, the background detail seeming more important than the personal story, and certainly very good to look at.

w Eula Seaton, Leon Heller   *novel The Awakening* by Kate Chopin   d Bob Graham   ph Robert Elswit   m Shirley Walker   pd Warren Jacobson, Erin Jo Jurow

Sally Sharp, Lilia Skala, David Marshall Grant, Kathleen Widdoes, Paul Roebling, Paul Shenar

'Reminiscent of nothing so much as the turning of pages in a family album.' – *Jo Imeson, MFB*

The End of St Petersburg **
USSR   1927   110m approx   bw   silent
Mezhrabpom-Russ
V
original title: *Konyets Sankt-Peterburga*

A peasant comes to live in St Petersburg in 1914, understands the workers' problems, and joins in the revolution.

Exhilarating propaganda, reprehensible but superbly conceived, with an especially rousing climax.

w Nathan Zarkhi   d V. I. Pudovkin   ph Anatoli Golovnya, K. Vents   ad S. Kozlovsky

Ivan Chuvelov, Vera Baranovskaya, A. P. Christiakov

† The film was officially commissioned as part of the 10th anniversary celebrations.

The End of the Affair
GB   1954   106m   bw
Columbia/Coronado (David Lewis)

In wartime London, a repressed wife has an affair with a writer but develops religious guilt which leads indirectly to her death.

Glum sinning in Greeneland; over-ambitious, miscast, and poor-looking.

w Lenore Coffee   *novel* Graham Greene   d Edward Dmytryk   ph Wilkie Cooper   m Benjamin Frankel

Deborah Kerr, Van Johnson, Peter Cushing, John Mills, Stephen Murray, Nora Swinburne, Charles Goldner

End of the Game *
US/West Germany   1976   104m   colour
TCF/Maximilian Schell

A retiring police inspector intensifies his vendetta against the crooked industrialist who thirty years earlier killed the woman they both loved.

Chess-like revenge melodrama very typical of its author, with no light relief and a few existentialist touches added for general confusion. Well made and sometimes fascinating, but finally annoying.

w Maximilian Schell, Friedrich Dürrenmatt   *novel The Judge and his Hangman* by Friedrich Dürrenmatt   d Maximilian Schell   ph Ennio Guarnieri, Klaus Koenig, Roberto Gerardi

Jon Voight, Robert Shaw, Martin Ritt, Jacqueline Bisset

'A more addled, overreaching, misjudged, ill-made, wasteful, posturizing, uninteresting and tedious little epic has not toddled into town in years.' – *Charles Champlin, Los Angeles Times*

The End of the Golden Weather
New Zealand   1992   103m   colour
Blue Dolphin/South Pacific/New Zealand Film Commission/TV New Zealand (Christina Milligan, Ian Mune)
V

During a summer holiday a lonely boy becomes friendly with a retarded youth with Olympic ambitions.

A slight and uninvolving movie of the dawning of maturity.

w Ian Mune, Bruce Mason   *play* Bruce Mason   d Ian Mune   ph Alun Bollinger   m Stephen McCurdy   pd Ron Highfield   ed Michael Horton

Stephen Fulford, Stephen Papps, Paul Gittins, Gabrielle Hammond, David Taylor, Alexandra Marshall

'An intimate and gentle coming-of-age comedy drama.' – *Variety*

End of the Rainbow: see *Northwest Outpost*

The End of the River *
GB   1947   83m   bw
GFD/The Archers (Michael Powell, Emeric Pressburger)

A South American Indian boy flees to the outside world and finds life in the city as dangerous as in the jungle.

Strange but oddly impressive departure for British film-makers at this time. A commercial and critical disaster.

w Wolfgang Wilhelm   *novel* Desmond Holdridge   d Derek Twist   ph Christopher Challis   m Lambert Williamson

Sabu, Esmond Knight, Bibi Ferreira, Robert Douglas, Antoinette Cellier, Raymond Lovell, Torin Thatcher, James Hayter

The End of the Road
GB   1936   71m   bw
Fox British

A travelling singer loses heart when he hears of the death of his daughter.

Stilted star vehicle of archival interest.

w Edward Dryhurst   d Alan Bryce   ph Stanley Grant

Harry Lauder, Ruth Haven, Ethel Glendinning, Bruce Seton

The End of the Road *
GB   1954   77m   bw
Group Three (Alfred Shaughnessy)

A retired engineer becomes frustrated by idleness, and his family contemplate sending him to an old people's home.

Reasonably absorbing study of old age, suffering from a contrived end.

w James Forsyth, Geoffrey Orme   d Wolf Rilla   ph Arthur Grant   m John Addison

Finlay Currie, Duncan Lamont, Naomi Chance, David Hannaford

End of the Road *
US   1970   110m   Eastmancolor
Contemporary/Allied Artists (Stephen F. Kesten, Terry Southern)
V*

Released from a sanitarium, a teacher takes a job at a local university and impregnates a professor's wife.

Determinedly offbeat, intermittently successful movie that was very much of its time, with the mad being regarded as truly sane.

w Aram Avakian, Dennis McGuire, Terry Southern   *novel* John Barth   d Aram Avakian   ph Gordon Willis   m Teo Macero   pd John K. Wright   ed Robert Q. Lovett

Stacy Keach, Harris Yulin, Dorothy Tristan, James Earl Jones, Grayson Hall, Ray Brock, James Coco

'The cinematography by Gordon Willis is often beautiful, the optical effects are sometimes elegant, and the sets and details are often remarkably fine, but the absurdist point of view has too self-congratulatory a tone.' – *Pauline Kael*

End of the World *
France   1930   105m   bw
Ecran d'Art (Abel Gance)
original title: *La Fin du Monde*

Social and economic panic is caused when a comet is about to hit the Earth.

Massive attempt by Gance to rival his *Napoleon* in scope. Made in German, French and English, it cost a phenomenal sum which it never regained; Gance found work hard to get in future, especially since he set himself up as a prophet.

wd Abel Gance

Abel Gance, Colette Darfeuil, Sylvia Grenade, Victor Francen

'A megalomaniac's effort turned out without consideration for financial results, and containing a strange mixture of crazy stuff, with successfully directed spectacular sequences.' – *Variety*

† The full title is *The End of the World as Seen, Heard and Rendered by Abel Gance.*

The End of the World (in our usual bed in a night full of rain)
Italy   1978   104m   colour
Gil Shiva/Liberty/Warner
V*

An American lady photographer has a bumpy romance with an Italian communist journalist with expensive tastes.

Pretentious talk-piece which slowly gets nowhere.

wd Lina Wertmuller

Candice Bergen, Giancarlo Giannini

Endangered Species
US   1982   97m   Metrocolor
MGM/Alive Enterprises (Carolyn Pfeiffer)

Citizens of a small Wyoming town discover that their cattle are being systematically murdered.

Curious melodrama which never really explains itself but seems to be carrying a message about chemical warfare. With a proper ending it could have been a good suspenser.

w Alan Rudolph, John Binder   *story* Judson Klinger, Richard Woods   *d* Alan Rudolph   *ph* Paul Lohmann   *m* Gary Wright   *pd* Trevor Williams

Robert Urich, Jobeth Williams, Paul Dooley, Hoyt Axton, Peter Coyote

'It's not over … it's not over!'

Endless Love
US   1981   110m   Technicolor
Polygram (Keith Barish)
V*, L

A high school student's love for a 15-year-old girl is thwarted by circumstance and accident.

Overheated melodrama with unbelievable and unlikeable characters. Why this director should choose to make it is mysterious.

w Judith Rascoe   *novel* Scott Spencer   *d* Franco Zeffirelli   *ph* David Watkin   *m* Jonathan Tunick   *pd* Ed Wittstein

Brooke Shields, Martin Hewitt, Shirley Knight, Don Murray, Richard Kiley, Beatrice Straight

AAN: title song (*m/y* Lionel Richie)

Endless Night *
GB   1971   99m   Eastmancolor
BL/EMI (Leslie Gilliat)
V*, L

An American girl buys an English stately home and marries a chauffeur, but is later frightened to death.

Bumpy British thriller, structurally weak and peopled by the dullest conceivable characters, but with watchably scary sequences.

wd Sidney Gilliat   *novel* Agatha Christie   *ph* Harry Waxman   *m* Bernard Herrmann

Hayley Mills, Hywel Bennett, George Sanders, Britt Ekland, Per Oscarsson, Lois Maxwell

The Endless Summer
US   1966   95m   Technicolor
Bruce Brown Films/Columbia
V*, L

A study of surfing round the world.

A documentary which became a cult for those influenced by this Californian obsession; smashing photography hardly atones for an approach so naïve as to become fatuous.

wd/ph/ed Bruce Brown

Die Ehe Der Maria Braun: see *The Marriage of Maria Braun*

Enemies, a Love Story *
US   1989   120m   colour
Fox/Morgan Creek Productions (Paul Mazursky)
V*, L, S

The life of a Jew who survived the concentration camps becomes tragically entangled with that of three women: his first wife, whom he thought was dead, his second wife and his mistress.

Rushed in its telling, despite its length, and lacking in conviction.

w Roger L. Simon, Paul Mazursky   *novel* Isaac Bashevis Singer   *d* Paul Mazursky   *ph* Fred Murphy   *m* Maurice Jarre   *pd* Pato Guzman   *ed* Stuart Pappe

Anjelica Huston, Ron Silver, Lena Olin, Margaret Sophie Stein, Judith Malina, Alan King, Rita Karin, Phil Leeds

AAN: Anjelica Huston, Lena Olin

Enemies of the Public: see *The Public Enemy*

Enemy Agent
US   1940   64m   bw
Universal

An aircraft worker is framed as a spy.

Nifty little topical support with not much sense but plenty of zest.

w Sam Robbins, Edmund L. Hartmann   *d* Lew Landers

Richard Cromwell, Philip Dorn, Helen Vinson, Marjorie Reynolds, Robert Armstrong, Vinton Haworth, Abner Biberman, Jack Carson, Jack La Rue

Enemy Agent (1940): see *British Intelligence*

Enemy Agents Meet Ellery Queen
US   1942   64m   bw
Columbia (Ralph Cohn)

Sailors and marines help Ellery to rout Nazi spies.

Uncoordinated extravaganza which signalled the end of the Queen series.

w Eric Taylor   *d* James Hogan

William Gargan, Margaret Lindsay, Charley Grapewin, Gale Sondergaard, Gilbert Roland, Sig Rumann

The Enemy Below *
US   1957   98m   Technicolor   Cinemascope
TCF (Dick Powell)
V, V*

During World War II an American destroyer in the South Atlantic is involved in a cat-and-mouse operation with a U-boat.

Well-staged, unsurprising naval thriller with good pace and a pat let's-not-be-nasty-to-each-other ending.

w Wendell Mayes   *novel* Commander D. A. Rayner   *d* Dick Powell   *ph* Harold Rosson   *m* Leigh Harline

Robert Mitchum, Curt Jurgens, Theodore Bikel, David Hedison

Enemy from Space: see *Quatermass II*

The Enemy General
US   1960   74m   bw
Columbia (Sam Katzman)

An American officer takes revenge on the German general who executed his fiancée.

Routine World War II heroics with a plot deserving a rather better production.

w Dan Pepper, Burt Picard   *d* George Sherman   *ph* Basil Emmott   *md* Mischa Bakaleinikoff

Van Johnson, Jean-Pierre Aumont, John Van Dreelen, Dany Carrel, Françoise Prévost

Enemy Mine
US   1985   108m   DeLuxe   Amiflex Widescreen
Kings Road/TCF (Stephen Friedman)
V, V*, S

A space pilot goes down on Dracon and makes friends with his lizard-like captor.

All talk and little action, this is a way-out piece of do-goodery which tests the patience.

w Edward Khmara   *story* Barry Longyear   *d* Wolfgang Petersen   *ph* Tony Imi   *m* Maurice Jarre   *pd* Rolf Zehetbauer   *ed* Hannes Nikel

Dennis Quaid, Lou Gossett Jnr, Brion James, Richard Marcus, Carolyn McCormick

An Enemy of the People *
US   1977   103m   Metrocolor
First Artists (George Schaefer)

A small-town doctor discovers that for commercial reasons his colleagues propose to conceal the fact that the local spa is contaminated by tannery waste.

Ibsen's plot is well intentioned but well worn – it more or less served as the starting point for *Jaws* – so in any modern version the acting is all. Here it isn't enough, though the star so badly wanted to do it that

arguments and sulks kept him off the screen for three years.

w Alexander Jacobs   *play* Arthur Miller's version of the play by Henrik Ibsen   *d* George Schaefer   *ph* Paul Lohmann   *m* Leonard Rosenman

Steve McQueen, Charles Durning, Bibi Andersson, Eric Christmas, Richard Bradford, Richard A. Dysart

'The main thing I was shooting for was not to make bucks but to have something I could believe in.' – *Steve McQueen*

An Enemy of the People *
India   1989   100m   Eastmancolor
Contemporary/Electric/National Film Development Corp of India (Anil Gupta)
V
original title: *Ganashatru*

A doctor encounters local hostility when he complains of polluted water supplies.

Less than successful transfer of Ibsen's play to modern-day India, in a studio-bound production.

wd Satyajit Ray   *play* Henrik Ibsen   *ph* Barun Raha   *m* Satyajit Ray   *ad* Ashok Bose   *ed* Dulal Dutta

Soumitra Chatterjee, Dhritiman Chatterjee, Ruma Guhathakurta, Mamata Shankar, Dipankar Dey, Subhendu Chatterjee

L'Enfance Nue **
France   1968   80m   colour
Stephan Films (Mag Bodard, François Truffaut, Claude Berri, Jo and Samy Siritzky)
aka: *Naked Childhood*; US title: *Me*

Rejected by his foster parents because of his difficult behaviour, a 10-year-old boy finds temporary refuge with an elderly couple.

A restrained, unsentimental account of a troubled and troublesome childhood, shot in a naturalistic style with a non-professional cast.

w Maurice Pialat, Arlette Langman   *d* Maurice Pialat   *ph* Claude Beausoleil

Michel Tarrazon, Rene Thierry, Marie-Louis Thierry, Henri Puff, Maurice Coussoneau, Marie Marc, Michel Soulé

L'Enfant Sauvage *
France   1970   84m   bw
UA/Films du Carrosse (Marcel Berbert)
US title: *The Wild Child*

In 1797, a scientist tames and studies a young boy who has mysteriously been living wild in the forest.

Slightly flat but generally interesting reconstruction of a true event, the same one which subsequently inspired TV projects such as *Stalk the Wild Child* and *Lucan*.

w François Truffaut, Jean Gruault   *d* François Truffaut   *ph* Nestor Almendros   *m* Vivaldi

Jean-Pierre Cargol, François Truffaut, Jean Dasté, Françoise Seigner

Les Enfants du Paradis ****
France   1945   195m   bw
Pathé (Fred Orain, Raymond Borderic)
V (W), V*, L
US title: *Children of Paradise*

In the 'theatre street' of Paris in the 1840s, a mime falls in love with the elusive Garance, but her problems with other men keep them apart.

A magnificent evocation of a place and a period, this thoroughly enjoyable epic melodrama is flawed only by its lack of human warmth and of a real theme. It remains nevertheless one of the cinema's most memorable films.

w Jacques Prévert   *d* Marcel Carné   *ph* Roger Hubert   *m* Maurice Thiriet, Joseph Kosma, G. Mouque   *ad* Alexandre Trauner, Léon Barsacq, Raymond Gabutti

Arletty, Jean-Louis Barrault, Pierre Brasseur, Marcel Herrand, Maria Casarès, Louis Salon, Pierre Renoir, Gaston Modot, Jane Marken

'A magnificent scenario . . . Prévert is as adept with wit as with poignancy . . . I don't believe a finer group of actors was ever assembled on film' – *John Simon*

AAN: Jacques Prévert

Les Enfants Terribles *
France 1950 100m bw
Jean-Pierre Melville
aka: *The Strange Ones*

The hothouse relationship of an adolescent brother and sister leads to tragedy.

Rough-edged, stage-bound but occasionally quite powerful exploration into familiar Cocteau territory.

wd Jean-Pierre Melville *novel* Jean Cocteau *ph* Henri Decaë *m* Bach, Vivaldi

Nicole Stéphane, Edouard Dermithe, Renée Cosima, Jacques Bernard

'The first story of the double-fisted DA who tore apart the evil dynasty that peddled murder for a price!'
The Enforcer ***
US 1950 87m bw
United States Pictures (Milton Sperling)
V, V*, L
GB title: *Murder, Inc*

A crusading District Attorney tracks down the leader of a gang which murders for profit.

Extremely suspenseful and well-characterized police yarn based on fact. One of the very best of its kind.

w Martin Rackin *d* Bretaigne Windust *ph* Robert Burks *m* David Buttolph

Humphrey Bogart, Everett Sloane, Zero Mostel, Ted de Corsia, Roy Roberts, King Donovan

'A tough, very slickly-made thriller with a host of fine character parts.' – *NFT, 1969*

'Absorbing and exciting, with little of the violence that so often disfigures films of this kind.' – *Richard Mallett, Punch*

'The first fifteen minutes is as powerful and rapid a sketch of tension as I can recall for seasons. The last fifteen might make Hitch weep with envy.' – *Observer*

The Enforcer
US 1976 96m DeLuxe Panavision
Warner/Malpaso (Robert Daley)
V, V*, L

Brutal Inspector Callahan of the San Francisco police redeems himself by rounding up a group of psychopathic hoodlums.

Dirty Harry, phase three: for hardened veterans only.

w Stirling Silliphant, Dean Riesner *d* James Fargo *ph* Richard Glouner *m* Jerry Fielding

Clint Eastwood, Tyne Daly, Harry Guardino, Bradford Dillman, John Mitchum, DeVeren Brookwalter, John Crawford

'A new low in mindless violence is reached in this film, which is so bad it would be funny if it were not for the gut-thumping killings from beginning to end.' – *William F. Fore, Film Information*

The Engagement *
GB 1970 44m Technicolor
Memorial (David Barber)

A young executive spends a devastating afternoon trying to borrow money to pay for an engagement ring which cost more than he expected.

Brisk little comedy which doesn't wear out its welcome.

w Tom Stoppard *d* Paul Joyce *ph* Tony Spratling *m* John Dankworth

David Warner, Michael Bates, George Innes, Juliet Harmer, Paul Curran, Barbara Couper, Peter Copley

England Made Me **
GB 1972 100m Eastmancolor Panavision
Hemdale/Atlantic (Jack Levin)

In 1935 a sponging Englishman becomes involved through his sister with a German financier.

Somewhat altered from the novel, this unusual film remains a lively, intelligent character melodrama.

w Desmond Cory, Peter Duffell *novel* Graham Greene *d* Peter Duffell *ph* Ray Parslow *m* John Scott

Peter Finch, Michael York, Hildegarde Neil, *Michael Hordern,* Joss Ackland

English without Tears *
GB 1944 89m bw
GFD/Two Cities (Anatole de Grunwald, Sydney Box)
US title: *Her Man Gilbey*

During World War II a rich ATS girl falls for her butler who has become a lieutenant.

Wispy satirical comedy with amusing moments, chiefly interesting for the pre-war League of Nations sequences.

w Terence Rattigan, Anatole de Grunwald *d* Harold French *ph* Bernard Knowles

Lilli Palmer, Michael Wilding, *Margaret Rutherford,* Penelope Dudley Ward, Albert Lieven, Roland Culver, Peggy Cummins

An Englishman's Home
GB 1939 79m bw
UA/Aldwych (Neville E. Neville, Sidney Harrison)
US title: *Madmen of Europe*

An English family plays unwitting host to a foreign spy.

Hilarious clinker, far too unintentionally funny to make the effective propaganda intended.

w (catch them all) Dennis Wheatley, Edward Knoblock, Ian Hay, Robert Edmunds, Dora Nirva, Clifford Grey, Richard Llewellyn, Rodney Ackland *play* Guy du Maurier *d* Albert de Courville *ph* Mutz Greenbaum, Henry Harris *ed* Lister Laurence

Edmund Gwenn, Mary Maguire, Paul Henreid, Geoffrey Toone, Richard Ainley, Desmond Tester

'There is nothing to be said for this film – though it might prove useful propaganda in enemy countries, purporting to illustrate the decadence of English architecture and taste.' – *Graham Greene*

Enid Is Sleeping
US 1989 102m DeLuxe
First Independent/Vestron/Davis (John A. Davis, Howard Malin)
V, V*
GB title: *Over Her Dead Body*

Having accidentally killed her sister, who discovered her in bed with her husband, a woman tries to dispose of the body without arousing suspicion.

Unoriginal attempt at a black comedy, lacking wit and timing; Hitchcock did it far better with *The Trouble With Harry*.

w Maurice Phillips, A. J. Tipping, James Whaley *d* Maurice Phillips *ph* Alfonso Beato *m* Craig Safan *pd* Paul Peters *ed* Malcolm Campbell

Elizabeth Perkins, Judge Reinhold, Jeffrey Jones, Rhea Perlman, Michael J. Pollard, Brion James, Charles Tyner

'Neither farcical enough nor sufficiently outrageous to justify the sterling efforts of the cast to inject some much-needed energy into the flatly directed scenes.' – *Nigel Floyd, Sight and Sound*

Enigma
GB/France 1982 101m colour
Embassy/Filmcrest/Peter Shaw
V, V*, L

An East German refugee is recruited by the CIA to return to East Berlin.

Threadbare spy stuff with an indecipherable plot.

w John Briley *novel* Michael Barak *d* Jeannot Szwarc *ph* Jean-Louis Picavet *m* Marc Wilkinson

Martin Sheen, Brigitte Fossey, Sam Neill, Derek Jacobi, Michel Lonsdale, Frank Finlay, Michael Williams, Warren Clarke

'Well made but insufficiently exciting.' – *Variety*

'The mystery is why they bothered.' – *Guardian*

The Enigma of Kaspar Hauser ****
West Germany 1974 110m colour
Contemporary/Zud Deutscher Rudfunk/Werner Herzog
V*
original title: *Jeder für sich und Gott gegen alle*; aka: *The Mystery of Kaspar Hauser; Every Man for Himself and God against All*

In the 1820s, a 16-year-old boy, who has spent his life isolated from others, is found abandoned in the town square of Nuremberg.

Based on a true story, a disturbing and affecting account of an untouched mind confronting humanity at its best and worst and exposing the limitations of society's response, with a fiercely convincing performance in the title role.

wd Werner Herzog *ph* Jörg Schmidt-Reitwein *m* Pachelbel, Albinoni and others *ad* Henning V. Gierke *ed* Beate Mainke-Jellinghaus

Bruno S., Walter Ladengast, Brigitte Mira, Willy Semmelrogge, Gloria Dör, Volker Prechtel, Hans Musaus

'A double fable, intermingling the stultifying effects of bourgeois society and the cruelty of a demonic universe.' – *Pauline Kael*

'Herzog's direction is not free of the hallmarks of contemporary German film-making, an estheticism, a slow pace, an arrogance toward dramatic concept that almost supply an imaginary soundtrack accompanying the picture saying: "You can see that this film was made by an intellectual, can't you?"' – *Stanley Kauffmann*

† The film was awarded the Special Jury Prize at the Cannes Film Festival in 1975.

Ensayo de un Crimen: see *The Criminal Life of Archibaldo de la Cruz*

Ensign Pulver
US 1964 104m Technicolor Panavision
Warner (Joshua Logan)
V*

Further naval misadventures of the character from *Mr Roberts*.

Threadbare naval comedy with every expected cliché.

w Joshua Logan, Peter S. Feibleman *play* Joshua Logan, Thomas Heggen *d* Joshua Logan *ph* Charles Lawton *m* George Duning

Robert Walker, Burl Ives, Walter Matthau, Tommy Sands, Millie Perkins, Kay Medford, Larry Hagman, James Farentino, James Coco, Al Freeman Jnr

Entebbe: Operation Thunderbolt: see *Operation Thunderbolt*

Entente Cordiale *
France 1939 95m bw Max Glass

A history of relations between England and France from Victorian times to the present day.

Ambitious pageant from the French point of view.

w Steve Passeur, Max Glass   *book Edward VII and His Times* by André Maurois   *d* Marcel l'Herbier   *ph* Ted Pahle, Marc Fossard   *m* Darius Milhaud

Victor Francen (Edward VII), Gaby Morlay (Queen Victoria), André Lefaur, Jean Perier, Jean d'Yd, Jean Worms

'One of the most outstanding productions of its type ever made in France.' – *Variety*

Enter Arsène Lupin

US   1944   72m   bw
Universal

A master thief protects a beautiful girl's emerald.

Stiff little second which failed to bring forth a series.

w Bertram Millhauser   *d* Ford Beebe

Charles Korvin, Ella Raines, J. Carrol Naish, George Dolenz, Gale Sondergaard, Miles Mander

Enter Inspector Duval

GB   1961   64m   bw
Bill Luckwell

A French detective helps Scotland Yard solve the murder of a socialite.

Dim mystery with no hope of becoming a series.

w J. Henry Piperno   *d* Max Varnel

Anton Diffring, Diane Hart, Mark Singleton

Enter Laughing *

US   1967   111m   Technicolor
Columbia/Acre/Sajo (Carl Reiner, Joseph Stein)
V*

In New York in the thirties, a young man about to train as a pharmacist decides to become an actor instead.

Strident Jewish comedy based on the writer-director's own youthful experiences, which might have been more effectively strained by another hand. The talent is there, though.

w Joseph Stein, Carl Reiner   *play* Carl Reiner
d Carl Reiner   *ph* Joseph Biroc   *m* Quincy Jones

Reni Santoni, José Ferrer, Shelley Winters, Elaine May, Jack Gilford, Janet Margolin, David Opatoshu, Michael J. Pollard

Enter Madame

US   1934   83m   bw
Paramount

A millionaire is humbled when he marries a glamorous opera singer.

Modest comedy operetta, with the star's voice dubbed by Nina Koshetz.

w Charles Brackett, Gladys Lehmann   *play* Gilda Varesi Archibald, Dorothea Donn-Byrne   *d* Elliott Nugent

Elissa Landi, Cary Grant, Lynne Overman, Sharon Lynne, Paul Porcasi

Enter the Dragon *

US/Hong Kong   1973   99m   Technicolor
Panavision
Warner/Concord (Fred Weintraub, Paul Heller)
V, V*, L, S

A master of martial arts is enlisted by British intelligence to stop opium smuggling.

The first Hollywood-based Kung Fu actioner; not bad, on the lines of a more violent James Bond.

w Michael Allin   *d* Robert Clouse   *ph* Gilbert Hubbs   *m* Lalo Schifrin

Bruce Lee, John Saxon, Shih Kien, Jim Kelly, Bob Wall

'A good-natured example of the pleasures of schlock art.' – *Pauline Kael*

The Entertainer *

GB   1960   96m   bw
BL/Bryanston/Woodfall/Holly (John Croydon)
V, V*

A faded seaside comedian reflects on his failure as an entertainer and as a man.

Even with Olivier repeating his stage triumph, or perhaps because of it, this tragi-comedy remains defiantly theatrical and does not take wing on film.

w John Osborne, Nigel Kneale   *play* John Osborne
d Tony Richardson   *ph* Oswald Morris   *m* John Addison

Laurence Olivier, Joan Plowright, Brenda de Banzie, *Roger Livesey*, Alan Bates, Shirley Anne Field, Albert Finney, Thora Hird, Daniel Massey

'No amount of deafening sound effects and speciously busy cutting can remove one's feeling that behind this distracting façade of heightened realism lurks a basic lack of confidence.' – *Peter John Dyer*

AAN: Laurence Olivier

Entertaining Mr Sloane *

GB   1969   94m   Technicolor
Pathé/Canterbury (Douglas Kentish)
V, V*

A lodger attracts the amorous attention of both the middle-aged daughter and older son of the house.

A Gothic *tour de force* of bad taste which worked better on the stage but has its moments.

w Clive Exton   *play* Joe Orton   *d* Douglas Hickox
ph Wolfgang Suschitzky   *m* Georgie Fame

Beryl Reid, Harry Andrews, Peter McEnery, Alan Webb

The Entity

US   1981   125m   Technicolor   Panavision
TCF/Pelleport Investors/American Cinema (Harold Schneider)

A young mother is attacked and raped by an invisible entity which may come from her own id.

Unpleasant nonsense, way overlong but with the occasional well-staged scene for those who can stay the course.

w Frank DeFelitta   *novel* Frank DeFelitta
d Sidney J. Furie   *ph* Stephen H. Burum
m Charles Bernstein   *pd* Charles Rosen   *ed* Frank J. Urioste

Barbara Hershey, Ron Silver, David Labiosa, George Coe, Jacqueline Brookes

Entr'acte **

France   1924   20m approx   bw   silent
Ballets Suédois

Various eccentric characters become involved in a crazy chase.

Hilarious nonsense short, devised originally to be shown between the acts of a Dadaist ballet. Very clearly the start of a famous directorial career.

w Francis Picabia   *d/ed René Clair   *ph* J. Berliet

Jean Borlin, Inge Fries, Francis Picabia, Man Ray, Georges Auric, Marcel Achard, Marcel Duchamp

Entre Nous: see *Coup de Foudre*

Entre Onze Heures et Minuit *

France   1948   103m   bw
Francinex (Jacques Roitfeld)

A police detective solves his case by impersonating one of the victims.

Twisty, elaborate murder mystery, very competently performed but a little overlong.

w Henri Decoin, Marcel Rivet   *novel Le Sosie de la Morgue* by Claude Luxel   *d* Henri Decoin
ph Nicolas Hayer   *m* Henri Saguet

Louis Jouvet, Madeleine Robinson, Robert Arnoux, Gisèle Casadesus

Entre Tinieblas: see *Dark Habits*

Entrée des Artistes *

France   1938   100m   bw
Regina

Jealousies among the students at the Paris Conservatory lead to murder.

Predictable but well-made audience pleaser.

w Henri Jeanson, André Cayatte   *d* Marc Allegret

Louis Jouvet, Odette Joyeux, Claude Dauphin, Janine Darcey, Carette, Dalio, Sylvie

'Everyone Has A Dark Side. Henry's About To Meet His.'

Equinox *

US   1992   110m   colour   Panavision
Metro Tartan/SC Entertainment (David Blocker)
V, V*, L, S

A shy and timid garage mechanic discovers that he has a twin brother who is a killer.

Quirky, stylized but insubstantial tale of people damaged by, or fearful of, life; but it cannot bear as much weight as its director intended.

wd Alan Rudolph   *ph* Elliot Davis
m Rachmaninov and others   *pd* Steven Legler
ed Michael Ruscio

Matthew Modine, Lara Flynn Boyle, Marisa Tomei, Fred Ward, Tyra Ferrell, Kevin J. O'Connor, Tate Donovan, Lori Singer, M. Emmet Walsh, Gailard Sartain

'A film which needs several viewings to be appreciated. Although the battle between dark and light is obvious, the finer touches are buried in a visual tapestry to be discovered by the devoted (perhaps obsessive) viewer.' – *Sight and Sound*

L'Equipage *

France   1935   107m   bw
Pathé-Natan

A World War I flyer finds that the love of his life is the wife of his colleague.

Tense romantic drama with aerial sequences, subsequently remade in Hollywood as *The Woman I Love*.

story Joseph Kessel   *d* Anatole Litvak

Charles Vanel, Jean-Pierre Aumont, Annabella

'A gripping human story, beautifully told.' – *Variety*

Equus *

GB   1977   137m   colour
UA/Winkast (Denis Holt)
V, V*, L

A middle-aged psychiatrist tries to find out why a 17-year-old boy blinded six horses.

Overlong film version of a play which was a *succès d'estime;* it makes the fatal mistake of showing the tragic events realistically instead of stylistically as was done on the stage, and as a study in abnormal psychology it is scarcely gripping or revealing.

w Peter Shaffer   *play* Peter Shaffer   *d* Sidney Lumet   *ph* Oswald Morris   *m* Richard Rodney Bennett   *pd* Tony Walton

Richard Burton, Peter Firth, Colin Blakely, Joan Plowright, Harry Andrews, Eileen Atkins, Jenny Agutter, Kate Reid

'It sets Peter Shaffer's worst ideas on a pedestal.' – *Pauline Kael*

AAN: Peter Shaffer; Richard Burton; Peter Firth

Eraserhead

US   1976   89m   bw
David Lynch
V, V*, S

A nondescript man has a number of increasingly nightmarish experiences including becoming pregnant and being consumed by a planet.

Tediously elongated piece of schlock surrealism. At least Buñuel and Dali didn't take so long about their nonsense.

wd David Lynch ph David Elmes, Herbert Cardwell

John Nance, Charlotte Stewart, Allen Joseph

'A compulsive hybrid mix of punk surrealism and B picture.' – Time Out

Ercole e la Regina di Lidia: see Hercules Unchained

L'Erdita Ferramonti: see The Inheritance

Erendira *
France/Mexico/Germany 1982 105m colour
Les Films du Triangle/A2/Cine Qua Non/Atlas Saskia Film (Alain Queffelean)
V*

An intolerant woman tries to restore the family fortune by prostituting her young granddaughter after she accidentally burns down their home.

Bizarre, surrealist fable of thwarted love and domination.

w Gabriel García Marquez d Ruy Guerra
ph Denys Clerval m Maurice Lecoeur pd Pierre Cadiou ed Kenout Peltier

Irene Papas, Claudia Ohana, Michel Lonsdale, Oliver Wehe, Rufus, Blanca Guerra, Ernesto Gomez Cruz

Erik the Viking
GB 1989 108m Technicolor
UIP/Erik The Viking Productions/Prominent Features/AB Svensk Filmindustri (Terry Glinwood)
V, V*, L

A Viking sails on an expedition to wake the Gods.

Uneasy mix of fantasy and humour.

wd Terry Jones novel Terry Jones ph Ian Wilson
m Neil Innes pd John Beard ed George Akers

Tim Robbins, Mickey Rooney, Eartha Kitt, Terry Jones, Imogen Stubbs, John Cleese, Tsutomu Sekine, Anthony Sher, Gary Cady, Charles McKeown, Tim McInnerny, John Gordon Sinclair

'A thunderous, unfunny jumble.' – MFB

Ernest Saves Christmas
US 1988 91m Metrocolor
Warner/Touchstone/Silver Screen Partners III (Stacy Williams, Doug Claybourne)
V*, L

Santa Claus goes to America to find someone to take over his job.

Inept and witless from start to finish.

w B. Kline, Ed Turner d John Cherry ph Peter Stein m Mark Snow ad Ian Thomas ed Sharyn L. Ross

Jim Varney, Douglas Seale, Oliver Clark, Noelle Parker, Gailard Sartain, Billie Bird, Bill Byrge, Robert Lesser, Key Howard

L'Eroe di Babylon: see The Hero of Babylon

Eroica *
Poland 1957 83m bw
Kadr
aka: Heroism

Two ironic episodes of war; in the 1944 Warsaw uprising and in a POW camp.

Nicely-judged little stories with a sting.

w Jerzy Stefan Stawinski novels Jerzy Stefan Stawinski d Andrzej Munk ph Jerzy Wojcik
m Jan Krenz

Barbara Polomska, L. Niemszyk, Edward Dziewonski, K. Rudzki, Roman Klosowski, Josef Nowak

Erotikon *
Sweden 1920 85m approx bw silent
Svensk Filmindustri

When a professor discovers that his wife is unfaithful, he consoles himself with his young niece.

Sophisticated comedy drama filled with material which might later have appealed to Lubitsch; a little faded now, but it still has charm.

w Gustav Molander, Mauritz Stiller play Franz Herzeg d Mauritz Stiller ph Henrik Jaenzon

Lars Hanson, Karin Molander, Tora Teje, Anders de Wahl

Erotikon *
Czechoslovakia 1929 85m approx bw silent
Gem Film

A stationmaster's daughter takes a rich lover.

Atmospheric little sex drama which sufficiently justified its title to be a big international success.

wd Gustav Machaty ph Vaclav Vich

Ita Rina, Karel Schleichert, Olaf Fjord, Theo Pistek

The Errand Boy
US 1961 92m bw
Paramount/Jerry Lewis (Ernest D. Glucksman)
V, V*, L

A dimwit paperhanger causes havoc in a Hollywood studio but is eventually signed up as a comic to rival Jerry Lewis.

Feeble comedy with the star at his self-satisfied worst.

wd Jerry Lewis ph W. Wallace Kelley m Walter Scharf

Jerry Lewis, Brian Donlevy, Sig Rumann, Fritz Feld, Isobel Elsom, Iris Adrian

Es Geschah am 20 Juli: see Jackboot Mutiny

Escapade
US 1935 87m bw
MGM (Bernard Hyman)

Affairs of a Viennese artist.

Turgid romantic drama copied from the more successful German film Maskerade.

w Herman J. Mankiewicz original Walter Reisch
d Robert Z. Leonard ph Ernest Haller
m Bronislau Kaper, Walter Jurmann

William Powell, Luise Rainer, Virginia Bruce, Mady Christians, Reginald Owen, Frank Morgan, Laura Hope Crews, Henry Travers

'A triumph of studio slickness.' – Variety

Escapade (1950): see Robinson Crusoeland

Escapade *
GB 1955 87m bw
Pinnacle (Daniel Angel)
V*

Parents row with a headmaster when their three sons steal an aeroplane, but all is well when it turns out that they are on a peace mission.

Whimsical comedy-drama with a rather foolish point; the cast however can hardly fail to provide entertaining moments.

w Gilbert Holland (Donald Ogden Stewart)
play Roger MacDougall d Philip Leacock ph Eric Cross m Bruce Montgomery

John Mills, Alastair Sim, Yvonne Mitchell, Colin Gordon, Marie Lohr

Escapade in Florence
US 1962 80m Technicolor
Walt Disney (Bill Anderson)

Two American students in Florence uncover art thefts.

Cheerful adventure for children, well enough produced on location, but quite unmemorable.

w Maurice Tombragel novel The Golden Doors by Edward Fenton d Steve Previn ph Kurt Grigoleit
m Buddy Baker

Ivan Desny, Tommy Kirk, Annette Funicello, Nino Castelnuovo

Escapade in Japan
US 1957 93m Technirama
RKO (Arthur Lubin)
V*

An American boy survives a plane crash in Tokyo and the crisis reunites his parents.

Nicely photographed travelogue with a thread of plot; pleasant but hardly sustaining.

w Winston Miller d Arthur Lubin ph William Snyder m Max Steiner

Cameron Mitchell, Teresa Wright, Jon Prevost, Philip Ober

Escape
GB 1930 69m bw
ATP (Basil Dean)

An escaped convict on Dartmoor is helped and hindered by various chance encounters.

Episodic, unsatisfactory drama from a stilted play.

wd Basil Dean play John Galsworthy ph Jack Mackenzie, Robert Martin md Ernest Irving
ad Clifford Pember ed Jack Kitchin

Gerald du Maurier, Edna Best, Madeleine Carroll, Gordon Harker, Horace Hodges, Mabel Poulton, Lewis Casson, Ian Hunter, Felix Aylmer

'A more careful work than most of the British talker product, but as an entertainment proposition it doesn't mean much.' – Variety

'There is a love from which no man can escape!'
Escape **
US 1940 104m bw
MGM (Lawrence Weingarten)
reissue title: When the Door Opened

An American gets his mother out of a Nazi concentration camp before World War II.

Ingenious but somewhat slow-moving melodrama with an exciting climax and good production values.

w Arch Oboler, Marguerite Roberts novel Ethel Vance d Mervyn Le Roy ph Robert Planck
m Franz Waxman

Norma Shearer, Robert Taylor, Conrad Veidt, Nazimova, Felix Bressart, Albert Basserman, Philip Dorn, Bonita Granville

'It takes an hour to get started and makes just another feeble fable from headlines.' – Otis Ferguson

'Far and away the most dramatic and hair-raising picture yet made on the sinister subject of persecution in a totalitarian land.' – Bosley Crowther, New York Times

'One of the most poignant dramatic films of the year.' – Modern Screen

'The director takes forever to set up the manoeuvres, and the villain is so much more attractive than the hero that the whole thing turns into a feeble, overproduced joke.' – Pauline Kael, 70s

'Some men are born to imperilled adventure! Some women are drawn to the most dangerous of loves!'
Escape
GB 1948 79m bw
TCF (William Perlberg)

Wholly artificial, predictable and uninteresting remake of the 1930 film.

w Philip Dunne d Joseph L. Mankiewicz
ph Frederick A. Young m William Alwyn

Rex Harrison, Peggy Cummins, William Hartnell, Norman Wooland, Jill Esmond

The Escape Artist *

US   1982   93m   Technicolor
Zoetrope Studios (Doug Claybourne, Buck Houghton)
V*

A young boy justifies his descent from 'the world's greatest escape artist'.

Curiously unfulfilled fable, too vague to satisfy the family audience it seems to aim at, but with pleasant moments.

w Melissa Mathison, Stephen Zito.   novel David Wagoner   d Caleb Deschanel   ph Stephen H. Burum   m Georges Delerue   pd Dean Tavoularis

Griffin O'Neal, Raul Julia, Teri Garr, Joan Hackett, Gabriel Dell, Desi Arnaz

Escape by Night

GB   1953   79m   bw
Tempean (Robert S. Baker, Monty Berman)

A tough reporter tries to get the inside story on a vice ring.

Formula thick ear with what now seems the world's most unlikely villain – Sid James.

wd John Gilling   ph Monty Berman   m Stanley Black

Bonar Colleano, Andrew Ray, Sidney James, Ted Ray, Simone Silva, Avice Landone, Patrick Barr

Escape from Alcatraz *

US   1979   112m   DeLuxe
Paramount/Malpaso (Don Siegel)
V, V*, L

The allegedly true story of a 1960 escape from the prison on a rock in San Francisco Bay.

A dour, terse, depressing prison movie which makes an uncomfortable star vehicle and not very much of an entertainment, but does preserve a certain integrity right to its ambiguous ending.

w Richard Tuggle   book J. Campbell Bruce   d Don Siegel   ph Bruce Surtees   m Jerry Fielding   pd Allen Smith

Clint Eastwood, Patrick McGoohan, Roberts Blossom, Jack Thibeau, Larry Hankin

'An almost entirely interior film masquerading as an exterior one.' – Tom Milne, MFB

Escape from Dartmoor *

GB   1930   77m   bw
Pro Patria

A barber murders his wife's lover.

Stilted melodrama, of interest only as an early British part-talkie. (The only words heard are from a film in a cinema which the characters visit.)

w Herbert Price   d Anthony Asquith

Norah Baring, Uno Henning, Hans Schlettow

'Morbid material, interesting only because of clever direction.' – Variety

Escape from East Berlin

Germany/US   1962   94m   bw
MGM/Walter Wood/Hans Albin
aka: Tunnel 28

An East German chauffeur is persuaded to help an escape attempt by digging and tunnelling under the Berlin Wall.

Cheerless escape melodrama, thinly based on fact but without much suspense.

w Gabrielle Upton, Peter Berneis, Millard Lampell   d Robert Siodmak   ph Georg Krause   m Hans-Martin Majewski

Don Murray, Christine Kaufmann, Werner Klemperer, Ingrid van Bergen

Escape from Fort Bravo *

US   1953   98m   Anscocolor
MGM (Nicholas Nayfack)

A girl helps her Confederate lover to escape from a Yankee fort in Arizona; the commander then tries to save them from Indians.

Grade A Western, effectively shot in Death Valley.

w Frank Fenton   d John Sturges   ph Robert Surtees   m Jeff Alexander

William Holden, Eleanor Parker, John Forsythe, William Demarest

Escape from New York *

US   1981   99m   Metrocolor   Panavision
Avco Embassy/International Film Investors/Goldcrest (Larry Franco, Debra Hill)
V, V*, L, S

In 1997 the whole of Manhattan Island has become a vast security prison; a president has to bale out over it and is taken hostage.

Inventive but too complex melodrama with unattractive detail; its director's biggest production but not his most rewarding.

w John Carpenter, Nick Castle   d John Carpenter   ph Jim Lucas   m John Carpenter   pd Joe Alves

Kurt Russell, Lee Van Cleef, Ernest Borgnine, Donald Pleasence, Isaac Hayes, Season Hubley, Adrienne Barbeau, Harry Dean Stanton

Escape from the Dark

GB   1976   104m   Technicolor
Walt Disney (Ron Miller)
V*

In 1909 Yorkshire, two boys save pit ponies from the slaughterhouse.

Efficient family fare with plenty of suspense and good character cameos.

w Rosemary Anne Sisson   d Charles Jarrott   ph Paul Beeson   m Ron Goodwin

Alastair Sim, Peter Barkworth, Maurice Colbourne, Susan Tebbs, Geraldine McEwan, Prunella Scales, Leslie Sands, Joe Gladwin

'A New Generation Of Incredible Apes In The Most Exciting Suspense Film Of Them All.'

Escape from the Planet of the Apes

US   1971   97m   DeLuxe   Panavision
TCF/APJAC (Arthur P. Jacobs, Frank Capra Jnr)
V, V*, L

Three educated apes travel back from the disaster-strewn future to warn mankind of what lies ahead. Mankind naturally misunderstands.

Predictable third in the series, with infantile humour alternating with a downbeat trend.

w Paul Dehn   d Don Taylor   ph Joseph Biroc   m Jerry Goldsmith

Roddy McDowall, Kim Hunter, Bradford Dillman, Ricardo Montalban, Natalie Trundy, Eric Braeden, William Windom, Sal Mineo

† See also Planet of the Apes.

Escape from Zahrain

US   1961   93m   Technicolor   Panavision
Paramount (Ronald Neame)

Prisoners escape across the desert from an oil sheikdom.

Slow, boring adventure film; good to look at, with James Mason unbilled in a tiny part.

w Robin Estridge   d Ronald Neame   ph Ellsworth Fredericks   m Lyn Murray

Yul Brynner, Sal Mineo, Madlyn Rhue, Jack Warden, Jay Novello

Escape If You Can: see St Benny the Dip

Escape in the Desert

US   1945   81m   bw
Warner (Alex Gottlieb)

An American flyer outwits renegade Nazis.

Oddball remake of The Petrified Forest, with Nazis sitting in for gangsters. Of no interest in itself.

w Thomas Job   play Robert E. Sherwood   d Edward A. Blatt   ph Robert Burks   m Adolph Deutsch

Philip Dorn, Helmut Dantine, Alan Hale, Jean Sullivan, Irene Manning, Samuel S. Hinds

Escape in the Fog

US   1945   65m   bw
Columbia

A nurse sees a man attacked in a dream, and helps to save him when the events recur in real life.

Muddy little spy story with premonition used as a book-end.

w Aubrey Wisberg   d Budd Boetticher

Nina Foch, Otto Kruger, William Wright

Escape Me Never *

GB   1935   95m   bw
B and D (Herbert Wilcox)

The mother of an illegitimate baby marries a composer who loves someone else.

Archetypal romantic weepie which has probably the star's most memorable and likeable performance.

w Carl Zuckerman, Robert Cullen   play Margaret Kennedy   d Paul Czinner   ph Georges Périnal

Elisabeth Bergner, Hugh Sinclair, Griffith Jones, Penelope Dudley Ward, Irene Vanbrugh, Leon Quartermaine, Lyn Harding

'Story stirs audience resentment, yet its able presentation commands attention.' – Variety

'That it is a thoroughly British film is proved by the fact that among the staff one can see names like Andrejiev, Allgeier and Strassner, that the principal actress is German, and the producer is German too.' – James Agate

AAN: Elisabeth Bergner

Escape Me Never

US   1947   104m   bw
Warner (Henry Blanke)
V*

Muddled remake of the above with shifted emphasis.

So ill-conceived it's like watching through frosted glass.

w Thomas Williamson   d Peter Godfrey   ph Sol Polito   m Erich Wolfgang Korngold

Errol Flynn, Ida Lupino, Eleanor Parker, Gig Young, Reginald Denny, Isobel Elsom, Albert Basserman, Ludwig Stossel, Helene Thimig

The Escape of Mechagodzilla: see Monsters from an Unknown Planet

Escape of the Amethyst: see Yangtse Incident

Escape Route

GB   1952   79m   bw
Banner/Eros
US title: I'll Get You

Man on the run turns out to be FBI agent on the spy trail.

A moderate co-feature, as unremarkable as its plot.

w John Baines, Nicholas Phipps   d Seymour Friedman, Peter Graham Scott

George Raft, Sally Gray, Clifford Evans, Reginald Tate

Escape to Athena

GB   1979   117m   Eastmancolor   Panavision
ITC/Pimlico (David Niven Jnr, Jack Wiener)
V*

Prisoners-of-war on a Greek island during World War II recruit the aid of their sympathetic camp commandant in harassing the SS.

Expensive but not very involving thick ear, hampered by tediously typecast actors and an uninventive script.

w Edward Anhalt, Richard S. Lochte   d George Pan Cosmatos   ph Gil Taylor   m Lalo Schifrin

Roger Moore, David Niven, Elliott Gould, Sonny Bono, Telly Savalas, Claudia Cardinale, Stefanie Powers, Richard Roundtree, Anthony Valentine

'Performing as though they had met up by chance on holiday . . . the clutch of box office stars do what they can in a situation where they are the stand-ins and the stuntmen (especially the motorcyclists) dominate the screen.' – Martyn Auty, MFB

Escape to Burma

US   1955   88m   Technicolor   Superscope
Benedict Bogeaus
V*

An adventurer suspected of murder hides out on the tea plantation of an indomitable American woman.

Far Eastern hokum in which the heroine has a way with elephants.

w Talbot Jennings, Herbert Donovan   d Allan Dwan   ph John Alton   m Louis Forbes

Barbara Stanwyck, Robert Ryan, David Farrar, Murvyn Vye, Reginald Denny

Escape to Danger

GB   1943   92m   bw
RKO (William Sistrom)

A British schoolmistress becomes a spy.

Adequate propaganda hokum.

w Wolfgang Wilhelm, Jack Whittingham   d Lance Comfort   ph Max Greene   m William Alwyn

Eric Portman, Ann Dvorak, Karel Stepanek, Ronald Ward, Ronald Adam, Lily Kann, David Peel, Felix Aylmer, A. E. Matthews

Escape to Glory

US   1940   74m   bw
Columbia (Sam Bischoff)
aka: Submarine Zone

A merchant ship with a variety of passengers is stalked by a Nazi submarine.

Minor Grand Hotel afloat: quite brisk and watchable.

w P. J. Wolfson   d John Brahm   ph Franz Planer

Pat O'Brien, Constance Bennett, John Halliday, Alan Baxter, Melville Cooper, Edgar Buchanan, Marjorie Gateson

Escape to Happiness: see Intermezzo

Escape to Victory: see Victory

Escape to Witch Mountain *

US   1974   97m   Technicolor
Walt Disney (Jerome Courtland)
V*, L

Two mysterious orphan children have extraordinary powers, are chased by a scheming millionaire, and prove to come from another planet.

Mildly ingenious story frittered away by poor scripting and special effects. A stimulating change in children's films, however.

w Robert Malcolm Young   novel Alexander Key
d John Hough   ph Frank Phillips   m Johnny Mandel   sp Art Cruickshank, Danny Lee

Ray Milland, Donald Pleasence, Eddie Albert, Kim Richards, Ike Eisenmann, Walter Barnes, Reta Shaw, Denver Pyle

Escapement

GB   1957   72m   bw
Anglo Amalgamated/Merton Park Studios (Alec C. Snowden)

An insurance investigator traces some mysterious deaths in France to a health clinic where doctors are experimenting with mind-altering techniques.

Efficient and slightly unconventional low-budget thriller.

w Charles Eric Maine, J. Maclaren-Ross
d Montgomery Tully   ph Bert Mason, Teddy Catford   md Richard Taylor   m Soundrama   ad Wilfred Arnold   ed Geoffrey Muller

Rod Cameron, Mary Murphy, Meredith Edwards, Peter Illing, Karl Jaffé, Kay Callard, Carl Duering, Roberta Huby

Escort West

US   1958   75m   bw   Cinemascope
Batjac/Romina/UA

An ex-Confederate soldier helps the survivors of a Union wagon train attack.

Watchable lower-berth Western.

w Leo Gordon, Fred Hartsook   d Francis D. Lyon

Victor Mature, Elaine Stewart, Faith Domergue, Noah Beery Jnr, Rex Ingram, John Hubbard

Eskimo *

US   1933   120m   bw
MGM

The life of an Eskimo hunter and his family.

Curious fated attempt by a major studio to do a northern version of the successful White Shadows in the South Seas. Despite a melodramatic plot and gripping documentary sequences, the locale chilled audiences to the marrow.

w John Lee Mahin   Peter Freuchen   d W. S. Van Dyke   ph Conrad Nevig

Mala, Peter Freuchen

'Igloo whoopee variations not sufficiently hotcha to spell b.o.' – Variety

AA: editing

L'Espion: see The Defector

Espionage *

US   1937   67m   bw
MGM (Harry Rapf)

Spies and counter spies mingle on the Orient Express.

Lively second feature on familiar lines.

w Manuel Seff, Leonard Lee, Ainsworth Morgan
play Walter Hackett   d Kurt Neumann   ph Ray June   m William Axt

Edmund Lowe, Madge Evans, Paul Lukas, Ketti Gallian, Skeets Gallagher, Leonid Kinskey, Barnett Parker, Frank Reicher

'Quite some laughs but chiefly for the duals.' – Variety

Espionage Agent

US   1939   83m   bw
Warner (Louis F. Edelmann)

An American diplomat falls in love with a spy.

Anti-isolationist, semi-documentary exposé, a rather sketchy cross between Foreign Correspondent and Confessions of a Nazi Spy.

w Warren Duff, Michael Fessier, Frank Donaghue, Robert Buckner   d Lloyd Bacon   ph Charles Rosher

Joel McCrea, Brenda Marshall, Jeffrey Lynn, George Bancroft, Stanley Ridges, James Stephenson, Nana Bryant

'War headlines dramatized. Lots of openings for exploitation.' – Variety

Les Espions

France   1957   136m   bw
Cinedis (L. de Mazure)
aka: The Spies

Spies from all sides converge on a psychiatric clinic where an atomic scientist is being hidden.

Unsatisfactory thriller with some aims to be both a whimsy and a parable. Not one of its director's successes.

w Henri-Georges Clouzot, Gerome Geronomi
d Henri-Georges Clouzot   ph Christian Matras
m Georges Auric

Martita Hunt, Peter Ustinov, Sam Jaffe, Vera Clouzot, Gabrielle Dorziat, Curt Jurgens, Gerard Sety, O. E. Hasse

El Espiritu de la Colmene: see The Spirit of the Beehive

Espoir *

France/Spain   1938–45   73m   bw
Cornignion/Moligniec
aka: Days of Hope; Man's Hope

Events of the Spanish Civil War, recreated by surviving combatants.

Anti-fascist propaganda which seems a good deal less inspiring than on its first release, but has some vivid cinematic ideas.

wd André Malraux   ph Louis Page   m Darius Milhaud

Mejuto, Nicolas Rodriguez, Jose Lado

'And it was written – gather together all the fair young virgins unto the palace – and let the maiden which pleaseth the king be queen.'

Esther and the King

US   1960   109m   Technicolor   Cinemascope
TCF/Galatea (Raoul Walsh)

A Persian king selects a new bride who helps defend him from his enemies.

Tedious biblical hokum with a muddled script and the usual co-production deficiencies.

w Raoul Walsh, Michael Elkins   d Raoul Walsh
ph Mario Bava   m Francesco Lavagnino, Roberto Nicolosi

Richard Egan, Joan Collins, Dennis O'Dea, Sergio Fantoni, Rik Battaglia

Esther Waters

GB   1947   108m   bw
GFD/Wessex (Ian Dalrymple)

In the 1870s, a maid is seduced by a squire but insists on bringing up her child without help.

Faded costumer with tentative performances and little else to recommend it.

w Michael Gordon, William Rose, Gerard Tyrrell
novel George Moore   d Ian Dalrymple, Peter Proud
ph C. Pennington-Richards, H. E. Fowle   m Gordon Jacob

Kathleen Ryan, Dirk Bogarde, Cyril Cusack, Ivor Barnard, Fay Compton, Mary Clare, Morland Graham

Et Dieu Créa la Femme: see And God Created Woman

Et Mourir de Plaisir: see Blood and Roses

L'Eté Meurtrier: see One Deadly Summer

Eternal Love

US   1929   110m approx   bw   silent
Feature/UA

Swiss lovers find their only option is to commit suicide.

Thin Romeo and Juliet stuff for which the star was too old.

w Hans Kraly   novel Jakob Beer   d Ernst Lubitsch

John Barrymore, Camilla Horn, Victor Varconi, Hobart Bosworth, Bodil Rosing

The Eternal Sea
US   1955   96m   bw
Republic (John H. Auer)

The career of an aircraft carrier captain in World War II and Korea.

Solemn biopic of John Hoskins: competent but quite uninspired.

w Allen Rivkin   d John H. Auer   ph John L. Russell Jnr   m Elmer Bernstein

Sterling Hayden, Alexis Smith, Dean Jagger, Virginia Grey

Eternally Yours *
US   1939   95m   bw
Walter Wanger
V*

A magician's wife thinks he is too interested in his tricks.

Slightly scatty romantic comedy, amiable if not quite good enough to stand the test of time, but with a great cast.

w Gene Towne, Graham Baker   d Tay Garnett
ph Merritt Gerstad   m Werner Janssen

Loretta Young, David Niven, Broderick Crawford, Hugh Herbert, Billie Burke, C. Aubrey Smith, Raymond Walburn, ZaSu Pitts, Virginia Field, Eve Arden, Herman the Rabbit

'Will have to depend on the name power to get it by.' – Variety

'An amusing and irresponsible picture, though on the whole more irresponsible than amusing.' – New York Times

AAN: Werner Janssen

L'Eternel Retour: see Love Eternal

L'Étoile du Nord *
France   1982   124m   Fujicolor
Gala/Sara Films/Antenne 2 (Alain Sarde)

A lodger entrances his landlady with stories of his Egyptian adventures, neglecting to mention his involvement in a murder there.

Two well-dovetailed performances lift this odd little thriller above the ordinary.

w Jean Aurenche, Michel Grisolia, Pierre Granier-Deferre   novel Le Locataire by Georges Simenon
d Pierre Granier-Deferre   ph Pierre-William Glenn
m Philippe Sarde   ad Dominique André   ed Jean Revel

Simone Signoret, Philippe Noiret, Fanny Cottençon, Julie Jezequel, Liliana Gerace, Gamil Ratib

Eureka
GB/USA   1982   129m   Technicolor
MGM/UA/RPC/JF (Jeremy Thomas)
V*

An immensely rich gold striker becomes a recluse and is murdered by Mafia hoods.

Unpleasant in detail and obscure in meaning, this is the sort of film of which the fact that it was financed at all is the most interesting thing about it.

w Paul Mayersberg   book Who Killed Sir Harry Oakes? by Marshall Houts   d Nicolas Roeg   ph Alex Thomson   m Stanley Myers   pd Michael Seymour

Gene Hackman, Theresa Russell, Rutger Hauer, Jane Lapotaire, Mickey Rourke, Ed Lauter

'A Roeg elephant film.' – Variety

'Between them Roeg and Mayersberg have worked an astonishing alchemy through which an abstraction of the basic patterns of human intercourse is rendered wholly concrete. Embodying Vico's cyclical theory of history, it expounds the despair of humanity's vicious circle from ecstasy to agony, as the impulse to love and possession leads inevitably to loss and destruction.' – Tom Milne, Monthly Film Bulletin

'I've a feeling it will become a cult movie, but no one will convince me that it isn't just the poshest kind of tosh.' – Margaret Hinxman, Daily Mail

Eureka Stockade
GB   1948   103m   bw
Ealing (Leslie Norman)
US title: Massacre Hill

In 1854, Australian gold miners revolt against a harsh governor.

Unconvincingly made historical actioner from Ealing's antipodean period.

w Harry Watt, Walter Greenwood, Ralph Smart
d Harry Watt   ph Gerald Heath   m John Greenwood

Chips Rafferty, Jane Barrett, Gordon Jackson, Jack Lambert, Peter Illing, Ralph Truman, Peter Finch

Europa **
Denmark   1991   114m   bw/colour   Scope
Electric/Nordisk/Eurimages (Peter Aalbaek Jensen, Bo Christensen)
V, V*, S
US title: Zentropa

In Germany in 1945, an idealistic young American finds work as a sleeping-car attendant and falls in love with a Nazi sympathizer.

Witty and exuberant tragi-comedy of the clash between New World innocence and European sophistication.

w Lars von Trier, Niels Vørsel, Tomas Gislason
d Lars von Trier   ph Henning Bendtsen, Jean-Paul Meurisse, Edward Klosinsky   m Joakim Holbek
pd Henning Bahs   ed Herve Schneid

Jean-Marc Barr, Barbara Sukowa, Udo Kier, Ernst-Hugo Järgård, Erik Mørk, Jørgen Reenberg, Henning Jensen, Eddie Constantine, Max von Sydow (as narrator)

Europa Europa **
France/Germany   1991   110m   Eastmancolor
Les Films du Losange/CCC Filmkunst/Perspektywa (Margaret Menegoz, Artur Brauner)
V, V*, L, S

A young Polish Jew, captured by the Germans, pretends to be a loyal Nazi in order to stay alive.

A fascinating true story with the qualities of a thriller, filmed with sensitivity.

wd Agnieszka Holland   book Salomon Perel
ph Jacek Petrycki   m Zbigniew Priesner   pd Allan Starski   ed Ewa Smal

Marco Hofschneider, Julie Delpy, André Wilms, Aschley Wanninger, Hanns Zischler, Klaus Kowatsch, Hanna Labornaska

'Filled with suspense and touches of humour, pic brings a fresh approach to familiar themes and should find an appreciative arthouse audience in many parts of the world.' – Variety

† Controversy erupted over the German committee's failure to nominate the film for an Oscar for best foreign film. Most leading German directors signed a letter protesting about its decision.

AAN: Agnieszka Holland (screenplay adaptation)

Europa 51 *
Italy   1952   110m   bw
Ponti/de Laurentiis

An American society woman living in Rome seeks vainly for truth in the chaotic post-war world and is committed to an asylum by her husband.

A despairing, ironic comment on a period which unfortunately does not convince on the personal level.

w Roberto Rossellini and others   d Roberto Rossellini   ph Aldo Tonti   m Renzo Rossellini

Ingrid Bergman, Alexander Knox, Ettore Giannini, Giulietta Masina

The Europeans *
GB   1979   83m   colour
Merchant Ivory (Ismail Merchant)
V*, L

In 1850, a European baroness arrives in Boston in search of a husband.

Charming if rather tentative period mood piece, probably the most professional and judicious of all the overpraised Merchant Ivory offerings.

w Ruth Prawer Jhabvala   novel Henry James
d James Ivory   ph Larry Pizer   m Richard Robbins
ad Jeremiah Rusconi

Lee Remick, Robin Ellis, Tim Woodward, Wesley Addy, Lisa Eichhorn

'A film of astonishing delicacy and richness in which the tiniest gesture or intonation reverberates with a world of meanings.' – Tom Milne, MFB

Eva
France/Italy   1962   135m   bw
Paris/Interopa (Robert and Raymond Hakim)
S

A raw Welsh novelist in Venice is humiliated by a money-loving Frenchwoman who erotically ensnares him.

Foolish story of a femme fatale; elegantly Freudian at moments, it long outstays its welcome.

w Hugo Butler, Evan Jones   novel James Hadley Chase   d Joseph Losey   ph Gianni di Venanzo
m Michel Legrand

Stanley Baker, Jeanne Moreau, Virna Lisi, James Villiers

'They don't hardly make 'em like Joseph Losey's Eva anymore, not even in Hollywood, not since Elinor Glyn passed from the script scene and Theda Bara quit as head vamp.' – Judith Crist

Eve Knew her Apples
US   1945   64m   bw
Wallace McDonald/Columbia

A radio singer sets off incognito for a vacation.

Mild musical support whose plot owes something to It Happened One Night.

w E. Elwin Moran   d Will Jason

Ann Miller, William Wright, Robert Williams, Ray Walker

The Eve of St Mark
US   1944   95m   bw
TCF (William Perlberg)

A small-town boy goes to war and his sweetheart waits for him.

Poetic propaganda based on a sticky play which however had a tragic ending that the film eschews. Smartly made is all one can say.

w George Seaton   play Maxwell Anderson   d John M. Stahl   ph Joseph LaShelle   m Cyril Mockridge

William Eythe, Anne Baxter, Michael O'Shea, Vincent Price, Ruth Nelson, Ray Collins, Stanley Prager, Henry Morgan

Eve Wants to Sleep *
Poland   1957   98m   bw
Film Polski (Wislaw Mincer)

An innocent country girl arrives in a city overrun by subversives.

Curious yet sympathetic black farce, like a cross between *Hellzapoppin* and *M*. One on its own.

wd Tadeusz Chmielewski *ph* Stefan Matyjaskiewicz *m* Henryk Czyz

Barbara Kwiatkowska, Stanislaw Mikulski, Ludwik Benoit

Evel Knievel
US 1971 90m Metrocolor
(MGM) Fanfare (George Hamilton)
V*

Episodes from the life of a motor-cycle stuntman.

Mildly entertaining ragbag of action sequences and fragments of philosophy which might have been more tolerable had EK played himself.

w Alan Caillou, John Milius *d* Marvin Chomsky *ph* David Walsh *m* Pat Williams

George Hamilton, Sue Lyon, Bert Freed, Rod Cameron

Evelyn Prentice
US 1934 80m bw
MGM (John W. Considine Jnr)

The wife of a criminal lawyer has an affair with a man who blackmails her.

Moderate domestic-cum-courtroom melodrama, heavily reliant on its popular stars.

w Lenore Coffee *novel* W. E. Woodward *d* William K. Howard *ph* Charles G. Clarke *md* Oscar Radin

Myrna Loy, William Powell, Una Merkel, Harvey Stephens, Isabel Jewell, Rosalind Russell, Henry Wadsworth, Edward Brophy

'Uneven film but extra heavy cast and strong femme sob yarn will put it in the money class.' – *Variety*

Even Dwarfs Started Small
West Germany 1970 96m bw
Werner Herzog
original title: *Auch Zwerge Haben Klein Angefangen*

Dwarfs in a prison settlement on a volcanic island stage an unsuccessful revolt.

Bizarre and off-putting movie that attempts to say something about the human condition but muddles its message.

wd Werner Herzog *ph* Thomas Mauch *m* Florian Fricke *ed* Beate Mainka-Jellinghaus

Helmut Doring, Paul Glauer, Gisela Hertwig, Hertel Minkner, Gertraud Piccini, Marianne Saar, Brigitte Saar

'There is little arresting in the visual images and the determined obliqueness of treatment is finally unsatisfying.' – *Films and Filming*

Evening Dress: see *Tenue de Soirée*

Evenings
Netherlands 1989 126m colour
Concorde/Praxino (René Solleveld, Peter Weijdeveld)
original title: *De Avonden*

In 1946 in Amsterdam a young man, unhappy at home and work, contemplates his unsatisfactory life before deciding to write about it.

Tiresome account of an obsessive adolescent's refusal to grow up.

w Jean Ummels, Rudolf van den Berg *novel* Gerard Reve *d* Rudolf van den Berg *ph* Willy Stassen *m* Bob Zimmerman *ad* Freek Bissiot *ed* Maria Steenburgen

Thom Hoffman, Rijk de Gooijer, Viviane de Muynck, Sylvia de Leur, Leen Jongewaard, Kees Coolen Pierre Bokma, Eljer Pelgrom, Jobet Schnibbe, Gija Scholten-van Aschat

Evenings for Sale
US 1932 68m bw
Paramount

An impoverished count becomes a dancing master.

Scented Viennese romance intended to extend the star's success in *Trouble in Paradise*.

w S. K. Lauren, Agnes Brand Leahy *novel* I. A. R Wylie *d* Stuart Walker

Herbert Marshall, Sari Maritza, Mary Boland, Charles Ruggles

'Fair entertainment but extremely doubtful on the draw.' – *Variety*

Evensong *
GB 1934 84m bw
Gaumont (Michael Balcon)

At the turn of the century, an Austrian prima donna gives up her career for love.

Well-made romantic drama of its type, notable as the best of its star's few films.

w Edward Knoblock, Dorothy Farnum *play* Beverley Nichols, Edward Knoblock *novel* Beverley Nichols *d* Victor Saville *ph* Max Greene *m/y* Mischa Spoliansky, Edward Knoblock *ad* Alfred Junge *ed* Otto Ludwig

Evelyn Laye, Fritz Kortner, Carl Esmond, Alice Delysia, Emlyn Williams, Muriel Aked

'A highly absorbing and intelligently produced musical . . . looks like money.' – *Variety*

Ever in My Heart
US 1933 70m bw
Warner

A Daughter of the American Revolution finds that her husband is a German spy.

Heavy romantic drama with a tragic finish.

w Bertram Millhauser *story* Beulah Marie Dix *d* Archie Mayo

Barbara Stanwyck, Otto Kruger, Ralph Bellamy, Ruth Donnelly, Frank Albertson

'A clean picture, more for the nabes than the first runs.' – *Variety*

'She'd say yes, but she no's him too well!'
Ever Since Eve
US 1937 80m bw
Warner (Earl Baldwin)

A publisher falls for a pretty girl, not realizing that she is his own plain secretary in disguise.

Silly romantic comedy which sadly lacks wit, style and believability.

w Lawrence Riley, Earl Baldwin, Lillie Hayward *d* Lloyd Bacon *ph* George Barnes *m* Heinz Roemheld

Marion Davies (her last film), Robert Montgomery, Frank McHugh, Patsy Kelly, Louise Fazenda, Barton MacLane, Mary Treen

'A highly incredible script, and badly handled . . . it just doesn't jell.' – *Variety*

Ever Since Venus
US 1944 74m bw
Columbia

The inventors of a new lipstick formula can't get production facilities.

Modestly effective wartime comedy with good talent not ill-used.

w Arthur Dreifuss, McElbert Moore *d* Arthur Dreifuss

Hugh Herbert, Billy Gilbert, Ina Ray Hutton, Glenda Farrell, Ann Savage, Ross Hunter, Alan Mowbray, Fritz Feld, Thurston Hall, Marjorie Gateson

Evergreen **
GB 1934 90m bw
Gaumont (Michael Balcon)
V, V*

A star's daughter takes her mother's place, with romantic complications.

Pleasant musical with more wit and style than might be expected.

w Emlyn Williams, Marjorie Gaffney *play Ever Green* by Benn W. Levy *d* Victor Saville *ph* Glen Mac Williams *md* Louis Levy *m/y* Rodgers and Hart ('Dancing on the Ceiling', 'Dear Dear'); all other songs Harry Woods *ad* Alfred Junge, Peter Proud *ed* Ian Dalrymple

Jessie Matthews, Sonnie Hale, Betty Balfour, Barry Mackay, Ivor McLaren, Hartley Power

Eversmile New Jersey
US/Argentina 1989 103m Technicolor
J&M Entertainment/Los Films del Camino (Oscar Kramer)
V, V*, L

A cavity-obsessed Irish dentist travelling around Patagonia acquires a female assistant en route.

An extraordinarily dreary attempt at a comic road movie, impossible to enjoy without anaesthetic.

w Jorge Goldenberg, Roberto Scheuer, Carlos Sorin *d* Carlos Sorin *ph* Esteban Courtalon *m* Steve Levine *ad* Coca Oderigo, Maria Julia Bertotto *ed* Bryan Oates

Daniel Day-Lewis, Mirjana Jokovic, Gabriela Acher, Julio de Grazia, Ignacio Quiros

Every Day's a Holiday *
US 1937 79m bw
Paramount (Emmanuel Cohen)

A confidence girl in the old Bowery sells Brooklyn Bridge to suckers.

The most satisfactory example of post-Legion of Decency Mae West, the smut being replaced by a lively cast of comedians.

w Mae West *d* A. Edward Sutherland *ph* Karl Struss *m/y* various *ad* Wiard Ihnen

Mae West, Edmund Lowe, Charles Butterworth, Charles Winninger, Walter Catlett, Lloyd Nolan, Herman Bing, Roger Imhof, Chester Conklin

'A lively, innocuously bawdy, and rowdy entertainment.' – *Variety*

AAN: Wiard Ihnen

Every Girl Should Be Married
US 1948 84m bw
RKO (Don Hartman, Dore Schary)
V*, L

A determined girl sets her cap at a bachelor pediatrician.

Woefully thin star comedy with few laughs.

w Stephen Morehouse Avery, Don Hartman *d* Don Hartman *ph* George E. Diskant *m* Leigh Harline

Cary Grant, Betsy Drake, Franchot Tone, Diana Lynn, Alan Mowbray, Elizabeth Risdon, Richard Gaines

'In the past, Cary Grant has shown a talent for quietly underplaying comedy. In this picture, he has trouble finding comedy to play.' – *Time*

Every Home Should Have One
GB 1970 94m Eastmancolor
British Lion/Example (Ned Sherrin)
V, V*

An advertising man goes berserk when he tries to think up an erotic way of selling porridge.

Tiresomely frenetic star comedy with the emphasis on smut.

w Marty Feldman, Barry Took, Denis Norden *d* James Clark *ph* Ken Hodges *m* John Cameron

Marty Feldman, Shelley Berman, Judy Cornwell, Julie Ege, Patrick Cargill, Jack Watson, Patience Collier, Penelope Keith, Dinsdale Landen

Every Little Crook and Nanny

US 1972 92m Metrocolor
MGM (Leonard J. Ackerman)

A Mafia chief finds his child's new nanny has a grudge against him.

Sporadically amusing farce.

w Cy Howard, Jonathan Axelrod, Robert Klane
d Cy Howard ph Philip Lathrop m Fred Karlin

Victor Mature, Lynn Redgrave, Paul Sand, Maggie Blye, Austin Pendleton, John Astin, Dom de Luise

Every Man for Himself: see *Sauve Qui Peut (La Vie)*

Every Man for Himself and God against All: see *The Enigma of Kasper Hauser*

Every Minute Counts: see *Count the Hours*

Every Night at Eight

US 1935 80m bw
Paramount (Walter Wanger)

Three sisters become a successful radio singing team.

Forgettable comedy musical with a mildly interesting cast.

w Gene Towne, Graham Baker d Raoul Walsh
ph James Van Trees m/y Dorothy Fields, Jimmy McHugh

George Raft, Alice Faye, Frances Langford, Patsy Kelly, The Radio Rogues, Walter Catlett, Herman Bing

'Looks like another case of missed opportunity . . . a routine show world romance.' – *Variety*

Every Other Inch a Lady: see *Dancing Co-Ed*

Every Saturday Night: see *The Jones Family*

Every Second Counts: see *Les Assassins du Dimanche*

Every Time We Say Goodbye

US 1986 95m colour
Tri-Star (Jacob Kotzky, Sharon Harel)
V, V*, L

In 1942 Jerusalem, an American pilot falls for a Sephardic Jewish girl.

Patchy and spasmodically developed story of love across the cultures: TV movie stuff.

w Moshe Mizrahi, Rachel Fabien, Leah Appet
d Moshe Mizrahi ph Giuseppe Lanci m Philippe Sarde ad Micky Zahar ed Mark Burns

Tom Hanks, Cristina Marsillach, Benedict Taylor, Anat Atzmon

Every Which Way but Loose

US 1978 114m DeLuxe
Warner/Malpaso
V, V*, L

A Los Angeles trucker wins an orang-utan in a prize fight and becomes involved in sundry brawls and chases.

Easy-going, shambling star vehicle which was liked by nobody but the public.

w Jeremy Joe Kronsberg d James Fargo
ph Rexford Metz md Steve Dorff

Clint Eastwood, Sondra Locke, Ruth Gordon, Geoffrey Lewis, Walter Barnes

† The 1980 sequel, almost indistinguishable, was *Any Which Way You Can*.

Every Woman's Man: see *The Prizefighter and the Lady*

Everybody Dance

GB 1936 74m bw
Gaumont/Gainsborough (Michael Balcon)

A night-club singer is forced to pose as a rural do-gooder.

Thin comedy vehicle.

w Stafford Dickens, Ralph Spence, Leslie Arliss
d Charles Riesner ph J. J. Cox md Louis Levy
m/y Mack Gordon, Harry Revel ad Vetchinsky
ed R. E. Dearing

Cicely Courtneidge, Ernest Truex, Charles Riesner Jnr, Billie de la Volta, Percy Parsons

Everybody Does It

US 1949 98m bw
TCF (Nunnally Johnson)

A stage-struck wife is chagrined to see her dull husband accidentally become an opera singer.

Very mild remake of *Wife, Husband and Friend*; everyone tries to be zany, but the result is often just silly.

w Nunnally Johnson d Edmund Goulding
ph Joseph LaShelle m Alfred Newman

Paul Douglas, Celeste Holm, Linda Darnell, Charles Coburn, Millard Mitchell, Lucile Watson, John Hoyt, George Tobias, Leon Belasco

'For sheer momentary enjoyment it would be hard to beat.' – *Richard Mallett, Punch*

Everybody Sing *

US 1937 80m bw
MGM (Harry Rapf)
V*, L

An eccentric theatrical family is upstaged by its servants, who put on a Broadway show.

Agreeably zany comedy with music.

w Florence Ryerson, Edgar Allan Woolf d Edwin L. Marin ph Joseph L. Ruttenberg m William Axt

Allan Jones, *Fanny Brice, Judy Garland*, Reginald Owen, Billie Burke, Lynne Carver, Monty Woolley, Reginald Gardiner, Henry Armetta

'Excellent film musical with fresh ideas and a corking cast . . . for the top spots.' – *Variety*

Everybody Wins

GB 1990 97m DuArt colour
Virgin/Recorded Picture Company (Jeremy Thomas)
V, V*, L, S

A private eye is seduced by the unstable woman who has hired him to clear a youth of a murder charge.

Old-fashioned, unsubtle and wordy exploration of small-town corruption.

w Arthur Miller d Karel Reisz ph Ian Baker
m Leon Redbone pd Peter Larkin ed John Bloom

Debra Winger, Nick Nolte, Will Patton, Judith Ivey, Jack Warden, Kathleen Wilhoite, Frank Converse

'For a brief period in the late sixties and early seventies, moviegoers seemed willing to be guided through a movie by their intuition and imagination; if this slyly funny movie about the spread of corruption had been released then, it might have been considered a minor classic.' – *Pauline Kael, New Yorker*

Everybody's All-American: see *When I Fall In Love*

Everybody's Cheering: see *Take Me Out to the Ball Game*

Everybody's Fine: see *Stanno Tutti Bene*

Everything But the Truth

US 1956 83m Technicolor
U-I (Howard Christie)

A small boy embarrasses his family by telling the truth at all times.

Dum-dum formula comedy made with jaded professionalism.

w Herb Meadow d Jerry Hopper ph Maury Gertsman m Milton Rosen

Maureen O'Hara, John Forsythe, Tim Hovey, Frank Faylen, Barry Atwater

Everything Happens at Night

US 1939 77m bw
TCF (Harry Joe Brown)

Two reporters fall for the daughter of a Nobel Peace Prize winner on the run from the Gestapo.

The star's sixth American film plays down the music and skating in favour of rather jaded spy comedy. Modest entertainment.

w Art Arthur, Robert Harari d Irving Cummings
ph Edward Cronjager m various

Sonja Henie, Ray Milland, Robert Cummings, Maurice Moscovitch, Leonid Kinskey, Alan Dinehart, Fritz Feld, Victor Varconi

'At no time does very much happen that is of interest.' – *Variety*

Everything Happens to Us: see *Hi Ya Chum*

Everything I Have Is Yours

US 1952 92m Technicolor
MGM (George Wells)

A song and dance team is disrupted when the wife decides to become a mother.

Uninventive but lively musical vehicle for the Champions.

w George Wells d Robert Z. Leonard ph William V. Skall md David Rose ch Nick Castle, Gower Champion

Marge and Gower Champion, Dennis O'Keefe, Eduard Franz

Everything Is Rhythm

GB 1936 73m bw
Joe Rock

A dance band leader wins a European princess.

Modest programme filler remarkable only for its record of a top band of its time.

w Syd Courtenay, Jack Byrd, Stanley Haynes
story Tom Geraghty d Alfred Goulding ph Ernest Palmer ad A. L. Mazzei, George Provis

Harry Roy and his Band, Princess Pearl, Ivor Moreton, Dave Kaye

Everything Is Thunder *

GB 1936 76m bw
Gaumont British (S. C. Balcon)

A German girl helps a British prisoner of war to escape.

Tolerable let's-not-be-beastly melodrama, quite unusual in its time.

w Marion Dix, John Orton novel Jocelyn L. Hardy
d Milton Rosmer ph Gunther Krampf ad Alfred Junge

Constance Bennett, Douglass Montgomery, Oscar Homolka, Roy Emerton, Frederick Lloyd, George Merritt

'Very good entertainment of a kind, the kind that deals with disguises and pursuits and incredible resourcefulness, with policemen on the stairs and hunted men in bathrooms.' – *Graham Greene*

Everything You Always Wanted to Know about Sex *

US 1972 87m DeLuxe
UA (Charles H. Joffe)
V, V*, L

Seven sketches on sexual themes.

Dishevelled revue with a reasonable number of laughs for broadminded audiences.

wd Woody Allen   *book* Dr David Reuben
ph David M. Walsh   *m* Mundell Lowe   *pd* Dale Hennesy

Woody Allen, Lynn Redgrave, Anthony Quayle, John Carradine, Lou Jacobi, Louise Lasser, Tony Randall, Burt Reynolds, Gene Wilder

Everything's Ducky
US   1961   81m   bw
Barboo/Columbia

Two naval ratings adopt a talking duck.

Anything-goes service farce, with material below the standard of the talent available.

w John Fenton Murray, Benedict Freedman   *d* Don Taylor

Mickey Rooney, Buddy Hackett, Jackie Cooper, Joanie Summers, Roland Winters

The Evictors
US   1979   92m   Movielab   Panavision
AIP (Charles B. Pierce)
V*

Axe murders abound when a young couple move into an old house with a history.

Old-hat horror, out of *Psycho* and *The Amityville Horror*: strictly for drive-ins.

w Charles B. Pierce, Gary Rusoff, Paul Fisk
d Charles B. Pierce   *ph* Chuck Bryant   *m* Jaimie Mendoza-Nava   *ed* Shirak Khojayan

Michael Parks, Jessica Harper, Vic Morrow, Sue Anne Langdon

The Evil
US   1978   89m   Movielab
New World/Rangoon (Ed Carlin)
V*

A psychologist takes a team to investigate a haunted house, and is soon sorry he meddled.

Another variation on the theme of *The Haunting* and *The Legend of Hell House*; more this time on the horror comic level, but reasonably effective.

w Donald G. Thompson   *d* Gus Trikonis
ph Mario Di Leo   *m* Johnny Harris

Richard Crenna, Joanna Pettet, Andrew Prine, Cassie Yates, Victor Buono, Lynne Moody

The Evil Dead
US   1980 (released 1983)   85m   DuArt
Palace/Renaissance (Robert G. Tapert)
V, V*, L, S

Five youngsters in a remote cabin find an old book which helps them summon up dormant demons from a nearby forest.

Semi-professional horror rubbish, blown up from 16mm and looking it. When released in England, it was prosecuted as unsuitable for public showing and gained a cult following. It was released on video in a cut version.

wd Sam M. Raimi   *ph* Tim Philo   *m* Joe LoDuca
ed Edna Ruth Paul

Bruce Campbell, Ellen Sandweiss, Betsy Baker, Hal Delrich

'The *ne plus ultra* of low-budget gore and shock effects.' – *Variety*

Evil Dead 2: Dead by Dawn
US   1987   85m   Technicolor
Renaissance/De Laurentiis (Robert G. Tapert)
V, V*, S

Trapped in a lonely cabin, a couple fight off ferocious hordes of the spirits of the dead.

Fast-moving horror movie with flashy camerawork and an exuberant taste in sick jokes.

w Sam Raimi, Scott Spiegel   *d* Sam Raimi
ph Peter Deming   *m* Joseph LoDuca   *ad* Philip Duffin, Randy Bennett   *sp* make-up: Mark Shostrom
ed Kaye Davis

Bruce Campbell, Sarah Berry, Dan Hicks, Kassie Wesley, Theodore Raimi, Denise Bixler

'More an absurdist comedy than a horror film.' – *Variety*

† It was followed by a sequel, *Army of Darkness* (qv).

'The monster's back and no one can stop him!'
The Evil of Frankenstein
GB   1964   94m   Eastmancolor
Rank/Hammer (Anthony Hinds)
V*, L

Frankenstein returns to his derelict castle and finds the Monster preserved in a glacier.

For their third Frankenstein film Hammer made a distribution deal with Universal and thus for the first time were able to use fragments of the old plots as well as something approximating to the Karloff make-up. Production and writing, however, are sadly dispirited except when relying on sadism.

w John Elder (Anthony Hinds)   *d* Freddie Francis
ph John Wilcox   *m* Don Banks   *ad* Don Mongaye
ed James Needs

Peter Cushing, Peter Woodthorpe, Sandor Eles, Kiwi Kingston (as the monster), Duncan Lamont, Katy Wild, David Hutcheson

The Evil that Men Do
US   1984   90m   CFI color
ITC/Capricorn/Zuleika Farms (Pancho Kohner)
V*, L

A professional killer is asked to eliminate a sadistic political torturer in Guatemala.

More than usually turgid and unpleasant vehicle for a star who is now too old for this kind of thing.

w David Lee Henry, John Crowther   *novel* R. Lance Hill   *d* J. Lee-Thompson   *ph* Javier Ruvalcaba Cruz   *m* Ken Thorne

Charles Bronson, Theresa Saldana, Joseph Maher, José Ferrer, René Enriquez, John Glover, Raymond St Jacques

Evil under the Sun
GB   1982   117m   Technicolor   Panavision
EMI/Mersham/Titan (John Brabourne, Richard Goodwin)
V*

Hercule Poirot solves the murder of a film star on an Adriatic holiday island.

Very competent but somehow too bland package in the Agatha Christie series, not quite so lively as *Death on the Nile*.

w Anthony Shaffer   *novel* Agatha Christie   *d* Guy Hamilton   *ph* Christopher Challis   *m* Cole Porter
pd Elliot Scott

Peter Ustinov, James Mason, Diana Rigg, Maggie Smith, Colin Blakely, Jane Birkin, Nicholas Clay, Roddy McDowall, Sylvia Miles, Dennis Quilley

'They have swapped elegant English menace for a splurge of theatrical camp.' – *Time Out*

'Temperance beverage Noël Coward.' – *Sunday Times*

Evils of Chinatown: see *Confessions of an Opium Eater*

'Forged by a god! Foretold by a wizard! Found by a king!'
'No mortal could possess it! No kingdom could command it!'
Excalibur *
US   1981   140m   Technicolor
Warner/Orion (John Boorman)
V, V*, L

The story of King Arthur, Merlin, Uther Pendragon, the Holy Grail and the Lady of the Lake.

Curiously pointless retelling of a legend with unexplained flashes of realism and bouts of gore alternating with romance and modern wisecracks. Of mainly visual interest.

w Rospo Pallenberg, John Boorman   *d* John Boorman   *ph* Alex Thomson   *m* Trevor Jones
pd Anthony Pratt

Nigel Terry, Helen Mirren, Nicol Williamson, Nicholas Clay, Cherie Lunghi, Paul Geoffrey

'Left entirely to his own devices, Boorman seems to run in self-defeating circles.' – *Richard Combs, MFB*

'It tries overhard to be simultaneously critical and credulous, magical and earthy, inspiring and entertaining.' – *Sunday Times*

'A record of the comings and goings of arbitrary, inconsistent, shadowy figures who are not heroes but simply giants run amok.' – *Roger Ebert*

AAN: Alex Thomson

Ex-Champ
US   1939   72m   bw
Universal

A retired boxer works as a doorman and has trouble with his ungrateful and semi-criminal son.

Father-love weepie, rather hard to take.

w Alex Gottleib, Edmund L. Hartmann, Gordon Kahn
d Phil Rosen

Victor McLaglen, Tom Brown, Nan Grey, William Frawley, Constance Moore

'Pathos and sentiment expertly mixed for satisfactory dualler.' – *Variety*

'Racket rule sweeps midwest city!'
Exclusive
US   1937   76m   bw
Paramount

Journalist sacrifices himself for daughter whose views he despises.

Solid newspaper drama jinxed by the excellent tragic performance of a star too long regarded as a comedian.

w John C. Moffitt, Sidney Salkow, Rian James
d Alexander Hall

Charles Ruggles, Fred MacMurray, Frances Farmer, Lloyd Nolan

'Hokey newspaper-gangster yarn of old-fashioned meller calibre.' – *Variety*

'In the tough race it falls behind – it can't make the 1937 speed in murder, and the result, like lavender, is not unagreeable.' – *Graham Greene*

Exclusive Story
US   1934   75m   bw
MGM

A newspaperman has a go at the numbers racket.

Tolerable anti-gangster crusade.

w Michael Fessier, Martin Mooney   *d* George B. Seitz

Franchot Tone, Madge Evans, *Joseph Calleia*, Stuart Erwin, J. Carrol Naish

'Publicity possibilities should put this one over, but it also has plenty of excitement to sell.' – *Variety*

Excuse My Dust *
US   1951   82m   Technicolor
MGM (Jack Cummings)

The inventor of a horseless carriage loves the daughter of a livery stable owner.

Innocuous small-town 1890s comedy with a race climax. Quite pleasant.

w George Wells   *d* Roy Rowland   *ph* Alfred Gilks
m Arthur Schwartz

Red Skelton, Sally Forrest, Macdonald Carey, William Demarest

'Every day he loves, somebody else dies!'

The Executioner *

GB 1970 107m Technicolor Panavision
Columbia/Ameran (Charles H. Schneer)
V*

A British spy suspects a colleague of being a double agent.

Dour espionage thriller with a reasonably holding narrative and predictable performances.

w Jack Pulman *d* Sam Wanamaker *ph* Denys Coop *m* Ron Goodwin

George Peppard, Nigel Patrick, Joan Collins, Judy Geeson, Oscar Homolka, Charles Gray, Keith Michell, George Baker, Alexander Scourby, Peter Bull, Ernest Clark, Peter Dyneley

'Does not escape from the well-worn shallow groove in which the contemporary spy film is in danger of becoming stuck.' – *Russell Campbell*

Executioner of Venice

Italy 1963 90m colour
Liber (Ottavio Poggi)
original title: *Il Boia di Venezia*

On the day of his marriage the son of the Doge of Venice discovers that his true father was a pirate and is arrested for treason on the orders of the power-hungry Grand Inquisitor.

Standard swashbuckler with glossy production values. *d* Luigi Capuano *ph* Alvardo Mancori *ed* Antonietta Zita

Lex Barker, Guy Madison, Alessandro Panaro, Alberto Farnese, Mario Petri, Guilo Marchetti

Executive Action *

US 1973 91m colour
EA Enterprises/Wakefield Orloff (Edward Lewis)
V*, L

An imaginative version of the facts behind the 1963 assassination of President Kennedy.

Interesting but rather messy mixture of fact and fiction; makes one sit up while it's unreeling.

w Dalton Trumbo *story* Mark Lane, Donald Freed *d* David Miller *ph* Robert Steadman *m* Randy Edelman

Burt Lancaster, Robert Ryan, Will Geer, Gilbert Green, John Anderson

'A dodo bird of a movie, the winner of the *Tora Tora Tora* prize.' – *Variety*

'High up in the skyscraper beauty and power clash in conflict!'

Executive Suite **

US 1954 104m bw
MGM (John Houseman)
V*

When the president of a big company dies, the boardroom sees a battle for control.

First of the boardroom films of the fifties, a calculatedly commercial mixture of business ethics and domestic asides, with an all-star cast working up effective tensions.

w Ernest Lehman, *novel* Cameron Hawley *d* Robert Wise *ph* George Folsey *m* none *ad* Cedric Gibbons, Edward Carfagno

Fredric March, William Holden, June Allyson, *Barbara Stanwyck*, Walter Pidgeon, Shelley Winters, Paul Douglas, *Louis Calhern*, Dean Jagger, *Nina Foch*, Tim Considine

'Not a classic, not a milestone in movie making, but it does suggest a standard of product that could bring back to the box office those vast audiences long alienated by trivia.' – *Arthur Knight*

'The only trouble with all these people is that they are strictly two-dimensional. They give no substantial illusion of significance, emotion or warmth.' – *Bosley Crowther, New York Times*

† A TV series followed in 1976.

AAN: George Folsey; Nina Foch; art direction

Ex-Flame

US 1930 68m bw
Liberty

A modernized version of *East Lynne*.

With so many American accents attached to the British peerage, this is mainly for laughs – unintentional ones.

wd Victor Halperin

Neil Hamilton, Marian Nixon, Norman Kerry, Roland Drew, Snub Pollard

'Old-fashioned mush stuff for the woman.' – *Variety*

The Exile *

US 1948 90m bw
U-I (Douglas Fairbanks Jnr)

The man who is to return to the English throne as Charles II hides in Holland, receives his friends and despatches his enemies.

Curious, talkative swashbuckler with only a few moments of action; the available talents are simply not used, though the director imposes a nice pictorial style.

w Douglas Fairbanks Jnr *novel His Majesty the King* by Cosmo Hamilton *d* Max Ophüls *ph* Franz Planer *m* Frank Skinner

Douglas Fairbanks Jnr, Maria Montez, Paula Corday, Henry Daniell, Nigel Bruce, Robert Coote

† Originally released in sepia.

Exile Express

US 1939 70m bw
Grand National

A lab assistant is innocently involved in the murder of her boss by a spy gang.

Lumpy comedy thriller taking place mainly on a train; very forgettable.

w Edwin Justus Mayer, Ethel La Blanche *d* Otis Garrett

Anna Sten, Alan Marshal, Jerome Cowan, Jed Prouty, Stanley Fields, Walter Catlett, Leonid Kinskey, Harry Davenport, Irving Pichel

'Both story and direction take it up all sorts of dull and impossible alleys.' – *Variety*

Exit Smiling **

US 1926 71m (24 fps) bw silent
MGM (Sam Taylor)

The worst actress in a stock company saves the show.

Amusing comedy for a star who never quite made it in films: this is the best of her vehicles.

w Sam Taylor, Tim Whelan *play* Marc Connelly *d* Sam Taylor *ph* André Barlatier

Beatrice Lillie, Jack Pickford, Harry Myers, Doris Lloyd, DeWitt Jennings, Louise Lorraine, Franklin Pangborn

'We don't dare tell you how daring it is!'

Ex-Lady *

US 1933 70m bw
Warner
V*

A lady artist has ultra-modern views on sex and marriage, but turns conventional when she falls in love.

Mildly shocking in its day, this romantic drama was one of the contributing factors to the onslaught of the Legion of Decency which transformed Hollywood output in the following year.

w David Boehm *story* Edith Fitzgerald, Robert Riskin *d* Robert Florey

Bette Davis (her first starring role), Gene Raymond, Frank McHugh, Monroe Owsley, Clare Dodd

† Previously filmed in 1931 as *Illicit*.

The Ex-Mrs Bradford *

US 1936 87m bw
RKO (Edward Kaufman)

A doctor's scatty ex-wife involves him in solving a murder plot.

Amusing crime comedy, just a little way behind *The Thin Man*.

w Anthony Veiller, James Edward Grant *d* Stephen Roberts *ph* J. Roy Hunt *m* Roy Webb

William Powell, Jean Arthur, James Gleason, Eric Blore, Robert Armstrong, Lila Lee, Grant Mitchell, Ralph Morgan

Exodus *

US 1960 220m Technicolor Super Panavision 70
UA/Carlyle/Alpha (Otto Preminger)
V*, L, S

The early years of the state of Israel, seen through various eyes.

Heavy-going modern epic, toned down from a passionate novel.

w Dalton Trumbo *novel* Leon Uris *d* Otto Preminger *ph* Sam Leavitt *m* Ernest Gold

Paul Newman, Eva Marie Saint, Ralph Richardson, Peter Lawford, Lee J. Cobb, Sal Mineo, John Derek, Hugh Griffith, Gregory Ratoff, Felix Aylmer, David Opatoshu, Jill Haworth, Alexandra Stewart, Martin Benson, Martin Miller

'Professionalism is not enough – after three and a half hours the approach seems more exhausting than exhaustive.' – *Penelope Houston*

† Jewish comedian Mort Sahl, invited by the director to a preview, is said to have stood up after three hours and said: 'Otto – let my people go!'

AA: Ernest Gold

AAN: Sam Leavitt; Sal Mineo

The Exorcist *

US 1973 122m Metrocolor
Warner/Hoya (William Peter Blatty)
V*, L

A small girl is unaccountably possessed by the devil and turned into a repellent monster who causes several violent deaths before she is cured.

Spectacularly ludicrous mishmash with uncomfortable attention to physical detail and no talent for narrative or verisimilitude. Its sensational aspects, together with a sudden worldwide need for the supernatural, assured its enormous commercial success.

w William Peter Blatty *novel* William Peter Blatty *d* William Friedkin *ph* Owen Roizman *m* Jack Nitzsche *pd* Bill Malley *ed* Jordan Leandopoulos, Evan Lottman, Norman Gay, Bud Smith

Ellen Burstyn, Max von Sydow, Jason Miller, Linda Blair, Lee J. Cobb, Kitty Winn, Jack McGowran

'No more nor less than a blood and thunder horror movie, foundering heavily on the rocks of pretension.' – *Tom Milne*

'*The Exorcist* makes no sense, [but] if you want to be shaken, it will scare the hell out of you.' – *Stanley Kauffmann*

'It exploits the subject of diabolic possession without telling you anything about it . . . just a stylistic exercise.' – *Michael Billington, Illustrated London News*

'There is a little exposition, some philosophy and theology, a quiet interlude, and then pandemonium reigns: rooms shake, heads turn full circle on bodies, wounds fester, vomit spews forth in bilious clouds besmirching a saintly priest, a possessed adolescent girl masturbates bloodily on a crucifix as she barks blasphemies and obscenities, and hoary demons freeze the soul.' – *Les Keyser, Hollywood in the Seventies*

'I know how to do it. I just throw everything at the audience and give them a real thrill. That's what they want. They don't want to go into a theater and treat it like a book. They don't even read books!' – *William Peter Blatty*

'This one was scheduled for 105 days. It wound up 200 days. We were plagued by strange and sinister things from the beginning.' – *William Peter Blatty*

'. . . raw and painful experience. Are people so numb that they need movies of this intensity in order to feel anything at all?' – *Roger Ebert*

† Published 1974: *The Story Behind the Exorcist* by Peter Travers and Stephanie Reiff.

AA: William Peter Blatty; sound (Robert Knudson, Chris Newman)

AAN: best picture; William Friedkin; Owen Roizman; Ellen Burstyn; Jason Miller; Linda Blair; Bill Malley; editing

'It's four years later. What does she remember?'
Exorcist II: The Heretic
US   1977   117m   Technicolor
Warner (Richard Lederer, John Boorman)
V, V*

Father Lamont, investigating the case related in *The Exorcist*, finds that the evil in Regan, apparently exorcized, is only dormant.

Highly unsatisfactory psychic melodrama which, far from the commercial route of the shocker followed by its predecessor, falls flat on its face along some wayward path of metaphysical and religious fancy. A commercial disaster, it was released in two versions and is unintelligible in either.

w William Goodhart *d* John Boorman
ph William A. Fraker *m* Ennio Morricone
pd Richard MacDonald

Richard Burton, Linda Blair, Louise Fletcher, Kitty Winn, Max von Sydow, Paul Henreid, James Earl Jones, Ned Beatty

'Do You Dare Walk These Steps Again?'
The Exorcist III
US   1990   110m   DeLuxe
Fox/Morgan Creek/Carter DeHaven (James G. Robinson, Joe Roth)
V, V*, L

A cop investigates a series of strange killings with the aid of an exorcist.

Unexciting and confused sequel that follows on from the first film in the series.

wd William Peter Blatty *novel Legion* by William Peter Blatty *ph* Gerry Fisher *m* Barry Deorzon
pd Leslie Dilley *ed* Tom Ramsay, Peter-Lee Thompson

George C. Scott, Ed Flanders, Brad Dourif, Jason Miller, Nicol Williamson, Scott Wilson, Nancy Fish, George Dienzo, Don Gordon

Experiment in Terror **
US   1962   123m   bw
Columbia/Geoffrey-Kate Productions (Blake Edwards)
V*, L
GB title: *The Grip of Fear*

An asthmatic stranger threatens the life of a bank teller and her sister if she does not help him commit a robbery.

Detailed, meticulous police thriller with San Francisco locations. Good stuff, a bit long.

w The Gordons *novel Operation Terror* by The Gordons *d* Blake Edwards *ph* Philip Lathrop
m Henry Mancini

Glenn Ford, Lee Remick, Ross Martin

Experiment Perilous *
US   1944   91m   bw
RKO (Warren Duff)
V*

A wealthy husband becomes insanely jealous of his wife.

Enjoyable mystery melodrama which takes itself with a pinch of salt.

w Warren Duff *novel* Margaret Carpenter
d Jacques Tourneur *ph* Tony Gaudio *m* Roy Webb
ad Albert S. D'Agostino, Jack Okey

Hedy Lamarr, Paul Lukas, George Brent, Albert Dekker, Margaret Wycherly

AAN: art direction

The Experts
US   1989   83m   Alpha Cine colour
Paramount (James Keach)
V*, L

Two trendy New Yorkers think they have been hired to open a night-club in Nebraska; in reality, they are transported to the USSR to teach American manners to Russian spies living in a replica of a US town.

Feeble and simple-minded comedy that is almost enough to restart the Cold War.

w Nick Thiel, Stephen Greene, Eric Alter *d* Dave Thomas *ph* Ronnie Taylor *m* Marvin Hamlisch
pd David Fischer *ed* Bud Molin

John Travolta, Arye Gross, Kelly Preston, Deborah Foreman, James Keach, Jan Rubes, Brian Doyle Murray, Mimi Maynard, Eve Brent, Charles Martin Smith

The Exploits of Elaine *
US   1914   14 episodes, each 20m approx   bw
      silent
Pathé/Wharton

Detective Craig Kennedy helps his girlfriend avenge her father's murder.

Archetypal cliffhanger serial following on the success of *The Perils of Pauline*. It was itself followed within a year by *The New Exploits of Elaine* and *The Romance of Elaine*. Chapter headings included such now familiar clichés as 'The Clutching Hand', 'The Vanishing Jewels', 'The Poisoned Room', 'The Death Ray' and 'The Devil Worshippers'. The films were much praised by critics for their pace and inventiveness.

w Charles W. Goddard, George B. Seitz
stories Arthur B. Reeve *d* Louis Gasnier, George B. Seitz

Pearl White, Creighton Hale, Sheldon Lewis, Arnold Daly

Explorers
US   1985   109m   Technicolor
Paramount/Edward S. Feldman/Industrial Light and Magic
V*, L, S

Two boys make off in a space craft and encounter an alien race whose culture consists of intercepted American television programmes.

Slightly interesting but overlong fantasy spoof, probably not for popular consumption.

w Eric Luke *d* Joe Dante *ph* John Hora
m Jerry Goldsmith *pd* Robert F. Boyle

Ethan Hawke, River Phoenix, Jason Presson, Amanda Peterson

'One of the weirdest and most endearingly offbeat alien pix to have surfaced in recent years.' – *Variety*

Exposed
US   1983   99m   Metrocolor
MGM-UA (James Toback)
V*

A fashion model falls for a concert violinist who turns out to be a notorious terrorist.

A glossy absurdity confected from reading too many indigestible headlines.

wd James Toback *ph* Henri Decae *m* Georges Delerue *pd* Brian Eatwell *ed* Robert Lawrence, Annie Charvein

Nastassja Kinski, Rudolf Nureyev, Harvey Keitel, Ian McShane, Bibi Andersson, Ron Randell, Pierre Clementi

'It often seems to be working out of a tension between sophisticated ambition and the capabilities of a tyro director, a kind of neo-primitivism (with a hint, perhaps, of Fuller, especially in its cultural name-dropping – Bach, Bosch, Dostoievsky, Heifetz, Perlman, Stern, to name a few).' – *Richard Combs, MFB*

'Johnny never had it so good – or lost it so fast!'
Expresso Bongo *
GB   1959   111m   bw   Dyaliscope
BL/Britannia/Conquest (Val Guest)
V, V*

A Soho agent turns a nondescript teenage singer into an international star.

Heavily vulgarized version of a stage skit on the Tommy Steele rock phenomenon, divested of most of its satirical barbs and only intermittently amusing.

w Wolf Mankowitz *play* Wolf Mankowitz *d* Val Guest *ph* John Wilcox *md* Robert Farnon
m/ly David Heneker, Monty Norman

Laurence Harvey, Sylvia Syms, Yolande Donlan, Cliff Richard, *Meier Tzelniker*, Gilbert Harding, Ambrosine Philpotts, Eric Pohlmann, Wilfrid Lawson, Hermione Baddeley, Reginald Beckwith, Martin Miller

'What the cinema offers is a sardonic rattle with music . . . The approach may be satirical or flippant; and yet one finds oneself half-beginning to believe in the subject; even minding about it.' – *Dilys Powell*

The Exquisite Sinner
US   1926   80m approx at 24 fps   bw   silent
MGM

A young French industrialist becomes bored with his society and takes off with a band of gypsies.

Curious and unsatisfactory farrago with extensive retakes by Phil Rosen (who also took credit the following year for an almost exactly similar film with a different title, *Heaven on Earth*, but featuring the same stars).

w Josef von Sternberg, Alice Duer Miller *d* Josef von Sternberg, Phil Rosen

Conrad Nagel, Renee Adoree

Extase *
Czechoslovakia   1932   90m   bw
Universal Elektra Film
V, V*
aka: *Ecstasy*

A country girl takes a lover.

Simple love story with Freudian sequences, quite successfully and cinematically done. It caused a sensation at the time and was issued in various censored versions; the star's husband later tried to destroy all the copies.

wd Gustav Machaty *story* Viteslav Nezval *ph* Jan Stallich *m* Giuseppe Becce

Hedy Kiesler (later Hedy Lamarr), Aribert Mog

'The first important film to come out of Czechoslovakia since *Erotikon*, and what a hornet's nest it has stirred up! Critics and public are divided into two camps. Some proclaim it the world's worst, others rank it among the best productions of the year. It would never get by the censor in America.' – *Variety*

The Exterminating Angel ***

Mexico 1962 95m bw
Uninci Films 59 (Gustavo Alatriste)
V*
original title: *El Angel Exterminador*

High society dinner guests find themselves unable to leave the room, stay there for days, and go totally to the bad before the strange spell is broken; when they go to church to give thanks, they find themselves unable to leave.

Fascinating surrealist fantasia on themes elaborated with even more panache in *The Discreet Charm of the Bourgeoisie*. Nevertheless, one of its director's key films.

wd Luis Buñuel (story assistance from Luis Alcoriza)
ph Gabriel Figueroa *ad* Jesus Bracho

Silvia Pinal, Enrique Rambal, Jacqueline Andere, Jose Baviera

'An unsound and unsightly mixture of spurious allegory and genuine craziness.' – *John Simon*

The Exterminator

US 1980 102m Movielab
Interstar (Mark Buntzman)
V, V*, L

An ex-Vietnam vet goes berserk when his friend is killed by a street gang, and vows revenge.

Vigilante movie with aspects of the modern horror-comic tradition; not much doubt that its real purpose is exploitation. It aroused some anger in America when a murder seemed to be based on its methods, but it was quickly succeeded by even more violent films.

wd James Glickenhaus *ph* Robert M. Baldwin
m Joe Renzetti

Robert Ginty, Christopher George, Samantha Eggar, Steve James

'Glickenhaus has plundered the iconographic treasury of recent American cinema, wrenching the images of war, sexuality and street crime out of their contexts and deploying them portentously so as to lend spurious significance to his film.' – *Martyn Auty, MFB*

Exterminator 2

US 1984 90m TVC colour
Cannon
V, V*

An unemployed Vietnam veteran in New York eliminates punks with a flame thrower.

Violence fantasy, an extreme form of *Death Wish*; quite reprehensible, and not for the squeamish.

w Mark Buntzman, William Sachs *d* Mark Buntzman

Robert Ginty, Deborah Geffner, Mario Van Peebles, Frankie Faison

The Extra Day

GB 1956 83m Eastmancolor
British Lion/William Fairchild (E. M. Smedley Aston)

The personal problems of five film extras who are recalled when a scene has to be reshot.

Thin excuse for portmanteau drama, only amusing in its depiction of a British movie being made with mostly foreign talent.

wd William Fairchild *ph* Arthur Grant *m* Philip Green

Richard Basehart, Simone Simon, Sid James, Josephine Griffin, George Baker, Colin Gordon, Laurence Naismith, Charles Victor, Olga Lindo, Beryl Reid, Dennis Lotis

The Extra Girl *

US 1923 69m bw silent
Mack Sennett
V*, L

A small town girl wins a beauty contest and goes to Hollywood.

A comparatively restrained comedy with slapstick interludes, this charming film shows its star at her best and admirably illustrates Hollywood in the early twenties.

d Mack Sennett *m* Jack Ward

Mabel Normand, Max Davidson, Ralph Graves, George Nicholls

The Extraordinary Seaman

US 1968 80m Metrocolor Panavision
MGM/John Frankenheimer/Edward Lewis (John H. Cushingham, Hal Dresner)

Four stranded sailors come upon the ghostly Royal Navy captain of a ghostly World War II ship.

Curious sixties attempt at forties fantasy; obviously, from its short running time and fragmented style, something went sadly adrift during its making, and the wide screen does not help, but there are scattered funny moments.

w Philip Rock, Hal Dresner *d* John Frankenheimer
ph Lionel Lindon *m* Maurice Jarre

David Niven, Faye Dunaway, Alan Alda, Mickey Rooney, Jack Carter, Juano Hernandez, Barry Kelley

'A cleverly made curiosity, not so much produced as manufactured.' – *Marjorie Bilbow*

Extreme Prejudice

US 1987 104m Technicolor
Carolco/Tri-Star (Buzz Feitshans)
V, V*, L, S

A Texas Ranger pins down a drug trafficker.

Ordinary urban thriller with overplayed violence.

w Deric Washburn, Harry Kleiner *story* John Milius, Fred Rexer *d* Walter Hill *ph* Matthew F. Leonetti *m* Jerry Goldsmith *pd* Albert Heschong *ed* Freeman Davies

Nick Nolte, Powers Boothe, Michael Ironside, Rip Torn, Clancy Brown, Maria Conchita Alonso

Extremities

US 1986 90m colour
Atlantic Releasing (Burt Sugarman)
V, V*, L

A girl takes revenge on the man who raped her.

Unpleasant when it's not verbose; anything but entertaining.

w William Mastrosimone *play* William Mastrosimone *d* Robert M. Young *ph* Curtis Clark *m* J. A. C. Redford *pd* Chester Kaczenski *ed* Arthur Coburn

Farrah Fawcett, James Russo, Diana Scarwid, Alfre Woodard

An Eye for an Eye

France/Italy 1956 93m Technicolor VistaVision
UGC/Jolly (André Cayatte)

A doctor finds himself trekking across the desert with a demented man whose wife has died in his care.

Initially striking melodrama which becomes increasingly unconvincing and has a tendency to harp on unpleasant detail.

wd André Cayatte *novel* Vahe Katcha
ph Christian Matras *m* Louiguy

Curt Jurgens, Folco Lulli, Lea Padovani

An Eye for an Eye

US 1981 104m CFI Color
Barber/Adams Apple/Avco Embassy (Frank Capra Jnr)
V*

An undercover cop resigns from the force but uncovers a drug ring.

Tedious and violent actioner with a martial arts champion for hero.

w William Gray, James Bruner *d* Steve Carver
ph Roger Shearman *m* William Goldstein
ad Vance Lorenzini *ed* Anthony Redman

Chuck Norris, Christopher Lee, Richard Roundtree, Matt Clark, Mako

'Terror that tears the scream right out of your throat!'

Eye of the Cat *

US 1969 102m Technicolor
Universal/Joseph M. Schenck (Bernard Schwarz, Philip Hazelton)

A young man who hates cats goes to stay with his crippled aunt who keeps a house full of them.

Odd, *Psycho*-like thriller (from the same screen writer) with plenty of scary sequences but an inadequate resolution.

w Joseph Stefano *d* David Lowell Rich *ph* Russell Metty, Ellsworth Fredericks *m* Lalo Schifrin *cat trainer* Ray Berwick

Eleanor Parker, Michael Sarrazin, Gayle Hunnicutt, Tim Henry, Laurence Naismith

'Not so much a good film as an extravagantly enjoyable one.' – *MFB*

Eye of the Devil *

GB 1967 92m bw
MGM/Filmways (John Calley, Ben Kadish)

A French nobleman is obsessed by a family tradition of pagan self-sacrifice.

Diabolical goings-on in a spooky castle, not really helped by a glittering supporting cast any more than by miscast stars, sluggish direction or a general atmosphere of gloom rather than suspense.

w Robin Estridge, Dennis Murphy *novel Day of the Arrow* by Philip Loraine *d* J. Lee-Thompson *ph* Erwin Hillier *m* Gary McFarland

David Niven, Deborah Kerr, Emlyn Williams, Flora Robson, Donald Pleasence, Edward Mulhare, David Hemmings, Sharon Tate, John Le Mesurier, Donald Bisset

'It is hard to say why the total effect is so constantly hilarious.' – *MFB*

† The film had a chequered career. The first attempt to make it was abandoned because of Kim Novak's inadequacy; it then went through three titles and a lot of trouble with the censor.

'To love a stranger is easy ... to kill a lover is not!'

Eye of the Needle

GB 1981 113m Technicolor
UA/Kings Road (Stephen Friedman)
V*

In London in 1940 a German agent murders his landlady but is eventually cornered by a girl on a Scottish island.

Listless espionage narrative with very little drive or interest: the shape of the story defies suspense.

w Stanley Mann *novel* Ken Follett *d* Richard Marquand *ph* Alan Hume *m* Miklos Rozsa

Donald Sutherland, Kate Nelligan, Christopher Cazenove, Ian Bannen, Alex McCrindle

Eye of the Tiger

US 1986 90m United color
Scotti Brothers (Tony Scotti)
V*

A vigilante avenges his wife's murder.

Predictable thriller with video in mind.

w Michael Montgomery *d* Richard Sarafian
ph Peter Collister *ad* Wayne Springfield *ed* Greg Prange

Gary Busey, Yaphet Kotto, Seymour Cassel, Bert Remsen, William Smith

Eye Witness (1950): see *Your Witness*

Eye Witness
GB   1956   82m   bw
Rank/Sydney Box

A maniacal burglar pursues a witness of his crime into the emergency ward of a local hospital.

Naïve but adequate suspenser with too many character cameos getting in the way of the plot.

w Janet Green   *d* Muriel Box   *ph* Reg Wyer   *m* Bruce Montgomery

Donald Sinden, Muriel Pavlow, Belinda Lee, Michael Craig, Nigel Stock, Susan Beaumont, David Knight, Ada Reeve

Eyes in the Night *
US   1942   80m   bw
MGM (Jack Chertok)

A blind detective sets out to discover whether a mysterious man engaged to an heiress is really a Nazi spy.

Tolerable wartime puzzler.

w Guy Trosper, Howard Emmett Rogers   *novel Odor of Violets* by Baynard Kendrick   *d* Fred Zinnemann   *ph* Robert Planck, Charles Lawton   *m* Lennie Hayton

Edward Arnold, Ann Harding, Donna Reed, Allen Jenkins, John Emery, Stephen McNally, Reginald Denny, Rosemary de Camp, Stanley Ridges

'They have converted a basically humdrum yarn into a tense and tingling little thriller.' – *New York Times*

† Edward Arnold appeared once more as Duncan Maclain, in *The Hidden Eye* (1944).

Eyes of Laura Mars
US   1978   104m   Metrocolor
Columbia/Jon Peters (Jack H. Harris)
V, V*, L

A fashion photographer has violent premonitions about a series of murders.

Silly and often unpleasant suspenser which despite its chic appearance never bothers to explain itself.

w John Carpenter, David Zelag Goodman   *d* Irvin Kershner   *ph* Victor J. Kemper   *m* Artie Kane

Faye Dunaway, Tommy Lee Jones, Brad Dourif, René Auberjonois, Raul Julia, Frank Adonis

'Long on trendy settings, high-priced actors and vicious murders, but devoid of narrative thrills.' – *Richard Schickel, Time*

'Perhaps the most austerely elegant horror film ever made.' – *New Yorker*

Eyes of the Underworld
US   1941   61m   bw
Universal

A crusading lawyer exposes an auto theft ring.

Efficient little support which was smart enough to play top on its original release.

w Michael L. Simmons, Arthur Strawn   *d* Roy William Neill

Richard Dix, Lon Chaney Jnr, Wendy Barrie, Don Porter, Billy Lee, Lloyd Corrigan

Eyes without a Face *
France/Italy   1959   90m   bw
Champs Elysées/Lux (Jules Borkon)
V*
original title: *Les Yeux sans Visage*; US title: *The Horror Chamber of Dr Faustus*

When his daughter is mutilated in a car accident, a mad professor murders young girls in the process of grafting their faces onto hers.

Unpleasant horror film which its director seems to have made as a joke; the years have made it a cult.

w Jean Redon   *novel* Jean Redon   *d* Georges Franju   *ph* Eugen Schüfftan   *m* Maurice Jarre

Pierre Brasseur, Alida Valli, Edith Scob, François Guérin

Eyewitness *
GB   1970   91m   Technicolor
ITC/ABP (Paul Maslansky)
V*

A boy is the sole witness to an assassination, but no one believes him except the assassins.

The Window all over again, the standard clichés being tricked out with fancy photography, sub-Hitchcock set-ups and Mediterranean locations, which make it all very tolerable.

w Ronald Harwood   *novel* Mark Hebden   *d* John Hough   *ph* David Holmes   *m* Fairfield Parlour, David Whitaker

Mark Lester, Lionel Jeffries, Susan George, Tony Bonner, Jeremy Kemp, Peter Vaughan, Peter Bowles, Betty Marsden

Eyewitness
US   1981   108m   Technicolor
TCF (Peter Yates)
V*, L
GB title: *The Janitor*

A bashful janitor with a crush on a TV star finds himself hunted down by a murderer afraid of identification.

Odd little character thriller which despite pleasant touches never really seems to have its mind on its plot.

w Steve Tesich   *d* Peter Yates   *ph* Matthew F. Leonetti   *m* Stanley Silverman   *pd* Philip Rosenberg

William Hurt, Christopher Plummer, Sigourney Weaver, Irene Worth, James Woods, Kenneth McMillan, Steven Hill

F

F for Fake *
France/Iran/West Germany 1973 85m colour
Astrophore/Saco/Janus (Dominique Antoine, François Reichenbach)
French title: *Vérités et Mensonges*

Orson Welles, at a railway station, lectures the audience in truth and falsehood, in art, in films and in life.

A ragbag of an entertainment, cannibalizing as it does more than one unsold documentary, shredded at the editing table to match the narrator's illusionist style. Despite the raptures of some critics, this is an irritating effusion, and Welles now looks more like a clever charlatan than a master film-maker.

w Orson Welles, Oja Palinkas *d* Orson Welles *ph* Gary Graver, Christian Odasso *m* Michel Legrand

'Welles stretches his material and his legend just about as thin as possible in this tedious treatise on truth and illusion.' – *Kevin Thomas, Los Angeles Times*

† Joseph Cotten, Paul Stewart and Laurence Harvey make fleeting appearances.

FBI Code 98
US 1964 94m bw
Warner

G-men track down a mad bomber.

Thin action thriller originally intended for TV.

w Stanley Niss *d* Leslie H. Martinson

Jack Kelly, Ray Danton, Andrew Duggan, Philip Carey, William Reynolds

The FBI Story *
US 1959 149m Technicolor
Warner (Mervyn Le Roy)

An FBI agent thinks back on his career with the bureau.

Predictable mix of domestic sentimentality (very trying) and competent crime capsules: mad bomber, Ku Klux Klan, thirties hoodlums, Nazi spy rings and the cold war.

w Richard L. Breen, John Twist *d* Mervyn Le Roy *ph* Joseph Biroc *m* Max Steiner *ad* John Beckman

James Stewart, Vera Miles, Larry Pennell, Nick Adams, Murray Hamilton

'Insufferably cosy.' – *MFB*

F.P.I *
GB/Germany 1933 93m bw
Gaumont/UFA (Erich Pommer)

Financiers try to destroy the first floating aerodrome.

'Futuristic' melodrama about an aircraft carrier. Very well done, and shot in two languages, but now dated in most respects.

w Curt Siodmak, Walter Reisch, Robert Stevenson, Peter Macfarlane *d* Karl Hartl *ph* Gunther Rittau, Konstantin Tochet

Conrad Veidt, Leslie Fenton, Jill Esmond, George Merritt, Donald Calthrop, Nicholas Hannen, Francis L. Sullivan

The Fabulous Adventures of Marco Polo
France/Italy/Yugoslavia/Egypt/Afghanistan 1964 115m
Eastmancolor Franscope
Ittac/Prodi/Avala/Mounir Rafla/Italaf Kaboul (Raoul Lévy)
aka: *Marco the Magnificent*

In 1271 Marco Polo carries a message of peace to Kubla Khan.

Curious mixture of melodrama and pantomime, with a star cast half playing for laughs.

w Raoul Lévy, Denys de la Patellière *d* Denys de la Patellière, Noel Howard *ph* Armand Thirard *m* George Garvarentz

Horst Buchholz, Anthony Quinn, Orson Welles, Akim Tamiroff, Robert Hossein, Omar Sharif, Elsa Martinelli, Grégoire Aslan, Massimo Girotti, Folco Lulli

The Fabulous Baker Boys *
US 1989 113m colour
Rank/Gladden (Paula Weinstein, Sydney Pollack, Mark Rosenberg)
V, V*, L, S

Two piano-playing brothers hire a female singer to enliven their dying night-club act.

Enjoyable excursion into the lower depths of showbusiness.

wd Steve Kloves *ph* Michael Ballhaus *m* Dave Grusin *pd* Jeffrey Townsend *ed* Bill Steinkamp

Jeff Bridges, *Michelle Pfeiffer*, Beau Bridges, Ellie Raab, Jennifer Tilly

AAN: Michelle Pfeiffer; Michael Ballhaus

The Fabulous Dorseys
US 1947 91m bw
UA (Charles R. Rogers)
V*, L

Two quarrelling bandleader brothers are reunited on the death of their father.

Slight, comedic biopic with the Dorseys playing well and trying hard.

w Richard English, Art Arthur, Curtis Kenyon *d* Alfred E. Green *ph* James Van Trees *m* Leo Shuken

Tommy Dorsey, Jimmy Dorsey (and their bands), Janet Blair, Paul Whiteman, William Lundigan

The Fabulous Texan
US 1947 97m bw
Republic

Confederate officers after the Civil War return home to find Texas overrun by carpetbaggers and despotic state police.

Fairly handsome Western which gets by without ever being memorable.

w Lawrence Hazard, Horace McCoy *d* Edward Ludwig

William Elliott, John Carroll, Catherine McLeod, Andy Devine, Albert Dekker, Ruth Donnelly, Harry Davenport, Douglass Dumbrille

Faccia a Faccia: see *Face to Face* (1967)

The Face ***
Sweden 1958 100m bw
Svensk Filmindustri (Allan Ekelund)
original title: *Ansiktet*; US title: *The Magician*

In 19th-century Sweden, a mesmerist and his troupe are halted at a country post to be examined by three officials. Partly exposed as a fraud, he takes a frightening revenge.

A virtually indecipherable parable which may be about the survival of Christianity (and may not), this wholly personal Bergman fancy has to be enjoyed chiefly for its surface *frissons*, for its acting and its look, which are almost sufficient compensation.

wd Ingmar Bergman *ph* Gunnar Fischer *m* Erik Nordgren *ad* P. A. Lundgren *ed* Oscar Rosander

Max von Sydow, Ingrid Thulin, *Gunnar Björnstrand*, Naima Wifstrand, Uke Fridell, Lars Ekborg, Bengt Ekerot

The Face at the Window *
GB 1939 65m bw
Pennant/Ambassador (George King)
V*

In 1880 Paris, a murderer uses his moronic half-brother to distract his victims but is foiled when a dead man apparently incriminates him.

Roistering melodrama which provided Tod Slaughter with one of his juiciest roles and is here effectively presented, which is more than can be said for the screen treatments of most of his other vehicles.

w A. R. Rawlinson, Randall Faye *play* F. Brooke Warren *d* George King *ph* Hone Glendinning *md* Jack Beaver

Tod Slaughter, Marjorie Taylor, John Warwick, Leonard Henry, Aubrey Mallalieu

'One of the best English pictures I have seen . . . leaves the American horror films far behind.' – *Graham Greene*

The Face behind the Mask *
US 1941 69m bw
Columbia (Wallace MacDonald)

When his face is disfigured in a fire, an immigrant turns to a life of crime.

Effective second feature melodrama with a good star performance.

w Allen Vincent, Paul Jarrico *play* Thomas O'Connell *d* Robert Florey *ph* Franz Planer *md* Sidney Cutner

Peter Lorre, Evelyn Keyes, *Don Beddoe*, George E. Stone

A Face in the Crowd ***
US 1957 126m bw
(Warner) Newton (Elia Kazan)
V*

A small-town hick becomes a megalomaniac when television turns him into a cracker-barrel philosopher.

Brilliantly cinematic melodrama of its time which only flags in the last lap and paints a luridly entertaining picture of modern show business.

w Budd Schulberg *story* Your Arkansas Traveller *by* Budd Schulberg *d* Elia Kazan *ph* Harry Stradling, Gayne Rescher *m* Tom Glazer

Andy Griffith, Lee Remick, Walter Matthau, Patricia Neal,
Anthony Franciosa, Percy Waram, Marshall Neilan

'Savagery, bitterness, cutting humour.' – *Penelope Houston*

'If Kazan and Schulberg had been content to make their case by implication, it might have been a completely sophisticated piece of movie-making. Instead, everything is elaborately spelled out, and the film degenerates into preposterous liberal propaganda.' – *Andrew Sarris*

'Some exciting scenes in the first half, but the later developments are frenetic, and by the end the film is a loud and discordant mess.' – *Pauline Kael, 70s*

A Face in the Rain *
US   1963   80m   bw
Filmways/Calvic (John Calley)

During World War II an American spy in Italy bungles his mission, and hides in the apartment of a professor's wife.

Offbeat, talkative melodrama with a few neat touches.

w Hugo Butler, Jean Rouverol   *d* Irvin Kershner
ph Haskell Wexler   *m* Richard Markowitz

Rory Calhoun, Marina Berti, Niall MacGinnis

Face in the Sky
US   1932   68m   bw
Fox

A sign painter falls for a farmer's daughter.

Curious, whimsical comedy romance which didn't work at any level.

w Humphrey Pearson   *story* Myles Connolly
d Harry Lachman

Spencer Tracy, Marian Nixon, Stuart Erwin, Sam Hardy, Lila Lee

'Why it was considered feature-length picture material is hard to understand.' – *Variety*

Face of a Fugitive *
US   1959   81m   Eastmancolor
Columbia/Morningside

A man falsely accused of murder makes a new life in a frontier town.

Lively Western melodrama with good atmosphere.

w David T. Chantler   *d* Paul Wendkos   *ph* Wilfrid M. Cline   *m* Jerry Goldsmith

Fred MacMurray, Lin McCarthy, Alan Baxter, James Coburn

Face of a Stranger: see The Promise

The Face of Fu Manchu **
GB   1965   96m   Techniscope
Anglo-EMI/Hallam (Harry Alan Towers)
V, V*

In the twenties, Nayland Smith of Scotland Yard links an oriental crime wave with evil mastermind Fu Manchu.

A splendidly light touch and attention to detail make this entertaining spoof like a tuppenny blood come to life.

w Peter Welbeck (Harry Alan Towers)   *d* Don Sharp
ph Ernest Steward   *m* Chris Whelan   *ad* Frank White

Nigel Green, Christopher Lee, Tsai Chin, Howard Marion Crawford

The Face of Marble
US   1946   70m   bw
Monogram (Jeffrey Bernard)

A scientist revives the dead through voodoo.

Grade Z shocker with entertaining moments.

w Michael Jacoby   *d* William Beaudine

John Carradine, Robert Shayne, Claudia Drake, Maris Wrixon

Face to Face
US   1952   89m   bw
RKO/Huntington Hartford

Two stories of confrontation, artificially presented by an independent company: *The Secret Sharer* by Joseph Conrad and *The Bride Comes to Yellow Sky* by Stephen Crane.

w Aeneas Mackenzie, James Agee   *d* John Brahm, Bretaigne Windust

James Mason, Gene Lockhart, Michael Pate; Robert Preston, Marjorie Steele, Minor Watson

Face to Face *
Italy/Spain   1967   110m   Technicolor   Techniscope
PEA/Arturo Gonzalez (Alberto Grimaldi)
original title: *Faccia a Faccia*

A consumptive university professor goes to Texas for a cure and becomes the ruthless leader of a gang of outlaws.

Political spaghetti Western that can be taken as an allegory for the rise of fascism and the doctrine that ten violent men are bandits, but hundreds are an army and thousands are history.

w Sergio Donati, Sergio Sollima   *d* Sergio Sollima
ph Raphael Pacheco   *m* Ennio Morricone
ad Carlo Simi   *ed* Eugenio Alabiso

Gian Maria Volonte, Tomas Milian, William Berger, Jolanda Modio, Gianni Rizzo, Carol André, Lidya Alfonsi

Face to Face ****
Sweden   1976   136m   Eastmancolor
Ingmar Bergman/De Laurentiis/Sveriges Radio (Ingmar Bergman, Lars-Owe Carlberg)

A psychiatrist staying with her grandparents finds herself in need of guidance.

Fascinating material edited down from a TV series; too long as a film.

wd Ingmar Bergman   *ph* Sven Nykvist   *m* Mozart
ad Anne Terselius-Hagegörd, Anna Asp, Maggie Strindberg   *ed* Siv Lundgren

Liv Ullmann, Erland Josephson, Gunnar Björnstrand, Aino Taube-Henrikson

'After one has detailed its shortcomings, a wonderful fact remains: it's a work possible only to a first-class artist who has invested his life with other artists.' – *Stanley Kauffmann*

AAN: Ingmar Bergman (as director); Liv Ullmann

Faces *
US   1968   130m   bw
Maurice McEndree
V, V*

A discontented Los Angeles executive tries but fails to go through with a divorce.

A personal, probing study of middle-aged loneliness, made with the director's usual long-winded relentlessness but quite frequently compelling.

wd John Cassavetes   *ph* Al Ruban   *m* Jack Ackerman

John Marley, Gena Rowlands, Lynn Carlin, Fred Draper, Seymour Cassel

'The cast are all painfully and overpoweringly real.' – *Jan Dawson*

AAN: John Cassavetes (as writer); Lynn Carlin; Seymour Cassel

Faces in the Dark *
GB   1960   85m   bw
Rank/Welbeck/Penington Eady (Jon Penington)

A blind man survives a plot against his life.

Unlikely but watchable puzzler, betrayed by lifeless handling. Hitchcock could have worked wonders with such a plot.

w Ephraim Kogan, John Tulley   *novel* Pierre Boileau
by Thomas Narcejac   *d* David Eady   *ph* Ken Hodges   *m* Edwin Astley

John Gregson, Mai Zetterling, Michael Denison, John Ireland, Tony Wright, Nanette Newman

The Facts of Life *
US   1960   103m   bw
UA/HLP (Norman Panama)

Two middle-aged married suburbanites have an abortive affair.

Star comedy with muted slapstick and earnest acting, a good try, but less effective than their normal pratfalls.

w Norman Panama, Melvin Frank   *d* Melvin Frank
ph Charles Lang Jnr   *m* Leigh Harline   *ad* Joseph McMillan Johnson, Kenneth A. Reid

Bob Hope, Lucille Ball, Ruth Hussey, Don Defore, Louis Nye, Philip Ober

'Random shots of mockery aimed effectively at the American middle-class way of life.' – *Peter John Dyer*

AAN: Norman Panama, Melvin Frank (script); Charles Lang Jnr; title song (*m/ly* Johnny Mercer); art direction

Fade to Black
US   1980   100m   colour
Compass International/Leisure Investment/Movie Ventures (George Braunstein, Ron Hamady)
V*

A film buff becomes known as the 'Celluloid Killer' for murdering his victims while disguised as his favourite movie characters.

Violent, off-beat thriller that makes black jokes at the expense of movies.

wd Vernon Zimmerman   *story* Irving Yablans
ph Alex Phillips Jnr   *sp* James Wayne   *ed* Howard Kunin

Dennis Christopher, Linda Kerridge, Tim Thomerson, Morgan Paull, Hennen Chambers, Marya Small, Mickey Rourke

The film won the Critics' Prize at the Avoriaz Festival of Fantastic Films in 1981.

Fahrenheit 451 *
GB   1966   112m   Technicolor
Rank/Anglo Enterprise/Vineyard (Lewis M. Allen)
V*, L

In a fascist future state, a fireman's job is to burn books.

1984 stuff, a little lacking in plot and rather tentatively directed, but with charming moments.

w François Truffaut, Jean-Louis Richard   *novel* Ray Bradbury   *d* François Truffaut   *ph* Nicolas Roeg
m Bernard Herrmann   *design consultant* Tony Walton

Oskar Werner, Julie Christie, Cyril Cusack, Anton Diffring, Jeremy Spenser

'He barely dramatizes the material at all, and though there are charming, childlike moments, the performers seem listless, and the whole enterprise is a little drab.' – *Pauline Kael*

† All the credits in this film are spoken.

'It will have you sitting on the brink of eternity!'
Fail Safe ***
US   1964   111m   bw
Columbia/Max E. Youngstein/Sidney Lumet
V*, L

An American atomic bomber is accidentally set to destroy Moscow, and the president has to destroy New York in retaliation.

Despite a confusing opening, this deadly earnest melodrama gets across the horror of its situation better than the contemporaneous *Dr Strangelove* which treated the same plot as black comedy. Here the details are both terrifying and convincing.

w Walter Bernstein   *novel* Eugene Burdick, Harvey Wheeler   *d* Sidney Lumet   *ph* Gerald Hirschfeld   *m* none

Henry Fonda, Walter Matthau, Dan O'Herlihy, Frank Overton, Fritz Weaver, Edward Binns, Larry Hagman, Russell Collins

Fair Game: see *Mamba*

Fair Warning
US   1937   70m   bw
TCF

A sheriff solves the murder of a Death Valley miner.

Very watchable little second feature.

wd Norman Foster   *story* Philip Wylie

J. Edward Bromberg, Betty Furness, John Howard Payne, Victor Kilian, Gavin Muir, Andrew Tombes

'Stereotype whodunit comedy.' – *Variety*.

'An hour of genuine entertainment and taut suspense.' – *Film Daily*

Fair Wind to Java
US   1952   92m   Trucolor
Republic (Joseph Kane)

A sailor with a mutinous crew seeks a South Sea treasure.

Routine adventure culminating in a volcanic explosion.

w Richard Tregaskis   *novel* Garland Roark
d Joseph Kane   *ph* Jack Marta   *m* Victor Young

Fred MacMurray, Vera Hruba Ralston, Robert Douglas, Victor McLaglen

Faithful in My Fashion
US   1946   81m   bw
MGM

A soldier on leave causes havoc in a department store where his girlfriend is manager.

Sentimental comedy, forgettable for itself but containing endearing performances by a number of favourite character actors.

w Lionel Houser   *d* Sidney Salkow

Tom Drake, Donna Reed, Edward Everett Horton, Spring Byington, Harry Davenport, Sig Rumann, Margaret Hamilton, Hobart Cavanaugh

Faithless
US   1932   76m   bw
MGM

A spoiled rich girl and her beau both descend to working-class level and almost further.

Would-be sensational drama ruined by censorship and miscasting.

w Carey Wilson   *novel* Tinfoil by Mildred Cram
d Harry Beaumont   *ph* Oliver T. Marsh

Tallulah Bankhead, Robert Montgomery, Hugh Herbert, Maurice Murphy, Louise Closser Hale, Lawrence Grant, Henry Kolker

'They pile the suffering on so thick that any but the most naive theatregoers are going to revolt and scoff.' – *Variety*

The Fake
GB   1953   81m   bw
Pax (Steven Pallos)

The Tate Gallery hires an American investigator who discovers that one of their da Vincis is a substitute.

Very standard co-feature mystery with pleasant touches.

w Patrick Kirwan   *d* Godfrey Grayson

Dennis O'Keefe, Coleen Gray, Hugh Williams, John Laurie, Guy Middleton

The Falcon

A debonair solver of crime puzzles allegedly created by Michael Arlen but owing much to The Saint and resulting from a need by RKO for more of the same. Helped by a tough/comic manservant, he flourished during the forties in sixteen second features (the last three for Film Classics). After three episodes George Sanders tired of the role and was written out by being 'shot' and having his real-life brother Tom Conway take over as his fictional one. The performances of these two actors are pleasant, though the films are now fairly unwatchable, but John Calvert who took over for the last three was not a success.

1941: THE GAY FALCON, A DATE WITH THE FALCON
1942: THE FALCON TAKES OVER (the plot was borrowed from Raymond Chandler's FAREWELL MY LOVELY), THE FALCON'S BROTHER
1943: THE FALCON STRIKES BACK, THE FALCON AND THE CO-EDS, THE FALCON IN DANGER
1944: THE FALCON IN HOLLYWOOD, THE FALCON IN MEXICO, THE FALCON OUT WEST
1945: THE FALCON IN SAN FRANCISCO
1946: THE FALCON'S ALIBI, THE FALCON'S ADVENTURE
1948: THE DEVIL'S CARGO, APPOINTMENT WITH MURDER, SEARCH FOR DANGER

The Falcon and the Co-Eds
US   1943   68m   bw
RKO (Maurice Geraghty)

The Falcon is called to a girl's school to investigate the murder of a teacher, forecast by a psychic student.

Flimsy programmer, with less wit and more implausibility than usual.

w Ardel Wray, Gerald Geraghty   *d* William Clemens   *ph* Roy Hunt   *md* C. Bakaleinikoff   *ad* Albert S. D'Agostino   *ed* Theron Warth

Tom Conway, Jean Brooks, Rita Corday, Amelita Ward, Isabel Jewell, George Givot, Cliff Clark, Ed Gargan

The Falcon and the Snowman
US   1984   123m   DeLuxe
Orion/Gabriel Katzka, John Schlesinger (John Daly)
V, V*, L, S

A college dropout and a drug pusher sell secrets to the Russians.

A true case is made to seem not merely impossible but uninteresting by flaccid cinematic treatment.

w Steven Zaillian   *book* Robert Lindsey   *d* John Schlesinger   *ph* Allen Daviau   *m* Pat Metheny, Lyle Mays   *pd* James D. Bissell   *ed* Richard Marden

Timothy Hutton, Sean Penn, David Suchet, Lori Singer, Pat Hingle, Dorian Harewood

The Falcon in Hollywood
US   1944   67m   bw
RKO (Maurice Geraghty)

Holidaying in Hollywood, the Falcon reluctantly investigates an actor's murder.

Light thriller, well enough done in its low-budget way, with a narrative device that prefigures *The Producers*.

w Gerald Geraghty   *d* Gordon Douglas
ph Nicholas Musuraca   *m* C. Bakaleinikoff
ad Albert S. D'Agostino, L. O. Croxton   *ed* Gene Milford

Tom Conway, Barbara Hale, Veda Ann Borg, John Abbott, Sheldon Leonard, Rita Corday

The Falcon in Mexico
US   1944   70m   bw
RKO (Maurice Geraghty)

The Falcon, suspected of murdering an art dealer and stealing a valuable painting, goes to Mexico to solve the mystery.

Moderate thriller, though the Falcon's capacity for being knocked unconscious at inopportune moments seems inexhaustible.

w George Worthing Yates, Gerald Geraghty
d William Berke   *ph* Frank Raimon   *md* C. Bakaleinikoff   *ad* Albert S. D'Agostino   *ed* Joseph Noriega

Tom Conway, Mona Maris, Martha MacVicar, Nestor Paiva, Mary Currier, Joseph Vitale

The Falcon in San Francisco
US   1945   66m   bw
RKO (Maurice Geraghty)

The Falcon goes to the rescue of a small girl and uncovers a smuggling ring.

One of the best of the series, an entertaining mix of thriller and comedy.

w Robert Kent, Ben Markson   *d* Joseph H. Lewis
ph Virgil Miller, William Sickner   *m* Paul Sawtell
ad Albert S. D'Agostino, Charles Pyke   *ed* Ernie Leadlay

Tom Conway, Rita Corday, Edward S. Brophy, Sharyn Moffett, Faye Helm, Robert Armstrong, Carl Kent

The Falcon Strikes Back
US   1943   66m   bw
RKO (Maurice Geraghty)

The Falcon, framed for stealing war bonds and shooting a bank messenger, tracks down the real culprit.

Thriller that tries rather too hard to be amusing, although it occasionally succeeds.

w Edward Dein, Gerald Geraghty   *story* Stuart Palmer   *d* Edward Dmytryk   *ph* Jack Mackenzie
md Roy Webb   *ad* Albert S. D'Agostino, Walter E. Keller   *ed* George Crone

Tom Conway, Harriet Hilliard, Jane Randolph, Edgar Kennedy, Cliff Edwards, Cliff Clark, Ed Gargan

The Fall *
Argentina   1958   86m   bw
Argentine Sono (Leopoldo Torre Nilsson)
original title: *La Caida*

A strictly brought-up college girl lodges with an eccentric family whose strange world comes to mean more to her than the love of a young lawyer.

Odd, claustrophobic melodrama from a very personal film-maker.

w Beatriz Guido, *Leopoldo Torre Nilsson*   *novel* Beatriz Guido   *d* Leopoldo Torre Nilsson   *ph* Alberto Etchebehere   *m* Juan Carlos Paz

Elsa Daniel, Duilio Marzia, Lydia Lamaison, Carlos Lopez Monet

Fall In
US   1943   48m   bw
Hal Roach

Two army sergeants resent each other.

Very mild farce, another of Hal Roach's middle-length 'screenliners'.

w Eugene Conrad, Edward E. Seabrook   *d* Kurt Neumann

William Tracy, Joe Sawyer, Robert Barrat, Jean Porter, Arthur Hunnicutt

The Fall of Berlin *
USSR   1949   160m   Agfacolor
Mosfilm
S

A steel worker turns soldier, sees all the major Russian battles of World War II, and has his hand shaken by Stalin.

Out-and-out propaganda, with caricatures of famous people and magnificently staged battles.

w M. Chiaureli, P. A. Pavlenko   d M. Chiaureli
ph L. V. Kosmatov   m Dmitri Shostakovich

B. Andreyev, M. Gelovani (as Stalin), V. Stanitsine (as Churchill), M. Kovaleva

The Fall of the House of Usher
France   1928   48m (24 fps)   bw   silent

Roderick Usher's sister, prone to catalepsy, is buried alive; her unexpected return to life is instrumental in setting the house ablaze.

The original story is not so much stated as inferred in this very impressionistic version, of limited interest only to art movie buffs.

wd Jean Epstein, Luis Buñuel   ad Pierre Kefer

Marguerite Gance, Jean Debucourt, Charles Lamy

The Fall of the House of Usher
GB   1949   70m   bw
GIB

Dismally inept low-budgeter, a pain to sit through.

w Kenneth Thompson, Dorothy Catt   d Ivan Barnett

Gwen Watford, Kay Tendeter, Irving Steen

The Fall of the House of Usher (1960): see: see
House of Usher

The Fall of the Roman Empire **
US/Spain   1964   187m   Technicolor   Ultra
            Panavision 70
Samuel Bronston
V, V*, S

After poisoning the Emperor Marcus Aurelius his mad son Commodus succumbs to dissipation and allows Rome to be ravaged by pestilence and the Barbarians.

Would-be distinguished epic with an intellectual first hour; unfortunately the hero is a priggish bore, the villain a crashing bore, the heroine a saintly bore, and the only interesting character is killed off early. A chariot race, a javelin duel, some military clashes and a mass burning at the stake keep one watching, and the production values are high indeed.

w Ben Barzman, Philip Yordan   d Anthony Mann
ph Robert Krasker, John Moore   m Dimitri Tiomkin
pd Venerio Colasanti

Alec Guinness, Christopher Plummer, Stephen Boyd, James Mason, Sophia Loren, John Ireland, Eric Porter, Anthony Quayle, Mel Ferrer, Omar Sharif

   Christopher Plummer to Sophia Loren: 'Sister! And I thought you'd retired as a vestal virgin!'

'The film works from a restricted palette, and the result is weirdly restraining and severe, a dignified curb on absurdities.' – *John Coleman*

'You have to hand it to Bronston for thinking and making it big – both in spectacle and silliness.' – *Judith Crist*

† The forum set in this film is said to be the largest ever built.

AAN: Dimitri Tiomkin

'Even now she stood between us – the taunt of her smile like a black curse on our love!'
Fallen Angel *
US   1945   97m   bw
TCF (Otto Preminger)

A man plans to get rid of his wife and marry another woman, but it is the latter who is murdered.

Oddly sleazy melodrama, not more successful then because it was unexpected than now because it is miscast. Some good sequences, though.

w Harry Kleiner   novel Marty Holland   d Otto Preminger   ph Joseph LaShelle   m David Raksin

Dana Andrews, Alice Faye, Linda Darnell, Charles Bickford, Anne Revere, Bruce Cabot, John Carradine, Percy Kilbride

'It holds you by its undertones of small-town life and frustration.' – *Richard Winnington*

'It isn't in the class of *Laura*, but it's tolerable, in a tawdry sort of way.' – *Pauline Kael, 70s*

The Fallen Idol ***
GB   1948   94m   bw
British Lion/London Films (Carol Reed)
V*, L
US title: *The Lost Illusion*

An ambassador's small son nearly incriminates his friend the butler in the accidental death of his shrewish wife.

A near-perfect piece of small-scale cinema, built up from clever nuances of acting and cinematic technique.

w Graham Greene   story The Basement Room by Graham Greene   d Carol Reed   ph Georges Périnal
m William Alwyn

Ralph Richardson, Michèle Morgan, *Bobby Henrey*, Sonia Dresdel, Jack Hawkins

'A short story has become a film which is compact without loss of variety in pace and shape.' – *Dilys Powell*

'It's too deliberate and hushed to be much fun . . . you wait an extra beat between the low-key lines of dialogue.' – *Pauline Kael, 70s*

AAN: Graham Greene; Carol Reed

The Fallen Sparrow *
US   1943   93m   bw
RKO (Robert Fellows)
V*, L

An American veteran of the Spanish Civil War finds himself hounded in New York by Nazis seeking the Spanish flag of freedom.

Obscure melodrama, very good to look at but hardly worth unravelling; a precursor of Hollywood's post-war *films noirs*.

w Warren Duff   novel Dorothy B. Hughes
d Richard Wallace   ph Nicholas Musuraca
md Roy Webb, Constantin Bakaleinikoff

John Garfield, Maureen O'Hara, Walter Slezak, Martha O'Driscoll, Patricia Morison, Bruce Edwards, John Banner, John Miljan

AAN: Roy Webb, Constantin Bakaleinikoff

Falling Down **
US   1992   112m   Technicolor
Warner (Arnold Kopelson, Herschel Weingrod, Timothy Harris)

A redundant defence worker abandons his car on the Los Angeles freeway and attempts to make his way to the home of his former wife and their daughter. Confronted with the problems of urban life, from recalcitrant shopkeepers to unnecessary roadworks and would-be muggers, his behaviour becomes increasingly violent.

A fascinating movie on urban life, with a protagonist who is both hero and villain. It can be seen as a vigilante film, an attempt to claim a position for White Anglo-Saxon Protestants as among the victims of modern society, or a satire on over-reaction to city living. It remains a slightly queasy but enjoyable experience.

w Ebbe Roe Smith   d Joel Schumacher   ph Andrzej Bartkowiak   m James Newton Howard
pd Barbara Ling   ed Paul Hirsch

Michael Douglas, *Robert Duvall*, Barbara Hershey, Rachel Ticotin, Tuesday Weld, Frederic Forrest, Lois Smith

'At first comes across like a mean-spirited black comedy and then snowballs into a reasonably powerful portrait of social alienation.' – *Variety*

'Glitzy, casually cruel, hip and grim. It's something very funny, and often nasty in the way it manipulates one's darkest feelings.' – *Vincent Canby, New York Times*

'It's hard to decide whether it's a fascist movie made by a liberal or a liberal film made by a fascist. Sometimes it's hard to tell the difference between a hawk on good behaviour or a dove on steroids.' – *Adam Mars-Jones*

Falling for You *
GB   1933   88m   bw
Gainsborough (Michael Balcon)

Fleet Street journalists in Switzerland try to outsmart each other.

Dated comedy very typical of the stars' extremely casual style, with immaculate set-pieces.

w Jack Hulbert, Douglas Furber, Robert Stevenson
story Sidney Gilliat   d Jack Hulbert, Robert Stevenson   ph Bernard Knowles   m/ly Vivian Ellis, Douglas Furber   ad Vetchinsky   ed R. E. Dearing

Jack Hulbert, Cicely Courtneidge, Tamara Desni, Garry Marsh, Alfred Drayton, O. B. Clarence, Morton Selten

Falling in Love *
US   1984   107m   Technicolor
Paramount/Marvin Worth
V*, L

Meeting as commuters, Frank and Molly, each married to someone else, think about having an affair.

Rather tedious rehash of *Brief Encounter*, with no real interest in the characters or their backgrounds.

w Michael Cristofer   d Ulu Grosbard   ph Peter Suschitzky   m Dave Grusin   pd Santo Loquasto
ed Michael Kahn

Robert de Niro, Meryl Streep, Harvey Keitel, Jane Kaczmarek, George Martin

'The effect of this talented pair acting in such a lightweight vehicle is akin to having Horowitz and Rubinstein improvise a duet on the theme of Chopsticks.' – *Variety*

Falling in Love Again *
US   1980   103m   colour
International Picture Show of Atlanta (Steven Paul)
V*

A middle-aged New Yorker remembers his young romances and his dreams of success.

Warm little independent production harking back to the days of *H. M. Pulham Esquire* and none the worse for that.

w Steven Paul, Ted Allan, Susannah York   d Steven Paul   ph Michael Mileham, Dick Bush, Wolfgang Suschitzky   m Michel Legrand

Elliott Gould, Susannah York, Stuart Paul, Kaye Ballard

Die Fälschung: see Circle of Deceit

False Faces: see Let 'Em Have It

False Witness: see Zigzag

Falstaff: see Chimes at Midnight

Fame *
US 1980 133m Metrocolor
MGM (David de Silva, Alan Marshall)
V, V*, L

Assorted teenagers attend Manhattan's High School for the Performing Arts.

Cleverly shot and edited slice of life which unfortunately features people whose language and personalities are fairly repellent. The result is like *A Chorus Line* without the music.

w Christopher Gore d Alan Parker ph Michael Seresin m Michael Gore pd Geoffrey Kirkland ed Gerry Hambling

Irene Cara, Lee Curreri, Laura Dean, Paul McCrane, Barry Miller, Gene Anthony Ray

'Our film, I hope, will be a microcosm of New York . . . a dozen races pitching in and having their own crack at the American dream.' – *Alan Parker*

'Its soft-centred view of human relationships is periodically undercut by what can only be described as the grotesque.' – *John Pym*

AA: Michael Gore; song 'Fame' (m Michael Gore, ly Dean Pitchford)

AAN: screenplay; song 'Out Here On My Own' (m Michael Gore, ly Lesley Gore); editing

Fame Is the Spur *
GB 1947 116m bw
GFD/Two Cities/Charter Films (John Boulting)

The rise to political eminence of a working-class socialist.

Disappointingly flat historical drama from a novel allegedly based on the career of Ramsay MacDonald. Interesting moments.

w Nigel Balchin novel Howard Spring d Roy Boulting ph Gunther Krampf, Harry Waxman m Alan Rawsthorne

Michael Redgrave, Rosamund John, Bernard Miles, Carla Lehmann, Hugh Burden, Marjorie Fielding, Seymour Hicks

La Famiglia: see *The Family* (1987)

The Family (1970): see
Violent City

The Family **
Italy/France 1987 127m colour
Maasfilm/Cinecitta/Cinemax/Ariane (Franco Committeri)
V*, L
original title: *La Famiglia*

A man of 80 recalls the events of his long life, centred on the Rome apartment where he and his family still live.

An intriguing family saga of love, laughter and disappointment that is both a character and a social study.

w Ruggero Maccari, Furio Scarpelli, Ettore Scola d Ettore Scola ph Ricardo Aronvich m Armando Trovajoli ad Luciano Ricceri ed Ettore Scola

Vittorio Gassman, Fanny Ardant, Stefania Sandrelli, Andrea Occhipinti, Jo Champa

A Family Affair *
US 1937 69m bw
MGM (Lucien Hubbard)

A small-town judge faces a few family problems.

The second feature that started the highly successful Hardy family series (qv under Hardy). In this case the judge and his wife were played by actors who did not persevere into the series, but the stage was otherwise set for a long run, and the town of Carvel came to mean home to many Americans abroad.

w Kay Van Riper play Skidding by Aurania Rouverol d George B. Seitz ph Lester White m David Snell

Lionel Barrymore, Spring Byington, *Mickey Rooney*, Eric Linden, Cecilia Parker, Sara Haden, Charles Grapewin, Julie Haydon

'Family trade and tops in dual locations.' – *Variety*

Family Business
US 1989 110m colour
Palace/Tri-Star (Lawrence Gordon)
V, V*, L

Three generations of crooks take part in a robbery.

Dull comedy that never convinces and certainly doesn't amuse.

w Vincent Patrick novel Vincent Patrick d Sidney Lumet ph Andrzej Bartowiak m Cy Coleman pd Philip Rosenberg ed Andrew Mondshein

Sean Connery, Dustin Hoffman, Matthew Broderick, Rosana DeSoto, Janet Carroll, Victoria Jackson, Bill McCutcheon, Deborah Rush, Marilyn Cooper

Family Doctor: see *RX Murder*

Family Honeymoon
US 1948 90m bw
U-I (John Beck, Z. Wayne Griffin)

A college professor marries a widow whose three children join them on their Grand Canyon honeymoon.

Very ordinary and predictable star comedy.

w Dane Lussier, Homer Croy d Claude Binyon ph William Daniels m Frank Skinner

Claudette Colbert, Fred MacMurray, Rita Johnson, Gigi Perreau, Peter Miles, Jimmy Hunt, Hattie McDaniel, Chill Wills

The Family Jewels
US 1965 100m Technicolor
Paramount/York/Jerry Lewis
V*

A child heiress chooses a new father from among her five uncles.

Unfunny star farce with multiple impersonations.

w Jerry Lewis, Bill Richmond d Jerry Lewis ph W. Wallace Kelley m Pete King

Jerry Lewis, Donna Butterworth, Sebastian Cabot, Robert Strauss

Family Life **
GB 1971 108m Technicolor
EMI/Kestrel (Tony Garnett)

A 19-year-old girl is driven into a mental collapse by emotional and family problems.

A slice of suburban life and an indictment of it, put together with unknown actors and probing TV techniques. Somewhat too harrowing for fiction, but extraordinarily vivid.

w David Mercer play In Two Minds by David Mercer d Ken Loach ph Charles Stewart m Marc Wilkinson

Sandy Ratcliff, Bill Dean, Grace Cave

'There's no body in the family plot!'
Family Plot **
US 1976 126m Technicolor
Universal (Alfred Hitchcock)
V*, L

A fake medium tries for easy money by producing a lost heir.

Talkative, complex, patchy, low-key but always interesting Hitchcock suspenser in an unusually friendly vein.

w Ernest Lehman novel The Rainbird Pattern by Victor Canning d Alfred Hitchcock ph Leonard J. South m John Williams pd Henry Bumstead

Karen Black, Bruce Dern, Barbara Harris, William Devane, Ed Lauter, Cathleen Nesbitt

'Full of benign mischief, beautiful craftsmanship and that elusive sense of cinematic rhythm that has always been Hitchcock's trump card.' – *Michael Billington, Illustrated London News*

'The picture bogs down in one talky, undramatic sequence after another, and the plot, with all its exposition and loose ends, is involved beyond belief.' – *De Witt Bodeen, Films in Review*

Family Portrait **
GB 1950 24m bw
Festival of Britain/Wessex (Ian Dalrymple)

A study of the English tradition and spirit through history.

The last work of a director-poet; not his most vivid movie, yet an accurate distillation of the themes which concerned him and of a dreamlike patriotism which now seems lost.

wd Humphrey Jennings ph Martin Curtis ed Stewart MacAllister commentary Michael Goodliffe

'Perhaps the most polished in style of all Jennings' films . . . continuously fascinating, sharp and evocative.' – *MFB*

The Family Secret
US 1951 85m bw
Columbia/Santana (Robert Lord, Henry S. Kesler)
V*

The son of a suburban family kills his best friend in a brawl, and his mother insists he conceal the truth even when another man is charged.

Television-style pattern play, not even very interesting at the time.

w Francis Cockrell, Andrew Solt d Henry Levin ph Burnett Guffey m George Duning

John Derek, Lee J. Cobb, Erin O'Brien Moore, Jody Lawrance, Henry O'Neill, Carl Benton Reid

'The general atmosphere is one of outward torment unbacked by inner emotion.' – *MFB*

Family Viewing
Canada 1988 86m colour
The Other Cinema/Ego Film (Atom Egoyan)

A television- and video-obsessed family live lives of quiet desperation.

Interesting low-budget film, originally shot on video, and as obsessed as its characters with electronic media.

wd Atom Egoyan ph Robert Macdonald m Michael Danna ad Linda del Rosario ed Atom Egoyan, Bruce Macdonald

David Hemblen, Aidan Tierney, Gabrielle Rose, Arsinee Khanjian, Selma Keklikian, Rose Sarkisyan, Jeanne Sabourin

'There are streaks of filmmaking talent visible through the pretentious murk of this disjointed story.' – *Variety*

The Family Way *
GB 1966 115m Eastmancolor
BL/Jambox (John Boulting)
V

There is consternation in a Lancashire family when the son cannot consummate his marriage.

Overstretched domestic farce-drama. Good scenes and performances, but it was all much sharper as a one-hour TV play.

w Bill Naughton play Honeymoon Deferred by Bill Naughton d Roy Boulting ph Harry Waxman m Paul McCartney

John Mills, *Marjorie Rhodes*, Hywel Bennett, Hayley Mills, *Avril Angers*, Murray Head, Wilfred Pickles, Barry Foster, Liz Fraser

The Famous Ferguson Case
US 1932 80m bw
Warner

Reporters on a small town paper expose their own hang-ups as they argue over the outcome of a current murder trial.

Generally unsuccessful attempt to do something mildly different.

w Harvey Thew story Courtenay Terrett, Granville Moore d Lloyd Bacon

Joan Blondell, Tom Brown, Adrienne Dore, Walter Miller, Leslie Fenton, J. Carrol Naish, Grant Mitchell

'Dull, trite, talky exposé of yellow journalism.' – *Variety*

The Fan *
US 1949 79m bw
TCF (Otto Preminger)
GB title: *Lady Windermere's Fan*

Scandal almost results when Lady Windermere loses her fan.

Reasonably polished, rather dull version of an old play, not really helped by modern bookends.

w Walter Reisch, Dorothy Parker, Ross Evans play *Lady Windermere's Fan* by Oscar Wilde d Otto Preminger ph Joseph LaShelle m Daniele Amfitheatrof

George Sanders, Madeleine Carroll, Jeanne Crain, Richard Greene, Martita Hunt, John Sutton, Hugh Dempster, Richard Ney

The Fan
US 1981 95m Technicolor
Paramount/Robert Stigwood/Filmways
V*, L

A Broadway actress is threatened by a disturbed admirer.

Ruthless, witless thriller with no suspense cliché unturned.

w Priscilla Chapman, John Hartwell d Edward Bianchi ph Dick Bush m Pino Donaggio pd Santo Loquasto

Lauren Bacall, James Garner, Maureen Stapleton, Hector Elizondo, Michael Biehn, Anna Maria Horsford

'Horror comic mechanics . . . the theatrical milieu fails to register, either individually or collectively.' – *Gilbert Adair, MFB*

Fanatic *
GB 1965 96m Technicolor
Hammer/Seven Arts (Anthony Hinds)
V*
US title: *Die! Die! My Darling*

An American girl in England visits the mother of her dead fiancé and finds herself the prisoner of a religious maniac.

Boringly overlong Grand Guignol which even defeats its gallantly unmade-up and deathly-looking star; mildly notable however as a record of one of her last performances.

w Richard Matheson novel *Nightmare* by Anne Blaisdell d Silvio Narizzano ph Arthur Ibbetson m Wilfrid Josephs pd Peter Proud ed James Needs, John Dunsford

Tallulah Bankhead, Stefanie Powers, Peter Vaughan, Yootha Joyce, Donald Sutherland

The Fanatics *
France 1957 92m bw
Cinégraphe-Regent (Pierre Lévy)

Patriots quarrel over the assassination by bomb of a South American dictator when he travels by public plane.

Suspense melodrama with many artificial twists, but slick and well acted.

w Alex Joffé, Jean Levitte d Alex Joffé ph L. H. Burel m Paul Misraki

Pierre Fresnay, Michel Auclair, Grégoire Aslan, Betty Schneider

Fancy Pants **
US 1950 92m Technicolor
Paramount (Robert Welch)
V*, L

A British actor stranded in the far west poses as a butler.

Lively Western comedy remake of *Ruggles of Red Gap* (qv), one of the star's better vehicles.

w Edmund Hartman, Robert O'Brien d George Marshall ph Charles Lang Jnr m Van Cleave

Bob Hope, Lucille Ball, Bruce Cabot, Jack Kirkwood, Lea Penman, Eric Blore, John Alexander, Norma Varden

Fandango
US 1985 91m Technicolor
Warner/Amblin (Tim Zinnemann)
V*

In the early 1970s, a group of college friends drive across Texas for a final weekend of fun before graduation and army service in Vietnam looms.

Slight but enjoyable movie that began life as a small student film before being expanded under the auspices of Steven Spielberg's production company.

wd Kevin Reynolds ph Thomas Del Ruth m Alan Silvestri ad Peter Lansdown Smith ed Arthur Schmidt, Stephen Semel

Kevin Costner, Judd Nelson, Sam Robards, Chuck Bush, Brian Cesak, Marvin J. McIntyre, Suzy Amis, Glenne Headly

Fanfan la Tulipe *
France 1951 98m bw
Filmsonor/Ariane/Amato (Alexandre Mnouchkine)

Recruited into the army of Louis XV by a prophecy that he will marry the king's daughter, a young braggart does everything he can to live up to it.

Rather like a spoof Errol Flynn effort, this likeable swashbuckler can't quite summon up enough buckle or swash to be the minor classic it clearly intends.

w Christian-Jaque, Henri Jeanson, René Wheeler story René Wheeler, René Fallet d Christian-Jaque ph Christian Matras m Georges Van Parys, Maurice Thiriet ad Robert Gys ed Jacques Desagneaux

Gérard Philipe, Gina Lollobrigida, Marcel Herrand, Olivier Hussenot, Henri Rollan, Nerio Bernardi, Jean Marc Tennberg, Jean Parédès, Noël Roquevert, Geneviève Page, Sylvia Pelayo

'A daring and delightful piece of work.' – *The Times*

† The film won Christian-Jaque the award for best director at the Cannes Film Festival in 1952.

Fängelse: see *The Devil's Wanton*

Fanny (Pagnol): see *Marius*

Fanny ***
France 1932 128m bw
Les Films Marcel Pagnol/Braunberger-Richebé

After her lover returns to sea, Fanny discovers that she is pregnant and agrees to marry a wealthy widower.

The second instalment of Pagnol's trilogy of Marseilles life, suffused with acute observation, warmth and humanity.

w Marcel Pagnol play Marcel Pagnol d Marc Allégret ph Nicolas Toporkoff, André Dantan, Roger Hubert, Georges Benoit, Coutelain m Vincent Scotto ed Raymond Lamy

Raimu, Orane Demazis, Pierre Fresnay, *Fernard Charpin,* Alida Rouffe, Robert Vattier, Auguste Mouriès, Milly Mathis, Maupi, Edouard Delmont

This was the first film Pagnol made as his own producer. After its success he was able to build his own studio. An Italian version, directed by Mario Almirante, was made in 1933 and a German version starring Emil Jannings in 1934. It followed on from *Marius* and was followed by a sequel, *César* (qqv).

'There are three men in her life. The one she married . . . the young adventurer . . . and the baby they all shared!'

Fanny *
US 1961 133m Technicolor
Warner/Mansfield (Joshua Logan)
V*

Life on the Marseilles waterfront, and in particular the story of two old men and two lovers.

Lumbering adaptation of three Pagnol films of the thirties (*Marius, Fanny, César* – see *Marius*) previously seen as a 1938 Hollywood film (*Port of Seven Seas*) and later as a Broadway musical. This is the dullest version despite fine photography and a couple of good performances.

w Julius J. Epstein play S. N. Behrman, Joshua Logan films Marcel Pagnol d Joshua Logan ph Jack Cardiff md Morris Stoloff, Harry Sukman m Harold Rome

Charles Boyer, Maurice Chevalier, Leslie Caron, Horst Buchholz, Georgette Anys, Salvatore Baccaloni, Lionel Jeffries, Raymond Bussières, Victor Francen

† The film was proudly advertised as 'Joshua Logan's Fanny' until the press pointed out the double meaning.

AAN: best picture; Jack Cardiff; Morris Stoloff, Harry Sukman; Charles Boyer

Fanny and Alexander ****
Sweden/France/West Germany 1982 188m Eastmancolor
AB Cinematograph/Swedish Film Institute/Swedish TV One/Gaumont/Persona Film/Tobis (Jörm Donner)
V, V*, L

A well-to-do Uppsala family comes together to celebrate Christmas 1907.

An interesting mixture of *Dear Octopus* and *Wild Strawberries* turns into something more akin to *The Face* or *The Night Comers.* A kind of Bergman compendium, and impossible to describe exactly for those who have not seen it.

wd Ingmar Bergman ph Sven Nykvist m Daniel Bell pd Anna Asp

Gunn Walgren, Ewa Fröling, Jarl Kulle, Erland Josephson, Allan Edwall, Börje Ahlstedt, Mona Malm, Gunnar Björnstrand, Jan Malmsjö

'It's as if Bergman's neuroses had been tormenting him for so long that he cut them off and went sprinting back to Victorian health and domesticity.' – *New Yorker*

AA: cinematography; best foreign-language film; art direction; costume

AAN: direction; screenplay

Fanny by Gaslight **
GB 1944 108m bw
GFD/Gainsborough (Edward Black)
V*
US title: *Man of Evil*

The illegitimate daughter of a cabinet minister is saved from a lustful Lord.

Highly-coloured Victorian romantic melodrama, enjoyably put over with no holds barred and a pretty high budget for the time.

w Doreen Montgomery, Aimée Stuart novel Michael Sadleir d Anthony Asquith ph Arthur Crabtree m Cedric Mallabey

James Mason, Phyllis Calvert, Stewart Granger, Wilfrid Lawson, John Laurie, Margaretta Scott, Stuart Lindsell, Jean Kent

'Seldom have I seen a film more agreeable to watch, from start to finish.' – *William Whitebait*

'Mr Asquith does not seem to have made much effort to freshen it by interesting treatment, so that the rare unusual device seems quite out of key among so much that is simple, obvious, hackneyed.' – *Richard Mallett, Punch*

† One of several costume melodramas patterned after the success of *The Man in Grey* (qv).

Fanny Foley Herself

US   1931   73m   Technicolor
RKO

A female vaudeville entertainer chooses between her profession and looking after her two daughters.

Rather disappointing comedy drama.

w Carey Wilson   *story* Juliet Wilbur Tompkins
d Melville Brown

Edna May Oliver, Hobart Bosworth, Helen Chandler, Rochelle Hudson, John Darrow

Fanny Hill

West Germany   1965   104m   bw
Albert Zugsmith/Pan World

Adventures of an 18th-century woman of pleasure.

Tacky exploitation piece half-spoofing a suddenly fashionable piece of pornography.

w Robert Heel   *d* Russ Meyer

Miriam Hopkins, Laetitia Roman, Walter Giller, Alex D'Arcy, Helmut Weiss

Fantasia ****

US   1940   135m   Technicolor
Walt Disney
V, V*, L

A concert of classical music is given cartoon interpretations. The pieces are:

Bach: Toccata and Fugue in D Minor
Tchaikovsky: The Nutcracker Suite
Dukas: The Sorcerer's Apprentice
Stravinsky: The Rite of Spring
Beethoven: The Pastoral Symphony
Ponchielli: Dance of the Hours
Mussorgsky: Night on a Bare Mountain
Schubert: Ave Maria

Brilliantly inventive for the most part, the cartoons having become classics in themselves. The least part (the Pastoral Symphony) can be forgiven.

supervisor Ben Sharpsteen   *md* Edward H. Plumb

Leopold Stokowski, the Philadelphia Orchestra, Deems Taylor

'Dull as it is towards the end, ridiculous as it is in the bend of the knee before Art, it is one of the strange and beautiful things that have happened in the world.' – *Otis Ferguson*

'It is ambitious, and finely so, and one feels that its vulgarities are at least unintentional.' – *James Agate*

'Disney sometimes at his worst, often at his very best; and the best is on a level which no other cinematographic designer has reached. It takes over two hours, but somehow or other I'm afraid you will have to find the time.' – *Dilys Powell*

† Multiplane cameras, showing degrees of depth in animation, were used for the first time. The film was re-released in a print restored to its original freshness in 1990.

AA: Special Award to Walt Disney, Leopold Stokowski

The Fantasist

Ireland   1987   98m   colour
Blue Dolphin (Mark Forstater)
V, V*

A psychopathic killer stalks a young country girl who goes to work in Dublin.

Occasionally suspenseful thriller, but it offers little out of the ordinary and is muddled in its intentions, attempting to be a more serious film than it actually is.

wd Robin Hardy   *novel* Goosefoot by Patrick McGinley   *ph* Frank Gell   *m* Stanislas Syrewicz   *ed* Thomas Schwalm

Moira Harris, Christopher Cazenove, Timothy Bottoms, John Kavanagh, Mick Lally

The Fantastic Disappearing Man: see *The Return of Dracula*

Fantastic Invasion of Planet Earth: see *The Bubble*

Fantastic Voyage *

US   1966   100m   DeLuxe   Cinemascope
TCF (Saul David)
V, V*, L

When a top scientist is shot and suffers brain damage, a team of doctors and a boat are miniaturized and injected into his blood stream . . . but one is a traitor.

Engagingly absurd science fiction which keeps its momentum but is somewhat let down by its décor.

w Harry Kleiner   *d* Richard Fleischer   *ph* Ernest Laszlo   *m* Leonard Rosenman   *ad* Dale Hennesy, Jack Martin Smith   *sp* L. B. Abbott, Art Cruickshank, Emil Kosa Jnr

Stephen Boyd, Raquel Welch, Edmond O'Brien, Donald Pleasence, Arthur Kennedy, Arthur O'Connell, William Redfield

'The process shots are so clumsily matted . . . that the actors look as if a child has cut them out with blunt scissors.' – *Pauline Kael*

AA: art direction; special visual effects (Art Cruickshank)

AAN: Ernest Laszlo

Fantomas *

France/Italy   1966   104m   bw
SNEG

A master crook is also a master of disguise.

One of several films made in the sixties in affectionate imitation of a French silent serial.

w Jean Halain, Pierre Foucaud   *d* André Hunebelle

Jean Marais, Louis de Funes, Mylene Demongeot, Jacques Dynam

Le Fantôme de la Liberté: see *The Phantom of Liberty*

Far and Away

US   1992   140m   DeLuxe   Panavision Super 70
UIP/Universal/Imagine (Brian Grazer, Ron Howard)
V, V*, L, S

A young Irish woman, daughter of a landowner, runs away to America, taking one of her father's tenants with her as an unwilling servant.

A romance conceived on an epic scale, but still-born; an uninteresting molehill of a movie.

w Bob Dolman   *story* Bob Dolman, Ron Howard   *d* Ron Grazer   *ph* Mikael Salomon   *m* John Williams   *pd* Jack T. Collis, Allan Cameron   *ed* Michael Hill, Daniel Hanley

Tom Cruise, Nicole Kidman, Thomas Gibson, Robert Prosky, Barbara Babcock, Cyril Cusack, Eileen Pollock, Colm Meaney, Niall Toibin

'A doddering bloated bit of corn, and its characters and situations so obviously hackneyed, that we can't

give in to the story and allow ourselves to be swept away.' – *Washington Post*

'The plot and characters sometimes seem to have been borrowed from a picture storybook for teenage girls.' – *Iain Johnstone, Sunday Times*

'Unrepentant and vapid nonsense, celebrated with inappropriate splendour.' – *Philip Strick, Sight and Sound*

The Far Country *

US   1954   97m   Technicolor
U-I (Aaron Rosenberg)

Two cowboys on their way to the Alaska goldfields are beset by swindlers.

Sturdy star Western with good production values.

w Borden Chase   *d* Anthony Mann   *ph* William Daniels   *m* Hans Salter

James Stewart, Walter Brennan, Ruth Roman, Corinne Calvet, John McIntire

Far East

Australia   1982   100m   colour
Filmco Australia/Alfred Road (Richard Mason)

An Australian bar owner in an Asian city rampant with violence is confronted by a girl from his past.

A disappointing attempt to redo *Casablanca* without the wit or style.

wd John Duigan   *ph* Brian Probyn   *m* Sharon Calcraft   *pd* Ross Major   *ed* Henry Dangar

Bryan Brown, Helen Morse, John Bell, Raina McKeon, Henry Duval Sinan Leong, Bill Hunter

Far from Home

US   1989   86m   CFI colour
Vestron/Lightning (Donald P. Borchers)
V, V*, L

While on holiday with her father, an adolescent girl is stalked by a serial killer.

Drear little film that follows the standard pattern for the over-familiar genre.

w Tommy Lee Wallace   *story* Ted Gershuny   *d* Meiert Avis   *ph* Paul Elliott   *m* Jonathan Elias   *ed* Marc Grossman

Matt Frewer, Drew Barrymore, Richard Masur, Karen Austin, Susan Tyrrell, Anthony Rapp, Jennifer Tilly, Dick Miller

Far from the Madding Crowd *

GB   1967   175m   Technicolor   Panavision 70
EMI/Vic/Appia (Joseph Janni)
V*, L, S

In Victorian Wessex a headstrong girl causes unhappiness and tragedy.

Good-looking but slackly handled version of a melodramatic and depressing novel.

w Frederick Raphael   *novel* Thomas Hardy   *d* John Schlesinger   *ph* Nicolas Roeg   *m* Richard Rodney Bennett   *pd* Richard Macdonald

Julie Christie, Peter Finch, Alan Bates, Terence Stamp, Prunella Ransome

'In this rather plodding film the insufficiency of the foreground is partly offset by the winsomeness of the backgrounds. The very sheep are so engaging as to entice our gaze into some extremely amiable woolgathering.' – *John Simon*

AAN: Richard Rodney Bennett

The Far Horizons

US   1955   108m   Technicolor   Vistavision
(Paramount) Pine-Thomas

The story of Lewis and Clark's 1803 expedition west through the Louisiana Purchase territory.

Flabbily-handled historical hokum; potential interest quickly dissipated.

w Winston Miller, Edmund H. North   *d* Rudolph Maté   *ph* Daniel L. Fapp   *m* Hans Salter

Fred MacMurray, Charlton Heston, Donna Reed, Barbara Hale, William Demarest

Far North
US   1988   89m   colour
Rank/Alive Films/Nelson/Circle JS (Malcolm R. Harding, Carolyn Pfieffer)
V, V*, L

A family squabbles around the bed of their sick father.

Inconsequential film that marked the directorial début of writer/actor Shepard.

wd Sam Shepard   *ph* Robbie Greenberg   *m* The Red Clay Ramblers, J. A. Deane   *pd* Peter Jamison   *ed* Bill Yahraus

Jessica Lange, Tess Harper, Charles Durning, Donald Moffat, Ann Wedgeworth, Patricia Arquette, Nina Draxten

A Far Off Place *
US   1993   116m   Technicolor
Buena Vista/Walt Disney/Amblin (Eva Monely, Elaine Sperber)
S

A teenage boy and girl, pursued by murderous ivory poachers, are guided across the Kalahari desert by a young bushman.

Old-fashioned children's movie about discovering maturity through an understanding of the natural world; the photography has charm.

w Robert Caswell, Jonathan Hensleigh, Sally Robinson   *book* A'Story Like the Wind and a Far Off Place by Laurens van der Post   *d* Mikael Salomon   *ph* Juan Ruiz-Anchia   *m* James Horner   *pd* Gemma Jackson   *ed* Ray Lovejoy

Reese Witherspoon, Ethan Randall, Jack Thompson, Sarel Bok, Robert Burke, Patricia Kalember, Maximilian Schell

'A coming-of-age yarn that should hold the attention of kids and patient adults.' – *Variety*

'Potential date movie material for environmentally aware 13-year-olds.' – *Matt Mueller, Empire*

Far Out Man
US   1990   85m   Foto-Kem colour
New Line/CineTel (Lisa M. Hansen)
V, V*, L

An ageing, permanently stoned hippie searches for his former girlfriend and their child.

A Chong family home movie inflicted upon a wider public, it is only worth watching if you are related to the writer/director and even then you must be prepared to be indulgent.

wd Tommy Chong   *ph* Greg Gardiner, Eric Woster   *m* Jay Chattaway   *ed* Stephen Myers, Gilberto Costa Nunes

Tommy Chong, C. Thomas Howell, Rae Dawn Chong, Shelby Chong, Paris Chong, Martin Mull, Bobby Taylor, Al Mancini, Judd Nelson, Cheech Marin, Paul Bartel

'Technically, pic is a mess. Two lensers are credited, so it may be that one held the camera while the other held the film and the director never came out of character long enough to tell them what to do with either.' – *Variety*

Farewell *
USSR   1981   126m   colour
Artificial Eye/Mosfilm (A. Rasskazov, G. Sokolova)
original title: Proshchanie

A peasant community is resettled, against its will, into modern apartments to make way for a new dam.

Emotional and detailed look at the destruction of a community and its relationships.

w Lorisa Shepitko, Rudolf Tyurin, German Klimov   *novel* Valentin Rasputin   *d* Elem Klimov   *ph* Alexei Rodionov, Yuri Skhirtladze, Sergei Taraskin   *m* V. Artyomov   *ad* V. Petrov   *ed* V. Byelova

Stefaniya Stayuta, Lev Durov, Alexe Petrenko, Leonid Kryuk, Vadim Yakovenko, Yuri Katin-Yartsev, Denis Luppov

Farewell Again **
GB   1937   85m   bw
Pendennis/London Films (Erich Pommer)
US title: Troopship

Soldiers returning from India have six hours' shore leave to sort out their problems.

Dated but sharply made compendium drama, a solid success of its time.

w Clemence Dane, Patrick Kirwan   *story* Wolfgang Wilhelm   *d* Tim Whelan   *ph* James Wong Howe, Hans Schneeberger   *m* Richard Addinsell   *ad* Frederick Pusey   *ed* Jack Dennis

Flora Robson, Leslie Banks, Robert Newton, René Ray, Patricia Hilliard, Sebastian Shaw, Leonora Corbett, Anthony Bushell, Edward Lexy, Wally Patch, Edmund Willard, Martita Hunt, John Laurie

Farewell My Concubine ***
Hong Kong/China   1993   156m   colour
Artificial Eye/Thomson/China Film/Beijing Film (Hsu Feng)
S

Two boys who train together at the Peking Opera form a lifelong relationship, both on-stage – one playing masculine roles, the other in feminine parts – and off, through the political upheavals from the 1930s onwards until their final performance in the 60s.

A beautiful and epic film that records the social changes of Chinese life with an unblinking eye and from the viewpoint of the endlessly persecuted.

w Lilian Lee, Lu Wei   *novel* Lilian Lee   *d* Chen Kaige   *ph* Gu Changwei   *m* Zhaao Jiping   *ad* Chen Huaikai   *ed* Pei Xiaonan

Leslie Cheung, Zhang Fengyi, Gong Li, Lu Qi, Ying Da, Ge You, Lin Chun, Lei Han, Tong Di

'Chinese cinema ceases to be an acquired taste and becomes a required one . . . Its vast running time contains some episodes of pleasure, pain, adventure, vice or instructive insight for every taste or brow – high and low.' – *Alexander Walker, London Evening Standard*

'Chen's attempt to reach a wider audience with a bigger, less ambiguous film is still a formidable success. It's a kind of opera in itself, conducted by a director whose visual power is matched by an emotional force that few others in world cinema can match.' – *Derek Malcolm*

'A big, eventful historical soap opera of the *Doctor Zhivago* school.' – *Terrence Rafferty, New Yorker*

The film was joint winner of the Palme d'Or at the Cannes Film Festival in 1993.

AAN: best foreign-language film; Gu Changwei

Farewell My Lovely ***
US   1944   95m   bw
RKO (Adrian Scott)
V*, L
aka: Murder My Sweet

A private eye searches for an ex-convict's missing girlfriend.

A revolutionary crime film in that it was the first to depict the genuinely seedy milieu suggested by its author. One of the first *films noirs* of the mid-forties, a minor masterpiece of expressionist film making, and a total change of direction for a crooner who suddenly became a tough guy.

w John Paxton   *novel* Raymond Chandler   *d* Edward Dmytryk   *ph* Harry J. Wild   *m* Roy Webb

Dick Powell, Claire Trevor, Anne Shirley, *Mike Mazurki*, Otto Kruger, Miles Mander, Douglas Walton, Ralf Harolde, Don Douglas, Esther Howard

MARLOWE (Dick Powell): '"Okay Marlowe," I said to myself. "You're a tough guy. You've been sapped twice, choked, beaten silly with a gun, shot in the arm until you're crazy as a couple of waltzing mice. Now let's see you do something really tough – like putting your pants on."'
MARLOWE: 'I caught the blackjack right behind my ear. A black pool opened up at my feet. I dived in. It had no bottom.'
MARLOWE: 'My fingers looked like a bunch of bananas.'

'A nasty, draggled bit of dirty work, accurately observed.' – *C. A. Lejeune*

Farewell My Lovely **
US   1975   95m   Technicolor
Avco Embassy/Elliott Kastner/ITC (George Pappas, Jerry Bruckheimer)
V*

A pretty sharp remake of the above, with the plot slightly rewritten but tightened, and an excellent performance from a rather over-age star.

w David Zelag Goodman   *d* Dick Richards   *ph* John A. Alonzo   *m* David Shire   *pd* Dean Tavoularis

Robert Mitchum, Charlotte Rampling, John Ireland, Sylvia Miles, Anthony Zerbe, Jack O'Halloran, Kate Murtagh

'A moody, bluesy, boozy recreation of Marlowe's tacky, neon-flashed Los Angeles of the early forties.' – *Judith Crist*

'A delicious remake with a nice, smoky 1940s atmosphere.' – *Michael Billington, Illustrated London News*

AAN: Sylvia Miles

A Farewell to Arms **
US   1932   78m   bw
(Paramount) Frank Borzage
V*, L

In World War I, a wounded American ambulance driver falls in love with his nurse.

Now very dated but important in its time, this romantic drama was one of the more successful Hemingway adaptations to be filmed.

w Benjamin Glazer, Oliver H. P. Garrett   *novel* Ernest Hemingway   *d* Frank Borzage   *ph* Charles Lang   *m* W. Franke Harling   *ad* Hans Dreier, Roland Anderson

Gary Cooper, *Helen Hayes*, Adolphe Menjou, Mary Philips, Jack La Rue, Blanche Frederici, Henry Armetta

'Too much sentiment and not enough strength.' – *Mordaunt Hall, New York Times*

'Borzage has invested the war scenes with a strange, brooding expressionist quality . . . indeed, the overall visual style is most impressive.' – *NFT, 1974*

'Corking femme film fare at any angle or price.' – *Variety*

† Remade as *Force of Arms* (qv) and see below.

AA: Charles Lang

AAN: best picture; art direction

A Farewell to Arms
US   1957   150m   DeLuxe   Cinemascope
TCF/David O. Selznick
V, V*, L

Elaborate ill-fated remake which tried to make an adventure epic out of a low-key war drama.

Its failure caused David O. Selznick to produce no more films.

w Ben Hecht   *d* Charles Vidor   *ph* Piero Portalupi, Oswald Morris   *m* Mario Nascimbene   *pd* Alfred Junge

Rock Hudson, Jennifer Jones, Vittorio de Sica, Alberto Sordi, Kurt Kasznar, Mercedes McCambridge, Oscar Homolka, Elaine Stritch, Victor Francen

AAN: Vittorio de Sica

Farewell to the King
US   1988   117m   Technicolor
Vestron/Orion/Film Plan Financing Number 1 (Albert S. Ruddy, Andre Morgan)
V, V*, L, S

In the Second World War, an American ruler of a tribe of headhunters in Borneo helps the British attack the Japanese.

Ineffectual Kiplingesque adventure with a confusing narrative.

wd John Milius   *novel* L'Adieu au Roi by Pierre Schoendoerffer   *ph* Dean Semler   *m* Basil Poledouris   *ed* Anne V. Coates, Timothy O'Meara

Nick Nolte, Nigel Havers, Frank McRae, James Fox, Marilyn Tokuda, Marius Weyers, William Wise, John Benett Perry, Elan Oberon, Gerry Lopez, Choy Chang Wing

'Thematically speaking, the admixture of the *Heart of Darkness* and *The Man Who Would Be King* promises a heady brew, but what emerges, alas, is a cup of weak tea.' – *Tom Milne, MFB*

Fargo
US   1964   99m   Technicolor
Universal/Pennebaker (Al Ruddy)
aka: *Wild Seed*

A teenage girl hitch-hikes from New York to Los Angeles and is befriended by a young tramp.

Peripatetic romance in the modern manner, with no conclusions drawn and not much entertainment value beyond the scenery.

w Les Pine   *d* Brian G. Hutton   *ph* Conrad Hall   *m* Richard Markowitz

Michael Parks, Celia Kaye, Ross Elliott, Woodrow Chambliss, Eva Novak

The Farmer Takes a Wife *
US   1935   91m   bw
TCF (Winfield Sheehan)
V*

By the Erie Canal in the 1820s, a wandering girl finds security with a farmer.

Pleasantly 'different' romantic drama, quite ably executed and introducing Henry Fonda to the screen.

w Edwin Burke   *play* Frank B. Elser, Marc Connelly   *novel* Rome Haul by Walter D. Edmonds   *d* Victor Fleming   *ph* John Seitz   *m* Arthur Lange

Janet Gaynor, Henry Fonda, Charles Bickford, Slim Summerville, Andy Devine, Roger Imhof, Jane Withers, Margaret Hamilton, Sig Rumann, John Qualen

'It will pull in the Gaynor fans, and do much to return her to favour.' – *Variety*

The Farmer Takes a Wife *
US   1953   81m   Technicolor
TCF (Frank P. Rosenberg)
V*

Musical remake with an agreeably stylized look, hampered by a slowish script and dull cast.

w Walter Bulloch, Sally Benson, Joseph Fields   *d* Henry Levin   *ph* Arthur E. Arling   *m* Cyril Mockridge   *m/y* Harold Arlen, Dorothy Fields   *ad* Lyle Wheeler, Addison Hehr

Betty Grable, Dale Robertson, Thelma Ritter, Eddie Foy Jnr, John Carroll

The Farmer's Daughter
US   1940   60m   bw
Paramount (William C. Thomas)

A stage struck country girl tries to horn in on a Broadway musical rehearsing nearby.

Feeble comedy for the sticks.

w Lewis R. Foster, Delmer Daves   *d* James Hogan   *ph* Leo Tover

Martha Raye, Charles Ruggles, Richard Denning, Gertrude Michael, William Frawley, William Demarest, Jack Norton

'Now she's raising eyebrows instead of corn!'

The Farmer's Daughter **
US   1947   97m   bw
RKO (Dore Schary)
V*

The Swedish maid of a congressman becomes a political force.

Well-made Cinderella story with a touch of asperity and top notch production values and cast.

w Allen Rivkin, Laura Kerr   *d* H. C. Potter   *ph* Milton Krasner   *m* Leigh Harline

Loretta Young, Joseph Cotten, Ethel Barrymore, Charles Bickford, Rose Hobart, Rhys Williams, Harry Davenport, Tom Powers

'Patricians, politicians, even peasants are portrayed with unusual perception and wit.' – *James Agee*

AA: Loretta Young

AAN: Charles Bickford

The Farmer's Wife
GB   1928   67m approx   bw   silent
BIP (John Maxwell)
V*

A farmer seeks a wife and after three disappointments settles for his housekeeper.

A simple and not very interesting silent screen version of a stage success which depended largely on dialogue.

wd Alfred Hitchcock   *play* Eden Philpotts   *ph* Jack Cox   *ed* Alfred Booth

Jameson Thomas, Gordon Harker, Lilian Hall-Davis, Maud Gill

'Some pleasant photography and a subtle impression of rural life rescued the picture from complete failure.' – *George Perry, 1966*

The Farmer's Wife
GB   1940   82m   bw
Associated British

Talkie remake of the above, a perfectly adequate photographed play.

w Norman Lee, Leslie Arliss, J. E. Hunter   *play* Eden Philpotts   *d* Norman Lee, Leslie Arliss

Basil Sydney, Wilfrid Lawson, Nora Swinburne, Patricia Roc, Michael Wilding

Farrebique **
France   1947   85m   bw
L'Ecran Français/Les Films Etienne Lallier

Problems of a peasant family in central France.

Superbly-filmed semi-documentary, acted by a real family.

wd Georges Rouquier   *ph* André Dantan   *m* Henri Sauguet

'Definitely a film for posterity.' – *MFB*

Fashions of 1934 *
US   1934   78m   bw
Warner (Henry Blanke)

A confidence trickster conquers the French fashion world.

Slight musical comedy with a couple of splendid Berkeley numbers.

w F. Hugh Herbert, Carl Brickson   *d* William Dieterle   *ch* Busby Berkeley   *ph* William Rees   *m/y* Sammy Fain, Irving Kahal   *ad* Jack Okey

William Powell, Bette Davis, Verree Teasdale, Frank McHugh, Reginald Owen, Hugh Herbert, Henry O'Neill

Fast and Furious: see *Fast Company* (1938)

Fast and Loose
US   1930   70m   bw
Paramount

A spoiled rich girl falls in love with a car mechanic.

Tiresome melodrama, dully scripted.

w Doris Anderson, Jack Kirkland, Preston Sturges   *play* The Best People by Avery Hopwood, David Gray   *d* Fred Newmeyer   *ph* William Steiner

Miriam Hopkins, Carole Lombard, Frank Morgan, Charles Starrett, Henry Wadsworth, David Hutcheson, Ilka Chase

Fast and Loose *
US   1939   80m   bw
MGM (Frederick Stephani)

Married detectives and rare book experts solve the mystery of a missing Shakespeare manuscript.

Pleasing comedy mystery in the wake of *The Thin Man*.

w Harry Kurnitz   *d* Edwin L. Marin   *ph* George Folsey

Robert Montgomery, Rosalind Russell, Ralph Morgan, Reginald Owen, Etienne Girardot, Alan Dinehart, Joan Marsh, Sidney Blackmer

Fast and Loose
GB   1954   75m   bw
Group Films/Rank

By a series of accidents, a married man has to spend a night at an inn with an old flame.

Spiritless and miscast remake of *A Cuckoo in the Nest*; all talents below form.

w A. R. Rawlinson, Ben Travers   *play* Ben Travers   *d* Gordon Parry

Brian Reece, Stanley Holloway, Kay Kendall, Reginald Beckwith, Charles Victor, June Thorburn

Fast Company *
US   1938   75m   bw
MGM

A couple in the rare book business are implicated in the murder of a rival.

First of three whodunnits featuring Joel and Garda Page, whose style was not at all dissimilar from that of Nick and Nora Charles in the *Thin Man* series. A polished time-passer.

w Marco Page (Harry Kurnitz)   *d* Edward Buzzell

Melvyn Douglas, Florence Rice, Clare Dodd, Louis Calhern, George Zucco

† The follow-ups had different stars as the pair of sleuths. *Fast and Loose* (qv) featured Robert Montgomery and Rosalind Russell; Sidney Blackmer, Ralph Morgan and Reginald Owen supported. *Fast and Furious*, also released in 1939, starred Franchot Tone and Ann Sothern, with Ruth Hussey, Lee Bowman and Allyn Joslyn.

Fast Company
US   1953   67m   bw
MGM

A girl inherits a racing stable and discovers a little chicanery.

Ho-hum support wasting a good cast.

w William Roberts   *d* John Sturges

Howard Keel, Nina Foch, Polly Bergen, Marjorie Main

The Fast Lady **
GB   1962   95m   Eastmancolor
Rank/Group Films (Teddy Baird)

A bashful suitor buys an old Bentley, becomes a roadhog, passes his test, captures some crooks and gets the girl.

Spirited if aimless farcical comedy which crams in all the jokes about cars anyone can think of.

w Jack Davies, Henry Blyth   d Ken Annakin   ph Reg Wyer   m Norrie Paramor

Stanley Baxter, James Robertson Justice, Leslie Phillips, Julie Christie, Dick Emery

Fast Talking
Australia   1984   95m   Eastmancolor
Ross Matthews/Oldata

The youngest son of a shiftless and semi-criminal Sydney family gets into trouble and finally drives off on his motor cycle to an uncertain future.

Depressingly downbeat comedy-drama about characters of whom any audience must quickly tire.
wd Ken Cameron

Rod Zuanic, Toni Allaylis, Chris Truswell, Gail Sweeny, Steve Bisley

Fast Times at Ridgemont High
US   1982   92m   Technicolor
Universal/Refugee (C. O. Erickson)
V*, L

Students at a California high school aim to lose their virginity.

The tiresome content of this teen comedy is slightly offset by bright handling. But only slightly.

w Cameron Crowe   book Cameron Crowe   d Amy Heckerling   ph Matthew F. Leonetti   m/songs Rob Fahey

Sean Penn, Jennifer Jason Leigh, Judge Reinhold, Phoebe Cates, Brian Backus, Robert Romanus, Ray Walston

Fast-Walking
US   1981   116m   Metrocolor
Lorimar
V*

Racial disharmony and violence prevail at a midwest state prison.

Curious black comedy dealing entirely with unpleasant types.

wd James B. Harris   novel The Rap by Ernest Brawley

James Woods, Tim McIntire, Kay Lenz, Robert Hooks, M. Emmet Walsh

'What do people think of when they write a script these days? Don't they have any sense of human values or human decency?' – Arthur Knight

Fast Workers
US   1933   68m   bw
MGM

Rivalries erupt among skyscraper workers.

Standard action programmer with which MGM terminated John Gilbert's contract after an illustrious rise and dramatic fall.

w Laurence Stallings   d Tod Browning

John Gilbert, Mae Clarke, Willard Mack, Robert Armstrong

The Fastest Guitar Alive
US   1968   87m   Metrocolor
Sam Katzman/MGM
V*

Inept Confederate soldiers are sent on a spy mission.

Ham-handed farce with music, unappealing on either count.

w Robert E. Kent   d Michael Moore

Roy Orbison, Sammy Jackson, Maggie Pierce, Joan Freeman, Lyle Bettger

The Fastest Gun Alive *
US   1956   89m   bw
MGM (Clarence Greene)

A mild-mannered Western storekeeper proves to be the son of a famous gunfighter, and is put to the test.

Flimsily contrived mini-Western helped by good performances.

w Frank D. Gilroy, Russel Rouse   d Russel Rouse   ph George Folsey   m André Previn

Glenn Ford, Broderick Crawford, Jeanne Crain, Russ Tamblyn, Allyn Joslyn, Leif Erickson, John Dehner

Fat City **
US   1972   96m   Eastmancolor
Columbia/Rastar (Ray Stark)
V*

In a small Californian town, a has-been boxer tries to get back to the top, but loses his self respect and becomes a hobo.

Vivid but over-casual exploration of failure, with more interest in the characters than the sport.

w Leonard Gardner   novel Leonard Gardner   d John Huston   ph Conrad Hall   md Marvin Hamlisch   pd Richard Sylbert

Stacy Keach, Jeff Bridges, Susan Tyrrell, Candy Clark

'Huston has confronted a piece of material and a milieu perfectly suited to his insights and talents. The result is his best film in years and one of the best he has ever done: a lean, compassionate, detailed, raucous, sad, strong look at some losers and survivors on the side streets of small-city Middle America.' – Charles Champlin

AAN: Susan Tyrrell

Fat Man and Little Boy: see Shadow Makers

The Fat Man
US   1950   77m   bw
U-I (Aubrey Schenck)

The murder of a dentist leads to the circus.

Dense murder mystery featuring a gourmet 17-stone detective; understandably, no series resulted.

w Harry Essex, Leonard Lee   d William Castle   ph Irving Glassberg   m Bernard Green

J. Scott Smart, Rock Hudson, Julie London, Clinton Sundberg, Jerome Cowan, Jayne Meadows

Fatal Attraction **
US   1987   119m   Technicolor
Paramount/Jaffe-Lansing (Stanley Jaffe, Sherry Lansing)
V (W), V*, L, CD, S

A married man finds it difficult to shed his nearly homicidal light of love.

A kind of rehash of Play Misty for Me, and a sensational success at the box-office: the timing must have been right, even if the details aren't always persuasive.

w James Dearden   d Adrian Lyne   ph Howard Atherton   m Maurice Jarre   pd Mel Bourne   ed Michael Kahn, Peter E. Berger

Michael Douglas, Glenn Close, Anne Archer, Fred Gwynne

'A predictable dog's dinner of thriller clichés – will appeal strongly to those who think women should be kept on a short leash.' – Time Out

'This shrewd film also touches on something deeper than men's fear of feminism: their fear of women, their fear of women's emotions, of women's hanging on to them. Fatal Attraction doesn't treat the dreaded

passionate woman as a theme; she's merely a monster in a monster flick.' – Pauline Kael

† A video release of the movie included an alternative ending to the film.

AAN: Glenn Close; Anne Archer; Adrian Lyne; best picture; James Dearden; film editing

Fatal Beauty
US   1987   104m   colour
Enterprise/MGM/CST Communications (Leonard Kroll)
V, V*, L

A female cop tracks down a drug dealer.

A violent formula film with nothing new to offer.

w Hilary Henkin, Dean Riesner   story Bill Svanoe   d Tom Holland   ph David M. Walsh   m Harold Faltermeyer   pd James William Newport   ed Don Zimmerman

Whoopi Goldberg, Sam Elliot, Ruben Blades, Harris Yulin, John P. Ryan, Jennifer Warren, Brad Dourif, Mike Jolly, Charles Hallahan, David Harris

The Fatal Glass of Beer *
US   1933   18m   bw
Paramount/Sennett

The prodigal son returns to a snowbound cabin in the Yukon.

Absurd star comedy with appeal to addicts only: most of the humour consists of repeats of one line, ' 'Taint a fit night out for man nor beast.'

w W. C. Fields   d Clyde Bruckman

W. C. Fields, Rosemary Theby, Rychard Cramer, George Chandler

Fatal Lady
US   1936   77m   bw
Walter Wanger/Paramount

An opera singer has trouble with men and becomes involved with murder.

Lively melodrama with songs, very much of its period.

w Jules Furthman   d Edward Ludwig

Mary Ellis, Walter Pidgeon, John Halliday, Ruth Donnelly, Alan Mowbray, Edgar Kennedy

The Fatal Night *
GB   1948   49m   bw
Anglofilm (Mario Zampi)

A joke haunting has unfortunate consequences.

A small, cheaply-made film which really thrilled.

w Gerald Butler   story The Gentleman from America by Michael Arlen   d Mario Zampi   ph Cedric Williams   m Stanley Black

Lester Ferguson, Jean Short, Leslie Armstrong, Brenda Hogan, Patrick MacNee

Fate Is the Hunter
US   1964   106m   bw   Cinemascope
TCF/Arcola (Aaron Rosenberg)

An airline executive investigates the cause of a fatal crash in which his friend the pilot was a victim.

Watchable how-did-it-happen melodrama marred by pretentious dialogue.

w Harold Medford   novel Ernest K. Gann   d Ralph Nelson   ph Milton Krasner   m Jerry Goldsmith

Glenn Ford, Rod Taylor, Nehemiah Persoff, Nancy Kwan, Suzanne Pleshette, Jane Russell

AAN: Milton Krasner

Father and Master: see Padre Padrone

Father and Son
Hong Kong   1981   96m   Eastmancolor
BFI/Feng Huang Motion Picture Company (Wong Kai-Chuen)
original title: Fuzi Qing

Returning home for his father's funeral, a film-maker reflects on his childhood.

A gently observant semi-autobiographical domestic drama, but lacking individuality.

w Chan Chiu, Cheung Kin-Ting, Lee Bik-Wah d Fong Yuk-Ping (Allen Fong) ph Patrick Wong m Violet Lam ad Wong Huk-Sun, Wong Kwai-Ping

Shek Lui, Lee Yu-Tin, Cheng Yu-Or, Chan Sun, Cheung Kwok-Ming, Kung Yee, Yan Sin-Mei, Yung Wai-Man, Chung Hung, Lo Tai-Wai

Father Brown ***
GB 1954 91m bw
Columbia/Facet (Vivian A. Cox)
V*
US title: The Detective

A Catholic clergyman retrieves a priceless church cross from master thief Flambeau.

Delightfully eccentric comedy based closely on the famous character, with a sympathetic if rather wandering script, pointed direction and some delicious characterizations. A thoroughly civilized entertainment.

w Thelma Schnee story The Blue Cross by G. K. Chesterton d Robert Hamer ph Harry Waxman m Georges Auric

Alec Guinness, Joan Greenwood, Peter Finch, Sidney James, Cecil Parker, Bernard Lee, Ernest Thesiger, Marne Maitland

'It has wit, elegance, and kindly humour – all somewhat rare commodities in the 1954 cinema.' – Star

Father Brown Detective *
US 1934 67m bw
Paramount

Flambeau, the thief, decides to steal Father Brown's blue cross.

Early attempt at the same story used in the 1954 Father Brown with Alec Guinness; quite pleasantly interesting.

story The Blue Cross by G. K. Chesterton d Edward Sedgwick

Walter Connolly, Paul Lukas, Gertrude Michael, Robert Loraine, Halliwell Hobbes, Una O'Connor, E. E. Clive

'Clean, but not strong enough to stand solo.' – Variety

Father Came Too
GB 1963 93m Eastmancolor
Rank/Independent Artists

Honeymooners agree to live with her overbearing actor-manager father.

Less funny sequel to The Fast Lady, with comic household disasters striking every couple of minutes. Easy-going, and predictably amusing in spots.

w Jack Davies, Henry Blyth d Peter Graham Scott ph Reg Wyer m Norrie Paramor

Stanley Baxter, James Robertson Justice, Leslie Phillips, Sally Smith, Ronnie Barker, Timothy Bateson, Philip Locke

Father Goose *
US 1964 116m Technicolor
U-I/Granox (Robert Arthur)
V, V*

During World War II a South Seas wanderer is compelled by the Australian navy to act as sky observer on a small island, where he finds himself in charge of six refugee schoolchildren and their schoolmistress.

Eager-to-please but unsatisfactory film which wanders between farce, adventure and sex comedy, taking too long about all of them.

w Peter Stone, Frank Tarloff d Ralph Nelson ph Charles Lang Jnr m Cy Coleman

Cary Grant, Leslie Caron, Trevor Howard

Cary Grant: 'Let me tell you I am not a father figure. I am not a brother figure or an uncle figure or a cousin figure. In fact, the only figure I intend being is a total stranger figure.'

'Reasoning would indicate a made-to-order Christmas package for the family trade. However, the more sophisticated may be bored and exasperated after some of the initial brightness wears off.' – Cue

'Cary Grant wrings what there is to be wrung from the role, but never quite enough to conceal the fact that Father Goose is a waste of his talent and the audience's time.' – Arthur Knight

AA: Peter Stone, Frank Tarloff

Father Is a Bachelor
US 1950 85m bw
Columbia (S. Sylvan Simon)

A young tramp cares for a family of orphaned children.

Boringly sentimental semi-Western.

w Aleen Leslie, James Edward Grant d Norman Foster, Abby Berlin ph Burnett Guffey m Arthur Morton

William Holden, Coleen Gray, Charles Winninger, Stuart Erwin, Sig Rumann

'Saccharine, paper thin. At least one spectator at the Palace yesterday couldn't take it – a tot of about four, wearing a cowboy suit, who aimed a toy pistol at the screen and popped off the cast one by one.' – New York Times

Father Is a Prince: see Big Hearted Herbert

'The bride gets the thrills! Father gets the bills!'
Father of the Bride **
US 1950 93m bw
MGM (Pandro S. Berman)
V, V*, L

A dismayed but happy father surveys the cost and chaos of his daughter's marriage.

Fragmentary but mainly delightful suburban comedy which finds Hollywood in its best light vein and benefits from a strong central performance.

w Frances Goodrich, Albert Hackett novel Edward Streeter d Vincente Minnelli ph John Alton m Adolph Deutsch

Spencer Tracy, Joan Bennett, Elizabeth Taylor, Don Taylor, Billie Burke, Moroni Olsen, Leo G. Carroll, Taylor Holmes, Melville Cooper

'The idealization of a safe sheltered existence, the good life according to MGM: 24 carat complacency.' – New Yorker, 1980

† Jack Benny badly wanted the role but was thought unsuitable.

AAN: best picture; Frances Goodrich, Albert Hackett; Spencer Tracy

'Love is wonderful. Until it happens to your only daughter.'
Father of the Bride
US 1991 105m Technicolor
Touchstone/Touchwood Pacific Partners I (Nancy Myers, Carol Baum, Howard Rosenman)
V, V*, L, S

A father is upset by his daughter's announcement that she is engaged – and even more horrified by the arrangements for an expensive wedding.

Lacklustre remake with flat or exaggerated performances, few jokes and a great deal of sentimentality.

w Frances Goodrich, Albert Hackett, Nancy Myers, Charles Shyer novel Edward Streeter d Charles

Shyer ph John Lindley m Alan Silvestri pd Sandy Veneziano ed Richard Marks

Steve Martin, Diane Keaton, Kimberley Williams, Martin Short, Kieran Culkin, George Newbern, B. D. Wong, Peter Michael Goetz

'Little more than a mildly entertaining diversion.' – Empire

Father Takes a Wife *
US 1941 80m bw
RKO (Lee S. Marcus)

A famous actress marries a shipping magnate and runs into resentment from her children.

Disappointing comedy with a script too flat for the stars to make interesting.

w Dorothy and Herbert Fields d Jack Hively ph Robert de Grasse m Roy Webb

Gloria Swanson, Adolphe Menjou, Desi Arnaz, John Howard, Helen Broderick, Florence Rice, Neil Hamilton

Father Was a Fullback
US 1949 84m bw
TCF (Fred Kohlmar)

The coach of a college football team has domestic problems.

Thin star comedy, strictly double bill.

w Aleen Leslie, Casey Robinson, Richard Sale, Mary Loos play Clifford Goldsmith d John M. Stahl ph Lloyd Ahern m Cyril Mockridge

Fred MacMurray, Maureen O'Hara, Betty Lynn, Natalie Wood, Rudy Vallee, Jim Backus

Father's Doing Fine
GB 1952 83m Technicolor
Marble Arch/ABP

An impoverished lady has trouble with her daughters, one of whom is pregnant.

Agreeable madcap farce from a long-running stage success (so why did they change the title?).

w Anne Burnaby play Little Lambs Eat Ivy by Noel Langley d Henry Cass

Heather Thatcher, Richard Attenborough, Susan Stephen, Noel Purcell, George Thorpe

Father's Little Dividend
US 1951 81m bw
MGM (Pandro S. Berman)

Sequel to Father of the Bride, in which the newlyweds have a baby.

A very flat follow-up, palatable enough at the time but quite unmemorable.

w Frances Goodrich, Albert Hackett d Vincente Minnelli ph John Alton m Albert Sendrey

Spencer Tracy, Joan Bennett, Elizabeth Taylor, Don Taylor, Billie Burke, Moroni Olsen, Frank Faylen, Marietta Canty, Russ Tamblyn

'The world's most uncovered undercover agent!'
Fathom
GB 1967 99m DeLuxe Franscope
TCF (John Kohn)

Adventures of a glamorous sky-diving spy.

Watchable romp with nothing memorable about it.

w Lorenzo Semple Jnr novel Larry Forrester d Leslie Martinson ph Douglas Slocombe, Ken Vos m Johnny Dankworth

Raquel Welch, Tony Franciosa, Clive Revill, Ronald Fraser, Greta Chi, Richard Briers, Tom Adams

'Belongs not in the category of High Camp but in that of Good Wholesome Fun.' – MFB

Le Fatiche di Ercole: see Hercules

Fatso
US   1980   93m   DeLuxe
TCF/Brooksfilms

A fat man fails to make much headway at slimming, and gives up.

Unappealing mixture of sentiment, satire, shouting and crude humour.

wd Anne Bancroft

Dom DeLuise, Anne Bancroft, Ron Carey, Candice Azzara

'As bumbling and sluggish as its title might suggest, a lamentable affair which ricochets uncontrollably between attempts at hilarity and pathos.' – *Variety*

Fatto di Sarigne fra due vomini per causa di una vedora – si sospettano moventi politici: see *Blood Feud*

Faust **
Germany   1926   100m approx   bw   silent
UFA
V

A superbly stylish version of the legend about a man who sells his soul to the devil.

The best of many silent versions; see also *All That Money Can Buy*.

w Hans Kyser   *d* F. W. Murnau   *ph* Carl Hoffman

Emil Jannings, Gosta Ekman, Camilla Horn, Yvette Guilbert, William Dieterle

Faustrecht der Freiheit: see *Fox*

Les Favoris de la Lune: see *Favourites of the Moon*

'A romantic comedy beyond normal experience.'
The Favour, the Watch & the Very Big Fish
France/GB   1991   87m   colour
Rank/Sovereign/Ariane/Fildebroc/Umbrella (Michelle de Broca)
V, V*

A religious photographer, who gets an ex-criminal to pose as Christ for him, falls in love with an actress who dubs pornographic films.

Flaccid farce in which most of the cast give the impression that they would rather be somewhere else.

wd Ben Lewin   *story* Rue Saint-Sulpice by Marcel Ayme   *ph* Bernard Zitzermann   *m* Vladimir Cosma   *pd* Carlos Conti   *ed* John Grover

Bob Hoskins, Jeff Goldblum, Natasha Richardson, Michel Blanc, Jacques Villeret, Jean-Pierre Cassel, Angela Pleasance

'Mildy intriguing title, stultifyingly dull film.' – *Empire*

Favourites of the Moon *
France   1984   102m   Eastmancolor
Philippe Dussart/FR3
original title: *Les Favoris de la Lune*

Characters in Paris find that their paths cross as they pursue their obsessions.

Buñuel-like surrealism without Buñuel's intensity of vision results in a film which sometimes pleases but eventually becomes tiresome.

w Otar Iosseliani, Gerard Brach   *d* Otar Iosseliani

Katia Rupe, Hans Peter Cloos, Alix de Montaigu, François Michel

Fear
US   1946   68m   bw
Monogram

A student kills his professor, and a detective taunts him to the point of confession.

Cheeky second feature version of *Crime and Punishment*, with a twist ending. Not too bad in its way.

---

w Alfred Zeisler, Dennis Cooper   *d* Alfred Zeisler   *ph* Jackson Rose

Warren William, Peter Cookson, Anne Gwynne, Nestor Paiva

'Your First Impulse. Your Last Sensation.'
Fear
US   1989   95m   CFI colour
First Independent/Richard Kobritz-Rockne S. O'Bannon
V, V*

A psychic detective discovers that the killer she is hunting is also a powerful psychic.

Mindless thriller that offers nothing new.

wd Rockne S. O'Bannon   *ph* Robert Stevens   *m* Henry Mancini   *pd* Joseph Nemec III   *ed* Kent Beyda

Ally Sheedy, Pruitt Taylor Vince, Lauren Hutton, Michael O'Keefe, Stan Shaw, Dinah Merrill, John Agar

'Treads an increasingly uninspiring road to nowhere.' – *MFB*

The Fear: see *City of The Living Dead*

Fear City
US   1985   93m   colour
Zupnik-Curtis Enterprises (Bruce Cohn Curtis)
V, V*, L

A psychopathic killer terrorizes strippers working in the Times Square area of New York.

Sleazy, violent, low-life thriller, of minimal interest despite an interesting cast.

w Nicholas St John   *d* Abel Ferrara   *ph* James Lemmo   *m* Dick Halligan   *ed* Jack Holmes, Anthony Redman

Tom Berenger, Billy Dee Williams, Jack Scalia, Melanie Griffith, Rossano Brazzi, Rae Dawn Chong, Joe Santos

Abel Ferrara said that the film was 'a big-budget movie that got caught up in the politics of the financing. Sometimes in these situations it's in the best interest of everyone that the film doesn't come out, if you know what I mean.'

Fear Eats the Soul *
West Germany   1974   92m   colour
Tango Film (Christian Hohoff)
V
original title: *Angst essen Seele auf*

A Moroccan immigrant in Munich comes up against social and racial prejudice when he marries a sixty-year-old charwoman.

Unexceptionable moral tale which can hardly have been necessary in view of the infrequency of such cases.

wd Rainer Werner Fassbinder   *ph* Jürgen Jürgesed   Thea Eymèsz

Brigitti Mira, El Hedi Ben Salem, Barbara Valentin, Irm Hermann, Rainer Werner Fassbinder

Fear in the Night **
US   1947   72m   bw
Paramount (William H. Pine, William C. Thomas)
V*

A man suffering from a strange nightmare discovers he has been hypnotized into committing a murder.

Intriguing small-scale puzzler later remade to less effect as *Nightmare* (qv). Adequate performances and handling, but the plot's the thing.

wd Maxwell Shane   *ph* Jack Greenhalgh   *m* Rudy Schrager

Paul Kelly, De Forrest Kelley, Ann Doran, Kay Scott

Fear in the Night *
GB   1972   85m   Technicolor
MGM-EMI/Hammer (Jimmy Sangster)
V*

A girl recovering from a nervous breakdown is deluded into committing a murder.

Yet another variant on *Les Diaboliques*, ingeniously worked out with good touches of detail to produce an air of general competence.

w Jimmy Sangster, Michael Syson   *d* Jimmy Sangster   *ph* Arthur Grant   *m* John McCabe   *ad* Don Picton   *ed* Peter Weatherley

Peter Cushing, Judy Geeson, Joan Collins, Ralph Bates

Fear Is the Key *
GB   1972   108m   Technicolor   Panavision
EMI/KLK (Alan Ladd Jnr, Elliott Kastner)
V, S

A man conceives an elaborate plot to track down those responsible for killing his wife and family in a plane crash.

Reasonably absorbing, surprise-plotted thriller.

w Robert Carrington   *novel* Alistair MacLean   *d* Michael Tuchner   *ph* Alex Thomson   *m* Roy Budd

Suzy Kendall, Barry Newman, John Vernon, Dolph Sweet, Ben Kingsley, Ray McAnally

Fear o' God: see *The Mountain Eagle*

Fear of a Black Hat *
US   1993   86m   colour
Oakwood (Darin Scott)

A mock documentary on the progress of a tough rap group, NWH (Niggas With Hats), and its members, Ice Cold, Taste Taste and Tone Def.

Witty demolition of rap's pretensions, in the style of *This Is Spinal Tap*, that hits the target more often than the similar, rival movie *CB4*.

wd Rusty Cundieff   *ph* John Demps   *m* Larry Robinson   *pd* Stuart Blatt   *ed* Karen Horn

Larry B. Scott, Christopher Lawrence, Rusty Cundieff, Kasi Lemmons, Howie Gold, Barry Heins, Eric Laneuville

'A midnight movie. But wild irreverent humor and exuberant music may also help this spoof find a larger, hip public.' – *Variety*

Fear Strikes Out
US   1957   100m   bw   Vistavision
Paramount/Alan Pakula
V*, L

A father wants his son to become a professional baseball player, and the son in consequence suffers a nervous breakdown.

Rather flat biopic of Jim Piersall; well-intentioned and careful in its psychological insights, but too often just plain dull.

w Ted Berkman, Raphael Blau   *d* Robert Mulligan   *ph* Haskell Boggs   *m* Elmer Bernstein

Anthony Perkins, Karl Malden, Norma Moore, Perry Wilson

Fearless Fagan
US   1952   78m   bw
MGM

A circus clown is enlisted and takes his pet lion along.

Rather silly comedy padded out with sentimentality.

w Charles Lederer   *d* Stanley Donen

Carleton Carpenter, Janet Leigh, Keenan Wynn, Richard Anderson, Ellen Corby

The Fearless Vampire Killers, or Pardon Me, Your Teeth Are in My Neck *

US 1967 124m Metrocolor Panavision
MGM/Cadre Films/Filmways (Gene Gutowski)
V*, L
aka: Dance of the Vampires

A professor and his assistant stake a Transylvanian vampire.

Heavy, slow spoof of *Dracula*, most of which shows that sense of humour is very personal; a few effective moments hardly compensate for the prevailing stodge.

w Gerard Brach, Roman Polanski d Roman Polanski ph Douglas Slocombe m Krzystof Komeda pd Wilfrid Shingleton

Jack MacGowran, Roman Polanski, Alfie Bass, Sharon Tate, *Ferdy Mayne*, Iain Quarrier, Terry Downes

'An engaging oddity . . . long stretches might have been lifted intact from any Hammer horror.' – *Tom Milne*

† A credit ran: Fangs by Dr Ludwig von Krankheit.

Fearless Young Boxer: see The Avenging Boxer

The Fearmakers

US 1958 85m bw
Pacemaker (Martin H. Lancer)

A brainwashed Korean War veteran returns to Washington and finds that his PR firm has been taken over by communist racketeers.

Unusual but cheaply made anti-Red propaganda, too talkative to be very entertaining.

w Elliot West, Chris Appley novel Darwin Teilhet d Jacques Tourneur ph Sam Leavitt m Irving Gertz

Dana Andrews, Dick Foran, Mel Tormé

A Feather in Her Hat

US 1935 72m bw
Columbia

A London widow with delusions of grandeur tells her son that his real mother was a famous actress.

Outmoded mother-love drama, interestingly cast.

w Lawrence Hazard story I. A. R. Wylie d Alfred Santell ph Joseph Walker

Pauline Lord, Basil Rathbone, Louis Hayward, Billie Burke, Wendy Barrie, J. M. Kerrigan, Victor Varconi, Nydia Westman, Thurston Hall

'Too British for general appeal, though well acted.' – *Variety*

Feather Your Nest *

GB 1937 86m bw
ATP (Basil Dean)

A gramophone record technician substitutes his own voice for a star and becomes world famous.

The star is in farcical vein than usual; this is the one in which he sings 'Leaning on a Lamp-post'.

w Austin Melford, Robert Edmunds, Anthony Kimmins story Ivar and Sheila Campbell d William Beaudine ph Ronald Neame m Leslie Sarony, Leslie Holmes and others ad R. Holmers Paul ed Ernest Aldridge

George Formby, Polly Ward, Enid Stamp Taylor, Val Rosing, Davy Burnaby

Federal Agents vs Underworld Inc

US 1949 bw serial: 12 eps
Republic

An archaeologist disappears after discovering the Golden Hands of Kurigal.

Routine thick ear for serial addicts.

d Fred Brannon

Kirk Alyn, Rosemary La Planche, Roy Barcroft, Carol Forman

Federal Operator 99

US 1945 bw serial: 12 eps
Republic

An underworld leader escapes from a prison train and plans to steal Princess Cornelia's jewels.

Nothing surprising, but the pot keeps boiling.

d Spencer Bennet, Wallace Grissell

Marten Lamont, Helen Talbot, George J. Lewis, Lorna Gray

Fedora *

West Germany/France 1978 110m Eastmancolor
Geria/SFP (Billy Wilder)
V*, L, S

An ageing star who seems miraculously to have kept her beauty comes out of retirement.

Sunset Boulevard revisited, with a less bitter approach and less effectiveness; but any civilized film is welcome in the late seventies.

w I. A. L. Diamond, Billy Wilder story Crowned Heads by Tom Tryon d Billy Wilder ph Gerry Fisher m Miklos Rozsa

William Holden, Marthe Keller, Hildegarde Knef, José Ferrer, Mario Adorf, Henry Fonda, Michael York

'Rife with Wilderean gallows humour and a sumptuous sense of decay in never-never land.' – *Sight and Sound*

Feds

US 1988 82m colour
Warner (Ilona Herzberg, Len Blum)
V, V*, L, S

Two women – one academic, the other athletic – meet masculine prejudice when they train to become FBI agents.

A mild, unarresting comedy, too predictable and unmemorable to cause more than a very occasional smile.

w Len Blum, Dan Goldberg d Dan Goldberg ph Timothy Suhrstedt m Randy Edelman pd Randy Ser ed Donn Cambern

Rebecca DeMornay, Mary Gross, Ken Marshall, Fred Dalton Thompson, Larry Cedar, Raymond Singer, James Luisi, Rex Ryon, Tony Longo

'A thrill a minute! A laugh a second! A comedy cyclone!'

Feet First **

US 1930 88m bw
Harold Lloyd
V*

A shoe salesman gets entangled with crooks and has a narrow escape when hanging from the side of a building.

Very funny early talkie comedy, probably the comedian's last wholly satisfactory film.

w Lex Neal, Felix Adler, Paul Gerard Smith d Clyde Bruckman ph Walter Ludin, Henry Kohler

Harold Lloyd, Robert McWade, Barbara Kent

'That Lloyd was a bit pressed for laughs may be guessed from the fact that he is again dangling from the front of a skyscraper.' – *Variety*

Feiying Gaiwak: see Operation Condor

Felix the Cat: The Movie

US 1989 82m colour
Transatlantic/Felix The Cat Creations/Productions Inc (Don Oriolo, Christian Schneider, Janos Schenk)
V

Felix rescues a princess from another dimension.

Laboured attempt to update the classic cartoon figure.

w Don Oriolo, Pete Brown d Tibor Hernadi ph Laszlo Radocsay pd Tibor A. Belay, Tibor Hernadi

voices of Chris Phillips, Maureen O'Connnell, Peter Neuman, Alice Playton, Susan Montanaro, Don Oriolo, Christian Schneider, David Kolin

'More likely to bury the ingratiating Felix beyond revival than to stimulate fresh legions of fans.' – *Philip Strick, MFB*

Fellini Satyricon: see Satyricon

Fellini's Casanova: see Casanova

Fellow Traveller **

GB/US 1989 97m colour
BFI/BBC Films/HBO (Michael Wearing)
V, V*

A blacklisted American scriptwriter ponders the suicide of his closest friend, a Hollywood star, and the role played in it by their Marxist psychotherapist.

Intelligent political thriller, despite some melodramatic moments.

w Michael Eaton d Philip Savile ph John Kenway m Colin Towns pd Gavin Davies ed Greg Miller

Ron Silver, Imogen Stubbs, Hart Bochner, Daniel J. Travanti, Katherine Borowitz, Julian Fellowes, Richard Wilson, Doreen Mantle, David O'Hara

'Thought-provoking, entertaining and visually pleasurable . . . one of the most original and impressive British films of the 80s' – *Julian Petley, MFB*

'One of the most politically sophisticated, visually imaginative British pictures of the past decade.' – *Philip French, Observer*

Female *

US 1933 60m bw
Warner
V*, L

A high-powered lady president of a motor car company has a secret night life.

Slick star vehicle reminiscent of *Peg's Paper* but absorbing while on screen.

w Gene Markey, Kathryn Scola story Donald Henderson Clarke d Michael Curtiz, William Dieterle

Ruth Chatterton, George Brent, Johnny Mack Brown, Ruth Donnelly, Douglass Dumbrille, Lois Wilson

'The story is worthy neither of this actress nor of the high-grade production.' – *Variety*

The Female Animal

US 1957 82m bw Cinemascope
U-I (Albert Zugsmith)

A beach bum becomes the lover of a film star, then falls in love with her daughter.

Dreary and humourless melodrama notable only for the comeback appearance of one of the screen's legendary glamour queens.

w Robert Hill d Harry Keller ph Russell Metty m Hans Salter

Hedy Lamarr, Jan Sterling, Jane Powell, George Nader, James Gleason

'Once she was too hungry for love to be afraid – but now – it was too late!'

The Female on the Beach

US 1955 97m bw
U-I (Albert Zugsmith)

A wealthy widow visits her late husband's beach house and falls for the gigolo next door, who later seems intent on murdering her.

Absurd and jaded melodrama, a rehash of *Love from a Stranger*, enlivened by some hilarious love-hate dialogue.

w Robert Hill, Richard Alan Simmons d Joseph Pevney ph Charles Lang m Joseph Gershenson

Joan Crawford, Jeff Chandler, Jan Sterling, Cecil Kellaway, Natalie Schafer

Joan Crawford to Jeff Chandler: 'I would have you if you were hung with diamonds, upside down!'

The Feminine Touch

US   1941   97m   bw
MGM (Joseph L. Mankiewicz)

A professor gets into woman trouble when he writes a book about jealousy.

Matrimonial comedy rather less interesting than its credits suggest.

w George Oppenheimer, Edmund L. Hartmann, Ogden Nash   d W. S. Van Dyke   m Franz Waxman

Rosalind Russell, Don Ameche, Kay Francis, Van Heflin, Donald Meek, Henry Daniell, Sidney Blackmer

The Feminine Touch

GB   1956   91m   Technicolor
Ealing (Jack Rix)
US title: The Gentle Touch

Five young student nurses arrive at St Augustine's Hospital.

Portmanteau soap opera of no absorbing interest.

w Ian McCormick   novel A Lamp is Heavy by Sheila Mackay Russell   d Pat Jackson   ph Paul Beeson   m Clifton Parker

George Baker, Belinda Lee, Delphi Lawrence, Adrienne Corri, Henryetta Edwards, Barbara Archer, Diana Wynyard, Mandy Miller

La Femme de l'Aviateur: see The Aviator's Wife

La Femme de Mon Pote: see My Best Friend's Girl

La Femme de Nulle Part *

France   1922   70m approx   bw   silent

aka: The Woman from Nowhere

A woman who feels that her life has been ruined through love returns home and persuades a young girl not to do the same.

A minor atmospheric piece of some power, comparable with Partie de Campagne and cinematically very interesting.

wd Louis Delluc   ph Lucas Gibory   ad F. Jourdain

Eve Francis, Roger Karl, Gine Avril

Une Femme Disparait *

France   1944   104m   bw
Mayer-Burstyn
aka: A Woman Disappeared; Portrait of a Woman

When a body is found, four people believe it to be that of a loved one who has disappeared; their stories are told in flashback.

Virtually a short story portmanteau to accommodate five performances by its star.

wd Jacques Feyder   novel Jacques Viot

Françoise Rosay, Henri Guisol, Jean Nohain, Claire Gérard

Une Femme Douce **

France   1969   88m   Eastmancolor
Academy/Parc/Marianne (Mag Bodard)
aka: A Gentle Creature

A husband attempts to explain to the maid the events of his married life which led to his wife's suicide.

A cool and subtle exploration of the gap between a person's understanding of life and reality.

wd Robert Bresson   story A Gentle Soul by Fyodor Dostoevsky   ph Chislain Cloquet   m Jean Wiener   ad Pierre Charbonnier   ed Raymond Lamy

Dominique Sanda, Guy Frangin, Jane Lobre

La Femme du Boulanger **

France   1938   110m   bw
Marcel Pagnol
aka: The Baker's Wife

Villagers put a stop to the infidelity of the baker's wife because her husband no longer has the heart to make good bread.

Best-known of Pagnol's rustic fables, this rather obvious and long-drawn-out joke is important because international critics hailed it as a work of art (which it isn't) and because it fixed an image of the naughty bucolic French.

wd Marcel Pagnol   novel Jean Le Bleu by Jean Giono   ph Georges Benoit, R. Lendruz, N. Daries   m Vincent Scotto   ed Suzanne de Troeye

Raimu, Ginette Leclerc, Charles Moulin, Charpin, Maximilienne

'It is a long film with a small subject, but the treatment is so authentic that it seems over far too soon, and the acting is superb.' – Graham Greene

Une Femme Est une Femme: see A Woman Is a Woman

'A secret life. A deadly passion.'
Femme Fatale

US   1991   96m   FotoKem colour
Republic/Gibraltar Entertainment (Andrew Lane, Nancy Rae Stone)
V*

After his wife leaves him at the start of their honeymoon, a husband discovers that she has more than one identity.

Anonymous thriller that stumbles to a lame conclusion.

w Michael Ferris, John D. Brancato   d André Guttfreund   ph Joey Forsyte   m Parmer Fuller   pd Pam Warner   ed Richard Candib

Colin Firth, Liza Zane, Billy Kane, Scott Wilson, Lisa Blount, Suzanne Snyder

La Femme Infidèle **

France/Italy   1968   98m   Eastmancolor
La Boëtie/Cinegay (André Génovès)
aka: The Unfaithful Wife

A middle-aged insurance broker, set in his ways, murders his wife's lover; when she suspects the truth, they are drawn closer together.

Almost a Buñuel-like black comedy, spare and quiet, with immaculate performances.

wd Claude Chabrol   ph Jean Rabier   m Pierre Jansen   ed Jacques Gaillard

Stéphane Audran, Michel Bouquet, Maurice Ronet

'On any level, this bizarre murder framed by whiskies emerges as Chabrol's most flawless work to date.' – Jan Dawson, MFB

Une Femme Mariée: see A Married Woman

La Femme Nikita: see Nikita

Une Femme ou Deux

France   1985   97m   colour
AAA/Hachette/Philippe Dussart/FR3/DD
aka: One Woman or Two

An advertising woman uses an archaeologist as basis for a new campaign, then falls in love with him.

Lighthearted, not to say light-headed, romantic comedy with silly asides: Doris Day and Rock Hudson, where are you?

w Daniel Vigne, Elisabeth Rappeneau   d Daniel Vigne

Gérard Depardieu, Sigourney Weaver, Michel Aumont, Dr Ruth Westheimer, Zabou, Jean-Pierre Bisson

'Unsatisfactory on all levels.' – Quentin Crisp

La Femme-flic *

France   1979   100m   Eastmancolor
Sara/Antenne 2 (Alain Sarde)
aka: The Lady Cop

A female police inspector who becomes a political embarrassment is transferred to the provinces, where she is subjected to high-level interference when she uncovers a child pornography racket.

Tough and cynical political thriller which comes to the conclusion that honesty is far from the best policy.

w Claude Veillot   story Claude Veillot, Yves Boisset   d Yves Boisset   ph Jacques Loiseleux   m Philippe Sarde   pd Maurice Sergent, Jimmy Vansteenkiste   ed Albert Jurgenson, Nadine Muse, Martine Fleury

Miou-Miou, Jean-Marc Thibault, Leny Escudero, Jean-Pierre Kalfon, François Simon, Alex Lacast, Niels Arestrup, Henri Garçin, Philippe Caubere

Femmes de Paris *

France   1954   85m approx   Agfacolor
Optimax-Lux (Edgar Bacquet)
aka: Ah! Les Belles Bacchantes

A touring revue is almost run out of town for indecency.

A rather crude but quite valuable record of Dhéry's stage revue, which convulsed London in the fifties.

w Robert Dhéry   d Jean Loubignac   ph René Colas   m Gérard Calvi

Robert Dhéry, Colette Brosset, Louis de Funès, Raymond Bussières, the Bluebell Girls

The Fencing Master ***

Spain   1992   88m   colour
Mayfair/Majestic/Origen/Altube Filmeak/ICAA (Antonio Cardenal, Pedro Olea)
V
original title: El Maestro de Esgrima

In Madrid in the 1860s, at a time of extreme political upheaval, a fencing master becomes involved with a beautiful woman and finds himself caught up in a situation he does not understand.

Elegant, erotically charged story of love and loyalty and of different codes of behaviour, told with subtlety, dash and elegance.

w Antonio Larreta, Francisco Prada, Arturo Pérez Reverte, Pedro Olea   novel Arturo Pérez Reverte   d Pedro Olea   ph Alfredo Mayo   m José Nieto   ad Luis Valles   ed José Salcedo

Omero Antonutti, Assumpta Serna, Joaquim de Almeida, José Luis Lopez Vázquez, Alberto Closas, Miguel Rellán

'Stellar performances . . . a distinguished and literate script, fine plot development and accomplished direction and lensing.' – Variety

'A deeply romantic Spanish thriller with two performances at its centre that do more than catch the eye. At times they catch the breath.' – Derek Malcolm, Guardian

La Ferme du Pendu *

France   1946   90m   bw
Corona
aka: Hanged Man's Farm

The lecherous son of a farming family brings tragedy to the lives of himself and his brothers and sister.

Cold Comfort Farm with a vengeance, appropriately played: arrant melodrama, but watchable.

w André-Paul Antoine   d Jean Dréville   ph André Thomas

Alfred Adam, Charles Vanel, Arlette Merry

FernGully: The Last Rainforest

Australia   1992   76m   DeLuxe
TCF/FAI/Youngheart (Wayne Young, Peter Faiman)
V, V*, L, S

A fairy, a fruit-bat and a miniaturized lumberjack save the rainforest from the evil spirit who would destroy it.

Moderately enjoyable animated feature with an ecological moral: be kind to trees.

w Jim Cox   story Diana Young   d Bill Kroyer
m Alan Silvestri   ad Susan Kroyer   ed Gillian Hutshing

voices of: Tim Curry, Samantha Mathis, Christian Slater, Jonathan Ward, Robin Williams, Grace Zabriskie, Geoffrey Blake, Robert Pastorelli, Cheech Marin, Tommy Chong, Tone-Loc

'As lectures on the environment go, this one is less likely to induce adult narcolepsy than most.' – Ian Johnstone, Sunday Times

'Pic will amply entertain tykes while feeding them an environmental lesson, and features enough amusing jokes and clever songs to make it palatable for adults.' – Variety

Ferris Bueller's Day Off *

US   1986   103m   Metrocolor   Panavision
Paramount/John Hughes, Tom Jacobson
V, V*, L

A teenage student enjoys an aimless day playing truant.

Aimless it is, and juvenile, but people have found pleasing things in it.

wd John Hughes   ph Tak Fujimoto   m Ira Newborn   pd John W. Corso   ed Paul Hirsch

Matthew Broderick, Alan Ruck, Mia Sara, Jeffrey Jones, Cindy Pickett, Jennifer Grey

Ferry to Hong Kong

GB   1958   113m   Eastmancolor   Cinemascope
Rank (George Maynard)
V*

An Austrian layabout can land at neither of the Hong Kong ferry's ports of call, but shows his true worth when a typhoon strikes.

Silly storyline and rampant bad acting ruin the Rank Organization's first attempt at an international epic.

w Vernon Harris, Lewis Gilbert   d Lewis Gilbert
ph Otto Heller   m Kenneth V. Jones

Curt Jurgens, Sylvia Syms, Orson Welles, Jeremy Spenser, Noel Purcell

La Fête à Henriette *

France   1952   113m   bw
Regina-Filmsonor
aka: Holiday for Henrietta

Two screenwriters disagree whether or not to give their hero and heroine a happy ending.

A rather heavy-handed romantic joke which does have its moments and was later – fatally – Americanized as Paris When It Sizzles.

w Julien Duvivier, Henri Jeanson   d Julien Duvivier   ph Roger Hubert   m Georges Auric

Dany Robin, Michel Auclair, Hildegarde Neff, Michel Roux, Saturnin Fabre, Julien Carette

Le Feu Follet ***

France   1963   107m   bw
Lux/Nouvelles Éditions (Jean Pieuchot)
V, V*
aka: Will-O'-The-Wisp; A Time to Live and a Time to Die; US title: The Fire Within

A recovering alcoholic, urged to be positive, visits his old friends and, horrified by the compromises they have made, kills himself.

A compassionate and fascinating film, shot in an understated way; though, with its downbeat ending, it is not easy viewing.

wd Louis Malle   novel Pierre Drieu La Rochelle
ph Ghislain Cloquet   m Erik Satie   ad Bernard Evein   ed Suzanne Baron, Monique Nana

Maurice Ronet, Léna Skerla, Jeanne Moreau, Yvonne Clech, Hubert Deschamps, Alexandra Stewart

'An epitaph for all the beautiful young men, the semi-intellectual "gilded mediocrities" who skim through their days to their doom unchanged save for a surface tarnish. A latter-day parable of a Dorian Gray, superbly acted and beautifully filmed.' – Judith Crist

The novel was based on the life and death of Jacques Rigaut, a surrealist poet who killed himself in 1929. Its author, Drieu La Rochelle, committed suicide in 1945.

Feudin', Fussin' and A-fightin'

US   1948   78m   bw
Universal-International

A fast-running travelling salesman is kidnapped by a hillbilly town which needs him in its annual sports.

Unpretentious lower-berth comedy for middle America.

w D. D. Beauchamp   d George Sherman

Donald O'Connor, Marjorie Main, Percy Kilbride, Penny Edwards, Joe Besser

A Fever in the Blood

US   1960   117m   bw
Warner (Roy Huggins)

Candidates for governor sharpen their campaigns on a murder trial.

Interestingly-cast, flabbily-written melodrama.

w Roy Huggins, Harry Kleiner   novel William Pearson   d Vincent Sherman   ph J. Peverell Marley   m Ernest Gold

Efrem Zimbalist Jnr, Angie Dickinson, Don Ameche, Herbert Marshall, Jack Kelly, Ray Danton, Jesse White, Rhodes Reason, Robert Colbert

Fever Pitch

US   1985   96m   Metrocolor
MGM-UA/Freddie Fields
V*

A compulsive Vegas gambler gets in deep with loan sharks.

You might think there was more to the plot than that, but no; and the whole thing is just glum.

wd Richard Brooks   ph William Fraker   m Thomas Dolby   pd Raymond G. Storey

Ryan O'Neal, Catherine Hicks, Giancarlo Giannini, Bridgette Andersen, Chad Everett, John Saxon

'The cards are stacked against it.' – Variety

A Few Good Men **

US   1992   138m   Technicolor
Columbia TriStar/Castle Rock (David Brown, Rob Reiner, Andrew Scheinman)
V, V (W), V*, L, S

A lawyer known for plea bargaining decides to defend two marines accused of killing a fellow marine, a case that depends on discrediting their martinet of a commanding officer.

Slick, engrossing courtroom drama, in which audiences can cheer the hero and hiss the villain, even though it seems little more than a more portentous re-run of The Caine Mutiny.

w Aaron Sorkin   play Aaron Sorkin   d Rob Reiner   ph Robert Richardson   m Marc Shaiman   pd J. Michael Riva   ed Robert Leighton

Tom Cruise, Jack Nicholson, Demi Moore, Kevin Bacon, Kiefer Sutherland, Kevin Pollak, James Marshall, J. T. Walsh, Christopher Guest, J. A. Preston

'A big-time, mainstream Hollywood movie par excellence.' – Variety

'A slick, entertaining, flashily-acted courtroom drama replete with all the standard ingredients.' – Philip French, Observer

AAN: Best picture; Jack Nicholson; Robert Leighton

ffoulkes: see North Sea Hijack

Fiddler on the Roof **

US   1971   180m   Technicolor   Panavision 70
UA/Mirisch (Norman Jewison)
V, V*, L, S

In a pre-revolutionary Russian village, Tevye the Jewish milkman survives family and political problems and when the pogroms begin cheerfully emigrates to America.

Self-conscious, grittily realistic adaptation of the stage musical, with slow and heavy patches in its grossly overlong celebration of a vanished way of life. The big moments still come off well though the songs tend to be thrown away and the photography is unnecessarily murky.

w Joseph Stein   play Joseph Stein   story Tevye and his Daughters by Sholom Aleichem   d Norman Jewison   ph Oswald Morris   md John Williams   pd Robert Boyle   m/ly Jerry Bock, Sheldon Harnick

Topol, Norma Crane, Leonard Frey, Molly Picon

'Jewison hasn't so much directed a film as prepared a product for world consumption.' – Stanley Kauffmann

AA: Oswald Morris; John Williams

AAN: best picture; Norman Jewison (as director); Topol; Leonard Frey

Fiddlers Three *

GB   1944   87m   bw
Ealing (Robert Hamer)

Sailors struck by lightning on Salisbury Plain are transported back to ancient Rome.

Sequel to Sailors Three; despite a harsh and unattractive look, every conceivable joke about old Romans is deftly mined and the good humour flows free.

w Diana Morgan, Angus Macphail   d Harry Watt
ph Wilkie Cooper   m Spike Hughes

Tommy Trinder, Sonnie Hale, Frances Day, Francis L. Sullivan, Ernest Milton, Diana Decker, Elizabeth Welch, Mary Clare

'It Owns Him. It Possesses Him. It Could Even Destroy Him.'
The Field *

GB   1990   110m   colour
Granada (Noel Pearson)
V, V*, L

A farmer is prepared to kill in order to keep a rented field which his family has farmed for generations and which an American wishes to buy.

Melodramatic domestic drama trying for a tragic dimension it cannot quite encompass.

wd Jim Sheridan   play John B. Keane   ph Jack Conroy   pd Frank Conway   ad Frank Hallinan Flood   ed J. Patrick Duffner

Richard Harris, John Hurt, Tom Berenger, Sean Bean, Frances Tomelty, Brenda Fricker

'Superb acting and austere visual beauty are offset by a somewhat overheated screenplay.' – Variety

Field of Dreams ***

US   1989   106m   DeLuxe
Guild/Universal/Carolco (Lawrence Gordon, Charles Gordon)
V, V*, L, S

A farmer builds a baseball pitch to summon the ghosts of past players.

A gentle fantasy with the power to charm.

wd Phil Alden Robinson *book* Shoeless Joe by W. P. Kinsella *ph* John Lindley, Ricky Bravo *m* James Horner *pd* Dennis Gassner *ed* Ian Crafford

Kevin Costner, Amy Madigan, James Earl Jones, Timothy Busfield, Ray Liotta, Burt Lancaster, Gaby Hoffmann, Frank Whaley, Dwier Brown

AAN: best film; best adapted screenplay; best original score

'Don't be ashamed to scream! Everyone in the theatre will be screaming with you!'

The Fiend Who Walked the West
US   1958   101m   bw   Cinemascope
TCF (Herbert B. Swope Jnr)
V*

A sadistic killer released from prison tracks down the associates of a cellmate and terrorizes the district.

Western remake of *Kiss of Death*, with babyface Robert Evans in the Widmark role. Violent and dull.

w Harry Brown, Philip Yordan *d* Gordon Douglas *ph* Joe MacDonald *m* Leon Klatzkin

Hugh O'Brian, Dolores Michaels, Robert Evans, Linda Cristal, Stephen McNally, Edward Andrews

The Fiend without a Face
GB   1957   75m   bw
Producers' Associates (John Croydon)
V*, L

A scientist working on materialized thought produces monsters from his own id.

Tepid shocker with well-organized mobile brains.

w H. J. Leder *d* Arthur Crabtree *ph* Lionel Banes *m* Buxton Orr *sp* Ruppel and Nordhoff

Kynaston Reeves, Terry Kilburn, Marshall Thompson

The Fiendish Plot of Dr Fu Manchu
US   1980   108m   Technicolor
Warner/Orion/Playboy (Hugh Hefner)
V*, L

The 'yellow peril' returns to the western world to mastermind diamond thefts.

Feeble spoof with a history of production troubles; clearly the only thing in anybody's mind was to get it over with.

w Jim Moloney, Rudy Dochtermann *d* Piers Haggard *ph* Jean Tournier *m* Marc Wilkinson *pd* Alexander Trauner

Peter Sellers, Helen Mirren, David Tomlinson, Sid Caesar, Simon Williams, Steve Franken, Stratford Johns, John Le Mesurier, Clive Dunn

The Fiends: see Les Diaboliques

The Fiercest Heart
US   1961   90m   DeLuxe   Cinemascope
TCF (George Sherman)

A British army deserter joins a Boer trek into South Africa.

Pioneer 'Western', poorly done but with novelty value.

w Edmund H. North *novel* Stuart Cloete *d* George Sherman *ph* Ellis Carter *m* Irving Gertz

Stuart Whitman, Juliet Prowse, Raymond Massey, Ken Scott, Geraldine Fitzgerald, Rafer Johnson

Fiesta
US   1947   102m   Technicolor
MGM (Jack Cummings)

A young Mexican wants to be a musician though his father insists he should be a bullfighter.

An extremely boring idea for a musical which at best is a tedious time-passer.

w George Bruce, Lester Cole *d* Richard Thorpe *ph* Sidney Wagner, Charles Rosner, William Cline *md* John Green *m* Aaron Copland

Esther Williams, Ricardo Montalban, Cyd Charisse, Mary Astor, John Carroll, Akim Tamiroff, Hugo Haas

AAN: John Green

Fièvre *
France   1921   50m approx   bw   silent
Alhambre

A brawl in a Marseilles bar ends in murder.

A dramatic sketch, filmed with remarkable detail and artistry.

wd Louis Delluc *ph* A. Gibory *ad* Bécan

Eve Francis, Edmond Van Daele, Gaston Modot

Fifi la Plume
France   1964   80m   bw
Les Films Montsouris (Albert Lamorisse)

A burglar becomes a circus bird-man, learns to fly, and is everywhere mistaken for an angel.

A likeable fantasy idea which doesn't quite come off, alternating uneasily between slapstick and sentiment.

wd Albert Lamorisse *ph* Pierre Petit *m* Jean-Michel Defaye

Philippe Avron, Mireille Nègre, Henri Lambert, Raoul Delfosse

Fifth Avenue Girl *
US   1939   83m   bw
RKO (Gregory La Cava)
V*, L

An unemployed girl is persuaded by a millionaire to pose as a gold digger and annoy his avaricious family.

Brightish comedy of the Cinderella kind.

w Allan Scott *d* Gregory La Cava *ph* Robert de Grasse

Ginger Rogers, Walter Connolly, Verree Teasdale, Tim Holt, James Ellison, Franklin Pangborn, Kathryn Adams, Louis Calhern

'Substantial comedy drama for top grosses.' – *Variety*

The Fifth Chair: see It's in the Bag

The Fifth Musketeer
Austria   1978   106m   Eastmancolor
Sascha-Wien Film/Ted Richmond
V*
aka: *Behind the Iron Mask*

Louis XIII and his twin brother Philippe vie for the crown of France.

Virtually a remake of *The Man in the Iron Mask*, with patchy style and a few excisable sex scenes added. The 1939 version was better.

w David Ambrose *d* Ken Annakin *ph* Jack Cardiff *m* Riz Ortolani

Beau Bridges, Sylvia Kristel, Ursula Andress, Cornel Wilde (as D'Artagnan), Lloyd Bridges, Alan Hale Jnr, José Ferrer (the ageing musketeers), Rex Harrison (Colbert), Olivia de Havilland (Queen Anne), Ian McShane, Helmut Dantine

55 Days at Peking *
US/Spain   1963   154m   Super Technirama 70
Samuel Bronston
V, V*, L

In 1900 Peking, Boxer fanatics are encouraged by the Empress to take over the city and besiege the international diplomatic quarter; an American major leads the defence.

Spasmodically lively action spectacular weighed down by romantic stretches.

w Philip Yordan, Bernard Gordon *d* Nicholas Ray, Andrew Marton *ph* Jack Hildyard, Manuel Berenguer *m* Dimitri Tiomkin *ad* Venerio Colasanti, John Moore

Charlton Heston, David Niven, Ava Gardner, Flora Robson, Robert Helpmann, Leo Genn, Paul Lukas, John Ireland, Harry Andrews, Elizabeth Sellars, Massimo Serrato, Jacques Sernas, Geoffrey Bayldon

'An open-air western in Chinese.' – *David Niven*

'Pictorially this is a beautiful film, but the characters are conventional siege figures.' – *Sunday Times*

AAN: Dimitri Tiomkin; song 'So Little Time' (*m* Dimitri Tiomkin, *ly* Paul Francis Webster)

Fifty Million Frenchmen
US   1931   68m   Technicolor
Warner

A rich American in Paris tries to prove that he was able to win a blonde without the aid of his bankroll.

Much changed and enfeebled version of a Broadway musical, with the Broadway talent transplanted.

w Al Boasberg, Eddie Welch, Joseph Jackson *d* Lloyd Bacon

Olsen and Johnson, William Gaxton, John Halliday, Helen Broderick, Claudia Dell, Lester Crawford

'Will have to depend mostly on its title for b.o. attraction.' – *Variety*

Fifty Roads to Town *
US   1937   80m   bw
TCF

Mistaken identities abound in a snowbound cabin.

Fairly funny minor comedy.

w George Marion Jnr, William Conselman *d* Norman Taurog

Don Ameche, Ann Sothern, Slim Summerville, Jane Darwell, John Qualen, Douglas Fowley, Stepin Fetchit

'Just about right for summer audiences . . . pleasant light romantic comedy demanding a minimum of concentration.' – *Variety*

52 Pick-up
US   1986   114m   TVC colour
Cannon (Henry T. Weinstein)
V*, L

A businessman rounds on blackmailers who take films of his sex life.

Uninteresting melodrama based on the same novel as *The Ambassador*, released two years earlier by the same company.

w Elmore Leonard, John Steppling *novel* Elmore Leonard *d* John Frankenheimer *ph* Jost Vacano *m* Gary Chang

Roy Scheider, Ann-Margret, Vanity, John Glover, Robert Trebor, Lonny Chapman

'There is no rush of energy to propel the film past its improbability.' – *Variety*

52nd Street
US   1937   83m   bw
Walter Wanger

A strictly-brought-up young woman shocks her family by falling for a singer.

Tame romantic comedy with musical items.

w Grover Jones *d* Harold Young

Kenny Baker, Ella Logan, Ian Hunter, ZaSu Pitts, Leo Carrillo

'It may have been a good idea to make a film about the metamorphosing of 52nd Street into a lane of niteries, but the conception doesn't come through . . . filmgoers are likely to wonder what it's all about, and why.' – *Variety*

Fight for Your Lady *

US 1937 67m bw
RKO

A jilted tenor is helped by a wrestling trainer.

Odd little comedy which contrives to amuse.

w Ernest Pagano, Harry Segall, Harold Kusell
d Ben Stoloff

John Boles, Jack Oakie, Ida Lupino, Margot
Grahame, Erik Rhodes, Billy Gilbert

'This picture is going to entertain whether it sells or
not.' – *Variety*

The Fighter

US 1952 78m bw
GH (Alex Gottlieb)
V*

A Mexican fisherman whose family is murdered by
government troops becomes a prizefighter to earn
money for the rebels.

A rather glum attempt to turn a few ringside clichés.

w Aben Kandel, Herbert Kline story *The Mexican* by
Jack London d Herbert Kline ph James Wong
Howe m Vincente Gomez

Richard Conte, Vanessa Brown, Lee J. Cobb, Frank
Silvera

Fighter Attack

US 1953 80m bw
Allied Artists
V*

Exploits of an American air base in Corsica.

Routine war action efficiently dispensed.

w Simon Wincelberg d Lesley Selander

Sterling Hayden, J. Carrol Naish, Joy Page, Kenneth
Tobey, Anthony Caruso

Fighter Squadron

US 1948 96m Technicolor
Warner (Seton I. Miller)

In World War II, a dedicated flyer risks his friends'
lives.

Routine aerial actioner.

w Seton I. Miller d Raoul Walsh ph Sid Hickox,
Wilfrid M. Cline m Max Steiner

Edmond O'Brien, Robert Stack, John Rodney, Tom
D'Andrea, Henry Hull, Walter Reed, Shepperd
Strudwick, Rock Hudson

'Enough is enough!'

Fighting Back

US 1982 98m Technicolor
Dino de Laurentiis (D. Constantine Conte)
V*
GB title: *Death Vengeance*

After his wife and mother are both injured in crimes
of violence, a delicatessen owner forms a vigilante
group and is backed to some extent by police and
businessmen.

Smartly made but ethically muddled urban shocker.

w Tom Hedley, David Zelag Goodman d Lewis
Teague ph Franco DiGiacomo m Piero Piccioni

Tom Skerritt, Michael Sarrazin, Patti LuPone, Yaphet
Kotto, David Rasche

Fighting Back

Australia 1982 100m Eastmancolor
Samson/Adams-Packer (Sue Milliken, Tom Jeffrey)

A teenager runs riot at home and at school.

Tolerable problem picture with no surprises.

w Tom Jeffrey, Michael Cove book *Tom* by John
Embling d Michael Caulfield

Lewis FitzGerald, Kris McQuade, Caroline Gillmer,
Paul Smith

Fighting Caravans

US 1931 91m bw
Paramount

A covered wagon party faces various dangers.

Slow-moving Western.

w E. E. Paramore Jnr, Keene Thompson, Agnes Leahy
novel Zane Grey d Otto Brower, David Burton
ph Lee Garmes, Henry Gerrard ad Robert Odell
ed William Shea

Gary Cooper, Lily Damita, Ernest Torrence, Fred
Kohler, Tully Marshall, Eugene Pallette

'Very mild western, rating de luxe house attention on
the cast names . . . lacks a punch.' – *Variety*

Fighting Devil Dogs

US 1938 bw serial: 12 eps
Republic

Marine lieutenants in a tropical protectorate fight
organized bandits led by The Lightning, who has
invented an electric thunderbolt.

Excessively juvenile shenanigans for Saturday
morning audiences.

d William Witney, John English

Lee Powell, Herman Brix, Eleanor Stewart, Montagu
Love

Fighting Father Dunne

US 1948 93m bw
RKO (Phil L. Ryan)
V*

A clergyman looks after unfortunate boys.

A slum melodrama which all concerned could have
made with their eyes closed, and probably did.

w Martin Rackin, Frank Davis d Ted Tetzlaff
ph George E. Diskant m Roy Webb

Pat O'Brien, Darryl Hickman, Charles Kemper, Una
O'Connor

The Fighting Guardsman

US 1945 84m bw
Columbia

Under the tyrannical reign of Louis XVI a young
nobleman leads a peasants' revolt.

Stiff swashbuckler in which the actors appear to have
been only recently introduced to their clothes.

w Franz Spencer, Edward Dein d Henry Levin

Willard Parker, Anita Louise, George Macready, John
Loder

The Fighting Kentuckian

US 1949 100m bw
Republic (John Wayne)
V*

In 1810 a farmer combats land-grabbing criminals.

Standard star Western for the family.

wd George Waggner ph Lee Garmes m George
Antheil

John Wayne, Vera Ralston, Oliver Hardy, Philip
Dorn, Marie Windsor, Mae Marsh

Fighting Mad

US 1976 90m DeLuxe
TCF/Santa Fe (Roger Corman)
V*

A rancher and his son are murdered by a local
industrialist who wants their land, and the rancher's
city-bred son takes revenge.

Another vigilante Western in modern dress, very
laborious and violent without being very exciting.

wd Jonathan Demme ph Bill Birch m Bruce
Langhorne

Peter Fonda, Lynn Lowry, John Doucette, Philip
Carey, Scott Glen

'Demme has allowed violence to outweigh ideas to
such a degree that the picture becomes a turnoff, little
more than a blatantly obvious play to the yahoo
mentality.' – *Kevin Thomas, Los Angeles Times*

Fighting Man of the Plains

US 1949 94m Cinecolor
Nat Holt/TCF

A reformed outlaw becomes marshal but is exposed.
Tolerable Western with familiar elements.

w Frank Gruber d Edwin L. Marin

Randolph Scott, Bill Williams, Victor Jory, Jane Nigh,
Douglas Kennedy

Fighting Marines

US 1935 bw serial: 12 eps
Mascot

A criminal called The Tiger Shark has an anti-gravity
gun . . .

Predictable cliffhanging heroics.

d B. Reeves Eason, Joseph Kane

Grant Withers, Ann Rutherford, Adrian Morris,
Robert Warwick

The Fighting O'Flynn

US 1949 94m bw
U-I (Douglas Fairbanks Jnr)

In 18th-century Ireland, a penniless young adventurer
aborts Napoleon's plan for invasion.

Lively minor-league adventure.

w Douglas Fairbanks Jnr, Robert Thoeren
novel Justin Huntly McCarthy d Arthur Pierson
ph Arthur Edeson m Frank Skinner

Douglas Fairbanks Jnr, Helena Carter, Richard
Greene, Patricia Medina, Arthur Shields, J. M.
Kerrigan

'Fairbanks plays the irrepressible O'Flynn with
unflagging energy and tongue in cheek good humour;
the rest of the cast stolidly refuses to see the joke.' –
MFB

The Fighting Pimpernel: see *Pimpernel Smith*

The Fighting Prince of Donegal

GB 1966 104m Technicolor
Walt Disney (Bill Anderson)
V*

Adventures of an Irish rebel in the reign of
Elizabeth I.

Adequate *Boys' Own Paper* romp.

w Robert Westerby novel *Red Hugh, Prince of Donegal*
by Robert T. Reilly d Michael O'Herlihy
ph Arthur Ibbetson m George Bruns

Peter McEnery, Susan Hampshire, Tom Adams,
Gordon Jackson, Andrew Keir, Norman Wooland,
Richard Leech

The Fighting Seabees

US 1944 100m bw
Republic (Albert J. Cohen)
V, V*

During World War II in the Pacific, construction
workers attack the Japanese.

Routine, studio-staged war melodrama, heavily
fleshed out with love interest.

w Borden Chase, Aeneas Mackenzie d Edward
Ludwig ph William Bradford m Walter Scharf,
Roy Webb

John Wayne, Susan Hayward, Dennis O'Keefe,
William Frawley, Duncan Renaldo, Addison
Richards, Leonid Kinskey, Paul Fix

AAN: Walter Scharf, Roy Webb

The Fighting Seventh: see *Little Big Horn*

The Fighting 69th *
US   1940   89m   bw
Warner (Hal B. Wallis)
V*

During World War I in the trenches, a cocky recruit becomes a hero and loses his life in the process.

Recruiting poster stuff, all well enough done but bewildering in its changes of mood.

w Norman Reilly Raine, Fred Niblo Jnr, Dean Franklin   d William Keighley   ph Tony Gaudio   m Adolph Deutsch

James Cagney, Pat O'Brien, George Brent, Jeffrey Lynn, Alan Hale, Frank McHugh, Dennis Morgan, Dick Foran, William Lundigan, Guinn Williams, John Litel, Henry O'Neill

'The picture is better if you can manage to forget the plot and think of it instead as the human, amusing and frequently gripping record of a regiment marching off to war.' – Frank Nugent, New York Times

Fighting Stock
GB   1935   68m   bw
Gaumont/Gainsborough (Michael Balcon)

The family gets together to save a girl from a blackmailer.

Fair example of the Aldwych farces, with the trio in good form.

w Ben Travers   d Tom Walls   ph Phil Tannura

Tom Walls, Ralph Lynn, Robertson Hare, Marie Lohr, Lesley Waring

The Fighting Sullivans: see The Sullivans

Fighting with Kit Carson
US   1933   bw   serial: 12 eps
Mascot

The famous wagon train scout survives an ambush and rounds up The Mystery Riders. Western serial with all the expected elements.

d Armand Schaefer, Colbert Clark

Johnny Mack Brown, Betsy King Ross, Noah Beery, Noah Beery Jnr, Robert Warwick

The Figurehead *
GB   1952   8m   Technicolor

A carved saint is turned into a figurehead and can't respond when a mermaid falls in love with him.

Pleasant whimsy, one of the better jobs from this team of animators.

animation John Halas, Joy Batchelor   poem Crosbie Garstin   pd John Halas, Joy Batchelor

narrator Robert Beatty

Figures in a Landscape
GB   1970   110m   Technicolor   Panavision
Cinecrest (John Kohn)

Two men on the run are pursued by soldiers and helicopters; only one crosses the frontier.

Portentous Pinterish parable, very long-winded and relentlessly boring though good to look at. Everything is symbolic, nothing is specific, not even the country.

w Robert Shaw   novel Barry England   d Joseph Losey   ph Henri Alekan   m Richard Rodney Bennett

Robert Shaw, Malcolm McDowell

The File of the Golden Goose
GB   1969   109m   DeLuxe
UA/Theme/Caralan/Dador (David E. Rose)

An American agent works with Scotland Yard to track down counterfeiters.

Incredibly predictable spy thriller which almost makes an eccentricity out of collecting so many clichés

and so many tourist views of London. Like ten TV episodes cut together.

w John C. Higgins, James B. Gordon   d Sam Wanamaker   ph Ken Hodges   m Harry Robinson

Yul Brynner, Edward Woodward, Charles Gray, John Barrie, Bernard Archard, Ivor Dean, Adrienne Corri, Graham Crowden, Karel Stepanek

'The film plods wearily homewards through an exceptionally uninteresting batch of fights, intrigues and sinister encounters.' – MFB

The File on Thelma Jordon *
US   1949   100m   bw
Paramount (Hal B. Wallis)
aka: Thelma Jordon

A district attorney falls for a murder suspect and has her acquitted by losing the case.

Stylishly made, murkily plotted melodrama and a superior star vehicle of its time.

w Ketti Frings   d Robert Siodmak   ph George Barnes   m Victor Young

Barbara Stanwyck, Wendell Corey, Paul Kelly, Joan Tetzel, Stanley Ridges, Richard Rober, Minor Watson, Barry Kelley

'An Ordinary Woman. An Extraordinary Love. A Daring Adventure.'
La Fille de l'Air **
France   1992   106m   colour
Ciby 2000/TF1 (Farid Chaouche)
V (W), S

A woman learns to fly a helicopter so that she can help her husband to break out of a Paris prison.

A unusual romantic drama, celebrating a wife's fierce and determined love and ignoring her dubious morality and that of her friends; it is nevertheless an extraordinary story, based on fact and told with conviction.

w Florence Quentin, Maroun Bagdadi, Dan Franck   book Nadine Vaujour   d Maroun Bagdadi   ph Thierry Arbogast   m Gabriel Yared   ad Michael Vandestien   ed Luc Barnier

Beatrice Dalle, Thierry Fortineau, Hippolyte Girardot, Roland Bertin, Jean-Claude Dreyfus, Catherine Jacob, Liliane Rovere, Jean-Paul Roussillon, Louis-Laure Mariani

'Delivers on action and suspense.' – Variety

La Fille du Puisatier *
France   1946   131m   bw
Marcel Pagnol
aka: The Well-Digger's Daughter

A stern old well-digger feels bound to send his daughter away when she becomes pregnant.

More country matters from Pagnol, this time with an East Lynne type plot getting in the way of some fine acting. Not much comedy.

wd Marcel Pagnol

Raimu, Fernandel, Charpin, Josette Day

'There is a feeling in France that such films are made for the foreigner and exploit the eccentricities of French rural life rather than the realities.' – MFB

Film
GB   1979   26m   Eastmancolor
BFI

No synopsis is possible for this speechless parable about a poor old man fighting (presumably) against personal obscurity, but its credits make it interesting; it was originally written for Buster Keaton.

w Samuel Beckett   d David Rayner Clark   ph Mike Tomlinson   pd Ariane Gastambide

Max Wall, Patricia Hayes

Film ohne Titel *
West Germany   1947   100m   bw
Camera Film (Erwin Gitt)
aka: Film without Title

Scriptwriters discuss how it is possible to make a comedy film in post-war Germany, and evolve a story with alternative endings.

Elegantly conceived but rather humourlessly executed, this interesting film was one of the first post-war German exports, but failed to start a trend. It has similarities to La Fête à Henriette and Rashomon.

w Helmut Kautner, Ellen Fechner, Rudolf Jugert   d Rudolf Jugert   ph Igor Oberberg   m Bernard Eichhorn

Hans Söhnker, Hildegarde Knef, Irene von Meyendorff, Willy Fritsch

Film without Title: see Film ohne Titel

Filofax: see Taking Care of Business

Fin de Semana para los Muertos: see The Living Dead at the Manchester Morgue

La Fin du Jour **
France   1939   106m   bw
Filmsonor/Regina

Tensions mount in a home for retired actors.

Fascinating opportunity for three fine actors to play off each other.

w Charles Spaak, Julien Duvivier   d Julien Duvivier   ph Christian Matras   m Maurice Jaubert

Michel Simon, Louis Jouvet, Victor Francen, Gabrielle Dorziat, Madeleine Ozeray, Sylvie

La Fin du Monde: see End of the World

'A psychiatrist and two beautiful sisters playing the ultimate mind game. Someone was seduced. Someone was set up. And before it was over . . . someone was dead.'
'Hot-blooded passion. Cold-blooded murder.'
Final Analysis
US   1992   124m   Technicolor
Warner/Roven-Cavallo (Charles Roven, Paul Junger Witt, Anthony Thomas)
V, V*, L, S

A psychiatrist begins a passionate affair with a patient's married sister, with the result that she decides she no longer wants her husband around.

Drearily derivative thriller that fails to engage the attention.

w Wesley Strick   story Robert Berger, Wesley Strick   d Phil Joanou   ph Jordan Cronenweth   m George Fenton   pd Dean Tavoularis   ed Thom Noble

Richard Gere, Kim Basinger, Uma Thurman, Eric Roberts, Paul Guilfoyle, Keith David, Robert Harper

'A crackling good melodrama in which star power and slick surfaces are used to potent advantage.' – Variety

'Nothing rings very true in this slick, vacuous Hitchcockian thriller.' – Newsday

'Any time, any place, at any game – Samson Shillitoe can outfox them all!'
'The power of evil is no longer in the hands of a child!'
The Final Conflict
US   1981   108m   DeLuxe   Panavision
TCF/Mace Neufeld (Harvey Bernhard)
V, V*, L, S

The Antichrist, now head of Thorn Industries, arranges to become US Ambassador in London.

The devil as an adult proves somehow less chilling than the devil as a child, and all the elaborate mayhem seems decidedly old hat in this sequel to The Omen and Damien: Omen II.

w Andrew Birkin d Graham Baker ph Robert Paynter, Phil Meheux m Jerry Goldsmith pd Herbert Westbrook

Sam Neill, Rossano Brazzi, Don Gordon, Lisa Harrow, Mason Adams, Robert Arden

'If Armageddon is as boring as this movie, we'll need a program to tell the players.' – *Roger Ebert*

The Final Countdown *
US 1980 105m TVC colour Panavision
UA/Bryna (Peter Vincent Douglas)
V, V*, L, S

An aircraft carrier on manoeuvres near Hawaii passes through a strange storm and finds itself back at Pearl Harbor.

Quite an enjoyable bit of schoolboy science fiction, but containing no more body than an episode of *Twilight Zone*. The ending, as so often, is impenetrable.

w David Ambrose, Gerry Davis, Thomas Hunter, Peter Powell d Don Taylor ph Victor J. Kemper m John Scott pd Fernando Carrere

Kirk Douglas, Martin Sheen, Katharine Ross, James Farentino, Ron O'Neal, Charles Durning

Final Impact
US 1992 102m Foto-Kem colour
PM (Richard Pepin, Joseph Merhi)
V, V*

A former kick-boxing champion trains his protégé to fight the new champion.

Undistinguished action flick, with the same moves and narrative that have been seen dozens of times before.

w Stephen Smoke d Joseph Merhi, Stephen Smoke m John Gonzalez pd Richard Dearborn ed Geraint Bell, John Weidner

Lorenzo Lamas, Kathleen Kinmont, Jeff Langton, Kathrin Lautner, Mike Toney, Michael Worth

The Final Option: see Who Dares Wins

'The future is cancelled!'
The Final Programme
GB 1973 89m Technicolor
Goodtimes/Gladiole (John Goldstone, Sanford Lieberson)
V*
US title: *The Last Days of Man on Earth*

In the future, when the world is torn by famine and war, a scientist awaits a new messiah.

Intellectualized sci-fi, hard to take as entertainment but very glossy.

wd Robert Fuest novel Michael Moorcock ph Norman Warwick m Paul Beaver, Bernard Krause

Jon Finch, Jenny Runacre, Sterling Hayden, Hugh Griffith

'Clumsy and almost incomprehensible.' – *Sight and Sound*

The Final Test
GB 1953 90m bw
Rank/ACT (R. J. Minney)

A cricketer looks forward to his last game but is out for a duck; he is however cheered by the crowd and comforted by his son.

Flat character study some way below the author's best style, cluttered up with real cricketers and stymied by lack of action.

w Terence Rattigan d Anthony Asquith ph Bill McLeod m Benjamin Frankel

Jack Warner, Robert Morley, George Relph

Finally, Sunday *
France 1983 111m bw
Films du Carrosse/Films A2/Soprofilms (Armand Barbault)
French title: Vivement Dimanche

When his friend is murdered, a small-town estate agent becomes a prime suspect.

Agreeable Hitchcock parody which goes on too long and runs out of steam.

w François Truffaut, Suzanne Schiffman, Jean Aurel novel The Long Saturday Night by Charles Williams d François Truffaut ph Nestor Almendros m Georges Delerue pd Hilton McConnico

Fanny Ardant, Jean-Louis Trintignant, Philippe Laudenbach, Caroline Sihol

'Devoid of interest or distinction, a comedy-thriller that is not funny and most emphatically not thrilling. Ardant and Trintignant fancy themselves as Carole Lombard and Fredric March, an illusion not likely to be shared by anyone else . . .' – *Gilbert Adair, MFB*

Find the Blackmailer
US 1943 55m bw
Warner

A private eye seeks a talking crow which may have evidence in a murder case.

Modest mystery filler.

w Robert E. Kent story G. E. Fleming-Roberts d D. Ross Lederman

Jerome Cowan, Faye Emerson, Gene Lockhart, Marjorie Hoshelle, Robert Kent

Finders Keepers
GB 1966 94m Eastmancolor
UA/Interstate (George H. Brown)

The Americans lose an atomic bomb off the Spanish coast, and it's found by a pop group.

Harmless youth musical without much style. Tunes poor, comedy rather too easy-going.

w Michael Pertwee d Sidney Hayers ph Alan Hume m The Shadows, Norrie Paramor

Cliff Richard, The Shadows, Robert Morley, Peggy Mount, Viviane Ventura, Graham Stark, John Le Mesurier, Robert Hutton

Finders Keepers
US 1984 96m Technicolor
CBS (Sandra Marsh, Terence Marsh)

On a train from California to New York, various factions try to grab stolen money hidden in a coffin.

Yawnworthy comedy-thriller with a zany streak; all the elements have been better done in other movies.

w Ronny Graham, Charles Dennis, Terence Marsh novel The Next to Last Train Ride by Charles Dennis d Richard Lester ph Brian West m Ken Thorne pd Terence Marsh

Michael O'Keefe, Beverly D'Angelo, Lou Gossett Jnr, Pamela Stephenson, Ed Lauter, David Wayne, Brian Dennehy, John Schuck

Fine and Dandy: see West Point Story

A Fine Madness *
US 1966 104m Technicolor
Warner Seven Arts (Jerome Hellman)
V*

A frustrated New York poet has outbursts of violence.

Patchy, interesting, with-it comedy which suffers from too many changes of mood.

w Elliot Baker novel Elliot Baker d Irvin Kershner ph Ted McCord m John Addison

Sean Connery, Jean Seberg, Joanne Woodward, Patrick O'Neal, Colleen Dewhurst, Clive Revill

'Straddling a no man's land somewhere between the nouvelle vague and the crazy comedies of Old Hollywood.' – *Tom Milne*

A Fine Mess
US 1985 88m DeLuxe Panavision
Columbia/BEE/Delphi V (Tony Adams)
V*, L

Two private eyes who accidentally know too much are chased by gangsters.

Not enough plot for a feature, and not enough comedy talent for a comedy, despite the dedication to Laurel and Hardy.

wd Blake Edwards ph Harry Stradling m Henry Mancini pd Rodger Maus ed John F. Burnett

Ted Danson, Howie Mandel, Richard Mulligan, Stuart Margolin, Paul Sorvino

'Word of mouth is unlikely to be favourable . . . mechanically contrived funny business, most of which falls pretty flat.' – *Variety*

'The plot needn't be the thing, but then the gags and setpieces aren't much either.' – *Sight and Sound*

A Fine Pair
Italy 1968 115m Technicolor Panavision
Vides (Franco Cristaldi)
original title: Ruba al Prossimo Tua

A New York detective falls for an Italian girl jewel thief.

Tedious, meandering comedy-thriller with nothing to offer apart from a good robbery sequence.

w Francesco Maselli, Luisa Montagnana, Larry Gelbart, Virgil C. Leone d Francesco Maselli ph Alfio Contino m Ennio Morricone

Rock Hudson, Claudia Cardinale, Tomas Milian, Leon Askin, Ellen Corby

The Finest Hours *
GB 1964 116m Technicolor
Jack Le Vien

The life of Winston Churchill is built up from newsreels plus a few feature film clips and some original location shooting.

Generally excellent documentary, a handy introduction to Churchill's own writing and rather more entertaining than the later *Young Winston*.

w Victor Wolfson d Peter Baylis

AAN: best documentary

Finger of Guilt: see The Intimate Stranger

The Finger Points
US 1931 88m bw
Warner

A crime reporter succumbs to pressures from the underworld.

Humourless and low-geared exposé-style melodrama.

w John Monk Saunders, W. R. Burnett, Robert Lord d John Francis Dillon

Richard Barthelmess, Clark Gable, Fay Wray, Regis Toomey

Fingerprints
US 1931 bw serial: 10 eps
Universal

Secret service agents catch a gang of smugglers.

Oddly-titled serial containing no memorable moments.

d Ray Taylor

Kenneth Harlan, Edna Murphy, Gayne Whitman, Gertrude Astor

Fingers *
US   1977   90m   Technicolor
Gala/Brut (George Barrie)
V*

A would-be concert pianist gets involved with his father's gangster friends, and violence results.

Lively and interesting skirmish with an overworked and essentially downbeat subject.

wd James Toback   *ph* Mike Chapman   *pd* Gene Rudolf   *ed* Robert Lawrence

Harvey Keitel, Tisa Farrow, Jim Brown, Marian Seldes, Danny Aiello

Fingers at the Window
US   1942   90m   bw
MGM (Irving Asher)

A stage magician hypnotizes lunatics into murdering all those who stand between him and an inheritance.

Slow-starting thriller which never achieves top gear.

w Rose Caylor, Lawrence P. Bachmann   *d* Charles Lederer   *ph* Harry Stradling, Charles Lawton   *m* Bronislau Kaper

Basil Rathbone, Lew Ayres, Laraine Day, Walter Kingsford, Miles Mander, Russell Gleason

'The kind of picture actors do when they need work.'
– *Lew Ayres*

Finian's Rainbow *
US   1968   140m   Technicolor   Panavision 70
Warner Seven Arts (Joseph Landon)
V (W), V*, L

A leprechaun tries to retrieve a crock of gold from an old wanderer who has taken it to America.

Musical whimsy-whamsy, a long way after a 1947 Broadway success; in this overlong and overblown screen version the elements and the style do not jell and there is too much sentimental chat, but moments of magic shine through.

w E. Y. Harburg, Fred Saidy   *play* E. Y. Harburg, Fred Saidy   *d* Francis Ford Coppola   *ph* Philip Lathrop   *md* Ray Heindorf   *pd* Hilyard M. Brown   *m/ly* Burton Lane, E. Y. Harburg

Fred Astaire, Petula Clark, Tommy Steele, Don Francks, Keenan Wynn, Barbara Hancock, Al Freeman Jnr

AAN: Ray Heindorf

Finis Terrae *
France   1929   90m approx   bw   silent
Société Générale des Films

A re-enacted account of the lives of fishermen on remote Brittany islands.

A feature documentary which was impressive at the time; very similar to Flaherty's *Man of Aran*.

wd Jean Epstein   *ph* Joseph Barth, Joseph Kottula

Finishing School
US   1934   73m   bw
RKO (Kenneth MacGowan)

A girl at an exclusive school falls for an intern.

Modest pap for the teenage audience.

w Wanda Tuchock, Laird Doyle   *d* George Nicholls Jnr   *ph* J. Roy Hunt   *m* Max Steiner

Frances Dee, Ginger Rogers, Billie Burke, Bruce Cabot, John Halliday, Beulah Bondi, Sara Haden

The Finishing Touch *
US   1928   20m   bw   silent
Hal Roach

Stan and Ollie accidentally destroy the house they are building.

Excellent early star slapstick with predictable but enjoyable gags.

w H. M. Walker   *d* Clyde Bruckman   *ph* George Stevens   *ed* Richard Currier

Laurel and Hardy, Edgar Kennedy, Dorothy Coburn

Finn and Hattie
US   1930   77m   bw
Paramount

A newly rich American takes his family to Paris.

Dodsworth-like comedy, fairly well regarded in its time but now looking very thin.

w Sam Mintz, Joseph L. Mankiewicz   *story* Donald Ogden Stewart   *d* Norman Taurog, Norman McLeod

Leon Errol, ZaSu Pitts, Mitzi Green, Jackie Searl, Regis Toomey, Lilyan Tashman

Finyé: see *The Wind*

Fire and Ice
US   1982   82m   colour
Fox/PSO (Ralph Bakshi, Frank Frazetta)
V*, L

Evil Lord Nekron uses black magic to subdue the good King Jarol.

Fair cartoon feature, using rotoscoping, in the mould of *Conan the Barbarian*.

w Roy Thomas, Gerry Conway   *d* Ralph Bakshi   *m* William Kraft   *ed* E. Davis Marshall

voices of Susan Tyrrell, Maggie Rosewell, William Ostrander, Stephen Mendel, Clare Nono, Alan Koss

'Three of the biggest in one of the best!'
Fire Down Below
GB   1957   116m   Technicolor   Cinemascope
Columbia/Warwick (Irving Allen, Albert Broccoli)
V*

Partners in a Caribbean fishing and smuggling business fall out over a woman.

Overheated melodrama with thin characters, predictable incident and ill-advised casting.

w Irwin Shaw   *novel* Max Catto   *d* Robert Parrish   *ph* Desmond Dickinson   *m* Arthur Benjamin

Rita Hayworth, Robert Mitchum, Jack Lemmon, Herbert Lom, Bonar Colleano, Bernard Lee, Edric Connor, Peter Illing

Fire Festival
Japan   1985   120m   Eastmancolor
Recorded Releasing/Gunro/Seibu/Cine Saison (Kazuo Shimizu)
original title: *Himatsuri*

A nature-loving lumberjack turns killer after observing the effects of pollution on the locality.

Fairly impenetrable to Western audiences, despite its ecological message.

w Kanji Nakagami   *d* Mitsuo Yanagimachi   *ph* Masaki Tamura   *m* Toru Takemitsu   *ad* Takeo Kimura   *ed* Sachiko Yamaji

Kinya Kitaoji, Kiwako Taichi, Ryota Nakamoto, Noribei Miki, Rikiya Yasuoka, Seiji Kurasaki, Maido Kawakami

A Fire Has Been Arranged
GB   1935   70m   bw
Twickenham (Julius Hagen)

Ex-convicts find a building in the field where they buried the loot.

Modest star comedy. Was this the first use of this well-worn plot?

w H. Fowler Mear, Michael Barringer, James Carter   *d* Leslie Hiscott   *ph* Sydney Blythe

Bud Flanagan, Chesney Allen, Alastair Sim, Robb Wilton, Mary Lawson, Harold French, C. Denier Warren

Fire in the Sky
US   1993   109m   DeLuxe   Panavision
Paramount (Joe Wizan, Todd Black)
V, V*, S

A lumberjack is suspected of murder when a friend goes to investigate a flying saucer and disappears.

A close encounter of the boring kind, in which small-town values are made to seem even more alien than tadpoles from outer space.

w Tracy Tormé   *book The Walton Experience* by Travis Walton   *d* Robert Lieberman   *ph* Bill Pope   *m* Mark Isham   *pd* Laurence Bennett   *sp* Industrial Light and Magic   *ed* Steve Mirkovich

D. B. Sweeney, Robert Patrick, Craig Sheffer, Peter Berg, Henry Thomas, Bradley Gregg, Noble Willingham, James Garner

'This unappealing pic is likely to attract only a few curiosity seekers.' – *Variety*

The Fire in the Stone
Australia   1983   100m   colour
South Australian Film Corp (Pamela H. Vanneck)

A teenager foils a murderer, finds some opals and re-unites her parents.

Unexceptional and undemanding entertainment.

w Graeme Koetsveld   *novel* Colin Thiele   *d* Gary Conway   *ph* Ross Berryman   *m* Garry and Anita Hardman   *ad* Derek Mills   *ed* Philip Reid

Alan Cassell, Paul Smith, Ray Meagher, Linda Hartley, Leo Taylor, Andrew Gaston, Theo Pertsinidis

'A world of women seeking male partners to carry on their race!'
Fire Maidens from Outer Space
GB   1956   80m   bw
Criterion Films/Eros
V*

Space explorers find that the thirteenth moon of Jupiter is inhabited solely by sixteen beautiful girls and an aged patriarch.

A strong contender for the title of worst movie ever made, with diaphanously clad English gals striking embarrassed poses against cardboard sets. Must be seen to be believed.

wd Cy Roth

Susan Shaw, Anthony Dexter, Harry Fowler, Sidney Tafler, Owen Berry, Paul Carpenter

'Even the most dedicated connoisseurs of the artless are likely to find this something of a strain on their patience.' – *MFB*

Fire over Africa: see *Malaga*

Fire over England **
GB   1937   92m   bw
London Films/Pendennis (Erich Pommer)
V*, L

Elizabeth I and her navy overcome the Spanish Armada.

Though the film has a faded air and the action climax was always a bath-tub affair, the splendid cast keeps this pageant afloat and interesting.

w Clemence Dane, Sergei Nolbandov   *novel* A. E. W. Mason   *d* William K. Howard   *ph* James Wong Howe   *m* Richard Addinsell   *ad* Lazare Meerson, Frank Wells   *ed* Jack Dennis

Flora Robson, Laurence Olivier, Leslie Banks, Vivien Leigh, Raymond Massey, Tamara Desni, Morton Selten, Lyn Harding, James Mason

'Should bring much artistic acclaim but, outside of the urban class spots, business will be stubborn . . . if it had marquee strength it would stand an excellent chance.' – *Variety*

'Pommer and Howard have done one remarkable thing: they have caught the very spirit of an English public schoolmistress's vision of history.' – *Graham Greene*

'Swashbuckling nonsense, but with a fine spirit.' – *Pauline Kael, 70s*

Fire over Rome

Italy 1968 94m colour
GMC (Giorgio Marzelli)
original title: *L'incendio di Roma*; aka: *Revenge of the Gladiators*

A Roman consul defies Nero's order to massacre Christians.

One of Italy's interminable gladiatorial epics of the period, consisting mainly of a series of sword fights, although Jesus gets a walk-on role right at the end.

d Guido Malatesta ph Aldo Greci ad Oscar D'Amico ed Enzo Alfonsi

Lang Jeffries, Cristina Gaioni, Moira Orfei, Mario Feliciani, Luciano Marin, Evi Maltagliati

Fire Sale *

US 1977 88m DeLuxe
TCF (Marvin Worth)

Misadventures of a frantic, eccentric New York-Jewish family who own a department store.

Frenzied black farce for ethnic audiences.

w Robert Klane novel Robert Klane d Alan Arkin ph Ralph Woolsey m Dave Grusin

Alan Arkin, Rob Reiner, Vincent Gardenia, Anjanette Comer, Kay Medford, Sid Caesar, Alex Rocco

'It moves fast enough to carry the occasional lapses from its own high standards of tastelessness.' – *Jan Dawson, MFB*

The Fire Within: see *Le Feu Follet*

The Fireball

US 1950 84m bw
Thor/TCF

A juvenile delinquent becomes a ruthless roller-skating champion.

Predictable and unattractive star character drama with sporting asides.

w Tay Garnett, Horace McCoy d Tay Garnett

Mickey Rooney, Pat O'Brien, Beverly Tyler, Glenn Corbett

The Firebird

US 1934 75m bw
Warner

An actor with the reputation of a Lothario is murdered.

Well cast but rather disappointing murder mystery.

w Charles Kenyon play Lajos Zilahy d William Dieterle

Verree Teasdale, Ricardo Cortez, Lionel Atwill, C. Aubrey Smith, Anita Louise, Dorothy Tree, Hobart Cavanaugh

'Padding in late reels keeps it from ace rating.' – *Variety*

Firecreek

US 1968 104m Technicolor Panavision
Warner Seven Arts (Philip Leacock)

The people of Firecreek protect themselves from wandering gunmen.

Dour, predictable little Western which does not show its stars at their best.

w Calvin Clements d Vincent McEveety ph William Clothier m Alfred Newman

James Stewart, Henry Fonda, Inger Stevens, Gary Lockwood, Dean Jagger, Ed Begley, Jay C. Flippen, Jack Elam, James Best, Barbara Luna

'This cramped and clumsy western grinds to a standstill in its attempts to give Firecreek symbolic status . . . while the gunmen roister like mad and the townsfolk rhubarb glumly in the background.' – *MFB*

Fired Wife

US 1943 75m bw
Universal

A radio actress has to keep her marriage a secret in order to preserve her job.

Decidedly humdrum comedy.

w Michael Fessier, Ernest Pagano d Charles Lamont

Louise Allbritton, Diana Barrymore, Robert Paige, Walter Abel, George Dolenz, Walter Catlett, Ernest Truex, Rex Ingram, Richard Lane

'It will make 1937 remembered always as the year of the first romantic dramatic musical film!'

The Firefly *

US 1937 131m bw
MGM (Hunt Stromberg)
V*

Adventures of a Spanish lady spy during the Napoleonic war.

Solid production of a romantic operetta; splendid stuff for connoisseurs.

w Frances Goodrich, Albert Hackett, Ogden Nash original book/ly Otto Harbach d Robert Z. Leonard ph Oliver Marsh md Herbert Stothart m Rudolf Friml

Jeanette MacDonald, *Allan Jones* (who sings the 'Donkey Serenade'), Warren William, Billy Gilbert, Henry Daniell, George Zucco, Douglass Dumbrille

'The sepia tint is monotonous . . . the length will seriously militate against popularity.' – *Variety*

'A lavish musical monstrosity.' – *New Yorker, 1978*

'The musical film par excellence . . . resplendent and gorgeous.' – *Evening News*

Firefox

US 1982 136m DeLuxe Panavision
Warner/Malpaso (Clint Eastwood)
V, V*, L

An American pilot is disguised as a businessman and sent to Moscow to steal a new supersonic Soviet fighter.

Dreary melodrama with doleful acting and very little action or suspense.

w Alex Lasker, Wendell Willman novel Craig Thomas d Clint Eastwood ph Bruce Surtees m Maurice Jarre sp John Dykstra

Clint Eastwood, Freddie Jones, David Huffman, Warren Clarke, Ronald Lacey, Kenneth Colley, Nigel Hawthorne

'What is most curious about this farrago is that Eastwood, the actor and the director, should have walked through it all with scarcely a thought for each other.' – *Richard Combs, MFB*

'Despite the tense mission being depicted, there's no suspense, excitement or thrills to be had, and lackadaisical pacing gives the viewer plenty of time to ponder the gaping implausibilities that skilful execution could have rendered irrelevant.' – *Variety*

'Immensely long, unfailingly dull, and not even silly enough to be funny.' – *Sunday Times*

Fireman Save My Child

US 1932 67m bw
Warner/First National

A fireman is more interested in baseball but becomes a hero all the same.

Thin star comedy.

w Ray Enright, Robert Lord, Arthur Caesar d Lloyd Bacon

Joe E. Brown, Evalyn Knapp, Lillian Bond, Guy Kibbee

Fireman Save My Child

US 1954 80m bw
U-I (Howard Christie)

In 1910 San Francisco, incompetent firemen accidentally catch a gang of crooks.

Slapstick farce intended for Abbott and Costello, taken over by a new team which did not catch on, played like the Keystone Kops. Mildly funny during the chases.

w Lee Loeb, John Grant d Leslie Goodwins ph Clifford Stine m Joseph Gershenson

Buddy Hackett, Spike Jones and the City Slickers, Hugh O'Brian, Adèle Jergens

The Firemen's Ball *

Czechoslovakia/Italy 1967 73m Eastmancolor
Barrandov/Carlo Ponti
V, V*
original title: *Hori, Ma Panenko*

In a small provincial town, arrangements for the firemen's annual ball go wrong at every turn.

Vaguely amusing Tati-esque comedy with not quite enough funny moments and a prevailing atmosphere of pessimism.

w Milos Forman, Ivan Passer, Jaroslav Papousek d Milos Forman ph Miroslav Ondricek m Karel Mares

Jan Vostrcil, Josef Kolb, Josef Svet, Frantisek Debelka

'A compendium of superb items.' – *Philip Strick*

AAN: best foreign film

Firepower

GB 1979 104m Technicolor
ITC/Michael Winner
V*

A chemist about to expose contaminated drugs is murdered; his widow persuades the US Justice Department to hire her ex-lover, a gangster, to track down his killers.

Globe-trotting kaleidoscope of the familiar patterns of violence; tolerable for those who haven't been here a hundred times before.

w Gerald Wilson d Michael Winner ph Robert Paynter, Dick Kratina md Jay Cattaway m Gato Barbieri pd John Blezard, Robert Gundlach ed Arnold Crust

Sophia Loren, James Coburn, Anthony Franciosa, O. J. Simpson, Eli Wallach, George Grizzard, Vincent Gardenia, Victor Mature

'The nearest thing yet to film-making by numbers, with identikit characters jet-setting across a travel brochure landscape to an orchestration of gunfire, car smashes and colourful explosions.' – *Clyde Jeavons, MFB*

Fires on the Plain **

Japan 1959 108m bw
Daiei (Masaichi Nagata)
V*
original title: *Nobi*

In the Philippines during World War II, a half-demented Japanese private takes to the hills, becomes a cannibal, and is shot by the Americans when he tries to surrender.

Stomach-turning anti-war epic with fine scenes and performances but dubious intent.

w Natto Wada novel Shohei O-oka d Kon Ichikawa ph Setsuo Kobayashi m Yasushi Akatagawa

Eiji Funakoshi, Osamu Takizawa, Micky Curtis

Fires Were Started **
GB   1943   63m   bw
Crown Film Unit (Ian Dalrymple)
aka: *I Was a Fireman*

One day and night in the life of a National Fire
Service unit during the London blitz.

Thoughtful, slow-moving, poetic documentary
originally intended as a training film but generally
released to boost morale. Not its director's finest
work, but perhaps his most ambitious.

wd Humphrey Jennings   *ph* C. Pennington- Richards
m William Alwyn

'An astonishingly intimate portrait of an isolated and
besieged Britain . . . an . . . unforgettable piece of
human observation, affectionate, touching, and yet
ironic.' – *Georges Sadoul*

'It transforms its observation into a personal, epic
celebration of the courage and dignity of ordinary
people in times of stress.' – *Time Out, 1984*

† The firemen were real firemen, but the scenes were
re-enacted.

Firestarter
US   1984   114m   Technicolor
Universal (Frank Capra Jnr)
V*, L, S

A young girl is capable of starting fires by
pyrokinesis, and the government wants to use her as a
weapon.

Complicated and dislikeable piece of political science
fiction.

w Stanley Mann   *novel* Stephen King   *d* Mark L.
Lester   *ph* Giuseppe Ruzzolini   *m* Tangerine
Dream

Drew Barrymore, George C. Scott, David Keith,
Martin Sheen, Freddie Jones, Heather Locklear, Art
Carney, Louise Fletcher, Moses Gunn

'The most astonishing thing in the movie is how
boring it is.' – *Roger Ebert*

Firewalker
US   1986   104m   TVC colour
Cannon (Menahem Golan, Yoram Globus)
V, V*, L

Adventurers seek gold in an Aztec temple.

Old hat heroics and violence in the wake of *Raiders of
the Lost Ark*. Not a happy outcome.

w Robert Gosnell   *d* J. Lee-Thompson   *ph* Alex
Philips   *m* Gary Chang   *pd* Jos Rodriguez
ed Richard Marx

Chuck Norris, Lou Gossett Jnr, Melody Anderson,
John Rhys-Davies, Will Sampson

The Firm *
US   1993   154m   DeLuxe
Paramount (Sydney Pollack, Scott Rudin, John Davis)
V, V*, L, S

A bright young lawyer finds himself trapped between
becoming an informant for the FBI and being killed
by the ruthless Mafia gangsters who control his firm.

An attention-holding thriller for the most part, though
its conclusion, diverging from the tougher stance of
the novel, is unsatisfactory.

w David Rabe, Robert Towne, David Rayfiel
novel John Grisham   *d* Sydney Pollack   *ph* John
Seale   *m* David Grusin   *pd* Richard Macdonald
ed William Steinkamp, Frederic Steinkamp

Tom Cruise, Jeanne Tripplehorn, Gene Hackman, Hal
Holbrook, Terry Kinney, Wilford Brimley, Ed Harris,
Holly Hunter, David Strathairn, Gary Busey, Stephen
Hill, Tobin Bell

'A vacuous upper-middle-class success story about a
fresh-faced lad outwitting both sides of the law while
securing wealth and safety for his family.' – *Michael
Sragow, New Yorker*

'There is sufficient conviction from everyone before
and behind the camera to provide an absorbing,
pulpy, old-fashioned movie experience.' – *Variety*

AAN: Holly Hunter; Dave Grusin

First a Girl
GB   1935   94m   bw
Gaumont (Michael Balcon)
V

A messenger girl attracts attention by posing as a boy,
and becomes a star.

Moderate light star vehicle.

w Marjorie Gaffney   *play* Viktor und Viktoria by
Reinhold Schunzel   *d* Victor Saville   *ph* Glen
MacWilliams   *md* Louis Levy   *ad* Oscar Werndorff
ed Al Barnes

Jessie Matthews, Sonnie Hale, Griffith Jones, Anna
Lee, Alfred Drayton, Martita Hunt, Eddie Gray

† Julie Andrews starred in a remake entitled *Victor/
Victoria* in 1982.

The First and the Last: see *Twenty-One Days*

First Blood
US   1982   94m   Technicolor   Panavision
Carolco (Buzz Feitshans)
V, V*, L, S

A former Green Beret gets into trouble in a small
Californian community and sets himself against the
forces of law.

Pure blood and thunder with some decent action
sequences.

w Michael Kozoll, William Sackheim, Sylvester
Stallone   *novel* David Marell   *d* Ted Kotcheff
ph Andrew Laszlo   *m* Jerry Goldsmith

Sylvester Stallone, Richard Crenna, Brian Dennehy,
David Caruso, Jack Starrett

'Socially irresponsible . . . there are enough nuts out
there without giving them a hero to cheer for.' –
Variety

† It was followed by two sequels: *Rambo: First Blood II*
and *Rambo III*.

First Comes Courage
US   1943   88m   bw
Columbia (Harry Joe Brown)

During World War II, a Norwegian girl appears to be
a Quisling but is really a spy getting information from
the Nazis by fraternizing with them.

Doleful war drama with little to commend it except
propaganda.

w Lewis Meltzer, Melvin Levy   *novel The Commandos*
by Elliott Arnold   *d* Dorothy Arzner   *ph* Joseph
Walker   *m* Ernst Toch

Merle Oberon, Brian Aherne, Carl Esmond, Fritz
Leiber, Erik Rolf, Reinhold Schunzel, Isobel Elsom

The First Deadly Sin
US   1980   112m   TVC color
Filmways/Artanis/Cinema Seven (Elliott Kastner)
V*, L

A police lieutenant tracks down a homicidal lunatic
but is unable to save his own wife who is dying in
hospital from an obscure ailment.

The two halves of this depressing cop show don't
seem to relate, and it offers little in the way of
entertainment value beyond the traditional tracking
down of the murderer.

w Mann Rubin   *novel* Lawrence Sanders   *d* Brian
G. Hutton   *ph* Jack Priestley   *m* Gordon Jenkins

Frank Sinatra, Faye Dunaway, David Dukes, George
Coe, Brenda Vaccaro, Martin Gabel, Anthony Zerbe,
James Whitmore

'An odd collection of pretensions seem to be rattling
round in an overlength TV film.' – *Mark Lefanu, MFB*

'Mystery without meaning, despite a froth of
intercutting and religious iconography.' – *Sight and
Sound*

The First Gentleman *
GB   1948   111m   bw
Columbia (Joseph Friedman)
US title: *Affairs of a Rogue*

The affairs and foibles of the Prince Regent.

Dullish adaptation of a successful West End play
about 18th-century court life; script and performances
still entertain.

w Nicholas Phipps, Reginald Long   *play* Norman
Ginsbury   *d* Cavalcanti   *ph* Jack Hildyard

Cecil Parker, Jean-Pierre Aumont, Joan Hopkins,
Margaretta Scott, Jack Livesey, Ronald Squire,
Athene Seyler, Hugh Griffith

The First Great Train Robbery *
GB   1978   108m   Technicolor   Panavision
UA/Starling (John Foreman)
V*, L, S
US title: *The Great Train Robbery*

In 1855, an elegant but ruthless crook picks out a
gang to help him rob the Folkestone express of gold
bullion.

Patchy but generally very likeable period crime story,
with just a few lapses of pace and taste.

wd Michael Crichton   *novel* Michael Crichton
ph Geoffrey Unsworth   *pd* Maurice Carter   *m* Jerry
Goldsmith

Sean Connery, Donald Sutherland, Lesley-Anne
Down, Alan Webb, Robert Lang, Malcolm Terris

'My dream was that the historical world was going to
be lovingly recreated, and then I was going to shoot
The French Connection inside it.' – *Michael Crichton*

The First Hundred Years
US   1938   75m   bw
MGM

A self-supporting wife is reluctant to give up her
career.

Tolerable matrimonial comedy resolved by
pregnancy.

w Melville Baker   *story* Norman Krasna   *d* Richard
Thorpe

Robert Montgomery, Virginia Bruce, Warren William,
Binnie Barnes, Alan Dinehart, Harry Davenport,
Nydia Westman

First Lady *
US   1937   82m   bw
Warner (Hal B. Wallis)

The President's wife is a power behind the scenes.

Solidly entertaining Washington comedy.

w Rowland Leigh   *play* George S. Kaufman,
Katherine Dayton   *d* Stanley Logan   *ph* Sid Hickox
m Max Steiner

Kay Francis, Preston Foster, Anita Louise, Walter
Connolly, Verree Teasdale, Victor Jory, Marjorie
Rambeau, Louise Fazenda

'Smart stuff but generally palatable.' – *Variety*

The First Legion *
US   1951   86m   bw
Sedif (Douglas Sirk)
V*

Priests are bewildered when one of their number is
the centre of an apparent miracle.

Talkative religious drama of a peculiarly American
kind which likes to have its cake and eat it; watchable
for the performances.

w Emmet Lavery   *play* Emmet Lavery   *d* Douglas
Sirk   *ph* Robert de Grasse   *m* Hans Sommer

Charles Boyer, William Demarest, Lyle Bettger, Barbara Rush, Leo G. Carroll, Walter Hampden, George Zucco, Taylor Holmes

First Love *
US   1939   84m   bw
Universal (Joe Pasternak)

An orphaned teenager goes to live with her uncle and his snobbish family, and falls for a local bigwig's son.

A vehicle carefully conceived to introduce its star to grown-up romance. The compromises show, but it's palatable enough.

w Bruce Manning, Lionel Houser   d Henry Koster
ph Joseph Valentine   md Charles Previn   m Frank Skinner   ad Jack Otterson, Martin Obzina

Deanna Durbin, Robert Stack, Eugene Pallette, Helen Parrish, Lewis Howard, Leatrice Joy

'A top-bracketer for general audiences in keys and subsequents.' – Variety

'The most obvious Cinderella story I ever met with, apart from Cinderella.' – Richard Mallett, Punch

'There is nothing at all to resent in the picture: it is admirably directed, amusingly written, and acted with immense virtuosity by a fine cast.' – Graham Greene

AAN: Charles Previn; art direction

First Man into Space
GB   1958   78m   bw
Producers' Associates (John Croydon)
V*

An astronaut runs into a cloud of meteor dust and returns to Earth a vampirish killer.

Quatermass-like shocker with modest budget but firm control.

w John C. Cooper, Lance Z. Hargreaves   d Robert Day   ph Geoffrey Faithfull   m Buxton Orr

Marshall Thompson, Marla Landi, Bill Edwards

First Men in the Moon *
GB   1964   103m   Technicolor   Panavision
Columbia/Ameran (Charles H. Schneer)
V, V*, L, S

A Victorian eccentric makes a voyage to the moon and is forced to stay there.

Rather slack in plot development, but an enjoyable schoolboy romp with a good eye for detail and tongue firmly in cheek.

w Nigel Kneale, Jan Read   novel H. G. Wells
d Nathan Juran   ph Wilkie Cooper   m Laurie Johnson   sp Ray Harryhausen

Lionel Jeffries, Edward Judd, Martha Hyer

† Uncredited, Peter Finch played the bit part of a process server.

'In the Supreme Court, there are only eight of them against all of her!'
First Monday in October
US   1981   99m   Metrocolor   Panavision
Paramount (Paul Heller, Martha Scott)
V*, L

Ruth Loomis becomes the first woman to be appointed to the US Supreme Court, and wins over her severest critic.

Fairly yawnworthy comedy which has nowhere to go from its initial situation, and has detail too complex for any but politically minded Americans.

w Jerome Lawrence, Robert E. Lee   play Jerome Lawrence, Robert E. Lee   d Ronald Neame
ph Fred J. Koenekamp   m Sousa, Handel, arr. Ian Fraser   pd Philip M. Jefferies

Jill Clayburgh, Walter Matthau, Barnard Hughes, Jan Sterling, James Stephens, Joshua Bryant

'Any attempts to inject a little healthy subversion or a few dangerous thoughts are soon smothered by the plot demands of middle-aged romantic whimsy.' – Sunday Times

First Name Carmen *
France   1983   85m   colour
Sara/A2/JLG Films (Alain Sarde)
V, V*, L
original title: Prénom Carmen

The niece of a mad film director pretends to be making a film in order to organize an armed robbery.

A quirky film, in which Godard enjoys himself playing a film director at the end of his tether, but which is otherwise disorganized and disjointed.

w Jean-Luc Godard, Anne-Marie Miéville   d Jean-Luc Godard   ph Raoul Coutard   m Beethoven

Maruschka Detmers, Jacques Bonnaffé, Myriem Roussel, Christophe Odent, Pierre-Alain Chapuis, Bertrand Liebert, Jean-Luc Godard

'From the way this new film is made, it appears that Godard feels hurt on some deep level and he thinks the movies did it to him – and he's not going to let himself be hurt again. He won't throw himself into this project. He gives the story a dry, flat treatment and entertains himself with Beethoven and the rolling surf and with a limited palette – soft, somber tones and subdued golden ones – that suggest the classics (but not of movies).' – Pauline Kael

It won the Lion d'Or for best film at the Venice Film Festival in 1983.

The First of the Few **
GB   1942   117m   bw
Melbourne/British Aviation (Leslie Howard, George King, Adrian Brunel, John Stafford)
V, V*
US title: Spitfire

The story of R. J. Mitchell who saw World War II coming and devised the Spitfire.

Low-key but impressive biopic with firm acting and good dialogue scenes. Production values slightly shaky.

w Anatole de Grunwald, Miles Malleson, Henry C. James, Katherine Strueby   d Leslie Howard
ph Georges Perinal   m William Walton

Leslie Howard, David Niven, Rosamund John, Roland Culver, David Horne

'Full of action, Schneider Trophy races, test flying and flashes from the Battle of Britain.' – Sunday Times

The First Power
US   1990   98m   DeLuxe
Castle Premier/Nelson Entertainment/Interscope Communications (David Madden)
V, V*, L

A serial killer comes back from the dead to continue his murders.

Silly, predictable tale of the supernatural.

wd Robert Resnikoff   ph Theo Van de Sande
pd Joseph T. Garrity   ed Michael Bloecher

Lou Diamond Phillips, Tracy Griffith, Jeff Kober, Mykel T. Williamson, Elizabeth Arlen, Dennis Lipscomb, Carmen Argenziano, Julianna McCarthy

The First Rebel: see Allegheny Uprising

The First Texan
US   1956   82m   Technicolor   Cinemascope
Allied Artists (Walter Mirisch)

The Governor of Tennessee helps Texas win its independence.

Generally well done biopic of Sam Houston, with the usual Western excitements.

w Daniel B. Ullman   d Byron Haskin   ph Wilfrid Cline   m Roy Webb

Joel McCrea, Felicia Farr, Jeff Morrow, Wallace Ford, Abraham Sofaer

The First Time
US   1968   90m   DeLuxe
UA/Mirisch/Rogallan (Roger Smith, Allan Carr)
V*
GB title: You Don't Need Pajamas at Rosie's

Three teenage boys who fantasize about sex help a stranded girl under the impression that she is a prostitute.

Embarrassingly sentimental teenage sex comedy, all the more irritating by its restraint. Not a patch on Summer of '42.

w Jo Heims, Roger Smith   d James Nielson
ph Ernest Laszlo   m Kenyon Hopkins

Jacqueline Bisset, Wes Stern, Rick Kelman, Wink Roberts, Sharon Acker

First to Fight
US   1967   97m   Technicolor   Panavision
Warner (William Conrad)

A World War II hero is taken home and fêted, but on returning to the front he loses his nerve.

War film in the guise of a psychological study; competently done but very American in its sentiments and a bit shaky on period detail.

w Gene L. Coon   d Christian Nyby   ph Harold Wellman   m Fred Steiner

Chad Everett, Gene Hackman, Dean Jagger, Marilyn Devon, Claude Akins

The First Traveling Saleslady
US   1956   92m   Technicolor
RKO (Arthur Lubin)

Two women set out to sell barbed wire in the old west.

Strained comedy with very few effective moments.

w Devery Freeman, Stephen Longstreet   d Arthur Lubin   ph William Snyder   m Irving Gertz

Ginger Rogers, Carol Channing, Barry Nelson, James Arness, David Brian, Clint Eastwood

First Yank into Tokyo
US   1945   82m   bw
RKO
V*

An army pilot undergoes plastic surgery so that he can infiltrate the Japanese lines.

Highly unconvincing spy fiction ripped off from the headlines as the war ended.

w J. Robert Bren   d Gordon Douglas

Tom Neal, Richard Loo, Marc Cramer, Barbara Hale, Keye Luke

The First Year *
US   1932   80m   bw
Fox

Problems of a couple in their first year of married life.

Pleasant star vehicle.

w Lynn Starling   play Frank Craven   d William K. Howard

Janet Gaynor, Charles Farrell, Minna Gombell, Dudley Digges, Leila Bennett

'Gaynor and Farrell in a story that's as close to perfection for them as any piece of screenwriting could be.' – Variety

Firstborn
US   1984   100m   Technicolor
Paramount (Paul Junger Witt, Tony Thomas)
V*, L

A divorced woman's children defend her against her malevolent second husband.

Heavy-handed melodrama with no clue to what inspired its making.

w Ron Koslow *d* Michael Apted *ph* Ralf D. Bode *m* Michael Small *pd* Paul Sylbert *ed* Arthur Schmidt

Teri Garr, Peter Weller, Christopher Collet, Corey Haim, Sarah Jessica Parker

A Fish Called Wanda **
US   1988   108m   Technicolor
MGM (Michael Shamberg)
V, V*, L, CD, S

Diamond-heist comedy depending on Anglo-American rivalries for its laughs.

Monty Python fans found it disappointing, but it went down well in the US.

w John Cleese, Charles Crichton *d* Charles Crichton *ph* Alan Hume *m* John Du Prez *pd* Roger Murray-Leach

John Cleese, Jamie Lee Curtis, Kevin Kline, Michael Palin, Maria Aitken

AA: Kevin Kline

AAN: Charles Crichton; best original screenplay

The Fish that Saved Pittsburgh
US   1979   104m   colour
United Artists (David Dashev, Gary Stromberg)
V*

An inept baseball team improves its performance by recruiting players born under the sign of Pisces.

Uninteresting comedy to a disco beat.

w Jaison Starkes, Edmond Stevens *d* Gilbert Moses *ph* Frank Stanley *m* Thom Bell *ad* Herbert Spencer Deverill *ed* Peter Zinner

Julius Erving, Jonathan Winters, Meadowlark Lemon, Jack Kehoe, Margaret Avery, James Bond III, Michael V. Gazzo, M. Emmet Walsh, Stockard Channing, Flip Wilson

'A Modern Day Tale About The Search For Love, Sanity, Ethel Merman And The Holy Grail.'

The Fisher King **
US   1991   137m   Technicolor
Columbia TriStar (Debra Hill, Linda Obst)
V, V*, L, S

A former disc jockey seeking salvation becomes involved in the mystic quest of a tramp who was once a medieval historian.

Enjoyable more for its director's extravagances than for its attempt at modern myth-making, and finally too diffuse to be taken seriously.

w Richard LaGravenese *d* Terry Gilliam *ph* Roger Pratt *m* George Fenton *pd* Mel Bourne *ed* Lesley Walker

Robin Williams, Jeff Bridges, Amanda Plummer, Mercedes Ruehl, Michael Jeter

'Has all the ingredients of a major critical and commercial event: two actors at the top of their form, and a compelling, well-directed and well-produced story.' – *Variety*

'At heart, the film is no different from a whole string of Hollywood movies centering on mysterious madmen who may be legendary heroes . . . A peculiarly irritating failure – a leaden piece of uplift.' – *New Yorker*

AA: Mercedes Ruehl

AAN: Robin Williams; Richard LaGravenese; George Fenton; Mel Bourne

Fisherman's Wharf
US   1939   72m   bw
Sol Lesser/RKO

The relationship of a boy and his foster father is upset by the arrival of relations on their fishing boat.

Family fare for addicts of the singing boy star.

w Bernard Schubert, Ian McLellan Hunter, Herbert Clyde Lewis *d* Bernard Vorhaus

Bobby Breen, Leo Carrillo, Lee Patrick, Henry Armetta, Tommy Bupp

'Lightweight entertainment which will find its level in the duals.' – *Variety*

F.I.S.T. *
US   1978   145m   Technicolor
UA/Norman Jewison (Gene Corman)
V, V*, L

The rise and fall of a union boss.

Reminiscent of *All the King's Men* and *On the Waterfront*, this much overlong melodrama has compelling passages, but the star is not quite equal to it and parts are both repetitive and obscure.

w Joe Eszterhas, Sylvester Stallone *d* Norman Jewison *ph* Laszlo Kovacs *m* Bill Conti *pd* Richard MacDonald

Sylvester Stallone, Rod Steiger, Peter Boyle, Melinda Dillon, David Huffman, Tony Lo Bianco, Cassie Yates, Peter Donat, Henry Wilcoxon

'Stallone exerts the same compulsive presence we saw in *Rocky* – and this time there is the added bonus that you can understand what he's saying.' – *Variety*

Fist of Fury (dubbed)
Hong Kong   1972   106m   Eastmancolor
                                    Dyaliscope
Cathay/Golden Harvest (Raymond Chow)
V, V*
aka: *The Chinese Connection; The Iron Hand*

A kung-fu fighter revenges himself on a gang of Japanese karate experts who have murdered his old teacher.

Violent martial arts movie, enlivened by Lee's style in the frequent fight scenes.

wd Lo Wei *ph* Chen Ching Cheh *m* Joseph Koo *pd* Lo Wei *ed* Chang Yao Chung

Bruce Lee, Nora Miao, James Tien, Robert Baker

Fist of the North Star (dubbed)
Japan   1986   112m   colour
Tohi (Shoji Kishimoto)
V.

In a world after a nuclear holocaust, grotesquely muscled thugs with mystic powers battle for supremacy.

Repellently violent animated feature, full of exploding heads, popping eyeballs and gushers of blood; as if that were not bad enough, it also lacks any narrative coherence.

w Buronson, Tetsuo Hara *novel* graphic novel by Buronson, Tetsuo Hara *d* Toyoo Ashida *ph* Tamiyo Hosoda *m* Katsuhisa Haltori *ad* Shiko Tanaka

voices of John Vickery, Michael McConnohie, Melodee Spivack, Dan Woren, Tony Oliver, Wally Burr, Gregory Snegoff

† The film was released direct to video.

A Fistful of Dollars ***
Italy/Germany/Spain   1964   100m   Techniscope
UA/Jolly/Constantin/Ocean (Arrigo Colombo, Georgio Papi)
V, V*, L, S
original title: *Per un Pugno di Dollari*

An avenging stranger, violent and mysterious, cleans up a Mexican border town.

A film with much to answer for: it began the craze for 'spaghetti Westerns', took its director to Hollywood, and made a TV cowboy into a world star. It turned the Western into a brutal baroque opera, a violent clash between individuals.

w Sergio Leone, Duccio Tessari *d* Sergio Leone *ph* Massimo Dallamano *m* Ennio Morricone

Clint Eastwood, Gian Maria Volonte, Marianne Koch

'A film with no purpose beyond its ninety-five-minute Technicolor close-up portrayals of men being shot, gouged, burned, beaten and stomped to death.' – *Judith Crist*

† Direct sequels by Leone, apart from numerous imitations, are *For a Few Dollars More* and *The Good, the Bad and the Ugly*.

A Fistful of Dynamite
Italy   1971   150m   Techniscope
UA/Rafran/San Marco/Miura (Fulvio Morsella)
V*, L, S
aka: *Duck, You Sucker*

In 1913 a Mexican bandit and an ex-IRA explosives expert join forces to rob a bank.

Overblown action spectacular, far too long to be sustained by its flashes of humour and excitement. A good instance of what happens to a small talent when success goes to its head.

wd Sergio Leone *ph* Giuseppe Ruzzolini *m* Ennio Morricone

Rod Steiger, James Coburn, Romolo Valli, Maria Monti

Fists in the Pocket *
Italy   1965   113m   bw
Doria (Ezio Passadore)
original title: *I Pugni in Tasca*

One of a family of epileptics murders most of the others in order to help his normal eldest brother.

Complex black melodrama which makes its points, if it has any, with great style.

wd Marco Bellocchio *ph* Alberto Marrama *m* Ennio Morricone

Lou Castel, Paola Pitagora, Liliona Gerace

'There have been few débuts as exciting as this in recent years.' – *Tom Milne, MFB*

Fists of Fury: see *The Big Boss*

Fit for a King
US   1937   73m   bw
RKO

A cub reporter falls for a princess.

Standard star comedy with action climax.

w Richard Flournoy *d* Edward Sedgwick

Joe E. Brown, Helen Mack, Halliwell Hobbes, Paul Kelly, Harry Davenport, John Qualen

Fitzcarraldo ****
West Germany   1982   158m   colour
Werner Herzog/ProjectFilmproduktion/Zweite Deutsches Fernsehen/Wildlife Films, Peru (Werner Herzog, Lucki Stipetic)
V, V*

In Peru at the turn of the century, an eccentric Irishman succeeds against all odds in establishing an opera house in the jungle.

A strange and brilliant film centring on the hero's successful attempt to drag his massive boat from one river to another.

wd Werner Herzog *ph* Thomas Mauch *m* Popol Vuh

Klaus Kinski, Claudia Cardinale, Jose Lewgoy, Paul Hittscher

† 'Fitzcarraldo' is the nearest the natives can get to 'Fitzgerald'.

Fitzwilly *
US   1967   102m   DeLuxe   Panavision
UA/Dramatic Features Inc/Walter Mirisch
GB title: *Fitzwilly Strikes Back*

A New York butler, in order to keep his lady in style, has to organize the staff into a crime syndicate.

Moderately inventive, good-looking comedy with rather too much plot and not enough funny lines.

w Isobel Lennart novel A Garden of Cucumbers by Poyntz Tyler d Delbert Mann ph Joseph Biroc m Johnny Williams

Dick Van Dyke, Edith Evans, Barbara Feldon, John McGiver, Harry Townes, John Fiedler, Norman Fell, Cecil Kellaway, Anne Seymour, Sam Waterston, Billy Halop

Fitzwilly Strikes Back: see Fitzwilly

Five
US 1951 89m bw
Columbia (Arch Oboler)

There are only five survivors of an atomic holocaust, and their political and racial tensions soon reduce the number to two.

Gutless talkfest which becomes interesting only when the camera moves out of doors; otherwise, too pretentious and dull by half.

wd Arch Oboler ph Lou Stoumen, Ed Spiegel, Sid Lubow m Henry Russell

William Phipps, Susan Douglas, James Anderson, Charles Lampkin, Earl Lee

'The talk leaves one with a strong impression that in this case the fittest did not survive.' – Penelope Houston

Five Against the House
US 1955 84m bw
Columbia (Sterling Silliphant, John Barnwell)

College students try to rob a casino.

Meandering caper melodrama with too much flabby dialogue.

w Sterling Silliphant, John Barnwell novel Jack Finney d Phil Karlson ph Leslie White m George Duning

Guy Madison, Kim Novak, Brian Keith, Kerwin Mathews, William Conrad

Five and Ten
US 1931 88m bw
MGM
GB title: Daughter of Luxury

A chain store heiress elopes with a married man, but is tamed by family misfortune.

Solid star drama which maintains points of interest.

w A. P. Younger, Edith Fitzgerald novel Fannie Hurst d Robert Z. Leonard

Marion Davies, Leslie Howard, Richard Bennett, Irene Rich, Kent Douglass, Halliwell Hobbes

Five Angles on Murder: see The Woman in Question

Five Boys from Barska Street *
Poland 1953 115m Agfacolor
Film Polski
original title: Piatka z Ulicy Barskiej

Five city boys are placed on probation and gradually change their attitudes towards life and society.

Rather dated propaganda piece with a plot which surprisingly follows Western models.

wd Aleksander Ford novel Kazimierz Kozniewski ph Jaroslav Tuzar m Kazimierz Serocki

Tadeusz Janczar, Aleksandra Slaska, Andrzej Kozak

Five Branded Women
Italy/US 1960 100m bw
Paramount/Dino de Laurentiis

Five Yugoslav girls have their heads shaved for associating with German soldiers, and after various adventures join the partisans.

Rough, tough war adventure which makes a few boring points about love and war.

w Ivo Perelli novel Ugo Pirro d Martin Ritt ph Giuseppe Rotunno m Francesco Lavagnino

Silvana Mangano, Van Heflin, Vera Miles, Barbara Bel Geddes, Jeanne Moreau, Richard Basehart, Harry Guardino, Steve Forrest, Alex Nicol

'For the most part the film is devoted to unexciting guerrilla action and uninviting partisan life . . . obstinately unreal despite lashings of blood, mutilation, childbirth and death.' – MFB

Five Came Back **
US 1939 75m bw
RKO (Robert Sisk)
V*, L

A passenger plane crashlands in the jungle. It can carry back only five survivors, and headhunters are coming closer . . .

A minor film which gradually achieved cult status and was remade as Back to Eternity as well as being the starting point for many variations. Still gripping in its dated way.

w Jerry Cady, Dalton Trumbo, Nathanael West d John Farrow ph Nicholas Musuraca m Roy Webb

Chester Morris, Lucille Ball, C. Aubrey Smith, Elizabeth Risdon, Wendy Barrie, John Carradine, Joseph Calleia, Allen Jenkins, Kent Taylor, Patric Knowles

'Exceptionally well-made adventure yarn, out of the B category and almost rates A . . . looks like a solid click.' – Variety

Five Card Stud
US 1968 103m Technicolor
Paramount/Hal. B. Wallis
V*

Members of a lynching party are murdered one by one.

Would-be nonchalant murder mystery Western: the stars just about hold it together, but it's an uphill fight.

w Marguerite Roberts novel Ray Gaulden d Henry Hathaway ph Daniel L. Fapp m Maurice Jarre

Dean Martin, Robert Mitchum, Inger Stevens, Roddy McDowall, Katherine Justice, John Anderson, Yaphet Kotto

'Marginally watchable . . . but destined to sink without trace minutes after one leaves the cinema.' – Gavin Millar

'So mediocre you can't get mad at it.' – Judith Crist

Five Corners *
US 1988 93m colour
Handmade Films (Tony Bill, Forest Murray)
V*

Four old friends meet again when one of them is released from prison.

Set in the 1960s, a perceptive period piece that unhappily segues into an unconvincing melodrama.

w John Patrick Shanley d Tony Bill ph Fred Murphy m James Newton Howard ed Andy Blumenthal

Jodie Foster, Tim Robbins, Todd Graff, John Turturro, Elizabeth Berridge, Rose Gregorio, Gregory Rozakis, John Seitz

Five Days One Summer *
US 1982 108m Technicolor
Warner/Ladd (Fred Zinnemann)
V*

In 1932 a middle-aged Scots doctor takes his young

mistress on an Alpine climbing holiday, and she falls for the guide.

Superbly photographed and crafted mountain movie, akin to the German epics of the early thirties. Alas, the content is very thin.

w Michael Austin story Maiden Maiden by Kay Boyle d Fred Zinnemann ph Giuseppe Rotunno m Elmer Bernstein pd Willy Holt ed Stuart Baird

Sean Connery, Betsy Brantley, Lambert Wilson, Jennifer Hilary, Isabel Dean, Anna Massey

'Dawdling and eventually silly, though the veteran director's tenacity and craftsmanship provide muted applause.' – Variety

Five Dolls for an August Moon (dubbed)
Italy 1970 88m colour
PAC
V
original title: Cinque Bambole per la Luna d'Agosto

A group of wealthy industrialists and their entourages are murdered one by one when they go to an island mansion to bid for the rights to a valuable formula.

Although the plot is based on Agatha Christie's Ten Little Indians, Bava shows little interest in its thriller aspects, preferring to concentrate on fashionable gloss, flashy photography and the occasional grisly image.

w Mario Di Nardo d Mario Bava ph Antonio Rinaldi m Piero Umiliani ad Giuseppe Aldobranc

William Berger, Ira Furstenberg, Edwige Fenech, Howard Ross (Renato Rossini), Helena Ronée, Teodoro Corrá, Maurice Poli

'A pleasure to watch even when the plot flags and the zooms proliferate.' – Tom Milne

The British video release runs for 80m.

Five Easy Pieces **
US 1970 98m Technicolor
Columbia/Bert Schneider (Bob Rafelson, Richard Wechsler)
V, V*, L

A middle-class drifter jilts his pregnant mistress for his brother's fiancée, but finally leaves both and hitches a ride to nowhere in particular.

Echoes of Easy Rider, The Graduate and Charlie Bubbles abound in this generally likeable but insubstantial modern anti-drama which at least takes place in pleasant surroundings and is firmly directed.

w Adrien Joyce d Bob Rafelson ph Laszlo Kovacs m various

Jack Nicholson, Karen Black, Susan Anspach, Lois Smith, Billy 'Green' Bush, Fannie Flagg

AAN: best picture; Adrien Joyce; Jack Nicholson; Karen Black

'There are many kinds of love, but are there any without guilt?'
Five Finger Exercise
US 1962 109m bw
Columbia/Sonnis (Frederick Brisson)

A snobbish wife falls in love with a young house guest, with dire effect on her husband and son.

This West End study of a neurotic family is probably not good film material, certainly not adaptable to California, and above all not suitable to this star's whizzbang dramatics. Numbing hysteria arrives early and stays till the end.

w Frances Goodrich, Albert Hackett play Peter Shaffer d Daniel Mann ph Harry Stradling m Jerome Moross

Rosalind Russell, Jack Hawkins, Maximilian Schell, Richard Beymer

Five Fingers **
US   1952   108m   bw
TCF (Otto Lang)
V*

The valet of the British ambassador in Ankara sells military secrets to the Germans, who pay him but never use the information.

Absorbing, lightweight film adaptation of a true story of World War II; civilized suspense entertainment with all talents contributing nicely.

w *Michael Wilson*   book Operation Cicero by L. C. Moyzich   d *Joseph L. Mankiewicz*   ph Norbert Brodine   m Bernard Herrmann   ad Lyle Wheeler, George W. Davis

James Mason, Danielle Darrieux, Michael Rennie, Walter Hampden, Oscar Karlweis, Herbert Berghof, John Wengraf, Michael Pate

'One of the highest, fastest and most absorbing spy melodramas since Hitchcock crossed the Atlantic.' – *Arthur Knight*

AAN: Michael Wilson; Joseph L. Mankiewicz

Five Gates to Hell
US   1959   98m   bw   Cinemascope
TCF

A Vietcong warlord carries off a nun and seven nurses; the latter escape by brutal means.

Unpleasant shocker showing no signs of talent in any department.   wd James Clavell

Dolores Michaels, Patricia Owens, Neville Brand, Kevin Scott, Nobu McCarthy, Nancy Kulp, Shirley Knight, Irish McCalla

'This grimly amateurish war film exploits sex and violence with an emotional arrest bordering on paranoia.' – *MFB*

Five Golden Dragons
GB   1965   92m   Techniscope
Harry Alan Towers
V, V*

An American playboy in Hong Kong becomes involved in the affairs of five master criminals preparing to sell out to the Mafia.

Anything-goes comedy-thriller, patchy at best, unintelligible at worst, and filled with ageing stars.

w Harry Alan Towers   d Jeremy Summers

Robert Cummings, Rupert Davies, Margaret Lee, Maria Perschy, Klaus Kinski, Dan Duryea, Brian Donlevy, Christopher Lee, George Raft

Five Golden Hours
GB/Italy   1960   90m   bw
Columbia/Anglofilm/Fabio Jegher (Mario Zampi)
V*

A con man tries to murder three widows who have invested money in one of his schemes.

Ill-judged black comedy, sadly lacking style.

w Hans Wilhelm   d Mario Zampi   ph Christopher Challis   m Stanley Black

Ernie Kovacs, Cyd Charisse, Kay Hammond, George Sanders, Dennis Price, Reginald Beckwith, Martin Benson, Ron Moody, Finlay Currie, Avis Landone, Sidney Tafler, John Le Mesurier, Clelia Matania

Five Graves to Cairo ***
US   1943   96m   bw
Paramount (Charles Brackett)

During the North Africa campaign, British spies try to destroy Rommel's secret supply dumps.

Intriguing spy melodrama set in a desert hotel, a notable example of Hollywood's ability to snatch polished drama from the headlines.

w *Charles Brackett, Billy Wilder*   play Lajos Biro   d *Billy Wilder*   ph John Seitz   m Miklos Rozsa   ad Hans Dreier, Ernst Fegte   ed Doane Harrison

Franchot Tone, Anne Baxter, *Erich von Stroheim* (as Rommel), Akim Tamiroff, Peter Van Eyck, Miles Mander

'Von Stroheim has all the other movie Huns backed completely off the screen.' – *Variety*

'Billy Wilder must have had something a little grander in mind: the cleverness lacks lustre.' – *New Yorker, 1978*

'A fabulous film fable, but it has been executed with enough finesse to make it a rather exciting pipe dream.' – *Howard Barnes, New York Herald Tribune*

† Locations representing the African desert include California's Salton Sea and Yuma, Arizona.

AAN: John Seitz; art direction; editing

Five Guns West
US   1955   78m   Pathecolor
Palo Alto (Roger Corman)

Five criminals are recruited into the Southern army to catch a traitor and some Union gold.

Western trial run for *The Dirty Dozen*; cheapjack actioner, quite tolerable of its kind.

w R. Wright Campbell   d Roger Corman   ph Floyd Crosby   m Buddy Bregman   ed Ronald Sinclair

John Lund, Dorothy Malone, Chuck Connors, Paul Birch

The Five Heartbeats *
US   1991   121m   DeLuxe
TCF (Loretha C. Jones)
V, V*, L

The ups and downs of a vocal group in the 1960s and 70s.

A dramatic and witty account of the tribulations of a black group fighting for recognition in a world controlled by whites.

w Robert Townsend, Keenen Ivory Wayans   d Robert Townsend   ph Bill Dill   m Stanley Clarke   pd Wynn Thomas   ed John Carter

Robert Townsend, Michael Wright, Leon, Harry J. Lennix, Tico Wells, Diahann Carroll, Harold Nicholas, Tressa Thomas, John Canada Terrell

'Convincing only in its sweet and dazzling musical sequences, this overly sincere effort otherwise misses its mark.' – *Variety*

Five Little Peppers and How They Grew
US   1939   58m   bw
Columbia

While Mrs Pepper is out working, eldest daughter Polly must take care of the other children.

Sentimental second feature which quickly spawned two others, *Five Little Peppers at Home* and *Five Little Peppers in Trouble*.

w Nathalie Bucknall, Jefferson Parker   novel Margaret Sidney   d Charles Barton

Edith Fellows, Clarence Kolb, Dorothy Peterson, Ronald Sinclair, Tommy Bond

Five Miles to Midnight *
France/Italy   1962   110m   bw
UA/Filmsonor/Dear Film (Anatole Litvak)

A neurotic believed dead forces his terrified wife to collect his life insurance.

Hysterical melodrama, smoothly made with all the familiar expressionist devices, but far too long for its content.

w Peter Viertel, Hugh Wheeler   d Anatole Litvak   ph Henri Alekan   m Mikis Theodorakis

Sophia Loren, Anthony Perkins, Gig Young, Jean-Pierre Aumont, Yolande Turner, Tommy Norden

'From the polished immediacy of the cars, streets, shop windows and café tables to the off-focus vertigo shots of panic, from the overhead view of neighbours

on stairs . . . to the close-ups of hands in filing trays touching off the details of fear and guilt, there is a thread of colour to keep you watching.' – *MFB*

'One of those movies without a country that are becoming as fixed a part of the international scene as the Duke and Duchess of Windsor.' – *Arthur Schlesinger Jnr, Show*

Five Million Years to Earth: see *Quatermass and the Pit*

Five of a Kind
US   1938   83m   bw
TCF

Two reporters compete for the best stories about the Dionne Quintuplets.

Third effort to exploit the famous quins, then four years old. Not otherwise remarkable.

w Lou Breslow, John Patrick   d Herbert I. Leeds

Jean Hersholt, Claire Trevor, Cesar Romero, Slim Summerville, Henry Wilcoxon, John Qualen, Jane Darwell

'Will find difficulty in generating much audience enthusiasm except in spots where women patronage predominates.' – *Variety*

The Five Pennies *
US   1959   117m   Technicolor   Vistavision
Paramount/Dena (Jack Rose)
V*

The rags-to-riches success story of cornet player Red Nichols.

The only touch of originality in this biopic is that the subject is given touches of irascibility. Production values reach a good standard.

w Jack Rose, Melville Shavelson   d Melville Shavelson   ph Daniel L. Fapp   md Leith Stevens   m cornet solos: Red Nichols   m/ly Sylvia Fine   ad Hal Pereira, Tambi Larsen

Danny Kaye, Barbara Bel Geddes, *Louis Armstrong*, Bob Crosby, Harry Guardino, Tuesday Weld, Ray Anthony

AAN: Daniel L. Fapp; Leith Stevens; title song

Five Savage Men: see *The Animals*

Five Star Final **
US   1931   89m   bw
Warner

A sensation-seeking newspaper causes tragedy.

Dated but still powerful melodrama which set the pattern for all the newspaper films of the thirties.

w *Robert Lord, Byron Morgan*   play Louis Weitzenkorn   d *Mervyn Le Roy*   ph Sol Polito   md Leo F. Forbstein

Edward G. Robinson, H. B. Warner, Marian Marsh, Anthony Bushell, George E. Stone, Ona Munson, Aline MacMahon, Boris Karloff

'All the elements to make a hit attraction.' – *Variety*

† Remade in 1936 with Humphrey Bogart, as *Two Against the World*.

AAN: best picture

Five Steps to Danger
US   1956   80m   bw
UA (Henry S. Kesler)

A girl possessing secret information from her dead scientist brother has a mental breakdown, and is pursued by spies.

Lively if cliché-ridden espionage melodrama, like an old-time serial.

wd Henry S. Kesler   novel Donald Hamilton   ph Kenneth Peach   m Paul Sawtell, Bert Shefter

Sterling Hayden, Ruth Roman, Werner Klemperer, Richard Gaines

The Five Thousand Fingers of Doctor T *
US   1953   88m   Technicolor
Columbia/Stanley Kramer

A boy who hates piano lessons dreams of his teacher as an evil genius who keeps five hundred boys imprisoned in a castle of musical instruments.

Badly scripted fantasy with gleaming sophisticated dream sequences which deserve a better frame. A real oddity to come from Hollywood at this time, even though Dr Seuss's books were and are bestsellers.

w Dr Seuss (Theodore Geisel), Alan Scott   d Roy Rowland   ph Franz Planer   m Frederick Hollander   ly Dr Seuss   pd Rudolph Sternad   ch Eugene Loring

Hans Conried, Tommy Rettig, Peter Lind Hayes, Mary Healy

AAN: Frederick Hollander

Five Weeks in a Balloon
US   1962   101m   DeLuxe   Cinemascope
TCF (Irwin Allen)
V*

In 1862 a professor is financed on a balloon trip into central Africa.

Would-be humorous semi-fantasy which strives to equal Journey to the Center of the Earth but unfortunately falls flat on its face despite the interesting talent available. Limp comedy situations, poor production values.

w Charles Bennett, Irwin Allen, Albert Gail   novel Jules Verne   d Irwin Allen   ph Winton Hoch   m Paul Sawtell   ad Jack Martin Smith, Alfred Ybarra

Cedric Hardwicke, Peter Lorre, Red Buttons, Fabian, Richard Haydn, Billy Gilbert, Herbert Marshall, Reginald Owen, Henry Daniell

Fixed Bayonets *
US   1951   93m   bw
TCF (Jules Buck)

An American division in Korea fights a rearguard action.

Downbeat war melodrama of a familiar kind, with more characterization than action.

wd Samuel Fuller   ph Lucien Ballard   m Roy Webb

Richard Basehart, Gene Evans, Michael O'Shea, Richard Hylton, Craig Hill

The Fixer
US   1968   130m   Metrocolor
MGM/Edward Lewis, John Frankenheimer

A Jew in Tsarist Russia denies his race but becomes a scapegoat for various crimes and is imprisoned without trial until he becomes a cause célèbre.

Worthy but extremely dreary realist melodrama.

w Dalton Trumbo   novel Bernard Malamud   d John Frankenheimer   ph Marcel Grignon   m Maurice Jarre

Alan Bates, Dirk Bogarde, Georgia Brown, Jack Gilford, Hugh Griffith, Elizabeth Hartman, Ian Holm, David Warner, Carol White, Murray Melvin, Peter Jeffrey, Michael Goodliffe

'The kind of film in which one has to admire much of the acting simply because it is all there is to admire.' – David Pirie

'A totally false film, devoid of a breath of human life or truth.' – Arthur Schlesinger Jnr

'Alan Bates's bare posterior, known to us from Georgy Girl and King of Hearts, makes another timely appearance here, thus becoming one of the most exposed arses in cinematic annals.' – John Simon

AAN: Alan Bates

The Fixer Uppers
US   1935   20m   bw
Hal Roach
V

Christmas card salesmen try to help a bored wife, but her jealous husband challenges Ollie to a duel.

Rather flat comedy marking a tailing-off from the stars' best period.

w uncredited   d Charles Rogers   ph Art Lloyded Bert Jordan

Laurel and Hardy, Mae Busch, Charles Middleton, Arthur Housman

† A remake of an early silent, Slipping Wives.

The Flag Lieutenant
GB   1933   85m   bw
British and Dominions (Herbert Wilcox)

A naval lieutenant, thought to be a coward, shows his true courage when a fort is beleaguered.

Boy's Own Paper stuff from a popular play previously filmed in 1919 (with George Wynn) and 1926 (with Henry Edwards).

w Joan Wentworth Wood   play W. P. Drury, Leo Trevor   d Henry Edwards   ph Stanley Rodwell   m Harris Weston   ad Wilfred Arnold   ed Michael Hankinson

Henry Edwards, Anna Neagle, Joyce Bland, Peter Gawthorne, Sam Livesey, O. B. Clarence, Abraham Sofaer

The Flame
US   1947   97m   bw
Republic (John H. Auer)

A nurse marries for money, but her ailing spouse recovers and she falls in love with him.

Turgid melodrama, ineptly presented.

w Lawrence Kimble   d John H. Auer   ph Reggie Lanning   m Heinz Roemheld

Vera Hruba Ralston, John Carroll, Robert Paige, Broderick Crawford, Henry Travers, Blanche Yurka, Constance Dowling, Hattie McDaniel, Sen Yung

'A good picture to stay away from, with or without a good book.' – Cue

The Flame and the Arrow *
US   1950   88m   Technicolor
Warner/Norma (Harold Hecht, Frank Ross)
V*, L

In medieval Italy, a rebel leader seeks victory over a tyrant.

Good-humoured Robin Hood stuff with the star at his most acrobatic.

w Waldo Salt   d Jacques Tourneur   ph Ernest Haller   m Max Steiner   ad Edward Carrere

Burt Lancaster, Virginia Mayo, Robert Douglas, Aline MacMahon, Frank Allenby, Nick Cravat

'I never found a Technicolor costume picture so entertaining.' – Richard Mallett, Punch

AAN: Ernest Haller; Max Steiner

The Flame and the Flesh
US   1954   104m   Technicolor
MGM (Joe Pasternak)

An unscrupulous American woman in Naples has a fatal fascination for the local menfolk.

Dreary remake of Naples au Baiser du Feu (France 1937), with the dullest possible handling all round.

w Helen Deutsch   novel Auguste Bailly   d Richard Brooks   ph Christopher Challis   m Nicholas Brodszky

Lana Turner, Carlos Thompson, Bonar Colleano, Pier Angeli, Charles Goldner, Peter Illing

A Flame In My Heart
France   1987   110m   bw
Mainline/Garance/Le Sept/Filmograph (Paulo Branco)

An actress ditches her working-class Arab lover for a journalist.

Pretentious and tasteless, always straining for the arty effect.

w Myriam Mezières, Alain Tanner   d Alain Tanner   ph Acacio de Almeida   m Bach   ed Laurent Uhler

Myriam Mezières, Benoit Regent, Aziz Kabouche, André Marcon, Jean-Gabriel Nordman, Jean-Yves Berteloot, Anne Rucki, Douglas Ireland

Flame in the Streets
GB   1961   93m   colour   Cinemascope
Rank/Somerset (Roy Baker)

A liberal-minded union man erupts when his daughter proposes to marry a black man.

Predictable East End problem picture, unconvincingly set and acted and boring into the bargain.

w Ted Willis   play Hot Summer Night by Ted Willis   d Roy Baker   ph Christopher Challis   m Phil Green

John Mills, Brenda de Banzie, Sylvia Syms, Earl Cameron, Johnny Sekka, Ann Lynn, Wilfred Brambell

'Its methods belong more to the writer's study than to life.' – John Gillett

'Adventure blazes across the burning sands!'
Flame of Araby
US   1951   76m   Technicolor
Universal-International

An Arabian princess, forced to marry, makes herself the prize in a horse race which she hopes her chosen man will win.

Trifling Eastern nonsense.

w Gerald Drayson Adams   d Charles Lamont

Maureen O'Hara, Jeff Chandler, Richard Egan, Susan Cabot, Lon Chaney Jnr, Buddy Baer, Maxwell Reed

Flame of Calcutta
US   1953   70m   Technicolor
Columbia (Sam Katzman)

In 18th-century India a mysterious girl leads attacks against a usurper.

Saturday matinée historical romp without much flair.

w Robert E. Kent   d Seymour Friedman

Denise Darcel, Patric Knowles, Paul Cavanagh, George Keymas

The Flame of New Orleans *
US   1941   79m   bw
Universal (Joe Pasternak)

A European adventuress settles in America.

Fluffy comedy romance with the exiled director scarcely in top form.

w Norman Krasna   d René Clair   ph Rudolph Maté   m Frank Skinner   ad Martin Obzina, Jack Otterson

Marlene Dietrich, Roland Young, Bruce Cabot, Mischa Auer, Andy Devine, Frank Jenks, Eddie Quillan, Laura Hope Crews, Franklin Pangborn

† Remade as Scarlet Angel.

AAN: art direction

Flame of the Barbary Coast
US   1945   97m   bw
Republic (Joseph Kane)

In old San Francisco, a cowboy becomes involved with a night-club queen, and their fortunes are resolved by the earthquake.

Tolerable period melodrama, and the one in which Wayne played a character named Duke: the nickname stuck.

w Borden Chase   d Joseph Kane   ph Robert de Grasse   m Dale Butts   sp Howard and Theodore Lydecker

John Wayne, Ann Dvorak, Joseph Schildkraut, William Frawley, Virginia Grey, Russell Hicks, Jack Norton, Paul Fix, Marc Lawrence

AAN: Dale Butts

Flame of the Islands
US   1955   90m   Trucolor
Republic (Edward Ludwig)

A girl invests a bequest in a Bahamas night-club, and there becomes involved with four men.

Barely competent time-filler.

w Bruce Manning   d Edward Ludwig   ph Bud Thackery   m Nelson Riddle

Yvonne de Carlo, Howard Duff, Zachary Scott, Kurt Kasznar, Barbara O'Neil, James Arness, Frieda Inescort

Flame Over India: see Northwest Frontier

The Flame Within
US   1935   73m   bw
MGM

A lady psychiatrist falls for the husband of one of her patients.

Decent star melodrama.   wd Edmund Goulding

Ann Harding, Maureen O'Sullivan, Louis Hayward, Henry Stephenson, Herbert Marshall

Flaming Feather
US   1951   78m   Technicolor
Nat Holt/Paramount

Arizona is harassed by an outlaw called The Sidewinder who leads a troupe of pillaging Indians.

Spot-the-villain Western; not much to detain one.

w Gerald Drayson Adams   d Ray Enright

Sterling Hayden, Forrest Tucker, Barbara Rush, Richard Arlen, Victor Jory, Edgar Buchanan

Flaming Frontiers
US   1938   bw   serial: 15 eps
Universal

An Indian scout helps his girlfriend to rid a town of outlaws.

Unremarkable serial fare.

d Ray Taylor, Alan James

Johnny Mack Brown, Eleanor Hansen, Ralph Bowman, Charles Middleton

Flaming Star *
US   1960   92m   DeLuxe   Cinemascope
TCF (David Weisbart)
V, V*

A half-breed family is torn between two loyalties.

Solemn, unusual Civil War Western with a downbeat ending.

w Clair Huffaker, Nunnally Johnson   d Don Siegel   ph Charles G. Clarke   m Cyril Mockridge

Elvis Presley, Dolores del Rio, Steve Forrest, Barbara Eden, John McIntire, Rodolpho Acosta

'Despite familiar absurdities, it has more than its share of good moments.' – MFB

The Flaming Torch: see The Bob Mathias Story

The Flamingo Kid
US   1984   100m   DeLuxe
Palace/Mercury/ABC (Michael Phillips)
V*, L

In 1963, a teenager comes of age while working at a beach club.

Innocent but unexciting comedy-drama about matters which scarcely concern grown-ups.

w Neal Marshall, Garry Marshall (no relation)   d Garry Marshall   ph James A. Kontner   pd Lawrence Miller   ed Priscilla Nedd

Matt Dillon, Richard Crenna, Hector Elizondo, Jessica Walter, Fisher Stevens

'A wrong girl from the right side of the tracks!'
Flamingo Road *
US   1949   94m   bw
Warner (Jerry Wald)
V*

A tough carnival dancer is stranded in a small town and soon affects the lives of the local politicians.

Standard melodrama from a bestseller, absurd but well performed.

w Robert Wilder   novel Robert Wilder   d Michael Curtiz   ph Ted McCord   m Max Steiner

Joan Crawford, David Brian, Sidney Greenstreet, Zachary Scott, Gladys George, Virginia Huston, Fred Clark

Une Flamme Dans Mon Coeur: see A Flame In My Heart

The Flanagan Boy
GB   1953   81m   bw
Exclusive/Hammer (Anthony Hinds)
US title: Bad Blonde

A young merchant seaman becomes a boxer and is corrupted by a hard-boiled blonde.

Competent British imitation of an American B movie.

w Guy Elmes, Richard Landau   novel Max Catto   d Reginald LeBorg   ph Walter Harvey   m Ivor Slaney   ad Wilfred Arnold   ed James Needs

Tony Wright, Barbara Payton, Sidney James, John Slater, Frederick Valk, Marie Burke

Flap
US   1970   106m   Technicolor   Panavision
Warner (Jerry Adler)
GB title: The Last Warrior

A drunken Indian on a dilapidated modern reservation starts a public relations war and leads a march on the city.

Unendearing comedy with a tragic end tacked on, not very entertaining as whimsy, farce or social conscience.

w Clair Huffaker   novel Nobody Loves a Drunken Indian by Clair Huffaker   d Carol Reed   ph Fred Koenekamp   m Marvin Hamlisch

Anthony Quinn, Claude Akins, Tony Bill, Victor Jory, Shelley Winters

Flare Up
US   1969   98m   Metrocolor
MGM/GMF (Leon Fromkes)

A man kills his wife and threatens her friends who he feels are responsible for the break-up of his marriage.

Sensationally violent melodrama with a plot that goes back to Sudden Fear and further. Adequately made.

w Mark Rodgers   d James Neilson   ph Andrew J. McIntyre   m Les Baxter

Raquel Welch, James Stacy, Luke Askew, Don Chastain, Ron Rifkin

Flash Gordon *
The hero of the 25th century was created in comic strip form by Alex Raymond and his chief claims to film fame are three wild and woolly serials made by Universal: Flash Gordon (1936), Flash Gordon's Trip to Mars (1938), and Flash Gordon Conquers the Universe

(1940), all starring Buster Crabbe with Charles Middleton as the wily Emperor Ming.

Their cheap and cheerful futuristic sets and their non-stop action have kept them popular with film buffs through the years. In 1974 a semi-porno spoof, Flesh Gordon, appeared.

Flash Gordon
GB   1980   115m   Technicolor   Todd-AO
EMI/Famous/Starling (Dino de Laurentiis)
V, V*, L, S

A football hero, his girlfriend, and Dr Zarkov have adventures on the planet Mongo.

Lively comic strip addition to the increasing numbers of such things being restaged at enormous expense fifty years after their prime.

w Lorenzo Semple Jnr, from characters created by Alex Raymond   d Michael Hodges   ph Gil Taylor   m Queen   pd Danilo Donati

Sam J. Jones, Melody Anderson, Topol, Max von Sydow, Timothy Dalton, Brian Blessed, Peter Wyngarde

'An expensively irrelevant gloss on its sources.' – Richard Combs, MFB

Flashback *
US   1990   108m   colour
Paramount (Marvin Worth)
V, V*, L

An uptight young FBI agent is chosen to escort to prison a hero of the counter-culture who has been caught after 20 years on the run.

A lightweight comedy of a culture clash, but too contrived to afford lasting amusement, particularly as everyone ends up on the same side.

w David Loughery   d Franco Amurri   ph Stefan Czapsky   m Barry Goldberg   pd Vincent Cresciman   ed C. Timothy O'Meara

Dennis Hopper, Kiefer Sutherland, Carol Kane, Paul Dooley, Cliff de Young, Richard Masur, Michael McKean, Kathleen York, Tom O'Brien

'Don't you understand? When you give up the dream, you die!'
Flashdance *
US   1983   98m   Movielab
Paramount/Polygram (Don Simpson, Jerry Bruckheimer)
V, V*, L, S

A female welder in a Pittsburgh factory has ambitions to be a ballet dancer.

Slickly-made, disco-style but dramatically empty entertainment.

w Tom Hedley, Joe Eszterhas   d Adrian Lyne   ph Don Peterman   m Giorgio Moroder   ed Bud Smith, Walt Mulconery

Jennifer Beals, Michael Nouri, Lilia Skala, Sunny Johnson, Kyle T. Heffner, Belinda Bauer

'It resembles an extended video for a record album.' – Observer

'A preposterous success.' – Guardian

'Basically, a series of rock videos.' – New Yorker

AA: song, 'Flashdance . . . What a Feeling' (m Giorgio Moroder, ly Keith Forsey, Irene Cara)

AAN: cinematography; editing; song, 'Maniac' (m/ly Michael Sembello, Dennis Matkosky)

Flashpoint
US   1985   94m   Metrocolor
Home Box Office/Silver Screen
V, V*, L

Border patrolmen discover treasure and decide to make off with it.

Competent action melodrama which doesn't quite hang together in the later stretches but has plenty of lively moments.

w Dennis Shryack, Michael Butler novel George La Fountaine d William Tannen ph Peter Moss m various, performed by Tangerine Dream

Kris Kristofferson, Treat Williams, Rip Torn, Kevin Conway

Flatliners

US 1990 114m DeLuxe Panavision
Columbia-Tri-Star/Stonebridge (Michael Douglas, Rick Bieber)
V, V*, L

Medical students experiment to discover whether there is life after death.

Hectic fantasy, filmed in a restless manner.

w Peter Filardi d Joel Schumacher ph Jan de Bont m James Newton Howard ed Robert Brown

Kiefer Sutherland, Julia Roberts, Kevin Bacon, William Baldwin, Oliver Platt, Kimberly Scott, Joshua Rudoy, Benjamin Mouton

'Filmed like an epic, packed with crisis, shock and suspense, it's a small tale that has been spectacularly escalated into a tall one.' – Philip Strick, MFB

Flavia Priestess of Violence: see Flavia the Heretic

Flavia the Heretic (dubbed)

Italy/France 1974 97m Technicolor
Eagle/PAC/ROC
V (W)
original title: Flavia la Monaca Musulmana; aka: Flavia la Nonne Musulmana; Flavia Priestess of Violence; The Rebel Nun

Forced to become a nun by her father and appalled by the violence of masculine society, a young woman takes her revenge by joining a force of invading Muslims.

An unpleasant mixture of religiosity and sadism, masquerading as a feminist tract. Some images are extraordinary – a naked woman crawling into the hanging carcase of a cow – but hardly compensate for its general lack of narrative drive.

w Fabrizio Onofri, Gianfranco Mingozzi, Bruno Di Geronimo, Sergio Tau story Raniero Di Giovanbattista, Sergio Tau, Francesco Vietri d Gianfranco Mingozzi ph Alfio Contini m Nicola Piovani ad Guido Josia ed Ruggero Mastroianni

Florinda Balkan, Maria Casares, Claudio Cassinelli, Anthony Corlan, Spiros Focas

Flaxy Martin

US 1948 86m bw
Warner (Saul Elkins)

A lawyer falls for a racketeer's girlfriend and finds himself framed for murder.

Flatly-handled melodrama with unsympathetic characters.

w David Lang d Richard Bare ph Carl Guthrie

Zachary Scott, Virginia Mayo, Dorothy Malone, Tom d'Andrea, Elisha Cook Jnr

A Flea in Her Ear *

US/France 1968 94m DeLuxe Panavision
TCF (Fred Kohlmar)

Various suspicious wives and husbands converge on the notorious Hotel Coq d'Or.

Disappointing filming of a Feydeau farce, which needs to be much more cleverly handled to come over with its full theatrical force.

w John Mortimer play La Puce à l'Oreille by Georges Feydeau d Jacques Charon ph Charles Lang m Bronislau Kaper pd Alexander Trauner

Rex Harrison, Rachel Roberts, Rosemary Harris, Louis Jourdan, John Williams, Grégoire Aslan, Edward Hardwicke, Frank Thornton, Victor Sen Yung

'The plunge into madness never comes, and one is left with the sight of a group of talented players struggling with alien material.' – Michael Billington, Illustrated London News

'Gobs of glee! A boatload of beauties! A shipful of songs!'
The Fleet's In *

US 1942 93m bw
Paramount (Paul Jones)

A sailor on leave in San Francisco takes a bet that he can kiss the glamorous singer at a swank night-club.

Mindless wartime musical which happened to set the seal of success on a number of young talents.

w Walter de Leon, Sid Silvers, Ralph Spence play Sailor Beware by Kenyon Nicholson story Monte Price, J. Walter Ruben d Victor Schertzinger ph William Mellor m/y Victor Schertzinger, Johnny Mercer ed Paul Weatherwax

songs: 'I Remember You'; 'When You Hear the Time Signal'; 'The Fleet's In'; 'Tomorrow You Belong to Uncle Sam'; 'Arthur Murray Taught Me Dancing in a Hurry'; 'If You Build a Better Mousetrap'; 'Tangerine'; 'Conga from Honga'

Dorothy Lamour, William Holden, Eddie Bracken, Betty Hutton, Cass Daley, Gil Lamb, Leif Erickson, Betty Jane Rhodes

'A slim and obvious comedy with some good tunes. Much of the film is a roughhouse; several reels towards the end are turned over to straight vaudeville.' – Eileen Creelman, New York Sun

† Previously a Clara Bow vehicle, it was later remade as Sailor Beware starring Dean Martin and Jerry Lewis.

The Flemish Farm

GB 1943 82m bw
Two Cities (Sydney Box)

An attempt is made to retrieve a buried flag from occupied Belgium.

Tolerable wartime flagwaver.

w Jeffrey Dell, Jill Craigie d Jeffrey Dell ph Eric Cross m Ralph Vaughan Williams

Clive Brook, Clifford Evans, Jane Baxter, Philip Friend, Brefini O'Rourke

'He sacrificed his career for the sake of a woman's lying lips!'
Flesh *

US 1932 95m bw
MGM

A German wrestler in the US falls for a street waif.

Unusual, rather unattractive, but vivid melodrama.

w Leonard Praskins, Edgar Allen Woolf, Moss Hart story Edmund Goulding d John Ford ph Arthur Edeson ed William S. Gray

Wallace Beery, Ricardo Cortez, Karen Morley, John Miljan, Jean Hersholt, Herman Bing, Edward Brophy

'Not bad, could have been better . . . that it takes 95 minutes to get home is the big fault.' – Variety

Flesh *

US 1968 105m colour
Vaughn/Score Movies (Andy Warhol)
V
aka: Andy Warhol's Flesh

A day in the life of a male prostitute.

A revelation at the time, for putting New York street life and unabashed sexuality on the screen. It wears better than most underground movies of its time.

wd Paul Morrissey

Joe Dallesandro, Geraldine Smith, Patti D'Arbanville, Candy Darling, Jackie Curtis, Geri Miller

'With this strangely kindly and sympathetic film obscenity is only in the beholder's eye.' – David Robinson, Financial Times

'Totally obscene from the conventional point of view.' – John Weightman, Encounter

Flesh and Blood

GB 1951 102m bw
BL/Harefield (Anatole de Grunwald)

Three generations of a family suffer from the effects of heredity.

Fragmented Scottish period piece which never settles down long enough to make an impact with any group of characters.

w Anatole de Grunwald play A Sleeping Clergyman by James Bridie d Anthony Kimmins ph Otto Heller m Charles Williams

Richard Todd, Glynis Johns, Joan Greenwood, André Morell, Ursula Howells, Freda Jackson, George Cole, James Hayter, Ronald Howard, Muriel Aked

Flesh & Blood

US 1985 126m DeLuxe Technovision
Riverside/Impala (Gys Versluys)
V, V*, L

In a dark medieval world, a young bride-to-be is kidnapped and raped, but grows to like it.

Unpleasant wallow in a decadent world of the imagination.

w Gerard Soeteman, Paul Verhoeven d Paul Verhoeven ph Jan de Bont m Basil Poledouris ad Felix Murcia ed Ine Schenkkan

Rutger Hauer, Jennifer Jason Leigh, Tom Burlinson, Jack Thompson, Susan Tyrrell, Ronald Lacey

Flesh and Fantasy *

US 1943 94m bw
Universal (Charles Boyer, Julien Duvivier)

A club bore tells three strange stories.

A portmanteau with ingredients of varying interest, attempting to emulate the success of Tales of Manhattan. The fourth episode planned was deleted and turned up as Destiny (qv). All quite stylish, the best section being Lord Arthur Savile's Crime.

w Ernest Pascal, Samuel Hoffenstein, Ellis St Joseph story Ellis St Joseph, Oscar Wilde, Laslo Vadnay d Julien Duvivier ph Paul Ivano, Stanley Cortez m Alexandre Tansman

Robert Benchley, Edward G. Robinson, Barbara Stanwyck, Charles Boyer, Betty Field, Robert Cummings, Thomas Mitchell, C. Aubrey Smith, Dame May Whitty, Edgar Barrier, David Hoffman

Flesh and Fury

US 1952 82m bw
Universal-International (Leonard Goldstein)

A young deaf mute becomes a successful prizefighter.

Totally unremarkable programmer with a happy ending.

w Bernard Gordon d Joseph Pevney

Tony Curtis, Jan Sterling, Mona Freeman, Wallace Ford, Connie Gilchrist

Flesh and the Devil *

US 1926 109m bw silent
MGM
V*

A temptress toys with three men.

Hokey but good-looking star melodrama, climaxing with death on an ice floe. A huge commercial success because of the off-screen Garbo-Gilbert romance.

w Benjamin Glazer novel The Undying Past by Hermann Sudermann d Clarence Brown ph William Daniels

Greta Garbo, John Gilbert, Lars Hanson, Marc McDermott, Barbara Kent

'A film of more than passing cleverness . . . the theme is sheer undiluted sex, and Brown uses a series of close-ups to get this across with considerable effect.' – *Paul Rotha, The Film Till Now*

The Flesh and the Fiends
GB 1959 97m bw Dyaliscope
Regal/Triad (Robert Baker, Monty Berman)
V*
US title: *Mania*

In 1820 Edinburgh, 'resurrection men' commit murders to keep anatomists supplied.

Dr Robert Knox rides again, in a version more bloody but less entertaining than *The Body Snatcher*.

w John Gilling, Leon Griffiths *d* John Gilling
ph Monty Berman *m* Stanley Black

Peter Cushing, June Laverick, George Rose, Donald Pleasence, Renée Houston, Billie Whitelaw, Dermot Walsh

The Flesh is Weak
GB 1957 88m bw
Eros (Raymond Stross)

A girl goes from bad to worse when she finds that her boyfriend is head of a vice ring.

Road to Ruin, fifties style; competently made, but neither shocking nor entertaining, just an exploitation piece.

w Leigh Vance *d* Don Chaffey

John Derek, Milly Vitale, William Franklyn, Martin Benson, Freda Jackson, Norman Wooland, Harold Lang, Patricia Jessel, John Paul

The Flesh of the Orchid
France/Italy/Germany 1974 100m Eastmancolor
VMP/Paris Cannes Productions/F. Meric/L'Astrophone/ORTF/
Oceana/TIT (Vincent Malle)
original title: *La Chair de l'Orchidée*

A young heiress, incarcerated in a mental institution by her aunt who wants her fortune, goes on the run with a man being hunted by contract killers.

A baroque and overwrought stew of sex and death, likely to be too rich for most tastes.

w Jean-Claude Carrière, Patrice Chéreau
novel James Hadley Chase *d* Patrice Chéreau
ph Pierre Lhomme *m* Fiorenzo Carpi *ad* Richard Peduzzi *ed* Pierre Gillette

Charlotte Rampling, Bruno Cremer, Edwige Feuillère, Alida Valli, Hans Christian Blech, François Simon, Hugues Quester, Simone Signoret

Fletch *
US 1985 96m Technicolor
Universal/Douglas/Greisman
V, V*, L

A newspaper columnist with a penchant for disguise tracks down a nefarious con man.

A lightness of touch unusual for the eighties makes this comedy mystery more welcome than most.

w Andrew Bergman *novel* Gregory McDonald
d Michael Ritchie *ph* Fred Schuler *m* Harold Faltermeyer

Chevy Chase, Dana Wheeler-Nicholson, Tim Matheson, Joe Don Baker, Richard Libertini, Kenneth Mars, M. Emmet Walsh

Fletch Lives
US 1989 95m colour
UIP/Universal/Greisman/Douglas)
V, V*, L

An investigative reporter inherits trouble along with a Southern mansion.

Dire comedy with nothing to recommend it.

w Leon Capetanos *d* Michael Ritchie *ph* John McPherson *m* Harold Flatermyer, Buckwheat Zydeco *ed* Richard A. Harris

Chevy Chase, Hal Holbrook, Julianne Phillips, R. Lee Ermey, Richard Libertini, Randall 'Tex' Cobb, Cleavon Little

Les Fleurs Sauvages
Canada 1982 153m col/bw
Cinegate/Cinak (Marguerite Duparc)

A seventy-year-old widow visits her married daughter for a holiday.

Excessively drawn-out and introspective view of family relationships that loses interest long before the end.

wd Jean Pierre Lefèbvre *ph* Guy Dufaux *m* Raoul Duguay, Jean Corriveau *ed* Marguerite Duparc

Marte Nadeau, Michell Magny, Pierre Curzi, Claudia Aubin, Eric Beausejour, Georges Belisle, Sarah Mills

Un Flic: see *Dirty Money*

'What would you do if the man you loved wanted you to love his pal?'
'The first all-talking drama of the air!'

Flight
US 1929 110m bw
Columbia (Harry Cohn)

Two rival flyers join a mission to rescue US Marines ambushed in Nicaragua.

Pale stuff now, but in its time an ambitious action movie showing a new suppleness in its young director.

w Frank Capra, Ralph Graves *d* Frank Capra
ph Joseph Walker *ad* Harrison Wiley

Jack Holt, Lila Lee, Ralph Graves, Alan Roscoe, Harold Goodwin, Jimmy de la Cruze

Flight Angels
US 1940 74m bw
Edmund Grainger/Warner

Airline stewardesses compete for the favours of a romantic pilot.

An efficient potboiler, now most interesting for its depiction of 1939 air travel.

w Maurice Leo *d* Lewis Seiler

Virginia Bruce, Dennis Morgan, Wayne Morris, Ralph Bellamy, Jane Wyman, John Litel

Flight Command
US 1940 116m bw
MGM (J. Walter Ruben)

A cocky recruit makes good in the naval air arm.

Routine flagwaver.

w Wells Root, Cmdr Harvey Haislip *d* Frank Borzage *ph* Harold Rosson *m* Franz Waxman

Robert Taylor, Ruth Hussey, Walter Pidgeon, Paul Kelly, Nat Pendleton, Red Skelton, Shepperd Strudwick, Dick Purcell

Flight Commander: see *The Dawn Patrol* (1930)

Flight for Freedom
US 1943 101m bw
RKO (David Hempstead)

Biography of an intrepid aviatrix and her husband.

Patchy job based on the life of Amelia Earhart, suggesting that her final disappearance was on a government mission. Dull production.

w Oliver H. P. Garrett, S. K. Lauren *d* Lothar Mendes *ph* Lee Garmes *m* Roy Webb
ad Albert S. D'Agostino, Carroll Clark

Rosalind Russell, Fred MacMurray, Herbert Marshall, Eduardo Ciannelli, Walter Kingsford

AAN: art direction

Flight from Ashiya *
US/Japan 1963 102m Eastmancolor Panavision
UA/Harold Hecht/Daiei

When a cargo vessel sinks off the coast of Japan during a typhoon, the helicopter rescue service springs into action.

Conventional Grade A action thriller with flashbacks to earlier disasters in the lives of its heroes.

w Elliott Arnold, Waldo Salt *d* Michael Anderson
ph Joe MacDonald, Burnett Guffey *m* Frank Cordell *pd* Eugène Lourié

Yul Brynner, Richard Widmark, George Chakiris, Shirley Knight, Daniele Gaubert, Suzy Parker

Flight from Destiny
US 1941 74m bw
Warner

An elderly professor with six months to live determines on one good deed . . . which includes murder.

Likeable minor melodrama, well put together.

w Barry Trivers *play* Anthony Berkeley
d Vincent Sherman

Thomas Mitchell, Geraldine Fitzgerald, Jeffrey Lynn, Mona Maris

Flight from Folly
GB 1944 93m bw
Warner

A chorus girl cures a playwright's amnesia.

Leadenly-titled and played variation on *Random Harvest*, with dreary musical numbers.

w Basil Woon, Lesley Storm, Katherine Strueby
d Herbert Mason

Pat Kirkwood, Hugh Sinclair, Sydney Howard, Marian Spencer, Tamara Desni, Jean Gillie, A. E. Matthews

Flight from Glory *
US 1937 66m bw
Robert Sisk/RKO
V*

Tensions mount among flyers who cross the Andes daily between secluded mines and their supply base.

Tense 'B' picture which looks like a trial run for *Only Angels Have Wings*.

w David Silverstein, John Twist *d* Lew Landers

Chester Morris, Whitney Bourne, Onslow Stevens, Van Heflin, Richard Lane, Paul Guilfoyle

'Better than the average programmer and worth strong exhibitor plugging. In tone the picture may be fairly described as semi-sophisticated, which for rank and file purposes is probably just the right amount of sophistication.' – *Variety*

Flight Lieutenant
US 1942 80m bw
Columbia (B. P. Schulberg)

A careless pilot crashes a plane, but atones heroically for his former misdeeds.

Inept wartime flagwaver.

w Michael Blankfort *d* Sidney Salkow

Glenn Ford, Pat O'Brien, Evelyn Keyes, Minor Watson, Jonathan Hale

Flight Nurse
US 1953 90m bw
Republic

An air force nurse is on the front line during the Korean War.

Routine mix of love and action.

w Alan LeMay d Allan Dwan

Joan Leslie, Forrest Tucker, Arthur Franz, Jeff Donnell, Ben Cooper

Flight of the Doves *

US 1971 101m colour
Columbia/Rainbow (Ralph Nelson)

Two children run away from their bullying stepfather to join their Irish grandmother, but are chased by a wicked uncle who knows they are heirs to a fortune.

Pantomimish whimsy which works in fits and starts, but has little real humour or charm.

w Frank Gabrielson, Ralph Nelson novel Walter Macken d Ralph Nelson ph Harry Waxman m Roy Budd

Ron Moody, Dorothy McGuire, Helen Raye, Dana, Jack Wild, Stanley Holloway, William Rushton

The Flight of the Dragon

US 1982 98m colour
Rankin/Bass Productions (Arthur Rankin Jnr, Jules Bass)

An author is plucked from modern times back into a mythic past to help save magic in the world.

Children's cartoon with an ecological message. By modern standards, the animation is above average.

w Romeo Muller book The Flight of Dragons by Peter Dickinson d Arthur Rankin Jnr, Jules Bass m Maury Laws pd Wayne Anderson

voices of Victor Bueno, James Gregory, James Earl Jones, Harry Morgan, John Ritter

Flight of the Innocent

Italy 1993 105m Technicolor
Buena Vista/Cristaldi/Fandango/Raitre/Fildebroc (Franco Cristaldi, Domenico Procacci)
S
original title: Corsa dell'Innocente

A 10-year-old boy, witness to a gang killing, goes on the run followed by killers.

An unoriginal and violent chase movie with a sickly ending, done with skill but hardly worth the doing; it represents the neo-realist tradition at its most decadent.

w Carlo Carlei, Gualtiero Rosella d Carlo Carlei ph Raffaele Mertes m Carlo Siliotto pd Franco Ceraolo ed Carlo Fontana, Claudio di Mauro

'Carlei has a strong eye for comic book images but he doesn't know when to stop, and the whole thing soon turns into a shapeless, hysterical melodrama.' – Derek Malcolm, Guardian

'This despicable docuthriller . . . the film's only agenda is finding pretexts to photograph people lifted out of their shoes and blown across the room, farmyard, or plaza by a shotgun blast to the chest, preferably in gold-suffused backlight.' – Richard T. Jameson, Film Comment

'The only thing they can count on is each other.'
Flight of the Intruder

US 1991 113m Technicolor Panavision
Paramount/Mace Neufeld, Robert Rehme
V, V (W), V*, L

Pilots aboard an aircraft carrier during the Vietnam war decide to bomb Hanoi.

Dated and dull, with nothing to recommend it.

w Robert Dillon, David Shaber novel Stephen Coonts d John Milius ph Fred J. Koenekamp m Basil Pouledouris pd Jack T. Collis ad E. Albert Heschong ed C. Timothy O'Mears, Steve Mirkovich, Peck Prior

Danny Glover, Willem Dafoe, Brad Johnson, Rosanna Arquette, Tom Sizemore, J. Kenneth Campbell

Flight of the Navigator *

US 1986 90m colour
Buena Vista/Walt Disney (Robby Wald, Dimitri Villard)
V*, L

Kidnapped by aliens, a 12-year-old boy returns home after an eight-year absence without having grown any older.

Science fiction aimed at a family audience and providing blandly innocuous, occasionally amusing entertainment.

w Michael Burton, Matt Macmanus story Mark H. Baker d Randal Kleiser ph James Glennon m Alan Silvestri pd William J. Creber ed Jeff Gourson

Joey Cramer, Veronica Cartwright, Cliff DeYoung, Sarah Jessica Parker, Matt Adler, Howard Hesseman, Paul Mall (Paul Reubens)

The Flight of the Phoenix *

US 1965 149m DeLuxe
TCF/Associates and Aldrich
V*, L

A cargo passenger plane crashes in the desert, and the survivors try to avert disaster.

Achingly slow character adventure; an all-star cast works desperately hard but the final flight of the rebuilt plane seems almost an anticlimax after the surfeit of personal melodramatics.

w Lukas Heller novel Elleston Trevor d Robert Aldrich ph Joseph Biroc m Frank de Vol

James Stewart, Richard Attenborough, Hardy Kruger, Peter Finch, Dan Duryea, Ernest Borgnine, Ian Bannen, Ronald Fraser, Christian Marquand, George Kennedy

AAN: Ian Bannen

The Flight of the White Stallions: see The Miracle of the White Stallions

The Flight that Disappeared

US 1961 73m bw
UA/Harvard (Robert E. Kent)

Atomic scientists on an airliner find themselves in 'heaven' being tried by people of the future.

Eccentric anti-bomb curiosity, a second feature Outward Bound.

w Ralph Hart, Judith Hart, Owen Harris d Reginald Le Borg ph Gilbert Warrenton m Richard La Salle

Gregory Morton, Addison Richards, Craig Hill, Paula Raymond, Dayton Lummis

Flight to Hong Kong

US 1956 88m bw
UA

A syndicate boss tries to two-time the mob.

Co-feature hokum which barely justifies its length.

w Leo Townsend, Leo G. O'Callaghan d Joseph M. Newman

Rory Calhoun, Barbara Rush, Dolores Donlon, Soo Young, Pat Conway, Werner Klemperer

Flight to Mars

US 1951 75m Cinecolor
Monogram
V*

After a rocket flight, four scientists discover that the inhabitants of Mars speak perfect American, learned by radio.

Pioneering science-fiction entry with nothing going for it but being first: writing, production and acting are alike abysmal.

w Arthur Strawn d Lesley Selander

Cameron Mitchell, Marguerite Chapman, Arthur Franz, Virginia Huston, John Litel

Flight to Tangier

US 1953 90m Technicolor 3-D
Paramount (Nat Holt)

A female FBI agent chases a three million dollar letter of credit.

Forced and boring action romance without much of either element.

wd Charles Marquis Warren ph Ray Rennahan m Paul Sawtell

Joan Fontaine, Jack Palance, Corinne Calvet, Robert Douglas, Marcel Dalio, Jeff Morrow, Murray Matheson, John Doucette

The Flim Flam Man *

US 1967 104m DeLuxe Panavision
TCF/Lawrence Turman
V*
GB title: One Born Every Minute

An army deserter joins forces with an elderly con man.

Folksy comedy in a small-town setting; none of it really comes to the boil after a couple of early chase sequences.

w William Rose novel Guy Owen d Irvin Kershner, Yakima Canutt ph Charles Lang m Jerry Goldsmith

George C. Scott, Michael Sarrazin, Sue Lyon, Harry Morgan, Jack Albertson, Alice Ghostley, Albert Salmi

Flipper

US 1963 87m Metrocolor
(MGM) Ivan Tors
V*

A fisherman's son on the Florida Keys befriends a dolphin.

Harmless boy-and-animal adventure which spawned two sequels and a TV series.

w Arthur Weiss d James B. Clark ph Lamar Boren, Joseph Brun m Henry Vars

Chuck Connors, Luke Halpin, Kathleen Maguire, Connie Scott

† Flipper's New Adventure followed in 1964.

Flirtation Walk *

US 1934 97m bw
Warner (Frank Borzage)
V*

Love affairs of West Point cadets.

Light musical very typical of its period, with a few agreeable numbers.

w Delmer Daves d Frank Borzage ch Bobby Connelly ph Sol Polito, George Barnes m/y Allie Wrubel, Mort Dixon

Dick Powell, Ruby Keeler, Pat O'Brien, Ross Alexander, John Arledge, Henry O'Neill, Guinn Williams

'A rousing recruiting poster . . . and a splendid laboratory specimen of the adolescent cinema.' – André Sennwald, New York Times

AAN: best picture

Flirting *

Australia 1989 99m colour
Warner/Kennedy Miller (George Miller, Doug Mitchell, Terry Hayes)
V, V*, L

A 17-year-old Australian schoolboy falls in love with a Ugandan girl at a neighbouring school.

A less effective, though occasionally affecting, sequel to The Year My Voice Broke.

wd John Duigan ph Geoff Burton pd Roger Ford ed Robert Gibson, Marcus D'Arcy

Noah Taylor, Thandie Newton, Nicole Kidman, Bartholomew Rose, Felix Nobis, Josh Picker, Kiri Paramore

'Such rites of passage movies are common currency nowadays, but Duigan's ability to summon up the past with conviction, get good performances from his cast and to apply a sense of humour as well as a feeling of horror at what Australians did to their young *circa* 1965, makes the film universal in its appeal.' – *Derek Malcolm, Guardian*

The Flirting Widow
US 1930 70m bw
First National

A girl invents a lover, then kills him off . . . but his friend shows up.

Whimsical comedy which outstays its welcome.

w John F. Goodrich story Green Stockings by A. E. W. Mason d William A. Seiter

Dorothy Mackaill, Basil Rathbone, Leila Hyams, Claude Gillingwater, William Austin

'Slim for the key houses and really built for neighbourhoods.' – *Variety*

Flirting with Fate
US 1938 70m bw
David L. Loew

A trailerized vaudeville troupe tours South America.

The setting is the only surprising thing about this rather dim comedy.

w Joseph Moncure March, Ethel La Blanche, Charlie Melson, Harry Clork d Frank McDonald

Joe E. Brown, Leo Carrillo, Beverly Roberts, Wynne Gibson, Steffi Duna, Stanley Fields, Leonid Kinskey, Charles Judels

Flood Tide
US 1958 82m bw 'Scope
Universal

A boy is jealous of his widowed mother's interest in a neighbour.

Modest melodrama, typical of its studio at the time.

w Dorothy Cooper d Abner Biberman

George Nader, Cornell Borchers, Michel Ray, Judson Pratt, Joanna Moore

Floods of Fear *
GB 1958 84m bw
Rank/Sydney Box

Two escaped convicts, a warder, and a pretty girl are trapped by floods in a lonely house.

Adequate melodrama with impressively gloomy production and performances but not many surprises.

wd Charles Crichton novel John and Ward Hawkins ph Christopher Challis m Alan Rawsthorne

Howard Keel, Anne Heywood, Harry H. Corbett, Cyril Cusack

Floodtide
GB 1949 90m bw
Aquila/Rank

A Clydebank apprentice becomes a ship designer.

Boring inspirational drama hindered by the Independent Frame method.

w Donald B. Wilson, George Blake d Frederick Wilson

Gordon Jackson, Rona Anderson, John Laurie, Jack Lambert, Elizabeth Sellars

The Floradora Girl
US 1930 75m bw (Technicolor sequence)
MGM
GB title: The Gay Nineties

The romance of the last remaining Floradora girl.

Not a musical but a period farce which laughs at rather than with the fashions of 1900. It doubtless succeeded with the audiences of its time.

w Gene Markey, Ralph Spence, Al Boasberg, Robert Hopkins d Harry Beaumont

Marion Davies, Lawrence Gray, Walter Catlett, Ilka Chase, Vivian Oakland, Jed Prouty

'Good hoke entertainment . . . an all-type audience picture with no limitations.' – *Variety*

The Florentine Dagger
US 1935 69m bw
Warner

A mysterious Borgia influence is brought to bear on the murder of an art dealer.

Vaguely unsatisfactory whodunnit with some intriguing and some pretentious elements.

w Brown Holmes, Tom Reed novel Ben Hecht d Robert Florey

Margaret Lindsay, Donald Woods, C. Aubrey Smith, Robert Barrat, Henry O'Neill

Florian
US 1940 91m bw
MGM (Winfield Sheehan)

In 1910 Austria, a poor boy and a rich girl are united by their love of a Lippizaner stallion.

Not kinky, but strangely dull.

w Noel Langley, Geza Herczeg, James K. McGuinness d Edwin L. Marin ph Karl Freund, Richard Rosson m Franz Waxman

Robert Young, Helen Gilbert, Charles Coburn, Lee Bowman, Reginald Owen, S. Z. Sakall, Lucile Watson, Irina Baronova

Flower Drum Song *
US 1961 133m Technicolor Panavision
U-I/Rodgers and Hammerstein/Joseph Fields (Ross Hunter)
V*, L

Romantic problems among the immigrants in San Francisco's Chinatown.

A Broadway musical which on the screen seems old-fashioned, remorselessly cute, and even insulting to the Chinese characters. Within its limits, however, it is well enough staged and performed.

w Joseph Fields d Henry Koster ph Russell Metty md Alfred Newman, Ken Darby m/ly Richard Rodgers, Oscar Hammerstein II ad Alexander Golitzen, Joseph Weight costumes Irene Sharaff d Hermes Pan

Nancy Kwan, James Shigeta, Juanita Hall, Myoshi Umeki, James Soo, Sen Yung

AAN: Alfred Newman, Ken Darby; Russell Metty

Flowers in the Attic
US 1987 92m colour
Entertainment/New World (Sy Levin, Thomas Fries)
V, V*, L, S

Four children are kept locked in an attic by their deranged grandmother.

Tame melodrama that tones down the horrors of the novel and settles for a soporific approach to its sensational material.

wd Jeffrey Bloom novel Virginia C. Andrews ph Frank Byers, Gil Hubbs m Christopher Young pd John Muto ed Gregory F. Plotts

Louise Fletcher, Victoria Tennant, Jeb Stuart Adams, Ben Ganger, Lindsay Parker, Marshall Colt, Nathan Davis

The Flowers of St Francis: see *Francis, God's Jester*

Flowing Gold
US 1940 82m bw
Warner

A fugitive from justice finds himself in a Western oilfield.

Routine melodrama with climactic heroics and nothing to remember next day.

w Kenneth Gamet d Alfred E. Green

John Garfield, Pat O'Brien, Frances Farmer, Raymond Walburn, Cliff Edwards

Fluffy
US 1964 92m Eastmancolor
U-I/Scarus (Gordon Kay)

A biologist manages to tame a lion.

Mindless, cheerful animal comedy.

w Samuel Rocca d Earl Bellamy ph Clifford Stine m Irving Gertz

Tony Randall, Shirley Jones, Edward Andrews, Ernest Truex, Howard Morris, Jim Backus, Frank Faylen

The Flute and the Arrow *
Sweden 1957 75m Technicolor Agascope
Sandrews (Arne Sucksdorff)
original title: En Djungelsaga

The story of a remote Indian tribe and a prowling leopard thought to be possessed by a demon.

Superbly photographed but rather dull: Sucksdorff failed to provide enough story for a feature.

wd/ph Arne Sucksdorff m Ravi Shankar

'Once it was human . . . even as you and I . . . this monster created by atoms gone wild!'
The Fly
US 1958 94m Eastmancolor Cinemascope
TCF (Kurt Neumann)
V, V*, L

A scientist invents a method of transmitting and reassembling atoms. He transmits himself and does not notice a fly in the compartment . . .

Unpleasant horror film which becomes ludicrous but not funny.

w James Clavell d Kurt Neumann ph Karl Struss m Paul Sawtell

David Hedison, Patricia Owens, Herbert Marshall, Vincent Price

'It might be possible, I suppose, to take this preposterous piece of merchandise as a monstrous joke. Even so, it would be a joke in deplorably bad taste.' – *C. A. Lejeune*

† Sequels were *Return of the Fly* (1959) and *Curse of the Fly* (1965), neither worth noting in detail. And see below.

'Be afraid. Be very afraid.'
The Fly *
US 1986 100m DeLuxe
TCF/Brooksfilm (Stuart Cornfeld)
V, V*, L, S

A deliberately gruesome update of the above, with much unpleasant detail carried along by a certain style.

w Charles Edward Pogue, David Cronenberg d David Cronenberg ph Mark Irwin m Howard Shore pd Carol Spier ed Ronald Sanders

Jeff Goldblum, Geena Davis, John Getz

'One does not have to be totally warped to appreciate this film, but it does take a particular sensibility to embrace it.' – *Variety*

'Stylish acrobatics, cowgum gore.' – *Sight and Sound*

AA: make-up (Chris Wales, Stephen Dupuis)

'Like father. Like son.'
The Fly II
US   1989   105m   colour
Fox/Brooksfilms (Steven-Charles Jaffe)
V, V*, L, S

The precocious son of The Fly takes his revenge on the scientist who exploits him.

An uneasy mix of sentimentality and gore, but otherwise a standard monster movie.

w Mick Garris, Jim and Ken Wheat, Frank Darabout d Chris Walas ph Robin Vidgeon m Christopher Young pd Michael S. Bolton sp Chris Walas ed Sean Barton

Eric Stoltz, Daphne Zuniga, Lee Richardson, Harley Cross, Gary Chalk, Ann Marie Lee, Frank C. Turner, John Getz

'Constructed with a refreshing intricacy and visual panache.' – Philip Strick, MFB

'Action that makes every pulse beat sound like thunder!'
Fly by Night *
US   1942   74m   bw
Paramount
GB title: Secrets of G32

A doctor, accused of murdering a scientist, goes on the run and uncovers a Nazi spy ring.

Hoary 39 Steps imitation, commendably done on a low budget to furnish wartime propaganda.

w Jay Dratler, F. Hugh Herbert d Robert Siodmak

Richard Carlson, Nancy Kelly, Albert Basserman, Walter Kingsford, Martin Kosleek, Miles Mander

The Flying Circus: see Flying Devils

The Flying Deuces *
US   1939   67m   bw
Boris Morros
V, V*, L

Laurel and Hardy join the Foreign Legion.

Patchy comedy from the end of the comedians' period of glory, and showing signs of decline.

w Ralph Spence, Harry Langdon, Charles Rogers, Alfred Schiller d Edward Sutherland ph Art Lloyd, Elmer Dyer md Edward Paul m Leo Shuken ed Jack Dennis

Stan Laurel, Oliver Hardy, Jean Parker, James Finlayson, Reginald Gardiner, Charles Middleton

'Mechanical stuff . . . seemed like Beau Hunks and Bonnie Scotland all over again.' – William K. Everson

Flying Devils
US   1933   62m   bw
RKO
GB title: The Flying Circus

Three war veteran pilots join a flying circus.

Smart little programmer which certainly provided money's worth and has no axe to grind.

w Byron Morgan, Louis Stevens d Russell Birdwell ph Nicholas Musuraca m Max Steiner

Arline Judge, Bruce Cabot, Ralph Bellamy, Eric Linden, Cliff Edwards

Flying Disc Men from Mars
US   1951   bw   serial: 12 eps
Republic

A young aviator uncovers a plot by Martians to take over Earth.

The title sets the level of this silly serial. d Fred C. Brannon

Walter Reed, Lois Collier, Gregory Gay, James Craven, Harry Lauter

Flying Down to Rio **
US   1933   89m   bw
RKO (Merian C. Cooper, Lou Brock)
V*, L

A dance band is a big success in Rio de Janeiro.

A thin musical electrified by the finale in which girls dance on the wings of moving airplanes, and by the teaming of Astaire and Rogers for the first time. Now an irresistible period piece.

w Cyril Hume, H. W. Hannemann, Erwin Gelsey play Anne Caldwell story Louis Brock d Thornton Freeland ph J. Roy Hunt md Max Steiner ch Dave Gould m/y Vincent Youmans, Edward Eliscu, Gus Kahn ad Van Nest Polglase, Carroll Clark ed Jack Kitchin

songs: 'Music Makes Me'; 'Orchids in the Moonlight'; 'Flying Down to Rio'

Dolores del Rio, Gene Raymond, Raul Roulien, Ginger Rogers, Fred Astaire, Blanche Frederici, Walter Walker, Franklin Pangborn, Eric Blore

'Its main point is the screen promise of Fred Astaire . . . the others are all hoofers after him.' – Variety

AAN: song 'The Carioca'

Flying Elephants
US   1927   20m   bw   silent
Hal Roach

A caveman has the toothache.

Fragmentary and generally unsatisfactory comedy starring Laurel and Hardy before they properly teamed, but released after their joint success.

w Hal Roach, H. M. Walker d Frank Butler

Laurel and Hardy, James Finlayson, Viola Richard, Dorothy Coburn

The Flying Fontaines
US   1959   73m   Eastmancolor
Columbia

Jealousy on the big top trapeze.

Old hat circus melodrama, not especially well presented.

w Donn Mullally, Lee Ewin d George Sherman

Michael Callan, Evy Norlund, Joan Evans, Rian Garrick, Joe DeSantis

Flying Fortress
GB   1942   110m   bw
Warner (Max Milner)

A Canadian becomes a hero of bombing missions over Berlin.

Cardboard propaganda with silly love interest and a hilarious climax in which the hero does his stuff on the wing of a flying plane.

w Brock Williams, Gordon Wellesley, Edward Dryhurst d Walter Forde ph Gus Drisse, Basil Emmott

Richard Greene, Carla Lehmann, Betty Stockfield, Donald Stewart, Charles Heslop, Sidney King, Basil Radford, John Stuart

Flying G-Men
US   1939   bw   serial: 15 eps
Columbia

Enemy spies strike at the nation's defences – until four stalwart G-men are assigned.

Lively nonsense with fast-moving thrill sequences.

d Ray Taylor and James W. Horne

Robert Paige (alias The Black Falcon), Robert Fiske, James Craig, Lorna Gray

Flying High
US   1931   80m   bw
MGM
GB title: Happy Landing

A zany inventor breaks a long-distance flight record because he doesn't know how to land.

Primitive comedy musical with inept dialogue and a static camera, partially salvaged by two early Busby Berkeley routines.

w Robert Hopkins, A. P. Younger, Charles Riesner d Charles Riesner

Bert Lahr, Charlotte Greenwood, Pat O'Brien, Charles Winninger, Guy Kibbee, Hedda Hopper

'Marine air-devils in hot pursuit . . . Blood-red trails streak the sky!'
'Bares the hearts of women who wait!'
Flying Leathernecks
US   1951   102m   Technicolor
RKO (Edmund Grainger)
V, V*, L

Two marine officers fight the Japs and each other on Guadalcanal.

Empty, violent war actioner full of phoney heroics.

w James Edward Grant d Nicholas Ray ph William E. Snyder m Roy Webb

John Wayne, Robert Ryan, Janis Carter, Don Taylor, Jay C. Flippen, William Harrigan, James Bell

'Ray's treatment is depressingly second rate and does nothing to alleviate the unpleasant impression of this disturbingly violent production.' – Penelope Houston

The Flying Missile
US   1950   92m   bw
Columbia (Jerry Bresler)

A submarine commander defies authority to prove that rockets can be launched from the deck of a submarine.

Dated semi-documentary melodrama which was pretty flat on first viewing.

w Richard English, James Gunn d Henry Levin ph William Snyder m George Duning

Glenn Ford, Viveca Lindfors, Henry O'Neill, Carl Benton Reid, Joe Sawyer, John Qualen

The Flying Scotsman
GB   1929   63m   bw
Warner/BIP

An ex-employee tries to wreck a crack train.

Fairly presentable example of an early talkie film originally shot silent; one or two climactic thrills.

w Victor Kendal, Garnett Weston story Joe Grossman d Castleton Knight ph Theodor Sparkuhl m Idris Lewis, John Reynders ad T. H. Gibbins ed A. C. Hammond

Moore Marriott, Pauline Jameson, Ray Milland, Alec Hurley, Dino Galvani

The Flying Serpent
US   1945   59m   bw
PRC (Sigmund Neufeld)
V*

A crazed archaeologist uses a rare bird as a murder instrument.

Ineffective low-key horror despite an always interesting star.

w John T. Neville d Sherman Scott

George Zucco, Ralph Lewis, Hope Kramer, Eddie Acuff

'A bomber squadron wouldn't get through . . . but one ship might make it!'
Flying Tigers
US   1942   100m   bw
Republic (Edmund Grainger)
V*, L

American airmen fight the Japs over World War II China.

More mock heroics with noisy but unconvincing action sequences.

w Kenneth Gamet, Barry Trivers   d David Miller   ph Jack Marta   m Victor Young

John Wayne, John Carroll, Anna Lee, Paul Kelly, Mae Clarke

AAN: Victor Young

FM

US   1978   104m   Technicolor
CIC/Universal (Rand Holston)
V*, L
aka: Citizens' Band

Problems of a commercial radio station whose disc jockeys seek integrity above commerce.

Footling cause-pleading is all this 'with-it' movie has to offer apart from its picture of commercial radio in the late seventies, which should be of interest to social historians.

w Ezra Sacks   d John A. Alonzo   ph David Myers   m Steely Dan, Linda Ronstadt, Jimmy Buffett and others   pd Lawrence G. Paull   ed Jeff Gourson

Michael Brandon, Eileen Brennan, Alex Karras, Cleavon Little, Martin Mull

Fog

US   1933   70m   bw
Columbia

Three murders occur on an ocean liner enveloped in fog.

Promising but increasingly inept mystery with an unconvincing solution.

w Ethel Hill, Dore Schary   story Valentine Williams, Dorothy Rice Sims   d Albert Rogell

Donald Cook, Mary Brian, Reginald Denny, Robert McQuade, Maude Eburne

'Ably directed but deficient on casting and story.' – Variety

The Fog *

US   1979   91m   Metrocolor   Panavision
Rank/Avco Embassy (Debra Hill)
V, V*, L, S

A small Californian town is invaded by the leprous ghosts of mariners wrecked on the coast a hundred years before.

Silly but beguiling horror film with shock effects typical of its director.

w John Carpenter, Debra Hill   d John Carpenter   ph Dean Cundey   m John Carpenter   pd Tommy Lee Wallace   ed Tommy Lee Wallace, Charles Bornstein

Adrienne Barbeau, Hal Holbrook, John Houseman, Janet Leigh, Jamie Lee Curtis, Tom Atkins

'An uneasy venture down a blind alley.' – Tom Milne, MFB

Fog Island

US   1945   70m   bw
PRC (Leon Fromkess)
V*

A wealthy ex-convict gathers on a foggy island all the people he considers responsible for his downfall.

Very tolerable minor mystery lifted without permission from Agatha Christie's And Then There Were None.

w Pierre Gendron   d Terry Morse

George Zucco, Lionel Atwill, Jerome Cowan, Sharon Douglas, Veda Ann Borg, Ian Keith

Fog over Frisco ***

US   1934   68m   bw
Warner (Henry Blanke)

A San Francisco heiress gets herself murdered.

Silly whodunnit highly notable for its cinematic style, all dissolves, wipes and quick takes. Probably the fastest moving film ever made, and very entertaining despite its plot inadequacy.

w Robert N. Lee   novel George Dyer   d William Dieterle   ph Tony Gaudio   md Leo F. Forbstein   ed Harold McLernon

Bette Davis, Donald Woods, Margaret Lindsay, Lyle Talbot, Hugh Herbert, Arthur Byron, Robert Barrat, Douglass Dumbrille, Henry O'Neill, Irving Pichel, Alan Hale

'Another racketeering story, mild in entertainment. No marked names of strength.' – Variety

'It reveals those qualities of pace and velocity and sharpness which make the Hollywood product acceptable even when the shallow content of ideas makes you want to scream.' – Robert Forsythe

'Its speed is artificially created by pacing, wipes, opticals, overlapping sound, camera movement and placing of characters, and by its habit of never having time really to begin or end scenes.' – William K. Everson

† Remade 1942 as Spy Ship, a second feature.

Folies Bergère ***

US   1935   84m   bw
Twentieth Century (William Goetz, Raymond Griffith)
GB title: The Man from the Folies Bergère

A Parisian banker persuades a music hall artist to impersonate him, but the wife and girlfriend become involved in the confusion.

Amusing star vehicle with inventive Berkeleyish numbers and some remarkably sexy dialogue.

w Bess Meredyth, Hal Long   play The Red Cat by Rudolph Lothar, Hans Adler   d Roy del Ruth   ph Barney McGill, Peverell Marley   md Alfred Newman   ch Dave Gould

Maurice Chevalier, Merle Oberon, Ann Sothern, Eric Blore

† Remade as That Night in Rio, with Don Ameche, and On the Riviera, with Danny Kaye (both qv).

AA: Dave Gould

Folks!

US   1992   106m   Technicolor
First Independent/Penta (Victor Drai, Malcolm R. Harding)
V, V*

At his ailing mother's suggestion, a businessman tries to kill her and his senile father for the insurance money.

Embarrassingly bad comedy, not merely tasteless but, what is worse, devoid of humour.

w Robert Klane   d Ted Kotcheff   ph Larry Pizer   m Michel Colombier   pd William J. Creber   ed Joan E. Chapman

Tom Selleck, Don Ameche, Anne Jackson, Christine Ebersole, Wendy Crewson, Robert Pastorelli, Michael Murphy

'Marking severe career setbacks for Ameche and Selleck, Folks! obviously miscalculates the low intelligence of the mass audience.' – Variety

Follies Girl

US   1943   71m   bw
PRC

An army private visits the forces canteen but falls for the burlesque dancer next door.

Feebly developed romance with music, mostly notable for its specialities.

w Marcy Klauber, Charles Robinson   d William Rowland

Wendy Barrie, Doris Nolan, Gordon Oliver, Anne Barrett, Cora Witherspoon

Follow a Star

GB   1959   104m   bw
Rank (Hugh Stewart)

A shy amateur singer allows a fading star to mime to his voice.

Star comedy with an antique plot and a superfluity of pathos.

w Jack Davies, Henry Blyth, Norman Wisdom   d Robert Asher   ph Jack Asher   m Philip Green

Norman Wisdom, Jerry Desmonde, June Laverick, Hattie Jacques, Richard Wattis, John Le Mesurier, Fenella Fielding, Ron Moody

'Such comedy as there is is mostly muffed by the lack of any sense of comic timing.' – MFB

Follow Me

GB   1971   93m   Technicolor   Panavision
Universal/Hal B. Wallis (Paul Nathan)
US title: The Public Eye

An eccentric private eye is hired to follow an accountant's wife, and she finds him fascinating.

Dullish, whimsical rendering of a dullish, whimsical one-act play; it never springs to life or interest.

w Peter Shaffer   play Peter Shaffer   d Carol Reed   ph Christopher Challis   m John Barry

Topol, Michael Jayston, Mia Farrow

'An uneasy mixture of broad comedy and high romance.' – Sight and Sound

Follow Me Boys

US   1966   132m   Technicolor
Walt Disney (Winston Hibler)

The domestic trials and tribulations of a smalltown schoolmaster.

Sentimental family saga full of patriotic fervour.

w Louis Pelletier   novel God and My Country by Mackinlay Kantor   d Norman Tokar   ph Clifford Stine   m George Bruns

Fred MacMurray, Vera Miles, Lillian Gish, Charlie Ruggles, Elliott Reid, Kurt Russell, Luana Patten, Ken Murray

'Demands an extremely strong stomach.' – MFB

'One of the worst films to emanate from the Disney studios, a near parody of all the lowbrow small-townery that has given Disney's features a bad name among intellectuals who never go to Disney movies. It is unworthy of the Disney trademark.' – Judith Crist

Follow Me Quietly *

US   1949   60m   bw
RKO (Herman Schlom)

Police track down a killer who strangles whenever it rains.

Effective little urban thriller with nice sense of detail.

w Lillie Hayward   d Richard Fleischer

William Lundigan, Dorothy Patrick, Jeff Corey, Nestor Paiva, Charles D. Brown, Paul Guilfoyle

Follow That Camel: see Carry On – Follow That Camel

Follow That Dream

US   1962   110m   DeLuxe   Panavision
UA/Mirisch (David Weisbart)
V, V*

A wandering family sets up house on a Florida beach.

Tiresomely cute comedy vehicle for a resistible star.

w Charles Lederer   novel Pioneer Go Home by Richard Powell   d Gordon Douglas   ph Leo Tover   m Hans Salter

Elvis Presley, Arthur O'Connell, Joanna Moore, Anne Helm, Jack Kruschen

Follow That Guy with the One Black Shoe:
see *Le Grand Blond avec une Chaussure Noire*

Follow the Band
US   1943   60m   bw
Universal (Paul Malvern)

A farm worker on his first visit to New York becomes a trombonist in a night-club.

Minor musical filler which packs in a surprising range of talent.

w Warren Wilson, Dorothy Bennett   *d* Jean Yarbrough

Eddie Quillan, Leon Errol, Mary Beth Hughes, Samuel S. Hinds, Robert Mitchum, Frances Langford, Leo Carrillo, Hilo Hattie, the King Sisters, Skinnay Ennis and his band

Follow the Boys *
US   1944   109m   bw
Universal (Charles K. Feldman)

A song and dance man organizes entertainment for the US troops during World War II.

Scrappy, unattractive propaganda tribute by the stars to the stars, enlivened only by a few guest spots.

w Lou Breslow, Gertrude Purcell   *d* A. Edward Sutherland   *ph* David Abel   *m* Leigh Harline and others

George Raft, Vera Zorina, Charley Grapewin, Grace MacDonald, Charles Butterworth, George Macready, Elizabeth Patterson; and Orson Welles, Marlene Dietrich, Jeanette MacDonald, Dinah Shore, Donald O'Connor, Peggy Ryan, W. C. Fields, the Andrews Sisters, Artur Rubenstein, Sophie Tucker, Ted Lewis and his band, etc

AAN: song 'I'll Walk Alone' (*m* Jule Styne, *ly* Sammy Cahn)

Follow the Boys
US   1963   95m   Metrocolor   Panavision
MGM/Franmet (Lawrence P. Bachmann)

An American warship is diverted from Cannes to Santa Margarita, and the waiting wives have to follow by road.

Harmless star comedy musical.

w David T. Chantler, David Osborn   *d* Richard Thorpe   *ph* Ted Scaife

Connie Francis, Paula Prentiss, Dany Robin, Russ Tamblyn, Richard Long

Follow the Fleet **
US   1936   110m   bw
RKO (Pandro S. Berman)
V*, L

Sailors on shore leave romance a couple of girl singers.

Amiable star musical which makes heavy weather of a listless and overlong script, but has good numbers for those who can wait.

w Dwight Taylor   *play* *Shore Leave* by Hubert Osborne, Allan Scott   *d* Mark Sandrich   *ph* David Abel   *md* Max Steiner   *m/ly* Irving Berlin

songs: 'I'm Putting All My Eggs in One Basket'; 'We Saw the Sea'; 'Let's Face the Music and Dance'; 'Let Yourself Go'; 'But Where Are You?'; 'I'd Rather Lead a Band'; 'Get Thee Behind Me Satan'; 'With a Smile on My Face'.

Fred Astaire, Ginger Rogers, Randolph Scott, Harriet Hilliard, Astrid Allwyn, Harry Beresford, Lucille Ball, Betty Grable, Tony Martin

'The running time is way overboard . . . dialogue is good and can be depended on for laughs, with the Astaire-Rogers dancing sure to do the rest. But cutting it would have helped a lot more.' – *Variety*

Follow the Leader
US   1930   76m   bw
Paramount

A saucy understudy replaces a kidnapped leading lady.

Broadway spoof rather tediously designed as a vehicle for the star's face-pulling.

w Sid Silvers, Gertrude Purcell from the Broadway musical *Manhattan Mary*   *d* Norman Taurog

Ed Wynn, Ginger Rogers, Ethel Merman, Lou Holtz, Stanley Smith

'First-run material and above average.' – *Variety*

Follow the Sun
US   1951   93m   bw
TCF (Samuel G. Engel)

Ben Hogan, a professional golfer, recovers slowly and painfully from a car crash and for the first time gains the affection of the crowd.

Modest sporting biopic, generally watchable but rising to no great heights.

w Frederick Hazlitt Brennan   *d* Sidney Lanfield   *ph* Leo Tover   *m* Cyril Mockridge

Glenn Ford, Anne Baxter, Dennis O'Keefe, June Havoc, Larry Keating, Nana Bryant, Roland Winters

Follow Thru
US   1930   93m   Technicolor
Paramount

Two women are after the same pro golfer.

Flat film version of a Broadway show.

w De Sylva, Brown, Henderson, from their show   *d* Laurence Schwab, Lloyd Corrigan

songs: 'Button Up Your Overcoat'; 'You Wouldn't Fool Me Would You'; 'I'm Hard to Please'; 'A Peach of a Pair'; 'It Must be You'.

Charles Rogers, Nancy Carroll, Zelma O'Neal, Jack Haley, Eugene Pallette, Thelma Todd

'Paramount has tossed away a heavy money picture.' – *Variety*

Folly to be Wise *
GB   1952   91m   bw
London Films/Launder and Gilliat

A brains trust at an army unit starts off a battle of the sexes.

Typical James Bridie comedy which starts brightly and whimsically, then peters out and is saved by the acting.

w Frank Launder, John Dighton   *play* *It Depends What You Mean* by James Bridie   *d* Frank Launder   *ph* Jack Hildyard   *m* Temple Abady

Alastair Sim, Roland Culver, Elizabeth Allan, Martita Hunt, Colin Gordon

'It seems to get funnier the longer it's spun out.' – *Pauline Kael, 70s*

Fontan **
USSR   1988   101m   colour
BFI/Lenfilm (Boris Pavlov-Silvanski)
aka: *The Fountain*

The eccentric inhabitants of a Leningrad apartment block take matters into their own hands when their water and electricity are cut off.

Satirical comedy poking fun at most aspects of Gorbachev's Russia.

w Vladimir Vardunas   *d* Yuri Mamin   *ph* Anatoli Lapshov   *m* Aleksei Zalivalow   *ad* Yuri Pugach   *ed* O. Adrianova

Asankul Kuttubaev, Sergei Dontsov, Zhanna Kerimtaeva, Viktor Mikhailov, Anatoli Kalmikov, Liudmila Samokhvalova

Fontane Effi Briest: see *Effi Briest*

The Food of the Gods
US   1976   88m   Movielab
AIP (Bert I. Gordon)

A curious substance which oozes out of the ground turns common beasts into monsters.

Rather crude horror movie which has little affinity with its literary original.

wd Bert I. Gordon   *story* H. G. Wells   *ph* Reginald Morris   *m* Elliot Kaplan

Marjoe Gortner, Pamela Franklin, Ida Lupino, Ralph Meeker, John McLiam

'Not only sick, but sickening.' – *Arthur Knight*

'I wish I hadn't seen the movie, so I could avoid it like the plague.' – *John Simon*

'More plot holes than any movie in recent memory, and enough dopey lines to make a Saturday night audience howl in all the wrong places.' – *David Sterritt, Christian Science Monitor*

Food of the Gods II
Canada   1989   91m   colour
Rose & Ruby (David Mitchell, Damian Lee)
V, V*, L

Giant man-eating rats are let loose on a college campus.

Risibly bad horror with a catch-penny title; it was not a sequel to the first film nor does it in any way resemble Wells's original story.

w Richard Bennet, E. Kim Brewster   *d* Damian Lee   *ph* Curtis Petersen   *sp* Ted Rae   *ed* David Mitchell

Paul Coufos, Lisa Schrage, Colin Fox, Frank Moore, Real Andrews, Jackie Burroughs

The British video release was cut to 82m.

The Fool **
GB   1990   140m   colour
Hobo/Sands Films/Richard Goodwin, Christine Edzard

A Victorian clerk enjoys a double life as a businessman moving in the best social circles.

Its meticulous evocation of Victorian life, drawing on the books of Henry Mayhew, sometimes overwhelms the slender plot, but it is never less than watchable.

w Christine Edzard, Olivier Stockman   *d* Christine Edzard   *ph* Robin Vidgeon   *m* Michael Sanvoisin   *ed* Olivier Stockman

Derek Jacobi, Cyril Cusack, Ruth Mitchell, Maria Aitken, Irina Brook, Paul Brooke, Richard Caldicot, James Cairncross, Jim Carter, Jonathan Cecil, Maria Charles

Fool for Love
US   1985   106m   colour
Cannon/Golan-Globus
V*

In a decaying motel, a half-brother and sister pick over the scab of their unsatisfactory, incestuous relationship.

Basically a filmed play, claustrophobic and taken at an excessively slow tempo.

w Sam Shepard   *play* Sam Shepard   *d* Robert Altman   *ph* Pierre Mignot   *m* George Burt   *pd* Stephen Altman   *ed* Luce Grunenwaldt, Steve Dunn

Sam Shepard, Kim Basinger, Randy Quaid, Harry Dean Stanton

The Fool Killer
US   1965   100m   bw
Landau/AA

An orphan suspects his friend is an axe murderer.

Post-Civil War fable with good performances but not much point.

w David Friedkin, Morton Fine   *novel* Helen Eustis
d Servando Gonzalez

Anthony Perkins, Edward Albert, Dana Elcar, Henry Hull, Salome Jens

A Fool There Was *
US   1914   67m (24 fps)   bw   silent
William Fox

A financier in Europe forsakes all for a *femme fatale*, and dies in her arms.

Antediluvian moral melodrama which made a star of Bara and added the word 'vamp' to the language.

wd Frank Powell   *play* Porter Emerson Browne suggested by Rudyard Kipling's poem *The Vampire*

Theda Bara, Edward Jose, Mabel Frenyer, May Allison

Foolin' Around
US   1979   101m   DeLuxe
Columbia/Arnold Kopelson

A country bumpkin wins a runaway heiress.

Uneasy harkback to the innocence of *It Happened One Night*, with willing performers in search of a script and setting.

w Mike Kane, David Swift   d Richard T. Heffron
ph Philip Lathrop   m Charles Bernstein

Gary Busey, Annette O'Toole, John Calvin, Eddie Albert, Cloris Leachman, Tony Randall

Foolish Wives **
US   1921   85m approx (24 fps); originally much longer
     bw   silent
Universal
V*, L

In Monte Carlo, a fake count seduces and blackmails rich women.

Weird melodrama with memorable moments and a vast set; Stroheim's most vivid star performance and one of his most lavish productions.

wd Erich von Stroheim   ph Ben Reynolds, William Daniels   ad Erich von Stroheim, Richard Day

Erich von Stroheim, Mae Busch, Maud George, Cesare Gravina

'A very superior piece of photoplay craftsmanship, original in ideas and treatment and deserving of higher rating than *Orphans of the Storm*, *Loves of Pharaoh*, *The Storm* and other second-class material which however brought forth applause and bravos from screen public and scribes.' – *Tamar Lane, What's Wrong with the Movies*

† The film was released in Latin America at a length of 6hrs 48m.

Fools
US   1970   93m   Eastmancolor
Translor
V*

An unsuccessful actor has an idyllic love affair with a girl he meets in a park; but her jealous millionaire husband shoots her dead.

Foolish is the word for those who concocted this tedious parable about the innocence of love and the sickness of society.

w Robert Rudelson   d Tom Gries

Jason Robards Jnr, Katharine Ross, Scott Hylands

Fools for Scandal *
US   1938   81m   bw
Warner (Mervyn Le Roy)

A Hollywood movie star falls in love with a French nobleman.

Disappointingly leaden romantic comedy.

w Herbert and Joseph Fields   *play Return Engagement* by Nancy Hamilton, Rosemary Casey, James Shute
d Mervyn Le Roy   ph Ted Tetzlaff   m/y Richard Rodgers, Lorenz Hart

Carole Lombard, Fernand Gravet, Ralph Bellamy, Allen Jenkins, Isabel Jeans, Marie Wilson, Ottola Nesmith

'Many diverting moments . . . will do average business.' – *Variety*

Fools of Fortune *
GB   1990   109m   Technicolor
Palace/Polygram/Working Title/Film Four International (Sarah Radclyffe)
V, V*, L, S

An Anglo-Irish family become caught up in the troubles of the 1920s.

Understated story of family tragedy, with a quiet appeal.

w Michael Hirst   *novel* William Trevor   d Pat O'Connor   ph Jerzy Zielinski   m Hans Zimmer
pd Jamie Leonard   ed Michael Bradsell

Iain Glen, Mary Elizabeth Mastrantonio, Julie Christie, Michael Kitchen, Niamh Cusack, Tom Hickey, John Kavanagh, Mick Lally, Niall Toibin

'A piece of classically-British film-making in the television style: restrained, elliptical, curiously reticent.' – *David Wilson, MFB*

Fools Parade **
US   1971   98m   Eastmancolor
Columbia/Stanmore/Penbar (Andrew V. McLaglen)
GB title: *Dynamite Man from Glory Jail*

An ex-con has trouble cashing a cheque for his prison savings, especially as outlaws are after it.

Curious admixture of comedy, adventure and violence with a thirties setting, from the author of *Night of the Hunter*; generally gripping entertainment.

w James Lee Barrett   *novel* Davis Grubb   d Andrew V. McLaglen   ph Harry Stradling Jnr   m Henry Vars
ad Alfred Sweeney   ed David Bretherton, Robert Simpson

James Stewart, George Kennedy, Strother Martin, Anne Baxter, Kurt Russell, William Windom, Mike Kellin

'A quintessentially American tribute to the quiet heroism of the self-made man.' – *Nigel Andrews*

Fools Rush In
GB   1949   82m   bw
Rank/Pinewood

A girl changes her mind on her wedding day, and causes repercussions through the family.

Thin, flat film version of a successful play.

w Geoffrey Kerr   *play* Kenneth Horne   d John Paddy Carstairs

Sally Ann Howes, Guy Rolfe, Nora Swinburne, Nigel Buchanan, Raymond Lovell, Thora Hird

Football Crazy
Italy   1974   106m   colour
Documento Films (Gianni Hecht Lucara)

A small-town football referee, who dreams of making the big time, has an affair with a glamorous journalist.

An ineffectual comedy that requires an audience to believe that referees are heroes in their community and that Joan Collins offers erotic promise.

w G. Scarniaci, R. Vianello, S. Continenza, Luigi Filipo D'Amico   d Luigi Filipo D'Amico   ph Sergio D'Offizi   m Guido and Maurizio de Angelis
pd Walter Patriarca   ed Marisa Mengoli

Lando Buzzanca, Joan Collins, Gabriella Pallotta, Ignazio Leone, Daniele Vargas

'Can you even think of missing it?'
'1,000 surprises! 300 beauties! 20 big stars!'

Footlight Parade ***
US   1933   104m   bw
Warner (Robert Lord)
V, V*, L

A determined producer of cine-variety numbers gets the show going despite great difficulty.

Classic putting-on-a-show musical distinguished by rapid-fire dialogue, New York setting, star performances and some of the best Busby Berkeley numbers.

w Manuel Seff, James Seymour   d Lloyd Bacon
ch Busby Berkeley   ph George Barnes   m/y Harry Warren, Al Dubin, Sammy Fain, Irving Kahal
ad Anton Grot, Jack Okey   ed George Amy

songs: 'By a Waterfall'; 'Ah, the Moon Is Here'; 'Sittin' on a Backyard Fence'; 'Shanghai Lil'; 'Honeymoon Hotel'

James Cagney, Joan Blondell, Ruby Keeler, Dick Powell, Frank McHugh, Guy Kibbee, Ruth Donnelly, Hugh Herbert, Claire Dodd, Herman Bing

'Bevies of beauty and mere males disport themselves in a Honeymoon Hotel, by (and in) a Waterfall, and over several acres of Shanghai.' – *C. A. Lejeune*

† The Chester Kent studio was a take-off of Fanchon and Marco, who had just such a studio on Sunset Boulevard.

Footlight Serenade
US   1942   80m   bw
TCF (William LeBaron)
V*

A boxer romances a showgirl.

Indifferent star musical.

w Robert Ellis, Helen Logan, Lynn Starling
d Gregory Ratoff   ph Lee Garmes   md Charles Henderson   m/y Ralph Rainger, Leo Robin

Betty Grable, John Payne, Victor Mature, James Gleason, Phil Silvers, Jane Wyman, Cobina Wright Jnr, June Lang, Mantan Moreland

'He's A Big-City Kid In A Small Town. They Said He'd Never Win. He Knew He Had To.'

Footloose
US   1984   107m   Movielab
Paramount/Indieprod (Lewis J. Rachmil, Craig Zadan)
V*, L, S

The domination of an old-fashioned local preacher is slackened by a young newcomer who insists on arranging a dance.

Odd fable which seeks to combine *Flashdance* with *Rebel without a Cause*, and misses out on both.

w Dean Pitchford   d Herbert Ross   ph Ric Waite
m various   pd Ron Hobbs

Kevin Bacon, Lori Singer, John Lithgow, Dianne Wiest, Christopher Penn

'The celebration of teenage frustration as dance reduces the issues to the level of platitude.' – *Donald Greig, MFB*

AAN: title song (m/y Kenny Loggins, Dean Pitchford); song 'Let's Hear It for the Boy' (m/y Dean Pitchford, Tom Snow)

Footsteps in the Dark
US   1941   96m   bw
Warner (Robert Lord)

A would-be detective novelist on the lookout for story material finds himself solving a murder.

Lethargic modern vehicle for Flynn between his swashbucklers, a poor imitation of the *Thin Man* style.

w Lester Cole, John Wexley   *play Blondie White* by Ladislas Fodor   d Lloyd Bacon   ph Ernest Haller
m Frederick Hollander

Errol Flynn, Brenda Marshall, Ralph Bellamy, Alan Hale, Lucile Watson, Allen Jenkins, Lee Patrick, William Frawley, Roscoe Karns, Grant Mitchell

'The footsteps were those of restless patrons on their way out to buy popcorn.' – *Clive Hirschhorn*

'When he comes to her room at midnight, is it to kiss or kill?'

Footsteps in the Fog *
GB   1955   90m   Technicolor
Film Locations/Mike Frankovich (Maxwell Setton)

A Victorian murderer plans to eliminate a blackmailing maid.

This variation on *Gaslight* turns into a black comedy without laughs, but it has effective moments and is efficiently if charmlessly made.

w Dorothy Reid, Lenore Coffee   *story* The Interruption by W. W. Jacobs   *d* Arthur Lubin   *ph* Christopher Challis   *m* Benjamin Frankel   *ad* Wilfrid Shingleton

Stewart Granger, Jean Simmons, Bill Travers, Ronald Squire, Finlay Currie, Peter Bull

For a Few Dollars More **
Italy/Spain/West Germany   1965   130m   Techniscope
PEA/Gonzales/Constantin (Alberto Grimaldi)
V, V*, L, S
original title: *Per Qualche Dollari in Più*

Bounty hunters in El Paso agree to work together.

Vague, inflated, sometimes good-looking sequel to *A Fistful of Dollars*, with customary violence and predictably mean performances.

wd Sergio Leone   *ph* Massimo Dallamano   *m* Ennio Morricone

Clint Eastwood, Lee Van Cleef, Gian Maria Volonte, Klaus Kinski

For Better For Worse
GB   1954   84m   Eastmancolor
Kenwood (Kenneth Harper)
US title: *Cocktails in the Kitchen*

Tribulations of a young married couple.

Undernourished comedy with an agreeable cast but no surprises.

wd J. Lee-Thompson   *play* Arthur Watkyn

Dirk Bogarde, Susan Stephen, Cecil Parker, Dennis Price, Athene Seyler, Eileen Herlie, Thora Hird, James Hayter, Pia Terri, Sid James, Charles Victor

For Freedom
GB   1940   88m   bw
GFD/Gainsborough (Edward Black, Castleton Knight)

Events surrounding the Battle of the River Plate and the sinking of the *Graf Spee*.

Economical wartime potboiler with much use of newsreel.

w Miles Malleson, Leslie Arliss   *d* Maurice Elvey, Castleton Knight   *ph* Arthur Crabtree

Will Fyffe, Anthony Hulme, E. V. H. Emmett, Guy Middleton, Albert Lieven

For Heaven's Sake
US   1950   92m   bw
TCF (William Perlberg)

Two angels are sent to earth to mend a Broadway producer's marriage.

Silly, flat whimsy of the *Here Comes Mr Jordan* school, and originating from the same author. Stale beer, but historically interesting.

wd George Seaton   *play* Harry Segall   *ph* Lloyd Ahern   *m* Alfred Newman

Clifton Webb, Edmund Gwenn, Robert Cummings, Joan Bennett, Joan Blondell, Gigi Perreau, Jack La Rue

For Keeps: see *Maybe Baby*

For Love of a Queen: see *The Dictator*

For Love of Ivy
US   1968   100m   Perfectcolor
Cinerama/Palomar (Edgar J. Scherick, Jay Weston)

An invaluable coloured maid gives notice, and the family blackmails a likeable black ne'er-do-well to make love to her so that she will stay.

Unhappy whimsy with an extremely laboured script and no jokes, notable only as Hollywood's first bow towards a black love affair.

w Robert Alan Aurthur   *story* Sidney Poitier   *d* Daniel Mann   *ph* Joseph Coffey   *m* Quincy Jones

Sidney Poitier, Abby Lincoln, Beau Bridges, Carroll O'Connor, Nan Martin, Lauri Peters

AAN: title song (*m* Quincy Jones, *ly* Bob Russell)

For Love or Money
US   1963   108m   Technicolor
U-I (Robert Arthur)

A rich widow hires a lawyer to look after the affairs of her three wayward daughters; he picks the eldest for himself.

Slow, thin, overlong comedy with a surfeit of witless chat.

w Larry Marks, Michael Morris   *d* Michael Gordon   *ph* Clifford Stine   *m* Frank de Vol

Kirk Douglas, Mitzi Gaynor, Thelma Ritter, William Bendix, Gig Young

For Love or Money
US   1993   96m   DeLuxe
Universal (Brian Grazer)
V, V*, S
GB title: *The Concierge*

A concierge's dreams of owning his own hotel come true.

A dim romantic comedy that wastes a likeable star.

w Mark Rosenthal, Lawrence Konner   *d* Barry Sonnenfeld   *ph* Oliver Wood   *m* Bruce Broughton   *pd* Peter Larkin   *ed* Jim Miller

Michael J. Fox, Gabrielle Anwar, Anthony Higgins, Michael Tucker, Bob Balaban, Isaac Mizrahi, Udo Kier, Dan Hedeya

'No amount of good humor can deter the thin tale from evaporating before the final clinch.' – *Variety*

'A faceless bit of professionalism, occasionally sparked by incidental bits of business, which coasts too heavily on Fox's boyish charm.' – *Kim Newman*

For Me and My Gal ***
US   1942   104m   bw
MGM (Arthur Freed)
V*, L

Just before World War I, a girl vaudevillian chooses between two partners.

A routine musical romance at the time of its production, this film now stands out because of its professional execution, its star value, and the fact that they don't make 'em like that any more.

w Richard Sherman, Sid Silvers, Fred Finklehoffe   *d* Busby Berkeley   *ph* William Daniels   *md* Georgie Stoll, Roger Edens

Judy Garland, Gene Kelly, George Murphy, Marta Eggerth, Ben Blue, Richard Quine, Stephen McNally

'A touch of imagination and a deal more than a touch of energy.' – *The Times*

AAN: Georgie Stoll, Roger Edens

For Men Only
US   1952   95m   bw
Lippert

A college professor is shocked when a death ensues from a freshman 'hazing' ceremony.

Weird exploitation study of supposed college rites.

w Lou Morheim, Herbert Margolies   *d* Paul Henreid

Paul Henreid, Robert Sherman, Russell Johnson, Margaret Field, Vera Miles

'Henreid allots himself an over-generous proportion of screen time – walking in and out of doors, smiling at the camera, being charming.' – *MFB*

For Pete's Sake *
US   1974   90m   Eastmancolor
Columbia/Rastar/Persky-Bright-Barclay (Martin Erlichmann, Stanley Shapiro)
V*

A New York taxi driver's wife borrows money and finds herself heavily committed to work off the debt.

Involved farcical comedy with amusing passages.

w Stanley Shapiro, Martin Richlin   *d* Peter Yates   *ph* Laszlo Kovacs   *m* Artie Butler

Barbra Streisand, Michael Sarrazin, Estelle Parsons, William Redfield, Molly Picon

'Revives memories of how much more inventively they used to do it thirty years ago.' – *Sight and Sound*

For Queen and Country
GB/US   1988   106m   Eastmancolor
UIP/Zenith/Atlantic/Working Title (Tim Bevan)

A black soldier returns to a squalid civilian life in Britain.

Turgid political drama that alienates the sympathies it attempts to arouse.

w Martin Stellman, Trix Worrell   *d* Martin Stellman   *ph* Richard Greatrex   *m* Michael Kamen, Geoff MacCormack, Simon Goldenberg   *pd* Andrew McAlpine   *ed* Stephen Singleton

Denzel Washington, Dorian Healy, Amanda Redman, Sean Chapman, Bruce Payne, Geff Francis, George Baker

'For The Laughter. For The Tears. For The Boys.'
For the Boys
US   1991   145m   DeLuxe
TCF/All Girl (Bette Midler, Bonnie Bruckheimer, Margaret South)
V, V*, L, S

A singer reminisces about her forty years in showbusiness and her partnership with a song-and-dance man.

Designed mainly as a showcase for Bette Midler, it becomes instead a sentimental wallow in cheap emotions.

w Marshall Brickman, Neil Jimenez, Lindy Laub   *d* Mark Rydell   *ph* Stephen Goldblatt   *m* Dave Grusin   *pd* Assheton Gorton   *ed* Jerry Greenberg, Jere Huggins

Bette Midler, James Caan, George Segal, Patrick O'Neal, Christopher Rydell, Ayre Gross, Norman Fell, Rosemary Murphy, Bud Yorke

'Strong on period décor, weak and dishonest on social history. What it makes you loathe is the ethos of show business.' – *Philip French, Observer*

AAN: Bette Midler

For the Defense *
US   1930   62m   bw
Paramount

Exploits of a New York criminal lawyer.

Slick programme picture of its day; it gave a lift to its star's career.

w Oliver H. P. Garrett (based on the career of William J. Fallon)   *d* John Cromwell

William Powell, Kay Francis, Scott Kolk, Thomas E. Jackson, William H. Davidson

'Certain to hold its head up on grosses.' – *Variety*

For the First Time
US   1959   97m   Technirama
MGM/Corona/Orion (Alexander Gruter)

A famous tenor slips off incognito to Capri and falls in love with a deaf girl.

Slipshod co-production (with West Germany) with a hoary sentimental plot, a fat star, and some agreeable picture postcard views.

w Andrew Solt   *d* Rudolph Maté   *ph* Aldo Tonti
md Georgie Stoll

Mario Lanza, Johanna von Koczian, Kurt Kasznar, Zsa Zsa Gabor, Hans Sohnker

For the Love of Benji
US   1977   84m   colour
Mulberry Square

A small dog gets lost in the Greek islands.

Adequate follow-up to *Benji;* what more can one say?

w Ben Vaughn, Joe Camp   *d* Joe Camp

Patsy Garrett, Cynthia Smith, Peter Bowles, Ed Nelson

For the Love of Mary
US   1948   90m   bw
Universal (Robert Arthur)

A White House switchboard operator gets tangled up in politics when the president helps cure her hiccups.

Tedious comedy with music, a hasty vehicle for a star past her peak.

w Oscar Brodney   *d* Frederick de Cordova
ph William Daniels   *m* Frank Skinner

Deanna Durbin, Edmond O'Brien, Harry Davenport, Don Taylor, Jeffrey Lynn, Ray Collins, Hugo Haas

'A warning to all interfering presidents.' – *MFB*

For the Love of Mike
US   1927   74m (24 fps)   bw   silent
First National

Three bachelors adopt an abandoned baby boy, who nearly (but not quite) lets them down when he grows up.

Sentimental comedy most notable now as the leading lady's first movie.

w Leland Hayward, J. Clarkson Miller   *story Hell's Kitchen* by John Moroso   *d* Frank Capra   *ph* Ernest Haller

Claudette Colbert, Ben Lyon, George Sidney, Ford Sterling, Hugh Cameron, Skeets Gallagher

For the Love of Mike *
US   1960   84m   DeLuxe   Cinemascope
TCF/Shergari (George Sherman)
GB title: *None But the Brave*

An Indian boy in New Mexico is helped by a priest to care for sick animals.

Sentimental outdoor film for young people with a pleasantly light touch.

w D. D. Beauchamp   *d* George Sherman   *ph* Alex Phillips   *m* Raul La Vista

Richard Basehart, Stuart Erwin, Arthur Shields, Armando Silvestre

For Them That Trespass
GB   1948   93m   bw
ABP (Victor Skutezky)

A man proves himself innocent of the crime for which he has served fifteen years in prison.

Tedious melodrama which served to introduce Richard Todd to the screen.

w J. Lee-Thompson   *d* Alberto Cavalcanti
ph Derick Williams   *m* Philip Green

Richard Todd, Stephen Murray, Joan Dowling, Patricia Plunkett, Michael Laurence, Rosalyn Boulter

For Those in Peril
GB   1943   67m   bw
Ealing

Exploits of the air/sea rescue service.

Standard semi-documentary morale-raiser.

w Harry Watt, J. O. C. Orton, T. E. B. Clarke
d Charles Crichton

David Farrar, Ralph Michael, Robert Wyndham, John Slater

For Those Who Think Young
US   1964   96m   Techniscope
UA/Aubrey Schenck-Howard W. Koch (Hugh Benson)

College students save their favourite club from closure.

Tedious beach party frolic, very typical of its day, with some odd cameo appearances.

w James and George O'Hanlon, Dan Beaumont
d Leslie H. Martinson   *ph* Harold E. Stine   *m* Jerry Fielding

James Darren, Pamela Tiffin, Woody Woodbury, Nancy Sinatra, Tina Louise, Paul Lynde, Bob Denver, Jack La Rue, George Raft, Allen Jenkins, Robert Armstrong, Roger Smith

For Valour *
GB   1937   95m   bw
GFD/Capitol (Max Schach)

Adventures in two wars of a major, his shady friend, and their sons.

Agreeable adult farce with the stars each playing father and son.

w Ben Travers   *d* Tom Walls   *ph* Phil Tannura
md Van Phillips   *ad* Oscar Werndorff   *ed* E. B. Jarvis

Tom Walls, Ralph Lynn, Veronica Rose, Joan Marion, Hubert Harben

'A very pleasant antidote to the Coronation, though a little marred by its inability to remain wholly flippant.' – *Graham Greene*

'168 minutes of breathless thrills and romance!'
For Whom the Bell Tolls **
US   1943   168m   Technicolor
Paramount (Sam Wood)
S

An American joins partisan fighters in the Spanish Civil War and falls in love with a refugee girl before going on a suicide mission.

Portentous, solemn adventure story based on a modern classic but without much cinematic impetus despite careful handling and useful performances. It looks expensive, though.

w Dudley Nichols   *novel* Ernest Hemingway
d Sam Wood   *ph* Ray Rennahan   *m* Victor Young
pd William Cameron Menzies   *ed* Sherman Todd, John Link

Gary Cooper, Ingrid Bergman, Akim Tamiroff, Arturo de Cordova, *Katina Paxinou*, Vladimir Sokoloff, Mikhail Rasumny, Victor Varconi, Joseph Calleia, Alexander Granach

MARIA (Ingrid Bergman): 'I do not know how to kiss, or I would kiss you. Where do the noses go?'

'Everybody must have thought they were making a classic . . . but what with the typical Hollywood compromises, plus the political pressures from Spain and from Catholics – or the fears of such pressures – the whole thing became amorphous and confused.' – *Pauline Kael, 70s*

'The rhythm of this film is the most defective I have ever seen in a super-production . . . colour is very nice for costume pieces and musical comedies, and has a great aesthetic future in films, but it still gets fatally in the way of any serious imitation of reality.' – *James Agee*

AA: Katina Paxinou

AAN: best picture; Ray Rennahan; Victor Young; Gary Cooper; Ingrid Bergman; Akim Tamiroff; Sherman Todd, John Link

For You Alone (1937): see *When You're in Love*

For You Alone
GB   1944   98m   bw
Butcher's

Romance of a naval officer and a vicar's daughter.

Sentimental drama with music; you can smell the lavender a mile off, but it was probably the most ambitious production of this indefatigable Poverty Row production company.

w Montgomery Tully   *d* Geoffrey Faithfull

Lesley Brook, Jimmy Hanley, Dinah Sheridan, G. H. Mulcaster, Manning Whiley

For Your Eyes Only *
GB   1981   127m   Technicolor   Panavision
UA/Eon (Albert R. Broccoli)
V, V*, L

James Bond traces a top secret device sunk in a surveillance vehicle off the Greek coast.

Lively set-pieces can't quite redeem this wholly uninventive addition to the Bond canon. Fun while it's on, but next morning there's nothing left to remember.

w Richard Maibaum, Michael G. Wilson   *d* John Glen   *ph* Alan Hume   *m* Bill Conti   *pd* Peter Lamont

Roger Moore, Carole Bouquet, Topol, Lynn-Holly Johnson, Julian Glover, Jill Bennett, Jack Hedley, Lois Maxwell, Desmond Llewellyn, Geoffrey Keen

'Roger Moore fronts for a succession of stunt men with all the relaxed, lifelike charm of a foyer poster of himself.' – *Sunday Times*

'Pretty boring between the stunts, as if the director isn't interested in actors, and Broccoli forgot to commission a screenplay.' – *Guardian*

† The first Bond in which original author Ian Fleming doesn't even rate a credit.

AAN: title song (*m* Bill Conti, *ly* Mick Leeson)

Forbidden
US   1931   83m   bw
Columbia

Our heroine loves the DA, but to save his marriage she marries someone else.

Turgid renunciation drama with some interest added by stars and director.

w Frank Capra, Jo Swerling   *d* Frank Capra

Barbara Stanwyck, Adolphe Menjou, Ralph Bellamy

'A cry picture for the girls, and on that presumption stands a good chance of going out and getting itself and the theatre some coin.' – *Variety*

Forbidden
GB   1949   87m   bw
Pennant/British Lion

A man in love with another woman tries to poison his extravagant wife.

Turgid melodrama with funfair background.

w Katherine Strueby   *d* George King

Douglass Montgomery, Hazel Court, Patricia Burke, Garry Marsh, Ronald Shiner, Kenneth Griffith

Forbidden
US 1953 85m bw
Universal-International

A detective falls in love with the woman a mobster has hired him to find.

Would-be intense *film noir*; talent does not enable it to register.

w William Sackheim, Gil Doud   d Rudolph Maté

Tony Curtis, Joanne Dru, Lyle Bettger, Marvin Miller, Sen Yung

Forbidden Alliance: see *The Barretts of Wimpole Street* (1934)

Forbidden Cargo
GB 1954 85m bw
Rank/London Independent Productions (Sydney Box)

A customs investigator prevents a large consignment of drugs from reaching its English outlets.

Routine British thick ear.

w Sydney Box   d Harold French   ph C. Pennington-Richards   m Lambert Williamson

Nigel Patrick, Elizabeth Sellars, Terence Morgan, Jack Warner

Forbidden Fruit *
France 1952 103m bw
Gray Film
original title: *Le Fruit Défendu*

A widowed doctor marries again, then falls for a prostitute.

One of the rather solemn romantic melodramas in which the star insisted from time to time in becoming involved.

w Jacques Companeez, Henri Verneuil, Jean Manse   novel *Lettre à Mon Juge* by Georges Simenon   d Henri Verneuil   ph Henri Alekan   m Paul Durand

Fernandel, Claude Nollier, Françoise Arnoul, Sylvie

Forbidden Games: see *Jeux Interdits*

Forbidden Music: see *Land without Music*

Forbidden Paradise
US 1924 60m (24 fps) bw silent
Paramount
GB title: *Czarina*

The amorous intrigues of Catherine the Great of Russia.

Seldom seen these days, this was judged at the time a scintillating satire, with its sly innuendo and modern references such as motor cars and bobbed hair. Remade, more or less, as *A Royal Scandal*

w Hans Kraly, Agnes Christine Johnston   play *The Czarina* by Melchior Lengyel, Lajos Biro   d Ernst Lubitsch   ph Charles Van Enger   ad Hans Dreier

Pola Negri, Adolphe Menjou, Rod La Rocque, Pauline Starke, Fred Malatesta

'Lubitsch's most brilliant film' – *Paul Rotha, 1949*

'More than a year in production!'
Forbidden Planet **
US 1956 98m Eastmancolor Cinemascope
MGM (Nicholas Nayfack)
V, V*, L, S

In AD 2200 a space cruiser visits the planet Altair Four to discover the fate of a previous mission.

Intriguing sci-fi with a plot derived from *The Tempest* and a Prospero who unwittingly creates monsters from his own id. High spirits and suspense sequences partially cancelled out by wooden playing from the younger actors and some leaden dialogue.

w Cyril Hume   d Fred M. Wilcox   ph George Folsey   m Louis and Bebe Barron   ad Cedric Gibbons, Arthur Lonergan

Walter Pidgeon, Anne Francis, Leslie Nielsen, Warren Stevens, Jack Kelly, Richard Anderson, Earl Holliman

'It's a pity they didn't lift some of Shakespeare's language.' – *New Yorker, 1977*

Forbidden Relations
Hungary 1983 92m Eastmancolor
Cinegate/Objektiv Filmstudio/Mafilm (Jozsef Marx)
original title: *Visszaesök*

In a peasant community, a step-brother and sister fall in love.

Relentless account of an uninteresting incest.

wd Zsolt Kézdi-Kovacs   ph János Kende   ad Tamas Banovich   ed Andrasne Karmento

Lili Monori, Miklós B. Székely, Mari Töröcsik, József Horváth, József Tóth, Tibor Molnar

The Forbidden Street: see *Britannia Mews*

The Forbin Project **
US 1969 100m Technicolor Panavision
Universal (Stanley Chase)
GB title: *Colossus, The Forbin Project*

An enormous computer takes over the defence of the western world; but it goes into collaboration with the Russian one.

Good-looking sci-fi for intellectual addicts.

w James Bridges   novel *Colossus* by D. F. Jones   d Joseph Sargent   ph Gene Polito   m Michel Columbier

Eric Braeden, Gordon Pinsent, Susan Clark, William Schallert

Force of Arms *
US 1951 100m bw
Warner (Anthony Veiller)

A soldier in the Italian campaign falls in love with his nurse.

Routine variation on *A Farewell to Arms*, adequately but unexcitingly mounted.

w Orin Jannings   story Richard Tregaskis   d Michael Curtiz   ph Ted McCord   m Max Steiner

William Holden, Nancy Olson, Frank Lovejoy, Gene Evans, Dick Wesson, Paul Picerni

'The romance rings true and the battle scenes are dangerously alive.' – *Variety*

Force of Evil ***
US 1948 78m bw
MGM/Enterprise (Bob Roberts)

A racketeer's lawyer finds that his boss has killed the lawyer's brother.

Involved, atmospheric melodrama about the numbers racket, moodily and brilliantly photographed in New York streets, gloweringly well acted and generally almost as hypnotic as *Citizen Kane*.

w Abraham Polonsky, Ira Wolfert   novel *Tucker's People* by Ira Wolfert   d Abraham Polonsky   ph George Barnes   m David Raksin

John Garfield, *Thomas Gomez*, Beatrice Pearson, Marie Windsor

'It credits an audience with intelligence in its ears as well as its eyes.' – *Dilys Powell*

A Force of One
US 1979 90m colour
American Cinema (Alan Belkin)

A karate expert tackles drug pushers in California.

Standard undistinguished action fare.

w Ernest Tidyman   story Pat Johnson, Ernest Tidyman   d Paul Aaron   ph Roger Shearman   m Dick Halligan   ad Norman Baron   ed Bert Lovitt

Chuck Norris, Jennifer O'Neill, Clu Glager, Ron O'Neal, James Whitmore Jnr, Clint Ritchie, Pepe Serna

† A sequel to *Good Guys Wear Black* (qv).

Force Ten from Navarone
GB 1978 118m Technicolor Panavision
Columbia/AIP/Guy Hamilton (Oliver A. Unger)
V, V*

During World War II, commandos are detailed to blow up a vital bridge separating the Germans and partisans in Yugoslavia.

Routine war hokum with plenty of explosions and sudden death, but not much sense. Nothing, really, to do with *The Guns of Navarone*.

w Robin Chapman   novel Alistair MacLean   d Guy Hamilton   ph Chris Challis   m Ron Goodwin   pd Geoffrey Drake

Robert Shaw, Edward Fox, Franco Nero, Harrison Ford, Barbara Bach, Richard Kiel

A Foreign Affair **
US 1948 116m bw
Paramount (Charles Brackett)

A deputation of American politicians goes to visit post-war Berlin and a congresswoman finds herself in an emotional triangle with a captain and his German mistress.

Bleakly sophisticated comedy from this team's headline-grabbing period; full of interest and amusement, it never quite sparkles enough to remove the doubtful taste.

w Charles Brackett, Billy Wilder, Richard Breen, story David Shaw   d Billy Wilder   ph Charles Lang Jnr   m Frederick Hollander

Jean Arthur, Marlene Dietrich, John Lund, Millard Mitchell, Peter von Zerneck, Stanley Prager

'This deliberately cynical political farce . . . often seems on the verge of being funny, but the humour is too clumsily forced.' – *New Yorker, 1980*

'What really shocks me about this Hollywood film is the attitude towards life that it reflects; the casual acceptance of irresponsibility and bad manners, of lawlessness and boorishness and mischief-making.' – *C. A. Lejeune*

AAN: script; Charles Lang Jnr

Foreign Affaires
GB 1935 71m bw
Gainsborough (Michael Balcon, Tom Walls)

A gambler and a car salesman get mixed up with a phoney casino.

Mild star farce.

w Ben Travers   d Tom Walls   ph Roy Kellino   md Louis Levy   ad Vetchinsky   ed Alfred Roome

Tom Walls, Ralph Lynn, Robertson Hare, Norma Varden, Marie Lohr, Diana Churchill, Cecil Parker

Foreign Correspondent ****
US 1940 120m bw
Walter Wanger
V*, L

An American journalist is sent to Europe in 1938 and becomes involved with spies.

Thoroughly typical and enjoyable Hitchcock adventure with a rambling script which builds up into brilliantly managed suspense sequences: an assassination, a windmill, an attempted murder in Westminster Cathedral, a plane crash at sea. The final speech was an attempt to encourage America into the war.

w *Charles Bennett, Joan Harrison, James Hilton, Robert Benchley* novel *Personal History* by Vincent Sheean *d* Alfred Hitchcock *ph* Rudolph Maté *m* Alfred Newman *pd* William Cameron Menzies *ad* Alexander Golitzen *sp* Lee Zavitz

Joel McCrea, Laraine Day, Herbert Marshall, Albert Basserman, Edmund Gwenn, George Sanders, Eduardo Ciannelli, Robert Benchley, Harry Davenport, Martin Kosleck

HAVERSTOCK (Joel McCrea): 'I've been watching a part of the world blown to pieces! I can't read the rest of the speech I had because the lights have gone out. It is as if the lights were out everywhere, except in America. Keep those lights burning there! Cover them with steel! Ring them with guns! Build a canopy of battleships and bombing planes around them! Hello, America! Hang on to your lights, they're the only lights left in the world!'

'If you have any interest in the true motion and sweep of pictures, watching that man work is like listening to music . . . If you would like a seminar in how to make a movie travel the lightest and fastest way, in a kind of beauty that is peculiar to movies alone, you can see this once, and then again to see what you missed, and then study it twice.' – *Otis Ferguson*

'The most excitingly shot and edited picture of the year.' – *Basil Wright*

'A masterpiece of propaganda, a first class production which no doubt will make a certain impression upon the broad masses of the people in enemy countries.' – *Joseph Goebbels*

'This juxtaposition of outright melodramatics with deadly serious propaganda is eminently satisfactory . . . Hitchcock uses camera tricks, cinematic rhythm and crescendo to make his points.' – *Howard Barnes, New York Herald Tribune*

'Easily one of the year's finest pictures.' – *Time*

AAN: best picture; script; Rudolph Maté; Albert Basserman; Alexander Golitzen

Foreign Intrigue *
US   1956   100m   Eastmancolor
UA/Sheldon Reynolds

A press agent investigates the death of a man who had been blackmailing potential traitors.

Location espionage melodrama of the cold war fifties, quite well done in a rather dismal vein, but a long way from *Foreign Correspondent*.

wd Sheldon Reynolds *ph* Bertil Palmgren *m* Paul Durand

Robert Mitchum, Genevieve Page, Ingrid Thulin, Eugene Deckers

The Foreman Went to France **
GB   1941   87m   bw
Ealing (Alberto Cavalcanti)
V*
US title: *Somewhere in France*

Before Dunkirk, a Welsh foreman is sent on a mission to salvage secret French machinery.

Fresh, appealing comedy drama based on a true incident of World War II.

w John Dighton, Angus Macphail, Leslie Arliss, Roger Macdougall, Diana Morgan *story* J. B. Priestley *d* Charles Frend *ph* Wilkie Cooper *m* William Walton

Tommy Trinder, Constance Cummings, Clifford Evans, Robert Morley, Gordon Jackson, Ernest Milton

'The thrilling story of women who play with fire, and men who fight it!'
The Forest Rangers *
US   1942   85m   Technicolor
Paramount (Robert Sisk)

A socialite marries a district ranger and rescues her disgruntled rival during a forest blaze.

Routine, competent, box-office actioner of its time, with popular stars, adequate plot, but precious little inventiveness.

w Harold Shumate *d* George Marshall *ph* Charles Lang *m* Victor Young

Fred MacMurray, Paulette Goddard, Susan Hayward, Lynne Overman, Albert Dekker, Eugene Pallette, Regis Toomey, Rod Cameron

'Another tale of the tall timbers, complete with conflagrations, he-men, and women like cats.' – *New York Times*

Forever Amber *
US   1947   137m   Technicolor
TCF (William Perlberg)
V*

Adventures of a desirable young lady during the reign of Charles II.

Much-bowdlerized version of a sensational novel of the forties; pretty but rather thin, with a colourless cast, saved by lively action sequences.

w Philip Dunne, Ring Lardner Jnr *novel* Kathleen Winsor *d* Otto Preminger *ph* Leon Shamroy *m* David Raksin *ad* Lyle Wheeler

Linda Darnell, Cornel Wilde, *George Sanders* (as Charles II), Richard Greene, Glenn Langan, Richard Haydn, Jessica Tandy, Anne Revere, Robert Coote, John Russell, Leo G. Carroll

AAN: David Raksin

Forever and a Day **
US   1943   104m   bw
RKO (Herbert Wilcox, Victor Saville)
V*

The history of a London house from 1804 to the blitz of World War II.

Made for war charities by a combination of the European talents in Hollywood, this series of sketches was unavoidably patchy but gave good opportunities to several familiar performers and stands as a likeable quick reference to their work at this period.

w Charles Bennett, C. S. Forester, Lawrence Hazard, Michael Hogan, W. P. Lipscomb, Alice Duer Miller, John Van Druten, Alan Campbell, Peter Godfrey, S. M. Herzig, Christopher Isherwood, Gene Lockhart, R. C. Sherriff, Claudine West, Norman Corwin, Jack Hartfield, James Hilton, Emmet Lavery, Frederick Lonsdale, Donald Ogden Stewart, Keith Winter *d* René Clair, Edmund Goulding, Cedric Hardwicke, Frank Lloyd, Victor Saville, Robert Stevenson, Herbert Wilcox *ph* Robert de Grasse, Lee Garmes, Russell Metty, Nicholas Musuraca *m* Anthony Collins *ad* Albert D'Agostino, Lawrence Williams, Al Herman

Anna Neagle, Ray Milland, *Claude Rains, C. Aubrey Smith,* Dame May Whitty, Gene Lockhart, Edmund Gwenn, Ian Hunter, *Jessie Matthews, Charles Laughton,* Montagu Love, *Cedric Hardwicke,* Reginald Owen, *Buster Keaton,* Wendy Barrie, Ida Lupino, *Brian Aherne,* Edward Everett Horton, June Duprez, Eric Blore, Merle Oberon, Una O'Connor, Nigel Bruce, *Roland Young, Gladys Cooper,* Robert Cummings, Richard Haydn, Elsa Lanchester, Sara Allgood, Robert Coote, Donald Crisp, Ruth Warrick, Kent Smith, Herbert Marshall, Victor McLaglen, many others in bit parts

'One of the most brilliant casts of modern times has been assembled to bolster up one of the poorest pictures.' – *James Agate*

'It is holding and entertaining . . . a production of outstanding quality.' – *CEA Film Report*

† The film is notable for having the longest-ever list of credited co-writers.

Forever Darling
US   1956   91m   Eastmancolor
MGM/Zanra (Desi Arnaz)
V*, L

A couple's matrimonial difficulties are solved by her guardian angel.

Cutesy-pie comedy with all concerned embarrassed by their material.

w Helen Deutsch *d* Alexander Hall *ph* Harold Lipstein *m* Bronislau Kaper

Lucille Ball, Desi Arnaz, James Mason (as the angel), John Emery, Louis Calhern, John Hoyt, Natalie Schafer

Forever England: see *Brown on Resolution*

Forever Female
US   1953   93m   bw
Paramount (Pat Duggan)

A young writer sells his play to a Broadway producer who wants to transform it into a vehicle for his ex-wife; she falls for the writer but eventually discourages him.

Talky romantic comedy without much style or sense of Broadway; a long way from *All About Eve.*

w Julius J. Epstein, Philip G. Epstein *play Rosalind* by J. M. Barrie *d* Irving Rapper *ph* Harry Stradling *m* Victor Young

Ginger Rogers, William Holden, Paul Douglas, James Gleason, Pat Crowley

Forever in Love: see *Pride of the Marines*

Forever Young
GB   1984   84m   colour
Goldcrest (Chris Griffin)

Father Michael finds himself influenced by sexual tensions among his flock.

Rather slight drama chiefly concerning a twelve-year-old boy who idolizes his fallible priest.

w Ray Connolly *d* David Drury *ph* Norman Langley *md* Anthony King

James Aubrey, Nicholas Gecks, Alec McCowen, Karen Archer

'Fifty years ago he volunteered for a dangerous experiment. All in the name of love.'
'Time waits for no man, but true love waits forever.'
Forever Young *
US   1992   102m   Technicolor
Warner/Icon (Bruce Davey)
V, V*, L, S

A pilot, who is frozen in an experiment in 1939, wakes up to find that it is 1992.

Pleasant, light-hearted romantic movie, a throwback to the past.

w Jeffrey Abrams *d* Steve Miner *ph* Russell Boyd *m* Jerry Goldsmith *pd* Gregg Fonseca *ed* Jon Poll

Mel Gibson, Jamie Lee Curtis, Elijah Wood, Isabel Glasser, George Wendt, Joe Morton, Nicholas Surovy, David Marshall Grant, Robert Hy Gorman, Mille Slavin

'A big, rousing, old-fashioned romance . . . A perfect "women's picture" alternative to action fare and kid-oriented sequels.' – *Variety*

Forever Yours: see *Forget Me Not*

Forfaiture: see *The Cheat*

Forget Me Not
GB   1936   72m   bw
UA/Itala/London Films (Alberto Giacolone, Alexander Korda)
US title: *Forever Yours*

On board ship, a young girl falls for a widowed tenor.

Bland romance, notable only for the star's singing.

w Hugh Gray, Arthur Wimperis   *d* Zoltan Korda, Stanley Irving   *ph* Hans Schneeberger   *m* Mischa Spoliansky

Beniamino Gigli, Joan Gardner, Ivan Brandt, Hugh Wakefield

'As a larynx exercise it possesses an appeal for those audiences which go for singing.' – *Variety*

Forgotten Commandments *

US   1932   75m   bw
Paramount

In a Russia which has renounced Christianity, a scientist who considers himself above emotion is led by jealousy into the murder of his mistress.

Vague, feeble and absurd modern parable which takes in its stride a 20-minute excerpt from de Mille's 1923 *The Ten Commandments*.

w J. B. Fagan, Agnes Brand Leahy   *d* Louis Gasnier, William Schoor

Gene Raymond, Sari Maritza, Irving Pichel, Marguerite Churchill, Edward Van Sloan, Harry Beresford

'Hardly a single dramatic sequence and not over three laughs at the New York opening – and one of them at, not with, the picture.' – *Variety*

Forgotten Faces

US   1936   70m   bw
Paramount

Jailed for killing his wife's lover, a man escapes to thwart his wife's further plans.

Slightly unusual melodrama which was remade as *A Gentleman After Dark*.

w Marguerite Roberts, Robert Yost, Brian Marlow   *d* E. A. Dupont

Herbert Marshall, Gertrude Michael, James Burke, Robert Cummings

Forgotten Girls

US   1940   68m   bw
Republic (Robert North)

A girl is convicted for a murder committed by her stepmother.

Minor saga of prison life, with an absurd method of proving the heroine's innocence.

w Joseph March, F. Hugh Herbert, Frank McDonald   *d* Phil Rosen

Louise Platt, Donald Woods, Wynne Gibson, Robert Armstrong, Eduardo Ciannelli, Jack La Rue

Forgotten Woman

US   1939   68m   bw
Universal (Edmund Grainger)

A woman wrongfully imprisoned has a baby in prison and emerges embittered.

Heavygoing tearjerker.

w Lionel Houser, Harold Buchman, John Kobler   *d* Harold Young

Sigrid Gurie, Eve Arden, Donald Briggs, William Lundigan, Elizabeth Risdon

The Formula

US   1980   117m   Metrocolor
MGM/CIP (Steve Shagan)

A cop follows a murder trail to West Germany and finds that it all hinges on a secret formula for turning coal into petrol.

Convoluted thriller which is all McGuffin and no interest.

w Steven Shagan   *novel* Steven Shagan   *d* John G. Avildsen   *ph* James Crabe   *m* Bill Conti

George C. Scott, Marlon Brando, Marthe Keller, John Gielgud, Beatrice Straight, Richard Lynch

AAN: James Crabe

Forsaking All Others *

US   1934   84m   bw
MGM (Bernard H. Hyman)

A woman almost marries the wrong man twice.

Star power carries this thin comedy drama.

w Joseph L. Mankiewicz   *play* Edward Barry Roberts, Frank Morgan Cavett   *d* W. S. Van Dyke   *ph* Gregg Toland, George Folsey   *m* William Axt

Clark Gable, Joan Crawford, Robert Montgomery, *Charles Butterworth*, Billie Burke, Frances Drake, Rosalind Russell, Arthur Treacher

'Stock romantic comedy despite some messy hokum.' – *Variety*

'Contrary to expectation, sophistication is at a minimum.' – *Time*

The Forsyte Saga: see *That Forsyte Woman*

'Where a woman meant more to a man than anywhere else in the world!'

Fort Algiers

US   1952   85m   bw
Erco/UA

A female French agent loves a fellow spy who turns up as a Foreign Legionnaire, working against an evil Emir.

Quite lively old-fashioned hokum, satisfactory on its level.

w Theodore St John   *d* Lesley Selander

Yvonne de Carlo, Carlos Thompson, Raymond Burr, Leif Erickson, Anthony Caruso

Fort Apache **

US   1948   127m   bw
RKO/Argosy (John Ford, Merian C. Cooper)
V, V*, L

In the old west, a military martinet has trouble with his family as well as the Indians.

Rather stiff and unsatisfactory epic Western which yet contains sequences in its director's best manner.

w Frank S. Nugent   *story* Massacre by James Warner Bellah   *d* John Ford   *ph* Archie Stout   *m* Richard Hageman   *ad* James Basevi   *ed* Jack Murray

Henry Fonda, John Wayne, Shirley Temple, Pedro Armendariz, Ward Bond, Irene Rich, George O'Brien, John Agar, Victor McLaglen, Anna Lee, Dick Foran, Guy Kibbee

'A visually absorbing celebration of violent deeds.' – *Howard Barnes*

'The whole picture is bathed in a special form of patriotic sentimentality: scenes are held so that we cannot fail to appreciate the beauty of the American past.' – *New Yorker, 1976*

'Shirley Temple and her husband handle the love interest as though they were sharing a soda fountain special, and there is enough Irish comedy to make me wish Cromwell had done a more thorough job.' – *James Agee*

Fort Apache, the Bronx

US   1980   123m   DeLuxe
Time Life/Producer Circle (David Susskind)
V*, L

A veteran policeman deals with various violent crimes in New York.

This instantly forgettable movie unspools like an ultra-violent *Dixon of Dock Green*, but Newman is no Jack Warner.

w Heywood Gould   *d* Daniel Petrie   *ph* John Alcott   *m* Jonathan Tunick   *pd* Ben Edwards

Paul Newman, Ed Asner, Ken Wahl, Danny Aiello, Rachel Ticotin, Pam Grier, Kathleen Beller

Fort Defiance

US   1951   81m   Cinecolor
Ventura/UA

Ben Shelby comes back from the Civil War to avenge his brother's death.

Complicated lower-berth Western, crudely executed.

w Louis Lantz   *d* John Rawlins

Dane Clark, Ben Johnson, Peter Graves, Tracey Roberts, George Cleveland

Fort Dobbs

US   1957   90m   bw
Warner

Man on the run rescues widow from Comanches and clears his name.

Very routine medium-scale Western showcasing a TV star.

w George W. George, Burt Kennedy   *d* Gordon Douglas

Clint Walker, Virginia Mayo, Brian Keith, Richard Eyer

Fort Massacre

US   1958   80m   DeLuxe   Cinemascope
Mirisch/UA

A cavalry sergeant becomes reckless when he has to lead to safety the survivors of an Indian attack.

Psychological Western without the skill necessary to realize its pretensions.

w Martin N. Goldsmith   *d* Joseph Newman

Joel McCrea, Forrest Tucker, Susan Cabot, John Russell

Fort Ti

US   1953   73m   Technicolor   3-D
Columbia (Sam Katzman)

In 1759 a platoon of Rogers' Rangers marches north to defend their territory against Indians.

Cheap and feeble Western memorable only for the amount of miscellaneous objects thrown at the audience via 3-D photography.

w Robert E. Kent   *d* William Castle   *ph* Lester E. White, Lathrop B. Worth   *md* Ross di Maggio

George Montgomery, Joan Vohs, Irving Bacon, James Seay

'The lack of restraint is remarkable. To the injury of tomahawks, rifle shots, cannon balls, flaming arrows, broken bottles and blazing torches is added the insult of grubby redskins hurled judo style into one's lap.' – *David Robinson*

Fort Utah

US   1967   84m   Technicolor   Techniscope
Paramount (A. C. Lyles)

Crazed killers take over a cavalry fort.

Muddled Western with the producer's usual roster of familiar old faces.

w Steve Fisher, Andrew Craddock   *d* Lesley Selander

John Ireland, Virginia Mayo, Scott Brady, John Russell, Robert Strauss, James Craig, Richard Arlen, Jim Davis, Donald Barry

Fort Vengeance

US   1953   75m   Cinecolor
Allied Artists (Walter Wanger)

A new Mountie recruit is an Indian killer.

Uninteresting Western with stock cast and situations.

w Dan Ullman   *d* Lesley Selander

James Craig, Rita Moreno, Keith Larsen, Reginald Denny, Morris Ankrum

Fort Worth

US 1951 80m Technicolor
Warner

A newspaper editor combats a would-be dictator.

Satisfying star Western.

w John Twist d Edwin L. Marin

Randolph Scott, Phyllis Thaxter, David Brian, Dick Jones, Paul Picerni

Fort Yuma

US 1955 78m colour
UA (Howard W. Koch)

Indians steal army uniforms and attack a fort.

Minor but efficient co-feature Western.

w Danny Arnold d Lesley Selander

Peter Graves, Joan Vohs, John Hudson, Joan Taylor, Addison Richards

Fortress

Australia/US 1993 89m CFI colour
Village Roadshow/Davis Entertainment (John Davis, John Flock)
V, V*

In the future, a couple who break the law by having more than one child are incarcerated in a huge underground prison, run by a harsh private corporation.

An efficient action film in a science-fiction setting, but one that is unable to escape from its own over-familiar scenario.

w Steve Feinberg, Troy Neighbors, Terry Curtis Fox d Stuart Gordon ph David Eggby m Frederic Talghorn pd David Copping sp Tad Pride, Paul Gentry ed Timothy Wellburn

Christopher Lambert, Kurtwood Smith, Loryn Locklin, Lincoln Kilpatrick, Clifton Gonzalez Gonzalez, Jeffrey Combs, Tom Towles, Vernon Wells

'A grim, sometimes bloody, futuristic prison picture that has been well produced and directed within the limitations of a predictable, uninspired screenplay.' – Variety

The Fortune

US 1975 88m Technicolor Panavision
Columbia (Hank Moonjean)

A twenties heiress elopes with her lover and his dim-witted friend but discovers that they mean to murder her for her money.

Bungled black comedy with top talent over-confident of carrying it.

w Adrien Joyce (Carol Eastman) d Mike Nichols ph John A. Alonzo m various songs pd Richard Sylbert

Jack Nicholson, Warren Beatty, Stockard Channing, Florence Stanley, Richard B. Shull, John Fiedler

'Like the ill-assorted styles of the film generally, the stars themselves frequently seem to belong in different movies.' – Richard Combs

'A silly, shallow, occasionally enjoyable comedy trifle . . . classy 20's production values often merit more attention than the plot.' – Variety

Fortune and Men's Eyes

Canada/US 1971 102m Metrocolor
MGM/Cinemex/CFD (Lester Persky, Lewis M. Allen)
V*

Life among homosexuals in a Canadian jail.

A welter of sensational incident outweighs any point the author may have had; this prison seems to be beyond reform.

w John Herbert play John Herbert d Harvey Hart ph Georges Dufaux m Galt McDermot

Wendell Burton, Michael Greer

The Fortune Cookie *

US 1966 125m bw Panavision
UA/Mirisch/Phalanx/Jalem (Billy Wilder)
V, V*, L
GB title: Meet Whiplash Willie

A crooked lawyer forces his slightly injured client to sue for a million dollars.

Flat, stretched-out, only occasionally effective comedy which relies too much on mordant attitudes and a single star performance.

w Billy Wilder, I. A. L. Diamond d Billy Wilder ph Joseph LaShelle m André Previn

Walter Matthau, Jack Lemmon, Ron Rich, Cliff Osmond, Lurene Tuttle

'A jackhammer of a film savagely applied to those concrete areas of human spirit where cupidity and stupidity have been so long entrenched.' – Richard Schickel

AA: Walter Matthau
AAN: Billy Wilder, I. A. L. Diamond (script); Joseph LaShelle

Fortune Is a Woman *

GB 1956 95m bw
Columbia/Frank Launder, Sidney Gilliat
US title: She Played with Fire

An insurance assessor investigates a fire, finds a murder, marries the victim's widow, and is blackmailed . . .

Slackly-handled mystery thriller, a disappointment from the talents involved.

w Frank Launder, Sidney Gilliat novel Winston Graham d Sidney Gilliat ph Gerald Gibbs m William Alwyn

Jack Hawkins, Arlene Dahl, Dennis Price, Geoffrey Keen, Violet Farebrother, John Robinson, Bernard Miles, Greta Gynt

Fortunes of Captain Blood

US 1950 91m bw
Columbia (Harry Joe Brown)

The famous Caribbean pirate eludes his pursuers by taking over their own ship.

Lethargic adventures on a low budget; the cast was there for something better.

w Michael Hogan, Robert Libbott, Frank Burt d Gordon Douglas

Louis Hayward, Patricia Medina, George Macready, Dona Drake, Alfonso Bedoya

Forty Carats *

US 1973 109m Metrocolor
Columbia/M. J. Frankovich
V*

A 40-year-old divorcee on holiday in Greece has a brief affair with a 22-year-old man.

Curiously miscast and mishandled comedy for the smart set; scores a laugh or two but never really takes off.

w Leonard Gershe play Pierre Barillet, Jean-Pierre Gredy d Milton Katselas ph Charles Lang Jnr m Michel Legrand

Liv Ullmann, Edward Albert, Gene Kelly, Billy 'Green' Bush, Binnie Barnes, Nancy Walker, Deborah Raffin, Don Porter, Natalie Schafer, Rosemary Murphy

Forty Eight Hours (1942): see Went the Day Well?

48 Hours

US 1982 96m Movielab
Paramount/Lawrence Gordon
V, V*, L

A cop and a criminal on parole combine to track down the latter's former associates.

Reasonable action melodrama with comedy asides and San Francisco locations; but too violent for its own good.

w Roger Spottiswoode, Walter Hill, Larry Gross, Steven E. de Souza d Walter Hill ph Ric Waite m James Horner pd John Vallone

Nick Nolte, Eddie Murphy, Annette O'Toole, Frank McRae

'It's like The French Connection, Dirty Harry and Butch Cassidy all put in a compactor and pressed into cartoon form.' – New Yorker

† It was followed, after a long gap, by a sequel Another 48 Hours (qv).

The Forty First *

USSR 1927 80m approx bw silent
Mezhrabpom
original title: Sorok Pervyi

During the Civil War in Turkestan, a girl sniper for the Reds becomes the companion in adventure of a White lieutenant. But in the end he becomes her 41st victim.

Strong action melodrama which found an international audience.

w Boris Lavryenov novel Boris Lavryenov d Yakov Protazanov ph Pyotr Yermolov

Ada Voitsik, Ivan Kovan-Samborsky

† Remade in 1956 by Grigori Chukrai, in colour.

Forty-Five Fathers

US 1937 71m bw
TCF (John Stone)

A show business orphan becomes the personal ward of the Gun and Spear Club.

Palatable vehicle for a growing child star.

w Frances Hyland, Albert Ray, Mary Bickel d James Tinling

Jane Withers, Paul and Grace Hartman, Thomas Beck, Louise Henry, Richard Carle, Nella Walker, Andrew Tombes

Forty Guns *

US 1957 80m bw Cinemascope
TCF/Globe (Samuel Fuller)

A powerful ranchwoman protects her hoodlum brother.

Heavily melodramatic and slow-moving Western with a few effective moments.

wd Samuel Fuller ph Joseph Biroc m Harry Sukman

Barbara Stanwyck, Barry Sullivan, Dean Jagger, Gene Barry, John Ericson

Forty Guns to Apache Pass

US 1967 95m Technicolor
Admiral/Columbia

A cavalry captain protects homesteaders when Cochise attacks.

Flat and overlong star Western compounded of excessively familiar elements.

w Willard and Mary Willingham d William Witney

Audie Murphy, Michael Burns, Kenneth Tobey, Laraine Stephens

Forty Little Mothers

US 1940 90m bw
MGM (Harry Rapf)

A teacher in a girls' school finds himself in charge of a baby.

Ill-advised star vehicle composed largely of whimsy . . . and no musical numbers.

w Dorothy Yost, Ernest Pagano   *d* Busby Berkeley   *ph* Charles A. Lawton Jnr

Eddie Cantor, Judith Anderson, Bonita Granville, Rita Johnson, Diana Lewis, Nydia Westman, Martha O'Driscoll

Forty Naughty Girls
US   1937   68m   bw
RKO (William Sistrom)

Hildegarde Withers solves a murder backstage.

Weak addition to a faltering series.

w John Grey, Stuart Palmer   *d* Edward Cline

ZaSu Pitts, James Gleason, Marjorie Lord, George Shelley, Joan Woodbury

'Decidedly tame, and won't cause much ripple on nether side of duals, where it'll undoubtedly land.' – *Variety*

The Forty Niners
US   1954   70m   bw
Allied Artists

A marshal tracks down three men who were accomplices to a murder.

Very tolerable minor Western.

w Dan Ullman   *d* Thomas Carr

Wild Bill Elliott, Virginia Grey, Henry Morgan, John Doucette, Lane Bradford

The Forty-Ninth Man
US   1953   73m   bw
Columbia (Sam Katzman)

Spies try to infiltrate a big bomb into the US.

Tolerable low-berth security thriller on semi-documentary lines.

w Harry Essex   *story* Ivan Tors   *d* Fred F. Sears

John Ireland, Richard Denning, Suzanne Dalbert, Touch Connors

Forty Ninth Parallel ***
GB   1941   123m   bw
GFD/Ortus (John Sutro, Michael Powell)
V, V*, L
US title: *The Invaders*

In Canada, five stranded U-boat men try to escape into the US.

Episodic, effective propaganda piece which develops some nice Hitchcockian touches and allows a range of star actors to make impact.

w Emeric Pressburger, Rodney Ackland   *d* Michael Powell   *ph* F. A. Young   *m* Ralph Vaughan Williams

Eric Portman, Laurence Olivier, Anton Walbrook, Leslie Howard, Raymond Massey, Glynis Johns, Niall MacGinnis, Finlay Currie, Raymond Lovell, John Chandos

'Some of the plotting and characterization look rather rusty at this remove, but the sense of landscape and figures passing through it remains authoritatively dynamic.' – *Tony Rayns, Time Out, 1979*

'An admirable piece of work from every point of view.' – *MFB*

AA: original story (Emeric Pressburger)

AAN: best picture; script

Forty Pounds of Trouble *
US   1963   105m   Eastmancolor   Panavision
U-I/Curtis Enterprises (Stan Margulies)

A casino manager is chased by his ex-wife's detective for alimony payments, and also has to look after an abandoned six-year-old girl.

Standard sentimental comedy with some verve and a lively climactic chase through Disneyland.

w Marion Hargrove   *d* Norman Jewison   *ph* Joe MacDonald   *m* Mort Lindsey

Tony Curtis, Phil Silvers, Suzanne Pleshette, Edward Andrews

'Mightier than Broadway ever beheld.'
'Most important entertainment event since Warner Bros gave you Vitaphone!'
42nd Street ***
US   1933   89m   bw
Warner (Hal B. Wallis)
V, V*, L

A Broadway musical producer has troubles during rehearsal but reaches a successful opening night.

Archetypal Hollywood putting-on-a-show musical in which the leading lady is indisposed and a chorus girl is told to get out there and come back a star. The clichés are written and performed with great zest, the atmosphere is convincing, and the numbers when they come are dazzlers.

w James Seymour, Rian James   *novel* Bradford Ropes   *d* Lloyd Bacon   *ch* Busby Berkeley   *ph* Sol Polito   *m/ly* Al Dubin, Harry Warren

songs: 'Forty-Second Street'; 'It Must Be June'; 'Shuffle Off to Buffalo'; 'Young and Healthy'; 'You're Getting to Be a Habit with Me'

Warner Baxter, Ruby Keeler, Bebe Daniels, George Brent, Una Merkel, Guy Kibbee, Dick Powell, Ginger Rogers (as Anytime Annie), Ned Sparks, George E. Stone, Allen Jenkins

(Warner Baxter): 'Sawyer, you listen to me, and you listen hard. Two hundred people, two hundred jobs, two hundred thousand dollars, five weeks of grind and blood and sweat depend upon you. It's the lives of all these people who've worked with you. You've got to go on, and you've got to give and give and give. They've got to like you. Got to. Do you understand? You can't fall down. You can't because your future's in it, my future and everything all of us have is staked on you. All right, now I'm through, but you keep your feet on the ground and your head on those shoulders of yours and go out, and Sawyer, you're going out a youngster but you've got to come back a star!'

'The story has been copied a hundred times since, but never has the backstage atmosphere been so honestly and felicitously caught.' – *John Huntley, 1966*

'It gave new life to the clichés that have kept parodists happy.' – *New Yorker, 1977*

AAN: best picture

Forty Thousand Horsemen
Australia   1940   100m   bw
Famous Feature Films (Charles Chauvel)

The story of the Australian Light Horse in Palestine during World War I.

One of the first Australian bids for the world market; in itself, just a competent little war movie, and too long.

w Charles Chauvel, Elsa Chauvel   *d* Charles Chauvel

Chips Rafferty, Betty Bryant, Grant Taylor, Pat Twohill

'Almost unbelievably primitive in these days of stream-lined talkies. It is also most uncannily exciting. I don't remember enjoying a film quite in this way since the first cowboys rode the range.' – *C. A. Lejeune*

Forward March: see *Doughboys*

Foul Play *
US   1978   116m   Movielab
Paramount/Thomas L. Miller, Edward K. Milkis
V, V*, L

Two innocents in San Francisco get involved in a plot to assassinate the visiting pope.

Sometimes sprightly, sometimes tired rehash of Hitchcock elements, rather on the level of the similar *Silver Streak*.

wd Colin Higgins   *ph* David M. Walsh   *m* Charles Fox

Goldie Hawn, Chevy Chase, Burgess Meredith, Rachel Roberts, Eugene Roche, Dudley Moore, Billy Barty

AAN: song, 'Ready to Take a Chance Again' (*m* Charles Fox, *ly* Norman Gimbel)

The Fountain
US   1934   84m   bw
RKO (Pandro S. Berman)

During World War I a British woman is tempted to forsake her mangled German air ace husband for her childhood sweetheart.

A slice of impenetrable gloom from an intractable novel.

w Jane Murfin, Samuel Hoffenstein   *novel* Charles Morgan   *d* John Cromwell   *ph* Henry W. Gerrard   *m* Max Steiner

Ann Harding, Brian Aherne, Paul Lukas, Jean Hersholt, Ralph Forbes, Violet Kemble-Cooper, Sara Haden

'One of the talkiest talkies yet.' – *Variety*

'Long and solemn and wonderfully empty.' – *Otis Ferguson*

The Fountain: see *Fontan*

The Fountainhead **
US   1949   114m   bw
Warner (Henry Blanke)
V*, L

An idealistic architect clashes with big business.

Overripe adaptation of a rather silly novel, full of Freudian symbols and expressionist techniques with which the star really can't cope; but an enjoyable field day for the director and the rest of the cast.

w Ayn Rand   *novel* Ayn Rand   *d* King Vidor   *ph* Robert Burks   *m* Max Steiner

Gary Cooper, Patricia Neal, Raymond Massey, Kent Smith, Robert Douglas, Henry Hull, Ray Collins, Moroni Olsen, Jerome Cowan

'If you like deep thinking, hidden meanings, plus pure modern architecture, then this is something for which you have been waiting a long time.' – *Screenland*

'The most bizarre movie in both Vidor's and Cooper's filmographies, this adaptation mutes Ms Rand's neo-Nietzschian philosophy of "objectivism" but lays on the expressionist symbolism with a "free enterprise" trowel.' – *Time Out, 1980*

Four Adventures of Reinette and Mirabelle **
France   1986   99m   colour
Artificial Eye/CER/Les Films du Losange (Eric Rohmer)
V, V*
original title: *Quatre Aventures de Reinette et Mirabelle*

Four stories involving two contrasted students, one from the country, the other from the city.

Charming small-scale work, full of incidental pleasures.

wd Eric Rohmer   *ph* Sophie Maintigneux   *m* Ronan Girre, Jean-Louis Valero   *ed* Marie-Luisa Garcia

Joëlle Miquel, Jessica Forde, Philippe Laudenbach, Yasmine Haury, Marie Rivière, Beatrice Romand, Gérard Courant, David Rocksavage

Four Against Fate: see *Derby Day*

Four Clowns **

US   1970   96m   bw
Robert Youngson Productions (Herb Gelbspan)

Studies of four silent comedians. Laurel and Hardy in excerpts from *Putting Pants on Philip, The Second Hundred Years, Their Purple Moment, Big Business, Two Tars* and *Double Whoopee;* Charley Chase in *Us, What Price Goofy, Fluttering Hearts, The Family Group* and *Limousine Love;* Buster Keaton in *Seven Chances*.

An essential compendium, especially for the Charley Chase revaluation which was long overdue.

w Robert Youngson   m Manny Alban

Narrator: Jay Jackson

Four Dark Hours: see *The Green Cockatoo*

Four Daughters ***

US   1938   90m   bw
Warner (Henry Blanke)
V*

Domestic and romantic adventures of a small-town family.

Standard small-town hearth-fire hokum, impeccably done and really quite irresistible.

w Julius Epstein, Lenore Coffee   *novel Sister Act* by Fannie Hurst   d Michael Curtiz   ph Ernest Haller   m Max Steiner

Claude Rains, John Garfield (a sensation in his first role), Priscilla Lane, Rosemary Lane, Lola Lane, Gale Page, Jeffrey Lynn, Frank McHugh, *May Robson*, Dick Foran

'It may be sentimental, but it's grand cinema.' – *New York Times*

'It simply, yet powerfully, brings into focus a panorama of natural but startling events.' – *Motion Picture Herald*

† An immediate sequel was required, but the Garfield character had been killed off, so to accommodate him a variation was written under the title *Daughters Courageous;* then came two proper sequels without him, *Four Wives* and *Four Mothers*. In 1955 the original was remade as *Young at Heart* (qv).

AAN: best picture; script; Michael Curtiz; John Garfield

The Four Days of Naples *

Italy   1962   119m   bw
Titanus-Metro (Goffredo Lombardo)

A reconstruction of the 1943 city battle in which the Nazis were driven out by civilian fury.

A kind of update of *Open City:* much admired, but a little ill-timed.

w Nanni Loy and others   d Nanni Loy   ph Marcello Gatti   m Carlo Rustichelli

Lea Massari, Frank Wolff, Domenico Formato, Raffaele Barbato

AAN: best foreign film; script

Four Desperate Men: see *The Siege of Pinchgut*

Four Faces West

US   1948   90m   bw
Enterprise (David Loewe, Charles Einfeld)
V*
aka: *They Passed This Way*

A young man turns bandit to save his father's ranch.

Thoughtful minor Western, nicely made.

w Graham Baker, Teddie Sherman   *novel Paso por aqui* by Eugene Rhodes   d Alfred E. Green   ph Russell Harlan   m Paul Sawtell

Joel McCrea, Frances Dee, Charles Bickford, Joseph Calleia

The Four Feathers **

US   1929   83m   bw
Paramount (David O. Selznick)

During the Sudan campaign of the 1890s, a stay-at-home receives four white feathers as a symbol of cowardice; but he goes undercover, becomes a hero, and rescues his best friend.

Ambitious early talkie based on a famous adventure novel, partly filmed in Africa; interesting but now very stilted.

w Howard Estabrook   *novel* A. E. W. Mason   d Lothar Mendes, Merian C. Cooper, Ernest Schoedsack   ph Robert Kurlle, Merian C. Cooper, Ernest Schoedsack   m William F. Peters

Richard Arlen, Fay Wray, Clive Brook, William Powell, George Fawcett, Theodore Von Eltz, Noah Beery

The Four Feathers ****

GB   1939   130m   Technicolor
London (Alexander Korda, Irving Asher)
V, V*, L

The standard version of the above, perfectly cast and presented, with battle scenes which have since turned up in a score of other films from *Zarak* to *Master of the World;* also a triumph of early colour.

w R. C. Sherriff, Lajos Biro, Arthur Wimperis   d Zoltan Korda   ph Georges Périnal, Osmond Borradaile, Jack Cardiff   m Miklos Rozsa   ad Vincent Korda   ed William Hornbeck, Henry Cornelius

John Clements, Ralph Richardson, C. Aubrey Smith, June Duprez, Allan Jeayes, Jack Allen, Donald Gray, Henry Oscar, John Laurie

'It cannot fail to be one of the best films of the year . . . even the richest of the ham goes smoothly down, savoured with humour and satire.' – *Graham Greene*

'Keeps the screen packed with movement, spectacle, and excitement. Beyond these box-office virtues, however, it has another quality. It tells a thumping good personal story.' – *C. A. Lejeune*

† Remade 1956 as *Storm over the Nile* (qv). An effective TV movie, *The Four Feathers*, was made in 1977, directed by Don Sharp and starring Beau Bridges, Robert Powell, Simon Ward, Richard Johnson, Jane Seymour and Harry Andrews.

Four for Texas

US   1963   124m   Technicolor
Warner/Sam Company (Robert Aldrich)
V*, L

Two survivors of a stagecoach raid doublecross each other for the loot and become rival saloon owners.

Flabby Western comedy, tediously directed and casually performed.

w Teddi Sherman, Robert Aldrich   d Robert Aldrich   ph Ernest Laszlo   m Nelson Riddle

Dean Martin, Frank Sinatra, Anita Ekberg, Ursula Andress, Charles Bronson, Victor Buono, the Three Stooges

'The major laughs come from the Three Stooges doing an ancient routine and an old lady falling out of her wheelchair. Zowie.' – *Judith Crist*

'One suspects that the most amusing antics were those that went on off-screen.' – *Films and Filming*

Four Friends

US   1981   115m   Technicolor
Filmways/Cinema 77/Geria (Arthur Penn, Gene Lasko)
V*
GB title: *Georgia's Friends*

A Yugoslavian boy grows up in Indiana and is influenced by the adult behaviour of his three friends.

Mildly interesting semi-autobiographical nostalgia movie, a vein which has been mined twice too often.

w Steve Tesich   d Arthur Penn   ph Ghislain Cloquet   m Elizabeth Swados   pd David Chapman

Craig Wasson, Jodi Thelen, Michael Huddleston, Jim Metzler

'They threw away conventions with their tattered clothes!'
Four Frightened People *

US   1934   78m   bw
Paramount/Cecil B. de Mille

A bubonic plague outbreak on board ship causes four survivors to escape via a lifeboat and trek through dangerous jungle.

Studio-bound but interesting action melodrama, of a type unusual from this director.

w Bartlett Cormack, Lenore Coffee   *novel* E. Arnot Robertson   d Cecil B. de Mille   ph Karl Struss   m Karl Hajos and others

Claudette Colbert, Herbert Marshall, William Gargan, Mary Boland, Leo Carrillo, Nella Walker, Tetsu Komai, Ethel Griffies

'The adventures are episodic and disjointed, running the gamut from stark tragedy to unbelievable farce.' – *Variety*

'A cumbersome sort of melodrama . . . despite some mildly entertaining jungle scenes.' – *Literary Digest*

Four Girls in Town

US   1956   85m   Technicolor   Cinemascope
U-I (Aaron Rosenberg)

Girls from various countries are chosen for Hollywood screen tests.

Formula romantic comedy adequately exposing young talent.

wd Jack Sher   ph Irving Glassberg   m Alex North

George Nader, Julie Adams, Marianne Cook, Elsa Martinelli, Gia Scala, Sidney Chaplin, Grant Williams, John Gavin

Four Girls in White

US   1938   88m   bw
MGM (Nat Levine)

Drama among the student nurses.

Standard hospital fare designed as a try-out for budding talent.

w Dorothy Yost   *story* Nathalie Bucknall, Endre Bohem   d S. Sylvan Simon

Florence Rice, Alan Marshal, Ann Rutherford, Una Merkel, Buddy Ebsen, Mary Howard, Kent Taylor, Jessie Ralph, Sara Haden, Philip Terry, Tom Neal

Four Guns to the Border

US   1954   83m   Technicolor
Universal-International

Things go wrong for four bank robbers after a raid.

Rather downbeat Western with insufficient excitement.

w George Van Marter, Franklin Coen   d Richard Carlson

Rory Calhoun, Walter Brennan, Coleen Miller, George Nader, Nina Foch, John McIntire, Charles Drake

The Four Horsemen of the Apocalypse **

US   1921   150m approx   bw   silent
Metro

A young Argentinian fights for his father's country, France, in World War I.

Highly derivative dramatic spectacle, almost a pageant, from a fairly unreadable novel. Despite its variable if exotic style, it made a star of Rudolph Valentino.

w June Mathis   *novel* Vicente Blasco-Ibanez   d Rex Ingram   ph John F. Seitz

Rudolph Valentino, Alice Terry, Nigel de Brulier, Alan Hale, Jean Hersholt, Wallace Beery

'A blend of exotic settings, striking composition, dramatic lighting, and colourful if sordid atmosphere.' – *Lewis Jacobs*

'Not only was it marvellously effective in its appeal to the eye, but the logical and dramatic unfolding of the basic story was a striking revelation of the valuable service that an expert scenario-writer may render to the professional writer of novels.' – *Edward S. Van Zile, That Marvel the Movie*

The Four Horsemen of the Apocalypse *
US   1961   153m   Metrocolor   Cinemascope
MGM (Julian Blaustein)
V*

In this ill-fated modernization, the idle grandson of an Argentinian beef tycoon finds his manhood at last as a member of the French resistance during World War II.

The visionary skyriding figures of death and pestilence simply do not fit in with bombs and concentration camps. Glum acting by a too elderly company, ugly colour and the usual hindrances of Cinemascope.

w Robert Ardrey, John Gay   d Vincente Minnelli   ph Milton Krasner   m André Previn

Glenn Ford, Ingrid Thulin, Charles Boyer, Paul Henreid, Lee J. Cobb, Paul Lukas, Karl Boehm, Yvette Mimieux

'An elephantine helping of hysteria and hokum.' – *Judith Crist, 1973*

Four Hours to Kill **
US   1935   74m   bw
Paramount (Arthur Hornblow Jnr)

A psychopathic gangster gets loose during an evening at the theatre.

Tense, well-handled melodrama making full use of its setting.

w Norman Krasna   play Small Miracle by Norman Krasna   d Mitchell Leisen   ph Theodor Sparkuhl

Richard Barthelmess, Ray Milland, Gertrude Michael, Joe Morrison, Helen Mack, Dorothy Tree, Roscoe Karns, Henry Travers

'It fails to grip and isn't long on laughs.' – *Variety*

The Four Hundred Blows **
France   1959   94m   bw   Dyaliscope
Films du Carrosse/SEDIF (Georges Charlot)
V, V*, L
original title: *Les Quatre Cents Coups*

A 12-year-old boy, unhappy at home, finds himself in a detention centre but finally escapes and keeps running.

Little more in plot terms than a piece of character observation, this engaging film is so controlled and lyrical as to be totally refreshing, and it gives a very vivid picture of the Paris streets.

wd François Truffaut   ph Henri Decaë   m Jean Constantin   ad Bernard Evein   ed Marie-Josèph Yoyotte

Jean-Pierre Léaud, Claire Maurier, Albert Rémy

'The narrative is boldly fluent. Sympathetic, amused, reminded, occasionally puzzled, you are carried along with it. I don't think you will get away before the end.' – *Dilys Powell*

† The film is said to be based on Truffaut's own childhood.

AAN: script

Four in a Jeep *
Switzerland   1951   96m   bw
Praesensfilm (Lazar Wechsler)
V*

In the post-war international zone of Vienna, the four nationals of a police patrol come to blows over the cases they encounter.

Historically interesting but rather bland illustration of an untenable and even tragic political situation which was treated more melodramatically in *The Third Man*.

w Richard Schweizer   d Leopold Lindtberg   ph Emil Barna   m Robert Blum

Viveca Lindfors, Ralph Meeker, Yoseph Yadin, Michael Medwin

Four in the Morning *
GB   1965   94m   bw
West One (John Morris)

Four personal stories are intercut during one London night.

Attractive minor effort which takes the eye without engaging the mind.

wd Anthony Simmons

Ann Lynn, Judi Dench, Norman Rodway, Brian Phelan, Joe Melia

Four Jacks and a Jill
US   1941   68m   bw
RKO (John Twist)
V*

Four struggling musicians adopt a down-and-out girl.

Flimsy remake of *That Girl from Paris;* the talent is given little opportunity to rise.

w John Twist   d Jack Hively   ph Russell Metty   m/ly Mort Greene, Harry Revel

Anne Shirley, Ray Bolger, Desi Arnaz, Jack Durant, June Havoc, Eddie Foy Jnr, Fritz Feld

Four Jills in a Jeep
US   1944   89m   bw
TCF (Irving Starr)

Four Hollywood glamour girls entertain the troops.

Condescending, dispirited 'semi-documentary' war musical.

w Robert Ellis, Helen Logan, Snag Werris   d William A. Seiter   ph Peverell Marley   md Emil Newman

Kay Francis, Martha Raye, Carole Landis, Mitzi Mayfair, Jimmy Dorsey and his band, John Harvey, Phil Silvers, Dick Haymes; guest stars Alice Faye, Betty Grable, Carmen Miranda, George Jessel

'It gives the painful impression of having been tossed together in a couple of hours.' – *Bosley Crowther*

The Four Just Men *
GB   1939   85m   bw
Ealing-Capad (Michael Balcon, S. C. Balcon)
US title: *The Secret Four*

To save the Empire, four stalwart Britishers agree to murder a villainous MP.

Bright, unusual but dated thriller from a popular novel.

w Roland Pertwee, Angus Macphail, Sergei Nolbandov   novel Edgar Wallace   d Walter Forde   ph Ronald Neame   m Ernest Irving   ad Wilfred Shingleton   ed Charles Saunders

Hugh Sinclair, Francis L. Sullivan, Frank Lawton, Griffith Jones, Anna Lee, Basil Sidney, Alan Napier, Athole Stewart, Edward Chapman, Garry Marsh, Ellaline Terriss, Lydia Sherwood, George Merritt

† The TV series of the late fifties restrained its heroes from criminal acts; the men were Jack Hawkins, Richard Conte, Dan Dailey, Vittorio de Sica.

Four Men and a Prayer *
US   1938   85m   bw
TCF (Kenneth MacGowan)

Four young Englishmen set out to clear the name of their dishonoured father.

Pleasantly performed mystery which improves after a slowish start.

w Richard Sherman, Sonya Levien, Walter Ferris   novel David Garth   d John Ford   ph Ernest Palmer   md Louis Silvers

Loretta Young, Richard Greene, George Sanders, David Niven, William Henry, C. Aubrey Smith, J. Edward Bromberg, John Carradine, Alan Hale, Reginald Denny, Barry Fitzgerald, Berton Churchill, John Sutton

'Better cast than story . . . the pace is so uneven that the general effect at times is bewildering.' – *Variety*

'Energetically told, compactly presented.' – *New York Times*

Four Mothers
US   1940   86m   bw
Warner (Henry Blanke)

The four Lemp sisters, all happily married, have financial problems.

Third and last in the *Four Daughters* trilogy; quite attractively made but very routine.

w Stephen Morehouse Avery   d William Keighley   m Heinz Roemheld

Priscilla Lane, Rosemary Lane, Lola Lane, Gale Page, Claude Rains, Dick Foran, Frank McHugh, Jeffrey Lynn, Eddie Albert, Vera Lewis

'What has eight legs, feathers, and is usually seen coming to the rescue?'

The Four Musketeers (The Revenge of Milady) *
Panama   1974   103m   Technicolor
TCF/Film Trust/Este (Alexander Salkind, Michael Salkind)
V*, S

Athos, Porthos, Aramis and D'Artagnan have a final battle with Rochefort.

Perfunctory sequel to the same team's *The Three Musketeers;* allegedly the two films were intended as one, but if so the first ten reels were by far the best, though this section has its regulation quota of high spirits and lusty action.

w George MacDonald Fraser   d Richard Lester   ph David Watkin   m Lalo Schifrin   pd Brian Eatwell

Michael York, Oliver Reed, Frank Finlay, Richard Chamberlain, Raquel Welch, Faye Dunaway, Charlton Heston, Christopher Lee, Simon Ward, Geraldine Chaplin, Jean-Pierre Cassel, Roy Kinnear

'The whole sleek formula has rolled over to reveal a very soft, very flabby underside.' – *Tony Rayns*

The Four-Poster
US   1952   103m   bw
Columbia/Stanley Kramer

The history of a marriage told in a series of bedroom scenes.

Hastily shot and rather tatty looking version of a stage play; unfortunately film can't contrast the comedy of the opening and the tragedy of the close within one small set, and the UPA cartoon bridges, though smart in themselves, are merely an irritation.

w Allan Scott   play Jan de Hartog   d Irving Reis   ph Hal Mohr   m Dimitri Tiomkin

Rex Harrison, Lilli Palmer

AAN: Hal Mohr

'Here's to our friends – and the strength to put up with them!'

The Four Seasons **
US   1981   108m   Technicolor
Universal (Martin Bregman)
V*, L

Three married couples take seasonal holidays together, and remain united despite various tensions.

Rueful sexual comedy which maintains considerable momentum and actually makes us laugh at its sympathetic characters.

wd Alan Alda   *ph* Victor J. Kemper   *m* Antonio Vivaldi

Alan Alda, Carol Burnett, Len Cariou, Sandy Dennis, Rita Moreno, Jack Weston, Bess Armstrong

'An odd mingling of perspicuity and histrionics . . . a real middle-of-the-road film.' – *Geoff Brown, MFB*

'Unfailingly amusing, touchingly honest, and in the end refreshingly decent.' – *Margaret Hinxman, Daily Mail*

'See! a strange and beautiful woman created before your eyes!'
Four Sided Triangle
GB   1953   81m   bw
Exclusive/Hammer (Michael Carreras, Alexander Paal)
V*

When a scientist's girlfriend marries another, he creates a clone but finds that it has the same preferences.

A very early entry in this field; not too well done, but faithful to its silly theme.

w Paul Tabori, Terence Fisher   *novel* William F. Temple   *d* Terence Fisher   *ph* Reg Wyer   *m* Malcolm Arnold   *ad* J. Elder Wills   *ed* Maurice Rootes

Stephen Murray, Barbara Payton, James Hayter, John Van Eyssen, Percy Marmont, Kynaston Reeves

The Four Skulls of Jonathan Drake
US   1959   70m   bw
UA/Vogue (Robert E. Kent)

A family is cursed by a head-hunting Equadorian medicine man.

Cheaply made but full-blooded occult horror, rather effectively done by a cast that knows how.

w Orville H. Hampton   *d* Edward L. Cahn   *ph* Maury Gertsman   *m* Paul Dunlap

Henry Daniell, Eduard Franz, Valerie French, Grant Richards, Paul Cavanagh

'Amazonian Indians may find the plot a shade far-fetched.' – *MFB*

Four Sons *
US   1940   89m   bw
TCF (Darryl F. Zanuck)

A Czech family is divided when the Nazis take over.

Predictable po-faced anti-Hitler melodrama released to an indifferent public well before America entered the war. A remake of a silent film set during World War I.

w John Howard Lawson   *d* Archie Mayo   *ph* Leon Shamroy   *m* David Buttolph

Don Ameche, Eugenie Leontovich, Mary Beth Hughes, Alan Curtis, George Ernest, Robert Lowery, Sig Rumann, Lionel Royce, Ludwig Stossel

'It partakes more of sentimental melodrama than of tragedy. . .. Neither in its performance nor its writing does the film ever rise to any passion.' – *New York Times*

Four Steps in the Clouds *
Italy   1942   90m   bw
Cines Amato
original title: *Quattro Passi fra le Nuvole*

A travelling salesman on a bus gets involved with the problems of a pregnant girl, but misunderstandings are finally cleared up to general satisfaction.

A comedy on the American model which was a great success in wartorn Italy. Not particularly remarkable in itself, it was remade in 1957, as *The Virtuous Bigamist*, with Fernandel. It does show the lighter side of Italian neo-realism.

w Cesare Zavattini, Giuseppe Amato, Piero Tellini, Aldo de Benedetti   *d* Alessandro Blasetti   *ph* Vaclav Vich   *m* Alessandro Cicognini

Gino Cervi, Adriana Benetti, Giuditta Rissone

Four Wives *
US   1939   110m   bw
Warner (Henry Blanke)

Three of the Lemp girls find a new husband for their widowed sister.

Lively and thickly textured sequel to *Four Daughters*; predecessor of the less interesting *Four Mothers*.

w Julius J. and Philip G. Epstein, Maurice Hanline   *novel* Sister Act by Fannie Hurst   *d* Michael Curtiz   *ph* Sol Polito   *m* Max Steiner

Claude Rains, Priscilla Lane, Rosemary Lane, Lola Lane, Gale Page, Jeffrey Lynn, Eddie Albert, May Robson, Frank McHugh, Dick Foran, John Garfield (briefly)

'Will ride along on momentum to excellent box office.' – *Variety*

Four's a Crowd
US   1938   91m   bw
Warner (Hal B. Wallis/David Lewis)

A public relations man has the job of promoting a mean-spirited millionaire, and falls in love with his daughter.

Floppy comedy, neither very witty nor as crazy as might have been expected. However, it ambles along quite engagingly.

w Casey Robinson, Sig Herzig   *d* Michael Curtiz   *ph* Ernest Haller   *m* Heinz Roemheld, Ray Heindorf

Errol Flynn, Rosalind Russell, Olivia de Havilland, Patric Knowles, Walter Connolly, Hugh Herbert, Melville Cooper, Franklin Pangborn, Herman Bing, Margaret Hamilton

'Goofy click comedy that moves along to a whirlwind laugh finish.' – *Variety*

Fourteen Hours ***
US   1951   92m   bw
TCF (Sol C. Siegel)

A man stands on the ledge of a tall building and threatens to jump.

Well-made documentary drama based on a true occurrence but given a happy ending. First class detail gives an impression of realism.

w John Paxton,   *article* Joel Sayre   *d* Henry Hathaway   *ph* Joe MacDonald   *m* Alfred Newman   *ad* Lyle Wheeler, Leland Fuller

Richard Basehart, Paul Douglas, Barbara Bel Geddes, Grace Kelly, Debra Paget, Agnes Moorehead, Robert Keith, Howard da Silva, Jeffrey Hunter, Martin Gabel, Jeff Corey

'A model of craftsmanship in all departments.' – *Penelope Houston*

'A highly enjoyable small scale picture, with a strength immensely greater than its size would suggest.' – *Richard Mallett, Punch*

AAN: art direction

'Centuries Before The Exploration Of Space, There Was Another Voyage Into The Unknown.'
1492: Conquest of Paradise **
US   1992   155m   colour   Panavision
Guild/Touchstone (Ridley Scott, Alain Goldman)
V, V (W), V*, L, S

Columbus persuades the Spanish court to back his expedition to reach the East by sailing west, but his attempts to live in peace with the natives in the New World are sabotaged by his followers.

A box-office flop, it is nevertheless a handsome-looking film and one that sustains one's interest throughout, despite some narrative ambiguity.

w Roselyne Bosch   *d* Ridley Scott   *ph* Adrian Biddle   *m* Vangelis   *pd* Norris Spencer   *ed* William Anderson, Françoise Bonnot

Gérard Depardieu, Armand Assante, Sigourney Weaver, Loren Dean, Angela Molina, Fernando Rey, Michael Wincott, Tcheky Karyo, Kevin Dunn, Frank Langella

The Fourth Man **
Netherlands   1983   102m   colour
Mainline/De Verenigde Nederlandse Filmcompagnie/ Spectrafilm (Rob Houwer)
original title: *De Vierde Man*

A novelist makes love to a widow as the first step to seducing her boyfriend.

Inventive, exuberant black comedy.

w Gerard Soeteman   *novel* Gerard Reve   *d* Paul Verhoeven   *ph* Jan de Bont   *m* Loek Dikker   *ad* Roland de Groot   *ed* Ine Schenkkan

Jerome Krabbé, Renee Soutendijk, Thom Hoffman, Dolf de Vries, Geert de Jong, Hans Veerman, Hero Muller, Caroline de Beus

'A highbrow debauch of depravity, destruction, sex and blasphemy.' – *Quentin Crisp*

The Fourth Protocol *
GB   1987   119m   Rank colour
Rank (Timothy Burrill)
V, V*, L

Vying masterspies narrowly avert nuclear disaster.

Very competent but somehow old hat espionage thriller, from a best seller.

w Frederick Forsyth   *novel* Frederick Forsyth   *d* John Mackenzie   *ph* Phil Meheux   *m* Lalo Schifrin   *pd* Alan Cameron

Michael Caine, Pierce Brosnan, Joanna Cassidy, Ned Beatty, Betsy Brantley, Ray McAnally, Ian Richardson, Anton Rodgers

'There is an uneasy feeling that the whole affair could have been better made into an excellent miniseries.' – *Daily Variety*

'It's no longer East vs West . . . Just two proud heroes with no one to fight . . . but each other.'
The Fourth War
US   1990   91m   DeLuxe
Kodiak (Wolf Schmidt)
V, V*, L

A violent feud develops between an American and a Soviet colonel, each in charge of a border post between Czechoslovakia and East Germany.

Moderate thriller, somewhat overtaken by events.

w Stephen Peters, Kenneth Ross   *novel* Stephen Peters   *d* John Frankenheimer   *ph* Gerry Fisher   *m* Bill Conti   *pd* Alan Manzer   *ed* Robert F. Shugrue

Roy Scheider, Jürgen Prochnow, Tim Reid, Lara Harris, Harry Dean Stanton, Dale Dye, Bill MacDonald

'A simple moral story, directly told without adornment and relying on old-fashioned effects.' – *MFB*

The Fourth Wish
Australia   1976   105m   colour
Galaxy/South Australian Film Corp (John Morris)

A single father sets out to grant three wishes to his 12-year-old son, who is dying from leukaemia.

Effective domestic drama, cut down from a three-part television series, held together by Meillon's strong central performance.

w Michael Craig   *d* Don Chaffey   *ph* Geoff Burton   *m* Tristram Cary   *ad* David Copping   *ed* G. Turney Smith

John Meillon, Robert Bettles, Michael Craig, Anne Haddy, Ron Haddrick, Robyn Nevin

Les Fous de Bassan: see *In the Shadow of the Wind*

'Between Ellen and Jill came Paul . . .'
The Fox *
US/Canada   1968   110m   DeLuxe
Warner/Raymond Stross/Motion Pictures International (Howard Koch)

On an isolated farm, two lesbians are disturbed by the arrival of a wandering seaman.

Rather obvious sexual high jinks full of symbolism and heavy breathing.

w Lewis John Carlino, Howard Koch   *novel* D. H. Lawrence   *d* Mark Rydell   *ph* Bill Fraker   *m* Lalo Schifrin

Anne Heywood, Sandy Dennis, Keir Dullea

AAN: Lalo Schifrin

Fox *
West Germany   1975   123m   Eastmancolor
Tango Film (Rainer Werner Fassbinder)
V*
aka: *Fox and His Friends*
original title: *Faustrecht der Freiheit*

The decline of a homosexual sideshow performer.

Ironic, semi-autobiographical melodrama in the *Blue Angel* tradition, with sidelong glances at Hollywood glamour. In its way very memorable, but overlong.

w Rainer Werner Fassbinder, Christian Hohoff   *d* Rainer Werner Fassbinder   *ph* Michael Ballhaus   *m* Peer Raben

Rainer Werner Fassbinder, Karl-Heinz Boehm, Peter Chatel, Harry Bär, Adrian Hoven, Ulla Jacobsen

Fox and His Friends: see *Fox*

The Fox and the Hound *
US   1981   83m   Technicolor
Walt Disney (Wolfgang Reitherman, Art Stevens)
S

A fox cub makes friends with a hound puppy, but their friendship is tested when they grow up.

Not unpleasant but somewhat heavy-going for a feature cartoon, made with some of the old Disney style but none of the old inventiveness.

w various   *novel* Daniel P. Mannix   *d* Art Stevens, Ted Berman, Richard Rich

voices of Mickey Rooney, Kurt Russell, Pearl Bailey, Jack Albertson, Sandy Duncan, Jeanette Nolan

'Laughs are few and far between . . . the whole enterprise lacks vitality.' – *Brenda Davies, MFB*

Fox Movietone Follies of 1929
US   1929   82m   bw/sequence in colour
Fox
GB title: *Movietone Follies of 1929*

An all-star review.

Every studio had its early talkie musical using up its contract stars; this was perhaps the least interesting.

wd David Butler, William K. Wells   *ph* Charles Van Enger   *md* Arthur Kay   *m* Con Conrad, Sidney Mitchell, Archie Gottlieb

Sue Carol, Lola Lane, Dixie Lee, Sharon Lynn, Stepin Fetchit

Foxes
US   1980   106m   Technicolor
UA/Polygram (David Puttnam, Gerald Ayres)
V*

Four teenage girls battle with sex, drugs and life in general.

Well-meaning but entirely resistible melodrama from behind the headlines.

w Gerald Ayres   *d* Adrian Lyne   *ph* Leon Bijou   *m* Giorgio Moroder   *ad* Michael Levesque   *ed* Jim Coblentz

Jodie Foster, Scott Baio, Sally Kellerman, Randy Quaid, Adam Faith

'Almost nil adult appeal.' – *Variety*

The Foxes of Harrow
US   1947   117m   bw
TCF (William A. Bacher)

In 1820 New Orleans, a philanderer seeks advancement by breaking up his marriage.

Tolerable but rather flat adaptation of a bestseller, stultified by central miscasting.

w Wanda Tuchock   *novel* Frank Yerby   *d* John M. Stahl   *ph* Joseph LaShelle   *m* Alfred Newman

Rex Harrison, Maureen O'Hara, Richard Haydn, Victor McLaglen, Vanessa Brown, Patricia Medina, Gene Lockhart, Hugo Haas

† Rex Harrison's role had been turned down by Tyrone Power.

'I don't care what they call you! I only care that you are all man – and all mine!'

Foxfire
US   1955   92m   Technicolor
U-I (Aaron Rosenberg)

A rich New York girl on holiday in Arizona is attracted to a half-Apache miner.

Romantic melodrama with action asides; watchable for those who like that sort of thing.

w Ketti Frings   *novel* Anya Seton   *d* Joseph Pevney   *ph* William Daniels   *m* Frank Skinner

Jane Russell, Jeff Chandler, Frieda Inescort, Dan Duryea

Foxhole in Cairo
GB   1960   80m   bw
Omnia (Steven Pallos, Donald Taylor)

A German agent in Libya is allowed to get back to Rommel with false information.

Interesting true spy story deflated by muddled handling.

w Leonard Mosley   *novel* The Cat and the Mice by Leonard Mosley   *d* John Moxey   *ph* Desmond Dickinson   *m* Wolfram Rohrig, Douglas Gamley, Ken Jones

James Robertson Justice, Adrian Hoven, Albert Lieven (as Rommel), Niall MacGinnis, Peter Van Eyck, Robert Urquhart, Fenella Fielding

Foxtrot
Mexico/Switzerland   1977   91m   Technicolor
New World (Gerald Green)
V*

Rich people retreat to a desert island to avoid World War II, but their servants revolt.

A more or less direct attempt to remake *La Règle du Jeu;* it sinks into boredom.

w Arturo Ripstein, José Emilio Pacheco, H. A. L. Craig   *d* Arturo Ripstein

Peter O'Toole, Charlotte Rampling, Max von Sydow, Jorge Luke, Helena Rojo, Claudio Brook

Fra Diavolo **
US   1933   90m   bw
MGM/Hal Roach
V*, L
aka: *The Devil's Brother*

Two incompetent bandits are hired as manservants by a real bandit.

Auber's 1830 operetta becomes a vehicle for Laurel and Hardy, setting a pattern they followed with *Babes in Toyland* and *The Bohemian Girl.* They have excellent sequences, but overall the film lacks pace.

w Jeanie McPherson   *d* Hal Roach, Charles Rogers   *ph* Art Lloyd, Hap Depew   *md* LeRoy Shield   *ed* Bert Jordan, William Terhune

Stan Laurel, Oliver Hardy, Dennis King, *James Finlayson,* Thelma Todd

'An early 19th-century comic opera doesn't make for particularly good film fare despite its hoking.' – *Variety*

La Fracture du Myocarde: see *Cross My Heart*

Fragment of an Empire *
USSR   1929   100m approx   bw   silent
Sovkino

A young man who lost his memory in World War I regains it in 1928 and surveys the changed social order.

Mildly satirical propaganda piece with a vivid impression of Leningrad at the time.

w Friedrich Ermier, Katerina Vinogradskaya   *d* Friedrich Ermier   *ph* Yevgeni Schneider

Fyoder Nikitin, Yakov Gudkin, Ludmila Semyonova

Fragment of Fear *
GB   1970   95m   Technicolor
Columbia (John R. Sloan)

A young writer investigates the murder of his aunt, but finds that he may himself be mad.

What appears to be a whodunnit turns into a flashy, fashionable, sub-Antonioni puzzle with no ending, but despite the considerable irritation this causes, the details and character cameos are excellent.

w Paul Dehn   *novel* John Bingham   *d* Richard C. Sarafian   *ph* Oswald Morris   *m* Johnny Harris

David Hemmings, Gayle Hunnicutt, Roland Culver, Daniel Massey, Flora Robson, Wilfrid Hyde-White, Adolfo Celi, Mona Washbourne

Framed
US   1947   82m   bw
Columbia
GB title: *Paula*

A drunken out-of-work engineer is used as fall guy by two thieves planning an elaborate coup.

Lugubrious mixture of puzzle, character drama and gloomy philosophizing, complete with femme fatale who is handed over to the cops at the end.

w Ben Maddow   *d* Richard Wallace

Glenn Ford, Janis Carter, Barry Sullivan

Framed
US   1974   106m   Metrocolor
Paramount
V*

A Tennessee gambler inadvertently kills a sheriff, is sent to prison, gets out on parole and wreaks revenge on those who framed him.

Violent thick-ear update of *The Count of Monte Cristo,* of interest only to connoisseurs of gratuitous nastiness.

w Mort Briskin   *d* Phil Karlson

Joe Don Baker, Conny Van Dyke, Gabriel Dell, Brock Peters, John Marley, John Larch

Frances
US   1982   140m   Technicolor
EMI/Brooksfilm (Jonathan Sanger)
V, V*, L

The downhill career of 30s actress Frances Farmer.

Long, glum, and not particularly convincing in its inferences, this exhaustive study of a person who didn't deserve all this fuss is illuminated only by a strong star performance.

w Eric Bergren, Christopher Devore, Nicholas Kazan   *d* Graeme Clifford   *ph* Laszlo Kovacs   *m* John Barry   *pd* Richard Sylbert

Jessica Lange, Kim Stanley, Sam Shepard, Bart Burns, Jeffrey de Munn

AAN: Jessica Lange; Kim Stanley

Francesco, Giullare di Dio: see *Francis, God's Jester*

The Franchise Affair *
GB 1950 88m bw
ABP (Robert Hall)

A young girl accuses two gentlewomen of kidnapping and ill-treating her.

Unusual and absorbing mystery based on a true 18th-century case; the treatment however is rather too mild.

w Robert Hall, Lawrence Huntington
novel Josephine Tey   d Lawrence Huntington
ph Gunther Krampf   m Philip Green

Michael Denison, Dulcie Gray, Anthony Nicholls, Marjorie Fielding, Athene Seyler, Ann Stephens, Hy Hazell, John Bailey, Kenneth More

Francis *
US 1950 90m bw
U-I (Robert Arthur)

An army private makes friends with a talking mule who causes him some embarrassment.

Simple-minded, quite agreeable if rather slow-moving fantasy farce which was popular enough to spawn several sequels and later a TV series called *Mister Ed.*

w David Stern   novel David Stern   d Arthur Lubin
ph Irving Glassberg   m Frank Skinner

Donald O'Connor, Patricia Medina, ZaSu Pitts, Ray Collins, John McIntire, Eduard Franz, Robert Warwick, and Chill Wills as Francis's voice. Sequels (the first six with Donald O'Connor):

1951: FRANCIS GOES TO THE RACES
1952: FRANCIS GOES TO WEST POINT
1953: FRANCIS COVERS BIG TOWN
1954: FRANCIS JOINS THE WACS
1955: FRANCIS IN THE NAVY (V*)
1956: FRANCIS IN THE HAUNTED HOUSE (with Mickey Rooney)

Francis, God's Jester **
Italy 1950 75m bw
Cineriz (Giuseppe Amato)
original title: *Francesco, Giullare di Dio*; aka: *The Flowers of St Francis*

An anecdotal and episodic account of the beginnings of the Franciscan order and its first members as they go to preach their faith.

Using mainly non-professional actors, and with Franciscan monks playing the founders of their order, Rossellini, with compassion and humour, affirms that the great virtues are innocence and simplicty.

w Roberto Rossellini, Federico Fellini   book The Little Flowers of St Francis and *The Life of Brother Ginepro*   d Roberto Rossellini   ph Otello Martelli
m Renzo Rossellini, Father Enrico Buondonno
ed Jolanda Benvenuti

Aldo Fabrizi, Arabella Lemaitre, Brother Nazario Gerardi (as St Francis)

Francis of Assisi
US 1961 107m DeLuxe Cinemascope
TCF/Perseus (Plato A. Skouras)

The son of a medieval cloth merchant takes a vow of poverty, cares for animals and dies a hermit.

Tedious biopic.

w Eugene Vale, Jack Thomas, James Forsyth
d Michael Curtiz   ph Piero Portalupi   m Mario Nascimbene

Bradford Dillman, Dolores Hart, Stuart Whitman, Eduard Franz, Pedro Armendariz, Cecil Kellaway, Finlay Currie, Mervyn Johns, Athene Seyler

Françoise Steps Out: see *Rue de l'Estrapade*

'A Terrifying Tale Of Sluts And Bolts.'
'Where Sex Can Cost You An Arm And A Leg.'
Frankenhooker
US 90m 1990 colour
Shapiro/Glickenhaus (Edgar Levens)
V

A mad scientist uses the bodies of prostitutes to rebuild his girlfriend, cut to pieces in a lawnmower accident.

Odd mix of uninventive comedy and gore, relying on its tastelessness to amuse.

w Robert Martin, Frank Henenlotter   d Frank Henenlotter   ph Robert M. Baldwin   m Joe Renzetti   sp Gabe Bartalos   ed Kevin Tent

James Lorintz, Patty Mullen, Charlotte Helmkamp, Shirley Stoler, Louise Lasser

† The film was cut to 81m on its British video release.

'To have seen it is to wear a badge of courage!'
'A monster science created but could not destroy!'
Frankenstein ****
US 1931 71m bw
Universal (Carl Laemmle Jnr)
V, L

A research scientist creates a living monster from corpses, but it runs amok.

Whole books have been written about this film and its sequels. Apart from being a fascinating if primitive cinematic work in its own right, it set its director and star on interesting paths and established a Hollywood attitude towards horror (mostly borrowed from German silents such as *The Golem*). A seminal film indeed, which at each repeated viewing belies its age.

w Garrett Fort, Francis Edward Faragoh, John L. Balderston
play Peggy Webling   novel Mary Wollstonecraft Shelley   d James Whale   ph Arthur Edeson
m David Broekman   ad Charles D. Hall

Boris Karloff, Colin Clive, Mae Clarke, John Boles, Edward Van Sloan, Frederick Kerr, Dwight Frye

'Still the most famous of all horror films, and deservedly so.' – *John Baxter, 1968*

'The horror is cold, chilling the marrow but never arousing malaise.' – *Carlos Clarens*

† Direct sequels by the same studio (all qv) include *The Bride of Frankenstein, Son of Frankenstein, Ghost of Frankenstein, Frankenstein Meets the Wolf Man, House of Frankenstein, House of Dracula, Abbott and Costello Meet Frankenstein*. The later Hammer series, which told the story all over again in gorier vein, includes (all qv) *The Curse of Frankenstein, The Revenge of Frankenstein, The Evil of Frankenstein, Frankenstein Created Woman, Frankenstein Must be Destroyed, Horror of Frankenstein, Frankenstein and the Monster from Hell*. Other Frankenstein films date from as early as 1908, and scores have been made in various languages. *Young Frankenstein* (qv) is a partly effective spoof on the Hollywood series; *The Munsters* was a sixties comedy series for TV which used the monster as its leading character in a domestic setting.
†† Robert Florey is said to have contributed to the script, having been the first choice for director.

Frankenstein and the Monster from Hell
GB 1973 99m Technicolor
Hammer/Avco (Roy Skeggs)
V*

The Baron turns an injured lunatic into a hairy ape man.

Cheaply made and very ghoulish horror comic in the unattractive setting of an asylum; very little entertainment is provided.

w John Elder (Anthony Hinds)   d Terence Fisher
ph Brian Probyn   ad Scott MacGregor   ed James Needs

Peter Cushing, Shane Briant, Madeleine Smith, John Stratton, Bernard Lee, Dave Prowse (as the monster)

'A beautiful woman with the soul of a devil!'
Frankenstein Created Woman
GB 1967 86m Technicolor
Warner/Hammer-Seven Arts (Anthony Nelson-Keys)

The Baron invests the body of a dead girl with the soul of her dead lover, and a murder spree results.

Crude and gory farrago, with the central laboratory sequence apparently excised at the last moment.

w John Elder (Anthony Hinds)   d Terence Fisher
ph Arthur Grant   m James Bernard   pd Bernard Robinson   ad Don Mingaye   ed James Needs, Spencer Reeve

Peter Cushing, Thorley Walters, Susan Denberg, Robert Morris, Duncan Lamont

'Titans of terror, clashing in mortal combat!'
Frankenstein Meets the Wolf Man **
US 1943 73m bw
Universal (George Waggner)
V*, L

Lawrence Talbot, the wolf man, travels to Vasaria in the hope of a cure, and finds the Frankenstein monster being reactivated.

Once one recovered from the bargain basement combination of two monsters in one picture, this was a horror comic with stylish sequences, weakened by cuts in the script and a miscast Bela Lugosi.

w Curt Siodmak   d Roy William Neill   ph George Robinson   m Hans Salter

Lon Chaney Jnr, Ilona Massey, Bela Lugosi (as the monster), Patric Knowles, *Maria Ouspenskaya*

Frankenstein Must Be Destroyed
GB 1969 96m Technicolor
Warner-Pathé/Hammer (Anthony Nelson-Keys)
V, V*, L

The Baron transplants the brain of one colleague into the body of another.

Spirited but decidedly unpleasant addition to the cycle, made more so by a genuine note of pathos.

w Bert Batt   d Terence Fisher   ph Arthur Grant
m James Bernard   ad Bernard Robinson
ed Gordon Hales

Peter Cushing, Freddie Jones, Veronica Carlson, Simon Ward, Thorley Walters, Maxine Audley

Frankenstein '70
US 1958 83m bw Cinemascope
Allied Artists (Aubrey Schenck)
V*

Television film-makers descend on Castle Frankenstein; the current Count needs the money to finance some monster making of his own.

Boringly talkative and very silly 'futuristic' blot on an honourable name, apart from a rather frightening pre-credits sequence.

w Richard Landau, G. Worthing Yates   d Howard W. Koch   ph Carl Guthrie   m Paul Dunlap

Boris Karloff, Tom Duggan, Jana Lund, Mike Lane (as the monster)

Frankenstein Unbound
US 1990 85m DeLuxe
Fox/Mount Company (Roger Corman, Thom Mount, Kabi Jaeger)
V, V*, L

A scientist is transported back in time to Switzerland in the 1800s where he meets Mary Godwin, Byron, Shelley and Dr Frankenstein and his monster.

Odd mix of science fiction and horror that fails to cohere.

w Roger Corman, F. X. Feeney novel Brian Aldiss d Roger Corman ph Armando Nannuzzi, Michael Scott m Carl Davis pd Enrico Tovaglieri ed Jay Cassidy, Mary Bauer

John Hurt, Raul Julia, Bridget Fonda, Nick Brimble, Catherine Rabett, Jason Patric, Michael Hutchence

'Competent but uninspired.' – Variety

Frankie and Johnny *
US   1966   87m   Technicolor
UA/F and J (Edward Small)
V, V*

On a Mississippi riverboat, a gambling singer is the despair of his lady partner.

Mildly amusing pastiche both of the old song and of the various riverboat dramas.

w Alex Gottlieb d Frederick de Cordova ph John Marquette m Fred Karger

Elvis Presley, Donna Douglas, Sue Ane Langdon, Harry Morgan, Nancy Kovack, Audrey Christie, Jerome Cowan

'He's no knight in shining armor. She's no princess. But who says life is a fairytale anyway?'

Frankie and Johnny *
US   1991   118m   Technicolor
UIP/Paramount (Garry Marshall)
V, V*, L, S

A short-order cook ardently woos a reluctant waitress.

Soft-centred romance with its stars trying hard to persuade an audience that they are damaged and unlovable until the final clinch.

w Terrence McNally play Frankie and Johnny in the Clair de Lune by Terrence McNally d Garry Marshall ph Dante Spinotti m Marvin Hamlisch pd Albert Brenner ed Battie Davis, Jacqueline Cambas

Al Pacino, Michelle Pfeiffer, Hector Elizondo, Nathan Lane, Jane Morris, Greg Lewis, Al Fann, Glenn Plummer, Sean O'Bryan, Kate Nelligan

'The layers of artifice are just too thick for the film's warm glow to last long.' – Geoff Brown, The Times

'This is a vehicle of Pacino and Pfeiffer, and they're more glamorous than the characters they're playing, but, in a weird way, their star power is perfectly appropriate here: it's the meat-and-potatoes stuff of big-budget movie entertainment.' – New Yorker

Frantic (1957): see Lift to the Scaffold

Frantic *
US   1988   120m   colour
Warner/Mount (Thom Mount, Tim Hampton)
V, V*, L

An American cardiologist in Paris hunting for his kidnapped wife becomes embroiled with Arab terrorists.

Amiable thriller with Hitchcockian touches, quite untypical of this director.

w Roman Polanski, Gérard Brach d Roman Polanski ph Witold Sobocinski m Ennio Morricone pd Pierre Guffroy ed Sam O'Steen

Harrison Ford, Betty Buckley, Emmanuelle Seigner, Alexandra Stewart

'Disappointingly conventional mystery.' – Variety

Fraternally Yours: see Sons of the Desert

Fraternity Row *
US   1977   101m   colour
Paramount (Charles Gary Allison)

In the early 1950s, students indulge in dangerous fraternity initiations at an exclusive Eastern university.

Efficient, well-acted drama of college life.

w Charles Gary Allison d Thomas J. Tobin ph Peter Gibbons m Michael Corner, Don McLean ad James Sbardellati ed Eugene A. Fournier

Peter Fox, Gregory Harrison, Scott Newman, Nancy Morgan, Wendy Phillips, Robert Emhardt, Robert Matthews, Bernard R. Kantor, Cliff Robertson

Frau im Mond: see The Woman in the Moon

'He's No Ordinary Insurance Man. You Can Bet Your Life On It!'
Frauds
Australia   1992   94m   colour
First Independent/Latent Image/AFFC (Andrena Finlay, Stuart Quin)
V

A manic practical-joke-playing insurance agent, who tosses dice to decide his next action, torments a couple who decide to play him at his own game.

A frantic comedy that remains unsympathetic viewing; it is simply not funny, despite the strenuous efforts of everyone involved.

wd Stephan Elliott ph Geoff Burton m Guy Gross pd Brian Thomson ed Frans Vandenburg

Phil Collins, Hugo Weaving, Josephine Byrnes, Peter Mochrie, Helen O'Connor, Rebel Russell, Colleen Clifford

'Chronically over-designed and over-directed, each angle containing something cute and clever.' – Sheila Johnston, Independent

'A comedy designed to set teeth on edge.' – Sight and Sound

Fräulein
US   1958   100m   Eastmancolor   Cinemascope
TCF (Walter Reisch)

During World War II an American prisoner of war escapes and is helped by the daughter of a German professor.

Studio-bound war heroics with little conviction achieved or aimed at.

w Lee Townsend novel James McGowan d Henry Koster ph Leo Tover m Daniele Amfitheatrof

Dana Wynter, Mel Ferrer, Margaret Hayes, Dolores Michaels, Theodore Bikel, Helmut Dantine

Fräulein Doktor
Italy/Yugoslavia   1968   104m   Technicolor
(Paramount) Dino de Laurentiis/Avala

In World War I, a German lady spy outwits British intelligence.

Rather glum international action melodrama.

w Diulio Coletti, H. A. L. Craig, Stanley Mann, Vittoriano Petrilli, Alberto Lattuada d Alberto Lattuada ph Luigi Kuveiller m Ennio Morricone

Suzy Kendall, Kenneth More, James Booth, Capucine, Alexander Knox, Nigel Green, Roberto Bisacco

† A similar story was filmed in 1936 as Mademoiselle Docteur.

Freaks **
US   1932   64m   bw
MGM (Tod Browning)
V*, L

A lady trapeze artist marries a midget, then poisons him for his money; his abnormal friends take revenge by turning her into a freak.

Made but disowned by MGM after accusations of tastelessness, this strident and silly melodrama has dated badly but has sequences of great power, especially the final massing of the freaks, slithering to their revenge in a rainstorm. It would have been better as a silent; the dialogue kills it.

w Willis Goldbeck, Leon Gordon novel Spurs by Tod Robbins d Tod Browning ph Merritt B. Gerstad

Wallace Ford, Olga Baclanova, Leila Hyams, Roscoe Ates

'Either too horrible or not sufficiently so.' – Variety

'It is a skilfully presented production but of a character which in consideration of the susceptibilities of mass audiences should be avoided.' – Martin Quigley

'For pure sensationalism it tops any picture yet produced.' – Louella Parsons

'I want something that out-horrors Frankenstein.' – Irving Thalberg

'Touching and funny and made with a miraculous delicacy.' – Evening Standard, 1964

Freaky Friday
US   1976   100m   Technicolor
Walt Disney (Ron Miller)
V*, L

A 13-year-old and her mother, each discontented with their lot, express a wish to change places – and do.

A trendy update of Vice Versa, padded out with Disney irrelevancies and long outstaying its welcome.

w Mary Rodgers novel Mary Rodgers d Gary Nelson ph Charles F. Wheeler m Johnny Mandel

Jodie Foster, Barbara Harris, John Astin, Patsy Kelly, Dick Van Patten, Sorrell Booke, Marie Windsor

Freckles
US   1935   69m   bw
RKO (Pandro S. Berman)

A mild teenager gets a job as a timber guard.

Unsensational version of a rustic classic.

w Dorothy Yost novel Gene Stratton-Porter d Edward Killy, William Hamilton

'The novel, published in 1875, is shown to have sold 2,000,000 copies. It will have a tough time making the same grade as a picture . . . its appeal is of a past generation.' – Variety

† A 1960 remake for Fox starred Martin West.

Freddie as F.R.0.7
GB   1992   91m   colour
Rank/Hollywood Road Films
V, V*, S

A human-sized frog, a French secret agent, investigates the disappearance of such British institutions as Buckingham Palace and the Tower of London.

Dated, animated parody of James Bond. It was intended as the first of a series starring Freddie, but its box-office failure led to a sequel being abandoned.

w Jon Acevski, David Ashton d Jon Acevski ph Rex Neville m/y David Dundas, Rick Wentworth, Don Black, Jon Acevski, David Ashton ad Paul Shardlow ed Alex Rayment, Mick Manning

voices of Ben Kingsley, Jenny Agutter, Brian Blessed, Nigel Hawthorne, Michael Hordern, Edmund Kingsley, Phyllis Logan, Victor Maddern, Jonathan Pryce, Prunella Scales, John Sessions, Billie Whitelaw

'This likeable enough saga of a super-agent frog looks unlikely to hop into the big time.' – Variety

'They saved the best . . . for last.'
Freddy's Dead: The Final Nightmare
US   1991   90m   DeLuxe   Part 3-D
Guild/New Line (Robert Shaye, Aron Warner)
V, V*, S

With the aid of some disturbed teenagers, Freddie Krueger's daughter ends her father's life.

Sixth and, with luck, the last of the *Nightmare On Elm Street* series, which has little to offer other than the gimmick of an ineffectual 3-D climax.

w Michael DeLuca story Rachel Talalay d Rachel Talalay ph Declan Quinn m Brian May pd C. J. Strawn ed Janice Hampton

Robert Englund, Lisa Zane, Shon Greenblatt, Lezlie Deane, Ricky Dean Logan, Breckin Meyer, Yaphet Kotto, Roseanne Arnold, Tom Arnold, Alice Cooper

'Delivers enough violence, black humor and even a final reel in 3-D to hit paydirt with horror-starved audiences.' – *Variety*

'The dream logic of Wes Craven's ground-breaking original has been reduced to sloppy plotting and a string of unrelated special-effects set-pieces. It is sadly apt therefore that the manner of Freddy's passing should be as unimaginative as the enervated sequels themselves.' – *Sight and Sound*

Free and Easy
US 1930 75m bw
MGM (Edward Sedgwick)
V*

A beauty contest winner is taken to Hollywood by her accident-prone manager.

Primitive talkie showing a great silent comedian all at sea with the new techniques, and the MGM studio offering entertainment on the level of a very bad school concert.

w Al Boasberg, Richard Schayer d Edward Sedgwick ph Leonard Smith

Buster Keaton, Anita Page, Robert Montgomery, Trixie Friganza

Free and Easy
US 1941 56m bw
MGM

In British high society, father and son both seek rich wives.

A remarkable cast is all at sea in a potted version of Ivor Novello's *The Truth Game*.

w Marvin Borowsky d George Sidney

Nigel Bruce, Robert Cummings, Ruth Hussey, Judith Anderson, C. Aubrey Smith, Reginald Owen, Tom Conway, Forrester Harvey

'This one must have slipped through the Metro wringer while the brains department was out to lunch.' – *Variety*

Free for All
US 1949 83m bw
U-I (Robert Buckner)

A young inventor finds a way of turning water into petrol.

Scatty comedy with mildly amusing moments.

w Robert Buckner d Charles T. Barton ph George Robinson m Frank Skinner

Robert Cummings, Ann Blyth, Percy Kilbride, Ray Collins, Donald Woods, Mikhail Rasumny

A Free Soul *
US 1931 91m bw
MGM
V*

An unconventional lawyer regrets allowing his daughter to consort with a gangster.

Heavy melodrama with outdated attitudes, but an impressive example of the studio's style in the early thirties.

w John Meehan novel Adela Rogers St John d Clarence Brown ph William Daniels m William Axt

Lionel Barrymore, Norma Shearer, Leslie Howard, Clark Gable, Lucy Beaumont, James Gleason

'An ungainly, rambling and preposterous theme, awkwardly brought to the screen.' – *Variety*

† Remade 1953 as *The Girl Who Had Everything*.

AA: Lionel Barrymore (who had a 14-minute speech)

AAN: Clarence Brown; Norma Shearer

Free to Live: see *Holiday* (1938)

'A 12 Year Old Street Kid. A 3 Ton Killer Whale. A Friendship You Could Never Imagine. An Adventure You'll Never Forget.'
Free Willy *
US 1993 112m Technicolor Panavision
Warner/Canal+/Regency/Alcor (Jennie Lew Tugend, Lauren Shuler-Donner)
V, V*, L, S

A young, disturbed boy forms a friendship with a killer whale threatened with death.

Sentimental animal story with a little charm and some appeal to the under-10s, but no more than a damp update of *Lassie*.

w Keith A. Walker, Corey Blechman d Simon Wincer ph Robbie Greenberg m Basil Poledouris pd Charles Rosen ed O. Nicholas Brown

Jason James Richter, Lori Petty, Jayne Atkinson, August Schellenberg, Michael Madsen, Michael Ironside, Keiko

'An exhilarating drama of boy and nature that unabashedly pulls at the heart-strings. Thankfully, its creators know just what to do emotionally and technically to pull off this old-fashioned sentimental yarn.' – *Variety*

'The movie hits every emotional button with a firm fist.' – *Richard Corliss, Time*

'Today they demolished 23 cars, four motor cycles and one apartment building. But don't call the cops. They *are* the cops!'
Freebie and the Bean *
US 1974 113m Technicolor Panavision
Warner (Richard Rush)
V*, L

Two vaguely incompetent cops try to link a mobster with the numbers racket.

Violent comedy melodrama with a high mortality rate, amoral outlook, and the usual seventies reliance on incoherent plot, bumbled dialogue and excessive background noise. Occasionally funny all the same.

w Richard Kaufman d Richard Rush ph Laszlo Kovacs m Dominic Frontière

Alan Arkin, James Caan, Loretta Swit, Jack Kruschen, Mike Kellin

'It summarizes Hollywood's favourite thematic elements of the early seventies: platonic male love affair, police corruption, comic violence, cynicism in high places, San Francisco, gay villains, the car chase. A return to the Keystone Kops, with character trimmings and lashings of sado-masochistic mayhem.' – *Clyde Jeavons*

'A tasteless film from a spitball script.' – *Variety*

'There is a beating or a killing, or at least a yelling scene, every couple of minutes.' – *New Yorker, 1980*

Freedom Is Paradise: see *SER*

Freedom Radio
GB 1941 95m bw
Columbia/Two Cities (Mario Zampi)
US title: *A Voice in the Night*

In Vienna during World War II, the husband of a Nazi actress runs a secret radio transmitter for Allied propaganda.

Moderate wartime flagwaver.

w Basil Wood, Gordon Wellesley, Louis Golding, Anatole de Grunwald, Jeffrey Dell, Bridget Boland,

Roland Pertwee d Anthony Asquith ph Bernard Knowles

Diana Wynyard, Clive Brook, Raymond Huntley, Joyce Howard, Derek Farr, Howard Marion Crawford, Morland Graham

Freejack
US 1992 108m Technicolor
Warner/Morgan Creek (Ronald Shusett, Stuart Oken)
V, V*, L, S

A racing-car driver on the point of death is taken eighteen years into the future so that his body can house the mind of a terminally ill millionaire.

Predictable science fiction about a sleazy future that lacks the wit and originality of the novel on which it is based.

w Steven Pressfield, Ronald Shusett, Dan Gilroy novel Immortality Inc by Robert Sheckley d Geoff Murphy ph Amir Mokri m Trevor Jones pd Joe Alves sp Richard Hoover ed Dennis Virkler

Emilio Estevez, Mick Jagger, René Russo, Anthony Hopkins, Jonathan Banks, David Johansen, Amanda Plummer

'Chalk it up as one of life's little ironies that a pic about mind transfers would be so mindless.' – *Variety*

French Can-Can **
France/Italy 1955 105m Technicolor
Franco-London/Jolly (Louis Wipf)
V*, L

How the can-can was launched in Paris night-clubs.

A dramatically thin vehicle splendidly evoking a vision of vanished Paris: a feast for the eyes.

w André-Paul Antoine d Jean Renoir ph Michel Kelber m Georges Van Parys

Jean Gabin, Françoise Arnoul, Maria Félix, Jean-Roger Caussimon, Edith Piaf, Patachou

'Doyle is bad news ... but a good cop!'
The French Connection ****
US 1971 104m DeLuxe
TCF/Philip D'Antoni
V, V*, L

New York police track down a consignment of drugs entering the country in a car.

Lively semi-documentary based on the true exploits of a tough cop named Eddie Egan who liked to break a few rules. Most memorable for a car chase scene involving an elevated railway, for showing the seamy side of New York more or less as it is.

w Ernest Tidyman book Robin Moore d William Friedkin ph Owen Roizman m Don Ellis

Gene Hackman, Roy Scheider, Fernando Rey, Tony Lo Bianco

'The only thing this movie believes in is giving the audience jolts, and you can feel the raw, primitive responses in the theater.' – *Pauline Kael, New Yorker*

AA: best picture; Ernest Tidyman; William Friedkin; Gene Hackman

AAN: Owen Roizman; Roy Scheider

French Connection II
US 1975 119m DeLuxe
TCF (Robert L. Rosen)
V, V*

The New York cop who in *The French Connection* smashed most of a drug ring arrives in Marseilles to track down its elusive leader.

Sleazy, virtually plotless and unattractive sequel which rises to a few good action moments but is bogged down by bad language, unconvincing characterization and an interminable and irrelevant 'cold turkey' sequence.

w Robert Dillon, Laurie Dillon, Alexander Jacobs
d John Frankenheimer   ph Claude Renoir   m Don
Ellis

Gene Hackman, Fernando Rey, Bernard Fresson,
Jean-Pierre Castaldi

'Visually as well as morally the film makes you
uncertain where its feet are.' – New Yorker

French Dressing
GB   1963   86m   bw
ABP/Kenwood (Kenneth Harper)

A deckchair attendant and a local reporter believe that
what Bardot can do for St Tropez they can do for
Gormleigh-on-Sea.

Cinema's enfant terrible directs this his first theatrical
film at breakneck speed with echoes of Tati, Keaton
and the Keystone Kops. Alas, lack of star comedians
and firm control make its exuberance merely
irritating.

w Peter Myers, Ronald Cass, Peter Britt   d Ken
Russell   ph Ken Higgins   m Georges Delerue

James Booth, Roy Kinnear, Marisa Mell, Bryan
Pringle

The French Key
US   1946   67m   bw
Republic

Private eyes, locked out of their hotel room for non-
payment of rent, use the fire escape and find a body
inside.

Minor mystery which seemed passable at the time.

w Frank Gruber   novel Frank Gruber   d Walter
Colmes

Albert Dekker, Mike Mazurki, Evelyn Ankers, John
Eldredge, Frank Fenton

French Leave
GB   1930   100m   bw
D and H (Louis Zimmerman)

In order to be near her husband, a British girl
pretends to be French and goes behind the trenches.

Flat picturization of a popular stage farce of the
twenties.

w W. P. Lipscomb, Reginald Berkeley
play Reginald Berkeley   d Jack Raymond
ph Bernard Knowles   ad G. T. Stoneham

Madeleine Carroll, Sydney Howard, Arthur Chesney,
Haddon Mason, Henry Kendall

† Remade in 1937 with Betty Lynne, Norman Lee, for
Welwyn.

'She was lost from the moment she saw him …'
The French Lieutenant's Woman *
GB   1981   123m   Technicolor
UA/Juniper (Leon Clore)
V, V*, L, S

In 1867 Lyme Regis, a gentleman forsakes his fiancée
for the abandoned mistress of a French seaman.

Vaguely unsatisfactory and muddily coloured
adaptation of a novel which set its thin story against
the entire social background of the Victorian age as
related to our own. The attempt to replace this by an
equally thin modern story about actors playing the
Victorian roles fails rather dismally; but the enterprise
supplies points of interest along the way.

w Harold Pinter   novel John Fowles   d Karel Reisz
ph Freddie Francis   m Carl Davis   pd Assheton
Gorton

Jeremy Irons, Meryl Streep, Leo McKern, Patience Collier,
Peter Vaughan, Hilton McRae

'Pinter's reduction not only shears away the sliding
historical perspective, but robs the narrative of its
Victorian charisma.' – Tom Milne, MFB

'There are some lovely moments, and a few have
magical undertones, but most of the picture might be
taking place in a glass case.' – Pauline Kael

'If you see the movie, the book will still surprise you,
and that's as it should be.' – Roger Ebert

AAN: Harold Pinter; editing (John Bloom); Meryl
Streep

best sound; Carl Davis; Meryl Streep

The French Line
US   1953   102m   Technicolor   3-D
RKO (Edmund Grainger)
V*

A cheery Texas oil heiress finds a husband while
travelling to France.

Very thinly plotted but quite attractive light musical
with a good-humoured star wearing costumes once
thought censorable.

w Mary Loos, Richard Sale   d Lloyd Bacon
ph Harry J. Wild   md Lionel Newman   ch Jack
Cole   m Walter Scharf

Jane Russell, Gilbert Roland, Arthur Hunnicutt, Mary
McCarty

'A slouching Amazon, her clothes appear to stay put
just as long as she agrees not to burst out of them;
essentially a good sort, she has an ever-annihilating
sneer for the false, the pretentious and the fresh.' –
MFB

A French Mistress
GB   1960   98m   bw
British Lion/Charter (John Boulting)

An attractive new mistress causes havoc at a boys'
school.

Sloppy, predictable comedy with practised performers
getting a few easy laughs. The producers tried to
excuse its imperfections by promoting it as 'a romp'.

w Roy Boulting, Jeffrey Dell   play Robert Monro
(Sonnie Hale)   d Roy Boulting   ph Max Greene
m John Addison

James Robertson Justice, Cecil Parker, Raymond
Huntley, Ian Bannen, Agnes Laurent, Thorley
Walters, Edith Sharpe, Athene Seyler, Kenneth
Griffith

The French They Are a Funny Race: see The
Diary of Major Thompson

A French Vampire in America: see Innocent
Blood

French without Tears **
GB   1939   85m   bw
Paramount/Two Cities (David E. Rose)

Young Britons at a French crammer fall for the young
sister of one of their number.

Pleasant light comedy from a successful West End
play.

w Terence Rattigan, Anatole de Grunwald, Ian
Dalrymple   play Terence Rattigan   d Anthony
Asquith   ph Bernard Knowles, Jack Hildyard
m Nicholas Brodszky   ad Paul Sheriff, Carmen
Dillon   ed David Lean

Ray Milland, Ellen Drew, Guy Middleton, Ronald Culver,
David Tree, Jim Gerald, Janine Darcy, Kenneth
Morgan

'There is always something a little shocking about
English levity. The greedy exhilaration of these blithe
young men when they learn that another fellow's girl
is to join them at the establishment where they are
learning French, the scramble over her luggage, the
light-hearted badinage, the watery and libidinous eye
– that national mixture of prudery and excitement –
would be unbearable if it were not for Mr Asquith's
civilized direction.' – Graham Greene

† Incredibly, Paramount had purchased the property
as a vehicle for Marlene Dietrich.

Frenchie
US   1950   80m   Technicolor
U-I (Michel Kraike)

A saloon queen sets up shop in Bottleneck, her real
aim being to track down her father's murderers.

Modest Western of the Destry Rides Again school.

w Oscar Brodney   d Louis King   ph Maury
Gertsman   m Hans Salter

Shelley Winters, Joel McCrea, Paul Kelly, Elsa
Lanchester, Marie Windsor, John Emery, George
Cleveland, John Russell

'For 24 reckless hours the arms of adventure embraced
her – and she knew the thrill of true love!'
Frenchman's Creek *
US   1944   112m   Technicolor
Paramount (B. G. de Sylva)

In Restoration England, a lady flees from a lascivious
nobleman to her family home in Cornwall, where she
falls in love with a French pirate.

Enjoyable Girls' Own Paper romance, dressed to kill
and entertaining despite its many palpable
absurdities.

w Talbot Jennings   novel Daphne du Maurier
d Mitchell Leisen   ph George Barnes   m Victor
Young   ad Hans Dreier, Ernst Fegte

Joan Fontaine, Arturo de Cordova, Basil Rathbone,
Nigel Bruce, Cecil Kellaway, Ralph Forbes, Moyna
McGill

'Masturbation fantasy triple distilled.' – James Agee

AA: art direction

Frenzy *
Sweden   1944   101m   bw
Svensk Filmindustri
V*
original title: Hets; aka: Torment

A sadistic Latin teacher and his sensitive pupil find
themselves competing for the same girl.

Hothouse melodrama of the Blue Angel school: it
seemed pretty powerful at the time.

w Ingmar Bergman   d Alf Sjöberg   ph Martin Bodin
m Hilding Rosenberg

Stig Jarrel, Alf Kjellin, Mai Zetterling

Frenzy (1945): see Latin Quarter

'From the master of shock, a shocking masterpiece!'
Frenzy *
GB   1972   116m   Technicolor
Universal/Alfred Hitchcock
V*, L

A disillusioned and aggressive ex-RAF officer is
suspected through circumstantial evidence of being
London's 'necktie murderer'.

Has-been, unconvincing, cliché-ridden thriller, an old
man's sex suspenser, which would have been derided
if anyone but Hitchcock had made it. As it is, a few
comic and suspenseful touches partly atone for the
implausibilities and lapses of taste.

w Anthony Shaffer   novel Goodbye Piccadilly, Farewell
Leicester Square by Arthur La Bern   d Alfred
Hitchcock   ph Gilbert Taylor   m Ron Goodwin
pd Syd Cain   ed John Jympson

Jon Finch, Alec McCowen, Barry Foster, Vivien Merchant,
Anna Massey, Barbara Leigh-Hunt, Billie Whitelaw

'Hitchcock's most stodgy piece since Dial M for Murder
and possibly his least interesting film from any
period.' – William S. Pechter

'There is suspense, and local colour, and always,
Hitchcock smacking his lips and rubbing his hands
and delighting in his naughtiness.' – Roger Ebert

Fresh Horses

US 1988 103m colour
Columbia TriStar/Weintraub Entertainment (Dick Berg)
V, V*, L

A wealthy student falls in love with a married 16-year-old girl.

Insignificant romance, no more than adequate.

w Larry Ketron play Larry Ketron d David Anspaugh ph Fred Murphy m David Foster, Patrick Williams pd Paul Sylbert ed David Rosenbloom

Molly Ringwald, Andrew McCarthy, Patti D'Arbanville, Ben Stiller, Leon Russom, Molly Hagen, Viggo Mortensen, Doug Hutchinson, Chiara Peacock

The Freshman **

US 1925 75m (24 fps) bw silent
Harold Lloyd
V, V*

An awkward college student accidentally becomes a star football player.

A rather slow but striking star vehicle with assured set-pieces. The football game climax was later used as the first reel of *Mad Wednesday*.

w Sam Taylor, Ted Wilde, Tim Whelan, John Grey d Fred Newmeyer, Sam Taylor ph Walter Lundin, Henry Kohler

Harold Lloyd, Jobyna Ralston, Brooks Benedict

'Next time they make you an offer you can't refuse . . . refuse!'

The Freshman **

US 1990 102m Technicolor
Tri-Star/Mike Lobell, Andrew Bergman
V, V*, L

A student of gangster movies goes to work for a real-life criminal.

A genial spoof of *The Godfather* films, with Brando parodying his own performance as an ageing patriarch of crime.

wd Andrew Bergman ph William A. Fraker m David Newman ed Barry Malkin

Marlon Brando, Matthew Broderick, Bruno Kirby, Penelope Ann Miller, Frank Whaley, Jon Polito, Paul Benedict, Richard Gant, Kenneth Welsh, Pamela Payton-Wright

Freud **

GB 1962 140m bw
U-I (Wolfgang Reinhardt)

Vienna 1885; Dr Sigmund Freud, a neurologist, uses hypnotism to treat hysteria, and finds new interest in the case of a boy whose hatred of his father springs from incestuous love of his mother, a failing which Freud finds in himself.

Earnest and competent biopic harking back to Warner's similar films of the 30s, with the addition of franker language. Generally absorbing, but undeniably hard tack.

w Charles Kaufman, Wolfgang Reinhardt d John Huston ph Douglas Slocombe m Jerry Goldsmith

Montgomery Clift, Larry Parks, Susannah York, Eileen Herlie, Susan Kohner, David McCallum

'The dream sequences, photographed mostly in negative or overexposure, belong not on the couch of Dr Freud but in the Cabinet of Dr Caligari.' – *John Simon*

'It is impossible, I would think, for any educated person to sit through *Freud* without bursting into laughter at least once.' – *Ernest Callenbach, Film Quarterly*

AAN: script: Jerry Goldsmith

Die Freudlose Gasse: see *Joyless Street*

Fric Frac *

France 1939 95m bw
Maurice Lehmann

A provincial jeweller's assistant falls in with underworld characters.

Well-prized French comedy with dialogue entirely in thieves' slang.

w Michel Duran play Edouard Bourdet d Maurice Lehmann

Michel Simon, Fernandel, Arletty, Helene Robert

Friday the Thirteenth ***

GB 1933 84m bw
Gainsborough (Michael Balcon)

Several people are involved in a bus crash, and we turn back the clock to see how they came to be there.

Highly competent compendium of comedies and dramas looking back to *The Bridge of San Luis Rey* and forward to the innumerable all-star films of the forties.

w G. H. Moresby-White, Sidney Gilliat, Emlyn Williams d Victor Saville ph Charles Van Enger ad Alfred Junge, Vetchinsky ed R. E. Dearing

Sonnie Hale, Cyril Smith, *Eliot Makeham*, Ursula Jeans, *Emlyn Williams*, Frank Lawton, Belle Chrystal, *Max Miller*, Alfred Drayton, Edmund Gwenn, Mary Jerrold, Gordon Harker, *Robertson Hare*, Martita Hunt, Leonora Corbett, Jessie Matthews, Ralph Richardson

Friday the Thirteenth

US 1980 95m colour
Georgetown (Sean S. Cunningham)
V, V*, L

When a summer camp is reopened after many years, the grisly murders which closed it down begin again.

Horror suspense story with no *raison d'être* but a series of inventively gory shock moments, which were enough for it to ring the box-office bell.

w Victor Miller d Sean S. Cunningham ph Barry Abrams m Harry Manfredini ad Virginia Field ed Bill Freda

Betsy Palmer, Adrienne King, Jeannine Taylor, Robbi Morgan

'An oversexed couple makes love in the bottom bunk, there's a dead body in the top bunk and the rest of the bunk is in the television commercials.' – *Variety*

Friday the Thirteenth Part II

US 1981 87m DeLuxe
CIC/Georgetown (Steve Miner, Dennis Murphy)
V, V*, L

The sole survivor of the massacre at Camp Crystal Lake is murdered, and five years later the mayhem begins again, the villain being the son of the woman who committed the former killings.

Virtually a remake of the first film, starting with a long flashback to it; short sharp shocks punctuate slabs of tedium.

w Ron Kurz d Steve Miner ph Peter Stein m Harry Manfredini pd Virginia Field ed Susan E. Cunningham

Amy Steel, John Furey, Adrienne King, Kirsten Baker, Stu Charno

Friday the Thirteenth Part III

US 1982 95m Movielab 3D
UIP/Jason Productions (Frank Mancuso Jnr)
V, V*, L

Crazy Jason is still murdering kids up at Crystal Lake.

No better than its predecessors for being in three dimensions; in fact, half as bad again.

w Martin Kitrosser, Carol Watson d Steve Miner ph Gerald Feil m Harry Manfredini ad Robb Wilson ed George Hively

Dana Kimmell, Richard Brooker, Catherine Parks, Paul Kratka

'The first was dreadful and took seventeen million. The second was just as bad and took more than ten million. No doubt the distributor will be happy to learn that the third is terrible too.' – *Variety*

Friday the Thirteenth: Final Chapter

US 1984 91m Movielab
Paramount (Frank Mancuso Jnr)
V, V*, L

Supposedly dead Jason escapes from cold storage at the morgue and goes on another rampage.

The awful mixture as before: would that the title meant what it says.

w Barney Cohen d Joseph Zito ph Joao Fernandes m Harry Manfredini pd Shelton H. Bishop III ed Joel Goodman

E. Erich Anderson, Judie Aronson, Peter Barton, Kimberly Beck

'Yet another catalogue of mindless slaughter which doesn't even offer the courtesy of a story.' – *Daily Mail*

'The censor says you have to be 18 to see it. I would suggest you merely have to be daft.' – *Sunday Times*

Friday the 13th Part V – A New Beginning

US 1985 92m colour
UIP/Paramount (Timothy Silver)
V, V*, L

A mass murderer stalks a private hospital, killing the inmates.

Gory return of a series that could only offer a repetition of its previous killings, poverty-stricken in imagination and everything else.

w Martin Kitrosser, David Cohen, Danny Steinmann d Danny Steinmann ph Stephen L. Posey m Harry Manfredini pd Robert Howland ed Bruce Green

John Shepard, Shavar Ross, Melanie Kinnaman, Richard Young, Corey Feldman, Corey Parker

Friday the 13th Part VI – Jason Lives

US 1986 87m Metrocolor
Paramount (Don Behrns)
V, V*, L

The corpse of the exhumed Jason is brought to life after being hit by lightning and, to the surprise only of the cast, begins killing teenagers yet again.

Tedious re-run of previous movies in the series without even a hint of originality to be discovered.

wd Tom McLoughlin ph Jon Kranhouse m Harry Manfredini pd Joseph T. Garrity sp Martin Becker ed Bruce Green

Thom Mathews, Jennifer Cooke, David Kagen, Renee Jones, C. J. Graham, Tony Goldwyn

'Jason Is Back. But This Time Someone's Waiting.'

Friday the 13th Part VII – The New Blood

US 1988 90m Technicolor
Paramount/Friday Four (Iain Paterson)
V, V*, L

A woman with telekinetic powers attempts to stop the axe-wielding Jason continuing his killing spree.

Lacklustre continuation, still offering no variation on its basic theme of killing teenagers, especially those who display any sexual feelings. There is, though, less gore than usual; perhaps make-up was in as short supply as imagination.

w Daryl Haney, Manuel Fidello d John Carl Buechler ph Paul Elliott m Harry Manfredini, Fred Mollin pd Richard Lawrence ed Barry Zetlin, Maureen O'Connell, Martin Jay Sadoff

Lar Park Lincoln, Kevin Blair, Susan Blu, Terry Kiser, Kane Hodder

Friday the 13th Part VIII – Jason Takes Manhattan

US   1989   96m   Technicolor
Paramount/Horror, Inc. (Randolph Cheveldave)
V, V*, L

An underwater electrical accident re-animates the corpse of Jason, who clambers aboard the cruise ship Lazarus to murder its young passengers.

The interminable story retold in the standard manner, though with less gore than usual; fans of the series, if any remain, are likely to be disappointed at the way the film cuts away from the action at the many moments of teenage death.

wd Rob Hedden   *ph* Bryan England   *m* Fred Mollin   *pd* David Fischer   *sp* make-up effects: Jamie Brown; mechanical effects: Martin Becker   *ed* Steve Mirkovich

Jensen Daggett, Scott Reeves, Barbara Bingham, Peter Mark Richman, Kane Hodder, Barbara Bingham, Sharlene Martin

'The secret of life? The secret's in the sauce.'

Fried Green Tomatoes at the Whistle Stop Café *

US   1991   130m   DeLuxe
Rank/Act III/Electric Shadow (Jordan Kerner, Jon Avnet)
V, V*, L, S

A middle-aged housewife is encouraged to be more self-assertive after listening to an old woman recalling her past.

A pleasant wallow in nostalgia for a less complicated age.

w Fannie Flagg, Carol Sobieski   *novel* Fannie Flagg   *d* Jon Avnet   *ph* Geoffrey Simpson   *m* Thomas Newman   *pd* Barbara Ling   *ed* Debra C. Neil

Kathy Bates, Jessica Tandy, Mary-Louise Parker, Mary Stuart Masterson, Cicely Tyson, Gailard Sartain, Stan Shaw

'Absorbing and life-affirming quality fare.' – *Variety*

AAN: Jessica Tandy; Fannie Flagg, Carol Sobieski

'Would you take Frieda into *your* home?'

Frieda *

GB   1947   97m   bw
Ealing (Michael Relph)
V*

An RAF officer marries and takes home a girl who helped him escape from a POW camp.

Stuffy and dated drama about how one English family learned to love one particular German. Timely when it appeared, however, and well made within its conventions.

w Angus Macphail, Ronald Millar   *play* Ronald Millar   *d* Basil Dearden   *ph* Gordon Dines   *m* John Greenwood

Mai Zetterling, David Farrar, Glynis Johns, Flora Robson, Albert Lieven

'Something of a cinema rarity – a film which stimulates intelligent thought and argument.' – *Dick Richards, Sunday Pictorial*

Friendly Enemies

US   1925   70m (24 fps)   bw   silent
PDC

Two German immigrants are divided when the United States enters the war.

Curious comedy-drama for two vaudevillians, based on a topical play of the time.

w Alfred A. Cohn   *play* Samuel Shipman, Aaron Hoffman   *d* George Melford

Joe Weber, Lew Fields, Virginia Brown Faire, Jack Mulhall

† Remade in 1942 with Charles Winninger.

Friendly Persuasion **

US   1956   139m   DeLuxe
AA (William Wyler)
V*, L

At the outbreak of the Civil War, a family of Quakers has to consider its position.

Sentimental, homespun Western fare, well done without being especially engrossing.

w Michael Wilson   *novel* Jessamyn West   *d* William Wyler   *ph* Ellsworth Fredericks   *m* Dimitri Tiomkin

Gary Cooper, Dorothy McGuire, Anthony Perkins, Marjorie Main, Richard Eyer, Robert Middleton, Walter Catlett

'The material is a little tenuous . . . but Wyler's sure-handed direction constantly illuminates it with a humour, a gentle charm and a feeling for fundamental values that are rare indeed.' – *Moira Walsh, America*

† It was successfully remade as a TV movie in 1975, directed by Joseph Sargent and starring Richard Kiley and Shirley Knight.

AAN: best picture; Michael Wilson; William Wyler; Anthony Perkins; song 'Thee I Love' (*m* Dimitri Tiomkin, *ly* Paul Francis Webster)

'Who needs the world when you own the moon and stars?'

Friends

GB   1971   102m   Technicolor
Paramount (Lewis Gilbert)
V*

Teenage lovers run away to a country cottage and have a child.

Peculiar idyll given corny 'poetic' treatment: a real non-starter.

w Jack Russell, Vernon Harris   *d* Lewis Gilbert   *ph* Andrew Winding   *m* Elton John

Sean Bury, Anicee Alvina, Toby Robbins, Ronald Lewis

'In a world ripped apart friends are all you can trust.'

Friends *

GB/France   1993   109m   Technicolor
Metro Tartan/Friends/Chrysalide/Rio/Channel4 (Judith Hunt)

Three friends from university – two white, one black – follow divergent paths in the political life of South Africa in the 1980s.

A complex film of an impossible situation and personal responses to it, although a schematic approach – the three female protagonists are an Afrikaner, a wealthy white who turns to terrorism, and a poor black – lessens its impact.

wd Elaine Proctor   *ph* Dominique Chapuis   *m* Rachel Portman   *pd* Carmel Collins   *ed* Tony Lawson

Kerry Fox, Dambisa Kente, Michele Burgers, Marius Weyers, Tertius Meintjes, Dolly Rathebe, Wilma Stockenstrom

'This powerful, moving and uplifting film uses its unfailingly human story to convey its anti-apartheid message without a hint of the righteousness which so often accompanies such statements. Intelligent, affecting and thoroughly thought-provoking cinema.' – *Yvette Huddleston, Empire*

Friends and Husbands **

West Germany   1982   106m   colour
Miracle/Bioskop/Les Films du Losange/Westdeutscher Rundfunk (Eberhard Junkersdorf)
original title: *Heller Wahn*

Two women engage in a friendship that destroys them both.

Slow-moving, but intense and absorbing.

wd Margarethe von Trotta   *ph* Michael Ballhaus   *m* Nicolas Economou   *ad* Jurgen Henze, Werner Mink   *ed* Dagmar Hirtz

Hanna Schygulla, Angela Winklet, Peter Striebeck, Christine Fersen, Franz Buchrieser, Jochen Striebeck, Therese Affolter, Werner Eichhorn

Friends and Lovers

US   1931   67m   bw
RKO (William Le Baron)
L

A society wife causes several hearts to flutter illicitly.

Unsatisfactory comedy-drama which lurches along from one mood to another and may have been intended as satire.

w Wallace Smith   *novel* The Sphinx Has Spoken by Maurice Dekobra   *d* Victor Schertzinger   *ph* J. Roy Hunt   *m* Victor Schertzinger, Max Steiner

Adolphe Menjou, Laurence Olivier, Lily Damita, Erich von Stroheim, Hugh Herbert, Frederick Kerr, Blanche Friderici

'Dumb sentimental romance . . . the people never once display motives that are understandable or reasonable.' – *Variety*

The Friends of Eddie Coyle *

US   1973   102m   Technicolor
Paramount (Paul Monash)

An ageing hoodlum agrees to become a police informer and is hunted down by his former associates.

Dour gangster melodrama held together by its central performance.

w Paul Monash   *novel* George V. Higgins   *d* Peter Yates   *ph* Victor J. Kemper   *m* Dave Grusin

Robert Mitchum, Peter Boyle, Richard Jordan, Steven Keats, Mitch Ryan, Alex Rocco

Friends of Mr Sweeney *

US   1934   68m   bw
Warner

A brow-beaten reporter gets drunk, faces life, and changes his personality.

Amusing minor comedy of a kind no longer made.

w Warren Duff, Sidney Sutherland   *novel* Elmer Davis   *d* Edward Ludwig

Charles Ruggles, Eugene Pallette, Berton Churchill, Robert Barrat, Ann Dvorak

'Old situations given a new comedy coating . . . positive all-round fun for every family.' – *Variety*

Fright

GB   1971   87m   Eastmancolor
Fantale/British Lion (Harry Fine, Michael Style)
V*

A babysitter is menaced by a psychotic.

Unattractive screamer which starts on a hysterical note and never lets up.

w Tudor Gates   *d* Peter Collinson

Susan George, Ian Bannen, Dennis Waterman, Honor Blackman, John Gregson, Maurice Kaufman

Fright Night

US   1985   105m   Metrocolor
Columbia/Vista (Herb Jaffe)
V, V*, L

A vampire moves in next door to a teenage horror film buff.

Fairly agreeable mixture of modest comedy and genuine scares; but no classic.

wd Tom Holland   *ph* Jan Kiesser   *m* Brad Fiedel   *pd* John DeCuir Jnr   *ed* Kent Beyda

Chris Sarandon, William Ragsdale, Amanda Bearse, Roddy McDowall

Fright Night Part 2

US 1988 104m DeLuxe Panavision
Columbia TriStar/Vista (Herb Jaffe, Mort Engelberg)
V, V*, L

A college student is attacked by vampires.

Virtually a remake of the first film, and much less
effective the second time around.

w Tim Metcalfe, Miguel Tejada-Flores, Tommy Lee
Wallace d Tommy Lee Wallace ph Mark
Irwin ed Jay Lash Cassidy, Jonathan P. Shaw,
Duwayne Dunham

Roddy McDowall, William Ragsdale, Traci Lin, Julie
Carmen, Jonathan Gries, Russell Clark, Brian
Thompson

'Strictly an identikit remake of Tom Holland's already
derivative original.' – *Kim Newman, MFB*

The Frightened Bride: see *The Tall Headlines*

Frightened City (1950): see *The Killer That Stalked
New York*

Frightened City

GB 1961 98m bw
Anglo Amalgamated/Zodiac (John Lemont)

Gangsters fall out over a protection racket.

Reasonably terse racketeer melodrama rather
surprisingly set in London.

w Leigh Vance d John Lemont ph Desmond
Dickinson m Norrie Paramour

Herbert Lom, Sean Connery, John Gregson, Alfred
Marks, Yvonne Romain, Kenneth Griffith

The Frightened Lady

GB 1932 87m bw
Gainsborough/British Lion (Michael Balcon)
US title: *Criminal at Large*

A mad young lord is protected by his mother.

Modest chiller remade later as *The Case of the Frightened
Lady* (qv).

w Angus McPhail, Bryan Edgar Wallace play *The
Case of the Frightened Lady* by Edgar Wallace d T.
Hayes Hunter ph Bernard Knowles, Alex Bryce
ad Norman Arnold ed Ralph Kemplen

Norman McKinnel, Cathleen Nesbit, Emlyn Williams,
Gordon Harker, Belle Chrystall, Finlay Currie

Frisco Jenny

US 1933 73m bw
Warner

A Barbary Coast lady is prosecuted for murder by her
own son.

Antediluvian melodramatic plot, borrowed from
Madame X, provides an adequate star vehicle.

w Wilson Mizner, Robert Lord d William A.
Wellman

Ruth Chatterton, Donald Cook, Louis Calhern, J.
Carrol Naish, James Murray

The Frisco Kid *

US 1935 77m bw
Warner (Samuel Bischoff)

A Shanghaied sailor rises to power among the riff raff
of the Barbary Coast in the 1860s.

Fair melodrama with the star in action and (less
interestingly) in love.

w Warren Duff, Seton I. Miller d Lloyd Bacon
ph Sol Polito md Leo F. Forbstein

James Cagney, Margaret Lindsay, Ricardo Cortez, Lili
Damita, Donald Woods, Barton MacLane, George E.
Stone, Addison Richards

'So similar to *Barbary Coast* as almost to be its twin . . .
nevertheless, good entertainment.' – *Variety*

The Frisco Kid

US 1979 108m Technicolor
Warner (Howard W. Koch Jnr)
V, V*

In the old west, a rabbi heading for San Francisco
makes friends with an outlaw.

Unsuccessful episodic comedy, unreasonably
alternating farce with sentimentality.

w Michael Elias, Frank Shaw d Robert Aldrich
ph Robert B. Hauser m Frank de Vol

Gene Wilder, Harrison Ford, Ramon Bieri, Leo Fuchs,
Penny Peyser

'A very forced comedy, made all the worse by the fact
that Aldrich seems to time and edit comedy as though
it were a melodrama only played a little slower.' –
Richard Combs, MFB

Frisco Lil

US 1942 62m bw
Universal

A girl law student traps a killer and clears her dad.

Formula second feature, quite adequate in its way.

w George Bricker, Michael Jacoby d Erle
C. Kenton

Irene Hervey, Kent Taylor, Minor Watson, Jerome
Cowan

Frisco Sal

US 1945 63m bw
Universal

A New England girl goes to California to avenge her
brother's murder.

Minor musical vehicle for a star being groomed as a
rival to Deanna Durbin.

w Curt Siodmak, Gerald Geraghty d George
Waggner

Susanna Foster, Turhan Bey, Alan Curtis, Andy
Devine, Thomas Gomez, Samuel S. Hinds

Le Frisson des Vampires (dubbed)

France 1970 90m colour
Films ABC/Filmes Modernes (Jean Rollin)
V
aka: *Sex and the Vampire; The Terror of the Vampires;
Vampire Thrills*

A newly married couple break their journey to stay at
an ancient chateau, where a vampire errant has
changed its two owners from vampire hunters into
bourgeois vampires.

A ridiculous, high-camp horror, which consists
mainly of actresses removing their clothes, usually to
indulge in a little lesbian lovemaking. An attempt at a
crepuscular atmosphere, all guttering candles and
flaming torches against old stone, is not helped by a
rock music soundtrack or by the trance-like acting and
banal dialogue.

wd Jean Rollin ph Jean-Jacques Renon
m Acanthus ad Michel Delesalles ed Olivier
Gregoire

Sandra Julien, Jean-Marie Durand, Jacques
Robiolles, Michel Delahaye, Marie-Pierre, Kuelan
Herce, Nicole Nancel, Dominique

'It combines the triteness of a typical Hammer plot
with stretches of decidedly unerotic skinflick
writhing, but is redeemed by Rollins' quirky descent
into surrealist imagery.' – *Empire*

Fritz the Cat **

US 1971 78m DeLuxe
Fritz Productions/Aurica (Steve Krantz)
V*

An alleycat student in New York seeks new and
varied experience.

Cartoon feature which applies the old
anthropomorphism to the contemporary scene, and

whips up more obscenity and violence than Disney
ever dreamed of. A fast-moving orgy of outrage which
could never have got by in live form.

wd/animator Ralph Bakshi comic strip R. H. Crumb
m Ed Bogas, Ray Shanklin

'A bitter and snarling satire that refuses to curl up in
anyone's lap.' – *Bruce Williamson*

The Frog *

GB 1937 75m bw
Herbert Wilcox

The mysterious leader of a criminal organization is
unmasked.

Lively old-fashioned mystery melodrama.

w Ian Hay, Gerald Elliott novel *The Fellowship of the
Frog* by Edgar Wallace d Jack Raymond
ph Frederick A. Young

Gordon Harker, Carol Goodner, Noah Beery, Jack
Hawkins, Richard Ainley, Esmé Percy, Felix Aylmer

'Badly directed, badly acted, it is like one of those
plays produced in country towns by stranded actors.
It has an old-world charm: Scotland Yard is laid up in
lavender.' – *Graham Greene*

† Sequel 1938: *The Return of the Frog.*

The Frog Prince *

GB 1984 90m Eastmancolor
Warner/Goldcrest/Enigma (Iain Smith)

In Paris in the early 1960s an English girl studying at
the Sorbonne decides to lose her virginity to a
handsome young Frenchman.

Quietly charming, though unmemorable, romantic
drama.

w Brian Gilbert, Posy Simmonds d Brian Gilbert
ph Clive Tickner m Enya Ni Bhraonain pd Anton
Furst ed Jim Clark

Jane Snowden, Alexandre Sterling, Diana Blackburn,
Oystein Wiik

The Frogmen

US 1951 96m bw
TCF (Samuel G. Engel)

Underwater demolition experts pave the way for the
invasion of a Japanese-held island.

Standard, efficient war fare.

w John Tucker Battle d Lloyd Bacon ph Norbert
Brodine m Cyril Mockridge

Richard Widmark, Dana Andrews, Gary Merrill,
Jeffrey Hunter, Warren Stevens, Robert Wagner,
Harvey Lembeck

'Competent, unpretentious and free from jingoism.' –
MFB

AAN: original story (Oscar Millard); Norbert Brodine

'Frogs lay millions and millions of eggs each year! What if
they all hatched? Today the pond – tomorrow the
world!'

Frogs *

US 1972 91m Movielab
AIP (George Edwards, Peter Thomas)
V*

A remote, inhabited island in the southern States is
overtaken by reptiles.

As Hitchcock might have said, the frogs is coming;
instead of monsters, ordinary creepy-crawlies in their
thousands devour most of the cast. Well enough done
for those with strong stomachs.

w Robert Hutchison, Robert Blees d George
McCowan ph Mario Tosi m Les Baxter

Ray Milland, Joan Van Ark, Sam Elliott, Adam
Roarke, Judy Pace

'One of the most remarkable and impressive
onslaughts since *King Kong*.' – *David Pirie*

'A mind is a terrible thing to waste.'

From Beyond *

US 1986 85m colour
Empire (Brian Yuzna)
V, V*, L

aka: *H. P. Lovecraft's From Beyond*

A physicist's experiment to stimulate the pineal gland and create a sixth sense summons man-eating monsters from another dimension.

Slickly directed, and extremely gory, horror that comes closer than most to recreating the nauseating, tentacled nightmares of Lovecraft's decadent imagination and an addiction to the search for forbidden knowledge.

w Dennis Paoli *story* H. P. Lovecraft, adapted by Brian Yuzna, Dennis Paoli, Stuart Gordon *d* Stuart Gordon *ph* Mac Ahlberg *m* Richard Band *pd* Giovanni Natalucci *sp* John Buechler, Mark Shostrom, John Naulin, Anthony Doublin *ed* Lee Percy

Jeffrey Combs, Barbara Crampton, Ken Foree, Ted Sorel, Carolyn Purdy-Gordon, Bunny Summers, Bruce McGuire

From Beyond the Grave *

GB 1973 98m Technicolor
Warner/Amicus (Milton Subotsky)
V*

The proprietor of an East End antique shop involves his customers in horrific situations.

Reasonably lively portmanteau of tall tales from a familiar stable.

w Robin Clarke, Raymond Christodoulou *d* Kevin Connor *ph* Alan Hume *m* David Gamley *pd* Maurice Carter

David Warner, Donald Pleasence, Ian Bannen, Diana Dors, Margaret Leighton, Ian Carmichael, Nyree Dawn Porter, Ian Ogilvy

From Headquarters

US 1933 63m bw
Warner (Sam Bischoff)

The police solve a murder by scientific methods.

Efficient, rather boring programmer.

w Robert N. Lee, Peter Milne *d* William Dieterle *ph* William Reese

George Brent, Margaret Lindsay, Eugene Pallette, Hugh Herbert, Hobart Cavanaugh, Robert Barrat, Henry O'Neill, Edward Ellis

From Hell It Came

US 1957 71m bw
Milner Brothers/Allied Artists

An executed native of Kalai returns to life in the form of a vengeful tree stump.

Absolute rubbish, just about worth sitting through for the unintentional laughs.

w Richard Bernstein *d* Dan Milner

Tod Andrews, Tina Carver, Linda Watkins

From Hell to Heaven

US 1933 67m bw
Paramount

Stories of a racetrack hotel.

Very minor *Grand Hotel*, neatly made for its time.

w Percy Heath, Sidney Buchman *story* Lawrence Hazard *d* Erle C. Kenton

Carole Lombard, Jack Oakie, Sidney Blackmer, Adrienne Ames, David Manners

From Hell to Texas

US 1958 100m Eastmancolor Cinemascope
TCF (Robert Buckner)
GB title: *Manhunt*

After accidentally killing a man, a cowboy is vengefully pursued by the victim's father.

Competent chase Western with a stand against violence.

w Robert Buckner, Wendell Mayes *d* Henry Hathaway *ph* Wilfrid Cline *m* Daniele Amfitheatrof

Don Murray, Diane Varsi, Chill Wills, Dennis Hopper, R. G. Armstrong, Margo, Jay C. Flippen

'The Boldest Book Of Our Time … Honestly, Fearlessly On The Screen!'

From Here to Eternity ***

US 1953 118m bw
Columbia (Buddy Adler)
V, V*, L

Life in a Honolulu barracks at the time of Pearl Harbor.

Cleaned up and streamlined version of a bestseller in which the mainly sexual frustrations of a number of unattractive characters are laid bare. As a production, it is Hollywood in good form, and certainly took the public fancy as well as establishing Sinatra as an acting force.

w Daniel Taradash *novel* James Jones *d* Fred Zinnemann *ph* Burnett Guffey *m* George Duning *ed* William Lyon

Burt Lancaster, Deborah Kerr, *Frank Sinatra*, Donna Reed, Ernest Borgnine, Montgomery Clift, Philip Ober, Mickey Shaughnessy

'This is not a theme which one would expect Zinnemann to approach in the hopeful, sympathetic mood of his earlier films; but neither could one expect the negative shrug of indifference with which he seems to have surrendered to its hysteria.' – *Karel Reisz, Sight and Sound*

† The story was remade for TV in 1979 as a six-hour mini-series.
†† Frank Sinatra got his key role after Eli Wallach dropped out.

AA: best picture; Daniel Taradash; Fred Zinnemann; Burnett Guffey; Frank Sinatra; Donna Reed; William Lyon

AAN: George Duning; Burt Lancaster; Deborah Kerr; Montgomery Clift

From Noon Till Three

US 1976 99m DeLuxe
UA/Frankovich-Self
V*

A bank robber becomes a local legend when he interrupts a raid to dally with an attractive widow. Later, when someone else is shot in mistake for him, he is reduced to penury, unable to prove his identity or live up to his own legend.

Curious, shapeless, lumpy Western satire, difficult to synopsize or analyse. Despite effort all round, it's just plain unsatisfactory.

wd Frank D. Gilroy *novel* Frank D. Gilroy *ph* Lucien Ballard *m* Elmer Bernstein

Charles Bronson, Jill Ireland, Douglas Fowley, Stan Haze, Damon Douglas

'It squanders its early sparkle for a pot of message.' – *Michael Billington, Illustrated London News*

'The main thing – hell, the only thing – worth noting about *From Noon Till Three* is that it is profoundly weird, which is not quite the same thing as being good.' – *Frank Rich, New York Post*

From Russia with Love ***

GB 1963 118m Technicolor
UA/Eon (Harry Saltzman, Albert Broccoli)
V, V*, L

A Russian spy joins an international crime organization and develops a plan to kill James Bond and steal a coding machine.

The second Bond adventure and possibly the best, with Istanbul and Venice for backdrops and climaxes involving a speeding train and a helicopter. Arrant nonsense with tongue in cheek, on a big budget.

w *Richard Maibaum, Johanna Harwood* *novel* Ian Fleming *d* Terence Young *ph* Ted Moore *m* John Barry *titles* Robert Brownjohn

Sean Connery, Robert Shaw, Pedro Armendariz, Daniela Bianchi, *Lotte Lenya,* Bernard Lee, Eunice Gayson, Lois Maxwell

From Soup to Nuts *

US 1928 20m bw silent
Hal Roach

Two temporary waiters wreck a dinner party.

Very funny slapstick which the stars subsequently reworked into *A Chump at Oxford.*

w H. M. Walker *story* Leo McCarey *d* Edgar Kennedy *ph* Len Powers*ed* Richard Currier

Laurel and Hardy, Anita Garvin, Tiny Sandford

From the Earth to the Moon

US 1958 100m Technicolor
Waverley (Benedict Bogeaus)
V*, L

In the 1880s an armaments millionaire finances a trip to the moon in a projectile fired by his own invention.

Cardboard science fiction, with an imposing cast at sea in an unspeakable script and an unseaworthy production.

w Robert Blees, James Leicester *novel* Jules Verne *d* Byron Haskin *ph* Edwin DuPar *m* Louis Forbes *ad* Hal Wilson Cox

Joseph Cotten, George Sanders, Henry Daniell, Carl Esmond, Melville Cooper, Don Dubbins, Debra Paget, Patric Knowles

From the Hip

US 1987 112m Technicolor
De Laurentiis Entertainment Group/Indian Neck (René Dupont, Bob Clark)
V*, L

An ambitious and unscrupulous young lawyer defends an academic accused of murder.

An unfortunate mix of courtroom drama and romantic comedy that fails on all levels.

w David E. Kelley, Bob Clark *d* Bob Clark *ph* Dante Spinotti *m* Paul Zaza *pd* Michael Stringer *ed* Stan Cole

Judd Nelson, Elizabeth Perkins, John Hurt, Darren McGavin, Dan Monahan, David Alan Grier, Ray Walston

From the Life of the Marionettes *

West Germany 1980 104m colour/bw
ITC/Personafilm (Horts Wendlandt, Ingrid Bergman, Richard Brick)
V*, L
original title: *Aus Dem Leben Der Marionetten*

An inquiry into the killing of a prostitute by a rich businessman.

A film somehow very typical of its director, but far from his most interesting work.

wd Ingmar Bergman *ph* Sven Nykvist *m* Rols Wilhelm *pd* Rolf Zehetbauer *ed* Petra von Oelffen, Geri Ashur

Robert Atzorn, Christine Buchegger, Martin Benrath

'In its unalloyed pessimism, its complete negation of hope, the film, stripped of the incidents, the excitements which have illumined the director's earlier work, is the purest of Bergman. He can go no farther.' – *Dilys Powell, Punch*

From the Mixed-Up Files of Mrs Basil E. Frankweiler

US 1973 105m colour
Cinema 5
V*

Two children hide out in New York's Metropolitan Museum of Art and befriend a rich woman.

An unusual idea makes ho-hum entertainment for well-brought-up children.

w Blanche Hanalis novel E. L. Konigsberg d Fielder Cook

Ingrid Bergman, Sally Prager, Johnny Doran, George Rose, Richard Mulligan

From the Terrace

US 1960 144m DeLuxe Cinemascope
TCF/Linebrook (Mark Robson)
V*, L

Life among Pennsylvania's idle rich.

Heavy-going family melodrama from a bestseller peopled with boorish characters.

w Ernest Lehman novel John O'Hara d Mark Robson ph Leo Tover m Elmer Bernstein

Paul Newman, Joanne Woodward, Myrna Loy, Ina Balin, Leon Ames, Felix Aylmer, George Grizzard, Patrick O'Neal, Elizabeth Allen

From This Day Forward ***

US 1946 95m bw
RKO (William L. Pereira)

After World War II, a New York couple think back to their early years in the poverty-stricken thirties.

Effective sentimental realism coupled with Hollywood professionalism made this film more memorable than it may sound.

w Hugo Butler, Garson Kanin novel All Brides Are Beautiful by Thomas Bell d John Berry ph George Barnes m Leigh Harline

Joan Fontaine, Mark Stevens, Rosemary de Camp, Henry Morgan, Wally Brown, Arline Judge, Bobby Driscoll, Mary Treen

'Distinguished from the usual film about Young Love and Young Marriage by irony, poetry and realism.' – Richard Winnington

The Front *

US 1976 95m Metrocolor
Columbia/Persky-Bright, Devon (Martin Ritt, Charles H. Joffe)
V, V*, L

For a small commission, a bookmaker puts his name to scripts by blacklisted writers.

Rather bland satire on the communist witch hunts of the fifties; interesting, but neither funny nor incisive enough.

w Walter Bernstein d Martin Ritt ph Michael Chapman m Dave Grusin

Woody Allen, Zero Mostel, Herschel Bernardi, Michael Murphy, Andrea Marcovicci, Lloyd Gough

'The pacing is off, the sequences don't flow, and the film seems sterile, unpopulated and flat.' – New Yorker

'A light comedy forged out of dark and authentic pain.' – Frank Rich, New York Post

'It catches the anguish of America's creative community with wit and feeling.' – Sunday Express

AAN: Walter Bernstein

The Front Page ***

US 1931 101m bw
Howard Hughes
V*

A Chicago reporter wants to retire and marry, but is tricked by his scheming editor into covering one last case.

Brilliant early talkie perfectly transferring into screen terms a stage classic of the twenties. Superficially a shade primitive now, its essential power remains.

w Bartlett Cormack, Charles Lederer play Charles MacArthur, Ben Hecht d Lewis Milestone ph Glen MacWilliams

Adolphe Menjou (Walter Burns), Pat O'Brien (Hildy Johnson), Mary Brian (Peggy), Edward Everett Horton (Bensinger), Walter Catlett (Murphy), George E. Stone (Earl Williams), Mae Clarke (Molly), Slim Summerville (Pincus), Matt Moore (Kruger), Frank McHugh (McCue)

'Sure money-getter . . . it will universally entertain and please.' – Variety

'The most riproaring movie that ever came out of Hollywood.' – Pare Lorentz

'It excelled most of the films of its day by sheer treatment. The speedy delivery of lines and business and the re-emphasis upon cutting as a prime structural element made the film a model of mobility for confused directors who did not know yet how to handle sound.' – Lewis Jacobs, The Rise of the American Film

† Remade in 1940 as His Girl Friday (qv) and in 1988 as Switching Channels (qv). And see below.

AAN: best picture; Lewis Milestone; Adolphe Menjou

The Front Page **

US 1974 105m Technicolor Panavision
U-I (Paul Monash)
V*, L

Disappointing Billy Wilder remake, relying overmuch on bad language and farcical intrusions, while tending to jettison the plot in the latter half. Some laughs nevertheless.

w Billy Wilder, I. A. L. Diamond d Billy Wilder ph Jordan S. Cronenweth m Billy May

Walter Matthau, Jack Lemmon, Susan Sarandon, David Wayne, Carol Burnett, Vincent Gardenia, Allen Garfield, Herb Edelman, Charles Durning, Austin Pendleton

'The signs of coarsening in Wilder's comedy technique are unmistakable.' – MFB

'I can't think of a better tonic for the winter glooms.' – Michael Billington, Illustrated London News

Front Page Story *

GB 1953 99m bw
British Lion/Jay Lewis

A day in the life of a Fleet Street newspaper, when the editor is torn between several big stories and nearly loses his wife.

Dogged 'slice of life' drama with few excitements but some incidental entertainment and a production of routine competence.

w Jay Lewis, Jack Howells d Gordon Parry ph Gilbert Taylor m Jackie Brown

Jack Hawkins, Elizabeth Allan, Derek Farr, Michael Goodliffe, Martin Miller

Front Page Woman **

US 1935 82m bw
Warner (Samuel Bischoff)

Rival reporters try to outshine each other.

Lively comedy-melodrama very typical of its style and time.

w Laird Doyle, Lillie Hayward, Roy Chanslor d Michael Curtiz ph Tony Gaudio md Leo Forbstein m Heinz Roemheld

Bette Davis, George Brent, Roscoe Karns, Wini Shaw, J. Carrol Naish, Walter Walker

'Completely screwy but will get fair b.o.' – Variety

'A swift-moving, unsensational, unsentimental, honest piece of cynicism which is really good value for money.' – MFB

Frontier: see Aerograd

Frontier Badmen

US 1943 74m bw
Ford Beebe Universal

Texas ranchers try to break a cattle-buying monopoly.

The good guys and the bad guys at it again, with fair results.

w Gerald Geraghty, Morgan B. Cox d William McGann

Robert Paige, Anne Gwynne, Lon Chaney Jnr, Noah Beery Jnr, Diana Barrymore, Leo Carrillo, Andy Devine, Thomas Gomez, William Farnum

Frontier Gal

US 1945 84m Technicolor
Universal (Michael Fessier, Ernest Pagano)
GB title: The Bride Wasn't Willing

An outlaw weds a saloon girl at pistol point; emerging five years later from prison, he finds he has a daughter.

Rambling Western with some pretensions to humour and sentiment; not a success, but it established de Carlo as a star.

w Michael Fessier, Ernest Pagano d Charles Lamont ph George Robinson, Charles Boyle m Frank Skinner

Yvonne de Carlo, Rod Cameron, Sheldon Leonard, Andy Devine, Fuzzy Knight, Andrew Tombes, Clara Blandick

Frontier Marshal *

US 1933 66m bw
Fox

A marshal cleans up Tombstone.

Interesting trial run for the 1939 film, which was subsequently done over as My Darling Clementine.

w William Conselman, Stuart Anthony book Stuart N. Lake d Lew Seiler

George O'Brien, Irene Bentley, George E. Stone, Ruth Gillette.

† For legal reasons in this version the marshal is called Michael Wyatt instead of Wyatt Earp.

Frontier Marshal *

US 1939 70m bw
TCF (Sol M. Wurtzel)

Wyatt Earp cleans up Tombstone.

Simple-minded, pleasing Western, later worked over by Ford as My Darling Clementine.

w Sam Hellman book Stuart N. Lake d Allan Dwan ph Charles Clarke m Samuel Kaylin

Randolph Scott, Nancy Kelly, Cesar Romero (as Doc Holliday), Binnie Barnes, John Carradine, Joe Sawyer, Lon Chaney Jnr, Ward Bond, Edward Norris, Eddie Foy Jnr

'Strong programme western, in-betweener for key duals, but a top biller in subsequents.' – Variety

† Eddie Foy Jnr appeared as his father, who historically did perform in Tombstone at the time. The equivalent in My Darling Clementine was the Shakespearean actor played by Alan Mowbray.

Frou Frou: see The Toy Wife

'At First Family Sperm Bank, she banks on babies, he banks on bucks.'

Frozen Assets

US 1992 93m Eastmancolor
RKO (Don Klein)
V, V*, S

A financial expert takes a job in a small town and discovers that he's expected to run a sperm bank.

A coy and extremely predictable comedy that treats its subject-matter with sniggers.

w Don Klein, Tom Kartozian d George Miller
ph Ron Lautore, Geza Sinkovics m Michael Tavera
pd Dorian Vernacchio ed Larry Bock

Shelley Long, Corbin Bernsen, Larry Miller, Dody Goodman, Matt Clark, Jeanne Cooper, Paul Sand, Gloria Camden, Teri Copley

'Yet another waste of the talents of Shelley Long, but she's the film's one real asset.' – Variety

It was released direct to video in Britain.

The Frozen Dead

GB 1966 95m Eastmancolor
Goldstar/Seven Arts

In an English laboratory, a scientist is trying to revive the frozen corpses of Nazi leaders.

Flatfooted horror piece providing very little of interest to pass the time.

wd Herbert J. Leder

Dana Andrews, Anna Palk, Philip Gilbert, Karel Stepanek, Kathleen Breck

The Frozen Ghost *

US 1945 61m bw
Universal

When a drunk dies while under his influence, a hypnotist fears he has the will and power to kill.

Absurdly titled and insufficiently vigorous entry in the Inner Sanctum series.

w Bernard Schubert, Luci Ward d Harold Young

Lon Chaney Jnr, Evelyn Ankers, Martin Kosleck, Milburn Stone, Tala Birell, Douglass Dumbrille

The Frozen Limits *

GB 1939 84m bw
Gainsborough (Edward Black)

Six impecunious comedians hear of the Yukon gold rush, and join it . . . forty years too late.

The Crazy Gang not quite at its best, but working hard, with a few hilarious moments and a special assist from Moore Marriott.

w Marriott Edgar, Val Guest, J. O. C. Orton d Marcel Varnel ph Arthur Crabtree md Louis Levy
ad Vetchinsky ed R. E. Dearing, Alfred Roome

Flanagan and Allen, Nervo and Knox, Naughton and Gold, Moore Marriott, Eileen Bell, Anthony Hulme, Bernard Lee, Eric Clavering

'The funniest English picture yet produced . . . it can bear comparison with Safety Last and The General.' – Graham Greene

Frühlingssinfonie: see Spring Symphony

Le Fruit Défendu: see Forbidden Fruit

The Fruit Machine

GB 1988 103m colour
Vestron/Granada/Ideal (Steve Morrison)
V, V*, L

Two mixed-up teenagers run away after witnessing a murder.

Unsuccessful mixture of fantasy and thriller.

w Frank Clarke d Philip Savile ph Dick Pope
m Hans Zimmer pd David Brockhurst ed Richard Bedford

Emile Charles, Tony Forsyth, Robert Stephens, Clare Higgins, Bruce Payne, Robbie Coltrane, Kim Christie, Julie Graham

Fu Manchu

The Yellow Peril, or evil Oriental master criminal, was created by Sax Rohmer in a 1911 novel, which led to 13 more plus some short stories.

A long series of British two-reelers was made in the twenties, and talking films are as follows:

1929: THE MYSTERIOUS DR FU MANCHU, with Warner Oland (Paramount)
1930: THE RETURN OF DR FU MANCHU (ditto)
1931: DAUGHTER OF THE DRAGON (ditto)
1932: THE MASK OF FU MANCHU (qv) with Boris Karloff (MGM)
1939: DRUMS OF FU MANCHU, with Henry Brandon (Republic serial)The remainder are British productions by Harry Alan Towers, with Christopher Lee:
1965: THE FACE OF FU MANCHU (qv)
1966: BRIDES OF FU MANCHU
1968: THE VENGEANCE OF FU MANCHU
1969: THE BLOOD OF FU MANCHU
1970: THE CASTLE OF FU MANCHU

Fuddy Duddy Buddy **

US 1952 7m Technicolor
UPA

Mr Magoo mistakes a walrus for his friend the colonel.

Top drawer Magoo adventure climaxing with the celebrated line: 'I don't care if he is a walrus. I like him. I like him!'

wd John Hubley m William Lava

The Fugitive (1939): see On the Night of the Fire

The Fugitive *

US 1947 104m bw
Argosy (Merian C. Cooper, John Ford)
V*, L

In an anti-clerical country, a priest is on the run.

Ford's attempt to do a Mexican Informer is slow and rather boring, but the pictures are nice to look at even though the original novel has been totally emasculated.

w Dudley Nichols novel The Power and the Glory by Graham Greene d John Ford ph Gabriel Figueroa
m Richard Hageman ad Alfred Ybarra ed Jack Murray

Henry Fonda, Dolores del Rio, Pedro Armendariz, J. Carrol Naish, Leo Carrillo, Ward Bond, Robert Armstrong, John Qualen

'A symphony of light and shade, of deafening din and silence, of sweeping movement and repose.' – Bosley Crowther

'The most pretentious travesty of a literary work since For Whom the Bell Tolls.' – Richard Winnington

'A murdered wife. A one-armed man. An obsessed detective. The chase begins.'

The Fugitive ***

US 1993 127m Technicolor
Warner (Keith Barish, Arnold Kopelson)
V, V*, L, S

A surgeon, unjustly accused of his wife's murder, goes on the run to find the real killer, while being hunted by a ruthless cop.

Tense and exciting thriller that sticks closely to the plot of the original television series and, despite its many improbabilities, remains compulsively watchable.

w Jeb Stuart, David Twohy story David Twohy, based on characters created by Roy Huggins for the TV series. d Andrew Davis ph Michael Chapman
m James Newton Howard pd Dennis Washington
ed Dennis Virkler, David Finfer, Dean Goodhill, Don Brochu, Richard Nord, Dov Hoenig

Harrison Ford, Tommy Lee Jones, Sela Ward, Joe Pantoliano, Jeroen Krabbé, Andreas Katsulas, Julianne Moore

'A consummate nail-biter that never flags, it leaves you breathless from the chase yet anxious for the next bit of mayhem or clever plot twist.' – Variety

'A remarkably successful Hollywood product, with a brilliantly contrived star double act pursuing different paths through the central plot.' – Kim Newman, Sight and Sound

The TV series ran from 1963 to 1967 and starred David Janssen.

AA: Tommy Lee Jones

AAN: best picture; Michael Chapman; James Newton Howard; editing; sound; sound effects editing

The Fugitive Kind

US 1960 121m bw
UA/Martin Jurow/Richard A. Shepherd/Pennebaker
V*

A Mississippi drifter in a small strange town runs into trouble with women.

Doom-laden melodrama, almost a parody of the author's works, full of cancer patients, nympho-dipsos, and cemetery seductions; we are however spared the final castration.

w Tennessee Williams, Meade Roberts play Orpheus Descending by Tennessee Williams d Sidney Lumet
ph Boris Kaufman m Kenyon Hopkins
pd Richard Sylbert

Marlon Brando, Anna Magnani, Joanne Woodward, Victor Jory, Maureen Stapleton, R. G. Armstrong

'A series of mythological engravings, determined by a literary text and a lurid concept of hell on earth.' – Peter John Dyer

'Sidney Lumet is usually clever at least part of the time – an acquisitive magpie who has picked up, along with the selly trash, a few small gems. This time he brings us nothing but bits of coloured glass.' – Stanley Kauffmann

Fugitive Lovers

US 1933 74m bw
MGM
V*

A convict escapes on a transcontinental bus.

Unsatisfactory comedy drama with a miscast star; chiefly interesting for showing the form of travel, but It Happened One Night did it better in the following year.

w Ferdinand Reyher, Frank Wead d Richard Boleslawski

Robert Montgomery, Madge Evans, Ted Healy and the Three Stooges, Nat Pendleton, C. Henry Gordon

'Acceptable for lesser houses but not de luxe quality.' – Variety

Fugitive Road

US 1934 69m bw
Chesterfield

A would-be immigrant into Austria has trouble with the patrol captain of a border garrison.

Curious, aimless, cheaply made drama which doesn't even provide a coherent role for its fallen star.

w Charles S. Belden, Robert Ellis d Frank Strayer

Erich von Stroheim, Wera Engels, Leslie Fenton, George Humbert

'Picture won't rate solo in many places.' – Variety

Full Circle

GB/Canada 1976 97m Eastmancolor
Paramount/Fetter-Classic (Peter Fetterman, Alfred Parisier)
V*

After the death of her small daughter, a woman leaves home to live in an old house which is haunted by the malevolent spirit of another dead child.

Unpleasant and incompetent supernatural nonsense, seeking a niche somewhere between *Don't Look Now* and *The Exorcist*.

w Dave Humphries *novel* *Julia* by Peter Straub d Richard Loncraine ph Peter Hannan m Colin Towns

Mia Farrow, Keir Dullea, Tom Conti, Jill Bennett, Robin Gammell, Cathleen Nesbitt, Mary Morris, Edward Hardwicke

Full Confession
US 1939 73m bw
RKO

A priest bound by the sanctity of confession urges a murderer to give himself up.

Neat little melodrama with a plot much copied subsequently.

wd John Farrow

Victor McLaglen, Barry Fitzgerald, Sally Eilers

'Rather interesting, but not strong enough for the upper bracket.' – *Variety*

A Full Day's Work *
France 1973 90m Eastmancolor
President/Cinetel/Euro International (Jacques-Eric Strauss)
original title: *Une Journée Bien Remplie*

A baker sets out to kill in one day the jurors who found his son guilty of murder.

Mildly amusing black comedy, though it is too self-conscious for its own good.

wd Jean-Louis Trintignant ph William Lubtchansky m Bruno Nicolai ed Nicole Lubtchansky

Jacques Dufilho, Luce Marquand, Denise Peron, Antoine Marin, Jacques Doniol-Valcroze, Vittorio Caprioli

Full House: see *O. Henry's Full House*

'In Vietnam The Wind Doesn't Blow. It Sucks.'
Full Metal Jacket **
GB 1987 116m Rank colour
Warner/Stanley Kubrick
V, V*, L, S

After rigorous training, US marines land in Vietnam.

Smartly ordered but rather ordinary and predictable war film to come from one of the cinema's acknowledged masters after seven years of silence.

w Stanley Kubrick, Michael Herr, Gustav Hasford *novel* *The Short Timers* by Gustav Hasford d Stanley Kubrick ph Douglas Milsome m Abigail Mead pd Anton Furst

Matthew Modine, Adam Baldwin, Vincent D'Onofrio, Lee Ermey, Dorian Harewood, Arliss Howard

AAN: best adapted screenplay

Full Moon in Blue Water
US 1988 95m Technicolor
Entertainment/Trans World Entertainment (Lawrence Turman, David Foster, John Turman)
V*, L

A Texan restaurateur foils plans by property developers to buy his diner.

Weak and sentimental comedy, resembling a TV sitcom.

w Bill Bozzone d Peter Masterson ph Fred Murphy m Phil Marshall ed Jill Savitt

Gene Hackman, Teri Garr, Burgess Meredith, Elias Koteas, Kevin Cooney, David Doty, Gil Glasgow, Becky Gelke, Marietta Marich, Lexie Masterson

'A comedy as soft-centred as they come . . . just about insufferable' – *MFB*

Full Moon in Paris *
France 1984 102m colour
V, V*
original title: *Les Nuits de la Pleine Lune*

Striving for independence, a girl divides her time between her boyfriend in the suburbs and a flat in Paris.

One of Rohmer's talkier Comedies and Proverbs, taking as its epigraph 'He who has two women loses his soul. He who has two houses loses his mind.'

w Eric Rohmer ph Renato Berta m Elli and Janco ed Cecile Decugis

Pascale Ogier, Tcheky Karo, Fabrice Luchini, Virginie Thevenet, Christian Vadim, Laszlo Szabo

Full of Life *
US 1956 91m bw
Columbia (Fred Kohlmar)

A poor New York/Italian couple expect a baby.

Domestic comedy drama with good scenes but fatally uncertain mood.

w John Fante *novel* John Fante d Richard Quine ph Charles Lawton Jnr m George Duning

Judy Holliday, Richard Conte, Esther Minciotti, Salvatore Baccaloni

'A new experience in screen suspense!'
The Full Treatment
GB 1960 109m bw Megascope
Columbia/Hilary/Falcon (Val Guest)
US title: *Stop Me Before I Kill*

A racing driver crashes and subsequently tries to murder his wife; psychiatric help leads to further gruesome goings-on.

Variation on *Les Diaboliques*, with very little mystery and too much talk from boring characters.

w Val Guest, Ronald Scott Thorn *novel* Ronald Scott Thorn d Val Guest ph Gilbert Taylor m Stanley Black

Ronald Lewis, Diane Cilento, Claude Dauphin, Françoise Rosay, Bernard Braden

The Fuller Brush Girl *
US 1950 85m bw
Columbia (S. Sylvan Simon)
GB title: *Affairs of Sally*

A cosmetics saleslady gets involved in murder.

Fairly amusing slapstick mystery with the star in good form.

w Frank Tashlin d Lloyd Bacon ph Charles Lawton m Heinz Roemheld

Lucille Ball, Eddie Albert, Carl Benton Reid, Gale Robbins, Jeff Donnell, John Litel, Jerome Cowan, Lee Patrick

The Fuller Brush Man *
US 1948 93m bw
Columbia (S. Sylvan Simon)
V*, L
GB title: *That Mad Mr Jones*

A door-to-door salesman gets involved in homicide.

Bright star comedy with slow patches.

w Frank Tashlin, Devery Freeman d S. Sylvan Simon ph Leslie White m Heinz Roemheld

Red Skelton, Janet Blair, Don McGuire, Adele Jergens

Fun and Fancy Free *
US 1947 73m Technicolor
Walt Disney (Ben Sharpsteen)

Cartoon stories told by and to Jiminy Cricket and Edgar Bergen.

Variable Disney ragbag including *Bongo* the Bear, and a lengthy version of *Jack and the Beanstalk*.

w various d various

Fun Down There
US 1988 88m colour
Metro/Angelina/Stigliano

A young homosexual leaves home to enjoy life in New York.

Full of grainy, low-budget sincerity, but slight to the point of boredom.

w Roger Stigliano, Michael Waite d Roger Stigliano ph Peggy Ahwesh d Roger Stigliano, Keith Sanbourn

Michael Waite, Nickolas Nagurney, Martin Goldin, Jeanne Sobkowski, Gretschen Somerville, Elizabeth Waite, Harold Waite

'Low-budget Woody Allen without the angst and wit.' – *MFB*

Fun in Acapulco
US 1963 97m Technicolor
Paramount/Hal B. Wallis
V

A trapeze artist becomes a lifeguard and is pursued by a lady bullfighter.

Dim comedy musical.

w Allan Weiss d Richard Thorpe ph Daniel Fapp m Joseph J. Lilley

Elvis Presley, Ursula Andress, Paul Lukas

Fun on a Weekend
US 1947 93m bw
United Artists

A girl with self-confidence persuades a penniless man to pose as a millionaire.

Weakish comedy with good moments.

w Andrew Stone

Eddie Bracken, Priscilla Lane, Tom Conway, Allen Jenkins, Arthur Treacher, Clarence Kolb

Fun with Dick and Jane
US 1976 100m Metrocolor
Columbia/Peter Bart, Max Pelevsky

When an aerospace executive is fired, in order to keep up with the Joneses he and his wife embark on a life of crime.

This being a 1970s satire, they actually get away with it, providing some, but not enough, fun on the way.

w David Giler, Jerry Belson, Mordecai Richler *story* Gerald Gaiser d Ted Kotcheff ph Fred J. Koenekamp m Ernest Gold

George Segal, Jane Fonda, Ed McMahon, Dick Gautier, Alan Miller

'A nitwit mixture of counterculture politics, madcap comedy and toilet humour.' – *New Yorker*

† The sequence in which the heroine discusses the family predicament while sitting on a toilet was later deleted, reducing the running time by two minutes.

The Funeral: see *Death Japanese Style*

Funeral in Berlin *
GB 1967 102m Technicolor
Paramount/Harry Saltzman (Charles Kasher)
V*, L

Harry Palmer is sent to Berlin to check a story that a Russian colonel wants to defect.

Initially intriguing, finally confusing, always depressing spy yarn in the sixties manner, i.e. with every character devious and no one a hero. Good production.

w Evan Jones *novel* *Funeral in Berlin* by Len Deighton d Guy Hamilton ph Otto Heller m Konrad Elfers pd Ken Adam

Michael Caine, *Oscar Homolka*, Eva Renzi, Paul Hubschmid, *Hugh Burden*, Guy Doleman, Rachel Gurney

'So many twists that even Sherlock Holmes might have been baffled . . . before long it becomes difficult to remember who is watching whom and why, or indeed whether anybody *was* watching anybody at any given moment.' – *Tom Milne*

† Second in the Harry Palmer series, of which the first was *The Ipcress File* and the third *Billion Dollar Brain* (both qv).

The Funhouse

US 1981 96m Technicolor Panavision
Universal/Mace Neufeld (Derek Power, Steven Bernhardt)
V, V*, L
aka: *Carnival of Terror*

Four teenagers decide to spend the night in the Haunted House of a travelling fair.

A violent, freak-show horror that tries for black humour but misses most of the time; it sticks to the usual equation: teenage sex equals gruesome death.

w Larry Block d Tobe Hooper ph Andrew Laszlo m John Beal pd Morton Rabinowitz sp Rick Baker, Craig Reardon ed Jack Hofstra

Elizabeth Berridge, Shawn Carson, Jeanne Austin, Jack McDermott, Cooper Huckabee, Largo Woodruff, David Carson, Sylvia Miles

The Funniest Man in the World *

US 1967 102m bw
Funnyman Inc

Moderately intelligent compilation of sequences from the films of Charlie Chaplin, including *Making a Living, Kid Auto Races at Venice, Tillie's Punctured Romance, The Tramp, A Night Out, The Rink, The Immigrant* and *Easy Street*. The later shorts and features, on which Chaplin himself claimed full copyright, are not included.

wd Vernon P. Becker

A Funny Dirty Little War **

Argentina 1983 79m Eastmancolor
ICA/Aries Cinematografica Argentina (Fernando Ayala, Luis Osvaldo)

Small town rebels defy the army as Perón is returned to power in 1974.

A brutal black farce of civilians succumbing to military terror, it won the special jury prize at the Berlin Film Festival in 1984.

w Roberto Cossa, Hector Olivera novel Osvaldo Soriano d Hector Olivera ph Leonardo Rodriguez m Oscar Cadoza Ocampo ed Eduaro Lopez

Federico Luppi, Hector Bidonde, Victor Laplace, Rodolfo Ranni, Miguel Angel Sola, Julio de Grazia, Lautaro Murua

Funny Face (1935): see *Bright Lights*

Funny Face **

US 1957 103m Technicolor Vistavision
Paramount (Roger Edens)
V, V*, L

A fashion editor and photographer choose a shy bookstore attendant as their 'quality woman'.

Stylish, wistful musical with good numbers but drawn-out dialogue; finally a shade too sophisticated and a whole lot too fey.

w Leonard Gershe d Stanley Donen ph Ray June m/ly George and Ira Gershwin ad Hal Pereira, George W. Davis

Fred Astaire, Audrey Hepburn, Kay Thompson, Michel Auclair, Robert Flemyng

AAN: Leonard Gershe; Ray June; art direction

Funny Girl **

US 1968 169m Technicolor Panavision 70
Columbia/Rastar (Ray Stark)
V, V*, L, S

Fanny Brice, an ugly Jewish girl from New York's east side, becomes a big Broadway star but loses her husband in the process.

Interminable cliché-ridden musical drama relieved by a few good numbers, high production gloss and the unveiling of a new powerhouse star.

w Isobel Lennart play Isobel Lennart d William Wyler ph Harry Stradling md Walter Scharf pd Gene Callahan m/ly Jule Styne, Bob Merrill

Barbra Streisand, Omar Sharif, Walter Pidgeon, Kay Medford, Anne Francis, Lee Allen, Gerald Mohr, Frank Faylen

AA: Barbra Streisand

AAN: best picture; Harry Stradling; Walter Scharf; Kay Medford; title song

Funny Lady *

US 1975 138m Eastmancolor Panavision
Columbia/Rastar/Persky-Bright/Vista (Ray Stark)
V, V*, L

Fanny Brice marries Billy Rose.

Unnecessary sequel to the above, entirely predictable and far from the truth, but with the occasional pleasures that a high budget brings.

w Jay Presson Allen, Arnold Schulman d Herbert Ross ph James Wong Howe md Peter Matz pd George Jenkins m/ly various

Barbra Streisand, James Caan, *Ben Vereen*, Omar Sharif, Roddy McDowall, Larry Gates

'The plot line is as slackly handled as the milieu.' – *Geoff Brown*

'As Fanny Brice, Streisand is no longer human; she's like a bitchy female impersonator imitating Barbra Streisand.' – *New Yorker*

AAN: James Wong Howe; Peter Matz; song 'How Lucky Can You Get' (m/ly Fred Ebb, John Kander)

A Funny Thing Happened on the Way to the Forum **

GB 1966 99m DeLuxe
UA/Quadrangle (Melvin Frank)
V, V*, L

In ancient Rome, a conniving slave schemes to win his freedom.

Bawdy farce from a Broadway musical inspired by Plautus but with a New York Jewish atmosphere. The film pays scant attention to the comic numbers that made the show a hit, but adds some style of its own, including a free-for-all slapstick climax.

w Melvin Frank, Michael Pertwee musical comedy Burt Shevelove, Larry Gelbart d Richard Lester ph Nicolas Roeg md Ken Thorne pd Tony Walton titles Richard Williams m/ly Stephen Sondheim

Zero Mostel, Phil Silvers, Michael Crawford, Jack Gilford, *Michael Hordern*, Buster Keaton, Patricia Jessel, Leon Greene, Beatrix Lehmann

'Actors have to be very fast and very sly to make themselves felt amid the flash and glitter of a characteristic piece of Lester film-mosaic.' – *John Russell Taylor*

'He proceeds by fits and starts and leaves jokes suspended in mid-air . . . like coitus interruptus going on forever.' – *Pauline Kael*

AA: Ken Thorne

Funnyman

US 1967 100m bw/colour
Korty Films (Hugh McGraw, Stephen Schmidt)

A satirical comedian seeks some better occupation in life, but finally agrees he's best as a comic.

One suspects Korty has seen *Sullivan's Travels* several times; but even though his film tries hard, it finally provides more yawns than appreciative chuckles.

w John Korty, Peter Bonerz d John Korty ph John Korty m Peter Schickele

Peter Bonerz, Sandra Archer, Carol Androsky, Gerald Hiken

'It has its dull patches, but it made me laugh louder and more often than any other film this year.' – *Michael Billington, Illustrated London News*

The Furies *

US 1950 109m bw
Paramount/Hal B. Wallis

A cattle baron feuds with his tempestuous daughter.

Interesting but heavy-going Western, more solemn than stimulating despite its Freudian excesses.

w Charles Schnee novel Niven Busch d Anthony Mann ph Victor Milner m Franz Waxman

Barbara Stanwyck, *Walter Huston*, Wendell Corey, Judith Anderson, Gilbert Roland, Thomas Gomez, Beulah Bondi, Wallace Ford, Albert Dekker, Blanche Yurka

'An immoral saga, capably mounted, with some pretentious psychological trimmings.' – *MFB*

AAN: Victor Milner

The Further Adventures of Tennessee Buck

US 1988 90m colour
Sarlui/Diamant/Sri Lanka Film Location Services (Gideon Amir)
V*, L

A big white hunter in Borneo leads a rich couple into cannibal country.

Charmless action adventure with a leering emphasis on the female body.

w Barry Jacobs, Stuart Jacobs, Paul Mason d David Keith ph Avraham Karpick m John Debney pd Errol Kelly ed Anthony Redman

David Keith, Kathy Shower, Brant Van Hoffmann, Sydney Lassick

The Further Perils of Laurel and Hardy ***

US 1967 99m bw
TCF/Robert Youngson
V*

A compilation of longish extracts from the stars' silent comedies, including *Early to Bed, The Second Hundred Years, Should Married Men Go Home, You're Darn Tootin', Habeas Corpus, That's My Wife*, and *Leave 'Em Laughing*. The producer is to be congratulated on refurbishing so many deteriorating negatives, though the commentary leaves much to be desired.

w/ed Robert Youngson m John Parker

Fury ***

US 1936 94m bw
MGM (Joseph L. Mankiewicz)
V*

A traveller in a small town is mistaken for a murderer and apparently lynched; he escapes in a fire but determines to have his persecutors hanged for his murder.

Powerful drama which becomes artificial in its latter stages but remains its director's best American film.

w Bartlett Cormack, Fritz Lang story Norman Krasna d Fritz Lang ph Joseph Ruttenberg m Franz Waxman

Spencer Tracy, Sylvia Sidney, Bruce Cabot, Walter Abel, Edward Ellis, Walter Brennan, Frank Albertson

'The surface of American life has been rubbed away: *Fury* gets down to the bones of the thing and shows them for what they are.' – *C. A. Lejeune*

'Since the screen began to talk, no other serious film except *The Front Page* has so clearly shown that here is a new art and what this new art can do.' – *John Marks*

'Everyday events and people suddenly took on tremendous and horrifying proportion; even the most insignificant details had a pointed meaning.' – *Lewis Jacobs*

'For half its length a powerful and documented piece of fiction about a lynching, and for the remaining half a desperate attempt to make love, lynching and the Hays Office come out even.' – *Otis Ferguson*

'Astonishing, the only film I know to which I have wanted to attach the epithet of *great*.' – *Graham Greene*

AAN: Norman Krasna

The Fury *
US　1978　117m　DeLuxe
TCF/Frank Yablans (Ron Preissman)
V*, L, S

The head of a government institute for psychic research finds that his own son is wanted by terrorists who wish to use his lethal psychic powers.

Flashy, kaleidoscopic nonsense which never even begins to make sense but is used as the basis for the director's showing-off, which is occasionally worth a glance for those with hardened stomachs.

w John Farris　*novel* John Farris　*d* Brian de Palma　*ph* Richard H. Kline　*m* John Williams

Kirk Douglas, John Cassavetes, Carrie Snodgress, Charles Durning, Andrew Stevens, Amy Irving, Fiona Lewis

'A conception of cinema that is closer to Ken Russell than Alfred Hitchcock.' – *Richard Combs, MFB*

Fury at Furnace Creek *
US　1948　88m　bw
TCF

A Westerner clears the name of his father, a general accused of diverting a wagon train into hostile Indian territory.

Adequate old-fashioned Western with a good story line and standard excitements.

w Charles G. Booth　*d* H. Bruce Humberstone　*ph* Harry Jackson　*md* Alfred Newman　*m* David Raksin

Victor Mature, Coleen Gray, Glenn Langan, Reginald Gardiner

Fury at Smugglers' Bay
GB　1960　96m　Eastmancolor　Panascope
Regal/Mijo (Michael Green, Joe Vegoda)

The squire of a Cornish village is being blackmailed by the vicious leader of a gang of wreckers.

Watchable, then forgettable variation on *Jamaica Inn*.

wd John Gilling　*ph* Harry Waxman　*m* Harold Geller

Peter Cushing, John Fraser, Bernard Lee, William Franklyn, June Thorburn, Miles Malleson, Michele Mercier, George Coulouris

Fuss over Feathers: see *Conflict of Wings*

Futtock's End *
GB　1969　49m　Eastmancolor
Paradine/Gannet/British Lion

Adventures of a weekend in an English country mansion.

A collection of visual gags, rather thinly spread, with dialogue replaced by squeaks and mumblings. Like all Barker's subsequent comedies on similar lines (*The Picnic, By the Sea*, etc) one chuckles in constant anticipation of guffaws which never come.

w Ronnie Barker　*d* Bob Kellett

Ronnie Barker, Michael Hordern, Roger Livesey, Julian Orchard, Kika Markham, Mary Merrall, Richard O'Sullivan

Future Cop: see *Trancers*

The Future of Emily
France/West Germany　1984　116m　colour
Mainline/Les Films du Losannge/Helma Sanders/Literarisches
　Colloquium/ ZDF/BMI/FFA/Berliner Film (Nicole Flipo,
　Ursula Ludwig)
original title: *L'Avenir D'Emilie*

Mother and daughter (a film star) discuss their attitudes to life.

Conversation piece of limited interest.

wd Helma Sanders-Brahms　*ph* Sacha Vierney　*m* Jürgen Knieper　*ad* Jean-Michel Hugon, Rainer Schaper　*ed* Ursula West

Brigitte Fossey, Hildegarde Knef, Ivan Desny, Herman Treusch, Camille Raymond, Mathieu Carrière

Futureworld *
US　1976　107m　Metrocolor
AIP (James T. Aubrey Jnr, Paul Lazarus III)
V*

The robot factory seen in *Westworld* (qv) now aims at world domination by duplicating influential figures.

Amusing and fairly suspenseful fantasy with a bigger budget than its predecessor.

w Mayo Simon, George Schenck　*d* Richard T. Heffron　*ph* Howard Schwartz, Gene Polito　*m* Fred Karlin

Peter Fonda, Blythe Danner, Arthur Hill, Yul Brynner, John Ryan, Stuart Margolin, Jim Antonio

Fuzi Qing: see *Father and Son*

Fuzz *
US　1972　93m　DeLuxe
UA/Filmways/Javelin (Jack Farren)
V*

Detectives of Boston's 87th precinct try to catch a rapist.

A black farce devoted to police incompetence, though taken from a straight 'Ed McBain' story. Brisk and sometimes funny.

w Evan Hunter ('Ed McBain')　*d* Richard A. Colla　*ph* Jacques Marquette　*m* Dave Grusin

Burt Reynolds, Raquel Welch, Jack Weston, Yul Brynner, Tom Skerritt, James McEachin

The Fuzzy Pink Nightgown
US　1957　88m　bw
UA/Russ-Field (Robert Waterfield)

A glamorous film star falls in love with her kidnapper.

Unendurable cheap romantic farce.

w Richard Alan Simmons　*novel* Sylvia Tate　*d* Norman Taurog　*ph* Joseph LaShelle　*m* Billy May

Jane Russell, Ralph Meeker, Keenan Wynn, Fred Clark, Adolphe Menjou, Una Merkel

F/X
US　1985　106m　Technicolor
Orion (Dodi Fayed, Jack Wiener)
V, V*, L
GB title: *Murder by Illusion*

A special effects man is paid to stage a phony assassination, then finds himself the target of hit men.

Initially mysterious premise settles down into a long chase, which of its kind isn't badly done but goes on forever.

w Robert T. Megginson, Gregory Fleeman　*d* Robert Mandel　*ph* Miroslav Ondricek　*m* Bill Conti　*pd* Mel Bourne　*ed* Terry Rawlings

Bryan Brown, Brian Dennehy, Diane Venora, Cliff DeYoung, Mason Adams, Jerry Orbach

'Delivers high-gear excitement from start to finish.' – *Bruce Williamson, Playboy*

'Outgunned by the mob, outmanned by the cops... their effects had better be special!'
F/X2: The Deadly Art of Illusion
US　1991　108m　DeLuxe
Columbia TriStar/Orion (Jack Wiener, Dodi Fayed)
V, V*, L

A former special effects man and a private eye team up to recover some stolen Michelangelo medallions.

Virtually a repeat of the first movie, but done with much less panache and little attempt at plausibility.

w Bill Condon　*d* Richard Franklin　*ph* Victor J. Kemper, David M. Walsh, Tonino Delli Colli　*m* Lalo Schifrin　*pd* John Jay Moore　*sp* Eric Allard　*ed* Andrew London, Michael Tronick

Bryan Brown, Brian Dennehy, Rachel Ticotin, Joanna Gleason, Philip Bosco, Keven J. O'Connor, Tom Mason

'With all the ingenuity that went into toys and gadgetry in this five-years-removed sequel, it's a shame no-one bothered to hook up a brain to the plot.' – *Variety*

G

GI Blues
US 1960 104m Technicolor
Paramount/Hal B. Wallis (Paul Nathan)
V

A guitar-playing gunner with the American army in West Germany falls for a cabaret dancer.

Routine star vehicle marking Presley's return from military service.

w Edmund Beloin, Henry Garson d Norman Taurog ph Loyal Griggs m Joseph J. Lilley

Elvis Presley, Juliet Prowse, Robert Ivers, Leticia Roman, Arch Johnson

G Man's Wife: see *Public Enemy's Wife*

G Men *
US 1935 85m bw
Warner (Lou Edelman)
V*

A young lawyer becomes a G-man to avenge the murder of his best friend, and finds himself tracking down another old friend who is a gangster.

In the face of mounting criticism of their melodramas making heroes of gangsters, Warner pulled a clever switch by showing the same crimes from a different angle, that of the law enforcer. As an action show it became pretty good after a slow start.

w Seton I. Miller d William Keighley ph Sol Polito md Leo F. Forbstein

James Cagney, Ann Dvorak, Margaret Lindsay, Robert Armstrong, Barton MacLane, Lloyd Nolan, William Harrigan

'Cagney joins the government and cleans up the gangsters. Just loads of action, knocked off in bing-bang manner. Strong b.o.' – *Variety*

'The gangster is back, racing madly through one of the fastest melodramas ever made.' – *New York Sun*

'The headiest dose of gunplay that Hollywood has unleashed in recent months.' – *André Sennwald, New York Times*

'It is not violence alone which is in the air; there is also a skilfully contrived and well-maintained suspense, and throughout a feeling of respect for the men who are paid to die in the execution of necessary work.' – *The Times*

'A swell show: the construction is swift and staccato.' – *New York World Telegraph*

'Not for the kiddies, but see it if your nerves are good.' – *Photoplay*

G-Men Never Forget
US 1948 bw serial: 12 eps
Republic

A criminal changes his face by plastic surgery and takes the place of the police commissioner.

Energetic serial thick ear.

d Fred Brannon, Yakima Canutt

Clayton Moore, Roy Barcroft, Ramsay Ames, Tom Steele, Dale Van Sickel

G-Men vs The Black Dragon
US 1943 bw serial: 15 eps
Republic

British, American and Chinese secret agents wipe out a Japanese sabotage ring.

Tolerable wartime propaganda serial.

d William Witney

Rod Cameron, Roland Got, Constance Worth, Nino Pipitone

'They had more than love ... they had fame!'
Gable and Lombard
US 1976 131m Technicolor
Universal (Harry Korshak)

After Carole Lombard's death in a 1942 air crash, Clark Gable recalls their years together.

Vulgar and inaccurate representation of two Hollywood stars of the thirties; it fails even as titillation.

w Barry Sandler d Sidney J. Furie ph Jordan S. Cronenweth m Michel Legrand pd Edward Carfagno

James Brolin, Jill Clayburgh, Allen Garfield (as Louis B. Mayer), Red Buttons, Joanne Linville

'A limply raunchy, meaningless movie with nothing to say about the movies, about love, or about stardom.' – *New Yorker*

'An uneven combination of smut and sentimentality.' – *Les Keyser, Hollywood in the Seventies*

'It comes like a marching army to thrill the nation!'
'The picture that will make 1933 famous!'
Gabriel over the White House *
US 1933 87m bw
MGM/Walter Wanger
V*

A crook becomes president and mysteriously reforms.

Pleasing, dated New Deal fantasy.

w Carey Wilson, Bertram Bloch novel *Rinehard* by T. F. Tweed d Gregory La Cava ph Bert Glennon m William Axt

Walter Huston, Karen Morley, Franchot Tone, C. Henry Gordon, Samuel S. Hinds, Jean Parker, Dickie Moore

'Flag-waving flapdoodle, shrewdly dished up for the man in the street and his best girl. Beautifully produced, cannily hoked, and looks like money all round.' – *Variety*

Gabriela
Brazil 1983 99m colour
Sultana
V*

In a coastal town in 1925, the sensual Gabriela marries a bar owner but becomes involved again with her old gangster cronies.

Ethnic melodrama of familiar type, a spin-off from an immensely popular Brazilian TV series.

w Leopoldo Sarran, Bruno Barreto novel Jorge Amada d Bruno Barreto

Sonia Braga, Marcello Mastroianni, Antonio Cantafora

Gaby
US 1956 97m Eastmancolor Cinemascope
MGM (Edwin H. Knopf)

Flabby remake of *Waterloo Bridge* (qv); saccharine, fussy and outmoded, despite updated settings and a happy ending.

w Albert Hackett, Frances Goodrich, Charles Lederer d Curtis Bernhardt ph Robert Planck m Conrad Salinger

Leslie Caron, John Kerr, Cedric Hardwicke, Taina Elg, Margalo Gillmore

Gaby – A True Story *
US 1987 114m colour
Columbia TriStar (Pinchas Perry)
V*, L

A Mexican girl suffering from cerebral palsy struggles to overcome her disabilities.

Well-acted and touching.

w Martin Salinas, Michael James Love d Luis Mandoki ph Lajos Koltai m Maurice Jarre ad Alejandro Luna ed Garth Craven

Liv Ullmann, Norma Aleandro, Robert Loggia, Rachel Levin, Lawrence Monoson, Robert Beltran, Beatriz Sheridan, Tony Goldwyn

AAN: Norma Aleandro

Gaiety George
GB 1946 98m bw
Embassy (George King)
US title: *Showtime*

The career in the London theatre of Irish impresario George Howard in the early part of the century.

Tepid musical biopic.

w Katherine Strueby d George King ph Otto Heller md Jack Beaver

Richard Greene, Ann Todd, Peter Graves, Hazel Court, Leni Lynn, Ursula Jeans, Morland Graham, Frank Pettingell

Gaiety Girls: see *Paradise for Two*

Gaily, Gaily *
US 1969 117m DeLuxe
UA/Mirisch/Cartier (Norman Jewison)
GB title: *Chicago, Chicago*

The early life on a Chicago newspaper of Ben Hecht.

Busy, farcical, melodramatic, always interesting biopic of the formative years of a celebrated literary figure.

w Abram S. Ginnes book Ben Hecht d Norman Jewison ph Richard Kline m Henry Mancini pd Robert Boyle

Beau Bridges, Melina Mercouri, *Brian Keith*, George Kennedy, Hume Cronyn, Margot Kidder, Wilfrid Hyde-White, Melodie Johnson, John Randolph

The Gal Who Took the West
US 1949 84m Technicolor
Universal-International

In 1890, an opera singer travels west and is the object of romantic rivalry.

Lame attempt to equal the splendid idiocy of *Salome Where She Danced.*

w William Bowers, Oscar Brodney d Frederick de Cordova

Yvonne de Carlo, Charles Coburn, Scott Brady, John Russell, James Millican

Galileo *

GB   1975   145m   Eastmancolor
Ely Landau/Cinevision

In the 17th century, a poor Italian mathematics teacher has trouble establishing his 'heretical' astronomical theories.

Overlong play-on-celluloid for the American Film Theatre: very decently made and acted, it lacks inspiration.

w Barbara Bray, Joseph Losey   play Bertolt Brecht
d Joseph Losey   ph Michael Reed   m Hanns Eisler

Topol, Edward Fox, Michel Lonsdale, Richard O'Callaghan, Tom Conti, Judy Parfitt, Patrick Magee, Michael Gough, John Gielgud, Colin Blakely, Margaret Leighton, Clive Revill

'The whole feeling is something like a modestly produced star touring-show. Without the star.' – *Stanley Kauffmann*

Gallant Bess

US   1946   99m   Cinecolor
MGM

A soldier's horse saves his life and becomes his peacetime friend.

Boy-and-horse story with a wartime setting; good for small towns.

w Jeanne Bartlett   d Andrew Marton

Marshall Thompson, George Tobias, Clem Bevans, Donald Curtis

The Gallant Blade

US   1948   81m   Cinecolor
Columbia

In France in 1648, a dashing young lieutenant rescues his general from the plot of a would-be revolutionary.

Pinchpenny swashbuckler which maintains a commendable verve.

w Walter Ferris, Morton Grant   d Henry Levin

Larry Parks, Marguerite Chapman, Victor Jory, George Macready

The Gallant Hours *

US   1959   115m   bw
UA/James Cagney/Robert Montgomery
V*

Episodes in the career of Admiral William F. Halsey.

Adulatory but physically restrained biopic which covers World War II with barely a scene outside control room sets: interesting but finally too talky.

w Beirne Lay Jnr, Frank D. Gilroy   d Robert Montgomery   ph Joe MacDonald   m Roger Wagner

James Cagney, Dennis Weaver, Richard Jaeckel, Ward Costello, Carl Benton Reid

'Imaginatively conceived but erroneously realized.' – *Robert Vas*

Gallant Journey

US   1946   86m   bw
Columbia (William A. Wellman)

The life of an early American aviation pioneer.

Curious biopic, very tentatively done, about an inventor so obscure as to be virtually fictitious. Sentimental, artificial, but harmless.

w Byron Morgan, William A. Wellman   d William A. Wellman   ph Burnett Guffey   m Marlin Skiles

Glenn Ford, Janet Blair, Charles Ruggles, Henry Travers, Arthur Shields

Gallant Lady

US   1933   84m   bw
UA/Twentieth Century (Darryl F. Zanuck)

A woman allows her illegitimate son to be adopted, but years later marries his stepfather.

A tearjerker very typical of its time, moderately well assembled; later remade as *Always Goodbye* (qv).

w Sam Mintz   story Gilbert Emery, Doug Doty
d Gregory La Cava   ph Peverell Marley   m Alfred Newman

Ann Harding, Clive Brook, Otto Kruger, Tullio Carminati, Dickie Moore, Janet Beecher

The Gallant Legion

US   1948   86m   bw
Republic

The Texas Rangers are formed but have to prove themselves.

Acceptable second-string Western with plenty of action and a strong cast.

w Gerald Drayson Adams   d Joseph Kane

William Elliott, Adrian Booth, Joseph Schildkraut, Bruce Cabot, Andy Devine, Jack Holt, Grant Withers, Adele Mara

Gallant Sons

US   1940   71m   bw
MGM

Schoolboys club together to get the father of one of them off a murder charge.

Unlikely and undemanding but pleasant filler.

w William R. Lipman, Marion Parsonnet   d George B. Seitz

Jackie Cooper, Bonita Granville, Gene Reynolds, Gail Patrick, Ian Hunter, June Preisser, Leo Gorcey, William Tracy, El Brendel

'From a place you may never have heard of, a story you'll never forget!'
Gallipoli *

Australia   1981   111m   Eastmancolor   Panavision
Associated R and R (Martin Cooper, Ben Gannon)
V, V (W), L

In 1915, two friends trek from Perth across the desert to join up, and one dies in the Dardanelles.

Consistently interesting aspects of the 1914—18 war, but rather broken-backed as a story.

w David Williamson   d Peter Weir   ph Russell Boyd
md Brian May

Mark Lee, Mel Gibson, Bill Hunter, Robert Grubb, Tim McKenzie, Bill Kerr

'Like so many of Weir's films it promises more than it delivers.' – *Time Out, 1984*

The Galloping Ghost

US   1931   bw   serial: 12 eps
Mascot

A school football hero begins a campaign to clear his name after an accusation of fixing.

Tedious and dated serial.   d B. Reeves Eason

Harold Grange, Dorothy Gulliver, Walter Miller, Francis X. Bushman

The Galloping Major *

GB   1951   82m   bw
British Lion/Romulus (Monja Danischewsky)

A group of suburbanites form a syndicate to buy a racehorse.

Rather contrived and imitative sub-Ealing comedy which fails to generate much steam.

w Monja Danischewsky, Henry Cornelius   d Henry Cornelius   ph Stan Pavey   m Georges Auric

Basil Radford, Janette Scott, Hugh Griffith, Jimmy Hanley, René Ray, Joyce Grenfell, Sidney Tafler, Charles Victor, A. E. Matthews

Gambit **

US   1966   109m   Techniscope
Universal (Leo L. Fuchs)
V*

A cockney thief conspires with a Eurasian girl to rob a multi-millionaire of a prize statue.

An enjoyably light pattern of cross and double cross is well sustained to the end.

w Jack Davies, Alvin Sargent   d Ronald Neame
ph Clifford Stine   m Maurice Jarre

Michael Caine, Shirley Maclaine, Herbert Lom, John Abbott, Roger C. Carmel, Arnold Moss

'He's been bruised, blackmailed, sliced and slammed. But nothing can stop him from going after the big money!'
The Gambler *

US   1975   111m   Eastmancolor
Paramount (Irwin Winkler, Robert Chartoff)
V*, L

A compulsive gambler has a will to lose.

Flashily made but basically uninteresting sub-Freudian study, vaguely based on Dostoievsky.

w James Tomack   d Karel Reisz   ph Victor J. Kemper   md Jerry Fielding   m Mahler

James Caan, Paul Sorvino, Lauren Hutton, Morris Carnovsky, Jacqueline Brookes, Burt Young

'The script is pretentious and empty. Reisz's quality, apparent in his early films and writings, seems to have atrophied with disuse and tension.' – *Stanley Kauffmann*

The Gambler and the Lady

GB   1952   74m   bw
Exclusive/Hammer (Anthony Hinds)

A tough American gambler and club-owner in London is ruined by his attempt to move in aristocratic circles.

Enjoyable if routine thriller with its contrast between a streetwise American losing his way among the upper-class English.

w uncredited   d Patrick Jenkins   ph Walter Harvey   m Ivor Slaney   ad J. Elder Wills
ed Maurice Rootes

Dane Clark, Kathleen Byron, Naomi Chance, Meredith Edwards, Anthony Forwood, Eric Pohlmann, Julian Somers, Thomas Gallagher, Max Bacon, Mona Washbourne

Terence Fisher has been named as the director, while American sources credit Sam Newfield as co-director. But Patrick Jenkins is given sole credit on the film itself. The American release ran for 71m.

Gambler from Natchez

US   1954   88m   Technicolor
TCF (Leonard Goldstein)

A professional gambler returns to New Orleans to avenge his father's murder, and disposes of his enemies one by one.

Mildly watchable semi-Western with a plot borrowed from *The Count of Monte Cristo.*

w Gerald Drayson Adams, Irving Wallace   d Henry Levin   ph Lloyd Ahern   md Lionel Newman

Dale Robertson, Debra Paget, Thomas Gomez, Kevin McCarthy

Gambling *

US   1934   82m   bw
Fox/Harold B. Franklin

A professional gambler ferrets out the killer of his ward.

Transcript of a George M. Cohan play, with the star in good form; but the presentation is uncinematic and tedious.

w Garrett Graham   *play* George M. Cohan   *d* Rowland V. Lee

George M. Cohan, Wynne Gibson, Dorothy Burgess, Theodore Newton

'It moves too slowly towards an intelligent but almost wholly mental climax.' – *Variety*

Gambling House
US   1950   80m   bw
RKO

An immigrant gambler is threatened with deportation when involved in a murder.

Heavy melodrama with assumed social conscience.

w Marvin Borowsky, Allen Rivkin   *d* Ted Tetzlaff

Victor Mature, Terry Moore, William Bendix, Basil Ruysdael

Gambling Lady *
US   1934   66m   bw
Warner (Henry Blanke)

The daughter of a gambling suicide follows in father's footsteps and becomes involved in murder.

Fast-paced melodrama with a happy ending: smart entertainment of its time.

w Ralph Block, Doris Malloy   *d* Archie Mayo   *ph* George Barnes

Barbara Stanwyck, Joel McCrea, Pat O'Brien, Claire Dodd, C. Aubrey Smith, Robert Barrat, Philip Reed

Gambling on the High Seas
US   1940   56m   bw
Warner

A reporter proves that a gambling ship owner is a murderer.

Unsurprising filler.

w Robert E. Kent   *d* George Amy

Wayne Morris, Jane Wyman, Gilbert Roland, William Pawley, John Litel

Gambling Ship
US   1933   70m   bw
Paramount

A big shot gambler annoys rivals by opening a gambling ship off Long Beach.

Any freshness this once had wore off long ago.

w Max Marcin, Seton I. Miller   *d* Max Marcin

Cary Grant, Benita Hume, Roscoe Karns, Glenda Farrell, Jack La Rue

'A fair flicker . . . but in toto it's a familiar formula of mob vs mob.' – *Variety*

A Game for Vultures
GB   1979   106m   colour
Columbia
V*

In Rhodesia, a sanctions-buster comes to understand a black freedom fighter.

After a lot of violence and attitudinizing, that is, in this unattractively pretentious piece of bloodthirsty hokum.

w Phillip Baird   *novel* Michael Hartmann   *d* James Fargo

Richard Harris, Richard Roundtree, Ray Milland, Joan Collins, Sven Bertil Taube, Denholm Elliott

A Game of Death
US   1945   72m   bw
RKO

Cheap remake of *The Most Dangerous Game* (qv); excitement dissipated by poor handling.

w Norman Houston   *d* Robert Wise   *ph* J. Roy Hunt   *m* Paul Sawtell

John Loder, Audrey Long, Edgar Barrier, Russell Wade, Russell Hicks

Games *
US   1967   100m   Techniscope
Universal (George Edwards)

A sophisticated New York couple play complex games, one of which turns out to have a deadly effect.

Tedious variation on *Les Diaboliques*, with interesting moments.

w Gene Kearney   *d* Curtis Harrington   *ph* William A. Fraker   *m* Samuel Matlovsky

Simone Signoret, James Caan, Katharine Ross, Don Stroud, Kent Smith, Estelle Winwood, Marjorie Bennett

'A cheap-jack mélange of *Angel Street* and *Diabolique* in a New York brownstone.' – *Judith Crist*

The Games *
GB   1970   97m   DeLuxe   Panavision
TCF (Lester Linsk)

Four men in various parts of the world prepare to take part in the marathon at the Rome Olympics.

Tepid multi-drama with good locations and a well-shot and exciting climactic race.

w Erich Segal   *novel* Hugh Atkinson   *d* Michael Winner   *ph* Robert Paynter   *m* Francis Lai

Stanley Baker, Michael Crawford, Ryan O'Neal, Charles Aznavour, Jeremy Kemp, Elaine Taylor, Kent Smith, Mona Washbourne

'Dramatically captures the tension, the physical agony and the almost religious fervour of the Olympics.' – *Daily Mail*

The Gamma People
GB   1955   79m   bw
Warwick/Columbia
V*

Journalists in a Balkan state uncover a plot by a mad scientist to control the minds of children by gamma rays.

Artless serial-like thriller with little suspense.

w John Gilling, John Gossage   *d* John Gilling

Paul Douglas, Leslie Phillips, Eva Bartok, Walter Rilla, Philip Leaver

Ganashatru: see *An Enemy of the People*

'His goal was freedom . . . his strategy was peace . . . his weapon was his humanity!'

Gandhi ***
GB   1982   188m   Technicolor   Panavision
Columbia/Goldcrest/Indo-British/International Film Investors/
    National Film Development Corporation of India (*Richard Attenborough*)
V, V*, L

The life of the young Indian advocate who became a revolutionary, a saint and a martyr.

A straightforward treatment with the odd twists and turns expected of this director; but the remarkable things about the film are first, that it was made at all in an age which regards inspirational epics as very old hat; and secondly, that it has brought into life so splendid a leading performance. Beside these factors the sluggish pace and the air of schoolbook history seem comparatively unimportant.

w John Briley   *d* Richard Attenborough   *ph* Billy Williams, Ronnie Taylor   *m* George Fenton   *pd* Stuart Craig   *ed* John Bloom

Ben Kingsley, Candice Bergen, Edward Fox, John Mills, John Gielgud, Trevor Howard, Martin Sheen, Ian Charleson, Athol Fugard, Saeed Jaffrey

'It reminds us that we are, after all, human, and thus capable of the most extraordinary and wonderful achievements, simply through the use of our imagination, our will, and our sense of right.' – *Roger Ebert*

† Opening dedication: 'No man's life can be encompassed in one telling . . . what can be done is to be faithful in spirit to the record and try to find one's way to the heart of the man.'

AA: best picture; Ben Kingsley; Richard Attenborough as director; John Briley; cinematography; costume design (John Mollo, Bhanu Athalya); art direction (Stuart Craig, Bob Laing); editing (John Bloom)

AAN: music

best film; best direction; best actor; best supporting actress (Rohini Hattangady); outstanding newcomer (Ben Kingsley)

Gang Buster *
US   1931   65m   bw
Paramount

A small-town sap defeats gangsters by accident.

Lively comedy which scored in the middle of the first gangster cycle.

w Joseph L. Mankiewicz   *story* Percy Heath   *d* A. Edward Sutherland

Jack Oakie, Jean Arthur, William Boyd, Wynne Gibson, Tom Kennedy

'First-rate week-stander . . . inlaid with surefire comic devices.' – *Variety*

Gang Busters
US   1942   bw   serial: 12 eps
Universal

Police run down a gang of city terrorists.

Lively serial antics which also survived as a 'potted' feature.

d Ray Taylor, Noel Smith

Kent Taylor, Irene Hervey, Ralph Morgan, Robert Armstrong, Joseph Crehan, Ralf Harolde

The Gang That Couldn't Shoot Straight
US   1971   96m   Metrocolor
MGM (Robert Chartoff, Irwin Winkler)

Members of the New York Mafia organize a cycle race and start antagonisms that end in mass murder.

Unfunny black comedy with all concerned gesticulating wildly.

w Waldo Salt   *novel* Jimmy Breslin   *d* James Goldstone   *ph* Owen Roizman   *m* Dave Grusin

Jerry Orbach, Leigh Taylor-Young, Jo Van Fleet, Lionel Stander, Robert de Niro, Herve Villechaize, Joe Santos

Gang War (1946): see *Odd Man Out*

Gang War *
US   1958   75m   bw   RegalScope
Fox (Harold E. Knox)

When his wife is killed by gangsters a reluctant witness seeks revenge.

Minor prototype for *Death Wish* and the star's other vehicles in similar vein.

w Louis Vittes   *novel* The Hoods Take Over by Ovid Demaris   *d* Gene Fowler Jnr

Charles Bronson, Kent Taylor, Jennifer Holden, John Doucette, Gloria Henry

The Gang's All Here *
GB   1939   77m   bw
ABPC/Jack Buchanan (Walter C. Mycroft)
US title: *The Amazing Mr Forrest*

An insurance investigator goes undercover among gangsters.

Lively comedy-melodrama.

w Ralph Spence d Thornton Freeland ph Claude Friese-Greene ad John Mead, Cedric Dawe ed E. B. Jarvis

Jack Buchanan, Googie Withers, Edward Everett Horton, Syd Walker, Otto Kruger, Jack La Rue, Walter Rilla

† Buchanan played the same character in Smash and Grab.

The Gang's All Here **
US   1943   103m   Technicolor
TCF (William Le Baron)
GB title: The Girls He Left Behind

A serviceman is caught between a fiery entertainer and a Park Avenue socialite.

Frenetic wartime musical with some of Busby Berkeley's most outré choreography (e.g. 'The Lady in the Tutti Frutti Hat') and gleamingly effective Technicolor.

w Walter Bullock d/ch Busby Berkeley ph Edward Cronjager md Alfred Newman m/ly Leo Robin, Harry Warren ad James Basevi, Joseph C. Wright

Alice Faye, Carmen Miranda, James Ellison, Phil Baker, Benny Goodman, Charlotte Greenwood, Eugene Pallette, Edward Everett Horton

'Those who consider Berkeley a master consider this film his masterpiece.' – New Yorker, 1976

'Mainly made up of Busby Berkeley's paroxysmic production numbers, which amuse me a good deal.' – James Agee

AAN: art direction

Gangs of New York *
US   1938   67m   bw
Republic

A cop infiltrates the mob and impersonates a tough gangster.

Highly unlikely but entertaining programmer, a good shot for a B studio.

w Wellyn Totman, Sam Fuller, Charles Francis Royal d James Cruze

Charles Bickford, Ann Dvorak, Alan Baxter, Wynne Gibson, Harold Huber, Willard Robertson, Maxie Rosenbloom, John Wray

'Rapid-fire gangster meller . . . sure to be a strong entry.' – Variety

Gangs of the Waterfront
US   1945   55m   bw
Republic

When his brother is killed, a taxidermist who looks like a gang leader assumes the leader's place and rounds up the mob.

Serial-like action antics; a reliable second feature.

w Albert Beich d George Blair

Robert Armstrong, Stephanie Batchelor, Martin Kosleck, Marion Martin

The Gangster
US   1947   84m   bw
Monogram/King Bros
V*

Rival gangs rub each other out.

Shoddy-looking Poverty Row melodrama with little rhyme, reason or interest.

w Daniel Fuchs d Gordon Wiles

Barry Sullivan, Akim Tamiroff, Belita, John Ireland

Gangway *
GB   1937   89m   bw
GFD/Gaumont (Michael Balcon)

A girl reporter poses as a star's maid and is accused of theft.

Mildly pleasing star vehicle.

w Lesser Samuels, Sonnie Hale d Sonnie Hale ph Glen MacWilliams

Jessie Matthews, Barry Mackay, Nat Pendleton, Noel Madison, Alastair Sim

Gangway for Tomorrow
US   1943   69m   bw
RKO

Five defence workers with problematical pasts unite in the cause of war.

Naïve but oddly stirring little propaganda piece.

w Arch Oboler d John H. Auer

Robert Ryan, Margo, John Carradine

Garbo Talks *
US   1984   103m   Technicolor
MGM-UA/Elliott Kastner (Burtt Harris)
V*

A dying woman's last obsession is to meet her idol Greta Garbo.

New Yorkish wry comedy which doesn't seem entirely clear of its point but is smartly acted and produced.

w Larry Grusin d Sidney Lumet ph Andrzej Bartkowiak m Cy Coleman pd Philip Rosenberg ed Andrew Mondshein

Anne Bancroft, Ron Silver, Carrie Fisher, Catherine Hicks, Steven Hill, Howard Da Silva, Harvey Fierstein, Dorothy Loudon, Hermione Gingold

'A sweet and sour film clearly not for all tastes.' – Variety

La Garce
France   1984   95m   colour
Sara Films/FR3 (Alain Sarde)
aka: The Bitch

Working as a private detective after serving a jail sentence for rape, an ex-cop is hired to investigate the girl he assaulted.

Slow-paced psychological thriller that hovers on the edge of risibility.

w Pierre Fabre, Laurent Heynemann, Christine Pascal, A. M. Delocque Fourcaud d Christine Pascal ph Raoul Coutard m Philippe Sarde ad Valerie Grall

Isabelle Huppert, Richard Berry, Vittorio Mezzogiorno, Jean Bengugli

Garde à Vue *
France   1981   88m   Eastmancolor
Ariane/TF1 (Georges Dancigers, Alexandre Mnouchkine)
GB title: The Inquisitor

In a French provincial town a wealthy lawyer is interrogated by police, who think he may be implicated in a rape case.

Basically a talk-piece, though with a twist ending, this is a smart little film which would undoubtedly have its best effect when not understood through sub-titles.

w Claude Miller, Jean Herman novel Brainwash by John Wainwright d Claude Miller ph Bruno Nuytten m Georges Delerue

Lino Ventura, Michel Serrault, Guy Marchand, Romy Schneider

'Not unlike a Twelve Angry Men from which all comfortable certainties have been withdrawn.' – Tom Milne, MFB

The Garden *
GB   1990   90m   colour
Artificial Eye/Basilisk/Channel 4/British Screen/ZDF/Uplink (James McKay)
V, V*, S

A sequence of images – of Jesus, the Last Supper, the director tending his garden, and a homosexual couple being persecuted – create the effect of a series of semi-religious tableaux.

AIDS and homosexual suffering are the main themes of an intensely personal film most likely to find favour with those who share the director's preoccupations or who can admire his visual flair.

wd Derek Jarman ph Christopher Hughes m Simon Fisher Turner pd Derek Brown, Christopher Hobbs ed Peter Cartwright

Kevin Collins, Roger Cook, Jody Graber, Pete Lee-Wilson, Philip Macdonald, Johnny Mills, Tilda Swinton

'Dangerous love in a desert paradise!'

The Garden of Allah **
US   1936   80m   Technicolor
David O. Selznick
V*, L

A disenchanted socialite falls in love with a renegade monk in the Algerian desert.

Arty old-fashioned romantic star vehicle; great to look at, and marking a genuine advance in colour photography, but dramatically a bit of a drag.

w W. P. Lipscomb, Lynn Riggs novel Robert Hichens d Richard Boleslawski ph W. Howard Greene, Harold Rosson m Max Steiner ad Sturges Carne, Lyle Wheeler, Edward Boyle

Marlene Dietrich, Charles Boyer, Basil Rathbone, Tilly Losch

'The last word in colour production, but a pretty dull affair.' – Variety

'Hopelessly dated folderol.' – J. R. Parish

'The juiciest tale of woe ever, produced in poshly lurid colour, with a Max Steiner score poured on top.' – Judith Crist

'Alas! my poor church, so picturesque, so noble, so superhumanly pious, so intensely dramatic. I really prefer the New Statesman view, shabby priests counting pesetas on their dingy fingers before blessing tanks.' – Graham Greene

† Previous, silent, versions had been made in 1917, with Tom Santschi and Helen Ware, and in 1927 with Ivan Petrovich and Alice Terry.

AA: special award for colour cinematography
AAN: Max Steiner

Garden of Evil *
US   1954   100m   Technicolor   Cinemascope
TCF (Charles Brackett)

En route to the Californian goldfields an ex-sheriff and a gambler help a woman to rescue her husband from a mine, but are trapped by Indians.

High-flying Western melodrama with the principals glowering at each other. Stock situations quite skilfully compiled.

w Frank Fenton d Henry Hathaway ph Milton Krasner m Bernard Herrmann

Susan Hayward, Gary Cooper, Richard Widmark, Hugh Marlowe, Cameron Mitchell

The Garden of the Finzi-Continis **
Italy/West Germany   1970   95m   Eastmancolor
Documento Film/CCC Filmkunst (Gianni Hecht Lucari, Arthur Cohn)
V*, L

In 1938, a family of wealthy Italian Jews sees its world collapse, with a concentration camp as the next destination.

A dreamlike, poignant, and very beautiful film.

w Tullio Pinelli, Valerio Zurlini, Franco Brusati, Ugo Pirro, Vittorio Bonicelli, Alain Katz novel Giorgio Bassani d Vittorio de Sica ph Ennio Guarnieri m Manuel de Sica

Dominique Sanda, Lino Capolicchio, Helmut Berger, Romolo Valli, Fabio Testi

'I lived through the period. The same feelings I experienced in life I transposed to the picture: that is the definition of the artist.' – Vittorio de Sica

'This extraordinary film, with its melancholy glamour, is perhaps the only one that records the halfhearted anti-Jewish measures of the Mussolini period.' – New Yorker

AA: best foreign film

AAN: script

Garden of the Moon

US 1938 94m bw
Warner (Lou Edelman)

A night-club owner vies with his bandleader for the affections of his leading singer.

Pleasant talent can't turn this script into anything but a tedious small-scale musical, especially since both director and songwriters are operating below par.

w Jerry Wald, Richard Macauley d Busby Berkeley m/ly Al Dubin, Harry Warren

Pat O'Brien, Margaret Lindsay, John Payne, Melville Cooper, Isabel Jeans

Gardens of Stone

US 1987 111m DeLuxe
Tri-Star/ML Delphi (Michael I. Levy, Francis Coppola)
V, V*, L

A soldier trains youngsters for the Vietnam War despite his conviction that the war is wrong.

Muddled talk-piece which fails to make any point.

w Ronald Bass novel Nicholas Proffitt d Francis Coppola ph Jordan Cronenweth m Carmine Coppola pd Dean Tavoularis ed Barry Malkin

James Caan, Anjelica Huston, James Earl Jones, D. B. Sweeney, Dean Stockwell, Mary Stewart Masterson, Dick Anthony Williams

The Garment Jungle *

US 1957 88m bw
Columbia (Harry Kleiner)

Union and gangster problems abound for a family in the New York clothing business.

Reasonably powerful melodrama fashioned from familiar material in the wake of On the Waterfront.

w Harry Kleiner d Robert Aldrich, Vincent Sherman ph Joseph Biroc m Leith Stevens

Lee J. Cobb, Kerwin Mathews, Gia Scala, Richard Boone, Valerie French, Robert Loggia, Joseph Wiseman

Gas Food Lodging **

US 1991 101m DeLuxe
Mainline/Cineville Partners (Daniel Hassid, Seth M. Willenson, William Ewart)
V, V*, S

A mother and her two disaffected daughters look for love in a small town.

Engrossing domestic drama of three women struggling to survive and searching for something to make life worthwhile.

wd Allison Anders novel Don't Look and It Won't Hurt by Richard Peck ph Dean Lent m J. Mascis pd Jane Ann Stewart ed Tracy S. Granger

Brooke Adams, Ione Syke, Fairuza Balk, James Brolin, Robert Knepper, David Landsbury, Jacob Vargas, Donovan Leitch, Chris Mulkey

'Anders's film is sometimes stilted, at times over-contrived, but it invariably rings true both socially and psychologically.' – Philip French, Observer

Gas House Kids

US 1946 71m bw
PRC

Young New Yorkers help a crippled veteran buy a chicken ranch.

First of three forgotten attempts to stretch out the Dead End Kids genre; not good. (The other titles, both in 1947, were Gas House Kids Go West and Gas House Kids in Hollywood.)

w Raymond Schrock, George and Elsie Bricker d Sam Newfield

Billy Halop, Alfalfa Switzer, Robert Lowery, Teala Loring, Rex Downing, David Reed

Gas! or It Became Necessary to Destroy the World in Order to Save It

US 1970 79m Movielab
AIP/San Jacinto (Roger Corman)
V, V*

A gas which speeds up the ageing process is accidentally released and kills everyone over twenty-five.

Psychedelic sci-fi for the Easy Rider set. Very mildly diverting.

w Graham Armitage d Roger Corman ph Ron Dexter m Country Joe and the Fish

Robert Corff, Elaine Giftos, Pat Patterson, Graham Armitage, Alex Wilson, Ben Vereen, Bud Cort

Gasbags *

GB 1940 77m bw
Gainsborough (Edward Black)

Airmen stranded in Germany by a barrage balloon return in a captured secret weapon.

Fast-moving knockabout from the Crazy Gang; often inventive despite reach-me-down script and production.

w Val Guest, Marriott Edgar d Marcel Varnel ph Arthur Crabtree md Louis Levy

Flanagan and Allen, Nervo and Knox, Naughton and Gold, Moore Marriott, Wally Patch, Peter Gawthorne, Frederick Valk

Gaslight ****

GB 1940 88m bw
British National (John Corfield)
V*
US title: Angel Street

A Victorian schizophrenic drives his wife insane when she seems likely to stumble on his guilty secret of an old murder and hidden rubies.

Modest but absolutely effective film version of a superb piece of suspense theatre.

w A. R. Rawlinson, Bridget Boland play Patrick Hamilton d Thorold Dickinson ph Bernard Knowles m Richard Addinsell

Anton Walbrook, Diana Wynyard, Frank Pettingell, Cathleen Cordell, Robert Newton, Jimmy Hanley

'For one who has seen the stage play, much of the tension is destroyed by the insistence on explaining everything rather than hinting at it.' – Dilys Powell

'The electric sense of tension and mid-Victorian atmosphere are entirely cinematic.' – Sequence, 1950

† MGM is said to have tried to destroy the negative of the film when it made its version four years later. See below.

'A melodrama of a strange love!'
'This is love … clouded by evil … darkened by a secret no one dared to guess! The strange drama of a captive sweetheart!'

Gaslight **

US 1944 114m bw
MGM (Arthur Hornblow Jnr)
V, V*, L
GB title: The Murder in Thornton Square

Grossly overblown and less effective version of the above, but with moments of power, effective performances and superior production.

w John Van Druten, Walter Reisch, John L. Balderston play Patrick Hamilton d George Cukor ph Joseph Ruttenberg m Bronislau Kaper ad Cedric Gibbons, William Ferrari

Charles Boyer, Ingrid Bergman, Joseph Cotten, Dame May Whitty, Barbara Everest, Angela Lansbury, Edmund Breon, Halliwell Hobbes

† Irene Dunne and Hedy Lamarr were previously offered the Ingrid Bergman part, and turned it down.

AA: Ingrid Bergman; art direction

AAN: best picture; script; Joseph Ruttenberg; Charles Boyer; Angela Lansbury

Gasoline Alley

US 1951 76m bw
Columbia (Milton Feldman)

Young marrieds open a diner.

Placid comedy-drama from a 30-year-old comic strip; the intended series did not materialize.

wd Edward Bernds comic strip Frank O. King

Scotty Beckett, Jimmy Lydon, Susan Morrow, Don Beddoe, Dick Wessel, Gus Schilling

The Gate

Canada 1987 92m colour
Vista (John Kemeny)
V, V*, L

Two young boys dig a hole in their back yard which opens a gate to hell.

Enjoyable low-budget horror, with some amusing moments.

w Michael Nankin d Tibor Takacs ph Thomas Vamos m Michael Hoenig, J. Peter Robinson pd William Beeton sp Randall William Cook ed Rit Wallis

Stephen Dorff, Christa Denton, Louis Tripp, Kelly Rowan, Jennifer Irwin, Scott Denton

'Sort of an Evil Dead for pre-teen nerds.' – Stefan Jaworzyn, Shock Xpress

Gate II

Canada 1992 95m Film House colour
Alliance/Andras Hamori
V, V*, L

A teenager and his two friends summon demons who possess them.

Predictable horror aimed at teen audiences, but too tame to attract them.

w Michael Nankin d Tibor Takacs ph Brian England m George Blondheim pd William Beeton sp Randall William Cook ed Ronald Sanders

Louis Tripp, Simon Reynolds, Pamela Segall, James Villemaire, Neil Munro

'An idiotic horror film boasting good monster effects.' – Variety

Gate of Hell *

Japan 1953 90m Eastmancolor
Daiei (Masaichi Nagata)
V*
original title: Jigokumon

After a 12th-century war, a soldier demands as his

prize a woman who has helped him; but she is married.

Curious traditional Japanese saga, its emphases strange to western eyes and ears. Its colour, however, is devastatingly beautiful. wd Teinosuke Kinugasa novel Kan Kikuchi ph Kohei Sugiyama m Yasushi Akutagawa

Machiko Kyo, Kazuo Hasegawa, Isao Yamagata

AA: best foreign film

Gate of Lilacs: see Porte des Lilas

Gates of Hell: see City of The Living Dead

Gates of Night: see Les Portes de la Nuit

Gates of Paris: see Porte des Lilas

Gateway *
US   1938   75m   bw
TCF (Darryl F. Zanuck)

An Irish girl emigrating to the US is helped on board ship by a war correspondent.

Brisk romantic drama which provides an interesting recreation of the Ellis Island procedures still effective in the thirties.

w Lamar Trotti d Alfred Werker ph Edward Cronjager m Arthur Lange, Charles Maxwell

Don Ameche, Arleen Whelan, Gregory Ratoff, Raymond Walburn, Binnie Barnes, Gilbert Roland, John Carradine, Harry Carey

'Grand Hotel treatment applied to Ellis Island . . . should look to fair b.o.' – Variety

A Gathering of Eagles
US   1963   115m   Eastmancolor
U-I (Sy Bartlett)
V*

A colonel becomes unpopular when he strives to improve the efficiency of a Strategic Air Command base.

Tame revamp of Twelve O'clock High without the justification of war; all strictly routine and perfectly dull.

w Robert Pirosh d Delbert Mann ph Russell Harlan m Jerry Goldsmith

Rock Hudson, Mary Peach, Rod Taylor, Barry Sullivan, Kevin McCarthy

'Come and get him!'
Gator
US   1976   116m   DeLuxe   Todd-AO 35
UA/Levy-Gardner-Laven
V*

A convicted moonshiner is blackmailed into becoming a government undercover man in the organization of a hoodlum.

Shambling mixture of action, violence, and raw humour.

w William Norton d Burt Reynolds ph William A. Fraker m Charles Bernstein

Burt Reynolds, Jack Weston, Lauren Hutton, Jerry Reed, Alice Ghostley, Dub Taylor, Mike Douglas

'The relentless violence, the sentimentality, the raucous stag party humour, the inability to cut off a scene once it has made its point, attest to the influence of Robert Aldrich.' – Philip French

Il Gattopardo: see The Leopard

The Gaucho *
US   1928   115m approx   bw   silent
Douglas Fairbanks

An outlaw reforms when he falls for the Girl of the Shrine.

Subdued star swashbuckler leading up to a fine climax.

w Lotta Woods story Douglas Fairbanks d F. Richard Jones

Douglas Fairbanks, Lupe Velez, Geraine Greear, Gustav von Seyffertitz

The Gaunt Stranger *
GB   1938   73m   bw
Northwood/Capad (Ealing) (Michael Balcon, S. C. Balcon)
US title: The Phantom Strikes

A criminal master of disguise threatens to kill a much more despicable criminal at an appointed hour . . . and does so despite police protection.

A highly reliable suspenser of which this is perhaps the best film version.

w Sidney Gilliat play and novel The Ringer by Edgar Wallace d Walter Forde ph Ronald Neame ad Oscar Werndorff ed Charles Saunders

Sonnie Hale, Wilfrid Lawson, Alexander Knox, Louise Henry, Patricia Roc, Patrick Barr, John Longden, George Merritt

'Dialogue, humour and suspense are effectively alternated . . . the film is in fact capital crime fiction.' – Kine Weekly

† Other versions, as The Ringer, appeared in 1931 and 1953.

The Gauntlet *
US   1977   109m   DeLuxe   Panavision
Warner/Malpaso (Robert Daly)
V, V*, L

A disreputable cop is assigned to escort a foul-mouthed prostitute to a courtroom across country, through the gauntlet of baddies who want them both dead.

The epitome of seventies violence, with no excuse except to stage one detailed shoot-up or explosion after another. Well done for those who like this sort of thing.

w Michael Butler, Dennis Shryack d Clint Eastwood ph Rexford Metz m Jerry Fielding

Clint Eastwood, Sondra Locke, Pat Hingle, William Prince

'At times the whole world seems to be firing at them. Buildings and cars are turned to lace. You look at the screen even though there's nothing to occupy your mind . . .' – Pauline Kael

† This was the first film to give a credit for first aid.

Gawain and the Green Knight *
GB   1973   93m   Technicolor   Panavision
UA/Sancrest (Philip Breen)

The medieval legend of a supernatural knight who challenges the king's men to kill him.

Enterprising if unsuccessful low-budget attempt to create a medieval world; too long by half.

w Philip Breen, Stephen Weeks d Stephen Weeks ph Ian Wilson m Ron Goodwin ad Anthony Woollard

Murray Head, Ciaran Madden, Nigel Green, Anthony Sharp, Robert Hardy, Murray Melvin

The Gay Bride
US   1934   80m   bw
MGM (John Considine Jnr)

A gold-digging chorus girl marries a racketeer but soon becomes a widow.

Misfiring satirical melodrama which quickly becomes tedious.

w Bella and Samuel Spewack story Repeal by Charles Francis Coe d Jack Conway ph Ray June

Carole Lombard, Chester Morris, ZaSu Pitts, Nat Pendleton, Leo Carrillo

'Gangster pictures are gone, and this won't do anything to bring them back.' – Variety

The Gay Deception *
US   1935   79m   bw
Fox (Jesse L. Lasky)

A Ruritanian prince becomes a doorman at a swank New York hotel, and marries a secretary.

Lightly-handled Cinderella story showing most of its director's accomplishment.

w Stephen Morehouse Avery, Don Hartman d William Wyler ph Joseph Valentine m Louis de Francesco

Francis Lederer, Frances Dee, Benita Hume, Alan Mowbray, Akim Tamiroff, Lennox Pawle, Richard Carle, Lionel Stander

'Doesn't lean too much to sophistication to miss appreciation in the hamlet houses.' – Variety

AAN: story

The Gay Desperado **
US   1936   85m   bw
Mary Pickford

An heiress is held for ransom by a romantic bandit.

Very light, quite amusing, sometimes irritatingly skittish musical spoof sparked by the director's ideas.

w Wallace Smith story Leo Birinski d Rouben Mamoulian ph Lucien Andriot m Alfred Newman

Ida Lupino, Nino Martini, Leo Carrillo, Harold Huber, Mischa Auer

'Fairly diverting Mexican western . . . it'll do spotty trade, depending on locale.' – Variety

'One of the best light comedies of the year . . . Mr Mamoulian's camera is very persuasive.' – Graham Greene

'While some of the show is fetching, the ideas mostly misfire and the spell is fitful and unsure.' – Otis Ferguson

'It has the lightness of touch which goes into the making of the perfect meringue.' – Basil Wright

The Gay Diplomat
US   1931   66m   bw
RKO

A Russian officer is sent to Bucharest to combat a woman superspy.

Thoroughly confused and inane mixture of romance, presumed sophistication and dark doings.

w Doris Anderson story Benn W. Levy d Richard Boleslawski

Ivan Lebedeff, Genevieve Tobin, Ilka Chase, Betty Compson

'A picture almost without a merit.' – Variety

The Gay Divorce: see The Gay Divorcee

'The gayest of mad musicals!'
'The dance-mad musical triumph of two continents!'
The Gay Divorcee **
US   1934   107m   bw
RKO (Pandro S. Berman)
V*, L
GB title: The Gay Divorce

A would-be divorcee in an English seaside hotel mistakes a dancer who loves her for a professional co-respondent.

Wildly and hilariously dated comedy musical with splendidly archaic comedy routines supporting Hollywood's great new dance team in their first big success. Not much dancing, but 'The Continental' is a show-stopper.

w George Marion Jnr, Dorothy Yost, Edward Kaufman musical comedy Samuel Hoffenstein, Kenneth Webb, Cole Porter play Dwight Taylor, J.

Hartley Manners   *d* Mark Sandrich   *ph* David Abel
md Max Steiner   *sp* Vernon Walker   *m/y* various
ad Van Nest Polglase, Carroll Clark   *sp* Vernon
Walker   *ed* William Hamilton

*Fred Astaire, Ginger Rogers, Edward Everett Horton, Alice
Brady, Erik Rhodes, Eric Blore, Lillian Miles, Betty
Grable*

'Cinch box office anywhere and certain of big foreign
grosses.' – *Variety*

'The plot is trivial French farce, but the dances are
among the wittiest and most lyrical expressions of
American romanticism on the screen.' – *New Yorker,*
1977

† 'Night and Day' was the only Cole Porter song to
survive from the stage musical.

AA: song 'The Continental' (*m* Con Conrad, *ly* Herb
Magidson)

AAN: best picture; musical score (Ken Webb, Samuel
Hoffenstein); art direction

The Gay Dog
GB   1954   87m   bw
Coronet/Eros

A miner trains a pet greyhound to win races.

Modest, set-bound regional comedy.

w Peter Rogers   *play* Joseph Colton   *d* Maurice
Elvey

*Wilfred Pickles, Petula Clark, Megs Jenkins, John
Blythe*

The Gay Duellist: see *Meet Me at Dawn*

The Gay Imposters: see *Gold Diggers in Paris*

The Gay Intruders
US   1948   68m   bw
TCF

Quarrelling stage marrieds consult psychiatrists, who
end up more confused than the patients.

Unusual second feature comedy with a few good
laughs; allegedly based on Tallulah Bankhead.

w Francis Swann   *d* Ray McCarey

*Tamara Geva, John Emery, Leif Erickson, Virginia
Gregg*

The Gay Lady: see *Trottie True*

The Gay Mrs Trexel: see *Susan and God*

The Gay Nineties: see *The Floradora Girl*

Gay Purree *
US   1962   85m   Technicolor
UPA (Henry Saperstein)
V*, L

A country cat goes to Paris and is Shanghaied.

Feature cartoon similar to Disney's later *The Aristocats*
and about as good, i.e. not quite up to the best
standards.

w Dorothy and Chuck Jones   *d* Abe Levitow
md Mort Lindsey   *m/y* Harold Arlen, E. Y. Harburg

voices of *Judy Garland, Robert Goulet, Hermione
Gingold*

The Gay Sisters *
US   1942   110m   bw
Warner (Henry Blanke)

Three sisters refuse to sell their aristocratic New York
mansion to make way for development.

Slowish but quite interesting family drama with
Chekhovian touches.

w Lenore Coffee   *novel* Stephen Longstreet
d Irving Rapper   *ph* Sol Polito   *m* Max Steiner

*Barbara Stanwyck, George Brent, Geraldine
Fitzgerald, Donald Crisp, Gig Young* (so named after
his part in this film; formerly Byron Barr), *Nancy
Coleman, Gene Lockhart, Larry Simms, Donald
Woods, Grant Mitchell*

The Gazebo *
US   1959   102m   bw
MGM/Avon (Lawrence Weingarten)

A TV writer kills a blackmailer (he thinks) and hides
his body in the garden.

Frenetic black comedy which must have worked
better on the stage but produces a few laughs.

w George Wells   *play* Alec Coppel   *d* George
Marshall   *ph* Paul C. Vogel   *m* Jeff Alexander

*Glenn Ford, Debbie Reynolds, Carl Reiner, John
McGiver, Mabel Albertson, Doro Merande, ZaSu
Pitts, Martin Landau*

The Geisha Boy
US   1958   98m   Technicolor   Vistavision
Paramount (Jerry Lewis)
V*

A third-rate magician joins a USO entertainment tour
in Japan.

Disconnected farce which amuses only fitfully, and
actively displeases when it becomes sentimental with
the star drooling over a baby.

wd Frank Tashlin   *ph* Haskell Boggs   *m* Walter
Scharf

*Jerry Lewis, Marie MacDonald, Barton MacLane,
Sessue Hayakawa, Suzanne Pleshette*

The Gene Krupa Story
US   1959   101m   bw
Columbia (Philip A. Waxman)
V*
GB title: *Drum Crazy*

A successful jazz drummer is convicted on a drugs
charge and falls from grace.

Dreary biopic with the expected music track.

w Orin Jannings   *d* Don Weis   *ph* Charles Lawton
Jnr   *m* Leith Stevens

*Sal Mineo, Susan Kohner, James Darren, Susan
Oliver, Yvonne Craig, Lawrence Dobkin, Celia
Lovsky;* and *Red Nichols, Shelly Manne, Buddy
Lester*

'Everybody laughs but Buster!'
The General ****
US   1926   80m approx (24 fps)   bw   silent
UA/Buster Keaton (Joseph M. Schenck)
V, V*, L

A confederate train driver gets his train and his girl
back when they are stolen by Union soldiers.

Slow-starting, then hilarious action comedy, often
voted one of the best ever made. Its sequence of sight
gags, each topping the one before, is an incredible joy
to behold.

w Al Boasberg, Charles Smith   *d* Buster Keaton, Clyde
Bruckman   *ph* J. Devereux Jennings, Bert Haines

Buster Keaton, Marion Mack, Glen Cavander

'It has all the sweet earnestness in the world. It is
about trains, frontier America, flower-faced girls.' –
New Yorker, 1977

'The production itself is singularly well mounted, but
the fun is not exactly plentiful . . . here he is more the
acrobat than the clown, and his vehicle might be
described as a mixture of cast iron and jelly.' –
Mordaunt Hall, New York Times

† The story is based on an actual incident of the Civil
War, treated more seriously in *The Great Locomotive
Chase* (qv).

†† The screenplay with 1,400 freeze frames was
issued in 1976 in the Film Classics Library (editor,
Richard Anobile).

'He strides recklessly into the vortex of cyclonic romantic
adventure, sweeping monarchs from their thrones to
suit a gypsy's whim!'
General Crack
US   1930   100m approx   bw/colour sequences
Warner

Exploits of an 18th-century brigand prince.

Elaborate swashbuckler which provided the star with
his first talkie but boringly demonstrates the technical
problems of films of this period, however highly
budgeted.

w J. Grubb Alexander and others   *d* Alan Crosland

*John Barrymore, Marian Nixon, Hobart Bosworth,
Armida, Lowell Sherman*

General Della Rovere **
Italy   1959   130m   bw
Gaumont/Zebra (Morris Ergas)
original title: *Il Generale Della Rovere*

A petty thief, forced by the Nazis to pose as a
Resistance leader to flush out the real leaders, begins
to take the role seriously.

De Sica's bravura performance saves a slickly made
but emotionally hollow film, one that its director
seems not to have liked.

w Sergio Amidei, Diego Fabbri, Indro Montanelli,
Roberto Rossellini   *d* Roberto Rossellini   *ph* Carlo
Carlini   *m* Renzo Rossellini   *ad* Piero Zuffi
ed Cesare Cavagna

*Vittorio de Sica, Hannes Messemer, Sandra Milo,
Giovanna Ralli*

The film was co-winner of the Golden Lion at the
Venice Film Festival in 1959.

'Gary goes to town for the best-looking gal in China!'
The General Died at Dawn **
US   1936   93m   bw
Paramount (William le Baron)
V*

A mercenary in China overcomes an evil warlord and
falls in love with a spy.

Heavy-going but very decorative studio-bound
intrigue which seems to take place on the old *Shanghai
Express* sets with an extra infusion of dry ice. An
intellectual's picture of its day.

w Clifford Odets   *novel* Charles Booth   *d* Lewis
Milestone   *ph* Victor Milner   *m* Werner Janssen,
Gerard Carbonara

*Gary Cooper, Madeleine Carroll, Akim Tamiroff, Dudley
Digges, Porter Hall, William Frawley*

'If it were not for a rather ludicrous ending, this
would be one of the best thrillers for some years.' –
Graham Greene

'In terms of cinematic invention, a fascinating
technical exercise.' – *John Baxter, 1968*

'A curious study in exoticism.' – *NFT, 1974*

'In direction and photography it has undeniable class
. . . but like most movies, it is empty of any ideas or
characters that stay with you longer than it takes to
reach the nearest subway entrance.' – *Brooklyn Daily
Eagle*

AAN: Victor Milner; Werner Janssen; Akim Tamiroff

The General Line **
USSR   1929   90m (24 fps)   bw   silent
Sovkino
V
original title: *Staroye i Novoye;* aka: *Old and New*

A country woman helps to start a village co-operative.

A slight piece of propaganda, put together with all of
Eisenstein's magnificent cinematic resources: the

cream separator demonstration is one of the most famous montage sequences in cinema history.

w Sergei Eisenstein *d* Sergei Eisenstein, Grigori Alexandrov *ph* Edouard Tissé

Marta Lapkina and a cast of non-professionals

General Spanky
US   1936   73m approx   bw
MGM/Hal Roach
V*, L

A small boy is instrumental in a famous Civil War victory.

Uneasy sentimental melodrama vehicle for one of the moppet stars of 'Our Gang'.

w Richard Flournoy, Hal Yates, John Guedel
d Gordon Douglas, Fred Newmeyer

Spanky McFarland, Phillips Holmes, Hobart Bosworth, Ralph Morgan, Irving Pichel

'Desultory, overlong . . . built for the lesser family trade.' – *Variety*

General Suvorov
USSR   1941   90m   bw
Mosfilm

The career of the general who turned back Napoleon at the gates of Moscow.

Competent propaganda piece, but not one of the Russian classics.

w G. Grebner   *d* V. I. Pudovkin

N. P. Cherkasov, A. Yachnitscki, S. Kiligin

Generation *
Poland   1954   90m   bw
Film Polski
V*
original title: *Pokolenie*

In occupied Warsaw in 1942 a teenager becomes hardened by life and joins the resistance.

Heavy-going but quite striking propaganda piece, amply demonstrating its director's talents.

w Bohdan Czeszko   *novel* Bohdan Czeszko
d Andrzej Wajda   *ph* Jerzy Lipman   *m* Andrzej Markowski

Tadeusz Lomnicki, Urszula Modrzynska, Roman Polanski, Zbigniew Cybulski

Generation
US   1969   104m   Technicolor
Avco Embassy/Frederick Brisson
V*
GB title: *A Time for Giving*

A Denver advertising executive is horrified by his daughter's ideas of modern marriage.

Lame generation-gap comedy centring on a couple who intend to deliver their own baby.

w William Goodhart   *play* William Goodhart
d George Schaefer   *ph* Lionel Lindon   *m* Dave Grusin

David Janssen, Kim Darby, Carl Reiner, Pete Duel, Andrew Prine, James Coco, Sam Waterston, Don Beddoe

'Slightly too sticky for comfort.' – *MFB*

Genevieve ****
GB   1953   86m   Technicolor
GFD/Sirius (Henry Cornelius)
V*

Two friendly rivals engage in a race on the way back from the Brighton veteran car rally.

One of those happy films in which for no very good or expected reason a number of modest elements merge smoothly to create an aura of high style and memorable moments. A charmingly witty script, carefully pointed direction, attractive actors and

locations, an atmosphere of light-hearted British sex and a lively harmonica theme turned it, after a slowish start, into one of Britain's biggest commercial hits and most fondly remembered comedies.

w William Rose   *d* Henry Cornelius   *ph* Christopher Challis   *md* Muir Mathieson   *m* Larry Adler (who also played it)   *ad* Michael Stringer

Dinah Sheridan, John Gregson, Kay Kendall, Kenneth More, Geoffrey Keen, Joyce Grenfell, Reginald Beckwith, Arthur Wontner

'One of the best things to have happened to British films over the last five years.' – *Gavin Lambert*

† On American prints, Muir Mathieson was credited as the composer and with the Oscar nomination rather than Larry Adler, who was blacklisted at the time.

AAN: William Rose; Larry Adler

'In the eight centuries since he ruled the world, no man has matched the magnificence of his adventure!'
Genghis Khan *
US   1964   126m   Technicolor   Panavision
Columbia/Irving Allen/CCC/Avala
V

Temujin raises a Mongol army and revenges himself on his old enemy Jamuga.

Meandering epic in which brutality alternates with pantomimish comedy and bouts of sex. Necessarily patchy but reasonably watchable.

w Clarke Reynolds, Beverley Cross   *d* Henry Levin
ph Geoffrey Unsworth   *m* Ducan Radic

Omar Sharif, Stephen Boyd, Françoise Dorléac, *James Mason*, Robert Morley, Telly Savalas, Woody Strode, Eli Wallach, Yvonne Mitchell

Genius at Work
US   1946   61m   bw
RKO

Radio detectives expose a killer.

Rackety vehicle for a comedy team which never even approached Abbott and Costello.

w Robert E. Kent, Monte Brice   *d* Leslie Goodwins

Wally Brown, Alan Carney, Anne Jeffries, Bela Lugosi, Lionel Atwill

A Genius in the Family: see *So Goes My Love*

Genou de Claire: see *Claire's Knee*

Les Gens du Voyage *
France   1938   123m   bw
Tobis

Trials and tribulations of circus people on the road.

Interesting but overlong multi-drama.

w Jacques Feyder, Jacques Viol   *d* Jacques Feyder

Françoise Rosay, André Brule, Fabien Loris, Marie Glory, Sylvia Bataille

'Boredom is unavoidably the impression.' – *Variety*

Gente di rispetto: see *The Masters*

Gentle Annie
US   1944   80m   bw
MGM

A marshal deals with a lady rancher who sees no harm in an occasional bank robbery to augment her income.

Tidy MGM second-string Western, originally intended for Robert Taylor.

w Lawrence Hazard   *novel* Mackinlay Kantor
d Andrew Marton

James Craig, Marjorie Main, Donna Reed, Henry Morgan, Paul Langton, Barton MacLane

A Gentle Creature: see *Une Femme Douce*

The Gentle Giant
US   1967   93m   Eastmancolor
Ivan Tors/Paramount
V*

A small boy in Florida befriends a bear, which later saves his disapproving father's life.

Lumbering family movie which provided the impetus for a TV series.

w Edward J. Lakso, Andy White   *novel* Gentle Ben by Walt Morey   *d* James Neilson

Dennis Weaver, Clint Howard, Vera Miles, Ralph Meeker, Huntz Hall

The Gentle Gunman
GB   1952   88m   bw
GFD/Ealing (Michael Relph)
V

Tensions mount in an IRA family where one brother believes in peace.

Stilted and unconvincing pattern play which wouldn't have done at all once the Troubles restarted.

w Roger MacDougall   *play* Roger MacDougall
d Basil Dearden   *ph* Gordon Dines   *m* John Greenwood   *ed* Peter Tanner

John Mills, Dirk Bogarde, Elizabeth Sellars, Barbara Mullen, Robert Beatty, Eddie Byrne, Joseph Tomelty, Gilbert Harding, Liam Redmond, Jack MacGowran

The Gentle Sergeant: see *Three Stripes in the Sun*

The Gentle Sex **
GB   1943   93m   bw
Rank/Two Cities/Concanen (Leslie Howard, Derrick de Marney)

Seven girls from different backgrounds are conscripted into the ATS.

Unassuming war propaganda, quite pleasantly done and historically very interesting.

w Moie Charles, Aimée Stuart, Phyllis Rose, Roland Pertwee   *d* Leslie Howard, Maurice Elvey
ph Robert Krasker   *m* John Greenwood

Rosamund John, Joan Greenwood, Joan Gates, Jean Gillie, Lilli Palmer, Joyce Howard, Barbara Waring, John Justin, Frederick Leister, Mary Jerrold, Everley Gregg

† Leslie Howard is heard as narrator and recognizably glimpsed in two scenes photographed from behind.

A Gentleman after Dark
US   1942   74m   bw
Edward Small

A jewel thief comes out of prison to pay back his vindictive wife for shopping him.

Efficient melodrama of a dated kind.

w Patterson McNutt, George Bruce   *story* A Whiff of Heliotrope by Richard Washburn Child   *d* Edwin L. Marin   *ph* Milton Krasner   *m* Dimitri Tiomkin

Brian Donlevy, Miriam Hopkins, Preston Foster, Harold Huber, Philip Reed, Gloria Holden, Douglass Dumbrille, Ralph Morgan

† Previously filmed in 1920 as *Heliotrope* with Fred Burton; in 1928 as *Forgotten Faces* with Clive Brook; and in 1936 as *Forgotten Faces* with Herbert Marshall.

A Gentleman at Heart
US   1942   66m   bw
TCF (Walter Morosco)

A racetrack bookie has aspirations to the art business but finds there are crooks there too.

Fairly lively second feature.

w Lee Loeb, Harold Buchman   *story* Paul Hervey Fox   *d* Ray Macarey

Cesar Romero, Carole Landis, Milton Berle, J. Carrol Naish, Rose Hobart, Jerome Cowan, Elisha Cook Jnr, Steve Geray

Gentleman for a Day: see *Union Depot*

The Gentleman in Room Six *
US 1951 11m bw
Meteor Films (George Brest)

In a seedy room in South America, a man we can't see gives orders to old associates. As he finally goes to shave, we see in the mirror that he is – *Adolf Hitler!*

A fairly sensational novelty at the time, and historically interesting still.

w Sidney Carroll *d* Alexander Hammid

Gentleman Jim **
US 1942 104m bw
Warner (Robert Buckner)
V, V*, L

The rise to fame of boxer Jim Corbett.

Cheerful biopic of an 1890s show-off, mostly played for comedy.

w Vincent Lawrence, Horace McCoy *book The Roar of the Crowd* by James J. Corbett *d* Raoul Walsh *ph* Sid Hickox *m* Heinz Roemheld

Errol Flynn, Alan Hale, Alexis Smith, John Loder, Jack Carson, *Ward Bond*, William Frawley, Rhys Williams, Arthur Shields

'Good-natured enough, but it lacks flavour.' – *New Yorker, 1976*

A Gentleman of Paris
GB 1931 76m bw
Stoll/Gaumont

A philandering French judge knows that the girl before him is innocent of murder, but dare not say so.

Tolerable melodrama of its time.

w Sinclair Hill, Sidney Gilliat, Sewell Collins *novel His Honour the Judge* by Niranjan Pal *d* Sinclair Hill *ph* Mutz Greenbaum *ad* A. L. Mazzei

Arthur Wontner, Hugh Williams, Vanda Greville, Phyllis Konstam, Sybil Thorndike

'Now! It comes to the screen with nothing left unsaid and no emotion unstressed!'

Gentleman's Agreement **
US 1947 118m bw
TCF (Darryl F. Zanuck)
V, V*, L

A journalist poses as a Jew in order to write about anti-semitism.

Worthy melodrama which caused a sensation at the time but as a film is alas rather dull and self-satisfied.

w Moss Hart *novel* Laura Z. Hobson *d* Elia Kazan *ph* Arthur Miller *m* Alfred Newman *ed* Harmon Jones

Gregory Peck, Dorothy McGuire, *John Garfield*, Celeste Holm, *Anne Revere*, June Havoc, Albert Dekker, Jane Wyatt, Dean Stockwell

AA: best picture; Elia Kazan; Celeste Holm

AAN: Moss Hart; Gregory Peck; Dorothy McGuire; Anne Revere; editing

Gentleman's Fate
US 1930 90m bw
MGM

A man goes to the bad after his wife walks out on him.

Dismal early talkie, one of several which killed off its star's career.

w Leonard Praskins *story* Ursula Parrott *d* Mervyn Le Roy

John Gilbert, Louis Wolheim, Leila Hyams, Anita Page, John Miljan, Marie Prevost

'It got a laugh at the Strand Saturday afternoon, where all of the audience probably thought the same thing, that Gilbert died too late as the picture had been dying since its start.' – *Variety*

A Gentleman's Gentleman
GB 1939 70m bw
Warner (Jerome Jackson)

A valet thinks his master is a murderer, and tries a little blackmail.

Uneasy serio-comic vehicle for a London stage character who had made his name in Hollywood.

w Austin Melford, Elizabeth Meehan *play* Philip MacDonald *d* Roy William Neill *ph* Basil Emmott

Eric Blore, Peter Coke, Marie Lohr, David Hutcheson

Gentlemen Are Born
US 1934 74m bw
Warner

College graduates find it hard to get jobs.

Tedious and uninventive quartet of linked stories.

w Eugene Solow, Robert Lee Johnson *d* Alfred E. Green

Franchot Tone, Ross Alexander, Dick Foran, Robert Light, Jean Muir, Margaret Lindsay, Ann Dvorak, Charles Starrett

Gentlemen Marry Brunettes
US 1955 95m Technicolor Cinemascope
UA/Russ-Field (Richard Sale, Robert Waterfield)

Two American shopgirls seek rich husbands in Paris, and find that their aunts were notorious there.

Jaded sequel to *Gentlemen Prefer Blondes*; it barely raises a smile and the numbers are dismal.

w Mary Loos, Richard Sale *d* Richard Sale *ph* Desmond Dickinson *m* Robert Farnon *ad* Paul Sheriff *ch* Jack Cole

Jane Russell, Jeanne Crain, Alan Young, Scott Brady, Rudy Vallee

Gentlemen Prefer Blondes *
US 1953 91m Technicolor
TCF (Sol. C. Siegel)
V, V*, L, S

A dumb blonde and a showgirl go to Paris in search of rich husbands.

Musicalized and updated version of the twenties satire; no real vigour, but not too bad.

w Charles Lederer *novel* Anita Loos *d* Howard Hawks *ph* Harry J. Wild *md* Lionel Newman *ch* Jack Cole *m/ly* Jule Styne, Leo Robin

Jane Russell, Marilyn Monroe, Charles Coburn, Tommy Noonan, Norma Varden, Elliott Reid, George Winslow

Geordie *
GB 1955 99m Technicolor
British Lion/Argonaut (Sidney Gilliat, Frank Launder)
US title: *Wee Geordie*

A weakly Scottish boy takes a physical culture course and becomes an Olympic hammer-thrower.

Slight comic fable, good to look at but without the necessary style to follow it through.

w Sidney Gilliat, Frank Launder *novel* David Walker *d* Frank Launder *ph* Wilkie Cooper *m* William Alwyn

Bill Travers, Alastair Sim, Norah Gorsen, Raymond Huntley, Brian Reece, Miles Malleson, Stanley Baxter

George and Margaret
GB 1940 77m bw
Warner

The frictions of a suburban family come to boiling point.

Fairly spruce film version of a stage comedy in which the title pair were much talked of but never seen.

w Brock Williams, Rodney Ackland *play* Gerald Savory *d* George King

Judy Kelly, Marie Lohr, Oliver Wakefield, Noel Howlett, Ann Casson, Arthur Macrae

George and Mildred
GB 1980 93m colour
Chips/ITC (Roy Skeggs)

A suburban husband on a weekend package holiday is mistaken for a hired killer.

Abysmal TV spinoff, seeming even more lugubrious since it was released after the death of the female star.

w Dick Sharples *d* Peter Frazer Jones *ph* Frank Watts *m* Philip Martell *ad* Carolyn Scott *ed* Peter Weatherley

Yootha Joyce, Brian Murphy, Stratford Johns, Norman Eshley, Sheila Fearn, Kenneth Cope

'Flaccid entertainment even by routine sit-com standards.' – *Martyn Auty, MFB*

George in Civvy Street
GB 1946 79m bw
Columbia (Marcel Varnel, Ben Henry)

A soldier returns to his country pub and finds himself in the middle of a beer war.

The star's last film was oddly lacklustre and compared very badly with his earlier successes.

w Peter Fraser, Ted Kavanagh, Max Kester, Gale Pedrick *d* Marcel Varnel *ph* Phil Grindrod

George Formby, Rosalyn Boulter, Ronald Shiner, Ian Fleming, Wally Patch

The George Raft Story
US 1961 105m bw
Allied Artists (Ben Schwab)
GB title: *Spin of a Coin*

In twenties New York, a dancer falls in with gangsters, but eludes them when he goes to Hollywood, where his acting career is harmed by temperament.

Tepid, unconvincing biopic, rather shoddily made but with flashes of interest.

w Crane Wilbur *d* Joseph M. Newman *ph* Carl Guthrie *m* Jeff Alexander

Ray Danton, Julie London, Jayne Mansfield, Frank Gorshin, Neville Brand (as Al Capone)

George Washington Slept Here
US 1942 93m bw
Warner (Jerry Wald)
V*

A New York couple move to a dilapidated country house.

Disappointingly stiff and ill-timed version of a play that should have been a natural.

w Everett Freeman *play* George Kaufman, Moss Hart *d* William Keighley *ph* Ernest Haller *m* Adolph Deutsch *ad* Max Parker, Mark-Lee Kirk

Jack Benny, Ann Sheridan, Percy Kilbride, Charles Coburn, Hattie McDaniel, William Tracy, Lee Patrick, John Emery, Charles Dingle

AAN: art direction

George White's Scandals *
US 1934 79m bw
Fox (Winfield Sheehan)

Romance blossoms backstage during the production of a big musical.

Revue with minimum plot and some impressive numbers.

w Jack Yellen, from the Broadway show directed by George White   d Thornton Freeland, Harry Lachman, George White   ph Lee Garmes, George Schneiderman   m/ly various

George White, Rudy Vallee, Alice Faye, Jimmy Durante, Dixie Dunbar, Adrienne Ames, Cliff Edwards, Gertrude Michael, Gregory Ratoff

George White's 1935 Scandals *
US   1935   83m   bw
Fox (Winfield Sheehan)

A small-town star is discovered by a Broadway producer.

Again, basic plot serves to introduce some pretty good acts.

w Jack Yellen, Patterson McNutt   d George White   ph George Schneiderman   m/ly various

George White, Alice Faye, James Dunn, Eleanor Powell, Ned Sparks, Lyda Roberti, Cliff Edwards, Arline Judge

George White's Scandals *
US   1945   95m   bw
RKO (Jack J. Gross, Nat Holt, George White)
V*

Ex-Scandals girls get together, and one disappears.

Lively comedy-musical with vaudeville orientations.

w Hugh Wedlock, Parke Levy, Howard Green   d Felix E. Feist   ph Robert de Grasse   m Leigh Harline   m/ly various

Joan Davis, Jack Haley, Philip Terry, Martha Holliday, Ethel Smith, Margaret Hamilton, Glenn Tryon, Jane Greer, Fritz Feld, Rufe Davis

Georgia's Friends: see Four Friends

Georgy Girl *
GB   1966   100m   bw
Columbia/Everglades (Otto Plaschkes, Robert A. Goldston)
V, V*, L

An unattractive girl is fancied by her middle-aged employer but escapes to look after the illegitimate baby of her ungrateful friend.

Frantic black farce which seems determined to shock, but has a few good scenes once you get attuned to the mood. A censorship milestone.

w Margaret Forster, Peter Nichols   novel Margaret Forster   d Silvio Narizzano   ph Ken Higgins   m Alexander Faris

James Mason, Lynn Redgrave, Charlotte Rampling, Alan Bates, Bill Owen, Clare Kelly, Rachel Kempson

'Another swinging London story filled with people running through London late at night, dancing madly in the rain, and visiting deserted children's playgrounds to ride on the roundabouts.' – MFB

'So glib, so clever, so determinedly kinky that everything seems to be devalued.' – Pauline Kael

'Its barrage of fashionable tricks proves exhausting.' – Sight and Sound

AAN: Ken Higgins; James Mason; Lynn Redgrave; title song (m Tom Springfield, ly Jim Dale)

Gerald McBoing Boing ***
US   1951   7m   Technicolor
UPA

A small boy becomes famous because he can't speak words: 'he goes boing-boing instead'.

Highly influential cartoon in what was then a new style; told with a light touch which is still extremely funny. Followed less successfully by Gerald McBoing Boing's Symphony and Gerald McBoing Boing On Planet Moo.

w Dr Seuss (Theodore Geisel)   d Robert Cannon   m Gail Kubik   pd John Hubley

AA: best cartoon

The German Sisters *
West Germany   1981   107m   Fujicolor
Bioskop Film/(Eberhard Junkersdorf)
original title: Die Bleierne Zeit

Based on a real-life case, this is a suppositional account of how two well-brought-up girls can develop so differently.

wd Margarethe von Trotta   ph Franz Rath   m Nicolas Economou   ed Dagmar Hirtz

Jutte Lampe, Barbara Sukowa, Rudiger Vogler, Doris Schade, Verenice Rudolph

'Beautifully acted and strikingly shot, it all has a calculated, crowd-pleasing fervour.' – Tom Milne, MFB

Germany Year Zero *
France/Italy   1947   78m   bw
Union Générale Cinématographique/DEFA
V
original title: Germana Anno Zero

Life in post-war Germany is so appalling that a boy kills his father and then himself.

Both realistic and pessimistic, this depressing film has a savage power of its own but totally fails to be constructive.

w Roberto Rossellini, Carlo Lizzani, Max Kolpet   d Roberto Rossellini   ph Robert Juillard   m Renzo Rossellini   ad Piero Filippone   ed Eraldo Da Roma

Edmund Moeschke, Ernst Pittschau, Franz Krüger, Ingetraud Hintze

'Sloppy, over-hasty and careless without even appearing to be informed by sincerity.' – Paul Dehn

'A film of inescapable irony and pity.' – William Whitebait

'Ten thousand red raiders roar into battle!'
Geronimo!
US   1939   89m   bw
Paramount

The seventh cavalry gives the Indians a run for their money.

Muddled Western of no discernible merit.

wd Paul H. Sloane   ph Henry Sharp   m Gerald Carbonara

Ellen Drew, Preston Foster, Andy Devine, Gene Lockhart, Ralph Morgan, William Henry

'Lusty and actionful melodrama geared to hit popular appeal.' – Variety

Geronimo
US   1962   101m   Technicolor   Panavision
UA/Laven-Gardner-Levy
V*

In 1883 Geronimo and his remaining Apaches seek peace but are betrayed.

Moderate Western held back by script and performances.

w Pat Fielder   d Arnold Laven   ph Alex Phillips   m Hugo Friedhofer

Chuck Connors, Ross Martin, Kamala Devi

Gertrud *
Denmark   1966   115m   bw
Pathé Contemporary/Palladium

A lawyer's wife leaves him for an unhappy affair with a young musician.

Austere psychological drama, better to look at than to listen to.

wd Carl Theodor Dreyer   play Hjalmar Soderberg

Nina Pens Rode, Bendt Rothe, Ebbe Rode, Axel Strobye

Gervaise *
France   1956   116m   bw
Agnès Delahaye-Silver Films-CLCC

In 19th-century Paris, a laundrymaid is deserted by her lover, settles with another man and is able to open her own laundry, but they both take to drink.

The French equivalent of David Lean's Dickens films, superbly detailed and wonderful to look at, but with a plot which finally seems worthless and depressing.

w Jean Aurenche, Pierre Bost   novel L'Assommoir by Emile Zola   d René Clément   ph René Juillard   m Georges Auric   ad Paul Bertrand

Maria Schell, François Périer, Suzy Delair, Mathilde Casadeus

'A tremendous tour de force of literal realism . . . a piece for the admiration of technicians, or for those whose consciences are purged and hands kept clean by the vicarious contemplation of how the other half lived – once upon a time.' – David Robinson, MFB

† Other French versions were made in 1902, 1909, 1911 and 1933.

AAN: best foreign film

Gestapo: see Night Train to Munich

Get Back
GB   1991   89m   colour/bw
Entertainment/Allied Filmmakers/Front Page/MPL (Henry Thomas, Philip Knatchbull)

Documentary of a world tour by Paul McCartney and his band.

An extended music video that is a far cry from Lester's exuberant earlier treatment of the Beatles; he and McCartney are obviously older and staider.

d Richard Lester   ph Jordan Cronenweth, Robert Paynter   d John Victor Smith

'Heavy on nostalgia and light on visual zap. Low-tech item will score limited biz in specialized play-off . . . By MTV standards, this is somewhere in a stone age.' – Variety

Get Carter **
GB   1971   112m   Metrocolor
MGM/Mike Klinger
V

A racketeer goes to Newcastle to avenge his brother's death at the hands of gangsters. He kills those responsible but is himself shot by a sniper.

Brutal British crime melodrama with faint echoes of Raymond Chandler. Sex and thuggery unlimited.

wd Mike Hodges   novel Jack's Return Home by Ted Lewis   ph Wolfgang Suschitzky   m Roy Budd

Michael Caine, John Osborne, Ian Hendry, Britt Ekland

'TV on the big screen – more sex, more violence, but no more attention to motivation or plot logic.' – Arthur Knight

'So calculatedly cool and soulless and nastily erotic that it seems to belong to a new era of virtuoso viciousness.' – Pauline Kael

Get Charlie Tully: see Ooh, You Are Awful

Get Cracking *
GB   1942   96m   bw
Columbia (Ben Henry)

George joins the home guard.

Adequate star comedy.

w L. DuGarde Peach   d Marcel Varnel   ph Stephen Dade   md Harry Bidgood

George Formby, Edward Rigby, Frank Pettingell, Dinah Sheridan, Ronald Shiner, Wally Patch, Irene Handl

Get Hep to Love
US   1942   79m   bw
Universal
GB title: She's My Lovely

A child concert prodigy is overworked by a mercenary aunt and goes off alone for a vacation.

Uninspired musical vehicle for young studio talents.

w Jay Dratler, M. M. Musselman   *d* Charles Lamont

Gloria Jean, Donald O'Connor, Peggy Ryan, Jane Frazee, Robert Paige, Nana Bryant, Edith Barrett, Cora Sue Collins

Get Off My Back: see *Synanon*

Get Off My Foot
GB   1935   83m   bw
Warner (Irving Asher)

A Smithfield porter becomes a butler, and later finds himself heir to a fortune.

The nearest Max Miller came to being a genuine film star was in this first of eight Warner comedies, but the screen simply couldn't contain him.

w Frank Launder, Robert Edmunds   *play Money By Wire* by Edward Paulton   *d* William Beaudine   *ph* Basil Emmott   *ad* Peter Proud

Max Miller, Chili Bouchier, Morland Graham, Jane Carr, Norma Varden, Reginald Purdell, Wally Patch

Get Out Your Handkerchiefs **
France   1978   108m   Eastmancolor
Les Films Ariane/CAPAC/Belga/SODEP (Georges Dancigers, Alexandre Minouchkine, Paul Claudon)
V, V*

original title: *Préparez Vos Mouchoirs*

A frigid wife is provided with a handsome lover by her doting husband but finds satisfaction only when she meets a bright 13-year-old boy.

Mildly amusing comedy, helped by some deft performances from the leading actors.

wd Bertrand Blier   *ph* Jean Penzer   *m* Georges Delerue   *ad* Eric Moulard   *ed* Claudine Merlin

Gérard Depardieu, Patrick Dewaere, Carole Laure, Michel Serrault, Eleanore Hirt, Jean Rougerie, Sylvie Jolly, Riton

AA: best foreign film

Get to Know Your Rabbit
US   1972   91m   Technicolor
Warner/Bernhardt-Gaer

A bored businessman enrols in a school of magic.

Whimsical satire which never takes off.

w Jordon Crittenden   *d* Brian DePalma

Tom Smothers, John Astin, Suzanne Zenor, Orson Welles, Samantha Jones, Allen Garfield, Katharine Ross

The Getaway
US   1941   89m   bw
MGM

A lawman goes to jail, gets to know an imprisoned mob leader, and breaks out with him.

Routine rehash of 1935's *Public Hero Number One*.

w Wells Root, W. R. Burnett   *d* Edward Buzzell

Robert Sterling, Dan Dailey, Donna Reed, Charles Winninger, Henry O'Neill

'It takes two to make it. The big two!'
The Getaway **
US   1972   122m   Technicolor   Todd-AO 35
Solar/First Artists (David Foster, Mitchell Brower)
V*

A convict leaves jail and promptly joins his wife in a bank robbery.

Violent, amoral, terse and fast-moving action melodrama which generally holds the interest despite its excesses.

w Walter Hill   *novel* Jim Thompson   *d* Sam Peckinpah   *ph* Lucien Ballard   *m* Quincy Jones

Steve McQueen, Ali MacGraw, Ben Johnson, Sally Struthers, Al Lettieri, Slim Pickens

'This pair have no mission or "meaning". As in all romances, *The Getaway* simply extracts one element of reality and dwells on it. Nor is the violence "American". Pictures like this don't fail overseas.' – *Stanley Kauffmann*

The Getaway *
US   1994   115m   DeLuxe   Panavision
Warner/Largo/JVC (David Foster, Lawrence Turman, John Alan Simon)

A crook, released from jail with the help of a gangster, promises his wife that their next robbery will be their last.

Slick, fast-moving thriller, an involved tale of duplicity and deception, but no improvement on the original and hardly worth re-making.

w Walter Hill, Amy Jones   *novel* Jim Thompson   *d* Roger Donaldson   *ph* Peter Menzies Jnr   *m* Mark Isham   *pd* Joseph Nemec III   *ed* Conrad Buff

Alec Baldwin, Kim Basinger, Michael Madsen, James Woods, David Morse, Jennifer Tilley, James Stephens, Richard Farnsworth

'A pretty good remake of a pretty good action thriller.' – *Variety*

'Like a digitally remastered CD of a Top Forty hit that you never much cared for.' – *Terrence Rafferty, New Yorker*

Getting Gertie's Garter
US   1945   73m   bw
UA (Edward Small)

A businessman tries all manner of wiles to retrieve an incriminating garter.

Silly variation on *Up in Mabel's Room*, with similar team and cast. A few laughs are inevitable.

w Allan Dwan, Karen de Wolf   *play* Wilson Collison, Avery Hopwood   *d* Allan Dwan

Dennis O'Keefe, Marie McDonald, Binnie Barnes, Barry Sullivan, J. Carrol Naish

Getting it Right
US   1989   102m   Fujicolor

A hairdresser becomes involved with three contrasting women.

Mildly amusing, old-fashioned, romp.

w Elizabeth Jane Howard   *novel* Elizabeth Jane Howard   *d* Randal Kleiser   *ph* Clive Tickner   *pd* Caroline Amies   *ad* Frank Walsh   *ed* Chris Kelly

Jesse Birdsall, Helena Bonham Carter, Peter Cook, John Gielgud, Jane Horrocks, Lynn Redgrave, Shirley Ann Field, Pat Heywood, Bryan Pringle, Nan Munro

'A contemporary London romance that vacillates between the relishable and the acutely embarrassing.' – *Kim Newman, MFB*

The Getting of Wisdom **
Australia   1977   101m   Eastmancolor
Southern Cross/AFC/Victorian Film Corporation/9 Television Network (Phillip Adams)
V*

In 1897 a backwoods girl is sent to an exclusive Melbourne ladies' college and eventually wins a music scholarship.

Praiseworthy period piece which thankfully seems to have no axe to grind and is all the better for it.

w Eleanor Witcombe   *novel* Henry Handel Richardson (Ethel Richardson)   *d* Bruce Beresford   *ph* Donald McAlpine   *m* various   *pd* John Stoddart

Susannah Fowle, Sheila Helpman, Patricia Kennedy, John Waters, Barry Humphries, Kerry Armstrong

Getting Straight *
US   1970   125m   Eastmancolor
Columbia/The Organization (Richard Rush)
V*

A political activist returns to college in order to teach and discovers the foolishness of most contemporary attitudes.

Modish comedy, too long, far too pleased with itself, and now irrevocably dated.

w Robert Kaufman   *novel* Ken Kolb   *d* Richard Rush   *ph* Laszlo Kovacs   *m* Ronald Stein

Elliott Gould, Candice Bergen, Robert F. Lyons, Jeff Corey, Max Julien, Cecil Kellaway

Ghare-Baire: see *The Home and the World*

Ghost **
US   1990   127m   Technicolor
UIP/Paramount/Howard W. Koch (Lisa Weinstein)
V, V*, L, S

A murdered stockbroker returns as a ghost to hunt down his killers.

Deftly made, romantic, sentimental, sometimes silly thriller that was the surprise hit of 1990, either because of its fundamentalist view of heaven and hell or its underlying theme that revenge is good for the soul.

w Bruce Joel Rubin   *d* Jerry Zucker   *ph* Adam Greenberg   *pd* Jane Musky   *sp* Industrial Light and Magic   *ed* Walter Murch

Patrick Swayze, Demi Moore, Tony Goldwyn, Whoopi Goldberg, Stanley Lawrence, Christopher J. Keene, Susan Breslau, Martina Degnan

'Amiable entertainment, even for those not looking for reassurances that the afterlife still permits use of the subway.' – *David Robinson, The Times*

AA: Whoopi Goldberg; Bruce Joel Rubin

AAN: best picture; best score; best film editing

The Ghost and Mr Chicken
US   1965   90m   Techniscope
Universal (Edward J. Montagne)

An incompetent small-town reporter finds ghosts in a local murder mansion.

Old-fashioned scare comedy starring a highly resistible comic. A big hit in American small towns.

w James Fritzell, Everett Greenbaum   *d* Alan Rafkin   *ph* William Margulies   *m* Vic Mizzy

Don Knotts, Skip Homeier, Joan Staley, Liam Redmond, Dick Sargent, Reta Shaw

'Doin' what comes supernaturally … it's the man-woman affair that's like nothing on earth!'
The Ghost and Mrs Muir *
US   1947   104m   bw
TCF (Fred Kohlmar)
V*, L

A widow refuses to be frightened away from her seaside home by the ghost of a sea captain, with whom she falls in love.

Charming sentimental fable in Hollywood's best style.

w Philip Dunne   *novel* R. A. Dick   *d* Joseph L. Mankiewicz   *ph* Charles Lang   *m* Bernard Herrmann   *ad* Richard Day, George Davis

Gene Tierney, Rex Harrison, George Sanders, Edna Best, Vanessa Brown, Anna Lee, Robert Coote, Natalie Wood, Isobel Elsom

'A not at all disagreeable piece of whimsy.' – *News Chronicle*

'A jolly caper, gently humorous and often sparkling.' – *New York Times*

† A half-hour TV series followed in 1968.

AAN: Charles Lang

The Ghost and the Guest

US   1943   59m   bw
PRC (Arthur Alexander)

A honeymooning couple find no peace in an eerie country house with hidden ghosts and gangsters.

Predictable, mildly amusing second feature comedy-thriller.

w Morey Amsterdam   *story* Milt Gross   *d* William Nigh

James Dunn, Florence Rice, Mabel Todd, Sam McDaniel, Robert Dudley

The Ghost Breakers ***

US . 1940   85m   bw
Paramount (Arthur Hornblow Jnr)

A girl inherits a West Indian castle and finds herself up to her neck in ghosts, zombies and buried treasure.

Archetypal comedy horror, very well done; a follow-up to the success of *The Cat and the Canary*, and just about as entertaining.

w Paul Dickey, Walter de Leon   *play* Paul Dickey, Charles W. Goddard   *d* George Marshall   *ph* Charles Lang   *m* Ernst Toch   *ad* Hans Dreier

Bob Hope, Paulette Goddard, Paul Lukas, Willie Best, Richard Carlson, Lloyd Corrigan, Anthony Quinn, Noble Johnson, Pedro de Cordoba

'Bob Hope can joke, apparently, even with a risen corpse.' – *MFB*

'Paramount has found the fabled formula for making audiences shriek with laughter and fright at one and the same time.' – *New York Times*

† Previously filmed in 1914 with H. B. Warner; in 1922 with Wallace Reid; and remade in 1953 as *Scared Stiff*.

The Ghost Camera

GB   1933   68m   bw
H & S Films/Real Art (Julius Hagen)

A chemist investigates how a camera containing film of a murder came into his possession.

Mundane, stagey thriller with much talk and little action.

w H. Fowler Mear   *story* Jefferson Farjeon
d Bernard Vorhaus   *ph* Ernest Palmer   *ad* James A. Carter   *ed* David Lean

Ida Lupino, Henry Kendall, John Mills, S. Victor Stanley, George Merrit, Felix Aylmer

Ghost Catchers

US   1944   68m   bw
Universal

A Southern colonel and his beautiful daughters have spooks in their mansion – or bats in the belfry.

Lower-case farce made when the stars' contract was being allowed to run out.

w Edmund L. Hartmann   *story* Milt Gross, Edward Cline   *d* Edward Cline

Ole Olsen, Chic Johnson, Gloria Jean, Leo Carrillo, Martha O'Driscoll, Andy Devine, Lon Chaney Jnr, Walter Catlett, Henry Armetta

Ghost Chase

West Germany   1987   89m   colour
Medusa/Contropolis/pro-ject Film/Hessischer Rundfunk (Dean Heyde)
V

Horror movie-makers summon a ghost to help them find treasure.

Its convoluted plot seems designed to confuse the young audience at which it is presumably aimed, though it misses the target anyway.

w Roland Emmerich, Thomas Kubisch   *story* Roland Emmerich, Oliver Eberle   *d* Roland Emmerich
ph Karl Walter Lindenlaub   *pd* Ekkehard Schroeer,

Sonja B. Zimmer   *sp* Joachim Grueninger, Hubert Bartholomae   *ed* Brigitte Pia Fritsche

Jason Lively, Jill Whitlow, Tim McDaniel, Paul Gleason, Chuck Mitchell, Leonard Lansink, Ian McNaughton, Toby Kaye, Cynthia Frost, Julian Curry

The Ghost Comes Home

US   1940   79m   bw
MGM

The return of a long-lost father causes embarrassment to his family.

Hoary hide-in-the-closet farce with all concerned straining at the leash.

w Richard Maibaum, Harry Ruskin   *d* William Thiele

Frank Morgan, Billie Burke, Ann Rutherford, John Shelton, Reginald Owen, Donald Meek, Nat Pendleton

Ghost Dad

US   1990   84m   DeLuxe
Universal/SAH (Terry Nelson)
V, V*, L

A frantic businessman, killed in a traffic accident, is given three days to sort out his affairs and see that his orphaned children are provided for.

A sentimental comedy dependent on its special effects for laughs; otherwise the jokes are so thin as to be almost invisible.

w Chris Reese, Brent Maddocks, S. S. Wilson
d Sidney Poitier   *ph* Andrew Laszlo   *m* Henry Mancini   *pd* Henry Bumstead   *ed* Pembroke Herring

Bill Cosby, Kimberley Russell, Denise Nicholas, Ian Bannen, Christine Ebersole, Barry Corbin, Salim Grant, Brooke Fontaine

The Ghost Goes West ***

GB   1935   85m   bw
London Films (Alexander Korda)
V, V*

When a millionaire buys a Scottish castle and transports it stone by stone to America, the castle ghost goes too.

Amusing whimsy which is always pleasant but never quite realizes its full potential; fondly remembered for its star performance.

w Robert E. Sherwood, Geoffrey Kerr   *story* Eric Keown   *d* René Clair   *ph* Harold Rosson
m Mischa Spoliansky

Robert Donat, Jean Parker, Eugene Pallette, Elsa Lanchester, Ralph Bunker, Patricia Hilliard, Morton Selten

'Fine business likely in the keys, but not for the tanks.' – *Variety*

'Although the film is not cast in the fluid, rapidly paced style of Clair's typical work, it has a sly wit and an adroitness of manner that make it delightful.' – *André Sennwald, New York Times*

'It is typical of the British film industry that M. René Clair should be brought to this country to direct a Scottish film full of what must to him be rather incomprehensible jokes about whisky and bagpipes, humorous fantasy without any social significance, realistic observation, or genuine satire.' – *Graham Greene*

The Ghost in the Invisible Bikini

US   1966   82m   Pathecolor
American International

A motor cycle gang gets mixed up with a rejuvenated corpse in a haunted mansion.

Mindless beach party stuff suffering under one of Hollywood's most inane titles.

w Louis M. Heyward, Elwood Ullman   *d* Don Weis

Boris Karloff, Basil Rathbone, Patsy Kelly, Tommy Kirk, Deborah Walley, Aron Kincaid, Quinn O'Hara, Jesse White

'You can't keep a good monster down!'
The Ghost of Frankenstein

US   1942   67m   bw
Universal (George Waggner)

Frankenstein's second son implants evil shepherd Igor's brain into the monster.

The rot set in with this flatly-handled potboiler, which had none of the literary mood or cinematic interest of *Bride* or *Son* which preceded it, and suffered from a particularly idiotic script.

w W. Scott Darling   *story* Eric Taylor   *d* Erle C. Kenton   *ph* Milton Krasner, Woody Bredell
md Hans J. Salter   *m* Charles Previn

Cedric Hardwicke, Lon Chaney Jnr (as the monster), Bela Lugosi, Lionel Atwill, Evelyn Ankers, Ralph Bellamy

† See *Frankenstein* for other episodes in the series.

The Ghost of St Michael's **

GB   1941   82m   bw
Ealing (Basil Dearden)

A school is evacuated to the Isle of Skye, and the local ghost turns out to be an enemy agent.

The star's schoolmaster character is here at its seedy best, and he is well supported in a comedy-thriller plot.

w Angus Macphail, John Dighton   *d* Marcel Varnel
ph Derek Williams

Will Hay, Claude Hulbert, Felix Aylmer, Raymond Huntley, Elliot Mason, Charles Hawtrey, John Laurie, Hay Petrie, Roddy Hughes, Manning Whiley

Ghost of Zorro *

US   1949   bw   serial: 12 eps
Republic

A survey engineer out west dons a mask in order to crusade against an outlaw empire.

Well-mounted serial typical of the genre's later days.

d Fred C. Brannon

Clayton Moore, Pamela Blake, Roy Barcroft, George J. Lewis, Gene Roth

The Ghost Ship

US   1943   69m   bw
RKO (Val Lewton)

The captain of a merchant ship is driven mad by isolation.

Long unavailable because of legal problems, this very minor Val Lewton thriller inevitably disappoints because it has no supernatural elements and must compare unfavourably with both *The Caine Mutiny* and *The Sea Wolf*, which plotwise it closely resembles.

w Donald Henderson Clarke   *d* Mark Robson
ph Nicholas Musuraca   *m* Roy Webb

Richard Dix, Russell Wade, Edith Barrett, Ben Bard, Edmund Glover, Skelton Knaggs

The Ghost Ship

GB   1952   74m   bw
Anglo Amalgamated
V*

A motor yacht proves to be haunted by the previous owner's murdered wife.

Mildly unusual second feature.

wd Vernon Sewell

Dermot Walsh, Hazel Court, Hugh Burden, John Robinson

'She'll never rest till her tale is told!'

Ghost Story *
GB 1974 89m Fujicolor
Stephen Weeks
V*

Former college acquaintances spend a weekend at a country house, and one of them is drawn into tragic events of forty years before.

Overlong chiller, ingeniously shot in India but very variably acted; aims for the M. R. James style and sometimes achieves it, but badly needs cutting.

w Rosemary Sutcliff, Stephen Weeks d Stephen Weeks ph Peter Hurst m Ron Geesin

Murray Melvin, Larry Dann, Vivian Mackerall, Marianne Faithfull, Anthony Bate, Leigh Lawson, Barbara Shelley

Ghost Story
US 1981 110m Technicolor
Universal (Ronald G. Smith)
V*, L, S

Four old men tell each other ghost stories, but are haunted by a guilty secret of their own.

Bizarre vehicle for four welcome old actors, ruined by the director's insistence on frequent shock cuts to the rotting spectre. A subtler treatment akin to that of The Uninvited might have produced a little masterpiece.

w Lawrence D. Cohen novel Peter Straub d John Irvin ph Jack Cardiff m Philippe Sarde

Fred Astaire, Melvyn Douglas, John Houseman, Douglas Fairbanks Jnr, Craig Wasson, Patricia Neal, Alice Krige, Jacqueline Brookes

The Ghost That Never Returns *
USSR 1929 80m approx (24 fps) bw silent
Sovkino
original title: Prividenie, Kotoroe ne Vozvrashchaetsya

After ten years' imprisonment for leading a strike, a South American worker is given a day's leave which may result in his death.

Unsatisfactory communist propaganda of its time, probably rescued from obscurity by its title. A few strikingly visual moments stand out, but the narrative is needlessly obscure.

w Valentin Turkin story Henri Barbusse d Abram Room ph Dmitri Feldman

B. Ferdinandov, Olga Zhizneva, Maxime Straukh

The Ghost That Walks Alone
US 1943 63m bw
Columbia

Honeymooners find a dead radio producer in their suite.

Ho-hum second feature mystery.

w Doris Shattuck, Clarence Upson Young d Lew Landers

Arthur Lake, Janis Carter, Frank Sully, Lynne Roberts

Ghost Town
US 1956 72m bw
Bel Air/UA

Stagecoach passengers are forced to spend the night in a ghost town beset by Indians.

Thin Western second with a few effectively restrained moments.

w Jameson Brewer d Allen Miner

Kent Taylor, John Smith, Marian Carr, John Doucette

The Ghost Train **
GB 1931 72m bw
Gainsborough (Michael Balcon)

Passengers stranded at a haunted station in Cornwall include a detective posing as a silly ass in order to trap smugglers.

Excellent early sound version of a comedy-thriller play which has not only been among the most commercially successful ever written but also provided the basic plot for many another comedy: Oh Mr Porter, The Ghost of St Michael's, Back Room Boy, Hold That Ghost, etc. Previously filmed as a silent in 1927, with Guy Newall.

w Angus Macphail, Lajos Biro play Arnold Ridley d Walter Forde ph Leslie Rowson ad Walter Murton ed Ian Dalrymple

Jack Hulbert, Cicely Courtneidge, Donald Calthrop, Ann Todd, Cyril Raymond, Angela Baddeley, Allan Jeayes

The Ghost Train *
GB 1941 85m bw
Gainsborough (Edward Black)

Adequate remake with the lead split into two characters, which doesn't work quite so well.

w Marriott Edgar, Val Guest, J. O. C. Orton d Walter Forde ph Jack Cox

Arthur Askey, Richard Murdoch, Kathleen Harrison, Morland Graham, Linden Travers, Peter Murray Hill, Herbert Lomas

The Ghost Walks
US 1934 70m bw
Chesterfield

A hired 'ghost' engaged for a party is scared off by a real one.

Cheeseparing spooky house comedy-thriller.

w Edward T. Lowe d Frank Strayer

John Miljan, June Collyer, Richard Carle

'Above the indie norm all round.' – Variety

Ghostbusters *
US 1984 105m Metrocolor Panavision
Columbia/Delphi (Ivan Reitman)
V, V*, L, S

Unemployed academic parapsychologists set themselves up as ghostbusters and destroy several monstrous apparitions on the streets of New York.

Crude farce with expensive special effects. It took more money – millions more – than Indiana Jones and the Temple of Doom, which must say something about the age we live in.

w Dan Aykroyd, Harold Ramis d Ivan Reitman ph Laszlo Kovacs, Herb Wagreitch m Elmer Bernstein pd John DeCuir ed Sheldon Kahn, David Blewitt

Bill Murray, Dan Aykroyd, Harold Ramis, Sigourney Weaver, Rick Moranis, Annie Potts, William Atherton

AAN: title song (m/ly Ray Parker)

Ghostbusters II
US 1989 108m DeLuxe Panavision
Columbia TriStar (Ivan Reitman)
V, V*, L

The disbanded Ghostbusters reform to deal with supernatural threats to New York.

Rambling, disjointed sequel of little amusement.

w Harold Ramis, Dan Aykroyd d Ivan Reitman ph Michael Chapman m Randy Edelman pd Bo Welch ed Sheldon Kahn, Donn Cambern

Bill Murray, Dan Aykroyd, Sigourney Weaver, Harold Ramis, Rick Moranis, Ernie Hudson, Annie Potts, Peter MacNichol, Harris Yulin, David Margulies

The Ghosts of Berkeley Square *
GB 1947 89m bw
British National (Louis H. Jackson)

Two 18th-century ghosts are doomed to haunt a London house until royalty visits.

Thin, skittish whimsy with pleasant moments.

w James Seymour novel No Nightingales by S. J. Simon, Caryl Brahms d Vernon Sewell ph Ernest Palmer

Robert Morley, Claude Hulbert, Felix Aylmer, Yvonne Arnaud, Abraham Sofaer, Ernest Thesiger, Marie Lohr, Martita Hunt, A. E. Matthews, John Longden, Ronald Frankau, Wilfrid Hyde-White, Esmé Percy, Mary Jerrold, Wally Patch, Martin Miller

Ghosts . . . of the Civil Dead
Australia 1988 93m colour
Electric/Correctional Services/Outlaw Values (Evan English)
V

Prisoners react violently against a repressive regime.

A confused narrative weakens a brutal drama, filmed in a documentary style.

w Gene Conkie, John Hillcoat, Evan English, Nick Cave, Hugo Race d John Hillcoat ph Paul Goldman, Graham Wood m Nick Cave, Mick Harvey, Blixa Bargeld pd Chris Kennedy ed Stewart Young

Dave Field, Mike Bishop, Chris de Rose, Nick Cave, Freddo Dierck, Vincent Gil, Bogdan Koca, Kevin Mackey, Dave Mason

The Ghoul **
GB 1933 79m bw
Gaumont (Michael Balcon)
V*

An Egyptologist returns from the tomb to uncover stolen jewels and a murderer.

Fascinating minor horror piece reminiscent of The Old Dark House, with many effective moments and a ripe cast.

w Frank King, Leonard Hines, L. DuGarde Peach, Roland Pertwee, John Hastings Turner, Rupert Downing novel Frank King d T. Hayes Hunter ph Gunther Krampf makeup Heinrich Heitfeld

Boris Karloff, Cedric Hardwicke, Ralph Richardson, Kathleen Harrison, Ernest Thesiger, Dorothy Hyson, Anthony Bushell, D. A. Clarke-Smith

'Lacks general US appeal because of bad plot mechanics, mostly bad acting, and colourless camerawork.' – Variety

† Remade after a fashion as What A Carve Up (1962).

The Ghoul
GB 1975 87m Eastmancolor
Tyburn (Kevin Francis)
V*

In the twenties, a group of stranded travellers is reduced in number when they take shelter in the house of a former clergyman.

The build-up is too slow, the revelation too nasty, and the whole thing is a shameless rip-off of the structure of Psycho.

w John Elder d Freddie Francis ph John Wilcox m Harry Robinson

Peter Cushing, Alexandra Bastedo, John Hurt, Gwen Watford, Veronica Carlson, Don Henderson

'Peter Cushing brings out his violin for a soothing spot of the classics, the local copper mutters veiled warnings before trundling off on his bike, and thick fog swirls round the exterior sets at the drop of a canister.' – Geoff Brown

Ghoulies
US 1985 88m colour
Empire (Jeffrey Levy)
V, V*

After a youth invokes a Satanic ritual, vicious imp-like creatures are loosed on the world.

Cheap and nasty rip-off of Gremlins, lacking wit and style and even failing at slapstick comedy.

w Luca Bercovici, Jeffrey Levy   *d* Luca Bercovici
ph Mac Ahlberg   *m* Richard Band, Shirley Walker

Peter Liapis, Lisa Pelikan, Michael Des Barres, Jack
Nance, Peter Risch, Tamara de Treaux

It was followed by *Ghoulies 2*, directed by Albert
Band, in 1988, and *Ghoulies 3: Ghoulies Go to College*,
directed by John Carl Buechler, in 1991, both
conforming to the usual law of diminishing returns.
Both were also released direct to video.

Giant **
US   1956   197m   Warnercolor
Warner (George Stevens, Henry Ginsburg)
V, V*, L

The life of a Texas cattle rancher through two
generations.

Sprawling, overlong family saga with unconvincing
acting but good visual style.

w Fred Guiol, Ivan Moffat   *novel* Edna Ferber
d George Stevens   *ph* William C. Mellor, Edwin DuPar
m Dimitri Tiomkin   *ad* Boris Leven   *ed* William
Hornbéck, Philip W. Anderson, Fred Bohanan

Rock Hudson, Elizabeth Taylor, James Dean,
Mercedes McCambridge, Carroll Baker, Chill Wills,
Jane Withers, Dennis Hopper, Sal Mineo, Rod Taylor,
Judith Evelyn, Earl Holliman, Alexander Scourby,
Paul Fix

AA: George Stevens

AAN: best picture; script; Dimitri Tiomkin; Rock
Hudson; James Dean; Mercedes McCambridge; art
direction; editing

The Giant Behemoth
GB   1959   70m   bw
Artistes Alliance/Stratford
aka: *Behemoth the Sea Monster*

A radioactive palaeosaurus menaces London.

Underfed monster, undercast melodramatics.

w Eugene Lourie   *d* Eugene Lourie, Douglas Hickox

Gene Evans, André Morell, Leigh Madison, John
Turner, Jack MacGowran

The Giant Claw
US   1957   71m   bw
Clover (Sam Katzman)
V*

A monstrous bird threatens New York.

Incompetent horror item: the bird is mostly talons and
sound track.

w Samuel Newman, Paul Gangelin   *d* Fred F. Sears

Jeff Morrow, Mara Corday, Morris Ankrum

The Giant Spider Invasion
US   1975   76m   Eastmancolor
Hemdale/Transcentury/Cinema Group 75 (Bill Rebane, Richard
L. Huff)
V*

Nuclear fall-out causes giant spiders to breed and go
on the rampage.

Thinly scripted reprise of one of those small-town
horror thrillers of the fifties.

w Richard L. Huff, Robert Easton   *d* Bill Rebane

Barbara Hale, Steve Brodie, Leslie Parrish, Alan Hale

Gideon of Scotland Yard: see *Gideon's Day*

Gideon's Day *
GB   1958   91m   Technicolor
Columbia/John Ford (Michael Killanin)
US title: *Gideon of Scotland Yard*

A Scotland Yard Inspector has an eventful but
frustrating day.

Pleasant, ordinary little TV style police yarn showing
no evidence of its director's particular talents.

w T. E. B. Clarke   *novel* John Creasey   *d* John Ford
ph Frederick A. Young   *m* Douglas Gamley
ad Ken Adam

Jack Hawkins, Dianne Foster, Anna Lee, Andrew
Ray, Anna Massey, Frank Lawton, John Loder, Cyril
Cusack

Gidget
US   1959   95m   Eastmancolor   Cinemascope
Columbia (Lewis J. Rachmil)
V*, L

A 16-year-old girl falls for a surfer; her parents
disapprove until he turns out to be the son of their
best friend.

Commercial mixture of domestic comedy and beach
athletics, for nice teenagers and their moms and pops.

w Gabrielle Upton   *novel* Frederick Kohner   *d* Paul
Wendkos   *ph* Burnett Guffey   *md* Morris Stoloff
m George Duning

Sandra Dee, Cliff Robertson, James Darren, Arthur
O'Connell

† Sequels include *Gidget Goes Hawaiian* (V*, 1961) with
Deborah Walley; *Gidget Goes to Rome* (V*, 1962) with
Cindy Carol; and two TV movies.

The Gift Horse *
GB   1952   100m   bw
British Lion/Molton (George Pitcher)
US title: *Glory at Sea*

In 1940 an old US destroyer is given to Britain, and an
officer reluctantly takes charge of it.

Conventional, popular seafaring war adventure.

w William Fairchild, Hugh Hastings, William Rose
d Compton Bennett   *ph* Harry Waxman   *m* Clifton
Parker

Trevor Howard, Richard Attenborough, Sonny Tufts,
James Donald, Joan Rice, Bernard Lee, Dora Bryan,
Hugh Williams, Robin Bailey

The Gift of Gab
US   1934   71m   bw
Universal

A conceited radio announcer gets his comeuppance.

Odd little comedy drama notable only for its long list
of stars making cameo appearances.

w Rian James, Lou Breslow   *d* Karl Freund
m Albert von Tilzer, Con Conrad, Charles Tobias

Edmund Lowe, Gloria Stuart, Ruth Etting, Phil Baker,
Alexander Woollcott, Ethel Waters, Victor Moore,
Boris Karloff, Bela Lugosi, Paul Lukas, Chester
Morris, Binnie Barnes, Douglass Montgomery, Wini
Shaw

'A hodge-podge, an elongated short.' – *Variety*

The Gift of Love
US   1958   105m   Eastmancolor   Cinemascope
TCF (Charles Brackett)

A dying wife adopts an orphan girl so that her
husband will not be lonely.

Incredibly cloying and miscast remake of *Sentimental
Journey* (qv).

w Luther Davis   *d* Jean Negulesco   *ph* Milton
Krasner   *m* Cyril Mockridge

Lauren Bacall, Robert Stack, Evelyn Rudie, Lorne
Greene

Gigi *
France   1948   109m   bw
Codo Cinema (Claude Dolbert)

In Paris in the 1890s, a young girl is trained by her
aunt to be a cocotte, but when married off to a rake
she reforms him.

Charming, overlong, non-musical version of a famous
story, chiefly memorable for its local colour.

w Pierre Laroche   *novel* Colette   *d* Jacqueline Audry
ph Gérard Perrin   *m* Marcel Landowski

Daniele Delorme, Gaby Morlay, Yvonne de Bray, Frank
Villard, Jean Tissier, Madeleine Rousset

Gigi ***
US   1958   119m   Metrocolor   Cinemascope
MGM (Arthur Freed)
V, V*, L, S

Laundered and musicalized version; delightfully set,
costumed and performed, but oddly lacking dance
numbers.

w Alan Jay Lerner   *d* Vincente Minnelli   *ph* Joseph
Ruttenberg   *md* André Previn   *pd/cos* Cecil Beaton
m/ly Frederick Loewe, Alan Jay Lerner   *ed* Adrienne
Fazan

*Leslie Caron, Louis Jourdan, Maurice Chevalier, Hermione
Gingold,* Isabel Jeans, Jacques Bergerac, Eva Gabor,
John Abbott

'It has the sureness expected when a group of the
most sophisticated talents are able to work together
on material entirely suited to them.' – *Penelope Houston*

AA: best picture; Alan Jay Lerner; Vincente Minnelli;
Joseph Ruttenberg; André Previn; Cecil Beaton;
editing; Preston Ames and William A. Horning (art
directors); title song; Maurice Chevalier (special
award)

Gigot
US   1962   104m   DeLuxe
TCF/Seven Arts (Kenneth Hyman)

The mute caretaker of a Montmartre boarding house
looks after an ailing prostitute and her child.

From Paris, Hollywood, comes a grotesque piece of
self-indulgence, the arch example of the clown who
wanted to play Hamlet. Plotless, mawkish and wholly
unfunny.

w John Patrick, Jackie Gleason   *d* Gene Kelly
ph Jean Bourgoin   *md* Michael Magne   *m* Jackie
Gleason   *ad* Auguste Capelier

Jackie Gleason, Katherine Kath, Gabrielle Dorziat,
Jean Lefebvre, Jacques Marin

'Chaplinesque pretensions have proved fatal before to
artists who will not accept their own limitations.' –
Gavin Lambert

AAN: Michael Magne

'There never was a woman like Gilda!'
Gilda ***
US   1946   110m   bw
Columbia (Virginia Van Upp)
V, V*, L

A gambler in a South American city resumes a love-
hate relationship with an old flame . . . but she is now
married to his dangerous new boss.

Archetypal Hollywood *film noir*, wholly studio-bound
and the better for it, with dialogue that would seem
risible if it did not happen to be dealt with in this
style and with these actors, who keep the mood
balanced between suspense and absurdity.

w Marion Parsonnet   *story* E. A. Ellington   *d* Charles
Vidor   *ph* Rudolph Maté   *md* Morris Stoloff, Marlin
Skiles   *m* Hugo Friedhofer

Rita Hayworth, Glenn Ford, George Macready, Steve Geray,
Joseph Calleia, Joe Sawyer, Gerald Mohr, Ludwig
Donath

'From a quietly promising opening the film settles
into an intractable obscurity of narrative through
which as in a fog three characters bite off at each other
words of hate.' – *Richard Winnington*

The Gilded Cage
GB   1955   72m   bw
Tempean/Eros (Robert S. Baker, Monty Berman)

In London a US airforce officer hunts for the killer of
his brother's girlfriend.

Routine thriller, slow and predictable.

w Brock Williams story Paul Erickson d John Gilling ph Monty Berman md Stanley Black ad Wilfred Arnold ed Jim Connock

Alex Nichol, Veronica Hurst, Clifford Evans, Ursula Howells, Elwyn Brook-Jones, John Stuart

'He fed her popcorn and kisses on a park bench!'
The Gilded Lily *
US 1935 85m bw
Paramount (Albert Lewis)

A poor stenographer who meets her reporter boyfriend on a park bench is wooed by a British peer.

Good depression era romantic comedy with the heroine inevitably choosing poverty.

w Claude Binyon d Wesley Ruggles ph Victor Milner

Claudette Colbert, Fred MacMurray, Ray Milland, C. Aubrey Smith, Luis Alberni, Donald Meek

'Breezy romance . . . should carry box-office draught.'
– Variety

'Altamont changed a lot of people's heads.'
Gimme Shelter ***
US 1970 90m colour
Cinema 5 (Ronald Schneider)
V*

Documentary of the Rolling Stones' free concert at Altamont Speedway in December 1969, when a member of the audience was killed by Hell's Angels who had been hired as security for the event.

An excellently photographed concert film that unexpectedly turned out to be the obverse of Woodstock, revealing the darker side of rock and the revolutionary fervour that once accompanied it.

d Albert Maysles, David Maysles, Charlotte Zwerin

The Rolling Stones, Ike and Tina Turner, Jefferson Airplane, The Flying Burrito Brothers

Ginger and Fred ***
Italy/France/West Germany 1986 126m colour
PEA/Revcom/Stella/RAI (Alberto Grimaldi)
V*, S

An ageing pair of dancers is brought out of retirement to appear on a TV show.

Melancholy comedy with resonances, chiefly taking the side of age against youth, with 'Fred' as an image of Fellini himself.

w Federico Fellini, Tonino Guerra, Tullio Pinelli d Federico Fellini ph Tonino Delli Colli, Ennio Guarnieri m Nicola Piovani pd Dante Ferretti

Giulietta Masina, Marcello Mastroianni, Franco Fabrizi, Frederick von Ledenberg

The Gipsy: see Le Gitan

A Girl, a Guy and a Gob
US 1941 91m bw
RKO/Harold Lloyd
V*
GB title: The Navy Steps Out

A secretary and her sailor boyfriend teach her stuffy boss how to enjoy life.

Did producer Lloyd intend himself for the role played by O'Brien? If so, he would have needed a stronger script to prevent this Capraesque comedy from falling flat.

w Frank Ryan, Bert Granet d Richard Wallace ph Russell Metty m Roy Webb

Lucille Ball, Edmond O'Brien, George Murphy, George Cleveland, Henry Travers, Franklin Pangborn, Marguerite Churchill, Lloyd Corrigan

The Girl and the General
Italy/France 1967 113m. Technicolor
MGM/Champion/Corcordia (Carlo Ponti)

During World War I, a captured Austrian general escapes with a girl partisan.

Turgid war epic veering from melodrama to comedy.

w Luigi Malerba, Pasquale Festa Campanile d Pasquale Festa Campanile ph Ennio Guarnieri m Ennio Morricone

Rod Steiger, Virna Lisi, Umberto Orsini

The Girl Can't Help It *
US 1956 97m Eastmancolor Cinemascope
TCF (Frank Tashlin)
V, V*, L, S

A theatrical agent grooms a gangster's dumb girlfriend for stardom.

Scatty, garish pop scene spoof with a plot borrowed from Born Yesterday and a lot of jokes about its new star's superstructure. Some scenes are funny, and it puts the first rock and roll stars in pickle for all time.

w Frank Tashlin, Herbert Baker story Do Re Mi by Garson Kanin d Frank Tashlin ph Leon Shamroy md Lionel Newman

Jayne Mansfield, Tom Ewell, Edmond O'Brien, Henry Jones, John Emery; and Julie London, Ray Anthony, Fats Domino, Little Richard, The Platters

Girl Crazy
US 1932 75m bw
RKO

Romance at a desert college.

Early talkie version of the musical comedy (see below), here redesigned as a weak vehicle for two comedy stars.

w Tim Whelan, Herman J. Mankiewicz d William A. Seiter

Bert Wheeler, Robert Woolsey, Eddie Quillan, Dorothy Lee, Mitzi Green, Arline Judge

'A weak sister . . . after a while it all becomes too silly.' – Variety

Girl Crazy *
US 1943 99m bw
MGM (Arthur Freed)
V*, L
aka: When the Girls Meet the Boys

Romance at a desert college.

Predictable star musical with good tunes.

w Fred F. Finklehoffe play Guy Bolton, Jack McGowan d Norman Taurog ph William Daniels, Robert Planck md Georgie Stoll m/ly George and Ira Gershwin

Judy Garland, Mickey Rooney, Guy Kibbee, Gil Stratton, Robert E. Strickland, Rags Ragland, June Allyson, Nancy Walker, Tommy Dorsey and his band

† Busby Berkeley was replaced as director during filming. Remade 1965 as When the Boys Meet the Girls.

The Girl Downstairs
US 1938 77m bw
MGM

A rich bachelor in Europe chooses the maid instead of the mistress.

Feeble rewrite of Cinderella.

w Harold Goldman, Felix Jackson, Karl Noti d Norman Taurog

Franchot Tone, Franciska Gaal, Walter Connolly, Rita Johnson, Reginald Owen, Reginald Gardiner, Franklin Pangborn, Robert Coote

'Keen direction and fine performances highlight moderate programmer.' – Variety

The Girl Friend
US 1935 67m bw
Columbia

An actor and two songwriters become rural con men.

Thin comedy with music.

w Gertrude Purcell, Benny Rubin d Eddie Buzzell

Ann Sothern, Jack Haley, Roger Pryor, Thurston Hall, Victor Kilian

'Enough hoke to make it a welcome laugh picture for lesser towns.' – Variety

The Girl Friends: see Le Amiche

The Girl from Avenue A
US 1940 73m bw
Sol M. Wurtzel/TCF

A slum brat is picked up by an author, who takes her home to use for reference.

Pygmalion did this far better, but the star was adolescent and the studio didn't know what else to do with her.

w Frances Hyland play The Brat by Maude Fulton d Otto Brower

Jane Withers, Kent Taylor, Katharine Aldridge, Elyse Knox, Laura Hope Crews, Jessie Ralph, Harry Shannon, Ann Shoemaker

The Girl from Jones Beach
US 1949 78m bw
Warner

A commercial artist meets a schoolteacher who is the real-life counterpart of his 'perfect girl'.

Predictable comedy with only the dimmest professional sparkle.

w I. A. L. Diamond d Peter Godfrey

Ronald Reagan, Virginia Mayo, Eddie Bracken, Dona Drake, Henry Travers, Florence Bates

A Girl from Lorraine
France 1980 112m colour
Gala/Phoenix/Gaumont/FR3/SSR (Yves Peyrot, Raymond Pousaz)
aka: La Provinciale

A woman from the country finds heartbreak in Paris.

Over-solemn in its determination to discover the disillusion of city life.

w Claude Goretta, Jacques Kirsner, Rosina Rochette d Claude Goretta ph Philippe Rousselot m Arié Dzierlatka ad Jacques Bufnoir ed Joele Van Effenterre

Nathalie Baye, Angela Winkler, Bruno Ganz, Pierre Vernier, Patrick Chesnais, Dominique Paturel, Roland Monod

The Girl from Manhattan
US 1948 81m bw
UA/Benedict Bogeaus

A model returns home to help her uncle with his mortgaged boarding house.

Mouldy comedy-drama full of kind thoughts, charming failures and worldly priests. Interesting for cast.

w Howard Estabrook d Alfred E. Green ph Ernest Laszlo md David Chudnow m Heinz Roemheld

Dorothy Lamour, Charles Laughton, George Montgomery, Ernest Truex, Hugh Herbert, Constance Collier, Sara Allgood, Frank Orth, Howard Freeman, Adeline de Walt Reynolds, George Chandler, Maurice Cass

The Girl from Maxim's
GB 1933 79m bw
UA/London Films (Alexander Korda, Ludovico Toeplitz)

Circumstances force a doctor to pass off a singer as his wife.

Tolerable period farce.

w Arthur Wimperis, Harry Graham *play* Georges Feydeau *d* Alexander Korda *ph* Georges Périnal *m* Kurt Schroeder *ad* Vincent Korda *ed* Harold Young, R. Bettinson

Leslie Henson, Frances Day, George Grossmith, Lady Tree, Stanley Holloway

† A French version, not released until 1934, was made simultaneously with a French cast in the leading roles; Odette Florelle replaced Frances Day and André Lefaur took the part played by Leslie Henson.

The Girl from Mexico: see *Mexican Spitfire*

The Girl from Missouri *
US   1934   75m   bw
MGM (Bernard H. Hyman)
V*
aka: *100% Pure*
original titles: *Born to be Kissed; Eadie was a Lady*

A chorus girl determines to remain virtuous until the right millionaire comes along.

Smart, amusing comedy very typical of its period.

w Anita Loos, *John Emerson* *d* Jack Conway *ph* Ray June *m* William Axt

Jean Harlow, Franchot Tone, Lionel Barrymore, Lewis Stone, Patsy Kelly, Alan Mowbray, Clara Blandick, Henry Kolker

'It's going to be in the money . . . one that plenty of purity crusaders will see and like.' – *Variety*

'Noisily defiant, rip-roaring and raucous in spots . . . fast and furious adult fare.' – *Photoplay*

The Girl from Petrovka
US   1974   103m   Technicolor
Universal/Richard Zanuck, David Brown
V*

An American correspondent in Moscow falls for a Russian girl.

Lugubrious and lethargic romantic comedy-drama.

w Allan Scott, Chris Bryant *d* Robert Ellis Miller *m* Henry Mancini

Goldie Hawn, Hal Holbrook. Anthony Hopkins, Grégoire Aslan, Anton Dolin

The Girl from Scotland Yard
US   1937   61m   bw
Paramount

A female agent tracks down the cause of mysterious explosions.

Lacklustre second feature.

w Doris Anderson, Dore Schary *d* Robert Vignola

Karen Morley, Robert Baldwin, Katherine Alexander, Eduardo Ciannelli

'Weak thriller . . . only for the back seat in duals.' – *Variety*

The Girl from Tenth Avenue
US   1935   69m   bw
Warner (Robert Lord)
GB title: *Men on Her Mind*

A jilted attorney drowns his sorrows and marries on the rebound.

Watchable 'woman's picture'.

w Charles Kenyon *play* Hubert Henry Davies *d* Alfred E. Green *m* James Van Trees

Bette Davis, Ian Hunter, Colin Clive, Alison Skipworth, Katherine Alexander, John Eldredge, Philip Reed

'Bette Davis' first starring venture . . . she should pull the picture through to good returns.' – *Variety*

The Girl-Getters: see *The System (GB)*

The Girl Habit
US   1931   77m   bw
Paramount

A mild Lothario tries to get arrested as protection from the gangster husband who has threatened him.

Easy-going farce which established Ruggles in Hollywood.

w Owen Davis, Gertrude Purcell *play* A. E. Thomas, Clayton Hamilton *d* Eddie Cline

Charles Ruggles, Tamara Geva, Margaret Dumont, Allen Jenkins, Donald Meek, Sue Conroy

'Hardly a dynamic b.o. prospect but nice entertainment.' – *Variety*

Girl Happy
US   1965   96m   Metrocolor   Panavision
MGM/Euterpe (Joe Pasternak)
V, V*

A pop singer in Florida is forced to chaperone a group of college girls including a gangster's daughter.

Standard star vehicle, quite professionally made and totally forgettable.

w Harvey Bullock, R. S. Allen *d* Boris Sagal *ph* Philip Lathrop *m* George Stoll

Elvis Presley, Harold J. Stone, Shelley Fabares, Gary Crosby, Nita Talbot

The Girl He Left Behind
US   1956   103m   bw
Warner (Frank P. Rosenberg)

The army makes a man of a spoiled youth.

Platitudinous recruiting comedy for dim American teenagers.

w Guy Trosper *book* Marion Hargrove *d* David Butler *ph* Ted McCord *m* Roy Webb

Tab Hunter, Natalie Wood, Jessie Royce Landis, Jim Backus, Henry Jones, Murray Hamilton, Alan King, James Garner, David Janssen

The Girl Hunters
GB   1963   100m   bw   Panavision
Present Day (Robert Fellows)
V*

Private eye Mike Hammer solves a few murders plus the disappearance of his own ex-secretary.

Comic strip thuggery with the author playing his own slouchy hero; the general incompetence gives this cheap production an air of Kafkaesque menace.

w Mickey Spillane, Roy Rowland, Robert Fellows *d* Roy Rowland *ph* Ken Talbot *m* Phil Green

Mickey Spillane, Shirley Eaton, Lloyd Nolan

Girl in a Boot
West Germany   1983   96m   colour
Cannon/Cinecom/Neue Filmproduktion/Sender Freies (Axel Bar, Franz Thies)
aka: *Einmal Ku'damm Und Zurück*

An East Berlin woman falls in love with a Swiss cook but opts to stay her side of the Wall.

Soberly shot romance which has dated more than somewhat.

w Jurgen Engert *d* Herbert Ballman *ph* Ingo Hamer *m* Jurgen Knieper *ed* Hans Otto Kruger, Ruth Kusche

Ursula Monn, Christian Kohlund, Evelyn Meyka, Peter Schiff

A Girl in a Million
GB   1946   90m   bw
Boca/British Lion

Having divorced a nagging wife, a chemist marries a dumb girl, but when he cures her . . .

Thin comedy which must have seemed funnier on the page than it does on the screen.

w Muriel and Sydney Box *d* Francis Searle

Joan Greenwood, Hugh Williams, Basil Radford, Naunton Wayne, Wylie Watson, Yvonne Owen

The Girl in Black
Greece   1955   93m   bw
Hermes
original title: *To Koritsi me ta Mavra*

A writer holidaying on a remote fishing island causes tension and tragedy when he falls for a local maiden.

Watchable mood piece benefiting from its star female performance.

wd Michael Cacoyannis *ph* Walter Lassally *m* Argyris Kounadis, Manos Hadji Bredkis

Elle Lambetti, George Foundas, Dimitri Horna

The Girl in Black Stockings
US   1957   71m   bw
Bel Air/UA

Suspects abound when a young woman is killed in a Utah hotel.

Tolerable murder mystery.

w Richard Landau *story* Wanton Murder by Peter Godfrey *d* Howard W. Koch

Anne Bancroft, Lex Barker, Mamie Van Doren, John Dehner, Ron Randell, Marie Windsor

Girl in Distress: see *Jeannie*

A Girl in Every Port *
US   1928   62m (24 fps)   bw   silent
Fox

Two sailors brawl over women.

Adventure comedy with themes typical of its director.

w Seton Miller, James K. McGuinness *story* Howard Hawks *d* Howard Hawks *ph* R. J. Berquist, L. William O'Connel*led* Ralph Dixon

Victor McLaglen, Robert Armstrong, Natalie Joyce, Dorothy Matthews, Maria Casajuana, Louise Brooks, Francis McDonald

'Brief and essentially anecdotal, it now looks more than anything else like a preliminary sketch for concerns which Hawks would later elaborate.' – *Tim Pulleine, MFB*

A Girl in Every Port
US   1951   87m   bw
RKO (Irwin Allen, Irving Cummings Jnr)
V*, L

Two accident-prone sailors have trouble with a racehorse.

Dismally mechanical farce.

wd Chester Erskine *ph* Nicholas Musuraca *m* Roy Webb

Groucho Marx, William Bendix, Marie Wilson, Don Defore, Gene Lockhart

The Girl in Overalls: see *Maisie (Swing Shift Maisie)*

The Girl in Pawn: see *Little Miss Marker (1934)*

The Girl in Room 17: see *Vice Squad*

The Girl in the Headlines *
GB   1963   93m   bw
Bryanston/Viewfinder (John Davis)
US title: *The Model Murder Case*

Scotland Yard investigates the murder of a model.

Standard police mystery, well enough done.

w Vivienne Knight, Patrick Campbell *novel The Nose on My Face* by Laurence Payne *d* Michael Truman *ph* Stan Pavey *m* John Addison

Ian Hendry, Ronald Fraser, Margaret Johnston, Natasha Parry

The Girl in the Kremlin

US   1957   81m   bw
Universal

An OSS agent infiltrates the Iron Curtain to assist a plot to overthrow Stalin.

Boring cold war nonsense with the leading lady for some reason playing three parts.

w Gene L. Coon, Robert Hill   *d* Russell Birdwell

Lex Barker, Zsa Zsa Gabor, Jeffrey Stone, Maurice Manson, William Schallert

The Girl in the News *

GB   1940   78m   bw
TCF (Edward Black)

A nurse is framed for the death of her employer.

Easy-going British mystery of the Agatha Christie school.

w Sidney Gilliat   *novel* Roy Vickers   *d* Carol Reed *ph* Otto Kanturek   *md* Louis Levy

Margaret Lockwood, Barry K. Barnes, Emlyn Williams, Margaretta Scott, Roger Livesey, Basil Radford, Wyndham Goldie, Irene Handl, Mervyn Johns, Kathleen Harrison, Richard Bird, Michael Hordern, Roland Culver, Edward Rigby

The Girl in the Painting: see *Portrait from Life*

The Girl in the Red Velvet Swing *

US   1955   109m   DeLuxe   Cinemascope
TCF (Charles Brackett)
V

In New York at the turn of the century, a rich unstable man shoots his mistress's former lover.

Plushy but not very interesting recounting of a celebrated murder case in which the victim was a famous architect, Stanford White.

w Walter Reisch, Charles Brackett   *d* Richard Fleischer   *ph* Milton Krasner   *m* Leigh Harline *ad* Lyle R. Wheeler, Maurice Ransford

Ray Milland, Farley Granger, Joan Collins, Glenda Farrell, Luther Adler, Cornelia Otis Skinner, Philip Reed, John Hoyt

'A needlessly long-winded piece of lush sensationalism.' – *Penelope Houston*

The Girl in the Taxi

GB   1937   72m   bw
ABFD/British Unity (Eugene Tuscherer, Kurt Bernhardt)

The head of the purity league is drawn into an adulterous flirtation.

Moderately piquant comedy shot in English and French versions.

w Austin Melford, Val Valentine and Fritz Gottfurcht *play* Georg Okonowsky   *d* André Berthomieu *ph* Roy Clark   *md* Jean Gilbert   *ad* D'Eaubonne *ed* Ray Pitt

Frances Day, Henri Garat, Lawrence Grossmith, Jean Gillie, Mackenzie Ward, Helen Haye, Albert Whelan

The Girl in White *

US   1952   93m   bw
MGM (Armand Deutsch)
GB title: *So Bright the Flame*

The story of Dr Emily Dunning, the first woman to become an intern in one of New York's hospitals.

Bland biopic, modestly produced, with predictable plot crises.

w Irmgard von Cube, Allen Vincent   *book Bowery to Bellevue* by Emily Dunning Barringer   *d* John Sturges   *ph* Paul C. Vogel   *m* David Raksin

June Allyson, Arthur Kennedy, Gary Merrill, Mildred Dunnock, Jesse White, Marilyn Erskine

The Girl Most Likely

US   1958   98m   Technicolor   RKOscope
RKO (Stanley Rubin)
V*, L

A girl finds herself engaged to three men at the same time, and envisions marriage with each.

Dully cast, quite brightly handled remake of *Tom, Dick and Harry*, with modest songs and dances.

w Devery Freeman   *d* Mitchell Leisen   *ph* Robert Planck   *m* Nelson Riddle   *m/y* Ralph Blane, Hugh Martin

Jane Powell, Cliff Robertson, Keith Andes, Tommy Noonan, Kaye Ballard, Una Merkel

† For Mitchell Leisen and RKO studios, their last film.

A Girl Must Live **

GB   1939   92m   bw
Gainsborough-20th Century (Edward Black)

A runaway schoolgirl falls among chorus girls planning to marry into the nobility.

Light, peppery comedy with a strong cast.

w Frank Launder, Michael Pertwee   *novel* Emery Bonnet   *d Carol Reed   ph* Jack Cox   *md* Louis Levy *m/y* Eddie Pola, Manning Sherwin   *ad* Vetchinsky *ed* R. E. Dearing

Margaret Lockwood, Renée Houston, Lilli Palmer, George Robey, Hugh Sinclair, Naunton Wayne, Moore Marriott, Mary Clare, David Burns, Kathleen Harrison, Martita Hunt, Helen Haye

'An unabashed display of undressed femininity, double-meaning dialogue alternating between piquancy and vulgarity, and hearty knockabout involving scantily attired young viragos who fight furiously in a whirligig of legs and lingerie.' – *Kine Weekly*

'He was half-oriental ... but he used the women of two continents without shame or guilt!'

A Girl Named Tamiko

US   1962   119m   Technicolor   Panavision
Paramount/Hal B. Wallis (Paul Newman)

A Eurasian photographer uses his women in an attempt to get American nationality.

Humdrum romantic melodrama with dim performances.

w Edward Anhalt   *novel* Ronald Kirkbride *d* John Sturges   *ph* Charles Lang Jnr   *m* Elmer Bernstein

Laurence Harvey, France Nuyen, Martha Hyer, Michael Wilding, Miyoshi Umeki

The Girl Next Door

US   1953   92m   Technicolor
TCF (Robert Bassler)

A Broadway musical star falls for her suburban neighbour.

Mild musical linked by UPA cartoon sequences.

w Isobel Lennart   *d* Richard Sale   *ph* Leon Shamroy   *md* Lionel Newman   *ch* Richard Barstow *m/y* Josef Myrow, Mack Gordon

Dan Dailey, June Haver, Natalie Schafer, Dennis Day, Cara Williams

The Girl of the Golden West

US   1930   81m   bw
Warner (Robert North)

A gun-toting, saloon-owning girl marries an outlaw and saves him from the sheriff.

Straight version of a dusty old Broadway success, later musicalized under the same title (see below).

w Waldemar Young   *play* David Belasco   *d* John Francis Dillon   *ph* Sol Polito

Ann Harding, James Rennie, Harry Bannister, Ben Hendricks Jnr, J. Farrell MacDonald

† A silent version was made in 1923 by First National, with Sylvia Breamer and J. Warren Kerrigan, directed by Edwin Carewe.

The Girl of the Golden West

US   1938   121m   bw/sepia release
MGM (William Anthony McGuire)
V*

In backwoods Canada, a girl loves a bandit who is being chased by the Mounties.

Solemn musical melodrama in which the stars seem miscast and a bit of pep is badly needed. Taken from a hoary David Belasco spectacular, and looks it.

w Isobel Dawn, Boyce DeGaw   *d* Robert Z. Leonard *ph* Oliver Marsh   *m/y* Sigmund Romberg, Gus Kahn

Jeanette MacDonald, Nelson Eddy, Walter Pidgeon, Leo Carrillo, Buddy Ebsen, Olin Howland

'This musical mustanger finds the stars not only out of their element, but hemmed in by a two-hour mélange of the great outdoors, Mexican bandits, early Spanish-Californian atmosphere and musical boredom . . . a spotty entry.' – *Variety*

Girl of the Limberlost

US   1934   86m   bw
Monogram

A girl of the swamps becomes a high school graduate.

Tearful rehash of an old sentimental warhorse.

w Adele Comandini   *novel* Gene Stratton Porter *d* Christy Cabanne

Louise Dresser, Ralph Morgan, Marian Marsh, Henry B. Walthall, Helen Jerome Eddy, Betty Blythe

'Wholesome to a fault. A family film good enough for anybody to see, but the fault lies in that not everybody will want to see it.' – *Variety*

Girl of the Night

US   1960   93m   bw
Vanguard/Warner

A streetwalker confesses all to her psychiatrist.

Stalwart exploitation picture of its time.

w Ted Berkman, Raphael Blau   *book The Call Girl* by Dr Harold Greenwald   *d* Joseph Cates

Anne Francis, Lloyd Nolan, Kay Medford, John Kerr, Arthur Storch, James Broderick

Girl of the Year: see *The Petty Girl*

Girl on a Motorcycle

GB/France   1968   91m   Technicolor
Mid Atlantic/Ares (William Sassoon)
V, V*
US title: *Naked under Leather*; French title: *La Motocyclette*

A married woman leaves her husband, zooms off on her motorcycle to see her lover, and crashes to her death while indulging in sexual reverie.

An incredibly plotless and ill-conceived piece of sub-porn claptrap, existing only as a long series of colour supplement photographs.

w Ronald Duncan   *novel La Motocyclette* by André Pieyre de Mandiargues   *d* Jack Cardiff   *ph* Jack Cardiff, René Guissart   *m* Les Reed

Marianne Faithfull, Alain Delon, Roger Mutton

Girl on Approval

GB   1962   75m   bw
Bryanston/Eyeline (Harold Orton)

A couple foster a difficult teenager whose mother is in prison.

Competent domestic drama of family tensions.

w Kathleen White d Charles Frend ph John Coquillon m Clifton Parker ad Herbert Smith, Malcolm Pride ed John Bloom

Rachel Roberts, James Maxwell, Annette Whiteley, Ellen McIntosh, John Dare, Michael Clarke

The Girl on the Boat
GB   1962   91m   bw
UA/Knightsbridge (John Bryan)

On a transatlantic liner in the twenties, two Englishmen fall in love.

Curious attempt to do something different with a star comic, who is clearly outclassed by the lighter talents at hand.

w Reuben Ship story P. G. Wodehouse d Henry Kaplan ph Denys Coop m Kenneth V. Jones

Norman Wisdom, *Richard Briers*, Millicent Martin, Athene Seyler, Sheila Hancock, Philip Locke

The Girl on the Canal: see *Painted Boats*

The Girl on the Front Page
US   1936   74m   bw
Universal

The lady owner of a newspaper gets a job on it under an assumed name, and helps the editor solve a mystery.

Fairly pleasing programmer.

w Austin Parker, Albert R. Perkins, Alice Duer Miller d Harry Beaumont

Edmund Lowe, Gloria Stuart, Spring Byington, Reginald Owen

The Girl Rosemarie
West Germany   1958   100m   bw
Roxy
original title: *Das Mädchen Rosemarie*

Corrupt industrialists and investigators alike are relieved when a girl who had been the mistress of all of them is murdered.

Slick melodrama based on an actual case; almost a documentary exposé.

w Erich Kuby, Rolf Thiele, Joe Herbst, Rolf Urich d Rolf Thiele ph Klaus von Rautenfeld m Norbert Schultze

Nadja Tiller, Peter Van Eyck, Carl Raddatz, Gert Frobe, Mario Adorf, Horst Frank

The Girl Rush
US   1955   85m   Technicolor   Vistavision
Paramount (Frederick Brisson, Robert Alton)

A gambler's daughter inherits a half share in a Las Vegas hotel.

Dull charmless semi-musical vehicle for a star who can't quite carry it.

w Phoebe and Henry Ephron d Robert Pirosh ph William Daniels m Herbert Spencer, Earle Hagen ch Robert Alton

Rosalind Russell, Eddie Albert, Fernando Lamas, James Gleason, Gloria de Haven, Marion Lorne

Girl Shy **
US   1924   65m   bw   silent
Pathé/Harold Lloyd

A bashful, stuttering apprentice tailor in a small town writes a book on love-making, despite being terrified of girls.

A comedy of character that only comes to life in its final slapstick chase sequence, one that has few rivals for invention and complexity as Lloyd transfers from car to horse, fire-engine, tram, speeding car,

motorcycle and collapsing horse and cart in order to get to the church on time.

story Sam Taylor, Ted Wilde, Tim Whelan d Fred Newmeyer, Sam Taylor ph Walter Ludin ad Liell K. Vedder ed Allen McNeil

Harold Lloyd, Jobyna Ralston, Richard Daniels, Carlton Griffin

The film was the first of Lloyd's own productions.

Girl Stroke Boy
GB   1971   88m   Eastmancolor
Hemdale/Virgin (Ned Sherrin, Terry Glinwood)

A well-to-do couple try to find out whether their son's house guest is male or female.

Initially funny but appallingly extended one-joke comedy which many will find merely embarrassing.

w Caryl Brahms, Ned Sherrin play *Girlfriend* by David Percival d Bob Kellett ph Ian Wilson m John Scott

Joan Greenwood, Michael Hordern, Clive Francis, Patricia Routledge, Peter Bull, Rudolph Walker, Elizabeth Welch

Girl Trouble
US   1942   82m   bw
TCF (Robert Bassler)

A South American in New York rents the apartment of a socialite who pretends to be his maid.

Thin romantic comedy with half-hearted screwball touches.

w Ladislas Fodor, Robert Riley Crutcher d Harold Schuster

Don Ameche, Joan Bennett, Billie Burke, Frank Craven, Alan Dinehart

A Girl Was Young: see *Young and Innocent*

The Girl Who Couldn't Quite
GB   1950   85m   bw
Argyle

Smile, that is. A tramp cures a teenager's amnesia and she fails to recognize him afterwards.

Sentimental bosh from a mildly popular play of its time.

w Norman Lee, Marjorie Deans play Leo Marks d Norman Lee

Bill Owen, Iris Hoey, Elizabeth Henson, Betty Stockfield

The Girl Who Couldn't Say No
Italy   1968   104m   Techniscope
INC/PC/Fulcro
original title: *Il Suo Modo di Fari*

A medical assistant has an on-off relationship with an eccentric girl.

Downright peculiar romantic comedy with an American star all at sea in the Mediterranean.

w Franco Brusati, Ennio de Concini d Franco Brusati

George Segal, Virna Lisi, Lila Kedrova

The Girl Who Had Everything
US   1953   69m   bw
MGM (Armand Deutsch)
V*

The daughter of a wealthy criminal lawyer falls in love with one of her father's crooked clients.

Glossy melodrama of purely superficial interest.

w Art Cohn novel Adela Rogers St John d Richard Thorpe ph Paul Vogel m André Previn

Elizabeth Taylor, William Powell, Fernando Lamas, Gig Young

† Remake of *A Free Soul*.

Girl with Green Eyes **
GB   1963   91m   bw
UA/Woodfall (Oscar Lewenstein)
V

An artless young Dublin girl falls for a middle-aged writer.

Lyrical romance which just about preserves its charm by good location sense.

w Edna O'Brien novel The Lonely Girl by Edna O'Brien d Desmond Davis ph Manny Wynn m John Addison

Peter Finch, Rita Tushingham, Lynn Redgrave

'A beautiful and eloquent first directorial effort . . . embodies all that is naive and silly and noble and wonderful and heartbreaking and funny about being young.' – *Judith Crist*

A Girl with Ideas
US   1937   70m   bw
Universal

A rich girl takes control of a daily paper which libelled her.

Lively comedy on familiar lines.

w Bruce Manning, Robert T. Shannon d S. Sylvan Simon

Wendy Barrie, Walter Pidgeon, Kent Taylor, George Barbier, Dorothea Kent, Samuel S. Hinds

'Bright and original comedy, suitable for the more important first runs.' – *Variety*

The Girl with Red Hair
Netherlands   1981   116m   Fujicolor
Blue Dolphin/Movies Filmproductions/VNU/Trio/Vara TV/ Querido/Meteor (Chris Brouwer, Haig Balian)
original title: *Het Meisje Met Het Rode Haar*

The life and death of a member of the Dutch resistance at the hands of the Nazis is recalled by a friend.

Muddled attempt to explain actions from a feminist point of view.

w Ben Verbong, Peter de Vos novel Theun de Vries d Ben Verbong ph Theo Van de Sande m Nicola Piovani ad Dorus Van Der Linden ed Ton de Graff

Renee Soutendijk, Peter Tuinman, Loes Luca, Johan Leysen, Robert Delhez, Ada Bouwman, Lineke Rijxman, Maria de Booy

The Girlfriend: see *La Amiga*

Girlfriends *
US   1978   86m   DuArt
Cyclops (Claudia Weill, Jan Saunders)
V*

A Jewish girl photographer in New York is ditched by her girlfriend and considers men.

Mild, amusing, well-observed little comedy-drama which goes nowhere in particular and slightly outstays its welcome.

w Vicki Polon d Claudia Weill ph Fred Murphy m Michael Small

Melanie Mayron, Eli Wallach, Anita Skinner, Bob Balaban

'A quiet triumph . . . There is no tedium, there is realization; involvement; pleasure. The more I think about this film, the warmer I feel.' – *Stanley Kauffmann*

Les Girls *
US   1957   114m   Metrocolor   Cinemascope
MGM (Sol. C. Siegel)
V, V*, L

One member of a dancing troupe sues another over her memoirs.

Disappointing, talent-laden comedy-musical with a *Rashomon*-like flashback plot and a curious absence of the expected wit and style.

w John Patrick *novel* Vera Caspary *d* George Cukor *ph* Robert Surtees *md* Adolph Deutsch *m/ly* Cole Porter *ch* Jack Cole

Gene Kelly, *Kay Kendall,* Mitzi Gaynor, Taina Elg, Jacques Bergerac, Leslie Phillips, Henry Daniell, Patrick MacNee

The Girls: see *Les Bonnes Femmes*

Girls about Town
US 1931 80m bw
Paramount

Gold diggers find true love.

A laugh, a tear and a wisecrack in the big city: very dated, but may have seemed fresh at the time.

w Raymond Griffith, Brian Marlow *story* Zoë Akins *d* George Cukor

Kay Francis, Joel McCrea, Lilyan Tashman, Eugene Pallette, Alan Dinehart, George Barbier

'Generally only fair b.o. as ultra sophistication may be small-town setback.' – *Variety*

Girls at Sea
GB 1958 80m Technicolor
ABP

After a shipboard party, three girls are left aboard a battleship.

Vulgarized remake of *The Middle Watch* (qv).

w T. J. Morrison, Gilbert Gunn, Walter C. Mycroft *d* Gilbert Gunn

Guy Rolfe, Ronald Shiner, Alan White, Michael Hordern, Anne Kimbell, Fabia Drake

Girls' Dormitory *
US 1936 66m bw
TCF

A college girl falls for her headmaster.

Old-fashioned romance for nice young people, smoothly produced in the Fox mid-30s manner.

w Gene Markey *story* Ladislaus Fodor *d* Irving Cummings *ph* Merritt B. Gerstad *m* Arthur Lange

Herbert Marshall, *Simone Simon,* Ruth Chatterton, Constance Collier, J. Edward Bromberg, Dixie Dunbar, Tyrone Power

'The Swingin'-est Elvis! The Fastest-Movin' Fun'n'Music! And The World's Curviest Girls! Girls! Girls!'
Girls, Girls, Girls
US 1962 106m Technicolor
Wallis-Hazen (Hal B. Wallis)
V, V*

A night-club singer runs a fishing boat as a hobby.

Empty-headed, lighter than air vehicle for star fans.

w Edward Anhalt, Allan Weiss *d* Norman Taurog *ph* Loyal Griggs *m* Joseph J. Lilley

Elvis Presley, Stella Stevens, Laurel Goodwin, Jeremy Slate

The Girls He Left Behind: see *The Gang's All Here* (1943)

Girls in the Night
US 1953 82m bw
Universal
GB title: *Life After Dark*

The son of a New York tenement family falls under suspicion of murder.

Very mildly sensational low-life melodrama, like a citified *Tobacco Road*.

w Ray Buffum *d* Jack Arnold

Glenda Farrell, Harvey Lembeck, Joyce Holden, Glen Roberts, Don Gordon

Girls in the Street: see *London Melody*

Girls in Uniform: see *Maedchen in Uniform*

Girls Never Tell: see *Her First Romance*

The Girls of Pleasure Island
US 1953 96m Technicolor
Paramount (Paul Jones)

In 1945 the Marines land on a tiny Pacific island, disturbing the life of an English gentleman and his three inexperienced but beautiful daughters.

Tedious and wholly artificial comedy with a leaden touch, devised as a try-out for young talent.

w F. Hugh Herbert *d* F. Hugh Herbert, Alvin Ganzer *ph* Daniel Fapp *m* Lyn Murray

Leo Genn, Gene Barry, Don Taylor, Elsa Lanchester, Dorothy Bromiley, Audrey Dalton, Joan Elan

The Girls of Summer: see *Satisfaction*

Girls on Probation
US 1938 63m bw
Warner

A lawyer falls in love with a young girl in trouble.

Formula B picture that was re-released a few years later when its two stars were more familiar to the public.

w Crane Wilbur *d* William McGann *ph* Arthur Todd *ad* Hugh Reticker *ed* Frederick Richards

Jane Bryan, Ronald Reagan, Sheila Bromley, Anthony Averill, Henry O'Neill, Elisabeth Risdon

'A creditable job.' – *Variety*

Girly: see *Mumsy, Nanny, Sonny and Girly*

Giro City *
GB 1982 102m colour
Silvarealm/Rediffusion/Channel 4 (Sophie Balhetchet, David Payne)

A television documentary team tries to present honest programmes about Ireland and about local government corruption.

Smartly made if somewhat predictably and stridently left-wing slice of so-called realism.

wd Karl Francis *ph* Curtis Clark *m* Alun Francis *ed* Kent Pan

Glenda Jackson, Jon Finch, Kenneth Colley, James Donnelly, Emrys James, Simon Jones

Le Gitan
France/Italy 1975 94m Eastmancolor
Lara/Adel (Raymond Danon, Alain Delon)
aka: *The Gipsy*

On the run from the police, an alienated gypsy commits a series of daring robberies with the aid of two accomplices.

A tired, plodding thriller-cum-protest about society's persecution of gypsies that settles for making its murderous hero into a figure of alluring glamour.

wd José Giovanni *novel* Histoire de Fou by José Giovanni *ph* Jean-Jacques Tarbes *m* Django Reinhardt, Claude Bolling, Lick *ad* Willy Holt *ed* Jacqueline Thiedot

Alain Delon, Annie Girardot, Paul Meurisse, Marcel Bozzuffi, Maurice Barrier, Maurice Giraud, Bernard Giraudeau, Renato Salvatori

Giulietta degli Spiriti: see *Juliet of the Spirits*

Giuseppina *
GB 1960 32m Technicolor
British Petroleum

The daughter of an Italian petrol station proprietor has an amusing afternoon watching customers.

Pleasing little Tatiesque sponsored comedy.

wd James Hill

Give a Girl a Break *
US 1953 84m Technicolor
MGM (Jack Cummings)

A Broadway star walks out on a show and three girls audition as replacements.

Minor musical vehicle for the Champions; an agreeable time-passer.

w Frances Goodrich, Albert Hackett *d* Stanley Donen *ph* William Mellor *md* André Previn *ch* Stanley Donen, Gower Champion *m/ly* Burton Lane, Ira Gershwin

Marge and Gower Champion, Debbie Reynolds, Bob Fosse, Kurt Kasznar

Give Her a Ring
GB 1934 79m bw
BIP (Walter Mycroft)

A telephonist falls for her employer.

Curious romantic comedy attempting to woo continental audiences.

w Clifford Grey, Ernst Wolff, Marjorie Deans, Wolfgang Wilhelm *play* H. Rosenfeld *d* Arthur Woods *ph* Claude Friese-Greene, Ronald Neame *md* Harry Acres *m/ly* Clifford Grey, Hans May *ad* Duncan Sutherland *ed* E. B. Jarvis

Clifford Mollison, Wendy Barrie, Zelma O'Neal, Erik Rhodes, Bertha Belmore, Stewart Granger (in a bit part)

'Delightful and unassuming' – *National Film Theatre, 1970*

Give Me a Sailor
US 1938 80m bw
Paramount (Jeff Lazarus)

An ugly girl envies her sister her beaux, but ends up winning a competition for beautiful legs.

One of the double bill comedies which got Bob Hope's career off to a shaky start.

w Doris Anderson, Frank Butler *play* Anne Nichols *d* Elliott Nugent *ph* Victor Milner *md* Boris Morros *m/ly* Leo Robin, Ralph Rainger

Martha Raye, Bob Hope, Betty Grable, Jack Whiting, Clarence Kolb

'Not so funny farce.' – *Variety*

Give Me the Stars
GB 1944 90m bw
British National

An American girl takes charge of her Scottish grandfather.

Half-hearted comedy of the music halls.

w Maclean Rogers, Austin Melford *d* Maclean Rogers

Will Fyffe, Leni Lynn, Jackie Hunter, Olga Lindo, Stanelli, Ronald Chesney

'Daringly intimate – it's strictly adult entertainment! The picture every woman will want some man to see!'
Give Me Your Heart
US 1936 88m bw
Warner
GB title: *Sweet Aloes*

A socialite has a child by a married man.

Dated tearjerker.

w Casey Robinson *play* Sweet Aloes by Joyce Carey *d* Archie Mayo

Kay Francis, George Brent, Patric Knowles, Roland Young, Henry Stephenson, Frieda Inescort

Give My Regards to Broad Street *
GB   1984   108m   colour
TCF/MPL (Andros Epimanondas)
V*, L

An international rock star fears that the priceless tapes of his new album have been stolen, and searches London for them.

An absurdly thin premise even for a musical which is essentially an ego trip for Paul McCartney, who at least squandered his own money on it and not the bank's. Some of the numbers have merit but the mood never connects.

w Paul McCartney   d Peter Webb   ph Ian McMillan   m Paul McCartney   pd Anthony Pratt

Paul McCartney, Bryan Brown, Ringo Starr, Barbara Bach, Tracey Ullman, Ralph Richardson, George Martin, John Bennett

Give My Regards to Broadway *
US   1948   89m   Technicolor
TCF (Walter Morosco)
L

An old-time vaudevillian yearns to get back into show business.

Pleasantly performed, sentimental family comedy with familiar tunes.

w Samuel Hoffenstein, Elizabeth Reinhardt
d Lloyd Bacon   ph Harry Jackson

Dan Dailey, *Charles Winninger*, Fay Bainter, Charles Ruggles, Nancy Guild

'Vaudeville is dead. I wish to God someone would bury it.' – *James Agee*

Give Out, Sisters
US   1942   65m   bw
Universal

For reasons of pure plot, the Andrews Sisters pose as wealthy old maids.

One of scores of musical seconds produced by Universal at this time; this one has an unusually strong cast.

w Paul Gerard Smith, Warren Wilson   d Edward F. Cline

The Andrews Sisters, Grace McDonald, Dan Dailey, Charles Butterworth, Walter Catlett, William Frawley, Donald O'Connor, Peggy Ryan

Give Us the Moon
GB   1944   95m   bw
GFD/Gainsborough (Edward Black)

In post-war London a club is opened for idle members only.

Whimsical comedy which fell with a dull thud.

wd Val Guest   novel *The Elephant is White* by Caryl Brahms, S. J. Simon

Margaret Lockwood, Vic Oliver, Peter Graves, Max Bacon, Roland Culver, Frank Cellier, Jean Simmons

Give Us This Day
GB   1949   120m   bw
Plantagenet (Rod E. Geiger, N. A. Bronsten)
US title: *Salt to the Devil*

Depression struggles of an Italian immigrant family in New York.

An unconvincing, self-pitying wallow, a very curious enterprise for a British studio.

w Ben Barzman   story *Christ in Concrete* by Pietro di Donato   d Edward Dmytryk   ph C. Pennington Richards   m Benjamin Frankel

Sam Wanamaker, Lea Padovani, Kathleen Ryan, Charles Goldner, Bonar Colleano, William Sylvester, Karel Stepanek, Sidney James

'Dmytryk insisted on cutting the film himself and he has left in at least three spare reels.' – *Richard Winnington*

'Worth making and worth seeing, but cramped by its symbolism and its language.' – *Richard Mallett, Punch*

Give Us Wings
US   1940   60m   bw
Universal

City boys become pilots in the Army Air Corps.

Undistinguished combining of the Dead End Kids with the East Side Kids.

w Arthur T. Horman, Robert Lee Johnson
d Charles Lamont

Billy Halop, Huntz Hall, Gabriel Dell, Bernard Punsley, Bobby Jordan, Wallace Ford, Anne Gwynne, Victor Jory, Shemp Howard

The Gladiator
US   1938   70m   bw
Columbia
V*

A poor boy wins a prize and becomes a college football hero.

Elementary star farce.

w Charles Melson, Arthur Sheekman   novel Philip Wylie   d Edward Sedgwick

Joe E. Brown, Man Mountain Dean, June Travis, Dickie Moore, Lucien Littlefield

'Goofy but a lot of fun.' – *Variety*

Gladiator *
US   1992   102m   Technicolor
Columbia TriStar/Columbia/Price Entertainment (Frank Price, Steve Roth)
V, V*, L, S

A white teenage amateur boxer is forced to turn professional by a crooked promoter and forms a friendship with a young black fighter.

Enjoyable boxing movie that nevertheless sticks to all the usual moves; it could never have been a contender but on its modest level it holds the interest.

w Lyle Kessler, Robert Mark Kamen   story Djordje Milicevic, Robert Mark Kamen   d Rowdy Herrington   ph Tak Fujimoto   m Brad Fiedel   pd Gregg Fonseca   ed Peter Zinner, Harry B. Miller III

James Marshall, Cuba Gooding Jnr, Brian Dennehy, Robert Loggia, Ossie Davis, Jon Seda, Cara Buono, Lance Slaughter

'An exercise in audience manipulation that probably will get a thumbs-down from the targetted younger audience.' – *Variety*

Glamorous Night
GB   1937   81m   bw
BIP/ABP (Walter C. Mycroft)

An opera singer and her gypsy friends save a Ruritanian king from his scheming prime minister.

Modest transcription of a popular stage musical.

w Dudley Leslie, Hugh Brooke, William Freshman   play Ivor Novello   d Brian Desmond Hurst   ph Fritz Arno Wagner   md Harry Acres   m/ly Ivor Novello, Christopher Hassall   ad Cedric Dawe   ed Flora Newton

Mary Ellis, Otto Kruger, Victor Jory, Barry Mackay, Trefor Jones, Finlay Currie, Felix Aylmer

† Although several of the original songs are either sung or heard, much of the background music is not Novello's.

Glamour
US   1934   74m   bw
Universal

A day in the life of a Broadway star.

Competent minor entertainment.

w Doris Anderson   story Edna Ferber   d William Wyler   ph George Robinson

Constance Cummings, Paul Lukas, Philip Reed, Joseph Cawthorne, Doris Lloyd, Olaf Hytten

'A good b.o. number with special pull for the femmes.' – *Variety*

Glamour Boy *
US   1941   79m   bw
Colbert Clark/Paramount
GB title: *Hearts in Springtime*

An ex-child star finds himself tutoring his successor.

Quite an appealing peep inside Hollywood, and especially wry at the time because the star was still a household word.

w Bradford Ropes, Val Burton   d Ralph Murphy

Jackie Cooper, Susanna Foster, Walter Abel, Darryl Hickman, Ann Gillis, William Demarest

'One of the happiest "idea" pictures turned out by Hollywood in a long time.' – *Variety*

'Underwater . . . undercover . . . under any circumstances . . . you must see the wildest, funniest new comedy!'
The Glass Bottom Boat
US   1966   110m   Metrocolor   Panavision
MGM/Arwin-Reame (Martin Melcher)
V*, L

A young widow gets involved with spies.

Frantic spy spoof, pleasantly set on the Californian coast, but overflowing with pratfalls, messy slapstick and pointless guest appearances.

w Everett Freeman   d Frank Tashlin   ph Leon Shamroy   m Frank de Vol

Doris Day, Rod Taylor, Arthur Godfrey, Paul Lynde, John McGiver, Edward Andrews, Eric Fleming, Dom de Luise

'He carries his love in his iron fists!'
The Glass Key **
US   1935   87m   bw
Paramount (E. Lloyd Sheldon)

A slightly corrupt but good-natured politician is saved by his henchman from being implicated in a murder.

Lively transcription of a zesty crime novel.

w Kathryn Scola, Kubec Glasmon, Harry Ruskin   novel *Dashiell Hammett*   d Frank Tuttle   ph Henry Sharp

Edward Arnold, George Raft, Claire Dodd, Rosalind Keith, Guinn Williams, Ray Milland

'Will have to struggle to strike above average grosses.' – *Variety*

The Glass Key **
US   1942   85m   bw
Paramount (Fred Kohlmar)
V*, L

Nifty remake of the above which finds some limited talents in their best form, helped by a plot which keeps one watching.

w Jonathan Latimer   d Stuart Heisler   ph Theodor Sparkuhl   m Victor Young

Brian Donlevy, Alan Ladd, Veronica Lake, Bonita Granville, *William Bendix*, Richard Denning, Joseph Calleia, Moroni Olsen

MADVIG (Brian Donlevy): 'I'm going to society. He's practically given me the key to his house.'
BEAUMONT (Alan Ladd): 'Yeah, a glass key. Be sure it doesn't break up in your hand.'

The Glass Menagerie **
US   1950   107m   bw
Warner/Charles K. Feldman (Jerry Wald)

A shy crippled girl seeks escape from the shabby reality of life in St Louis and from her mother's fantasies.

Pleasantly moody version of one of its author's lighter and more optimistic plays; fluent and good-looking production, memorable performances.

w *Tennessee Williams*, Peter Berneis *play* Tennessee Williams *d* Irving Rapper *ph* Robert Burks *m* Max Steiner

Gertrude Lawrence, Jane Wyman, Kirk Douglas, Arthur Kennedy

† An excellent TV movie of the play, directed by Anthony Harvey and starring Katharine Hepburn, was made in 1973.

The Glass Menagerie *
US 1987 135m DuArt
Cineplex (Burtt Harris)
V*, L

A son longs to escape from his stifling home, where his genteel mother worries about the future prospects of his lame, shy sister.

Well-acted and faithful to the original stage play, this version still obstinately refuses to come to life on the screen.

w *Tennessee Williams* *play* Tennessee Williams *d* Paul Newman *ph* Michael Ballhaus *m* Henry Mancini *pd* Tony Walton *ed* David Ray

Joanne Woodward, John Malkovich, Karen Allen, James Naughton

The Glass Mountain
GB 1949 98m bw
Victoria (John Sutro, Joseph Janni, Fred Zelnik)

In the Dolomites, a married composer loves an Italian girl who saved his life during the war.

Tedious sudser, ineptly produced; an enormous British box-office success because of its theme music.

w Joseph Janni, John Hunter, Emery Bonnet, Henry Cass, John Cousins *d* Henry Cass *ph* Otello Martelli, William McLeod *m* Nino Rota

Michael Denison, Dulcie Gray, Valentina Cortese, Tito Gobbi, Sebastian Shaw

The Glass Slipper
US 1954 94m Eastmancolor
MGM (Edwin H. Knopf)
V*

The story of Cinderella.

To those used to the pantomime version this is dull, dreary, high-flown stuff: limbo sets, ballets, psychological rationalization and virtually no comedy.

w/ly Helen Deutsch *d* Charles Walters *ph* Arthur E. Arling *m* Bronislau Kaper *ch* Roland Petit

Leslie Caron, Michael Wilding, Elsa Lanchester, Barry Jones, *Estelle Winwood* (as Fairy Godmother)

The Glass Sphinx
Spain/Italy 1968 98m colour
AIP

An archaeologist is in danger because of his discoveries.

Multi-national mish-mash only notable as one of the last films of its star.

w Adriano Bolzoni, Louis M. Heyward *d* Fulvio Lucisano

Robert Taylor, Anita Ekberg, Gianna Sera, Jack Stuart

The Glass Web
US 1953 81m bw 3-D
U-I (A. J. Cohen)

A TV executive kills a blackmailing actress and allows a young scriptwriter to be accused.

Boring thriller set in a TV studio.

w Robert Blees, Leonard Lee *d* Jack Arnold *ph* Maury Gertsman *m* Joseph Gershenson

Edward G. Robinson, John Forsythe, Marcia Henderson, Richard Denning

Gleaming the Cube
US 1988 105m Deluxe colour
Rank/Gladden Entertainment (Lawrence Turman)
V, V*, L

A teenage skateboarder tracks down the killers of his adopted Vietnamese brother.

Likely to appeal only to those who know what the film's title means.

w Michael Tolkin *d* Graeme Clifford *ph* Reed Smoot *m* Jay Ferguson *pd* John Muto *ed* John Wright

Christian Slater, Steven Bauer, Richard Herd, Le Tuan, Min Luong, Art Chudabala, Ed Lauter, Micole Mercurio, Peter Kwong

Glen or Glenda
US 1953 61m bw
Edward D. Wood Jnr
V*
aka: *I Changed My Sex; He or She; The Transvestite; I Led Two Lives*

A doctor relates stories about transvestites and sex-change operations.

Notorious grade Z exploitation piece, often counted among the worst films ever made. See for yourself.

wd Edward D. Wood Jnr

Lyle Talbot, Timothy Farrell, Bela Lugosi

'A Story For Everyone Who Works For A Living.'
Glengarry Glen Ross **
US 1992 100m Eastmancolor
Rank/Zupnik Enterprises (Jerry Tokofsky, Stanley R. Zupnik)
V, V*, L, S

Four real-estate salesmen are in competition to see who can sell the most, with the sack facing the two losers.

A brilliant stage play seems a little claustrophobic on its transfer to the screen, but provides opportunities for some excellent acting.

w *David Mamet* *play* David Mamet *d* James Foley *ph* Juan Ruiz Anchia *m* James Newton Howard *pd* Jane Musky *ed* Howard Smith

Al Pacino, Jack Lemmon, Alec Baldwin, Ed Harris, Alan Arkin, Kevin Spacey, Jonathan Pryce

'The prize-winning comedy of outrage is brought to the screen, intact and enhanced.' – *Time*

'An entertaining but slightly uncomfortable marriage both of different stage traditions and of movie ways of dealing with them.' – *Richard Combs, Sight and Sound*

† Jack Lemmon won the best actor award at the 1992 Venice Film Festival for his performance.

AAN: Al Pacino

The Glenn Miller Story **
US 1953 116m Technicolor
U-I (Aaron Rosenberg)
V, V*, L, S

The life of the unassuming trombonist and bandleader whose plane disappeared during World War II.

Competent musical heartwarmer with a well-cast star and successful reproduction of the Miller sound. A big box-office hit.

w Valentine Davies, Oscar Brodney *d* *Anthony Mann* *ph* *William Daniels* *md* Henry Mancini, Joseph Gershenson

James Stewart, June Allyson, Harry Morgan, Charles Drake, Frances Langford, Louis Armstrong, Gene Krupa

AAN: script; music direction

Gli Occhi, La Bocca: see *Those Eyes, That Mouth*

A Global Affair
US 1963 84m bw
Seven Arts/Hall Bartlett

A United Nations official has to look after an abandoned baby.

Flat sentimental farce which embarrassingly tries to say something about the UN.

w Arthur Marx, Bob Fisher, Charles Lederer *d* Jack Arnold *ph* Joseph Ruttenberg *m* Dominic Frontière

Bob Hope, Lilo Pulver, Michèle Mercier, Yvonne de Carlo

'Squaresville incarnate, with a side trip into Leersville.' – *Judith Crist, 1973*

La Gloire de Mon Père *
France 1990 110m Eastmancolor
Palace/Gaumont International/La Guéville/TF1 (Marc Goldstaub, Guy Azzi)
V, V*, L
aka: *My Father's Glory*

A young city boy goes on holiday to Provence with his family and falls in love with the countryside.

Charm and nostalgia are laid on thickly in a movie based on the childhood of Marcel Pagnol, who grew up to become an influential film-maker.

w Jérôme Tonnere, Louis Nucera, Yves Robert *autobiography* Marcel Pagnol *d* Yves Robert *ph* Robert Alazraki *m* Vladimir Cosma *ad* Jacques Dugied *ed* Pierre Gillette

Philippe Caubère, Nathalie Roussel, Didier Pain, Thérèse Liotard, Julien Ciamaca, Victorien Delamare, Joris Molinas, Paul Crauchet, Jean-Pierre Darras (as narrator)

'The weave of inner drama, family album, and discursive sceneries is gentle and lightly enchanting.' – *Raymond Durgnat, Sight and Sound*

† The story is continued in a sequel, *Le Château de Ma Mère* (qv).

Gloria *
US 1980 121m Technicolor
Columbia (Sam Shaw)
V, V*, L

In the Bronx, an innocent woman finds she has to meet violence with violence in order to protect a small boy from the mob.

Overlong but lively and oddly entertaining; however, one is never quite sure what if anything it is getting at.

wd John Cassavetes *ph* Fred Schuler *m* Bill Conti *ad* Rene D'Auriac *ed* George C. Villasenor

Gena Rowlands, John Adames, Buck Henry, Julie Carmen, Tony Knesich, Gregory Cleghorn

AAN: Gena Rowlands

Glorifying the American Girl *
US 1929 87m bw/colour sequence
Paramount (Florenz Ziegfeld)
V*

A chorus girl rejects her boyfriend for the sake of stardom.

Archetypal show-must-go-on musical.

w J. P. McEvoy, Millard Webb *d* Millard Webb, John Harkrider *ph* George Folsey *md* Frank Tours

Mary Eaton, Edward Crandall; and as guests Eddie Cantor, Helen Morgan, Rudy Vallee, Florenz Ziegfeld, Adolph Zukor, Otto Kahn, Texas Guinan, Mayor Jimmy Walker, Ring Lardner, Noah Beery, Johnny Weissmuller

The Glorious Adventure *
GB 1921 100m (approx) Prizmacolor silent
Stoll/J.Stuart Blackton

Various lives are affected by the Great Fire of London in 1666.

Stagey costume drama, notable only as the first British film in colour.

w Felix Orman   d J. Stuart Blackton   ph William T. Crespinal

Lady Diana Manners, Victor McLaglen, Gerald Lawrence, Cecil Humphreys, Alex Crawford, Lennox Pawle (as Pepys)

Glorious Betsy
US 1928 90m approx bw silent
Warner

Napoleon's younger brother loves an American girl.

Popular period romance of its day.

w Anthony Coldeway   play Rida Johnson Young
d Alan Crosland

Conrad Nagel, Dolores Costello, John Miljan, Betty Blythe

† The happy ending is not historical. It was remade in 1936 as *Hearts Divided* (qv).

AAN: Anthony Coldeway

Glory
US 1955 100m Technicolor Superscope
RKO/David Butler

Girl loves horse more than boy.

Conventional young love/Kentucky Derby marshmallow.

w Peter Milne   d David Butler   ph Wifrid Cline
m Frank Perkins

Margaret O'Brien, Walter Brennan, Charlotte Greenwood, John Lupton

Glory **
US 1989 122m Technicolor Panavision
Columbia TriStar (Freddie Fields)
V, V (W), V*, L, S

A young and inexperienced Union officer is given command of the first black regiment recruited to fight in the Civil War.

Moving, if sometimes sanitised, account of the stirrings of black freedom.

w Kevin Jarre   book Lay This Laurel by Lincoln Kirstein, *One Gallant Rush* by Peter Burchard, the letters of Robert Gould Shaw   d Edward Zwick
ph Freddie Francis   m James Horner   pd Norman Garwood   ed Steven Rosenblum

Matthew Broderick, Denzel Washington, Cary Elwes, Morgan Freeman, Jihmi Kennedy, Andre Braugher, John Finn, Donovan Leitch, John David Cullum

AA: Freddie Francis; Denzel Washington

AAN: art direction; editing

Glory Alley
US 1952 79m bw
MGM (Nicholas Nayfack)

A sullen young boxer has trouble with his girl, her father and the demon rum.

Flat, boring second feature with musical interludes.

w Art Cohn   d Raoul Walsh   ph William Daniels
md Georgie Stoll

Leslie Caron, Ralph Meeker, Kurt Kasznar, Gilbert Roland, John McIntire, Louis Armstrong, Jack Teagarden

'This is the kind of film that contains bits of everything. New Orleans night life and an episode of the Korean war; an arty French ballet sequence and jazz from Louis Armstrong; a boxer who acquired a neurosis in childhood when his father hit him over

the head and a blind old father with a French accent, who knows all about everything.' – MFB

Glory at Sea: see The Gift Horse

The Glory Brigade
US 1953 82m bw
TCF (William Bloom)

Greek soldiers fight in Korea alongside the Americans.

Modest war adventure with predictable racial tensions.

w Franklin Coen   d Robert D. Webb   ph Lucien Andriot   md Lionel Newman

Victor Mature, Alexander Scourby, Lee Marvin, Richard Egan

The Glory Guys *
US 1965 112m DeLuxe Panavision
UA/Levy-Gardner-Laven
V*

Officers of the US cavalry disagree about dealing with the Indians.

Standard big-budget Western.

w Sam Peckinpah   novel The Dice of God by Hoffman Birney   d Arnold Laven   ph James Wong Howe
m Riz Ortolani

Tom Tryon, Harve Presnell, Senta Berger, Andrew Duggan, James Caan, Slim Pickens, Michael Anderson Jnr

G'mar Giviya: see Cup Final

The Gnome-Mobile *
US 1967 90m Technicolor
Walt Disney (James Algar)
V*

A millionaire and his family go for a forest picnic and help a colony of gnomes.

Cheerful adventures for small children, with good trick work.

w Ellis Kadison   novel Upton Sinclair   d Robert Stevenson   ph Edward Colman   m Buddy Baker

Walter Brennan, Matthew Garber, Karen Dotrice, Richard Deacon, Sean McClory, Ed Wynn, Jerome Cowan, Charles Lane

Go Chase Yourself
US 1938 70m bw
RKO (Robert Sisk)

A bank clerk gets involved with gangsters.

Mild comedy for a radio star.

w Paul Yawitz, Bert Granet   d Edward F. Cline

Joe Penner, Lucille Ball, June Travis, Richard Lane, Fritz Feld, Tom Kennedy

Go for a Take
GB 1972 90m colour
Rank/Century Films (Roy Simpson)

Two waiters in debt to a gangster take refuge in a film studio.

Painful British farce.

w Alan Hackney   d Harry Booth   ph Mark McDonald   m Glen Mason

Reg Varney, Norman Rossington, Sue Lloyd, Dennis Price, Julie Ege, Patrick Newell, David Lodge

Go for Broke
US 1951 93m bw
MGM (Dore Schary)

World War II exploits of Japanese-American soldiers.

Absolutely unsurprising war film with all the anti-Japs converted by the end. Production quite good.

wd Robert Pirosh   ph Paul C. Vogel   m Alberto Colombo

Van Johnson, Lane Nakano, George Miki, Akira Fukunaga, Warner Anderson, Don Haggerty

AAN: Robert Pirosh (as writer)

Go into Your Dance **
US 1935 89m bw
Warner (Sam Bischoff)
L
GB title: Casino de Paree

A big-headed star gets his come-uppance and finds happiness.

Moderate backstage musical notable for the only teaming of Jolson and Keeler, who were then married.

w Earl Baldwin   d Archie Mayo   ph Tony Gaudio, Sol Polito   m/ly Harry Warren, Al Dubin   ch Bobby Connolly

Al Jolson, Ruby Keeler, Glenda Farrell, Benny Rubin, Phil Regan, Barton MacLane, Sharon Lynne, Akim Tamiroff, Helen Morgan, Patsy Kelly

'It has everything for the box office.' – Variety

AAN: Bobby Connolly

Go, Johnny Go!
US 1958 75m bw
Hal Roach (Alan Freed)
V*, L

A former choirboy becomes a rock singer.

Typical teen fare of its time; if it retains any interest, it is due to Berry singing the title song, 'Little Queenie' and 'Memphis Tennessee', and to Ritchie Valens's only film performance.

w Gary Alexander   d Paul Landres

Alan Freed, Chuck Berry, Jimmy Clanton, Sandy Stewart, Herb Vigran, Eddie Cochrane, Ritchie Valens

Go Man Go
US 1954 82m bw
Alfred Palca (Anton M. Leader)

How Abe Saperstein moulded and trained the Harlem Globetrotters basketball team.

Not so much a film as an athletic demonstration with some actors round the edges.

w Arnold Becker   d James Wong Howe   ph Bill Steiner   m Alex North

Dane Clark, Sidney Poitier, Pat Breslin, Edmon Ryan

Go Naked in the World
US 1960 103m Metrocolor Cinemascope
MGM/Arcola (Aaron Rosenberg)

A prostitute causes a rift between son and millionaire father.

Antediluvian melodrama with overblown performances.

wd Ranald MacDougall   novel Tom Chamales
ph Milton Krasner   m Adolph Deutsch

Gina Lollobrigida, Tony Franciosa, Ernest Borgnine, Luana Patten, Will Kuluva, Philip Ober

'A good example of how the increased liberation of Hollywood can be misused.' – MFB

Go Tell the Spartans
US 1978 114m CFI color
Spartan Company (Allan F. Bodoh, Mitchell Cannold)
L

In Vietnam, a seasoned commander tries to get a platoon of raw soldiers out of a Vietcong ambush.

We have been here before, in other wars, and since there is little heroism to be had from Vietnam it is difficult to see why we are invited again.

w Wendell Mayes   *story* Daniel Ford   *d* Ted Post
ph Harry Stradling Jnr   *m* Dick Halligan

Burt Lancaster, Craig Wasson, Jonathan Goldsmith,
Marc Singer

'No earth-shaking masterpieces, but in its small-scale
way it's strong, hard, forthright.' – *Stanley Kauffmann*

'Has the virtues of its defects. It is understated,
lacking in powerful dramatic incidents and high
human emotion, and rather flatly written and
directed. As a result, it has about it a realistically
antiheroic air that is rare enough in any movie about
any war.' – *Richard Schickel, Time*

Go to Blazes

GB   1961   84m   Technicolor   Cinemascope
ABP (Kenneth Harper)
V

Ex-convicts become firemen, intending to use the
engine for smash and grab raids.

Mild comedy ruined by wide screen.

w Patrick Campbell, Vivienne Knight   *d* Michael
Truman   *ph* Erwin Hillier   *m* John Addison

Dave King, Daniel Massey, Norman Rossington,
Wilfrid Lawson, Maggie Smith, Robert Morley, Coral
Browne

'Laughter is what it has nothing else but!'
Go West *

US   1925   70m (24 fps)   bw   silent
Metro-Goldwyn/Buster Keaton (Joseph M. Schenck)

A tenderfoot makes friends with a cow and takes it
everywhere.

Disappointingly slow star comedy with splendid
moments.

w Raymond Cannon   *d* Buster Keaton   *ph* Bert
Haines, E. Lessley

Buster Keaton, Howard Truesdall, Kathleen Myers

Go West **

US   1940   82m   bw
MGM (Jack Cummings)
V

Three zanies tackle a Western villain.

Minor Marx comedy with a good start (the ticket
office sketch) and a rousing finale as they take a
moving train to bits, but some pretty soggy stuff in
between.

w Irving Brecher   *d* Edward Buzzell   *ph* Leonard
Smith   *md* Georgie Stoll   *m* Bronislau Kaper

Groucho Marx, Harpo Marx, Chico Marx, John
Carroll, Diana Lewis, Robert Barrat

Go West Young Lady

US   1940   70m   bw
Columbia

A lawless Western town expects a sheriff who turns
out to be a girl.

Mildly pleasing variation on *Destry Rides Again*.

w Karen de Wolf, Richard Flournoy   *d* Frank
Strayer

Glenn Ford, Penny Singleton, Charles Ruggles

'How you gonna keep 'em down on the farm, after they've
seen Mae West?'
Go West Young Man

US   1936   80m   bw
Paramount (Emanuel R. Cohen)

A movie star has a car breakdown in Pennsylvania
and falls for a local lad.

Cleaned-up Mae West vehicle, all rather boring.

w Mae West   *play Personal Appearance* by Lawrence
Riley   *d* Henry Hathaway   *ph* Karl Struss
m George Stoll

Mae West, Randolph Scott, Warren William, Lyle
Talbot, Alice Brady, Isabel Jewell, Elizabeth Patterson

'On the way to snug profits.' – *Variety*

'Quite incredibly tedious, as slow and wobbling in its
pace as Miss West's famous walk. The wisecracks lack
the old impudence, and seldom have so many feet of
film been expended on a mere dirty look.' – *Graham
Greene*

The Goalie's Anxiety at the Penalty Kick: see
The Goalkeeper's Fear of the Penalty Kick

The Goalkeeper's Fear of the Penalty Kick **

West Germany   1971   101m   colour
Filmverlag der Autoren/Osterreichischer Telefilm (Thomas
   Schamoni, Peter Genee)
V, V*
original title: *Die Angst des Tormanns beim Elfmeter*

Sent off during a game, an ageing goalkeeper commits
a motiveless murder.

Disturbing film of the failure of communication;
difficult but rewarding for the patient.

wd Wim Wenders   *story* Peter Handke   *ph* Robby
Muller   *m* Jurgen Knieper   *ed* Peter Przygodda

Arthur Brauss, Kai Fischer, Erika Pluhar, Libgart
Schwartz, Rudiger Vogler, Marie Bardischewski

The Go-Between **

GB   1970   116m   Technicolor
EMI/World Film Services (John Heyman, Norman Priggen)
V*

Staying at a stately home around the turn of the
century, 12-year-old Leo carries love letters from a
farmer to his friend's sister.

A rather tiresome plot sustains a rich picture of the
Edwardian gentry, a milieu with which however the
director is not at home and treats far too slowly and
tricksily.

w Harold Pinter   *novel* L. P. Hartley   *d* Joseph
Losey   *ph* Geoffrey Fisher   *m* Michel Legrand
ad Carmen Dillon

Alan Bates, Julie Christie, Michael Redgrave,
Dominic Guard, Michael Gough, Margaret Leighton,
Edward Fox

'It's an almost palpable recreation of a past
environment, and that environment is the film's real
achievement, not the drama enacted within it.' –
Stanley Kauffmann

AAN: Margaret Leighton

God Gave Him a Dog: see *The Biscuit Eater* (1940)

God Is My Co-Pilot

US   1945   89m   bw
Warner (Robert Buckner)

Pacific air adventures during World War II.

Adequate flagwaver.

w Peter Milne, Abem Finkel   *book* Col. Robert Lee
Scott Jnr   *d* Robert Florey   *ph* Sid Hickox
m Franz Waxman

Dennis Morgan, Dane Clark, Raymond Massey, Alan
Hale, Andrea King, John Ridgely, Stanley Ridges,
Craig Stevens

'A slapped-together attraction . . . all the flashbacks,
supposedly emotional scenes, and fragments of
philosophy which punctuate the aerial action vitiate a
tale which might have been a notable addition to the
screen's extensive considerations of the far-flung
theatres of the war.' – *Howard Barnes, New York Herald
Tribune*

God Is My Partner

US   1957   82m   bw   Regalscope
TCF (Sam Hersh)

A surgeon retires and begins to give his money away

to religious causes; members of his family file suit
against him.

Rather obvious fable in the *Mr Deeds* tradition.

w Charles Francis Royal   *d* William F. Claxton

Walter Brennan, John Hoyt, Marion Ross, Jesse White

God Needs Men: see *Dieu a Besoin des Hommes*

God Told Me To

US   1976   89m   colour
Larco
GB title: *Demon*

A detective investigates the death of a mad sniper and
finds it to be a case of demonic possession.

Unsavoury mix of several genres, insufficiently well
written to compel.

wd Larry Cohen

Tony Lo Bianco, Deborah Raffin, Sandy Dennis,
Sylvia Sidney, Sam Levene, Robert Drivas, Richard
Lynch, Harry Bellaver

The Goddess *

US   1958   105m   bw
Columbia/Carnegie (Milton Perlman)
V*, L

A small-town girl becomes a Hollywood sex symbol
and lives to regret it.

Savage attack on the Marilyn Monroe cult, a bit
lachrymose and compromised by miscasting, but with
interesting detail.

w Paddy Chayevsky   *d* John Cromwell   *ph* Arthur J.
Ornitz   *m* Virgil Thompson

Kim Stanley, Lloyd Bridges, Steven Hill, Betty Lou
Holland

AAN: Paddy Chayevsky

The Goddess (1960): see *Devi*

The Godfather ****

US   1972   175m   Technicolor
Paramount/Alfran (Albert S. Ruddy)
V, V*, L, S

When, after ruling for two generations, the Mafia's
New York head dies of old age, his son takes over
reluctantly but later learns how to kill.

A brilliantly-made film with all the fascination of a
snake pit: a warm-hearted family saga except that the
members are thieves and murderers. Cutting would
help, but the duller conversational sections do
heighten the cunningly judged moments of suspense
and violence.

w Francis Ford Coppola, Mario Puzo   *novel* Mario
Puzo   *d Francis Ford Coppola*   *ph* Gordon Willis
m Nino Rota   *pd* Dean Tavoularis

Marlon Brando, Al Pacino, Robert Duvall, James Caan,
Richard Castellano, Diane Keaton, Talia Shire,
Richard Conte, John Marley

'The immorality lies in his presentation of murderers
as delightful family men – the criminal is the salt of
the earth – and to our shame we rub it into the
wounds of our Watergate-world mortality and even
ask for more.' – *Judith Crist, 1974*

'They have put pudding in Brando's cheeks and
dirtied his teeth, he speaks hoarsely and moves stiffly,
and these combined mechanics are hailed as great
acting . . . Like star, like film, the keynote is inflation.
The Godfather was made from a big bestseller, a lot of
money was spent on it, and it runs over three hours.
Therefore it's important.' – *Stanley Kauffmann*

'The greatest gangster picture ever made.' – *Pauline
Kael*

AA: best picture; script; Marlon Brando

AAN: Francis Ford Coppola (as director); Al Pacino; Robert Duvall; James Caan

The Godfather of Harlem: see *Black Caesar*

The Godfather Part II ****
US   1974   200m   Technicolor
Paramount/the Coppola Company (Francis Ford Coppola)
V, V*, L, S

In 1958, Michael Corleone reflects on the problems of himself and his father before him.

Complex gangster movie, explaining the present in terms of the past and providing a comprehensive view of American society, full of good scenes and performances.

w Francis Ford Coppola, Mario Puzo   d Francis Ford Coppola   ph Gordon Willis   m Nino Rota, Carmine Coppola   pd Dean Tavoularis

Al Pacino, *Robert de Niro*, Diane Keaton, Robert Duvall, John Cazale, Lee Strasberg, Michael V. Gazzo, Talia Shire, Troy Donahue

'The daring of Part II is that it enlarges the scope and deepens the meaning of the first film . . . It's an epic vision of the corruption of America.' – *Pauline Kael, New Yorker*

† The two films were eventually combined and extended for television into a ten-hour serial, *The Godfather Saga*.

AA: best picture; script; Francis Ford Coppola (as director); Nino Rota, Carmine Coppola; Robert de Niro

AAN: Al Pacino; Lee Strasberg; Michael V. Gazzo; Talia Shire

'Real Power Can't Be Given. It Must Be Taken.'
The Godfather Part III **
US   1990   161m   Technicolor
Paramount/Zoetrope (Francis Ford Coppola)
V, V*, L, S

Michael Corleone attempts to become a legitimate businessman while grooming his brother's violent and illegitimate son as his successor.

Overlong, often confusing to those who cannot remember the earlier films, and hampered by at least one wretched performance, it fails to reach the standard of the first two movies in the series. But for all that it retains one's interest most of the time.

w Mario Puzo, Francis Ford Coppola   d Francis Ford Coppola   ph Gordon Willis   m Carmine Coppola, Nino Rota   pd Dean Tavoularis   ad Alex Tavoularis   ed Barry Malkin, Lisa Fruchtman, Walter Murch

Al Pacino, Diane Keaton, Talia Shire, Andy Garcia, Eli Wallach, Joe Mantegna, George Hamilton, Bridget Fonda, Sofia Coppola, Raf Vallone, Franc D'Ambrosio, Donal Donnelly, Richard Bright, Helmut Berger, Don Novello

'While certain flaws may prevent it from being regarded as the full equal of its predecessors . . . it nonetheless matches them in narrative intensity, epic scope, sociopolitical analysis, physical beauty and deep feeling for its characters and milieu.' – *Variety*

'This engrossing movie is conceived and executed on a grand scale. In these inflationary times, the numbers of killings and the sums of money under discussion are much greater than before. But, oddly enough, Michael seems to shrink in stature as the picture proceeds and the *Lear*-like tragedy at which Coppola aims is not realised.' – *Philip French, Observer*

'As in the second film, a fearful price is paid for power, and Michael is left alone to consider the cost. It is here, in the ruined face of such a man, that *The Godfather Part III* locates an emotional gravity rare in American movies. The film is a slow fuse with a big bang – one that echoes through every family whose own tragedy is an aching for things past and loved ones lost.' – *Richard Corliss, Time*

AAN: best picture; best song 'Promise Me You'll Remember'; best art direction; best cinematography; best film editing

God's Country and the Woman
US   1936   80m   Technicolor
Warner (Lou Edelman)

The junior partner of a lumber company goes to work undercover in an opponent's camp, causes trouble, and falls in love.

Adequate outdoor melodrama in early colour.

w Norman Reilly Raine   novel James Oliver Curwood   d William Keighley   ph Tony Gaudio   m Max Steiner

George Brent, Beverly Roberts, Barton MacLane, Robert Barrat, Alan Hale, Addison Richards, El Brendel, Roscoe Ates, Billy Bevan

'Great outdoors in Technicolor, but not likely for much b.o.' – *Variety*

God's Gift to Women
US   1931   72m   bw
Warner

In Paris, a descendant of Don Juan is pursued by numerous women but falls for an American girl.

Tedious comedy with a star out of his element.

w Joseph Jackson, Raymond Griffith   play *The Devil Was Sick* by Jane Hinton   d Michael Curtiz

Frank Fay, Joan Blondell, Laura la Plante, Charles Winninger, Louise Brooks

'No gift to audiences.' – *Variety*

'The story that no one dared film till now becomes the most adult motion picture ever made!'
God's Little Acre *
US   1958   110m   bw
Security (Sidney Harmon)
V*

A poor white farmer in Georgia neglects his land in a fruitless search for gold.

Tobacco Road under another name, and not so lively: bowdlerized and eventually tedious despite a welter of sensational incident and depraved characters.

w Philip Yordan   novel Erskine Caldwell   d Anthony Mann   ph Ernest Haller   m Elmer Bernstein

Robert Ryan, Aldo Ray, Tina Louise, Buddy Hackett, Jack Lord, Vic Morrow, Rex Ingram

The Gods Must Be Crazy
South Africa   1980   109m   colour   Panavision
New Realm/Mimosa/CAT (Jamie Uys)
V, V*, L

A Coca-Cola bottle falls from a plane and becomes a religious object to Kalahari bushmen.

Unexpected throwback farce with the blacks behaving almost as stupidly as Mantan Moreland in an old Charlie Chan movie. One for the Race Relations Board.

wd Jamie Uys   ph Jamie Uys, Buster Reynolds   m John Boshoff   ad Caroline Burls

N'xau, Marius Weyers, Sandra Prinsloo, Nic de Jager, Michael Thys

The Gods Must Be Crazy II
South Africa   1988   98m   colour
Fox/Elrina Investment Corp (Boet Troskie)
V, V*, L

A bushman searching for his lost children finds a New York lawyer in the desert.

Implausible tale, as condescending as the first film to its black cast.

wd Jamie Uys   ph Buster Reynolds   m Charles Fox   ed Renee Engelbrecht, Ivan Hall

N'xau, Lena Farugia, Hans Strydom, Eiros, Nadies, Erick Bowen, Treasure Tshabalala, Pierre Van Pletzen, Lournes Swanepoel, Richard Loring

The Godson: see *The Samurai*

'The gospel according to today!'
Godspell *
US   1973   102m   TVC color
Columbia/Lansbury/Duncan/Beruh (Edgar Lansbury)

The Gospel according to St Matthew played out musically by hippies in the streets of New York.

Wild and woolly film version of the successful theatrical fantasy, surviving chiefly by virtue of its gleaming photography.

w David Greene, John Michael Tebelak   play John Michael Tebelak   d David Greene   ph Richard G. Heimann   m/ly Stephen Schwartz

Victor Garber, David Haskell, Jerry Sroka, Lynne Thigpen, Robin Lamont

'A patch of terra incognita somewhere between *Sesame Street* and the gospel according to *Laugh-In*.' – *Bruce Williamson*

Godzilla
Japan   1955   80m (dubbed version)   bw
Toho (Tomoyuki Tanaka)
V*
original title: *Gojira*

A prehistoric monster is awakened by H-bomb tests and menaces Tokyo.

Tepid forerunner of scores of Japanese monster movies peopled by men in rubber suits.

w Takeo Murato, Inoshiro Honda   d Inoshiro Honda   ph Masao Tamai   m Akira Ifukube

Raymond Burr, Takashi Shimura, Momoko Kochi

† Sequels included *Godzilla vs the Thing, King Kong vs Godzilla, Godzilla vs the Sea Monster, Godzilla vs the Smog Monster, Destroy All Monsters*. Other monstrous creations included *Rodan, Manda* and *Mothra*.

Godzilla on Monster Island: see *Godzilla versus Gigan*

Godzilla versus Gigan
Japan   1972   89m (dubbed)   colour
Toho Productions (Tomoyuki Tanaka)
aka: *Godzilla on Monster Island*

With the aid of Godzilla and his friends, a comic-book artist foils a plot by giant alien cockroaches to take over the world.

The usual nonsense, with the novelty of talking monsters, although their dialogue is no more interesting than that of the humans.

w Shinichi Sekizawa   d Jun Fukuda   m Akira Ifukube   pd Yoshifumi Honda   sp Akiyoshi Nakano   ed Yoshio Tamura

Hiroshi Ishikawa, Tomoko Umeda, Yuriko Hishimi, Minora Takashima, Zan Fujita, Toshiaki Nishizawa, Kunio Murai

Godzilla versus Megalon
Japan   1976   80m (dubbed)   colour
Toho Studios (Tomoyuki Tanaka)
V*

Angered by nuclear tests, the ruler of an underwater world sends a monster, a sort of winged lobster, to destroy Tokyo.

Most ridiculous, and, for that reason, the most enjoyable of the *Godzilla* series, notable for the Seatopians, a submarine race given to wearing togas with knee-length boots, and the tag-team wrestling style of the monster combats.

w Shinichi Sekizawa   d Jun Fukuda   ph Yuzuru Aizawa   m Riichiro Manabe   ad Yoshibumi Honda   sp Akiyoshi Nakano   ed Michiko Ikeda

Katsuhiko Sasaki, Yutaka Hayashi, Hiroyuki Kawase

Godzilla versus Monster Zero: see *Invasion of the Astro-Monsters*

Gog *
US 1954 85m Color Corporation 3D
Ivan Tors

In an underground laboratory in New Mexico, a giant computer controls two robots, and a spy programs it to kill.

Brisk, imaginative low-budget sci-fi in gleaming colour, well staged and developed.

w Tom Taggart   d Herbert B. Strock   ph Lothrop B. Worth   m Harry Sukman

Richard Egan, Constance Dowling, Herbert Marshall

The Go-Getter
US 1937 90m bw
Warner (Sam Bischoff)

A one-legged navy veteran is determined that his injury will not prevent him from becoming a success.

Moderate comedy-drama, agreeably played.

w Delmer Daves, Peter B. Kyne   d Busby Berkeley   ph Arthur Edeson   md Leo F. Forbstein

George Brent, Charles Winninger, Anita Louise, John Eldredge, Henry O'Neill, Willard Robertson, Eddie Acuff

'A fair amount of comedy within a story bordering on the ridiculous.' – *Variety*

Goha
France/Tunisia 1957 90m Agfacolor
Films Franco-Africains

A young Arab helps a blind musician and falls in love with a wise man's young bride.

Curiously winning, good-looking little romance which, apart from an unexpected sad ending, plays like an update of the Arabian Nights.

w Georges Schéhadé   novel Le Livre de Goha le Simple by A. Ades, A. Jospiovici   d Jacques Baratier   ph Jean Bourgoin   m Maurice Ohana

Omar Chérif (later Sharif), Zina Bouzaiane, Lauro Gazzolo

Going Bye Bye **
US 1934 20m bw
Hal Roach

A violent convict escapes to take vengeance on the two innocents whose evidence sent him up.

Splendid star comedy displaying most of the team's most endearing aspects.

w Anon   d Charles Rogers   ph Francis Corbyed   Bert Jordan

Laurel and Hardy, Walter Long, Mae Busch

Going Highbrow
US 1935 68m bw
Warner

Two *nouveaux riches* people try to trick their way into society.

Agreeably cast farce that outstays its welcome.

w Edward Kaufmann, Sy Bartlett, Ralph Spence   d Edward Florey

Edward Everett Horton, Guy Kibbee, ZaSu Pitts, Ross Alexander, Judy Canova

'So-so flicker for the lesser spots.' – *Variety*

Going Hollywood *
US 1933 80m bw
MGM
V*, L

A crooner is pursued by a girl who poses as a French maid.

Lively comedy with a studio setting; anything goes.

w Donald Ogden Stewart   d Raoul Walsh

Bing Crosby, Marion Davies, Patsy Kelly, Stuart Erwin

'Lavishly produced musical with everything but a story.' – *Variety*

Going Home
US 1971 98m colour
MGM
L

An ex-convict who killed his wife while drunk assumes an ambivalent relationship with his son.

Thoroughly uninteresting melodrama which was barely released.

w Lawrence Marcus   d Herbert B. Leonard

Robert Mitchum, Jan-Michael Vincent, Brenda Vaccaro

Going in Style
US 1979 97m Technicolor
Warner/Tony Bill

Three bored elderly men decide to plan a bank robbery.

Curiously aimless sentimental comedy-drama which is simply neither funny enough, thrilling enough or moving enough to hold the interest.

wd Martin Brest   ph Billy Williams   m Michael Small

George Burns, Art Carney, Lee Strasberg

Going My Way **
US 1944 126m bw
Paramount (Leo McCarey)
V*, L

A young priest comes to a New York slum parish and after initial friction charms the old pastor he is to succeed.

Sentimental comedy which got away with it wonderfully at the time, largely through careful casting, though it seems thin and obvious now.

w Frank Butler, Frank Cavett, Leo McCarey   d Leo McCarey   ph Lionel Lindon   m Robert Emmett Dolan   m/ly Johnny Burke, James Van Heusen, J. R. Shannon   ed Leroy Stone

Bing Crosby, Barry Fitzgerald, Rise Stevens, Frank McHugh, James Brown, Gene Lockhart, Jean Heather, Porter Hall

'I should not feel safe in recommending it to anyone but a simple-hearted sentimentalist with a taste for light music.' – *Richard Mallett, Punch*

'The lessons, if I read them right, are that leisureliness can be excellent, that if you take a genuine delight in character the universe is opened to you, and perhaps above all that a movie, like any other genuine work of art, must be made for love. But I am willing to bet that the chief discernible result of *Going My Way* will be an anxiety-ridden set of vaudeville sketches about Pat and Mike in cassocks.' – *James Agee*

† Father O'Malley reappeared in *The Bells of St Mary's* and *Say One for Me* (both qv).

AA: best picture; script; original story (Leo McCarey); Leo McCarey (direction); Bing Crosby; Barry Fitzgerald (best supporting actor); song, 'Swinging on a Star' (m James Van Heusen, ly Johnny Burke)

AAN: Lionel Lindon; Barry Fitzgerald (best actor); Leroy Stone

Going Places
US 1938 84m bw
Warner (Hal Wallis)

A sporting goods salesman poses as a jockey and has to ride a horse to victory.

Thin musical spurred by the hit song 'Jeepers Creepers', here sung by Louis Armstrong to the race horse.

w Jerry Wald, Sig Herzig, Maurice Leo   play The Hottentot by Victor Mapes, William Collier   d Ray Enright   ph Arthur L. Todd   md Leo F. Forbstein   ad Hugh Reticker   ed Clarence Kolster

Dick Powell, Anita Louise, Ronald Reagan, Louis Armstrong, Allen Jenkins, Walter Catlett

'Satisfactory but not smash.' – *Variety*

AAN: song 'Jeepers Creepers' (m Harry Warren, ly Johnny Mercer)

'Saved from the hangman for a fate worse than death!'
Goin' South
US 1978 101m Metrocolor
Paramount (Henry Gittes, Harold Schneider)
V, V*, L

An unwashed outlaw is saved from the rope when a young girl promises to marry and reform him . . .

. . . for no very good reason. Curious semi-comic Western which might have made a good two-reeler.

w John Herman Shaner, Al Ramrus, Charles Shyer, Alan Mandel   d Jack Nicholson   ph Nestor Almendros   m Van Dyke Parks, Perry Botkin Jnr

Jack Nicholson, Mary Steenburgen, Christopher Lloyd, John Belushi, Veronica Cartwright, Richard Bradford

'Mae's a lady now and she'll lick anyone in the house who says she ain't!'
Goin' To Town *
US 1935 74m bw
Paramount (William Le Baron)

A Western oil heiress moves into society.

Reasonably satisfactory Mae West vehicle, but not in the old bawdy style.

w Mae West   d Alexander Hall   ph Karl Struss   md Andrea Setaro   m/ly Sammy Fain, Irving Kahal

Mae West, Paul Cavanagh, Ivan Lebedeff, Tito Coral, Marjorie Gateson, Fred Kohler Snr, Monroe Owsley

'No amount of epigrammatic hypoing can offset the silly story.' – *Variety*

Gold *
Germany 1934 105m bw
UFA

Scientists invent a machine that will make synthetic gold.

Overlong melodrama made in German and French, boring when the equipment is off the screen.

w Rolf E. Vanloo   d Karl Hartl

Hans Albers, Brigitte Helm, Lien Deyers, Michael Bohnen

† The central sequences were reused years later for the climax of *The Magnetic Monster* (qv).

Gold *
GB 1974 124m Technicolor Panavision
Hemdale/Avton (Michael Klinger)
V*

A South African mining engineer falls for the boss's granddaughter and exposes a conspiracy.

Old-fashioned thick ear with spectacular underground sequences and a rousing finale.

w Wilbur Smith, Stanley Price   novel Goldmine by Wilbur Smith   d Peter Hunt   ph Ousama Rawi   m Elmer Bernstein

Roger Moore, Susannah York, Ray Milland, Bradford Dillman, John Gielgud, Tony Beckley

AAN: song 'Wherever Love Takes Me' (m Elmer Bernstein, ly Don Black)

'Exceeds in pretentiousness and beauty anything which has yet appeared on the screen!'

Gold Diggers of Broadway *
US 1929 98m Technicolor
Warner

Three Broadway chorus girls seek rich husbands.

Fascinating primitive musical that includes the songs 'Tiptoe Through the Tulips' and 'Painting the Clouds With Sunshine'.

w Robert Lord play The Gold Diggers by Avery Hopwood d Roy del Ruth ph Barney McGill, Ray Rennahan m/y Al Dubin, Joe Burke

Nancy Welford, Conway Tearle, Winnie Lightner, Ann Pennington, Lilyan Tashman, William Bakewell, Nick Lucas

† Other versions of the play include *The Gold Diggers* (1923), *Gold Diggers of 1933* (qv), *Painting the Clouds with Sunshine* (qv).

'Your dream of perfect beauty come true!'

Gold Diggers of 1933 ***
US 1933 96m bw
Warner (Robert Lord)
V*, L

Cheerful, competent, well-cast remake of the above; numbers include 'My Forgotten Man', 'We're in the Money' and 'Pettin' in the Park'.

w Erwin Gelsey, James Seymour, David Boehm, Ben Markson play The Gold Diggers by Avery Hopwood d Mervyn Le Roy ch Busby Berkeley ph Sol Polito m/y Harry Warren, Al Dubin

Warren William, Joan Blondell, *Aline MacMahon*, Ruby Keeler, Dick Powell, Guy Kibbee, Ned Sparks, Ginger Rogers, Clarence Nordstrom

'It sums up what is meant by the phrase "pure thirties": electrically wired chorus girls singing "In the Shadows Let Me Come and Sing to You" merge to form a big illuminated violin.' – *New Yorker, 1979*

'It is memorable chiefly because Busby Berkeley created a mad geometry of patterned chorines. . . . The innocent vulgarity of the big numbers is charming and uproarious, and aesthetically preferable to the pretentious ballet finales of fifties musicals like *An American in Paris*. Even those of us who were children at the time did not mistake *Gold Diggers* for art – and certainly no one took it for life.' – *Pauline Kael, 1968*

Gold Diggers of 1935 **
US 1935 95m bw
Warner (Robert Lord)
V, V*, L

A socialite puts on a Broadway show at her country home, and is taken in by a swindler.

Heavy-handed but laugh-provoking comedy with familiar faces of the day, climaxed by big numbers including 'Lullaby of Broadway'.

w Manuel Seff, Peter Milne, Robert Lord d/ch Busby Berkeley ph George Barnes md Ray Heindorf m/y Harry Warren, Al Dubin

Dick Powell, Adolphe Menjou, Gloria Stuart, Alice Brady, Hugh Herbert, Glenda Farrell, Frank McHugh, Grant Mitchell, Wini Shaw

'Busby Berkeley, the master of scenic prestidigitation, continues to dazzle the eye and stun the imagination.' – *André Sennwald, New York Times*

'A decidedly heady mixture.' – *Pare Lorentz*

AA: song 'Lullaby of Broadway'

AAN: choreography

Gold Diggers of 1937 *
US 1936 100m bw
Warner (Hal B. Wallis)

A group of insurance salesmen back a show.

Mild tailing-off of the Gold Diggers series, though with the accustomed production polish.

w Warren Duff play Richard Maibaum, Michael Wallach, George Haight d Lloyd Bacon ch Busby Berkeley ph Arthur Edeson m/y Harry Warren, Al Dubin, E. Y. Harburg, Harold Arlen

Dick Powell, Joan Blondell, Glenda Farrell, Victor Moore, Lee Dixon, Osgood Perkins, Charles D. Brown

AAN: Busby Berkeley

Gold Diggers in Paris *
US 1938 95m bw
Warner (Sam Bischoff)
GB title: *The Gay Imposters*

Three girls chase rich husbands abroad.

A thin end to the series, saved by an agreeable cast.

w Earl Baldwin, Warren Duff d Ray Enright ph Sol Polito, George Barnes ch Busby Berkeley m/y Harry Warren, Al Dubin, Johnny Mercer

Rudy Vallee, Rosemary Lane, Hugh Herbert, Allen Jenkins, Gloria Dickson, Melville Cooper, Fritz Feld, Ed Brophy, Curt Bois

Gold Dust Gertie
US 1931 66m bw
Warner
GB title: *Why Change Your Husband?*

A tough divorcee tries to sponge on her former spouses.

Silly and unattractive comedy.

w W. K. Wells, Ray Enright play The Life of the Party by Len D. Hollister d Lloyd Bacon

Winnie Lightner, Chic Johnson, Ole Olsen, Dorothy Carlisle, Claude Gillingwater

'Roughest kind of comedy dialogue; in need of careful surgery.' – *Variety*

Gold Is Where You Find It *
US 1938 90m Technicolor
Warner (Sam Bischoff)

Gold rush miners settle as California farmers.

Agreeable Western in excellent early colour.

w Warren Duff, Clements Ripley, Robert Buckner d Michael Curtiz ph Sol Polito m Max Steiner

George Brent, Olivia de Havilland, Claude Rains, Margaret Lindsay, John Litel, Marcia Ralston, Barton MacLane, Tim Holt, Sidney Toler

Gold of Naples
Italy 1955 135m bw
Ponti-de Laurentiis
original title: *L'Oro di Napoli*

Six sketches, comic and tragic, give an impression of Naples today.

A variable collection, mainly shown around the world in abridged versions.

w Cesare Zavattini, Vittorio de Sica, Giuseppe Marotta d Vittorio de Sica ph Otello Martelli m Alessandro Cicognini

Vittorio de Sica, Eduardo de Filippo, Toto, Sophia Loren, Paolo Stoppa, Silvana Mangano

Gold of the Seven Saints
US 1961 89m bw Warnerscope
Warner (Leonard Freeman)

Cowboys compete in a search for lost gold.

Adequate minor Western using TV stars.

w Leigh Brackett, Leonard Freeman d Gordon Douglas ph Joseph Biroc m Howard Jackson

Clint Walker, Roger Moore, Leticia Roman, Robert Middleton, Chill Wills, Gene Evans

The Gold Rush ***
US 1925 72m (sound version 1942) bw
Charles Chaplin
V, V*, L

A lone prospector in the Yukon becomes rich after various adventures.

Essentially a succession of slowly but carefully built visual gags, this is Chaplin's finest example of comedy drawn from utter privation; as such it appealed vastly to the poor of the world. As a clown, Chaplin himself is near his best, though as usual there is rather too much straining for pathos.

wd/p/m Charles Chaplin ph Rollie Totheroh md Max Terr (1942 version) ad Charles D. Hall ed Harold McGhean (1942 version)

Charles Chaplin, Georgia Hale, Mack Swain, Tom Murray

AAN: Max Terr

The Golden Age of Buster Keaton **
US 1975 97m bw
Jay Ward (Raymond Rohauer)

A useful introductory package to the shorts and features of Buster Keaton, with most of the great silent scenes present.

commentary: Bill Scott

The Golden Age of Comedy ****
US 1957 78m bw
Robert Youngson Productions
V*

First of the scholarly compilations of silent comedy which saved many negatives from destruction, this is a fast-paced general survey which despite a facetious sound track does provide a laugh a minute.

It particularly brought Laurel and Hardy back into public notice, and includes sections from *Two Tars* and *The Battle of the Century*.

wd Robert Youngson narrators Dweight Weist, Ward Wilson m George Steiner

Stan Laurel, Oliver Hardy, Harry Langdon, Ben Turpin, Will Rogers, Billy Bevan, Charlie Chase, Andy Clyde

Golden Arrow
US 1936 68m bw
Warner

An heiress tricks a newspaper reporter into a marriage of convenience.

Dull, schematic romantic comedy.

w Charles Kenyon, Michael Arlen d Alfred E. Green

Bette Davis, George Brent, Eugene Pallette, Dick Foran

Golden Arrow
GB 1952 82m bw
Anatole de Grunwald
US title: *The Gay Adventure*

On a transcontinental train, three men have different daydreams about the same girl.

Transparent portmanteau comedy which didn't click.

w Paul Darcy, Sid Colin d Gordon Parry

Jean Pierre Aumont, Paula Valenska, Burgess Meredith, Richard Murdoch, Kathleen Harrison, Karel Stepanek, Edward Lexy

'His blade of gold, a legend in battle – her kiss of surrender, the prize of victory!'

The Golden Blade
US 1953 80m Technicolor
U-I (Richard Wilson)

With the help of a magic sword, Harun saves a princess and captures a rebel.

Standard cut-rate Arabian Nights adventure, very typical of its studio during the fifties.

w John Rich d Nathan Juran ph Maury Gertsman m Joseph Gershenson

Rock Hudson, Piper Laurie, George Macready, Gene Evans, Kathleen Hughes

Golden Boy *
US   1939   101m   bw
Columbia (William Perlberg)
V*, L

A poor boy is torn between two absorbing interests: prizefighting and the violin.

Personalized version of a socially conscious play; moderately effective with smooth production and good cast.

w Lewis Meltzer, Daniel Taradash, Sarah Y. Mason, Victor Heerman play Clifford Odets d Rouben Mamoulian ph Nicholas Musuraca, Karl Freund md Morris Stoloff m Victor Young ad Lionel Banks ed Otto Meyer

Barbara Stanwyck, William Holden, Adolphe Menjou, Joseph Calleia, Lee J. Cobb, Sam Levene, Edward Brophy, Don Beddoe

'Strong entertainment with general audience appeal.' – Variety

'A slick, swift, exciting but insensitive movie.' – Gordon Sager

'Interesting, entertaining, dramatic, but scarcely first-rate.' – Frank Nugent, New York Times

AAN: Victor Young

Golden Braid *
Australia   1990   91m   colour
Artificial Eye/Illumination/Australian Film Commission/Film Victoria (Paul Cox, Paul Ammitzboll, Santhana Naidu)
V

A clock restorer, obsessed by death and time, falls in love with a braid of hair he discovers in the secret drawer of an antique cabinet.

Slow-paced account of a man trying to decide between fantasy and reality that at times comes near to showing that one man's obsession is another's tedium.

w Paul Cox, Barry Dickens story La Chevelure by Guy de Maupassant d Paul Cox ph Nino G. Marinetti pd Neil Angwin ed Russell Hurley

Chris Haywood, Gosia Dobrowolska, Paul Chubb, Norman Kaye, Marion Heathfield, Monica Maughan, Robert Menzies, Jo Kennedy

The Golden Child
US   1986   93m   Metrocolor
Paramount/Feldman-Meeker/Eddie Murphy
V, V*, L

A social worker is assigned to look for a mystic child who will bring peace to the Earth.

Astonishingly inept fantasy.

w Dennis Feldman d Michael Ritchie ph Donald E. Thorin m Michael Colombier

Eddie Murphy, Charles Dance, Charlotte Lewis, Victor Wong

The Golden Coach
Italy/France   1953   100m   Technicolor
Hoche/Panaria (Valentine Brosio, Giuseppe Bordognoi)
V*, L
original title: Le Carrosse d'Or

In Spanish South America in the 18th century, the leading lady of a band of strolling players turns all heads including that of the viceroy, who scandalizes all by making her a present of his official golden coach.

The director seems to have been chiefly interested in the colour and the backgrounds: the story is a bore and the leading lady ill-chosen.

w Jean Renoir, Jack Kirkland, Renzo Avanzo, Giulio Macchi play Prosper Merimée d Jean Renoir ph Claude Renoir m Vivaldi

Anna Magnani, Duncan Lamont, Paul Campbell, Ricardo Rioli, William Tubbs

Golden Dawn
US   1930   81m   Technicolor
Warner

An English regiment holds the blacks at bay.

An operetta outmoded even in 1930, stagily brought to the screen.

w Walter Anthony d Ray Enright m/ly Emmerich Kalman, Herbert Stothart

Walter Woolf, Vivienne Segal, Noah Beery, Alice Gentle, Lupino Lane

'Everybody seems to sing, even Noah Beery in blackface.' – Variety

'Now you know the way a gypsy loves!'

Golden Earrings *
US   1947   95m   bw
Paramount (Harry Tugend)

A British Intelligence officer is helped by a gypsy to sneak a poison gas formula out of Nazi Germany.

One of the silliest stories of all time, despite the presence of Quentin Reynolds asserting that he believed it; also lacking in the humour which might have saved it, but produced with polish and interesting for the two stars at this stage in their careers.

w Abraham Polonsky, Frank Butler, Helen Deutsch novel Yolanda Foldes d Mitchell Leisen ph Daniel L. Fapp m Victor Young

Ray Milland, Marlene Dietrich, Murvyn Vye, Bruce Lester, Dennis Hoey, Reinhold Schunzel, Ivan Triesault

'A good deal of torso work goes on which I can't help feeling they're a bit old for.' – Richard Winnington

The Golden Falcon (dubbed)
1955   Italy   90m   colour
Ottavio Poggi
original title: Il Falco d'Oro

Rivalry between two powerful Italian families becomes more intense when plans go wrong over an arranged marriage to end the fighting.

Comic swashbuckler, performed without much panache and not helped by unsympathetic dubbing.

d Carlo Ludovico Bragaglia ph Alvaro Mancori

Anna Maria Ferrero, Nadia Gray, Massimo Serato

The Golden Fleecing
US   1940   68m   bw
MGM (Edgar Selwyn)

A timid insurance salesman becomes embroiled with gangsters.

Modestly effective double-bill comedy.

w S. J. and Laura Perelman d Leslie Fenton

Lew Ayres, Lloyd Nolan, Virginia Grey, Leon Errol, Rita Johnson, Nat Pendleton, William Demarest, Marc Lawrence

Golden Girl *
US   1951   108m   Technicolor
TCF (George Jessel)

The story of Lotta Crabtree, who after the Civil War determined to become a great musical star.

Harmless semi-Western biopic with good tunes.

w Walter Bullock, Charles O'Neal, Gladys Lehman d Lloyd Bacon ph Charles G. Clarke md Lionel Newman ch Seymour Felix

Mitzi Gaynor, Dale Robertson, Dennis Day, James Barton, Una Merkel, Raymond Walburn, Gene Sheldon

AAN: song 'Never' (m Lionel Newman, ly Eliot Daniel)

Golden Gloves
US   1939   69m   bw
Paramount

A sports reporter cleans up a boxing racket.

Competent second feature.

w Maxwell Shane, Lewis R. Foster d Edward Dmytryk

Richard Denning, Jeanne Cagney, William Frawley, Robert Ryan

The Golden Hawk
US   1952   83m   Technicolor
Columbia

A pirate determines to avenge his mother's death at the hands of the governor of Cartagena.

Clean-cut period romp for boys who don't demand realism.

w Robert E. Kent novel Frank Yerby d Sidney Salkow

Sterling Hayden, Rhonda Fleming, John Sutton, Helena Carter, Paul Cavanagh

The Golden Head
US/Hungary   1964   115m   Technirama 70
Cinerama/Hungarofilm (Alexander Paal)

Passengers on a Danube pleasure boat become involved in the theft of the golden head of St Laszlo.

Travelogue with a thin plot, somewhat slow moving but suitable for children.

w Stanley Boulder, Ivan Boldizsar d Richard Thorpe ph Istvan Hildebrand m Peter Fenyes

George Sanders, Buddy Hackett, Douglas Wilmer, Jess Conrad, Robert Coote

The Golden Heist: see Inside Out

The Golden Horde
US   1951   76m   Technicolor
U-I (Howard Christie)
aka: The Golden Horde of Genghis Khan

Crusaders meet Mongols in Samarkand, and Sir Guy wins a princess.

Rather priceless idiocies are perpetrated in this variation on the studio's favourite Arabian Nights theme, but somehow they fail to make one laugh, which should be the only possible response to such a farrago.

w Gerald Drayson Adams d George Sherman ph Russell Metty m Hans Salter

David Farrar, Ann Blyth, George Macready, Henry Brandon, Richard Egan, Marvin Miller

The Golden Horde of Genghis Khan: see The Golden Horde

The Golden Hour: see Pot o' Gold

The Golden Madonna
GB   1949   88m   bw
IFP/Pendennis (John Stafford)

Two young people search Italy for a religious painting stolen by thieves.

Stilted but eager to please, this romantic comedy-drama seemed a bit lacking in drive.

w Akos Tolnay d Ladislas Vajda ph Anchise Brizzi

Phyllis Calvert, Michael Rennie, Tullio Carminati, David Greene, Aldo Silvani

Golden Marie: see Casque d'Or

The Golden Mask: see South of Algiers

The Golden Mistress *
US   1954   80m   Technicolor
UA/RK (Richard Kay, Harry Rybnick)

An American and his girlfriend search the sea bed for the forbidden treasure of a Haitian tribe.

Curious independent production, an adventure in the style of silent serials; amateur in many ways, yet with a freshness of photography and location plus some powerful voodoo scenes.

wd Joel Judge (Abner Biberman)   ph William
C. Thompson   m Raoul Kraushaar

John Agar, Rosemarie Bowe, Abner Biberman

'Whoever owns them can rule the world!'
Golden Needles
US   1974   92m   Movielab   Panavision
AIP/Sequoia (Fred Weintraub, Paul Heller)

Various factions seek a Hong Kong statue showing seven miraculous acupuncture points.

Youth/sex/Kung Fu/James Bond action amalgam.

w S. Lee Pogostin, Sylvia Schneble   d Robert
Clouse   ph Gilbert Hubbs   m Lalo Schifrin

Joe Don Baker, Elizabeth Ashley, Jim Kelly, Burgess Meredith, Ann Sothern

Golden Rendezvous
US   1977   109m   colour
Film Trust/Milton Okun (Andre Pieterse)
V*

Murderous mercenaries take over a freighter, but reckon without the courageous first officer.

Blood-and-thunder hokum with many casualties but not much sense.

w Stanley Price   novel Alistair MacLean   d Ashley
Lazarus   ph Ken Higgins   m Jeff Wayne

Richard Harris, Ann Turkel, David Janssen, Burgess Meredith, John Vernon, Gordon Jackson, Keith Baxter, Dorothy Malone, John Carradine, Robert Flemyng, Leigh Lawson, Robert Beatty

The Golden Salamander
GB   1949   87m   bw
GFD/Pinewood (Ronald Neame, Alexander Galperson)

An Englishman in Tunis defeats gun runners.

Boring and unconvincing action hokum.

w Lesley Storm, Victor Canning, Ronald Neame
novel Victor Canning   d Ronald Neame
ph Oswald Morris   m William Alwyn

Trevor Howard, Anouk Aimée, Herbert Lom, Miles Malleson, Walter Rilla, Jacques Sernas, Wilfrid Hyde-White, Peter Copley

The Golden Seal *
US   1983   94m   Metrocolor
Samuel Goldwyn Jnr (Russell Thatcher)
L

On a bleak Aleutian island a boy stops hunters from killing a seal once thought mythical.

Rather chilling and thinly plotted moral fable for children, who may, however, be bored. The seals, the scenery and the music just about save it.

w John Groves   novel A River Ran out of Eden by
James Vance Marshall   d Frank Zuniga   ph Eric
Saarinen   m Dana Kaproff, John Barry

Steve Railsback, Michael Beck, Penelope Milford, Torquil Campbell

The Golden Virgin: see The Story of Esther Costello

The Golden Voyage of Sinbad *
GB   1973   105m   Eastmancolor
Columbia/Morningside (Charles H. Schneer)
V, V*, L

Sinbad finds a strange map and crosses swords with a great magician.

Routine, rather uninspired fantasy enlivened by grotesque trick effects.

w Brian Clemens, Ray Harryhausen   d Gordon
Hessler   ph Ted Moore   m Miklos Rozsa
pd John Stoll   sp Ray Harryhausen

John Philip Law, Caroline Munro, Tom Baker, Douglas Wilmer, Grégoire Aslan

Goldengirl
US   1979   104m   colour
Avco Embassy (Danny O'Donovan)
V*

A scientist uses experimental drugs on his daughter to turn her into an Olympic champion runner.

Ridiculous and overblown fantasy with a cast busily distancing themselves from the script.

w John Kohn   novel Peter Lear   d Joseph Sargent
ph Steven Larner   m Bill Conti   ad Syd Litwack
ed George Nicholson

Susan Anton, James Coburn, Curt Jurgens, Leslie Caron, Robert Culp, James A. Watson Jnr, Harry Guardino, Ward Costello, Michael Lerner

'James Bond 007 Back In Action!'
Goldfinger ***
GB   1964   112m   Technicolor
UA/Eon (Harry Saltzman, Albert R. Broccoli)
V, V*, L

James Bond prevents an international gold smuggler from robbing Fort Knox.

Probably the liveliest and most amusing of the Bond spy spoofs, with a fairly taut plot between the numerous highlights. The big budget is well used.

w Richard Maibaum, Paul Dehn   novel Ian Fleming
d Guy Hamilton   ph Ted Moore   m John Barry
pd Ken Adam   titles Robert Brownjohn

Sean Connery, Honor Blackman, Gert Frobe, Harold Sakata, Shirley Eaton, Bernard Lee, Lois Maxwell, Desmond Llewellyn

'A dazzling object lesson in the principle that nothing succeeds like excess.' – Penelope Gilliatt

'A diverting comic strip for grown-ups.' – Judith Crist

Goldie
US   1931   58m   bw
Fox

A carnival girl causes a rift between two sailors.

Curious comedy-drama notable only for its stars.

w Gene Towne, Paul Perez   d Ben Stoloff

Spencer Tracy, Jean Harlow, Warren Hymer, Lina Basquette, Maria Alba

The Goldwyn Follies **
US   1938   115m   Technicolor
Samuel Goldwyn
V*

A Hollywood producer seeks the average girl to test his scripts.

Goldwyn's failure to become Ziegfeld, chiefly due to a lack of humour in the script, still has a soupçon of effective Hollywood satire and some excellent numbers.

w Ben Hecht   d George Marshall   ph Gregg
Toland   m Alfred Newman   ch George Balanchine
ad Richard Day

Kenny Baker, Vera Zorina, the Ritz Brothers, Adolphe Menjou, Edgar Bergen and Charlie McCarthy, Helen Jepson, Phil Baker, Ella Logan, Bobby Clark, Jerome Cowan, Nydia Westman, Andrea Leeds

'An advance glimpse at next Sunday's amusement section from any metropolitan newspaper.' – Variety

'The bizarre in musical pretentiousness.' – Commonweal

'Many features to suit all tastes and not enough of them to suit anybody's.' – Time

AAN: Alfred Newman; Richard Day

The Golem ***
Germany   1920   75m approx   bw   silent
UFA

In 16th-century Prague a Jewish Rabbi constructs a man of clay to defend his people against a pogrom.

There were several versions of this story (Germany 1913, sequel 1917; Czechoslovakia 1935 and 1951), but this is almost certainly the best, its splendid sets, performances and certain scenes all being clearly influential on later Hollywood films, especially Frankenstein.

w Paul Wegener, Henrik Galeen   d Paul Wegener,
Carl Boese   ph Karl Freund, Guido Seeber   ad Hans
Poelzig

Paul Wegener, Albert Steinruck, Ernst Deutsch

The Golem *
Czechoslovakia   1936   95m   bw
AB
GB title: The Legend of Prague

Rather disappointing remake with entirely French crew.

w André Paul Antoine, Julien Duvivier   d Julien
Duvivier

Harry Baur, Roger Karl, Ferdinand Hart, Charles Dorat

'Sequences are scattered; there's no build-up, and no human interest is created.' – Variety

'It is all rich and spacious, and rather exquisite, and the big scene at the end should do nicely. If one can forget that Wegener once did it so much better, with nothing but a robot, a child and a flower.' – C. A. Lejeune

The Golf Specialist **
US   1930   18m   bw
RKO

A film version of a classic vaudeville golfing sketch (also reprised in You're Telling Me).

d Monte Brice

W. C. Fields

Golgotha *
France   1935   100m   bw
D'Agular
S

The trial and passion of Jesus Christ.

Impressive version made at a time when the portrayal of Christ was still virtually taboo.

wd Julien Duvivier   m Jacques Ibert

Harry Baur (Herod), Jean Gabin (Pilate), Robert le Vigan (Jesus), Charles Granval (Caiaphas), Edwige Feuillère (Claudia)

'An accomplishment that should bring world-wide prestige to the French film industry.' – Variety

Goliath, King of Slaves: see The Hero of Babylon

Golpes a Mi Puerta: see Knocks at My Door

Gomar the Human Gorilla: see Night of the Bloody Apes

Gone to Earth
GB   1950   110m   Technicolor
London Films/David O. Selznick (Michael Powell, Emeric Pressburger)
US title: The Wild Heart

In the 1890s, a wild Shropshire girl is desired by the local squire.

Unintentionally funny film version of an intractable novel.

wd Michael Powell, Emeric Pressburger novel Mary Webb ph Christopher Challis m Brian Easdale pd Hein Heckroth

Jennifer Jones, David Farrar, Cyril Cusack, Esmond Knight, Sybil Thorndike, Edward Chapman, George Cole, Hugh Griffith, Beatrice Varley

'It tries hard to be a powerful work of art, but it is intrinsically artificial and pretentious.' – *Richard Mallett, Punch*

† For the version shown in US, additional scenes were directed by Rouben Mamoulian.

'The most magnificent picture ever!'
Gone with the Wind ****
US 1939 220m Technicolor
MGM/Selznick International (David O. Selznick)
V, V*, L

An egotistic Southern girl survives the Civil War but finally loses the only man she cares for.

The only film in history which could be profitably revived for forty years: 'still pure gold', said the *Daily Mirror* in 1975. Whole books have been written about it; its essential appeal is that of a romantic story with strong characters and an impeccable production. The widescreen version produced in the late sixties ruined its composition and colour, but it is to be hoped that the original negative still survives.

w Sidney Howard (and others) novel Margaret Mitchell d Victor Fleming (and George Cukor, Sam Wood) ph Ernest Haller, Ray Rennahan m Max Steiner pd William Cameron Menzies ad Lyle Wheeler sp Jack Cosgrove, Fred Albin, Arthur Johns ed Hal C. Kern, James E. Newcom

Clark Gable, Vivien Leigh, Olivia de Havilland, Leslie Howard, Thomas Mitchell, Barbara O'Neil, Hattie McDaniel, Butterfly McQueen, Victor Jory, Evelyn Keyes, Ann Rutherford, Laura Hope Crews, Harry Davenport, Jane Darwell, Ona Munson, Ward Bond

'A major event in the history of the industry but only a minor event in motion picture art. There are moments when the two categories meet on good terms, but the long stretches between are filled with mere spectacular efficiency.' – *Franz Hoellering, The Nation*

'Shakespeare's *The Taming of the Shrew* seems to have got mixed up with one of the novels of Ethel M. Dell.' – *James Agate*

'Perhaps the key plantation movie.' – *Time Out, 1980*

'Forget it, Louis, no Civil War picture ever made a nickel.' – *Irving Thalberg to Louis B. Mayer, 1936*

† The best account of the film's making is in Gavin Lambert's 1975 book, *GWTW*.
†† In the early seventies a stage musical version toured the world, with music by Harold Rome.

AA: best picture; Sidney Howard; Victor Fleming; best cinematography; Lyle Wheeler; Vivien Leigh; Hattie McDaniel; best film editing; William Cameron Menzies (special award)

AAN: Max Steiner; Clark Gable; Olivia de Havilland; special effects

The Gong Show Movie
US 1980 89m colour
Chuck Barris Productions (Bud Granoff)

The trials and tribulations of the host of a TV talent show for untalented amateurs.

A once-successful television show transfers unsuccessfully to the screen.

w Chuck Barris, Robert Downey d Chuck Barris ph Richard C. Glouner m Milton Delugg ad Robert J. Kinoshita ed James Mitchell

Chuck Barris, Robin Altman, Brian O'Mullin, Mabel King, James B. Douglas, Jaye P. Morgan

The Good Companions **
GB 1933 113m bw
Gaumont/Welsh-Pearson (Michael Balcon, George Pearson)

Three ill-assorted people take to the road and in various capacities join the Dinky Doos pierrot troupe.

Gallant, mini-budgeted version of Priestley's popular picaresque novel. A little faded now, it retains some of its vigour, and the performances please.

w W. P. Lipscomb, Angus Macphail, Ian Dalrymple play J. B. Priestley, Edward Knoblock novel J. B. Priestley d Victor Saville ph Bernard Knowles md Louis Levy m/ly George Posford, Douglas Furber ad Alfred Junge ed Frederick Y. Smith

Edmund Gwenn, Mary Glynne, John Gielgud, Jessie Matthews, Percy Parsons, A. W. Baskomb, Dennis Hoey, Richard Dolman, Frank Pettingell, Finlay Currie, Max Miller, Jack Hawkins, George Zucco

'Has come to the screen just as it was written, honest and sentimental and episodic, with the smell of the tarmac and the railway buffet, the tinny rapture of the pavilion piano, the jostling pageantry of insignificant faces.' – *C. A. Lejeune*

The Good Companions *
GB 1956 104m Technicolor Cinemascope
ABP (Hamilton Inglis, J. Lee-Thompson)

Faint-hearted remake of the above, unwisely Cinemascoped and leaving no impression.

w T. J. Morrison d J. Lee-Thompson ph Gilbert Taylor m Laurie Johnson

Eric Portman, Celia Johnson, John Fraser, Janette Scott, Hugh Griffith, Bobby Howes, Rachel Roberts, John Salew, Thora Hird

† A stage musical version (m André Previn, ly Johnny Mercer) had moderate success in London in 1974.

Good Dame
US 1934 77m bw
Paramount
GB title: *Good Girl*

A penniless chorus girl falls for a cardsharp.

Unsurprising pattern play for two miscast stars.

w William K. Lipman, Vincent Lawrence, Frank Partos, Sam Hellman d Marion Gering

Sylvia Sidney, Fredric March, Jack La Rue, Noel Francis, Russell Hopton

Good Day for a Hanging
US 1959 85m Columbia Color
Columbia

A young outlaw is arrested and seems destined to be lynched; the marshal tries to see fair play.

Moody Western in which the protected hero turns out to be very guilty after all.

w Daniel B. Ullman, Maurice Zimm d Nathan Juran

Fred MacMurray, Robert Vaughn, Maggie Hayes, Joan Blackman, James Drury

The Good Die Young *
GB 1954 98m bw
Remus (Jack Clayton)

Four crooks, all with private problems, set out to rob a mail van.

Glum all-star melodrama which set a pattern for such things; worth waiting for is the climactic chase through underground stations.

w Vernon Harris, Lewis Gilbert d Lewis Gilbert ph Jack Asher m Georges Auric

Laurence Harvey, Margaret Leighton, Gloria Grahame, Richard Basehart, Joan Collins, John Ireland, René Ray, Stanley Baker, Robert Morley

'To the memory of Irving Grant Thalberg we dedicate this picture – his last great achievement!'
The Good Earth ***
US 1937 138m bw
MGM (Irving Thalberg)
V*, L

A Chinese peasant grows rich but loses his beloved wife.

A massive, well-meaning and fondly remembered production which is nevertheless artificial, unconvincing and pretty undramatic in the second half. The star performances impress to begin with, then wear thin, but the final locust attack is as well done as it originally seemed. Historically valuable as a Hollywood prestige production of the thirties.

w Talbot Jennings, Tess Schlesinger, Claudine West play Owen and Donald Davis novel Pearl S. Buck d Sidney Franklin ph Karl Freund m Herbert Stothart montage Slavko Vorkapich ad Cedric Gibbons ed Basil Wrangell

Paul Muni, Luise Rainer, Walter Connolly, Tilly Losch, Jessie Ralph, Charley Grapewin, Keye Luke, Harold Huber

'A true technical achievement with names enough to send it across. But it's not going to be easy to get the three-million-dollar investment back. And if it does come back it's going to take a long time.' – *Variety*

'Performances, direction and photography are of a uniform excellence, and have been fused perfectly into a dignified, beautiful, but soberly dramatic production.' – *New York Times*

'One of the superb visual adventures of the period.' – *John Baxter, 1968*

'Prestigious boredom, and it goes on for a very long time.' – *New Yorker, 1977*

AA: Karl Freund; Luise Rainer

AAN: best picture; Sidney Franklin; Basil Wrangell

The Good Fairy *
US 1935 90m bw
Universal (Henry Henigson)

A beautiful but naïve cinema usherette ensnares three rich men.

Unusual, rather lumpy romantic comedy using top talent.

w Preston Sturges, play Ferenc Molnar d William Wyler ph Norbert Brodine

Margaret Sullavan, Herbert Marshall, Frank Morgan, Reginald Owen, Alan Hale, Beulah Bondi, Cesar Romero, Eric Blore, Al Bridge

'It's rather slapsticking a master but it's for the box office. It will not please those who cherish memories of the play but it will please a more important audience.' – *Variety*

† Remade as *I'll Be Yours* (qv).

The Good Fellows
US 1943 70m bw
Paramount

A family man spends too much time with his fraternal order.

Mild, pleasant family comedy.

w Hugh Wedlock Jnr, Howard Snyder play George S. Kaufman, Herman Mankiewicz d Jo Graham

Cecil Kellaway, Helen Walker, James Brown, Mabel Paige

Good Girl: see *Good Dame*

Good Girls Go To Paris *
US 1939 75m bw
Columbia (William Perlberg)

After several zany adventures, a Greek professor marries a gold digger.

Amusingly crazy comedy, one of the last of its type.

w Gladys Lehman, Ken Englund   *d* Alexander Hall
ph Henry Freulich   *md* Morris Stoloff

Melvyn Douglas, Joan Blondell, Walter Connolly,
Alan Curtis, Joan Perry, Isabel Jeans, Alexander
D'Arcy, Clarence Kolb

'It can't stand analysis much, but it pleases while
you're there.' – *Variety*

The Good Guys and the Bad Guys *
US   1969   90m   Technicolor   Panavision
Warner (Robert M. Goldstein)

An ageing sheriff and a train robber have one last
showdown.

Good-humoured, black-flavoured Western set in the
early days of automobiles.

w Ronald M. Cohen, Dennis Shyrack   *d* Burt
Kennedy   *ph* Harry Stradling Jnr   *m* William Lava

Robert Mitchum, George Kennedy, David Carradine,
Tina Louise, Douglas Fowley, Martin Balsam, Lois
Nettleton, John Davis Chandler, John Carradine,
Marie Windsor

Good Guys Wear Black
US   1977   95m   CFI Color
Enterprise/Mar Vista/Action One Film Partners (Allan F. Bodoh)
V*, L

The former leader of a commando raid into North
Vietnam sets out to discover who in Washington
betrayed him and his men.

Lacklustre martial arts action in an unsuccessful
American attempt to create a local star to replace
Bruce Lee.

w Bruce Cohn, Mark Medoff   *story* Joseph Fraley
d Ted Post   *ph* Bob Steadman   *m* Craig Safan
ad B. B. Neal   *ed* William and Millie Moore

Chuck Norris, Anne Archer, James Franciscus, Lloyd
Haynes, Dana Andrews, Jim Backus

† The film was followed by a sequel, *A Force of One*
(qv).

A Good Marriage: see *Le Beau Mariage*

Good Morning Babylon *
Italy/France   1987   115m   colour
Filmtre/MK2/Pressman/RAI/Films A2 (Giuliani G. de Negri)
V, V*, L, S

Italian film-makers set out for Hollywood to restore
the family fortunes.

Likeable but sometimes inept fantasia on
Hollywood's early silent days.

wd Paolo and Vittorio Taviani   *ph* Giuseppe Lanci
m Nicola Piovani   *ad* Gianni Shara   *ed* Roberto
Perpignanni

Vincent Spano, Joaquim de Almeida, Greta Scacchi,
Desiree Becker, Charles Dance (as D. W. Griffith)

'They have made a molehill of a picture out of a
mountain of an idea.' – *Daily Variety*

Good Morning Boys **
GB   1937   79m   bw
GFD/Gainsborough (Edward Black)

A schoolmaster takes his troublesome pupils to Paris
and becomes involved with an art theft.

Sprightly vehicle for the star's seedy schoolmaster
persona: it established him as a major draw in British
films.

w Marriott Edgar, Val Guest, Anthony Kimmins   *d* Marcel
Varnel   *ph* Arthur Crabtree   *md* Louis Levy
ad Vetchinsky   *ed* R. E. Dearing, Alfred Roome

Will Hay, Graham Moffatt, Lilli Palmer, Mark Daly,
Peter Gawthorne, Martita Hunt, Charles Hawtrey,
Will Hay Jnr

† Remade with Ronald Shiner as *Top of the Form*.

Good Morning, Doctor: see *You Belong to Me*

Good Morning, Judge
US   1943   66m   bw
Paul Malvern/Universal

A music publisher falls for the lady lawyer suing him
for plagiarism.

Light, predictable comedy for double billing.

w Maurice Geraghty, Warren Wilson   *d* Jean
Yarbrough

Dennis O'Keefe, Louise Allbritton, J. Carrol Naish,
Mary Beth Hughes, Louise Beavers, Samuel S. Hinds

Good Morning, Miss Dove
US   1955   107m   Eastmancolor   Cinemascope
TCF (Samuel G. Engel)

While recovering from an operation, a small-town
schoolmistress looks back on her career.

A fairly spirited weepie with a happy ending and a
strong sense of cynicism behind the scenes.

w Eleanore Griffin   *novel* Frances Gray Patton
d Henry Koster   *ph* Leon Shamroy   *m* Leigh
Harline

Jennifer Jones, Robert Stack, Robert Douglas, Kipp
Hamilton, Peggy Knudsen, Marshall Thompson,
Chuck Connors, Mary Wickes

'Mr Chips has changed sex and habitat while
preserving intact his ability to provoke epidemics of
sentimentality.' – *MFB*

Good Morning, Vietnam *
US   1987   120m   DeLuxe
Touchstone (Mark Johnson, Larry Brezner)
V, V*, L, S

Exploits of an Armed Forces Radio disc-jockey in
Saigon at the height of the Vietnam War.

Largely a vehicle for the frenetic irreverence of Robin
Williams, enjoyed by many for the 60s hits used
copiously on the soundtrack.

w Mitch Markowitz   *d* Barry Levinson   *ph* Peter
Sova   *m* Alex North   *pd* Roy Walker

Robin Williams, Forest Whitaker, Tung Thanh Tran,
Chintara Sukapatana, Bruno Kirby

AAN: Robin Williams

The Good Mother
US   1988   103m   colour
Warner/Touchstone/Silver Screen Partners IV (Arnold
   Glimcher)
V*, L

A separated husband claims his daughter has been
sexually abused by his wife's lover.

Dull domestic drama.

w Michael Bortman   *novel* Sue Miller   *d* Leonard
Nimoy   *m* Elmer Bernstein   *pd* Stan Jolley
ed Peter Berger

Diane Keaton, Liam Neeson, Jason Robards, Ralph
Bellamy, Teresa Wright, James Naughton, Asia Vieira,
Joe Morton, Katey Sagal, Margaret Bard, Nancy
Beatty

'An over-simplified addendum to a series of recent
works in which mothers are taken to task and
sometimes pilloried.' – *MFB*

Good Neighbour Sam
US   1964   130m   Eastmancolor
Columbia/David Swift
V*

A prissy suburban advertising man becomes
innocently involved in a pretence to be the husband
of the divorcee next door.

A promising comic idea is here ruined by lengthiness,
lack of funny lines, and no apparent idea of how to

film a farce. The actors are driven to repeating every
trick a dozen times.

w James Fritzell, Everett Greenbaum, David Swift
novel Jack Finney   *d* David Swift   *ph* Burnett
Guffey   *m* Frank de Vol

Jack Lemmon, Romy Schneider, Dorothy Provine,
Senta Berger, Edward G. Robinson, Mike Connors,
Edward Andrews, Louis Nye

Good News
US   1930   85m approx   bw
MGM

Fraternity tensions are sorted out in time for the big
football game.

Spirited early talkie musical.

w Frances Marion, Joe Farnham   *d* Nick Grinde,
Edgar McGregor   *ph* Percy Hilburn   *md* Abe
Lyman   *m/ly* De Sylva, Brown, Henderson and
others

songs: 'He's a Ladies' Man'; 'The Best Things in Life
Are Free'; 'Varsity Drag'; 'Good News'; 'Tait Song';
'Students Are We'; 'If You're Not Kissing Me';
'Football'; 'I Feel Pessimistic'; 'I'd Like to Make You
Happy'

Bessie Love, Stanley Smith, Gus Shy, Mary Lawlor,
Lola Lane, Dorothy McNulty (Penny Singleton), Cliff
Edwards

'Not the smash hit the show was. Too fast, too peppy,
too entertaining to flop, though.' – *Variety*

Good News *
US   1947   83m   Technicolor
MGM (Arthur Freed)
V*, L

Bright, good-humoured remake of the above.

w Betty Comden, Adolph Green   *d* Charles Walters
ph Charles Schoenbaum   *md* Lennie Hayton
m/ly De Sylva, Brown, Henderson and others
ad Cedric Gibbons, Edward Carfagno   *ed* Albert
Akst

June Allyson, Peter Lawford, Patricia Marshall, *Joan
McCracken*, Mel Tormé

AAN: song 'Pass that Peace Pipe' (*m/ly* Ralph Blane,
Hugh Martin, Roger Edens)

The Good Old Days
GB   1939   79m   bw
Warner (Jerome Jackson)

A noble child is kidnapped by a chimney sweep and
saved by strolling players.

Curious Victorian vehicle for a snappy 20th-century
star.

w Austin Melford, John Dighton   *story* Ralph Smart
d Roy William Neill   *ph* Basil Emmott

Max Miller, Hal Walters, Kathleen Gibson, H. F.
Maltby, Martita Hunt, Allan Jeayes, Roy Emerton

Good Old Schooldays: see *Those Were the Days*

Good Old Soak
US   1937   67m   bw
MGM

A small-town drunk beats a teetotal banker guilty of a
shady transaction.

Amiable star comedy.

w A. E. Thomas   *play* The Old Soak by Don Marquis
d J. Walter Ruben

Wallace Beery, Una Merkel, Eric Linden, Judith Barrett,
Betty Furness, Janet Beecher, Robert McWade,
Margaret Hamilton

'A melodramatic sentimentality that will probably do
okay.' – *Variety*

Good Sam

US   1948   114m   bw
Rainbow (Leo McCarey)

A small-town business man is so charitable that he finds himself bankrupt.

Poor, disjointed, overlong and obvious comedy in the Capra style.

w Ken Englund   d Leo McCarey   ph George Barnes   m Robert Emmett Dolan

Gary Cooper, Ann Sheridan, Ray Collins, Edmund Lowe, Joan Lorring, Ruth Roman, Clinton Sundberg

'A bit too long, but in its incidentals often very enjoyable.' – Richard Mallett, Punch

The Good Son

US   1993   87m   DeLuxe   Panavision
TCF (Mary Anne Page, Joseph Ruben)
S

A sweet-seeming 10-year-old boy is actually an amoral, murderous child.

A slick but uninvolving updating of the themes of The Bad Seed

w Ian McEwan   d Joseph Reuben   ph John Lindley   m Elmer Bernstein   pd Bill Groom   ed George Bowers

Macaulay Culkin, Elijah Wood, Wendy Crewson, David Morse, Daniel Hugh Kelly, Jacqueline Brooks, Quinn Culkin

'This rather peculiar thriller doesn't deliver enough jolts to leave the audience screaming.' – Variety

'If this film were a teenager, it would be the one who always did his homework, never pranged the family car, and then one day quietly shot everyone with a rifle made in his metalwork class.' – Leslie Felperin Sharman, Sight and Sound

The Good, the Bad and the Ugly ***

Italy   1966   180m   Techniscope
PEA (Alberto Grimaldi)
V, V*, L, S
original title: Il Buono, il Brutto, il Cattivo

During the American Civil War, three men seek hidden loot.

Intermittently lively, very violent, and interminably drawn-out Western with a number of rather hilarious stylistic touches.

w Age Scarpelli, Luciano Vincenzoni, Sergio Leone   d Sergio Leone   ph Tonino delli Colli   m Ennio Morricone

Clint Eastwood, Eli Wallach, Lee Van Cleef

Good Time Girl

GB   1948   93m   bw
Triton/Rank

A girl escapes from a remand home and starts on the road to ruin.

Risible vehicle for a rising star; at the time it set the box-offices clicking.

w Muriel and Sidney Box, Ted Willis   novel Night Darkens the Street by Arthur La Bern   d David MacDonald

Jean Kent, Dennis Price, Flora Robson, Griffith Jones, Herbert Lom, Bonar Colleano

Good Times

US   1967   92m   DeLuxe
Motion Picture International

A singing duo in Hollywood imagines starring in films of various types.

Mildly agreeable light fantasy.

w Tony Barrett   d William Friedkin

Sonny and Cher, George Sanders, Norman Alden, Larry Duran

The Good Wife

Australia   1987   92m   Eastmancolor
Entertainment/Laughing Kookaburra (Jan Sharp, Helen Watts)
Australian title: The Umbrella Woman

In 1939, a wife is bored with her backwater life, and takes a lover.

Heavy-going domestic drama with an interesting setting.

w Peter Kenna   d Ken Cameron   ph James Bartle   m Cameron Allan   pd Sally Campbell   ed John Scott

Rachel Ward, Bryan Brown, Sam Neill, Steven Vidler

Goodbye Again

US   1933   66m   bw
Warner

An author's secretary is jealous of his rekindled interest in an old flame.

Unassuming star comedy which entertained at the time.

w Ben Markson   play George Haight, Allan Scott   d Michael Curtiz

Warren William, Joan Blondell, Genevieve Tobin, Hugh Herbert, Helen Chandler, Ruth Donnelly

† Honeymoon for Three in 1941 (qv) was a leaden remake.

Goodbye Again *

US   1961   120m   bw
UA/Mercury/Argus/Anatole Litvak
V*

A woman of forty swaps her rich lover for a young law student.

Melancholy romantic drama, well produced and staged on Paris locations.

w Samuel Taylor   novel Aimez-vous Brahms by Françoise Sagan   d Anatole Litvak   ph Armand Thirard   m Georges Auric

Ingrid Bergman, Anthony Perkins, Yves Montand, Jessie Royce Landis, Jackie Lane

'A grey-toned Sagan novella, spread wide and lush over two hours of screen time.' – MFB

'The kind of "woman's picture" that gives women a bad name.' – Judith Crist, 1973

Goodbye Charlie *

US   1964   116m   DeLuxe   Cinemascope
TCF/Venice (David Weisbart)

A philandering gangster, shot dead by an irate husband, is reincarnated in his friend's house as a dishy blonde.

Overlong but amusing Broadway comedy for wisecrackers, uninventively adapted.

w Harry Kurnitz   play George Axelrod   d Vincente Minnelli   ph Milton Krasner   m André Previn

Debbie Reynolds, Pat Boone, Walter Matthau, Tony Curtis

'Every father's daughter is a virgin!'
Goodbye Columbus **

US   1969   105m   Technicolor
Paramount/Willow Tree (Stanley Jaffe)
V*

A young Jewish librarian has an affair with the wilful daughter of a nouveau riche family.

An amusing and well-observed delineation of two kinds of Jewish life in New York; the story, despite its frank talk of penises and diaphragms, leaves much to be desired, and the style is post-Graduate.

w Arnold Schulman   novel Philip Roth   d Larry Peerce   ph Gerald Hirschfeld   m Charles Fox

Richard Benjamin, Ali MacGraw, Jack Klugman, Nan Martin, Michael Meyers, Lori Shelle

AAN: Arnold Schulman

Goodbye Gemini

GB   1970   89m   colour
Cinerama/Josef Shaftel (Peter Snell)

A 20-year-old brother and sister share a world of petulant fantasy which leads to murder.

Abysmally over-the-top melodrama with a swinging London backdrop. Its immaculate appearance only makes matters worse.

w Edmund Ward   novel Ask Agamemnon by Jenni Hall   d Alan Gibson   ph Geoffrey Unsworth   m Christopher Gunning   pd Wilfrid Shingleton

Judy Geeson, Martin Potter, Michael Redgrave, Alexis Kanner, Mike Pratt, Freddie Jones, Peter Jeffrey

'Every man she ever loved thought a permanent relationship was a three-day weekend!'
The Goodbye Girl *

US   1977   110m   Metrocolor
Warner/Rastar (Ray Stark)
V, V*, L

A misunderstanding about the lease of an apartment results in a girl dancer agreeing to share it with a would-be actor.

A very moderate script assisted by excellent acting and the usual array of Neil Simon one-liners. Nothing at all new, but enjoyable.

w Neil Simon   d Herbert Ross   ph David M. Walsh   m Dave Grusin

Richard Dreyfuss, Marsha Mason, Quinn Cummings, Paul Benedict, Barbara Rhoades

AA: Richard Dreyfuss

AAN: best picture; Neil Simon; Marsha Mason; Quinn Cummings

Goodbye Mr Chips ***

GB   1939   114m   bw
MGM (Victor Saville)
V*, L

The life of a shy schoolmaster from his first job to his death.

Sentimental romance in MGM's best style, a long-standing favourite for its performances and humour; but the production seems slightly unsatisfactory these days.

w R. C. Sherriff, Claudine West, Eric Maschwitz   novel James Hilton   d Sam Wood   ph Frederick A. Young   m Richard Addinsell   ed Charles Frend

Robert Donat, Greer Garson, Paul Henreid, Lyn Harding, Austin Trevor, Terry Kilburn, John Mills, Milton Rosmer, Judith Furse

'Charming, quaintly sophisticated . . . more for the big situations than the smaller towns.' – Variety

'The whole picture has an assurance, bears a glow of popularity like the face of a successful candidate on election day. And it is wrong to despise popularity in the cinema.' – Graham Greene

'The picture has no difficulty in using two hours to retell a story that was scarcely above short story length. Mr Chips is worth its time.' – New York Times

'The novel became an American best seller when that old sentimentalist Alexander Woollcott touted it on the radio . . . the movie clogs the nose more than necessary.' – Pauline Kael, 70s

AA: Robert Donat

AAN: best picture; script; Sam Wood; Greer Garson; editing

'He is a shy schoolmaster. She is a music hall star. They marry and immediately have 283 children – all boys!'

Goodbye Mr Chips *
GB   1969   147m   Metrocolor   Panavision 70
MGM/APJAC (Arthur P. Jacobs)
V, V*, L

Elaborate musical remake of the above.

Slow and slushy, with no improvement visible whatever; but a few of the trimmings please.

w Terence Rattigan   d Herbert Ross   ph Oswald Morris   md John Williams   m Leslie Bricusse   pd Ken Adam

Peter O'Toole, Petula Clark, Michael Bryant, Michael Redgrave, George Baker, Jack Hedley, Sian Phillips, Alison Leggatt

'The sum total is considerably less than the parts.' – Variety

'An overblown version with songs where they are not needed (and Leslie Bricusse's songs are never needed).' – Pauline Kael, New Yorker

† Originally sought for the title role, in order of preference, were Richard Burton and Rex Harrison; for the female lead, Samantha Eggar and Lee Remick.

AAN: Leslie Bricusse, John Williams; Peter O'Toole

Goodbye My Fancy
US   1951   107m   bw
Warner (Henry Blanke)

A congresswoman returns to her old college for an honorary degree, and falls in love.

Tolerable romantic flim-flam.

w Ivan Goff, Ben Roberts   play Fay Kanin   d Vincent Sherman   ph Ted McCord   m Daniele Amfitheatrof

Joan Crawford, Robert Young, Frank Lovejoy, Eve Arden, Janice Rule

Goodbye My Lady *
US   1956   95m   bw
Warner/Batjac (William Wellman)

A Mississippi swamp boy finds a valuable dog but eventually returns it to its owner.

Reliable, slightly unusual family film.

w Sid Fleischman   novel James Street   d William Wellman   ph William H. Clothier, Archie Stout   m Laurindo Almeida, George Field

Brandon de Wilde, Walter Brennan, Phil Harris, Sidney Poitier, William Hopper, Louise Beavers

The Goodbye People
US   1984   104m   DeLuxe
Embassy/Coney Island (David V. Picker)
V*, L

Middle-aged eccentrics meet on a beach.

Saroyanesque talk piece which never quite comes off, and will probably be seen only at festivals.

wd Herb Gardner   play Herb Gardner   ph John Lindley   pd Tony Walton   ed Rick Shaine

Martin Balsam, Judd Hirsch, Pamela Reed, Ron Silver, Michael Tucker, Gene Saks

Goodbye Pork Pie *
New Zealand   1980   105m   Eastmancolor
NZ Film Commission/NZ United Corporation/Nigel
    Hutchinson, Geoff Murphy
V*

Three young people go on an illegal road spree and are arrested one by one.

Familiar high jinks with a moral conclusion. Fun up to a point, and good to look at.

w Geoff Murphy, Ian Mune   d Geoff Murphy   ph Alun Bollinger   m John Charles

Tony Barry, Kelly Johnson, Claire Oberman

'Displays encouraging physical flair in its cross-country sweep of action.' – Tim Pulleine, MFB

'Three Decades of Life in the Mafia.'

GoodFellas ****
US   1990   146m   Technicolor
Warner (Irwin Winkler)
V, V*, L

An Irish-Italian boy grows up to become a gangster.

Brilliant, unsparing delineation of the sub-culture of crime and the corruption of the spirit it entails.

w Martin Scorsese, Nicholas Pileggi   novel Wiseguy by Nicholas Pileggi   d Martin Scorsese   ph Michael Ballhaus   pd Kristi Zea   ad Maher Ahmad   ed Thelma Schoonmaker

Robert de Niro, Ray Liotta, Joe Pesci, Lorraine Bracco, Paul Sorvino, Frank Sivero, Tony Darrow, Mike Starr, Frank Vincent, Chuck Low

'Simultaneously fascinating and repellent.' – Variety

'In its own narrow, near-claustrophobic perspective, however, driven along by a classic soundtrack and with no shortage of master directorial brush strokes, it is hard to imagine a bigger picture than this.' – Empire

AA: Joe Pesci

AAN: Lorraine Bracco; best adapted screenplay; film editing; best picture

Goodnight Vienna
GB   1932   76m   bw
British and Dominions (Herbert Wilcox)
US title: Magic Night

In 1913 Vienna, a general's son falls for a shopgirl.

Already dated when it was made, this thin musical romance nevertheless made a star of Anna Neagle and re-established Jack Buchanan on the screen.

w Holt Marvel, George Posford   play Holt Marvel, George Posford   d Herbert Wilcox   ph F. A. Young   m George Posford, Eric Maschwitz   ad L. P. Williams   ed E. Aldridge

Jack Buchanan, Anna Neagle, Gina Malo, Clive Currie, William Kendall

The Goonies
US   1985   111m   Technicolor   Panavision
Warner/Steven Spielberg
V, V*, L

Kids discover a pirate map and set out on a fantasy treasure hunt.

The bottomless pit of the Spielberg genre, a silly tale which takes forever to get going and is acted by children who have not studied elocution. The trick effects when they come are OK, but it's a long annoying haul to that point.

w Chris Columbus   story Steven Spielberg   d Richard Donner   ph Nick McLean   m Dave Grusin   pd J. Michael Riva   ed Michael Kahn

Sean Astin, Josh Brolin, Jeff Cohen, Corey Feldman, Kerri Green, Martha Plimpton, Ke Huy Kwan

The Goose and the Gander
US   1935   65m   bw
Warner

A divorcee can't leave her ex-husband's life alone.

Tolerable farcical goings-on which just fail to come to the boil.

w George Kenyon   d Alfred E. Green

Kay Francis, George Brent, Genevieve Tobin, John Eldredge, Claire Dodd

'Well-played little farce with too much story for its own good.' – Variety

The Goose Steps Out *
GB   1942   79m   bw
Ealing (S. C. Balcon)

To steal a secret weapon, an incompetent teacher is sent into Germany in place of his Nazi double.

Quite amusing star vehicle, not up to his best standards.

w Angus Macphail, John Dighton   d Will Hay, Basil Dearden   ph Ernest Palmer   m Bretton Byrd

Will Hay, Charles Hawtrey, Frank Pettingell, Julien Mitchell, Peter Croft, Jeremy Hawk, Peter Ustinov, Raymond Lovell, Barry Morse

The Goose Woman
US   1925   90m approx   bw   silent
Universal

A young actress falls for the son of an embittered old one.

Interesting character melodrama of which prints have survived.

w Melville Brown   story Rex Beach   d Clarence Brown   ph Milton Moore

Louise Dresser, Jack Pickford, Constance Bennett, James Barrows

The Gorbals Story
GB   1949   75m   bw
Eros/New World (Ernest Gartside)

A successful artist remembers his unhappy youth in a tenement in the slums of Glasgow.

Well-meaning, low-budget proletarian melodrama, featuring actors from the Glasgow Unity theatre. Set mainly in a couple of tenement rooms, it would have benefitted from opening up with more exterior scenes; as it is, it remains a photographed stage play.

w David MacKane   play Robert McLeish   d David MacKane   ph Stanley Clinton   m John Bath   ad George Haslam   ed Helen Wiggins

Russell Hunter, Betty Henderson, Howard Connell, Marjorie Thomson, Roddy McMillan, Isobel Campbell, Carl Williamson, Lothar Lewinsohn, Andrew Keir

Gordon of Ghost City
US   1933   bw   serial: 12 eps
Universal

A cowboy hunts down cattle rustlers.

Simple-minded serial with a stalwart hero.

d Ray Taylor

Buck Jones, Madge Bellamy, Walter Miller, Hugh Enfield, William Desmond

Gordon's War
US   1973   90m   TVC color
TCF/Palomar (Robert L. Schaffel)

A black Vietnam veteran returns to Harlem and avenges the death of his wife.

Violent vigilante melodrama with vivid locations.

w Howard Friedlander, Ed Spielman   d Ossie Davis   ph Victor J. Kemper   m Andy Bodale, Al Ellis

Paul Winfield, Carl Lee, David Downing

A Gorgeous Bird Like Me: see Une Belle Fille comme Moi

'An unbeatable cast in an unequalled drama! Metro's successor to The Great Ziegfeld!'

The Gorgeous Hussy *
US   1936   105m   bw
MGM (Joseph L. Mankiewicz)

The love life of Peggy O'Neal, protégée of President Andrew Jackson.

Bowdlerized all-star historical drama; the production values are better than the script.

w Ainsworth Morgan, Stephen Morehouse Avery   novel Samuel Hopkins Adams   d Clarence Brown   ph George Folsey   m Herbert Stothart

Joan Crawford, Lionel Barrymore, Franchot Tone, Melvyn Douglas, Robert Taylor, James Stewart, Alison Skipworth, Louis Calhern, Beulah Bondi, Melville Cooper, Sidney Toler, Gene Lockhart

† A Foreword read: 'This story of Peggy Eaton and her times is not presented as a precise account of either, rather as fiction founded upon historical fact.'

AAN: George Folsey; Beulah Bondi

'This is the big one! Two years in the making!'

Gorgo
GB   1960   78m   Technicolor
King Brothers (Wilfrid Eades)
V*, L

A prehistoric monster is caught in Irish waters and brought to London, but rescued by its mother.

Amiable monster hokum with a happy ending but not much technical resource.

w John Loring, Daniel Hyatt   d Eugene Lourié
ph Frederick A. Young   m Angelo Lavagnino
sp Tom Howard

Bill Travers, William Sylvester, Vincent Winter, Christopher Rhodes, Joseph O'Conor, Bruce Seton, Martin Benson

The Gorgon *
GB   1964   83m   Technicolor
Columbia/Hammer (Anthony Nelson-Keys)
V, V*, L

A castle ruin near a German village is infested by Megaera, the gorgon of ancient myth, whose gaze turns people to stone and who can take over the form of an unknowing villager.

Writhing snakes in the hair-do being too great a challenge to the make-up man, the monster is barely glimpsed and the film becomes a who-is-it, all quite suspenseful despite the central idea being too silly for words.

w John Gilling   story J. Llewellyn Devine
d Terence Fisher   ph Michael Reed   m James Bernard   ad Bernard Robinson   ed James Needs, Eric Boyd-Perkins

Peter Cushing, Christopher Lee, Barbara Shelley, Richard Pasco, Patrick Troughton, Michael Goodliffe, Jack Watson

The Gorilla *
US   1939   66m   bw
TCF (Harry Joe Brown)
V*, L

A murderer blames an escaped gorilla for his crimes.

Spooky house mystery comedy revamped as a Ritz Brothers vehicle; not much suspense, but it all looks good and the cast is highly satisfactory.

w Rian James, Sid Silvers   play Ralph Spence
d Allan Dwan   ph Edward Cronjager   md David Buttolph

The Ritz Brothers, Bela Lugosi, Lionel Atwill, Patsy Kelly, Joseph Calleia, Anita Louise, Edward Norris, Wally Vernon

'A good programmer that will get by for normal biz where the Ritzes can attract.' – Variety

† There were two previous versions, in 1927 with Charlie Murray and 1931 with Joe Frisco.

'Get out of the way – before it's too late!'

Gorilla at Large
US   1954   93m   Technicolor   3-D
TCF/Panoramic (Robert L. Jacks)

A circus gorilla is used as a cover for murder.

Silly thriller with the gorilla as unconvincing as the story.

w Leonard Praskins, Barney Slater   d Harmon Jones
ph Lloyd Ahern   m Lionel Newman

Anne Bancroft, Lee J. Cobb, Cameron Mitchell, Lee Marvin, Raymond Burr, Charlotte Austin, Peter Whitney, Warren Stevens

The Gorilla Man
US   1942   63m   bw
Warner

A wounded commando discovers that his hospital is run by Nazis, who then try to prove him insane so that he won't be believed.

There must have been less laborious ways, one assumes, but at least this farrago is good for a few unintentional laughs.

w Anthony Coldeway   d D. Ross Lederman

John Loder, Ruth Ford, Richard Fraser, Paul Cavanagh, John Abbott

Gorillas in the Mist *
US   1988   129m   Technicolor
UIP/Warner (Arnold Glimcher, Terence Clegg)
V, V*, L, S

Researching into the lives of gorillas, a reclusive female scientist antagonizes local poachers.

Respectful, unenlightening biopic.

w Anna Hamilton Phelan   story Anna Hamilton Phelan, Tab Murphy   book Dian Fossey, article by Harold T. P. Hayes   d Michael Apted   ph John Seale   m Maurice Jarre   pd John Graysmark
sp Rick Baker   ed Stuart Baird

Sigourney Weaver, Bryan Brown, Julie Harris, John Omirah Miluwi, Iain Cuthbertson, Constantin Alexandrov, Waigwa Wachira, Iain Glenn, David Lansbury

AAN: Sigourney Weaver; Maurice Jarre; Anna Hamilton Phelan; Stuart Baird; best sound

Gorky Park *
US   1983   128m   Technicolor
Orion/Eagle (Gene Kirkwood, Howard W. Koch Jnr)
V, V*, L, S

The Moscow police link murders with a sable-smuggling operation.

Bleak thriller which doggedly makes its way through a conventional plot but fails to convey the book's detail of life in Moscow today. (The film was shot in Helsinki.)

w Dennis Potter   novel Martin Cruz Smith
d Michael Apted   ph Ralf D. Bode   m James Horner   pd Paul Sylbert

Lee Marvin, William Hurt, Brian Dennehy, Ian Bannen, Joanna Pacula, Michael Elphick, Richard Griffiths, Alexander Knox

The Gospel According to St Matthew *
Italy/France   1964   142m   bw
Arco/Lux (Alfredo Bini)
V, V*, L
original title: Il Vangelo Secondo Matteo

The life of Christ seen almost as a ciné-vérité documentary.

The tone is realist but not notably iconoclastic.

wd Pier Paolo Pasolini   ph Tonino delli Colli
md Luis Enrique Bacalov   m Bach, Mozart, Prokofiev

Enrique Irazoqui, Susanna Pasolini, Mario Socrate

AAN: Luis Enrique Bacalov

Gösta Berlings Saga: see The Atonement of Gösta Berling

Gothic
GB   1986   90m   Eastmancolor
Virgin Visions (Penny Corke)
V, V*, L, S

Byron, the Shelleys and Dr Polidori spend a weekend thinking up ghost stories.

Somewhat unhinged version of a famous occurrence in 1816, full of nauseous detail typical of its director.

w Stephen Volk   d Ken Russell   ph Mike Southon
m Thomas Dolby   pd Christopher Hobbs

Gabriel Byrne, Julian Sands, Natasha Richardson, Miriam Cyr, Timothy Spall

'The thinking man's Nightmare on Elm Street.' – Daily Variety

Götterdämmerung: see The Damned (1969)

Goupi Mains Rouges *
France   1943   95m   bw
Minerva
US title: It Happened at the Inn

A French village is largely populated by members of the same family, and one of them murders another.

An odd little black comedy which strengthened its director's reputation.

w Pierre Véry, Jacques Becker   novel Pierre Véry
d Jacques Becker   ph Pierre Montazel, Jean Bourgoin   m Jean Alfaro

Fernand Ledoux, Georges Rollin, Blanchette Brunoy, Robert Le Vigan

Government Agents vs The Phantom Legion
US   1951   bw   serial: 12 eps
Republic

A G-man goes undercover as a truck driver in order to expose hijackers.

Routine serial thick ear showing a touch of desperation in the title department.

d Fred C. Brannon

Walter Reed, Mary Ellen Kay, Dick Curtis, John Pickard, Fred Coby

Government Girl
US   1943   94m   bw
RKO

War Department secretaries find their love lives confused in wartime Washington, where rooms have to be shared.

Thin variation on a theme curiously dear to Hollywood at the time.

wd Dudley Nichols   story Adela Rogers St John, Budd Schulberg

Olivia de Havilland, Sonny Tufts, Anne Shirley, James Dunn, Paul Stewart, Agnes Moorehead, Harry Davenport, Una O'Connor, Sig Rumann, Jane Darwell

The Grace Moore Story: see So This Is Love

Grace Quigley
US   1984   95m   colour
Cannon/Northbrook (Christopher Pearce)
V*
aka: The Ultimate Solution of Grace Quigley

An aged widow blackmails a hit man into performing his services for all her elderly and miserable friends.

Yukky black comedy which ill befits its star and is an embarrassment from start to finish.

w A. Martin Zwieback   d Anthony Harvey
ph Larry Pizer   m John Addison

Katharine Hepburn, Nick Nolte, Elizabeth Wilson, Walter Abel, Kit Le Fever, Chip Zuen

† The Grace Quigley version has a contrived happy ending. In the original, Grace walks into the sea and the hit man is drowned trying to save her.

The Gracie Allen Murder Case *
US   1939   74m   bw
George K. Arthur/Paramount

Gracie Allen helps Philo Vance solve the murder of an escaping convict.

At the time of Gracie Allen's radio eminence, this was a cute comedy idea.

w Nat Perrin   novel S. S. Van Dine   d Alfred E. Green

Gracie Allen, Warren William, Ellen Drew, Kent Taylor, Jed Prouty, Jerome Cowan, Donald McBride, H. B. Warner, William Demarest

'Smacko for general audiences . . . one of the top comedies of the season.' – Variety

'This is Benjamin . . . he's a little worried about his future!'
The Graduate ****
US   1967   105m   Technicolor   Panavision
UA/Embassy (Lawrence Turman)
V, V*, L, S

A rich Californian ex-student is led into an affair with the wife of his father's friend, then falls in love with her daughter.

Richly reflecting the anything-goes mood of the late sixties, this lushly-filmed sex comedy opened a few new doors, looked ravishing, was well acted and had a popular music score. A comedy of its time, it has also stood the test of time.

w Calder Willingham, Buck Henry   novel Charles Webb   d Mike Nichols   ph Robert Surtees   m Dave Grusin   pd Richard Sylbert   m/y Paul Simon (sung by Simon and Art Garfunkel)

Dustin Hoffman, Anne Bancroft, Katharine Ross, Murray Hamilton, William Daniels, Elizabeth Wilson

BENJAMIN: 'Mrs Robinson, if you don't mind my saying so, this conversation is getting a little strange.'

'Seeing The Graduate is a bit like having one's most brilliant friend to dinner, watching him become more witty and animated with every moment, and then becoming aware that what one may really be witnessing is the onset of a nervous breakdown.' – Renata Adler

'Yes, there are weaknesses . . . But in cinematic skill, in intent, in sheer connection with us, The Graduate is a milestone in American film history.' – Stanley Kauffmann

AA: Mike Nichols

AAN: best picture; script; Robert Surtees; Dustin Hoffman; Anne Bancroft; Katharine Ross

Graffiti Bridge
US   1990   95m   colour
Warner/Paisley Park (Arnold Stiefel, Randy Phillips)
V, V*, L

Two clubowners quarrel over the type of music they should be featuring.

Little more than an excuse for Prince to perform his songs, and strictly for fans.

wd Prince   ph Bill Butler   m Prince   pd Vance Lorenzini   ed Rebecca Rose

Prince, Ingrid Chavez, Morris Day, Jerome Benton, Mavis Staples

'A half-baked retread of tired MTV imagery and childish themes that will have even fans of the music eyeing the exit signs.' —Variety

Le Grand Blond avec une Chaussure Noire (dubbed) *
France   1972   89m   Eastmancolor
Fox-Rank/Gaumont International/Productions de la Guéville/
Madeleine (Alain Poire, Yves Robert)
aka: Follow That Guy with the One Black Shoe

A disaster-prone violinist is the victim of a set-up by the head of the secret service who is attempting to discredit his second-in-command.

Mildly amusing comedy that makes fun of spies and their suspicious attitudes, though it suffers from being dubbed.

w Yves Robert, Francis Véber   d Yves Robert
ph René Mathelin   m Vladimir Cosma
ed Ghislaine Desjonquères

Pierre Richard, Bernard Blier, Jean Rochefort, Mireille Darc, Jean Carmet, Colette Castel

Grand Canary
US   1934   76m   bw
Fox (Jesse Lasky)

In the Canary Islands, a missionary girl tries to reform a derelict doctor, who finds true love elsewhere.

Curiously slack adaptation; one feels that something grandly philosophical was attempted and failed.

w Ernest Pascal   novel A. J. Cronin   d Irving Cummings

Warner Baxter, H. B. Warner, Madge Evans, Marjorie Rambeau, Juliette Compton, Zita Johann

'Essentially dull and slow . . . nothing very much happens.' – Variety

Grand Canyon *
US   1991   134m   DeLuxe   Panavision
TCF (Lawrence Kasdan, Charles Okun, Michael Grillo)
V, V*, L, S

After a black truck driver comes to the aid of a white lawyer, the two men form a friendship despite the disparity between them.

A sentimental account of urban unease, and one that offers glib answers to the questions it raises, but at least it does raise questions.

w Meg and Lawrence Kasdan   d Lawrence Kasdan
ph Owen Roizman   m James Newton Howard
pd Bo Welch   ed Carol Littleton

Danny Glover, Kevin Kline, Steve Martin, Mary McDonne, Mary-Louise Parker, Alfred Woodard

'As a study of survival strategies in a disintegrating metropolis, pic brings a welcome seriousness and maturity to subject matter too often treated with flippancy and mindless romanticism.' – Variety

'It is hard to think of another American movie that has so directly, even naively, confronted the basic source of our existential unease.' – Richard Schickel, Time

AAN: Meg and Lawrence Kasdan (screenplay)

Grand Central Murder
US   1942   72m   bw
MGM (B. F. Zeidman)

A murder is solved in New York's giant railway station.

Very moderate time-filler with a rather lethargic script.

w Peter Ruric   novel Sue McVeigh   d S. Sylvan Simon   ph George F. Folsey   m David Snell

Van Heflin, Cecilia Parker, Sam Levene, Connie Gilchrist, Millard Mitchell, Tom Conway, Virginia Grey, Samuel S. Hinds

Le Grand Chemin **
France   1987   107m   colour
Warner/Flach/Selena Audio Visuel/TF1 (Pascal Hommais, Jean-
François Lepetit)
S

A nine-year-old boy spends the summer with a childless couple.

Charming account of a child trying to cope with the adult world which was a big hit in France.

wd Jean-Loup Hubert   ph Claude Lecomte
m Georges Granier   pd Farid Chaouche
ed Raymonde Guyot

Anemone, Richard Bohringer, Antoine Hubert, Vanessa Guedi, Christine Pascal, Raoul Billerey, Pascale Roberts, Marie Matheron, Daniel Railet

The Grand Duchess and the Waiter *
US   1926   90m approx   bw   silent
Famous Players

A millionaire becomes a servant in order to win the heart of a titled lady.

Sophisticated silent comedy with a good reputation.

w Pierre Collings, John Lynch   play Alfred Savoir
d Malcolm St Clair   ph Lee Garmes

Adolphe Menjou, Florence Vidor, Lawrence Grant, Andre Beranger

Grand Exit
US   1935   68m   bw
Columbia

An insurance company sleuth traps an arson fiend.

Lively co-feature mystery.

w Gene Towne, Graham Baker, Bruce Manning, Lionel Houser   d Erle C. Kenton

Edmund Lowe, Ann Sothern, Onslow Stevens, Robert Middlemass, Selmer Jackson, Edward Van Sloan

'Novel story, crisp dialogue, distinguished direction.' – Variety

'The greatest cast in stage or screen history!'
Grand Hotel **
US   1932   115m   bw
MGM (Irving Thalberg)
V, V*, L

The lives of various hotel guests become intertwined and reach their climaxes.

It's a little faded now, but much of the magic still works in this first of the portmanteau movies; the production is opulent yet somehow stiff, and the performances have survived with varying success.

w William A. Drake   novel Vicki Baum   d Edmund Goulding   ph William Daniels   ad Cedric Gibbons

Greta Garbo, John Barrymore, Lionel Barrymore, Joan Crawford, Wallace Beery, Jean Hersholt, Lewis Stone

DOCTOR (Lewis Stone): 'Grand Hotel. Always the same. People come, people go. Nothing ever happens.'
GRUSINSKAYA (Greta Garbo): 'I want to be alone . . . I think I have never been so tired in my life.'

† Remade as Weekend at the Waldorf (qv).

AA: best picture

Le Grand Jeu *
France   1934   115m   bw
Films de France

A young man joins the Foreign Legion to forget a woman, meets another who reminds him of her, and is condemned to death for murdering the second woman's lover.

Hokey melodrama whose great interest lay in its picture of life in the Legion.

w Charles Spaak, Jacques Feyder   d Jacques Feyder
ph Harry Stradling, Maurice Forster   m Hanns Eisler

Pierre-Richard Wilm, Marie Bell (in a dual role), Françoise Rosay, Charles Vanel

'At last a good French film.' – Variety

† A remake appeared in 1953, directed by Robert Siodmak and starring Jean-Claude Pascal, Gina Lollobrigida and Arletty. Sometimes known as Card of Fate, it is of little interest.

Le Grand Meaulnes **
France   1967   110m   Eastmancolor   Techniscope
Fair Enterprises/Madeleine/Awa (Gilbert de Goldschmidt)
aka: The Wanderer

An adolescent's frantic search for a beautiful young girl he met by chance ends in tragedy.

A bitter-sweet romance that is faithful to the original but, for all its attractions, lacks imagination in its transfer to the screen.

w Isabelle Rivière, Jean-Gabriel Albicocco
novel Alain-Fournier   d Jean-Gabriel Albicocco
ph Quinto Albicocco   m Jean-Pierre Bourtayre
ad Daniel Louradour   ed Georges Klotz

Brigitte Fossey, Jean Blaise, Alain Libolt, Alain Noury, Juliette Villard, Christian de Tillière

'Photographed for the most part in unforgettable scenery, and acted with convincing delicacy and charm, it carries a real poetic power and retains an amazing amount of the original's intensely romantic quality of loss and fragile innocence.' – *David Pirie, MFB*

Le Grand Méliès *
France   1952   30m   bw
Armor Films (Fred Orain)

The life of Georges Méliès, conjuror and pioneer film maker, is told in a series of vignettes separated by clips from his films.

An interesting documentary reconstruction.

wd Georges Franju

André Méliès

Grand National Night
GB   1953   80m   bw
Talisman (George Minter)
US title: *The Wicked Wife*

A stable owner accidentally kills his drunken wife, but fate and a complex series of events clear him.

Slightly dubious morally, but otherwise an adequate detective story with the outcome hinging on train timetables and the like.

w Dorothy and Campbell Christie   *play* Dorothy and Campbell Christie   d Bob McNaught   ph Jack Asher   m John Greenwood

Nigel Patrick, Moira Lister, Beatrice Campbell, Betty Ann Davies, Michael Hordern, Noel Purcell, Leslie Mitchell, Barry Mackay, Colin Gordon

Grand Prix *
US   1966   179m   Metrocolor   Super Panavision
MGM/Douglas and Lewis (Edward Lewis)
V*, L

Motor racers converge on Monte Carlo and other European centres.

Seemingly endless montage, mostly in multisplit screens, of motor races, with some very jaded personal footage between. It looks a dream but quickly becomes a bore.

w Robert Alan Aurthur   d John Frankenheimer
ph Lionel Lindon   m Maurice Jarre   pd Richard Sylbert

James Garner, Eva Marie Saint, Brian Bedford, Yves Montand, Toshiro Mifune, Jessica Walter, Françoise Hardy, Adolfo Celi, Claude Dauphin, Genevieve Page

'The same old story with the same types we've seen flying planes and riding horses in dozens of fast, cheap, hour-and-a-quarter movies.' – *Pauline Kael*

'Nothing more nor less than a paean to the racing car . . . off the track, though, the film is firmly stuck in bottom gear.' – *MFB*

Grand Rue: see *Calle Mayor*

Il Grand Silencio: see *The Big Silence*

Grand Slam
US   1933   65m   bw
Warner

A Russian waiter is called in to make a fourth at bridge and proves to be an expert.

Able spoof of the bridge craze then sweeping America; precise knowledge unnecessary.

w David Boehm, Ernest Gelsey   *novel* B. Russell Herts   d William Dieterle

Paul Lukas, Loretta Young, Frank McHugh, Glenda Farrell, Helen Vinson, Walter Byron, Ferdinand Gottschalk

'It just about makes three spades doubled, which isn't bad when you're vulnerable, and that should be enough to show a profit.' – *Variety*

Grand Slam
Italy/Spain/West Germany   1967   120m   Techniscope
Paramount/Jolly-Coral-Constantin (Harry Columbo, George Papi)
original title: *Ad Ogni Costo*

A retired professor has a plan for a diamond robbery, but recruits his aides unwisely.

Long-drawn-out caper melodrama with good sequences but nothing at all new; a very poor man's *Rififi*.

w Mino Roli, Caminito, Marcello Fondato, Antonio de la Loma   d Giuliano Montaldo   ph Antonio Macasoli   m Ennio Morricone

Janet Leigh, Edward G. Robinson, Klaus Kinski, Robert Hoffman, Georges Rigaud, Adolfo Celi

La Grande Bouffe: see *Blow-Out*

La Grande Illusion ***
France   1937   117m   bw
Réalisations d'Art Cinématographique (Frank Rollmer, Albert Pinkovitch)
V, V*, L

During World War I, three captured French pilots have an uneasy relationship with their German commandant.

Celebrated mood piece with much to say about war and mankind; more precisely, it is impeccably acted and directed and has real tragic force.

w Jean Renoir, Charles Spaak   d Jean Renoir
ph Christian Matras   m Joseph Kosma
m/ly Vincent Telly, Albert Valsien   ad Eugène Lourie   ed Marguerite Renoir, Marthe Huguet

Pierre Fresnay, Erich von Stroheim, Jean Gabin, Julien Carette, Marcel Dalio, Gaston Modot, Jean Dasté, Dita Parlo

'The story is true. It was told to me by my friends in the war . . . notably by Pinsard who flew fighter planes. I was in the reconnaissance squadron. He saved my life many times when the German fighters became too persistent. He himself was shot down seven times. His escapes are the basis for the story.' – *Jean Renoir*

'Artistically masterful.' – *Variety*

'One of the true masterpieces of the screen.' – *Pauline Kael, 70s*

AAN: best picture

La Grande Vadrouille: see *Don't Look Now ... We're Being Shot At!*

Les Grandes Manoeuvres *
France/Italy   1955   106m   Eastmancolor
Filmsonor/Rizzoli
aka: *Summer Manoeuvres*

In 1913, an army lieutenant takes a bet that he can win any woman in the town in which his regiment is quartered during manoeuvres.

An elegant, but surprisingly unwitty film from this director, saddled with a well-worn and very predictable plot.

wd René Clair   ph Robert Le Fèbvre, Robert Juillard   m Georges Van Parys

Gérard Philipe, Michèle Morgan, Brigitte Bardot, Yves Robert, Jean Desailly, Pierre Dux

Grandma's Boy *
US   1922   50m approx (24 fps)   bw   silent
Associated Exhibitors

Inspired by the heroism of his own grandpa, a meek and mild young fellow subdues a terrifying tramp.

Modest second-feature-length comedy of a burgeoning star, no great shakes by his later standards.

d Fred Newmeyer

Harold Lloyd, Dick Sutherland, Anna Townsend

Granny Get Your Gun
US   1939   56m   bw
Warner

An indomitable old lady turns sheriff to get her granddaughter off the hook for murder.

Energetic second feature comedy mystery from a Perry Mason story; pleasant performances.

w Kenneth Gamet   d George Amy

May Robson, Harry Davenport, Margot Stevenson, Hardie Albright

'The thousands who have read the book will know why WE WILL NOT SELL ANY CHILDREN TICKETS to see this picture!'

The Grapes of Wrath ****
US   1940   128m   bw
TCF (Darryl Zanuck, Nunnally Johnson)
V, V*, L

After the dust-bowl disaster of the thirties, Oklahoma farmers trek to California in the hope of a better life.

A superb film which could scarcely be improved upon. Though the ending is softened from the book, there was too much here for filmgoers to chew on. Acting, photography, direction combine to make this an unforgettable experience, a poem of a film.

w Nunnally Johnson   novel John Steinbeck   d John Ford   ph Gregg Toland   m Alfred Newman
ad Richard Day, Mark Lee Kirk   ed Robert Simpson

Henry Fonda, Jane Darwell, John Carradine, Charley Grapewin, Dorris Bowdon, Russell Simpson, Zeffie Tilbury, O. Z. Whitehead, John Qualen, Eddie Quillan, Grant Mitchell

TOM (Henry Fonda) reading grave marker: 'This here's William James Joad, died of a stroke, old, old man. His fokes bured him because they got no money to pay for funerls. Nobody kilt him. Just a stroke and he died.'

MA (Jane Darwell): 'Rich fellas come up, an' they die, an' their kids ain't no good, an' they die out. But we keep a-comin'. We're the people that live. Can't lick us. We'll go on forever, Pa, because we're the people.'

MA: 'Well, Pa, woman can change bettern a man. Man lives – well, in jerks. Baby born or somebody dies, that's a jerk. Gets a farm or loses one, an' that's a jerk. With a woman, it's all one flow, like a stream – little eddies, little waterfalls – but the river, it goes right on. Woman looks at it that way.'

'A genuinely great motion picture which makes one proud to have even a small share in the affairs of the cinema.' – *Howard Barnes*

'The most mature motion picture that has ever been made, in feeling, in purpose, and in the use of the medium.' – *Otis Ferguson*

'A sincere and searing indictment of man's cruel indifference to his fellows.' – *Basil Wright*

AA: John Ford; Jane Darwell

AAN: best picture; Nunnally Johnson; Henry Fonda; Robert Simpson

Grass *

US 1925 50m approx bw silent
Famous Players-Lasky

Nomadic Iranian tribes make an annual migration in search of fresh pasture.

Striking early documentary marred by facetious subtitles.

wd/ph Merian C. Cooper, Ernest Schoedsack
titles Terry Ramsaye

The Grass Is Greener *

GB 1960 104m Technirama
Grandon (Stanley Donen)
V

The wife of an English earl falls for an American millionaire tourist.

Heavy-going and unsuitably widescreened version of an agreeable piece of West End fluff. Performances just about save it.

w Hugh and Margaret Williams *play* Hugh and Margaret Williams *d* Stanley Donen
ph Christopher Challis *md* Muir Mathieson
m/y Noël Coward

Cary Grant, Deborah Kerr, Robert Mitchum, *Jean Simmons, Moray Watson*

'It's too bad Coward couldn't have written the wisecracks too.' – *Philip T. Hartung*

'The stars do not glitter or even glow. Instead of being liberated and propelled by the screenplay, they are chained and sunk. It is one of the year's most disappointing films.' – *James Powers, Hollywood Reporter*

The Grasshopper

US 1969 98m Technicolor
NGP (Jerry Belson, Barry Marshall)
V*

A small-town girl goes from man to man in Los Angeles and Las Vegas, finally becoming a call girl.

The road to ruin in modern dress; nicely made and quite entertaining in its gaudy way.

w Jerry Belson *novel* The Passing of Evil by Mark MacShane *d* Jerry Paris *ph* Sam Leavitt *m* Billy Goldenberg

Jacqueline Bisset, Jim Brown, Joseph Cotten, Corbett Monica

Graveyard Shift

US 1990 86m DeLuxe
Columbia TriStar/Graveyard Inc (William J. Dunn, Ralph S. Singleton)
V, V*, L

Workers in a rat-infested, run-down mill investigate a mysterious killer beast in the cellars.

Dreary, badly made horror movie that fails on every level.

w John Esposito *story* Stephen King *d* Ralph S. Singleton *ph* Peter Stein *m* Anthony Marinelli, Brian Banks *pd* Gary Wissner *ed* Jim Gross, Randy Jon Morgan

David Andrews, Kelly Wolf, Stephen Macht, Andrew Divoff, Vic Polizos, Brad Dourif, Robert Alan Beuth, Ilona Margolis

'Miserably inept.' – *Sight and Sound*

'Aside from being so dark and murky as to be almost unwatchable, the pic's sole distinction is that it employs more rats – largely of the puppy-sized variety – than perhaps any film since Ben.' —*Variety*

The Gravy Train *

US 1974 96m Eastmancolor
Columbia-Warner/Tomorrow Entertainment (Jonathan T. Taplin)
aka: *The Dion Brothers*

Two working-class brothers throw up their jobs and take to crime with bloody results.

Moderately entertaining caper, which manages to mix comedy and mayhem with some success.

w Bill Kerby, David Whitney (Terrence Malick)
d Jack Starrett *ph* Jerry Hirshfeld *pd* Stan Jolley
ed John Horger

Stacy Keach, Frederic Forrest, Margot Kidder, Barry Primus, Richard Romanus, Denny Miller

Gray Lady Down

US 1978 111m Technicolor Panavision
Universal/Mirisch (Walter Mirisch)
V*

After a collision, an American submarine lodges in the neck of an underwater canyon.

A rather boring update of *Morning Departure* with added technology.

w James Whittaker, Howard Sackler *novel* Event 1000 by David Levallee *d* David Greene
ph Stevan Larner *m* Jerry Fielding

Charlton Heston, David Carradine, Stacy Keach, Ned Beatty, Stephen McHattie, Ronny Cox, Dorian Harewood, Rosemary Forsyth

'The crew eventually reach the surface, but the film deserves to sink without trace.' – *Nicholas Wapshott, The Times*

Grease **

US 1978 110m Metrocolor Panavision
Paramount/Robert Stigwood, Allan Carr
V, V (W), V*, L, S

The path of true love in a fifties high school does not run smoothly.

Amiable 'period' musical for teenagers: a highly fashionable exploitation of the new star John Travolta, its commercialism is undeniable, and it carefully built in appeal to older age groups.

w Bronte Woodard *stage musical* Jim Jacobs, Warren Casey *d* Randal Kleiser *ch* Patricia Birch
ph Bill Butler *md* Louis St Louis *pd* Phil Jefferies
titles John Wilson *m/y* Jim Jacobs, Warren Casey
ed John F. Burnett

John Travolta, Olivia Newton-John, Stockard Channing, Eve Arden, Frankie Avalon, Joan Blondell, Edd Byrnes, Sid Caesar, Alice Ghostley, Sha Na Na, Jeff Conaway, Barry Pearl, Michael Tucci

'A bogus, clumsily jointed pastiche of late fifties high school musicals, studded with leftovers from *West Side Story* and *Rebel Without A Cause.*' – *New Yorker*

AAN: song, 'Hopelessly Devoted to You' (*m/y* John Farrar)

Grease 2

US 1982 114m Metrocolor Panavision
Paramount (Robert Stigwood, Allan Carr)
V, V (W), V*, L

In 1961 an English boy causes emotional problems when he joins the senior class of Rydell High School.

Despite the mixture as before, this sequel was a resounding flop in all departments, perhaps proving that the success of the original was only a fluke of timing.

w Ken Finkleman *d* Patricia Birch *ph* Frank Stanley *md* Louis St Louis *songs* various

Maxwell Caulfield, Michele Pfeiffer, Adrian Zmed, Lorna Luft, Eve Arden, Sid Caesar, Tab Hunter, Connie Stevens

'It's like being cooped up for two hours inside a combination of juke box and pinball machine, with you as the ball.' – *Daily Mail*

Greased Lightning

US 1977 96m Movielab
Third World (Hannah Weinstein)

A black Virginian moonshiner becomes a famous stock car racer.

Fashionable action hokum based on a real character.

w Kenneth Vose, Lawrence DuKore, Melvin Van Peebles, Leon Capetanos *d* Michel Schultz
ph George Bouillet *m* Fred Karlin

Richard Pryor, Beau Bridges, Pam Grier, Cleavon Little, Vincent Gardenia

The Great Adventure (1950): see: see
The Adventurers

The Great Adventure **

Sweden 1953 73m bw
Arne Sucksdorff
V*

Two boys on a farm rescue an otter and keep it as a pet.

Superbly photographed wildlife film featuring a variety of small animals.

wd/ed/ph Arne Sucksdorff *m* Lars Erik Larsson

Anders Norberg, Kjell Sucksdorff, Arne Sucksdorff

The Great Adventures of Captain Kidd

US 1953 bw serial: 15 eps
Columbia

Naval officers assigned to track down Captain Kidd the pirate realize that he is really a patriot.

Unhistorical serial charade, not really in the most entertaining tradition.

d Derwin Abbe, Charles Gould

Richard Crane, David Bruce, John Crawford, George Wallace

The Great Adventures of Wild Bill Hickok

US 1938 bw serial: 15 eps
Columbia

The marshal of Abilene opposes the Phantom Raiders.

Standard serial exploits.

d Mack V. Wright, Sam Nelson

Gordon Elliott, Monte Blue, Carole Wynne, Frankie Darro

The Great Alaskan Mystery *

US 1944 bw serial: 13 eps
Universal

Dr Miller invents a defence weapon called the Peratron, and goes to Alaska, followed by evil fascists, in search of the one element which will make it work.

Good serial stuff with a remarkably recognizable cast, and Ralph Morgan for once not the villain.

d Ray Taylor, Lewis D. Collins

Milburn Stone, Marjorie Weaver, Edgar Kennedy, Ralph Morgan, Samuel S. Hinds, Martin Kosleck, Joseph Crehan, Fuzzy Knight, Harry Cording

The Great American Broadcast *

US 1941 90m bw
TCF (Kenneth MacGowan)
V*

A romantic triangle set against the burgeoning years of the radio industry.

Pleasant musical, amusing if historically inaccurate.

w Don Ettlinger, Edwin Blum, Robert Ellis, Helen Logan *d* Archie Mayo *ph* Leon Shamroy, Peverell Marley *m/y* Mack Gordon, Harry Warren

Alice Faye, John Payne, Jack Oakie, Cesar Romero, The Ink Spots, The Nicholas Brothers, The Wiere Brothers

The Great American Pastime

US 1956 89m bw
MGM (Henry Berman)

A mild lawyer takes over a junior baseball team but incurs parental jealousy.

Thin lower-bracket comedy.

w Nathaniel Benchley d Herman Hoffman
ph Arthur E. Arling m Jeff Alexander

Tom Ewell, Anne Francis, Ann Miller, Dean Jones,
Raymond Bailey

The Great Awakening: see New Wine

Great Balls of Fire!
US 1989 107m colour
Rank/Orion (Adam Fields)
V, V*, L, S

Biopic of the country rock singer Jerry Lee Lewis.

Unimaginative, unfactual treatment that conveys little
of the performer's qualities.

w Jack Baran, Jim McBride book Myra Lewis,
Murray Silver d Jim McBride ph Affonso Beato
pd David Nichols ed Lisa Day, Pembroke Herring,
Bert Lovitt

Dennis Quaid, Winona Ryder, John Doe, Joe Bob
Briggs, Stephen Tobolowsky, Trey Wilson, Alec
Baldwin, Steve Allen, Lisa Blount, Joshua Sheffield

The Great Bank Robbery *
US 1969 98m colour Panavision
Warner (Malcolm Stuart)

Would-be bank robbers turn up in a Western town
disguised as priests.

Western spoof without the courage of its convictions,
but easy enough to watch.

w William Peter Blatty novel Frank O'Rourke
d Hy Averback ph Fred J. Koenekamp m Nelson
Riddle

Kim Novak, Zero Mostel, Clint Walker, Claude Akins,
Akim Tamiroff, Larry Storch, John Anderson, Sam
Jaffe, Ruth Warrick, Elisha Cook Jnr

The Great Barrier
GB 1937 85m bw
Gaumont British (Gunther Stapenhorst)
US title: Silent Barriers

A professional cardplayer gets involved in the
building of the Canadian Pacific Railway.

Forgotten epic which has scenes of some grandeur.

w Ralph Spencer, Michael Barringer, Milton Rosmer
novel The Great Divide by Alan Sullivan d Milton
Rosmer, Geoffrey Barkas ph Glen MacWilliams,
Robert Martin, Sidney Bonnett md Louis Levy
m Hubert Bath ad Walter Murton ed Charles
Frend

Richard Arlen, Antoinette Cellier, Lilli Palmer, Barry
Mackay, Roy Emerton

'Authentic history done sensitively . . . ranks with the
best made anywhere . . . will certainly achieve
commercial and artistic success throughout the
world.' – Variety

The Great Caruso **
US 1951 109m Technicolor
MGM (Joe Pasternak)
V, V*, L, S

Semi-fictional biography of the Italian tenor.

Dramatically flat but opulently staged biopic, turned
into a star vehicle and a huge commercial success.

w Sonya Levien, William Ludwig d Richard
Thorpe ph Joseph Ruttenberg md Johnny Green,
Peter Herman Adler

Mario Lanza, Ann Blyth, Dorothy Kirsten, Jarmila
Novotna, Carl Benton Reid, Eduard Franz, Richard
Hageman, Ludwig Donath, Alan Napier

'Sounds like a recorded programme of excerpts from
"Operas You Have Loved" which indeed it is.' – C. A.
Lejeune

AAN: Johnny Green, Peter Herman Adler

Great Catherine
GB 1968 98m Technicolor
Warner/Keep Films (Jules Buck)

An English captain visits the court of Catherine the
Great.

Chaos results from the attempt to inflate an ill-
considered Shavian whimsy into a feature film: the
material is simply insufficient and the performances
flounder in irrelevant production values.

w Hugh Leonard play Bernard Shaw d Gordon
Flemyng ph Oswald Morris m Dimitri Tiomkin
pd John Bryan

Jeanne Moreau, Peter O'Toole, Zero Mostel, Jack
Hawkins, Marie Lohr, Akim Tamiroff, Marie Kean,
Kenneth Griffith

'All Shaw's jokes work very well, but the film has
been padded out with Cossack dances, frantic chases,
and unfunny slapstick.' – Michael Billington, Illustrated
London News

The Great Chase
US 1963 82m bw
Continental
V*

A compendium of chase sequences from silent films.

w Harvey Kort, Paul Killiam, Saul Turrell

William S. Hart, Douglas Fairbanks Snr and Buster
Keaton (in The General)

The Great Commandment
US 1940 78m bw
John T. Coyle

In AD 30, with Judaea still under Roman rule, a
village scholar preaches the teachings of Jesus.

Thin little religious fable, independently produced
and without much going for it.

w Dana Burnet d Irving Pichel

John Beal, Albert Dekker, Maurice Moscovich,
Marjorie Cooley, Lloyd Corrigan

The Great Dan Patch
US 1949 92m bw
United Artists (W. R. Frank)
V*

The career of a famous racehorse at the turn of the
century.

Modest small-town crowd-pleaser.

w John Taintor Foote d Joseph Newman

Dennis O'Keefe, Gail Russell, Ruth Warrick,
Charlotte Greenwood, Henry Hull, John Hoyt, Arthur
Hunnicutt

Great Day
GB 1945 79m bw
RKO British (Victor Hanbury)
V*

A village Women's Institute prepares for a visit by
Mrs Roosevelt.

Modestly pleasing little drama from a successful play.

w Wolfgang Wilhelm, John Davenport play Lesley
Storm d Lance Comfort ph Erwin Hillier

Eric Portman, Flora Robson, Sheila Sim, Isabel Jeans,
Walter Fitzgerald, Philip Friend, Marjorie Rhodes,
Maire O'Neill, Beatrice Varley

Great Day in the Morning
US 1955 92m Technicolor Superscope
RKO/Edmund Grainger

At the outbreak of the Civil War, Denver has divided
loyalties.

Solemn semi-Western without much excitement.

w Lesser Samuels novel Robert Hardy Andrews
d Jacques Tourneur ph William Snyder m Leith
Stevens

Robert Stack, Virginia Mayo, Ruth Roman, Alex
Nicol, Raymond Burr, Regis Toomey

The Great Diamond Robbery
US 1954 69m bw
MGM

Crooks convince a dumb jewellery apprentice to help
them.

Tedious second feature comedy, the star's last for the
studio.

w Laslo Vadnay d Robert Z. Leonard

Red Skelton, Cara Williams, James Whitmore, Kurt
Kasznar, Reginald Owen

The Great Dictator **
US 1940 129m bw
United Artists/Charles Chaplin
V, V*

A Jewish barber is mistaken for dictator Adenoid
Hynkel.

Chaplin's satire on Hitler has a few funny moments,
but the rest is heavy going, the production is
cheeseparing, and the final speech to the world is a
grave mistake.

wd Charles Chaplin ph Karl Struss, Rollie Totheroh
m Meredith Willson ad J. Russell Spencer
ed Willard Nico

Charles Chaplin, Paulette Goddard, Jack Oakie (as
Napaloni), Reginald Gardiner, Henry Daniell, Billy
Gilbert, Maurice Moscovich

'For this film he takes on more than a mimed
representation of common humanity; he states, and
accepts, the responsibility of being one of humanity's
best and most widely-known representatives.' – Basil
Wright

'The last impassioned speech about peace and
serenity still wrecks everything that has gone before:
Chaplin mawkish can always overrule Chaplin the
innocent mime.' – New Yorker, 1978

'You must go back to Intolerance for another motion
picture that is so completely one man's personal
expression of his attitude on something about which
he feels deeply and passionately.' – James Shelley
Hamilton, National Board of Review

'No time for comedy? Yes, I say, time for comedy.
Time for Chaplin comedy. No time ever for Chaplin to
preach as he does in those last six minutes, no matter
how deeply he may feel what he wrote and says. He is
not a good preacher. Indeed, he is frighteningly bad.'
– John O'Hara

'Some moments actually work, but they are very few
and far between.' – Time Out, 1984

AAN: Charles Chaplin (as writer and actor);
Meredith Willson; Jack Oakie

The Great Escape **
US 1963 173m DeLuxe Panavision
UA/Mirisch/Alpha (John Sturges)
V, V*, L, S

Allied prisoners plan to escape from a German prison
camp.

Pretty good but overlong POW adventure with a
tragic ending.

w James Clavell, W. R. Burnett book Paul Brickhill
d John Sturges ph Daniel Fapp m Elmer Bernstein

James Garner, Steve McQueen, Richard Attenborough,
James Donald, Charles Bronson, Donald Pleasence,
James Coburn, David McCallum, Gordon Jackson,
John Leyton, Nigel Stock

Great Expectations
US 1934 100m bw
Universal
V*

A poor boy becomes unexpectedly rich and mistakes the source of his good fortune.

Solidly carpentered but never inspired version of a sprawling novel later tackled with much more style by David Lean. See below.

w Gladys Unger *novel* Charles Dickens *d* Stuart Walker *m* Edward Ward

Phillips Holmes (Pip), Jane Wyatt (Estella), Henry Hull (Magwitch), Florence Reed (Miss Havisham), Alan Hale (Joe Gargery), Rafaela Ottiano (Mrs Joe), Francis L. Sullivan (Jaggers)

'First half represents a fine achievement . . . and then it all falls apart.' – *Variety*

Great Expectations ****
GB 1946 118m bw
Rank/Cineguild (Anthony Havelock-Allan)
V, V*, L

A boy meets an escaped convict on the Romney Marshes, with strange consequences for both of them.

Despite the inevitable simplifications, this is a superbly pictorial rendering of a much-loved novel, with all the famous characters in safe hands and masterly judgement in every department.

w Ronald Neame, David Lean, Kay Walsh, Cecil McGivern, Anthony Havelock-Allan *d* David Lean *ph* Guy Green *m* Walter Goehr *ad* John Bryan

John Mills, Bernard Miles, *Finlay Currie, Martita Hunt,* Valerie Hobson, *Jean Simmons,* Alec Guinness, Francis L. Sullivan, Anthony Wager, Ivor Barnard, Freda Jackson, Hay Petrie, O. B. Clarence, George Hayes, Torin Thatcher, Eileen Erskine

'The first big British film to have been made, a film that sweeps our cloistered virtues out into the open.' – *Richard Winnington*

'The best Dickens adaptation, and arguably David Lean's finest film.' – *NFT, 1969*

'It does for Dickens what *Henry V* did for Shakespeare. That is, it indicates a sound method for translating him from print to film . . . almost never less than graceful, tasteful and intelligent, and some of it better than that.' – *James Agee*

† It was remade as a less than memorable TV movie in 1974, directed by Joseph Hardy and starring Michael York, Sarah Miles and James Mason.

AA: Guy Green; John Bryan

AAN: best picture; script; David Lean (as director)

The Great Flamarion
US 1945 78m bw
Republic
V*

A jealous vaudeville sharpshooter hunts down and kills the woman he loves because she prefers another.

Heavy-handed melodrama reminiscent of German silents but without their flair.

w Heinz Harald, Ann Widton, Richard Weil *d* Anthony Mann

Erich von Stroheim, Dan Duryea, Mary Beth Hughes

The Great Flirtation
US 1934 71m bw
Paramount

An actor is jealous of his wife's stardom.

Would-be sophisticated comedy with far too many loose ends.

w Humphrey Pearson *story* Gregory Ratoff *d* Ralph Murphy

Adolphe Menjou, Elissa Landi, David Manners, Lynne Overman, Raymond Walburn, Paul Porcasi, Akim Tamiroff

'Hardly a picture of strong audience appeal.' – *Variety*

The Great Gabbo
US 1929 88m bw
Sono Art

A ventriloquist's personality is taken over by that of his dummy.

Yes, that old chestnut, here in tedious and primitive early talkie form.

w F. Hugh Herbert *story* Ben Hecht *d* James Cruze

Erich von Stroheim, Betty Compson, Margie Kane

The Great Gambini
US 1937 70m bw
Paramount

A mindreader's efforts to solve a murder only point to his own guilt.

Talkative twister which doesn't quite work.

w Frederick Jackson, Frank Partos, Howard Irving Young *d* Charles Vidor

Akim Tamiroff, John Trent, Marian Marsh, Genevieve Tobin, Reginald Denny, William Demarest, Edward Brophy

'Not enough punch to produce better than ordinary entertainment.' – *Variety*

The Great Game
GB 1952 80m bw
Advance

A football club chairman gets involved in crooked deals.

Dismal comedy drama which gives few opportunities to anybody.

w Wolfgang Wilhelm *play Shooting Star* by Basil Thomas *d* Maurice Elvey

James Hayter, Diana Dors, Thora Hird, Sheila Shand Gibbs, John Laurie, Glyn Houston

The Great Garrick **
US 1937 91m bw
Warner (Mervyn Le Roy)

When Garrick goes to act in Paris, members of the Comédie Française take over a wayside inn and try to teach him a lesson, but the plan goes awry.

A pleasant unhistorical conceit makes a rather literary film to have come from Hollywood, but it is all very winning and cast and director keep the fun simmering happily.

w Ernest Vajda *d James Whale ph* Ernest Haller *m* Adolph Deutsch

Brian Aherne, Edward Everett Horton, Olivia de Havilland, Lionel Atwill, *Melville Cooper, Luis Alberni, Étienne Girardot*, Marie Wilson, Lana Turner, Albert Dekker, Fritz Leiber, Dorothy Tree, Chester Clute

'Finely made period romantic comedy, but its reception at the paygate is extremely problematical.' – *Variety*

'As elegantly witty as anything Whale ever did.' – *Tom Milne*

'A jestful and romantic piece.' – *Frank S. Nugent, New York Times*

The Great Gatsby *
US 1949 90m bw
Paramount (Richard Maibaum)

Events leading to the death of a retired gangster and mysterious Long Island plutocrat.

Rather bland and uninteresting attempt to accommodate a unique author to a formula star.

w Richard Maibaum *novel* F. Scott Fitzgerald *d* Elliott Nugent *ph* John Seitz *m* Robert Emmett Dolan

Alan Ladd, Macdonald Carey, Betty Field, Barry Sullivan, Howard da Silva

† A silent version in 1926 had starred Warner Baxter.

The Great Gatsby **
US 1974 146m Eastmancolor
Paramount/Newdon (David Merrick)
V, V*, L

Plush version with lavish production values and pleasing period sense but not much grip on the story or characters. Overlong footage is not made to seem shorter by snail's pace and dull performances.

w Francis Ford Coppola *d* Jack Clayton *ph* Douglas Slocombe *m* Nelson Riddle *pd* John Box

Robert Redford, Mia Farrow, Karen Black, Scott Wilson, *Sam Waterston*, Lois Chiles

'Pays its creator the regrettable tribute of erecting a mausoleum over his work.' – *Richard Combs*

'Leaves us more involved with six-and-a-half-million dollars' worth of trappings than with human tragedy.' – *Judith Crist*

'A total failure of every requisite sensibility.' – *Stanley Kauffmann*

'Profoundly unfilmable: a poetic and ultimately pessimistic comment on the American dream is transformed by cinematic realism into pure prose.' – *Michael Billington, Illustrated London News*

AA: Nelson Riddle; costumes (Theoni V. Aldredge)

The Great Gilbert and Sullivan: see *The Story of Gilbert and Sullivan*

The Great Gildersleeve
US 1942 61m bw
RKO (Herman Schlom)
V*

A small town loudmouth is always in hot water.

Unremarkable film début for a radio character from Fibber McGee and Molly. Three more second features followed.

w Jack Townley, Joseph Josephson *d* Gordon Douglas

Harold Peary, Jane Darwell, Nancy Gates, Charles Arnt, Thurston Hall

Great Guns *
US 1941 74m bw
TCF (Sol M. Wurtzel)
V, V*

A young millionaire's retainers join the army with him.

Disappointing Laurel and Hardy comedy, their first for Fox and the beginning of their decline. A few good jokes, but no overall control or inventiveness.

w Lou Breslow *d* Monty Banks *ph* Glen MacWilliams *m* Emil Newman *ed* Al de Gaetano

Stan Laurel, Oliver Hardy, Sheila Ryan, Dick Nelson, Edmund Macdonald, Charles Trowbridge, Ludwig Stossel, Mae Marsh

Great Guy *
US 1936 73m bw
Grand National (Douglas Maclean)
V*
GB title: *Pluck of the Irish*

An ex-prizefighter joins the bureau of weights and measures and fights corruption.

Rather tame racket film, Cagney's first independent venture away from Warner. He atones for rather thin production values.

w Henry McCarthy, Henry Johnson, James Edward Grant, Harry Ruskin *d* John G. Blystone *ph* Jack McKenzie *m* Marlin Skiles

James Cagney, Mae Clarke, James Burke, Edward Brophy, Henry Kolker

'It's all typical Cagney stuff, and that's the trouble with it. Cagney apparently is doing the things he likes best, but they're repetitious and apt to disappoint a public anticipating something finer from this star after his quite lengthy absence.' – *Variety*

The Great Hospital Mystery

US 1937 59m bw
TCF

The lady superintendent of a hospital has a busy night including impersonation and murder.

Confused but watchable second feature.

w Bess Meredyth, William Conselman, Jerry Cady *novel* Mignon G. Eberhart d James Tinling

Jane Darwell, Joan Davis, Sig Rumann, Sally Blane, Thomas Beck, William Demarest

The Great Hotel Murder

US 1934 70m bw
TCF

Rival sleuths find the truth about a murder less important than being first to find it out.

Lively programme filler of its day, with the stars still doing their Flagg and Quirt act.

w Arthur Kober *story* Vincent Starrett d Eugene Forde

Edmund Lowe, Victor McLaglen, Rosemary Ames, Mary Carlisle

The Great Impersonation *

US 1935 81m bw
Universal (Edmund Grainger)

During World War I, a German murders an English nobleman and, being his double, takes over.

Reliable espionage melodrama with atmospheric country house asides, from a sturdily compelling novel.

w Frank Wead, Eve Greene *novel* E. Phillips Oppenheim d Alan Crosland ph Milton Krasner m Franz Waxman

Edmund Lowe, Valerie Hobson, Vera Engels, Henry Mollison, Lumsden Hare, Spring Byington, Charles Waldron, Dwight Frye

'They giggled a bit when Lowe went to bed with candles, and an hour later a sliding panel attempt on his life has him pushing an electric light switch . . . probably doesn't matter that the 1914 characters are dressed throughout in 1935 modishness and drive around in streamlined automobiles.' – *Variety*

† It was previously filmed in 1921 with James Kirkwood.

The Great Impersonation *

US 1942 71m bw
Universal (Paul Malvern)

Okay quickie updating of the above, serviceable rather than inventive.

w W. Scott Darling d John Rawlins ph George Robinson m Hans Salter

Ralph Bellamy, Evelyn Ankers, Aubrey Mather, Edward Norris, Karen Verne, Henry Daniell, Ludwig Stossel

The Great Imposter *

US 1961 112m bw
U-I (Robert Arthur)
V*

The career of Ferdinand Waldo Demara, a marine and Trappist monk who also impersonated a Harvard research fellow, a prison warden, a naval doctor and a schoolteacher.

Uncertain mood hampers this biopic of a likeable fantasist.

w Liam O'Brien *book* Robert Crichton d Robert Mulligan ph Robert Burks m Henry Mancini

Tony Curtis, Raymond Massey, Karl Malden, Edmond O'Brien, Arthur O'Connell, Gary Merrill, Frank Gorshin, Joan Blackman, Robert Middleton

Great – Isambard Kingdom Brunel *

GB 1975 28m Eastmancolor
British Lion

A musical, animated biography of the great Victorian engineer.

Quite unexpected, and therefore the more delightful.

w Bob Godfrey d Bob Godfrey

The Great Jasper

US 1933 83m bw
RKO

An Irish motorman becomes a fortune teller, and has his way with lots of women.

Curious comedy-melodrama which never quite hits the right style.

w Sam Ornitz, H. W. Hanemann *novel* Fulton Oursler d J. Walter Ruben

Richard Dix, Wera Engels, Edna May Oliver, Florence Eldridge, Bruce Cabot

'Okay as a critics' film but looks like an in-and-outer.' – *Variety*

The Great Jesse James Raid

US 1953 70m Ansco Color
Lippert

Jesse James comes out of retirement for one last haul.

Boring two-bit Western, all preparation and no action.

w Richard Landau d Reginald Le Borg

Willard Parker, Barbara Payton, Tom Neal, Wallace Ford, Jim Bannon

The Great Jewel Robber

US 1950 91m bw
Warner

The exploits of real-life society thief Gerald Graham Dennis.

Surprisingly acceptable and entertaining reconstruction.

w Borden Chase d Peter Godfrey

David Brian, Marjorie Reynolds, John Archer, Jacqueline de Wit

The Great John L.

US 1945 96m bw
UA/Bing Crosby Productions (Frank Mastroly, James Edward Grant)
GB title: *A Man Called Sullivan*

Women in the life of prizefighter John L. Sullivan.

Very mild period biopic without the zest of *Gentleman Jim*.

w James Edward Grant d Frank Tuttle ph James Van Trees m Victor Young

Greg McClure, Linda Darnell, Barbara Britton, Lee Sullivan, Otto Kruger, Wallace Ford, Robert Barrat

'Sometimes there's a terrible penalty for telling the truth

The Great Lie ***

US 1941 107m bw
Warner (Hal B. Wallis, Henry Blanke)
V*, L

A determined girl loses the man she loves, believes him dead in a plane crash, and takes over the baby which his selfish wife does not want.

Absurd melodrama becomes top-flight entertainment with all concerned in cracking form and special attention on the two bitchy female leads, splendidly played. Classical music trimmings, too.

w Leonore Coffee *novel* January Heights by Polan Banks d Edmund Goulding ph Tony Gaudio m Max Steiner

Bette Davis, Mary Astor, George Brent, Lucile Watson, Hattie McDaniel, Grant Mitchell, Jerome Cowan

AA: Mary Astor

The Great Locomotive Chase *

US 1956 76m Technicolor Cinemascope
Walt Disney (Lawrence Edward Watkin)
V*

During the Civil War, Union spies steal a train and destroy track and bridges behind them.

A serious version of Buster Keaton's *The General*, based on a true incident; good sequences but no overall pace.

w Lawrence Edward Watkin d Francis D. Lyon ph Charles Boyle m Paul Smith

Fess Parker, Jeffrey Hunter, Jeff York, John Lupton, Kenneth Tobey

The Great Lover

US 1931 77m bw
MGM

Capers of a philandering opera star.

Satisfactory drama-comedy vehicle for a durable star.

w Gene Markey d Harry Beaumont

Adolphe Menjou, Irene Dunne, Neil Hamilton, Olga Baclanova

'Appeal limited to the mature fan.' – *Variety*

The Great Lover *

US 1949 80m bw
(Paramount) Hope Enterprises (Edmund Beloin)
V*

On a transatlantic liner, a timid scoutmaster catches a strangler.

Amusing suspense comedy, a good star vehicle.

w Edmund Beloin, Melville Shavelson, Jack Rose d Alexander Hall ph Charles Lang m Joseph J. Lilley

Bob Hope, Rhonda Fleming, *Roland Young,* Jim Backus, Roland Culver, George Reeves

'He'll give you the biggest heart sock, laugh shock you ever thrilled to!'

The Great McGinty **

US 1940 83m bw
Paramount (Paul Jones)
V*, L
GB title: *Down Went McGinty*

A hobo and a crook have a hectic political career.

Lively comedy-drama which signalled the arrival as director of a new and stimulating Hollywood talent.

wd Preston Sturges ph William C. Mellor m Frederick Hollander

Brian Donlevy, Akim Tamiroff, Muriel Angelus, Louis Jean Heydt, Arthur Hoyt

PROLOGUE: 'This is the story of two men who met in a banana republic. One of them never did anything dishonest in his life except for one crazy minute. The other never did anything honest in his life except for one crazy minute. They both had to leave the country.'

'This is his first directing job and where has he been all our lives? He has that sense of the incongruous which makes some of the best gaiety.' – *Otis Ferguson*

'The tough dialogue is matched by short, snappy scenes; the picture seems to have wasted no time, no money.' – *Gilbert Seldes*

'A director as adroit and inventive as any in the business . . . it starts like a five-alarm fire and never slackens pace for one moment until its unexpected conclusion.' – *Pare Lorentz*

'Sturges takes the success ethic and throws it in the face of the audience.' – *James Orsini*

'Capra with the gloves off.' – *Raymond Durgnat*

AA: script

The Great McGonagall

GB 1974 89m Eastmancolor
Darlton

An unemployed Scot aims to become Queen Victoria's Poet Laureate.

Appalling tribute to a minor figure of sub-literature.

w Joe McGrath, Spike Milligan   d Joe McGrath

Spike Milligan, Peter Sellers, Julia Foster, Julian Chagrin, John Bluthal, Valentine Dyall, Victor Spinetti

The Great Man **

US 1956 92m bw
U-I (Aaron Rosenberg)

A memorial programme to a much-loved TV personality turns into an exposé.

Patchy melodrama with a *Citizen Kane* framework; the best bits are very effective.

w *José Ferrer, Al Morgan   novel* Al Morgan   d José Ferrer   ph Harold Lipstein   m Herman Stein

José Ferrer, Dean Jagger, Keenan Wynn, *Julie London,* Joanne Gilbert, *Ed Wynn,* Jim Backus

'Its distinction is in its unwavering tone – one of blunt and frequently savage irony and cynicism.' – *MFB*

'The movie is almost over before one realizes what a slick, fast sell it is (resembling nothing so much as what it is attacking).' – *Pauline Kael, 1968*

The Great Man Votes *

US 1938 72m bw
RKO (Cliff Reid)

A drunken professor turns out to have the casting vote in a local election.

Slow-starting but progressively funny political comedy with some favourite talents in good form.

w John Twist   *story* Gordon Malherbe Hillman   d *Garson Kanin*   ph Russell Metty   m Roy Webb

John Barrymore, Virginia Weidler, Peter Holden, *William Demarest,* Donald MacBride

'It will be hailed by class audiences as a fine example of the film art, yet carrying sock appeal for mass patronage.' – *Variety*

The Great Manhunt (1949): see: see

The Doolins of Oklahoma

The Great Manhunt (1950): see: see

State Secret

The Great Man's Lady *

US 1941 90m bw
Paramount (William A. Wellman)

A Western pioneer is inspired and encouraged by his wife.

Adequate but unsurprising flashback family drama starting with its star as a lady of 109.

w W. L. Rivers   *story* Vina Delmar   d William A. Wellman   ph William C. Mellor   m Victor Young

Barbara Stanwyck, Joel McCrea, Brian Donlevy, Katharine Stevens, Thurston Hall, Lloyd Corrigan

The Great Meadow

US 1931 80m bw
MGM

Early settlers from Virginia walk to Kentucky.

Dim pioneering fable, without even a covered wagon.

w Edith Ellis, Charles Brabin   *novel* Elizabeth Madox Roberts   d Charles Brabin

John Mack Brown, Eleanor Boardman, Lucille La Verne, Anita Louise, Gavin Gordon, Guinn Williams

'Rather a sorry mess . . . cannot be depended on for an average gross.' – *Variety*

The Great Missouri Raid

US 1950 81m Technicolor
Nat Holt/Paramount
V*

Jesse and Frank James are seen as Civil War guerrillas, subsequently forced into crime by a vengeful officer.

Unsuccessful whitewash job, tediously told.

w Frank Gruber   d Gordon Douglas

Macdonald Carey, Wendell Corey, Ward Bond, Ellen Drew, Bruce Bennett, Bill Williams, Anne Revere, Edgar Buchanan

The Great Mr Handel *

GB 1942 103m Technicolor
Rank/GHW (James B. Sloan)
V

How the 18th-century composer came to write the Messiah.

Earnest, unlikely biopic, naïve but rather commendable.

w Gerald Elliott, Victor MacClure   *play* L. DuGarde Peach   d Norman Walker   ph Claude Friese-Greene, Jack Cardiff   md Ernest Irving

Wilfrid Lawson, Elizabeth Allan, Malcolm Keen, Michael Shepley, Hay Petrie, A. E. Matthews

'A graceful addition to the ranks of prestige pictures.' – *Kine Weekly*

The Great Mr Nobody

US 1941 71m bw
Warner

A classified ad salesman is too prone to let colleagues take the credit for his ideas.

Thin character comedy which did nobody concerned any good.

w Ben Markson, Kenneth Gamet   d Ben Stoloff

Eddie Albert, Joan Leslie, Alan Hale, William Lundigan, John Litel

The Great Moment **

'They booed him to greatness!'

US 1944 83m bw
Paramount
V*

How anaesthetics may have been invented.

Curious biopic of Dr W. T. G. Morgan, poised somewhere between utter seriousness and pratfall farce. The beginning of its director's decline, but always interesting in itself.

wd *Preston Sturges   book* Triumph over Pain by René Fulop-Miller   ph Victor Milner   m Victor Young

Joel McCrea, Betty Field, William Demarest, Harry Carey, Franklin Pangborn, Porter Hall, Grady Sutton

'Mr Sturges has triumphed over stiffness in screen biography.' – *New York Times*

'The careless, careful authority is there . . . the contrivance is smart enough.' – *Sunday Times*

The Great Mouse Detective *

US 1986 80m Technicolor
Walt Disney/Silver Screen Partners II (Burny Mattinson)
V, V*, L, S
GB title: *Basil, The Great Mouse Detective*

A mouse who has studied Sherlock Holmes solves the mystery of a missing mouse toymaker and outwits the evil Professor Rattigan.

One of the better recent Disney cartoon features, but the texture will probably never again be so rich as in the days of *Pinocchio* and *Bambi.*

w Pete Young, Steven Hulett, John Musker, Matthew O'Callaghan, Dave Michener, Vane Gerry, Ron Clements, Bruce M. Morris, Melvin Shaw, Burny Mattinson   *novel Basil of Baker Street* by Eve Titus   d John Musker, Ron Clements, Dave Michener and Burny Mattinson   ph Ed Austin   m Henry Mancini   pd Guy Vasilovich   ed Roy M. Brewer Jnr, James Melton

voices of Barrie Ingham, Vincent Price, Val Bettin, Alan Young

The Great Muppet Caper **

GB 1981 97m Technicolor
ITC (David Lazer, Frank Oz)
V, V*, L, S

Kermit and Fozzie are reporters sent to solve a jewel robbery.

Considerably livelier than *The Muppet Movie* but a badly timed flop at the box-office, this genial caper has a pleasant collection of guest stars as well as showing the familiar puppets at their most typical.

w Tom Patchett, Jay Tarses, Jerry Juhl, Jack Rose   d Jim Henson   ph Oswald Morris   m Joe Raposo   pd Harry Lange

Diana Rigg, Charles Grodin, John Cleese, Robert Morley, Trevor Howard, Peter Ustinov, Jack Warden

'Large chunks are pleasingly daft.' – *Sight and Sound*

AAN: song 'The First Time It Happened' (m/ly Joe Raposo)

The Great Northfield Minnesota Raid *

US 1971 91m Technicolor
Universal/Robertson and Associates/Jennings Lang
V*

In 1876 a gang of bandits, technically pardoned, plan a bank robbery.

'Realistic' Western in which the settings and photography have an impressively rough look but the script leaves much to be desired.

wd Philip Kaufman   ph Bruce Surtees   m Dave Grusin

Cliff Robertson, Robert Duvall, Luke Askew, Elisha Cook Jnr

The Great O'Malley

US 1937 77m bw
Warner (Harry Joe Brown)

An overzealous cop cares for the wife and child of a petty criminal whom he has sent to prison.

Considering the talent involved, an astonishingly routine programmer.

w Milton Krims, Tom Reed   *story The Making of O'Malley* by Gerald Beaumont   d William Dieterle   ph Ernest Haller   m Heinz Roemheld

Pat O'Brien, Humphrey Bogart, Ann Sheridan, Sybil Jason, Frieda Inescort, Donald Crisp, Henry O'Neill, Hobart Cavanaugh, Mary Gordon

'Familiar sentimental police theme: little action or appeal.' – *Variety*

† Previously filmed in 1923 with Milton Sills, as *The Making of O'Malley.*

The Great Outdoors

US 1988 90m CFI Panavision
Universal/Hughes Entertainment (Arne L. Schmidt)
V, V*, L

A family's holiday in the woods is disrupted by a surprise visit from their wealthy in-laws.

Broad and tiresome comedy in which its participants flail around noisily to no particular purpose.

w John Hughes *d* Howard Deutch *ph* Ric Waite *m* Thomas Newman *pd* John W. Corso *ed* Tom Rolf, William Gordean, Seth Flaum

Dan Aykroyd, John Candy, Stephanie Faracy, Annette Bening, Chris Young, Ian Giatti, Hilary Gordon, Rebecca Gordon, Robert Prosky

The Great Profile *
US 1940 82m bw
TCF (Raymond Griffith)

A dissipated actor disgraces his family and becomes an acrobat.

Shapeless farce in which a great talent on his last legs parodies himself.

w Milton Sperling, Hilary Lynn *d* Walter Lang *ph* Ernest Palmer *m* Cyril Mockridge

John Barrymore, Mary Beth Hughes, Gregory Ratoff, Anne Baxter, John Payne, Lionel Atwill, Edward Brophy, Willie Fung

'The greatest comedy ever made!'
The Great Race ***
US 1965 163m Technicolor Super Panavision
Warner/Patricia/Jalem/Reynard (Martin Jurow)
V*, L, S

In 1908, the Great Leslie and Professor Fate are leading contenders in the first New York to Paris car race.

Elaborate comedy spectacular with many good moments, notably the early disasters, a Western saloon brawl, and a custard pie fight. Elsewhere, there is more evidence of an oversize budget than of wit or finesse, and the entire *Prisoner of Zenda* spoof could have been omitted. Excellent production detail and general good humour.

w Arthur Ross *d* Blake Edwards *ph* Russell Harlan *m* Henry Mancini *pd* Fernando Carrere

Jack Lemmon, Tony Curtis, Peter Falk, Natalie Wood, George Macready, Ross Martin, Vivian Vance, Dorothy Provine

AAN: Russell Harlan; song 'The Sweetheart Tree' (*m* Henry Mancini, *ly* Johnny Mercer)

The Great Rupert
US 1950 87m bw
Eagle Lion (George Pal)
V*

A family of impoverished acrobats are assisted by a pet squirrel which proves lucky in more ways than one.

Modest whimsical comedy which outstays its welcome.

w Laslo Vadnay *d* Irving Pichel

Jimmy Durante, Terry Moore, Tom Drake, Sara Haden, Frank Orth

† The squirrel was part puppet.

The Great St Trinian's Train Robbery
GB 1966 94m Eastmancolor
British Lion/Braywild (Leslie Gilliat)
V, V*

The staff of St Trinian's is infiltrated by would-be train robbers.

Flat-footed farce with a sense of strain evident from first to last shot.

w Frank Launder, Ivor Herbert *d* Frank Launder, Sidney Gilliat *ph* Ken Hodges *m* Malcolm Arnold

Frankie Howerd, Dora Bryan, Reg Varney, Desmond Walter-Ellis, Raymond Huntley, Richard Wattis, George Benson, Eric Barker, Godfrey Winn, George Cole, Colin Gordon, Barbara Couper, Elspeth Duxbury

The Great Santini *
US 1979 115m Technicolor
Warner/Orion/Bing Crosby Productions (Charles A. Pratt)
V*

A crack fighter pilot has difficulty adjusting to peacetime domestic life.

Overlong but generally absorbing star character drama.

wd Lewis John Carlino *novel* Pat Conway *ph* Ralph Woolsey *m* Elmer Bernstein *pd* Jack Poplin

Robert Duvall, Blythe Danner, Michael O'Keefe, Lisa Jane Persky, Julie Anne Haddock

AAN: Robert Duvall; Michael O'Keefe (supporting actor)

'They were not forgotten by history – they were left out on purpose!'
The Great Scout and Cathouse Thursday
US 1976 102m Technicolor
AIP (Jules Buck and David Korda)
V*
reissue title: *Wildcat*

While trying to revenge himself on an absconding partner, an old cowboy falls for a young prostitute.

Downright peculiar comedy Western which never seems to make up its mind what it's trying to be, and too often is merely embarrassing.

w Richard Shapiro *d* Don Taylor *ph* Alex Phillips Jnr *m* John Cameron *pd* Jack Martin Smith

Lee Marvin, Oliver Reed, Kay Lenz, Robert Culp, Elizabeth Ashley, Strother Martin, Sylvia Miles

'It takes more than a dollop or two of sentiment and acres of dirty talk to make a movie.' – *Michael Billington, Illustrated London News*

'It sounds like the latest in the cute twosome series launched by *Butch Cassidy and the Sundance Kid*. In fact it features not two but seven wacky westerners who all seem addicted to stealing, hee-hawing, falling into puddles and punching each other in the privates.' – *Janet Maslin, Newsweek*

The Great Sinner *
US 1949 110m bw
MGM (Gottfried Reinhardt)

A serious young writer becomes a compulsive gambler.

Rather pointless and heavy-handed but extremely good-looking and splendidly cast period drama vaguely based on Dostoievsky.

w Ladislas Fodor, Christopher Isherwood *d* Robert Siodmak *ph* George Folsey *m* Bronislau Kaper *ad* Cedric Gibbons, Hans Peters

Gregory Peck, *Walter Huston*, Ava Gardner, Agnes Moorehead, Ethel Barrymore, Melvyn Douglas, Frank Morgan

The Great Sioux Massacre
US 1965 93m Eastmancolor Cinemascope
Columbia/FF (Leon Fromkess)

Two officers are court-martialled after Custer's last stand.

Fragmentary flashback Western let down by production and performances.

w Fred C. Dobbs *d* Sidney Salkow *ph* Irving Lippman *m* Emil Newman, Edward B. Powell

Joseph Cotten, Darren McGavin, Phil Carey, Nancy Kovack, Julie Sommars, Michael Pate

The Great Sioux Uprising
US 1953 80m Technicolor
U-I (Albert J. Cohen)

Indians rebel when their horses are stolen for sale to the commander of Fort Laramie.

Moderate Western programmer.

w Richard Breen, Gladys Atwater *d* Lloyd Bacon *ph* Maury Gertsman *m* Joseph Gershenson

Jeff Chandler, Faith Domergue, Lyle Bettger

The Great Smokey Roadblock
US 1976 106m colour
Marvista (Ingo Preminger, Allan F. Bodoh)
V*
original title: *The Last Of The Cowboys*

A truckdriver avoiding the finance company picks up an assortment of eccentrics and starts on a wild chase.

What possessed Henry Fonda to appear in this hick action melodrama will be forever unclear.

wd John Leone *ph* Ed Brown Snr *m* Craig Safan *ed* Corky Ehlers

Henry Fonda, Eileen Brennan, John Byner, Dub Taylor, Susan Sarandon, Dana House, Robert Englund, Melanie Mayron, Valerie Curtin

The Great Spy Mission: see *Operation Crossbow*

The Great Stone Face *
US 1968 93m bw
Funnyman Productions

A very acceptable biography of Buster Keaton, with unusual emphasis on the very early films.

wd Vernon P. Becker

The Great Train Robbery ***
US 1903 10m approx bw silent
Edison

Bandits tie up a telegraph operator and rob a train, but are arrested.

In its day this was a real pioneer. It was among the longest films then made, it had the most complicated story line, it was the first Western and it used new technical tricks such as the pan and the close-up. Needless to say, it must now be viewed with sympathy.

wd Edwin S. Porter

Marie Murray, Broncho Billy Anderson, George Barnes

The Great Train Robbery (1978): see *The First Great Train Robbery*

'The grandest of love stories told to the tunes of the grandest musical score ever written!'
The Great Victor Herbert *
US 1939 91m bw
Paramount (Andrew L. Stone)

At the turn of the century a famous composer plays cupid to two young singers.

Pleasant minor musical with excellent songs and an infectious cheerfulness.

w Russel Crouse, Robert Lively *d* Andrew L. Stone *ph* Victor Milner *md* Phil Boutelje, Arthur Lange

Walter Connolly, Allan Jones, Mary Martin, Susanna Foster, Lee Bowman

'Elaborately produced, visually effective . . . but audiences will learn from it very little about Victor Herbert.' – *Variety*

'Not highbrow, not lowbrow, but strictly on the beam for both mass and class audiences.' – *Motion Picture Herald*

AAN: Phil Boutelje, Arthur Lange

'What do you do when the war is over and you're the second best pilot in the world?'
The Great Waldo Pepper *
US 1975 108m Technicolor Todd-AO 35
Universal (George Roy Hill)
V, V*, L

In the twenties, a World War I flyer becomes an aerial stuntman.

Whimsical spectacular which concentrates less on the mystique of flying than on a series of splendid stunts.

w William Goldman　*d* George Roy Hill　*ph* Robert Surtees　*m* Henry Mancini

Robert Redford, Bo Svenson, Bo Brundin, Susan Sarandon, Geoffrey Lewis

'Charged with enthralling balletic precision.' – *Tom Milne*

'One hundred per cent pure plastic adolescent male fantasy.' – *New Yorker*

A Great Wall

US　1987　102m　colour
Mainline/W and S/Nanhai (Shirley Sun)
V, V*, L

A Chinese-American executive takes his family to visit China and the sister he has not seen for twenty years.

The first American film to be made in China since the revolution turns out to be a small and pleasant comedy of cultural misunderstandings.

w Peter Wang, Shirley Sun　*d* Peter Wang *ph* Peter Stein, Robert Primes　*m* David Laing, Ge Ganru　*ad* Wing Lee, Feng Yuan, Moing Ming Cheung　*ed* Graham Weinbren

Peter Wang, Sharon Iwai, Kelvin Han Yee, Li Qinqin, Hu Xiaoguang, Shen Guanglan

'Miliza Korjus – rhymes with gorgeous!'
The Great Waltz ***

US　1938　103m　bw
MGM (Bernard Hyman)
V*

Young Johann Strauss becomes Vienna's waltz king.

Exhilarating old-fashioned studio-set musical located in Hollywood's endearing vision of Old Vienna, assisted by streamlined production and excellent cast. Musical schmaltz.

w Walter Reisch, Samuel Hoffenstein *story* Gottfried Reinhardt　*d* Julien Duvivier *ph* Joseph Ruttenberg　*m* Dimitri Tiomkin *ed* Tom Held

Fernand Gravet, Luise Rainer, Miliza Korjus, Lionel Atwill, Hugh Herbert, Herman Bing, Curt Bois

'Should click nicely, but in these swingaroo days the waltz part may slow down anticipated b.o. enthusiasm.' – *Variety*

'A film to set the feet itching, and to make you want to grab a partner and join in.' – *Film Weekly*

AA: Joseph Ruttenberg

AAN: Miliza Korjus; Tom Held

The Great Waltz *

US　1972　134m　Metrocolor　Panavision 70
MGM (Andrew L. Stone)

Heavy-going remake set on real locations and hampered by them, styled in the manner of the same director's *Song of Norway*, i.e. with no real style at all.

The music survives.

wd Andrew L. Stone　*ph* David Boulton　*m* the Strauss family, adapted by Robert Wright, Chet Forrest　*ch* Onna White　*ad* William Albert Havenmeyer

Horst Buchholz, Nigel Patrick, Mary Costa, Rossano Brazzi, Yvonne Mitchell

'Take a box of chocolates – soft-centred, of course.' – *Michael Billington, Illustrated London News*

'He could beat any white man in the world. He just couldn't beat all of them!'
The Great White Hope **

US　1970　103m　DeLuxe　Panavision
TCF (Lawrence Turman)
V*

In 1910, a black boxer becomes world heavyweight champ but has trouble through his affair with a white girl.

Vivid, slightly whitewashed biopic of Jack Johnson (called Jefferson). Dramatic deficiencies outweighed by excellent period detail and a spellbinding central performance.

w Howard Sackler　*play* Howard Sackler　*d* Martin Ritt　*ph* Burnett Guffey　*md* Lionel Newman *pd* John DeCuir

James Earl Jones, Jane Alexander, Lou Gilbert, Joel Fluellen, Chester Morris, Robert Webber, Hal Holbrook

AAN: James Earl Jones; Jane Alexander

The Great Ziegfeld **

US　1936　179m　bw
MGM (Hunt Stromberg)
V*, L

The growth and Broadway fame of impresario Florenz Ziegfeld.

Mammoth biopic which despite a few show-stopping numbers never takes off dramatically and becomes something of an endurance test; interesting, however, as a spectacular of its time.

w William Anthony McGuire　*d* Robert Z. Leonard *ph* Oliver T. Marsh, Ray June, George Folsey *md* Arthur Lange　*ad* Cedric Gibbons, Eddie Imazu, Edwin B. Willis　*ch* Seymour Felix

William Powell, Luise Rainer (as Anna Held), Myrna Loy (as Billie Burke), Frank Morgan, Reginald Owen, Nat Pendleton, Virginia Bruce, *Ray Bolger*, Harriett Hoctor, Ernest Cossart, *Fanny Brice*, Robert Greig, Gilda Gray, Leon Errol, Stanley Morner (Dennis Morgan)

'This huge inflated gas-blown object bobs into the critical view as irrelevantly as an airship advertising somebody's toothpaste at a south coast resort. It lasts three hours. That is its only claim to special attention.' – *Graham Greene*

'Everything should have been tightened – not in the team job of cutting those miles of negative, but in boiling down the script, saving a line here, combining two scenes into one.' – *Otis Ferguson*

AA: best picture; Luise Rainer; Seymour Felix

AAN: William Anthony McGuire; Robert Z. Leonard; art direction

The Greatest

US/GB　1977　101m　Metrocolor
Columbia/EMI (John Marshall)

The life and times of Muhammad Ali.

Bland confection of rags to riches in the boxing ring, its only plus being that Ali plays himself and offers a predictable array of enjoyable one-liners.

w Ring Lardner Jnr　*book* The Greatest by Muhammad Ali　*d* Tom Gries　*ph* Harry Stradling *m* Michael Masser

Muhammed Ali, Ernest Borgnine, Roger E. Mosley, Lloyd Haynes, Malachi Throne, John Marley, Robert Duvall, David Huddleston, Ben Johnson, James Earl Jones, Dina Merrill, Paul Winfield

The Greatest Attack

France　1978　96m　colour
Adel Productions/Films 21/Eota Films/Antenne 2
original title: *Le Toubib*

An introspective surgeon falls for a sickly nurse during a European war in the 1980s.

Moodily self-indulgent melodrama.

w Pascal Jardin, Pierre Granier-Deferre *novel Harmonie ou les horreurs de la guerre* by Jean Freustie　*d* Pierre Granier-Deferre　*ph* Claude Renoir　*m* Phillipe Sarde　*ad* Maurice Sargent *ed* Jean Revel

Alain Delon, Veronique Jannot, Bernard Giraudeau, Bernard Le Coq, Catherine Lachens, Francine Berge, Michael Auclair

The Greatest Show on Earth *

US　1952　153m　Technicolor
Paramount/Cecil B. de Mille (Henry Wilcoxon)
V, V*, L

Various dramas come to a head under the big top.

Moribund circus drama with bad acting, stilted production, an irrelevant train crash climax and a few genuinely spectacular and enjoyable moments.

w Fredric M. Frank, Theodore St John, Frank Cavett, Barre Lyndon　*d* Cecil B. de Mille　*ph* George Barnes, Peverell Marley, Wallace Kelley　*m* Victor Young　*ad* Hal Pereira, Walter Tyler　*ed* Anne Bauchens

Betty Hutton, Cornel Wilde, James Stewart, Charlton Heston, Dorothy Lamour, Gloria Grahame, Lyle Bettger, Henry Wilcoxon, Emmett Kelly, Lawrence Tierney, John Kellogg, John Ringling North

AA: best picture; original story (Fredric M. Frank, Theodore St John, Frank Cavett)

AAN: Cecil B. de Mille (as director); editing

The Greatest Story Ever Told **

US　1965　225m　Technicolor　Ultra Panavision 70
UA/George Stevens
V*, S

Solemn spectacular with an elephantine pace, shot in Utah because allegedly it looked more like Palestine than Palestine did.

All frightfully elegant and reverent, but totally unmoving, partly because of the fatal casting of stars in bit parts. (John Wayne looks in merely to say 'Truly this man was the son of God.')

w James Lee Barrett, George Stevens　*d* George Stevens　*ph* William C. Mellor, Loyal Griggs　*m* Alfred Newman　*ad* Richard Day, William Creber

Max von Sydow, Dorothy McGuire, Claude Rains, José Ferrer, David McCallum, Charlton Heston, Sidney Poitier, Donald Pleasence, Roddy McDowall, Gary Raymond, Carroll Baker, Pat Boone, Van Heflin, Sal Mineo, Shelley Winters, Ed Wynn, John Wayne, Telly Savalas, Angela Lansbury, Joseph Schildkraut, Victor Buono, Nehemiah Persoff

'George Stevens was once described as a water buffalo of film art. What this film more precisely suggests is a dinosaur.' – *MFB*

'God is unlucky in *The Greatest Story Ever Told*. His only begotten son turns out to be a bore . . . the photography is inspired mainly by Hallmark Cards . . . as the Hallelujah Chorus explodes around us stereophonically and stereotypically it becomes clear that Lazarus was not so much raised from the tomb as blasted out of it. As for pacing, the picture does not let you forget a single second of its four hours.' – *John Simon*

'No more than three minutes have elapsed before we suspect that Stevens' name and fame have been purchased by the Hallmark Greeting Card Company, and that what we are looking at is really a lengthy catalogue of greeting cards for 1965 – for Those Who Care Enough to Send the Very Best.' – *Stanley Kauffmann*

'Who but an audience of diplomats could sit through this thing? As the picture ponderously unrolled, it was mainly irritation that kept me awake.' – *Shana Alexander, Life*

'If the subject-matter weren't sacred, we would be responding to the picture in the most charitable way by laughing at it from start to finish.' – *Brendan Gill, New Yorker*

'A big windy bore.' – *Bruce Williamson, Playboy*

† The film was originally released at 4 hours 20 minutes. Subsequent versions were at 3 hours 58 minutes, 3 hours 17 minutes, 2 hours 27 minutes and 2 hours 7 minutes.

AAN: William C. Mellor, Loyal Griggs; Alfred Newman

Greed ***
US 1924 110m (24 fps) bw silent
MGM/Goldwyn Company (Erich von Stroheim, Irving Thalberg)
V*, L

An ex-miner dentist kills his avaricious wife. Later in Death Valley he also kills her lover, but is bound to him by handcuffs.

This much-discussed film is often cited as its director's greatest folly: the original version ran eight hours. Re-edited by June Mathis, it retains considerable power sequence by sequence, but is necessarily disjointed in development. However, it must be seen to be appreciated.

wd Erich von Stroheim *novel* McTeague by Frank Norris *ph* Ben Reynolds, William Daniels *ad* Richard Day, Cedric Gibbons, Erich von Stroheim *ed* Erich Von Stroheim, Rex Ingram, June Mathis, Jos W. Farnham

Gibson Gowland, ZaSu Pitts, *Jean Hersholt*, Chester Conklin, Dale Fuller

'The end leaves one with an appalling sense of human waste, of futility, of the drabness and cruelty of lives stifled by genteel poverty. Every character in the film is overwhelmed by it.' – *Gavin Lambert*

'Von Stroheim is a genius – *Greed* established that beyond all doubt – but he is badly in need of a stopwatch.' – *Robert E. Sherwood*

'Nothing more morbid and senseless, from a commercial picture standpoint, has been seen on the screen for a long time . . . Never has there been a more out-and-out box-office flop.' – *Variety*

† In 1972 Herman G. Weinberg published a complete screenplay with 400 stills.
†† The original length at the première is said to have been 420m.

The Greed of William Hart
GB 1948 78m bw
Bushey (Gilbert Church)

In old Edinburgh, grave robbers procure corpses for an anatomist.

Cheapie version of a much filmed subject. This scenario was refurbished eleven years later by the same writer as *The Flesh and the Fiends;* see also *The Body Snatcher, Burke and Hare.*

w John Gilling *d* Oswald Mitchell *ph* S. D. Onions

Tod Slaughter, Henry Oscar, Aubrey Woods, Arnold Bell

The Greek Tycoon
US 1978 106m Technicolor Panavision
Universal/ABKCO (Allan Klein, Ely Landau)
V*

A billionaire shipping tycoon marries the widow of an American president.

Rather messy 'faction' based on Onassis and Jacqueline Kennedy; entirely uninteresting save for glossy backgrounds and the relentlessness with which the characters swear at each other.

w Mort Fine *d* J. Lee-Thompson *ph* Tony Richmond *m* Stanley Myers *pd* Michael Stringer

Anthony Quinn, Jacqueline Bisset, Raf Vallone, Edward Albert, James Franciscus, Camilla Sparv

† Among its other idiocies, this is the first film to credit 'Assistant to the assistant to the Unit Publicist'.

The Greeks Had a Word for Them *
US 1932 77m bw
UA/Samuel Goldwyn
V*

Adventures of three New York gold diggers.

Smart early talkie which helped launch the *Gold Diggers* series and TCF's parallel *Three Little Mice/Moon over Miami/How to Marry a Millionaire* series.

w Sidney Howard *play* Zoe Akins *d* Lowell Sherman *ph* George Barnes *m* Alfred Newman

Joan Blondell, Madge Evans, Ina Claire, David Manners, Lowell Sherman, Phillips Smalley, Betty Grable

'Grand rowdy comedy . . . a revel in femme clothes and a picture calculated to fascinate women. Backwater clienteles questionable.' – *Variety*

The Green Archer
US 1940 bw serial: 15 eps
Columbia

A villain unjustly imprisons his brother and takes over the family castle, only to be stalked by a mysterious green archer.

Richly absurd serial which doesn't quite exploit its possibilities. *d* James W. Horne

Victor Jory (a hero for once), Iris Meredith, James Craven, Robert Fiske

'Their badge of honour was a green beret, and it said they had lived it all . . . the night jumps, the ambushes, the hand-to-hand combat, and the long nights of terror they filled with courage!'

The Green Berets
US 1968 141m Technicolor Panavision
Warner/Batjac (Michael Wayne)
V, V*, L

After extensive training, two tough army detachments see service in Vietnam.

Overlong actioner criticized for unquestioningly accepting the Vietnam cause; in itself, violent, exhausting and dull.

w James Lee Barrett *novel* Robin Moore *d* John Wayne, Ray Kellogg *ph* Winton C. Hoch *m* Miklos Rozsa

John Wayne, David Janssen, Jim Hutton, Aldo Ray, Raymond St Jacques, Jack Soo, Bruce Cabot, Patrick Wayne, Irene Tsu, Jason Evers, Luke Askew

'Propaganda as crude as this can only do damage to its cause.' – *David Wilson*

'A film best handled from a distance and with a pair of tongs.' – *Penelope Gilliatt*

The Green Buddha
GB 1954 62m bw
Republic

A charter pilot finds his clients are thieves and rounds them up.

Fair second-feature thick ear.

w Paul Erickson *d* John Lemont

Wayne Morris, Mary Germaine, Walter Rilla, Arnold Marle

Green Card *
Australia/France 1991 108m Technicolor
Touchstone (Peter Weir)
V, V*, L, S

A Frenchman marries a New Yorker in order to stay in the United States.

Amiable romantic tale of an odd couple.

wd Peter Weir *ph* Geoffrey Simpson *m* Hans Zimmer *pd* Wendy Stites *ad* Christopher Nowak *ed* William Anderson

Gérard Depardieu, Andie MacDowell, Bebe Neuwirth, Gregg Edelman, Robert Prosky, Jessie Keosian, Ethan Phillips, Mary Louise Wilson, Lois Smith, Conrad McLaren

The Green Cockatoo
GB 1940 65m bw
TCF/New World (Robert T. Kane)
aka: *Four Dark Hours; Race Gang*

A man seeks revenge on the gangsters who killed his brother.

Sleazy little Soho-set thriller, mainly remarkable for cast and credits.

w Edward O. Berkman, Arthur Wimperis *story* Graham Greene *d* William Cameron Menzies *ph* Osmond Borradaile *m* Miklos Rozsa

John Mills, Robert Newton, Rene Ray, Bruce Seton, Charles Oliver

† The film was made in 1937 but not shown for three years.

'A fiery girl dares the dangers of the sea and a strange land – fighting for the love of a bold adventurer!'

Green Dolphin Street
US 1947 141m bw
MGM (Carey Wilson)
V*, L

A Channel Islander emigrates to New Zealand and sends home for the wrong bride.

Silly 19th-century romance climaxed by rather a good earthquake. Expensively but falsely produced.

w Samson Raphaelson *novel* Elizabeth Goudge *d* Victor Saville *ph* George Folsey *m* Bronislau Kaper *ed* George White

Lana Turner, Richard Hart, Edmund Gwenn, Van Heflin, Donna Reed

'The actors in this stupefyingly flimsy epic seem to be in competition for booby prizes.' – *Pauline Kael, 70s*

AAN: George Folsey; George White

Green Eyed Woman: see *Take a Letter Darling*

Green Fingers
GB 1946 83m bw
British National (Louis H. Jackson)

An unqualified osteopath tries to achieve respectability.

Unsurprising and flatly made drama of eventual success against all odds.

w Jack Whittingham *novel* Persistent Warrior by Edith Arundel *d* John Harlow *m* Hans May

Robert Beatty, Carol Raye, Nova Pilbeam, Felix Aylmer, Moore Marriott, Edward Rigby

Green Fire
US 1954 100m Eastmancolor Cinemascope
MGM (Armand Deutsch)

Two engineers disagree over their mining of Colombia emeralds.

Routine adventure story with good action highlights including landslide, flood and storm, all deadened by dull dialogue and romantic complications.

w Ivan Goff, Ben Roberts *d* Andrew Marton *ph* Paul Vogel *m* Miklos Rozsa

Stewart Granger, Paul Douglas, Grace Kelly

Green for Danger ***
GB 1946 93m bw
Rank/Individual (Frank Launder, Sidney Gilliat)
V*, L

A mysterious murderer strikes on the operating table at a wartime emergency hospital.

Classic comedy-thriller, with serious detection balanced by excellent jokes and performances, also by moments of fright.

w Sidney Gilliat, Claud Guerney novel Christianna Brand *d Sidney Gilliat ph Wilkie Cooper m* William Alwyn *pd* Peter Proud *ed* Thelma Myers

Alastair Sim, Sally Gray, Rosamund John, Trevor Howard, Leo Genn, Megs Jenkins, Judy Campbell, Ronald Ward, Moore Marriott

'Slick, witty and consistently entertaining.' – *Daily Telegraph*

'Launder and Gilliat have told an exciting story excitingly.' – *Times*

The Green Glove

US/France 1952 89m bw
UA/Benagoss (George Maurer)
V*

A paratrooper against all odds returns a jewelled relic to its proper place in a French church.

An unsatisfactory concoction by people who have clearly seen *The Maltese Falcon* as well as lots of Hitchcock films, this interestingly cast and credited independent production never really takes off.

w Charles Bennett *d* Rudolph Maté *ph* Claude Renoir *m* Joseph Kosma

Glenn Ford, Cedric Hardwicke, Geraldine Brooks, George Macready, Gaby André, Roger Treville

The Green Goddess *

US 1930 80m bw
Warner

An Indian potentate holds Britishers prisoner.

Early talkie star vehicle which was also successful on the stage and as a silent but has little appeal now.

w Julian Josephson *play* William Archer *d* Alfred E. Green *ph* James Van Trees

George Arliss, Alice Joyce, H. B. Warner, Ralph Forbes, David Tearle

'Nice programme fare, but it suggests too many synthetic thrillers that have gone before.' – *Variety*

† Remade 1942 as *Adventure in Iraq.*

AAN: George Arliss

Green Grass of Wyoming

US 1948 88m Technicolor
TCF

A rancher captures his runaway white stallion and wins the local trotting races.

Predictable, good-looking family film shot on location; a second sequel to *My Friend Flicka.*

w Martin Berkeley *novel* Mary O'Hara *d* Louis King *ph* Charles G. Clarke *m* Cyril Mockridge

Peggy Cummins, Charles Coburn, Robert Arthur, Lloyd Nolan

AAN: Charles G. Clarke

Green Grow the Rushes

GB 1951 77m bw
ACT Films (John Gossage)
V*

Civil servants discover that a Kentish village is devoted to smuggling.

Amiable but disappointingly feeble imitation of Ealing comedy by a company formed from the technicians' union; it simply hasn't got the right snap in any department.

w Derek Twist, Howard Clewes *novel* Howard Clewes *d* Derek Twist *ph* Harry Waxman *m* Lambert Williamson

Roger Livesey, Richard Burton, Honor Blackman, Frederick Leister, John Salew, Colin Gordon, Geoffrey Keen, Harcourt Williams, Vida Hope

Green Hell *

US 1940 87m bw
Universal (Harry Edgington)

Explorers seek Inca treasure in the South American jungle.

Studio-bound potboiler unworthy of its director but mainly enjoyable as a romp.

w Frances Marion *d* James Whale *ph* Karl Freund

Douglas Fairbanks Jnr, Joan Bennett, George Sanders, Vincent Price, Alan Hale, Gene Garrick, George Bancroft, John Howard

'It's the old nickelodeon mellerdrammer, at higher prices.' – *Picture Play*

† The temple set was re-used the same year in *The Mummy's Hand.*

The Green Helmet

GB 1961 88m bw
MGM (Charles Francis Vetter)

A race driver with shattered nerves makes his last job the introduction of an American car of new design.

Totally conventional motor racing thriller. Most of the work could just as effectively have been phoned in.

w Jon Cleary *novel* Jon Cleary *d* Michael Forlong *ph* Geoffrey Faithfull *m* Ken Jones

Bill Travers, Ed Begley, Sidney James, Nancy Walters, Ursula Jeans, Megs Jenkins

The Green Hornet

US 1940 bw serial: 13 eps
Universal

A crusading publisher in disguise fights various rackets.

Archetypal serial in the Batman and Robin mould; the assistant here is a judo expert.

d Ford Beebe, Ray Taylor

Gordon Jones, Wade Boteler, Keye Luke, Anne Nagel, Philip Trent

The Green Hornet Strikes Again

US 1940 bw serial: 13 eps
Universal

See above, but with Warren Hull in the lead.

d Ford Beebe, John Rawlins

Green Ice

GB 1981 116m colour
ITC/Lew Grade (Jack Wiener)
V*, L

An aimless American in Mexico becomes involved with emerald thieves.

Dismally routine punch-ups and car chases are enlivened by a mildly original theft by balloon, but the overall effect is soporific.

w Edward Anhalt, Ray Hassett, Anthony Simmons, Robert de Laurentiis *novel* Gerald Browne *d* Ernest Day *ph* Gilbert Taylor *m* Bill Wyman

Ryan O'Neal, Anne Archer, Omar Sharif, Philip Stone

'It should not tempt anyone away from doubtlessly superior versions of the same material on television.' – *Geoff Brown, MFB*

The Green Light *

US 1937 85m bw
Warner (Henry Blanke)

A dedicated doctor gives up his practice when a patient dies.

Adequate star melodrama.

w Milton Krims *novel* Lloyd C. Douglas *d* Frank Borzage *ph* Byron Haskin *m* Max Steiner

Errol Flynn, Anita Louise, Margaret Lindsay, Cedric Hardwicke, Henry O'Neill, Spring Byington

'Customer lure in the title and the player names . . . it will carry a weak sister nicely.' – *Variety*

The Green Man *

GB 1956 80m bw
BL/Grenadier (Frank Launder, Sidney Gilliat)
V

A professional assassin stalks a pompous politician.

Cheerful but not very subtle black comedy, suffering from the attempt to make a star part out of a very minor character.

w Sidney Gilliat, Frank Launder *play Meet a Body* by Sidney Gilliat, Frank Launder *d* Robert Day *ph* Gerald Gibbs *m* Cedric Thorpe Davie

Alastair Sim, George Cole, Jill Adams, Terry-Thomas, Avril Angers, John Chandos, Dora Bryan, Colin Gordon, Raymond Huntley

Green Mansions

US 1959 104m Metrocolor Cinemascope
MGM/Avon (Edmund Grainger)

In a remote Amazon forest an adventurer encounters Rima, a child of nature who takes him on a quest for truth.

Absurd studio-bound Shangri-La story based on an Edwardian fantasy that may well have suited the printed page, but not the wide screen. Dismally photographed in shades of green, with all concerned looking acutely uncomfortable.

w Dorothy Kingsley *novel* W. H. Hudson *d* Mel Ferrer *ph* Joseph Ruttenberg *m* Bronislau Kaper, Hector Villa-Lobos

Anthony Perkins, Audrey Hepburn, Lee J. Cobb, Henry Silva

The Green Pastures ***

US 1936 93m bw
Warner (Henry Blanke)
V*

Old Testament stories as seen through simple-minded negro eyes.

Though recently attacked as setting back the cause of black emancipation, this is a brilliantly sympathetic and humorous film, very cunningly adapted for the screen in a series of dramatic scenes which make the material work even better than it did on the stage.

w Marc Connelly *play* Marc Connelly *stories* Roark Bradford *d* William Keighley, Marc Connelly *ph* Hal Mohr *m* Erich Wolfgang Korngold

Rex Ingram, Oscar Polk, Eddie Anderson, Frank Wilson, George Reed

'I imagine God has a sense of humour, and I imagine that He is delighted with *The Green Pastures.*' – *Don Herold*

'That disturbance around the Music Hall yesterday was the noise of shuffling queues and the sound of motion picture critics dancing in the street.' – *Bosley Crowther, New York Times*

'This is as good a religious play as one is likely to get in this age from a practised New York writer.' – *Graham Greene*

Green Promise

US 1949 88m bw
RKO/Glenn McCarthy (Robert Paige, Monty F. Collins)
V*
GB title: *Raging Waters*

A farmer refuses to move from the dust bowl area, and a landslide causes a flood.

Curiously stilted independent production which doesn't really bear comparison with *The Grapes of Wrath.*

w Monty F. Collins *d* William D. Russell *ph* John Russell *m* David Chudnow

Marguerite Chapman, Walter Brennan, Robert Paige, Natalie Wood, Ted Donaldson, Connie Marshall

The Green Ray **
France 1986 98m colour
Les Films du Losange (Margaret Menegoz)
V
original title: *Le Rayon Vert*; aka: *Summer*

A lonely secretary goes on holiday alone and, after days of tedium, falls in love.

With its improvised dialogue and less than sympathetic heroine, the movie lacks the precision and interest of Rohmer's best work, even if the theme remains the same.

w Eric Rohmer, Marie Rivière d Eric Rohmer ph Sophie Maintigneux m Jean-Louis Valero ed Marie-Luisa Garcia

Marie Rivière, Lisa Heredia, Béatrice Romand, Vincent Gautier, Eric Hamm, Rosette, Vanessa Leleu, Irene Skobline, Carita

The Green Scarf
GB 1954 96m bw
B and A (Bertram Ostrer, Albert Fennell)

An elderly French lawyer takes on the defence of a blind, deaf and dumb murder suspect.

Plodding courtroom drama with familiar faces in unconvincing French guise.

w Gordon Wellesley novel *The Brute* by Guy des Cars d George More O'Ferrall ph Jack Hildyard m Brian Easdale

Michael Redgrave, Ann Todd, Leo Genn, Kieron Moore

The Green Years *
US 1946 127m bw
MGM (Leon Gordon)

A young boy brought up strictly in Ireland makes friends with his mischievous grandfather.

Period family film in familiar style, sparked only by its scene-stealing star performance.

w Robert Ardrey, Sonya Levien novel A. J. Cronin d Victor Saville ph George Folsey m Herbert Stothart ad Cedric Gibbons, Hans Peters

Charles Coburn, Dean Stockwell, Tom Drake, Beverly Tyler, Hume Cronyn, Gladys Cooper, Selena Royle, Jessica Tandy, Richard Haydn, Andy Clyde

'It has been described in the ads as "wonderful" by everyone within Louis B. Mayer's purchasing power except his horses, so I hesitate to ask you to take my word for it: the picture is awful.' – *James Agee*

AAN: George Folsey; Charles Coburn

The Greengage Summer *
GB 1961 99m Technicolor
Columbia/PKL (Victor Saville, Edward Small)
US title: *Loss of Innocence*

A young girl staying at a hotel falls in love with a jewel thief but is accidentally responsible for his capture.

Old-fashioned and not very interesting story with an appeal, one supposes, to well-brought-up young women. Decently made.

w Howard Koch novel Rumer Godden d Lewis Gilbert ph Frederick A. Young m Richard Addinsell

Kenneth More, Danielle Darrieux, Susannah York, Claude Nollier, Jane Asher, Elizabeth Dear, Maurice Denham

Greenwich Village *
US 1944 82m Technicolor
TCF (William Le Baron)

In the twenties, a hick composer in New York allows his concerto to be used in a jazz musical.

Lightweight musical romp.

w Michael Fessier, Ernest Pagano d Walter Lang ph Leon Shamroy, Harry Jackson m/y Leo Robin, Nacio Herb Brown

Carmen Miranda, Don Ameche, William Bendix, Vivian Blaine, Felix Bressart, Tony and Sally de Marco, Adolph Green, Betty Comden, Alvin Hammer, Judy Holliday

Greetings *
US 1968 88m Eastmancolor
West End Films
V*, L

A draftee tries every which way to be exempted, then subjects himself to a whirl of physical experience.

Kaleidoscopic stringing together of fleeting satirical bits; talent undeniable but equally uncontrolled.

w Charles Hirsch, Brian de Palma d Brian de Palma ed Brian de Palma

Jonathan Warden, Robert de Niro, Gerrit Graham, Megan McCormick

Gregorio
Peru 1985 95m colour
Grupo Chaski (Maria Barea)

The young son of a peasant farmer turns to crime in the big city.

The documentary-style work of a film collective, well-meaning but only intermittently interesting.

w Maria Barea, Fernando Espinoza, Stefan Kaspar, Alejandro Legaspi, Margreth Noth, Susi Pastor d Alejandro Legaspi m Arturo Ruiz del Pozo ad Rafael Hernandez ed Alejandro Legaspi, Stefan Kaspar, Gaby Faura

Marino Leon de La Torre, Vetzy Perez-Palma, Augusto Varillas, Manuel Acosta Ojeda, Rafael Hernandez

Gregory's Girl **
GB 1980 91m colour
Lake/NFFC/STV (Davina Belling, Clive Parsons)
V, V*

In a Scottish new town, a school footballer becomes aware of sex.

Curiously diverting comedy peopled by dreamers but handicapped by impenetrable accents. An unexpected world-wide success.

wd Bill Forsyth ph Michael Coulter m Colin Tully

Gordon John Sinclair, Dee Hepburn, Jake D'Arcy, Claire Grogan

BFA: best script

Gremlins *
US 1984 106m Technicolor
Warner/Amblin (Michael Finnell)
V, V*, L, S

Small furry creatures called mogwais prove to be immensely prolific and dangerous when wet.

Juvenile horror comic, a kind of deliberate inversion of *E.T.* Slow to start, and a little too knowingly nasty, with variable special effects; but a pretty hot commercial success.

w Chris Columbus d Joe Dante ph John Hora m Jerry Goldsmith sp Gremlin designer: Chris Walas ed Tina Hirsch

Zach Galligan, Phoebe Cates, Hoyt Axton, Polly Holliday, Keye Luke, Scott Brady, Edward Andrews

'Don't go if you still believe in Santa Claus.' – *Roger Ebert*

Gremlins 2: The New Batch **
US 1990 105m Technicolor
Warner/Amblin (Michael Finnell)
V, V*, L, S

A mogwai, captured by mad research scientists, produces hundreds of violent gremlins who run amuck in a megalomaniac property developer's skyscraper.

A sequel more entertaining than the original, stuffed with in-jokes for movie buffs.

w Charlie Haas d Joe Dante ph John Hora m Jerry Goldsmith pd James Spencer ad Joe Lucky sp Gremlin and mogwai effects: Rick Baker ed Kent Beyda

Zach Galligan, Phoebe Cates

'An hilarious sequel featuring equal parts creature slapstick and satirical barbs for adults.' – *Variety*

The Grey Fox *
Canada 1982 91m Eastmancolor
Mercury (Peter O'Brian)
V, V*, L

The more or less true story of a turn-of-the-century stagecoach bandit who in 1901 was released from a long prison term, genially committed more crimes, and disappeared.

Likeable semi-Western with an excellent sense of place and time.

w John Hunter d Philip Borsos ph Frank Tidy m Michael Conway

Richard Farnsworth, Jackie Burroughs, Ken Pogue, Wayne Robson

Greyfriars Bobby *
GB 1960 91m Technicolor
Walt Disney (Hugh Attwooll)
V*

A Skye terrier keeps persistent vigil over his master's grave and is made a freeman of the city of Edinburgh.

Adequately produced film of a charming old Victorian story.

w Robert Westerby book Eleanor Atkinson d Don Chaffey ph Paul Beeson m Francis Chagrin

Donald Crisp, Laurence Naismith, Alexander Mackenzie, Kay Walsh, Andrew Cruickshank, Vincent Winter, Moultrie Kelsall, Duncan Macrae

'The better Disney qualities of exact period detail and childlike directness are apparent.' – *MFB*

† The story was previously filmed as *Challenge to Lassie*.

Greystoke: The Legend of Tarzan, Lord of the Apes
GB 1984 130m Eastmancolor Panavision
Warner/WEA Records (Hugh Hudson, Stanley S. Canter)
V, V*, L

In the 1880s, an English lord and lady are killed in Africa, and their son is brought up by apes.

An absurd attempt to treat the story seriously after 70 years of hokum, this meandering chronicle, cut down from something much longer and even less endurable, has men in ape suits, an eye for unpleasant detail, and Ralph Richardson sliding down the stairs on a tray. The attempt to moralize at the end is emetic.

w P. H. Vazak (Robert Towne), Michael Austin novel *Tarzan of the Apes* by Edgar Rice Burroughs d Hugh Hudson ph John Alcott m John Scott pd Stuart Craig

Ralph Richardson, Ian Holm, James Fox, Christopher Lambert, Andie MacDowell, Cheryl Campbell, Paul Geoffrey, John Wells, Nigel Davenport, Ian Charleson, Richard Griffiths

'A unique mixture of pomposity and ineptitude . . . in the second half the movie simply loses its mind, and dribbles to a pathetically indecisive conclusion.' – *Pauline Kael, New Yorker*

† Andie MacDowell's voice was dubbed by Glenn Close.

AAN: Ralph Richardson (supporting actor); adapted screenplay

Il Grido *

Italy 1957 102m bw
SPA Cinematografica/Robert Alexander
aka: *The Cry*

A man whose wife has left him travels across the Po Valley with his daughter in search of new happiness, but fails to find it and commits suicide.

Watchable but rather aimlessly depressing character drama.

w Michelangelo Antonioni, Elio Bartolini, Ennio de Concini d Michelangelo Antonioni ph Gianni di Venanzo m Giovanni Fusco

Steve Cochran, Alida Valli, Dorian Gray, Betsy Blair, Lynn Shaw

La Grieta

Spain 1989 83m (dubbed) colour
Warner/Dister (Jose Escriva, Francesca de Laurentiis)
V
aka: *The Rift*

Submariners discover mutated monsters under the sea.

Feeble fantasy with poor special effects.

w J. P. Simon, Mark Klein d J. P. Simon ph Manuel Rojas m Joel Goldsmith pd Gonzalo Gonzalo ed Isaac Sehayek, Earl Watson

Jack Scalia, R. Lee Ermey, Ray Wise, Deborah Adair, John Toles Bey, Ely Pouget, Emilio Linder, Tony Isbert, Alvaro Labra, Luis Lorenzo

'The characterisation is predictably shallow and the romantic interest distinctly soggy, while the model work and creature effects plumb new depths of ineptitude.' – *Nigel Floyd, MFB*

'Just another day of lying, cheating and stealing.'
The Grifters ***

US 1990 110m CFI
Palace/Cineplex Odeon (Martin Scorsese, Robert Harris)
V, V*, L, S

A mother, who is robbing her gangster boss, is reunited with her son and his girlfriend, both confidence tricksters.

Bleakly invigorating vision of the underside of the American dream.

w Donald Westlake novel Jim Thompson d Stephen Frears ph Oliver Stapleton m Elmer Bernstein pd Dennis Casner ed Mike Audsley

Anjelica Huston, John Cusack, Annette Bening, Pat Hingle, Henry Jones, Michael Laskin, Eddie Jones, J. T. Walsh, Charles Napier

'A brilliant, immensely seductive mix of *Kammerspiel*, film noir and naturalistic slice-of-life.' – *Tom Milne, MFB*

AAN: Angelica Huston; Annette Bening; Donald Westlake

Grim Prairie Tales *

US 1990 94m colour
East West Film Partners (Richard Hahn)
V*

Two drifters, who meet by chance on the prairie, pass the night by telling each other stories.

A clever compendium movie, a mix of Western and atmospheric horror, which is stylish and imaginative enough to rise above its low-budget limitations, helped by strong performances from its two leads.

wd Wayne Coe ph Janusz Kaminski m Steve Dancz pd Anthony Zierhut ed Earl Ghaffari

James Earl Jones, Brad Dourif, William Atherton, Lisa Eichhorn, Marc McClure, Scott Paulin, Will Hare, Michelle Joyner, Wendy Cooke

The Grip of Fear: see *Experiment in Terror*

Grip of the Strangler *

GB 1958 78m bw
Producers' Associates (John Croydon)
US title: *The Haunted Strangler*

A novelist investigating an old murder case finds that he was himself the murderer.

Moderate thriller with a predictable but efficient plot.

w Jan Read d Robert Day ph Lionel Banes m Buxton Orr

Boris Karloff, Elizabeth Allan, Jean Kent, Vera Day, Anthony Dawson

Grissly's Millions

US 1945 71m bw
Republic

An heiress is in danger from less successful relations.

Watchable co-feature.

w Muriel Roy Bolton d John English

Paul Kelly, Virginia Grey, Don Douglas, Elisabeth Risdon, Robert Barrat, Clem Bevans

The Grissom Gang

US 1971 128m Metrocolor
Associates and Aldrich/ABC
V*

In 1931, a New York heiress is kidnapped by gangsters and comes to like it.

Unpleasant remake of *No Orchids for Miss Blandish* (previously filmed under that title, incredibly badly, in GB in 1948), with too much footage of lush blonde being slobbered over by psychotic thug, and an inevitable emphasis on violence.

w Leon Griffiths novel James Hadley Chase d Robert Aldrich ph Joseph Biroc m Gerald Fried ad James Dowell Vance

Scott Wilson, Kim Darby, Tony Musante, Robert Lansing, Irene Dailey, Connie Stevens, Wesley Addy

'Offensive, immoral and perhaps even lascivious.' – *Vincent Canby*

Gritos en la Noche: see *The Awful Dr Orloff*

'18 feet of towering fury! The most dangerous jaws on land!'
Grizzly

US 1976 91m Movielab Todd-AO 35
Film Ventures International (David Sheldon, Harvey Flaxman)
V*
aka: *Killer Grizzly*

A mammoth bear preys upon campers in a national park.

Inept and boring shocker in the wake of *Jaws*.

w Harvey Flaxman, David Sheldon d William Girdler ph William Asman m Robert O. Ragland

Christopher George, Andrew Prine, Richard Jaeckel, Joan McCall

The Groom Wore Spurs

US 1951 81m bw
Universal (Howard Welsch)

A supposed tough cowboy star gets into trouble in Las Vegas.

Tedious star comedy.

w Robert Carson novel *Legal Bride* by Robert Carson d Richard Whorf

Ginger Rogers, Jack Carson, Joan Davis, Stanley Ridges, James Brown

Gross Anatomy

US 1989 107m Technicolor
Touchstone/Silver Screen Partner IV (Howard Rosenman, Debra Hill)
V*, L
aka: *A Cut Above*

A fisherman's son, who becomes a medical student because he wants to be rich, discovers compassion and love in his first year.

A light romantic comedy that cannot encompass the darker moments it attempts, relying too heavily on the charm of its star to compensate for the conceited brat he plays.

w Ron Nyswaner, Mark Spragg story Mark Spragg, Howard Rosenman, Alan Jay Glueckman, Stanley Isaacs d Thom Eberhardt ph Steve Yaconelli m David Newman pd William F. Matthews ed Bud Smith, Scott Smith

Matthew Modine, Daphne Zuniga, Christine Lahti, Todd Field, John Scott Clough, Alice Carter, Robert Desiderio, Zakes Mokae

Ground Zero *

Australia 1987 109m Eastmancolor Panavision
BDB/Pattinson-Burrowes
V*, L

A cinematographer stumbles on dangerous secrets when investigating his father's death 30 years previously.

Smart contemporary thriller with a political theme.

w Jan Sardi, Mac Gudgeon d Michael Pattinson, Bruce Myles

Colin Friels, Jack Thompson, Donald Pleasence, Natalie Bate

'He's having the day of his life ... over and over again.'
Groundhog Day ***

US 1993 101m Technicolor Panavision
Columbia TriStar/Columbia (Trevor Albert, Harold Ramis)
V, V*, L, S

A cynical weatherman, sent to cover an annual small-town Ground Hog ceremony, finds himself reliving his day over and over again until he becomes a better person.

A 90s version of *It's A Wonderful Life*: tougher, smarter, more knowing and successfully avoiding corn to provide an unexpectedly witty and warming comedy.

w Danny Rubin, Harold Ramis d Harold Ramis ph John Bailey m George Fenton pd David Nichols. ed Pembroke J. Herring

Bill Murray, Andie MacDowell, Chris Elliott, Stephen Tobolowsky, Brian Doyle-Murray, Marita Geraghty, Angela Paton, Rick Ducommun

'A major studio Hollywood comedy that both delights and surprises.' – *Sight and Sound*

'Something of a comedy classic, and a film which, for sheer entertainment value, you'd be hard pushed to beat.' – *Empire*

Grounds for Marriage

US 1950 90m bw
MGM

A divorced couple meet again and find they have strange effects on each other.

Stolid romantic comedy with second team talent.

w Allen Rivkin, Laura Kerr d Robert Z. Leonard

Van Johnson, Kathryn Grayson, Paula Raymond, Lewis Stone, Reginald Owen, Barry Sullivan

'We challenge you to guess the ending!'
The Groundstar Conspiracy *

US 1972 96m Technicolor Panavision
Universal/Hal Roach International (Trevor Wallace)
V*

An explosion rips apart a top secret space project, and the surviving scientist loses his memory.

Gimmicky but generally compulsive sci-fi mystery yarn, with an effective though predictable climax.

w Matthew Howard novel *The Alien* by L. P. Davies d Lamont Johnson ph Michael Reed m Paul Hoffert

George Peppard, Michael Sarrazin, James Olson, Christine Belford, Tim O'Connor, James McEachin

The Group ***

US 1966 152m DeLuxe
UA/Famous Artists (Sidney Buchman)
V*

The subsequent love lives of a group of girls who graduate from Vassar in 1933.

Patchy but generally fascinating series of interwoven sketches and character studies, with mainly tragic overtones; good attention to period detail, and dazzling array of new talent.

w Sidney Buchman, novel Mary McCarthy d Sidney Lumet ph Boris Kaufman m Charles Gross pd Gene Callahan

Joanna Pettet, Candice Bergen, Jessica Walter, Joan Hackett, Elizabeth Hartman, Mary Robin-Redd, Kathleen Widdoes, Shirley Knight, Larry Hagman, Hal Holbrook, Robert Emhardt, Richard Mulligan, James Congdon, James Broderick

'Although it is a strange, inclusive, no-holds-barred movie that runs the gamut from scenes that are almost soap-operaish, to amusing scenes that are almost satire, to outrageously frank scenes that are almost voyeuristic, it is still greatly exhilarating while it provokes thought and pushes the viewer into examining his own conscience.' – Philip T. Hartung, Commonweal

Grumpy

US 1930 74m bw
Paramount

A very elderly gentleman is still in control of his family.

Interesting but not exciting transcript of a production which was having surprising success on Broadway with English players, though a very musty vehicle even then.

w Doris Anderson play Horace Hodges, Thomas Wigney Percyval d George Cukor, Cyril Gardner

Cyril Maude, Phillips Holmes, Paul Cavanagh, Frances Dade, Halliwell Hobbes, Paul Lukas

'Its box office fate is in the balance.' – Variety

Grumpy Old Men

US 1993 104m Technicolor
Warner/Lancaster Gate (John Davis, Richard C. Berman)

A long feud between two ageing neighbours is intensified when an attractive widow moves into the neighbourhood.

Mildy amusing comedy, providing an opportunity for Lemmon, Matthau and Meredith to do their party pieces, which they do as well as their somewhat thin material will allow.

w Mark Steven Johnson d Donald Petrie ph Johnny E. Jensen m Alan Silvestri pd David Chapman ed Bonnie Koehler

Jack Lemmon, Walter Matthau, Ann-Margret, Burgess Meredith, Daryl Hannah, Kevin Polack, Ossie Davis, Buck Henry, Christopher McDonald

'Light, reasonably pleasant and undoubtedly sappy holiday entertainment.' – Variety

Gruppo di Famiglia in un Interno: see
Conversation Piece

Guadalcanal Diary *

US 1943 93m bw
TCF (Bryan Foy)

Marines fight for a vital Pacific base.

Standard war propaganda, with good action scenes.

w Lamar Trotti book Richard Tregaskis d Lewis Seiler ph Charles G. Clarke m David Buttolph

Preston Foster, Lloyd Nolan, William Bendix, Richard Conte, Anthony Quinn, Richard Jaeckel, Roy Roberts, Minor Watson, Ralph Byrd, Lionel Stander, Miles Mander, Reed Hadley

'Tonight, while the world is asleep … an ancient evil is about to awaken.'

The Guardian

US 1990 93m Technicolor
UIP/Universal (Joe Wizan)
V, V*, L

A nanny sacrifices her charges to a tree.

Ridiculous horror of no discernible interest.

w Stephen Volk, Dan Greenburg novel The Nanny by Dan Greenburg d William Friedkin m Jack Hues pd Gregg Fonseca sp Phil Cory, Ray Svedin, Hans Metz ed Seth Flaum

Jenny Seagrove, Dwier Brown, Carey Lowell, Brad Hull, Miguel Ferrer, Natalia Nogulich, Pamela Brull, Gary Swanson

'An ill-conceived, simple-minded horror flick' – Variety

The Guardsman *

US 1931 83m bw
MGM (Albert Lewin)

A jealous actor tests his wife's fidelity.

Theatrically effective comedy filmed for the sake of its stars; later remade as a musical, The Chocolate Soldier (qv).

w Ernest Vajda, Claudine West play Ferenc Molnar d Sidney Franklin ph Norbert Brodine

Alfred Lunt, Lynn Fontanne, Roland Young, ZaSu Pitts, Maude Eburne, Herman Bing, Ann Dvorak

'Looks like a smash engagement on Broadway and less than moderate returns on general release.' – Variety

AAN: Alfred Lunt; Lynn Fontanne

Guelwaar **

Senegal/France 1992 115m colour
Domireew/Galatee/FR3 (Ousmane Sembène, Jacques Perrin)

A Catholic family discover when they come to bury their father that his corpse has disappeared and he has been given a Muslim funeral by mistake.

A comic and ironic tone pervades an engaging tale of bureaucratic bungling, chauvinism, parochial intransigence and civic and national corruption.

wd Ousmane Sembène ph Dominique Gentil m Baaba Mall pd François Laurent Sulva ed Marie-Aimée Debril

Omar Seck, Ndiawar Diop, Mame Ndoumbe Diop, Isseu Niang, Thierno Niaye, Joseph Baloma Sane, Abou Camara, Samba Wane, Moustapha Diop

'One of the more accessible African films to emerge in the last couple of years.' – Variety

† Sample dialogue: Man to young widow, 'For you, I'll divorce my four wives.'

Les Guerisseurs

Ivory Coast/France 1988 90m colour
Afriki Projection/Cote d'Ivoire Films/DEA/Alain Depardieu (Ayala Bakaba)
aka: Aduefue, Lords of the Street

In order to get money to finance his extravagant lifestyle, a black businessman plans a robbery with the aid of a French pimp.

A rambling, ill-constructed narrative on corruption, semi-satirical in tone and influenced for the worse by American action movies.

wd Sijiri Bakaba ph Mohammed Soudani m Serge Franklin ad Alama Kanate ed Olivier Morel

Pierre Loup Rajot, Georges T. Benson, Nayanka Bell, Mory Traore, Sijiri Bakaba, Alpha Blondy, Salifou Keita

La Guerra di Troia: see The Trojan War

La Guerre Est Finie

France/Sweden 1966 122m bw
Sofracima/Europa Film
aka: The War Is Over

A Spanish revolutionary maintains his ideals even though he is warned that he will be sold out.

Dreary drama with romantic interludes and a fussy technique involving what appears to be the first use of flashforwards.

w Jorge Semprun d Alain Resnais ph Sacha Vierny m Giovanni Fusco

Yves Montand, Ingrid Thulin, Geneviève Bujold, Michel Piccoli

'The most sophisticated work Alain Resnais has yet provided us, perfecting his technique in dealing cinematically with the interrelation of time and place, and never before has he brought such lyricism to the harshness of everyday living or given such scope to the probing of the inner man – all this within the framework of a suspense thriller.' – Judith Crist

AAN: Jorge Semprun

Guess Who's Coming to Dinner **

US 1967 112m Technicolor
Columbia/Stanley Kramer
V, V*, L

A well-to-do San Francisco girl announces that she is going to marry a black man, and her parents find they are less broad-minded than they thought.

The problem picture that isn't really, since everyone is so nice and the prospective bridegroom is so eligible. It looks like a photographed play, but isn't based on one; the set is unconvincing; but the acting is a dream.

w William Rose d Stanley Kramer ph Sam Leavitt md Frank de Vol pd Robert Clatworthy

Spencer Tracy, Katharine Hepburn, Katharine Houghton (Hepburn's niece), Sidney Poitier, Cecil Kellaway, Roy E. Glenn Snr, Beah Richards, Isabel Sanford, Virginia Christine

'Suddenly everybody's caught up in a kind of integrated drawing-room comedy, and unable to decide whether there's anything funny in it or not.' – Ann Birstein, Vogue

'A load of embarrassing rubbish. In the circumstances there is little that director Stanley Kramer can do but see that his camera plod from room to room and make the most of people sitting down and getting up again.' – Penelope Mortimer

'What Rose and Kramer have done is to create a number of elaborate Aunt Sallies, arrange them in attractive patterns, and dispose of them with the flick of a feather.' – Basil Wright, 1972

'Mendacious and sanctimonious drivel.' – John Simon

AA: William Rose; Katharine Hepburn

AAN: best picture; Stanley Kramer; Frank de Vol; Spencer Tracy; Cecil Kellaway; Beah Richards

The Guest: see The Caretaker

Guest in the House *

US 1944 121m bw
Hunt Stromberg

A seemingly pleasant young woman is invited to stay with a family and brings tragedy and hatred to them.

Theatrical and rather unconvincing melodrama.

w Ketti Frings play Dear Evelyn by Dale Eunson, Hagar Wilde d John Brahm ph Lee Garmes m Werner Janssen pd Nicolai Remisoff

Anne Baxter, Ralph Bellamy, Aline MacMahon, Ruth Warrick, Scott McKay, Jerome Cowan, Marie McDonald, Percy Kilbride, Margaret Hamilton

AAN: Werner Janssen

Guest Wife

US 1945 90m bw
UA/Greentree (Jack H. Skirball)

For business purposes a man allows his wife to pretend to be the wife of another.

Stereotyped star farce which seemed tolerable at the time.

w Bruce Manning, John Klorer   d Sam Wood
ph Joseph Valentine   md Daniele Amfitheatrof

Claudette Colbert, Don Ameche, Dick Foran, Charles Dingle, Grant Mitchell

'Mr Wood is a big gun to be trained on so trivial a target, but the result justifies the choice.' – Richard Mallett, Punch

AAN: Daniele Amfitheatrof

'For the married man who's thinking single – or the single man who's just thinking!'

A Guide for the Married Man **

US 1967 91m DeLuxe Panavision
TCF (Frank McCarthy)
V*

A practised wolf explains to a perfect husband how to be unfaithful.

Generally funny revue with as many hilarious moments as flat spots.

w Frank Tarloff   d Gene Kelly   ph Joe Macdonald
m Johnny Williams

Walter Matthau, Inger Stevens, Robert Morse, Sue Anne Langdon, Lucille Ball, Art Carney, Jack Benny, Polly Bergen, Joey Bishop, Sid Caesar, Wally Cox, Jayne Mansfield, Carl Reiner, Phil Silvers, Jeffrey Hunter, Terry-Thomas, Ben Blue

'One of the funniest films of the last several seasons . . . it has sense enough to sit down when it's through.' – Robert Windeler

Guilt Is My Shadow

GB 1950 86m bw
ABPC (Ivan Foxwell)

A girl kills her villainous husband and is helped by a farmer.

Tedious melodrama, stiffly told and not helped by rural surroundings.

w Ivan Foxwell, Roy Kellino, John Gilling
novel You're Best Alone by Peter Curtis   d Roy Kellino

Patrick Holt, Elizabeth Sellars, Peter Reynolds, Lana Morris, Avice Landone

The Guilt of Janet Ames

US 1947 83m bw
Columbia

A paralysed war widow seeks to discover whether her husband's sacrifice was worthwhile.

Embarrassing attempt by a comedienne to play Hamlet.

w Louella Macfarlane, Allen Rivkin, Devery Freeman
story Lenore Coffee   d Henry Levin   ph Joseph Walker   m Morris Stoloff

Rosalind Russell, Melvyn Douglas, Sid Caesar, Betsy Blair, Nina Foch, Harry von Zell, Arthur Space

'If you're willing to swallow the hypnotic idea, the substance of the film is lively and entertaining, and includes a gem of a cabaret turn by Sid Caesar.' – Fred Majdalany, Daily Mail

Guilty?

GB 1956 93m bw
Grand National/Gibraltar (Charles A. Leeds)

An ex-resistance heroine is on trial for murder at the Old Bailey; her young solicitor goes to Avignon to prove her innocence.

Solidly cast old-fashioned mystery with a courtroom climax.

w Maurice J. Wilson   novel Death Has Deep Roots by Michael Gilbert   d Edmond Greville   ph Stan Pavey   m Bruce Montgomery

John Justin, Barbara Laage, Donald Wolfit, Stephen Murray, Norman Wooland, Frank Villard, Sydney Tafler, Betty Stockfield

Guilty as Charged

US 1991 95m Foto-Kem
Copeland/Colichman (Randolph Gale)
V*

A mad tycoon turned vigilante sets up his own electric chair to execute murderers who escape the law.

Over-the-top performances help distract attention from the predictable events.

w Charles Gale   d Sam Irvin   ph Richard Michalak   m Steve Bartek   pd Byrnadette DiSanto
ed Kevin Tent

Rod Steiger, Lauren Hutton, Heather Graham, Lyman Ward, Isaac Hayes, Zelda Rubinstein, Irwin Keyes, Michael Beach

Guilty as Hell *

US 1932 82m bw
Paramount

A doctor commits what he hopes is the perfect murder.

Smart murder story with two points of interest: the audience knows who done it from the start, and the detective and reporter roles are worked over to fit the actors who played Flagg and Quirt. It certainly pleased at the time.

w Arthur Kober, Frank Partos   play Riddle Me This by Daniel Rubin   d Erle C. Kenton

Edmund Lowe, Victor McLaglen, Richard Arlen, Ralph Ince, Adrienne Ames, Henry Stephenson, Elizabeth Patterson

'Excellent entertainment and should do a good business where the title does not hurt.' – Variety

† It was remade in 1937 as Night Club Scandal, with John Barrymore in the lead as the doctor.

Guilty as Sin

US 1993 107m Technicolor
Buena Vista/Hollywood (Martin Ransohoff)

An ambitious lawyer agrees to defend a man accused of murdering his wife and discovers that he is a serial killer.

Elegant but empty thriller, taken at too easy a tempo to create any suspense or tension.

w Larry Cohen   d Sidney Lumet   ph Andrzej Bartkowiak   m Howard Shore   pd Philip Rosenberg   ed Evan Lottman

Rebecca DeMornay, Don Johnson, Stephen Lang, Jack Warden, Dana Ivey, Ron White

'This has the empty, varnished vacuity of any old American TV movie, masquerading as one of those lesser Hitchcock courtroom sagas. The director is Sidney Lumet. I have absolutely no idea why he dunnit.' – Derek Malcolm, Guardian

'All it took was a whisper.'

Guilty by Suspicion *

US 1990 105m DeLuxe
Warner (Arnon Milchan)
V, V*, L, S

In the 1950s, a successful film director finds himself without work after refusing to co-operate with the House Un-American Activities Committee investigating 'communist subversion' in Hollywood.

A weak, if well-meaning, attempt to deal with the period of blacklisting in Hollywood, but one that comes close to ignoring the complicity of the majority of studios in HUAC's activities. Martin Scorsese makes a brief appearance playing Joe Lesser, a director based on Joseph Losey, who fled to Europe to avoid testifying to the committee.

wd Irwin Winkler   ph Michael Ballhaus   m James Newton Howard   pd Leslie Dilley   ed Priscilla Nedd

Robert de Niro, Annette Bening, George Wendt, Patricia Wettig, Sam Wanamaker

'Once again, a producer has confused earnestness with seriousness, and felt that displaying good intentions could serve as a substitute for the low cunning of entertainment.' – Sight and Sound

The Guilty Generation

US 1931 82m bw
Columbia

A gangster has social ambitions for his daughter's sake.

Rather heavy melodrama which didn't catch on.

play Jo Milward, J. Kerby Hawkes   d Rowland V. Lee

Leo Carrillo, Constance Cummings, Robert Young, Boris Karloff, Emma Dunn

'Merits a fair showing . . . will do average or better.' – Variety

Guilty Hands

US 1931 60m bw
MGM

A district attorney commits murder and tries to frame a girl, but is killed when rigor mortis makes the gun go off in his victim's hand.

Risible melodrama which might with better writing have been effective.

w Bayard Veiller   d W. S. Van Dyke

Lionel Barrymore, Kay Francis, Madge Evans, William Bakewell, C. Aubrey Smith, Polly Moran, Alan Mowbray

'Someone missed here, and plenty.' – Variety

Guilty of Treason

US 1950 86m bw
Eagle Lion
GB title: Treason

An account of the trial by the Russians of the Hungarian primate Cardinal Mindzenty.

Gutter press version of real events, with cheap production and fictional frills.

w Emmet Lavery   d Felix Feist

Charles Bickford, Paul Kelly, Bonita Granville, Richard Derr, Berry Kroeger, Elisabeth Risdon

The Guinea Pig **

GB 1948 97m bw
Pilgrim (John Boulting)
US title: The Outsider

The first poor boy to win a scholarship to a famous public school has a hard time.

Enjoyable though unrealistic school drama with chief interest centring on the staff. A rude word ('kick up the arse') ensured its popularity.

w Bernard Miles, Warren Chetham Strode
play Warren Chetham Strode   d Roy Boulting
ph Gilbert Taylor   m John Wooldridge

Richard Attenborough, Robert Flemyng, Cecil Trouncer, Sheila Sim, Bernard Miles, Joan Hickson

Guling Jie Shaonian Sha Ren Shijan: see A Brighter Summer Day

Gulliver's Travels **

US 1939 74m Technicolor
Paramount/Max Fleischer
V*, L

Animated cartoon version which invents a Romeo-Juliet romance between Lilliput and Blefuscu and has the usual trouble with romantic humans.

At the time it represented a genuine challenge to Disney, but has not worn well in terms of pace or inventiveness. Fleischer made one more feature cartoon, *Mr Bug Goes to Town.*

d Dave Fleischer *m* Victor Young *m/ly* Ralph Rainger, Leo Robin

'Effective entertainment, but may not reach the grosses of *Snow White.*' – *Variety*

AAN: song 'Faithful Forever'; Victor Young

Gulliver's Travels

GB 1976 81m Eastmancolor
EMI/Valeness-Belvision (Josef Shaftel)

An ineffective treatment, again aimed at children, in which Gulliver is the only human element and all the Lilliputians are cartooned.

w Don Black *d* Peter Hunt *ph* Alan Hume *m* Michel Legrand *pd* Michael Stringer

Richard Harris, Catherine Schell, Norman Shelley

'Bonelessly inoffensive.' – *Sight and Sound*

The Gumball Rally

US 1976 107m Technicolor
Warner/First Artists (Chuck Bail)
V*

A variety of vehicles take part in a crazy race from New York to Long Beach.

The stuntmen are the real stars of this good-looking but dramatically deficient chase and destruction extravaganza.

w Leon Capetanos *d* Chuck Bail *ph* Richard Glouner *m* Dominic Frontière *stunt coordinator* Eddie Donno

Michael Sarrazin, Normann Burton, Gary Busey, John Durren, Susan Flannery

Gumshoe **

GB 1971 85m Eastmancolor
Columbia/Memorial (David Barber)
V, V*

A Liverpool bingo caller dreams of becoming a Bogart-like private eye and finds himself in the middle of a murder case.

A likeable spoof which is never quite as funny as it means to be. *Billy Liar* did it better, but there's plenty of amusing detail.

w Neville Smith *d* Stephen Frears *ph* Chris Menges *m* Andrew Lloyd Webber

Albert Finney, Billie Whitelaw, Fulton Mackay, Frank Finlay, Janice Rule

Gun Crazy *

US 1950 87m bw
King Brothers/Universal-International
V*
reissue title: *Deadly Is the Female*

A boy and girl set off on a trail of armed robbery and murder.

Modernized Bonnie and Clyde story which has become a minor cult film.

w Dalton Trumbo *story* Mackinlay Kantor *d* Joseph H. Lewis *ph* Russell Harlan *m* Victor Young

John Dall, Peggy Cummins, Morris Carnovsky, Berry Kroeger, Annabel Shaw, Harry Lewis

Gun for a Coward

US 1956 88m Technicolor Cinemascope

Three brothers join forces on a cattle drive, but one is killed.

Slightly pretentious Western co-feature.

w R. Wright Campbell *d* Abner Biberman

Fred MacMurray, Jeffrey Hunter, Dean Stockwell, Chill Wills, Janice Rule

Gun Fury

US 1953 80m Technicolor 3-D
Columbia (Lewis J. Rachmil)
V*, L

Outlaws rob a stagecoach and abduct a girl; her fiancé follows and takes revenge.

Adequate Western programmer.

w Irving Wallace, Roy Huggins *d* Raoul Walsh *ph* Lester H. White *md* Mischa Bakaleinikoff

Rock Hudson, Donna Reed, Phil Carey, Lee Marvin, Neville Brand

Gun Glory

US 1957 89m Metrocolor Cinemascope
MGM (Nicholas Nayfack)

A gunfighter returns home to settle down, but finds his wife dead and his son resentful.

Dull, unexciting star Western.

w William Ludwig *novel* *Man of the West* by Philip Yordan *d* Roy Rowland *ph* Harold J. Marzorati *m* Jeff Alexander

Stewart Granger, Rhonda Fleming, Chill Wills, Steve Rowland, James Gregory

'She Was Nobody Until Somebody Found . . .'
The Gun in Betty Lou's Handbag

US 1992 89m Technicolor
Buena Vista/Touchstone/Interscope/Nomura Babcock & Brown (Scott Kroopf)
V, V*

An unassertive librarian, tired of being ignored by everyone, confesses to a murder she did not commit.

Drear and dim-witted comedy, short on laughs, long on longueurs and with a few moments of unpleasant violence to ensure its failure as entertainment.

w Grace Cary Bickley *d* Allan Moyle *ph* Charles Minsky *m* Richard Gibbs *pd* Michael Corenblith *ed* Janice Hampton, Erica Huggins

Penelope Ann Miller, Eric Thal, William Forsythe, Cathy Moriarty, Julianne Moore, Alfre Woodard

'Figures to fire a blank into the box-office till' – *Variety*

The Gun Runner: see *Santiago*

The Gun Runners *

US 1958 82m bw
UA/Seven Arts (Clarence Greene)

The owner of a Florida motor cruiser innocently rents it to a gun merchant.

Modestly effective action melodrama, the third version of *To Have and Have Not* (qv).

w Daniel Mainwaring, Paul Monash *d* Don Siegel *ph* Hal Mohr *m* Leith Stevens

Audie Murphy, Eddie Albert, Patricia Owens, Everett Sloane

Guncrazy

US 1992 93m Foto-Kem colour
Zeta/First Look (Zane W. Levitt, Diane Firestone)
V, V*

A parentless 16-year-old marries a paroled murderer and the two take to the road, robbing and killing as they go.

An uninvolving thriller set in a depressed and depressing red-neck community; it may interest for the light it sheds on the darker edges of American society, but it is hardly entertaining.

w Matthew Bright *d* Tamra Davis *ph* Lisa Rinzler *m* Ed Tomney *ed* Kevin Tent

Drew Barrymore, James LeGros, Billy Drago, Rodney Harvey, Joe Dallesandro, Michael Ironside, Ione Sky

'A shoot-'em-up exploitationer with a few interesting ideas . . . settles into a surprisingly somber mood that suppresses the possibilities latent in the story and actors.' – *Variety*

Guney's The Wall: see *The Wall*

'In the bullring at Bajo Rio, Mexico, on Saturday at 4 pm, they'll pay to see two men kill each other!'
A Gunfight *

US 1970 94m Technicolor
Harvest/Thoroughbred/Bryna (Ronnie Lubin, Harold Jack Bloom)
V*

Two famous gunfighters on their uppers stage a duel for money.

Austere and anti-climactic Western supposedly against popular blood lust.

w Harold Jack Bloom *d* Lamont Johnson *ph* David M. Walsh *m* Laurence Rosenthal

Kirk Douglas, Johnny Cash, Karen Black, Raf Vallone, Jane Alexander

Gunfight at Comanche Creek

US 1963 90m DeLuxe Panavision
Allied Artists

In 1875 a detective goes undercover to unmask the brains behind a robber gang with complex methods.

Ingenious but over-emphatic Western programmer.

w Edward Bernds *d* Frank McDonald

Audie Murphy, Ben Cooper, Coleen Miller, John Hubbard, DeForrest Kelley

Gunfight at Dodge City

US 1958 81m DeLuxe Cinemascope
UA/Mirisch

After various problems, Bat Masterson is elected sheriff of Dodge City.

Fair standard Western with emphasis on plot and character.

w Daniel B. Ullman, Martin M. Goldsmith *d* Joseph M. Newman *ph* Carl Guthrie *m* Hans Salter

Joel McCrea, Julie Adams, John McIntire, Richard Anderson, Nancy Gates

Gunfight at the OK Corral **

US 1957 122m Technicolor Vistavision
Paramount/Hal Wallis
V*, L

Wyatt Earp and Doc Holliday defeat the Clanton Gang.

Watchable, ambitious, but vaguely disappointing super-Western.

w Leon Uris *d* John Sturges *ph* Charles B. Lang *m* Dimitri Tiomkin

Burt Lancaster, Kirk Douglas, Jo Van Fleet, Rhonda Fleming, John Ireland, Frank Faylen, Kenneth Tobey, Earl Holliman

'Carefully and lavishly mounted, but overlong and overwrought.' – *John Cutts*

† The legendary gunfight was tackled again in the 1994 Western *Tombstone* (qv).

Gunfight in Abilene

US 1967 86m Technicolor
Universal

After the Civil War, an officer goes home to find strife between farmers and cattlemen.

Fairly sensible and pleasing lower-berth Western.

w Berne Giler, John D. F. Black   *d* William Hale

Bobby Darin, Emily Banks, Leslie Nielsen, Donnelly Rhodes, Don Galloway, Michael Sarrazin

'His only friend was his gun – his only refuge, a woman's heart!'

The Gunfighter **
US   1950   84m   bw
TCF (Nunnally Johnson)
V*, L

A gunfighter fails to shake off his past.

Downbeat, small-scale but very careful adult Western set in a believable community.

w William Bowers, William Sellers   *d* Henry King
ph Arthur Miller   *m* Alfred Newman

Gregory Peck, Helen Westcott, Millard Mitchell, Jean Parker, Karl Malden, Skip Homeier, Mae Marsh

'Preserves throughout a respectable level of intelligence and invention.' – *Lindsay Anderson*

'Not merely a good western, a good film.' – *Richard Mallett, Punch*

'The movie is done in cold, quiet tones of gray, and every object in it – faces, clothing, a table, the hero's heavy moustache – is given an air of uncompromising authenticity, suggesting those dim photographs of the nineteenth-century west . . .' – *Robert Warshow, The Immediate Experience*

AAN: original story (William Bowers, André de Toth)

Gunfighters
US   1947   87m   Cinecolor
Columbia
GB title: *The Assassin*

A retired gunfighter is suspected of the murder of his best friend.

Presentable star Western.

w Alan Le May   *novel* Twin Sombreros by Zane Grey
d George Waggner

Randolph Scott, Barbara Britton, Dorothy Hart, Bruce Cabot, Forrest Tucker

Gunfighters of the Northwest
US   1954   bw   serial: 15 eps
Columbia

The Royal Canadian Mounties ride into action.

Just what you'd expect of a serial with this title.

d Spencer Bennet

Jack Mahoney (later Jock), Clayton Moore, Phyllis Coates, Marshall Reed, Lyle Talbot

Gunfire: see *China 9, Liberty 37*

Gung Ho!
US   1943   88m   bw
Universal/Walter Wanger
V*

Adventures of the Marines in the Pacific War.

Trite flagwaver, popular at the time.

w Lucien Hubbard, based on the experiences of Captain W. S. LeFrançois USMC   *d* Ray Enright
ph Milton H. Krasner   *m* Frank Skinner, Hans Salter

Randolph Scott, Grace MacDonald, Alan Curtis, Noah Beery Jnr, J. Carrol Naish, David Bruce, Peter Coe, Robert Mitchum

Gung Ho
US   1986   111m   Technicolor   Panavision
Paramount (Tony Ganz, Deborah Blum)
V*, L

Japanese management takes over an American small town.

Basically old-fashioned hands-across-the-sea stuff, without any very clear attitude except gentle fun. It rapidly led to a TV series, which folded, and that's about its level.

w Lowell Ganz, Babaloo Mandel   *d* Ron Howard
ph Don Peterman   *m* Thomas Newman   *pd* James Schoppe   *ed* Daniel Hanley, Michael Hill

Michael Keaton, Gedde Watanabe, George Wendt, Mimi Rogers, John Turturro

'A film that's not much of anything except two hours long.' – *People*

'Thrills for a thousand movies plundered for one mighty show!'
'Romance aflame through dangerous days and nights of terror! In a land where anything can happen – most of all to a beautiful girl alone!'

Gunga Din ***
US   1939   117m   bw
RKO (George Stevens)
V*, L

Three cheerful army veterans meet adventure on the North-West Frontier.

Rousing period actioner with comedy asides, one of the most entertaining of its kind ever made.

w Joel Sayre, Fred Guiol, Ben Hecht, Charles MacArthur   *poem* Rudyard Kipling   *d* George Stevens
ph Joseph H. August   *m* Alfred Newman   *ad* Van Nest Polglase

Cary Grant, Victor McLaglen, Douglas Fairbanks Jnr, Sam Jaffe, Eduardo Ciannelli, Joan Fontaine, Montagu Love, Robert Coote, Cecil Kellaway, Abner Biberman, Lumsden Hare

'One of the big money pictures this year . . . will recoup plenty at the box office window.' – *Variety*

'One of the most enjoyable nonsense-adventure movies of all time.' – *Pauline Kael, 1968*

'Bravura is the exact word for the performances, and Stevens' composition and cutting of the fight sequences is particularly stunning.' – *NFT, 1973*

Gunhed (dubbed)
Japan   1989   99m   colour
Manga/Toho/Sunrise (Yoshishige Shimatani, Tetsuhisha Yamada)

In 2039, engineers patch up warrior-robots to disarm a super-computer that is trying to take over the world.

Comic-book science fiction, frequently risible and always over the top.

w Masato Harada, James Bannon   *d* Masato Harada
ph Jinichi Fujisawa   *m* Toshiyuki Honda
sp Koichi Kawakita, Imagica Group   *ed* Yoshitami Kuroiwa

Masahiro Takashima, Brenda Bakke, Yujin Harada, Kaori Mizushima, Aya Enyoji, Mickey Curtis, James B. Thompson, Doll Nguyen, Landy Leyes

'A hokey slab of Nipponese sci-fi that's OK for buffs but not high-key enough to break into wider markets.' – *Variety*

'This is the computer game as cinema.' – *Derek Malcolm, Guardian*

The film was given a British release in 1994.

Gunman's Walk *
US   1958   97m   Technicolor   Cinemascope
Columbia (Fred Kohlmar)

A tough Westerner has two sons, one of whom follows too literally in his footsteps.

Competent action melodrama with good characterization.

w Frank Nugent   *d* Phil Karlson   *ph* Charles Lawton   *m* George Duning

Van Heflin, Tab Hunter, James Darren, Kathryn Grant

Gunn *
US   1967   95m   Technicolor
Paramount/Geoffrey (Owen Crump)

A private eye is hired to find a gangster's killer.

Tongue-in-cheek violence from the television series, with Craig Stevens doing a Cary Grant imitation.

w Blake Edwards, William Peter Blatty   *d* Blake Edwards   *ph* Philip Lathrop   *m* Henry Mancini

Craig Stevens, Laura Devon, Ed Asner, Sherry Jackson, Helen Traubel, J. Pat O'Malley, Regis Toomey

'Falters between parody and straight action.' – *MFB*

Gunpoint: see *At Gunpoint*

Gunpoint
US   1966   86m   Technicolor
Universal

A Colorado sheriff goes after train robbers.

Simple-minded but quite professional and good-looking Western programmer.

w Mary and Willard Willingham   *d* Earl Bellamy

Audie Murphy, Joan Staley, Warren Stevens, Edgar Buchanan, Denver Pyle

Guns at Batasi *
GB   1964   103m   bw   Cinemascope
TCF/George H. Brown
V*

The headquarters of an Anglo-African regiment is threatened by rebels.

Basically the old chestnut about a group of disparate types trapped in a dangerous situation, this is given shape and stature by the star's lively performance as the martinet of an RSM.

w Robert Hollis   *novel* The Siege of Battersea by Robert Hollis   *d* John Guillermin   *ph* Douglas Slocombe
m John Addison

Richard Attenborough, Flora Robson, Mia Farrow, Jack Hawkins, Cecil Parker, Percy Herbert, Errol John, John Leyton, Earl Cameron

Guns for San Sebastian
France/Mexico/Italy   1967   111m   Metrocolor   Franscope
MGM/Cipra/Filmes/Ernesto Eniques (Jacques Bar)
S

In Mexico in 1746, a rebel on the run stays to defend a besieged village.

Multi-national actioner, violent but quite undistinguished.

w James R. Webb   *book* A Wall for San Sebastian by William B. Flaherty   *d* Henri Verneuil   *ph* Armand Thirard   *m* Ennio Morricone

Anthony Quinn, Charles Bronson, Sam Jaffe, Anjanette Comer, Silvia Pinal, Fernand Gravet

Guns in the Afternoon: see *Ride the High Country*

Guns in the Heather
US   1968   90m   Technicolor
Walt Disney

An American schoolboy in Ireland finds that his elder brother is a CIA agent.

Tolerable kiddie-fodder from the Disney treadmill; later desiccated for TV.

w Herman Groves   *d* Robert Butler

Glenn Corbett, Alfred Burke, Kurt Russell, Patrick Barr

Guns of Darkness
GB   1962   102m   bw
ABP/Cavalcade (Thomas Clyde)

A British plantation boss in Latin America escapes with his wife when rebels strike.

Chase/escape film with a few tiny comments about violence.

w John Mortimer novel Act of Mercy by Francis Clifford d Anthony Asquith ph Robert Krasker m Benjamin Frankel

David Niven, Leslie Caron, James Robertson Justice, David Opatoshu

The Guns of Fort Petticoat

US 1957 79m Technicolor
Columbia/Brown-Murphy (Harry Joe Brown)

During the Civil War, a wandering Texan trains townswomen into a fighting force.

Unlikely Western which passes the time.

w Walter Doniger d George Marshall ph Ray Rennahan m Mischa Bakaleinikoff

Audie Murphy, Kathryn Grant, Hope Emerson, Jeff Donnell, Isobel Elsom

The Guns of Loos *

GB 1927 89m (24 fps) bw silent
Stoll/New Era

A blinded hero of the war returns home to run an industrial empire and is confronted by a strike.

One of the better British silents, with a strong plot and an interesting cast.

w L. H. Gordon, Reginald Fogwell, Sinclair Hill d Sinclair Hill ph Desmond Dickinson

Henry Victor, Madeleine Carroll, Bobby Howes, Hermione Baddeley

The Guns of Navarone **

GB 1961 157m Technicolor Cinemascope
Columbia/Open Road/Carl Foreman (Cecil F. Ford)
V, V*, L, S

In 1943 a sabotage team is sent to destroy two giant guns on a Turkish Island.

Ambitiously produced Boy's Own Paper heroics, with lots of noise and self-sacrifice; intermittently exciting but bogged down by philosophical chat.

w Carl Foreman novel Alistair Maclean d J. Lee-Thompson ph Oswald Morris m Dimitri Tiomkin ad Geoffrey Drake

Gregory Peck, David Niven, Stanley Baker, Anthony Quinn, Anthony Quayle, James Darren, Gia Scala, James Robertson Justice, Richard Harris, Irene Papas, Bryan Forbes

'A desperate imbalance: the moral arguments cut into the action without extending it.' – Penelope Houston

AAN: best picture; Carl Foreman; J. Lee-Thompson; Dimitri Tiomkin; special effects (Bill Warrington, Vivian C. Greenham)

Guns of the Magnificent Seven

US 1969 106m DeLuxe Panavision
UA/Mirisch (Vincent M. Fennelly)
V*

Seven mercenaries rescue a Mexican Robin Hood.

Stale, flat and unprofitable third serving of this particular hash.

w Herman Hoffman d Paul Wendkos ph Antonio Macasoli m Elmer Bernstein

George Kennedy, Monte Markham, Joe Don Baker, James Whitmore, Bernie Casey, Scott Thomas, Reni Santoni, Michael Ansara, Wende Wagner, Fernando Rey, Frank Silvera

Guns of the Timberland

US 1960 91m Technicolor
Jaguar (Aaron Spelling)

Loggers are opposed by cattle interests.

Routine star Western with tolerable production values.

w Joseph Petracca, Aaron Spelling novel Louis L'Amour d Robert D. Webb ph John Seitz m David Buttolph

Alan Ladd, Jeanne Crain, Gilbert Roland, Frankie Avalon, Lyle Bettger, Noah Beery Jnr

Guns of Wyoming: see Cattle King

Gunsmoke

US 1953 79m Technicolor
Universal

A cowboy befriends the rancher he has been hired to kill.

Moderate Western with too many pauses for sentiment.

w D. D. Beauchamp d Nathan Juran

Audie Murphy, Paul Kelly, Susan Cabot, Mary Castle, Charles Drake

The Guru

US/India 1969 112m DeLuxe
TCF/Arcadia (Ismail Merchant)

In India, an English pop singer succumbs to the local atmosphere.

Pleasant, affectionate but forgettable anecdote of modern India.

w Ruth Prawer Jhabvala, James Ivory d James Ivory ph Subrata Mitra m Ustad Vilayat Khan

Michael York, Rita Tushingham, Utpal Dutt, Aparna Sen, Barry Foster

Gus

US 1976 96m Technicolor
Walt Disney (Ron Miller)
V*, L

A football team co-opts a mule which can kick a hundred yard ball.

Predictable Disney fantasy comedy with a direct line back to The Absent Minded Professor.

w Arthur Alsberg, Don Nelson d Vincent McEveety ph Frank Phillips m Robert F. Brunner

Ed Asner, Don Knotts, Gary Grimes, Tim Conway, Liberty Williams, Bob Crane, Harold Gould, Tom Bosley, Dick Van Patten

'In the current comedy climate, when humour so often hinges on a four-letter word or its lengthier variant, a light-hearted football game spoof is a breath of fresh air.' – Tatiana Balkoff Lipscomb, Films in Review

The Guv'nor

GB 1935 88m bw
Gaumont (Michael Balcon)
US title: Mr Hobo

By chance a tramp becomes a bank director.

Predictable star vehicle with Arliss a most unlikely tramp.

w Maude Howell, Guy Bolton d Milton Rosmer ph Max Greene md Louis Levy

George Arliss, Gene Gerrard, Viola Keats, Patric Knowles, Frank Cellier, Mary Clare, George Hayes

'His admirers need not fear that he has lost any of his usual refinement or sentiment, his cultured English accent, his Universal certificate.' – Graham Greene

A Guy Named Joe

US 1944 120m bw
MGM (Everett Riskin)
V*

A flyer is killed but comes back as a ghost to supervise his ex-girl's new romance.

Icky romantic comedy-drama with strong propaganda intent; the stars make it tolerable.

w Dalton Trumbo d Victor Fleming ph George Folsey, Karl Freund m Herbert Stothart

Spencer Tracy, Irene Dunne, Ward Bond, Van Johnson, James Gleason, Lionel Barrymore, Barry Nelson, Don Defore, Henry O'Neill

'As far as I could judge, the audience loved it: melodrama, farce, fake philosophy, swimming eyes and all.' – Richard Mallett, Punch

'It neatly obtunds death's sting as ordinary people suffer it by not only assuming but photographing a good, busy, hearty hereafter.' – James Agee

† The title was explained by one of the characters who observed that 'in the Army Air Corps, any fellow who is a right fellow is called Joe'.

AAN: original story (David Boehm, Chandler Sprague)

The Guy Who Came Back

US 1951 92m bw
TCF

A pro football player hates the thought of retiring.

Sentimental sporting drama without much life in it.

w Allan Scott d Joseph Newman

Paul Douglas, Joan Bennett, Linda Darnell, Don Defore, Zero Mostel

Guys and Dolls *

US 1955 149m Eastmancolor Cinemascope
Samuel Goldwyn
V, V*, L

A New York gangster takes a bet that he can romance a Salvation Army lady.

The artifices of Runyonland are made more so by a defiantly studio-bound production and thoroughly flat handling; but the songs and sometimes the performances survive.

wd Joseph L. Mankiewicz musical Jo Swerling, Abe Burrows ph Harry Stradling md Cyril Mockridge, Jay Blackton ch Michael Kidd pd Oliver Smith m/ly Frank Loesser ad Joseph Wright

Frank Sinatra, Marlon Brando, Jean Simmons, Vivian Blaine, Stubby Kaye, B. S. Pully, Robert Keith, Sheldon Leonard, George E. Stone

'Quantity has been achieved only at the cost of quality.' – Penelope Houston

AAN: Harry Stradling; Cyril Mockridge, Jay Blackton; art direction

Gycklarnas Afton: see Sawdust and Tinsel

Gymkata

US 1985 90m Metro colour
MGM/UA (Fred Weintraub)
V, V*

An American gymnast trains to win a contest of skill and strength in a small Asian country, mainly populated by ninjas, in order that the US can install a spy satellite there.

Disagreeable and ridiculous gung-ho martial arts nonsense.

w Charles Robert Carner novel The Terrible Game by Dan Tyler Moore d Robert Clouse ph Godfrey Godar m Alfi Kabiljo pd Veljko Despotovic ed Robert A. Ferretti

Kurt Thomas, Tetchie Agbayani, Richard Norton, Edward Bell, John Barrett, Conan Lee

Gypsy

GB 1936 78m bw
Warner (Irving Asher)

An ageing playboy marries a gypsy but gives her back to her true love.

Hard-to-swallow drama with insufficient comedy relief for its star.

w Brock Williams, Terence Rattigan *novel Tsigane* by Lady Eleanor Smith *d* Roy William Neill

Roland Young, Chili Bouchier, Hugh Williams, Frederick Burtwell

'The girl who became the greatest show in show business!'
Gypsy *
US 1962 149m Technirama
Warner (Mervyn Le Roy)
V*, L

The early days of stripteaser Gypsy Rose Lee, and the exploits of her ambitious mother.

A vaudeville musical that is nowhere near raucous enough, or brisk enough, for its subject, and is miscast into the bargain. The songs are great, but not here: Miss Russell is as boring as an electric drill in a role that should have been reserved for Ethel Merman.

w Leonard Spigelgass *play* Arthur Laurents *d* Mervyn Le Roy *ph* Harry Stradling *md* Frank Perkins *m/y* Jule Styne, Stephen Sondheim *ad* John Beckman

Rosalind Russell, Natalie Wood, *Karl Malden*, James Milhollin

AAN: Harry Stradling; Frank Perkins

The Gypsy and the Gentleman
GB 1957 107m Eastmancolor
Rank (Maurice Cowan)

A penniless Regency rake marries a tempestuous gypsy, with melodramatic and tragic results.

Expensive and typically mistimed Rank attempt to re-do *The Man in Grey;* a barnstormer notable only for waste of talent.

w Janet Greene *novel Darkness I Leave You* by Nina Warner Hooke *d* Joseph Losey *ph* Jack Hildyard *m* Hans May *ad* Ralph Brinton

Melina Mercouri, Keith Michell, Patrick McGoohan, June Laverick, Flora Robson, Helen Haye

Gypsy Colt
US 1954 72m Ansco Color
MGM

A cherished colt has to be sold, but makes its way back home.

Disguised second feature remake of *Lassie Come Home;* good for children.

w Martin Berkeley *d* Andrew Marton

Donna Corcoran, Ward Bond, Frances Dee, Larry Keating, Lee Van Cleef

Gypsy Girl: see Sky West and Crooked

The Gypsy Moths *
US 1969 110m Metrocolor
MGM/Frankenheimer-Lewis (Hal Landers, Bobby Roberts)

Sky-diving stuntmen find love and death on a small-town tour.

Brilliantly breathtaking actioner which too frequently gets grounded, and does not find a reason for being so glum.

w William Hanley *novel* James Drought *d* John Frankenheimer *ph* Philip Lathrop *aerial ph* Carl Boenisch *m* Elmer Bernstein

Burt Lancaster, Deborah Kerr, Gene Hackman, Scott Wilson, William Windom, Bonnie Bedelia, Sheree North

'A Bergmanesque world of inner emotions and ambiguous means. . .. As in many of Frankenheimer's films it rains, and the wind in the trees in the park and the sound of traffic all contribute to the realism that makes his work so satisfying.' – *Gerald Pratley*

Gypsy Wildcat
US 1944 77m Technicolor
Universal (George Waggner)

A Transylvanian gypsy girl is really a long lost countess.

Universal's Frankenstein sets are put to lighter use in a quite incredible piece of downright hokum.

w James Hogan, Gene Lewis, James M. Cain *d* Roy William Neill *ph* George Robinson, W. Howard Greene *m* Edward Ward

Maria Montez, Jon Hall, Leo Carrillo, Gale Sondergaard, Douglass Dumbrille, Nigel Bruce, Peter Coe, Curt Bois

'The picture's so bad, it's bound to make money.' – *Cue*

'Never rises to the wild camp of *Cobra Woman;* it's just *opéra bouffe* without music.' – *Pauline Kael, 70s*

H

H. M. Pulham Esquire **

US 1940 120m bw
MGM (King Vidor)

A moderately successful Bostonian businessman
looks back over his rather stuffy life and has a fling.

Solidly upholstered drama which does not quite do
justice to the book on which it is based.

w King Vidor, Elizabeth Hill novel John P.
Marquand d King Vidor ph Ray June
m Bronislau Kaper

Robert Young, Ruth Hussey, Hedy Lamarr, Charles
Coburn, Van Heflin, Fay Holden, Bonita Granville

HMS Defiant *

GB 1962 101m Technicolor Cinemascope
Columbia/GW (John Brabourne)
US title: Damn the Defiant

Mutiny erupts on an 18th-century British sailing ship.

Rather unpleasant and unenterprising sea fare
reminiscent of the goings-on aboard the Bounty. Well
enough staged and acted but not very remarkable or
memorable.

w Nigel Kneale, Edmund H. North novel Mutiny by
Frank Tilsley & Lewis Gilbert ph Christopher
Challis m Clifton Parker

Alec Guinness, Dirk Bogarde, Anthony Quayle, Tom
Bell, Nigel Stock, Murray Melvin, Victor Maddern,
Maurice Denham, Walter Fitzgerald

'It authentically if superficially recreates the days of
press gangs, maggots and the cat.' – Peter John Dyer

H. P. Lovecraft's From Beyond: see From Beyond

H. P. Lovecraft's The Unnamable Returns: see
The Unnamable Returns

Habeas Corpus *

US 1928 20m bw silent
Hal Roach

A mad professor sends two vagabonds out to look for
a body.

Unusual star comedy, more grotesque and
pantomimish than any of the others.

w H. M. Walker story Leo McCarey d James
Parrott ph Len Powers ed Richard Currier

Laurel and Hardy, Charles Carle

Hachigatsu-no-Kyoshikyoku: see Rhapsody in
August

Hadaka no Shima: see The Island

Hail the Conquering Hero ***

US 1944 101m bw
Paramount (Preston Sturges)
V*

An army reject is accidentally thought a hero when he
returns to his small-town home.

Skilfully orchestrated Preston Sturges romp, slightly
marred by an overdose of sentiment but featuring his
repertory of comic actors at full pitch.

wd Preston Sturges ph John Seitz m Werner
Heymann

Eddie Bracken, William Demarest, Ella Raines, Franklin
Pangborn, Elizabeth Patterson, Raymond Walburn, Alan
Bridge, Georgia Caine, Freddie Steele, Jimmy Conlin,
Torben Meyer

'Mob scenes, rough-houses and sharply serious
passages are played for all the pantomime they are
worth . . . one of the happiest, heartiest comedies in a
twelvemonth.' – Otis L. Guernsey Jnr

'First rate entertainment, a pattern of film making, not
to be missed.' – Richard Mallett, Punch

'The energy, the verbal density, the rush of Americana
and the congestion seen periodically in The Miracle of
Morgan's Creek stagger the senses in this newest film.' –
James Ursini

'It tells a story so touching, so chock-full of human
frailties and so rich in homely detail that it achieves a
reality transcending the limitations of its familiar
slapstick.' – James Agee

'He uses verbal as well as visual slapstick, and his
comic timing is so quirkily effective that the dialogue
keeps popping off like a string of firecrackers.' – New
Yorker, 1977

AAN: Preston Sturges (as writer)

Hair *

US 1979 121m Technicolor Panavision
UA/CIP (Lester Persky, Michael Butler)
V, V*, L

An Oklahoman on his way to enlist for Vietnam
service stops off in New York and becomes embroiled
with the flower people.

Slick, vigorous but eventually unsatisfying version of
a quickly dated musical frolic with some obvious
points to make.

w Michael Weller musical play Galt MacDermot
(music) and Gerome Ragni/James Rado (book)
d Milos Forman ph Miroslav Ondricek, Richard
Kratina, Jean Talvin m/ly Galt MacDermot, Gerome
Ragni, James Rado

John Savage, Treat Williams, Beverly D'Angelo,
Annie Golden, Dorsey Wright

'The makers of Hair have given us some high-spirited
reminders of splendid things that film can do and,
these days, isn't often asked to.' – Stanley Kauffmann

The Hairdresser's Husband **

France 1990 80m colour Panavision
Palace/Lambart/TF1/Investimage 2 and 3/Sofica (Thierry de
Ganay)
V, V*, S
original title: Le Mari de la Coiffeuse

A middle-aged man fulfils his childhood erotic
fantasy of marrying a hairdresser.

Quirky, witty drama of an obsessive relationship.

w Claude Klotz, Patrice Leconte d Patrice Leconte
ph Eduardo Serra m Michael Nyman ad Ivan
Maussion ed Joëlle Hache

Jean Rochefort, Anna Galiena, Roland Bertin,
Maurice Chevit, Philippe Clevenot, Jacques Mathou,
Claude Aufaure, Henry Hocking

'Made with a light comic touch, but always peering
through the droll surface is a darker suggestion of
danger and perversity.' —Philip French, Observer

Hairspray

US 1988 90m colour
Palace (Rachel Talalay)
V, V*, L

A fat teenager becomes the star of a local TV dance
show.

Drear and campy comedy, set in the early days of rock
and beehive hair-styles.

wd John Waters ph David Insley m Kenny Vance
pd Vincent Peranio ed Janice Hampton

Sonny Bono, Ruth Brown, Divine, Colleen
Fitzpatrick, Jo Ann Havrilla, Michael St Gerard,
Debbie Harry, Ricki Lake, Leslie Ann Powers

The Hairy Ape

US 1944 91m bw
Jules Levy
V*

A ship's stoker aims to kill a socialite who has
insulted him.

Patchy treatment of an intractable and dated play.

w Jules Levy play Eugene O'Neill d Alfred
Santell ph Lucien Andriot m Michel Michelet,
Edward Paul

William Bendix, Susan Hayward, John Loder,
Dorothy Comingore, Roman Bohnen, Alan Napier

AAN: Michel Michelet, Edward Paul

Hakayitz Shel Aviya: see The Summer of Aviya

Half a Hero

US 1953 71m bw
MGM

A timid journalist has problems with wife, baby, boss
and new house.

Aimless comedy quite unsuited to its star.

w Max Shulman d Don Weis

Red Skelton, Jean Hagen, Charles Dingle, Mary
Wickes, Polly Bergen

Half a Sinner

US 1934 70m bw
Universal

A cheerful elderly cardsharp masquerades as a
deacon.

Midwestern pleaser not too well made here, but later
remade under its original title as a Bob Burns vehicle.

w Earle Snell, Clarence Marks play Alias the Deacon
by John B. Hymer and LeRoy Clemens d Kurt
Neumann

Berton Churchill, Joel McCrea, Sally Blane, Mickey
Rooney, Spencer Charters

'Little marquee strength, but sufficient punch to
please 'em once they're in.' – Variety

'It's everything a motion picture can be!'
Half a Sixpence *

GB 1967 148m Technicolor Panavision
Paramount/Ameran (Charles H. Schneer, George Sidney)
V*

A draper's assistant inherits a fortune and moves into
society.

Mildly likeable but limp and overlong musical which would have benefited from more intimate, sharper treatment than the wide screen can give. The period decor and lively numbers seem insufficient compensation for the longueurs.

w Beverley Cross *play* Beverley Cross *novel Kipps* by H. G. Wells *d* George Sidney *ph* Geoffrey Unsworth *pd* Ted Haworth *ch* Gillian Lynne *m/ly* David Heneker

Tommy Steele, Julia Foster, Cyril Richard, Penelope Horner, Elaine Taylor, Hilton Edwards, Pamela Brown, James Villiers

'The confessions of a female sleepwalker!'
Half Angel
US   1951   80m   Technicolor
TCF

A prim and proper nurse has a more forthright personality when she sleepwalks.

Silly romantic comedy with amusing moments.

w Robert Riskin   *d* Richard Sale

Loretta Young, Joseph Cotten, Cecil Kellaway, Basil Ruysdael, Jim Backus, Irene Ryan

The Half-Breed
US   1952   81m   Technicolor
RKO
V*

A gambler helps a half-breed and wins the respect of the Apaches.

Half-hearted Western which could never be more than the bottom half of a double bill.

w Harold Shumate, Richard Wormser   *d* Stuart Gilmore

Robert Young, Jack Buetel, Janis Carter, Barton MacLane, Reed Hadley, Porter Hall, Connie Gilchrist

Half Moon Street
US   1986   90m   Technicolor
RKO/Edward R. Pressman (Geoffrey Reeve)
V, V*, L

A lady PhD turns to prostitution to augment her income, and becomes involved in Middle Eastern schemes.

Totally muddled compromise between thriller and exploitation piece; its message seems to have got left on the cutting room floor.

w Bob Swaim, Edward Behr   *novel Dr Slaughter* by Paul Theroux   *d* Bob Swaim   *ph* Peter Hannan *m* Richard Harvey   *pd* Anthony Curtis   *ed* Richard Marden

Sigourney Weaver, Michael Caine, Patrick Kavanaugh, Keith Buckley

'A half-baked excuse for a film.' – *Variety*

The Half Naked Truth *
US   1932   67m   bw
RKO (David O. Selznick)

A publicity agent has trouble with a temperamental actress whose schemes are always over the top.

Amusing wisecracking comedy.

w Bartlett Cormack, Corey Ford   *d* Gregory La Cava *ph* Bert Glennon   *m* Max Steiner

Lee Tracy, Lupe Velez, Eugene Pallette, Frank Morgan, Bob McKenzie

Half Shot at Sunrise *
US   1930   78m   bw
RKO

Allegedly one of the best representations of a star comedy duo who went into a decline after 1932.

w James Ashmore Creelman   *d* Paul Sloane

Bert Wheeler, Robert Woolsey, Edna May Oliver, Dorothy Lee, John Rutherford

'Laugh programmer beyond ordinary . . . it will do business, including de luxers.' – *Variety*

Half Way to Shanghai
US   1942   61m   bw
Universal (Paul Malvern)

Spies are included among the passengers on a Burma night train before the Japanese invasion.

Watchable if muddled mystery with a good cast; Shanghai is neither relevant nor mentioned.

w Stuart Palmer   *d* John Rawlins

Kent Taylor, Irene Hervey, Henry Stephenson, J. Edward Bromberg, George Zucco, Alexander Granach, Lionel Royce

Halfaouine
Tunisia/France   1990   98m   colour
Cine Tele/France Media/Scarabee/RTT/La Sept/WDR (Ahmed Attia, Hassen Daldoul, Elaine Stutterheim)
aka: *The Rooftop Hopper*

In Tunis, a young boy begins to discover sex, a subject that also obsesses his elders.

Slight, episodic narrative of minor interest.

w Férid Boughedir, Maryse Léon Garcia, Nouri Bouzid, Taoufik Jebali   *d* Férid Boughedir *ph* George Barsky   *m* Anouar Braham   *ed* Moufida Tlatli

Mohamed Driss, Mustafa Adueni, Rabia Ben Abdallah, Fatma Ben Saidane, Helène Catazaras, Fathi Al Hadawi, Sélim Boughedir

'Boughedir is a director of broad ideas more than a stylist, yet the pic manages to capture and hold viewers from start to finish.' – *Variety*

The Halfway House *
GB   1944   99m   bw
Ealing (Cavalcanti)

Overnight guests at an inn find it was bombed a year before and they have all been given a supernatural chance to reconsider their lives.

Interesting pattern play which would have benefited from lighter handling.

w Angus Macphail, Diana Morgan   *play* Denis Ogden   *d* Basil Dearden   *ph* Wilkie Cooper *m* Lord Berners

Françoise Rosay, Tom Walls, Alfred Drayton, Sally Ann Howes, Mervyn Johns, Glynis Johns, Esmond Knight, Richard Bird, Guy Middleton

Hallelujah! **
US   1929   106m   bw
MGM (King Vidor)
V*, L

A black cotton worker accidentally kills a man and decides to become a preacher.

Hollywood's unique black melodrama now seems stilted because of its early talkie technique, but at the time its picture of negro life had a freshness and truth which was not reached again for thirty years.

w Wanda Tuchock, King Vidor   *d* King Vidor *ph* Gordon Avil   *md* Eva Jessye

Daniel Haynes, Nina Mae McKinney, William Fountaine, Fannie Belle de Knight, Harry Gray

'The central theme became swamped by the forty or so singing sequences of folk songs, spirituals, baptism wails, love songs and blues.' – *Peter Noble, The Negro in Films*

AAN: King Vidor

Hallelujah, I'm a Bum **
US   1933   80m   bw
Lewis Milestone
V*
GB titles: Hallelujah I'm a Tramp; Lazy Bones

The leader of a group of Central Park tramps smartens

himself up for love of a lady who lost her memory. When she recovers it, he becomes a tramp again.

Curious whimsy expressed mainly in recitative, with embarrassing stretches relieved by moments of visual and verbal inspiration. Very typical of the Depression, with the tramps knowing best how life should be lived.

w S. N. Behrman, Ben Hecht   *d* Lewis Milestone *ph* Lucien Andriot   *rhymes/m/ly* Richard Rodgers, Lorenz Hart   *ad* Richard Day

songs: 'Hallelujah I'm a Bum'; 'You Are Too Beautiful'; 'I'll do It Again'; 'What Do You Want with Money?'; 'I've Got to Get Back to New York'

Al Jolson, Harry Langdon, Madge Evans, Frank Morgan, Chester Conklin

'It must rise or fall by Al Jolson's rep . . . it won't bore, once in, but it's not a mass play picture.' – *Variety*

'Given a scene or two of high sentiment, he still has you wrapped round his little finger.' – *The Times, 1973*

Hallelujah, I'm a Tramp: see *Hallelujah, I'm a Bum*

The Hallelujah Trail
US   1965   167m   Technicolor   Ultra Panavision 70
UA/Mirisch/Kappa (John Sturges)
V, V*, L

In 1867 a wagonload of whisky bound for Denver is waylaid by Indians, temperance crusaders and the civilian militia.

Absurdly inflated, prolonged, uninventive comedy Western with poor narrative grip; all dressed up and nowhere to go.

w John Gay   *novel* Bill Gulick   *d* John Sturges *ph* Robert Surtees   *m* Elmer Bernstein

Burt Lancaster, Lee Remick, Brian Keith, Jim Hutton, Donald Pleasence, Martin Landau

The Halliday Brand *
US   1956   78m   bw
UA/Collier Young

A tough farmer/sheriff conflicts with his son over his attitude to Indians.

Dour, reliable Western melodrama with a good cast.

w George W. George, George S. Slavin   *d* Joseph H. Lewis   *ph* Ray Rennahan   *m* Stanley Wilson

Joseph Cotten, Viveca Lindfors, Ward Bond, Betsy Blair, Bill Williams, Jay C. Flippen

Halloween *
US   1978   91m   Metrocolor   Panavision
Falcon International (Irwin Yablans)
V, V*, L, S

In a small Illinois town, a mad killer escapes from the asylum.

Single-minded shocker with virtually no plot, just a succession of bloody attacks in semi-darkness. Very well done if you like that kind of thing, though the final suggestion of the supernatural is rather baffling.

w John Carpenter, Debra Hill   *d* John Carpenter *ph* Dean Cundey   *m* John Carpenter   *pd* Tommy Wallace

Donald Pleasence, Jamie Lee Curtis, Nancy Loomis, P. J. Soles

'One of the cinema's most perfectly engineered devices for saying Boo!' – *Richard Combs, MFB*

Halloween Two
US   1981   92m   Metrocolor   Panavision
Dino de Laurentiis (Debra Hill, John Carpenter)
V, V*, L, S

The motiveless murderer from *Halloween* escapes from the asylum fifteen years later.

A totally unnecessary sequel which seems merely an excuse for assorted mayhem at close quarters.

w John Carpenter, Debra Hill   *d* Rick Rosenthal
ph Dean Cundey   *m* John Carpenter, Alan Howarth

Donald Pleasence, Jamie Lee Curtis, Charles Cyphers, Jeffrey Kramer

Halloween Three: Season of the Witch
US   1983   98m   Technicolor   Panavision
Dino de Laurentiis (Debra Hill, John Carpenter)
V*, L, S

A malicious toy maker intends to restore Halloween to its witch cult origins through magic masks made at his Santa Mira factory. The Halloween zombie-killer makes no appearance: this is a fresh story inspired by *Invasion of the Body Snatchers*.

Alas, its good intentions flounder in a bath of gore.

wd Tommy Lee Wallace   *ph* Dean Cundey
m John Carpenter, Alan Howarth   *pd* Peter Jamison

Tom Atkins, Stacey Nelkin, Dan O'Herlihy, Ralph Strait, Michael Currie

† Nigel Kneale wrote the original script but asked to have his name removed from the credits.

Halloween Four: The Return of Michael Myers
US   1988   88m   colour   Panavision
Fox/Trancas International/Halloween 4 Partnership (Paul Freeman)
V, V*, L, S

The motiveless murderer emerges from a coma to kill again, and again, and again.

A further unnecessary sequel, poorly made.

w Alan B. McElroy   *story* Dhani Lipsius, Larry Rattner, Benjamin Ruffner   *d* Dwight H. Little
ph Peter Lyons Collister   *m* Alan Howarth
ad Roger S. Crandall   *ed* Curtiss Clayton

Donald Pleasence, Ellie Cornell, Danielle Harris, Michael Pataki, Beau Starr, Kathleen Kinmont, Sasha Jenson, George R. Wilbur, Gene Ross, Carmen Filpi

Halloween Five: The Revenge of Michael Myers
US   1989   96m   CFI colour
Magnum (Ramsey Thomas)
V*, L, S

A small girl senses when the Halloween killer is going to strike again.

Lacklustre sequel that goes to some lengths to set up a further instalment of mindless killings at its end.

w Michael Jacobs, Dominique Othenin-Girard, Shem Bitterman   *d* Dominique Othenin-Girard
ph Robert Draper   *m* Alan Howarth, John Carpenter
pd Steven Lee   *ed* Jerry Brady

Donald Pleasence, Danielle Harris, Wendy Kaplan, Ellie Cornell, Donald L. Shanks, Jeffrey Landman, Beau Starr

'Pretty stupid and boring fare.' – *Variety*

Halls of Anger
US   1969   99m   DeLuxe
UA/Mirisch (Herbert Hirschman)

A black basketball star goes to teach in his home town and faces segregation problems.

Schematic melodrama, as well meaning as it is boring.

w John Shaner, Al Ramrus   *d* Paul Bogart
ph Burnett Guffey   *m* Dave Grusin

Calvin Lockhart, Janet McLachlan, Jeff Bridges

Halls of Montezuma *
US   1950   113m   Technicolor
TCF (Robert Bassler)

Marines fight World War II in the Pacific.

Well-mounted, simple-minded actioner.

w Michael Blankfort   *d* Lewis Milestone
ph Winton C. Hoch, Harry Jackson   *md* Lionel Newman   *m* Sol Kaplan

Richard Widmark, Jack Palance, Reginald Gardiner, Robert Wagner, Karl Malden, Richard Hylton, Richard Boone, Skip Homeier, Jack Webb, Bert Freed, Neville Brand, Don Hicks, Martin Milner

'By far the noisiest war film I ever encountered.' – *Richard Mallett, Punch*

Ham and Eggs at the Front
US   1927   70m approx at 24 fps   bw   silent
Warner

Two black soldiers have adventures in the trenches.

Irresistibly-titled war farce with our heroes played by whites in blackface.

w Darryl F. Zanuck   *d* Roy Del Ruth

Tom Wilson, Charlie Conklin, Myrna Loy

Hambone and Hillie
US   1983   90m   colour   Panavision
Sandy Howard/Adams Apple (Gary Gillingham)
V*

A small dog is lost at New York airport and tracks his aged mistress on foot to California.

Basically a revamp of *Lassie Come Home*, with a cute dog and some attractive exteriors, but made unsuitable for its presumably intended family audience by the death of a second dog and a horrific pitchfork sequence in which a heavily pregnant woman is attacked by marauders.

w Sandra K. Bailey, Michael Murphey, Joel Soisson
d Roy Watts   *ph* Jon Kranhouse   *m* George Garvarentz

Lillian Gish, Timothy Bottoms, Candy Clark, Robert Walker, O. J. Simpson, Jack Carter, Alan Hale

Hamburger Hill *
US   1987   110m   Technicolor
Paramount/RKO (Marcia Nasatir, Jim Carabatsos)
V, V*, L

An untried squad goes into action in Vietnam.

One of several Vietnam pics released almost simultaneously; neither the worst nor the best.

w Jim Carabatsos   *d* John Irvin   *ph* Peter MacDonald   *m* Philip Glass   *pd* Austen Spriggs
ed Peter Tanner

Anthony Barrie, Michael Patrick Boatman, Don Cheadle, Michael Dolan, Don James

'Had the filmmakers resisted the temptation to politicise their material they might have made a great war movie. They might also have thought to give us some indication of the strategic significance of the hill. As it is, they've managed to create a deeply affecting, highly accomplished film.' – *Hal Hinson, Washington Post*

Hamlet **
GB   1948   142m   bw
Rank/Two Cities (Laurence Olivier)
V, V*, L

Prince Hamlet takes too long making up his mind to revenge his father's death.

The play is sharply cut, then time is wasted having the camera prowl pointlessly along gloomy corridors . . . but much of the acting is fine, some scenes compel, and the production has a splendid brooding power.

w Alan Dent   *play* William Shakespeare
d Laurence Olivier   *ph* Desmond Dickinson
m William Walton   *pd* Roger Furse   *ad* Carmen Dillon

Laurence Olivier, Eileen Herlie, Basil Sydney, Jean Simmons, Felix Aylmer, Norman Wooland, Terence Morgan, *Stanley Holloway,* Peter Cushing, Esmond Knight, Anthony Quayle, Harcourt Williams, John Laurie, Niall MacGinnis, Patrick Troughton

'Be you 9 or 90, a PhD or just plain Joe, *Hamlet* is the movie of the year.' – *Washington Times*

'By the end one no longer thinks of the piece as filmed Shakespeare, but accepts it simply as a splendid production of a masterpiece.' – *Dilys Powell*

AA: best picture; Laurence Olivier (as actor)

AAN: Laurence Olivier (as director); William Walton; Jean Simmons; art direction

Hamlet *
USSR   1964   150m   bw   Sovscope
Lenfilm

A Russian version of the play, with lowering sets, brooding photography and strong acting.

play William Shakespeare (translation Boris Pasternak)   *d* Grigori Kozintsev   *ph* I. Gritzys
m Dmitri Shostakovich

Innokenti Smoktunovsky, Mikhail Nazvanov, Elsa Radzin, Anastasia Vertinskaya

'An opportunity almost deliberately missed.' – *Basil Wright, 1972*

Hamlet *
GB   1969   119m   Technicolor
Woodfall/Filmways/Columbia (Neil Hartley)
V, V*

A version which has its moments but fails to impress as a whole.

d Tony Richardson

Nicol Williamson, Anthony Hopkins, Gordon Jackson, Judy Parfitt, Marianne Faithfull, Mark Dignam, Roger Livesey

Hamlet *
US   1991   135m   colour
Warner/Nelson Entertainment/Icon (Dyson Lovell)
V, V*, L, S

A son, inspired by his father's ghost, vows to kill his murdering uncle, who has married his mother and usurped the throne of Denmark.

Decent, unadventurous adaptation that does not challenge Olivier's version.

w Christopher de Vore, Franco Zeffirelli
play William Shakespeare   *d* Franco Zeffirelli
ph David Watkin   *m* Ennio Morricone   *pd* Dante Ferretti   *ad* Michael Lamont   *ed* Richard Marden

Mel Gibson, Glenn Close, Alan Bates, Paul Scofield, Ian Holm, Helena Bonham-Carter, Stephen Dillane, Nathaniel Parker, Sean Murray, Michael Maloney, Trevor Peacock, John McEnery

'A generally flat-footed production, an illustrated gloss on the full Shakespearean text.' – *Variety*

'Funny thing is, Hamlet almost is perfect for Gibson, with his neurotic physicality and urgent baritone . . . Zeffirelli goes for the grand. His aim here – nicely realised in a sumptuous production – is to make *Hamlet* so vigorous that the kids will forget it's poetry.' – *Richard Corliss, Time*

AAN: best art direction; best costume design

Hamlet Goes Business **
Finland   1987   86m   bw
Electric/Villealfa Productions/Aki Kaurismäki
original title: *Hamlet Liikemaailmassa*

A son whose father is murdered takes revenge on the killer.

Bizarre and enjoyable modern-day version of Shakespeare's play, which is treated as black comedy and set in the world of business, with company directors attempting to control the rubber duck industry.

wd Aki Kaurismäki   *ph* Tino Salminen
m Shostakovich, Tchaikovsky, Elmore James and others   *ed* Raija Talvio

Pirkka-Pekka Petelius, Esko Salminen, Kati Outinen, Elina Salo, Esko Nikkari, Kari Vaananen, Hannu Valtonen, Mari Rantasila

Hamlet Liikemaailmassa: see *Hamlet Goes Business*

Hammerhead
GB 1968 99m Technicolor
Columbia (Irving Allen)

An American secret agent captures a master criminal.

Jaded James Bond imitation, full of would-be fashionable detail.

w William Best, Herbert Baker *novel* James Mayo *d* David Miller *ph* Kenneth Talbot *m* David Whitaker

Vince Edwards, Peter Vaughan, Judy Geeson, Diana Dors, Michael Bates, Beverly Adams, Patrick Cargill, Patrick Holt

Hammersmith Is Out *
US 1972 114m DuArt Color
Cinerama/J. Cornelius Cream (Alex Lucas)
V*

With the help of a male nurse, a homicidal mental inmate escapes and becomes the most influential man in the country.

Pretentious updating of Faust into a kind of black farce that seldom amuses but is interesting in fits and starts.

w Stanford Whitmore *d* Peter Ustinov *ph* Richard Kline *m* Dominic Frontière

Richard Burton, Elizabeth Taylor, Peter Ustinov, Beau Bridges, Leon Ames, John Schuck, George Raft

Hammett *
US 1982 97m Technicolor
Orion/Zoetrope (Francis Coppola)
V*

San Francisco 1928: Dashiell Hammett is asked to locate a missing Chinese girl and gets involved in sinister goings-on which provide the basis for another mystery book.

Careful and interesting crime thriller in which, however, the rather pretentious framework is largely irrelevant, leaving a detective story slightly off-beat in treatment but otherwise indistinguishable from many others.

w Ross Thomas, Dennis O'Flaherty *novel* Joe Gores *d* Wim Wenders *ph* Philip Lathrop, Joseph Biroc *m* John Barry *pd* Dean Tavoularis, Eugene Lee *ed* Barry Malkin, Marc Laub, Robert Q. Lovett, Randy Roberts

Frederic Forrest, Peter Boyle, Marilu Henner, Roy Kinnear, Elisha Cook Jnr, R. G. Armstrong, Richard Bradford, Sylvia Sidney, Royal Dano, Samuel Fuller

'A symbolic liquidation by Wenders of the massive, but ambivalent patrimony of the American cinematic and cultural tradition that has increasingly dominated his work.' – *Sheila Johnston, MFB*

† The film was actually in pre-production from 1975, though shooting did not begin until 1980. This version was abandoned in rough cut and two-thirds of it was shot again in 1981 with a different crew. Sylvia Miles and Brian Keith were in the first version and not the second.

The Hammond Mystery: see *The Undying Monster*

Hamnstad: see *Port of Call*

The Hand
GB 1960 60m bw
Bill and Michael Luckwell/Butcher's
V*

When an old man has his hand severed and is

subsequently murdered, the trail leads to a doctor who subsequently commits suicide.

Confused second feature which seems to have been badly edited but might otherwise have been quite entertaining.

w Ray Cooney, Tony Hilton *d* Henry Cass

Derek Bond, Ronald Leigh-Hunt, Reed de Rouen, Ray Cooney, Harold Scott

The Hand
US 1981 104m Technicolor
Warner/Orion (Edward R. Pressman)
V*

A cartoonist loses his hand, which takes on a life of its own to wreak vengeance on his enemies.

Pale imitation of *The Beast with Five Fingers*, which wasn't all that good to begin with.

wd Oliver Stone *novel* The Lizard's Tail by Oliver Stone *ph* King Baggot *m* James Horner *pd* John Michael Riva *sp* Carlo Rambaldi *ed* Richard Marks

Michael Caine, Andrea Marcovicci, Viveca Lindfors, Rosemary Murphy, Bruce McGill

Hand in Hand *
GB 1960 80m bw
ABP (Helen Winston)

The friendship of two 7-year-olds is affected by racial prejudice because one is Catholic and the other Jewish; but after misunderstandings their friendship is confirmed by priest and rabbi.

Pleasant, well-meaning drama apparently intended for older children.

w Diana Morgan *d* Philip Leacock *ph* Frederick A. Young *m* Stanley Black

Lorette Parry, Phillip Needs, Sybil Thorndike, John Gregson, Finlay Currie

The Hand of Night
GB 1966 73m Technicolor
Associated British Pathé (Harry Field)
US title: *Beast of Morocco*

In order to recover from the death of his wife and children, an architect holidays in Morocco, where a vampire princess sets out to seduce him.

A psychological horror film, long on talk and short on action.

w Bruce Stewart *d* Frederic Goode *ph* William Jordan *m* Joan Shakespeare *ad* Peter Moll *ed* Frederick Ives

William Sylvester, Diane Clare, William Dexter, Alizia Gur, Edward Underdown, Terence de Marney

'Relies heavily on old Hammer production tricks without contributing any original variations of its own.' – *MFB*

The Hand that Rocks the Cradle *
US 1991 110m Alpha Cine
Buena Vista/Hollywood Pictures/Interscope/Nomura, Babcock & Brown (David Madden)
V, V*, L, S

After her husband's suicide and her miscarriage, a woman becomes nanny to the family she blames for her misfortunes.

A predictable thriller that just manages to hold an audience's interest.

w Amanda Silver *d* Curtis Hanson *ph* Robert Elswit *m* Graeme Revell *pd* Edward Pisoni *ed* John F. Link

Annabella Sciorra, Rebecca de Mornay, Matt McCoy, Ernie Hudson, Julianne Moore, Madeline Zima, John de Lancie, Kevin Skousen

'Diagrammatic script channels the action in a predictable direction toward an inevitable climax, but fine performances and a refusal to pander to the

audience's grosser instincts raise this a notch or two above the norm.' – *Variety*

'A rabble-rousing hit, and so adept is the movie at exploiting the sinister potential in ordinary domestic surroundings.' – *Gary Arnold, Washington Times*

A Handful of Clouds: see *Doorway to Hell*

A Handful of Dust **
GB 1988 118m colour
Premier (Derek Granger)
V, V*

An aristocratic wife, frustrated by the old-fashioned habits of her stately home-owning husband, begins an affair with a young man-about-town.

Glossy production, impeccably acted, although it loses some of the satire of the original.

w Charles Sturridge, Tim Sullivan, Derek Granger *novel* Evelyn Waugh *d* Charles Sturridge *ph* Peter Hannan *m* George Fenton *pd* Eileen Diss *ed* Peter Coulson

James Wilby, Kristin Scott Thomas, Rupert Graves, Anjelica Huston, Judi Dench, Alec Guinness, Stephen Fry, Graham Crowden

AAN: best costume design (Jane Robinson)

Handgun *
US 1982 101m DuArt
EMI/Kestrel (Tony Garnett)
V*

A schoolmistress, raped at gunpoint, takes her revenge.

Novel, feminist revenge drama with a neat twist at the end.

wd Tony Garnett *ph* Charles Stewart *m* Mike Post *pd* Lilly Kilvert

Karen Young, Clayton Day, Suzie Humphreys, Helena Humann

Handle with Care *
US 1958 82m bw
MGM (Morton Fine)

Small-town college students stage a mock trial and come up with some embarrassing answers.

Interesting melodrama with a disappointing ending; a well done second feature.

w Morton Fine, David Friedkin *d* David Friedkin *ph* Harold J. Marzorati *m* Alexander Courage

Dean Jones, Joan O'Brien, Thomas Mitchell, Walter Abel, John Smith

Handle with Care *
US 1977 98m colour
Paramount (Paul Brickman)
aka: *Citizens Band*

An enthusiast of Citizen's Band radio tries to prevent it being abused in his home town.

Lively and often sharp comedy, but one that failed to find an audience at the time.

w Paul Brickman *d* Jonathan Demme *ph* Jordan Cronenweth *m* Bill Conti *pd* Bill Malley *ed* John F. Link II

Paul LeMat, Candy Clark, Ann Wedgeworth, Bruce McGill, Marcia Rodd, Charles Napier, Alix Elias, Roberts Blossom, Ed Begley Jnr

'A palmy, elegantly deadpan comedy; the jokes aren't pushed, so it takes viewers a few minutes to settle into the comic style, which has the mellow, light touch of thirties Renoir.' – *Pauline Kael, New Yorker*

'For once, the intelligentsia are right about an American genre film; this one is worth serious consideration.' – *Richard Schickel, Time*

The Handmaid's Tale

US/Germany 1990 109m colour
Virgin/Cinecom/Bioskop Film (Daniel Wilson)
V, V*, L, S

In the near future, a woman revolts against her role as child-bearer for the controlling elite.

Barren feminist fantasy.

w Harold Pinter novel Margaret Atwood d Volker Schlondorff ph Igor Luther m Ryuichi Sakamoto pd Tom Walsh ed David Ray

Natasha Richardson, Robert Duvall, Faye Dunaway, Aidan Quinn, Elizabeth McGovern, Victoria Tennant, Blanche Baker, Traci Lind, David Dukes

Hands across the Table *

US 1935 81m bw
Paramount (E. Lloyd Sheldon)

A manicurist determines to marry a rich man.

Lively romantic comedy, smoothly made and typical of its time.

w Norman Krasna, Vincent Lawrence, Herbert Fields d Mitchell Leisen ph Ted Tetzlaff m Sam Coslow, Frederick Hollander

Carole Lombard, Fred MacMurray, Ralph Bellamy, Astrid Allwyn, Ruth Donnelly, Marie Prévost, William Demarest, Ed Gargan

'Snappy comedy that should satisfy all over.' – Variety

'A happy mixture of brainwork and horseplay and a reminder that when intelligence goes for a walk among even the oldest props, the props may come to life.' – Otis Ferguson

† Ray Milland was originally cast, but bowed out saying that he couldn't play comedy.

The Hands of Orlac (1935): see Mad Love

The Hands of Orlac

GB/France 1960 105m bw
Riviera/Pendennis (Steven Pallos, Don Taylor)
V*

A concert pianist's hands are crushed in an accident, and a mad surgeon grafts on those of an executed murderer.

Flatulent remake of the 1926 German silent and the 1935 American Mad Love. Stilted, hammy, threadbare and overlong.

w John Baines, Edmond T. Gréville novel Maurice Renard d Edmond T. Gréville ph Desmond Dickinson m Claude Bolling

Mel Ferrer, Donald Wolfit, Christopher Lee, Dany Carel, Felix Aylmer, Basil Sydney, Donald Pleasence

Hands of the Ripper

GB 1971 85m Technicolor
Rank/Hammer (Aida Young)
V, V*

Jack the Ripper stabs his wife to death in view of his small daughter, who grows up a sexually repressed murderess.

Gory Hammer horror with well done scenes.

w L. W. Davidson story Edward Spencer Shew d Peter Sasdy ph Kenneth Talbot m Christopher Gunning ad Roy Stannard ed Christopher Barnes

Angharad Rees, Eric Porter, Dora Bryan, Jane Merrow, Derek Godfrey

Hands off the Loot: see Touchez pas au Grisbi

Hands over the City

Italy 1963 105m bw Galatea
original title: Le Mani sulla Città

A property tycoon wangles local politicians so that he gets development on the property he controls.

An angry political film which is too strident to have much entertainment value.

w Enzo Provencale, Enzo Forcella, Raffaele La Capria, Francesco Rosi d Francesco Rosi ph Gianni di Venanzo m Piero Piccioni

Rod Steiger, Salvo Randone, and non-professionals

Hands Up *

US 1926 65m (24 fps) bw silent
Paramount

General Lee assigns a spy to prevent a Union man from getting his hands on a gold cache.

Pleasant Civil War comedy with a curious Mormon happy ending.

w Monty Brice, Lloyd Corrigan d Clarence Badger

Raymond Griffith, Marion Nixon, Virginia Lee Corbin, Mack Swain, Montagu Love

Handsome Antonio: see Il Bell'Antonio

Handy Andy

US 1934 82m bw
Fox

A midwestern druggist is married to a snob.

Competent star vehicle overflowing with crackerbarrel philosophy.

w William Conselman, Henry Johnson play Merry Andrew by Lewis Beach d David Butler ph Arthur Miller

Will Rogers, Peggy Wood, Conchita Montenegro, Mary Carlisle, Roger Imhof, Robert Taylor (his first film), Paul Harvey

'They made two mistakes – they hanged the wrong man, and they didn't finish the job!'

Hang 'em High

US 1967 114m DeLuxe
UA/Malpaso/Leonard Freeman
V, L, S

A cowboy is rescued from lynching and takes revenge on his persecutors.

Hollywood's first attempt to imitate the gore and brutality of spaghetti Westerns and to take back its own errant star. Emetic and interminable.

w Leonard Freeman, Mel Goldberg d Ted Post ph Leonard South, Richard Kline m Dominic Frontière

Clint Eastwood, Inger Stevens, Ed Begley, Pat Hingle, James MacArthur, Arlene Golonka, Charles McGraw, Ben Johnson, L. Q. Jones

Hangar 18

US 1980 97m Technicolor
Sunn Classic

A UFO crashlands and is cared for in secret by the American government.

A cinematic equivalent to the yellow press, supposing villainous behaviour by all concerned but eager only to provide low grade thriller entertainment.

w Steven Thornley d James L. Conway

Darren McGavin, Robert Vaughn, Gary Collins, Philip Abbott

Hanged Man's Farm: see La Ferme du Pendu

'It's gonna be one hell of a night.'

Hangin' with the Homeboys **

US 1991 89m Metrocolor
Palace/New Line (Richard Brick)
V, V*, L, S

In the Bronx, four youths get together for an eventful night out on the town and end up in the unfamiliar surroundings of Manhattan.

Acute and humorous portrait of the immature discovering the beginnings of maturity and self-knowledge.

wd Joseph B. Vasquez ph Anghel Decca ad Isabel Bau Madden ed Michael Schweitzer

Doug E. Doug, Mario Joyner, John Leguizamo, Nestor Serrano, Kimberly Russell, Mary B. Ward, Reggie Montgomery, Christine Claravall, Rosemary Jackson

'The performances here are hip, funny and smart, the situations embarrassingly recognizable and the pace energetic and assured.' —Angie Errigo, Empire

The Hanging Tree *

US 1959 106m Technicolor
Warner/Baroda (Martin Jurow, Richard Shepherd)
V*

Life is tough in a Montana gold-mining camp, especially for a doctor who has killed his unfaithful wife.

Lowering Western with a feeling for place and period, plus a welter of melodramatic incident.

w Wendell Mayes, Halstead Welles novel Dorothy M. Johnson d Delmer Daves ph Ted McCord m Max Steiner

Gary Cooper, Maria Schell, Karl Malden, Ben Piazza, George C. Scott

AAN: title song (m Jerry Livingston, ly Mack David)

The Hangman

US 1959 86m bw
Paramount (Frank Freeman Jnr)

A marshal with a reputation for getting his man deliberately allows one to escape.

Dour, low-key Western, competent but rather flat and uninteresting.

w Dudley Nichols d Michael Curtiz ph Loyal Griggs m Harry Sukman

Robert Taylor, Jack Lord, Fess Parker, Tina Louise, Mickey Shaughnessy

Hangman's House

US 1928 72m (24 fps) bw silent
Fox

To please her dying father, an Irish girl marries a wastrel instead of the man she loves, but her husband is killed in a duel.

Blarney-filled melodrama, like a sober Quiet Man. John Wayne can be glimpsed as an extra.

w Marion Orth story Don Byrne d John Ford ph George Schneiderman

June Collyer, Larry Kent, Earle Foxe, Victor McLaglen, Hobart Bosworth

Hangman's Knot

US 1952 81m Technicolor
Columbia (Harry Joe Brown)
V*

Confederate soldiers returning home with Union booty are waylaid at a way station by renegades.

Adequate suspense Western.

wd Roy Huggins

Randolph Scott, Donna Reed, Claude Jarman Jnr, Frank Faylen, Glenn Langan, Richard Denning, Lee Marvin, Jeanette Nolan

Hangmen Also Die *

US 1943 131m bw
Arnold Pressburger/Fritz Lang (T. W. Baumfield)
reissue title: Lest We Forget

The Nazis take revenge for the killing of Heydrich.

Disappointingly heavy-handed, though deeply felt war propaganda set in Hollywood's idea of Czechoslovakia. Only moments of interest remain.

w John Wexley   *story* Fritz Lang, Bertolt Brecht
d *Fritz Lang*   *ph* *James Wong Howe*   *m* Hanns Eisler

Brian Donlevy, Anna Lee, Walter Brennan, Gene
Lockhart, Dennis O'Keefe, Alexander Granach,
Margaret Wycherly, Nana Bryant, Hans von
Twardowski (as Heydrich), Jonathan Hale, Lionel
Stander

'Lang, working with American actors on an American
theme, has produced *Fury*. Lang trying to recreate his
own Central Europe on a Hollywood set is completely
at sea.' – *Paul Rotha, 1949*

'Directed with a skill which excites and delights . . .
brilliant use of the tiny, shocking detail.' – *Dilys Powell*

'They have chosen to use brutality, American gangster
idiom, and middle high German cinematic style to get
it across, and it is rich with clever melodrama, over-
maestoso directional touches, and the sort of
Querschnitt sophistication for detail which Lang
always has.' – *James Agee*

† Working titles included *The Silent City* and *Never
Surrender*.

AAN: Hanns Eisler

Hangover Square *
US   1945   77m   bw
TCF (Robert Bassler)

In 1903 London, a psychopathic composer murders
pretty women.

This rather empty melodrama has almost nothing to
do with the book from which it is allegedly taken, but
the Hollywoodian evocation of gaslit London is richly
entertaining and good to look at.

w Barre Lyndon   *novel* Patrick Hamilton   *d* John
Brahm   *ph* Joseph LaShelle   *m* Bernard Herrmann
ad Lyle Wheeler, Maurice Ransford

Laird Cregar, Linda Darnell, George Sanders, Glenn
Langan, Faye Marlowe, Alan Napier, Frederick
Worlock

'Cregar lumbers around with a Karloffian glare in the
spacious mists which happily blur the architectural
decor.' – *Richard Winnington*

'Distinguished photography gets the last glint of fancy
fright out of the pomps and vanities of the turn of the
century.' – *Time*

'A half-chewed collection of reminiscences of *Dr Jekyll
and Mr Hyde* and *The Lodger*.' – *Richard Mallett, Punch*

'The worst betrayal of a first class novel that I can
remember.' – *James Agate*

'A better than average horror picture up to, but not
including, its wildly overloaded climax.' – *James Agee*

† Tragically, Laird Cregar died after slimming for this
role, to which he was in any case unsuited.

Hanky Panky
US   1982   107m   Metrocolor
Columbia (Martin Ransohoff)
V*, L

A girl on a spy mission is pursued by assassins and
enlists the reluctant aid of an architect she meets in a
taxi.

Frantic spoof of *North by Northwest*, which was itself as
spoofy as all get out. This strained effort lacks wit,
substituting shouting, violence and an exasperating
hero.

w Henry Rosenbaum, David Taylor   *d* Sidney
Poitier   *ph* Arthur Ornitz   *m* Tom Scott   *pd* Ben
Edwards   *ed* Harry Keller

Gene Wilder, Gilda Radner, Kathleen Quinlan,
Richard Widmark

'The plot, rather like Mr Wilder, rushes hither and
yon at the slightest excuse without ever adding up to
very much. Even McGuffins are supposed to make
more sense than this.' – *Richard Combs, MFB*

'A comedy thriller designed solely as a vehicle for
Wilder's uninhibited hysteria is bad enough; one that
so thoroughly submerges everyone else is so much
worse.' – *Sight and Sound*

'One long screech.' – *Ibid.*

Hannah and Her Sisters ***
US   1986   106m   Technicolor
Orion/Charles R. Joffe, Jack Rollins (Robert Greenhut)
V, V*, L

Relationships intermingle for a New York family over
a two-year period between Thanksgiving dinners.

Even though it has nowhere in particular to go, and
certain scenes are over the top, this is a brilliantly
assembled and thoroughly enjoyable mélange of fine
acting and New Yorkish one-liners, with particularly
sharp editing and a nostalgic music score.

wd Woody Allen   *ph* Carlo di Palma   *m* popular and
classical extracts   *pd* Stuart Wurtzel   *ed* Susan E.
Morse

Woody Allen, Mia Farrow, Dianne Wiest, Michael Caine,
Carrie Fisher, Barbara Hershey, Maureen O'Sullivan,
Lloyd Nolan, Max von Sydow, Daniel Stern, Sam
Waterston, Tony Roberts

'A loosely knit canvas of Manhattan interiors and
exteriors.' – *Sight and Sound*

'One of Woody Allen's great films.' – *Variety*

AA: best original screenplay; Dianne Wiest; Michael
Caine

AAN: best picture; Woody Allen (as director); Susan
E. Morse; art direction

Hanna's War
US   1988   148m   colour
Cannon (Menahem Golan, Yoram Globus)
V*, L

A Jewish poetess, working for the British secret
service, is parachuted into Yugoslavia, captured and,
after being taken to Budapest, is tortured and
executed.

A true and tragic story diminished by its clumsy
telling.

wd Menahem Golan   *books* The Diaries of Hanna
Senesh by Hanna Senesh; A Great Wind Cometh by Yoel
Palgi   *ph* Elemer Ragalyi   *m* Dov Seltzer   *pd* Kuli
Sander   *ed* Alain Jakubowicz

Ellen Burstyn, Maruschka Detmers, Anthony
Andrews, Donald Pleasence, David Warner, Vincenzo
Ricotta, Christopher Fairbank

Hannibal
Italy   1959   103m   Technicolor   Supercinescope
Liber Film (Ottavio Poggi)

Hannibal crosses the Alps and falls for the daughter of
a Roman senator.

Unhistorical farrago which totally fails to entertain on
any level.

w Mortimer Braus   *d* Carlo Ludovico Bragaglia,
Edgar G. Ulmer   *ph* Raffaele Masciocchi   *m* Carlo
Rustichelli

Victor Mature, Rita Gam, Gabriele Ferzetti, Milly
Vitale, Rik Battaglia

'Not even the elephants emerge with dignity.' – *MFB*

Hannibal Brooks
GB   1968   102m   DeLuxe
UA/Scimitar (Michael Winner)

A British POW in Germany escapes over the Alps
with an elephant.

Curious action adventure which seems undecided
whether to take itself seriously. Some passable
sequences.

w Dick Clement, Ian La Frenais   *d* Michael Winner
ph Robert Paynter   *m* Francis Lai

Oliver Reed, Michael J. Pollard, Wolfgang Preiss,
Karen Baal

Hannie Caulder
GB   1971   85m   colour   Panavision
Tigon/Curtwel (Tony Tenser)
V*

Raped by three outlaws who murdered her husband,
a Western woman takes revenge.

Unintentionally comical action melodrama with the
star defeating all comers.

w Z. X. Jones (Burt Kennedy, David Haft)   *d* Burt
Kennedy   *ph* Ted Scaife   *m* Ken Thorne

Raquel Welch, Robert Culp, Ernest Borgnine, Strother
Martin, Jack Elam, Christopher Lee, Diana Dors

Hanover Street
GB   1979   108m   Technicolor   Panavision
Columbia (Paul N. Lazarus III)
V

In 1943, an American bomber pilot meets a Red Cross
nurse in a bus queue.

Wartime romance of a rather sticky sort, which turns
with little warning into escape adventure, with our
hero rescuing his loved one's husband from certain
death.

wd Peter Hyams   *ph* David Watkin   *m* John Barry
pd Philip Harrison

Harrison Ford, Lesley-Anne Down, Christopher
Plummer, Alec McCowen, Richard Masur, Michael
Sacks, Max Wall

Hans Christian Andersen *
US   1952   112m   Technicolor
Samuel Goldwyn
V*, L

A storytelling cobbler leaves his village to make shoes
for the prima ballerina in Copenhagen.

Artificial, sugary confection with little humour and far
too little magic of any kind; the star carries it nicely,
but he is on his own apart from the songs.

w Moss Hart   *d* Charles Vidor   *ph* Harry Stradling
md Walter Scharf   *m/ly* Frank Loesser   *ad* Richard Day
ch Roland Petit

Danny Kaye, Zizi Jeanmaire, Farley Granger, John
Qualen, Joey Walsh

'I found it such a charming entertainment, full of
happiness and pathos, expert in interpretation yet
swinging along with a gay holiday spirit that, when it
was all over, I wanted to sit still for a minute and
think about it, and then go away and sing its praises.'
– *C. A. Lejeune*

† 16 screenplays were written before this one was
chosen. Moira Shearer was signed for the role of
ballerina but became pregnant. Gary Cooper was
thought of for the lead, with William Wyler as
director.

AAN: Harry Stradling; Walter Scharf; song
'Thumbelina'

Hanussen *
Hungary/West Germany   1988   117m   Eastmancolor
Columbia TriStar/Objektiv/Mafilm/CCC Filmkunst/ZDF (Arthur
Brauner)
V, V*, L

An Austrian clairvoyant's predictions are used as Nazi
propaganda.

Unusual, if somewhat insubstantial, political drama.

w István Szabó, Péter Dobai   *d* István Szabó
ph Lajos Koltai   *m* György Vukan   *ed* Zsuzsa
Csákány, Eva Szentandrási, Brigitta Kajdácsi, Bettina
Rekuc

Klaus Maria Brandauer, Erland Josephson, Ildikó
Bánsági, Walter Schmidinger, Károly Eperjes

AAN: best foreign film

The Happening

US 1967 101m Technicolor
Columbia/Horizon/Dover (Jud Kinberg)

Four young hippies kidnap a wealthy businessman and don't know what to do with him; he turns the tables.

Freewheeling irresponsible comedy which even at the time of swinging cities seemed very irritating.

w Frank R. Pierson, James D. Buchanan, Ronald Austin d Eliot Silverstein ph Philip Lathrop m Frank de Vol pd Richard Day

Anthony Quinn, George Maharis, Michael Parks, Faye Dunaway, Robert Walker, Oscar Homolka, Martha Hyer, Milton Berle, Jack Kruschen

'A wacky comedy à la mode, oddly mixed and only spasmodically effective.' – Variety

Happidrome

GB 1943 87m bw
Aldwych

A play intended seriously becomes a comedy hit.

A theme later used by The Producers forms the background for this naïve screen version of a wartime radio series.

w Tom Arnold, James Seymour d Phil Brandon

Harry Korris, Robbie Vincent, Cecil Frederick, Bunty Meadows, Lisa Lee, 'Hutch', the Cairoli Brothers

The Happiest Days of Your Life ***

GB 1950 81m bw
British Lion/Individual (Frank Launder)
V

A ministry mistake billets a girls' school on a boys' school.

Briskly handled version of a semi-classic postwar farce, with many familiar talents in excellent form.

w Frank Launder, John Dighton play John Dighton d Frank Launder ph Stan Pavey m Mischa Spoliansky

Alastair Sim, Margaret Rutherford, Joyce Grenfell, Richard Wattis, Edward Rigby, Guy Middleton, Muriel Aked, John Bentley, Bernadette O'Farrell

'Absolutely first rate fun.' – Richard Mallett, Punch

'Launder couldn't have knocked another laugh out of the situation if he'd used a hockey stick.' – Sunday Express

'The best mixed comedy pairing since Groucho Marx and Margaret Dumont.' – Sunday Chronicle

The Happiest Millionaire

US 1967 159m Technicolor
Walt Disney (Bill Anderson)
V*

In 1916, a sporting millionaire has several surprising interests but finds time to sort out family problems.

Drearily inept family entertainment with a couple of good songs and an amusing alligator sequence but acres of yawning boredom in between.

w A. J. Carothers play Kyle Crichton book My Philadelphia Father by Cornelia Drexel Biddle d Norman Tokar ph Edward Colman md Jack Elliott m/ly Richard M. and Robert B. Sherman

Fred MacMurray, Tommy Steele, Greer Garson, John Davidson, Gladys Cooper, Lesley Anne Warren, Geraldine Page, Hermione Baddeley

Happiness Ahead

US 1934 80m bw
First National

A rich girl finds her true love in a singing window cleaner.

Not anybody's idea of a big attraction, but it passed the time for small towns.

w Ralph Spence, Philip Dunne d Mervyn Le Roy

Dick Powell, Josephine Hutchinson, John Halliday, Dorothy Dare, Frank McHugh, Allen Jenkins, Ruth Donnelly

'Pleasant comedy, bound to amuse.' – Variety

The Happiness of Three Women

GB 1954 78m bw
Advance

A village postman and busybody adopts various subterfuges to improve the future happiness of his clients.

Minor Welsh waffle which pleased naïve audiences at the time.

w Eynon Evans play Wishing Well by Eynon Evans d Maurice Elvey

Brenda de Banzie, Eynon Evans, Petula Clark, Donald Houston, Patricia Burke, Patricia Cutts

Happy Anniversary

US 1959 83m bw
UA/Ralph Fields

A television set causes family trouble.

Marital farce designed to take a few sideswipes at TV.

w Joseph Fields, Jerome Chodorov play Anniversary Waltz by Joseph Fields, Jerome Chodorov d David Miller ph Lee Garmes m Sol Kaplan, Robert Allan

David Niven, Mitzi Gaynor, Carl Reiner, Loring Smith, Patty Duke, Phyllis Povah

Happy Anniversary *

France 1961 13m bw
Capac

A husband is late for his anniversary dinner because of a traffic jam.

Amusing gag comedy, virtually silent and all the better for it.

wd Pierre Etaix

Pierre Etaix, Loriot, Nono Zammit

Happy Birthday to Me

Canada 1980 111m Metrocolor
Birthday/CFDC/Famous Players (John Dunning, Andre Link)
V*, L

Members of the senior class at Crawford Academy are killed off one at a time by one of their number.

Abysmal teenage shocker which grinds on relentlessly for nearly two hours.

w Timothy Bond, Peter Jobin, John Saxton d J. Lee-Thompson ph Miklos Lente m Bo Harwood, Lance Rubin

Melissa Sue Anderson, Glenn Ford, Laurence Dane, Sharon Acker, Frances Hyland

Happy Birthday Wanda June *

US 1971 105m Technicolor
Columbia (Lester Goldsmith)

An adventurer believed dead returns just as his wife is about to choose one of two suitors.

A farcical situation becomes in this writer's hands an investigation of the hero cult, with many zany jokes, episodes in heaven, and bad language. Interesting in spots, but it would have worked better with a more fluent cinematic technique.

w Kurt Vonnegut Jnr play Kurt Vonnegut Jnr d Mark Robson ph Fred J. Koenekamp

Rod Steiger, Susannah York, George Grizzard, Don Murray

'We can only assume that Mr Robson deserted the filmic instincts that brought him commercial success because here he was, finally, in the presence of Art.' – Hollis Alpert

'Nothing more than a miscast film record of the dialogue and plot outline of the stage work.' – Judith Crist

Happy Days

US 1930 86m bw Grandeur
Fox

A showboat singer is a hit in New York and helps her old friends.

Virtually a revue, with spectacular effects on the giant screen.

w Sidney Lanfield, Edwin Burke d Benjamin Stoloff ph Lucien Andriot and others m Hugo Friedhofer m/ly various

Marjorie White; and Janet Gaynor, Charles Farrell, Victor McLaglen, Edmund Lowe, El Brendel, Walter Catlett, James J. Corbett, Tom Patricola, Dixie Lee, Sharon Lynn, Whispering Jack Smith

'We don't love. We just make love. And damn little of that!'

The Happy Ending *

US 1969 112m Technicolor Panavision
UA/Pax Films (Richard Brooks)
V*

A middle-aged woman reflects over sixteen years of unhappy marriage.

Sometimes glib, sometimes trenchant sophisticated drama with enough interesting scenes to make it more than merely a 'woman's picture'.

wd Richard Brooks ph Conrad Hall m Michel Legrand

Jean Simmons, John Forsythe, Shirley Jones, Lloyd Bridges, Teresa Wright, Dick Shawn, Nanette Fabray, Bobby Darin, Tina Louise

'Packed with punchy little epigrams floating in a vacuum of glossy superficiality.' – David Wilson

'The truth about the process of ageing is what binds this film together like cement.' – Alexander Walker

AAN: Jean Simmons; song 'What Are You Doing the Rest of Your Life' (m Michel Legrand, ly Alan and Marilyn Bergman)

Happy Ever After

GB/Germany 1932 86m bw
UFA (Erich Pommer)

Window-cleaners put a young actress on the way to stardom.

Cheerful comedy, set and made in Germany by mainly British talent.

w Jack Hulbert, Douglas Furber story Walter Reisch, Billy Wilder d Paul Martin, Robert Stevenson

Lilian Harvey, Jack Hulbert, Cicely Courtneidge, Sonnie Hale, Edward Chapman

Happy Ever After *

GB 1954 87m Technicolor
ABP/Mario Zampi
V
US title: Tonight's the Night

Irish villagers draw lots for the privilege of murdering their rascally squire.

Fairly hilarious black comedy with a good cast entering into the spirit of the thing.

w Jack Davies, Michael Pertwee, L. A. G. Strong d Mario Zampi ph Stan Pavey m Stanley Black

David Niven, Yvonne de Carlo, A. E. Matthews, Michael Shepley, George Cole, Barry Fitzgerald

Happy Family (1934): see The Merry Frinks

The Happy Family

GB 1952 86m bw
London Independent
US title: Mr Lord Says No

A shopkeeper refuses to move and provide a site for the Festival of Britain.

Pale Ealing imitation with amiable cast.

w Muriel and Sydney Box play Michael Clayton Hutton d Muriel Box

Stanley Holloway, Kathleen Harrison, Naunton Wayne, George Cole, Dandy Nichols, Miles Malleson

Happy Go Lovely

GB 1950 97m Technicolor
Excelsior (Marcel Hellman)
V*

A chorus girl meets a millionaire during the Edinburgh Festival.

For a semi-official contribution to the Festival of Britain this is a lamentably unspontaneous musical with no use of cinema techniques or natural locales. Even allowing for the flat handling, it is tedious.

w Val Guest d Bruce Humberstone ph Erwin Hillier m Mischa Spoliansky

David Niven, Vera-Ellen, Cesar Romero, Bobby Howes, Diane Hart, Gordon Jackson, Barbara Couper, Gladys Henson, Joyce Carey

† A remake of Paradise for Two.

Happy Go Lucky

US 1937 69m bw
Nat Levine/Republic

A musical comedy singer is mistaken for an aviator and kidnapped.

Thin vehicle for a star who didn't last.

w Raymond Schrock, Olive Cooper and others d Aubrey Scotto

Phil Regan, Evelyn Venable, Jed Prouty, William Newell

Happy Go Lucky

US 1942 81m Technicolor
Paramount (Harold Wilson)

A cigarette girl chases a millionaire to a Caribbean island.

Flimsy musical for those who like the stars.

w Walter de Leon, Melvin Frank, Norman Panama d Curtis Bernhardt ph Karl Struss, Wilfrid Cline m/ly Frank Loesser, Jimmy McHugh

Mary Martin, Dick Powell, Betty Hutton (singing 'Murder He Says'), Rudy Vallee, Eddie Bracken, Mabel Paige, Eric Blore, Clem Bevans

Happy Gypsies *

Yugoslavia 1967 90m Eastmancolor
Avala
US title: I Even Met Happy Gypsies

A handsome, cruel-natured gypsy and his wife have violent adventures and find themselves on the run from the police.

The first film in the gypsy language does not make one too sympathetic to their cause, but some scenes are well managed and the colour is fine.

wd Alexander Petrovic ph Tomislav Pinter m gypsy melodies

Bekim Fehmiu, Olivera Vuco, Bata Zivojinovic

AAN: best foreign film

The Happy Hooker

US 1975 98m Movielab
Double H/Cannon-Happy (Fred Caruso)
V*, L

A Dutch girl in New York starts a career as a prostitute and finds she enjoys it.

Glum sex comedy based on the supposed exploits of a real madam; crude and not very funny. If this is emancipation, Shirley Temple seems more attractive by the minute.

w William Richert book Xaviera Hollander d Nicholas Sgarro ph Dick Kratina m Don Elliott

Lynn Redgrave (hilariously miscast), Jean-Pierre Aumont, Lovelady Powell, Nicholas Pryor, Elizabeth Wilson, Tom Poston, Conrad Janis, Richard Lynch

† Follow-ups: The Happy Hooker Goes to Washington (1977), The Happy Hooker Goes to Hollywood (1980).

Happy Is the Bride *

GB 1957 84m bw
Panther/Paul Soskin

A couple planning a quiet summer wedding reckon without the intervention of her parents.

Tame remake of Quiet Wedding; the right spirit but not much sparkle.

w Jeffrey Dell, Roy Boulting play Esther McCracken d Roy Boulting ph Ted Scaife m Benjamin Frankel

Ian Carmichael, Janette Scott, Cecil Parker, Joyce Grenfell, Terry-Thomas, John Le Mesurier, Eric Barker, Edith Sharpe, Athene Seyler

Happy Land *

US 1943 75m bw
TCF (Kenneth MacGowan)

Grandfather's ghost comes back to comfort a family which has lost its son at war.

Sentimental flagwaver very typical of its time; well made, it ensured not a dry eye in the house.

w Kathryn Scola, Julien Josephson novel Mackinlay Kantor d Irving Pichel ph Joseph LaShelle m Cyril Mockridge

Don Ameche, Frances Dee, Harry Carey, Ann Rutherford, Cara Williams, Henry Morgan, Richard Crane, Dickie Moore

Happy Landing (1931): see Flying High

Happy Landing *

US 1938 102m bw
TCF (David Hempstead)

A Norwegian girl falls for an American flyer who crashes near her home.

Lightweight skating musical, well put together.

w Milton Sperling, Boris Ingster d Roy del Ruth ph John Mescall md Louis Silvers

Sonja Henie, Don Ameche, Cesar Romero, Ethel Merman, Jean Hersholt, Billy Gilbert, Wally Vernon, El Brendel

'Just about everything to ensure entertainment value, shrewdly blended.' – Variety

Happy New Year *

France/Italy 1973 115m Eastmancolor
Films 13/Rizzoli (Claude Lelouch)
V*
original title: La Bonne Année

A thief is paroled on New Year's Eve in the hope that he will lead police to his confederates. In fact he learns a lot about the world and himself.

Bitter comedy apparently intended to distance the director from the romantic fervour of A Man and a Woman, a clip from which is screened for the convicts at the beginning.

wd/ph Claude Lelouch m Francis Lai

Lino Ventura, Françoise Fabian, Charles Gérard, André Falcon

Happy New Year *

US 1987 85m DeLuxe
Columbia/Delphi IV (Jerry Weintraub)

Two middle-aged jewel thieves head for a big score in Florida.

Loose remake of Lelouch's La Bonne Année, quite watchable in its familiar way.

w Warren Lane d John G. Avildsen ph James Crabe m Bill Conti pd William J. Cassidy ed Jane Kuson

Peter Falk, Charles Durning, Wendy Hughes, Tom Courtney, John Copeland

The Happy Road *

US/France 1956 100m bw
MGM/Thor (Gene Kelly)

Two children run away from a Swiss school and are pursued by the American father of one of them.

Whimsical peripatetic comedy which fails to come off despite charming passages.

w Arthur Julian, Joseph Morhaim, Harry Kurnitz d Gene Kelly ph Robert Juillard m George Van Parys

Gene Kelly, Barbara Laage, Michael Redgrave, Bobby Clark, Brigitte Fossey

The Happy Thieves

US 1962 88m bw
UA/Hillworth (James Hill, Rita Hayworth)

A gentleman thief and his accomplice become unwittingly involved in murder.

Dreary comedy which turns into equally dreary drama and makes its European backgrounds look ugly.

w John Gay novel The Oldest Confession by Richard Condon d George Marshall ph Paul Beeson m Mario Nascimbene

Rex Harrison, Rita Hayworth, Grégoire Aslan, Joseph Wiseman, Alida Valli

The Happy Time ***

US 1952 94m bw
Columbia/Stanley Kramer (Earl Felton)

Domestic misadventures of a family of French Canadians during the twenties.

Basically concerned with adolescent sexual stirrings, this very agreeable film has a light touch and is most deftly directed and acted.

w Earl Felton, play Samuel A. Taylor d Richard Fleischer ph Charles Lawton Jnr m Dimitri Tiomkin pd Rudolph Sternad

Charles Boyer, Louis Jourdan, Bobby Driscoll, Marsha Hunt, Marcel Dalio, Kurt Kasznar, Linda Christian, Jeanette Nolan, Jack Raine, Richard Erdman

Happy Times: see The Inspector General

Happy Together

US 1990 96m Metrocolor
Seymour Borde (Jere Henshaw)
V, V*, L

Due to a mix-up, a prudish college student finds himself sharing a room with an attractive girl.

Predictable teenage wish-fulfilment comedy unlikely to interest anyone over school-going age.

w Craig J. Nevius d Mel Damski ph Joe Pennella m Robert Folk pd Marcia Hinds ed O. Nicholas Brown

Patrick Dempsey, Helen Slater, Dan Schneider, Kevin Hardesty, Marius Weyers, Barbara Babcock

The Happy Years

US 1950 86m bw
MGM (Carey Wilson)

The taming of an unruly pupil at a turn-of-the-century American school.

A curiously unrealized piece of Americana, with only moments to suggest what was being aimed at.

w Harry Ruskin   novel *The Lawrenceville School Stories* by Owen Johnson   d William Wellman   ph Paul C. Vogel   m Leigh Harline

Dean Stockwell, Leo G. Carroll, Darryl Hickman, Scotty Beckett, Leon Ames, Margalo Gillmore

Hara Kiri (1934): see *The Battle*

Hara Kiri *
Japan   1962   135m   bw   Grandscope
Shochiku (Tatsuo Hosoya)
original title: *Seppuku*

17th-century samurai often pretend to commit hara kiri so that a grand lord will have sympathy and take them on. One of them is forced to go through with it.

Strange, traditional, slow and explicitly brutal costume piece, for specialized western eyes only.

w Shinodu Hashimoto   d Masaki Kobayashi   ph Yoshio Miyajima   m Toru Takemitsu   ad Junichi Ozumi

Tatsuya Nakadai, Shimai Iwashita, Akira Isahama

'As a cop, he has brains, brawn and an instinct to kill.'
Hard-Boiled *
Hong Kong   1992   126m   colour
Golden Princess/Milestone (Linda Kuk, Terence Chang)
V, V (W), V*
original title: *Lashou Shentan*

A gun-happy cop smashes a smuggling ring.

Spectacularly violent gangster movie, with a body-count in the hundreds and stylishly choreographed, slow-motion deaths and stunts; possibly the best example of John Woo's particular talents for large-scale mayhem.

w Barry Wong   story John Woo   d John Woo   ph Wang Wing-Heng   m Michael Gibbs, James Wong   ad James Leung, Joel Chong   ed John Woo, David Wu, Kai Kit-Wai, Jack

Chow Yun-Fat, Tony Leung, Teresa Mo, Philip Chan, Philip Kwok, Anthony Wong, Kwan Hoi-Shan, Tung Wai, Y. Yonemura

'Superbly choreographed violence . . . Pic delivers ample ammunition with a good dose of humor.' – *Variety*

'A vivid cartoon version of the kinetics and twisted-loyalty themes of Sam Peckinpah.' – *Michael Sragow, New Yorker*

The film was released on video in a subtitled wide-screen and a dubbed version.

The Hard Boiled Canary
US   1941   80m   bw
Paramount (Andrew Stone)
GB title: *There's Magic in Music*

A young burlesque singer is softened at a summer music school.

Another Pygmalion enterprise, but the story is only a slim vehicle for the songs.

w Frederick Jackson   story Andrew L. Stone, Robert Lively, Ann Ronell   d Andrew Stone

Susanna Foster, Allan Jones, Margaret Lindsay, Lynne Overman, William Collier Snr

Hard Contract
US   1969   106m   DeLuxe   Panavision
TCF (Marvin Schwarz)

A professional killer has sexual hang-ups.

Heavy-going modern thriller with lively scenes separated by too much self-analytical chat, not to mention a tour of Europe.

wd S. Lee Pogostin   ph Jack Hildyard   m Alex North

James Coburn, Lilli Palmer, Lee Remick, Burgess Meredith, Patrick Magee, Sterling Hayden, Helen Cherry, Karen Black, Claude Dauphin

'Behind it one glimpses a much better film than its surface suggests.' – *MFB*

'Like a flat-footed James Bond story that soaked its feet in a hot bath of existentialism.' – *John Simon*

Hard Country
US   1981   104m   CFI Color
AFD (David Greene, Mack Bing)
V*, L

An urban cowboy has no ambitions until he falls in love.

Simple modern Western with music, not at all bad but with a scant potential audience.

w Michael Kane   d David Greene   ph Dennis Dalzell   m Michael Martin Murphey, Jimmie Haskell   pd Edward Richardson   ed John A. Martinelli

Jan-Michael Vincent, Kim Basinger, Michael Parks, Tanya Tucker, Gailard Sartain

A Hard Day's Night ****
GB   1964   85m   bw
UA/Proscenium (Walter Shenson)
V, V*, L, S

Harassed by their manager and Paul's grandpa, the Beatles embark from Liverpool by train for a London TV show.

Comic fantasia with music; an enormous commercial success with the director trying every cinematic gag in the book, it led directly to all the kaleidoscopic swinging London spy thrillers and comedies of the later sixties, and so has a lot to answer for; but at the time it was a sweet breath of fresh air, and the Beatles even seemed willing and likeable.

w Alun Owen   d Richard Lester   ph Gilbert Taylor   md George Martin   m/ly The Beatles

The Beatles, Wilfrid Brambell, Norman Rossington, Victor Spinetti

'A fine conglomeration of madcap clowning . . . with such a dazzling use of camera that it tickles the intellect and electrifies the nerves.' – *Bosley Crowther*

'All technology was enlisted in the service of the gag, and a kind of nuclear gagmanship exploded.' – *John Simon*

'The *Citizen Kane* of Jukebox movies' – *Andrew Sarris*

† It has also been released on CD-ROM for Apple Macintosh computers, together with the script and an essay on the movie.

AAN: Alun Owen; George Martin

Hard Driver: see *The Last American Hero*

Hard, Fast and Beautiful
US   1951   76m   bw
RKO/The Filmmakers (Collier Young)

A girl tennis player is influenced by her ambitious mother.

Unusual but not very effective melodrama.

w Martha Wilkerson   novel John R. Tunis   d Ida Lupino   ph Archie Stout   m Roy Webb

Claire Trevor, Sally Forrest, Carleton Young, Robert Clarke, Kenneth Patterson, Joseph Kearns

Hard Promises
US   1991   95m   DeLuxe
Columbia/Stone/High Horse (Cindy Chvatal, William Petersen)
V*, L

An absentee husband, discovering that his wife has divorced him, returns home to prevent her remarriage.

Drear domestic comedy in which it is hard to sympathize with any of the main characters.

w Jule Selbo   d Martin Davidson   ph Andrzej Bartkowiak   m Kenny Vance   pd Dan Leigh   ed Bonnie Koehler

Sissy Spacek, William Petersen, Brian Kerwin, Mare Winningham, Jeff Perry, Olivia Burnette, Peter MacNichol

Hard Steel
GB   1942   86m   bw
GFD/GHW (James B. Sloan)
reissue title: *What Shall It Profit*

A steel worker is promoted and loses his humanity, but comes to his senses when his wife leaves him.

Modest moral drama from the uplift side of the Rank empire.

w Lydia Hayward   novel *Steel Saraband* by Roger Dataller   d Norman Walker   ph Claude Friese-Greene

Wilfrid Lawson, Betty Stockfield, John Stuart, George Carney, Joan Kemp-Welch, Hay Petrie

'Don't hunt what you can't kill.'
Hard Target
US   1993   97m   DeLuxe
UIP/Alphaville/Renaissance (James Jacks, Sean Daniel)
V, V*, L, S

In New Orleans, a wealthy man organizes the hunting and killing of men for sport.

John Woo, Hong Kong's influential director of action films, makes his American debut with yet another remake of *The Most Dangerous Game*; the experience seems not to have been a happy one for him, or for his audience.

w Chuck Pfarrer   d John Woo   ph Russell Carpenter   m Graeme Revell   pd Phil Dagort   ed Bob Murawski

Jean-Claude Van Damme, Lance Henriksen, Yancy Butler, Arnold Vosloo, Kasil Lemmons, Wilford Brimley, Chuck Pfarrer

'A thuggish, badly scripted thriller.' – *Philip French, Observer*

'Giggles seem as appropriate as shocked gasps. For this film has nothing to do with real life or real violence.' – *Nigel Andrews, Financial Times*

Hard Times *
US   1975   93m   Metrocolor   Panavision
Columbia (Lawrence Gordon)
V, V*, L
GB title: *The Streetfighter*

In New Orleans in the Depression-hit thirties, a prizefighter and a promoter help each other.

Interesting, atmospheric melodrama on the lone stranger theme.

w Walter Hill, Bryan Gindorff, Bruce Henstell   d Walter Hill   ph Philip Lathrop   m Barry DeVorzon

Charles Bronson, James Coburn, Jill Ireland, Strother Martin, Maggie Blye

Hard Times *
Portugal/GB   1988   96m   bw
Artificial Eye/Joã Botelho
original title: *Tempos dificeis, este tempo*

A circus child is brought up in the loveless household of a pedant who teaches his children to revere facts.

Dickens is scaled down, but effectively translated to modern-day Portugal.

wd Joã Botelho   novel Charles Dickens   ph Elso Roque   m António Pinho Vargas   ad Jasmin Matos   ed Joã Botelho

Luis Estreka, Julia Britton, Isabel de Castro, Ruy Furtado, Inês Medeiros, Henrique Viana, Lia Gama, Joaquim Mendes, Isabel Ruth

Hard to Get
US   1938   80m   bw
Warner

An architect is reduced to working at a gas station; here he meets and falls in love with a millionairess.

Arch romantic comedy which failed to enhance its stars.

w Jerry Wald, Maurice Leo, Richard Macauley *d* Ray Enright

Dick Powell, Olivia de Havilland, Charles Winninger, Thurston Hall, Isabel Jeans, Penny Singleton, Allen Jenkins

'Will carry in top brackets mainly due to selling names.' – *Variety*

Hard to Handle **
US   1933   75m   bw
Warner (Robert Lord)

The success story of a cheerful public relations man.

Punchy star comedy with interesting sidelights on the social fads of the early thirties including marathon dancing, get-rich-quick schemes and grapefruit diets.

w Wilson Mizner, Robert Lord   *d* Mervyn Le Roy *ph* Barney McGill

James Cagney, Ruth Donnelly, Mary Brian, Allen Jenkins, Claire Dodd

'Hokum this time instead of the realism that boosted him to stardom.' – *Variety*

'A violent, slangy, down-to-the-pavement affair which has many a mirthful moment.' – *Mordaunt Hall*

Hard to Kill
US   1989   96m   Technicolor
Warner/Lee Rich Productions/Adelson-Todman-Simon
V, V*, L

Reviving from a seven-year coma, a former cop and martial arts expert seeks revenge for the massacre of his family.

Formula action film.

w Steve McKay   *d* Bruce Malmuth   *ph* Matthew F. Leonetti   *m* David Michael Frank   *pd* Robb Wilson King   *ed* John F. Link

Steven Seagal, Kelly Le Brock, Bill Sadler, Frederick Coffin, Bonnie Burroughs, Andrew Bloch, Branscombe Richmond, Charles Boswell

'There are two sides to every story – and every woman!'
The Hard Way *
US   1942   109m   bw
Warner (Jerry Wald)

A strong-willed girl pushes her reluctant sister to the heights of show business.

Unconvincing but well-mounted drama.

w Daniel Fuchs, Peter Viertel   *d* Vincent Sherman *ph* James Wong Howe   *md* Leo F. Forbstein *m* Heinz Roemheld

Ida Lupino, Joan Leslie, Dennis Morgan, Jack Carson, Gladys George, Faye Emerson, Paul Cavanagh, Roman Bohnen

The Hard Way *
US   1991   111m   DeLuxe
UIP/Universal/Badham/Cohen (William Sackheim)
V, V*, L, S

A Hollywood actor who plans to play a cop in his new film teams up with a real-life New York policeman who is obsessed with catching a serial killer.

Amusing comedy that pokes fun at buddy-buddy and cop movies while being both itself.

w Daniel Pyne, Lem Dobbs   *story* Lem Dobbs, Michael Kozoll   *d* John Badham   *ph* Robert Primes, Don McAlpine   *m* Arthur B. Rubinstein *pd* Philip Harrison   *ed* Frank Morris, Tony Lombardo

Michael J. Fox, James Woods, Stephen Lang, Annabella Sciorra, Delroy Lindo, Luis Guzman, Mary Mara, Penny Marshall

'Proves that sometimes the system, fuelled here by self-mocking jibes, can turn out films appreciable and enjoyable without adding anything to the cinema.' – *Kim Newman, Sight and Sound*

Hardcore *
US   1978   108m   Metrocolor
Columbia/A-Team (John Milius)
GB title: *The Hardcore Life*

A religious man from Michigan journeys to Los Angeles in search of his daughter, who has taken to acting in porno films.

Intense and solemn treatment of a situation that could have gone over the top, and very nearly does; the acting saves it.

wd Paul Schrader   *ph* Michael Chapman   *m* Jack Nitzsche

George C. Scott, Peter Boyle, Season Hubley, Dick Sargent, Leonard Gaines

'Flawed and uneven, it contains moments of pure revelation.' – *Roger Ebert*

The Hardcore Life: see *Hardcore*

'No Punches Pulled!'
'If you thought "On the Waterfront" hit hard ... wait till you see this one!'
The Harder They Fall *
US   1956   109m   bw
Columbia (Philip Yordan)
V*

A press agent exposes the crooked fight game.

Wearily efficient sporting melodrama.

w Philip Yordan   *novel* Budd Schulberg   *d* Mark Robson   *ph* Burnett Guffey   *m* Hugo Friedhofer

Humphrey Bogart (his last performance), Rod Steiger, Jan Sterling, Mike Lane, Max Baer, Edward Andrews, Harold J. Stone

AAN: Burnett Guffey

Hardware *
GB/US   1990   92m   colour
Palace/Miramax/British Screen/BSB/Wicked Films (Joanne Sellar, Paul Trybits)
V, V*, L, S

Scavengers in a radioactive wasteland unknowingly recover a killer robot.

A low-budget science-fiction horror story, filmed in the style of a rock music video.

wd Richard Stanley   *story* SHOK! by Steve McManus, Kevin O'Neill   *ph* Steven Chivers *m* Simon Boswell   *pd* Joseph Bennett   *sp* Image Animation   *ed* Derek Trigg

Dylan McDermott, Stacey Travis, John Lynch, William Hootkins, Iggy Pop

'A cacophonic, nightmarish variation on the postapocalyptic cautionary genre.' – *Variety*

The Hardy Family

America's favourite fictional characters just before and during World War II were the family of a small-town judge, who seemed to personify all that everyone was fighting for, especially as the young son was always getting into amusing scrapes. Designed by a delighted MGM as low-budgeters, they paid for many an expensive failure, and introduced, as young Andy's girlfriends, a series of starlets who went on to much bigger things. The basic family was Lewis Stone, Fay Holden, Mickey Rooney, Cecilia Parker and Sara Haden (as the spinster aunt); but in the very first episode Lionel Barrymore and Spring Byington played the judge and his wife. MGM was given a special Academy Award in 1942 'for representing the American Way of Life' in the films.

A FAMILY AFFAIR (1936); 69m; *d* George B. Seitz; *w* Kay Van Riper; *play* Aurania Rouverol

YOU'RE ONLY YOUNG ONCE (1938); 78m; *d* George B. Seitz; *w* Kay Van Riper; introducing Ann Rutherford (who became a regular)
JUDGE HARDY'S CHILDREN (1938); 78m; *d* George B. Seitz; *w* Kay Van Riper; *with* Ruth Hussey
LOVE FINDS ANDY HARDY (1938); 90m; *d* George B. Seitz; *w* William Ludwig; *with* Judy Garland, Lana Turner
OUT WEST WITH THE HARDYS (1938); 90m; *d* George B. Seitz; *w* Kay Van Riper, Agnes Christine Johnston, William Ludwig
THE HARDYS RIDE HIGH (1939); 81m; *d* George B. Seitz; *w* as above
ANDY HARDY GETS SPRING FEVER (1939); 85m; *d* W. S. Van Dyke II; *w* Kay Van Riper
JUDGE HARDY AND SON (1939); 90m; *d* George B. Seitz; *w* Carey Wilson; *with* June Preisser, Maria Ouspenskaya
ANDY HARDY MEETS A DEBUTANTE (1940); 89m; *d* George B. Seitz; *w* Annalee Whitmore, Thomas Seller; *with* Judy Garland, Ian Hunter
ANDY HARDY'S PRIVATE SECRETARY (1941); 101m; *d* George B. Seitz; *w* Jane Murfin, Harry Ruskin; *with* Kathryn Grayson, Ian Hunter
LIFE BEGINS FOR ANDY HARDY (1941); 100m; *d* George B. Seitz; *w* Agnes Christine Johnston; *with* Judy Garland
THE COURTSHIP OF ANDY HARDY (1942); 93m; *d* George B. Seitz; *w* Agnes Christine Johnston; *with* Donna Reed
ANDY HARDY'S DOUBLE LIFE (1942); 92m; *d* George B. Seitz; *w* Agnes Christine Johnston; *with* Esther Williams, Susan Peters
ANDY HARDY'S BLONDE TROUBLE (1944); 107m; *d* George B. Seitz; *w* Harry Ruskin, William Ludwig, Agnes Christine Johnston; *with* Bonita Granville, Jean Porter, Herbert Marshall, the Wilde twins
LOVE LAUGHS AT ANDY HARDY (1946); 94m; *d* Willis Goldbeck; *w* Harry Ruskin, William Ludwig; *with* Bonita Granville
ANDY HARDY COMES HOME (1958); 80m; *d* Howard Koch; *w* Edward Everett Hutshing, Robert Morris Donley; *without* Lewis Stone

Harem
US/France   1985   113m   colour
UGC/Sara (Alain Sarde)
V*, L

A New York girl is abducted and taken to an Arabian prince's harem.

Weird and unsatisfactory romantic fantasy; the sheikh, it turns out, is only making a romantic gesture and foists no demands on the girl. Any significance is submerged in yawns.

w Arthur Joffe, Tom Rayfiel, Richard Prieur *d* Arthur Joffe

Nastassja Kinski, Ben Kingsley, Dennis Goldson, Zohra Segal

Harem Girl
US   1952   70m   bw
Columbia

The secretary to a princess vanquishes her employer's Arab ill-wishers.

Dispirited pratfall farce, its star's last movie.

w Edward Bernds, Ellwood Ullman   *d* Edward Bernds

Joan Davis, Peggie Castle, Arthur Blake, Paul Marion

Harem Holiday: see *Harum Scarum*

Harlem Nights
US   1989   116m   Technicolor
UIP/Paramount/Eddie Murphy Productions (Robert D. Wachs, Mark Lipsky)
V, V*, L

Two night-club owners fight off a takeover bid by gangsters.

Witless display of self-indulgence by its overparted director-author-star.

wd Eddie Murphy *ph* Woody Omens *m* Herbie Hancock *pd* Lawrence G. Paull *ed* George Bowers, Alan Balsam

Eddie Murphy, Richard Pryor, Redd Foxx, Danny Aiello, Michael Lerner, Della Reese, Berlinda Tolbert, Stan Shaw, Jasmine Guy, Vic Polizos

AAN: best costume design (Joe I. Tompkins)

Harlequin
Australia 1980 93m Eastmancolor Panavision
FG Films/Far Flight (Anthony Ginnane)
V*

A faith healer cures a politician's son, seduces his wife, and proves to be of supernatural origin.

Muddled and unsatisfactory fantasy in the manner of *The Passing of the Third Floor Back;* in this case far too much is left unexplained, and the film is scarcely entertaining despite effort all round.

w Everett de Roche *d* Simon Wincer

Robert Powell, David Hemmings, Carmen Duncan, Broderick Crawford

Harley Davidson and the Marlboro Man
US 1991 98m DeLuxe
UIP/MGM (Jere Henshaw)
V, V*, L

In the near future, two drifters rob a bank to save their favourite bar from being re-developed.

Tiresome action film on the side of lawlessness and disorder.

w Don Michael Paul *d* Simon Wincer *ph* David Eggby *m* Basil Poledouris *pd* Paul Peters *ed* Corky Ehlers

Mickey Rourke, Don Johnson, Chelsea Field, Daniel Baldwin, Giancarlo Esposito, Vanessa Williams, Robert Ginty, Tia Carrere, Julius Harris, Eloy Casados

'Bone-headed biker Western.' – *Variety*

'She was famous for light dresses, loose living, and trips to the bottom between pictures!'
Harlow
US 1965 125m Technicolor Panavision
Paramount/Embassy/Prometheus (Joseph E. Levine)
V*

In 1929, starlet Jean Harlow is shot to fame by her agent Arthur Landau.

Absurdly whitewashed and excruciatingly boring rags-to-riches yarn with most of the characters fictitious and little to do with the real Jean Harlow. Only the studio scenes are mildly interesting.

w John Michael Hayes *d* Gordon Douglas *ph* Joseph Ruttenberg *m* Neal Hefti *ad* Hal Pereira, Roland Anderson *costumes* Edith Head

Carroll Baker, Peter Lawford, Mike Connors, Red Buttons, Raf Vallone, Angela Lansbury, *Martin Balsam*

'Hollywood once again succeeds in reducing one of its few fascinating realities to the sleazy turgid level of its more sordid fictions.' – *Judith Crist*

† A rather better television tape drama of the same title, starring Carol Lynley and Ginger Rogers, was made almost simultaneously. It was converted to film ('Electronovision') but had few bookings.

Harmony Heaven *
GB 1930 61m bw/colour
BIP

A composer becomes famous with the help of his girlfriend.

Unbelievably naïve musical, notable only as British and in colour. Not tolerable today as entertainment.

w Arthur Wimperis, Randall Faye *d* Thomas Bentley *ph* Theodor Sparkuhl *md* John Reynders *m/ly* Edward Brandt, Eddie Pola *ad* John Mead *ed* Sam Simmonds

Polly Ward, Stuart Hall, Trilby Clark, Jack Raine

Harmony Lane
US 1935 85m bw
Mascot (Colbert Clark)

The life of Stephen Foster.

Heavygoing biopic from an independent studio; for rural audiences only. *wd* Joseph Santley *story* Milton Krims

Douglass Montgomery, Evelyn Venable, Adrienne Ames, Joseph Cawthorn, William Frawley, Clarence Muse

Harmony Parade: see *Pigskin Parade*

Harold and Maude *
US 1971 92m Technicolor
Paramount/Mildred Lewis/Colin Higgins
V*, L

A repressed young man, fixated on death and funerals, has an affair with an 80-year-old woman.

Often hilarious black comedy for those who can stand it; the epitome of bad taste, splashed around with wit and vigour, it became a minor cult.

w Colin Higgins *d* Hal Ashby *ph* John A. Alonzo *m* Cat Stevens

Bud Cort, Ruth Gordon, Vivian Pickles, Cyril Cusack

Harold Lloyd's Funny Side of Life ***
US 1963 99m bw
Harold Lloyd (Duncan Mansfield)

Excerpts from twenties comedies plus a shortened version of *The Freshman* (1925).

Excellent compilation, though the mini-feature makes it a little unbalanced.

w Arthur Ross *m* Walter Scharf

Harold Lloyd

Harold Lloyd's World of Comedy ****
US 1962 97m bw
Harold Lloyd
S

Generous clips from the comic climaxes of Lloyd's best silent and sound comedies including *Safety Last, The Freshman, Hot Water, Why Worry, Girl Shy, Professor Beware, Movie Crazy* and *Feet First.*

As Lloyd's work lends itself well to extract, this can hardly fail to be a superb anthology capsuling the appeal of one of America's greatest silent comedians. The timing is just perfect.

w Walter Scharf

commentary: Art Ross

Harold Teen
US 1934 66m bw
Warner
GB title: *Dancing Fool*

A young reporter saves a small-town bank from collapse.

Teenage romantic comedy.

w Paul Gerard Smith, Al Cohn *comic strip* Carl Ed *d* Murray Roth

Hal Le Roy, Rochelle Hudson, Patricia Ellis, Guy Kibbee, Hobart Cavanaugh

† Previously filmed in 1928 (with Arthur Lake and Mary Brian, directed by Mervyn Le Roy) and here reduced to second feature status.

The Harp of Burma: see *The Burmese Harp*

Harper *
US 1966 121m Technicolor Panavision
Warner/Gershwin-Kastner
V*, L
GB title: *The Moving Target*

A Los Angeles private eye is hired by a rich woman to find her missing husband.

Formula Californian detection distinguished by its cast rather than by any special talent in the writing or presentation. It seemed likely to produce a new Chandleresque school, but imitations proved very sporadic; the star repeated the role less successfully in *The Drowning Pool* (qv).

w William Goldman *novel* The Moving Target by John Ross Macdonald *d* Jack Smight *ph* Conrad Hall *m* Johnny Mandel

Paul Newman, Lauren Bacall, Shelley Winters, Arthur Hill, Julie Harris, Janet Leigh, Pamela Tiffin, Robert Wagner, Robert Webber, Strother Martin

'It isn't a bad try, but it never really slips into overdrive.' – *Penelope Houston*

'Nothing needs justification less than entertainment; but when something planned only to entertain fails, it has no justification. A private-eye movie without sophistication and style is ignominious.' – *Pauline Kael, 1968*

Harper Valley P.T.A.
US 1978 93m colour
April Fools (George Edwards)
V*

An independent woman takes her revenge on those who disapprove of her free-wheeling ways.

A feeble-minded comedy that cannot sustain interest for any longer than the hit song of the 1960s on which it is based.

w George Edwards, Barry Schneider *d* Richard Bennett *ph* Willy Kurant *m* Nelson Riddle *ed* Michael Economu

Barbara Eden, Ronny Cox, Nanette Fabray, Susan Swift, Louis Nye, Pat Paulsen

The Harrad Experiment
US 1973 97m Eastmancolor
Cinerama/Cinema Arts (Dennis F. Stevens)
V*

A college professor conducts a series of tests on sexual relationships.

Low-keyed Kinsey Report for the seventies, pleasantly made but not very stimulating.

w Michael Werner, Ted Cassidy *novel* Robert H. Rimmer *d* Ted Post *ph* Richard Kline *m* Artie Butler

James Whitmore, Tippi Hedren, Don Johnson, Laurie Walters, Robert Middleton

'Ludicrously sober-sided amalgam of nude yoga and extra-curricular groping, which should set sex educational theory back ten years.' – *Sight and Sound*

Harrad Summer
US 1974 105m colour
Cinerama (Dennis F. Stevens)
V*

Students at a sex-education college return home to put their knowledge into practice.

Dull, if inoffensive, drama that never rises above the level of an average soap opera.

w Morth Thaw, Steven Zacharias *d* Steven Hillard Stern *ph* Richard Kline *m* Pat Williams *ed* Bill Brame

Robert Reiser, Laurie Walters, Richard Doran, Victoria Thompson, Emaline Henry, Bill Dana

† A sequel to *The Harrad Experiment* (qv).

Harriet Craig

US 1950 94m bw
Columbia (William Dozier)

A wife's only real love is her meticulously kept and richly appointed house.

Ho-hum remake of a sturdy thirties film *Craig's Wife* (qv).

w Anne Froelick, James Gunn *play Craig's Wife* by George Kelly d Vincent Sherman ph Joseph Walker md Morris Stoloff m George Duning

Joan Crawford, Wendell Corey, Allyn Joslyn, Lucile Watson, William Bishop, K. T. Stevens, Raymond Greenleaf

'They're two men with nothing in common – they're father and son!'

Harry and Son

US 1984 117m Technicolor
Orion/Paul Newman
V*, L

An ageing construction worker is at odds with his twenty-one-year-old son, who lives with him.

One can't imagine why Paul Newman wanted to make this boring shouting match between people no one can care for.

w Ronald L. Buck, Paul Newman *novel A Lost King* by Raymond DeCapite d Paul Newman ph Donald McAlpine m Henry Mancini

Paul Newman, Robby Benson, Ellen Barkin, Wilford Brimley

Harry and the Hendersons

US 1987 110m DeLuxe
Universal/Amblin (Richard Vane, William Dear)
V*, L
GB title: *Big Foot and the Hendersons*

A camping family meets a docile Big Foot.

Elementary kiddie/family pic in the wake of *E.T.*

w William Dear, William E. Martin, Ezra D. Rappaport d William Dear m Bruce Broughton pd James Bissell sp Harry designed by Rick Baker ed Donn Cambern

John Lithgow, Melinda Dillon, David Suchet, Don Ameche, Margaret Langrick, Joshua Rudoy

AA: best make-up

Harry and Tonto *

US 1974 115m DeLuxe
TCF (Paul Mazursky)
V*

An elderly New York widower and his cat are evicted and trek to Chicago.

Amiable character study, very watchable but rather pointless.

w Paul Mazursky, Josh Greenfield d Paul Mazursky ph Michael Butler m Bill Conti

Art Carney, Ellen Burstyn, Chief Dan George, Geraldine Fitzgerald, Larry Hagman, Arthur Hunnicutt, Herbert Berghof

'A vivacious and affectionate folk tale.' – *New Yorker*

'It has a life-affirming quality as welcome contrast to the destructive delirium of most modern movies.' – *Michael Billington, Illustrated London News*

AA: Art Carney

AAN: Paul Mazursky (as writer)

Harry and Walter Go to New York

US 1976 120m Metrocolor Panavision
Columbia (Don Devlin, Harry Gittes)
V, V*, L

In oldtime New York, two carnival entertainers get involved with suffragettes and a safecracker.

Extended period romp in which the high humour soon palls and a general lack of talent makes itself felt.

w John Byrum, Robert Kaufman d Mark Rydell ph Laszlo Kovacs m David Shire pd Harry Horner

James Caan, Elliott Gould, Michael Caine, Diane Keaton, Charles Durning, Lesley Ann Warren, Jack Gilford

'A charmless mishmash.' – *Sight and Sound*

'This film fails to work as a light comedy, as a period piece, as a jigsaw puzzle . . . mainly, it just sits there and dies.' – *Frank Rich, New York Post*

'Strictly for those who'll laugh at anything.' – *Kevin Thomas, Los Angeles Times*

'The woman or the tiger? He can't have them both!'

Harry Black

GB 1958 117m Technicolor Cinemascope
Mersham (John Brabourne)
V*
US title: *Harry Black and the Tiger*

A famous tiger hunter allows his best friend to prove himself a hero, and falls in love with the friend's wife.

Lethargic melodrama with good Indian backgrounds.

w Sydney Boehm *novel* David Walker d Hugo Fregonese ph John Wilcox m Clifton Parker

Stewart Granger, Anthony Steel, Barbara Rush, I. S. Johar

Harry Black and the Tiger: see *Harry Black*

Harry in Your Pocket

US 1973 103m DeLuxe Panavision
UA/Cinema Video (Bruce Geller)

Adventures of a young, a middle-aged and an old pickpocket.

Partly pleasant but rather aimless comedy drama, agreeably set in Seattle and Salt Lake City.

w Ron Austin, James Buchanan d Bruce Geller ph Fred Koenekamp m Lalo Schifrin

James Coburn, *Walter Pidgeon*, Michael Sarrazin, Trish Van Devere

Harry Munter **

Sweden 1969 101m Eastmancolor
Gala/Sandrew (Göran Lindgren)

A schoolboy inventor rejects the opportunity to move to America with his discontented parents and make his fortune because he feels a responsibility to help the people around him.

Affecting and witty account of the difficulties of adolescent idealism.

wd Kjell Grede ph Lars Björne m Dvorak ed Lars Hagström

Jan Nielsen, Carl-Gustaf Lindstedt, Gun Jönsson, Georg Adelly, Al Simon, Elina Salo

'Some kind of personal vision does emerge to save the film from undiluted monotony.' – *Films and Filming*

Harum Scarum

US 1965 95m Metrocolor
Sam Katzman/MGM
V, V*, L
GB title: *Harem Holiday*

An American star on the way to the Middle Eastern première of his latest film is kidnapped by assassins.

Flavourless comedy with music; before dull backgrounds the star performs adequately.

w Gerald Drayson Adams d Gene Nelson

Elvis Presley, Mary Ann Mobley, Fran Jeffries, Michael Ansara, Theo Marcuse, Jay Novello, Billy Barty

Harvest

France 1937 122m bw
Marcel Pagnol
original title: *Regain*

A poacher and an itinerant girl set up house in a deserted village and bring it back to life.

Somewhat charming but interminably slow rustic parable.

wd Marcel Pagnol *novel* Jean Giono ph Willy m Arthur Honegger

Gabriel Gabrio, Fernandel, Orane Demazis, E. Delmont

Harvest of Hate

Australia 1979 80m colour
South Australian Film Corp./Nine Network/Australian Film Commission (Jane Scott)

In the Australian desert Arab guerrillas training to attack Israel take prisoner a couple visiting an isolated house.

Tepid thriller with a ridiculous plot, not helped by its percussive, over-insistent score which attempts to suggest excitement where there is none.

w uncredited d Michael Thornhill ph David Sanderson m uncredited ad David Copping ed G. Turney Smith

Dennis Grosvenor, Kris McQuade, Richard Meikle, Michael Atkins, Leon Cosak, Moshe Kedein, John Oresik

Harvey ***

US 1950 104m bw
U-I (John Beck)
V, V*, L

A middle-aged drunk has an imaginary white rabbit as his friend, and his sister tries to have him certified.

An amiably batty play with splendid lines is here transferred virtually intact to the screen and survives superbly thanks to understanding by all concerned, though the star is as yet too young for a role which he later made his own.

w Mary Chase (with Oscar Brodney) *play* Mary Chase d Henry Koster ph William Daniels m Frank Skinner

James Stewart, Josephine Hull, Victoria Horne, Peggy Dow, *Cecil Kellaway,* Charles Drake, *Jesse White,* Nana Bryant, Wallace Ford

VETA LOUISE (Josephine Hull): 'Myrtle Mae, you have a lot to learn, and I hope you never learn it.'

ELWOOD (James Stewart): 'I've wrestled with reality for 35 years, and I'm happy, doctor, I finally won out over it.'

ELWOOD: 'Harvey and I have things to do . . . we sit in the bars . . . have a drink or two . . . and play the juke box. Very soon the faces of the other people turn towards me and they smile. They say: "We don't know your name, mister, but you're all right, all right." Harvey and I warm ourselves in these golden moments. We came as strangers – soon we have friends. They come over. They sit with us. They drink with us. They talk to us. They tell us about the great big terrible things they've done and the great big wonderful things they're going to do. Their hopes, their regrets. Their loves, their hates. All very large, because nobody ever brings anything small into a bar. Then I introduce them to Harvey, and he's bigger and grander than anything they can offer me. When they leave, they leave impressed. The same people seldom come back.'

ELWOOD (describing his first meeting with Harvey): 'I'd just helped Ed Hickey into a taxi. Ed had been mixing his drinks, and I felt he needed conveying. I started to walk down the street when I heard a voice saying: "Good evening, Mr Dowd". I turned, and there was this big white rabbit leaning against a lamp-post. Well, I thought nothing of that! Because when you've lived in a town as long as I've lived in this one, you get used to the fact that everybody knows your name . . .'

AA: Josephine Hull

AAN: James Stewart

The Harvey Girls **
US 1946 101m Technicolor
MGM (Arthur Freed)
V*, L

A chain of 19th-century restaurants hires young ladies to go out west as waitresses.

Sprightly if overlong musical based on fact; a good example of an MGM middle-budget extravaganza.

w Edmund Beloin, Nathaniel Curtis d George Sidney ph George Folsey md Lennie Hayton m/y Johnny Mercer, Harry Warren

Judy Garland, Ray Bolger, John Hodiak, Preston Foster, Virginia O'Brien, Angela Lansbury, Marjorie Main, Chill Wills, Kenny Baker, Selena Royle

'Anybody who did anything at all in America up to 1900 is liable to be made into a film by MGM.' – Richard Winnington

'An abundance of chromatic spectacle and an uncommonly good score.' – New York Times

'A perfect example of what Hollywood can do with its vast resources when it wants to be really showy.' – New York Herald Tribune

AA: song 'On the Atcheson, Topeka and the Santa Fe'

AAN: Lennie Hayton

Harvey Middleman Fireman *
US 1965 76m Eastmancolor
Columbia (Robert L. Lawrence)

A frustrated middle-aged fireman begins an affair; the resulting guilt complex drives him to a psychiatrist.

Grotesque satirical comedy from one of the sixties' most fashionable cartoonists. Mild, quite pleasing, occasionally crude.

wd Ernest Pintoff ph Karl Malkames m Bernard Green

Gene Troobnick, Hermione Gingold, Pat Harty

Has Anybody Seen My Gal? **
US 1952 89m Technicolor
U-I (Ted Richmond)

A multi-millionaire pretends to be poor and moves in with distant relatives to test their worthiness.

Very agreeable comedy set in the twenties and centring on a satisfying star performance.

w Joseph Hoffman d Douglas Sirk ph Clifford Stine m Joseph Gershenson ad Bernard Herzbrun, Hilyard Brown

Charles Coburn, Piper Laurie, Rock Hudson, Gigi Perreau, Lynn Bari, Larry Gates, William Reynolds, Skip Homeier, James Dean

The Hasty Heart *
GB 1949 104m bw
ABP (Vincent Sherman)

At an army hospital in Burma, attitudes to an arrogant young Scot change when it is learned that he has only a few weeks to live.

Flat, adequate filming of a successful sentimental stage play.

w Ranald MacDougall play John Patrick d Vincent Sherman ph Wilkie Cooper m Jack Beaver

Richard Todd, Patricia Neal, Ronald Reagan, Orlando Martins, Howard Marion-Crawford

AAN: Richard Todd

Hat Check Honey
US 1944 66m bw
Universal (Will Cowan)

A veteran comic wants his son to click, but is not so sure when the boy gets a Hollywood contract.

Lightweight musical filler with more numbers than plot.

w Maurice Leo, Stanley Davis, Al Martin d Edward F. Cline

Leon Errol, Grace McDonald, Richard Davis, Walter Catlett, Milburn Stone

Hat, Coat and Glove
US 1934 64m bw
RKO

A New York lawyer accidentally kills an old flame.

Tiresome courtroom melodrama, told in a rather stilted manner.

w Francis Faragoh play Wilhelm Speyer d Worthington Miner

Ricardo Cortez, Barbara Robbins, John Beal, Margaret Hamilton, Sara Haden, Samuel S. Hinds

Hatari! *
US 1962 158m Technicolor
Paramount/Malabar (Howard Hawks)
V*, L

International hunters in Tanganyika catch game to send to zoos.

Plotless adventure film with good animal sequences but no shape or suspense; a typical folly of its director, whose chief interest is seeing smart men and women in tough action. The elephants steal this overlong show.

w Leigh Brackett d Howard Hawks ph Russell Harlan m Henry Mancini

John Wayne, Elsa Martinelli, Red Buttons, Hardy Kruger

'Hawks was taking his friends and cast and crew on a trip he wanted to make personally, and the film is both the incidental excuse for and the record of that experience.' – Joseph Gelmis, 1970

AAN: Russell Harlan

'A beautiful butterfly broken on the wheel of life!'
The Hatchet Man
US 1932 74m bw
Warner
GB title: The Honourable Mr Wong

The executioner of a San Francisco tong dutifully kills his best friend but promises to care for his daughter.

Unconvincing Chinese-American melodrama.

w J. Grubb Alexander play The Honourable Mr Wong by Achmed Abdullah, David Belasco d William A. Wellman ph Sid Hickox

Edward G. Robinson, Loretta Young, Dudley Digges, Leslie Fenton, Edmund Breese, Tully Marshall, J. Carrol Naish, Noel Madison, Blanche Frederici

'Mild gang stuff in oriental trappings . . . dynamic action or high voltage drama is missing.' – Variety

The Hatchet Murders: see Deep Red

A Hatful of Rain *
US 1957 108m bw Cinemascope
TCF/(Buddy Adler)

A war veteran becomes a drug addict and upsets his wife and family.

One of the first drug dramas: straightforward, well acted, and quite powerful.

w Michael V. Gazzo, Alfred Hayes play Alfred Hayes d Fred Zinnemann ph Joe Macdonald m Bernard Herrmann

Eva Marie Saint, Don Murray, Anthony Franciosa, Lloyd Nolan, Henry Silva

AAN: Anthony Franciosa

'Are you shockproof? Then you will dare to see this famous drama of violence – of hate – of men who teach women the terror of cruelty and mad obsession!'
Hatter's Castle **
GB 1941 102m bw
Paramount British (Isadore Goldsmith)

In the 1890s, a megalomaniac Scottish hatter ruins the lives of his wife and daughter.

Enjoyable period melodrama with a rampant star performance and pretty good detail.

w Rodney Ackland novel A. J. Cronin d Lance Comfort ph Max Greene m Horace Shepherd

Robert Newton, Deborah Kerr, James Mason, Beatrice Varley, Emlyn Williams, Henry Oscar, Enid Stamp-Taylor, Brefni O'Rourke

The Haunted and the Hunted: see Dementia 13

Haunted Harbor
US 1944 bw serial: 15 eps
Republic

Heroes and villains sort out the truth of sea monster stories near an ocean trading post.

Muddled serial with a poor monster.

d Spencer Bennet, Wallace Grissell

Kane Richmond, Kay Aldridge, Roy Barcroft

Haunted Honeymoon (1940): see Busman's Honeymoon

Haunted Honeymoon
US 1986 82m Rank Colour
Orion/Susan Ruskin
V*, L

A radio actor takes his fiancée to the family's gloomy country estate, where werewolves and transvestites are some of the creatures which abound.

Mainly unfunny spoof: all concerned should have taken a closer look at The Cat and the Canary.

w Gene Wilder, Terence Marsh d Gene Wilder ph Fred Schuler m John Morris pd Terence Marsh ed Christopher Greenbury

Gene Wilder, Gilda Radner, Dom DeLuise, Jonathan Pryce, Peter Vaughan, Bryan Pringle

'Faintly amusing but singularly uncompelling.' – Variety

The Haunted House of Horror
GB/US 1969 90m Eastmancolor
Tigon/AIP (Tony Tenser)
US title: The Horror House; aka: The Dark

A group of young people try to cover up the murder of one of their number, killed during a night spent at a haunted house.

Wretched attempt to combine a youth movie of swinging London and low-budget horror; neither element works.

w Michael Armstrong, Peter Marcus d Michael Armstrong ph Jack Atchelor m Reg Tilsley ad Haydon Pearce ed Peter Pitt

Frankie Avalon, Jill Haworth, Dennis Price, George Sewell, Gina Warwick, Richard O'Sullivan, Carol Dilworth, Julian Barnes, Mark Wynter

The Haunted Palace
US 1963 85m Pathecolor Panavision
AIP/Alta Vista (Roger Corman)
V*, L

In 1875 a New Englander claims an old mansion as his inheritance and is haunted by his vicious ancestor.

Plodding horror comic, too slow to give opportunities to its stalwart cast.

w Charles Beaumont, from material by H. P. Lovecraft and Edgar Allan Poe d Roger Corman ph Floyd Crosby m Ronald Stein

Vincent Price, Lon Chaney Jnr, Debra Paget, Frank Maxwell, Leo Gordon, Elisha Cook Jnr, John Dierkes

'For those of ghoulish bent, or lovers of the perfectly awful.' – Judith Crist

The Haunted Strangler: see Grip of the Strangler

Haunted Summer
US 1988 106m colour
Pathé/Cannon (Martin Poll)
V*, L

Byron, Shelley, Mary Godwin and others indulge in drugs and sex in Switzerland.

Unconvincing as history or cinema.

w Lewis John Carlino novel Anne Edwards d Ivan Passer ph Giuseppe Rotunno m Christopher Young pd Stephen Grimes ed Cesare D'Amico, Richard Fields, Steve Peck

Philip Anglim, Laura Dern, Alice Krige, Eric Stoltz, Alexander Winter, Peter Berling, Don Hodson

'You may not believe in ghosts, but you cannot deny terror!'
The Haunting *
GB 1963 112m bw Panavision
MGM/Argyle (Robert Wise)

An anthropologist, a sceptic and two mediums spend the weekend in a haunted Boston mansion.

Quite frightening but exhausting and humourless melodrama with a lot of suspense, no visible spooks, and not enough plot for its length. The wide screen is a disadvantage.

w Nelson Gidding novel The Haunting of Hill House by Shirley Jackson d Robert Wise ph David Boulton m Humphrey Searle pd Elliot Scott

Richard Johnson, Claire Bloom, Russ Tamblyn, Julie Harris, Lois Maxwell, Valentine Dyall

Havana
US 1990 145m DeLuxe
UIP/Universal/Mirage (Sydney Pollack, Richard Roth)
V, V*, L, S

An American gambler becomes involved in left-wing Cuban politics in the last days of the Batista regime.

Inconsequential, rambling tale with no perceptible point.

w Judith Rascoe, David Rayfiel d Sydney Pollack ph Owen Roizman m Dave Grusin pd Terence Marsh ad George Richardson ed Frederic Steinkamp, William Steinkamp

Robert Redford, Lena Olin, Alan Arkin, Tomas Milian, Raul Julia, Daniel Davis, Tony Plana, Betsy Brantley

'A hollow, handsomely designed reworking of Casablanca.' – Philip French, Observer

AAN: Dave Grusin

Havana Widows *
US 1933 63m bw
First National

Gold diggers seek millionaires in Havana.

Lively second feature with the Warner repertory company.

w Stanley Logan, Earl Badwin d Ray Enright

Joan Blondell, Glenda Farrell, Guy Kibbee, Lyle Talbot, Allen Jenkins, Frank McHugh, Ruth Donnelly, Hobart Cavanaugh

'Hasn't been a picture in weeks with the same content of rapid-fire laughs, all legitimately gained and inescapable.' – Variety

Have a Heart
US 1934 75m bw
MGM

A dancing instructress becomes a cripple and is deserted by her boyfriend.

Family drama with comedy asides, plus a dog and a mystery element.

w Florence Ryerson, Edgar Allen Woolf d David Butler

Jean Parker, James Dunn, Una Merkel, Stuart Erwin, Willard Robertson

'Such a barrage of sobbing hokum is a novelty in itself in this supposedly sophisticated age.' – Variety

Having a Wild Weekend: see Catch Us If You Can

Having Wonderful Crime
US 1945 70m bw
RKO
V*

Three amateur detectives solve the mystery of a disappearing magician.

Easy-going comedy thriller.

w Howard J. Green, Stewart Sterling, Parke Levy d Eddie Sutherland

Pat O'Brien, Carole Landis, George Murphy

Having Wonderful Time
US 1938 70m bw
RKO (Pandro S. Berman)
V*, L

A New York girl falls in love at a summer camp.

Mild comedy which, robbed of its original Jewish milieu, falls resoundingly flat.

w Arthur Kober play Arthur Kober d Alfred Santell ph Robert de Grasse m Roy Webb

Ginger Rogers, Douglas Fairbanks Jnr, Peggy Conklin, Lucille Ball, Lee Bowman, Eve Arden, Red Skelton, Donald Meek, Jack Carson

Hawaii *
US 1966 186m DeLuxe Panavision
UA/Mirisch (Lewis J. Rachmil)
V*, L, S

In 1820 a pious Yale divinity student becomes a missionary to the Hawaiian islands.

Ambitious attempt to contrast naïve dogma with native innocence, ruined by badly handled sub-plots, storms, a childbirth sequence and other distractions, all fragments of an immense novel. Heavy going.

w Daniel Taradash, Dalton Trumbo novel James A. Michener d George Roy Hill ph Russell Harlan m Elmer Bernstein second unit Richard Talmadge pd Cary Odell

Max von Sydow, Julie Andrews, Richard Harris, Jocelyn La Garde, Carroll O'Connor, Torin Thatcher, Gene Hackman

'Consistently intelligent humanism gives it a certain stature among the wide screen spectacles.' – Brenda Davies

AAN: cinematography; Elmer Bernstein; Jocelyn La Garde; song 'My Wishing Doll' (m Elmer Bernstein, ly Mack David)

Hawaii Calls
US 1938 73m bw
RKO (Sol Lesser)

Boy stowaways catch a steamer from San Francisco to Hawaii.

Slight vehicle for a singing star.

w Wanda Tuchock novel Stowaways in Paradise by Don Blanding d Edward F. Cline

Bobby Breen, Ned Sparks, Irvin S. Cobb, Warren Hull, Gloria Holden, Pua Lani

'Okay musically but light on romance.' – Variety

The Hawaiians
US 1970 132m DeLuxe Panavision
UA/Mirisch (Walter Mirisch)
GB title: Master of the Islands

A young scion of a shipping business leaves after an argument and strikes oil in terrain supposedly barren.

More fragments from Michener, covering 1870 to 1900 and comprising an absolutely uninteresting family chronicle with moments of spectacle.

w James R. Webb d Tom Gries ph Philip Lathrop m Henry Mancini pd Cary Odell

Charlton Heston, Tina Chen, Geraldine Chaplin, John Phillip Law, Alec McCowen, Mako, Ann Knight, Lyle Bettger, Keye Luke

'A quickfire succession of corruption, revolution, plague, fire and questions of moral responsibility.' – MFB

'Total relaxation – preferably of the brain – is recommended.' – Judith Crist

'The First Person You Want To Trust. The Last Person You Want To Suspect.'
The Hawk
GB 1992 86m Rank Film colour
Feature Film/BBC/Initial (Ann Wingate, Eileen Quinn)
V

A wife begins to suspect that her husband is a serial killer.

A thriller that fails to grip the attention and provides little insight.

w Peter Ransley novel Peter Ransley d David Hayman ph Andrew Dunn m Nick Bicat pd David Myerscough-Jones ed Justin Krish

Helen Mirren, George Costigan, Rosemary Leach, Owen Teale, Christopher Madin, Marie Hamer, Melanie Hill, Helen Ryan

'A small film without too much ambition.' – Derek Malcolm, Guardian

Hawk of the Wilderness
US 1938 bw serial: 12 eps
Republic

A shipwreck on an unknown island kills two scientists: their baby grows up with a lost tribe. He's called Kioga, not Tarzan, but this serial follows predictable paths.

d William Witney, John English

Herman Brix, Mala, Monte Blue, Noble Johnson

Hawk the Slayer
GB 1980 93m colour
ITC/Chips (Harry Robertson)
V, V*, L

Good and evil brothers compete for possession of a magical flying sword.

Curiously unexciting and rather gloomy sword-and-sorcery epic.

w Terry Marcel, Harry Robertson d Terry Marcel ph Paul Beeson m Harry Robertson

Jack Palance, John Terry, Bernard Bresslaw, Ray Charleson, Annette Crosbie, Cheryl Campbell, Peter O'Farrell

Hawks
GB 1988 109m colour
Rank (Stephen Lanning, Keith Cavele)

Two terminal cancer patients escape from hospital to have a final fling.

Black comedy that lacks the courage of its convictions.

w Roy Clarke *d* Robert Ellis Miller *ph* Doug Milsome *m* Barry Gibb, John Cameron *pd* Peter Howitt *ed* Malcolm Cooke

Timothy Dalton, Anthony Edwards, Janet McTeer, Camille Coduri, Jill Bennett, Robert Lang, Pat Starr, Bruce Boa, Sheila Hancock, Geoffrey Palmer

Hawmps
US 1976 127m colour
Mulberry Square
V*

The Texas cavalry experiments with the use of camels in the South-western desert.

Incredibly overstretched and tedious period comedy with some bright patches.

w William Bickley, Michael Warren *d* Joe Camp

James Hampton, Christopher Connelly, Slim Pickens, Denver Pyle, Jennifer Hawkins, Jack Elam

Häxan: see *Witchcraft Through the Ages*

Hazard
US 1948 95m bw
Paramount (Mel Epstein)

A compulsive lady gambler agrees to marry the winner of a dice game, but runs away and is chased by a private detective.

Silly, unamusing romantic comedy-drama.

w Arthur Sheekman, Roy Chanslor *d* George Marshall *ph* Daniel L. Fapp *m* Frank Skinner

Paulette Goddard, Macdonald Carey, Fred Clark, Stanley Clemens, Maxie Rosenbloom, Charles McGraw

'A good bit this side of inspired.' – *New York Times*

He Found a Star
GB 1941 88m bw
John Corfield

A theatrical agent loses his star singer and thinks again about his secretary.

A strong contender for the Golden Turkey Award (British Division); the ineptitude has to be sampled to be believed.

w Austin Melford, Bridget Boland *d* John Paddy Carstairs

Vic Oliver, Sarah Churchill, Joan Greenwood, Evelyn Dall, Robert Atkins

He Knows You're Alone
US 1980 92m Metrocolor
MGM (Lansbury-Beruh)
V*

A sex-starved maniac attacks teenage girls.

Cheapjack horror comic full of fashionable slashing and screaming; of no cinematic interest whatever.

w Scott Parker *d* Armand Mastroianni

Don Scardino, Elizabeth Kemp

'At this point in the killer-with-a-knife sweepstakes, every company in Hollywood is getting into the act . . . more ingenuity is going into the titles and campaigns than into the films.' – *Variety*

He Laughed Last *
US 1956 77m Technicolor
Columbia (Jonie Taps)

In the twenties, New York gangsters battle for control of a night-club.

Small-scale gangster burlesque which comes off rather better than its credits suggest.

wd Blake Edwards *ph* Henry Freulich *m* Arthur Morton

Frankie Laine, Lucy Marlow, Anthony Dexter, *Jesse White*

He Married His Wife
US 1940 83m bw
TCF (Raymond Griffith)

A divorced wife falls back in love with her husband.

Pleasant minor comedy with screwball touches.

w Sam Hellman, Darrell Ware, Lynn Starling, John O'Hara *story* Erna Lazarus, Scott Darling *d* Roy Del Ruth *ph* Ernest Palmer *m* David Buttolph

Joel McCrea, Nancy Kelly, Roland Young, Mary Boland, Cesar Romero, Lyle Talbot, Elisha Cook Jnr

He or She: see *Glen or Glenda*

'Dynamite fills the screen with their kind of love!'
He Ran All the Way *
US 1951 78m bw
UA/Bob Roberts

A hoodlum on the run from the police virtually picks up a girl and hides in her family's apartment.

Uninteresting situation melodrama helped by intelligent acting and handling.

w Guy Endore, Hugo Butler *novel* Sam Ross *d* John Berry *ph* James Wong Howe *m* Franz Waxman

John Garfield, Shelley Winters, Wallace Ford, Selena Royle, Gladys George, Norman Lloyd, Bobby Hyatt

He Rides Tall
US 1964 84m bw
Universal

A marshal postpones his marriage after being forced to kill his stepbrother.

Semi-adult Western, of no particular consequence.

w Charles W. Irwin, Robert Creighton *d* R. G. Springsteen

Tony Young, Dan Duryea, Madlyn Rhue, Jo Morrow, R. G. Armstrong

He Said, She Said
US 1991 115m Technicolor
Paramount (Frank Mancuso Jnr)
V, V*, L

A couple of TV journalists break up during a programme.

An unusual idea – the story is told first from the man's point of view and then from the woman's – fails to work, owing to a script that provides neither insight nor humour.

w Brian Hohlfeld *d* Ken Kwapis, Marisa Silver *ph* Stephen H. Burum *m* Miles Goodman *pd* Michael Corenblith *ed* Sidney Levin

Kevin Bacon, Elizabeth Perkins, Nathan Lane, Anthony LaPaglia, Sharon Stone, Stanley Anderson, Charlayne Woodard, Danton Stone

'Two awful films rolled into one.' – *Variety*

He Snoops to Conquer
GB 1944 103m bw
Columbia (Ben Henry, Marcel Varnel)

A local handyman exposes a corrupt council.

Spotty star comedy with insufficient zest for its great length.

w Stephen Black, Howard Irving Young, Norman Lee, Michael Vaughan, Langford Reed *d* Marcel Varnel *ph* Roy Fogwell

George Formby, Robertson Hare, Elizabeth Allan, Aubrey Mallalieu

He Stayed for Breakfast
US 1940 89m bw
Columbia (B. P. Schulberg)

A Parisian communist waiter hides out in the apartment of American capitalists, and learns from them.

Post-*Ninotchka* comedy, not bad but somehow rather uninteresting and mechanical.

w P. J. Wolfson, Michael Fessier, Ernest Vajda *play Liberté Provisoire* by Michel Duran *d* Alexander Hall *ph* Joseph Walker *m* Werner Heymann

Melvyn Douglas, Loretta Young, Alan Marshal, Eugene Pallette, Una O'Connor, Curt Bois, Leonid Kinskey

He Walked by Night *
US 1948 80m bw
Eagle-Lion/Bryan Foy
V*, L

A burglar becomes a cop-killer and is hunted down by the police.

Interesting if rather flatly handled documentary melodrama in clear imitation of *Naked City.*

w John C. Higgins, Crane Wilbur *d* Alfred Werker *ph* John Alton *m* Leonid Raab

Richard Basehart, Scott Brady, Roy Roberts, Whit Bissell

He Was Her Man
US 1934 70m bw
Warner

A safecracker goes straight in order to get even with old rivals.

Sassy comedy-drama, not quite smart enough to match its star.

w Niven Busch, Tom Buckingham *d* Lloyd Bacon

James Cagney, Joan Blondell, Victor Jory, Frank Craven, Harold Huber

'No help will be President Roosevelt's pronunciamento of last Saturday (May 19) in which he decried the public penchant for romanticizing crime.' – *Variety*

He Who Gets Slapped *
US 1924 80m approx (24 fps) bw silent
MGM

A scientist starts a new life as a circus clown.

Odd poetic tragedy, Metro-Goldwyn-Mayer's very first production; the public took to it surprisingly well.

w Victor Sjostrom, Carey Wilson *play* Leonid Andreyev *d* Victor Sjostrom

Lon Chaney, Norma Shearer, John Gilbert, Tully Marshall, Ford Sterling

'For dramatic value and a faultless adaptation of a play, this is the finest production we have yet seen.' – *New York Times*

He Who Must Die *
France/Italy 1957 126m bw Cinemascope
Indusfilms
original title: *Celui Qui Doit Mourir*

In a Greek village in 1921, preparations for a passion play are interrupted by the arrival of refugees from the mountains.

Occasionally striking, but mainly arty and pretentious parable; however well meant, a bore to watch.

w Ben Barzman, Jules Dassin *novel* Nikos Kazantzakis *d* Jules Dassin *ph* Jacques Natteau *m* Georges Auric

Jean Servais, Carl Mohner, Pierre Vaneck, Melina Mercouri, Fernand Ledoux

He Who Rides a Tiger
GB 1965 103m bw
British Lion/David Newman

A feckless burglar comes out of prison and returns to the old life.

Cliché crime yarn which tries rather desperately after fresh detail but bogs down in romantic asides.

w Trevor Peacock   *d* Charles Crichton   *ph* John von Kotze   *m* Alexander Faris

Tom Bell, Judi Dench, Paul Rogers, Kay Walsh, Ray McAnally, Jeremy Spenser

He Who Shoots First: see *Django Spara per Primo*

Head *
US   1968   85m   Technicolor
Columbia (Bert Schneider)
V, V*, L

Fantasia on the life of a sixties pop group.

A psychedelic trip of a movie which does for the Monkees what *A Hard Day's Night* and *Yellow Submarine* did for the Beatles, and what *Monty Python* did for us all. Sometimes funny, slick and clever; often just plain silly.

w Jack Nicholson, Bob Rafaelson   *d* Bob Rafaelson   *ph* Michael Hugo   *m* Ken Thorne   *sp* Chuck Gaspar

The Monkees, Victor Mature, Annette Funicello, Timothy Carey

'Random particles tossed around in some demented jester's wind machine.' – *Richard Combs, MFB, 1978*

'A mind-blowing collage of mixed media, a free-for-all freakout of rock music and psychedelic splashes of colour.' – *Daily Variety*

Head over Heels *
GB   1937   81m   bw
Gaumont (S. C. Balcon)
US title: *Head Over Heels in Love*

A singing star can't make up her mind between two men.

Interestingly dated light star vehicle.

w Dwight Taylor, Fred Thompson, Marjorie Gaffney *play Pierre ou Jack* by François de Croisset   *d* Sonnie Hale   *ph* Glen McWilliams   *md* Louis Levy *m/ly* Harry Revel, Mack Gordon   *ad* Alfred Junge

Jessie Matthews, Robert Flemyng, Louis Borell, Romney Brent, Helen Whitney Bourne, Eliot Makeham

Head over Heels
US   1980   97m   Technicolor
UA/Triple Play (Mark Metcalf, Allen Joseph, Griffin Dunne)
V*
aka: *Chilly Scenes of Winter*

A government office worker thinks back on his on-again off-again relationship with the woman he loves.

Quirky comedy drama without the zest of *Annie Hall*, which it much resembles; too much like a television play for box-office success.

wd Joan Macklin Silver   *novel Chilly Scenes of Winter* by Ann Beattie   *ph* Bobby Byrne   *m* Ken Lauber *pd* Peter Jamison   *ed* Cynthia Scheider

John Heard, Mary Beth Hurt, Peter Riegert, Kenneth McMillan, Gloria Grahame

Head over Heels in Love: see *Head over Heels* (1937)

Heads Up
US   1930   76m   bw
Paramount

A coastguard ensign is assigned to a private yacht under suspicion of rum-running.

Tedious, flat musical, only interesting for starring the 'boop boop a doop girl', who soon outstays her welcome.

w Jack McGowan, Jack Kirkland   *d* Victor Schertzinger

Charles Rogers, Helen Kane, Victor Moore, Margaret Breen

'Holds nothing to pull above average grosses and will slide many a house below that mark.' – *Variety*

Health *
US   1979   102m   DeLuxe
TCF/Robert Altman

Complications result when a health foods convention is staged in a Florida hotel.

Zany satirical all-star romp on the lines of *A Wedding* but by no means as likeable or laughable, considering its cast, as it should be.

w Robert Altman, Paul Dooley, Frank Barhydt *d* Robert Altman   *ph* Edmond L. Koons   *m* Joseph Byrd

Lauren Bacall, Glenda Jackson, James Garner, Dick Cavett, Carol Burnett, Paul Dooley, Henry Gibson, Donald Moffat

Hear Me Good
US   1957   82m   bw   VistaVision
Paramount

Adventures of a confidence trickster in the beauty contest racket. Sub-Damon Runyon goings on, featuring a brash new comedian who was subsequently little heard from.

wd Don McGuire

Hal March, Jean Willes, Joe E. Ross, Merry Anders, Milton Frome

Hear My Song **
GB   1991   105m   Fujicolor
Palace/Film Four/Vision/Limelight/British Screen/Windmill Lane (Alison Owen-Allen)
V, V*, L, S

To revive his flagging business, a 1980s Liverpudlian night-club manager hires a singer who may, or may not, be Joseph Locke, a romantic tenor who was once a variety theatre headliner and fled to Ireland to avoid charges of tax evasion.

A small-scale delight, a film of charm and wit.

w Peter Chelsom, Adrian Dunbar   *d* Peter Chelsom *ph* Sue Gibson   *m* John Altman   *pd* Caroline Hanania   *ed* Martin Walsh

Ned Beatty, Adrian Dunbar, Shirley Anne Field, Tara Fitzgerald, William Hootkins, Harold Berens, David McCallum, John Dair, Stephen Marcus

'One of the year's most delightful films.' – *Kevin Thomas, Los Angeles Times*

'Far from making an innovative contribution to British cinema, *Hear My Song* relies for the most part on nostalgia, whimsy and sleight of hand.' – *Tom Charity, Sight and Sound*

Hear No Evil
US   1993   97m   Technicolor
TCF/Great Movie Ventures (David Matalon)

A deaf fitness trainer becomes a target for crooks trying to recover a stolen priceless coin.

Dull and pointless thriller that looks as if it's made to be sandwiched between television commercials.

w R. M. Badat, Kathleen Rowell   *d* Robert Greenwood   *ph* Steven Shaw   *m* Graeme Revell *pd* Bernt Capra   *ed* Eva Gardos

Marlee Matlin, D. B. Sweeney, Martin Sheen, John C. McGinley, Christina Carlisi, Greg Elam, Charley Lang

'This is filming by numbers, the algebra of the inane.' – *Sight and Sound*

The Hearse
US   1980   95m   Metrocolor
Crown International/Marimark (Mark Tenser)
V*

A woman moves into a house that is reputed to be haunted.

Tedious and interminable, lacking suspense and interest.

w Bill Bleich   *d* George Bowers   *ph* Mori Kawa *m* Webster Lewis   *ad* Keith Michl   *ed* George Berndt

Trish Van Devere, Joseph Cotten, David Gautreaux, Donald Hotton, Med Flory, Donald Petrie, Christopher McDonald, Perry Lang

Heart and Souls
US   1993   104m   DeLuxe
Universal/Alphaville/Stampede (Nancy Roberts, Sean Daniel)
S

Passengers killed in a car and coach crash become guardian angels to the child born of a couple who survive the accident, but he grows up to become a sleazy banker.

Curious and uninvolving movie of obscure intentions.

w Brent Maddock, S. S. Wilson, Gregory and Erik Hansen   *d* Ron Underwood   *ph* Michael Watkins *m* Marc Shaiman   *pd* John Muto   *ed* O. Nicholas Brown

Robert Downey Jnr, Charles Grodin, Alfre Woodard, Kyra Sedgwick, Tom Sizemore, David Paymer, Elisabeth Shue

'That the effort is at all watchable is a tribute largely to its performers.' – *Variety*

Heart Beat
US   1979   109m   Technicolor
Orion/Warner (Alan Greisman, Michael Shamberg)

The literary career of Jack Kerouac is paralleled with his curious sex life. Hesitant and generally unsatisfactory analysis of the so-called beat generation.

w John Byrum   *ph* Laszlo Kovacs   *m* Jack Nitzsche *pd* Jack Fisk   *ed* Eric Jenkins

John Heard, Nick Nolte, Sissy Spacek, Ray Sharkey, Tony Bill

Heart Condition
US   1990   95m   DeLuxe
Enterprise/New Line Cinema (Steve Tisch)
V, V*, L

A bigoted white cop who has a heart transplant is haunted by the organ's donor, a suave black lawyer.

Dire comedy, despite likeable performances by its stars.

wd James D. Parriott   *ph* Arthur Albert   *m* Patrick Leonard   *pd* John Muto   *ed* David Finfer

Bob Hoskins, Denzel Washington, Chloe Webb, Robert Apisa, Jeffrey Meek, Frank R. Roach, Kieran Mulroney, Lisa Stahl, Ray Baker, Eva Larue, Roger E. Mosley

Heart Divided
US   1936   76m   bw
Warner

Napoleon's brother weds a Baltimore beauty.

Uneasy remake of *Glorious Betsy* (qv) with a couple of musical numbers added; a splendid cast retires defeated.

w Laird Doyle, Casey Robinson   *d* Frank Borzage

Marion Davies, Dick Powell, Edward Everett Horton, Claude Rains, Charles Ruggles, Arthur Treacher, Henry Stephenson

A Heart in Winter: see *Un Coeur en Hiver*

The Heart Is a Lonely Hunter *
US 1968 123m Technicolor
Warner Seven Arts (Joel Freeman)
V*

Incidents in the life of a gentle deaf mute in a small
Southern town.

Wispy film of a wistful novel; quite well done but
overlong and hard to cheer at.

w Thomas C. Ryan   novel Carson McCullers
d Robert Ellis Miller   ph James Wong Howe
m Dave Grusin

Alan Arkin, Sondra Locke, Stacy Keach, Laurinda
Barrett, Chuck McCann, Biff McGuire, Percy
Rodriguez, Cicely Tyson

AAN: Alan Arkin; Sondra Locke

Heart Like a Wheel *
US 1983 113m CFI colour
Aurora (Charles Rovin)
V*, L

The wife of a service station owner stops at nothing to
become a racing driver.

Well-made study of an obsession, with the usual
racing thrills.

w Ken Friedman   d Jonathan Kaplan   ph Tak
Fujimoto   m Laurence Rosenthal   pd James
William Newport

Bonnie Bedelia, Beau Bridges, Leo Rossi, Hoyt Axton,
Bill McKinney

'An Americanized Chariots of Fire for the drive-in
market.' – Observer

Heart of a Nation **
France 1940 111m bw
Paul Graetz
original title: Untel Père et Fils

The story of a Paris family from the Franco-Prussian
war to 1939.

Uneven and episodic but consistently interesting
piece completed just as the Nazis moved into Paris
and suppressed by them, but later released from
America with linking narrative by Charles Boyer.

w Charles Spaak   d Julien Duvivier   ph Jules
Kruger   m Jean Wiener

Louis Jouvet, Raimu, Suzy Prim, Lucien Nat, Michèle
Morgan

Heart of Dixie
US 1989 105m DeLuxe
Orion (Steve Tisch)
V, V*, L

The civil rights movement impinges on the lives of
three friends at a college in Alabama in the 1950s.

Trivial stuff, presumably aimed at a teen audience that
no longer exists for such mild and inoffensive drama.

w Tom McCown   novel Heartbreak Hotel by Anne
Rivers Siddons   d Martin Davidson   ph Robert
Elswit   m Kenny Vance, Phillip Namanworth
pd Glenda Ganis   ed Bonnie Koehler

Ally Sheedy, Virginia Madsen, Phoebe Cates, Treat
Williams, Don Michael Paul, Kyle Secor, Francesca
Roberts

'A messy goo of nostalgia, rites of passage and clumsy
social conscience with an almost exclusive emphasis
on Sheedy's eager smile and breathless enthusiasm.' –
Empire

Heart of Glass *
West Germany 1976 94m Eastmancolor
Werner Herzog
V, V*
original title: Herz aus Glas

A wandering herdsman with special powers supplies
a factory owner with the secret of making a very
precious glass.

Apocalyptic visionary parable which may mean
everything, or nothing, but amuses fitfully while it's
on the screen.

w Werner Herzog, Herbert Achternbusch   d Werner
Herzog   ph Jörg Schmidt-Reitwin, Michael Gast
m Popol Vuh   ed Beate Mainka-Jellinghaus

Josef Bierbichler, Stefan Güttler, Clemens Scheitz,
Sonja Skiba

Heart of Midnight
US 1988 105m TVC Color
Vestron/AG Productions (Jon Kurtis)
V*, L, S

An emotionally disturbed woman uncovers the dark
secrets of a night-club left to her by her uncle.

Unattractive psychological horror.

wd Matthew Chapman   ph Ray Rivas   m Yanni
pd Gene Rudolph   ed Penelope Shaw

Jennifer Jason Leigh, Denise Dummont, Gale
Mayron, James Rebhorn, Sam Schacht, Frank
Stallone, Brenda Vaccaro, Peter Coyote, Jack Hallett,
Nick Love

Heart of New York *
US 1932 74m bw
Warner

A plumber invents a washing machine and becomes a
millionaire.

Ethnic farce set in New York's Jewish quarter; of
considerable curiosity value.

w Arthur Caesar, Houston Branch   play Mendel Inc by
David Freedman   d Mervyn Le Roy

Smith and Dale, George Sidney, Anna Apfel, Aline
MacMahon, Donald Cook

'Gabby to an extreme . . . too much dialect and too
little animation.' – Variety

The Heart of the Matter *
GB 1953 105m bw
British Lion/London Films (Ian Dalrymple)

In 1942 in an African colony a police officer has an
affair while his wife is away, is blackmailed, and
plans suicide despite his staunch Catholic belief.

Rather stodgy attempt to film Graham Greene;
perhaps everyone tries a little too hard, and in any
case the ending is compromised.

w Ian Dalrymple, Lesley Storm   novel Graham
Greene   d George More O'Ferrall   ph Jack
Hildyard   m Brian Easdale

Trevor Howard, Maria Schell, Elizabeth Allan,
Denholm Elliott, Peter Finch, Gérard Oury, George
Coulouris, Earl Cameron, Michael Hordern, Colin
Gordon, Cyril Raymond, Orlando Martins

'A curious choice for commercial filming.' – Lindsay
Anderson

Heart of the North
US 1938 74m Technicolor
Warner (Bryan Foy)

The Canadian Mounties chase after gold and fur
thieves.

Routine adventure utilizing early developments in
colour processing.

w Lee Katz, Vincent Sherman   novel William Byron
Mowery   d Lew Seiler

Dick Foran, Gloria Dickson, Gale Page, Allen Jenkins,
Patric Knowles, James Stephenson

Heart of the West *
US 1975 103m Metrocolor
MGM/Bill-Zieff (Tony Bill)
GB title: Hollywood Cowboy

In the early thirties a naïve midwesterner almost
accidentally becomes a Hollywood star.

Overstretched comedy poking gentle fun at old
Hollywood: likeable but finally disappointing, as it
obviously needed a Buster Keaton.

w Rob Thompson   d Howard Zieff   ph Mario Tosi
m Ken Lauber

Jeff Bridges, Alan Arkin, Andy Griffith, Blythe Danner,
Donald Pleasence, Richard B. Shull, Herb Edelman

Heartbeat
US 1946 102m bw
RKO/Robert and Raymond Hakim

A French gamin released from reform school becomes
a professional pickpocket.

Unamusing remake of Battement de Coeur, with script
and most performances very strained.

w Hans Wilhelm, Max Kolpe, Michel Duran, Morrie
Ryskind   d Sam Wood   ph Joe Valentine   m Paul
Misraki

Ginger Rogers, Jean-Pierre Aumont, Adolphe
Menjou, Basil Rathbone, Mikhail Rasumny, Melville
Cooper, Mona Maris, Henry Stephenson

'The heartbeat is irregular and sadly ailing.' –
Photoplay

The Heartbreak Kid *
US 1972 106m DeLuxe
(TCF) Palomar (Edgar J. Scherick)
V, V*, L, S

Disappointed with his honeymoon, a sporting goods
salesman promptly sets his cap at a richer, prettier
prospective spouse.

Heartless modern comedy reminiscent of The Graduate;
quite well done but unsympathetic and somehow too
American to export satisfactorily.

w Neil Simon   story A Change of Plan by Bruce Jay
Friedman   d Elaine May   ph Owen Roizman
m Garry Sherman

Charles Grodin, Cybill Shepherd, Jeannie Berlin,
Eddie Albert, Audra Lindley, William Prince, Art
Metrano

'The latest in a relatively new kind of American film –
glittery trash.' – Stanley Kauffmann

AAN: Jeannie Berlin; Eddie Albert

Heartbreak Ridge
US 1986 130m Technicolor
Warner/Malpaso/Jay Weston (Clint Eastwood)
V, V*, L

An ageing gunnery sergeant transforms raw recruits
into fighting men who become heroes in Grenada.

Dismayingly predictable potboiler with nothing but
foul language to pass the time.

w James Carabatsos   d Clint Eastwood   ph Jack
N. Green   m Lennie Niehaus

Clint Eastwood, Marsha Mason, Everett McGill,
Moses Gunn, Eileen Heckart, Bo Svenson

'Now looking increasingly like an Easter Island
statue, he has a voice pickled in Bourbon, a tongue
like razor wire and a body so full of shrapnel he can't
walk through airport metal detectors.' – Time Out

Heartbreakers
US 1984 98m DeLuxe
Orion/Jethro Films (Bob Weis, Bobby Roth)

Two old friends, one an artist, the other a
businessman, worry about their relationship, their
careers and their love-life.

Mundane drama of male bonding.

wd Bobby Roth   ph Michael Ballhaus
m Tangerine Dream   pd David Nichols   ed John
Carnochan

Peter Coyote, Nick Mancuso, Carole Laure, Max Gail,
James Laurenson, Carol Wayne, Jamie Rose, Kathryn
Harrold

Heartburn *
US   1986   108m   Technicolor
Paramount/Mike Nichols, Robert Greenhut
V, V*, L

Romantic problems of a busy professional couple.

Rather ordinary and overstretched scripting is
enlivened by star playing, but the overall feeling is
one of disappointment.

w Nora Ephron novel Nora Ephron d Mike
Nichols ph Nestor Almendros m Carly Simon
pd Tony Walton ed Sam O'Steen

Meryl Streep, Jack Nicholson, Jeff Daniels, Maureen
Stapleton, Stockard Channing, Richard Masur, Steven
Hill, Milos Forman, Catherine O'Hara

'A movie of colossal inconsequence. Heartburn? No,
just a bad attack of wind.' – Time Out

Heartland *
US   1979   96m   DuArt
Wilderness Women Productions/Filmhaus (Annick Smith)
V*

In 1910 Wyoming, a woman with a small daughter
takes up her arduous duties as housekeeper to a dour
rancher.

Impressive if not very likeable semidocumentary
which certainly rubs one's nose in the unfairness of
life.

w Beth Ferris, from the papers of Elmore Randall
Stewart d Richard Pearce ph Fred Murphy
m Charles Gross

Conchata Ferrell, Rip Torn, Barry Primus, Lila Skala

Heart's Desire
GB   1935   82m   bw
BIP (Walter Mycroft)

In old Vienna, a tenor finds that a glamorous socialite
wants him for his voice rather than himself.

Dated operetta, but the star still reigns supreme.

w Clifford Grey, L. DuGarde Peach, Jack Davies,
Roger Burford and Bruno Frank story Lioni Pickard
d Paul Stein ph J. J. Cox md Idris Lewis,
Stanford Robinson m Schumann and others
ad Clarence Elder ed Leslie Norman

Richard Tauber, Leonora Corbett, Diana Napier, Frank
Vosper

Hearts in Springtime: see Glamour Boy

Hearts of Darkness: A Filmmaker's
     Apocalypse **
US   1991   96m   colour
Blue Dolphin/Zaloom Mayfield/Zoetrope (George Zaloom, Les
   Mayfield)
V, V (W), V*, L

A documentary on the making of Francis Ford
Coppola's Apocalypse Now in 1976.

Fascinating glimpse not only of filmmaking on a
troubled location with oversized egos in collision, but
also of Hollywood attitudes of the time. It bears out
Coppola's own summation, 'We had access to too
much money, too much equipment, and little by little
we went insane.'

wd Fax Bahr, George Hickenlooper ph Larry
Carney, Eleanor Coppola, Bill Neal, Doug Ryan, Les
Blank and others m Todd Boekelheide
ed Michael Hreer, Jay Miracle

Hearts of Fire
US   1987   95m   colour   Cinemascope
UKFD/Lorimar/Phoenix Entertainment/Fox (Richard Marquand,
   Jennifer Miller, Jennifer Alward)
V, V*, L

A female rock singer succeeds with the aid of a
reclusive star and a weary British rocker.

Tedious exposé of the world of rock music, lacking in
excitement and a sad end to the career of Marquand,
who died soon after finishing it.

w Scott Richardson, Joe Esterhas d Richard
Marquand ph Alan Hume m John Barry
pd Roger Murray-Leach ed Sean Barton

Fiona Flanagan, Bob Dylan, Rupert Everett, Lesley
Donaldson, Barbara Barnes-Hopkins, Maury Chakin,
Ian Dury, Richie Havens, Julian Glover

Hearts of the World *
US   1918   80m (24 fps)   bw   silent
Artcraft (David Wark Griffith)
V*

Of various people involved in World War I, the
patriotic and dutiful ones come out best.

Rather dim patriotic propaganda made by Griffith at
the request of the British government and using a
good deal of newsreel as well as reconstruction. The
personal stories are on the predictable side.

wd David Wark Griffith ph Billy Bitzer ed James
Smith

Lillian Gish, Dorothy Gish, Robert Harron, Josephine
Crowell, Erich von Stroheim, Noël Coward

'Here we have an art of pure emotion which can go
beneath thought, beneath belief, beneath ideals,
down to the brute fact of emotional psychology, and
make a man or a woman who has hated war, all war,
even this war, feel the surge of group emotion, group
loyalty and group hate.' – Kenneth MacGowan, The New
Republic (1918)

† For the screenplay credit Griffith used the
pseudonym of Gaston de Tolignac.

Heat *
US   1972   100m   colour
Score/Sarx (Andy Warhol)
V, V*
aka: Andy Warhol's Heat

An out-of-work television actor and singer moves into
a run-down Los Angeles motel and begins an affair
with an older, fading actress.

Perverse variation on Sunset Boulevard, casually
presented but offering amusement along the way.

wd Paul Morrissey story from an idea by John
Hallowell ph Paul Morrissey m John Cale
ed Lan Jokel, Jed Johnson

Joe Dallesandro, Sylvia Miles, Andrea Feldman, Pat
Ast, Ray Vestal, P. J. Lester, Eric Emerson

'An unsavoury piece of work, laced with sex,
lesbianism, self-abuse and perversion.' – Daily Record,
Glasgow

'Succeeds in being both funny and effortlessly
truthful.' – Derek Malcolm, Guardian

Heat
US   1987   101m   Technicolor
Vista/New Century (Keith Rotman, George Pappas)
V*, L

A Las Vegas gambler gets into trouble with gangsters.

Unremarkable toughie with the star at his most
predictable.

w William Goldman novel William Goldman d R.
M. Richards ph James Contner m Michael Gibbs
ed Jeffrey Wolf

Burt Reynolds, Karen Young, Peter MacNicol,
Howard Hesseman, Diana Scarwid

Heat and Dust **
GB   1982   130m   colour
Merchant Ivory (Ismail Merchant)
V, V*

A woman discovers India's past through her great-
aunt's letters.

Much praised by those who admire the work of this
team, but found (as usual) mildly bewildering by
others, this has at least a large enough budget to
produce interest in its historically re-created
backgrounds if not its complex plot structure.

w Ruth Prawer Jhabvala novel Ruth Prawer
Jhabvala d James Ivory ph Walter Lassally
m Richard Robbins

Julie Christie, Christopher Cazenove, Shashi Kapoor,
Greta Scacchi, Nikolas Grace, Jennifer Kendal, Julian
Glover, Susan Fleetwood

'A likeable patchwork of concepts and cameos.' –
Philip Strick, MFB

BFA: screenplay

Heat and Sunlight
US   1987   98m   bw
Stutz/Snowball/New Front Alliance (Steve Burns, Hildy Burns)

A photographer becomes confused when he discovers
that his love affair with a dancer is coming to an end.

An improvised low-budget study in neurosis, of
interest mainly to its participants.

wd Rob Nilsson ph Tomas Tucker m David
Byrne, Brian Eno pd Hildy Burns, Steve Burns
ed Henk Van Eeghen

Robb Nilsson, Don Bejema, Consuelo Faust, Ernie
Fosselius

Heat Lightning
US   1934   63m   bw
Warner

A lady gas station attendant in the hot South-west
becomes involved with two murderers on the run.

Cautionary tale which does not quite jell despite
effort all round.

w Brown Holmes, Warren Duff play George
Abbott, Leon Abrams d Mervyn Le Roy

Aline MacMahon, Ann Dvorak, Preston Foster, Lyle
Talbot, Glenda Farrell, Frank McHugh, Ruth
Donnelly

'Drab background, little sex appeal and not enough
tension. It's a sluffo for deluxers, but can get by
elsewhere.' – Variety

† Remade in 1941 as Highway West.

Heathers
US   1988   103m   DeLuxe
Premier Releasing/New World/Cinemarque Entertainment
   (Denise Di Novi)
V, V*, L, S

A high-school student begins to systematically
murder his fellow students.

Black joke that rapidly runs out of interest.

w Daniel Waters d Michael Lehmann ph Francis
Kenny m David Newman pd Jon Hutman
ed Norman Hollyn

Winona Ryder, Christian Slater, Shannen Doherty,
Lisanne Falk, Kim Walker, Penelope Milford, Glenn
Shadix

'The film is not seriously a comedy about high school
as a metaphor for society – its false values, its power-
hungry cliques, its emotional exploitation.' – Richard
Coombs, MFB

The Heat's On
US   1943   79m   bw
Columbia (Milton Carter)
GB title: Tropicana

A star seeks financial backing from an elderly angel
whose sister runs the Legion of Purity.

Dim musical vehicle for a fading star; her last film for
twenty-seven years.

w Fitzroy Davis, George S. George, Fred Schiller *d* Gregory Ratoff *ph* Franz Planer *md* Yasha Bunchuk *m* John Leipold

Mae West, Victor Moore, William Gaxton, Almira Sessions, Lester Allan, Mary Roche, Hazel Scott, Alan Dinehart, Lloyd Bridges, Xavier Cugat and his Orchestra

'A stale-ale musical in which a lot of good people apathetically support the almost equally apathetic Mae West.' – *James Agee*

Heatwave *
Australia 1982 95m Eastmancolor
M and L Enterprises/Preston Crothers (Hilary Linstead)
V*

Community activists move to prevent the schemes of a Sydney developer.

Rather like an Ealing drama descending into melodrama; a polished piece of committed film journalism masquerading as fiction.

w Marc Rosenberg, Phillip Noyce *d* Phillip Noyce *ph* Vincent Monton *m* Cameron Allan *pd* Ross Major

Judy Davis, Richard Moir, Chris Haywood, Bill Hunter, John Meillon, John Gregg

† A similarly themed Australian film, *The Killing of Angel Street,* came out almost simultaneously.

Heaven *
US 1987 80m colour
Island Pictures/RVP Productions (Joe Kelly)
V*, L

Interviews with a variety of people about death, after-life and heaven are interspersed with clips from old Hollywood movies and TV programmes that illustrate or contradict the statements made.

Documentary demonstrating the optimism and vagueness of our views on the subject, entertaining in its offbeat fashion despite the manner in which the interviewees are photographed in distracting patterns of light and shade.

d Diane Keaton *ph* Frederick Elmes, Joe Kelly *m* Howard Shore *ad* Barbara Ling *ed* Paul Barnes

'From Vietnam to America, one woman's journey from hope, to love, to discovery.'

Heaven & Earth *
US 1993 140m Technicolor Panavision
Warner/Regency/Canal+/Alcor (Oliver Stone, Arnon Milchan, Robert Kline, A. Kitman Ho)
V, V*, L, S

A Vietnamese peasant woman endures hardships and torment from both sides in the war, and life is slow to improve after she goes to America as the wife of a US marine.

An ambitious and epic film, but too strident to be successful and one that, although ostensibly dealing with the life of a Vietnamese woman, still manages to make the subject-matter that of the American experience in Vietnam and its aftermath; the balance shifts from the moment Tommy Lee Jones's damaged marine enters the picture.

wd Oliver Stone *books When Heaven and Earth Changed Place* by Le Ly Hayslip, Jay Wurts; *Child of War, Woman of Peace* by Le Ly Hayslip, James Hayslip *ph* Robert Richardson *m* Kitaro *pd* Victor Kempster *ed* David Brenner, Sally Menke

Tommy Lee Jones, Joan Chen, Haing S. Ngor, Hiep Thi Le, Debbie Reynolds, Supak Pititam, Thuan K. Nguyen

'The sledgehammer approach to storytelling merely results in audience numbness and distance from the potentially moving material.' – *Variety*

'Thematically grotesque but visually gorgeous . . . if Stone simplifies and distorts, he often does so brilliantly, like a cartoonist with a Fauvist's eye for the drama in color and character.' – *Richard Corliss, Time*

'Cry? I could have wept with boredom.' – *Alexander Walker*

Heaven Can Wait ***
US 1943 112m Technicolor
TCF (Ernst Lubitsch)
V*, L

On arrival in Hades, an elderly playboy reports his peccadilloes to Satan, who sends him Upstairs.

Charming period piece with fantasy bookends; the essence of the piece is its evocation of American society in the 1890s, and in its director's waspish way with a funny scene.

w Samson Raphaelson *play Birthday* by Lazlo Bus-Fekete *d* Ernst Lubitsch *ph* Edward Cronjager *m* Alfred Newman *ad* James Basevi, Leland Fuller

Don Ameche, Gene Tierney, *Laird Cregar, Charles Coburn, Marjorie Main*, Eugene Pallette, *Allyn Joslyn*, Spring Byington, Signe Hasso, Louis Calhern

'It was so good I half believed Lubitsch could still do as well as he ever did, given half a chance.' – *James Agee*

AAN: best picture; Ernst Lubitsch; Edward Cronjager

Heaven Can Wait *
US 1978 100m Movielab
Paramount/Warren Beatty (Howard W. Koch Jnr, Charles H. McGuire)
V*, L

A football star finds himself accidentally in heaven after a car accident; when he is allowed to return, his body has been cremated, so he has to find another.

Unexpectedly commercially successful (the late seventies clearly needed religion) remake of 1941's *Here Comes Mr Jordan.* It lacks the sharpness and style of its predecessor, and despite amusing moments is often merely tacky.

w Warren Beatty, Elaine May *play* Harry Segall *d* Warren Beatty, Buck Henry *ph* William A. Fraker *m* Dave Grusin *pd* Paul Sylbert

Warren Beatty, Julie Christie, James Mason (as Mr Jordan), Jack Warden, Charles Grodin, *Dyan Cannon*, Buck Henry, Vincent Gardenia, Joseph Maher

AAN: best picture; script; direction; photography; music; Warren Beatty (as actor); Jack Warden; Dyan Cannon

Heaven Fell That Night
France/Italy 1958 90m Eastmancolor
Cinemascope
IENA/CEIAP (Raoul Levy)
original title: *Les Bijoutiers du Clair de Lune*

A young girl becomes involved in a revenge plot and finds herself on the run with a killer.

Heavy going sex-and-violence hokum.

w Roger Vadim, Peter Viertel *novel* Albert Vidalie *d* Roger Vadim *ph* Armand Thirard *m* Georges Auric

Brigitte Bardot, Alida Valli, Stephen Boyd, Pepe Nieto

Heaven Help Us
US 1985 104m Metrocolor
Tri-Star/HBO/Silver Screen (Dan Wigutow, Mark Carliner)
V*, L

In mid-sixties Brooklyn, a new priest has trouble with teenagers at a Catholic boys' school.

Lively if rather wearing exploration of teenage sex pranks and Catholic guilt, treated rather uncertainly as comedy.

w Charles Purpura *d* Michael Dinner *ph* Miroslav Ondricek *m* James Horner *pd* Michael Molly *ed* Stephen A. Rotter

Donald Sutherland, John Heard, Andrew McCarthy, Mary Stuart Masterson, Kevin Dillon, Kate Reid

Heaven Is Round the Corner
GB 1943 94m bw
British National/Fred Zelnick

A war veteran is helped to find his long-lost love.

Sentimental tosh with music, a second team effort which went down well enough in wartime.

w Austin Melford *d* Maclean Rogers

Will Fyffe, Leni Lynn, Austin Trevor, Magda Kun, Peter Glenville

Heaven Knows Mr Allison *
US 1957 105m Technicolor Cinemascope
TCF (Buddy Adler, Eugene Franks)

Marooned on a small Pacific island during World War II, a marine and a nun, antagonistic to each other, combine to outwit the Japs.

Silly adventure story with predictably well-handled action sequences separated by even more predictable dialogue, lots of it.

w John Lee Mahin, John Huston *novel* Charles Shaw *d* John Huston *ph* Oswald Morris *m* Georges Auric

Robert Mitchum, Deborah Kerr

AAN: script; Deborah Kerr

Heaven on Earth (1927): see *The Exquisite Sinner*

Heaven on Earth
US 1931 78m bw
Universal

Mississippi steamship owners feud with the shanty houseboaters who line the riverbank.

Oddly titled melodrama with a conscience; it doesn't really work.

w Ray Doyle *novel Mississippi* by Ben Lucian Burman *d* Russel Mack

Lew Ayres, Anita Louise, Harry Beresford, Elizabeth Patterson, Slim Summerville

'Needs strong stage support wherever chanced.' – *Variety*

Heaven Only Knows
US 1947 98m bw
UA (Seymour Nebenzal)

An angel is sent to the old west to reform a bad man.

Whimsical comedy-drama which doesn't work at all, even as a distant cousin of *Here Comes Mr Jordan.*

w Art Arthur, Rowland Leigh *d* Albert S. Rogell *ph* Karl Struss *m* Heinz Roemheld

Robert Cummings, Brian Donlevy, Marjorie Reynolds, Bill Goodwin, John Litel, Stuart Erwin

Heaven with a Barbed Wire Fence
US 1939 61m bw
TCF (Sol M. Wurtzel)

A New York clerk hitch-hikes his way to Arizona, where he has bought a piece of land.

Subdued flagwaver with everybody behaving just swell in God's own country.

w Dalton Trumbo, Leonard Hoffman, Ben Grauman Kohn *d* Ricardo Cortez *ph* Edward Cronjager *md* Samuel Kaylin

Glenn Ford (his first film), Jean Rogers, Richard Conte, Marjorie Rambeau, Raymond Walburn, Eddie Collins, Ward Bond

'A slightly clouded title, with little possibility of propelling many customers through the front door.' – *Variety*

Heaven with a Gun
US 1969 101m Metrocolor Panavision
MGM (King Brothers)

The determined new preacher of a small Western town is an ex-gunfighter.

Solidly carpentered half-a-bill Western.

w Richard Carr   *d* Lee Katzin

Glenn Ford, Carolyn Jones, David Carradine, J. D. Cannon, Barbara Hershey, Noah Beery Jnr

The Heavenly Body

US   1943   93m   bw
MGM (Arthur Hornblow Jnr)

An astronomer is too busy to notice his wife, so she takes up astrology and meets a dark handsome stranger as predicted.

Thin romantic comedy which despite crazy touches never actually makes one laugh.

w Michael Arlen, Walter Reisch   *d* Alexander Hall
ph Robert Planck   *m* Bronislau Kaper

William Powell, Hedy Lamarr, James Craig, Fay Bainter, Henry O'Neill, Spring Byington, Morris Ankrum, Connie Gilchrist

Heavenly Days

US   1944   72m   bw
RKO (Robert Fellows)

Fibber McGee and Molly go to Washington.

Extension of a radio comedy series about a man who simply can't tell the truth; amusing at the time, but with topical references which mean little today.

wd Howard Estabrook

Jim Jordan, Marion Jordan, Eugene Pallette, Gordon Oliver, Raymond Walburn, Barbara Hale, Don Douglas, Frieda Inescort

Heavenly Pursuits

GB   1986   91m   colour
Island Films/Skreba/Film Four (Michael Relph)
V

A sceptical Scottish teacher is involved with seemingly miraculous happenings at a Catholic school.

Well acted, ineffectual satire on education and religion.

wd Charles Gormley   *ph* Michael Coulter   *m* B. A. Robinson   *pd* Rita McGurn   *ed* John Gow

Tom Conti, Helen Mirren, Brian Pettifer, David Hayman, Dave Anderson, Jennifer Black

Heavens Above *

GB   1963   118m   bw
British Lion/Charter (Roy Boulting)
V, V*

A northern parson with proletarian sympathies is accidentally appointed to a snobby village where he converts the dowager aristocrat to works of absurd charity. Eventually he has the whole country in an uproar and takes the place of an astronaut.

Patchy satirical comedy which takes unsteady aim at too many targets but scores some predictable laughs.

w Frank Harvey, John Boulting   *d* John Boulting
ph Max Greene   *m* Richard Rodney Bennett

Peter Sellers, Isabel Jeans, Cecil Parker, Brock Peters, Ian Carmichael, Irene Handl, Eric Sykes, Bernard Miles

'What one loves about life are the things that fade ...'
'The most talked-about film of the decade!'
'The only thing greater than their passion for America ... was their passion for each other!'

Heaven's Gate

US   1980   219m   Technicolor   Panavision
UA (Joan Carelli)
V, V*, L

1890 Wyoming: established cattlemen fight immigrants.

Totally incoherent, showy Western which was lambasted by the critics and quickly withdrawn. A vital turning point in Hollywood policy, hopefully marking the last time a whiz kid with one success behind him is given a blank cheque to indulge in self-abuse.

wd Michael Cimino   *ph* Vilmos Zsigmond
m David Mansfield   *ad* Tambi Larsen   *ed* Tom Rolf, William Reynolds, Lisa Fruchtman, Gerald Greenberg

Kris Kristofferson, Christopher Walken, John Hurt, Sam Waterston, Brad Dourif, Isabelle Huppert, Joseph Cotten, Jeff Bridges

'The trade must marvel that directors now have such power that no one, in the endless months since work on the picture began, was able to impose some structure and sense.' – *Variety*   'All too much and not enough.' – *Sunday Times*

'A film which John Ford would have brought in on time and on budget with quite as much social, critical and political comment – and much more entertainment value.' – *Margaret Hinxman, Daily Mail*

'It fails so completely that you might suspect Mr Cimino sold his soul to the devil to obtain the success of *The Deer Hunter*, and the devil has just come around to collect.' – *Vincent Canby, New York Times*

† The film was budgeted at $7.5 million and cost $36 million. The story of what happened is told in Stephen Bach's *Final Cut: Dreams and Disaster in the Making of Heaven's Gate*, published in 1985.

AAN: Tambi Larsen

'A step beyond science fiction!'
Heavy Metal *

US   1981   90m   Metrocolor
Columbia/Ivan Reitman, Leonard Vogel

A complicated comic strip/science fiction story, with soft core jokes in the modern manner, is told by international teams of animators each working on an episode.

The experiment is interesting rather than successful.

w Dan Goldberg, Len Blum   *story* Richard Corben, Angus McKie, Dan O'Bannon, Thomas Warkentin, Berni Wrightson   *d* Gerald Potterton   *m* Leonard Bernstein and others

'Something of a hodge-podge ... the script is a skeletal, whimsically mystical affair ...' – *John Pym, MFB*

Heavy Petting *

US   1988   80m   bw/colour
ICA/Fossil (Obie Benz, Carol Noblitt)
V*, L

An examination of the sexual customs and habits of the 1950s as seen in films of the time and as recalled by interviews with celebrities. It includes excerpts from *Highschool Hellcats, Blackboard Jungle, Because They're Young* and *Rebel Without a Cause* and from educational films.

An entertaining documentary, although many of the interviews are less revealing than the films of the time.

d Obie Benz, Josh Waletzky   *ph* Sandi Sisseled Josh Waletzky, Judith Sobol, Edith Becker

Laurie Anderson, Sandra Bernhard, William Burroughs, Allen Ginsberg, David Byrne, Spalding Gray, Abbie Hoffman, Josh Mostel

Hedd Wynn *

Wales   1992   125m   colour
S4C (Shân Davis)

A Welsh farmer wins a prize for his poetry after he is killed in the First World War.

Glossy period piece, well done but too long for comfort.

w Alan Llwyd   *d* Paul Turner   *m* John E. R. Hardy
pd Jane Roberts, Martin Morley   *ed* Chris Lawrence

Huw Garmon, Sue Roderick, Judith Humphreys, Nia Dryhurst, Gwen Ellis, Grey Evans, Emlyn Gomer

'With its emphasis on veracity and immaculate production design and costuming, pic lacks enough dramatic smarts to go the two-hour-plus distance.' – *Variety*

AAN: best foreign-language film

Hedda *

GB   1975   102m   Technicolor
Brut (Robert Enders)
V*

A selfish pregnant woman is bored by her husband and revolted at the idea of carrying his child. She takes an opportunity to revenge herself on an old lover, but the scheme rebounds on herself.

Rather flat rendering of a play which has received more than its due share of attention.

wd Trevor Nunn   *play* Henrik Ibsen   *ph* Douglas Slocombe   *m* Laurie Johnson

Glenda Jackson, Peter Eyre, Timothy West, Jennie Linden, Patrick Stewart

AAN: Glenda Jackson

Heidi *

US   1937   88m   bw
TCF (Raymond Griffith)
V, V*, L

An orphan is sent to stay with her crusty grandfather in a mountain village.

Star-tailored version of a favourite children's story; just what the box-office ordered at the time.

w Walter Ferris, Julian Josephson   *novel* Johanna Spyri   *d* Allan Dwan   *ph* Arthur Miller
md Louis Silvers

Shirley Temple, Jean Hersholt, Arthur Treacher, Helen Westley, Pauline Moore, Mary Nash, Thomas Beck, Sidney Blackmer, Mady Christians, Sig Rumann, Marcia Mae Jones, Christian Rub

'Good for the average Temple draw or better.' – *Variety*

Heimat **

West Germany   1984   924m   bw/colour
Edgar Reitz/WDR/SFB
aka: *Homeland*

An epically conceived story of life in a German village between 1919 and 1982.

Essentially a superior soap opera with pretensions of grandeur, this beautifully photographed serial has moments of magic amid much that is merely pretentious and unexplained. Despite the symbolism and the irony (a village idiot is ever present), an eager if arty audience found that it had much to say, though no one could explain its lapses from colour to black-and-white and back again.

w Edgar Reitz, Peter Steinbach   *d* Edgar Reitz
ph Gernot Roll   *m* Nikos Mamangakis

Marita Breuer, Michael Lesch, Dieter Schaad, Karin Kienzler, Eva Maria Bayerswaltes, Rüdiger Weigang, Karin Rasenach

The Heir to Genghis Khan: see *Storm Over Asia*

'She was taught to love and hate – by masters!'
The Heiress **

US   1949   115m   bw
Paramount (William Wyler)
V*

A plain but rich young woman takes revenge on her fortune-seeking lover.

Richly-decorated and generally pleasing version of a stage success based on a Henry James story set in the 1890s.

w Ruth and Augustus Goetz   *play Washington Square* by Ruth and Augustus Goetz   *novel Washington Square* by Henry James   *d* William Wyler   *ph* Leo Tover   *m* Aaron Copland   *ad* John Meehan

Olivia de Havilland, Ralph Richardson, Montgomery Clift, Miriam Hopkins, Vanessa Brown, Mona Freeman, Ray Collins

'Wyler is that rarest of craftsmen who can take such a drama, already completely fulfilled in theatre terms, and convert it to film without ever permitting the play-form to dominate the screen.' – *Hermione Isaacs, Films in Review*

AA: Aaron Copland; Olivia de Havilland; John Meehan

AAN: best picture; William Wyler; Leo Tover; Ralph Richardson

The Heist: see *Dollars*

'No star ever climbed higher – no woman ever fell lower!'
The Helen Morgan Story
US   1957   118m   bw   Cinemascope
Warner (Martin Rackin)
GB title: *Both Ends of the Candle*

A young singer rises from vaudeville to Broadway but becomes an alcoholic.

Moderately truthful biopic with effective 20s trimmings.

w Oscar Saul, Dean Riesner, Stephen Longstreet, Nelson Gidding   *d* Michael Curtiz   *ph* Ted McCord   *m* various   *ad* John Beckman

Ann Blyth, Paul Newman, Richard Carlson, Gene Evans, Alan King, Cara Williams, Walter Woolf King (as Ziegfeld)

'All the tumultuous wonder and tremendous drama in the story of history's most famous runaway lovers! Soon the whole world will know of its greatness!'
Helen of Troy
US/Italy   1955   118m   Warnercolor   Cinemascope
Warner (Robert Wise)

Helen is kidnapped by Paris and regained by use of the Trojan Horse.

Dingy historical spectacular, stultifyingly boring until the final spectacle, with the actors obviously wishing themselves doing anything but mouthing the doggerel dialogue.

w John Twist, Hugh Gray   *d* Robert Wise   *ph* Harry Stradling   *m* Max Steiner

Rosanna Podesta, Jacques Sernas, Cedric Hardwicke, Niall MacGinnis, Stanley Baker, Nora Swinburne, Robert Douglas, Torin Thatcher, Harry Andrews, Janette Scott, Ronald Lewis, Brigitte Bardot

The Helicopter Spies
US   1967   90m   Metrocolor
MGM/Arena (Anthony Spinner)

Spies recruit an expert criminal to open a safe containing a thermal prism, or heat ray, that can destroy the world.

The usual comic-strip mad-scientist scenario with two mad scientists, but entertaining in its undemanding way.

w Dean Hargrove   *d* Boris Sagal   *ph* Fred Koenekamp   *m* Richard Shores   *ad* George W. Davis, James W. Sullivan   *ed* Joseph Dervin, John B. Rogers

Robert Vaughn, David McCallum, Carol Lynley, Bradford Dillman, Lola Albright, John Dehner, John Carradine, Leo G. Carroll, Julie London, H. M. Wynant

The film was edited from episodes of the TV series *The Man from U.N.C.L.E.*

Hell and High Water *
US   1954   103m   Technicolor   Cinemascope
TCF (Raymond A. Klune)

A privately-financed anti-Red scientific expedition sets off for Alaska to prevent a Chinese anti-American plot.

Early scoper which mixes deviously plotted schoolboy fiction with submarine spectacle and cold war heroics.

wd Samuel Fuller   *ph* Joe MacDonald   *m* Alfred Newman

Richard Widmark, Bella Darvi, Victor Francen, David Wayne, Cameron Mitchell, Gene Evans

'Out of the warm arms of women – into the cold grip of the sea!'
Hell Below
US   1933   105m   bw
MGM

Tensions mount at a Mediterranean submarine base during World War I.

Adequate war actioner with appropriate trimmings of heroism, tragedy, comedy and romance.

w John Lee Mahin, John Meehan, Laird Doyle, Raymond Schrock   *novel Pigboats* by Commander Edward Ellsberg   *d* Jack Conway   *ph* Harold Rosson

Robert Montgomery, Walter Huston, Madge Evans, Jimmy Durante, Eugene Pallette, Robert Young, Edwin Styles, John Lee Mahin, Sterling Holloway

'Not a two dollar picture, but will be more than oke in the grinds.' – *Variety*

Hell Below Zero
GB   1954   91m   Technicolor
Columbia/Warwick (Irving Allen, Albert Broccoli)

An American adventurer accompanies the daughter of a whaling captain to the Antarctic to discover who killed her father.

Adequate outdoor thick ear with an unusual setting and lively cast.

w Alec Coppel, Max Trell   *novel The White South* by Hammond Innes   *d* Mark Robson   *ph* John Wilcox   *m* Clifton Parker

Alan Ladd, Joan Tetzel, Basil Sydney, Stanley Baker, Jill Bennett, Niall MacGinnis

Hell Bent for Glory: see *Lafayette Escadrille*

Hell Boats
GB   1970   95m   Technicolor
UA/Oakmont

An American commander with the British navy is assigned to blockade Malta.

Decently made small-scale war epic.

w Anthony Spinner, Donald and Derek Ford   *d* Paul Wendkos

James Franciscus, Elizabeth Shepherd, Ronald Allen, Inigo Jackson

Hell Comes to Frogtown
US   1987   82m   Technicolor
New World Entertainment (Donald G. Jackson, Randall Frakes)
V, V*, L

In the future, one of the few potent men is sent on a mission to rescue women captured by mutants and impregnate them to provide cannon-fodder for another world war.

Adolescent, misogynistic comedy not helped by having a slob as its hero.

w Donald G. Jackson, Randall Frakes   *d* R. J. Kizer, Donald G. Jackson   *ph* Donald G. Jackson, Enrico Picard   *m* David Shapiro   *ed* James Metheny, R. J. Kizer

Roddy Piper, Sandahl Bergman, William Smith, Rory Calhoun, Nicholas Worth, Kristi Somers, Cec Verrell

Hell Divers *
US   1931   113m   bw
MGM

Friendly rivalry exists between two officers in the Naval Air Force.

Routine romantic melodrama with action highlights; a crowdpuller of its day.

w Harvey Gates, Malcolm Stuart Boylan   *story* Frank 'Spig' Wead   *d* George Hill   *ph* Harold Wenstrom

Wallace Beery, Clark Gable, Conrad Nagel, Dorothy Jordan, Marjorie Rambeau, Marie Prévost, Cliff Edwards

'Fine technical naval aviation display, and no story . . . unusually long on footage and short on entertainment.' – *Variety*

'It's a matter of squadron after squadron of planes, the mechanics attached thereto, the cutting in and around newsreel material, which Metro does so well, and Beery's excellent personal performance.' – *Hollywood Reporter*

Hell Drivers *
GB   1957   108m   bw   Vistavision
Rank/Aqua (Ben Fisz)

Fast driving on death-trap roads is required of rival lorry drivers for a cheapjack haulage firm.

Absurd, violent, hilarious and constantly surprising melodrama with the silliest of premises backed by a good cast and well handled thrill sequences.

w John Kruse, C. Raker Endfield   *d* C. Raker Endfield   *ph* Geoffrey Unsworth   *m* Hubert Clifford

Stanley Baker, Patrick McGoohan, Herbert Lom, Peggy Cummins, William Hartnell, Wilfrid Lawson, Sidney James, Jill Ireland, Alfie Bass, Gordon Jackson

'This extraordinary film may interest future historians for its description of road haulage and masculine social behaviour in the mid-20th century . . . though produced with efficiency and assurance it is disagreeable and occasionally vicious.' – *MFB*

Hell Harbor
US   1930   90m   bw
United Artists

Derelicts congregate in a Caribbean harbour.

Low-life dramatics and scenery, but not much story interest.

w Clarke Silvernall   *story* Rida Johnson Young   *d* Henry King

Lupe Velez, Jean Hersholt, Gibson Gowland, John Holland, Al St John

'Production of great beauty retarded by a story which fails to retain interest.' – *Variety*

Hell, Heaven and Hoboken: see *I Was Monty's Double*

Hell in Korea: see *A Hill in Korea*

Hell in the Heavens
US   1934   79m   bw
Fox

In the 1918 air war, an American helps a French unit to get an ace German flyer.

Routine *Dawn Patrol* stuff which somehow fails to make an impact.

w Byron Morgan, Ted Parsons   *play The Ace* by Herman Rossmann   *d* John G. Blystone

Warner Baxter, Conchita Montenegro, Herbert Mundin, Russell Hardie, Andy Devine, Ralph Morgan

'Interesting but probably too familiar at this date.' –
Variety

Hell in the Pacific *
US   1969   104m   Technicolor   Panavision
Cinerama/Selmur (Reuben Bercovitch)
V, V*, L

During World War II, an American pilot and a
Japanese naval officer who are stranded on the same
tiny Pacific island almost become friends.

Highly artificial and pretentious allegorical two-parter
which is occasionally well acted and good to look at.

w Alexander Jacobs, Eric Bercovici   d John
Boorman   *ph Conrad Hall*   m Lalo Schifrin

Lee Marvin, Toshiro Mifune

'No real reverberation and no real excitement,
intellectual or physical.' – *Tom Milne*

Hell Is a City *
GB   1959   93m   bw   Hammerscope
ABP/Hammer (Michael Carreras)

A jewel thief breaks jail and is hunted by the
Manchester police.

Lively semi-documentary, cameo-filled cop thriller
filmed on location.

wd Val Guest   novel Maurice Proctor   *ph Arthur
Grant*   m Stanley Black

Stanley Baker, John Crawford, Donald Pleasence,
Maxine Audley, Billie Whitelaw, Joseph Tomelty,
George A. Cooper, Vanda Godsell

'A hectic pace, with frequent scene changes, mobility
of camera and performers, and much rapid, loud,
intense dialogue.' – *MFB*

Hell Is for Heroes *
US   1962   90m   bw
Paramount (Henry Blanke)
V*, L

In 1944, embittered GIs fight and die while taking a
German pillbox near the Siegfried line.

Fairly routine anti-war film with a strong cast and
effectively-directed moments battling a generally
artificial look.

w Robert Pirosh, Richard Carr   d Don Siegel
ph Harold Lipstein   m Leonard Rosenman

Steve McQueen, Bobby Darin, Fess Parker, James
Coburn, Bob Newhart, Harry Guardino

Hell Is Sold Out
GB   1951   84m   bw
Zelstro (Raymond Stross)

A novelist returns from the supposed dead to find that
a glamorous woman is posing as his widow and
issuing best-sellers under his name.

Downright peculiar comedy-drama which never jells
for long enough to be enjoyable. ('Hell Is Sold Out' is
the title of a book in the story.)

w Guy Morgan, Moie Charles   d Michael Anderson

Herbert Lom, Mai Zetterling, Richard Attenborough

Hell Night
US   1981   101m   Metrocolor
BLT (Irwin Yablans, Bruce Cohn Curtis)
V, V*

As an initiation ceremony, four students spend a night
in an old mansion where 12 years earlier a man
murdered his demented wife and deformed children
and then committed suicide, witnessed by his mute
son, who then disappeared.

Direly unimaginative teen horror, presumably made
for the mentally challenged.

w Randolph Feldman   d Tom de Simone   ph Mac
Ahlberg   m Dan Wyman   ad Steven C. Legler
sp Court Wizard productions; make-up: Kenneth
Horn, Tom Schwartz   ed Tony Di Marco

Linda Blair, Vincent Van Patten, Kevin Brophy, Jenny
Neumann, Suki Goodwin, Jimmy Sturtevant, Peter
Barton

Hell on Frisco Bay
US   1955   98m   Warnercolor   Cinemascope
Jaguar (George Berthelon)
V*

An ex-cop sets out to find the man who framed him
for manslaughter.

Tedious actioner enlivened by the character parts and
a violent climax.

w Sidney Boehm, Martin Rackin   novel William P.
McGivern   d Frank Tuttle   ph John Seitz   m Max
Steiner

Alan Ladd, Edward G. Robinson, Joanne Dru, *Paul
Stewart*, William Demarest, Fay Wray

Hell to Eternity
US   1960   132m   bw
Allied Artists/Atlantic (Irving H. Levin)

Marine Guy Gabaldon, brought up by Japanese foster
parents, has divided loyalties after Pearl Harbor.

Battle-strewn biopic which after two hours seems to
lose its point, if it ever had one, but is efficiently
made.

w Ted Sherdeman, Walter Roeber Schmidt   d Phil
Karlson   ph Burnett Guffey   m Leith Stevens

Jeffrey Hunter, David Janssen, Vic Damone, Patricia
Owens, Richard Eyer, Sessue Hayakawa

Hell up in Harlem
US   1973   96m   colour
AIP (Larry Cohen)

A gangster attempts to clean up Harlem by killing
everyone.

Tediously violent exploitation movie, showing little
of its director's usual quirky style.

wd Larry Cohen   ph Fenton Hamilton   m Fonce
Mizell, Freddie Perren   pd Larry Lurin   ed Franco
Guerri, Peter Holmes

Fred Williamson, Julius W. Harris, Gloria Hendry,
Margaret Avery, D'Urville Martin.

† A sequel to *Black Caesar* (qv).

'They all had something to sell – courage – sex –
corruption!'
The Hell with Heroes
US   1968   102m   Techniscope
Universal (Stanley Chase)

Air cargo experts find themselves unwittingly
smuggling cigarettes into France, and American
counter-intelligence steps in.

Unremarkable, totally predictable action melodrama.

w Halsted Welles, Harold Livingston   d Joseph
Sargent   ph Bud Thackery   m Quincy Jones

Rod Taylor, Claudia Cardinale, Harry Guardino,
Kevin McCarthy, Pete Deuel, William Marshall

Hellbound: Hellraiser II
GB   1988   93m   Technicolor
Premier Releasing/Film Futures/New World Pictures
   (Christopher Figg)
V, V*, L, S

A crazed psychiatrist resurrects a dead woman and
ventures into hell with her.

Confused and bloody sequel to *Hellraiser* (qv).

w Pete Atkins   story Clive Barker   d Tony Randel
ph Robin Vidgeon   m Christopher Young
pd Mike Buchanan   ed Richard Marden

Clare Higgins, Ashley Laurence, Kenneth Cranham,
Imogen Boorman, Sean Chapman, William Hope,
Doug Bradley, Barbie Wilde, Simon Bamford,
Nicholas Vince

Hellcats of the Navy
US   1957   82m   bw
Columbia (Charles H. Schneer)

Exploits of a daring submarine commander in the war
against Japan.

Flimsy jingoistic potboiler.

w David Lang, Raymond Marcus   book Charles A.
Lockwood, Hans Christian Adamson   d Nathan
Juran   ph Irving Lippman   md Mischa
Bakaleinikoff   ad Rudi Feld   ed Jerome Thoms

Ronald Reagan, Nancy Davis, Arthur Franz, Robert
Arthur

Helldorado
US   1934   75m   bw
Fox (Jesse L. Lasky)

A penniless hitchhiker finds a ghost town with a gold
mine.

Feeble fable unpersuasively presented.

w Frances Hyland, Rex Taylor   story Frank M. Dazey
d James Cruze

Richard Arlen, Madge Evans, Henry B. Walthall,
Ralph Bellamy, James Gleason, Helen Jerome Eddy

'Incredible story poorly cast and not at all likely at the
b.o.' – *Variety*

Heller in Pink Tights *
US   1960   100m   Technicolor   Vistavision
Paramount (Carlo Ponti, Marcello Girosi)

Adventures of a dramatic company touring the west in
the 1880s.

Genteel spoof Western which does not quite come off.

w Dudley Nichols, Walter Bernstein   novel Heller
with a Gun by Louis L'Amour   d George Cukor
ph Harold Lipstein   m Daniele Amfitheatrof
ad Hal Pereira, Eugene Allen

Sophia Loren, Anthony Quinn, Steve Forrest, Eileen
Heckart, Edmund Lowe, Margaret O'Brien, Ramon
Novarro

'It has a welcome individuality which is never quite
smothered by its lapses into convention.' – *Penelope
Houston*

Heller Wahn: see *Friends and Husbands*

Hellfighters
US   1969   120m   Technicolor   Panavision
Universal (Robert Arthur)
V*, L

Oil well fire-fighting specialists have problems
among themselves and with their womenfolk.

Ham-fisted story line and performances are slightly,
but only slightly, compensated by excellent special
effects.

w Clair Huffaker   d Andrew V. McLaglen
ph William H. Clothier   m Leonard Rosenman

John Wayne, Jim Hutton, Katharine Ross, Vera Miles,
Jay C. Flippen, Bruce Cabot, Barbara Stuart

'The overall effect is unpardonably tedious.' – *MFB*

The Hellfire Club *
GB   1960   93m   Eastmancolor   Dyaliscope
Regal/New World (Robert S. Baker, Monty Berman)

In the 18th century, a nobleman's child escapes from
his degenerate father, joins a travelling circus, and
later returns to claim his inheritance.

Sprightly historical romantic melodrama lightly based
on the nefarious activities of the real Hellfire Club;
energetic and entertaining if slightly too jokey.

w Leon Griffiths, Jimmy Sangster   d/ph Robert
S. Baker, Monty Berman   m Clifton Parker

Keith Michell, Peter Arne, Adrienne Corri, Kai Fischer,
Bill Owen, Peter Cushing, David Lodge, Francis
Matthews

Hellgate

US 1952 87m bw

Commander Films/Lippert

In the 1860s a veterinary surgeon is wrongly convicted and sent to a savage prison.

Competent exploitation melodrama, not apparently based on truth.

wd Charles Marquis Warren

Sterling Hayden, Ward Bond, Joan Leslie, Jim Arness, Peter Coe

The Hellhounds of Alaska (dubbed)

West Germany 1973 90m colour

A fur-trapper solves a mystery of a missing gold shipment and a lost child.

A snow- and cliché-bound Western, attempting the baroque style of the Italians and missing it entirely.

w Johannes Weiss *d* Harald Reinl *ph* Heinz Hölscher *m* Bruno Nicolai *ad* Zeljko Senecic *ed* Eva Zeyn

Doug McClure, Harald Leipnitz, Angelica Ott, Roberto Blanco, Kristina Nel, Klaus Löwitsch, Kurt Bülau, Heinz Reincke

The Hellions

GB 1961 80m Technirama

Columbia/Irving Allen, Jamie Uys (Harold Huth)

In the 1860s, a family of South African outlaws starts a reign of terror in a small village.

A British attempt to restage the OK Corral; it goes sadly awry.

w Harold Swanton, Patrick Kirwan, Harold Huth *d* Ken Annakin *ph* Ted Moore *m* Larry Adler

Richard Todd, Lionel Jeffries, James Booth, Jamie Uys, Ronald Fraser, Anne Aubrey, Zena Walker, Marty Wilde, Colin Blakely

'Unconvincingly staged and plotted, tediously violent, uncertainly directed and very badly acted.' – *MFB*

Hello Again

US 1987 96m colour

Warner/Touchstone (Frank Perry)

V, V*, L, S

A year after dying, a housewife is brought back by her sister, a medium, to discover that life has changed in her absence.

Moribund comedy that fails to get much mileage from its material.

w Susan Isaacs *d* Frank Perry *ph* Jan Weincke *m* William Goldstein *pd* Edward Pisoni *ed* Peter C. Frank, Trudy Ship

Shelly Long, Judith Ivey, Thor Fields, Corbin Bernsen, Gabriel Byrne, Sela Ward, Austin Pendleton, Carrie Nye

Hello Beautiful: see *The Powers Girl*

Hello Dolly **

US 1969 129m DeLuxe Todd-AO

TCF/Chenault (Ernest Lehman)

V, V*, L

In 1890 New York, a widowed matchmaker has designs on a wealthy grain merchant.

Generally agreeable but overblown musical based on a slight but much worked-over farce, fatally compromised by the miscasting of a too-young star. Some exhilarating moments.

w Ernest Lehman *musical* Jerry Herman (m/l), *Michael Stewart* (book), *play The Matchmaker* by *Thornton Wilder* *ph* Harry Stradling *md* Lennie Hayton, Lionel Newman *pd* John DeCuir *ch* Michael Kidd

Barbra Streisand, Walter Matthau, *Michael Crawford, Marianne McAndrew*, E. J. Peaker, Tommy Tune, David Hurst

'The film leaves an oddly negative impression; a good deal of synthetic effervescence . . . but very little real vitality.' – *David Wilson*

† Carol Channing, Ginger Rogers and Betty Grable all fought to get the title role.

AA: music direction; art direction; sound (Jack Solomon, Murray Spivack)

AAN: best picture; photography

Hello Down There

US 1969 98m Eastmancolor

MGM (Ivan Tors)

The designer of an underwater house volunteers to live in it for a month.

Curious comedy with predictable obstacles to the happy ending.

w Frank Telford, John McGreevey *d* Jack Arnold

Tony Randall, Janet Leigh, Jim Backus, Roddy McDowall, Merv Griffin, Ken Berry, Richard Dreyfuss

'A lady bountiful with a ready song on her lips to hide the ache of emptiness in her own heart!'

Hello Everybody

US 1932 69m bw

Paramount

An overweight girl becomes a national radio celebrity.

Slim vehicle in which its star sings nine times.

w Dorothy Yost, Lawrence Hazard *story* Fannie Hurst *d* William Seiter

Kate Smith, Randolph Scott, Sally Blane, Jerry Tucker, George Barbier

'Should do okay outside big cities.' – *Variety*

Hello Frisco Hello *

US 1943 98m Technicolor

TCF (Milton Sperling)

On the Barbary Coast, a girl singer becomes a star.

Moderately pleasing period musical with plenty going on but nothing very striking.

w Robert Ellis, Helen Logan, Richard Macauley *d* Bruce Humberstone *ph* Charles Clarke, Allen Davey *m/y* various *ad* James Basevi, Boris Leven

Alice Faye, John Payne, Jack Oakie, Lynn Bari, Laird Cregar, June Havoc, Ward Bond, Aubrey Mather, George Barbier, Frank Orth

AA: song 'You'll Never Know' (*m* Harry Warren, *ly* Mack Gordon)

AAN: Charles Clarke, Allen Davey

Hello Goodbye

US 1970 101m DeLuxe

TCF (André Hakim)

A cheerful young Englishman falls for a mysterious Frenchwoman who turns out to be the wife of a Baron.

Modest, aimless, forgettable romantic comedy, full of old-fashioned clichés imperfectly remembered.

w Roger Marshall *d* Jean Negulesco *ph* Henri Decaë *m* Francis Lai *pd* John Howell *ad* Auguste Capelier

Michael Crawford, Geneviève Gilles, Curt Jurgens, Ira Furstenberg

Hello Hemingway **

Cuba 1990 88m colour

Metro/ICAIC (Ricardo Guila)

In the 1950s a teenage girl from a poor Havana family enters an examination to win a scholarship to an American university.

Modest and enjoyable movie that marries Hemingway's *The Old Man and the Sea* to a narrative of adolescent striving.

w Maydo Royero *d* Fernando Perez *ph* Julio Valdes *m* Edesio Alejandro *ad* Onelio Larraldi *ed* Jorge Abello

Laura de la Uz, Raul Paz, Herminia Sanchez, Caridad Hernandez, Enrique Molina, Maria Isabel Diaz, Marta Del Rio, Micheline Calvert

'A thoughtful, lovely little film.' – *Variety*

Hello Sister *

US 1933 62m bw

Fox (Winfield Sheehan)

aka: *Walking Down Broadway*

Boy meets girl in New York.

A mild little romance, only notable because it was edited down from an original by Erich von Stroheim, and touches of his work remain.

w Erich von Stroheim, Leonard Spigelgass *novel* Dawn Powell *d* Erich von Stroheim, Alfred Werker *ph* James Wong Howe

James Dunn, Boots Mallory, ZaSu Pitts, Minna Gombell

Hellraiser

GB 1987 93m Technicolor

Cannon/Film Futures/New World Entertainment (Christopher Figg)

V, V (W), V*, L, S

A woman tries to bring back her lover from the tortures of hell.

Gloatingly sadistic and unnecessarily gory horror movie.

wd Clive Barker *novel The Hellbound Heart* by Clive Barker *ph* Robin Vidgeon *m* Christopher Young *ad* Jocelyn James *ed* Richard Marden

Andrew Robinson, Clare Higgins, Ashley Laurence, Sean Chapman, Oliver Smith, Robert Hines, Antony Allen, Leon Davis, Michael Cassidy

† It was followed by a sequel, *Hellbound: Hellraiser II* (qv).

'What Began In Hell Will End On Earth.'

Hellraiser III: Hell on Earth

US 1992 93m colour

Arrow/Nostradamus (Lawrence Mortorff)

V, V*, S

A television journalist battles with Pinhead, a creature from hell.

Gore-filled horror, in which the main intention seems to be to create in Pinhead a demonic figure capable of sustaining a long-running series of such movies.

w Peter Atkins *story* Peter Atkins, Tony Randel *d* Anthony Hickox *ph* Gerry Lively *m* Randy Miller, Christopher Young *pd* Steve Hardie *sp* Bob Keen; Cinema Research Corporation *ed* Christopher Cibelli, James D. R. Hickox

Terry Farrell, Doug Bradley, Paula Marshall, Kevin Bernhardt, Ken Carpenter, Peter Boynton, Aimee Leigh, Lawrence Mortorff

'Film's extremely grotesque gore effects and negative tone will turn off mainstream viewers but hold a hypnotic appeal for hardcore horror aficionados.' – *Variety*

'It is competent and accomplishes the small feat of being better than its predecessor.' – *Sheila Johnston, Independent*

Hell's Angels ***

US 1930 135m bw/part colour

Howard Hughes

V*

Two Americans become flyers in World War I.

Celebrated early talkie spectacular, with zeppelin and flying sequences that still thrill. The dialogue is another matter, but all told this expensive production, first planned as a silent, is a milestone of cinema history.

w Howard Estabrook, Harry Behn *d* Howard Hughes *ph* Tony Gaudio, Harry Perry, E. Burton Steene *m* Hugo Reisenfeld

Ben Lyon, James Hall, Jean Harlow, John Darrow, Lucien Prival

'That it will ever pay off for its producer is doubtful . . . he's in so deep it can't really matter to him now. Minus blue nose interference, it can't miss, but it's up to the brim with sex.' – *Variety*

'It is not great, but it is as lavish as an eight-ring circus, and when you leave the theatre you will know you have seen a movie and not a tinny reproduction of a stage show.' – *Pare Lorentz*

† The film was reissued in 1940 in a 96m version which has not survived.

AAN: Tony Gaudio, Harry Perry, E. Burton Steene

Hell's Five Hours
US   1958   75m   bw
Allied Artists

A psychopath takes hostages and threatens to blow up a rocket fuel plant.

Standard suspense programmer; tolerable but entirely forgettable.

wd Jack L. Copeland

Stephen McNally, Vic Morrow, Coleen Gray

Hell's Half Acre
US   1953   91m   bw
Republic

A soldier missing after Pearl Harbor turns up years later in Hawaii under a different identity.

Complex melodrama ending in self-sacrifice; amusing bits don't make it hang together.

w Steve Fisher *d* John H. Auer

Wendell Corey, Evelyn Keyes, Elsa Lanchester, Nancy Gates, Philip Ahn, Keye Luke

Hell's Heroes
US   1930   65m   bw
Universal

Three cowboys find an abandoned baby.

Yet another version of *Three Godfathers;* maybe not the best but the shortest.

w Tom Reed *novel* Peter Kyne *d* William Wyler *ph* George Robinson

Charles Bickford, Raymond Hatton, Fred Kohler, Fritzi Ridgeway

† Photographed in the Mojave and Panamint Deserts.

Hell's Highway *
US   1932   62m   bw
RKO

A convict plans escape from a forced labour gang, under the threat of the lash and the sweatbox.

Well-made but heavy-going melodrama without light relief.

w Samuel Ornitz, Robert Tasker, Rowland Brown *d* Rowland Brown

Richard Dix, Rochelle Hudson, Tom Brown, C. Henry Gordon, Louise Carter

'The story is too sodden to carry a general appeal.' – *Variety*

Hell's House
US   1932   72m   bw
Capital Films

A boy is wrongly sentenced to a corrupt reform school.

Primitive cheapie notable only for the early appearance of Bette Davis.

w Paul Gangelin, B. Harrison Orkow *d* Howard Higgin

Bette Davis, Pat O'Brien, Junior Durkin, Junior Coghlan, Emma Dunn, Charley Grapewin

Hell's Island *
US   1955   84m   Technicolor   Vistavision
Paramount/Pine-Thomas

Crooks congregate on a Caribbean island in search of a famous ruby.

Cheeky rehash of *The Maltese Falcon,* not bad in its own routine way.

w Maxwell Shane *d* Phil Karlson *ph* Lionel Lindon *md* Irvin Talbot

John Payne, Mary Murphy, *Francis L. Sullivan,* Arnold Moss

Hell's Kitchen
US   1939   82m   bw
Warner (Mark Hellinger, Bryan Foy)

Boys revolt under the cruel headmaster of a reformatory.

Dreary vehicle for the Dead End Kids.

w Crane Wilbur, Fred Niblo Jnr *d* Lewis Seiler, E. A. Dupont *ph* Charles Rosher *ad* Hugh Reticker *ed* Clarence Kolster

Billy Halop, Leo Gorcey, Bobby Jordan, Huntz Hall, Gabriel Dell, Bernard Punsley, Ronald Reagan, Margaret Lindsay, Stanley Fields, Grant Mitchell

'A quagmire of misplaced sentimentality hokum and general incredulousness.' – *Variety*

The Hellstrom Chronicle
US   1971   90m   CFI colour
David Wolper
V*

A scientist explains the range and variety of insect life.

Odd documentary in fictional bookends; smart and quite sensational for those with strong stomachs.

w David Seltzer *d* Walon Green

Laurence Pressman (as Nils Hellstrom)

AA: best documentary

Hellzapoppin ***
US   1942   84m   bw
Universal/Mayfair (Glenn Tryon, Alex Gottlieb)

Two incompetent comics make a picture.

Zany modification of a smash burlesque revue; the crazy jokes are toned down and a romantic interest is added (and tentatively sent up). The result is patchy but often hilarious, and the whole is a handy consensus of forties humour and pop music.

w Nat Perrin, Warren Wilson *d* H. C. Potter *ph* Woody Bredell *md* Charles Previn *m* Frank Skinner

Ole Olsen, Chic Johnson, Hugh Herbert, Martha Raye, Mischa Auer, Robert Paige, Jane Frazee, Shemp Howard, Elisha Cook Jnr, Richard Lane

'Alive with good gags, mechanical surprise effects, and novelty touches.' – *CEA Report*

† The Frankenstein monster and Man Who Falls into Pool were played by Dale Van Sickel.

Help! *
GB   1965   92m   Eastmancolor
UA/Walter Shenson/Suba Films
V, V*, L

An oriental high priest chases the Beatles around the world because one of them has a sacred ring.

Exhausting attempt to outdo *A Hard Day's Night* in lunatic frenzy, which goes to prove that some talents work better on low budgets. The humour is a frantic cross between *Hellzapoppin,* the Goons, Bugs Bunny and the shade of Monty Python to come. It looks good but becomes too tiresome to entertain.

w Charles Wood, Marc Behm *d* Dick Lester *ph* David Watkin *m* The Beatles *ad* Ray Simm

The Beatles, Leo McKern, Eleanor Bron, Victor Spinetti

Helpmates ***
US   1932   20m   bw
Hal Roach
V

Stan helps Ollie clean up after a wild party while the wife was away.

A brilliant succession of catastrophe gags in the stars' best tradition.

w H. M. Walker *d* James Parrott *ph* Art Lloyd *ed* Richard Currier

Laurel and Hardy, Blanche Payson, Robert Callahan

Helter Skelter
GB   1949   75m   bw
GFD/Gainsborough (Anthony Damborough)

An heiress with hiccups is helped by the staff of the BBC.

Scatty comedy which tries everything, from custard pies and guest stars to a clip from a silent Walter Forde comedy. It isn't the British *Hellzapoppin* it sets out to be, but hardened buffs will find it worth a look.

w Patrick Campbell *d* Ralph Thomas *ph* Jack Asher *m* Francis Chagrin

Carol Marsh, David Tomlinson, Mervyn Johns, Peter Hammond, Jimmy Edwards, Richard Hearne, Jon Pertwee, Terry-Thomas

Helter Skelter
US   1976   92m   Movielab
Hemdale/Lorimar (Tom Gries)

Charles Manson and his followers are charged with the murders of actress Sharon Tate and others.

Dull re-telling of a horrific series of killings from the viewpoint of the prosecutor.

w J. B. Miller *book* The Manson Murders by Vincent Bugliosi with Curt Gentry *d* Tom Gries *ph* Jules Brenner *m* Billy Goldenberg *ad* Phil Barber *ed* Bud S. Isaacs, Byron 'Buzz' Brandt

George DiCenzo, Steve Railsback, Nancy Wolf, Marilyn Burns, Christina Hart, Cathey Paine

Hemingway's Adventures of a Young Man *
US   1962   145m   DeLuxe   Cinemascope
TCF (Jerry Wald)
aka: *Adventures of a Young Man*

The son of a weak doctor and a religious mother breaks away from his family circle on a voyage of discovery.

Curious mélange of ill-assimilated Hemingway stories based on his Nick Adams character. The film has good intentions but no shape or style, and the guest stars don't help.

w A. E. Hotchner *stories* Ernest Hemingway *d* Martin Ritt *ph* Lee Garmes *m* Franz Waxman

Richard Beymer, Diane Baker, Corinne Calvet, Fred Clark, Dan Dailey, James Dunn, Juano Hernandez, Arthur Kennedy, Ricardo Montalban, Susan Strasberg, Paul Newman, Jessica Tandy, Eli Wallach

'They had killed a woman and destroyed his life. Now he will kill a woman and destroy their nation!'

Hennessy
GB   1975   104m   colour
AIP/Marseilles (Peter Snell)
V*

Angered at the death of his family in the Belfast troubles, an Irish revolutionary hurries to London to blow up the Houses of Parliament.

Unattractive, uninventive thriller with a silly script and not an ounce of real suspense.

w John Gay   *story* Richard Johnson   *d* Don Sharp   *ph* Ernest Steward   *m* John Scott   *pd* Ray Simm

Rod Steiger, Richard Johnson, Lee Remick, Trevor Howard, Eric Porter, Peter Egan, David Collings

Henry Aldrich

Henry was originally a radio character created by Ezra Stone, an awkward small-town youth who like Andy Hardy was always getting into scrapes. Clifford Goldsmith wrote the original play which hit Broadway as well as the radio waves before starting a Hollywood series of amiable Paramount second features, most of them starring Jimmy Lydon with Charles Smith as his friend Dizzy.

1939: WHAT A LIFE (with Jackie Cooper)
1941: LIFE WITH HENRY (with Jackie Cooper), HENRY ALDRICH FOR PRESIDENT
1942: HENRY AND DIZZY, HENRY ALDRICH EDITOR
1943: HENRY ALDRICH GETS GLAMOUR, HENRY ALDRICH SWINGS IT, HENRY ALDRICH HAUNTS A HOUSE
1944: HENRY ALDRICH BOY SCOUT, HENRY ALDRICH PLAYS CUPID, HENRY ALDRICH'S LITTLE SECRET

Henry and June *

US   1990   136m   colour
UIP/Universal/Walrus & Associates (Peter Kaufman)
V, V*, L, S

Anais Nin, married to a banker, has affairs with the writer Henry Miller and his wife.

Complex film of shifting relationships and their transmutation into literature, graphically portrayed.

w Philip Kaufman, Rose Kaufman   *book* Anais Nin   *d* Philip Kaufman   *ph* Philippe Rousselot   *m* Mark Adler   *pd* Guy-Claude François   *ed* Vivien Hillgrove, William S. Scharf, Dede Allen

Fred Ward, Uma Thurman, Maria de Medeiros, Richard E. Grant, Kevin Spacey, Jean-Philippe Ecoffey, Bruce Myers, Jean-Louis Buñuel, Feodor Atkine

'It's like a well-wrapped and luxurious parcel that contains just what you don't want for Christmas.' – *Derek Malcolm, Guardian*

AAN: Philippe Rousselot

Henry VIII and His Six Wives *

GB   1972   125m   Technicolor
EMI (Roy Baird)

Dullish historical account of the king's reign, staged as recollections from his deathbed but lacking any of the sparkle of *The Private Life of Henry VIII* made forty years previously.

Accurate sets and costumes fail to compensate for lack of film flair.

w Ian Thorne   *d* Waris Hussein   *ph* Peter Suschitzky   *m* David Munro

Keith Michell, Frances Cuka (Aragon), Charlotte Rampling (Boleyn), Jane Asher (Seymour), Jenny Bos (Cleves), Lynne Frederick (Howard), Barbara Leigh-Hunt (Parr), Donald Pleasence (Thomas Cromwell)

† The production was stimulated by a highly successful BBC TV series, *The Six Wives of Henry VIII.*

Henry V ****

GB   1944   137m   Technicolor
Rank/Two Cities (Laurence Olivier)
V, V*

Shakespeare's historical play is seen in performance

at the Globe Theatre in 1603; as it develops, the scenery becomes more realistic.

Immensely stirring, experimental and almost wholly successful production of Shakespeare on film, sturdy both in its stylization and its command of more conventional cinematic resources for the battle.

w Laurence Olivier, Alan Dent   *play* William Shakespeare   *d* *Laurence Olivier*   *ph* Robert Krasker   *m* *William Walton*   *ad* *Paul Sheriff, Carmen Dillon*

Laurence Olivier, *Robert Newton, Leslie Banks, Esmond Knight*, Renée Asherson, George Robey, *Leo Genn*, Ernest Thesiger, Ivy St Helier, Ralph Truman, Harcourt Williams, Max Adrian, Valentine Dyall, Felix Aylmer, John Laurie, Roy Emerton

'His production – it was his first time out as a director – is a triumph of colour, music, spectacle, and soaring heroic poetry, and, as actor, he brings lungs, exultation, and a bashful wit to the role.' – *Pauline Kael, 70s*

'What Shakespeare wrote in *Henry V*, and what the film has splendidly caught in its own fashion, is a fanfare; a flourish; a salute to high adventure; a kind of golden and perennially youthful exaltation of man's grim work.' – *C. A. Lejeune*

AA: Special Award to Laurence Olivier

AAN: best picture; William Walton; Laurence Olivier (as actor); art direction

Henry V ***

GB   1989   137m   Technicolor
Curzon/Renaissance Films (Bruce Sharman)
V, V (W), V*, L, S

After his claim to the throne of France is refused, King Henry invades the country and wins a famous victory.

A darker film than Olivier's, with which it can stand comparison, stressing the brutality of war.

w Kenneth Branagh   *play* William Shakespeare   *d* Kenneth Branagh   *ph* Kenneth MacMillan   *m* Patrick Doyle   *pd* Tim Harvey   *ed* Mike Bradsell

Kenneth Branagh, Derek Jacobi, Simon Shepherd, James Larkin, Brian Blessed, James Simmons, Paul Gregory, Charles Kay, Alec McCowen, Edward Jewesbury, Ian Holm, Michael Williams, Geoffrey Hutchings, Robert Stephens, Judi Dench, Paul Scofield, Harold Innocent, Emma Thompson, Geraldine McEwan

'The film's visual tedium, vulgarity and musical mediocrity would be more bearable if Branagh himself were a more persuasive lead actor.' – *MFB*

'The more I thought about it, the more convinced I became that here was a play to be reclaimed from jingoism and its World War Two associations.' – *Kenneth Branagh*

AA: best costume design (Phyllis Dalton)

AAN: Kenneth Branagh (as best actor and best director)

Henry Nine Till Five *

GB   1970   6m   colour
British Lion

A commuter spends his working days fantasizing about sex.

Typical and very lively cartoon.

w Stan Heyward   *d* Bob Godfrey

Henry: Portrait of a Serial Killer **

US   1990   83m   colour
Electric/Maljack (John McNaughton, Lisa Dedmond, Steven A. Jones)
V, V*

Documentary-style account of the life and methods of a motiveless mass murderer.

Oddly compelling, it is often hard to watch because of its violence and, perversely, hard not to watch.

w Richard Fire, John McNaughton   *d* John McNaughton   *ph* Charlie Lieberman   *m* John McNaughton, Ken Hale, Steven A. Jones   *pd* Rick Paul   *ed* Elena Maganini

Michael Rooker, Tom Towles, Tracy Arnold

'A film of clutching terror that's meant to heighten our awareness instead of dulling it . . . This film gives off a dark chill that follows you all the way home.' – *Peter Travers, Rolling Stone*

Henry the Rainmaker

US   1948   64m   bw
Monogram (Peter Scully)

A concerned citizen runs for mayor and calls in a rainmaker to solve a drought.

Pleasant homely comedy which ran to a brief series.

w Lane Beauchamp   *d* Jean Yarbrough

Raymond Walburn, Walter Catlett, William Tracy, Mary Stuart, Barbara Brown

Her Adventurous Night

US   1946   75m   bw
Universal (Marshall Grant)

An imaginative boy spreads a story which lands his headmaster in jail, but absolves himself by solving a murder mystery.

Agreeable minor comedy for the hinterlands.

w Jerry Warner   *d* John Rawlins

Dennis O'Keefe, Helen Walker, Tom Powers, Fuzzy Knight, Scotty Beckett

Her Alibi

US   1989   94m   colour
Warner (Keith Barish)
V, V*, L

A thriller writer provides a false alibi for a woman accused of murder.

A romantic comedy without laughs or much love.

w Charlie Peters   *d* Bruce Beresford   *ph* Freddie Francis   *m* Georges Delerue   *pd* Henry Bumstead   *ed* Anne Goursaud

Tom Selleck, Paulina Porizkova, William Daniels, James Farentino, Hurd Hatfield, Ronald Guttman, Victor Argo, Patrick Wayne, Tess Harper

'Lacking a script able to go beyond the obvious, and direction able to make up for the lack of wit and sophistication.' – *MFB*

Her Cardboard Lover *

US   1942   93m   bw
MGM (J. Walter Ruben)

A flirtatious lady hires a lover to make her fiancé jealous.

Paper-thin comedy previously filmed in 1932 with Buster Keaton. It did nobody any good, but preserves some style despite a witless script.

w Jacques Deval, John Collier, Anthony Veiller, William H. Wright   *play* Jacques Deval   *d* George Cukor   *ph* Harry Stradling, Robert Planck   *m* Franz Waxman

Norma Shearer, Robert Taylor, George Sanders, Frank McHugh, Elizabeth Patterson, Chill Wills

Her Favourite Husband

GB   1950   79m   bw
Orlux/Renown
US title: *The Taming of Dorothy*

A wife finds that her husband has been replaced by a gangster who aims to rob a bank.

Rather tiresome Italian-set comedy with funny moments.

w Noel Langley, W. F. Templeton   *play* Pepine de Felipe   *d* Mario Soldati

Jean Kent, Robert Beatty, Gordon Harker, Margaret Rutherford, Rona Anderson, Max Adrian

Her First Beau
US   1941   76m   bw
Columbia (B. B. Kahane)

A teenage girl finds her childhood sweetheart is taking her for granted.

Mild family comedy, but the star did not easily take to semi-adult roles.

w Gladys Lehman, Karen DeWolf   d Theodore Reed

Jane Withers, Jackie Cooper, Edith Fellows, Josephine Hutchinson, William Tracy, Una O'Connor, Edgar Buchanan

Her First Romance
US   1951   73m   bw
Columbia
GB title: *Girls Never Tell*

A schoolgirl pursues an older boy to a summer camp.

Flat little adolescent comedy which did no good for a star in her awkward age.

w Albert Mannheimer   d Seymour Friedman

Margaret O'Brien, Allen Martin Jnr, Jimmy Hunt, Sharyn Moffett

Her Highness and the Bellboy
US   1945   112m   bw
MGM (Joe Pasternak)

A hotel bellboy forsakes his crippled sweetheart to woo a visiting princess.

Glutinous sentimental mishmash; one waits for musical numbers which never happen.

w Richard Connell, Gladys Lehman   d Richard Thorpe   ph Harry Stradling   m Georgie Stoll

Hedy Lamarr, Robert Walker, June Allyson, Rags Ragland, Agnes Moorehead, Carl Esmond, Warner Anderson, Ludwig Stossel

Her Husband Lies
US   1937   74m   bw
Paramount

A New York gambler tries to ensure that his kid brother is not contaminated.

Adequate remake of *Street of Chance*.

w Wallace Smith, Eve Brown   story O. H. P. Garrett   d Edward Ludwig

Ricardo Cortez, Gail Patrick, Akim Tamiroff, Tom Brown, Louis Calhern

'Superb direction and expert acting.' – *Variety*

Her Husband's Affairs *
US   1947   83m   bw
Columbia (Raphael Hakim)
V*

A husband and wife team of advertising agents promote a depilatory which turns out to grow hair instead.

Mildly amiable crazy comedy.

w Ben Hecht   d S. Sylvan Simon   ph Charles Lawton Jnr   m George Duning

Lucille Ball, Franchot Tone, Edward Everett Horton, Mikhail Rasumny, Gene Lockhart, Nana Bryant, Jonathan Hale, Mabel Paige

'See the mystical hypnotic rites of the white goddess of the jungle! See the plane crash in the tragic typhoon! See the ravening charge of the hundred sacred crocodiles!'
Her Jungle Love *
US   1938   81m   Technicolor
Paramount (George M. Arthur)

An aviator crashlands in the jungle, where he is comforted by a lovely lady, a chimp and a lion but distressed by an earthquake, a volcano and assorted villains.

Second of Dorothy Lamour's jungle hokum shows, and the first in colour; despite its fair technical proficiency, the fact that it once packed 'em in is tribute to the changing tastes of mankind.

w Joseph M. March, Lillie Hayward, Eddie Welch   d George Archainbaud   ph Ray Rennahan   m Gregory Stone

Dorothy Lamour, Ray Milland, Lynne Overman, J. Carrol Naish, Dorothy Howe

'Splendid colour job, but there's little more . . . only slightly varied from the type of a bygone era.' – *Variety*
† The Lynne Overman character wisecracks: 'Those *Esquire* cartoons must be right: there's always just one girl on a desert island.'
†† The lion cub in this case is called Meewa, the chimp Gaga.

Her Kind of Man
US   1946   78m   bw
Warner

A singer finds a gangster irresistible but eventually settles for a newspaper columnist.

Shiny, nondescript forties copy of a thirties style; more yawns than thrills.

w Gordon Kahn, Leopold Atlas   d Frederick de Cordova

Dane Clark, Zachary Scott, Janis Paige, Faye Emerson, George Tobias, Sheldon Leonard

Her Majesty Love
US   1931   76m   bw
Warner

A well-born Berliner finds it easier to court the barmaid he loves after she has married a baron.

Heavy-handed musical comedy worth excavating for the odd talents involved.

w Robert Lord, Arthur Caesar   d William Dieterle

Marilyn Miller, Ben Lyon, W. C. Fields, Leon Errol, Chester Conklin, Ford Sterling

'An exceptionally dismal musical.' – *Clive Hirschhorn, 1983*

Her Man *
US   1930   85m   bw
Pathé

The story of Frankie and Johnnie is transposed to a French apache setting.

Comedy melodrama which has its adherents.

w Howard Higgin, Tay Garnett   d Tay Garnett

Helen Twelvetrees, Ricardo Cortez, Marjorie Rambeau, James Gleason, Franklin Pangborn, Philips Holmes, Thelma Todd

'Looks like box office . . . full of action.' – *Variety*

Her Man Gilbey: see *English without Tears*

Her Master's Voice
US   1936   75m   bw
Paramount (Walter Wanger)

Henpecked by his wife and her mother, a man makes a name for himself as a radio troubadour.

Mild comedy from a stage success.

w Dore Schary, Harry Sauber   play Clare Kummer   d Joseph Santley

Edward Everett Horton, Peggy Conklin, Laura Hope Crews, Elizabeth Patterson, Grant Mitchell

'Suitable because of frothy humour for family and nabe audiences solo.' – *Variety*

Her Panelled Door: see *The Woman with No Name*

Her Primitive Man
US   1944   87m   bw
Universal

An author disguises himself as a savage in order to denounce a woman trying to prove his theories a fraud.

Very silly comedy partly salvaged by a few good lines.

w Michael Fessier, Ernest Pagano   d Charles Lamont

Robert Paige, Louise Allbritton, Robert Benchley, Edward Everett Horton, Helen Broderick, Ernest Truex, Walter Catlett, Nydia Westman

Her Sister's Secret
US   1946   86m   bw
PRC (Henry Brash)

A pregnant girl hands over her child to her sister; but what will the sister's husband say?

Peg's Paper in modern dress, but an ambitious project for this Poverty Row company.

w Anne Green   novel *Dark Angel* by Gina Kaus   d Edgar G. Ulmer

Nancy Coleman, Margaret Lindsay, Philip Reed, Felix Bressart, Regis Toomey, Henry Stephenson, Fritz Feld

Her Sweetheart: see *Christopher Bean*

Her Twelve Men
US   1954   91m   Anscocolor
MGM (John Houseman)

A woman teacher in a boys' school reforms a difficult class.

Predictable, sugary and artificial school story with the star exuding sweetness and light.

w William Roberts, Laura Z. Hobson   d Robert Z. Leonard   ph Joseph Ruttenberg   m Bronislau Kaper

Greer Garson, Robert Ryan, Richard Haydn, Barry Sullivan

Her Wedding Night
US   1930   78m   bw
Paramount

On the Italian riviera a man marries his friend's wife under the impression that they are only booking rooms for the night.

Spicy bedroom farce which crested the wave of its star's notoriety.

w Henry Myers   play Avery Hopwood   d Frank Tuttle

Clara Bow, *Charles Ruggles,* Ralph Forbes, Skeets Gallagher

'Deftly handled for smartness and taste . . . ought to make women talk.' – *Variety*

Herbie Goes Bananas
US   1980   100m   Technicolor
Walt Disney
V*

Two Americans take their magical Volkswagen on a South American holiday.

Listless addition to a series which has already gone on too long.

w Don Tait   d Vincent McEveety

Charles Martin Smith, Stephan W. Burns, Cloris Leachman, John Vernon

Herbie Goes to Monte Carlo
US   1977   105m   Technicolor
Walt Disney (Ron Miller)
V*

The Volkswagen with a mind of its own enters the Monte Carlo rally and routs a gang of thieves.

Utterly predictable, patchily made family comedy.

w Arthur Alsberg, Don Nelson *d* Vincent McEveety
ph Leonard J. South *m* Frank de Vol

Dean Jones, Don Knotts, Julie Sommars, Jacques Marin, Roy Kinnear, Bernard Fox

† Second sequel to *The Love Bug*.

Herbie Rides Again

US 1974 88m Technicolor
Walt Disney (Bill Walsh)
V*, L

A Volkswagen with a mind of its own helps an old lady to rout a property developer.

Acceptable sequel to *The Love Bug*.

w Bill Walsh *d* Robert Stevenson

Helen Hayes, Ken Berry, Stefanie Powers, John McIntyre, Keenan Wynn, Huntz Hall

Hercules

Italy 1957 105m Eastmancolor Dyaliscope
Oscar/Galatea (Federico Teti)
V*, L

original title: *Le Fatiche di Ercole*

Hercules helps Jason find the golden fleece.

The strong man epic which started a genre; of little interest in itself.

w Pietro Francisci, Ennio de Concini, Gaio Frattini
d Pietro Francisci *ph* Mario Bava *m* Enzo Masetti

Steve Reeves, Sylva Koscina, Gianna Maria Canale, Fabrizio Mione

Hercules against Rome (dubbed)

France/Italy 1965 87m Eastmancolor
Totalscope
Romana/Regina (Fortunato Misiano)
original title: *Ercole contro Roma*; aka: *Hercules in Rome*

Hercules, a blacksmith, goes to the aid of the daughter of the Emperor, in the power of the commander of the Praetorian Guard.

Standard muscle-bound epic, with our hero fighting, not too convincingly, against state corruption.

w Piero Pierotti, Arpad de Riso *story* Arpad de Riso, Nino Scolaro *d* Piero Pierotti (American version *d* Robert Spafford) *ph* Augusto Tiezzi *m* A. F. Lavagnino *ad* Salvatore Giancotti *ed* Iolanda Benvenuti

Alan Steel, Wandisa Guida, Daniele Vargas, Livio Lorenzon, Andrea Aureli, Dina de Santis, Mimmo Palmara

Hercules Goes Bananas: see *Hercules in New York*

Hercules in New York

US 1969 91m Eastmancolor
RAF Industries (Aubrey Wisberg)
V*, L
aka: *Hercules Goes Bananas*; *Hercules – the Movie*

Hercules drops in on modern-day New York and becomes involved with wrestlers and gamblers.

Schwarzenegger's first film, a dim comedy – and one that no doubt returns to haunt him, particularly his dubbed all-American high tenor voice and the way his muscles do the acting.

w Aubrey Wisberg *d* Arthur A. Seidelman
ph Leo Lebowitz *m* John Balamos *ad* Perry Watkins *ed* Donald Finamore

Arnold Stang, Arnold Strong (Schwarzenegger), Deborah Loomis, James Karen, Ernest Graves, Tanny McDonald, Tania Elg, Michael Lipton

'Schwarzenegger as Herc wrestled with a man in a bear suit and when I tell you that the suit was a better actor you will have some conception.' – *Nancy Banks-Smith, Guardian*

Hercules in Rome: see *Hercules against Rome*

Hercules – the Movie: see *Hercules in New York*

Hercules Unchained

Italy/France 1959 105m Eastmancolor
Dyaliscope
Lux/Galatea (Bruno Vailati)
V*, L
original title: *Ercole e la Regina di Lidia*

Hercules has problems with the king of Thebes and the queen of Lidia.

More comic-strip versions of old legends. This item had more spent on it in publicity than in production cost, and consequently was seen by vast audiences around the world. It isn't very good.

w Pietro Francisci, Ennio di Concini *d* Pietro Francisci *ph* Mario Bava *m* Enzo Masetti

Steve Reeves, Sylva Koscina, Sylvia Lopez, Primo Carnera

† Many sequels followed, the hero sometimes being known as Ursus or Goliath.

Here Come the Coeds

US 1945 88m bw
Universal (John Grant)

Janitors help to forestall a mortgage foreclosure on a college for women.

Routine star vehicle with few highlights.

w Arthur T. Horman, John Grant *d* Jean Yarbrough
ph George Robinson *m/y* Jack Brooks, Edgar Fairchild

Bud Abbott, Lou Costello, Lon Chaney Jnr, Peggy Ryan, Martha O'Driscoll, Donald Cook, June Vincent, Charles Dingle

Here Come the Girls *

US 1953 78m Technicolor
Paramount/Hope Enterprises (Paul Jones)
original title: *Champagne for Everybody*

In the 1890s an ageing chorus boy traps a mysterious murderer.

Spotty, ineptly titled star comedy with music; in fact among the last of his passable vehicles, with excellent production backing.

w Edmund Hartmann, Hal Kanter *d* Claude Binyon
ph Lionel Lindon *md* Lyn Murray *ad* Hal Pereira, Roland Anderson

Bob Hope, Rosemary Clooney, Tony Martin, Arlene Dahl, Millard Mitchell, Fred Clark, William Demarest, Robert Strauss

Here Come the Huggetts *

GB 1948 93m bw
Rank/Gainsborough (Betty Box)

A suburban family has its ups and downs.

Cosy domestic comedy drama, a presage of TV soap operas to come, or Britain's answer to the Hardys, depending how you look at it. Tolerable at the time.

w Mabel and Denis Constanduros, Muriel and Sydney Box, Peter Rogers *d* Ken Annakin *ph* Reg Wyer *m* Anthony Hopkins

Jack Warner, Kathleen Harrison, Jane Hylton, Susan Shaw, Petula Clark, Jimmy Hanley, David Tomlinson, Diana Dors, Peter Hammond, John Blythe

† The Huggetts had actually originated in *Holiday Camp* the previous year, and appeared again in *Vote for Huggett* and *The Huggetts Abroad*; Warner and Harrison became an inseparable duo for many years.

Here Come the Nelsons

US 1951 76m bw
Universal

The sons of an advertising agent get involved with gangsters.

Empty-headed family comedy based on the long-running TV show *The Adventures of Ozzie and Harriet*.

w Ozzie Nelson, Donald Nelson, William Davenport
d Frederick de Cordova

Ozzie Nelson, Harriet Hilliard, David and Ricky Nelson, Rock Hudson, Barbara Lawrence, Ann Doran, Jim Backus

Here Come the Waves

US 1944 98m bw
Paramount (Mark Sandrich)

A sailor falls in love with identical twin Waves.

Empty-headed, professionally executed musical recruiting poster.

w Allen Scott, Ken Englund, Zion Myers *d* Mark Sandrich *ph* Charles Lang *md* Robert Emmett Dolan *m/y* Harold Arlen, Johnny Mercer

Bing Crosby, Betty Hutton, Sonny Tufts, Ann Doran, Gwen Crawford

'An almost totally negligible musical.' – *James Agee*

AAN: song 'Accentuate the Positive'

Here Comes Cookie

US 1935 65m bw
Paramount (William le Baron)

Gracie comes into money and opens a theatre-cum-hotel for vaudevillians.

Slight star comedy with its share of laughs.

w Sam Mintz, Don Hartman *d* Norman Z. McLeod

George Burns, Gracie Allen, George Barbier, Betty Furness, Andrew Tombes

'Situation and gag pounding without an ounce of seriousness or sense.' – *Variety*

Here Comes Mr Jordan ***

US 1941 93m bw
Columbia (Everett Riskin)
V, V*, L

A prizefighter who is also an amateur saxophonist crashes in his private plane and goes to heaven by mistake: he was supposed to survive and live another forty years. Unfortunately when he goes back for his body it has been cremated, so he has to find another one, recently deceased . . .

Weird heavenly fantasy which succeeded because of its novelty and because heaven in wartime was a comforting vision. As a movie taken on its own merits, it suffers from illogicalities, a miscast star and a wandering plot, but scene for scene there is enough firmness and control to make it memorable. It certainly had many imitations, including *Angel on My Shoulder*, *Down to Earth*, *A Guy Named Joe*, *Heaven Only Knows*, *The Horn Blows at Midnight* and *That's the Spirit*.

w Seton I. Miller, Sidney Buchman *play Halfway to Heaven* by Harry Segall *d* Alexander Hall *ph* Joseph Walker *md* Morris Stoloff *m* Frederick Hollander

Robert Montgomery, Evelyn Keyes, Rita Johnson, *Claude Rains*, *James Gleason*, *Edward Everett Horton*, John Emery, *Donald MacBride*, Halliwell Hobbes, Don Costello

'There is something about this original so sweet-spirited and earnest that it transcends its plot devices and shines through its comedic asides to become a true morality play without once becoming either preachy or mawkish.' – *Kit Parker catalogue, 1980*

'Audiences loved this chunk of whimsy . . . the slickly hammy Rains gives Mr Jordan a sinister gloss, as if he were involved in some heavenly racket, like smuggling Chinese.' – *Pauline Kael, 70s*

† Remade 1978 as *Heaven Can Wait*.

AA: original story (Harry Segall); script

AAN: best picture; Alexander Hall; Joseph Walker; Robert Montgomery; James Gleason

Here Comes the Band

US   1935   82m   bw
MGM

Buddies from an army band are stuck in the taxi business.

Shapeless comedy with interesting numbers. But not very.

w Paul Sloane, Ralph Spence, Victor Mansfield
d Paul Sloane

Ted Lewis and his Band, Ted Healy, Nat Pendleton, Virginia Bruce, Harry Stockwell, Donald Cook, Spanky McFarland

'Not punchy enough for the de luxe trade . . . best as second stringer.' – *Variety*

Here Comes the Groom *

US   1951   114m   bw
Paramount (Frank Capra)
V*, L

A journalist adopts war orphans and reforms his selfish fiancée.

Tired attempt by Capra to recapture his prewar mood; despite intermittent pleasures it has neither the right style nor the topical substance.

w Virginia Van Upp, Myles Connelly, Liam O'Brien   *story* Robert Riskin   *d* Frank Capra   *ph* George Barnes   *md* Joseph Lilley   *m/ly* Jay Livingston, Ray Evans

Bing Crosby, Jane Wyman, Franchot Tone, Alexis Smith, James Barton, Connie Gilchrist, Robert Keith, Anna Maria Alberghetti

'The general impression is of a loud, strident, rather vulgar comedy in which technique is used to disappointingly mechanical ends, and which a few bright lines of dialogue cannot rescue from tedium.' – *Penelope Houston*

AA: song 'In the Cool Cool Cool of the Evening' (*m* Hoagy Carmichael, *ly* Johnny Mercer)

AAN: Robert Riskin

Here Comes the Navy *

US   1934   86m   bw
Warner (Lou Edelman)

An aggressive young naval rating fights with his former friend, now Petty Officer.

Breezy comedy melodrama teaming Cagney and O'Brien for the first time and offering star heroics as a sop to the Legion of Decency.

w Ben Markson, Earl Baldwin   *d* Lloyd Bacon
ph Arthur Edeson   *m* Leo F. Forbstein

James Cagney, Pat O'Brien, Dorothy Tree, Gloria Stuart, Frank McHugh, Robert Barrat

'It's a bit too masculine for matinée appeal and it'll have to be a case of the kids and men dragging the womenfolk along.' – *Variety*

'Rapid and reasonably authentic, a satisfactory addition to a series of cinema cartoons which, because their colour and mood are indigenous and timely, may be more interesting twenty years from now.' – *Time*

AAN: best picture

Here Comes the Sun

GB   1946   91m   bw
Universal (John Baxter)
V

Racetrack touts help to breathe fresh life into a provincial newspaper.

Amiable comedy with a touch of do-goodery, very typical of this producer.

w Geoffrey Orme   *d* John Baxter

Bud Flanagan, Chesney Allen, Joss Ambler, Dick Francis, Horace Kenney

Here I Am a Stranger

US   1939   82m   bw
TCF (Harry Joe Brown)

A rich woman tries to prevent her son being influenced by her once-drunken ex-husband.

Predictable family drama which was catnip to 1939 audiences.

w Sam Hellman and Milton Sperling   *story* Gordon Malherbe Hillman   *d* Roy del Ruth   *ph* Arthur Miller   *md* Louis Silvers

Gladys George, Richard Dix, Richard Greene, Brenda Joyce, Roland Young, Russell Gleason, George Zucco

'Strong programme drama will catch many top key spots.' – *Variety*

Here Is a Man: see *All That Money Can Buy*

Here Is My Heart

US   1934   73m   bw
Paramount

An American radio crooner on the riviera pretends to be a waiter in order to court a princess.

Musical remake of *The Grand Duchess and the Waiter;* not bad of its type.

w Edwin Justus Mayer, Harlan Thompson   *d* Frank Tuttle   *m/ly* Leo Robin, Ralph Rainger

songs: 'Love Is Just Around the Corner'; 'With Every Breath I Take'; 'June in January'; 'Here Is My Heart'; 'You Can't Make a Monkey of the Moon'.

Bing Crosby, Kitty Carlisle, Roland Young, Alison Skipworth, Reginald Owen, Akim Tamiroff

'First-class entertainment . . . though it seems they adapted it by running it through the electric fan.' – *Variety*

Here We Go Again

US   1942   75m   bw
RKO (Allan Dwan)

Various radio celebrities congregate at Silvertip Lodge.

Random excuse for a variety show, with top talent of its day; a sequel to *Look Who's Laughing.*

w Paul Gerard Smith, Joe Bigelow   *d* Allan Dwan

Jim Jordan, Marion Jordan (Fibber McGee and Molly), Edgar Bergen, Charlie McCarthy, Harold Peary (The Great Gildersleeve), Ginny Simms, Gale Gordon, Ray Noble and his orchestra

Here We Go Round the Mulberry Bush *

GB   1967   96m   Technicolor
UA/Giant (Larry Kramer, Clive Donner)

A school-leaver is obsessed by sex and determines to lose his virginity.

Repetitive comedy which certainly opened new avenues in British humour and seemed pretty permissive at the time (pre-*Graduate*). In itself, however, more modish than sympathetic.

w Hunter Davies, Larry Kramer   *novel* Hunter Davies   *d* Clive Donner   *ph* Alex Thomson
m various groups

Barry Evans, Judy Geeson, Angela Scoular, Adrienne Posta, Sheila White, Vanessa Howard, Denholm Elliott, Maxine Audley, Moyra Fraser, Michael Bates

'The only incongruity is that it should have been made by adults, so completely does it enter into the teenager's view of himself.' – *MFB*

Here's To Romance

US   1935   82m   bw
TCF (Jesse L. Lasky)

A young tenor who finds a patron in Paris is pursued by the wealthy wife.

Amiable piece of musical froth which somehow failed to make a big singing star of Martini.

w Ernest Pascal, Arthur Richman   *d* Alfred E. Green

Nino Martini, Genevieve Tobin, Reginald Denny, Anita Louise, Mme Schumann-Heink, Maria Gambarelli

'Given a sturdier story he might have emerged as a Grace Moore for talkers.' – *Variety*

Hero *

US   1992   116m   Technicolor
Columbia TriStar (Laura Ziskin)
V, V*, L, S
GB title: *Accidental Hero*

A drifter claims to be the saviour of a plane crash while the real hero, a petty crook, goes unrecognized.

An interesting central situation is inadequately developed and finally frittered away.

w David Webb Peoples   *story* Laura Ziskin, Alvin Sargent   *d* Stephen Frears   *ph* Oliver Stapleton   *m* George Fenton   *pd* Dennis Gasner   *ed* Mick Audsley

Dustin Hoffman, Geena Davis, Andy Garcia, Joan Cusack, Kevin J. O'Connor, Maury Chaykin, Stephen Tobolowsky

'Peppered with occasional gems but one has to sift through a lot of wreckage to find them.' – *Variety*

The Hero: see *Bloomfield*

A Hero Ain't Nothing but a Sandwich

US   1977   107m   CFI color
New World/Radnitz-Mattel (Robert B. Radnitz)
V*, L

Problems for an urban family in the black ghetto.

Well-intentioned but ultimately wearisome and cliché-strewn melodrama.

w Alice Childress   *novel* Alice Childress   *d* Ralph Nelson   *ph* Frank Stanley   *m* Tom McIntosh

Cicely Tyson, Paul Winfield, Larry B. Scott, Helen Martin, Glynn Turman

'The sort of dreaded wholesome film that cultural and societal groups heavily endorse but nobody pays money to go see.' – *Variety*

Hero at Large

US   1980   98m   Metrocolor
MGM (Stephen Freedman)
V, V*

An actor playing Captain Avenger accidentally becomes a real-life hero, but his fans turn against him when they find he's just an ordinary guy.

Muddled satirical comedy-melodrama with too many pauses for love interest.

w A. J. Carothers   *d* Martin Davidson

John Ritter, Anne Archer, Bert Convy, Kevin McCarthy, Harry Bellaver

The Hero of Babylon

Italy/France   1964   90m   Eastmancolor   Euroscope
FIA/Gladiator Film (Albino Morandini)
original title: *L'Eroe di Babylone*; aka: *Goliath, King of Slaves*

Prince Nipur returns home to find that his cousin has usurped the throne of Babylon and is ruling as a tyrant.

Typical product of the Italian cycle of movies with an Old Testament setting, given over to sword fights.

w Gianpaolo Callegari, Siro Marcellini, Albert Valentin   *d* Siro Marcellini   *ph* Pierludovico Pavoni   *m* Carlo Franzi   *pd* Vittorio Marchi   *ed* Nella Nannuzzi

Gordon Scott, Moira Orfei, Geneviève Grad, Piero Lulli, Andrea Scotti, Mario Petri

The Heroes

Italy/France/Spain 1972 110m Telecolour Scope
Paladin/Gerico Sound/Finarco/Corona/Transinter/Atlantida
(Alfredo Bini)
original title: *Gli Eroi*

In North Africa during the Second World War a
former prostitute makes off with £2 million, pursued
by German soldiers, a British officer and assorted
allies.

Dull caper movie of predictable unoriginality.

w Luciano Vincenzoni, Sergio Donati   *novel* Albert
Kantof, René Harvard   d Duccio Tessari   ph Carlo
Carlini   m Riz Ortolani   ad Walter Patriarca,
Andrea Crisanti   ed Mario Morra

Rod Steiger, Rosanna Schiaffino, Rod Taylor, Claude
Brasseur, Terry-Thomas

'Treads a well-worn path with a handful of stock
characters.' – *Tom Milne, MFB*

The film was cut to 99m for its British release.

Heroes

US 1977 113m Technicolor
Universal (David Foster, Lawrence Turman)
V*

A Vietnam veteran, made slightly kooky by his
experiences, settles down after several adventures
when he falls in love.

Just plain awful: a would-be star vehicle that doesn't
work.

w James Carabatsos (David Freeman, uncredited)
d Jeremy Paul Kagan   ph Frank Stanley   m Jack
Nitzsche, Richard Hazard

Henry Winkler, Sally Field, Harrison Ford, Val Avery

The Heroes Are Tired

France 1955 101m bw
Cila-Terra
original title: *Les Héros Sont Fatigués*

Two ex-wartime pilots, one Free French and the other
German, set up an air charter service in Liberia but
come to grief over stolen diamonds.

Gloomy post-war *film noir* set in a peculiarly
depressing atmosphere, and not really sharp enough
to overcome its squalid plot.

w Yves Ciampi, Jacques-Laurent Bost
novel Christine Garnier   d Yves Ciampi   ph Henri
Alekan   m Louiguy

Yves Montand, Maria Félix, Jean Servais, Curt
Jurgens, Gérard Oury

Heroes for Sale

US 1933 73m bw
Warner
V*

A war veteran becomes in turn a drug addict, a
millionaire and the central figure in a labour dispute.

Minor social-conscience melodrama with watchable
elements.

w Robert Lord, Wilson Mizner   d William A.
Wellman

Richard Barthelmess, Aline MacMahon, Loretta
Young, Berton Churchill, Robert Barrat

'This attempted satire on unemployment conditions
just prior to the Roosevelt election is not well told . . .
b.o. doubtful.' – *Variety*

The Heroes of Telemark *

GB 1965 131m Technicolor Panavision
Rank/Benton (Ben Fisz)
V

Norwegian resistance workers in World War II help
the Allies to smash a heavy water plant.

Ambling narrative with big action sequences which
often seem irrelevant, so that the story as a whole fails
to excite.

w Ivan Moffat, Ben Barzman   d Anthony Mann
ph Robert Krasker   m Malcolm Arnold

Kirk Douglas, Richard Harris, Ulla Jacobsson, Roy
Dotrice, Anton Diffring, Michael Redgrave

Heroes of the West

US 1932 bw serial: 12 eps
Universal

Young Noah Blaine helps his father to build the
transcontinental railroad.

Fairly ambitious serial of its time.   d Ray Taylor

Noah Beery Jnr, Diane Duval, Onslow Stevens,
William Desmond

The Heroin Gang: see *Sol Madrid*

Heroism: see *Eroica*

Hero's Island *

US 1962 94m Technicolor Panavision
UA/Daystar/Portland (James Mason, Leslie Stevens)

In 1718 bondslaves settle on a Carolina island, are
attacked by fishermen and protected by one of the
aides of Blackbeard the Pirate.

An oddly personal, patchy, rather mysterious film
with a rhetorical script and rather good action
sequences.

wd Leslie Stevens   ph Ted McCord   m Dominic
Frontière

James Mason, Kate Manx, Neville Brand, Rip Torn

Les Héros Sont Fatigués: see *The Heroes Are Tired*

Herr Puntila and His Servant Matti *

Austria 1955 95m Agfacolor
Bauerfilm

A rich landowner, usually drunk, is rescued from
scrapes by his patient valet.

A cogent comedy which its author is said to have
approved in this version.

w Alberto Cavalcanti, Vladimir Pozner, Ruth Wieden
play Bertolt Brecht   d Alberto Cavalcanti
ph André Bac, Arthur Hämmerer   m Hanns Eisler

Curt Bois, Hans Engelmann, Maria Emo, Edith Prager

Hers to Hold

US 1943 94m bw
Universal (Felix Jackson)

A girl decides whether or not to marry a serviceman.

Limp star vehicle, a sequel to *Three Smart Girls* (qv).

w Lewis R. Foster   d Frank Ryan   ph Elwood
Bredell   md Charles Previn   m Frank Skinner

Deanna Durbin, Joseph Cotten, Charles Winninger,
Nella Walker, Gus Schilling, Ludwig Stossel

AAN: song 'Say a Prayer for the Boys Over There' (m
Jimmy McHugh, ly Herb Magidson)

Herz aus Glas: see *Heart of Glass*

He's a Cockeyed Wonder

US 1950 77m bw
Columbia

An orange sorter goes into the magic business.

Energetic low-budget comedy vehicle for
unsophisticated audiences.

w Jack Henley   d Peter Godfrey

Mickey Rooney, Terry Moore, William Demarest,
Charles Arnt, Mike Mazurki

Hester Street *

US 1974 89m bw
Midwest Films (Raphael D. Silver)

How Jewish immigrants settled in East Side New
York in the 1890s.

Modest, humorous, but not always smooth or
dramatically emphatic chronicle of a familiar
background; the detail however is excellent.

wd Joan Micklin Silver   story Yekl by Abraham
Cahan   ph Kenneth Van Sickle   m William Bolcom

Steven Keats, Carol Kane, Mel Howard, Dorrie
Kavanaugh, Doris Roberts

'A small, beautifully detailed, slightly shaggy
independent film of charm and substance.' – *Judith
Crist*

'For old diehards who still go to the cinema seeking
humanity, tenderness and insight.' – *Michael Billington,
Illustrated London News*

AAN: Carol Kane

Hets: see *Frenzy*

Hexen geschändet und zu Tode gequält: see
Mark of the Devil

Hey, Good-Lookin'

US 1982 76m Technicolor
Warner (Ralph Bakshi)

Life in 1953 Brooklyn centres round two young
womanizers.

Enterprising attempt to use animation to tell a youth
melodrama; interesting but not successful.
wd Ralph Bakshi

voices of Richard Romanus, David Proval, Jesse
Welles, Tina Bowman

Hey! Hey! USA

GB 1938 92m bw
Gainsborough (Edward Black)

An education expert sails to America, falls in with
gangsters, and saves a boy from being kidnapped by
them.

Misconceived star vehicle which provides some
laughs, but not of the expected kind.

w J. O. C. Orton, Val Guest, G. Marriott Edgar
story Howard Irving Young, Ralph Spence   d Marcel
Varnel   ph Arthur Crabtree   md Louis Levy
m Cecil Milner   ad Vetchinsky   ed R. E. Dearing

Will Hay, Edgar Kennedy, David Burns, Fred Duprez

Hey Rookie

US 1944 71m bw
Columbia (Irving Briskin)

A musical comedy producer in the army puts on a
show.

Virtually a non-stop revue.

w Henry Myers, Edward Ellsen, Jay Gurney
play K. B. and Doris Culvan   d Charles Barton

Ann Miller, Joe Besser, Larry Parks, Joe Sawyer, the
Condos Brothers, Jack Gilford, the Hal McIntyre
Orchestra

'Brief, to the point, and will do.' – *Variety*

Hi Buddy

US 1943 66m bw
Universal (Paul Malvern)

Soldiers stage a benefit show at a boys' club.

Luckily the sentiment does not get in the way of the
numbers; ordinary modest musical filler.

w Warren Wilson   d Harold Young

Dick Foran, Harriet Hilliard, Robert Paige, Marjorie
Lord, the King's Men, the Four Sweethearts, Dolores
Diane

Hi Diddle Diddle *

US 1943 72m bw
UA/Andrew Stone
aka: *Try and Find It*

Young lovers are hampered by con artist parents.

Scatty comedy with amusing patches and some zest in the telling.

w Edmund L. Hartmann   d Andrew L. Stone
ph Charles Van Enger   m Phil Boutelje

Adolphe Menjou, Pola Negri, Dennis O'Keefe, Billie Burke, Martha Scott, June Havoc

AAN: Phil Boutelje

Hi Gang

GB   1941   100m   bw
Rank/Gainsborough (Edward Black)

American expatriates in London get involved in a case of mistaken identity.

Icky farce based faintly on a wartime radio variety series, notable only for preserving the three stars involved.

w Val Guest, Marriott Edgar, J. O. C. Orton, Howard Irving Young   d Marcel Varnel   ph Jack Cox

Bebe Daniels, Ben Lyon, Vic Oliver, Graham Moffatt, Moore Marriott, Felix Aylmer, Sam Browne

Hi, Mom! *

US   1969   86m   Movielab
West End Films

Adventures of a young porno film maker and of the eccentrics who live in the same building.

Busy comedy of the drop-out life, full of random satirical jabs and *hommages* to other film makers.

wd Brian de Palma

Robert de Niro, Allen Garfield, Gerrit Graham, Jennifer Salt

Hi Nellie *

US   1934   79m   bw
Warner (Robert Presnell)

An ex-editor is demoted to advice to the lovelorn and gets involved in city rackets.

Minor, effective star comedy-melodrama.

w Abem Finkel, Sidney Sutherland   d Mervyn Le Roy   ph Sol Polito

Paul Muni, Glenda Farrell, Ned Sparks, Robert Barrat, Hobart Cavanaugh, Berton Churchill, Donald Meek, Douglass Dumbrille, Edward Ellis

'Barely gets by as fair entertainment . . . it's a better Muni performance than a picture.' – *Variety*

† Remade in 1935 as *Front Page Woman*; 1937 as *Love Is on the Air*; 1942 as *You Can't Escape Forever*; 1949 as *The House across the Street*.

Hi Ya Chum

US   1943   61m   bw
Universal
GB title: *Everything Happens to Us*

On their way to Hollywood, variety performers are stranded in a small town.

Thin star comedy support.

w Edmund L. Hartmann   d Harold Young

The Ritz Brothers, Jane Frazee, Robert Paige, June Clyde

Hiawatha

US   1952   80m   Cinecolor
Allied Artists

A young brave prevents war between three Indian tribes.

Muddled actioner which has little to do with Longfellow's poem.

w Arthur Strawn, Dan Ullman   d Kurt Neumann

Vincent Edwards, Yvette Dugay, Keith Larsen, Morris Ankrum, Ian MacDonald

Hickey and Boggs

US   1972   111m   DeLuxe
UA/Film Guarantors Ltd (Fouad Said)

Two down and out private eyes, hired to find a girl, keep falling over dead bodies.

Extraordinarily confused thriller with moments of humour and well staged action sequences.

w Walter Hill   d Robert Culp   ph Wilmer Butler   m Ted Ashford

Robert Culp, Bill Cosby, Rosalind Cash

The Hidden

US   1988   97m   DeLuxe
Palace/New Line-Heron/Third Elm Street Venture (Robert Shaye, Gerald T. Olson, Michael Meltzer)
V*, L

Detectives hunt down a murderous slug-like alien who possesses the bodies of humans.

Standard action fare, somewhat sillier than the norm.

w Bob Hunt   d Jack Sholder   ph Jacques Haitkin   m Michael Convertino   pd C. J. Strawn, Mick Strawn   ed Michael N. Knue

Kyle MacLachlan, Michael Nouri, Claudia Christian, Clarence Felder, Clu Gulager, Ed O'Ross, William Boyett, Richard Brooks, Larry Cedar

'The film appears to suggest that the universe is entirely peopled with strange creatures who nevertheless conform to American stereotypes.' *Kim Newman, MFB*

Hidden Agenda **

GB   1990   108m   Eastmancolor
Enterprise/Hemdale (Eric Fellner)
V, V*, L

A police officer discovers that members of the Royal Ulster Constabulary are responsible for murders of IRA sympathisers in Belfast.

Powerful political film, based in part on actual events, that sometimes descends into hectoring agit-prop. It won the Jury Prize at the Cannes Film Festival in 1990.

w Jim Allen   d Ken Loach   ph Clive Tickner   m Stewart Copeland   pd Martin Johnson   ed Jonathan Morris

Brian Cox, Frances McDormand, Brad Dourif, Mai Zetterling, Bernard Bloch, John Benfield, Jim Norton, Patrick Kavanagh, Bernard Archard

'*Hidden Agenda*, though it attempts to make an acceptable theatrical entertainment out of a complex political saga, lacks big-screen impact.' – *Variety*

The Hidden Eye

US   1945   69m   bw
MGM

A blind detective gets on the trail of a murderer who deliberately leaves confusing clues.

Thin successor to *Eyes in the Night*: no style at all.

w George Harmon Coxe, Harry Ruskin   d Richard Whorf

Edward Arnold, Frances Rafferty, William Phillips, Ray Collins, Thomas Jackson

Hidden Fear

US   1957   83m   bw
UA (St Aubrey-Kohn)

An American cop in Copenhagen clears his sister of a murder charge.

Patchy, tough thriller with some pretensions to style sabotaged by a muddled script.

w André de Toth, John Ward Hawkins   d André de Toth

John Payne, Anne Neyland, Alexander Knox, Conrad Nagel, Elsy Albiin

The Hidden Fortress *

Japan   1958   123m   bw   Tohoscope
Toho (Masumi Fujimoto)
V*, L
original title: *Kakushi Toride No San-Akunin*

In medieval Japan, the heiress of a feudal lord is saved from a bandit by a samurai.

Roistering eastern Western.

w Ryuzo Kikushima, Hideo Oguni, Shinobu Hashimoto, Akira Kurosawa   d Akira Kurosawa   ph Ichio Yamazaki   m Masaru Sato

Toshiro Mifune, Misa Uehara, Minoru Chiaki

The Hidden Hand

US   1942   67m   bw
Warner

Murders proliferate in the house of a wealthy old spinster.

Heavy-going spoof of the thunderstorm mystery; sometimes amusing for connoisseurs of the genre.

w Anthony Coldeway   d Ben Stoloff

Craig Stevens, Elisabeth Fraser, Julie Bishop, Willie Best, Milton Parsons

The Hidden Room: see *Obsession* (1948)

Hide and Seek

GB   1963   90m   bw
British Lion/Albion/Spectrum (Hal E. Chester)

A research scientist is the centre of a kidnap plan designed to make it appear that he has defected.

Too many mysterious happenings with too little explanation sink this comedy-thriller from the start.

w David Stone   d Cy Endfield   ph Gilbert Taylor   m Muir Mathieson, Gary Campbell

Ian Carmichael, Janet Munro, Curt Jurgens, Hugh Griffith, George Pravda, Kieron Moore, Edward Chapman

Hide in Plain Sight

US   1980   92m   Metrocolor   Panavision
MGM (Robert Christiansen, Rick Rosenberg)
V*

A factory worker searches for his children when his former wife is hidden by the government to protect her husband, an informer.

Unpersuasive melodrama with little more than its unusual plot to commend it.

w Spencer Eastman   book Leslie Waller   d James Caan   ph Paul Lohmann   m Leonard Rosenman

James Caan, Jill Eikenberry, Robert Viharo

Hideaway Girl

US   1936   71m   bw
Paramount (A. M. Botsford)

A girl suspected of stealing a necklace goes on the run.

Humdrum comedy melodrama with songs: a hotchpotch.

w Joseph Moncure March   d George Archainbaud

Martha Raye, Shirley Ross, Robert Cummings, Monroe Owsley

'Rowdy, nonsensical lightweight, geared for doubles.' – *Variety*

The Hideous Sun Demon

US   1959   74m   bw
Clarke-King Enterprises/Robert Clarke
V*
GB title: *Blood on His Lips*

Subjected to a high level of radiation, a scientist turns into a giant two-legged lizard when exposed to sunlight.

Simple-minded science fiction featuring the producer-director-star in an ill-fitting monster costume.

w E. S. Seeley Jnr, Doane Hoag d Robert Clarke, Tom Boutrous ph John Morrill, Vilis Lapenieks, Stan Follis m John Seely ad Gianbattista Cassarino ed Tom Boutrous

Robert Clarke, Patricia Manning, Nan Peterson, Patrick White

Hideout
US 1934 83m bw
MGM
V*

An injured racketeer takes refuge with a farm family and is reformed by the simple life and true love.

Schematic eat-your-cake-and-have-it melodrama which pleased audiences at the time.

w Frances Goodrich, Albert Hackett story Mauri Grashin d W. S. Van Dyke

Robert Montgomery, Maureen O'Sullivan, Mickey Rooney, Edward Arnold, C. Henry Gordon, Elizabeth Patterson, Edward Brophy, Herman Bing

AAN: original story

The Hideout (1948): see *The Small Voice*

Hideout in the Alps: see *Dusty Ermine*

Hider in the House
US 1989 108m CFI color
Vestron/Precision Films (Edward Teets, Michael Taylor)
V*, L, S

A murderer, hiding in the attic of a house, spies on the family that lives there.

A thriller lacking in suspense and with nothing else to recommend it.

w Lem Dobbs d Matthew Patrick ph Jeff Jur m Christopher Young pd Victoria Paul ed Debra T. Smith

Gary Busey, Mimi Rogers, Michael McKean, Kurt Christopher Kinder, Candy Hutson, Elizabeth Ruscio, Chuck Lafont, Bruce Glover

The Higgins Family
US 1938 65m bw
Republic

An advertising man is driven almost to divorce when his wife becomes a radio personality.

Modest family comedy which ran to a short series.

w Paul Gerard Smith, Jack Townley, Richard English d Gus Meins

James Gleason, Lucile Gleason, Russell Gleason, Lynne Roberts, Harry Davenport

'Shows fine promise.' – *Variety*

High and Dry: see *The Maggie*

High and Low **
Japan 1963 142m bw Tohoscope
Toho (Tomoyuki Tanaka)
V*, L

A wealthy shoe manufacturer's chauffeur's son is kidnapped in mistake for his own, and he faces a moral dilemma.

Interesting, rather gloomy Japanese version of a light American thriller with all the style expected of the director.

w Hideo Oguni, Ryuzo Kikushima, Eijiro Hisaito, Akira Kurosawa novel *The King's Ransom* by Ed McBain d Akira Kurosawa ph Asakazu Makai, Takao Saito m Masaru Sato

Toshiro Mifune, Kyoko Kagawa, Tatsuya Nakadai

'A tapestry of crime, detection and punishment, with vivid vignettes of various strata of society, haunting moments on the waterfront, in an all-night saloon, in an opium den, right down to the confrontation between victim and criminal in the death cell.' – *Judith Crist*

The High and the Mighty *
US 1954 147m Warnercolor Cinemascope
Wayne – Fellows

A big passenger plane is in trouble over the Pacific, and its occupants react in various ways to the prospect of a crash landing.

Compendium fiction with even the pilot having a personal problem which could cloud his judgement. Tolerable, well made hokum.

w Ernest K. Gann novel Ernest K. Gann d William Wellman ph William Clothier m Dimitri Tiomkin

John Wayne, Robert Newton, Robert Stack, Doe Avedon, Claire Trevor, Laraine Day, Jan Sterling, Phil Harris, Sidney Blackmer, John Howard

AA: Dimitri Tiomkin

AAN: William Wellman; Claire Trevor; Jan Sterling; title song (m Dimitri Tiomkin, ly Ned Washington)

High Anxiety *
US 1977 94m DeLuxe
TCF/Crossbow (Mel Brooks)
V, V*, L

A psychologist taking up a new appointment suspects that his predecessor may have been murdered.

Elementary but somewhat entertaining spoof of various Hitchcock movies (*Spellbound, North by Northwest, The Birds*), with the level of humour as unsubtle and lavatorial as one has come to expect.

w Mel Brooks, Ron Clark, Rudy DeLuca, Barry Levinson d Mel Brooks ph Paul Lohmann m John Morris

Mel Brooks, Madeline Kahn, Cloris Leachman, Harvey Korman, Ron Carey, Howard Morris, Dick Van Patten

'It basically just shambles along, in search of the next big set-piece to send up.' – *Richard Combs, MFB*

'Brooks has no idea of how to build a sequence, how to tell a story, when to leave well enough (or ill enough) alone.' – *Philip French, Observer*

'A child's idea of satire – imitations, with a comic hat and a leer.' – *New Yorker*

High-Ballin'
US 1978 100m Movielab
AIP/Stanley Chase/Pando (Jan Slan)
V*

An independent trucker battles hijackers as well as pressures from a giant trucking firm.

Routine action hokum, a long way behind 1948's *Thieves' Highway* and even less entertaining than TV's *Movin' On*.

w Paul Edwards d Peter Carter ph René Verzier m Paul Hoffert

Peter Fonda, Jerry Reed, Helen Shaver, Chris Wiggins

High Barbaree
US 1947 91m bw
MGM (Everett Riskin)
V*

A pilot crashlands in the Pacific and finds himself drifting towards a Utopian island fancifully described by his favourite uncle.

Thin Hollywood mysticism on Shangri-La lines but without the solid virtues of plot, dialogue and imagination.

w Anne Morrison Chapin, Whitfield Cook, Cyril Hume d Jack Conway ph Sidney Wagner m Herbert Stothart

Van Johnson, June Allyson, Thomas Mitchell, Marilyn Maxwell

The High Bright Sun
GB 1965 114m Technicolor
Rank (Betty Box)
US title: *McGuire Go Home*

In 1957 Cyprus the British army is beleaguered by partisans, and an officer tries to contact a leading rebel.

Confused and boring attempt to make romantic drama out of an intractably sad situation.

w Ian Stuart Black novel Ian Stuart Black d Ralph Thomas ph Ernest Steward m Angelo Lavagnino

Dirk Bogarde, Susan Strasberg, George Chakiris, Denholm Elliott

The High Command *
GB 1936 88m bw
ABFD/Fanfare/Wellesley/(Gordon Wellesley)
V*

The general of a West African garrison has a guilty secret known to his young medical officer.

Dated melodrama, rather interestingly performed and directed.

w Katherine Strueby, Walter Meade, Val Valentine novel *The General Goes Too Far* by Lewis Robinson d Thorold Dickinson ph Otto Heller, James Rogers md Ernest Irving ad R. Holmes Paul ed Sidney Cole

James Mason, Lionel Atwill, Lucie Mannheim, Steve Geray, Leslie Perrins

The High Commissioner: see *Nobody Runs Forever*

High Conquest
US 1947 79m bw
Monogram (Irving Allen)

A young man tries to climb the Matterhorn, on which his father was killed.

Unsatisfactory and ill-edited drama filmed partly in Switzerland and Austria. A good cast is largely wasted.

w Max Troll, Eben Kandel d Irving Allen

Anna Lee, Gilbert Roland, Warren Douglas, Beulah Bondi, C. Aubrey Smith, John Qualen, Helene Thimig

The High Cost of Loving *
US 1958 87m bw Cinemascope
MGM (Milo O. Frank Jnr)

A happily married middle class couple have doubts about their future.

Pleasant, mildly satirical romantic comedy which doesn't really get anywhere.

w Rip Van Ronkel d José Ferrer ph George J. Folsey m Jeff Alexander

José Ferrer, Gena Rowlands, Joanne Gilbert, Jim Backus, Bobby Troup, Philip Ober, Edward Platt, Werner Klemperer

The High Country
Canada 1981 101m colour Panavision
Crown International/Gene Slott (Bruce Mallen)

An escaped convict heads for the mountains accompanied by a simple-minded girl on the run from home.

Tedious drama that will test the patience of the most tolerant; it has nothing to recommend it.

w Bud Townsend d Harvey Hart ph Robert Ryan m Eric Robertson ad Reuben Freed ed Ron Wisman

Timothy Bottoms, Linda Purl, George Sims

High Encounters of the Ultimate Kind: see *Cheech and Chong's Next Movie*

High Flight

GB 1957 102m Technicolor Cinemascope
Columbia/Warwick (Phil C. Samuel)

Cadets train at the Royal Air Force College.

Simple-minded peacetime flagwaver.

w Joseph Landon, Ken Hughes   d John Gilling
ph Ted Moore   md Muir Mathieson   m Kenneth V.
Jones, Douglas Gamley   title march Eric Coates

Ray Milland, Bernard Lee, Kenneth Haigh, Anthony
Newley, Kenneth Fortescue, Sean Kelly, Helen
Cherry

High Flyers

US 1937 70m bw
RKO (Lee Marcus)

Two incompetents are duped into smuggling
contraband gems.

Feeble finale to the career of two comedians.

w Benny Rubin, Bert Granet   play Victor Mapes
d Edward Cline   ph Jack Mackenzie   m Roy
Webb   m/ly Herman Ruby, Dave Dreyer

Bert Wheeler, Robert Woolsey, Lupe Velez, Marjorie
Lord, Margaret Dumont, Jack Carson, Paul Harvey

High Fury: see White Cradle Inn

'A mother, a daughter, a lover. Relationships can be
murder.'
High Heels

Spain 1991 Eastmancolor
El Deseo/Ciby 2000 (Agustin Almadóvar)
V, V*, S
original title: Tacones Lejanos

A singer restarts an affair with a former lover, who is
now married to her daughter.

Camp extravaganza of a showbiz mother-daughter
relationship that tries too hard to shock and titillate.

wd Pedro Almodóvar   ph Alfredo Mayo
m Ryuichi Sakamoto   ad Pierre-Louis Thevenet
ed José Salcedo

Victoria Abril, Marisa Paredes, Miguel Bosé, Feodor
Atkine, Pedro Díez del Corral, Ana Lizarán

'One of the finest, most high fashion portrayals of loss
and mourning' – Stuart Klawans, The Nation

'It's got mad love, a bad-seed child, acrobatic sex, an
anchor-woman's on-air announcement of her own
arrest for murder, a chorus line in a woman's prison
and, of course, cross-dressing. It careers like a
runaway circus train over the rickety trestle of
melodrama. Yet it already has even true believers –
Almodóvar's own camp followers – asking, "Is that
all there is?"' – Richard Corliss, Time

High Hopes

GB 1988 112m Eastmancolor
Palace/Portman/Film Four International/British Screen (Simon
Channing-Williams, Victor Glynn)
V, V*

A family of contrasting types gather to celebrate their
mother's birthday.

A comedy of caricatures.

wd Mike Leigh   m Andrew Dixon   pd Diana
Charnley   ed Jon Gregory

Philip Davis, Ruth Sheen, Edna Dore, Philip Jackson,
Heather Tobias, Lesley Manville, David Bamber,
Jason Watkins, Judith Scott

High Lonesome

US 1950 80m Technicolor
Eagle Lion

A young man believed to be crazed and homicidal
flees into the desert and returns to establish his
innocence.

Thinly stretched Western not helped by an
exhibitionist star performance.

wd Alan Le May

John Barrymore Jnr, Chill Wills, Kristine Miller, Lois
Butler

'When the hands point up ... the excitement starts!'
High Noon ****

US 1952 85m bw
Stanley Kramer
V, V*, L

A marshal gets no help when he determines to defend
his town against revengeful badmen.

A minor Western with a soft-pedalled message for the
world, this turned out to be a classic simply because it
was well done, with every scene and performance
clearly worked out. Cinematically it was pared to the
bone, and the theme tune helped.

w Carl Foreman   story The Tin Star by John W.
Cunningham   d Fred Zinnemann   ph Floyd Crosby
m Dimitri Tiomkin   singer Tex Ritter   ed Elmo
Williams, Harry Gerstad

Gary Cooper, Grace Kelly, Thomas Mitchell, Lloyd
Bridges, Katy Jurado, Otto Kruger, Lon Chaney,
Henry Morgan

'The western form is used for a sneak civics lesson.' –
Pauline Kael, 70s

'Like nearly all the Kramer productions, this is a neat,
well-finished and literate piece of work, though its
limitations are more conventional than most.' – Gavin
Lambert

'A western to challenge Stagecoach for the all-time
championship.' – Bosley Crowther

'A series of crisp and purposeful scenes that interpret
each other like the pins on a strategist's war map.' –
Robert L. Hatch

'It is astonishing how much of the simple western
story is told visually by rapid cross-cutting.' – Films in
Review

'Few recent westerns have gotten so much tension
and excitement into the classic struggle between good
and evil.' – Life

AA: Dimitri Tiomkin; Gary Cooper; title song (m
Dimitri Tiomkin, ly Ned Washington); editing

AAN: best picture; Carl Foreman; Fred Zinnemann

'They'll never forget the day he drifted into town!'
High Plains Drifter *

US 1972 105m Technicolor Panavision
Universal/Malpaso (Robert Daley)
V, V*, L

A mysterious stranger rides into town and terrifies the
inhabitants.

Semi-supernatural, mystical revenge Western with an
overplus of violence. Very watchable, but irritating.

w Ernest Tidyman   d Clint Eastwood   ph Bruce
Surtees   m Dee Barton   ad Henry Bumstead

Clint Eastwood, Verna Bloom, Marianna Hill, Mitch
Ryan, Jack Ging

'Ritualized violence and plodding symbolism make
for heavy going.' – Sight and Sound

'A nervously humorous, self-conscious near-satire on
the prototype Eastwood formula.' – Variety

High Pressure *

US 1932 74m bw
Warner

A would-be tycoon believes there's a fortune to be
made in artificial rubber.

Amusing con man comedy with good work all round.

w Joseph Jackson   play Hot Money by Abem Kandel
d Mervyn Le Roy

William Powell, Evelyn Brent, George Sidney, Guy
Kibbee, Frank McHugh

'Well acted, but lacks strength to attract much
business.' – Variety

'Getting In Was Easy ... Getting Out Was War!!!'
High Risk

US 1981 94m colour
American Cinema (Joe Raffill, Gerard Green)
V*

A documentary film-maker enlists three buddies to
steal a million dollars from a South American drugs
dealer.

Moderately entertaining caper movie which stops too
often for action and occasionally for comedy.

wd Stewart Raffill   ph Alex Phillips Jnr   m Mark
Snow   ed Tom Walls Jnr

James Brolin, Cleavon Little, Lindsay Wagner, Ernest
Borgnine, Bruce Davison, Chick Vennera, Anthony
Quinn, James Coburn

High Road to China

US 1983 105m Technicolor
Golden Harvest/Pan Pacific (Fred Weintraub)
V, V*, L

In the twenties, an American heiress in Afghanistan
has adventures with a drunken flyer.

Abysmal attempt to mate James Bond with a cut-price
Raiders of the Lost Ark. It comes up with nothing at all,
and is on the lowest level for continuity, dialogue and
direction.

w Sandra Weintraub Roland, S. Lee Pogostin
novel Jon Cleary   d Brian G. Hutton   ph Ronnie
Taylor   m John Barry   pd Robert Laing

Tom Selleck, Bess Armstrong, Jack Weston, Robert
Morley, Wilford Brimley, Brian Blessed

'An attempt to revive the sort of comedy-adventure
romance in which Clark Gable and Jean Harlow
would squabble furiously but you knew they were
really in love. But as scripted and abominably
directed, the thing is as flat as a pancake.' – Guardian

High Season

GB 1987 92m colour
Curzon/British Screen/Film Four/Michael White/Hemdale
(Clare Downs)
V*, L

A female photographer meets strange friends in
Rhodes.

Spies, thieves and tourists make an odd lightweight
mixture in a movie best suited to TV.

w Mark and Clare Peploe   d Clare Peploe
ph Chris Menges   m Jason Osborn   pd Andrew
McAlpine   ed Gabriella Cristiani

Jacqueline Bisset, James Fox, Irene Papas, Sebastian
Shaw, Kenneth Branagh, Robert Stephens

'The blazing mountain manhunt for Killer Mad-Dog Earle!'
High Sierra *

US 1941 96m bw
Warner (Hal. B. Wallis, Mark Hellinger)
V*, L

An ex-con gangster plans one last heist in the
Californian mountains, but is mortally wounded
through his involvement with two women.

Rather dreary action melodrama which gave Bogart
his first real star part (after George Raft turned it
down). Remade 1955 as I Died a Thousand Times (qv);
also in 1949 as a Western, Colorado Territory.

w John Huston, W. R. Burnett   novel W. R. Burnett
d Raoul Walsh   ph Tony Gaudio   m Adolph
Deutsch

Humphrey Bogart, Ida Lupino, Joan Leslie, Alan Curtis,
Arthur Kennedy, Henry Hull, Henry Travers, Jerome
Cowan

'The last swallow, perhaps, of the gangsters' summer.'
– William Whitebait

'Like it or not, I'll be damned if you leave before the end, or go to sleep.' – *Otis Ferguson*

'As gangster pictures go, this one has everything – speed, excitement, suspense, and that ennobling suggestion of futility which makes for irony and poetry.' – *New York Times*

High Society

US   1956   107m   Technicolor   Vistavision
MGM (Sol C. Siegel)
V, V*, L

A haughty rich girl chooses between several suitors.

Cold, flat, dull musical reworking of *The Philadelphia Story* (qv), with ill-cast performers and just a few bright moments.

w John Patrick   d Charles Walters   ph Paul C. Vogel   md Johnny Green, Saul Chaplin   m/y Cole Porter   ad Cedric Gibbons, Hans Peters

songs: 'Well, Did You Evah'; 'High Society'; 'Who Wants to be a Millionaire?'; 'I Love You, Samantha'; 'Now You Has Jazz'

Bing Crosby, Grace Kelly, Frank Sinatra, Celeste Holm, Louis Armstrong, Sidney Blackmer, Margalo Gillmore, Louis Calhern, Lydia Reed, John Lund

'The principals perform, most of the time, with a kind of glum cheeriness.' – *Hollis Alpert*

'Simply not Top Drawer.' – *Time*

AAN: Johnny Green, Saul Chaplin; song 'True Love'

High Society Blues

US   1930   102m   bw
Fox

A girl ditches a French count in favour of an all-American hero.

Frothy musical romance which did nothing for its stars and is now unwatchable.

w Howard J. Green   d David Butler   ph Charles Van Enger   m/y Joe McCarthy, James Hanley

Janet Gaynor, Charles Farrell, William Collier Snr, Hedda Hopper, Louise Fazenda, Lucien Littlefield, Joyce Compton

'Certain to please the average fan . . . commercial product of the first programme grade.' – *Variety*

High Spirits

GB   1988   96m   colour
Palace/Vision PDG (Stephen Woolley, David Saunders)
V, V*, L, S

In order to attract tourists, the owner of an Irish castle fakes ghosts and then discovers that he has summoned up some real ones.

Insubstantial comedy that lurches unsuccessfully into supernatural romance.

wd Neil Jordan   ph Alex Thomson   m George Fenton   pd Alex Furst   ed Michael Bradsell

Peter O'Toole, Donald McCann, Mary Koughlan, Liz Smith, Steve Guttenberg, Beverly D'Angelo, Jennifer Tilly, Peter Gallagher, Daryl Hannah, Liam Neeson, Ray McAnally

High Tension

US   1936   63m   bw
TCF

Exploits of a cable layer in Hawaii.

Routine brawling comedy.

w Lou Breslow, Edward Eliscu, John Patrick   d Allan Dwan

Brian Donlevy, Norman Foster, Glenda Farrell, Helen Wood, Robert McWade

The High Terrace

GB   1956   82m   bw
CIPA/Robert S. Baker

A theatrical producer is murdered, and members of the cast protect their leading lady; but she is guilty.

Rather solemn, enclosed little mystery which evokes no compulsion to go on watching.

w Alfred Shaughnessy, Norman Hudis   d Henry Cass

Lois Maxwell, Dale Robertson, Derek Bond, Eric Pohlmann, Mary Laura Wood, Lionel Jeffries

High Tide *

Australia   1987   104m   colour
Ritzy/FGH/STL/Hemdale (Sandra Levy)
V, V*, L

An unsuccessful singer meets the teenage daughter she abandoned years before.

Unsentimental and well acted study of maternal stirrings.

w Laura Jones   d Gillian Armstrong   ph Russell Boyd   m Peter Best   pd Sally Campbell   ed Nicholas Beauman

Judy Davis, Jan Adele, Claudia Karvan, Colin Friels, John Clayton, Frankie J. Holden

'There have never been characters like Ally and her mom in movies, and there has never been a film like this emotional riptide.' – *Carrie Rickey, Philadelphia Inquirer*

High Tide at Noon

GB   1957   111m   bw
Rank (Julian Wintle)

Passions run high among lobster fishermen in Nova Scotia.

Neat, clean romantic melodrama in agreeable surroundings.

w Neil Paterson   d Philip Leacock   ph Eric Cross   m John Veale

Betta St John, Michael Craig, Patrick McGoohan, William Sylvester, Flora Robson, Alexander Knox, Peter Arne, Patrick Allen, Susan Beaumont

High Time

US   1960   103m   DeLuxe   Cinemascope
TCF/Bing Crosby (Charles Brackett)

A middle-aged widower goes back to college.

Flaccid comedy-musical with some undergraduatish jokes.

w Tom and Frank Waldman   d Blake Edwards   ph Ellsworth Fredericks   m Henry Mancini   *songs* Jimmy Van Heusen, Sammy Cahn

Bing Crosby, Tuesday Weld, Fabian, Richard Beymer, Nicole Maurey

AAN: song 'The Second Time Around'

High Treason

GB   1929 •   90m   bw
Gaumont

In 1940, women unite to prevent a second world war.

Tired little prophetic fable with primitive techniques.

w L'Estrange Fawcett   *play* Noel Pemberton-Billing   d Maurice Elvey

Jameson Thomas, Benita Hume, Basil Gill, Humberston Wright

High Treason *

GB   1951   93m   bw
GFD/Conqueror (Paul Soskin)

Saboteurs are routed by the London police.

Unconvincing documentary melodrama which moves fast enough to be entertaining.

w Frank Harvey, Roy Boulting   d Roy Boulting   ph Gilbert Taylor   m John Addison

Liam Redmond, André Morell, Anthony Bushell, Kenneth Griffith, Patric Doonan, Joan Hickson,

Anthony Nicholls, Mary Morris, Geoffrey Keen, Dora Bryan

High Vermilion: see *Silver City*

High Wall

US   1947   99m   bw
MGM (Robert Lord)

A war veteran is put in an asylum after confessing to killing his wife, but later events prove that he was drugged into saying so.

Adequately entertaining, supremely unconvincing mystery melodrama.

w Sydney Boehm   d Curtis Bernhardt   ph Paul C. Vogel   m Bronislau Kaper

Robert Taylor, Herbert Marshall, Audrey Totter, Dorothy Patrick, H. B. Warner, Warner Anderson

High, Wide and Handsome *

US   1937   110m   bw
Paramount (Arthur Hornblow Jnr)

Pennsylvania 1859: a travelling showgirl falls in love with a farmer.

Disappointingly stilted period musical with most of the talent ill at ease until the final reel.

w Oscar Hammerstein II   d Rouben Mamoulian   ph Victor Milner, Theodore Sparkuhl   ch Le Roy Prinz   md Boris Morros   m/y Jerome Kern, Oscar Hammerstein II   ad Hans Dreier, John Goodman

Irene Dunne, Randolph Scott, Dorothy Lamour, Raymond Walburn, Alan Hale, Elizabeth Patterson, Charles Bickford, William Frawley, Akim Tamiroff, Ben Blue, Irving Pichel, Lucien Littlefield

'Not a road show, but a big picture, and should get nice returns.' – *Variety*

'There are two hours of this long, dumb and dreary picture . . . one is left with a few dim distressing memories.' – *Graham Greene*

'Irene Dunne at her cornball primmest, singing alongside a farmhorse when Randolph Scott isn't around.' – *Pauline Kael, 70s*

A High Wind in Jamaica *

GB   1965   104m   DeLuxe   Cinemascope
TCF (John Croydon)

In Victorian days, English children en route home from Jamaica are captured by pirates and influence their lives.

Semi-serious adventure story with a highly unlikely ending in which the chief pirate allows himself to be executed for a murder committed by a child. There are however pleasures along the way.

w Stanley Mann, Ronald Harwood, Denis Cannan   *novel* Richard Hughes   d Alexander Mackendrick   ph Douglas Slocombe   m Larry Adler

Deborah Baxter, Anthony Quinn, James Coburn, Isabel Dean, Nigel Davenport, Gert Frobe, Lila Kedrova

The High Window: see *The Brasher Doubloon*

Higher and Higher *

US   1943   90m   bw
RKO (Tim Whelan)

Servants have an elaborate plan to restore the family fortune.

Unamusing musical which undernourishes several talents.

w Jay Dratler, Ralph Spence   *play* Gladys Hurlbut, Joshua Logan   d Tim Whelan   ph Robert de Grasse   md Constantin Bakaleinikoff   m/y Jimmy McHugh, Harold Adamson

Michele Morgan, Jack Haley, *Frank Sinatra*, Leon Errol, Marcy McGuire, *Victor Borge*, Mary Wickes, Barbara Hale, Elizabeth Risdon

'There may be some folks who can't figure out the reasons for Sinatra's meteoric rise, or might be wondering whether he's here to stay or not, but in his first screen starring role he at least gets in no one's way.' – *Variety*

AAN: Constantin Bakaleinikoff; song 'I Couldn't Sleep a Wink Last Night'

The Highest Honour
Australia   1982   143m   colour
Southern International Films (Lee Robinson)
aka: *Southern Cross*

In 1942, an Australian spy befriends his captor and finally executioner.

Sombre true story, far too long in the telling.

w Lee Robinson   *d* Peter Maxwell

George Mallaby, Michael Aitkens, John Howard, Atsuo Nakamura, Stuart Wilson, Steve Bisley

'Largely fails to ignite.' – *Julian Petley, MFB*

Highlander
GB/US   1986   111m   Technicolor
EMI/Highlander (Peter S. Davis, William N. Panzer)
V*, L

A 14th-century Scotsman apparently dies in battle but finds he is an immortal, and is still crossing swords with his enemy the Kurgan in 20th-century Manhattan.

Muddled, violent and noisy fantasy: the explanation doesn't come until most people will have given up.

w Gregory Widden, Peter Bellwood, Larry Ferguson *d* Russell Mulcahy   *ph* Gerry Fisher   *m* Michael Kamen   *pd* Allan Cameron   *ed* Peter Honess

Christopher Lambert, Roxanne Hart, Clancy Brown, Sean Connery

'While there are entertaining moments, total work is a mess.' – *Variety*

'A moody combination of *Blade Runner*, *The Terminator* and your last really good nightmare.' – *People*

'It's Time For A New Kind Of Magic.'
Highlander II – The Quickening
US   1990   100m   Eastmancolor
Entertainment/Lamb Bear/Peter S. Davis, William Panzer
V, V*

Two immortal aliens join forces to defeat a dictator who controls the Earth.

Incoherent and inconsequential sequel.

w Peter Bellwood   *story* Brian Clemens, William Panzer   *d* Russell Mulcahy   *ph* Phil Meheux *m* Stewart Copeland   *pd* Roger Hall   *sp* John Richardson   *ed* Hubert C. de la Bouillerie, Anthony Redman

Christopher Lambert, Sean Connery, Virginia Madsen, Michael Ironside, Allan Rich, John C. McGinley

'A terrible mess. The film's organization at all levels, from plot down to the cutting of individual action sequences, is so full of holes that there is nothing solid for it to adhere to.' – *Sight and Sound*

Highly Dangerous
GB   1950   88m   bw
Rank/Two Cities (Anthony Darnborough)

A lady entomologist in a Balkan country is suspected of spying but manages to outwit her enemies.

Odd blend of straight adventure and spoof; it doesn't quite come off.

w Eric Ambler   *d* Roy Baker   *ph* Reg Wyer *m* Richard Addinsell

Margaret Lockwood, Dane Clark, Marius Goring, Naunton Wayne, Eugene Deckers, Wilfrid Hyde-White, Michael Hordern, Gladys Henson

Highpoint
Canada   1984 (filmed 1979)   88m   Eastmancolor
Highpoint/New World

An industrialist is on the run from both the Mafia and the CIA.

Routine thriller with a finale atop Toronto's CN Tower.

w Richard Guttman, Ian Sutherland   *d* Peter Carter

Richard Harris, Christopher Plummer, Beverly D'Angelo, Kate Reid, Peter Donat

Highway Dragnet
US   1954   71m   bw
Allied Artists (William F. Broidy)

A lady photographer gives a lift to an ex-marine who may or may not be a murderer.

Twisty lower-berth thriller in which all is not as it seems.

w Herb Meadow, Jerome Odlum   *d* Nathan Juran

Joan Bennett, Richard Conte, Wanda Hendrix, Reed Hadley, Mary Beth Hughes, Iris Adrian

Highway 301 *
US   1950   83m   bw
Warner (Bryan Foy)

The Tri-State Gang is apprehended by police.

Actionful gangster melodrama of the *Bonnie and Clyde* type with plenty of suspenseful situations and slick camerawork.

wd Andrew Stone   *ph* Carl Guthrie   *m* William Lava

Steve Cochran, Virginia Grey, Gaby Andre, Edmon Ryan, Richard Egan, Robert Webber

'Several good suspense sequences, some good comic observation, and many pleasing visual moments of the wet-streets-at-night category.' – *Richard Mallett, Punch*

Highway to Freedom: see *Joe Smith American*

'Where the toll is your soul.'
Highway to Hell
US   1992 (made 1989)   93m   CFI colour
Sovereign/Hemdale (Mary Anne Page, John Byers)
V, V*

An eloping couple on the way to Las Vegas run into a demonic cop who abducts the girl.

Hell is an uninventive horror flick.

w Brian Helgeland   *d* Ate de Jong   *ph* Robin Vidgeon   *m* Hidden Faces   *pd* Phillip Dean Foreman   *ed* Todd Ramsay, Randy Thornton

Patrick Bergin, Adam Storke, Chad Lowe, Kristy Swanson, Pamela Gidley, Jarrett Lennon, C. J. Graham, Richard Farnsworth

'A failed horror comedy in search of a bigger budget and far better script.' – *Variety*

The Highwayman
US   1951   82m   Cinecolor
Allied Artists/Jack Dietz (Hal. E. Chester)

A 17th-century nobleman disguises himself as a Quaker and becomes a highwayman to right wrongs.

Curious Poverty Row period actioner with ideas generally above its station, not to mention an unexpected tragic ending.

w Jan Jeffries   *poem* Alfred Noyes   *d* Lesley Selander   *ph* Harry Neumann   *m* Herschel Burke Gilbert

Philip Friend, Charles Coburn, Victor Jory, Wanda Hendrix, Cecil Kellaway, Scott Forbes, Virginia Huston, Dan O'Herlihy

Highways by Night
US   1942   62m   bw
RKO

A millionaire drafts legal resources to round up hi-jackers.

Formula thick ear with romance.

w Lynn Root, Frank Fenton   *story* Clarence Budington Kelland   *d* Peter Godfrey

Richard Carlson, Jane Randolph, Jane Darwell, Barton MacLane, Ray Collins

'I want to live like a man – and still be a woman!'
Hilda Crane
US   1956   87m   Technicolor   Cinemascope
TCF (Herbert B. Swope Jnr)

An unhappy woman marries for the third time and convinces herself it won't work.

Emotional melodrama of the old school: very moderate in all departments.

wd Philip Dunne   *play* Samson Raphaelson *ph* Joe MacDonald   *m* David Raksin

Jean Simmons, Guy Madison, Jean-Pierre Aumont, *Evelyn Varden*, Judith Evelyn, Peggy Knudsen

'They went up like men! They came down like animals!'
The Hill **
GB   1965   122m   bw
MGM/Seven Arts (Kenneth Hyman)
L

Prisoners rebel against the harsh discipline of a British military detention centre in North Africa during World War II.

Lurid melodrama which descends fairly quickly into black farce with a number of sweaty actors outshouting each other. Enjoyable on this level when you can hear the dialogue through the poor sound recording.

w Ray Rigby   *play* Ray Rigby   *d* Sidney Lumet *ph* Oswald Morris   *m* none

Sean Connery, Harry Andrews, Michael Redgrave, Ian Bannen, Alfred Lynch, *Ossie Davis*, Roy Kinnear, Jack Watson, Ian Hendry

A Hill in Korea
GB   1956   81m   bw
British Lion/Wessex (Anthony Squire)
V
US title: *Hell in Korea*

During the Korean war, a small patrol guards a hill.

Minor war talk-piece, shot in Surrey and looking it.

w Ian Dalrymple, Anthony Squire, Ronald Spencer *novel* Max Catto   *d* Julian Amyes   *ph* Freddie Francis   *m* Malcolm Arnold

George Baker, Harry Andrews, Stanley Baker, Michael Medwin, Ronald Lewis, Stephen Boyd, Victor Maddern, Harry Landis

'Character is adequately sketched into a suitably laconic script.' – *MFB*

Hill 24 Doesn't Answer
Israel   1954   101m   bw
Sikor (Thorold Dickinson, Peter Frye)

Four friends defend Hill 24 against the Arabs on the eve of the cease-fire, and are all killed.

Israel's first feature film, a curious amalgam of the slick and the amateur, with long flashbacks which make it resemble *The Bridge of San Luis Rey*.

w Zvi Kolitz, Peter Frye, Joanna and Thorold Dickinson   *d* Thorold Dickinson   *ph* Gerald Gibbs *m* Paul Ben-Haim

Michael Wager, Edward Mulhare, Haya Harareet, Arie Lavi, Michael Shilo

Hill's Angels: see *The North Avenue Irregulars*

The Hills Have Eyes

US 1977 90m Movielab
New Realm/Blood Relations (Peter Locke)
V, V*, L

Holidaymakers are waylaid and killed by a family of desert cannibals.

Low-grade shocker which mysteriously achieved some cult status.

wd Wes Craven ph Eric Saarinen m Don Peake
ad Robert Burns ed Wes Craven

John Steadman, Janus Blythe, Arthur King, Russ Grieve, Virginia Vincent

'Simultaneously risible and nauseating.' – Tim Pulleine, MFB

The Hills of Home

US 1948 95m Technicolor
MGM
GB title: Master of Lassie

A doctor returns to his Scottish village to practise medicine, and brings his faithful collie.

Adequate addition to the Lassie saga, with competent work all round.

w William Ludwig d Fred Wilcox

Edmund Gwenn, Tom Drake, Donald Crisp, Rhys Williams, Reginald Owen

Himatsuri: see Fire Festival

Der Himmel Über Berlin: see Wings of Desire

The Hindenburg *

US 1975 125m Technicolor Panavision
Universal/Filmmakers (Robert Wise)
V*, L

In 1937, sabotage causes the airship Hindenburg to crash on arrival at New York.

An extremely uninteresting guess at the cause of this famous disaster. The plot and dialogue are leaden, and such actors as have more than a couple of lines look extremely glum. The special effects, however, are fine despite curious blue-rinse photographic processing.

w Nelson Gidding novel Michael M. Mooney
d Robert Wise ph Robert Surtees m David Shire
pd Edward Carfagno sp Albert Whitlock

George C. Scott, Anne Bancroft, Burgess Meredith, William Atherton, Roy Thinnes, Gig Young, Charles Durning, Robert Clary, René Auberjonois

'The tackiest disaster movie yet – a cheap and chaotic collage of painted drops, wooden actors and not-so-special effects that manages to make one of this century's most sensational real-life catastrophes seem roughly as terrifying as a badly stubbed toe.' – Frank Rich

AAN: Robert Surtees

Hindle Wakes

GB 1952 82m bw
Monarch
US title: Holiday Week

A Lancashire millgirl spends a week at Blackpool with the master's son but causes a scandal when she refuses to marry him.

Modestly competent version of a semi-classic play about class distinctions.

w John Baines play Stanley Houghton d Arthur Crabtree

Lisa Daniely, Leslie Dwyer, Brian Worth, Sandra Dorne, Ronald Adam

† A probably better, but unavailable version was made in 1931 by Victor Saville for Gaumont, with Belle Chrystall, Edmund Gwenn, John Stuart, Ruth Peterson, Norman McKinnel and Sybil Thorndike.

Hips Hips Hooray

US 1934 68m bw
RKO

Two salesmen pitch flavoured lipstick to a beauty parlour chain.

Tired star comedy.

w Harry Ruby, Bert Kalmar d Mark Sandrich

Bert Wheeler, Robert Woolsey, Ruth Etting, Thelma Todd, Dorothy Lee, George Meeker

'Femme display chief asset.' – Variety

The Hired Hand

US 1971 93m Technicolor
Universal/Pando (William Hayward)
V*

Two Western drifters avenge the killing of their friend and settle down to work on a farm; but violence follows them.

A potentially enjoyable small-scale Western is spoiled by pretentious direction and effects which bore the spectator to death.

w Alan Sharp d Peter Fonda ph Vilmos Zsigmond m Bruce Langhorne

Peter Fonda, Warren Oates, Verna Bloom, Severn Darden

'The first slow-motion western, with endless artsy photography not quite succeeding in obscuring the rambling plot.' – Judith Crist, 1973

'When a film begins with a "lyrical" shot, your heart has a right to sink.' – Stanley Kauffmann

Hired Wife

US 1940 96m bw
Universal

A secretary who loves her boss saves his company by marrying him so that it can be transferred to her name.

After which the plot has absolutely nowhere to go.

w Richard Connell, Gladys Lehman d William A. Seiter

Rosalind Russell, Brian Aherne, Virginia Bruce, Robert Benchley, John Carroll, Hobart Cavanaugh

The Hireling *

GB 1973 108m colour
Columbia/World Film Services (Ben Arbeid)

In the twenties, a lady's chauffeur falls in love with her.

Talkative drama, elegant but not much fun.

w Wolf Mankowitz novel L. P. Hartley d Alan Bridges ph Michael Reed m Marc Wilkinson pd Natasha Kroll

Sarah Miles, Robert Shaw, Peter Egan, Elizabeth Sellars, Caroline Mortimer

Hiroshima Mon Amour *

France/Japan 1959 91m bw
Argos/Comei/Pathé/Daiei
V, V*

A French actress working in Hiroshima falls for a Japanese architect and remembers her tragic love for a German soldier during the occupation.

Jumbled mixture of flashbacks and flashforwards which can now be recognized as typical of this director and on its first appearance was hailed as a work of art in an innovative new style.

w Marguerite Duras d Alain Resnais ph Sacha Vierny, Takahashi Michio m Giovanni Fusco, Georges Delerue

Emmanuele Riva, Eiji Okada

'Suddenly a new film. Really new, first-hand: a work which tells a story of its own in a style of its own. One is almost afraid to touch it.' – Dilys Powell

AAN: Marguerite Duras

His Affair: see This Is My Affair

His and Hers

GB 1960 90m bw
Eros (Hal E. Chester)

An author gets lost with the Bedouin while on a research trip, and by the time he gets home his personality is transformed.

The thinnest of comedy ideas becomes a film of almost no substance at all.

w Stanley Mann, Jan and Mark Lowell d Brian Desmond Hurst

Terry-Thomas, Janette Scott, Wilfrid Hyde- White, Nicole Maurey, Joan Sims, Kenneth Connor, Kenneth Williams, Meier Tzelniker, Joan Hickson, Colin Gordon, Oliver Reed, Francesca Annis

His Brother's Wife

US 1936 91m bw
MGM (Lawrence Weingarten)

A young scientist is helped out of trouble by his brother, on condition he disappears; the brother then weds the scientist's girlfriend.

Heavy romantic melodrama containing everything including jungle fever, flung together to take advantage of the stars' real-life romance.

w Leon Gordon, John Meehan story George Auerbach d W. S. Van Dyke II ph Oliver T. Marsh m Franz Waxman

Robert Taylor, Barbara Stanwyck, Joseph Calleia, John Eldredge, Jean Hersholt, Samuel S. Hinds, Leonard Mudie, Jed Prouty

His Butler's Sister *

US 1943 94m bw
Universal (Felix Jackson)

A temporary maid falls for her sophisticated boss.

Pleasant comedy musical: no great shakes, but the principals give the air of enjoying themselves.

w Samuel Hoffenstein, Betty Reinhardt d Frank Borzage ph Elwood Bredell m Hans Salter

Deanna Durbin, Franchot Tone, Pat O'Brien, Evelyn Ankers, Walter Catlett, Alan Mowbray, Akim Tamiroff, Elsa Janssen, Iris Adrian

His Double Life *

US 1933 63m bw
Paramount (Eddie Dowling)
V*

A famous painter, when his valet dies, takes his identity.

Adequate transcription of a novel later redone as Holy Matrimony.

w Arthur Ellis novel Arnold Bennett d Arthur Hopkins

Roland Young, Lillian Gish, Lumsden Hare, Lucy Beaumont

'Pleasant little film; big grosses unlikely.' – Variety

His Excellency

GB 1951 84m bw
Ealing (Michael Truman)

The Labour government sends a trade union official to govern a Mediterranean colony.

Disappointingly tacky-looking and stagebound version of an unpersuasive West End comedy.

w Robert Hamer, W. P. Lipscomb play Dorothy and Campbell Christie d Robert Hamer ph Douglas Slocombe md Ernest Irving m Handel

Eric Portman, Cecil Parker, Helen Cherry, Susan Stephen, Edward Chapman, Clive Morton, Robin Bailey, Geoffrey Keen

His Family Tree

US   1935   59m   bw
RKO

An Irishman migrates to America and gets involved in politics.

Lively second feature for the Irish halls.

w Joel Sayre, John Twist   play Old Man Murphy by Patrick Kearney, Henry Wagstaff Gribble   d Charles Vidor

James Barton, Margaret Callahan, Maureen Delany, Addison Randall, William Harrigan

'With more care, this might have been much better.' – Variety

His Girl Friday ****

US   1940   92m   bw
Columbia (Howard Hawks)
V, V*

A remake of The Front Page (qv), with Hildy Johnson turned into a woman.

Frantic, hilarious black farce with all participants at their best; possibly the fastest comedy ever filmed, and one of the funniest.

w Charles Lederer   play The Front Page by Charles MacArthur, Ben Hecht   d Howard Hawks   ph Joseph Walker   md Morris Stoloff   m Sydney Cutner

Rosalind Russell, Cary Grant, Ralph Bellamy, Gene Lockhart, Porter Hall, Ernest Truex, Cliff Edwards, Clarence Kolb, Roscoe Karns, Frank Jenks, Abner Biberman, Frank Orth, John Qualen, Helen Mack, Billy Gilbert, Alma Kruger

'The kind of terrific verbal slam-bang that has vanished from current film-making.' – New Yorker, 1975

'One of the fastest of all movies, from line to line and from gag to gag.' – Manny Farber, 1971

'Overlapping dialogue carries the movie along at breakneck speed; word gags take the place of the sight gags of silent comedy, as this vanished race of brittle, cynical, childish people rush around on corrupt errands.' – Pauline Kael, 1968

'The main trouble is that when they made The Front Page the first time, it stayed made.' – Otis Ferguson

† The Rosalind Russell role had first been turned down by Jean Arthur, Ginger Rogers, Claudette Colbert and Irene Dunne.

His Glorious Night

US   1929   85m   bw
MGM
GB title: Breath of Scandal

A princess falls in love with a commoner.

Soporific early talkie, remade in 1960 as A Breath of Scandal. The movie which first exposed its star's high-pitched voice and is credited with killing his career.

w Willard Mack   play Olimpia by Ferenc Molnar   d Lionel Barrymore   ph Percy Hilburn

John Gilbert, Catherine Dale Owen, Hedda Hopper, Gustav von Seyffertitz, Nance O'Neil

His Kind of Woman *

US   1951   120m   bw
RKO (Howard Hughes, Robert Sparks)
V*

At a remote Mexican ranch resort, a gangster on the run holds up residents including a fortune-hunting girl and a fading matinee idol.

Agreeable tongue-in-cheek melodrama which slightly outstays its welcome but is generally good fun.

w Frank Fenton   d John Farrow   ph Harry J. Wild   md Constantin Bakaleinikoff   m Leigh Harline

Robert Mitchum, Jane Russell, Vincent Price, Raymond Burr, Tim Holt, Charles McGraw, Marjorie Reynolds, Jim Backus

His Lordship *

GB   1936   71m   bw
Gaumont (S. C. Balcon)
US title: Man of Affairs

A politician's twin takes his place to expose an old murder.

Comfortable star comedy-drama.

w Maude Howell, Edwin Greenwood, L. DuGarde Peach   play The Nelson Touch by Neil Grant   d Herbert Mason   ph Gunther Krampf   md Louis Levy   ad Alfred Junge

George Arliss, Rene Ray, Romilly Lunge, Jessie Winter, Allan Jeayes

His Majesty Bunker Bean: see Bunker Bean

His Majesty O'Keefe

GB   1954   90m   Technicolor
Warner/Norma (Harold Hecht)

Native islanders are taught by an easygoing mariner how to exploit their natural resources and defend themselves against pirates.

Thin adventure romance with too little for its star to do.

w Borden Chase, James Hill   novel Lawrence Kingman, Gerald Green   d Byron Haskin   ph Otto Heller   m Robert Farnon

Burt Lancaster, Joan Rice, André Morell, Abraham Sofaer, Benson Fong, Archie Savage

His Night Out

US   1935   74m   bw
Universal

A henpecked office help saves the bonds from gangsters.

Typical star farce, a remake of The Mollycoddle.

w Doris Malloy, Harry Clork   d William Nigh

Edward Everett Horton, Irene Hervey, Robert McWade, Jack La Rue, Willard Robertson

His Other Woman: see Desk Set

'From the ends of the earth . . . a darling baby brings them together!'

His Woman

US   1931   80m   bw
Paramount (Albert Kaufman)

The captain of a tramp freighter finds himself in charge of an abandoned baby and a runaway girl.

Slow, indifferent comedy drama, previously filmed in 1929 as Sal of Singapore.

w Adelaide Heilbron, Melville Baker   novel The Sentimentalist by Dale Collins   d Edward Sloman   ph William Steiner, Arthur Ellis

Gary Cooper, Claudette Colbert, Averill Harris, Richard Spiro, Douglass Dumbrille, Joseph Calleia, Harry Davenport

'Actionless picture . . . too many barnacles cling to the script.' – Variety

Une Histoire D'Amour *

France   1951   95m   bw
Jacques Roitfeld/Cité Films
GB title: Love Story

A police inspector discovers that a young couple killed themselves because of parental opposition.

A rather soggy little drama made watchable by its careful detail and immaculate leading performance.

w Michel Audiard   d Robert Clavel   ph Louis Page   m Paul Misraki

Louis Jouvet, Daniel Gélin, Dany Robin

Une Histoire Inventée: see An Imaginary Tale

Histoires Extraordinaires *

France/Italy   1968   120m   Eastmancolor
Les Films Marceau/Cocinor/PEA (Raymond Eger)
GB title: Tales of Mystery and Imagination; aka: Spirits of the Dead

Episodic film based on three stories by Edgar Allan Poe.

Only Fellini provides entertainment, and that by abandoning all pretence to be faithful to the original, with a story about a drunken English actor working in Rome.

w Metzengerstein: Roger Vadim, Pascal Cousin, Clement Biddlewood; William Wilson: Louis Malle, Clement Biddlewood; Toby Dammit: Federico Fellini, Bernardo Zapponi   stories Edgar Allan Poe   d Metzengerstein: Roger Vadim; William Wilson: Louis Malle; Toby Dammit: Federico Fellini   ph Metzengerstein: Claude Renoir; William Wilson: Tonino Delli Colli; Toby Dammit: Guiseppe Rotundo   m Metzengerstein: Jean Prodromides; William Wilson: Diego Masson; Toby Dammit: Nino Rota   ad William Wilson: Carlo Leva; Toby Dammit: Fabrizio Clerici   ed Metzengerstein: Helene Plemiannikov; William Wilson: Franco Arcalli, Susanne Baron; Toby Dammit: Ruggiero Mastroianni

Metzengerstein: Jane Fonda, Peter Fonda, Carla Marlier, James Robertson Justice; William Wilson: Alain Delon, Brigitte Bardot, Katia Christina; Toby Dammit: Terence Stamp, Salvo Randone

History Is Made at Night *

US   1937   97m   bw
Walter Wanger
V*, L

A divorcee and her new love have trouble from her ex-husband.

Atmospheric, artificial, generally entertaining romantic comedy-drama of a kind which went out of fashion long ago.

w Gene Towne, Graham Baker   d Frank Borzage   ph Gregg Toland   m Alfred Newman

Charles Boyer, Jean Arthur, Leo Carrillo, Colin Clive

'A weird and unbelievable melodrama . . . mildly entertaining with good scenes.' – Variety

'So souped up with demonic passions and tender glances and elegant photography that it's rather fun.' – New Yorker, 1978

'Frank Borzage, who could turn Frankenstein Meets the Wolf Man into a romantic reverie, is quite undeterred by the venality rampant in the script and interjects his vision of what Andrew Sarris called love over probability. Oh, there's an iceberg disaster too.' – Kit Parker catalogue

The History of Mr Polly *

GB   1949   94m   bw
GFD/Two Cities (John Mills)

A draper's assistant buys a small shop but tires of his nagging wife and decides the time has come for a change.

Patchy but generally amusing version of a popular comic novel, very English and rather appealingly done.

w Anthony Pelissier   novel H. G. Wells   d Anthony Pelissier   ph Desmond Dickinson   m William Alwyn

John Mills, Sally Ann Howes, Megs Jenkins, Finlay Currie, Betty Ann Davies, Edward Chapman

History of the World Part One

US   1981   92m   DeLuxe   Panavision
Brooksfilms (Mel Brooks)
V, V*, L

Episodes from world history are presented with the author's usual lack of taste or wit: a woeful collection of schoolboy scatology.

wd Mel Brooks   *ph* Woody Omens, Paul Wilson
m John Morris

Mel Brooks, Dom de Luise, Madeline Kahn, Cloris
Leachman, Harvey Korman, Ron Carey, Sid Caesar,
Pamela Stephenson, Henny Youngman

'Most of the time it's just expensive sets sitting around
waiting for Brooks to do something funny in front of
them.' – *Roger Ebert*

Hit!

US   1973   134m   Technicolor   Panavision
Paramount (Harry Korshak)
V*

A federal agent takes personal action against a drug
ring which caused his daughter's death.

Black vigilante melodrama, very violent and
interminably padded out with irrelevancies.

w Alan Trustman, David M. Wolf   *d* Sidney J. Furie
ph John A. Alonzo   *m* Lalo Schifrin

Billy Dee Williams, Richard Pryor, Paul Hampton,
Gwen Welles

'No more under-the-armpit shots, but obscurity is still
the keynote of this Sidney Furie effort in the urban
vigilante genre.' – *Sight and Sound*

The Hit

GB   1984   98m   Technicolor
Zenith/Central/The Recorded Picture Company (Jeremy
    Thomas)
V*, L

A supergrass hiding in Spain is sought by two gang
executioners.

Old hat thuggery shown in new-style detail. Violently
suspenseful but not otherwise interesting.

w Peter Prince   *d* Stephen Frears   *ph* Mike Molloy
m Paco de Lucia   *pd* Andrew Sanders

John Hurt, Terence Stamp, Tim Roth, Laura del Sol,
Fernando Rey, Bill Hunter

'Sensitive editing and seductive camerawork can't
disguise that the exercise is heading nowhere, a road
movie without fuel.' – *Philip Strick, MFB*

Hit Man

US   1972   90m   colour
MGM (Gene Corman)

A professional killer returns home to avenge his
brother's death.

An ineffectual reworking of the superior *Get Carter*,
with an American setting and a black cast.

wd George Armitage   *novel* *Jack's Return Home* by Ted
Lewis   *ph* Andrew Davis   *m* H. B. Barnum
ad Lynn Griffin   *ed* Morton Tubor

Bernie Casey, Pamela Grier, Lisa Moore, Bhetty
Waldron, Sam Laws, Don Diamond

The Hit Parade

US   1937   77m   bw
Republic (Nat Levin)

An agent tries to get a new star into radio.

An excuse for a line-up of acts, some quite tolerable.

w Bradford Ropes, Sam Ornitz   *d* Gus Meins

Frances Langford, Phil Regan, Louise Henry, Pert
Kelton, Al Pearce, Ed Brophy, William Demarest,
Duke Ellington and his Band, Eddy Duchin and his
Band, Max Terhune, Monroe Owsley, Inez Courtney,
the Tic Toc Girls

'Should gather plenty of de luxe dates . . . the tempo
guarantees that the average fan will find it diverting.'
– *Variety*

Hit Parade of 1941

US   1940   83m   bw
Republic (Sol C. Siegel)

The young owner of a radio station subs his singer
girlfriend for the sponsor's daughter.

Moderate musical in need of a better script.

w Bradford Ropes, F. Hugh Herbert (no relation),
Maurice Leo   *d* John H. Auer   *m* Cy Feuer

Kenny Baker, Frances Langford, Hugh Herbert, Mary
Boland, Ann Miller, Patsy Kelly, Phil Silvers, Sterling
Holloway, Donald MacBride, Barnett Parker, Franklin
Pangborn, Six Hits and a Miss, Borrah Minevitch and
his Harmonica Rascals

AAN: Cy Feuer; song 'Who Am I?' (*m* Jule Styne, *ly*
Walter Bullock)

Hit Parade of 1943

US   1943   90m   bw
Republic (Albert J. Cohen)
aka: *Change of Heart*

A plagiaristic songwriter becomes a model swain.

Lively comedy musical, third and best of the series.

w Frank Gill Jnr   *d* Albert S. Rogell   *m* Walter
Scharf

John Carroll, Susan Hayward, Gail Patrick, Eve
Arden, Melville Cooper, Walter Catlett, Mary Treen,
Tom Kennedy, Dorothy Dandridge, the Golden Gate
Quartet, Count Basie and his orchestra

AAN: Walter Scharf; song 'Change of Heart' (*m* Jule
Styne, *ly* Harold Adamson)

Hit Parade of 1947

US   1947   90m   bw
Republic (Frank McDonald)

A struggling songwriter tries in vain to become
sophisticated.

Tolerable musical jamboree with too thin a storyline.

w Mary Loos, Parke Levy   *d* Frank McDonald

Eddie Albert, Constance Moore, Joan Edwards, Gil
Lamb, Bill Goodwin, William Frawley, Richard Lane,
Roy Rogers and Trigger, Woody Herman and his
orchestra

Hit the Deck

US   1930   93m   bw/colour sequences
RKO

Navy recruits have girl trouble.

Lumpy production of a stage musical already well
worn.

wd Luther Reed   *play* Herbert Fields

Jack Oakie, Polly Walker, Roger Gray, Harry Sweet

'No reason why this one should run into trouble on
week stands or less.' – *Variety*

Hit the Deck

US   1954   112m   Eastmancolor   Cinemascope
MGM (Joe Pasternak)
V*, L

Romantic adventures of three sailors on shore leave in
San Francisco.

Boring situations and performances reduce the
temperature of this youth musical which is not
another *On the Town*.

w Sonya Levien, William Ludwig   *musical
play* Herbert Fields   *novel Shore Leave* by Hubert
Osborn   *d* Roy Rowland   *ph* George Folsey
md George Stoll   *ch* Hermes Pan   *m/ly* Vincent
Youmans, Leo Robin

Tony Martin, Jane Powell, Ann Miller, Debbie
Reynolds, Walter Pidgeon, Vic Damone, Gene
Raymond

Hitch-hike Lady

US   1935   77m   bw
Republic

An English housekeeper saves enough money to visit

her son in the US, not aware that he is in San
Quentin.

Easy-going sentimental comedy, shot on the road.

w Gordon Rigby, Lester Cole   *story* Wallace
MacDonald   *d* Aubrey Scotto

Alison Skipworth, Arthur Treacher, Mae Clarke,
James Ellison, Warren Hymer, Beryl Mercer

'Happy intermingling of humour and heart tugs.' –
Variety

Hitler

US   1961   107m   bw
Three Crown/E. Charles Straus

A sex-oriented, semi-fictional biopic of the German
dictator, from the murder of his niece to his final
madness and suicide.

Enterprising sensationalism which deserves a nod for
sheer audacity.

w Sam Neuman   *d* Stuart Heisler   *ph* Joseph Biroc
m Hans Salter

Richard Basehart, Maria Emo, Martin Kosleck, John
Banner

Hitler – Beast of Berlin

US   1939   87m   bw
PRC
aka: *Beasts of Berlin*

A spy among Hitler's storm troopers escapes to
Switzerland.

Feeble exploitation item which succeeded only as
propaganda. Hitler is not seen.

w Shepard Traube   *story* Goose Step by Shepard
Traube   *d* Sherman Scott

Roland Drew, Steffi Duna, Alan Ladd, Greta
Granstedt, Lucien Prival

'There are doubtless powerful pictures to be made on
the anti-Nazi theme, but this isn't one.' – *Variety*

Hitler – Dead or Alive

US   1942   72m   bw
Ben Judell/Charles House

Three Alcatraz graduates try to collect a prize for the
capture of Hitler.

Silly mix of farce and propaganda.

w Sam Neumann, Karl Brown   *d* Nick Grinde

Ward Bond, Dorothy Tree, Warren Hymer, Paul Fix,
Russell Hicks, Bobby Watson

'More morphine for Herr Goering! The greatest gangster
    picture of all!'
'Did Hitler kill the one woman he loved? What was Hess
    to Hitler?'

The Hitler Gang **

US   1944   101m   bw
Paramount (B. G. de Sylva)

The rise to power of Hitler and his henchmen.

Though at the time it seemed rather like a serious
cabaret turn, this fictionalization of historical fact has
some good impersonations and dramatically effective
scenes.

w Frances Goodrich, Albert Hackett   *d* John Farrow
ph Ernest Laszlo   *m* David Buttolph

Robert Watson, Martin Kosleck (Goebbels), Victor
Varconi (Hess), Luis Van Rooten (Himmler),
Alexander Pope (Goering), Roman Bohnen, Ivan
Triesault, Helene Thimig, Reinhold Schunzel, Sig
Rumann, Alexander Granach

Hitler – The Last Ten Days

GB/Italy   1973   104m   Technicolor
MGM/Wolfgang Reinhardt/Westfilm
V*

With Adolf and Eva in the bunker.

Claustrophobic historical reconstruction with an uncomfortable star.

w Ennio de Concini, Maria Pia Fusco, Wolfgang Reinhardt, Ivan Moffat   *d* Ennio de Concini *ph* Ennio Guarnieri   *m* Mischa Spoliansky

Alec Guinness, Simon Ward, Doris Kunstmann, Adolfo Celi, Diane Cilento, Eric Porter, Joss Ackland

'The truth about the Nazis from the cradle to the battlefront!'

Hitler's Children *
US   1943   83m   bw
RKO (Edward A. Golden)
V*

A family reacts to Hitler and the Hitler Youth.

Artificial melodrama set in an unlikely Germany but successful at the time because of its topicality and its refusal to play the Nazis as idiots, which was the usual Hollywood line.

w Emmet Lavery   *book* Education for Death by Gregor Ziemer   *d* Edward Dmytryk   *ph* Russell Metty *m* Roy Webb

Tim Holt, Bonita Granville, Otto Kruger, Kent Smith, H. B. Warner, Lloyd Corrigan, Erford Gage, Gavin Muir, Hans Conried

'A curiously compromised production . . . strong anti-Nazi propaganda, it has not been woven into a defined and moving show.' – *Howard Barnes, New York Herald Tribune*

Hitler's Gold: see *Inside Out*

Hitler's Hangman: see *Hitler's Madman*

Hitler's Madman *
US   1943   84m   bw
MGM/PRC (Seymour Nebenzal)
aka: Hitler's Hangman

Heydrich is assassinated in Czechoslovakia and the Nazis take revenge on the village of Lidice.

Cheapjack sensationalism based on a horrifying incident of World War II; despite its imperfections it generates a certain raw power.

w Peretz Hirshbein, Melvin Levy, Doris Malloy *d* Douglas Sirk   *m* Karl Hajos

Patricia Morison, *John Carradine*, Alan Curtis, Ralph Morgan, Ludwig Stossel, Edgar Kennedy, Al Shean, Jimmy Conlin, Blanche Yurka, Victor Kilian

'Newspaper accounts of the bombing of German cities will be pleasant antidotes for the unhappy feeling brought on by the final grim scenes of *Hitler's Madman*.' – *New York Herald Tribune*

'Even in its poorly depicted scenes of brutality, it inflames a common anger.' – *Theodore Strauss, New York Times*

Ho! (dubbed)
France/Italy   1968   107m   Eastmancolor
Golden Era/Filmsonor/Marceau/Cocinor/Mega Film
aka: Criminal Face

A racing driver turned crook decides to go straight. The title refers to the hero's nickname of Ho.

Ho-hum drama.

w Pierre Pelegri, Lucienna Hamon, Robert Enrico *novel* José Giovanni   *d* Robert Enrico   *ph* Jean Boffety   *m* François de Roubaix   *ad* Jacques Saulnier   *ed* Jacqueline Meppiel

Jean-Paul Belmondo, Joanna Shimkus, Paul Crauchet, Stéphane Fey, Tony Taffin, Sydney Chaplin

Hobson's Choice ***
GB   1953   107m   bw
British Lion/London (Norman Spencer)
V, V*, L

In the 1890s a tyrannical Lancashire bootmaker is

brought to heel by his plain-speaking daughter and her simple-minded husband.

Brilliantly played version of a famous working-class comedy, memorably set and photographed; one regrets only the slight decline of the predictable third act.

w Norman Spencer, Wynard Browne   *play* Harold Brighouse   *d* David Lean   *ph* Jack Hildyard *m* Malcolm Arnold   *ad* Wilfrid Shingleton

Charles Laughton, Brenda de Banzie, John Mills, Richard Wattis, Helen Haye, Daphne Anderson, Prunella Scales

† Previously filmed in 1931 by Thomas Bentley for BIP from a screenplay by Frank Launder, with James Harcourt, Viola Lyel and Frank Pettingell.

Hocus Pocus
US   1993   96m   Technicolor
Buena Vista/Walt Disney (David Kirschner, Steven Haft)
V*, L, S

In Salem, three children inadvertently conjure up three wicked witches.

A mildly comic vehicle for Bette Midler, though a kiddies' film is not the best setting for her talents.

w Mick Garris, Neil Cuthbert   *story* David Kirschner, Mick Garris   *d* Kenny Ortega   *ph* Hiro Narita   *m* John Debney   *pd* William Sandell *ed* Peter E. Berger

Bette Midler, Sarah Jessica Parker, Kathy Najimy, Omri Katz, Thora Birch, Vinessa Shaw, Amanda Shepherd

'The blend of witchcraft and comedy should divert kids without driving the patience of their parents to the boiling point.' – *Variety*

Hoffa
US   1992   140m   colour   Panavision
TCF/Jersey (Edward R. Pressman, Danny DeVito, Caldecot Chubb)
V, V*, L, S

An aggressive agitator for the Teamster's Union accepts the aid of gangsters and becomes its leader before mysteriously vanishing.

A creakingly old-fashioned biopic that reaches few conclusions and makes no judgements.

w David Mamet   *d* Danny DeVito   *ph* Stephen H. Burum   *m* David Newman   *pd* Ida Random *ed* Lynzee Klingman, Ronald Roose

Jack Nicholson, Danny DeVito, Armand Assante, J. T. Walsh, John C. Reilly, Frank Whaley, Kevin Anderson, John P. Ryan, Robert Prosky, Cliff Gorman

'As is so often the case with biopics that attempt to convey decades, something gets sacrificed. Here, it's a human drama one can relate to.' – *Variety*

AAN: Stephen H. Burum

'Hope never dies for a man with a good dirty mind.'
Hoffman
GB   1970   113m   Technicolor
ABP/Longstone (Ben Arbeid)
V

A middle-aged misfit blackmails a typist into spending a week with him.

Interminable sex comedy padded out from a short TV play; it quickly becomes claustrophobic, tasteless, and boring.

w Ernest Gebler   *play* Ernest Gebler   *novel* Ernest Gebler   *d* Alvin Rakoff   *ph* Gerry Turpin   *m* Ron Grainer

Peter Sellers, Sinead Cusack, Jeremy Bulloch, Ruth Dunning

Hog Wild ***
US   1930   20m   bw
Hal Roach
V

Stan helps Ollie to put a radio aerial on the roof of his house.

Brilliantly sustained slapstick makes this one of the best star comedies of Laurel and Hardy.

w H. M. Walker, Leo McCarey   *d* James Parrott *ph* George Stevens*d* Richard Currier

Laurel and Hardy, Fay Holderness, Dorothy Granger

Hohenfeuer: see *Alpine Fire*

The Holcroft Covenant
GB   1985   112m   colour
EMI/Ely and Edie Landau
V*, L

One of the architects of Hitler's Third Reich leaves a bequest which may fall into the wrong hands.

Muddled political thriller which tends to provoke unintended laughs.

w George Axelrod, Edward Anhalt, John Hopkins *novel* Robert Ludlum   *d* John Frankenheimer *ph* Gerry Fisher   *m* Stanislas   *pd* Peter Mullins

Michael Caine, Anthony Andrews, Victoria Tennant, Lilli Palmer, Mario Adorf, Michael Lonsdale, Bernard Hepton

'A narrative deficient in thrills or plausibility.' – *Variety*

'Master of love! He is to all women what each desires him to be!'
Hold Back the Dawn *
US   1941   115m   bw
Paramount (Arthur Hornblow Jnr)

A would-be immigrant into the US via Mexico marries a schoolteacher he does not love.

Surprisingly effective romantic melodrama with a nice style and some mordant lines in the script.

w Charles Brackett, Billy Wilder   *d* Mitchell Leisen *ph* Leo Tover   *m* Victor Young   *ad* Hans Dreier, Robert Usher

Charles Boyer, Olivia de Havilland, Paulette Goddard, Victor Francen, Walter Abel, Curt Bois, Rosemary de Camp, Nestor Paiva, Mitchell Leisen

'All those years with all the others I closed my eyes and thought of you.' – *sample dialogue spoken by Paulette Goddard*

'It has all the vitamins for mass popular appeal.' – *Variety*

† The story is told by Boyer to Mitchell Leisen on a film set where he has just shot a scene from *I Wanted Wings*.

AAN: best picture; Charles Brackett, Billy Wilder; Leo Tover; Victor Young; Olivia de Havilland; art direction

Hold Back the Night
US   1956   80m   bw
Allied Artists

From World War II to Korea, a marine commander carries with him a lucky whisky bottle.

Pointlessly titled war heroics, competently mounted.

w John C. Higgins, Walter Doniger   *novel* Pat Frank *d* Allan Dwan

John Payne, Mona Freeman, Peter Graves, Chuck Connors, Audrey Dalton

Hold Back Tomorrow
US   1956   75m   bw
Universal-International (Hugo Haas)

A convicted killer's last request is for a woman to

spend his last night with him. They fall in love before he is executed.

A ripe example of the higher tosh, indifferently made and acted.

wd Hugo Haas

Cleo Moore, John Agar, Frank de Kova, Dallas Boyd

Hold 'em Yale
US 1935 61m bw
Paramount

Four con men find themselves looking after a disinherited heiress.

Thin filming of a Damon Runyon story; strictly supporting material.

w Paul Gerard Smith, Eddie Welch *d* Sidney Lanfield

Patricia Ellis, Cesar Romero, Larry Crabbe, William Frawley, Andy Devine, George E. Stone, Warren Hymer

Hold Everything
US 1930 78m Technicolor
Warner

A comedian becomes a prizefighter.

Pleasant comedy musical which established Joe E. Brown in Hollywood, as it had established Bert Lahr on stage.

w Robert Lord *play* B. G. De Sylva, John McGowan *d* Roy del Ruth

Joe E. Brown, Winnie Lightner, Georges Carpentier, Sally O'Neil, Bert Roach

'Pip laugh picture, the best comedy Warners has turned out since talkers came in.' – *Variety*

Hold My Hand
GB 1938 76m bw
Associated British (Walter C. Mycroft)

A businessman is engaged to an aristocrat's daughter but marries his secretary instead.

Routine light comedy with a few songs that must have worked better on the stage. It ends with one of the most absurd dance sequences on film.

w Clifford Grey, Bert Lee, William Freshman *play* Stanley Lupino *d* Thornton Freeland *ph* Otto Kanturek *md* Harry Acres *ad* Ian White *ed* E. B. Jarvis

Stanley Lupino, Fred Emney, Syd Walker, Barbara Blair, Sally Gray, Polly Ward, Bartha Belmore, Jack Melford, John Wood

Hold That Blonde
US 1945 75m bw
Paramount (Paul Jones)

A psychiatrist suggests that romance may cure a kleptomaniac, but the patient unfortunately chooses a jewel thief.

Thin comedy which erupts into frantic farce, with some energetic slapstick and a Harold Lloyd style finale.

w Walter de Leon, Earl Baldwin, E. Edwin Moran *d* George Marshall *ph* Daniel L. Fapp *m* Werner Heymann

Eddie Bracken, Veronica Lake, Albert Dekker, Frank Fenton, George Zucco, Donald MacBride, Norma Varden, Willie Best

Hold That Co-Ed *
US 1938 80m bw
TCF (David Hempstead)
GB title: *Hold That Girl*

A girl dressed as a boy wins a university football match and thereby helps a governor get re-elected.

Intriguingly-cast crazy comedy which works up into a fine frenzy.

w Karl Tunberg, Don Ettinger, Jack Yellen *d* George Marshall *ph* Robert Planck *md* Arthur Lange

John Barrymore, Joan Davis, George Murphy, Marjorie Weaver, Jack Haley, George Barbier, Donald Meek, Johnny Downs, Guinn Williams

'On the wacky side and fairly amusing, but not quite making the big league.' – *Variety*

Hold That Ghost *
US 1941 86m bw
Universal (Burt Kelly, Glenn Tryon)
V*

A group of strangers are stranded in an apparently haunted house.

Long thought of as Abbott and Costello's best comedy, this now seems pretty strained and slow to start, but it has its classic moments.

w Robert Lees, Fred Rinaldo, John Grant *d* Arthur Lubin *ph* Elwood Bredell, Joe Valentine *m* Hans Salter

Bud Abbott, Lou Costello, Joan Davis, the Andrews Sisters, Richard Carlson, *Ted Lewis* and his band, Evelyn Ankers, Marc Lawrence, Mischa Auer

Hold That Girl: see *Hold That Co-Ed*

Hold That Kiss
US 1938 75m bw
MGM

A man and woman each believe the other to be wealthy.

Elementary comedy of misunderstandings, of no abiding interest.

w Stanley Rauh *d* Edwin S. Marin

Maureen O'Sullivan, Dennis O'Keefe, Mickey Rooney, George Barbier, Jessie Ralph, Ed Brophy

'Pleasant but undistinguished.' – *Variety*

Hold Your Man *
US 1933 89m bw
MGM (Sam Wood)

A hard-boiled young woman falls for a confidence man, has his baby, and waits for him to emerge from prison.

Briskly-fashioned star comedy-drama with entertaining moments.

w Anita Loos, Howard Emmett Rogers *d* Sam Wood *ph* Harold Rosson *m/ly* Nacio Herb Brown, Arthur Freed

Jean Harlow, Clark Gable, Stuart Erwin, Dorothy Burgess, Muriel Kirkland, Paul Hurst

'A real money picture . . . most promising box office prospect in months.' – *Variety*

'The sudden transition from wise-cracking romance to sentimental penitence provides a jolt.' – *Frank S. Nugent*

The Hole *
France/Italy 1959 123m bw
Play-Art/Filmsonor/Titanus (Serge Silberman)
original title: *Le Trou*

Four convicts in a Paris prison dig a tunnel to freedom and almost make it.

Meticulous escape drama nicely shot in very limited sets: hypnotic for those with the patience to adjust to its pace.

w Jacques Becker, José Giovanni, Jean Aurel *novel* José Giovanni *d* Jacques Becker *ph* Ghislain Cloquet

Philippe Leroy, Mark Michel, Jean Kéraudy, Michel Constantine

The Hole (1964): see *Onibaba*

A Hole in the Head *
US 1959 120m DeLuxe Cinemascope
UA/Sincap (Frank Sinatra)
V*, L

A Miami hotelier is threatened with foreclosure and tries to raise the money from his provident elder brother.

Easy-going comedy without much point, but various amusing facets artfully deployed.

w Arnold Shulman *play* Arnold Shulman *d* Frank Capra *ph* William H. Daniels *m* Nelson Riddle

Frank Sinatra, Edward G. Robinson, Eleanor Parker, Eddie Hodges, Carolyn Jones, Thelma Ritter, Keenan Wynn, Joi Lansing

AA: song 'High Hopes' (*m* Jimmy Van Heusen, *ly* Sammy Cahn)

The Hole in the Wall
US 1929 73m bw
Paramount

A gangster falls for a phony fortune teller on a revenge scheme.

Involved melodrama, a primitive talkie notable chiefly for its stars.

w Pierre Collings *play* Fred Jackson *d* Robert Florey *ph* George Folsey

Edward G. Robinson, Claudette Colbert, David Newell, Nelly Savage, Donald Meek, Louise Closser Hale

Holiday *
US 1930 99m bw
Pathé (E. B. Derr)

A bright-minded rich girl steals her sister's fiancé, a struggling young lawyer.

Competent early talkie version of a hit play.

w Horace Jackson *play* Philip Barry *d* Edward H. Griffith *ph* Norbert Brodine *m* Josiah Zuro

Ann Harding, Robert Ames, Mary Astor, Edward Everett Horton, Hedda Hopper, Monroe Owsley, William Holden

'A comedy of wide appeal in a finished style.' – *Variety*

AAN: Horace Jackson; Ann Harding

'So daring – so tender – so human – so true – that everyone in love will want to see it!'

Holiday ***
US 1938 93m bw
Columbia (Everett Riskin)
V, V*, L
GB titles: *Free to Live*; *Unconventional Linda*

Elegant, highly successful remake of the above; still a stage play on film, but subtly devised to make the very most of the lines and performances.

w Donald Ogden Stewart *d* George Cukor *ph* Franz Planer *m* Sidney Cutner *ad* Stephen Goosson, Lionel Banks

Katharine Hepburn, Cary Grant, Doris Nolan, *Edward Everett Horton* (same role), *Ruth Donnelly, Lew Ayres*, Henry Kolker, Binnie Barnes

'Corking comedy . . . exhibitors will pencil in some extra days.' – *Variety*

'The comedy is full of the best of humour, edged with pathos never allowed to drop into sentimentality. It is played with the greatest cheerfulness and a winning skill.' – *Arthur Pollock, Brooklyn Daily Eagle*

'I suppose actually it is a neat and sometimes elegant job, but under its surface of too much brightness and too many words it seems so deadly bored and weary. Hell, save your money and yawn at home.' – *Otis Ferguson*

'Played with the greatest cheerfulness and a winning skill.' – *Brooklyn Daily Eagle*

AAN: art direction

Holiday Affair
US   1949   87m   bw
RKO (Don Hartman)

A young widow falls for an easy-going boat builder.

Flimsy star-shaped romantic comedy with nice touches.

w Isobel Lennart   *d* Don Hartman   *ph* Milton Krasner   *m* Roy Webb

Robert Mitchum, Janet Leigh, Wendell Corey, Griff Barnett, Esther Dale, Gordon Gebert, Henry O'Neill, Harry Morgan

Holiday Camp *
GB   1947   97m   bw
GFD/Gainsborough (Sydney Box)

At a summer holiday camp, a murderer on the prowl affects people's enjoyment in various ways.

Seminal compendium comedy drama, a bore in itself but establishing several post-war norms of the British cinema, including the Huggetts.

w Muriel and Sidney Box, Ted Willis, Peter Rogers, Mabel and Denis Constanduros   *story* Godfrey Winn   *d* Ken Annakin   *ph* Jack Cox   *m* Bob Busby

Jack Warner, Kathleen Harrison, Flora Robson, Dennis Price, Hazel Court, Emrys Jones, Yvonne Owen, Esmond Knight, Jimmy Hanley, Peter Hammond, Esma Cannon, John Blythe, Susan Shaw

'It is real – and true – and it will be a smash at the box office.' – *Sunday Chronicle*

Holiday for Henrietta: see *La Fête à Henriette*

Holiday for Lovers
US   1959   103m   DeLuxe   Cinemascope
TCF (David Weisbart)

To distract his teenage daughter from boys, a Boston psychiatrist organizes a family holiday in South America.

Frail old-fashioned family comedy with entirely predictable situations culminating in a drunk scene for stuffy father.

w Luther Davis   *d* Henry Levin   *ph* Charles G. Clarke   *m* Leigh Harline

Clifton Webb, Jane Wyman, Paul Henreid, Carol Lynley, Jill St John, Gary Crosby, José Greco

Holiday for Sinners
US   1952   72m   bw
MGM (John Houseman)

In New Orleans during the Mardi Gras three old friends meet crises in their lives.

Slightly curious but not very interesting portmanteau drama.

w A. I. Bezzerides   *novel* Hamilton Basso   *d* Gerald Mayer   *ph* Paul Vogel   *md* Alberto Colombo

Gig Young, Keenan Wynn, Janice Rule, Richard Anderson, William Campbell, Michael Chekhov, Sandro Giglio, Edith Barrett, Porter Hall

'It gives an impression of blurred, rather heavy-going sincerity.' – *MFB*

Holiday in Mexico
US   1946   127m   Technicolor
MGM (Joe Pasternak)

The daughter of the American Ambassador to Mexico falls for Jose Iturbi.

Travel brochure musical in which the occasional plums do not redeem the sogginess of the pudding.

w Isobel Lennart   *d* George Sidney   *ph* Harry Stradling   *m* André Previn

Walter Pidgeon, Ilona Massey, Jane Powell, Jose Iturbi, Roddy McDowall

Holiday in Spain: see *Scent of Mystery*

Holiday Inn **
US   1942   101m   bw
Paramount (Mark Sandrich)
V, V*, L

The joint proprietors of a roadhouse hotel love the same girl.

Plain, simple-minded musical which provided a peg for pleasant performances and good numbers. It hit the box-office spot, especially as it introduced 'White Christmas'.

w Claude Binyon, Elmer Rice   *d* Mark Sandrich   *ph* David Abel   *md* Robert Emmett Dolan   *m/ly* Irving Berlin

Bing Crosby, Fred Astaire, Walter Abel, Marjorie Reynolds, Virginia Dale, Louise Beavers, Irving Bacon, James Bell

'The best musical drama of the year.' – *New York Post*

† Marjorie Reynolds was dubbed by Martha Mears

AA: song 'White Christmas'

AAN: original story (Irving Berlin); Robert Emmett Dolan

Holiday on the Buses
GB   1973   85m   Technicolor
MGM-EMI/Hammer (Ronald Wolfe, Ronald Chesney)

After losing their jobs on the buses, two drivers and an inspector find work at a holiday camp.

Tired sitcom spin-off in which the cast go half-heartedly through their familiar, poorly timed slapstick routines.

w Ronald Wolfe, Ronald Chesney from their TV series   *d* Bryan Izzard   *ph* Brian Probyn   *m* Denis King   *ad* Don Picton   *ed* James Needs

Reg Varney, Stephen Lewis, Doris Hare, Michael Robbins, Anna Karen, Bob Grant, Wilfred Brambell, Arthur Mullard, Henry McGee

'The only concession Wolfe and Chesney have made to avoid being accused of compiling the entire scripts from old *Carry On* situations involves a subsidiary romance between Doris Hare and Wilfred Brambell. One could probably conceive of a more revolting spectacle than Brambell panting after Miss Hare and making jokes about cutting notches on his walking stick, but nothing comes immediately to mind.' – *David McGillivray, Films and Filming*

Hollow Triumph: see *The Scar*

The Holly and the Ivy *
GB   1952   83m   bw
British Lion/London (Anatole de Grunwald)

Christmas brings family revelations in a remote Norfolk rectory.

A badly-filmed stage success which succeeds because of its performances.

w Anatole de Grunwald   *play* Wynard Browne   *d* George More O'Ferrall   *ph* Ted Scaife   *m* Malcolm Arnold

Ralph Richardson, Celia Johnson, Margaret Leighton, Denholm Elliott, John Gregson, Hugh Williams, Margaret Halstan, Maureen Delany, William Hartnell, Robert Flemyng, Roland Culver

'This type of direct translation to the screen, using none of the cinema's resources, can only do harm to the play itself.' – *Penelope Houston*

Hollywood and Vine
US   1945   59m   bw
PRC (Leon Fromkess)
GB title: *Daisy Goes to Hollywood*

A New York writer is ordered to Hollywood to script a film for a dog.

Mild satire which works in fits and starts.

w Edith Watkins, Charles Williams   *d* Alexis Thurn-Taxis

James Ellison, Wanda McKay, June Clyde, Ralph Morgan, Emmett Lynn, Franklin Pangborn, Leon Belasco

Hollywood Boulevard *
US   1936   75m   bw
Paramount (A. M. Botsford)

A washed-up Hollywood actor writes a sensational memoir for publication, but lives to regret it.

Entertaining melodrama with famous names in bit parts.

w Marguerite Roberts   *d* Robert Florey   *ph* Karl Struss   *m* Gregory Stone

John Halliday, Marsha Hunt, Robert Cummings, C. Henry Gordon, Frieda Inescort, Esther Dale; and Gary Cooper, Francis X. Bushman, Maurice Costello, Mae Marsh, Charles Ray, Jane Novak, Bryant Washburn, Jack Mulhall, Creighton Hale, Bert Roach

'A pretty hoary melodrama and a slight enough excuse for a whole series of homilies upon the uncertainty of fame and fortune in the glamour city.' – *New York Times*

Hollywood Boulevard
US   1977   83m   colour
New World (Jon Davison)
V*

An inexperienced actress goes to work for makers of low-budget exploitation movies with violent results.

Bizarre action film spoof, with dialogue and a slim narrative added to action sequences taken from previous Roger Corman movies; it will mainly interest fans of Corman or of the other talents involved.

w Patrick Hobby   *d* Allan Arkush, Joe Dante   *ph* Jamie Anderson   *m* Andrew Stein   *ad* Jack DeWolfe   *ed* Allan Arkush, Joe Dante, Amy Jones

Candice Rialson, Mary Woronov, Rita George, Jeffrey Kramer, Dick Miller, Paul Bartel, Jonathan Kaplan, Charles B. Griffith

† The film began as a bet which Davison made with Roger Corman that he could produce a picture for $90,000, which was less than any other New World movie, providing he could use stock footage from other Corman productions. It was shot in ten days at a cost of $80,000.

Hollywood Canteen *
US   1944   123m   bw
Warner (Alex Gottlieb)
V*, L

The stars give their evenings to entertaining soldiers.

Shoddily made but sociologically fascinating record of Hollywood doing its bit in World War II.

wd Delmer Daves   *ph* Bert Glennon   *md* Leo F. Forbstein   *m* Ray Heindorf

Joan Leslie, Robert Hutton, Dane Clark, Janis Paige; and The Andrews Sisters, Jack Benny, Joe E. Brown, Eddie Cantor, Joan Crawford, Bette Davis, John Garfield, Sidney Greenstreet, Paul Henreid, Peter Lorre, Ida Lupino, Dennis Morgan, Roy Rogers, S. Z. Sakall, Alexis Smith, Barbara Stanwyck, Jane Wyman, etc etc

'The corporal steps slowly backwards, in his eyes that look of glazed ecstasy which Jennifer Jones wore all through *The Song of Bernadette.* He has just been kissed by Joan Leslie.' – *Richard Winnington*

AAN: Ray Heindorf; song 'Sweet Dreams, Sweetheart' (*m* M. K. Jerome, *ly* Ted Koehler)

'It does for the motion picture what Alexander's Ragtime Band did for popular music!'

Hollywood Cavalcade *
US 1939 96m Technicolor
TCF (Harry Joe Brown)

The career of an old-time Hollywood producer.

A lively first half with amusing re-staging of early slapstick comedies gives way depressingly to personal melodrama, but there is enough historical interest to preserve the balance.

w Ernest Pascal d Irving Cummings ph Allen M. Davey, Ernest Palmer md Louis Silvers m David Raksin, David Buttolph, Cyril Mockridge ad Richard Day, Wiard B. Ihnen

Don Ameche, Alice Faye, J. Edward Bromberg, Alan Curtis, Stuart Erwin, Jed Prouty, Buster Keaton, Donald Meek, and the original Keystone Kops

'Surefire . . . should score heavily in theatres of every type.' – Variety

† Alice Faye did not sing. The Keystone Kops sequence was directed by Mal St Clair. The Ameche/Faye characters were supposedly based on Mack Sennett and Mabel Normand; Mack Sennett's appearance under his own name seemed to be an effort to throw people off the scent.

Hollywood Cowboy: see Hearts of the West

Hollywood Hotel
US 1938 109m bw
Warner (Sam Bischoff)

A Hollywood radio show has its problems.

Half-hearted, overlong Warner musical with little of the expected zip.

w Jerry Wald, Maurice Leo, Richard Macauley d Busby Berkeley ph Charles Rosher, George Barnes m/ly Johnny Mercer, Richard Whiting

Dick Powell, Rosemary Lane, Lola Lane, Hugh Herbert, Ted Healy, Glenda Farrell, Louella Parsons, Alan Mowbray, Frances Langford, Allyn Joslyn, Benny Goodman, Edgar Kennedy

Hollywood or Bust
US 1956 95m Technicolor Vistavision
Paramount/Hal Wallis

Two halfwits win a car and drive across country to Hollywood.

Dopey comedy with more misses than hits; the last film of Martin and Lewis as a team.

w Erna Lazarus d Frank Tashlin ph Daniel Fapp m Walter Scharf

Dean Martin, Jerry Lewis, Pat Crowley, Maxie Rosenbloom, Anita Ekberg

Hollywood Party
US 1934 68m bw/Technicolor sequence
MGM (Harry Rapf, Howard Dietz)
V*

A mad Russian throws a party which ends in disaster.

Dismal 'all-star' comedy relieved by guest appearances.

w Howard Dietz, Arthur Kober d (uncredited) Richard Boleslawski, Allan Dwan, Roy Rowland, George Stevens m/ly Rodgers, Hart and others ed George Boemler

Laurel and Hardy, Jimmy Durante, Lupe Velez, Charles Butterworth, Eddie Quillan, Ted Healy and the Stooges, Polly Moran

'A big short . . . averagely passable screen divertissement.' – Variety

'The picture hardly rates the time and money that MGM has expended.' – Hollywood Reporter

† The film was dogged by disaster and was in production for a year. At least eight directors were involved, but no one wanted a credit on the finished film.

The Hollywood Revue of 1929 **
US 1929 116m part-Technicolor
MGM (Harry Rapf)
L

A variety show featuring most of MGM's talent in slightly surprising acts, this is something of a bore to sit through but an archival must; and just occasionally it boasts surprising vitality.

w Al Boasberg, Robert E. Hopkins d Charles F. Reisner ph John Arnold, Irving Ries, Maximilian Fabian ch Sammy Lee m/ly various

Jack Benny, Buster Keaton, Joan Crawford, John Gilbert, Norma Shearer, Laurel and Hardy, Marion Davies, Marie Dressler, William Haines, Lionel Barrymore, Conrad Nagel, Bessie Love, Cliff Edwards, Nils Asther

AAN: best picture

Hollywood Shuffle *
US 1987 82m colour
Samuel Goldwyn Company/Conquering Unicorn (Robert Townsend)
V*, L

A young black actor looks for work in films.

A loosely connected series of satirical sketches that provide fun at the expense of current movie genres and the stereotyping of black actors as gangsters or pimps.

w Robert Townsend, Keenen Ivory Wayans d Robert Townsend ph Peter Deming m Patrice Rushen, Udi Harpaz ad Melba Katzman Farquhar ed W. O. Garrett

Robert Townsend, Anne-Marie Johnson, Starletta Dupois, Helen Martin, Craigus R. Johnson, John Witherspoon, Keenen Ivory Wayans, Jimmy Woodard

'Scattershot humor misses as much as it hits.' – Variety

Hollywood Speaks
US 1932 71m bw
Columbia

A Los Angeles columnist exposes Hollywood corruption.

Superficial exploitation piece of no interest apart from glimpses of studios.

w Norman Krasna, Jo Swerling d Eddie Buzzell

Pat O'Brien, Genevieve Tobin, Lucien Prival, Rita Leroy

'Its field is really the split weeks . . . good bet for the less educated clientele.' – Variety

Hollywood Story *
US 1951 76m bw
U-I (Leonard Goldstein)

A young producer solves a 20-year-old studio murder mystery.

Adequate potboiler with a reasonably absorbing plot and glimpses of silent stars.

w Frederick Kohner, Fred Brady d William Castle ph Carl Guthrie m Joseph Gershenson

Richard Conte, Julie Adams, Richard Egan, Henry Hull, Fred Clark, Jim Backus, Paul Cavanagh; and Francis X. Bushman, William Farnum, Betty Blythe, Helen Gibson, Joel McCrea

Holocaust 2000
GB/Italy 1977 102m Technicolor Technovision
Rank/Aston/Embassy (Edmondo Amati)
V*
aka: The Chosen

The executive in charge of a thermonuclear plant in the Middle East is drawn into a legend about the rebirth of the anti-Christ, and discovers that the evil one is his own son.

Extraordinary mishmash of horror, religiosity and social conscience which scarcely works on any level.

w Sergio Donati, Alberto de Martino, Michael Robson d Alberto de Martino ph Erico Menczer m Ennio Morricone

Kirk Douglas, Simon Ward, Agostina Belli, Anthony Quayle, Virginia McKenna, Spiros Focas, Alexander Knox, Adolfo Celi

'The wildest farrago yet to have come out of the demonology genre.' – Richard Combs, MFB

Holt of the Secret Service
US 1941 bw serial: 15 eps
Columbia

The FBI tracks down counterfeiters.

Handy serial thick ear.

d James W. Horne

Jack Holt, Evelyn Brent, Montague Shaw, Tristram Coffin

Holy Matrimony *
US 1943 87m bw
TCF (Nunnally Johnson)

A famous painter comes back from exile for a knighthood; but when his valet dies of pneumonia, has him buried as himself in Westminster Abbey.

Slightly stilted but generally warmly amusing version of a favourite novel, with excellent star performances.

w Nunnally Johnson novel Buried Alive by Arnold Bennett d John Stahl ph Lucien Ballard m Cyril Mockridge

Monty Woolley, Gracie Fields, Laird Cregar, Eric Blore, Una O'Connor

'A pleasant hour and a half, very well produced and acted.' – James Agate

AAN: Nunnally Johnson

Holy Terror: see Communion (1978)

The Holy Terror
US 1936 66m bw
TCF

A child is a mischief-maker at a naval air station.

Lightweight star vehicle for Shirley Temple's only competitor.

w Lou Breslow, John Patrick d James Tinling

Jane Withers, Tony Martin, Leah Ray, Joan Davis, El Brendel, John Eldredge

'Nicely paced for laughs . . . strong dual bill attraction.' – Variety

Hombre **
US 1967 111m DeLuxe Panavision
TCF/Hombre Productions (Martin Ritt, Irving Ravetch)
V*, L

Stagecoach passengers at the mercy of a robber are helped by a despised half-caste.

Slow but suspenseful Western melodrama which works up to a couple of good climaxes but falls away in an unnecessary tragic ending.

w Irving Ravetch, Harriet Frank novel Elmore Leonard d Martin Ritt ph James Wong Howe m David Rose

Paul Newman, Diane Cilento, Fredric March, Richard Boone, Martin Balsam, Barbara Rush, Cameron Mitchell

'A fine array of quirkish characters . . . and some unusually literate dialogue.' – Tom Milne

Hombre Mirando al Sudeste *

Argentina   1986   100m   Eastmancolor
Cinequanon (Hugo E. Lauria)

A saxophone-playing psychiatrist is confronted by a patient who claims to come from another planet.

An interesting, if portentously told, fable of a Christ-like character meeting with incomprehension in the modern world.

wd Eliseo Subiela   *ph* Ricardo de Angelis *m* Pedro Aznar   *pd* Marta Albertinazzi   *ed* Luis Cesar D'Angiolillo

Lorenzo Quinteros, Hugo Soto, Ines Vernengo

El Hombre que Vino de Ummo: see *Dracula versus Frankenstein*

Home Alone *

US   1990   102m   DeLuxe
TCF/John Hughes
V, V*, L, S

A young boy, inadvertently left behind at Christmas when his parents go on holiday, foils some inept house-breakers.

Swinging uneasily between heavy-handed slapstick and sentimental domestic comedy, this unpretentious movie was, inexplicably, the biggest box-office success of 1990.

w John Hughes   *d* Chris Columbus   *ph* Julio Macat   *m* John Williams   *pd* John Muto   *ed* Raja Gosnell

Macaulay Culkin, Joe Pesci, Daniel Stern, Catherine O'Hara, John Heard, Roberts Blossom, John Candy

'What is astonishing is that a cute family comedy which takes over an hour really to get going should have provoked such an enthusiastic audience response and gained such a phenomenal word-of-mouth reputation.' – *MFB*

AAN: John Williams; best song 'Somewhere In My Memory'

'He's Up Past His Bedtime In The City That Never Sleeps!'
Home Alone 2: Lost in New York

US   1992   120m   colour
TCF (John Hughes)
V, V*, L, S

Separated from his family after boarding the wrong plane, a young boy alone in New York thwarts the same two robbers he met at home.

Virtually a re-make of the first film, though the humour has a far more unpleasantly sadistic edge to it. This undistinguished comedy was among the biggest box-office successes of 1992.

w John Hughes   *d* Chris Columbus   *ph* Julio Macat   *m* John Williams   *pd* Sandy Veneziano *ed* Raja Gosnell

Macaulay Culkin, Joe Pesci, Daniel Stern, Catherine O'Hara, John Heard, Devin Ratray, Hillary Wolf, Maureen Elisabeth Shay, Brenda Fricker

'An interesting example of formula film-making, making use of a higher budget than before but even lower expectations.' – *Derek Malcolm, Guardian*

Home and the World **

India   1984   140m   Eastmancolor
Artificial Eye/National Film Development Corp of India
V*
original title: *Ghare-Baire*

A wealthy landowner brings his wife out from purdah into the world, with fatal results.

Elegant and impressively acted, with an undercurrent of despair.

wd Satyajit Ray   *novel* Rabindranath Tagore *ph* Soumendu Roy   *m* Satyajit Ray   *ad* Ashoke Bose   *ed* Dulal Dutt

Soumitra Chatterjee, Victor Banerjee, Swatilekha Chatterjee, Gopa Aich, Jennifer Kapoor, Manoj Mitra, Indrapramit Roy, Bimal Chatterjee

Home at Seven

GB   1952   85m   bw
British Lion/London (Maurice Cowan)
V*
US title: *Murder on Monday*

A clerk suffers a 24-hour loss of memory and may have been involved in a murder.

Intriguing suburban mystery, well acted but all too flatly transferred from the stage, and with a weak solution.

w Anatole de Grunwald   *play* R. C. Sherriff *d* Ralph Richardson   *ph* Jack Hildyard, Edward Scaife   *m* Malcolm Arnold

Ralph Richardson, Margaret Leighton, Jack Hawkins, Campbell Singer, Michael Shepley, Margaret Withers, Meriel Forbes, Frederick Piper

'A film with a notable absence of imagination in conception, direction and acting is not vindicated because it was made very cheaply in fifteen days . . . it seems ominous that the technique closely resembles that of television.' – *MFB*

Home before Dark

US   1958   137m   bw
Warner (Mervyn Le Roy)

A college professor brings his wife home after a year in a mental hospital, but trouble starts again as the circumstances are unchanged.

Overlong, heavygoing, well-made soap opera, quite unconvincing despite firm performances and a suitably gloomy *mise-en-scène*.

w Eileen and Robert Bassing   *d* Mervyn Le Roy *ph* Joseph Biroc   *md* Ray Heindorf   *m* Franz Waxman

Jean Simmons, Efrem Zimbalist Jnr, Dan O'Herlihy, Rhonda Fleming, Mabel Albertson

Home from the Hill

US   1959   150m   Metrocolor   Cinemascope
MGM/Sol C. Siegel (Edmund Grainger)

A Southern landowner with a voracious sexual appetite has trouble with his two sons, legitimate and illegitimate.

Shades of *Cold Comfort Farm* and *Tobacco Road* . . . and this solemn family saga does go on a bit.

w Irving Ravetch, Harriet Frank   *novel* William Humphrey   *d* Vincente Minnelli   *ph* Milton Krasner   *m* Bronislau Kaper

Robert Mitchum, George Hamilton, George Peppard, Eleanor Parker, Luana Patten, Everett Sloane, Constance Ford, Ray Teal

Home in Indiana

US   1944   103m   Technicolor
TCF (André Daven)

Farmers compete in trotting races and their progeny fall in love.

Archetypal homespun Americana, well enough made according to its lights, but now like something from another world . . . an innocent one.

w Winston Miller   *novel* *The Phantom Filly* by George Agnew Chamberlain   *d* Henry Hathaway *ph* Edward Cronjager   *md* Emil Newman   *m* Hugo Friedhofer

Jeanne Crain, June Haver, Lon McCallister, Walter Brennan, Charlotte Greenwood, Ward Bond, Charles Dingle, Willie Best

† Remade as *April Love*.

AAN: Edward Cronjager

Home of the Brave *

US   1949   86m   bw
Stanley Kramer
V*

During World War II, a black man finds himself the butt of racist behaviour from the rest of his platoon.

One of the first films to touch the subject of anti-black bias, this now seems pretty tame and dated, and in fact never was much more than a filmed play (in which the butt was originally a Jew).

w Carl Foreman   *play* Arthur Laurents   *d* Mark Robson   *ph* Robert de Grasse   *m* Dimitri Tiomkin

Frank Lovejoy, Lloyd Bridges, Douglas Dick, James Edwards, Steve Brodie, Jeff Corey, Cliff Clark

A Home of Your Own *

GB   1965   44m   bw
Dormar/British Lion

Calamities pile up on a building site.

Genuinely funny silent comedy, with bits from a variety of familiar faces.

w Jay Lewis, John Whyte   *d* Bob Kellett

Ronnie Barker, George Benson, Richard Briers, Janet Brown, Peter Butterworth, Bernard Cribbins, Fred Emney, Bill Fraser, Ronnie Stevens

Home Sweet Homicide

US   1946   90m   bw
TCF

Children solve a murder mystery with the help of their mother, a detective novelist.

Mild family fare.

w F. Hugh Herbert   *novel* Craig Rice   *d* Lloyd Bacon   *ph* John Seitz   *m* David Buttolph

Lynn Bari, Randolph Scott, Peggy Ann Garner, Connie Marshall, Dean Stockwell, Barbara Whiting

Home to Danger

GB   1951   66m   bw
New World (Lance Comfort)

An heiress returns after her father's death and finds herself pursued by a murderer.

Tuppenny shocker, quite amusing in its way.

w Francis Edge, Guy Temple-Smith   *d* Terence Fisher

Rona Anderson, Guy Rolfe, Stanley Baker, Francis Lister, Alan Wheatley

The Home Towners

US   1928   84m   bw
Warner

A wealthy man falls for a girl half his age and is warned by a hometown friend that she may be a gold digger.

Fairly fluent early talkie which pleased at the time.

w Addison Burkhart   *play* George M. Cohan *d* Bryan Foy

Richard Bennett, Robert McWade, Doris Kenyon, Stanley Taylor

† Remakes include *Times Square Playboy* (1936) with Warren William, Gene Lockhart and June Travis, *d* William McGann; and *Ladies Must Live* (1940) with Wayne Morris, Priscilla Lane and Roscoe Karns; both for Warner.

Homebodies

US   1973   96m   colour
Essential/Cinema Entertainment (Marshall Backlar)

Among the old people living in a tenement scheduled for redevelopment are homicidal maniacs.

Bizarre and tasteless horror of little visible merit.

w Larry Yust, Howard Kaminsky, Bennett Sims
d Larry Yust ph Isidore Mankofsky m Bernardo
Segall ad John Retsek ed Peter Parasheles

Peter Brocco, Frances Fuller, William Hansen, Ruth
McDevitt, Paula Trueman

'The film never finds its right level (and, incidentally,
seems at a loss to know how to conclude itself).' –
David McGillivray

Homeboy

US 1988 116m Technicolor
TCF/Homeboy Productions/Redruby (Alan Marshall, Elliott
Kastner)
V, V*, L

A down-and-out boxer gets one last chance at the big
time.

Dim melodrama of the low life.

w Eddie Cook story Mickey Rourke d Michael
Seresin ph Gale Tattersall m Eric Clapton,
Michael Kamen pd Brian Morris ed Ray Lovejoy

Mickey Rourke, Christopher Walken, Debra Feuer,
Thomas Quinn, Kevin Conway, Anthony Alda, Jon
Polito, Bill Slayton, David Taylor, Joseph Ragno

Homecoming

US 1948 113m bw
MGM (Sidney Franklin)
V*

A ruthless society doctor is called up in World War II
and has his life changed by a brief affair with a nurse
who is killed in action.

Ho-hum romantic melodrama which stumbles most
badly when it aims to be serious.

w Paul Osborn d Mervyn Le Roy ph Harold
Rosson md Charles Previn m Bronislau Kaper

Clark Gable, Lana Turner, Anne Baxter, John Hodiak,
Ray Collins, Gladys Cooper, Cameron Mitchell,
Marshall Thompson

'Its basic substance, like the base of a perfume, has a
terrible smell; but to many moviegoers the end-
product will seem quite pleasant.' – Time

The Homecoming *

GB 1973 114m colour
American Express/Ely Landau

Tensions mount and sexual revelations abound in the
house of a retired London butcher.

Plain treatment of an anything-but-plain Pinter play.
The result is a record of a performance rather than a
film.

w Harold Pinter play Harold Pinter d Peter Hall
ph David Watkin m Thelonious Monk pd John
Bury

Paul Rogers, Cyril Cusack, Michael Jayston, Ian
Holm, Vivien Merchant, Terence Rigby

'Shocking in its own lucidity, and fascinating as an
arrangement of mutually reflecting prisms . . . the
remarkable control of Pinter's language guarantees
that the dramatic situations are revealed to be even
more abstract and diagrammatic as they steadily
accumulate psychological density.' – Jonathan
Rosenbaum

The Homestretch

US 1947 97m Technicolor
TCF (Robert Bassler)

A racing enthusiast neglects his wife.

Thin romantic drama, handsomely photographed on
various racecourses.

w Wanda Tuchock d H. Bruce Humberstone
ph Arthur Arling m David Raksin

Cornel Wilde, Maureen O'Hara, Glenn Langan, Helen
Walker, James Gleason, Henry Stephenson

Homeward Bound: The Incredible Journey

US 1993 85m Technicolor
Buena Vista/Walt Disney/Touchwood Pacific Partners I
(Franklin R. Levy, Jeffrey Chernov)
S

Two dogs and a cat, separated from their human
family, run off to find them.

A remake of Disney's The Incredible Journey with
human voices added for the animals, in the manner of
the Look Who's Talking films; speech adds a feeling of
unreality to the proceedings, but probably young
audiences will not mind.

w Caroline Thompson, Linda Wolverton book The
Incredible Journey by Sheila Burnford d Duwayne
Durham ph Reed Smoot m Bruce Broughton
pd Roger Cain ed Jonathan P. Shaw, Jay Cassidy,
Michael Kelly, Brian Berdan

voices of Michael J. Fox, Sally Field, Don Ameche

'A sprightly little entertainment that should enthrall
tots without straining the patience of parents.' –
Variety

Homework: see La Tarea

'Can your heart stand the challenge when the clock starts
the countdown?'
'All those too timid to take the climax will be welcomed to
the cowards' corner!'

Homicidal

US 1961 87m bw
Columbia/William Castle

A murderous blonde and a very strange young man
both live in the house of a paralysed old lady.

Transvestite horror comic allegedly based on a true
case; made on a low budget and played for cheap
shocks.

w Robb White d William Castle ph Burnett
Guffey m Hugo Friedhofer

Jean Arless, Glenn Corbett, Patricia Breslin, Eugenie
Leontovitch, Alan Bunce, Richard Rust

† The film was played with a 'fright break' during
which faint-hearted members of the audience might
leave before the final onslaught.

Homicide

US 1949 76m bw
Warner

A murder witness is intimidated by the killers.

Stiff little crime yarn which slowly recovers after a
dull beginning.

w William Sackheim d Felix Jacoves

Robert Douglas, Robert Alda, Helen Westcott

'Bob Gold is a cop. A good cop. But tonight, he will betray
his friends, disgrace the force, and commit an act of
violence because he believes it is the only right thing to
do.'

Homicide **

US 1991 102m colour
First Independent/J&M Entertainment/Cinehaus (Michael
Hausman, Edward R. Pressman)
V, V*, L

A Jewish cop investigating the murder of a
storekeeper suspects an anti-Semitic conspiracy.

Engrossing study of one man's disintegration.

wd David Mamet ph Roger Deakins m Alaric
Jans pd Michael Merritt ed Barbara Tulliver

Joe Mantegna, William H. Macy, Natalija Nogulich,
Ving Rhames, Rebecca Pidgeon, J. J. Johnston, Jack
Wallace

'Portrayed with a spell-binding skill and precision,
the pace of an action-thriller off-set by unexpected
patterns of colour and speech, part documentary, part
theatrical melodrama.' – Philip Strick, Sight and Sound

'A genre picture with delusions of grandeur . . . The
funereal pace and the melancholy, reflective tone
seem intended to mask the story's essential
recklessness and irresponsibility, and perhaps also to
conceal the trite cop-movie mechanics of its
construction.' —Terrence Rafferty, New Yorker

Homicide Bureau

US 1938 56m bw
Columbia

A tough small-town cop deals with racketeers.

Routine programme filler.

w Earle Snell d C. C. Coleman Jnr

Bruce Cabot, Rita Hayworth, Marc Lawrence, Moroni
Olsen

'Hits new low . . . every department of production
way below par.' – Variety

Un Homme Amoureux: see A Man in Love

L'Homme au Chapeau Rond *

France 1946 91m bw
Alcina

When his wife dies, a man becomes obsessed with
causing the downfall of her two lovers.

Heavy-going melodrama without much in the way of
light relief; chiefly memorable for its central
performance.

w Charles Spaak, Jean Loubignic novel The Eternal
Husband by Dostoevsky d Pierre Billon
ph Nicolas Torporkoff m Maurice Thiriet

Raimu, Aimé Clariond, Lucy Valnor

L'Homme de Ma Vie *

France/Canada 1992 104m colour
Optima/Cineroux/Ciné Cinq/Prodeve (Gabriel Boustani)
V (W)
aka: The Man of My Life

Determined to find a rich husband, a young Parisian
woman marries a bad-tempered restaurant critic and
suffers in style before deciding that love is better than
comfort.

A light and frothy account of male–female
relationships.

wd Jean Charles Tacchella ph Dominique Le
Rigoleur m Raymond Alessandrini ad Serge
Douy ed Marie-Aimée Debril

Maria de Medeiros, Thiérry Fortineau, Anne
Letourneau, Ginette Garcin, Ginette Mathieu, Alain
Doutey, Jean-Pierre Bacri

L'Homme de Rio: see That Man from Rio

Un Homme est Mort: see The Outside Man

Un Homme et une Femme: see A Man and a
Woman

Hondo *

US 1953 93m Warnercolor 3-D
Wayne-Fellows

In 1874 New Mexico a cavalry despatch rider stops to
defend a lonely widow and her son against Indians.

Overwritten but pleasant-looking Western, clearly
patterned after Shane.

w James Edward Grant novel Louis L'Amour
d John Farrow ph Robert Burks, Archie Stout
m Emil Newman, Hugo Friedhofer

John Wayne, Geraldine Page, Ward Bond, Michael
Pate

AAN: Geraldine Page

Honey

US 1930 75m bw
Paramount

A brother and sister rent out their Southern mansion and decide to become the butler and cook.

Comedy with music, a little heavier than it should have been.

w Herman J. Mankiewicz   play *Come Out of the Kitchen* by Alice Duer Miller, A. E. Thomas   d Wesley Ruggles

Nancy Carroll, Skeets Gallagher, Stanley Smith, Lillian Roth, Harry Green, Mitzi Green, ZaSu Pitts

'Not worthy of a big rave but should satisfy the mob.' – *Variety*

Honey, I Blew Up the Kid
US   1992   89m   Technicolor
Buena Vista/Walt Disney (Dawn Steel, Edward S. Feldman)
V, V*, L, S

An inventor inadvertently exposes his two-year-old son to a ray that causes him to grow to 50 feet tall.

Predictable and dull comedy that fails to develop its central notion in interesting ways.

w Thom Eberhardt, Peter Elbling, Garry Goodrow   d Randal Kleiser   ph John Hora   m Bruce Broughton   pd Leslie Dilley   ed Michael A. Stevenson, Harry Hitner, Tina Hirsch

Rick Moranis, Marcia Strassman, Robert Oliveri, Daniel Shalikar, Joshua Shalikar, Lloyd Bridges, John Shea, Keri Russell, Ron Canada, Amy O'Neill

'A romp, escapism at its breeziest.' – *Variety*

'Proclaims in its every move that particular blend of crassness and technical expertise that is so often used for Hollywood's more down-market popular successes.' – *Derek Malcolm, Guardian*

Honey, I Shrunk the Kids *
US   1989   93m   Metrocolor
Warner/Walt Disney/Doric (Penny Finkelman Cox)
V, V*, L

An inventor inadvertently miniaturises his children and dumps them in the garden.

Amusing comedy with Disney's winsomeness kept at bay for the most part, apart from a brave little ant.

w Ed Naha, Tom Schulman   story Stuart Gordon, Brian Yuzna, Ed Naha   d Joe Johnston   ph Hiro Narita   pd Gregg Fonseca   ed Michael A. Stevenson

Rick Moranis, Matt Frewer, Marcia Strassman, Kristine Sutherland, Thomas Brown, Jared Rushton, Amy O'Neil, Robert Oliveri, Carl Steven

'You are cordially invited to a perfectly elegant case of murder!'
The Honey Pot *
US   1966   150m   Technicolor
UA/Famous Artists (Charles K. Feldman) (Joseph L. Mankiewicz)
V*

A millionaire pretends to be dying in order to trick three former mistresses; but one of them is murdered.

Uneasy variation, via two other interludes, on Ben Jonson's *Volpone;* despite bright moments, the mood is fatally inconsistent, and a cloud of pseudo-sophisticated dialogue hangs over the whole thing like a pall.

wd Joseph L. Mankiewicz   play *Mr Fox of Venice* by Frederick Knott   novel *The Evil of the Day* by Thomas Sterling   ph Gianni di Venanzo   m John Addison   pd John DeCuir

Rex Harrison, Susan Hayward, *Maggie Smith*, Cliff Robertson, Capucine, Edie Adams, Adolfo Celi, Herschel Bernardi

'One of the talkiest pictures ever made.' – *Stephen Farber*

Honeychile
US   1951   89m   Trucolor
Republic

A music publisher tries to cheat a country composer.

Hayseed shenanigans for small-town consumption.

w R. G. Springsteen

Judy Canova, Eddie Foy Jnr, Alan Hale Jnr, Walter Catlett, Claire Carleton, Leonid Kinskey

'Miss Glamorous and Mr Amorous in a gay elopement adventure that makes Mexico City blush!'
Honeymoon
US   1947   74m   bw
RKO (Warren Duff)
GB title: *Two Men and a Girl*

An 18-year-old elopes to Mexico City with an army corporal but meets a sophisticated older man.

Emaciated comedy, one of the reasons for Shirley Temple's early retirement.

w Michael Kanin   story Vicki Baum   d William Keighley   ph Edward Cronjager   m Leigh Harline

Shirley Temple, Franchot Tone, Guy Madison, Lina Romay, Gene Lockhart, Grant Mitchell

Honeymoon
Spain/GB   1959   109m   Technicolor   Technirama/Dimension 180
Suevia/Everdene (Cesario Gonzalez, Michael Powell)
Spanish title: *Luna de Miel*

An ex-ballerina in Spain with her new husband is tempted to return to the boards.

Incredibly shapeless travel poster with some dancing and two interpolated ballets to provide moments of musical interest. An unbelievable disaster from the co-creator of *The Red Shoes*.

w Michael Powell, Luis Escobar   d Michael Powell   ph Georges Périnal, Gerry Turpin   m Mikis Theodorakis

Anthony Steel, Ludmila Tcherina, Antonio, Leonide Massine

Honeymoon Deferred
US   1940   84m   bw
Universal

An insurance investigator is called away from honeymoon when his boss is murdered.

Unremarkable star programmer.

w Roy Chanslor, Eliot Gibbons   d Lew Landers

Edmund Lowe, Margaret Lindsay, Elizabeth Risdon, Joyce Compton, Chick Chandler

Honeymoon Deferred
GB   1951   79m   bw
Vic Films

A war veteran returns for his honeymoon to the Italian village he helped to liberate, but finds himself accused of ruining the crops.

Curious hybrid comedy which fails to jell on all levels.

w Suso d'Amico, A. Pietrangeli   d Mario Camerini

Griffith Jones, Sally Ann Howes, Kieron Moore, Lea Padovani

Honeymoon for Three
US   1941   77m   bw
Warner

An author is protected from adoring females by his secretary.

Fairly flaccid romantic comedy, a remake of *Goodbye Again* (1933).

w Julius J. Epstein, Philip G. Epstein, Earl Baldwin   d Lloyd Bacon

George Brent, Ann Sheridan, Osa Massen, Charles Ruggles, Jane Wyman, Lee Patrick

Honeymoon Hotel
US   1964   98m   Metrocolor   Cinemascope
MGM/Avon (Lawrence Weingarten)

A jilted swain goes off with a philandering friend on what was to have been his honeymoon trip . . . only to be followed by his repentant fiancée.

Rather unattractive farce with insufficient funny moments.

w R. S. Allen, Harvey Bulloch   d Henry Levin   ph Harold Lipstein   m Walter Scharf

Nancy Kwan, Robert Goulet, Robert Morse, Jill St John, Elsa Lanchester, Keenan Wynn

Honeymoon in Bali
US   1939   95m   bw
Paramount (Jeff Lazarus)
GB title: *Husbands or Lovers?*

A department store head intends to pursue her career without marriage, but two swains try to prove her wrong.

Thin romantic comedy which got by on its stars.

w Virginia Van Upp   d Edward H. Griffith

Madeleine Carroll, Fred MacMurray, Allan Jones, Akim Tamiroff, Helen Broderick, Osa Massen

'Infectiously sparkling . . . will click substantially in the regular runs.' – *Variety*

† The original title, *Are Husbands Necessary?*, was discarded when Miss Carroll became involved in a divorce suit.

'A comedy about one bride, two grooms, and 34 flying Elvises.'
Honeymoon in Vegas *
US   1992   96m   Technicolor
First Independent/Castle Rock/New Line/Lobell/Bergman (Mike Lobell)
V, V*, L, S

In a poker game a Las Vegas gambler wins a weekend with the fiancée of a New York detective.

Moderately enjoyable comedy, with an amusing running gag about Elvis impersonators.

wd Andrew Bergman   ph William A. Fraker   m David Newman   pd William A. Elliott   ed Barry Malkin

James Caan, Nicolas Cage, Sarah Jessica Parker, Pat Morita, Johnny Williams, Anne Bancroft, Peter Boyle

'A virtually nonstop scream of benign delirium, pop entertainment as revivifying as anything you're likely to see this year.' – *Vincent Canby, New York Times*

'A very good comedy indeed, a dynamite throwback to those 40s screwball numbers.' – *Jeff Dawson, Empire*

The Honeymoon Killers *
US   1969   108m   bw
Warren Steibel
V, V*, L

A gigolo and a nurse team up to prey upon women looking for a husband.

Unsparing low-budget film, based on a true story of multiple murderers, that has gained a cult following.

wd Leonard Kastle

Shirley Stoler, Tony Lo Bianco, Mary Jane Higby, Doris Roberts, Kip McArdle

The Honeymoon Machine
US   1961   91m   Metrocolor   Cinemascope
MGM/Avon (Lawrence Weingarten)

A naval lieutenant uses the ship's computer to break the bank at the Venice casino.

Stolid, expensive-looking comedy which barely raises a laugh.

w George Wells *play* The Golden Fleecing by Lorenzo Semple Jnr *d* Richard Thorpe *ph* Joseph LaShelle *m* Leigh Harline

Steve McQueen, Brigid Bazlen, Jim Hutton, Paula Prentiss, Dean Jagger, Jack Weston, Jack Mullaney

Honeysuckle Rose

US 1980 119m Technicolor
Warner (Sydney Pollack)
V*, L

A happily married country and western star takes to the bottle whenever he goes on the road.

Glum modern drama with music, a semi-autobiographical star vehicle; for fans only.

w Carol Sobieski, William D. Wittliff, John Binder *d* Jerry Schatzberg *ph* Robby Muller *pd* Joel Schiller *m/y* Willie Nelson *ed* Aram Avakian, Norman Gay, Marc Laub, Evan Lottman

Willie Nelson, Dyan Cannon, Amy Irving, Slim Pickens

AAN: song 'On the Road Again'

Hong Gaoliang: see Red Sorghum

Hong Kong

US 1951 91m Technicolor
Paramount/Pine-Thomas

An ex-GI has various adventures with a Chinese orphan and a golden idol.

And a plot that seems to make itself up as they go along. Corn-fed hokum.

w Winston Miller *d* Lewis R. Foster *ph* Lionel Lindon *m* Lucien Cailliet *ad* Lewis H. Creber *ed* Howard Smith

Ronald Reagan, Rhonda Fleming, Nigel Bruce, Marvin Miller, Lowell Gilmore

The Honkers *

US 1971 102m DeLuxe
UA/Levy-Gardner-Laven

An ageing rodeo rider has trouble with his wife.

Quiet, carefully accomplished study of a man and his milieu.

w Steve Ihnat, Stephen Lodge *d* Steve Ihnat *ph* John Crabe *m* Jimmie Haskell

James Coburn, Lois Nettleton, Slim Pickens, Richard Anderson

Honky Tonk

US 1929 80m bw
Warner

A night-club entertainer sacrifices everything for her daughter's education.

Primitive cross between Applause and Imitation of Life, with spirited moments from Sophie Tucker the only plus.

w C. Graham Baker, Jack Yellen *d* Lloyd Bacon

Sophie Tucker, Lila Lee, Audrey Ferris, George Duryea, Mahlon Hamilton

'Every kiss a thrill!'

Honky Tonk *

US 1941 104m bw
MGM (Pandro S. Berman)

A Western con man meets his match in the daughter of a fake judge.

Generally amusing comedy melodrama that ambles along between two styles but leaves a pleasant after-effect.

w Marguerite Roberts, John Sanford *d* Jack Conway *ph* Harold Rosson *m* Franz Waxman

Clark Gable, Lana Turner, Frank Morgan, Claire Trevor, Marjorie Main, Albert Dekker, Henry O'Neill, Chill Wills, Betty Blythe

'A lively, lusty western that makes you wish you had been there.' – Variety

Honky Tonk Freeway

US 1981 107m Technicolor
EMI/Kendon/HTF Company (Don Boyd, Howard W. Koch Jnr)
V, V*

The mayor of a small Florida resort town has it painted pink to attract tourists . . . but too many of the wrong kind come in.

Zany farce, rather like It's a Mad Mad Mad Mad World without a proper hook to the story. Not an audience-pleaser, and very expensive.

w Edward Clinton *d* John Schlesinger *ph* John Bailey *m* George Martin, Elmer Bernstein

William Devane, Beau Bridges, Teri Garr, Beverly D'Angelo, Hume Cronyn, Jessica Tandy, Howard Hesseman, Geraldine Page, George Dzundza

'A shambles, and a more convincing one than the half-hearted affair which brings it to a close.' – Richard Combs, MFB

'A film for "now" which seems almost endearingly bereft of any real ideas about the messed-up contemporary world it inhabits.' – Guardian

Honkytonk Man

US 1982 122m Technicolor
Warner/Malpaso (Clint Eastwood)
V, V*, L

In the thirties, an ageing and alcoholic country singer turns to his rural family for help.

Yet another occasion when the star should have asked for help instead of doing all the chores himself. Not much real entertainment here, just a very few moments that amuse.

w Clancy Carlile *novel* Clancy Carlile *d* Clint Eastwood *ph* Bruce Surtees *m* Steve Dorff *pd* Edward Carfagno

Clint Eastwood, Kyle Eastwood, John McIntire, Verna Bloom, Alexa Kenin, Matt Clark

Honolulu

US 1938 83m bw
MGM (Jack Cummings)

A movie star is mistaken for his double.

Sloppy comedy with a few musical numbers.

w Herbert Fields, Frank Partos *d* Edward Buzzell *ph* Ray June *m* Franz Waxman

Robert Young, Eleanor Powell, George Burns, Gracie Allen, Rita Johnson, Ruth Hussey, Clarence Kolb, Sig Rumann, Eddie Anderson

'Fairly amusing comedy for top brackets in duals.' – Variety

'The whole thing seems to have been thrown together so that Eleanor Powell can do a frenetic hula.' – New Yorker, 1977

Honor Among Lovers

US 1931 76m bw
Paramount

A young businessman complicates his life when he decides to marry his secretary.

Smart comedy unfolding a complex plot, but slow by modern standards.

w Austin Parker, Gertrude Purcell *d* Dorothy Arzner

Claudette Colbert, Fredric March, Monroe Owsley, Charlie Ruggles, Ginger Rogers

'A sweet piece of work hiding behind a faulty title.' – Variety

Honor Bound

US 1989 102m Technicolor
Pacific/FilmAccord (Tim Van Relim, Eric A. Weymueller)

Two American soldiers investigate a mysterious happening at a Soviet missile base in East Germany.

Cold War thriller of limited interest.

w Aiken Woodruff *novel* Recovery by Steven L.Thompson *d* Jeannot Szwarc *ph* Robert Stevens *m* Mark Shreeve *pd* John Graysmark *ed* John Jympson

John Philbin, Tom Skerritt, Gabrielle Lazure, George Dzunda, Lawrence Pressman, Gene Davis

Honor of the Family

US 1931 66m bw
First National

The young mistress of an aged Budapest resident is after his money.

Tiresome comedy drama.

play Emil Fabre *story* Balzac *d* Lloyd Bacon

Bebe Daniels, Warren William, Frederick Kerr, Alan Mowbray, Blanche Friderici

The Honorary Consul

GB 1983 104m Movielab
World Film Services (Norma Heyman)
US title: Beyond the Limit

In northern Argentina, a doctor is drawn into the kidnapping by activists of a drunken British consul.

Self-parodic visit to Greeneland, with everybody drunk or depressed. Bouts of explicit sex don't help much, if at all.

w Christopher Hampton *novel* Graham Greene *d* John MacKenzie *ph* Phil Meheux *m* Stanley Myers *pd* Allan Cameron

Michael Caine, Richard Gere, Bob Hoskins, Elpidia Carrillo, Joaquim de Almeida

'Some very old friends: exhausted passion, moral betrayal and relics of religious faith.' – Sight and Sound

'All it takes is the character to decide he is a burnt-out case, sleeping with all women but capable of loving none, for all the familiar icons to be ranged in battle array.' – Tom Milne, MFB

Honour Among Thieves: see Touchez pas au Grisbi

The Honourable Mr Wong: see The Hatchet Man

An Honourable Murder *

GB 1959 70m bw
Warner/Danzigers (Edward J. Danziger, Harry Lee Danziger)

Boardroom executives scheme to be rid of their chairman.

Oddball, interesting attempt to play Julius Caesar in modern dress. Not entirely successful, but full marks for trying.

w Brian Clemens, Eldon Howard *d* Godfrey Grayson *ph* James Wilson

Norman Wooland, Margaretta Scott, Lisa Daniely, Douglas Wilmer, Philip Saville, John Longden

The Hoodlum

US 1951 63m bw
Jack Schwarz Productions
V*

A convict is paroled but continues his criminal career.

Toughish crime support with interesting moments.

w Sam Neumann, Nat Tanchuck *d* Max Nosseck

Lawrence Tierney, Liza Golm, Edward Tierney, Allene Roberts

Hoodlum Empire

US 1952 98m bw
Republic (Joseph Kane)
V*

A Congressional committee investigates a racketeer.

Moderate semi-documentary potboiler inspired by the Kefauver investigations.

w Bruce Manning, Bob Considine   d Joseph Kane
ph Reggie Lanning   m Nathan Scott

Brian Donlevy, Forrest Tucker, Claire Trevor, Vera Ralston, Luther Adler, John Russell, Gene Lockhart, Grant Withers, Taylor Holmes

'Familiar gangster melodramatics and repentances, played out in a rigmarole of flashbacks.' – MFB

The Hoodlum Priest *
US   1961   100m   bw
UA/Don Murray-Walter Wood

A Jesuit teacher tries to help young criminals, especially a condemned murderer.

Moderately well done, very depressing and downbeat chunk of social conscience based on the life of Charles Dismas Clark.

w Don Mankiewicz, Joseph Landon, 'Don Deer' (i.e. Don Murray)   d Irvin Kershner   ph Haskell Wexler   m Richard Markowitz

Don Murray, Keir Dullea, Larry Gates, Cindi Wood, Logan Ramsey

The Hoodlum Saint
US   1946   93m   bw
MGM (Cliff Reid)

A cynical newspaperman turns to religion and succours thieves.

Hard-boiled sentimentality, a downright peculiar and doleful comedy drama in deflated post-war mood.

w Frank Wead, James Hill   d Norman Taurog
ph Ray June   m Nathaniel Shilkret

William Powell, Esther Williams, Angela Lansbury, James Gleason, Lewis Stone, Rags Ragland, Frank McHugh, Slim Summerville, Roman Bohnen, Louis Jean Heydt, Charles Arnt, Charles Trowbridge, Henry O'Neill

The Hook
US   1962   98m   bw   Panavision
MGM/Perlberg-Seaton

Three GIs escaping from Korea are ordered to execute a prisoner but cannot bring themselves to do it.

Predictable, claustrophobic drama which becomes a slick exercise in morality.

w Henry Denker   novel The Hameçon by Vahe Katcha
d George Seaton   ph Joe Ruttenberg   m Larry Adler

Kirk Douglas, Robert Walker, Nick Adams, Nehemiah Persoff

Hook *
US   1991   144m   DeLuxe   Panavision
Columbia TriStar/Amblin (Kathleen Kennedy, Frank Marshall, Gerald R. Molen)
V, V*, L, S

Peter Pan, who has returned to the ordinary world to become a father and a corporate lawyer, returns to Neverland to fight Captain Hook.

Sprawling, overlong, often camp extravaganza with splendid special effects and settings that may appeal to the small child in most of us, even if it is time that Spielberg himself grew up.

w Jim V. Hart, Malia Scotch Marmo   play Peter Pan by J. M. Barrie   story Jim V. Hart, Nick Castle   d Steven Spielberg   ph Dean Cundey   m John Williams   pd Norman Garwood (John Napier was visual consultant)   sp Industrial Light and Magic   ed Michael Kahn

Dustin Hoffman, Robin Williams, Julia Roberts, Bob Hoskins, Maggie Smith, Caroline Goodall, Charlie Korsmo, Amber Scott, Laurel Cronin, Phil Collins, David Crosby

'Spirited, rambunctious, often messy and undisciplined, this determined attempt to recast the Peter Pan story in contemporary terms splashes every bit of its megabudget (between $60 and $80 million) onto the screen; commercial elements overflow in such abundance that major hit status seems guaranteed.' – Variety

'Peel away the expensive, special effects surface and there's nothing but formula.' – Washington Post

† Glenn Close appears in an uncredited role as a bearded pirate.

AAN: song 'When You're Alone' (m John Williams, ly Leslie Bricusse); Norman Garwood; visual effects

Hook Line and Sinker
US   1930   72m   bw
RKO
L

Two insurance agents run a derelict hotel.

Feeble comedy vehicle.

w Tim Whelan, Ralph Spence   d Eddie Cline

Bert Wheeler, Robert Woolsey, Hugh Herbert, Dorothy Lee, Jobyna Howland, Ralf Harolde

'Will tickle most in those spots where the price is least.' – Variety

Hook, Line and Sinker
US   1968   92m   Technicolor
Columbia/Jerry Lewis

A salesman who thinks he is dying goes on a spending spree; when he learns the truth, he has to disappear because of his huge debts.

Miserable comedy with frantic slapstick interludes. The plot might have served Preston Sturges.

w Rod Amateau   d George Marshall   ph W. Wallace Kelley   m Dick Stabile

Jerry Lewis, Peter Lawford, Anne Francis, Pedro Gonzales Gonzales

Hooper *
US   1978   99m   Metrocolor
Warner/Burt Reynolds, Lawrence Gordon (Hank Moonjean)
V, V*, L

An ageing stunt man decides on one last sensational stunt before retiring.

There are some agreeably striking moments, but you can't make a movie out of stunts and loud camaraderie. This one palls half way through.

w Thomas Rickman, Bill Kerby   d Hal Needham
ph Bobby Byrne   m Bill Justis

Burt Reynolds, Sally Field, Brian Keith, Jan-Michael Vincent, John Marley, Robert Klein, James Best, Adam West

'Burt Reynolds's annual Kleenex of a movie: something to use and throw away without any thought beyond a certain gratitude for the convenience of the thing.' – Richard Schickel, Time

'Clara Bow ... red-headed warm-blooded dynamite ... again releases the torrent of her genius in the most colorful performance of her life.'

Hoopla
US   1933   85m   bw
Fox

A hardboiled carnival dancer agrees to seduce the son of the show's manager, but ends by marrying him.

Strained melodrama with the star, in her last film, at the end of her tether.

w Bradley King, J. M. March   play The Barker by Kenyon Nicholson   d Frank Lloyd

Clara Bow, Richard Cromwell, Preston Foster, Herbert Mundin, James Gleason, Minna Gombell, Roger Imhof

'Miss Bow seems ripe to come back strongly.' – Variety

Hooray for Love
US   1935   75m   bw
RKO (Felix Young)

A rich college boy plays angel to a musical comedy.

Thin pot-pourri of familiar elements.

w Lawrence Hazard, Ray Harris   story Marc Lachmann   d Walter Lang   ph Lucien Andriot   md Albert Colombo   m/ly Dorothy Fields, Jimmy McHugh   ad Van Nest Polglase   ed George Crone

Ann Sothern, Gene Raymond, Bill Robinson, Thurston Hall, Pert Kelton, Lionel Stander, Fats Waller

'Trouble is entirely traceable to its terribly lethargic tempo and lack of any real production numbers.' – Variety

The Hoosegow **
US   1929   20m   bw
Hal Roach
V

Stan and Ollie, in prison, contrive to fell a tree on the cook's tent and to smother the governor in boiled rice.

Splendid slapstick leading up to one of their best tit-for-tat routines.

w Leo McCarey, H. M. Walker   d James Parrott
ph George Stevens, Len Powers, Glenn Robert Kershner   ed Richard Currier

Laurel and Hardy, James Finlayson, Tiny Sandford

Hoosier Schoolboy
US   1937   62m   bw
Monogram (Ken Goldsmith)

A rural boy defends his drunken father, shell-shocked in the war.

Simple tale for rural audiences.

w Robert Lee Johnson   novel Edward Eggleston
d William Nigh

Mickey Rooney, Anne Nagel, Frank Shields, Edward Pawley

'A compelling film which word of mouth might turn into a sleeper.' – Variety

Hoosiers
US   1986   114m   CFI colour
Orion/Hemdale/Carter de Haven
V*, L
GB title: Best Shot

The training and triumph of an Indiana high school basketball team.

Expertise expended on a subject of very limited interest.

w Angelo Pizzo   d David Anspaugh   ph Fred Murphy   m Jerry Goldsmith

Gene Hackman, Barbara Hershey, Dennis Hopper, Sheb Wooley, Fern Persons

'Both rousing and too conventional.' – Variety

AAN: Jerry Goldsmith; Dennis Hopper

Hoots Mon *
GB   1939   77m   bw
Warner

A cockney comedian starts a popularity contest with a female impressionist.

Tolerable comedy whose value is that it preserves, albeit in cleaned-up form, portions of Max Miller's variety act. Florence Desmond isn't bad either.

w Roy William Neill, Jack Henley, John Dighton
d Roy William Neill   ph Basil Emmott   md Bretton Byrd   ad Norman Arnold   ed Leslie Norman

Florence Desmond, Max Miller, Hal Walters, Davina Craig, Garry Marsh

Hop Harrigan

US   1946   bw   serial: 15 eps
Columbia

Civil aviators fight a death-ray-wielding villain called
The Chief Pilot.

More than faintly absurd action shenanigans, with
more yawns than thrills.

d Derwin Abrahams

William Blakewell, Jennifer Holt, Robert 'Buzz'
Henry

Hopalong Cassidy

Cassidy, a creation of Clarence E. Mulford, was a
fictitious gentleman cowboy who oddly enough wore
black; 26 books about him were published between
1912 and 1956 when Mulford died. 66 films were
made starring William Boyd as Hoppy, with either
George Gabby Hayes or Andy Clyde as comic
sidekick: Harry Sherman produced them, first for
Paramount and then for UA, and they were later
edited down for TV, in which medium Boyd became a
folk hero and eventually made a further series. The
films were easy-going, slow-moving second features
which always pointed an admirable moral for
children; their main directors were Howard
Bretherton, Nate Watt, Lesley Selander and George
Archainbaud.

1935: HOPALONG CASSIDY, THE EAGLE'S
   BROOD, BAR 20 RIDES AGAIN
1936: CALL OF THE PRAIRIE, THREE ON THE
   TRAIL, HEART OF THE WEST, HOPALONG
   CASSIDY RETURNS, TRAIL DUST
1937: BORDERLAND, HILLS OF OLD WYOMING,
   NORTH OF THE RIO GRANDE, RUSTLERS'
   VALLEY, HOPALONG RIDES AGAIN, TEXAS
   TRAIL
1938: HEART OF ARIZONA, BAR 20 JUSTICE,
   PRIDE OF THE WEST, IN OLD MEXICO,
   SUNSET TRAIL, THE FRONTIERSMAN,
   PARTNERS OF THE PLAINS, CASSIDY OF
   BAR 20
1939: RANGE WAR, LAW OF THE PAMPAS,
   SILVER ON THE SAGE, RENEGADE TRAIL
1940: SANTA FE MARSHAL, THE SHOWDOWN,
   HIDDEN GOLD, STAGECOACH WAR, THREE
   MEN FROM TEXAS
1941: DOOMED CARAVAN, IN OLD COLORADO,
   BORDER VIGILANTES, PIRATES ON
   HORSEBACK, WIDE OPEN TOWN,
   OUTLAWS OF THE DESERT, RIDERS OF THE
   TIMBERLINE, SECRETS OF THE
   WASTELAND, STICK TO YOUR GUNS,
   TWILIGHT ON THE TRAIL
1942: UNDERCOVER MAN
1943: COLT COMRADES, BAR 20, LOST CANYON,
   HOPPY SERVES A WRIT, BORDER PATROL,
   THE LEATHER BURNERS, FALSE COLOURS,
   RIDERS OF THE DEADLINE
1944: MYSTERY MAN, FORTY THIEVES, TEXAS
   MASQUERADE, LUMBERJACK
1946: THE DEVIL'S PLAYGROUND
1947: FOOL'S GOLD, HOPPY'S HOLIDAY,
   MARAUDERS, UNEXPECTED GUEST,
   DANGEROUS VENTURE
1948: SINISTER JOURNEY, SILENT CONFLICT,
   STRANGE GAMBLE, BORROWED TROUBLE,
   THE DEAD DON'T DREAM, FALSE
   PARADISE

Hope and Glory **

GB   1987   113m   Technicolor
Columbia/Goldcrest/Nelson (John Boorman)
V, V*, L, S

Adventures of a small boy and his family during
World War II in suburban London.

Generally appealing but not too accurate
reminiscences of an exciting and emotional time.

wd John Boorman   *ph* Philippe Rousselot   *m* Peter
Martin   *pd* Anthony Pratt   *ad* Don Dossett

Sarah Miles, Susan Wooldridge, Ian Bannen, David
Hayman, Derrick O'Connor, Sebastian Rice-Edwards

AAN: Philippe Rousselot; John Boorman as director;
best picture; best original screenplay; best art
direction – set decoration

Hoppity Goes to Town: see *Mr Bug Goes to Town*

Hopscotch *

US   1980   104m   Movielab
Avco/Edie and Ely Landau (Otto Plaschkes)
V, V*, L

An ex-CIA man writes a revealing book and foils the
consequent attempts on his life.

Genial but patchy spy comedy caper; a filler for all
concerned.

w Brian Garfield, Bryan Forbes   *novel* Brian Garfield
d Ronald Neame   *ph* Arthur Ibbetson   *m* Ian
Fraser

Walter Matthau, Glenda Jackson, Ned Beatty, Sam
Waterston, Herbert Lom, George Baker

Hori, Ma Panenko: see *The Firemen's Ball*

Horizons West

US   1952   81m   Technicolor
U-I (Albert J. Cohen)

After the Civil War, a rancher builds an empire on
greed and ruthlessness, and his brother has to bring
him to trial.

Rather lugubrious Western with the usual quota of
effective action scenes.

w Louis Stevens   *d* Budd Boetticher   *ph* Charles P.
Boyle   *md* Joseph Gershenson

Rock Hudson, Robert Ryan, Julia Adams, John
McIntire, Raymond Burr, Dennis Weaver, Judith
Braun

The Horizontal Lieutenant

US   1962   90m   Metrocolor   Cinemascope
MGM/Euterpe (Joe Pasternak)

World War II Hawaii; an amorous intelligence officer
accidentally captures a Japanese guerrilla.

Very moderate army farce of no great skill or
memorability.

w George Wells   *d* Richard Thorpe   *ph* Robert
Bronner   *m* George Stoll

Jim Hutton, Paula Prentiss, Jim Backus, Miyoshi
Umeki, Jack Carter

L'Horloger de St Paul: see *The Watchmaker of St
Paul*

The Horn Blows at Midnight *

US   1945   80m   bw
Warner (Mark Hellinger)
V*

An angel is sent to earth to destroy the planet with
Gabriel's horn.

Wacky comedy inspired by *Here Comes Mr Jordan*, but
on a broader slapstick level; much better than its star
always pretended.

w Sam Hellman, James V. Kern   *d* Raoul Walsh
ph Sid Hickox   *m* Franz Waxman

Jack Benny, Alexis Smith, Dolores Moran, Allyn
Joslyn, Guy Kibbee, Reginald Gardiner, *Franklin
Pangborn*, John Alexander, Margaret Dumont

Hornet's Nest

US   1969   109m   DeLuxe
UA/Triangle (Stanley S. Kanter)

In World War II Italy, a wounded US army
demolitions expert is nursed back to health by child
partisans, who help him destroy a German-held dam.

Overlong war exploits with the children used as a
tiresome gimmick.

w S. S. Schweitzer   *d* Phil Karlson   *ph* Gabor
Pogani   *m* Ennio Morricone

Rock Hudson, Sergio Fantoni, Sylva Koscina, Jacques
Sernas

Horriplante Bestia Humana: see *Night of the
Bloody Apes*

Horror Express *

GB/Spain   1972   88m   Technicolor
Gala/Granada/Benmar (Bernard Gordon)

An alien intelligence, trapped in a humanoid fossil for
centuries, escapes and goes on a killing spree in
which it absorbs the memories of its victims.

Moderately effective and ingenious low-budget
horror.

w Arnaud d'Usseau, Julian Halevy   *story* Eugenio
Martin   *d* Gene Martin   *ph* Alejandro Ulloa
m John Cavacas   *ad* Ramiro Gomez Guadiana
sp Pablo Perez   *ed* Robert Dearberg

Christopher Lee, Peter Cushing, Telly Savalas, Silvia
Tortosa, Jorge Rigaud, Alberta de Mondoza

'The script unwinds itself with sufficient cunning to
keep interest alive, always one step ahead of the
audience with a new revelation to come.' – Tom Milne,
MFB

Horror Hotel: see *City of the Dead*

The Horror House: see *The Haunted House of
Horror*

Horror Island

US   1941   60m   bw
Universal

Various people travel to an island where buried
treasure might be hidden.

Feeble little mystery with very little interest in who
done what to whom.

w Maurice Tombragel, Victor McLeod   *d* George
Waggner

Dick Foran, Leo Carrillo, Peggy Moran, Fuzzy Knight,
John Eldredge, Walter Catlett, Hobart Cavanaugh

Horror of Dracula: see *Dracula* (1958)

The Horror of Frankenstein

GB   1970   95m   Technicolor
EMI/Hammer (Jimmy Sangster)
V, V*, L

Victor Frankenstein is not above murdering his
acquaintances for the sake of his experiments in
bringing the dead back to life.

Ill-advised attempt to remake the original story as a
black comedy, with Frankenstein frankly villainous
from the start. The last in the Hammer series.

w Jeremy Burnham, Jimmy Sangster   *d* Jimmy
Sangster   *ph* Moray Grant   *m* Malcolm Williamson
ad Scott MacGregor   *ed* Chris Barnes

Ralph Bates, Kate O'Mara, Graham James, Veronica
Carlson, Bernard Archard, Dennis Price, Joan Rice,
Dave Prowse

Horror of Snape Island: see *Tower of Evil*

Horror Planet: see *Inseminoid*

The Horror Show

US   1989   95m   DeLuxe
UA (Sean S. Cunningham)
V, V*
aka: *House III*

A cop and his family become the target for a dead
homicidal maniac, resurrected through electricity.

Muddled and confused horror that never sparks into life.

w Alan Smithee, Leslie Bohem   *d* James Isaac
ph Mac Ahlberg   *m* Harry Manfredini   *pd* Stewart
Campbell   *ed* Edward Anton

Lance Henriksen, Brion James, Rita Taggart, Dedee
Pfeiffer, Thom Bray, Matt Clark, Lawrence Tierney

Horrors of the Black Museum
GB   1959   81m   Eastmancolor   Cinemascope
Herman Cohen
V

A crime writer is fascinated by murder, and works out
his own plots by practice beforehand.

Crude shocker.

w Aben Kandel, Herman Cohen   *d* Arthur Crabtree

Michael Gough, Graham Curnow, Shirley Ann Field,
Geoffrey Keen

Hors La Vie
French/Italian/German   1991   97m   colour
Galatee/A2/Filmalpha/Lamy/Canal Plus/Raidue (Jacques Perrin)
S

A French photographer working in Beirut is taken
hostage.

Based on fact, this is an unsensational but not
illuminating account of what it is to be held prisoner.

w Maroun Bagdadi, Didier Decoin, Elias Khoury
book Roger Auque, Patrick Forestier   *d* Maroun
Bagdadi   *ph* Patrick Blossier   *m* Nicola Piovani
ad Dan Weil   *ed* Luc Barnier

Hippolyte Girardot, Rafic Ali Ahmad, Hussein Sbetty,
Habib Hammoud, Magdi Machmouchi, Hassan
Farhat, Hamzah Nasrullah, Nidal El Achkar

'Sober, uncompromising but never excessive
treatment conveys the mental and physical horrors of
detention while delineating delicate balance between
captors and victim.' – *Variety*

'An assembly-kit political thriller. In a moment of
madness the Cannes Jury gave it a Special Jury Prize.
Perhaps they liked the telegraphic simplicity of the
story.' – *Nigel Andrews, Financial Times*

'A scandalous record of low Marx at college – or life
    among the thirsty co-eds!'
Horse Feathers ***
US   1932   69m   bw
Paramount (Herman J. Mankiewicz)
V*, L

A college needs to win at football, and its corrupt new
president knows just how to do it.

Possibly the Marxes' wildest yet most streamlined
kaleidoscope of high jinks and irreverence, with at
least one bright gag or line to the minute and lively
musical interludes to boot. A classic of zany comedy.

w Bert Kalmar, Harry Ruby, S. J. Perelman, Will B.
Johnstone   *d* Norman Z. McLeod   *ph* Ray June
m/ly Bert Kalmar, Harry Ruby

Groucho, Chico, Harpo, Zeppo, *Thelma Todd,* Robert Greig

    GROUCHO: 'You have the brain of a four-year-old
child, and I'll bet he was glad to get rid of it.'
    CHICO: 'There's a man outside with a big black
moustache.'
    GROUCHO: 'Tell him I've got one.'
    GROUCHO (to Zeppo): 'You're a disgrace to our
family name of Wagstaff, if such a thing is possible.'
    GROUCHO: 'For years before my son was born I
used to yell from night till morn Whatever it is – I'm
against it! And I've been yelling since I
first commenced it – I'm against it!'

'The current Marx comedy is the funniest talkie since
the last Marx comedy, and the record it establishes is
not likely to be disturbed until the next Marx comedy
comes along. As for comparisons, I was too busy
having a good time to make any.' – *Philip K. Scheuer*

The Horse in the Grey Flannel Suit
US   1969   112m   Technicolor
Walt Disney
V*

A teenager's horse becomes the central figure in an
advertising campaign for a stomach pill.

Interminable kiddie movie which in its virtual
absence of plot or excitement is likely to bore kiddies
to death.

w Louis Pelletier   *novel* The Year of the Horse by Eric
Hatch   *d* Norman Tokar

Dean Jones, Fred Clark, Diane Baker, Lloyd Bochner,
Morey Amsterdam

The Horse Soldiers *
US   1959   119m   DeLuxe
UA/Mirisch (John Lee Mahin, Martin Rackin)
V, V*, L

In 1863 a Union cavalry officer is sent three hundred
miles into Confederate territory to demolish a railroad
junction.

Typically sprawling John Ford cavalry Western with
not too many high spots and more sombre ingredients
than usual.

w John Lee Mahin, Martin Rackin   *d* John Ford
ph William Clothier   *m* David Buttolph

John Wayne, William Holden, Constance Towers,
Hoot Gibson

    HOLDEN: 'Look here, colonel, I didn't ask to be
assigned to this mission . . .'

'Blemished as many of his films are blemished:
patches of horseplay, too much manly chest-beating.
But the blemishes proceed from the quality which
gives his work its frequent splendours. The horseplay
and the over-emphasised masculinity belong to his
romantic vision.' – *Dilys Powell*

Horse Thief **
China   1986   88m   colour
Xi'an Film Studio (Li Changqing)

Trying to feed his family, a peasant becomes a thief
and outcast.

Its stunning visuals, of exotic rituals and broad
landscapes, and exuberant style compensate for the
slightness of narrative.

w Zhang Rui   *d* Tian Zhuangzhuang   *ph* Hou Yong,
Zhao Fei   *m* Qu Xiaosong   *ad* Huo Jianqi   *ed* Li
Jingzhong

Tseshang Rinzim, Dan Jiji, Jayang Jamco

The Horse without a Head **
GB   1963   89m   Technicolor
Walt Disney (Hugh Attwooll)

Stolen money is hidden in an old toy horse, and
crooks trying to get it back clash with police and
children.

Excellent children's adventure with scenes on trains
and in a toy factory.

w T. E. B. Clarke   *d* Don Chaffey   *ph* Paul Beeson
m Eric Rogers

Leo McKern, Jean-Pierre Aumont, Herbert Lom,
Pamela Franklin, Vincent Winter

The Horsemen
US   1970   109m   colour   Super Panavision
Columbia/John Frankenheimer-Edward Lewis
V*

An Afghan tribesman is determined to rival his father
at horsemanship.

Rather tedious variant on *Taras Bulba;* plenty of action
but not much characterization, or taste, or interest.

w Dalton Trumbo   *novel* Joseph Kessel   *d* John
Frankenheimer   *ph* Claude Renoir   *m* Georges
Delerue

Omar Sharif, Jack Palance, Leigh Taylor-Young, Peter
Jeffrey, Eric Pohlmann, Despo, David de Keyser

The Horse's Mouth *
GB   1958   93m   Technicolor
UA/Knightsbridge (John Bryan)
V*, L

An obsessive painter is a liability to his friends.

Thin but fitfully amusing light study of a social
outcast, with a background of London river and
streets. Too slight for real success.

w Alec Guinness   *novel* Joyce Cary   *d* Ronald
Neame   *ph Arthur Ibbetson   *m* K. V. Jones from
Prokofiev   *paintings* John Bratby

Alec Guinness, Kay Walsh, Renée Houston, Robert
Coote, Arthur Macrae, Michael Gough, Ernest
Thesiger

'Immensely and joyously successful at what it sets out
to do.' – *Evening Standard*

'A work of genius.' – *News of the World*

AAN: Alec Guinness (as writer)

The Hospital **
US   1971   101m   DeLuxe   Panavision
UA/Simcha (Howard Gottfried)
V*

A city hospital is beset by weird mishaps, and it
transpires that a killer is on the loose.

Black comedy with the emphasis on sex and medical
ethics; in the same genre as *M*A*S*H,* and very funny
if you can take it.

w Paddy Chayevsky   *d* Arthur Hiller   *ph* Victor
Kemper   *m* Morris Surdin

George C. Scott, Diana Rigg, Barnard Hughes, Nancy
Marchand, Richard Dysart

AA: Paddy Chayevsky

AAN: George C. Scott

The Hostage
GB   1956   86m   bw
Westridge/Eros

A South American president condemns a
revolutionary to death; in London, sympathizers
kidnap the president's daughter.

Tolerable support.

w Alfred Shaughnessy   *d* Harold Huth

Ron Randell, Mary Parker, Carl Jaffe, Margaret
Diamond, Cyril Luckham

'They're blasting the Nazis – from inside!'
Hostages
US   1943   88m   bw
Paramount (Sol C. Siegel)

In occupied Prague, the Nazis seize a variety of
hostages and threaten them with death as a reprisal
for underground activities.

Modest morale-builder, unfortunately padded out
with melodramatics and overacting.

w Lester Cole, Frank Butler   *novel* Stefan Heym
d Frank Tuttle   *ph* Victor Milner   *m* Victor Young

Luise Rainer, Paul Lukas, William Bendix, Oscar
Homolka, Arturo de Cordova, Katina Paxinou, Roland
Varno

Hostile Guns
US   1967   91m   Techniscope
Paramount (A. C. Lyles)
V*, L

A marshal has to deliver four dangerous convicts to
the penitentiary.

Rather crude addition to the A. C. Lyles series
distinguished only by nostalgic casting.

w Steve Fisher, Sloan Nibley   *d* R. G. Springsteen

George Montgomery, Tab Hunter, Yvonne de Carlo, Brian Donlevy, Fuzzy Knight, John Russell, Leo Gordon, Robert Emhardt, Richard Arlen

Hostile Witness

GB   1968   101m   DeLuxe
UA/Caralan/Dador (David E. Rose)

A barrister suffers a nervous breakdown after the death of his daughter and finds himself accused of murder.

Complex courtroom thriller, filmed in a flatly boring way with stagey sets and performances. The plot is the only interest.

w Jack Roffey   play Jack Roffey   d Ray Milland
ph Gerry Gibbs

Ray Milland, Sylvia Sims, Felix Aylmer, Raymond Huntley, Geoffrey Lumsden, Norman Barrs, Percy Marmont, Ewan Roberts

'Be there when Jane Russell shakes her tambourines!'
'If you'd hit me and given me orders on our wedding night, I would have kissed your hand!'

Hot Blood

US   1955   85m   Technicolor   Cinemascope
Columbia (Howard Welsch)

A dying gypsy king wants his young brother to get married and succeed him.

What promises to be a boring musical proves to be a boring melodrama. Artificial Romany hokum.

w Jesse Lasky Jnr   d Nicholas Ray   ph Ray June
m Les Baxter

Cornel Wilde, Jane Russell, Joseph Calleia, Helen Westcott, Mikhail Rasumny

The Hot Box

US   1972   89m   Metrocolor
New Realm/New World (Jonathan Demme)

Three American nurses are kidnapped by a revolutionary leader in Latin America.

Ridiculous exploitation film providing sex and violence.

w Joe Viola, Jonathan Demme   d Joe Viola
ph Felipe Sacdalan   m Resti Umali   ad Ben Otico
ed Ben Barcelon

Andrea Cagan, Margaret Markov, Rickey Richardson, Laurie Rose, Carmen Argenziano, Charles Dierkop

'The film emerges as an honourable solution to the problem of taking a left-wing position in an essentially capitalist industry.' – Tony Rayns, MFB

The film was cut to 86m on its British release.

Hot Enough for June

GB   1963   98m   Eastmancolor
Rank (Betty E. Box)
US title: Agent 8 3/4

A penniless writer is sent to Czechoslovakia on a goodwill mission and finds himself being used as a spy.

Very moderate spoof, neither very funny nor very thrilling.

w Lukas Heller   novel The Night before Wenceslas by Lionel Davidson   d Ralph Thomas   ph Ernest Steward   m Angelo Lavagnino

Dirk Bogarde, Sylva Koscina, Robert Morley, Leo McKern, John Le Mesurier

Hot Lead and Cold Feet

US   1978   90m   colour
Buena Vista (Ron Miller)

Twin brothers, one a tough gunfighter, the other a pacifist, compete in a race to inherit a Western town.

Comic Western showcasing Dale in three differing roles – as the father and his two sons – but with a script that runs out of ideas long before the end.

w Arthur Alsberg, Joe McEveety, Don Nelson
story Rod Piffath   d Robert Butler   ph Frank Phillips   m Buddy Baker   ad John Mansbridge, Frank T. Smith   ed Ray de Leuw

Jim Dale, Karen Valentine, Don Knots, Jack Elam, Darren McGaven, John Williams, Warren Vanders

Hot Millions *

US   1968   106m   colour
MGM/Mildred Freed Alberg

A confidence trickster makes a fortune out of fictitious companies.

Elaborate, talky, overlong comedy with irresistible star performances.

w Ira Wallach, Peter Ustinov   d Eric Till   m Laurie Johnson

Peter Ustinov, Maggie Smith, Bob Newhart, Karl Malden, Robert Morley, Cesar Romero

AAN: Ira Wallach, Peter Ustinov (script)

The Hot One: see Corvette Summer

Hot Pepper

US   1933   76m   bw
Fox

Ex-Marines Flagg and Quirt become bootleggers and quarrel over a fiery South American entertainer.

Fourth and last in the comedy-melodrama series stemming from What Price Glory? Mild, stereotyped entertainment.

w Barry Connors, Philip Klein, Dudley Nichols
d John G. Blystone   ph Charles G. Clarke

Edmund Lowe, Victor McLaglen, Lupe Velez, El Brendel, Lillian Bond

Hot Pursuit

US   1987   93m   Metrocolor
Paramount/RKO (Theodore R. Parvin, Pierre David)
V*, L

Delayed at the start of a Caribbean holiday, a student tries to catch up with his girlfriend and her family who have gone on ahead.

Predictable and uninteresting teen comedy that veers into unexpected and unnecessary violence at its climax.

w Stephen Lisberger, Steven Carabatsos   d Stephen Lisberger   ph Frank Tidy   m Rareview
pd William J. Creber   ed Mitchell Sinoway

John Cusack, Robert Loggia, Wendy Gazelle, Jerry Stiller, Monte Markham, Shelley Fabares

The Hot Rock ***

US   1972   105m   DeLuxe   Panavision
TCF (Hal Landers, Bobby Roberts)
V*, L
GB title: How to Steal a Diamond in Four Uneasy Lessons

Four crooks plan to rob the Brooklyn Museum of a priceless diamond.

Enjoyable variation on the caper theme, with relaxed comic performances and highly skilled technical back-up. It's refreshing to come across a film which hits its targets so precisely.

w William Goldman   novel Donald E. Westlake
d Peter Yates   ph Ed Brown   m Quincy Jones

Robert Redford, George Segal, Zero Mostel, Paul Sand, Ron Leibman, Moses Gunn, William Redfield

'A funny, fast-paced, inventive and infinitely clever crime comedy, almost as if The French Connection had been remade as a piece of urban humour.' – Michael Korda

'Her lips offered what her heart denied!'
Hot Saturday

US   1932   73m   bw
Paramount

Malicious gossip in a small town causes a girl to lose her job.

Small town, small potatoes; interesting chiefly for its two budding male stars.

w Seton I. Miller   novel Harvey Ferguson
d William A. Seiter

Nancy Carroll, Cary Grant, Randolph Scott, Edward Woods, Lillian Bond, Jane Darwell, William Collier Snr

'Fairly agreeable as entertainment, but will not get preferred playing time.' – Variety

'There's Something Funny In The Air.'
Hot Shots!

US   1991   85m   DeLuxe
TCF (Bill Badalato)
V, V*, L, S

A young disturbed pilot joins an élite group to take part in a raid on a nuclear plant or, as secondary target, an accordion factory.

A hit-and-miss send-up of Top Gun and other Hollywood hits, in which most of the targets are missed.

w Jim Abrahams, Pat Proft   d Jim Abrahams
ph Bill Butler   m Sylvester Levay   pd William A. Elliott   ed Jane Kurson, Eric Sears

Charlie Sheen, Cary Elwes, Valeria Golino, Lloyd Bridges, Jon Cryer, Kevin Dunn, Bill Irwin, William O'Leary, Kristy Swanson, Efrem Zimbalist Jnr

'Re-Armed, Re-United . . . Re-Diculous!'
Hot Shots!: Part Deux

US   1993   88m   DeLuxe
TCF (Bill Badalato)
V, V*, L, S

A special forces mission is sent to the Middle East to rescue a special forces mission whose mission it was to rescue hostages.

A send-up of Rambo, if that is possible, which also takes in references to dozens of other movies, but without providing much in the way of laughs.

w Jim Abrahams, Pat Proft   d Jim Abrahams
ph John R. Leonetti   m Basil Pouledouris
pd William A. Elliott   ed Malcolm Campbell

Charlie Sheen, Lloyd Bridges, Valeria Golina, Richard Crenna, Brenda Bakke, Miguel Ferrer, Rowan Atkinson

'To truly enjoy it, the viewer must abandon his or her dignity for at least 90 minutes, and accept the inherent silliness.' – John Anderson, Newsday

Hot Spell *

US   1958   86m   bw   Vistavision
Paramount/Hal Wallis

In a small Southern town, a husband seeks to leave his wife and family for a 20-year-old girl.

Overwrought domestic drama slipping perilously close to farce at times, but a good theatrical vehicle for its stars.

w James Poe   play Next of Kin by Lonnie Coleman
d Daniel Mann   ph Loyal Griggs   m Alex North

Anthony Quinn, Shirley Booth, Shirley Maclaine, Earl Holliman, Eileen Heckart

Hot Spot (1941): see I Wake Up Screaming

The Hot Spot *

US   1990   130m   colour
Rank/Orion (Paul Lewis)
V, V*, L

A car dealer's wife seduces a drifter and petty crook who goes to work for her husband.

Effective melodrama, much in the manner of a 1940s *film noir*.

w Nona Tyson, Charles Williams   novel *Hell Hath No Fury* by Charles Williams   d Dennis Hopper   ph Ueli Steiger   m Jack Nitzsche   pd Cary White   ed Wende Phifer Mate

Don Johnson, Virginia Madsen, Jennifer Connelly, Charles Martin Smith, William Sadler, Jerry Hardin, Barry Corbin, Leon Rippy, Jack Nance

Hot Stuff
US   1979   91m   Metrocolor
Columbia/Rastar/Mort Engleberg
V, V*, L

Members of a Burglary Task Force need convictions, so they set up fences in order to lure criminals, and are embarrassed by the results.

Slightly unusual but rather frantically assembled comedy which wears out its welcome long before the end.

w Michael Kane, Donald E. Westlake   d Dom DeLuise   ph James Pergola   m Patrick Williams

Dom DeLuise, Suzanne Pleshette, Ossie Davis, Jerry Reed, Luis Avalos, Marc Lawrence

'Heavy farce in which a bright comedy is struggling to escape.' – *Tom Milne, MFB*

Hot Summer Night *
US   1957   85m   bw
MGM (Morton S. Fine)

A foolhardy reporter determines on an interview with a notorious outlaw, and has to be rescued.

Interesting but disappointing low-budget experiment.

w Morton S. Fine, David Friedkin   d David Friedkin   ph Harold S. Marcorati   m André Previn

Leslie Nielsen, Colleen Miller, Edward Andrews, Jay C. Flippen, James Best, Paul Richards, Robert Wilke, Claude Akins

Hot Water *
US   1924   50m approx (24 fps)   bw   silent
Harold Lloyd

A young husband has trouble with a turkey, a new car and his in-laws.

Casually structured star comedy with brilliant sequences.

w Harold Lloyd, Sam Taylor   d Fred Newmeyer, Sam Taylor

Harold Lloyd, Jobyna Ralston, Josephine Crowell

Hotel *
US   1967   124m   Technicolor
Warner (Wendell Mayes)
V*

Guests at a luxurious New Orleans hotel have various problems.

Old-fashioned omnibus drama from a bestseller, quite brightly done.

w Wendell Mayes   novel Arthur Hailey   d Richard Quine   ph Charles Lang   m Johnny Keating

Rod Taylor, Catherine Spaak, Karl Malden, Melvyn Douglas, Merle Oberon, Richard Conte, Michael Rennie, Kevin McCarthy, Alfred Ryder

Hotel Berlin *
US   1945   98m   bw
Warner (Louis F. Edelman)

Various lives intertwine in a Berlin hotel towards the end of the war.

After five years of total war this view of life on the other side can hardly fail to be unconvincing, but the actors gleefully seize on moments of melodrama.

w Thomas Job   novel Vicki Baum   d Peter Godfrey   ph Carl Guthrie   m Franz Waxman

Raymond Massey, Peter Lorre, Faye Emerson, Helmut Dantine, Andrea King, Alan Hale, George Coulouris, Henry Daniell, Helene Thimig, Kurt Kreuger, Steve Geray, Frank Reicher

'The most heavily routine of Warners' political melodramas, stuffed with sympathetic veterans.' – *James Agee*

Hotel du Nord **
France   1938   110m   bw
Sedif/Imperial

People with problems congregate at a small hotel.

Melancholy, studio-confined character drama which has its adherents but technically seemed a throwback to earlier standards. The acting rescues it.

w Henri Jeanson, Eugene Dabit   d Marcel Carné   ph Armand Thirard   m Maurice Jaubert

Annabella, *Louis Jouvet*, Jean-Pierre Aumont, *Arletty*, Jeanne Marken, Bernard Blier

'An outstander in this country and possesses good chance abroad.' – *Variety (Paris)*

Hotel du Paradis
GB/France   1986   113m   Eastmancolor
Umbrella-Portman Films/Pierson/Film Four/London Trust/
Antenne 2 (Simon Perry)

An ageing actor, planning a comeback in a one-man show, revisits a small Parisian hotel that he loves.

Slow, atmospheric but inconsequential drama.

wd Jana Bokova   ph Gerard de Battista   m Rodolfo Mederos   pd Patrick Weibel   ed Bill Shapter

Fernando Rey, Fabrice Luchini, Berangere Bonvoisin, Hugues Quester, Marika Rivera, Carola Regnier, Raul Gimenez, Michael Medwin, Georges Geret

Hotel for Women
US   1939   83m   bw
TCF (Raymond Griffith)

Young city gold diggers are encouraged by a matron.

Slight comedy drama notable for the acting debut of hostess Elsa Maxwell.

w Katherine Scola, Darrell Ware   d Gregory Ratoff   ph Peverell Marley   m David Buttolph

Elsa Maxwell, Linda Darnell, Ann Sothern, James Ellison, John Halliday, Lynn Bari, Alan Dinehart

'Synthetic Cinderella story . . . fluffed up with a generous display of latest fashions.' – *Variety*

Hotel Haywire
US   1937   66m   bw
Paramount (Harold Hurley)

An astrologer makes eyes at a dentist's wife, and causes much confusion in a hotel.

Frantic farce which might have been funnier if it had stuck to the original script and cast (it was intended for Burns and Allen).

w Preston Sturges (before studio revision)   d George Archainbaud   ph Henry Sharp

Leo Carrillo, Lynne Overman, Mary Carlisle, Benny Baker, Spring Byington, George Barbier, Porter Hall, Lucien Littlefield, John Patterson

'Broad comedy applied with sufficient skill and effect to make the journey on the dual route fairly safe.' – *Variety*

'Flaming love drama of the war-torn Balkans!'
'Her beauty sent men marching to their death with a smile!'
Hotel Imperial
US   1939   78m   bw
Paramount

Balkans, 1916: a Polish dancer suspects a Hungarian officer of being responsible for her sister's death.

Dim romantic melodrama with espionage trimmings.

w Gilbert Gabriel, Robert Thoeren   play Lajos Biro   d Robert Florey   ph William Mellor   md Boris Morros

Ray Milland, Isa Miranda, Reginald Owen, Gene Lockhart, J. Carrol Naish, Curt Bois, Henry Victor, Albert Dekker

'Nothing much to be done about this one . . . a weak sister, dated and inconclusive . . . never seems to generate any interest.' – *Variety*

'A very competent rehash . . . for the unexacting the picture has its moments.' – *Graham Greene*

† Previously made in 1926 by Mauritz Stiller, with Pola Negri. This version was originally announced in 1936 as *I Loved a Soldier*, to star Marlene Dietrich (or Margaret Sullavan) and Charles Boyer.

The Hotel New Hampshire
US   1984   108m   Technicolor
Orion/Woodfall (Neil Hartley, Pieter Kroonenburg, David Patterson)
V, V*, L

A schoolmaster and his family are obsessed by the fantasy of living in a hotel, and this fantasy is performed with variations.

A parable of life in the manner of Thornton Wilder's *The Skin of Our Teeth*, and sometimes even more obscure, but generally quite entertaining along the way.

wd Tony Richardson   novel John Irving   ph David Watkin   m Jacques Offenbach   pd Jocelyn Herbert   ed Robert K. Lambert

Rob Lowe, Jodie Foster, Paul McCrane, Beau Bridges, Nastassja Kinski, Wallace Shawn, Wilford Brimley

Hotel Paradiso *
US   1966   99m   Metrocolor   Panavision
MGM (Peter Glenville)

Various romantic affairs come to a head one evening at a seedy hotel.

A famous boulevard farce seems jellied in aspic in this good-looking but very flatly handled film version, in which famous artists are left to caper about on an unsuitable wide screen with no help from the director.

w Peter Glenville, Jean-Claude Carrière   play Georges Feydeau   d Peter Glenville   ph Henri Decaë   m Laurence Rosenthal   pd François de Lamothe

Alec Guinness, Gina Lollobrigida, Robert Morley, Peggy Mount, Douglas Byng, Akim Tamiroff, Robertson Hare

Hotel Reserve
GB   1944   89m   bw
RKO (Victor Hanbury)

An Austrian refugee in the south of France is asked by the police to track down a spy among his fellow hotel guests.

Slow, obvious and poorly made suspenser from a good novel.

w John Davenport   novel *Epitaph for a Spy* by Eric Ambler   d Victor Hanbury, Lance Comfort, Max Greene   ph Max Greene

James Mason, Lucie Mannheim, Raymond Lovell, Julien Mitchell, Martin Miller, Herbert Lom, Frederick Valk, Valentine Dyall

Hotel Sahara *
GB 1951 96m bw
GFD/Tower (George H. Brown)

In North Africa during World War II, a small hotel changes its loyalties to suit its occupiers.

Overstretched, studio-bound, fitfully amusing comedy.

w George H. Brown, Patrick Kirwan d Ken Annakin ph Jack Hildyard m Benjamin Frankel

Peter Ustinov, Yvonne de Carlo, David Tomlinson, Roland Culver, Albert Lieven, Bill Owen, Sidney Tafler, Ferdy Mayne

'Cheerful, uncomplicated empty stuff . . . no more subtle than a music hall sketch.' – Richard Mallett, Punch

The Hottentot
US 1929 77m bw
Warner

A horse lover is forced to masquerade as a champion jockey.

Early talkie version of a well-worn theme which had previously appeared as a silent in 1923 with Douglas MacLean; it later turned up as a Joe E. Brown vehicle and in 1938 became Going Places, a Dick Powell musical.

w Harvey Thew play Victor Mapes, Willie Collier d Roy del Ruth

Patsy Ruth Miller, Douglas Gerrard

Houdini *
US 1953 106m Technicolor
Paramount (George Pal)
V*

In the 1890s a fairground magician shows a passionate talent for escapology and finally kills himself by undertaking increasingly impossible tricks.

Superficial biopic with more attention to romance than to interesting detail. Some zest in the playing is killed by claustrophobic studio sets.

w Philip Yordan d George Marshall ph Ernest Laszlo m Roy Webb

Tony Curtis, Janet Leigh, Torin Thatcher, Sig Rumann, Angela Clarke

The Hound Dog Man
US 1959 87m DeLuxe Cinemascope
TCF/Company of Artists (Jerry Wald)

An irresponsible country boy gets his come-uppance.

Mild, competent backwoods comedy drama introducing a teenage rave.

w Fred Gipson, Winston Miller d Don Siegel ph Charles G. Clarke m Cyril Mockridge

Fabian, Stuart Whitman, Carol Lynley, Arthur O'Connell, Betty Field, Royal Dano, Jane Darwell, Edgar Buchanan, Claude Akins

The Hound of the Baskervilles **
US 1939 80m bw
(TCF) Gene Markey
V*, L

Sherlock Holmes solves the mystery of a supernatural hound threatening the life of a Dartmoor baronet.

Basil Rathbone's first appearance as Sherlock Holmes is in a painstaking studio production which achieves good atmosphere and preserves the flavour if not the letter of the book but is let down by a curious lack of pace.

w Ernest Pascal novel Arthur Conan Doyle d Sidney Lanfield ph Peverell Marley m Cyril Mockridge ad Thomas Little

Basil Rathbone, Nigel Bruce, Richard Greene, Wendy Barrie, Lionel Atwill, Morton Lowry, John Carradine,

Barlowe Borland, Beryl Mercer, Ralph Forbes, E. E. Clive, Eily Malyon, Mary Gordon

'A startling mystery-chiller . . . will find many bookings on top spots of key duallers.' – Variety

'Lush dialogue, stagey sets and vintage supporting cast make it a delectable Hollywood period piece.' – Judith Crist, 1980

† For Rathbone's other appearances as Holmes see under Sherlock Holmes.

The Hound of the Baskervilles *
GB 1959 86m Technicolor
UA/Hammer (Anthony Hinds)
V, V*

Spirited remake let down by dogged Hammer insistence on promises of horror and sex; good atmosphere also let down by poor colour.

w Peter Bryan novel Arthur Conan Doyle d Terence Fisher ph Jack Asher m James Bernard ad Bernard Robinson ed James Needs

Peter Cushing, André Morell, Christopher Lee, Marla Landi, Ewen Solon, Francis de Wolff, Miles Malleson, John Le Mesurier

The Hound of the Baskervilles
GB 1977 85m Technicolor
Hemdale/Michael White Ltd (John Goldstone)
V*

A pointless, pitiful and vulgar spoof of an enjoyable original.

w Dudley Moore, Peter Cook, Paul Morrissey d Paul Morrissey ph Dick Bush, John Wilcox m Dudley Moore

Peter Cook (Sherlock Holmes), Dudley Moore (Watson), Denholm Elliott (Stapleton), Terry-Thomas (Mortimer), Joan Greenwood, Max Wall, Irene Handl, Kenneth Williams, Hugh Griffith, Roy Kinnear, Penelope Keith, Dana Gillespie, Prunella Scales, Jessie Matthews, Spike Milligan

Hounded: see Johnny Allegro

The Hounds of Zaroff: see The Most Dangerous Game

'As I held her in my arms, how could I know that she was as vicious as she was beautiful?'
The Hour before the Dawn
US 1944 75m bw
Paramount (William Dozier)

When a pacifist English nobleman discovers during World War II that he has married a Nazi spy, he strangles her and joins the forces.

Stultifyingly absurd, badly made and acted melodrama which its author clearly wished he had never written, as it was later withdrawn from his canon.

w Michael Hogan, Lester Samuels novel W. Somerset Maugham d Frank Tuttle ph John F. Seitz m Miklos Rozsa

Franchot Tone, Veronica Lake, John Sutton, Binnie Barnes, Henry Stephenson, Philip Merivale, Nils Asther, Edmund Breon

'Tedious and generally uneventful . . . a weak entry for the duals.' – Variety

The Hour of Decision
GB 1957 81m bw
Tempean/Eros
V*

A reporter is assigned to investigate the death of a columnist.

A familiar type of second feature whodunnit, with little about it to spark enthusiasm.

w Norman Hudis d C. Pennington-Richards

Jeff Morrow, Hazel Court, Lionel Jeffries, Anthony Dawson, Mary Laura Wood

Hour of Glory: see The Small Back Room

'Wyatt Earp – hero with a badge, or cold-blooded killer?'
Hour of the Gun **
US 1967 101m DeLuxe Panavision
UA/Mirisch/Kappa (John Sturges)
V*, S

After the gunfight at the OK Corral, Wyatt Earp tracks down the rest of the Clanton gang.

Vividly set, slowly developed Western which makes an ambiguous but forceful figure of Earp. Generally confident and interesting.

w Edward Anhalt d John Sturges ph Lucien Ballard m Jerry Goldsmith

James Garner, Jason Robards Jnr, Robert Ryan, Steve Ihnat, Michael Tolan, Frank Converse, Sam Melville, Monte Markham, Albert Salmi, Jon Voight, William Windom, Charles Aidman

'The case is a dog. The defendant is a pig. And the law is an ass.'
The Hour of the Pig *
GB/France 1993 117m colour
Mayfair/BBC/CiBy 2000 (David M. Thompson)

In medieval France, a young city lawyer is sent to a backward, rural area, to defend a pig on the charge of murdering a Jewish boy.

An original film that manages to cram in comedy, traces of thriller, and high-level corruption in its depiction of the superstitious past; it doesn't work as well as it might, but at least it tries something a little different from the endless reworking of over-familiar material.

wd Leslie Megahey ph John Hooper m Alexandre Desplat pd Bruce Macadie ed Isabelle Dedieu

Colin Firth, Ian Holm, Donald Pleasence, Amina Annabi, Nicol Williamson, Michael Gough, Harriet Walter, Jim Carter, Lysette Anthony

'The picture is an off-beat one. A pity that the mix is too rich and the cooking of it frequently too muddled and a lot of the acting is mummery dressed in drama-school accents.' – Alexander Walker

The Hour of the Wolf *
Sweden 1968 89m bw
Svensk Filmindustri (Lars-Owe Carlberg)
V*
original title: Vargtimmen

A painter, at his summer island home with his wife, is terrorized by monstrous nightmares and by memories of his own adulterous past.

Rather like the gloomy side of Smiles of a Summer Night, this very typical Bergman melodrama doesn't quite flow as intended, and whatever its meaning may be, its surface is less entertaining than usual.

wd Ingmar Bergman ph Sven Nykvist m Lars Johan Werle ad Marik Vos-Lundh ed Ulla Ryghe

Max von Sydow, Liv Ullmann, Ingrid Thulin, Georg Rydeberg, Erland Josephson

The Hour of Thirteen
GB 1952 78m bw
MGM (Hayes Goetz)

Edwardian London is shocked when policemen are stabbed one by one.

Jaded Hollywood-English thriller, a remake of The Mystery of Mr X (qv).

w Leon Gordon, Howard Emmett Rogers novel X vs Rex by Philip MacDonald d Harold French ph Guy Green m John Addison

Peter Lawford, Dawn Addams, Roland Culver, Derek Bond, Leslie Dwyer, Michael Hordern, Colin Gordon, Heather Thatcher

† Originally to be called *T for Terror.*

The Hours and Times *
US   1991   60m   bw
ICA/Antarctic Pictures
V, V*

On holiday in Spain with Beatle John Lennon, his manager Brian Epstein tries to get him into bed and is as unsuccessful in seducing a hotel bellboy.

Interesting, very low-budget feature exploring the ambivalent relationship of men divided by sex and class.

wd Christopher Münch   *ph* Christopher Münch
ed Christopher Münch

David Angus, Ian Hart, Stephanie Pack, Robin McDonald, Sergio Moreno, Unity Grimwood

'A quality piece of film-making.' – *Derek Malcolm, Guardian*

'A touching, perceptive film and well worth seeing.' – *Philip French, Observer*

House
US   1986   93m   colour
New World/Sean Cunningham
V, V*, L, S

An old lady is found dead in her spooky house; her nephew moves in and endures various apparitions.

Silly film in which the creatures look ridiculous and the psychology makes no sense, especially when the whole thing attempts to be a protest about Vietnam.

w Ethan Wiley   *d* Steve Miner   *ph* Mac Ahlberg
m Harry Manfredini   *pd* Gregg Fonseca

William Katt, George Wendt, Richard Moll, Kay Lenz

House II: The Second Story
US   1988   88m   colour
Entertainment/New World (Sean S. Cunningham)
V, V*, L, S

A former Vietnam veteran moves into an old house where his parents were killed 25 years before and searches for a valuable Aztec skull buried with one of his ancestors.

A movie that has little relationship to the original, other than in its general silliness and incoherence.

wd Ethan Wiley   *ph* Mac Ahlberg   *m* Harry Manfredini   *pd* Gregg Fonseca   *ed* Marty Nicholson

Arye Gross, Jonathan Stark, Royal Dano, Bill Maher, Lar Park Lincoln, John Ratzenberger

'Sluggish, nonsensical and a generally pointless venture, replete with animated monsters, unresolved plot convolutions and totally forgettable characters. Ridiculous.' – *Stefan Jaworzyn, Shock Xpress*

House III: see *The Horror Show*

'Home Deadly Home.'
House IV
US   1992   93m   DeLuxe
Sean S. Cunningham Films
V*

A widow's brother-in-law attempts to frighten her into abandoning the family mansion.

An improvement over its predecessors, it maintains interest despite its unoriginality.

w Geof Miller, Deirdre Higgins   *story* Jim Wynorski, R. J. Robinson   *d* Lewis Abernathy   *ph* James Mathers   *m* Harry Manfredini   *ed* Seth Gaven

Terry Treas, William Katt, Scott Burkholder, Melissa Clayton, Denny Dillon, Dabbs Greer, Mark Gash

'The emphasis . . . is on scares rather than comedy, and the result is satisfying.' – *Variety*

'Representing yet another in the seemingly endless parade of artistically-bankrupt genre sequels . . . It's really sad that given the high-gloss resources afforded this production, the filmmakers couldn't have done any better.' – *Fangoria*

The House across the Bay
US   1940   88m   bw
UA/Walter Wanger
V*

To protect her racketeer husband from his enemies, his wife has him convicted of income tax evasion.

Unpersuasive melodrama, a star potboiler.

w Kathryn Scola   *d* Archie Mayo   *ph* Merritt Gerstad   *m* Werner Janssen

Joan Bennett, George Raft, Lloyd Nolan, Walter Pidgeon, Gladys George, June Knight

The House across the Street
US   1949   69m   bw
Warner (Saul Elkins)

A racketeer brings pressure on a newspaper, and a crusading reporter is relegated to giving advice to the lovelorn.

Tepid remake of *Hi Nellie.*

w Russell Hughes, Roy Chanslor   *d* Richard Bare

Wayne Morris, Janis Paige, James Mitchell, Alan Hale, Bruce Bennett

House by the River *
US   1950   88m   bw
Republic/Fidelity (Howard Welsch)

A weak and lecherous writer murders his maid and persuades his brother to help cover up the deed.

Intriguing little thriller, atmospheric and suspenseful for the most part, until it topples into melodrama.

w Mel Dinelli   *novel* A. P. Herbert   *d* Fritz Lang
ph Edward Cronjager   *m* George Antheil   *ad* Boris Leven   *ed* Arthur D. Hilton

Louis Hayward, Lee Bowman, Jane Wyatt, Dorothy Patrick, Ann Shoemaker, Jody Gilbert, Peter Brocco, Howland Chamberlin

House Calls *
US   1978   98m   Technicolor
Universal/Jennings Lang (Alex Winitsky, Arlene Sellers)
V*, L

A middle-aged doctor finds himself widowed and seeks a new mate.

Spotty comedy which tries to combine conventional romantic spats with medical satire, and comes off only in fits and starts.

w Max Shulman, Julius J. Epstein, Alan Mandel, Charles Shyer   *d* Howard Zieff   *ph* David M. Walsh   *m* Henry Mancini

Walter Matthau, Glenda Jackson, Art Carney, Richard Benjamin, Candice Azzara, Thayer David, Dick O'Neill

A House Divided *
US   1931   70m   bw
Universal (Paul Kohner)

A tough widowed fisherman seeks a new wife, but she falls in love with his son.

Glum variation on *Desire under the Elms,* interesting for early Wyler touches.

w John P. Clymer, Dale Van Every, John Huston
story Heart and Hand by Olive Edens   *d* William Wyler
ph Charles Stumar

Walter Huston, Kent Douglass, Helen Chandler, Vivian Oakland, Frank Hagney, Mary Foy

The House in Nightmare Park *
GB   1973   95m   Technicolor
EMI/Associated London/Extonation (Clive Exton, Terry Nation)
V

In 1907, a ham actor is asked to perform at an old dark house in the country where an axe murderer prowls during the night.

Standard creepy house comedy thriller, well enough done though it would have been better with Bob Hope.

w Clive Exton, Terry Nation   *d* Peter Sykes   *ph* Ian Wilson   *m* Harry Robinson

Frankie Howerd, Ray Milland, Hugh Burden, Kenneth Griffith, John Bennett, Rosalie Crutchley, Ruth Dunning

The House in the Square *
GB   1951   91m   Technicolor/b/w endpieces
TCF (Sol C. Siegel)
US title: *I'll Never Forget You*

An American atomic chemist living in London becomes his own ancestor of two hundred years ago, and falls in love.

Slow-starting but thereafter quite acceptable remake of *Berkeley Square* (qv), with some interesting dialogue and a genuinely affecting fade-out.

w Ranald MacDougall   *play* John L. Balderston
d Roy Baker   *ph* Georges Périnal   *m* William Alwyn   *ad* C. P. Norman

Tyrone Power, Ann Blyth, Michael Rennie, Beatrice Campbell, Dennis Price, Raymond Huntley, Irene Browne, Robert Atkins (as Dr Johnson)

A House Is Not a Home
US   1964   98m   bw
Paramount/Embassy (Clarence Greene)

The life story of New York's most famous madam, Polly Adler.

Dismal, unappealing, laundered biopic, cheaply made in an unconvincing period setting.

w Russel Rouse, Clarence Greene   *d* Russel Rouse
ph Harold Stine   *m* Joseph Weiss

Shelley Winters, Robert Taylor, Cesar Romero, Ralph Taeger, Broderick Crawford

The House of a Thousand Candles
US   1936   54m   bw
Republic

A young man must live in an unfinished mansion to inherit under the terms of his grandfather's will.

Odd but basically unremarkable little mystery; the title is more interesting than the movie.

w H. W. Hanemann, Endre Bohem   *novel* Meredith Nicholson   *d* Arthur Lubin

Phillips Holmes, Mae Clarke, Irving Pichel, Rosita Moreno

House of Angels **
Sweden   1992   119m   colour
Mayfair/Memfis/Sveriges Television/TV2/Svenska Filminstitute/
Danmarks Radio/Nordisk Film and TV (Lars Jönsson, Lars Dahlquist)
V
original title: *Änglagård*

Villagers are scandalized when a landowner dies and his farm is inherited by his hitherto unknown granddaughter, a night-club singer who has a bisexual boyfriend.

Highly enjoyable comedy of a culture clash, full of a generosity of spirit.

wd Colin Nutley   *ph* Jens Fischer   *m* Björn Isfält
pd Ulla Herdin   *ed* Perry Schaffer

Helena Bergström, Rikard Wolff, Sven Wolter, Reine Brynolfsson, Ernst Gunter, Viveka Seldahl, Per Oscarsson, Tord Peterson, Ing-Marie Carlsson

'Nutley's achievement is in finding a delicate balance between satire and sentiment . . . a surprising delight.' – *Angie Errigo, Empire*

'The story Tokyo couldn't hide, and Washington couldn't hold back!'

House of Bamboo **
US   1955   102m   DeLuxe   Cinemascope
TCF (Buddy Adler)

Japanese and American authorities move into undercover action against Tokyo gangsters.

Routine big-budget crime drama given a novel twist by its location and vaguely adapted from *The Street with No Name* (qv).

w Harry Kleiner, Samuel Fuller   *d* Samuel Fuller   *ph* Joe MacDonald   *m* Leigh Harline   *pd* Lyle R. Wheeler, Addison Hehr   *ed* James B. Clark

Robert Stack, Robert Ryan, Shirley Yagamuchi, Cameron Mitchell, Sessue Hayakawa

House of Cards
US   1968   100m   Techniscope
Universal/Westward (Dick Berg)

An American becomes tutor in the Paris household of a French general's widow, and finds himself a pawn in a high-powered game of international intrigue.

Good-looking location thriller which after an intricate opening settles into a *39 Steps*-style chase, but makes little of it.

w James P. Bonner   *novel* Stanley Ellin   *d* John Guillermin   *ph* Piero Portalupi   *m* Francis Lai

George Peppard, Inger Stevens, Orson Welles, Keith Michell, William Job, Maxine Audley, Peter Bayliss

House of Cards
US   1993   107m   Technicolor
Penta/A&M Films (Dale Pollock, Lianne Halfon, Wolfgang Glattes)
V, V*

After the sudden death of her husband, a woman struggles with the fact that her daughter has stopped talking and begun to act in strange ways.

Mundane domestic drama that veers unerringly towards the sentimental.

wd Michael Lessac   *ph* Victor Hammer   *m* James Horner   *pd* Peter Larkin   *ed* Walter Murch

Kathleen Turner, Tommy Lee Jones, Asha Menina, Shiloh Strong, Esther Rolle, Park Overall, Michael Horse, Anne Pitoniak

'Plays like a top-of-the-line disease-of-the-week TV movie.' – *Variety*

† The film was released direct to video in Britain.

House of Connelly: see *Carolina*

House of Dark Shadows *
US   1970   97m   Metrocolor
MGM (Dan Curtis)
V, V*, L

A 200-year-old vampire is released from the crypt of an old mansion and tries to find a cure for his affliction.

Effectively creepy little horror, done with some style.

w Sam Hall, Gordon Russell   *d* Dan Curtis   *ph* Arthur Ornitz   *pd* Trevor Williams   *m* Robert Cobert   *ed* Arline Garson

Jonathan Frid, Joan Bennett, Roger Davis, Grayson Hall, Kathryn Leigh Scott, Nancy Barrett, Thayer David

'Despite a few awkward moments in the photography and editing (betraying under-budgeting and hasty shooting), the result is the most satisfyingly convulsive traditional horror film in years.' – *Tony Rayns, MFB*

The film had its origins in a daytime television series, *Dark Shadows*, which ran from 1966 to 1971 and was briefly revived as a prime-time series in 1991. It was followed by the less successful *Night of Dark Shadows* (qv).

House of Doom: see *The Black Cat*

House of Dracula *
US   1945   67m   bw
Universal (Paul Malvern)

As a result of being visited in one evening by Count Dracula, the Wolf Man and the Frankenstein monster, a sympathetic doctor goes on the rampage. Mind-boggling finale to the first Universal monster cycle, with a happy ending for the Wolf Man.

Cheaply made and not really inventive, but has to be seen to be believed.

w Edward T. Lowe   *d* Erle C. Kenton   *ph* George Robinson   *m* Edgar Fairchild

Onslow Stevens, John Carradine, Lon Chaney Jnr, Glenn Strange, Lionel Atwill, Martha O'Driscoll, Jane Adams

The House of Fear: see *The Last Warning* (1929)

The House of Fear
US   1939   65m   bw
Universal

Murder in a haunted theatre: an actor dies and the corpse disappears.

Lively Crime Club whodunnit, a remake of *The Last Warning* (1929).

w Peter Milne   *d* Joe May

William Gargan, Irene Hervey, Dorothy Arnold, Alan Dinehart, Harvey Stephens, Walter Woolf King, Robert Coote, El Brendel, Tom Dugan

'Sufficient edge-of-seat suspense to catch lower-bracket bookings in the nabe duallers.' – *Variety*

The House of Fear *
US   1945   68m   bw
Universal
V*, L

Members of a club are murdered one by one.

A knotty problem for Sherlock Holmes, but rather tediously unravelled. Despite the orange pips it owes virtually nothing to Conan Doyle.

w Roy Chanslor   *d* Roy William Neill

Basil Rathbone, Nigel Bruce, Dennis Hoey, Aubrey Mather, Paul Cavanagh, Holmes Herbert, Gavin Muir

'Mighty monsters, locked in mortal combat!'
House of Frankenstein *
US   1944   71m   bw
Universal (Paul Malvern)
V*

A mad doctor thaws out the monster and the Wolf Man (frozen at the end of *Frankenstein Meets the Wolf Man*) but comes to a sticky end.

Originally called *Chamber of Horrors*, this was the studio's first attempt to package its monsters (the first two reels are about Dracula). It could have been pacier in view of the possibilities, but it has its interest.

w Edward T. Lowe, Curt Siodmak   *d* Erle C. Kenton   *ph* George Robinson   *m* Hans Salter

Boris Karloff, John Carradine, Lon Chaney Jnr, George Zucco, J. Carrol Naish, Anne Gwynne, Elena Verdugo, Lionel Atwill, Sig Rumann, Glenn Strange

'A chiller-diller meller.' – *Variety*

House of Fright: see *The Two Faces of Dr Jekyll*

House of Games ***
US   1987   102m   Du Art Color
Filmhaus/Orion (Michael Hausman)
V, V*, L

A psychiatrist becomes involved with a confidence trickster.

Stylish directorial debut, playing dazzling tricks with its audiences' expectations, by a respected Broadway playwright.

wd David Mamet   *ph* Juan Ruiz Anchia   *m* Alaric Jans

Lindsay Crouse, Joe Mantegna, Mike Nussbaum, Lilia Skala

House of Horrors
US   1946   65m   bw
Universal
GB title: *Joan Medford Is Missing*

An incompetent sculptor tricks a psychopathic killer into murdering his critics.

Grade Z thriller with a monster element; crude beyond belief.

w George Bricker   *d* Jean Yarbrough

Martin Kosleck, Rondo Hatton, Robert Lowery, Virginia Grey, Bill Goodwin

House of Long Shadows: see *House of the Long Shadows*

House of Menace: see *Kind Lady*

House of Mortal Sin
GB   1975   104m   Technicolor
Columbia-Warner/Pete Walker

A sexually obsessed and murderous Catholic priest attempts to blackmail a young woman over her confession.

A horror film of some originality, but feebly directed and acted.

w David McGillivray   *story* Pete Walker   *d* Pete Walker   *ph* Tony Imi   *m* Stanley Myers   *ad* Chris Burke   *ed* Matt McCarthy

Anthony Sharp, Susan Penhaligon, Stephanie Beauchamp, Norman Eshley, Sheila Keith, Mervyn Johns, Bill Kerr, Andrew Sachs

House of Mystery: see *Night Monster*

House of Numbers
US   1957   92m   bw   Cinemascope
MGM (Charles Schnee)

A man helps his thuggish twin brother escape from prison.

An original melodramatic idea is frittered away through slow pacing.

w Russel Rouse, Don M. Mankiewicz   *novel* Jack Finney   *d* Russel Rouse   *ph* George J. Folsey   *m* André Previn

Jack Palance, Barbara Lang, Harold J. Stone, Edward Platt

The House of Rothschild **
US   1934   87m   bw   (Technicolor sequence)
Twentieth Century (William Goetz, Raymond Griffith)

The chronicles of the famous banking family at the time of the Napoleonic Wars.

Lavish historical pageant with interesting scenes and performances.

w Nunnally Johnson   *play* George Humbert Westley   *d* Alfred Werker   *ph* Peverell Marley   *m* Alfred Newman

George Arliss, Loretta Young, Boris Karloff, Robert Young, C. Aubrey Smith, Arthur Byron, Helen Westley, Reginald Owen, Florence Arliss, Alan Mowbray, Holmes Herbert

'A fine picture on all counts . . . one of those occasional 100% smashes which Hollywood achieves.' – *Variety*

'A good dramatic photoplay, finely presented, packed with ripe incident and quite beautiful photography.' – *C. A. Lejeune*

AAN: best picture

House of Secrets

GB   1956   97m   Technicolor   Vistavision
Rank/Julian Wintle (Vivian A. Cox)
US title: *Triple Deception*

A naval officer is asked to impersonate a lookalike counterfeiter and work undercover to expose the gang.

Old-hat *Boys' Own Paper* adventure story, mindlessly watchable.

w Robert Buckner, Bryan Forbes   *d* Guy Green
ph Harry Waxman   *m* Hubert Clifford

Michael Craig, Julia Arnall, Brenda de Banzie, David Kossoff, Barbara Bates, Gerard Oury, Geoffrey Keen, Anton Diffring

House of Settlement: see *Mr Soft Touch*

The House of Seven Gables

US   1940   89m   bw
Universal (Burt Kelly)

In 17th-century New England, a jealous brother sends his sister's fiancé to prison.

Flat adaptation of a grim, brooding novel; it never grips.

w Lester Cole   *novel* Nathaniel Hawthorne   *d* Joe May   *ph* Milton Krasner   *m* Frank Skinner

George Sanders, Margaret Lindsay, Vincent Price, Alan Napier, Nan Grey, Cecil Kellaway, Dick Foran, Miles Mander

AAN: Frank Skinner

House of Strangers **

US   1949   101m   bw
TCF (Sol C. Siegel)
V*

An Italian-American banker who rigidly controls his three sons is arrested for illegal practices, and the family ties slacken.

Interesting ethnic melodrama with good script and performances; much remade, e.g. as *Broken Lance.*

w *Philip Yordan*   *novel* Jerome Weidman   *d* Joseph L. Mankiewicz   *ph* Milton Krasner   *m* Daniele Amfitheatrof

Edward G. Robinson, Richard Conte, Susan Hayward, *Luther Adler,* Paul Valentine, Efrem Zimbalist Jnr, Debra Paget, Hope Emerson, Esther Minciotti, Diana Douglas

The House of Tao Lin: see *Dangerous Millions*

The House of the Angel **

Argentina   1957   73m   bw
Argentina Sono Film (Leopoldo Torre Nilsson)
original title: *La Casa del Angel*

A repressed girl is obsessed for life by the shame of her first love affair.

Fascinating minor classic in a heavily Wellesian style.

w Beatriz Guido, *Leopoldo Torre Nilsson,* Martin Rodriguez Mentasti   *novel* Beatriz Guido
d Leopoldo Torre Nilsson   *ph* Anibal Gonzalez Paz   *m* Juan Carlos Paz

Elsa Daniel, Lautaro Murua, Guillermo Battaglia

'The first major work of a director of individual vision and strongly national style.' – *Robert Vas, MFB*

The House of the Arrow

GB   1940   66m   bw
ABPC
US title: *Castle of Crimes*

A wealthy Frenchwoman is murdered and her English companion is under suspicion.

A case for Inspector Hanaud; very tolerable whodunnit.

w Doreen Montgomery   *novel* A. E. W. Mason   *d* Harold French

Kenneth Kent, Diana Churchill, Belle Chrystall, Peter Murray Hill, Clifford Evans, Catherine Lacey

† A previous version in 1930 starred Dennis Neilson Terry and was directed by Leslie Hiscott. A further version in 1953 with Oscar Homolka as Hanaud was directed by Michael Anderson for Associated British.

House of the Damned *

US   1963   63m   bw
TCF/Associated Producers (Maury Dexter)

An architect is asked to make a survey of an old empty castle, but he and his wife find that someone or something is in hiding there.

Corny but mildly effective second feature with a few neat touches.

w Harry Spalding   *d* Maury Dexter   *ph* John Nickolaus Jnr   *m* Henry Vars

Ronald Foster, Merry Anders

House of the Long Shadows

GB   1983   101m   colour
Cannon (Jenny Craven)

An author takes a bet to isolate himself in a dilapidated house and write a Gothic novel within 24 hours . . .

Semi-spoof variation on an old chestnut, with aged horror practitioners interrupting the silence. Too restricted in script and production to be really effective.

w Michael Armstrong   *play* Seven Keys to Baldpate by George M. Cohan   *novel* Earl Derr Biggers   *d* Pete Walker   *ph* Norman Langley   *m* Richard Harvey

Christopher Lee, Peter Cushing, Vincent Price, Desi Arnaz Jnr, John Carradine, Sheila Keith, Julie Peasgood, Richard Todd

'Golan and Globus seem to have inherited Lord Grade's habit of assembling advertising packages with movies appended as an afterthought.' – *Kim Newman, MFB*

'A horror flick which basks in the Hammer tradition without in any way understanding it.' – *Guardian*

House of the Seven Hawks

GB   1959   92m   bw
MGM/David E. Rose

An American adventurer becomes involved in a search by criminals for buried Nazi loot.

Cliché-ridden thick ear, adequately produced but of no interest.

w Jo Eisinger   *novel* The House of Seven Flies by Victor Canning   *d* Richard Thorpe   *ph* Ted Scaife   *m* Clifton Parker

Robert Taylor, Nicole Maurey, Linda Christian, Donald Wolfit, David Kossoff, Eric Pohlmann, Gerard Heinz

'Every Passion . . . Every Obsession . . . Caught In The Fire Of Revolution.'

The House of the Spirits

Germany/Denmark/Portugal   1993   138m   colour
Panavision
Entertainment/Neue Constantin/Spring Creek/House of Spirits/ Costa do Castelo (Bernd Eichinger)
S

In Chile, a saga of a family's rise to power and its fall

is played out against a background of political upheaval.

Miscast and misconceived, this tale of magic realism is turned into a stolid drama of mundane fantasy; a disappointment.

wd Bille August   *novel* Isabel Allende   *ph* Jörgen Persson   *m* Hans Zimmer   *pd* Anna Asp   *ed* Janus Billeskov Jansen

Jeremy Irons, Meryl Streep, Glenn Close, Winona Ryder, Antonio Banderas, Vanessa Redgrave, Maria Conchita Alonso, Armin Mueller-Stahl

'Turgid, overlong, silly, hysterical (and that spells TOSH).' – *Adam Mars-Jones, Independent*

'What we get is a romantic drama set against the tide of history, that looks more and more like Latin-American melodrama traversed by a cast of talented strangers to the culture.' – *Derek Malcolm, Guardian*

House of Usher *

US   1960   85m   Eastmancolor   Cinemascope
AIP/Alta Vista (Roger Corman)
V*
GB title: *The Fall of the House of Usher*

The last of the Usher line, prone to catalepsy, is buried alive by her brother and returns to wreak vengeance.

Stylish but grottily-coloured low-budget horror which started the Poe cycle of the sixties. A bit slow, it would have worked better in the standard screen ratio, but there is a tense and spectacular finale.

w Richard Matheson   *story* Edgar Allan Poe   *d* Roger Corman   *ph* Floyd Crosby   *m* Les Baxter   *ad* Daniel Haller

Vincent Price, Myrna Fahey, Mark Damon, Harry Ellerbe

House of Usher

US   1990   90m   Rank colour
21st Century/Breton (Harry Alan Towers)
V*, L

Roderick Usher attempts to force his nephew's girlfriend to bear his child.

Tedious version of the oft-filmed tale, lacking style and substance.

w Michael J. Murray   *story* The Fall of the House of Usher by Edgar Allan Poe   *d* Alan Birkinshaw   *ph* Jossi Wein   *m* George S. Clinton, Gary Chang   *pd* Leonardo Coen Cagli   *ed* Michael J. Duthie

Oliver Reed, Donald Pleasence, Romy Windsor, Rufus Swart, Norman Coombes, Anne Stradi

'This remake offers no suspense and a very weak cast.' – *Variety*

'The most astounding motion picture since motion pictures began! Man turned monster stalking show-world beauties! The ultimate dimension in terror!'
'You've never been scared until you've been scared in 3-D!'

House of Wax **

US   1953   88m   Warnercolor   3-D
Warner (Bryan Foy)
V*, L

Mutilated in a fire at his wax museum, a demented sculptor arranges a supply of dead bodies to be covered in wax for exhibition at his new showplace.

Spirited remake of *The Mystery of the Wax Museum* (qv); as a piece of screen narrative it leaves much to be desired, but the sudden shocks are well managed, perhaps because this is the first Grade-A 3-D film, packed with gimmicks irrelevant to the story and originally shown with stereophonic sound.

w Crane Wilbur   *d* André de Toth   *ph* Bert Glennon   *m* David Buttolph

Vincent Price (whose horror career began here), Carolyn Jones, Paul Picerni, Phyllis Kirk, Frank Lovejoy

† The director could not see the 3-D effect, being blind in one eye.

House of Whipcord *
GB   1974   101m   Eastmancolor
Miracle/Peter Walker

An elderly couple and their son, who run their own private penal system, sentence to death a French model on charges of immorality.

Low-budget psychological horror that stylishly achieves its object: to disturb.

w David McGillivray   story Peter Walker   d Peter Walker   ph Peter Jessop   m Stanley Myers   ad Mike Pickwode   ed Matt McCarthy

Barbara Markham, Patrick Barr, Ray Brooks, Anne Michelle, Penny Irving, Sheila Keith, Celia Imrie

'Shows that something worthwhile in the entertainment-horror market can be done for the tiny sum of £60,000.' – Derek Elley, Films and Filming

House of Women
US   1962   85m   bw
Warner

A pregnant woman is sent to prison for a robbery she didn't commit.

Loose remake of Caged, with very little sense or vigour.

w Crane Wilbur   d Walter Doniger

Shirley Knight, Andrew Duggan, Constance Ford, Barbara Nichols, Margaret Hayes

The House on Carroll Street *
US   1988   100m   colour
Rank/Orion (Peter Yates, Robert F. Colesberry)
V*, L

A journalist, forced out of her job in McCarthyite America, uncovers a right-wing political conspiracy.

Moderately effective thriller, in a style close to Hitchcock.

w Walter Bernstein   d Peter Yates   ph Michael Ballhaus   m Georges Delerue   pd Stuart Wurtzel   ed Ray Lovejoy

Kelly McGillis, Jeff Daniels, Mandy Patinkin, Christopher Rhode, Jessica Tandy, Jonathan Hogan

House on Haunted Hill
US   1958   75m   bw
Allied Artists/William Castle
V*, L

An old house which has seen several murders is the setting for a millionaire's party.

Gimmick ghost story with some (unexplained) gruesome moments; the most outlandish of its producer's cheapjack trick films (Thirteen Ghosts, The Tingler, Macabre, etc), it was originally billed as being in Emergo, which meant that at an appropriately horrific moment an illuminated skeleton on wires was suddenly trundled over the heads of the audience.

w Robb White   d William Castle   ph Carl Guthrie   m Von Dexter

Vincent Price, Richard Long, Carol Ohmart, Alan Marshal, Elisha Cook Jnr

The House on 92nd Street ***
US   1945   88m   bw
TCF (Louis de Rochemont)

During World War II in New York, the FBI routs Nazi spies after the atomic bomb formula.

Highly influential documentary-style 'now it can be told' spy drama, which borrowed the feel of its producer's March of Time series and applied them to a fairly true story set on genuine locations though with a modicum of fictional mystery and suspense.

Highly effective in its own right, it looked forward to The Naked City three years later; the later film unaccountably got most of the credit for taking Hollywood out into the open air.

w Barre Lyndon, Charles G. Booth, John Monks Jnr   d Henry Hathaway   ph Norbert Brodine   m David Buttolph

William Eythe, Lloyd Nolan, Signe Hasso, Leo G. Carroll, Gene Lockhart, Lydia St Clair, Harry Bellaver

'Recommended entertainment for those who believe that naïve Americans are no match for wily Europeans in the spy trade, and for those who just like their movies to move.' – Time

'Imagine an issue of The March of Time. The hard agglomeration of fact; the road drill style; the voice. Prolong it to four times its usual length, throw in a fictional climax, and there you have The House on 92nd Street.' – William Whitebait, New Statesman

AA: original story (Charles G. Booth)

The House on Telegraph Hill
US   1951   93m   bw
TCF (Robert Bassler)

A woman in a concentration camp assumes her dead friend's identity so that on release she can be sent to America; but murder threatens there.

Modernized amalgam of Gaslight and Suspicion, not as good as either, but the complexities of the story hold adequate interest.

w Elick Moll, Frank Partos   novel Dana Lyon   d Robert Wise   ph Lucien Ballard   m Sol Kaplan   ad Lyle Wheeler, John DeCuir

Richard Basehart, Valentina Cortesa, William Lundigan, Fay Baker, Gordon Gebert, Steve Geray

AAN: art direction

House Party
US   1990   104m   Metrocolor
Enterprise/Hudlin Brothers/New Line (Gerald Olsen)
V, V*, L, S

A teenager, whose parents are away, throws a party for his friends.

Low-budget youth movie, likeable enough but unlikely to rouse much enthusiasm on the adult side of the generation gap.

wd Reginald Hudlin   ph Peter Deming   m Marcus Miller   pd Bryan Jones   ed Earl Watson

Christopher Reid, Robin Harris, Christopher Martin, Martin Lawrence, Tisha Campbell, A. J. Johnson, Paul Anthony

House Party 2
US   1991   94m   DeLuxe
New Line (Doug McHenry, George Jackson)
V, V*, L, S

Two rappers leave high school and consider their future.

Dull sequel, as if no one was quite sure of what to do next.

w Rusty Cundieff, Daryl G. Nickens   d Doug McHenry, George Jackson   ph Francis Kenny   m Vassal Benford   pd Michelle Minch   ed Joel Goodman

Christopher Reid, Christopher Martin, Tisha Campbell, Iman, Martin Lawrence, D. Christopher Judge, Queen Latifah

'The crowd's the same, but the atmosphere's different in this disappointing followup.' – Variety

'Terror Waits For You In Every Room.'
The House that Dripped Blood *
GB   1970   102m   Eastmancolor
Amicus (Milton Subotsky)
V*

A Scotland Yard man investigating a disappearance is led to a house with a murderous history.

Quartet of stories in Dead of Night style, neatly made and generally pleasing despite a low level of originality in the writing.

w Robert Bloch   d Peter John Duffell   ph Robert Parslow   m Michael Dress

John Bennett, Christopher Lee, Peter Cushing, Denholm Elliott, Joanna Dunham, Nyree Dawn Porter, Jon Pertwee, Ingrid Pitt

Houseboat
US   1958   110m   Technicolor   Vistavision
Paramount/Scribe (Jack Rose)
V, V*, L

A widower with three children engages a maid who is really a socialite, and they all set up house on a boat.

Artificial sentimental comedy with A-1 credits but little style or bite.

w Melville Shavelson, Jack Rose   d Melville Shavelson   ph Ray June   m George Duning

Cary Grant, Sophia Loren, Martha Hyer, Eduardo Ciannelli, Harry Guardino

'The kind of picture to which you can take your stuffy maiden aunt, your wicked sophisticated uncle and your ten-year-old child, and they will all have a wonderful time.' – Ruth Waterbury, Los Angeles Examiner

AAN: script; song 'Almost In Your Arms' (m/ly Jay Livingston, Ray Evans)

The Housekeeper's Daughter *
US   1939   71m   bw
Hal Roach

A gangster's moll returns to mama for a visit and falls in love with the stuffy son of the household.

Zany crime farce which too often lets its zip fade, but atones in a crazy firework finale.

w Rian James, Gordon Douglas   novel Donald Henderson Clarke   d Hal Roach   ph Norbert Brodine   m Amedeo de Filippi

Joan Bennett, John Hubbard, Adolphe Menjou, William Gargan, George E. Stone, Peggy Wood, Donald Meek, Marc Lawrence, Lilian Bond, Victor Mature, Luis Alberni

'A smacko laugh generator due for profitable biz up and down the line.' – Variety

Housekeeping *
US   1987   115m   colour
Columbia (Robert F. Colesberry)

Two orphaned sisters are brought up by their wayward aunt.

In his first American feature, Forsyth's pawky humour is overlaid with a bleaker view and his characters seem more conventional and less well-observed.

wd Bill Forsyth   novel Marilynne Robinson   ph Michael Coulter   m Michael Gibbs   pd Adrienne Atkinson   ed Michael Ellis

Christine Lahti, Sara Walker, Andrea Burchill, Anne Pitoniak, Barbara Reese, Bill Smillie, Margo Pinvidic, Wayne Robson

'I wouldn't call it a great film, but it comes very close to being a perfect one in everything that it sets out to do.' – Jonathan Rosenbaum, Chicago Reader

Housemaster *
GB   1938   95m   bw
ABPC (Walter Mycroft)

A schoolmaster sides with his boys against the new headmaster's dictatorial methods.

Pleasing photographed play with all concerned in good form.

w Dudley Leslie, Elizabeth Meehan   play Bachelor Born by Ian Hay   d Herbert Brenon   ph Otto Kanturek   ad Cedric Dawe   ed Flora Newton

Otto Kruger, Diana Churchill, Phillips Holmes, Joyce Barbour, Kynaston Reeves, Rene Ray, Walter Hudd, John Wood, Cecil Parker, Michael Shepley, Jimmy Hanley

Housesitter

US   1992   102m   DeLuxe
UIP/Imagine/Universal (Brian Grazer)
V, V*, L

After a one-night stand with an architect, a waitress decides to move into his new house, claiming to be his wife.

A farcical comedy that is too leisurely to provoke laughter.

w Mark Stein, Brian Grazer   d Frank Oz   ph John A. Alonzo   m Miles Goodman   pd Ida Random   ed John Jympson

Steve Martin, Goldie Hawn, Dana Delany, Julie Harris, Donald Moffat, Peter MacNicol, Richard B. Shull, Laurel Cronin

'A tediously unfunny screwball comedy . . . a career misstep both for Steve Martin and Goldie Hawn.' – *Variety*

Housewife

US   1934   69m   bw
Warner (Robert Lord)

For an advertising copywriter, success almost brings divorce.

Modestly efficient romantic programmer of its day.

w Manuel Seff, Lillie Hayward   d Alfred E. Green   ph William Rees   m Leo. F. Forbstein

Bette Davis, George Brent, Ann Dvorak, John Halliday, Ruth Donnelly, Hobart Cavanaugh, Robert Barrat, Phil Regan

'The dramatic punches are not merely telegraphed, but radioed.' – *Frank S. Nugent*

The Houston Story

US   1956   80m   bw
Columbia (Sam Katzman)

An oil worker has a plan for stealing oil, and is employed by the syndicate.

Racketeering melodrama of the least interesting kind.

w James B. Gordon   d William Castle

Gene Barry, Barbara Hale, Edward Arnold, Paul Richards, Frank Jenks

How Do I Love Thee

US   1970   109m   Metrocolor
ABC (Robert Enders, Everett Freeman)

A philosophy professor recalls the odd career of his atheist father.

Curious comedy about an eccentric and his family relationships, a kind of *Cheaper by the Dozen* with religion added. Not on in 1970.

w Everett Freeman   novel *Let Me Count the Ways* by Peter de Vries   d Michael Gordon   ph Russell Metty   m Randy Sparks

Jackie Gleason, Maureen O'Hara, Shelley Winters, Rick Lenz, Rosemary Forsyth

'Nauseated embarrassment for participants and onlookers alike.' – *Judith Crist*

'Rich is their humor! Deep are their passions! Reckless are their lives! Mighty is their story!'
'"What are you? A man or a saint? I don't want him, I want you!" Her desire scorched both their lives with the vicious breath of scandal!'

How Green Was My Valley ***

US   1941   118m   bw
TCF (Darryl F. Zanuck)
V, V*, L, S

Memories of childhood in a Welsh mining village.

Prettified and unconvincing but dramatically very effective tearjerker in the style which lasted from Cukor's *David Copperfield* to *The Green Years*. High production values here add a touch of extra class, turning the result into a Hollywood milestone despite its intrinsic inadequacies.

w Philip Dunne   novel Richard Llewellyn   d John Ford   ph Arthur Miller   m Alfred Newman   ad Richard Day, Nathan Juran   ed James B. Clark

Walter Pidgeon, Maureen O'Hara, Roddy McDowall, Donald Crisp, Sara Allgood, Anna Lee, John Loder, Barry Fitzgerald, Patric Knowles, Morton Lowry, Arthur Shields, Frederic Worlock

'Perfection of cinematic narrative . . . pure visual action, pictures powerfully composed, dramatically photographed, smoothly and eloquently put together.' – *James Shelley Hamilton*

† The unseen narrator was Irving Pichel.

AA: best picture; John Ford; Arthur Miller; Donald Crisp; art direction

AAN: Philip Dunne; Alfred Newman; Sara Allgood; James B. Clark

How He Lied to Her Husband

GB   1930   33m   bw
BIP

An early film version of Shaw's playlet about a minor flirtation.

Of historical interest only.

w Frank Launder   play George Bernard Shaw   d Cecil Lewis   ph J. J. Cox   ad Gladys Calthrop   ed Sam Simmonds

Edmund Gwenn, Robert Harris, Vera Lennox

How I Got Into College

US   1989   89m   colour
TCF (Michael Shamberg)
V, V*, L

Dim student applies to go to the same difficult-to-enter college as the girl he loves.

Mildy amusing teenage comedy.

w Terrel Seltzer   d Savage Steve Holland   m Joseph Vitarelli   pd Ida Ransom   ed Sonya Sones Tramer, Kaja Fehr

Anthony Edwards, Corey Parker, Lara Flynn Boyle, Finn Carter, Charles Rocket, Christopher Rydell, Brian-Doyle Murray

How I Won the War

GB   1967   110m   Eastmancolor
UA/Petersham (Richard Lester)
V*, L

During World War II an earnest young man becomes an officer and survives many tribulations including the death of his comrades.

Appalling kaleidoscope of black comedy and the director's own brand of uncontrolled cinematic zaniness, with echoes of *Candide* and *Oh What a Lovely War!* Just the way to alienate a paying audience.

w Charles Wood   novel Patrick Ryan   d Richard Lester   ph David Watkin   m Ken Thorne

Michael Crawford, John Lennon, Roy Kinnear, Lee Montague, Jack McGowran, Michael Hordern, Jack Hedley, Karl Michael Vogler, Ronald Lacey, James Cossins, Alexander Knox

'Pretentious tomfoolery.' – *John Simon*

'One feels that Lester has bitten off more than he can chew . . . the ideas misfire, lost somewhere between the paper on which they were conceived and the celluloid on which they finally appear.' – *MFB*

How Sweet It Is *

US   1968   98m   Technicolor   Panavision
Warner/Cherokee/National General (Garry Marshall, Jerry Belson)
V*

Suspicious of their son's intentions towards his girlfriend on a European holiday, a middle-aged American couple decide to follow.

Good-looking, rather silly comedy, plain spoken in the modern manner but without much entertainment value except when farce gets the upper hand.

w Garry Marshall, Jerry Belson   novel *The Girl in the Turquoise Bikini* by Muriel Resnik   d Jerry Paris   ph Lucien Ballard   m Pat Williams

James Garner, Debbie Reynolds, Maurice Ronet, Paul Lynde, Marcel Dalio, Terry-Thomas, Donald Losby, Hilarie Thompson

'One of those slender marital farces in which the behaviour of the adults is consistently more juvenile than that of the teenagers.' – *MFB*

How the West Was Won *

US   1962   162m   Technicolor   Cinerama
MGM/Cinerama (Bernard Smith)
V, V*, L, S

Panoramic Western following the daughter of a pioneering family from youth (1830) to old age, with several half-relevant stories along the way.

Muddled spectacular with splendid set-pieces but abysmal dullness in between, especially if not seen in three-strip Cinerama (the Cinemascope prints are muddy and still show the dividing lines). An all-star fairground show of its time.

w James R. Webb   d Henry Hathaway (first half), John Ford (Civil War), George Marshall (train)   ph William Daniels, Milton Krasner, Charles Lang Jnr, Joseph LaShelle   m Alfred Newman   ad George W. Davis, William Ferrari, Addison Hehr

Debbie Reynolds, Carroll Baker, Lee J. Cobb, Henry Fonda, Carolyn Jones, Karl Malden, Gregory Peck, George Peppard, Robert Preston, James Stewart, Eli Wallach, John Wayne, Richard Widmark, Brigid Bazlen, Walter Brennan, David Brian, Andy Devine, Raymond Massey, Agnes Moorehead, Henry Morgan, Thelma Ritter, Russ Tamblyn, Spencer Tracy (narrator)

'That goddamned Cinerama . . . do you know a waist shot is as close as you could get with that thing?' – *Henry Hathaway*

AA: James R. Webb

AAN: best picture; photography; music

How to Be Very Very Popular

US   1955   89m   DeLuxe   Cinemascope
TCF (Nunnally Johnson)

Two belly dancers on the run from gangsters hide out in a co-ed college.

Wacky remake of *She Loves Me Not* (qv); tries hard for a vein of freewheeling lunacy but only occasionally achieves it. A few numbers might have helped.

wd Nunnally Johnson   ph Milton Krasner   m Cyril Mockridge

Betty Grable, Sheree North, *Charles Coburn*, Robert Cummings, Orson Bean, Fred Clark, Tommy Noonan

How to Beat the High Cost of Living

US   1980   110m   Movielab
Filmways

Three middle-class women take to robbery when they can't make the housekeeping balance.

Undercast, reprehensible and almost totally unfunny alleged comedy.

w Robert Kaufman   d Robert Scheerer

Susan Saint James, Jane Curtin, Jessica Lange, Richard Benjamin, Fred Willard, Eddie Albert

How to Commit Marriage

US   1969   98m   Technicolor
Cinerama/Naho (Bill Lawrence)
V*

A couple decide to divorce, with repercussions on their family and in-laws.

Tiresome generation-gap comedy.

w Ben Starr, Michael Kanin   d Norman Panama   ph Charles Lang   m Joseph J. Lilley

Bob Hope, Jackie Gleason, Jane Wyman, Leslie Nielsen, Maureen Arthur, Paul Stewart, Tina Louise

How to Get Ahead in Advertising

GB   1989   94m   colour
Virgin/HandMade Films (David Wimbury)
V, V*, L, S

An advertising man, in revolt against salesmanship, grows a boil that turns into an alternative head.

Unsuccessful diatribe on the consumer society.

wd Bruce Robinson   ph Peter Hannan   m David Dundas, Rick Wentworth   pd Michael Pickwoad   ed Alan Strachan

Richard E. Grant, Rachel Ward, Richard Wilson, Jacqueline Tong, John Shrapnel, Susan Wooldridge, Mick Ford, Jacqueline Pearce, Roddy Maude-Roxby

How to Make It: see Target Harry

How to Marry a Millionaire **

US   1953   96m   Technicolor   Cinemascope
TCF (Nunnally Johnson)
V, V*, L

Three girls rent an expensive New York apartment and set out to trap millionaires.

Cinemascope's first attempt at modern comedy was not quite as disastrous as might have been expected, largely because of the expensiveness of everything and the several stars still brightly twinkling, but the handling of this variation on the old Golddiggers theme, while entirely amiable, is dramatically very slack.

w Nunnally Johnson   d Jean Negulesco   ph Joe MacDonald   md Alfred Newman   m Cyril Mockridge

Lauren Bacall, Marilyn Monroe, Betty Grable, William Powell, Cameron Mitchell, David Wayne, Rory Calhoun, Alex D'Arcy, Fred Clark

'Not only educational, but great fun.' – Star

† The film has an eight-minute pre-credits concert sequence, which is pretty unnerving when it unspools on TV.

'The last word in do-it-yourself!'

How to Murder a Rich Uncle

GB   1957   80m   bw   Cinemascope
Columbia/Warwick (Ronald Kinnoch)

An impoverished nobleman decides to murder his rich old uncle.

Feebly-handled black comedy which does not come off at all despite a highly talented cast.

w John Paxton   play Il Faut Tuer Julie by Didier Daix   d Nigel Patrick   ph Ted Moore

Nigel Patrick, Charles Coburn, Katie Johnson, Wendy Hiller, Anthony Newley, Athene Seyler, Michael Caine, Noel Hood, Kenneth Fortescue

How to Murder Your Wife *

US   1964   118m   Technicolor
UA/Murder Inc (George Axelrod)
V, V*, L

A strip cartoonist tests out his violent scenes in real life; when his wife disappears he finds himself accused of murder.

Amusing preliminaries give way to dreary plot complications and an overlong courtroom scene. Leave after the first hour.

w George Axelrod   d Richard Quine   ph Harry Stradling   m Neal Hefti   pd Richard Sylbert

Jack Lemmon, Virna Lisi, Terry-Thomas, Eddie Mayehoff, Sidney Blackmer, Claire Trevor

How to Rob a Bank: see A Nice Little Bank That Should Be Robbed

How to Save a Marriage and Ruin Your Life

US   1968   102m   Technicolor   Panavision
Columbia/Nob Hill (Stanley Shapiro)

An attorney takes it upon himself to convince his friend of the infidelity of the friend's mistress . . .

Tedious sex antics without any sex; a few smiles are not enough to endear it.

w Stanley Shapiro, Nate Monaster   d Fielder Cook   ph Lee Garmes   m Michel Legrand

Dean Martin, Eli Wallach, Stella Stevens, Anne Jackson, Betty Field, Jack Albertson, Katharine Bard

'Another variation on Hollywood's patent version of the Restoration comedy, which as usual abandons the lustiness of its 17th-century prototype in favour of guilt-ridden lechery and a fundamental respect for the married state.' – MFB

How to Steal a Diamond in Four Uneasy Lessons: see The Hot Rock

How to Steal a Million *

US   1966   127m   DeLuxe   Panavision
TCF/World Wide (Fred Kohlmar)
V*

The daughter of an art forger mistakenly involves a private detective in a robbery.

High-class but rather boring romantic comedy; the credits promise much but interest wanes quickly owing to uncertain handling.

w Harry Kurnitz   d William Wyler   ph Charles Lang   m Johnny Williams

Audrey Hepburn, Peter O'Toole, Charles Boyer, Hugh Griffith, Eli Wallach, Fernand Gravet, Marcel Dalio

'Terribly wordy and slow . . . Wyler hasn't got the touch nowadays.' – Sight and Sound

'The picture isn't offensive, and it's handsome enough, but it's just blah.' – Pauline Kael, New Yorker

How to Steal the World

US   1968   90m   Metrocolor
MGM/Arena (Anthony Spinner)

A renegade American agent sets out to end war by kidnapping six leading scientists to create a special gas that will allow him to control the minds of everyone else.

Glossily vacuous spy caper, rarely rising above an atmosphere of genial stupidity amid mass slaughter.

w Norman Hudis   d Sutton Roley   ph Robert B. Hauser   m Richard Shores   ad George W. Davis, James W. Sullivan   ed Joseph Dervin, Harry Knapp

Robert Vaughn, David McCallum, Barry Sullivan, Eleanor Parker, Leslie Nielsen, Tony Bill, Mark Richman, Daniel O'Herlihy, Leo G. Carroll

The film was edited from an episode from the television series The Man from U.N.C.L.E. Its scriptwriter is better known for having written the first six Carry On movies.

How to Succeed in Business without Really Trying **

US   1967   121m   DeLuxe   Panavision
UA/Mirisch (David Swift)
V*, L

A window cleaner cajoles his way to the top of a New York company.

Cinematically uninventive but otherwise brisk and glowing adaptation of a sharp, slick Broadway musical.

w David Swift   musical book Abe Burrows, Jack Weinstock, Willie Gilbert   book Shepherd Mead   d David Swift   ph Burnett Guffey   m/ly Frank Loesser   ch Dale Moreda after Bob Fosse

Robert Morse, Rudy Vallee, Michele Lee, Anthony Teague, Maureen Arthur, Murray Matheson

'Shows how taste and talent can succeed in bringing a stage musical to the screen with its virtues intact.' – John Cutts

Howard, a New Breed of Hero: see Howard the Duck

Howard the Duck

US   1986   111m   DeLuxe
Universal/Gloria Katz/George Lucas
V, V*, L
GB title: Howard, a New Breed of Hero

A duck from outer space comes to Earth and has various uncomfortable adventures.

Toned down from an adult comic strip, this peculiar film has nowhere to go because it's too sexy for kids and too stupid for adults.

w Willard Huyck, Gloria Katz from Steve Gerber's character   d Willard Huyck   ph Richard H. Kline   m John Barry   pd Peter Jamison

Lea Thompson, Jeffrey Jones, Paul Guilfoyle

Howards End ***

GB   1992   140m   Technicolor   Super35   Widescreen
Merchant Ivory/Film Four (Ismail Merchant)
V, V*, L, S

The fortunes of two middle-class families overlap and interlock.

The best of the adaptations of Forster's novels, in which the nostalgia is undercut by an examination of the moral bankruptcy of the ruling class.

w Ruth Prawer Jhabvala   novel E. M. Forster   d James Ivory   ph Tony Pierce-Roberts   m Richard Robbins   pd Luciana Arrighi   ed Andrew Marcus

Anthony Hopkins, Vanessa Redgrave, Helena Bonham Carter, Emma Thompson, James Wilby, Sam West, Jemma Redgrave, Nicola Duffet, Prunella Scales, Simon Callow

'A most compelling drama, perhaps the best film made during the 30-year partnership of Ismail Merchant and James Ivory.' – Variety

'A handsome and intelligent piece of work: a faithful, well-paced, and carefully crafted dramatization of a very good story.' – Terrence Rafferty, New Yorker

AA: Emma Thompson; Ruth Prawer Jhabvala; Luciana Arrighi

AAN: Best picture; James Ivory; Vanessa Redgrave; Tony Pierce-Roberts; Richard Robbins; Sheena Napier (costume design)

The Howards of Virginia

US   1940   117m   bw
Columbia (Frank Lloyd)
V, V*
GB title: The Tree of Liberty

A Virginian surveyor finds himself involved in the Revolutionary War.

Historical cavalcade in which central miscasting seems to cast a shadow of artifice over the whole. Interesting but seldom stimulating.

w Sidney Buchman   novel The Tree of Liberty by Elizabeth Page   d Frank Lloyd   ph Bert Glennon   m Richard Hageman

Cary Grant, Martha Scott, Cedric Hardwicke, Alan Marshal, Richard Carlson, Paul Kelly, Irving Bacon, Elizabeth Risdon

AAN: Richard Hageman

'Imagine your worst fear a reality!'
The Howling *
US   1980   90m   CFI Color
Avco Embassy/International Film Investors/Wescom (Ron Bottin)
V, V*, L

A lady newscaster discovers that the medical retreat at which she stays to recover from a nervous breakdown is likely to give her another.

A plethora of werewolves and a glut of in-jokes pale beside a gallery of convincing and horrifying special effects.

w John Sayles, Terence H. Winkless novel Gary Brandner d Joe Dante ph John Hora m Pino Donaggio make-up Rick Baker

Dee Wallace, Patrick MacNee, Dennis Dugan, Christopher Stone, Kevin McCarthy, John Carradine, Slim Pickens

† Some of the character names: George Waggner, R. William Neill, Sam Newfield, Fred Francis, Terry Fisher, Erle Kenton, Charlie Barton, Lew Landers . . .

Howling II . . . Your Sister Is a Werewolf
US   1985   90m   colour
Thorn-EMI /Granite/Hemdale (Steven Lane)
V, V*, L

An expert goes to Transylvania to track down the werewolf queen.

Thin attempt at comedy-horror, which barely got released.

w Robert Sarno, Gary Brandner d Philippe Mora

Christopher Lee, Annie McEnroe, Reb Brown, Ferdy Mayne

† The film, which was shot in Czechoslovakia, has no relation whatsoever to The Howling.

The Howling III
Australia   1987   94m   colour
Baccanial (Charles Waterstreet, Philippe Mora)
V, V*, L

A mad scientist goes in search of marsupial werewolves, which resemble fierce koala bears.

Bizarre horror spoof that somehow manages to incorporate the drag act of Barry Humphries as Australian super-housewife Dame Edna Everage – the result is below average.

wd Philippe Mora novel Gary Brandner ph Louis Irving m Allan Zavod pd Ross Major sp Bob McCarron ed Lee Smith

Barry Otto, Imogen Annesley, Dasha Blahova, Max Fairchild, Ralph Cotterill, Barry Humphries, Michael Pate, Frank Thring

Howling IV: The Original Nightmare
GB   1988   92m   colour
IVE (Harry Alan Towers)
V, V*, L

A best-selling author has visions of a werewolf and goes to an isolated cottage for a rest cure.

Like the rest of this series, this movie bears little resemblance to its predecessors, other than in its low-budget mediocrity.

w Clive Turner, Freddie Rowe d John Hough ph Godfrey Godar m David George, Barrie Guard sp Steve Johnson ed Claudia Finkle, Malcolm Burns-Errington

Romy Windsor, Michael T. Weiss, Anthony Hamilton, Suzanne Severeid, Lamya Derval, Norman Anstey, Kate Edwards, Clive Turner

'Poor horror fare.' – Films and Filming

Howling V: The Rebirth
US   1989   99m   colour
Allied Vision (Clive Turner)
V, V*, L

A group of tourists are invited to spend a weekend in an ancient castle in Budapest – and discover that one of them is a werewolf.

Dismal horror that attempts to take the myth more seriously than other films in the series, but succeeds only in being a boring variation on Agatha Christie's Ten Little Indians.

w Clive Turner, Freddie Rowe novel The Howling 1—3 by Gary Brandner d Neal Sundstrom ph Arledge Armenaki m The Factory

Ben Cole, William Shockley, Mark Siversen, Philip Davis, Elizabeth She, Victoria Catlin, Stephanie Faulkner, Mary Stavin, Clive Turner

Huang Tudi: see Yellow Earth

Huckleberry Finn
US   1931   71m   bw
Paramount

The river adventures of Mark Twain's scapegrace hero.

Adequate early talkie family film.

w Grover Jones, William Slavens McNutt d Norman Taurog ph David Abel

Jackie Coogan, Junior Durkin, Mitzi Green, Jackie Searl, Eugene Pallette

Huckleberry Finn **
US   1939   90m   bw
MGM (Joseph L. Mankiewicz)
V*

Solidly competent remake with excellent production values and several entertaining sequences.

w Hugo Butler d Richard Thorpe ph John Seitz m Franz Waxman

Mickey Rooney, Walter Connolly, William Frawley, Rex Ingram

Huckleberry Finn *
US   1960   107m   Metrocolor   Cinemascope
MGM (Samuel Goldwyn Jnr)
aka: The Adventures of Huckleberry Finn

Another patchy remake.

w James Lee d Michael Curtiz ph Ted McCord m Jerome Moross

Eddie Hodges, Tony Randall, Archie Moore, Neville Brand, Judy Canova, Buster Keaton, Andy Devine

Huckleberry Finn
US   1974   118m   DeLuxe   Panavision
UA/Apjac/Readers Digest (Robert Greenhut)
V*

Ambitious but lustreless version of the famous story, with songs.

w/m/ly Richard M. Sherman, Robert B. Sherman d J. Lee-Thompson ph Laszlo Kovacs pd Philip Jeffries

Jeff East, Paul Winfield, David Wayne, Harvey Korman, Arthur O'Connell, Gary Merrill, Natalie Trundy

'It expires in a morass of treacle.' – Tom Milne

'It transforms a great work of fiction into something bland, boring and tasteless.' – Michael Billington, Illustrated London News

The Hucksters **
US   1947   115m   bw
MGM (Arthur Hornblow Jnr)
V*, L

Back from the war, an advertising executive finds it difficult to put up with his clients' tantrums.

Good topical entertainment which still entertains and gives a good impression of its period.

w Luther Davis novel Frederic Wakeman d Jack Conway ph Harold Rosson m Lennie Hayton

Clark Gable, Deborah Kerr, Ava Gardner, Sidney Greenstreet, Adolphe Menjou, Keenan Wynn, Edward Arnold, Aubrey Mather

'A good picture, quick and to the point.' – Photoplay

Hud ****
US   1963   112m   bw   Panavision
Paramount/Salem/Dover (Martin Ritt, Irving Ravetch)
V*, L

Life is hard on a Texas ranch, and the veteran owner is not helped by his sexually arrogant ne'er-do-well son, who is a bad influence on the household.

Superbly set in an arid landscape, this incisive character drama is extremely well directed and acted.

w Irving Ravetch, Harriet Frank novel Horseman Pass By by Larry McMurtry d Martin Ritt ph James Wong Howe m Elmer Bernstein

Paul Newman, Patricia Neal, Melvyn Douglas, Brandon de Wilde

'So uncompromising in its portrait of an amoral man and his impact upon three people that I am tempted to reach for that dangerous adjective "unique".' – Judith Crist

AA: James Wong Howe; Patricia Neal; Melvyn Douglas

AAN: script; Martin Ritt; Paul Newman

Huddle
US   1932   104m   bw
MGM
GB title: The Impossible Lover

A steel worker's son makes good at Harvard, and wants to marry out of his class.

Would-be serious class drama which fell over its own feet.

w Robert Johnson, C. Gardner Sullivan, Arthur Hyman, Walton Smith d Sam Wood

Ramon Novarro, Madge Evans, Una Merkel, Conrad Nagel, Arthur Byron, Cliff Edwards

'Football film doing much to defeat its own purpose by extreme length . . . the Metro foreign production end is substituting soccer for the football portions for European screenings.' – Variety

'For the world's greatest cat burglar nine lives may just not be enough . . .'
Hudson Hawk
US   1991   100m   Technicolor
Columbia TriStar/Silver Pictures/Ace Bone (Joel Silver)
V, V*, L, S

A cat burglar is hired to steal from the Vatican an alchemical formula for turning lead into gold.

Direly unsuccessful attempt at a comedy thriller that was a box-office flop.

w Steven E. de Souza, Daniel Waters story Bruce Willis, Robert Kraft d Michael Lehmann ph Dante Spinotti m Michael Kamen, Robert Kraft pd Jack DeGovia ed Chris Lebenzon, Michael Tronick

Bruce Willis, Danny Aiello, Andie MacDowell, James Coburn, Richard E. Grant, Sandra Bernhard, Donald Burton, Don Harvey, David Caruso

'Ever wondered what a Three Stooges short would look like with a $40 million budget? Then meet Hudson Hawk, a relentlessly annoying clay duck that crash-lands in a sea of wretched excess and silliness.' – Variety

'Its utter failure can only be explained by some form of madness having overcome the people involved in its making.' – Philip French, Observer

Hudson's Bay **
US   1940   95m   bw
TCF (Kenneth MacGowan)

Pierre Radisson, a French Canadian trapper, opens up
millions of acres of northern wilderness for England.

Well-made historical saga with good production and
performances.

w Lamar Trotti   *d* Irving Pichel   *ph* Peverell Marley,
George Barnes   *m* Alfred Newman   *ad* Richard
Day, Wiard B. Ihnen

Paul Muni, Laird Cregar, Gene Tierney, John Sutton,
Virginia Field, Vincent Price (as King Charles II),
Nigel Bruce, Morton Lowry, Robert Greig, Frederic
Worlock, Montagu Love

Hue and Cry ***
GB   1946   82m   bw
Ealing (Michael Balcon)
V, V*

East End boys discover that their favourite boys'
paper is being used by crooks to pass information.

The first 'Ealing comedy' uses vivid London locations
as background for a sturdy comic plot with a climax in
which the criminals are rounded up by thousands of
boys swarming over dockland.

w T. E. B. Clarke   *d* Charles Crichton   *ph* Douglas
Slocombe, John Seaholme   *m* Georges Auric

Alastair Sim, Jack Warner, Harry Fowler, Valerie
White, Frederick Piper

'Refreshing, bloodtingling and disarming.' – *Richard
Winnington*

Hugo the Hippo
US   1975   78m   colour
Brut (Robert Halmi)
V*

An independently-minded hippo combats a Zanzibar
magician.

Uninventive cartoon feature, endearing neither in
characterization nor in draughtsmanship.

w Thomas Baum   *d* William Feigenbaum   *md* Bert
Keyes

voices of Burl Ives, Marie Osmond, Jimmy Osmond,
Robert Morley, Paul Lynde

Hugs and Kisses *
Sweden   1966   96m   bw
Sandrews (Göran Lindgren)
original title: *Puss och Kram*

A destitute bohemian takes over the house and the
wife of the old executive friend who shelters him out
of pity.

Rather like a comedy version of the Dirk Stroeve
section of *The Moon and Sixpence*, this sophisticated film
came under censorship fire for depicting the first full
frontal female. *wd* Jonas Cornell   *ph* Lars
Swanberg   *m* Bengt Ernryd

Sven-Bertil Taube, Agneta Ekmanner, Hakan Serner

'The brilliance of the film lies in the way humour and
sadness are kept in perfect equilibrium.' – *MFB*

Huis Clos *
France   1954   99m   bw
Films Marceau

Two women and a man die, go to hell, and are locked
up for ever in an elegant room.

Rather flat intellectual fantasy from a play which
made great waves when first performed.

w Pierre Laroche   *play* Jean-Paul Sartre
d Jacqueline Audry   *ph* Robert Juillard   *m* Joseph
Kosma

Arletty, Frank Villard, Gaby Sylvia

'Without the ecstasy, terror and poetic imagination of
a Cocteau, the subject becomes a fatally stationary
one.' – *Peter John Dyer, MFB*

Huk!
US   1956   83m   Eastmancolor
UA (Collier Young)

In 1951, an American fights Philippine guerrillas who
murdered his father.

Crude action melodrama which served a purpose.

w Stirling Silliphant   *novel* Stirling Silliphant
d John Barnwell

George Montgomery, Mona Freeman, John Baer,
James Bell

Hullabaloo
US   1940   77m   bw
MGM (Louis K. Sidney)

A veteran actor goes into radio and causes a furore
with a broadcast about men from Mars.

Slim framework for a variety show encasing some
young MGM talents.

w Nat Perrin   *d* Edwin L. Marin

Frank Morgan, Virginia Grey, Dan Dailey Jnr, Billie
Burke, Nydia Westman, Donald Meek, Reginald
Owen, Leni Lynn, Virginia O'Brien, Sara Haden

The Human Beast: see *La Bête Humaine*

The Human Comedy *
US   1943   117m   bw
MGM (Clarence Brown)
V*, L

In a small town during the war, a telegram boy brings
tragedy to others and is touched by it himself.

Gooey, sentimental morale booster in the best MGM
tradition, a variant on the Hardy family series but
with all the pretensions of its author.

w Howard Estabrook   *novel* William Saroyan
d Clarence Brown   *ph* Harry Stradling   *m* Herbert
Stothart

Mickey Rooney, Frank Morgan, James Craig, Marsha
Hunt, Jackie Jenkins, Fay Bainter, Ray Collins, Van
Johnson, Donna Reed

Opening narration by Ray Collins: 'I am Matthew
Macauley. I have been dead for two years. So much of
me is still living that I know now the end is only the
beginning. As I look down on my homeland of Ithaca,
California, with its cactus, vineyards and orchards, I
see that so much of me is still living there – in the
places I've been, in the fields and streets and church
and most of all in my home, where my hopes, my
dreams, my ambitions still live in the daily life of my
loved ones.'

'The dignity and simplicity of the ideas shade off into
cheap pretentiousness.' – *Bosley Crowther*

'The best one can say of it . . . is that it tries on the
whole to be "faithful" to Saroyan; not invariably a
good idea.' – *James Agee*

'The Saroyan touch leaves nothing ordinary: the film
is electric with the joy of life.' – *Time*

AA: original story

AAN: best picture; Clarence Brown; Harry Stradling;
Mickey Rooney

Human Desire *
US   1954   90m   bw
Columbia (Lewis J. Rachmil)
V*

A jealous railway official forces his wife to help him
murder her suspected lover.

Drab and unattractive remake of *La Bête Humaine*.

w Alfred Hayes   *d* Fritz Lang   *ph* Burnett Guffey
m Daniele Amfitheatrof

Gloria Grahame, Glenn Ford, Broderick Crawford,
Edgar Buchanan

The Human Factor
GB   1975   95m   Technicolor
Eton (Terry Lens)
V*

The family of a NATO war planner in Italy is
slaughtered by terrorists.

Violent revenge drama, of little interest.

w Tom Hunter, Peter Powell   *d* Edward Dmytryk

George Kennedy, John Mills, Raf Vallone, Arthur
Franz, Rita Tushingham, Frank Avianca, Barry
Sullivan

The Human Factor
GB   1979   114m   Technicolor   Panavision
Rank/Wheel/Sigma/Otto Preminger

An innocent man is suspected of being the 'mole' in
the Foreign Office.

Quietly sardonic scenes of diplomatic chess are
played far too broadly and literally in this ill-advised
and poorly executed foray into the serious spy scene,
which despite its stars becomes merely risible before
the end.

w Tom Stoppard   *novel* Graham Greene   *d* Otto
Preminger   *ph* Mike Malloy   *m* Richard and Gary
Logan

Nicol Williamson, Richard Attenborough, Derek
Jacobi, Robert Morley, John Gielgud, Ann Todd,
Richard Vernon, Joop Doderer, Iman

'Unfortunately, Preminger stages it all as if he was just
trying to get all the actors through their line readings
in under two hours, allowing no breathing room or
time for character nuance in a tale which resolutely
calls for quiet moments.' – *Variety*

The Human Jungle
US   1954   82m   bw
Allied Artists

A new police captain cleans up a gangster-ridden
slum district.

Adequate low-life actioner of the kind later taken
over by TV.

w William Sackheim, Daniel Fuchs   *d* Joseph M.
Newman

Gary Merrill, Jan Sterling, Paula Raymond, Emile
Meyer, Regis Toomey, Lamont Johnson, Chuck
Connors

The Human Monster: see *Dark Eyes of London*

The Human Side
US   1934   60m   bw
Universal

A philandering theatrical producer returns to his
family.

Pleasant light comedy, instantly forgettable.

w Frank Craven, Ernest Pascal   *play* Christine Ames
d Eddie Buzzell

Adolphe Menjou, Doris Kenyon, Charlotte Henry,
Dickie Moore, Reginald Owen, Joseph Cawthorn

'Homely, wholesome domestic comedy that should
find beaucoup favour with the family trade.' – *Variety*

Humanoids from the Deep
US   1980   81m   Metrocolor
New World (Martin B. Cohen)
V*
GB title: *Monster*

Gruesome amphibious creatures rise from the ocean to
stalk and destroy the most nubile women in sight.

Lurid, nonsensical but very violent horror flick, with much rape and nudity; like a Corman quickie of the fifties but with added gore.

w Frederick James d Barbara Peeters (sic)
ph Daniele Lacambre m James Horner
costumes Rob Bottin

Vic Morrow, Doug McClure, Ann Turkel

Humoresque **
US 1946 125m bw
Warner (Jerry Wald)
V*, L

An ambitious violinist gets emotionally involved with his wealthy patroness.

Lush soaper about suffering in high society, complete with tragic end and lashings of classical music (Isaac Stern on the sound track).

w Clifford Odets, Zachary Gold novel Fannie Hurst
d Jean Negulesco ph Ernest Haller md Franz
Waxman

Joan Crawford, John Garfield, Oscar Levant, J. Carrol Naish, Joan Chandler, Tom D'Andrea, Craig Stevens, Ruth Nelson

'This brilliantly executed but less well-conceived picture functions like a beautifully made piece of machinery, fascinating to watch in action, powerful, but cold and insensitive.' – Jympson Harman, London Evening News

AAN: Franz Waxman

The Hunchback of Notre Dame **
US 1923 120m approx (24 fps) bw silent
Universal
V, V*, L

The deformed Notre Dame bellringer rescues a gypsy girl from the evil intentions of her guardian.

Victorian gothic version with a riveting star performance.

w Percy Poore Sheehan, Edward T. Lowe Jnr
novel Notre Dame de Paris by Victor Hugo d Wallace
Worsley ph Robert S. Newhard, Tony Kornman

Lon Chaney, Patsy Ruth Miller, Norman Kerry, Ernest Torrence, Gladys Brockwell, Kate Lester, Brandon Hurst, Tully Marshall

The Hunchback of Notre Dame ****
US 1939 117m bw
RKO (Pandro S. Berman)
V, V*, L

This superb remake is one of the best examples of Hollywood expertise at work: art direction, set construction, costumes, camera, lighting and above all direction brilliantly support an irresistible story and bravura acting.

w Sonya Levien, Bruno Frank d William Dieterle
ph Joseph H. August m Alfred Newman ad Van Nest
Polglase

Charles Laughton, Cedric Hardwicke, Maureen O'Hara, Edmond O'Brien, Thomas Mitchell, Harry Davenport, Walter Hampden, Alan Marshal, George Zucco, Katherine Alexander, Fritz Leiber, Rod la Rocque

'A super thriller-chiller. Will roll up healthy grosses at the ticket windows.' – Variety

'Has seldom been bettered as an evocation of medieval life.' – John Baxter, 1968

'It exceeds in sheer magnificence any similar film in history. Sets are vast and rich in detail, crowds are immense, and camera uses of both are versatile, varied and veracious.' – Motion Picture Herald

† Other versions: Esmeralda (1906, French); Notre Dame de Paris (1911, French); The Darling of Paris (1917, US, with Theda Bara); and see above and below.

AAN: Alfred Newman

The Hunchback of Notre Dame
France/Italy 1956 107m Eastmancolor
Cinemascope
Paris Films/Panitalia (Robert and Raymond Hakim)
original title: Notre Dame de Paris

Crude international rehash with nothing to commend it, though the script before dubbing may have been interesting.

w Jacques Prévert, Jean Aurenche d Jean Delannoy
ph Michel Kelber m Georges Auric

Anthony Quinn, Gina Lollobrigida, Jean Danet, Alain Cuny, Robert Hirsch

The Hundred Pound Window
GB 1943 84m bw
Warner (Max Milder)

A racecourse clerk becomes involved with gamblers who bribe him to rig the totalizator, but he finally exposes them.

Routine programmer notable only for giving a leading role to an old character actor.

w Abem Finkel, Brock Williams, Rodney Ackland
d Brian Desmond Hurst ph Otto Heller m Hans
May

Frederick Leister, Mary Clare, Anne Crawford, Richard Attenborough, David Farrar, Niall MacGinnis, David Hutcheson

'The Hunger is a mood, a look, an ambience created by Tony Scott. It is the lighting of Stephen Goldblatt, it is the production design of Brian Morris, it is the clothes created by Milena Canonero.'

The Hunger
US 1983 99m Metrocolor Panavision
MGM-UA/Richard Shepherd
V, V*, L, S

A couple of ageless vampires are desperate for blood.

Absurd attempt to update Dracula with lashings of sex, rock music and flashy photography. An ordeal.

w Ivan Davis, Michael Thomas novel Whitley
Strieber d Tony Scott ph Stephen Goldblatt, Tom
Mangravite m Michael Rubini, Denny Jaeger
pd Brian Morris

Catherine Deneuve, Susan Sarandon, David Bowie, Cliff de Young

'One of the most incoherent and foolish pictures of recent months.' – Observer

Hungry for Love: see Adua e le Compagne

Hungry Hill
GB 1946 92m bw
GFD/Two Cities (William Sistrom)

An Irish family feud spans three generations.

Rather uninteresting costume melodrama.

w Daphne du Maurier, Terence Young, Francis
Crowdy d Brian Desmond Hurst ph Desmond
Dickinson m John Greenwood

Margaret Lockwood, Dennis Price, Cecil Parker, Michael Denison, F. J. McCormick, Dermot Walsh, Jean Simmons, Eileen Herlie, Eileen Crowe, Barbara Waring, Eileen Herlie

'It has got everything – costume, Irish brogues, Irish scenery, family feuds, family curses, love, hate, murder, fights, drink and drugs – everything, in fact, but life, movement and conviction, everything but the power to hold your interest.' – Richard Winnington, News Chronicle

'Deadly. Silent. Stolen.'
The Hunt for Red October **
US 1990 137m Technicolor Panavision
Paramount/Mace Neufeld/Jerry Sherlock
V, V (W), V*, L, CD, S

The Soviet commander of a top-secret submarine attempts to defect to the West in his vessel.

An intermittently suspenseful thriller, stronger on hardware than human interest.

w Larry Ferguson, Donald Stewart novel Tom
Clancy d John McTiernan ph Jan de Bont
m Basil Poledouris pd Terence Marsh ad Dianne
Wager sp Industrial Light & Magic ed Dennis
Virkler, John Wright

Sean Connery, Alec Baldwin, Scott Glenn, Sam Neill, James Earl Jones, Joss Ackland, Richard Jordan, Peter Firth, Tim Curry

'A terrific adventure yarn, excitingly filmed.' – Variety

AA: best sound effects editing

AAN: best film editing; best sound

Hunted *
GB 1952 84m bw
GFD/Independent Artists (Julian Wintle)
US title: The Stranger in Between

A runaway boy joins forces with a runaway murderer, and the latter sacrifices himself for the boy's safety.

Predictable pattern melodrama, nicely made and acted.

w Jack Whittingham d Charles Crichton ph Eric
Cross m Hubert Clifford

Dirk Bogarde, Jon Whiteley, Kay Walsh, Elizabeth Sellars, Frederick Piper, Geoffrey Keen, Julian Somers

Hunted Men *
US 1938 67m bw
Paramount

A killer on the run moves into a private home and is outwitted by the head of the house.

Competent second feature which sticks in the memory.

w Horace McCoy, William R. Lipman d Louis King
ph Victor Milner

Lloyd Nolan, Lynne Overman, Mary Carlisle, J. Carrol Naish, Anthony Quinn, Dorothy Peterson

The Hunter
US 1980 117m Metrocolor
Paramount/Rastar/Mort Engelberg
V*, L

Episodes in the violent career of an urban bounty hunter.

The action scenes salvage a mysteriously banal screenplay full of continuity lapses and unexplained characters.

w Ted Leighton, Peter Hyams book Christopher
Keane, and the life of Ralph Thorson d Buzz Kulik
ph Fred J. Koenekamp m Michel Legrand

Steve McQueen (his last film), Eli Wallach, Kathryn Harrold, LeVar Burton, Ben Johnson

'The final impression is of an extended TV pilot for yet another police-boosting serial with more action than sense.' – Sunday Times

The Hunters
US 1958 108m DeLuxe Cinemascope
TCF (Dick Powell)
V*

A fearless American pilot is sent to Korea on a special mission.

Standard war thriller, good to look at when airborne but pretty boring on the ground; propaganda element very strong.

w Wendell Mayes novel James Salter d Dick
Powell ph Charles G. Clarke, Tom Tutwiler
m Paul Sawtell

Robert Mitchum, Robert Wagner, Richard Egan, May Britt

The Hunting Party

US 1971 108m DeLuxe
UA/Brighton/Levy-Gardner-Levy

A sadistic Texas baron sets out to shoot one by one the outlaws who have kidnapped his wife.

Crude, brutish and repellent melodrama: the epitome of permissiveness, replete with gore, rape and sadism.

w William Norton, Gilbert Alexander, Lou Morheim d Don Medford ph Cecilio Paniagua m Riz Ortolani

Gene Hackman, Candice Bergen, Oliver Reed

Las Hurdes: see Land Without Bread

'Through miles of raging ocean he defied man's law!'
The Hurricane **

US 1937 110m bw
Samuel Goldwyn (Merritt Hulburd)
V*, L

The simple life on a South Pacific island is disrupted, not only by a vindictive governor but by a typhoon.

Tolerable island melodrama with a spectacular climax and a generally good cast.

w Dudley Nichols, Oliver H. P. Garrett novel Charles Nordhoff, James Norman Hall d John Ford, Stuart Heisler ph Bert Glennon m Alfred Newman

Dorothy Lamour, Jon Hall, C. Aubrey Smith, Mary Astor, Raymond Massey, Thomas Mitchell, John Carradine, Jerome Cowan

'A big money picture . . . a production masterpiece.' – Variety

'There's a hurricane all right. It's magnificent . . . Few people will bother to remember what the rest of the film is about. It goes with the wind.' – C. A. Lejeune

† Remade in 1979.

AAN: Alfred Newman; Thomas Mitchell

Hurricane

US 1979 120m Technicolor Todd-AO 70
Dino de Laurentiis/Famous Films (Lorenzo Semple Jnr)
V*

A remake of the 1937 film, lacking the style, the innocence, and even the technical splendour.

w Lorenzo Semple Jnr d Jan Troell ph Sven Nykvist m Nino Rota pd Danilo Donati

Jason Robards, Mia Farrow, Trevor Howard, Max von Sydow, Dayton Ka'ne, Timothy Bottoms, James Keach

Hurricane Island

US 1951 71m Supercinecolor
Sam Katzman/Columbia

Spaniards colonizing Florida are beset by evil spirits.

Saturday matinee hokum in poor colour.

w David Matthews d Lew Landers

Jon Hall, Edgar Barrier, Marie Windsor, Marc Lawrence

Hurricane Smith

US 1952 90m Technicolor
Paramount/Nat Holt

An adventurer charters a boat to find a South Sea treasure but the boat owner turns the tables on him.

Standard thick ear with plenty of action.

w Frank Gruber d Jerry Hopper ph Ray Rennahan m Paul Sawtell

John Ireland, Yvonne de Carlo, James Craig, Forrest Tucker

Hurry Up, or I'll Be 30 *

US 1973 88m colour
Avco Embassy (Joseph Jacoby)
V*

A failure attempts to find success and love before he reaches the beginning of middle age.

Gentle and sometimes perceptive comedy of manners.

w Joseph Jacoby, David Wiltse d Joseph Jacoby ph Burleigh Wartes m Stephen Lawrence ed Stan Warnow

John Lefkowitz, Linda de Coff, Ronald Anton, Maureen Byrnes, Danny DeVito, David Kirk, Frank Quinn

'Will the south overcome the bigotry of the hate-laden white aristocrats?'
Hurry Sundown

US 1967 146m Technicolor Panavision
Paramount/Sigma (Otto Preminger)

Post-war racial problems in Georgia farmland, with degenerate whites and noble blacks.

Incredibly cliché-ridden epic melodrama with action and sex asides, from a rock bottom bestseller. It long outstays its welcome even for unintentional hilarity.

w Thomas C. Ryan, Horton Foote novel K. B. Gilden d Otto Preminger ph Loyal Griggs, Milton Krasner m Hugo Montenegro

Jane Fonda, Michael Caine, Rex Ingram, Diahann Carroll, Burgess Meredith, John Phillip Law, Robert Hooks, Faye Dunaway, Beah Richards, George Kennedy, Madeleine Sherwood

'Critic Wilfrid Sheed wrote recently that no film is ever so bad that you can't find some virtue in it. He must not have seen Hurry Sundown.' – Rex Reed

'To criticize it would be like tripping a dwarf.' – Wilfrid Sheed

'A pantomime version of Greek tragedy.' – MFB

'Preminger's taste is atrocious. His idea of erotic symbolism is Jane Fonda caressing Michael Caine's saxophone.' – Cue

'A comedy about love, death, and freedom!'
Husbands *

US 1970 154m DeLuxe
Columbia/Faces Music Inc (Al Ruban)

Three married men, shocked by the death of their friend, impulsively get drunk, fly to London and set out on a weekend of dissipation.

Irritatingly rough hewn and insanely overlong, this half-improvised tragi-comedy forces three good actors to overplay embarrassingly; but its best moments are memorable.

wd John Cassavetes ph Victor Kemper m none

Peter Falk, John Cassavetes, Ben Gazzara

Husbands and Wives ***

US 1992 108m DuArt
Columbia TriStar/TriStar (Jack Rollins, Charles H. Joffe)
V, V*, L

After their best friends announce that they are splitting up, a writer and his wife decide to separate and he becomes infatuated with a young student.

One of Allen's best films, a clever and insightful examination of the insecurities and often self-destructive behaviour of couples, though the nervy camera-work irritates.

wd Woody Allen ph Carlo Di Palma pd Santo Loquasto ed Susan E. Morse

Woody Allen, Judy Davis, Mia Farrow, Juliette Lewis, Liam Neeson, Blythe Danner, Sydney Pollack, Lysette Anthony

'The thing that moviegoers will realize decades hence is that Husbands and Wives is a damn fine film.' – Richard Corliss, Time

'Rich in characterisation, waspishly witty and profound in its observations about the frailty and fallibilities of modern marriage.' – Ian Johnstone, Sunday Times

AAN: Judy Davis; Woody Allen (as writer)

Husband's Holiday

US 1931 70m bw
Paramount

A wife takes a passive attitude to her husband's affair.

Tepid sophisticated comedy which doesn't register.

w Ernest Pascal play The Marriage Bed by Ernest Pascal d Robert Milton

Clive Brook, Vivienne Osborne, Charles Ruggles, Juliette Compton, Charles Winninger, Elizabeth Patterson

'Mild drawing-room problem play made even milder by repressed acting.' – Variety

'It starts with the most shocking scene of all time – and that's only the beginning!'
Hush Hush Sweet Charlotte *

US 1964 133m bw
TCF/Associates and Aldrich
V, V*, L

A Southern belle lives 37 years in a lonely mansion tormented by nightmarish memories of her fiancé's murder. Suddenly, after a series of apparent hauntings and other strange events, she finds she didn't do it.

Padded but generally enjoyable replay of elements from Whatever Happened to Baby Jane, with a large helping of Les Diaboliques. The stars help more than the director.

w Henry Farrell, Lukas Heller d Robert Aldrich ph Joseph Biroc m Frank de Vol ad William Glasgow

Bette Davis, Olivia de Havilland, Joseph Cotten, Cecil Kellaway, Victor Buono, William Campbell, Mary Astor, Agnes Moorehead

'The blood is on the cleaver, the madwoman is on the loose, the headless corpse is on the prowl and the Guignol is about as grand as it can get.' – Judith Crist

'Aldrich only just manages to keep this side of being disgusting and that side of being ridiculous.' – Films and Filming

AAN: Joseph Biroc; Frank de Vol; Agnes Moorehead; title song (m Frank de Vol, ly Mack David)

Hush Money

US 1931 68m bw
Fox

A girl serves a jail term, but afterwards gets involved with a racketeer.

Underworld comedy-drama which paid its way.

w Dudley Nichols, Courtney Terrett d Sidney Lanfield

Joan Bennett, Owen Moore, Hardie Albright, Myrna Loy, C. Henry Gordon, George Raft

'A light programmer for fair grosses.' – Variety

Hussy

GB 1979 94m Eastmancolor
Boyd/Watchgrove (Jeremy Watt)
V*

A high-class prostitute becomes involved with gangsters but eventually finds a new life for herself and her offspring.

Tedious exploitation melodrama, shot like a ninety-minute commercial.

wd Matthew Chapman ph Keith Goddard pd Hazel Peizer ed Bill Blunden

Helen Mirren, John Shea, Daniel Chasin, Jenny Runacre, Murray Salem, Patti Boulaye, Sandy Ratcliff

Hustle

US 1975 118m Eastmancolor
Paramount/RoBurt (Robert Aldrich)
V*

A police lieutenant lives with a call girl and is drawn into her corrupt life.

Doleful crime melodrama with both eyes in the gutter.

w Steve Shagan d Robert Aldrich ph Joseph Biroc m Frank de Vol

Burt Reynolds, Catherine Deneuve, Ben Johnson, Paul Winfield, Eileen Brennan, Eddie Albert, Ernest Borgnine, Catherine Bach, Jack Carter

'A fine companion piece to *Kiss Me Deadly* in its vision of a journey to the end of the night in quest of a myth.' – *Tim Milne*

'Even with such a meandering script as this, one expects more than the paltry fare Aldrich offers.' – *Paul Coleman*

The Hustler ****

US 1961 135m bw Cinemascope
TCF/Robert Rossen
V, V*, L

A pool room con man comes to grief when he falls in love.

Downbeat melodrama with brilliantly handled and atmospheric pool table scenes; the love interest is redundant.

w Robert Rossen, Sidney Carroll *novel* Walter Tevis d Robert Rossen ph Eugene Schufftan m Kenyon Hopkins

Paul Newman, Jackie Gleason, George C. Scott, Piper Laurie, Myron McCormick, Murray Hamilton, Michael Constantine

'There is an overall impression of intense violence, and the air of spiritual decadence has rarely been conveyed so vividly.' – *David Robinson*

'The supreme classic of that great American genre, the low-life movie.' – *Observer*

AA: Eugene Schufftan

AAN: best picture; script; Robert Rossen (as director); Paul Newman; Jackie Gleason; George C. Scott; Piper Laurie

Hyde Park Corner

GB 1935 84m bw
Grosvenor (Harcourt Templeman)

Events of 1780 at Hyde Park Corner seem to happen again in modern times.

Half-hearted reincarnation romance with good moments.

w D. B. Wyndham-Lewis *play* Walter Hackett d Sinclair Hill ph Cyril Bristow ad Aubrey Hammond

Gordon Harker, Binnie Hale, Gibb McLaughlin, Harry Tate, Eric Portman, Donald Wolfit

Hyenes

Senegal/France/Germany 1992 95m colour
ADR/Thelma/Maag Daan/MK2 (Pierre-Alain Meier, Alain Rozanes)
aka: *Hyenas*

Returning to her poverty-stricken home town, a rich old woman offers a fortune to the people if they will kill the man who wronged her 30 years before.

A naïve and melodramatic version of a familiar story.

wd Djibril Diop Mambéty *play The Visit* by Friedrich Dürrenmatt ph Matthias Kälin m Wasis Diop ed Loredana Cristelli

Mansour Diouf, Ami Diakhate, Mamadou Mahouredia Gueye, Mbaba Diop de Rufisque, Abdoulaye Yama Diop, Calgou Fall, Djibril Diop Mambéty

The Hypnotic Eye

US 1960 79m bw
Allied Artists

A mad killer hypnotizes pretty girls into defacing themselves.

Unattractive thriller including much mumbo-jumbo about hypnotism.

w Gitta and William Read Woodfield d George Blair

Jacques Bergerac, Allison Hayes, Merry Anders, Marcia Henderson

The Hypnotist: see *London After Midnight*

Hysteria

GB 1965 85m bw
MGM/Hammer (Jimmy Sangster)

An American suffering from amnesia is discharged from a London clinic and walks into a murder plot.

Complicated and rather unsympathetic Hammer twister.

w Jimmy Sangster d Freddie Francis ph John Wilcox m Don Banks pd Edward Carrick ed James Needs

Robert Webber, Lelia Goldoni, Anthony Newlands, Jennifer Jayne, *Maurice Denham,* Peter Woodthorpe

I

IP5
France 1992 119m colour
Artificial Eye/Cargo/Gaumont (Jean-Jacques Beineix)
S

A black rap performer and a graffiti artist steal a car on a trip across France and discover an old man on the back seat.

A road movie that covers a lot of ground without getting anywhere; it attempts romance but achieves whimsy.

w Jean-Jacques Beineix, Jacques Forgeas d Jean-Jacques Beineix ph Jean-François Robin m Gabriel Yared ad Dan Weil ed Joëlle Hache

Yves Montand, Olivier Martinez, Sekkou Sall, Géraldine Pailhas, Colette Renard, Sotigui Kouyate

'Beineix specialises in a grandiloquent glossiness that masquerades as art.' – Nigel Andrews, Financial Times

'A dismal French road movie.' – Philip French, Observer

† It was Yves Montand's last film.

I Accuse *
GB 1958 99m bw Cinemascope
MGM (Sam Zimbalist)

In 1894 Paris, Alfred Dreyfus is tried for treason and later defended by Emile Zola.

A well tried historical incident is stolidly retold and unsuitably wide-screened; the star cast tends to flounder for lack of assistance.

w Gore Vidal d José Ferrer ph Frederick A. Young m William Alwyn

José Ferrer (Dreyfus), Anton Walbrook (Esterhazy), Emlyn Williams (Zola), Viveca Lindfors, David Farrar, Leo Genn, Herbert Lom, Harry Andrews, Felix Aylmer, George Coulouris, Donald Wolfit

I Aim at the Stars
US 1960 107m bw
Columbia/Morningside/Fama (Charles H. Schneer)

The story of German rocket expert Wernher von Braun and his later work on American space vehicles.

Shaky biopic of a controversial scientist who changed sides.

w Jay Dratler d J. Lee-Thompson ph Wilkie Cooper m Laurie Johnson

Curt Jurgens, Herbert Lom, James Daly, Gia Scala, Victoria Shaw, Adrian Hoven, Karel Stepanek

'Mannered panning shots and crafty cutting abound, leading to a stylistic St Vitus' Dance.' – John Gillett

'The biggest double exposure since Adam and Eve!'
I Am a Camera
GB 1955 99m bw
Romulus (Jack Clayton)
V*

A young English writer observes life in Berlin in the early thirties, and has a platonic relationship with an amoral and reckless young English girl.

A rather flat and flabby treatment of the stories by Christopher Isherwood and the play by John Van Druten, all better known these days in the form of Cabaret. Disappointingly unstylish.

w John Collier d Henry Cornelius ph Guy Green m Malcolm Arnold

Julie Harris, Laurence Harvey, Shelley Winters, Ron Randell, Anton Diffring

'Six sticks of dynamite that blasted his way to freedom . . . and awoke America's conscience!'
I Am a Fugitive from a Chain Gang ****
US 1932 90m bw
Warner (Hal B. Wallis)
V*, L

An innocent man is convicted and after brutal treatment on the chain gang becomes a vicious criminal on the run.

Horrifying story in the semi-documentary manner; a milestone in Hollywood history and still a fairly compelling piece of shock entertainment.

w Sheridan Gibney, Brown Holmes, Robert E. Burns d Mervyn Le Roy ph Sol Polito m Bernhard Kaun

Paul Muni, Glenda Farrell, Helen Vinson, Preston Foster, Allen Jenkins, Edward J. Macnamara, Berton Churchill, Edward Ellis

'A picture with guts . . . everything about it is technically 100% . . . shy on romantic angles, but should get nice money all over.' – Variety

'To be enthusiastically commended for its courage, artistic sincerity, dramatic vigour, high entertainment concept and social message.' – Wilton A. Barrett

'I quarrel with the production not because it is savage and horrible, but because each step in an inevitable tragedy is taken clumsily, and because each character responsible for the hero's doom is shown more as a caricature than as a person.' – Pare Lorentz

AAN: best picture; Paul Muni

I Am a Thief
US 1934 64m bw
Warner (Henry Blanke)

Robbery and murder on the Orient Express.

Involved programmer which becomes as tiresome as its library footage.

w Ralph Block, Doris Malloy d Robert Florey

Mary Astor, Ricardo Cortez, Dudley Digges, Robert Barrat, Irving Pichel

'Should be able to top on a double bill but will have a tough time singling.' – Variety

I Am Not Afraid
US 1939 59m bw
Warner (Bryan Foy)
GB title: The Man Who Dared

An old man testifies against political terrorists.

Tepid remake of Star Witness.

w Lee Katz story Lucien Hubbard d Crane Wilbur

Charley Grapewin, Jane Bryan, Henry O'Neill, Elizabeth Risdon

'Filler for the duals.' – Variety

I Am Suzanne *
US 1933 99m bw
Fox (Jesse L. Lasky)

A dancer in love with a puppeteer comes under the influence of gangsters.

Curious but vaguely endearing mixture of music and mayhem, with the puppets used as symbolic furtherers of the plot.

w Edwin Justus Mayer, Rowland V. Lee d Rowland V. Lee

Lilian Harvey, Gene Raymond, Leslie Banks, Georgia Caine, Halliwell Hobbes

'Not a wow, but rates fairly well.' – Variety

I Am the Law *
US 1938 83m bw
Columbia (Everett Riskin)
V*, L

A law professor is asked by a civic leader to become a special prosecutor cleaning up rackets.

Adequate star potboiler, quite enjoyable.

w Jo Swerling d Alexander Hall ph Henry Freulich md Morris Stoloff

Edward G. Robinson, Otto Kruger, John Beal, Barbara O'Neil, Wendy Barrie, Arthur Loft, Marc Lawrence

'A slam-bang, rip-roaring meller that has all the elements of previous films inspired by District Attorney Thomas E. Dewey's career.' – Variety

'The liveliest melodrama in town.' – New York Times

I Became a Criminal: see They Made Me a Fugitive

I Believe in You *
GB 1952 95m bw
Ealing (Michael Relph)

Interwoven stories of probation officers.

Watchable and reasonable but not very compelling.

w Michael Relph, Basil Dearden, Jack Whittingham, Nicholas Phipps d Basil Dearden ph Gordon Dines m Ernest Irving

Celia Johnson, Cecil Parker, Godfrey Tearle, Harry Fowler, George Relph, Joan Collins, Laurence Harvey, Ernest Jay, Ursula Howells, Sidney James, Katie Johnson, Ada Reeve, Brenda de Banzie

I Believed in You
US 1934 69m bw
Fox

A wife is driven to leave her radical agitator husband.

Initially interesting but unsatisfactory romantic melodrama.

w William Conselman d Irving Cummings

Rosemary Ames, Victor Jory, John Boles, Gertrude Michael, George Meeker

'Some idea, but lacking punch in plot and direction.' – Variety

'Most Motorcycles Run on Petrol. This One Runs on Blood!'
I Bought a Vampire Motorcycle
GB 1989 105m colour
Hobo/Dirk Productions (Mycal Miller, John Wolskel)
V

A biker acquires a motorbike possessed by an evil spirit.

Low-budget tongue-in-cheek horror, full of ancient music-hall jokes.

w Mycal Miller   *d* Dirk Campbell   *ph* Tom Ingle   *m* Dean Friedman   *pd* Jose Furtado   *sp* Image Animation   *ed* Mycal Miller

Neil Morrissey, Amanda Noar, Michael Elphick, Anthony Daniels, Andrew Powell, George Rossi, Midge Taylor, Daniel Peacock, Burt Kwouk

'An exuberant tribute to British comedy culture.' – *Screen International*

'The most spinechilling cry that can freeze the blood!'
I Bury the Living
US   1957   77m   bw
Maxim/UA
V*

The honorary chairman of a cemetery seems to have the power to mark people for death.

Unusual enough to be encouraging, sloppy enough to disappoint even mystery lovers.

w Louis Garfinkle   *d* Albert Band

Richard Boone, Theodore Bikel, Herbert Anderson, Peggy Maurer

I Call First: see *Who's That Knocking at My Door*

I Can Get It for You Wholesale *
US   1951   89m   bw
TCF (Sol C. Siegel)
GB title: *This Is My Affair*; American TV title: *Only the Best*

An ambitious young mannequin starts her own dressmaking firm and sets her sights high.

Watchable comedy-drama which quickly sheds the edge of satire which might have made it the dressmaker's *All About Eve*.

w Abraham Polonsky   *novel* Jerome Weidman   *d* Michael Gordon   *ph* Milton Krasner   *md* Lionel Newman   *m* Sol Kaplan

Susan Hayward, Dan Dailey, George Sanders, Sam Jaffe, Randy Stuart, Marvin Kaplan, Harry von Zell

'There is nothing remarkable about the film, except perhaps the carefree abandon with which pearl necklaces are broken, and the curious sidelight that is cast on the ethics of cutters and salesmen. It hadn't occurred to me before that the male partners of a modest costume house would go into voluntary bankruptcy sooner than let their dress designer live in sin, but I haven't moved much in wholesale circles of the garment trade.' – *C. A. Lejeune*

I Changed My Sex: see *Glen or Glenda*

I Cheated the Law
US   1948   71m   bw
TCF (Sam Baerwitz)

An attorney wins a murder case but finds he has been tricked into providing an alibi.

Meandering crime story which fails to hold the attention.

w Richard G. Hubler   *story* Sam Baerwitz   *d* Edward L. Cahn   *ph* Jackson A. Rose   *md* Edward J. Kay

Tom Conway, Steve Brodie, Robert Osterloh, Barbara Billingsley, Russell Hicks

I Come in Peace: see *Dark Angel*

'Crushed lips don't talk!'
I Confess **
US   1953   94m   bw
Warner/Alfred Hitchcock
V, V*, L

A priest hears the confession of a murderer and cannot divulge it to the police even though he is himself suspected.

Hitchcock is always worth watching, and although this old chestnut gives him very restricted scope he

imbues the story with a strong feeling for its setting (Quebec) and an overpowering sense of doom.

w George Tabori, William Archibald   *play* Paul Anthelme   *d* Alfred Hitchcock   *ph* Robert Burks   *m* Dimitri Tiomkin

Montgomery Clift, Anne Baxter, Brian Aherne, Karl Malden, Dolly Haas, O. E. Hasse

'Whatever its shortcomings, it has the professional concentration of effect, the narrative control, of a story teller who can still make most of his rivals look like amateurs.' – *MFB*

I Could Go on Singing *
GB   1963   99m   Eastmancolor   Panavision
UA/Barbican (Lawrence Turman)
V*, L

An American singing star in Britain looks up an old lover and tries to take over their illegitimate son, but the call of the footlights proves stronger.

The star enjoys her last specially-tailored role; a banal, old-fashioned agreeable one-woman show.

w Mayo Simon   *d* Ronald Neame   *ph* Arthur Ibbetson   *m* Mort Lindsey

Judy Garland, Dirk Bogarde, Aline MacMahon, Jack Klugman

'Merely standard fare in an age without standards.' – *John Simon*

I Cover the Waterfront *
US   1933   75m   bw
Reliance (Edward Small)
V*

A reporter uses a girl's friendship to expose her father's smuggling activities.

In its time a tough, even daring melodrama, this plot has now become the stuff of every other TV series episode.

w Wells Root, Jack Jevne, Max Miller   *d* James Cruze   *ph* Ray June   *m* Alfred Newman

Claudette Colbert, Ben Lyon, Ernest Torrence, Hobart Cavanaugh

'Combination of title, picturesque background and three good performances should offset inferior story for favourable business.' – *Variety*

'A bit raw and a bit sentimental and a bit routine, the film does let life in through the cracks.' – *Graham Greene*

† Credited with being the origin of the phrase, 'Not tonight, Josephine!'

I Didn't Do It
GB   1945   97m   bw
Columbia (Ben Henry, Marcel Varnel)

Murder in a theatrical boarding house, with suspicion pointing at Our George.

One of the star's last vehicles: not too bad at all, but without the sweet smell of success.

w Howard Irving Young, Stephen Black, Norman Lee, Peter Fraser, Michael Vaughan   *d* Marcel Varnel   *ph* Roy Fogwell

George Formby, Billy Caryll, Hilda Mundy, Gaston Palmer, Jack Daly, Carl Jaffe, Marjorie Browne, Wally Patch

I Died a Thousand Times
US   1955   109m   Warnercolor   Cinemascope
Warner (Willis Goldbeck)
V*, L

An ex-convict plans a big hotel robbery, but things go wrong within his gang.

Overlong, heavygoing, tedious gangster melodrama with too much talk.

w W. R. Burnett   *d* Stuart Heisler   *ph* Ted McCord   *m* David Buttolph

Jack Palance, Shelley Winters, Lori Nelson, Lon Chaney Jnr, Lee Marvin, Gonzales Gonzales, Earl Holliman, Perry Lopez

'This remake of *High Sierra* is scarcely more inspired than its title.' – *MFB*

'It is an insult to the intelligence to pull this old mythological hero out of the archives and set him on a mountaintop again.' – *New York Times*

The I Don't Care Girl *
US   1953   78m   Technicolor
TCF (George Jessel)

The life of musical entertainer Eva Tanguay, at her height during World War I, as told by three men in her life.

Breezy, conventional backstage musical biopic.

w Walter Bullock   *d* Lloyd Bacon   *ph* Arthur Arling   *md* Lionel Newman   *ch* Jack Cole, Seymour Felix

Mitzi Gaynor, David Wayne, Oscar Levant, *George Jessel*, Warren Stevens

I Don't Kiss: see *J'Embrasse Pas*

I Don't Want to Be Born
GB   1975   94m   Eastmancolor
Rank/Unicapital (Norma Corney)
V*
US title: *The Devil within Her*

An ex-stripper gives birth to a monstrous baby which goes on a murderous rampage.

Sick horror stuff with a high death rate and no notable credits.

w Stanley Price   *d* Peter Sasdy   *ph* Ken Talbot   *m* Ron Grainer

Joan Collins, Ralph Bates, Donald Pleasence, Eileen Atkins, George Claydon

I Dood It!
US   1943   102m   , bw
MGM (Jack Cummings)
V*
GB title: *By Hook or by Crook*

A tailor falls for a Hollywood star.

Boring star comedy with interpolated musical numbers.

w Sig Herzig, Fred Saidy   *d* Vincente Minnelli   *ph* Ray June   *md* George Stoll

Red Skelton, Eleanor Powell, John Hodiak, Lena Horne, Jimmy Dorsey and his Orchestra, Hazel Scott, Richard Ainley

I Dream of Jeannie
US   1952   90m   Trucolor
Republic

The loves and financial problems of songwriter Stephen Foster.

Low-key musical biopic covering exactly the same ground as *Swanee River*.

w Alan Le May   *d* Allan Dwan

Ray Middleton (as E. P. Christy), Bill Shirley, Muriel Lawrence, Rex Allen

I Dream Too Much
US   1935   95m   bw
RKO (Pandro S. Berman)
V*

A French girl singer marries an American composer.

Forgettable vehicle for an operatic star.

w Edmund North, James Gow   *d* John Cromwell   *ph* David Abel   *md* Max Steiner   *m/y* Jerome Kern, Dorothy Fields

Lily Pons, Henry Fonda, Eric Blore, Osgood Perkins, Lucien Littlefield, Lucille Ball, Esther Dale, Mischa Auer, Paul Porcasi

'It will be a winner at the box office without breaking any records.' – *Variety*

I Escaped from Devil's Island
US 1973 81m DeLuxe
UA (Roger Corman, Gene Corman)

In 1918, a black convict makes his plans for escape.

Rough, brutish melodrama which plainly aimed to beat *Papillon* to the box-office.

w Richard L. Adams   d William Witney
ph Rosalio Solano   m Les Baxter

Jim Brown, Christopher George, Rick Ely, James Luisi, Richard Rust

'Exploitation's own *Papillon*, mercifully free from big brother's pretentiousness.' – *Sight and Sound*

I Escaped from the Gestapo
US 1943 74m bw
Monogram/King Brothers

An expert counterfeiter is sprung from jail by American Nazis, but he turns the tables on them.

Mediocre second feature dramatics; the propaganda is incidental.

w Henry Blankfort, Wallace Sullivan   d Harold Young

Dean Jagger, John Carradine, Sidney Blackmer, Mary Brian

I Even Knew Happy Gypsies: see *Happy Gypsies*

I Found Stella Parish
US 1935 85m bw
Warner (Harry Joe Brown)

An actress tries to keep her naughty past from her child, but a blackmailer strikes.

One for the ladies, who flocked to it in its day.

w Casey Robinson   d Mervyn Le Roy

Kay Francis, Paul Lukas, Ian Hunter, Sybil Jason, Jessie Ralph, Barton MacLane

'Will receive widespread support at the box office all the way from the best runs down to the subsequents, in the big keys and in the smallest towns.' – *Variety*

I Give My Love
US 1934 68m bw
Universal

A mother goes to prison for killing her no-good husband.

Tedious mother-love story with a happy ending.

w Doris Anderson   novel Vicki Baum   d Karl Freund

Paul Lukas, Wynne Gibson, Eric Linden, Anita Louise

'Good, clean, wholesome, although wholly unoriginal entertainment.' – *Variety*

I Have a New Master: see *L'Ecole Buissonière*

I Hired a Contract Killer
Finland/Sweden 1990 79m Metrocolor
Electric/Contemporary/Villealfa/Swedish Film Institute (Aki Kaurismäki)

An unhappy man hires someone to kill him, and then decides he wants to live.

Lacklustre comedy.

wd Aki Kaurismäki   ph Timo Salminen   pd John Ebden   ed Aki Kaurismäki

Jean-Pierre Léaud, Margi Clarke, Kenneth Colley, Trevor Bowen, Imogen Clare, Angela Walsh, Cyril Epstein, Nicky Tesco

I, Jane Doe
US 1948 85m bw
Republic
GB title: *Diary of a Bride*

A French girl comes to America in search of the flyer she married during the war. When she finds he was already married, she shoots him.

Melodrama for women, culminating in an unconvincing trial scene.

w Lawrence Kimble   d John H. Auer

Ruth Hussey, John Carroll, Vera Ralston, Gene Lockhart, John Howard

I Killed Rasputin
France/Italy 1967 100m Eastmancolor Franscope
Copernic/CGC (Raymond Danon)

The evil monk of the Russian court is killed by Prince Yusopov.

Dull version of a much told story. One of the big international films that never seem to get shown anywhere.

w Alain Decaux, Claude Desailly, Robert Hossein
d Robert Hossein   ph Henri Persin   m André Hossein

Gert Frobe, Peter McEnery, Robert Hossein, Geraldine Chaplin, Ira Furstenberg, Patrick Balkany

'A tedious illustrated history lesson which actually manages to obscure the motivation behind the murder.' – *MFB*

† The script was authorized by Prince Yusopov.

I Killed the Count
GB 1939 89m bw
Grafton (Isadore Goldschmidt)
US title: *Who is Guilty?*

Four people confess to the murder of a philanderer.

Inept version of a West End success.

w Alec Coppel, Lawrence Huntington   play Alec Coppel   d Fred Zelnik   ph Bryan Langley
ed Sam Simmonds

Syd Walker, Ben Lyon, Terence de Marney, Barbara Blair, Antoinette Cellier, Kathleen Harrison, Athole Stewart, Leslie Perrins, Ronald Shiner

I Know Where I'm Going **
GB 1945 91m bw
GFD/The Archers (Michael Powell, Emeric Pressburger)
V, V*

A determined girl travels to the Hebrides to marry a wealthy old man, but is stranded on Mull and marries a young naval officer instead.

A strange assembling of attractive but disparate elements: romance, comedy, bleak scenery, a trained hawk and a dangerous whirlpool. At the time it seemed to represent the Elizabethan age of the British cinema, and remains entertaining for its parts though a bit of a puzzle as a whole.

wd Michael Powell, Emeric Pressburger   ph Erwin Hillier

Wendy Hiller, Roger Livesey, Pamela Brown, Nancy Price, Finlay Currie, John Laurie, George Carney, Walter Hudd

'Continuously fresh and interesting, intelligently written and played, and full of beautiful photography.' – *Richard Mallett, Punch*

'The sensitive photography and the intelligent if not very imaginative use of sound do more than enough to make eloquent the influence of place on people; and the whole thing is undertaken with taste and modesty.' – *James Agee*

I Led Two Lives: see *Glen or Glenda*

I Like Money: see *Mr Topaze*

I Like Your Nerve
US 1931 70m bw
First National

A bookworm goes to Central America and becomes a romantic adventurer.

Junior aspiring to Senior's seven league boots; he doesn't quite make it, and that's the script's fault.

w Houston Branch   story Roland Pertwee
d William McGann

Douglas Fairbanks Jnr, Loretta Young, Claude Allister, Henry Kolker, Edmund Breon, Boris Karloff

'Mediocre, unimpressive and implausible story . . . strictly an off-day booking.' – *Variety*

I Live for Love
US 1935 83m bw
Warner (Bryan Foy)
GB title: *I Live For You*

A socialite has show business leanings.

Minor musical.

w Jerry Wald, Julius Epstein, Robert Andrews   d/ch Busby Berkeley   ph George Barnes   md Leo F. Forbstein

Dolores del Rio, Everett Marshall, Allen Jenkins, Eddie Conrad, Guy Kibbee, Berton Churchill

I Live for You: see *I Live for Love*

I Live in Grosvenor Square
GB 1945 113m bw
ABP (Herbert Wilcox)
US title: *A Yank in London*

A duke's daughter falls in love with an American air force sergeant.

Sloppily-made topical romance which was hot box-office at the time and started the producer's 'London' romances: *Piccadilly Incident, Spring in Park Lane, Maytime in Mayfair*, etc.

w Nicholas Phipps, William D. Bayles, Maurice Cowan   d Herbert Wilcox   ph Max Greene
m Anthony Collins

Anna Neagle, *Dean Jagger*, Rex Harrison, Robert Morley, Jane Darwell, Nancy Price, Irene Vanbrugh, Edward Rigby, Walter Hudd

I Live My Life
US 1935 85m bw
MGM (Bernard H. Hyman)
V*

A bored society girl falls for a working-class archaeologist.

Standard star romance.

w Joseph L. Mankiewicz   story Claustrophobia by A. Carter Goodloe   d W. S. Van Dyke II   ph George Folsey   m Dimitri Tiomkin

Joan Crawford, Brian Aherne, Frank Morgan, Aline MacMahon, Eric Blore, Jessie Ralph, Arthur Treacher, Hedda Hopper, Etienne Girardot, Ed Brophy

'An amusing romance is backgrounded by clothes, cocktails and butlers.' – *Variety*

I Lived with You
GB 1933 100m bw
Twickenham (Julius Hagen)

A cockney family find that their lodger is an exiled Russian prince.

Overlong whimsy from a successful West End play.

w G. A. Cooper, H. Fowler Mear   play Ivor Novello
d Maurice Elvey   ph Sydney Blyth   m W. L. Trytel
ad James Carter   ed Jack Harris

Ivor Novello, Ursula Jeans, Ida Lupino, Minnie Rayner, Eliot Makeham, Jack Hawkins

I Love a Mystery *
US   1945   68m   bw
Columbia

An eastern secret society offers a businessman a large sum for his head when he dies, as he resembles their founder whose embalmed head is deteriorating.

Start of a short series of mysteries from a radio series; the production was never up to the ingenious plots.

w Charles O'Neal   d Henry Levin   ph Burnett Guffey   m Mario Castelnuovo-Tedesco

George Macready, Jim Bannon, Nina Foch

'She kissed the boys goodbye – until Sonny said hello!'
I Love a Soldier
US   1944   106m   bw
Paramount (Mark Sandrich)

A San Francisco girl thinks hard before embarking on a wartime marriage.

Glossy, insubstantial sudser chiefly memorable for casting its leading lady as a welder.

w Allan Scott   d Mark Sandrich   ph *Charles Lang*   m Robert Emmett Dolan

Paulette Goddard, Sonny Tufts, Beulah Bondi, Walter Sande, Mary Treen, Ann Doran, Barry Fitzgerald

I Love Melvin *
US   1953   77m   Technicolor
MGM (George Wells)
V*, L

A photographer's assistant falls for a high-born chorus girl.

Zippy little musical with all concerned working hard with thin material.

w George Wells   d Don Weis   ph Harold Rosson   md George Stoll   ch Robert Alton   m/ly Josef Myrow, Mack Gordon

Donald O'Connor, Debbie Reynolds, Una Merkel, Allyn Joslyn

I Love My Wife
US   1970   95m   Technicolor
Universal (Robert Kaufman)

The affairs of a successful doctor with a guilt complex about sex.

Frantic, fashionable comedy drama with wildly erratic treatment and performances.

w Robert Kaufman   d Mel Stuart   ph Vilis Lapenieks   m Lalo Schifrin

Elliott Gould, Brenda Vaccaro, Angel Tompkins

'A leer-laden, anti-feminist tract disguised as a comedy.' – *Judith Crist*

I Love Trouble
US   1947   93m   bw
Columbia/S. Sylvan Simon

A private eye tries to trace the background of a politician's wife.

Standard urban mystery with loose ends, a few notches below Raymond Chandler.

w Roy Huggins   novel *The Double Take* by Roy Huggins   d S. Sylvan Simon

Franchot Tone, Janet Blair, Janis Carter, Adele Jergens, Glenda Farrell, Steve Geray, Tom Powers

I Love You Again *
US   1940   99m   bw
MGM (Lawrence Weingarten)
V*, L

A much married man gets amnesia and turns into a gay Lothario.

Sprightly romantic comedy with all concerned letting rip until the pace slows.

w Charles Lederer, George Oppenheimer, Harry Kurnitz   d W. S. Van Dyke II   ph Oliver T. Marsh   m Franz Waxman

William Powell, Myrna Loy, Frank McHugh, Edmund Lowe, Donald Douglas, Nella Walker, Pierre Watkin

I Love You, Alice B. Toklas *
US   1968   93m   Technicolor
Warner Seven Arts/Paul Mazursky, Larry Tucker

An asthmatic Los Angeles lawyer escapes his bullying fiancée by joining the flower people.

Quite amusing satirical farce about the dangers of marijuana, Gertrude Stein and Jewish mothers, thrown together with no great sense of style but achieving hilarious moments among the longueurs.

w *Paul Mazursky, Larry Tucker*   d Hy Averback   ph Philip Lathrop   m Elmer Bernstein   pd Pato Guzman

Peter Sellers, Jo Van Fleet, Joyce Van Patten, Leigh Taylor-Young, David Arkin, Herb Edelman

I Love You No More: see *Je T'Aime Moi Non Plus*

I Love You to Death
US   1990   97m   Technicolor
Columbia TriStar/Chestnut Hill (Jeffrey Lurie, Ron Moler)
V, V*, L

Discovering her husband's philandering, a wife decides to have him killed.

Black comedy that runs out of jokes.

w John Kostmayer   d Lawrence Kasdan   ph Owen Roizman   m James Horner   pd Lilly Kilvert   ed Anne V. Coates

Kevin Kline, Tracey Ullman, Joan Plowright, River Phoenix, William Hurt, Keanu Reeves, James Gammon, Jack Kehler, Victoria Jackson

'Over-the-top farce.' – *David Robinson, The Times*

'A stillborn attempt at black comedy that wastes considerable acting talent.' – *Variety*

'Lips of thunder on lips of fire!'
I Loved a Woman *
US   1933   90m   bw
Warner (Henry Blanke)

The career of a Chicago meat packer is hampered by his social-climbing wife.

Potboiling star melodrama which still holds some interest.

w Charles Kenyon, Sidney Sutherland   d Alfred E. Green   ph James Van Trees

Edward G. Robinson, Kay Francis, Genevieve Tobin, J. Farrell MacDonald, Henry Kolker, Robert Barrat

'E.G.R. out of his class; may cut biz.' – *Variety*

I Loved You Wednesday
US   1933   77m   bw
Fox

A man vies with a married friend for a lady's favour.

Mildly amusing comedy of the second rank.

w Philip Klein, Horace Jackson   play Molly Ricardei, William Dubois   d Henry King, William Cameron Menzies

Warner Baxter, Elissa Landi, Victor Jory, Miriam Jordan, Laura Hope Crews

'A romantic comedy-drama of first-rate possibilities, beautifully made and abundantly provided with class.' – *Variety*

I, Madman *
US   1989   89m   colour
Sarlui/Diamant (Rafael Eisenman)
V*, L

A bookshop assistant finds that the trashy novel she is reading about a mad, murderous doctor is coming true.

Above average horror, sillier than most in its premise, but performed and directed with some style.

w David Chaskin   d Tibor Takacs   ph Bryan England   m Michael Hoenig   sp Randall William Cook   ed Marcus Manton

Jenny Wright, Clayton Rohner, Randall William Cook, Steven Memel, Stephanie Hodge, Michelle Jordan

I Married a Communist: see *The Woman on Pier 13*

I Married a Dead Man
France   1983   110m   colour
Sara/TF1 (Alain Sarde)
original title: *J'ai Épousé Une Ombre*; aka: *I Married a Shadow*

Following a train crash, an abandoned pregnant woman assumes the identity of a wealthy mother-to-be.

Moderately effective remake of *No Man of Her Own*, which was made in 1950.

w Patrick Laurent, Robin Davis   novel William Irish   d Robin Davis   ph Bernard Zitzermann   m Philippe Sarde   ad Ivan Maussion   ed Marie Castro Vazquez

Nathalie Baye, Francis Huster, Richard Bohringer, Madeleine Robinson, Guy Trejan, Victoria Abril

I Married a Doctor
US   1936   87m   bw
Warner (Harry Joe Brown)

An idealistic city girl marries a small-town doctor.

Solidly carpentered version of *Main Street*.

w Casey Robinson, Harriet Ford, Harvey O'Higgin   novel Sinclair Lewis   d Archie Mayo

Josephine Hutchinson, Pat O'Brien, Ross Alexander, Guy Kibbee, Louise Fazenda

† *Main Street* was filmed under its own title in 1923, with Florence Vidor.

I Married a Monster from Outer Space *
US   1958   78m   bw
Paramount/Gene Fowler Jnr
V*

A young man is taken over by alien invaders but his wife helps to destroy them and bring him back to normal.

Decent, plodding, reasonably effective low-budget science fiction on a well-trampled theme; its minor virtues have been effaced by its silly title.

w Louis Vittes   d Gene Fowler Jnr   ph Haskell Boggs   sp John P. Fulton

Tom Tryon, Gloria Talbott, Robert Ivers

'Carries imaginative plottage which makes it strong fare.' – *Variety*

'Its underlying messages about society and, more specifically, women, are important ones that are particularly relevant today.' – *Cinefantastique, 1974*

I Married a Nazi: see *The Man I Married*

I Married a Shadow: see *I Married a Dead Man*

'She knows all about love potions . . . and lovely motions!'
I Married a Witch ***
US   1942   82m   bw
UA/Cinema Guild/René Clair
V*, L

A Salem witch and her sorcerer father come back to haunt the descendant of the Puritan who had them burned.

Delightful romantic comedy fantasy which shows all concerned at the top of their form. Hollywood moonshine, impeccably distilled.

w Robert Pirosh, Marc Connelly   novel The Passionate Witch by Thorne Smith   d René Clair   ph Ted Tetzlaff   m Roy Webb

Fredric March, Veronica Lake, Cecil Kellaway, Robert Benchley, Susan Hayward, Elizabeth Patterson, Robert Warwick

'A delightful sense of oddity and enchantment.' – New York World Telegram

AAN: Roy Webb

I Married a Woman
US   1956   85m   bw/colour sequence   RKOscope
RKO
V*, L

A nervous young advertising executive neglects his wife, who determines to make him jealous.

Simple-minded comedy tailored to unsympathetic stars.

w Goodman Ace   d Hal Kanter   ph Lucien Ballard   m Cyril Mockridge

George Gobel, Diana Dors, Adolphe Menjou, Jessie Royce Landis, Nita Talbot

'It brings laughter and song to the screen as this pair from paradise is joyously reunited!'
I Married an Angel
US   1942   84m   bw
MGM (Hunt Stromberg)

An attractive angel lures a playboy from his earthly girlfriends.

Silly musical fantasy which spelled the end of a great musical star partnership.

w Anita Loos   play Vilismary Janos   d W. S. Van Dyke   ph Ray June   m/ly Richard Rodgers, Lorenz Hart

Jeanette MacDonald, Nelson Eddy, Edward Everett Horton, Binnie Barnes, Reginald Owen, Douglass Dumbrille

'As bland as operetta but without its energy.' – New Yorker, 1978

I Met a Murderer *
GB   1939   78m   bw
Grand National/Gamma (Roy Kellino, Pamela Kellino, James Mason)

A murderer on the run meets a girl novelist who is touring in her motor caravan.

Semi-professional location melodrama which won commendation at the time but now seems very faded.

w Pamela Kellino, James Mason   d Roy Kellino   ph Roy Kellino   m Eric Ansell   ed Fergus McDonnell

James Mason, Pamela Kellino, Sylvia Coleridge, William Devlin, Peter Coke

'Graceful, gallant, resourceful . . . better and more enjoyable than most studio pictures.' – James Agee

'That it has a number of defects does not mean that it is not worthy of serious consideration.' – Basil Wright

I Met Him in Paris *
US   1937   86m   bw
Paramount (Wesley Ruggles)

A fashion designer spends five years' savings on a fling in Paris and finds herself pursued to Switzerland by two philanderers.

Not very witty but likeable romantic comedy with polished performers near their best.

w Claude Binyon   d Wesley Ruggles   ph Leo Tover   md Boris Morros   m John Leopold

Claudette Colbert, Melvyn Douglas, Robert Young, Lee Bowman, Mona Barrie

'A money picture . . . laughs are piled on laughs.' – Variety

'At least half the footage is a perfect scream, and if you miss it you are an old sobersides, and who cares.' – Otis Ferguson

I Met My Love Again
US   1937   77m   bw
Walter Wanger
V*

A small-town girl marries a drunken writer, but on his death returns to her first love, a biology professor.

Mildly pleasing, rather dated romantic drama with good local colour.

w David Hertz   novel Summer Lightning by Aileen Corliss   d Joshua Logan, Arthur Ripley   ph Hal Mohr   m Heinz Roemheld

Henry Fonda, Joan Bennett, Alan Marshal, Dorothy Stickney, Dame May Whitty, Alan Baxter, Louise Platt, Tim Holt, Florence Lake

'Sentimentally as sticky as a gum drop, this sugar-coated romance will have to find its favour with the femmes.' – Variety

I, Mobster
US   1958   80m   bw   Cinemascope
Edward L. Alperson (Roger Corman, Gene Corman)
V*

A slum teenager becomes a top gangster.

Routine gangland thriller.

w Steve Fisher   novel Joseph Hilton Smith   d Roger Corman   ph Floyd Crosby   m Gerald Fried   ad Daniel Haller   ed William B. Murphy

Steve Cochran, Lita Milan, Robert Strauss, Celia Lovsky, Grant Withers

I, Monster *
GB   1970   75m   Eastmancolor
Amicus (Milton Subotsky)

A straight remake of Dr Jekyll and Mr Hyde, holding closely to the original novel but mysteriously using different names.

Interesting minor work.

w Milton Subotsky   d Stephen Weeks   ph Moray Grant   m Carl Davis   ad Tony Curtis

Christopher Lee, Peter Cushing, Richard Hurndall, George Merritt

I Never Promised You a Rose Garden
US   1977   96m   colour
New World/Imorh/Fadsin (Roger Corman)
V*

A suicidal teenage girl is treated in a psychiatric hospital.

Careful, thoughtful case history which can't help, after so many TV movies of the kind, seeming rather too simple for a theatrical feature, as well as too heavy-going despite the upbeat ending.

w Gavin Lambert, Lewis John Carlino   novel Hannah Green   d Anthony Page   ph Bruce Logan   m Paul Chihara   pd Toby Rafelson

Kathleen Quinlan, Bibi Andersson, Sylvia Sidney, Ben Piazza, Lorraine Gary, Reni Santoni, Signe Hasso

AAN: best adapted screenplay

I Never Sang for My Father *
US   1969   92m   Technicolor
Columbia/Jamel (Gilbert Cates)
V*, L

When his mother dies, a middle-aged widower is saddled with his cantankerous father, who tries to prevent him from remarrying.

Literal transcription of a Eugene O'Neillish play, a fascinating if depressing character study.

w Robert Anderson   play Robert Anderson   d Gilbert Cates   ph Morris Hartzband, George Stoetzel   m Al Gorgoni, Barry Mann

Melvyn Douglas, Gene Hackman, Dorothy Stickney, Estelle Parsons

AAN: Robert Anderson; Melvyn Douglas; Gene Hackman

I Ought to Be in Pictures *
US   1982   107m   DeLuxe
TCF (Herbert Ross, Neil Simon)

A young actress hitch-hikes to Hollywood to break into pictures and also to see her estranged scriptwriter father.

Fairly agreeable comedy-drama in the Neil Simon manner, with the studio background an extra plus.

w Neil Simon   play Neil Simon   d Herbert Ross   ph David M. Walsh   m Marvin Hamlisch   pd Albert Brenner

Walter Matthau, Ann-Margret, Dinah Manoff, Lance Guest, Lewis Smith

I Passed for White
US   1960   92m   bw
Allied Artists (Fred M. Wilcox)

A light-skinned Negress comes to New York but fails to achieve happiness by pretending to be white.

Earnest, rather dreary social drama which doesn't get anywhere.

d Fred M. Wilcox   ph George J. Folsey   m Johnny Williams

Sonya Wilde, James Franciscus, Pat Michon, Elizabeth Council

I Promise to Pay
US   1937   68m   bw
Columbia

An office worker finds himself at the wrong end of the loan shark racket.

Competent programmer from the headlines.

w Mary McCall Jnr, Lionel Houser   d D Ross Lederman

Chester Morris, Leo Carrillo, Helen Mack, Thomas Mitchell, Thurston Hall

'Just average . . . if placed on a dual bill, it'll be found more than enough to float its end.' – Variety

'The sweetest movie anyone would ever wish to see!'
I Remember Mama **
US   1948   134m   bw
RKO (Harriet Parsons)
V*, L

A novelist remembers some of the adventures of growing up with her Norwegian-American family.

Overlong, but well-upholstered nostalgia: warm-hearted, sentimental, nicely detailed, richly acted but just a little boring in spots.

w De Witt Bodeen   play John Van Druten   book Mama's Bank Account by Kathryn Forbes   d George Stevens   ph Nicholas Musuraca   m Roy Webb

Irene Dunne, Barbara Bel Geddes, Oscar Homolka, Edgar Bergen, Philip Dorn, Ellen Corby, Florence Bates, Cedric Hardwicke, Barbara O'Neil, Rudy Vallee

AAN: Nicholas Musuraca; Irene Dunne; Barbara Bel Geddes; Oscar Homolka; Ellen Corby

I Saw What You Did
US   1965   82m   bw
Universal/William Castle

A murderer thinks that two playful teenagers have witnessed his deed, and sets out to kill them too.

Predictable and long-winded suspenser, very short of inventive detail.

w William McGivern   *novel* Ursula Curtiss
d William Castle   *ph* Joseph Biroc   *m* Van
Alexander

John Ireland, Joan Crawford, Leif Erickson

I See a Dark Stranger **
GB   1945   112m   bw
GFD/Individual (Frank Launder, Sidney Gilliat)
V, V*
US title: *The Adventuress*

An Irish colleen who hates the English comes to
England to spy for the Germans but falls in love with
a young English officer.

Slipshod plotting does not quite destroy the jolly
atmosphere of this comedy-thriller which has the
cheek to take an IRA member as its heroine. Good
fun, very well staged.

w Frank Launder, Sidney Gilliat, Wolfgang Wilhelm
d Frank Launder   *ph* Wilkie Cooper   *m* William
Alwyn

Deborah Kerr, Trevor Howard, Raymond Huntley,
Norman Shelley, Michael Howard, Brenda Bruce,
Liam Redmond, Brefni O'Rourke

'It is the cinematic equivalent of Irish blarney which
inspires most of this picture.' – *MFB*

'There is some intelligence, grace and fun here, but
essentially this seems to me a supercilious drama, as if
it had been made by bright young men who had
decided to package and toss a bone to the
groundlings.' – *James Agee*

I See Ice
GB   1938   81m   bw
ATP

The property man in an ice ballet company is a keen
amateur photographer who accidentally snaps crooks
at work.

Fair star comedy with good production.

w Anthony Kimmins, Austin Melford   *d* Anthony
Kimmins

George Formby, Kay Walsh, Betty Stockfield, Cyril
Ritchard, Garry Marsh

I Sell Anything
US   1935   70m   bw
First National

An auctioneer rises in the business.

Mildly interesting comedy-drama with character
progress but not much plot.

w Brown Holmes, Sidney Sutherland   *d* Robert
Florey

Pat O'Brien, Ann Dvorak, Claire Dodd, Roscoe Karns,
Hobart Cavanaugh

'Nicely made and played, but all in one key.' – *Variety*

I Sent a Letter to My Love **
France   1981   102m   colour
Cineproductions (Lise Fauyolles, Giorgio Silvagni)
V*
original title: *Chère Inconnue*

A crippled brother unknowingly carries on a love
affair by letter with his sister.

Gentle tale of two lonely people finding an
unexpected release from each other.

w Moshe Mizrahi, Gérard Brach   *novel* Bernice
Rubens   *d* Moshe Mizrahi   *ph* Ghislain Cloquet
m Philippe Sarde   *ad* Bernard Evein   *ed* Françoise
Bonnot

Simone Signoret, Jean Rochefort, Delphine Seyrig,
Genevieve Fontanel, Dominique Labourier

'Insensitive direction and unconvincing performances
ruin an interesting dramatic idea.' – *Variety*

'This muted, smouldering French film first teases and
eventually clutches our emotions.' – *Judith Crist,
Saturday Review*

I Shall Return: see *An American Guerrilla in the
Philippines*

I Shot Jesse James *
US   1948   81m   bw
Lippert/Screen Guild (Carl K. Hittleman)
V*

The story of Bob Ford, who gunned down the famous
outlaw.

Doubtfully historical but quite lively Western
melodrama.

wd Samuel Fuller   *story* Homer Croy   *ph* Ernest
Miller   *m* Albert Glasser   *ad* Frank Hotaling
ed Paul Landres

Preston Foster, John Ireland, Barbara Britton, Reed
Hadley, J. Edward Bromberg, Victor Kilian, Tom
Tyler

I Stand Condemned: see *Moscow Nights*

I Start Counting
GB   1969   105m   DeLuxe
UA/Triumvirate (David Greene)

A young girl thinks her foster-brother may be the sex
murderer known to be rampant in the locality. But
after a great many red herrings, of course, he is not.

Strained psychological suspenser with good moments
between the *longueurs*.

w Richard Harris   *novel* Audrey Erskine Lindop
d David Greene   *ph* Alex Thomson   *m* Basil
Kirchin   *pd* Brian Eatwell

Jenny Agutter, Bryan Marshall, Clare Sutcliffe, Simon
Ward, Lana Morris, Billy Russell, Fay Compton, Lally
Bowers

I Stole a Million
US   1939   89m   bw
Universal (Burt Kelly)

A cab driver cheated by a finance company becomes a
criminal to support his family.

Ho-hum star melodrama.

w Nathanael West   *story* Lester Cole   *d* Frank
Tuttle   *ph* Milton Krasner

George Raft, Claire Trevor, Dick Foran, Henry
Armetta, Victor Jory, Joe Sawyer, Stanley Ridges

'Crime drama neatly packaged . . . topper for key
duals at normal b.o.' – *Variety*

I Take This Woman
US   1931   74m   bw
Paramount (Hector Turnbull)

A reckless society girl falls for a cowhand and agrees
to live in his ramshackle house.

Patchy romantic comedy-drama of little remaining
interest.

w Vincent Lawrence   *novel* Lost Ecstasy by Mary
Roberts Rinehart   *d* Marion Gering, Slavko
Vorkapich   *ph* Victor Milner

Gary Cooper, Carole Lombard, Helen Ware, Lester
Vail, Charles Trowbridge, Clara Blandick

I Take This Woman
US   1939   97m   bw
MGM (Louis B. Mayer)

A doctor marries a beautiful European and decides too
late that he does not love her.

Thin comedy-drama which Louis B. Mayer
unaccountably took it into his head to produce
personally. The results had to be re-shot so much and
so often that Hollywood dubbed the film I Re-Take

This Woman. It offers little in the way of
entertainment.

w James Kevin McGuinness   *story* Charles
MacArthur   *d* W. S. Van Dyke   *ph* Harold Rosson
m Bronislau Kaper

Spencer Tracy, Hedy Lamarr, Verree Teasdale, Kent
Taylor, Laraine Day, Mona Barrie, Jack Carson, Paul
Cavanagh, Marjorie Main

I Thank a Fool
GB   1962   100m   Metrocolor   Cinemascope
MGM (Anatole de Grunwald)

A woman found guilty of the murder of her lover is
offered a fresh start in the home of the prosecutor's
family . . . but another nightmare situation builds up.

Jane Eyre melodrama of the loonier type, with good
actors struggling through a wild but unrewarding
script.

w Karl Tunberg   *novel* Audrey Erskine Lindop
d Robert Stevens   *ph* Harry Waxman   *m* Ron
Goodwin

Peter Finch, Susan Hayward, Diane Cilento, Cyril
Cusack, Kieron Moore, Athene Seyler

I Thank You
GB   1941   81m   bw
Gainsborough

Actors seeking a backer become servants to a titled
ex-star.

Acceptable comedy vehicle.

w Howard Irving Young, Val Guest, Marriott Edgar
d Marcel Varnel

Arthur Askey, Richard Murdoch, Lily Morris, Moore
Marriott, Graham Moffatt, Kathleen Harrison

I the Jury
US   1953   87m   bw   3-D
Parklane (Victor Saville)

Private eye Mike Hammer avenges the murder of his
friend.

Charmless toughie, roughly made and devoid of plot
or character interest.

wd Harry Essex   *ph* John Alton   *m* Franz Waxman

Biff Elliott, Peggie Castle, Preston Foster, Elisha Cook
Jnr, John Qualen

I the Jury
US   1982   109m   colour
American Cinema/Larco/Solofilm (Robert Solo)

An amoral private eye avenges the murder of his
Vietnam buddy.

Hard, brutal thriller more in line than the previous
version with the tone of the novel.

w Larry Cohen   *d* Richard T. Heffron   *ph* Andrew
Laszlo   *m* Bill Conti   *pd* Robert Gundlach

Armand Assante, Barbara Carrera, Luarene London,
Alan King, Geoffrey Lewis, Paul Sorvino

'The repellent formula as usual, with the gun and the
penis as interchangeable instruments of quick-fire
tough-guy virility.' – *Sunday Times*

I, the Worst of All **
Argentina   1990   105m   colour
Electric/Assai Communications/Screening 22/GEA (Lita Stantic)
original title: *Yo, la peor de todas*

In Mexico in the 17th century, the Church forces
Sister Juana, a nun who is also a gifted poet and
playwright, to forswear literature and the intellectual
life.

An austere and moving account, based on fact and
with an appeal wider than feminism, of a talent
overwhelmed by religious and masculine prejudice
and oppression.

w Maria Luisa Bemberg, Antonio Larreta *book* Sor Juana: Her Life and Her World (*Sor Juana Ines de la Cruz o Las Trampas de la Fe*) by Octavio Paz *d* Maria Luisa Bemberg *ph* Felix Monti *m* Luis Maria Serra *pd* Voytek *ed* Juan Carlos Macias

Assumpta Serra, Dominique Sanda, Hector Alterio, Lautaro Murua, Alberto Segado, Franklin Caicedo, Graciela Araujo, Hugo Soto, Gerardo Romano

I Wake Up Screaming **
US 1941 79m bw
TCF (Milton Sperling)
V, V*
GB and alternative title: *Hot Spot*

A model is murdered and her sister joins forces with the chief suspect to find the real killer.

Moody thriller with plenty going for it including one memorable performance.

w Dwight Taylor *novel* Steve Fisher *d* H. Bruce Humberstone *ph* Edward Cronjager *m* Cyril Mockridge

Betty Grable, Victor Mature, Carole Landis, *Laird Cregar,* William Gargan, Alan Mowbray, Allyn Joslyn, Elisha Cook Jnr

† Remade as *Vicki* (qv).

I Walk Alone *
US 1947 98m bw
Paramount (Hal B. Wallis)

An ex-smuggler comes out seeking vengeance after fourteen years in prison.

Dreary gangster drama unworthy of its stars.

w Charles Schnee *play Beggars Are Coming to Town* by Theodore Reeves *d* Byron Haskin *ph* Leo Tover *m* Victor Young

Burt Lancaster, Kirk Douglas, Lizabeth Scott, Wendell Corey, Kristine Miller, George Rigaud, Marc Lawrence, Mike Mazurki

'The picture deserves, like four out of five other movies, to walk alone, tinkle a little bell, and cry Unclean, unclean.' – *James Agee*

I Walk the Line *
US 1970 97m Eastmancolor Panavision
Columbia/Frankenheimer/Lewis/Halcyon/Atticus (Harold D. Cohen)

A Tennessee sheriff protects moonshiners for the favours of their daughter; when an investigator arrives, bloodshed results.

Competent but uninteresting hothouse melodrama in which only the plot twists compel attention.

w Alvin Sargent *novel An Exile* by Madison Jones *d* John Frankenheimer *ph* David M. Walsh *md* Robert Johnson

Gregory Peck, Tuesday Weld, Estelle Parsons, Ralph Meeker

'She's Alive . . . Yet Dead! She's Dead . . . Yet Alive!'
I Walked with a Zombie *
US 1943 68m bw
RKO (Val Lewton)
V*

A nurse is retained by a Caribbean planter to care for his voodoo-sick wife.

Mild horror from the famous Lewton package; some style, but generally thin stuff, the plot having been mirthfully borrowed from *Jane Eyre.*

w Curt Siodmak, Ardel Wray *d Jacques Tourneur* *ph* J. Roy Hunt *m* Roy Webb

Frances Dee, James Ellison, Tom Conway, Christine Gordon, Edith Barrett, James Bell, Sir Lancelot

I Wanna Hold Your Hand
US 1978 104m Technicolor
Universal/Steven Spielberg (Tamara Asseyev, Alex Rose)
V*, L

A day in 1964 finds assorted New Jersey teenagers eagerly awaiting the Beatles' appearance on the Ed Sullivan Show.

Modest period comedy utilizing fresh young talent.

w Robert Zemeckis, Bob Gale *d* Robert Zemeckis *ph* Donald M. Morgan *m* Meredith Willson

Nancy Allen, Bobby diCicco, Marc McClure, Susan Kendall Newman

I Want a Divorce
US 1940 74m bw
Paramount

A young law student marries rashly, but is prevented from doing anything about it by examples of the unhappiness brought by divorce.

Peculiar comedy-drama which never seems to make up its mind to any particular course.

w Frank Butler *story* Adela Rogers St John *d* Ralph Murphy *ph* Ted Tetzlaff *m* Victor Young

Dick Powell, Joan Blondell, Frank Fay, Gloria Dickson, Jessie Ralph, Conrad Nagel, Harry Davenport, Sidney Blackmer, Louise Beavers

I Want to Live *
US 1958 120m bw
UA/Walter Wanger
V*, L

A vagrant prostitute is executed in the gas chamber despite growing doubt as to her guilt.

Sober, harrowing treatment of the Barbara Graham case, uneasily adapted to provide a star role amid the tirade against capital punishment.

w Nelson Gidding, Don Mankiewicz *d* Robert Wise *ph* Lionel Lindon *m* John Mandel *ed* William Hornbeck

Susan Hayward, Simon Oakland, Virginia Vincent, Theodore Bikel, Wesley Lau, Philip Coolidge

'An inconclusive amalgam of variously unexplored themes.' – *Peter John Dyer*

AA: Susan Hayward

AAN: Nelson Gidding, Don Mankiewicz; Robert Wise; Lionel Lindon; editing

I Want What I Want
GB 1971 105m Eastmancolor
Marayan (Raymond Stross)
V*

Roy has a sex change operation and becomes Wendy.

Although based on an actual trans-sexual experience, this film confuses more than it informs, and provokes unintentional mirth when its glamorous star is playing a boy.

w Gillian Freeman *novel* Geoff Brown *d* John Dexter *ph* Gerry Turpin *m* Johnny Harris

Anne Heywood, Paul Rogers, Harry Andrews, Jill Bennett

I Want You
US 1951 101m bw
Samuel Goldwyn

A family reacts to the Korean war.

Glossy small-town flagwaver; no *Best Years of Our Lives.*

w Irwin Shaw *d* Mark Robson *ph* Harry Stradling *m* Leigh Harline *ad* Richard Day

Dorothy McGuire, Dana Andrews, Farley Granger, Peggy Dow, Robert Keith, Ray Collins, Mildred Dunnock, Martin Milner, Jim Backus

'A recruiting picture which seems to accept a third world war almost as a present reality.' – *Penelope Houston*

'Below the entertaining surface it has very little of value to offer.' – *Richard Mallett, Punch*

'Blonde bomber – she flew them into the ground!'
I Wanted Wings *
US 1941 131m bw
Paramount (Arthur Homblow Jnr)

The fortunes of three recruits to the American Air Force.

Cheerful, overlong recruiting poster with concessions to melodrama.

w Richard Maibaum, Beirne Lay Jnr, Sig Herzig *d* Mitchell Leisen *ph* Leo Tover, Elmer Dyer *m* Victor Young

Ray Milland, William Holden, Brian Donlevy, Wayne Morris, Veronica Lake, Constance Moore, Harry Davenport, Phil Brown

'Far more a poster than a drama.' – *Howard Barnes, New York Herald Tribune*

'All the life and death moments a man can know!'
I Was a Communist for the FBI
US 1951 83m bw
Warner (Bryan Foy)

Matt Cvetic, a Pittsburgh steel worker, is actually an FBI agent working undercover to trap communists.

Crude and shoddy Red-baiting melodrama, a kind of updating of *Confessions of a Nazi Spy* but using a sadly deteriorated technique.

w Crane Wilbur, Matt Cvetic *d* Gordon Douglas *ph* Edwin DuPar *m* Max Steiner

Frank Lovejoy, Dorothy Hart, Phil Carey, James Millican, Richard Webb, Paul Picerni, Konstantin Shayne

'It seems that this is a subject which Hollywood is incapable of tackling even at its customary level of journalistic efficiency.' – *Penelope Houston*

AAN: documentary feature

I Was a Fireman: see Fires Were Started

I Was a Male War Bride **
US 1949 105m bw
TCF (Sol C. Siegel)
V*
GB title: *You Can't Sleep Here*

A WAC in Europe marries a French officer and can't get him home.

High-spirited farce against realistic backgrounds of war-torn Europe, which scarcely accord with Cary Grant's pretending to be a Frenchman (and later a Frenchwoman). Funny, though.

w Charles Lederer, Hagar Wilde, Leonard Spigelgass *d Howard Hawks* *ph* Norbert Brodine, Osmond Borradaile *md* Lionel Newman *m* Cyril Mockridge

Cary Grant, *Ann Sheridan,* Marion Marshall, Randy Stuart

'It is excellent light entertainment but it is not likely to appeal to the prudish and some discretion should be exercised in booking it.' – *CEA Film Report*

I Was a Prisoner on Devil's Island
US 1941 71m bw
Columbia (Wallace MacDonald)

A young American seaman is involved in a brawl in which his captain dies; result, three years on Devil's Island.

Hokey but boring melodrama with production values at low level.

w Karl Brown *d* Lew Landers

Donald Woods, Sally Eilers, Edward Ciannelli, Victor Kilian, Charles Halton

I Was a Spy **
GB   1933   89m   bw
Gaumont (Michael Balcon)
V*

In Belgium 1914, a nurse is trained as a spy.

Good standard war espionage melodrama.

w W. P. Lipscomb, Ian Hay   book Marthe McKenna
d Victor Saville   ph Charles Van Enger   md Louis Levy   ad Alfred Junge   ed Frederick Y. Smith

Madeleine Carroll, Conrad Veidt, Herbert Marshall, Gerald du Maurier, Edmund Gwenn, Donald Calthrop, Nigel Bruce, Anthony Bushell, Martita Hunt

'Body of a boy! Mind of a monster! Soul of an unearthly thing!'

I Was a Teenage Frankenstein
US   1957   72m   bw
American International (Herman Cohen)
V, V*
GB title: Teenage Frankenstein

Professor Frankenstein fashions a creature from selected morsels of old corpses, and kills a teenager to give it a more handsome head.

It seemed gruesome enough at the time, but by 1980 standards this is tame, cheap stuff, only notable for its occasional bravura.

w Kenneth Langtry   d Herbert J. Strock
ph Lothrop Worth   m Paul Dunlap

Whit Bissell, Phyllis Coates, Gary Conway, Robert Burton

   PROFESSOR TO MONSTER: 'Answer me! I know you have a civil tongue in your head, because I sewed it in there!'

† In-joke: when the professor crates up the monster to send it to London, the address is 113 Wardour Street, which was Hammer House.

'The most amazing motion picture of our time!'

I Was a Teenage Werewolf
US   1957   76m   bw
AIP/Sunset (Herman Cohen)
V, V*

A scientist experiments on an aggressive student and turns him into a werewolf.

Hilarious farrago with a title which achieved a splendour of its own.

w Ralph Thornton   d Gene Fowler Jnr   ph Joseph LaShelle   m Paul Dunlap

Michael Landon, Whit Bissell, Yvonne Lime

I Was an Adventuress *
US   1940   81m   bw
TCF (Darryl F. Zanuck)

A ballerina works as decoy for a pair of confidence tricksters.

Pleasing comedy drama with striking cast.

w Karl Tunberg, Don Ettlinger, John O'Hare
d Gregory Ratoff   ph Leon Shamroy, Edward Cronjager   md David Buttolph

Vera Zorina, Erich von Stroheim, Peter Lorre, Richard Greene, Sig Rumann, Fritz Feld, Cora Witherspoon

I Was an American Spy
US   1951   84m   bw
Allied Artists (David Diamond)

Stranded in Manila after occupation, an American girl assumes Italian identity and charms Japanese officers.

Fairly gripping co-feature, remotely based on fact.

w Sam Rocca, from articles in Reader's Digest
d Lesley Selander

Ann Dvorak, Gene Evans, Douglas Kennedy, Richard Loo, Philip Ahn

I Was Happy Here *
GB   1965   91m   bw
Partisan (Roy Millichip)
US title: Time Lost and Time Remembered

A girl leaves her husband in London and returns to the little Irish port of her childhood.

Nicely made, over-mannered study in nostalgia and lost illusions.

w Edna O'Brien, Desmond Davis   d Desmond Davis
ph Manny Wynn   m John Addison

Sarah Miles, Cyril Cusack, Julian Glover, Sean Caffrey, Marie Kean

I Was Monty's Double **
GB   1958   100m   bw
Film Traders/Maxwell Setton
V
US title: Hell, Heaven and Hoboken

To distract the Nazis in Africa, an actor is hired to pose as General Montgomery.

An amusing and intriguing first hour gives way to spy chases, but the overall provides solid entertainment.

w Bryan Forbes   book M. E. Clifton-James   d John Guillermin   ph Basil Emmott   m John Addison

John Mills, Cecil Parker, M. E. Clifton-James, Patrick Allen, Leslie Phillips, Michael Hordern, Marius Goring

'Silva Is Alone In New York … But Not For Long …'
I Was on Mars *
Germany/Switzerland/US   1991   87m   Eastmancolor
Metro Tartan/Luna/Fama/Balthazar/Good Machine (Gudrun Ruzickova-Steiner)
V

A young Polish woman, alone and reduced to penury in New York, follows a con man who has stolen all her savings.

An entertainingly eccentric and baleful account, made on a small budget, of an innocent abroad, with the city seen in close-up as a threatening, decaying slum populated by hustlers of one kind or another.

w Dani Levy, Maria Schrader   d Dani Levy
ph Carl-F. Koschnick   m Niki Reiser   pd Dan Ouellette   ed Susann Lahaye

Maria Schrader, Dani Levy, Mario Giacalone, Antonia Rey

'There's no denying Levi's eye for comic detail, and the film abounds in resonant little scenes.' – Sight and Sound

I Will … I Will … for Now
US   1975   108m   Technicolor
Brut (C. O. Erickson)
V*

Divorcees with sex problems eventually get together again.

Witless soft-core farrago of coy jokes, as clumsy and unappealing as its title.

w Norman Panama, Albert E. Lewin   d Norman Panama   ph John A. Alonzo   m John Cameron   pd Fernando Carrere

Elliott Gould, Diane Keaton, Paul Sorvino, Victoria Principal, Warren Berlinger, Candy Clark, Robert Alda

I Wonder Who's Kissing Her Now *
US   1947   104m   Technicolor
TCF (George Jessel)

The career of 1890s songwriter Joseph E. Howard.

Routine biopic, quite pleasantly handled.

w Lewis R. Foster   d Lloyd Bacon   ph Ernest Palmer   md Alfred Newman   ad Richard Day, Boris Leven   ch Hermes Pan

Mark Stevens, June Haver, Martha Stewart, Reginald Gardiner, Lenore Aubert, William Frawley, Gene Nelson

Ice-Capades
US   1941   88m   bw
Republic

A newsreel cameraman fakes an ice show in Central Park.

Tepid musical entertainment.

w Jack Townley and others   d Joseph Santley
md Cy Feuer

James Ellison, Phil Silvers, Jerry Colonna, Dorothy Lewis, Barbara Jo Allen, Alan Mowbray

AAN: Cy Feuer

Ice-Capades Revue
US   1942   79m   bw
Republic (Robert North)

A New England farm girl inherits a bankrupt ice show.

Thin excuse for an ice revue, which is tolerable.

w Bradford Ropes, Gertrude Purcell   d Bernard Vorhaus

Ellen Drew, Richard Denning, Jerry Colonna, Barbara Jo Allen, Harold Huber, Vera Hruba, Joe Jackson Jnr

Ice Castles
US   1978   109m   Metrocolor
Columbia/International Cinemedia Center (John Kemeny)
V, V*

Nick and Lexie meet and fall in love at the ice rink. He goes into professional ice hockey; she becomes an Olympic champion but an accident leaves her blind.

Slick, empty, three-handkerchief wallow in the modern manner; well made but instantly forgettable.

w Donald Wrye, Gary L. Baim   d Donald Wrye
ph Bill Butler   m Marvin Hamlisch   pd Joel Schiller

Robby Benson, Lynn-Holly Johnson, Colleen Dewhurst, Tom Skerritt, Jennifer Warren, David Huffman

AAN: song 'Through the Eyes of Love' (m Marvin Hamlisch, ly Carole Bayer Sager)

Ice Cold in Alex **
GB   1958   132m   bw
ABP (W. A. Whittaker)
V
US title: Desert Attack

In 1942 Libya, the commander of a motor ambulance gets his vehicle and passengers to safety despite the hazards of minefields and a German spy.

Engrossing desert adventure with plenty of suspense sequences borrowed from The Wages of Fear; long, but very well presented.

w T. J. Morrison, Christopher Landon   d J. Lee-Thompson   ph Gilbert Taylor   m Leighton Lucas

John Mills, Sylvia Sims, Anthony Quayle, Harry Andrews

Ice Follies of 1939
US   1939   82m   bw/Technicolor sequence
MGM (Harry Rapf)

A Hollywood star goes east to help her old ice-skating friends put on a show.

The downright peculiar sight of these particular stars on ice is backed by good turns and practically no story.

w Florence Ryerson, Edgar Allan Woolf d Reinhold Schunzel ph Joseph Ruttenberg, Oliver T. Marsh m Franz Waxman

Joan Crawford, James Stewart, Lew Ayres, Lewis Stone, Lionel Stander, Bess Ehrhardt, Charles D. Brown, the International Ice Follies

Ice Palace

US 1960 143m Warnercolor
Warner (Henry Blanke)

After World War I, two men set up a fishery business in Alaska, and their subsequent lives are tied up with the political development of the state.

Tedious saga from a bestseller, with entertaining incidents but no real grip.

w Harry Kleiner novel Edna Ferber d Vincent Sherman ph Joseph Biroc m Max Steiner ad Malcolm Bert

Richard Burton, Robert Ryan, Martha Hyer, Carolyn Jones, Jim Backus, Ray Danton, Diane McBain, Karl Swenson

The Ice Pirates

US 1984 94m Metrocolor
MGM-UA (John Foreman)
V*, L

On a distant planet in the future, water has become precious, and the evil Templars have cornered it.

Extraordinarily talkative and unpersuasive space opera: pretentious hokum.

w Stewart Raffill, Stanford Sherman d Stewart Raffill ph Matthew F. Leonetti m Bruce Broughton ad David M. Haber, Ronald Kent Foreman ed Tom Walls

Robert Urich, Mary Crosby, Michael D. Roberts, Anjelica Huston, Ron Perlman, John Carradine

Ice Station Zebra

US 1968 148m Metrocolor Super Panavision
MGM/Filmways (James C. Pratt)
V, V*, L

Russian and American agents speed towards the North Pole to recover a lost capsule containing vital military information.

Talky and unconvincingly staged spy adventure with a disappointing lack of action and a great many cold war platitudes.

w Douglas Heyes, Harry Julian Fink novel Alistair MacLean d John Sturges ph Daniel L. Fapp m Michel Legrand

Rock Hudson, Patrick McGoohan, Ernest Borgnine, Jim Brown, Tony Bill, Lloyd Nolan, Gerald S. O'Loughlin, Alf Kjellin

'It's terrible in such a familiar way that at some level it's pleasant. We learn to settle for so little, we moviegoers.' – Pauline Kael

AAN: Daniel L. Fapp; special effects (Hal Miller, J. McMillan Johnson)

Iceland

US 1942 79m bw
TCF (William LeBaron)
GB title: Katina

A marine in Reykjavik falls for a local belle.

Superficial musical with a stage farce plot and unreal musical numbers.

w Robert Ellis, Helen Logan d Bruce Humberstone

Sonja Henie, John Payne, Jack Oakie, Felix Bressart, Osa Massen

Iceman

US 1984 99m Technicolor
Universal (Patrick Palmer, Norman Jewison)
V*, L, S

An oil-drilling team in the Arctic discovers the

perfectly preserved body of a Neanderthal man, who having been returned to civilization wakes up and creates havoc.

All civilization's fault, of course: initial suspense gives way to boredom when morals are preached.

w Chip Proser, John Drimmer d Fred Schepisi ph Ian Baker m Bruce Smeaton ad Leon Ericksen, Josan Russo ed Billy Weber

Timothy Hutton, Lindsay Crouse, John Lone, Josef Sommer, Danny Glover

Ichabod and Mr Toad **

US 1949 68m Technicolor
Walt Disney
aka: The Adventures of Ichabod and Mr Toad

Cartoon versions of stories by Washington Irving and Kenneth Grahame.

An uncomfortable double bill; the story of Ichabod, though well narrated by Bing Crosby, is macabre without being very interesting; The Wind in the Willows, however, is charmingly pictured, and Mr Toad is splendidly voiced by Eric Blore.

d Jack Kinney, Clyde Geronimi, James Algar supervisor Ben Sharpsteen

The Icicle Thief **

Italy 1989 85m colour
Metro/Bambú/Reitalia (Ernesto Di Sarro)
V, V*, L
original title: Ladri Di Saponette

Watching the television screening of his new film, a director enters the movie when he discovers his characters are changing their lines and leaving the action to appear in commercials.

Witty parody of neo-realistic cinema (the title recalls de Sica's classic Bicycle Thieves), commercialism and TV's treatment of films.

w Maurizio Nichetti, Mauro Monti d Maurizio Nichetti ph Maria Battistoni m Manuel de Sica pd Ada Legori ed Rita Rossi, Anna Missoni

Maurizio Nichetti, Caterina Sylos Labini, Federico Rizzo, Renato Scarpa, Heidi Komarex, Carlina Torta, Massimi Sacilotto, Claudio G. Fava

'An unqualified treat . . . This sophisticated satire on the undifferentiated tap-flow of television is also a passionate declaration of love for the movies.' – David Robinson, The Times

I'd Climb the Highest Mountain *

US 1951 88m Technicolor
TCF (Lamar Trotti)

A Methodist preacher and his wife face the problems of life in a remote part of North Georgia.

Pleasant, rambling, adequately serious and old-fashioned family entertainment, well presented in Hollywood's medium style.

w Lamar Trotti novel Corra Harris d Henry King ph Edward Cronjager md Lionel Newman m Sol Kaplan

Susan Hayward, William Lundigan, Rory Calhoun, Barbara Bates, Gene Lockhart, Lynn Bari, Ruth Donnelly, Alexander Knox

I'd Rather Be Rich *

US 1964 96m Eastmancolor
U-I/Ross Hunter

To comfort her dying grandfather, an heiress introduces an eligible stranger as her fiancé . . . but the old man recovers and begins matchmaking.

Reasonably zesty remake of It Started with Eve, kept afloat by Chevalier's performance.

w Oscar Brodney, Leo Townsend, Norman Krasna d Jack Smight ph Russell Metty m Percy Faith

Maurice Chevalier, Sandra Dee, Robert Goulet, Andy Williams, Gene Raymond, Hermione Gingold, Charles Ruggles

An Ideal Husband *

GB 1947 96m Technicolor
British Lion/London Films (Alexander Korda)

In the 1890s, the career of a London diplomat is threatened by the reappearance of an old flame.

A slight, stiff play is swamped by the cast, the decor, and very garish colour, but there are moments of enjoyment along the way.

w Lajos Biro play Oscar Wilde d Alexander Korda ph Georges Périnal m Arthur Benjamin ad Vincent Korda, Cecil Beaton

Paulette Goddard, Hugh Williams, Michael Wilding, Diana Wynyard, C. Aubrey Smith, Constance Collier, Glynis Johns, Christine Norden

'The composing and cutting of this fine raw material is seldom above medium grade.' – James Agee

Identification of a Woman

Italy 1982 130m Technicolor Technovision
Artificial Eye/Iter Film/Gaumont (Giorgio Nocella, Antonio Macri)
original title: Identificazione di una Donna

A film director searches for an ideal woman to spark off his new film.

A quest that the audience will tire of long before the end.

w Michelangelo Antonioni, Gérard Brach, Tonino Guerra d Michelangelo Antonioni ph Carlo di Palma ad Andrea Crisanti ed Michelangelo Antonioni

Tomas Milian, Daniela Silverio, Christine Boisson, Sandra Monteleoni, Giampaolo Saccarola, Alessandro Ruspoli, Giada Gerini, Sergio Tardioli

Identity Unknown

US 1945 71m bw
Republic/Walter Colmes

An amnesiac soldier comes back from the war.

Curious propaganda piece with everything but roses round the door.

w Richard Weil, Robert Newman d Walter Colmes

Richard Arlen, Cheryl Walker, Roger Pryor, Bobby Driscoll, Lola Lane, Ian Keith

Idiot's Delight *

US 1939 105m bw
MGM (Hunt Stromberg)
V*, L

At the outbreak of World War II, in a hotel on the Swiss border, a hoofer with an all-girl troupe meets an old flame masquerading as a Russian countess.

Interesting but quite unsuccessful film version of a highly artificial play which had been carried off superbly by the Lunts but was now somewhat less well cast, though it did represent an early Hollywood challenge to Hitler. The flagwaving in fact made it more than a little boring.

w Robert E. Sherwood play Robert E. Sherwood d Clarence Brown ph William Daniels m Herbert Stothart

Clark Gable, Norma Shearer, Edward Arnold, Charles Coburn, Burgess Meredith, Joseph Schildkraut, Laura Hope Crews, Skeets Gallagher, Pat Paterson, Fritz Feld

'Exceptionally entertaining comedy, a b.o. sock.' – Variety

'The fun and excitement are still there, however filtered it may be.' – Film Daily

'The mood of the whole thing is forced and cheap – the coming world war staged by Maurice Chevalier.' – Otis Ferguson

'Exactly the same pseudo-qualities as *The Petrified Forest*: a moral pretentiousness, a kind of cellophaned intellectuality.' – *Graham Greene*

The Idle Class *
US   1922   30m approx   bw   silent
First National/Charles Chaplin
V

A tramp dreams of the rich life and is mistaken for the husband of a lady.

Rather slight later Chaplin without the full-blooded farcical elements which made him so popular around 1917.

wd Charles Chaplin   ph Rollie Totheroh

Charles Chaplin, Edna Purviance, Mack Swain

The Idol
GB   1966   111m   bw
Embassy (Leonard Lightstone)
V*

A divorced woman falls in love with her son's friend.

Stupefyingly boring generation-gap sex drama.

w Millard Lampell   d Daniel Petrie   ph Ken Higgins   m Johnny Dankworth

Jennifer Jones, Michael Parks, John Leyton, Jennifer Hilary, Guy Doleman, Natasha Pyne

Idol of Paris
GB   1948   105m   bw
Premier (R. J. Minney)

In old Paris, a ragman's daughter becomes queen of the demi-mondaines.

Unintentionally hilarious copy of the Gainsborough period romances which had been so popular; much criticized because the leading ladies fight a duel with whips, but that's the least of its faults.

w Norman Lee, Stafford Dickens, Henry Ostrer   novel *Paiva Queen of Love* by Alfred Shirkauer   d Leslie Arliss   ph Jack Cox   m Mischa Spoliansky

Beryl Baxter, Christine Norden, Michael Rennie, Margaretta Scott, Kenneth Kent, Henry Oscar, Miles Malleson, Andrew Osborn, Andrew Cruickshank

The Idolmaker
US   1980   119m   Technicolor
United Artists/Gene Kirkwood, Howard W. Koch
V*, L

A songwriter accurately sums up his own limited talent and turns agent and starmaker.

Sharp but padded look behind the scenes of the pop industry; in the end of interest only to initiates.

w Edward Di Lorenzo   d Taylor Hackford   ph Adam Holender   m Jeff Barry

Ray Sharkey, Tovah Feldshuh, Peter Gallagher, Paul Land

Idols in the Dust: see *Saturday's Hero*

If . . . ****
GB   1968   111m   Eastmancolor
Paramount/Memorial (Lindsay Anderson, Michael Medwin)
L

Discontent at a boys' public school breaks out into rebellion.

Allegorical treatment of school life with much fashionable emphasis on obscure narrative, clever cutting, variety of pace, even an unaccountable changing from colour to monochrome and vice versa. It catches perfectly a mood of rebellion and dissatisfaction with the status quo.

w *David Sherwin*   d Lindsay Anderson   ph Miroslav Ondricek   m Marc Wilkinson   pd Jocelyn Herbert

Malcolm McDowell, David Wood, Richard Warwick, Robert Swann, Christine Noonan, Peter Jeffrey, Arthur Lowe, Anthony Nicholls

'The school . . . is the perfect metaphor for the established system all but a few of us continue to accept.' – *David Wilson*

'It's something like the Writing on the Wall.' – *Lindsay Anderson*

'Combines a cold and queasy view of youth with a romantic view of violence.' – *New Yorker*

If a Man Answers
US   1962   102m   Technicolor
Universal/Ross Hunter

A wife decides to make her husband jealous.

Derivative second-team matrimonial comedy, all dressed up but with nowhere to go.

w Richard Morris   novel Winifred Wolfe   d Henry Levin   ph Russell Metty   m Hans Salter

Sandra Dee, Bobby Darin, Micheline Presle, John Lund, Cesar Romero, Stephanie Powers

If Ever I See You Again
US   1978   105m   colour
Columbia (Joe Brooks)

A songwriter attempts to win back the love of an old girlfriend.

Almost a one-man band of a movie that plays too long on one note and is better never seen at all.

w Joe Brooks, Martin Davidson   d Joe Brooks   ph Adam Holender   m Joe Brooks   ed Rich Shaine

Joe Brooks, Shelley Hack, Jimmy Breslin, Jerry Keller, George Plimpton, Michael Decker

If I Had a Million **
US   1932   88m   bw
Paramount (Benjamin Glazer, Louis D. Lighton)

Various people each receive a million dollars from an eccentric who wants to test their reactions.

Interesting, dated multi-part comedy drama remembered chiefly for the brief sequence in which Laughton blows a raspberry to his boss and Fields chases road hogs. As an entertainment it's patchy, lacking an overall style.

w Claude Binyon, Whitney Bolton, Malcolm Stuart Boylan, John Bright, Sidney Buchman, Lester Cole, Isabel Dawn, Boyce DeGaw, Walter de Leon, Oliver H. P. Garrett, Harvey Gates, Grover Jones, Ernst Lubitsch, Lawton Mackaill, Joseph L. Mankiewicz, William Slavens McNutt, Seton I. Miller, Tiffany Thayer   story Robert D. Andrews   d Ernst Lubitsch, Norman Taurog, Stephen Roberts, Norman Z. McLeod, James Cruze, William A. Seiter, H. Bruce Humberstone

W. C. Fields, *Charles Laughton, May Robson*, Richard Bennett, Alison Skipworth, Gary Cooper, Wynne Gibson, George Raft, Jack Oakie, Frances Dee, Charles Ruggles, Mary Boland, Roscoe Karns, Gene Raymond, Lucien Littlefield

'Not uninteresting, but spotty in retrospect . . . the cinematic porridge is naturally replete with a diversity of seasonings.' – *Variety*

'It develops an obvious idea in an obvious way.' – *Time*

If I Had My Way *
US   1940   82m   bw
Universal (David Butler)

Two vaudevillians help an orphan girl and open a new night-club.

Quite likeable and very typical star vehicle of its period.

w William Conselman, James V. Kern   d David Butler   ph George Robinson   m Frank Skinner

Bing Crosby, Charles Winninger, Gloria Jean, El Brendel, Allyn Joslyn, Donald Woods, Eddie Leonard, Claire Dodd, Blanche Ring

If I Were Free
US   1933   65m   bw
RKO

A man and woman, each unhappily married, try to get together.

Rather soppy drama which fails to develop.

w Dwight Taylor   play *Behold We Live* by John Van Druten   d Elliott Nugent

Irene Dunne, Clive Brook, Nils Asther, Henry Stephenson, Laura Hope Crews

'Thin in texture, it never reaches a pace that really counts.' – *Variety*

'His love-making was as dangerous as his swordplay!'
If I Were King *
US   1938   101m   bw
Paramount (Frank Lloyd)

The 14th-century poet and rascal François Villon matches wits with Louis XI and leads an uprising of the people.

A story which we have grown used to seeing with music as *The Vagabond King* is here well presented but somehow rings hollow, with insufficient derring-do; it is the wrong kind of swashbuckling for its star, who is for once outacted by Rathbone in an unusual wily characterization.

w Preston Sturges   d Frank Lloyd   ph Theodor Sparkuhl   m Richard Hageman   ad Hans Dreier, John Goodman

Ronald Colman, *Basil Rathbone*, Frances Dee, Ellen Drew, C. V. France, Heather Thatcher, Henry Wilcoxon, Sidney Toler

'Healthy box office that will hit extended runs right down the line.' – *Variety*

'A well mounted and splendid production that carries along at a fascinating pace.' – *Daily Variety*

AAN: Richard Hageman; Basil Rathbone; art direction

If I'm Lucky
US   1945   79m   bw
TCF (Bryan Foy)

A singer runs for state governor and exposes corruption.

Lacklustre remake of *Thanks a Million,* with decidedly dispirited elements.

w Snag Werris, Robert Ellis, Helen Logan, George Bricker   d Lewis Seiler   ph Glen MacWilliams   md Emil Newman   m/ly Edgar de Lange, Joseph Myrow

Vivian Blaine, Perry Como, Carmen Miranda, Harry James, Phil Silvers, Edgar Buchanan, Reed Hadley

If It's Tuesday, This Must Be Belgium *
US   1969   98m   DeLuxe
UA/Wolper (Stan Margulies)
V*, L

A group of American tourists have various adventures during a lightning tour of Europe.

Amusing comedy which does pretty well by a good idea.

w David Shaw   d Mel Stuart   ph Vilis Lapenieks   m Walter Scharf

Suzanne Pleshette, Ian McShane, Mildred Natwick, Murray Hamilton, Michael Constantine, Sandy Baron, Norman Fell, Peggy Cass, Marty Ingels, Pamela Britton, Luke Halpin, Aubrey Morris

If Looks Could Kill: see *Teen Agent*

If This Be Sin: see *That Dangerous Age*

If Winter Comes
US 1948 97m bw
MGM (Victor Saville)

A sentimental idealist, unhappily married, finds himself at the mercy of village gossip when he takes in a pregnant girl.

Artificial romantic nonsense, unconvincingly staged and modernized from a very dated bestseller.

w Marguerite Roberts, Arthur Wimperis   novel A. S. M. Hutchinson   d Victor Saville   ph George Folsey   m Herbert Stothart

Walter Pidgeon, Deborah Kerr, Janet Leigh, Angela Lansbury, Binnie Barnes, Dame May Whitty, Reginald Owen

If You Could Only Cook
US 1935 72m bw
Columbia

A young millionaire meets a poor girl and they get jobs as cook and butler.

Whimsical comedy-romance; thin but moderately beguiling.

w F. Hugh Herbert, Gertrude Purcell, Howard J. Green   d William A. Seiter

Jean Arthur, Herbert Marshall, Leo Carrillo, Lionel Stander, Frieda Inescort

'Plenty of chuckles . . . offers particularly strong promise for the nabes.' – Variety

† This was the film which enabled Frank Capra to get out of his Columbia contract, because they accidentally promoted it in Europe as being directed by him.

If You Feel Like Singing: see Summer Stock

If You Knew Susie *
US 1948 90m bw
RKO (Eddie Cantor)
V*

A vaudeville couple retire to his ancestral home in New England.

Mild family comedy capitalizing on the team established in Show Business.

w Warren Wilson, Oscar Brodney   d Gordon Douglas   ph Frank Redman

Eddie Cantor, Joan Davis, Allyn Joslyn, Bobby Driscoll, Charles Dingle

Ikiru *
Japan 1952 143m bw
Toho
aka: Living; Doomed

A clerk learns that he is dying and spends his last months creating a children's playground.

A moving and beautifully made personal drama which also gives an interesting background of modern Japan.

w Hideo Oguni, Shinobu Hashimoto, Akira Kurosawa   d Akira Kurosawa   ph Asaishi Nakai   m Fumio Hayasaka

Takashi Shimura, Nobuo Kaneko, Kyoko Seki

Il Faut Vivre Dangereusement
France 1975 100m colour
Fox/ORFT (Nelly Kaplan)
aka: You've Got to Live Dangerously

A private eye, hired to investigate a young woman, uncovers a plot to find a fabulous diamond.

Baroque thriller with more corpses than Hamlet, but one that fails to sustain interest, despite its recourse to naked flesh at every possible opportunity.

w Nelly Kaplan   d Claude Makovsky   m Claude Bolling   ad Jacques Dugied   ed Jocelyne Triquet

Claude Brasseur, Anne Girardot

Il mio nome è Nessuno: see My Name Is Nobody

L'Ile au trésor: see Treasure Island

'Both living a secret – each afraid to tell!'
I'll Be Seeing You **
US 1944 85m bw
David O. Selznick (Dore Schary)

A lady convict at home on parole for Christmas meets and falls for a shell-shocked soldier.

Schmaltzy, middle-American romantic drama with some nicely handled moments and plenty of talent on hand. In the Hollywood mainstream.

w Marion Parsonnet   novel Charles Martin   d William Dieterle   ph Tony Gaudio   m Daniele Amfitheatrof

Ginger Rogers, Joseph Cotten, Shirley Temple, Spring Byington, Tom Tully, Chill Wills

'A sentimental, improbable picture, but unexpectedly rewarding in detail.' – Richard Mallett, Punch

I'll Be Your Sweetheart
GB 1945 104m bw
Gainsborough (Louis Levy)

In 1900, songwriters fight with copyright pirates.

Studio-bound musical romance without the necessary resonance.

w Val Guest, Val Valentine   d Val Guest   ph Phil Grindrod   md Louis Levy

Margaret Lockwood, Michael Rennie, Vic Oliver, Peter Graves, Moore Marriott, Frederick Burtwell, Maudie Edwards, Garry Marsh

I'll Be Yours
US 1947 90m bw
Universal (Felix Jackson)

A small-town girl tries to make good in the big city.

Slackly handled remake of The Good Fairy. A doubtful 'A' production which did nothing for its star's ailing career.

w Preston Sturges (adapted anonymously from his previous screenplay based on the Molnar original)   d William A. Seiter   ph Hal Mohr   m Frank Skinner

Deanna Durbin, Tom Drake, William Bendix, Adolphe Menjou, Walter Catlett, Franklin Pangborn

I'll Cry Tomorrow *
US 1955 119m bw
MGM (Lawrence Weingarten)
V*, L

Lillian Roth, a Broadway/Hollywood star of the early thirties, becomes an alcoholic.

Fictionalized biopic, pretty well done of the True Confessions kind.

w Helen Deutsch, Jay Richard Kennedy   book Lillian Roth, Gerold Frank   d Daniel Mann   ph Arthur E. Arling   m Alex North   ad Cedric Gibbons, Randall Duell

Susan Hayward, Richard Conte, Eddie Albert, Jo Van Fleet, Don Taylor, Ray Danton, Margo

'By emphasizing physical degradation in almost every frame, the film makes her less an object of acutely personal concern than a street casualty seen remotely from the top of a bar.' – Alexander Walker

AAN: Arthur E. Arling; Susan Hayward; art direction

I'll Get By
US 1950 86m Technicolor
TCF (William Perlberg)

Two songwriters meet success, then join the marines and are reunited with their former girlfriends.

Fair standard musical, a modernization of Tin Pan Alley.

w Mary Loos, Richard Sale   d Richard Sale   ph Charles G. Clarke   md Lionel Newman

June Haver, Gloria de Haven, William Lundigan, Dennis Day, Harry James, Thelma Ritter

AAN: Lionel Newman

I'll Get You for This
GB 1950 83m bw
Romulus
US title: Lucky Nick Cain

An American gambler in Italy goes after the gangsters who framed him.

Second-grade star thick ear.

w George Callahan, William Rose   novel High Stakes by James Hadley Chase   d Joseph M. Newman

George Raft, Coleen Gray, Charles Goldner, Walter Rilla, Greta Gynt, Enzo Staiola

I'll Give a Million *
US 1938 70m bw
TCF (Darryl F. Zanuck)

A millionaire becomes a tramp and disappears, letting it be known that he will give a fortune for genuine acts of kindness. Tramps are then royally entertained all over town.

Amusing depression comedy with satirical touches.

w Boris Ingster, Milton Sperling   d Walter Lang   ph Lucien Andriot   md Louis Silvers

Warner Baxter, Peter Lorre, Marjorie Weaver, Jean Hersholt, John Carradine, J. Edward Bromberg, Lynn Bari, Fritz Feld, Sig Rumann

'Not worth that much . . . the plot sags at the halfway mark and the wind-up is disappointing.' – Variety

Ill Met by Moonlight
GB 1956 104m bw Vistavision
Rank/Vega (Michael Powell, Emeric Pressburger)
US title: Night Ambush

In Crete during the German occupation, British agents work with partisans to capture a German general.

Disappointingly dreary war adventure with too many night locations, too little suspense and characterization, and photography which seems to be deliberately unattractive.

wd Michael Powell, Emeric Pressburger   book W. Stanley Moss   ph Christopher Challis   m Mikis Theodorakis

Dirk Bogarde, Marius Goring, David Oxley, Cyril Cusack, John Cairney, Laurence Payne, Wolfe Morris, Michael Gough

I'll Never Forget Whatshisname *
GB 1967 96m Technicolor
Universal/Scimitar (Michael Winner)

An advertising executive gives up power and money for integrity on a small literary magazine, but is won back by a mogul.

Vivid yet muddled tragi-comedy of the sixties, with splashes of sex and violence in trendy settings, a hero one really doesn't believe in, and a title which seems to have no meaning whatsoever.

w Peter Draper   d Michael Winner   ph Otto Heller   m Francis Lai

Oliver Reed, Orson Welles, Carol White, Harry Andrews, Michael Hordern, Wendy Craig, Marianne Faithfull

I'll Never Forget You: see The House in the Square

I'll See You in My Dreams *
US 1952 112m bw
Warner (Louis F. Edelman)
V, V*, L

The domestic and professional life of songwriter Gus Kahn.

Quiet-toned, well made, quite forgettable musical.

w Melville Shavelson, Jack Rose   d Michael Curtiz
ph Ted McCord   md Ray Heindorf   ch Le Roy
Prinz

Doris Day, Danny Thomas, Frank Lovejoy, Patrice
Wymore, James Gleason

I'll Take Romance
US   1937   85m   bw
Columbia (Everett Riskin)

When an opera singer refuses to fulfil a South
American contract, her impresario kidnaps her.

Moderate star vehicle.

w George Oppenheimer, Jane Murfin   d Edward H.
Griffith   ph Lucien Andriot   m/ly various

Grace Moore, Melvyn Douglas, Helen Westley, Stuart
Erwin, Margaret Hamilton, Walter Kingsford, Esther
Muir

I'll Take Sweden
US   1965   96m   Technicolor
UA/Edward Small

A widowed oil company executive accepts a
Stockholm posting to remove his teenage daughter
from an unsuitable attachment.

Feeble comedy which unwisely attempts to be with it,
but is bogged down by amateurish handling and wit-
wise is sadly without it.

w Nat Perrin, Bob Fisher, Arthur Marx   d Frederick
de Cordova   ph Daniel L. Fapp   m Jimmy Haskell

Bob Hope, Tuesday Weld, Frankie Avalon, Dina
Merrill, Jeremy Slate, John Qualen, Walter Sande

I'll Tell the World
US   1945   76m   bw
Universal

A small-town sports announcer starts a lonely hearts
programme.

Amiable second feature, a reworking of the star's
earlier Advice to the Lovelorn.

w Henry Blankfort   d Leslie Goodwins

Lee Tracy, Brenda Joyce, Raymond Walburn, June
Preisser, Thomas Gomez

'Feasible b.o., but not a strong drafter where the Tracy
name can't help.' – Variety

Illegal *
US   1955   88m   bw
Warner (Frank P. Rosenberg)
V*

A disillusioned District Attorney becomes a
racketeer's lawyer but finally denounces him at the
cost of his own life.

Competent remake of The Mouthpiece (qv), a good star
melodrama.

w W. R. Burnett, James R. Webb   story Frank J.
Collins   d Lewis Allen   ph Peverell Marley
m Max Steiner

Edward G. Robinson, Nina Foch, Albert Dekker,
Hugh Marlowe, Jayne Mansfield, Howard St John,
Ellen Corby

'Hard-hitting stuff in the old gangster tradition.' –
MFB

Illegal Entry
US   1949   84m   bw
Universal-International

Undercover agents investigate a smuggling racket.

Routine, quite entertaining alleged exposé.

w Joel Malone   d Frederick de Cordova

Howard Duff, George Brent, Marta Toren, Tom Tully,
Paul Stewart, Gar Moore

Illegal Traffic
US   1938   67m   bw
Paramount

The FBI tracks down an organization devoted to
smuggling criminals away from danger.

Smart second feature based on J. Edgar Hoover's
Persons in Hiding.

w Robert Yost, Lewis Foster, Stuart Anthony
d Louis King

J. Carrol Naish, Mary Carlisle, Robert Preston

'Good racketeer film . . . should do better than average
business.' – Variety

Illegally Yours
US   1988   102m   Technicolor
UA/Crescent Moon/DEG (Peter Bogdanovich)
V, V*

A juror sets out to prove the innocence of a woman he
has loved from afar, who is accused of murder and
blackmail.

Screwed-up attempt at a screwball comedy, painful to
watch.

w M. A. Stewart, Max Dickens   d Peter
Bogdanovich   ph Dante Spinotti   m Phil Marshall
pd Jane Musky   ed Richard Fields, Ronald Krehel

Rob Lowe, Colleen Camp, Kenneth Mars, Harry
Carey Jnr, Kim Myers, Marshall Colt

Illicit
US   1931   81m   bw
Warner

A disillusioned wife walks out on her husband and
seeks solace elsewhere.

Undistinguished weepie, which later became Ex-Lady.

w Harvey Thew   d Archie Mayo

Barbara Stanwyck, Ricardo Cortez, Joan Blondell,
Charles Butterworth

'Lacks a wallop and action.' – Variety

'Don't dare stare at . . .'
The Illustrated Man *
US   1969   103m   Technicolor   Panavision
Warner/SKM (Howard B. Kreitsek, Ted Mann)
V, V*, L

A strange wanderer tells weird stories based on the
tattooed pictures which cover him from tip to toe.

Oddball compendium based rather insecurely on Ray
Bradbury stories; in this form they don't amount to
much but the presentation is assured.

w Howard B. Kreitsek   d Jack Smight   ph Philip
Lathrop   m Jerry Goldsmith   ad Joel Schiller

Rod Steiger, Claire Bloom, Robert Drivas, Don
Dubbins, Jason Evers

'A curiously passionless affair – efficient enough,
meaty enough, but without poetry, without charm,
without beauty.' – Philip Strick

'A pretentious comic strip of maudlin and muddled
fantasies.' – Judith Crist

Illustrious Corpses *
Italy/France   1975   120m   Technicolor
PEA/UA (Alberto Grimaldi)
original title: Cadaveri Eccellenti

A right-wing conspiracy to arouse feelings against
dissidents is found to be behind the murders of public
figures.

Elegant police melodrama on an unlikely political
thesis.

w Francesco Rosi, Tonino Guerra, Lino Jannuzzi
novel Il Contesto by Leonardo Sciascia   d Francesco Rosi
ph Pasqualino de Santis   m Piero Piccioni

Lino Ventura, Alain Cuny, Maolo Bonacelli, Marcel
Bozzuffi, Max von Sydow, Fernando Rey, Charles
Vanel, Tina Aumont

'Like watching layer after layer peeled off some
diseased flower until the poisoned root is reached.' –
Michael Billington, Illustrated London News

I'm All Right Jack ***
GB   1959   104m   bw
British Lion/Charter (Roy Boulting)
V*

A world-innocent graduate takes a job in industry; by
starting at the bottom he provokes a national strike.

Satirical farce which manages to hit most of its
widespread targets and finds corruption in high, low
and middle places. A not inaccurate picture of aspects
of British life in the fifties, and a presage of the satire
boom to come with Beyond the Fringe and That Was the
Week That Was.

w Frank Harvey, John Boulting   novel Private Life by
Alan Hackney   d John Boulting   ph Max Greene
m Ken Hare

Ian Carmichael, Peter Sellers, Irene Handl, Richard
Attenborough, Terry-Thomas, Dennis Price, Margaret
Rutherford, Liz Fraser, John Le Mesurier, Sam Kydd

I'm Dancing as Fast as I Can
US   1982   106m   Movielab
Paramount/Edgar J. Scherick/Scott Rudin
V*, L

A documentary film-maker is rehabilitated after
dependence on drugs.

Unabsorbing case history more suitable as a TV movie
except that the acting for TV would not have been so
far over the top.

w David Rabe   book Barbara Gordon   d Jack
Hofsiss   ph Jan de Bont   m Stanley Silverman

Jill Clayburgh, Nicol Williamson, Dianne Wiest, Joe
Pesci, Geraldine Page, James Sutorius, Richard
Masur, Kathleen Widdoes

I'm from Missouri
US   1939   77m   bw
Paramount

The wife of a Missouri farmer and mule breeder has
social aspirations.

Rural comedy patterned after the Will Rogers
successes.

w John C. Moffitt, Duke Atterbury   d Theodore
Reed

Bob Burns, Gladys George, Gene Lockhart, Judith
Barrett, William Henry, Patricia Morison, E. E. Clive,
Melville Cooper

'Moderate grosser for family trade.' – Variety

I'm Gonna Git You, Sucka
US   1988   89m   DeLuxe
UIP/United Artists/Ivory Way/Raymond Katz/Front Films (Peter
McCarthy, Carl Craig)
V*, L, S

Black heroes are recruited to overthrow a white
gangster.

Good-natured parody of black action movies such as
Shaft.

wd Keenen Ivory Wayans   ph Tom Richmond
m David Michael Frank   pd Melba Farquhar,
Catherine Hardwicke   ed Michael R. Miller

Keenen Ivory Wayans, Bernie Casey, Antonio Fargas,
Steve James, Isaac Hayes, Jim Brown, Janet DuBois,
Dawnn Lewis, John Vernon, Clu Gulagher

Im Innern des Wals: see In the Belly of the Whale

Im Lauf der Zeit: see Kings of the Road

'Just a sensitive gal who climbed the ladder of success ...
wrong by wrong! A story about a gal who lost her
reputation – and never missed it!'

I'm No Angel ***
US   1933   88m   bw
Paramount (William Le Baron)

A carnival dancer gets off a murder charge, moves into
society and sues a man for breach of promise.

The star's most successful vehicle, credited with
saving the fortunes of Paramount, remains a highly
diverting side show with almost a laugh a minute.
Released before the Legion of Decency was formed, it
also contains some of Mae's fruitiest lines.

w *Mae West*   d Wesley Ruggles   ph Leo Tover
m/ly Harvey Brooks, Gladys Dubois

Mae West, Edward Arnold, Cary Grant, Gregory Ratoff,
Ralf Harolde, Kent Taylor, Gertrude Michael

'The most freewheeling of all Mae's screen vehicles,
and the most satisfying of the lot.' – *James Robert Parish*

'A quality of balance and proportion which only the
finest films attain.' – *Views and Reviews*

Images
Eire   1972   101m   Technicolor   Panavision
Lions Gate/Hemdale (Tommy Thompson)

A semi-hysterical woman is confronted by the images
of her former lovers.

Pretentious psycho-drama which might have made a
good half-hour.

wd Robert Altman   ph Vilmos Zsigmond   m John
Williams

Susannah York, René Auberjonois, Marcel Bozzuffi

AAN: John Williams

Imaginary Sweetheart: see *Professional Sweetheart*

An Imaginary Tale
France   1990   100m   colour
Mayfair/C. M. Luca/Téléscène/National Film Board of Canada
    (Claudio Luca, Robin Spry)
French title: *Une histoire inventée*

In Montreal, a jazz trumpeter falls in love with an
actress, to the annoyance of her actor-lover.

Performances of Shakespeare's *Othello* form a
background to this tale of jealousy, treated as comic
rather than tragic.

w André Forcier, Jacques Marcotte   d André Forcier
ph George Dufaux   m Serge Fiore   ad Réal
Ouellette   ed François Gill

Jean Lapointe, Louise Marleau, Charlotte Laurier,
Marc Messier, Jean-François Pichette, France Castel,
Toni Nardi

'Too hermetic to be much more than a light diversion.'
– *Sight and Sound*

Imitation General
US   1958   88m   bw
MGM (William Hawks)

France 1944: when a general is killed, a sergeant takes
his place to preserve morale.

Odd, rather unpalatable war comedy-drama.

w William Bowers   d George Marshall   ph George
Folsey

Glenn Ford, Red Buttons, Taina Elg, Dean Jones,
Kent Smith

Imitation of Life **
US   1934   109m   bw
Universal (John M. Stahl)

A woman becomes rich through the pancake recipe of
her black servant, but the latter has a tragic life
because her daughter passes for white.

Monumentally efficient tearjerker, generally well
done.

w William Hurlbut   novel Fannie Hurst   d John
Stahl   ph Merritt Gerstad   m Heinz Roemheld

Claudette Colbert, Warren William, *Louise Beavers*, Ned
Sparks, Rochelle Hudson, Fredi Washington, Alan
Hale, Henry Armetta

'Grim and harsh stuff . . . its reception in the south
cannot be judged or guessed by a northerner.' – *Variety*

'Classic, compulsively watchable rags-to-riches-and-
heartbreak weeper.' – *New Yorker, 1977*

AAN: best picture

Imitation of Life *
US   1959   124m   Eastmancolor
U-I (Ross Hunter)
V*

Glossy remake of the above with its heroine now an
actress; stunningly produced but dully acted, making
its racially sensitive plot seem insincere.

w Eleanore Griffin, Allan Scott   d Douglas Sirk
ph Russell Metty   m Frank Skinner

Lana Turner, Juanita Moore, John Gavin, Susan
Kohner, Dan O'Herlihy, Sandra Dee, Robert Alda

AAN: Juanita Moore; Susan Kohner

Immaculate Conception *
GB   1991   120m   Metrocolor
Feature/Dehlavi Films/Film on Four (Jamil Dehlavi)
V

In Pakistan, a childless American woman is told that
she will conceive if she returns to a shrine with her
English husband, although she suspects him of
having an affair with an Indian friend.

Tangled tale of adultery amid a clash of cultures,
rendered exotic by its setting of a fertility cult
administered by priestly eunuchs.

wd Jamil Dehlavi   ph Nic Knowland   m Richard
Harvey   pd Mike Porter   ed Chris Barnes

James Wilby, Melissa Leo, Shabana Azmi, Zia
Mohyeddin, James Cossins, Shreeram Lagoo, Ronny
Jhutti, Tim Choate

'Well worth a look, if for no other reason than
Western audiences rarely get a chance to see anything
(vaguely) Asian. – *Kim Newman, Empire*

Immediate Family
US   1989   95m   DeLuxe
Columbia (Sarah Pillsbury, Midge Sanford)
V, V*, L

A rich but childless couple arrange to adopt the
newborn baby of a poor, unmarried teenager.

Well-meaning, predictable problem movie that fails to
involve an audience.

w Barbara Benedek   d Jonathan Kaplan   ph John
W. Lindley   m Brad Fiedel   ed Jane Kurson

Glenn Close, James Woods, Mary Stuart Masterson,
Kevin Dillon, Linda Darlow, Jane Greer, Jessica
James

The Immigrant **
US   1917   20m approx   bw   silent
Mutual

A penniless immigrant befriends a girl on the boat
and later helps her in a café.

One of the most inventive early Chaplins, with
touches of sentiment and social comment which for
once only strengthen and do not antagonize.

wd Charles Chaplin   ph William C. Foster, Rollie
Totheroh

Charles Chaplin, Edna Purviance, Albert Austin,
Henry Bergman, Eric Campbell

'In its roughness and apparent simplicity it is as much
a jewel as a story by O. Henry.' – *Photoplay*

Immoral Tales
France   1974   103m   Eastmancolor
Argos (Anatole Dauman)

Four bawdy stories, ranging from 1498 to 1970.

The usual sex portmanteau with a little more strength
in the detail and interest in human behaviour than
usual.

wd Walerian Borowczyk   ph Bernard Daillencourt,
Guy Durban, Michel Zolat, Noel Véry   m Maurice Le
Roux

Lise Danvers, Charlotte Alexandra, Paloma Picasso,
Florence Bellamy

'You come out having learned something about the
waywardness of life and love and having been taken
on a mystery tour into the present, the past, and the
enigmatic strangeness of womanhood.' – *Michael
Billington, Illustrated London News*

Immortal Battalion: see *The Way Ahead*

The Immortal Sergeant *
US   1943   90m   bw
TCF (Lamar Trotti)
V*

In the North African campaign, a battle-toughened
sergeant is killed after inspiring the raw recruits
under his command.

'Inspirational' war adventure, quite neatly done but a
shade embarrassed by its own poetic leanings.

w Lamar Trotti   novel John Brophy   d John Stahl
ph Arthur Miller   m David Buttolph

Henry Fonda, Thomas Mitchell, Maureen O'Hara,
Allyn Joslyn, Reginald Gardiner, Melville Cooper,
Branwell Fletcher, Morton Lowry

'By the time the first soldier has bit the sand, the film
identifies itself: it is none other than Hollywood's old
friend the Foreign Legion of Beau Geste vintage,
jerked from the shelf and clothed in a new uniform.' –
Time

The Immortal Story
France   1968   60m   Eastmancolor
Albina/ORTF (Micheline Rozan)

In 19th-century Macao, a rich merchant tries to make
an old seaman's story come true.

Muddled and stiltedly told fable which would have
excited no attention if it had not been associated with
the elusive Mr Welles.

wd Orson Welles   story Isak Dinesen   ph Willy
Kurant   m Erik Satie

Orson Welles, Jeanne Moreau, Roger Coggio, Norman
Eshley

Impact
US   1949   111m   bw
(UA) Harry M. Popkin
V*

A woman and her lover plan the murder of her rich
industrialist husband, but things go wrong and the
husband survives under another name . . .

Curiously elongated but watchable melodrama, with
the impression of a second team doing its best.

w Dorothy Reid   d Arthur Lubin   ph Ernest Laszlo

Brian Donlevy, Ella Raines, Charles Coburn, Helen
Walker

Impact
GB   1963   61m   bw
Butcher's (John I. Phillips)

An investigative reporter is framed by a crooked
night-club owner.

Efficient, unmemorable second feature.

w Conrad Phillips, Peter Maxwell   d Peter Maxwell
ph Gerald Moss   m Johnny Gregory   ad Harry
White   ed David Hawkins

Conrad Phillips, George Pastell, Ballard Berkeley, Linda Marlowe, Richard Klee, Anita West

The Impatient Maiden
US   1932   78m   bw
Universal

A romantic maidservant learns the difference between life and fantasy.

Solidly made comedy-drama which doesn't seem to have inspired its director.

w Richard Schayer, Winifred Dunn   *novel The Impatient Virgin* by Donald Henderson Clarke   d James Whale

Mae Clarke, Lew Ayres, Una Merkel, John Halliday, Andy Devine, Berton Churchill

'Trashy stuff . . . aims at smartness and sophistication, and achieves but crudity.' – *Variety*

The Impatient Years
US   1944   91m   bw
Columbia (Virginia Van Upp)

A soldier finds difficulty in adjusting to his civilian matrimonial state.

Thin star comedy.

w Virginia Van Upp   d Irving Cummings   ph Hal Mohr   m Marlin Skiles

Jean Arthur, Lee Bowman, Charles Coburn, Edgar Buchanan, Harry Davenport, Grant Mitchell, Jane Darwell

The Imperfect Lady (1935): see *The Perfect Gentleman*

'Scandal seeks her out – even on her wedding night!'
The Imperfect Lady
US   1946   97m   bw
Paramount (Karl Tunberg)
GB title: *Mrs Loring's Secret*

In 1890s London, an MP marries a lady with a past.

Dusty melodrama, adequately produced.

w Karl Tunberg   story Ladislas Fodor   d Lewis Allen   ph John F. Seitz   m Victor Young

Ray Milland, Teresa Wright, Cedric Hardwicke, Virginia Field, Anthony Quinn, Reginald Owen, Melville Cooper, George Zucco, Rhys Williams, Charles Coleman, Miles Mander, Edmund Breon, Frederick Worlock

The Impersonator *
GB   1961   64m   bw
Bryanston/Herald (Anthony Perry)

Americans at a British air base are suspected when a murderous prowler strikes.

Well made second-feature thriller with effective locations, suspense sequences and village atmosphere.

wd Alfred Shaughnessy   ph John Coquillon   m de Wolfe

John Crawford, Jane Griffith, Patricia Burke, John Salew

The Importance of Being Earnest **
GB   1952   95m   Technicolor
Rank/Javelin/Two Cities (Teddy Baird)
V*

Two wealthy and eligible bachelors of the 1890s have problems with their marriage prospects.

Disappointingly stagey rendering (when compared, say, with *Occupe-toi d'Amélie*) of Britain's most wondrously witty lighter-than-air comedy of manners. As a record of a theatrical performance, however, it is valuable.

w Anthony Asquith   play Oscar Wilde   d Anthony Asquith   ph Desmond Dickinson   m Benjamin Frankel   ad Carmen Dillon

Michael Redgrave, Michael Denison, Edith Evans, Margaret Rutherford, Joan Greenwood, Miles Malleson, Dorothy Tutin, Walter Hudd

'A more positive decision on style should have been taken. A film of this kind must be either an adaptation or a piece of filmed theatre. This one, being partially both, is not wholly either.' – *Gavin Lambert*

The Impossible Lover: see *Huddle*

The Impossible Years
US   1968   98m   Metrocolor   Panavision
MGM/Marten (Lawrence Weingarten)

A university psychiatrist has trouble controlling his nubile 17-year-old daughter.

Wacky farce which veers between the tasteless and the ludicrous, and is never more than momentarily entertaining.

w George Wells   play Bob Fisher, Arthur Marx   d Michael Gordon   ph William H. Daniels   m Don Costa

David Niven, Lola Albright, Chad Everett, Ozzie Nelson, Cristina Ferrare, Don Beddoe

'A comedy of the generation gap which didn't bridge it but fell right into it.' – *Gerald Garrett*

The Impostor
US   1944   92m   bw
Universal
TV title: *Strange Confession*

A French convict escapes during a Nazi bombing raid, and in the guise of a dead man fights bravely for France.

Propagandist melodrama, more stiffly made than its talent would suggest.

wd Julien Duvivier

Jean Gabin, Ellen Drew, Richard Whorf, Allyn Joslyn, Peter Van Eyck, Ralph Morgan

Impromptu *
GB   1989   107m   colour
Rank/Sovereign/Governor/Les Films Ariane (Stuart Oken, Daniel A. Sherkow)
V, V*, L

George Sand chases after Chopin to a country house-party and succeeds in seducing him later in Paris.

Lively re-telling of a well-known romance, but the modern, slangy dialogue makes it seem like a fancy-dress party, and it runs out of energy halfway through.

w Sarah Kernochan   d James Lapine   ph Bruno de Keyzer   md Chris Walker   ad Gérard Daoudal   ed Michael Ellis

Judy Davis, Hugh Grant, Mandy Patinkin, Bernadette Peters, Julian Sands, Ralph Brown, Georges Corraface, Anton Rodgers, Emma Thompson, Anna Massey

'Not wholly successful, this is nevertheless a surprisingly perky addition to the mainly dreary catalogue of films about the loves of deadweight famous names from the past.' – *Kim Newman, MFB*

Improper Channels
Canada   1979   91m   colour

A father runs into administrative trouble when he takes his injured daughter to hospital.

Salutary but not very commanding tale for our times, with a leading performance that suffers from overfamiliarity.

w Morrie Rubinsky, Ian Sutherland, Adam Arkin   d Eric Till   ph Anthony Richmond   m Maribeth Solomon, Micky Erbe

Alan Arkin, Mariette Hartley, Monica Parker, Harry Ditson

An Impudent Girl **
France   1985   97m   colour
Artificial Eye/Oliane/A2/Telema/Monthyon (Marie-Laure Reyre)
V
original title: *L'Effrontée*

An awkward 13-year-old girl begins to grow up.

Charming film of adolescent trauma, owing much to Carson McCuller's *The Member of the Wedding* and superior to the US movie version.

w Claude Miller, Luc Beraud, Bernard Stora, Annie Miller   d Claude Miller   ph Dominique Chapuis   m Alain Jomy   pd Jean-Pierre Kohut Svelko   ed Albert Jurgenson

Charlotte Gainsbourg, Bernadette Lafont, Jean-Claude Braily, Raoul Billerey, Clothilde Baudon, Jean-Philippe Ecoffey

Impulse
US   1984   99m   DeLuxe
Tim Zinnemann/ABC Motion Pictures

After an earthquake, a small farming community is menaced by a mysterious underground substance which makes people self-destructive.

Modest, mildly humorous sci-fi which has its fun without explaining anything at all.

w Bart Davis, Don Carlos Dunaway   d Graham Baker

Tim Matheson, Meg Tilly, Hume Cronyn, John Karlen, Amy Stryker

Impulse
US   1990   108m   Technicolor
Warner (Albert S. Ruddy)
V*, L

An undercover cop keeps quiet about the murder of a missing witness.

Implausible thriller.

w John de Marco, Leigh Chapman   d Sondra Locke   ph Deam Semler   m Michel Colombier   pd William A. Elliott   ed John W. Wheeler

Theresa Russell, Jeff Fahey, George Dzundza, Alan Rosenberg, Nicholas Mele, Eli Danker, Charles McCaughan, Lynne Thigpen, Swan Elliott

In a Lonely Place *
US   1950   93m   bw
Columbia/Santana (Robert Lord)

An embittered Hollywood scriptwriter escapes a murder charge but loses his girlfriend through his violent temperament.

Curious character melodrama which intrigues without satisfying.

w Andrew Solt   novel Dorothy B. Hughes   d Nicholas Ray   ph Burnett Guffey   m George Antheil

Humphrey Bogart, Gloria Grahame, Frank Lovejoy, Carl Benton Reid, Art Smith, Jeff Donnell

'It remains better than average, but lacks the penetration which would make it really interesting.' – *Gavin Lambert*

In a Year with 13 Moons
West Germany   1978   124m   colour
Tango/Project/Filmverlag der Autoren
original title: *In einem Jahr mit 13 Monden*

Ordeals of a man who undergoes a sex change.

Unattractive case history with expressionist decoration.

wd Rainer Werner Fassbinder   ph Rainer Werner Fassbinder   m Peter Raben

Volker Spengler, Ingrid Caven, Gottfried John, Elisabeth Trissenaar, Eva Mattes

In Bed with Madonna: see *Truth or Dare*

In Caliente

US 1935 85m bw
Warner

In a Mexican horse racing resort, a dancer falls for the magazine editor who criticized her act.

Very slim storyline fails to make this a major musical despite attractive numbers including 'The Lady in Red'.

w Jerry Wald, Julius Epstein d Lloyd Bacon
ph Sol Polito, George Barnes ch Busby Berkeley
m/ly various

Dolores del Rio, Pat O'Brien, Edward Everett Horton, Leo Carrillo, Glenda Farrell, Judy Canova, Phil Regan, Wini Shaw, Herman Bing

In Celebration

GB 1974 131m Eastmancolor
Ely Landau/Cinevision

Three sons travel north for their miner father's fortieth wedding anniversary.

Sharply observant but fairly predictable dramatics, plainly filmed.

w David Storey play David Storey d Lindsay Anderson ph Dick Bush m Christopher Gunning

Alan Bates, James Bolam, Brian Cox, Constance Chapman, Bill Owen

In Cold Blood ***

US 1967 134m bw Panavision
Columbia/Richard Brooks
V*, L

An account of a real life crime in which an entire family was brutally murdered by wandering gunmen.

Unnecessarily complicated as narrative, and uncompromisingly brutal in treatment, this well-meaning film is hard to take in many ways.

wd Richard Brooks book Truman Capote
ph Conrad Hall m Quincy Jones

Robert Blake, Scott Wilson, John Forsythe, Paul Stewart, Gerald S. O'Loughlin, Jeff Corey

'It marks a slight step up for its director, best remembered for reducing Lord Jim to pablum and The Brothers Karamazov to pulp.' – John Simon

AAN: Richard Brooks (as writer); Richard Brooks (as director); Conrad Hall; Quincy Jones

In Country

US 1989 115m DuArt
Warner (Norman Jewison, Richard Roth)
V, V*, L

A young girl attempts to discover more about her father, a soldier who died in Vietnam.

Mundane account of a child coming to terms with her life.

w Frank Pierson, Cynthia Cidre novel Bobbie Ann Mason d Norman Jewison ph Russell Boyd
m James Horner pd Jackson DeGovia ed Antony Gibbs, Lou Lombardo

Bruce Willis, Emily Lloyd, Joan Allen, Kevin Anderson, Richard Hamilton, Judith Ivey, Peggy Rea, John Terry, Dan Jenkins

In Enemy Country

US 1968 107m Techniscope
Universal (Harry Keller)

In 1939 Paris, the French secret service evolves an elaborate four-year undercover plan.

Standard, overlong espionage melodrama with no surprises.

w Edward Anhalt story Sy Bartlett d Harry Keller
ph Loyal Griggs m William Lava

Tony Franciosa, Anjanette Comer, Guy Stockwell, Paul Hubschmid, Tom Bell, Harry Townes, Michael Constantine, John Marley

'To Some, Losing Control Is ... Everything.'
In Excess

Italy 1991 94m Fotocinema
Metrofilm/PAC (Galliano Juso)
V

An English screenwriter grows increasingly jealous of his wife after she insists on spending her weekends with a sadistic lover.

Glossy, sterile, would-be erotic thriller that fails to satisfy on any level.

w Sergio Bazzini novel Alberto Moravia d Mauro Bolognini ph Giuseppi Lanci m Ennio Morricone
pd Claudio Cinini ed Sergio Montanari

Julian Sands, Joanna Pacula, Tcheky Karyo, Lara Wendel, Mario Di Stefano

'A pretentious Euro-production which shifts between haunting lyricism and self-indulgence.' – Sight and Sound

'Humourless tosh.' – Empire

In Gay Madrid

US 1930 78m bw
MGM

A Spanish blade is torn between two women.

Feeble star vehicle, presumably aimed at the Spanish market.

w Bess Meredyth, Edwin Justus Mayer, Salisbury Field novel Alejandro Perez Lugin d Robert Z. Leonard

Ramon Novarro, Dorothy Jordan, Lettice Howell, Claude King, Eugenie Besserer

'Unreal story, poor acting, ditto direction and general lack of popular appeal.' – Variety

In God We Trust

US 1980 97m Technicolor
Universal

A monk leaves his monastery to raise some ready cash.

Dismal and tasteless attempt at religious satire.

w Marty Feldman, Chris Allen d Marty Feldman

Marty Feldman, Peter Boyle, Louise Lasser, Richard Pryor, Wilfrid Hyde-White

'A rare achievement – a comedy with no laughs. Its energy is prodigious. But only rarely is it matched by invention.' – Variety

In Harm's Way *

US 1965 167m bw Panavision
Paramount/Sigma (Otto Preminger)
V*, S

The American navy retaliates after Pearl Harbor.

Odd mix of all-star action, spectacle (mostly models) and personal romances, with a few interesting scenes; shorn of colour it seems rather half-hearted.

w Wendell Mayes novel James Bassett d Otto Preminger ph Loyal Griggs m Jerry Goldsmith
titles Saul Bass

John Wayne, Kirk Douglas, Patricia Neal, Tom Tryon, Paula Prentiss, Brandon de Wilde, Stanley Holloway, Burgess Meredith, Henry Fonda, Dana Andrews, Franchot Tone, Jill Haworth, George Kennedy, Hugh O'Brian, Carroll O'Connor, Patrick O'Neal, Slim Pickens, Bruce Cabot, Larry Hagman, James Mitchum

'Lacks even a touch of the touch.' – Stanley Kauffmann

AAN: Loyal Griggs

In Like Flint

US 1967 107m DeLuxe Cinemascope
TCF (Saul David)
V*, L

Top agent Derek Flint unmasks a subversive female spy ring which has kidnapped the President.

This sequel to Our Man Flint (qv) is silly rather than funny, a spy spoof which becomes irritatingly hard to take.

w Hal Fimberg d Gordon Douglas ph William Daniels m Jerry Goldsmith

James Coburn, Lee J. Cobb, Jean Hale, Andrew Duggan, Anna Lee

'It gently founders in yards of flat dialogue, lavishly uninteresting sets, fuzzy colour processing, and a supporting cast in which all the girls look alarmingly mass produced.' – MFB

In Love and War

US 1958 111m Eastmancolor Cinemascope
TCF (Jerry Wald)

Three men from different backgrounds join the US Marines and see service in the Pacific.

Self-conscious propaganda concoction of bare routine interest.

w Edward Anhalt novel Anton Myrer d Philip Dunne ph Leo Tover m Hugo Friedhofer

Jeffrey Hunter, Robert Wagner, Bradford Dillman, Dana Wynter, Hope Lange, Sheree North, France Nuyen

In Name Only *

US 1939 94m bw
RKO (Pandro S. Berman)

A rich man falls in love but his wife refuses a divorce.

The stars seem unhappy in this sombre matrimonial drama, but of its kind it's surprisingly well made.

w Richard Sherman novel Memory of Love by Bessie Brewer d John Cromwell ph J. Roy Hunt m Roy Webb

Cary Grant, Carole Lombard, Kay Francis, Charles Coburn, Helen Vinson

'Sock romantic drama . . . will get maximum playing time and the best dating the country offers.' – Variety

'Shot with a refined taste for interior decoration . . . it is oversweetened with the material for tears.' – Graham Greene

'The talking picture reaches perfection!'
In Old Arizona **

US 1929 95m bw
Fox

Adventures of the Cisco Kid.

Primitive sound Western, a sensation in its day but now of purely historical interest.

w Tom Barry stories O. Henry d Raoul Walsh, Irving Cummings ph Arthur Edeson

Warner Baxter, Edmund Lowe, Dorothy Burgess, J. Farrell MacDonald

† See also The Cisco Kid.

AA: Warner Baxter

AAN: best picture; Tom Barry; Irving Cummings; Arthur Edeson

In Old California

US 1942 89m bw
Republic
V*

A Boston pharmacist heads west towards gold rush California.

Moderate star Western with parsimonious budget.

w Gertrude Purcell, Frances Hyland d William McGann

John Wayne, Binnie Barnes, Albert Dekker, Helen Parrish, Patsy Kelly, Edgar Kennedy, Dick Purcell, Charles Halton

In Old Chicago ***

US   1937   115m   bw
TCF (Kenneth MacGowan)
V*

Events leading up to the great Chicago fire include a
torrid romance between a gambler and a café singer.

Spectacular melodrama which with its two-million-
dollar budget was a deliberate attempt to outdo *San
Francisco*, and only failed because the cast was less
interesting. A splendid studio super-production.

w Lamar Trotti, Sonya Levien   *novel We the O'Learys*
by Niven Busch   d Henry King   ph Peverell Marley
m Louis Silvers   ad William Darling   sp H. Bruce
Humberstone, Daniel B. Clark, Fred Sersen, Louis J. Witte

Tyrone Power, Alice Faye, Don Ameche, *Alice Brady*,
Andy Devine, Brian Donlevy, Phyllis Brooks, Tom
Brown, Sidney Blackmer, Berton Churchill, Paul
Hurst, Rondo Hatton, Eddie Collins

'Sock spectacle film . . . an elaborate and liberally
budgeted entertainment.' – *Variety*

AA: Alice Brady

AAN: best picture; Niven Busch (original story);
Louis Silvers

In Old Kentucky

US   1935   85m   bw
TCF (Edward Butcher)

A family feud is settled by a horse race.

Warm-hearted, old-fashioned stuff, and the star's last
film.

w Sam Hellman, Gladys Lehmann   *play* Charles T.
Dazey   d George Marshall

Will Rogers, Bill Robinson, Dorothy Wilson, Russell
Hardie

In Old Mexico

US   1938   62m   bw
Paramount (Harry Sherman)

Hopalong Cassidy rides out in search of the outlaw
who shot the son of a friend and is now trying to kill
him.

Slow-moving Western, strictly for fans of our hero.

w Harrison Jacobs   d Edward D. Venturini
ph Russell Harlan   m Gregory Stone   ad Lewis J.
Rachmil   ed Robert Warwick

William Boyd, George Hayes, Russell Hayden, Paul
Sutton, Allen Garcia, Jane Clayton, Glenn Strange

In Old Oklahoma: see War of the Wildcats

In Our Time *

US   1944   110m   bw
Warner (Jerry Wald)

English girl marries Polish count and helps defy the
Nazis.

Ambitious, would-be meaningful melodrama that
doesn't quite come off.

w Ellis St Joseph, Howard Koch   d Vincent
Sherman   ph Carl Guthrie   m Franz Waxman

Ida Lupino, Paul Henreid, Nancy Coleman, *Nazimova*,
Mary Boland, Victor Francen, Michael Chekhov

'The story starts a good many hares but prudently
refrains from following them.' – *Richard Mallett, Punch*

In Person

US   1935   85m   bw
RKO (Pandro S. Berman)

A glamorous but exhausted film star tries to escape
her public by fleeing incognito to the country.

Mild star comedy.

w Allan Scott   *novel* Samuel Hopkins Adams
d William A. Seiter   ph Edward Cronjager   m Roy
Webb   *songs* Oscar Levant, Dorothy Fields

Ginger Rogers, George Brent, Alan Mowbray, Grant
Mitchell, Samuel S. Hinds, Spencer Charters

'Inept starring debut for Ginger Rogers . . . a very
weak affair.' – *Variety*

In Praise of Older Women

Canada   1978   108m   colour
Warner/Canadian Film Development/Famous Players & TSM
Investments (Robert Lantos, Claude Héroux)
V*

A young Hungarian has affairs with older women in
his homeland and, following the revolution, in
Canada.

Episodic movie that soon becomes numbingly
repetitious.

w Paul Gottlieb   *novel* Stephen Vizinczey
d George Kaczender   ph Miklos Lente   m Tibor
Polgar   ad Wolf Kroeger   ed George Kaczender,
Peter Wintonick

Tom Berenger, Karen Black, Susan Strasberg, Helen
Shaver, Marilyn Lightstone, Alexandra Stewart

In Rosie's Room: see Rosie the Riveter

In Search of Gregory

GB   1969   90m   Technicolor
Universal/Vic Films/Vera Films (Joe Janni, Daniele Senatore)

A girl attends her father's wedding to meet a
mysterious guest named Gregory, whom she never
quite contacts.

Irritatingly pretentious Pinterish puzzle-drama with
apparently no hidden depths except the urge to be
clever.

w Tonino Guerra, Lucile Laks   d Peter Wood
ph Otto Heller, Giorgio Tonti   m Ron Grainer

Julie Christie, Michael Sarrazin, John Hurt, Adolfo
Celi, Roland Culver, Tony Selby

'Moments in a vacuum: however lively the surface,
the centre remains depressingly inert.' – *MFB*

'A thousand thrills . . . and Hayley Mills'
In Search of the Castaways ***

GB   1961   100m   Technicolor
Walt Disney (Hugh Attwooll)

With the aid of an eccentric professor, three children
seek their lost explorer father in some geographically
fantastic regions of South America.

Engaging Victorian fantasy which starts realistically
but builds up to sequences in the manner of *The
Wizard of Oz* and concludes in *Treasure Island* vein.
Jaunty juvenile fare.

w Lowell S. Hawley   *novel Captain Grant's Children*
by Jules Verne   d Robert Stevenson   ph Paul
Beeson   m William Alwyn   ad Michael Stringer

Maurice Chevalier, Hayley Mills, George Sanders, Wilfrid
Hyde-White, *Wilfrid Brambell*

In Society *

US   1944   74m   bw
Universal (Edmund Hartmann)

Two incompetent plumbers ruin a mansion.

One of the better A & C romps, with little padding
between the comedy highlights, though the
trimmings are fearsomely dated.

w John Grant, Hal Fimberg, Edmund L. Hartmann
d Jean Yarbrough   ph Jerome Ash   m Edgar
Fairchild

Bud Abbott, Lou Costello, Kirby Grant, Ann Gillis,
Arthur Treacher, Steve Geray, George Dolenz, Marion
Hutton

In the Belly of the Whale *

West Germany   1985   96m   colour
DNS Film/Haro Senft/NDR
original title: *Im Innern des Wals*

Fleeing from her violent father, an adolescent girl
goes in search of the mother she has not seen for ten
years.

Teenage angst is set against adult violence and
unhappy love affairs.

w Michael Junker, Doris Dörrie   d Doris Dörrie
ph Alex Block   m Claus Bantzer   ad Jörg Neuman
ed Raimund Barthelmes

Janna Marangosoff, Eisi Gulp, Peter Saltmann, Silvia
Reize

In the Cool of the Day

GB   1962   91m   Metrocolor   Panavision
MGM (John Houseman)

The frail wife of a New York publisher dies in Greece
after an affair with his colleague.

Travelogue with romantic asides; a pretty glum
business.

w Meade Roberts   *novel* Susan Ertz   d Robert
Stevens   ph Peter Newbrook   m Francis Chagrin
ad Ken Adam

Jane Fonda, Peter Finch, Arthur Hill, Angela
Lansbury, Constance Cummings

In the Doghouse

GB   1961   93m   bw
Rank (Hugh Stewart)

Misadventures of a newly qualified vet.

Easy-going farce with animal interest and a great
many familiar faces.

w Michael Pertwee   *novel It's a Vet's Life* by Alex
Duncan   d Darcy Conyers   ph Alan Hume
m Philip Green

Leslie Phillips, Peggy Cummins, Hattie Jacques,
James Booth, Dick Bentley, Colin Gordon, Joan Heal,
Fenella Fielding, Esma Cannon, Richard Goolden,
Joan Hickson, Vida Hope, Harry Locke, Kynaston
Reeves

'Anywhere but Paris it would have been a scandal!'
In the French Style *

US/France   1962   105m   bw
Columbia/Casanna/Orsay (Robert Parrish, Irwin Shaw)

An American girl in Paris has affairs with a young boy
and with a divorced newspaperman.

Smooth, episodic, romantic character study, well
made but with no perceptible dramatic point.

w Irwin Shaw   d Robert Parrish   ph Michel Kelber
m Josef Kosma

Jean Seberg, Stanley Baker, Philippe Fouquet

In the Good Old Summertime *

US   1949   102m   Technicolor
MGM (Joe Pasternak)
V*, L

In a Chicago music store in 1906, a salesgirl
corresponds through a dating service with a man who
turns out to be the manager she detests.

Cheerful remake of *The Shop around the Corner* (qv),
with agreeable music, garish colour and not much
style.

w Albert Hackett, Frances Goodrich, Ivan Tors
play Miklos Laszlo   d Robert Z. Leonard   ph Harry
Stradling   md George Stoll   ad Randell Duell
ch Robert Alton

Judy Garland, Van Johnson, S. Z. Sakall, Spring
Byington, Clinton Sundberg, Buster Keaton, Lillian
Bronson

In the Heat of the Night ****

US   1967   109m   DeLuxe
UA/Mirisch (Walter Mirisch)
V, V*, L

In a small Southern town, the bigoted and bombastic

sheriff on a murder hunt grudgingly accepts the help of a black detective.

A tense and exciting thriller that also explores racism through the explosive clash of two contrasting personalities.

w Sterling Silliphant *d* Norman Jewison *ph* Haskell Wexler *m* Quincy Jones *ad* Paul Groesse *ed* Hal Ashby

Sidney Poitier, Rod Steiger, Warren Oates, Quentin Dean, William Schallert

'A very nice film and a very good film and yes, I think it's good to see a black man and a white man working together . . . but it's not going to take the tension out of New York City; it's not going to stop the riots in Chicago.' – *Rod Steiger*

† Poitier subsequently starred in a couple of very inferior sequels, *They Call Me Mister Tibbs* and *The Organization* (both qv).

AA: best picture; Sterling Silliphant; Rod Steiger; Hal Ashby; sound

AAN: Norman Jewison; sound effects (James A. Richard)

In the Line of Fire *
US 1993 129m Technicolor Panavision
Columbia (Jeff Apple)
V, V*, L, S

A secret service agent, who is haunted by his failure to save President Kennedy, is taunted by a ruthless killer who announces he intends to assassinate the current US President.

An enjoyable thriller that provides Eastwood the opportunity to develop an unstereotypical character, but which also lets Malkovich go over the top as a carpet-chewing baddie and lacks suspense.

w Jeff Maguire *d* Wolfgang Petersen *ph* John Bailey *m* Ennio Morricone *pd* Lilly Kilvert *ed* Anne V. Coates

Clint Eastwood, John Malkovich, Rene Russo, Dylan McDermott, Gary Cole, Fred Dalton Thompson, John Mahoney, Greg Alan-Williams

'Meat-and-potatoes genre-picture entertainment: nothing fancy, nothing unusual.' – *Terrence Rafferty, New Yorker*

'The story is from recycled thrillersville, but it's snappy and appealing in its fast, tense treatment.' – *Angie Errigo, Empire*

AAN: John Malkovich; Jeff Maguire; Anne V. Coates

In the Meantime, Darling
US 1944 72m bw
TCF (Otto Preminger)

A wealthy bride lives in an overcrowded boarding house to be near her husband's army camp.

Unassuming wartime soaper of very little interest.

w Arthur Kober, Michael Uris *d* Otto Preminger *ph* Joe MacDonald *md* Emil Newman *m* David Buttolph

Jeanne Crain, Frank Latimore, Mary Nash, Eugene Pallette, Stanley Prager, Gale Robbins, Jane Randolph

In the Mood: see The Woo Woo Kid

In the Name of the Father **
Eire/GB 1993 133m Technicolor
Universal/Hell's Kitchen/Gabriel Byrne (Jim Sheridan)
S

Four young Irish friends are framed by the police for planting an IRA bomb that blows up a Guildford pub.

A true story, filled with a righteous indignation and deftly told, but debasing its own authenticity with its final, hollow court-room scene which is not only completely invented and inaccurate in its portrayal of British procedure, but is played like the climax from a

Perry Mason movie; it is at its best when exploring the relationship between father and son.

w Terry George, Jim Sheridan *d* Jim Sheridan *ph* Peter Biziou *m* Trevor Jones *pd* Caroline Amies *ed* Gerry Hambling

Daniel Day-Lewis, Pete Postlethwaite, Emma Thompson, John Lynch, Mark Sheppard, Beatie Edney, Marie Jones, Britta Smith, Corin Redgrave

'Solid and well-crafted, with moments of great power.' – *Adam Mars-Jones, Independent*

'Unashamed Irish myth-making. But considering the sensitivity of the issues involved, it is a bit odd that Sheridan has taken quite such liberties with the truth. This is, after all, a film about a man who spent 14 years in prison because people made up stories about him.' – *Martin Bright, Sight and Sound*

AAN: Daniel Day-Lewis; Pete Postlethwaite; Emma Thompson; Jim Sheridan (as director); Terry George, Jim Sheridan; Gerry Hambling

In the Navy *
US 1941 86m bw
Universal (Alex Gottlieb)
V*, L

Two incompetents and a singing heart-throb are naval recruits.

A basically feeble follow-up to *Buck Privates* which outgrossed its predecessor and now stands as an interesting pointer to how mass entertainment has changed since 1941.

w John Grant, Arthur T. Horman *d* Arthur Lubin *ph* Joseph Valentine *m/ly* Gene de Paul, Don Raye

Bud Abbott, Lou Costello, Dick Powell, The Andrews Sisters, Claire Dodd, Dick Foran, Shemp Howard

In the Shadow of the Wind
French/Canadian 1987 107m colour
Cinevideo/Les Film Ariane/TFI Films (Justine Héroux)
original title: *Les Fous de Bassan*

A middle-aged artist recalls an earlier time when he disrupted the life of a small, puritanical fishing community.

Slow-moving movie that tries for, and misses, a tragic dimension.

w Sheldon Chad, Marcel Beaulieu, Yves Simoneau *novel* Anne Hébert *d* Yves Simoneau *ph* Alain Dostie *m* Richard Grégoire *ad* Michel Proulx *ed* Joele Van Effenterre

Steve Banner, Charlotte Valandrey, Laure Marsac, Angèle Coutu, Paul Hébert, Marie Tifo, Bernard-Pierre Donnadieu, Lothaire Bluteau, Jean Louis Millette

In the Soup
GB 1936 72m bw
Twickenham (Julius Hagen)

A solicitor and his wife are forced to pose as their own servants.

Undernourished star comedy.

w H. Fowler Mear *play* Ralph Lumley *d* Henry Edwards *ph* Sydney Blythe, William Luff *md* W. L. Trytel *ad* James Carter *ed* Jack Harris, Michael Chorlton

Ralph Lynn, Judy Gunn, Morton Selten, Nelson Keyes, Bertha Belmore

In the Soup **
US/Japan/Germany/France 1992 93m bw
Will Alliance/Pandora/Why Not/Odessa/Alta/Mikado (Jim Stark, Hank Blumenthal)
V, V*

A con-man uses an independent film director trying to raise the money to finance his screenplay as a front for his schemes.

An amusing off-beat comedy about the education of an innocent.

w Alexandre Rockwell, Tim Kissell *d* Alexandre Rockwell *ph* Phil Parmet *m* Mader *pd* Mark Friedberg *ed* Dana Congdon

Steve Buscemi, *Seymour Cassel,* Jennifer Beals, Pat Moya, Will Patton, Jim Jarmusch, Carol Kane

'Winning performances and gentle, self-deprecating humor put this across as an audience pleaser for the specialized film crowd.' – *Variety*

† Although the cinema release was in black and white, the film was issued on video in a colour print.

In the White City *
Portugal/Switzerland 1983 108m colour
Contemporary/Metro filme/Filmograph/WDR/Channel 4
(Paulo Branco, Alain Tanner, Antonio Vaz da Silver)
original title: *Dans La Ville Blanche*

Jumping ship in Lisbon, a married sailor falls in love with a local girl and sends home movies of the city to his wife.

A study in masculine alienation, dependent on its images to carry its message of distintegration and illusory freedom.

wd Alain Tanner *ph* Acacio de Almeida *m* Jean-Luc Barbier *ad* Maria Jose Branco *ed* Laurent Uhler

Bruno Ganz, Teresa Madruga, Julia Vonderlinn, José Carvalho, Victor Costa, Francisco Baiao, José Wallenstein, Lidia Franco

In the Woods: see Rashomon

'No one is as good as Bette when she's bad!'
In This Our Life **
US 1942 101m bw
Warner (David Lewis)

A neurotic girl steals her sister's husband, leaves him in the lurch, dominates her hapless family and is killed while on the run from the police.

Splendid star melodrama with good supporting acting and background detail.

w Howard Koch *novel* Ellen Glasgow *d* John Huston *ph* Ernest Haller *m* Max Steiner

Bette Davis, Charles Coburn, Olivia de Havilland, Frank Craven, George Brent, Dennis Morgan, Billie Burke, Hattie McDaniel, Lee Patrick, Walter Huston (uncredited)

In Which We Serve ****
GB 1942 114m bw
Rank/Two Cities (Noël Coward)
V*

Survivors from a torpedoed destroyer recall their life at sea and on leave.

Dated but splendid flagwaver; an archetypal British war film of almost limitless propaganda value.

w Noël Coward *d* Noël Coward, David Lean *ph* Ronald Neame *m* Noël Coward

Noël Coward, Bernard Miles, *John Mills,* Richard Attenborough, *Celia Johnson,* Kay Walsh, Joyce Carey, Michael Wilding, Penelope Dudley Ward, Kathleen Harrison, Philip Friend, George Carney, Geoffrey Hibbert, James Donald

COMMANDER (Noël Coward): 'The Torrin has been in one scrap after another, but even when we've had men killed, the majority survived and brought the old ship back. Now she lies in 1500 fathoms and with her more than half our shipmates. If they had to die, what a grand way to go! And now they lie all together with the ship we loved, and they're in very good company. We've lost her, but they're still with her. There may be less than half the Torrin left, but I feel that we'll all take up the battle with even stronger heart. Each of us knows twice as much about fighting, and each of us has twice as good a reason to fight. You will all be sent to replace men who've been killed in other ships, and the next time you're in action, remember the Torrin! I should like to add that there isn't one of you that I wouldn't be proud and honoured to serve with again.'

'One of the screen's proudest achievements at any time and in any country.' – *Newsweek*

'Never at any time has there been a reconstruction of human experience which could touch the savage grandeur and compassion of this production.' – *Howard Barnes, New York Herald Tribune*

† The story and the Coward character were based on the experiences of Louis Mountbatten, whose ship, HMS *Kelly*, was sunk under him.

AA: Special Award to Noël Coward

AAN: best picture; Noël Coward (as writer)

Inadmissible Evidence **
GB 1968 96m bw
Paramount/Woodfall (Ronald Kinnoch)

A frustrated 40-year-old solicitor is on the verge of a nervous breakdown.

Interesting and surprisingly successful transcription of a difficult play which was virtually an anti-humanity soliloquy.

w *John Osborne* play John Osborne d *Anthony Page* ph *Kenneth Hodges* m *Dudley Moore* ad *Seamus Flannery*

Nicol Williamson, Eleanor Fazan, Jill Bennett, Peter Sallis, Eileen Atkins, Isobel Dean

'A play that was conceived as an increasingly bad dream has been made into a grittily detailed, naturalistic film.' – *Stanley Kauffmann*

'She was the biggest sucker of them all!'
Incendiary Blonde *
US 1945 112m Technicolor
Paramount (Joseph Sistrom)

The life of twenties night-club queen Texas Guinan.

Laundered biopic with guns, girls and gangsters as well as songs.

w Claude Binyon, Frank Butler d George Marshall ph *Ray Rennahan* m Robert Emmett Dolan

Betty Hutton, Arturo de Cordova, Charles Ruggles, Albert Dekker, Barry Fitzgerald, Mary Phillips, Bill Goodwin, Eduardo Ciannelli, Maurice Rocco

'It runs its noisy but high-minded course through steamy emotion, painful misunderstanding and dramatic self-sacrifice, winding up in the snow among the blood of dead gangsters. Have we ever seen gangsters in Technicolor before?' – *Richard Mallett, Punch*

'A brassy synthesis of colour, song and dance, spattered with laughs.' – *Daily Herald*

AAN: Robert Emmett Dolan

L'incendio di Roma: see *Fire over Rome*

Incense for the Damned
GB 1970 87m Eastmancolor
Grand National/Lucinda/Titan (Graham Harris)
aka: *Bloodsuckers*

An Oxford academic holidays in Greece and becomes a vampire.

A moderately successful attempt to create a modern-day vampire story, substituting sexual perversion for the usual occult approach.

w *Julian More* novel *Doctors Wear Scarlet* by Simon Raven d Michael Burrowes (Robert Hartford-Davis) ph *Desmond Dickinson* m Bobby Richards pd George Provis

Patrick Macnee, Peter Cushing, Alex Davion, Johnny Sekka, Madeline Hinde, Patrick Mower, Imogene Hassall, Edward Woodward, William Mervyn, David Lodge

'Well enough constructed to amount to a richly subversive exercise in the genre.' – *David Pirie, MFB*

† The film was cut by four minutes for its British release and disowned by its director, who did not regard it as finished. It was given a trade show in 1972 but did not receive a London showing until 1976.

Inchon
US 1981 140m colour
One Way Productions (Mitsuharu Ishii)
S

General MacArthur is affected by divine guidance during a major battle of the Korean war.

A very curious enterprise apparently financed by the Moonies. The religious angle sits oddly with the war scenes, and the result is an unsatisfactory mess.

w Robin Moore, Laird Koenig d Terence Young ph Bruce Surtees m Jerry Goldsmith

Laurence Olivier (as MacArthur), Jacqueline Bisset, David Janssen, Ben Gazzara, Toshiro Mifune, Richard Roundtree, Gabriele Ferzetti, Rex Reed

'A near total loss as well as a laugh.' – *Bruce Williamson, Playboy*

'The worst movie ever made, a turkey the size of Godzilla.' – *Jack Kroll, Newsweek*

'Quite possibly the worst movie ever made . . . stupefyingly incompetent.' – *Peter Rainer, Los Angeles Herald Examiner*

'As military spectacles go, one of the sorriest in military history.' – *Richard Schickel, Time*

Incident at Owl Creek *
France 1961 27m bw
Marcel Ichac/Films de Centaure/Paul de Roubaix
original title: *La Rivière du Hibou*
US title: *An Occurrence At Owl Creek*

During the American Civil War a man is about to be hanged, and imagines how he might escape.

Intriguing but somewhat overpraised short with a rather obvious solution.

wd Robert Enrico story Ambrose Bierce ph Jean Boffety m Henri Lanoë

Roger Jacquet, Anne Cornaly, Anker Larsen

'A powerful and remarkable film.' – *MFB*

AA: best short film

Incident at Phantom Hill
US 1966 88m Technicolor
Universal

Two men face desperate odds to reach one million dollars in gold.

Full-blooded Western programmer with useful performances.

w Frank Nugent d Earl Bellamy

Robert Fuller, Dan Duryea, Jocelyn Lane, Claude Akins, Noah Beery Jnr

Les Inconnus dans la Maison *
France 1941 94m bw
Continental

An embittered ex-barrister saves his teenage daughter from a murder charge.

Unlikely melodrama remade as *Stranger in the House*; this version has more compelling writing and acting.

w *Henri-Georges Clouzot* novel Georges Simenon d Henri Decoin ph Jules Kruger m Roland Manuel

Raimu, Juliette Faber, Jacques Baumer, Jean Tissier

The Incredible Journey **
US 1963 80m Technicolor
Walt Disney (James Algar)
V*

Two dogs and a cat, separated from their owners, escape and travel 250 miles home.

A novelty attraction which keeps going purely on its animal interest, which is considerable.

w James Algar book Sheila Burnford d Fletcher Markle ph Kenneth Peach, Jack Couffer, Lloyd Beebe m Oliver Wallace

The Incredible Melting Man
US 1977 84m Movielab
AIP/Quartet (Max J. Rosenberg)
V, V*

The survivor of a space flight is rushed to hospital with radiation burns and an infection which causes his flesh to melt.

Unpleasant and nonsensical horror film with a few unintentional laughs and a plot borrowed from *The Quatermass Experiment*.

wd William Sachs ph Willy Curtis m Arlon Ober

Alex Rebar, Burr DeBenning, Myron Healey, Michael Alldredge

The Incredible Mr Limpet
US 1964 102m Technicolor
Warner (John C. Rose)
V*, L

A meek but patriotic clerk is turned down by the navy and turns into a fish. In this form he becomes a radar assistant to a warship.

Sentimental sub-Disney goo, part animated.

w Jameson Bewer, John C. Rose novel Theodore Pratt d Arthur Lubin ph Harold Stine m Frank Perkins

Don Knotts, Andrew Duggan, Larry Keating, Jack Weston

The Incredible Sarah *
GB 1976 105m Technicolor Panavision
Readers Digest (Helen M. Strauss)
V*, L

The career of French actress Sarah Bernhardt up to the age of thirty-five.

Mildly pleasing old-fashioned biopic with remarkably unreliable detail and a regrettably bland approach to its fascinating subject.

w Ruth Wolff d Richard Fleischer ph Christopher Challis m Elmer Bernstein pd Elliot Scott

Glenda Jackson, Daniel Massey, Yvonne Mitchell, Douglas Wilmer, David Langton, Simon Williams, John Castle, Edward Judd, Peter Sallis

'An incredibly old-fashioned movie full of the most unforgettable moments you have ever tried to forget.' – *Andrew Sarris, Village Voice*

'A job lot of obligatory Hollywood platitudes strung together with all the skill of Captain Hook trying to thread a needle.' – *Benny Green, Punch*

'In the stupefying tradition of *Song of Norway*.' – *Pauline Kael*

'So incredible you'll talk about it for years to come!'
The Incredible Shrinking Man *
US 1957 81m bw
U-I (Albert Zugsmith)
V*, L

After being caught in a radioactive mist, a man shrinks inexorably to micro-size.

Horrifyingly inevitable sci-fi with imaginative touches gracing a cheap production.

w *Richard Matheson* d Jack Arnold ph Ellis W. Carter m Joseph Gershenson m Hans Salter sp *Clifford Stine, Roswell A. Hoffman, Everett H. Bronssard*

Grant Williams, Randy Stuart, April Kent, Paul Langton

'It opens up new vistas of cosmic terror.' – *Peter John Dyer*

'One hails a science fiction film which is both inventive and humane.' – *Sunday Times*

'Simple, ingenious, effective.' – *The Times*

The Incredible Shrinking Woman
US   1981   88m   Technicolor
Universal/Lija (Hank Moonjean)
V*, L

A housewife finds herself shrinking after using a new perfume . . .

Hamfisted spoof on *The Incredible Shrinking Man*, with flat jokes and rather poor trick photography.

w Jane Wagner   d Joel Schumacher   ph Bruce Logan   m Suzanne Ciani

Lily Tomlin, Charles Grodin, Ned Beatty, Henry Gibson, Elizabeth Wilson

'Leaden satire on consumerism . . . even the special effects are barely passable.' – *Time Out, 1984*

The Incredible Two-Headed Transplant
US   1970   88m   DeLuxe
Mutual General/Trident/American International (John Lawrence)
V*

A mad doctor grafts an extra head onto a homicidal maniac.

Full-blooded nonsense on a low budget; utterly repellent to some, but done with sufficient verve to be a minor cult title to others.

w James Gordon White, John Lawrence   d Anthony M. Lanza   ph John Steely, Glen Gano, Paul Hipp   m John Barber

Bruce Dern, Pat Priest, Casey Kasem, Berry Kroeger

The Incredibly Strange Creatures who Stopped Living and Became Mixed-up Zombies
US   1963   82m   colour
Morgan Steckler Productions
V, V*

A gypsy fortune-teller keeps monsters of her own making at the back of her tent.

Murder and mayhem at the carnival: cheap exploitation item which for long was thought to be a fragment of someone's imagination, but turns out really to exist.

w Gene Pollock, Robert Silliphant   d Cash Flagg (Ray Dennis Steckler)

Cash Flagg, Carolyn Brandt, Brett O'Hara

'The Dreams. The Nightmares. The Desires. The Fears. The Mystery. The Revelation. The Warning.'
Incubus
Canada   1981   92m   colour
Guardian Trust Company
V*, L

Women are raped by a rampant demon.

Utterly distasteful horror film.

w George Franklin   novel Ray Russell   d John Hough

John Cassavetes, Kerrie Keane, Helen Hughes, Erin Flannery, John Ireland

'A husband. A wife. A billionaire. A proposal.'
Indecent Proposal
US   1993   117m   DeLuxe
Paramount (Sherry Lansing)
V, V*, L, CD, S

In Las Vegas, after her husband has lost the last of his money in a desperate gamble, a wealthy man offers a woman a million dollars to spend a night with him.

Glutinous problem drama of transcendent silliness; perhaps the dilemma would have seemed more interesting if the millionaire had been less personable than Redford, although it would still have remained a ridiculous enterprise.

w Amy Holden Jones   novel Jack Engelhard   d Adrian Lyne   ph Howard Atherton   m John Barry   pd Mel Bourne   ed Joe Hutshing

Robert Redford, Demi Moore, Woody Harrelson, Seymour Cassel, Oliver Platt, Billy Bob Thornton, Rip Taylor, Billy Connolly

'One of those high-concept pictures with a big windup and weak delivery.' – *Variety*

'Unredeemingly awful.' – *Philip French, Observer*

'300,000 volts of horror!'
Indestructible Man
US   1956   70m   bw
Allied Artists

The dead body of a vicious killer is given new life by a mad doctor.

Low-budget horror mayhem with no style at all.

w Vy Russell, Sue Bradford   d Jack Pollexfen

Lon Chaney Jnr, Robert Shayne, Casey Adams, Marian Carr

The Indian Fighter
US   1955   88m   Technicolor   Cinemascope
UA/Bryna (William Schorr)

An Indian fighter protects a wagon train from the Sioux.

Simple-minded Western with touches of philosophy and not much drive.

w Frank Davis, Ben Hecht   d André de Toth   ph Wilfrid M. Cline   m Franz Waxman

Kirk Douglas, Elsa Martinelli, Walter Abel, Walter Matthau, Diana Douglas, Eduard Franz, Lon Chaney Jnr, Alan Hale Jnr, Elisha Cook Jnr

The Indian Runner
US   1991   126m   DeLuxe
Columbia TriStar/Mount Film Group/Mico/NHK Enterprises (Don Philips)
V, V*, L

A small-town cop has a stormy relationship with his criminally inclined brother.

Glum and talky drama drawn out to an inordinate length, long after it has exhausted any interest.

wd Sean Penn   song 'Highway Patrolman' by Bruce Springsteen   ph Anthony B. Richmond   m Jack Nitzsche   pd Michael Haller   ed Jay Cassidy, Phil Linson

David Morse, Viggo Mortensen, Valerie Golino, Patricia Arquette, Charles Bronson, Sandy Dennis, Dennis Hopper, Jordan Rhodes

'More than two hours' worth of predictable characters and plot developments visible at a distance of some miles.' – *Kim Newman, Empire*

Indian Scout
US   1949   70m   bw
Edward Small

Episodes in the life of Davy Crockett.

Minor Western which hit the spot with small-town audiences, and in the late fifties, after the success of the Disney film, was reissued as *Davy Crockett, Indian Scout*.

w Richard Schayer   d Ford Beebe

George Montgomery, Ellen Drew, Philip Reed, Noah Beery Jnr

Indian Summer: see *The Judge Steps Out*

'The Man With The Hat Is Back. And This Time He's Bringing His Dad.'
Indiana Jones and the Last Crusade **
US   1989   127m   DeLuxe
UIP/Paramount/Lucasfilm (Robert Watts)
V, V*, L, S

Indiana Jones goes in search of his father who disappeared while looking for the Holy Grail.

The formula as before, which still works thanks to some splendid set-pieces and the genial interplay between Ford and Connery.

w Jeffrey Boam   story George Lucas, Menno Meyjes   d Steven Spielberg   ph Douglas Slocombe   m John Williams   pd Elliot Scott   ed Michael Kahn

Harrison Ford, Sean Connery, Denholm Elliott, Alison Doody, John Rhys-Davies, Julian Glover, River Phoenix, Michael Byrne, Kevork Malikyan, Robert Eddison, Richard Young, Alexei Sayle

'The hero is back!'
Indiana Jones and the Temple of Doom **
US   1984   118m   Rank/DeLuxe   Panavision
Paramount/Lucasfilm (Robert Watts)
V, V*, L, S

A prequel to *Raiders of the Lost Ark*: Jones in 1935 finds the sacred Sankara stone.

Slow-starting adventure romp with much ingenuity and too much brutality and horror. In the US it caused the creation of a new censor certificate: PG(13).

w Willard Huyck, Gloria Katz   story George Lucas   d Steven Spielberg   ph Douglas Slocombe, Allan Daviau   m John Williams   pd Elliot Scott

Harrison Ford, Kate Capshaw, Ke Huy Kwan, Philip Stone

'One of the most sheerly pleasurable physical comedies ever made.' – *Pauline Kael, New Yorker*

'A thin, arch, graceless affair.' – *Observer*

'A two-hour series of none too carefully linked chase sequences . . . sitting on the edge of your seat gives you a sore bum but also a numb brain.' – *Guardian*

AAN: music

Indianapolis Speedway
US   1939   82m   bw
Warner

A racetrack driver wants his kid brother to continue in college, but he has the racing fever.

Editor's-bench mélange of *The Crowd Roars* (1932) and *Here Comes the Navy;* this doesn't star Cagney.

w Sig Herzig, Wally Klein   d Lloyd Bacon

Pat O'Brien, Ann Sheridan, John Payne, Gale Page, Frank McHugh, Regis Toomey

'It contains just about every cliché such type melodrama can have.' – *Variety*

† Frank McHugh played the same role in the 1932 version.

The Indians Are Coming
US   1930   bw   serial: 12 eps
Universal

A cowboy escorts two friends to a wagon train, deflecting attacks from villains and outlaws en route.

Unremarkable Western chapters.

d Henry McRae

Tim McCoy, Allene Ray, Charles Royal, Francis Ford

Indio Black, Sai che ti Dico: Sei un Gran Figlio di . . .: see *The Bounty Hunters*

'Through one indiscretion ... a woman with a future became a woman with a past!'

Indiscreet
US   1931   92m   bw
Art Cinema Corporation (Joseph M. Schenck)

A socialite endangers her own romance when she tries to protect her younger sister.

Embarrassing and slow-moving farce which helped to kill its star's career.

w/songs Brown, de Sylva and Henderson   d Leo McCarey   ph Ray June, Gregg Toland   m Alfred Newman

Gloria Swanson, Ben Lyon, Monroe Owsley, Barbara Kent, Arthur Lake, Maude Eburne, Henry Kolker

'How dare he make love to me – and not be a married man!'

Indiscreet **
GB   1958   100m   Technicolor
Grandon (Stanley Donen)
V, V*

An American diplomat in London falls in love with an actress but protects himself by saying he is married.

Affairs among the ultra rich, amusing when played by these stars but with imperfect production values which the alarmingly thin plot allows one too much time to consider.

w Norman Krasna   play Kind Sir by Norman Krasna   d Stanley Donen   ph Frederick A. Young   m Richard Bennett, Ken Jones

Cary Grant, Ingrid Bergman, Phyllis Calvert, Cecil Parker, David Kossoff, Megs Jenkins

'One is often on the point of being bored, but one never is, quite.' – Richard Roud

'A film to which you would not hesitate to take your jeweller, your architect, your home decorator, your dressmaker and your domestic staff.' – Alexander Walker

Indiscretion (1945): see Christmas in Connecticut

Indiscretion (1954): see Indiscretion of an American Wife

Indiscretion of an American Wife *
Italy/US   1954   75m   bw
David O. Selznick (Vittorio de Sica)
V*
aka: Terminus Station; Indiscretion

An American woman and an Italian professor say goodbye in Rome's terminal station.

Strained attempt to re-do Brief Encounter against the busy background of a great railway station; moments of interest, but artificiality prevails, and the plot never gets up enough steam.

w Cesare Zavattini, Truman Capote, etc   d Vittorio de Sica   ph G. R. Aldo   m Aldo Cicognini

Jennifer Jones, Montgomery Clift, Gino Cervi, Richard Beymer

Indochine **
France   1992   158m   colour
Paradis/La Générale d'Images/BAC/Orly/Ciné Cinq (Eric Heumann)
V, L, S

In the unsettled Indochina of the 1930s, the adopted Indochinese daughter of the female head of a rubber plantation runs away to be with the French naval officer loved by her and her mother.

A glossy romantic drama dominated by Deneuve's performance.

w Erik Orsenna, Louis Gardeal, Catherine Cohen, Régis Wargnier   d Régis Wargnier   ph François Catonne   m Patrick Doyle   ed Genevieve Winding

Catherine Deneuve, Vincent Perez, Linh Dan Pham, Jean Yanne, Dominique Blanc, Henri Marteau, Mai Chau

'A riveting romantic saga.' – Variety

'It has the breadth and intelligence of the David Lean epics from whose plots it borrows so freely ... And in Deneuve the movie has a star of epic glamour and gravity. Her presence is like some handsome monument to the French spirit miraculously preserved on the streets of Vietnam.' – Richard Corliss, Time

AA: foreign language film

AAN: Catherine Deneuve

Inferno **
US   1953   83m   Technicolor   3-D
TCF (William Bloom)

When a millionaire breaks his leg in the desert, his wife and her lover leave him to die; but he contrives to catch up with them.

An outdoor melodrama which made better use of 3-D than any other film, suggesting the lone handicapped figure in the vast spaces; but the lovers are dull and the fire climax perfunctory.

w Francis Cockrell   d Roy Baker   ph Lucien Ballard   m Paul Sawtell

Robert Ryan, William Lundigan, Rhonda Fleming

'Its chief merit is a strong and simple story.' – C. A. Lejeune

Inferno
Italy   1980   107m   Technicolor
TCF
V*

A New York apartment house is occupied by satanists who murder those who learn their secret.

Absurdly overplotted and mainly incomprehensible shocker with some small pretensions to style.

wd Dario Argento

Leigh McCloskey, Irene Miracle, Eleonora Giorgi

The Informer ***
US   1935   91m   bw
RKO (Cliff Reid)
V*, L

An IRA leader is betrayed by a simple-minded hanger-on who wants money to emigrate; he is hounded by fellow rebels and his own conscience.

A tedious plot is turned into brilliant cinema by full-blooded acting and a highly stylized yet brilliantly effective mise en scène which never attempts reality.

w Dudley Nichols   novel Liam O'Flaherty   d John Ford   ph Joseph H. August   m Max Steiner   ad Van Nest Polglase   ed George Hively

Victor McLaglen, Heather Angel, Margot Grahame, Una O'Connor, Wallace Ford, Preston Foster, J. M. Kerrigan, Joe Sawyer, Donald Meek

'A tough subject, a sure critic's picture, but dubious box office.' – Variety

'As impressive as Scarface, or anything in the whole powerful literature redolent of fog and grime and dreariness which the Germans gave to the Americans.' – Bardèche and Brasillach

'Among the best five pictures since the coming of sound.' – Baltimore Sun

† An early British sound version was made in 1929 by Arthur Robison for BIP, with Lars Hansen and Lya de Putti. Dudley Nichols became the first person to refuse to accept an Oscar, due to a quarrel between the Academy and some industry organizations.

AA: Dudley Nichols; John Ford; Max Steiner; Victor McLaglen

AAN: best picture; editing

The Informers
GB   1963   104m   bw
Rank (William MacQuitty)
US title: Underworld Informers

A police informer is murdered and his brother takes revenge.

Basic police melodrama, with clumsy script and jaded direction.

w Alun Falconer   novel Death of a Snout by Douglas Warner   d Ken Annakin   ph Reg Wyer   m Clifton Parker

Nigel Patrick, Colin Blakely, Derren Nesbitt

L'Ingénue Libertine
France   1950   88m approx   bw
Codo-Cinéma (Jean Velter)

A romantic girl lives in an imaginary world of affairs, but can't bring herself to consummate her marriage.

Minor period sex comedy which has the distinction of being Britain's first 'X' film, though the naughtiness is more implied than stated.

w P. Laroche   novel Colette   d Jacqueline Audry   ph Grignon   m Vincent Scotto

Daniele Delorme, Frank Villard, Jean Tissier

Inherit the Wind **
US   1960   127m   bw
UA/Lomitas (Stanley Kramer)
V, V*, L

A fictionalized account of the 1925 Scopes 'monkey trial', when a schoolmaster was accused of teaching the theory of evolution.

Splendid theatrics with fine performances, marred by boring subplots but enhanced by a realistic portrait of a sweltering Southern town.

w Nathan E. Douglas, Harold Jacob Smith   play Jerome Lawrence, Robert E. Lee   d Stanley Kramer   ph Ernest Laszlo   m Ernest Gold   ed Frederic Knudtson

Spencer Tracy, Fredric March, Florence Eldridge, Gene Kelly, Dick York, Donna Anderson, Harry Morgan, Elliott Reid, Claude Akins

AAN: script; Ernest Laszlo; Spencer Tracy; editing

The Inheritance (1947): see Uncle Silas

The Inheritance
Italy   1976   121m   Eastmancolor
Flag Productions (Gianni Hecht Lucari)
original title: L'Eredità Ferramonti

In Rome of the 1880s, a wealthy father disinherits his children but succumbs to the wiles of his daughter-in-law.

Sumptuous period soap opera, for which Sanda won a best actress award at the Cannes Film Festival.

w Ugo Pirro, Sergio Bazzini   novel Gaetano Carlo Chelli   d Mauro Bolognini   ph Ennio Guarnieri   m Ennio Morricone   ad Luigi Scaccianoce   ed Nino Baragli

Anthony Quinn, Fabio Testi, Dominique Sanda, Luigi Proietti, Adriana Asti, Paolo Bonacelli, Rosella Rusconi, Harold Bromley

The In-Laws
US   1979   103m   Technicolor
Warner (Alan Arkin)
V*, L

A timorous dentist and a CIA spy, whose children are to marry, find themselves unwillingly linked together in gunplay in a South American republic.

Two charismatic actors can't fail to get some laughs, but the extended script makes it a bumpy ride.

w Andrew Bergman   d Arthur Hiller   ph David M. Walsh   m John Morris   pd Pato Guzman

Peter Falk, Alan Arkin, Richard Libertini, Penny Peyser, Nancy Dussault

'It seems incapable either of adhering to the conventions of a comedy-thriller plot or of mustering sufficient invention to abandon plot altogether for a farcical free-for-all.' – *Tim Pulleine, MFB*

Inn for Trouble

GB   1960   90m   bw
Film Locations/Eros

A suburban couple become country publicans.

Amiable extension of a popular TV series, *The Larkins*.

w Fred Robinson   d C. M. Pennington-Richards

Peggy Mount, David Kossoff, Leslie Phillips, Glyn Owen, Charles Hawtrey, A. E. Matthews, Yvonne Monlaur

The Inn of the Sixth Happiness **

GB   1958   158m   DeLuxe   Cinemascope
TCF (Mark Robson)
V, V*

An English servant girl becomes a missionary and spends many arduous years in China.

Romanticized biopic of Gladys Aylward, with lots of children, a happy ending, and everyone sensationally miscast. Somehow it all works, even North Wales standing in for China.

w Isobel Lennart   book The Small Woman by Alan Burgess   d Mark Robson   ph Frederick A. Young   m Malcolm Arnold

Ingrid Bergman, Curt Jurgens, Robert Donat, Athene Seyler, Ronald Squire, Richard Wattis, Moultrie Kelsall

AAN: Mark Robson

The Inner Circle

Italy   1991   137m   Technicolor
Columbia TriStar/Numero Uno (Claudio Bonivento)
V, S
Italian title: *Il Proiezionista*

A cinema projectionist goes to work for Stalin, an act that has a devastating effect on his marriage.

A movie that attempts to explain the appeal to the Russian people of Stalin, but achieves only a trivialization of history.

w Andrei Konchalovsky, Anatoli Usov   d Andrei Konchalovsky   ph Ennio Guarnieri   m Eduard Artemyev   pd Ezio Frigerio   ed Henry Richardson

Tom Hulce, Lolita Davidovich, Bob Hoskins, Alexandre Zbruev, Feodor Chaliapin Jnr, Bess Meyer, Maria Baranova, Irina Kuptchenko

'A dramatically messy, momentarily compelling look at Stalin's tyranny.' – *Variety*

'The umpteenth film to turn truth-based political tragedy into dial-a-cliché melodrama. Overacted by almost everyone in sight and scripted for stark risibility . . . it comes to life only when raiding history direct.' – *Nigel Andrews, Financial Times*

Inner Sanctum

The title was taken from a radio show featuring mystery stories with a last minute twist. The films were introduced rather oddly by a misshapen head in a crystal ball on the empty table of a boardroom. The head belonged to David Hoffman, and he introduced each film: 'This . . . is the inner sanctum . . .' (The original reference was presumably to the innermost working of the human mind.) The films, made for Universal, all starred Lon Chaney Jnr (who alternated as hero and villain); they were among the most boring and badly made second feature thrillers of the forties.

1943: CALLING DR DEATH
1944: WEIRD WOMAN, DEAD MAN'S EYES
1945: STRANGE CONFESSION (remake of THE MAN WHO RECLAIMED HIS HEAD), THE FROZEN GHOST
1946: PILLOW OF DEATH

Innerspace *

US   1987   120m   Technicolor
Warner/Amblin/Steven Spielberg/Guber-Peters (Michael Finnell)
V, V*, L, S

A miniaturized air force flyer is injected into the body of a grocery clerk.

Derivative comedy with clever twists; very tolerable of its kind, but no *Back to the Future*.

w Jeffrey Boam, Chip Proser   d Joe Dante   ph Andrew Laszlo   m Jerry Goldsmith   pd James H. Spencer

Dennis Quaid, Martin Short, Meg Ryan, Kevin McCarthy, Fiona Lewis

AA: special visual effects (Dennis Muren)

Innocence is Bliss: see *Miss Grant Takes Richmond*

The Innocent ***

Italy   1976   125m   colour   Technovision
Rizzoli (Giovanni Bertolucci)
V*
original title: *Innocente*; aka: *The Intruder*

In Rome in the 1890s, a Sicilian aristocrat who keeps his wife informed of his own affair takes a terrible revenge when he discovers she also has a lover.

An elegant account of decadence and sexual politics, one that subverts the intentions of the novel on which it is based.

w Suso Cecchi D'Amico, Luchino Visconti, Enrico Medioli   novel Gabriele d'Annunzio   d Luchino Visconti   ph Pasqualino De Santis   m Chopin, Liszt, Mozart, Gluck   ad Mario Garbuglia   ed Ruggero Mastroianni

Giancarlo Giannini, Laura Antonelli, Jennifer O'Neill, Rina Morelli, Didier Haudepin, Massimo Girotti, Marie Dubois

'An outstanding example of what Hemingway would have called grace under pressure.' – *Sight and Sound*

'The protagonist is meant to be an atheist hero, a brave anarch who pays the price for his amorality. But he comes out only a sordid, spoiled sensualist swine, with no kind of depth, so this story has no involvement for the viewer.' – *Stanley Kauffmann*

† Visconti had wanted Alain Delon and Romy Schneider for the two leads. He directed the film from a wheelchair and died just before its release.

'For generations, the Mafia preyed on the innocent. Tonight, someone's feasting on them.'
Innocent Blood

US   1992   113m   Technicolor
Warner (Lee Rich, Leslie Belzberg)
V, V*
aka: *A French Vampire in America*

A female vampire regrets turning a Mafia hoodlum into a vampire.

Haphazard and anaemic vampire movie with comic elements which never really works on any level.

w Michael Wolk   d John Landis   ph Mac Ahlberg   m Ira Newborn   pd Richard Sawyer   sp Steve Johnson, Syd Dutton, Bill Taylor   ed Dale Beldin

Anne Parillaud, Robert Loggia, Anthony LaPaglia, Don Rickles, Elaine Kagan, David Proval, Chazz Palminteri

'Teens and genre fans should eat up John Landis' latest mix of horror and camp comedy.' – *Variety*

'A gloomy, almost oppressive film.' – *Geoff Brown, The Times*

† Directors who make brief appearances in the movie include Dario Argento, Frank Oz, Sam Raimi, Michael Ritchie and Tom Savini.

Innocent Bystanders *

GB   1972   110m   Eastmancolor
Sagittarius (George H. Brown)

The British secret service sends three agents to trace a Russian traitor.

Confused and violent espionage thriller; rather a waste of good production.

w James Mitchell   d Peter Collinson   ph Brian Probyn   m John Keating

Stanley Baker, Geraldine Chaplin, Dana Andrews, Donald Pleasence

An Innocent Man

US   1989   113m   Technicolor
Warner/Touchstone/Silver Screen Partners IV (Ted Field, Robert W. Cort)
V, V*

Framed by crooked cops, an engineer learns lessons of survival in prison, which he applies to seeking vengeance on his release.

Undistinguished melodrama.

w Larry Brothers   d Peter Yates   ph William A. Fraker   m Howard Shore   pd Stuart Wurtzel   ed Stephen A. Rotter, William S. Scharf

Tom Selleck, F. Murray Abraham, Laila Robins, David Rasche, Richard Young, Badja Djola, Todd Graff, M. C. Gainey

Innocent Moves: see *Searching for Bobby Fischer*

Innocent Sinners **

GB   1957   95m   bw
Rank (Hugh Stewart)

A 13-year-old London girl builds a garden in the rubble of a bombed church, and gets into trouble with the police.

Likeable, slightly unfinished, mildly astringent little human drama full of well-observed character sketches.

w Neil Paterson   novel An Episode of Sparrows by Rumer Godden   d Philip Leacock   ph Harry Waxman   m Philip Green

Flora Robson, Catherine Lacey, David Kossoff, Barbara Mullen, June Archer

The Innocents **

GB   1961   99m   bw   Cinemascope
TCF/Achilles (Jack Clayton)

In Victorian times, a spinster governess in a lonely house finds her young charges possessed by evil demons of servants now dead.

Elaborate revamping of Henry James's *The Turn of the Screw*, the ghosts being now (possibly) the figments of a frustrated woman's imagination. The *frissons* would have worked better on a normal-shaped screen, but the decor, lighting and general handling are exceptional.

w William Archibald, Truman Capote   d Jack Clayton   ph Freddie Francis   m Georges Auric   ad Wilfrid Shingleton

Deborah Kerr, Megs Jenkins, Pamela Franklin, Martin Stephens, Michael Redgrave, Peter Wyngarde

Les Innocents aux Mains Sales: see *Innocents with Dirty Hands*

Innocents in Paris

GB   1953   102m   bw
Romulus (Anatole de Grunwald)

British tourists spend a weekend in the gay city.

Strained compendium of anecdotes which misses an easy target.

w Anatole de Grunwald   d Gordon Parry   ph Gordon Lang   m Josef Kosma

Alastair Sim, Margaret Rutherford, Jimmy Edwards, Claire Bloom, Laurence Harvey, Ronald Shiner

Innocents of Paris

US   1929   69m   bw
Paramount/Jesse L. Lasky

A Parisian junk dealer saves a boy's life and falls for his aunt.

Heavygoing and dated musical comedy which introduced Chevalier to world audiences.

w Ethel Doherty, Ernest Vajda   play Flea Market by Charles Andrews   d Richard Wallace   ph Charles Lang   m/ly Leo Robin, Richard A. Whiting

Maurice Chevalier, Sylvia Beecher, Russell Simpson, George Fawcett

Innocents with Dirty Hands **

France/West Germany/Italy   1975   125m   Eastmancolor
Fox-Rank/Films la Boétie/Terra/Juppiter (André Génovès)
original title: Les Innocents aux Mains Sales

An unhappy wife and her new young lover decide to kill her alcoholic husband, but he is aware of their plan.

An enjoyable, teasing thriller that keeps its audience, as well as its characters, guessing as one double-cross quickly follows upon another.   wd Claude Chabrol   novel The Damned Innocents by Richard Neely   ph Jean Rabier   m Pierre Jansen   ad Guy Littaye   ed Jacques Gaillard

Romy Schneider, Rod Steiger, Paolo Giusti, Jean Rochefort, François Maistre, Pierre Santini, François Perrot

'One of cinema's most enjoyable charades.' – Richard Combs, MFB

Inquest *

GB   1939   60m   bw
Charter (John Boulting)

A coroner has his suspicions as to who murdered the deceased.

Modest courtroom suspenser which marked the Boultings' first attempt (the second was Suspect) to raise the standard of second features.

w Francis Miller   play Michael Barringer   d Roy Boulting   ph D. P. Cooper   ad John Maxted   ed Roy Boulting

Elizabeth Allan, Herbert Lomas, Hay Petrie, Barbara Everest, Olive Sloane

The Inquisitor **

France   1981   90m   Eastmancolor
Gala/Ariane/TFI (Georges Dancigers, Alexandre Mnouchkine)
original title: Garde à Vu

On New Year's Eve, a police inspector questions a rich lawyer suspected of killing a child.

Excellently acted, engrossing contest of wits.

w Claude Miller, Jean Herman, Michel Audiard   novel Brainwash by John Wainwright   d Claude Miller   ph Bruno Nuytten   m Georges Delerue   ad Eric Moulard   ed Albert Jurgenson

Lino Ventura, Michel Serrault, Guy Marchand, Romy Schneider, Didier Agostini. Patrick Depeyrat, Pierre Maguelon, Serge Malik

Inseminoid

GB   1980   92m   colour
Brent Walker/Jupiter (Richard Gordon, David Speechley)
V, V*
US title: Horror Planet

On a far-off planet a scientist is raped by an alien and gives birth to monsters.

Cheap and nasty rip-off of Alien that is full of disgusting effects and violent deaths but lacks any suspense.

w Nick Maley, Gloria Maley   d Norman J. Warren   ph John Metcalfe   m John Scott   pd Hayden Pearce

Robin Clarke, Jennifer Ashley, Stephanie Beacham, Judy Geeson, Victoria Tennant, Steven Grives, Barry Houghton

† Six minutes were cut from the film on its US release.

'A degenerate film with dignity!'

Inserts

GB   1975   117m   DeLuxe
UA/Film and General (Davina Belling, Clive Parsons)
V*

In 1930 Hollywood, a fading silent queen and a has-been director take to drugs.

Curious, interesting semi-porno melodrama with Pinterish asides and an inaccurate but stimulating feel of the film city at its height.

wd John Byrum   ph Denys Coop   md Jessica Harper

Richard Dreyfuss, Jessica Harper, Veronica Cartwright, Bob Hoskins, Stephen Davies

'The ludicrous plot and the painfully obvious symbolism make it tempting to interpret Inserts as a comedy. Yet to assume that a bad movie about the making of a bad movie is somehow good by virtue of its badness is to be guilty of a kind of mimetic fallacy.' – Robert Asahina, New Leader

'This is the story of Daisy Clover … Love at 15. Married at 16. Divorced at 17.'

Inside Daisy Clover *

US   1965   128m   Technicolor   Panavision
Warner/Pakula-Mulligan (Alan J. Pakula)
V (W), V*, L

Tribulations of an adolescent movie star in thirties Hollywood.

Amusing, rather hysterical variant on A Star Is Born; agreeably wacky in spots, glum in others. Would have benefited from the greater permissiveness possible a few years later.

w Gavin Lambert   novel Gavin Lambert   d Robert Mulligan   ph Charles Lang Jnr   m André Previn   ch Herbert Ross   ad Robert Clatworthy

Natalie Wood, Robert Redford, Ruth Gordon, Christopher Plummer, Roddy MacDowall

'The movie is short on characters, detail, activity, dialogue, even music; it's as if it's so determined to be stylish and sophisticated that rather than risk vulgarity or banality, it eliminates almost everything.' – Pauline Kael, 1968

AAN: Ruth Gordon

Inside Detroit

US   1955   82m   bw
Columbia (Sam Katzman)

A racketeer comes out of prison and tries to regain control of the car workers' union.

Tedious support, like a grossly extended Crime Does Not Pay.

w Robert E. Kent, James B. Gordon   d Fred F. Sears

Pat O'Brien, Dennis O'Keefe, Tina Carver, Mark Damon

Inside Moves

US   1980   113m   colour
Goodmark (Mark M. Tanz, R. W. Goodwin)
V*, L

A failed suicide makes friends in Max's bar with other handicapped people.

Curious tragi-comedy which generally settles for sentimentality but provides a few funny moments along the way.

w Valerie Curtin, Barry Levinson   novel Todd Walton   d Richard Donner   ph Laszlo Kovacs   m John Barry

John Savage, David Morse, Diana Scarwid, Amy Wright, Tony Burton, Harold Russell

'A dismal contribution in the Year of the Disabled Person.' – John Pym, MFB

'If you imagine The Iceman Cometh rewritten by William Saroyan as a tribute to Frank Capra, that's about it.' – Sunday Times

AAN: Diana Scarwid (supporting actress)

Inside Out *

GB/West Germany   1975   97m   Technicolor
Warner/Kettledrum (Judd Bernard)
V*
TV title: The Golden Heist; aka: Hitler's Gold

A German ex-commandant of a POW camp enlists the aid of Americans in a daring plan to kidnap a Nazi war criminal from East Germany and find buried Nazi loot.

Entertaining but very silly actioner with too many changes of mood, though some sequences please.

w Judd Bernard, Stephen Schneck   d Peter Duffell   ph John Coquillon   m Konrad Elfers

Telly Savalas, James Mason, Robert Culp, Aldo Ray, Gunter Meisner, Adrian Hoven, Charles Korvin, Richard Warner

Inside Straight

US   1951   89m   bw
MGM (Richard Goldstone)

The life of a 19th-century tycoon is revealed in flashbacks during a poker game.

Solid melodrama which doesn't quite have the required spark.

w Guy Trosper   d Gerald Mayer   ph Ray June   m Lennie Hayton

David Brian, Arlene Dahl, Barry Sullivan, Mercedes McCambridge, Paula Raymond, Claude Jarman Jnr, Lon Chaney Jnr, John Hoyt

Inside the Walls of Folsom Prison

US   1951   87m   bw
Bryan Foy/Warner

A prison riot results in the death of the governor; when a replacement with more humane ideas is appointed, this does not stop violence from breaking out again.

Old-fashioned prison movie on highly predictable lines.

wd Crane Wilbur

Steve Cochran, David Brian, Phil Carey, Ted de Corsia, Scott Forbes

Insignificance

GB   1985   108m   colour
Zenith/Recorded Picture Company (Jeremy Thomas)
V*, L

On a hot night in 1953, a professor, an actress, a senator and a ballplayer meet in a New York hotel room.

Presumably meaningful but very boring talk piece in which the audience is supposed to recognize not merely well-known figures but a cross-section of America at the time.

w Terry Johnson   play Terry Johnson   d Nicolas Roeg   ph Peter Hannan   m Stanley Myers

Gary Busey, Tony Curtis, Theresa Russell, Michael Emil

Inspecteur Lavardin

France   1986   100m   colour
Artificial Eye/MK2/Antenne 2/Suisse Romande TV (Marin Karmitz)

A detective investigates the murder of a respected writer.

Sequel to *Cop Au Vin*, featuring an unorthodox cop, but less effective this time around.

w Claude Chabrol, Dominique Roulet d Claude Chabrol ph Jean Rabier m Matthieu Chabrol ed Monique Fardoulis, Angela Braga-Marmet

Jean Poiret, Jean-Claude Brialy, Bernadette Lafont, Jean-Luc Bideau, Jacques Dacqmine, Hermine Clair

The Inspector *
GB 1961 111m DeLuxe Cinemascope
TCF (Mark Robson)
US title: *Lisa*

In 1946 a Dutch policeman rescues a Jewish girl from an ex-Nazi and helps smuggle her to Palestine.

Peripatetic melodrama with surface suspense and subdued thoughts of ideology and race. Moments of interest, but generally dully developed and acted.

w Nelson Gidding novel Jan de Hartog d Philip Dunne ph Arthur Ibbetson m Malcolm Arnold

Stephen Boyd, Dolores Hart, Leo McKern, Hugh Griffith, Donald Pleasence, Harry Andrews, Robert Stephens, Marius Goring

'A sluggish mélange of melodrama, romance, mystery and what the inactive might call action.' – *Judith Crist*

An Inspector Calls **
GB 1954 79m bw
British Lion/Watergate (A. D. Peters)

In 1912 a prosperous Yorkshire family is visited by a mysterious inspector who proves that each of them was partly responsible for the death of a young girl.

Tactful, enjoyable record of a celebrated play in its author's most typical manner.

w Desmond Davis play J. B. Priestley d Guy Hamilton ph Ted Scaife m Francis Chagrin ad Joseph Bato

Alastair Sim, Jane Wenham, Arthur Young, Olga Lindo, Brian Worth, Eileen Moore, Bryan Forbes

Inspector Clouseau
GB 1968 105m Eastmancolor Panavision
UA/Mirisch (Lewis J. Rachmil)
V

An incompetent French policeman is brought to London to investigate the aftermath of the Great Train Robbery.

Tiresome charade with all the jokes well telegraphed, and a background of swinging London.

w Tom and Frank Waldman d Bud Yorkin ph Arthur Ibbetson m Ken Thorne

Alan Arkin, Delia Boccardo, Frank Finlay, Patrick Cargill, Beryl Reid, Barry Foster

The Inspector General **
US 1949 101m Technicolor
Warner (Jerry Wald)
V*
aka: *Happy Times*

An assistant elixir salesman with a travelling fair is mistaken by villagers for the dreaded inspector general.

Well wrought but basically boring version of a basically boring classic farce full of rhubarbing Old Russians. Nice production and hilarious moments do not quite atone for the dull stretches.

w Philip Rapp, Harry Kurnitz play Nikolai Gogol d Henry Koster ph Elwood Bredell m John Green songs Sylvia Fine ad Robert Haas

Danny Kaye, Walter Slezak, Barbara Bates, Elsa Lanchester, Gene Lockhart, Alan Hale, Benny Baker, Walter Catlett

Inspector Hornleigh *
GB 1938 87m bw
TCF (Robert T. Kane)

The Chancellor of the Exchequer's bag is stolen.

First of three police comedy-dramas based on a character created for the radio series *Monday Night at Eight* by Hans Priwin. Not bad, but the thinnest of the trio.

w Bryan Wallace, Gerald Elliott, Richard Llewellyn d Eugene Forde ph Derrick Williams, Phil Tannura md Bretton Byrd

Gordon Harker, Alastair Sim, Miki Hood, Hugh Williams, Steve Geray, Wally Patch, Edward Underdown, Gibb McLaughlin, Ronald Adam

'The opening shots – the murder in the squalid lodging and the stamp auction with the rows of poker faces and the elaborately mute bids – are not only good cinema, they are good English cinema, as national as a shot, say, from a Feyder, a de Mille or a Pommer.' – *Graham Greene*

'Interest is well sustained from the exciting opening shots to the crescendo at the close.' – *MFB*

Inspector Hornleigh Goes to It *
GB 1940 87m bw
TCF (Edward Black)
US title: *Mail Train*

Hornleigh and Bingham track down a fifth columnist.

Zestful comedy thriller climaxing on an express train: good fun for addicts of the genre.

w Val Guest, J. O. C. Orton, Frank Launder d Walter Forde ph John Cox md Louis Levy

Gordon Harker, Alastair Sim, Phyllis Calvert, Edward Chapman, Charles Oliver, Raymond Huntley, Percy Walsh, David Horne, Peter Gawthorne

Inspector Hornleigh on Holiday *
GB 1939 87m bw
TCF (Edward Black)

The inspector and his sergeant solve the death of a fellow boarder at a seaside hotel.

Lively Hitchcockian comedy-thriller romp with an excellent script and plenty of variety of location.

w Frank Launder, Sidney Gilliat, J. O. C. Orton d Walter Forde ph John Cox md Louis Levy

Gordon Harker, Alastair Sim, Linden Travers, Wally Patch, Edward Chapman, Philip Leaver, Kynaston Reeves

Inspiration
US 1930 74m bw
MGM
V*, L

A French artists' model renounces her lover in case she harms his career.

Inane romantic melodrama.

w Gene Markey d Clarence Brown ph William Daniels

Greta Garbo, Robert Montgomery, Lewis Stone, Marjorie Rambeau, Beryl Mercer, John Miljan

'As an adult problem it holds and never offends . . . box office certainly, and a cinch for women.' – *Variety*

'Camille without the cough.' – *Motion Picture*

The Intelligence Men
GB 1965 104m Eastmancolor
Rank/Hugh Stewart
US title: *Spylarks*

Two incompetent spies blunder through a series of adventures.

Inept and rather embarrassing big-screen debut for two excellent television comedians.

w S. C. Green, R. M. Hills d Robert Asher ph Jack Asher m Phillip Green

Eric Morecambe, Ernie Wise, William Franklyn, April Olrich, Richard Vernon, David Lodge, Warren Mitchell, Francis Matthews

Intent to Kill *
GB 1958 89m bw Cinemascope
TCF/Zonic (Adrian Worker)
V*, L

In a Montreal hospital, attempts are made on the life of a South American dictator recovering from a brain operation.

Solidly entertaining suspenser.

w Jimmy Sangster d Jack Cardiff ph Desmond Dickinson m Kenneth V. Jones

Richard Todd, Betsy Drake, Herbert Lom, Warren Stevens, Alexander Knox

Interference
US 1929 75m bw
Paramount

To prevent his wife from being blackmailed, a dying man commits murder and turns himself in.

Dreary drama with the distinction of being Paramount's first talking picture.

w Ernest Pascal, Hope Loring play Roland Pertwee, Harold Dearden d Lothar Mendes, Roy Pomeroy

William Powell, Evelyn Brent, Clive Brook, Doris Kenyon

Interiors *
US 1978 95m Technicolor
UA/Jack Rollins-Charles H. Joffe
V*, L

Everybody in a well-heeled American family has problems.

Curious attempt by Woody Allen to make his own version of the Bergmanesque psycho-dramas he usually satirizes. Apparently this is the real Woody, and the comedian was a mask. Oh, well.

wd Woody Allen ph Gordon Willis m none

Kristin Griffith, Marybeth Hurt, Richard Jordan, Diane Keaton, E. G. Marshall, Geraldine Page, Maureen Stapleton, Sam Waterston

'As dull as toothache and as predictable as a metronome.' – *Barry Took, Punch*

AAN: script; direction; Geraldine Page; Maureen Stapleton

Interlude
US 1957 89m Technicolor Cinemascope
U-I (Ross Hunter)

An American girl in Munich falls in love with an orchestral conductor but leaves him because of his insane wife.

Dull remake of *When Tomorrow Comes* (qv), with poor script and performances.

w Daniel Fuchs, Franklin Coen d Douglas Sirk ph R. F. Schoengarth m Frank Skinner

Rossano Brazzi, June Allyson, Françoise Rosay, Marianne Cook, Keith Andes, Jane Wyatt

'Contains every cliché known to romantic fiction.' – *MFB*

Interlude *
GB 1968 113m Technicolor
Columbia/Domino (David Deutsch, Jack Hanbury)

A girl reporter falls for a celebrated orchestral conductor; they have an affair but he finally goes back to his wife.

Intermezzo remade for the swinging London set, quite agreeable in parts because of the acting but generally rather soggy.

w Lee Langley, Hugh Leonard d Kevin Billington ph Gerry Fisher m Georges Delerue pd Tony Woollard

Oskar Werner, Barbara Ferris, *Virginia Maskell, John Cleese*, Donald Sutherland, Nora Swinburne, Alan Webb

'If you laughed at *Brief Encounter* you will roar over this one.' – *Wilfrid Sheed*

'It's got all the schmaltz and none of the style of the tearjerkers of yesteryear.' – *Judith Crist, 1973*

'Wild longings . . . fierce desires he could not name . . . for an interlude of stolen love! To one woman he gave his memories – to another he gave his dreams!'

Intermezzo ***
US 1939 69m bw
David O. Selznick
V, V*, L
GB title: *Escape to Happiness*

A renowned, married violinist has an affair with his musical protégée.

Archetypal cinema love story, Hollywoodized from a Swedish original but quite perfect in its brief, sentimental way.

w George O'Neil *original scenario* Gosta Stevens, Gustav Molander *d* Gregory Ratoff *ph* Gregg Toland *m* Robert Henning, Heinz Provost *m* Lou Forbes

Leslie Howard, Ingrid Bergman, John Halliday, Edna Best, Cecil Kellaway

† William Wyler is said to have assisted in the direction.

AAN: Lou Forbes

'Trust me . . . I'm a cop.'
Internal Affairs
US 1990 115m Technicolor Panavision
UIP/Paramount (Frank Mancuso Jnr)
V, V*, L

A duel to the death develops between an honest and a corrupt cop.

Unconvincing melodrama in which loud voices substitute for passion and feeling.

w Henry Bean *d* Mike Figgis *ph* John A. Alonso *m* Mike Figgis, Anthony Marinelli, Brian Banks *pd* Waldemar Kalinowski *ed* Robert Estrin

Richard Gere, Andy Garcia, Nancy Travis, Laurie Metcalf, Richard Bradford, William Baldwin, Michael Beach

'Where *Internal Affairs* really succeeds is in its cracking narrative drive, moody atmospherics, and excellent performances, even in the smallest roles.' – *MFB*

'Stars of stage, screen, radio and boudoir throw a party for your entertainment!'
International House *
US 1933 73m bw
Paramount
V*, L

A weird variety of travellers are quarantined in a Shanghai hotel where a local doctor has perfected television.

Madcap farce which succeeds in hits and misses.

w Francis Martin, Walter de Leon, Lou Heifetz, Neil Brant *d* Edward Sutherland *ph* Ernest Haller *m/ly* Ralph Rainger, Leo Robin

W. C. Fields, George Burns, Gracie Allen, Peggy Hopkins Joyce, Stuart Erwin, Sari Maritza, Bela Lugosi, Edmund Breese, Lumsden Hare, Rose Marie, Rudy Vallee, Sterling Holloway, Cab Calloway and his band, Colonel Stoopnagle and Budd

'Cast includes enough names to offset the effects of an otherwise second-rate picture.' – *Variety*

'Constructed along the lines of a mammoth vaudeville show, the motivating story often is sidetracked entirely to permit a lot of unrelated hokum comedy.' – *Motion Picture Herald*

'A thousand thrills as two men battle across a continent!'
International Lady *
US 1941 102m bw
Edward Small

An FBI man falls for the lady Axis agent he is chasing.

Cliché-ridden melodrama partially saved by light comedy touches.

w Howard Estabrook *d* Tim Whelan *ph* Hal Mohr *m* Lucien Moraweck

George Brent, Basil Rathbone, Ilona Massey, Gene Lockhart, George Zucco, Francis Pierlot, Martin Kosleck, Marjorie Gateson

International Settlement
US 1938 75m bw
TCF (Darryl F. Zanuck)

An adventurer becomes involved in Shanghai gun-running during the war between China and Japan.

Brisk action romance with good technical credits.

w Lou Breslow, John Patrick *d* Eugene Forde *ph* Lucien Andriot *md* Samuel Kaylin

George Sanders, Dolores del Rio, June Lang, Dick Baldwin, Ruth Terry, John Carradine, Keye Luke, Harold Huber, Pedro de Cordoba

'Strong supporting picture for double bills.' – *Variety*

International Squadron *
US 1941 87m bw
Warner (Edmund Grainger)

A playboy becomes a fighting air ace.

Standard war story, quite well done; remake of *Ceiling Zero* (qv).

w Barry Trivers, Kenneth Gamet *story* Frank Wead *d* Lothar Mendes *ph* James Van Trees, Ted McCorded Frank McGee

Ronald Reagan, James Stephenson, Julie Bishop, Cliff Edwards, Reginald Denny, Olympe Bradna, William Lundigan, John Ridgely

International Velvet
GB 1978 125m Metrocolor
MGM (Bryan Forbes)
V*

A hostile orphan becomes an international horsewoman.

Disappointing attempt to produce a sequel to 1944's *National Velvet*; none of it coheres, one is not clear to whom it is intended to appeal, and some of the dialogue is fearsome.

wd Bryan Forbes *ph* Tony Imi *m* Francis Lai *pd* Keith Wilson

Nanette Newman, Tatum O'Neal, Anthony Hopkins, Christopher Plummer, Peter Barkworth, Dinsdale Landen

The Internecine Project *
GB 1974 89m Eastmancolor
Maclean and Co/Lion International/Hemisphere (Barry Levinson, Andrew Donally)
V*

A Harvard professor arranges the mutual extermination of four people who could spoil a politician's presidential chances.

Coldly murderous romp with plenty of style.

w Barry Levinson, Jonathan Lynn *novel* Mort W. Elkind *d* Ken Hughes *ph* Geoffrey Unsworth *m* Roy Budd

James Coburn, Lee Grant, Harry Andrews, Ian Hendry, Michael Jayston, Keenan Wynn

'He risked his life to save a rat – and what did he get for it?'
Internes Can't Take Money *
US 1937 75m bw
Paramount (Benjamin Glazer)
GB title: *You Can't Take Money*

A hospital doctor persuades a gangster friend to help a woman find her missing child.

Quite interesting minor melodrama, first of the Dr Kildare series which was subsequently recast and restyled by MGM.

w Rian James, Theodore Reed *story* Max Brand *d* Alfred Santell *ph* Theodor Sparkuhl *m* Gregory Stone

Joel McCrea, Barbara Stanwyck, Lloyd Nolan, Stanley Ridges, Lee Bowman, Irving Bacon

'Satisfactory melodrama with a tear . . . better than average standing at the box office.' – *Variety*

'Their nights are as fast and frantic as their days! Don't miss the wildest party ever filmed!'
The Interns *
US 1962 130m bw
Columbia/Interns Co./Robert Cohn
V*, L

In an American hospital, newly qualified doctors have personal and career problems.

Birth, abortion, sudden death, drugs and women's lib all figure in this melodramatic compendium which succeeds well enough on its own level and spawned a sequel (*The New Interns*) and an unsuccessful TV series.

w Walter Newman, David Swift *novel* Richard Frede *d* David Swift *ph* Russell Metty *m* Leith Stevens

Cliff Robertson, Michael Callan, James MacArthur, Nick Adams, Suzy Parker, Buddy Ebsen, Telly Savalas

Interpol
GB 1957 92m bw Cinemascope
Columbia/Warwick (Irving Allen, Albert R. Broccoli)
US title: *Pickup Alley*

The US Anti-Narcotics Squad trails across Europe the insane and ruthless leader of a drug ring.

Drearily routine thick ear electrified by one performance but not helped by wide screen.

w John Paxton *d* John Gilling *ph* Ted Moore *m* Richard Bennett

Victor Mature, Anita Ekberg, *Trevor Howard*, Bonar Colleano, Marne Maitland, Eric Pohlmann, Alec Mango, Peter Illing, Sydney Tafler

Interrogation ***
Poland 1982 120m colour
Gala/Zespol Filmowy 'X' (Tadeusz Drewno)
original title: *Przesluchanie*

In the 1950s, a fun-loving singer is arrested, questioned and tortured by the secret police.

Harrowing, but uplifting in its depiction of an unquenchable human spirit. The film was banned by the authorities, its director moving to work in North America, and not released until 1990.

wd Ryszard Bugajski *ph* Jacek Petrycki *pd* Janusz Sosnowski *ed* Katarzyna Maciejko

Krystyna Janda, Adam Ferency, Janusz Gajos, Agnieszka Holland, Anna Romantowska, Bozena Dykiel, Olgierda Lukaszewicza, Tomasz Dedek

The Interrupted Journey
GB 1949 80m bw
Valiant (Anthony Havelock-Allan)
V*

An author leaves his wife for another woman, changes his mind on the journey, pulls the communication cord and causes a train crash. Or does he?

Minor melodrama with expressionist tendencies and a dream explanation. Interesting for its parts rather than its whole.

w Michael Pertwee *d* Daniel Birt *ph* Erwin Hillier

Richard Todd, Valerie Hobson, Christine Norden, Tom Walls, Ralph Truman, Vida Hope

Interrupted Melody

US 1955 106m Eastmancolor Cinemascope
MGM (Jack Cummings)

The story of Marjorie Lawrence, an Australian opera singer who fell victim to polio.

Standard biopic which jells less well than some.

w William Ludwig, Sonya Levien d Curtis Bernhardt ph Joe Ruttenberg, Paul Vogel music supervisor Saul Chaplin

Eleanor Parker, Glenn Ford, Roger Moore, Cecil Kellaway, Stephen Bekassy

AA: script

AAN: Eleanor Parker

'Make every move as if it were your last.'

Intersection

US 1994 98m DeLuxe
Paramount (Bud Yorkin, Mark Rydell)
V, V*, S

An architect's love-life goes awry after a car crash.

Dim and glossy melodrama about the meaning of life; if you value every moment, then don't waste time watching it.

w David Rayfiel, Marshall Brickman novel Paul Guimard d Mark Rydell ph Vilmos Zsigmond m James Newton Howard pd Harold Michelson ed Mark Warner

Richard Gere, Sharon Stone, Lolita Davidovich, Martin Landau, David Selby, Jenny Morrison

'A misguided attempt to retool a French art film as a Hollywood big-star vehicle.' – Variety

† It is a remake of Les Choses de la Vie (qv), directed in 1969 by Claude Sautet and starring Michel Piccoli and Romy Schneider.

Intervista *

Italy 1987 105m Eastmancolor
Aljosha/RAI Uno/Cinecittà (Ibrahim Moussa)
V, V*

Part autobiographical reminiscence, part celebration of the fiftieth anniversary of Cinecittà, part interview by Japanese television.

Fascinating, though also self-indulgent, trip through Fellini's past.

w Federico Fellini, Gianfranco Angelucci d Federico Fellini ph Tonino Delli Colli m Nicola Piovani ad Danilo Donati, Paul Mazursky, Leon Capetanos ed Nino Baragli

Federico Fellini, Marcello Mastroianni, Anita Ekberg, Sergio Rubini, Lara Wendel, Paola Liguori, Nadai Ottaviani, Tonino Delli Colli, Danilo Donati

Intimacy *

US 1965 87m bw
Goldstone (David Heilwell)

A businessman in need of a government contract tries to compromise the official concerned.

Unusual minor melodrama, interesting but not quite successful.

w Eva Wolas d Victor Stoloff ph Ted Saizis m Geordie Hormel

Barry Sullivan, Nancy Malone, Jack Ging, Joan Blackman, Jackie Shannon

Intimate Relations: see Les Parents Terribles

The Intimate Stranger *

GB 1956 95m bw
Anglo-Guild (Alec Snowden)
US title: Finger of Guilt

An American film producer in England is plagued by a strange girl who claims to have been his mistress.

Acceptable mystery thriller which holds the interest and has good detail.

w Peter Howard novel Pay the Piper by Peter Howard d Joseph Walton (Joseph Losey) ph Gerald Gibbs m Trevor Duncan

Richard Basehart, Mary Murphy, Mervyn Johns, Constance Cummings, Roger Livesey, Faith Brook

Into the Blue

GB 1950 83m bw
Imperadio
US title: Man in the Dinghy

A cheerful stowaway on a yacht helps the owners catch smugglers.

Emaciated comedy which never gets going.

w Pamela Wilcox Bower, Donald Taylor, Nicholas Phipps d Herbert Wilcox

Michael Wilding, Odile Versois, Jack Hulbert, Constance Cummings, Edward Rigby

Into the Night

US 1985 115m Technicolor
Universal/George Folsey Jnr, Ron Koslow
V*, L

A harassed husband becomes even more so when one night at the airport he meets a dizzy girl with six smuggled emeralds.

A kind of nocturnal road film into which for some reason the director has crammed a number of his colleagues. None of it really works, even as an in-joke.

w Ron Koslow d John Landis ph Robert Paynter m Ira Newborn pd John Lloyd

Jeff Goldblum, Michelle Pfeiffer, Richard Farnsworth, Irene Papas, Paul Mazursky, Roger Vadim, David Bowie

Into the Sun

US 1991 100m Foto-Kem
Trimark (Kevin M. Kallberg, Oliver G. Hess)
V, V*

A top pilot is assigned to demonstrate his skills for the benefit of a Hollywood star of action movies.

Pleasant but unmemorable movie that becomes ridiculous towards the end.

w John Brancato, Michael Ferris d Fritz Kiersch ph Steve Grass m Randy Miller pd Gary T. New ed Barry Zetlin

Anthony Michael Hall, Michael Paré, Deborah Maria Moore, Terry Kiser, Brian Haley, Michael St Gerard, Linden Ashby

'Where myth and magic walk the earth.'
Into the West *

Eire 1992 102m Technicolor
Entertainment/Little Bird/Parallel/Majestic/Miramax/Film Four/Newcomm (Jonathan Cavendish, Tim Palmer)
V, V*, S

A father, a former traveller, hunts for his two sons who have run away from their Dublin home with a magical white horse, Tir na nOg.

An odd, likeable film, despite its not always successful mythic overtones, and one that should have an appeal to the young.

w Jim Sheridan, David Keating story Michael Pearce d Mike Newell ph Tom Sigel m Patrick Doyle pd Jamie Leonard ed Peter Boyle

Gabriel Byrne, Ellen Barkin, Ciarán Fitzgerald, Ruaidhri Conroy, David Kelly, Johnny Murphy, Colm Meaney, John Kavanagh, Brendan Gleeson, Jim Norton

'Its heady mix of Irish myth and gritty realism will effortlessly capture the imaginations of all ages.' – Empire

Intolerance ****

US 1916 115m approx (24 fps) bw silent
D. W. Griffith
V, V*, L

Four stories – including Belshazzar's feast and the massacre of St Bartholomew – of intolerance through the ages are intercut and linked by the image of a mother and her baby: 'out of the cradle, endlessly rocking'.

A massive enterprise of which audiences at the time and after were quite intolerant. Hard to take in parts, it rises to a fine climax as all the stories come to a head, including a modern one with a race between a car and train, and has been called 'the only film fugue'. At the time, by far the most expensive film ever made.

wd D. W. Griffith ph Billy Bitzer, Karl Brown

Mae Marsh, Lillian Gish, Constance Talmadge, Robert Harron, Elmo Lincoln, Eugene Pallette

'A mad, brilliant, silly extravaganza. Perhaps the greatest movie ever made. In it one can see the source of most of the major traditions of the screen: the methods of Eisenstein and von Stroheim, the Germans and the Scandinavians, and, when it's bad, de Mille.' – New Yorker, 1980

Intrigue

US 1947 90m bw
UA/Star (Sam Bischoff)

In Shanghai after the war, a civilian pilot becomes unwittingly involved in drug smuggling.

Tedious and flashy pot-boiler.

w Barry Trivers, George Slavin d Edwin L. Marin ph Lucien Andriot m Louis Forbes

George Raft, June Havoc, Tom Tully, Helena Carter

Intrigue in Paris: see Miss V from Moscow

The Intruder *

GB 1953 84m bw
British Lion/Ivan Foxwell

An ex-army officer surprises a burglar and recognizes his old comrade who has been ill-served by society.

Watchable but rather mechanical compendium drama in which a series of cameos supposedly sum up the problems of life in post-war Britain.

w Robin Maugham, John Hunter novel Line on Ginger by Robin Maugham d Guy Hamilton ph Ted Scaife m Francis Chagrin

Jack Hawkins, Michael Medwin, Hugh Williams, George Cole, Dennis Price, Dora Bryan

The Intruder *

US 1961 84m bw
Filmgroup (Roger Corman)
V, V*
GB title: The Stranger

A mild-mannered stranger arrives in a Southern town and stirs up racist trouble.

Cheaply-made social melodrama with many effective moments.

w Charles Beaumont novel Charles Beaumont d Roger Corman ph Taylor Byars m Herman Stein

William Shatner, Frank Maxwell, Beverly Lunsford, Robert Emhardt, Jeanne Cooper, Leo Gordon, Charles Beaumont

The Intruder (1976): see The Innocent

Intruder in the Dust ***

US 1949 87m bw
MGM (Clarence Brown)
V*

In a Southern town, a boy and an old lady solve a mystery and prevent a black man from being lynched.

Excellent character drama which also offers vivid local colour, a murder puzzle and social comment. A semi-classic.

w Ben Maddow *novel* William Faulkner *d* Clarence Brown *ph* Robert Surtees *m* Adolph Deutsch

Juano Hernandez, Elizabeth Patterson, David Brian, Claude Jarman Jnr, *Porter Hall,* Will Geer

'It is surely the years of range and experience which have given him a control of the medium so calm, sure and – apparently – easy that he can make a complex story seem simple and straightforward.' – *Pauline Kael*

'A really good movie that is also and incidentally the first honestly worked out "racial" film I have seen.' – *Richard Winnington*

'An example of gripping film craftsmanship.' – *News of the World*

The Invaders: see *49th Parallel*

'From out of space – came hordes of green monsters!'
Invaders from Mars
US 1953 82m Cinecolor
Edward L. Alperson
V*, L

Martian invaders use hypnotized humans as saboteurs.

Poverty Row sci-fi partly redeemed by its erratic but talented designer who provides flashes of visual imagination.

w Richard Blake *d/pd* William Cameron Menzies *ph* John Seitz *m* Raoul Kraushaar

Helena Carter, Arthur Franz, Leif Erickson, Hillary Brooke

Invaders from Mars
US 1986 100m TVC colour Panavision
Cannon (Menaham Golan, Yoram Globus)
V*, L

A boy one night sees a space ship land in his back yard.

Astonishingly witless remake of a show that was a cheap second feature in 1953.

w Dan O'Bannon, Don Jakoby *d* Tobe Hooper *ph* Daniel Pearl *m* Christopher Young

Karen Black, Hunter Carson, Timothy Bottoms, Louise Fletcher, Bud Cort

Invasion *
GB 1966 82m bw
AA/Merton Park (Jack Greenwood)
V*

An English village is beset one night by invaders from outer space.

Understated, effective little suspenser, well done in all departments.

w Roger Marshall *d* Alan Bridges *ph* James Wilson *m* Bernard Ebbinghouse

Edward Judd, Valerie Gearon, Lyndon Brook, Yoko Tani, Tsai Chin, Barrie Ingham, Arthur Sharp

'A modest but highly intelligent science fiction thriller.' – *Financial Times*

Invasion of Planet X: see *Invasion of the Astro-Monsters*

Invasion of the Astro-Monsters
Japan 1967 90m (dubbed) colour
Toho/Henry G. Saperstein Enterprises (Tomoyuki Tanaka)
aka: *Monster Zero; Invasion of Planet X; Godzilla vs Monster Zero*

Aliens program three monsters, Godzilla, Rodan and Ghidrah, to attack the Earth.

Dull monster movie, its only novelty being its American leading man.

w Shinichi Sekizawa *d* Inoshiro Honda *ph* Hajime Koizumi *m* Akira Ifukube *ad* Takeo Kita *sp* Eiji Tsuburaya *ed* Rhyohei Fujii

Nick Adams, Akira Takarada, Kumi Mizuno, Keiki Sawai, Jun Tazaki, Yoshio Tsuchiya, Akira Kubo

'The world as they knew it was slipping away from them. Time was running out for the human race. And there was nothing to hold on to – except each other!'
Invasion of the Body Snatchers ****
US 1956 80m bw Superscope
Allied Artists/Walter Wanger
V, V*, L

A small American town is imperceptibly taken over by an alien force.

Persuasive, thoroughly satisfying, low-budget science fiction, put across with subtlety and intelligence in every department.

w Daniel Mainwaring *novel* Jack Finney *d* Don Siegel *ph* Ellsworth Fredericks *m* Carmen Dragon

Kevin McCarthy, Dana Wynter, Larry Gates, King Donovan, Carolyn Jones, Virginia Christine, Sam Peckinpah

Invasion of the Body Snatchers *
US 1978 115m Technicolor
UA/Robert H. Solo
V*, L

Flashy updating of the 1956 classic, mistakenly set in a big city (San Francisco) and confusingly unravelled, with nobody for the audience to empathize with.

Its nicest effect is to have Kevin McCarthy repeat his old role in a cameo.

w W. D. Richter *d* Philip Kaufman *ph* Michael Chapman *m* Denny Zeitlin *pd* Charles Rosen

Donald Sutherland, Brooke Adams, Leonard Nimoy, Veronica Cartwright, Jeff Goldblum, Art Hindle, Lelia Goldoni, Kevin McCarthy, Don Siegel

Invasion of the Saucermen
US 1957 90m bw
AIP/Malibu (James H. Nicholson, Robert J. Gurney Jnr)
V*

Little green aliens who land on Earth in a flying saucer are defeated by teenagers.

Science fiction with comic overtones, though done with so little finesse that it is difficult to know what is intentionally funny and what is accidentally so.

w Robert J. Gurney Jnr, Al Martin *story* Paul Fairman *d* Edward L. Cahn *ph* Fred West *m* Ronald Stein *ad* Don Ament *ed* Ronald Sinclair

Steve Terrell, Gloria Castillo, Frank Gorshin

Invasion Quartet
GB 1961 87m bw
MGM (Ronald Kinnoch)

An ill-assorted foursome of officers and a boffin take on the dangerous mission of silencing a Nazi gun trained on Dover.

A plot which could have been handled any way is played unsatisfactorily for farce, and all concerned are understandably uneasy.

w Jack Trevor Story, John Briley *story* Norman Collins *d* Jay Lewis *ph* Geoffrey Faithfull, Gerald Moss *m* Ron Goodwin

Bill Travers, Spike Milligan, Grégoire Aslan, John Le Mesurier, Thorley Walters, Maurice Denham, Millicent Martin, Cyril Luckham

'America wasn't ready – but he was!'
Invasion USA
US 1952 70m bw
Columbia (Albert Zugsmith)

A hypnotist in a New York bar gives a group of people a foretaste of what might happen to them under atomic attack.

Ludicrous, dangerous, hilarious low-budget exploitationer composed mainly of rubber rocks and old newsreels.

w Robert Smith *d* Alfred E. Green *ph* John L. Russell *m* Albert Glasser

Dan O'Herlihy, Gerald Mohr, Peggie Castle

Invasion USA
US 1985 107m TVC colour
Cannon (Menahem Golan, Yoram Globus)
V, V*, L

Ruthless foreign mercenaries invade the southern US.

Brainless farrago of violence which goes out of its way to be unpleasant but ends up being rather funny.

w James Bruner, Chuck Norris *d* Joseph Zito *ph* Joao Fernandes *m* Jay Chattaway

Chuck Norris, Richard Lynch, Melissa Prophet, Alexander Zale

Investigation of a Citizen above Suspicion *
Italy 1970 115m Technicolor
Vera (Daniele Senatore)
S

A successful police inspector kills his mistress and, paranoically considering himself above suspicion, plants clues leading to himself and even confesses the crime.

Fairly engrossing character study with political undertones; cinematically quite striking, too.

w Ugo Pirro, Elio Petri *d* Elio Petri *ph* Luigi Kuveiller *m* Ennio Morricone

Gian Maria Volonte, Florinda Bolkan, Salvo Randone, Gianni Santuccio

AA: best foreign film

AAN: script

An Investigation of Murder: see *The Laughing Policeman*

Invisible Adversaries
Austria 1977 109m colour
Valie Export
original title: *Unsichtbare Gegner*

A female photographer becomes convinced that aliens are taking over people's bodies and robbing them of their humanity.

Bizarre images of alienation – a man urinating on a woman's head, a fish head gasping after it has been severed from its body, a baby in a fridge – reinforce an attack on conformity. But *Invasion of the Body Snatchers* it isn't.

w Peter Weibel *d* Valie Export *ph* Wolfgang Simon

Susanne Widl, Peter Weibel, Dr Josef Plavek, Monica Helfer-Friedrich, Helke Sander, Dominick Dusek, Herbert Schmid, Edward Neversal

Invisible Agent *
US 1942 84m bw
Universal (George Waggner)

Nazi and Japanese spies seek the secret of invisibility from its inventor.

Lively fantasy thriller with a cast more distinguished than it deserves.

w Curt Siodmak *d* Edwin L. Marin *m* Hans Salter *sp* John P. Fulton

Cedric Hardwicke, Peter Lorre, Ilona Massey, Jon Hall, Albert Basserman, J. Edward Bromberg, John Litel

Invisible Boy
US 1957 89m bw
MGM/Pan (Nicholas Nayfack)

A scientist allows his 10-year-old son to repair a robot, which comes under the control of an alien force.

Minor sci-fi utilizing the robot from *Forbidden Planet*.

w Cyril Hume   *d* Herman Hoffman   *ph* Harold Wellman   *m* Les Baxter

Richard Eyer, Philip Abbott, Harold J. Stone, Diane Brewster

'Even the moon is frightened of me – frightened to death!'
The Invisible Man ****
US   1933   71m   bw
Universal (Carl Laemmle Jnr)
V*, L

A scientist discovers a means of making himself invisible, but in the process becomes a megalomaniac.

Superb blend of eccentric character comedy, melodrama and trick photography in a Hollywood English setting; remarkably faithful to the spirit of the book. It made a star of Claude Rains in his first film, even though he is seen for only a couple of seconds.

w R. C. Sherriff, Philip Wylie,   novel H. G. Wells
d James Whale   *ph* Arthur Edeson   *m* W. Frank Harling   *sp* John P. Fulton

Claude Rains, Gloria Stuart, William Harrigan, Henry Travers, E. E. Clive, Una O'Connor, Forrester Harvey, Dudley Digges, Holmes Herbert

GRIFFIN (Claude Rains): 'We'll start with a few murders. Big men, little men – just to show we make no distinction.'

'Well made and full of intentional and unintentional laughs. Should do well.' – *Variety*

'Taken either as a technical exercise or as a sometimes profoundly moving retelling of the Frankenstein fable, it is one of the most rewarding of recent films.' – *William Troy*

† Sequels, successively less interesting, were (all qv) *The Invisible Man Returns* (1940), *Invisible Woman* (1941), *Invisible Agent* (1942), *The Invisible Man's Revenge* (1944), *Abbott and Costello Meet the Invisible Man* (1951) and *Memoirs of an Invisible Man* (1992). A TV series with an anonymous hero was made by ATV in 1955; a Universal one with David McCallum followed in 1975, and was restructured as *The Gemini Man* in 1976. †† Boris Karloff had been first choice for the role, but he turned it down.

The Invisible Man Returns
US   1940   81m   bw
Universal (Ken Goldsmith)
V*

A man convicted of killing his brother uses the secret of invisibility to find the real culprit.

Second in the series takes itself too seriously: a slow starter which works its way to a strong climax.

w Curt Siodmak, Lester Cole, Cedric Belfrage   *d* Joe May   *ph* Milton Krasner   *m* Hans Salter, Frank Skinner   *sp* John P. Fulton

Vincent Price, Cedric Hardwicke, John Sutton, Nan Grey, Cecil Kellaway, Alan Napier, Forrester Harvey

'Though the film has its bright moments, and some weird ones too, the first freshness is gone. Even the effects seem repetitive.' – *Pauline Kael, 70s*

The Invisible Man's Revenge
US   1944   77m   bw
Universal (Ford Beebe)

A psychopathic killer on the run takes refuge with a doctor who has discovered the secret of invisibility.

Curious reversion to the original story in that the invisible man is now again the villain; but otherwise there's no flavour at all to this horror comic set in a phoney England.

w Bertram Millhauser   *d* Ford Beebe   *m* Hans Salter   *sp* John P. Fulton

Jon Hall, Leon Errol, John Carradine, Alan Curtis, Evelyn Ankers, Gale Sondergaard, Halliwell Hobbes

The Invisible Menace
US   1938   55m   bw
Warner

Murder at an army base brings strange revelations of the past.

Standard mystery in which the star seems misplaced.

w Crane Wilbur   *play* Ralph S. Zink   *d* John Farrow

Boris Karloff, Regis Toomey, Marie Wilson, Henry Kolker

'Undistinguished mystery meller, for bottom-lining the duals.' – *Variety*

† It was remade in 1943 as *Murder at the Waterfront*.

The Invisible Monster
US   1950   bw   serial: 12 eps
Republic

Alien smuggling is the new pastime of a scientific criminal who calls himself The Phantom Ruler.

Cheerful serial nonsense.

d Fred C. Brannon

Richard Webb, Aline Towne, Lane Bradford, Stanley Price, John Crawford

The Invisible Ray *
US   1935   79m   bw
Universal (Edmund Grainger)
V*, L

A scientist discovers a superpowerful element which makes him homicidal.

Slow-moving science fiction with a touch of horror, and the pattern for its star's many later roles as a sympathetic man who turns into a monster. Interesting rather than stimulating.

w John Colton   *story* Howard Higgin, Douglas Hodges   *d* Lambert Hillyer   *ph* George Robinson   *m* Franz Waxman   *sp* John P. Fulton

Boris Karloff, Bela Lugosi, Frances Drake, Frank Lawton, Walter Kingsford, Beulah Bondi, Violet Kemble Cooper, Nydia Westman

'An easy number to sell, it should do pretty good business.' – *Variety*

Invisible Stripes
US   1939   82m   bw
Warner (Hal B. Wallis)

An ex-con finds it difficult to go straight.

By 1940 Warner must have been able to make rip-offs of *Angels with Dirty Faces* in their sleep, and this one, despite its cast, suggests that they did.

w Warren Duff   *book* Warden Lewis E. Lawes
d Lloyd Bacon   *ph* Ernest Haller   *m* Heinz Roemheld

George Raft, Humphrey Bogart, William Holden, Flora Robson, Jane Bryan, Paul Kelly, Lee Patrick, Henry O'Neill, Moroni Olsen

'It's a familiar cinematic yarn but strengthened by a zippy pace, excellent performances and direction.' – *Variety*

The Invisible Woman
US   1941   72m   bw
Universal (Burt Kelly)

A mad scientist turns a model invisible.

Screwball comedy with a deteriorating star at his hammiest: generally very laboured, but with some funny moments.

w Robert Lees, Fred Rinaldo, Gertrude Purcell   *d* A. Edward Sutherland   *ph* Elwood Bredell
md Charles Previn

John Barrymore, Charles Ruggles, Virginia Bruce, John Howard, Oscar Homolka, Donald MacBride,

Edward Brophy, Shemp Howard, Margaret Hamilton, Maria Montez

Invitation
US   1952   81m   bw
MGM (Lawrence Weingarten)

When a millionaire's daughter believes she is dying, revelations ensue about her beloved husband's original intentions.

Competently idiotic weepie with a happy ending.

w Paul Osborn   *story* Jerome Weidman
d Gottfried Reinhardt   *ph* Ray June   *m* Bronislau Kaper

Dorothy McGuire, Van Johnson, Ruth Roman, Louis Calhern, Ray Collins, Michael Chekhov

'The dialogue is stagey and the treatment indeterminate, with overmuch reliance on the dubious emotional reinforcement of loud background music.' – *Penelope Houston*

L'Invitation *
Switzerland/France   1973   100m   colour
Groupe 5/Television Suisse/Citel Films/Planfilm

Following his mother's death, a middle-aged bachelor buys a home in the country and invites his office colleagues to a garden party.

Delightful comedy of manners that won a Special Jury Prize at the Cannes Film Festival.

w Claude Goretta, Michel Viala   *d* Claude Goretta   *ph* Jean Zeller   *m* Patrick Moraz   *ad* Yanko Hodjis   *ed* Joelle Van Effenterre

Jean-Luc Bideau, Jean Champion, Corinne Coderey, Pierre Collet, Neige Dolsky, Jacques Rispal, Michel Robin, Rosine Rochette, François Simon, Cecile Vassort

Invitation to a Gunfighter *
US   1964   92m   DeLuxe
UA/Stanley Kramer (Richard Wilson)
V*

A small-town tyrant hires a smooth gunfighter to keep down the farmers he has cheated.

Predictable, rather self-satisfied little Western with a studio look. Smart script and performances.

w Elizabeth and Richard Wilson   *d* Richard Wilson   *ph* Joseph MacDonald   *m* David Raksin

Yul Brynner, George Segal, Janice Rule, Pat Hingle

Invitation to Happiness
US   1939   95m   bw
Paramount (Wesley Ruggles)

A society girl marries a prizefighter.

Routine star romantic drama.

w Claude Binyon   *d* Wesley Ruggles   *ph* Leo Tover   *m* Frederick Hollander

Irene Dunne, Fred MacMurray, Charles Ruggles, Billy Cook, William Collier Snr, Marion Martin

'Heartthrob drama, geared for good biz.' – *Variety*

Invitation to the Dance **
GB   1954   92m   Technicolor
MGM (Arthur Freed)
V*

Three stories in dance and mime.

Unsuccessful ballet film which closed its star's great period and virtually ended the heyday of the Hollywood musical. The simple fact emerged that European ballet styles were not Kelly's forte; yet there was much to enjoy in *Circus, Ring around the Rosy* and *The Magic Lamp*.

wd/ch Gene Kelly   *ph* Frederick A. Young
m Jacques Ibert, André Previn, Rimsky-Korsakov
ad Alfred Junge

Gene Kelly, Igor Youskevitch, Tommy Rall, Belita, Tamara Toumanova

Invitation to the Wedding
GB 1985 90m colour widescreen
Chancery Lane (Joseph Brooks)

An aristocratic wedding causes trouble when the bride's uncle, the bishop, marries her to the wrong man at rehearsal.

A situation which could have been mildly amusing in the *Quiet Wedding* vein is botched by an unfunny script and wildly eccentric casting.

w William Fairchild *d* Joseph Brooks *ph* Freddie Young *m* Joseph Brooks

Ralph Richardson, John Gielgud (as an American evangelist), Paul Nicholas, Elizabeth Shepherd, Ronald Lacey (as two people for some reason), John Standing, Susan Brooks

The Ipcress File **
GB 1965 109m Techniscope
Rank/Steven/Lowndes (Harry Saltzman)
V, V*

An intelligence man traces a missing scientist and finds that one of his own superiors is a spy.

The attempt to present a low-key James Bond (glasses, good at cookery, supermarket shopper) is frustrated by flashy direction and a confused plot. It did herald a new genre though the whole ambiance is now sadly dated, like an old copy of *The Sunday Times* Colour Supplement.

w Bill Canaway, James Doran *novel* Len Deighton
d Sidney J. Furie *ph* Otto Heller *m* John Barry
ad Ken Adam

Michael Caine, Nigel Green, Guy Doleman, Sue Lloyd, Gordon Jackson

'The deglamorized espionage story, but with plenty of tingle and zest, both in plot and camerawork.' – *Judith Crist*

† Two sequels appeared starring 'Harry Palmer' (never named in the books): *Funeral in Berlin* and *Billion Dollar Brain* (both qv).

Irene
US 1940 101m bw/colour sequence
RKO/Imperator (Herbert Wilcox)
V*

A New York Irish shopgirl moves into society.

Fairly dim picturization of the old musical: the cast does its best.

w Alice Duer Miller *play* James H. Montgomery
d Herbert Wilcox *ph* Russell Metty *md* Anthony Collins *m/y* Harry Tierney, Joseph McCarthy

Anna Neagle, Ray Milland, Roland Young, Alan Marshal, May Robson, Billie Burke, Arthur Treacher, Marsha Hunt, Isabel Jewell, Ethel Griffies

'This pre-camp version tries to be innocuously charming, and the effort is all too evident.' – *New Yorker, 1976*

† Previously filmed in 1926 with Colleen Moore.

AAN: Anthony Collins

Irish Eyes Are Smiling **
US 1944 90m Technicolor
TCF (Damon Runyon)

The life and times of an 1890s songwriter, Ernest R. Ball.

Standard musical biopic, handsomely mounted.

w Earl Baldwin, John Tucker Battle *d* Gregory Ratoff *ph* Harry Jackson *md* Alfred Newman, Charles Henderson

Dick Haymes, June Haver, Monty Woolley, Anthony Quinn, Beverly Whitney, Maxie Rosenbloom, Veda Ann Borg, Clarence Kolb

AAN: Alfred Newman, Charles Henderson

The Irish in Us
US 1935 84m bw
Warner (Samuel Bischoff)

Adventures of three New York brothers.

Routine, good-natured star action frolic.

w Earl Baldwin *d* Lloyd Bacon *ph* George Barnes
md Leo F. Forbstein

James Cagney, Pat O'Brien, Olivia de Havilland, Mary Gordon, Frank McHugh, Allen Jenkins, J. Farrell MacDonald, Thomas Jackson

'A hokey laugh ensemble that will be oke.' – *Variety*

'A story of bloodshed, passion, desire and death . . . everything in fact that makes life worth living!'

Irma La Douce *
US 1963 146m Technicolor Panavision
UA/Phalanx/Mirisch/Edward L. Alperson (Billy Wilder)
V*, L

A Paris policeman falls for a prostitute and becomes her pimp.

A saucy yarn originally presented inventively as a small-scale stage musical becomes a tasteless yawn on the big screen, especially when presented at such length and without the songs. Minor compensations abound but are insufficient.

w Billy Wilder, I. A. L. Diamond *d* Billy Wilder
ph Joseph LaShelle *md* André Previn
m Marguerite Monnot *ad* Alexander Trauner

Shirley Maclaine, Jack Lemmon, Lou Jacobi, Herschel Bernardi, Joan Shawlee, Bruce Yarnell

AA: André Previn

AAN: Joseph LaShelle; Shirley Maclaine

Iron Claw
US 1941 bw serial: 15 eps
Columbia

A newspaper reporter reveals the identity of the infamous Iron Claw.

Serial hi-jinks in the *Clutching Hand* tradition.

d James W. Horne

Charles Quigley, Walter Sande, Joyce Bryant, Forrest Taylor

The Iron Curtain
US 1948 87m bw
TCF (Sol C. Siegel)

A Russian official in Ottawa becomes disillusioned and reveals to the US authorities details of a spy ring.

Cold war biopic of Igor Gouzenko; not badly done in the semi-documentary mould.

w Milton Krims *d* William Wellman *ph* Charles G. Clarke *md* Alfred Newman, using Russian themes

Dana Andrews, Gene Tierney, Berry Kroeger, Edna Best

The Iron Duke *
GB 1934 88m bw
Gaumont (Michael Balcon)

After Waterloo, the Duke of Wellington defeats a French scheme to discredit him.

A popular historical star vehicle of its time and a good example of British pre-war production in the Korda mould.

w Bess Meredyth *story* H. M. Harwood *d* Victor Saville *ph* Curt Courant *md* Louis Levy
ad Alfred Junge *ed* Ian Dalrymple

George Arliss, Gladys Cooper, Emlyn Williams, Ellaline Terriss, A. E. Matthews, Edmund Willard, Felix Aylmer

Iron Eagle
US 1986 119m Metrocolor
Tri-Star (Ron Samuels, Joe Wizan)
V, V*, L

A young man rescues his hostage father from a Middle Eastern country.

Increasingly suspenseful adventure drama which suited America's mood.

w Kevin Elders, Sidney J. Furie *d* Sidney J. Furie
ph Adam Greenberg *m* Basil Poledouris *pd* Robb Wilson King *ed* George Grenville

Louis Gossett Jnr, Jason Gedrick, David Suchet, Tim Thomerson, Larry B. Scott

'Theaters may have to stay open from high noon to red dawn to handle the crowd.' – *Variety*

Iron Eagle II
Canada 1988 100m Bellevue Pathé
Guild/Alliance Entertainment/Harkot Productions (Jacob Kotzky, Sharon Harel, John Kemeny)
V, V*, L

American and Russian pilots co-operate to destroy a nuclear missile base in the Middle East.

Silly fantasy, made occasionally bearable by its airborne sequences.

w Kevin Elders, Sydney J. Furie *d* Sidney J. Furie
ph Alain Dostie *m* Amin Bhatia *ad* Ariel Roshko
ed Rit Wallis

Louis Gosset Jnr, Mark Humphrey, Stuart Margolin, Alan Scarfe, Sharon H. Brandon, Maury Chaykin, Colm Feore, Clark Johnson, Jason Blicker

The Iron Glove
US 1954 77m Technicolor
Columbia

A staunch supporter of the Old Pretender meets friends and enemies in London at the court of George I.

Stilted costume piece, unsuitably cast and flatly written.

w Jesse L. Lasky Jnr, De Vallon Scott, Douglas Heyes
d William Castle

Robert Stack, Ursula Thiess, Richard Stapley, Alan Hale Jnr

The Iron Hand: see *Fist of Fury*

The Iron Horse *
US 1924 119m (24 fps) bw silent
Fox

A man seeking to avenge his father's murder works on the first transcontinental railroad.

Archetypal Western, very slow to start but with an authentic cast of thousands.

w Charles Kenyon, John Russell *d* John Ford
ph George Schneidermann

George O'Brien, Madge Bellamy, Cyril Chadwick, Fred Kohler

'At last a film has come from America which trusts the railroad, and sees magic in it, and power; which honours the railroad and holds it mightier than man; which loves the railroad and is content to follow it into the heart of romance.' – *C. A. Lejeune*

The Iron Maiden
GB 1962 98m Eastmancolor
Anglo Amalgamated/GHW (Peter Rogers)
US title: *The Swinging Maiden*

An aircraft designer gets into trouble because of his affection for traction engines.

Feeble attempt to duplicate the success of *Genevieve*, this time starring a steamroller. Very English.

w Vivian Cox, Leslie Bricusse   *d* Gerald Thomas   *ph* Alan Hume   *m* Eric Rogers

Michael Craig, Alan Hale Jnr, Jeff Donnell, Cecil Parker, Noel Purcell, Roland Culver, the Duke of Bedford, Anne Helm

The Iron Major

US   1943   85m   bw
RKO
V*

The life of Frank Cavanaugh, football coach and hero of World War I.

Sub-standard biopic.

w Aben Kandel, Warren Duff   *d* Ray Enright

Pat O'Brien, Ruth Warrick, Robert Ryan, Leon Ames

'A respectful, rather dull picture . . . all the talk is in words of less than one syllable.' – *James Agee*

The Iron Man

US   1931   73m   bw
Universal (Carl Laemmle Jnr)

A prizefighter is spurred on by his money-hungry wife.

Competent, routine, ringside melodrama.

w Francis Edward Faragoh   *novel* W. R. Burnett   *d* Tod Browning   *ph* Percy Hilburn

Lew Ayres, Jean Harlow, Robert Armstrong, John Miljan, Eddie Dillon, Ned Sparks

† Remade in 1937 as *Some Blondes Are Dangerous* and in 1951 under the original title.

Iron Man

US   1951   81m   bw
Universal-International

A coal miner is persuaded to become a prizefighter, but success changes his character.

A somewhat changed version of the 1931 film; no better.

w George Zuckerman, Borden Chase   *d* Joseph Pevney

Jeff Chandler, Evelyn Keyes, Stephen McNally, Joyce Holden, Rock Hudson, Jim Backus, James Arness

The Iron Mask *

US   1929   97m   bw   talking sequences, sound and
music score
UA/Douglas Fairbanks
V*, L

The true prince of France is kidnapped and imprisoned, but the villains reckon without D'Artagnan and the three musketeers.

Spirited star rendition of Dumas, the last big silent costume drama of the twenties.

w Elton Thomas (Douglas Fairbanks)   *novel Ten Years After* by Alexandre Dumas   *d* Allan Dwan   *ph* Henry Sharp   *m* Hugo Riesenfeld   *pd* Maurice Leloir

Douglas Fairbanks, Nigel de Brulier, Belle Bennett, Marguerite de la Motte

'. . . a labyrinth of deception.'

Iron Maze

US/Japan   1991   102m   CFI colour
First Independent/Trans-Tokyo/J & M Entertainment (Ilona Herzberg, Hidenori Ueki)
V, V*, L

A police-chief in a Pennsylvania steel town investigates the attempted murder of a Japanese businessman, who wants to build an amusement park on the site of the mill; the chief suspects are the man's American wife and her lover.

Based on the same story that Kurosawa used as an inspiration for *Rashomon*, which was first filmed in Hollywood as *The Outrage*, this seems little more than a muddled protest at the Japanese takeover of US businesses (and, perhaps, of Hollywood studios).

w Tim Metcalfe   *story* In A Grove by Ryunosuke Akutagawa   *d* Hiroaki Yoshida   *ph* Morio Saequsa   *m* Stanley Myers   *pd* Toby Corbett, Toro Ueno   *ed* Bonnie Koehler

Jeff Fahey, Bridget Fonda, Hiroaki Murakami, J. T. Walsh, Gabriel Damon, John Randolph, Peter Allas, Carmen Filpi

'A mess from beginning to end, presenting three cardboard characters and a flashback-infested narrative which rivals *Passage to Marseille* and *Millennium* as one of the most inelegant ever committed to film.' – *Empire*

The Iron Mistress

US   1952   107m   Technicolor
Warner (Henry Blanke)

The life of Westerner Jim Bowie and his famous knife.

Stolid actioner with uninspired script and performances.

w James R. Webb   *novel* Paul I. Wellman   *d* Gordon Douglas   *ph* John Seitz   *m* Max Steiner

Alan Ladd, Virginia Mayo, Joseph Calleia, Phyllis Kirk, Alf Kjellin, Douglas Dick, Tony Caruso, George Voskovec

The Iron Petticoat

GB   1956   96m   Technicolor   Vistavision
Remus/Harry Saltzman (Betty E. Box)
V

An American air force officer persuades a Russian lady flyer of the advantages of the western way of life.

Feeble imitation of *Ninotchka* with a saucy star team which simply doesn't jell.

w Ben Hecht   *d* Ralph Thomas   *ph* Ernest Steward   *m* Benjamin Frankel

Bob Hope, Katharine Hepburn, James Robertson Justice, Robert Helpmann, David Kossoff, Alan Gifford, Paul Carpenter, Noelle Middleton

'They seem amazed to find themselves in a comedy that has no humour, and they go through the motions grimly, like children at dancing school, hoping it will all be over soon.' – *William K. Zinsser*

The Iron Road: see *Buckskin Frontier*

The Iron Triangle

US   1988   91m   colour
Medusa/Eurobrothers/International Video Entertainment (Angela P. Schapiro, Tony Scotti)
V, V*, L

An American officer is captured by two Vietcong, one idealistic, the other murderous.

War film more concerned with humanity than action, and effective enough in its small way.

w Eric Weston, John Bushelman, Lawrence Hilbrand   *book* based on the diary of an unknown Vietcong soldier   *d* Eric Weston   *ph* Irv Goodnoff   *m* Michael Lloyd, John D'Anrea, Nick Strimple   *pd* Errol Kelly   *ed* Roy Watts

Beau Bridges, Haing S. Ngor, Liem Whatley, Johnny Hallyday, Jim Ishida, Ping Wu, Jack Ong, Sophie Trang

Ironweed

US   1987   143m   Technicolor
Taft Entertainment/Keith Barish/Home Box Office
V, V*, L

An alcoholic down-and-out returns to his home town, where he is haunted by his violent past. Although forgiven by his family, he takes to the road again.

Relentlessly gloomy and ploddingly faithful re-creation of a Pulitzer prizewinner.

w William Kennedy   *novel* William Kennedy   *d* Hector Babenco   *ph* Lauro Escorel   *m* John Morris   *pd* Jeannine C. Oppewall

Jack Nicholson, Meryl Streep, Carroll Baker, Michael O'Keefe, Diane Venora, Tom Waits

AAN: Jack Nicholson; Meryl Streep

Irreconcilable Differences

US   1984   113m   Technicolor
Lantana/Warner
V*, L

Nine-year-old Casey interferes in her parents' planned divorce.

An ancient wheeze for a romantic comedy, here decked out with modern trimmings but no better intrinsically than it was in the thirties.

w Nancy Meyers, Charles Shyer   *d* Charles Shyer

Ryan O'Neal, Shelley Long, Drew Barrymore, Sam Wanamaker, Allen Garfield, Sharon Stone

Is Everybody Happy?

US   1929   80m   bw
Warner

The life of a clarinettist who rises from poverty.

Or, The Ted Lewis Story, a primitive musical.

w Joseph Jackson, James A. Starr   *d* Archie Mayo

Ted Lewis, Alice Day, Ann Pennington, Lawrence Grant

Is Everybody Happy?

US   1943   73m   bw
Columbia

A virtual remake of the above, with the star fourteen years older.

Low-budget filler with a few good numbers.

w Monte Brice   *d* Charles Barton

Ted Lewis, Larry Parks, Michael Duane, Nan Wynn

Is Paris Burning?

France/US   1965   165m   bw   Panavision (colour sequence)
Paramount/Transcontinental/Marianne (Paul Graetz)
V*, S

A multi-storied account of the 1944 liberation of Paris.

Muddled, scribbled, tedious and confusing attempt at a thinking man's all-star war epic.

w Francis Ford Coppola, Gore Vidal   *book* Paris, brûle-t-il? by Larry Collins and Dominique Lapierre   *d* René Clément   *ph* Marcel Grignon   *m* Maurice Jarre

Leslie Caron, Gert Frobe, Charles Boyer, Yves Montand, Orson Welles, Alain Delon, Jean-Pierre Cassel, Jean-Paul Belmondo, Kirk Douglas, Glenn Ford, Claude Dauphin, Daniel Gélin, Anthony Perkins, Simone Signoret, Robert Stack, George Chakiris

'An incoherent, ponderous and shallow tribute to one of the great experiences of our time, an insult to those with intimate knowledge of or experience with the liberation of Paris, an embarrassment for those interested in spectacular moviemaking.' – *Judith Crist*

AAN: Marcel Grignon

Isadora *

GB   1968   138m   Eastmancolor
Universal (Robert and Raymond Hakim)
V*
US title: *The Loves of Isadora*

Eccentric character dancer Isadora Duncan reflects on her crowded and unconventional life.

Ambitious and expensive but finally unsatisfactory biopic of a controversial figure of the twenties.

w Melvyn Bragg, Clive Exton   *d Karel Reisz*
ph Larry Pizer   *m* Maurice Jarre   *pd* Jocelyn
Herbert   *ad* Michael Seymour, Ralph Brinton

Vanessa Redgrave, Jason Robards Jnr, James Fox,
Ivan Tchenko, John Fraser, Bessie Love

'A brave attempt at a daunting task.' – *Tom Milne*

AAN: Vanessa Redgrave

Ishtar
US   1987   107m   Technicolor
Columbia/Delphi V (Warren Beatty)
V, V*, L

Two untalented songwriters get involved with
Middle Eastern turmoil.

Bitty rehash of old jokes and situations, vaguely
resembling a Hope-Crosby Road picture of long ago,
but far less funny despite costing 50 million dollars.

wd Elaine May   *ph* Vittorio Storaro   *pd* Paul
Sylbert

Dustin Hoffman, Warren Beatty, Isabelle Adjani,
Charles Grodin, Jack Weston, Tess Harper

'One can't help but wonder whether the camel was
the only blind creature who had something to do with
this picture.' – *Daily Variety*

The Island *
Japan   1961   92m   bw
Kindai Eiga Kyokai (Kaneto Shindo)
V*
original title: *Hadaka no Shima*

The quiet tenor of life for the only family inhabiting a
tiny island is eventually broken by illness and death.

Slow, controlled, beautiful film in which not a single
word of dialogue is spoken. The artificiality of this
concept eventually diminishes its stature.

wd Kaneto Shindo   *ph* Kiyoshi Kuroda   *m* Hikaru
Hayashi

Nobuko Otowa, Taiji Tonoyama, Shinji Tanaka,
Masanori Horimoto

'A visual poem which mirrors tedium without ever
inducing it.' – *MFB*

'For 300 years a terrifying secret has been kept from the
outside world!'
The Island
US   1980   114m   Technicolor
Universal (Richard Zanuck and David Brown)
V*, L

A journalist is in fear of his life on a Caribbean island
inhabited by the bloodthirsty descendants of 17th-
century buccaneers.

Ridiculous shocker from the *Jaws* people; stupidly
plotted and gruesome in detail.

w Peter Benchley   *novel* Peter Benchley   *d* Michael
Ritchie   *ph* Henri Decaë   *m* Ennio Morricone

Michael Caine, David Warner, Angela Punch
McGregor, Frank Middlemass, Dudley Sutton, Clyde
Jeavons

'Suspense gives way to gut-level sadism aimed at the
lowest common audience denominator.' – *Variety*

The Island at the Top of the World **
US   1974   93m   Technicolor
Walt Disney (Winston Hibler)
V*

In 1907, a rich Englishman commissions an airship to
take him to a mythical arctic Shangri-La in search of
his lost son.

Generally brisk and effective adventure fantasy whose
trick effects are sufficiently splendid to redeem a sag
in the middle and an overplus of Viking chatter which
has to be laboriously translated.

w John Whedon   *novel The Lost Ones* by Ian Cameron
d Robert Stevenson   *ph* Frank Phillips   *m* Maurice

Jarre   *pd Peter Ellenshaw*   *sp Art Cruickshank, Danny Lee*

Donald Sinden, David Hartman, Jacques Marin,
Mako

Island Escape: see *No Man Is an Island*

Island in the Sky *
US   1953   109m   bw
Wayne-Fellows (Robert Fellows)

A transport plane makes a forced landing north of
Greenland, and the crew must survive till help comes.

Well-made outdoor suspenser shot in the California
Sierras.

w Ernest K. Gann   *novel* Ernest K. Gann
d William Wellman   *ph* Archie Stout   *md* Emil
Newman   *m* Hugo Friedhofer

John Wayne, Lloyd Nolan, Walter Abel, Allyn Joslyn,
Andy Devine, James Arness

Island in the Sun *
GB   1957   119m   Technicolor   Cinemascope
TCF (Darryl F. Zanuck)

Sexual and racial problems erupt on a West Indian
island.

Portmanteau romantic melodrama which generally
misfires, especially in an attempt to parallel *Crime and
Punishment;* but the cast is interesting.

w Alfred Hayes   *novel* Alec Waugh   *d* Robert
Rossen   *ph* Frederick A. Young   *m* Malcolm
Arnold

James Mason, Joan Fontaine, Harry Belafonte, John
Williams, Dorothy Dandridge, Joan Collins, Michael
Rennie, Patricia Owens, Stephen Boyd, Basil Sydney,
Diana Wynyard, Ronald Squire, John Justin

Island of Crime (dubbed)
Italy   1968   85m   Eastmancolor   Scope
Golden Era/Clesi (Silvio Clementelli)
original title: *Sequestro di Persona*

When a rich young man is kidnapped and killed in
Sardinia, his friend decides to seek revenge.

A confusing story of murder and ransom demands,
treated as an everyday happening, but never fully
explained; it is a film that does not travel well.

w Ugo Pirro, Gianfranco Mingozzi   *d* Gianfranco
Mingozzi   *ph* Ugo Piccone   *m* Riz Ortolani
ad Sergio Canevari   *ed* Ruggero Mastroianni

Franco Nero, Charlotte Rampling, Frank Wolff, Ennio
Balbo, Pier Luigi Aprè, Steffen Zacharias

† The Italian version ran for 95m.

Island of Desire: see *Saturday Island*

The Island of Dr Moreau *
US   1977   98m   Movielab
AIP/Cinema 77 (Skip Steloff, John Temple-Smith)
V*

In 1911, shipwrecked sailors land on a Pacific island
where a mad doctor experiments with animal
mutations.

A sprightly version of an old story; unfortunately it
lacks any sense of the sinister, and the star is no match
for Charles Laughton in *Island of Lost Souls*.

w John Herman Shaner, Al Ramrus   *story* H. G.
Wells   *d* Don Taylor   *ph* Gerry Fisher
m Laurence Rosenthal

Burt Lancaster, Michael York, Nigel Davenport,
Barbara Carrera, Richard Basehart, Nick Cravat

'Cursed with lush colour photography instead of
black and white atmospherics, and Lancaster's stolid
mania instead of Laughton's manic zeal.' – *Sight and
Sound*

Island of Lost Men
US   1939   64m   bw
Paramount

An Oriental girl seeks her lost father in waterfront
dives and finds him on a prison island.

Adequate action programmer.

w William R. Lipman, Horace McCoy   *d* Kurt
Neumann

Anna May Wong, Broderick Crawford, Anthony
Quinn, J. Carrol Naish

† A remake of *White Woman.*

'Out of the dark fantastic madness of his science he
created her – the panther woman – throbbing to the
hot flush of new-found love!'
Island of Lost Souls *
US   1932   74m   bw
Paramount

On a remote South Sea island, mad Dr Moreau
transforms animals into humans by vivisection.

Unchilling but interesting thriller with a rolling-eyed
star performance.

w Waldemar Young, Philip Wylie   *story* The Island
of Dr Moreau by H. G. Wells   *d* Erle C. Kenton
ph Karl Struss

Charles Laughton, Bela Lugosi, Richard Arlen,
Kathleen Burke, Leila Hyams

Island of Lost Women
US   1958   72m   bw
Jaguar/Warner
V*

A newspaperman lands on a remote island where a
scientist has retired from the world with his
daughters.

Unexciting hokum with more talk than action.

w Ray Buffum   *d* Frank Tuttle

Jeff Richards, Venetia Stevenson, John Smith, Alan
Napier

Island of Love
US   1963   101m   Technicolor   Panavision
Warner/Belgrave (Morton da Costa)

A gangster finances a film providing his girlfriend
stars, but when it flops he chases the producers to a
Greek island.

Dismally unfunny comedy wasting a talented cast.

w David R. Schwartz   *d* Morton da Costa
ph Harry Stradling   *m* George Duning

Robert Preston, Tony Randall, Walter Matthau,
Giorgia Moll

Island of Terror
GB   1966   89m   Eastmancolor
Planet (Tom Blakeley)
V*

On an Irish island, a scientist makes monsters who
thrive on bone.

Horror hokum, moderately done.

w Edward Andrew Mann, Alan Ramsen   *d* Terence
Fisher   *ph* Reg Wyer   *m* Malcolm Lockyer
sp John St John Earl

Peter Cushing, Edward Judd, Carole Gray, Eddie
Byrne, Sam Kydd, Niall MacGinnis

Island of the Blue Dolphins
US   1964   93m   Eastmancolor
U-I/Robert B. Radnitz

Two orphaned children grow up alone on a
Californian island, protected by wild dogs.

Pleasant if unconvincing family film based on a true
story.

w Ted Sherdeman, Jane Klove *novel* Scott O'Dell
d James B. Clark *ph* Leo Tover *m* Paul Sawtell

Celia Kaye, Larry Dornasin, George Kennedy

Island of The Living Dead: see *Zombie Flesh Eaters*

Island of the Lost
US 1968 92m colour
Ivan Tors
V*

An anthropologist sets sail for an uncharted island and is shipwrecked on it.

Good-looking but singularly plotless action adventure.

w Richard Carlson, Ivan Tors *d* Richard Carlson

Richard Greene, Luke Halpin, Mark Hulswit

Island Rescue: see *Appointment with Venus*

Islands in the Stream
US 1977 105m Metrocolor Panavision
Paramount (Peter Bart, Max Palevsky)
V*, L, S

On a Bahamian island in 1940, an expatriate American artist welcomes his three sons and reflects on the futility of life.

Shapeless semi-autobiographical fragments culminating unpersuasively in an action climax of heroic self-sacrifice. A film on which no expense has been spared and which doesn't work at all.

w Denne Bart Petitclerc *novel* Ernest Hemingway
d Franklin Schaffner *ph* Fred J. Koenekamp
m Jerry Goldsmith

George C. Scott, David Hemmings, Gilbert Roland, Susan Tyrrell, Richard Evans, Claire Bloom, Hart Bochner, Julius Harris

'It is all too awful for words.' – *Benny Green, Punch*

AAN: photography

Isle of Forgotten Sins
US 1943 82m bw
PRC (Peter R. Van Duinen)

In the South Seas, villains congregate in search of sunken treasure.

Patchy tropical melodrama with a cast more interesting than the script.

w Raymond L. Schrock *story* Edgar G. Ulmer
d Edgar G. Ulmer

John Carradine, Gale Sondergaard, Sidney Toler, Frank Fenton, Rita Quigley, Veda Ann Borg

Isle of Fury
US 1936 60m bw
Warner

A fugitive from justice finds temporary peace on a South Sea island.

Limp remake of *The Narrow Corner* (qv); its star later pretended he hadn't made it.

w Robert Andrews, William Jacobs *d* Frank McDonald

Humphrey Bogart, Margaret Lindsay, Donald Woods

Isle of Missing Men
US 1942 67m bw
Monogram

Convicts on a prison island try to make a break.

The very poor man's *Papillon*.

w Richard Oswald, Robert Chapin *d* Richard Oswald

Gilbert Roland, Helen Gilbert, John Howard

Isle of Sinners: see *Dieu a Besoin des Hommes*

Isle of the Dead **
US 1945 72m bw
RKO (Val Lewton)
V*, L

On a Balkan island in 1912 a group of people shelter from the plague and fear that one of their number is a vampire.

Glum, ghoulish melodrama with some neatly handled shocks; quite different from any other horror film.

w Ardel Wray, Josef Mischel *d* Mark Robson
ph Jack Mackenzie *m* Leigh Harline

Boris Karloff, Ellen Drew, Helene Thimig, Marc Cramer, Katherine Emery, Alan Napier, Jason Robards

Isn't It Romantic *
US 1948 87m bw
Paramount (Daniel Dare)

Romance hits the household of an ex-Civil War colonel in Indiana.

Pleasant but forgettable period semi-musical.

w Theodore Strauss, Josef Mischel, Richard Breen
d Norman Z. McLeod *ph* Lionel Lindon
m Joseph J. Lilley

Veronica Lake, Mona Freeman, Mary Hatcher, Roland Culver, Billy de Wolfe, Patric Knowles, Richard Webb, Kathryn Givney, Pearl Bailey

Isn't Life Wonderful? *
US 1924 99m (24 fps) bw silent
UA/David Wark Griffith

The life of a family in post-war Germany.

An unpopular subject, and a grey-looking film, but the director shows a lot of his strength in it.

wd D. W. Griffith *story* Geoffrey Moss

Carol Dempster, Neil Hamilton, Helen Lowell, Frank Puglia, Marcia Harris, Lupino Lane

Isn't Life Wonderful? *
GB 1952 83m Technicolor
ABP (Warwick Ward)

In 1902, drunken Uncle Willie runs a bicycle shop and manages to reconcile a lovers' quarrel.

Engaging, well-cast family comedy.

w Brock Williams *novel* Uncle Willie and the Bicycle Shop by Brock Williams *d* Harold French
ph Erwin Hillier *m* Philip Green *ad* Terence Verity

Donald Wolfit, Eileen Herlie, Cecil Parker, Eleanor Summerfield, Robert Urquhart, Cecil Trouncer

Istanbul
US 1956 84m Technicolor Cinemascope
U-I (Albert J. Cohen)

Various adventurers and an amnesiac girl seek stolen diamonds in Istanbul.

Dim remake of a flat-footed piece of thick ear called *Singapore*.

w Seton I. Miller, Barbara Gray, Richard Alan Simmons *d* Joseph Pevney *ph* William Daniels
m Joseph Gershenson

Errol Flynn, Cornell Borchers, John Bentley, Torin Thatcher, Leif Erickson, Martin Benson, Vladimir Sokoloff, Werner Klemperer, Nat King Cole, Peggy Knudsen

Istoria Asi Klyachinoi, kotoraya lyubila, da nie vshla zamuzh: see *Asya's Happiness*

It *
US 1927 72m (24 fps) bw silent
Famous Players-Lasky/Paramount (B. P. Schulberg)
V*, L

A shopgirl tries to live by the tenets of Elinor Glyn's book, and finally marries her boss.

In its day a fast and funny spoof, and the years have not dealt too unkindly with it.

w Hope Loring, Louis D. Lighton *adaptation* Elinor Glyn *d* Clarence Badger *ph* H. Kinley Martin

Clara Bow, Antonio Moreno, William Austin, Jacqueline Gadsdon, Gary Cooper, Elinor Glyn

It Ain't Hay
US 1943 79m bw
Universal (Alex Gottlieb)
GB title: *Money for Jam*

When a racehorse dies, a New York cabbie and his friend try to find a new one for the impecunious owners.

Formula Abbot and Costello with a small injection of sentiment and Runyonese. Not their best by a mile.

w Allen Boretz, John Grant *story* Princess O'Hara by Damon Runyon *d* Erle C. Kenton *ph* Charles von Enger *m/ly* Harry Revel, Paul Francis Webster

Bud Abbott, Lou Costello, Grace McDonald, Cecil Kellaway, Patsy O'Connor, Eugene Pallette, Shemp Howard, Eddie Quillan

It All Came True *
US 1940 97m bw
Warner (Mark Hellinger)

A gangster hides out in a boarding house and puts it back on its feet.

Competent New York fairy story full of sweetness and light.

w Michael Fessier, Lawrence Kimble *story* Better Than Life by Louis Bromfield *d* Lewis Seiler
ph Ernest Haller *m* Heinz Roemheld

Humphrey Bogart, Ann Sheridan, Jeffrey Lynn, ZaSu Pitts, Una O'Connor, Jessie Busley, John Litel, Grant Mitchell, Felix Bressart

It Always Rains on Sunday ***
GB 1947 92m bw
Ealing (Henry Cornelius)

An escaped convict takes refuge in his married mistress's house in East London.

Influential slumland melodrama, now dated – the stuff of every other television play – but at the time electrifyingly vivid and very well done.

w Angus Macphail, Robert Hamer, Henry Cornelius,
novel Arthur La Bern *d* Robert Hamer *ph* Douglas Slocombe *m* Georges Auric

Googie Withers, John McCallum, Jack Warner, Edward Chapman, Susan Shaw, Sydney Tafler

'Let me pay it the simplest of compliments and say that it has the persuasiveness of an exciting story professionally told.' – *Sunday Times*

It Came from beneath the Sea
US 1955 80m bw
Columbia/Sam Katzman (Charles Schneer)
V, V*, L

A giant octopus half destroys San Francisco.

Tepid monster movie; special effects only fair.

w George Worthing Yates, Hal Smith *d* Robert Gordon *ph* Henry Freulich *md* Mischa Bakaleinikoff

Kenneth Tobey, Faith Domergue, Donald Curtis, Ian Keith

It Came from Outer Space **
US 1953 80m bw 3-D
U-I (William Alland)
V*

A young astronomer sees a space ship land in the Arizona desert and tracks down the occupants who can adopt human appearance at will.

Quite bright science fiction, the first to use this theme of borrowing bodies and the first to utilize the Western desert locations. 3-D adds a shock moment or two.

w Harry Essex, *story* Ray Bradbury *d* Jack Arnold *ph* Clifford Stine *md* Joseph Gershenson *m* Herman Stein

Richard Carlson, Barbara Rush, Charles Drake, Kathleen Hughes

'A solid piece of eerie entertainment, replete with wild screams and bug-eyed monsters guaranteed to send scared customers out of this world.' – *Hollywood Reporter*

'Desert was Arnold's favourite location, and he used it consistently to create a sense of strangeness and menace otherwise much restricted by his budgets.' – *Time Out, 1982*

It Can't Be Winter, We Haven't Had Summer Yet
Canada   1980   84m   colour
La Maison de Quatre (Louise Carré)
original title: *Ça Peut Pas Être l'Hiver, On n'a Même Pas Êu d'Été*

A middle-aged woman, much to the apprehension of her children, enjoys a new lease of life after her husband's death.

Too pat and comfortable to be plausible, though it has some charm, apart from a dire excursion into a pop video halfway through.

wd Louise Carré *ph* Robert Vanherweghem *m* Marc O'Farrell *ed* André Théberge

Charlotte Boisjoli, Jacques Galipeau, Céline Lomez, Serge Bélair, Mireille Thibault, Daniel Matte, Marie-Eve Doré, Martin Neufeld

It Comes Up Love
US   1942   64m   bw
Ken Goldsmith/Universal
GB title: *A Date With an Angel*

A businessman tries to bring up two motherless daughters.

A slim plotline serves as an excuse for a brief but snappy 'B' musical.

w Dorothy Bennett, Charles Kenyon *d* Charles Lamont

Gloria Jean, Donald O'Connor, Ian Hunter, Frieda Inescort, Louise Allbritton, Charles Coleman

It Conquered the World
US   1956   68m   bw
AIP
V, V*

Something from another planet is sheltered by a well-meaning scientist who discovers too late that its intentions are evil.

Tolerable horror comic on a risibly low budget.

w Lou Rusoff *d* Roger Corman

Peter Graves, Beverly Garland, Lee Van Cleef, Sally Fraser, Charles B. Griffith

It Could Happen to You
US   1939   73m   bw
TCF

After a stag party, an advertising man finds a body in his car.

Neat second-feature mystery.

w Allen Rivkin, Lou Breslow *d* Alfred Werker

Stuart Erwin, Gloria Stuart, Raymond Walburn, Douglas Fowley

It Grows on Trees
US   1952   84m   bw
U-I (Leonard Goldstein)

A housewife finds a money tree in her backyard.

Protracted fantasy comedy.

w Leonard Praskins, Barney Slater *d* Arthur Lubin *ph* Maury Gertsman *m* Frank Skinner

Irene Dunne (her last film), Dean Jagger, Joan Evans, Richard Crenna, Edith Meiser, Dee Pollock

It Had to Be You
US   1947   98m   bw
Columbia/Don Hartman

A dizzy dame runs out on three prospective husbands and is pursued by an Indian.

Weak sex farce without the courage of its lack of convictions.

w Norman Panama, Melvin Frank *d* Don Hartman, Rudolph Maté *ph* Rudolph Maté *md* Morris Stoloff *m* Heinz Roemheld

Ginger Rogers, Cornel Wilde, Percy Waram, Spring Byington, Thurston Hall, Ron Randell

It Had to Happen
US   1936   80m   bw
TCF/Raymond Griffith

An Italian immigrant becomes the political boss of New York City.

Unconvincing melodrama with star appeal.

w Howard Ellis Smith, Kathryn Scola, Rupert Hughes *d* Roy del Ruth *ph* Peverell Marley *md* Arthur Lange

George Raft, Rosalind Russell, Leo Carrillo, Arline Judge, Alan Dinehart, Andrew Tombes

'Incredible story precludes its b.o. chances.' – *Variety*

It Happened at the Inn: see *Goupi Mains Rouges*

It Happened at the World's Fair
US   1962   104m   Metrocolor   Panavision
MGM/Ted Richmond
V*

At the Seattle World's Fair, two crop-dusting pilots have romantic intrigues.

Routine star vehicles.

w Si Rose, Seaman Jacobs *d* Norman Taurog *ph* Joseph Ruttenberg *m* Leith Stevens

Elvis Presley, Gary Lockwood, Joan O'Brien, Yvonne Craig, Ginny Tiu

It Happened Here **
GB   1963   99m   bw
UA/Kevin Brownlow, Andrew Mollo

What might have happened if the Germans had invaded England in 1940.

A remarkable semi-professional reconstruction which took seven years to film and is totally convincing in detail, but unfortunately rather confused and padded as drama.

wd Kevin Brownlow, Andrew Mollo *ph* Peter Suschitsky *m* Jack Beaver

Sebastian Shaw, Pauline Murray, Fiona Lekland, Honor Fehrson

'For a grain of artistic truth, we can forgive even the grainy photography and wavering sound with which part of it is afflicted.' – *John Simon*

It Happened in Athens
US   1961   100m   DeLuxe   Cinemascope
TCF (James S. Elliott)

At the first revival of the Olympic Games in 1896 a publicity-seeking actress announces that she will marry whoever wins the Marathon.

Witless extravagant romp, well mounted but adding up to zero.

w Laszlo Vadnay *d* Andrew Marton *ph* Curt Courant *m* Manos Hadjidakis

Jayne Mansfield, Trax Colton, Bob Mathias

It Happened in Brooklyn *
US   1947   103m   bw
MGM (Jack Cummings)
V*, L

Young New Yorkers with musical talents find their way to fame.

Well-handled routine musical of its time.

w Isobel Lennart *d* Richard Whorf *ph* Robert Planck *m* Johnny Green *songs* Jule Styne, Sammy Cahn

Frank Sinatra, Jimmy Durante, Kathryn Grayson, Peter Lawford, Gloria Grahame

'Aside from Sinatra and Durante the show amounts to practically nothing, but there is a general kindliness about it which I enjoyed.' – *James Agee*

It Happened in Hollywood
US   1937   67m   bw
Columbia

A silent cowboy star is washed up when talkies come in.

Indifferent studio story.

w Ethel Hill, Harvey Ferguson, Sam Fuller, Myles Connolly *d* Harry Lachman

Richard Dix, Fay Wray, Victor Kilian, Franklin Pangborn, Charles Arnt, Granville Bates

'It will have difficulty fitting in . . . won't particularly satisfy 'em in the duals.' – *Variety*

It Happened on Fifth Avenue *
US   1947   115m   bw
Allied Artists (Roy del Ruth)

A child of divorce finds amiable squatters in her millionaire father's house.

Curious, overlong, cheerful Capraesque comedy with the mildest of social pretensions.

w Everett Freeman, Frederick Stephani, Herbert Clyde Lewis *d* Roy del Ruth *ph* Henry Sharp

Gale Storm, Ann Harding, Victor Moore, Charles Ruggles, Don Defore

AAN: original story

'Together For The First Time!'
It Happened One Night ***
US   1934   105m   bw
Columbia (Frank Capra)
V, V*, L

A runaway heiress falls in love with the reporter who is chasing her across America.

Highly successful and influential romantic comedy, the first to use buses and motels as background and still come up sparkling; it remains superlative in patches, but overall has a faded, dated air.

w Robert Riskin, *story* Night Bus by Samuel Hopkins Adams *d* Frank Capra *ph* Joseph Walker *md* Louis Silvers

Clark Gable, Claudette Colbert, Walter Connolly, Roscoe Karns, Alan Hale, Ward Bond, Jameson Thomas, Arthur Hoyt

'A laughing hit that will mean important coin.' – *Variety*

'It will be a long day before we see so little made into so much.' – *Otis Ferguson*

'Something to revive your faith in a medium which could belong among the great arts.' – *Robert Forsythe*

'We may look askance at Capra's sententious notions about the miserable rich and the happy poor, but there's no doubting the chord he struck in depression audiences.' – *Time Out, 1980*

'It made audiences happy in a way that only a few films in each era do. In the mid-30s, the Colbert and Gable of this film became Americans' idealized view of themselves – breezy, likeable, sexy, gallant, and maybe just a little harebrained. It was the *Annie Hall* of its day – before the invention of anxiety.' – *Pauline Kael, 70s*

'One of the most entertaining films that has ever been offered to the public.' – *Observer*

† Remade 1956 (badly) as *You Can't Run Away From It.* †† Robert Montgomery was the first choice for the Gable role, but he refused it because he had been on a bus in *Fugitive Lovers*. The Colbert role was first offered to Myrna Loy, Margaret Sullavan and Constance Bennett. Colbert was lured by a 40,000-dollar fee.

AA: best picture; Robert Riskin; Frank Capra; Clark Gable; Claudette Colbert

It Happened One Summer: see *State Fair* (1945)

It Happened One Sunday
GB   1943   99m   bw
ABPC

In Liverpool, a Canadian seaman falls for an Irish maid.

Overlong romantic comedy with nowhere to go.

w Victor Skutezky, Friedrich Gotfurt, Stephen Black d Karel Lamac

Robert Beatty, Barbara White, Marjorie Rhodes, Ernest Butcher, Judy Kelly, Irene Vanbrugh

It Happened to Jane
US   1959   98m   Technicolor   Cinemascope
Columbia/Arwin (Richard Quine)

A lady lobster dealer becomes involved in a battle with the railroad whose inefficiency affects her business.

Witless, wholesome farce which promises more than it delivers.

w Norman Katkov   d Richard Quine   ph Charles Lawton Jnr   m George Duning

Doris Day, Jack Lemmon, *Ernie Kovacs*, Steve Forrest

It Happened Tomorrow ***
US   1944   84m   bw
UA/Arnold Pressburger

A reporter meets an old man with the power to show him tomorrow's newspaper headlines, so that he always gets scoops – including his own death . . .

Engaging fantasy, flawlessly made and quietly very entertaining.

w *Dudley Nichols, René Clair*   d *René Clair*   ph Archie Stout   m Robert Stolz

Dick Powell, Linda Darnell, Jack Oakie, *John Philliber*, Edgar Kennedy, Ed Brophy, George Cleveland, Sig Rumann

'Students of cinematic style will find many shrewdly polished bits to admire and enjoy.' – *James Agee*

'Diverting escapist entertainment for all audiences.' – *Variety*

AAN: Robert Stolz

It Happens Every Spring
US   1949   80m   bw
TCF (William Perlberg)

A chemistry teacher discovers a formula that makes baseballs repellent to wood.

Smartly produced but rather desperate fantasy comedy.

w Valentine Davies   d Lloyd Bacon   ph Joe MacDonald   m Leigh Harline

Ray Milland, Jean Peters, Paul Douglas, Ed Begley, Ted de Corsia, Ray Collins, Jessie Royce Landis, Alan Hale Jnr

AAN: original story (Shirley W. Smith, Valentine Davies)

It Happens Every Thursday *
US   1953   80m   bw
U-I (Anton Leader)

The new owner of a small-town newspaper becomes unpopular through his attempts to boost the circulation.

Pleasant comedy with amusing scenes.

w Dane Lussier   d Joseph Pevney   ph Russell Metty   m Joseph Gershenson

Loretta Young, John Forsythe, Jimmy Conlin, Frank McHugh, Edgar Buchanan, Jane Darwell

It Hurts Only When I Laugh: see *Only When I Laugh*

It Lives Again
US   1978   91m   colour
Warner/Larco (Larry Cohen)
V*, S
aka: *It's Alive II*

Three mutant killer babies are protected by a scientist from a cop determined to kill them.

A sequel to *It's Alive* that is less effective because the babies are too visible for too much of the time.

wd Larry Cohen   ph Fenton Hamilton   m Bernard Herrmann   ed Curt Burch, Louis Friedman, Carol O'Blath

Frederic Forrest, Kathleen Lloyd, John P. Ryan, John Marley, Andrew Duggan, Eddie Constantine, James Dixon

† It was followed by *It's Alive III* (qv).

It Pays to Advertise
US   1931   66m   bw
Paramount

A mild youth is turned by his girl into a business success.

Fair film version of a popular stage comedy.

w Arthur Kober   play Walter Hackett   d Frank Tuttle

Norman Foster, Carole Lombard, Skeets Gallagher, Eugene Pallette, Louise Brooks, Lucien Littlefield

'Good enough programme material.' – *Variety*

It Rains on Our Love *
Sweden   1946   95m   bw
Sveriges Folkbiografer (Lorens Marmstedt)
original title: *Det Regnar Pa Var Kärlek; Man with an Umbrella*

A pregnant girl meets an ex-prisoner while waiting for a train and they decide to live together.

A mainly light-hearted movie about two irresponsible people making the best of the worst that life has to offer.

w Ingmar Bergman, Herbert Grevenius   play Oscar Braathen   d Ingmar Bergman   ph Göran Strindberg, Hilding Bladh   m Erland von Koch   ad P. A. Lundgren   ed Tage Holmberg

Barbro Kollberg, Birger Malmsten, Gösta Cederlund, Ludde Gentzel, Douglas Hage, Hjördis Pettersson, Benkt-Ake Benktsson, Sture Ericson

It Should Happen to You **
US   1954   87m   bw
Columbia (Fred Kohlmar)

A slightly daffy New York model with an urge to be famous rents a huge billboard and puts her name on it.

Likeable comedy which starts brightly and slowly falls apart, disappointing considering the credentials of the talents involved and the satiric possibilities of the plot.

w Ruth Gordon, Garson Kanin   d George Cukor   ph Charles Lang   m Frederick Hollander

Judy Holliday, Jack Lemmon, Peter Lawford, Michael O'Shea

It Shouldn't Happen to a Dog
US   1946   70m   bw
TCF (William Girard)

A lady detective, her dog and a reporter solve a murder case more by good luck than good management.

Acceptable comedy support.

w Eugene Ling, Frank Gabrielson   story Edwin Lanham   d Herbert I. Leeds   ph Glen MacWilliams   m David Buttolph

Allyn Joslyn, Carole Landis, Margo Woode, Henry Morgan, Reed Hadley, John Alexander

It Shouldn't Happen to a Vet
GB   1976   93m   Technicolor
EMI/Talent Associates/Readers Digest
US title: *All Things Bright and Beautiful*

Adventures of a Yorkshire vet just before World War II.

Competent sequel to *All Creatures Great and Small* (qv).

w Alan Plater   books James Herriot   d Eric Till   ph Arthur Ibbetson   m Laurie Johnson

John Alderton, Colin Blakely, Lisa Harrow, Bill Maynard, Richard Pearson, Raymond Francis, John Barrett, Paul Shelley

It Started in Naples *
US   1960   100m   Technicolor   Vistavision
Paramount/Capri (Jack Rose)
V*

A Philadelphia lawyer goes to Naples to settle his dead brother's affairs, and falls for his nephew's aunt.

Nicely made, formula romantic comedy which started life as a vehicle for Gracie Fields.

w Melville Shavelson, Jack Rose, Susi Cecchi d'Amico   d Melville Shavelson   ph Robert Surtees   m Alessandro Cicognini   ad Hal Pereira, Roland Anderson

Clark Gable, Sophia Loren, Vittorio de Sica, Marietto, Paulo Carlini

AAN: art direction

It Started in Paradise
GB   1952   94m   Technicolor
GFD/British Film Makers (Leslie Parkyn, Sergei Nolbandov)

The career of an ambitious dress designer.

Stilted and garishly coloured but often amusing backstage melodrama of the fashion world: a Hollywood-style star vehicle which seems faintly surprising as a British product.

w Marghanita Laski   d Compton Bennett   ph Jack Cardiff   m Malcolm Arnold   ad Edward Carrick

Jane Hylton, Ian Hunter, Terence Morgan, Muriel Pavlow, Brian Worth, *Martita Hunt, Ronald Squire, Harold Lang*, Joyce Barbour, Kay Kendall

It Started with a Kiss
US   1959   104m   Metrocolor   Cinemascope
MGM/Arcola (Aaron Rosenberg)
V*

An army sergeant posted to Spain is embarrassed when his wife follows him.

Flabby comedy with the emphasis on sex and pratfalls.

w Charles Lederer   d George Marshall   ph Robert Bronner   m Jeff Alexander

Glenn Ford, Debbie Reynolds, Fred Clark, Edgar Buchanan, Eva Gabor

It Started with Eve **

US 1941 93m bw

Universal (Joe Pasternak)

A dying millionaire wants to see his grandson engaged, so a waitress obliges for an hour . . . but the old man recovers.

Charming comedy which was probably the star's best film; remade as *I'd Rather be Rich* (qv).

w Norman Krasna, Leo Townsend *d* Henry Koster *ph* Rudolph Maté *md* Charles Previn, Hans Salter

Deanna Durbin, Charles Laughton, Robert Cummings, Margaret Tallichet, Guy Kibbee, Walter Catlett, Catherine Doucet

'The perfect 8 to 80 picture.' – *Variety*

AAN: Charles Previn, Hans Salter

It! The Terror from Beyond Space

US 1958 69m bw

Vogue/United Artists

V*

A space ship returning from Mars is invaded by a worm-like monster.

Laughable but lively precursor of *Alien;* rather more fun on the whole.

w Jerome Bixby *d* Edward L. Cahn

Marshall Thompson, Shawn Smith, Kim Spaulding, Ann Doran, Dabbs Greer

The Italian Job **

GB 1969 100m Eastmancolor Panavision

Paramount/Oakhurst (Michael Deeley)

V, V*

Crooks stage a traffic jam in Turin in order to pull off a bullion robbery.

Lively caper comedy which provides a good measure of entertainment.

w Troy Kennedy Martin *d* Peter Collinson *ph* Douglas Slocombe, Norman Warwick *m* Quincy Jones

Michael Caine, Noël Coward, Benny Hill, Raf Vallone, Tony Beckley, Rossano Brazzi, Maggie Blye, Irene Handl, John Le Mesurier, Fred Emney

An Italian Straw Hat ***

France 1927 74m (24 fps) bw silent

Albatross

original title: *Un Chapeau de Paille d'Italie*

The hero is prevented from getting to a wedding when his horse chews up a lady's straw hat and her escort demands that it be replaced.

Lively but gentle comedy of errors, a stage farce expanded for the screen and filled with visual gags. A very influential and still amusing piece.

wd René Clair, play Eugène Labiche *ph* Maurice Desfassiaux, Nicolas Roudakoff *ad Lazare Meerson*

Albert Préjean, Olga Tschekowa, Marise Maia, Alice Tissot

'The very springtime of screen comedy.' – *Tatler*

'One of the funniest films ever made.' – *Tribune, 1945*

'Still one of the funniest films in the world.' – *Sunday Times, 1948*

ItalianAmerican

US 1974 45m colour/bw

National Communications Foundation (Saul Rubin, Elaine Attias)

V

Martin Scorsese's affectionate portrait of his parents, as they talk about their upbringing, and their enjoyment of food, showing holiday snaps mainly of people at dinner.

A sophisticated home movie, rooting a family in their environment. The credits include the recipe for Mrs Scorsese's meatball sauce.

wd Martin Scorsese *ph* Alex Hirshfeld

Catherine and Charles Scorsese

† It was released on video with three other shorts under the title *4 x Scorsese.*

It's a Big Country

US 1952 89m bw

MGM (Robert Sisk)

Seven stories show the diversity of the US and the glory of being one of its citizens.

Stultifying flagwaver memorable chiefly as a waste of good actors.

w William Ludwig, Helen Deutsch, George Wells, Allen Rivkin, Dorothy Kingsley, Isobel Lennart *d* Richard Thorpe, Don Weis, John Sturges, Don Hartman, William Wellman, Charles Vidor, Clarence Brown *ph* John Alton, Ray June, William Mellor, Joseph Ruttenberg *m* Bronislau Kaper, Rudolph G. Kopp, David Raksin, David Rose

Ethel Barrymore, Keefe Brasselle, Nancy Davis, Van Johnson, Gene Kelly, Janet Leigh, Marjorie Main, Fredric March, George Murphy, William Powell, S. Z. Sakall, Lewis Stone, James Whitmore

It's a Boy

GB 1933 80m bw

Gainsborough (Michael Balcon)

A blackmailer claims to be a bridegroom's long-lost illegitimate son.

Heavy-footed version of a popular stage farce.

w John Paddy Carstairs, L. H. Gordon *play* Franz Arnold, Ernst Bach and Austin Melford *d* Tim Whelan *ph* Mutz Greenbaum *ad* Vetchinsky *ed* Harold M. Young

Leslie Henson, Edward Everett Horton, Heather Thatcher, Alfred Drayton, Albert Burdon, Robertson Hare, Wendy Barrie

It's a Date *

US 1940 100m bw

Universal/Joe Pasternak

V*

The daughter of a Broadway musical heroine has stage ambitions of her own, and chases an older man who is more interested in her mother.

Fairly pleasant but unduly elongated star comedy.

w Norman Krasna *d* William Seiter *ph* Joe Valentine *m* Charles Previn

Deanna Durbin, Walter Pidgeon, Kay Francis, Eugene Pallette, Henry Stephenson, Cecilia Loftus, Samuel S. Hinds, S. Z. Sakall

'A natural which will roll grosses of upper bracket proportions.' – *Variety*

It's a Dog's Life: see *The Bar Sinister*

It's a Gift **

US 1934 73m bw

Paramount (William Le Baron)

V*, L

A general store proprietor buys an orange ranch by mail and transports his family to California.

Roughly assembled comedy of disasters which happens to show the star more or less at his best, though the expected climax is lacking.

w Jack Cunningham *story* W. C. Fields, J. P. McEvoy *d* Norman Z. McLeod *ph* Henry Sharp

W. C. Fields, Kathleen Howard, Jean Rouverol, Julian Madison, Tommy Bupp, Baby LeRoy

'An enormously amusing succession of rough and ready gags.' – *Literary Digest*

It's a Grand Life

GB 1953 102m bw

Mancunian/John E. Blakeley

A nitwit army private plays Cupid.

Senseless and under-rehearsed farce which has interest for fans of the usually drunken star.

w H. F. Maltby, Frank Randle *d* John E. Blakeley

Frank Randle, Diana Dors, Dan Young, Michael Brennan, Jennifer Jayne, John Blythe

It's a Great Feeling *

US 1949 85m Technicolor

Warner (Alex Gottlieb)

V*, L

No one will direct a Jack Carson movie, so he has to do it himself.

Amiable studio farce with plenty of guest appearances.

w Jack Rose, Mel Shavelson *d* David Butler *ph* Wilfrid M. Cline *m* Ray Heindorf *songs* Jule Styne, Sammy Cahn

Jack Carson, Doris Day, Dennis Morgan, Bill Goodwin, Gary Cooper, Joan Crawford, Errol Flynn, Sidney Greenstreet, Danny Kaye, Patricia Neal, Edward G. Robinson, Jane Wyman, Eleanor Parker, Ronald Reagan

AAN: title song

It's a Mad Mad Mad Mad World **

US 1963 192m Technicolor Ultra Panavision 70

UA/Stanley Kramer

V, V*, L

An assortment of people including a frustrated cop are overcome by greed when they hear of buried loot.

Three hours of frantic chasing and violent slapstick is too much even when done on this scale and with this cast, but one must observe that scene for scene it is extremely well done and most of the players are in unusually good form though they all outstay their welcome and are upstaged by the stunt men.

w William and Tania Rose *d Stanley Kramer* *ph* Ernest Laszlo *m Ernest Gold, stunts* Carey Loftin *titles Saul Bass*

Spencer Tracy, Jimmy Durante, *Milton Berle*, Sid Caesar, Ethel Merman, Buddy Hackett, Mickey Rooney, Dick Shawn, *Phil Silvers, Terry-Thomas,* Jonathan Winters, Edie Adams, Dorothy Provine, Eddie Anderson, Jim Backus, William Demarest, Peter Falk, Paul Ford, Leo Gorcey, Ben Blue, Edward Everett Horton, Buster Keaton, Joe E. Brown, Carl Reiner, the Three Stooges, ZaSu Pitts, Sterling Holloway, Jack Benny, Jerry Lewis

'To watch on a Cinerama screen in full colour a small army of actors inflict mayhem on each other with cars, planes, explosives and other devices for more than three hours with stereophonic sound effects is simply too much for the human eye and ear to respond to, let alone the funny bone.' – *Dwight MacDonald*

AAN: Ernest Laszlo; Ernest Gold; title song (*m* Ernest Gold, *ly* Mack David)

It's a Pleasure

US 1945 90m Technicolor

International/RKO

The career of an ice-skating couple is interrupted when he takes to drink.

Unimpressive vehicle from the star's waning years: the numbers are good but the rest very soggy.

w Lynn Starling, Elliot Paul *d* William A. Seiter

Sonja Henie, Michael O'Shea, Marie McDonald

It's a Small World

US 1935 72m bw

Fox

A man and woman fall in love after being stranded by a car crash in a small Louisiana town.

Mildly amusing comedy.

w Sam Hellman, Gladys Lehman   *d* Irving Cummings

Spencer Tracy, Wendy Barrie, Raymond Walburn, Virginia Sale, Irving Bacon

'Very weak entertainment, strictly for double bills.' – *Variety*

It's a 2'6" above the Ground World
GB   1972   96m   Eastmancolor
British Lion/Welbeck/Betty E. Box-Ralph Thomas
aka: *The Love Ban*

A Roman Catholic couple go on the pill.

Smutty, not very funny sex comedy.

w Kevin Laffan   *play* Kevin Laffan   *d* Ralph Thomas   *ph* Tony Imi   *m* Stanley Myers

Nanette Newman, Hywel Bennett, Russell Lewis, Simon Henderson, Milo O'Shea

It's a Wise Child
US   1931   73m   bw
Cosmopolitan/MGM

When a girl is thought to be pregnant, her family hunts the father.

Tasteless comedy with too few laughs.

w Laurence E. Johnson   *play* Laurence E. Johnson   *d* Robert Z. Leonard

Marion Davies, Sidney Blackmer, James Gleason, Polly Moran, Marie Prevost, Lester Vail

'No subject matter here for family audiences . . . it must prove embarrassing to young unmarried couples attending the theatre together.' – *Variety*

It's a Wonderful Life ****
US   1946   129m   bw
RKO/Liberty Films (Frank Capra)
V, V (C), V*, L, S

A man is prevented from committing suicide by an elderly angel, who takes him back through his life to show him what good he has done.

Superbly assembled small-town comedy drama in a fantasy framework; arguably Capra's best and most typical work.

w Frances Goodrich, Albert Hackett, Frank Capra   *d* Frank Capra   *ph* Joseph Walker, Joseph Biroc   *m* Dimitri Tiomkin   *ed* William Hornbeck

James Stewart, Henry Travers, Donna Reed, Lionel Barrymore, Thomas Mitchell, Beulah Bondi, Frank Faylen, Ward Bond, Gloria Grahame, H. B. Warner, Frank Albertson, Samuel S. Hinds, Mary Treen

   CLARENCE (Henry Travers): 'Every time you hear a bell ring, it means that some angel's just got his wings.'

'One of the most efficient sentimental pieces since *A Christmas Carol*.' – *James Agee*

'The most brilliantly made motion picture of the 1940s, so assured, so dazzling in its use of screen narrative.' – *Charles Higham*

'In its own icky, bittersweet way, it's terribly effective.' – *New Yorker, 1977*

'At its best all this seems to me insipid, and at its worst an embarrassment to both flesh and spirit.' – *Richard Winnington, News Chronicle*

AAN: best picture; Frank Capra; James Stewart; editing

It's a Wonderful World *
US   1939   86m   bw
MGM (Frank Davis)

Kidnapped by a suspected murderer, a girl helps him track down the real criminal.

Madcap comedy mystery which now seems much fresher and funnier than it did at the time. A highlight of the crazy comedy cycle.

w Ben Hecht, Herman J. Mankiewicz   *d* W. S. Van Dyke II   *ph* Oliver Marsh   *m* Edward Ward

Claudette Colbert, James Stewart, Guy Kibbee, Nat Pendleton, Frances Drake, Edgar Kennedy, Ernest Truex, Richard Carle, Sidney Blackmer, Andy Clyde, Cliff Clark, Hans Conried

'It's right down the alley for general audiences.' – *Variety*

'One of the few genuinely comic pictures in a dog's age.' – *Otis Ferguson*

'Save your screams till you see its face!'
It's Alive
US   1974   91m   Technicolor
Warner/Larco (Larry Cohen)
V, V*

A new-born baby turns out to be a vicious monster.

Exploitation horror flick in the worst of taste, with a good central performance.

wd Larry Cohen   *ph* Fenton Hamilton   *m* Bernard Herrmann   *ed* Peter Honess

John Ryan, Sharon Farrell, Andrew Duggan, Guy Stockwell, James Dixon, Michael Ansara

'The best horror movie ever.' – *Quentin Crisp, Christopher Street*

† It was followed by *It Lives Again* and *It's Alive III: Island of The Alive* (qv).

It's Alive II: see *It Lives Again*

It's Alive III: Island of the Alive
US   1988   91m   Technicolor
Warner/Larco (Paul Stader)
V*

A mutant baby, whose father has gone to court to protect his right to live, swiftly grows to adulthood on a remote island with others of his kind and then heads back to America with his own child.

Wild, undisciplined horror film full of satirical thrusts at everything from attitudes to AIDS to media exploitation.

wd Larry Cohen   *ph* Daniel Pearl   *m* Laurie Johnson, Bernard Herrmann   *ad* George Stoll   *sp* Steve Neill, Rick Baker, William Hedge   *ed* David Kern

Michael Moriarty, Karen Black, Laurene Landon, James Dixon, Neal Israel, Art Lund, Ann Dane, Macdonald Carey, Gerrit Graham

'This is from the Cohen home-movie stable and non-aficionados should beware: production values and special effects are as hokey as ever.' – *Anne Billson, Shock Xpress*

† The film was shot in four weeks in Hawaii and Los Angeles.

It's All Happening
GB   1963   101m   Eastmancolor
British Lion/Magna/KNP (Norman Williams)
US title: *The Dream Maker*

A talent scout for a recording agency helps to save an orphanage and makes himself a star in the process.

Unassuming, jolly little comedy with music; a better title would have made it more memorable.

w Leigh Vance   *d* Don Sharp   *ph* Ken Hodges   *m* Philip Green

Tommy Steele, Angela Douglas, Michael Medwin, Bernard Bresslaw, Walter Hudd, Jean Harvey, Richard Goolden

It's All Yours
US   1937   80m   bw
Columbia

A millionaire leaves a fortune to his favourite secretary, hoping that it will make his nephew take notice of her.

Unpersuasive romantic comedy with slightly crazy touches.

w Mary C. McCall Jnr   *d* Elliott Nugent

Madeleine Carroll, Francis Lederer, Mischa Auer, Grace Bradley

'Of the whimsy, gay school currently in vogue . . . too light to figure importantly at solo b.o.' – *Variety*

It's Always Fair Weather **
US   1955   101m   Eastmancolor   Cinemascope
MGM (Arthur Freed)
V*, L

In 1945 three army veterans vow to meet ten years on, but they find each other dull failures until they go on a wild spree.

Rather dejected New Yorkish comedy with musical sequences; some of it works very well, but the colour is crude and the wide screen doesn't help.

w/m/ly Betty Comden, Adolph Green   *d* Gene Kelly, Stanley Donen   *ph* Robert Bronner   *md* André Previn

Gene Kelly, Dan Dailey, Michael Kidd, Dolores Gray, Cyd Charisse

AAN: Betty Comden, Adolph Green (as writers); André Previn

It's Great to Be Young *
GB   1956   93m   Technicolor
AB-Pathé/Marble Arch (Victor Skutezky)

A popular teacher falls foul of the new headmaster who tries to disband the school orchestra.

Very acceptable but totally forgettable star comedy.

w Ted Willis   *d* Cyril Frankel   *ph* Gilbert Taylor   *m* Ray Martin, Lester Powell, John Addison

John Mills, Cecil Parker, Jeremy Spenser, Dorothy Bromiley, John Salew, Derek Blomfield, Eleanor Summerfield, Bryan Forbes

It's Hard to Be Good
GB   1948   93m   bw
GFD/Two Cities (Jeffrey Dell)

A demobbed war hero determines to spread peace and goodwill, but comes one cropper after another.

Well intended but somehow unprofessional comedy which irritates more than it amuses.

wd Jeffrey Dell   *ph* Laurie Friedman   *m* Antony Hopkins

Jimmy Hanley, Anne Crawford, Raymond Huntley

It's Hot in Hell: see *A Monkey in Winter*

It's in the Air *
GB   1938   86m   bw
ATP (Basil Dean)
US title: *George Takes the Air*

Adventures of an accident-prone RAF recruit.

Amiable star comedy with good situations and songs.

wd Anthony Kimmins   *ph* Gordon Dines, Ronald Neame

George Formby, Garry Marsh, Polly Ward, Julien Mitchell, Jack Hobbs, Hal Gordon

It's in the Bag (1932): see *L'Affaire est dans le Sac*

It's in the Bag **
US   1945   87m   bw
(UA) Manhattan Productions
GB title: *The Fifth Chair*

The owner of a flea circus seeks a legacy hidden in one of five chairs which have been sold to a variety of people.

Patchily amusing, star-studded comedy which was also filmed as *Keep Your Seats Please* and *The Twelve*

Chairs. Full enjoyment requires some knowledge of American radio characters.

w Jay Dratler, Alma Reville   d Richard Wallace   ph Russell Metty   m Werner Heymann

Fred Allen, Binnie Barnes, *Jack Benny*, Robert Benchley, Don Ameche, Victor Moore, Rudy Vallee, William Bendix, Jerry Colonna

'An untidy piece that doesn't make the most of itself but is full of fun.' – *Richard Mallett, Punch*

It's Love Again *
GB   1936   83m   bw
Gaumont (Michael Balcon)
V*

A chorus girl poses as a socialite who has hit the headlines without ever existing.

Delightfully dated comedy musical.

w Lesser Samuels, Marion Dix, Austin Melford   d *Victor Saville*   ph Glen MacWilliams   md Louis Levy   m Louis Levy, Bretton Byrd   songs Harry Woods, Sam Coslow   ad Alfred Junge   ed A. L. Barnes

Jessie Matthews, Robert Young, Sonnie Hale, Ernest Milton, Robb Wilton, Sara Allgood, Athene Seyler, Cyril Raymond

'Mr Saville has directed it with speed, efficiency and a real sense of the absurd.' – *Graham Greene*

'The tops in topsy-turvy romance!'
It's Love I'm After *
US   1937   90m   bw
Warner (Harry Joe Brown)

A beloved stage star couple fight like cat and dog behind the scenes.

Amusing romantic farce which has worn rather less well than might have been expected but does present two stars at their peak.

w Casey Robinson   d Archie Mayo   ph James Van Trees   m Heinz Roemheld

Bette Davis, Leslie Howard, Olivia de Havilland, Patric Knowles, Eric Blore, George Barbier, Spring Byington, Bonita Granville, E. E. Clive

'Smash comedy hit. Arrange extra playing time for this one.' – *Variety*

'One of the most delightful and diverting comedies the madcap cinema has yet turned out.' – *New York World Telegram*

'Proceeds like a somewhat deranged *Taming of the Shrew* . . . [BD and LH] are surrounded by that set of millionaires, valets and heiresses that were at one time as much of a convention in American comedy as the fops of Restoration theatre.' – *American Film Institute*

It's Magic: see *Romance on the High Seas*

It's My Turn
US   1980   90m   Metrocolor
Columbia/Rastar/Martin Elfand
V*, L

A lady mathematics professor decides to seize her chances when she falls for the son of her father's new wife.

Unattractive and rather uninteresting comedy-drama with strong overtones of women's lib.

w Eleanor Bergstein   d Claudia Weill   ph Bill Butler   m Patrick Williams

Jill Clayburgh, Michael Douglas, Charles Grodin, Beverly Garland, Steven Hill

It's Never Too Late
GB   1956   95m   Eastmancolor
Park Lane/ABP

A mother considered dull by her family starts a new career as a scriptwriter.

Acceptable but quite unexciting matinée comedy.

w Edward Dryhurst   play Felicity Douglas   d Michael McCarthy

Phyllis Calvert, Guy Rolfe, Susan Stephen, Patrick Barr, Delphi Lawrence, Sarah Lawson, Peter Hammond

It's Never Too Late to Mend
GB   1937   67m   bw
George King

An evil squire schemes for the hand of the farmer's beautiful daughter.

Archetypal melodrama of the 'Fie, Sir Jasper' school, mainly interesting in this version for the antics of its heavy-breathing star.

w H. F. Maltby   play Charles Reade, Arthur Shirley   d David MacDonald   ph Hone Glendinning

Tod Slaughter, Marjorie Taylor, Jack Livesey, Lawrence Hanray

It's Not Cricket
GB   1948   77m   bw
GFD/Gainsborough (Betty Box)

Bowler-hatted officers catch a Nazi spy.

Over-spoofed comedy which barely allows the stars a real chance.

w Lyn Lockwood, Bernard MacNab   d Alfred Roome   ph Gordon Lang   m Arthur Wilkinson

Basil Radford, Naunton Wayne, Maurice Denham, Susan Shaw, Nigel Buchanan

It's Not Just You Murray! *
US   1964   16m   bw
New York University
V

A crook describes how he made it to the top.

An exuberant short, revealing Scorsese's interest in American low-life and European film directors, expressed here in a light-hearted style with an ironic voice-over that rarely matches the truth of what is shown on-screen.

w Martin Scorsese, Mardik Martin   d Martin Scorsese   ph Richard H. Coll   m Richard H. Coll   ed Eli F. Bleich

Ira Rubin, Sam DeFazio, Andrea Martin, Catherine Scorsese

† It was released on video with three other shorts under the title *4 x Scorsese*.

It's Only Money (1951): see
Double Dynamite

It's Only Money
US   1962   84m   bw
Paramount/York/Jerry Lewis Productions (Paul Jones)

A TV repair mechanic hampers his detective friend in a search for a missing heir, which turns out to be himself.

Patchy mystery spoof with the star in rather better form than usual, and a memorable scene in which he is chased by an army of lawnmowers.

w John Fenton Murray   d Frank Tashlin   ph W. Wallace Kelley   m Walter Scharf

Jerry Lewis, Zachary Scott, Joan O'Brien, Jesse White, Jack Weston

It's That Man Again **
GB   1942   84m   bw
GFD/Gainsborough (Edward Black)

The Mayor of Foaming-at-the-Mouth puts on a show to save a bombed theatre.

Smart, fast-moving comedy which no longer seems particularly funny in itself but is an invaluable record of the characters and wisecracks of a radio show which proved a prime morale booster during World War II.

w Howard Irving Young, *Ted Kavanagh*   d Walter Forde

Tommy Handley, Jack Train, Greta Gynt, Dino Galvani, Dorothy Summers, Horace Percival, Sidney Keith, Clarence Wright

It's Tough to be Famous
US   1932   81m   bw
First National

A young naval hero finds that fame destroys his private life.

Unco-ordinated comedy-drama.

w Robert Lord, Mary McCall Jnr   d Alfred E. Green

Douglas Fairbanks Jnr, Mary Brian, Walter Catlett, J. Carrol Naish

'Lightweight feature possessing sufficient entertainment value to give theatres a moderate week.' – *Variety*

Ivan Groznyi: see *Ivan the Terrible*

Ivan the Terrible **
USSR   1942—6   100m (part one), 88m (part two)
   bw/some Agfacolor in part two
Mosfilm
V, V*, L, S
original title: *Ivan Groznyi*

The life of a 16th-century tsar.

A heavy-going film overflowing with grim, gloomy and superbly composed images: the plot is by the way, and part two (also known as *The Boyars' Plot*) is not up to the standard of part one, in which the coronation sequence alone is a masterpiece of cinema.

wd/ed *Sergei Eisenstein*   ph Edouard Tissé (exteriors), Andrei Moskvin (interiors)   m *Sergei Prokofiev*   ad Isaac Shpinel, L. Naumova

Nikolai Cherkassov, Ludmilla Tselikovskaya, Serafima Birman

'A visual opera, with all of opera's proper disregard of prose-level reality . . . an extraordinarily bold experiment, fascinating and beautiful to look at.' – *James Agee*

Ivanhoe *
GB   1952   106m   Technicolor
MGM (Pandro S. Berman)
V, V*, L

Derring-do among the knights of medieval England.

Tolerable, big-budget spectacular based on Sir Walter Scott's novel.

w Noel Langley, Aeneas Mackenzie   d Richard Thorpe   ph F. A. Young   m Miklos Rozsa

Robert Taylor, Joan Fontaine, Elizabeth Taylor, Emlyn Williams, George Sanders, Robert Douglas, Finlay Currie, Felix Aylmer, Francis de Wolff, Guy Rolfe, Norman Wooland, Basil Sydney

AAN: best picture; F. A. Young; Miklos Rozsa

Ivanovo Detstvo: see *Ivan's Childhood*

Ivan's Childhood ***
USSR   1962   95m   bw
Mosfilm (G. Kuznetsov)
V*, L
original title: *Ivanovo Detstvo*

A vengeful 12-year-old escapes from a concentration camp and joins the partisans after his family is killed by the Nazis.

Probably Tarkovsky's most accessible film, a tragic tale beautifully told.

w Vladimir Bogomolov, Mikhail Papava   novel Vladimir Bogomolov   d *Andrei Tarkovsky*   ph Vadim Yusov   m Vyacheslav Ovchinnikov   ad Evgeni Cherniaev   ed G. Natanson

Kolya Burlyaev, Irma Takovskaya, Valentin Zubkov, E. Zharikov, S. Krylov, Nikolai Grinko, L. Malyavina, Andrey Mikhalkov-Konchalovsky

'The film is not disfigured by the unnaturally cheery or the conventionally hysterical. With one blow it annuls a whole cinémathèque of the war films of all lands.' – *Ivor Montagu, Sight and Sound*

† It won the Golden Lion for best film at the Venice Film Festival in 1962.

I've Always Loved You
US 1946 116m Technicolor
Republic
V*, L
GB title: *Concerto*

A brilliant pianist becomes jealous of his girl pupil, despite his love for her.

High-flown romantic tosh with music, an unusual departure for this studio; most notable for Arthur Rubenstein on the sound track.

w Borden Chase *d* Frank Borzage *ph* Tony Gaudio *m* Walter Scharf

Philip Dorn, Catherine McLeod, Felix Bressart, Maria Ouspenskaya, William Carter

I've Got Your Number
US 1934 68m bw
Warner

Telephone service engineers help prove a girl innocent of burglary.

Cheerful, fast-moving programmer typical of its studio at the time.

w Warren Duff, Sidney Sutherland *d* Ray Enright

Joan Blondell, Pat O'Brien, Allen Jenkins, Glenda Farrell, Eugene Pallette

I've Heard the Mermaids Singing *
Canada 1987 84m colour
Contemporary/Electric/Ontario Arts Council/Canada Council/
  National Film Board/Ontario Film Development Corp/
  Telefilm Canada (Patricia Rozema)
V*, L

An untalented woman falls in love with the owner of the art gallery where she works.

Gentle, quirky and enjoyable romance.

wd Patricia Rozema *ph* Douglas Koch *m* Mark Korven *ad* Valanne Ridgeway *ed* Patricia Rozema

Sheila McCarthy, Ann-Marie MacDonald, John Evans, Brenda Kamino, Richard Monette

I've Lived Before
US 1956 82m bw
U-I (Howard Christie)

After a plane crash, the pilot recovers but believes himself to be another airman who died in 1918.

Dullish, talky drama which wastes its interesting reincarnation theme.

w Norman Jolley, William Talman *d* Richard Bartlett *ph* Maury Gertsman *m* Herman Stein

Jock Mahoney, Leigh Snowden, Ann Harding, John McIntire, Raymond Bailey, Jerry Paris

Ivory Hunter: see *Where No Vultures Fly*

Ivy *
US 1947 99m bw
Universal (William Cameron Menzies)

In Edwardian society England, a lady poisoner gets her come-uppance.

Curiously ineffective period thriller in which the star is the elegant but artificial production design: the script is deadly dull.

w Charles Bennett *novel* Mrs Belloc Lowndes *d* Sam Wood *ph* Russell Metty *m* Daniele Amfitheatrof *pd* William Cameron Menzies

Joan Fontaine, Herbert Marshall, Patric Knowles, Richard Ney, Cedric Hardwicke, Lucile Watson, Sara Allgood, Henry Stephenson, Rosalind Ivan, Lilian Fontaine, Una O'Connor, Isobel Elsom, Alan Napier, Paul Cavanagh, Gavin Muir, Norma Varden

'The real star is whoever was responsible for the dressing, setting, lighting and shooting, and that, I infer from past performance, is the producer, William Cameron Menzies.' – *James Agee*

'He's a District Attorney. He will risk his life, the lives of his family, everything he holds dear for the one thing he holds sacred . . . the truth.'

JFK **
US   1991   189m   DuArt   Panavision
Warner/Le Studio Canal+/Regency Enterprises/Alcor (A. Kitman Ho, Oliver Stone)
V, V*, L, S

New Orleans DA Jim Garrison investigates the assassination of President Kennedy and uncovers what amounts to a *coup d'état* to kill him because he wanted to pull out of Vietnam.

Bad history and a bullying, though engrossing, movie, mixing fact and dubious speculation indiscriminately.

w Oliver Stone, Zachary Sklar   book Trail of the Assassins by Jim Garrison; Crossfire: The Plot That Killed Kennedy by Jim Marrs   d Oliver Stone   ph Robert Richardson   m John Williams   pd Victor Kempster   ed Joe Hutshing, Pietro Scalia

Kevin Costner, Sissy Spacek, Joe Pesci, Tommy Lee Jones, Gary Oldman, Jay O. Sanders, Michael Rooker, Laurie Metcalf, Gary Grubbs, John Candy, Jack Lemmon, Walter Matthau, Ed Asner, Donald Sutherland, Kevin Bacon, Brian Doyle-Murray, Sally Kirkland, Jim Garrison

'A rebuke to official history and a challenge to continue investigating the crime of the century, Oliver Stone's *JFK* is electric muckraking filmmaking.' – *Variety*

'The first thing to be said about *JFK* is that it is a great movie, and the next is that it is one of the worst great movies ever made. It is great in spite of itself, and such greatness owes more to the moxie of the director than to his special talents' – *Norman Mailer, Vanity Fair*

'Courageous, gripping, reckless . . . the culmination or apotheosis of the paranoid political thriller.' – *Philip French, Observer*

'Shortchanges the audience and at the end plays like a bait-and-switch scam.' – *Vincent Canby, New York Times*

AA: Robert Richardson; editing

AAN: film; Oliver Stone; Tommy Lee Jones; Oliver Stone, Zachary Sklar (screenplay adaptation); John Williams; sound

J. R.: see *Who's That Knocking at My Door*

J. W. Coop *
US   1971   112m   Eastmancolor
Columbia/Robertson and Associates (Cliff Robertson)

After ten years in prison, a rodeo rider returns to his home town.

Well-made but rather inconsequential drama with attractive locations.

w Cliff Robertson, Gary Cartwright, Bud Shrake   d Cliff Robertson   ph Frank Stanley   m Don Randi, Louie Shelton

Cliff Robertson, Cristina Ferrare, Geraldine Page, R. G. Armstrong

Jabberwocky
GB   1977   101m   Technicolor
Umbrella (John Goldstone, Sandy Lieberson)
V*, L

A medieval cooper's apprentice is mistaken for a prince and slays the dragon which is terrorizing the neighbourhood.

An intellectual Carry On film, with very little more taste and a great deal more unpleasant imagery. Despite much re-editing, the laughs are very intermittent.

w Charles Alverson, Terry Gilliam   d Terry Gilliam   ph Terry Bedford   m De Wolfe   pd Roy Smith

Michael Palin, Max Wall, Deborah Fallender, Warren Mitchell, John Le Mesurier, Harry H. Corbett, Rodney Bewes, Bernard Bresslaw

'The constant emphasis on blood, excrement, dismemberment and filth ultimately becomes rather wearing.' – *Michael Billington, Illustrated London News*

J'Accuse *
France   1939   95m   bw
Forrester-Parant
V*

A scientist intends his invention to end war; when it is put to a contrary purpose, he calls the war dead to rise from their graves and accuse humanity.

Stern, well acted, but (as it proved) ineffective propaganda.

wd Abel Gance

Victor Francen, Jean Max, Renée Devilliers

Jack Ahoy
GB   1934   82m   bw
Gaumont (Michael Balcon)

An accident-prone naval rating routs bandits and wins the girl.

Tailor-made star comedy with skilful moments.

w Jack Hulbert, Leslie Arliss, Gerald Fairlie, Austin Melford   story Sidney Gilliat, J. O. C. Orton   d Walter Forde   ph Bernard Knowles   m Bretton Byrd   ed Ralph Kemplen

Jack Hulbert, Nancy O'Neil, Alfred Drayton, Tamara Desni

'Mr Hulbert is equal to all his occasions . . . his abounding energy and high spirits are never monotonous or wearisome.' – *E. V. Lucas, Punch*

Jack and the Beanstalk
US   1952   78m   Supercinecolor
Warner/Alex Gottlieb
V*

A babysitter dreams the story he is reading aloud.

Rather feeble star comedy aimed entirely at the kiddie set, and with none of the familiar routines. The 'bookends', as is customary, are in black and white.

w Nat Curtis   d Jean Yarbrough   ph George Robinson   m Heinz Roemheld

Bud Abbott, Lou Costello, Buddy Baer, Dorothy Ford, William Farnum

Jack Armstrong
US   1947   bw   serial: 15 eps
Columbia

An aviation company developing atom-powered motors is threatened by enemy agents.

Rousing serial stuff for the kids.

d Wallace Fox

John Hart, Rosemary La Planche, Charles Middleton, Claire James, Pierre Watkin

Jack Be Nimble
New Zealand   1992   95m   colour
Metro Tartan/Essential/New Zealand Film Commission (Jonathan Dowling, Kelly Rogers)

An unhappy youth, separated from his psychic sister, invents a machine to hypnotize and kill his cruel, adopted parents, but their spirits seek revenge.

Ghoulish and disturbing horror, offering nothing in the way of comfort.

wd Garth Maxwell   ph Donald Duncan   m Chris Neal   pd Grant Major   sp Kevin Chisnall   ed John Gilbert

Alexis Arquette, Sarah Smuts-Kennedy, Bruno Lawrence, Tony Barry, Elizabeth Hawthorne, Brenda Simmons, Gilbert Goldie

'This deeply weird melodrama . . . at once affecting, funny and horrifying.' – *Kim Newman, Empire*

Jack London
US   1943   93m   bw
Samuel Bronston/United Artists

Jack London seeks various kinds of adventure, writes a book about the Klondike, and warns the world of the Japanese menace.

Occasionally bright but generally faltering biopic, obviously made on the cheap.

w Ernest Pascal   d Alfred Santell

Michael O'Shea, Susan Hayward, Osa Massen, Harry Davenport, Virginia Mayo, Jonathan Hale

AAN: Frederick E. Rich (music)

Jack McCall Desperado
US   1952   75m   Technicolor
Columbia (Sam Katzman)

A Union officer is forced into outlawry but redeems himself.

Tolerable minor Western.

w John O'Dea   d Sidney Salkow

George Montgomery, Angela Stevens, Douglas Kennedy, James Seay, Jay Silverheels

Jack of All Trades *
GB   1936   76m   bw
Gainsborough (Michael Balcon)

A cheerful con man talks his way into a top job in an international firm.

Odd amalgam of star comedy, musical numbers of the Astaire/Rogers type, shafts of satire from the original play, and finally some flat-footed farce. Certainly worth a look.

w Jack Hulbert, Austin Melford, J. O. C. Orton   play Youth at the Helm by Hubert Griffith, Paul Vulpuis   d Jack Hulbert, Robert Stevenson   ph Charles Van Enger   md Louis Levy   ad Vetchinsky   ed T. R. Fisher

Jack Hulbert, Gina Malo, Robertson Hare, Athole Stewart, Felix Aylmer, H. F. Maltby

Jack of Diamonds
US/West Germany   1967   105m   Metrocolor
Harris/Bavaria Atelier/MGM

A retired jewel thief introduces a brilliant pupil into society.

Repetitive and rather glum comedy-drama which perks up occasionally.

w Jack de Witt, Sandy Howard   d Don Taylor

George Hamilton, Joseph Cotten, Marie Laforet, Maurice Evans, Wolfgang Preiss, Lilli Palmer, Carroll Baker, Zsa Zsa Gabor

Jack Slade

US   1953   90m   bw
Allied Artists
GB title: Slade

A Western gunman becomes a psychopathic killer.

Cliché-ridden but rather brutish Western, thought sensationally violent at the time.

w Warren Douglas   d Harold Schuster

Mark Stevens, Dorothy Malone, Barton MacLane, John Litel, Paul Langton, Harry Shannon

'A Father. Two Sons. A Love Story.'
'Every Family Needs A Hero.'

Jack the Bear

US   1993   99m   DeLuxe
TCF/American Filmworks/Lucky Dog (Bruce Gilbert)
V, V*

In the 1970s, following the death of his wife, an actor begins to drink heavily as he tries to cope with his two young sons and unbalanced neighbour.

Family drama that veers towards melodrama without becoming very interesting.

w Steven Zaillian   novel Dan McCall   d Marshall Herskovitz   ph Fred Murphy   m James Horner   pd Lilly Kilvert   ed Steven Rosenblum

Danny DeVito, Robert J. Steinmiller Jnr, Miko Hughes, Gary Sinise, Art LaFleur, Stefan Gierasch, Erica Yohn, Andrea Marcovicci

'Its effect is that of a TV series that has been telescoped and packed, with each of its rather glib resolutions, into an hour and a half. Despite a surfeit of material, nothing is thorny enough to sustain and the result is a long haul.' – Amanda Lipman, Sight and Sound

Jack the Giant Killer **

US   1961   94m   Technicolor
Zenith/Edward Small (Robert E. Kent)
V*, L

Demon Pendragon kidnaps the princess of Cornwall but she is rescued by a farmer's son.

Very creditable fairy tale, with the right style and atmosphere assisted by vigorous acting, good pace and excellent trick effects. Unfortunately it turned out rather scary for a child audience and so fell between two stools.

w Orville Hampton, Nathan Juran   d Nathan Juran   ph David S. Horsley   m Paul Sawtell, Bert Shefter   ad Fernando Carere, Frank McCoy   sp Howard Anderson

Kerwin Mathews, Judi Meredith, Torin Thatcher, Don Beddoe, Walter Burke, Barry Kelley

'He baffled the great Scotland Yard, the celebrated Arthur Conan Doyle, and Robert Louis Stevenson!'

Jack the Ripper

GB   1958   84m   bw
Mid Century (Baker and Berman)
V*

In Victorian London the Ripper murders are finally attributed to a demented surgeon.

Flat and rather flabby treatment of a cause célèbre, saved by a reasonably convincing period look.

w Jimmy Sangster   d/ph Robert S. Baker, Monty Berman   m Stanley Black

Ewen Solon, Lee Patterson, Eddie Byrne, Betty McDowell, John Le Mesurier

Jackass Mail

US   1942   80m   bw
MGM (John Considine Jnr)

A horse thief marries the proprietress of a gambling saloon in the hope of hijacking her mail line, but she reforms him.

Boisterously conceived but anaemically scripted Western comedy with the stars in full throttle.

w Lawrence Hazard   d Norman Z. McLeod   ph Clyde de Vinna   m David Snell, Earl Brent

Wallace Beery, Marjorie Main, J. Carrol Naish, Darryl Hickman, William Haade, Hobart Cavanaugh

'This time at least they are repeating their variation on the Min-and-Bill routine among companions whose resemblance to burlesque is as unabashed as their own.' – Bosley Crowther, New York Times

Jackboot Mutiny

Germany   1955   77m   bw
Arca-Ariston
original title: Es Geschah am 20 Juli

An account of the army officers' plot to assassinate Hitler.

Documentary-like treatment without much attempt at characterization. An important historical document nevertheless.

w W. P. Zibaso, Gustav Machaty   d G. W. Pabst   ph Kurt Hasse   m Johannes Weissenbach

Bernhard Wicki, Karl Ludwig Diehl, Carl Wery

Jacknife

US   1988   103m   Technicolor
Vestron/Kings Road Entertainment (Robert Schaffel, Carol Baum)
V, V*, L

A Vietnam veteran begins a relationship with the sister of an old army friend.

Well-acted but only occasionally interesting.

w Stephen Metcalfe   play Strange Snow by Stephen Metcalfe   d David Jones   ph Brian West   pd Edward Pisoni   ed John Bloom

Robert de Niro, Ed Harris, Kathy Baker, Charles Dutton, Elizabeth Franz, Tom Isbell, Loudon Wainwright III, Sloane Shelton, Ivan Brogger

The Jackpot **

US   1950   85m   bw
TCF (Samuel G. Engel)

A suburban husband finds that life becomes complicated when winning the jackpot on a radio quiz makes him a celebrity.

Modest, skilful comedy in Hollywood's best manner.

w Phoebe and Henry Ephron   d Walter Lang   ph Joseph LaShelle   md Lionel Newman

James Stewart, Barbara Hale, James Gleason, Fred Clark, Alan Mowbray, Patricia Medina, Natalie Wood, Tommy Rettig, Robert Gist, Lyle Talbot

Jack's the Boy *

GB   1932   91m   bw
Gainsborough (Michael Balcon)
US title: Night and Day

The police commissioner's son proves his worth in rounding up a smash-and-grab gang.

Dated but lively farce which established its star as a British box-office attraction of the 30s.

w W. P. Lipscomb   story Jack Hulbert, Douglas Furber   d Walter Forde   ph Leslie Rowson   md Louis Levy   m/ly Vivian Ellis, Douglas Furber   ad Vetchinsky   ed Ian Dalrymple, John Goldman

Jack Hulbert, Cicely Courtneidge, Francis Lister, Winifred Shotter, Peter Gawthorne, Ben Field

'A riotously funny, good, clean, honest British picture.' – Sydney Carroll, Sunday Times

† The film in which Hulbert sang 'The Flies Crawled Up the Window'.

Jackson County Jail

US   1976   84m   Metrocolor
UA/New World (Roger Corman)
V*

A lady driver is hijacked, attacked, disbelieved by the local police, thrown into jail and raped by the jailer, whom she brains with a stool.

An exploitation piece with social pretensions which it in no way justifies: it is however quite competently entertaining in its mindlessly violent way.

w Donald Stewart   d Michael Miller   ph Bruce Logan   m Loren Newkirk

Yvette Mimieux, Tommy Lee Jones, Robert Carradine, Frederic Cook, Severn Darden, Howard Hesseman

Jacob's Ladder

US   1990   113m   Technicolor
Tri-Star/Carolco (Alan Marshall)
V, V*, L, S

A Vietnam veteran is unwittingly the subject of secret experiments with chemical weapons.

Exceedingly silly on every level, particularly in its supernatural dabblings.

w Bruce Joel Rubin   d Adrian Lyne   ph Jeffrey L. Kimball   m Maurice Jarre   pd Brian Morris   ed Tom Rolf

Tim Robbins, Elizabeth Pena, Danny Aiello, Matt Craven, Pruitt Taylor Vince, Jason Alexander, Patricia Kalember

'Dull, unimaginative and pretentious.' – Variety

Jacqueline *

GB   1956   93m   bw
Rank (George H. Brown)

A Belfast shipyard worker cannot stand heights, takes to drink, and is helped by his small daughter.

Convincing, well-made, realistically set domestic comedy-drama.

w Patric Kirwan, Liam O'Flaherty   d Roy Baker   ph Geoffrey Unsworth   m Cedric Thorpe Davie

John Gregson, Kathleen Ryan, Jacqueline Ryan, Noel Purcell, Cyril Cusack, Marie Kean, Liam Redmond, Maureen Delany

Jacqueline Susann's Once Is Not Enough: see Once Is Not Enough

Jacquot de Nantes **

France   1991   119m   bw/colour
Cine-Tamaris/Canal+/La Sept/La Sofiarp (Agnes Varda, Perrine Baudin)
V

Biopic of the early years of the life of director Jacques Demy, combined with clips from his films and interviews with him, based on his own memoirs.

A labour of love from Demy's wife that is both moving as a tribute and fascinating in its exploration of a youthful obsession.

wd Agnes Varda   ph Patrick Blosier, Agnes Godard, Georges Strouve   m Joanna Bruzdowicz   pd Robert Nardone, Olivier Radot   ed Marie-Jo Audiard

Philippe Maron, Edouard Joubeaud, Laurent Monnier, Brigitte de Villepoix, Daniel Dublet, Guillaume Navaud

'A delightful, if overlong, depiction of the formative years of a youngster determined to make films when he grows up.' – Variety

The Jade Box

US   1930   bw   serial: 10 eps
Universal

Members of an Eastern cult determine to recover a mystical stolen box.

Primitive talkie serial. *d* Ray Taylor

Louise Morraine, Jack Perrin, Francis Ford

Jagged Edge **
US   1985   108m   Metrocolor
Columbia/Marvin Ransohoff
V, V*, L

A lady lawyer defends a newspaper publisher who may or may not be guilty of murder.

Well-crafted courtroom mystery with fashionable violence and a few unexpected twists.

w Joe Eszterhas *d* Richard Marquand
ph Matthew F. Leonetti *m* John Barry *pd* Gene Callahan *ed* Sean Barton, Conrad Buff

Jeff Bridges, Glenn Close, Peter Coyote, Robert Loggia, Leigh Taylor-Young, John Dehner

AAN: Robert Loggia (supporting actor)

Jaguar Lives
US   1979   90m   Eastmancolor
Jaguar (Sandy Howard)
V*

Exploits of an international secret agent with skill in the martial arts.

Flashy, violent, James Bond rip-off, years behind its time.

w Yabo Yablonsky *d* Ernest Pintoff

Joe Lewis, Christopher Lee, Donald Pleasence, Capucine, Barbara Bach, Joseph Wiseman, Woody Strode, John Huston

J'ai Épousé une Ombre: see I Married a Dead Man

Jailbirds: see Pardon Us

Jailhouse Rock *
US   1957   96m   bw   Cinemascope
MGM (Pandro S. Berman)
V, V*, L

An ex-convict becomes a pop star.

Reasonably competent star vehicle, sourer in tone than most.

w Guy Trosper *d* Richard Thorpe *ph* Robert Bronner *md* Jeff Alexander

Elvis Presley, Judy Tyler, Mickey Shaughnessy, Vaughn Taylor, Dean Jones

Jakarta
Indonesia/US   1988   95m   colour   Panavision
Medusa/Parkit Films/Troma

An ex-CIA agent is taken to Indonesia to put an end to a local big-time drug dealer.

Inconsequential thriller.

w Charles Kaufman, Ralph Soll *d* Charles Kaufman *ph* Robert Chappell, Kasiyo Hadiwijoyo *m* Jay Chattaway *pd* Susan Kaufman *ed* Michael Spence, Norman Benny

Christopher Noth, Sue Francis Pai, Franz Tumbuan, Ronald Hunter, Zoraya Perucha, David Sharp, David Gale

Jake Speed
US   1986   100m   Technicolor
Crawford/Lane/Foster/Balcor
V*, L

A famous hero tracks down an American girl abducted in Paris.

Adventure hokum with spoof elements which don't come off.

w Wayne Crawford, Andrew Lane *d* Andrew Lane

Wayne Crawford, John Hurt, Donnis Christopher, Karen Kopins, Leon Ames

Jalna
US   1935   75m   bw
RKO

Episodes in the life of the Whiteoaks family.

Flat adaptation of a Canadian bestseller.

w Anthony Veiller, Garrett Fort, Larry Bachmann *novel* Mazo de la Roche *d* John Cromwell

Kay Johnson, Ian Hunter, C. Aubrey Smith, Jessie Ralph, Nigel Bruce, David Manners, Peggy Wood, Halliwell Hobbes

'Nice production of a not very good adaptation.' – *Variety*

Jalsaghar: see The Music Room

Jamaica Inn *
GB   1939   107m   bw
Mayflower (Erich Pommer)
V*

In old Cornwall, an orphan girl becomes involved with smugglers.

Stagey, stilted adventure story which never loses its studio feel or takes fire as a Hitchcock picture. The cast keeps it interesting.

w Sidney Gilliat, Joan Harrison, J. B. Priestley *novel* Daphne du Maurier *d* Alfred Hitchcock *ph* Harry Stradling, Bernard Knowles *m* Eric Fenby *ad* Tom Morahan *ed* Robert Hamer

Charles Laughton, Maureen O'Hara, Leslie Banks, Robert Newton, Emlyn Williams, Wylie Watson, Marie Ney, Morland Graham

'Should get good but not outstanding b.o. Superb direction, excellent casting, expressive playing and fine production offset an uneven screenplay.' – *Variety*

'I was irresistibly reminded of an all-star charity matinee.' – *Graham Greene*

Jamaica Run
US   1953   92m   Technicolor
Paramount/Pine-Thomas

A search for documents, which may apportion a great house to another branch of the family, leads to murder.

Plot-bound romantic mystery in period, with elements of a Caribbean *Rebecca*. Watchable medium-budget hokum. *wd* Lewis R. Foster *novel* Max Murray *ph* Lionel Lindon *m* Lucien Cailliet

Ray Milland, Arlene Dahl, Wendell Corey, Patric Knowles

The James Brothers: see The True Story of Jesse James

The James Brothers of Missouri
US   1950   bw   serial: 12 eps
Republic

Jesse and Frank determine to re-establish themselves as members of society.

Another serial contravention of history. *d* Fred C. Brannon

Keith Richards, Robert Bice, Noel Neill, Roy Barcroft

'A Film Where Women Eat Men And Men Eat Ham.'
Jamón Jamón *
Spain   1992   91m   colour
Metro Tartan/Lolafilms/Ovideo/Sogepaq (Andrés Vicente Gómez)
V (W), S

A wealthy mother decides she wants a local stud for herself after hiring him to seduce her son's girlfriend.

Broad and enjoyable comedy of sex and male virility, not to be taken seriously despite its downbeat, partner-swapping finale.

w Cuca Canals, Bigas Luna, Quim Monzó *d* Bigas Luna *ph* José Luis Alcaine *m* Nicola Piovani

pd Chu Uroz, Noemi Campano *ad* Julio Esteban *ed* Teresa Font

Stefania Sandrelli, Anna Galiena, Juan Diego, Penélope Cruz, Javier Bardem, Jordi Molla

'Racy and surreal farce.' – *Empire*

'His storytelling wanders too arbitrarily between slapstick eroticism and an exaggerated neo-realism to achieve any clarity of focus.' – *Philip Strick, Sight and Sound*

Jana-Aranya: see The Middle Man

Jane and the Lost City
GB   1988   92m   colour
Blue Dolphin/Marcel-Robertson (Harry Robertson)

A girl with a penchant for stripping becomes a British agent during the Second World War.

Based on a once-famous *Daily Mirror* strip cartoon, a tatty, low-budget romp of no perceptible interest, other than to students of the decline of British cinema.

w Mervyn Haisman *story* Mervyn Haisman, Terry Marcel, Harry Robertson *d* Terry Marcel *ph* Paul Beeson *m* Harry Robertson *pd* Michael Pickwoad *ed* Alan Jones

Sam Jones, Maud Adams, Jasper Carrott, Kirsten Hughes, Graham Stark, Robin Bailey, Ian Roberts, Elsa O'Toole

Jane Eyre
US   1934   62m   bw
Monogram

A Poverty Row transcription of the Charlotte Brontë novel: see below.

w Adele Comandini *d* Christy Cabanne

Virginia Bruce, Colin Clive, Beryl Mercer, Jameson Thomas, Aileen Pringle

'The cast appear to have considered their tasks with considerable melancholy.' – *Variety*

'A love story every woman would die a thousand deaths to live!'
Jane Eyre ***
US   1943   96m   bw
TCF (William Goetz)
V, V*, L, S

In Victorian times, a harshly treated orphan girl becomes governess in a mysterious Yorkshire mansion with a brooding master.

Sharply paced, reasonably faithful and superbly staged Hollywood version of Charlotte Brontë's archetypal romantic novel which stimulated so many imitations, including *Rebecca*.

w Aldous Huxley, Robert Stevenson, John Houseman *d* Robert Stevenson *ph* George Barnes *m* Bernard Herrmann *ad* Wiard B. Ihnen, James Basevi *sp* Fred Sersen

Joan Fontaine, Orson Welles, Margaret O'Brien, *Henry Daniell*, John Sutton, Agnes Moorehead, Elizabeth Taylor, Peggy Ann Garner, Sara Allgood, Aubrey Mather, Hillary Brooke, Edith Barrett, Ethel Griffies, Barbara Everest, *John Abbott*

'A careful and tame production, a sadly vanilla-flavoured Joan Fontaine, and Orson Welles treating himself to broad operatic sculpturings of body, cloak and diction, his eyes glinting in the Rembrandt gloom, at every chance, like side orders of jelly.' – *James Agee*

'The essentials are still there; and the non-essentials, such as the gloom, the shadows, the ground mist, the rain and the storms, have been expanded and redoubled and magnified to fill up the gaps.' – *Richard Mallett, Punch*

Jane Eyre
GB   1970   110m   Eastmancolor
British Lion/Omnibus/Sagittarius (Frederick H. Brogger)

A Victorian governess discovers that the master she comes to love hides a secret in his attic.

A generally lacklustre version of a classic story, enlivened by Scott's performance.

w Jack Pulman novel Charlotte Brontë d Delbert Mann ph Paul Beeson m John Williams ad Alex Vetchinsky ed Peter Boita

George C. Scott, Susannah York, Ian Bannen, Jack Hawkins, Nyree Dawn Porter, Rachel Kempson, Kenneth Griffith, Peter Copley, Michele Dotrice, Clive Morton, Constance Cummings

'A pleasant if unispired reminder of Charlotte's most successful novel.' – David Pirie, MFB

Janice Meredith
US   1924   153m   bw   silent
Metro-Goldwyn/Cosmopolitan
GB title: The Beautiful Rebel

Vicissitudes of the coquettish daughter of a New Jersey family through the War of Independence.

Marathon melodrama not unlike Gone with the Wind in subject matter, but of no remaining interest.

w Lillie Hayward novel Paul Leicester Ford d E. Mason Hopper ph Ira H. Morgan, George Barnes m Deems Taylor ad Joseph Urban

Marion Davies, Harrison Ford, Macklyn Arbuckle, Joseph Kilgour, George Nash, Tyrone Power Snr, May Vokes, W. C. Fields, Olin Howland

Janie
US   1944   106m   bw
Warner (Brock Pemberton)

The teenage daughter of a middle-class American household gets into innocent scrapes with the army.

Deafening tomboy farce.

w Agnes Christine Johnston, Charles Hoffman play Josephine Bentham, Herschel V. Williams Jnr d Michael Curtiz ph Carl Guthrie m/ly Lee David, Sammy Cahn, Jule Styne ed Owen Marks

Joyce Reynolds, Robert Hutton, Ann Harding, Edward Arnold, Robert Benchley, Claire Foley, Hattie McDaniel

† Janie Gets Married, made the following year and running 89m, had almost identical credits except that Joan Leslie replaced Joyce Reynolds and Dorothy Malone joined the cast.

AAN: Owen Marks

The Janitor: see Eye Witness (1981)

The January Man
US   1989   97m   DeLuxe
UIP/MGM (Norman Jewison, Ezra Swerdlow)
V*, L

A disgraced policeman tracks down a serial killer.

Ludicrously implausible thriller.

w John Patrick Shanley d Pat O'Connor ph Jerzy Zielinksy m Marvin Hamlisch pd Philip Rosenberg ed Lou Lombardo

Kevin Kline, Susan Sarandon, Mary Elizabeth Mastrantonio, Harvey Keitel, Danny Aiello, Rod Steiger, Alan Rickman, Faye Grant, Ken Welsh

Japanese War Bride *
US   1952   94m   bw
TCF/Bernhard (Joseph Bernhard)

An officer wounded in Korea marries his Japanese nurse and takes her home to California.

Predictable domestic drama very similar to the British Frieda, marginally interesting for sociological reasons.

w Catherine Turney d King Vidor ph Lionel Lindon md Emil Newman m Arthur Lange

Shirley Yamaguchi, Don Taylor, Cameron Mitchell, Marie Windsor, James Bell, Louise Lorimer

Jarrapellejos **
Spain   1987   108m   colour
Penelope/Television Española (Jose G. Blanco Sola, Jose Joaquin Aguirre)

In the early 1900s, a corrupt landowner in a small town covers up the rape and murder of a mother and daughter.

Devastating exposé of social and sexual hypocrisy, shot in a stately fashion.

w Antonio Gimenez Rico, Manuel Gutierrez Aragon novel Felipe Trigo d Antonio Gimenez Rico ph Jose Luis Alcaine m Carmelo A. Bernaola ad Rafael Palmero ed Miguel Gonzalez Sinde

Antonio Ferrandis, Juan Diego, Lydia Bosch, Amparo Larrañaga, Joaquin Hinojosa, Miguel A. Rellan, Aitana Sanchez-Gijon, Carlos Tristancho, Florinda Chico, Jose Coronado

Jason and the Argonauts ***
GB   1963   104m   Technicolor
Columbia/Charles H. Schneer
V, V*, L

With help and hindrance from the gods, Jason voyages in search of the Golden Fleece and meets all kinds of monsters.

Rambling semi-classic mythological fantasy which keeps its tongue firmly in its cheek and provides a framework for some splendid stop-frame animation.

w Jan Read, Beverley Cross d Don Chaffey ph Wilkie Cooper m Bernard Herrmann sp Ray Harryhausen

Todd Armstrong, Honor Blackman, Niall MacGinnis, Andrew Faulds, Nancy Kovack

Jason Goes to Hell: The Final Friday
US   1993   88m   DeLuxe
New Line (Sean S. Cunningham)
V, V*

Jason attempts to kill his relatives so that he can live forever.

The series ends, but does not even manage a whimper on the way out; it simply fades away into witless, boring nonsense. The most frightening moment comes at the end, with the hint that he and Freddy, hero of the Nightmare on Elm Street series, may be teamed in a new movie.

w Dean Lorey, Jay Huguely d Adam Marcus ph William Dill m Harry Manfredini pd W. Brooke Wheeler ed David Handman

Jon D. LeMay, Kari Keegan, Kane Hodder, Steve Williams, Steven Culp, Erin Gray, Rusty Schwimmer

'Jason goes to hell and not a moment too soon.' – Variety

† The film was the ninth and last film in the Friday the 13th series (qv).

Jassy
GB   1947   102m   Technicolor
GFD/Gainsborough (Sydney Box)

A gypsy servant girl falls in love with her master but is accused of murder.

Period romantic melodrama of the Man in Grey school; poor of its kind despite high production values.

w Dorothy and Campbell Christie, Geoffrey Kerr novel Norah Lofts d Bernard Knowles ph Jack Asher

Margaret Lockwood, Patricia Roc, Dennis Price, Basil Sydney, Dermot Walsh, Nora Swinburne, Linden Travers, Ernest Thesiger, Cathleen Nesbitt, John Laurie, Jean Cadell, Clive Morton

'As a piece of unabashed romantic hokum, I found it more and more diverting as the plot thickened.' – Evening Standard

Java Head *
GB   1934   85m   bw
ATP (Basil Dean)

In 1850 Bristol, a shipbuilder forsakes his Manchu wife for an English girl.

Rather obvious period melodrama with full-blooded acting.

w Martin Brown, Gordon Wellesley novel Joseph Hergesheimer d J. Walter Ruben ph Robert Martin md Ernest Irving ad Edward Carrick ed Thorold Dickinson, David Lean

Anna May Wong, John Loder, Ralph Richardson, Elizabeth Allan, Edmund Gwenn, Herbert Lomas, George Curzon, Roy Emerton

Jaws **
US   1975   125m   Technicolor   Panavision
Universal/Zanuck-Brown (William S. Gilmore Jnr)
V, V*, L

A man-eating shark causes havoc off the Long Island coast.

In the exploitation-hungry seventies this film took more money than any other. In itself, despite genuinely suspenseful and frightening sequences, it is a slackly narrated and sometimes flatly handled thriller with an over-abundance of dialogue and, when it finally appears, a pretty unconvincing monster.

w Peter Benchley, Carl Gottlieb novel Peter Benchley d Steven Spielberg ph Bill Butler m John Williams ad Joseph Alves Jnr ed Verna Fields

Robert Shaw, Roy Scheider, Richard Dreyfuss, Lorraine Gary, Murray Hamilton, Carl Gottlieb

'A mind-numbing repast for sense-sated gluttons. Shark stew for the stupefied.' – William S. Pechter

'The opening sequences have few parallels in modern cinema; like the shower scene in Psycho they will haunt a whole generation.' – Les Keyser, Hollywood in the Seventies

AA: John Williams; Verna Fields; sound

AAN: best picture

Jaws: The Revenge
US   1987   100m   colour
UIP/Universal (Joseph Sargent)
V, V*, L, S

Superfluous fourth story in the Jaws series, almost indistinguishable from the others once you accept that the sharks are after Brody's widow.

w Michael de Guzman d Joseph Sargent ph John McPherson m Michael Small pd John Lloyd ed Michael Brown

Lorraine Gary, Lance Guest, Mario von Peebles, Karen Young, Michael Caine

Jaws 2
US   1978   117m   Technicolor   Panavision
Universal/Richard Zanuck, David Brown (Joe Alves)
V, V*, L, S

Another man-eating shark menaces teenagers in the Long Island resort of Amity.

Repetitive and feeble sequel aimed directly at the popcorn market.

w Carl Gottlieb, Howard Sackler, Dorothy Tristan d Jeannot Szwarc ph David Butler, Michael McGowan m John Williams

Roy Scheider, Lorraine Gary, Murray Hamilton, Joseph Mascolo, Collin Wilcox

'A manipulation of the audience, in the best sense of the term' – Jeannot Szwarc, director

'The third dimension is terror!'
Jaws 3-D
US   1983   99m   Technicolor   ArriVision 3-D
Alan Landsburg/Universal (Rupert Hitzig)
V, V*, L

A man-eating shark turns up in a Florida theme park.

Noisy additional chapter to this string of shocks.

w Richard Matheson, Carl Gottlieb   story Guerdon Trueblood   d Joe Alves   ph James A. Cotner   m Alan Parker   pd Woods Macintosh   ed Randy Roberts, Corky Ehlers

Dennis Quaid, Bess Armstrong, Simon MacCorkindale, Louis Gossett Jnr, John Putch, Lea Thompson

The Jayhawkers
US   1959   110m   Technicolor   Vistavision
Paramount/Panama and Frank
V*

Before the Civil War, a farmer defeats a militant posse of private raiders.

Unconvincing but rather unusual Western, flat patches alternating with striking ones.

w Melvin Frank, Joseph Petracca, Frank Fenton, A. I. Bezzerides   d Melvin Frank   ph Loyal Griggs   m Jerome Moross

Fess Parker, Jeff Chandler, Nicole Maurey, Henry Silva, Herbert Rudley

Jazz Comedy *
USSR   1934   93m   bw
Mosfilm
original title: Vesolye Rebyata

A shepherd is frequently mistaken for a famous conductor.

Peripatetic comedy with many sight gags and western slapstick: Russian comedy being still a rare thing, it seems something of a revelation.

w Grigori Alexandrov, Nikolai Erdman, V. Mass   d Grigori Alexandrov   ph Vladimir Nilsen   m Isaac Dunayevsky

Lubov Orlova, Leonid Utyosov, Maria Strelkova

Jazz on a Summer's Day ***
US   1959   85m   DeLuxe
Galaxy/Raven (Allan Green)
V, V*

Exemplary documentary about the Newport Jazz Festival, incorporating many excellent performances from the musicians involved.

Made by a famous fashion photographer, this is visually as interesting as it is musically. With its witty juxtaposition of images and sound, it remains probably the best documentary of its kind so far.

w Arnold Pearl, Albert D'Annibale   d Bert Stern   ph Bert Stern, Courtney Hafela, Ray Phealan   md George Avakian   ed Aram Avakian

Louis Armstrong, Mahalia Jackson, Gerry Mulligan, Dinah Washington, Chico Hamilton, Anita O'Day, George Shearing, Chuck Berry, Jack Teagarden, Thelonius Monk, Big Maybelle, Sonny Stitt

'New songs and old favourites sung by Mr Jolson during the action of the story on the Vitaphone!'
The Jazz Singer ****
US   1927   89m   bw
Warner
V, V*, L, S

A cantor's son makes it big in show business.

Archetypal Jewish weepie which became of absorbing interest as the first talkie film (songs and a few fragments of speech) and in its way, surprisingly, is not half bad.

w Alfred A. Cohn   play Samson Raphaelson   d Alan Crosland   ph Hal Mohr   md Louis Silvers

Al Jolson, May McAvoy, Warner Oland, Eugenie Besserer, Otto Lederer

'A beautiful period piece, extravagantly sentimental . . . yet entirely compelling in its own conviction.' – NFT, 1969

'The Jazz Singer definitely establishes the fact that talking pictures are imminent. Everyone in Hollywood can rise up and declare that they are not, and it will not alter the fact. If I were an actor with a squeaky voice I would worry.' – Welford Beaton, The Film Spectator

AA: Special Award to Warner for producing 'the pioneer outstanding talking picture'

AAN: Alfred A. Cohn

The Jazz Singer
US   1953   107m   Technicolor
Warner (Louis F. Edelman)

Ill-considered, schmaltzy remake of the above.

w Frank Davis, Leonard Stern, Lewis Meltzer   d Michael Curtiz   ph Carl Guthrie   md Ray Heindorf   m Max Steiner

Danny Thomas, Peggy Lee, Mildred Dunnock, Eduard Franz

AAN: Ray Heindorf; Max Steiner

The Jazz Singer
US   1980   115m   DeLuxe
EMI/Jerry Leider
V, V*, L, S

Oddly-timed reprise of the above, with doting mum replaced by patient wife.

A good basis for a best-selling album, otherwise a pointless enterprise.

w Herbert Baker, Stephen H. Foreman   d Richard Fleischer   ph Isidore Mankofsky   m Leonard Rosenman   pd Harry Horner

Neil Diamond, Laurence Olivier, Lucie Arnaz, Catlin Adams, Sully Boyar

'What is jazz to Neil Diamond and what is Neil Diamond to jazz? Old title has nothing to do with music on display here and would seem meaningless to modern audiences.' – Variety

Jazzboat
GB   1959   96m   bw   Cinemascope
Warwick/Columbia

A jazz musician pretends to be a crook and leads the police to an important gang.

Flimsy comedy with a background of pop acts. Very dated.

w Ken Hughes, John Antrobus   d Ken Hughes

Anthony Newley, Anne Aubrey, David Lodge, Lionel Jeffries, Bernie Winters, James Booth, Al Mulock, Joyce Blair, Leo McKern, Ted Heath and his Music

Je T'Aime, Je T'Aime **
France   1967   94m   Eastmancolor
TCF/Parc/Fox Europa (Mag Bodard)

During experiments with a time-machine, a suicidal man relives the experience of an unhappy love affair that led him to attempt to take his own life.

A fascinating, if sometimes confusing, speculation on the nature of time and the fact that there are no second chances in life.

w Jacques Sternberg   d Alain Resnais   ph Jean Boffety   m Krzysztof Penderecki, Jean-Claude Pelletier, Jean Dandeny   ad Jacques Dugied, Auguste Pace   ed Albert Jurgenson, Colette Leloup

Claude Rich, Olga Georges-Picot, Anouk Ferjac, Annie Fargue, Bernard Fresson, Yvette Etievant

'A work that deserves to be studied and discussed: to see it is essential.' – Gordon Gow, Films and Filming

Je T'Aime Moi Non Plus
France   1975   90m   Eastmancolor
President/Renn (Jacques-Eric Strauss)
V
aka: I Love You No More

A gay truck driver begins an affair with a boyish girl which proves difficult to consummate and also upsets his jealous Italian boyfriend.

Rambling, inconsequential, intermittently entertaining tale that gives the impression that the actors made it up as they went along.

wd Serge Gainsbourg   ph Willy Kurant   m Serge Gainsbourg   ad Theo Meurisse   ed Kenout Peltier

Jane Birkin, Joe Dallesandro, Hugues Quester, Rene Kolldehoff, Gérard Depardieu, Michel Blanc

Je Vous Aime
France   1981   105m   Eastmancolor
Renn Productions/FR3 (Pierre Grunstein)

A woman changes husbands as if they were dresses.

Shallow depiction of an incurable romantic, or obsessive promiscuity, depending on your viewpoint. From either, it makes for a dull movie.

w Claude Berri, Michel Grisolla   d Claude Berri   ph Etienne Becker   m Serge Gainsbourg   ad Pierre Guffroy   ed Arlette Langmann

Catherine Deneuve, Jean-Louis Trintignant, Gérard Depardieu, Serge Gainsbourg, Alain Souchon, Christian Marquand

Jealousy
US   1929   66m   bw
Paramount

A young artist is jealous of his wife's older friend, and kills him.

Turgid adaptation of a two-character play; interesting only for its cast, though the star died before it was released.

w Garrett Fort, John D. Williams   play Louis Verneuil   d Jean de Limur

Jeanne Eagels, Fredric March, Halliwell Hobbes, Henry Daniell

Jealousy
US   1934   66m   bw
Columbia

A boxer is knocked out and dreams that his jealousy has landed him in the electric chair.

Disagreeable melodrama not saved by its tricks.

w Kubec Glasmon, Joseph Moncure March   d Roy William Neill

Nancy Carroll, George Murphy, Donald Cook, Raymond Walburn

Jealousy *
US   1945   70m   bw
Republic

A failed writer, jealous of his wife's friendship with another man, is found murdered.

Curious but interesting melodrama with much talent breaking through.

w Arnold Phillips, Gustav Machaty, Dalton Trumbo   d Gustav Machaty   m Hanns Eisler

Nils Asther, John Loder, Jane Randolph, Karen Morley

'It is a sympathetic film, and in spite of its overall failure, contains enough sincerity and enough artistry to make most of the other films mentioned here look sick.' – James Agee

Jealousy Italian Style *

Italy/Spain 1970 106m Technicolor Panavision
Dean/Jupiter Generale/Midega (Pio Angeletti, Adriano de
Micheli)

original title: *Dramma della Gelosia – Tutti i Particolari in
Cronaca*; aka: *A Drama of Jealousy; The Pizza Triangle*

Two friends – a married bricklayer and a pizza cook –
fall in love with the same woman, who cannot choose
between them, resulting in disaster for all three.

Mildly amusing, if over-loud and vociferous, comedy
that takes swipes at, among other targets, male–
female relationships, modern Italian design, politics,
and Fellini's liking for grotesques.

w Furio Scarpelli, Agenore Incrocci, Ettore Scola
d Ettore Scola *ph* Carlo Di Palma *m* Armando
Trovaioli *ad* Luciano Ricceri *ed* Alberto Gallitti

Marcello Mastroianni, Giancarlo Giannini, Monica
Vitti, Manolo Zarzo, Marisa Merlini, Hercules Cortes

† Mastroianni's performance won him the Best Actor
award at the Cannes Film Festival in 1970.

Jean de Florette **

France 1986 121m Eastmancolor Technovision
Renn/Films A2/RAI2/DD
V, V*, L, S

Elemental story of feuding over water supplies in
rural France in the 20s.

Stunning performances and detailed depiction of
Provençal farming life made it a wild success in
France, repeated to a remarkable extent abroad.

w Claude Berri, Gérard Brach *novel* Marcel Pagnol
d Claude Berri *ph* Bruno Nuytten *m* Jean-Claude
Petit *pd* Bernard Vezat

Yves Montand, Gérard Depardieu, Daniel Auteuil,
Elisabeth Depardieu

† The saga continued in *Manon des Sources* (qv), from
Pagnol's sequel *L'eau de collines*.

Jeanne Eagels *

US 1957 114m bw
Columbia (George Sidney)

A sideshow dancer becomes a Broadway star of the
twenties but dies of drugs.

Well-upholstered but basically too conventional
showbiz biopic.

w Daniel Fuchs, Sonya Levien, John Fante *d* George
Sidney *ph* Robert Planck *m* George Duning

Kim Novak, Jeff Chandler, Agnes Moorehead,
Charles Drake, Larry Gates, Virginia Grey

Jeanne's House **

France 1987 94m colour
MDG/FR3 (Marie-Dominique Girodet)
original title: *La Maison de Jeanne*

A restaurateur, driven to the point of breakdown by
her passive husband, demanding mother and noisy
children, falls in love with her new landlord.

Witty movie of domestic conflict that comes to a
surprising conclusion.

wd Magali Clement *ph* Pierre Novion
m Raymond Alessandrini *ad* Bruno Bruneau
ed Amina Mazani

Christine Boisson, Benoit Regent, Jean-Pierre Bisson,
Marie Trintignant, Michelle Goddet, Maxime Leroux,
Pascale Audret, Jacques Richard

Jeannie *

GB 1941 101m bw
GFD/Tansa (Marcel Hellman)
US title: *Girl in Distress*

A Scots girl comes into money and takes a European
holiday.

Mildly astringent, generally amusing comedy which
overcomes shaky production. Remade as *Let's Be
Happy* in 1952.

w Anatole de Grunwald, Roland Pertwee
play Aimée Stuart *d* Harold French *ph* Bernard
Knowles *m* Mischa Spoliansky

Barbara Mullen, Michael Redgrave, Albert Lieven,
Wilfrid Lawson, Kay Hammond, Edward Chapman,
Googie Withers, Gus MacNaughton

'One of the easiest, sweetest of light comedies.' –
James Agee

'As enchanting a bit of rue and nonsense as we've
succumbed to in many a month.' – *New York Times*

Jeder für sich und Gott gegen alle: see *The
Enigma of Kaspar Hauser*

J'Embrasse Pas *

France 1991 115m colour
President/BAC/Salome/Ciné Cinq/Canal Plus (Maurice Benart,
Jacques Eric-Strauss, Jean Labadie)
V
aka: *I Don't Kiss*

An ill-educated but ambitious youth from the country
comes to Paris, finds success as a male prostitute and
falls for a whore.

Dour moral tale of disillusioned youth that comes to
no satisfactory conclusion.

w Jacques Nolot, André Téchiné, Michel Grisolia
d André Téchiné *ph* Thierry Arbogast
m Philippe Sarde *ed* Claudine Merlin, Edith
Vassard

Philippe Noiret, Emmanuelle Béart, Manual Blanc,
Hélène Vincent, Yvan Desni

Jennie: see *Portrait of Jennie*

'The drama of all women who meet the demands of love!'
Jennie Gerhardt

US 1933 85m bw
Paramount (B. P. Schulberg)

An unmarried mother is hard done by but gets the
man she loves in the end.

Archetypal weepie, adequately put across.

w Josephine Lovett, Joseph M. March, S. K. Lauren,
Frank Partos *novel* Theodore Dreiser *d* Marion
Gering *ph* Leon Shamroy

Sylvia Sidney, Donald Cook, Mary Astor, Edward
Arnold, H. B. Warner, Theodor von Eltz

'Doesn't look to become a general b.o. favourite
because it is a story without action.' – *Variety*

Jennifer

US 1953 73m bw
AA (Berman Swartz)

The lady housekeeper of a California mansion broods
on the mysterious disappearance of her predecessor.

Slight, quietly effective suspenser with a letdown
ending.

w Virginia Myers *d* Joel Newton *ph* James Wong
Howe *m* Ernest Gold

Ida Lupino, Howard Duff, Robert Nicholas, Mary
Shipp

'On the trail of a serial killer, Detective John Berlin has no
clues and no suspects. And no alibi.'
Jennifer Eight

US 1992 120m DeLuxe
Paramount (Gary Lucchesi, David Wimbury)
V, V*, L

A burnt-out cop, moving to a new small-town job,
faces local derision when he decides a murder has
been committed by a serial killer who targets blind
women.

A drawn-out, predictable thriller that becomes more
ridiculous the longer it lasts; and it lasts a long time.

wd Bruce Robinson *ph* Conrad L. Hall
m Christopher Young *pd* Richard Macdonald
ed Conrad Buff

Andy Garcia, Uma Thurman, John Malkovich, Lance
Henriksen, Kathy Baker, Kevin Conway, Graham
Beckel

'Although initially menacing, Robinson's addition to
the serial killer genre falls back on clichés.' – *Sight and
Sound*

'A sombre character-oriented suspense mystery, this
is notable both for its stunningly atmospheric
cinematography and the dark psychological
undercurrents lurking beneath the surface.' – *Empire*

† The film was released direct to video in Britain.

Jenny Lind: see *A Lady's Morals*

Jeopardy

US 1952 69m bw
MGM (Sol Baer Fielding)

A man on a camping holiday falls off a jetty and gets
stuck in the timbers while the water rises; his wife
frantically seeks help from an escaped convict.

Panic melodrama enjoyable for its clichés.

w Mel Dinelli *d* John Sturges *ph* Victor Milner
m Dimitri Tiomkin

Barbara Stanwyck, Barry Sullivan, Ralph Meeker

'Some say he's dead … some say he never will be!'
Jeremiah Johnson **

US 1972 107m Technicolor Panavision
Warner (Joe Wizan)
V, V*, L

In the 1850s an ex-soldier becomes a mountain
trapper.

Splendidly made if rather desultorily plotted
adventure story with the feel of raw reality.

w John Milius, Edward Anhalt *d* Sydney Pollack
ph Andrew Callaghan *m* John Rubinstein, Tim
McIntire

Robert Redford, Will Geer, Allyn McLerie

Jeremy

US 1973 90m DeLuxe
UA/Kenasset (George Pappas)

A music student falls in love with a ballet dancer.

Sentimental love story with nothing positive to
commend it, chiefly interesting because for
commercial release it was blown up from 16mm.

wd Arthur Barron *ph* Paul Goldsmith *m* Lee
Holdridge

Robby Benson, Glynnis O'Connor, Len Bari,
Leonardo Cimino

Jericho

GB 1937 77m bw
Buckingham (Walter Futter, Max Schach)
US title: *Dark Sands*

A court-martialled officer pursues a murderous
deserter across Africa.

Lively star vehicle of its day.

w Frances Marion, George Barraud, Peter Ruric,
Robert N. Lee *d* Thornton Freeland *ph* John W.
Boyle

Paul Robeson, Henry Wilcoxon, Wallace Ford, John
Laurie, James Carew

'Can't fail to interest audiences throughout the world.'
– *Variety*

The Jerk

US 1979 94m Technicolor
Universal/Aspen (Peter MacGregor-Scott)
V, V*, L

An innocent white man brought up by black

sharecroppers goes out into the world and first makes, then loses a fortune.

Hit-or-miss star vehicle with flashes of satire and fallen aspirations to be a modern *Candide*.

w Steve Martin, Carl Gottlieb, Michael Elias   *d* Carl Reiner   *ph* Victor J. Kemper   *m* Jack Elliott

Steve Martin, Bernadette Peters, Catlin Adams, Bill Macy, Maurice Evans

'Goofy, dumb, innocent, loud, uncoordinated, bashful and quite dirty.' – *Variety*

Jersey Girl
US   1992   95m   Technicolor
Entertainment/Electric/Interscope
V, V*

A New Jersey teacher crashes her Volkswagen into a Mercedes belonging to the kind of person that she needs to improve her life: a successful and handsome man from Manhattan.

Amiable comedy of class differences with true love winning out in the end, to no one's surprise.

w Gina Wendkos   *d* David Burton Morris   *ph* Ron Fortunato   *m* Misha Segal   *pd* Lester Cohen   *ed* Norman Hollyn

Jami Gertz, Dylan McDermott, Molly Price, Aida Turturro, Star Jasper, Sheryl Lee, Joseph Bologna, Joseph Mazzello, Philip Casnoff

'Pic has the potential to warm the hearts of ancillary viewers, especially young women.' – *Variety*

The Jerusalem File
US/Israel   1971   96m   Metrocolor
MGM/Sparta (Ram Ben Efraim)

American archaeologists in Jerusalem become involved in Arab/Israeli espionage.

Muddled mixture of action and politics.

w Troy Kennedy Martin   *d* John Flynn   *ph* Raoul Coutard   *m* John Scott

Bruce Davison, Nicol Williamson, Donald Pleasence, Ian Hendry

Jesse James **
US   1938   106m   Technicolor
TCF (Nunnally Johnson)
V, V*, L

After the Civil War, two brothers take to train robbing when railroad employees harass their family.

The life of an outlaw turns into family entertainment when Hollywood bathes it in sentiment, soft colour, family background and warm humour. It works dangerously well, and the action sequences are splendid.

w Nunnally Johnson   *d* Henry King   *ph* George Barnes   *md* Louis Silvers   *ad* William Darling, George Dudley

Tyrone Power, Henry Fonda, Nancy Kelly, Jane Darwell, Randolph Scott, Henry Hull, Slim Summerville, Brian Donlevy, J. Edward Bromberg, John Carradine, Donald Meek

'Sock outdoors meller, vigorous and intensely dramatic in its unfolding . . . box office smacko.' – *Variety*

'An authentic American panorama.' – *New York Times*

† Sequel 1940: *The Return of Frank James*. Remake 1957: *The True Story of Jesse James*.

Jesse James Meets Frankenstein's Daughter
US   1965   82m   Pathé Color
Avco Embassy/Circle/Embassy (Carroll Case)
V*

Baron Frankenstein's granddaughter moves to a Mexican village where she sets up in the family business and falls in love with Jesse James.

Low-budget nonsense, played and directed with little sense of style or purpose.

w Carl K. Hittleman   *d* William Beaudine
ph Lothrop Worth   *m* Raoul Kraushaar   *ad* Paul Sylos, Harry Reif   *ed* Roy Livingston

John Lupton, Estelita, Cal Bolder, Narda Onyx, Steven Geray, Raymond Barnes

'With script and direction proving equally frail, the film is only prevented from becoming the camper's delight promised by the title by the fact that the cast plod through it all with gravity hardly befitting the occasion.' – *Tom Milne, MFB*

† The same director was also responsible for *Billy the Kid vs Dracula* (qv).

Jesse James Rides Again
US   1947   bw   serial: 13 eps
Republic

A reformed Jesse James tries to go straight.

Unlikely serial heroics.

d Fred C. Brannon, Thomas Carr

Clayton Moore, Linda Stirling, Roy Barcroft, Tristram Coffin

Jessica
France/Italy/US   1962   105m   Technicolor
Panavision
UA/Ariane/Dear Film (Jean Negulesco)
V*

The attractive midwife in a Sicilian village causes the women to go on a sex strike.

Synthetic rustic naughtiness showing several influences imperfectly assimilated.

w Edith Sommer   novel *The Midwife of Pont Clery* by Flora Sundstrom   *d* Jean Negulesco   *ph* Piero Portalupi   *m* Mario Nascimbene

Angie Dickinson, Maurice Chevalier, Noel Noel, Gabriele Ferzetti, Sylva Koscina, Agnes Moorehead, Marcel Dalio

Jesus Christ Superstar *
US   1973   107m   Technicolor   Todd-AO 35
Universal (Norman Jewison, Robert Stigwood)
V, V (W), V*, L, S

Young tourists in Israel re-enact episodes of the life of Christ.

Location-set fantasia based on the phenomenally successful rock opera; some of it works, but the original concept was a theatrical one.

w Melvyn Bragg, Norman Jewison   *d* Norman Jewison   *ph* Douglas Slocombe   *md* André Previn   *m/ly* Andrew Lloyd Webber, Tim Rice

Ted Neeley, Carl Anderson, Yvonne Elliman, Barry Dennen

'One of the true fiascos of modern cinema.' – *Paul D. Zimmerman*

AAN: André Previn

Jesus of Montreal ***
Canada/France   1989   120m   colour
Max Films/Gérard Mital Productions/NFB Canada (Roger Frappier, Pierre Gendron)
V, V*, L
original title: *Jésus de Montréal*

An actor, chosen to play Christ in a religious play, finds himself in conflict with the church authorities.

A modern morality, surprisingly effective despite sometimes forced parallels between the actor's experiences and those of Jesus, and fuelled by a passionate irony.

wd Denys Arcand   *ph* Guy Dufaux   *m* Yves Laferrière, François Dompierre, Jean-Marie Benoît   *ad* François Seguin   *ed* Isabelle Dedieu

Lothaire Bluteau, Catherine Wilkening, Johanne-Marie Tremblay, Rémy Girard, Robert Lepage, Gilles Pelletier, Yves Jacques

'Arcand is a master of tone, a sympathetic director of actors, and an unsanctimonious moralist, who locates his fable within a well-observed society.' – *Philip French, Observer*

AAN: best foreign film

Jet Men of the Air: see *Air Cadet*

Jet over the Atlantic
US   1958   95m   bw
Warner/Inter Continental (Benedict Bogeaus)
V*

A noble British passenger on a plane from Madrid to New York has planted a gas bomb in the luggage compartment.

Mechanical airborne suspenser with the usual assortment of unconvincing types making unconvincing gestures.

w Irving H. Cooper   *d* Byron Haskin   *ph* George Stahl   *m* Lou Forbes

Guy Madison, Virginia Mayo, George Raft, George Macready, Ilona Massey, Anna Lee, Margaret Lindsay, Venetia Stevenson, Mary Anderson, Brett Halsey, Frederic Worlock

Jet Pilot
US   1957   112m   Technicolor
Howard Hughes (Jules Furthman)
V*, L

A Russian lady spy falls for an American pilot.

Lamentably dull and stupid romantic actioner of which all concerned should be thoroughly ashamed, especially as it took seven years to complete and is not even technically competent.

w Jules Furthman   *d* Josef von Sternberg (and others)   *ph* Winton C. Hoch   *m* Bronislau Kaper

John Wayne, Janet Leigh, Jay C. Flippen, Paul Fix, Richard Rober, Roland Winters, Ivan Triesault, Hans Conried

'One of the most childish, tedious and futile cold war spy dramas yet concocted by a Hollywood screenwriter.' – *John Gillett*

Jet Storm *
GB   1959   99m   bw
British Lion/Britannia/Pendennis (Steven Pallos)

An airliner in flight from London to New York is discovered to have a bomb on board.

All-star slice-of-life suspenser with competently handled dialogue and situations.

w Cy Endfield, Sigmund Miller   *d* Cy Endfield   *ph* Jack Hildyard   *m* Thomas Rajna

Richard Attenborough, George Rose, Hermione Baddeley, Mai Zetterling, Diane Cilento, Stanley Baker, Harry Secombe, Virginia Maskell, Elizabeth Sellars, Sybil Thorndike, Bernard Braden, Cec Linder, David Kossoff

Jetsons: The Movie
US   1990   83m   CFI color
UIP/Universal/Hanna-Berbera/Wang/Cuckoo's Nest Studios (Bruce David Johnson)
V*, L, S

The Jetson family solve the problem of alien saboteurs who object to their asteroid being the site of a mining factory.

Poorly animated situation comedy that would be better suited to television and best suited to the nearest garbage disposal unit.

w Dennis Marks, Carl Sautter   *d* William Hanna, Joseph Barbera   *ph* Daniel Bunn   *m* John Debney

voices of George O'Hanlon, Mel Blanc, Penny Singleton, Tiffany, Patric Zimmerman, Don Messick, Jean Vanderpyl

'This exercise in high-tech tedium might prove more bewildering than charming to its pre-teen audience.' – *MFB*

Jeu de Massacre *

France 1967 94m colour
Coficitel/A. J. Films/Films Modernes/Francinor (René Thevenet)
US title: *The Killing Game*; aka: *Comic Strip Hero*

An impoverished comic-book writer and his artist wife become involved with a wealthy young fantasist.

Witty games-playing on the themes of illusion and reality.

wd Alain Jessua   *ph* Jacques Robin   *m* Jacques Loussier   *ad* Claire Forestier   *ed* Nicole Marko

Claudine Auger, Jean-Pierre Cassel, Michel Duchaussoy, Eleonore Hirt, Guy Saint-Jean, Anna Gaylor, Nancy Holloway

La Jeune Fille Assassinée: see *Charlotte*

Jeux Interdits ***

France 1952 84m bw
Robert Dorfmann (Paul Joly)
aka: *Forbidden Games*; *The Secret Game*

In 1940, the little daughter of refugee parents sees her parents killed, and takes refuge with a peasant family, the small son of which helps her bury her dead puppy. They make a game of building a cemetery, which leads to a village feud . . .

Poignant anti-war tract which seemed a masterpiece at the time and is full of marvellous moments, but no longer holds up as a whole.

w Jean Aurenche, Pierre Bost   *novel* François Boyer   *d* René Clément   *ph* Robert Julliard   *m* Narciso Yepes

Brigitte Fossey, Georges Poujouly, Amédée, Laurence Badie, Jacques Marin, Suzanne Courtal, Lucien Hubert

'A truly imposing achievement of blending several seemingly unrelated elements into a totally meaningful whole.' – *John Simon, 1967*

AA: best foreign film

AAN: François Boyer (original story)

Les Jeux Sont Faits *

France 1947 91m bw
Films Gibe

Falling in love in Purgatory, two murdered people get a second chance to return to earth, but spend their time quarrelling.

Somewhat despondent romantic fantasy with morsels of wit.

w Jean-Paul Sartre   *d* Jean Delannoy   *ph* Christian Matras   *m* Georges Auric

Micheline Presle, Marcel Pagliero, Marguerite Moreno, Charles Dullin

Jew Suss **

GB 1934 109m bw
Gaumont (Michael Balcon)
US title: *Power*

In old Württemberg, a Jew gains power to help his people, then finds he is Gentile.

Interesting, heavy-handed historical satire on the pointlessness of race distinctions, made partly in answer to Nazi oppression in Germany.

w Dorothy Farnum, A. R. Rawlinson   *novel* Lion Feuchtwanger   *d* Lothar Mendes   *ph* Bernard Knowles, Roy Kellino   *md* Louis Levy   *ad* Alfred Junge   *ed* Otto Ludwig

Conrad Veidt, Benita Hume, Frank Vosper, Cedric Hardwicke, Gerald du Maurier, Pamela Ostrer

'Powerful as an artistic film achievement . . . but may have to struggle for commercial contentment.' – *Variety*

Jew Suss *

Germany 1940 85m bw
Terra

Celebrated travesty of the above, in which the Jew is wholly evil and rapes Aryan girls.

w Ludwig Metzger, Veit Harlan, Eberhard Wolfgang Möller   *d* Veit Harlan   *ph* Bruno Mondi   *m* Wolfgang Zeller

Ferdinand Marian, Werner Krauss, Heinrich George, Kristina Söderbaum

'The epitome of anti-semitic propaganda . . . the most notorious film of the Third Reich and one which brought disgrace on almost everyone connected with it.' – *Georges Sadoul*

'Highly recommended for its artistic value and, to serve the politics of the State, recommended for young people.' – *Josef Goebbels*

'When the going gets tough, the tough get going!'

Jewel of the Nile *

US 1985 104m Technicolor
TCF/Michael Douglas
V, L

A lady novelist gets into trouble when she accepts an invitation from a Middle Eastern potentate.

Moderate sequel to *Romancing the Stone;* plenty of action, but dull spots in between.

w Mark Rosenthal, Lawrence Konner   *d* Lewis Teague   *ph* Jan DeBont   *m* Jack Nitzsche   *pd* Richard Dawking, Terry Knight

Michael Douglas, Kathleen Turner, Danny DeVito, Spiros Focas

'Mass destruction, endless gunfire and a fiery finish . . . the only box office question is whether the film comes late in the cycle for Saturday matinee revivals.' – *Variety*

Jewel Robbery *

US 1932 68m bw
Warner

A jewel thief and a millionaire's wife fall in love in Vienna.

Good sparkling fun in the shadow of *Trouble in Paradise* (qv).

w Erwin Gelsey   *play* Ladislaus Fodor   *d* William Dieterle   *ph* Robert Kurrle

William Powell, Kay Francis, Hardie Albright, André Luguet, Henry Kolker, Spencer Charters, Alan Mowbray, Helen Vinson, Lawrence Grant

'The Greatest Actress Of The Screen . . . In The Greatest Romance Of The South!'

Jezebel ***

US 1938 104m bw
Warner (Henry Blanke)
V, V*, L

Before the Civil War, a Southern belle stirs up trouble among the menfolk by her wilfulness and spite, but atones when a plague strikes.

Superb star melodrama, tossed to her in compensation for losing *Gone with the Wind*, and dealt with in high style by all concerned.

w Clements Ripley, Abem Finkel, John Huston   *play* Owen Davis Snr   *d* William Wyler   *ph* Ernest Haller   *m* Max Steiner

Bette Davis, Henry Fonda, George Brent, Margaret Lindsay, Fay Bainter, Richard Cromwell, Donald Crisp, Henry O'Neill, John Litel, Spring Byington, Eddie Anderson, Gordon Oliver, Irving Pichel

'Good femme film, assured of okay results.' – *Variety*

'Its excellences come from many sources – good plotting and writing, a director and photographer who know how to make the thing flow along with dramatic pictorial effect, and a cast that makes its story

a record of living people.' – *James Shelley Hamilton, National Board of Review*

'Without the zing Davis gave it, it would have looked very mossy indeed.' – *Pauline Kael, 1968*

AA: Bette Davis; Fay Bainter

AAN: best picture; Ernest Haller; Max Steiner

Jigokumon: see *Gate of Hell*

Jigsaw

US 1949 72m bw
UA/Tower (The Danzigers)
V*

An assistant District Attorney uncovers a mob stirring up racial hatred.

Undistinguished piece of do-goodery, curiously decorated by guest stars doing bit parts as a gesture of goodwill.

w Fletcher Markle, Vincent McConnor   *d* Fletcher Markle   *ph* Don Malkames   *m* Robert Stringer

Franchot Tone, Jean Wallace, Myron McCormick, Marc Lawrence, Marlene Dietrich, Henry Fonda, John Garfield, Marsha Hunt, Leonard Lyons, Burgess Meredith

Jigsaw **

GB 1962 107m bw Cinemascope
British Lion/Britannia/Figaro (Val Guest)

Brighton policemen track down the murderer of a woman found in a lonely house on the beach.

Absorbing and entertaining little murder mystery which sustains its considerable length with interesting detail and plays as fair as can be with the audience. Excellent unassuming entertainment.

wd Val Guest   *play* *Sleep Long My Love* by Hilary Waugh   *ph* Arthur Grant   *m* none

Jack Warner, Ronald Lewis, *Michael Goodliffe*, Yolande Donlan, John Barron

The Jigsaw Man

GB 1985 98m colour
J & M
V*, L

A British traitor in Moscow is given a new face and sent back home, where he becomes a double agent.

Somewhat elementary cold war chicanery with an abundance of talk before a routine action finish. Production was interrupted by financial crises, and the final result is patchy to say the least.

w Jo Eisinger   *d* Terence Young   *ph* Freddie Francis   *m* John Cameron

Michael Caine, Laurence Olivier, Robert Powell, Susan George, Michael Medwin, Vladek Sheybal

Jim Thorpe, All-American

US 1951 105m bw
Warner (Everett Freeman)
V*, L
GB title: *Man of Bronze*

A Red Indian becomes a star footballer, but later succumbs to drink.

Adequate sporting biopic.

w Douglas Morrow, Everett Freeman   *d* Michael Curtiz   *ph* Ernest Haller   *m* Max Steiner

Burt Lancaster, Charles Bickford, Steve Cochran, Phyllis Thaxter, Dick Wesson

Jimmy Reardon

US 1988 92m colour
Island/Enterprise/Fox (Russell Schwartz)
V*, L
original title: *A Night in the Life of Jimmy Reardon*

A romantic youth finds he has a rival for the girl he loves.

Teenage angst, deftly done but lacking a wider perspective.

wd William Richert *novel Aren't You Ever Gonna Kiss Me Goodbye* by William Richert *ph* John J. Connor *m* Bill Conti *pd* Norman Newberry *ed* Suzanne Fenn

River Phoenix, Ann Magnuson, Meredith Salenger, Matthew Perry, Ione Skye, Jane Hallaren, Matthew L. Perry, Paul Koslo, Jason Court

Jimmy the Gent *
US 1934 67m bw
Warner (Robert Lord)

A racketeer supplies heirs for unclaimed estates.

Adequate star crime comedy.

w Bertram Millhauser *d* Michael Curtiz *ph* Ira Morgan *md* Leo F. Forbstein

Jimmy Cagney, Bette Davis, Alice White, Allen Jenkins, Arthur Hohl, Mayo Methot, Alan Dinehart, Hobart Cavanaugh, Ralf Harolde, Philip Reed, Joe Sawyer

'Fast and flip, rough and rowdy.' – *New York American*

Jingcha Gushi: see *Police Story*

Jinxed!
US 1982 103m Technicolor
MGM-UA/Herb Jaffe
V*

A frustrated blackjack dealer seduces the girl of a frequent winner.

Unfunny gambling comedy which never begins to cohere.

w Bert Blessing, David Newman *d* Don Siegel *ph* Vilmos Zsigmond *m* Bruce Roberts, Miles Goodman

Bette Midler, Ken Wahl, Rip Torn, Val Avery, Jack Elam, Benson Fong, Jacqueline Scott

Jit *
Zimbabwe 1990 92m bw
ICA/FilmAfrica/Makuvisi (Rory Kilalea)

A youth takes various jobs in order to raise the money he needs to buy the bride he wants.

Lively low-budget comedy, the first feature film to be made in Zimbabwe, with an engaging soundtrack of local popular music.

wd Michael Raeburn *ph* João Costa *m* Oliver Mtukudzi *pd* Lindie Pankiv *ed* Justin Krish

Dominic Makuvachuma, Sibongile Nene, Farai Sevenzo, Winnie Ndemera, Oliver Mtukudzi, Lawrence Simbarashe

Jitterbugs *
US 1943 75m bw
TCF (Sol M. Wurtzel)

Laurel and Hardy help a night-club singer to fight off gangsters.

The last Laurel and Hardy film to contain any good scenes, and almost the only one of their TCF films that did.

w Scott Darling *d* Mal St Clair *ph* Lucien Andriot *md* Emil Newman *m/y* Charles Newman, Lew Pollack *ed* James Bashevi, Chester Gore

Stan Laurel, Oliver Hardy, Vivian Blaine, Bob Bailey, Douglas Fowley, Noel Madison, Lee Patrick

Jivaro
US 1953 91m Technicolor 3D
Paramount/William H. Pine, William C. Thomas
GB title: *Lost Treasure of the Amazon*

A mixed party of Americans follows a drunken treasure seeker into the jungle.

Elementary treasure hunt adventure, hampered by studio foliage, bad script and half-hearted acting.

w Winston Millerm *story* David Duncan *d* Edward Ludwig *ph* Lionel Lindon *m* Gregory Stone

Fernando Lamas, Rhonda Fleming, Brian Keith, Lon Chaney Jnr, Marvin Miller, Richard Denning

Joan Medford Is Missing: see *House of Horrors*

Joan of Arc
US 1948 145m Technicolor
RKO/Sierra/Walter Wanger
V*, L

The last campaign of the Maid of Orleans.

Strictly from Dullsville; one studio set-piece follows another, and a group of talented people clearly thought that prestige would sell itself without the hard work that goes into more commercial productions.

w Maxwell Anderson, Andrew Solt *play Joan of Lorraine* by Maxwell Anderson *d* Victor Fleming *ph* Joe Valentine *md* Emil Newman *m* Hugo Friedhofer *ad* Richard Day *ed* Frank Sullivan

Ingrid Bergman, José Ferrer, George Coulouris, Francis L. Sullivan, Gene Lockhart, Ward Bond, John Ireland, Hurd Hatfield, Cecil Kellaway, George Zucco, J. Carrol Naish

'A bad film with one or two good things. It is childishly oversimplified, its battles *papier mâché*, its heroine far too worldly, its spiritual content that of a chromo art calendar.' – *Herman G. Weinberg*

AA: Joe Valentine; Walter Wanger (Special Award for 'adding to the moral stature' of the industry by his production)

AAN: Hugo Friedhofer; Ingrid Bergman; José Ferrer; art direction; editing

Joan of Ozark
US 1942 82m bw
Republic
GB title: *The Queen of Spies*

A hillbilly sharpshooter becomes a national spy heroine.

Scatty comedy of moderate liveliness.

w Robert Harari, Eve Greene and Jack Townley *d* Joseph Santley

Judy Canova, Joe E. Brown, Eddie Foy Jnr, Jerome Cowan, Alexander Granach

Joan of Paris
US 1942 95m bw
RKO (David Hempstead)
V*

A French resistance leader sacrifices herself so that Allied pilots can escape.

Well-made propaganda adventure dignified by excellent cast.

w Charles Bennett, Ellis St Joseph *story* Jacques Thery, Georges Kessel *d* Robert Stevenson *ph* Russell Metty *m* Roy Webb

Michele Morgan, Paul Henreid, Thomas Mitchell, Laird Cregar, May Robson, Alexander Granach, Alan Ladd

AAN: Roy Webb

Joan the Woman **
US 1916 125m approx bw silent
Cardinal

The story of Joan of Arc.

An epic spectacle typical of its director.

w Jeanie Macpherson *d* Cecil B. DeMille

Geraldine Farrar, Raymond Hatton, Wallace Reid, Hobart Bosworth, Theodore Roberts

Joanna
GB 1968 122m DeLuxe Panavision
TCF/Laughlin (Michael S. Laughlin)
S

A girl art student comes to London and quickly finds the road to ruin.

Antediluvian rubbish tarted up with swinging London settings.

wd Michael Sarne *ph* Walter Lassally *m* Rod McKuen

Genevieve Waite, Christian Doermer, Calvin Lockhart, Donald Sutherland

'An unnecessarily protracted punishing of a very dead quadruped.' – *MFB*

The Job **
Italy 1961 90m bw
24 Horses Films (Alberto Soffientini)
original title: *Il Posto*

A teenage boy gets his first job, and progresses from office boy to clerk when a senior man dies.

Appealingly observant social comedy, very simple and extremely effective.

wd Ermanno Olmi *ph* Lamberto Caimi

Sandro Panzeri, Loredana Detto

'Rueful and funny and honest . . . the players have been encouraged not so much to act as to behave. Olmi stalks them like a naturalist, and the result is a small, unique and perfect achievement in film-making.' – *Penelope Houston, MFB*

Jób Lázadása: see *The Revolt of Job*

Joe *
US 1970 107m DeLuxe
Cannon (David Gil)

A construction worker in a bar meets a businessman who has just killed his daughter's drug addicted lover; they become buddies in their hatred of hippies.

Highly successful in America as a backlash against permissiveness, this rough-hewn opportunistic melodrama is vivid enough but moves in fits and starts.

w Norman Wexler *d/ph* John G. Avildsen *m* Bobby Scott

Peter Boyle, Dennis Patrick, Audrey Caire, Susan Sarandon

'A bad film disfigured by brute strokes of tendentiousness.' – *Penelope Gilliatt*

AAN: Norman Wexler

Joe Butterfly
US 1957 90m Technicolor Cinemascope
U-I (Aaron Rosenberg)

Shortly after World War II, American occupying troops are conned by a Japanese interpreter.

Dull comedy intent on healing old wounds.

w Sy Gomberg, Jack Sher, Marion Hargrove *d* Jesse Hibbs *ph* Irving Glassberg *m* Joseph Gershenson

Burgess Meredith, Audie Murphy, George Nader, Keenan Wynn, Fred Clark, John Agar, Charles McGraw

Joe Dakota
US 1957 90m Technicolor Cinemascope
U-I (Howard Christie)

A stranger appears in a Western town in search of his Indian friend, who turns out to have been murdered by the townspeople so that they can share the profits from his oil well.

Feeble rip-off of *Bad Day at Black Rock*.

w William Talman, Norman Jolley   *d* Richard Bartlett   *ph* George Robinson   *md* Joseph Gershenson   *m* Hans Salter

Jock Mahoney, Luana Patten, Charles McGraw, Barbara Lawrence, Claude Akins, Lee Van Cleef

Joe Hill: see *The Ballad of Joe Hill*

Joe Kidd

US   1972   87m   Technicolor   Panavision
Universal/Malpaso (Sidney Beckerman)
V*, L

A disreputable bounty hunter tracks down the leader of a tribe of Mexican bandits.

Rough-and-tumble star Western with untenable moral attitudes.

w Elmore Leonard   *d* John Sturges   *ph* Bruce Surtees   *m* Lalo Schifrin

Clint Eastwood, Robert Duvall, John Saxon, Don Stroud, James Wainwright

Joe Macbeth

GB   1955   90m   bw
Film Locations/Frankovich (George Maynard)

A gangster is urged by his wife to rub out his boss.

Almost too bad to be funny, this effort to update Shakespeare has actors behaving as though they were stuck in treacle, and its gimmick quality is quickly dissipated by an indifferent production.

w Philip Yordan   *d* Ken Hughes   *ph* Basil Emmott   *m* Trevor Duncan

Paul Douglas, Ruth Roman, Grégoire Aslan, Bonar Colleano, Sidney James

Joe Palooka, Champ

US   1946   72m   bw
Monogram (Hal E. Chester)

A boxing promoter grooms a young dope for the ring.

Modest series opener with plenty to be modest about.

w George Moskov, Albert de Pina   *d* Reginald Le Borg

Leon Errol, Joe Kirkwood, Elyse Knox, Eduardo Ciannelli, Joe Sawyer, Elisha Cook Jnr

Joe Smith American *

US   1942   63m   bw
MGM (Jack Chertok)
GB title: *Highway to Freedom*

An aircraft factory worker with special knowledge is kidnapped by Nazis but leads the FBI to his captors.

Watchable propaganda thriller credited with easing Americans into a war mood.

w Allen Rivkin   *story* Paul Gallico   *d* Richard Thorpe   *ph* Charles Lawton Jnr   *m* Daniele Amfitheatrof

Robert Young, Marsha Hunt, Darryl Hickman, Harvey Stephens, Jonathan Hale, Noel Madison, Joseph Anthony

'Not a high-powered movie, it is a first rate die for the new propaganda models which Hollywood is readying for mass production.' – *Time*

Joe versus the Volcano

US   1990   102m   Technicolor   Panavision
Warner/Amblin Entertainment (Teri Schwartz)
V, V*, L

Told that he has only a few months to live, a man agrees to jump into a volcano to prevent an eruption and save an island for an entrepreneur.

Weak whimsy, directed without flair.   *wd* John Patrick Shanley   *ph* Stephen Goldblatt   *pd* Bo Welch   *ed* Richard Halsey

Tom Hanks, Meg Ryan, Lloyd Bridges, Robert Stack, Abe Vigoda, Dan Hedaya, Barry McGovern, Amanda Plummer, Ossie Davis, Jayne Haynes

Joey Boy

GB   1965   91m   bw
British Lion/Launder-Gilliat

In 1941, a group of petty crooks join the army.

Abysmal service comedy, incredibly cheap and tatty and the nadir of several of the talents involved.

wd Frank Launder   *ph* Arthur Lavis   *m* Philip Green

Harry H. Corbett, Stanley Baxter, Bill Fraser, Reg Varney, Percy Herbert, Lance Percival

'As visually shoddy as it is unfunny . . . the final shot (Corbett pulling a lavatory chain) is all too crudely apt.' – *MFB*

Johann Mouse ***

US   1952   8m   Technicolor
MGM (Fred Quimby)

Strauss's mouse dances to his master's music; the cat, to lure him out, learns to play the piano.

Splendid Tom and Jerry cartoon from the great period of this neglected art.

AA: best cartoon

John and Julie

GB   1955   82m   Eastmancolor
Group Three (Herbert Mason)

Two children run away to see the coronation.

Genial little family comedy full of stock comic characters.

wd William Fairchild   *ph* Arthur Grant   *m* Philip Green

Colin Gibson, Leslie Dudley, Peter Sellers, Moira Lister, Wilfrid Hyde-White, Sidney James, Andrew Cruickshank

John and Mary *

US   1969   92m   DeLuxe   Panavision
TCF/Debrod (Ben Kadish)

Two New Yorkers have a one-night affair and cannot decide whether to continue.

Slight, disappointing sex comedy vehicle for two stars who were very hot at the time.

w John Mortimer   *novel* Mervyn Jones   *d* Peter Yates   *ph* Gayne Rescher   *m* Quincy Jones   *pd* John Robert Lloyd

Dustin Hoffman, Mia Farrow, Michael Tolan, Sunny Griffin, Tyne Daly

'The emphasis is not on action but on acting, which although skilful and subtly nuanced does not in this case amount to the same thing as character.' – *Jan Dawson*

'Despite all the "now" sets and surfaces, it's like an old comedy of the thirties – minus the comedy.' – *Judith Crist*

John Goldfarb Please Come Home

US   1965   96m   DeLuxe   Cinemascope
TCF/Steve Parker/J. Lee-Thompson

An American spy pilot crashlands near the palace of a Middle Eastern potentate at the same time as a girl reporter arrives for an interview.

Would-be satire on the cold war, anti-feminism, American football, American/Arab relations, etc. None of it works for a minute, and the actors' desperation can be plainly seen.

w William Peter Blatty   *d* J. Lee-Thompson   *ph* Leon Shamroy   *m* Johnny Williams

Shirley Maclaine, Richard Crenna, Peter Ustinov, Fred Clark, Wilfrid Hyde-White, Jim Backus

John Loves Mary

US   1948   87m   bw
Warner (Jerry Wald)

A GI returns home to get married, but unfortunately,

to help a friend, he has already entered into a marriage of convenience.

Moderately amusing comedy with an excess of complications.

w Phoebe and Henry Ephron   *play* Norman Krasna   *d* David Butler   *ph* Peverell Marley   *m* David Buttolph

Ronald Reagan, Patricia Neal, Jack Carson, Virginia Field

John Meade's Woman

US   1937   82m   bw
Paramount

A timber industrialist marries a farm girl.

Solemn star drama.

w Vincent Lawrence, Herman J. Mankiewicz   *d* Richard Wallace

Edward Arnold, Francine Larrimore, Gail Patrick, George Bancroft

'One more picture with a message. Edward Arnold's pictures are beginning to look alike.' – *Variety*

John Paul Jones

US   1959   126m   Technirama
Warner/Samuel Bronston

At the time of the American revolution a young Scotsman rises to great heights in the American navy.

Fragmented biopic with a succession of guest stars which turn it into a charade almost as silly as *The Story of Mankind*. On that level it is not unentertaining.

wd John Farrow   *ph* Michel Kelber   *m* Max Steiner

Robert Stack, Charles Coburn (as Benjamin Franklin), Bette Davis (as Catherine the Great), Marisa Pavan, Jean-Pierre Aumont, Peter Cushing, Bruce Cabot, Macdonald Carey

Johnny Allegro *

US   1949   81m   bw
Columbia (Irving Starr)
GB title: *Hounded*

A private eye eliminates a counterfeiter and marries his wife.

Cheeky variation on the plot of *Gilda*, with Macready repeating his role; later stages borrow from *The Most Dangerous Game*. All mildly diverting.

w Karen de Wolf, Guy Endore, James Edward Grant   *d* Ted Tetzlaff   *ph* Joseph Biroc   *m* George Duning

George Raft, George Macready, Nina Foch, Will Geer, Ivan Triesault

'Without any particular distinction, but certainly not boring.' – *Richard Mallett, Punch*

Johnny Angel *

US   1945   79m   bw
RKO (William L. Pereira)
V*, L

A seaman solves the mystery of his father's ship, found empty and adrift in the Gulf of Mexico.

Very watchable mystery with plenty of plot twists and efficient presentation.

w Steve Fisher   *d* Edwin L. Marin   *ph* Harry J. Wild   *m* Leigh Harline

George Raft, Claire Trevor, Signe Hasso, Lowell Gilmore, Hoagy Carmichael, Marvin Miller

Johnny Apollo

US   1940   93m   bw
TCF (Harry Joe Brown)
V*

A well-heeled young man turns crook.

Moderate crime melo, impeccably turned out.

w Philip Dunne, Rowland Brown   *d* Henry Hathaway   *ph* Arthur Miller   *md* Alfred Newman   *m* Cyril Mockridge

Tyrone Power, Dorothy Lamour, Edward Arnold, Lloyd Nolan, Charles Grapewin, Lionel Atwill, Marc Lawrence, Jonathan Hale

'There was temptation in her helpless silence – and then torment!'

Johnny Belinda **
US   1948   103m   bw
Warner (Jerry Wald)
V*

In a remote fishing community, a deaf mute girl is raped and the sympathetic local doctor is suspected of being the father of her baby.

Melodrama of the old school which in 1948 seemed oddly to mark a new permissiveness and made a big star of Jane Wyman; the production and locations were also persuasive.

w Irmgard von Cube, Allen Vincent   *play* Elmer Harris   *d* Jean Negulesco   *ph* Ted McCord   *md* Leo F. Forbstein   *m* Max Steiner   *ad* Robert Haas

Jane Wyman, Lew Ayres, Charles Bickford, Agnes Moorehead, Stephen McNally, Jan Sterling, Rosalind Ivan, Mabel Paige

'Hollywood has tried something dangerously different here, and succeeded in making a powerful and sensitive job of it.' – *Observer*

'An atmosphere in which the hokey, tearjerking elements are used for more than mere pathos – an example of technique over subject matter.' – *Pauline Kael, 70s*

AA: Jane Wyman

AAN: best picture; script; Jean Negulesco; Ted McCord; Max Steiner; Lew Ayres; Charles Bickford; Agnes Moorehead; art direction

Johnny Come Lately *
US   1943   97m   bw
Cagney Productions (William Cagney)
V, V*, L
GB title: *Johnny Vagabond*

A travelling newspaperman is jailed for vagrancy in a small town and stays to expose corrupt politicians.

A turn-of-the-century folksy drama seemed an odd choice for a Cagney independent production, and it was not very persuasively made, but the star produced moments of his old charisma.

w John Van Druten   *novel* McLeod's Folly by Louis Bromfield   *d* William K. Howard   *ph* Theodor Sparkuhl   *m* Leigh Harline

James Cagney, *Grace George*, Marjorie Main, Marjorie Lord, Hattie McDaniel, Edward McNamara, Bill Henry, Robert Barrat, George Cleveland, Margaret Hamilton, Lucien Littlefield, Irving Bacon

'The kind of business that might result if Jimmy Cagney, the immortal Hollywood movie star, had returned to play the lead in the annual production of his old high school's Masque and Film Club.' – *John T. McManus*

'The film does show a fatal commercial uneasiness and, I half suspect, radical loss or atrophy of cinematic judgment. But . . . there is a general ambience of hope and pleasure about the production which, regrettably, loses its glow.' – *James Agee*

AAN: Leigh Harline

Johnny Comes Flying Home
US   1946   65m   bw
Aubrey Schenck/TCF

Three discharged flyers build an air freight company.

The Best Years of Our Lives it isn't, not on this budget, but it clumsily expresses some of the same concerns.

w Jack Andrews, George Bricker   *d* Ben Stoloff

Richard Crane, Faye Marlowe, Martha Stewart, Roy Roberts, Henry Morgan

Johnny Concho
US   1956   84m   bw
UA/Kent (Frank Sinatra)

A coward runs Cripple Creek because he has a gunfighter brother, but when the latter is shot another gunman takes over.

Unexpected small-scale Western, pleasantly made but no *High Noon*.

w David P. Harmon, Don McGuire   *d* Don McGuire   *ph* William Mellor   *m* Nelson Riddle

Frank Sinatra, *William Conrad*, Phyllis Kirk, Wallace Ford, John Qualen

Johnny Cool *
US   1963   101m   bw
UA/Chrislaw (William Asher)

A Sicilian bandit is sent to the US on a mission of vengeance.

Chilling gangster thriller, the callousness of which is apparently meant to be counterpointed by the humorous cameo appearances of several well-known faces. This does not work.

w Joseph Landon   *novel* John McPartland   *d* William Asher   *ph* Sam Leavitt   *m* Billy May

Henry Silva, Elizabeth Montgomery, Jim Backus, Marc Lawrence, John McGiver, Sammy Davis Jnr, Mort Sahl, Telly Savalas, Joseph Calleia, Robert Armstrong, Douglass Dumbrille, Elisha Cook Jnr

'Organized crime has never been so disorganized!'

Johnny Dangerously
US   1984   90m   DeLuxe
TCF/Edgewood (Michael Hertzberg)
V, V*

A boy takes up crime to pay for an operation for his ailing mother.

1930s gangster send-up which fails to register, and is filled with unnecessary excesses.

w Norman Steinberg, Bernie Kukoff, Harry Colomby, Jeff Harris   *d* Amy Heckerling   *ph* David M. Walsh   *m* John Morris   *pd* Joseph R. Jennings   *ed* Pembroke J. Herring

Michael Keaton, Joe Piscopo, Marilu Henner, Maureen Stapleton, Peter Boyle, Griffin Dunne, Richard Dmitri, Glynnis O'Connor, Dom DeLuise, Ray Walston

'The material given all of them just gets worse and worse.' – *Variety*

Johnny Dark
US   1954   85m   Technicolor
U-I (William Alland)

A motor company produces a new sports car designed by an employee, who drives it in a race.

Competent, unremarkable action melodrama tailor-made for its star.

w Franklin Coen   *d* George Sherman   *ph* Carl Guthrie   *m* Hans Salter

Tony Curtis, Piper Laurie, Don Taylor, Paul Kelly, Ilka Chase, Sidney Blackmer

Johnny Doesn't Live Here Any More
US   1944   77m   bw
Monogram (Maurice and Frank King)

A girl using her army boyfriend's Washington flat finds that he has loaned keys to several friends.

Tepid farce which presumably amused at the time.

w Philip Yordan, John H. Kafka   *d* Joe May

Simone Simon, James Ellison, William Terry, Minna Gombell, Chick Chandler, Alan Dinehart, Robert Mitchum

Johnny Doughboy
US   1943   64m   bw
Republic

A teenage girl star runs away, falls for a middle-aged playwright, and joins an acting troupe called The Hollywood Victory Caravan.

Curious attempt to make a child star grow up, with a supporting cast laced with others of her ilk.

w Lawrence Kimble   *d* John H. Auer   *m* Walter Scharf

Jane Withers, Henry Wilcoxon, William Demarest, Ruth Donnelly; and Bobby Breen, Baby Sandy, Butch and Buddy, Spanky McFarland, etc

AAN: Walter Scharf

'The flaming drama of a high-born beauty who blindly loved the most icy-hearted big shot gangland ever knew!'

Johnny Eager *
US   1942   107m   bw
MGM (John W. Considine)

A gangster makes a play for a society girl.

Well-made, rather unattractive gangster melodrama.

w John Lee Mahin, James Edward Grant   *d* Mervyn Le Roy   *ph* Harold Rosson   *m* Bronislau Kaper

Robert Taylor, Van Heflin, Lana Turner, Edward Arnold, Robert Sterling, Patricia Dane, Glenda Farrell, Henry O'Neill

AA: Van Heflin

Johnny Frenchman
GB   1945   111m   bw
Ealing (S. C. Balcon)

Rivalry between the fishermen of Cornwall and Brittany prevents the course of true love from running smooth.

Rhubarbing extras and studio sets make this an unreal and disappointing Ealing melodrama, and all the actors look helpless.

w T. E. B. Clarke   *d* Charles Frend   *ph* Roy Kellino   *m* Clifton Parker

Françoise Rosay, Tom Walls, Patricia Roc, Paul Dupuis, Ralph Michael, Frederick Piper, Arthur Hambling

Johnny Got His Gun
US   1971   111m   colour
World Entertainments Ltd (Bruce Campbell)
V*, L

In 1918 a soldier is so badly wounded as to lose arms, legs, eyes, ears, mouth and nose, and begs his doctors to kill him.

A horrifying and fascinating premise turns out to have nowhere to go, at least not in this talky treatment which the author has nurtured too long.

wd Dalton Trumbo   *ph* Jules Brenner   *m* Jerry Fielding

Timothy Bottoms, Jason Robards Jnr, Marsha Hunt, Donald Sutherland, Kathy Fields, Diane Varsi

Johnny Guitar *
US   1953   110m   Trucolor
Republic (Nicholas Ray)
V*, L, S

In old Arizona, the proprietress of a gambling saloon stakes a claim to valuable land and incurs the enmity of a lady banker.

Weird Freudian Western notable for a running catfight between its lady protagonists; the title character is decidedly secondary. Not exactly a good movie, but memorable because it's almost always over the top.

w Philip Yordan   *novel* Roy Chanslor   *d* Nicholas Ray   *ph* Harry Stradling   *m* Victor Young

Joan Crawford, Mercedes McCambridge, Sterling Hayden, Ernest Borgnine, Ward Bond, John Carradine, Scott Brady

'A very rum western, with cockeyed feminist attitudes.' – *New Yorker,* 1975

Johnny Handsome
US 1989 94m Technicolor
Guild/Carolco Pictures/Guber-Peters (Charles Roven)
V, V*, L, S

A deformed petty criminal undergoes surgery to give him a new appearance.

A thriller of betrayal and double-cross that never fully engages the attention.

w Ken Friedman *novel The Three Worlds of Johnny Handsome* by John Godey *d* Walter Hill *ph* Matthew F. Leonetti *m* Ry Cooder *pd* Gene Rudolf *ed* Freeman Davies, Carmel Davies, Donn Aron

Mickey Rourke, Ellen Barkin, Elizabeth McGovern, Morgan Freeman, Forest Whitaker, Lance Henriksen, Scott Wilson, David Schramm, Yvonne Bryceland

'A taut, violent, moody thriller.' – *Philip French, Observer*

'A faintly risible mess, torn between a dozen stools and never managing to settle squarely on any of them.' – *Tom Milne, MFB*

Johnny Holiday
US 1949 92m bw
United Artists (R. W. Alcorn)

A reform school boy becomes a goodie through devotion to his sergeant.

Sentimental mush.

w Jack Andrews, Willis Goldbeck, Frederick Stephani *d* Willis Goldbeck

William Bendix, Stanley Clements, Allen Martin Jnr, Herbert Newcomb, Hoagy Carmichael

Johnny in the Clouds: see *The Way to the Stars*

Johnny Nobody
GB 1960 88m bw Warwickscope
Columbia/Viceroy (Irving Allen, Albert Broccoli)
V*

A drunken Irish author challenges God to strike him dead for blasphemy. When an amnesiac shoots him, a nationwide religious controversy begins, but the deed is found to have a mercenary motive.

A mysterious rigmarole which irritates more than it entertains.

w Patrick Kirwan *story The Trial of Johnny Nobody* by Albert Z. Carr *d* Nigel Patrick *ph* Ted Moore *m* Ron Goodwin

Nigel Patrick, Aldo Ray, Yvonne Mitchell, William Bendix, Cyril Cusack, Niall MacGinnis, Bernie Winters, Noel Purcell, Jimmy O'Dea

'The more one thinks of it, the more one is amazed that anyone should have thought a plot and players as uniformly unlikely as these could have worked out satisfactorily.' – *Peter John Dyer, MFB*

Johnny O'Clock
US 1946 95m bw
Columbia

A gambler appears to be involved in the death of a crooked policeman, but a girl helps to clear him.

Tawdry material made palatable by surface slickness.

wd Robert Rossen *ph* Burnett Guffey

Dick Powell, Ellen Drew, Lee J. Cobb, Evelyn Keyes

Johnny One-Eye
US 1950 80m bw
United Artists (Benedict Bogeaus)

Two gangsters out to get each other are led together by a small girl and a dog.

Unpalatable mixture of violence and sentiment.

w Richard E. Landau *story* Damon Runyon *d* Robert Florey

Pat O'Brien, Wayne Morris, Dolores Moran, Gayle Reed

Johnny Rocco
US 1958 83m bw
Allied Artists

The small son of a gangster is affected by his father's notoriety.

Awful sentimental melodrama with tear-stained ending; for connoisseurs of cliché.

w James O'Hanlon, Samuel F. Roeca *d* Paul Landres

Richard Eyer, Stephen McNally, Coleen Gray, Russ Conway

'Their bullets talked where law stopped!'
Johnny Stool Pigeon
US 1949 75m bw
U-I (Aaron Rosenberg)

A detective releases a convict on condition that he leads him to a drug smuggling gang.

Competent low budget addition to the documentary police cycle.

w Robert L. Richards *d* William Castle *ph* Maury Gertsman *m* Milton Schwarzwald

Howard Duff, Shelley Winters, Dan Duryea, Gar Moore, Tony Curtis, John McIntire, Barry Kelley, Leif Erickson

'A Smooth Comedy...'
Johnny Suede *
US/Switzerland/France 1991 97m Fujicolor
Artificial Eye/Vega/Balthazar/Starr/Arena (Yoram Mandel, Ruth Waldburger)
V, V*

After a pair of suede shoes drops on top of a phone booth he's using, an ineffectual young man with an exaggerated quiff puts them on and tries to become a rock star.

Stylish exploration of pop style, although a certain tedium sets in before the end.

wd Tom DiCillo *ph* Joe DeSalvo *m* Jim Farmer, Link Wray *pd* Patricia Woodbridge *ed* Geraldine Peroni

Brad Pitt, Catherine Keener, Calvin Levels, Alison Moir, Nick Cave, Peter McRobbie, Ashley Gardner, Dennis Parlato, Ron Vawter, Tina Louise

'There are moments of quirky charm and humor in this odd, stylized fable.' – *Stephen Farber, Movieline*

Johnny Tiger
US 1966 102m colour
Nova Hook (John Hugh)
V*

A repressed schoolteacher learns to trust his feelings after working on an Indian reservation and encouraging a wild young half-breed Seminole to study.

Formulaic confrontational drama of minimal interest.

w Paul Crabtree, John Hugh *d* Paul Wendkos *ph* Charles Straumer *m* John Green *ed* Harry Coswick

Robert Taylor, Geraldine Brooks, Chad Everett, Brenda Scott, Marc Lawrence

Johnny Tremain
US 1957 81m Technicolor
Walt Disney
V*

In 1773 Boston an apprentice silversmith joins the Sons of Liberty and helps start the War of Independence.

Schoolbook history with little vitality.

w Tom Blackburn *novel* Esther Forbes *d* Robert Stevenson *ph* Charles B. Boyle *m* George Bruns

Hal Stalmaster, Luana Patten, Jeff York, Sebastian Cabot, Richard Beymer, Walter Sande

Johnny Trouble
US 1956 88m bw
Clarion (John H. Auer)

An elderly widow becomes involved with a boys' college and thinks she has found her lost grandson.

Sentimental, whimsical star vehicle.

w Charles O'Neal, David Lord *d* John H. Auer *ph* Peverell Marley *m* Frank de Vol

Ethel Barrymore, Stuart Whitman, Cecil Kellaway, Carolyn Jones, Jesse White

Johnny Vagabond: see *Johnny Come Lately*

The Johnstown Flood *
US 1926 70m approx (24 fps) bw silent
Fox

A construction worker is warned by his girlfriend of an approaching flood, in which she dies.

Curious melodrama with mild spectacle.

w Edfrid Bingham, Robert Lord *d* Irving Cummings

George O'Brien, Janet Gaynor (her first film), Paul Panzer, George Harris

The Joker Is Wild *
US 1957 126m bw Vistavision
Paramount/Charles Vidor

Joe E. Lewis, a twenties night-club singer, loses his voice after an attack by gangsters, and becomes a comedian.

Reasonably lively showbiz biopic in jaundiced vein; good atmosphere but far too long.

w Oscar Saul *book* Art Cohn *d* Charles Vidor *ph* Daniel L. Fapp *m* Walter Scharf

Frank Sinatra, Mitzi Gaynor, Eddie Albert, Jeanne Crain, Beverly Garland, Jackie Coogan, Ted de Corsia

AA: song 'All the Way' (*m* Jimmy Van Heusen, *ly* Sammy Cahn)

The Jokers **
GB 1967 126m Technicolor
Universal/Adastra/Gildor/Scimitar (Maurice Foster, Ben Arbeid)

Two young brothers in London society plan to create a sensation by borrowing (and replacing) the crown jewels.

Bright suspense comedy which sums up the swinging London era pretty well and is generally amusing though it finally lacks aplomb.

w Dick Clement, Ian La Frenais *d* Michael Winner *ph* Ken Hodges *m* Johnny Pearson

Michael Crawford, Oliver Reed, Harry Andrews, *James Donald,* Daniel Massey, Michael Hordern, Gabriella Licudi, Frank Finlay, Warren Mitchell, Rachel Kempson, Peter Graves

A Jolly Bad Fellow *
GB 1964 95m bw
British Lion/Pax/Tower/Michael Balcon (Donald Taylor)
US title: *They All Died Laughing*

A brash chemistry don tries a new poison on his enemies.

Interesting but finally irritating comedy of murders with a punnish rather than a donnish script and only moments of genuine sub-Ealing hilarity.

w Robert Hamer, Donald Taylor   *novel Don Among the Dead Men* by C. E. Vulliamy   *d* Don Chaffey *ph* Gerald Gibbs   *m* John Barry

Leo McKern, Janet Munro, Maxine Audley, Duncan Macrae, Dennis Price, Miles Malleson, Leonard Rossiter

Jolson Sings Again **
US   1949   96m   Technicolor
Columbia (Sidney Buchman)
V, V*, L

Al Jolson's later career and second marriage to a nurse he met while entertaining troops in World War II.

Breezy, routine, rather empty sequel to the following.

w Sidney Buchman   *d* Henry Levin   *ph* William Snyder   *md* Morris Stoloff, George Duning

Larry Parks, Barbara Hale, William Demarest, Ludwig Donath, Bill Goodwin, Tamara Shayne, Myron McCormick

'Just relax and enjoy yourself.' – *Daily Express*

'I love it now – every last sentimental showbiz cliché, every oversung song.' – *Daily Telegraph, 1969*

† 3rd biggest moneyspinner of 1946, after *The Best Years of Our Lives* and *Duel in the Sun*

AAN: Sidney Buchman; William Snyder; Morris Stoloff, George Duning

The Jolson Story ****
US   1946   129m   Technicolor
Columbia (Sidney Skolsky)
V*, L

Asa Yoelson, son of a cantor, becomes Al Jolson, the great entertainer of the twenties; but showbiz success brings marital difficulties.

Whitewashed biopic in impeccable Hollywood style, with everything working shamelessly right, a new star in the leading role, perfect if unambitious production values, and a deluge of the best songs ever written.

w Stephen Longstreet   *d* Alfred E. Green, Joseph H. Lewis *ph* Joseph Walker   *md* Morris Stoloff   *ed* William Lyon

Larry Parks (using Jolson's own voice), *William Demarest, Evelyn Keyes, Ludwig Donath, Tamara Shayne, Bill Goodwin, Scotty Beckett,* John Alexander

'I have nothing in the world against this picture except that at least half of it seemed to me enormously tiresome.' – *James Agee*

AA: Morris Stoloff

AAN: Joseph Walker; Larry Parks; William Demarest; William Lyon

'Everyone's book is now everyone's motion picture!'
Jonathan Livingston Seagull
US   1973   114m   DeLuxe   Panavision
Paramount/JLS Partnership/Hall Bartlett
V, V*, S

The life of a seagull who aims to fly faster than any of his peers and eventually arrives in a perfect world.

Weird 'family' fantasy based on a phenomenally successful book which clearly could not translate easily to the screen. The bird photography is much more successful than the mysticism.

w Richard Bach   *novel* Richard Bach   *d* Hall Bartlett   *ph Jack Couffer   ph* Boris Leven   *m* Neil Diamond, Lee Holdridge

'A parable couched in the form of a nature film of overpowering beauty and strength in which, perhaps to our horror, we are forced to recognize ourselves in a seagull obsessed with the heights.' – *Michael Korda*

'It may be that the creature best qualified to review it is another seagull.' – *Benny Green, Punch*

'If one must spend two hours following the adventures of a bird, far better that the hero be Donald Duck.' – *Jay Cocks, Time*

'The sort of garbage that only a seagull could love.' – *Judith Crist*

AAN: Jack Couffer

The Jones Family
Less human, more farcical than the Hardy films (qv), this series was TCF's second feature answer to MGM's money-makers, and pleased a lot of people at the time. Pop was Jed Prouty, Mom was Spring Byington, Grandma was Florence Roberts, and the youngsters included Kenneth Howell, George Ernest, Billy Mahan, June Carlson and June Lang. The first script was from a play by Katharine Cavanaugh, and the principal director was Frank Strayer.

1936: EVERY SATURDAY NIGHT, EDUCATING FATHER, BACK TO NATURE
1937: OFF TO THE RACES, BORROWING TROUBLE, HOT WATER
1938: LOVE ON A BUDGET, TRIP TO PARIS, SAFETY IN NUMBERS, DOWN ON THE FARM
1939: EVERYBODY'S BABY, QUICK MILLIONS, THE JONES FAMILY IN HOLLYWOOD, TOO BUSY TO WORK
1940: ON THEIR OWN

† An earlier series with different actors was abandoned after two episodes: *Young as You Feel* (1931), *Business and Pleasure* (1932).

'The epic love story in which everybody has a great role and a big part.'
Joseph Andrews
GB   1977   104m   Eastmancolor
UA/Woodfall (Neil Hartley)

Adventures of a naïve 18th-century footman.

Woebegone attempt to restage *Tom Jones*.

w Allan Scott, Chris Bryant   *d* Tony Richardson *ph* David Watkin   *m* John Addison   *pd* Michael Annals

Peter Firth, Ann-Margret, Michael Hordern, Beryl Reid, Jim Dale, Peter Bull, John Gielgud, Hugh Griffith, Timothy West, Wendy Craig, Peggy Ashcroft, James Villiers, Karen Dotrice, Ronald Pickup

'Even the incidental pleasures cannot offset the sense of *déjà vu* which pervades this musty enterprise.' – *John Pym, MFB*

Josephine and Men
GB   1955   98m   Eastmancolor
Charter (John and Roy Boulting)

The three romances of a determined young woman.

Alarmingly thin, old-fashioned romantic comedy with all resolved in a country cottage. Nothing quite works, especially the colour.

w Nigel Balchin, Roy Boulting, Frank Harvey *d* Roy Boulting   *ph* Gilbert Taylor   *m* John Addison

Glynis Johns, *Jack Buchanan*, Donald Sinden, Peter Finch, Heather Thatcher, Ronald Squire

Josette
US   1938   73m   bw
TCF (Gene Markey)

A New Orleans coquette teases two men.

Very minor musical, well enough presented but adding up to almost nothing.

w James Edward Grant   *d* Allan Dwan   *ph* John Mescall   *m/ly* Harry Revel, Mack Gordon

Simone Simon, Don Ameche, Robert Young, Joan Davis, Bert Lahr, Paul Hurst, William Collier Snr, Lynn Bari, William Demarest

'Rollicking farce with music . . . a corking good entertainment.' – *Variety*

'The hunted has become the hunter. And there will be no mercy.'
Joshua Tree
US   1993   94m   Foto-Kem colour
Vision International (Illana Diamant, Andy Armstrong)
V, V*

A trucker escapes from prison, takes a female cop as hostage and goes to seek revenge on those who killed his partner and framed him for murder.

An action film with a familiar plot but also possessing a slight sense of irony, with a little bow along the way to Bogart and a violent confrontation with Chinese crooks straight out of a Hong Kong movie.

w Steven Pressfield   *d* Vic Armstrong   *ph* Dan Turrett   *m* Joel Goldsmith   *pd* John J. Moore *ed* Paul Morton

Dolph Lundgren, George Segal, Kristian Alfonso, Geoffrey Lewis, Bert Remsen, Michelle Phillips

'Serviceable action-suspense pic.' – *Sight and Sound*

Jour de Fête ***
France   1948   87m   bw
Francinex (Fred Orain)
V, V*, L

A village postman sees a film about the efficiency of the American postal service and decides to smarten himself up.

First, and some say best, of Tati's comedy vehicles: two-thirds superb local colour, one-third hilarious slapstick.

w Jacques Tati, Henri Marquet   *d* Jacques Tati *ph* Jacques Mercanton   *m* Jean Yatove

Jacques Tati, Guy Decomble, Paul Fankeur, Santa Relli

'You could watch it with a bout of toothache and it would make you laugh.' – *Daily Express*

'It is not progressive; it won't be a landmark in the history of the cinema; but it gives me more pleasure than any film for the last five years.' – *Dilys Powell*

† A reissue version had colour items hand-painted in each frame, and proved quite effective.

Le Jour Se Lève ***
France   1939   95m   bw
Sigma
aka: *Daybreak*

A murderer is besieged by police in his attic room, remembers his past through the night, and shoots himself.

A model of French poetic realism, and a much-praised film which was almost destroyed when it was bought for an American remake (*The Long Night*).

w Jacques Viot, Jacques Prévert   *d* Marcel Carné *ph* Curt Courant, Philippe Agostini, André Bac *m* Maurice Jaubert   *ad* Alexander Trauner

Jean Gabin, Jules Berry, Arletty, Jacqueline Laurent

'The man walks about his room, moves a few things, lies on his bed, looks out of the window, chain-smokes . . . and one is genuinely interested in him all the time (remembering afterwards that there exist directors who contrive to be boring even when they use fifteen characters in a motor car chase crackling with revolver shots).' – *Richard Mallett, Punch*

Le Journal de Lady M: see *The Diary of Lady M*

Journal d'un Curé de Campagne: see *The Diary of a Country Priest*

Le Journal d'une Femme de Chambre: see *The Diary of a Chambermaid*

Journal of a Crime
US   1934   65m   bw
Warner

A woman shoots her husband's mistress and gets amnesia before she can confess.

Melodramatic farrago which entertains by its very excesses.

w F. Hugh Herbert, Charles Kenyon   play Jacques Deval   d William Keighley

Ruth Chatterton, Adolphe Menjou, Claire Dodd, Douglass Dumbrille, George Barbier

'High in sympathetic interest and force.' – Variety

Une Journée Bien Remplie: see A Full Day's Work

The Journey
US   1959   125m   Technicolor
MGM/Alby (Anatole Litvak)

During the 1956 Hungarian uprising, a busload of international passengers is detained overnight by a Russian major.

Pretentious, predictable and dull multi-melodrama peopled by uninteresting characters; different handling might have made a Casablanca of it.

w George Tabori   d Anatole Litvak   ph Jack Hildyard   m Georges Auric

Yul Brynner, Deborah Kerr, Jason Robards Jnr, Anouk Aimée, Robert Morley, E. G. Marshall, Anne Jackson, David Kossoff, Kurt Kasznar, Gerard Oury

'Ten minutes of this and we know where we are: we are back in the 1930s with Alfred Hitchcock and that glamorous band of international characters trapped in Mitteleuropa.' – Steven Marcus

Journey Back to Oz *
US   1964 (released 1974)   90m   colour
Norm Prescott and Lou Scheimer/Filmation
V*

Dorothy makes a return journey over the rainbow to fight the wicked witch's sister.

Competent cartoon version of Frank Baum themes from The Wizard of Oz.

d Hal Sutherland

voices of Liza Minnelli, Milton Berle, Ethel Merman, Margaret Hamilton, Mickey Rooney, Paul Ford

Journey for Margaret *
US   1942   81m   bw
MGM (B. P. Fineman)
V*

An American correspondent brings home an orphan from the London blitz.

Efficient tearful propaganda which coincidentally made a star of little Margaret O'Brien.

w David Hertz, William Ludwig   book William L. White   d W. S. Van Dyke   ph Ray June   m Franz Waxman

Robert Young, Laraine Day, Margaret O'Brien, Billy Severn, Fay Bainter, Signe Hasso, Nigel Bruce, Halliwell Hobbes

Journey into Autumn *
Sweden   1954   86m   bw
Sandrews (Rune Waldekrantz)
V*
original title: Kvinnodrøm

Two business women visiting Gothenburg have difficult relationships to settle.

Moody, impressionist sex drama which succeeds by fits and starts.

wd Ingmar Bergman   ph Hilding Bladh

Eva Dahlbeck, Harriet Andersson, Gunnar Bjornstrand, Ulf Palme, Inga Landgre, Naima Wifstrand

'Scenes of austere anti-romanticism and painful irony.' – Peter John Dyer, MFB

Journey into Fear ***
US   1942   71m   bw
RKO (Orson Welles)
V*, L

A munitions expert finds himself in danger from assassins in Istanbul, and has to be smuggled home.

Highly enjoyable impressionist melodrama supervised by Orson Welles and full of his touches and excesses.

w Joseph Cotten, Orson Welles   novel Eric Ambler   d Norman Foster (and Orson Welles)   ph Karl Struss   md Constantin Bakaleinikoff   m Roy Webb

Joseph Cotten, Dolores del Rio, Jack Moss, Orson Welles, Ruth Warrick, Agnes Moorehead

'Brilliant atmosphere, the nightmare of pursuit, eccentric encounters on the way, and when the shock comes it leaps at eye and ear.' – William Whitebait

† A 1976 remake, much heralded, was for obscure legal reasons hardly seen. Directed by Daniel Mann for New World, it starred Zero Mostel, Shelley Winters, Stanley Holloway, Vincent Price, Donald Pleasence, Sam Waterston, Joseph Wiseman, Scott Marlowe and Yvette Mimieux.

Journey into Light
US   1951   87m   bw
TCF/Joseph Bernhard

A minister loses his faith, becomes a derelict, and is reformed by a blind girl.

An old-fashioned tract in pictures. Has to be seen to be believed, but quite nicely made.

w Stephanie Nordli, Irving Schulman   d Stuart Heisler   m Paul Dunlap

Sterling Hayden, Viveca Lindfors, Thomas Mitchell, H. B. Warner, Ludwig Donath, Jane Darwell, Charles Evans

'Slow, inept, and often extremely embarrassing.' – MFB

Journey of Hope *
Switzerland   1990   110m   colour
Mainline/Catpics/Condor/SRG/RTSI/Film Four (Alfi Sinniger, Peter Fueter)
V, V*, L
original title: Reise der Hoffnung

A Turkish father and mother and their young son, part of a group of illegal immigrants abandoned by their guide, try to make their way across a mountain pass into Switzerland.

Moving, almost documentary account of refugees seeking a better life.

w Xavier Koller, Feride Çiçekoğlu, Heike Hubert   d Xavier Koller   ph Elemer Ragalyi   ad Luigi Pelizzo, Kathrin Brunner   ed Galip Iyitanir

Necmettin Čobanoğlu, Nur Srer, Emin Sivas, Erdinç Akbas, Yaman Okay, Yasar Gner, Hseyin Mete, Yaman Tarcan

AA: best foreign film

The Journey of Natty Gann
US   1985   105m   colour
Walt Disney (Michael Lobell)
V*, L

During the Chicago depression, a girl follows her father west and hitch-hikes across America.

A kind of human Lassie Come Home: doggedly watchable but not inspiring, especially since it was shot in Canada.

w Jeanne Rosenberg   d Jeremy Kagan   ph Richard Bush   m James Horner

Meredith Salenger, John Cusack, Ray Wise, Scatman Crothers

'Cut to an hour, it would make a fine Disney telepic.' – Variety

AAN: costumes (Albert Wolsky)

Journey to Italy: see Voyage to Italy

Journey to Shiloh
US   1967   101m   Techniscope
Universal

Seven young Texans leave home to fight in the Civil War.

Episodic Western which failed in its ambition to reach epic stature.

w Gene Coon   novel Fields of Honour by Will Henry   d William Hale

James Caan, Michael Sarrazin, Brenda Scott, Paul Petersen, Don Stroud, Michael Burns, Michael Vincent, Harrison Ford, John Doucette, Noah Beery Jnr

Journey to the Center of the Earth ***
US   1959   132m   DeLuxe   Cinemascope
TCF (Charles Brackett)
V, V*, L, S

An Edinburgh professor and assorted colleagues follow an explorer's trail down an extinct Icelandic volcano to the Earth's centre.

Enjoyable hokum which gets more and more fantastic but only occasionally misses its footing; it ends splendidly with the team being catapulted out of Stromboli on a tide of lava.

w Walter Reisch, Charles Brackett   novel Jules Verne   d Henry Levin   ph Leo Tover   m Bernard Herrmann   ad Lyle R. Wheeler, Franz Bachelin, Herman A. Blumenthal

James Mason, Arlene Dahl, Pat Boone, Peter Ronson, Diane Baker, Thayer David

'The attraction of a Jules Verne fantasy . . . is in the endearing contrast between the wildest adventures and the staidest Victorian propriety on the part of those undergoing them . . . There is about the whole film a good-natured enjoyment of its own excesses.' – Penelope Houston

AAN: art direction

'Caught in a fantastic time trap.'
Journey to the Center of Time
US   1967   82m   colour
Ember/Flamingo/Borealis-Dorad (Ray Dorn, David L. Hewitt)

Scientists inadvertently send themselves to the year 5000 AD, at a time of a war with aliens, and then travel to 1,000,000 BC where they are attacked by monsters.

Low-budget, unexciting sci-fi, with the prehistoric world represented by one medium-sized lizard, dry ice and coloured lights.

w David Prentiss   d David L. Hewitt   ph Robert Caramico   pd Edward D. Engoron   sp Modern Film Effects   ed Bill Welburn

Scott Brady, Gigi Perreau, Anthony Eisley, Abraham Sofaer, Poupee Gamin

Journey to the Far Side of the Sun *
GB   1969   99m   DeLuxe   Cinemascope
Universal/Century 21 Productions (Gerry Anderson)
aka: Doppelgänger

An astronaut on a mission to a hitherto undetected planet discovers it to be an exact duplicate of Earth, and his own double returns in his place.

Intriguing, impeccably produced, but rather dull science fiction.

w Gerry and Sylvia Anderson, Donald James   d Robert Parrish   ph John Read   m Barry Gray   sp Harry Oakes   models Derek Meddings

Ian Hendry, Roy Thinnes, Patrick Wymark, Lynn Loring, Herbert Lom, George Sewell, Ed Bishop

Journey to the South (dubbed)
Argentina/Yugoslavia 1988 90m colour
Art Film 80/Smart Egg/CFS (Jorge Estrada Mora, Aleksandar Stojanović)
V
original title: El Camino del Sur

In the 1920s, a young Yugoslavian girl thinks she is marrying a wealthy European who lives in Buenos Aires, but discovers instead that she has been sold to work in a brothel.

Episodic treatment of the once-flourishing white slave trade in East European women, a colourful but unconvincing melodrama.

w Juan Bautista Stagnaro, Elida Cecconi story Beda Docampo Feijoo d Juan Bautista Stagnaro ph Karpo A. Godina m Zoran Simjanović ad Nikola Lazarevski, Santijago Eider ed Enrique Muzio, Snezana Ivanović

Mirjana Joković, Adrian Ghio, Zarko Lausević, Mira Furlan, Osvaldo Santoro

Journey Together *
GB 1944 95m bw
RAF Film Unit (John Boulting)
V*

Trainee pilots receive instruction in England and America before going on their first bombing mission.

Modest wartime semi-documentary, pleasingly done.

w Terence Rattigan d John Boulting ph Harry Waxman m Gordon Jacob pd John Howell

Richard Attenborough, Jack Watling, David Tomlinson, Edward G. Robinson, Hugh Wakefield, Sebastian Shaw, Ronald Adam, Bessie Love

'It has a natural dignity as well as a natural fun.' – Listener

'One of the most realistic and brilliant films of the war in the air.' – News Chronicle

Journey's End *
GB/US 1930 120m bw
Gainsborough/Welsh-Pearson/Tiffany-Stahl (George Pearson)

France 1917: personal tensions mount as men die in the trenches.

Primitive early sound version (made in Hollywood because of better equipment) of a justly celebrated play first performed a year earlier. Cinematically uninteresting, with acting generally over the top, but it kept Whale and Clive in Hollywood where they shortly collaborated on Frankenstein.

w Joseph Moncure March, Gareth Gundrey play R. C. Sherriff d James Whale ph Benjamin Kline m none ad Harvey Libbert ed Claude Berkeley

Colin Clive, Ian MacLaren, David Manners, Billy Bevan, Anthony Bushell, Robert Adair

'No crystal gazing required to forecast a big measure of success.' – Variety

'It has been transferred to the screen with the greatest possible tact and discretion.' – James Agate

'Hollywood has produced its first sex-appeal-less film. Mr George Pearson is to be congratulated on his restraint.' – Punch

'Almost painfully English . . . I cannot believe that the strangulated emotions which resulted can have meant much to audiences outside the English-speaking world.' – Basil Wright, 1972

† It was the first Anglo-American co-production.

Joy House
France 1964 98m bw Franscope
MGM (Jacques Bar)
V*
aka: The Love Cage

The husband of a wealthy American woman in France tries to kill her boyfriend.

Weird hothouse drama, an unsuccessful attempt to combine French and American styles.

w René Clément, Pascal Jardin, Charles Williams novel Day Keene d René Clément ph Henri Decae m Lalo Schifrin ad Jean Andre ed Fedora Zincone

Jane Fonda, Alain Delon, Lola Albright

Joy in the Morning
US 1965 103m Metrocolor
MGM (Henry T. Weinstein)

Early episodes in the marriage of a poor teenage student.

Glutinous romantic drama, quite well made.

w Sally Benson, Alfred Hayes, Norman Lessing novel Betty Smith d Alex Segal ph Ellsworth Fredricks m Bernard Herrmann

Richard Chamberlain, Yvette Mimieux, Arthur Kennedy, Oscar Homolka, Joan Tetzel, Sidney Blackmer

'Between every mother and daughter there is a story that must be told.'

The Joy Luck Club
US 1993 139m Technicolor
Buena Vista/Hollywood Pictures (Wayne Wang, Amy Tan, Ronald Bass, Patrick Markey)
V*, L, S

The relationships of four Chinese-American daughters with their Chinese mothers are recalled.

A long, slick, mostly sentimental wallow in the past that fails to throw much light on the present or the future; it lacks the sense of culture clash and quirky humour evident in the director's earlier, low-budget films.

w Amy Tan, Ronald Bass novel Amy Tan d Wayne Wang ph Amir Mokri m Rachel Portman pd Donald Graham Burt ed Maysie Hoy

Kieu Chinh, Tsai Chin, France Nuyen, Lisa Lu, Ming-Na Wen, Tamlyn Tomita, Lauren Tom, Victor Wong

'Beautifully made and acted and emotionally moving into the bargain.' – Variety

'Delivers neither subtlety nor heart-warming ebullience. Everything is shoe-horned into the fake conflicts and resolutions of soap opera . . . If you go to this film with a date whom you want to impress with your sensitivity, bring onions.' – Adam Mars-Jones, Independent

Joy of Living *
US 1938 90m bw
RKO (Felix Young)
V*, L

A practical-minded Broadway songstress succumbs to the charms of an aristocratic freewheeler.

Zany romantic comedy, not quite zippy enough to make one forget its irritating archness, but socio-historically very interesting, in the mould of You Can't Take It with You.

w Gene Towne, Allan Scott, Graham Baker d Tay Garnett ph Joseph Walker md Frank Tours m/ly Jerome Kern, Dorothy Fields

Irene Dunne, Douglas Fairbanks Jnr, Alice Brady, Guy Kibbee, Lucille Ball, Eric Blore, Jean Dixon, Warren Hymer, Billy Gilbert

'Fair farce . . . bereft of sufficient novelty or comedy plot to sustain itself through an hour and a half of gags.' – Variety

Joyless Street *
Germany 1925 139m (24 fps) bw silent
Sofar Film
V*, L
original title: Die Freudlose Gasse

Problems of the inhabitants of a street in Vienna after World War I.

Realistic but studio-set melodrama which brought its director and Greta Garbo to international fame. In itself the film begins by stimulating and ends by boring.

w Willy Haas novel Hugo Bettauer d G. W. Pabst ph Guido Seeber, Curt Oertel, Robert Lach

Asta Nielsen, Werner Krauss, Greta Garbo, Valeska Gert, Agnes Esterhazy

'Moments of searing pain, of mental anguish, of sheer unblemished beauty.' – Paul Rotha, The Film Till Now

Joyriders
GB 1988 96m Technicolor
Pathé/Granada/British Screen/Little Bird/Film Four (Emma Hayter)

A battered wife runs away with a petty criminal.

Road movie that, for all its squalor, never comes near to reality.

w Andy Smith story Aisling Walsh, Andy Smith d Aisling Walsh ph Gabriel Beristain pd Leigh Malone ed Thomas Schwalm

Patricia Kerrigan, Andrew Connolly, Billie Whitelaw, David Kelly, John Kavanagh, Deirdre Donoghue, Tracy Peacock, Rolf Saxon, Otto Jarman

Ju Dou **
Japan/China 1990 94m Eastmancolor
ICA/Tokuma Shoten/China Film/X'ian Film Studio (Shigeru Mori, Hiroyuki Kato, Zhao Hangao)
V, V*

An impotent old man succeeds in revenging himself on his adulterous wife and her lover, his nephew, through their son.

A tragic folk-tale, colourfully told.

w Liu Heng story Fuxi Fuxi by Liu Heng d Zhang Yimou, Yang Fengliang ph Gu Changwei, Yang Lun m Zhao Jiping ad Cao Jiuping, Xia Rujin ed Du Yuan

Li Wei, Gong Li, Li Baotian, Zhang Yi, Zheng Jian

'A film where the images do the talking, and almost everything they have to say is deeply cautionary.' – MFB

† The film was banned in China.

AAN: best foreign film

'See it now! Remember it always!'A story so momentous it required six Academy Award stars and a cast of 1,186 players!'

Juarez **
US 1939 132m bw
Warner (Hal. B. Wallis, Henry Blanke)
V*

A revolutionary leader causes the downfall of Emperor Maximilian of Mexico.

Spectacular historical drama with many fine moments which do not quite coalesce into a dramatic whole, chiefly owing to the lack of a single viewpoint.

w John Huston, Wolfgang Reinhardt, Aeneas Mackenzie d William Dieterle ph Tony Gaudio m Erich Wolfgang Korngold

Brian Aherne, Bette Davis, Paul Muni, Claude Rains, John Garfield, Donald Crisp, Gale Sondergaard, Joseph Calleia, Gilbert Roland, Henry O'Neill, Pedro de Cordoba, Montagu Love, Harry Davenport

'With such potent box office values, its success at theatres seems assured.' – Variety

'A million dollars' worth of ballroom sets, regimentals, gauze shots and whiskers.' – Otis Ferguson

'Dramatically by far the most effective of Warners' biographical films of the thirties.' – Graham Greene

'Muni's big-star solemn righteousness is like a dose of medicine.' – New Yorker, 1977

† Based vaguely on two novels: *The Phantom Crown* by Bertita Harding, and *Maximilian and Carlotta* by Franz Werfel.

†† According to Brian Aherne the film was to have been called *The Phantom Crown*, but Muni's contract enabled him to insist that the name of his character should appear in the title.

AAN: Brian Aherne

Jubal
US 1955 101m Technicolor Cinemascope
Columbia (William Fadiman)
V*, L

A rancher's wife causes trouble when she falls in love with a wandering cowhand.

Solid sex Western, moderately interestingly done.

w Russell S. Hughes, Delmer Daves *novel Jubal Troop* by Paul Wellman d Delmer Daves ph Charles Lawton m David Raksin

Glenn Ford, Ernest Borgnine, Felicia Farr, Rod Steiger, Valerie French, Charles Bronson, Noah Beery Jnr

Jubilee *
GB 1978 104m colour
Whaley-Malin/Megalovision
V

Queen Elizabeth I is transported by her astrologer into the latter part of the 20th century, and is appalled by what she sees.

Outrageous dissection of modern urban life, full of black jokes: it has the right attitudes but is not free of a determination to shock at all costs.

w Derek Jarman and others d Derek Jarman ph Peter Middleton m Brian Eno

Jenny Runacre, Little Nell, Toyah Willcox, Jordan, Hermine Demoriane

'One of the most intelligent and interesting films to be made in Britain in a long time.' – *Scott Meek, MFB*

Jubilee Trail *
US 1954 103m Trucolor
Republic (Joseph Kane)
V*

Jealousy and murder by covered wagon en route from New Orleans to the California gold fields.

Bumpy adventure melodrama, generally quite entertaining.

w Bruce Manning *novel* Gwen Bristow d Joseph Kane ph Jack Marta m Victor Young

Vera Hruba Ralston, Forrest Tucker, Joan Leslie, Pat O'Brien, John Russell, Ray Middleton

Judas Was a Woman: see *La Bête Humaine*

Judex **
France 1916 12 episodes totalling 5 hours approx
bw silent
Gaumont

A Robin Hood type crimefighter destroys the empire of an evil banker.

Stylishly enjoyable serial from the maker of *Les Vampires* and *Fantômas*.

w Arthur Bernade, Louis Feuillade d *Louis Feuillade*

René Creste, Musidora, Yvette Andreyor, Louis Leubas

† Another *Judex* serial was made in 1917, and in 1933 came a feature version directed by Maurice Champreux, with René Ferte. In 1963 Georges Franju directed another feature remake with Channing Pollock, and this was extremely well received.

'Enough laughs to make your head spin!'
Judge Priest *
US 1934 79m bw
Fox (Sol M. Wurtzel)
V*

A political judge sees fair play through a criminal case.

Mainly effective star vehicle.

w Dudley Nichols, Lamar Trotti *stories* Irvin S. Cobb d John Ford ph George Schneiderman m Samuel Kaylin

Will Rogers, Tom Brown, Anita Louise, *Henry B. Walthall*, David Landau, Rochelle Hudson

'A great part for Will Rogers and a box office bet.' – *Variety*

The Judge Steps Out *
US 1947 91m bw
RKO
V*
GB title: *Indian Summer*

A middle-aged judge leaves his wife and sets off on an aimless journey in the course of which he falls in love with a café proprietress.

A pleasing human story, simply told in a manner which at the time seemed more French than American.

w Boris Ingster, Alexander Knox d Boris Ingster ph Robert de Grasse m Constantin Bakaleinikoff

Alexander Knox, Ann Sothern, George Tobias, Sharyn Moffett

'The things you'll see and the things you'll feel are the things that will be part of you as long as you live!'
Judgment at Nuremberg **
US 1961 190m bw
UA/Roxlom (Stanley Kramer)
V*, L

A fictionalized version of the 1948 trial of the Nazi leaders for crimes against humanity.

Interminable, heavy-going dramatic documentary expanded from a succinct TV play into a courtroom marathon with philosophical asides. All good stuff, but too much of it.

w Abby Mann *play* Abby Mann d Stanley Kramer ph Ernest Laszlo m Ernest Gold pd Rudolph Sternad

Spencer Tracy, Marlene Dietrich, Burt Lancaster, Richard Widmark, *Maximilian Schell*, Judy Garland, Montgomery Clift, William Shatner, Edward Binns, Werner Klemperer, Torben Meyer, Alan Baxter, Ray Teal

'Some believe that by tackling such themes Kramer earns at least partial remission from criticism. How much? 20 per cent off for effort?' – *Stanley Kauffmann*

† Burt Lancaster replaced Laurence Olivier, who was originally cast.

AA: Abby Mann; Maximilian Schell

AAN: best picture; Stanley Kramer; Ernest Laszlo; Spencer Tracy; Judy Garland; Montgomery Clift

Judgment Deferred
GB 1951 88m bw
Group Three (John Baxter)

A collection of Dorset eccentrics brings to book the head of a dope smuggling ring who has framed one of their associates.

An unusual story can't compensate for stagey handling in this first disappointing production of a company set up by the National Film Finance Corporation to make low budget films with top talent.

w Geoffrey Orme, Barbara Emary, Walter Meade d John Baxter ph Arthur Grant m Kennedy Russell

Hugh Sinclair, Helen Shingler, Abraham Sofaer, Leslie Dwyer, Joan Collins, Harry Locke, Elwyn Brook Jones, Bransby Williams, Maire O'Neill, Harry Welchman

† This was an expanded remake of *Dosshouse*.

Judgment in Berlin
US 1988 96m Eastmancolor
Hobo/Bibo TV/January Enterprises/Sheen-Greenblatt (Joshua Sinclair, Ingrid Windisch)
V, V*, L

An East German is tried by an American court in Berlin after hijacking a Polish airliner.

Despite being based on an actual incident, this courtroom drama lacks conviction.

w Joshua Sinclair, Leo Penn *book* Herbert J. Stern d Leo Penn ph Gabor Pogany ad Jan Schlubach, Peter Alteneder ed Teddy Darvas

Martin Sheen, Sam Wanamaker, Max Gail, Juergen Heinrich, Heinz Hoenig, Carl Lumbly, Max Volkert Martens, Christine Rose, Sean Penn

Judith
US 1965 109m Technicolor Panavision
Paramount/Cumulus/Command (Kurt Unger)

In 1947 Israel, loyalists rescue the wife of an escaped war criminal and ask her to identify him, but she takes her own revenge.

Glowering kibbutz adventures, well enough made but adding up to neither one thing nor the other, and rather confusing to non-Jews.

w John Michael Hayes *story* Lawrence Durrell d Daniel Mann ph John Wilcox m Sol Kaplan pd Wilfrid Shingleton

Sophia Loren, Peter Finch, Jack Hawkins, Hans Verner, André Morell

'Tasteless and pretentious . . . Here is tragedy and glory being used as window dressing for some cheap little undercover-agent episodes and fleshly exploitation.' – *Judith Crist*

Judith of Bethulia
US 1913 42m (24 fps) bw silent
Biograph (D. W. Griffith)

A widow in a city attacked by the Assyrians courts their leader and beheads him.

Semi-biblical melodrama in Griffith's most Victorian style.

w Frank Woods d D. W. Griffith ph Billy Bitzer

Blanche Sweet, Henry B. Walthall, Lillian Gish, Dorothy Gish, Lionel Barrymore, Mae Marsh, Robert Harron

Juggernaut
GB 1937 64m bw
Ambassador (Julius Hagen)

A scientist lacking funds for his experiments agrees to commit murder.

Tedious melodrama which wastes Karloff's time.

w Cyril Campion, H. Fowler Mear, H. Fraenkel d Henry Edwards ph Sidney Blythe

Boris Karloff, Mona Goya, Joan Wyndham, Arthur Margetson, Anthony Ireland, Morton Selten

'It gets into motion slowly and reaches the meat of the plot after numerous distractions.' – *Variety*

Juggernaut **
GB 1974 110m DeLuxe Panavision
United Artists/David E. Picker (Richard Alan Simmons)
V*

A transatlantic liner is threatened by a mad bomber.

Elaborate suspense spectacular, most of which works pretty well.

w Richard Alan Simmons   *d* Richard Lester
ph Gerry Fisher   *m* Ken Thorne   *pd* Terence Marsh

Richard Harris, David Hemmings, Omar Sharif,
Anthony Hopkins, Ian Holm, Shirley Knight, Roy
Kinnear, Cyril Cusack, Freddie Jones

'However unoriginal its basic ingredients, it hardly
ever slackens its pace or diverts attention from its
central premise.' – *Jonathan Rosenbaum*

'Jaunty, cynical slapstick.' – *New Yorker*

The Juggler
US   1953   88m   bw
Columbia/Stanley Kramer

A Jewish refugee in Palestine has a horror of being
imprisoned, and runs away from a transit camp with a
small wandering boy.

Well-meaning cheapie, a curiously aimless topical
drama which fails to make any of its several points.

w Michael Blankfort   *novel* Michael Blankfort
d Edward Dmytryk   *ph* Roy Hunt   *m* Georges
Antheil

Kirk Douglas, Milly Vitale, Paul Stewart, Joey Walsh

'Power. Respect.'
Juice **
US   1992   91m   Technicolor
Electric/Paramount/Island World (David Heyman, Neal H.
Moritz, Peter Frankfort)
V, V*, L

Four young friends from Harlem find their
relationship alters after they rob a store and kill its
owner.

Gripping tale of inner-city despair and the dead end
offered by violence.

w Gerard Brown, Ernest R. Dickerson   *d* Ernest
R. Dickerson   *ph* Larry Banks   *m* Hank Shocklee &
The Bomb Squad   *pd* Lester Cohen   *ed* Sam
Pollard, Brunilda Torres

Omar Epps, Tupac Shakur, Jermaine Hopkins, Khalil
Kain, Cindy Herron, Vincent Laresca, Samuel L.
Jackson, George O. Gore, Grace Garland, Queen
Latifah

'A vivid slice of everyday fun and mortal danger in
young Harlem.' – *Joe Brown, Washington Post*

'Demonstrates the black community's untapped talent
waiting for opportunities on both sides of the camera,
but it also reflects the confined realm within which
the filmmakers and performers are forced to operate.'
– *Variety*

Jujiro: see *Crossroads*

Juke Girl
US   1942   90m   bw
Warner (Jack Saper, Jerry Wald)

Fruit workers in Florida get involved in murder.

Hokum melodrama with all concerned treading water.

w A. I. Bezzerides   *novel* Theodore Pratt   *d* Curtis
Bernhardt   *ph* Bert Glennon   *m* Adolph Deutsch

Ann Sheridan, Ronald Reagan, Richard Whorf, Gene
Lockhart, Faye Emerson, George Tobias, Alan Hale,
Howard da Silva, Donald McBride, Fuzzy Knight,
Willie Best

Jules et Jim ****
France   1962   105m   bw   Franscope
Films du Carrosse/SEDIF (Marcel Berbert)
V, V*, L, S

Before World War I, in Paris, a girl alternates between
a French and a German student, and after the war they
meet again to form a constantly shifting triangle.

Charming, quintessentially French period romance,
technically interesting, emotionally up-lifting, and
acted and directed with verve and feeling.

w François Truffaut, Jean Gruault   *novel* Henri-Pierre
Roche   *d* François Truffaut   *ph* Raoul Coutard
m Georges Delerue

Oskar Werner, Jeanne Moreau, Henri Serre

'The sense is of a director intoxicated with the
pleasure of making films.' – *Penelope Houston, MFB*

'A story of turmoil, of courage, of love!'
Julia **
US   1977   117m   Technicolor
TCF (Julien Derode)
V*, L

Lillian Hellman reflects on the fortunes of her friend
Julia, filled with enthusiasm for European causes and
finally killed by the Nazis.

Thoughtful, elegant patchwork of thirties memories, a
vehicle for actors and a subtle, self-effacing director.

w Alvin Sargent   *book* Pentimento by Lillian Hellman
d Fred Zinnemann   *ph* Douglas Slocombe
m Georges Delerue   *pd* Carmen Dillon, Gene
Callahan, Willy Holt

Jane Fonda, Vanessa Redgrave, Jason Robards Jnr,
Maximilian Schell, Hal Holbrook, Rosemary Murphy,
Cathleen Nesbitt, Maurice Denham

'After a while it becomes apparent that Zinnemann
and Sargent are trafficking in too many quotations
and flashbacks because they can't find the core of the
material.' – *Pauline Kael*

AA: script; Vanessa Redgrave; Jason Robards Jnr

AAN: best picture; Fred Zinnemann; Douglas
Slocombe; Georges Delerue; Jane Fonda; Maximilian
Schell

'An erotic comedy about life on the line.'
Julia Has Two Lovers
US   1990   85m   colour
Oneira (Bashar Shbib)
V, V*

A woman, who has ambivalent feelings about her
current lover, begins a romance with a man who dials
her number by mistake.

Low-budget romance that fails to ring bells.

w Daphna Kastner, Bashar Shbib   *d* Bashar Shbib
ph Stephen Reizes   *m* Emilio Kauderer   *ed* Dan
Foegelle, Bashar Shbib

Daphna Kastner, David Duchoveny, David Charles,
Tim Ray

Julia Misbehaves
US   1948   99m   bw
MGM (Everett Riskin)
V*

An actress returns to her stuffy husband when her
daughter is about to marry.

Desperate attempt to find a vehicle for a fading star
team.

w William Ludwig, Arthur Wimperis, Harry Ruskin
novel The Nutmeg Tree by Margery Sharp   *d* Jack
Conway   *ph* Joseph Ruttenberg   *m* Adolph
Deutsch

Greer Garson, Walter Pidgeon, Elizabeth Taylor, Peter
Lawford, Cesar Romero, Lucile Watson, Nigel Bruce,
Mary Boland, Reginald Owen, Ian Wolfe, Edmund
Breon, Fritz Feld, Aubrey Mather, Henry Stephenson

Julie *
US   1956   97m   bw
MGM/Arwin (Marty Melcher)

A concert pianist plans to murder his wife.

Wildly improbable but entertaining suspenser in
which the lady finally has to assume control of an
airplane.

wd Andrew Stone   *ph* Fred Jackman Jnr   *m* Leith
Stevens

Doris Day, Louis Jourdan, Barry Sullivan, Frank
Lovejoy, John Gallaudet

'Some of the dialogue reaches a fine pitch of banality.'
– *MFB*

AAN: Andrew Stone (as writer); title song (*m* Leith
Stevens, *ly* Tom Adair)

Juliet of the Spirits *
Italy/France   1965   145m   Technicolor
Federiz/Francoriz (Clemente Fracassi)
V*, S
original title: *Giulietta degli Spiriti*

A bored middle-aged woman finds she can conjure up
spirits who lead her into a life of sensual gratification.

A fascinating patchwork of autobiographical
flashbacks, the distaff side of *Eight and a Half*.

w Federico Fellini, Tullio Pinnelli, Brunello Rondi,
Ennio Flaiano   *d* Federico Fellini   *ph* Gianni di
Venanzo   *m* Nino Rota

Giulietta Masina, Mario Pisu, Sandra Milo, Valentina
Cortese, Sylva Koscina

'A kaleidoscope of fantasy, a series of cerebral
inventions, of which only a few are artistically
justified . . . an extravagant illusion, a huge confidence
trick, with little new to say and an often pedantic way
of saying it.' – *David Wilson, MFB*

'Greater than Ivanhoe!'
'Thrill to ruthless men and their goddess-like women in a
sin-swept age!'
'Thrill to traitors and heroes, killings and conspiracies,
passions and violence in Rome's most exciting age!'
Julius Caesar **
US   1953   121m   bw
MGM (John Houseman)
V, V*

Cassius and Brutus lead the conspirators who murder
Caesar, but are themselves routed by Mark Antony.

Straightforward, rather leaden presentation of
Shakespeare's play, lit by effective moments in the
acting, but the sudden change from talk to battle is
not smoothed over.

wd Joseph L. Mankiewicz   *ph* Joseph Ruttenberg
m Miklos Rozsa   *ad* Cedric Gibbons, Edward
Carfagno

John Gielgud, James Mason, Marlon Brando, Greer
Garson, Deborah Kerr, Louis Calhern, Edmond
O'Brien, George Macready, Michael Pate, John Hoyt,
Alan Napier

AA: art direction

AAN: best picture; Joseph Ruttenberg; Miklos Rozsa;
Marlon Brando

Julius Caesar
GB   1969   116m   Technicolor   Panavision
Commonwealth United (Peter Snell)
V*, L

Elementary production with a surprising number of
faults and very few merits.

w Robert Furnival   *d* Stuart Burge   *ph* Ken
Higgins   *m* Michael Lewis   *pd* Julia Trevelyan
Oman

Richard Johnson, Jason Robards Jnr, *John Gielgud,*
Charlton Heston, Robert Vaughn, Richard
Chamberlain, Diana Rigg, Jill Bennett, Christopher
Lee, Alan Browning, Andrew Crawford

'Ugly, ill-spoken, ham-fisted.' – *Sight and Sound*

Jumbo *
US   1962   124m   Metrocolor   Panavision
MGM (Joe Pasternak, Martin Melcher)
V*
aka: *Billy Rose's Jumbo*

In 1910, the daughter of the owner of a shaky circus
prevents a take-over bid.

Hoary circus story with music. General effect disappointing: the elephant steals the show.

w Sidney Sheldon play Ben Hecht, Charles MacArthur d Charles Walters ph William H. Daniels md George Stoll ch Busby Berkeley m/y Richard Rodgers, Lorenz Hart

Doris Day, Jimmy Durante, Stephen Boyd, Martha Raye, Dean Jagger

AAN: George Stoll

Jump for Glory
GB 1937 89m bw
Criterion (Douglas Fairbanks Jnr, Marcel Hellman)
US title: When Thief Meets Thief

Adventures of a cat burglar who accidentally kills his ex-partner.

Curious star comedy drama with pleasing scenes.

w John Meehan Jnr, Harold French novel Gordon MacDonnell d Raoul Walsh ph Cedric Williams

Douglas Fairbanks Jnr, Valerie Hobson, Alan Hale, Edward Rigby, Barbara Everest, Jack Melford, Anthony Ireland

'Starts off at a commendable pace but doesn't carry through.' – Variety

Jump into Hell
US 1955 93m bw
Warner (David Weisbart)

Paratroops relieve a fort in Indo-China.

Mediocre semi-documentary war heroics.

w Irving Wallace d David Butler ph Peverell Marley m David Buttolph

Jacques Sernas, Kurt Kasznar, Arnold Moss, Peter Van Eyck, Pat Blake

Jumpin' Jack Flash
US 1986 100m DeLuxe
TCF (Lawrence Gordon-Joel Silver)
V, V*, L

A black office worker finds herself plunged into espionage.

Tiresome, dirty-talking, would-be wild and woolly comedy which fails to establish itself.

w David H. Franzoni, J. W. Melville, Patricia Irving, Christopher Thompson d Penny Marshall ph Matthew F. Leonetti m Thomas Newman pd Robert Boyle ed Mark Goldblatt

Whoopi Goldberg, Stephen Collins, John Wood, Carol Kane, Annie Potts, Roscoe Lee Browne

Jumping for Joy
GB 1955 88m bw
Rank/Raymond Stross

A track attendant acquires a winning greyhound and exposes a group of crooks.

Totally predictable star comedy which needs livening up.

w Jack Davies, Henry E. Blyth d John Paddy Carstairs ph Jack Cox m Larry Adler

Frankie Howerd, Stanley Holloway, A. E. Matthews, Tony Wright, Alfie Bass, Joan Hickson, Lionel Jeffries

Jumping Jacks *
US 1952 96m bw
Paramount/Hal B. Wallis

Two cabaret comedians join the paratroops.

Standard star farce, one of Martin and Lewis's best.

w Robert Lees, Fred Rinaldo, Herbert Baker d Norman Taurog ph Daniel L. Fapp m Joseph J. Lilley

Dean Martin, Jerry Lewis, Mona Freeman, Robert Strauss, Don Defore

June Bride
US 1948 97m bw
Warner (Henry Blanke)
V*

Two bickering reporters are sent to cover a small-town wedding.

Sloppily structured romantic farce in which nothing ever comes together.

w Ranald MacDougall play Feature for June by Eileen Tighe, Graeme Lorimer d Bretaigne Windust ph Ted McCord m David Buttolph

Bette Davis, Robert Montgomery, Fay Bainter, Tom Tully, Betty Lynn, Barbara Bates, Jerome Cowan, Mary Wickes, Debbie Reynolds

Jungfrukällan: see The Virgin Spring

'More thrilling than the deeds of man … more beautiful than the love of woman … more wonderful than the dreams of children!'

The Jungle Book *
US 1942 109m Technicolor
Alexander Korda (W. Howard Greene)
V*, L, S
aka: Rudyard Kipling's Jungle Book

Growing up with animals in an Indian forest, a boy forestalls the getaway of three thieves.

High-budgeted but rather boring live action version with stiff-jointed model animals.

w Laurence Stallings stories Rudyard Kipling d Zoltan Korda, André de Toth ph Lee Garmes, W. Howard Greene m Miklos Rozsa ad Vincent Korda

Sabu, Joseph Calleia, John Qualen, Frank Puglia, Rosemary de Camp

AAN: cinematography; Miklos Rozsa; Vincent Korda

Jungle Book *
US 1967 78m Technicolor
Walt Disney
V, V*, L

Cartoon version relying less on action than on songs and voices; patchily successful but no classic.

d Wolfgang Reitherman m/y Richard and Robert Sherman, Terry Gilkyson

voices of George Sanders, Phil Harris, Louis Prima, Sebastian Cabot, Sterling Holloway

AAN: song 'The Bare Necessities' (m/y Terry Gilkyson)

Jungle Captive
US 1945 63m bw
Universal

A mad doctor steals the body of Paula the ape woman and restores it to life.

Arrant rubbish, a sequel to Captive Wild Woman and Jungle Woman.

w M. Coates Webster, Dwight V. Babcock d Harold Young

Otto Kruger, Phil Brown, Rondo Hatton, Jerome Cowan, Amelita Ward

Jungle Drums of Africa
US 1953 bw serial: 12 eps
Republic

A mining engineer puts paid to a villainous hunter who is on the trail of uranium deposits.

Routine serial exploits with a wildlife background (by courtesy of the stock shot library).

d Fred C. Brannon

Clayton Moore, Phyllis Coates, Johnny Spencer, Roy Glenn

Jungle Fever **
US 1991 132m DuArt
UIP/Universal/Forty Acres and A Mule Filmworks (Spike Lee)
V, V*, L, S

A black architect leaves his wife and child to live with his Italian-American secretary.

Sharply observed drama of racism and prejudice that raises more questions than it attempts to answer.

wd Spike Lee ph Ernest Dickerson m Terence Blanchard, Stevie Wonder pd Wynn Thomas ed Sam Pollard, Brunilda Torres

Wesley Snipes, Annabella Sciorra, Spike Lee, Ossie Davis, Ruby Dee, Samuel L. Jackson, Lonette McKee, John Turturro, Frank Vincent, Anthony Quinn, Tim Robbins, Brad Dourif

'An inspired and very welcome return to form.' – Empire

Jungle Fighters: see The Long and the Short and the Tall

Jungle Girl
US 1941 bw serial: 15 eps
Republic

A scientist's daughter grows up with natives and outwits her wicked uncle.

Exploits of a female Tarzan. d William Witney, John English

Frances Gifford, Tom Neal, Trevor Bardette, Gerald Mohr, Eddie Acuff

Jungle Jim
US 1937 bw serial: 12 eps
Universal

A white hunter leads a safari in search of an American heiress raised in the jungle.

Naïve adventures with a villain called The Cobra.

d Ford Beebe, Cliff Smith

Grant Withers, Betty Jane Rhodes, Raymond Hatton, Henry Brandon, Evelyn Brent, Al Bridge

Jungle Jim

When Johnny Weissmuller began to show his middle-age spread, Columbia put him in a jacket and more or less redid his Tarzan thing in a series of second features which appeared to be shot in producer Sam Katzman's back garden and gradually indulged in wilder and wilder plots. None of them has more than curiosity value.

1948: JUNGLE JIM
1949: THE LOST TRIBE
1950: CAPTIVE GIRL, MARK OF THE GORILLA, PYGMY ISLAND
1951: FURY OF THE CONGO, JUNGLE MANHUNT
1952: JUNGLE JIM IN THE FORBIDDEN LAND, VOODOO TIGER
1953: SAVAGE MUTINY, VALLEY OF THE HEADHUNTERS, KILLER APE
1954: JUNGLE MANEATERS, CANNIBAL ATTACK
1955: JUNGLE MOON MEN, DEVIL GODDESS

w main scriptwriters were Carroll Young, Dwight Babcock, Sam Newman d main directors William Berke, Lee Sholem, Spencer G. Bennet

Jungle Menace
US 1937 bw serial: 15 eps
Columbia

A Malayan rubber-planter's crop is attacked by rover pirates, and an adventurer hastens to help.

Unusual setting for routine adventures.

d George Melford, Harry Fraser

Frank Buck, John St Polis, Charlotte Henry, William Bakewell

The Jungle Mystery

US 1932 bw serial: 12 eps
Universal

Americans in Africa combat ivory hunters.

Early talkie serial with footage which now seems hilarious.

d Ray Taylor

Tom Tyler, Cecilia Parker, William Desmond, Noah Beery Jnr

'Men staked their lives for just one look at the thrilling beauty of this tiger woman!'

The Jungle Princess *

US 1936 84m bw
Paramount (E. Lloyd Sheldon)

A British hunter is injured on a tropical island and rescued by a native girl and her animal retinue.

Dorothy Lamour's first film role cast her as the female Tarzan she was to play (in a sarong, of course) a dozen times again. This is strictly a programmer, but after its success it was all done again, rather better, as *Her Jungle Love*.

w Cyril Hume, Gerald Geraghty, Gouverneur Morris d William Thiele ph Harry Fischbeck md Boris Morros

Dorothy Lamour, Ray Milland, Akim Tamiroff, Lynne Overman, Molly Lamont, Hugh Buckler

'Fairly palatable entertainment most of the way.' – *Variety*

'Poor Mr Lynne Overman is expected to lend humorous relief to a film already richly comic.' – *Graham Greene*

† On this trip the tiger was Liamu and the chimp Bogo.

Jungle Queen

US 1945 bw serial: 13 eps
Universal

Nazis stir up African tribes against the Allies, who have a friend in a mysterious queen.

Echoes of *She* abound in this tried-and-tested serial.

d Ray Taylor, Lewis D. Collins

Ruth Roman, Eddie Quillan, Edward Norris, Douglass Dumbrille, Lois Collier, Tala Birell

Jungle Raiders

US 1945 bw serial: 15 eps
Columbia

An evil trader holds captive a doctor who knows the whereabouts of secret treasure.

Standard jungle hazards, including crocodile swamps, volcanoes and landslides, lend colour to this listless serial.

d Lesley Selander

Kane Richmond, Eddie Quillan, Veda Ann Borg, Carol Hughes, Charles King, I. Stanford Jolley

Jungle Woman

US 1944 54m bw
Universal

A mad doctor restores an ape to life. It turns into a beautiful woman.

Middle section of a talentless trio of which the first is *Captive Wild Woman* and the third *Jungle Captive*.

w Bernard Schubert, Henry Sucher, Edward Dein d Reginald LeBorg

J. Carrol Naish, Acquanetta, Evelyn Ankers, Milburn Stone, Richard Davis, Lois Collier

Junior Army

US 1943 70m bw
Columbia (Colbert Clark)

An English boy goes to an American military academy.

Routine propaganda item which might almost have been titled *David Copperfield Meets the Dead End Kids*.

w Albert Bein, Paul Gangelin d Lew Landers

Freddie Bartholomew, Billy Halop, Huntz Hall, Bobby Jordan, Don Beddoe, Peter Lawford, Boyd Davis

Junior Bonner *

US 1972 105m Movielab Todd-AO 35
ABC/Booth-Gardner/Joe Wizan/Solar
V, V*

An ageing rodeo star returns to his home town and finds his family in trouble.

Well-made, rather downcast and not very interesting drama, remarkably gentle from this director.

w Jeb Rosebrook d Sam Peckinpah ph Lucien Ballard m Jerry Fielding

Steve McQueen, Ida Lupino, Robert Preston, Joe Don Baker, Ben Johnson

Junior G-Men

US 1940 bw serial: 12 eps
Universal

The son of a G-man enlists street friends to track down a vanished military leader.

Serial situations retailored for reformed Dead End Kids.

d Ford Beebe, John Rawlins

Billy Halop, Huntz Hall, Gabriel Dell, Bernard Punsley, Philip Terry, Russell Hicks

Junior G-Men of the Air

US 1942 bw serial: 13 eps
Universal

The son of an airplane junkyard owner recruits friends to unmask a fifth-column organization.

Fairly lively wartime serial.

d Ray Taylor, Lewis D. Collins

Billy Halop, Gene Reynolds, Lionel Atwill, Frank Albertson, Richard Lane, Huntz Hall, Gabriel Dell, Bernard Punsley, Frankie Darro, Turhan Bey

Junior Miss *

US 1945 94m bw
TCF (William Perlberg)

A teenager causes trouble by meddling in the lives of her family.

Amusing family comedy from a hit play.

w George Seaton play Jerome Chodorov, Joseph Fields stories Sally Benson d George Seaton ph Charles Clarke m David Buttolph

Peggy Ann Garner, Allyn Joslyn, Faye Marlowe, Mona Freeman, Michael Dunne, John Alexander

Juno and the Paycock

GB 1930 85m bw
British International (John Maxwell)
V*
US title: *The Shame of Mary Boyle*

During the Irish troubles of the early twenties, tragedy comes to a poor Dublin family.

A plainly done film version of a modern classic whose changes of mood would not in any case have worked well on the screen.

w Alfred Hitchcock, Alma Reville play Sean O'Casey d Alfred Hitchcock ph Jack Cox ad Norman Arnold ed Émile de Ruelle

Sara Allgood, Edward Chapman, Maire O'Neill, Sidney Morgan, John Longden

'A film which completely justifies the talkies.' – *James Agate*

'Just a photograph of a stage play.' – *Alfred Hitchcock*

Jupiter's Darling *

US 1954 96m Eastmancolor Cinemascope
MGM (George Wells)
V*, L

Advancing on Rome, Hannibal falls in love with the dictator's fiancée.

A splendid example of the higher lunacy, with coloured elephants decorating an MGM musical about the fall of the Roman Empire. Small elements can be salvaged, and the gall is enough to be divided into three parts.

w Dorothy Kingsley play *The Road to Rome* by Robert E. Sherwood d George Sidney ph Paul C. Vogel, Charles Rosher m David Rose ch Hermes Pan m/ly Burton Lane, Harold Adamson ad Cedric Gibbons, Uric McCleary

Esther Williams, Howard Keel, George Sanders, Marge and Gower Champion, Richard Haydn, William Demarest

'An adventure 65 million years in the making.'

Jurassic Park **

US 1993 127m colour
UIP/Universal/Amblin (Kathleen Kennedy, Gerald R. Molen)
V, V*, L, S

Genetically re-created from blood taken from ancient mosquitoes, dinosaurs run amok in a theme park.

The dinosaurs are amazing: living, breathing, believable creatures, which is more than you can say for the actors in this otherwise cardboard creation, hung up on toilet jokes and often seeming no more than an elongated commercial for all the merchandise associated with the movie, which includes a long, shameless pan along shelves of the toys and books available. The film was distributed with a warning that it might upset sensitive children. Sensitive adults are likely to be disappointed, too.

w Michael Crichton, David Koepp novel Michael Crichton d Steven Spielberg ph Dean Cundey m John Williams pd Rick Carter sp Dennis Muren, Stan Winston, Phil Tippett, Pamela Easley ed Michael Kahn

Sam Neill, Laura Dern, Jeff Goldblum, Richard Attenborough, Bob Peck, Martin Ferrero, B. D. Wong, Joseph Mazello, Ariana Richards, Samuel L. Jackson

'Doesn't have the imagination – or the courage – to take us any place we haven't been a thousand times before. It's just a creature feature on amphetamines.' – *Terrence Rafferty, New Yorker*

'The dinosaurs are wonderful, but they aren't on the set enough of the time (yes, I know how much more they cost than human actors). Unfortunately, the plot line for the human actors reduces to pap and romantic drivel of the worst kind, the very antithesis of the book's grappling with serious themes.' – *Stephen Jay Gould*

† Among the many inconsistencies in the narrative, Sam Neill warns that the Tyrannosaurus Rex reacts to movement when he can have no knowledge or experience of this fact.

AA: sound; sound effects editing; visual effects

Jury's Evidence

GB 1935 71m bw
British Lion (Herbert Smith)

The jury in a murder trial disagrees.

Courtroom drama with an unsatisfactory finish.

w Ian Dalrymple play Jack de Leon, Jack Celestin d Ralph Ince ph George Stretton

Hartley Power, Margaret Lockwood, Nora Swinburne, Sebastian Shaw

The Jury's Secret

US 1937 64m bw
Universal

The guilty man in a murder case is on the jury.

Slow-moving courtroom drama with an unsatisfactory twist.

w Lester Cole, Newman Levy d Edward Sloman

Kent Taylor, Fay Wray, Jane Darwell, Nan Grey, Larry Blake, Fritz Leiber

'Doomed for no honours such as b.o.' – *Variety*

Just a Gigolo

US 1931 71m bw
MGM

A young lord masquerades as a gigolo to avoid being the prey of gold diggers.

Slackly handled comedy which doesn't come off.

w Hans Kraly, Richard Schayer, Claudine West
d Jack Conway

William Haines, Irene Purcell, C. Aubrey Smith, Lillian Bond

'Too much talk, too little action.' – *Variety*

Just a Gigolo

West Germany 1978 147m colour
Leguan (Rolf Thiele)
V*, L

A young Prussian veteran of World War I intends to succeed, but stumbles through the Berlin underworld and is accidentally shot in a street skirmish.

An international misadventure whose English version is not only interminable and badly dubbed but extremely clumsily made.

w Ennio de Concini, Joshua Sinclair d David Hemmings ph Charly Steinberger m Gunther Fischer pd Peter Rothe

David Bowie, Sydne Rome, Kim Novak, Marlene Dietrich, David Hemmings, Maria Schell, Curt Jurgens, Erika Pluhar

'It often goes for laughs it hasn't a hope of getting; sometimes it aspires to tragic dignity and looks truly inept. It would be kinder to yourself and to everybody involved to overlook it.' – *Time Out*

Just Across the Street

US 1952 78m bw
Universal-International/Leonard Goldstein

Complications arise when a plumber's secretary pretends to be rich.

Silly and pointless comedy which provides its talent with nothing to do.

w Rosell Rogers, Joel Malone d Joseph Pevney

Ann Sheridan, John Lund, Robert Keith, Cecil Kellaway, Harvey Lembeck, Natalie Schafer, Alan Mowbray

'If you think you know her, think again.'
Just Another Girl on the I.R.T.

US 1992 97m colour
Metro Tartan/Miramax/Truth 24 F.P.S. (Erwin Wilson)
V

A 17-year-old rebellious black Brooklyn girl with aspirations to be a doctor becomes pregnant by a boy she meets at a party.

A sympathetic portrait of a teenager refusing to come to terms with reality, brightly performed but hampered by a script that sticks to the obvious and settles for an easy resolution.

wd Leslie Harris ph Richard Connors m Eric Sadler, Willie Bruno II pd Michael O'Dell Green ed Jack Haigis

Ariyan A. Johnson, Kevin Thigpen, Ebony Jerido, Jerard Washington, Chequita Jackson

'A crude but disturbing exposé of teenage ignorance and denial about the facts of life on the streets and in the bedroom.' – *Variety*

'The movie's only strong point is its sharp and zappy cast. But hazy vision finally saps even their energy –

just as the pasted-on happy ending mocks their efforts to keep things real.' – *Cynthia Rose, Sight and Sound*

Just Around the Corner

US 1938 70m bw
TCF (David Hempstead)
V*

A little girl helps her dad to get on in business.

Tedious Little Miss Fixit tale from the period when Shirley's star was sliding.

w Ethel Hill, J. P. McEvoy, Darrel Ware d Irving Cummings ph Henry Sharp md Louis Silvers

Shirley Temple, Charles Farrell, Bert Lahr, Joan Davis, Amanda Duff, Bill Robinson, Franklin Pangborn, Cora Witherspoon

'Top flight for general all-round entertainment.' – *Variety*

Just Before Dawn

US 1980 90m Movielab
Oakland

Visitors to a mountain area are terrorized by a cleaver-wielding killer.

Teenage shocker with just a little more style than most.

w Mark Arywitz, Gregg Irving d Jeff Lieberman

George Kennedy, Mike Kellin, Chris Lemmon, Gregg Henry, Deborah Benson

Just Between Friends

US 1986 120m DeLuxe
Orion/MTM (Edward Teets, Allan Burns)
V*

A middle-aged woman finds little excitement in her household, and fancies a lesbian relationship; but her husband dies and she finds herself pregnant.

Ho-hum melodrama of our time.

wd Allan Burns ph Jordan Cronenweth m Patrick Williams pd Sydney Z. Litwack

Mary Tyler Moore, Ted Danson, Christine Lahti, Sam Waterston, Salome Jens

'The main difference between this and a TV movie is that this doesn't have commercials.' – *Variety*

Just for You

US 1952 104m Technicolor
Paramount (Pat Duggan)

A successful songwriter finds that his troublesome teenage son is in love with his own fiancée.

Tiresomely scripted, pleasantly played romantic comedy with music.

w Robert Carson novel *Famous* by Stephen Vincent Benet d Elliott Nugent ph George Barnes md Emil Newman m Hugo Friedhofer m/y Harry Warren, Leo Robin

Bing Crosby, Jane Wyman, Bob Arthur, Ethel Barrymore, Natalie Wood, Cora Witherspoon, Regis Toomey

AAN: song 'Zing a Little Zong'

Just Imagine

US 1930 102m bw
Fox

A man who dies in 1930 is revived in 1980 and can't get used to the pace of life.

Famous fantasy which doesn't live up to its reputation and can now be seen as hampered by poor sets, script and acting. Futuristic sets are few but choice.

d David Butler w/songs De Sylva, Brown, Henderson ch Seymour Felix ph Ernest Palmer md Arthur Kay m Hugo Friedhofer ad Stephen Gooson, Ralph Hammeras

El Brendel, Maureen O'Sullivan, John Garrick, Frank Albertson, Marjorie White, Hobart Bosworth, Mischa Auer, Wilfred Lucas

'Needs to be sold in advance on its novelty angle . . . it seems essential that something be done to make them say "Go down and take a look at that crazy picture".' – *Variety*

AAN: art direction

Just Like a Woman

GB 1966 89m Eastmancolor
Dormar (Bob Kellett)

A TV director's wife leaves him and gets ideas above her station.

Curious comedy which aims at sophistication but starts flagging in the first five minutes. Familiar performers just about keep it afloat.

wd Bob Fuest ph Billy Williams m Ken Napper

Wendy Craig, Francis Matthews, John Wood, Dennis Price, Miriam Karlin, Peter Jones, Clive Dunn, Ray Barrett

'She stole his heart. He stole her clothes.'
Just Like a Woman

GB 1992 106m Eastmancolor
Rank/Zenith/LWT/British Screen (Nick Evans)
V, S

An American living in London moves into lodgings after his wife throws him out, and reveals to his landlady that he is a transvestite.

Tedious comedy of minimal interest, even to cross-dressers.

w Nick Evans novel *Geraldine, for the Love of a Transvestite* by Monica Jay d Christopher Monger ph Alan Hume m Michael Storey pd John Box ed Nicolas Gaster

Julie Walters, Adrian Pasdar, Paul Freeman, Susan Woolridge, Gordon Kennedy, Ian Redford, Shelley Thompson

'The film remains poky, parochial, and its message is clear – no sex, please, we're British.' – *Geoff Brown, The Times*

'A tepid comedy of Anglo-Saxon inhibition.' – *Philip French, Observer*

Just My Luck

GB 1957 86m bw
Rank (Hugh Stewart)

A jeweller's assistant becomes involved in horse racing.

Flat star vehicle.

w Alfred Shaughnessy d John Paddy Carstairs ph Jack Cox m Philip Green

Norman Wisdom, Jill Dixon, Leslie Phillips, Margaret Rutherford, Delphi Lawrence

Just Off Broadway

US 1942 66m bw
TCF/Sol M. Wurtzel

Michael Shayne investigates a court case on which he is sitting as a juror.

Standard second feature mystery, reasonably well made.

w Arnaud D'Usseau d Herbert I. Leeds

Lloyd Nolan, Marjorie Weaver, Phil Silvers, Janis Carter, Richard Derr, Chester Clute

Just Tell Me What You Want

US 1980 112m Technicolor
Warner/Jay Presson Allen, Sidney Lumet
V*

A powerful tycoon starts to weave plots when one of his harem wants to go independent.

Thoroughly silly melodrama with a few incidental humours.

w Jay Presson Allen   *novel* Jay Presson Allen *d* Sidney Lumet   *ph* Oswald Morris   *m* Charles Strouse   *pd* Tony Walton

Ali MacGraw, Alan King, Myrna Loy, Keenan Wynn, Tony Roberts, Dina Merrill, Peter Weller

'Jay Presson Allen has adapted her trashy novel into a trashy picture . . . Myrna Loy looks as if she's constantly amazed at the kinds of films getting made these days, and she's absolutely right.' – *Variety*

Just the Way You Are
US   1984   95m   Metrocolor
MGM-UA (Leo L. Fuchs)
V*

A young fluteplayer tries to carve a career for herself while overcoming a physical disability.

Odd little comedy-drama with little plot beyond the central character's crippled leg; not likely to make much headway.

w Allan Burns   *d* Edouard Molinaro   *ph* Claude Lecomte   *m* Vladimir Cosmar   *ad* François de Lamotte   *ed* Claudio Ventura, Georges Klotz

Kristy McNichol, Michael Ontkean, Kaki Hunter, André Dussolier, Robert Carradine

Just William
GB   1939   94m   bw
Associated British (Walter C. Mycroft)

William, hunting for bomb-carrying spies, foils a con man and helps his father in his campaign to become a local councillor.

The first and best of the *William* series, with a good cast and a genuine feeling for children's fantasy and anarchy.

w Graham Cutts, Doreen Montgomery, Ireland Wood *novel* Richmal Crompton   *d* Graham Cutts *ph* Walter Harvey   *ad* Cedric Dawe   *ed* E. B. Jarvis

Fred Emney, Basil Radford, Iris Hoey, Amy Veness, Dicky Lupino, Roddy McDowall, Norman Robinson, Peter Miles, Jenny Laird, David Tree

Just William's Luck
GB   1947   85m   bw
Alliance (James Carter)

William tries to marry off his brother so that he can inherit his bicycle, and succeeds in foiling a gang of smugglers.

Limp comedy that fails to translate to the screen the verbal exuberance and mayhem of the novels.

wd Val Guest   *novel* Richmal Crompton   *ph* Bert Mason   *m* Robert Farnon   *ad* Harry Moore *ed* Anne Barker

William Graham, Leslie Bradley, Garry Marsh, Jane Walsh, Hugh Cross, Kathleen Stuart, Muriel Aked, Joan Hickson, A. E. Matthews

† It was followed by a sequel, *William at the Circus* (qv).

Just You and Me, Kid
US   1979   93m   Metrocolor
Columbia/Irving Fein-Jerome M. Zeitman

An elderly comedian reluctantly takes care of a naked teenager on the run from a dope pusher.

Virtually a one-set comedy which quickly tires the eye and ear; not a good idea despite the veteran star.

w Oliver Hailey, Leonard Stern   *d* Leonard Stern *ph* David Walsh   *m* Jack Elliott

George Burns, Brooke Shields, Burl Ives, Lorraine Gary, John Schuck, Keye Luke, Leon Ames, Ray Bolger, Carl Ballantine

Justice Est Faite *
France   1950   105m   bw
Silver Films

The personal lives of jurors in a mercy killing case affect their verdict.

Absorbing courtroom drama with a message.

w Charles Spaak, André Cayatte   d André Cayatte ph Jean Bourgoin   m Raymond Legrand

Valentine Tessier, Claude Nollier, Jacques Castelot, Michel Auclair

Justice for Sale: see *Night Court*

Justine
US   1969   116m   DeLuxe   Panavision
TCF/Pandro S. Berman
V*

In Alexandria in the thirties, the beautiful wife of a wealthy banker influences the lives of all who meet her.

Disastrous condensed version of a very unusual set of novels whose atmosphere has not translated at all well. The result is like a bad rehearsal for a film, which is not surprising in view of the number of producers variously involved. The author feared 'a sort of *Peyton Place* with camels', and got it.

w Lawrence B. Marcus   *novels The Alexandria Quartet* by Lawrence Durrell   *d* George Cukor   *ph* Leon Shamroy   *m* Jerry Goldsmith

Anouk Aimée, Michael York, Dirk Bogarde, Anna Karina, John Vernon, George Baker, Philippe Noiret, Robert Forster, Jack Albertson, Michael Dunn, Barry Morse, Cliff Gorman, Severn Darden

'Could well stand as a model of what can happen when Hollywood gets to grips with a celebrated literary property.' – *David Wilson*

'Despite leaden forays into homosexuality, transvestitism, incest, and child prostitution, it remains as naively old-fashioned in its emotional and intellectual vocabulary as in its actual verbiage and cinematic technique.' – *John Simon*

† The film is said to have been eight years in preparation. Joseph Strick was fired as director when the cast and crew returned to Los Angeles after shooting exteriors in Tunisia. Cukor, reported Michael York, 'made his disapproval of some of his inherited cast quite unambiguous. At the mention of our leading lady his face would flush.'

K

K2
US 1991 111m Technicolor
Entertainment/Trans Pacific/Majestic (Jonathan Taplin, Marilyn Weiner, Tim Van Rellim)
V, V*, L, S

Two friends join an ill-assorted expedition to climb the Himalayan mountain K2.

A tame buddy-buddy movie that has nowhere to go but down.

w Patrick Myers, Scott Roberts   play Patrick Myers   d Franc Roddam   ph Gabriel Beristain   m Chaz Jankel   pd Andrew Sanders   ed Sean Barton

Michael Biehn, Mattr Craven, Raymond J. Barry, Hiroshi Fujioka, Luca Bercovici, Patricia Charbonneau, Julia Nickson-Soul, Jamal Shah

'Begins as mindlessly as it means to – and does – go on.' – Sight and Sound

'On this evidence, climbing K2 can't be any harder than sitting through it.' – Kim Newman, Empire

K-9
US 1988 102m DeLuxe
UIP/Universal (Lawrence Gordon, Charles Gordon)
V, V*, L

A narcotics cop teams up with an Alsatian.

A not-so-shaggy dog story with a couple of laughs.

w Steven Siegel, Scott Myers   d Rod Daniel   ph Dean Semler   m Miles Goodman   pd George Costello   ed Lois Freeman-Fox

James Belushi, Mel Harris, Kevin Tighe, Ed O'Neill, Jerry Lee, James Handy, Daniel Davis, Cotter Smith, John Snyder, Pruitt Taylor Vince

K9000
US 1989 90m colour
Fries Entertainment (J. Rickley Dunn)

A cop teams up with a cybernetic dog to bust a crime syndicate.

Witless compendium of action picture clichés.

w Stephen E. de Souza, Michael Part   d Kim Manners   ph Frank Raymond   m Jan Hammer   pd Elliott Gilbert   ed J. P. Farrell

Chris Mulkey, Catherine Oxenburg, Dennis Haysbert, Dana Gladstone, Jerry Houser, Judson Scott, Anne Haney, Thom McFadden

Kafka *
US/France 1991 98m bw/colour
Guild/Renn/Baltimore/Pricel (Stuart Cornfeld, Harry Benn)
S

A timid insurance clerk finds himself drawn into an anarchist plot when he investigates the disappearance of a friend.

An intriguing attempt to create a paranoid fiction combining elements of Kafka's life and his stories; it is stylish though not entirely successful, closer to the basics of a horror movie than to its author's works.

w Lem Dobbs   d Steven Soderbergh   ph Walt Lloyd   m Cliff Martinez   pd Gavin Bocquet   ed Steven Soderbergh

Jeremy Irons, Theresa Russell, Joel Grey, Ian Holm, Jeroen Krabbé, Armin Mueller-Stahl, Alec Guinness, Brian Glover, Robert Flemyng

'Soderbergh's film has few surprises because he sticks too matter-of-factly to Kakfa basics, where others have spun out their own distinctive take.' – Nick James, Sight and Sound

'Soderbergh's most entertaining, least pretentious film to date, this is weirdly recommended.' – Kim Newman, Empire

Kagemusha **
Japan 1980 179m Eastmancolor
TCF/Toho (Akira Kurosawa)
V, V*
aka: The Double; Shadow Warrior

On the death of a clan chief his place is taken by the lookalike hired to overlook battlefields while the chief is really busy elsewhere.

Fascinating Japanese epic centring on stately ritual and court intrigue, with the occasional battle for spectacular action; one of the director's most impressive works.

w Akira Kurosawa, Masato Ide   d Akira Kurosawa   ph Kazuo Miyagawa, Asaiachi Nakai   m Shinichiro Ikebe

Tatsura Nakadai, Tsutomu Yamazaki, Kenichi Hagiwara

AAN: best foreign film; art direction

BFA: direction; costume design

Kakushi Toride No San-Akunin: see The Hidden Fortress

El Kalaa *
Algeria 1988 98m Eastmancolor
Metro/Le Centre Algérien de l'Art et l'Industrie Cinématographique (Tahar Harhoura)
aka: The Citadel

A merchant runs into opposition when he decides to take a fourth wife.

Successful on the level of a village soap opera.

wd Mohamed Chouikh   ph Allel Yahyaoui   ad Zerrouki Boukhari, Ahmed Kobbi   ed Yamina Chouikh

Khaled Barkat, Djillali Ain Tedelles, Fettouma Ousliha, Fatima Belhadj, Momo

Kaleidoscope *
GB 1966 103m Technicolor
Warner/Winkast (Elliott Kastner)
reissue title: The Bank Breaker

An American playboy breaks into a playing card factory and marks the designs so that he can win in every European casino.

Would-be swinging comedy-thriller which in fact is entertaining only when it stops trying to dazzle.

w Robert and Jane Howard-Carrington   d Jack Smight   ph Christopher Challis   m Stanley Myers   ad Maurice Carter

Warren Beatty, Susannah York, Clive Revill, Eric Porter, Murray Melvin

'A "groovie movie" it certainly is, with a battery of fashionable camera tricks, kaleidoscopic dissolves, and virtually every scene introduced from behind an irrelevant piece of furniture.' – David Wilson

Kalifornia
US 1993 118m DeLuxe Cinemascope
Rank/Propaganda/Polygram/Viacom (Tim Clawson)
V*, L

A couple driving across America to write about and photograph sites of murders unwittingly have as travelling companions a killer and his girlfriend.

An unlovely road movie, simultaneously violent and smug – and too knowing for its own good.

w Tim Metcalfe   d Dominic Sena   ph Bojan Bazelli   m Carter Burwell   pd Michael White   ed Martin Hunter

Brad Pitt, Juliette Lewis, David Duchovny, Michelle Forbes, Sierra Pecheur, Gregory Mars Martin

'An extremely handsome production imbued with a chilling surrealistic sensibility.' – Variety

'Looks a treat, tells what ought to be a fascinating story but ends up wallowing in its own pretensions.' – Derek Malcolm, Guardian

Kameradschaft *
Germany 1931 92m bw
Nerofilm
aka: Comradeship

On the Franco-German border French miners are imprisoned below ground and Germans burrow to free them.

Salutary message film with good dramatic pointing.

w Laszlo Vajda, Karl Otten, Peter Martin Lampel   d G. W. Pabst   ph Fritz Arno Wagner, Robert Baberski

Ernst Busch, Alexander Granach, Fritz Kampers, Gustav Puttjer

Kamikaze
France 1986 89m Eastmancolor Cinemascope
Blue Dolphin/Les Films du Loup/ARP/Gaumont (Luc Besson)

An electronics engineer develops a deadly weapon that can kill anyone appearing live on television.

Weak thriller that fails to make anything of its silly central concept.

w Luc Besson, Didier Grousset   d Didier Grousset   ph Jean-François Robin   m Eric Serra   ed Olivier Mauffroy

Richard Bohringer, Michel Galabru, Dominique Lavanant, Riton Leibman, Kim Massee, Harry Cleven, Romane Bohringer, Etienne Chicot, Philippe Girard

'When the action stops and the talking starts, the amiable triviality of the whole exercise becomes tediously apparent.' – Philip Strick, MFB

Kanal *
Poland 1956 97m bw
Film Polski (Stanislaw Adler)
V*
aka: They Loved Life

In 1944, an anti-Nazi resistance group is trapped in a sewer.

A suffocatingly unpleasant film to watch; its message and technical excellence are undoubted.

w Jerzy Stawinski   novel Kloakerne by Jerzy Stawinski   d Andrzej Wajda   ph Jerzy Lipman   m Jan Krenz

Teresa Izewska, Tadeusz Janczar, Emil Kariewicz, Wienczylaw Glinski

Kanchenjungha **
India   1962   102m   colour
NCA Productions

During an afternoon on holiday in Darjeeling, a domineering father tries to arrange his daughter's marriage to an older, eligible bachelor.

Leisurely examination of attitudes to love and marriage and of the relationship between the sexes. It was Ray's first film in colour.

wd Satyajit Ray   *ph* Subrata Mitra   *m* Satyajit Ray
ad Bansi Chandragupta   *ed* Dulal Dutta

Chhabi Biswas, Anil Chatterjee, Karuna Banerjee, Anubha Gupta, Subrata Sen, Sibani Singh, Alaknanda Roy, Arun Mukherjee, N. Viswanathan

'Under the primitive working circumstances, the story about love and ambition and the collision of cultures was perhaps too complex, but the setting and the beautiful women help to compensate for the awkwardness and naiveté.' – *Pauline Kael*

Kangaroo
US   1952   84m   Technicolor
TCF (Robert Bassler)

In old Australia, a con man pretends to be a rancher's long-lost heir, then complicates things by falling in love with the rancher's daughter.

Standard romantic action hokum.

w Harry Kleiner   *d* Lewis Milestone   *ph* Charles G. Clarke   *m* Sol Kaplan

Maureen O'Hara, Peter Lawford, Finlay Currie, Richard Boone, Chips Rafferty, Charles Tingwell

'I'll make this town keep the peace – if I have to blow it to pieces!'

The Kansan
US   1943   79m   bw
UA (Harry Sherman)
V*

A wandering marksman stops off to become marshal of a frontier town.

Solid routine Western with good performances.

w Harold Shumate   *book* Frank Gruber   *d* George Archainbaud   *m* Gerard Carbonara

Richard Dix, Albert Dekker, Jane Wyatt, Eugene Pallette, Victor Jory, Robert Armstrong, Clem Bevans, Hobart Cavanaugh, Willie Best

AAN: Gerard Carbonara

Kansas
US   1988   106m   colour
Cannon/Trans World Entertainment (George Litto)
V, V*, L

A drifter falls foul of a crook and in love with a farmer's daughter.

Well-photographed wide open spaces that are empty of interest.

w Spencer Eastman   *d* David Stevens   *ph* David Eggby   *m* Pino Donnagio   *pd* Matthew Jacobs
ed Robert Barrere

Andrew McCarthy, Matt Dillon, Leslie Hope, Brent Jennings, Kyta Sedwick, Harry Northup, Arlen Dean Snyder

Kansas City Bomber
US   1972   99m   Metrocolor
MGM/Levy-Gardner-Laven/Raquel Welch (Marty Elfand)

A roller skating star finds time between affairs to beat her rival in a big match.

Vulgar melodrama with good action scenes.

w Thomas Rickman, Calvin Clements   *d* Jerrold Freedman   *ph* Fred Koenekamp   *m* Don Ellis

Raquel Welch, Kevin McCarthy, Norman Alden, Jeanne Cooper

Kansas City Confidential
US   1952   98m   bw
United Artists/Edward Small
V*
GB title: *The Secret Four*

An ex-detective plans a perfect crime, and recruits three confederates who all remain unknown to each other by wearing masks.

Moderately lively if violent thriller which gets less inventive as it goes along but satisfies the action buffs.

w George Bruce, Harry Essex   *d* Phil Karlson
ph George Diskant   *m* Paul Sawtell

Preston Foster, John Payne, Coleen Gray, Lee Van Cleef, Neville Brand, Jack Elam, Dona Drake

Kansas City Princess
US   1934   64m   bw
Warner (Lou Edelman)

Gold diggers go to Paris.

Light farce comedy, somewhat lacking in punch.

w Sy Bartlett, Manuel Seff   *d* William Keighley

Joan Blondell, Glenda Farrell, Hugh Herbert, Robert Armstrong, Osgood Perkins, Hobart Cavanaugh

'Just a comedy, good for better than moderate biz.' – *Variety*

Kansas Raiders
US   1951   80m   Technicolor
Universal-International

During the Civil War, Jesse James joins Quantrill's Raiders.

Fast-moving, fairly violent Western only remotely based on fact.

w Robert L. Richards   *d* Ray Enright

Audie Murphy, Brian Donlevy, Marguerite Chapman, Scott Brady, Tony Curtis, Richard Arlen, James Best, Richard Long

Kaos **
Italy   1984   188m   Eastmancolor
RAI-TV/Filmtre (Giuliano de Negri)

Five stories by Pirandello are combined in settings near his birthplace.

Generally fascinating mixture of tales which range from comedy to horror, styled by master film-makers.
wd *Paolo and Vittorio Taviani*   *ph* *Giuseppe Lanci*
m Nicola Piovanni   *ed* Roberto Perignani

Margarita Lozano, Claudio Bigagli, Enrica Maria Modugno, Ciccio Ingrassia, Franco Franchi, Biagio Barone, Omero Antonutti

Kapo
Italy/France   1960   115m   bw
Vides/Zebra/Francinex

A French Jewess survives the horrors of a Nazi concentration camp and becomes camp guard.

Curious exploitation piece which turns tragedy into melodrama, and doesn't even do that with much flair.

w Franco Solinas, Gillo Pontecorvo   *d* Gillo Pontecorvo   *ph* Goffredo Bellisario, Alexander Sekulovic   *m* Carlo Rustichelli

Susan Strasberg, Laurent Terzieff, Emmanuelle Riva

AAN: best foreign film

The Karate Kid *
US   1984   127m   Metrocolor
Columbia/Delphi II (Jerry Weintraub)
V, V*, L

A teenage boy, new to California, joins a karate club and defeats the local bullies.

A kind of amateur *Rocky*, not bad in its way, but its huge commercial success in the US remains mystifying.

w Robert Mark Kamen   *d* John G. Avildsen
ph James Crabe   *m* Bill Conti   *pd* William J. Cassidy   *ed* Bud Smith, Walt Mulconery

Ralph Macchio, Noriyuki 'Pat' Morita, Elizabeth Shue, Martin Kove, Randee Heller, William Zabka

AAN: Pat Morita (supporting actor)

The Karate Kid Part II
US   1986   113m   DeLuxe
Columbia/Delphi II (Jerry Weintraub)
V, V*, L

Daniel's teacher heads back to Okinawa where his father is gravely ill.

Tedious attempt to spin out a surprise hit; no surprises this time.

w Robert Mark Kamen   *d* John G. Avildsen
ph James Crabe   *m* Bill Conti   *pd* William J. Cassidy   *ed* David Garfield, Jane Kurson, John G. Avildsen

Pat Morita, Ralph Macchio, Nobu McCarthy, Danny Kamekona

AAN: song 'Glory of Love'

Karate Kid III
US   1989   112m   DeLuxe
Columbia TriStar (Jerry Weintraub)
V, V*, L

The karate kid defeats villains who attempt to humiliate him.

Even less interesting than Part II.

w Robert Mark Kamen   *d* John G. Avildsen
ph Stephen Yaconelli   *m* Bill Conti   *pd* William F. Matthews   *ed* John Carter, John G. Avildsen

Ralph Macchio, Noriyuki 'Pat' Morita, Robyn Lively, Thomas Ian Griffith, Martin L. Kove, Sean Kanan, Jonathan Avildsen

'Young love, meanwhile, has rarely been shown so boringly on screen.' – *MFB*

The Karate Killers
US   1967   90m   Metrocolor
MGM/Arena (Boris Ingster)

The men from U.N.C.L.E. foil enemy agents who steal a formula for making gold out of sea water.

Comic-strip spy spoof, featuring two incompetent agents who are forever being knocked out by the opposition, even when it's no stronger than geisha girls; a starry cast is given very little to do.

w Norman Hudis   *story* Boris Ingster   *d* Barry Shear   *ph* Fred Koenekamp   *m* Richard Shores
ad George W. Davis

Robert Vaughn, David McCallum, Joan Crawford, Curt Jurgens, Telly Savalas, Herbert Lom, Terry-Thomas, Leo G. Carroll, Kim Darby, Diane McBain

† The film was edited from episodes of the television series *The Man from U.N.C.L.E.*

Käre John: see *Dear John*

Kate Plus Ten
GB   1938   81m   bw
Wainwright (Richard Wainwright)

A police inspector falls for the attractive female leader of a bullion gang.

Curious comedy thriller with insufficient of either commodity.

w Jack Hulbert, Jeffrey Dell   *novel* Edgar Wallace
d Reginald Denham   *ph* Roy Kellino   *m* Allan Gray   *ad* D. L. W. Daniels   *ed* E. M. Hunter

Jack Hulbert, Genevieve Tobin, Noel Madison, Francis L. Sullivan, Arthur Wontner, Frank Cellier,

Googie Withers, Peter Haddon, Felix Aylmer, Leo Genn, Edward Lexy

Kathleen

US   1941   88m   bw   MGM (George Haight)

A neglected daughter finds a new wife for her widowed father.

One of the reasons for Shirley Temple's early retirement.

w Mary McCall Jnr   *story* Kay Van Riper   *d* Harold S. Bucquet   *ph* Sidney Wagner   *m* Franz Waxman

Shirley Temple, Herbert Marshall, Laraine Day, Gail Patrick, Felix Bressart, Nella Walker, Lloyd Corrigan

Kathy O

US   1958   99m   Eastmancolor   Cinemascope
U-I (Sy Gomberg)

A temperamental child star befriends a lonely columnist.

Overlong Hollywood comedy drama with amusing moments.

w Jack Sher, Sy Gomberg   *d* Jack Sher   *ph* Arthur E. Arling   *m* Frank Skinner   *m/ly* Charles Tobias, Ray Joseph

Patty McCormack, Dan Duryea, Jan Sterling, Sam Levene

Katie Did It

US   1951   81m   bw
Universal-International (Leonard Goldstein)

A small town is shocked when young Katie comes back having posed in scanty attire for a commercial artist.

Feeble comedy which totters to a lame conclusion.

w Jack Henley   *d* Frederick de Cordova, Russell Metty   *m* Frank Skinner

Ann Blyth, Mark Stevens, Cecil Kellaway, Elizabeth Patterson, Jesse White, Harold Vermilyea, Craig Stevens

Katina: see *Iceland*

Katinka *

Denmark/Sweden   1988   96m   colour
Nordisk Film/AB Svensk Filmindustri (Bo Christensen)

The wife of a village station master and a new farm foreman fall in love.

Intense domestic tragedy, in the manner of Ingmar Bergman.

w Klaus Rifberg   *novel* Ved Vejen by Herman Bang   *d* Max von Sydow   *ph* Sven Nykvist   *m* Georg Riedel   *ed* Janus Billeskov Jansen

Tammi Øst, Ole Ernest, Kurt Ravn

The Keep

US   1983   93m   Metrocolor   Scope
Paramount (Gene Kirkwood, Howard W. Koch Jnr)
V*, L

German troops in 1941 occupy a castle in the Carpathian Alps, and discover that it contains an evil force.

Extraordinary combination of war and fantasy fiction, not entirely dissimilar from *Castle Keep* which had a similar exposition.   *wd* Michael Mann   *novel* F. Paul Wilson   *ph* Alex Thomson   *m* Tangerine Dream

Scott Glenn, Alberta Watson, Jurgen Prochnow, Robert Prosky, Gabriel Byrne, Ian McKellen

Keep an Eye on Amelia: see *Occupe-Toi d'Amélie*

Keep 'Em Flying

US   1941   86m   bw
Universal (Glenn Tryon)
V*, L

Two incompetents in the Army Air Corps get mixed up with identical twin girls.

A big moneymaker of its day, this comedy now seems especially resistible.

w True Boardman, Nat Perrin, John Grant   *d* Arthur Lubin   *ph* Joseph Valentine   *m* Frank Skinner

Bud Abbott, Lou Costello, Martha Raye, Carol Bruce, William Gargan, Dick Foran, Charles Lang

AAN: song 'Pig Foot Pete' (*m* Gene de Paul, *ly* Don Raye)

Keep Fit *

GB   1937   82m   bw
ATP (Basil Dean)

A barber mistaken for an athlete finally excels at sport and also catches a thief.

Good star vehicle with snappy songs and fast comedy scenes.

w Anthony Kimmins, Austin Melford   *d* Anthony Kimmins   *ph* Ronald Neame, Gordon Dines   *m/ly* Harry Gifford, Fred. E. Cliffe   *ad* Wilfred Shingelton   *ed* Ernest Aldridge

George Formby, Kay Walsh, Guy Middleton, Gus McNaughton, Edmund Breon, George Benson, C. Denier Warren, Hal Gordon, Hal Walters, Leo Franklyn

Keep It Up Downstairs

GB   1976   94m   Technicolor
EMI/Pyramid (Hazel Adair)

A bed-hopping aristocratic family are faced with losing their ancestral home.

Dire sex farce that apes but fails to emulate the low style of the *Carry On* movies.

w Hazel Adair   *d* Robert Young   *ph* Alan Pudney   *m* Michael Nyman   *ad* Jacqueline Charrott-Lodwige   *ed* Mike Campbell

Diana Dors, Jack Wild, William Rushton, Aimi MacDonald, Françoise Pascal, Neil Hallett, Julian Orchard

'The cast, required to bare breasts and buttocks at regular intervals, is able to make no headway against the inane script and consistently mistimed direction.' – *Verina Glaessner, MFB*

Keep Smiling *

GB   1938   91m   bw
TCF (Robert T. Kane)
US title: *Smiling Along*

Problems of a touring concert party.

Pretty good star vehicle, though with unfortunate signs of an attempt to glamorize Our Gracie.

w Val Valentine, Rodney Ackland   *story* Sandor Farago, Alexander G. Kemedi   *d* Monty Banks   *ph* Max Greene   *md* Bretton Byrd   *ad* Oscar Werndorff   *ed* James B. Clark

Gracie Fields, Roger Livesey, Mary Maguire, Peter Coke, Jack Donohue, Tommy Fields, Eddie Gray, Edward Rigby, Hay Petrie

Keep Smiling

US   1938   77m   bw
TCF (John Stone)

The niece of a Hollywood director finds him on the skids.

More than usually substantial star comedy-drama.

w Frances Hyland, Albert Ray   *story* Frank Fenton, Lynn Root   *d* Herbert I. Leeds   *ph* Edward Cronjager   *md* Samuel Kaylin

Jane Withers, Henry Wilcoxon, Gloria Stuart, Helen Westley, Jed Prouty, Pedro de Cordoba, Douglas Fowley

'A kids' picture with an adult punch.' – *Variety*

Keep Your Powder Dry

US   1945   93m   bw
MGM (George Haight)

Three girls from different backgrounds join the WACS.

Totally uninteresting and unconvincing female flagwaver.

w Mary C. McCall Jnr, George Bruce   *d* Edward Buzzell   *ph* Ray June   *m* David Snell

Lana Turner, Laraine Day, Susan Peters, Agnes Moorehead, Bill Johnson, Natalie Schafer, June Lockhart, Lee Patrick

Keep Your Seats Please *

GB   1936   82m   bw
ATP (Basil Dean)

A prospective heir seeks a fortune hidden in one of six chairs.

Good star comedy on a theme later reworked in *It's in the Bag* (qv) and *The Twelve Chairs* (qv).

w Tom Geraghty, Ian Hay, Anthony Kimmins   *play* Twelve Chairs by Elie Ilf, Eugene Petrov   *d* Monty Banks   *ph* John W. Boyle   *m/ly* Harry Parr-Davies, Harry Gifford, Fred. E. Cliffe   *ad* R. Holmes Paul   *ed* Jack Kitchin

George Formby, Florence Desmond, Alastair Sim, Gus McNaughton, Harry Tate

Keeper of the Bees

US   1935   76m   bw
Monogram (Trem Carr)

A country boy makes good.

Victorian-style fable for rural audiences.

w Adele Buffington   *novel* Gene Stratton Porter   *d* Christy Cabanne

Neil Hamilton, Betty Furness, Emma Dunn, Edith Fellows, Hobart Bosworth

'For discriminating patronage, a washout . . . a calico narrative for the crossroads.' – *Variety*

Keeper of the Flame *

US   1942   100m   bw
MGM (Victor Saville)

A reporter befriends the widow of a politician and forces her to disclose her husband's guilty secret.

Well-acted but over-solemn melodrama which badly needs a sting in the tail.

w Donald Ogden Stewart   *novel* I. A. R. Wylie   *d* George Cukor   *ph* William Daniels   *m* Bronislau Kaper

Spencer Tracy, Katharine Hepburn, Richard Whorf, Margaret Wycherly, Donald Meek, Stephen McNally, Audrey Christie, Frank Craven

'An expensive testimonial to Hollywood's inability to face a significant theme.' – *Time*

'Unorthodox and on the whole absorbing drama. Ominous portents and overtones take the place of physical action.' – *Christian Science Monitor*

'A gothic wet blanket of a movie.' – *Pauline Kael, 70s*

Keepers of Youth

GB   1931   70m   bw
BIP (John Maxwell)

A young schoolmaster finds his fresh ideas make him unpopular, especially when he is found in a compromising position with the assistant matron.

Old-fashioned drama with a few lively scenes.

w Frank Launder, Thomas Bentley, Walter Mycroft   *play* Arnold Ridley   *d* Thomas Bentley   *ph* James Wilson, Bert Ford

Garry Marsh, Ann Todd, Robin Irvine, John Turnbull, O. B. Clarence, Mary Clare

Keeping Company
US 1940 80m bw
MGM

A young man announces his engagement but has trouble when his ex-girlfriend returns to town.

Amiable family comedy which was announced to be the first of a series, but stayed lonely.

w James Hill, Harry Ruskin, Adrian Scott d S. Sylvan Simon

Frank Morgan, Irene Rich, John Shelton, Ann Rutherford, Virginia Weidler, Dan Dailey, Gene Lockhart, Virginia Grey

Kelly and Me
US 1956 86m Technicolor Cinemascope
U-I (Robert Arthur)

The ups and downs of a song and dance man and the dog who shares his act.

Mild vaudeville saga with totally predictable twists.

w Everett Freeman d Robert Z. Leonard
ph Maury Gertsman m Joseph Gershenson

Van Johnson, Piper Laurie, Martha Hyer, Onslow Stevens

Kelly the Second
US 1936 71m bw
MGM

A determined lady trains a dimwitted prizefighter.

Easy-going farce from a studio which knew how to make them; but this wasn't one of the best.

w Jack Jevne, Gordon Douglas d Hal Roach

Patsy Kelly, Guinn Williams, Charley Chase, Pert Kelton, Harold Huber

Kelly's Heroes
US/Yugoslavia 1970 143m Metrocolor Panavision
MGM/The Warriors/Avala (Irving Leonard)
V, V*, L

During World War II, an American platoon abducts a German general and accidentally discovers the whereabouts of a fortune in gold.

Crude slam-bang actioner for the obvious market.

w Troy Kennedy Martin d Brian G. Hutton
ph Gabriel Figueroa second unit Andrew Marton
m Lalo Schifrin

Clint Eastwood, Telly Savalas, Don Rickles, Donald Sutherland, Carroll O'Connor, Stuart Margolin, Dick Davalos

'Over two hours of consistently devastating explosions, pyrotechnics and demolition.' – MFB

'Made for no possible reason other than a chance to use the Yugoslav army at cut rates.' – Judith Crist, 1973

The Kennel Murder Case **
US 1933 73m bw
Warner (Robert Presnell)
V*

Philo Vance proves that an apparent suicide is really murder.

Complex murder mystery, very smartly handled and often cited as a classic of the genre; later remade as Calling Philo Vance.

w Robert N. Lee, Peter Milner novel S. S. Van Dine
d Michael Curtiz ph William Reese

William Powell, Mary Astor, Eugene Pallette, Ralph Morgan, Helen Vinson, Jack La Rue, Paul Cavanagh, Robert Barrat

'Entertaining all the way.' – Variety

'Players are cast so inevitably to type that the film is like a demonstration of the principles of running a stock company.' – New Yorker, 1978

'Stylistically a little gem.' – Clive Hirschhorn

† See also Philo Vance.

The Kentuckian
US 1955 104m Technicolor Cinemascope
UA/Hecht-Lancaster (Howard Hecht)
V, V*, S

A Kentucky backwoodsman takes his small son to settle in Texas.

Ambling mid-Western with moments of interest.

w A. B. Guthrie Jnr novel The Gabriel Horn by Felix Holt d Burt Lancaster ph Ernest Laszlo
m Bernard Herrmann

Burt Lancaster, Dianne Foster, Diana Lynn, Walter Matthau, John McIntire, Una Merkel, John Carradine

Kentucky *
US 1938 95m Technicolor
TCF (Gene Markey)

Horse-breeding rivalry prevents the smooth running of true love.

Harmless family entertainment, more professionally handled than its innumerable later imitations. Remade as April Love.

w Lamar Trotti novel The Look of Eagles by John Taintor Foote d David Butler ph Ernest Palmer
md Louis Silvers

Loretta Young, Richard Greene, Walter Brennan, Douglass Dumbrille, Karen Morley, Moroni Olsen, Russell Hicks

'An outstanding effort, geared for top money.' – Variety

AA: Walter Brennan

The Kentucky Fried Movie
US 1977 90m colour
Alpha/Kentucky Fried Theatre (Robert K. Weiss)
V, V*

Comedy sketches from the University of Wisconsin parodying television programmes and commercials.

The writers later gave us Airplane. Enough said?

w David and Jerry Zucker, Jim Abrahams d John Landis ph Stephen M. Katz ad Rick Harvel
ed George Folsey Jnr

Marilyn Joi, Saul Kahan, Marcy Goldman, Joe Medalis

Kentucky Kernels
US 1934 74m bw
RKO
GB title: Triple Trouble

An orphan left with two musicians proves to be the heir to a fortune, but the way to it is through feuding hillbilly country.

Fairly funny Wheeler and Woolsey comedy, in other words one of their better efforts.

w Bert Kalmar, Harry Ruby and Fred Guiol
d George Stevens

Bert Wheeler, Robert Woolsey, Mary Carlisle, Spanky McFarland, Noah Beery, Willie Best

Kentucky Moonshine *
US 1938 87m bw
TCF (Darryl F. Zanuck)

In the hope of a radio contract, the Ritz Brothers masquerade as hillbillies and find themselves in the middle of a feud.

One of the trio's best solo vehicles.

w Art Arthur, M. M. Musselman d David Butler
ph Robert Planck md Louis Silvers m/ly Lew Pollack, Sidney Mitchell

The Ritz Brothers, Tony Martin, Marjorie Weaver, Slim Summerville, John Carradine, Wally Vernon, Berton Churchill, Eddie Collins

'It's crazy and it's wild, but it's funny and grand entertainment.' – Variety

La Kermesse Héroïque **
France 1935 115m bw
Tobis
aka: Carnival in Flanders

When Spaniards invade a Flemish town in 1616, the men make themselves scarce and the women find other ways of conquering.

Sprightly though overlong comedy which seemed risqué at the time and therefore enjoyed international success.

w Charles Spaak, Jacques Feyder novel Charles Spaak
d Jacques Feyder ph Harry Stradling m Louis Beydts ad Lazare Meerson

Françoise Rosay, Louis Jouvet, Jean Murat, Alfred Adam, André Alerme

'A mixture of gay absurdity and shrewd comment, selecting its own pitch and holding it – comedy, you might say, self-contained.' – Otis Ferguson

'Everything fits perfectly into the pattern of cultured and sophisticated entertainment. Nowhere is there a false touch.' – The Times, 1952

Kes ****
GB 1969 109m Technicolor
UA/Woodfall (Tony Garnett)
V

In a northern industrial town, a boy learns about life from the fate of his pet bird.

Realistic family drama that is one of the key British films of its period.

w Barry Hines, Ken Loach, Tony Garnet novel A Kestrel for a Knave by Barry Hines d Ken Loach
ph Chris Menges m John Cameron

David Bradley, Lynne Perrie, Colin Welland, Freddie Fletcher, Brian Glover

'There emerges a most discouraging picture of life in the industrial north . . . infinitely sad in its total implications, it is also immensely funny in much of its detail.' – Brenda Davies

'Particularly to be admired is the way in which the dialogue has been kept flowing, as if it were always spontaneous, something proceeding from the moment.' – Dilys Powell

The Kettles
The rustic couple evolved from characters in The Egg and I (qv); Marjorie Main and Percy Kilbride went on to play them in a cheap but very popular series for Universal, variously scripted and directed.

1949: MA AND PA KETTLE
1950: MA AND PA KETTLE GO TO TOWN
1951: MA AND PA KETTLE BACK ON THE FARM
1952: MA AND PA KETTLE AT THE FAIR
1953: MA AND PA KETTLE ON VACATION
1954: MA AND PA KETTLE AT HOME
1955: MA AND PA KETTLE AT WAIKIKI
1956: THE KETTLES IN THE OZARKS (Arthur Hunnicutt instead of Kilbride)
1957: THE KETTLES ON OLD MACDONALD'S FARM (Parker Fennelly instead of Kilbride)

The Key *
US 1934 71m bw
Warner

In Ireland in the twenties, a British army captain falls for the wife of an intelligence officer.

Heroics among the black and tans; interesting but dated drama.

w Laird Doyle play R. Gore-Brown, J. L. Hardy
d Michael Curtiz

William Powell, Edna Best, Colin Clive, Hobart Cavanaugh, Halliwell Hobbes, Henry O'Neill, Arthur Treacher, Donald Crisp

'The door opened into a haven from hell ... and the girl came with the key!'

The Key *
GB   1958   134m   bw   Cinemascope
Columbia/Open Road (Carl Foreman)
V*, L

World War II tugboat skippers, about to embark on dangerous missions, pass on the key to an apartment and a girl to go with it.

Rather foolish symbolic melodrama which never makes its purpose clear but along the way provides fragments of love story, chunks of the supernatural and dollops of war action, rather languidly assembled with great technical competence but little real feeling. The talent occasionally shows through.

w Carl Foreman   novel Stella by Jan de Hartog
d Carol Reed   ph Oswald Morris   m Malcolm Arnold

William Holden, Sophia Loren, Trevor Howard, Oscar Homolka, Kieron Moore

The Key
Italy   1984   116m   Technicolor
Enterprise/San Francisco Film (Giovanni Bertolucci)
V

As Mussolini begins his rise to power, an art professor keeps a diary concerning his frustration over his wife's prudery; in turn she begins a diary of her affair with her daughter's boyfriend.

Atrocious soft-core porn that takes in transvestism, necrophilia and urolagnia and includes Finlay dressed in bra, panties, suspenders and stockings having a heart attack while making love. Avoid.

wd Tinto Brass   novel Kagi by Junichiro Tanizaki
ph Silvano Ippoliti   m Ennio Morricone   ad Paolo Biagetti   ed Tinto Brass

Frank Finlay, Stefania Sandrelli, Franco Branciaroli, Barbara Cupisti, Armando Marra, Maria Grazia Bon, Gino Cavalieri

'Where there's muck, there's brass; and where there's cinematic muck, there's Tinto Brass.' – Virgin Film Yearbook

'A storm of fear and fury in the sizzling Florida keys!'

Key Largo ***
US   1948   101m   bw
Warner (Jerry Wald)
V, V*, L

A returning war veteran fights gangsters on the Florida keys.

Moody melodrama on similar lines to To Have and Have Not: it sums up the post-war mood of despair, allows several good acting performances, and builds up to a pretty good action climax.

w Richard Brooks, John Huston   play Maxwell Anderson   d John Huston   ph Karl Freund   m Max Steiner

Humphrey Bogart, Lauren Bacall, Claire Trevor, Edward G. Robinson, Lionel Barrymore, Thomas Gomez, Marc Lawrence

'It's a confidently directed, handsomely shot movie, and the cast go at it as if the nonsense about gangsters and human dignity were high drama.' – New Yorker, 1977

'A completely empty, synthetic work.' – Gavin Lambert

AA: Claire Trevor

Key to the City
US   1950   101m   bw
MGM (Z. Wayne Griffin)

At a San Francisco convention, two mayors get involved in several escapades and fall in love.

Routine romantic comedy.

w Robert Riley Crutcher   d George Sidney
ph Harold Rosson   m Bronislau Kaper

Clark Gable, Loretta Young, Frank Morgan, James Gleason, Marilyn Maxwell, Raymond Burr, Lewis Stone, Raymond Walburn, Pamela Britton

'A comedy made to measure . . . the script concerns itself with wringing every possible laugh from a number of stock situations.' – Variety

'Don't come if you're afraid to see what's on the other side of ...'

The Keyhole *
US   1933   70m   bw
Warner (Hal Wallis)

A divorce investigator falls for the wife he is commissioned to frame.

Unsavoury little drama, unusual enough to be interesting.

w Robert Presnell   novel Adventures by Alice Duer Miller   d Michael Curtiz

Kay Francis, George Brent, Glenda Farrell, Allen Jenkins, Monroe Owsley

The Keys of the Kingdom *
US   1944   137m   bw
TCF (Joseph L. Mankiewicz)
V*

The life of a 19th-century Scottish priest in China.

Studio-made missionary melodrama, a big hit for its new star but otherwise an undistinguished piece of work with a shuffling pace and not much by way of climax.

w Joseph L. Mankiewicz, Nunnally Johnson
novel A. J. Cronin   d John M. Stahl   ph Arthur Miller   m Alfred Newman   ad James Basevi, William Darling

Gregory Peck, Thomas Mitchell, Vincent Price, Rose Stradner, Roddy McDowall, Edmund Gwenn, Cedric Hardwicke, Peggy Ann Garner, James Gleason, Anne Revere

'Long, earnest, long, worthy, interesting and long.' – Richard Mallett, Punch

AAN: Arthur Miller; Alfred Newman; Gregory Peck; art direction

'Where the Nile divides, their mighty conflict begins!'

Khartoum *
GB   1966   134m   Technicolor   Ultra Panavision
UA/Julian Blaustein
V*, L

The last years of General Gordon.

Dullish history book stuff which fails to explain Gordon the man but occasionally erupts into glowing action.

w Robert Ardrey   d Basil Dearden   ph Edward Scaife, Harry Waxman   m Frank Cordell

Charlton Heston, Laurence Olivier, Ralph Richardson, Richard Johnson, Hugh Williams, Alexander Knox, Johnny Sekka, Nigel Green, Michael Hordern

'Academic accuracy and spectacular battles are unhappy partners.' – MFB

'Beautifully photographed, lavishly mounted, intelligently acted, but ultimately dull.' – Sight and Sound

AAN: Robert Ardrey

Kickboxer
US   1989   103m   Technicolor
Entertainment/Kings Road Entertainment (Mark DiSalle)
V*, L

After his brother is crippled in a fight, an American kickboxer seeks revenge.

Standard martial arts adventure.

w Glenn Bruce   story Mark DiSalle, Jean Claude Van Damme   d Mark DiSalle, David Worth
ph Jon Kranhouse   m Paul Hertzog   pd Shay Austin   ed Wayne Wahrman

Jean Claude Van Damme, Dennis Alexio, Dennis Chan, Tong Po (Michel Qissi), Haskell Anderson, Rochelle Ashana, Steve Lee, Richard Foo, Ricky Lui

Kickboxer II: The Road Back
US   1990   89m   colour
Entertainment/Kings Road (Tom Karnowksi)
V, V*

A retired kickboxer is forced back into the ring to defeat a Thai gangster's champion.

Direly inept sequel.

w David S. Goyer   d Albert Pyun   ph Mark Emery Moore   m Tony Riparetti, James Saad   ad Nicholas T. Prevost   ed Alan E. Baumgarten

Sasha Mitchell, Peter Boyle, Dennis Chan, Cary-Hiroyuki Tagawa, John Diehl, Michel Qissi, Heather McComb, Vince Murducco, Matthias Hues

'Has all the faults of many Stateside chop-socky carbons: slow pacing, fortune-cookie philosophy and fight sequences shot from all the wrong angles.' – Variety

Kickboxer III: The Art of War
US   1992   92m   DeLuxe
Vision International (Michael Pariser)
V*

In Rio de Janeiro, an American kick-boxer takes revenge on a fight promoter who is also a white slaver.

Only a slight variation here on the single plot that seems to serve for every martial arts movie, and there is no variation at all on the usual high-kicking and predictable action.

w Dennis Pratt   d Rick King   ph Edgar Moura   m Harry Manfredini   pd Clovis Bueno   ed Dan Lowenthal

Sasha Mitchell, Dennis Chan, Richard Comar, Noah Verduzco, Milton Goncalves, Alethea Miranda, Miguel Orniga

'A routine martial arts pic that benefits from attractive Brazilian location photography.' – Variety

Kicking the Moon Around
GB   1938   78m   bw
Vogue (Howard Welsch)
US titles: The Playboy; Millionaire Merry Go Round

A millionaire goes into show business to establish a career for his singing protégée.

Mild, frothy comedy, dated but quite fluent.

w Angus McPhail, Roland Pertwee, Michael Hogan, Harry Fowler Mear   story Tom Geraghty   d Walter Forde   ph Francis Carver   ad John Bryan   ed Derek Twist

Ambrose and his Orchestra, Evelyn Dall, Hal Thompson, Florence Desmond, Harry Richman, C. Denier Warren, Max Bacon

'6 Reels of Joy.'

The Kid ***
US   1921   52m approx (24 fps)   bw   silent
First National/Charles Chaplin
V, V*, L

A tramp brings up an abandoned baby, and later loses him to his mother; but there is a happy ending.

Sentimental comedy set in the slums. The comedy is very sparingly laid on, but the effect of the whole is much less painful than the synopsis would suggest, the production is comparatively smooth, the child actor is sensational, and the film contains much of the quintessential Chaplin.

wd Charles Chaplin   ph Rollie Totheroh

Charles Chaplin, Jackie Coogan, Edna Purviance

Kid

US   1990   91m   Alpha Cine
Entertainment/Tapestry Films (Robert L. Levy, Peter Abrams, Nathan Zahavi)
V, V*

A teenager returns to his home town for revenge on the locals who killed his parents.

Dull, morally confused modern Western.

w Leslie Bohem   d John Mark Robinson
ph Robert Yeoman   m Tim Truman   pd Sharon Seymour   ed Nathan Zahavi

C. Thomas Howell, Sarah Trigger, Brian Austin Green, R. Lee Ermey, Dale Dye, Michael Bowen, Damon Bowen, Lenore Kasdorf

'Ludicrously recasts a barely stubbled youth in the role of the outsider-avenger.' – *MFB*

Kid Auto Races at Venice

US   1914   6m approx   bw   silent
Keystone/Mack Sennett

This much-mentioned film is no more than a few candid camera shots of a children's car race on the California beach. It so happened that the young Charles Chaplin was called upon to liven up proceedings by causing a nuisance, and hastily conceived his tramp costume to do so. His fragments of comedy, primitive though they now seem, made him a star.

wd Henry Lehrman   ph Frank D. Williams

Kid Blue

US   1973   100m   DeLuxe   Panavision
TCF/Marvin Schwarz Productions

In 1902 Texas a young outlaw tries to go straight.

Deliberately myth-deflating Western with agreeably rich detail.

w Edwin Shrake   d James Frawley   ph Billy Williams   m Tim McIntire, John Rubinstein
pd Joel Schiller

Dennis Hopper, Warren Oates, Peter Boyle, Ben Johnson, Lee Purcell, Janice Rule, Clifton James

The Kid Brother ****

US   1927   83m   bw   silent
Paramount/Lloyd (Harold Lloyd)

The youngest son in the family proves that he is more than the household drudge.

Lively, slapstick comedy with the star at his best.

w John Grey, Tom Crizer, Ted Wilde   d Ted Wilde, J. A. Howe, Lewis Milestone   ph Walter Lundin, Henry N. Kohler   ad Liell K. Vedder   ed Allen McNeil

Harold Lloyd, Jobyna Ralston, Walter James, Leo Willis, Olin Francis, Constantine Romanoff

'As gaggy a gag picture as he has ever done.' – *Variety*

The Kid Comes Back

US   1937   61m   bw
Warner (Bryan Foy)

A tenderfoot from Texas is trained by an ex-champion prizefighter.

Not really a sequel to *Kid Galahad*, but a second feature in its wake; as such, fair.

w George Bricker, E. J. Flanagan   d B. Reeves Eason

Wayne Morris, Barton MacLane, June Travis, Maxie Rosenbloom

'Brisk, fast, strong dualler.' – *Variety*

A Kid for Two Farthings *

GB   1955   96m   Eastmancolor
London Films (Carol Reed)
V*

Among the colourful characters of London's Petticoat Lane market moves a boy whose pet goat seems to have the magical power of a unicorn.

Whimsical character comedy-drama made with some style but too insubstantial and unconvincing to be affectionately remembered.

w Wolf Mankowitz   d Carol Reed   ph Ted Scaife
m Benjamin Frankel

Celia Johnson, Diana Dors, David Kossoff, Brenda de Banzie, Sidney Tafler, Primo Carnera, Joe Robinson, Jonathan Ashmore

The Kid from Brooklyn

US   1946   114m   Technicolor
Samuel Goldwyn
V*, L

A timid milkman becomes a prizefighter.

Yawn-provoking comedy, a remake of Harold Lloyd's *The Milky Way;* the first indication that Danny Kaye could be a bore.

w Grover Jones, Frank Butler, Richard Connell
d Norman Z. McLeod   ph Gregg Toland
md Carmen Dragon   m/ly Jule Styne, Sammy Cahn

Danny Kaye, Virginia Mayo, Vera-Ellen, Steve Cochran, Eve Arden, Walter Abel, Lionel Stander, Fay Bainter, Clarence Kolb

† Lionel Stander played the same role in *The Milky Way.*

The Kid from Kokomo

US   1939   92m   bw
Warner (Sam Bischoff)

A farm boy's fight manager decides that for publicity purposes he must acquire a family.

Yet another follow-up to *Kid Galahad*, this time on the farcical side. Not bad, but too long.

w Jerry Wald, Richard Macauley, Dalton Trumbo
d Lewis Seiler

Pat O'Brien, Wayne Morris, Joan Blondell, May Robson, Jane Wyman, Stanley Fields, Maxie Rosenbloom, Sidney Toler, Ed Brophy

'Full of laughs, and a very probable money-getter.' – *Variety*

The Kid from Left Field

US   1953   80m   bw
TCF (Leonard Goldstein)

A big league basketball player is reduced to selling peanuts at the games, but passes on advice through his small son, who is appointed team manager.

Half-hearted whimsy for addicts.

w Jack Sher   d Harmon Jones   ph Harry Jackson
m Lionel Newman

Dan Dailey, Billy Chapin, Anne Bancroft, Lloyd Bridges, Ray Collins, Richard Egan

The Kid from Spain **

US   1932   90m   bw
Samuel Goldwyn

A simpleton is mistaken for a celebrated bullfighter.

Charmingly dated star musical which, though primitive in some respects, is a splendid reminder of its period.

w William Anthony McGuire, Bert Kalmar, Harry Ruby   d Leo McCarey   ph Gregg Toland   ch Busby Berkeley   m/ly Bert Kalmar, Harry Ruby

Eddie Cantor, Lyda Roberti, Robert Young, Ruth Hall, John Miljan, Noah Beery, J. Carrol Naish, Stanley Fields, Betty Grable, Paulette Goddard

'A corking comedy . . . it'll get a lot of money.' – *Variety*

The Kid from Texas

US   1950   85m   Technicolor
Universal-International
GB title: *Texas Kid, Outlaw*

The last rampage of Billy the Kid.

Surprisingly violent Western for its time; otherwise unremarkable.

w Robert Hardy Andrews, Karl Kamb   d Kurt Neumann

Audie Murphy, Gale Storm, Albert Dekker, Shepperd Strudwick, Will Geer, William Talman

Kid Galahad *

US   1937   101m   bw
Warner (Samuel Bischoff)
V, V*
TV title: *Battling Bellhop*

A bellhop is groomed as a prizefighter, and his trainer grows jealous.

Good standard prizefight melodrama, remade as *The Wagons Roll at Night* and later as *Kid Galahad* with Elvis Presley (see below).

w Seton I. Miller   novel Francis Wallace
d Michael Curtiz   ph Tony Gaudio   m Heinz Roemheld, Max Steiner

Edward G. Robinson, Bette Davis, Wayne Morris, Jane Bryan, Humphrey Bogart, Harry Carey

'Good prizefight picture with action, melodrama and names. Unusual in that women will like it.' – *Variety*

Kid Galahad

US   1962   96m   DeLuxe   Panavision
UA/Mirisch (David Weisbart)

Tolerable light-hearted musical remake of the above.

w William Fay   d Phil Karlson   ph Burnett Guffey
m Jeff Alexander

Elvis Presley, Lola Albright, Gig Young, Joan Blackman, Charles Bronson, Ned Glass, David Lewis, Robert Emhardt

Kid Glove Killer *

US   1942   73m   bw
MGM (Jack Chertok)

A police laboratory scientist tracks down the murderer of the mayor and finds his best friend is the culprit.

Professional police suspenser of the kind now tackled by television.

w John Higgins, Allen Rivkin   d Fred Zinnemann
ph Paul C. Vogel   m David Snell

Van Heflin, Lee Bowman, Marsha Hunt, Samuel S. Hinds, Eddie Quillan

Kid Millions *

US   1935   90m   bw/Technicolor sequence
Samuel Goldwyn

An East Side kid inherits a fortune and has the time of his life.

Dated star musical with moments which still please.

w George Oppenheimer, William Anthony McGuire, Nunnally Johnson   d Roy del Ruth   ph Gregg Toland   md Alfred Newman   m/ly various
ad Richard Day

Eddie Cantor, Ethel Merman, Ann Sothern, George Murphy, Warren Hymer

'Goldwyn-Cantor girl-and-gag socko.' – *Variety*

Kid Nightingale

US   1939   56m   bw
Warner

A waiter is promoted into a prizefighter, and sings as he knocks out each opponent.

Self-spoofing comedy with some laughs.

w Charles Belden, Raymond Schrock, Lee Katz
d George Amy

John Payne, Jane Wyman, Walter Catlett, Ed Brophy, Charles D. Brown

'It's so absolutely silly it's almost good.' – *Variety*

'One man had been like any other to Nora. Then she met the kid.'

Kid Rodelo

US/Spain   1966   91m   bw
Trident/Fenix/Paramount

An outlaw fresh from prison races his former partners for the hidden loot.

Dull Western.

w Jack Natteford   story Louis L'Amour   d Richard Carlson

Don Murray, Janet Leigh, Richard Carlson, Broderick Crawford, Jose Nieto

Kidco

US   1984   105m   colour
TCF (Frank Yablans, David Niven Jnr)
V*

A boy who thinks up a series of money-making schemes in the hope of getting rich while young finds himself in trouble with the law.

Mildly amusing comedy, said to be based on a true story, but one without a natural audience: its concerns are too old for kids, and too silly for adults.

w Bennett Tramer   d Ronald F. Maxwell   ph Paul Lohmann   m Michael Small   pd Fred Price
ed David E. McKenna

Scott Schwartz, Clifton James, Charles Hallahan, Maggie Blye, Basil Hoffman, Phil Rubenstein, Cinnamon Idles, Tristine Skyler, Elizabeth Gorcey

Kidnapped (1933): see
Miss Fane's Baby Is Stolen

Kidnapped *

US   1938   93m   bw
TCF (Kenneth MacGowan)

During the Jacobite rebellion a young boy is sold by his wicked uncle as a slave, and is helped by an outlaw.

Much altered version of a classic adventure story, exciting enough in its own right, and well made in the thirties tradition.

w Sonya Levien, Richard Sherman, Walter Ferris   novel Robert Louis Stevenson   d Alfred L. Werker   ph Bert Glennon   m Arthur Lange

Warner Baxter, Freddie Bartholomew, Arleen Whelan, John Carradine, C. Aubrey Smith, Nigel Bruce, Reginald Owen

'Strange modifications have been wrought . . . ambitious effort which misses top rating.' – *Variety*

Kidnapped *

GB   1959   95m   Technicolor
Walt Disney (Hugh Attwooll)
V*, L

A remake fairly faithful to the book, which results in a few *longueurs;* but in general the action is spirited.

wd Robert Stevenson   ph Paul Beeson   m Cedric Thorpe Davie

Peter Finch, James MacArthur, Bernard Lee, John Laurie, Finlay Currie, Niall MacGinnis, Peter O'Toole, Miles Malleson, Oliver Johnston, Duncan Macrae, Andrew Cruickshank

Kidnapped *

GB   1971   107m   Movielab   Panavision
Omnibus (Frederick H. Brogger)

Remake incorporating sections of *Catriona.* Not particularly exciting, but the acting helps.

w Jack Pulman   d Delbert Mann   ph Paul Beeson   m Roy Budd

Michael Caine, Lawrence Douglas, Trevor Howard, Jack Hawkins, Donald Pleasence, Gordon Jackson, Freddie Jones, Jack Watson

The Kidnappers *

GB   1953   95m   bw
Rank/Nolbandov-Parkyn
US title: *The Little Kidnappers*

In a Nova Scotian village at the turn of the century a stern old man denies his young grandchildren a pet, so they borrow a baby and hide it in the woods.

Fairly pleasing and popular whimsy for family audiences.

w Neil Paterson   d Philip Leacock   ph Eric Cross   m Bruce Montgomery

Duncan Macrae, Vincent Winter, Jon Whiteley, Theodore Bikel, Jean Anderson

The Kidnapping of the President *

Canada   1980   113m   DeLuxe
Sefel (George Mendeluk, John Ryan)
V*

Third-world terrorists devise a plot to bring America to its knees by kidnapping the president.

Spirited political thriller which suffers chiefly from overlength.

w Richard Murphy   novel Charles Templeton   d George Mendeluk   ph Mike Malloy   m Paul J. Zaza

Hal Holbrook, William Shatner, Van Johnson, Ava Gardner, Miguel Fernandez, Cindy Girling, Elizabeth Shepherd

The Kid's Last Fight: see *The Life of Jimmy Dolan*

Kiki

US   1931   96m   bw
UA/Mary Pickford (Joseph M. Schenck)

A tomboyish chorus girl sets her cap at her divorced producer.

Long unseen star musical.

w Sam Taylor   play David Belasco   d Sam Taylor   ph Karl Struss   m Alfred Newman

Mary Pickford, Reginald Denny, Joseph Cawthorn, Margaret Livingston

'Too long and too light . . . what was to have been a cocktail has turned out to be a soda.' – *Variety*

Kikuchi

Japan   1990   68m   colour
ICA/Vortex Japan (Shuichi Ohi)

A laundry worker, who leads an aimless life, becomes obsessed with a check-out girl at a supermarket.

Quirky small film, with little in the way of action or dialogue.

wd Kenchi Iwamoto   ph Hideo Fukuda   pd Takashi Iwai   ed Keiichi Okada

Jiro Yoshimura, Yasuhiro Oka, Misa Kukuma, Papa Akiyama, Mama Akiyama, Masaya Yasumura

Kill and Pray (dubbed) *

Italy/W. Germany   1967   102m   colour
Castor/Mancor Chretien/Luce/Tefi (Carlo Lizzani)
V (W)
original title: *Requiescant*

The adopted son of a preacher discovers that he is the sole survivor of a massacre, instigated by an American in order to steal land promised to the Mexican peasants.

Stylish Marxist spaghetti Western, though the politics are subsumed in the usual ingredients of plangent music, over-the-top confrontations, bizarre

happenings and multiple deaths. Pasolini pops up unexpectedly as a revolutionary priest.

w Andrew Baxter, Denis Greene, Edward Williams   story Arnold Elias, Frank Mills   d Carlo Lizzani   ph Alexander Clark   m Roger Higgins   ad Geoffrey Bailey   ed Frank Rubien

Lou Castel, Mark Damon, Pier Paolo Pasolini, Barbara Frey, Rossana Krisman, Mary Ellen Maxwell

Kill Her Gently

GB   1958   75m   bw
Fortress/Columbia

A madman hires two convicts to murder his wife.

Very mild and unmemorable thriller.

w Paul Erickson   d Charles Saunders

Griffith Jones, Maureen Connell, Marc Lawrence, George Mikell

Kill Me Again

US   1989   96m   DeLuxe
Palace/Propaganda Films/ITC (David W. Warfield, Sigurjon Sighvatsson, Steve Golin)
V

On the run from her boyfriend, whom she robbed, a woman pays a private eye to fake her death.

Not very successful attempt to recreate the style of 1940s *film noir.*

w John R. Dahl, David W. Warfield   d John R. Dahl   ph Jacques Steyn   m William Olvis   pd Michelle Minch   ed Frank Jiminez, Jonathan Shaw, Eric Beason

Val Kilmer, Joanne Whalley-Kilmer, Michael Madsen, Jonathan Gries, Pat Mulligan, Nick Dimitri

Kill Me Tomorrow

GB   1957   80m   bw
Delta

A down-and-out reporter confesses to murder in order to obtain cash for his son's operation.

Tepid melodrama without much chemistry.

w Robert Falconer, Manning O'Brine   d Terence Fisher

Pat O'Brien, Lois Maxwell, George Coulouris, Wensley Pithey, Tommy Steele

Kill or Cure

GB   1962   88m   bw
MGM (George H. Brown)

A series of murders at a nature clinic are solved by a bumbling private detective.

Flatfooted and unprofessional murder farce whose only pace is slow.

w David Pursall, Jack Seddon   d George Pollock   ph Geoffrey Faithfull   m Ron Goodwin

Terry-Thomas, Eric Sykes, Dennis Price, Lionel Jeffries, Moira Redmond, David Lodge, Ronnie Barker

Kill the Umpire

US   1950   78m   bw
Columbia

An over-age baseball player can't get the game out of his mind, and returns as an argumentative umpire.

Minor comedy of presumed pleasure to sports addicts.

w Frank Tashlin   d Lloyd Bacon

William Bendix, Una Merkel, Ray Collins, Gloria Henry, William Frawley

The Killer *

Hong Kong   1989   111m   colour
Palace/Film Workshop/Golden Princess/Magnum (Tsui Hark)
V, V*
original title: *Diexue Shuang Xiong*

A hired killer is double-crossed by his employer.

Excessively violent imitation of Hollywood gangster movies.

wd John Woo   *ph* Wong Wing-Hang, Peter Pao   *m* Lowell Lowe   *ad* Luk Man-Wah   *ed* Fan Kung-Ming

Chow Yun-Fat, Danny Lee, Sally Yeh, Chu Kong, Kenneth Tsang, Lam Chung, Shing Fui-On

'In its serenely overstated way, it is as resonant and emotive as the "classics" it refers to.' – *Tony Rayns, MFB*

The Killer Elite
US   1975   120m   DeLuxe   Panavision
UA/Exeter-Persky Bright (Martin Baum, Arthur Lewis)
V*, L

A private crime fighting organization handles cases which the CIA prefers not to.

Smooth, fashionable violence which seems to proclaim the end of a cycle.

w Marc Norman, Stirling Silliphant   *novel Monkey in the Middle* by Robert Rostand   *d* Sam Peckinpah   *ph* Philip Lathrop   *m* Jerry Fielding

James Caan, Robert Duvall, Arthur Hill, Gig Young, Mako, Bo Hopkins, Burt Young, Tom Clancy

'Merely a commercial chore.' – *Tom Milne*

'A mysterious, elliptical, visually triumphant film about personal survival in a world of mean-minded machination.' – *Michael Billington, Illustrated London News*

Killer Fish
France/Brazil   1978   101m   colour
Victoria/Filmar do Brazil/Fawcett-Majors
V*

The leader of a burglary gang hides their haul in a dammed reservoir which he stocks with piranha fish.

Heavy-going underwater shocker, with no fun while the fish are off-screen.

w Michael Rogers   *d* Antonio Margheriti

Lee Majors, Karen Black, Margaux Hemingway, Marisa Berenson, James Franciscus

'A slapdash actioner which casts its rod in water so overfished of late that it's amazing there's still anything down there biting.' – *Variety*

Killer Grizzly: see *Grizzly*

The Killer Inside Me
US   1976   99m   Metrocolor   Panavision
Devi (Michael W. Leighton)
V, V*

A well-respected small-town deputy sheriff in Montana, seriously disturbed by memories of his violent childhood, finds that his life is out of control.

Unimpressive and implausible psychological study of a man's disintegration, lacking the sleazy authenticity of the novel.

w Edward Mann, Robert Chamblee   *novel* Jim Thompson   *d* Burt Kennedy   *ph* William A. Fraker   *m* Tim McIntire, John Rubinstein   *ed* Danford B. Greene, Aaron Stell

Stacy Keach, Susan Tyrell, Tisha Sterling, Keenan Wynn, John Carradine, Don Stroud, Charles McGraw, John Dehner, Pepe Serna, Royal Dano, Julie Adams

The Killer Is Loose
US   1956   73m   bw
Crown/United Artists

A bank robber swears revenge on a policeman who accidentally killed his wife.

Star potboiler, just about tolerable.

w Harold Medford   *d* Budd Boetticher

Joseph Cotten, Wendell Corey, Rhonda Fleming, Alan Hale Jnr, Michael Pate

The Killer Is on the Phone
Italy   1972   102m   Eastmancolor   Cinescope
Cathay/Difnei (Vittorio Bartattolo, Aldo Scavarda)
original title: *Assassino … è al telefono*

An unstable actress is stalked by a killer.

A dull and unimaginative thriller.

w Alberto de Martino, Vincenzo Mannino, Adriano Bolzoni, Renato Izzo   *d* Alberto de Martino   *ph* Aristide Massaccesi   *m* Stelvio Cipriani   *ad* Antonio Visone   *ed* Otello Colangeli

Anne Heywood, Telly Savalas, Rossella Falk

† The film was cut to 83m for its British release.

Killer McCoy
US   1947   104m   bw
MGM (Sam Zimbalist)

A prizefighter becomes involved in a murder.

Grade A production applied to a grade B script.

w Frederick Hazlitt Brennan, Thomas Lennon, George Bruce, George Oppenheimer   *d* Roy Rowland   *ph* Joseph Ruttenberg   *m* David Snell

Mickey Rooney, Ann Blyth, Brian Donlevy, James Dunn, Tom Tully, Sam Levene, James Bell, Gloria Holden

Killer Meets Killer: see *Each Dawn I Die*

'From the secret archives of the Vatican.'
Killer Nun
Italy   1978   90m   colour
Cinesud (Enzo Gallo)
V
original title: *Suor Omicidi*

In a lunatic asylum, a nun kills the male patients while framing another nun for the murders.

An over-the-top melodramatic horror, given matching histrionics by the cast.

w Giulio Berruti, Alberto Tarallo   *d* Giulio Berruti   *ph* Tonino Maccoppi

Anita Ekberg, Alida Valli, Massimo Serato, Lou Castel, Joe Dallesandro, Laura Nucci

'This hits all the proper lurid notes. But like many Italian exploitation movies, it's torn between sleaze and artiness.' – *Empire*

Killer of Killers: see *The Mechanic*

Killer on a Horse: see *Welcome to Hard Times*

The Killer That Stalked New York
US   1950   75m   bw
Columbia (Robert Cohn)
GB title: *Frightened City*

New York is on the alert for a girl smallpox carrier.

Absurdly-titled minor thriller, quite competent but wholly unsurprising.

w Harry Essex   *d* Earl McEvoy   *ph* Joseph Biroc   *m* Hans Salter

Charles Korvin, Evelyn Keyes, William Bishop, Dorothy Malone, Lola Albright, Barry Kelley, Carl Benton Reid, Ludwig Donath

The Killers ***
US   1946   105m   bw
U-I (Mark Hellinger)
TV title: *A Man Alone*

In a small sleazy town a gangster waits for two assassins to kill him, and we later find out why.

Elaborate tale of cross and double-cross, stunningly executed.

w Anthony Veiller   *story* Ernest Hemingway   *d* Robert Siodmak   *ph* Elwood Bredell   *m* Miklos Rozsa   *ed* Arthur Hilton

Burt Lancaster, Edmond O'Brien, Ava Gardner, Albert Dekker, Sam Levene, John Miljan, Virginia Christine, Vince Barnett, Charles B. Brown, Donald MacBride, Phil Brown, Charles McGraw, William Conrad

'About one tenth is Hemingway's, the rest is Universal-International's.' – *Richard Winnington*

'Seldom does a melodrama maintain the high tension that distinguishes this one.' – *Variety*

'There is nothing unique or even valuable about the picture, but energy combined with attention to form and detail doesn't turn up every day; neither does good entertainment.' – *James Agee*

† John Huston contributed to the script but is not credited.

AAN: Anthony Veiller; Robert Siodmak; Miklos Rozsa; Arthur Hilton

The Killers ***
US   1964   95m   Pathecolor
U-I (Don Siegel)
V*

Zesty, brutal remake intended for TV, but released theatrically because of its violence.

w Gene L. Coon   *story* Ernest Hemingway   *d* Don Siegel   *ph* Richard L. Rawlings   *m* Johnny Williams   *ad* Frank Arrigo, George Chan   *ed* Richard Belding

John Cassavetes, Lee Marvin, Clu Gulager, Angie Dickinson, Ronald Reagan, Claude Akins

† This was Ronald Reagan's last feature film and the first in which he played a bad guy.

'Her soft mouth was the road to sin-smeared violence!'
Killer's Kiss
US   1955   64m   bw
UA/Stanley Kubrick
V*, L

A prizefighter rescues a girl from her gangster lover, and is marked for death.

Tedious low-budget indie which first brought its director into notice.

wd/ph Stanley Kubrick   *m* Gerald Fried

Frank Silvera, Irene Kane, Jamie Smith

The Killers of Kilimanjaro
GB   1959   91m   Technicolor   Cinemascope
Columbia/Warwick (John R. Sloan)
US title: *Adamson of Africa*

A railroad engineer helps a girl find her lost father and fiancé.

Old-fashioned safari adventure full of action and animals.

w Richard Maibaum, Cyril Hume   *d* Richard Thorpe   *ph* Ted Moore   *m* William Alwyn

Robert Taylor, Anne Aubrey, Grégoire Aslan, Anthony Newley

The Killing **
US   1956   83m   bw
UA/Harris-Kubrick (J. B. Harris)
V*, L

An ex-convict recruits helpers to steal two million dollars from a racetrack.

Incisive, entertaining, downbeat caper movie clearly influenced by *The Asphalt Jungle* and *Rififi*.

wd Stanley Kubrick   *novel Clean Break* by Lionel White   *ph* Lucien Ballard   *m* Gerald Fried

Sterling Hayden, Marie Windsor, Jay C. Flippen, Elisha Cook Jnr, Coleen Gray, Vince Edwards, Ted de Corsia, Joe Sawyer, Tim Carey

'The visual authority constantly dominates a flawed script.' – *Arlene Croce*

'The camera watches the whole shoddy show with the keen eye of a terrier stalking a pack of rats.' – *Time*

Killing Cars (dubbed)

West Germany 1985 94m colour
Sentana (Mario Krebs)

The designer of a car that runs without petrol finds himself enmeshed in an international conspiracy to bury his invention.

Heavy-handed ecological thriller, more interested in slick surfaces and fashionable posturing than in its ostensible message.

wd Michael Verhoeven *ph* Jacques Steyn *ad* Norbert Scherer *ed* Fred Srp

Jurgen Prochnow, Senta Berger, Agnes Soral, Daniel Gélin, Bernhard Wicki, William Conrad

Killing Dad

GB 1989 93m Technicolor Panavision
Palace/Scottish TV Film Enterprises/British Screen/Applecross (Iain Smith)
V, S

When a down-at-heel father tries to return to the family he abandoned more than twenty years before, his ineffectual son decides to kill him.

Limp, forced and unfunny attempt at a black comedy.

wd Michael Austin *novel* *Berg* by Anna Quinn *d* Michael Austin *ph* Gabriel Beristain *m* Chaz Jankel, David Storrs *pd* Adrienne Atkinson *ed* Edward Marner, Derek Trigg

Denholm Elliott, Julie Walters, Richard E. Grant, Anna Massey, Laura de Sol

'Signally fails to amuse.' – *MFB*

The Killing Fields ***

GB 1984 141m colour
Goldcrest/Enigma (*David Puttnam*)
V, V*, L

An American journalist is engulfed in the horror of Cambodia, and his native adviser disappears and is thought to be dead.

Brilliantly filmed, but probably too strong for a commercial audience to stomach, this true adventure tosses one into the horror of modern war and leaves one reeling despite its comparatively happy ending.

w Bruce Robinson, from the article 'The Death and Life of Dith Pran' by Sidney Schanberg *d* Roland Joffe *ph* Chris Menges *m* Mike Oldfield *pd* Roy Walker *ed* Jim Clark

Sam Waterston (as Sidney Schanberg), *Haing S. Ngor* (as Dith Pran), John Malkovich, Julian Sands, Craig T. Nelson

AA: Haing S. Ngor (supporting actor); photography; editing

AAN: best picture; Sam Waterston; adapted screenplay; Roland Joffe

BFA: best picture; adapted screenplay; Haing S. Ngor (supporting actor)

The Killing Game: see Jeu de Massacre

The Killing of a Chinese Bookie

US 1976 113m colour
John Cassavetes
V, V*

A Los Angeles night-club owner is prevailed upon by gangsters to pay off his debt by eliminating a troublesome Chinese.

Another unendurable slab of Cassavetes pretentiousness; why he goes on trying, in the face of twenty years of public indifference, is beyond imagining.

wd John Cassavetes

Ben Gazzara, Timothy Carey, Seymour Cassel, Morgan Woodward

The Killing of Angel Street

Australia 1981 100m colour
Forest Home Films
V*

Residents fight to save old terraced houses from demolition.

Rather routine light drama, like an Ealing comedy without laughs.

w Michael Craig, Cecil Holmes, Evan Jones *d* Donald Crombie

Elizabeth Alexander, John Hargreaves, Reg Lye, David Downer

The Killing of Sister George *

US 1969 138m Metrocolor
Associates and Aldrich/Palomar
V, V*

An ageing lesbian actress is fired from a TV serial and her life collapses around her.

Heavily handled film version of an amusing and moving play; everything is clumsily spelt out, including the love scenes, and the actresses are forced to repeat themselves.

w Lukas Heller *play* Frank Marcus *d* Robert Aldrich *ph* Joseph Biroc *m* Gerald Fried

Beryl Reid, Susannah York, Coral Browne, Roland Fraser, Patricia Medina, Hugh Paddick, Cyril Delevanti

'The play was second-rate, but with its nice blend of the homely and the chilling, the absurdist and the perverse, it had the quality of a Kraft-Ebbing comic book. Aldrich and Heller have turned this material into a crawling tear-jerker, the lines spoken at a speed adjusted to non-English or non-language-speaking audiences.' – *John Simon*

'A clumpingly archaic piece of film-making.' – *New Yorker, 1982*

The Kill-Off *

US 1989 97m Technicolor
Palace/Filmworld International (Lydia Dean Pilcher)
V

Three men set out to kill a vindictive, bed-ridden town gossip.

Low-life thriller that manages an authentic sleaziness.

wd Maggie Greenwald *novel* Jim Thompson *d* Maggie Greenwald *ph* Declan Quinn *m* Evan Lurie *pd* Pamela Woodbridge *ed* James Y. Kwei

Loretta Gross, Andrew Lee Barrett, Jackson Sims, Steve Monroe, Cath Haase, William Russell, Jorjan Fox, Sean O'Sullivan, Ellen Kelly

Kilroy Was Here

US 1947 68m bw
Monogram (Sid Luft)

A hellraiser of the Pacific war goes to college.

Mild comedy reuniting two former child stars, but without many other ideas.

w Dick Irving Hyland *d* Phil Karlson

Jackie Cooper, Jackie Coogan, Wanda McKay, Frank Jenks

Kim *

US 1950 112m Technicolor
MGM (Leon Gordon)
V, V*

The orphaned son of a British soldier in India has adventures with his horseman friend who belongs to the British secret service.

Colourful *Boys' Own Paper* high jinks, quite lively but never convincing.

w Leon Gordon, Helen Deutsch, Richard Schayer *novel* Rudyard Kipling *d* Victor Saville *ph* William Skall *m* André Previn

Errol Flynn, Dean Stockwell, Paul Lukas, Robert Douglas, Thomas Gomez, Cecil Kellaway, Arnold Moss, Reginald Owen

'Ornate, lavish, but curiously lacking in genuine atmosphere, vitality or period sense.' – *Penelope Houston*

Kind Hearts and Coronets ***

GB 1949 106m bw
Ealing (Michael Relph)
V, V*, L

An impecunious heir eliminates eight D'Ascoynes who stand between him and the family fortune.

Witty, genteel black comedy well set in the stately Edwardian era and quite deserving of its reputation for wit and style; yet the effect is curiously muffled and several opportunities are missed.

w Robert Hamer, John Dighton *novel* Noblesse Oblige by Roy Horniman *d* Robert Hamer *ph* Douglas Slocombe *md* Ernest Irving

Dennis Price, Alec Guinness (in eight roles), *Valerie Hobson, Joan Greenwood, Miles Malleson, Arthur Lowe*

'A brilliant misfire for the reason that its plentiful wit is literary and practically never pictorial.' – *Richard Winnington*

'Enlivened with cynicism, loaded with dramatic irony and shot through with a suspicion of social satire.' – *Daily Telegraph*

'The film in general lacks a visual style equal to its script . . . All the same, *Kind Hearts and Coronets* is a very funny film and it gets away with a great deal. With so much, in fact, that its makers deserve salutation as pioneers in the little-explored territory of adult British cinema.' – *Lindsay Anderson*

'A film which can be seen and seen again with undiminished pleasure.' – *Basil Wright, 1972*

Kind Lady *

US 1935 76m bw
MGM/Lucien Hubbard
aka: House of Menace

A confidence trickster insinuates himself and his criminal friends into the house of an invalid lady.

Unusual but unconvincing melodrama with overwrought leading performances.

w Bernard Schubert *play* Edward Chodorov *story* Hugh Walpole *d* George B. Seitz *ph* George Folsey *m* Edward Ward

Basil Rathbone, Aline MacMahon, Mary Carlisle, Frank Albertson, Dudley Digges, Doris Lloyd

'Leisurely pace cramps effectiveness.' – *Variety*

Kind Lady *

US 1951 78m bw
MGM (Armand Deutsch)

Edwardian-set remake of the above, rather more subtly acted but failing to extract all possible *frissons*.

w Jerry Davis, Edward Chodorov, Charles Bennett *d* John Sturges *ph* Joseph Ruttenberg *m* David Raksin

Maurice Evans, Ethel Barrymore, Angela Lansbury, Keenan Wynn, Betsy Blair, John Williams

'A curiously tame melodrama whose shocks, when they do come, are muffled and ineffectual.' – *Penelope Houston*

A Kind of Loving ****

GB 1962 112m bw
Anglo-Amalgamated/Waterhall/Vic Films (Joe Janni)
V, V*

A young north country draughtsman is forced into marriage, has to live with his dragon-like mother in law, and finally sorts out a relationship with his unhappy wife.

Blunt melodrama with strong kinship to *Saturday Night and Sunday Morning*, strikingly directed and photographed amid urban grime and suburban conformity.

w *Keith Waterhouse, Willis Hall*   novel *Stan Barstow*
d *John Schlesinger*   ph *Denys Coop*   m Ron Grainer

Alan Bates, June Ritchie, Thora Hird, Bert Palmer, Gwen Nelson

'You will be shocked by this highly moral film only if you are shocked by life.' – *Evening News*

Kindergarten Cop
US   1990   110m   colour
Universal (Ivan Reitman, Brian Grazer)
V, V*, L, S

A cop, attempting to catch a drug dealer, works undercover as a teacher.

Muscle-bound would-be comedy, with an undercurrent of brutality and objectionable morality.

w Murray Salem, Herschel Weingrod, Timothy Harris
d Ivan Reitman   ph Michael Chapman   m Randy Edelman   pd Bruno Rubeo   ed Sheldon Kahn, Wendy Bricmont

Arnold Schwarzenegger, Penelope Ann Miller, Pamela Reed, Linda Hunt, Richard Tyson, Carroll Baker, Joseph Cousins, Christian Cousins

The Kindred
US   1987   97m   Technicolor
Norkat/F-M Entertainment (Jeffrey Obrow)

Young scientists fall foul of a genetically engineered monster.

Unoriginal and uninteresting.

w Jeffrey Obrow, Stephen Carpenter, John Penney, Earl Ghaffari, Joseph Stefano   d Jeffrey Obrow, Stephen Carpenter   ph Stephen Carpenter
m David Newman   pd Chris Hopkins   ed John Penney, Earl Ghaffari

David Allen Brooks, Rod Steiger, Amanda Pays, Talia Balsam, Kim Hunter, Timothy Gibbs, Peter Frechette, Julia Montgomery

King and Country *
GB   1964   86m   bw
BHE (Norman Priggen, Joseph Losey)
V

In the trenches during World War I, a private is court-martialled and shot for desertion.

Neat cinematic treatment of a very downbeat play.

w Evan Jones   play *Hamp* by John Wilson
d Joseph Losey   ph *Denys Coop*   m Larry Adler
pd Richard Macdonald

Tom Courtenay, *Dirk Bogarde*, Leo McKern, Barry Foster, James Villiers, Peter Copley

The King and Four Queens
US   1956   86m   DeLuxe   Cinemascope
UA/Russ/Field/Gabco (David Hempstead)
V*

A cowboy braves the wrath of a lady sharpshooter to gain gold and the hand of one of her four daughters.

Tawdry sex Western sporadically enlivened by good-humoured playing.

w Margaret Fitts, Richard Alan Simmons   d Raoul Walsh   ph Lucien Ballard   m Alex North

Clark Gable, Eleanor Parker, Jo Van Fleet, Jean Willes, Barbara Nichols, Sara Shane, Roy Roberts

'A superficially cynical exercise in the rival attractions of sex and money.' – *MFB*

The King and I *
US   1956   133m   Eastmancolor   Cinemascope 55
TCF (Charles Brackett)
V, V (W), V*, L, S

Musical remake of *Anna and the King of Siam* (qv), from the highly successful stage production.

The film is opulent in lush detail but quite lacking in style.

w Ernest Lehman   d Walter Lang   ph Leon Shamroy   md Alfred Newman, Ken Darby
m *Richard Rodgers   book/ly* Oscar Hammerstein II
ad Lyle Wheeler, John DeCuir

Deborah Kerr, Yul Brynner, Rita Moreno, Martin Benson, Alan Mowbray, Geoffrey Toone, Terry Saunders

'Gaiety has something of a struggle to survive.' – *Penelope Houston*

AA: Yul Brynner; Alfred Newman, Ken Darby; art direction

AAN: best picture; Walter Lang; Leon Shamroy; Deborah Kerr

The King and the Chorus Girl
US   1937   94m   bw
Warner (Mervyn Le Roy)
GB title: *Romance Is Sacred*

A European prince on the spree falls for a New York chorine.

Reasonably lively romantic comedy.

w Norman Krasna, Groucho Marx   story *Grand Passion* by Norman Krasna, Groucho Marx
d Mervyn Le Roy   ph Tony Gaudio   m Werner Heymann

Joan Blondell, Fernand Gravet, Edward Everett Horton, Jane Wyman, Alan Mowbray, Mary Nash, Kenny Baker

'Sure word of mouth and a shoo-in for dough.' – *Variety*

King Arthur Was a Gentleman
GB   1942   99m   bw
GFD/Gainsborough (Edward Black)

A soldier becomes a hero when he believes he has King Arthur's sword.

Not-too-successful attempt to turn a music hall comedian into a figure of Chaplinesque pathos.

w Val Guest, Marriott Edgar   d Marcel Varnel
ph Arthur Crabtree

Arthur Askey, Evelyn Dall, Anne Shelton, Max Bacon, Jack Train, Peter Graves, Vera Frances, Ronald Shiner, Brefni O'Rourke

King Creole
US   1958   116m   bw   Vistavision
Paramount/Hal B. Wallis
V, V*, L

A failed graduate becomes a singer in a New Orleans night-club, and gets involved with gangsters.

Disagreeable crook melodrama turned into a musical star vehicle.

w Herbert Baker, Michael V. Gazzo   novel *A Stone for Danny Fisher* by Harold Robbins   d Michael Curtiz
ph Russell Harlan   m Walter Scharf

Elvis Presley, Carolyn Jones, Dean Jagger, Walter Matthau, Dolores Hart, Paul Stewart

King David
GB/US   1985   114m   Rank colour   Panavision
Paramount/Martin Elfand
V, V*, L

The biblical story of David's involvements with Saul, Goliath and Bathsheba.

Astonishingly tedious, confused and inept retelling of familiar tales, especially so for an audience which needs to be lured back to them.

w Andrew Birkin, James Costigan   d Bruce Beresford   ph Donald McAlpine   m Carl Davis
pd Ken Adam   ed William Anderson

Richard Gere, Edward Woodward, Denis Quilley, Jack Klaff, Cherie Lunghi, Alice Krige, Hurd Hatfield, John Castle, Niall Buggy

King for a Night
US   1933   78m   bw
Universal

A minister's son becomes a boxer and goes to the electric chair for a murder committed by his sister.

Glum and incredible moral saga.

w W. A. McGuire and others   d Kurt Neumann

Chester Morris, Helen Twelvetrees, Grant Mitchell, Alice White, John Miljan, George E. Stone

A King in New York *
GB   1957   109m   bw
Attica (Charles Chaplin)
V*

A penniless European king finds himself at odds with the American way of life.

Feeble Chaplin comedy from his anti-American period; tedious dialogue and poor physical production allow only momentary flashes of the satire intended.

wd/m Charles Chaplin   ph Georges Périnal

Charles Chaplin, Michael Chaplin, *Oliver Johnston*, Dawn Addams, Jerry Desmonde, Harry Green, Maxine Audley, Sid James

'Unhappily he is a sadder and an older man; the real punch is gone. His dethroned king is an ironically apt image.' – *Marvin Felheim*

'Maybe the worst film ever made by a celebrated film artist.' – *New Yorker, 1977*

'It shows how the coming of sound was a curse to Chaplin; how its freedoms dissipated his strengths; how his attempts to exploit it intellectually and ideologically played to his weaknesses; how, in short, he was much more grievously hurt by history in art than by history in politics.' – *Stanley Kauffmann*

'An overblown, self-piteous excursion into autobiography.' – *Time Out, 1984*

King Kong ****
US   1933   100m   bw
RKO (Merian C. Cooper)
V, V*, L, S

A film producer on safari brings back a giant ape which terrorizes New York.

The greatest monster movie of all, a miracle of trick work and suspense, with some of the most memorable moments in film history.

w James Creelman, Ruth Rose   story Edgar Wallace
d Merian C. Cooper, Ernest Schoedsack   ph Edward Linden, Vernon Walker, L. O. Taylor   sound effects Murray Spivak   chief technician Willis J. O'Brien   m Max Steiner

Robert Armstrong, Fay Wray, Bruce Cabot, Frank Reicher

CARL DENHAM (Robert Armstrong): 'It wasn't the airplanes. It was beauty killed the beast.'

'If properly handled, should gather good grosses in a walk . . . and may open up a new medium for scaring babies via the screen.' – *Variety*

'Just amusing nonsense punctuated by such reflections as why, if the natives wanted to keep the monster on the other side of the wall, they should have built a door big enough to let him through.' – *James Agate*

'The most exciting motion picture event of all time!'

King Kong

US 1976 135m Metrocolor Panavision
Dino de Laurentiis
V, V*, L

Semi-spoof remake with added sexual overtones; though launched on a massive wave of publicity, it lacks both the charm and the technical resources of its predecessor.

w Lorenzo Semple Jnr d John Guillermin
ph Richard H. Kline m John Barry pd Dale Hennesy, Mario Chiari

Jeff Bridges, Charles Grodin, Jessica Lange, John Randolph, René Auberjonois, Julius Harris, Ed Lauter

'The one and original lovable monster is lost amid all the hydraulic manipulations in what now emerges as the story of a dumb blonde who falls for a huge plastic finger.' – Judith Crist, Saturday Review

'Even with colour, the settings of Kong II are no match for the rich black-and-white chiaroscuro of Kong I, with its echoes of artists like Gustave Doré and Max Ernst and its sensitivity to the emotional values of tone and texture.' – Jack Kroll, Newsweek

† King Kong Lives (L) crept out minimally in 1986.

AA: visual effects (Carlo Rambaldi, Glen Robinson, Frank Van Der Veer)

AAN: Richard H. Kline

King Lear *

GB/Denmark 1970 137m bw
Columbia/Filmways-Laterna (Michael Birkett)
V, V*

Tragedy ensues when an old king prematurely divides his kingdom between his daughters.

Miserably photographed in freezing Jutland, this is a deliberately downbeat version which despite its varied points of interest is extremely hard to sit through.

wd Peter Brook play William Shakespeare
ph Henning Kristiansen m none pd Georges Wakhevitch

Paul Scofield, Irene Worth, Alan Webb, Tom Fleming, Susan Engel, Cyril Cusack, Patrick Magee, Jack MacGowran

King Lear

US 1987 90m colour
Cannon (Menahem Globus, Yoram Golan)
V*

A culture expert travelling in France thinks of a mad old man and his daughter as subjects for a film.

Sheer nonsense doodled by the director with someone else's money.

wd Jean-Luc Godard play William Shakespeare
ph Sophie Maintigneux d Jean-Luc Godard

Burgess Meredith, Peter Sellars, Molly Ringwald, Jean-Luc Godard, Norman Mailer, Kate Mailer, Woody Allen

King of Alcatraz *

US 1938 56m bw
Paramount (William C. Thomas)

Convicts escape on a freighter, but one needs surgery.

Pacy programmer with a stalwart cast.

w Irving Reis d Robert Florey ph Harry Fischbeck md Boris Morros

Gail Patrick, J. Carrol Naish, Lloyd Nolan, Harry Carey, Robert Preston, Anthony Quinn, Dennis Morgan, Porter Hall

'Good gangster actioner . . . will please those liking crime cinematics.' – Variety

King of Burlesque *

US 1935 88m bw
TCF (Kenneth MacGowan)
V*

A vaudeville impresario overcomes his troubles.

Well-written musical with plenty of variety talent.

w James Seymour, Gene Markey, Harry Tugend
d Sidney Lanfield ph Peverell Marley
m/ly various ch Sammy Lee

songs: 'I've Got My Fingers Crossed'; 'Lovely Lady'; 'Spreadin' Rhythm Around'; 'Whose Big Baby Are You?'; 'I'm Shooting High'; 'I Love to Ride the Horses'

Warner Baxter, Alice Faye, Jack Oakie, Mona Barrie, Arline Judge, Dixie Dunbar, Gregory Ratoff, Herbert Mundin, Fats Waller, Kenny Baker

'Big-time musical, with production, material and cast making up for story shortcomings.' – Variety

† It was remade as Hello Frisco Hello.

AAN: Sammy Lee

King of Chinatown

US 1939 56m bw
Paramount (Stuart Walker)

A top racketeer is double-crossed by his henchman.

Smartly paced underworld melodrama.

w Lillie Hayward, Irving Reis, Herbert Biberman
d Nick Grinde

Anna May Wong, Akim Tamiroff, Sidney Toler, J. Carrol Naish, Philip Ahn, Anthony Quinn

'Good support for key duals.' – Variety

King of Comedy ****

US 1983 109m Technicolor
TCF/Embassy International (Arnon Milchan)
V*, L

Obsessed with becoming a chat show host, an aspiring comedian kidnaps his idol and ransoms him for a spot in the show.

Amusing, underplayed farce with a tragic lining: a very convincing picture of the media today.

w Paul D. Zimmermann d Martin Scorsese ph Fred Shuler md Robbie Robertson m various
pd Boris Leven

Robert de Niro, Jerry Lewis, Diahnne Abbott, Sandra Bernhard

'This is a very frightening film, and in retrospect nothing about it seems funny at all.' – Variety

'Unquestionably one of the films of the year.' – Guardian

'A most eerie and memorable picture.' – Spectator

BFA: best original screenplay

King of Gamblers

US 1937 79m bw
Paramount
aka: Czar of the Slot Machines

A ruthless gangster loves a singer who loves a reporter who is out to expose him.

A muddled script mars this pacy lower-birth item.

w Doris Anderson d Robert Florey ph Harry Fischbeck m Boris Morros

Akim Tamiroff, Claire Trevor, Lloyd Nolan, Buster Crabbe, Porter Hall

'Well enough done to rate okay in the smaller spots solo.' – Variety

King of Hearts

France/Italy 1966 110m Eastmancolor
UA/Fildebroc/Montoro (Philippe de Broca)
original title: Le Roi de Coeur

In World War I, a Scottish soldier finds a war-torn town occupied only by lunatics who have escaped from the asylum and who want to make him their king.

Heavy-handed whimsy which never catches fire despite the talents involved.

w Daniel Boulanger d Philippe de Broca
ph Pierre Lhomme m Georges Delerue

Alan Bates, Geneviève Bujold, Jean-Claude Brialy, Françoise Christophe, Pierre Brasseur, Micheline Presle, Adolfo Celi, Julien Guiomar

King of Jazz ***

US 1930 101m Technicolor
Universal (Carl Laemmle Jnr)
V*

Musical revue.

Stylish, spectacular, revelatory early musical: a treasure trove.

devised/d John Murray Anderson w Harry Ruskin, Charles MacArthur, Harry Mohr, Ray Rennahan, Jerome Ash ad Herman Rose songs: 'Happy Feet'; 'A Bench in the Park'; 'My Bridal Veil'; 'Song of the Dawn'; 'I Like to Do Things for You'; 'Music Has Charms'; 'My Lover'; 'It Happened in Monterey'; 'Ragamuffin Romeo'; 'So the Bluebirds and the Blackbirds Got Together'

Paul Whiteman and his orchestra, John Boles, Bing Crosby (with the Rhythm Boys), Laura la Plante, Glenn Tryon, Slim Summerville, Walter Brennan

'A box office picture anywhere for one week.' – Variety

AAN: Herman Rose

'Under a master director and the reverent genius of great players, the story of Christ has taken human form and greater understanding!'
'Dramatic magnificence, spectacular splendour, riotous joy, tigerish rage, undying love, terrifying tempests, appalling earthquakes!'

King of Kings **

US 1927 155m approx (24 fps) (various versions)
bw silent
Pathé/Cecil B. de Mille
V*, L

The life of Jesus, seen more or less from the viewpoint of Mary Magdalene.

A patchy but frequently moving and pictorially effective work, ranging from the sublime (the first view of Jesus as a blind man regains his sight) to the ridiculous ('Harness my zebras, gift of the Nubian king!' says the Queen of Sheba in a sub-title).

w Jeanie Macpherson d Cecil B. de Mille ph J. Peverell Marley

H. B. Warner, Jacqueline Logan, Joseph Schildkraut (Judas), Ernest Torrence (Peter), Victor Varconi (Pilate), Dorothy Cumming (Mary, mother of Jesus), Rudolph Schildkraut (Caiaphas)

'The most impressive of all motion pictures.' – Mordaunt Hall, New York Times

'A picture which will tend to standardize the world's conception of the New Testament . . . de Mille has one of the best business minds in pictures and making King of Kings was the most brilliant stroke of his successful business career.' – Welford Beaton, The Film Spectator

'A story of the Christ! The glory of his spoken words!'

King of Kings *

US 1961 161m Super Technirama
MGM/Samuel Bronston
V*, L, S

The life of Jesus Christ.

Known in the trade as I Was a Teenage Jesus, this good-looking but rather tedious film is neither vulgar nor very interesting; a solemn, decent, bible-in-pictures pageant.

w Philip Yordan   *d* Nicholas Ray   *ph* Franz Planer, Manuel Berenger   *m* Miklos Rozsa   *ad* Georges Wakhevitch

Jeffrey Hunter, Robert Ryan, Siobhan McKenna, Frank Thring, Hurd Hatfield, Rip Torn, Harry Guardino, Viveca Lindfors, Rita Gam

'I have decided to confer on *King of Kings* both my 1961 Scripture Prizes: (1) Dullest; (2) Most Undenominational.' – *Dilys Powell*

† Nicholas Ray's reaction to film critics who attacked the film was, 'They are not hip enough with the times of Christ.'

The King of Marvin Gardens *
US   1972   104m   Eastmancolor
Columbia/BBS (Bob Rafelson)
V*

The host of a late night radio talk show gets embroiled in his brother's schemes.

Thoughtful tragi-comedy overweighted by talk, but with good performances.

w Jacob Brackman   *d* Bob Rafelson   *ph* Laszlo Kovacs

Jack Nicholson, Bruce Dern, Ellen Burstyn, Julia Anne Robinson

'Indecipherable dark nonsense about brothers and goals and the American dream. An unqualified disaster.' – *New Yorker*

'Glum news from the people who made *Five Easy Pieces*, which had a lot of good work in it along with some pretentious flab. In their new picture the flab has taken over.' – *Stanley Kauffmann*

King of New York
US   1990   103m   colour
Rank/Reteitalia/Scena/Caminito (Mary Kane)
V, V*, L

Released from prison, a New York gangster takes over the city's drug trafficking by murdering his rivals.

Excessively violent and sadistic fantasy, with a mannered leading performance.

w Nicholas St John   *d* Abel Ferrara   *ph* Bojan Bazelli   *m* Joe Delia   *pd* Alex Tavoularis *ed* Anthony Redman

Christopher Walken, David Caruso, Larry Fishburne, Victor Argo, Wesley Snipes, Janet Julian, Joey Chin, Giancarlo Esposito

'Executed with the mix of splatter and gallows humour that Ferrara has made his own.' – *Sight and Sound*

'A nihilistic exercise in designer pessimism stating that the American system is corrupt from top to bottom.' – *Philip French, Observer*

King of Paris
GB   1935   75m   bw
British and Dominions (Herbert Wilcox)

The story of a French stage impresario, supposedly based on Sacha Guitry.

Interesting try for a minority audience.

w W. P. Lipscomb, John Drinkwater, Paul Gangelin *play La Voie Lactée* by Alfred Savoir, John van Druten *d* Jack Raymond   *ph* Freddie Young   *ad* L. P. Williams

Cedric Hardwicke, Marie Glory, Ralph Richardson, Phillis Monkman

'Nothing much to be desired in this picture, excepting a story.' – *Variety*

King of the Carnival
US   1955   bw   serial: 12 eps
Republic

Circus acrobats help the treasury department to track down counterfeiters.

A lively background prevents this serial from becoming tedious.

d Franklin Adreon

Harry Lauter, Fran Bennett, Keith Richards, Robert Shayne

King of the Children *
China   1988   107m   colour
ICA/Xi'an Film Studio (Wu Tianming)

A youth, first sent from the city to work on a farm during the Cultural Revolution, is transferred to teach at a remote school where he uses unconventional methods which soon cause trouble.

Pleasant film with much of interest, though its deeper implications are likely to be understood only by a Chinese audience.

w Chen Kaige, Wan Zhi   *story Haizi Wang* by Ah Cheng   *d* Chen Kaige   *ph* Gu Changwei   *m* Qu Xiaosong   *ad* Chen Shaohua   *ed* Liu Miaomiao

Xie Yuan, Yank Xuewen, Chen Shaohua, Zhang Camimei, Xu Guoqing

King of the Congo
US   1952   bw   serial: 15 eps
Columbia

An air force captain assumes the identity of a dead pilot taking secret microfilm to a subversive group in Africa; but he is captured by The Rock People.

Rather splendid serial with all the trimmings.

d Spencer Bennet, Wallace Grissell

Buster Crabbe, Gloria Dee, Leonard Penn, Jack Ingram

King of the Damned *
GB   1935   76m   bw
Gaumont (Michael Balcon)

On a South Seas convict settlement, harsh treatment leads to mutiny.

A downright peculiar project for a British studio at this time, but technically very competent for those who like this kind of thing.

w Charles Bennett, Sidney Gilliat, Noel Langley *play* John Chancellor   *d* Walter Forde   *ph* Bernard Knowles   *md* Louis Levy   *ad* Oscar Werndorff *ed* C. Randell

Conrad Veidt, Helen Vinson, Noah Beery, Cecil Ramage, Edmund Willard, Raymond Lovell, Allan Jeayes, Percy Parsons

'Goes so far overboard on gloom that it defeats its own end.' – *Variety*

King of the Forest Rangers
US   1946   bw   serial: 12 eps
Republic

Strange prehistoric towers hold the key to vast wealth, and the Forest Rangers prevent villains from getting it.

He-man stuff, adequately mounted.

d Spencer Bennet, Fred Brannon

Larry Thompson, Helen Talbot, Stuart Hamblen, Anthony Warde

King of the Gypsies
US   1978   112m   Technicolor
Paramount/Dino de Laurentiis (Anna Gross)
V*

A gypsy leader is denied the hand in marriage of the daughter of a rival, so he kidnaps her.

Ethnic melodrama which despite its vigorous insistence on tradition – or perhaps because of it – plays like a mad musical without any songs.

w Frank Pierson   *novel* Peter Maas   *d* Frank Pierson   *ph* Sven Nykvist, Edward Lachman *m* David Grisman   *pd* Gene Callahan

Sterling Hayden, Brooke Shields, Shelley Winters, Susan Sarandon, Judd Hirsch, Eric Roberts

King of the Hill *
US   1993   102m   DeLuxe   Panavision
Wildwood/Bona Fide/Gramercy (Albert Berger, Barbara Maltby, Ron Yerxa)
S

A 10-year-old boy grows up in St Louis during the Depression of the 30s.

A gentle, sometimes touching drama of an observant boy trying to make the best of life, but steeped in a somewhat rosy nostalgia.

wd Steven Soderbergh   *book* A. E. Hotchner *ph* Elliot Davis   *m* Cliff Martinez   *pd* Gary Frutkoff   *ed* Steven Soderbergh

Jesse Bradford, Jeroen Krabbé, Lisa Eichhorn, Karen Allen, Spalding Gray, Elizabeth McGovern, Joseph Krest, Cameron Boyd

'This densely detailed, superbly acted evocation of a resourceful boy's life during the depths of the Depression animates another time and place, while quietly underlining the parallels to contemporary problems.' – *Variety*

'Body of a Greek god! Strength of a Hercules!'
King of the Jungle
US   1933   73m   bw
Paramount

A small boy grows up with lions; he is captured with them and sold to an American circus.

Sub-Tarzan hokum which cheered up the kids.

w Philip Wylie, Fred Niblo Jnr, C. T. Stoneham *d* H. Bruce Humberstone, Max Marcin

Buster Crabbe, Frances Dee, Douglass Dumbrille, Robert Adair, Robert Barrat

'Minus any help from the marquee it will have to attract on merit alone, and on merit it rates fair business.' – *Variety*

King of the Khyber Rifles
US   1954   100m   Technicolor   Cinemascope
TCF (Frank Rosenberg)

In 1857 a British garrison in India is threatened by the forces of Kuuram Khan but saved by a half-caste officer.

Standard North-West Frontier adventure, old-fashioned and rather dull.

w Ivan Goff, Ben Roberts   *d* Henry King   *ph* Leon Shamroy   *m* Bernard Herrmann

Tyrone Power, Terry Moore, Michael Rennie, Guy Rolfe, John Justin

King of the Mounties
US   1942   bw   serial: 12 eps
Republic

Activities of the Canadian Fifth Column result in that country being mercilessly bombed by a new craft called The Falcon.

The Mounties once more get their man.

d William Witney

Allan Lane, Gilbert Emery, Russell Hicks, Douglass Dumbrille, Peggy Drake, Abner Biberman, Duncan Renaldo

King of the Roaring Twenties
US   1961   106m   bw
Warner/AA/Bischoff-Diamond
V*
GB title: *The Big Bankroll*

A gambler, Arnold Rothstein, becomes powerful among twenties gangsters.

Routine crime drama, shoddily made.

w Jo Swerling   *d* Joseph M. Newman   *ph* Carl Guthrie   *m* Franz Waxman

David Janssen, Dianne Foster, Mickey Rooney, Mickey Shaughnessy, Diana Dors, Dan O'Herlihy, Jack Carson, Keenan Wynn, William Demarest, Joseph Schildkraut, Regis Toomey, Murvyn Vye

'Superficial, shopworn biography of an infamous bookie.' – MFB

King of the Rocket Men
US   1949   bw   serial: 12 eps
Republic

Diabolical Dr Vulcan menaces a desert research project, but is foiled by The Rocket Man.

Irresistible serial nonsense with all the ingredients.

d Fred Brannon

Tristram Coffin, Mae Clarke, Don Haggerty, House Peters Jnr, I. Stanford Jolley

King of the Royal Mounted
US   1940   bw   serial: 12 eps
Republic

A new discovery called Compound X is sought by enemy agents.

Just what you expect from a serial about the Mounties.

d William Witney, John English

Allan Lane, Robert Strange, Robert Kellard, Lita Conway, Harry Cording, Bryant Washburn

King of the Texas Rangers
US   1941   bw   serial: 12 eps
Republic

The son of a Texas Ranger avenges his father's death by routing a gang of saboteurs.

Fair average serial.

d William Witney, John English

Sammy Baugh, Neil Hamilton, Pauline Moore, Duncan Renaldo, Charles Trowbridge, Monte Blue

King of the Turf
US   1939   88m   bw
Edward Small

A gambler out of luck befriends a small boy who turns out to be his own son.

Hard to take even at the time, this sentimental tariddiddle does not bear later scrutiny.

wd George Bruce

Adolphe Menjou, Dolores Costello, Walter Abel, Roger Daniel

'Dandy racetrack yarn . . . it has a refreshing appeal and the dialogue is excellent.' – Variety

King of the Underworld
US   1938   69m   bw
Warner (Bryan Foy)

When her husband is killed by gangsters, a doctor takes her own steps to round them up.

Sex-change remake of Dr Socrates; certainly no better.

w George Bricker, Vincent Sherman   d Lewis Seiler

Kay Francis, Humphrey Bogart, James Stephenson, John Eldredge

'It will have trouble even in the duals.' – Variety

King of the Wild
US   1931   bw   serial: 12 eps
Mascot

Several adventurers search for a diamond mine.

Early talkie serial with little of the later style.

d Richard Thorpe

Walter Miller, Nora Lane, Boris Karloff, Dorothy Christy, Tom Santschi

King of the Wind
US   1989   102m   Technicolor
Enterprise/Davis Panzer/HTV International (Michael Guest, Paul Sarony, Peter S. Davis, William Panzer)
V, V*, S

Adventures in France and England of a young Arab groom and his horse.

Lamely told and a waste of everyone's time.

w Phil Frey   novel Marguerite Henry   d Peter Duffell   ph Brian Morgan   m John Scott   pd Ken Sharp   ed Lyndon Matthews

Frank Finlay, Jenny Agutter, Nigel Hawthorne, Navin Chowdhry, Ralph Bates, Neil Dickson, Barry Foster, Jill Gascoine, Joan Hickson, Anthony Quayle, Ian Richardson, Norman Rodway, Peter Vaughan, Richard Harris, Glenda Jackson

King, Queen, Knave *
US/West Germany   1972   92m   Eastmancolor
Wolper/Maran (Lutz Hengst)
V*

The wife of a Munich bookseller falls for his adolescent nephew.

Amusing, capriciously directed sex comedy.

w David Shaw, David Seltzer   novel Vladimir Nabokov   d Jerzy Skolimowski   ph Charly Steinberger   m Stanley Myers

Gina Lollobrigida, David Niven, John Moulder-Brown, Mario Adorf, Carl Fox-Duering

King Ralph
US   1991   97m   Eastmancolor
UIP/Universal/Mirage/Ibro (Jack Brodsky)
V, V*, L

A Las Vegas entertainer becomes King of England when the Royal Family is electrocuted.

Witless farce, set in an England that even P.G. Wodehouse would have found quaintly old hat.

wd David S. Ward   novel Headlong by Emlyn Williams   ph Kenneth MacMillan   m James Newton Howard   pd Simon Holland   ed John Jympson

John Goodman, Peter O'Toole, John Hurt, Camille Coduri, Richard Griffiths, Leslie Phillips, James Villiers, Joely Richardson, Niall O'Brian, Julian Glover, Judy Parfitt

'As the man who wouldn't be King if he could help it, Goodman redeems what might have been just another high-concept comedy for the party of humanity.' – Richard Schickel, Time

'Even Hell had to have a monarch!'
King Rat **
US   1965   134m   bw
Columbia/Coleytown (James Woolf)
V*

In Singapore's Changi Gaol during World War II an American corporal lives more comfortably than the other prisoners by shabby dealings with the camp guards.

Overlong but generally gripping character melodrama – 'not a story of escape but a story of survival'.

wd Bryan Forbes   novel James Clavell   ph Burnett Guffey   m John Barry

George Segal, Tom Courtenay, John Mills, James Fox, Denholm Elliott, Todd Armstrong, Patrick O'Neal, James Donald, Alan Webb, Leonard Rossiter, Geoffrey Bayldon

AAN: Burnett Guffey

King Richard and the Crusaders
US   1954   113m   Warnercolor   Cinemascope
Warner (Henry Blanke)
V*

During the Crusades, the dreaded Saladin arrives in

England in disguise and falls in love with Lady Edith . . .

Crudely confected comic strip version of Sir Walter Scott's The Talisman, ineptly written and cast, with poor production values.

w John Twist   d David Butler   ph Peverell Marley   m Max Steiner

Rex Harrison (as Saladin), Virginia Mayo, George Sanders, Laurence Harvey, Robert Douglas

LADY EDITH (Virginia Mayo): 'Fight, fight, fight! That's all you think of, Dick Plantagenet!'

'Do not adjust your set – the sound you hear is Sir Walter Scott turning in his grave.' – Sunday Express

'It shows why the Crusades never really amounted to much.' – Time

King Solomon of Broadway
US   1935   72m   bw
Universal

A night-club owner gambles away money he has borrowed from the mob.

Stale underworld melodrama.

w Harry Clork, Doris Malloy   d Alan Crosland

Edmund Lowe, Dorothy Page, Pinky Tomlin, Louise Henry, Charles Grapewin

'Won't go very far; mostly for doubles.' – Variety

King Solomon's Mines *
GB   1937   80m   bw
Gainsborough (Geoffrey Barkas)

Explorers in Africa persuade an exiled chief to help them find a diamond mine.

Rather somnolent though well-cast version of a favourite adventure novel, with a splendid final reel.

w Michael Hogan, A. R. Rawlinson, Roland Pertwee, Ralph Spence, Charles Bennett   novel H. Rider Haggard   d Robert Stevenson   ph Glen MacWilliams   m Mischa Spoliansky

Cedric Hardwicke, Paul Robeson, Roland Young, John Loder, Anna Lee, Sydney Fairbrother, Robert Adams

'If the pop houses can accept its half-throttle speed, they'll get all the thrills and entertainment they want.' – Variety

'They kept the eye of the camera open for every form of wild and savage life and crammed it all into the picture, so one gets the impression that Allan Quartermain is delivering a lecture with illustrations rather than taking part in an adventure.' – Richard Mallett, Punch

King Solomon's Mines *
US   1950   102m   Technicolor
MGM (Sam Zimbalist)
V*, L

A remake which is largely travelogue with the merest trimmings of story.

w Helen Deutsch   d Compton Bennett   ph Robert Surtees   ed Ralph E. Winters, Conrad A. Nervig

Stewart Granger, Deborah Kerr, Richard Carlson, Hugo Haas, Lowell Gilmore

† Andrew Marton directed the second unit sequences.

AA: Robert Surtees; editing

AAN: best picture

King Solomon's Mines
US   1985   100m   colour   Cinemascope
Cannon
V, V*

Quartermain is hired by a girl who wants to find her kidnapped father.

Adaptation in the vein of Indiana Jones and then some: the leading characters are almost boiled in a pot. Enjoyment depends on your sense of humour.

w Gene Quintano, James R. Silke   *d* J. Lee-Thompson

Richard Chamberlain, Sharon Stone, Herbert Lom, John Rhys-Davies, Ken Gampu

'The cinema's equivalent to junk food.' – *Sunday Mail*

The King Steps Out *
US   1936   85m   bw
Columbia (William Perlberg)
V*

Emperor Franz Josef falls in love with the sister of the princess to whom he is betrothed.

Rather heavy-handed romance with music, not in its director's best style but showing flashes of his decorative talent.

w Sidney Buchman   *operetta* Cissy by Herbert and Ernst Marischka   *d* Josef von Sternberg   *ph* Lucien Ballard   *m/ly* Fritz Kreisler, Dorothy Fields
ad Stephen Goossen

Grace Moore, Franchot Tone, Walter Connolly, Raymond Walburn, Herman Bing, Victor Jory, Elizabeth Risdon, Nana Bryant, Frieda Inescort, Thurston Hall

'Josef von Sternberg asked that it not be included in retrospectives of his work, but he really did make the damned thing.' – *New Yorker, 1977*

Kingdom of the Spiders
US   1977   95m   colour
Arachnid/Dimension (Henry Fownes)

In an Arizona valley the death rate soars when tarantulas begin preying in groups on humans instead of singly on each other.

The spiders is coming, as Hitch might have remarked, and not even giant-size. Standard shudders, efficiently presented.

w Richard Robinson, Alan Caillou   *d* John Cardos   *ph* John Morrill, John Wheeler   *md* Igo Kantor

William Shatner, Tiffany Bolling, Woody Strode, David MacLean

Kings and Desperate Men
Canada   1983   118m   colour
Alexis Kanner

A radio talk show host is held hostage by a group of unpredictable, idealistic terrorists.

Indulgently scripted, directed and acted, and dreary to watch.

w Edmund Ward, Alexis Kanner   *d* Alexis Kanner   *ph* Henry Lucas, Paul Van der Linden   *m* Michel Robidoux, Pierre F. Brault   *ad* Will McCrow
ed Henry Lucas

Patrick McGoohan, Alexis Kanner, Andrea Marcovicci, Margaret Trudeau

Kings Go Forth
US   1958   109m   bw
UA/Ross-Eton (Frank Ross)
S

August 1944: two American soldiers fall out over a black French woman who is torn between them.

Heavy-going war melodrama, well enough done for those who can take it.

w Merle Miller   *novel* Joe David Brown   *d* Delmer Daves   *ph* Daniel Fapp   *m* Elmer Bernstein

Frank Sinatra, Tony Curtis, Natalie Wood, Leora Dana, Karl Swenson

Kings of the Road
Germany   1975   176m   bw
Wim Wenders Productions
V, V*
original title: *Im Lauf der Zeit*

Two men on a bus talk of their past lives, their problems, their hopes and their fears.

Impossibly tedious two-hander which doubtless says something about life for those with the patience to sit it out.

wd Wim Wenders   *ph* Robby Müller, Martin Schäfer   *m* Alex Linstädt   *ed* Peter Pryzgodda

Rüdiger Vogler, Hanns Zischler, Lisa Kreuzer

Kings of the Sun
US   1963   108m   DeLuxe   Panavision
UA/Mirisch (Lewis J. Rachmil)

A Mayan tribe emigrates from Mexico to Texas and makes peace with the local Indian chief.

Ponderous dark age epic replete with human sacrifice, high-mindedness and solemn pauses. The actors and sets carry it as far as it will go.

w Elliott Arnold, James R. Webb   *d* J.Lee-Thompson   *ph* Joe MacDonald   *m* Elmer Bernstein
ad Alfred Ybarra

Yul Brynner, George Chakiris, Shirley Anne Field, Richard Basehart, Brad Dexter, Barry Morse

'The king's ships . . . the king's gold . . . the king's girls . . . were the treasure!'

The King's Pirate
US   1967   100m   Technicolor
Universal (Robert Arthur)

An American in the 18th-century British navy infiltrates a pirate stronghold in Madagascar.

Tatty remake of *Against All Flags*, rising to a few minor heights of swashbuckling.

w Paul Wayne   *d* Don Weis   *ph* Clifford Stine   *m* Ralph Ferraro

Doug McClure, Jill St John, Guy Stockwell, Kurt Kasznar, Torin Thatcher, Richard Deacon, Sean McClory

King's Rhapsody
GB   1955   93m   Eastmancolor   Cinemascope
Everest (Herbert Wilcox)

An exiled Ruritanian king leaves his mistress to return home to a political marriage.

Love versus duty in a ludicrously inept film of Ivor Novello's highly theatrical musical drama, cheaply made and killed stone dead by casting and wide screen.

w Pamela Bower, Christopher Hassall, A. P. Herbert   *d* Herbert Wilcox   *ph* Max Greene

Errol Flynn, Anna Neagle, Patrice Wymore, Martita Hunt, Finlay Currie

'Out of the hushed strangeness of these lives, and out of the shadows that hid their shame, filmdom has fashioned a drama most unusual, most touching and most wonderful!'
'The town they talk of in whispers!'

King's Row ****
US   1942   127m   bw
Warner (Hal B. Wallis)
V*, L, S

In a small American town during the early years of the century, three children grow up into a world of cruelty and madness.

Superb Hollywood melodrama, a Peyton Place with great visual strength, haunting music and a wholly absorbing if incredible plot.

w Casey Robinson   *novel* Henry Bellamann   *d* Sam Wood   *ph* James Wong Howe   *m* Erich Wolfgang Korngold   *pd* William Cameron Menzies

Ann Sheridan, Robert Cummings, Ronald Reagan, *Claude Rains,* Betty Field, Charles Coburn, Nancy Coleman, *Maria Ouspenskaya,* Harry Davenport, Judith Anderson, Karen Verne

DRAKE (Ronald Reagan): 'Where's the rest of me?'

'Half masterpiece and half junk.' – *James Agate*

'Tranquilly accepting many varieties of psychopathic behaviour as the simple facts of life, this film has its own kind of sentimental glow, yet the melodramatic incidents are surprisingly compelling.' – *New Yorker, 1982*

'One of the great melodramas, a veritable Mount Rushmore of physical and emotional cripples.' – *Time Out, 1981*

† The film was made in 1941, but its release was delayed for a year because the studio thought it too downbeat. It was not a great box-office success.

AAN: best picture; Sam Wood; James Wong Howe

A King's Story *
GB   1965   102m   Technicolor
Le Vien Films (Jack Le Vien)

Interviews with the Duke and Duchess of Windsor are interspersed with newsreels of the abdication crisis.

Earnest popular documentary with many points in its favour, including a resounding commentary by Orson Welles.

w Glyn Jones   *d* Harry Booth   *m* Ivor Slaney

AAN: best documentary

The King's Thief
US   1955   79m   Eastmancolor   Cinemascope
MGM (Edwin H. Knopf)

The Duke of Brampton plots treason against Charles II but a highwayman robs him of an incriminating notebook.

Dismal swashbuckler with neither zest nor style, just a cast of unhappy-looking actors.

w Charles Knopf   *d* Robert Z. Leonard   *ph* Robert Planck   *m* Miklos Rozsa

David Niven, Edmund Purdom, Ann Blyth, George Sanders, Roger Moore

The King's Vacation
US   1933   62m   bw
Warner

A king abdicates to seek the simple life.

Pleasing fable with a few theatrical ironies.

w Ernest Pascal, Maude T. Howell   *d* John Adolfi

George Arliss, Florence Arliss, Dick Powell, Marjorie Gateson, Dudley Digges

The King's Whore *
France/GB/Austria/Italy   1990   138m   colour
ASC/FR3/Cinema e Cinema/Umbrella (Maurice Benart, Wieland Schullz-Keil, Paolo Zaccaria)
V*, L

The beautiful wife of a courtier is forced to become a king's mistress.

Sumptuously romantic drama, conceived on a grand scale, but ultimately failing to live up to it.

w Daniel Vigne, Frederic Raphael, Axel Corti, Derek Marlowe   *novel* Jeanne, Putain du Roi by Jacques Tournier   *d* Axel Corti   *ph* Gernot Roll   *m* Gabriel Yared   *pd* Francesco Frigeri   *ed* Joelle Van Effenterre

Timothy Dalton, Valeria Golino, Stephane Freiss, Robin Renucci, Feodor Chaliapin, Eleanor David, Margaret Tyzack, Paul Crauchet

'The 17th century melodrama is less magnificent than it first appears, as it proves to be built around the small and inflexible obsessions of less-than-heroic characters.' – *Variety*

'A movie that makes one glad to have missed the 17th century.' – *Derek Malcolm, Guardian*

Kinjite: Forbidden Subjects
US   1989   97m   TVC
Cannon/Golan Globus (Pancho Kohner)
V, V*, L

A cop goes after a pimp specializing in child prostitutes.

Depressingly violent and nasty thriller, little more than a rerun of the star's *Death Wish* vigilante series.

w Harold Nebenzal d J. Lee-Thompson
ph Gideon Porath*ed* Peter Lee-Thompson, Mary E. Jochem

Charles Bronson, Perry Lopez, Juan Fernandez, Peggy Lipton, James Pax, Sy Richardson, Marion Kodama Yue, Bill McKinney

Kipps ***

GB 1941 112m bw
TCF (Edward Black)
V*
US title: *The Remarkable Mr Kipps*

In 1906, a draper's assistant comes into money and tries to crash society.

Charming, unassuming film of a well-loved novel, later musicalized as *Half a Sixpence.*

w Sidney Gilliat novel H. G. Wells d Carol Reed
ph Arthur Crabtree m Charles Williams

Michael Redgrave, Phyllis Calvert, Diana Wynyard, *Arthur Riscoe,* Max Adrian, Helen Haye, Michael Wilding, Lloyd Pearson, Edward Rigby, Hermione Baddeley, Frank Pettingell, Beatrice Varley, Kathleen Harrison, Felix Aylmer

'It has the old fashioned charm of wax roses under a glass bell.' – *New York Times*

Kisenga, Man of Africa: see *Men of Two Worlds*

Kismet

US 1930 90m bw 65mm Vitascope
Warner

An Oriental magician overcomes a wicked vizier.

Rather tame filming of a spectacular which belongs on the stage.

w Howard Estabrook play Edward Knoblock
d John Francis Dillon ph John Seitz

Otis Skinner, Loretta Young, David Manners, Mary Duncan, Sidney Blackmer, Fred Sterling, Edmund Breese, Montagu Love

Kismet *

US 1944 100m Technicolor
MGM (Everett Riskin)
TV title: *Oriental Dream*

Hollow and humourless but striking-looking remake of the above.

w John Meehan d William Dieterle ph Charles Rosher m Herbert Stothart ad Cedric Gibbons, Daniel B. Cathcart

Ronald Colman, Marlene Dietrich, James Craig, Edward Arnold, Hugh Herbert, Joy Ann Page, Florence Bates, Harry Davenport, Hobart Cavanaugh, Robert Warwick

'Enormous sets and crowding players are handled with such a clarity of line and colour that their gorgeousness never becomes untidy.' – *MFB*

AAN: Charles Rosher; Herbert Stothart; art direction

Kismet

US 1955 113m Eastmancolor Cinemascope
MGM (Arthur Freed)
V, V*, L, S

Unlucky musical remake from the stage show with Borodin music.

w Charles Lederer, Luther Davis musical play Charles Lederer, Luther Davis d Vincente Minnelli ph Joseph Ruttenberg ch Jack Cole
ad Cedric Gibbons, Preston Ames

Howard Keel, Ann Blyth, Dolores Gray, Vic Damone, Monty Woolley, Sebastian Cabot, Jay C. Flippen, Mike Mazurki, Jack Elam

The Kiss *

US 1929 64m approx (24 fps) bw silent
MGM (Albert Lewin)
V*, L

A woman is accused of the murder of her jealous husband.

A wisp of a melodrama, enlivened by its star; otherwise only notable as MGM's last silent picture.

w Hans Kraly d Jacques Feyder ph William Daniels

Greta Garbo, Lew Ayres, Conrad Nagel, Holmes Herbert, Anders Randolf

The Kiss

US 1988 98m colour
Columbia TriStar/Trilogy Entertainment/Astral Film Enterprises (Pen Densham, John Watson)
V, V*, L

A glamorous model is possessed by a demonic snake-like creature.

Unimaginative horror movie.

w Stephen Volk, Tom Ropelewski d Pen Densham
ph François Protat m J. Peter Robinson pd Roy Forge Smith sp Chris Walas ed Stan Cole

Pamela Collyer, Peter Dvorsky, Joanna Pacula, Meredith Salenger, Mimi Kuzyk, Nicholas Kilbertus, Sabrina Boudot, Shawn Levy, Jan Rubes, Celine Lomez

'Women were putty in his hands!'
Kiss and Make Up

US 1934 80m bw
Paramount (B. P. Schulberg)

A Parisian beauty specialist forsakes a rich client for his loyal secretary.

Forgettable romantic comedy.

w Harlan Thompson, George Marion Jnr
play Stephen Bekeffi d Harlan Thompson
ph Leon Shamroy

Cary Grant, Genevieve Tobin, Helen Mack, Edward Everett Horton, Lucien Littlefield, Mona Maris

'More gags than romance . . . a nice picture lacking sufficient strength to wow, but should do all right.' – *Variety*

Kiss and Tell *

US 1945 92m bw
Columbia (Sol C. Siegel)

To protect another girl, an irrepressible teenager pretends to be pregnant.

Good-humoured farcical comedy which at the time was thought pretty shocking, especially with the infant darling of the thirties in the lead.

w F. Hugh Herbert play F. Hugh Herbert d Richard Wallace ph Charles Lawton m Werner Heymann

Shirley Temple, Robert Benchley, Walter Abel, Jerome Courtland, Katherine Alexander, Porter Hall, Tom Tully

'All brilliantly characteristic of the worst anyone could think of American life.' – *James Agee*

A Kiss before Dying *

US 1956 94m DeLuxe Cinemascope
UA/Crown (Robert Jacks)

A college boy kills women who get in his way.

Reasonably absorbing exercise in psychopathology which would have been more effective on a smaller screen.

w Lawrence Roman novel Ira Levin d Gerd Oswald ph Lucien Ballard m Lionel Newman

Jeffrey Hunter, Joanne Woodward, Robert Wagner, Virginia Leith, Mary Astor, George Macready

A Kiss before Dying *

US 1991 93m Eastmancolor
UIP/Universal/Initial (Robert Lawrence)
V, V*, L

A woman discovers that the man she married is a multiple murderer.

Moderately effective thriller, though it offers a considerable simplification of the novel on which it is based.

wd James Dearden novel Ira Levin ph Mike Southon m Howard Shore pd Jim Clay
ed Michael Bradsell

Matt Dillon, Sean Young, Max von Sydow, Jim Fyfe, Ben Browder, Diane Ladd, James Bonfanti

'As exciting as watching someone go bald.' – *Anthony Lane, Independent on Sunday*

The Kiss before the Mirror

US 1933 66m bw
Universal

A lawyer defends a man who killed his wife from jealousy, then finds that the same thing is happening to him.

Stilted drama which was thought stylish at the time but is now a disappointment from this director; miscast, too.

w William Anthony McGuire play Lazslo Fodor
d James Whale

Frank Morgan, Nancy Carroll, Gloria Stuart, Paul Lukas, Charles Grapewin

'Direction and adaptation lift this one into passable entertainment.' – *Variety*

† It was remade in 1938 as *Wives Under Suspicion.*

A Kiss for Corliss

US 1949 88m bw
UA/Strand/James Nasser (Colin Miller)
V*
aka: *Almost a Bride*

A teenager develops a crush on a middle-aged roué.

Dismal sequel to *Kiss and Tell* in the shadow of *The Bachelor and the Bobby Soxer.*

w Howard Dimsdale d Richard Wallace
ph Robert de Grasse m Werner Heymann

David Niven, Shirley Temple, Tom Tully, Darryl Hickman, Virginia Welles

'A disastrous teenage potboiler.' – *David Niven*

'I sometimes think that David Niven Should not take all the parts he's given; While of the art of Shirley Temple I, for the moment, have had ample.'
– *C. A. Lejeune*

A Kiss in the Dark

US 1949 87m bw
Warner (Harry Kurnitz)

A concert pianist finds romance in a boarding house peopled with zany characters.

Paper-thin romantic comedy.

w Harry Kurnitz d Delmer Daves ph Robert Burks m Max Steiner

David Niven, Jane Wyman, Broderick Crawford, Maria Ouspenskaya, Victor Moore, Wayne Morris, Joseph Buloff, Curt Bois

Kiss Me Again **

US 1925 77m approx (24 fps) bw silent
Warner

A bored wife is tempted to stray, but doesn't.

Excellent silent comedy from an old boulevard farce, remade to less effect in the forties as *That Uncertain Feeling.*

w Hans Kraly   *play Divorçons* by Victorien Sardou, Emile de Najac   *d* Ernst Lubitsch   *ph* Charles von Enger

Marie Prévost, Monte Blue, John Roche, Willard Louis, Clara Bow

'Another sex masterpiece from the Attila of Hollywood . . . Continental high comedy done in the central European manner with Germanic harshness and irony of attack.' – *Ted Shane, New Yorker*

'Perhaps the most exquisite light screen comedy ever made on the subject of l'amour.' – *Herman G. Weinberg*

Kiss Me Again

US   1931   74m   Technicolor
Warner
GB title: *Toast of the Legion*

A French lieutenant and a cabaret singer chase each other half across the world.

Modest musical from Victor Herbert's *Mademoiselle Modiste;* popular at the time as a vehicle for two-colour Technicolor.

w Julien Josephson, Paul Perez   *d* William A. Seiter

Walter Pidgeon, Bernice Claire, Frank McHugh, Edward Everett Horton

'Doubtful as strong b.o. but clean, deserving, and may get a break.' – *Variety*

'I don't care what you do to me, Mike – just do it fast!'
Kiss Me Deadly ***

US   1955   105m   bw
UA/Parklane (Robert Aldrich)
V*, L

By helping a girl who is nevertheless murdered, Mike Hammer prevents crooks from stealing a case of radio-active material.

Exuberant and harsh thriller set in an unlovely world and shot with brutal close-ups and unusual camera angles that create a disquieting effect. It is as unremittingly tough as its thuggish hero.

w A. I. Bezzerides   *novel* Mickey Spillane *d* Robert Aldrich   *ph* Ernest Laszlo   *m* Frank de Vol

Ralph Meeker, Albert Dekker, Cloris Leachman, Paul Stewart, Juano Hernandez, Wesley Addy, Maxene Cooper

'This meeting of "art" and pulp literature is, to say the least, curious.' – *MFB*

Kiss Me Goodbye

US   1982   101m   DeLuxe
TCF/Boardwalk/Burt Sugarman/Keith Barish (Robert Mulligan)
V*

A widow planning to marry again is harassed by the ghost of her first husband.

It worked in *Blithe Spirit,* but this is on a different level, a toned-down rendering of the heavy-breathing Brazilian farce *Donna Flor and Her Two Husbands,* and it doesn't work on any level.

w Charlie Peters   *d* Robert Mulligan   *ph* Donald Peterman   *m* Ralph Burns   *pd* Philip M. Jefferies *ed* Sheldon Kahn

James Caan, Sally Field, Jeff Bridges, Paul Dooley, Claire Trevor, Mildred Natwick, William Prince

Kiss Me Kate **

US   1953   111m   Anscocolor   3-D
MGM (Jack Cummings)
V, V*, L, S

The married leading players of a musical version of *The Taming of the Shrew* lead an equally tempestuous life backstage.

Brisk, bright screen version of the Broadway musical hit.

w Dorothy Kingsley   *play* Samuel and Bella Spewack   *d George Sidney*   *ph* Charles Rosher

md André Previn, Saul Chaplin   *m/y Cole Porter ch Hermes Pan*

Howard Keel, Kathryn Grayson, Ann Miller, Keenan Wynn, Bobby Van, Tommy Rall, James Whitmore, Bob Fosse, Kurt Kasznar

AAN: André Previn, Saul Chaplin

Kiss Me Stupid *

US   1964   124m   bw   Panavision
UA/Mirisch/Phalanx/(Billy Wilder)
V, V*, L

A womanizing pop singer stops overnight in a small California desert town and shows interest in an unsuccessful songwriter in order to get at his wife.

Draggy, tasteless, surprisingly unamusing smoking room story, with the actors behaving as though driven against their will (apart from Dean Martin, ideally cast as the idol who gets a headache if he doesn't have sex every night). Some good wisecracks, but it should have been much faster and funnier.

w Billy Wilder, I. A. L. Diamond   *play L'oro della fantasia* by Anna Bonacci   *d* Billy Wilder *ph* Joseph LaShelle   *m* André Previn *pd* Alexander Trauner   *m/y* George and Ira Gershwin

Dean Martin, Kim Novak, Ray Walston, Cliff Osmond

'A work of ferocious tastelessness . . . Swiftian in its relentless disgust.' – *Peter Barnes*

'You know what I do to squealers? I let them have it in the belly. So they can roll around for a long time thinking it over!'
Kiss of Death **

US   1947   98m   bw
TCF (Fred Kohlmar)
V*

A captured thief informs on his own gang, and a psychopathic killer is sent to extract vengeance.

Gloomy, well-made semi-location thriller which descends into heavy melodrama. Remade as *The Fiend Who Walked the West.*

w Ben Hecht, Charles Lederer   *d* Henry Hathaway *ph* Norbert Brodine   *m* David Buttolph

Victor Mature, Richard Widmark, Brian Donlevy, Coleen Gray, Karl Malden, Taylor Holmes

'A tense, terrifying crime melodrama with an unusually authentic seamy atmosphere.' – *New Yorker, 1980*

'Economy of narration enhances the compactness and tautness of the whole and achieves that rarity, a picture minus unnecessary footage.' – *National Board of Review*

'It illustrates a new and vigorous trend in US moviemaking. One of the best things that is happening in Hollywood is the tendency to move out of the studio – to base fictional pictures on fact, and to shoot them not in painted studio sets but in actual places.' – *James Agee*

AAN: original story (E. Lipsky); Richard Widmark

Kiss of Evil: see *Kiss of the Vampire*

Kiss of Fire

US   1955   86m   Technicolor
Universal-International (Samuel Marx)

An ex-soldier escorts an exiled princess on a dangerous journey through Mexico.

Slightly unusual but rather clumsy swashbuckler of no especial merit.

w Franklin Coen, Richard Collins   *novel The Rose and the Flame* by Jonreed Lauritzen   *d* Joseph M. Newman   *ph* Carl Guthrie   *md* Joseph Gershenson *m* Hans Salter

Jack Palance, Barbara Rush, Martha Hyer

Kiss of the Spider Woman **

US/Brazil   1985   119m   MGM Color
HB/Sugarloaf (David Weisman)
V, V*, L

Fantasies of two prisoners in a South American jail.

One of those lucky flukes, an opening up of a fringe novel about the relationship between a flagrant homosexual and a political prisoner; the former entertains the latter with accounts of his favourite pulp movies. Not for Aunt Edna.

w Leonard Schrader   *novel* Manuel Puig   *d* Hector Babenco   *ph* Rodolfo Sanchez   *m* John Neschling *pd* Clovis Bueno

William Hurt, Raul Julia

AA: William Hurt

AAN: best picture; direction; adapted screenplay

William Hurt

Kiss of the Tarantula

US   1976   84m   Eastmancolor
New Realm/Manson (Daniel B. Cady)
V*
GB title: *Shudder*

A young girl kills those she does not like with her pet spiders.

Excessively dim horror movie without thrills or shudders.

w Warren Hamilton Jnr   *story* Daniel B. Cady *d* Chris Munger   *ph* Henning Schellerup *m* Phillan Bishop   *ed* Warren Hamilton Jnr

Suzanne Ling, Eric Mason, Herman Wallner, Patricia Landon, Beverly Eddins, Jay Scott Neal, Rebecca Eddins, Rita French

'The spiders are good for one or two mild sensations as they crawl lovingly over their initial victims, but even they are gradually overcome by the appalling banality of the script and the general lethargy of the direction.' – *Tom Milne*

Kiss of the Vampire *

GB   1964   88m   Eastmancolor
Rank/Hammer (Anthony Hinds)
US title: *Kiss of Evil*

In 1910 a Bavarian disciple of Dracula lures a British honeymoon couple.

This unsubtle variation on *Dracula* is handled in lively fashion, with a splendid climax in which assorted white-robed vampires are destroyed by bats.

w John Elder (Anthony Hinds)   *d Don Sharp ph* Alan Hume   *m* James Bernard   *pd* Bernard Robinson   *ed* James Needs

Noel Willman, Clifford Evans, Edward de Souza, Jennifer Daniel, Isobel Black

PROF. ZIMMER (Noel Willman): 'You must not expect your Queensberry rules here, Mr Harcourt.'

'They won't stop us – nobody can stop us!'
Kiss the Blood Off My Hands

US   1948   80m   bw
Universal/Hecht-Norma (Harold Hecht)
GB title: *Blood on My Hands*

A nurse helps a seaman on the run for murder.

Risible romantic melodrama in never-was London docks setting, with Newton large as life and twice as villainous.

w Leonardo Bercovici   *novel* Gerald Butler *d* Norman Foster   *ph* Russell Metty   *m* Miklos Rozsa

Joan Fontaine, Burt Lancaster, Robert Newton, Lewis Russell, Aminta Dyne

Kiss the Boys Goodbye *

US   1941   85m   bw
Paramount (Paul Jones)

A Broadway producer falls for one of his chorines.

Moderately smart musical entertainment of its time.

w Harry Tugend, Dwight Taylor   play Clare Boothe
d Victor Schertzinger ph Ted Tetzlaff m/y Victor
Schertzinger, Frank Loesser

Don Ameche, Mary Martin, Oscar Levant, Rochester,
Raymond Walburn, Connie Boswell, Virginia Dale,
Barbara Jo Allen, Elizabeth Patterson

Kiss the Bride Goodbye
GB   1944   89m   bw
Butcher

A runaway couple are unwittingly abetted by her
uncle.

Unsubtle family farce.

w Jack Whittingham   d Paul Stein

Patricia Medina, Jimmy Hanley, Frederick Leister,
Marie Lohr, Claud Allister, Ellen Pollock, Wylie
Watson

Kiss the Girls and Make Them Die
Italy   1966   106m   Technicolor
Dino de Laurentiis
original title: Si Tutte le Donne del Mondo . . .

A rich industrialist has a plan to sterilize the whole
male population of the world and restock it with his
own mistresses, whom he keeps in suspended
animation.

Patchy James Bond spoof.

w Jack Pulman, Dino Maiuri   d Henry Levin, Dino
Maiuri   ph Aldo Tonti   m Mario Nascimbene

Michael Connors, Dorothy Provine, Raf Vallone,
Terry-Thomas

Kiss Them for Me
US   1957   105m   Eastmancolor   Cinemascope
TCF (Jerry Wald)

Three navy pilots spend a weekend's unofficial leave
in San Francisco, and get into various kinds of
trouble.

Based on a novel which also served as source for the
musical Hit the Deck, this very heavy-footed comedy
with serious asides is most unsuitably cast and
generally ill-timed and unattractive.

w Julius Epstein   novel Shore Leave by Frederick
Wakeman   d Stanley Donen   ph Milton Krasner
m Lionel Newman

Cary Grant, Jayne Mansfield, Suzy Parker, Ray
Walston, Larry Blyden, Leif Erickson, Werner
Klemperer

Kiss Tomorrow Goodbye
US   1950   102m   bw
Cagney Productions (William Cagney)
V*, L

A violent criminal breaks jail and plans several daring
robberies.

Surprisingly brutal star melodrama which failed to
repeat the success of White Heat.

w Harry Brown   novel Horace McCoy   d Gordon
Douglas   ph Peverell Marley   m Carmen Dragon

James Cagney, Barbara Payton, Ward Bond, Luther
Adler, Helena Carter, Steve Brodie, Rhys Williams,
Barton MacLane, Frank Reicher, John Litel

'The mixture as before without an ingredient
changed.' – Otis Guernsey Jnr

Kisses for Breakfast
US   1941   81m   bw
Warner

A man just married loses his memory and marries
again.

Poorly developed farce comedy with stars who can't
help.

w Kenneth Gamet   play Seymour Hicks   d Lewis
Seiler

Dennis Morgan, Jane Wyatt, Shirley Ross, Lee
Patrick, Jerome Cowan, Una O'Connor, Barnett
Parker, Cornel Wilde

Kisses for My President
US   1964   113m   bw
Warner/Pearlayne (Curtis Bernhardt)

America's first woman president causes problems for
her husband.

Solidly-carpentered comedy with too few ideas for its
length.

w Claude Binyon, Robert G. Kane   d Curtis
Bernhardt   ph Robert Surtees   m Bronislau Kaper

Polly Bergen, Fred MacMurray, Arlene Dahl, Eli
Wallach, Edward Andrews

Kissin' Cousins
US   1963   96m   Metrocolor   Panavision
MGM/Four Leaf (Sam Katzman)
V, V*

The USAF wants to build a missile base on Smokey
Mountain, and their PR man discovers that one of the
hillbillies is his double.

A feeble production in every sense, even below its
star's usual standard.

w Gerald Drayson Adams, Gene Nelson   d Gene
Nelson   ph Ellis W. Carter   md Fred Karger

Elvis Presley, Arthur O'Connell, Glenda Farrell, Jack
Albertson

The Kissing Bandit
US   1948   102m   Technicolor
MGM (Joe Pasternak)

In old California, a young businessman finds he is
expected to keep up his bandit father's criminal and
romantic reputation.

Silly, witless musical which never settles into gear;
mocked by its star as Benny mocked The Horn Blows at
Midnight.

w Isobel Lennart, John Briard Harding   d Laslo
Benedek   ph Robert Surtees   m Georgie Stoll
m/y Nacio Herb Brown, Earl Brent, Edward Heyman

Frank Sinatra, Kathryn Grayson, J. Carrol Naish,
Mildred Natwick, Mikhail Rasumny, Billy Gilbert,
Clinton Sundberg

Kit Carson
US   1940   95m   bw
Edward Small
V*

Adventures of the pioneer Indian scout.

Thinly scripted Western imaginings with a sturdy but
not alluring cast.

w George Bruce   d George B. Seitz

Jon Hall, Lynn Bari, Dana Andrews, Harold Huber,
Ward Bond, Renee Riano, Raymond Hatton

The Kitchen Toto *
GB   1987   95m   colour
Cannon/Skreba/British Screen/Film Four (Ann Skinner)
V*, L

1950: in Kenya, a police officer agrees to take in the
son of a black priest murdered by the Mau Mau.

Rather lumpy but well-meaning drama with a tragic
ending.

wd Harry Hook   ph Roger Deakins   m John Keane
pd Jamie Leonard   ed Tom Priestley

Bob Peck, Phyllis Logan, Edwin Mahinda, Robert
Urquhart

Kitten with a Whip
US   1964   83m   bw
Universal

A girl escaped from reform school takes refuge with a
politician whose wife is away.

Over-the-top melodrama thought bannable at the
time.

wd Douglas Heyes   book Wade Miller

Ann-Margret, John Forsythe, Patricia Barry, Ann
Doran, Audrey Dalton

Kitty
GB   1928   90m (24 fps)   bw   silent
BIP/Burlington (Victor Saville)

A shopgirl loves a paralysed amnesiac, but his mother
interferes.

Uninteresting romantic melodrama, notable only as
Britain's first sound film: a few dialogue sequences
were quickly added (in New York).

w Violet Powell, Benn W. Levy   novel Warwick
Deeping   d Victor Saville   ph Karl Puth

John Stuart, Estelle Brody, Dorothy Cumming, Marie
Ault, Olaf Hytten

'She had all London on a MARRY-go-round!'
Kitty ***
US   1945   103m   bw
Paramount (Karl Tunberg)

In 18th-century London, an aristocrat makes a
duchess of a guttersnipe.

Well-detailed period Pygmalion which works much
better than one would expect.

w Darrell Ware, Karl Tunberg   novel Rosamund
Marshall   d Mitchell Leisen   ph Daniel L. Fapp
m Victor Young   ad Hans Dreier, Walter Tyler

Paulette Goddard, Ray Milland, Cecil Kellaway, Constance
Collier, Reginald Owen, Patric Knowles, Dennis Hoey,
Sara Allgood, Eric Blore, Gordon Richards, Michael
Dyne

'Enough sex, wit and urbane cynicism to make one
forget a footling ending.' – Peter John Dyer, MFB

'It is excellently cast, delightfully acted, and the rather
sordid story is told with subtlety and skill.' – Picture
Show

'The most glamorous study of unrelieved sordidness
that the screen has presented.' – Motion Picture Herald

AAN: art direction

'The most daring novel ever written by a man about a
woman!'
Kitty Foyle **
US   1940   108m   bw
RKO (Harry E. Edgington, David Hempstead)
V*, L

A white-collar girl has a troubled love life.

Solid entertainment of its time, especially aimed at
ambitious young ladies.

w Dalton Trumbo, Donald Ogden Stewart
novel Christopher Morley   d Sam Wood   ph Robert
de Grasse   m Roy Webb

Ginger Rogers, Dennis Morgan, James Craig, Eduardo
Ciannelli, Ernest Cossart, Gladys Cooper, Mary Treen

AA: Ginger Rogers

AAN: best picture; Dalton Trumbo; Sam Wood

The Klansman
US   1974   112m   Technicolor
Paramount/Atlanta (William Alexander)
V*

An Alabama sheriff confronts the Ku Klux Klan.

Violent melodrama, all noise, brutality and bad
acting.

w Millard Kaufman, Samuel Fuller   novel William
Bradford Huie   d Terence Young   ph Lloyd Ahern,
Aldo Tonti   m Stax Organization

Lee Marvin, Richard Burton, Cameron Mitchell, O. J. Simpson, Lola Falana, David Huddleston, Luciana Paluzzi, Linda Evans

'There's not a shred of quality, dignity, relevance or impact in this yahoo-oriented bunk.' – *Variety*

'Mae goes north and Alaska goes west!'
Klondike Annie
US   1936   83m   bw
Paramount (William Le Baron)

A torch singer on the run disguises herself as a missionary and revivifies a Klondike mission.

Laundered Mae West vehicle, from her fading period but not too bad.

w Mae West, Marion Morgan, George B. Dowell
d Raoul Walsh   *ph* George Clemens

Mae West, Victor McLaglen, Philip Reed, Helen Jerome Eddy, Harry Beresford, Harold Huber, Esther Howard

Klute ***
US   1971   114m   Technicolor   Panavision
Warner (Alan J. Pakula)
V, V*, L

A policeman leaves the force to investigate the disappearance of a research scientist, and takes up with a call girl who is involved.

Excellent adult thriller with attention to detail and emphasis on character.

w Andy K. Lewis, Dave Lewis   *d* Alan J. Pakula
ph Gordon Willis   *m* Michael Small

Jane Fonda, Donald Sutherland, Charles Cioffi, Roy Scheider, Rita Gam

AA: Jane Fonda

AAN: Andy K. Lewis, Dave Lewis

The Knack ****
GB   1965   84m   bw
UA/Woodfall (Oscar Lewenstein)

A sex-starved young teacher lets one room of his house to a successful womanizer, another to an innocent girl from the north.

An excuse for an anarchic series of visual gags, a kaleidoscope of swinging London in which anything goes. Brilliantly done in the style of *A Hard Day's Night*.

w Charles Wood   *play* Ann Jellicoe   *d* Richard Lester   *ph* David Watkin   *m* John Barry

Michael Crawford, Ray Brooks, Rita Tushingham, Donal Donnelly

'The whole film has the anarchic quality modish today and at all times appealing to a new generation understandably bent on overturning the ideas which have hardened in the minds of their elders.' – *Dilys Powell*

'The running jokes and gags never come off.' – *Pauline Kael*

Knave of Hearts *
GB   1954   103m   bw
Transcontinental (Paul Graetz)
aka: *Monsieur Ripois et Son Nemesis*
US title: *Lover Boy*

A born philanderer confesses all his affairs to his wife.

Well-observed though strangely flat and disappointing sex comedy, something of a pioneer in its time and therefore perhaps too diffident in its approach.

w René Clément, Hugh Mills   *d* René Clément
ph Oswald Morris   *m* Roman Vlad

Gérard Philipe, Margaret Johnston, Joan Greenwood, Natasha Parry, Valerie Hobson

Knickerbocker Holiday *
US   1944   84m   bw
UA/PCA/Harry Joe Brown
V*

In old New Amsterdam, a one-legged tyrant finally sees the light.

Artificial musical from a famous Broadway original, staged in 1938, with engaging moments including Charles Coburn singing 'September Song'.

w David Boehm, Harry Goldman, Roland Leigh, Thomas Lennon   *novel* Father Knickerbocker's History of New York by Washington Irving   *d* Harry Joe Brown
ph Phil Tannura   *m* Werner Heymann   *m/ly* Kurt Weill, Maxwell Anderson

Charles Coburn, Nelson Eddy, Constance Dowling, Ernest Cossart, Shelley Winters, Otto Kruger

AAN: Werner Heymann, Kurt Weill

Knife in the Water *
Poland   1962   94m   bw
ZRF Kamera (Stanislaw Zylewicz)
V, V*, L
original title: *Noz w Wodzie*

A young couple ask a hitchhiker to spend a weekend on their yacht, and regret it.

Detached little melodrama in which the sex and violence hover beneath the surface. All very watchable, but in a minor key.

w Jerzy Skolimowski, Roman Polanski, Jakub Goldberg   *d* Roman Polanski   *ph* Jerzy Lipman
m Krzystof Komeda

Leon Niemczyk, Jolanta Umecka, Zygmunt Malanowicz

AAN: best foreign film

Knight Moves
US/Germany   1992   116m   Eastmancolor
Columbia TriStar/Knight Moves/Cine Vox (Ziad El Khoury, Jean-Luc Defait)
V, V*, L, S

A chess champion is suspected of being a serial killer.

Lacklustre thriller with little suspense or sense of reality.

w Brad Mirman   *d* Carl Schenkel   *ph* Dietrich Lohmann   *md* Anne Dudley   *pd* Graeme Murray
ed Norbert Herzner

Christopher Lambert, Diane Lane, Tom Skerritt, Daniel Baldwin, Ferdinand Mayne, Katherine Isobel, Charles Bailey-Gates, Arthur Strauss

'Mannered, heavy-handed and rather ridiculous.' – *Philip French, Observer*

Knight without Armour **
GB   1937   107m   bw
London Films (Alexander Korda)
V*

During the Russian Revolution of 1917, a widowed countess is helped to safety by a British translator.

Underrated romantic adventure with big production values and some splendid moments.

w Lajos Biro, Arthur Wimperis, Frances Marion
novel James Hilton   *d* Jacques Feyder   *ph* Harry Stradling, Bernard Browne, Jack Cardiff   *md* Muir Matheson   *m* Miklos Rozsa   *ad* Lazare Meerson
ed William Hornbeck, Francis Lyon

Robert Donat, Marlene Dietrich, Irene Vanbrugh, Herbert Lomas, Austin Trevor, Basil Gill, David Tree, John Clements, Lawrence Hanray

'Another feather in the cap of Alexander Korda for his series of artistic film productions. There is relatively little to find fault with and much to praise.' – *Variety*

'A first-class thriller, beautifully directed, with spare and convincing dialogue and a nearly watertight scenario.' – *Graham Greene*

Knightriders
US   1981   155m   colour
V*

A group of wandering hippies, led by a man obsessed with notions of chivalry, re-enact medieval tournaments on motor-bikes.

A glum and wordy movie, revealing little point or purpose.

wd George A. Romero   *ph* Michael Gornick
m Donald Rubinstein   *pd* Cletus Anderson
ed George A. Romero, Pasquala Buba

Ed Harris, Gary Lahti, Tom Savini, Amy Ingersoll, Patricia Tallman, Christine Forrest

Knights and Emeralds
GB   1986   94m   colour
Warner/Goldcrest/Enigma (Susan Richards, Raymond Day)

A young white drummer joins a rival black band for the national marching bands championship.

Dull teen drama of racial relationships, accompanied by a great deal of uninteresting music.

wd Ian Emes   *ph* Richard Greatrex   *m* Colin Towns   *ad* Deborah Gillingham   *ed* John Victor-Smith

Christopher Wild, Beverley Hills, Warren Mitchell, Bill Leadbitter, Rachel Davies

Knights of the Round Table *
GB   1953   115m   Eastmancolor   Cinemascope
MGM (Pandro S. Berman)
V*, L

Lancelot, banished from King Arthur's court for loving Guinevere, returns to defeat the evil Modred.

Disappointingly flat, pageant-like adaptation of the legends, with a few lively strands insufficiently firmly drawn together.

w Talbot Jennings, Jan Lustig, Noel Langley
d Richard Thorpe   *ph* Frederick A. Young, Stephen Dade   *m* Miklos Rozsa   *ad* Alfred Junge, Hans Peters

Robert Taylor, Mel Ferrer, Ava Gardner, Anne Crawford, Stanley Baker, Felix Aylmer, Robert Urquhart, Niall MacGinnis

AAN: art direction

Knights of the Teutonic Order *
Poland   1960   180m   Eastmancolor   Dyaliscope
Studio Unit (Zygmunt Krol)
original title: *Krzyzacy*

Teutonic knights pillage Poland on the pretext of converting the inhabitants to Christianity; when they kill a noblewoman, her daughter swears revenge.

Medieval epic differing little from those of Hollywood, but splendid to look at.

w Jerzy Stafan Stawinski, Aleksander Ford
novel Henryk Sienkiewicz   *d* Aleksander Ford
ph Mieczyslaw Jahoda   *m* Kazimierz Serocki

Urszula Modrzynska, Grazyna Staniszewska, Andrzej Szalawski

Knock on Any Door *
US   1949   100m   bw
Columbia/Santana (Robert Lord)
V*, L

A defence lawyer pleads with the jury for the life of a slum boy on a murder charge.

Smartly-made but empty melodrama making facile social points.

w Daniel Taradash, John Monks Jnr   *novel* Willard Motley   *d* Nicholas Ray   *ph* Burnett Guffey
m George Antheil

Humphrey Bogart, John Derek, George Macready, Allene Roberts

Knock on Wood **
US 1954 103m Technicolor
Paramount (Norman Panama, Melvin Frank)

Stolen plans are hidden inside the dummy of an unsuspecting ventriloquist.

Excellent star comedy with good script and production (but some strange ideas of London's geography).

wd *Norman Panama, Melvin Frank* ph Daniel Fapp
m Leith Stevens ch Michael Kidd m/ly Sylvia Fine

Danny Kaye, Mai Zetterling, David Burns, Torin Thatcher, Leon Askin, Abner Biberman, Steve Geray

AAN: Norman Panama, Melvin Frank (script)

Knockout: see *Knute Rockne, All American*

Knocks at My Door **
Venezuela/Cuba/Argentina (Liz Mago) 1993 106m
Agfa colour
Foncine/CONAC/ASP/ICAIC/Channel 4 (Alejandro Saderman)
original title: *Golpes a Mi Puerta*

Two nuns face execution for sheltering a young radical being hunted by a military death-squad.

Gripping and timely drama of courage and obduracy, political expediency and state brutality.

w Juan Carlos Gene, Alejandro Saderman
play Juan Carlos Gene d Alejandro Saderman
ph Jonny Semeco, Adriano Moreno m Julio D'Escrivan ad Marietta Perroni ed Claudia Uribe

Véronica Oddó, Elba Escobar, Juan Carlos Gené, José Antonio Rodriguez, Ana Castell, Mirta Ibarra, Frank Spano

Knute Rockne, All American
US 1940 98m bw
Warner (Robert Fellows)
V*
GB titles: *Knockout; A Modern Hero*

The career of a famous Notre Dame football coach.

Standard sporting biopic.

w Robert Buckner d Lloyd Bacon ph Tony Gaudio m Ferde Grofé

Pat O'Brien, Ronald Reagan, Gale Page, Donald Crisp, Albert Basserman, John Qualen, John Sheffield

Koenigsmark
France 1935 114m bw
Roger Richebé/Capitol

A princess falls for a commoner.

Rather elementary royal romance in a Ruritanian background, filmed simultaneously in French and English by the same principals.

novel Pierre Benoit d Maurice Tourneur

Elissa Landi, Pierre Fresnay, John Lodge

Koks I Kulissen: see *Ladies on the Rocks*

Komissar **
USSR 1967 108m colour Cinemascope
Artificial Eye/Gorky Studios (V. Levin, L. Prilutzkaya)
aka: *The Commissar*

During the Civil War of the 1920s, a pregnant soldier of the Red Army moves in with a poor Jewish family to have her child.

First publicly shown twenty years after it was made, the film's events indict anti-Semitism and foreshadow the later treatment of the Jews within the context of a simple domestic story.

wd Alexander Askoldov novel *In the Town of Berdichev* by Vasily Grossman ph Valery Ginsburg m Alfred Schnittke ad Sergei Serebrennikov ed V. Isayeva, N. Loginova, S. Lyashinskaya

Nonna Mordyukova, Rolan Bykov, Raisa Niedashkovskaya, Vasily Shukshin

Komitas
West Germany 1988 106m colour
ICA/Margarita Woskanjan Filmproduction/WDR/SFB/Channel 4

Visually striking meditation on an Armenian monk and composer traumatized into silence by the Turkish massacre of his countrymen in 1915.

Limited in its appeal.

wd Don Askarjan ph Jorgos Arvanitis, Martin Gressmann, Eberhard Geik m Komitas and others ad Jurgen Kiebach, Michael Poladian ed Rene Perraudin, Marion Regentrop

Samvel Ovasapain, Margarita Woskanjan, Onig Saadetian, Yeghishe Mougikian

Koneko Monogatari: see *The Adventures of Milo and Otis*

Kongbufenzi: see *The Terrorizer*

Kongo
US 1932 86m bw
MGM

An embittered African recluse takes revenge on the daughter of his former enemy.

No-holds-barred melodrama which never really exerts the right grip; a remake of the Lon Chaney silent *West of Zanzibar.*

w Leon Gordon play Chester de Vonde, Kilbourn Gordon d William Cowen ph Harold Rosson

Walter Huston, Lupe Velez, Virginia Bruce, Conrad Nagel, C. Henry Gordon

'Horror and tropical stuff combined . . . chiefly for the daily grinds.' – *Variety*

Der Kongress Tanzt: see *Congress Dances*

Kontrakt: see *The Contract*

Konyets Sankt-Peterburga: see *The End of St Petersburg*

Korczak
Poland/Germany/France/GB 1990 118m colour
Artificial Eye/Filmstudio 'Perspektywa'/Regina Ziegler Filmproduktion/Erato Films/BBC Films/Telmar Film International (Regina Ziegler, Janusz Morgenstern, Daniel Tocsan du Plantier)
V*

The director of a Polish orphanage attempts to protect his charges from the Nazis.

Despite, or perhaps because of, being based on reality, the film fails to engage satisfactorily with its subject matter.

w Agnieszka Holland d Andrzej Wajda ph Robby Müller m Wojciech Kilar pd Allan Starski ed Ewa Smal

Wojtek Pszoniak, Ewa Dalkowska, Piotr Kozlowski, Marzena Trybala, Wojciech Klata, Adam Siemion, Karolina Czernicka, Agnieszka Kruk

To Koritsi me ta Mavra: see *The Girl in Black*

Korkalen: see *Thy Soul Shall Bear Witness*

Koroshi No Rakuin: see *Branded to Kill*

Korotkie Vstrechi: see *Short Encounters*

Koshikei: see *Death by Hanging*

Kotch *
US 1971 114m Metrocolor
ABC/Kotch Company (Richard Carter)
V*

An eccentric 72-year-old widower is at odds with his family and helps a pregnant babysitter.

Variously amusing, moving and sentimental, this generally likeable film about a crotchety grandpa is sustained by its star performance.

w John Paxton novel Katherine Topkins d Jack Lemmon ph Richard H. Kline m Marvin Hamlisch

Walter Matthau, Deborah Winter, Felicia Farr, Charles Aidman

AAN: Walter Matthau; song 'Life Is What You Make It' (m Marvin Hamlisch, ly Johnny Mercer)

Koyaanisqatsi *
US 1983 86m DeLuxe
Island Alive/Blue Dolphin/Institute for Regional Education (Godfrey Reggio)
V, V*, S

A panoramic view of contemporary America without commentary or narrative, using time-lapse photography. The title is an Indian word meaning 'a state of life that calls for another way of living'.

A rather pointless, very beautiful, and finally rather boring experience.

w Ron Fricke, Godfrey Reggio, Michael Hoenig, Alton Walpole d Godfrey Reggio ph Ron Fricke m Philip Glass ed Anton Walpole, Ron Fricke

'Arrogant bombast, provoking no response except "wow".' – *Sight & Sound*

† It was followed by *Powaqqatsi* (qv), which gave a similar treatment to the Third World.

Krakatoa, East of Java
US 1968 136m Technicolor Cinerama
ABC/Cinerama (Lester A. Sansom)

In 1883 the SS *Batavia Queen* leaves Singapore and is engulfed by the Krakatoa eruption.

Mindless spectacular, technically quite impressive but with no dramatic interest whatsoever. (Krakatoa is actually west of Java.)

w Clifford Newton Gould, Bernard Gordon d Bernard Kowalski ph Manuel Berenguer m Frank de Vol pd/sp Eugene Lourié

Maximilian Schell, Diane Baker, Brian Keith, Rossano Brazzi, Barbara Werle, John Leyton, Sal Mineo, J. D. Cannon, Marc Lawrence

'Apparently designed to disprove the old adage, "they don't make them like that any more". At a conservative count it includes such sure-fire cinematic ingredients as hidden treasure, deep-sea divers with shattered lungs and claustrophobia, mutiny and fire on board ship, nuns, convicts, a lost orphan boy, girl divers and even a little striptease, climaxing in the biggest explosion and the greatest tidal wave known to history.' – *MFB*

AAN: special visual effects

'There are three sides to this love story!'
Kramer versus Kramer ***
US 1979 105m Technicolor
Columbia/Stanley Jaffe (Richard C. Fischoff)
V, V*, L, S

A divorced advertising executive gets temporary custody of his seven-year-old son.

New-fashioned tearjerker, as slick as a colour supplement and catnip to the emotion-starved masses.

wd *Robert Benton* novel Avery Corman ph Nestor Almendros md Erma E. Levin pd Paul Sylbert ed Jerry Greenberg

Dustin Hoffman, Justin Henry, Meryl Streep, Jane Alexander, Howard Duff

'Pastel colours, a cute kid and a good script made this one of the most undeserved successes of the year: wall-to-wall sentiment.' – *Time Out*

AA: best picture; Robert Benton (as director); Dustin Hoffman; Meryl Streep; screenplay adapted from another medium

AAN: Justin Henry; Jane Alexander; Nestor Almendros; editing

'When people are afraid of you ... You can do everything. Remember that.'

The Krays **
GB   1990   119m   colour
Rank/Parkfield (Dominic Anciano, Ray Burdis)
V, V*, CD, L

Twins, who grow up in a mother-dominated household, become feared and fearsome East End thugs.

Made with the cooperation of its real-life protagonists, it stays within a gangster milieu and comes close to glamourizing them both.

w Philip Ridley d Peter Medak ph Alex Thomson m Michael Kamen pd Michael Pickwoad ed Martin Walsh

Billie Whitelaw, Gary Kemp, Martin Kemp, Susan Fleetwood, Charlotte Cornwall, Jimmy Jewel, Avis Bunnage, Kate Hardie, Alfred Lynch, Tom Bell, Steven Berkoff

'The direction does not flinch, as do most other British crime-class-nostalgia movies, from graphic violence.' – MFB

'The movie comes over like a collaboration between Joan Littlewood's Theatre Workshop, an ungifted follower of Sigmund Freud and the postcard artist Donald McGill.' – Philip French, Observer

Kreitzerova Sonata
USSR   1987   135m   colour
Cannon/Mosfilm (Maria Zakharova)
aka: The Kreutzer Sonata

A jealous husband tells a fellow traveller how he came to kill his wife.

Restlessly faithful to the book, but failing to engage its audience.

w Mikhail Schweitzer novel Leo Tolstoy
d Mikhail Schweitzer, Sofia Milkina ph Mikhail Agraovich m Sofia Gubaidulina pd Igor Lemeshev, Vladimir Fabrikov ed Lyudmila Feiginova

Oleg Yankovsky, Aleksandr Trofimov, Irina Seleznyova, Dmitri Pokrovsky

'If you miss the first five minutes you miss one suicide, two executions, one seduction and the key to the plot!'

The Kremlin Letter
US   1970   122m   DeLuxe   Panavision
TCF (Carter de Haven, Sam Wiesenthal)

An American intelligence team is sent undercover to Moscow to retrieve an arms treaty mistakenly signed.

Tediously violent cold war mystifier: a few good performances do not make it worth unravelling.

w John Huston, Gladys Hill novel Noel Behn
d John Huston ph Ted Scaife m Robert Drasnin pd Ted Haworth

Richard Boone, Orson Welles, Bibi Andersson, Max von Sydow, Patrick O'Neal, Ronald Radd, George Sanders, Dean Jagger, Nigel Green, Barbara Parkins, Lila Kedrova, Michael MacLiammoir, Sandor Eles, Niall MacGinnis, John Huston

'One of those all-star international spy sagas that trick out an indecipherably tortuous plot with a series of vignettes in which the pleasures of star-spotting are expected to compensate for any narrative longueurs.' – Nigel Andrews

Krótki Film o Milości: see A Short Film about Love

Krótki Film o Zabijaniu: see A Short Film about Killing

Krull
GB   1983   121m   Metrocolor
Columbia/Ted Mann-Ron Silverman
V, V*, L

Prince Colwyn's bride-to-be is abducted by the Beast of the Black Fortress.

Old-fashioned derring-do taking place on a somewhat unattractive planet; nevertheless fairly lively in its action and trick effects.

w Stanford Sherman d Peter Yates ph Peter Suschitzky m James Horner pd Stephen Grimes

Ken Marshall, Lysette Anthony, Freddie Jones, Francesca Annis, Alun Armstrong, David Battley, Bernard Bresslaw, John Welsh, Tony Church, Bernard Archard

'Nearly everything in it has been done before, in some cases rather better, but rarely quite so likeably.' – Nick Roddick, MFB

'Not really thrilling enough to be a blockbuster and not light enough to be anything else.' – Sight and Sound

Krzyzacy: see Knights of the Teutonic Order

'When you have attitude, who needs experience?'
Kuffs
US   1992   101m   Technicolor
Universal/EvansGideon (Raynold Gideon)
V, V*, L, S

A high-school dropout inherits his murdered brother's private police business and sets out to avenge his death.

Messily coarse comedy not helped by the star's direct addresses to the camera.

w Bruce A. Evans, Raynold Gideon d Bruce A. Evans ph Thomas Del Ruth m Harold Faltermeyer pd Victoria Paul, Armin Ganz ed Stephen Semel

Christian Slater, Tony Goldwyn, Milla Jovovich, Bruce Boxleitner, Troy Evans, George de la Pena, Leon Rippy

'Film veers from ultra-violence to slapstick comedy in an arbitrary and irritating fashion. Hokey camera angles and flashy dissolves fail to pump up the action.' – Variety

'The film comes to resemble the bastard child of Miami Vice and an especially bad movie-of-the-week.' – New York Times

Kumonosu-Jo: see Throne of Blood

Kung Fu Street Fighter (dubbed)
Japan   1974   74m   Eastmancolor   Actionscope
Eural/Toei-Kyoto Eiga/Titan (Norimichi Matsudaira)
original title: Gekitotsu! Satsujinken

A Japanese hitman offers his services to protect an oil heiress, who is threatened by Chinese businessmen with Mafia connections.

An unsavoury martial arts movie with a thuggish hero, whose behaviour is excused because his father was killed by a Chinese firing squad.

w Koji Yakada, Motohiro Torii d Shigehiro Ozawa ph Kenji Horikoshi m Tony Tsushima ad Takatoshi Suzuki ed Kozo Horiike

Sonny Chiba, Gerald Yamada, Doris Nakajima, Tony Cetera, Tatsuro Endo, Masashi Ishibashi

'The plentiful fight scenes are choreographed and stage-managed with unusual vigour, rising to operatic delirium for the climax.' – Tony Rayns, MFB

† It was followed by a sequel, Blood of the Dragon (qv).

Kuroi Ame: see Black Rain

Kvinnodrom: see Journey into Autumn

Kwaidan ****
Japan   1964   164m   Eastmancolor   Tohoscope
Ninjin Club/Bungei
V*, L

Four elegant ghost stories by Lafcadio Hearn.

A literally haunting film that is among the most beautiful ever made, with its succession of exotic, perfectly composed images and strange narratives.

w Yoko Mizuki d Masaki Kobayashi ph Yoshio Miyajima m Toru Takemitsu ad Shigemasa Toda

Rentaro Mikuni, Ganjiro Nakamura, Katsuo Nakamura

AAN: best foreign film

L

'Something Funny Is Happening In L.A.'

L.A. Story *
US   1991   95m   Technicolor
Guild/Rastar (Daniel Melnick, Michael Rachmil)
V, V*, L

A TV weather forecaster in Los Angeles falls for a
visiting English journalist.

A pleasant romantic comedy, though the love affair is
mainly with Los Angeles itself.

w Steve Martin   d Mick Jackson   ph Andrew
Dunn   m Peter Melnick   pd Lawrence Miller
ed Richard A. Harris

Steve Martin, Victoria Tennant, Richard E. Grant,
Marilu Henner, Sarah Jessica Parker, Susan Forristal,
Kevin Pollak, Patrick Stewart

'A light-headed joyride for an audience.' – *Pauline
Kael, New Yorker*

The L-Shaped Room *
GB   1962   142m   bw
British Lion/Romulus (James Woolf, Richard Attenborough)
V

A girl intending to have an abortion takes a room in a
London suburban house which is none too clean but
full of characters.

Watchable, mildly sensational low-life melodrama of
the pre-swinging London era when well-to-dos
thought it amusing to live in garrets. Hellishly
overlong but enjoyable in patches because of the
professionalism with which it is made.

w Bryan Forbes   novel Lynne Reid Banks   d Bryan
Forbes   ph Douglas Slocombe   m Brahms, John
Barry

Leslie Caron, Tom Bell, *Brock Peters, Cicely Courtneidge,
Bernard Lee, Avis Bunnage, Patricia Phoenix, Emlyn
Williams*

'It would be hard to imagine a more unlikely, or
commercially more sure-fire group of lodgers living
under a single roof than this pregnant French girl,
maladjusted negro, lesbian actress, couple of
prostitutes, and unpublished writer who finally
commits it all to paper – shades of *I Am a Camera* as
well as *A Taste of Honey*.' – *MFB*

AAN: Leslie Caron

L.627 **
France   1992   146m   colour
Artificial Eye/Little Bear (Alain Sarde)

A dedicated Paris cop joins a newly established team
set up to deal with drug dealers.

A documentary-style film of police at work that
inevitably reveals the grim underside of urban life,
and problems that defy solution.

w Michel Alexandre   d Bertrand Tavernier   ph Alain
Choquart   m Philippe Sarde   pd Guy-Claude
François   ed Ariane Boeglin

Didier Bezace, Charlotte Kady, Philippe Torreton, Nils
Tavernier, Jean-Paul Comart, Jean-Roger Milo, Lara
Guirao, Cécile Garcia-Fogel, Claude Brosset

'With extraordinary documentary realism, the director
has produced one of his best and most challenging
films.' – *Variety*

† The title refers to the legislation against the
possession and use of narcotics.

La Bamba: see *Bamba*

La Conga Nights
US   1940   59m   bw
Universal

An elderly music moron helps to found a night-club.

Flimsy excuse for a musical, with the star playing
himself, four sisters and his mother.

w Jay Dratler, Harry Clork, Paul Smith   d Lew
Landers

Hugh Herbert, Dennis O'Keefe, Constance Moore,
Eddie Quillan

Laberinto de Pasiones: see *Labyrinth of Passion*

Laburnum Grove **
GB   1936   73m   bw
ATP (Basil Dean)

A suburban father reveals he is a forger.

Agreeable worm-turns comedy melodrama, much
copied since.

w Gordon Wellesley, Anthony Kimmins   play J. B.
Priestley   d Carol Reed   ph John W. Boyle

Cedric Hardwicke, Edmund Gwenn, Victoria Hopper,
Ethel Coleridge, Katie Johnson, Francis James

'Here at last is an English film one can unreservedly
praise.' – *Graham Greene*

Labyrinth
US   1986   101m   colour
Tri-Star/Eric Rattray, George Lucas
V, V*, L, S

A young girl embarks on a fantasy adventure to save
her stepbrother from the clutches of the Goblin King.

Bizarre but tedious attempt to create a new *Alice in
Wonderland*, with the inventor of the Muppets in
charge. Unfortunately his creatures become less
attractive with each attempt, and the script is
emaciated.

w Terry Jones, from script by Dennis Less and Jim
Henson   d Jim Henson   ph Alex Thomson
m Trevor Jones   pd Elliot Scott   conceptual
design Brian Froud

David Bowie, Jennifer Connelly, Toby Froud, Shelley
Thompson

'A crashing bore . . . no real charm or texture to
capture the imagination.' – *Variety*

Labyrinth of Passion
Spain   1982   99m   colour
Metro/Alphaville/Ha Sido Producida (Andrés Santana)
V, V*, L
original title: *Laberinto de Pasiones*

The sexual adventures of a nymphomaniac and the
gay son of an emperor.

The Spanish equivalent of an Andy Warhol movie: a
delirious farrago of sex and psychobabble intended to
shock and amuse.

wd Pedro Almodóvar   ph Angel L. Fernandez
pd Pedro Almodóvar   ed José Salcedo

Cecilia Roth, Imanol Arias, Helga Liné, Marta
Fernandez-Muro, Angel Alcazar, Antonio Banderas,
Agustin Almodóvar

'The quintessential Spanish cult movie.' – *Sight and
Sound*

The Lacemaker
France/Switzerland/West Germany   1977   107m
   Eastmancolor
Action/FR3/Citel/Janus (Yves Gasser)
V
original title: *La Dentellière*

An 18-year-old girl becomes ill and withdrawn when
her first affair breaks up.

Careful social character study, witty and observant
but in memory insufficiently differentiated from
numerous exploitation pieces with similar plots.

w Pascal Lainé, Claude Goretta   novel Pascal Lainé
d Claude Goretta   ph Jean Boffety   m Pierre
Jansen   ad Serge Etter, Claude Chevant   ed Joelle
van Henterre, Nelly Meunier, Martine Charasson

Isabelle Huppert, Yves Beneyton, Florence Giorgetti,
Anne Marie Düringer

Lacombe, Lucien ****
France   1974   141m   Eastmancolor
Rank/NEF/UPF/Vides/Hallelujah Films (Louis Malle)
V

A boy is rejected for the French resistance and joins
the Gestapo instead.

Tragic fable, a mite overlong, which caused its creator
to migrate to America because of criticism received in
France.

w Louis Malle, Patrick Modiano   d Louis Malle
ph Tonino Delli Colli   m Django Reinhardt

Pierre Blaise, Aurore Clement, Holger Lowenadler,
Thérèse Gieshe

'Malle's film is a long, close look at the banality of
evil; it is – not incidentally – one of the least banal
movies ever made.' – *Pauline Kael, New Yorker*

AAN: best foreign film

The Lad
GB   1935   74m   bw
Univeral (Julius Hagen)

A good-natured con man discovers that the
inhabitants of a stately home have all got secrets to
hide.

Old-fashioned, stagey but neatly plotted and quite
watchable comedy thriller.

w Gerard Fairlie   play Edgar Wallace   d Henry
Edwards   ph Sydney Blythe   md William L. Trytel
ad James A. Carter   ed Lister Laurance

Gordon Harker, Betty Stockfeld, Jane Carr, Gerald
Barry, Michael Shepley, Geraldine Fitzgerald,
Sebastian Shaw, Barbara Everest

Ladder of Swords *
GB   1988   98m
Hobo/Film Four International/British Screen/Arden (Jennifer
Howarth)
V

A circus performer is investigated by a policeman
convinced that he has murdered his wife.

Well acted but rarely believable with its contrivances of a convenient death and a dim cop.

w Neil Clarke story Norman Hull, Neil Clarke d Norman Hull ph Thaddeus O'Sullivan m Stanley Myers pd Caroline Hanania ed Scott Thomas

Martin Shaw, Eleanor David, Juliet Stevenson, Bob Peck, Simon Molloy, Pearce Quigley, Anthony Benson, Graham Rigby

'The whole enterprise is marked by a nimble, self-confident energy.' – MFB

Laddie
US 1935 70m bw
Pandro S. Berman/RKO

A young farmer loves the squire's daughter, but the squire says no.

Rather dim old-fashioned rural romance.

w Ray Harris, Dorothy Yost play Gene Stratton Porter novel Gene Stratton Porter d George Stevens

John Beal, Gloria Stuart, Virginia Weidler, Charlotte Henry, Donald Crisp

† Remade in 1940 by Cliff Reid for RKO, with Tim Holt, Virginia Gilmore.

Ladies Courageous
US 1944 88m bw
Universal (Walter Wanger)

Girls ferry war planes from base for the USAF.

Absolutely predictable propaganda potboiler.

w Norman Reilly Raine, Doris Gilbert d John Rawlins ph Hal Mohr m Dimitri Tiomkin

Loretta Young, Geraldine Fitzgerald, Diana Barrymore, Evelyn Ankers, Anne Gwynne, Philip Terry, David Bruce, Lois Collier, Samuel S. Hinds

'Needs exploitation hype to catch nominal biz . . . wandering continuity fails to generate much punch.' – Variety

Ladies' Day
US 1943 62m bw
Bert Gilroy/RKO

A baseball pitcher loses his touch when he falls in love, so has to be kept away from his latest girl.

Mildly wacky comedy with a fairly nimble touch.

w Charles E. Roberts, Dane Lussier play Robert Considine, Edward C. Lilley and Bertrand Robinson d Leslie Goodwins

Lupe Velez, Eddie Albert, Patsy Kelly, Max Baer, Jerome Cowan, Iris Adrian

Ladies in Love *
US 1936 97m bw
TCF (B. G. de Sylva)

Man-hunting girls in Budapest form a joint plan.

Amusing romantic nonsense.

w Melville Baker play Ladislaus Bus-Fekete d Edward H. Griffith ph Hal Mohr md Louis Silvers

Janet Gaynor, Loretta Young, Constance Bennett, Simone Simon, Don Ameche, Paul Lukas, Tyrone Power, Alan Mowbray, Wilfred Lawson, J. Edward Bromberg, Virginia Field

Ladies in Retirement **
US 1941 92m bw
Columbia (Lester Cowan)

A housekeeper murders her employer for the sake of her two mentally disturbed sisters.

Splendidly effective Grand Guignol, from a well-written play but filmically quite interesting. Remade with lots of gore as The Mad Room (qv).

w Reginald Denham, Edward Percy, Garrett Fort play Reginald Denham, Edward Percy d Charles Vidor ph George Barnes m Ernst Toch, Morris Stoloff ad Lionel Banks

Ida Lupino, Louis Hayward, Isobel Elsom, Edith Barrett, Elsa Lanchester, Emma Dunn

'General excellence of script, direction, acting and mounting . . . but too strong to catch general audience reaction on favourable plane.' – Variety

AAN: Ernst Toch, Morris Stoloff; Lionel Banks

Ladies Love Brutes
US 1930 83m bw
Paramount

A gangster tries to improve himself to marry a socialite.

Uneasy comedy-drama with good moments.

w Waldemar Young, Herman J. Mankiewicz play Pardon My Glove by Zoë Akins d Rowland V. Lee ph Harry Fischbeck

George Bancroft, Mary Astor, Fredric March, Margaret Quimby, Stanley Fields

Ladies Love Danger
US 1935 69m bw
Fox

A playwright and amateur sleuth solves a series of murders.

Light, bright whodunnit.

w Samson Raphaelson story Ilya Zorn d H. Bruce Humberstone

Gilbert Roland, Mona Barrie, Donald Cook, Adrienne Ames, Hardie Albright, Herbert Mundin

'Stronger marquee strength would have sent it into ace spots. As is, looks best for secondaries.' – Variety

Ladies' Man *
US 1931 70m bw
Paramount

A man of the world preys successfully on rich women until one grows jealous when her daughter falls for him.

Vivid, hard melodrama showing the blacker side of early thirties high society living.

w Herman J. Mankiewicz d Lothar Mendes ph Victor Milner

William Powell, Kay Francis, Carole Lombard, Gilbert Emery, Olive Tell

'He's a hit with the misses, they go for his kisses!'

Ladies' Man
US 1947 90m bw
Paramount

A poor farmer strikes oil, becomes a millionaire, and finds himself a prize for the ladies.

Below-par comedy which wastes an agreeable cast.

w Edmund Beloin, Jack Rose and Lewis Meltzer d William D. Russell

Eddie Bracken, Cass Daley, Virginia Welles, Spike Jones and his City Slickers

Ladies' Man
US 1961 106m Technicolor
Paramount/York (Jerry Lewis)
V*, L

The adventures of an accident-prone houseboy at a Hollywood hotel for aspiring actresses.

Hit-or-miss collection of comic scraps which might have benefited from being put together on a less grandiose scale.

w Jerry Lewis, Bill Richmond d Jerry Lewis ph W. Wallace Kelley m Walter Scharf

Jerry Lewis, Helen Traubel, Jack Kruschen, Doodles Weaver, Gloria Jean

'Regression into infantilism cannot be carried much further than this.' – MFB

Ladies Must Live: see The Home Towners

Ladies of Leisure
US 1930 98m bw
Columbia

A gold digger gets an attack of conscience and gives up her rich fiancé.

Only fitfully interesting early Capra, with little sparkle in any department.

w Milton Herbert Gropper and Jo Swerling d Frank Capra

Barbara Stanwyck, Lowell Sherman, Ralph Graves, Marie Prevost

Ladies of the Big House
US 1931 77m bw
Paramount

A married couple are framed on a murder charge and sent to prison.

Melodramatic nonsense in the wake of The Big House.

w Louis Weitzenkorn d Marion Gering ph David Abel

Sylvia Sidney, Gene Raymond, Wynne Gibson, Rockcliffe Fellows, Earle Foxe

'Powerful in heart appeal and should do very well.' – Variety

Ladies of the Chorus
US 1949 61m bw
Columbia
V*

A Broadway burlesque queen falls for a socialite.

Threadbare backstage support, notable only for the first leading performance of Marilyn Monroe.

w Harry Sauber and Joseph Carole d Phil Karlson

Adele Jergens, Rand Brooks

Ladies of the Jury
US 1932 64m bw
RKO

A lady changes the minds of a murder jury to 'not guilty'.

Light-hearted early variation on Twelve Angry Men.

play Frederick Ballard d Lowell Sherman

Edna May Oliver, Ken Murray, Roscoe Ates, Kitty Kelly, Guinn Williams, Cora Witherspoon

'A highly satisfying B house release.' – Variety

Ladies of the Park: see Les Dames du Bois de Boulogne

Ladies on the Rocks *
Denmark 1983 110m colour
Artificial Eye/Komme Films/Danish Film Institute
original title: Koks I Kulissen

Two women take their cabaret act on the road.

Small but well-observed film, with good performances.

w Christian Braad Thomsen, Helle Ryslinge, Annemarie Helger d Christian Braad Thomsen ph Dirk Bruel m Helle Ryslinge, Pernille Grumme, Annemarie Helger ed Grete Moldrup

Helle Ryslinge, Annemarie Helger, Flemming Quist Moller, Hans Henrick Clemmensen, Gyda Hansen, Aksel Erhardsen

Ladies Should Listen
US 1934 63m bw
Paramount (Douglas MacLean)

A knowledgeable switchboard operator helps a financier with his problems.

Moderately beguiling, instantly forgettable romantic frou-frou.

w Claude Binyon, Frank Butler, Guy Bolton
d Frank Tuttle   ph Harry Sharp

Cary Grant, Frances Drake, Edward Everett Horton, Rosita Moreno, George Barbier, Nydia Westman, Charles Ray

'Synthetic farce that strains too hard for laughs.' – Variety

Ladies They Talk About *
US   1933   69m   bw
Warner
V*

Trouble in a women's prison.

Entertaining comedy-melodrama which had some brushes with the Hays Office because of its frankly man-hungry characters.

w Sidney Sutherland, Brown Holmes   play Women in Prison by Dorothy Mackaye, Carlton Miles
d Howard Bretherton, William Keighley   ph John Seitz

Barbara Stanwyck, Lyle Talbot, Preston Foster, Dorothy Burgess, Lillian Roth, Maude Eburne, Ruth Donnelly, Harold Huber

'Will get average business if sold to the hilt.' – Variety

Ladies Who Do
GB   1963   85m   bw
British Lion/Bryanston/Fanfare (George H. Brown)

Charladies form a successful company from tips they salvage from wastepaper baskets.

Mild farce sustained by familiar actors.

w Michael Pertwee   d C. M. Pennington-Richards
ph Geoffrey Faithfull   m Ron Goodwin

Peggy Mount, Miriam Karlin, Robert Morley, Harry H. Corbett, Dandy Nichols

Ladri di Biciclette: see Bicycle Thieves

Ladri di Saponette: see The Icicle Thief

Il Ladro di Bambini: see The Stolen Children

The Lady and the Bandit
US   1951   78m   bw
Harry Joe Brown/Columbia
GB title: Dick Turpin's Ride

A highwayman sacrifices his own life to avenge his father and protect his wife.

Fairly pathetic example of historical whitewashing to provide minor excitements.

w Robert Libbott and Frank Burt   d Ralph Murphy

Louis Hayward, Patricia Medina, Suzanne Dalbert, Tom Tully, John Williams, Alan Mowbray

The Lady and the Doctor: see The Lady and the Monster

The Lady and the Mob
US   1939   65m   bw
Columbia (Fred Kohlmar)

A lady bank owner menaced by gangsters forms her own mob.

Weak comedy.

w Richard Maibaum, Gertrude Purcell   d Ben Stoloff   ph John Stumar

Fay Bainter, Ida Lupino, Lee Bowman, Henry Armetta, Warren Hymer, Harold Huber

'Neat, entertaining farce; rates exploitation.' – Variety

The Lady and the Monster
US   1944   86m   bw
Republic (George Sherman)
aka: Tiger Man
GB title: The Lady and the Doctor

A scientist keeps alive the brain of a mortally injured financier, and it comes to dominate him.

Fair, over-padded version of a much filmed thriller (see also Donovan's Brain, Vengeance).

w Dane Lussier, Frederick Kohner   novel Donovan's Brain by Curt Siodmak   d George Sherman
ph John Alton   m Walter Scharf

Erich von Stroheim, Richard Arlen, Vera Hruba Ralston, Mary Nash, Sidney Blackmer, Helen Vinson

The Lady and the Outlaw: see Billy Two Hats

Lady and the Tramp **
US   1955   76m   Technicolor   Cinemascope
Walt Disney (Erdmann Penner)
V*, L

A pedigree spaniel falls foul of two Siamese cats and has a romantic adventure with a mongrel who helps her.

Pleasant cartoon feature in Disney's cutest and most anthropomorphic vein.

d Hamilton Luske, Clyde Geronimi, Wilfred Jackson
m Oliver Wallace   m/ly Peggy Lee, Sonny Burke

voices of Peggy Lee, Barbara Luddy, Bill Thompson, Bill Baucon, Stan Freberg

Lady Be Good
US   1941   111m   bw
MGM (Arthur Freed)
V*, L

Married songwriters produce a musical.

Thin musical with good talent and tunes; very little connection with the 1924 musical show.

w Jack McGowan, Kay Van Riper, John McClain
d Norman Z. McLeod   ph George J. Folsey, Oliver T. Marsh   md George Stoll   songs various

Eleanor Powell, Robert Young, Ann Sothern, Red Skelton, Dan Dailey, Virginia O'Brien, Reginald Owen, John Carroll, Lionel Barrymore, Jimmy Dorsey and his Orchestra

'A molasses-paced picture that extravagantly wastes talent and time . . . poor direction, unimaginative story-telling and slipshod photography.' – Variety

† Songs include: 'Hang on to Me'; 'Fascinating Rhythm'; 'Lady Be Good'; 'You'll Never Know'; 'Your Words and My Music'.

AA: song 'The Last Time I Saw Paris' (m Jerome Kern, ly Oscar Hammerstein II)

Lady By Choice *
US   1934   78m   bw
Columbia

A publicity-mad dancer adopts an old rummy as a Mother's Day stunt.

Amusing sentimental comedy in the wake of Lady for A Day.

w Jo Swerling, Dwight Taylor   d David Burton
ph Ted Tetzlaff

Carole Lombard, May Robson, Walter Connolly, Roger Pryor, Arthur Hohl, Raymond Walburn, James Burke, Henry Kolker

'Can very well stand on its own outside the deluxers if properly sold.' – Variety

Lady Caroline Lamb *
GB   1972   123m   Eastmancolor   Panavision
EMI/GEC/Pulsar/Video Cinematographica (Fernando Ghia)
V, V*, S

In 1805, impulsive Lady Caroline Ponsonby marries

William Lamb, later Lord Melbourne, and then disgraces him by her wildness.

Pale, disappointing historical fiction with good spots but no reverence for fact; slackly written and handled, and not helped by the wide screen.

wd Robert Bolt   ph Oswald Morris   m Richard Rodney Bennett   ad Carmen Dillon

Sarah Miles, Jon Finch, Richard Chamberlain (as Byron), Margaret Leighton, John Mills (as Canning), Ralph Richardson (as George III), Laurence Olivier (as Wellington)

Lady Chatterley's Lover
France   1955   101m/84m (English version)   bw
Regie du Film/Orsay Film (Gilbert Cohen-Séat)

The wife of a crippled and impotent mine-owner has an affair with a coarse gamekeeper and enjoys it.

Hilariously po-faced transcription of a notorious novel, of no cinematic interest whatever.

w Gaston Bonheur, Philippe de Rothschild, Marc Allégret   novel D. H. Lawrence   d Marc Allégret
ph Georges Périnal   m Joseph Kosma

Danielle Darrieux, Leo Genn, Erno Crisa

'The classic of erotic literature!'
Lady Chatterley's Lover
GB/France   1981   104m   colour
Cannon/Producteurs Associés
V, V*, L

A 'period' remake, lovingly photographed but with some risible soft porn episodes and no great interest in the acting.

w Christopher Wicking, Just Jaeckin   d Just Jaeckin   ph Robert Fraisse   m Stanley Myers, Richard Harvey   pd Anton Furst   ed Eunice Mountjoy

Sylvia Kristel, Nicholas Clay, Shane Briant, Ann Mitchell, Elizabeth Spriggs

The Lady Consents
US   1936   76m   bw
RKO (Edward Kaufman)

When a doctor's wife sees that he is in love with another woman, she makes it easy for him to get a divorce; but he finally comes back to her.

Unbelievable matinée drama for star fans.

w P. J. Wolfson, Anthony Veiller   play The Indestructible Mrs Talbot by P. J. Wolfson   d Stephen Roberts   ph J. Roy Hunt   m Roy Webb

Ann Harding, Herbert Marshall, Margaret Lindsay, Walter Abel, Edward Ellis, Hobart Cavanaugh, Ilka Chase

'Pretty fair entertainment; good woman's picture.' – Variety

The Lady Cop: see La Femme-flic

'Eve Sure Knows Her Apples!'
The Lady Eve ***
US   1941   97m   bw
Paramount (Paul Jones)
V*, L

A lady cardsharper and her father are outsmarted on a transatlantic liner by a millionaire simpleton; she plans an elaborate revenge.

Hectic romantic farce, the first to show its director's penchant for mixing up sexual innuendo, funny men and pratfalls. There are moments when the pace drops, but in general it's scintillating entertainment, especially after viewing its weak remake The Birds and the Bees (qv).

wd Preston Sturges   play Monckton Hoffe   ph Victor Milner   m Leo Shuken, Charles Bradshaw
ad Hans Dreier, Ernest Fegte   ed Stuart Gilmore

Barbara Stanwyck, Henry Fonda, Charles Coburn, Eugène Pallette, William Demarest, Eric Blore, Melville Cooper, Martha O'Driscoll, Janet Beecher, Robert Greig, Luis Alberni, Jimmy Conlin

'The whole theme, with all its variations of keys, is played to one end, to get laughs, and at several different levels it gets them.' – *National Board of Review*

'Preston Sturges, they tell me, is known in Hollywood as "the streamlined Lubitsch". This needn't put you off, because if he goes on producing films as lively as this one he will one day come to be known as Preston Sturges.' – *William Whitebait*

'This time Preston Sturges has wrapped you up another package that is neither very big nor very flashy, but the best fun in months.' – *Otis Ferguson*

'A mixture of visual and verbal slapstick, of high artifice and pratfalls . . . it represents the dizzy high point of Sturges' writing.' – *New Yorker, 1977*

'The brightest sort of nonsense, on which Preston Sturges' signature is written large. The result has a sustained comic flavour and an individual treatment that are rarely found in Hollywood's antic concoctions.' – *New York Herald Tribune*

'A more charming or distinguished gem of nonsense has not occurred since It Happened One Night.' – *New York Times*

AAN: Monckton Hoffe (original story)

Lady for a Day ***
US   1933   95m   bw
Columbia (Frank Capra)
V, V*, L

Gangsters help an old apple seller to pose as a rich woman when her daughter visits.

Splendid sentimental comedy full of cinematic resource; the best translation of Runyon to the screen.

w Robert Riskin   *story* Madame La Gimp by Damon Runyon   *d* Frank Capra   *ph* Joseph Walker

May Robson, Warren William, Guy Kibbee, Glenda Farrell, Ned Sparks, Jean Parker, Walter Connolly, Nat Pendleton

'Exceptionally adroit direction and scenario . . . sell it with plenty of adjectives as it will please everybody.' – *Variety*

AAN: best picture; Robert Riskin; Frank Capra; May Robson

Lady for a Night
US   1941   87m   bw
Republic (Albert J. Cohen)
V*

The lady owner of a gambling boat determines to break into society.

Moderate period comedy with a belated murder plot.

w Isabel Dawn, Boyce DeGaw   *d* Leigh Jason   *ph* Norbert Brodine   *m* David Buttolph

Joan Blondell, John Wayne, Ray Middleton, Philip Merivale, Blanche Yurka, Edith Barrett, Leonid Kinskey, Montagu Love

The Lady from Cheyenne
US   1941   87m   bw
Universal (Frank Lloyd)

In 1860 Wyoming, a schoolmistress fights for women's rights.

Mild Western star romance.

w Kathryn Scola, Warren Duff   *d* Frank Lloyd   *ph* Milton Krasner   *m* Frank Skinner

Loretta Young, Robert Preston, Gladys George, Edward Arnold, Frank Craven, Jessie Ralph, Spencer Charters, Alan Bridge

Lady from Lisbon
GB   1942   75m   bw
Shaftesbury/British National

A millionaire spies for the Nazis in return for the promise of art treasures.

Modest potboiling comedy-melodrama.

w Michael Barringer   *d* Leslie Hiscott

Jane Carr, Francis L. Sullivan, Martita Hunt, Charles Victor, Antony Holles

Lady from Louisiana
US   1941   84m   bw
Republic (Bernard Vorhaus)

In old Mississippi, a lottery-owner's daughter falls in love with a lawyer employed to make her father's business illegal.

Curious pot-boiler containing everything but the kitchen stove, including murder and a raging storm.

w Vera Caspary, Guy Endore, Michael Hogan   *d* Bernard Vorhaus   *ph* Jack Marta   *m* Cy Feuer

John Wayne, Ona Munson, Ray Middleton, Henry Stephenson, Helen Westley, Dorothy Dandridge, Jack Pennick

The Lady from Nowhere
US   1936   60m   bw
Columbia

A manicurist tries to lose her identity after witnessing a gangland killing.

A silly plot robs this second feature of the interest it might otherwise deserve.

w Fred Niblo Jnr, Ben G. Kohn, Arthur Strawn, Joseph Krumgold   *d* Gordon Wiles

Mary Astor, Charles Quigley, Thurston Hall, Victor Kilian, Spencer Charters

'Mild entertainment.' – *Variety*

The Lady from Shanghai **
US   1948   87m   bw
Columbia (Richard Wilson, William Castle)
V*, L

A seaman becomes involved in the maritime wanderings of a crippled lawyer and his homicidal frustrated wife.

Absurd, unintelligible, plainly much cut and rearranged, this thriller was obviously left too much in Welles's hands and then just as unfairly taken out of them; but whole sequences of sheer brilliance remain, notably the final shoot-out in the hall of mirrors.

wd Orson Welles   *novel* If I Die Before I Wake by Sherwood King   *ph* Charles Lawton Jnr   *m* Heinz Roemheld

Orson Welles, Rita Hayworth, *Everett Sloane, Glenn Anders,* Ted de Corsia, Erskine Sanford, Gus Schilling

'The slurred social conscience of the hero leads him to some murky philosophizing, all of which with many individualities of diction clog the issue and the sound track. Sub-titles, I fear, would have helped.' – *Richard Winnington*

The Lady from Texas
US   1951   78m   Technicolor
Universal-International (Leonard Goldstein)

A Civil War widow is thought to be committable.

Mild comedy of insanity, a pale shadow of *Harvey* whose star it borrows.

w Gerald Drayson Adams and Connie Lee Bennett   *d* Joseph Pevney

Josephine Hull, Mona Freeman, Howard Duff, Gene Lockhart, Craig Stevens, Ed Begley

The Lady from the Shanghai Cinema
Spain   1988   117m   colour
Metro/Star/Raiz/Embrafilme/Chroma (Assunção Hernandes
original title: *A dama do cine Shanghai*

After becoming obsessed with the wife of a lawyer

who may also be a criminal, a cinema-going estate agent contemplates murder.

Murky pastiche of *film noir* that deliberately confuses fantasy and reality; the central character might have been spared a great deal of misery if he had been better acquainted with Welles's *The Lady from Shanghai.*

wd Guilherme Del Almeida Prado   *ph* Cláudio Portioli, José Roberto Eliezer   *m* Hermelino Neder   *pd* Hector Gomez

Maite Proença, Antonio Fagundes, José Lewgoy, Jorge Doria, José Mayer, Miguel Falabella, Paulo Villaca

'The relentless drama of a woman driven to the depths of emotion by a craving beyond control!'

The Lady Gambles
US   1949   99m   bw
U-I (Michael Kraike)

A happy woman destroys her marriage when she becomes addicted to gambling.

Boring, overwrought, underplotted fiction for women.

w Roy Huggins   *story* Lewis Meltzer, Oscar Saul   *d* Michael Gordon   *ph* Russell Metty   *m* Frank Skinner

Barbara Stanwyck, Robert Preston, Stephen McNally, Edith Barrett, John Hoyt

'A kind of Lost Weekend of the gaming tables.' – *Ella Smith*

Lady Godiva
US   1955   89m   Technicolor
U-I (Robert Arthur)
GB title: *Lady Godiva of Coventry*

Lord Leofric tames a Saxon shrew but she suspects his motives and rides naked through the streets of Coventry to prove the loyalty of the Saxons.

Comic strip historical legend, reliably turned out for midwestern family audiences.

w Oscar Brodney, Harry Ruskin   *d* Arthur Lubin   *ph* Carl Guthrie   *m* Hans Salter

George Nader, Maureen O'Hara, Victor McLaglen, Eduard Franz, Torin Thatcher

Lady Godiva of Coventry: see *Lady Godiva*

Lady Godiva Rides Again
GB   1951   90m   bw
British Lion/London Films/Sidney Gilliat, Frank Launder

A waitress wins a local beauty contest and becomes a charm school starlet and later a stripteaser.

Disappointing satirical comedy with good credentials.

w Frank Launder, Val Valentine   *d* Frank Launder   *ph* Wilkie Cooper   *m* William Alwyn

Pauline Stroud, Stanley Holloway, Diana Dors, Alastair Sim, George Cole, Dennis Price, John McCallum, Bernadette O'Farrell, Kay Kendall, Dora Bryan

Lady Hamilton: see *That Hamilton Woman*

The Lady Has Plans
US   1942   77m   bw
Paramount (Fred Kohlmar)

A lady reporter in Lisbon is mistaken for a Nazi spy.

Competent fluff which veers between comedy and melodrama.

w Harry Tugend   *d* Sidney Lanfield   *ph* Charles Lang   *m* Leo Shuken, Leigh Harline

Paulette Goddard, Ray Milland, Albert Dekker, Roland Young, Margaret Hayes, Cecil Kellaway, Addison Richards, Edward Norris

Lady Ice

US   1973   92m   Technicolor   Panavision
Tomorrow Entertainment (Harrison Starr)
V*

An insurance investigator steals a diamond and goes into partnership with a gangster's daughter.

Unamusing Miami-based thriller.

w Alan Trustman, Harold Clemins   d Tom Gries   ph Lucien Ballard   m Perry Botkin Jnr

Donald Sutherland, Jennifer O'Neil, Robert Duvall, Patrick Magee

'Because of its frank nature, we urge you – do not see it alone!'

Lady in a Cage

US   1964   97m   bw
American Entertainments Corp. (Luther Davis)
V*

A rich widow is trapped by roving marauders in her private elevator.

Unpleasant and boring suspenser with nasty details.

w Luther Davis   d Walter Grauman   ph Lee Garmes   m Paul Glass   pd Rudolf Sternad

Olivia de Havilland, James Caan, Ann Sothern, Jeff Corey

'The film parades its pretensions on a note of high-pitched hysteria.' – MFB

Lady in a Jam

US   1942   78m   bw
Universal (Gregory La Cava)

A scatterbrained socialite loses her money and inherits an Arizona farm.

A very thin vehicle for a star who deserved better.

w Eugene Thackrey, Frank Cockrell, Otho Lovering   d Gregory La Cava   ph Hal Mohr   m Frank Skinner

Irene Dunne, Patric Knowles, Ralph Bellamy, Eugene Pallette, Robert Homans, Samuel S. Hinds

Lady in Cement

US   1968   93m   DeLuxe   Panavision
TCF/Arcola/Millfield (Aaron Rosenberg)
V*, L

A Florida private eye on his morning swim finds a dead blonde.

Routine private eye stuff with fashionable sex and violence added.

w Marvin H. Albert, Jack Guss   d Gordon Douglas   ph Joseph Biroc   m Hugo Montenegro

Frank Sinatra, Raquel Welch, Richard Conte, Martin Gabel, Lainie Kazan, Pat Henry, Steve Peck

'While Tony Rome seemed to herald a return to the forties thriller, Lady in Cement marks nothing more exciting than a return to Tony Rome.' – MFB

Lady in Distress: see A Window in London

The Lady in Question *

US   1940   81m   bw
Columbia

A Parisian shopkeeper on a jury is responsible for getting a girl acquitted of a murder charge, but begins to worry when his son falls in love with her.

Stagey but quite satisfying Hollywood remake of the French drama Gribouille, with Raimu and Michele Morgan.

w Lewis Meltzer   story Marcel Achard   d Charles Vidor   ph Lucien Andriot   m Lucien Moraweck

Brian Aherne, Rita Hayworth, Glenn Ford, Irene Rich, George Coulouris, Lloyd Corrigan, Evelyn Keyes, Edward Norris, Curt Bois, Frank Reicher

The Lady in Red

US   1979   93m   Metrocolor
New World

The story of Dillinger's mistress.

Okay but uninspired gangster drama from a fresh angle.

w John Sayles   d Lewis Teague

Pamela Sue Martin, Robert Conrad, Louise Fletcher, Robert Hogan, Rod Gist

The Lady in the Car with Glasses and a Gun

France/US   1969   105m   Eastmancolor   Panavision
Lira Film/Columbia (Anatole Litvak)

An English secretary in Paris decides to drive to the coast but has various adventures which make her believe she is either mad or amnesiac.

Muddled, tedious suspenser with a totally implausible 'explanation'.

w Richard Harris, Eleanor Perry   novel Sebastien Japrisot   d Anatole Litvak   ph Claude Renoir   m Michel Legrand

Samantha Eggar, Oliver Reed, John McEnery, Stéphane Audran

'The minx in mink with a yen for men!'

Lady in the Dark **

US   1944   100m   Technicolor
Paramount (Richard Blumenthal)

The editress of a fashion magazine is torn between three men, has worrying dreams, and takes herself to a psychoanalyst.

Lush, stylish and frequently amusing version of a Broadway musical, lacking most of the songs; despite its faults, an excellent example of studio spectacle and a very typical forties romantic comedy.

w Frances Goodrich, Albert Hackett   play Moss Hart   d Mitchell Leisen   ph Ray Rennahan   md Robert Emmett Dolan   m Kurt Weill   ly Ira Gershwin   ad Hans Dreier, Raoul Pene du Bois   sp Gordon Jennings

Ginger Rogers, Warner Baxter, Ray Milland, Jon Hall, Mischa Auer, Mary Phillips, Barry Sullivan

† The film was completed in 1942 but held up because of overstock.

† Paramount chief Buddy de Sylva is credited with ruining the film by cutting the theme song, 'My Ship', which is the key to the psychoanalysis.

AAN: Ray Rennahan; Robert Emmett Dolan; art direction

Lady in the Iron Mask

US   1952   78m   Natural Colour
Wanger-Frenke/TCF

Princess Anne's twin sister is kept in an iron mask to prevent dispute about the succession.

Naïve twist on a well-worn legend; production values below par.

w Jack Pollexfen and Aubrey Wisberg   d Ralph Murphy

Louis Hayward, Patricia Medina, Alan Hale Jnr, Judd Holdren, Steve Brodie, John Sutton

The Lady in the Lake *

US   1946   103m   bw
MGM (George Haight)
V*

A private eye is assigned to find a missing wife . . .

Complex private eye yarn which makes the original Chandler dialogue sound childish by over-reliance on the subjective camera method: we see the hero's face only when he looks in a mirror. An experiment that failed because it was not really understood.

w Steve Fisher   novel Raymond Chandler   d Robert Montgomery   ph Paul C. Vogel   m David Snell

Robert Montgomery, Audrey Totter, Lloyd Nolan, Tom Tully, Leon Ames

Lady in the Morgue *

US   1938   70m   bw
Universal
GB title: The Case of the Missing Blonde

A private eye investigates a suicide and uncovers three murders.

Smart 'B' feature frequently cited as a model of its kind.

w Eric Taylor and Robertson White   novel Jonathan Latimer   d Otis Garrett

Preston Foster, Frank Jenks, Patricia Ellis, Thomas Jackson

† A previous film with the same characters and actors was The Westland Case, directed by Christy Cabanne in 1937.

Lady in White *

US   1988   113m   DeLuxe
Virgin/New Sky Productions/Samuel Goldwyn Company
   (Andrew G. La Marca, Frank LaLoggia)
V*, L

After seeing the ghost of a murdered girl, a young boy discovers the identity of her killer.

Modest, but rewarding, movie in its depiction of childhood traumas.

wd Frank LaLoggia   ph Russell Carpenter   m Frank LaLoggia   pd Richard K. Hummel   ed Steve Mann

Lukas Haas, Len Cariou, Alex Rocco, Katherine Helmond, Jason Presson, Renata Vanni, Angelo Bertolini, Joelle Jacobi, Jared Rushton

'A ghost movie with an overcomplicated plot, but it has a poetic feeling that makes up for much of the clutter.' – Pauline Kael, New Yorker

The Lady Is a Square

GB   1958   99m   bw
ABP/Wilcox-Neagle

An impoverished socialite widow tries to keep her husband's symphony orchestra going and is helped by a pop singer.

Strained attempt to carry on the Spring in Park Lane tradition, with a few inspirations from Joe Pasternak and One Hundred Men and a Girl. Earnest performances, obvious jokes.

w Harold Purcell, Pamela Bower, Nicholas Phipps   d Herbert Wilcox   ph Gordon Dines   md Wally Stott

Anna Neagle, Frankie Vaughan, Anthony Newley, Janette Scott, Wilfrid Hyde-White

The Lady Is Willing

GB   1933   74m   bw
Columbia British

An ex-officer becomes a detective and takes his revenge on the financier who ruined him.

Interesting comedy-melodrama with strong cast.

w Guy Bolton   play Louis Verneuil   d Gilbert Miller

Leslie Howard, Cedric Hardwicke, Binnie Barnes, Nigel Playfair, Nigel Bruce

The Lady Is Willing

US   1942   91m   bw
Columbia (Mitchell Leisen)

A musical comedy star adopts a baby and falls in love with its pediatrician.

Dull mixture of light drama and heavy comedy, with all concerned ill at ease.

w James Edward Grant, Albert McCleery
d Mitchell Leisen *ph* Ted Tetzlaff *m* W. Franke
Harling

Marlene Dietrich, Fred MacMurray, Aline
MacMahon, Stanley Ridges, Arline Judge, Marietta
Canty

Lady Jane

GB 1986 142m Technicolor
Paramount/Peter Snell
V, V*, L

After the death in 1553 of Edward VI, a faction pushes
into power his second cousin Lady Jane Grey.

The puzzle is why this dreary and overlong historical
piece was made in an unsympathetic age; and why
such an unsuitable leading lady was cast.

w David Edgar, Chris Bryant *d* Trevor Nunn
ph Douglas Slocombe *m* Stephen Oliver
pd Allan Cameron *ed* Anne V. Coates

Helena Bonham Carter, Cary Elwes, John Wood,
Michael Hordern, Jill Bennett, Jane Lapotaire, Sara
Kestelman, Joss Ackland, Patrick Stewart, Richard
Vernon

† The story was previously told in 1936 as *Tudor Rose*.

Lady Killer ***

US 1933 76m bw
Warner (Henry Blanke)
V*, L

A cinema usher turns to crime, flees to Hollywood,
and becomes a movie star.

Hectic slam-bang action comedy with melodramatic
moments. Great fun.

w Ben Markson *novel* *The Finger Man* by Rosalind
Keating Shaffer *d* Roy del Ruth *ph* Tony Gaudio
md Leo F. Forbstein

James Cagney, Mae Clarke, Leslie Fenton, Margaret
Lindsay, Henry O'Neill, Willard Robertson, Raymond
Hatton, Russell Hopton

'An all-time high in roughneck character work even
for this rough-and-tumble star.' – *Variety*

'A kind of résumé of everything he has done to date in
the movies.' – *New York Evening Post*

'Sprightly, more or less daring, thoroughly
entertaining.' – *New York World Telegram*

The Lady Killers: see *The Ladykillers*

Lady L

France/Italy/US 1965 124m Eastmancolor
Panavision
Concordia/Champion/MGM (Carlo Ponti)

An 80-year-old lady recalls her romantic life from her
youth as a Paris laundress.

Unhappy, lumbering, styleless attempt to recapture
several old forms, indifferently though expensively
made and acted.

wd Peter Ustinov *novel* Romain Gary *ph* Henri
Alekan *m* Jean Françaix *ad* Jean D'Eaubonne,
Auguste Capelier

Sophia Loren, David Niven, Paul Newman, Peter
Ustinov, Claude Dauphin, Philippe Noiret, Michel
Piccoli, Marcel Dalio, Cecil Parker, Eugène Deckers

Lady, Let's Dance

US 1943 86m bw
Scott R. Dunlap/Monogram

An entertainment director for a California resort needs
a new star.

Thin musical with production values ambitious for its
source.

w Peter Milne and Paul Gerard Smith *d* Frank
Woodruff

Belita, James Ellison, Frick and Frack, Walter Catlett,
Lucien Littlefield

AAN: Edward Kay (music); song 'Silver Shadows
and Golden Dreams' (*m* Lew Pollack, *ly* Charles
Newman)

The Lady Lies

US 1929 75m bw
Paramount

A wealthy widowed attorney courts a working-class
girl and offends his children.

Dated melodrama in primitive talkie technique.

w John Meehan and Garrett Fort *d* Hobart Henley

Walter Huston, Claudette Colbert, Charles Ruggles,
Tom Brown

Lady Luck

US 1946 97m bw
RKO (Warren Duff)

The daughter of a long line of ill-fated gamblers
marries one and tries to reform him, but the reverse
happens.

Tedious comedy drama.

w Lynn Root, Frank Fenton *d* Edwin L. Marin
ph Lucien Andriot *m* Leigh Harline

Robert Young, Barbara Hale, Frank Morgan, James
Gleason, Don Rice, Harry Davenport, Lloyd Corrigan

Lady of Burlesque *

US 1943 91m bw
Hunt Stromberg
V*
GB title: *Striptease Lady*

A burlesque dancer solves a number of backstage
murders.

Agreeable murder mystery with strong injections of
comedy.

w James Gunn *novel* *The G-String Murders* by Gypsy
Rose Lee *d* William A. Wellman *ph* Robert de
Grasse *m* Arthur Lange

Barbara Stanwyck, Michael O'Shea, J. Edward
Bromberg, Iris Adrian, Gloria Dickson, Charles
Dingle

AAN: Arthur Lange

Lady of Deceit: see *Born to Kill*

Lady of Scandal

US 1930 67m bw
MGM

The son of a noble house wants to marry an actress,
but the family is nasty to her.

Dated melodrama with sophisticated comedy asides.

w Hans Kraly *play* *The High Road* by Frederick
Lonsdale *d* Sidney Franklin

Ruth Chatterton, Basil Rathbone, Ralph Forbes,
Nance O'Neil, Frederick Kerr, Herbert Bunston

'Should register well in any but the lowest grind.' –
Variety

Lady of Secrets

US 1936 73m bw
B. P. Schulberg/Columbia

A rich girl's father prevents her marriage without
knowing that she is pregnant.

Complicated and very boring mother-love yarn with
the faint perfume of a bygone age.

w Joseph Anthony, Zoe Akins, Katherine Brush
d Marion Gering

Ruth Chatterton, Otto Kruger, Lionel Atwill, Lloyd
Nolan, Marion Marsh, Elizabeth Risdon

'Chatterton, back to the screen after a long absence, is
still having trouble with her offspring. This time she

is also having trouble with the play, the direction, and
the photography.' – *Variety*

Lady of the Boulevards: see *Nana*

Lady of the Tropics

US 1939 92m bw
MGM (Sam Zimbalist)

An American playboy in Saigon marries a half-caste
girl but her former admirer prevents her from getting
a passport.

Interminable romantic melodrama with stars
apparently straight from the taxidermist.

w Ben Hecht *d* Jack Conway *ph* George Folsey
m Franz Waxman

Robert Taylor, Hedy Lamarr, Joseph Schildkraut,
Gloria Franklin, Ernest Cossart

'Mediocre and stagey romance, but stars should pull it
through.' – *Variety*

Lady on a Train *

US 1945 84m bw
Universal (Felix Jackson)

A girl arriving in New York by train sees a murder
committed and can't make anyone believe her.

Cheerful mystery which starts in the right spirit but
does not progress too satisfactorily.

w Edmund Beloin, Robert O'Brien *novel* Leslie
Charteris *d* Charles David *ph* Elwood Bredell
m Miklos Rozsa

Deanna Durbin, Ralph Bellamy, David Bruce, Edward
Everett Horton, George Coulouris, Allen Jenkins, Dan
Duryea, Patricia Morison

The Lady Pays Off

US 1951 80m bw
Universal-International

A gambling schoolteacher agrees to pay off her debts
by tutoring the casino owner's daughter.

Flat and unprofitable romantic comedy-drama.

w Frank Gill Jnr and Albert J. Cohen *d* Douglas
Sirk

Linda Darnell, Stephen McNally, Gigi Perreau,
Virginia Field, Ann Codee

'The sort of thing that people who shun the cinema
imagine all films to be.' – *C. A. Lejeune*

Lady Possessed

US 1952 86m bw
Republic/Portland (James Mason)

An unbalanced woman imagines she is destined to
take the place of a pianist's dead wife.

Weary melodramatic nonsense dating from
Hollywood's first obsession with psychiatry.

w Pamela Kellino, James Mason *novel* *Del Palma* by
Pamela Kellino *d* William Spier, Roy Kellino
ph Karl Struss *m* Nathan Scott

James Mason, June Havoc, Stephen Dunne, Fay
Compton, Pamela Kellino, Steven Geray

The Lady Says No

US 1951 83m bw
UA/Stillman (Frank Ross, John Stillman Jnr)
V*

A magazine photographer tames a female chauvinist
author.

Very silly comedy with neither wit nor style.

w Robert Russell *d* Frank Ross *ph* James Wong
Howe *m* Emil Newman

Joan Caulfield, David Niven, James Robertson
Justice, Lenore Lonergan, Henry Jones

Lady Scarface
US 1941 69m bw
RKO (Cliff Reid)

A police lieutenant captures a dangerous female gangster.

Weird gangster second feature with too many domestic comedy asides; notable only for the appearance in it of its dignified lead, fresh from *Rebecca*.

w Arnaud D'Usseau, Richard Collins d Frank Woodruff ph Nicholas Musuraca

Judith Anderson, Dennis O'Keefe, Frances Neal, Mildred Coles, Eric Blore, Marc Lawrence

Lady Sings the Blues *
US 1972 144m Eastmancolor Panavision
Paramount/Motown/Weston/Furie (Jay Weston, James S. White)
V*, L, S

The disastrous private life of jazz singer Billie Holliday.

Old-fashioned showbiz biopic with new-fashioned drugs, sex and squalor.

w Terence McCloy, Chris Clark, Suzanne de Passe d Sidney J. Furie ph John Alonzo md Gil Askey m Michel Legrand

Diana Ross, Billy Dee Williams, Richard Pryor, James Callahan, Sid Melton

AAN: script; Gil Askey; Diana Ross

A Lady Surrenders
US 1930 95m bw
Universal

A misunderstanding turns an innocent husband into a bigamist after his wife has supposedly divorced him.

Totally effete romantic drama with no comedy relief.

w Gladys Lehman novel Sincerity by John Erskine d John Stahl

Conrad Nagel, Genevieve Tobin, Basil Rathbone, Rose Hobart, Carmel Myers

'It fails from all angles: too stilted, slow, talky and punchless.' – *Variety*

A Lady Surrenders: see *Love Story* (1944)

A Lady Takes a Chance
US 1943 86m bw
RKO (Frank Ross)
V*
aka: *The Cowboy and the Girl*

A New York office girl on holiday in Oregon falls for a rodeo rider.

Slender star action romance.

w Robert Ardrey d William A. Seiter ph Frank Redman m Roy Webb

Jean Arthur, John Wayne, Charles Winninger, Phil Silvers, Mary Field, Don Costello, John Philliber, Grady Sutton, Hans Conried

The Lady Takes a Flyer
US 1958 95m Eastmancolor Cinemascope
Universal-International (William Alland)

A pilot's wife finds that life at home is not easy, especially with a baby.

Heavy comedy or light drama; on either count a bore.

w Danny Arnold d Jack Arnold

Lana Turner, Jeff Chandler, Richard Denning, Chuck Connors, Andra Martin

The Lady Takes a Sailor *
US 1949 99m bw
Warner

A girl devoted to telling the truth insists on proving

her story of a mysterious submarine which saved her after a sailing accident.

Curious romantic farce with echoes of the old slapstick tradition.

w Everett Freeman d Michael Curtiz

Jane Wyman, Dennis Morgan, Eve Arden, Allyn Joslyn, Robert Douglas, William Frawley

A Lady to Love
US 1930 92m bw
MGM

An ageing grape grower spots an attractive waitress, sends her a marriage proposal by mail, but encloses a photo of his handsome foreman.

Rather primitive but well-acted version of a subject later filmed more fluently under the title of the original play.

w Sidney Howard play They Knew What They Wanted by Sidney Howard d Victor Seastrom ph Merritt B. Gerstad

Edward G. Robinson, Vilma Banky, Robert Ames, Richard Carle

'A hit as a talker: well directed, acted and treated.' – *Variety*

Lady Tubbs
US 1935 69m bw
Universal

An ex-cook crashes society and shows up the pretenders.

Mildly agreeable sentimental farce.

w Barry Trivers novel Homer Croy d Alan Crosland

Alice Brady, Douglass Montgomery, Anita Louise, Alan Mowbray, Minor Watson, Russell Hicks, Hedda Hopper

'Solid laugh fare for the nabes.' – *Variety*

The Lady Vanishes ****
GB 1938 97m bw
Gaumont British/Gainsborough (Edward Black)
V, V*, L

En route back to England by train from Switzerland, an old lady disappears and two young people investigate.

The disappearing lady trick brilliantly refurbished by Hitchcock and his screenwriters, who even get away with a horrid model shot at the beginning. Superb, suspenseful, brilliantly funny, meticulously detailed entertainment.

w Sidney Gilliat, Frank Launder, novel The Wheel Spins by Ethel Lina White d Alfred Hitchcock ph Jack Cox md Louis Levy

Margaret Lockwood, Michael Redgrave, Dame May Whitty, Paul Lukas, Basil Radford, Naunton Wayne, Catherine Lacey, Cecil Parker, Linden Travers, Googie Withers, Mary Clare, Philip Leaver

'If it were not so brilliant a melodrama, we should class it as a brilliant comedy.' – *Frank S. Nugent*

'No one can study the deceptive effortlessness with which one thing leads to another without learning where the true beauty of this medium is to be mined.' – *Otis Ferguson*

'Directed with such skill and velocity that it has come to represent the very quintessence of screen suspense.' – *Pauline Kael, 70s*

† Hitchcock was actually second choice as director. The production was ready to roll as *Lost Lady*, directed by Roy William Neill, with Charters and Caldicott already in place, when Neill became unavailable and Hitch stepped in.

The Lady Vanishes
GB 1979 97m Eastmancolor Panavision
Rank/Hammer (Michael Carreras, Tom Sachs)
V*, L

A remake of the above in which everything goes wrong: wrong shape, wrong actors, wrong style (or lack of it).

Reasonable adherence to the original script can't save it.

w George Axelrod d Anthony Page ph Douglas Slocombe m Richard Hartley pd Wilfred Shingleton

Cybill Shepherd, Elliott Gould, Angela Lansbury, Herbert Lom, Arthur Lowe, Ian Carmichael, Gerald Harper, Jenny Runacre, Jean Anderson

The Lady Wants Mink
US 1953 92m Trucolor
Republic (Herbert J. Yates)

A wife causes domestic upsets when she decides to start a mink farm in order to get the fur coat that she has always wanted.

A by-the-numbers comedy which comes to the predictable conclusions that the rural life is better than an urban existence and that money can't buy happiness; it fails to convince or even amuse.

w Dane Lussier, Richard Alan Simmons story Leonard Neubauer, Lou Schor d William A. Seiter ph Reggie Lanning m Stanley Wilson ad Martin Obzina ed Fred Allen

Dennis O'Keefe, Ruth Hussey, Eve Arden, William Demarest, Gene Lockhart, Hope Emerson, Hilary Brooke, Tommy Rettig

Lady Windermere's Fan *
US 1925 80m (24 fps) bw silent
Warner

The mysterious Mrs Erlynne almost causes a scandal in London society.

Oscar Wilde's play transposed to the twenties, with the Lubitsch touch daringly displacing Wildean epigrams. Still more amusing than the sound remake, *The Fan*.

w Julien Josephson d Ernst Lubitsch ph Charles Van Enger

Ronald Colman, May McAvoy, Irene Rich, Bert Lytell, Edward Martindel

'Lubitsch's best silent film, full of incisive details, discreet touches, nuances of gestures, where behaviour betrays the character and discloses the sentiment of the personages.' – *Georges Sadoul*

Lady Windermere's Fan (1949): see *The Fan*

The Lady with a Lamp *
GB 1951 110m bw
British Lion/Imperadio (Herbert Wilcox)

The life of Florence Nightingale and her work in reforming the nursing service in 19th-century England.

Solid biopic, not quite in accord with history.

w Warren Chetham Strode play Reginald Berkeley d Herbert Wilcox ph Max Greene m Anthony Collins ad William C. Andrews

Anna Neagle, Michael Wilding, Gladys Young, Felix Aylmer, Julian D'Albie, Arthur Young, Edwin Styles, Barbara Couper, Cecil Trouncer, Rosalie Crutchley

'A slow, sedate, refined chronicle . . . Herbert Wilcox is a good deal more at ease with the balls and dinners, than with anything that happens later.' – *Penelope Houston*

'It may please fans of Anna Neagle and Michael Wilding, but not fans of Florence Nightingale.' – *Richard Mallett, Punch*

Lady with a Past *
US 1932 80m bw
RKO (Charles R. Rogers)
GB title: *Reputation*

A wealthy but shy girl almost accidentally finds
herself with a reputation as a scarlet woman, and the
men flock around her.

Moderately enjoyable star comedy drama.

w Horace Jackson *novel* Harriet Henry d Edward
H. Griffith ph Hal Mohr m Max Steiner

Constance Bennett, Ben Lyon, David Manners, Astrid
Allwyn, Merna Kennedy, Blanche Frederici, Nella
Walker

'Light and satisfying material for the women.' – *Variety*

Lady with Red Hair *
US 1940 78m bw
Warner (Edmund Grainger)

The life of actress Mrs Leslie Carter and her
association with impresario David Belasco.

Mildly interesting but unsatisfying biopic of a lady
scarcely remembered.

w Charles Kenyon, Milton Krims, N. Brewster Morse,
Norbert Faulkner d Curtis Bernhardt ph Arthur
Edeson m Heinz Roemheld

Miriam Hopkins, Claude Rains, Richard Ainley, John
Litel, Laura Hope Crews, Helen Westley, Mona Barrie,
Victor Jory, Cecil Kellaway, Fritz Leiber, Halliwell
Hobbes

The Lady with the Little Dog *
USSR 1959 90m bw
Lenfilm
original title: *Dama s Sobachkoi*

In Yalta at the turn of the century, an unhappily
married woman and a married man start an affair
which lasts secretly over the years.

Modestly pleasing, subtly acted anecdote.

wd Josef Heifits, story Anton Chekhov ph Andrei
Moskvin m Jiri Sternwald ed D. Meschiev

Ya Savvina, Alexei Batalov, Ala Chostakova

A Lady without Passport *
US 1950 84m bw
MGM (Samuel Marx)

A secret service undercover man tracks down aliens
being smuggled into the US, and falls in love with
one of them.

Routine material, very well handled.

w Howard Dimsdale d Joseph H. Lewis ph Paul
C. Vogel m David Raksin

Hedy Lamarr, John Hodiak, James Craig, George
Macready, Steve Geray

'A Comedy With Balls.'
Ladybugs
US 1992 90m DeLuxe
Warner/Morgan Creek (Albert S. Ruddy, Andre E. Morgan)
V, V*, L

A salesman takes over managership of a women's
soccer team and has his son join it in drag.

Dismayingly stupid comedy that is embarrassing to
watch.

w Curtis Burch d Sidney J. Furie m Richard
Gibbs pd Robb Wilson King ed John W.
Wheeler, Timothy N. Board

Rodney Dangerfield, Jackée, Jonathan Brandis, Ilene
Graff, Vinessa Shaw, Tom Parks

'This picture doesn't deserve any respect. Sexist,
homophobic and woefully unfunny to boot, Rodney
Dangerfield's latest starring effort is a waste of comic
talent.' – *Variety*

'This week's candidate for the worst film in history.' –
Geoff Brown, The Times

'Cursed for eternity! No force in heaven will release them
… no power on earth can save them!'
Ladyhawke
US 1985 124m Technicolor
Warner/Richard Donner, Lauren Schuler
V, V*, L

Medieval boy and girl lovers have been changed
respectively into a wolf and a hawk, never
simultaneously to resume their true forms.

Unpersuasive legend, dolefully told at excessive
length.

w Edward Khmara, Michael Thomas, Tom
Mankiewicz d Richard Donner ph Vittorio
Storaro m Andrew Powell pd Wolf Kroeger
ed Stuart Baird

Matthew Broderick, Rutger Hauer, Michelle Pfeiffer,
Leo McKern, John Wood

The Ladykillers ***
GB 1955 97m Technicolor
Ealing (Seth Holt)
V, V*

An old lady takes in a sinister lodger, who with his
four friends commits a robbery. When she finds out,
they plot to kill her, but are hoist with their own
petards.

Witty black comedy, shot in muted colours, which
approaches the grotesque without damaging its
acerbic humour or sense of fantasy; it is one of the few
films where death is both shocking and funny.

w William Rose d Alexander Mackendrick
ph Otto Heller m Tristam Cary

Alec Guinness, *Katie Johnson*, Peter Sellers, Cecil
Parker, Herbert Lom, Danny Green, Jack Warner,
Frankie Howerd, Kenneth Connor

'To be frivolous about frivolous matters, that's merely
boring. To be frivolous about something that's in
some way deadly serious, that's true comedy.' –
Alexander Mackendrick

'The acting is triumphant . . . Artistically, I suspect,
The Ladykillers needs a shade more of the macabre; it
would be a better film if it were blacker. But I am
beginning to find that I can see a joke better in
twilight than midnight.' – *Dilys Powell*

'This sinister black comedy of murder accelerates until
it becomes a grotesque fantasy of murder. The actors
seem to be having a boisterous good time getting
themselves knocked off.' – *Pauline Kael*

'One of the neatest blends of the mirthful and
macabre I can remember.' – *Fred Majdalany, Time and
Tide*

'Undoubtedly the most stylish, inventive and funniest
British comedy of the year.' – *Alan Brien, London
Evening Standard*

† The role of Professor Marcus, played by Alec
Guinness, was originally intended for Alistair Sim. It
has been claimed, though Guinness has denied it, that
his toothy appearance was based on the critic
Kenneth Tynan who worked for Ealing as a script
editor.

AAN: William Rose

The Lady's from Kentucky
US 1939 75m bw
Jeff Lazarus/Paramount

A crooked bookie is reformed by a lady horse breeder.

Yawnworthy drama with an unattractive hero.

w Malcolm Stuart Boylan d Alexander Hall

George Raft, Ellen Drew, Hugh Herbert, ZaSu Pitts,
Louise Beavers, Forrester Harvey

'It starts with promise, stumbles in the middle
section, and drags itself across the line for the finish.'
– *Variety*

A Lady's Morals
US 1930 86m bw
MGM
GB titles: *Jenny Lind; The Soul Kiss*

The 'Swedish nightingale' learns that love is more
important than a singing career.

Cliché-strewn romance with music.

w Hans Kraly, Claudine West, John Meehan, Arthur
Richman d Sidney Franklin m Herbert Stothart

Grace Moore, Reginald Denny, Wallace Beery, Jobyna
Howland

'Class production of money potentialities.' – *Variety*

† Wallace Beery played P. T. Barnum, a role he was to
repeat four years later in *The Mighty Barnum*.

A Lady's Profession
US 1933 65m bw
Paramount

A British nobleman comes to America to retrieve his
lost fortune, and starts a speakeasy.

Rather silly farce which generally disappoints.

w Walter de Leon, Malcolm Stuart Boylan
d Norman McLeod

Alison Skipworth, Roland Young, Sari Maritza, Kent
Taylor, Roscoe Karns

'Slow. Some bright spots, but too widely spaced.' –
Variety

Lafayette
France/Italy 1961 158m Super Technirama 70
Copernic/Cosmos (Maurice Jacquin)

French officers help America in the revolutionary war
of 1776.

Nerveless international epic, interesting only for its
star cameos.

w Jean-Bernard Luc, Suzanne Arduini, Jacques
Sigurd, François Ponthier, Jean Dréville, Maurice
Jacquin d Jean Dréville ph Claude Renoir, Roger
Hubert m Steve Laurent, Pierre Duclos

Michel Le Royer, Jack Hawkins, Orson Welles,
Howard St John, Vittorio de Sica, Edmund Purdom,
Jacques Castelot, Folco Lulli

'It looks, sounds and smells like nothing so much as
the same old indigestible, ill-dubbed, co-produced
continental spectaculars which have already turned
the stomach in a whole range of lesser screen ratios.' –
MFB

Lafayette Escadrille
US 1957 93m bw
Warner (William Wellman)
GB title: *Hell Bent for Glory*

Early in World War I, a young American joins the
French air force.

The director's valedictory film, on a subject close to
his heart, is a curiously disappointing, flat and
disjointed affair, partly salvaged by a good period
feel.

w A. S. Fleischmann d William A. Wellman
ph William Clothier m Leonard Rosenman

Tab Hunter, Etchika Choreau, David Janssen, Clint
Eastwood, Will Hutchins, Paul Fix

The Lair of the White Worm
GB 1988 93m Technicolor
Vestron (Ken Russell)
V, V*, L

A female vampire attempts to make human sacrifices
to an ancient snake god.

Grotesque horror done without finesse or subtlety.

wd Ken Russell novel Bram Stoker ph Dick Bush
m Stanislas Syrewicz sp Geoff Portass ed Peter
Davies

Amanda Donoghue, Hugh Grant, Catherine Oxenberg, Peter Capaldi, Sammi Davis, Stratford Johns, Paul Brooke, Imogen Claire, Christopher Gable

'He proves incapable of handling straight suspense, horror, or supernatural sequences.' – *MFB*

Lake Consequence

US   1992   90m   colour
Rank/10dB/Zalman King (Avram Butch Kaplan)

A housewife who was gang-raped by a rock band wants more of the same.

Glossy, cliché-ridden would-be erotica for the easily pleased.

w Zalman King, Melanie Finn, Henry Cobbold   story MacGregor Douglas   d Rafael Eisenman   ph Harris Savides   m George S. Clinton   pd Dominic Watkins   ed James Gavin Bedford, Curtis Edge

Billy Zane, Joan Severance, May Karasun, Whip Hubley, Courtland Mead, Dan Reed, Christi Allen

'Slickly shot, but over dramatised (some of the editing is positively epileptic) at the expense of any remotely believable dialogue or acting, this, given its pedigree, is high on sauce but low on just about everything else.' – *Empire*

Lake Placid Serenade

US   1944   85m   bw
Harry Grey/Republic

A Czech girl skater is sent to America to represent her country.

Simple-minded entertainment overloaded with musical numbers.

w Dick Irving Hyland and Doris Gilbert   d Steve Sekely

Vera Hruba Ralston, Robert Livingston, Eugene Pallette, Vera Vague, Walter Catlett, Lloyd Corrigan, William Frawley

Lamb

GB   1986   110m   Eastmancolor
Cannon/Flickers/Limehouse/Channel 4 (Neil Zeiger)

A young priest at a harsh Irish reform school absconds with a 14-year-old pupil, an act with tragic consequences for them both.

Rather wearisome transcription of religious thesis into makeshift drama: disturbing but not satisfying.

w Bernard MacLaverty   novel Bernard MacLaverty   d Colin Gregg   ph Mike Garfath   m Van Morrison   pd Austen Spriggs   ad Peter Delfgou

Liam Neeson, Hugh O'Conor, Harry Towb, Frances Tomelty, Ian Bannen

Lambada

US   1990   98m   Alpha-Cine   Panavision
Warner/Cannon/Film and Television Company (Peter Shepherd)
V, V*, L

A teacher spends his nights as a lambada dancer so that he can give lessons to a gang of dropouts.

Dismal attempt to cash in on a short-lived American dance craze.

w Joel Silberg, Sheldon Renan   d Joel Silberg   ph Roberto D'Ettore Piazzoli   m Greg DeBelles   pd Bill Cornfield   ed Marcus Manton

J. Eddie Peck, Melora Hardin, Shabba-Doo, Ricky Paul Goldin, Basil Hoffman, Dennis Burkley, Keene Curtis

The Lambeth Walk

GB   1939   84m   bw
CAPAD/Pinebrook (Anthony Havelock-Allan)

A cockney bloke inherits a dukedom.

Mild screen version of a popular musical play and a song which became a nationwide hit.

w Clifford Grey, John Paddy Carstairs, Robert Edmunds   play Me and My Girl by Louis Rose, Douglas Furber, Noel Gay   d Albert de Courville   ph Francis Carver

Lupino Lane, Sally Gray, Seymour Hicks, Enid Stamp Taylor, Wilfrid Hyde-White, Charles Heslop, Norah Howard

The Lamp Still Burns

GB   1943   90m   bw
GFD/Two Cities (Leslie Howard)

Adventures of wartime probationary nurses.

Understated wartime morale-builder, no longer very interesting.

w Elizabeth Baron, Roland Pertwee   novel One Pair of Feet by Monica Dickens   d Maurice Elvey   ph Robert Krasker

Rosamund John, Stewart Granger, Godfrey Tearle, Sophie Stewart, John Laurie, Margaret Vyner, Cathleen Nesbitt, Joyce Grenfell

Lan Fengzheng: see *The Blue Kite*

Lancashire Luck

GB   1937   74m   bw
Paramount British

A poor girl's life is changed when her father wins the pools.

Modest comedy which started its star's career.

w A. R. Rawlinson   story Ronald Gow   d Henry Cass

Wendy Hiller, George Carney, Muriel George, Nigel Stock, George Galleon

Lancelot and Guinevere *

GB   1962   117m   Eastmancolor   Panavision
Emblem (Cornel Wilde)
US title: *Sword of Lancelot*

Sir Lancelot covets the wife of his beloved King Arthur, but after Arthur's death she takes the veil.

Decently made, rather tame transcription of the legends, with all concerned doing quite creditably but not brilliantly.

w Richard Schayer, Jefferson Pascal   d Cornel Wilde   ph Harry Waxman   m Ron Goodwin

Cornel Wilde, Jean Wallace, Brian Aherne, George Baker, John Barrie

Lancer Spy *

US   1937   80m   bw
TCF

A German spy is captured and his English double is sent back to replace him.

World War I yarn on the lines of *The Great Impersonation* (qv). Excellent production and a good beginning and end, but a slow middle.

w Philip Dunne   novel Marthe McKenna   d Gregory Ratoff   ph Barney McGill   m Arthur Lange

George Sanders, Dolores del Rio, Peter Lorre, Joseph Schildkraut, Virginia Field, Sig Rumann, Fritz Feld

'Sometimes exciting, always absorbing, and played with serious intensity.' – *Variety*

The Land before Time

US   1988   69m   Technicolor
UIP/Universal/Amblin (Don Bluth, Gary Goldman, John Pomeroy)
V*, L, S

An orphaned dinosaur sets out with friends to find the way to a valley of plenty.

Over-cute, immensely sentimental animated feature.

w Stu Krieger   story Judy Freudberg, Tony Geiss   d Don Bluth   ph Jim Mann   m James Horner

Voices of Gabriel Damon, Helen Shaver, Bill Erwin, Candice Houston, Pat Hingle, Burke Barnes, Judith Barsi, Will Ryan

Land of Desire: see *A Ship to India*

Land of Fury: see *The Seekers*

Land of Liberty *

US   1939   137m   bw
Motion Picture Producers and Distributors of America

A compilation of footage from American historical films, amounting hopefully to a history of America as seen by Hollywood.

A pretty impressive job of selection and editing, compiled for the New York World's Fair.

w Jeannie McPherson, Jesse Lasky Jnr ed Cecil B. de Mille and others

'Her treachery stained every stone of the pyramid!' '20,000 workers and technicians! 1,600 camels! 104 specially built barges! 9,753 players in one scene alone!'

Land of the Pharaohs *

US   1955   105m   Warnercolor   Cinemascope
Warner/Continental (Howard Hawks)
V*, L

Pharaoh is obsessed with life after death and builds a great pyramid for himself and his treasures . . . but his wife is ambitious . . .

Unexpected, interesting excursion into Ancient Egypt, distended by Cinemascope; basically a macabre melodrama with a final spectacular twist. The engineering details would make a fascinating documentary.

w William Faulkner, Harry Kurnitz, H. Jack Bloom   d Howard Hawks   ph Lee Garmes, Russell Harlan   m Dimitri Tiomkin   ad Alexander Trauner

Jack Hawkins, Joan Collins, Alexis Minotis, James Robertson Justice, Sidney Chaplin

The Land that Time Forgot *

GB   1974   91m   Technicolor
Amicus (John Dark)
V, V*

In 1916, survivors from a torpedoed supply ship find themselves on a legendary island full of prehistoric monsters.

Lively old-fashioned adventure fantasy with good technical credits.

w James Cawthorne, Michael Moorcock   novel Edgar Rice Burroughs   d Kevin Connor   ph Alan Hume   m Douglas Gamley   pd Maurice Carter   sp Derek Meddings, Roger Dicken

Doug McClure, John McEnery, Susan Penhaligon, Keith Barron, Anthony Ainley

The Land Unknown *

US   1957   78m   bw   Cinemascope
U-I (William Alland)

A plane is forced down into a strange Antarctic valley where dinosaurs still roam.

Efficient adventure fantasy on *King Kong* lines but without any of that film's panache.

w Laslo Gorog   d Virgil Vogel   ph Ellis Carter   m Hans Salter   sp Roswell Hoffman, Fred Knoth, Orien Ernest, Jack Kevan

Jock Mahoney, Shawn Smith, William Reynolds, Henry Brandon

Land without Bread *

Spain   1932   27m   bw
Ramon Acin
aka: *Las Hurdes*

A famous documentary showing the poorest region of

northern Spain, notable for some stunningly unpleasant images impeccably staged.

wd/ed Luis Buñuel   *ph* Eli Lotar

Land without Music *
GB   1936   80m   bw
Capitol Films (Max Schach)
US title: *Forbidden Music*

The ruler of a Ruritanian country bans music because her subjects are too busy singing to make money. A revolutionary singer however wins the duchess's hand and reverses her decision.

Artless but attractively played operetta with the star in excellent form.

w Marian Dix, L. Du Garde Peach   *d* Walter Forde   *ph* John Boyle   *m* Oscar Straus

Richard Tauber, Jimmy Durante, Diana Napier, June Clyde, Derrick de Marney, Esme Percy, George Hayes, Edward Rigby

Landfall
GB   1949   88m   bw
ABPC (Victor Skuzetzky)

A test pilot mistakenly believes that he accidentally sank a British submarine.

Second-rate transcription of a popular novel.

w Talbot Jennings, Gilbert Gunn, Anne Burnaby   *novel* Nevil Shute   *d* Ken Annakin   *ph* Wilkie Cooper

Michael Denison, Patricia Plunkett, Kathleen Harrison, David Tomlinson, Joan Dowling, Maurice Denham, A. E. Matthews, Margaretta Scott, Sebastian Shaw, Laurence Harvey

The Landlord *
US   1970   110m   DeLuxe
United Artists/Mirisch/Carter (Norman Jewison)

A tycoon's son buys a tenement in Brooklyn's black ghetto, and conscience diverts him into improving the lot of his tenants.

Overlong satirical comedy, good on detail but short on structure.

w Bill Gunn   *novel* Kristin Hunter   *d* Hal Ashby   *ph* Gordon Willis   *m* Al Kooper   *pd* Robert Boyle

Beau Bridges, Lee Grant, Pearl Bailey, Diana Sands

'Bad taste from start to finish . . . not an avenue of offensiveness to any race is left unexplored.' – *Judith Crist*

AAN: Lee Grant

Landru
France/Italy   1962   115m   Eastmancolor
Rome-Paris/CC Champion (Carlo Ponti, Georges de Beauregard)
aka: *Bluebeard*

The true story of a furniture dealer who murdered women for financial gain, also treated by Chaplin in *Monsieur Verdoux.*

A curious artificial style has been adopted, making a tragi-comedy look like a farce which isn't very funny, and falls on very stony ground indeed despite the all star cast.

w Françoise Sagan   *d* Claude Chabrol   *ph* Jean Rabier   *m* Pierre Jansen

Charles Denner, Michèle Morgan, Danielle Darrieux, Hildegarde Knef, Stéphane Audran, Catherine Rouvel

Landscape in a Mist *
Greece/France/Italy   1988   125m   colour
Artificial Eye/Paradis Films/ET-1/Basicinematografica/Channel 4 (Theo Angelopoulos)
S
original title: *Topio Stin Omichli*

Two children, an eleven-year-old girl and her five-year-old brother, travel through Greece in an attempt

to reach Germany and the father they have never known.

Lyrical, but slow-moving account of a child's discovery of the world that would have been as meaningful at half its length.

w Theo Angelopoulos, Tonino Guerra, Thanassis Valtinos   *d* Theo Angelopoulos   *ph* Giorgos Arvanitis   *m* Eleni Karaindrou   *ad* Mikes Karapiperis   *ed* Yannis Tsitsopoulos

Michalis Zeke, Tania Palaiologou, Stratis Tzortzoglou

Larceny
US   1948   89m   bw
Universal (Aaron Rosenberg)

A con man fleeces a war widow into paying for a memorial to her husband, but falls in love with her.

Drearily predictable melodrama.

w Herbert F. Margolis, Louis Markein, William Bowers   *novel* The Velvet Fleece by Lois Ely, John Fleming   *d* George Sherman   *ph* Irving Glassberg   *m* Leith Stevens

Joan Caulfield, John Payne, Dan Duryea, Shelley Winters, Dorothy Hart, Richard Rober, Dan O'Herlihy

Larceny, Inc
US   1942   95m   bw
Warner (Jack Saper, Jerry Wald)

An ex-convict tries to rob a bank but finds that honesty pays best.

Tepid comedy-drama from the period when Warner were taming their gangster image.

w Everett Freeman, Edwin Gilbert   *play* The Night before Christmas by Laura and S. J. Perelman   *d* Lloyd Bacon   *ph* Tony Gaudio

Edward G. Robinson, Jane Wyman, Broderick Crawford, Anthony Quinn, Jack Carson, Edward Brophy, Harry Davenport, John Qualen, Barbara Jo Allen, Jackie Gleason, Grant Mitchell, Andrew Tombes

Larceny Lane: see *Blonde Crazy*

The Las Vegas Story
US   1952   88m   bw
RKO (Robert Sparks)

When an investment broker and his new wife stop at Las Vegas, her shady past begins to emerge.

So-so programmer with some eccentric talents in average form, capped by a desert helicopter chase.

w Earl Felton, Harry Essex   *d* Robert Stevenson   *ph* Harry J. Wild   *md* Constantin Bakaleinikoff   *m* Leigh Harline

Jane Russell, Victor Mature, Vincent Price, Hoagy Carmichael, Colleen Miller, Brad Dexter, Jay C. Flippen

The Laser Man
Hong Kong   1988   90m   colour
Peter Wang Films/Hong Kong Film Workshop (Peter Wang)

An out-of-work laser scientist is hired by a mysterious corporation to develop a deadly weapon.

Quirky thriller – the Chinese hero has a Jewish mother – but lacking anything other than its deliberate eccentricity.   *wd* Peter Wang   *ph* Ernest Dickerson   *m* Mason Daring   *pd* Lester Cohen   *ed* Graham Weinbren

Marc Hayashi, Maryann Urbano, Joan Copeland, Tony Ka-Fei Leung, Neva Small, David Chan, Sally Yeh, Peter Wang

The Lash
US   1930   76m   bw
First National

Adventures of a Spanish-Californian Robin Hood.

Or, *The Mark of Zorro* in all but name: a stalwart early talkie.

w Bradley King   *story* Adios by Lanier Virginia Bartlett   *d* Frank Lloyd

Richard Barthelmess, Mary Astor, James Rennie, Marian Nixon

'A good action talker in the western romantic strain.' – *Variety*

† Filmed in VitaScope (65mm).

Lashou Shentan: see *Hard-Boiled*

Lasky Jedne Plavovlasky: see *Loves of a Blonde*

Lassie
The official Lassie series, made by MGM, was as follows:

1943: LASSIE COME HOME (qv)
1945: SON OF LASSIE (*d* S. Sylvan Simon *with* Peter Lawford, Donald Crisp, Nigel Bruce)
1946: COURAGE OF LASSIE (*d* Fred M. Wilcox *with* Elizabeth Taylor, Frank Morgan, Tom Drake)
1948: THE HILLS OF HOME¹ (*d* Fred M. Wilcox *with* Edmund Gwenn, Donald Crisp, Tom Drake)
1949: THE SUN COMES UP (*d* Richard Thorpe *with* Jeanette MacDonald, Lloyd Nolan)
1949: CHALLENGE TO LASSIE (*d* Richard Thorpe *with* Edmund Gwenn, Donald Crisp)
1951: THE PAINTED HILLS (*d* Harold F. Kress *with* Paul Kelly, Bruce Cowling)

† Later 'Lassie' features were taken from episodes of the long-running TV series.
¹GB title: *Master of Lassie.*

Lassie Come Home *
US   1943   88m   Technicolor
MGM (Samuel Marx)
V*, L

A poor family is forced to sell its beloved dog, but she makes a remarkable journey to return to them.

First of the Lassie films and certainly the best: an old-fashioned heartwarmer.

w Hugo Butler   *novel* Eric Knight   *d* Fred M. Wilcox   *ph* Leonard Smith   *m* Daniele Amfitheatrof

Roddy McDowall, Elizabeth Taylor, Donald Crisp, Edmund Gwenn, Dame May Whitty, Nigel Bruce, Elsa Lanchester, J. Pat O'Malley

'The late Eric Knight wrote this immortal essay in Doggery-Woggery. MGM finished it off.' – *Richard Winnington*

AAN: Leonard Smith

Lassiter
US   1984   100m   Technicolor
Pan Pacific/Golden Harvest (Albert S. Ruddy)
V, V*, L

An American detective in pre-war London is forced by Scotland Yard to steal papers from the German Embassy.

Flat to the point of stultification, this marks yet another failure to make a big screen star of Tom Selleck.

w David Taylor   *d* Roger Young   *ph* Gil Taylor   *m* Ken Thorne   *pd* Peter Mullins   *ed* Benjamin Weissman, Richard Hiscott

Tom Selleck, Jane Seymour, Lauren Hutton, Bob Hoskins, Joe Regalbuto, Ed Lauter, Warren Clarke

Last Action Hero
US   1993   131m   Technicolor   Panavision
Columbia TriStar/Columbia (Steve Roth, John McTiernan)
V, V*, L, S

A magic ticket enables a boy to enter the world of an action movie, but it also allows the villain to escape into the real world, where he is followed by the boy and the film's muscular hero.

A film that tries to have it both ways, simultaneously mocking and celebrating the conventions of action movies, which leaves audiences, as well as the actors and director, in a state of bewildered confusion.

w Shane Black, David Arnott   *story* Zack Penn, Adam Leff   *d* John McTiernan   *ph* Dean Semler   *m* Michael Kamen   *pd* Eugenio Zanetti   *ed* John Wright

Arnold Schwarzenegger, F. Murray Abraham, Art Carney, Charles Dance, Frank McRae, Tony Noonan, Robert Prosky, Anthony Quinn, Mercedes Ruehl, Ian McKellan, Joan Plowright, Tina Turner

'A joyless, soulless machine of a movie.' – *Variety*

'A perfect example of cinematic self-hatred.' – *Sight and Sound*

† The film's production costs were reportedly $100 million. It took around $28 million at the US box-office, though better results elsewhere meant that its final loss was reckoned to be some $20 million, although some estimates put it much higher.

The Last Adventurers
GB   1937   77m   bw
Conway (H. Fraser Passmore)

Adventures on board a fishing trawler.

Acceptable low-budget outdoor drama.

w Denison Clift   *d* Roy Kellino   *ph* Eric Cross   *m* Eric Ansell   *ad* W. R. Brinton   *ed* David Lean

Niall MacGinnis, Linden Travers, Roy Emerton, Kay Walsh, Peter Gawthorne, Katie Johnson

The Last American Hero *
US   1973   95m   DeLuxe   Panavision
TCF/Wizan/Rojo (John Cutts, William Roberts)
V*

The adventures of an illicit whisky distiller with a passion for fast cars.

Observant, amusing hillbilly comedy drama based on the early life of racing driver Junior Johnson.

w William Roberts   *d* Lamont Johnson   *ph* George Silano   *m* Charles Fox

Jeff Bridges, Valerie Perrine, Geraldine Fitzgerald, Ned Beatty, Art Lund, Gary Busey

'A pop saga phrased with rough vernacular authenticity.' – *Bruce Williamson, Playboy*

† Reissue title: *Hard Driver*

The Last Angry Man *
US   1959   100m   bw
Columbia (Fred Kohlmar)
V*

An old doctor in a Brooklyn slum is made the subject of a TV documentary.

Self-confidently sentimental wallow which just about works.

w Gerald Green   *novel* Gerald Green   *d* Daniel Mann   *ph* James Wong Howe   *m* George Duning   *ad* Carl Anderson

Paul Muni, David Wayne, Betsy Palmer, Luther Adler, Dan Tobin, Robert F. Simon

AAN: Paul Muni; art direction

The Last Battle
France   1983   92m   bw   Cinemascope
ICA/Les Films du Loup (Luc Besson)
original title: *Le Dernier Combat*

A samurai swordsman runs amok in a world destroyed by nuclear war.

Chic, virtually silent film that borrows from dozens of other works on the same theme.

wd Luc Besson   *ph* Carlo Varini   *m* Eric Serra   *ed* Sophie Schmit

Pierre Jolivet, Jean Bouise, Fritz Wepper, Jean Reno, Maurice Lany, Pierre Carrive, Jean-Michel Castanie, Michel Doset

The Last Blitzkrieg
US   1959   84m   bw
Columbia/Sam Katzman

During the Battle of the Bulge a German leads a squad of American saboteurs.

Weakly pacifist, technically incompetent war adventure.

w Lou Morheim   *d* Arthur Dreifuss   *ph* Ted Scaife   *m* Hugo de Groot

Van Johnson, Kerwin Mathews, Dick York, Larry Storch

'They're two fallen heroes up against the gambling syndicate in pro sports. Everyone had counted them out. But they're about to get back into the game.'

The Last Boy Scout
US   1991   105m   Technicolor   Panavision
Warner/Geffen/Silver (Joel Silver, Michael Levy)
V, V*, L

A too-honest secret agent turned private eye is hired by a former football player to protect his girlfriend, a stripper.

Standard buddy-buddy action movie with high-budget special effects and non-stop violence.

w Shane Black   *story* Shane Black, Greg Hicks   *d* Tony Scott   *ph* Ward Russell   *m* Michael Kamen   *pd* Brian Morris   *ed* Mark Goldblatt, Mark Helfrich

Bruce Willis, Damon Wayans, Chelsea Field, Noble Willingham, Taylor Negron, Danielle Harris, Halle Berry, Bruce McGill

'Entertaining if mindless shoot-'em-up . . . the Boy Scouts' ''Be Prepared'' motto could be taken as a warning to check one's brain at the door.' – *Variety*

'To give it a negative review would be dishonest. To be positive is to seem to approve its sickness.' – *Roger Ebert*

† Shane Black was reportedly paid $1.75 million for his screenplay.

The Last Bridge
Austria/Yugoslavia   1953   95m   bw
Cosmopol/UFUS (Carl Szokoll)

During World War II, a German nurse in Yugoslavia is captured by partisans and turns to their point of view.

Message melodrama, very ably put together with a bleakly tragic climax; but nothing at all new.

w Helmut Kautner, Norbert Kunze   *d* Helmut Kautner   *ph* Elio Carniel   *m* Carl de Groof

Maria Schell, Bernhard Wicki, Barbara Rütting, Carl Möhner

The Last Chance *
Switzerland   1945   105m   bw
Praesens Film

In 1943 an Englishman and an American escape from a fascist camp in northern Italy and with the help of refugees cross the mountains into Switzerland.

Earnest propaganda piece which struck the spot at the time: cinematically rather plodding, but with some exciting scenes.

w Richard Schweizer   *d* Leopold Lindtberg   *ph* Emil Berna   *m* Robert Blum

E. G. Morrison, Ray Reagan, John Hoy, Luisa Rossi

The Last Command **
US   1928   100m approx (24 fps)   bw   silent
Paramount

An exiled Russian general goes berserk when given a

role in a movie which virtually involves playing himself.

Fascinating ironic comedy tailored for an international star who was not to survive the talkies.

w John S. Goodrich   *story* Lajos Biro   *d* Josef von Sternberg   *ph* Bert Glennon   *ad* Hans Dreier

Emil Jannings, William Powell, Evelyn Brent, Nicholas Soussanin

AA: Emil Jannings

AAN: Lajos Biro

The Last Command *
US   1955   110m   Trucolor
Republic (Frank Lloyd)
V*

Jim Bowie returns to Texas in the 1830s and dies at the Alamo alongside other famous men.

Reasonably interesting Western on a subject which has often figured but seldom worked.

w Warren Duff   *d* Frank Lloyd   *ph* Jack Marta   *m* Max Steiner

Ernest Borgnine, Sterling Hayden, Anna Maria Alberghetti, Arthur Hunnicutt, Richard Carlson, J. Carrol Naish

Last Days of Chez Nous *
Australia   1992   96m   Eastmancolor
Metro/Jan Chapman/Australian Film Finance Corp.
V, V*, S

In Sydney, while a wife is away on holiday, her sister has an affair with her French husband and her daughter goes to bed with the lodger.

A slight but perceptive domestic drama.

w Helen Garner   *d* Gillian Armstrong   *ph* Geoffrey Simpson   *m* Paul Grabowsky   *pd* Janet Patterson   *ed* Nicholas Beauman

Lisa Harrow, Bruno Ganz, Kerry Fox, Mirando Otto, Kiri Paramore, Bill Hunter

'Beautifully acted and crafted.' – *Variety*

'Poignantly observed and dry-humoured account of emotional blundering and bruising.' – *Lizzie Franke, Sight and Sound*

The Last Days of Dolwyn *
GB   1949   95m   bw
London/BLPA (Anatole de Grunwald)
V*
US title: *Woman of Dolwyn*

A Welsh valley is flooded to make a reservoir and a village has to be evacuated.

Interesting but rather stagey drama based on an actual 19th-century event, with personal melodrama added.

wd Emlyn Williams   *ph* Otto Heller   *m* John Greenwood

Edith Evans, Emlyn Williams, Richard Burton, Hugh Griffith, Barbara Couper, Allan Aynesworth

'The conventionally picturesque Welsh flavour and mounting probabilities apart, the treatment is stiff and episodic.' – *MFB*

The Last Days of Man on Earth: see *The Final Programme*

'Pompeii . . . drunk with wealth and power . . . rotten with pagan pleasures . . . doomed to fiery death from the skies!'

The Last Days of Pompeii *
US   1935   96m   bw
RKO (Merian C. Cooper)
V*

In ancient Pompeii, various personal dramas are submerged in the eruption of Vesuvius.

Starchy melodrama capped by a reel of spectacular disaster.

w Ruth Rose, Boris Ingster   *novel* Lord Lytton
d Merian C. Cooper, Ernest Schoedsack   *ph* Eddie
Linden Jnr, J. Roy Hunt   *m* Roy Webb   *sp Vernon
Walker, Harry Redmond*

Preston Foster, Basil Rathbone, Alan Hale, Dorothy
Wilson

'Well-done spectacle minus romance and cast names.
Should do all right generally.' – *Variety*

The Last Detail **
US   1973   104m   Metrocolor
Columbia/Acrobat/Persky-Bright (Gerald Ayres)
V, V*, L

Two hardened naval petty officers escort a young
recruit, sentenced for thieving, from Virginia to a New
Hampshire jail, and give him a wild last night.

Foul-mouthed weekend odyssey, with a few well-
observed moments for non-prudes. Technically the
epitome of Hollywood's most irritating seventies
fashion, with fuzzy sound recording, dim against-the-
light photography, and a general determination to
show up the ugliness of everything around us.

w Robert Towne   *novel* Darryl Ponicsan   *d* Hal
Ashby   *ph* Michael Chapman   *m* Johnny Mandel

Jack Nicholson, Otis Young, Randy Quaid, Clifton
James, Carol Kane

'Visually it is relentlessly lower-depths gloomy, and
the material, though often very funny, is programmed
to wrench your heart.' – *New Yorker*

AAN: Robert Towne; Jack Nicholson; Randy Quaid

The Last Dinosaur
US   1977   100m   colour
Rankin-Bass Productions
V*

An oil-drilling team discovers a *tyrannosaurus rex*
while probing the polar oil-cap.

Inept monster saga with poorish special effects from a
Japanese team.

w William Overgard   *d* Alex Grasshof, Tom Kotani
ph Shoshi Ueda   *m* Maury Laws

Richard Boone, Joan Van Ark, Steven Keats

'He thinks someone is trying to kill him. He's dead right!'
Last Embrace
US   1979   101m   Technicolor
UA (Michael Taylor, Dan Wigutow)
V*

An investigator survives a number of attacks on his
life, though his wife is killed in the first of them.

Hitchcockian mystery without the master's zest or
humour, though it leads to a pretty exciting climax at
Niagara Falls.

w David Shaber   *novel* The 13th Man by Murray
Teigh Bloom   *d* Jonathan Demme   *ph* Tak
Fujimoto   *m* Miklos Rozsa

Roy Scheider, Janet Margolin, Sam Levene, John
Glover, Charles Napier, Christopher Walken,
Jacqueline Brookes

'A case study of late seventies movie-making which
does everything in its power to avoid taking risks.' –
John Pym, MFB

The Last Emperor **
Italy/Hong Kong/GB   1987   160m approx
Technicolor   Technovision
Columbia/Yanco Films/Tao Films/Recorded Picture Company/
   Screenframe/AAA Soprofilm (Jeremy Thomas)
V, V*, L, S

The life of China's last imperial ruler, from ascending
the throne as a puppet-like 3-year-old, to serene old
age as a gardener in Mao's People's Republic.

A lavish spectacle which caught the imagination of
audiences, though many found the compression of 60
years of Chinese politics baffling.

w Mark Peploe, Bernardo Bertolucci   *d Bernardo
Bertolucci*   *ph* Vittorio Storaro   *m* Ryuichi
Sakamoto, David Byrne, Cong Su   *pd* Ferdinando
Scarfiotti   *ad* Bruno Cesari   *ed* Gabriella Cristiani

John Lone, Joan Chen, Peter O'Toole, Ying Ruocheng

AA: best picture; best director; best adapted
screenplay; best cinematography; best original score;
best film editing; best art direction; best costume
design; best sound

The Last Escape
GB   1970   90m   DeLuxe
Oakmont/UA

An American officer in Munich tries to rescue a
German scientist from the Nazis.

Standard World War II actioner.

w Herman Hoffman   *d* Walter Grauman

Stuart Whitman, John Collin, Martin Jarvis, Pinkas
Braun

Last Exit to Brooklyn ***
West Germany   1989   98m   colour
Guild/Neue Constantin Film Produktion/Bavaria Film/Allied
   Filmmakers (Bernd Eichinger)
V, V*, L, S

Striking workers and their families and a prostitute
lead thwarted lives in Brooklyn in the early 1950s.

True to the spirit of Selby's grim, but compassionate,
low-life novel, with some brilliant ensemble acting.

w Desmond Nakano   *novel* Hubert Selby Jnr   *d* Uli
Edel   *ph* Stefan Czapsky   *m* Mark Knopfler
pd David Chapman   *ad* Mark Haak   *ed* Peter
Przygodda

Stephen Lang, Jennifer Jason Leigh, Burt Young,
Peter Dobson, Christopher Murney, Jerry Orbach,
Alexis Arquette

'Edel surprisingly has managed to capture exactly the
horrified yet tender tone of Selby's book.' – *MFB*

The Last Flight ***
US   1931   80m   bw
Warner

In 1919, four veteran American flyers stay on in Paris
in the hope of calming their shattered physical and
emotional states.

Fascinatingly offhand study on post-war cynicism and
the faint hope of a better world, beautifully written
and directed in a manner more effective than *The Sun
Also Rises.*

w John Monk Saunders   novel Single Lady by John
Monk Saunders   *d William Dieterle   ph* Sid Hickox

Richard Barthelmess, Helen Chandler, David Manners,
John Mack Brown, *Elliott Nugent,* Walter Byron

'If the crowd can understand that girl character in this
picture the film is an undoubted grosser.' – *Variety*

'A narrative as tight and spare as a Racine tragedy . . .
unique in Hollywood of that time in its persistent,
calculated understatement.' – *Tom Milne, 1975*

† In magazine form the story was known as 'Nikki
and her War Birds'.

The Last Flight of Noah's Ark
US   1980   98m   Technicolor
Walt Disney
V*

An impecunious pilot reluctantly flies an orphanage
worker and a cargo of animals across the Pacific, only
to be stranded with them on a desert island.

It must have sounded like a good idea, but if it was to
work at all it needed much sharper handling.

w Steven W. Carabatsos, Sandy Glass, George Arthur
Bloom   *story The Gremlin's Castle* by Ernest K. Gann
d Charles Jarrott   *ph* Charles F. Wheeler
m Maurice Jarre

Elliott Gould, Geneviève Bujold, Ricky Schroder,
Tammy Lauren, Vincent Gardenia

The Last Frontier
US   1932   bw   serial: 12 eps
RKO

A Western newspaper battles a gang of outlaws.

Routine serial, a rare commodity from this studio.

d Spencer Bennet

Creighton Chaney (Lon Chaney Jnr), Dorothy
Gulliver, Mary Jo Desmond

The Last Frontier (1956): see *Savage Wilderness*

'The big fellow is out of Alcatraz – ready to show them no
mercy!'
The Last Gangster *
US   1937   81m   bw
MGM (J. J. Cohn)

A gangster is released from Alcatraz and plans
vengeance on his wife for deserting him.

Clean-cut star melodrama which suddenly turns
sentimental.

w John Lee Mahin   *d* Edward Ludwig
ph William Daniels   *montage Slavko Vorkapich*
m Edward Ward

Edward G. Robinson, Rose Stradner, James Stewart,
Lionel Stander, Douglas Scott, John Carradine,
Sidney Blackmer, Edward Brophy

'May indeed be the last gangster movie . . . a good
film which will blossom at the b.o.' – *Variety*

'A lot of water has flowed under the bridge since *Little
Caesar,* but Mr Robinson has breasted the tides to
make his impersonation of a 1937 thug as persuasive
as was his portrait of a killer in that earlier classic of
rats and rackets.' – *Frank Nugent*

The Last Gangster (1944): see *Roger Touhy,
Gangster*

The Last Gentleman
US   1934   80m   bw
Fox

The career of a New England millionaire.

Pleasing star family drama.

w Leonard Praskins   *d* Sidney Lanfield

George Arliss, Edna May Oliver, Ralph Morgan, Janet
Beecher, Charlotte Henry

'A prolonged monologue . . . mediocre film which
must depend on the star's rep.' – *Variety*

The Last Grenade
GB   1969   93m   Eastmancolor   Panavision
Cinerama/Dimitri de Grunwald/Josef Shaftel

An army mercenary is betrayed by an ex-friend in the
Congo and pursues him to Hong Kong.

Violent action melodrama with few redeeming
qualities.

w Kenneth Ware   *novel The Ordeal of Major Grigsby* by
John Sherlock   *d* Gordon Flemyng   *ph* Alan Hume
m Johnny Dankworth

Stanley Baker, Alex Cord, Honor Blackman, Richard
Attenborough, Rafer Johnson, Andrew Keir, Ray
Brooks, Julian Glover, John Thaw

The Last Hard Men
US   1976   97m   DeLuxe   Panavision
TCF/Belasco-Seltzer-Thatcher

A train robber breaks jail and sets out to revenge
himself on the now-retired lawman who committed
him.

Tough action adventure without much sense except to
paint the end of the golden days of the west.

w Guerdon Trueblood *novel Gun Down* by Brian Garfield *d* Andrew V. McLaglen *ph* Duke Callaghan *m* Jerry Goldsmith

Charlton Heston, James Coburn, Barbara Hershey, Christopher Mitchum, Michael Parks, Jorge Rivero, Thalmus Rasulala

'Script and direction seem equally tired.' – *Sight and Sound*

'The action proceeds slackly from one setpiece shoot-up to the next, barely providing the voltage for the two leads to expand their stereotyped roles into displays of star power.' – *Richard Combs, MFB*

The Last Harvest *
Argentina 1992 91m colour
Arenas/Jorge Estrada Mora (Julio Lencina, Ricardo Freixa)
original title: *La Ultima Siembra*

On an Argentinian ranch, conflict grows between an Indian miner turned maize farmer and the American-educated son of the landowner who wants to replace the cattle with a tobacco plantation.

Leisurely examination of a clash between races, classes and entrenched attitudes, coming heavily down on the side of conservatism.

wd Miguel Pereira *novel Los Humilides* by Miguel Angel Pereira *ph* Pablo Esteban Courtalón *m* Ariel Petrocelli, Tukuta Gordillo Isamara *ad* Mirta Spagarino *ed* Miguel Perez

Patricio Contreras, Leonor Manso, Mario Pasik, Alberto Benegas, Gonzalo Morales, Antonio Paleari

Last Holiday *
GB 1950 88m bw
ABPC/Watergate (Stephen Mitchell, A. D. Peters, J. B. Priestley)
V*

A man with a short time to live has a thoroughly enjoyable and useful final fling.

Slight, amusing and moving comedy drama spoiled by an unnecessary double twist.

w J. B. Priestley *d* Henry Cass *ph* Ray Elton *m* Francis Chagrin

Alec Guinness, Kay Walsh, Beatrice Campbell, Grégoire Aslan, Bernard Lee, Wilfrid Hyde-White, Helen Cherry, Sidney James, Muriel George

'To Avoid Fainting Keep Repeating, It's Only A Movie … Only A Movie … A Movie … Only A Movie.'

Last House on the Left
US 1972 91m colour
Hallmark (Sean S. Cunningham)
V*, L

Parents seek revenge after their daughter is raped and killed by a gang of escaped convicts.

Low-budget shocker, updating and debasing Ingmar Bergman's *Virgin Spring*.

wd Wes Craven *ph* Victor Hurwitz *m* Steve Chapin, David Hess *ed* Wes Craven

David Hess, Lacy Grantham, Sandra Cassel, Marc Sheffler, Jeramie Rain, Fred Lincoln

Last House on the Left Part II: see *A Bay of Blood*

The Last Hunt *
US 1956 103m Eastmancolor Cinemascope
MGM (Dore Schary)

Buffalo hunters fall out with each other.

Terse, brutish outdoor Western with something to say about old Western myths and a famous ending in which the bad guy freezes to death while waiting to gun down the hero.

wd Richard Brooks *ph* Russell Harlan *m* Daniele Amfitheatrof

Stewart Granger, Robert Taylor, Debra Paget, Lloyd Nolan, Russ Tamblyn, Constance Ford

The Last Hurrah **
US 1958 125m bw
Columbia (John Ford)
V*, L

The political boss of a New England town fights his last campaign.

Enjoyable if disjointed melodrama, an old man's film crammed with cameo performances from familiar faces: important as one of Hollywood's great sentimental reunions.

w Frank Nugent, *novel* Edwin O'Connor *d* John Ford *ph* Charles Lawton Jnr

Spencer Tracy, Jeffrey Hunter, Dianne Foster, *Pat O'Brien*, Basil Rathbone, Edward Brophy, Donald Crisp, James Gleason, John Carradine, Ricardo Cortez, Wallace Ford, Frank McHugh, Frank Albertson, Anna Lee, Jane Darwell, Willis Bouchey, Basil Ruysdael

† A TV version was subsequently made with Carroll O'Connor.

Last Images of the Shipwreck
Argentina/Spain 1989 129m colour
Palace/Cinequanon/TVE (Hugo Lauria)
V
original title: *Ultimas Imagenes del Naufragio*

A would-be writer befriends a prostitute and her crooked brother in order to gather material for a novel.

Playing rather unsuccessful games with illusion and reality, this odd movie soon loses its way.

wd Eliseo Subiela *ph* Alberto Basail *m* Pedro Aznar *pd* Abel Facello *ed* Mercela Saenz

Lorenzo Quniteros, Noemi Frenkel, Hugo Soto, Pablo Brichta, Sara Benitez, Andres Tiengo, Alicia Aller, Alfredo Stuart

The Last Journey *
GB 1935 66m bw
Twickenham (Julius Hagen)

The driver of an express train, driven mad with jealousy, goes berserk.

Workmanlike little train suspenser with an exciting climax.

w John Soutar, H. Fowler Mear *story* J. Jefferson Farjeon *d* Bernard Vorhaus

Godfrey Tearle, Hugh Williams, Julien Mitchell, Judy Gunn, Nelson Keys, Frank Pettingell, Olga Lindo, Sydney Fairbrother

The Last Laugh ***
Germany 1924 73m approx (24 fps) bw silent
UFA
V*
original title: *Der Letzte Mann*

The old doorman of a luxury hotel is given the job of lavatory attendant but comes into a fortune and gets his revenge.

Ironic anecdote made important by its virtual abandonment of dialogue and whole-hearted adoption of the camera eye technique which gives some thrilling dramatic effects.

w Carl Mayer *d* F. W. Murnau *ph* Karl Freund

Emil Jannings, Max Hiller, Maly Delschaft, Hans Unterkirchen

'A marvellous picture – marvellous in its simplicity, its economy of effect, its expressiveness, and its dramatic power.' – *Life*

† A German remake of 1955 had Hans Albers in the lead and was of no interest.

The Last Man to Hang?
GB 1956 75m bw
ACT Films/Columbia

Sir Roderick Strood is on trial for the murder of his neurotic wife.

Reasonably interesting co-feature based on Gerald Bullett's *The Jury*; the title refers to the no-hanging bill then passing through Parliament.

w Gerald Bullett and others *d* Terence Fisher

Tom Conway, Elizabeth Sellars, Eunice Gayson, Freda Jackson, Hugh Latimer, Anthony Newley, Margaretta Scott

The Last Married Couple in America
US 1979 102m Technicolor
Universal/Cates Brothers (John Shaner)
V*

A Los Angeles couple resist the efforts of their friends to involve them in the swinging life.

Tolerable sex comedy of modern mores, a shade too long delayed after *Bob and Carol and Ted and Alice*.

w John Herman Shaner *d* Gilbert Cates *ph* Ralph Woolsey *m* Charles Fox *pd* Gene Callahan

Natalie Wood, George Segal, Richard Benjamin, Arlene Golonka, Alan Arbus, Marilyn Sokol, Dom DeLuise, Valerie Harper

The Last Metro ****
France 1980 131m Fujicolor
Les Films du Carrosse/Andrea/SEDIF/TF1/SFP (Jean-José Richer)
V, V*, S
original title: *Le Dernier Métro*

In occupied Paris, the Jewish manager of a theatre hides in the cellar of the building.

Tightly enclosed symbolic melodrama of oppression and release that concentrates on individual lives caught up in a moment of mass madness and seeking refuge in their dedication to their art.

w François Truffaut, Suzanne Schiffman *d* François Truffaut *ph* Nestor Almendros *m* Georges Delerue *ad* Jean-Pierre Kohut Svelko *ed* Martine Barraque

Catherine Deneuve, Gérard Depardieu, Jean Poiret, Heinz Bennent

AAN: best foreign film

The Last Mile *
US 1932 84m bw
World Wide (E. W. Hammons)
V*

Tensions mount in jail as the execution of Killer Mears approaches.

Strident melodrama which works up quite a head of hysteria.

w Seton I. Miller *play* John Wexley *d* Sam Bischoff *ph* Arthur Edeson

Preston Foster, Howard Phillips, George E. Stone, Noel Madison

'Subject's lure is confined to the morbid-minded sensation seeker . . . without feminine interest.' – *Variety*

The Last Mile
US 1959 81m bw
UA/Vanguard (Milton Subotsky)

Even more hysterical remake, retaining the original period.

A cheerless, though literally electrifying, entertainment.

w Milton Subotsky, Seton I. Miller *d* Howard W. Koch *ph* Joseph Brun *m* Van Alexander

Mickey Rooney, Clifford David, Frank Conroy, Frank Overton, Leon Janney

The Last Movie
US 1971 108m Technicolor
Universal
V*

Moviemakers go to Peru to film a Western.

Muddled and pretentious melodrama following the success of *Easy Rider*.

w Stewart Stern   d Dennis Hopper   m Kris Kristofferson

Dennis Hopper, Julie Adams, Peter Fonda, Kris Kristofferson, Rod Cameron, Daniel Ades, Michael Anderson Jnr, Sam Fuller

The Last of England

GB   1987   87m   bw and colour
Blue Dolphin/Anglo International/British Screen/Channel 4/
   ZDF-Tartan Films (James Mackay, Don Boyd)
L, S

Impressionistic mix of home movies and images of urban disintegration.

Too personal to communicate much, even to a sympathetic audience.

d Derek Jarman   ph Derek Jarman, Christopher Hughes, Cerith Wyn Evans, Richard Heslop   m Simon Turner, Andy Gill, Mayo Thompson, Albert Oehlen, Barry Adamson, El Tito   pd Christopher Hobbs   ed Peter Cartwright, Angus Cook, Sally Yeadon, John Maybury

Spring, John Phillips, Gay Gaynor, Gerrard McArthur, Matthew Hawkins, Tilda Swinton, Spencer Leigh

The Last of His Tribe

US   1992   90m   CFI colour
HBO Pictures/River City (John Levoff, Robert Lovenheim)
V, V*

In the early 1900s a Californian anthropologist forms a friendship with Ishi, the last surviving Yahi Indian who still lives in the traditional way.

Well-meaning but dull re-telling of a fascinating true story.

w Stephen Harrigan   d Harry Hook   ph Martin Fuhrer   m John E. Keane   pd Michael Baugh   ed Bill Yahraus

Jon Voight, Graham Greene, David Ogden Stiers, Jack Blessing, Anne Archer

† The film was made for cable television in the States and released direct to video in Britain.

The Last of Mrs Cheyney

US   1929   94m   bw
MGM

A confidence woman in British high society falls in love.

Old theatrical warhorse, much filmed but never very satisfactorily. (See below.)

w Hans Kraly, Claudine West   play Frederick Lonsdale   d Sidney Franklin   ph William Daniels

Norma Shearer, Basil Rathbone, George Barraud, Hedda Hopper, Maude Turner Gordon, Herbert Bunston

AAN: Hans Kraly

The Last of Mrs Cheyney

US   1937   98m   bw
MGM (Lawrence Weingarten)

Adequate, unexciting remake.

w Leon Gordon, Samson Raphaelson, Monckton Hoffe   d Richard Boleslawski   ph George Folsey   m William Axt

Joan Crawford, Robert Montgomery, William Powell, Frank Morgan, Jessie Ralph, Nigel Bruce, Benita Hume, Melville Cooper, Sara Haden

'Good film fodder, although not particularly socko.' – *Variety*

† A further remake was *The Law and the Lady* (qv).

'Any number can play; any number can die!'

The Last of Sheila *

US   1973   123m   Technicolor
Warner (Herbert Ross)
V*

A Hollywood star is killed by a hit-and-run driver; a year later her husband invites six friends to his yacht, and murders begin.

Confused, in-jokey showbiz whodunnit with flashes of interest.

w Stephen Sondheim, Anthony Perkins   d Herbert Ross   ph Gerry Turpin   m Billy Goldenberg   ad Ken Adam

Richard Benjamin, Dyan Cannon, James Coburn, James Mason, Joan Hackett, Ian MacShane, Raquel Welch

'The most teasing riddles for an audience are likely to be the real identities of the personalities being satirized.' – *MFB*

Last of the Bad Men

US   1957   79m   DeLuxe   Cinemascope
Allied Artists (Vincent M. Fennelly)

In the 1870s, a Chicago detective poses as a wanted man in order to infiltrate a gang of outlaws in Colorado.

A mediocre Western in which much of the narrative consists of a portentous voice-over in the documentary style of *Dragnet*, turning it into more of an illustrated lecture than a movie.

w Daniel B. Ullman, David Chantler   d Paul Landres   ph Ellsworth Fredricks   m Paul Sawtell   ad David Milton   ed William Austin

George Montgomery, James Best, Douglas Kennedy, Keith Larsen, Robert Foulk, Willis Bouchey, Michael Ansara

The Last of the Buccaneers

US   1950   79m   Technicolor
Columbia

The story of Jean Lafitte, French privateer in the war of 1812.

Cheerful low-budget swashbuckler.

w Robert E. Kent   d Lew Landers

Paul Henreid, Jack Oakie, Karin Booth, Edgar Barrier, Mary Anderson, John Dehner

The Last of the Comanches *

US   1953   85m   Technicolor
Columbia (Buddy Adler)
V*
GB title: *The Sabre and the Arrow*

Survivors of an Indian raid take refuge in an abandoned mission until help arrives.

Competent Western remake of *Sahara* (which was a remake of *The Lost Patrol*).

w Kenneth Gamet   d André de Toth   ph Charles Lawton Jnr   m George Duning

Broderick Crawford, Barbara Hale, Lloyd Bridges, Martin Milner

Last of the Fast Guns

US   1959   82m   Eastmancolor   Cinemascope
Universal-International

Rival gunfighters form a friendship but fall out over their mission.

Mildly unusual Western programmer.

w David P. Harmon   d George Sherman

Gilbert Roland, Jock Mahoney, Linda Cristal, Eduard Franz, Lorne Greene, Carl Benton Reid

The Last of the Finest: see *Blue Heat*

The Last of the Mohicans

US   1936   91m   bw
Edward Small
V*, L

Incidents during colonial America's French-Indian war.

Vigorous if rough-and-ready Western, later remade (poorly) as *Last of the Redmen* and as a Canadian TV series.

w Philip Dunne, John Balderston, Paul Perez, Daniel Moore   novel James Fenimore Cooper   d George B. Seitz   ph Robert Planck   m Roy Webb

Randolph Scott, Binnie Barnes, Bruce Cabot, Henry Wilcoxon, Heather Angel, Hugh Buckler

The Last of the Mohicans *

US   1992   122m   colour   Scope
Warner/Morgan Creek (Michael Mann, Hunt Lowry)
V, V*, L, S

The white, adopted son of an Indian rescues a British officer's two daughters from hostile Indians and falls in love with one of them.

An ambitious but flawed epic adventure: the characterization is as shallow as the photography, the action is repetitious, the narrative lacks suspense and the romance is unconvincing, with Cooper's self-reliant woodsman here tamed into domesticity.

w Michael Mann, Christopher Crowe   novel James Fenimore Cooper   story screenplay by Philip Dunne   d Michael Mann   ph Dante Spinotti   m Trevor Jones, Randy Edelman   pd Wolf Kroeger   ed Dov Hoenig, Arthur Schmidt

Daniel Day-Lewis, Madeleine Stowe, Russell Means, Eric Schweig, Jodhi May, Steven Waddington, Wes Studi, Maurice Roeves, Patrice Chereau

'Whether it was because we were young or the movies were young or the world was at least youngish, old-fashioned Hollywood history was exhilarating. In retrospect there is something alarming about its simplicities and the enthusiasm we brought to it. It is the great virtue of this grandly scaled yet deliriously energetic movie that it reanimates that long-ago feeling without patronizing it – and without making us think we will wake up some day once again embarrassed by it.' – *Richard Schickel, Time*

'Michael Mann has been aiming all along at two very different targets, trying to turn an adventure story into a responsible account of Native American life, while also making it lovey-dovey enough for the market place.' – *Adam Mars-Jones, Independent*

AAN: sound

Last of the Red Hot Lovers *

US   1972   98m   Technicolor
Paramount (Howard W. Koch)
V*, L

A middle-aged fish restaurateur feels the need for an extra-marital spree.

Modest, plainly-filmed sex comedy from a reliable stable.

w Neil Simon   play Neil Simon   d Gene Saks   ph Victor J. Kemper   m Neal Hefti

Alan Arkin, Paula Prentiss, Sally Kellerman, Renée Taylor

Last of the Redmen

US   1947   78m   Vitacolor
Sam Katzman/Columbia
GB title: *Last of the Redskins*

British soldiers escort a general's children through Indian country.

Tinpot rendition of *The Last of the Mohicans*.

w Herbert Dalmas, George H. Plympton   d George Sherman

Jon Hall, Michael O'Shea, Evelyn Ankers, Julie Bishop, Buster Crabbe

Last of the Secret Agents

US 1966 90m Technicolor
Paramount

Two odd job men are recruited as spies.

Pratfall comedy featuring a briefly existing comedy double act.

w Mel Tolkin d Norman Abbott

Marty Allen, Steve Rossi, John Williams, Nancy Sinatra, Lou Jacobi, Theo Marcuse, Sig Rumann

'Open war between a handful of English and swarming tribesmen! Hidden war between fellow-officers who love the same woman!'

The Last Outpost *

US 1935 75m bw
Paramount (E. Lloyd Sheldon)

A British officer is captured by the Kurds and freed by an adventurer whose wife he covets.

Patchy, unusual adventure story with good moments.

w Philip MacDonald story F. Britten Austin d Charles Barton, Louis Gasnier ph Theodor Sparkuhl

Cary Grant, Claude Rains, Gertrude Michael, Kathleen Burke, Colin Tapley, Akim Tamiroff, Billy Bevan, Jameson Thomas

'Loosely-woven melodramatic mélange.' – Variety

'Half of it is remarkably good and half of it quite abysmally bad. One can even put one's finger on the joins.' – Graham Greene

The Last Outpost

US 1951 89m Technicolor
Paramount/Pine-Thomas

A Civil War colonel finds his brother fighting on the other side.

Routine historical action romance.

w Geoffrey Homes, G. Worthing Yates, Winston Miller d Lewis R. Foster ph Loyal Griggs m Lucien Cailliet

Ronald Reagan, Bruce Bennett, Rhonda Fleming, Noah Beery Jnr

The Last Page

GB 1952 84m bw
Hammer-Lippert
US title: Manbait

A bookseller is framed for the death of a blackmailer.

Curious English mystery with American stars.

w Frederick Knott play James Hadley Chase d Terence Fisher

George Brent, Marguerite Chapman, Diana Dors, Raymond Huntley, Peter Reynolds, Eleanor Summerfield

The Last Parade

US 1931 82m bw
Columbia

A detective and a racketeer are buddies in the war, but not afterwards.

Predictable character melodrama with no remaining interest.

w Dorothy Howell, Casey Robinson d Erle C. Kenton

Jack Holt, Constance Cummings, Tom Moore, Gaylord Pendleton

'In for money, but not that strong for a holdover.' – Variety

The Last Picture Show ****

US 1971 118m bw
Columbia/LPS/BBS (Stephen J. Friedman)
V, V*, L, S

Teenage affairs in a small Texas town in 1951, ending with the hero's embarkation for Korea and the closing of the tatty cinema.

Penetrating nostalgia with over-emphasis on sex; the detail is the attraction.

w Larry McMurtry, Peter Bogdanovich d Peter Bogdanovich ph Robert Surtees m original recordings pd Polly Platt

Timothy Bottoms, Jeff Bridges, Cybill Shepherd, Ben Johnson, Cloris Leachman, Ellen Burstyn

'The most important work by a young American director since Citizen Kane.' – Paul D. Zimmerman

'So many things in it are so good that I wish I liked it more.' – Stanley Kauffmann

'Colour always had a tendency to prettify, and I didn't want that. I didn't want it to be a nostalgic piece.' – Peter Bogdanovich

† Texasville, a sequel featuring many of the same actors, was filmed by Bogdanovich in 1990.

AA: Ben Johnson; Cloris Leachman

AAN: best picture; script; Peter Bogdanovich (as director); Robert Surtees; Jeff Bridges; Ellen Burstyn

The Last Posse

US 1953 73m bw
Columbia

Members of a thief-catching posse fall out on the way and return in disgrace.

Stumbling little Western, a poor return to the star after All the King's Men.

w Seymour and Connie Lee Bennett, Kenneth Gamet d Alfred Werker

Broderick Crawford, John Derek, Wanda Hendrix, Charles Bickford

'A different kind of love story!'

The Last Remake of Beau Geste

US 1977 85m Technicolor
Universal (William S. Gilmore Jnr)
V*

The Geste brothers find themselves in the Foreign Legion after the theft of the Blue Water sapphire.

Woebegone spoof of a romantic original, with most of the jokes totally irrelevant to the purpose and seldom at all funny.

w Marty Feldman, Chris J. Allen d Marty Feldman ph Gerry Fisher m John Morris

Marty Feldman, Michael York, Ann-Margret, Peter Ustinov, Trevor Howard, James Earl Jones, Henry Gibson, Terry-Thomas, Roy Kinnear, Spike Milligan, Hugh Griffith, Irene Handl

'A ragbag of a film which looks like nothing so much as a Monty Python extravaganza in which inspiration has run dry and the comic timing gone sadly awry.' – Tom Milne, MFB

Last Rites

US 1988 103m DeLuxe
MGM (Donald P. Bellisario, Patrick McCormick)
V*, L

A Catholic priest falls in love with a woman whom his gangster father wishes to kill.

Turgid thriller, slow-paced and uninteresting despite its hints of incest and emphasis on sex.

wd Donald P. Bellisario ph David Watkin m Bruce Broughton ed Pembroke J. Herring

Tom Berenger, Daphne Zuniga, Chick Vennera, Anne Twomey, Paul Dooley, Dane Clark, Vassili Lambrinos

The Last Run *

US 1971 92m Metrocolor Panavision
MGM (Carter de Haven)

An ex-Chicago gangster retired to a Portuguese fishing village undertakes one last fatal job.

Well-made, rather uninteresting downbeat melodrama.

w Alan Sharp d Richard Fleischer ph Sven Nykvist m Jerry Goldsmith

George C. Scott, Tony Musante, Trish Van Devere

The Last Safari

GB 1967 110m Technicolor
Paramount (Henry Hathaway)
V*

A disillusioned white hunter takes on one last safari.

Dullsville adventure story with good animal photography redeeming some of the clichés.

w John Gay novel Gilligan's Last Elephant by Gerald Hanley d Henry Hathaway ph Ted Moore m Johnny Dankworth

Stewart Grainger, Kaz Garas, Gabriella Licudi, Johnny Sekka, Liam Redmond, Eugene Deckers

The Last Shot You Hear

GB 1970 90m bw
Lippert-TCF (Jack Parsons)

Lovers plot murder, but the scheme backfires.

Unassuming mystery programmer from a West End success.

w Tim Shields play The Sound of Murder by William Fairchild d Gordon Hessler

Hugh Marlowe, Zena Walker, Patricia Haines, William Dysart, Thorley Walters

The Last Stage *

Poland 1947 110m bw
Film Polski
original title: Ostatni Etap

Women suffer but one is finally rescued from the Nazi concentration camp at Auschwitz.

A dour, obsessive, horrifying record of human inhumanity, set in the actual camp and made by two former inmates.

w Wanda Jakubowska, Gerda Schneider d Wanda Jakubowska ph Borys Monastyrski m R. Palester

Huguette Faget, W. Bartowna, T. Gorecka

The Last Starfighter *

US 1984 101m Technicolor Panavision
Lorimar/Universal (Gary Adelson, Edward O. Denault)
V*, L, S

A teenage whiz at video games is abducted by the survivors of a distant planet who need his skills if they are to outwit their enemies.

A surprisingly pleasant variation on the Star Wars boom, with sharp and witty performances from two reliable character actors and some elegant gadgetry to offset the teenage mooning.

w Jonathan Betuel d Nick Castle ph King Baggot m Craig Safan pd Ron Cobb ed C. Timothy O'Meara

Lance Guest, Robert Preston, Dan O'Herlihy, Catherine Mary Stewart, Barbara Bosson, Norman Snow

Last Summer *

US 1969 97m Eastmancolor
Alsid/Francis (Alfred Crown, Sidney Beckerman)
V*

Well-to-do teenagers have sexual adventures on a summer seaside holiday.

Striking off-beat melodrama with vividly sketched characters.

w *Eleanor Perry*, *novel* Evan Hunter   *d* Frank Perry
ph Gerald Hirschfeld   *m* John Simon

Barbara Hershey, Richard Thomas, Bruce Davison, Cathy Burns, Ernesto Gonzales, Ralph Waite

AAN: Cathy Burns

The Last Sunset
US   1961   112m   Eastmancolor
U-I (Brynaprod) (Eugene Frenke, Edward Lewis)

A killer and his hunter learn a lot about each other before the final showdown.

Slow psycho-Western with pretensions to tragedy.

w Dalton Trumbo   *novel Showdown at Crazy Horse* by Howard Rigsby   *d* Robert Aldrich   *ph* Ernest Laszlo   *m* Ernest Gold

Rock Hudson, Kirk Douglas, Dorothy Malone, Carol Lynley, Joseph Cotten, Regis Toomey, Neville Brand

The Last Supper *
Cuba   1976   125m   colour
Cuban Film Institute (Santiago Llapin, Camilo Vives)
original title: *La Ultima Cena*

In 18th-century Cuba, an aristocratic plantation owner attempts to get on better terms with his slaves.

Intermittently powerful, if overlong, political drama on the corruption of power and the acquiesence of the Church in the requirements of the State.

w Tomás Gonzalez, Maria Eugenia Haya, T. G. Alea   *d* T. G. Alea   *ph* Mario García Joya   *m* Leo Brouwer   *ad* Carlos Arditi   *ed* Nelson Rodriguez

Nelson Villagra, Silvano Rey, Luis Alberto García, José Antonio Rodriguez, Mario Balmaseda

'A laborious historical analogy, clumsy in the making and in implication, ineffectual esthetically and, for that matter, politically.' – *Stanley Kauffmann*

Last Tango in Paris *
France/Italy/US   1972   129m   Technicolor
Les Artistes Associés/PEA/UA (Alberto Grimaldi)
V, V*, L

A middle-aged man and a young French girl have a doomed love affair.

Pretentious sex melodrama mainly notable for being banned.

w Bernardo Bertolucci, Franco Arcalli   *d* Bernardo Bertolucci   *ph* Vittorio Storaro   *m* Gato Barbieri

Marlon Brando, Maria Schneider, Jean-Pierre Léaud

'An intense meditation on the realization of mortality.' – *Sight and Sound*

AAN: Bernardo Bertolucci (as director); Marlon Brando

The Last Temptation of Christ *
US/Canada   1988   163m   Technicolor
Universal/Cineplex Odeon (Harry Ufland)
V, V*, L, S

On the cross, Jesus dreams of escaping his destiny and living the life of an ordinary man.

Beautifully shot and strikingly acted, but wordy and too long; pre-release notoriety muffled consideration of the film's intentions.

w Paul Schrader   *novel* Nikos Kazantzakis   *d* Martin Scorsese   *ph* Michael Ballhaus   *m* Peter Gabriel   *pd* John Beard

Willem Dafoe, Harvey Keitel, Barbara Hershey, Harry Dean Stanton, David Bowie

'A film of challenging ideas and not salacious provocations.' – *Variety*

AAN: Martin Scorsese

The Last Time I Saw Archie
US   1961   98m   bw
UA/Mark VII/Manzanita/Talbot (Jack Webb)

Adventures of a con man amid overage civilian pilots at an army/air force base.

Patchy service comedy.

w William Bowers   *d* Jack Webb   *ph* Joe MacDonald   *m* Frank Comstock

Jack Webb, Robert Mitchum, Martha Hyer, France Nuyen, Louis Nye, Jimmy Lydon, Richard Arlen, Don Knotts, Robert Strauss, Joe Flynn

The Last Time I Saw Paris
US   1954   116m   Technicolor
MGM (Jack Cummings)
V*, L

A writer recalls his romance with a wealthy American girl in Paris.

Dull romantic drama which very deadeningly and predictably updates F. Scott Fitzgerald's *Babylon Revisited*.

w Julius J. and Philip G. Epstein, Richard Brooks   *d* Richard Brooks   *ph* Joseph Ruttenberg   *m* Conrad Salinger

Elizabeth Taylor, Van Johnson, Walter Pidgeon, Donna Reed, Eva Gabor

Last Train (dubbed)
France/Italy   1973   100m   Eastmancolor/bw
          Panavision
Lira/Capitolina (Raymond Danon)
original title: *Le Train*

In 1941, on a train fleeing from the Germans, a Frenchman becomes separated from his pregnant wife and young daughter and begins an affair with a German Jewish refugee.

Somewhat glum romance, set against a background of war and casual death, with a downbeat ending.

w Pascal Jardin, Pierre Granier-Deferre   *novel* Georges Simenon   *d* Pierre Granier-Deferre   *ph* Walter Wottitz   *m* Philippe Sarde   *ad* Jacques Saulnier   *ed* Jean Ravel

Jean-Louis Trintignant, Romy Schneider, Maurice Biraud, Regine, Serge Marquand, Anne Wiazemsky, Nike Arrighi

Last Train from Bombay
US   1952   72m   bw
Sam Katzman/Columbia

A diplomat in Bombay is falsely accused of the murder of an old friend.

Stilted melodrama culminating in a hectic train ride.

w Robert Yale Libbott   *d* Fred F. Sears

Jon Hall, Christine Larson, Lisa Ferraday, Douglas Kennedy

Last Train from Gun Hill *
US   1959   98m   Technicolor   Vistavision
(Paramount) Hal B. Wallis/Bryna
V, V*

A marshal tracks down the man who raped and murdered his wife; it turns out to be the son of an old friend.

Good suspense and action Western culminating in a *High Noon* situation.

w James Poe   *d John Sturges*   *ph* Charles Lang Jnr   *m* Dimitri Tiomkin

Kirk Douglas, Anthony Quinn, Earl Holliman, Carolyn Jones, Brian Hutton

'Flaming love drama set against the background of Spain's Civil War!'

The Last Train from Madrid
US   1937   85m   bw
Paramount (George M. Arthur)

A variety of people escape the fighting in the Spanish Civil War.

Tawdry topical melodrama with cliché characters and situations.

w Louis Stevens, Robert Wyler   *d* James Hogan   *ph* Harry Fischbeck   *md* Boris Morros

Dorothy Lamour, Lew Ayres, Gilbert Roland, Karen Morley, Lionel Atwill, Helen Mack, Robert Cummings, Olympe Bradna, Anthony Quinn, Lee Bowman, George Lloyd

'It is probably the worst film of the decade and should have been the funniest.' – *Graham Greene*

'Simply a topical and different background for a glib little fiction.' – *Frank S. Nugent*

The Last Tycoon
US   1976   124m   Technicolor
Paramount/Academy/Sam Spiegel
V*, L

The production head of a Hollywood studio in the thirties has his troubles complicated when he falls in love with a girl who reminds him of his dead wife.

Astonishingly inept and boring big budget all-star melodrama which doesn't even begin promisingly (the scenes from supposed thirties films are woefully inaccurate in style); it then bogs down in interminable dialogue scenes, leaving its famous cast all at sea.

w Harold Pinter   *novel* F. Scott Fitzgerald   *d* Elia Kazan   *ph* Victor Kemper   *m* Maurice Jarre   *pd* Eugene F. Callahan

Robert de Niro, Robert Mitchum, Tony Curtis, Jeanne Moreau, Jack Nicholson, Ingrid Boulting, Donald Pleasence, Ray Milland, Dana Andrews, John Carradine

'So enervated it's like a vampire movie after the vampires have left.' – *New Yorker*

'That the result is incoherent is no surprise; that it is so hollow and visually graceless adds a kind of wonder to the disappointment.' – *Sight and Sound*

'The breathless reverence that informs the movie kills it stone dead.' – *Michael Billington, Illustrated London News*

'It seems to me that Kazan and Pinter have failed disastrously, but then perhaps the task is impossible anyway.' – *Benny Green, Punch*

The Last Valley
GB   1970   128m   Eastmancolor   Todd-AO
ABC/Season/Seamaster (James Clavell)
V*

In 1641 during the Thirty Years War a scholar tries to defend a remote and prosperous Swiss valley against a horde of mercenaries.

Big-scale historical action picture crammed with pillage, torture, rape, death at the stake, throat cutting and general carnage; reasonably literate for all that, and convincingly set.

wd James Clavell   *novel* J. B. Pick   *ph* Norman Warwick   *m* John Barry   *ad* Peter Mullins

Michael Caine, Omar Sharif, Florinda Bolkan, Nigel Davenport, Per Oscarsson, Arthur O'Connell, Brian Blessed

The Last Voyage *
US   1960   91m   Metrocolor
MGM/Andrew and Virginia Stone
V*

A boiler room explosion causes an old passenger liner to sink.

Spectacular if dramatically deficient actioner for which a genuine liner (awaiting scrapping) was sunk.

wd Andrew L. Stone   *ph* Hal Mohr   *m* Rudy Schrager

Robert Stack, Dorothy Malone, Edmond O'Brien, George Sanders, Woody Strode, Jack Kruschen

'A prolonged nerve stretcher.' – *MFB*

'They pitted the fire of their youth against the flame of the frontier – when America was moving west!'

The Last Wagon
US   1956   99m   Eastmancolor   Cinemascope
TCF (William B. Hawks)

A half-breed wanted for murder joins an 1875 wagon train.

Heavy-going big-scale Western.

w James Edward Grant, Delmer Daves, Gwen Bagni   d Delmer Daves   ph Wilfrid Cline   m Lionel Newman

Richard Widmark, Felicia Farr, Tommy Rettig, Susan Kohner, Ray Stricklyn, Nick Adams, Carl Benton Reid

The Last Waltz
US   1978   115m   DeLuxe
UA/Martin Scorsese, Jonathan Taplin
V*, L, S

Rock documentary featuring the last concert of The Band.

An occasion for specialists, very adequately packaged.

d Martin Scorsese   ph Michael Chapman   pd Boris Leven

The Last Warning *
US   1929   88m   bw
Universal

Murder backstage.

Shot as a silent film, with sound hurriedly added, this remains a stylish comedy-thriller with all the familiar ingredients of the whodunnit.

w Alfred A. Cohn   d Paul Leni   ph Hal Mohr

Laura La Plante, Montagu Love, Roy D'Arcy, John Boles, Mack Swain, Slim Summerville, Margaret Livingston

† Remade in 1938 as The House of Fear, a William Gargan second feature.

The Last Warning
US   1938   62m   bw
Universal (Irving Starr)

A private eye mystery.

Better-than-average second feature.

w Edmund L. Hartmann   novel The Dead Don't Care by Jonathan Latimer   d Albert S. Rogell

Preston Foster, Joyce Compton, Frank Jenks

The Last Warrior: see Flap

The Last Wave *
Australia   1977   106m   Atlab
(UA) Ayer/MacElroy/Derek Power
V*

During a spell of freak weather, a lawyer has recurrent dreams which give him the key to an Aborigine prophecy about the world being destroyed by flood . . .

Curious supernatural drama successfully played as a mystery, with excellent atmosphere and special effects.

w Peter Weir, Tony Morphett, Petru Popescu   d Peter Weir   ph Russell Boyd   m Charles Wain   pd Goran Warff

Richard Chamberlain, Olivia Hamnet, Frederick Parslow

'A Hitchcockian sense of minatory dislocation.' – Tim Pulleine, MFB

The Last Word
US   1979   105m   colour
Variety International Pictures

An Irish inventor by wily stratagems prevents the demolition of the apartment block he occupies.

Oddly old-fashioned comedy drama of little obvious appeal.

w Michael Varhol, Greg Smith and Kit Carson   d Roy Boulting

Richard Harris, Karen Black, Martin Landau, Biff McGuire

Last Year at Marienbad ***
France/Italy   1961   94m   bw   Dyaliscope
Terra/Tamara/Cormoran/Precitel/Como/Argos/Cinetel/Silver/Cineriz(Raymond Froment)
V, V*

original title: L'Année Dernière à Marienbad

In a vast old-fashioned hotel, a man meets a woman who may or may not have had an affair with him the previous year in Marienbad – or was it Frederiksbad?

A dreamy, elegant film which presents a puzzle with no solution. It has its attractions for film buffs and cryptogram addicts, but is not for anyone who simply wants to be told a story.

w Alain Robbe-Grillet   d Alain Resnais   ph Sacha Vierny   m Francis Seyrig   ad Jacques Saulnier

Delphine Seyrig, Giorgio Albertazzi, Sacha Pitoeff

'Elaborate, ponderous and meaningless.' – Newsweek

'Clearly the film's creators know exactly what they want to do and have done it with complete success. Whether one responds to the result is entirely a matter of temperament.' – John Russell Taylor, MFB

AAN: Alain Robbe-Grillet

The Late Edwina Black *
GB   1951   78m   bw
IFD/Elvey-Gartside (Ernest Gartside)
L
US title: Obsessed

When a schoolteacher's wife is found dead, the police have three suspects.

Adequately suspenseful Victorian thriller from a successful play.

w Charles Frank, David Evans   play William Dinner, William Morum   d Maurice Elvey   ph Stephen Dade   m Allan Gray

Geraldine Fitzgerald, David Farrar, Roland Culver, Jean Cadell, Mary Merrall, Harcourt Williams, Charles Heslop, Ronald Adam

'Tomorrow wasn't just another day.'
Late for Dinner
US   1991   93m   DeLuxe
First Independent/New Line/Castle Rock (Dan Lupovitz, W. D. Richter)
V, V*

After being unwittingly frozen for 19 years, a man and his retarded brother-in-law wake up to discover that the world has moved on to 1991.

Rip van Winkle without a twinkle.

w Mark Andrus   d W. D. Richter   ph Peter Sova   m David Mansfield   pd Lilly Kilvert   ed Richard Chew, Robert Leighton

Brian Wimmer, Peter Berg, Marcia Gay Harden, Peter Gallagher, Colleen Flynn, Kyle Secor, Michael Beach

The Late George Apley *
US   1946   96m   bw
TCF (Fred Kohlmar)

The uneventful family life of a Boston blueblood.

Pleasant but tame family comedy-drama, solidly carpentered.

w Philip Dunne   novel John P. Marquand   d Joseph L. Mankiewicz   ph Joseph LaShelle   m Cyril Mockridge

Ronald Colman, Edna Best, Vanessa Brown, Richard Haydn, Peggy Cummins, Charles Russell

The Late Show *
US   1977   93m   Metrocolor
Warner (Robert Altman)
V*, L

An ageing private eye in Los Angeles finds that his ex-partner's death and a lost cat have a complex connection.

A more-or-less engaging spoof of, or perhaps a valediction to, the private eye genre, with engaging scenes marred by poor colour and occasional excesses of violent action.

wd Robert Benton   ph Chuck Rosher   m Ken Wannberg   ed Lou Lombardo, Peter Appleton

Art Carney, Lily Tomlin, Bill Macy, Ruth Nelson, Howard Duff, Joanna Cassidy, Eugene Roche

'On its own terms, it's perfectly executed. The squalid settings stink of decay; the spare pacing captures the tough style of Hammett prose; and the stylized use of blood puts some sting into murder.' – Frank Rich, New York Post

AAN: Robert Benton (for script)

Latin Lovers
US   1953   104m   Technicolor
MGM (Joe Pasternak)
V*

An heiress on holiday in Brazil looks for a man who will love her for herself alone.

Barren romantic drama, flatfooted and drawn out.

w Isobel Lennart   d Mervyn Le Roy   ph Joseph Ruttenberg   m George Stoll

Lana Turner, Ricardo Montalban, John Lund, Louis Calhern, Jean Hagen

Latin Quarter *
GB   1945   80m   bw
British National (Louis H. Jackson, Derrick de Marney)
US title: Frenzy

In 1890s Paris a mad sculptor murders his fiancée and hides her inside his latest exhibit.

Artificial-looking but melodramatically effective thriller with a chilling climax and a detailed Degas-period background.

wd Vernon Sewell   play L'Angoisse by Pierre Mills, Charles Vylars   ph Gunther Krampf

Derrick de Marney, Joan Greenwood, Beresford Egan, Frederick Valk, Lily Kann, Martin Miller

Laugh and Get Rich
US   1931   72m   bw
RKO

A man invests his wife's money in a tyre with a whistling valve.

Inconsequential comedy with ancient jokes.

w Ralph Spence, Gregory La Cava   d Gregory La Cava

Hugh Herbert, Edna May Oliver, Dorothy Lee, Robert Emmett Keane

'Entertainment for the willing.' – Variety

Laugh with Max Linder **
France   1963   88m   bw
Films Max Linder
original title: En Compagnie de Max Linder

Excerpts from three of the dapper comedian's most famous American comedies: Be My Wife (1921), The Three Must-Get-Theres (1922), Seven Years' Bad Luck (1923).

A compilation which must serve as a consensus of this almost forgotten comedian's work. The gag with a broken mirror in particular was borrowed by innumerable other comedians, notably the Marx Brothers in Duck Soup. Audiences new to Linder's work will find him not especially sympathetic but capable of many felicities. He wrote, produced and directed all three films.

compiler Maud Max Linder

Laugh Your Blues Away
US   1943   65m   bw
Jack Fier/Columbia

Jobless actors pose as guests at a society party.

Feeble filler.

w Harry Sauber   d Charles Barton

Jinx Falkenberg, Bert Gordon (radio's 'mad Russian'), Isobel Elsom, Douglass Drake

Laughing Anne
GB   1953   90m   Technicolor
Republic/Wilcox-Neagle

French Anne and her boxing lover are characters of the Javanese waterfront; he kills her after she has fallen for a sea captain.

Cheap and turgid adaptation of a Joseph Conrad story; the author would not recognize it. Studio settings put the lid on hilariously bad work all round.

w Pamela Bower   d Herbert Wilcox   ph Max Greene   m Anthony Collins

Margaret Lockwood, Forrest Tucker, Ronald Shiner, Wendell Corey, Robert Harris

Laughing at Trouble
US   1937   60m   bw
Max Golden/TCF

A small town newspaper editress untangles personal problems.

Acceptable second feature which almost became a series.

w Robert Ellis and Helen Logan   d Frank R. Strayer

Jane Darwell, Sara Haden, Lois Wilson, Margaret Hamilton, Allan Lane, John Carradine

Laughing Boy
US   1934   80m   bw
MGM

A young Navajo brave marries an outcast maiden.

Misguided and absurd melodrama for unsuitable stars.

w John Colton and John Lee Mahin   novel Oliver La Farge   d W. S. Van Dyke

Ramon Novarro, Lupe Velez, Chief Thunderbird, William Davidson

'Touchy theme and plot . . . below par as entertainment.' – *Variety*

Laughing Gravy ***
US   1931   20m   bw
Hal Roach
V (C)

Stan and Ollie retrieve their dog when the landlord throws it out into the snow.

One of the most endearing comedies of these stars, and one of the simplest.

w H. M. Walker   d James W. Horne

Laurel and Hardy, Charlie Hall

The Laughing Lady
GB   1946   93m   Technicolor
Louis H. Jackson/British National

During the French revolution, an artist under sentence is required to steal an English lady's pearls.

Heavy-going operetta with the sense that all concerned have bitten off more than they can chew.

w Jack Whittingham   play Ingram d'Abbes   d Paul Stein

Anne Ziegler, Webster Booth, Peter Graves, Felix Aylmer, Francis L. Sullivan, Paul Dupuis, Ralph Truman

'Eight people know who the killer is – and they're all dead!'
The Laughing Policeman *
US   1973   112m   DeLuxe
TCF (Stuart Rosenberg)
V*
GB title: *An Investigation of Murder*

A mad machine-gunner eludes the San Francisco police.

Downbeat, semi-documentary police thriller with pretensions. Too complex by half, with an overplus of characterization, but the location work is excellent.

w Thomas Rickman   novel Maj Sjowall, Per Wahloo   d Stuart Rosenberg   ph David Walsh   m Charles Fox

Walter Matthau, Bruce Dern, Lou Gossett, Albert Paulsen, Anthony Zerbe

Laughing Sinners
US   1931   71m   bw
MGM

A girl with a past joins the Salvation Army.

Glum romance which however started an effective star combination.

w Bess Meredyth and Martin Flavin   d Harry Beaumont

Joan Crawford, Clark Gable, Neil Hamilton, Marjorie Rambeau, Guy Kibbee

Laughter **
US   1930   99m   bw
Paramount (Herman J. Mankiewicz)

An ex-Follies girl marries a millionaire but later goes on a spree with the composer she once loved.

Sharply observed, before its time romantic comedy reminiscent now of the later *Philadelphia Story* in its attitudes to wealth and love. A precursor of the smart crazy comedies of the mid-thirties.

w Donald Ogden Stewart   d Harry d'Abbabie d'Arrast   ph George Folsey

Fredric March, Nancy Carroll, Frank Morgan, Glenn Anders, Diane Ellis

'One of the best talking pictures I have ever seen.' – *James Agate*

'A talkie with so fast a pace that it crowds the comprehension of half the customers . . . marked at intervals by superb dialogue and the quick hand of a smart director.' – *Pare Lorentz*

'A lovely sophisticated comedy.' – *New Yorker, 1977*

AAN: original story (Donald Ogden Stewart, Harry d'Abbadie d'Arrast, Douglas Doty)

Laughter in Paradise *
GB   1951   93m   bw
Transocean (Mario Zampi)

An eccentric leaves in his will a fortune for each of his relations providing they will perform certain embarrassing or criminal acts.

A funny idea gets half-hearted treatment, but the good bits are hilarious.

w Michael Pertwee, Jack Davies   d Mario Zampi   ph William McLeod   m Stanley Black

Alastair Sim, Joyce Grenfell, Hugh Griffith, Fay Compton, John Laurie, George Cole, Guy Middleton, Ronald Adam, Leslie Dwyer, A. E. Matthews, Beatrice Campbell

† Remade 1972 as *Some Will, Some Won't.*

Laughter in the Dark *
GB/France   1969   104m   DeLuxe
UA/Woodfall/Winkast/Marceau (Neil Hartley)

A wealthy art dealer is taken in by an ambitious usherette and her lover, and after being blinded in a car accident tries to kill them.

Unsatisfactory adaptation of a novel with a very specialized appeal: conventional swinging London and Riviera settings only confuse the spectator. Moments do work, though.

w Edward Bond   novel Vladimir Nabokov   d Tony Richardson   ph Dick Bush   m Raymond Leppard   ad Julia Trevelyan Oman

Nicol Williamson, Anna Karina, Jean-Claude Drouot, Peter Bowles, Sian Phillips

'It fails to create the slightest interest in its trio of repulsive characters.' – *Philip Strick*

Laughterhouse *
GB   1984   93m   colour
Greenpoint/Film Four International (Ann Scott)

A Norfolk farmer decides to walk his fattened geese to market.

An attempt to revive the tradition of Ealing comedy lands up somewhere on the wrong side of Group Three. Not enough plot, almost no jokes, and the geese are almost the only pleasant creatures.

w Brian Glover   d Richard Eyre   ph Clive Tickner   m Dominic Muldowney

Ian Holm, Penelope Wilton, Bill Owen, Richard Hope, Stephen Moore, Rosemary Martin

Laura ***
US   1944   85m   bw
TCF (Otto Preminger)
V, V*, L

A beautiful girl is murdered . . . or is she? A cynical detective investigates.

A quiet, streamlined little murder mystery that brought a new adult approach to the genre and heralded the mature *film noir* of the later forties. A small cast responds perfectly to a classically spare script, and in Clifton Webb a new star is born.

w Jay Dratler, Samuel Hoffenstein, Betty Reinhardt, novel Vera Caspary   d Otto Preminger   ph Joseph LaShelle   m David Raksin   ad Lyle Wheeler, Leland Fuller

Dana Andrews, Clifton Webb, Gene Tierney, Judith Anderson, Vincent Price, Dorothy Adams, James Flavin

WALDO LYDECKER (Clifton Webb): 'It's lavish, but I call it home.'
WALDO: 'I shall never forget the weekend Laura died. A silver sun burned through the sky like a huge magnifying glass. It was the hottest Sunday in my recollection. I felt as if I were the only human being left in New York . . . I had just begun Laura's story when another of those detectives came to see me. I had him wait.'
WALDO: 'In my case, self-absorption is completely justified. I have never discovered any other subject quite so worthy of my attention.'

'Everybody's favourite chic murder mystery.' – *New Yorker, 1977*

† Rouben Mamoulian directed some scenes before handing over to Preminger.

AA: Joseph LaShelle

AAN: script; Otto Preminger; Clifton Webb; art direction

Laurel and Hardy in Toyland: see *Babes in Toyland* (1934)

The Laurel and Hardy Murder Case
US   1930   30m   bw
Hal Roach

Heirs to a fortune are menaced by a mad murderer.

Empty spoof on *The Cat and the Canary* which affords little scope to Laurel and Hardy.

w H. M. Walker   d James Parrott

Laurel and Hardy's Laughing Twenties **
US 1965 90m bw
MGM/Robert Youngson
V, V*, L

Excerpts from lesser comedians of the period – Max Davidson, Charlie Chase – are interspersed with highlights from Laurel and Hardy's silent two-reelers.

A hilarious and craftsmanlike compilation, perhaps a little too long for its own good.

w/ ed Robert Youngson   m Skeets Alquist
commentator Jay Jackson

† Films extracted include *Putting Pants on Philip, From Soup to Nuts, Wrong Again, The Finishing Touch, Liberty, Double Whoopee, Leave 'Em Laughing, You're Darn Tooting* and the custard pie climax from *The Battle of the Century*.

The Lavender Hill Mob ****
GB 1951 78m bw
Ealing (Michael Truman)
V, V*, L

A timid bank clerk conceives and executes a bullion robbery.

Superbly characterized and inventively detailed comedy, one of the best ever made at Ealing or in Britain.

w T.E.B. Clarke   d Charles Crichton   ph Douglas Slocombe   m Georges Auric

Alec Guinness, Stanley Holloway, Sidney James, Alfie Bass, Marjorie Fielding, Edie Martin, John Gregson, Gibb McLaughlin

'Amusing situations and dialogue are well paced and sustained throughout: the climax is delightful.' – *MFB*

'An outrageous comedy, of course, but the observations of detail and character are so true, the sense of a familiar place so sharp, that few will resent the gusto with which the outrage is perpetrated.' – *C. A. Lejeune*

AA: T. E. B. Clarke

AAN: Alec Guinness

The Law: see *Where the Hot Wind Blows*

Law and Disorder (1939): see *Spies of the Air*

Law and Disorder
GB 1940 73m bw
K. C. Alexander/British Consolidated

A solicitor's partner unmasks saboteurs.

Light topical comedy thriller, capably performed.

w Roger MacDonald   d David MacDonald

Barry K. Barnes, Diana Churchill, Alastair Sim, Edward Chapman, Austin Trevor, Leo Genn

Law and Disorder *
GB 1958 76m bw
British Lion/Hotspur (Paul Soskin)

Crooks rally round a confederate about to be arrested, to prevent his son from learning of his father's real career.

Amusing, well-pointed caper on sub-Ealing lines.

w T. E. B. Clarke   novel *Smuggler's Circuit* by Denys Roberts   d Charles Crichton   ph Ted Scaife   m Humphrey Searle

Michael Redgrave, Robert Morley, Joan Hickson, Lionel Jeffries, Ronald Squire, Elizabeth Sellars

Law and Disorder *
US 1974 102m Technicolor Panavision
Memorial/Leroy Street/Ugo Fadsin (William Richert)
V, V*

New York suburbanites aghast at escalating violence form themselves into a vigilante patrol.

Bewilderingly uneven comedy drama which starts as satirical comedy and ends with one of the heroes dead and the other moralizing. Sporadically interesting, and certainly topical.

w Ivan Passer, William Richert, Kenneth Harris Fishman   d Ivan Passer   ph Arthur J. Ornitz   m Andy Badale

Ernest Borgnine, Carroll O'Connor, Karen Black, Ann Wedgeworth, Leslie Ackerman, David Spielberg

The Law and Jake Wade *
US 1958 86m Metrocolor Cinemascope
MGM (William Hawks)

A marshal helps an old outlaw friend to escape from jail, and lives to regret it.

Good standard Western, enjoyable throughout but with no outstanding merits.

w William Bowers   d John Sturges   ph Robert Surtees

Robert Taylor, Richard Widmark, Patricia Owens, Robert Middleton, Henry Silva

Law and Order *
US 1932 80m bw
Universal

A cowboy becomes marshal and cleans up Tombstone.

Drily effective fictionalization of Wyatt Earp's exploits, with a good star performance.

w John Huston   novel *Saint Johnson* by W. R. Burnett   d Edward L. Cahn

Walter Huston, Harry Carey, Raymond Hatton, Russell Simpson, Russell Hopton

Law and Order
US 1953 80m Technicolor
Universal-International

Curious belated sequel to the above with Johnson moving on to tame Cottonwood; actual presentation rather dull.

w John and Gwen Bagni and D. D. Beauchamp   d Nathan Juran

Ronald Reagan, Dorothy Malone, Preston Foster, Alex Nicol, Russell Johnson

The Law and the Lady
US 1951 104m bw
MGM (Edwin H. Knopf)

A couple of confidence tricksters inveigle themselves into the house of a vulgar millionairess, but one of them has an attack of conscience.

Dreary remake of *The Last of Mrs Cheyney* (qv) with the locale altered, the plot simplified, and the level of wit diluted.

w Leonard Spigelgass, Karl Tunberg   d Edwin H. Knopf   ph George Folsey   m Carmen Dragon

Greer Garson, Michael Wilding, Fernando Lamas, Marjorie Main, Hayden Rorke, Margalo Gillmore, Ralph Dumke

Law of Desire *
Spain 1987 101m colour
Other Cinema/El Deseo/Laurenfilm (Ester Garcia)
V
original title: *La Ley del Deseo*

A glamorous homosexual film director is pursued by a male would-be lover while sharing his apartment with his former brother, who has undergone a sex change, and her transvestite lover's daughter.

Delirious, stylish mix of sex and passion, though many may regard it as too camp and overdone.

wd Pedro Almodovar   ph Angel Luis Fernandez   pd Javier Fernandez   ed Jose Salcedo

Eusebio Poncela, Carmen Maura, Antonio Banderas, Miguel Molina, Manuela Velasco, Bibi Andersen, Fernando Guillen

'Almodovar's tone is not like anyone else's; the film has the exaggerated plot of an absurdist Hollywood romance . . . The film is festive. It doesn't disguise its narcissism; it turns it into bright-coloured tragicomedy.' – *Pauline Kael, New Yorker*

The Law of the Lawless
US 1963 87m Techniscope
Paramount/A. C. Lyles

A judge arrives in a small Western town to conduct the murder trial of a former friend.

Jaded Western of interest only for the producer's custom of packing the bit roles with former stars.

w Steve Fisher   d William F. Claxton   ph Lester Shorr

Dale Robertson, Yvonne de Carlo, William Bendix, Bruce Cabot, Barton MacLane, John Agar, Richard Arlen, Kent Taylor, Lon Chaney Jnr

Law of the Tropics
US 1941 76m bw
Warner (Ben Stoloff)

A café singer on the run from a murder charge marries a South American rubber plantation owner.

Hackneyed melodrama born from a mating of *Oil for the Lamps of China* and *Tropic Zone*.

w Charles Grayson   d Ray Enright   ph Sid Hickox   m Howard Jackson

Constance Bennett, Jeffrey Lynn, Regis Toomey, Mona Maris, Frank Puglia, Thomas Jackson, Craig Stevens

The Law of the Wild
US 1934 bw serial: 12 eps
Mascot

A young rancher tames the king of the wild horses.

Modest serial with strong animal interest.

d Armand Schaefer and B. Reeves Eason

Rex, Rin Tin Tin Jnr, Bob Custer, Ben Turpin

'Out of the most exciting pages of frontier history!'
The Law Versus Billy the Kid
US 1954 73m Technicolor
Sam Katzman/Columbia

Billy the Kid is driven into crime to avenge a friend.

Technicolor seems wasted on this two-bit Western which can't even manage to tell a clear story.

w John T. Williams   d William Castle

Scott Brady, Betta St John, James Griffith, Alan Hale Jnr, Paul Cavanagh

The Lawless
US 1949 83m bw
Paramount/Pine-Thomas
GB title: *The Dividing Line*

The editor of a California small-town newspaper defends a Spanish boy who is being victimized by the racist element.

Well-meaning 'realistic' melodrama, unfortunately among the dullest of the socially conscious movies of this period.

w Geoffrey Homes   d Joseph Losey   ph Roy Hunt   m Mahlon Merrick

Macdonald Carey, Gail Russell, John Sands, John Hoyt, Lee Patrick, Lalo Rios

The Lawless Breed
US 1952 83m Technicolor
U-I (William Alland)

The adventures and repentance of badman John Wesley Hardin.

Standard Western programmer with the star in an unlikely role.

w Bernard Gordon d Raoul Walsh ph Irving Glassberg m Joseph Gershenson

Rock Hudson, Julie Adams, John McIntire, Dennis Weaver, Hugh O'Brian

A Lawless Street
US 1955 78m Technicolor
Columbia (Harry Joe Brown)

A marshal marries a dance hall entertainer, and loses interest in his job when she leaves him.

Enjoyable minor Western.

w Kenneth Gamet novel Marshal of Medicine Bend by Brad Ward d Joseph H. Lewis ph Ray Rennahan m Paul Sawtell

Randolph Scott, Angela Lansbury, Warner Anderson, Jean Parker, Wallace Ford, John Emery, James Bell, Ruth Donnelly, Michael Pate, Jeanette Nolan, Don Megowan

Lawman *
US 1970 99m Technicolor
UA/Scimitar (Michael Winner)
V*

When a marshal tracks down drunken cowboys who have killed an old man, the townsfolk's resistance leads to a bloodbath.

Terse, violent Western with a good cast.

w Gerald Wilson d Michael Winner ph Bob Paynter m Jerry Fielding

Burt Lancaster, Robert Ryan, Lee J. Cobb, Sheree North, Robert Duvall, Joseph Wiseman, John McGiver, Albert Salmi, J. D. Cannon

'God Made Him Simple. Science Made Him A God.'
The Lawnmower Man *
GB/US 1992 108m DeLuxe
First Independent/Allied Vision/Lane Pringle/Fuji Eight (Gimel Everett)
V, V*, L
aka: Stephen King's The Lawnmower Man

A doctor experiments with drugs and computer technology to improve the mind of his retarded gardener, with startling and unforeseen results.

Some impressive special effects, simulating 'virtual reality' – a computer-created world – enliven an otherwise drab and predictable science fiction movie.

w Brett Leonard, Gimel Everett story Stephen King d Brett Leonard ph Russell Carpenter m Dan Wyman pd Alex McDowell sp Angel Studios, Xaos Inc. ed Alan Baumgarten

Jeff Fahey, Pierce Brosnan, Jenny Wright, Geoffrey Lewis, Mark Bringleson, Jeremy Slate, Dean Norris

'It all works surprisingly well, with interesting and well-integrated visual effects, some nice humour and a few genuinely visionary effects.' – Kim Newman, Empire

† Stephen King was granted an injunction forbidding the film's producers from using his name in connection with the film.
†† A director's cut of the film was also released on video with a running time of 142m.

Lawrence of Arabia ****
GB 1962 221m Technicolor Super Panavision 70
Columbia/Horizon (Sam Spiegel)
V (W), V*, L, S

An adventurer's life with the Arabs, told in flashbacks after his accidental death in the thirties.

Sprawling epic which manages after four hours to give no insight whatever into the complexities of character of this mysterious historic figure, but is often spectacularly beautiful and exciting along the way.

w Robert Bolt d David Lean ph Frederick A. Young m Maurice Jarre pd John Box ad John Stoll

Peter O'Toole, Omar Sharif, Arthur Kennedy, Jack Hawkins, Donald Wolfit, Claude Rains, Anthony Quayle, Alec Guinness, Anthony Quinn, José Ferrer, Michel Ray, Zia Mohyeddin

'Grandeur of conception is not up to grandeur of setting.' – Penelope Houston

'Lean has managed to market epics as serious entertainment rather than as the spectacles they are.' – Time Out, 1980

† Albert Finney turned down the role before O'Toole was offered it.
AA: best picture; David Lean; Frederick A. Young; Maurice Jarre
AAN: Robert Bolt; Peter O'Toole; Omar Sharif

Laws of Gravity *
US 1992 98m colour
Oasis/The Shooting Gallery (Bob Gosse, Larry Meistrich)

In Brooklyn, friendship between two young, petty crooks is strained when they become involved with a gangster who is trying to sell guns.

Down-beat drama of losers, effectively filmed and acted in a documentary style although it does cover familiar territory.

wd Nick Gomez ph Jean de Segonzac m Douglas Cuomo pd Monica Bretherton ed Tom McArdle

Peter Greene, Edie Falco, Adam Trese, Arabella Field, Paul Schulze, Saul Stein, James McCauley

'Reasonably acted with some funny, protracted conversations.' – Empire

The Lawyer *
US 1970 120m Technicolor
Paramount (Brad Dexter)

An ambitious young Italian-American defence lawyer takes on a murder case.

Smartly scripted, perfectly ordinary courtroom drama in a well-detailed Western setting. The star subsequently played the same character in a TV series, Petrocelli.

w Sidney J. Furie, Harold Buchman d Sidney J. Furie ph Ralph Woolsey m Malcolm Dodds

Barry Newman, Harold Gould, Diana Muldaur, Robert Colbert, Kathleen Crowley, Booth Colman

Lawyer Man
US 1932 68m bw
Warner

An honest lawyer becomes corrupted by success.

Smart, cynical melodrama, dated but sufficiently fast-paced to remain interesting.

w Rian James, James Seymour novel Max Trell d William Dieterle ph Robert Kurrle

William Powell, Joan Blondell, Helen Vinson, Alan Dinehart, Allen Jenkins, David Landau, Claire Dodd

'Good picture in the lawyer cycle.' – Variety

Laxdale Hall
GB 1952 77m bw
Group Three (Alfred Shaughnessy)
US title: Scotch on the Rocks

MPs are sent to investigate a tiny Hebridean island which refuses to pay road tax.

Thin rehash of Whisky Galore put together without the Ealing style. Minor compensations can be found.

w John Eldridge, Alfred Shaughnessy d John Eldridge ph Arthur Grant m Frank Spencer

Raymond Huntley, Ronald Squire, Sebastian Shaw, Fulton Mackay, Kathleen Ryan, Kynaston Reeves

'Constantly amusing in its quiet and wry fashion.' – Cinema

Lazy Bones: see Hallelujah I'm a Bum

Lazy River
US 1934 75m bw
MGM

Ex-convicts go to work in a shrimp cannery and defeat a Chinese smuggler.

Curious comedy drama which defeats all participants.

w Lucien Hubbard play Ruby by Lea David Freeman d George B. Seitz

Jean Parker, Robert Young, Ted Healy, C. Henry Gordon, Nat Pendleton

Le Mans *
US 1971 108m DeLuxe Panavision
Solar/Cinema Center (Jack N. Reddish)

A sullen American enters for the 24-hour race.

Almost no plot and little documentary examination; what's left is a multitude of racing shots with Steve McQueen at the wheel. For some this may be enough.

w Harry Kleiner d Lee H. Katzin ph Robert B. Hauser, René Gruissart Jnr m Michel Legrand

Steve McQueen, Siegfried Rauch, Elga Anderson, Ronald Leigh-Hunt

Leadbelly *
US 1976 126m Eastmancolor
CIC/Brownstone/David Paradine (Marc Merson)

Biopic of the tough folk and blues singer and guitarist Huddie Ledbetter, concentrating on his earlier years and his times in chain gangs.

Pleasing, if stolid, account of a fascinating performer who sang his way out of prison.

w Ernest Kinoy d Gordon Parks ph Bruce Surtees m Fred Karlin pd Robert Boyle m/y Huddie Ledbetter ed Harry Howard

Roger E. Mosley, Paul Benjamin, Madge Sinclair, Alan Manson, Albert P. Hall, Art Evans, James E. Brodhead, John Henry Falk

'Little more than the traditional biopic molasses.' – MFB

† Leadbelly's songs are sung by HiTide Harris.

League of Frightened Men
US 1937 71m bw
Columbia

Nero Wolfe solves another murder case from his armchair.

Fair dectective story, but a negation of film.

w Eugene Solow, Guy Endore novel Rex Stout d Alfred E. Green

Walter Connolly, Lionel Stander, Eduardo Ciannelli, Irene Hervey, Victor Kilian, Nana Bryant

'Hardly any audience likes to watch a character who just sits and thinks.' – Variety

The League of Gentlemen ***
GB 1960 112m bw
Rank/Allied Film Makers (Michael Relph)
V*

An ex-army officer recruits high-class misfits with guilty secrets to help him in a bank robbery.

Delightfully handled comedy adventure, from the days (alas) when crime did not pay; a lighter ending would have made it a classic.

w Bryan Forbes, novel John Boland d Basil Dearden ph Arthur Ibbetson m Philip Green

Jack Hawkins, Richard Attenborough, Roger Livesey, Nigel Patrick, Bryan Forbes, Kieron Moore, Terence Alexander, Norman Bird, Robert Coote, Melissa

Stribling, Nanette Newman, Gerald Harper, Patrick Wymark, David Lodge, Doris Hare, Lydia Sherwood

'Once in a lifetime you get a chance to do something different.'

A League of Their Own *
US   1992   128m   Technicolor
Columbia/Parkway
V, V*, L, S

During the Second World War, women are recruited to play in an all-female baseball league.

A comedy that trundles along in a predictable fashion, settling for sentimentality rather than humour.

w Lowell Ganz, Babaloo Mandel   story Kim Wilson, Kelly Candaele   d Penny Marshall   ph Miroslav Ondricek   m Hans Zimmer   pd Bill Groom   ed George Bowers

Tom Hanks, Geena Davis, Madonna, Lori Petty, Jon Lovitz, David Strathairn, Gerry Marshall, Bill Pullman, Megan Cavanagh, Tracy Reiner, Rosie O'Donnell, Ann Cusack

'This movie aims for the tear ducts and the funny bone as ruthlessly as the summer's big action-fantasy hits go after the viscera. It unfolds in field-of-dreams land – complete with cornstalks.' – *Michael Sragow, New Yorker*

'Awash in sentimentality and manic energy but only occasionally bubbling over with high humor.' – *Variety*

Lean on Me
US   1989   108m   Technicolor
Warner (Norman Twain)
V, V*, L

A stern teacher tames the pupils at New Jersey's toughest school.

Given its subject matter, a surprisingly soft-centred drama, based on a true story.

w Michael Schiffer, Douglas Seelig   d John G. Avildsen   ph Victor Hammer   m Bill Conti   pd Doug Kraner   ed John Carter, John G. Avildsen

Morgan Freeman, Beverly Todd, Robert Guillaume, Alan North, Lynne Thigpen, Robin Bartlett, Ethan Phillips

Lease of Life *
GB   1954   94m   Eastmancolor
Ealing (Jack Rix)

A poor clergyman is given a year to live, and puts it to good use.

Somewhat depressing but well-acted drama with excellent village atmosphere.

w Eric Ambler   d Charles Frend   ph Douglas Slocombe   m Alan Rawsthorne

Robert Donat, Kay Walsh, Adrienne Corri, Denholm Elliott

The Leather Boys *
GB   1963   108m   bw   Cinemascope
British Lion/Garrick (Raymond Stross)
V, V*

Two working-class teenagers marry for sex; she becomes a drudge and he develops a relationship with a homosexual motorcyclist.

Sharply-observed slice of low life which now seems quite dated, the central figures no longer being of the 'heroic' interest given them at the time. Technically the film is tediously and fashionably flashy.

w Gillian Freeman   novel Elliot George   d Sidney J. Furie   ph Gerald Gibbs   m Bill McGuffie

Rita Tushingham, Dudley Sutton, Colin Campbell, Gladys Henson

The Leather Saint
US   1955   86m   bw   Vistavision
Paramount (Norman Retchin)

To provide his parish hospital with medical equipment, a Catholic priest becomes a commercial prizefighter.

Unlikely piece of religiosity, not too badly done.

w Norman Retchin, Alvin Ganzer   d Alvin Ganzer   ph Haskell Boggs   md Irvin Talbot

Paul Douglas, John Derek, Cesar Romero, *Ernest Truex*, Jody Lawrance

Leathernecking
US   1930   80m   bw (colour sequence)
RKO (Louis Sarecky)
GB title: *Present Arms*

A Honolulu socialite falls for a marine, but grows cool when she discovers that he is a private and not an officer as he pretended.

Curiously cast, spasmodically funny non-musical version of a Rodgers and Hart Broadway hit.

w Alfred Jackson, Jane Murfin   play Present Arms by Herbert Fields, Rodgers and Hart   d Edward Cline   ph J. Roy Hunt   m Oscar Levant

Irene Dunne (her first role), Ken Murray, Eddie Foy Jnr, Louise Fazenda, Ned Sparks, Lilyan Tashman
'Weak medley of horseplay and romantic musical, and both poor.' – *Variety*

Leave All Fair *
New Zealand   1984   88m   colour
Pacific Films (John O'Shea)

At the end of his life, John Middleton Murry recalls his relationship with his first wife, the writer Katherine Mansfield.

Intelligent and ambivalent drama, leaving open the question of whether Murry was the betrayer or saviour of his wife's reputation.

w Stanley Harper, Maurice Pons, Jean Betts, John Reid   d John Reid   ph Bernard Lutic   m Stephen McCurdy   ad Joe Bleakley   ed Ian John

John Gielgud, Jane Birkin, Feodor Atkine, Simon Ward

Leave 'Em Laughing *
US   1928   20m   bw   silent
Hal Roach

Stan has toothache, visits the dentist, and accidentally causes all concerned to inhale an overdose of laughing gas.

The earlier sequences are only mildly funny, but the laughing finale is irresistible.

w Hal Roach and Reed Heustis   d Clyde Bruckman

Laurel and Hardy, Edgar Kennedy, Charlie Hall

'The sum total of all human emotion!'
Leave Her to Heaven
US   1945   111m   Technicolor
TCF (William A. Bacher)

A selfish, jealous woman causes unhappiness for those around her, even in her suicide.

No-holds-barred melodrama of the old school; what seemed lush production at the time now looks tatty.

w Jo Swerling   novel Ben Ames Williams   d John M. Stahl   ph Leon Shamroy   m Alfred Newman   ad Lyle Wheeler, Maurice Ransford

Gene Tierney, Cornel Wilde, Jeanne Crain, Vincent Price, Mary Philips, Ray Collins, Gene Lockhart, Reed Hadley, Chill Wills

'The story's central idea might be plausible enough in a dramatically lighted black and white picture . . . but in the rich glare of Technicolor, all its rental library characteristics are doubly glaring.' – *James Agee*

AA: Leon Shamroy
AAN: Gene Tierney; art direction

The Leavenworth Case
US   1935   66m   bw
Republic

Police investigate the murder of a wealthy man.

Sluggish transcription of what claims to be the first American detective story.

w Albert DeMond, Sidney Sutherland   novel Anna Katherine Green

Donald Cook, Jean Rouverol, Norman Foster, Erin O'Brien-Moore, Maude Eburne, Warren Hymer

'Just another detective meller.' – *Variety*

Leaves from Satan's Book *
Denmark   1919   80m approx (24 fps)   bw   silent
Nordisk

Episodes from the activities of Satan through the ages: with Christ, the Inquisition, the French Revolution and the Russian Revolution.

Vaguely propagandist short-story compilation with effective moments.

w Edgar Hoyer, Carl Dreyer   novel The Sorrows of Satan by Marie Corelli   d Carl Dreyer   ph George Schneevoigt

Lebenszeichen: see *Signs of Life*

La Lectrice **
France   1988   98m   colour
Curzon Films/Elefilm/AAA/TSF/Ciné 5/Sofimage (Rosalinde Deville)
V*, L

A beautiful young woman, hired to read books out loud to people who are disabled in some way, has unexpected effects on her customers.

Witty games-playing comedy.

w Michel Deville, Rosalinde Deville   novel Raymond Jean   d Michel Deville   ph Dominique Le Rigoleur   m Beethoven   pd Thierry Leproust   ed Raymonde Guyot

Miou-Miou, Régis Royer, Christian Ruché, Maria Cesars, Patrick Chesnais, Marianne Denicourt, Pierre Dux

'A frothy conceit, a true jeu d'esprit, but when it has said all that it has to say, albeit with panache, it has said nothing.' – *MFB*

'You can count the truly daring concepts in the making of motion pictures on the fingers of your right hand. Now add . . .'
The Left Hand of God
US   1955   87m   DeLuxe   Cinemascope
TCF (Buddy Adler)
V*

China, 1947: a Catholic priest newly arrived in a small village proves to be an American flyer on the run from a warlord; but he contrives to work a small 'miracle'.

Hollywood religiosity at its most contrived, put together without distinction; the players have a wary look.

w Alfred Hayes   novel William E. Barrett   d Edward Dmytryk   ph Franz Planer   m Victor Young

Humphrey Bogart, Gene Tierney, Lee J. Cobb, E. G. Marshall, Agnes Moorehead

The Left Handed Gun *
US   1958   102m   bw
Warner/Haroll (Fred Coe)
V, V (W), V*, L

Billy the Kid sets out to shoot four men who have killed his friend.

'Method'-oriented Western, efficiently made but somewhat downcast.

w Leslie Stevens, TV play Gore Vidal   d Arthur Penn   ph Peverell Marley   m Alexander Courage

Paul Newman, John Dehner, Lita Milan, Hurd
Hatfield

'Top of the poll for laughs!'
Left Right and Centre *
GB   1959   95m   bw
Vale/Launder and Gilliat

A TV personality becomes Tory candidate at a by-
election.

Scrappy political comedy with the saving grace of a
large number of comic talents.

w Sidney Gilliat, Val Valentine   d Sidney Gilliat
ph Gerald Gibbs   m Humphrey Searle

Ian Carmichael, Alastair Sim, Patricia Bredin, Richard
Wattis, Eric Barker, Gordon Harker, George Benson,
Frederick Leister

The Legacy
GB   1978   102m   colour
Columbia/Pethurst/Turman-Foster (David Foster)

An American designer goes to stay with her employer
and finds herself in the middle of an occult murder
plot.

Cliché-ridden screamer which will please the easily
pleased.

w Jimmy Sangster, Patrick Tilley, Paul Wheeler
d Richard Marquand   ph Dick Bush, Alan Hume
m Michael J. Lewis   pd Disley Jones   ed Anne
Coates

Katharine Ross, Sam Elliott, Roger Daltrey, John
Standing, Ian Hogg, Margaret Tyzack, Charles Gray,
Lee Montague, Hildegard Neil

'Like father, like son . . .'
Legacy of Rage (dubbed)
Hong Kong   1987   82m   colour
Imperial (John Sham, Linda Kuk)

After six years in jail for a crime he did not commit, a
former waiter teams up with a cell-mate to seek
revenge on the gangster who framed him.

Standard martial arts adventure, notable only for
Brandon Lee's debut.

wd Ronny Yu

Brandon Lee, Onno Boelee (Bolo Yeung), Michael
Wong, Regina Kent, Tanya George

'Offers too few thrills to satisfy hard-core action fans.'
– Film Review

Legal Eagles
US   1986   114m   Technicolor   Panavision
Universal/Northern Lights (Ivan Reitman)
V, V*, L

An assistant DA becomes involved for the defence in
an arson case.

Sophisticated but messy comedy with odd unrelated
asides, reminiscent of the TV series Moonlighting but
with top production values.

w Jim Cash, Jack Epps Jnr   d Ivan Reitman
ph Laszlo Kovacs   m Elmer Bernstein

Robert Redford, Debra Winger, Daryl Hannah, Brian
Dennehy, Terence Stamp, Steven Hill

Legend *
GB   1985   94m   Fujicolour   Panavision
(TCF/Universal) Legend Productions (Arnon Milchan)
V, V*, L, S

Young peasant Jack takes his sweetheart on a quest to
see the last surviving unicorns, but Satan uses them as
pawns in his own game.

Elegant fairy tale for the few grown-ups who have use
for such a thing. More to look at than to listen to.

w William Hjortsberg   d Ridley Scott   ph Alex
Thomson   m Jerry Goldsmith   pd Assheton Gorton
ed Terry Rawlings

Tim Curry, Mia Sara, Tom Cruise, David Bennent

'The dying gasp of the sword and sorcery cycle.' –
Philip French, Observer

'The enchanted forests constantly threaten to sell us
something – most frequently soft toilet paper.' – Ibid.

AAN: make-up (Rob Bottin, Peter Robb-King)

The Legend of Billie Jean
US   1985   96m   Metrocolor
Tri-Star/Rob Cohen (Jon Peters, Peter Guber)
V*

While protecting her brother, a girl becomes an
outlaw by accident.

Unattractive and even distasteful farrago which is
presumably intended to teach kids, so far as the law is
concerned, how to eat their cake and have it.

w Mark Rosenthal, Lawrence Konner   d Matthew
Robbins   ph Jeffrey L. Kimball   m Craig Safan
pd Ted Haworth   ed Cynthia Schneider

Helen Slater, Keith Gordon, Christian Slater, Richard
Bradford, Peter Coyote

'The germ of an idea, but hardly a reason for a film.' –
Variety

'For the sake of your sanity, pray it isn't true!'
The Legend of Hell House *
GB   1973   94m   DeLuxe
TCF/Academy (Albert Fennell, Norman T. Herman)
V*, L

Four people arrive at a haunted house in which
several psychic investigators have been killed.

Harrowing thriller, a less solemn but more frightening
version of The Haunting.

w Richard Matheson   novel Richard Matheson
d John Hough   ph Alan Hume   m Brian Hodgson,
Delia Derbyshire

Pamela Franklin, Roddy McDowall, Clive Revill,
Gayle Hunnicutt, Roland Culver, Peter Bowles,
Michael Gough

'One of the most absorbing, goose-fleshing and mind-
pleasing ghost breaker yarns on film.' – Judith Crist,
1977

The Legend of Lobo *
US   1962   67m   Technicolor
Walt Disney (James Algar)
V*

The life of a forest wolf.

Anthropomorphic entertainment in which a dreaded
animal becomes something of a hero and finally saves
his mate from bounty hunters. Impeccably contrived,
like a live-action Bambi.

w Dwight Hauser, James Algar   story Ernest
Thompson Seton   d James Algar   ph Jack Couffer,
Lloyd Beebe   m Oliver Wallace

The Legend of Lylah Clare *
US   1968   130m   Metrocolor   Panavision
MGM/Robert Aldrich

A mad director brings an unknown actress to
Hollywood because of her resemblance to a former
star, his creation, who had died mysteriously.

Unintentionally risible melodrama with echoes of
Svengali and Sunset Boulevard; not to the public's taste,
or anyone else's, in the late sixties.

w Hugo Butler, Jean Rouverol   TV play Robert
Thom, Edward de Blasio   d Robert Aldrich
ph Joseph Biroc   m Frank de Vol

Peter Finch, Kim Novak, Ernest Borgnine, Coral
Browne, Milton Seltzer, Rossella Falk, Gabriele Tinti,
Valentina Cortesa, George Kennedy

Legend of the Demon Womb
Japan   1990   84m   colour
Toshio Maeda/West Cape
original title: Urotsukidoji II

Demons and man-beasts fight to prevent the son of a
mad Nazi from gaining ultimate power by killing the
boy who is destined to be the over-fiend, the god of
gods.

† Extremely gruesome animated fantasy,
concentrating on graphic sex, from masturbation,
fellatio and lesbianism to rape, and much violence,
including decapitations, multiple murders and human
sacrifice.

w Noboru Aikawa   story Toshio Maeda   d Hideki
Takayama   ph Hideo Okazaki   m Masamichi
Amano   ad Hitoshi Nagao   ed Shigeru Nishiyama

voices of Christopher Courage, Rebel Joy, Danny
Bush, Lucy Morales, Rose Palmer

† A sequel to the equally gruesome Legend of the
Overfiend (qv). It was followed by the video releases of
Urotsukidoji III: Episode 1 and Urotsukidoji III: Episode 2,
which both continue the mixture as before with an
unintelligible narrative, an impenetrable mythology,
a comic-book style of animation, and much sex and
violence.

Legend of the Holy Drinker **
Italy   1988   128m   colour
Artificial Eye/Aura Film/Cecchi Gori Group/Tiger
Cinematografica/RAI Uno (Roberto Cicutto, Vincenzo de
Leo)
V
original title: La Leggenda del Santo Bevitore

An alcoholic tramp is repeatedly frustrated in his
attempts to repay money to the shrine of a saint.

An odd fable, beautifully presented.

w Tullio Kezich, Ermanno Olmi   novel Die Legende
des Heiligen Trinkers by Joseph Roth   d Ermanno
Olmi   ph Dante Spinotti   m Stravinsky
pd Gianni Quaranta   ed Ermanno Olmi

Rutger Hauer, Anthony Quayle, Sandrine Dumas,
Dominique Pinon, Sophie Segalen, Jean Maurice
Chanet, Cecile Paoli, Joseph de Medina

'The film where you hiss the villain and cheer the hero!'
The Legend of the Lone Ranger
US   1981   98m   Technicolor   Panavision
ITC/Jack Wrather (Walter Coblenz)
V*

A much-betrayed young Texan, almost killed in an
ambush, is nursed back to health by an Indian and
becomes a masked avenger.

Extremely ill-constructed and moody Western,
apparently photographed through brown Windsor
soup, which doesn't slip into the right gear until
twenty minutes before the end.

w Ivan Goff, Ben Roberts, Michael Kane, William
Roberts   d William A. Fraker   ph Laszlo Kovacs
m John Barry

Klinton Spilsbury, Michael Horse, Christopher Lloyd,
Matt Clark

'Wallows in endless sentiment before switching to
what may possibly have been intended as parody.' –
Sight and Sound

'Tedious hokum . . . the kind of film that closes
cinemas.' – Sunday Times

Legend of the Lost
US   1957   107m   Technirama
UA/Batjac/Robert Haggiag/Dear (Henry Hathaway)

Two adventurers and a slave girl seek a lost city in the
Sahara.

Tediously vague and underplotted desert adventure
with a few attractive moments.

w Robert Presnell Jnr, Ben Hecht   d Henry
Hathaway   ph Jack Cardiff   m A. F. Lavagnino

John Wayne, Sophia Loren, Rossano Brazzi

Legend of the Overfiend (dubbed)

Japan 1989 96m colour
West Cape Corp (Yasuhito Yamaki)
V
original title: Urotsukidōji

Creatures from two parallel universes battle to become supreme rulers of the Earth.

Revolting and thoroughly nasty animated feature, full of rape, masturbation, mutilation and grotesque mutations, with heads exploding and eyeballs popping. What narrative there is amid the sex and violence makes little sense.

w Noboru Aikawa story Toshio Maeda d Hideki Takayama m Masamichi Amano ad Shigemi Ikeda ed Shigeru Nishiyma

voices of Christopher Courage, Rebel Joy, Danny Bush, Lucy Morales, Rose Palmer

'Formula heroics, facile science fiction futurism, slavering monsters and tediously repetitive violence – the animated fantasies of the Manga school have everything to satisfy the adolescent mind.' – Sight and Sound

The Legend of the Seven Golden Vampires

GB/Hong Kong 1974 89m Eastmancolor Panavision
Hammer-Shaw (Don Houghton, Vee King Shaw)
US title: The Seven Brothers Meet Dracula

In 1904 Chungking, Professor Van Helsing finds his old enemy Dracula behind a Chinese vampire cult.

Hectic, outlandish mix of Hammer horror and Kung Fu; plenty of gusto but not much sense.

w Don Houghton d Roy Ward Baker ph John Wilcox, Roy Ford m James Bernard

Peter Cushing, David Chiang, Julie Ege, Robin Stewart, John Forbes Robertson

Legend of the Suram Fortress *

USSR 1984 87m colour
Poseidon/Georgianfilm Studio (X. Gogiladze, M. Simxaev)
V
original title: Legenda Suramskoi Kreposti

A youth lets himself be immured in the walls of a fortress to stop it from crumbling.

Colourful re-enactment of a folk tale, though not up to the director's best work.

w Vazha Gigashvili book D. Tchonghadze d Sergo Paradjanov, Dodo Abashidze ph Sergo Sixarulidze m Dzhansugh K'axidze ad Alexandr Dzhanishiev ed K'ora Ts'ereteli

Venerik'o Andzhaparidze, Dodo Abashidze, Sopik'o Ch'iaureli, Duduxana Ts'erodze, Tamar Tsitsishuili

The Legend of Tom Dooley

US 1959 77m bw
Columbia/Shpetner

At the end of the Civil War, Confederate youths take the law into their own hands and attack Unionists.

Youthful rebellion in historical mould, decently but rather dully delivered, based on a folk ballad.

w Stan Shpetner d Ted Post ph Gilbert Warrenton m Ronald Stein

Michael Landon, Richard Rust, Jo Morrow

The Lemon Drop Kid *

US 1951 91m bw
Paramount (Robert A. Welch)
V*, L

A gangster forces a bookie to find the money which he has lost on a horse through the bookie's incompetence.

Amusing Bob Hope/Runyon vehicle despite heavy sentiment about an old folks' home. The Santa Claus sequences are memorable.

w Edmund Hartmann, Frank Tashlin, Robert O'Brien story Damon Runyon d Sidney Lanfield ph Daniel L. Fapp m Victor Young

Bob Hope, Marilyn Maxwell, Lloyd Nolan, Jane Darwell, Andrea King, Fred Clark, Jay C. Flippen, William Frawley, Harry Bellaver

† The previous 1934 version starred Lee Tracy, Helen Mack and William Frawley; ran 60m; and was directed by Marshall Neilan for Paramount

Lenin in October *

USSR 1937 111m bw
Mosfilm
original title: Lenin v Octiabrye

The activities of Lenin during the revolution.

Stalwart propaganda piece, of solid but not outstanding cinematic interest.

w Alexei Kapler d Mikhail Romm ph Boris Volchok m Anatoli Alexandrov

Boris Shchukin

† The success of this film provoked Lenin in 1918, made in the following year (132m) by the same talents, with Cherkassov as Gorky. Many other Russian films on Lenin have followed.

'Somewhere in the tundra lived the worst rock'n'roll band in the world...'

Leningrad Cowboys Go America **

Finland/Sweden 1989 78m
Artificial Eye/Villealfa/Swedish Film Institute/Finnish Film Foundation (Aki Kaurismäki, Klas Olofsson, Katinka Farago)
V, V*, L

An inept rock band travels through America in search of fame and fortune, which prove elusive.

Engagingly ramshackle comedy, with keen observation of the underside of the American dream

wd Aki Kaurismäki story Sakke Järvenpää, Aki Kaurismäki, Mato Valtonen ph Timo Salminen m Mauri Sumén ed Raija Talvio

Matti Pellonpää, Kari Väänänen, Sakke Jarvenpää, Hiekki Keskinen, Pimme Oinonen, Silu Seppälä, Mauri Sumén, Mato Valtonen, Pekka Virtanen, Jim Jarmusch

Lenin v Octiabrye: see Lenin in October

Lenny **

US 1974 111m bw
UA (Marvin Worth)
V, V*, L

The career of obscene comedian Lenny Bruce and his struggles with the law.

Old-fashioned rags-to-riches-to-rags story, rampant with the new permissiveness. Filmically extremely clever, emotionally hollow.

w Julian Barry play Julian Barry d Bob Fosse ph Bruce Surtees md Ralph Burns pd Joel Schiller

Dustin Hoffman, Valerie Perrine, Jan Miner, Stanley Beck, Gary Morton

'For audiences who want to believe that Lenny Bruce was a saintly gadfly who was martyred for having lived before his time.' – New Yorker

AAN: best picture; Julian Barry; Bob Fosse; Bruce Surtees; Dustin Hoffman; Valerie Perrine

Leo the Last

GB 1969 104m DeLuxe
UA/Char/Wink/Boor (Irwin Winkler, Robert Chartoff)

An alienated aristocrat brings his retinue to a London slum and has an effect on most of the inhabitants.

Infuriating symbolic fantasy; only the writer-director (presumably) has any idea what it is about.

w William Stair, John Boorman d John Boorman ph Peter Suschitsky m Fred Myrow pd Tony Woollard

Marcello Mastroianni, Billie Whitelaw, Calvin Lockhart, Glenna Forster Jones, Graham Crowden, Gwen Ffrangcon Davies, David de Keyser, Vladek Sheybal, Kenneth J. Warren

'One must be grateful for the bold, high-spirited experiments and surprises . . . They are never boring.' – Dilys Powell

'Léolo's fantasy is of Bianca and Sicily. His reality is Murder and Madness.'

Léolo *

Canada/France 1992 103m colour
Alliance/Verseau/Flach/Canal+ (Lyse Lafontaine, Aimée Danis)
V

In a poor part of Montreal, a dreamy small boy, growing up at odds with his mainly demented family, retreats from reality.

A dark tragi-comic account of the flowering and the failure of an imagination.

wd Jean-Claude Lauzon ph Guy Dufaux ad François Séguin ed Michel Arcand

Ginette Reno, Pierre Bourgault, Maxime Collin, Giuditta Del Vecchio, Julien Guiomar

'A semi-autobiographical phantasmagoria about growing up in a 1960s East-Montreal French-Canadian tenement populated by Fellini-esque grotesques.' – Philip French, Observer

Léon Morin, Priest *

France/Italy 1961 117m bw
Rome – Paris Films (Georges de Beauregard)

During the German occupation of France a young widow finds herself falling in love with the young priest who is converting her to religion.

An intellectual romance, sharp and witty for the most part, with vivid wartime backgrounds.

wd Jean-Pierre Melville novel Béatrix Beck ph Henri Decaë m Martial Solal, Albert Raisner

Jean-Paul Belmondo, Emmanuele Riva, Irène Tunc, Marielle Gozzi

Leon the Pig Farmer

GB 1992 104m colour
Electric/Leon the Pig Farmer Production (Gary Sinyor, Vadim Jean)
V, S

A Jewish estate agent discovers that his real father is a Yorkshire pig farmer.

Laboured low-budget comedy of racial stereotypes.

w Gary Sinyor, Michael Norman d Vadim Jean, Gary Sinyor ph Gordon Hickie m John Murphy pd Simon Hicks ed Ewa Lind

Mark Frankel, Gina Bellman, Janet Suzman, Brian Glover, Connie Booth, Maryam D'Abo

'Overall, flashes of inspiration are outweighed by laboured skits that fall somewhat flat, but this is a worthy and promising effort.' – Empire

'The comedy has wit and pace. It has originality that Mel Brooks might envy.' – Alexander Walker, London Evening Standard

† The film was made on a budget of £160,000. It won the International Critics' Prize at the Venice Film Festival and an award for best first film at the Edinburgh Film Festival.

The Leopard ****

US/Italy 1963 205m Technirama
TCF/Titanus/SNPC/GPC (Goffredo Lombardo)
S
original title: Il Gattopardo

The family life of an Italian nobleman at the time of Garibaldi.

Elaborate, complex family saga, painted like an old master with great care and attention to detail, but with not much chance outside Italy of delivering its original dramatic force. Visconti had asked for Lancaster, so TCF picked up the international release but couldn't make head or tail of it commercially; they even ruined its high quality by releasing a dubbed, shortened version in Cinemascope and DeLuxe colour of poor standard.

wd Luchino Visconti, *novel* Giuseppe de Lampedusa *ph* Giuseppe Rotunno *m* Nino Rota *ad* Mario Garbuglia

Burt Lancaster, Claudia Cardinale, Alain Delon, Paolo Stoppa, Serge Reggiani, Leslie French

Leopard in the Snow
GB/Canada 1977 94m Technicolor
Seastone/Leopard in the Snow (W. Laurence Heisey)
V*

A girl caught in a Cumberland blizzard is rescued by a mysterious stranger with a pet leopard. He turns out to be a disfigured racing driver, and she falls in love with him.

A deliberate cross between *Jane Eyre* and a shopgirl's romance, adequately produced for its intended audience.

w Anne Mather, Jill Hyem *novel* Anne Mather *d* Gerry O'Hara *ph* Alfie Hicks *m* Kenneth V. Jones

Keir Dullea, Susan Penhaligon, Jeremy Kemp, Kenneth More, Billie Whitelaw

The Leopard Man **
US 1943 59m bw
RKO (Val Lewton)

Murders in a Mexican border town are attributed to an escaped leopard.

Effective minor piece in the Lewton horror gallery; poor plot countered by highly effective suspense sequences.

w Ardel Wray, Edward Dein *novel* Black Alibi by Cornell Woolrich *d* Jacques Tourneur *ph* Robert de Grasse *m* Roy Webb

Dennis O'Keefe, Jean Brooks, Margo, James Bell, Isabel Jewell

'It's all confusion, too much for an audience to follow.' – *Variety*

Lepke
US 1974 110m DeLuxe Panavision
Warner/AmeriEuro Pictures (Menahem Golan)
V, V*

After World War I a small-time crook becomes head of Murder Incorporated.

Violent but totally uninteresting gangster melodrama; fidelity to fact is not enough.

w Wesley Lau, Tamar Hoffs *d* Menahem Golan *ph* Andrew Davis *m* Ken Wannberg *pd* Jack Degovia

Tony Curtis, Anjanette Comer, Michael Callan, Warren Berlinger, Milton Berle, Gianni Russo

'A kosher version of The Godfather.' – *Verina Glaessner*

Leprechaun
US 1992 92m CFI color
Trimark (Jeffrey B. Mallian)
V, V*, S

A leprechaun terrorizes a household while searching for gold that was stolen from him.

Lugubrious, trivial horror with some nasty moments of violence.

wd Mark Jones *ph* Levie Isaacs *m* Kevin Kiner *pd* Naomi Slodki *ed* Christopher Roth

Warwick Davis, Jennifer Anniston, Mark Holton, Ken Olandt, Mark Holton, Robert Gorman, John Sanderford

'A dull, unscary horror movie whose sole selling point is some extraneous gore footage.' – *Variety*

Les Girls: see Girls

Les Misérables: see Misérables

Les Patterson Saves the World
Australia 1987 90m
Recorded Releasing/Humpstead (Sue Milliken)
V

A coarse and slobbish Australian diplomat foils a dastardly plot to unleash a deadly virus.

Gross and tasteless comedy, without wit or style.

w Barry Humphries, Diane Milstead *d* George Miller *ph* David Connell *m* Tim Finn *pd* Graham 'Grace' Walker *ed* Tim Wellburn

Barry Humphries, Pamela Stephenson, Thaao Penghlis, Andrew Clarke, Henri Szeps, Hugh Keays-Byrne

Less than Zero
US 1987 98m DeLuxe
TCF (Jon Avnet, Jordan Kerner)
V*, L, S

A group of the rich young and upwardly mobile in Los Angeles become hooked on a meaningless round of drugs, parties and sex.

Limp attempt to film a best-selling novel of the blank generation, concentrating not so much on the despair and self-pity of the participants as on their enviable life-style.

w Harley Peyton *novel* Bret Easton Ellis *d* Marek Kanievska *ph* Edward Lachman *m* Thomas Newman *pd* Barbara Ling *ed* Peter E. Berger, Michael Tronick

Andrew McCarthy, Jami Gertz, Robert Downey Jnr, James Spader, Tony Bill, Nicholas Pryor, Donna Mitchell

A Lesson in Love
Sweden 1954 95m bw
Svensk Filmindustri (Allan Ekelund)
original title: En Lektion I Kärlek

A gynaecologist and his wife grow bored and turn to other partners, but are reconciled.

Slight comedy, surprisingly unsubtle for its creator, but passable.

wd Ingmar Bergman *ph* Martin Bodin, Bengt Nordwal *m* Dag Wirén *ad* P. A. Lundgren *ed* Oscar Rosander

Gunnar Björnstrand, Eva Dahlbeck, Harriet Andersson, Yvonne Lombard, Ake Grönberg

Lest We Forget: see Hangmen Also Die

Let 'Em Have It *
US 1935 90m bw
Edward Small
GB title: False Faces

The FBI go after criminals on a terror spree.

Lively cops and robbers with some starkly effective moments.

w Joseph Moncure March, Elmer Harris *d* Sam Wood *ph* J. Peverell Marley, Robert Planck

Richard Arlen, Virginia Bruce, Alice Brady, Bruce Cabot, Harvey Stephens, Eric Linden, Joyce Compton, J. Farrell MacDonald

Let Freedom Ring
US 1939 100m sepia
MGM (Harry Rapf)

A Westerner returns to his home town and clears it of corruption.

Elementary Hollywood actioner with curious credits, climaxed by Eddy singing *The Star Spangled Banner*.

w Ben Hecht *d* Jack Conway *ph* Sidney Wagner *m* Arthur Lange

Nelson Eddy, Victor McLaglen, Virginia Bruce, Lionel Barrymore, H. B. Warner, Raymond Walburn, Edward Arnold, Guy Kibbee, Charles Butterworth, Billy Bevan

'Big box office . . . lusty patriotic meller. Cinch for exploitation.' – *Variety*

Let George Do It **
GB 1940 82m bw
Ealing (Basil Dearden)

A ukelele player accidentally goes to Bergen instead of Blackpool and is mistaken for a spy.

Generally thought to be the best George Formby vehicle, with plenty of pace, good situations and catchy tunes.

w John Dighton, Austin Melford, Angus MacPhail, Basil Dearden *d* Marcel Varnel *ph* Gordon Dines, Ronald Neame

George Formby, Phyllis Calvert, Garry Marsh, Romney Brent, Bernard Lee, Coral Browne, Torin Thatcher, Hal Gordon

'The shocking true story of an unbelievable miscarriage of justice.'

Let Him Have It **
GB 1991 115m colour
First Independent/Vivid/Le Studio Canal Plus/British Screen (Luc Roeg, Robert Warr)
V, V*, S

Derek Bentley, an 18-year-old with a low IQ, is hanged for a murder committed by another.

Affecting drama that keeps its focus on its central character.

w Neal Purvis, Robert Wade *d* Peter Medak *ph* Oliver Stapleton *m* Michael Kamen *pd* Michael Pickwoad *ed* Ray Lovejoy

Christopher Eccleston, Paul Reynolds, Tom Bell, Eileen Atkins, Clare Holman, Michael Elphick, Mark McGann, Tom Courtenay, Michael Gough

'A powerful mix of social conscience and solid entertainment.' – *Variety*

'The straightforward, chronological narrative of this often moving naturalistic drama is both its major emotional strength and its chief dramatic weakness.' – *Nigel Floyd, Sight and Sound*

Let It Ride
US 1989 86m Technicolor
Paramount (David Giler)
V, V*, L

A compulsive and unsuccessful gambler comes good at the race-track.

A comedy that limps along for most of its length.

w Ernest Morton (Nancy Dowd) *book* Good Vibes by Jay Cronley *d* Joe Pykta *ph* Curtis J. Wehr *m* Giorgio Moroder *pd* Wolf Kroeger *ed* Dede Allen

Richard Dreyfuss, David Johansen, Teri Garr, Allen Garfield, Jennifer Tilly, Michelle Phillips, Mary Woronov, Robbie Coltrane

Let No Man Write My Epitaph
US 1960 106m bw
Columbia/Boris D. Kaplan

A slum boy wants to become a concert pianist but falls in with gangsters.

Squalid, predictable melodrama without many redeeming features.

w Robert Presnell Jnr   *novel* Willard Motley
d Philip Leacock   *ph* Burnett Guffey   *m* George
Duning

James Darren, Shelley Winters, Burl Ives, Jean
Seberg, Jeanne Cooper, Ricardo Montalban, Ella
Fitzgerald

Let the People Sing *
GB   1942   105m   bw
British National (John Baxter)

An out-of-work comedian persuades a drunken
nobleman to join a protest against the closing of a
village hall.

A development of *The Good Companions* which
compares quite nicely with the Capra films from
across the water: naïve but entertaining, with good
star performances.

w John Baxter, Barbara K. Emery, Geoffrey Orme
novel J. B. Priestley   *d* John Baxter   *ph* James Wilson

Alastair Sim, Fred Emney, Edward Rigby, Patricia Roc,
Oliver Wakefield, Marian Spencer, Olive Sloane, Gus
McNaughton, Charles Hawtrey

Let Them Live
US   1937   71m   bw
Universal

A young man matches wits with a crooked town boss.

Tepid second-feature drama.

w Bruce Manning, Lionel Houser   *d* Harold Young

John Howard, Nan Grey, Edward Ellis, Judith Barrett

'Better than many of its kind . . . should please in
nabes.' – *Variety*

Let Us Be Gay
US   1930   79m   bw
MGM

Divorcees meet again, many years later, in Paris.

Predictable star romance, now very dated, like its
title.

w Frances Marion   *play* Rachel Crothers   *d* Robert
Z. Leonard

Norma Shearer, Rod La Rocque, Marie Dressler, Sally
Eilers, Raymond Hackett, Hedda Hopper

'Strong on all counts, romance, comedy, human
sympathy and gorgeous clothes against a glamorous
setting.' – *Variety*

Let Us Live
US   1937   67m   bw
Columbia

An innocent taxi driver is convicted of murder.

Intense little melodrama which served its purpose.

w Joseph F. Dineen, Anthony Veiller and Allen
Rivkin   *d* John Brahm

Maureen O'Sullivan, Henry Fonda, Ralph Bellamy

'Heavy dramatic preachment with limited appeal.' –
Variety

Lethal Weapon *
US   1987   110m   Technicolor
Warner/ Richard Donner, Joel Silver
V, V (W), V*, L

A slightly unhinged cop uncovers a drug smuggling
operation.

Extremely violent *policier* which caters to the Rambo
crowd but has enough pizazz to recommend it to most
classes.

w Shane Black   *d* Richard Donner   *ph* Stephen
Goldblatt   *m* Michael Kamen, Eric Clapton

Mel Gibson, Danny Glover, Gary Busey, Mitchell
Ryan, Tom Atkins, Darlene Love

'Style masquerading as content.' – *Daily Variety*

Lethal Weapon 2
US   1989   111m   colour   Panavision
Warner/Silver Pictures (Richard Donner, Joel Silver)
V, V (W), V*, L, S

Two cops hunt down drug smugglers protected by
diplomatic immunity.

Slick action film with South Africans as the villains,
fast-paced enough for the many implausibilities of
plot and character to flash by.

w Jeffrey Boam   *story* Shane Black, Warren Murphy
d Richard Donner   *ph* Stephen Goldblatt
m Michael Kamen, Eric Clapton, David Sanborn
pd J. Michael Riva   *ed* Stuart Baird

Mel Gibson, Danny Glover, Joe Pesci, Joss Ackland,
Derrick O'Connor, Patsy Kensit

'The magic is back again.'

Lethal Weapon 3
US   1992   118m   Technicolor   Panavision
Warner/Silver Pictures (Richard Donner, Joel Silver)
V, V*. L, S

Two detectives expose a former cop who is running
an arms racket.

A succession of violent set pieces substitutes for
narrative and character in this increasingly cynical
series.

w Jeffrey Boam, Robert Mark Kamen   *d* Richard
Donner   *ph* Jan de Bont   *m* Michael Kamen, Eric
Clapton, David Sanborn   *pd* James Spencer
ed Robert Brown, Battle Davis

Mel Gibson, Danny Glover, Joe Pesci, Rene Russo,
Stuart Wilson, Steve Kahan, Darlene Love, Traci
Wolfe

'A pic that's really more about moments – comic or
thrilling – than any sort of cohesive whole.' – *Variety*

'It celebrates a luxurious kind of destruction and
disorder that can only appear mindless amid today's
realities.' – *Vincent Canby, New York Times*

Let's Be Famous
GB   1939   83m   bw
Ealing (Michael Balcon)

A stage-struck Irish lad and Lancashire lass have
various adventures in London.

Easy-going comedy introducing radio personalities of
the day.

w Roger MacDougall, Allan MacKinnon   *d* Walter
Forde   *ph* Ronald Neame, Gordon Dines
md Ernest Irving

Jimmy O'Dea, Betty Driver, Sonnie Hale, Patrick Barr,
Basil Radford, Milton Rosmer, Garry Marsh

Let's Be Happy
GB   1957   107m   Technicolor   Cinemascope
ABP/ Marcel Hellman

Footling musical remake of *Jeannie* (qv).

w Diana Morgan   *d* Henry Levin   *ph* Erwin Hillier
md Louis Levy   *songs* Nicholas Brodszky, Paul
Francis Webster   *m* Nicholas Brodszky

Vera-Ellen, Tony Martin, Robert Flemyng, Zena
Marshall, Guy Middleton, Katherine Kath, Jean
Cadell, Gordon Jackson

'Success still eludes the Anglo-American musical.' –
MFB

Let's Dance
US   1950   112m   Technicolor
Paramount (Robert Fellows)

Show business partners reunite after five years of
private life.

Tediously plotted musical with a couple of good
numbers.

w Allan Scott   *story* Maurice Zolotow   *d* Norman
Z. McLeod   *ph* George Barnes   *m* Robert Emmett
Dolan   *songs* Frank Loesser

Fred Astaire, Betty Hutton, Roland Young, Ruth
Warrick, Lucile Watson, Barton MacLane, Shepperd
Strudwick, Melville Cooper, Harold Huber, George
Zucco

Let's Do It Again
US   1953   95m   Technicolor
Columbia (Oscar Saul)

A songwriter and his wife plan a divorce but call it off
in the nick of time.

Tame musical remake of *The Awful Truth* (qv), pleasant
enough but lacking style and punch.

w Mary Loos, Richard Sale   *d* Alexander Hall
ph Charles Lawton Jnr   *md* Morris Stoloff
songs Lester Lee, Ned Washington   *m* George
Duning

Jane Wyman, Ray Milland, Aldo Ray, Leon Ames

Let's Do It Again
US   1975   113m   Technicolor
Warner/First Artists/Verdon (Melville Tucker, Pembroke J.
Herring)
V*

Three Atlanta workers conceive a zany plan to raise
money for their church by hypnotizing a boxer into
winning a big fight.

Lively but overlong farce reassembling the black
talents of *Uptown Saturday Night*.

w Richard Wesley   *d* Sidney Poitier   *ph* Donald
M. Morgan   *m* Curtis Mayfield

Sidney Poitier, Bill Cosby, Calvin Lockhart, John
Amos, Denise Nicholas, Ossie Davis, Jimmy Walker

Let's Face It
US   1943   76m   bw
Paramount (Fred Kohlmar)

A smart-alec soldier has a plot involving a ladies'
health camp, but finds himself up to his neck in spies.

Tepid star comedy which unaccountably ditches
almost all the numbers from the musical on which it
was based.

w Harry Tugend   *musical play* Dorothy and Herbert
Fields, Cole Porter   *play* Cradle Snatchers by Norma
Mitchell, Russell Medcraft   *d* Sidney Lanfield
ph Lionel Lindon   *songs* Cole Porter

Bob Hope, Betty Hutton, Eve Arden, Phyllis Povah,
Dona Drake, ZaSu Pitts, Marjorie Weaver, Raymond
Walburn, Joe Sawyer

Let's Fall in Love
US   1934   67m   bw
Columbia

A film director passes off a circus attendant as a
glamorous foreign star.

Lightweight comedy with music which did okay.

w Herbert Fields   *d* David Burton

Edmund Lowe, Ann Sothern, Miriam Jordan,
Gregory Ratoff

'No chorus, no legs, no undressing for a change . . .
moderately geared for moderate income.' – *Variety*

Let's Get Lost *
US   1988   120m   bw
Mainline/Little Bear (Bruce Weber)
V, V*, S

Documentary on the life of jazz trumpeter and drug
addict Chet Baker.

Fascinating series of interviews with friends,
associates and lovers, interspersed with film from
Baker's earlier life and some modern-day
performances.

w Susan Stribling   *d* Bruce Weber   *ph* Jeff Preiss
m Chet Baker   *ad* Sam Shahid, Donald Sterzin, Rise
Daniels   *ed* Angelo Corrao

Let's Get Married
US   1937   68m   bw
Columbia

A politician's daughter falls for the weather bureau chief.

Aimless romantic comedy which gets by on its performers.

w Ethel Hill   *story* A. H. Z. Carr   *d* Alfred E. Green

Ida Lupino, Walter Connolly, Ralph Bellamy, Reginald Denny, Raymond Walburn

'Mediocre dualler.' – *Variety*

Let's Go Native
US   1930   75m   bw
Paramount

Various people are shipwrecked on a South Sea island.

Easy-going farce comedy with music.

w George Marion Jnr, Percy Heath   *d* Leo MacCarey

Jack Oakie, Jeanette MacDonald, Skeets Gallagher, James Hall, Kay Francis

'Hokum laughs with songs and dances.' – *Variety*

Let's Go Places
US   1930   70m   bw
Fox

A young tenor goes to Hollywood, is mistaken for someone more famous and becomes a star.

Lightweight comedy with mildly interesting studio scenes.

w William K. Wells   *d* Frank Strayer

Joseph Wagstaff, Lola Lane, Sharon Lynn, Ilka Chase, Walter Catlett, Dixie Lee

'Plenty of music, no drawing names. Rates moderate for the big houses.' – *Variety*

Let's Hope It's a Girl *
Italy/France   1985   119m   colour
Artificial Eye/Clemi Cinematografica/Producteurs Associes/
    Soprofilms/A2 (Raimondo Castelli, Bruno Ridolfi)
original title: *Speriamo Che Sia Femmina*

A countess strives, with the help of other women of the household, to keep running the family farm.

Gently amusing, rambling comedy.

w Leo Benvenuti, Tullio Pinelli, Suso Cecchi D'Amico, Piero de Bernardi, Mario Monicelli
d Mario Monicelli   *ph* Camillo Bazzoni   *m* Nicola Piovani   *ad* Enrico Fiorentini   *ed* Ruggero Mastroianni

Liv Ullmann, Catherine Deneuve, Philippe Noiret, Bernard Blier, Giuliana de Sio, Stefania Sandrelli, Athina Cenci, Lucrezia Lante Della Rovere

Let's Kill Uncle
US   1966   92m   colour
Universal/William Castle

A boy is threatened by his wicked uncle, and retaliates.

Mildly intriguing black comedy, leadenly handled.

w Mark Rodger   *novel* Rohan O'Grady   *d* William Castle   *ph* Harold Lipstein   *m* Herman Stein

Nigel Green, Mary Badham, Pat Cardi, Robert Pickering

Let's Live a Little
US   1948   85m   bw
Eagle-Lion/United California Productions

An advertising agent falls for his lady psychiatrist, and after many vicissitudes they and their former partners make it to the altar.

Mild comedy which just about bubbles along despite a rather uncomfortable cast.

w Albert J. Cohen, Jack Harvey   *d* Richard Wallace
ph Ernest Laszlo   *m* Werner Heymann

Hedy Lamarr, Robert Cummings, Anna Sten, Robert Shayne, Mary Treen

Let's Live Tonight
US   1935   75m   bw
Columbia

Two millionaire brothers in Monte Carlo love the same girl.

Flimsy romantic comedy which gets by on its music.

w Gene Markey, Bradley King   *d* Victor Schertzinger

Lilian Harvey, Tullio Carminati, Hugh Williams, Janet Beecher, Tala Birell, Luis Alberni

'A parrot gets most of the laughs, which tips off the script.' – *Variety*

Let's Make a Night of It
GB   1937   92m   bw
Associated British

In Nice, a husband and wife own rival night-clubs.

Slim musical with rather too many interpolated turns.

w Hugh Brooke   *radio play* The Silver Spoon by Henrik Ege   *d* Graham Cutts

Buddy Rogers, June Clyde, Claire Luce, Fred Emney, Iris Hoey, Steve Geray, and Syd Walker, Afrique, Oliver Wakefield, Brian Michie, Joe Loss and his Band, Sidney Lipton and his Band

'Definitely no appeal for the US.' – *Variety*

Let's Make It Legal
US   1951   77m   bw
TCF

An attractive grandmother divorces her gambler husband and takes up with an old boyfriend.

Unremarkable but competent star comedy.

w F. Hugh Herbert, I. A. L. Diamond   *d* Richard Sale

Claudette Colbert, Zachary Scott, Macdonald Carey, Barbara Bates, Robert Wagner, Marilyn Monroe

Let's Make Love *
US   1960   118m   DeLuxe   Cinemascope
TCF (Jerry Wald)
V, V*, L

A multi-millionaire, learning that he is to be burlesqued in a Broadway show, joins the cast as an actor.

Complex, moderately sophisticated, occasionally funny musical inspired by *On The Avenue* (qv); lively characterizations but poor numbers.

w Norman Krasna   *d* George Cukor   *ph* Daniel L. Fapp   *ch* Jack Cole   *md* Lionel Newman, Earl H. Hagen   *songs* Sammy Cahn, Jimmy Van Heusen

Yves Montand, Marilyn Monroe, Tony Randall, Wilfrid Hyde-White, Frankie Vaughan, David Burns, and guests Bing Crosby, Gene Kelly, Milton Berle

AAN: Lionel Newman, Earl H. Hagen

Let's Make Music
US   1940   85m   bw
RKO (Howard Benedict)

An old maid of a teacher writes a school song that unexpectedly becomes a novelty hit.

Slight but pleasant time-filler that includes a performance of Crosby's hit 'Big Noise from Winnetka'. Its only surprise is that it was written by the acerbic novelist Nathanael West during his time as an ill-paid Hollywood hack.

w Nathanael West; special dialogue for Bob Crosby by Helen Phillips, Bernard Dougall   *d* Leslie Goodwins   *ph* Jack Mackenzie   *ad* Van Nest Polglase   *ed* Desmond Marquette

Bob Crosby, Jean Rogers, Elisabeth Risdon, Joseph Buloff, Joyce Compton, Bob Crosby's Orchestra featuring The Bobcats

Let's Make Up: see Lilacs in the Spring

Let's Scare Jessica to Death
US   1971   89m   colour
Paramount/Jessica Co (Charles B. Moss Jnr)
V*

Back home after a nervous breakdown, our heroine is troubled by voices and visions, not to mention an ambulant corpse and a vampire or two.

Competent screamie.

w Norman Jonas, Ralph Rose   *d* John Hancock
ph Bob Baldwin   *m* Orville Stoeber

Zohra Lampert, Barton Heyman, Kevin O'Connor

Let's Spend the Night Together
US   1982   94m   Technicolor
Embassy (Ronald L. Schwary)
V*

A concert film shot on the Rolling Stones' tour of America in 1981, including performances from the Sun Devil Stadium in Tempe, Arizona and the Brendan Byrne Arena in Rutherford, New Jersey.

Fan material, providing nothing of backstage interest, and performances, in the large and impersonal arenas favoured by rock stars, which seem strictly by rote despite their energy.

d Hal Ashby   *ph* Caleb Deschanel, Gerald Feil
m/ly Mick Jagger, Keith Richards and others   *ed* Lisa Day, Sonya Sones, Lorinda Hollingshead

† Songs performed include 'All Down the Line', 'Beast of Burden', 'Black Limousine', 'Brown Sugar', 'Hang Fire', 'Honky Tonk Woman', 'Jumpin' Jack Flash', 'Let It Bleed', 'Let's Spend the Night Together', 'Satisfaction', 'Under My Thumb' and 'You Can't Always Get What You Want'.

Let's Try Again
US   1934   64m   bw
RKO

A doctor and his wife drift apart, then get back together again.

Formula high-life drama without much conviction.

w Worthington Miner and Allen Scott   *play* Vincent Lawrence   *d* Worthington Miner

Diana Wynyard, Clive Brook, Irene Hervey, Helen Vinson

'Talky, tedious and far from original: where the cast doesn't mean anything the picture will have plenty of worries.' – *Variety*

The Letter *
US   1929   61m   bw
Paramount

Early talkie version of a solid piece of theatre.

See below.

play W. Somerset Maugham   *story* W. Somerset Maugham   *d* Jean de Limur

Jeanne Eagels, O. P. Heggie, Reginald Owen, Herbert Marshall, Irene Browne

AAN: Jeanne Eagels

'With all my heart, I still love the man I killed!'
The Letter ****
US   1940   95m   bw
Warner (Robert Lord)
V*, L

A rubber plantation owner's wife kills a man in what seems to have been self-defence; but a letter from her proves it to have been a crime of passion, and becomes an instrument of blackmail.

Excellent performances and presentation make this the closest approximation on film to reading a Maugham story of the Far East, though censorship forced the addition of an infuriating moral ending.

w Howard Koch,   *story* W. Somerset Maugham
d William Wyler   *ph* Tony Gaudio   *m* Max Steiner
ed Warren Low

Bette Davis, Herbert Marshall, James Stephenson, Sen Yung, Frieda Inescort, Gale Sondergaard, Bruce Lester, Tetsu Komai

'The writing is taut and spare throughout . . . the unravelling of Maugham's story is masterly and the presentation visual and cinematic . . . the audience at the trade show did not move a finger.' – *James Agate*

† Herbert Marshall played the lover in the first version and the husband in the second.

AAN: best picture; William Wyler; Tony Gaudio; Max Steiner; Bette Davis; James Stephenson; Warren Low

A Letter for Evie
US   1945   88m   bw
William H. Wright/MGM

A girl starts confusion when she writes a letter to an unknown soldier; a wimp writes back but sends his he-man buddy's photograph.

Predictable comedy with longueurs.

w De Vallon Scott, Alan Friedman   *d* Jules Dassin

Marsha Hunt, John Carroll, Hume Cronyn, Spring Byington, Pamela Britton, Norman Lloyd

'The story that will live . . . as long as there is love!'
Letter from an Unknown Woman ***
US   1948   89m   bw
Universal/Rampart (John Houseman)
V*, L

A woman wastes her life in unrequited love for a rakish pianist.

Superior 'woman's picture' which gave its director his best chance in America to recreate his beloved Vienna of long ago. Hollywood production magic at its best.

w Howard Koch,   *novel* Stefan Zweig   *d* Max Ophuls
ph Franz Planer   *m* Daniele Amfitheatrof
ad Alexander Golitzen

Joan Fontaine, Louis Jourdan, Mady Christians, Art Smith, Marcel Journet

'A film full of snow, sleigh bells, lights gleaming in ornamental gardens and trysts at night.' – *Charles Higham, 1972*

'It is fascinating to watch the sure deft means by which Ophuls sidetracks seemingly inevitable clichés and holds on to a shadowy, tender mood, half buried in the past. Here is a fragile filmic charm that is not often or easily accomplished.' – *Richard Winnington*

'Film narrative of a most skilled order.' – *William Whitebait*

'Probably the toniest "woman's picture" ever made.' – *Pauline Kael, 70s*

Letter of Introduction *
US   1938   100m   bw
Universal (John M. Stahl)

A young actress is encouraged by an ageing star whom she does not know is her father.

Commercial melodrama with luxury trimmings, all very neatly packaged.

w Sheridan Gibney, Leonard Spigelgass   *d* John M. Stahl   *ph* Karl Freund   *m* Charles Previn

Adolphe Menjou, Andrea Leeds, Edgar Bergen (and Charlie McCarthy), George Murphy, Eve Arden, Rita Johnson, Ernest Cossart, Ann Sheridan

'Headed for big business everywhere.' – *Variety*

A Letter to Brezhnev **
GB   1985   95m   colour
Yeardream/Film Four International/Palace Productions (Janet Goddard)
V

Two girls from Liverpool spend a busy night with Russian sailors; when one of them receives no subsequent letters, she writes to Brezhnev and is invited to Moscow.

Vivid it is, but also raucous and seedy until true love enters as a redeeming factor. The critics loved it, thinking it about unemployment and urban decline; it certainly paints a low picture of Liverpool.

w Frank Clarke   *d* Chris Bernard   *ph* Bruce McGowan   *m* Alan Gill   *ed* Lesley Walker

Alfred Molina, Peter Firth, Margi Clarke, Tracy Lea, Alexandra Pigg

'Fast-moving, funny, entertaining and poignant . . . in short how to make a British film.' – *Jill Forbes, MFB*

'A peek into the other woman's male!'
A Letter to Three Wives **
US   1949   102m   bw
TCF (Sol C. Siegel)
V*, L

Three wives on a picnic receive word from a friend that she has run off with one of their husbands.

Amusing short-story compendium which seemed more revelatory at the time than it does now, and paved the way for its writer-director's heyday.

wd Joseph L. Mankiewicz,   *novel* John Klempner
ph Arthur Miller   *m* Alfred Newman

Jeanne Crain, Ann Sothern, Linda Darnell, Jeffrey Lynn, Kirk Douglas, *Paul Douglas*, Barbara Lawrence, Connie Gilchrist, Florence Bates, Hobart Cavanaugh, and the voice of Celeste Holm

'A mere shadow of those acid Hollywood comedies of the thirties . . . over-written and under-directed . . . but it has a supply of ironies and makes a certain alkaline comment on present-day American customs and manners.' – *Richard Winnington*

'Replete with sharp dialogue. He aims barbed darts at the country's favourite institutions, and makes them score with telling effect.' – *Variety*

AA: Joseph L. Mankiewicz (as writer); Joseph L. Mankiewicz (as director)

AAN: best picture

Letters from a Dead Man *
USSR   1986   87m   colour/bw
Artificial Eye/Lenfilm/Sovexportfilm
original title: *Pisma Myortvovo Cheloveka*

After a nuclear holocaust, a scientist composes letters to his missing son while trying to rescue young survivors thrown out of the central shelter.

Grim and powerful for the most part, although not always easy to watch.

w Konstantin Lopushansky, Vyacheslav Rybakov, Boris Strugatsky   *d* Konstantin Lopushansky   *ph* Nikolai Pokoptsev   *m* Alexander Zhurbin, Faure   *ad* Yelema Amshinskaya, Viktor Ivanov

Rolan Bykov, I. Ryklin, V. Mikailov, A. Sabinin, V. Lobanov, N. Gryakalova, V. Mayorova, V. Dvorzhetski

Letty Lynton
US   1932   84m   bw
MGM

When one lover is murdered, Letty turns to another to prove her innocent.

Bad girl drama which established the star's box-office appeal.

w John Meehan and Wanda Tuchock   *d* Clarence Brown

Joan Crawford, Robert Montgomery, Nils Asther, May Robson, Lewis Stone

'Big grosses are written all over this one.' – *Variety*

Letyat Zhuravli: see *The Cranes are Flying*

Der Letzte Mann: see *The Last Laugh*

Leviathan
US/Italy   1989   98m   Technicolor
Fox/Gordon Company/Filmauro (Luigi de Laurentiis, Aurelio de Laurentiis)
V, V*, L, S

Deep sea miners are the victims of a monstrous genetic experiment gone wrong.

An underwater variation on *Alien*, lacking originality and suspense.

w David Peoples, Jeb Stuart   *d* George P. Cosmatos   *ph* Alex Thomson   *m* Jerry Goldsmith   *pd* Ron Cobb   *sp* Perpetual Motion Pictures, Stan Winston Studios   *ed* Roberto Silvi, John F. Burnett

Peter Weller, Richard Crenna, Amanda Pays, Daniel Stern, Ernie Hudson, Michael Carmine, Meg Foster, Lisa Eilbacher, Hector Elizondo

'Given the familiarity of it all, Leviathan is at least an enjoyable rip-off.' – *MFB*

La Ley del Deseo: see *Law of Desire*

Les Liaisons Dangereuses *
France   1959   106m   bw
Films Marceau

Valmont and his wife compare notes on each other's affairs.

Showy modernization of a notorious minor classic.

w Roger Vailland, Roger Vadim, Claude Brulé   *novel* Choderlos de Laclos   *d* Roger Vadim   *ph* Marcel Grignon   *m* Jack Murray, Thelonius Monk

Gérard Philipe, Jeanne Moreau, Annette Vadim, Jeanne Valerie, Simone Renant, Jean-Louis Trintignant

'A woman's picture par excellence.' – *John Russell Taylor, MFB*

Lianlian Feng Chen: see *Dust in the Wind*

Lianna
US   1983   112m   DuArt
Winwood

A wife and mother becomes a lesbian.

That's all there is, folks, not much in the way of plot, and barely enough for a TV movie; but some good observation and acting come through.   *wd* John Sayles

Linda Griffiths, Jane Hallaren, Jon de Vries, Jo Henderson

Libel *
GB   1959   100m   bw
MGM/Comet (Anatole de Grunwald)

An ex-POW baronet is accused of being an impostor.

Old-fashioned courtroom spellbinder, quite adequately done though occasionally creaky.

w Anatole de Grunwald, Karl Tunberg   *play* Edward Wooll   *d* Anthony Asquith   *ph* Robert Krasker   *m* Benjamin Frankel

Dirk Bogarde, Olivia de Havilland, Paul Massie, Wilfrid Hyde-White, Robert Morley, Anthony Dawson, Richard Wattis, Martin Miller, Millicent Martin

Libeled Lady **
US   1936   98m   bw
MGM (Lawrence Weingarten)
V*, L

An heiress sues a newspaper, and the editor hires a friend to compromise her.

Lively four-star romantic comedy which sums up its era as well as any.

w Maurine Watkins, Howard Emmett Rogers, George Oppenheimer d Jack Conway ph Norbert Brodine m William Axt

Jean Harlow, Myrna Loy, Spencer Tracy, William Powell, Walter Connolly, Charley Grapewin, Cora Witherspoon, E. E. Clive, Charles Trowbridge

'Handsomely mounted and produced, lavishly costumed, cleverly written and artfully directed, *Libeled Lady* is entirely worthy of the noble comedians who head its cast.' – *Bland Johaneson, New York Daily Mirror*

† Remade as *Easy to Wed* (qv); central situation borrowed for *Man's Favorite Sport* (qv).

AAN: best picture

'All she wanted was her black man's money and her white man's love!'
The Liberation of L. B. Jones *
US   1970   102m   Technicolor
Columbia/Liberation Co (Ronald Lubin)
V*

Racial murder is the result when a black undertaker wants a divorce in a small Tennessee town.

Violent, pointless but well-made melodrama which really does not take matters much further than *Intruder in the Dust*.

w Stirling Silliphant, Jesse Hill Ford, from Ford's novel d William Wyler ph Robert Surtees m Elmer Bernstein

Lee J. Cobb, Anthony Zerbe, Roscoe Lee Browne, Lola Falana, Lee Majors, Barbara Hershey, Yaphet Kotto, Arch Johnson, Chill Wills

'With its genuinely ferocious climax it adds up to probably the most powerful, if not the most sophisticated, race-war film the commercial studios have yet produced.' – *Nigel Andrews*

Liberty **
US   1929   20m   bw   silent
Hal Roach
V

Two convicts escape and have adventures high on a construction site.

Amusing gags are succeeded by breathtaking thrills in the Harold Lloyd style.

w Leo McCarey and H. M. Walker d Leo McCarey

Laurel and Hardy, James Finlayson

Licence to Kill *
US   1989   133m   Technicolor   Panavision
UIP/United Artists/Danjaq (Albert R. Broccoli, Michael G. Wilson)
V, V*, L, S

James Bond goes after a drug dealer who has injured his best friend.

The mixture is much as usual, though the action is more violent and Bond has become more of a free agent.

w Michael G. Wilson, Richard Maibaum d John Glen ph Alec Mills m Michael Kamen pd Peter Lamont ed John Grover

Timothy Dalton, Carey Lowell, Robert Davi, Talisa Soto, Anthony Zerbe, Frank McRae, Everett McGill, Wayne Newton, Benicio del Toro

Licensed to Kill
GB   1965   97m   Eastmancolor
Alistair Films (Estelle E. Richmond)
US title: *The Second Best Secret Agent in the Whole Wide World*

The Foreign Office calls in agent Charles Vine to protect a top international scientist.

Cheap copy of James Bond which wins no laurels but produces a few efficient routine thrills.

w Howard Griffiths, Lindsay Shonteff d Lindsay Shonteff ph Terry Maher m Bertram Chappell

Tom Adams, Veronica Hurst, Karel Stepanek, Felix Felton, Peter Bull

The Lie: see *Mensonge*

Eine Liebe in Deutschland: see *A Love in Germany*

Liebelei *
Austria   1932   85m   bw
Fred Lissa

A young army officer falls in love; but he is killed in a duel and his girl commits suicide.

Semi-classic romantic novelette, like a warm-up for *Letter from an Unknown Woman*.

w Hans Wilhelm, Kurt Alexander story Arthur Schnitzler d Max Ophuls ph Franz Planer m Theo Macheber

Magda Schneider, Wolfgang Liebeneiner, Luise Ullrich, Willy Eichberger, Gustaf Gruendgens, Paul Hoerbiger

† A revised French version played as *Une Histoire d'Amour*. The story had previously been shot under the same title in Germany in 1927; and in the sixties Romy Schneider and Alain Delon appeared in a French remake called *Christine*.

Liebestraum
US   1991   113m   DuArt
UIP/MGM/Initial (Eric Fellner)
V, V*, L, S

An architectural writer, returning home to visit his dying mother, unwittingly uncovers her violent past which has repercussions in the present.

Involved thriller that leaves a lot of questions unanswered.

wd Mike Figgis ph Juan Ruiz Anchia m Mike Figgis pd Waldemar Kalinowski ed Martin Hunter

Kevin Anderson, Pamela Gidley, Bill Pullman, Kim Novak, Graham Beckel, Zach Grenier, Thomas Kopache

'Seldom has the gulf between artistic intentions and end result yawned so protractedly.' – *Empire*

† A central scene, set in a brothel and lasting eleven minutes, was cut from the film before its release in America.

Lien-lien feng-ch'en: see *Dust in the Wind*

Les Liens du Sang: see *Blood Relatives*

Lies My Father Told Me
Canada   1975   102m   colour
Columbia/Pentimento/Pentacle (Anthony Bedrich, Harry Gulkin)
V*

Adventures of a poor Jewish boy and his grandfather in Montreal in the twenties.

Effectively if rather dishonestly sentimental, this is the kind of family picture for which critics are always clamouring but which few people in the seventies would pay to see.

w Ted Allan book Ted Allan d Jan Kadar ph Paul Van der Linden m Sol Kaplan

Yossi Yadin, Len Birman, Marilyn Lightstone, Jeffrey Lynas 'Sentiment by numbers . . . a lovable child awakening to discovery of the world; a lovable, whimsical old grandfather; a lovable, ne'er-do-well father; a lovable, long-suffering mother; a lovable, broken-down horse; lovable neighbours; a lovable whore across the way. It all strives so hard to be

lovable that you want to scream.' – David Robinson, The Times

† A British low-budgeter was made from the same story in 1940, changing the venue to Ireland and the race to Irish.

AAN: Ted Allan

Lt Robin Crusoe USN
US   1966   114m   Technicolor
Walt Disney (Bill Walsh, Ron Miller)

A navy pilot parachutes on to a Pacific island and gets involved in the local women's lib movement.

Slow-paced family comedy with very few laughs.

w Bill Walsh, Don da Gradi d Byron Paul ph William Snyder m Bob Brunner

Dick Van Dyke, Nancy Kwan, Akim Tamiroff

The Lieutenant Wore Skirts
US   1955   99m   Eastmancolor   Cinemascope
TCF (Buddy Adler)

When a TV writer joins the service, his wife enlists to be near him; but he is rejected on medical grounds.

Raucous, tasteless farce which tries far too hard to raise laughs.

w Albert Beich, Frank Tashlin d Frank Tashlin ph Leo Tover m Cyril Mockridge

Tom Ewell, Sheree North, Rita Moreno, Rick Jason, Les Tremayne

Life After Dark: see *Girls in the Night*

The Life and Death of a Hollywood Extra *
US   1927   11m (24 fps)   bw   silent
(Robert Florey and Slavko Vorkapich)

A nonentity arrives in Hollywood and dreams of becoming a star.

Avant-garde short, still interesting if less revolutionary than it seemed at the time.

wd Robert Florey and Slavko Vorkapich ph Slavko Vorkapich and Gregg Toland ad/ed Slavko Vorkapich

Jules Raucort, Georges Voya

The Life and Death of Colonel Blimp ***
GB   1943   163m   Technicolor
GFD/Archers (Michael Powell, Emeric Pressburger)
V*, L
US title: *Colonel Blimp*

A British soldier survives three wars and falls in love with three women.

Not the Blimp of the cartoon strip, but a sympathetic figure in a warm, consistently interesting if idiosyncratic love story against a background of war. The Archers as usual provide a sympathetic German lead (friend of the hero); quite a coup in wartime.

wd Michael Powell, Emeric Pressburger ph Jack Cardiff m Allan Gray ad Alfred Junge

Roger Livesey, Anton Walbrook, Deborah Kerr, Roland Culver, James McKechnie, Albert Lieven, Arthur Wontner, A. E. Matthews, David Hutcheson, Ursula Jeans, John Laurie, Harry Welchman

'There is nothing brilliant about the picture, but it is perceptive, witty and sweet-tempered.' – *James Agee*

'No one else has so well captured English romanticism banked down beneath emotional reticence.' – *Time Out, 1985*

Life and Nothing But **
France   1989   134m   colour   Panavision
Artificial Eye/Hachette Première et Cie/AB Films/Little Bear/A2 (René Cleitman)
V (W), V*, L, S
original title: *La Vie Et Rien D'Autre*

Two women, one searching for her missing husband, the other for her lover among the patients at a military hospital, discover that they are looking for the same man.

Complex and affecting movie of love and disillusion, of individual tragedy and national pride, set at the end of the First World War.

w Jean Cosmos, Bertrand Tavernier *d* Bertrand Tavernier *ph* Bruno de Keyzer *m* Oswald d'Andrea *pd* Guy-Claude François *ed* Armand Psenny

Philippe Noiret, Sabine Azéma, Pascale Vignal, Maurice Barrier, François Perrot, Jean-Pol Dubois, Daniel Russo, Michael Duchaussoy, Arlette Gilbert

'I want peace – and I don't care who I kill to get it!'

The Life and Times of Judge Roy Bean *
US   1972   124m   Technicolor   Panavision
National General/First Artists (John Foreman)
V*, L

A fantasia on the famous outlaw judge of the old west.

Sporadically entertaining but schematically messy mixture of burlesqued folklore and violent action, not in the same league as *Butch Cassidy*.

w John Milius *d* John Huston *ph* Richard Moore *m* Maurice Jarre

Paul Newman, Ava Gardner, Jacqueline Bisset, Tab Hunter, Stacy Keach, Roddy McDowall, Anthony Perkins, John Huston

AAN: song 'Marmalade, Molasses and Honey' (*m* Maurice Jarre, *ly* A. and M. Bergman)

Life at the Top *
GB   1965   117m   bw
Columbia/Romulus (James Woolf)

Ten years after marrying into money, Joe Lampton is dissatisfied, and he and his wife both have affairs.

Rough-talking but basically predictable and old-fashioned sequel to *Room at the Top*, a bit compromised by having to reflect the sixties London scene; the early Yorkshire sequences are the best.

w Mordecai Richler *d* Ted Kotcheff *ph* Oswald Morris *m* Richard Addinsell

Laurence Harvey, Jean Simmons, Honor Blackman, Michael Craig, Donald Wolfit, *Margaret Johnston*, Allan Cuthbertson, Ambrosine Philpotts, Robert Morley, Nigel Davenport, George A. Cooper

'Another thoroughly mean-spirited film of a kind which has been taking root in the British cinema.' – *Tom Milne*

† The character of Joe Lampton was later used in a long-running TV series called *Man at the Top*, which sprouted a film of its own under that title.

Life Begins
US   1932   72m   bw
Warner (Ray Griffith)
GB title: *Dream of Life*

A night in a maternity hospital.

Multi-melodrama later remade as *A Child Is Born*. Passable.

w Earl Baldwin *play* Mary McDougal Axelson *d* James Flood *ph* James Van Trees

Loretta Young, Eric Linden, Aline MacMahon, Preston Foster, Glenda Farrell, Frank McHugh, Clara Blandick, Elizabeth Patterson, Gilbert Roland

'Splendid women's picture promising at least solid matinee business.' – *Variety*

Life Begins at Eight-Thirty *
US   1942   85m   bw
TCF (Nunnally Johnson)
GB title: *The Light of Heart*

A distinguished actor is reduced through drink to being a street corner Santa Claus.

Diluted and sentimentalized version of an agreeable play.

w Nunnally Johnson *play* The Light of Heart by Emlyn Williams *d* Irving Pichel *ph* Edward Cronjager *m* Alfred Newman

Monty Woolley, Ida Lupino, Cornel Wilde, Sara Allgood, Melville Cooper, J. Edward Bromberg

Life Begins in College *
US   1937   80m   bw
TCF
GB title: *The Joy Parade*

Three zanies save the honour of the college football team.

Another of the myriad college football stories of the thirties, but this time enlivened by comedians in the leads.

w Karl Tunberg and Don Ettlinger *d* William A. Seiter

The Ritz Brothers, Joan Davis, Tony Martin, Gloria Stuart, Fred Stone, Nat Pendleton

'The Ritzes soar to stardom; a box office touchdown.' – *Variety*

Life Dances On: see *Un Carnet de Bal*

Life for Ruth *
GB   1962   91m   bw
Rank/Allied Film Makers (Michael Relph, Basil Dearden)
US title: *Condemned to Life*

A little girl dies because her parents' religion forbids blood transfusions.

Dramatized from the headlines, this little case history is small beer as film-making, and not exactly entertainment, but absorbing as a comment on human behaviour.

w Janet Green, John McCormick *d* Basil Dearden *ph* Otto Heller *md* Muir Mathieson *m* William Alwyn

Michael Craig, Patrick McGoohan, Janet Munro, Paul Rogers, Megs Jenkins, Frank Finlay, Maureen Pryor

Life Force
GB   1985   101m   Rank colour   Dunton vision
Cannon (Menahem Golan, Yoram Globus)
L

Zombies from outer space wreak havoc in London town.

Tacky vampire saga which takes ages to get going, then expires in a welter of bad acting and absurd visuals.

w Dan O'Bannon, Don Jakoby *novel* The Space Vampires by Colin Wilson *d* Tobe Hooper *ph* Alan Hume *m* Henry Mancini *pd* John Graysmark *ed* John Grover

Steve Railsback, Peter Firth, Frank Finlay, Patrick Stewart, Nicholas Ball, Mathilda May

'The unintentional laff-fest of the season.' – *Variety*

Life in Danger
GB   1959   63m   bw
Butchers/Parroch (Jack Parsons)

Angry villagers hunt for a murderer who has escaped from a nearby mental hospital.

Competent thriller with a twist in its tail.

w Malcolm Hulke, Eric Paice *d* Terry Bishop *ph* Peter Hennessy *m* William Davies *ad* Peter Proud *ed* John Trumper

Derren Nesbit, Julie Hopkins, Howard Marion Crawford, Victor Brooks, Jack Allen, Christopher Witty, Carmel McSharry, Bruce Seton

Life in Emergency Ward 10
GB   1959   84m   bw
Eros Films (Ted Lloyd)

A new consultant at the hospital causes controversy by introducing an experimental modification to heart

surgery techniques and becoming involved with a colleague's wife.

A spin-off from a popular TV series, though still looking as if it were made for the small screen and scripted as a series of anecdotal episodes that mix comedy and sentimentality in predictable ways.

w Tessa Diamond, Hazel Adair *d* Robert Day *ph* Geoffrey Faithfull *m* Philip Green *ad* George Beech *ed* Lito Carruthers

Michael Craig, Wilfrid Hyde-White, Dorothy Alison, Glyn Owen, Charles Tingwell, Frederick Bartman, Rosemary Miller, Joan Sims

A Life in the Balance *
US   1954   75m   bw
TCF/Panoramic (Leonard Goldstein)

A Mexican widower springs into action when his young son is kidnapped by a murderer.

Taut little melodrama taking place during one night in Mexico City; made with vigour on a low budget.

w Robert Presnell Jnr, Leo Townsend *d* Harry Horner *ph* J. Gomez Urquiza *m* Raul Lavista

Ricardo Montalban, Anne Bancroft, Lee Marvin

Life Is a Bed of Roses *
France   1983   111m   Eastmancolor
Philippe Dusart/Soprofilms/Films A2/Fideline/Ariane/Filmedis/ Ministry of Culture (Philippe Dusart)
original title: *La Vie est un Roman*

A count opens a temple of happiness and starts to re-educate his friends.

Dense fantasy which never really explains itself but provides pleasant moments along the way.

w Jean Gruault *d* Alain Resnais *ph* Bruno Nuytten *m* M. Philippe-Gerard

Vittorio Gassman, Ruggero Raimondi, Geraldine Chaplin, Fanny Ardant, Pierre Arditi

Life Is a Circus
GB   1958   84m   bw
Vale Film (M. Smedley Aston)

An odd-job man in a rundown circus finds Aladdin's lamp.

Feeble comedy by the Crazy Gang in a state of geriatric disrepair, simply going through the motions, which is an understandable reaction given the script. Chesney Allen makes a brief appearance to sing 'Underneath the Arches' with his old partner, Bud Flanagan.

wd Val Guest *m* Philip Green *ad* Tony Masters *ed* Bill Lenny

Bud Flanagan, Nervo and Knox, Naughton and Gold, Monsewer Eddie Gray, Shirley Eaton, Michael Holliday, Joseph Tomelty, Lionel Jeffries

Life Is a Long Quiet River: see *La Vie Est un Long Fleuve Tranquille*

Life Is Cheap . . . But Toilet Paper Is Expensive *
US   1990   88m   colour
ICA/Forever Profit Investments/Far East Stars (Winnie Fredriksz)
V*, L

Travelling from San Francisco to Hong Kong to deliver a gift to a local gangster, an Asian-American is plunged into a society he fails to understand and circumstances that lead to his humiliation.

Inventive, low-budget thriller of cultural bewilderment, mixed in with documentary-style monologues from the locals.

w Spencer Nakasako *story* Amir Mokri, Spencer Nakasako, Wayne Wang *d* Wayne Wang *ph* Amir Mokri *m* Mark Adler *ad* Colette Koo *ed* Chris Sanderson, Sandy Nervig

Chan Kim Wan, Spencer Nakasako, Victor Wong, Cheng Kwan Min, Cora Miao, Lam Chung

'Audaciously stylish and visually mesmerizing . . . Wayne Wang's take on the conundrum of Chinese identity has all the narrative logic of a tilted pinball machine.' – *Variety*

Life Is Sweet

GB   1990   103m   Metrocolor
Palace/Thin Man/Film Four International/British Screen (Simon Channing-Williams)
V, V*, L

An unexceptional couple and their grown-up children survive minor disasters.

Mildly amusing suburban comedy, though the actors' attitude to their characters ranges from condescension to caricature.

wd Mike Leigh   *ph* Dick Pope   *m* Rachel Portman   *pd* Alison Chitty   *ed* Jon Gregory

Alison Steadman, Jim Broadbent, Claire Skinner, Jane Horrocks, Stephen Rea, Timothy Spall

The Life of Adolf Hitler *

West Germany   1961   102m   bw
Real Film

A documentary culled from newsreel material; somehow less arresting than one would have hoped, though undoubtedly worthy.

w Helga Koppel   *d* Paul Rotha   *ed* Paul Rotha

'He plucked from the gutter a faded rose and made an immortal masterpiece!'

The Life of Emile Zola ***

US   1937   116m   bw
Warner (Henry Blanke)
V*

The French writer intervenes in the case of Alfred Dreyfus, condemned unjustly to Devil's Island.

The box-office success of this solidly-carpentered piece of Hollywood history was compounded in equal parts of star power and the sheer novelty of having such a thing turn up at the local Odeon.

w Norman Reilly Raine   *story* Heinz Herald and Geza Herczeg   *d* William Dieterle   *ph* Tony Gaudio   *m* Max Steiner   *ad* Anton Grot

Paul Muni, Joseph Schildkraut, Gale Sondergaard, Gloria Holden, Donald Crisp, Erin O'Brien Moore, John Litel, Henry O'Neill, Morris Carnovsky, Ralph Morgan, Louis Calhern, Robert Barrat, Vladimir Sokoloff, Harry Davenport, Robert Warwick, Walter Kingsford

'Destined to box office approval of the most substantial character. It is finely made and merits high rating as cinema art and significant recognition as major showmanship.' – *Variety*

'Along with Louis Pasteur, it ought to start a new category – the Warner crusading films, costume division.' – *Otis Ferguson*

'A grave story told with great dignity and superbly played and produced.' – *Pare Lorentz*

'One of the fine ones which begin as a film and end as an experience.' – *John Grierson*

'Rich, dignified, honest and strong, it is at once the finest historical film ever made and the greatest screen biography.' – *New York Times*

AA: best picture; script; Joseph Schildkraut

AAN: original story; William Dieterle; Max Steiner; Paul Muni; Anton Grot

A Life of Her Own

US   1950   108m   bw
MGM (Voldemar Vetluguin)

An innocent girl from Kansas becomes one of New York's top models.

Road to ruin, American style, from the pages of a women's magazine.

w Isobel Lennart   *d* George Cukor   *ph* George Folsey   *m* Bronislau Kaper

Lana Turner, Ray Milland, Tom Ewell, Louis Calhern, Ann Dvorak, Barry Sullivan, Jean Hagen

'This story belongs to the realms of soap opera – extremely artificial, highly moral in tone, and deliberately concocted to combine luxurious settings with an elementary assault on the audience's emotions.' – *MFB*

The Life of Jimmy Dolan

US   1933   85m   bw
Warner (Hal B. Wallis)
GB title: *The Kid's Last Fight*

An amiable wanderer is mistaken for a prize fighter wanted for murder.

Modest character romance, later remade as *They Made Me a Criminal*.

w David Boehm, Erwin Gelsey   *play* Bertram Millhauser, Beulah Marie Dix   *d* Archie Mayo   *ph* Arthur Edeson

Douglas Fairbanks Jnr, Loretta Young, Aline MacMahon, Guy Kibbee, Lyle Talbot, Fifi D'Orsay, Harold Huber, George Meeker

The Life of Oharu ***

Japan   1952   110m   bw
Shin Toho
original title: *Saikaku Ichidai Onna*

In the 1680s the daughter of a samurai recalls her descent into prostitution through her love for a servant.

Superbly photographed and acted tragedy of a woman trapped by a remorseless fate.

w Yoshikata Yoda, Kenji Mizoguchi   *novel* Saikaku Ihara   *d* Kenji Mizoguchi   *ph* Yoshima Kono, Yoshimi Hirano   *m* Ichiro Saito

Kinuyo Tanaka, Hisako Yamane, Toshiro Mifune, Yuriko Hamada

The Life of Riley

US   1948   87m   bw
Universal-International (Irving Brecher)

The trials of a family man in a low-paid job.

Adequate transcription from a radio series.

wd Irving Brecher

William Bendix, James Gleason, Rosemary de Camp, Bill Goodwin, Beulah Bondi, Richard Long

Life of the Party

US   1930   78m   Technicolor
Warner

Two gold-digging shop girls operate from a modiste's.

Half-hearted vulgar comedy, rather oddly given colour status.

w Arthur Caesar   *story* Melville Crossman (Darryl F. Zanuck)   *d* Roy del Ruth

Winnie Lightner, Irene Delroy, Charles Butterworth, Jack Whiting

'Spotty for laughs and business.' – *Variety*

Life of the Party

US   1937   86m   bw
RKO

A girl tries to evade suitors arranged by her mother.

Very thin comedy with several second-bracket names; not at all memorable.

w Bert Kalmar, Harry Ruby, Viola Brothers Shore   *d* William A. Seiter

Joe Penner, Harriet Hilliard, Gene Raymond, Parkyakarkus, Victor Moore, Helen Broderick, Billy Gilbert, Ann Miller

'Should prove fairish entertainment and do fairly at the b.o.' – *Variety*

The Life of Vergie Winters

US   1934   82m   bw
RKO (Pandro S. Berman)

A rising politician marries for position but keeps watch over his mistress and their child.

Archetypal soap opera, a cross between *Stella Dallas* and *Back Street*.

w Jane Murfin   *novel* Louis Bromfield   *d* Alfred Santell   *ph* Lucien Andriot   *m* Max Steiner

Ann Harding, John Boles, Helen Vinson, Frank Albertson, Lon Chaney Jnr, Sara Haden, Ben Alexander, Donald Crisp

Life on a String **

GB/Germany/China   1991   120m   Eastmancolor
Serene/Pandora/Beijing Film Studio/Herald Ace/Film Four/Berlin Filmforderung (Don Ranvaud)
original title: *Bian Zhou Bian Chang*

Accompanied by a blind youth, an elderly blind musician wanders the countryside waiting for a cure for his affliction which will come when he has broken a thousand strings while playing his three-stringed guitar.

Beautiful to look at, full of spectacular and striking images, this sedately-paced movie remains obscure to the end.

wd Chen Kaige   *story* Shi Tiesheng   *ph* Gu Changwei   *m* Qu Xiaosong   *pd* Shao Ruigang   *ed* Pei Xiaonan

Li Zhongyuan, Huang Lei, Xu Qing, Ma Ling, Zhang Zhengyuan

'A rich film experience, but its length and lack of conventional narrative will be factors to overcome in getting the film across to arthouse audiences.' – *Variety*

Life Returns

US   1938   62m   bw
Scienart

A fictional story leads up to the actual experiment performed in 1934 by Dr Robert E. Cornish when he brought a dead dog back to life.

Weird mélange of fact and fiction; despite the achievement, the presentation never catches fire. The film was banned in Britain.

w Arthur Horman, John F. Goodrich   *d* Eugen Frenke

Onslow Stevens, George Breakston, Valerie Hobson, Lois Wilson

'A picture much longer to the audience than its accredited running time would indicate.' – *Variety*

Life Stinks

US   1991   95m   DeLuxe
TCF/Brooks Films/Le Studio Canal Plus (Mel Brooks)
V, V*, L

A rich property developer takes a bet that he can survive on his own on the streets of a slum for thirty days.

Crass, tasteless comedy in which the jokes are poor.

w Mel Brooks, Rudy de Luca, Steve Haberman   *story* Mel Brooks, Ron Clark, Rudy de Luca, Steve Haberman   *d* Mel Brooks   *ph* Steven Poster   *m* John Morris   *pd* Peter Larkin   *ed* David Rawlins

Mel Brooks, Lesley Ann Warren, Jeffrey Tambor, Stuart Pankin, Howard Morris, Rudy de Luca, Teddy Wilson, Billy Barty

'Antic comedy has more laughs than the filmmaker's last couple of efforts, and presents an amiably sympathetic, if unreliable, look at the homeless.' – *Variety*

Life Upside Down *
France   1964   92m   bw
A.J. Films
original title: La Vie à l'Envers

A pleasant, ordinary young man discovers the joy of being absolutely alone, and begins to detach himself from his surroundings, ending up in a barren flat and a private hospital ward.

Engaging semi-comic case history which generates much sympathy for its eccentric hero.

wd Alain Jessua   ph Jacques Robin   m Jacques Loussier

Charles Denner, Anna Gaylor, Guy Saint-Jean, Nicole Gueden

'The tone is civilized, quiet, infinitely peaceful and often brilliantly funny.' – Brenda Davies, MFB

'Amusing or disturbing depending on whether it is viewed from the outside or the inside, but perceptive and artistic whichever way one views it.' – John Simon

'Take your cookie to see the picture that takes the cake for laughs!'

Life with Father *
US   1947   118m   Technicolor
Warner (Robert Buckner)
V*

Turn-of-the-century anecdotes of an irascible well-to-do paterfamilias who won't be baptized.

Well-upholstered screen version of a long- running play; oddly tedious considering the talent involved.

w Donald Ogden Stewart   play Howard Lindsay, Russel Crouse   d Michael Curtiz   ph Peverell Marley, William V. Skall   m Max Steiner
ad Robert Haas

William Powell, Irene Dunne, Edmund Gwenn, ZaSu Pitts, Elizabeth Taylor, Martin Milner, Jimmy Lydon, Emma Dunn, Moroni Olsen, Elizabeth Risdon

'Everybody seems to be trying too hard . . . the director is totally out of his element in this careful, deadly version.' – New Yorker, 1978

† Censorship of the day absurdly clipped Father's famous last line: 'I'm going to be baptized, damn it!'

AAN: Peverell Marley, William V. Skall; Max Steiner; William Powell; Robert Haas

Lifeboat **
US   1944   96m   bw
TCF (Kenneth MacGowan)
V, V*, L

Survivors from a torpedoed passenger ship include the U-Boat commander responsible.

Propaganda gimmick melodrama interesting for the casting and for Hitchcock's response to the challenge of filming in one cramped set.

w Jo Swerling   story John Steinbeck   d Alfred Hitchcock   ph Glen MacWilliams   m Hugo Friedhofer

Tallulah Bankhead, Walter Slezak, Henry Hull, John Hodiak, Canada Lee, William Bendix, Mary Anderson, Heather Angel, Hume Cronyn

'The initial idea – a derelict boat and its passengers as microcosm – is itself so artificial that . . . it sets the whole pride and brain too sharply to work on a tour de force for its own sake.' – James Agee

AAN: John Steinbeck; Alfred Hitchcock; Glen MacWilliams

Lifeforce
US   1985   101m   Eastmancolor
Cannon (Menahem Golan, Yoram Globus)
V*, L, S

An Anglo-American space expedition investigating Halley's Comet discovers that it hides a two-mile-high alien spaceship containing the bodies of giant,

bat-like creatures and three humanoids in suspended animation.

Extraordinarily bizarre mix of science fiction and vampire movie, more likely to provoke derision than any other emotion.

w Dan O'Bannon, Don Jakoby   novel Space Vampires by Colin Wilson   d Tobe Hooper   ph Alan Hume   m Henry Mancini, Michael Kamen, James Guthrie   pd John Graysmark   sp John Dykstra, Nick Maley, John Gant   ed John Grover

Steve Railsback, Peter Firth, Frank Finlay, Patrick Stewart, Michael Gothard, Nicholas Ball, Mathilda May, Aubrey Morris

Lifeguard
US   1976   96m   CFI colour
Paramount

A beach guard at 30 reviews his life and his future.

Odd but not unlikeable little personal drama which barely got released.

w Ron Koslow   d Daniel Petrie

Sam Elliott, Anne Archer, Stephen Young, Parker Stevenson, Kathleen Quinlan

The Lift
Netherlands   1983   99m   Eastmancolor
Warner/Sigma Films (Matthijs Van Heijningen)
V*, L

An office block elevator seems to assume deadly powers. After a murderous car, a murderous lift.

Slick but rather empty semi-horror.

wd Dick Maas   ph Marc Felperlaan   m Dick Maas   ad Harry Ammerlaan   ed Hans Van Dongen

Huub Stapel, Willeke Van Ammelrooy, Josine Van Dalsum

Lift to the Scaffold *
France   1957   89m   bw
Nouvelles Editions de Films (Jean Thuillier)
V, V*, S
original title: Ascenseur pour l'Echafaud; US title: Frantic

An executive murders his employer but is trapped in the building all night; meanwhile his car is stolen and he is arrested for a murder committed by the thief.

Complex, watchable suspenser with pretensions.

w Roger Nimier, Louis Malle   novel Noel Calef   d Louis Malle   ph Henri Decaë   m Miles Davis

Maurice Ronet, Jeanne Moreau, Georges Poujouly, Yori Bertin, Lino Ventura

'Cold, clever and rather elegant.' – Penelope Houston, MFB

The Light across the Street
France   1955   99m   bw
EGC/Fernand Rivers (Jacques Gauthier)
original title: La Lumière d'en Face

A lorry driver, injured in an accident, becomes insanely jealous of his young wife.

Low-life melodrama tailored for the sultry attractions of its new star.

w Louis Cahavance, René Masson, René Lefèvre   d Georges Lacombe   ph Louis Page   m Norbert Glanzberg

Brigitte Bardot, Raymond Pellégrin, Roger Pigaut, Claude Romain

The Light at the Edge of the World
US/Spain/Liechtenstein   1971   120m   Eastmancolor
   Panavision
Bryna/Jet/Triumfilm (Kirk Douglas, Ilya Salkind)
V*, S

A lighthouse keeper near Cape Horn resists a band of wreckers.

Pretentious, disaster-prone version of a simple adventure story; one wonders not so much what went wrong as whether anything went right in this international venture.

w Tom Rowe   novel Jules Verne   d Kevin Billington   ph Henri Decaë   m Piero Piccioni

Kirk Douglas, Yul Brynner, Samantha Eggar, Jean-Claude Drouot, Fernando Rey, Renato Salvatori

The Light Fantastic: see Love Is Better Than Ever

The Light in the Forest
US   1958   92m   Technicolor
Walt Disney
V*

Kidnapped by Indians as an infant, a teenager is returned to his parents but finds the white man's ways disturbing.

Modest frontier drama with a moral.

w Lawrence Edward Watkin   novel Conrad Richter   d Herschel Daugherty   ph Ellsworth Fredericks   m Paul Smith

James MacArthur, Carol Lynley, Jessica Tandy, Wendell Corey, Fess Parker, Joanne Dru, Joseph Calleia

The Light in the Piazza
GB   1962   101m   Metrocolor   Cinemascope
MGM (Arthur Freed)

An American matron in Florence tries to marry off her mentally retarded daughter to a wealthy Italian.

Puzzling romantic drama in which one is never quite sure why the characters behave as they do; in the end all one appreciates is the tour of northern Italy.

w Julius J. Epstein   novel Elizabeth Spencer   d Guy Green   ph Otto Heller   m Mario Nascimbene

Olivia de Havilland, Yvette Mimieux, George Hamilton, Rossano Brazzi, Barry Sullivan

Light of Day
US   1987   107m   Astro Color
Taft/Keith Barish/Tri-Star
V

A Cleveland family is upset by illness and rock'n'roll.

Drab musical wallow which seems to have little point.

wd Paul Schrader   ph John Bailey   m Thomas Newman   pd Jeannine Claudia Oppewall   ed Jacqueline Cambas

Michael J. Fox, Joan Jett, Gena Rowlands, Michael McKean

The Light of Heart: see Life Begins at Eight-Thirty

Light Sleeper *
US   1991   103m   DuArt
Guild/Grain of Sand (Linda Reisman)
V, V*, L

A drug delivery man and former addict contemplates his future as his employer decides to give up the business and go straight.

An intelligent and occasionally gripping thriller.

wd Paul Schrader   ph Ed Lachman   m Michael Been   pd Richard Hornung   ed Kristina Boden

Willem Dafoe, Susan Sarandon, Mary Beth Hurt, Dana Delany, David Clennon, Victor Garber, Jane Adams, Paul Jabara   'Contemplative and violent by turns, this quasi-thriller about a long-time drug dealer leaving the business has a great deal to recommend it but could have been significantly better had Schrader done some fresh plotting and not relied on his standby gunplay to resolve issues.' – Variety

'Laugh, you little fool, laugh... for I'm giving you something
you never had before – a soul... on canvas!'

The Light that Failed *
US   1939   97m   bw
Paramount (William A. Wellman)

A London artist is going blind as the result of a war
wound, and must finish the portrait of the little
cockney whom he loves.

Nicely-made but rather boring star romance; no
surprises in plot or performance.

w Robert Carson   story Rudyard Kipling
d William Wellman   ph Theodor Sparkuhl
m Victor Young

Ronald Colman, Walter Huston, Ida Lupino, Dudley
Digges, Muriel Angelus, Fay Helm

'Production fine for moderate b.o. Will catch attention
of the carriage trade, the literati crowd and the critics.'
– Variety

† Previously filmed in 1916 and 1923.

The Light Touch
US   1951   107m   bw
MGM (Pandro S. Berman)

An elegant art thief tries to doublecross the gangster
who employs him.

Elongated and witless romantic charade on European
locations.

wd Richard Brooks   story Jed Harris, Tom Reed
ph Robert Surtees   m Miklos Rozsa

Stewart Granger, George Sanders, Pier Angeli, Kurt
Kasznar, Larry Keating, Rhys Williams, Norman
Lloyd, Mike Mazurki

'A comedy thriller which moves far too slowly for its
imperfections to be overlooked.' – Penelope Houston,
MFB

The Light Touch (1955): see Touch and Go

Light Up the Sky
GB   1960   90m   bw
British Lion/Bryanston (Lewis Gilbert)

Life on a searchlight battery during World War II.

Wartime comedy-drama with accent on the laughs but
adding dollops of tragedy and sentiment. A very
patchy entertainment.

w Vernon Harris   play Touch It Light by Robert Storey
d Lewis Gilbert   ph John Wilcox   m Douglas
Gamley

Ian Carmichael, Tommy Steele, Benny Hill, Sydney
Tafler, Victor Maddern, Harry Locke, Johnny Briggs,
Dick Emery

The Lighthorsemen *
Australia   1988   110m   colour
Medusa/RKO (Simon Wincer, Ian Jones)
V, V*, S

Comrades take part in the cavalry charge on the
fortified city of Beersheba in the First World War.

Intermittently exciting re-creation of a historic event,
at its best in the battle scenes.

w Ian Jones   d Simon Wincer   ph Dean Semler
m Mario Millo   pd Bernard Hides   ed Adrian Carr

Jon Blake, Peter Phelps, Tony Bonner, Bill Kerr, John
Walton, Gary Sweet, Tim McKenzie, Sigrid Thornton,
Anthony Andrews

Lightnin' *
US   1930   94m   bw
Fox

A country fellow is wiser than he seems, and in
between setting other folks' lives right, persuades his
own wife not to divorce him.

Archetypal Will Rogers star part which he played on
the stage; now his first big talkie hit.

play Frank Bacon and Winchell Smith   d Henry
King

Will Rogers, Louise Dresser, Joel McCrea, Sharon Lynn,
J. M. Kerrigan

'A production of the highest quality in all its phases.'
– Variety

The Lightning Express
US   1930   bw   serial: 10 eps
Universal

A railroad owner's son guards the crack express
against saboteurs.

Primitive adventure exploits.

d Henry McRae

Lane Chandler, Louise Lorraine, Al Ferguson

Lightning Over Water
West Germany/Sweden   1980   91m   Movielab
Road Movies/Viking Film (Renée Gunde-Lach, Pierre Cottrell,
  Chris Sievernich)
aka: Nick's Movie

A record of the last months of Nicholas Ray's life,
when he was hoping to revive his career while visibly
dying from cancer.

Unique and uneasy, something for film buffs to chew
over.

wd Nicholas Ray, Wim Wenders   m Ronee Blakley
ed Wim Wenders, Peter Przygodda

Lightning Strikes Twice
US   1951   91m   bw
Warner (Henry Blanke)

A woman decides to clear her lover of suspicion of
murder, but later has her own doubts.

Silly melodrama with no credibility, little suspense,
and too much talk.

w Lenore Coffee   novel Margaret Echard   d King
Vidor   ph Sid Hickox   m Max Steiner

Richard Todd, Ruth Roman, Mercedes McCambridge,
Zachary Scott, Darryl Hickman, Frank Conroy,
Kathryn Givney

The Lightning Warrior
US   1931   bw   serial: 12 eps
Mascot

A dog unmasks The Wolf Man, who is terrorizing
pioneer settlers.

One of the last Rin Tin Tin serials: it satisfied at the
time.

d Armand Schaefer and Ben Kline

Frankie Darro, Georgia Hale, George Brent, Pat
O'Malley

Lights of New York ***
US   1928   57m   bw
Warner

A chorus girl becomes involved with gangsters.

The first '100 per cent all-talking' film, dramatically
primitive but historically important.

w F. Hugh Herbert, Murray Roth   d Bryan Foy
ph E. B. DuPar

Helene Costello, Cullen Landis, Wheeler Oakman,
Eugene Pallette, Tom Dugan, Gladys Brockwell, Mary
Carr

'100 per cent crude.' – Variety

Lights of Old Broadway
US   1925   80m approx at 24 fps   bw   silent
MGM

Twin orphan girls find very different routes to
happiness.

One of the star's most popular vehicles.

w Carey Wilson   d Monta Bell

Marion Davies, Conrad Nagel, George K. Arthur,
Julia Swayne Gordon

Lights of Variety *
Italy   1950   94m   bw
Film Capitolium (Alberto Lattuada)
V, V*

A stage-struck young girl forsakes the manager of the
troupe in which she found stardom for the bright
lights of the city.

Tragi-comical backstage story in which the bits of
detail are more entertaining than the plot.

w Federico Fellini   d Alberto Lattuada   ph Otello
Martelli   m Felice Lattuada

Peppino de Filippo, Carla del Poggio, Giulietta
Masina, John Kitzmiller, Folco Lulli

'Told with the humor and compassion, the subtlety
and sensitivity, and marked by the satiric eye, the
keenness of insight, the appreciation of human frailty,
that are Fellini's strong points.' – Judith Crist

Lights Out: see Bright Victory

The Lightship
US   1985   89m   colour
Rank/CBS (Moritz Borman, Bill Benenson)

A lightship is taken over by a gang of psychopathic
crooks on the run.

Echoes of Key Largo abound in this dreary suspense
melodrama which aspires to more meaning than is
evident.

w William Mai, David Taylor   novel Siegfried Lenz
d Jerzy Skolimowski   ph Charly Steinberger
m Stanley Myers   ad Holger Gross   ed Barry
Vince, Scott Hancock

Robert Duvall, Klaus Maria Brandauer, Tom Bower,
Robert Constanzo

Like Father Like Son
US   1987   98m   Technicolor
Grazer-Valdes/Tri-Star
V*, L

A surgeon and his son find themselves in each other's
bodies.

Role-reversal comedy at the beginning of a trend; in
itself a bore.

w Lorne Cameron, Steven L. Bloom   d Rod Daniel
ph Jack N. Green   m Miles Goodman   pd Dennis
Gassner   ed Lois Freeman-Fox

Dudley Moore, Kirk Cameron, Sean Astin, Patrick
O'Neal, Margaret Colin

'A Delicious Love Story.'

Like Water for Chocolate **
Mexico   1991   114m   colour
Electric/Cinevista/NCCA/NTDF/Alfonso Arau
V, V*, L
original title: Como agua para chocolate

In Mexico in the early 1900s, forced to stay at home to
look after her mother and to see the man she loves
marry her sister, the youngest of three daughters puts
all her emotions into her cooking.

Part soap opera, part delightful fable and wholly
enjoyable, this is a sweet, rich but not indigestible
romantic drama.

w Laura Esquivel   novel Laura Esquivel   d Alfonso
Arau   ph Emmanuel Lubezki, Steve Bernstein
m Leo Brower   pd Marco Antonio Arteaga, Mauricio
de Aguinaci, Denise Pizzini   ed Carlos Bolado,
Francisco Chiu

Marco Leonardi, Lumi Cavazos, Regina Torne, Mario
Ivan Martinez, Ada Carrasco, Yareli Arizmendi,
Claudette Maille, Pilar Aranda

'This classic love story bridging generations is so
compelling and splendidly expressed in the script that

the frustrated filmgoer can only shake his head at the incompetent handling.' – *Variety*

'The film acts as a kind of palliative for the middle-class audiences with which it has been so successful. Despite all the changes brought about in Mexican society by the Revolution and its aftermath, they can still feel comfortable with those things that have remained the same: the servants in their kitchens.' – *John Kraniauskas, Sight and Sound*

† The title refers to the heroine's temper, kept just below boiling point – like water for chocolate.

The Likely Lads *

GB 1976 90m bw
EMI (Aida Young)
V

Two Geordie friends, with wife and mistress, go on a touring holiday.

Valuable as a record of an excellent and long-running TV series, this big-screen version finds most of the humour regrettably broadened.

w Dick Clement, Ian La Frenais   d Michael Tuchner
ph Tony Imi   m Mike Hugg

Rodney Bewes, James Bolam, Brigit Forsyth, Mary Tamm, Sheila Fearn, Zena Walker

A Likely Story

US 1947 88m bw
RKO (Richard H. Berger)

A man thinks he has only a short time to live, and in trying to do his best for a girlfriend gets mixed up with gangsters.

Even a star cast could not have made much of this zany comedy script.

w Bess Taffel   d H. C. Potter   ph Roy Hunt
md Constantin Bakaleinikoff   m Leigh Harline

Barbara Hale, Bill Williams, Lanny Rees, Sam Levene, Dan Tobin, Nestor Paiva

Li'l Abner *

US 1959 113m Technicolor Vistavision
Paramount/Panama-Frank (Norman Panama)
V*

The hillbilly town of Dogpatch, tagged the most useless community in America, fights being used as a test site for A-bombs.

Set-bound, intrinsically American, but bright and cheerful film of a stage show about Al Capp's famous comic strip characters.

wd Norman Panama, Melvin Frank from the musical show (*ly Johnny Mercer, words* Gene de Paul)
ph Daniel L. Fapp   md Joseph Lilley, Nelson Riddle
m Gene de Paul   ch Dee Dee Wood, Michael Kidd

Peter Palmer, Leslie Parrish, Billie Hayes, Howard St John, Stubby Kaye, Stella Stevens, Julie Newmar, Robert Strauss

'As joyous, screwy, dancin' and jokin' a musical show as Hollywood has sent us for a long time.' – *Sunday Dispatch*

AAN: Joseph Lilley, Nelson Riddle

The Lilac Domino

GB 1937 79m bw
Grafton-Capitol-Cecil

A Hungarian count is attracted at the gambling tables by a masked girl.

Surprisingly undercast version of a popular operetta.

w Basil Mason, Neil Gow, R. Hutter and Derek Neame   play Rudolf Bernauer, E. Gatti and B. Jenbach   d Fred Zelnik

June Knight, Michael Bartlett, Athene Seyler, Richard Dolman, S. Z. Sakall, Fred Emney, Jane Carr

Lilac Time *

US 1928 90m approx bw   silent with sound effects
First National
GB title: *Love Never Dies*

A French girl promises to wait for an American flyer, but his stern father tells her he is dead.

Popular war romance which retains moments of interest.

w Carey Wilson   play Jane Cowl, Jane Murfin   d/p George Fitzmaurice   ph Sid Hickox   m Nathaniel Shilkret

Colleen Moore, Gary Cooper, Eugenie Besserer, Burr McIntosh, Arthur Lake

Lilacs in the Spring

GB 1954 94m Trucolor
Republic/Everest (Herbert Wilcox)
US title: *Let's Make Up*

During the London blitz a young actress is knocked unconscious and dreams of herself as Nell Gwyn, Queen Victoria and her own mother before waking up to deal with her personal problems.

Good-humoured theatrical charade deadened by poorish production and colour, strengthened by the star's game run-through of her staple characters. How Mr Flynn came to be involved is anybody's guess.

w Miles Malleson (uncredited)   play *The Glorious Days* by Harold Purcell   d Herbert Wilcox   ph Max Greene   m Robert Farnon

Anna Neagle, Errol Flynn, Peter Graves, David Farrar, Kathleen Harrison

Lili *

US 1953 81m Technicolor
MGM (Edwin H. Knopf)
V*

A 16-year-old orphan girl joins a carnival and falls in love with the magician.

Romantic whimsy dependent entirely on treatment, which is sometimes heavy-handed. Charm, ballet and puppets are provided, but a little cheerful song and dance would not have been amiss.

w Helen Deutsch   novel Paul Gallico   d/ch Charles Walters   ph Robert Planck   m Bronislau Kaper
ad Cedric Gibbons, Paul Groesse

Leslie Caron, Jean-Pierre Aumont, Mel Ferrer, Kurt Kasznar

'A lovely and beguiling little film, touched with the magic of romance.' – *Bosley Crowther*

AA: Bronislau Kaper

AAN: Helen Deutsch; Charles Walters; Robert Planck; Leslie Caron; art direction

Lili Marleen *

West Germany 1980 116m colour
Roxy/CIP/Rialto/Bayerische Rundfunk (Luggi Waldleitner)
S

A German girl singer becomes famous and notorious during World War II by her rendition of an old song.

Curious mixture of melodrama and satire which doesn't really work but is always lively to watch.

w Manfred Purzer, Joshua Sinclair, Rainer Werner Fassbinder   novel *The Sky Has Many Colours* by Lale Andersen   d Rainer Werner Fassbinder   ph Xaver Schwarzenberger   m Peer Raben   ed Juliane Lorenz, Rainer Werner Fassbinder

Hanna Schygulla, Giancarlo Giannini, Mel Ferrer, Karl Heinz

Lilies of the Field

US 1930 60m bw
First National

A chorus girl has been robbed of her child by framed divorce court evidence.

Backstage melodrama with music, very dated now but with interesting credits.

w John Goodrich   play William Hurlbut
d Alexander Korda

Corinne Griffith, Ralph Forbes, John Loder, Patsy Paige, Freeman Wood, Virginia Bruce

'Big revue sequences in backstage locale. Better than average programmer.' – *Variety*

Lilies of the Field *

US 1963 94m bw
UA/Rainbow/Ralph Nelson
V*, S

An itinerant black workman in New Mexico helps a group of German nuns to build a chapel.

Liberal, sentimental, under-dramatized little comedy with everyone coming to understand each other's point of view, so that the audience feels improved if not especially entertained.

w James Poe   novel William E. Barrett   d Ralph Nelson   ph Ernest Haller   m Jerry Goldsmith

Sidney Poitier, Lilia Skala

AA: Sidney Poitier

AAN: best picture; James Poe; Ernest Haller; Lilia Skala

Liliom *

US 1930 94m bw
Fox

A Budapest carnival man is killed in a fight but later comes back from heaven to see how his family is doing.

Ingeniously-staged fantasy, very dated but a lot more interesting than its musical remake *Carousel* (qv).

w S. N. Behrman   play Ferenc Molnar   d Frank Borzage   ph Chester Lyons   m Richard Fall

Charles Farrell, Rose Hobart, Estelle Taylor, Lee Tracy, Walter Abel, Guinn Williams, H. B. Warner, Dawn O'Day (Anne Shirley)

'Beyond the depth of Farrell's dramatic ability . . . shapes up as passable for a week-stand in the keys.' – *Variety*

Lilith *

US 1964 126m bw
Columbia/Centaur (Robert Rossen)
V*

A trainee therapist at an asylum falls in love with a patient.

Strange, wistful, poetic and rather soporific character melodrama.

wd Robert Rossen   novel J. R. Salamanca
ph Eugene Schufftan   m Kenyon Hopkins
pd Richard Sylbert

Warren Beatty, Jean Seberg, Peter Fonda, Kim Hunter, Anne Meacham, James Patterson, Jessica Walter, Gene Hackman

'A remarkable attempt to dig a little deeper in an almost untilled field, and to throw some light on the relationship between madness and the creative imagination.' – *Tom Milne*

Lillian Russell *

US 1940 130m bw
TCF (Gene Markey)

The life and loves of the famous 1890s entertainer.

Flabby and inaccurate biopic, worth seeing for its highlights but flatly and incompetently written.

w William Anthony McGuire   d Irving Cummings
ph Leon Shamroy   md Alfred Newman
ad Richard Day, Joseph C. Wright

Alice Faye, Don Ameche, Edward Arnold, Warren William, Henry Fonda, Leo Carrillo, Helen Westley, Dorothy Peterson, Ernest Truex, Nigel Bruce, Claud

Allister, Lynn Bari, Weber and Fields, Eddie Foy Jnr, Una O'Connor

AAN: art direction

Lilly Turner
US   1933   65m   bw
Warner

A girl unwittingly marries a bigamist, then a drunk who will give her baby a name.

Turgid mother-love saga.

w Gene Markey, Kathryn Scola   play Philip Dunning, George Abbott   d William A. Wellman

Ruth Chatterton, George Brent, Frank McHugh, Ruth Donnelly, Guy Kibbee, Robert Barrat

'Spotty returns most probable.' – *Variety*

Lily in Love
US/Hungary   1985   103m   colour
Robert Halmi

Denied the lead in a film scripted by his wife, an actor disguises himself as an Italian in order to get the part.

A weak comedy, done with some style.

w Frank Cucci   d Karoly Makk   ph John Lindley   m Szaboks Fenyes   ad Tamas Vayer   ed Norman Gay

Christopher Plummer, Maggie Smith, Elke Sommer, Adolph Green

Limbo *
US   1972   111m   Technicolor
Universal (Linda Gottlieb)
aka: *Chained to Yesterday*

Women wait for their husbands to return from Vietnam.

Worthy but dramatically uninteresting multi-storied semi-propaganda piece with an untried cast.

w Joan Silver, James Bridges   d Mark Robson   ph Charles Wheeler   m Anita Kerr

Kate Jackson, Katherine Justice, Stuart Margolin, Hazel Medina, Kathleen Nolan

'Romantic ruler of London's half-world!'
Limehouse Blues *
US   1934   65m   bw
Paramount
aka: *East End Chant*

In London's shady quarter, an oriental roustabout tries to leave his jealous mistress for a girl with a shady past.

Artificial, atmospheric melodrama set in a never-never Limehouse redolent of *Broken Blossoms*. Interesting for its very excesses.

w Arthur Phillips, Cyril Hume, Grover Jones   d Alexander Hall   ph Harry Fischbeck

George Raft, Anna May Wong, Jean Parker, Kent Taylor, Billy Bevan

'Weak and slow-moving . . . won't satisfy the average fan.' – *Variety*

Limelight
GB   1935   80m   bw
GFD/Herbert Wilcox
US title: *Backstage*

A chorus girl helps a street singer to become a star.

Highly predictable backstage musical drama which made a nine days wonder of 'The Street Singer'.

w Laura Whettier   d Herbert Wilcox   ph Henry Harris

Anna Neagle, *Arthur Tracy*, Jane Winton, Ellis Jeffreys, Muriel George

'A syrupy concatenation to win all British hearts.' – *James Agate*

Limelight ***
US   1952   144m   bw
Charles Chaplin
V, V*

A broken-down music hall comedian is stimulated by a young ballerina to a final hour of triumph.

Sentimental drama in a highly theatrical London East End setting. In other hands it would be very hokey, but Chaplin's best qualities, as well as his worst, are in evidence, and in a way the film sums up his own career.

wd Charles Chaplin   ph Karl Struss   m Charles Chaplin, Raymond Rasch, Larry Russell   ad Eugene Lourié   photographic consultant Rollie Totheroh

Charles Chaplin, Claire Bloom, Buster Keaton, Sydney Chaplin, Nigel Bruce, Norman Lloyd   'From the first reel it is clear that he now wants to talk, that he loves to talk . . . where a development in the story line might easily be conveyed by a small visual effect, he prefers to make a speech about it . . . it is a disturbing rejection of the nature of the medium itself.' – *Walter Kerr*

'Surely the richest hunk of self-gratification since Huck and Tom attended their own funeral.' – *New Yorker, 1982*

'His exhortations about life, courage, consciousness and "truth" are set in a self-pitying, self-glorifying story.' – *Pauline Kael, 70s*

AA: Charles Chaplin, Raymond Rasch, Larry Russell

Limit Up
US   1989   88m   colour
Medusa/Management Company Entertainment (Jonathan D. Krane)

A woman sells her soul to an apparent demon in exchange for a successful career on the stock exchange.

A dull fantasy, dimly directed.

w Richard Martini, Luana Anders   d Richard Martini   ph Peter Lyons Collier   m John Tesh   pd R. Clifford Searcy   ed Sonny Baskin

Nancy Allen, Dean Stockwell, Brad Hall, Danitra Vance, Ray Charles, Rance Howard, Sandra Bogan

The Limping Man
GB   1953   74m   bw
Banner/Eros (Donald Ginsberg)
V*

An American leaving his plane at Heathrow sees another passenger shot by a limping man.

Initially intriguing thriller which gives up the ghost and tacks on a dream ending.

w Ian Stuart and Reginald Long   d Charles de Lautour

Lloyd Bridges, Moira Lister, Helene Cordet, Bruce Beeby, Alan Wheatley, Leslie Phillips

Linda *
GB   1960   61m   bw
Independent Artists

A teenage girl falls for a member of a street gang.

Nicely atmospheric low-life romance; no real content but plenty of raw style.

w Bill MacIlwraith   d Don Sharp

Carol White, Alan Rothwell, Cavan Malone, Lois Dane, Edward Cast

The Lineup *
US   1958   86m   bw
Columbia (Frank Cooper)

San Francisco police trap a gunman who is also a drug contact.

Energetic, polished movie version of a popular TV series, *San Francisco Beat*.

w Stirling Silliphant   d Don Siegel   ph Hal Mohr   m Mischa Bakaleinikoff

Warner Anderson, Robert Keith, Eli Wallach

'He wants to be tied down. She wants to be tied up. It's not what you think.'
The Linguini Incident
US   1992   98m   CFI colour
Rank/Isolar (Arnold Orgolini)
V, V*, S

A waitress who wants to be an escape artist and a barman seeking a wife set out to rob an antique shop of a ring that once belonged to Houdini.

No escape from boredom in this trivial and lacklustre comedy.

w Richard Shepard, Tamar Brott   d Richard Shepard   ph Robert Yeoman   m Thomas Newman   pd Marcia Hinds-Johnson   ed Sonya Polonsky

Rosanna Arquette, David Bowie, Eszter Balint, André Gregory, Buck Henry, Viveca Lindfors, Marlee Matlin

'Energetic actors can't overcome the uninspired, poverty-row production values.' – *Variety*

Link
GB   1986   103m   Technicolor
Cannon/EMI (Richard Franklin)
V*

A scientist in a lonely house educates chimpanzees, but one proves malevolent.

Not much plot for a long film, and no suspense either.

w Everett DeRoche   d Richard Franklin   ph Mike Malloy   m Jerry Goldsmith

Terence Stamp, Elisabeth Shue, Steven Pinner, Richard Garnett

'What is missing from Link is a reason to see it.' – *Variety*

The Lion
GB   1962   96m   DeLuxe   Cinemascope
TCF (Samuel G. Engel)

An American lawyer goes to Africa to visit his ex-wife and their child.

Unabsorbing marital drama with child and animal interest.

w Irene and Louis Kamp   novel Joseph Kessel   d Jack Cardiff   ph Ted Scaife   m Malcolm Arnold

William Holden, Trevor Howard, Capucine, Pamela Franklin

'The main fault must be attributed to the spiritless direction of Jack Cardiff, whose recent change of métier has resulted in the industry losing a great lighting cameraman.' – *John Gillett*

The Lion Has Wings *
GB   1939   76m   bw
London Films (Alexander Korda)

A documentary drama tracing the steps leading up to the outbreak of war.

Once-inspiring propaganda piece, now regrettably hilarious. Valuable social history, though.

w Adrian Brunel, E. V. H. Emmett   d Michael Powell, Brian Desmond Hurst, Adrian Brunel   ph Harry Stradling   m Richard Addinsell

Merle Oberon, Ralph Richardson, June Duprez, Robert Douglas, Anthony Bushell, Derrick de Marney, Brian Worth, Austin Trevor

'As a statement of war aims, one feels, this leaves the world beyond Roedean still expectant.' – *Graham Greene*

The Lion in Winter *
GB   1968   134m   Eastmancolor   Panavision
Avco Embassy/Haworth (Martin Poll)
V, V*, L

Henry II and Eleanor of Aquitaine celebrate Christmas together and have a family row.

An acting feast for two principals and assorted supports, a talking marathon in which not all the talk is good, a smart comedy with sudden lapses into melodrama; stimulating in parts but all rather tiresome by the end, especially as there is not much medieval splendour.

w James Goldman play James Goldman
d Anthony Harvey ph Douglas Slocombe m John Barry

Katharine Hepburn, Peter O'Toole, Jane Merrow, John Castle, Anthony Hopkins, Nigel Terry, Timothy Dalton

'He is not writing a factual movie about the Plantagenets but an interpretation in which he combines their language and ours.' – *Philip T. Hartung*

AA: James Goldman; John Barry; Katharine Hepburn

AAN: best picture; Anthony Harvey; Peter O'Toole

A Lion Is in the Streets *
US 1953 88m Technicolor
Warner/Cagney Productions (William Cagney)
V*

An itinerant confidence trickster becomes a defender of the people, is nominated for governor, and becomes corrupt.

Busy melodrama which came a bit soon after *All the King's Men*.

w Luther Davis novel Adria Locke Langley
d Raoul Walsh ph Harry Stradling m Franz Waxman pd Wiard Ihnen

James Cagney, Barbara Hale, Anne Francis, Warner Anderson, John McIntire, Jeanne Cagney, Lon Chaney Jnr, Frank McHugh, Larry Keating, Onslow Stevens, James Millican, Sara Haden

'A headlong and dynamic drama which offers Mr Cagney one of his most colourful and meaningful roles.' – *Bosley Crowther*

Lion of the Desert
US 1980 163m Eastmancolor Panavision
Falcon International (Moustapha Akkad)
V, V*, S

In 1929 an Italian general in Libya withstands the attacks of rebel leader Omar Mukhtar.

Whitewashed account of the activities of a patriarchal partisan who was hanged in 1931. Of interest primarily to Arab zealots.

w H. A. L. Craig d Moustapha Akkad ph Jack Hildyard m Maurice Jarre pd Mario Garbuglia, Syd Cain

Anthony Quinn, Oliver Reed, Irene Papas, Raf Vallone, Rod Steiger, John Gielgud, Andrew Keir

Lionheart
US 1987 104m colour
Orion (Stanley O'Toole, Talia Shire)
V, V*, L

On his way to join King Richard the Lionheart's crusade, a young knight rescues a band of children from a slave trader.

Aimed at a family audience, it lacks excitement and pace and is best treated as a soporific.

w Menno Meyjes, Richard Outten d Franklin J. Schaffner ph Alec Mills m Jerry Goldsmith pd Gil Parrondo ed David Bretherton, Richard Haines

Eric Stoltz, Gabriel Byrne, Nicola Cowper, Dexter Fletcher, Deborah Barrymore, Nicholas Clay, Bruce Purchase, Neil Dickson, Chris Pitt

'High on heart-warming ideals, but low in every other department.' – *Empire*

Lionheart (1990): see AWOL

The Lion's Den: see *La Boca del Lobo*

'Rape was only the beginning!'
Lipstick
US 1976 90m Technicolor
Paramount/Dino de Laurentiis (Freddie Fields)
V*, L, S

A girl is raped but gets nowhere in court until her sister lures the man to rape her too.

Franker but not very interesting extension of a fifties co-feature, with all the developments well telegraphed.

w David Rayfiel d Lamont Johnson ph Bill Butler m Michel Polnareff

Margaux Hemingway, Perry King, Anne Bancroft, Chris Sarandon, Mariel Hemingway, Robin Gammell

'One of Lipstick's points is that voyeurism encourages senseless crime, but it unfortunately ignores its own lesson.' – *Marsha McCreadie, Films in Review*

Liquid Sky
US 1982 118m TVC colour
Z Films (Slava Tsukerman)
V, S

Aliens in a flying saucer land on the roof of a New York skyscraper in search of a heroin-like drug, which they obtain by killing people during orgasm.

A film with an undeserved cult reputation, presumably because it is set among punks and junkies; otherwise it is tediously plotted and poorly written and acted, dealing with unattractive characters in an unpleasant environment.

w Slava Tsukerman, Anne Carlisle, Nina V. Kerova
d Slava Tsukerman ph Yuri Neyman m Slava Tsukerman, Brenda L. Hutchinson, Clive Smith
pd Marina Levikova-Neyman ed Sharyn Leslie Ross

Anne Carlisle, Paula E. Sheppard, Bob Brady, Susan Doukas, Elaine C. Grove, Stanley Knap, Jack Adalist, Otto von Wernherr

'By turns self-consciously bizarre and beautiful.' – *Sight and Sound*

The Liquidator *
GB 1965 104m Metrocolor Panavision
MGM/Leslie Elliott (Jon Pennington)

An ex-war hero is recruited by the secret service as an eliminator of security risks.

Fairly lively James Bond spoof which is never quite as funny as it imagines.

w Peter Yeldham novel John Gardner d Jack Cardiff ph Ted Scaife m Lalo Schifrin

Rod Taylor, Trevor Howard, *David Tomlinson*, Jill St John, Wilfrid Hyde-White, Derek Nimmo, Eric Sykes, Akim Tamiroff

Lisa: see The Inspector

Lisa and the Devil
Italy 1974 93m Technicolor
Leone International (Alfred Leone)
V, V*
original title: *Il Diavolo e il Morto*

A tourist stranded in a small town takes refuge in an old, dark villa.

Baroque thriller that constantly teeters on the edge of absurdity before finally falling.

w Mario Bava, Alfred Leone d Mario Bava ph Cecilio Paniagua m Carlo Savina ad Nedo Azzini ed Carlo Reali

Telly Savalas, Elke Sommer, Silva Koscina, Alessio Orano, Alida Valli, Gabriele Tinti, Kathy Leone

'Not quite in the first rank of the director's work, it's still a bizarre gem.' – *Empire*

Lisbon
US 1956 90m Trucolor Naturama
Republic (Ray Milland)
V*

An international crook negotiates an Iron Curtain prisoner's release, but the man's wife has other ideas.

Glossy international intriguer with smart performances.

w John Tucker Battle d Ray Milland ph Jack Marta m Nelson Riddle

Ray Milland, *Claude Rains*, Maureen O'Hara, Yvonne Furneaux, Francis Lederer, Percy Marmont, Edward Chapman

The Lisbon Story
GB 1946 103m bw
British National

Spies in 1940 Lisbon rescue a French atom scientist.

Flat filming of a musical show which kept Britons humming 'Pedro the Fisherman' throughout World War II.

w Jack Whittingham play Harold Purcell and Harry Parr-Davies d Paul Stein

Patricia Burke, David Farrar, Walter Rilla, *Richard Tauber*, Austin Trevor, Harry Welchman

The List of Adrian Messenger **
US 1963 98m bw
U-I/Joel (Edward Lewis)
V*

An intelligence officer traps a mass murderer with a penchant for disguise.

Old-fashioned mystery thriller, as though Holmes and Watson were combating a modern Moriarty (and a rough-hewn production). The whole thing is camped up like an end-of-term treat, and as a further gimmick four guest stars allegedly appear under heavy disguise in cameo parts.

w Anthony Veiller novel Philip MacDonald
d John Huston ph Joe MacDonald m Jerry Goldsmith

George C. Scott, Kirk Douglas, Clive Brook, Dana Wynter, Jacques Roux, Walter Tony Huston, Herbert Marshall, Bernard Archard, Gladys Cooper; and Robert Mitchum, Frank Sinatra, Burt Lancaster, Tony Curtis

'A leisurely, underplayed thriller with some good performances and a gimmick which turns it into a guessing contest.' – *L.A. Times*

Listen Darling
US 1938 70m bw
MGM (Jack Cummings)
V*

Children try to find their widowed mother a new husband.

Slight domestic comedy chiefly notable for its young talent.

w Elaine Ryan, Anne Morrison Chapin
story Katherine Brush d Edwin L. Marin
ph Charles Lawton Jnr md George Stoll
m George Axt

Mary Astor, Judy Garland, Freddie Bartholomew, Walter Pidgeon, Alan Hale, Scotty Beckett, Charley Grapewin, Barnett Parker, Gene Lockhart

'Inauspicious start for the Garland-Bartholomew team . . . mediocre story hurts.' – *Variety*

Listen to Britain ****
GB 1941 20m bw
Ministry of Information (Crown Film Unit)

Images of Britain at war.

A brilliant compilation of almost poetic sights and sounds which distil the essence of a year.

d Humphrey Jennings

Listen to Me
US   1989   110m   CFI
Columbia TriStar/Weintraub Entertainment/Martin Bregman (Marykay Powell)
V*, L

Two students fall in love while being members of their college debating team.

Of limited interest, unless you happen to be a member of a debating team, and even then it is unlikely to hold your attention for long.

wd Douglas Day Stewart   *ph* Fred J. Koenekamp   *m* David Foster   *pd* Gregory Pickrell   *ed* Anne V. Coates

Kirk Cameron, Jami Gertz, Roy Scheider, Amanda Peterson, Tim Quill, George Wyner, Anthony Zerbe, Christopher Atkins

Listen Up: The Lives of Quincy Jones
US   1990   115m   Technicolor
Warner/Cort (Courtney Sale Ross)
V*, L, S

Documentary on the life of the influential record producer, arranger and composer who began as a big-band trumpeter.

Distractingly edited, as if intended for an audience with a very short attention span, and mainly given over to performances and uninformative interviews with those with whom Jones has worked, from jazz musicians such as Lionel Hampton, Miles Davis and Ella Fitzgerald to rock singer Michael Jackson and rapper Big Daddy Kane.

d Ellen Weissbrod   *ph* Stephen Kazmierski   *m* Quincy Jones   *ed* Milton Moses

Lisztomania
GB   1975   104m   colour   Panavision
Warner/VPS/Goodtimes (Roy Baird, David Puttnam)
V, V*, L

The life of Liszt seen in terms of a modern pop performer.

The most excessive and obscene of all this director's controversial works, incapable of criticism on normal terms except that it seems unusually poor in production values.

wd Ken Russell   *ph* Peter Suschitsky   *md* John Forsyth

Roger Daltrey, Sara Kestelman, Paul Nicholas, Fiona Lewis, John Justin, Ringo Starr

Sample dialogue: 'Piss off, Brahms!'

'Ken Russell's first completely unmitigated catastrophe in several years . . . a welter of arbitrary gags, manic self-references and frantic exploitation-movie clichés.' – *Tony Rayns*

'Oscar Wilde once said "Each man kills the thing he loves", and the remark perfectly suits Ken Russell's film treatments of classical composers . . . he has bludgeoned into pulp some of the finest music civilization has produced.' – *Patrick Snyder*

'This gaudy compendium of camp, second-hand Freud and third-rate pastiche is like a bad song without end.' – *Sight and Sound*

Liten Ida: see *Little Ida*

Little Accident
US   1930   82m   bw
Universal

A man is about to marry again when he finds that his first wife is having his baby.

Stretched-out comedy which fumbles its way along.

w Gladys Lehman   *play* Floyd Dell and Thomas Mitchell   *d* William James Craft

Douglas Fairbanks Jnr, Anita Page, Sally Blane, ZaSu Pitts, Joan Marsh, Roscoe Karns, Slim Summerville

'If anybody thinks 82 minutes is the proper time for this film, they should be made to sit through it twice.' – *Variety*

Little Accident
US   1939   65m   bw
Universal

A baby is passed from hand to hand after her father abandons her.

Simple-minded comedy bearing little relation to the above; it's now a vehicle for the baby.

w Paul Yawitz, Eve Greene   *d* Charles Lamont

Baby Sandy, Hugh Herbert, Richard Carlson, Florence Rice, Ernest Truex, Fritz Feld, Edgar Kennedy

'Elemental comedy for supporting attraction in nabes.' – *Variety*

Little Annie Rooney *
US   1925   99m (24 fps)   bw   silent
United Artists/Mary Pickford
V*, L

A 12-year-old tomboy in a New York slum rounds up the killer of her policeman father.

Sentimental melodrama tailored for a 32-year-old star who liked playing kids. Of minor historical interest.

w Hope Loring, Louis D. Lighton   *d* William Beaudine   *ph* Charles Rosher, Hal Mohr   *m* Joseph Plunkett

Mary Pickford, William Haines, Walter James, Gordon Griffith

The Little Ark
US   1971   86m   DeLuxe   Panavision
Cinema Center/Robert B. Radnitz

Two war orphans and their pets, trapped in a flood, sail to safety in a houseboat.

Well-meaning, somewhat allegorical family film, too desultory to maintain interest and rather too frightening for children.

w Joanna Crawford   *novel* Jan de Hartog   *d* James B. Clark   *ph* Austin Dempster, Denys Coop   *m* Fred Karlin

Theodore Bikel, Philip Frame, Genevieve Ambas

AAN: song 'Come Follow Follow Me' (*m* Fred Karlin, *ly* Marsha Karlin)

Little Big Horn *
US   1951   86m   bw
Lippert (Carl K. Hittleman)
V*
GB title: *The Fighting Seventh*

A cavalry squad sets out to warn Custer about Little Big Horn, but all the men are massacred before Custer arrives.

Dour, impressive low-budget Western.

wd Charles Marquis Warren   *ph* Ernest Miller   *m* Paul Dunlap

Lloyd Bridges, John Ireland, Marie Windsor, Reed Hadley, Hugh O'Brian, Wally Cassell, King Donovan

'The Cavalry Against The Indians And Dustin Hoffman Is On Both Sides!'

Little Big Man *
US   1970   147m   Technicolor   Panavision
Stockbridge/Hiller/Cinema Center (Stuart Millar)
V, V*, L

An aged veteran of the old west recounts his life story – with elaborations.

A number of episodes varying from stark tragedy to satirical farce are framed for no good reason by the

star in heavy disguise; the intention is hard to guess but there are goodies along the way.

w Calder Willingham   *novel* Thomas Berger   *d* Arthur Penn   *ph* Harry Stradling   *m* John Hammond   *pd* Dean Tavoularis

Dustin Hoffman, Martin Balsam, Faye Dunaway, *Chief Dan George*, Richard Mulligan, Jeff Corey

'A hip epic, with an amiable first hour. Then the massacres and messages take over.' – *New Yorker, 1976*

'A tangy and, I think, unique film with American verve, about some of the things American verve has done.' – *Stanley Kauffmann*

AAN: Chief Dan George

Little Big Shot
US   1935   80m   bw
Warner

A gangster's child is orphaned and cared for by two con men.

Reasonably lively vehicle for a new child star who didn't last.

w Jerry Wald, Julius J. Epstein, Robert Andrews   *d* Michael Curtiz

Sybil Jason, Glenda Farrell, Robert Armstrong, Edward Everett Horton, Jack La Rue, J. Carrol Naish, Edgar Kennedy

'Should pave the way handily for young Miss Jason's future.' – *Variety*

A Little Bit of Heaven
US   1940   87m   bw
Universal (Joe Pasternak)

A 12-year-old girl becomes a singing sensation but runs into family opposition.

Predictable vehicle for a young star being built up as a stop-gap Deanna Durbin.

w Daniel Taradash, Gertrude Purcell, Harold Goldman   *story* Grover Jones   *d* Andrew Marton   *ph* John Seitz   *m* Charles Previn

Gloria Jean, Robert Stack, Hugh Herbert, C. Aubrey Smith, Stuart Erwin, Nan Grey, Eugene Pallette, Billy Gilbert, Butch and Buddy

Little Boy Lost
US   1953   95m   bw
Paramount (William Perlberg)

An American returns to Paris after the war to find his wife dead and his small son missing.

Rather dull tearjerker.

wd George Seaton   *novel* Marghanita Laski   *ph* George Barnes   *m* Victor Young

Bing Crosby, Claude Dauphin, Christian Fourcade, Gabrielle Dorziat, Nicole Maurey

Little Caesar ****
US   1931   77m   bw
Warner
V, V*, L

The rise and fall of a vicious gangster.

Its central character clearly modelled on Al Capone, this also has historical interest as vanguard of a spate of noisy gangster films. The star was forever identified with his role, and the film, though technically dated, moves fast enough to maintain interest over sixty years later.

w Francis Faragoh, Robert E. Lee   *novel* W. R. Burnett   *d* Mervyn Le Roy   *ph* Tony Gaudio   *m* Erno Rapee

Edward G. Robinson, Douglas Fairbanks Jnr, Glenda Farrell, William Collier Jnr, Ralph Ince, George E. Stone, Thomas Jackson, Stanley Fields, Sidney Blackmer

'It has irony and grim humour and a real sense of excitement and its significance does not get in the way of the melodrama.' – *Richard Dana Skinner*

'One of the best gangster talkers yet turned out . . . a swell picture.' – *Variety*

AAN: Francis Faragoh, Robert E. Lee

The Little Colonel **

US   1935   80m   bw (colour sequence)
Fox (B. G. de Sylva)
V*, L

In a Southern household after the Civil War, a little girl ends a family feud, plays Cupid to her sister, routs a few villains and mollifies her cantankerous grandfather.

First-class Temple vehicle, the first to boast an expensive production.

w William Conselman   *novel* Annie Fellows Johnson   *d* David Butler   *ph* Arthur Miller   *md* Arthur Lange

Shirley Temple, Lionel Barrymore, Evelyn Venable, John Lodge, Bill Robinson, Hattie McDaniel, Sidney Blackmer

The Little Damozel

GB   1933   73m   bw
British and Dominions

A gambler marries a young singer for a bribe, but falls in love with her.

Lavender-tinted romance with music; notable as its star's first major role.

w Donovan Pedelty   *play* Monckton Hoffe   *d* Herbert Wilcox

Anna Neagle, James Rennie, Benita Hume, Athole Stewart, Alfred Drayton

Little Darlings

US   1980   92m   Metrocolor
Paramount/Stephen J. Friedman
V*, L

Teenage girls at a summer camp take bets on who will lose her virginity first.

Crass and tasteless comedy with only prurient appeal.

w Kimi Peck, Dalene Young   *d* Ronald F. Maxwell   *ph* Fred Batka   *m* Charles Fox   *pd* William Hiney   *ed* Pembroke J. Herring

Tatum O'Neal, Kristy McNichol, Krista Errickson, Armand Assante

Little Dorrit **

GB   1987   Part 1 176m/Part 2 181m   Technicolor
Sands/Cannon (John Brabourne)
V, V*, L

Faithful adaptation of classic novel.

Lovingly made by a large team, economically and authentically re-creating Dickens's London, with a starry cast giving their all. Adored by audiences who could take the length.

wd Christine Edzard   *novel* Charles Dickens   *ph* Bruno de Keyzer   *m* Giuseppe Verdi

Derek Jacobi, Joan Greenwood, Max Wall, *Alec Guinness,* Cyril Cusack, Sarah Pickering, Eleanor Bron, Robert Morley

AAN: Alec Guinness; best adapted screenplay

The Little Drummer Girl *

US   1984   130m   Technicolor
Warner/Pan Arts (Robert L. Crawford)
V, V*, L

An American actress in Britain is persuaded by Israeli agents to lose her Arab sympathies and spy for them.

Tediously protracted and unexciting version of a novel which was generally agreed to have been based on Vanessa Redgrave. Interesting for its quality look

and surface style only: the intricate plotting of the Le Carré manner is surely no longer fashionable.

w Loring Mandel   *novel* John Le Carré   *d* George Roy Hill   *ph* Wolfgang Treu   *m* Dave Grusin   *pd* Henry Bumstead   *ed* William Reynolds

Diane Keaton, Yorgo Voyagis, Klaus Kinski, Sami Frey, Michael Cristofer, David Suchet, Eli Danker, Thorley Walters, Anna Massey

Little Egypt

US   1951   81m   Technicolor
Universal-International (Jack Gross)
GB title: *Chicago Masquerade*

An American girl poses as an Egyptian princess at the Chicago World's Fair.

Sluggish turn-of-the-century romantic melodrama based on a factual swindle involving a phoney Nile reclamation project.

w Oscar Brodney, Doris Gilbert   *d* Frederick de Cordova   *ph* Russell Metty   *md* Joseph Gershenson

Rhonda Fleming, Mark Stevens, Nancy Guild, Charles Drake, Tom D'Andrea, Minor Watson, Steve Geray

Little Fauss and Big Halsy

US   1970   99m   Movielab   Panavision
Paramount/Alfran/Furie (Albert S. Ruddy)

Two motor cycle track racers team up and have violent adventures round the country.

Rather pointless capers in the wake of *Easy Rider*, neither interesting nor well done.

w Charles Eastman   *d* Sidney J. Furie   *ph* Ralph Woolsey   *m* Johnny Cash, Bob Dylan, Carl Perkins

Robert Redford, Michael J. Pollard, *Noah Beery Jnr,* Lauren Hutton

'A sort of *Batman and Robin* on wheels.' – *Rex Reed*

The Little Foxes ***

US   1941   116m   bw
Samuel Goldwyn
V, V*, L

A family of schemers in post-Civil War days will stop at nothing to outwit each other.

Superb film of a brilliant play; excellent to look at and listen to, with a compelling narrative line and memorable characters.

w Lillian Hellman   *play* Lillian Hellman   *d* William Wyler   *ph* Gregg Toland   *m* Meredith Willson   *ad* Stephen Goosson   *ed* Daniel Mandell

Bette Davis, Herbert Marshall, Teresa Wright, Richard Carlson, *Charles Dingle, Dan Duryea, Carl Benton Reid, Patricia Collinge,* Jessica Grayson, Russell Hicks

HORACE GIDDENS (Herbert Marshall): 'Maybe it's easy for the dying to be honest. I'm sick of you, sick of this house, sick of my unhappy life with you. I'm sick of your brothers and their dirty tricks to make a dime. There must be better ways of getting rich than building sweatshops and pounding the bones of the town to make dividends for you to spend. You'll wreck the town, you and your brothers. You'll wreck the country, you and your kind, if they let you. But not me, I'll die my own way, and I'll do it without making the world any worse. I leave that to you.'

'One of the really beautiful jobs in the whole range of movie making.' – *Otis Ferguson*

'No one knows better than Wyler when to shift the camera's point of view, when to cut, or how to relate the characters in one shot to those in the next . . . you never have to wonder where you are in a Wyler picture.' – *Arthur Knight*

AAN: best picture; Lillian Hellman; William Wyler; Meredith Willson; Bette Davis; Teresa Wright; Patricia Collinge; Stephen Goosson; Daniel Mandell

Little Friend

GB   1934   85m   bw
Gaumont

A girl is driven to attempt suicide by her parents' proposed divorce.

Fairly well written but rather stilted domestic drama which maintained a small reputation.

w Margaret Kennedy, Christopher Isherwood and Berthold Viertel   *novel* Ernst Lothar   *d* Berthold Viertel

Nova Pilbeam, Matheson Lang, Lydia Sherwood, Arthur Margetson, Allan Aynesworth, Jean Cadell, Jimmy Hanley

The Little Giant

US   1933   74m   bw
Warner

At the end of Prohibition, a beer baron moves to California and tries to break into society.

Disappointingly unfunny gangster comedy which never really gets going.

w Robert Lord, Wilson Mizner   *d* Roy del Ruth   *ph* Sid Hickox   *md* Leo F. Forbstein

Edward G. Robinson, Mary Astor, Helen Vinson, Kenneth Thomson, Russell Hopton, Donald Dillaway

'It makes Robinson a comedy character surrounded by semi-travesty and the fans are likely to resent it.' – *Variety*

'From homicide to house parties – from dames to debutantes!'

Little Giant

US   1946   91m   bw
Universal (Joseph Gershenson)
GB title: *On the Carpet*

Misadventures of a vacuum cleaner salesman.

Curious, unsatisfactory Abbott and Costello comedy in which the boys play separate characters instead of working as a team. They should have waited for a better script before experimenting.

w Paul Jarrico, Richard Collins, Walter de Leon   *d* William A. Seiter   *ph* Charles van Enger   *m* Edgar Fairchild

Bud Abbott, Lou Costello, Brenda Joyce, George Cleveland, Elena Verdugo

The Little Girl Who Lives Down the Lane

US/Canada/France   1976   94m   colour
Zev Braun/ICL/Filmedis-Filmel (Zev Braun)
V*, L

A 13-year-old girl, when her father dies, is discovered to be keeping her mother's corpse in the cellar, and doesn't stop at more murders to keep her secret.

Tasteless piece of grand guignol, badly directed and over-acted.

w Laird Koenig   *novel* Laird Koenig   *d* Nicolas Gessner   *ph* Rene Verzier   *m* Christian Gaubert

Jodie Foster, Alexis Smith, Martin Sheen, Scott Jacoby

† Originally intended as a TV movie.

The Little Hut

US   1957   90m   Eastmancolor
MGM/Herbson S A (F. Hugh Herbert, Mark Robson)

A man, his wife and her lover are shipwrecked on a desert island.

Sophisticated French farce which falls resoundingly flat in this bowdlerized Hollywood version in bilious colour, fatally compromising itself at the beginning with a 'realistic' London prologue.

w F. Hugh Herbert   *play* André Roussin and Nancy Mitford   *d* Mark Robson   *ph* Frederick A. Young   *m* Robert Farnon   *ad* Elliot Scott

Stewart Granger, David Niven, Ava Gardner, Walter Chiari, Finlay Currie, Jean Cadell

Little Ida **
Norway 1981 79m Eastmancolor
Minema/Norsk Film/Svenska Filminstituten (Harald Ohrvik, Sven Johansen)
original title: *Liten Ida*

A seven-year-old girl is ostracized because of her mother's relationship with a Nazi soldier.

Unsentimental, excellently acted account of childhood suffering.

w Marit Paulsen, Laila Mikkelsen *novel* Marit Paulsen *d* Laila Mikkelsen *ph* Hans Welin, Kjell Vassdal *m* Eyvind Solas *ad* Anders Barreus *ed* Peter Falck

Sunniva Lindekleiv, Howard Halvorsen, Lise Fjeldstad, Arne Lindtner Ness, Ellen Westerfjell, Roennaug Alten

Little Johnny Jones
US 1930 73m bw
First National

An American jockey wins the Derby.

Mild comedy with music from the old George M. Cohan play.

w Adelaide Heilbron and Eddie Buzzell *d* Mervyn Le Roy

Eddie Buzzell, Alice Day, Edna Murphy, Robert Edeson

'Familiar formula but done nicely.' – *Variety*

The Little Kidnappers: see *The Kidnappers*

Little Lord Fauntleroy *
US 1921 11m (24 fps) bw silent
United Artists/Mary Pickford

An American boy who lives with his widowed mother discovers he is heir to an English dukedom.

Over-upholstered sentimental extravaganza tailored for a star in her twenties playing both young Cedric and his mother, a curious double. One can now only wonder at the immense appeal this film had in its own time; but that is not to diminish the vitality of its star.

w Bernard McConville *novel* Frances Hodgson Burnett *d* Jack Pickford, Alfred E. Green *ph* Charles Rosher *m* Louis F. Gottschalk

Mary Pickford, Claude Gillingwater, Kate Price, James A. Marcus, Emmet King

Little Lord Fauntleroy *
US 1936 98m bw
David O. Selznick
V*

A sound remake which did surprisingly well at the box-office and is still very watchable.

w Richard Schayer, Hugh Walpole, David O. Selznick *d* John Cromwell *ph* Charles Rosher *m* Max Steiner

Freddie Bartholomew, C. Aubrey Smith, Mickey Rooney, Dolores Costello, Jessie Ralph, Guy Kibbee

† A TV movie version appeared in 1980, with Ricky Schroder and Alec Guinness.

Little Man Tate *
US 1991 99m DeLuxe
Columbia TriStar/Orion (Scott Rudin, Peggy Rajski)
V, V*, L, S

A battle develops over the future of a precociously bright child between his working-class mother and a teacher of gifted children.

A drama of family tensions that might have worked better on television.

w Scott Frank *d* Jodie Foster *ph* Mike Southon *m* Mark Isham *pd* Jon Hutman *ed* Lynzee Klingman

Jodie Foster, Dianne Wiest, Adam Hann-Byrd, Harry Connick Jnr, David Pierce, Debi Mazar, P. J. Ochlan

'A nice little film, but what audience it is meant to appeal to is, frankly, something of a mystery.' – *Angie Errigo, Empire*

Little Man, What Now? *
US 1934 95m bw
Universal

Problems of Germany in the grip of unemployment.

One of the studio's several 'sequels' to *All Quiet on the Western Front,* poignant at the time but now very dated.

w William Anthony McGuire *novel* Hans Fallada *d* Frank Borzage *ph* Norbert Brodine

Margaret Sullavan, Douglass Montgomery, Alan Hale, Muriel Kirkland, Alan Mowbray, Mae Marsh

'Human, homely and romantic . . . should get ample b.o. attention.' – *Variety*

Little Men
US 1935 77m bw
Mascot

Joe and her professor run a school for boys.

Slapdash sequel to *Little Women;* not an ambitious production.

w Gertrude Orr *novel* Louisa M. Alcott *d* Phil Rosen

Ralph Morgan, Erin O'Brien-Moore, Junior Durkin, Cora Sue Collins, Frankie Darro, Dickie Moore

'Goes overboard on pathos . . . tears flow over the most insignificant matters.' – *Variety*

† A remake emerged from RKO in 1940, but was ill received. Running 84 minutes, it starred Kay Francis, Jack Oakie, James Lydon, and Ann Gillis, not to mention Elsie the cow. Mark Kelly and Arthur Caesar wrote it, Norman Z. McLeod directed; for Graham Towne and Gene Baker.

The Little Mermaid **
US 1989 83m
Warner/Walt Disney/Silver Screen Partners IV (Howard Ashman, John Musker)
V, V*, L, S

A mermaid falls in love with a prince and longs to be human.

A return to Disney's classic manner, with some excellent animation, though sentimentality is rampant.

wd John Musker, Ron Clements *story* Hans Christian Andersen *m* Alan Menken *m/ly* Howard Ashman, Alan Menken

Voices of Rene Auberjonois, Christopher Daniel Barnes, Jodi Benson, Pat Carroll, Paddi Edwards, Buddy Hackett, Jason Marin, Kenneth Mars, Edie McClurg, Will Ryan, Ben Wright, Samuel E. Wright

AA: best original score; best song

The Little Minister
US 1934 110m bw
RKO (Pandro S. Berman)

In 1840 Scotland, the gypsy girl with whom the new pastor falls unsuitably in love is really the local earl's wayward daughter.

Tedious film version of a cloyingly whimsical play.

w Jane Murfin, Sarah Y. Mason, Victor Heerman *play* J. M. Barrie *d* Richard Wallace *ph* Henry Gerrard *m* Max Steiner

Katharine Hepburn, John Beal, Alan Hale, Donald Crisp, Lumsden Hare, Andy Clyde, Beryl Mercer, Dorothy Stickney, Frank Conroy, Reginald Denny

'Fine production of an old favourite.' – *Variety*

'Although dear Babbie's elfin whimsies are likely to cause teeth-gnashing among unsympathetic moderns, Miss Hepburn plays the part with likeable sprightliness and charm.' – *André Sennwald, New York Times*

Little Miss Broadway
US 1938 70m bw
TCF (David Hempstead)
V*

A small girl is adopted by the owner of a hotel for vaudeville artistes.

One of the child star's more casual vehicles, but quite pleasing.

w Harry Tugend, Jack Yellen *d* Irving Cummings *ph* Arthur Miller *md* Louis Silvers

Shirley Temple, George Murphy, Jimmy Durante, Edna May Oliver, Phyllis Brooks, George Barbier, Edward Ellis, Jane Darwell, El Brendel, Donald Meek, Claude Gillingwater, Russell Hicks

'It can't be old age, but it does look like weariness.' – *New York Times*

'Shirley is better than her new vehicle, which in turn is better than her last one.' – *Variety*

Little Miss Marker **
US 1934 80m bw
Paramount (B. P. Schulberg)
GB title: *The Girl in Pawn*

A cynical racetrack gambler is forced to adopt a little girl, who not only softens him but saves him from his enemies.

The twin appeals of Temple (a new hot property) and Runyon made this a big hit of its time.

w William R. Lipman, Sam Hellman, Gladys Lehman *story* Damon Runyon *d* Alexander Hall *ph* Alfred Gilks *songs* Leo Robin, Ralph Rainger

Shirley Temple, Adolphe Menjou, Dorothy Dell, Charles Bickford, Lynne Overman, Frank McGlynn Snr, Willie Best

'A good response to that element which claims there is nothing good in pictures. Clean, funny, with thrills and heart appeal all nicely blended.' – *Variety*

'No one can deny that the infant was a trouper: she delivers her lines with a killer instinct.' – *Pauline Kael, 70s*

† Remade as *Sorrowful Jones* (qv).

Little Miss Marker
US 1980 103m Technicolor
Universal (Jennings Lang)
V*

Mainly glutinous remake of the above, with acerbic asides from the star.

wd Walter Bernstein *ph* Philip Lathrop *m* Henry Mancini

Walter Matthau, Julie Andrews, Tony Curtis, Bob Newhart, Sara Stimson, Lee Grant, Brian Dennehy

Little Mr Jim
US 1946 92m bw
Orville O. Dull/MGM

The plight of a youngster when mother dies and father takes to drink.

Unabashed tearjerker with a fairly resistible child star.

w George Bruce *novel Army Brat* by Tommy Wadelton *d* Fred Zinnemann

Jackie 'Butch' Jenkins, James Craig, Frances Gifford, Luana Patten, Spring Byington

Little Murders
US 1971 108m DeLuxe
TCF/Brodsky-Gould (Jack Brodsky)
V*

A young photographer rises above all the urban

horror of New York life, but when his wife is killed by a sniper he takes to violence.

This adaptation of an ultrablack comedy would have worked better as a comic strip, for its characters are satirical puppets, and when played by human beings the whole thing seems violently silly.

w Jules Feiffer play Jules Feiffer d Alan Arkin ph Gordon Willis m Fred Kaz

Elliott Gould, Marcia Rodd, Elizabeth Wilson, Vincent Gardenia, Alan Arkin

Little Nellie Kelly *
US 1940 100m bw
MGM (Arthur Freed)

The daughter of a New York Irish cop patches up a family feud.

Sentimental nostalgic vehicle for young Judy Garland, who plays both wife and daughter and sings plenty of standard melodies.

w Jack McGowan play George M. Cohan d Norman Taurog songs George M. Cohan, Roger Edens, Nacio Herb Brown, Arthur Freed ph Ray June

Judy Garland, George Murphy, Charles Winninger, Douglas McPhail, Arthur Shields, Forrester Harvey

A Little Night Music *
Austria/West Germany 1977 125m Eastmancolor
Sascha Film/S & T (Elliott Kastner)
V*, L

In Vienna at the turn of the century, a middle-aged lawyer, frustrated by the virginity of his young wife, turns to an old actress flame.

Fumbled version of a rather splendid Broadway musical based on Ingmar Bergman's *Smiles of a Summer Night*. The locale is changed, several of the songs are cut, and the leads are miscast.

w Hugh Wheeler play Hugh Wheeler d Harold Prince ph Arthur Ibbetson m/ly Stephen Sondheim

Elizabeth Taylor, Diana Rigg, Len Cariou, Lesley-Anne Down, Hermione Gingold, Christopher Guard, Laurence Guittard

AA: Jonathan Tunick (music adaptation)

Little Old New York
US 1940 100m bw
TCF (Raymond Griffith)

The story of Robert Fulton and his invention of the steamboat.

Romantic hokum with a veneer of fact; good production.

w Harry Tugend play Rida Johnson Young d Henry King ph Leon Shamroy m Alfred Newman

Alice Faye, Richard Greene, Fred MacMurray, Henry Stephenson, Brenda Joyce, Andy Devine, Fritz Feld, Ward Bond

Little Orphan Annie
US 1932 60m bw
RKO

A girl orphan charms a millionaire.

Ineffective early version of the comic strip used many years later (equally ineffectively) as the basis for *Annie*.

w Wanda Tuchock, Tom McNamara d John Robertson

Mitzi Green, Edgar Kennedy, May Robson, Buster Phelps

The Little Prince
US 1974 89m Technicolor
Paramount/Stanley Donen
V*, L

A small boy leaves the asteroid he rules to learn of life on Earth.

A whimsical bestseller turns into an arch musical which falls over itself early on and never recovers; in any case it fatally lacks the common touch, though it has pleasing moments.

w Alan Jay Lerner novel Antoine de St-Exupery d Stanley Donen ph Christopher Challis pd John Barry m/ly Frederick Loewe, Alan Jay Lerner

Richard Kiley, Steven Warner, Bob Fosse, Gene Wilder, Joss Ackland, Clive Revill, Victor Spinetti, Graham Crowden

'Handsome production cannot obscure limited artistic achievement.' – Variety

† Kiley replaced Frank Sinatra, who backed out.

AAN: title song; musical adaptation (Angela Morley, Douglas Gamley)

The Little Princess **
US 1939 93m Technicolor
TCF (Gene Markey)
V*, L

In Victorian London a little girl is left at a harsh school when her father goes abroad.

One of the child star's plushest vehicles, a charming early colour film complete with dream sequence and happy ending.

w Ethel Hill, Walter Ferris novel Frances Hodgson Burnett d Walter Lang ph Arthur Miller, William Skall md Louis Silvers

Shirley Temple, Richard Greene, Anita Louise, Ian Hunter, Cesar Romero, Arthur Treacher, Mary Nash, Sybil Jason, Miles Mander, Marcia Mae Jones, Beryl Mercer, E. E. Clive

A Little Romance
US 1979 108m Technicolor
Warner/Orion (Patrick Kelley)
V*, L, S

A French teenager elopes with an American girl, encouraged by a garrulous old pickpocket.

Treacly juvenile romance enriched by in-jokes and an enjoyably over-the-top star performance.

w Allan Burns novel Patrick Cauvin d George Roy Hill ph Pierre William Glenn m Georges Delerue pd Henry Bumstead

Laurence Olivier, Diane Lane, Thelonious Bernard, Arthur Hill, Sally Kellerman, Broderick Crawford, David Dukes

AA: Georges Delerue

AAN: Allan Burns

A Little Sex
US 1982 94m Technicolor
Universal/MTM (Robert de Laurentiis, Bruce Paltrow)

A young husband has a wandering eye.

Very thin comedy drama more suitable for TV if it were a little less outspoken.

w Robert de Laurentiis d Bruce Paltrow ph Ralf D. Bode m Georges Delerue

Tim Matheson, Kate Capshaw, Edward Herrmann, John Glover

Little Shop of Horrors **
US 1960 70m bw
Santa Clara (Roger Corman)
V*

A dim flower-shop assistant nurtures a man-eating plant.

A Corman quickie, allegedly shot in two days, that is a lively, if occasionally ramshackle, comic delight with a notable cameo from Nicholson as a masochist.

w Charles B. Griffiths d Roger Corman ph Arch Dalzell m Fred Katz ad Daniel Haller ed Marshall Neilan Jnr

Jonathan Haze, Jack Nicholson, Jackie Joseph, Mel Welles, Myrtle Vail, Dick Miller, Leola Wendorff

'One big sick joke, but it's essentially harmless and good-natured.' – Variety

Little Shop of Horrors *
US 1986 88m Technicolor
Warner (David Geffen)
V, V*, L, S

Workers in a flower shop are menaced by a plant with sinister intent.

Transcript of the off-Broadway musical curiously inspired by a 1961 Roger Corman horror flick which few people saw. A strange item with occasional effective moments.

w Howard Ashman play Howard Ashman d Frank Oz ph Robert Paynter m Alan Menken pd Roy Walker ed John Jympson, Derek Trigg, Bob Gavin

Rick Moranis, Ellen Greene, Vincent Gardenia, Steve Martin

'The best movie ever made about a man-eating plant.' – People

AAN: song 'Mean Green Mother from Outer Space'

Little Tokyo USA
US 1942 64m bw
Bryan Foy/TCF

A cop ferrets out Japanese espionage agents in Los Angeles.

Tolerable wartime second feature.

w George Bricker d Otto Brower

Preston Foster, Brenda Joyce, June Duprez, Harold Huber, Don Douglas, George E. Stone, Abner Biberman

Little Tough Guy
US 1938 83m bw
Universal
V*

A New York slum boy gets involved with a gang and is sent to reform school.

A development of the Dead End Kids, with attitudes not yet crystallized, the overall tone being heavy.

w Gilson Brown and Brenda Weisburg d Harold Young

Billy Halop, Helen Parrish, Marjorie Main, Huntz Hall, Gabriel Dell, Bernard Punsley, Jackie Searl, Hally Chester

Little Tough Guys in Society
US 1938 75m bw
Universal

A society matron invites slum boys to her mansion as a corrective for her stuffy son.

The cast makes it plain that the Dead End Kids/Little Tough Guys are now headed for comedy, the reason being that their 'serious' films were thought to set a bad example.

w Edward Eliscu and Mortimer Offner d Erle C. Kenton

Mary Boland, Mischa Auer, Edward Everett Horton, Helen Parrish, Jackie Searl, Frankie Thomas, Billy Benedict, Hally Chester, David Gorcey

Little Vera *
USSR 1988 134m colour
Mainline/Gorky Studios (Yuri Prober)
V*, L, S
original title: Malenkaya Vera

A young woman in a grim Russian town leads a disaffected life.

With its drunken father, promiscuous daughter and nagging mother, it will bring a sense of *déjà vu* to anyone familiar with the British kitchen sink dramas of the 1960s.

w Mariya Khmelik   *d* Vasili Pichul   *ph* Yefim Reznikov   *m* Vladimir Matetski   *ad* Vladimir Pasternak   *ed* Yelena Zabolotskaya

Natalya Negoda, Ludmilla Zaitseva, Andrei Sokolov, Yuri Nazarov, Alexander Alexeyev-Negreba, Alexandra Tabakova

'They leap from the book and live!'
Little Women ***
US   1933   115m   bw
RKO (David O. Selznick, Merian C. Cooper, Kenneth MacGowan)
V*, L

The growing up of four sisters in pre-Civil War America.

Charming 'big picture' of its day, with excellent production and performances.

w Sarah Y. Mason, Victor Heerman   *novel* Louisa May Alcott   *d George Cukor*   *ph* Henry Gerrard   *m* Max Steiner

Katharine Hepburn, Paul Lukas, Joan Bennett, Frances Dee, Jean Parker, *Spring Byington*, Edna May Oliver, Douglass Montgomery, Henry Stephenson, Samuel S. Hinds, John Lodge, Nydia Westman

'If to put a book on the screen with all the effectiveness that sympathy and good taste and careful artifice can devise is to make a fine motion picture, then *Little Women* is a fine picture.' – *James Shelley Hamilton*

'One of the most satisfactory pictures I have ever seen.' – *E. V. Lucas, Punch*

'A reminder that emotions and vitality and truth can be evoked from lavender and lace as well as from machine guns and precision dances.' – *Thornton Delehanty, New York Post*

AA: script

AAN: best picture; George Cukor

Little Women *
US   1949   122m   Technicolor
MGM (Mervyn Le Roy)
V, V*, L

Syrupy Christmas-card remake, notably lacking the light touch.

w Andrew Solt, Sarah Y. Mason, Victor Heerman   *d* Mervyn Le Roy   *ph* Robert Planck, Charles Schoenbaum   *m* Adolph Deutsch (after Max Steiner)   *ad* Cedric Gibbons, Paul Groesse

June Allyson, Elizabeth Taylor, Peter Lawford, Margaret O'Brien, Janet Leigh, Mary Astor

'It will raise a smile and draw a tear from the sentimental.' – *MFB*

AA: art direction

AAN: cinematography

The Little World of Don Camillo *
France/Italy   1952   106m   bw
Rizzoli-Amato-Francinex (Giuseppe Amato)
V*

In a small Italian village the parish priest and the communist mayor are in a constant state of amiable feud.

Slightly lethargic character comedy with a mild message for its times, popular enough to warrant several sequels.

w Julien Duvivier, René Barjavel   *novel* Giovanni Guareschi   *d* Julien Duvivier   *ph* Nicolas Hayer   *m* Alessandro Cicognini

Fernandel, Gino Cervi, Sylvie, Manara, Vera Talqui, Franco Interlenghi

'Cute and cosy.' – *MFB*

The Littlest Rebel *
US   1935   70m   bw
TCF (B. G. de Sylva)
V

A small Southern girl persuades President Lincoln to release her father.

Charming, archetypal early Temple vehicle, very well produced.

w Edwin Burke   *play* Edward Peple   *d* David Butler   *ph* John Seitz   *m* Cyril Mockridge

Shirley Temple, John Boles, Jack Holt, Karen Morley, *Bill Robinson*, Guinn Williams, Willie Best, Frank McGlynn Snr

'Shirley Temple as the public likes her . . . which means money.' – *Variety*

Live a Little, Steal a Lot
US   1974   102m   CFI
American International (Dominick Galate)
aka: *Murph the Surf*

Jewel thieves go from success to success, but the police finally force them to strike a bargain and return the gems.

Elaborate but rather unattractive caper story based on the exploits of two real criminals.

w E. Arthur Kean   *story* Allan Dale Kuhn   *d* Marvin Chomsky   *ph* Michael Hugo   *m* Philip Lambro

Robert Conrad, Don Stroud, Donna Mills, Robyn Miller, Luther Adler, Paul Stewart

Live and Let Die *
GB   1973   121m   Eastmancolor
UA/Eon (Harry Saltzman)
V, V*, L, S

James Bond chases a black master criminal and becomes involved in West Indian Voodoo.

Standard tongue-in-cheek spy adventure with a new lightweight star and an air of *déjà vu*. Professional standards high.

w Tom Mankiewicz   *novel* Ian Fleming   *d* Guy Hamilton   *ph* Ted Moore   *m* George Martin   *titles* Maurice Binder

Roger Moore, Yaphet Kotto, Jane Seymour, Clifton James, David Hedison, Bernard Lee, Lois Maxwell

'Plot lines have descended further to the level of the old Saturday afternoon serial, and the treatment is more than ever like a cartoon.' – *Variety*

'A Bond movie is not made. It is packaged. Like an Almond Joy. So much coconut to this much chocolate and a dash of raisins.' – *Joseph Gelmis*

AAN: title song (*m/ly* Paul and Linda McCartney)

Live for Life
France/Italy   1967   130m   Eastmancolor
UA/Ariane/Vides
original title: *Vivre pour Vivre*

A news reporter forsakes his wife for a fashion model.

Interminable and unoriginal romantic drama against Sunday supplement backgrounds.

w Pierre Uytterhoeven, Claude Lelouch   *d/ph* Claude Lelouch   *m* Francis Lai

Yves Montand, Candice Bergen, Annie Girardot, Irene Tunc

'The overall effect is of *Gone with the Wind* remade by Jacopetti.' – *New Yorker*

AAN: best foreign film

The Live Ghost
US   1934   20m   bw
Hal Roach

Two reluctant sailors think they have murdered one of their mates.

Somewhat unyielding material for Stan and Ollie, but still funnier than any of their rivals at the time.

w H. M. Walker   *d* Charles Rogers

Laurel and Hardy, Walter Long, Arthur Housman

Live, Love and Learn
US   1937   78m   bw
MGM (Harry Rapf)

A bohemian painter is tamed by marriage.

Tiresome romantic trifle.

w Charles Brackett, Cyril Hume, Richard Maibaum   *d* George Fitzmaurice   *ph* Ray June   *m* Edward Ward

Robert Montgomery, Rosalind Russell, Robert Benchley, Helen Vinson, Mickey Rooney, Monty Woolley, E. E. Clive, Maude Eburne

'Mildly entertaining mixture of slapstick and drama around the theme of art vs material success.' – *Variety*

Live Now, Pay Later
GB   1962   104m   bw
(Regal) Woodlands/Jay Lewis (Jack Hanbury)

A credit store salesman is himself heavily in debt, and his private life is in ruins; but even after a chapter of unexpected and tragic events he remains irrepressibly optimistic.

A satirical farce melodrama which lets fly in too many directions at once and has a cumulatively cheerless effect despite funny moments.

w Jack Trevor Story   *d* Jay Lewis   *ph* Jack Hildyard   *m* Ron Grainer

Ian Hendry, John Gregson, June Ritchie, Geoffrey Keen, Liz Fraser

Live Today for Tomorrow: see *An Act of Murder* (1964)

'1750 to 1! Always outnumbered! Never outfought!'
Lives of a Bengal Lancer **
US   1934   119m   bw
Paramount (Louis D. Lighton)
V*, L

Adventures on the North-West Frontier.

British army heroics are here taken rather solemnly, but the film is efficient and fondly remembered.

w Waldemar Young, John F. Balderston, Achmed Abdullah, Grover Jones, William Slavens McNutt   *book* Francis Yeats-Brown   *d* Henry Hathaway   *ph* Charles Lang   *m* Milan Roder   *ad* Hans Dreier, Roland Anderson   *ed* Ellsworth Hoagland

Gary Cooper, *Franchot Tone*, Richard Cromwell, *Sir Guy Standing*, C. Aubrey Smith, Monte Blue, Kathleen Burke, Colin Tapley, *Douglass Dumbrille*, Akim Tamiroff, Noble Johnson

'The best army picture ever made.' – *Daily Telegraph*

AAN: best picture; script; Henry Hathaway; art direction; editing

Living: see *Ikiru*

The Living Corpse *
Germany/USSR   1928   108m (24 fps)   bw   silent
Prometheus/Mezhrabpomfilm
original title: *Zhivoi Trup*

An unhappy husband, whose wife loves another, tries all manner of means to give her a divorce. Refused by both church and state, he kills himself.

Heavy-going dramatic tract, photographed and directed with stirring style.

w B. Gusman, Anatoly Marienhof play Leo Tolstoy
d Fedor Ozep ph Anatoly Golovnya

Vsevolod Pudovkin, Maria Jacobini, V. Garden, Gustav Diessl

'One of the really few achievements of the Russian industry: a picture so gripping that it will hold any audience.' – Variety

The Living Daylights **
GB 1987 130m Technicolor Panavision
MGM-UA/Eon (Albert R. Broccoli, Michael G. Wilson)
V, V*, L

James Bond helps the Soviets chase a KGB defector with sinister intent.

25th-anniversary Bond heroics with more adult style than usual, and all technical aspects up to par.

w Richard Maibaum, Michael G. Wilson d John Glen ph Alec Mills m John Barry pd Peter Lamont

Timothy Dalton, Maryam d'Abo, Jeroen Krabbe, Joe Don Baker, John Rhys-Davies, Art Malik, Robert Brown

The Living Dead at the Manchester Morgue (dubbed) *
Spain/Italy 1974 93m Eastmancolor
Miracle/Star/Flaminia (Edmundo Amati)
V

original title: Fin de Semana para los Muertos; aka: Don't Open the Window

The dead are brought back to life as flesh-eating zombies by insects infected by an experimental crop-dusting machine.

An effectively creepy variation on The Night of the Living Dead, filmed in England.

w Sandro Continenza, Marcello Coscia d Jorge Grau ph Francisco Sempere m Giuliano Sorgini pd Carlo Leva sp Giannetto de Rossi, Luciano Bird ed Vincenzo Tomassi

Ray Lovelock, Christine Galbo, Arthur Kennedy, Aldo Massasso, Giorgio Trestini, Roberto Posse

'A director with a genuine talent for the macabre mood and unsettling detail.' – Verina Glaessner

The Living Dead Girl *
France 1982 98m colour
ABC/Aleriaz/Du Yaka/Sam Selsky
V

original title: La Morte Vivante

Toxic waste, released by an earthquake, revives the corpse of a young woman who needs blood to survive.

Spooky movie with some original touches, including a reluctant zombie, but containing rather too much gore for most tastes.

w Jean Rollin, Jacques Ralf d Jean Rollin ph Max Monteillet m Philippe d'Aram sp Benoit Lestang ed Janette Kronegger

Marina Pierro, Françoise Blanchard, Mike Marshall, Carina Barone, Fanny Magieri, Patricia Besnard-Rousseau, Veronique Pinson

'This has a weird feel achieved by combining pastoral visions of an idyllic French countryside with oddly-staged tableaux of blood sacrifice and monstrous innocence. Very violent but not really scary.' – Empire

† The British video release runs for 86m.

The Living Desert ***
US 1953 72m Technicolor
Walt Disney (James Algar)
V*

A light-hearted documentary showing the animals and insects which live in American desert areas.

The aim is entertainment and Disney is not above faking, i.e. the famous sequence in which scorpions

appear to do a square dance, but on its level the thing is brilliantly done.

w James Algar, Winston Hibler, Ted Sears d James Algar ph N. Paul Kenworthy Jnr, Robert H. Grandall m Paul Smith special processes Ub Iwerks

'The film has the same cosy anthropomorphism as a Disney cartoon and its facetious commentary and vulgar music score are typical of others in the series.' – Georges Sadoul

† The other 'True Life Adventures' were: Seal Island 49 (2 reels), Beaver Valley 50 (2 reels), Nature's Half Acre 51 (2 reels), Water Birds 52 (2 reels), Bear Country 53, Prowlers of the Everglades 53, The Vanishing Prairie 54, The African Lion 55, Secrets of Life 56, White Wilderness 58, Jungle Cat 60.

AA: Documentary

'A gleeful journey of sex and violence.'
The Living End
US 1992 84m colour
Mainline/Strand Releasing/Desperate Pictures (Marcus Hu, Jon Gerrans)
V, V*

Two HIV-positive homosexuals – one a drifter, the other a film critic – head for San Francisco, indulging in casual sex and slaughter along the way.

A movie that its director has defined as 'irresponsible', although deliberately unpleasant and self-pitying would seem a more accurate description.

wd Gregg Araki ph Gregg Araki m Cole Coonce ed Gregg Araki

Mike Dytri, Craig Gilmore, Mark Finch, Mary Woronov, Johanna Went, Darcy Marta, Paul Bartel

'Mark this down as the first, worst film of a director who may improve when he empties his system of gay special pleading and camp melodramatics.' – Nigel Andrews, Financial Times

Living Free
GB 1972 92m colour
Columbia/Open Road/High Road (Paul Radin)
V, V*

On the death of Elsa the lioness, George and Joy Adamson capture her three cubs and transfer them for their own safety to Serengeti.

Sloppy sequel to Born Free, depending very heavily on the appeal of the cubs.

w Millard Kaufman d Jack Couffer ph Wolfgang Suschitzky m Sol Kaplan

Susan Hampshire, Nigel Davenport, Geoffrey Keen

'Amazing adventures beneath the curse of the jaguar god!'
The Living Idol
Mexico/US 1956 100m Eastmancolor Cinemascope
MGM (Albert Lewin)

A Mexican girl becomes possessed by the spirit of the jaguar to whom local maidens were once sacrificed.

Pretentious but rather enjoyable highbrow hokum of the heady kind expected from this producer.

wd Albert Lewin ph Jack Hildyard m Rodolpho Halffter

James Robertson Justice, Steve Forrest, Liliane Montevecchi

Living in a Big Way
US 1947 103m bw
MGM (Pandro S. Berman)

A demobbed GI finds he can't get on with his rich selfish wife and opens up a charity home for the families of war casualties.

Odd mixture of comedy, drama and a few songs and dances, not forgetting a message or two. It mostly falls flat on its face.

w Gregory La Cava, Irving Ravetch d Gregory La Cava ph Harold Rosson m Lennie Hayton

Gene Kelly, Marie McDonald, Charles Winninger, Phyllis Thaxter, Spring Byington, Clinton Sundberg

Living It Up *
US 1954 95m Technicolor
Paramount/Hal B. Wallis (Paul Jones)

A suspected victim of radium poisoning is played up by the press into a national hero.

Remake of Nothing Sacred with Lewis as Carole Lombard; deserves a mark for cheek.

w Jack Rose, Mel Shavelson d Norman Taurog ph Daniel Fapp m Walter Scharf

Dean Martin, Jerry Lewis, Janet Leigh, Edward Arnold, Fred Clark, Sheree North, Sig Rumann

Living on Velvet *
US 1935 77m bw
Warner (Edward Chodorov)

A happy-go-lucky aviator changes his life style when he narrowly escapes death in a crash.

Reasonably interesting 'serious' drama of its period.

w Jerry Wald, Julius Epstein d Frank Borzage ph Sid Hickox md Leo F. Forbstein

George Brent, Kay Francis, Warren William, Helen Lowell, Henry O'Neill, Samuel S. Hinds, Russell Hicks, Edgar Kennedy

'Three good names but doubtful of pulling above ordinary business.' – Variety

Lizzie
US 1957 81m bw
MGM/Bryna (Jerry Bresler)

Murder and rape turn a girl into a triple personality.

Preposterous cash-in on The Three Faces of Eve, too silly to be even funny.

w Mel Dinelli novel The Bird's Nest by Shirley Jackson d Hugo Haas ph Paul Ivano m Leith Stevens

Eleanor Parker, Richard Boone, Joan Blondell, Hugo Haas

'Ruddy peculiar.' – MFB

Lloyd's of London **
US 1936 115m bw
TCF (Kenneth MacGowan)

A young messenger boy in the 18th century grows up to found a great insurance company.

Thoroughly well mounted, if unconvincing and slightly boring, historical charade in which the Prince of Wales, Lord Nelson, Dr Johnson and other personages make guest appearances. An archetypal prestige film of its time which also turned out to be box-office.

w Ernest Pascal, Walter Ferris book Curtis Kenyon d Henry King ph Bert Glennon md Louis Silvers ad William S. Darling

Tyrone Power, Madeleine Carroll, George Sanders, Freddie Bartholomew, C. Aubrey Smith, Guy Standing, Virginia Field, Montagu Love, Gavin Muir, Miles Mander, Una O'Connor, E. E. Clive

'Fictional history with fine production but weak from marquee standpoint . . . basically it's the story of the beginning and rise of an insurance company, and how can average audiences be asked to get excited about that?' – Variety

'The name of England is so freely on the characters' lips that we recognize at once an American picture. These people live, make love, bear children all from the most patriotic motives, and it's all rather like London in coronation week.' – Graham Greene

AAN: art direction

Loan Shark *
US 1952 79m bw
Lippert
V*

A detective goes undercover as a tyre worker in order to undermine a loan shark operation.

Competent co-feature with technical aspects in good shape.

w Martin Rackin, Eugene Ling   d Seymour Friedman

George Raft, Dorothy Hart, Paul Stewart, Helen Westcott, John Hoyt

Local Hero **
GB 1983 111m colour
Enigma/Goldcrest (David Puttnam)
V, V*, L, S

A young American executive meets various difficulties when he is sent to a Scottish coastal village to arrange for the building of a new refinery.

Reminiscent of various Ealing comedies, especially *Whisky Galore* and *The Maggie,* this ambitious comedy is really not funny enough for its great length.

wd Bill Forsyth   ph Chris Menges   m Mark Knopfler

Burt Lancaster, Peter Riegert, *Denis Lawson,* Peter Capaldi, Fulton Mackay, Jenny Seagrove

'Little in the way of obvious commercial hooks . . . dominated by a constantly surprising sense of whimsicality.' – *Variety*

BFA: direction

Le Locataire: see *The Tenant*

Lock Up
US 1989 109m Technicolor
Guild/White Eagle/Carolco/Gordon Company (Lawrence Gordon, Charles Gordon)
V, V*, L

A tough prison warden tries to break the spirit of a tougher prisoner.

Nasty and sadistic, with no redeeming qualities.

w Richard Smith, Jeb Stuart, Henry Rosenbaum   d John Flynn   ph Donald E. Thorin   m Bill Conti   pd Bill Kenney   ed Michael N. Knue, Donald Brochu

Sylvester Stallone, Donald Sutherland, John Amos, Sonny Landham, Tom Sizemore, Frank McRae, Darlanne Fluegel, William Allen Young

'The restoration comedy about what cannot be restored!'
Lock Up Your Daughters
GB 1969 103m Technicolor
Columbia/Domino (David Deutsch)

In 18th-century London an aristocratic rake and various lower orders are all in search of female companionship and get their wires crossed.

Noisy, vulgar, ill-acted version (without music) of a successful musical based on two old theatrical warhorses.

w Keith Waterhouse, Willis Hall   play Bernard Miles based on *Rape upon Rape* by Henry Fielding and *The Relapse* by John Vanbrugh   d Peter Coe   ph Peter Suschitzky   m Ron Grainer   pd Tony Woollard

Christopher Plummer, Roy Kinnear, Georgia Brown, Susannah York, Glynis Johns, Ian Bannen, Tom Bell, Elaine Taylor, Jim Dale, Kathleen Harrison, Roy Dotrice, Vanessa Howard, Fenella Fielding, Peter Bayliss, *Richard Wordsworth,* Peter Bull, Fred Emney

'Subtlety is neither required nor displayed.' – *Jack Ibberson*

Lock Your Doors: see *The Ape Man*

The Locked Door
US 1929 70m bw
United Artists

Husband and wife try to save each other by assuming guilt for a murder.

Rather static filmed play.

w C. Gardner Sullivan   play The Sign on the Door by Channing Pollock   d George Fitzmaurice

Barbara Stanwyck, Rod la Rocque, William Boyd, Betty Bronson, ZaSu Pitts, Mack Swain

The Locket
US 1946 85m bw
RKO (Bert Granet)

A *femme fatale* is bent on destroying men, and eventually we discover why.

Dark, confusing melodrama very typical of the immediate post-war years; it has little to say but says it dourly, even achieving flashbacks within flashbacks within flashbacks.

w Sheridan Gibney   d John Brahm   ph Nicholas Musuraca   m Roy Webb

Laraine Day, Robert Mitchum, Brian Aherne, Gene Raymond, Ricardo Cortez

The Lodger ***
GB 1926 84m approx (24 fps) bw silent
Gainsborough (Michael Balcon)
V*

Subtitle: *A Story of the London Fog;* US title: *The Case of Jonathan Drew*

A modern version of the novel about a stranger who is (in this case) wrongly thought to be Jack the Ripper.

The first true Hitchcock film, full of his familiar dramatic visual touches. Oddly enough it was followed by three years during which he seemed to forget them.

w Eliot Stannard, Alfred Hitchcock   novel Mrs Belloc Lowndes   d Alfred Hitchcock   ph Baron Ventimigliaed   Ivor Montagu

Ivor Novello, June, Marie Ault, Arthur Chesney, Malcolm Keen

'It was the first time I exercised my style . . . you might almost say it was my first picture.' – *Alfred Hitchcock, 1966*

The Lodger *
GB 1932 85m bw
Twickenham (Julius Hagen)
US title: *The Phantom Fiend*

The upstairs lodger is suspected of being Jack the Ripper . . .

Modernized version of a story already tackled by Hitchcock as a silent and to be done again in costume in 1944. Not bad, for a minor British film of the time.

w Ivor Novello, Miles Mander, Paul Rotha, H. Fowler Mear   novel Mrs Belloc Lowndes   d Maurice Elvey   ph Stanley Blythe, Basil Emmott

Ivor Novello, Elizabeth Allan, A. W. Baskcomb, Jack Hawkins, Barbara Everest, Peter Gawthorne, Kynaston Reeves

'They can make pictures in England . . . the only point for discussion is why they do not make them oftener.' – *Variety*

The Lodger *
US 1944 84m bw
TCF (Robert Bassler)

1880s version of the above in which the lodger is Jack the Ripper.

Nicely mounted apart from some anachronisms, but a little dull.

w Barre Lyndon   d John Brahm   ph Lucien Ballard   m Hugo Friedhofer

Laird Cregar, Merle Oberon, George Sanders, Cedric Hardwicke, Sara Allgood, Aubrey Mather, Queenie Leonard, Helena Pickard, Lumsden Hare, Frederick Worlock

'The only thing you can't have in this perfect world of total pleasure is your 30th birthday. . . Logan is 29.'
Logan's Run *
US 1976 118m Metrocolor Todd-AO
MGM (Saul David)
V, V*, L, S

In the future, people try to escape from a society which dooms everyone to death at thirty.

Interesting and quite exciting fantasy melodrama which mercifully moves instead of preaching.

w David Zelag Goodman,   novel William F. Nolan   d Michael Anderson   ph Ernest Laszlo   m Jerry Goldsmith   pd Dale Hennesy

Michael York, Richard Jordan, Jenny Agutter, Roscoe Lee Browne, Farrah Fawcett-Majors, Peter Ustinov, Michael Anderson Jnr

'A science fiction film made by people who don't understand science fiction for the amusement of people who don't care one way or the other.' – *S. Frank, L. A. Panorama*

'It puts the future back two thousand years.' – *Benny Green, Punch*

AAN: Ernest Laszlo

La Loi: see *Where the Hot Wind Blows*

Lola *
France/Italy 1960 91m bw Franscope
Rome-Paris/Euro-International
V (W), V*

A cabaret dancer in Nantes chooses between three men.

A slight romance which was much admired for its decoration and visual style, which reminded many of Max Ophuls.

wd Jacques Demy   ph Raoul Coutard   m Michel Legrand

Anouk Aimée, Jacques Harden, Marc Michel, Elina Labourdette

'Like an adolescent's dream of romance, formed from old movies.' – *Pauline Kael, 70s*

Lola (1969): see *Twinky*

Lola *
West Germany 1982 113m colour
Rialto-Trio (Horst Wendlandt)
S

A cabaret singer leads a double life.

Blue Angel country is the setting for this over-predictable fable from a director whose films always have interest.

w Peter Martesheimer, Pea Froelich, Rainer Werner Fassbinder   d Rainer Werner Fassbinder   ph Xaver Schwarzenberger   m Peer Raben   ed Juliane Lorenz, Rainer Werner Fassbinder

Barbara Sukowa, Mario Adorf, Armin Mueller-Stahl, Matthias Fuchs

Lola Montes *
France/Germany 1955 140m Eastmancolor
Cinemascope
Gamma/Florida/Oska
V*, L

The life of the famous courtesan and her romance with the King of Bavaria, told in diverting fragments by a circus ringmaster.

An elaborate, expensive and trickily presented historical charade which confused the public and bankrupted its production company; but the various shorter versions released didn't help.

w Max Ophuls, Annette Wademant, Franz Geiger *novel* Cécil Saint-Laurent *d* Max Ophuls *ph* Christian Matras *m* Georges Auric *ad* Jean d'Aubonne, Willy Schatz

Martine Carol, Anton Walbrook, Peter Ustinov, Ivan Desny, Oskar Werner, Will Quadflieg

'If you want to know what form can really do for content, rush along.' – *Derek Malcolm, Guardian*

Lolita **
GB   1962   152m   bw
MGM/Seven Arts/AA/Anya/Transworld (James B. Harris)
V*, L

A middle-aged lecturer falls for a 14-year-old girl and marries her mother to be near her.

Fitfully amusing but slightly plotted and very lengthy screen version of a sensational novel in which the heroine is only twelve, which makes a difference. The flashback introduction and various comic asides are pretentious and alienating.

w Vladimir Nabokov   *novel* Vladimir Nabokov *d* Stanley Kubrick   *ph* Oswald Morris   *m* Nelson Riddle

James Mason, Shelley Winters, Sue Lyon, Peter Sellers

'The director's heart is apparently elsewhere. Consequently, we face the problem without the passion, the badness without the beauty, the agony without the ecstasy.' – *Andrew Sarris*

'A diluted Blue Angel with a teenage temptress instead of a tart.' – *Stanley Kauffmann*

'So clumsily structured that you begin to wonder whether what was shot and then cut out, whether the beginning was intended to be the end; and it is edited in so dilatory a fashion that after the first hour, almost every scene seems to go on too long.' – *Pauline Kael*

† Before Mason was cast, Noël Coward and Laurence Olivier were sought for the role of Humbert Humbert.

AAN: Vladimir Nabokov

The Lolly Madonna War: see *Lolly Madonna XXX*

Lolly Madonna XXX
US   1973   105m   Metrocolor
MGM (Rodney Carr-Smith)
GB title: *The Lolly Madonna War*

Tennessee hillbilly farmers fight over a meadow.

Violent feudin' melodrama, technically accomplished but of limited interest to non hillbillies.

w Rodney Carr-Smith, Sue Grafton   *novel* Sue Grafton   *d* Richard C. Sarafian   *ph* Philip Lathrop *m* Fred Myrow

Rod Steiger, Robert Ryan, Scott Wilson, Jeff Bridges, Season Hubley

London After Midnight *
US   1927   approx 75m   bw   silent
MGM (Tod Browning)
GB title: *The Hypnotist*

A creepy house murder is solved by hypnotism, and a grinning monster proves to be a red herring.

Famous star thriller of which lamentably no prints survive; remade as *Mark of the Vampire.*

w Tod Browning, Waldemar Young   *d* Tod Browning   *ph* Merritt Gerstad

Lon Chaney, Marceline Day, Conrad Nagel, Henry B. Walthall, Polly Moran

London Belongs to Me **
GB   1948   112m   bw
GFD/Individual (Frank Launder, Sidney Gilliat)
US title: *Dulcimer Street*

A young boy is arrested on a murder charge and his boarding-house friends rally to his defence.

Unconvincing but highly entertaining sub-Dickensian comedy-drama with a rousing finish and an abundance of character roles.

w Sidney Gilliat, J. B. Williams   *novel* Norman Collins   *d* Sidney Gilliat   *ph* Wilkie Cooper *m* Benjamin Frankel

Alastair Sim, Stephen Murray, Richard Attenborough, Fay Compton, Wylie Watson, Susan Shaw, Ivy St Helier, Joyce Carey, Andrew Crawford, Eleanor Summerfield, Hugh Griffith, Gladys Henson

'Memorable for its character-drawing and for the excellence of its writing and acting.' – *Dilys Powell*

The London Blackout Murders
US   1942   58m   bw
Republic
GB title: *Secret Motive*

A mild tobacconist murders people who are sabotaging the war effort.

Curious, set-bound little melodrama with an interesting lead performance.

w Curt Siodmak   *d* George Sherman

John Abbott, Mary McLeod, Lloyd Corrigan, Lester Matthews, Anita Bolster, Billy Bevan, Frederick Worlock

London by Night *
US   1937   70m   bw
MGM

Apparent murders are really part of a blackmail scheme.

Reasonably intriguing mystery with good cast and atmosphere.

w George Oppenheimer   *play* The Umbrella Man by Will Scott   *d* William Thiele

George Murphy, Rita Johnson, Leo G. Carroll, George Zucco, Virginia Field, Montagu Love, Eddie Quillan, Leonard Mudie

'Quality is there, but drawing power isn't.' – *Variety*

London Can Take It ****
GB   1940   9m   bw
The Ministry of Information

Quentin Reynolds, an American war correspondent, shows Americans what the London blitz was like.

Historically significant short, credited with inclining Americans towards participation. In its own right, a brilliant job of editing and presentation.

w Quentin Reynolds   *d* Harry Watt

London Kills Me
GB   1991   107m   colour
Rank/Working Title/Polygram/Film Four (Tim Bevan)
V, V*

A drug pusher, down on his luck, is told that he can have a job as a waiter providing he acquires a good pair of shoes.

Aimless drama of young drug addicts and hangers-on that goes nowhere slowly.

wd Hanif Kureishi   *ph* Ed Lachman   *m* Mark Springer, Sarah Sarhandi   *pd* Stuart Walker *ed* Jon Gregory

Justin Chadwick, Steven Mackintosh, Emer McCourt, Roshan Seth, Fiona Shaw, Brad Dourif, Tony Haygarth, Alun Armstrong   'The motivation is often obscure, the action is sometimes lacking in simple credibility, which is not to be blamed on the performers, and ultimately Kureishi fails to make his people interesting either as individuals or as social types. Nevertheless, he has attempted to take us into an unfamiliar subculture without making us feel that we are slumming.' – *Philip French, Observer*

'An amazing, hypnotizing, mind-bending shambles . . . Photographed like a home video that has been savaged by the cat, the film is earnestly ugly and passionately shapeless.' – *Nigel Andrews, Financial Times*

London Melody
GB   1937   75m   bw
GFD/Herbert Wilcox
V*
US title: *Girls in the Street*

A diplomat falls for a dancer.

Light but rather humourless musical drama.

w Florence Tranter, Monckton Hoffe   *d* Herbert Wilcox   *ph* F. A. Young

Anna Neagle, Tullio Carminati, Robert Douglas, Horace Hodges

'Excellent compilation of bromidial mush, beautifully produced and directed, which should satisfy.' – *Variety*

The London Nobody Knows *
GB   1967   53m   Eastmancolor
Norcon/British Lion

James Mason wanders round the capital's by-ways in search of relics from former ages.

Unhurried but generally delightful documentary.

w Geoffrey Fletcher   *book* Geoffrey Fletcher *d* Norman Cohen

London Town *
GB   1946   126m   Technicolor
GFD/Wesley Ruggles
US title: *My Heart Goes Crazy*

An understudy finally achieves stardom thanks to his daughter's schemes.

Disastrous and expensive attempt to make a major British musical without a single new idea. Tasteless, tawdry and sluggish, but it does record for posterity four of the star's sketches.

w Elliot Paul, Siegfried Herzig, Val Guest   *d* Wesley Ruggles   *ph* Erwin Hillier

Sid Field, Greta Gynt, Kay Kendall, Tessie O'Shea, Claude Hulbert, Sonnie Hale, Mary Clare, Petula Clark, Jerry Desmonde

'I can't see the point of importing an American director and giving him all the time and money in the world to play with when we can make bad musicals on our own, and quicker.' – *Richard Winnington*

The Lone Defender
US   1930   bw   serial: 12 eps
Mascot

A dog avenges the death of his prospector owner.

More hard work for Rin Tin Tin, nearing the end of his career.

d Richard Thorpe

Walter Miller, June Marlowe, Buzz Barton

The Lone Hand
US   1953   80m   Technicolor
Universal-International

A quiet Western farmer is really a Pinkerton detective.

Slightly unusual Western in which the happy ending is not however in doubt.

w Joseph Hoffman   *d* George Sherman

Joel McCrea, Barbara Hale, Alex Nicol, Charles Drake, James Arness

The Lone Ranger

This high-minded Western character, with his black mask, his horse Silver and his Indian friend Tonto, originated (complete with 'William Tell' overture) as a 1933 radio serial in which he was played by George Seaton.

In 1938 he came to film via a Republic serial with a sequel in 1939 (see below). In 1949 Clayton Moore brought him to TV in innumerable half-hour adventures. These eventually encouraged two feature versions; see below. Also, *The Legend of the Lone Ranger* (qv).

The Lone Ranger
US   1938   bw   serial: 15 eps
Republic

A mysterious masked rider turns out to be one of five lawmen combating a ruthless outlaw gang.

The original Lone Ranger serial, with Lee Powell (and Chief Thundercloud as Tonto).   *d* William Witney and John English

Herman Brix, Lynne Roberts, Stanley Andrews, William Farnum

The Lone Ranger
US   1955   85m   Warnercolor
Jack Wrather

The masked do-gooder foils a ranchers' plot to destroy an Indian reservation.

Tolerably watchable adventures.

w Herb Meadow   *d* Stuart Heisler

Clayton Moore, Jay Silverheels, Lyle Bettger, Bonita Granville, Perry Lopez

The Lone Ranger and the Lost City of Gold
US   1958   81m   colour
Jack Wrather

The masked rider solves murders which have been committed for a mysterious medallion.

Lively Western for kids.

w Robert Schaefer and Eric Freiwald   *d* Lesley Selander

Clayton Moore, Jay Silverheels, Douglas Kennedy, Charles Watts

The Lone Ranger Rides Again
US   1939   bw   serial: 15 eps
Republic

A powerful cattleman wages a campaign of violence against innocent settlers.

Sequel serial with a new star.

d William Witney and John English

Robert Livingston, Chief Thundercloud, Duncan Renaldo, Jinx Falken, Ralph Dunn, J. Farrell McDonald

Lone Star
US   1952   90m   bw
MGM (Z. Wayne Griffin)

Andrew Jackson enlists the aid of a Texas adventurer to persuade Sam Houston to change his mind about an agreement with Mexico.

Slow-moving semi-Western, hard to follow for non-Americans. Production values quite high.

w Borden Chase, Howard Estabrook   *d* Vincent Sherman   *ph* Harold Rosson   *m* David Buttolph

Clark Gable, Ava Gardner, Lionel Barrymore, Broderick Crawford, Ed Begley, Beulah Bondi, James Burke, William Farnum, Lowell Gilmore, Moroni Olsen, Russell Simpson, William Conrad

The Lone Wolf
The jewel thief turned sleuth was created by Louis Joseph Vance and turned up in several silent films. During the talkie period several actors played Michael Lanyard; the role of his valet passed from Raymond Walburn to Eric Blore to Alan Mowbray. All the films were made for Columbia, but only the first was anything like a main feature.

1935: THE LONE WOLF RETURNS (*d* Roy William Neill with Melvyn Douglas)
1938: THE LONE WOLF IN PARIS (*d* Albert S. Rogell with Francis Lederer)

1939: THE LONE WOLF SPY HUNT (*d* Peter Godfrey with Warren William)
1940: THE LONE WOLF STRIKES (*d* Sidney Salkow with Warren William)
1941: THE LONE WOLF MEETS A LADY, THE LONE WOLF TAKES A CHANCE, THE LONE WOLF KEEPS A DATE (all as above), SECRETS OF THE LONE WOLF (*d* Edward Dmytryk; WW)
1943: ONE DANGEROUS NIGHT (*d* Michael Gordon: WW), PASSPORT TO SUEZ (*d* André de Toth: WW)
1946: THE NOTORIOUS LONE WOLF (*d* D. Ross Lederman; with Gerald Mohr)
1947: THE LONE WOLF IN LONDON (*d* Leslie Goodwins: GM), THE LONE WOLF IN MEXICO (*d* D. Ross Lederman: GM)
1949: THE LONE WOLF AND HIS LADY (*d* John Hoffman: Ron Randell)

Lone Wolf McQuade
US   1983   107m   DeLuxe
1818/Top Kick/Orion (Yoram Ben-Ami, Steve Carver)
V, L

A tough Texas Ranger takes on horse rustlers and hijackers.

Adults-only action rubbish, disarmingly competently made.

w B. J. Nelson   *d* Steve Carver   *ph* Roger Shearman   *m* Francesco de Masi   *pd* Norm Baron   *ed* Anthony Redman

Chuck Norris, David Carradine, Barbara Carrera, Leon Isaac Kennedy

'A winningly ludicrous mish-mash of mayhem-movie rudiments and action-man reputations.' – *Paul Taylor, MFB*

The Loneliness of the Long Distance Runner ***
GB   1962   104m   bw
British Lion/Bryanston/Woodfall (Tony Richardson)
V, V*, L

The only thing a Borstal boy does well is run, and as he trains he thinks back to his depressing life.

Rather pale study of a social outcast; interesting scenes do not quite form a compelling whole.

w Alan Sillitoe   *story* Alan Sillitoe   *d* Tony Richardson   *ph* Walter Lassally   *m* John Addison

Tom Courtenay, Michael Redgrave, James Bolam, Avis Bunnage, Alec McCowen, Joe Robinson, Julia Foster

Lonely Are the Brave *
US   1962   107m   bw   Panavision
U-I/Joel (Edward Lewis)
V*

The last of the cowboy rebels is no match for pursuit by jeep and helicopter.

A strange, sad, rather moving fable, with very good performances and action scenes, but a shade too unrelenting in its downbeat tone to become a popular classic.

w Dalton Trumbo   *novel* *Brave Cowboy* by Edward Abbey   *d* David Miller   *ph* Philip Lathrop   *m* Jerry Goldsmith

Kirk Douglas, Walter Matthau, Gena Rowlands, Michael Kane, Carroll O'Connor, Karl Swenson, George Kennedy, Bill Raisch

'Above all a portrait to remember and cherish, alive, doomed, tragic, by Kirk Douglas.' – *Dilys Powell*

The Lonely Guy
US   1984   90m   Technicolor
Universal (Arthur Hiller)
V, V*, L

After being thrown out by his girlfriend, a writer discovers a secret society of single men.

Glossy but heavy-handed comedy, attempting satire but not succeeding in its aim.

w Ed Weinberger, Stan Daniels, Neil Simon *book* *The Lonely Guy's Book of Life* by Bruce J. Friedman   *d* Arthur Hiller   *ph* Victor J. Kemper   *m* Jerry Goldsmith   *pd* James D. Vance   *ed* William Reynolds

Steve Martin, Charles Grodin, Judith Ivey, Steven Lawrence, Robyn Douglass, Merv Griffin, Dr Joyce Brothers

'Generally likeable, but it makes you feel as though you were watching television.' – *Pauline Kael, New Yorker*

Lonely Hearts *
Australia   1981   95m   Eastmancolor
Adams Packer Films (John B. Murray)
V, V*, L

When his mother dies, a 50-year-old attempts to go on a belated romantic spree.

Unexpectedly amusing comedy reminiscent of a New Yorker cartoon.

w Paul Cox, John Clarke   *d* Paul Cox   *ph* Yuri Sokol   *m* Norman Kaye

Wendy Hughes, *Norman Kaye*, John Finlayson, Julia Blake, Jonathan Hardy

The Lonely Lady
US   1982   92m   Technicolor
KGA Industries/Harold Robbins International
V*, L

A girl graduate in Los Angeles suffers various setbacks and assaults on her way to being a film star.

Risible concoction designed to show off the non-talents of a non-star in a film financed by her husband.

w John Kershaw, Shawn Randall   *novel* Harold Robbins   *d* Peter Sasdy

Pia Zadora, Lloyd Bochner, Bibi Besch, Joseph Cali, Anthony Holland, Jared Martin

The Lonely Man
US   1957   87m   bw   Vistavision
Paramount (Pat Duggan)

An outlaw hopes to regain social recognition and contacts the son who abhors him.

Dullish psycho Western.

w Harry Essex, Robert Smith   *d* Henry Levin   *ph* Lionel Lindon   *m* Van Cleave

Jack Palance, Anthony Perkins, Elaine Aiken, Neville Brand, Lee Van Cleef, Elisha Cook Jnr, Robert Middleton

The Lonely Passion of Judith Hearne **
GB   1987   116m   Fuji Color
HandMade (George Harrison, Denis O'Brien)
V, V*

A middle-aged piano teacher's hopeless life in Dublin boarding houses.

Inevitably gloomy tale, intelligently crafted and with wonderfully detailed performances.

w Peter Nelson   *novel* Brian Moore   *d* Jack Clayton   *ph* Peter Hannan   *m* Georges Delerue   *pd* Michael Pickwoad

Maggie Smith, Bob Hoskins, Wendy Hiller, Marie Kean, Prunella Scales

The Lonely Woman: see *Voyage to Italy*

Lonelyhearts *
US   1958   103m   bw
UA/Dore Schary
V*

A young journalist finds himself engrossed, appalled and sickened by his work on the agony column.

Episodic, occasionally interesting but generally too vaguely liberal; an intellectual reshaping of a despairing novel. The producer as usual is well meaning but doesn't quite make it.

w Dore Schary *novel* Nathanael West *d* Vincent J. Donehue *ph* John Alton *m* Conrad Salinger

Montgomery Clift, Robert Ryan, Myrna Loy, Dolores Hart, Maureen Stapleton

AAN: Maureen Stapleton

Lonesome *

US 1928 69m (24 fps) bw silent
Universal (Carl Laemmle Jnr)

Young lovers lose each other at Luna Park but later discover that they are neighbours.

Amiable exploration of the life of city workers, comparable with *The Crowd* but showing a lighter touch.

w Edmund T. Lowe *d* Paul Fejos *ph* Gilbert Warrenton

Glenn Tryon, Barbara Kent

† Had sound effects and some talking sequences.

Lonesome Cowboys

US 1968 105m colour
Andy Warhol Films
V
aka: *Andy Warhol's Lonesome Cowboys*

A gang of outlaws rides into town, where the only inhabitants are a wealthy woman, her male nurse and a transvestite sheriff.

A sort of improvised and inspired home movie, a gay Western made by city lovers who regard wide-open spaces and horses with great suspicion. *wd* Paul Morrissey

Viva, Taylor Mead, Tom Hompertz, Louis Waldron, Joe Dallesandro, Eric Emerson

The Long Absence: see *Une Aussi Longue Absence*

Long Ago Tomorrow: see *The Raging Moon*

The Long and the Short and the Tall *

GB 1960 105m bw
ABP/Michael Balcon
V
US title: *Jungle Fighters*

In Malaya during World War II a Japanese scout is captured by a British patrol.

Stark war melodrama with the emphasis on character. Vivid at the time, it now seems very routine.

w Wolf Mankowitz *play* Willis Hall *d* Leslie Norman *ph* Erwin Hillier *m* Stanley Black

Laurence Harvey, Richard Todd, David McCallum, Richard Harris, Ronald Fraser, John Meillon, John Rees, Kenji Takaki

The Long Arm **

GB 1956 96m bw
Ealing (Tom Morahan)
V
US title: *The Third Key*

A Scotland Yard superintendent solves a series of robberies.

Good straightforward police thriller with careful detail.

w Janet Green, Robert Barr *d* Charles Frend *ph* Gordon Dines *m* Gerbrand Schurmann

Jack Hawkins, Dorothy Alison, John Stratton, Michael Brooke, Geoffrey Keen, Sidney Tafler, Meredith Edwards, Ralph Truman, Ursula Howells

'A generally efficient example of popular British film-making.' – *MFB*

The Long Dark Hall

GB 1951 86m bw
British Lion/Five Oceans (Anthony Bushell)

A chorus girl is murdered and her married lover is accused.

Miserable mystery with a trick ending, most inappropriately cast.

w Nunnally Johnson, W. E. C. Fairchild *d* Anthony Bushell, Reginald Beck *ph* Wilkie Cooper *m* Benjamin Frankel

Rex Harrison, Lilli Palmer, Raymond Huntley, Denis O'Dea, Anthony Bushell, Henry Longhurst, Patricia Wayne, Meriel Forbes, Brenda de Banzie, Anthony Dawson

The Long Day Closes ***

GB 1992 85m colour
Mayfair/Palace/Film Four/BFI (Olivia Stewart)
V, V*, L

A man remembers growing up in working-class Liverpool of the mid-1950s as a solitary, movie-obsessed 11-year-old.

Remarkable, atmospheric, understated, nostalgic movie, dealing with emotional repression and the release offered by the cinema.

wd Terence Davies *ph* Michael Coulter *md* Robert Lockhart *pd* Christopher Hobbs *ed* William Diver

Marjorie Yates, Leigh McCormack, Anthony Watson, Nicholas Lamont, Ayse Owens, Tina Malone, Jimmy Wilde, Robin Polley

'A technically elaborate, dryly witty mood piece.' – *Variety*

'A warm and oddly moving experience.' – *Empire*

'Davies' best film yet testifies to the vigour and flexibility of cinematic realisms.' – *Raymond Durgnat, Sight and Sound*

The Long Day's Dying

GB 1968 95m Techniscope
Paramount/Junction Films (Harry Fine)

Three British paratroopers in Europe are cut off from their unit and die pointlessly.

Violent, irritating anti-war film which resurrects all the clichés and makes itself unpleasant into the bargain.

w Charles Wood *novel* Alan White *d* Peter Collinson *ph* Brian Probyn *m* Malcolm Lockyer *pd* Disley Jones

David Hemmings, Tom Bell, Tony Beckley, Alan Dobie

'It is typical of all that is wrong with the film that it should end on a frozen frame of a soldier in the act of dying while heavily ironic patriotic music swells on the sound track.' – *David Wilson*

Long Day's Journey into Night **

US 1962 174m bw
Ely Landau
V*

Connecticut 1912: days in the life of an ageing actor, his drug addicted wife and their sons, one of whom is an alcoholic and the other Eugene O'Neill.

Heavy going, nicely handled, superbly acted version of a play which can be a player's triumph and certainly is here; but it still has more effect in the theatre.

w Eugene O'Neill *d* Sidney Lumet *ph* Boris Kaufman *m* André Previn *pd* Richard Sylbert

Ralph Richardson, Katharine Hepburn, Jason Robards Jnr, *Dean Stockwell*

'Letting his players have their head, lighted miraculously so that every flicker of emotion is preserved, and pursuing them with Kaufman's unobtrusive camera, Lumet illuminates the play, line

by line, and gives it all the impact of a live performance.' – *Brenda Davies*

'A very great play has been not translated to the screen but reverently put behind glass.' – *John Simon*

AAN: Katharine Hepburn

The Long Duel

GB 1967 115m Technicolor Panavision
Rank (Ken Annakin)

On the North-West Frontier in the twenties, British officers disagree about handling the natives, and one of them forms a strong regard for the native leader.

Unconvincing cut-price Indian adventure with little cohesion and less entertainment value.

w Peter Yeldham *d* Ken Annakin *ph* Jack Hildyard *m* Patrick John Scott

Trevor Howard, Yul Brynner, Harry Andrews, Charlotte Rampling, Virginia North, Andrew Keir, Laurence Naismith, Maurice Denham

'The dialogue seems to have been written by a computer fed a programme of execrable films on the same theme.' – *MFB*

The Long Good Friday *

GB 1980 105m colour
Black Lion/Calendar (Barry Hanson)
V, V*, S

A gangland boss faces violent reprisals from the competition.

Heavily melodramatic stylish updating of *Scarface* in a London East End setting. A critical success despite vicious detail and IRA plot involvement.

w Barrie Keefe *d* John Mackenzie *ph* Phil Meheux *m* Francis Monkman

Bob Hoskins, Helen Mirren, Dave King, Bryan Marshall, Eddie Constantine, Stephen Davis

'Nothing says goodbye like a bullet!'
The Long Goodbye

US 1973 111m Technicolor Panavision
UA/Lions Gate (Jerry Bick)
V*, L

Philip Marlowe helps an eccentric friend who is suspected of murdering his wife.

Ugly, boring travesty of a well-respected detective novel, the apparent intention being to reverse the author's attitudes completely and to substitute dullness and incomprehensibility.

w Leigh Brackett *novel* Raymond Chandler *d* Robert Altman *ph* Vilmos Zsigmond *m* John T. Williams

Elliott Gould, Nina Van Pallandt, Sterling Hayden, Mark Rydell, Henry Gibson

'Altman's fragmentation bomb blows up itself rather than the myths he has said he wants to lay to rest.' – *Sight and Sound*

'The trouble is that this Marlowe is an untidy, unshaven, semi-literate dimwit slob who could not locate a missing skyscraper and who would be refused service at a hot dog stand.' – *Charles Champlin*

'A spit in the eye to a great writer.' – *Michael Billington, Illustrated London News*

The Long Gray Line *

US 1955 138m Technicolor Cinemascope
Columbia (Robert Arthur)
V*

The career of an athletics trainer at West Point.

Dim biopic, the kind of true life yarn that Americans like, produced in the cheerful, sentimental, sparring way that John Ford likes.

w Edward Hope *book* Bring Up the Brass by Marty Maher *d* John Ford *ph* Charles Lawton Jnr *md* Morris Stoloff *m* George Duning

Tyrone Power, Maureen O'Hara, Donald Crisp, Ward Bond, Robert Francis, Betsy Palmer, Phil Carey, Harry Carey Jnr, Patrick Wayne, Sean McClory

'Its celebration of the codes and ideals of West Point vexatiously combines sentimental cosiness and a kind of religious awe.' – *Gavin Lambert*

The Long Hot Summer *
US   1958   118m   Eastmancolor   Cinemascope
TCF (Jerry Wald)
V*, L

Conflict arises between a Mississippi town boss and a tenant farmer.

Busy Peyton Place-style family brawling saga with sex on the side, flabby as narrative but compulsive as character study.

w Irving Ravetch, Harriet Frank   *stories* William Faulkner   *d* Martin Ritt   *ph* Joseph LaShelle   *m* Alex North

Orson Welles, Paul Newman, Joanne Woodward, Tony Franciosa, Lee Remick, Angela Lansbury

Long John Silver
Australia   1953   106m   Eastmancolor
Cinemascope
TI Pictures (Joseph Kaufman)
V*

Back from Treasure Island, Silver and Hawkins plan a return visit with fresh clues to the treasure.

Cheaply produced, bitsy-piecy adventure fragments with no one to restrain the star from eye-rolling.

w Martin Rackin   *d* Byron Haskin   *ph* Carl Guthrie   *m* David Buttolph

Robert Newton, Connie Gilchrist, Kit Taylor, Rod Taylor

Long Live Life **
France   1984   Eastmancolor
UGC/Les Films 13/Top No. 1 (Eugene Bellin)

Police and scientists investigate after a businessman and an actress are both unable to account for a three-day absence from their homes.

Tricksy whodunnit in the shadow of the nuclear holocaust, mixing dreams and reality and with several twists in its tale.

wd *Claude Lelouch*   *ph* Bernard Lutic   *m* Didier Barbelivien   *pd* Jacques Bufnoir   *ed* Hugues Darmois, Pauline Leroy

Charlotte Rampling, Michel Piccoli, Jean-Louis Trintignant, Evelyne Bouix, Charles Aznavour, Laurent Malet, Tanya Lopert, Anouk Aimee

Long Live the Lady! **
Italy   1987   106m   colour
Artificial Eye/Rai Channel 1 Cinemaundici (Giampietro Bonamigo)
original title: *Lunga Vita Alla Signora!*

Six catering students go to a hotel converted from a mysterious castle to help prepare a grand banquet presided over by a spectral old lady.

Innocence and inexperience meet sophistication and tradition in a witty, deliberately ambiguous film.

wd *Ermanno Olmi*   *ph* Maurizio Zaccaro, Ermanno Olmi   *m* George Philip Teleman   *ed* Giulia Ciniselli, Ermanno Olmi

Marco Esposito, Simona Brandalise, Stefania Busarello, Simone Dalla Rosa, Lorenzo Paolini, Tarcisio Tosi, Marisa Abbate

The Long Long Trailer *
US   1954   96m   Anscocolor
MGM (Pandro S. Berman)
V*

A construction engineer and his bride buy a trailer for their honeymoon, and wish they hadn't.

Disaster comedy with long bright periods and the inevitable saggy bits.

w Frances Goodrich, Albert Hackett   *novel* Clinton Twiss   *d* Vincente Minnelli   *ph* Robert Surtees   *m* Adolph Deutsch

Lucille Ball, Desi Arnaz, Marjorie Main, Keenan Wynn, Moroni Olsen

Long Lost Father
US   1934   63m   bw
RKO

A restaurant owner saves his daughter from a theft charge.

Competent minor star drama.

w Dwight Taylor   *novel* G. B. Stern   *d* Ernest B. Schoedsack   *ph* Nicholas Musuraca   *m* Max Steiner

John Barrymore, Helen Chandler, Donald Cook, Alan Mowbray, Claude King

'A mild piece with an unbelievable story . . . British background and dialogue, mostly dull.' – *Variety*

The Long Memory
GB   1952   96m   bw
Rank/Europa (Hugh Stewart)

An ex-con, framed for a murder he did not commit, plots revenge but instead uncovers a fresh crime.

Slow and dreary melodrama set largely on a barge, never rising to anything like excitement.

w Robert Hamer, Frank Harvey   *novel* Winston Clewes   *d* Robert Hamer   *ph* Harry Waxman   *m* William Alwyn

John Mills, John McCallum, Elizabeth Sellars, Geoffrey Keen

'Love that promised the world – and paid off in bullets!'
The Long Night *
US   1947   97m   bw
(RKO) Anatole Litvak

A young man shoots the seducer of his sweetheart and barricades himself in a room against the police.

Good-looking but empty remake of *Le Jour se Lève.*

w John Wexley   *story* Jacques Viot   *d* Anatole Litvak   *ph* Sol Polito   *m* Dimitri Tiomkin

Henry Fonda, Barbara Bel Geddes, Vincent Price, Ann Dvorak, Queenie Smith

'This film faithfully reproduces the letter while altering the spirit of the original almost beyond recognition.' – *MFB*

'It would be interesting to see it on a double bill with its French original. Both films clearly rate themselves as tragedies; they are merely intelligent trash. But the old one is much more discreet with its self-pity and much more sharply edged.' – *James Agee*

'A classic of the bashful age!'
Long Pants *
US   1927   58m (24 fps)   bw   silent
First National/Harry Langdon

A country bumpkin has trouble in the city.

Far from the best Langdon comedy, but funny in flashes.

w Arthur Ripley   *d* Frank Capra   *ph* Elgin Lessley

Harry Langdon, Gladys Brockwell, Alan Roscoe, Alma Bennett

The Long Ride Home: see *A Time for Killing*

'All the world loves an outlaw. For some damn reason they remember 'em!'
The Long Riders
US   1980   99m   Technicolor
UA/Huka (Tim Zinnemann)
V, V*, L, S

The story of Western outlaw brothers named Younger, Miller and James.

Well-worn territory with new-fangled violent detail. Not much of an attraction despite the gimmick of having the various anti-heroes played by real brothers.

w Bill Bryden, Steven Philip Smith, Stacy Keach, James Keach   *d* Walter Hill   *ph* Ric Waite   *m* Ry Cooder   *pd* Jack T. Collis

Stacy Keach, James Keach, David Carradine, Keith Carradine, Robert Carradine, Dennis Quaid, Randy Quaid

The Long Ships
GB/Yugoslavia   1963   126m   Technirama
Columbia/Warwick/Avila (Irving Allen)
V

A Viking adventurer and a Moorish prince fall out over a golden bell.

Stilted medieval epic with some visual compensations but more chat than action.

w Berkely Mather, Beverley Cross   *novel* Frank G. Bengtsson   *d* Jack Cardiff   *ph* Christopher Challis   *m* Dusan Radic

Richard Widmark, Sidney Poitier, Russ Tamblyn, Rosanna Schiaffino, Oscar Homolka, Colin Blakely

'To say it was disastrous is a compliment.' – *Sidney Poitier*

The Long, the Short and the Tall: see *The Long and the Short and the Tall*

'The love of woman in their eyes – the salt of the sea in their blood!'
The Long Voyage Home **
US   1940   104m   bw
Walter Wanger
V*, L

Merchant seamen on shore leave get drunk, philosophize and have adventures.

Stagey-looking but dramatically interesting amalgam of four one-act plays by Eugene O'Neill, with talent abounding.

w Dudley Nichols   *d John Ford*   *ph* Gregg Toland   *m* Richard Hageman   *ed* Sherman Todd

John Wayne, Thomas Mitchell, Ian Hunter, Ward Bond, Barry Fitzgerald, Wilfrid Lawson, *Mildred Natwick,* John Qualen, Arthur Shields, Joe Sawyer

'One of the finest of all movies that deal with life at sea.' – *Pauline Kael, 70s*

AAN: best picture; Dudley Nichols; Gregg Toland; Richard Hageman; Sherman Todd

The Long Wait
US   1954   93m   bw
UA/Parklane (Lesser Samuels)

An amnesia victim returns home to solve a murder in which he was involved.

Flatulent version of a Mickey Spillane novel, over-plotted and inadequately motivated.

w Alan Green, Lesser Samuels   *d* Victor Saville   *ph* Franz Planer   *m* Mario Castelnuovo Tedesco

Anthony Quinn, Charles Coburn, Gene Evans, Peggie Castle, Dolores Donlan

Long Weekend
Australia   1977   100m   colour   Panavision
Dugong Films (Colin Eggleston)

Wild life appears to gang up on a couple with marital problems who go for a camping trip to an isolated beach.

Didactic thriller, too predictable to hold anyone's interest for long.

w Everett de Roche   *d* Colin Eggleston
ph Vincent Monton   *m* Michael Carlos   *pd* Larry Eastwood   *ed* Brian Kavanagh

John Hargreaves, Briony Behets

The Longest Day **
US   1962   169m   bw   Cinemascope
TCF (Darryl F. Zanuck, Elmo Williams)
V, V (W), V*, L

A multi-faceted account of the landings in Normandy in June 1944.

Extraordinarily noisy war spectacular, enjoyable as a violent entertainment once one has caught all the threads, but emotionally unaffecting because every part is played by a star.

w Cornelius Ryan, Romain Gary, James Jones, David Pursall, Jack Seddon   *book* Cornelius Ryan
d Andrew Marton, Ken Annakin, Bernhard Wicki
ph Henri Persin, Walter Wottitz, Pierre Levent, Jean Bourgoin   *m* Maurice Jarre, Paul Anka

John Wayne, Robert Mitchum, Henry Fonda, Robert Ryan, Rod Steiger, Robert Wagner, Paul Anka, Fabian, Tommy Sands, Richard Beymer, Mel Ferrer, Jeffrey Hunter, Sal Mineo, Roddy McDowall, Stuart Whitman, Steve Forrest, Eddie Albert, Edmond O'Brien, Red Buttons, Tom Tryon, Alexander Knox, Ray Danton, Ron Randell, Richard Burton, Donald Houston, Kenneth More, Peter Lawford, Richard Todd, Leo Genn, John Gregson, Sean Connery, Michael Medwin, Leslie Phillips, Irina Demich, Bourvil, Jean-Louis Barrault, Christian Marquand, Arletty, Curt Jurgens, Paul Hartmann, Gert Frobe, Wolfgang Preiss, Peter Van Eyck, Christopher Lee, Eugene Deckers, Richard Wattis

AA: photography

AAN: best picture

The Longest Yard
US   1974   122m   Technicolor
Paramount/Long Road (Albert S. Ruddy)
V, V*, L
GB title: The Mean Machine

Imprisoned for drunkenness and car theft, a football star is blackmailed into training a prison football team of hulking misfits.

Violent, meandering comedy-drama with murderous jokes but no narrative grip.

w Tracy Keenan Wynn   *d* Robert Aldrich
ph Joseph Biroc   *m* Frank de Vol

Burt Reynolds, Eddie Albert, Ed Lauter, Michael Conrad, Jim Hampton

The Longshot
US   1986   89m   DeLuxe
Orion/Longshot (Lang Elliott)
V*

Four disgruntled punters borrow money from a local gangster to bet on a horse that a con man has told them is a certain winner.

An also-ran of a comedy, inconsequential and witless.

w Tim Conway   *d* Paul Bartel   *ph* Robby Muller
m Charles Fox   *ad* Joseph M. Altadonna   *ed* Adam Toomayan

Tim Conway, Harvey Korman, Jack Weston, Ted Wass, Stella Stevens, Jonathan Winters, Anne Meara, George DiCenzo, Jorge Cervera

Longtime Companion *
US   1990   99m   colour
Palace/Companion Productions/American Playhouse (Stan Wlodkowski)
V, V*

A group of homosexuals, watching their lovers and friends dying of AIDS, decide to become actively involved in fighting the disease.

While tracing its characters' lives from the beginning to the end of the 1980s, the film avoids easy emotion and sentimentality, though it stays with the somewhat sexless affluent middle-classes who are able to articulate their concerns.

w Craig Lucas   *d* Norman Rene   *ph* Tony Jannelli
m Greg DeBelles   *pd* Andrew Jackness
ed Katherine Wenning

Stephen Caffrey, Patrick Cassidy, Brian Cousins, Bruce Davison, John Dossett, Mark Lamos, Dermot Mulroney, Mary-Louise Parker

AAN: Bruce Davison

Look Back in Anger *
GB   1959   99m   bw
ABP/Woodfall (Gordon L. T. Scott)
V, V*

A bad-tempered young man with a grudge against life and the government runs a market stall, lives in a squalid flat, and has an affair with his wife's best friend.

Well-made version of a play whose sheer dreariness was theatrically stimulating but in terms of film realism becomes only depressing and stupid despite competence all round. It also set shoddy standards for its many less proficient imitators.

w Nigel Kneale   *play* John Osborne   *d* Tony Richardson   *ph* Oswald Morris   *m* Chris Barber

Richard Burton, Mary Ure, Claire Bloom, Edith Evans, Gary Raymond, Glen Byam Shaw, Phyllis Neilson-Terry, Donald Pleasence, George Devine

Look Before You Love
GB   1948   96m   bw
Burnham/Rank

Romance in Rio for a girl of the embassy staff.

Abysmal romantic comedy with little of either commodity in evidence.

w Reginald Long   *d* Harold Huth

Margaret Lockwood, Griffith Jones, Norman Wooland, Phyllis Stanley, Michael Medwin, Maurice Denham

'The sunshine story of Broadway's glory girl!'
Look for the Silver Lining *
US   1949   106m   Technicolor
Warner (William Jacobs)

The life story of twenties stage star Marilyn Miller.

Harmless musical biopic with a sense of humour.

w Phoebe and Henry Ephron, Marian Spitzer, Bert Kalmar, Harry Ruby   *d* David Butler   *ph* Peverell Marley   *md* Ray Heindorf

June Haver, *Ray Bolger, Charles Ruggles,* Gordon Macrae, Rosemary de Camp, S. Z. Sakall, Walter Catlett

AAN: Ray Heindorf

Look in Any Window
US   1961   87m   bw
Allied Artists

A rich but psychotic youth despises his friends and relations and is arrested as a peeping tom.

Psychiatric case history which also wags a social finger. Not particularly convincing.

w Laurence E. Mascott   *d* William Alland

Paul Anka, Ruth Roman, Alex Nicol, Gigi Perreau, George Dolenz, Jack Cassidy

Look Up and Laugh *
GB   1935   82m   bw
ATP (Basil Dean)

Market stallholders defy a big chain store.

Good star comedy with music.

w Gordon Wellesley   *story* J. B. Priestley   *d* Basil Dean   *ph* Robert G. Martin   *md* Ernest Irving

Gracie Fields, Douglas Wakefield, Harry Tate, Alfred Drayton, Morris Harvey, Vivien Leigh, Robb Wilton

Look Who's Laughing
US   1941   75m   bw
RKO (Allan Dwan)
See also: Here We Go Again

Fibber McGee and Molly act as unexpected hosts to Edgar Bergen and Charlie McCarthy.

Exploitation of radio sitcoms, acceptable at the time.With Lucille Ball.

w James V. Kern and others   *d* Allan Dwan

Look Who's Talking
US   1989   96m   Technicolor
Columbia TriStar (Jonathan D. Krane)
V, V*, L

A baby comments on the growing relationship between his unmarried mother and a taxi driver.

Indifferent comedy that enjoyed a great success through the novelty of adult speech and attitudes issuing from the mouth of a baby.   *wd* Amy Heckerling   *ph* Thomas Del Ruth   *m* David Kitay
ad Reuben Freed, Graeme Murray   *ed* Debra Chiate

John Travolta, Kirstie Alley, Olympia Dukakis, George Segal, Abe Vigoda, Bruce Willis, Twink Caplan, Joy Boushel, Don S. Davis

'Carelessly put together, ugly to look at and mawkish and stupid in turn.' – Derek Malcolm, Guardian

Look Who's Talking Too
US   1990   81m   Technicolor
Columbia TriStar (Jonathan D. Krane)
V, V*, L

Small babies comment on the disagreements between a husband and wife.

All that this sad comedy has to recommend it is the novelty of adult voices issuing from the mouths of babes, a joke that quickly outstays its welcome.

w Amy Heckerling, Neal Israel   *d* Amy Heckerling
ph Thomas Del Ruth   *m* David Kitay   *pd* Reuben Freed   *ed* Debra Chiate

John Travolta, Kirstie Alley, Olympia Dukakis, Elias Koteas, Twink Caplan and voices of Bruce Willis, Roseanne Barr, Damon Wayans, Mel Brooks

'Whenever Heckerling runs out of inspiration, which is every couple of minutes, she slaps an old rock 'n' roll record on the turntable and transforms the film into a music-video.' – Philip French, Observer

Looker
US   1981   94m   colour
Warner/The Ladd Company (Howard Jeffrey)
V*, L

A plastic surgeon investigates the murders of beautiful models who were his clients.

Unconvincing, paranoid science-fiction thriller about advertising.

wd Michael Crichton   *ph* Paul Lohmann   *m* Barry DeVorzon   *pd* Dean Edward Mitzner   *ed* Carl Kress

Albert Finney, James Coburn, Susan Dey, Leigh Taylor-Young, Dorian Harewood, Tim Rossovich

Lookin' to Get Out
US   1982   105m   colour
Lorimar/North Star/Voight-Schaffel (Robert Schaffel)

A couple of inveterate gamblers take on the Las Vegas establishment.

Fairly pleasant, mindless, quite forgettable comedy.

w Al Schwartz, Jon Voight   *d* Hal Ashby
ph Haskell Wexler   *m* Johnny Mandel   *pd* Robert Boyle

Jon Voight, Ann-Margret, Burt Young, Bert Remsen, Jude Farese, Richard Bradford

Looking for Love

US   1964   83m   Metrocolor   Panavision
Joe Pasternak/MGM

A talented girl can't decide between show business
and marriage.

Limp, would-be-cute romantic nonsense with poor
musical numbers.

w Ruth Brooks Flippen   d Don Weis

Connie Francis, Jim Hutton, Susan Oliver, Joby
Baker, Barbara Nichols, Jay C. Flippen, Jesse White,
Charles Lane

Looking for Mr Goodbar

US   1977   136m   Metrocolor   Panavision
Paramount (Freddie Fields)
V*, L

A teacher of deaf children leads a sordid secret night
life.

Exploitative and very boring sex melodrama which
doesn't even make one believe in its central character.
wd Richard Brooks   novel Judith Rossner
ph William A. Fraker   m Artie Kane   ad Edward
Carfagno

Diane Keaton, Tuesday Weld, William Atherton,
Richard Kiley

'Brooks has laid a windy jeremiad about permissive
sex on top of fractured film syntax.' – Judith Crist

AAN: William A. Fraker; Tuesday Weld

Looking for Trouble

US   1933   77m   bw
UA/Darryl F. Zanuck

Two telephone engineers brawl over a girl.

Early star vehicle, quite watchable.

w Leonard Praskins and Elmer Harris   d William
Wellman

Spencer Tracy, Jack Oakie, Constance Cummings,
Morgan Conway, Arline Judge

'Too much of a plug for the phone company . . . plus
an overpacked plot and certain dialogue failings.' –
Variety

Looking Forward

US   1933   76m   bw
MGM

A shop owner finds he must sell his property and fire
valued staff.

Depression fable from Dodie Smith's play Service,
adequately mounted.

w Bess Meredyth, H. M. Harwood   d Clarence
Brown

Lewis Stone, Lionel Barrymore, Benita Hume,
Elizabeth Allan, Phillips Holmes, Colin Clive

The Looking Glass War

GB   1969   107m   Technicolor   Panavision
Columbia/M. J. Frankovich (John Box)
V*

The British secret service sends a young Pole into East
Germany to find a top secret film.

Jaundiced spy story which aims for irony and tragedy
but becomes merely verbose and irritating.

wd Frank R. Pierson   novel John Le Carré
ph Austin Dempster   m Wally Stott

Christopher Jones, Pia Degermark, Ralph Richardson,
Anthony Hopkins, Paul Rogers, Susan George, Ray
McAnally, Robert Urquhart, Maxine Audley, Anna
Massey

'There are a lot of incidental pleasures, but in the final
analysis they only add up to half a film.' – Nigel
Andrews

Looking on the Bright Side *

GB   1931   81m   bw
ATP (Basil Dean)

A songwriter gets ideas above his station but
eventually returns to the manicurist who loves him.

Dated but lively musical which helped confirm
Gracie's stardom.

w Basil Dean, Archie Pitt, Brock Williams   d Basil
Dean   ph Robert G. Martin   md Carroll Gibbons

Gracie Fields, Richard Dolman, Julian Rose, Wyn
Richmond

Loophole

GB   1980   105m   colour
Brent Walker (Julian Holloway, David Korda)

A safecracker plans to rob the vault of a London bank.

Dim caper yarn which can't make its mind up how
serious it means to be. As it stands, it is all very old
hat and has a cop-out finish.

w Jonathan Hales   novel Robert Pollock   d John
Quested   ph Michael Reed   m Lalo Schifrin

Albert Finney, Martin Sheen, Susannah York, Colin
Blakeley, Jonathan Pryce, Robert Morley, Alfred
Lynch

Loose Ankles

US   1930   66m   bw
First National

A girl's inheritance will be cancelled if she is involved
in scandal. Rival claimants try to ensure that she is.

Thin, amiable comedy based on a Broadway success.

w Gene Towne   play Sam Janney   d Ted Wilde

Loretta Young, Douglas Fairbanks Jnr, Louise
Fazenda, Otis Harlan, Daphne Pollard, Inez Courtney

'Will bring a chuckle to the most hard-boiled
metropolite.' – Variety

Loose Connections *

GB   1983   96m   colour
Umbrella/Greenpoint (Simon Perry)

Adventures on a drive to Munich.

Thin, easy-going road comedy. Pleasant enough, but
no Genevieve.

w Maggie Brooks   d Richard Eyre   ph Clive
Tickner   m Dominic Muldowney

Lindsay Duncan, Stephen Rea, Carole Harrison,
Frances Low

Loot *

GB   1970   101m   Eastmancolor
Performing Arts Ltd (Arthur Lewis)
V, V*

A crook hides his mother's body and uses the coffin to
carry the proceeds of a robbery.

Breakneck black farce which still can't move quite fast
enough to cover up its bad taste, though well done by
all concerned.

w Ray Galton, Alan Simpson   play Joe Orton
d Silvio Narizzano   ph Austin Dempster   m Keith
Mansfield, Richard Willing-Denton   ad Anthony
Pratt

Richard Attenborough, Lee Remick, Hywel Bennett,
Milo O'Shea, Dick Emery

The Looters

US   1955   87m   bw
Universal

A plane crashes on Pike's Peak, and rescuers fall out
about whether to loot the wreckage.

Competent co-feature of its period and style.

w Richard Alan Simmons   d Abner Biberman

Rory Calhoun, Ray Danton, Thomas Gomez, Julie
Adams, Frank Faylen, Rod Williams

Lord Camber's Ladies

GB   1932   80m   bw
BIP

A nobleman tries to murder his way out of a romantic
tangle.

Rather dull suspenser notable only for its stagey cast
and the fact that Alfred Hitchcock produced it.

w Benn W. Levy, Edwin Greenwood and Gilbert
Wakefield   novel The Case of Lady Camber by Horace
Annesley Vachell   d Benn W. Levy

Gerald du Maurier, Gertrude Lawrence, Benita Hume,
Nigel Bruce, Clare Greet, A. Bromley Davenport

Lord Edgware Dies

GB   1934   81m   bw
Real Art

Hercule Poirot proves that an elderly nobleman was
not killed by his young wife.

Modest whodunnit: the intended series did not catch
on.

w H. Fowler Mear   novel Agatha Christie   d Henry
Edwards

Austin Trevor, Jane Carr, Richard Cooper, John
Turnbull, Michael Shepley

Lord Jeff

US   1938   78m   bw
MGM (Frank Davis)
GB title: The Boy from Barnardo's

A well-brought-up boy gets into trouble and is sent
under supervision to a naval school.

Adequate family film with absolutely no surprises.

w James K. McGuinness   story Bradford Ropes, Val
Burton, Endré Bohem   d Sam Wood   ph John Seitz
m Edward Ward

Freddie Bartholomew, Mickey Rooney, Charles
Coburn, Herbert Mundin, Terry Kilburn, Gale
Sondergaard, Peter Lawford

Lord Jim *

GB   1964   154m   Technicolor   Super Panavision
Columbia/Keep (René Dupont)
V*

Adventures of a sailor who prowls the Far East
looking for truth; he helps enslaved natives, is raped
by a tribal chief, and finally sacrifices his life.

Lush and very boring farrago of miscellaneous
incident, with a central character about whose fate no
one can care. However, an expensive production must
have its points of interest, and the belated
introduction of a gentleman villain gives a little edge.

wd Richard Brooks   novel Joseph Conrad
ph Frederick A. Young   m Bronislau Kaper
pd Geoffrey Drake

Peter O'Toole, James Mason, Eli Wallach, Paul Lukas,
Jack Hawkins, Daliah Lavi, Curt Jurgens, Akim
Tamiroff

Lord Love a Duck *

US   1966   105m   bw
UA/Charleston (George Axelrod)

A senior Los Angeles student practises hypnotism on
his girlfriend.

Rather sloppy satire on American culture and fancies,
dressed up as crazy comedy; occasional laughs.

w Larry H. Johnson, George Axelrod   novel Al Hine
d George Axelrod   ph Daniel Fapp   m Neal Hefti

Roddy McDowall, Tuesday Weld, Lola Albright, Ruth
Gordon, Harvey Korman, Max Showalter

Lord of the Flies

GB   1963   91m   bw
Allen-Hogdon Productions/Two Arts (Lewis M. Allen)
V*

After a plane crash, a party of English schoolboys are

stranded on an uncharted tropical island and gradually turn savage.

Semi-professional production of a semi-poetic novel which worked well on the printed page but on screen seems crude and unconvincing.

wd Peter Brook *novel* William Golding *ph* Tom Hollyman, Gerald Feil *m* Raymond Leppard

James Aubrey, Tom Chapin, Hugh Edwards, Roger Elwin, Tom Gaman

'A Classic Story of Conflict and Survival'
Lord of the Flies

US 1990 90m DeLuxe Panavision
Columbia/Castle Rock/Nelson/Jack's Camp/Signal Hill (Ross Milloy)
V, V*, L, S

Boys from a US military school, survivors of an air crash on an uninhabited tropical island, revert to savagery.

Dull remake, with crude melodrama substituting for the subtle social disintegration of the original.

w Sara Schiff *novel* William Golding *d* Harry Hook *ph* Martin Fuhrer *m* Philippe Sarde *pd* Jamie Leonard *ed* Harry Hook

Balthazar Getty, Chris Furth, Danuel Pipoly, Badgett Dale, Edward Taft, Andrew Taft, Bob Peck, Bill Schoppert, Michael Greene

'Individual performances mostly never rise above the semi-amateur level.' – *Variety*

'A Technicolor travel brochure in which a pack of already uncivilized kids act rough and talk dirty like children temporarily freed from the vigilance of their parents.' – *Alexander Walker, London Evening Standard*

Lord of the Rings *

US 1978 133m DeLuxe
UA/Fantasy (Saul Zaentz)
V*, S

In Middle Earth the Dark Lord loses a powerful ring, and a Hobbit tries to prevent him from getting it back.

Disappointingly stolid, overlong and confused cartoon version of a modern classic which may well deserve all those adjectives. Parts of it are charming, and the method of making cartoons from film of actors photographed in the ordinary way is certainly ingenious though it denies the cartoon characters their own full richness.

w Chris Conkling, Peter S. Beagle *books* J. R. R. Tolkien *d* Ralph Bakshi *ph* Timothy Galfas *m* Leonard Rosenman *voices* Christopher Guard, John Hurt, William Squire, Michael Scholes

The Lords of Discipline

US 1982 103m Eastmancolor
Paramount (Herb Jaffe, Gabriel Katzka)
V*, L

Murky goings-on at the Carolina Military Institute.

Strictly for those interested in army cadets being unpleasant to each other.

w Thomas Pope, Lloyd Fonvielle *novel* Pat Conroy *d* Franc Roddam *ph* Brian Tufano *m* Howard Blake *pd* John Graysmark *ed* Michael Ellis

David Keith, Robert Prosky, G. D. Spradlin, Barbara Babcock, Michael Biehn, Rick Rossovich

The Lords of Flatbush *

US 1974 86m Technicolor
Columbia (Stephen F. Verona)
V*, L

Adventures of Brooklyn street gangs.

Not quite the violent movie one might think, and interesting for its cast as well as some thoughtful passages.

w Stephen F. Verona, Martin Davidson, Gayle Glecker, Sylvester Stallone *d* Stephen F. Verona, Martin Davidson

Perry King, Henry Winkler, Sylvester Stallone, Paul Mace, Susan Blakely, Maria Smith

Lorenzo's Oil **

US 1992 135m Technicolor
UIP/Universal/Kennedy Miller (Doug Mitchell, George Miller)
V, V*, L, S

After they are told their young son has a fatal disease, his parents defy medical opinion to find a cure.

An inspiring true story of faith and determination, but acted and directed as an all-out emotional assault that some will find wearying before the end.

w George Miller, Nick Enright *d* George Miller *ph* John Seale *pd* Kristi Zea *ed* Richard Francis-Bruce, Marcus D'Arcy, Lee Smith

Nick Nolte, *Susan Sarandon,* Peter Ustinov, Kathleen Wilhoite, Gerry Bamman, Margo Martindale, James Rebhorn, Ann Hearn, Maduka Steady, Zack O'Malley Greenburg

'As gruelling a medical case study as any audience would ever want to sit through . . . A one-of-a-kind film that will devastate some viewers and prove too overbearing and clinical for others, it is as obsessive and relentless as its leading characters.' – *Variety*

† Medical research released in 1993 claimed that the oil produced 'no detectable clinical improvement' in sufferers from the brain disease.

AAN: Susan Sarandon; George Miller (as writer), Nick Enright

Lorna Doone **

GB 1934 90m bw
ATP (Basil Dean)

In 1625 on Exmoor, a farmer comes to love an outlaw's daughter who proves to be in reality a kidnapped heiress.

Simple, straightforward, effective version of the famous romance, with refreshing use of exteriors.

w Dorothy Farnum, Miles Malleson, Gordon Wellesley *novel* R. D. Blackmore *d* Basil Dean *ph* Robert Martin

Victoria Hopper, John Loder, Margaret Lockwood, *Roy Emerton,* Edward Rigby, Mary Clare, Roger Livesey, George Curzon, D. A. Clarke-Smith, Lawrence Hanray, Amy Veness, Eliot Makeham

'It has polish, but it lacks drama and grip.' – *Variety*

Lorna Doone

US 1951 89m Technicolor
Columbia (Edward Small)

Grotesque remake which treats the story like a cheap Western.

w Jesse L. Lasky Jnr, Richard Schayer *d* Phil Karlson *ph* Charles Van Enger *m* George Duning

Barbara Hale, Richard Greene, Anne Howard, William Bishop, Carl Benton Reid, Ron Randell, Sean McClory, Onslow Stevens, Lester Matthews, John Dehner

Loser Takes All

GB 1956 88m Eastmancolor Cinemascope
British Lion/John Stafford

An accountant and his wife are invited to Monte Carlo but the high life estranges them.

Tedious taradiddle from an unexpected quarter; not a success by any standard.

w Graham Greene *novel* Graham Greene *d* Ken Annakin *ph* Georges Périnal *m* Alessandro Cicognini

Glynis Johns, Rossano Brazzi, Robert Morley, Joyce Carey, A. E. Matthews, Tony Britton, Felix Aylmer, Albert Lieven, Geoffrey Keen

Loss of Innocence: see *The Greengage Summer*

Lost *

GB 1955 89m Technicolor
Rank (Vivian A. Cox)
US title: *Tears for Simon*

The police go on the trail of a stolen child.

Mildly effective semi-documentary police story, with good use of locations.

w Janet Green *d* Guy Green *ph* Harry Waxman *m* Benjamin Frankel

David Farrar, David Knight, Julia Arnall, Anthony Oliver, Thora Hird, Eleanor Summerfield, Marjorie Rhodes, Joan Sims

Lost and Found

US 1979 105m Technicolor Panavision
Columbia/Gordon (Melvin Frank)
V, V*

A widowed American professor meets an English divorcee on a skiing holiday, but after marriage they prove to be incompatible.

Unattractive romantic comedy-drama which despite capable stars degenerates into a series of wounding slanging matches.

w Melvin Frank, Jack Rose *d* Melvin Frank *ph* Douglas Slocombe *m* John Cameron *pd* Trevor Williams

Glenda Jackson, George Segal, Maureen Stapleton, Paul Sorvino, John Cunningham, Hollis McLaren

Lost Angel *

US 1943 91m bw
MGM (Robert Sisk)

A lost little girl is adopted by a reporter.

Good star vehicle for the sentimentally-inclined, with solid production and casting back-up.

w Isabel Lennart *d* Roy Rowland *ph* Robert Surtees *m* Daniele Amfitheatrof

Margaret O'Brien, James Craig, Marsha Hunt, Philip Merivale, Henry O'Neill, Donald Meek, Keenan Wynn

'A beautiful opportunity for true satire is offered and, I regret to say, thrown away. For our little Gulliver is rapidly decivilized by all the familiar bromidic palliatives: love, crooning, fairies and night clubs.' – *Richard Winnington*

Lost Angels: see *The Road Home*

Lost Boundaries *

US 1949 105m bw
Film Classics (Louis de Rochemont)

In a New Hampshire town in the forties, a beloved doctor and his wife are found to have negro blood.

Well-meaning but dramatically ineffective racial drama which meanders along allowing an occasional burst of genuine feeling to come through.

w Virginia Shaler, Eugene Ling *d* Alfred Werker *ph* William J. Miller *m* Louis Applebaum

Mel Ferrer, Beatrice Pearson, Richard Hylton, Susan Douglas, Canada Lee, Grace Coppin

'It cannot be said to betray its subject, but is, rather, unequal to it.' – *Gavin Lambert*

The Lost Boys

US 1987 92m Technicolor Panavision
Warner (Harvey Bernhard)
V, V*, L, S

Vampiric bikers corrupt innocent teenagers.

Wild nonsense which affronts all classes by its sheer excesses.

w Janice Fischer, James Jeremias, Jeffrey Boam *d* Joel Schumacher *ph* Michael Chapman *m* Thomas Newman *pd* Bo Welch *ed* Robert Brown

Jason Patric, Corey Haim, Dianne Wiest, Barnard Hughes, Kiefer Sutherland

The Lost City

US 1935 bw serial: 12 eps
Krellberg

Electrical storms disrupt the world, and an engineer tracks the source to Central Africa, where a wizard named Zolok runs a city with the Magnetic Mountain.

Agreeably lunatic free-for-all in serial form.

d Harry Revier

Kane Richmond, William 'Stage' Boyd, Claudia Dell

Lost City of the Jungle

US 1946 bw serial: 13 eps
Universal

A warmonger finds an antidote to the atom bomb inside the African tomb of The Glowing Goddess.

Absurdities pile on each other in a serial which was clearly the starting point for *Raiders of the Lost Ark:* when the chest is opened, the evil element inside disintegrates those present.

d Ray Taylor and Lewis D. Collins

Russell Hayden, Jane Adams, Lionel Atwill, Keye Luke, Helen Bennett, John Eldredge, John Miljan

'Wherever their feet touched ground, a new adventure was born!'

Lost Command

US 1966 128m Technicolor Panavision
Columbia/Red Lion (Mark Robson)
V*

Adventures of a French paratroop regiment in Indo-China and Algeria.

Anti-war war adventure; noisy but scarcely inspired.

w Nelson Gidding *novel* The Centurions by Jean Larteguy *d* Mark Robson *ph* Robert Surtees *m* Franz Waxman

Anthony Quinn, Alain Delon, George Segal, Michèle Morgan, Maurice Ronet, Claudia Cardinale, Grégoire Aslan, Jean Servais

The Lost Continent *

GB 1968 98m Technicolor
Hammer (Michael Carreras)
V*

The captain of a tramp steamer illegally carries dynamite, and he and his passengers are stranded in a weird Sargasso Sea colony run by the Spanish Inquisition.

Hilariously imaginative hokum with splendid art direction and some of the grottiest monsters on film; but memorable moments do not quite add up to a classic of the genre.

w Michael Nash *novel* Uncharted Seas by Dennis Wheatley *d* Michael Carreras *ph* Paul Beeson *m* Gerard Schurmann *ad* Arthur Lawson *sp* Robert A. Mattey, Cliff Richardson

Eric Porter, Hildegarde Neff, Suzanna Leigh, Tony Beckley, Nigel Stock, Neil McCallum, Jimmy Hanley, James Cossins, Victor Maddern

'One of the most ludicrously enjoyable bad films since Salome Where She Danced.' – *MFB*

Lost Honeymoon

US 1947 70m bw
Eagle-Lion
V*

An amnesiac GI fails to remember either his wife or his young family.

Artificial comedy which the actors can't carry off.

w Joseph Fields *d* Leigh Jason

Franchot Tone, Ann Richards, Tom Conway

Lost Horizon ****

US 1937 130m (released at 118m) bw
Columbia (Frank Capra)
V, V*, L

Escaping from a Chinese revolution, four people are kidnapped by plane and taken to an idyllic civilization in a Tibetan valley, where the weather is always kind and men are not only gentle to each other but live to a very advanced age.

Much re-cut romantic adventure which leaves out some of the emphasis of a favourite Utopian novel but stands up pretty well on its own, at least as a supreme example of Hollywood moonshine, with perfect casting, direction and music. If the design has a touch of Ziegfeld, that's Hollywood.

w Robert Riskin, *novel* James Hilton *d* Frank Capra *ph* Joseph Walker *m* Dmitri Tiomkin *ad* Stephen Goosson

Ronald Colman, H. B. Warner, Thomas Mitchell, Edward Everett Horton, Sam Jaffe, Isabel Jewell, Jane Wyatt, Margo, John Howard

'One of the most impressive of all thirties films, a splendid fantasy which, physically and emotionally, lets out all the stops.' – *John Baxter, 1968*

'One is reminded of a British critic's comment on Mary of Scotland, "the inaccuracies must have involved tremendous research".' – *Robert Stebbins*

'The best film I've seen for ages, but will somebody please tell me how they got the grand piano along a footpath on which only one person can walk at a time with rope and pickaxe and with a sheer drop of three thousand feet or so?' – *James Agate*

'If the long dull ethical sequences had been cut to the bone there would have been plenty of room for the real story: the shock of western crudity and injustice on a man returned from a more gentle and beautiful way of life.' – *Graham Greene*

† A 1943 reissue trimmed down the negative still further, to 109 minutes; but in 1979 the American Film Institute restored a print of the original length.

AA: Stephen Goosson

AAN: best picture; Dimitri Tiomkin; H. B. Warner

'The adventure that will live forever has been transformed into spectacular musical drama!'
'Come to Shangri-La and a new world of love!'

Lost Horizon *

US 1972 143m Panavision Technicolor
Columbia/Ross Hunter
L

Torpid remake with a good opening followed by slabs of philosophizing dialogue and an unbroken series of tedious songs.

w Larry Kramer *d* Charles Jarrott *ph* Robert Surtees *m* Burt Bacharach *songs* Burt Bacharach, Hal David *ad* Preston Ames

Peter Finch, Liv Ullmann, Sally Kellerman, *Bobby Van*, George Kennedy, Michael York, Olivia Hussey, James Shigeta, John Gielgud, Charles Boyer

'It will never play again outside of Shangri-La.' – *Les Keyser, Hollywood in the Seventies*

'Only Ross Hunter would remake a 1937 movie into a 1932 one.' – *Judith Crist*

'It can't even be enjoyed as camp.' – *Newsweek*

'The narrative has no energy, and the pauses for the pedagogic songs are so awkward that you feel the director's wheelchair needs oiling.' – *Pauline Kael*

The Lost Illusion: see *The Fallen Idol*

Lost in a Harem **

US 1944 89m bw
MGM (George Haight)

Two travelling entertainers in the Middle East get mixed up with a conniving sultan, who hypnotizes them.

Lively, well-staged romp which shows the comedians at their best and uses astute borrowings from burlesque, pantomime, and Hollywood traditions of fantasy and running jokes.

w Harry Ruskin, John Grant, Harry Crane *d* Charles Reisner *ph* Lester White *m* David Snell

Bud Abbott, Lou Costello, Douglass Dumbrille, Marilyn Maxwell, John Conte, Jimmy Dorsey and his Orchestra

Lost in Alaska: see *Abbott and Costello Lost in Alaska*

Lost in America *

US 1985 91m Technicolor Panavision
Warner/Geffen Company (Marty Katz)
V*, L

A successful couple drop out of their expensive life-style to discover that poverty has its disadvantages.

Witty demolition of yuppie attitudes to the simple life.

w Albert Brooks, Monica Johnson *d* Albert Brooks *ph* Eric Saarinen *m* Arthur B. Rubinstein *pd* Richard Sawyer *ed* David Finfer

Albert Brooks, Julie Hagerty, Michael Greene, Garry K. Marshall, Maggie Roswell, Tom Tarpey

Lost in Siberia *

GB/USSR 1992 108m Eastmancolor
Winstone/Spectator/Mosfilm
V
aka: *Zateriannyi v Sibiri*

In the late 40s an English archaeologist working on the border between Persia and Russia is accused of being a spy and sent to Siberia.

One of an unsuccessful series of co-productions with the West; this has the effect of diminishing the Russian experience of the gulags in favour of a thriller-like movie, but it has its moments.

w James Brabazon, Alexander Mitta, Valery Fried, Yuri Korotkov *d* Alexander Mitta *ph* Vladimir Shevtsik *m* Leonid Desyatnikov *ad* Valery Yurkevitch, Vatali Klimenkov *ed* Anthony Sloman, Nadezhda Veselovskaya

Anthony Andrews, Yelena Mayorova, Vladimir Ilyin, Ira Mikhalyova, Yevgeni Mironov, Alexei Zharkov, Valentin Gaft, Alexander Bureyev

Lost in Time: see *Waxwork II: Lost in Time*

The Lost Jungle

US 1934 bw serial: 12 eps
Mascot

An animal trainer rescues his girlfriend's father from the jungle.

Slightly anaemic serial adventures. *d* Armand Schaefer and David Howard

Clyde Beatty, Cecilia Parker, Syd Saylor, Mickey Rooney

A Lost Lady

US 1934 71m bw
Warner

A girl falls in love with a much older man.

Empty-headed and over-familiar romantic melodrama.

w Gene Markey, Kathryn Scola *novel* Willa Cather *d* Alfred E. Green

Barbara Stanwyck, Frank Morgan, Ricardo Cortez, Lyle Talbot, Philip Reed, Hobart Cavanaugh, Henry Kolker

'Lightweight in story and interesting only as a femme style display.' – *Variety*

'He crowded a lifetime into 37 suspenseful hours!'
The Lost Man
US   1969   113m   Technicolor   Panavision
Universal (Ernest B. Wehmeyer)

After a robbery, a crook is pursued by the police and goes into hiding.

Odd Man Out made over as a vehicle for polemics about civil rights for blacks: too shiny, too long, too talky to have any grip.

wd Robert Alan Aurthur   *ph* Jerry Finnerman
m Quincy Jones

Sidney Poitier, Joanna Shimkus, Al Freeman Jnr, Michael Tolan, Leon Bibb, Richard Dysart, David Steinberg, Paul Winfield

'In a strange house of hate – they loved where love had never dared to live before!'
The Lost Moment *
US   1947   89m   bw
Universal/Walter Wanger (Martin Gabel)
V*, L

An American publisher goes to Venice to recover love letters written by a famous poet to a lady now aged 105.

Slightly absurd but memorable period drama with a guilty secret eventually coming to light, all put across with apparently deliberate artificiality.

w Leonardo Bercovici   *novel* *The Aspern Papers* by Henry James   *d* Martin Gabel   *ph* Hal Mohr
m Daniele Amfitheatrof

Robert Cummings, Susan Hayward, *Agnes Moorehead*, Joan Lorring, Eduardo Ciannelli

'A compelling piece, highly stylized and very personal, with a beautifully photographed studio recreation of Venice.' – *NFT, 1973*

'Boiling passions in the burning sands!'
The Lost Patrol *
US   1934   74m   bw
RKO (Cliff Reid)
V*, L

A small British army group is lost in the Mesopotamian desert under Arab attack.

Much-copied adventure story of a small patrol under attack (compare *Sahara, Bataan* and *The Last of the Comanches* for a start). The original now seems pretty starchy but retains moments of power.

w Dudley Nichols,   *story* Patrol by Philip MacDonald
d John Ford   *ph* Harold Wenstrom   *m* Max Steiner

Victor McLaglen, Boris Karloff, Wallace Ford, Reginald Denny, J. M. Kerrigan, Billy Bevan, Alan Hale

'Although the running time is long, there's nothing draggy about it.' – *Variety*

† A silent British version was released in 1929, written and directed by Walter Summers for British Instructional, with Cyril McLaglen, Sam Wilkinson and Terence Collier.

AAN: Max Steiner

The Lost People
GB   1949   89m   bw
GFD/Gainsborough (Gordon Wellesley)

Displaced persons gather for comfort in a disused German theatre.

Once again a very flat film has been unsuitably made from an effective piece of theatre, with all possible types present and all views represented. Not on.

w Bridget Boland   *play* Cockpit by Bridget Boland
d Bernard Knowles   *ph* Jack Asher   *m* John Greenwood

Richard Attenborough, Mai Zetterling, Siobhan McKenna, Dennis Price, Maxwell Reed, William Hartell, Gerard Heinz, Harcourt Williams, Marcel Poncin

The Lost Planet
US   1953   bw   serial: 15 eps
Columbia

Reporters are captured by aliens and taken to the planet Ergro.

Plenty going on in this silly serial fantasy, but it could have been more effective if played for laughs.

d Spencer Bennet

Judd Holdren, Vivian Mason, Ted Thorpe, Forrest Taylor, Gene Roth, I. Stanford Jolley

The Lost Special
US   1932   bw   serial: 12 eps
Universal

A train filled with gold disappears.

Amiable serial remotely based on a Conan Doyle story.

d Henry McRae

Frank Albertson, Cecilia Parker, Francis Ford, Ernie Nevers

'Shot at only by cameras – yet falling in flames!'
The Lost Squadron *
US   1932   79m   bw
RKO (David O. Selznick)
V*, L

World War I pilots find work stunting for a movie studio.

Unusual comedy-drama with several points of interest.

w Herman J. Mankiewicz, Wallace Smith   *d* George Archainbaud   *ph* Leo Tover, Edward Cronjager
m Max Steiner

Richard Dix, Mary Astor, Erich von Stroheim, Joel McCrea, Dorothy Jordan, Hugh Herbert, Robert Armstrong

'A pretty good show . . . whether it will get back what it cost is something else again.' – *Variety*

Lost Treasure of the Amazon: see *Jivaro*

'From the best-seller that was talked about in whispers!'
'The picture that dares to bare a man's soul'
The Lost Weekend ****
US   1945   101m   bw
Paramount (Charles Brackett)
V*, L

Two days in the life of a young dipsomaniac writer.

Startlingly original on its release, this stark little drama keeps its power, especially in the scenes on New York streets and in a dipso ward. It could scarcely have been more effectively filmed.

w Charles Brackett, Billy Wilder,   *novel* Charles Jackson
d Billy Wilder   *ph* John F. Seitz   *m* Miklos Rozsa
ed Doane Harrison

Ray Milland, Jane Wyman, Philip Terry, *Howard da Silva*, Frank Faylen

DON BIRNAM (Ray Milland): 'It shrinks my liver, doesn't it, Nat? It pickles my kidneys, yeah. But what does it do to my mind? It tosses the sandbags overboard so the balloon can soar. Suddenly I'm above the ordinary. I'm competent, supremely competent. I'm walking a tightrope over Niagara Falls. I'm one of the great ones. I'm Michelangelo, moulding the beard of Moses. I'm Van Gogh, painting pure sunlight. I'm Horowitz, playing the Emperor Concerto. I'm John Barrymore before the movies got

him by the throat. I'm Jesse James and his two brothers – all three of 'em. I'm W. Shakespeare. And out there it's not Third Avenue any longer – it's the Nile, Nat, the Nile – and down it moves the barge of Cleopatra.'

'A reminder of what celluloid is capable of achieving when used by a good director.' – *Spectator*

'I undershtand that liquor interesh; innerish; intereshtsh are rather worried about thish film. Thatsh tough.' – *James Agee*

'Most to be admired are its impressions of bare dreadful truth: the real crowds in the real streets as the hero-victim lugs his typewriter to the pawnshop, the trains screaming overhead, the awful night as he makes his escape from the alcoholics' ward.' – *Dilys Powell*

'A distinguished film, rich in cinematic ingenuity.' – *The Times*

AA: best picture; script; Billy Wilder (as director); Ray Milland

AAN: John F. Seitz; Miklos Rozsa; editing

'Sir Arthur Conan Doyle's Stupendous Story of Adventure and Romance.'
The Lost World **
US   1925   60m   bw
First National
V, V*, L

The irascible Professor Challenger leads an expedition to prove his claim that prehistoric creatures are still living on a remote plateau in South America.

A sensational film of its time, complete with dinosaurs, an apeman, a volcanic eruption, a forest fire and a brontosaurus running wild in the streets of London, destroying Tower Bridge. It still retains a naïve charm, as well as a providing a narrative that has served as a prototype for dozens of similar films since.

novel Arthur Conan Doyle   *d* Harry O. Hoyt
sp Willis O'Brien

Wallace Beery, Lewis Stone, Bessie Love, Lloyd Hughes, Alma Bennett, Arthur Hoyt, Margaret McWade, Bull Montana

'This has precious few touches to visual imagination to complement its wonderful monsters and stirring romance.' – *Empire*

'In the middle of the twentieth century you fall off the brink of time!'
The Lost World
US   1960   98m   DeLuxe   Cinemascope
TCF/Saratoga (Irwin Allen)

Professor Challenger is financed by a newspaper to confirm the report of prehistoric life on a South African plateau.

Pitiful attempt to continue the success of *Journey to the Center of the Earth*, with the story idiotically modernized, unconvincing monsters, a script which inserts conventional romance and villainy, and fatal miscasting of the central part.

w Irwin Allen, Charles Bennett   *novel* Sir Arthur Conan Doyle   *d* Irwin Allen   *ph* Winton C. Hoch
m Bert Shefter, Paul Sawtell

Claude Rains, *Michael Rennie*, David Hedison, *Richard Haydn*, Fernando Lamas, Jill St. John, Ray Stricklyn

'Resembles nothing so much as a ride on a rundown fairground Ghost Train.' – *MFB*

The Lottery Bride
US   1930   85m   bw
Arthur Hammerstein/United Artists
V*

A girl goes on the run when she finds herself first prize in a lottery.

Dismal operetta from the period when silent techniques were still giving way to sound.

w Horace Jackson, Howard Emmett Rogers *story* Henry Stothart *d* Paul Stein

Jeanette MacDonald, Joe E. Brown, John Garrick, ZaSu Pitts

'One of the worst of the really very bad features released since sound.' – *Variety*

Lottery Lover
US 1935 80m bw
Fox

A shy sailor wins a lottery prize, an introduction to a Folies Bergère star, but falls in love with the public relations girl organizing the stunt.

Faded romantic comedy of little surviving interest.

w Sig Herzig *d* William Thiele

Lew Ayres, Reginald Denny, Pat Paterson, Sterling Holloway

The Loudest Whisper: see *The Children's Hour*

Louisa *
US 1950 90m bw
Universal-International

A much-married man finds that both his daughter and his mother have boyfriend trouble.

Friendly generation gap comedy with practised talent.

w Stanley Roberts *d* Alexander Hall

Ronald Reagan, Spring Byington, Charles Coburn, Ruth Hussey, Edmund Gwenn, Piper Laurie, Scotty Beckett

Louise *
France 1939 99m bw
European Film Distributors

A seamstress is rescued from a life of shame.

Ill-advised venture into film opera for an American star.

w Steve Passeur, *opera* Gustave Charpentier *d* Abel Gance

Grace Moore, Georges Thill, André Pernet

'Tedious and unconvincing.' – *Variety*

Louisiana
US 1947 82m bw
Lindsley Parsons/Monogram

A poor singing farmer becomes governor.

Musical biopic of only historical interest.

w Jack de Witt *d* Phil Karlson

Jimmie Davis, Margaret Lindsay, John Gallaudet, Freddie Stewart

Louisiana Purchase *
US 1941 98m Technicolor
Paramount (Harold Wilson)

Efforts are made to compromise a politician.

Quite lively transcription of a Broadway musical success with elements of political satire including a climactic filibuster scene.

w Jerome Chodorov, Joseph Fields *play* Morrie Ryskind *songs* Irving Berlin *d* Irving Cummings *ph* Harry Hallenberger, Ray Rennahan *ad* Raoul Pene du Bois

Bob Hope, Vera Zorina, *Victor Moore*, Irene Bordoni, Dona Drake, Raymond Walburn, Maxie Rosenbloom, Frank Albertson, Donald MacBride, Andrew Tombes

AAN: Harry Hallenberger, Ray Rennahan; Raoul Pene du Bois

Louisiana Story *
US 1948 77m bw
Standard Oil Company (Robert Flaherty)
V*

In the Louisiana bayous a young native boy watches as oil drillers make a strike.

Quite beautiful but over-extended semi-documentary.

w Robert and Frances Flaherty *d* Robert Flaherty *ph* Richard Leacock *m* Virgil Thomson *ed* Helen Van Dongen

Joseph Boudreaux, Lionel Leblanc, Frank Hardy

'The film will be remembered, not for its content, but for the sustained beauty of photography and music, harmonised in shots recalling the delicacy of Chinese landscape painting.' – *Campbell Dixon*

AAN: original story

Loulou
France 1980 105m Eastmancolor
Gaumont/Action Films
V

A smart young business woman sets up an uneasy menage with a working-class layabout.

Curious but not particularly interesting character study, watchable mainly for its detail.

w Arlette Langmann *d* Maurice Pialat *ph* Pierre-William Glenn, Jacques Loiseleux *md* Philippe Sarde

Isabelle Huppert, Gérard Depardieu, Guy Marchand, Humbert Balsan

'Caught in the swirl of passions and sacrifice!'
Love *
US 1927 82m (24 fps) bw silent
MGM (Edmund Goulding)
V*

Anna Karenina leaves her husband and child for Count Vronsky.

Marginally interesting first shot at a famous subject by a star who came back to it in 1935.

w Frances Marion, Lorna Moon *novel* Leo Tolstoy *d* Edmund Goulding *ph* William Daniels *m* Ernst Luz *ad* Cedric Gibbons, Alexander Toluboff

Greta Garbo, John Gilbert, Brandon Hurst, Philippe de Lacy, George Fawcett, Emily Fitzroy

† An alternative happy ending was provided for exhibitors who wanted it.

Love Affair
US 1932 68m bw
Columbia

An heiress falls for a flying instructor.

Mild romantic comedy drama.

w Jo Swerling *story* Ursula Parrott *d* Thornton Freeland *ph* Ted Tetzlaff

Dorothy Mackaill, Humphrey Bogart, Jack Kennedy, Astrid Allwyn, Halliwell Hobbes, Barbara Leonard

'A neighbourhood operation, that's about its worth.' – *Variety*

Love Affair ***
US 1939 89m bw
RKO (Leo McCarey)
V*

On a transatlantic crossing, a European man of the world meets a New York girl, but their romance is flawed by misunderstanding and physical accident.

The essence of Hollywood romance, and one of the most fondly remembered films of the thirties, perhaps because of the easy comedy sense of the first half.

w Delmer Daves, Donald Ogden Stewart, *story* Mildred Cram, Leo McCarey *d* Leo McCarey *ph* Rudolph Maté *m* Roy Webb *ad* Van Nest Polglase, Al Herman

Charles Boyer, Irene Dunne, Maria Ouspenskaya, Lee Bowman, Astrid Allwyn, Maurice Moscovich

'Production is of grade A quality . . . its b.o. chances look good.' – *Variety*

'Those excited over the mastery of form already achieved in pictures, will like to follow this demonstration of the qualities of technique and imagination the films must always have and keep on recruiting to their service . . . Clichés of situation and attitude are lifted almost beyond recognition by a morning freshness of eye for each small thing around.' – *Otis Ferguson* 'McCarey brought off one of the most difficult things you can attempt with film. He created a mood, rather than a story; he kept it alive by expert interpolations; he provided comedy when he needed comedy and poignancy when he needed substance; and he did it with the minimum of effort.' – *Pare Lorentz*

† Remade as *An Affair to Remember* (qv).

AAN: best picture; original story; Irene Dunne; Maria Ouspenskaya; art direction; song 'Wishing' (*m/y* Buddy de Sylva)

Love among the Millionaires
US 1930 70m bw
Paramount

A waitress falls for the son of a railroad president.

Ho-hum star vehicle without much get-up-and-go.

w Grover Jones, William Conselman, Joseph L. Mankiewicz *d* Frank Tuttle

Clara Bow, Stanley Smith, Mitzi Green, Skeets Gallagher, Stuart Erwin

'It will call for a lot of faith from the Clara Bow admirers to accept her in this kind of a part, the sweet wishy-washy thing, after the bum publicity she's been getting.' – *Variety*

Love and Bullets
US 1978 103m Metrocolor
ITC (Pancho Kohner)

A gangster's mistress is brought back from Switzerland by a revengeful Phoenix cop.

Downbeat bang-bang with a high death rate and a glum finale; generally low-grade stuff.

w Wendell Mayes, John Melson *d* Stuart Rosenberg *ph* Fred Koenekamp *m* Lalo Schifrin *pd* John DeCuir

Charles Bronson, Jill Ireland, Rod Steiger, Henry Silva, Strother Martin, Bradford Dillman, Michael V. Gazzo

'A relatively dismaying example of the Lew Grade entertainment formula: as locations, production values and clichéd set-pieces proliferate, scripts increasingly look like shaggy dog stories desperately in search of a point, and actors are left to do their own thing as characters disintegrate.' – *Richard Combs, MFB*

'Love and bullets my eye: embarrassment and tedium would be more like it.' – *Time Out*

Love and Death *
US 1975 85m DeLuxe Panavision
UA/Jack Rollins, Charles H. Joffe
V, V*, L

In 1812 Russia, a man condemned reviews the follies of his life.

Personalized comedy fantasia inspired by *War and Peace*, Ingmar Bergman and S. J. Perelman. Basically only for star fans.

wd Woody Allen *ph* Ghislain Cloquet *m* Prokofiev

Woody Allen, Diane Keaton, Georges Adel, Despo, Frank Adu

'I have a feeling that one of these days Allen will get it most dreadfully together and make a film which is more than a string of funny one-liners and set-pieces. He hasn't quite done it here.' – *Benny Green, Punch*

Love and Hisses *
US   1937   84m   bw
TCF (Kenneth MacGowan)

A gossip columnist and a bandleader continue their feud.

Moderate sequel to *Wake Up and Live* (qv); it got by.

w Art Arthur, Curtis Kenyon   d Sidney Lanfield
ph Robert Planck   m Louis Silvers

Walter Winchell, Ben Bernie and his orchestra, Joan Davis, Bert Lahr, Simone Simon, Ruth Terry

Love and Learn
US   1947   83m   bw
Warner

Two impoverished songwriters are secretly helped by a rich girl.

Tame comedy with few laughs.

w Eugene Conrad, Francis Swann and I. A. L. Diamond   d Frederick de Cordova

Jack Carson, Robert Hutton, Martha Vickers, Janis Paige, Otto Kruger

Love and Money
US   1980   95m   Metrocolor
Lorimar

A banker kidnaps a financier's wife, and finds himself in dead trouble.

Incoherent light melodrama which barely got released.

wd James Toback

Ray Sharkey, Ornella Muti, Klaus Kinski, Armand Assante, King Vidor (as the hero's senile grandfather), William Prince

Love and Pain and the Whole Damn Thing
US   1972   113m   Eastmancolor
Columbia/Gus (Alan J. Pakula)

An asthmatic young American on holiday in Spain has an affair with an older woman suffering from an incurable disease.

Dreary doomed romance studiously treated as tourist comedy.

w Alvin Sargent   d Alan J. Pakula   ph Geoffrey Unsworth   m Michael Small

Maggie Smith, Timothy Bottoms

Love and Sacrifice: see *America*

Love at First Bite *
US   1979   96m   colour
Simon (Joel Freeman)
V, V*, L

Count Dracula flees from the communists and settles in New York.

Energetic spoof, with jokes on the sexy side; good work all round.

w Robert Kaufman   d Stan Dragoti   ph Edward Rosson   m Charles Bernstein   pd Serge Krizman

George Hamilton, Susan St James, Richard Benjamin, Dick Shawn, Arte Johnson

'Love is so hard to find you have to hire a detective'
Love at Large *
US   1990   97m   DeLuxe
Rank/Orion (David Blocker)
V, V*, L

A private eye checks on the wrong man, while a female detective is hired by his girlfriend to check on him.

Enjoyably light-hearted treatment of an intricate plot of double-cross and double lives.

wd Alan Rudolph   ph Elliot Davis   m Mark Isham   pd Stephen Legler   ed Lisa Churgin

Tom Berenger, Elizabeth Perkins, Anne Archer, Kate Capshaw, Annette O'Toole, Ted Levine, Ann Magnuson, Kevin J. O'Connor, Ruby Dee, Barry Miller, Neil Young

The Love Ban: see *It's a 2' 6" Above the Ground World*

Love before Breakfast
US   1936   90m   bw
Universal

Two Park Avenue beaux vie for a socialite.

Thinly plotted but quite amusing romantic comedy.

w Herbert Fields   novel *Spinster Dinner* by Faith Baldwin   d Walter Lang

Carole Lombard, Preston Foster, Cesar Romero, Janet Beecher, Bert Roach

A Love Bewitched
Spain   1985   98m   colour
Emiliano Piedra
original title: *El Amor Brujo*

The future marriage of two children is arranged by their gypsy fathers with tragic results.

A dance drama likely to appeal only to aficionados of the genre.

w Carlos Saura, Antonio Gades   d Carlos Saura   ph Teo Escamilla   m Manuel de Falla   pd Gerardo Vera   ed Pedro Del Rey

Antonio Gades, Cristina Hoyos, Laura Del Sol, Juan Antonio Jiminez, Emma Penella, La Polaca, Gomez de Jerez

The Love Bug **
US   1968   107m   Technicolor
Walt Disney (Bill Walsh)
V*, L

An unsuccessful racing driver finds that his small private Volkswagen has a mind of its own.

Amusing, pacy period fantasy in the best Disney style.

w Bill Walsh, Don da Gradi   d Robert Stevenson   ph Edward Colman   m George Bruns   sp Eustace Lycett

David Tomlinson, Dean Jones, Michele Lee, Buddy Hackett, Joe Flynn, Benson Fong, Joe E. Ross

The Love Cage: see *Joy House*

The Love Child
GB   1987   101m   colour
BFI/Frontroom Pro/Channel 4/VPRO TV (Angela Topping)

An orphaned South London youth falls in love with an artist living in a squat.

Weak whimsy of working-class life.

w Gordon Hann   d Robert Smith   ph Thaddeus O'Sullivan   m Colin Gibson, Kenny Craddock   pd Caroline Hanania   ed John Davies

Sheila Hancock, Peter Capaldi, Percy Herbert, Lesley Sharp, Alexei Sayle, Arthur Hewlett, Cleo Sylvestre, Stephen Lind

Love Crazy *
US   1941   100m   bw
MGM (Pandro S. Berman)

When his wife threatens to divorce him, a businessman hatches all manner of crazy schemes, including disguising himself as his own sister.

Zany romantic comedy, over-stretched but with a fair share of hilarity.

w William Ludwig, Charles Lederer, David Hertz   d Jack Conway   ph Ray June   m David Snell

William Powell, Myrna Loy, Gail Patrick, Jack Carson, Florence Bates, Sidney Blackmer, Vladimir Sokoloff, Donald MacBride, Sig Rumann, Sara Haden, Elisha Cook Jnr, Kathleen Lockhart

Love Crimes
US   1991   90m   DeLuxe
Rank/Sovereign/Miramax (Lizzie Borden, Rudy Langlais)
V

An assistant DA goes undercover so that she can trap a photographer who is raping the women who pose for him.

Confused thriller that seems uncertain as to what kind of film it wants to be; it finally settles for mediocrity.

w Allan Moyle, Laurie Frank   d Lizzie Borden   ph Jack N. Green   m Graeme Revell, Roger Mason   pd Armin Ganz   ed Nicholas C. Smith, Mike Jackson

Sean Young, Patrick Bergin, Arnetia Walker, James Read, Ron Orbach, Fern Dorsey, Tina Hightower, Donna Biscoe

Love Eternal *
France   1943   111m   bw
André Paulvé
original title: *L'Eternel Retour*

The love story of Tristan and Isolde.

This modernized version had a Teutonic look and was respected rather than admired.

w Jean Cocteau   d Jean Delannoy   ph Roger Hubert   m Georges Auric   ad Wakhevitch

Jean Marais, Madeleine Sologne, Jean Murat, Yvonne de Bray

Love Field
US   1992   104m   DeLuxe
Orion (Sarah Pillsbury, Midge Sanford)
V, V*, L, S

A hairdresser in Dallas who identifies with Jacqueline Kennedy goes to attend President Kennedy's funeral and is attracted to a black man she meets on the way.

Intensely American movie that is too parochial to be rewarding.

w Don Roos   d Jonathan Kaplan   ph Ralf Bode   m Jerry Goldsmith   pd Mark Freeborn   ed Jane Kurson

Michelle Pfeiffer, Dennis Haysbert, Stephanie McFadden, Brian Kerwin, Louise Latham, Peggy Rea, Beth Grant

AAN: Michelle Pfeiffer

Love Finds a Way: see *Alias French Gertie*

Love from a Stranger *
GB   1936   90m   bw
Trafalgar (Max Schach)
V*

A young woman realizes she may have married a maniac.

Stalwart suspenser from a popular novel and play.

w Frances Marion   play Frank Vosper   story *Philomel Cottage* by Agatha Christie   d Rowland V. Lee   ph Philip Tannura   m Benjamin Britten

Ann Harding, Basil Rathbone, Binnie Hale, Bruce Seton, Jean Cadell, Bryan Powley, Joan Hickson, Donald Calthrop

'Gorgeously photographed and splendidly cut . . . takes front rank with the long list of gruesome films produced in recent years.' – *Variety*

Love from a Stranger
US   1947   81m   bw
Eagle Lion (James J. Geller)
V*
GB title: *A Stranger Walked In*

Stilted period remake.

w Philip MacDonald   d Richard Whorf   ph Tony Gaudio   m Hans Salter

Sylvia Sidney, John Hodiak, Ann Richards, John Howard, Isobel Elsom, Frederick Worlock

The Love God?

US 1969 103m Techniscope
Universal (Edward J. Montagne)

A meek ornithologist is thought to be the brains behind a girlie magazine, and becomes a national sex symbol.

Dispiriting and very talkative star farce which would have been long at half the time.

wd Nat Hiken ph William Margulies m Vic Mizzy

Don Knotts, Edmond O'Brien, Anne Francis, James Gregory, Maureen Arthur

'Strictly for admirers of Don Knotts. Can there really be many?' – MFB

The Love Goddesses **

US 1965 87m bw
Paramount/Walter Reade/Sterling

A light-hearted account of female sexuality on the Hollywood screen.

Sharp-eyed compilation film which is worth a dozen books on the subject.

w Saul J. Turell, Graeme Ferguson m Percy Faith narrator Carl King

'A compilation of shrapnel from old sex-bomb movies, full of deliciously improbable moments.' – Newsweek

† Clips include *Blonde Venus, Morocco, True Heart Susie, Cleopatra* (1934), *Intolerance, The Cheat, The Sheik, Blood and Sand, The Sorrows of Satan, The Love of Sunya, Diary of a Lost Girl, Ecstasy, L'Atlantide, Peter the Tramp, Cabin in the Cotton, Platinum Blonde, Gold Diggers of 1933, No Man of Her Own, Professional Sweetheart, Love Me Tonight, I'm No Angel, Baby Face, They Won't Forget, College Swing, Her Jungle Love, Gilda, A Place in the Sun, Some Like it Hot.*

Love Happy *

US 1949 85m bw
Lester Cowan/Mary Pickford
V, V*, L

A group of impoverished actors accidentally gets possession of the Romanov diamonds.

The last dismaying Marx Brothers film, with Harpo taking the limelight and Groucho loping in for a couple of brief, tired appearances. A roof chase works, but Harpo tries too hard for sentiment, and the production looks shoddy.

w Ben Hecht, Frank Tashlin, Mac Benoff d David Miller ph William Mellor m Ann Ronell

Groucho, Harpo, Chico, Eric Blore, Ilona Massey, Marilyn Monroe, Vera-Ellen

Love Has Many Faces

US 1964 104m Eastmancolor
Columbia/Jerry Bresler
V*

A rich woman marries a beach boy and has an affair with another, who is murdered.

Hilarious but unentertaining sex melodrama built around an overage star.

w Marguerite Roberts d Alexander Singer ph Joseph Ruttenberg m David Raksin

Lana Turner, Cliff Robertson, Hugh O'Brian, Stefanie Powers, Ruth Roman, Virginia Grey

'For connoisseurs of perfectly awful movies.' – Judith Crist

Love Hate: see L'Albatross

'A big comedy about life's little heartaches'
Love Hurts

US 1990 115m CFI
Vestron/Love Hurts Production (Bud Yorkin, Doro Bachrach)
V, V*

Returning home for his sister's wedding, a philanderer puts his past behind him.

A botched attempt, with unsympathetic characters, to return to comic style of Capra.

w Ron Nyswaner d Bud Yorkin ph Adam Greenberg m Frank DeCaro pd Armin Ganz ed John C. Horger

Jeff Daniels, Judith Ivey, John Mahoney, Cynthia Sikes, Amy Wright, Cloris Leachman, Mary Griffin, Thomas Allen

Love in a Goldfish Bowl

US 1961 88m Technicolor Panavision
Paramount/Jurow-Shepherd

On holiday in Honolulu, two teenagers get into mischief.

Tiresome youth-oriented family comedy with pleasant backgrounds. wd Jack Sher

Tommy Sands, Fabian, Jan Sterling, Toby Michaels, Edward Andrews, John McGiver

Love in Bloom

US 1934 76m bw
Paramount

A carnival owner's daughter marries a songwriter.

Lame little romance broken up by crosstalk from Burns and Allen; an ill-considered entertainment.

w J. P. McEvoy, Keene Thompson d Elliott Nugent

George Burns, Gracie Allen, Dixie Lee, Joe Morrison

'Radio pair may save their latest celluloid effort, but it won't help their future on the screen.' – Variety

AAN: song 'She Loves Me Not' (m Ralph Rainger, ly Leo Robin)

Love in Exile

GB 1936 78m bw
Capitol

A Ruritanian king is induced to abdicate but fights back.

Airy comedy with little general appeal.

w Herman Mankiewicz, Roger Burford and Ernest Betts novel His Majesty's Pajamas by Gene Markey d Alfred L. Werker

Clive Brook, Helen Vinson, Mary Carlisle, Will Fyffe, Ronald Squire, Tamara Desni, Henry Oscar

A Love in Germany *

West Germany/France 1983 107m colour
Artificial Eye/CCC Filmkunst/Gaumont/TFL/Stand'Art (Arthur Brauner)
V*
original title: Eine Liebe in Deutschland

A German woman and a Jewish prisoner-of-war fall in love during the Second World War.

Powerful drama, though it lacks a tragic dimension.

w Boleslaw Michalek, Agnieszka Holland novel Rolf Hochhuth d Andrzej Wajda ph Igor Luther m Michel Legrand ad Allan Starski, Gotz Heymann, Jurgen Henze ed Halina Prugar-Ketling

Hanna Schygulla, Marie-Christine Barrault, Armin Mueller-Stahl, Elisabeth Trissenaar, Daniel Olbrychski, Piotr Lysak

Love in Las Vegas: see Viva Las Vegas

Love in the Afternoon

US 1957 126m bw
AA (Billy Wilder)
V*

The daughter of a private detective warns an American philanderer in Paris that an enraged husband is en route to shoot him.

Tired and dreary romantic sex comedy, miscast and far too long. With the talent around, there are of course a few compensations.

w Billy Wilder, I. A. L. Diamond novel Ariane by Claude Anet d Billy Wilder ph William Mellor m Franz Waxman ad Alexander Trauner

Gary Cooper, Audrey Hepburn, Maurice Chevalier, John McGiver

Love in the Afternoon: see L'Amour, L'Après-midi

Love Is a Ball

US 1962 112m Technicolor Panavision
UA/Oxford/Gold Medal (Martin H. Poll)
GB title: All This and Money Too

A Riviera matchmaker recruits instructors to train his star pupil, but one of them walks away with the lady.

Forgettable comedy in which more effort goes into the glamorous background than the script.

w David Swift, Tom and Frank Waldman novel The Grand Duke and Mr Pimm by Lindsay Hardy d David Swift ph Edmond Séchan m Michel Legrand

Glenn Ford, Charles Boyer, Ricardo Montalban, Telly Savalas, Ruth McDevitt, Ulla Jacobsson

Love is a Headache

US 1938 73m bw
MGM

An actress on hard times gets a break through freak publicity.

Wholly artificial comedy, hammed up to little avail.

w Marion Parsonnet, Harry Ruskin, William Lipman, Lou Heifetz, Herbert Klein d Richard Thorpe

Franchot Tone, Gladys George, Mickey Rooney, Ralph Morgan, Jessie Ralph, Ted Healy, Barnett Parker, Frank Jenks, Virginia Weidler, Fay Holden

'Dialogue is pungent, but fails to cover up slap-happy situations.' – Variety

'A love that defied five thousand years of tradition!'
Love Is a Many Splendored Thing *

US 1955 102m DeLuxe Cinemascope
TCF (Buddy Adler)
V, V*, L

During the Korean War, a Eurasian lady doctor in Hong Kong falls in love with a war correspondent.

Self-admittedly sentimental soaper with a tragic ending; the theme tune kept it popular for years.

w John Patrick novel Han Suyin d Henry King ph Leon Shamroy m Alfred Newman ad Lyle Wheeler, George W. Davis

Jennifer Jones, William Holden, Torin Thatcher, Isobel Elsom, Murray Matheson, Virginia Gregg, Richard Loo

AA: Alfred Newman; title song (m Sammy Fain, ly Paul Francis Webster)

AAN: best picture; Leon Shamroy; Jennifer Jones; art direction

Love Is a Racket

US 1932 72m bw
Warner
GB title: Such Things Happen

A newspaperman covers up for a girl suspected of murder, but she lets him down.

Jaundiced comedy-drama of Broadway night life; quite effective.

w Courtney Terrett d William Wellman

Douglas Fairbanks Jnr, Frances Dee, Ann Dvorak, Lee Tracy, Lyle Talbot, Warren Hymer

Love Is Better Than Ever

US   1951   81m   bw
MGM (William H. Wright)
V*
GB title: *The Light Fantastic*

A small-town girl falls for a New York theatrical agent.

Only moderate production values are brought to bear on this wispy plot which shows no signs of development.

w Ruth Brooks Flippen   *d* Stanley Donen
ph Harold Rosson   *md* Lennie Hayton

Larry Parks, Elizabeth Taylor, Josephine Hutchinson, Tom Tully, Ann Doran

Love Is My Profession: see *En Cas de Malheur*

Love Is News *

US   1937   78m   bw
TCF (Earl Carroll, Harold Wilson)

An heiress marries a scoop-hunting reporter just to show him how embarrassing publicity can be.

Silly romantic comedy with plenty of laughs.

w Harry Tugend, Jack Yellen   *d* Tay Garnett
ph Ernest Palmer

Tyrone Power, Loretta Young, Don Ameche, Slim Summerville, Dudley Digges, Walter Catlett, Jane Darwell, Stepin Fetchit, George Sanders, Frank Conroy, Elisha Cook Jnr

'Fast-moving comedy and good star names. Surefire.' – *Variety*

† Remade as *Sweet Rosie O'Grady* and *That Wonderful Urge*.

'Blood on her hands ... love in her heart!'
Love Letters *

US   1945   101m   bw
Paramount (Hal B. Wallis)

A girl who has lost her memory through war shock is threatened by more physical danger.

Oddly unexciting romantic melodrama directed and designed in heavy but satisfying style. Typical post-war depressive fare.

w Ayn Rand   *novel* *Pity My Simplicity* by Chris Massie
d William Dieterle   *ph* Lee Garmes   *m* Victor Young
ad Hans Dreier, Roland Anderson

Jennifer Jones, Joseph Cotten, Ann Richards, Gladys Cooper, Anita Louise, Cecil Kellaway, Robert Sully, Byron Barr, Reginald Denny, Lumsden Hare

AAN: Jennifer Jones; title song (*m* Victor Young, *ly* Edward Heyman); Victor Young; art direction

Love Letters *

US   1983   89m   DeLuxe
Roger Corman/Millennium
V, V*, L

Affected by her mother's old letters revealing an unconsummated love, a twenty-two-year-old girl begins an affair with an older man.

Low-budget drama which might have worked better as a television play; but it has its memorable aspects.
wd Amy Jones

Jamie Lee Curtis, James Keach, Matt Clark, Bonnie Bartlett, Bud Cort, Amy Madigan

Love Letters of a Star

US   1936   66m   bw
Universal

A blackmailed rich girl takes poison.

Complicated but efficient murder mystery.

w Lewis R. Foster, Milton Carruth, James Mulhauser
novel *The Case of the Constant God* by Rufus King
d Lewis R. Foster and Milton Carruth

Henry Hunter, Polly Rowles, C. Henry Gordon, Walter Coy, Hobart Cavanaugh, Mary Alice Rice

'Good family entertainment . . . ought to do all right.' – *Variety*

Love, Life and Laughter *

GB   1934   83m   bw
ATP (Basil Dean)

A film actress catches the eye of a Ruritanian prince.

Lively star vehicle ranging from sentiment to slapstick.

w Robert Edmunds   *d* Maurice Elvey

Gracie Fields, John Loder, Norah Howard, Allan Aynesworth, Esme Percy, Robb Wilton, Fred Duprez, Horace Kenney, Veronica Brady

The Love Lottery

GB   1953   83m   Technicolor
Ealing (Monja Danischewsky)

A British film star is persuaded to offer himself as first prize in a lottery.

Satirical farce which doesn't come off, mainly owing to paucity of comedy ideas.

w Harry Kurnitz   *d* Charles Crichton   *ph* Douglas Slocombe   *m* Benjamin Frankel   *pd* Tom Morahan

David Niven, Herbert Lom, Peggy Cummins, Anne Vernon, Charles Victor, Gordon Jackson, Felix Aylmer, Hugh McDermott

The Love Machine

US   1971   110m   Eastmancolor
Columbia/Mike Frankovich

Megalomaniac TV reporter progresses to network programme controller but is finally undone by his vivid sex life.

Stodgy, silly melodrama from a bestseller whose inspiration was well known in TV circles.

w Samuel Taylor   *novel* Jacqueline Susann   *d* Jack Haley Jnr   *ph* Charles Lang Jnr   *m* Artie Butler

John Philip Law, Dyan Cannon, Robert Ryan, Jackie Cooper, David Hemmings, Shecky Greene

The Love Match *

GB   1955   85m   bw
British Lion/Beaconsfield (Maclean Rogers)

A North Country train driver's enthusiasm for his local football team lands him in trouble at home and work.

A regional farce, full of stock characters and situations, but given some individuality by the likeable performances of its cast.

w Godfrey Orme, Glenn Melvyn   *play* Glenn Melvyn   *d* David Paltenghi   *ph* Arthur Grant
m Wilfred Burns   *ad* Bernard Robinson   *ed* J. M. Sterling

Arthur Askey, Thora Hird, Glenn Melvyn, Robb Wilton, Shirley Eaton, Edward Chapman, William Franklyn, Patricia Hayes, Maurice Kaufmann

Love Me Darling

Denmark   1971   88m   Eastmancolor
Cinecenta/Gabriel Axel
original title: *Med Kaerlig Hilsen*

Two lovers journey through time, enjoying themselves from the Garden of Eden onwards.

A series of farcical sketches on the subject of sex, without any evidence of humour or eroticism.

wd Gabriel Axel   *ph* Rolf Rønne   *m* B. Fabricius Bjerre   *ad* Erik Bjoric   *ed* Anders Refn

Buster Larsen, Birte Tove, Christian Sarvig, Lone Helmer

'Completely lacking in style or originality, the film also fails to titillate, since its actors project about as

---

much sex-appeal as damp cardboard.' – *Carol Howard, MFB*

Love Me Forever

US   1935   92m   bw
Columbia
GB title: *On Wings of Song*

A down and out singer makes good.

Fair star vehicle.

w Jo Swerling, Sidney Buchman   *d* Victor Schertzinger   *ph* Joe Walker   *md* Louis Silvers

Grace Moore, Leo Carrillo, Robert Allen, Spring Byington, Michael Bartlett, Thurston Hall, Douglas Dumbrille, Luis Alberni

'Gangsters and grand opera are tough to mix, but . . . should be all right in major towns.' – *Variety*

Love Me or Leave Me **

US   1955   122m   Eastmancolor   Cinemascope
MGM (Joe Pasternak)
V*, L

Twenties singer Ruth Etting is befriended by a racketeer who pushes her to the top but drives her to drink and despair in the process.

Agreeably bitter showbiz biopic which gives the impression of being not too far from the truth.

w Daniel Fuchs, Isobel Lennart   *d* Charles Vidor
ph Arthur E. Arling   *md* Percy Faith, George Stoll
ad Cedric Gibbons, Urie McCleary

Doris Day, James Cagney, Cameron Mitchell, Robert Keith, Tom Tully, Harry Bellaver, Richard Gaines

AA: original story (Daniel Fuchs)

AAN: script; Percy Faith, George Stoll; James Cagney; song 'I'll Never Stop Loving You' (*m* Nicholas Brodszky, *ly* Sammy Cahn)

Love Me Tender

US   1956   95m   bw   Cinemascope
TCF (David Weisbart)
V, V*

Three brothers fall out over loot they have brought home from the Civil War.

Odd Western designed (perhaps after shooting began) as Presley's introductory vehicle; he sings four songs before getting shot, and reappears in ghostly form at the end.

w Robert Buckner   *d* Robert D. Webb   *ph* Leo Tover   *m* Lionel Newman

Richard Egan, Debra Paget, Elvis Presley, Robert Middleton, William Campbell, Neville Brand, Mildred Dunnock, Bruce Bennett, James Drury, Ken Clark, Barry Coe

Love Me Tonight ****

US   1932   104m   bw
Paramount (Rouben Mamoulian)

A Parisian tailor accidentally moves into the aristocracy.

The most fluently cinematic comedy musical ever made, with sounds and words, lyrics and music, deftly blended into a compulsively and consistently laughable mosaic of sophisticated nonsense; one better than the best of Lubitsch and Clair.

w Samuel Hoffenstein, Waldemar Young, George Marion Jnr,   *play* Tailor in the Château by Leopold Marchand and Paul Armont   *d* Rouben Mamoulian   *ph* Victor Milner   *songs* Rodgers and Hart

Maurice Chevalier, Jeanette MacDonald, Charles Butterworth, Charles Ruggles, Myrna Loy, C. Aubrey Smith, Elizabeth Patterson, Ethel Griffies, Blanche Frederici, Robert Greig

'A musical frolic, whimsical in its aim and delicately carried out in its pattern.' – *Variety*

'Gay, charming, witty, it is everything that the Lubitsch musicals should have been but never were.' – *John Baxter, 1968*

'With the aid of a pleasant story, a good musician, a talented cast and about a million dollars, he has done what someone in Hollywood should have done long ago – he has illustrated a musical score.' – *Pare Lorentz*

'It has that infectious spontaneity which distinguishes the American musical at its best.' – *Peter Cowie, 1970*

'A rich amalgam of filmic invention, witty decoration and wonderful songs.' – *NFT, 1974*

'What a picture! First you have Chevalier, and last you have Chevalier!' – *Photoplay*

The Love Nest

US   1923   22m (24 fps)   bw   silent
Buster Keaton Productions

Buster dreams of a solitary voyage in a small boat.

Long lost but ultimately disappointing Keaton short.
wd Buster Keaton and Eddie Cline

Buster Keaton, Joe Roberts, Virginia Fox

Love Nest

US   1951   84m   bw
TCF

A writer and his wife invest in an apartment building but find their tenants time-consuming.

Fairly lively comedy with varied talent.

w I. A. L. Diamond   *novel* Scott Corbett   *d* Joseph Newman

William Lundigan, June Haver, Frank Fay, Marilyn Monroe, Jack Paar, Leatrice Joy

Love Never Dies: see *Lilac Time*

The Love of Jeanne Ney *

Germany   1927   98m (24 fps)   bw   silent
UFA

In the Crimea during the Russian Revolution, a political observer is accidentally killed by his daughter's lover.

Inconsistently-styled contemporary melodrama. The abiding interest is in the detailed treatment rather than the story or acting.

w Ladislas Vajda, Rudolph Leonhardt, Ilya Ehrenberg   *d* G. W. Pabst   *ph* Fritz Arno Wagner, Walter Robert Lach

Edith Jehane, Uno Henning, Fritz Rasp, Brigitte Helm

The Love of Sunya

US   1927   80m (24 fps)   bw   silent
Swanson Producing Corporation

A yogi recognizes two young lovers as people he wronged in a previous existence, and warns them of impending disaster.

Star tosh of its period, unthinkable now as a screen attraction.

w Earle Brown   *play* The Eyes of Youth by Max Marcin, Charles Guernon   *d* Albert Parker
ph Robert Martin   *ad* Hugo Ballin

Gloria Swanson, John Boles, Anders Randolph, Hugh Miller, Flobelle Fairbanks, Raymond Hackett

† Previously filmed as *Eyes of Youth* with Clara Kimball Young.

Love on the Dole ***

GB   1941   100m   bw
British National (John Baxter)
V*

Life among unemployed cotton workers in industrial Lancashire between the wars.

Vividly characterized, old-fashioned social melodrama, well made on a low budget; a rare problem picture for Britain at this time.

w Walter Greenwood, Barbara K. Emery, Rollo Gamble   *novel* Walter Greenwood   *d* John Baxter
ph James Wilson   *m* Richard Addinsell

Deborah Kerr, Clifford Evans, *George Carney*, Joyce Howard, Frank Cellier, Geoffrey Hibbert, *Mary Merrall*, Maire O'Neill, *Marjorie Rhodes*, A. Bromley Davenport, Marie Ault, Iris Vandeleur, Kenneth Griffith

'Kissing and kidding their way from Mayfair to the Mediterranean in a transcontinental caravan of jollity!'

Love on the Run *

US   1936   81m   bw
MGM (Joseph L. Mankiewicz)
V*, L

Rival newspapermen help an heiress to escape an unwanted wedding and in the process uncover a ring of spies.

Harebrained star farce, smoothly assembled and still fairly funny.

w John Lee Mahin, Manuel Seff, Gladys Hurlbut
d W. S. Van Dyke   *ph* Oliver T. Marsh   *m* Franz Waxman

Clark Gable, Joan Crawford, Franchot Tone, Reginald Owen, Mona Barrie, Ivan Lebedeff, William Demarest

'Should collect its share at the gate through the sheer momentum of the Gable–Crawford combo.' – *Variety*

'A slightly daffy cinematic item of absolutely no importance.' – *New York Times*

Love on the Run *

France   1979   95m   Eastmancolor
Les Films du Carrosse (François Truffaut)
V*

Antoine Doinel, separated from his family, is still having girl trouble.

Amorous adventure of the character first glimpsed in *Les Quatre Cent Coups* and presumably based on the director; fair sophisticated fun for those who appreciate the joke.

w François Truffaut, Marie-France Pisier, Jean Aurel, Suzanne Schiffman   *d* François Truffaut   *ph* Nestor Almendros   *m* Georges Delerue   *pd* Jean-Pierre Kohut Svelko   *ed* Martine Barraqué

Jean-Pierre Léaud, Marie-France Pisier, Claude Jade, Rosy Varte

Love on Wheels

GB   1932   87m   bw
Gainsborough

A department store assistant becomes publicity-conscious.

Zippy little comedy of its day.

w Victor Saville, Angus Macphail, Robert Stevenson and Douglas Furber   *d* Victor Saville

Jack Hulbert, Edmund Gwenn, Leonora Corbett, Gordon Harker, Percy Parsons, Roland Culver, Miles Malleson

The Love Parade **

US   1929   112m   bw
Paramount (Ernst Lubitsch)

The prince of Sylvania marries.

Primitive sound operetta set among the idle European rich, with clear but faded instances of the Lubitsch touch.

w Ernest Vajda, Guy Bolton   *play* The Prince Consort by Leon Xanrof and Jules Chancel   *d* Ernst Lubitsch
ph Victor Milner   *songs* Victor Schertzinger, Clifford Grey   *ad* Hans Dreier

Maurice Chevalier, Jeanette MacDonald, Lupino Lane, Lillian Roth, Edgar Norton, Lionel Belmore, Eugene Pallette

'The first truly cinematic screen musical in America.' – *Theodore Huff*

AAN: best picture; Ernst Lubitsch; Victor Milner; Maurice Chevalier; Hans Dreier

'Imagine if sex appeal came in a bottle.'
'If you've got it – you get it!'

Love Potion No. 9

US   1992   97m   CFI colour
TCF (Dale Launer)
V, V*

Unattractive scientists discover a chemical that makes the user irresistible to the opposite sex.

Occasionally amusing teen comedy, but one that fails to develop its central idea to any effect.

wd Dale Launer   *ph* William Wages   *m* Jed Leiber
pd Linda Pearl   *ed* Suzanne Petit

Tate Donovan, Sandra Bullock, Mary Mara, Dale Midkiff, Hillary Bailey Smith, Dylan Baker, Anne Bancroft

'A light-hearted one-joke romantic comedy that tries too hard to be cute.' – *Variety*

Love, Soldiers and Women

France/Italy   1953   96m   bw
Franco-London/Continental
original title: *Destinées*; US title: *Daughters of Destiny*

Three stories of women in war: Joan of Arc, Lysistrata, and a modern American war widow visiting her husband's grave.

Uninteresting patchwork with Lysistrata predictably stealing the show.'Jeanne':

w Jean Aurenche, Pierre Bost   *d* Jean Delannoy *with* Michèle Morgan'Elizabeth':

w Sergio Amedei   *d* Marcel Pagliero *with* Claudette Colbert, Eleanora Rossi Drago'Lysistrata':

w Jean Ferry, Henri Jeanson, Carlo Rim
play Aristophanes   *d* Christian-Jaque *with* Martine Carol, Raf Vallone, Paolo Stoppa

Love Story

GB   1944   112m   bw
GFD/Gainsborough (Harold Huth)
US title: *A Lady Surrenders*

In Cornwall during World War II, a half-blind airman falls for a pianist with a weak heart.

Novelettish love story which became popular because of its Cornish Rhapsody.

w Leslie Arliss, Doreen Montgomery, Rodney Ackland   *novel* J. W. Drawbell   *d* Leslie Arliss
ph Bernard Knowles   *m* Hubert Bath

Margaret Lockwood, Stewart Granger, Patricia Roc, Tom Walls, Reginald Purdell, Moira Lister

'A splendid, noble and fatuous piece.' – *C. A. Lejeune*

'In psychology and dialogue this is straight out of Mabel's Weekly.' – *Richard Winnington*

Love Story (1951): see *Une Histoire d'Amour*

Love Story *

US   1970   100m   Movielab
Paramount (David Golden)
V, V*, L, S

Two students marry; she dies.

A barrage of ripe old Hollywood clichés spiced with new-fangled bad language. In the circumstances, well enough made, and certainly astonishingly popular.

w Erich Segal   *novelette* Erich Segal   *d* Arthur Hiller   *ph* Dick Kratina   *md* Francis Lai   *m* Bach, Mozart, Handel

Ali MacGraw, Ryan O'Neal, Ray Milland, John Marley

'Camille with bullshit.' – *Alexander Walker*

AA: Francis Lai

AAN: best picture; Erich Segal; Arthur Hiller; Ali MacGraw; Ryan O'Neal; John Marley

Love Streams

US 1984 141m Metrocolor
Cannon (Menahem Golan, Yoram Globus)
V*

A distraught woman whose marriage has gone sour
moves in with her philandering brother.

Elongated study of two life styles, not so shapeless as
most Cassavetes films, but not exactly dramatic or
endearing either.

w Ted Allan, John Cassavetes play Ted Allan
d John Cassavetes ph Al Ruban m Bo Harwood
ad Phedon Papamichael ed George C. Villasenor

Gena Rowlands, John Cassavetes, Dianne Abbott,
Seymour Cassel, Margaret Abbott

The Love Test

GB 1935 63m bw
Fox British (Leslie L. Landau)

Research scientists plot to prevent a woman from
taking over as head of the laboratory by selecting one
of their number to seduce her.

Competent, if unoriginal, comedy with an occasional
directorial touch that lifts it out of the very ordinary.

w Selwyn Jepson story Jack Celestin d Michael
Powell ph Arthur Crabtree

Judy Gunn, Louis Hayward, David Hutcheson,
Googie Withers, Morris Harvey, Aubrey Dexter,
Gilbert Davis, Bernard Miles

'A light, bright romantic comedy.' – Variety

Love That Brute

US 1950 85m bw
TCF (Fred Kohlmar)

A ruthless Chicago gangleader is actually a softy,
leaving his supposedly rubbed-out enemies in a
comfortable cellar; a young governess persuades him
to reform.

Rickety, dully-scripted gangster farce.

w Darrell Ware, John Lee Mahin, Karl Tunberg
d Alexander Hall ph Lloyd Ahern m Cyril
Mockridge

Paul Douglas, Jean Peters, Cesar Romero, Joan Davis,
Arthur Treacher

Love Thy Neighbour *

US 1940 81m bw
Paramount

Two radio comics fall out.

Curious mixture of fact and fiction, basing its plot on
the publicity feud between Benny and Allen, who
appear 'in character' as themselves.

w William Morrow, Edmund Beloin, Ernest Pagano,
Z. Myers pd Mark Sandrich

Jack Benny, Fred Allen, Mary Martin, Eddie
Anderson, Verree Teasdale, Virginia Dale, Richard
Denning

Love Thy Neighbour

GB 1973 85m Technicolor
EMI/Hammer (Roy Skeggs)
V

A prejudiced white worker has coloured neighbours.

Elongated screen version of the popular TV series in
which the West Indians smile through all the insults
and come out top in the end. It might have been
worse, but not much.

w Vince Powell, Harry Driver d John Robins
ph Moray Grant m Albert Elms

Jack Smethurst, Kate Williams, Rudolph Walker,
Nina Baden-Semper, Bill Fraser, Charles Hyatt, Keith
Marsh, Patricia Hayes, Arthur English

Love Time

US 1934 72m bw
Fox

Franz Schubert falls for a duke's daughter.

Curious, off-putting costumer with music.

w William Conselman, Henry Johnson d James
Tinling

Pat Paterson, Nils Asther, Herbert Mundin, Harry
Green, Henry B. Walthall, Lucien Littlefield

'Thin story, and slim chances.' – Variety

Love under Fire

US 1937 75m bw
TCF (Nunnally Johnson)

A detective catches up with a lady jewel thief in
Madrid during the Spanish Civil War.

Adequately entertaining but rather tasteless
adventure comedy.

w Gene Fowler, Allen Rivkin, Ernest Pascal
play Walter Hackett d George Marshall ph Ernest
Palmer m Arthur Lange

Loretta Young, Don Ameche, Frances Drake, Walter
Catlett, John Carradine, Borrah Minevitch and his
Rascals, Sig Rumann, Harold Huber, E. E. Clive,
Katherine de Mille

'Melodrama with music cooked up for the duals.' –
Variety

'There is a moment … a long moment … when everything
is risked with the proper stranger!'

Love with the Proper Stranger **

US 1964 100m bw
Paramount/Boardwalk (Alan J. Pakula)
V*, L

A musician tries to help his pregnant shopgirl friend
get an abortion, but they decide to get married
instead.

Oddly likeable comedy drama set on New York's
Italian East Side, with an excellent location sense.

w Arnold Schulman d Robert Mulligan ph Milton
Krasner m Elmer Bernstein

Steve McQueen, Natalie Wood, Tom Bosley, Edie Adams,
Herschel Bernardi

AAN: Arnold Schulman; Milton Krasner; Natalie
Wood

The Loved One *

US 1965 118m bw
MGM/Filmways (Neil Hartley)
V*, L

A young English poet in California gets a job at a very
select burial ground.

A pointed satire on the American way of death has
been allowed to get out of hand, with writer and
actors alike laying it on too thick; but there are
pleasantly waspish moments in a movie advertised as
'the motion picture with something to offend
everybody'.

w Terry Southern, Christopher Isherwood
novel Evelyn Waugh d Tony Richardson
ph Haskell Wexler m John Addison pd Rouben
Ter-Arutunian

Robert Morse, John Gielgud, Rod Steiger, Liberace,
Anjanette Comer, Jonathan Winters, Dana Andrews,
Milton Berle, James Coburn, Tab Hunter, Margaret
Leighton, Roddy McDowall, Robert Morley, Lionel
Stander

'Even a chaotic satire like this is cleansing, and it's
embarrassing to pan even a bad movie that comes out
against God, mother and country.' – Pauline Kael, 1968

'A spineless farrago of collegiate gags.' – Stanley
Kauffmann

'A sinking ship that makes it to port because everyone
on board is too giddy to panic.' – New Yorker, 1978

'The Meanest … Roughest … Toughest … Gang Ever To
Hit The Screen! Muscles Clad In Black Leather … Incest
… And Murder!'
'Sworn To Fun … Loyal To None!!!'

The Loveless

US 1983 83m colour
Mainline/Pioneer Films (Grafton Nunes, A. Kitman Ho)

In the 1950s, a gang of bikers cause problems in a
small Southern town.

Arty (the settings are reminiscent of the paintings of
Edward Hopper), derivative and inconsequential
drama.

wd Kathryn Bigelow, Monty Montgomery
ph Doyle Smith m Robert Gordon pd Lilly Kivert
ed Nancy Kantner

Willem Dafoe, Robert Gordon, Marin Kanter, J. Don
Ferguson, Tina L'Hotsky

Lovely to Look At (1937): see Thin Ice

Lovely to Look At *

US 1952 102m Technicolor
MGM (Jack Cummings)
V*, L, S

Three Broadway producers inherit a Paris fashion
house.

Lavish but dullish remake of Roberta (qv), in itself no
great shakes as a storyline; again the fashions and the
numbers are the thing.

w George Wells, Harry Ruby d Mervyn Le Roy
ph George J. Folsey m Jerome Kern ad Cedric
Gibbons, Gabriel Scognamillo

Howard Keel, Kathryn Grayson, Ann Miller, Red
Skelton, Marge and Gower Champion, Zsa Zsa Gabor,
Kurt Kasznar

A Lovely Way to Die

US 1968 98m Techniscope
Universal (Richard Lewis)
GB title: A Lovely Way to Go

An ex-cop becomes bodyguard to a suspected
murderess, but proves her innocent.

Offbeat mélange of caper comedy, black farce, private
eye detection, courtroom drama, spectacular action
and routine thick ear. Doesn't work.

w A. J. Russell d David Lowell Rich ph Morris
Hartzband m Kenyon Hopkins

Kirk Douglas, Sylva Koscina, Eli Wallach, Martyn
Green, Kenneth Haigh, Sharon Farrell

'The net result is rather as though Philip Marlowe had
met Doris Day on his not very inspiring way to the
forum.' – MFB

A Lovely Way to Go: see A Lovely Way to Die

The Lover: see L'Amant

Lover Boy: see Knave of Hearts

Lover Come Back

US 1946 90m bw
Universal (Howard Benedict)

When a war correspondent returns, his wife discovers
that he hasn't been so lonely overseas as he might
have been.

Very tolerable star comedy which at the time seemed
quite fresh.

w Michael Fessier, Ernest Pagano d William A.
Seiter ph Joseph Valentine m Hans J. Salter

George Brent, Lucille Ball, Vera Zorina, Charles
Winninger, Carl Esmond, Raymond Walburn,
Franklin Pangborn, Louise Beavers

'Should chalk up good grosses in most situations.' –
Variety

Lover Come Back **

US   1961   107m   Eastmancolor
U-I/Seven Pictures/Nob Hill/Arwin (Stanley Shapiro, Marty Melcher)
V*

Rival executives find themselves advertising a non-existent product.

Fairly sharp advertising satire disguised as a romantic comedy; the most entertaining of the Day-Hudson charmers.

w Stanley Shapiro, Paul Henning   *d* Delbert Mann
ph Arthur E. Arling   *m* Frank de Vol

Doris Day, Rock Hudson, *Tony Randall,* Jack Oakie, Edie Adams

AAN: Stanley Shapiro, Paul Henning

Loverboy

US   1989   99m   Technicolor
Columbia TriStar/Crescent Film Enterprises (Gary Foster, Willie Hunt)
V, V*, L

A pizza delivery boy pays his way through college by becoming a lover to his female customers.

Feeble comedy with little wit or sense.

w Robin Schiff, Tom Ropelewski, Leslie Dixon
d Joan Micklin Silver   *ph* John Davis   *m* Michel Colombier   *pd* Dan Leigh   *ed* Rick Shaine

Patrick Dempsey, Kate Jackson, Kirstie Alley, Carrie Fisher, Robert Ginty, Nancy Valen, Charles Hunter Walsh, Barbara Carrera

'The material often suggests a crude and juvenile variation on The Graduate.' – *MFB*

The Lovers (1958): see Les Amants

The Lovers

GB   1972   89m   Eastmancolor
British Lion/Gildor (Maurice Foster)

A Manchester bank clerk with a prim girlfriend finds it difficult to lose his virginity.

Well-written but rather arch comedy which seemed much funnier and fresher as a TV series.

w Jack Rosenthal   *d* Herbert Wise   *ph* Bob Huke
m Carl Davis

Richard Beckinsale, Paula Wilcox, Joan Scott, Susan Littler, John Comer, Stella Moray, Nikolas Simmonds

'This landlady has more than just rent on her mind.'

Lovers *

Spain   1991   103m   colour
Mainline/TVE/Pedro Costa
V, V*, S
original title: *Amantes*

In the 1950s, a young Spanish man finds himself torn between his virginal fiancée and the sexy, sophisticated widow with whom he lodges.

Overheated and old-fashioned drama that becomes increasingly melodramatic as it continues.

w Carlos Perez, Alvaro Del Amo, Vicente Aranda
d Vicente Aranda   *ph* José Luis Alcaine   *m* José Nieto   *ad* Josep Rosell   *ed* Teresa Font

Victoria Abril, Jorge Sanz, Maribel Verdu, Enrique Cerro, Mabel Escano, José Cerro, Gabriel Latorre

'A nicely photographed, well-dressed, at times distinctly tedious love triangle thriller.' – *Empire*

Lovers and Other Strangers ***

US   1970   104m   Metrocolor
ABC/David Susskind
V*

After living together for eighteen months, Susan and Mike decide to get married, and find their parents have sex problems of their own.

Wise, witty and well-acted sex farce, with many actors making the most of ample chances under firm directorial control.

w Renée Taylor, Joseph Bologna, David Zelag Goodman
d Cy Howard   *ph* Andrew Laszlo   *m* Fred Karlin

Gig Young, Anne Jackson, Richard Castellano, Bonnie Bedelia, Michael Brandon, *Beatrice Arthur,* Robert Dishy, Harry Guardino, Diane Keaton, Cloris Leachman, Anne Meara, Marian Hailey

'An extremely engaging comedy.' – *Gillian Hartnoll*

AA: song 'For All We Know' (*m* Fred Karlin, *ly* Robb Wilson, Arthur James)

AAN: script, Richard Castellano

Lovers Courageous

US   1932   78m   bw
MGM

An unsuccessful playwright covets the admiral's daughter.

Heavily-titled comedy with good performances of the period.

w Frederick Lonsdale   *d* Robert Z. Leonard

Robert Montgomery, Madge Evans, Roland Young, Frederick Kerr, Reginald Owen, Halliwell Hobbes, Alan Mowbray

Lovers Like Us: see Call Him Savage

Lovers Must Learn: see Rome Adventure

The Lovers of Lisbon *

France   1954   112m   bw
EGC/Hoche/Fides (Jacques Gauthier)
original title: *Les Amants du Tage*

A man who has killed his unfaithful wife is acquitted of murder, gets a job as a taxi driver in Lisbon, and falls for a rich Englishwoman who has killed her husband and is being pursued by a police inspector.

Pretentious tosh with a few compensations.

w Marcel Rivet   *novel* Joseph Kessel   *d* Henri Verneuil   *ph* Roger Hubert   *m* Lucien Legrand

Daniel Gélin, Françoise Arnoul, Trevor Howard, Ginette Leclerc, Marcel Dalio

Lovers of Montparnasse *

France   1958   110m   bw
Franco London Films (Ralph Baum)
original title: *Les Amants de Montparnasse;* US title: *Modigliani of Montparnasse*

Alcoholic and ill, Modigliani pursues his art and the young woman who inspires him to paint.

Moderate biopic, though with an unconvincing performance from Philipe.

w Jacques Becker, Max Ophuls, Henri Jeanson
novel Les Montparnos by Michel Georges Michel
d Jacques Becker   *ph* Christian Matras   *m* Paul Misraki   *pd* J. A. d'Eaubonne   *ed* Marguerite Renoir

Gérard Philipe, Lilli Palmer, Léa Padovani, Lino Ventura, Anouk Aimée

The Lovers of Toledo

Italy/France/Spain   1952   82m   bw
EGE/Lux/Athenea (Raymond Eger)

In 1825 a cruel police chief releases a political prisoner in return for the hand in marriage of his mistress.

Curiously unpersuasive period melodrama with good credits but too many international cooks.

w Claude Vermorel   *story* Le Coffre et le Revenant by Stendhal   *d* Henri Decoin   *ph* Michel Kelber
m Jean-Jacques Grunenwald

Pedro Armendariz, Alida Valli, Gérard Landry, Françoise Arnoul

The Lovers of Verona: see Les Amants de Vérone

Lovers on the Pont-Neuf: see Les Amants du Pont-Neuf

Loves of a Blonde *

Czechoslovakia   1965   82m   bw
Barrandov Studios
V, V*, L
original title: *Lasky Jedne Plavovlasky;* aka: *A Blonde in Love*

A factory girl falls for a visiting musician but meets suspicion from his family when she pursues him.

Mild anecdote with excellent humorous detail which endeared it to international critics.

w Milos Forman, Jaroslav Papousek, Ivan Passer
d Milos Forman   *ph* Miroslav Ondricek   *m* Evzen Illin

Hanna Brejchova, Vladimir Pucholt

'It depends on an instinctive sense of timing and a consistent vision of life and people.' – *Georges Sadoul*

AAN: best foreign film

The Loves of a Dictator: see The Dictator

The Loves of Carmen

US   1948   99m   Technicolor
Columbia (Charles Vidor)
V*

In 1820s Seville, a dragoon corporal is enslaved by a gypsy, kills her husband and becomes an outlaw.

Unrewarding version of the original much-filmed story, with both stars plainly wishing they were elsewhere.

w Helen Deutsch   *novel* Prosper Mérimée
d Charles Vidor   *ph* William Snyder   *m* Mario Castelnuovo-Tedesco

Rita Hayworth, Glenn Ford, Victor Jory, Ron Randell, Luther Adler, Arnold Moss, Margaret Wycherly, Bernard Nedell

AAN: William Snyder

The Loves of Edgar Allan Poe

US   1942   67m   bw
TCF (Bryan Foy)

The famous writer marries his childhood sweetheart but becomes an alcoholic.

A curiosity which fails to bring out the bizarre truth and emerges as a stilted charade.

w Samuel Hoffenstein, Tom Reed   *d* Harry Lachman
ph Lucien Andriot   *m* Emil Newman

John Shepperd, Linda Darnell, Virginia Gilmore, Jane Darwell, Frank Conroy, Henry Morgan

The Loves of Isadora: see Isadora

The Loves of Joanna Godden

GB   1947   89m   bw
Ealing (Sidney Cole)

On Romney Marsh at the turn of the century, a woman farmer has three suitors.

Dullish 'woman's picture'.

w H. E. Bates, Angus Macphail   *novel* Sheila Kaye-Smith   *d* Charles Frend   *ph* Douglas Slocombe
m Ralph Vaughan Williams

Googie Withers, John McCallum, Jean Kent, Derek Bond, Chips Rafferty, Henry Mollison, Sonia Holm, Edward Rigby, Josephine Stuart

'Made with sincerity, and its outdoor backgrounds abound in freshness and beauty, but I felt that it faltered because the script writers and the director permitted themselves to become so obsessed by the landscape and local colour that they regarded the plot as somewhat of a hindrance to their documentary explorations.' – Ewart Hodgson, News of the World

† Robert Hamer directed some scenes.

Lovesick
US 1983 96m Technicolor
Warner/Ladd (Charles Okun)
V*, L

A New York psychiatrist in love with a patient is guided by the ghost of Sigmund Freud.

Depressing comedy with a non-star and supporting players who must have been embarrassed.

wd Marshall Brickman   ph Gerry Fisher
m Philippe Sarde   pd Philip Rosenberg

Dudley Moore, Elizabeth McGovern, Alec Guinness (as Freud), John Huston, Larry Rivers, Gene Saks, Renee Taylor, Alan King

'Flat, lamebrained and indigestible.' – Geoff Brown, MFB

Lovin' Molly *
US 1973 98m Movielab
Stephen Friedman (David Golden)

In Texas between 1925 and 1945, two men friends and an accommodating lady have a shifting relationship.

Odd little drama compendium, with fragments told by each in turn; too slight in structure and substance for complete success, but interesting most of the way.

w Stephen Friedman   novel Leaving Cheyenne by Larry McMurtry   d Sidney Lumet   ph Edward Brown   m Fred Hellerman

Blythe Danner, Anthony Perkins, Beau Bridges, Edward Binns, Susan Sarandon

Loving **
US 1970 90m Eastmancolor
Columbia/Brooks Ltd (Don Devlin)

A commercial artist reaches crisis point with both his wife and his mistress.

Smart New Yorkish sex comedy, typical of many but better than most.

w Don Devlin   novel Brooks Wilson Ltd by J. M. Ryan
d Irvin Kershner   ph Gordon Willis   m Bernardo Segall   pd Walter Scott Herndon

George Segal, Eva Marie Saint, Sterling Hayden, Keenan Wynn, Nancie Phillips, Janis Young, David Doyle

Loving Couples *
Sweden 1964 118m bw
Sandrew (Rune Waldekranz)
original title: Älskande Par

Three expectant mothers think back over their sex lives.

Superbly made, rather hollow diatribe against sex, presented as a series of intricate flashbacks. Along the way, there is much to enjoy, but the result is not really a film of importance.

w Mai Zetterling, David Hughes   novel Froknarna von Pahlen by Agnes von Krusenstjerna   d Mai Zetterling
ph Sven Nykvist   m Rodger Wallis

Harriet Andersson, Gunnel Lindblom, Anita Bjork, Gunnar Bjornstrand, Eva Dahlbeck, Frank Sundstrom, Inga Landgre

'. . . that air of packaged neurosis so peculiar to the Swedish cinema.' – Tom Milne, MFB

Loving Couples
US 1980 98m Metrocolor
Time Life (Renee Valente)
V*

Man-and-wife doctors decide to liven up their lives by having affairs.

Embarrassingly with-it romantic charade.

w Martin Donovan   d Jack Smight   ph Philip Lathrop   m Fred Karlin

Shirley Maclaine, James Coburn, Susan Sarandon, Stephen Collins, Sally Kellerman

Loving in the Rain
France/Italy/West Germany 1973 90m
Eastmancolor
Lira Films/Terra Film (Raymond Danon)
original title: Un Amour de Pluie

A mother and her teenage daughter both experience a holiday love affair.

An inconsequential romance involving inconsequential people.

w Jean-Claude Brialy, Yves Simon   d Jean-Claude Brialy   ph Andreas Winding   m Francis Lai
ed Eva Zorn

Romy Schneider, Nino Castelnuovo, Mehdi, Benedicte Bucher, Suzanne Flon

Loving You
US 1957 101m Technicolor Vistavision
Paramount/Hal B. Wallis
V, L

A press agent signs a young hillbilly singer to give zest to her husband's band.

Empty-headed, glossy star vehicle.

w Herbert Baker, Hal Kanter   d Hal Kanter
ph Charles Lang Jnr   m Walter Scharf

Elvis Presley, Lizabeth Scott, Wendell Corey, Dolores Hart, James Gleason

The Lower Depths (1936): see
Les Bas-fonds

The Lower Depths **
Japan 1957 124m bw
Toho
V, V*
original title: Donzoko

An elderly pilgrim moves into a hovel and changes the lives of the derelicts who live there.

Effectively unsentimental, claustrophobic version of life at the bottom, although it betrays its theatrical origins, with more talk than action.

w Akira Kurosawa, Hideo Oguni   play Maxim Gorky   d Akira Kurosawa   ph Ichio Yamazaki
m Masaru Sato

Isuzu Yamada, Toshiro Mifune, Bokuzen Hidari, Kyoko Kagawa, Akemi Nigishi, Nijiko Kiyokawa

'Lesser Kurosawa, but still high-quality cinema.' – Empire

Loyalties
GB 1934 74m bw
Associated British

A vengeful Jew turns the tables when his wallet is stolen at a society party.

Badly made film version of a significant play.

w W. P. Lipscomb   play John Galsworthy   d Basil Dean

Basil Rathbone, Miles Mander, Heather Thatcher, Joan Wyndham, Philip Strange

Luci del Varieta: see Lights of Variety

The Luck of Ginger Coffey *
Canada/US 1964 100m bw
Crawley/Roth-Kershner (Leon Roth)

An Irish layabout in Canada finds it difficult to keep a job or protect his family.

Mildly interesting character study with good background detail of Montreal.

w Brian Moore   novel Brian Moore   d Irvin Kershner   ph Manny Wynn   m Bernardo Segall

Robert Shaw, Mary Ure, Liam Redmond

The Luck of the Irish *
US 1948 99m bw
TCF (Fred Kohlmar)

A New York newsman's love life is complicated by a helpful leprechaun he meets in Ireland.

Hollywood moonshine, second class: the will and the players are there, but the script is not funny enough.

w Philip Dunne   novel There Was a Little Man by Constance and Guy Jones   d Henry Koster
ph Joseph LaShelle   m Cyril Mockridge

Tyrone Power, Cecil Kellaway, Anne Baxter, Lee J. Cobb, James Todd, Jayne Meadows, J. M. Kerrigan, Phil Brown

AAN: Cecil Kellaway

The Luckiest Girl in the World
US 1936 75m bw
Charles R. Rogers/Universal

A rich girl bets her father that she can live in New York for a month on 150 dollars.

Lighthearted comedy with farcical trimmings.

w Herbert Fields, Henry Myers, Anne Jordan
d Eddie Buzzell

Jane Wyatt (who really was from the social register), Louis Hayward, Eugene Pallette, Nat Pendleton, Catherine Doucet, Philip Reed

'Speed and gags offset story absurdity.' – Variety

Lucky Boy
US 1929 97m bw part silent
Tiffany-Stahl

A young Jewish boy makes it big on Broadway.

Simple-minded fable inspired by The Jazz Singer (which Jessel is said to have turned down).

w George Jessel   d Norman Taurog and others

George Jessel, Rosa Rosanova, William K. Strauss, Margaret Quimby

Lucky Devils
US 1933 63m bw
David O. Selznick/RKO

Hollywood stuntmen rescue an actress from a suicide attempt.

Tolerable action special with interesting sidelights.

w Agnes Christine Johnston, Ben Markson, Casey Robinson, Bob Rose   d Ralph Ince

William Boyd, Dorothy Wilson, William Gargan, Robert Rose, Roscoe Ates, Bruce Cabot

Lucky Jim **
GB 1957 95m bw
British Lion/Charter (Roy Boulting)
V, V*

At a provincial university, an accident-prone junior lecturer has a disastrous weekend with his girlfriend and his professor.

Quite funny in its own right, this is a vulgarization of a famous comic novel which got its effects more subtly, with more sense of place, time and character.

w Jeffrey Dell, Patrick Campbell   novel Kingsley Amis   d John Boulting   ph Max Greene   m John Addison

Ian Carmichael, Hugh Griffith, Terry-Thomas, Sharon Acker, Jean Anderson, Maureen Connell, Clive Morton, John Welsh, Reginald Beckwith, Kenneth Griffith

'An almost endless ripple of comfortable laughter.' – News Chronicle

'When he smiles, it's not because he likes you – it's because he likes what he's going to do to you!'

Lucky Jordan
US   1942   83m   bw
Paramount (Fred Kohlmar)

A con man is drafted and overcomes Nazi agents.

Forgettable star cheapie.

w Darrell Ware, Karl Tunberg   d Frank Tuttle   ph John F. Seitz   m Adolph Deutsch

Alan Ladd, Helen Walker, Sheldon Leonard, Marie McDonald, Mabel Paige, Lloyd Corrigan, Dave Willock, Miles Mander

'It's still cops and robbers, no matter how you slice it . . . Mr Ware and Mr Tunberg are not above dragging in mother love as the reason the gangster changes from a selfish killer to a patriot.' – *Joseph Pihodna, New York Herald Tribune*

Lucky Lady
US   1975   118m   DeLuxe
TCF/Gruskoff/Venture (Michael Gruskoff)

A cabaret girl in 1930 Tijuana joins two adventurers in smuggling liquor into the US by boat.

Whatever can be done wrong with such a story has been done, including irritatingly washed out photography, kinky sex, and sudden switches from farce to gore. None of it holds the interest for a single moment.

w Willard Huyck, Gloria Katz   d Stanley Donen   ph Geoffrey Unsworth   m Ralph Burns   pd John Barry

Liza Minnelli, Gene Hackman, Burt Reynolds, Michael Hordern, Geoffrey Lewis, Robby Benson

'A manic mess that tries to be all things to all people and ends up offering nothing to anyone.' – *Frank Rich*

'It sports its calculations on its sleeve like rhinestones.' – *Sight and Sound*

'They're all rumrunners in the early 30s, and they're meant to be adorable. This is a big expensive movie for people who don't mind being treated like hicks: the audience is expected to shudder with delight every time it hears an obscenity or sees a big movie star grin.' – *Pauline Kael, New Yorker*

Lucky Mascot: see *The Brass Monkey*

Lucky Me *
US   1954   100m   Warnercolor   Cinemascope
Warner (Henry Blanke)

Theatrical entertainers stranded in Florida get a lucky break.

Watchable, forgettable musical.

w James O'Hanlon, Robert O'Brien, Irving Elinson   d Jack Donohue   ph Wilfrid M. Cline   md Ray Heindorf

Doris Day, Robert Cummings, Phil Silvers, Eddie Foy Jnr, Nancy Walker, Martha Hyer, Bill Goodwin, Marcel Dalio

'The first Cinemascope musical . . . pleasant, light-hearted, frothy entertainment.' – *MFB*

Lucky Nick Cain: see *I'll Get You for This*

Lucky Night
US   1939   90m   bw
MGM (Louis D. Lighton)

An heiress goes out into the world to make a life for herself, and falls for a man she finds on a park bench.

Tedious pattern romance which did neither of its stars any good.

w Vincent Laurence, Grover Jones   d Norman Taurog   ph Ray June   m Franz Waxman

Myrna Loy, Robert Taylor, Joseph Allen, Henry O'Neill, Douglas Fowley, Marjorie Main, Charles Lane, Bernard Nedell

'Light romantic comedy, okay for box office . . . but certain sections might object to so much liquor-imbibing.' – *Variety*

Lucky Partners *
US   1940   101m   bw
RKO (George Haight)
V*

Two strangers share a sweepstake ticket and fall in love.

A very thin comedy kept afloat by its stars.

w Allan Scott, John Van Druten   story *Bonne Chance* by Sacha Guitry   d Lewis Milestone   ph Robert de Grasse   m Dimitri Tiomkin

Ronald Colman, Ginger Rogers, Jack Carson, Spring Byington, Cecilia Loftus, Harry Davenport

The Lucky Star *
Canada   1980   110m   colour
Tele Metropole International/Claude Leger

During World War II a Dutch Jewish boy studies wild west films and captures a German colonel.

Unusual and likeable family adventure story with an unnecessary downbeat ending.

w Max Fischer, Jack Rosenthal   d Max Fischer   ph Frank Tidy   m Art Philipps

Rod Steiger, Louise Fletcher, Brett Marx, Lou Jacobi, Helen Hughes

The Lucky Stiff
US   1948   101m   bw
Amusement Enterprises/UA

A cabaret singer sentenced to death for murder is secretly reprieved but comes back as a 'ghost' to scare the real culprit into confession.

Weird comedy-melodrama which seems to embarrass all concerned.

wd Lewis R. Foster   novel Craig Rice

Dorothy Lamour, Brian Donlevy, Claire Trevor, Irene Hervey

The Lucky Texan
US   1933   56m   bw
Monogram/Lone Star (Paul Malvern)
V*

Two crooked assayers try to cheat an old man out of his ranch and gold mine, but the son of his former partner saves the day.

Brisk programmer, with some novel stunts, including Wayne almost walking on water, 'Gabby' Hayes beginning to perfect the comic role of a whiskery and garrulous sidekick which he was to play for the next 18 years, and an unusual final chase involving horses, an automobile and a railcar.

wd Robert N. Bradbury   ph Archie Stout   ed Carl Pierson

John Wayne, Barbara Sheldon, Lloyd Whitlock, George Hayes, Yakima Canutt, Ed Parker, Gordon Demaine, Earl Dwire

Lucretia Borgia
France/Italy   1952   105m approx   Technicolor
Ariane/Filmsonor/Rizzoli

Cesare Borgia uses his beautiful sister as a political pawn.

Well-mounted but rather boring period barnstormer.

w Cécil Saint-Laurent, Jacques Sigurd, Christian-Jaque   d Christian-Jaque   ph Christian Matras   m Maurice Thiriet

Martine Carol, Pedro Armendariz, Massimo Serato, Ventine Tessier

Lucy Gallant *
US   1955   104m   Technicolor   Vistavision
Paramount/Pine-Thomas

The success story of a dressmaker who comes to run a group of fashion shops but neglects her love life.

Efficient, smartly-handled woman's picture.

w John Lee Mahin, Winston Miller   novel *The Life of Lucy Gallant* by Margaret Cousins   d Robert Parrish   ph Lionel Lindon   m Van Cleave

Jane Wyman, Charlton Heston, Claire Trevor, Thelma Ritter, William Demarest, Wallace Ford, Tom Helmore, Mary Field

Ludwig *
Italy/France/West Germany   1972   186m
Technicolor   Panavision
Mega/Cinetel/Dieter Gessler/Divina (Robert Gordon Edwards)

The 19th-century King of Bavaria becomes involved in scandal and goes mad.

A stylish but historically questionable and highly coloured view of events; it drags its heels long before history did.

w Luchino Visconti, Enrico Medioli   d Luchino Visconti   ph Armando Nannuzzi   md Franco Nannino

Helmut Berger, Romy Schneider, Trevor Howard, Silvana Mangano, Helmut Griem, Nora Ricci, Gert Frobe, John Moulder Brown

The Lullaby: see *The Sin of Madelon Claudet*

'Happiness is busting out all over!'
Lullaby of Broadway *
US   1951   92m   Technicolor
Warner (William Jacobs)
V, V*, L

The daughter of a faded Broadway star becomes the new toast of the town.

Reasonably lively musical with solid production values but little style or wit.

w Earl Baldwin   d David Butler   ph Wilfrid Cline   md Ray Heindorf

Doris Day, Billy de Wolfe, Gene Nelson, Gladys George, Florence Bates, S. Z. Sakall

Lulu: see *Pandora's Box*

Lulu Belle
US   1948   87m   bw
Benedict Bogeaus/Columbia

A selfish singer has a bad effect on one man after another.

Dreary melodrama with a miscast star.

w Everett Freeman   play Charles MacArthur, Edward Sheldon   d Leslie Fenton

Dorothy Lamour, George Montgomery, Otto Kruger, Albert Dekker, Glenda Farrell

La Lumière d'en Face: see *The Light Across the Street*

Lumière d'Eté *
France   1943   112m   bw
Discina (André Paulvé)

The idle and decadent rich in a mountain hotel are affected in various ways by workmen in the valley below.

Unusual and generally interesting character melodrama.

w Jacques Prévert, Pierre Laroche   d Jean Grémillion   ph Louis Page   m Roland Manuel

Madeleine Renaud, Pierre Brasseur, Madeleine Robinson, Paul Bernard, Jane Marken, Georges Marchal

La Luna
Italy   1979   142m   Eastmancolor
TCF/Fiction Cinematografica (Giovanni Bertolucci)

A singer has an incestuous relationship with her teenage son.

Interminable catalogue of events few people wanted to experience; the kindest description would be 'pretentious claptrap'.

w Giuseppe and Bernardo Bertolucci, Clare Peploe *d* Bernardo Bertolucci *ph* Vittorio Storaro *m* operatic excerpts

Jill Clayburgh, Matthew Barry, Laura Betti, Renato Salvatori, Fred Gwynne

Luna de Miel: see *Honeymoon*

'A seriously wicked comedy hot from Jamaica'
The Lunatic
US 1992 93m CFI
Island (Paul Heller, John Pringle)
V

A German photographer visiting Jamaica falls for a local butcher and a boy who talks to the trees.

Whimsical fable that passes an idle hour or so.

w Anthony C. Winkler *novel* Anthony C. Winkler *d* Lol Creme *ph* Richard Greatrex *m* Wally Badarou *ad* Giorgio Ferrarri *ed* Michael Connell

Julie T. Wallace, Paul Campbell, Reggie Carter, Carl Bradshaw, Winston Stona, Linda Gambrill, Rosemary Murray, Lloyd Reckord

'An annoyingly cute fable.' – *Variety*

Lunch Hour
GB 1962 64m bw
Eyeline (John Mortimer, Harold Orton)

An executive's affair with a young woman at work goes wrong when he hires a hotel room for a lunchtime meeting.

Amusing little anecdote about thwarted love.

w John Mortimer *d* James Hill *ph* Wolfgang Suschitzky *m* James Hill *ad* Jack Stevens *ed* Ted Hooker

Shirley Anne Field, Robert Stephens, Kay Walsh, Michael Robbins, Nigel Davenport

Lunch on the Grass **
France 1959 91m Eastmancolor
Compagnie Jean Renoir
original title: *Déjeuner sur l'Herbe*

An international scientist hears the pipes of Pan, embarks on a country idyll and impregnates a housemaid whom he later marries.

Charming if overlong frolic with ideas, a harking back to earlier Renoir themes such as in *Boudu Sauvé des Eaux*.

wd Jean Renoir *ph* Georges Leclerc *m* Joseph Kosma

Paul Meurisse, Catherine Rouvel, Fernand Sardou, Ingrid Nordine

'A warm, loving, garrulous, undisciplined film.' – *Penelope Houston, MFB*

La Lune dans le Caniveau: see *The Moon in the Gutter*

Lunes de fiel: see *Bitter Moon*

Lunga Vita All Signora!: see *Long Live the Lady*

Lure of the Wilderness
US 1952 92m Technicolor
TCF (Robert L. Jacks)

A man falsely accused of murder hides for eight years in Georgia's Okefenokee swamp.

Remake of *Swamp Water*, with Walter Brennan playing the same part. The plot works fairly well still, but colour doesn't suit the scenery.

w Louis Lantz *story* Vereen Bell *d* Jean Negulesco *ph* Edward Cronjager *m* Franz Waxman

Jeffrey Hunter, Jean Peters, Walter Brennan, Constance Smith, Jack Elam

Lured *
US 1947 102m bw
(UA) Hunt Stromberg (James Nasser)
GB title: *Personal Column*

An American dancer stranded in London helps Scotland Yard catch a killer.

Minor murder mystery with a pleasing cast.

w Leo Rosten, from the French film *Pièges* *d* Douglas Sirk *ph* William Daniels *m* Michel Michelet *pd* Nicolai Remisoff

Lucille Ball, George Sanders, Charles Coburn, Boris Karloff, Cedric Hardwicke, Alan Mowbray, George Zucco, Joseph Calleia, Robert Coote, Alan Napier

Lust for a Vampire
GB 1970 95m Technicolor
Hammer (Harry Fine, Michael Style)
L

In 1830 an English writer discerns that a pupil in an exclusive mid-European girls' school is a reincarnated vampire.

Moderate Hammer horror.

w Tudor Gates *novel Carmilla* by J. Sheridan Le Fanu *d* Jimmy Sangster *ph* David Muir *m* Harry Robinson

Ralph Bates, Michael Johnson, Barbara Jefford, Suzanna Leigh, Yutte Stensgaard, Mike Raven, Helen Christie

Lust for Gold
US 1949 90m bw
Columbia (S. Sylvan Simon)
V*

A young man goes to Arizona to search for a lost gold mine discovered by his grandfather.

Moderate Western drama consisting largely of flashback.

w Ted Sherdeman, Richard English *novel Thunder God's Gold* by Barry Storm *d* S. Sylvan Simon *ph* Archie Stout *m* George Duning

Ida Lupino, Glenn Ford, Gig Young, William Prince, Edgar Buchanan, Will Geer, Paul Ford

Lust for Life **
US 1956 122m Metrocolor Cinemascope
MGM (John Houseman)
V, V*, L, S

The life of Vincent Van Gogh.

Fairly absorbing, not inaccurate, but somehow uninspiring biopic, probably marred by poor colour and wide screen; despite good work all round, it simply doesn't fall into a classic category.

w Norman Corwin *book* Irving Stone *d* Vincente Minnelli *ph* F. A. Young, Russell Harlan *m* Miklos Rozsa *ad* Cedric Gibbons, Hans Peters, Preston Ames

Kirk Douglas, Anthony Quinn (as Gauguin), James Donald, Pamela Brown, Everett Sloane, Niall MacGinnis, Noel Purcell, Henry Daniell, Lionel Jeffries, Madge Kennedy, Jill Bennett, Laurence Naismith

'Two hours of quite shattering and exciting entertainment.' – *Alan Dent, Illustrated London News*

† Anthony Quinn was on the screen for a total of eight minutes in his Oscar-winning role.

AA: Anthony Quinn

AAN: Norman Corwin; Kirk Douglas; art direction

Lust in the Dust
US 1984 87m CFI colour
Fox Run (Allan Glaser, Tab Hunter)
V, V*

In the old west, a strong silent man and a drag queen beat the baddies to the gold.

Fitfully funny spoof for adults.

w Philip Taylor *d* Paul Bartel *ph* Paul Lohmann *m* Peter Matz *ed* Alan Toomayan

Tab Hunter, Divine, Lainie Kazan, Geoffrey Lewis, Henry Silva, Cesar Romero, Woody Strode

Lust in the Sun (dubbed)
France/Spain 1971 84m Eastmancolor
Golden Era/Kerfrance/IMF
original title: *Dans la Poussiére du Soleil*

A son, who is regarded by many as a coward, revenges his father's death by killing his uncle.

Enjoyably bizarre updating of *Hamlet* to a cowboy setting, with Polonius becoming the town's sheriff, and faithful enough to the original to include the 'play within the play'.

wd Richard Balducci *play Hamlet* by William Shakespeare *ph* Tadusu G. Suzuki *m* Francis Lai *pd* Santiago Ontanon *ed* Liliane Fattori

Maria Schell, Bob Cunningham, Daniel Beretta, Karin Meier, Pépé Calvo, Colin Drake

'The inherent silliness of the conception . . . quickly converts the film into a variety skit.' – *MFB*

The Lusty Men *
US 1952 113m bw
RKO/Wald-Krasna (Jerry Wald)

Tensions lead to the death of one of a pair of rider friends on a rodeo tour.

Standard melodrama with semi-documentary detail and star performances.

w Horace McCoy, David Dortort *d* Nicholas Ray *ph* Lee Garmes *m* Roy Webb

Robert Mitchum, Arthur Kennedy, Susan Hayward, Arthur Hunnicutt

Luther *
GB 1973 112m Eastmancolor
American Express/Ely Landau/Cinevision
V*

In 1525, the teachings of Luther culminate in the Peasants' Revolt.

Hard-to-watch filming by the American Film Theatre of a singularly theatrical play, and not a very good one at that. Some good acting.

w Edward Anhalt *play* John Osborne *d* Guy Green *m* Freddie Young *m* John Addison *pd* Peter Mullins

Stacy Keach, Patrick Magee, Hugh Griffith, Robert Stephens, Alan Badel, Julian Glover, Judi Dench, Leonard Rossiter, Maurice Denham

Luv
US 1967 95m Technicolor Panavision
Columbia/Jalem (Martin Manulis)
V*, L

When a man prevents an old friend from jumping off the Brooklyn Bridge and brings him home, a sexual square dance develops.

A modern comedy that should have stayed in the theatre.

w Elliott Baker *play* Murray Shisgal *d* Clive Donner *ph* Ernest Laszlo *m* Gerry Mulligan

Jack Lemmon, Peter Falk, Elaine May, Nina Wayne, Eddie Mayehoff, Paul Hartman, Severn Darden

'A light but incisive comedy about the patterns and language of love in a Freud-ridden society has become an inept and lethally unamusing film farce.' – *MFB*

Luxury Liner
US   1933   72m   bw
Paramount

Stories of various passengers on a liner bound from New York to Bremerhaven.

Interesting minor multi-drama, like a rough sketch for *Ship of Fools* (qv).

w Gene Markey, Kathryn Scola   *novel* Gina Kaus
d Lothar Mendes   *ph* Victor Milner

George Brent, Zita Johann, Vivienne Osborne, Alice White, Verree Teasdale, C. Aubrey Smith, Frank Morgan, Henry Wadsworth, Billy Bevan

'Not even the frank hook-up with Grand Hotel will help this entry much . . . a loose and thin catch-as-catch-can affair.' – *Variety*

Luxury Liner
US   1948   98m   Technicolor
MGM (Joe Pasternak)
L

The captain of a liner has trouble with his teenage daughter.

Minor shipboard musical with pleasing talents applied.

w Gladys Lehmann, Richard Connell   *d* Richard Whorf   *ph* Ernest Laszlo   *md* George Stoll

George Brent, Jane Powell, Lauritz Melchior, Frances Gifford, Marina Koshetz, Xavier Cugat, Richard Derr, Connie Gilchrist

'The girl who thought she knew all about love!'
Lydia *
US   1941   104m   bw
Alexander Korda (Lee Garmes)

An ageing lady recalls her former beaux.

Pleasing remake of *Carnet du Bal*, with excellent production values.

w Ben Hecht, Samuel Hoffenstein   *story* Julien Duvivier, Laszlo Bus-Fekete   *d* Julien Duvivier

ph Lee Garmes   *m* Miklos Rozsa   *pd* Vincent Korda

Merle Oberon, Joseph Cotten, Alan Marshal, Edna May Oliver, Hans Yaray, George Reeves, John Halliday, Sara Allgood

AAN: Miklos Rozsa

Lydia Bailey
US   1952   89m   Technicolor
TCF (Jules Schermer)

In 1802 a Boston lawyer visits Haiti to obtain the signature of a wayward heiress, and becomes involved in the negro fight against the French.

Standard adventure romance with plenty of excitements.

w Michael Blankfort, Philip Dunne   *novel* Kenneth Roberts   *d* Jean Negulesco   *ph* Harry Jackson   *m* Hugo Friedhofer

Dale Robertson, Anne Francis, Charles Korvin, William Marshall, Adeline de Walt Reynolds

M

M ***
Germany 1931 118m bw
Nero Film (Seymour Nebenzal)
V, V (W), V*, L

A psychopathic murderer of children evades the police but is caught by the city's criminals who find his activities getting them a bad name.

An unmistakable classic whose oddities are hardly worth criticizing, this is part social melodrama and part satire, but entirely unforgettable, with most of its sequences brilliantly staged.

w Thea von Harbou, Paul Falkenberg, Adolf Jansen, Karl Vash *d* Fritz Lang *ph* Fritz Arno Wagner *m* Adolf Jansen *ad* Karl Vollbrecht, Emil Hasler

Peter Lorre, Otto Wernicke, Gustav Gründgens

'Visual excitement, pace, brilliance of surface and feeling for detail.' – *New Yorker, 1977*

† Of Lang's later work, *Fury* comes closest to the feeling and style of *M.*

M *
US 1951 82m bw
Columbia (Seymour Nebenzal)

Faithful but fated remake; without the heavy expressionist techniques, the story seems merely silly and the atmosphere is all wrong.

w Norman Reilly Raine, Leo Katcher *d* Joseph Losey *ph* Ernest Laszlo *m* Michel Michelet *pd* John Hubley *ed* Edward Mann

David Wayne, Howard Da Silva, Luther Adler, Martin Gabel, Glenn Anders, Karen Morley, Norman Lloyd, Walter Burke

'I consciously repeated only one shot . . . essentially Lang's villain was my hero.' – *Joseph Losey*

M. Butterfly
US 1993 100m colour
Warner/Geffen (Gabriella Martinelli)
S

In the 1960s a French diplomat has a long affair with a Chinese woman, who turns out to be a male spy.

A successful play translates poorly to the screen, where close-ups make the deception seem incredible, even though the story has a basis in fact.

w David Henry Hwang *play* David Henry Hwang *d* David Cronenberg *ph* Peter Suschitzky *m* Howard Shore *pd* Carol Spier *ed* Ronald Sanders

Jeremy Irons, John Lone, Ian Richardson, Annabel Leventon, Shizuko Hoshi, Richard McMillan, Vernon Dobtcheff

'Icy, surprisingly conventional and never truly convincing.' – *Variety*

Ma and Pa Kettle *
US 1949 75m bw
U-I (Leonard Goldstein)

Pa Kettle wins a house in a contest and is accused of cheating.

First of a series of low-budget comedies which, based on characters from *The Egg and I* (qv), had astonishing commercial success in America. The standard varied from adequate to painful.

w Herbert Margolis, Louis Morheim, Al Lewis *d* Charles Lamont *ph* Maury Gertsman *m* Milton Schwarzwald

Marjorie Main, Percy Kilbride, Richard Long, Meg Randall

'Not exactly Noël Coward.' – *Leonard Maltin*

† For others in the series, see under *The Kettles.*

Ma Nuit Chez Maud *
France 1969 110m bw
Films du Losange (Pierre Cottreill)
V, L
aka: *My Night at Maud's*

A Catholic clerk in a small town falls in love with an elegant divorcee but can't bring himself to court her openly and marries someone else.

Subdued, literate talk-piece which finally exhausts rather than stimulates.

wd Eric Rohmer *ph* Nestor Almendros

Jean-Louis Trintignant, Françoise Fabian, Marie-Christine Barault

AAN: best foreign film; Eric Rohmer (as writer)

'Every success has its story. And its price.'
Mac *
US 1992 118m Technicolor
Entertainment/Macfilm (Nancy Tenenbaum, Brenda Goodman)

A construction worker, irritated by the sloppy standards of his foreman, decides to start his own business, working to the best of his ability; his two brothers join him but then leave.

A drama of obsession and integrity, with splendid ensemble acting and a gritty reality.

w John Turturro, Brandon Cole *d* John Turturro *ph* Ron Fortunato *m* Richard Termini, Vin Tese *pd* Robert Standefer *ed* Michael Berenbaum

John Turturro, Katherine Borowitz, Michael Badalucco, Carl Capotorto, Ellen Barkin, John Amos, Dennis Farina

'Obviously made as a labour of love. But it is a bit of a labour to sit through.' – *Alexander Walker, London Evening Standard*

'A film of old-fashioned virtues – sincerity, worthiness, and probity – used in an unpatronising way.' – *Philip French*

Mac and Me
US 1988 99m
Guild/R. J. Louis
V*, L

A family of aliens is inadvertently dumped in California.

A cardboard confection, copying much of the plot of *E.T.,* that is little more than a dull and extended commercial for fast foods.

w Steven Feke, Stewart Raffill *d* Stewart Raffill *ph* Nick McLean *m* Alan Silvestri *pd* W. Stewart Campbell *ed* Tom Walls

Christine Ebersole, Jonathan Ward, Tina Caspary, Lauren Stanley, Jade Calegory, Vinnie Torrente, Martin West

'See it with someone who can carry you home!'
'So terrifying we have to insure your life!'
Macabre
US 1958 73m bw
AA (William Castle)

When a small-town doctor's daughter is kidnapped, he fears she may have been buried alive in the cemetery.

Genuine but unsuccessful attempt to film a horror comic; incredibly stodgy writing, acting and direction put the lid on it.

w Robb White *d* William Castle *ph* Carl Guthrie *m* Les Baxter

William Prince, Jim Backus, Jacqueline Scott, Philip Tonge, Ellen Corby

'A ghoulish but totally ineffective horror piece, set mainly in undertakers' offices and an atmosphere of graveyards and swirling fog.' – *MFB*

† When first released, admission carried insurance against death by fright. Some said it should have been death by boredom.

Macao
US 1952 81m bw
RKO (Alex Gottlieb)
V*, L

A wandering American in the Far East helps a detective catch a gangster.

A few flashy decorative touches show the director's hand, otherwise this is routine, murky thick ear.

w Bernard C. Schoenfeld, Stanley Rubin *d* Josef von Sternberg (and Nicholas Ray) *ph* Harry J. Wild *m* Anthony Collins

Robert Mitchum, Jane Russell, William Bendix, Gloria Grahame, Thomas Gomez

MacArthur the Rebel General *
US 1977 130m Technicolor
Universal/Richard D. Zanuck, David Brown (Frank McCarthy)
V*, L

The exploits of General MacArthur during the Pacific wars and his strained relationships with two presidents.

Sober, earnest political biography with war sequences; very well done but somehow unsympathetic.

w Hal Barwood, Matthew Robbins *d* Joseph Sargent *ph* Mario Tosi *m* Jerry Goldsmith

Gregory Peck, Dan O'Herlihy (as Roosevelt), Ed Flanders (as Truman), Ward Costello, Marj Dusay, Ivan Bonar

'A biopic that begins when its subject is sixty lacks roots – and in this case revelation.' – *Judith Crist*

'Taking on the drug lords is impossible. Taking on a country is insane.'
McBain
US 1991 102m TVC colour
Shapiro Glickenhaus (J. Boyce Harman Jnr)
V, V*

A former soldier agrees to help the sister of a friend overthrow the corrupt government in Colombia.

Predictable and interminable, lacking any sense of reality.

wd James Glickenhaus *ph* Robert M. Baldwin Jnr *m* Christopher Franke *pd* Charles C. Bennett *ed* Jeffrey Wolf

Christopher Walken, Maria Conchita Alonso, Michael Ironside, Steve James, Jay Patterson, T. G. Waites, Victor Argo, Hechter Ubarry, Russell Dennis Baker, Chick Vennera

'A silly action film geared mainly to overseas audiences.' – *Variety*

Macbeth *
US 1948 89m bw
Republic/Mercury (Orson Welles)
V*, L, S

A famous – or infamous – attempt to film Shakespeare in twenty-one days in papier mâché settings running with damp; further hampered by the use of a form of unintelligible bastard Scots.

A few striking moments at the beginning remain; the rest should be silence.

w Orson Welles *play* William Shakespeare *d* Orson Welles *ph* John L. Russell *m* Jacques Ibert *ad* Fred Ritter *ed* Louis Lindsay

Orson Welles, Jeanette Nolan, Dan O'Herlihy, Roddy McDowall, Edgar Barrier, Erskine Sanford

Macbeth
GB 1972 140m Technicolor Todd-AO 35
Playboy/Caliban (Andrew Braunsberg)
V, V*, L

A sharpened and brutalized version; the blood swamps most of the cleverness and most of the poetry.

w Roman Polanski, Kenneth Tynan *play* William Shakespeare *d* Roman Polanski *ph* Gilbert Taylor *m* the Third Ear Band *pd* Wilfrid Shingleton

Jon Finch, Francesca Annis, Martin Shaw, Nicholas Selby, John Stride

McCabe and Mrs Miller
US 1971 120m Technicolor Panavision
Warner (David Foster, Mitchell Brower)
V (W), V*, L

At the turn of the century a gambling gunfighter comes to a northwest mining town and uses his money to set up lavish brothels.

Obscurely scripted, muddy-coloured and harshly recorded Western melodrama whose squalid 'realism' comes as close to fantasy as does *The Wizard of Oz*.

w Robert Altman, Brian McKay *novel* McCabe by Edmund Naughton *d* Robert Altman *ph* Vilmos Zsigmond *pd* Leon Ericksen

Warren Beatty, Julie Christie, René Auberjonois, Shelley Duvall, John Schuck

'A fleeting, diaphanous vision of what frontier life might have been.' – *Pauline Kael*

'Altman directed *M*A*S*H*, which wandered and was often funny; then *Brewster McCloud*, which wandered and was not funny; now this, which wanders and is repulsive. The thesis seems to be that if you take a corny story, fuzz up the exposition, vitiate the action, use a childishly ironic ending, and put in lots of profanity and nudity, you have Marched On with Time.' – *Stanley Kauffmann*

AAN: Julie Christie

The McConnell Story
US 1955 107m Warnercolor Cinemascope
Warner (Henry Blanke)
V*, L
GB title: *Tiger in the Sky*

The career and accidental death of a jet ace of the Korean war.

Crude, obvious and saccharine biopic.

w Ted Sherdeman, Sam Rolfe *d* Gordon Douglas *ph* John Seitz, Ted McCord *m* Max Steiner

Alan Ladd, June Allyson, James Whitmore, Frank Faylen, Willis Bouchey

MacDonald of the Canadian Mounties: see Pony Soldier

McFadden's Flats
US 1935 65m bw
Paramount

The quarrel between a bricklayer and a barber affects their children.

Modest working-class comedy from a well-worn play.

w Arthur Caesar, Edward Kaufman, Casey Robinson, Andy Rice *play* Gus Hill *d* Ralph Murphy

Walter C. Kelly, Andy Clyde, Richard Cromwell, Jane Darwell, Betty Furness, George Barbier

'Better-than-average family picture.' – *Variety*

McGuire Go Home: see The High Bright Sun

'Even the Mafia calls him Mister!'
Machine Gun McCain
Italy 1970 94m Techniscope
Euroatlantica/Columbia
S

The Mafia springs a hardened criminal from jail and puts him to use.

Dull but violent Las Vegas-set mobster story with some echoes of *Bonnie and Clyde*.

w Giuliano Montaldo, Mino Roli *d* Giuliano Montaldo *m* Ennio Morricone

John Cassavetes, Peter Falk, Britt Ekland, Gabriele Ferzetti

Macho Callahan
US 1970 100m Movielab Panavision
Avco/Felicidad (Bernard Kowalski, Martin C. Schute)

A vengeful cowboy annihilates all who stand in his way.

Squalid Mexican-made Western with unremitting emphasis on violence.

w Clifford Newton Gould *d* Bernard Kowalski *ph* Gerry Fisher *m* Pat Williams

David Janssen, Lee J. Cobb, David Carradine, James Booth, Jean Seberg

MacKenna's Gold *
US 1969 136m Technicolor Super Panavision
Columbia/Highroad (Carl Foreman, Dimitri Tiomkin)
V, V*, L

A dying Indian entrusts a sheriff with a map of the legendary Valley of Gold, and when the news breaks the map is in demand.

Curious serial-like Western melodrama packed with stars and pretensions above its station. On a lower level, it is quite enjoyable.

w Carl Foreman *novel* Will Henry *d* J. Lee-Thompson *ph* Joseph MacDonald, Harold Wellman *m* Quincy Jones *pd* Geoffrey Drake

Gregory Peck, Omar Sharif, Telly Savalas, Camilla Sparv, Keenan Wynn, Julie Newmar, Ted Cassidy, Eduardo Ciannelli, Eli Wallach, Edward G. Robinson, Raymond Massey, Burgess Meredith, Anthony Quayle, Lee J. Cobb

'Preposterous hotch-potch of every cliché known to the gold lust book.' – *MFB*

'Twelve-year-olds of all ages might tolerate it.' – *Judith Crist*

'A western of truly stunning absurdity, a thriving example of the old Hollywood maxim about how to succeed by failing big.' – *Vincent Canby*

The McKenzie Break *
GB 1970 106m DeLuxe
UA/Levy-Gardner-Laven

During World War II, German prisoners at a Scottish camp stage an escape.

Effective little action suspenser.

w William Norton *d* Lamont Johnson *ph* Michael Reed *m* Riz Ortolani

Brian Keith, Helmut Griem, Ian Hendry, Jack Watson, Patrick O'Connell, Horst Janson

'Only Mackintosh can save them now – and Mackintosh is dead!'
The Mackintosh Man *
GB 1973 99m Technicolor
Warner/Newman-Foreman/John Huston
V*

A government agent is sent to prison to contact a criminal gang.

Convoluted but entertaining spy thriller with good performances and action sequences.

w Walter Hill *novel* The Freedom Trap by Desmond Bagley *d* John Huston *ph* Oswald Morris *m* Maurice Jarre

Paul Newman, James Mason, Dominique Sanda, Nigel Patrick, Harry Andrews, Michael Hordern, Ian Bannen, Peter Vaughan, Roland Culver, Percy Herbert, Robert Lang, Leo Genn

McLintock *
US 1963 127m Technicolor Panavision
UA/Batjac (Michael Wayne)
V*

A cattle baron can control a whole town but not his termagant wife.

Sub-Ford Western farce borrowed from *The Taming of the Shrew*, with much fist-fighting and mud-splattering, and rather too much chat in between.

w James Edward Grant *d* Andrew V. McLaglen *ph* William H. Clothier *m* Frank de Vol

John Wayne, Maureen O'Hara, Yvonne de Carlo, Patrick Wayne, Stefanie Powers, Chill Wills, Bruce Cabot, Jack Kruschen

The McMasters
US 1969 90m Technicolor
JayJen (Dimitri de Grunwald)
V*

A black man returning home from the Civil War gets unexpected help from a tough landowner.

Racial Western with black, white and red points of view, all very violently expressed.

w Harold Jacob Smith *d* Alf Kjellin *ph* Lester Shorr *m* Coleridge-Taylor Parkinson

Brock Peters, Burl Ives, David Carradine, Nancy Kwan, Jack Palance, Dane Clark, John Carradine, L. Q. Jones, R. G. Armstrong

The Macomber Affair *
US 1947 89m bw
(UA) Benedict Bogeaus (Casey Robinson)

The wife of a bullying big game hunter falls for their guide.

Safari melodrama with a plot which has become a cliché but seemed fresh enough at the time. Goodish writing and acting.

w Casey Robinson *story* The Short Happy Life of Francis Macomber by Ernest Hemingway *d* Zoltan Korda *ph* Karl Struss *m* Miklos Rozsa

Gregory Peck, Joan Bennett, Robert Preston, Reginald Denny, Carl Harbord, Jean Gillie

'The best movie job on Hemingway to date.' – *James Agee*

'It has survived the hazardous crossing from brilliant short story to film with practically no casualties.' – *Daily Mail*

Macon County Line

US 1973 89m Eastmancolor
Sam Arkoff/Max Baer
V*

In mid-fifties Louisiana, a couple of hell-raisers are harassed by a local sheriff, and much bloodshed results.

Shapeless melodrama more or less in the wake of *Easy Rider*; an unattractive film which unaccountably had great box-office success.

w Max Baer, Richard Compton *d* Richard Compton *ph* Daniel Lacambre *m* Stu Phillips

Alan Vint, Cheryl Waters, Geoffrey Lewis, Joan Blackman, Jesse Vint, Max Baer

'He's a busted cop, his gun is unlicensed, his methods unlawful, his story incredible!'
McQ

US 1974 111m Technicolor Panavision
Warner/Batjac/Levy-Gardner
V, V*, L

A Seattle police detective goes after the gangster who killed his friend.

Rambling, violent thriller with good sequences but no cohesion.

w Lawrence Roman *d* John Sturges *ph* Harry Stradling Jnr *m* Elmer Bernstein

John Wayne, Eddie Albert, Diana Muldaur, Colleen Dewhurst, Clu Gulager, David Huddleston, Julie Adams

Macu, the Policeman's Wife

Venezuela 1987 102m colour
Macu Films/Cinearte (Olegario Barrera)
original title: *Macu*

The young wife of a policeman suspects her husband of having murdered her lover and his friends.

Slice-of-life drama that was a big hit in its own country, but does not travel well.

w Solveig Hoogesteijn, Milagros Rodríguez *d* Solveig Hoogesteijn *ph* Andrés Agusti *m* Victor Cuica *ed* José Alcalde

Maria Luisa Mosquera, Daniel Alvarado, Frank Hernández, Tito Aponte, Ana Castell, Carmen Palma, Iván Feo

McVicar

GB 1980 112m Eastmancolor
The Who Films/Brent-Walker (Bill Curbishley, Roy Baird, Roger Daltrey)
V, V*, L

The true story of the escapes from prison of a violent criminal who was subsequently reformed and rehabilitated.

Some smart sequences don't prevent this from being an exploitation item.

w John McVicar and Tom Clegg *d* Tom Clegg *ph* Vernon Layton *m* Jeff Wayne *ad* Fred Carter *ed* Peter Boyle

Roger Daltrey, Adam Faith, Cheryl Campbell, Billy Murray, Georgina Hale, Steven Berkoff

Mad about Men

GB 1954 90m Technicolor
GFD/Group Films (Betty Box)

By mutual agreement, a sports mistress and a mermaid change places for a while.

Laborious rehash of *Miranda* with familiar jokes.

w Peter Blackmore *d* Ralph Thomas *ph* Ernest Steward *m* Benjamin Frankel

Glynis Johns, Donald Sinden, Anne Crawford, Margaret Rutherford, Dora Bryan, Nicholas Phipps, Irene Handl

Mad about Music *

US 1938 98m bw
Universal (Joe Pasternak)

A girl at a Swiss school adopts a personable visitor as her father.

Pleasing star vehicle with charm and humour; badly remade as *Toy Tiger* (qv).

w Bruce Manning, Felix Jackson *d* Norman Taurog *ph* Joseph Valentine *m* Frank Skinner, Charles Previn *m/y* Harold Adamson, Jimmy McHugh

Deanna Durbin, Herbert Marshall, Gail Patrick, Arthur Treacher, Helen Parrish, Marcia Mae Jones, William Frawley

'Another Durbin smash . . . will mop up at the b.o.' – *Variety*

AAN: original story (Marcella Burke, Frederick Kohner); Joseph Valentine; Frank Skinner, Charles Previn

The Mad Adventures of 'Rabbi' Jacob: see *Les Aventures de Rabbi Jacob*

The Mad Bomber *

US 1972 91m Movielab colour
Scotia-Barber/College (Bert I. Gordon)
V*

A detective tries to track down a bomber who is killing people by dynamiting buildings in Los Angeles in order to punish society.

Low-budget thriller, effective in a harsh and unpolished way. *wd* Bert I. Gordon *story* Marc Behm *m* Michel Mention *ed* Gene Ruggerio

Vince Edwards, Chuck Connors, Neville Brand, Christina Hart, Faith Quabius

'An attempt not to be sneezed at.' – *Tom Milne, MFB*

The film was cut to 87m for its British release.

'She knew the ecstasy and terror of loving him!'
The Mad Doctor

US 1940 90m bw
Paramount (George Arthur)
GB title: *A Date with Destiny*

A doctor marries wealthy women and then murders them.

Naïve melodrama of little interest except as a vehicle for its star.

w Howard J. Green *d* Tim Whelan *ph* Ted Tetzlaff *m* Victor Young

Basil Rathbone, Ellen Drew, John Howard, Barbara Allen, Ralph Morgan, Martin Kosleck

The Mad Doctor of Blood Island

Philippines/USA 1969 86m colour
Westland/Hemisphere (Eddie Romero)
V*
aka: *Tomb of the Living Dead*

Visitors to a Pacific island discover that a scientist searching for the secret of eternal life has created a vegetable monster.

Dreary horror that receives the inept treatment it deserves from all those concerned in its making.

w Reuben Candy *d* Gerardo de Leon, Eddie Romero *ph* Justo Paulino *m* Tito Arevalo

John Ashley, Angelique Pettyjohn, Ronald Remy, Alicia Alonso

'The script is trite, the dramatic structure slack and the violence unconvincing.' – *Paul Joannides, MFB*

The Mad Doctor of Market Street

US 1942 61m bw
Universal

Shipwrecked people on a tropical island find that one of their number is a dangerous paranoiac.

Dull and misleadingly titled second-feature melodrama.

w Al Martin *d* Joseph H. Lewis

Lionel Atwill, Nat Pendleton, Una Merkel, Claire Dodd

Mad Dog and Glory

US 1992 97m Technicolor
UIP/Universal (Barbara DeFina, Martin Scorsese)
V, V*, S

A timid and conventional Chicago cop is embarrassed when a gangster he inadvertently helps gives him a present of a beautiful woman for a week.

A movie that promises much but fails to deliver, quickly dwindling into something inconsequential, though it occasionally amuses; the problem lies in the passivity of its two central characters, including a female role that is totally inert.

w Richard Price *d* John McNaughton *ph* Robby Müller *m* Elmer Bernstein *pd* David Chapman *ed* Craig McKay, Elena Maganini

Robert de Niro, Uma Thurman, Bill Murray, David Caruso, Mike Starr, Tom Towles, Kathy Baker

'A pleasurably offbeat picture that manages the rare trick of being both charming and edgy.' – *Variety*

'Price's macho fantasy smells way past its dwell-by date.' – *Ian Penman, Sight and Sound*

Mad Dog Coll

US 1961 87m bw
Columbia-Warner/Thalia (Edward Schreiber)

Biopic about a violent gangster of the 1930s.

Predictable low-budget exploitation movie, offering no new insights into the times and the vicious mobsters it bred.

w Edward Schreiber *story* Leo Lieberman *d* Burt Balaban *ph* Gayne Reschner *m* Stu Phillips *ad* Richard Sylbert *ed* Ralph Rosenblum

John Davis Chandler, Neil Nephew, Brooke Hayward, Jerry Orbach, Telly Savalas, Vincent Gardenia, Gene Hackman

The Mad Game

US 1933 73m bw
Fox

A gangster turns stool pigeon to round up kidnappers.

Fairly lively crime melodrama.

w William Conselman, Henry Johnson *d* Irving Cummings

Spencer Tracy, Claire Trevor, Ralph Morgan, J. Carrol Naish, John Miljan

'Enough romance and action to satisfy.' – *Variety*

'Adults Only! Censor's orders!'
The Mad Genius

US 1931 81m bw
Warner

A crippled puppeteer adopts a boy and makes him into a great dancer.

Curious variation on *Trilby*, filmed as *Svengali* the previous year with much the same cast. Not a great success: the script is dreadful.

w J. Grubb Alexander, Harvey Thew *play The Idol* by Martin Brown *d* Michael Curtiz *ph* Barney McGill *ad* Anton Grot

John Barrymore, Marian Marsh, Donald Cook, Luis Alberni, Carmel Myers, Charles Butterworth, Boris Karloff, Frankie Darro

'Magnificent acting, but not the sort of thing that will panic the fans.' – *Variety*

† Many of the sets in this production had ceilings, ten years before the idea was supposed to have been invented for *Citizen Kane*.

The Mad Ghoul

US 1943 65m bw
Universal (Ben Pivar)

A mad scientist needs fresh hearts to keep alive the victims of his experiments with a poison vapour.

Stagey, tasteless horror melodrama.

w Brenda Weisberg, Paul Gangelin story Hans Kraly d James Hogan ph Milton Krasner md Hans Salter

George Zucco, David Bruce, Evelyn Ankers, Turhan Bey, Robert Armstrong, Charles McGraw, Milburn Stone

Mad Holiday

US 1936 72m bw
MGM

A rebellious film actor goes on a cruise and gets involved in a murder.

Spotty mystery comedy in which the elements don't really jell.

w Florence Ryerson and Edgar Allen Woolf story Murder in a Chinese Theatre by Joseph Santley d George B. Seitz

Edmund Lowe, Elissa Landi, Edmund Gwenn, ZaSu Pitts, Ted Healy, Edgar Kennedy

'Very draggy . . . largely a bore.' – Variety

Mad Little Island: see Rockets Galore

Mad Love **

US 1935 83m bw
MGM (John Considine Jnr)
V*
GB title: The Hands of Orlac

A pianist loses his hands in an accident; a mad surgeon, in love with the pianist's wife, grafts on the hands of a murderer.

Absurd Grand Guignol done with great style which somehow does not communicate itself in viewer interest, only in cold admiration.

w Guy Endore, P. J. Wolfson, John Balderston novel The Hands of Orlac by Maurice Renard d Karl Freund ph Chester Lyons, Gregg Toland m Dmitri Tiomkin

Colin Clive, Peter Lorre, Frances Drake, Ted Healy, Edward Brophy, Isabel Jewell, Sara Haden

'The results in screen potency are disappointing . . . will probably do fair biz.' – Variety

'Mr Lorre cuts deeply into the darkness of the morbid brain.' – New York Times

The Mad Magician

US 1954 72m bw
Columbia (Bryan Foy)

A magician's star-struck inventor murders his employer and several others who stand between him and the big time.

Hokey horror flick set in the eighties and originally shown in 3-D.

w Crane Wilbur d John Brahm ph Bert Glennon m Emil Newman

Vincent Price, Mary Murphy, Eva Gabor, John Emery, Patrick O'Neal

The Mad Martindales

US 1942 55m bw
Walter Morosco/TCF

In 1900 San Francisco, an eccentric family gets out of debt.

The star's last film for a major studio is a filler of unrelieved tedium.

w Francis Edwards Faragoh d Alfred Werker

Jane Withers, Alan Mowbray, Marjorie Weaver, Jimmy Lydon, Byron Barr, George Reeves

Mad Masquerade: see Washington Masquerade

Mad Max *

Australia 1979 100m Eastmancolor Todd-AO 35
Warner/Mad Max Pty (Byron Kennedy)
V, V (W), V*, L, S

In the future, motor cycle gangs combat the police.

Violent extravaganza with no real merit save its enthusiasm for destruction of both bikes and bodies.

w James McCausland, George Miller d George Miller ph David Eggby m Brian May ad John Dowding ed Tony Paterson, Cliff Hayes

Mel Gibson, Joanne Samuel, Hugh Keays-Byrne, Steve Bisley

'Ruthless . . . Savage . . . Spectacular'

Mad Max 2 *

Australia 1981 96m colour Panavision
Warner/Kennedy Miller Entertainment (Byron Kennedy)
V, V*, L, S
US title: The Road Warrior

A shortage of petrol causes all-out war between police and bikers.

Not much more than a retread of the above, but a more expensive, spectacular and violent one.

w Terry Hayes, George Miller, Brian Hannant d George Miller ph Dean Semler m Brian May ad Graham Walker ed David Stiven, Tim Wellburn, Michael Chirgwin

Mel Gibson, Bruce Spence, Vernon Wells, Emil Minty

'Essentially just another display of vehicles smashing into each other.' – David McGillivray, MFB

Mad Max beyond Thunderdome

Australia 1985 106m colour Panavision
Warner/Kennedy Miller (George Miller)
V, V*, L, S

More violent futuristic rubbish in similar vein to its predecessors.

w Terry Hayes, George Miller d George Miller and George Ogilvie ph Dean Semler m Maurice Jarre pd Graham Walker ed Richard Francis-Bruce

Mel Gibson, Tina Turner, Angelo Rossitto, Helen Buday

The Mad Miss Manton *

US 1938 80m bw
RKO (Pandro S. Berman)
V*, L

A zany socialite involves her friends in a murder mystery.

Mildly funny comedy-thriller without too much of either, but a good example of the style of thirties craziness at its zenith.

w Philip G. Epstein d Leigh Jason ph Nicholas Musuraca m Roy Webb

Barbara Stanwyck, Henry Fonda, Sam Levene, Frances Mercer, Stanley Ridges, Whitney Bourne, Hattie McDaniel, Miles Mander

'Something ground out by people in a desperate mood.' – Pauline Kael, 70s

The Mad Monkey

Spain 1990 108m Eastmancolor Panavision
Hobo/Iberoamericana Films/Emmanuel Schlumberger (Andres Vincente Gomez)
V, S
original title: El Mono Loco

A screenwriter becomes involved with a young, incestuous brother and sister.

Ridiculous farrago of sex and drugs, devoid of sense and sensuality.

w Fernando Trueba, Manolo Matji novel The Dream of the Mad Monkey by Christopher Frank d Fernando Trueba ph Jose Luis Alcaine m Antoine Duhamel ad Pierre-Louis Thevenet ed Carmen Frias

Jeff Goldblum, Miranda Richardson, Anemone, Dexter Fletcher, Daniel Ceccaldi, Liza Walker, Jerome Natali, Arielle Dombasle, Micaela Sebastian

The Mad Monster

US 1942 77m bw
Sigmund Neufeld/PRC
V*

A mad scientist injects wolf blood into a man, who goes around at night killing people.

Inept and uncontrolled shocker, the kind of thing that gives horror films a bad name.

w Fred Myton d Sam Newfield

George Zucco, Johnny Downs, Glenn Strange, Anne Nagel

Mad Monster Party

US 1967 94m Eastmancolor Animagic
Embassy/Videocraft (Arthur Rankin Jnr)

Baron von Frankenstein invites Dracula, the Mummy, the Werewolf, the Hunchback of Notre Dame and other monsters to a party to celebrate his new invention.

A children's film that uses stop-motion animated figures, it is harmless but trivial entertainment.

w Len Korobkin, Harvey Kurtzman story Arthur Rankin Jnr d Jules Bass m Maury Laws m/ly Maury Laws, Jules Bass sp character design: Jack Davis

voices of Boris Karloff, Phyllis Diller, Alan Swift, Gale Garnett

The Mad Parade

US 1931 62m bw
Liberty/Paramount

A story told by women about the effect of the war on their sex.

Not really strong enough to be taken seriously, this was played as a novelty.

w Henry McCarthy and Frank R. Conkin story Gertrude Orr and Doris Malloy d William Beaudine

Evelyn Brent, Irene Rich, Louise Fazenda, Lilyan Tashman, Marceline Day

'Chances for disappointing business greater than the opposite.' – Variety

The Mad Room

US 1969 92m Berkeley Pathecolor
Columbia/Norman Mauer
V*

A companion kills her wealthy employer so that her mentally retarded brother and sister will have a home.

Tasteless remake of Ladies in Retirement, in the brutalized vein which audiences are supposed by producers to want. In modern dress and sharp locations, it succeeds only in being nauseating.

w Bernard Girard, A. Z. Martin d Bernard Girard ph Harry Stradling Jnr m Dave Grusin

Stella Stevens, Shelley Winters, Skip Ward, Carol Cole, Severn Darden

Mad Wednesday *

US 1947 77m bw
Howard Hughes
V*

A middle-aged book-keeper is sacked and goes on the town.

Woolly and unattractive farce which proved something of a disaster for all the talents concerned but historically is of considerable interest. It begins with an excerpt from *The Freshman* and continues to comic adventures with a lion.

wd/pd Preston Sturges (re-edited by others) *ph* Robert Pittack *m* Werner Richard Heymann

Harold Lloyd, Jimmy Conlin, Raymond Walburn, Franklin Pangborn, Al Bridge, Margaret Hamilton, Edgar Kennedy

Madam Satan *

US 1930 105m bw
MGM (C. B. de Mille)
V*

When her husband strays, a socialite disguises herself as a mysterious *femme fatale* and wins him back.

Abysmal comedy in which both director and principals appear frozen until the closing reels present a crazy, spectacular party on a dirigible which crashes but allows a happy ending.

w Jeanie Macpherson, Gladys Unger, Elsie Janis *d* C. B. de Mille *ph* Harold Rosson *m* Herbert Stothart *m/ly* Clifford Grey, Herbert Stothart, Elsie Janis, Jack King *ad* Cedric Gibbons, Mitchell Leisen *ed* Anne Bauchens

Kay Johnson, Reginald Denny, Lillian Roth, Roland Young

'A strange conglomeration of unreal incidents that are sometimes set forth with no little technical skill.' – *Mordaunt Hall, New York Times*

Madame: see *Madame Sans-Gêne* (1962)

'Whatever it is that French women have – Madame Bovary had more of it!'

Madame Bovary

US 1949 114m bw
MGM (Pandro S. Berman)
V*, L

A passionate girl marries a dull husband, takes a lover, and commits suicide.

Dull, emasculated version of a classic.

w Robert Ardrey *novel* Gustave Flaubert *d* Vincente Minnelli *ph* Robert Planck *m* Miklos Rozsa *ad* Cedric Gibbons, Jack Martin Smith

Jennifer Jones, Van Heflin, James Mason, Louis Jourdan, Christopher Kent, Gene Lockhart, Gladys Cooper, John Abbott, George Zucco

'If you hadn't read the book, you wouldn't guess what it was about from this film.' – *Pauline Kael, 70s*

† Previously filmed in 1932 as *Unholy Love*.

AAN: art direction

Madame Bovary

France 1991 120m colour
Arrow/MK2/CED/FR3 (Marin Karmitz)
V

A bored housewife with social pretensions, married to a doctor, indulges in self-destructive behaviour.

A reasonably faithful, but lifeless, adaptation, which seems as stultifying as the middle-class existence it portrays. *novel* Gustave Flaubert *d* Claude Chabrol *ph* Jean Rabier *m* Matthieu Chabrol *ad* Michèle Abbé *ed* Monique Fardoulis

Isabelle Huppert, Jean-François Balmer, Christophe Malavoy, Jean Yanne, Lucas Belvaux, Christiane Minazzoli

'Respectful, luxurious and eminently forgettable.' – *Sight and Sound*

'One of the world's magnificent romances of great, unselfish love!'

Madame Butterfly

US 1932 88m bw
Paramount (B. P. Schulberg)

A Japanese geisha commits hara kiri when an American lieutenant passes her up for a western girl.

Drearily modernized version of the opera without its music; an odd idea to say the least.

w Josephine Lovett, Joseph M. March *play* David Belasco, John Luther Long *d* Marion Gering *ph* David Abel *md* W. Franke Harling

Sylvia Sidney, Cary Grant, Charlie Ruggles, Sandor Kallay, Irving Pichel, Helen Jerome Eddy

'The long-drawn tragedy might be bearable if it were expressed in music or poetry, without any such embellishment it is apt to be painfully pathetic.' – *The Times*

'Travels slow and makes for only fair entertainment.' – *Variety*

'Mr and Mrs Miniver together again!'

Madame Curie *

US 1943 124m bw
MGM (Sidney Franklin)
V*, L

The life and marriage of the woman who discovered radium.

Dignified and rather dull biopic which well exemplifies MGM's best production style of the forties.

w Paul Osborn, Paul H. Rameau *book* Eve Curie *d* Mervyn Le Roy *ph* Joseph Ruttenberg *m* Herbert Stothart *ad* Cedric Gibbons, Paul Groesse

Greer Garson, Walter Pidgeon, Henry Travers, Albert Basserman, Robert Walker, C. Aubrey Smith, Dame May Whitty, Van Francen, Elsa Basserman, Reginald Owen, Van Johnson

'It achieves a notable triumph in making the discovery of a new element seem almost as glamorous as an encounter with Hedy Lamarr.' – *C. A. Lejeune*

AAN: best picture; Joseph Ruttenberg; Herbert Stothart; Greer Garson; Walter Pidgeon; art direction

Madame De *

France/Italy 1953 102m bw
Franco-London/Indus/Rizzoli
US title: *The Earrings of Madame de*

Tragic misunderstandings arise when a society wife sells her earrings and tells her husband she has lost them.

Elegant, rather heavy-handed but superbly glossy extension of a fashionable novelette.

w Marcel Achard, Max Ophuls, Annette Wademant *novel* Louise de Vilmorin *d* Max Ophuls *ph* Christian Matras *m* Oscar Straus, Georges Van Parys *ad* Jean d'Eaubonne

Charles Boyer, Danielle Darrieux, Vittorio de Sica, Lea di Lea, Jean Debucourt

Madame Dubarry **

Germany 1919 85m (24 fps) bw silent
Union-UFA
US title: *Passion*

The life and times of the glamorous courtesan of Louis XV.

Milestone silent film which introduced to the cinemas of America and Britain not only the subtleties of the European cinema but the more adaptable subtleties of a key director, here dealing rather heavy-handedly with material which he should later have re-used.

w Fred Orbing, Hans Kraly *d* Ernst Lubitsch *ph* Theodor Sparkuhl

Pola Negri, Emil Jannings, Harry Liedtke, Reinhold Schünzel

Madame Dubarry

US 1934 77m bw
Warner

The life of the legendary courtesan at Versailles.

Utterly unpersuasive but sometimes decorative historical charade.

w Edward Chodorov *d* William Dieterle

Dolores del Rio, Reginald Owen, Victor Jory, Anita Louise, Osgood Perkins, Verree Teasdale

'A lavish but not particularly distinguished production.' – *Variety*

Madame Pimpernel: see *Paris Underground*

Madame Racketeer

US 1932 68m bw
Paramount

Tactics of a middle-aged lady larcenist.

Light crime comedy drama, not bad but overlookable.

w Malcolm Stuart Boylan and Harvey Gates *d* Alexander Hall and Harry Wagstaff Gribble

Alison Skipworth, Richard Bennett, Evalyn Knapp, George Raft, Robert McWade

'The subtle high comedy that flows so gently through the script is likely to pass over the hats of the peasantry.' – *Variety*

Madame Rosa

France 1977 120m Eastmancolor
Lira Films
V*
original title: *La Vie Devant Soi*

An elderly Jewish prostitute runs an unofficial nursery school and cares especially for a fourteen-year-old Arab.

Splendidly acted but basically dreary fable twisted from a novel which took the child's point of view.

wd Moshe Mizrahi *novel* Emile Ajar

Simone Signoret, Claude Dauphin, Samy Ben Youb

AA: best foreign film

Madame Sans-Gêne

US 1925 110m (24 fps) bw silent
Paramount

During the French Revolution, Napoleon plays Cupid to a laundry-maid and her lover.

The story formed the basis of one of Gloria Swanson's last successes; but it was made in France and did not have the zip of her Hollywood productions.

w Forrest Halsey *d* Léonce Perret

Charles de Roche, Emile Drain

Madame Sans-Gêne

France/Italy/Spain 1962 100m Technirama
TCF/Cine Alliance/Gesi/Champion/Agata (Maleno Malenotti)
GB and US title: *Madame*

Historical romp based on an old theatrical warhorse.

Pretty stilted in this version; especially when dubbed.

w Henri Jeanson and others *play* Victorien Sardou *d* Christian-Jaque *ph* Roberto Gerardi *m* Francesco Lavagnino

Sophia Loren, Robert Hossein, Julien Bertheau, Marina Berti

Madame Sousatzka

GB 1988 122m Eastmancolor
Curzon/Sousatzka Productions (Robin Dalton)
V, V*, L, S

A piano teacher is reluctant to let go of her star pupil.

A parade of eccentrics is mixed with a little domestic drama, but it all remains inert and uninteresting.

w Ruth Prawer Jhabvala, John Schlesinger *novel* Bernice Rubens *d* John Schlesinger *ph* Nat Crosby *m* Gerald Gouriet *pd* Luciana Arrighi *ed* Peter Honess

Shirley MacLaine, Peggy Ashcroft, Twiggy, Shabana Azmi, Leigh Lawson, Geoffrey Bayldon, Lee Montague, Robert Rietty, Navin Chowdhry

'No amount of technical finesse, or polite musical trappings, can make the film seem other than an unswallowable, old-fashioned, overlong slab of confectionery.' – *Geoff Brown, MFB*

Madame Spy
US   1934   70m   bw
Universal

Russian and Austrian spies are married to each other.

Absurd melodrama which never gets a grip.

w William Hurlbut from a German film, *Under False Flags*   d Karl Freund

Fay Wray, Nils Asther, Edward Arnold, John Miljan, David Torrence

'Story too hopeless to mean money anywhere.' – *Variety*

Madame Spy
US   1942   63m   bw
Universal

A glamorous Nazi spy turns out to be an American secret agent.

Elementary espionage stuff without much in the way of plot development.

w Lynn Riggs and Clarence Upson Young   d Roy William Neill

Constance Bennett, Don Porter, John Litel, Edward Brophy, John Eldredge

Madame X *
US   1929   95m   bw
MGM
L
TV title: *Absinthe*

After an accidental death, a wealthy woman disappears and goes down in the world; at a subsequent murder trial she is defended by her unrecognizing son.

Two silent versions (with Dorothy Donnelly and Pauline Frederick) had been made of this old theatrical warhorse; two sound versions followed this one. The thing defies criticism.

w Willard Mack   play Alexandre Bisson   d Lionel Barrymore

Ruth Chatterton, Raymond Hackett, Mitchell Lewis, Sidney Toler, Carroll Nye, Lewis Stone, Richard Carle

'Works like this confound the reformers, elevate the name of pictures, and tell the world that there is an art in film making.' – *Variety*

AAN: Lionel Barrymore; Ruth Chatterton

Madame X *
US   1937   72m   bw
MGM (James K. McGuinness)

Competent remake with an excellent cast.

w John Meehan   d Sam Wood   ph John B. Seitz   m David Snell

Gladys George, John Beal, Warren William, Reginald Owen, Lynne Carver, Henry Daniell, Emma Dunn, Ruth Hussey, George Zucco

'An upper bracketer when played with a strong companion.' – *Variety*

'A fine old play, dated and outmoded. Audiences will leave the theatre expecting to find the coachman with horse and buggy.' – *Variety*

'One man drove her to it – one man tempted her – one man degraded her – one man defended her!'

Madame X
US   1965   100m   Technicolor
Universal/Ross Hunter/Eltee
V*

An elaborately dressed remake which suffered from a wooden lead; the more expensive the production, the more obvious the holes in the plot and the psychology.

w Jean Holloway   d David Lowell Rich   ph Russell Metty   m Frank Skinner

Lana Turner, John Forsythe, Ricardo Montalban, *Constance Bennett*, Burgess Meredith, Keir Dullea, Virginia Grey, Warren Stevens

'One is free to enjoy a luxurious wallow in emotions that are all the more enjoyable for having no connection whatever with reality.' – *Brenda Davies*

The Madcap Adventures of Mr Toad: see
Ichabod and Mr Toad

Das Mädchen Rosemarie: see *The Girl Rosemarie*

Made for Each Other *
US   1938   90m   bw
David O. Selznick
V*

Problems of a lawyer and his new wife culminate in the near-death of their infant son.

Smooth star tearjerker.

w Jo Swerling   d John Cromwell   ph Leon Shamroy   m Hugo Friedhofer, David Buttolph   theme Oscar Levant   pd William Cameron Menzies

Carole Lombard, James Stewart, Charles Coburn, Lucile Watson, Harry Davenport, Eddie Quillan, Esther Dale, Louise Beavers

'Made to order for strong box office.' – *Variety*

Made for Each Other *
US   1971   107m   DeLuxe
TCF/Wylde Films (Roy Townshend)

Romance between two New Yorkers with inferiority complexes.

Elongated cabaret sketch, a Brooklynesque comedy of flashy brilliance but limited general interest.

w Renée Taylor, Joe Bologna   d Robert B. Bean   ph William Storz

Renée Taylor, Joe Bologna

'At the sperm-bank, she asked for a tall, intelligent, black man. One out of three ain't bad.'

Made in America
US   1993   110m   Technicolor
Warner/Stonebridge/Kalola/Regency/Canal+ (Arnon Milchan, Michael Douglas, Rick Bieber)
V, V*, L, S

A black teenager, born by artificial insemination, discovers that her father is a white car-salesman with a crass manner.

An occasionally amusing comedy, owing more to the performances than the script, which skirts all the racial issues it raises to settle for a comforting situation comedy.

w Holly Goldberg Sloan   story Marcia Brandwynne, Nadine Schiff   d Richard Benjamin   ph Ralf Bode   m Mark Isham   pd Evelyn Sakash   ed Jacqueline Cambas

Whoopi Goldberg, Ted Danson, Will Smith, Nia Long, Paul Rodriguez, Jennifer Tilly, Peggy Rae, Clyde Kusatsu

'It's a likeable effort, good enough for a sultry summer evening at the multiplex when the film you came to see is sold out.' – *Sight and Sound*

Made in Heaven
GB   1952   81m   Technicolor
Fanfare/Rank

Married couples compete for the Dunmow Flitch.

Easy-going family comedy which aims to be liked.

w William Douglas Home   d John Paddy Carstairs

David Tomlinson, Petula Clark, Sonja Ziemann, A. E. Matthews, Charles Victor, Sophie Stewart, Richard Wattis, Athene Seyler

Made in Heaven
US   1987   103m   colour
Rudolph-Blocker/Lorimar (Raynold Gideon, Bruce A. Evans, David Blocker)
V*, L

A boy is sent back from heaven to find his lost love.

Droopy fantasy on the lines of *Here Comes Mr Jordan* but without the wit.

w Bruce A. Evans, Raynold Gideon   d Alan Rudolph   ph Jan Kiesser   m Mark Isham   pd Paul Peters   ed Tom Walls

Timothy Hutton, Kelly McGillis, Maureen Stapleton, Don Murray, Marj Dusay, Debra Winger (as Emmett, incognito)

Made on Broadway
US   1933   65m   bw
MGM
GB title: *The Girl I Made*

A public relations man deals with the mayor's dirty linen.

Flat and unconvincing political comedy drama.

w Gene Markey   book Public Relations by Courtney Terrett   d Harry Beaumont

Robert Montgomery, Sally Eilers, Madge Evans, Eugene Pallette, C. Henry Gordon, Jean Parker

Madeleine *
GB   1949   114m   bw
GFD/David Lean/Cineguild (Stanley Haynes)
V*

In Victorian Glasgow a well-to-do young woman is accused of murdering her lover, but the verdict is 'not proven'.

Dramatically dead because of its ambiguous ending, this lavish and good-looking treatment of a *cause célèbre* was a mistake for all concerned, but its incidental pleasures are considerable.

w Nicholas Phipps, Stanley Haynes   d David Lean   ph Guy Green   m William Alwyn   pd John Bryan   costumes Margaret Furse

Ann Todd, Leslie Banks, Elizabeth Sellars, Ivor Barnard, Ivan Desny, Norman Wooland, Edward Chapman, Barbara Everest, André Morell, Barry Jones, Jean Cadell, John Laurie, Eugene Deckers

Mademoiselle Docteur *
GB   1937   84m   bw
Grafton/Trafalgar (Max Schach)

A German lady spy falls for a British agent.

War melodrama vaguely based on fact and later remade as *Fräulein Doktor*.

w Jacques Natanson, Marcel Achard, Ernest Betts   d Edmond Greville   ph Otto Heller

Dita Parlo, John Loder, Erich von Stroheim, Claire Luce, Gyles Isham, Clifford Evans, John Abbott

Mademoiselle Fifi *
US   1944   69m   bw
RKO (Val Lewton)
V*, L

During the Franco-Prussian war a stagecoach is held up because a prostitute, despite the urging of her fellow passengers, refuses to sleep with a Prussian officer. When she gives in, they shun her, and she kills him.

Interesting low budget version of a story which inspired many films.

w Josef Mischel, Peter Ruric   stories Boule de Suif/ Mademoiselle Fifi by Guy de Maupassant   d Robert Wise   ph Harry Wild   m Werner Heymann

Simone Simon, Kurt Kreuger, John Emery, Alan Napier, Jason Robards Sr, Norma Varden, Helen Freeman, Fay Helm

'There is a gallant, fervent quality about the whole picture, faults and all, which gives it a peculiar kind of life and likeableness, and which signifies that there is one group of men working in Hollywood who have neither lost nor taken care to conceal the purity of their hope and intention.' – *James Agee*

Mademoiselle France: see *Reunion in France*

Madhouse *
GB   1974   92m   Eastmancolor
AIP/Amicus (Milton Subotsky)
V*

A reluctant horror actor makes a comeback and finds himself involved in a series of grisly murders.

In-jokey horror piece with clips from old AIP chillers; quite likeable.

w Greg Morrison   *novel Devilday* by Angus Hall
d Jim Clark   ph Ray Parslow   m Douglas Gamley

Vincent Price, Peter Cushing, Robert Quarry, Adrienne Corri, Natasha Pyne, Linda Hayden, Barry Dennen

Madhouse
US   1990   90m   colour
Rank/Orion/A Boy of the Year (Leslie Dixon)
V

Unwanted friends and neighbours move in as house guests of a young couple.

Remarkably unfunny domestic comedy, directed with a heavy hand.

wd Tom Ropelewski   ph Denis Lewiston
m David Newman   pd Dan Leigh   ed Michael Jablow

John Larroquette, Kirstie Alley, Alison LaPlaca, John Diehl, Jessica Lundy, Bradley Gregg, Dennis Miller, Robert Ginty, Wayne Tippit

Madigan *
US   1968   100m   Techniscope
Universal (Frank P. Rosenberg)
V*

A Brooklyn police detective brings in a dangerous escaped criminal at the cost of his own life.

Lively, well-characterized police thriller with excellent locations.

w Henri Simoun, Abraham Polonsky   *novel The Commissioner* by Richard Dougherty   d Don Siegel
ph Russell Metty   m Don Costa

Richard Widmark, Henry Fonda, Michael Dunn, Inger Stevens, Harry Guardino, James Whitmore, Susan Clark, Steve Ihnat, Don Stroud, Sheree North, Warren Stevens, Raymond St Jacques

† The character was later resurrected for a TV series also starring Richard Widmark.

Madison Avenue
US   1961   94m   bw   Cinemascope
TCF (Bruce Humberstone)

An advertising executive plans to revenge himself on his treacherous boss.

Predictable melodrama with an adequate plot but dismal acting and presentation.

w Norman Corwin   *novel The Build-Up Boys* by Jeremy Kirk   d Bruce Humberstone   ph Charles G. Clarke   m Harry Sukman

Dana Andrews, Jeanne Crain, Eleanor Parker, Eddie Albert, Howard St John, Henry Daniell, Kathleen Freeman

'Simply nowhere near grand enough.' – *MFB*

Madness of the Heart
GB   1949   105m   bw
GFD/Two Cities (Richard Wainwright)

A blind girl marries a French aristocrat and has to cope with a jealous neighbour.

Heavily disguised version of the *Rebecca* theme, with a happy ending after many alarums and excursions, most of them irrelevant. As film-making, very thin.

wd Charles Bennett   *novel* Flora Sandstrom
ph Desmond Dickinson   m Allan Gray

Margaret Lockwood, Paul Dupuis, Kathleen Byron, Maxwell Reed

Madonna of the Seven Moons
GB   1944   110m   bw
GFD/Gainsborough (R. J. Minney)
V

Affected by childhood rape, a demure lady has a second life as a daring gypsy.

Novelettish balderdash killed stone dead by stilted presentation; but highly successful in its day.

w Roland Pertwee, Brock Williams   *novel* Margery Lawrence   d Arthur Crabtree   ph Jack Cox

Phyllis Calvert, Stewart Granger, Patricia Roc, Peter Glenville, John Stuart, Jean Kent, Nancy Price, Peter Murray Hill, Reginald Tate

'One of the most diverting British films of the forties.' – *Richard Roud*

'The purplest production English cinema has yet achieved.' – *Time and Tide*

The Madonna's Secret
US   1946   79m   bw
Stephen Auer/Republic

Women attracted to a Parisian painter are all found dead.

Slow-moving mystery which manages to remain suspenseful.

w Bradbury Foote, William Thiele   d William Thiele

Francis Lederer, Gail Patrick, Ann Rutherford, Edward Ashley, Linda Stirling, John Litel

The Madwoman of Chaillot *
GB   1969   142m   Technicolor
Warner/Commonwealth United (Ely Landau)
V*, L

An eccentric Parisian lady has equally eccentric friends, but her real life is in the past.

A highly theatrical whimsy which somewhat lacks humour, this should never have been considered as a film, certainly not as an all-star extravaganza; but it was, and it falls flat on its face in the first reel of tedious conversation.

w Edward Anhalt   *play* Jean Giraudoux   d Bryan Forbes   ph Claude Renoir, Burnett Guffey
m Michael J. Lewis   pd Ray Simm

Katharine Hepburn, Yul Brynner, Danny Kaye, Edith Evans, Charles Boyer, Claude Dauphin, John Gavin, Paul Henreid, Nanette Newman, Oscar Homolka, Margaret Leighton, Giulietta Masina, Richard Chamberlain, Donald Pleasence, Fernand Gravet

'One finds oneself too often longing for the drop of the curtain.' – *Brenda Davies*

'The intentions are honourable – defeat is inevitable.' – *Rex Reed*

'One of Giraudoux's less good and most fragile plays has been rewritten, bloated with inept contemporary references, drawn out to gigantic proportions of humourless vacuity, and peopled with a barrelful of nonacting stars.' – *John Simon*

'The remnants of Giraudoux' slight, whimsical play can still be perceived in Edward Anhalt's vile modernization, and a lot of famous actors can be

recognized even in the performances they give here.' – *Pauline Kael, New Yorker*

Maedchen in Uniform *
Germany   1931   90m   bw
Deutsche Film-Gemeinschaft
V*
aka: *Girls in Uniform*

A girl at a strict boarding school falls in love with one of the teachers and commits suicide.

Famous early stab at lesbianism, remade in 1958 with Romy Schneider and Lilli Palmer. Interesting for content, not style.

w F. D. Andam, Christa Winsloe   *play Gestern und Heute* by Christa Winsloe   d Leontine Sagan
ph Reimar Kuntze   m Hansen Milde-Meissner

Dorothea Wieck, Ellen Schwannecke, Hertha Thiele, Emilie Lunde

'At once a strident warning against the consequences of Hitler's regime and the first truly radical lesbian film.' – *Time Out, 1981*

Il Maestro
Belgium/France   1989   92m   Fujicolor
Man's Films/Flach Film/RTBF/BTR (Marion Hänsel, François Lepetit)
aka: *The Maestro*

Returning to Italy to conduct *Madame Butterfly*, a Jewish conductor reveals a wartime betrayal that brings on a breakdown.

Small-scale, overstretched drama.

wd Marion Hänsel   *story La Giacca Verde* by Mario Soldati   ph Acacio de Almeida   m Frederick Devreese   ad Ernita Frigato, Antonello Geleng

Malcolm McDowell, Charles Aznavour, Andréa Ferréol, Francis Lemaire

El Maestro de Esgrima: see *The Fencing Master*

Il Maestro di Don Giovanni: see *Crossed Swords*

Maestro – Ma Non Troppo
French   1985   90m   colour
Antenne 2

A provincial orchestral conductor is kidnapped to prevent him from performing at a concert for world peace.

Farcical attempt at political satire.

w Christian Watton, Serge Korber   d Serge Korber
ph André Dumaître, Bernard Dumont   m Greco Casadesus   ed Claude Dufour

Alain Doutey, Sophie Barjac, Claude Villers, Joelle Guillaud, Jean Gaven, Jacques Spiesser, Jess Hahn, Clément Harari

The Maggie **
GB   1953   93m   bw
Ealing (Michael Truman)
US title: *High and Dry*

An American businessman is tricked into sending his private cargo to a Scottish island on an old puffer in need of repair.

Mildly amusing comedy about the wily Scots; not the studio at its best, but pretty fair.

w William Rose   d Alexander Mackendrick   ph Gordon Dines   m John Addison

Paul Douglas, *Alex Mackenzie*, James Copeland, Abe Barker, Dorothy Alison, Hubert Gregg, Geoffrey Keen, Andrew Keir, Tommy Kearins

Magic
US   1978   107m   Technicolor
TCF/Joseph E. Levine
V, V*, L

A ventriloquist obsessed by his dummy is impelled to murder.

Pretentious and occasionally unpleasant version of an oft-told tale.

w William Goldman   *novel* William Goldman
d Richard Attenborough   *ph* Victor J. Kemper
m Jerry Goldsmith   *pd* Terence Marsh

Anthony Hopkins, Ann-Margret, Burgess Meredith, Ed Lauter, E. J. Andre, David Ogden Stiers

'The gloomily withdrawn Hopkins has no vulgarity in his soul – nothing that suggests any connection with the world of entertainment – and the picture grinds along.' – *New Yorker*

The Magic Bow
GB   1946   106m   bw
GFD/Gainsborough (R. J. Minney)

Episodes in the life of the violin virtuoso Paganini.

Poor costumer, dramatically and historically unpersuasive.

w Norman Ginsbury, Roland Pertwee   *d* Bernard Knowles   *ph* Jack Cox   *violin solos* Yehudi Menuhin

Stewart Granger, Jean Kent, Phyllis Calvert, Dennis Price, Cecil Parker, Felix Aylmer, Frank Cellier, Marie Lohr, Henry Edwards

The Magic Box *
GB   1951   118m   Technicolor
Festival Films (Ronald Neame)
V

The life of William Friese-Greene, a British cinema pioneer who died in poverty.

A joint British film industry venture to celebrate the Festival of Britain, this rather downbeat and uneventful story takes on the nature of a pageant or a series of charades, with well-known people appearing to no good purpose. But it means well.

w Eric Ambler   *d* John Boulting   *ph* Jack Cardiff
m William Alwyn   *pd* John Bryan

Robert Donat, Margaret Johnson, Maria Schell, John Howard Davies, Renée Asherson, Richard Attenborough, Robert Beatty, Michael Denison, Leo Genn, Marius Goring, Joyce Grenfell, Robertson Hare, Kathleen Harrison, Jack Hulbert, Stanley Holloway, Glynis Johns, Mervyn Johns, Barry Jones, Miles Malleson, Muir Mathieson, A. E. Matthews, John McCallum, Bernard Miles, Laurence Olivier, Cecil Parker, Eric Portman, Dennis Price, Michael Redgrave, Margaret Rutherford, Ronald Shiner, Sybil Thorndike, David Tomlinson, Cecil Trouncer, Peter Ustinov, Kay Walsh, Emlyn Williams, Harcourt Williams, Googie Withers

'An honest and often a very moving film.' – *Daily Express*

'Patriotic, sentimental, overlong and faintly embarrassing.' – *Time Out, 1984*

The Magic Carpet
US   1951   84m   Supercinecolor
Sam Katzman/Columbia

The caliph's son returns as the Scarlet Falcon to rout the usurper.

Hopeless kid's matinée rubbish, not even performed with verve.

w David Matthews   *d* Lew Landers

Lucille Ball, Raymond Burr, John Agar, Patricia Medina, George Tobias

The Magic Christian
GB   1969   95m   Technicolor
Commonwealth United/Grand Films (Dennis O'Dell)
V, V*, L

An eccentric millionaire spends his wealth deflating those who pursue money or power.

A series of variably funny but always unpleasant sketches, climaxing with citizens delving for spoils in a vat of blood and manure. In its aim to be satirical, very typical of its time.

w Terry Southern, Joseph McGrath, Peter Sellers
novel Terry Southern   *d* Joseph McGrath
ph Geoffrey Unsworth   *m* Ken Thorne
pd Assheton Gorton

Peter Sellers, Ringo Starr, Richard Attenborough, Laurence Harvey, Christopher Lee, Spike Milligan, Yul Brynner, Roman Polanski, Raquel Welch, Wilfrid Hyde-White, Fred Emney, John Le Mesurier, Dennis Price, Patrick Cargill, John Cleese, Graham Chapman

The Magic Face
US   1951   90m   bw
Columbia (Mort Briskin, Robert Smith)

A brilliant German impersonator kills Hitler, takes his place, and leads Germany deliberately into defeat.

Hilariously unlikely anecdote 'as told to William Shirer', performed with vigour but handicapped by a shoddy production.

w Mort Briskin, Robert Smith   *d* Frank Tuttle
ph Tony Braun   *m* Herschel Burke Gilbert

Luther Adler, Patricia Knight, Ilka Windish, William L. Shirer

'If Shirer believed this story, then he must be the only person in the world to do so.' – *Gavin Lambert*

Magic Fire
US   1954   94m   Trucolor
Republic (William Dieterle)

The life and loves of Richard Wagner.

Remarkably boring biopic with much music but little story or characterization. Ugly colour minimizes German locations.

w Bertita Harding, E. A. Dupont, David Chantler
d William Dieterle   *ph* Ernest Haller   *md* Erich Wolfgang Korngold

Alan Badel, Yvonne de Carlo, Peter Cushing, Frederick Valk, Carlos Thompson, Valentina Cortesa

Magic Night: see *Goodnight Vienna*

The Magic of Lassie
US   1978   99m   colour
Lassie Productions (Bonita Granville Wrather, William Beaudine)

A collie dog is sold but makes its way back home.

Downright peculiar revamp of *Lassie Come Home* with music and an ageing all-star cast.

w Jean Holloway, Richard B. Sherman, Robert M. Sherman   *d* Don Chaffey   *m* Irwin Kostal
songs Richard and Robert Sherman

James Stewart, Alice Faye, Mickey Rooney, Pernell Roberts, Stephanie Zimbalist, Gene Evans

AAN: song 'When You're Loved'

The Magic Sword
US   1962   80m   Eastmancolor
UA/Bert I. Gordon
V*

The son of a well-meaning witch rescues a princess from the clutches of an evil sorcerer.

Shaky medieval fantasy on too low a budget.

w Bernard Schoenfeld   *d* Bert I. Gordon   *ph* Paul Vogel   *m* Richard Markowitz   *sp* Milt Rice

Basil Rathbone, Estelle Winwood, Gary Lockwood, Anne Helm

'The guy with the dynamite heart meets the girl with the firecracker eyes!'

Magic Town
US   1947   103m   bw
Robert Riskin Productions
V*, L

An opinion pollster discovers a small town which exactly mirrors the views of the USA at large.

A bright Capraesque idea is extraordinarily dully scripted, the production looks dim, and all concerned are operating one degree under.

w Robert Riskin   *d* William A. Wellman
ph Joseph Biroc   *m* Roy Webb

James Stewart, Jane Wyman, Kent Smith, Regis Toomey, Donald Meek, Ned Sparks, Wallace Ford

The Magic Toyshop *
GB   1986   107m   colour
Granada (Steve Morrison)

Three children are left in the care of their uncle, a puppet-maker.

Weird, sometimes grotesque fantasy focusing on an adolescent girl's sexual awakening.

w Angela Carter   *novel* Angela Carter   *d* David Wheatley   *ph* Ken Morgan   *m* Bill Connor
pd Stephen Fineren   *ed* Anthony Ham

Tom Bell, Caroline Milmoe, Kilian McKenna

The Magician *
US   1926   approx 80m   bw   silent
MGM

A dabbler in the occult comes to grief when he tries to influence a young girl.

A melodrama with interesting credits; unfortunately no prints remain.   *novel* Somerset Maugham
d Rex Ingram

Paul Wegener, Ivan Petrovitch, Alice Terry

The Magician (1958): see: see *The Face*

The Magician of Lublin
West Germany/Israel   1979   114m   colour
Geria-Golan-Globus (Harry N. Blum)

In 1901 an itinerant magician with an active sex life dreams of being able really to fly.

Curious muddled fable with apparent correspondences to the Christ story, like Bergman's *The Face*. In the end it does not confidently address itself to any audience, despite clever moments.

w Irving S. White, Menahem Golan   *novel* Isaac Bashevis Singer   *d* Menahem Golan   *ph* David Gurfinkel   *m* Maurice Jarre   *pd* Jürgen Kiebach

Alan Arkin, Louise Fletcher, Valerie Perrine, Shelley Winters, Lou Jacobi, Warren Berlinger

'California Polish accents grapple with hamfisted direction and a script of surpassing banality.' – *Sight and Sound*

The Magnet
GB   1950   79m   bw
Ealing (Sidney Cole)

A small boy steals a magnet and accidentally becomes a hero.

Very mild Ealing comedy, not really up to snuff.

w T. E. B. Clarke   *d* Charles Frend   *ph* Lionel Banes   *m* William Alwyn

Stephen Murray, Kay Walsh, William Fox, Meredith Edwards, Gladys Henson, Thora Hird, Wylie Watson

The Magnetic Monster *
US   1953   75m   bw
UA/Ivan Tors

A new radio-active element causes 'implosions' of increasing size by drawing energy from the area around it.

Well-told low-budget sci-fi with the audience kept abreast of all developments; the undersea lab scenes are borrowed from an old German film, *Gold*.

w Curt Siodmak, Ivan Tors   d Curt Siodmak
ph Charles Van Enger   m Blaine Sanford
pd George Van Marter

Richard Carlson, King Donovan, Jean Byron, Byron Foulger

'A crackling mixture of science and fiction.' – Time

'Real life screened more daringly than it's ever been before!'
The Magnificent Ambersons ****
US   1942   88m   bw
RKO/Mercury (Orson Welles)
V*, L, S

A proud family loses its wealth and its control of the neighbourhood, and its youngest male member gets his come-uppance.

Fascinating period drama told in brilliant cinematic snippets; owing to studio interference the last reels are weak, but the whole is a treat for connoisseurs, and a delight in its fast-moving control of cinematic narrative.

wd Orson Welles,   novel Booth Tarkington   ph Stanley Cortez   m Bernard Herrmann   ad Mark-Lee Kirk   ed Robert Wise, Mark Robson

Joseph Cotten, Dolores Costello, Agnes Moorehead, Tim Holt, Anne Baxter, Ray Collins, Richard Bennett, Erskine Sanford, Donald Dillaway

NARRATOR (Welles): 'And now Major Amberson was engaged in the profoundest thinking of his life, and he realized that everything which had worried him or delighted him during his lifetime – all his buying and building and trading and banking – that it was all a trifle and a waste beside what concerned him now, for the Major knew now that he had to plan how to enter an unknown country where he was not even sure of being recognized as an Amberson.'
NARRATOR: 'Something had happened. A thing which years ago had been the eagerest hope of many, many good citizens of the town. And now it had come at last: George Amberson Minafer had got his come-uppance. He got it three times filled and running over. But those who had so longed for it were not there to see it, and they never knew it. Those who were still living had forgotten all about it and all about him.'

'Rich in ideas that many will want to copy, combined in the service of a story that few will care to imitate.' – C. A. Lejeune

'Nearly every scene is played with a casual perfection which could only come from endless painstaking planning and rehearsals, and from a wonderful sense of timing.' – Basil Wright, 1972

'Even in this truncated form it's amazing and memorable.' – Pauline Kael, 70s

† Previously filmed in 1925 as Pampered Youth.

† The credits are all at the end and all spoken, ending with: 'I wrote and directed the picture. My name is Orson Welles.'

AAN: best picture; Stanley Cortez; Agnes Moorehead

The Magnificent Brute
US   1936   77m   bw
Universal

A blast furnace boss becomes involved with stolen money.

Star character drama; very predictable.

w Owen Francis, Lewis J. Foster and Bertram Millhauser   d John G. Blystone   ad Albert S. Agostino, Jack Otterson

Victor McLaglen, Binnie Barnes, Billy Burrud, William Hall, Jean Dixon

AAN: art direction

'The whisper of every woman – the toast of every man!'
Magnificent Doll
US   1946   95m   bw
Universal/Hallmark (Jack H. Skirball, Bruce Manning)

Dolly Madison, wife of the President, finds that traitor Aaron Burr is a memory from her own past.

Uneasy historical semi-fiction, badly cast and rather boring, yet with some sense of period style.

w Irving Stone   d Frank Borzage   ph Joseph Valentine   m Hans Salter

Ginger Rogers, David Niven, Burgess Meredith, Stephen McNally, Peggy Wood, Robert Barrat

'No duller case has ever been made out for liberty.' – Daily Mail

'Some day the moviemakers will discover that they can make history wonderfully believable and exciting by just sticking roughly to the facts.' – The Times

The Magnificent Dope
US   1942   83m   bw
TCF (William Perlberg)
V*

As a publicity stunt a success school brings the nation's most complete failure to New York, and he outsmarts them all.

Dim sub-Capra comedy.

w George Seaton   d Walter Lang   ph Peverell Marley   md Emil Newman   m David Raksin and others

Henry Fonda, Lynn Bari, Don Ameche, Edward Everett Horton, George Barbier, Frank Orth, Hobart Cavanaugh

The Magnificent Fraud
US   1939   78m   bw
Paramount

The president of a Latin American republic is murdered, and an impersonator takes his place.

Sharply played dramatic hokum.

w Gilbert Gabriel and Walter Ferris   d Robert Florey

Akim Tamiroff, Lloyd Nolan, Patricia Morison, Mary Boland

'Dull drama; no marquee names; filler fodder for duals.' – Variety

The Magnificent Matador
US   1955   94m   Eastmancolor   Cinemascope
Edward L. Alperson
V*
GB title: The Brave and the Beautiful

A matador trains his illegitimate son to follow in his footsteps but has a premonition of his death in the ring.

Dreary bullfighting drama with romantic interludes.

w Charles Lang   d Budd Boetticher   ph Lucien Ballard   m Raoul Kraushaar

Anthony Quinn, Maureen O'Hara, Manuel Rojas, Richard Denning, Thomas Gomez, Lola Albright

Magnificent Obsession **
US   1935   112m   bw
Universal (John M. Stahl)

The playboy who is half-responsible for the death of a woman's husband and for her own blindness becomes a surgeon and cures her.

Absurd soaper which was phenomenally popular and is certainly well done.

w George O'Neil, Sarah Y. Mason, Victor Heerman   novel Lloyd C. Douglas   d John M. Stahl   ph John Mescall   m Franz Waxman

Irene Dunne, Robert Taylor, Ralph Morgan, Sara Haden, Charles Butterworth, Betty Furness, Arthur Hoyt, Gilbert Emery, Arthur Treacher

'Capital romance, a cinch for the femme trade.' – Variety

Magnificent Obsession **
US   1954   108m   Technicolor
Universal (Ross Hunter)
V*

Glossy remake which sent Ross Hunter to the commercial heights as a remaker of thirties weepies.

This one worked best.

w Robert Blees   d Douglas Sirk   ph Russell Metty   m Frank Skinner

Jane Wyman, Rock Hudson, Agnes Moorehead, Barbara Rush, Otto Kruger, Gregg Palmer, Paul Cavanagh, Sara Shane

AAN: Jane Wyman

The Magnificent Rebel
US   1960   94m   Technicolor
Walt Disney (Peter V. Herald)

Episodes in the life of the young Beethoven.

Solid Disney biopic, shot in Vienna with good period detail.

w Joanne Court   d Georg Tressler   ph Göran Strindberg   md Frederick Stark

Karl Boehm, Ernst Nadhering, Ivan Desny, Gabriele Porks

'They were seven – and they fought like seven hundred!'
The Magnificent Seven **
US   1960   138m   DeLuxe   Panavision
UA/Mirisch-Alpha (John Sturges)
V, V*, L

A Mexican village hires seven American gunmen for protection against bandits.

Popular Western based on the Japanese Seven Samurai; good action scenes, but the rest is verbose and often pretentious.

w William Roberts   d John Sturges   ph Charles Lang Jnr   m Elmer Bernstein

Yul Brynner, Steve McQueen, Robert Vaughn, James Coburn, Charles Bronson, Horst Buchholz, Eli Wallach, Brad Dexter, Vladimir Sokoloff, Rosenda Monteros

AAN: Elmer Bernstein

The Magnificent Seven Deadly Sins
GB   1971   107m   colour
Tigon (Graham Stark)
V

Compendium of comedy sketches, a very variable ragbag of old jokes.

w Bob Larbey, John Esmonde, Dave Freeman, Barry Cryer, Graham Chapman, Graham Stark, Marty Feldman, Alan Simpson, Ray Galton, Spike Milligan   d Graham Stark   ph Harvey Harrison Jnr   m Roy Budd

Bruce Forsyth, Joan Sims, Roy Hudd, Harry Secombe, Leslie Phillips, Julie Ege, Harry H. Corbett, Ian Carmichael, Alfie Bass, Spike Milligan, Ronald Fraser

The Magnificent Seven Ride
US   1972   100m   DeLuxe
UA/Mirisch (William A. Calihan)

Tired finale to a patchy series (Return of the Seven, Guns of the Magnificent Seven) in which the original leader returns to save a Mexican village once again from bandits.

Very modest.

w Arthur Rowe   d George McCowan   ph Fred Koenekamp   m Elmer Bernstein

Lee Van Cleef, Stefanie Powers, Mariette Hartley, Pedro Armendariz Jnr, Luke Askew

The Magnificent Showman: see Circus World

The Magnificent Two
GB   1967   100m   Eastmancolor
Rank (Hugh Stewart)

One of two incompetent travelling salesmen in a Latin American banana republic is persuaded to pose as a dead rebel leader.

More or less a Bob Hope vehicle, adapted for the less realistic Morecambe and Wise with unhappy results: too few sight gags and a curious emphasis on violence. The third and last of their attempts to find film vehicles.

w S. C. Green, R. M. Hills, Michael Pertwee, Peter Blackmore d Cliff Owen ph Ernest Steward m Ron Goodwin

Eric Morecambe, Ernie Wise, Margit Saad, Cecil Parker, Virgilio Texeira, Isobel Black, Martin Benson

The Magnificent Yankee *
US   1950   88m   bw
MGM (Armand Deutsch)
GB title: *The Man with Thirty Sons*

Episodes in the later life of Judge Oliver Wendell Holmes.

Vaguely well-meaning biopic without much dramatic sense.

w Emmet Lavery play Emmet Lavery d John Sturges ph Joseph Ruttenberg m David Raskin

Louis Calhern, Ann Harding, Eduard Franz, Philip Ober, Richard Anderson, Edith Evanson

AAN: Louis Calhern

Magnum Force
US   1973   124m   Technicolor   Panavision
Warner/Malpaso (Robert Daley)
V, V*, L

Inspector Harry Callahan has to track down his partner who is slaughtering gangsters in cold blood.

Toned-down sequel to *Dirty Harry;* the violence is still there but the hero no longer commits it.

w John Milius, Michael Cimino d Ted Post ph Frank Stanley m Lalo Schifrin

Clint Eastwood, Hal Holbrook, Mitch Ryan, Felton Perry, David Soul

'A ragbag of western mythology and head-on thuggery.' – *Sight and Sound*

The Magus
GB   1968   116m   DeLuxe   Panavision
TCF/Blazer (John Kohn, Jud Kinberg)

An English schoolmaster on a Greek island is influenced by the local magician.

Fashionable philosophical nonsense, an elaborate mystery with no solution; the kind of film that all concerned begin to wish they had never thought of, especially as the presentation has nothing like the panache required, so that not even the critics liked it.

w John Fowles novel John Fowles d Guy Green ph Billy Williams m Johnny Dankworth pd Don Ashton

Michael Caine, Anthony Quinn, Candice Bergen, Anna Karina, Paul Stassino, Julian Glover, George Pastell

'Faintly ludicrous some of the time and painfully unexciting all of the time.' – *MFB*

'This may not be the most misguided movie ever made, but it's in there pitching.' – *Rex Reed*

'There's enough incoherence pretending to be enigma, sex play and chat about existentialism and self-discovery to make teenagers think they're having an experience; for grown-ups it's an ordeal.' – *Judith Crist*

'It has much of the fascination of a Chinese puzzle, but it would have been infinitely more enthralling if it hadn't been quite so flatly acted and directed.' – *Michael Billington, Illustrated London News*

'Probably the only movie in which one will ever see a copy of Empson's Seven Types of Ambiguity.' – *Pauline Kael, New Yorker*

The Mahabharata *
France   1989   171m   colour
Virgin/Les Productions du 3ème Etage (Michel Propper)

A boy listens to the story of a great war between competing tribes.

The vast Indian epic poem of 100,000 couplets in this condensed cinematic form results in a complex incident-crammed narrative, in which the significance of specific events can be hard to comprehend.

w Peter Brook, Jean-Claude Carrière, Marie-Hélène Estienne play Jean-Claude Carrière d Peter Brook ph William Lubtchansky m Toshi Tsuchitori, Djamchid Cherirani, Kudsi Erguner, Kim Menzer, Mahmoud Tabrizi-Zadeh pd Chloe Oboloensky ed Nicholas Gaster

Urs Biher, Ryszard Cieslak, Georges Carraface, Mamadou Dioumé, Miriam Goldschmidt, Jeffrey Kissoon, Sotigui Kouyate, Tuncel Kurtiz, Robert Langdon Lloyd

Mahanagar: see *The Big City* (1963)

Mahler *
GB   1974   115m   Technicolor
Goodtimes Enterprises (Roy Baird)
V, V*

Fantasia on the life and times of the Jewish composer.

Fairly successful Ken Russell musical biopic on the lines of his early BBC specials. wd Ken Russell ph Dick Bush

Robert Powell, Georgina Hale, Richard Morant, Lee Montague, Rosalie Crutchley, Benny Lee, David Collings

'A piece of movie making that sets my pulses racing.' – *Michael Billington, Illustrated London News*

'Whether the title of the opus happens to be *Strauss* or *Tchaikovsky* or *Elgar* or *Brubeck,* the real title is always Russell.' – *Benny Green, Punch*

Mahogany
US   1975   109m   colour   Panavision
Paramount/Nikor (Rob Cohen, Jack Ballard)
V*, L

The love life of a model and fashion designer.

Virtually a Joan Crawford vehicle redesigned for a black heroine who creates her own clothes. Fairly hilarious.

w John Byrum d Berry Gordy ph David Watkin m Michael Masser ly Gerry Goffin

Diana Ross, Billy Dee Williams, Anthony Perkins, Jean-Pierre Aumont, Nina Foch, Beah Richards, Marisa Mell

'The level of silliness rises steadily.' – *Geoff Brown*

'Movies as frantically bad as Mahogany can be enjoyed on at least one level; the spectacle of a lot of people making fools of themselves.' – *Time*

'What *Mahogany* does so fascinatingly and sometimes hilariously is to pilfer certain stock clichés of 50's Hollywood and adapt them to a black milieu.' – *Molly Haskell*

AAN: song 'Do You Know Where You're Going To?' (m Michael Masser, ly Gerry Goffin)

'Love so glorious it was denounced as sin!'
Maid of Salem *
US   1937   86m   bw
Paramount (Frank Lloyd)

In 1692 Salem, a young girl is accused of witchcraft but saved by her lover.

Remarkably solemn period melodrama, unfortunately betrayed by amiable but miscast leads.

w Bradley King, Walter Ferris, Durward Grinstead d Frank Lloyd ph Leo Tover m Victor Young

Claudette Colbert, Fred MacMurray, Harvey Stephens, Gale Sondergaard, Louise Dresser, Edward Ellis, Beulah Bondi, Bonita Granville

'Weak and slow saga of witchcraft: stars the only hope.' – *Variety*

'Once the panic of witchcraft starts you are carried along on a vicious crescendo of madness and terror.' – *Stage*

Maid to Order
US   1987   96m   DeLuxe
Vista/New Century (Herb Jaffe, Mort Engelberg)
V, V*, L

A spoiled rich girl takes work as a maid but finds she has a fairy godmother.

Weird semi-fantasy which wasn't wanted in the 80s, Cinderella being out of fashion. wd Amy Jones (co-writers Perry and Randy Howze) ph Shelly Johnson m Georges Delerue pd Jeffrey Townsend ed Sidney Wolinski

Ally Sheedy, Michael Ontkean, Beverly D'Angelo, Valerie Perrine, Dick Shawn, Tom Skerritt

Maiden Voyage: see *Bridal Suite*

The Maids
GB   1974   95m   Technicolor
Ely Landau/Cinevision
V*

Two Paris maids evolve a sado-masochistic ritual involving the death of their employer, but never go through with it.

Unbalanced and dreary film version of an essentially theatrical play.

w Robert Enders, Christopher Miles play Jean Genet d Christopher Miles ph Douglas Slocombe m Laurie Johnson

Glenda Jackson, Susannah York, Vivien Merchant, Mark Burns

'In view of the huge technical, stylistic and even metaphysical difficulties, I think it succeeds very well.' – *Stanley Kauffmann*

Maid's Night Out
US   1937   65m   bw
RKO

A wealthy girl falls for the milkman, who is really a rich man who thinks she's the maid.

Skittish second-feature comedy which helped to build a new star.

w Bert Granet d Ben Holmes

Joan Fontaine, Allan Lane, Billy Gilbert, Cecil Kellaway, Hedda Hopper

Maigret Sets a Trap *
France/Italy   1957   119m   bw
Intermondia/J. P. Guibert/Jolly Film

Maigret sets a policewoman as decoy for a knife murderer . . .

Probably the best Maigret film, with excellent Parisian atmosphere and excellent acting.

w Michel Audiard, novel Georges Simenon d Jean Delannoy ph Louis Page m Paul Misraki ad René Renoux

Jean Gabin, Annie Girardot, Jean Desailly, Oliver Hussenot, Alfred Adam, Lino Ventura

'It is puzzling, it is intermittently exciting, it is not offensive to a modest intelligence, not at any rate a modest intelligence used to crime stories.' – *Dilys Powell*

Mail Order Bride
US   1963   83m   Metrocolor   Panavision
MGM (Richard E. Lyons)
GB title: *West of Montana*

An old Westerner tries to find a bride for a wild young man in his charge.

Mild Western comedy drama; quite tolerable.

wd Burt Kennedy *ph* Paul C. Vogel *m* George Bassman

Buddy Ebsen, Lois Nettleton, Keir Dullea, Warren Oates, Marie Windsor

Mail Train: see *Inspector Hornleigh Goes To It*

The Main Attraction
GB 1962 90m Metrocolor
Seven Arts (John Patrick)

A wandering singer causes emotional problems backstage at a circus.

Limp melodrama with the star miscast as a fatal charmer.

w John Patrick *d* Daniel Petrie *ph* Geoffrey Unsworth *m* Andrew Adorian

Pat Boone, Mai Zetterling, Nancy Kwan, Yvonne Mitchell, John Le Mesurier

The Main Event
US 1979 112m Technicolor
Warner/First Artists/Barwood (Jon Peters, Barbra Streisand)
V, V*, L, S

A lady entrepreneur takes on a prizefighter.

Thin and very patchy comedy for confirmed addicts of its star.

w Gail Parent, Andrew Smith *d* Howard Zieff *ph* Mario Tosi *m* Michael Melvoin *pd* Charles Rosen

Barbra Streisand, Ryan O'Neal, Paul Sand, Whitman Mayo, James Gregory

Main Street: see *I Married a Doctor*

Main Street After Dark
US 1944 57m bw
Jerry Bresler/MGM

The police launch an assault on con men and petty thieves preying on returning ex-servicemen.

Watchable crime filler.

w Karl Kamb, John C. Higgins *d* Edward L. Cahn

Edward Arnold, Selena Royle, Tom Trout, Audrey Totter, Dan Duryea, Hume Cronyn

Main Street to Broadway *
US 1953 102m bw
Lester Cowan Productions
V*

After several reverses a young playwright sees his work through to a Broadway opening night; it fails, but he has learned several lessons.

Curious, flat attempt to show the public how Broadway works, with big stars playing themselves in cameo roles.

w Samson Raphaelson *d* Tay Garnett *ph* James Wong Howe

Tom Morton, Mary Murphy, Ethel Barrymore, Lionel Barrymore, Shirley Booth, Rex Harrison, Lilli Palmer, Helen Hayes, Henry Fonda, Tallulah Bankhead, Mary Martin, Louis Calhern, John Van Druten, Cornel Wilde, Joshua Logan, Agnes Moorehead, Gertrude Berg

Les Mains Sales
France 1951 103m bw
Fernand Rivers
aka: *Dirty Hands*

A young communist intellectual, required to kill a traitor, finds he can do so only when he suspects the man of making love to his wife.

Verbose and dull version of a play which had some international success as *Crime Passionel.*

wd Fernand Rivers *play* Jean-Paul Sartre *ph* Jean Bachelet

Pierre Brasseur, Daniel Gélin, Claude Nollier

Maisie
US 1939 74m bw
MGM (J. Walter Ruben)

Adventures of a Brooklyn showgirl.

Acceptable programmer which led to a series, all quite watchable and absolutely forgettable.

w Mary McCall Jnr *novel Dark Dame* by Wilson Collison *d* Edwin L. Marin *ph* Leonard Smith

Ann Sothern, Robert Young, Ian Hunter, Ruth Hussey, Anthony Allan (John Hubbard), Cliff Edwards

The succeeding titles, mostly written by Mary McCall and directed by Marin or Harry Beaumont or Roy del Ruth, were:

1940: CONGO MAISIE (with John Carroll; a remake of RED DUST), GOLD RUSH MAISIE (with Lee Bowman), MAISIE WAS A LADY (with Lew Ayres, Maureen O'Sullivan)
1941: RINGSIDE MAISIE (with George Murphy; GB title CASH AND CARRY)
1942: MAISIE GETS HER MAN (with Red Skelton; GB title SHE GOT HER MAN)
1943: SWING SHIFT MAISIE (with James Craig; GB title THE GIRL IN OVERALLS)
1944: MAISIE GOES TO RENO (with John Hodiak; GB title YOU CAN'T DO THAT TO ME)
1946: UP GOES MAISIE (with George Murphy; GB title UP SHE GOES)
1947: UNDERCOVER MAISIE (with Barry Nelson; GB title UNDERCOVER GIRL)

La Maison de Jeanne: see *Jeanne's House*

Le Maître de Musique: see *The Music Teacher*

'Is she a kid – or is she kidding?'
The Major and the Minor **
US 1942 100m bw
Paramount (Arthur Hornblow Jnr)

A girl poses as a child in order to travel half fare on a train, and is helped by an officer who falls for her.

Moderately smart comedy showing the writer-director's emergent style. Remade as *You're Never Too Young* (qv).

w Charles Brackett, Billy Wilder *d* Billy Wilder *ph* Leo Tover *m* Robert Emmett Dolan

Ginger Rogers, Ray Milland, Rita Johnson, Robert Benchley, Diana Lynn, Edward Fielding, Frankie Thomas, Charles Smith

OSBORNE (Robert Benchley): 'Why don't you get out of that wet coat and into a dry martini?'

'The script seems to have been concocted after the title.' – *New Yorker, 1977*

Major Barbara ***
GB 1941 121m bw
Gabriel Pascal
V*

The daughter of an armaments millionaire joins the Salvation Army but resigns when it accepts her father's donation.

Stagey but compulsive version of a play in which the author takes typical side swipes at anything and everything within reach, allowing for some gorgeous acting (and overacting) by an impeccable cast.

w Anatole de Grunwald, Gabriel Pascal *play Bernard Shaw* *d* Gabriel Pascal, Harold French, David Lean *ph* Ronald Neame *m* William Walton *ad* Vincent Korda, John Bryan *ed* Charles Frend *costumes* Cecil Beaton

Wendy Hiller, Rex Harrison, Robert Morley, Robert Newton, Marie Lohr, Emlyn Williams, Sybil Thorndike, Deborah Kerr, David Tree, Felix Aylmer, Penelope

Dudley Ward, Walter Hudd, Marie Ault, Donald Calthrop

'Shaw's ebullience provides an unslackening fount of energy . . . his all-star cast of characters are outspoken as no one else is in films except the Marx Brothers.' – *William Whitebait*

'To call it a manifest triumph would be an arrant stinginess with words.' – *New York Times*

Major Dundee *
US 1965 134m Eastmancolor Panavision
Columbia (Jerry Bresler)
V*

A small group of men from a US cavalry post sets out to annihilate marauding Indians.

Large-scale, rough-and-ready Western which rambles along in humourless vein but rises to some spectacularly bloodthirsty climaxes.

w Harry Julian Fink, Oscar Saul, Sam Peckinpah *d* Sam Peckinpah *ph* Sam Leavitt *m* Daniele Amfitheatrof

Charlton Heston, Richard Harris, Jim Hutton, James Coburn, Michael Anderson Jnr, Warren Oates, Senta Berger, Slim Pickens

Major League
US 1989 106m Technicolor
Braveworld/Fox (Mark Rosenberg)
V, V*, L, S

A hopeless baseball team turn winners when they learn their owner wants them to lose.

Broad and often tasteless comedy, too predictable to be funny.

wd David S. Ward *ph* Reynaldo Villalobos *m* James Newton Howard *pd* Jeffrey Howard *ed* Dennis M. Hill, Tony Lombardo

Tom Berenger, Charlie Sheen, Corbin Bernsen, Margaret Whitton, James Gammon, Rene Russo, Wesley Snipes, Charles Cyphers

A Majority of One
US 1961 156m Technicolor
Warner (Mervyn Le Roy)

A Jewish widow has a shipboard romance with a Japanese businessman.

Interminable stage-bound comedy-drama, boringly assembled and fatally compromised by the casting of stars who are neither Jewish nor Japanese.

w Leonard Spigelgass *play* Leonard Spigelgass *d* Mervyn Le Roy *ph* Harry Stradling *m* Max Steiner

Rosalind Russell, Alec Guinness, Ray Danton, Madlyn Rhue

AAN: Harry Stradling

Make a Wish
US 1937 75m bw
(RKO) Sol Lesser
V*

A composer discovers a boy singer at a summer camp.

Acceptable family entertainment.

w Gertrude Berg, Bernard Schubert, Earle Snell *d* Kurt Neumann *ph* John Mescall *songs* Oscar Straus *m* Hugo Riesenfeld

Basil Rathbone, Bobby Breen, Marion Claire, Leon Errol, Henry Armetta, Ralph Forbes, Donald Meek

AAN: Hugo Riesenfeld

Make Haste to Live
US 1954 89m bw
Republic (William A. Seiter)

A lady newspaper owner is embarrassed, to say the least, by the reappearance of her murderer husband, long thought dead.

Competent but rather dull programmer.

w Warren Duff *novel The Gordons* d William A.
Seiter *ph* John L. Russell *m* Elmer Bernstein

Dorothy McGuire, Stephen McNally, Mary Murphy,
Edgar Buchanan, John Howard

Make Me a Star
US   1932   80m   bw
Paramount (Lloyd Sheldon)

A grocery clerk goes to Hollywood and becomes a film
star.

Modest remake of a silent success; see also *Merton of
the Movies*.

w Sam Mintz, Walter de Leon, Arthur Kober
novel Merton of the Movies by Harry Leon Wilson
d William Beaudine *ph* Allen Siegler

Stuart Erwin, Joan Blondell, ZaSu Pitts, Ben Turpin,
Florence Roberts; and Tallulah Bankhead, Clive
Brook, Gary Cooper, Maurice Chevalier, Claudette
Colbert, Fredric March, Jack Oakie, Charlie Ruggles,
Sylvia Sidney

'Packed with laughs which offsets the longish
running time.' – *Variety*

Make Me an Offer *
GB   1954   88m   Eastmancolor
Group Three (W. P. Lipscomb)
V*

An antique dealer has an ambition to own a famous
vase.

Mildly pleasant Jewish comedy with interesting
sidelights on the antique business.

w W. P. Lipscomb *novel* Wolf Mankowitz d Cyril
Frankel *ph* Denny Densham *m* John Addison

Peter Finch, Adrienne Corri, *Meier Tzelniker*, Rosalie
Crutchley, Finlay Currie, *Ernest Thesiger*, Wilfrid
Lawson, Alfie Bass

Make Mine a Million
GB   1959   82m   bw
British Lion/Elstree Independent/Jack Hylton (John Baxter)

A TV make-up man strikes it rich by showing
advertisements on non-commercial television.

Amiable, low-key comedy, relying heavily on the
personality of its star.

w Peter Blackmore, Arthur Askey, Talbot Rothwell
story Jack Francis d Lance Comfort *ph* Arthur
Grant *m* Stanley Black *ad* Dennis Wreford
ed Peter Pitt

Arthur Askey, Sidney James, Dermot Walsh, Olga
Lindo, Clive Morton, Sally Barnes, Leigh Madison,
Bernard Cribbins, Gillian Lynee, The Penge
Formation Dancers

Make Mine Mink **
GB   1960   101m   bw
Rank (Hugh Stewart)
V*

Members of a high-class boarding establishment steal
furs to give the proceeds to charity.

Enjoyable comedy, expertly performed.

w Michael Pertwee, Peter Blackmore *play Breath of
Spring* by Peter Coke d Robert Asher *ph* Reginald
Wyer *m* Philip Green *ad* Carmen Dillon
ed Roger Cherrill

Terry-Thomas, Athene Seyler, Hattie Jacques, Billie
Whitelaw, Raymond Huntley, Irene Handl, Kenneth
Williams, Noel Purcell, Sydney Tafler

† The film was reissued with 21m cut.

Make Mine Music **
US   1946   74m   Technicolor
Walt Disney (Joe Grant)

A programme of cartoon shorts: JOHNNY FEDORA,
ALL THE CATS JOIN IN, WITHOUT YOU, TWO

SILHOUETTES, CASEY AT THE BAT, THE
MARTINS AND THE COYS, BLUE BAYOU, AFTER
YOU'VE GONE, WILLIE THE SINGING WHALE,
PETER AND THE WOLF

An insubstantial banquet, sometimes arty and
sometimes chocolate boxy, which occasionally rises to
the expected heights.

w various d various

'There is enough genuine charm and imagination and
humour to make up perhaps one good average Disney
short.' – *James Agee*

Make Way for a Lady
US   1936   63m   bw
Zion Myers/RKO

A girl determines to find a mate for her widowed
father.

Rather irritating comedy of embarrassment.

w Gertrude Purcell *novel Daddy and I* by Elizabeth
Jordan d David Burton

Herbert Marshall, Anne Shirley, Gertrude Michael,
Margot Grahame, Clara Blandick, Taylor Holmes,
Willie Best

'It lacks suspense, surprise, and plausibility.' – *Variety*

'Grandpa moves in! Daughter moves out! And the riot
starts!'

Make Way for Tomorrow **
US   1937   94m   bw
Paramount (Leo McCarey)

An elderly couple are in financial difficulty and have
to be parted because their children will not help.

Sentimental drama which had a devastating effect at
the time but now seems oversimplified and
exaggerated.

w Vina Delmar *novel The Years Are So Long* by
Josephine Lawrence d Leo McCarey *ph* William
C. Mellor *m* George Antheil

Victor Moore, Beulah Bondi, Thomas Mitchell, Fay
Bainter, Porter Hall, Barbara Read, Maurice
Moscovich, Elizabeth Risdon, Gene Lockhart

'Needs special exploitation: even so, business is apt to
be spotty where played solo.' – *Variety*

'The most brilliantly directed and acted film of the
year.' – *John Grierson*

'A sense of misery and inhumanity is left vibrating in
the nerves.' – *Graham Greene*

Make Your Own Bed
US   1944   82m   bw
Warner

A detective and his girlfriend pretend to be servants
in order to protect an inventor from Nazis.

Mirthless pratfall farce.

w Francis Swann and Edmund Joseph d Peter
Godfrey

Jack Carson, Jane Wyman, Irene Manning, Ricardo
Cortez, Alan Hale, George Tobias

Making Love
US   1982   111m   DeLuxe
TCF/IndieProd (Allen Adler, Danny Melnick)
V*

A young married doctor declares that he is gay and
moves in with a friend.

Would-be daring melodrama whose producers
quickly found that nobody was interested.

w Barry Sandler *story* A. Scott Berg d Arthur
Hiller *ph* David M. Walsh *m* Leonard Rosenman
pd James D. Vance *ed* William H. Reynolds

Michael Ontkean, Kate Jackson, Harry Hamlin,
Wendy Hiller, Arthur Hill, Nancy Olson

Making Mr Right
US   1987   98m   colour
Rank/Orion (Mike Wise, Joel Tuber)
V*, L, S

An android falls in love with a public relations
consultant.

Slight comedy that soon runs out of anywhere to go.

w Floyd Byars, Laurie Frank d Susan Seidelman
ph Edward Lachman *m* Chaz Jankel *pd* Barbara
Ling *ed* Andrew Mondshein

Ann Magnuson, John Malkovich, Glenne Headly,
Ben Masters, Laurie Metcalf, Polly Bergen, Harsh
Nayyar, Hart Bochner

Mala Noche *
US   1988   78m   bw
The Other Cinema/Northern Film/Respectable (Gus Van Sant)

A homosexual store worker falls for a heterosexual
illegal Mexican immigrant.

Interesting first feature, a study in obsession, shot on a
minimal budget.

wd Gus Van Sant *story* Walt Curtis *ph* John
Campbell *m* Creighton Lindsay

Tim Streeter, Doug Cooeyate, Ray Monge, Nyla
McCarthy

Malachi's Cove
GB   1973   75m   Technicolor
Penrith/Impact Quadrant Films (Andrew Sinclair, Kent Walwin)
aka: *The Seaweed Children*

In 1880 Cornwall, a 14-year-old girl lives by selling
seaweed.

Slimly-plotted film for the family, pleasant without
being very interesting.

wd Henry Herbert *story* Anthony Trollope
ph Walter Lassally *m* Brian Gascoigne

Donald Pleasence, Dai Bradley, Veronica Quilligan,
Arthur English, David Howe

Malaga
GB   1954   84m   Technicolor
M. J. Frankovich/Film Locations
US title: *Fire Over Africa*

An American woman agent catches drug smugglers in
Tangier.

Routine international thick ear.

w Robert Westerby d Richard Sale

Maureen O'Hara, Macdonald Carey, Binnie Barnes,
Guy Middleton, Leonard Sachs

Malaga (1962): see *Moment of Danger*

Malaya *
US   1949   95m   bw
MGM (Edwin H. Knopf)
GB title: *East of the Rising Sun*

An adventurer attempts to smuggle rubber out of
Japanese-occupied Malaya.

Dour action melodrama, unworthy of its considerable
cast but watchable.

w Frank Fenton d Richard Thorpe *ph* George
Folsey *m* Bronislau Kaper

Spencer Tracy, James Stewart, Sidney Greenstreet,
John Hodiak, Valentina Cortesa, Lionel Barrymore,
Gilbert Roland

Malcolm
Australia   1986   86m   colour
Enterprise/Cascade (David Parker, Nadia Tass)
V*, L

A retarded but mechanically talented youth lives
alone in a Melbourne suburb and takes in a petty
criminal and his girlfriend.

Initially interesting but mishandled character study which never settles into a comfortable groove.

w David Parker d Nadia Tass ph David Parker m Simon Jeffes ed Ken Sallows

Colin Friels, John Hargreaves, Lindy Davies, Chris Haywood, Charles Tingwell

Malcolm X **
US 1992 201m DuArt
Warner/Largo/Forty Acres and a Mule (Marvin Worth, Spike Lee)
V, V*, L

Biopic of the turbulent life and violent death of the black revolutionary leader.

Despite Washington's powerful performance in the title role, an overlong and somewhat subdued treatment that seems anxious not to offend.

w Arnold Perl, Spike Lee book The Autobiography of Malcolm X as told to Alex Haley d Spike Lee ph Ernest Dickerson m Terence Blanchard pd Wynn Thomas ed Barry Alexander Brown

Denzel Washington, Angela Bassett, Albert Hall, Al Freeman Jnr, Delroy Lindo, Spike Lee, Theresa Randle, Kate Vernon, Lonette McKee, Tommy Hollis

'A disappointingly sluggish and conventional film.' – Variety

'Always watchable even if one can't call it memorable.' – Derek Malcolm, Guardian

AAN: Denzel Washington; Ruth Carter (costume design)

The Male Animal *
US 1942 101m bw
Warner (Wolfgang Reinhardt)

A dry college professor emancipates himself when his wife becomes attracted to a football star.

Stagebound but amusing college comedy with pleasant humour and good performances. Remade as She's Working Her Way through College (qv).

w Julius J. and Philip G. Epstein, Stephen Morehouse Avery play James Thurber and Elliott Nugent d Elliott Nugent ph Arthur Edeson m Heinz Roemheld

Henry Fonda, Olivia de Havilland, Jack Carson, Joan Leslie, Eugene Pallette, Don Defore, Herbert Anderson, Hattie McDaniel

Malenkaya Vera: see Little Vera

'Deception. Betrayal. Murder. Some Things You Never See Coming.'
Malice
US 1993 107m Technicolor
Rank/Castle Rock/New Line (Rachel Pfeffer, Charles Mulvehill, Harold Becker)
S

An academic finds that he is the victim of a confidence trick.

Elaborate, involved, over-heated thriller that makes little sense and provides less enjoyment.

w Aaron Sorkin, Scott Frank, Jonas McCord d Harold Becker ph Gordon Willis m Jerry Goldsmith pd Philip Harrison ed David Bretherton

Alec Baldwin, Nicole Kidman, Bill Pullman, Bob Neuwirth, George C. Scott, Anne Bancroft, Peter Gallagher, Josef Sommer, Tobin Bell

'A virtual scrapbook of elements borrowed from other suspense pics, but no less enjoyable for being so familiar.' – Variety

'One of the most shameless pieces of unadultered trash.' – Alexander Walker, London Evening Standard

Malone
US 1987 92m DeLuxe
Orion (Leo L. Fuchs)
V, V*, L

A disillusioned CIA hit man is not allowed to go 'straight'.

Moody but not unwatchable thriller largely set in Oregon.

w Christopher Frank novel Shotgun by William Wingate d Harley Cokliss ph Gerald Hirschfield m David Newman pd Graeme Murray ed Todd Ramsay

Burt Reynolds, Cliff Robertson, Kenneth McMillan, Cynthia Gibb, Scott Wilson, Lauren Hutton

Malou *
West Germany 1980 93m colour
Regina Ziegler

A teacher goes on a journey to discover more about her dead mother and, ultimately, herself.

This simple story of a woman trying to come to terms with the past and the present is sometimes too didactic, but often rewarding.

wd Jeanine Meerapfel ph Michael Ballhaus m Peer Raben ad Rainer Schaper ed Dagmar Hirtz

Ingrid Caven, Grischa Huber, Helmut Griem, Ivan Desny, Marie Colbin, Peter Chatel, Margarita Calahorra

The Malta Story
GB 1953 103m bw
GFD/British Film Makers (Peter de Sarigny)
V*

An English flyer is involved in the defence of Malta during World War II.

Glib propaganda piece which is not very excitingly written or characterized, and fails to convince on any but the most elementary level.

w William Fairchild, Nigel Balchin d Brian Desmond Hurst ph Robert Krasker m William Alwyn

Alec Guinness, Anthony Steel, Muriel Pavlow, Jack Hawkins, Flora Robson, Renée Asherson, Ralph Truman, Reginald Tate, Hugh Burden

The Maltese Bippy
US 1969 92m Metrocolor Panavision
MGM

A skin flick star thinks he is turning into a werewolf.

Failed attempt to construct a crazy comedy for the stars of Laugh-In; even the spooky house sequences don't go.

w Everett Freeman, Ray Singer d Norman Panama

Dan Rowan, Dick Martin, Carol Lynley, Julie Newmar, Mildred Natwick, Fritz Weaver, Robert Reed

The Maltese Falcon **
US 1931 80m bw
Warner
V*
TV title: Dangerous Female

After the death of his partner, private eye Sam Spade is dragged into a quest for a priceless statuette.

Excellent crime melodrama with smart pace and performances. Remade as Satan Met a Lady (1936); and see below.

w Maude Fulton, Lucien Hubbard, Brown Holmes novel Dashiell Hammett d Roy del Ruth ph William Rees

Ricardo Cortez, Bebe Daniels, Dudley Digges, Dwight Frye, Robert Elliott, Thelma Todd, Oscar Apfel

'Any type of audience will enjoy it.' – Variety

'The best mystery thriller of the year.' – New York Times

'A nice blend of humour, intelligence and suspense.' – Clive Hirschhorn, 1979

'A guy without a conscience! A dame without a heart!'
'He's as fast on the draw as he is in the drawing room!'
The Maltese Falcon ****
US 1941 101m bw
Warner (Henry Blanke)
V, V*, L

A remake which shows the difference between excellence and brilliance; here every nuance is subtly stressed, and the cast is perfection. wd John Huston ph Arthur Edeson m Adolph Deutsch

Humphrey Bogart, Mary Astor, Sidney Greenstreet, Elisha Cook Jnr, Barton MacLane, Lee Patrick, Peter Lorre, Gladys George, Ward Bond, Jerome Cowan

GUTMAN (Sidney Greenstreet): 'I distrust a close-mouthed man. He generally picks the wrong time to talk and says the wrong things. Talking's something you can't do judiciously, unless you keep in practice. Now, sir, we'll talk if you like. I'll tell you right out, I'm a man who likes talking to a man who likes to talk.'

SPADE (Humphrey Bogart) to Cairo (Peter Lorre): 'When you're slapped, you'll take it and like it!'

SPADE to Brigid (Mary Astor): 'Don't be too sure I'm as crooked as I'm supposed to be.'

GUTMAN: 'I distrust a man who says when. If he's got to be careful not to drink too much, it's because he's not to be trusted when he does.'

'The first crime melodrama with finish, speed and bang to come along in what seems like ages.' – Otis Ferguson

'A work of entertainment that is yet so skilfully constructed that after many years and many viewings, it has the same brittle explosiveness – and some of the same surprise – that it had in 1941.' – Pauline Kael, 1968

'The trick which Mr Huston has pulled is a combination of American ruggedness with the suavity of the English crime school – a blend of mind and muscle – plus a slight touch of pathos.' – Bosley Crowther, New York Times

'Admirable photography of the sort in which black and white gives full value to every detail, every flicker of panic.' – Francis Wyndham

AAN: best picture; John Huston (as writer); Sidney Greenstreet

Mama Loves Papa *
US 1933 70m bw
Paramount

A middle-class wife decides to do some social climbing.

Slight but amusing comedy which put together a useful team.

w Arthur Kober, Nunnally Johnson, Douglas MacLean, Keene Thompson d Norman Z. McLeod

Charles Ruggles, Mary Boland, Lilyan Tashman, George Barbier, Morgan Wallace

'Exceptionally funny comedy . . . a cinch builder.' – Variety

† A second film under this title was a Leon Errol vehicle of 1945.

La Maman et la Putain: see The Mother and the Whore

Mamba
US 1930 76m Technicolor
Tiffany

Germans in East Africa go to the bad during World War I.

Absurd melodrama climaxing with a Zulu uprising.

w Tom Miranda, Winifred Dunn   *story* F. Schumann-Heink and John Reinhardt   *d* Al Rogell

Jean Hersholt, Eleanor Boardman, Ralph Forbes, Josef Swickard

'It has its lowlights and highlights; in between it's not a bad programmer.' – *Variety*

Mamba
Italy   1988   81m   colour
Medusa/Eidoscope/Reteitalia (Mario Orfini)
V

A woman is locked in a room with a deadly snake by her murderous ex-boyfriend.

Modest, moderately suspenseful thriller that just manages to eke out its length.

w Lidia Ravera, Mario Orfini   *d* Mario Orfini
ph Dante Spinotti   *m* Giorgio Moroder
pd Ferdinando Scarfiotti   *ed* Claudio Cutry

Trudie Styler, Gregg Henry, Bill Moseley

Mambo
Italy/USA   1954   92m (English version), 107m (Italian version)   bw
Paramount/Ponti/De Laurentiis
V*

A Venetian shopgirl loves a worthless gambler, is romanced by a haemophiliac count, and joins a dance troupe.

Patchy melodrama with plenty going on but no grip.

w Guido Piovene, Ivo Perelli, Ennio de Concini, Robert Rossen   *d* Robert Rossen   *ph* Harold Rosson   *m* Nino Rota, Francesco Lavagnino   *sets* Andrei Andrejew   *ch*: Katherine Dunham

Silvana Mangano, Michael Rennie, Shelley Winters, Vittorio Gassman, Eduardo Ciannelli, Mary Clare, Katherine Dunham and her troupe

The Mambo Kings *
US   1992   104m   DeLuxe
Warner/Canal+/Regency/Alcor (Arnon Milchan, Arne Glimcher)
V, V*, L, S

In the 1950s, a Cuban trumpeter and his brother, a singer, leave home to seek their fortunes in New York.

Energetic but dull version of a best-selling novel.

w Cynthia Cidre   *novel* The Mambo Kings Play Songs of Love by Oscar Hijuelos   *d* Arne Glimcher
ph Michael Ballhaus   *m* Robert Kraft, Carlos Franzetti   *pd* Stuart Wurtzel   *ed* Claire Simpson

Armand Assante, Antonio Banderas, Cathy Moriarty, Maruschka Detmers, Pablo Calogero, Scott Cohen, Mario Grillo, Desi Arnaz Jnr, Roscoe Lee Browne, Tito Puente

'An ambitious, old-fashioned Hollywood film . . . is bound to win converts to the intoxicating rhythms of Latino music.' – *Variety*

AAN: Song: 'Beautiful Maria of My Soul' (*m* Robert Kraft, *ly* Arne Glimcher)

'She'll coax the blues right out of your heart'
Mame *
US   1974   131m   Technicolor   Panavision
Warner/ABC (Robert Fryer, James Cresson)
V, V*, L

In 1928, a 10-year-old boy goes to live with his eccentric, sophisticated aunt.

Old-fashioned and rather bad film of a much overrated Broadway musical, inept in most departments but with occasional show-stopping moments.

w Paul Zandel   *play* Jerome Lawrence, Robert E. Lee   *book* Patrick Dennis   *d* Gene Saks   *ph* Philip Lathrop   *pd* Robert F. Boyle   *m/ly* Jerry Herman

Lucille Ball, Beatrice Arthur, Robert Preston, Bruce Davison, Jane Connell, Joyce Van Patten, John McGiver

'It makes one realize afresh the parlous state of the Hollywood musical, fighting to survive against misplaced superstars and elephantine budgets matched with minuscule imagination.' – *Geoff Brown*

'The cast seem to have been handpicked for their tone-deafness, and Lucille Ball's close-ups are shot blatantly out of focus.' – *Sight and Sound*

'So terrible it isn't boring; you can get fixated staring at it and wondering what Lucille Ball thought she was doing.' – *New Yorker, 1977*

Mammy *
US   1930   84m   bw
Warner (Walter Morosco)
L

Murder backstage at a minstrel show.

One of the star's better musicals.

w L. G. Rigby, Joseph Jackson   *d* Michael Curtiz   *ph* Barney McGill   *m* Irving Berlin

Al Jolson, Lowell Sherman, Hobart Bosworth, Louise Dresser, Lee Moran

'Looks like money . . . a lively picture playing fast.' – *Variety*

A Man, a Woman and a Bank
Canada   1979   101m   CFI color
Bennett/McNichol
V*

A civil engineer and a computer expert devise a foolproof way of robbing a bank.

We have been here before, except that these days the criminals are allowed to get away with it. Ho-hum.

w Raynold Gideon, Bruce A. Evans and Stuart Margolin   *d* Noel Black

Donald Sutherland, Brooke Adams, Paul Mazursky

A Man about the House
GB   1947   95m   bw
British Lion (Edward Black)
V*

Two English ladies inherit an Italian villa and fall under the spell of the handsome handyman, who marries one of them and proceeds slowly to poison her.

Now clearly dull, at the time this seemed a fairly enterprising rehash of *Gaslight, Kind Lady* and *Rebecca*.

w J. B. Williams, Leslie Arliss   *play* John Perry   *novel* Francis Brett Young   *d* Leslie Arliss   *ph* Georges Perinal   *m* Nicholas Brodszky

Margaret Johnston, Dulcie Gray, Kieron Moore, Felix Aylmer, Lilian Braithwaite

A Man about the House
GB   1974   90m   colour
EMI/Hammer (Roy Skeggs)
V

Two young women, their male flatmate and their landlords combine forces to prevent the terrace from being razed for redevelopment.

Mild and rather exhausting sex comedy from the TV series, as relentlessly single-minded as a 'Carry On'.

w Johnnie Mortimer, Brian Cooke   *d* John Robins   *ph* Jimmy Allen   *m* Christopher Gunning

Richard O'Sullivan, Paula Wilcox, Sally Thomsett, Yootha Joyce, Brian Murphy, Peter Cellier, Patrick Newell, Spike Milligan, Arthur Lowe

Man about Town
US   1932   75m   bw
Fox

A society gambler is really a secret service man.

Flabby melodrama which practically dislocates the long arm of coincidence.

w Leon Gordon   *novel* Denison Clift   *d* John Francis Dillon

Warner Baxter, Karen Morley, Conway Tearle, Lawrence Grant, Leni Stengel, Alan Mowbray, Lillian Bond, Halliwell Hobbes

'Plenty of hodge-podge, and doubtful b.o. Will need strong support almost everywhere.' – *Variety*

Man about Town *
US   1939   85m   bw
Paramount (Arthur Hornblow Jnr)

A Broadway producer in London makes his girlfriend jealous.

Fairly amusing comedy-musical programmer.

w Morrie Ryskind   *d* Mark Sandrich   *ph* Ted Tetzlaff   *md* Victor Young

Jack Benny, Dorothy Lamour, Edward Arnold, Binnie Barnes, Phil Harris, Eddie Anderson, Monty Woolley, Isabel Jeans, Betty Grable, E. E. Clive

'Good comedy, rates okay biz.' – *Variety*

Man Afraid
US   1957   84m   bw   Cinemascope
Universal-International

A priest is forced to kill a hoodlum in self-defence, and is then threatened by the dead man's psychopathic father.

Heavy-going melodrama not helped at all by the very wide screen.

w Herb Meadow   *d* Harry Keller

George Nader, Phyllis Thaxter, Harold J. Stone, Tim Hovey, Eduard Franz

Man Alive
US   1945   70m   bw
RKO

A husband thought to be dead comes back as a 'ghost' and frightens away his wife's new suitor.

Curious and rather tasteless comedy.

w Edwin Harvey Blum   *d* Ray Enright

Pat O'Brien, Ellen Drew, Adolphe Menjou, Rudy Vallee, Jack Norton

A Man Alone: see The Killers (1946)

A Man Alone *
US   1955   96m   Trucolor
Republic

A wandering gunman is framed by other badmen.

Solemn, slow-moving but generally interesting Western, the star's first attempt at direction.

w John Tucker Battle   *d* Ray Milland   *ph* Lionel Lindon   *m* Victor Young

Ray Milland, Mary Murphy, Ward Bond, Raymond Burr, Arthur Space, Lee Van Cleef, Alan Hale Jnr

A Man and a Woman **
France   1966   102m   Eastmancolor
Les Films 13
V, V*, S
original title: *Un Homme et une Femme*

A racing driver and a script girl, both of whose spouses are dead, meet while visiting their children, and an affair leads to marriage.

Slight romantic drama so tricked out with smart images that it looks like a series of expensive commercials. A great box-office success, but its director never again succeeded in this vein which he made his own.

w Claude Lelouch, Pierre Uytterhoeven   *d* Claude Lelouch   *ph* Jean Columb, Patrice Pouget   *m* Francis Lai

Anouk Aimée, Jean-Louis Trintignant

'When in doubt, Lelouch's motto seems to be, use a colour filter or insert lyrical shots of dogs and horses; when in real doubt, use both.' – *Tom Milne, MFB*

'A slick item with all the Hollywood ingredients.' – *John Simon*

AA: best foreign film; Claude Lelouch, Pierre Uytterhoeven

AAN: Claude Lelouch (as director); Anouk Aimée

A Man and a Woman: Twenty Years Later

France 1986 120m Eastmancolor
Films 13/Warner
V*

original title: *Un Homme Et Une Femme: Vingt Ans Déjà*

Slightly macabre attempt to extend the appeal with the same actors, the same technique, and even shots from Lelouch's other movies.

A bit of a wallow.

w Claude Lelouch, Pierre Uytterhoeven, Monique Lange, Jérôme Tonnerre   *d* Claude Lelouch
ph Jean-Yves Le Mener   *m* Francis Lai

Anouk Aimée, Jean-Louis Trintignant, Evelyne Bouix, Marie-Sophie Pochat

Man and His Mate: see *One Million BC*

The Man at the Gate

GB 1941 48m bw
GHW
V

The war takes its toll of Cornish fishermen.

Modest family drama which strives to be inspirational via a speech made by King George VI.

w Lydia Hayward and Harold Simpson
story Manning Haynes   *poem* Louise Haskin
d Norman Walker

Wilfred Lawson, Mary Jerrold, Kathleen O'Regan

† The film has been released on video together with *Turn of the Tide*.

Man at the Top *

GB 1973 87m Technicolor
Hammer/Dufton (Peter Charlesworth)
V

A pharmaceutical executive finds that his firm is marketing an unsafe drug.

Further adventures of the belligerent hero of *Room at the Top* (qv), this time following a popular television series. All very fashionable and predictable.

w Hugh Whitemore   *d* Mike Vardy   *ph* Bryan Probyn   *m* Roy Budd

Kenneth Haigh, Nanette Newman, Harry Andrews, John Quentin, Charlie Williams

The Man Behind the Gun

US 1952 82m Technicolor
Warner

A cavalry officer is sent to quell a rebellion and helps to found Los Angeles.

Cheerful Western programmer.

w John Twist   *d* Felix Feist

Randolph Scott, Patrice Wymore, Dick Wesson, Phil Carey

The Man Behind the Mask

GB 1936 79m bw
Joe Rock

A mad scientist kidnaps a nobleman's daughter.

Serial-like hokum with interesting credits.

w Ian Hay, Syd Courtenay, Jack Byrd and Stanley Haynes   *d* Michael Powell

Hugh Williams, Maurice Schwartz, Jane Baxter, Donald Calthrop, Henry Oscar

A Man Betrayed

US 1941 82m bw
Armand Schaefer/Republic
V*

GB title: *Citadel of Crime*

A hick lawyer in the big city smashes corruption.

Somewhat inconsequential melodrama which fails to come through with the powerful entertainment it promises.

w Isabel Dawn   *d* John Auer

John Wayne, Frances Dee, Edward Ellis, Wallace Ford, Ward Bond, Harold Huber, Alexander Granach, Barnett Parker

The Man Between *

GB 1953 101m bw
British Lion/London Films (Carol Reed)
V

Ivo Kern operates successfully as a West Berlin racketeer; love causes a softening of his attitudes and leads to his death.

Imitation *Third Man* with an uninteresting mystery and a solemn ending. Good acting and production can't save it.

w Harry Kurnitz   *d* Carol Reed   *ph* Desmond Dickinson   *m* John Addison   *ad* Andrei Andreiev

James Mason, Hildegarde Neff, Claire Bloom, Geoffrey Toone, Ernst Schroeder

'Reed's love of photogenic corruption, his technical finesse, and his feeling for atmospheric intrigue almost make something really good out of a synthetic script.' – *Variety*

'A cold-hearted film about people with cold feet.' – *Daily Express*

Man Bites Dog **

Belgium 1992 96m bw
Metro/Les Artistes Anonymes (Rémy Belvaux, André Bonzel, Benoît Poelvoorde)
V, V*, S

original title: *C'est arrivé près de chez vous*

A documentary film crew begin by recording the activities of a motiveless serial killer and end by helping him with his murders.

A black comedy that makes some effective points about the relationship between cinema (or TV) and exploitation and voyeurism but which becomes ever harder to watch or enjoy, with its scenes of gang rape and murder. A remarkable, if sometimes repellent, first feature, nevertheless.

w Rémy Belvaux, André Bonzel, Benoît Poelvoorde, Vincent Tavier   *d* Rémy Belvaux, André Bonzel, Benoît Poelvoorde   *ph* André Bonzel   *m* Jean-Marc Chenut   *ed* Rémy Belvaux, Eric Dardill

Benoît Poelvoorde, Jacqueline Poelvoorde-Pappaert, Nelly Pappaert, Jenny Drye, Malou Madou, Willy Vandenbroeck

'To encounter Man Bites Dog is to submit to a torrent of hilariously cruel humour, enacted without fuss or rancour, and inconceivably authentic.' – *Philip Strick, Sight and Sound*

'Offbeat, darkly hilarious . . . Violent yet trenchant, potential sleeper should attract a cult following and will look just right on video.' – *Variety*

'Carefully shaped to draw us in and repel us, to make us laugh and wipe the smiles off our faces. The most horrendous scenes are calculated to force us into asking how we can bear to watch such things.' – *Philip French, Observer*

A Man Called Gannon

US 1969 105m Technicolor
Universal

A wandering cowboy helps a widow rancher in her fight against encroaching cattlemen.

Adequate remake of *The Man Without a Star*, which somehow had much more stature.

w Gene Kearney, D. D. Beauchamp and Borden Chase   *d* James Goldstone

Tony Franciosa, Michael Sarrazin, Judi West, Susan Oliver, John Anderson

A Man Called Horse *

US 1970 114m Technicolor Panavision
Cinema Center/Sanford Howard
V, V*

In 1825 an English aristocrat is captured by Indians, lives with them and eventually becomes their leader.

Harrowing account of tribal life and customs, with much bloodshed and torture and most of the dialogue in Indian. Occasionally impressive but not exactly entertaining.

w Jack di Witt   *story* Dorothy M. Johnson   *d* Elliot Silverstein   *ph* Robert Hauser   *m* Leonard Rosenman

Richard Harris, Judith Anderson, Jean Gascon, Manu Tupou

† Sequels 1976: *The Return of a Man Called Horse*. 1984: *Triumphs of a Man Called Horse*.

The Man Called Noon

GB/Spain/Italy 1973 95m Technicolor
Frontier/Montana/Finarco (Euan Lloyd)

A Western gunslinger loses his memory.

Childish Western melodrama in the violent manner.

w Scot Finch   *novel* Louis L'Amour   *d* Peter Collinson   *ph* John Cabrera   *m* Luis Bacalov

Richard Crenna, Stephen Boyd, Rosanna Schiaffino, Farley Granger

A Man Called Peter *

US 1955 119m DeLuxe Cinemascope
TCF (Samuel G. Engel)
V*

The life of Peter Marshall, a Scottish clergyman who became chaplain to the US Senate.

Careful but rather dreary biopic.

w Eleanore Griffin   *book* Catherine Marshall
d Henry Koster   *ph* Harold Lipstein   *m* Alfred Newman

Richard Todd, Jean Peters, Marjorie Rambeau, Jill Esmond, Les Tremayne, Robert Burton

AAN: Harold Lipstein

A Man Called Sledge

Italy 1970 92m Techniscope
Dino de Laurentiis (Carl Olsen)
V*

A bandit tries in vain to mastermind a bank robbery.

Curious change of pace for a genial star. A spaghetti Western without style but with plenty of violence, the result doesn't linger in the memory.

w Vic Morrow, Frank Kowalsky   *d* Vic Morrow
ph Luigi Kuveiller

James Garner, Dennis Weaver, Claude Akins, John Marley

A Man Called Sullivan: see *The Great John L.*

A Man Could Get Killed *

US 1966 98m Technicolor Panavision
Universal/Cherokee (Ernest Wehmeyer)

An American businessman in Lisbon is mistaken for a secret agent.

Minor thrill comedy with a confused plot and a willing cast.

w T. E. B. Clarke, Richard Breen   novel Diamonds Are Danger by David Walker   d Ronald Neame, Cliff Owen   ph Gabor Pogany   m Bert Kaemfert

James Garner, Melina Mercouri, Sandra Dee, Tony Franciosa, Robert Coote, Roland Culver, Cecil Parker, Grégoire Aslan, Dulcie Gray, Martin Benson, Niall MacGinnis

A Man for All Seasons ****
GB   1966   120m   Technicolor
Columbia/Highland (Fred Zinnemann)
V, V*, L

Sir Thomas More opposes Henry VIII's divorce, and events lead inexorably to his execution.

Irreproachable film version of a play which has had its narrative tricks removed but stands up remarkably well. Acting, direction, sets, locations and costumes all have precisely the right touch.

w Robert Bolt,   play Robert Bolt   d Fred Zinnemann   ph Ted Moore   m Georges Delerue   pd John Box

Paul Scofield, Wendy Hiller, Susannah York, Robert Shaw, Orson Welles, Leo McKern, Nigel Davenport, John Hurt, Corin Redgrave, Cyril Luckham, Jack Gwillim

'Mr Zinnemann has crystallized the essence of this drama in such pictorial terms as to render even its abstractions vibrant.' – New York Times

'A beautiful and satisfying film, the ultimate demonstration, perhaps, of how a fine stage play can be transcended and, with integrity and inspiration, turned into a great motion picture.' – Judith Crist

† Reports indicate that Charlton Heston badly wanted the role of Sir Thomas More.

AA: best picture; Robert Bolt; Fred Zinnemann; Ted Moore; Paul Scofield

AAN: Wendy Hiller; Robert Shaw

'If you've read the book, forget it!'
Man Friday
GB   1975   115m   Eastmancolor   Panavision
Avco-Embassy/ITC/ABC/Keep Films (Jules Buck)
V*

The story of Robinson Crusoe told so that Friday appears the more intelligent.

A pointless and not very entertaining exercise which wears out its welcome very early.

w Adrian Mitchell   d Jack Gold   ph Alex Phillips   m Carl Davis

Peter O'Toole, Richard Roundtree

'Liberal intentions trail sadly through every sequence and cause absurd fluctuations of tone, since no one seems to have decided whether laborious slapstick, heavy portentousness or method acting is the best vehicle for the message.' – Jill Forbes

The Man from Bitter Ridge
US   1955   80m   Technicolor
Universal-International

A special agent goes undercover to nail stagecoach bandits, but himself comes under suspicion.

Adequate Western programmer.

w Lawrence Roman   d Jack Arnold

Lex Barker, Mara Corday, Stephen McNally, Trevor Bardette, John Dehner

The Man from Blankley's
US   1930   67m   bw
Warner

A drunken aristocrat goes to the wrong party and teaches those present, and himself, a thing or two.

Amusing star trifle, previously filmed as a silent.

w Harvey Thew, Joseph Jackson   story F. Anstey   d Alfred E. Green   ph James Van Trees

John Barrymore, Loretta Young, William Austin, Albert Gran, Emily Fitzroy

'Dickens comedy, in the Sennett vein, with the Barrymore finesse.' – Variety

The Man from Colorado
US   1949   99m   Technicolor
Columbia (Jules Schermer)
V*

A maladjusted Civil War veteran becomes a Western judge and rules by the gun.

Slightly unusual, watchable star Western.

w Robert D. Andrews, Ben Maddow, Borden Chase   d Henry Levin   ph William Snyder   m George Duning

Glenn Ford, William Holden, Ellen Drew, Ray Collins, Edgar Buchanan, Jerome Courtland, James Millican, Jim Bannon

'No more humour than a lawyer's shingle, but it has suspense and some exciting shots of fist fights and burning houses.' – Time

The Man from Dakota *
US   1940   75m   bw
MGM
GB title: Arouse and Beware

A Yankee soldier is taken prisoner by the South and becomes a spy.

Good period action piece.

w Laurence Stallings   novel Mackinlay Kantor   d Leslie Fenton

Wallace Beery, Dolores Del Rio, John Howard, Donald Meek, H. B. Warner, Victor Varconi

Man from Del Rio
US   1956   82m   bw
UA/Robert L. Jacks

A Mexican hobo becomes sheriff and forces the local badman to leave town.

Modest, efficient, rather brutal little Western.

w Richard Carr   d Harry Horner   ph Stanley Cortez   m Fred Steiner

Anthony Quinn, Katy Jurado, Peter Whitney, Douglas Fowley

The Man from Down Under
US   1943   103m   bw
MGM

A veteran of World War I smuggles two orphans back into Australia.

Appallingly indulgent sentimental star vehicle, a mistake for all concerned.

w Wells Roots, Thomas Seller   d Robert Z. Leonard

Charles Laughton, Binnie Barnes, Donna Reed, Richard Carlson, Horace McNally, Arthur Shields

'He came a thousand miles to kill someone he'd never seen!'
The Man from Laramie **
US   1955   104m   Technicolor   Cinemascope
Columbia (William Goetz)
V, V*

A wandering cowman seeks revenge on those who killed his brother.

Grade-A Western with new-fangled touches of brutality touching off the wide screen spectacle.

w Philip Yordan, Frank Burt   d Anthony Mann   ph Charles Lang Jnr   md Morris Stoloff   m George Duning

James Stewart, Arthur Kennedy, Donald Crisp, Cathy O'Donnell, Alex Nicol, Aline MacMahon, Wallace Ford, Jack Elam

The Man from Majorca *
Sweden   1984   105m   colour
Cannon/Drakfilm (Göran Lindström)
original title: Mannen Fròn Mallorca

Two policemen are thwarted in their attempt to uncover a political and sexual scandal.

A taut thriller that maintains its suspense until the end.

wd Bo Widerberg   novel Grisfesten by Leif G. W. Persson   ph Thomas Wahlberg   m Björn Jason Lindh   ad Jan Öquist   ed Bo Widerberg

Sven Wollter, Tomas von Brömssen, Hòkan Serner, Ernst Günther, Thomas Hellberg, Ingvar Hirdvall, Niels Jensen

The Man from Morocco
GB   1944   116m   bw
ABP (Warwick Ward)

Members of the international brigade are captured and later sent by Vichy to build a Sahara railway for the Germans; one escapes to London with vital information.

Stilted, meandering and extremely unconvincing melodrama with a star ill at ease.

w Warwick Ward, Edward Dryhurst, Marguerite Steen   story Rudolph Cartier   d Max Greene   ph Basil Emmott

Anton Walbrook, Margaretta Scott, Mary Morris, Reginald Tate, Peter Sinclair, David Horne

The Man from Nevada: see The Nevadan

The Man from Planet X
US   1951   70m   bw
Sherrill Corwin/United Artists (Aubrey Wisberg and Jack Pollexfen)

On a remote Scottish island a spacecraft deposits a strange creature with a large head and mesmeric powers.

Early, minor, moderately pleasing fragment in the Close Encounters cycle.

w Aubrey Wisberg and Jack Pollexfen   d Edgar G. Ulmer

Margaret Field, Raymond Bond, William Schallert

The Man from Snowy River
Australia   1982   104m   Eastmancolor   Panavision
Cambridge Films/Michael Edgley International (Geoff Burrowes)
V, V*, L

In 1888, an orphan boy grows up with an obsession about wild horses.

Essentially no more than an Audie-Murphy-style Western given full down-under treatment. An Australian smash, a programmer elsewhere.

w John Dixon, Fred Cullen   poem A. B. Paterson   d George Miller   ph Keith Wagstaff   m Bruce Rowland

Kirk Douglas, Jack Thompson, Sigrid Thornton, Tom Burlinson, Terence Donovan, Lorraine Bayly

The Man from the Alamo *
US   1953   79m   Technicolor
U-I (Aaron Rosenberg)
V*

A survivor of the Alamo is thought to be a deserter but proves his story and exposes a villain.

Satisfying Western programmer.

w Steve Fisher, D. D. Beauchamp   d Budd Boetticher   ph Russell Metty   m Frank Skinner

Glenn Ford, Victor Jory, Julia Adams, Hugh O'Brian

The Man from the Diners' Club *
US   1963   96m   bw
Columbia/Dena/Ampersand (Bill Bloom)

A clerk accidentally lets a credit card go to a notorious gangster, and makes desperate efforts to retrieve it.

Minor star comedy with funny moments surviving a slapdash script.

w Bill Blatty   *d* Frank Tashlin   *ph* Hal Mohr
m Stu Philips

Danny Kaye, Telly Savalas, Martha Hyer, Cara
Williams, Everett Sloane, George Kennedy

The Man from the Folies Bergère: see *Folies
Bergère*

The Man from Tokyo: see *Tokyo Drifter*

The Man from U.N.C.L.E

This long-running one-hour TV series (1964—68)
began as a spoof of James Bond, which was itself a
spoof.

Not much more serious or convincing than *Batman*,
they caused a lot of people to suspend their disbelief.

Robert Vaughn played Napoleon Solo, David
McCallum Ilya Kuryakin, and Leo G. Carroll Mr
Waverly

† Several feature films were made up from various
episodes, and did well in cinemas in some countries.
They were: TO TRAP A SPY, THE SPY WITH MY
FACE, THE KARATE KILLERS, THE SPY IN THE
GREEN HAT, ONE OF OUR SPIES IS MISSING,
THE HELICOPTER SPIES, HOW TO STEAL THE
WORLD and ONE SPY TOO MANY.

The Man from Utah

US   1934   55m   bw
Lone Star (Paul Malvern)
L

At the urging of a US Marshal, a cowboy goes
undercover to expose a gang organizing a crooked
rodeo.

Dull Western, with some moderately interesting
rodeo footage. It opens, uncharacteristically, with
Wayne as a guitar-toting cowboy on a white horse,
singing a love song in an unpleasing baritone.

w Lindsley Parsons   *d* Robert Bradbury
ph Archie Stout   *m* William Barber   *ed* Carl
Pierson

John Wayne, Polly Ann Young, Anita Compillo,
Edward Peil, George Hayes, Yakima Canutt, George
Cleveland

A Man from Wyoming

US   1930   70m   bw
Paramount

A slow-speaking engineer joins the army, serves
overseas and marries an ambulance driver.

Uncertain star vehicle which helped to mould his
screen character.

w John Weaver and Albert Shelby Le Vino
d Rowland V. Lee

Gary Cooper, June Collyer, Regis Toomey, E. H.
Calvert, Morgan Farley

'Bad enough to be good entertainment if taken as
farce.' – *New York Evening Post.*

'Her body ached for the man she loved!'
The Man from Yesterday

US   1932   71m   bw
Paramount

A man is reported missing in World War I, but years
later his wife and her new fiancé find him in
Switzerland, dying of gas poisoning.

Enoch Arden rides again, and very boringly.

w Oliver H. P. Garrett   *d* Berthold Viertel   *ph* Karl
Struss

Claudette Colbert, Clive Brook, Charles Boyer, Andy
Devine, Alan Mowbray, Christian Rub

'Rather too late in the day to expect war scenes, and
when the war peters out, there is only scenery and
conversation.' – *Variety*

Man Hunt

US   1932   65m   bw
Warner

A cub reporter hunts a bank robber.

Standard support action fare of its time.

w Roy Chanslor, Earl Felton   *d* William Clemens

William Gargan, Ricardo Cortez, Marguerite
Chapman, Chic Sale, Maude Eburne

'Script never lives up to the title's promise.' – *Variety*

Man Hunt **

US   1941   98m   bw
TCF (Kenneth MacGowan)

A big game hunter misses a shot at Hitler and is
chased back to England by the Gestapo.

Despite hilariously inaccurate English backgrounds,
this is perhaps its director's most vivid Hollywood
thriller, though watered down in tone from the
original novel.

w Dudley Nichols   *novel* *Rogue Male* by Geoffrey
Household   *d* Fritz Lang   *ph* Arthur Miller
m Alfred Newman

Walter Pidgeon, Joan Bennett, *George Sanders*, John
Carradine, Roddy McDowall, Ludwig Stossel,
Heather Thatcher, Frederick Worlock

'A tense and intriguing thriller that is both
propaganda and exciting entertainment.' – *Paul M.
Jensen, 1969*

'In its manipulation of these dark and intent forces on
a checkerboard, it manages to take your breath away.'
– *Otis Ferguson*

† Remade for TV in 1976 as *Rogue Male.*

The Man I Killed: see *Broken Lullaby*

The Man I Love

US   1946   76m   bw
Warner (Arnold Albert)

A night-club singer is involved with a mobster.

Dreary little melodrama which never really gets
going.

w Catherine Turney   *d* Raoul Walsh   *ph* Sid
Hickox   *m* Max Steiner

Ida Lupino, Robert Alda, Andrea King, Martha
Vickers, Bruce Bennett, Alan Hale, Dolores Moran,
John Ridgely

The Man I Married *

US   1940   79m   bw
TCF (Raymond Griffith)
aka: *I Married a Nazi*

When an American couple take a European vacation,
the wife is horrified to find her husband, who is of
German parentage, agreeing with the Nazis.

Naïve but striking melodrama exploring attitudes of
its time.

w Oliver H. P. Garrett   *novel* *Swastika* by Oscar
Shisgall   *d* Irving Pichel   *ph* Peverell Marley
m David Buttolph

Joan Bennett, Francis Lederer, Lloyd Nolan, Anna
Sten, Otto Kruger, Maria Ouspenskaya, Ludwig
Stossel, Johnny Russell

Man in a Cocked Hat: see *Carlton-Browne of the FO*

The Man in Grey **

GB   1943   116m   bw
GFD/Gainsborough (Edward Black)
V*

In Regency times, an aristocratic girl's love for her less
fortunate friend is repaid by jealousy, treachery and
murder.

Rather dully performed flashback costume melodrama
which caught the public imagination in the middle of

a dreary world war, especially as its evil leading
characters were played by stars who rapidly went
right to the top. The several imitations which
followed, including *The Wicked Lady, Jassy* and *Hungry
Hill*, became known as the Gainsborough school.

w Margaret Kennedy, Leslie Arliss, Doreen
Montgomery   *novel* Lady Eleanor Smith   *d* Leslie
Arliss   *ph* Arthur Crabtree   *m* Cedric Mallabey
ad Walter Murton

*James Mason, Margaret Lockwood, Phyllis Calvert, Stewart
Granger*, Helen Haye, Nora Swinburne, Raymond
Lovell, Martita Hunt

'There was not a moment when I would not gladly
have dived for my hat.' – *James Agate*

'All the time-tested materials: gypsy fortune-teller;
scowling, black-browed villain; gushy diary kept by a
doe-eyed girl who munches candied violets; fire-
breathing adventuress who dotes on discord and low-
cut gowns . . .' – *Time*

'Even the one girl who loved enough to ask no questions –
had to face the fearful truth!'
The Man in Half Moon Street

US   1944   91m   bw
Paramount (Walter MacEwen)

A mysteriously handsome young scientist is actually a
90-year-old who has discovered a surgical method of
preserving youth.

Boring screen version of a play which was conceived
in an almost romantic vein; Hollywood has taken it
too literally.

w Charles Kenyon   *play* Barre Lyndon   *d* Ralph
Murphy   *ph* Henry Sharp   *m* Miklos Rozsa

Nils Asther, Helen Walker, Brandon Hurst, *Reinhold
Schunzel*

† Remade in straight horror vein as *The Man Who Could
Cheat Death* (qv).

Man in Love *

France/Italy   1987   110m   colour
Virgin/Fox/Camera One/Alexandra Films/JMS (Michel Seydoux,
Diane Kurys)
V*, L
original title: *Un Homme Amoureux*

A married American film star falls in love with an
actress while making a movie in Italy.

Overlong romantic melodrama that generates little
heat.

w Diane Kurys, Olivier Schatzky   *d* Diane Kurys
ph Bernard Zitzermann   *m* Georges Delerue
ad Dean Tavoularis   *ed* Joelle Van Effenterre

Peter Coyote, Greta Scacchi, Peter Riegert, Claudia
Cardinale, John Berry, Vincent Lindon, Jamie Lee
Curtis

The Man in Possession

US   1931   81m   bw
MGM

A lady falls in love with the bailiff's man in temporary
charge of her establishment.

Light comedy subsequently remade as *Personal
Property*; quite tolerable.

w Sarah Y. Mason   *play* H. M. Harwood   *d* Sam
Wood

Robert Montgomery, Irene Purcell, Charlotte
Greenwood, C. Aubrey Smith, Beryl Mercer, Reginald
Owen, Alan Mowbray

'Should have no trouble where the censors don't
interfere . . . where it gets by with the dirt, the dirt
should get it over.' – *Variety*

The Man in Possession (1937): see *Personal
Property*

The Man in the Attic

US   1953   82m   bw
TCF

Remake of the much-remade *The Lodger*, this time with parsimonious production values and no style.

w Robert Presnell Jnr and Barre Lyndon   *d* Hugo Fregonese

Jack Palance, Constance Smith, Bryron Palmer, Frances Bavier, Rhys Williams

The Man in the Back Seat *

GB   1961   57m   bw
Independent Artists (Julian Wintle, Leslie Parkyn)

Two robbers fail to separate a bookie from the locked bag chained to his wrist, at first taking him with them they finally kill him and are apparently haunted by him.

Taut, downbeat little crime thriller which won a few critical plaudits.

w Malcolm Hulke, Eric Paice   *d* Vernon Sewell
ph Reg Wyer   *m* Stanley Black

Derren Nesbitt, Keith Faulkner, Carol White, Harry Locke

'Death at the carnival – as a killer takes over the switchback!'

Man in the Dark *

US   1953   70m   bw   3-D
Columbia (Wallace Macdonald)

A convict submits to a brain operation which will remove his criminal tendencies. Unfortunately it also removes his memory, and on his release he is bewildered when gangsters expect him to know where the loot is hidden.

Silly low-budgeter which is only notable as the 3-D film which most exploited the short-lived medium. Apart from a roller coaster ride, objects hurled at the audience include scissors, spiders, knives, forceps, fists and falling bodies.

w George Bricker, Jack Leonard   *d* Lew Landers
ph Floyd Crosby   *md* Ross de Maggio

Edmond O'Brien, Audrey Totter, Ted de Corsia, Horace MacMahon

The Man in the Gray Flannel Suit *

US   1956   152m   Eastmancolor   Cinemascope
TCF (Darryl F. Zanuck)
V*, L

A young New York executive is offered a demanding job but decides that his first loyalty is to his wife and children.

An amusingly accurate novel of Madison Avenue mores becomes a marathon emotional melodrama in which the mordant bits quickly give way to domestic problems and a guilt complex about a wartime affair, shown in lengthy flashback. It's all too much.

wd Nunnally Johnson   *novel* Sloan Wilson
ph Charles G. Clarke   *m* Bernard Herrmann

Gregory Peck, Fredric March, Jennifer Jones, Ann Harding, *Arthur O'Connell, Henry Daniell,* Marisa Pavan, Lee J. Cobb, Keenan Wynn, Gene Lockhart, Gigi Perreau, Connie Gilchrist, Joseph Sweeney

The Man in the Iron Mask **

US   1939   110m   bw
Edward Small
V*, L

King Louis XIV keeps his twin brother prisoner.

Exhilarating swashbuckler based on a classic novel, with a complex plot, good acting and the three musketeers in full cry.

w George Bruce   novel Alexandre Dumas   *d James Whale   ph* Robert Planck   *m* Lucien Moraweck, Lud Gluskin

Louis Hayward, Warren William (as D'Artagnan), Alan Hale, Bert Roach, Miles Mander, Joan Bennett, *Joseph Schildkraut,* Walter Kingsford, Marion Martin, Montagu Love, Albert Dekker

'Substantial entertainment for general appeal and satisfaction.' – *Variety*

'A sort of combination of *The Prisoner of Zenda* and *The Three Musketeers,* with a few wild west chases thrown in . . . not unentertaining.' – *Richard Mallett, Punch*

† Remade 1976 as a TV movie with Richard Chamberlain, and 1978 as *The Fifth Musketeer* (qv).

AAN: Lucien Moraweck, Lud Gluskin

The Man in the Middle *

GB   1964   94m   bw   Cinemascope
TCF/Pennebaker/Belmont (Walter Seltzer)

In India during World War II, an American lieutenant is indicted for murder and the defence counsel is instructed to lose the case.

Courtroom melodrama with unusual angles; quite intriguing, though the wide screen doesn't help.

w Keith Waterhouse, Willis Hall   *novel The Winston Affair* by Howard Fast   *d* Guy Hamilton   *ph* Wilkie Cooper   *m* John Barry

Robert Mitchum, Trevor Howard, Keenan Wynn, Barry Sullivan, France Nuyen, Alexander Knox

'For once Mitchum seems to have an excuse for keeping his eyes at half mast.' – *Judith Crist*

The Man in the Mirror

GB   1936   82m   bw
JH Productions (Julius Hagen)

A timid man's reflection steps out of the mirror and organizes him.

Modest comedy with a pleasing star.

w F. McGrew Willis, Hugh Mills   *novel* William Garrett   *d* Maurice Elvey   *ph* Curt Courant

Edward Everett Horton, Geneviève Tobin, Garry Marsh, Ursula Jeans, Alastair Sim, Aubrey Mather, Felix Aylmer

'High speed sequences of comic incident put over in fine style.' – *Cinema*

Man in the Moon

GB   1960   99m   bw
Allied Film Makers/Excalibur (Michael Relph)
L

A man who earns his living as Mr Normal, a human guinea pig for scientific research, is chosen as the first astronaut.

Dated comedy which rather dismayingly turns from mild satire to outright farce and fantasy.

w Michael Relph, Bryan Forbes   *d* Basil Dearden
ph Harry Waxman   *m* Philip Green

Kenneth More, Shirley Anne Field, Michael Hordern, John Phillips, John Glyn-Jones, Charles Gray, Norman Bird

The Man in the Moon *

US   1991   99m   Eastmancolor
UIP/MGM/Pathé (Mark Rydell)
V, V*, L, S

In the 1950s, a 14-year-old girl falls in love with a 17-year-old boy, but he prefers her sister.

Weepy period account of growing-up, handled with skill.

w Jenny Wingfield   *d* Robert Mulligan
ph Freddie Francis   *m* James Newton Howard
pd Gene Callahan   *ed* Trudy Ship

Sam Waterson, Tess Harper, Gail Strickland, Reese Witherspoon, Jason London, Emily Warfield

'A disappointing return by Mulligan to the well-ploughed cliché.' – *Philip Strick, Sight and Sound*

'One of the most delicate and heart-warming movies of the year.' – *Roger Ebert*

The Man in the Net

US   1958   96m   bw
UA/Mirisch-Jaguar (Walter Mirisch)

When a painter is accused of murdering his wife, he goes into hiding and is helped by children.

Extremely tedious and inept mystery, doubly disappointing in view of the credits.

w Reginald Rose   *novel* Patrick Quentin
d Michael Curtiz   *ph* John Seitz   *m* Hans Salter

Alan Ladd, Carolyn Jones, Diane Brewster, John Lupton, Charles McGraw, Tom Helmore, John Alexander

The Man in the Road

GB   1957   83m   bw
Gibraltar

An amnesiac scientist is deceived by communists.

Mildly diverting spy caper with a good cast.

w Guy Morgan   *novel He Was Found in the Road* by Anthony Armstrong   *d* Lance Comfort

Derek Farr, Ella Raines, Donald Wolfit, Lisa Daniely, Karel Stepanek, Cyril Cusack

Man in the Saddle

US   1951   87m   Technicolor
Harry Joe Brown/Columbia
GB title: *The Outcast*

A small rancher is victimized by his wealthy neighbour.

Fairly lively Western which develops into a series of gunfights.

w Kenneth Gamet   *d* André de Toth

Randolph Scott, Alexander Knox, Joan Leslie, Ellen Drew, Richard Rober

Man in the Shadow *

US   1957   80m   bw   Cinemascope
U-I (Albert Zugsmith)
GB title: *Pay the Devil*

The sheriff of a small western town investigates a murder against the wishes of a powerful local rancher.

Mini-social drama in which the honest man wins out at last . . . and who would expect anything different. A brooding melodrama which delivers less than it promises.

w Gene L. Coon   *d* Jack Arnold   *ph* Arthur E. Arling   *m* Hans Salter

Jeff Chandler, Orson Welles, Colleen Miller, John Larch, Joe Schneider, Leo Gordon

The Man in the Sky *

GB   1956   87m   bw
Ealing (Seth Holt)
US title: *Decision against Time*

A test pilot refuses to bale out when an engine catches fire; his plight is interwoven with scenes of his family, friends and associates.

Thin suspense drama with some effective moments but too many irrelevant asides.

w William Rose, John Eldridge   *d* Charles Crichton
ph Douglas Slocombe   *m* Gerbrand Schurmann

Jack Hawkins, Elizabeth Sellars, Walter Fitzgerald, Eddie Byrne, John Stratton, Victor Maddern, Lionel Jeffries, Donald Pleasence

The Man in the Trunk

US   1942   70m   bw
TCF

The ghost of a murder victim helps a young attorney to nail the culprit.

Slightly uneasy spook comedy with a good star performance.

w John Larkin   d Malcolm St Clair

Raymond Walburn, Lynne Roberts, George Holmes, J. Carrol Naish, Dorothy Peterson

The Man in the White Suit ****

GB   1951   81m   bw
Ealing (Sidney Cole)
V, V*, L

A scientist produces a fabric that never gets dirty and never wears out. Unions and management are equally aghast.

Brilliant satirical comedy played as farce and put together with meticulous cinematic counterpoint, so that every moment counts and all concerned give of their very best.

w *Roger Macdougall, John Dighton, Alexander Mackendrick* d *Alexander Mackendrick*   ph *Douglas Slocombe* m *Benjamin Frankel*

Alec Guinness, Joan Greenwood, Cecil Parker, Vida Hope, *Ernest Thesiger*, Michael Gough, Howard Marion Crawford, Miles Malleson, *George Benson, Edie Martin*

'The combination of an ingenious idea, a bright, funny and imaginative script, skilful playing and perceptive brisk direction has resulted once more in a really satisfying Ealing comedy.' – *Richard Mallett, Punch*

AAN: script

Man in the Wilderness *

US   1971   105m   Technicolor   Panavision
Warner/Wilderness (Sanford Howard)
V*

In 1820 in the Canadian northwest, a fur trapper is mauled by a grizzly and left for dead, but he learns to survive and sets out for revenge.

Endurance melodrama modelled after *A Man Called Horse*; a bit stretched and only for the hardened, but taking an agreeably unromantic view of nature.

w Jack de Witt   d Richard Sarafian   ph Gerry Fisher   m Johnny Harris

Richard Harris, John Huston, John Bindon, Prunella Ransome, Henry Wilcoxon, Ben Carruthers

The Man Inside

GB   1958   97m   bw   Cinemascope
Columbia/Warwick (Harold Huth)
L

A jeweller's book-keeper steals a priceless diamond and is trailed by various factions half across Europe.

Fairly modest and unenterprising British thriller which hadn't much hope of the world market it was aiming at.

w John Gilling, David Shaw   novel M. E. Chaber d John Gilling   ph Ted Moore   m Richard Bennett

Nigel Patrick, Jack Palance, Anita Ekberg, Anthony Newley, Bonar Colleano, Sid James, Donald Pleasence

A Man is Ten Feet Tall: see *Edge of the City*

A Man Like Eva *

West Germany   1983   89m   colour
Blue Dolphin/Cinevista/Schier-Straub/Trio/Impuls/Maran (Horst Schier, Laurens Straub)
original title: *Ein Mann Wie Eva*

While making a film, its director marries the female star and seduces the male star.

Based on the messy, manipulative life of bisexual film director Rainer Werner Fassbinder, it has one of his leading ladies, Eva Mattes, in the role of the male director, surprising casting that works well and adds an extra spice to an already over-heated narrative.

w Radu Gabrea, Laurens Straub   d Radu Gabrea ph Horst Schier   m Verdi   ad Herbert Buchenberger   ed Dragos-Emmanuel Witowski

Eva Mattes, Lisa Kreuzer, Werner Stocker, Charles Regnier, Carlo Regnier, Charly Muhamed Huber, Albert Kitzl

Man Made Monster *

US   1940   57m   bw
Universal (Jack Bernard)
GB title: *The Electric Man*

A scientist experiments with a man who is impervious to electric shock, and turns him into a walking robot.

A smart little semi-horror originally planned for Karloff and Lugosi.

w Joseph West   d George Waggner   ph Elwood Bredell   md Charles Previn   m Hans Salter sp John P. Fulton

Lon Chaney Jnr, Lionel Atwill, Anne Nagel, Frank Albertson, Samuel S. Hinds

'Who were the women who twisted his life and love – gutting the flame of his incredible genius?'
Man of a Thousand Faces **

US   1957   122m   bw   Cinemascope
U-I (Robert Arthur)
V*, L

The rise to fame of silent screen character actor Lon Chaney.

Moderately commendable biopic with a strong sense of period Hollywood, an excellent star performance, but too much sudsy emoting about deaf mute parents and an ungrateful wife.

w R. Wright Campbell, Ivan Goff, Ben Roberts d Joseph Pevney   ph Russell Metty   m Frank Skinner   ad Alexander Golitzen

James Cagney, Dorothy Malone, Robert Evans (as Irving Thalberg), Roger Smith, *Marjorie Rambeau*, Jane Greer, Jim Backus

'The script and conception are so maudlin and degrading that Cagney's high dedication becomes somewhat oppressive.' – *Pauline Kael, 70s*

AAN: script

Man of Affairs (1936): see *His Lordship*

Man of Affairs

GB   1937   70m   bw
Gaumont British

When the foreign secretary is kidnapped, his twin brother impersonates him.

Lighthearted star vehicle which satisfied.

w Maude Howell and L. Du Garde Peach   play *The Nelson Touch* by Neil Grant   d Herbert Mason

George Arliss, Romilly Lunge, Rene Ray, Jessie Winter, Allan Jeayes

'Business possibilities only moderate.' – *Variety*

Man of Aran **

GB   1934   75m   bw
Gainsborough (Michael Balcon)
V, V*

The primitive life of crofting and fishing folk in the west of Ireland.

A lowering documentary very typical of its maker: highly impressive scene for scene, but tedious as a whole; still, highly remarkable that it was made at all for the commercial cinema.

w Robert and Frances Flaherty   d *Robert Flaherty*

Colman King, Maggie Dirane (amateurs)

'In so far as it is a rendering of the efforts of the Atlantic to overwhelm and demolish a wall of rock, it is magnificent; but the human note is inadequate and unnecessary.' – *E. V. Lucas, Punch*

'However real, it would have made better truth if it had been handled with more of the art of fiction.' – *Otis Ferguson*

'Six thousand feet of such fine and purposeful pictorial composition have seldom been seen on the screen.' – *Observer*

Man of Bronze: see *Jimmy Thorpe, All American*

Man of Conquest

US   1939   99m   bw
Republic (Sol C. Siegel)

The life of Western hero Sam Houston, who became president of Texas.

Competent action/domestic biopic.

w Wells Root, E. E. Paramore Jnr   d George Nicholls Jnr   ph Joseph H. August   m Victor Young   ad John Victor Mackay

Richard Dix, Joan Fontaine, Gail Patrick, Edward Ellis, Victor Jory, Robert Barrat, George Hayes, Ralph Morgan, Robert Armstrong, C. Henry Gordon, Janet Beecher

'A grown-up hoss opera, based on authentic and colorful history, with fairly believable characters, ample action and reasonable suspense.' – *Variety*

AAN: Victor Young; art direction

Man of Evil: see *Fanny by Gaslight*

Man of Flowers *

Australia   1983   91m   Fujicolor
Flowers International (Jane Ballantyne, Paul Cox)
V*, L

A model's relationship with her lover, a blackmailing, cocaine-snorting artist, and her admirer, a wealthy, repressed, middle-aged aesthete, leads to violence.

A study of sexual hang-ups that teeters on the edge of black farce.

w Paul Cox, Bob Ellis   d Paul Cox   ph Yuro Sokol ad Asher Bilu   ed Tim Lewis

Norman Kaye, Alyson Best, Chris Haywood, Sarah Walker, Werner Herzog

Man of Iron

US   1935   62m   bw
Warner

A steel works foreman rises to the boardroom, but doesn't like it.

Rather obvious moral tale without much excitement.

w William Wister Haines, Dawn Powell   d William McGann

Barton MacLane, Mary Astor, John Eldredge, Dorothy Peterson, Joseph Crehan

'Unimportant programme material.' – *Variety*

Man of Iron *

Poland   1981   152m   colour and bw
PRF/Filmowy X
original title: *Czowiek Z Zelaza*

The events of 1980 in Poland are seen through the eyes of a strike leader.

A stirring companion piece to *Man of Marble*; hard tack for the entertainment seeker but as honest a piece of history as one is likely to get from a so-called fiction film.

w *Aleksander Scibor-Rylski*   d *Andrzej Wajda* ph Edward Klosinski   m Andrzej Korzynski

Jerzy Radziwilowicz, Krystyna Janda, Marian Opania

AAN: best foreign film

Man of La Mancha *

US   1972   132m   DeLuxe
UA/PEA (Arthur Hiller)
V, V*, L

Arrested by the Inquisition and thrown into prison, Miguel de Cervantes relates the story of Don Quixote.

Unimaginative but generally good-looking attempt to recreate on the screen an essentially theatrical experience.

w Dale Wasserman   *play* Dale Wasserman
d Arthur Hiller   *ph* Goffredo Rotunno   *md* Laurence Rosenthal   *m* Mitch Leigh   *ly* Joe Darion
ad Luciano Damiani

Peter O'Toole, Sophia Loren, James Coco, Harry Andrews, John Castle, Brian Blessed

'Needful of all the imagination the spectator can muster.' – *Variety*

AAN: Laurence Rosenthal

Man of Marble *
Poland   1978   165m   colour
PRF/Zespol X (Andrzej Wajda)
V*
original title: *Czlowiek Z Marmur*

Young film makers gather material on a political hero of the fifties.

An extended drama on the style of *Citizen Kane* but with much more relevance to contemporary history. A key film to students of Poland, but too specialized for general entertainment.

w Aleksander Scibor-Rylski   *d* Andrzej Wajda
ph Edward Klosinski   *m* Andrzej Korzinski

Jerzy Radziwilowicz, Krystyna Janda, Michael Tarkowski, Tadeusz Lomnicki

The Man of My Life: see *L'Homme de Ma Vie*

Man of the East (dubbed)
Italy/France   1972   125m   Technicolor
    Techniscope
UA/PEA/Artistes Associés (Alberto Grimaldi)
original title: *... E Poi Lo Chiamarono Il Magnifico*

An English fop is taught how to fight and shoot by three outlaws.

Over-long comedy Western, in which the jokes are few and far between.

w Enzo Barboni   *d* E. B. Clutcher (Enzo Barboni)
ph Aldo Giordani   *m* Guido de Angelis, Maurizio de Angelis   *ad* Enzo Bulgarelli   *ed* Eugenio Alabiso

Terence Hill (Mario Girotti), Yanti Somer, Gregory Walcott, Harry Carey, Dominici Barto, Riccardo Pizzuti

'A predictable plot ... is strung out to almost interminable length by the director's own script which never misses an opportunity to employ five sequences where one would do.' – *David Pirie, MFB*

Man of the Hour: see *Colonel Effingham's Raid*

Man of the Moment
GB   1935   82m   bw
Warner

An engaged young man saves a girl from suicide and falls in love with her.

Minor romantic comedy of predictable development.

w Roland Pertwee, Guy Bolton and A. R. Rawlinson
play Yves Mirande   *d* Monty Banks

Douglas Fairbanks Jnr, Laura La Plante, Claude Hulbert, Margaret Lockwood, Donald Calthrop, Monty Banks

Man of the People
US   1937   80m   bw
Lucien Hubbard/MGM

An Italian immigrant works for a law degree but is forced in with crooks.

Political power play without much zest despite good acting.

w Frank Dolan   *d* Edwin L. Marin

Joseph Calleia, Thomas Mitchell, Florence Rice, Ted Healy, Catherine Doucet

'Patently primed for duals, where it can hold its own.' – *Variety*

Man of the West
US   1958   100m   DeLuxe   Cinemascope
UA/Ashton (Walter M. Mirisch)
V*

In 1874 Arizona, a reformed gunman is cajoled by his old buddies to help them rob a bank.

Talkative, set-bound, cliché-ridden star Western with minor compensations.

w Reginald Rose   *novel* Will C. Brown   *d* Anthony Mann   *ph* Ernest Haller   *m* Leigh Harline

Gary Cooper, Lee J. Cobb, Julie London, Arthur O'Connell, Jack Lord, John Dehner, Royal Dano, Robert Wilke

Man of the World
US   1931   71m   bw
Paramount

A gentleman racketeer operates on American playboys in Paris.

Predictable but smooth star vehicle.

w Herman J. Mankiewicz   *d* Richard Wallace

William Powell, Carole Lombard, Wynne Gibson, Guy Kibbee, Lawrence Gray

'Anything better than moderate for gross must come through the star's personal pull.' – *Variety*

Man of Two Worlds
US   1933   92m   bw
RKO

An Eskimo is temporarily civilized, but returns to the Arctic wild.

Uneventful and somewhat chilly drama which fails to convince.

w Howard and Ainsworth Morgan   *novel* Ainsworth Morgan   *d* J. Walter Ruben

Francis Lederer, Elissa Landi, Henry Stephenson, J. Farrell MacDonald, Walter Byron

Man on a String
US   1960   92m   bw
Columbia/Louis de Rochemont
GB title: *Confessions of a Counterspy*

A Russian-born Hollywood producer is asked by the Russians to work as a spy but becomes a double agent.

Slightly unbelievable biopic about Boris Morros, rather childlike in its simplicity and not too entertaining either.

w John Kafka, Virginia Shaler   *book* Ten Years a Counterspy by Boris Morros   *d* André de Toth
ph Charles Lawton Jnr and others   *m* George Duning

Ernest Borgnine, Kerwin Mathews, Colleen Dewhurst, Alexander Scourby, Glenn Corbett, Vladimir Sokoloff

Man on a Swing
US   1975   108m   Technicolor
Paramount (Howard B. Jaffe)

Investigations into a murder are helped by a would-be medium.

Overlong and confused psycho-mystery with one stand-out performance.

w David Zelag Goodman   *d* Frank Perry   *ph* Adam Holender   *m* Lalo Schifrin

Cliff Robertson, *Joel Grey*, Dorothy Tristan, Peter Masterson

'Runs out of interest long before it runs out of film.' – *Variety*

Man on a Tightrope *
US   1953   105m   bw
TCF (Robert L. Jacks)

A Czech circus owner has trouble with the communist authorities and tries to escape.

Adventure story with cold war pretensions which virtually kill it.

w Robert Sherwood   *d* Elia Kazan   *ph* Georg Krause   *m* Franz Waxman

Fredric March, Cameron Mitchell, Adolphe Menjou, Gloria Grahame, Terry Moore, Richard Boone, John Dehner, Dorothea Wieck

The Man on America's Conscience: see *Tennessee Johnson*

Man on Fire
US   1957   95m   bw
MGM (Sol C. Siegel)

When his wife divorces him, a middle-aged man refuses to hand over their son.

Low-key personal drama of very moderate interest and modest budget.   *wd* Ranald MacDougall
ph Joseph Ruttenberg   *m* David Raksin

Bing Crosby, Inger Stevens, Mary Fickett, E. G. Marshall

A Man on the Beach
GB   1956   29m   Eastmancolor
Anthony Hinds/Exclusive

A man on the run is cared for and handed over to the police by a blind recluse.

Modest featurette which scarcely justifies its credits. *story* Victor Canning   *d* Joseph Losey

Donald Wolfit, Michael Medwin, Michael Ripper

The Man on the Eiffel Tower *
US   1949   82m   Anscocolor
A & T (Irving Allen)
V*

A crazy killer defies Inspector Maigret to discover his identity.

Early independent production, an unsatisfactory crime melodrama with international talent and Paris locations. Some quirky acting carries it through.

w Harry Brown   *novel* A Battle of Nerves by Georges Simenon   *d* Burgess Meredith   *ph* Stanley Cortez
m Michel Michelet

Charles Laughton, Burgess Meredith, Franchot Tone, Robert Hutton, Jean Wallace, Patricia Roc, Wilfrid Hyde-White, Belita

† Some scenes were directed by Charles Laughton and some by Franchot Tone.

The Man on the Flying Trapeze *
US   1935   65m   bw
Paramount (William Le Baron)
GB title: *The Memory Expert*

Adventures of an oppressed family man who is useful to his boss because of his prodigious memory.

Plotless rigmarole of shapeless comedy sketches, for star fans.

w Ray Harris, Sam Hardy, Jack Cunningham, Bobby Vernon   *story* Charles Bogle (W. C. Fields)
d Clyde Bruckman   *ph* Al Gilks

W. C. Fields, Kathleen Howard, Mary Brian, Grady Sutton, Vera Lewis, Lucien Littlefield, Oscar Apfel

'A series of gags unrelated to the title. Under average.' – *Variety*

The Man on the Roof *

Sweden   1976   109m   Eastmancolor
Svensk Filmindustri (Per Berglund)
original title: *Mannen pò Taket*

A brutal policeman is murdered, and a rooftop sniper turns out to be the culprit.

Alternately vivid and lumbering police thriller with a regrettable tendency to moralize.

wd Bo Widerberg   *novel* The Abominable Man by Max Sjöwall, Max Wahlöös   *ph* Odd Geir Saether, Per Kallberg, others   *m* Björn Lindh

Carl Gustav Lindstedt, Gunnel Wadner, Hòkan Serner, Sven Wollter

Man on the Run

GB   1949   82m   bw
ABPC

A deserter becomes innocently involved in a jewel robbery.

Competent crime programmer.

wd Lawrence Huntington

Derek Farr, Joan Hopkins, Edward Chapman, Laurence Harvey, John Stuart

Man Proof

US   1937   74m   bw
MGM (Louis D. Lighton)

In trying to win back her man a woman discovers she really loves someone else.

Modest romantic comedy which leaves its stars at sea.

w Vincent Lawrence, Waldemar Young, George Oppenheimer   *novel* The Four Marys by Fanny Heaslip Lea   *d* Richard Thorpe   *ph* Karl Freund   *m* Franz Waxman

Myrna Loy, Franchot Tone, Walter Pidgeon, Rosalind Russell, Nana Bryant, Ruth Hussey

'A smartly produced, well-directed and excellently acted society comedy drama.' – *Variety*

The Man They Could Not Hang

US   1939   65m   bw
Columbia
V*

A scientist working on a mechanical heart causes the death of a volunteer student. He is executed, but his assistant restores him to life and he determines to murder those who convicted him.

Predictable horror hokum which set Karloff on his mad doctor cycle.

w Karl Brown   *d* Nick Grinde   *ph* Benjamin Kline   *md* Morris Stoloff

Boris Karloff, Lorna Gray, Robert Wilcox, Roger Pryor, Don Beddoe, Byron Foulger

A Man to Remember *

US   1938   80m   bw
RKO (Robert Sisk)

At a small-town doctor's funeral, his life is remembered by mourners.

Modestly effective family film.

w Dalton Trumbo   *novel* Failure by Katharine Haviland-Taylor   *d* Garson Kanin   *ph* J. Roy Hunt   *m* Roy Webb

Edward Ellis, Anne Shirley, Lee Bowman, William Henry, Granville Bates

'No sock for the marquee but a fine, well-made little picture.' – *Variety*

A Man to Respect

Italy/West Germany   1972   108m   Technicolor
Techniscope
Eagle/Verona Cinematografica/Paramount-Orion (Marina Cicogna)
aka: *Un Uomo da Rispettare*

On his release from jail, a safebreaker trains a young acrobat in his skills so that they can commit a double robbery.

An ingeniously plotted thriller that indulges in over-statement.

w Mino Roli   *story* Franco Bucceri, Roberto Leoni   *d* Michele Lupo   *ph* Tonino Delli Colli   *m* Ennio Morricone   *ad* Francesco Bronzi   *ed* Tony Zila

Kirk Douglas, Giuliano Gemma, Florinda Bolkan

'A small triumph of dehumanised style.' – *Richard Combs, MFB*

'She Put Her Life In His Hands. Unfortunately, His Hands Have A Life Of Their Own.'

Man Trouble

US   1992   100m   DeLuxe
First Independent/Penta/American Filmworks/Budding Grove
(Bruce Gilbert, Carole Eastman)
V, V*, L

A dog-trainer becomes involved with an opera singer when she decides she needs a guard dog to protect her home.

An unlikely romance is at the centre of an even unlikelier narrative – and even if you swallow the implausibilities, the result is still sickly.

w Carole Eastman   *d* Bob Rafelson   *ph* Stephen H. Burum   *m* Georges Delerue   *pd* Mel Bourne   *ed* William Steinkamp

Jack Nicholson, Ellen Barkin, Harry Dean Stanton, Beverly D'Angelo, Michael McKean, Saul Rubineck, Viveka Davis

'An insultingly trivial star vehicle.' – *Variety*

'Unredeemedly awful.' – *Philip French, Observer*

The Man Upstairs *

GB   1958   88m   bw
British Lion/ACT (Robert Dunbar)
V

A mild-mannered lodger becomes violent, injures a policeman, and barricades himself in his room.

Character melodrama reminiscent of both *Fourteen Hours* and *Le Jour se Lève*, but not so interesting as either.

w Alun Falconer   *d* Don Chaffey   *ph* Gerald Gibbs

Richard Attenborough, Bernard Lee, Donald Houston, Dorothy Alison, Maureen Connell, Kenneth Griffith, Virginia Maskell, Patricia Jessel

Man Wanted

US   1932   60m   bw
Warner

A business woman takes on a male secretary.

Yawnworthy comedy drama with no surprises.

w Robert Lord   *d* William Dieterle

Kay Francis, David Manners, Andy Devine, Una Merkel, Kenneth Thompson

'Threadbare plot weakens this for the big theatres and makes it extremely light and familiar entertainment for the others.' – *Variety*

The Man Who Broke the Bank at Monte Carlo *

US   1935   67m   bw
Twentieth Century (Nunnally Johnson)

A Russian émigré becomes a taxi driver, wins a fortune at roulette, loses it all again, and returns happily to his cab.

Very mild, unconvincing and not very entertaining malarkey which rested squarely on its star, who carried it with aplomb.

w Nunnally Johnson   *d* Stephen Roberts   *ph* Ernest Palmer   *md* Oliver Bradley

Ronald Colman, Joan Bennett, Colin Clive, Nigel Bruce, Montagu Love, Frank Reicher, Ferdinand Gottschalk

'Nice production though lacks dash . . . Colman at times seems to be playing under wraps. Should do fairly well.' – *Variety*

'The richest roles of romance and redemption they ever played!'

The Man Who Came Back

US   1930   74m   bw
Fox

A reckless young man is reformed when he finds his erstwhile sweetheart now a drug addict in Hong Kong.

Earnest melodrama which not surprisingly damaged the talkie success of a celebrated screen team, and must now seem risible in the extreme.

w Edwin J. Burke   *play* Jules Eckert Goo   *story and novel* John Fleming Wilson   *d* Raoul Walsh   *ph* Arthur Edeson   *pd* Joseph Urban

Janet Gaynor, Charles Farrell, Kenneth MacKenna, William Holden, Mary Forbes, Peter Gawthorne

'Gripping old melodrama of drugs and degradation tamed down and made into a cheerful sentimental piece. Co-star names make it a strong bid.' – *Variety*

'Sophisticates will give it one big horse laugh.' – *Photoplay*

The Man Who Came Back (1941): see *Swamp Water*

The Man Who Came to Dinner ***

US   1941   112m   bw
Warner (Jack Saper, Jerry Wald)
V*, L

An acid-tongued radio celebrity breaks his hip while on a lecture tour, and terrorizes the inhabitants of the suburban home where he must stay for several weeks.

Delightfully malicious caricature of Alexander Woollcott which, though virtually confined to one set, moves so fast that one barely notices the lack of cinematic variety, and certainly provides more than a laugh a minute, especially for those old enough to understand all the references.

w Julius J. and Philip G. Epstein   *play George S. Kaufman, Moss Hart*   *d* William Keighley   *ph* Tony Gaudio   *m* Frederick Hollander

Monty Woolley, Bette Davis, Ann Sheridan, *Jimmy Durante* (spoofing Chico Marx), *Reginald Gardiner* (spoofing Noël Coward), Richard Travis, *Billie Burke, Grant Mitchell, Ruth Vivian, Mary Wickes,* George Barbier, Elisabeth Fraser

WHITESIDE (Monty Woolley) to his nurse, who won't let him eat chocolates: 'I had an aunt who ate a box of chocolates every day of her life. She lived to be a hundred and two, and when she had been dead three days, she looked healthier than you do now!'

NURSE (Mary Wickes): 'I am not only walking out on this case, Mr Whiteside, I am leaving the nursing profession. I became a nurse because all my life, ever since I was a little girl, I was filled with the idea of serving a suffering humanity. After one month with you, Mr Whiteside, I am going to work in a munitions factory. From now on, anything I can do to help exterminate the human race will fill me with the greatest of pleasure. If Florence Nightingale had ever nursed YOU, Mr Whiteside, she would have married Jack the Ripper instead of founding the Red Cross!'

WHITESIDE (introducing his secretary): 'This ageing debutante, Mr Jefferson, I retain in my employ only because she is the sole support of her two-headed brother.'

BANJO (Jimmy Durante): 'Did you ever get the feeling that you wanted to stay, and still get the feeling that you wanted to go?'

BEVERLY CARLTON (Reginald Gardiner impersonating Noël Coward): 'Don't tell me how you are, Sherry, I want none of the tiresome details. I've very little time, and so the conversation will be entirely about me, and I shall love it. Shall I tell you how I glittered through the South Seas like a silver scimitar, or would you rather hear how I finished a three-act play with one hand and made love to a maharaja's daughter with the other?'

The Man Who Changed His Mind
GB   1936   66m   bw
Gainsborough
US title: *The Man Who Lived Again*

A scientist dabbles in brain transplants.

Mild British-style horror piece; not a success.

w John L. Balderston, L. DuGarde Peach and Sidney Gilliat   *d* Robert Stevenson

Boris Karloff, Anna Lee, Donald Calthrop, John Loder, Frank Cellier, Cecil Parker

'A spine-freezer of routine construction. The accents are very limey and the way laboratory is pronounced may have American schoolchildren wondering.' – *Variety*

The Man Who Changed His Name
GB   1934   80m   bw
Universal/Twickenham (Julius Hagen)

A wife begins to suspect that her husband is trying to murder her and her former lover.

Tepid comedy thriller that betrays its stage origins and is not helped by being somnambulistically acted and directed.

w H. Fowler Mear, Edgar Wallace   *play* Edgar Wallace   *d* Henry Edwards   *ph* Sydney Blythe   *md* W. L. Trytel   *ad* James A. Carter   *ed* Jack Harris, Michael C. Chorlton

Lyn Harding, Betty Stockfield, Leslie Perrins, Ben Welden, Aubrey Mather, Stanley Vine

The Man Who Cheated Himself
US   1950   81m   bw
TCF (Jack M. Warner)

A woman shoots her husband and her homicide detective lover covers up for her.

Efficient crime melodrama.

w Seton I. Miller, Philip MacDonald   *d* Felix Feist   *ph* Russell Harlan   *m* Louis Forbes

Lee J. Cobb, Jane Wyatt, John Dall, Terry Frost

The Man Who Could Cheat Death
GB   1959   83m   Technicolor
Paramount/Hammer (Anthony Nelson-Keys)

A surgeon looks 35 but is really 104, having had a series of gland operations performed on himself.

Vulgar, gory, gruesomely coloured Hammer version of a rather attractive play, previously filmed under its original title *The Man in Half Moon Street* (qv). The shocks are routine, and entertainment value is minimal.

w Jimmy Sangster   *play* Barrie Lyndon   *d* Terence Fisher   *ph* Jack Asher   *m* Richard Rodney Bennett

Anton Diffring, Hazel Court, Christopher Lee, Arnold Marle, Delphi Lawrence, Francis de Wolff

The Man Who Could Work Miracles ***
GB   1936   82m   bw
London (Alexander Korda)
V*, L

A city clerk discovers he has the power to work miracles (given him by sportive gods) and nearly causes the end of the Earth.

Slow-moving but rather pleasing variation on a simple theme.

w Lajos Biro   *story* H. G. Wells   *d* Lothar Mendes   *ph* Harold Rosson   *m* Mischa Spoliansky

Roland Young, Ralph Richardson, Ernest Thesiger, Edward Chapman, Joan Gardner, Sophie Stewart, Robert Cochrane, George Zucco, Lawrence Hanray, George Sanders

'Supposedly a comedy. A weakling: little draw power on this side.' – *Variety*

'Sometimes fake poetry, sometimes unsuccessful comedy, sometimes farce, sometimes sociological discussion, without a spark of creative talent or a trace of film ability.' – *Graham Greene*

The Man Who Couldn't Get Enough: see
Confessions of a Sex Maniac

The Man Who Cried Wolf
US   1937   67m   bw
Universal

An actor continually confesses to crimes he didn't commit in the hope that when he does commit one he won't be believed.

An attractive idea rather poorly handled.

w Charles Grayson and Sy Bartlett   *d* Lewis R. Foster

Lewis Stone, Tom Brown, Barbara Read, Marjorie Main, Forrester Harvey

'Will get by as the number two feature on dual bills.' – *Variety*

The Man Who Dared
US   1933   72m   bw
Fox

The life of a local politician, based on Mayor Cermak of Chicago.

Episodic but not unpleasant biopic; it adds up to very little, though.

w Dudley Nichols, Lamar Trotti   *d* Hamilton McFadden

Preston Foster, Zita Johann, Joan Marsh, Irene Biller, Leon Waycoff

'The most flattering account ever written of any man's life . . . but as a commercial talker it's not likely to get very far. Even in Chicago they didn't care for it.' – *Variety*

The Man Who Fell to Earth *
GB   1976   138m   colour   Panavision
British Lion (Michael Deeley, Barry Spikings)
V, V*, L

A visitor from another planet tries to colonize Earth, but his powers are destroyed and he ends an alcoholic cripple.

A weird piece of intellectual science fiction made weirder by longueurs of all varieties: obscure narrative, voyeuristic sex, pop music and metaphysics. Not an easy film or a likeable one, despite its great technical skill.

w Paul Mayersburg   *novel* Walter Tevis   *d* Nicolas Roeg   *ph* Anthony Richmond   *md* John Phillips

David Bowie, Rip Torn, Candy Clark, Buck Henry

'Once you have pierced through its glittering veneer, you find only another glittering veneer underneath.' – *Michael Billington, Illustrated London News*

'There is a punch line, but it takes forever, and great expectations slump away.' – *Charles Champlin, L.A. News*

'You feel finally that all that has been achieved has been to impose an aura of mystery and enigma where essentially there is none; to turn a simple tale into the sort of accumulation of sensations that has become fashionable.' – *David Robinson, The Times*

The Man Who Finally Died
GB   1962   100m   bw   Cinemascope
British Lion/Magna/White Cross (Norman Williams)

A German-born Englishman returns to Bavaria for

news of his father, and becomes involved in a spy plot.

Busy adaptation of a TV serial with a convoluted plot which might have been more pacily developed and better explained.

w Lewis Greifer, Louis Marks   *d* Quentin Lawrence   *ph* Stephen Dade   *m* Philip Green

Stanley Baker, Peter Cushing, Mai Zetterling, Eric Portman, Niall MacGinnis, Nigel Green, Barbara Everest, Harold Scott

The Man Who Found Himself
US   1937   67m   bw
RKO (Cliff Reid)

A nurse helps a downcast doctor face his problems and renew his enthusiasm for life.

Simple-minded programmer.

w J. Robert Bren, Edmund Hartmann, G. V. Atwater   *d* Lew Landers   *ph* Roy Hunt

John Beal, Joan Fontaine, Philip Huston, Jane Walsh, George Irving

'No names in this hokey B session . . . flapdoodle with a capital F.' – *Variety*

The Man Who Had His Hair Cut Short *
Belgium   1966   94m   bw
Belgian Cultural Ministry

A frustrated law clerk has an aberration after attending an autopsy and meeting again an old love.

Pessimistic case history with unpleasant details often brilliantly recorded.

w Anna de Pagter, André Delvaux   *d* André Delvaux   *ph* Ghislain Cloquet   *m* Freddy Devreese

Seene Rouffaer, Beata Tyszkiewicz, Hector Camerlynck

The Man Who Had Power over Women
GB   1970   89m   Eastmancolor
Kettledrum/Avco
V*

A successful public relations man comes to hate himself, his job and what it has done to his marriage.

Fashionable wallow in guilt and luxury, not very convincingly done.

w Alan Scott and Chris Bryant   *novel* Gordon Williams   *d* John Krish

Rod Taylor, Carol White, James Booth, Penelope Horner, Charles Korvin, Alexandra Stewart, Keith Barron

The Man Who Haunted Himself
GB   1970   94m   Technicolor
ABP/Excalibur (Michael Relph)
V, V*

After recovering from a road accident, a staid businessman finds that he has an evil doppelganger who steals his wife and his job.

Mildly effective if inexplicable story idea which served more suitably as a Hitchcock TV half hour and here, despite adequate production, outstays its welcome.

w Basil Dearden, Michael Relph   *story* The Case of Mr Pelham by Anthony Armstrong   *d* Basil Dearden   *ph* Tony Spratling   *m* Michael Lewis

Roger Moore, Hildegarde Neil, Olga-Georges Picot, Anton Rodgers, Freddie Jones, Thorley Walters, John Carson, John Welsh

The Man Who Knew Too Much ***
GB   1934   84m   bw
GFD/Gaumont British (Ivor Montagu)
V*, L

A child is kidnapped by spies to ensure her father's silence, but he springs into action.

Splendid early Hitchcock which after a faded start moves into memorable sequences involving a dentist, an East End mission and the Albert Hall. All very stagey by today's standards, but much more fun than the expensive remake.

w A. R. Rawlinson, Charles Bennett, D. B. Wyndham Lewis, Edwin Greenwood, Emlyn Williams d Alfred Hitchcock ph Curt Courant m Arthur Benjamin

Leslie Banks, Edna Best, Peter Lorre, Nova Pilbeam, Frank Vosper, Hugh Wakefield, Pierre Fresnay

'A natural and easy production that runs smoothly and has the hallmark of sincerity.' – Variety

'The film's mainstay is its refined sense of the incongruous.' – Peter John Dyer, 1964

'A single clash of cymbals that will rock the lives of an American family!'
The Man Who Knew Too Much *
US 1956 120m Technicolor Vistavision
(Paramount) Alfred Hitchcock
V, V*, L

Flaccid remake of the above, twice as long and half as entertaining, though it does improve after a very slow start.

w John Michael Hayes, Angus MacPhail d Alfred Hitchcock ph Robert Burks m Bernard Herrmann

James Stewart, Doris Day, Bernard Miles, Brenda de Banzie, Daniel Gelin, Ralph Truman, Mogens Wieth, Alan Mowbray, Hillary Brooke

'The balance between character and incident in the earlier film makes a far better thriller.' – Observer

'The remake is heavy and oppressive, the suspense often risible, and the moments of comic relief fall flat.' – Sunday Times

'Let's say the first version is the work of a talented amateur and the second was made by a professional.' – Alfred Hitchcock

AA: song 'Que Sera Sera' (m/ly Jay Livingston, Ray Evans)

The Man Who Lived Again: see The Man Who Changed His Mind

The Man Who Lost Himself
US 1941 71m bw
Universal

A man back from the tropics finds himself playing the part of a lookalike millionaire.

Pleasantly nimble farce; not original but agreeable to watch.

w Eddie Moran novel H. DeVere Stacpoole d Edward Ludwig

Brian Aherne, Kay Francis, S. Z. Sakall, Henry Stephenson, Nils Asther, Sig Rumann

The Man Who Loved Cat Dancing
US 1973 114m Metrocolor Panavision
MGM (Martin Poll, Eleanor Perry)
V, V*

A runaway wife is kidnapped by train thieves and comes to love one of them.

Outdoor variation on No Orchids for Miss Blandish, remarkably lacking in any kind of entertainment value.

w Eleanor Perry novel Marilyn Dunham d Richard Sarafian ph Harry Stradling Jnr m John Williams

Sarah Miles, Burt Reynolds, Lee J. Cobb, Jack Warden, George Hamilton, Bo Hopkins, Robert Donner, Jay Silverheels

'Any number of things have gone wrong with this peculiarly dreary western.' – Tom Milne

'Sarah Miles undergoes more perils than Pauline.' – Variety

The Man Who Loved Redheads
GB 1954 90m Eastmancolor
British Lion/London Films (Josef Somlo)

Throughout his career, a diplomat seeks women who resemble the redhead with whom in youth he had had an idyllic affair.

West End theatrical moonshine, poorly filmed in ugly colour but saved by the cast.

w Terence Rattigan play Who Is Sylvia? by Terence Rattigan d Harold French ph Georges Périnal m Benjamin Frankel

John Justin, Moira Shearer, Roland Culver, Gladys Cooper, Denholm Elliott, Harry Andrews, Patricia Cutts, Moira Fraser, Joan Benham, Jeremy Spenser

'Deciding which woman in the world he loved most is driving him out of his mind!'
The Man Who Loved Women
France 1977 119m Eastmancolor
Les Films du Carrosse/PAA (Marcel Bebert)
V*

A man spends his life in pursuit of women and dies in the chase.

Sour comedy which doesn't quite come off.

w François Truffaut, Michel Fermaud, Suzanne Schiffman d François Truffaut ph Nestor Almendros m Maurice Jaubert

Charles Denner, Brigitte Fossey, Leslie Caron, Nelly Borgeaud, Nathalie Baye

'Doesn't just miss: it has virtually nothing.' – Stanley Kauffmann

The Man Who Loved Women
US 1983 110m Metrocolor
Columbia/Delphi/Blake Edwards (Blake Edwards, Tony Adams)
V*, L

An American remake of the above, with even less success.

w Blake Edwards, Milton Wexler, Geoffrey Edwards d Blake Edwards ph Haskell Wexler m Henry Mancini

Burt Reynolds, Julie Andrews, Kim Basinger, Marilu Henner, Cynthia Sikes, Jennifer Edwards

'The strangest story in the annals of naval espionage!'
The Man Who Never Was **
GB 1955 102m DeLuxe Cinemascope
Sumar/André Hakim
V*

In 1943, the British secret service confuses the Germans by dropping a dead man into the sea with false documents.

Mainly enjoyable true life war story marred by an emotional romantic sub-plot with a double twist but helped by an equally fictitious spy hunt which cheers up the last half hour.

w Nigel Balchin book Ewen Montagu d Ronald Neame ph Oswald Morris m Alan Rawsthorne

Clifton Webb, Robert Flemyng, Gloria Grahame, Stephen Boyd, Laurence Naismith, Josephine Griffin

The Man Who Played God *
US 1932 81m bw
Warner
GB title: The Silent Voice

A musician goes deaf but finds satisfaction in helping a young student.

Stagey but effective star vehicle which Arliss also played as a silent film. Remade as Sincerely Yours (qv).

w Julian Josephson, Maude Howell play The Silent Voice by Jules Eckert Goodman d John G. Adolfi ph James Van Trees

George Arliss, Violet Heming, Ivan Simpson, Bette Davis, Louise Closser Hale, Donald Cook, Ray Milland

'Will need all the Arliss name strength to pull average returns.' – Variety

The Man Who Reclaimed His Head *
US 1934 81m bw
Universal (Henry Henigson)

A writer who feels he has been betrayed and his brain sapped by his publisher takes a gruesome revenge.

Oddball period melodrama tailored rather unsuccessfully for a new star. Remade as Strange Confession (see Inner Sanctum).

w Jean Bart, Samuel Ornitz play Jean Bart d Edward Ludwig ph Merrit Gerstad m Heinz Roemheld

Claude Rains, Joan Bennett, Lionel Atwill, Juanita Quigley, Henry O'Neill, Lawrence Grant

'Interesting screen diversion . . . Far from a smash, but good enough to keep to the average level or above.' – Variety

The Man Who Shot Liberty Valance ***
US 1962 122m bw
Paramount/John Ford (Willis Goldbeck)
V*, L

A tenderfoot becomes a hero for shooting a bad man, but the shot was really fired by his friend and protector.

Clumsy, obvious Western with the director over-indulging himself but providing some good scenes in comedy vein.

w James Warner Bellah, Willis Goldbeck d John Ford ph William H. Clothier m Cyril Mockridge

James Stewart, John Wayne, Vera Miles, Lee Marvin, Edmond O'Brien, Andy Devine, Jeanette Nolan, John Qualen, Ken Murray, Woody Strode, Lee Van Cleef, Strother Martin, John Carradine

'Like Queen Victoria, John Wayne has become lovable because he stayed in the saddle into a new era.' – Judith Crist

'A heavy-spirited piece of nostalgia.' – Pauline Kael, 1975

'A film whose fascination lies less in what it is itself than in what it reveals about the art of its maker.' – William S. Pechter

'When truth becomes legend, print the legend!'
The Man Who Talked Too Much
US 1940 75m bw
Warner (Edmund Grainger)

A smart defence attorney gets the goods on a gangster and decides to turn him in.

Below-par remake of The Mouthpiece (qv), later filmed again as Illegal (qv).

w Walter de Leon, Tom Reed play The Mouthpiece by Frank J. Collins d Vincent Sherman ph Sid Hickox

George Brent, Brenda Marshall, Richard Barthelmess, Virginia Bruce, William Lundigan, John Litel, George Tobias, William Armetta, Alan Baxter

'Human or inhuman, no woman is safe!'
The Man Who Turned to Stone
US 1957 71m bw
Clover/Columbia
V*

A girls' reformatory is taken over by a group of zombie scientists born in the 18th century.

Cheap horror item with a few choice moments for connoisseurs of the absurd.

w Raymond T. Marcus d Leslie Kardos

Victor Jory, Ann Doran, Charlotte Austin, William Hudson, Paul Cavanagh

The Man Who Understood Women

US 1959 105m Eastmancolor Cinemascope
TCF (Nunnally Johnson)

An arrogant, exhibitionist film producer finally alienates his long-suffering wife.

Something of an aberration, with good scenes submerged in an unholy mixture of sharp comedy and sentimental melodrama.

wd Nunnally Johnson   *novel* Colours of the Day by Romain Gary   *ph* Milton Krasner   *m* Robert Emmett Dolan

Henry Fonda, Leslie Caron, Myron McCormick, Cesare Danova, Marcel Dalio, Conrad Nagel, Harry Ellerbe

'A pretentious extravaganza on a romantic theme.' – *MFB*

The Man Who Watched Trains Go By

GB 1952 80m Technicolor
Raymond Stross
V*
aka: *Paris Express*

A clerk steals money in order to fulfil his wish of world travel, and this leads to murder.

Miscast minor Simenon, not exactly badly made but with no spark of excitement or suspense.   *wd* Harold French   *novel* Georges Simenon   *ph* Otto Heller   *m* Benjamin Frankel

Claude Rains, Marius Goring, Marta Toren, Anouk Aimée, Herbert Lom, Ferdy Mayne

The Man Who Would Be King *

US 1975 129m colour Panavision
Columbia/Allied Artists/Persky-Bright/Devon (John Foreman)
V, V*, L, S

In India in the 1880s, two adventurers find themselves accepted as kings by a remote tribe, but greed betrays them.

After an ingratiating start this ambitious fable becomes more predictable, and comedy gives way to unpleasantness. Despite its sporadic high quality, one does not remember it with enthusiasm.

w John Huston, Gladys Hill   *story* Rudyard Kipling   *d* John Huston   *ph* Oswald Morris   *m* Maurice Jarre   *pd* Alexander Trauner

Sean Connery, Michael Caine, Christopher Plummer (as Kipling), Saeed Jaffrey, Jack May, Shakira Caine

'Huston has now made a good picture – not up to the standard of his early best but with sweep and guts and with nicely overblown cinematic eloquence.' – *Stanley Kauffmann*

AAN: script

The Man Who Wouldn't Talk

US 1940 72m bw
Sol M. Wurtzel/TCF

A man on trial for murder has such a mysterious background that he may even be the victim.

Efficient remake of Paul Muni's *The Valiant.*

w Robert Ellis, Helen Logan, Lester Ziffren and Edward Ettinger   *d* David Burton

Lloyd Nolan, Jean Rogers, Richard Clarke, Eric Blore, Mae Marsh

The Man Who Wouldn't Talk

GB 1957 97m bw
British Lion/Everest (Herbert Wilcox)

A lady QC gets an acquittal for a man who can't defend himself on a murder charge because of loyalty to a scientist on the run.

Efficient courtroom melodrama based on a somewhat incredible and even uninteresting situation.

w Edgar Lustgarten   *story* Stanley Jackson   *d* Herbert Wilcox   *ph* Gordon Dines   *m* Stanley Black

Anna Neagle, Anthony Quayle, Zsa Zsa Gabor, Katherine Kath, Dora Bryan, Patrick Allen

The Man with a Cloak *

US 1951 81m bw
MGM (Stephen Ames)

In 1848 New York, a mysterious stranger (who turns out to be Edgar Allan Poe) helps a young French girl to keep her inheritance.

Curious domestic melodrama set on MGM's choicest sets; its playful literary allusion causes it to fall between suspense thriller and character drama, but the acting keeps one watching.

w Frank Fenton   *story* John Dickson Carr   *d* Fletcher Markle   *ph* George Folsey   *m* David Raksin

Joseph Cotten, Barbara Stanwyck, Leslie Caron, Louis Calhern, Joe de Santis, Jim Backus, Margaret Wycherly

The Man with a Hundred Faces: see *Crackerjack*

Man with a Million: see *The Million Pound Note*

The Man with an Umbrella: see *It Rains on Our Love*

The Man with Bogart's Face

US 1980 106m CFI color
TCF/Melvin Simon (Andrew J. Fenady)
V*

An unremarkable private eye gets lots of assignments because he looks like Humphrey Bogart.

Amiably nostalgic romp, not too spoofy to be enjoyable for its own sake, but notably underproduced.

w Andrew J. Fenady   *novel* Andrew J. Fenady   *d* Robert Day   *ph* Richard C. Glouner   *m* George Duning

Robert Sacchi, Misty Rowe, Michelle Phillips, Franco Nero, Olivia Hussey, Victor Buono, Herbert Lom, George Raft, Yvonne de Carlo, Jay Robinson, Mike Mazurki, Henry Wilcoxon, Victor Sen Yung

The Man with My Face

US 1951 77m bw
UA/Edward F. Gardner

A successful young man finds a double in his place at both home and office, and himself branded as an impostor.

Intriguing yarn which deserved a better production.

w Samuel W. Taylor, Edward J. Montagne, T. J. McGowan and Vincent Bogart   *novel* Samuel W. Taylor   *d* Edward J. Montagne

Barry Nelson, Lynn Ainley, John Harvey, Carole Matthews, Jack Warden

The Man with Nine Lives *

US 1940 73m bw
Columbia
GB title: *Behind the Door*

A scientist believes he can cure cancer by freezing, but accidentally locks himself and his patients in an underground ice chamber for seven years, and goes berserk when thawed out.

Interesting, rather prophetic science fiction thriller which rather lacks the style required to put it over.

w Karl Brown   *story* Harold Shumate   *d* Nick Grinde   *ph* Benjamin Kline

Boris Karloff, Byron Foulger, Roger Pryor, Jo Ann Sayers

The Man with One Red Shoe

US 1985 93m colour
TCF (Victor Drai)
V, V*

A violinist wearing odd shoes is mistaken for a spy

and becomes a pawn in a battle being waged by rival factions for control of the CIA.

Farcical comedy that rarely achieves the right tempo or timing for its occasional jokes.

w Robert Klane   *d* Stan Dragoti   *ph* Richard H. Kline   *m* Thomas Newman   *pd* Dean E. Mitzner   *ed* Bud Molin, O. Nicholas Brown

Tom Hanks, Dabney Coleman, Lori Singer, Charles Durning, Jim Belushi, Carrie Fisher, Ed Herrmann, Irving Metzman, Tom Noonan, David Ogden Stiers

† It was a remake of the French film *Le Grand Blond avec une Chaussure Noire* (qv), written by Francis Veber and Yves Robert.

The Man with the Deadly Lens: see *Wrong Is Right*

The Man with the Golden Arm *

US 1956 119m bw
Otto Preminger
V, V*, S

A Chicago poker dealer finally kicks the drug habit.

Sensational on its first release, with its cold turkey scenes, this now seems a muddled impressionist melodrama with echoes of the silent German cinema and much over-acting and miscasting all round. But Sinatra is good; and it is different . . .

w Walter Newman, Lewis Meltzer   *novel* Nelson Algren   *d* Otto Preminger   *ph* Sam Leavitt   *m* Elmer Bernstein   *pd* Joe Wright   *titles* Saul Bass

Frank Sinatra, Kim Novak, Eleanor Parker, Darren McGavin, Arnold Stang, Robert Strauss, John Conte, Doro Merande, George E. Stone

'Nothing very surprising or exciting . . . a pretty plain and unimaginative look-see at a lower depths character.' – *Bosley Crowther*

'A very inferior film . . . the script is inexcusably clumsy, the sets are unbelievable and the casting is ridiculous.' – *Diana Willing, Films in Review*

'It has the same running time as Citizen Kane but it seems a whole lot longer.' – *Robert James*

AAN: Elmer Bernstein; Frank Sinatra; art direction

The Man with the Golden Gun *

GB 1974 125m Eastmancolor
UA/Eon (Harry Saltzman, Albert R. Broccoli)
V, V*, L, S

James Bond goes to the Far East to liquidate a professional assassin named Scaramanga.

Thin and obvious Bond extravaganza with conventional expensive excitements.

w Richard Maibaum, Tom Mankiewicz   *novel* Ian Fleming   *d* Guy Hamilton   *ph* Ted Moore, Oswald Morris   *m* John Barry   *pd* Peter Murton

Roger Moore, Christopher Lee, Britt Ekland, Maud Adams, Hervé Villechaize, Clifton James, Richard Loo, Marc Lawrence

'The script lacks satiric insolence and the picture grinds on humourlessly.' – *New Yorker*

The Man with the Green Carnation: see *The Trials of Oscar Wilde*

Man with the Gun *

US 1955 83m bw
UA/Samuel Goldwyn Jnr
aka: *Deadly Peacemaker*

A gunfighter is hired to clean up a town overrun by hired guns.

A well-made Western, tough, grim and suspenseful.

w N. B. Stone Jnr, Richard Wilson   *d* Richard Wilson   *ph* Lee Garmes   *m* Alex North   *ad* Hilyard Brown   *ed* Gene Milford

Robert Mitchum, Jan Sterling, Karen Sharpe, Henry Hull, Emile Meyer, John Lupton, Barbara Lawrence, Ted DeCorsia, Leo Gordon, James Westerfield

The Man with the Movie Camera **
USSR   1928   60m approx   bw   silent
VUFKU
original title: Chelovek s Kinoapparatom

A 'camera eye' documentary without any plot, showing, through a succession of street and interior scenes, all the tricks of which the instrument is capable; it takes a bow at the end.

Unique documentary which was understandably a sensation when it first appeared but now often seems merely quaint.

wd/ed Dziga Vertov   ph Mikhail Kaufman

The Man with the Steel Whip
US   1954   bw   serial: 12 eps
Republic

A young rancher opposing troublemakers disguises himself as El Latigo, a legendary masked rider.

Routine serial in imitation of The Mark of Zorro.
d Franklin Adreon

Richard Simmons, Barbara Bestar, Dale Van Sickel, Lane Bradford

The Man with Thirty Sons: see The Magnificent Yankee

The Man with Two Brains
US   1983   93m   colour
Warner/Aspen (David V. Picker, William E. McEuen)
V*, L

A surgeon, trapped in a frustrating marriage, falls in love with a brain in a jar.

Offbeat, broad comedy that is never as funny as it promises to be.

w Carl Reiner, Steve Martin, George Gipe   d Carl Reiner   ph Michael Chapman   m Joel Goldsmith   ad Polly Platt   ed Bud Molin

Steve Martin, Kathleen Turner, David Warner, Paul Benedict, Richard Brestoff, James Cromwell, Sissy Spacek (voice)

'Indefensible by any known standard of comedy form – or formlessness. It's not much of anything, but it moves along enjoyably.' – Pauline Kael, New Yorker

The Man with Two Faces *
US   1934   72m   bw
Warner

An actor takes revenge on a scoundrel who had preyed on his sister.

Pleasing melodrama hinging on disguise; the Hays Office surprisingly allowed the hero to get away with it.

w Tom Reed, Niven Busch   play The Dark Tower by George S. Kaufman, Alexander Woollcott   d Archie Mayo   ph Tony Gaudio

Edward G. Robinson, Mary Astor, Ricardo Cortez, Louis Calhern, Mae Clarke, John Eldredge

'Fair fodder, but undistinguished in the main, and in spots very confusing.' – Variety

The Man with X-Ray Eyes: see X—The Man with X-Ray Eyes

The Man Within *
GB   1947   88m   Technicolor
GFD/Production Film Service (Muriel and Sydney Box)
US title: The Smugglers

An orphan boy discovers that his mysterious new guardian is a smuggler.

Unconvincing period yarn which has managed to drain every vestige of subtlety from the novel, but at least looks good.

w Muriel and Sydney Box   novel Graham Greene   d Bernard Knowles   ph Geoffrey Unsworth   m Clifton Parker

Michael Redgrave, Richard Attenborough, Jean Kent, Joan Greenwood

'With more style this might have been rather good. Outside of life more private than I am normally party to I can't recall hearing so many men so often say, to other men, I hate him! or I hate you!' – James Agee

The Man without a Body
GB   1957   80m   bw
Filmplays Guido Coen/Eros

A tycoon with a brain tumour steals the head of Nostradamus and has it kept alive to replace his own.

Hilarious horror comic, inept in every department.

w William Grote   d W. Lee Wilder and Charles Saunders

George Coulouris, Robert Hutton, Nadja Regin, Julia Arnall

Man without a Face
US   1993   115m   Technicolor
Entertainment/Icon (Bruce Davey)
V, V*, L, S

A boy remembers how he was helped to enter a military academy by a disfigured former teacher who had become an outcast in the community.

A well-meaning but rather dull movie that makes heavy weather of a not very affecting drama.

w Malcolm MacRury   novel Isabelle Holland   d Mel Gibson   ph Donald M. McAlpine   m James Horner   pd Barbara Dunphy   ed Tony Gibbs

Mel Gibson, Margaret Whitton, Fay Masterson, Gaby Hoffman, Geoffrey Lewis, Richard Masur, Nick Stahl, Viva

'The overall effect is sincere, sentimental and slightly uneasy.' – Philip French, Observer

'A contrived story, overloaded with pop psychology, that would never reach the big screen unless a major star insisted. As director, Mel Gibson proves no visual stylist.' – Geoff Brown, The Times

The Man without a Star *
US   1955   89m   Technicolor
U-I (Aaron Rosenberg)

A wandering cowboy helps settlers to put up barbed wire against an owner of vast cattle herds.

Conventional but entertaining star Western.

w Borden Chase, D. D. Beauchamp   novel Dee Linford   d King Vidor   ph Russell Metty   m Hans Salter

Kirk Douglas, Jeanne Crain, Claire Trevor, William Campbell, Jay C. Flippen, Mara Corday, Richard Boone

† Remade for TV as A Man Called Gannon.

Man, Woman and Child
US   1982   100m   DeLuxe
Gaylord

A married professor discovers that he has a son by his only infidelity.

Angst among the well-to-do, from the author of Love Story.

w Erich Segal, David Selag Goodman   novel Erich Segal   d Dick Richards

Martin Sheen, Blythe Danner, Craig T. Nelson, David Hemmings, Nathalie Nell

Man, Woman and Sin
US   1927   85m approx at 24 fps   bw   silent
MGM

A reporter has an affair with his boss's mistress.

Glossy romantic drama marking the first screen appearance of a sensational stage star; her effect on screen was more muted.

w Alice Duer Miller   d Monta Bell

Jeanne Eagels, John Gilbert, Marc McDermott

Manbait: see The Last Page

The Manchurian Candidate ****
US   1962   126m   bw
UA/MC (Howard W. Koch)
V, V*, L

A Korean war 'hero' comes back a brainwashed zombie triggered to kill a liberal politician, his control being his own monstrously ambitious mother.

Insanely plotted but brilliantly handled spy thriller, a mixture of Hitchcock, Welles and All the King's Men.

w George Axelrod   novel Richard Condon   d John Frankenheimer   ph Lionel Lindon   m David Amram   pd Richard Sylbert

Frank Sinatra, Laurence Harvey, Janet Leigh, James Gregory, Angela Lansbury, Henry Silva, John McGiver

'The unAmerican film of the year.' – Penelope Houston

'An intelligent, funny, superbly written, beautifully played, and brilliantly directed study of the all-embracing fantasy in everyday social, emotional and political existence.' – Philip Strick, 1973

'Although it's a thriller, it may be the most sophisticated political satire ever to come out of Hollywood.' – Pauline Kael, 70s

AAN: Angela Lansbury

Mandalay
US   1934   65m   bw
Warner

A lady of the tropics murders her lover and pushes his body through a porthole.

Steamy melodrama which the masses found absorbing.

w Austin Parker and Charles Kenyon   d Michael Curtiz

Kay Francis, Ricardo Cortez, Lyle Talbot, Ruth Donnelly, Shirley Temple, Warner Oland, Lucien Littlefield, Reginald Owen

Manden I Manen: see The Dark Side of the Moon

Mandingo
US   1975   126m   Technicolor
Dino de Laurentiis (Peter Herald)
V*, L

On a slave-breeding plantation in 1840 Louisiana, passions ride high.

Like Gone with the Wind with all the characters on heat, this exuberant and unpleasant melodrama goes several points over the top from start to finish but proved to have wide appeal for the groundlings, in the Tobacco Road tradition of a wallow in other people's depravities.

w Norman Wexler   play Jack Kirkland   novel Kyle Onstott   d Richard Fleischer   ph Richard H. Kline   m Maurice Jarre   pd Boris Leven

James Mason, Susan George, Perry King, Richard Ward, Brenda Sykes, Ken Norton

Mandrake the Magician
US   1939   bw   serial: 12 eps
Columbia

A world-famous magician trails an underworld leader called The Wasp.

Rather stylish serial exploits with the added effect of illusions.   d Sam Nelson and Norman Denning

Warren Hull, Doris Weston, Al Kikume, Rex Downing, Don Beddoe

'She'll find a home in every heart! She'll reach the heart of every home!'

Mandy ***
GB 1952 93m bw
Ealing (Leslie Norman)
V, V*
US title: *The Crash of Silence*

A little girl, born deaf, is sent to a special school.

Carefully wrought and very sympathetic little semi-documentary film in which all the adults underplay in concession to a new child star who alas did not last long at the top.

w Nigel Balchin, Jack Whittingham novel *This Day Is Ours* by Hilda Lewis d Alexander Mackendrick
ph Douglas Slocombe m William Alwyn

Jack Hawkins, Terence Morgan, Phyllis Calvert, *Mandy Miller*, Godfrey Tearle, Dorothy Alison

'An extremely touching film, in spite of occasional obviousness in a plot never dull, and in spite of its subject never saccharine.' – *Dilys Powell*

Maneater of Kumaon
US 1948 78m bw
Monty Shaff-Frank Rosenberg/Universal

A doctor in the Himalayas helps track down a man-eating tiger.

Slightly unusual adventure story based on a currently popular book.

w Jeanne Bartlett and Lewis Meltzer book Jim Corbett d Byron Haskin

Sabu, Wendell Corey, Joanne Page, Morris Carnovsky

Manèges *
France 1950 90m bw
Films Modernes-Discina (Emil Natan)
GB title: *The Wanton*

A scheming girl marries the middle-aged owner of a riding school and, with her greedy mother, milks him of his money.

A neat little melodrama with flashbacks so arranged that the girl, paralysed in an accident, seems for the first half to have an angelic character.

w Jacques Sigurd d Yves Allégret ph Jean Bourgoin

Simone Signoret, Bernard Blier, *Frank Villard*, Jane Marken

Manhandled
US 1949 97m bw
Paramount/Pine-Thomas

The secretary of a bogus psychiatrist becomes involved in a murder and finds herself in danger from all comers.

Modest, overlong suspenser with adequate production values.

w Lewis R. Foster, Whitman Chambers novel *The Man Who Stole a Dream* by L. S. Goldsmith d Lewis R. Foster ph Ernest Laszlo m David Chudnow

Dorothy Lamour, Dan Duryea, Sterling Hayden, Irene Hervey, Harold Vermilyea, Philip Reed, Alan Napier, Art Smith, Irving Bacon

Manhattan ****
US 1979 96m bw Panavision
UA/Jack Rollins/Charles H. Joffe
V, V*, L, S

Episodes in the sex life of a TV comedy writer with an obsession about New York.

As close to a summation of Woody Allen's views and *oeuvre* as anybody needs; some smart jabs about the lives we lead are sometimes bogged down in earnestness and half-comic despair.

w Woody Allen, Marshall Brickman d Woody Allen
ph Gordon Willis md Tom Pierson

Woody Allen, Diane Keaton, Meryl Streep, Mariel Hemingway, Michael Murphy

'Given that the identity of his films has increasingly been determined by his compulsion to talk about the things he finds important, but also by his fear of having them come out as anything but a joke, it is not surprising that he has scarcely been able to decide on a form for his "art": from the anything-for-a-laugh skittering of his early films, to the broad parodies and pastiches of his middle period, to the recent confessional/psychoanalytical mode.' – *Richard Combs, MFB*

'A masterpiece that has become a film for the ages by not seeking to be a film of the moment.' – *Andrew Sarris*

AAN: script; Mariel Hemingway

Manhattan Heartbeat
US 1940 71m bw
Sol M. Wurtzel/TCF

A husband is reluctant to assume the responsibilities of fatherhood.

Oddly-titled support, a remake of *Bad Girl*; no great shakes from any angle.

w Harold Buchman, Clark Andrews, Jack Jungmeyer Jnr, Edith Skouras d David Burton

Robert Sterling, Virginia Gilmore, Joan Davis, Edmund MacDonald, Don Beddoe

Manhattan Madness: see *Adventure in Manhattan*

Manhattan Melodrama **
US 1934 93m bw
MGM (David O. Selznick)
V*, L

Two slum boys grow up friends, one as district attorney and the other as a gangster.

Archetypal American situation drama (cf *Angels with Dirty Faces, Cry of the City*, etc), with the bad guy inevitably indulging in self-sacrifice at the end. An all-star cast makes it palatable in this case, though the film is inevitably dated.

w Oliver H. P. Garrett, Joseph L. Mankiewicz
story Arthur Caesar d W. S. Van Dyke ph James Wong Howe m William Axt

William Powell, Clark Gable, Myrna Loy, Leo Carrillo, Nat Pendleton, George Sidney, Isabel Jewell, Thomas E. Jackson

'Action meller of the big town . . . replete with punchy, popularly-appealing ingredients.' – *Variety*

† *Manhattan Melodrama* gained some irrelevant fame as the movie John Dillinger was watching when he was cornered and shot.

AA: Arthur Caesar

Manhattan Merry-go-round *
US 1937 82m bw
Republic
V*

A sound recording studio is taken over by a band of racketeers.

Sufficient comedy plot to sustain a revue of historical interest.

w Harry Sauber, Frank Hummert d Charles F. Reisner ad Victor MacKay

Phil Regan, Leo Carrillo, Ann Dvorak, Tamara Geva, James Gleason, Ted Lewis and his Orchestra, Cab Calloway and his Orchestra, the Kay Thompson Ensemble, Louis Prima and his Band, Gene Autry, Joe Di Maggio

'So much talent and novelty has been compressed within the limits of the film that customers dare not sneeze for fear of missing something . . . for the

territorial distributors and independent theatres it is something to get excited about.' – *Variety*

AAN: Victor MacKay

Manhattan Murder Mystery *
US 1993 105m Technicolor
TriStar (Robert Greenhut)

A husband becomes concerned when his wife decides that the woman who lives next door has been murdered.

Amiable comedy whodunnit that jogs along nicely without arriving anywhere that is particularly interesting.

w Woody Allen, Marshall Brickman d Woody Allen ph Carlo Di Palma pd Santo Loquasto
ed Susan E. Morse

Woody Allen, Alan Alda, Anjelica Huston, Diane Keaton, Jerry Adler, Joy Behar, Ron Rifkin, Lynn Cohen, Melanie Norris

'Light, insubstantial and utterly devoid of the heavier themes Allen has grappled with in most of his recent outings, this confection keeps the chuckles coming and is mainstream enough in sensibility to be a modest success.' – *Variety*

'God, it's good to get a film which gives you only fun to worry about.' – *Alexander Walker*

Manhattan Parade
US 1931 77m Technicolor
Warner

Behind the scenes as a theatrical costumier tries to get into the revue business.

Aimless backstage comedy with turns.

w Robert Lord and Houston Branch play Sam Shipman d Lloyd Bacon

Smith and Dale, Winnie Lightner, Charles Butterworth, Walter Miller, Luis Alberni

'A few laughs dot the scenery, and they're all this musical possesses in value.' – *Variety*

Manhunt: see *From Hell to Texas*

Manhunt of Mystery Island
US 1945 bw serial: 15 eps
Republic

A criminologist searches the tropics for a missing scientist, and comes up against a supernatural Captain Mephisto.

Serial mumbo-jumbo, all quite tolerable.

d Spencer Bennet, Wallace Grissell, Yakima Canutt

Richard Bailey, Linda Stirling, Roy Barcroft

Manhunter **
US 1986 120m Technicolor Panavision
Recorded Releasing/Red Dragon/De Laurentiis Entertainment (Richard Roth)
V, V*, L

An FBI agent with an ability to think like a killer tracks down a serial murderer.

Slick and glossy thriller, enjoyable enough if you can accept its premise.

wd/p Michael Mann novel *Red Dragon* by Thomas Harris ph Dante Spinotti m Michael Rubini, The Reds pd Mel Bourne ed Dov Hoenig

William Peterson, Kim Greist, Joan Allen, Brian Cox, Dennis Farina, Stephen Lang, Tom Noonan, David Seaman, Benjamin Hendrickson

Le Mani sulla Città: see *Hands over the City*

Maniac
GB 1963 86m bw Hammerscope
Columbia/Hammer (Jimmy Sangster)
V*

Murders by oxyacetylene torch in the Camargue, with the wrong lunatic going to the asylum.

Hammer's mark two plot, the shuddery murder mystery in which someone is not quite what he seems; feebly done in this case, with a fatally slow start.

w Jimmy Sangster   d Michael Carreras   ph Wilkie Cooper

Kerwin Mathews, Donald Houston, Nadia Gray, Justine Lord

Maniac Cop
US   1988   85m   colour
Medusa/Shapiro Glickenhaus Entertainment (Larry Cohen)
V, V*

A former cop turns killer in New York.

Excessively violent thriller that is too implausible to be enjoyable.

w Larry Cohen   d William Lustig   ph Vincent J. Rabe   m Jay Chataway   ad Jonathan Hodges, Ann Cudworth   ed David Kern

Tom Atkins, Bruce Campbell, Laurence Landon, Richard Roundtree, William Smith, Robert Z'Dar, Sheree North

Maniac Cop 2
US   1990   88m   Foto-Kem   Panavision
Medusa/Movie House Sale/Fadd Enterprises (David Hodgins, Frank D'Alessio)
V, V*

A murderous and deranged former policeman teams up with a mass murderer to terrorize New York.

Limply directed sequel that offers nothing new, but just increases the body count.

w Larry Cohen   d William Lustig   ph James Lemmo   m Jay Chattaway   pd Gene Abel, Charles Logola   ed David Kern

Robert Davi, Claudia Christian, Michael Lerner, Bruce Campbell, Laurene Landon, Robert Z'Dar, Clarence Williams III, Leo Rossi

'The Wrong Arm Of The Law Is Back.'
Maniac Cop 3: Badge of Silence
US   1992   81m   Foto-Kem colour
Neo/First Look (Larry Cohen)
V, V*

Resurrected by occult methods, a dead cop acts as a vigilante to protect the reputation of a policewoman, shot during a hold-up and accused of killing an innocent hostage.

An action adventure rather than a horror movie, with the maniac cop remaining a shadowy figure; it avoids predictability, has an inventive car chase and manages a moderate amount of suspense.

w Larry Cohen   d William Lustig   ph Jacques Haitkin   m Joel Goldsmith   pd Clark Hunter   ed David Kern, Michael Eliot

Robert Davi, Caitlin Dulany, Gretchen Becker, Paul Gleason, Jackie Earle Haley, Julius Harris, Grand Bush, Doug Savant, Robert Z'Dar

'A promising exploitation sequel, laced with Cohen's dark humour, which collapses in its final act into a series of dull stunts.' – Sight and Sound

Maniacs on Wheels: see Once a Jolly Swagman

Manifesto
US   1988   94m   colour
Cannon/Menahem Golan, Yoram Globus
V*, S

In an Eastern European village in the 1920s, a lecherous secret policeman waylays revolutionaries before a visit by a king.

Sex-obsessed black comedy that muffs its climaxes.
wd Dusan Makavejev   story For a Night of Love by

Emile Zola   ph Tomislav Pinter   m Nicola Piovani
pd Velijo Despotovic   ed Tony Lawson

Alfred Molina, Camilla Soeberg, Simon Callow, Lindsay Duncan, Eric Stoltz, Rade Serbedzija, Chris Haywood, Linda Marlowe, Ronald Lacey

Manila Calling
US   1942   82m   bw
Sol M. Wurtzel/TCF

Americans in the Philippines try to install a short-wave radio transmitter before the Japs take over.

Acceptable thick ear with professional trimmings.

w John Larkin   d Herbert I. Leeds

Lloyd Nolan, Carole Landis, Cornel Wilde, James Gleason, Martin Kosleck, Ralph Byrd

The Manitou
US   1978   104m   CFI Color
Herman Weist/Melvin Simon (William Girdler)
V, V*, L

A fake spiritualist finds his girlfriend is possessed by the demon of a 400-year-old Indian.

Boring retread of The Exorcist.

w William Girdler, Jon Cedar, Tom Pope
novel Graham Masterton   d William Girdler
ph Michel Hugo   m Lalo Schifrin

Tony Curtis, Susan Strasberg, Michael Ansara, Stella Stevens, Jon Cedar, Ann Sothern, Burgess Meredith, Paul Mantee

Mannen pò Taket: see The Man on the Roof

Mannequin
US   1937   95m   bw
MGM (Joseph L. Mankiewicz)
V*

The wife of a small-time crook gets a modelling job and falls for a shipping magnate.

Competent star melodrama about a working girl's harassments.

w Lawrence Hazard   d Frank Borzage   ph George Folsey   m Edward Ward

Joan Crawford, Spencer Tracy, Alan Curtis, Ralph Morgan, Mary Philips, Elizabeth Risdon, Leo Gorcey

'A star vehicle in which the star is so solemnly noble that you want to strangle her.' – New Yorker

AAN: song 'Always and Always' (m Edward Ward, ly Chet Forrest, Bob Wright)

Mannequin
US   1987   89m   DuArt
TCF/Gladden (Art Levinson)
V, V*, L

A window dresser falls in love with a mannequin who changes into a real live girl.

Feeble and never less than idiotic fantasy.

w Edward Rugoff, Michael Gottlieb   d Michael Gottlieb   ph Tim Suhrstedt   m Sylvester Levay
pd Josan Russo   ed Richard Halsey, Frank Jiminez

Andrew McCarthy, Kim Cattrall, Estelle Getty, James Spader, G. W. Bailey, Carole Davis, Stephen Vinovich, Christopher Maher, Meshach Taylor

Mannequin Two: On the Move
US   1991   95m   colour
Rank/Gladden (Edward Rugoff)
V, V*, L

A window dresser discovers that a mannequin holds the imprisoned spirit of a bewitched peasant girl.

Even less enjoyable than the original, if that's possible.

w Edward Rugoff, David Isaacs, Ken Levine, Betty Israel   d Stewart Raffill   ph Larry Pizer   m David

McHugh   ad Norman B. Dodge Jnr   ed Joan Chapman

Kristy Swanson, William Ragsdale, Meshach Taylor, Terry Kizer, Stuart Pankin, Cynthia Harris, Andrew Hill Newman

'If this stiff ever shows any life, it will be a wonder indeed.' – Variety

'A messy rehash of clichés and tired jokes.' – Empire

Männer . . .: see Men . . .

Mano dello Straniero: see The Stranger's Hand

Manon *
France   1949   96m   bw
Alcina (P. E. Decharme)

After the liberation, a girl who has been a collaborator becomes involved in the black market, passes from man to man, and ends up being shot by Arabs in the Sahara desert.

Oddball modernized version of Manon Lescaut, with post-war pessimism and the glamour of sin going hand in hand. Worth comparing with Gilda.

w H. G. Clouzot, J. Ferry   novel L'Abbé Prévost
d H. G. Clouzot   ph Armand Thirard   m Paul Misraki

Michel Auclair, Cécile Aubry, Serge Reggiani, Gabrille Dorziat

'A clever idea, handled cleverly, but without depth of feeling.' – Penelope Houston

'Though I have been going to the pictures since I wore rompers, I do not recall a more horrible film.' – Leonard Mosley

Manon des Sources
France   1952   190m   bw
Films Marcel Pagnol

A Provençal girl who lives in the hills with her goats is thought to be a witch, and takes her revenge on the populace by stopping the water supply.

Insanely long idyll of the countryside with the writer-director unintentionally caricaturing himself.

wd Marcel Pagnol   ph Willy   m Raymond Legrand

Jacqueline Pagnol, Raymond Péllégrin, Henri Vibert

'Something of an endurance test for all but the most enthusiastic Pagnol admirers.' – John Gillett, MFB

† Pagnol later expanded the story into two novels which were the basis for a two-part film, Jean de Florette (qv) and Manon des Sources (1986) (qv).

Manon des Sources ***
France   1986   114m   colour
Renn Productions/A2/RAI 2/DD Productions (Roland Thenot)
V, V*, L, S

A young girl avenges the wrong done to her father by a farmer and his nephew.

Absorbing drama of rural life, impeccably performed and directed.

w Claude Berri, Gérard Brach   novel Marcel Pagnol
d Claude Berri   ph Bruno Nuytten   m Jean-Claude Petit   pd Bernard Vizat   ed Geneviève Louveau, Hervé de Luze

Yves Montand, Daniel Auteuil, Emmanuelle Béart, Hippolyte Girardot, Margarita Lozano, Gabriel Bacquier

Manpower *
US   1941   103m   bw
Warner (Mark Hellinger)

Power linesmen fall out over a night-club hostess.

Yet another variation on Tiger Shark, with vivid fisticuff and storm sequences supporting the star performers.

w Richard Macaulay, Jerry Wald   *d* Raoul Walsh
ph Ernest Haller   *m* Adolph Deutsch

Edward G. Robinson, George Raft, Marlene Dietrich, Alan Hale, Frank McHugh, Eve Arden, Barton MacLane, Walter Catlett, Joyce Compton, Ward Bond

'The pace and cutting are those of the best gangster films . . . the climax outdoes anything the Lyceum may have known.' – *William Whitebait*

Man's Best Friend

US   1993   87m   DeLuxe
Guild/New Line/Roven-Cavello (Bob Engelman)
V, V*

A reporter releases from an experimental laboratory a genetically altered dog that combines size and intelligence with the ability of a chameleon and the instincts of a killer.

A moderately entertaining, but gory, thriller that at least provides a welcome antidote to the *Beethoven* series.

wd John Lafia   *ph* Mark Irwin   *m* Joel Goldsmith
pd Jaymes Hinkle   *sp* Kevin Yagher   *ed* Michael N. Knue

Ally Sheedy, Lance Henriksen, Robert Constanzo, Frederic Lehne, John Cassini, J. D. Daniels, William Sanderson

'Combines increasingly gory black-comic bits . . . with a plethora of gimmicks. The mixture is far from boring, but it coarsens the comedy about the hidden life of dogs.' – *Michael Sragow, New Yorker*

'How we all laughed at this movie's awful lines and clichéd plot contrivances, down to the closing, sequel-bound litter of pyscho puppies.' – *Sheila Johnston, Independent*

Man's Castle *

US   1933   70m   bw
Columbia (Frank Borzage)

Romance blooms among the unemployed who live in a shanty town on the banks of the East River.

Depression moonshine which at the time was taken for realism; sociologically very interesting but very faded as entertainment.

w Jo Swerling   *play* Lawrence Hazard   *d* Frank Borzage   *ph* Joseph August   *m* W. Franke Harling

Spencer Tracy, Loretta Young, Glenda Farrell, Walter Connolly, Arthur Hohl, Marjorie Rambeau, Dickie Moore

'A picture that goes contrary to normal entertainment appetites and tastes, its possibilities of going places look slender at best.' – *Variety*

'Heavily sentimental yet magically romantic.' – *New Yorker, 1977*

Man's Favourite Sport? *

US   1963   120m   Technicolor
Universal/Gibraltar/Laurel (Howard Hawks)
V*

A star salesman of fishing tackle finds his bluff called when he has to enter a fishing competition.

Over-extended romantic farce drawn by the director from memories of older and better films, such as *Libeled Lady* and his own *Bringing Up Baby*.

w John Fenton Murray   *d* Howard Hawks
ph Russell Harlan   *m* Henry Mancini

Rock Hudson, Paula Prentiss, Maria Perschy, Charlene Holt, John McGiver, Roscoe Karns

'Hawks' deadpan documentation of a physical gag is as effective as ever, but the overall pace of his direction is curiously contemplative, as though he were savoring all his past jokes for the last time.' – *Andrew Sarris*

Man's Hope: see *Espoir*

Manslaughter *

US   1922   80m approx (24 fps)   bw   silent
Paramount/Famous Players (Cecil B. de Mille)

An idle rich girl accidentally kills a man while driving, and is sent to prison, but falls for the district attorney who convicted her.

De Mille was here testing out his *Ten Commandments* format, with a long flashback during the DA's speech to the idle rich of ancient Rome. It worked like a charm at the box-office.

w Jeanie McPherson   *novel* Alice Duer Miller
d Cecil B. de Mille   *ph* Alvin Wyckoff

Leatrice Joy, Thomas Meighan, Lois Wilson, John Miltern

† A 1930 sound remake for Paramount was directed by George Abbott, who also tried in vain to modernize the screenplay (by omitting the flashback). Claudette Colbert and Fredric March starred.

Mantrap

US   1943   57m   bw
Republic (George Sherman)

A retired Scotland Yard man helps the DA's office in a murder case.

Entertaining second feature with a geriatric hero; alas, the clues don't play quite fair.

w Curt Siodmak   *d* George Sherman

Henry Stephenson, Lloyd Corrigan, Joseph Allen Jnr, Dorothy Lovett

Mantrap

US   1961   93m   bw   Panavision
Paramount/Tiger (Edmond O'Brien, Stanley Frazen)

An honest man is lured by an old Marine friend into a hi-jack attempt which leads to the death of his wife.

Rather uninteresting melodrama, played and directed for more than it's worth.

w Ed Waters   *novel* Taint of the Tiger by John D. Macdonald   *d* Edmond O'Brien   *ph* Loyal Griggs
m Leith Stevens

Jeffrey Hunter, David Janssen, Stella Stevens, Hugh Sanders

Manuela *

GB   1957   95m   bw
British Lion/Ivan Foxwell
US title: *Stowaway Girl*

In a South American port, the engineer of a tramp steamer smuggles aboard a half caste girl, but it is the disillusioned captain who falls in love with her.

Downbeat seafaring melodrama, fine for those seeking a mood piece.

w William Woods   *novel* William Woods   *d* Guy Hamilton   *ph* Otto Heller   *m* William Alwyn

Trevor Howard, Elsa Martinelli, Pedro Armendariz, Donald Pleasence

The Manxman

GB   1929   90m (24 fps)   bw   silent
British International (John Maxwell)

A fisherman thought drowned comes back to find that his girl is expecting his best friend's baby.

Stern romantic melodrama of virtually no interest despite its director.

w Eliot Stannard   *novel* Hall Caine   *d* Alfred Hitchcock   *ph* Jack Cox

Carl Brisson, Malcolm Keen, Anny Ondra, Randle Ayrton, Clare Greet

† Previously filmed in 1916 with Henry Ainley and Elizabeth Risdon.

Many Happy Returns

US   1934   62m   bw
Paramount

A scatty girl jinxes her father's department store and a Hollywood studio.

Silly comedy with stops for vaudeville.

w J. P. McEvoy, Claude Binyon, Keene Thompson, Ray Harris, Lady Mary Cameron(!)   *d* Norman Z. McLeod

George Burns, Gracie Allen, Guy Lombardo and his Band, Veloz and Yolanda, Ray Milland, George Barbier, Joan Marsh, Franklin Pangborn, William Demarest, Larry Adler

'Often very funny, at other moments it lags.' – *Variety*

Many Rivers to Cross *

US   1955   94m   Eastmancolor   Cinemascope
MGM (Jack Cummings)

A trapper bound for Canada is helped by a sharp-shooting girl, and in return he saves her from marauding Indians.

Simple-minded, cheerful, quite refreshing Western compounded of equal parts comedy and action.

w Harry Brown, Guy Trosper   *d* Roy Rowland
ph John Seitz   *m* Cyril Mockridge

Robert Taylor, Eleanor Parker, Victor McLaglen, Josephine Hutchinson, Jeff Richards, Russ Tamblyn, James Arness, Alan Hale Jnr

'From a Kingdom of Ice to a Land of Fire . . . A Love That Knows No Boundaries.'

Map of the Human Heart *

GB/Australia   1992   109m   colour
Rank/Working Title/Map/Sunrise/Polygram/AFFC/Vincent Ward
V, V*, S

An elderly Eskimo recalls to a surveyor the events of his life: how he helped map his remote part of the Arctic as a boy, was sent to Canada to cure his tuberculosis, served in the RAF and loved and lost a girl he met in hospital and later in England.

An ambitious, sprawling and flawed film that attempts to take in too much, in time and emotion – with a 'feel-good' ending that seems out of place with the tragic story that has gone before.

w Louis Nowra   *story* Vincent Ward   *d* Vincent Ward   *ph* Eduardo Serra   *m* Gabriel Yared
pd John Beard   *ed* John Scott, Frans Vandenburg

Patrick Bergin, Anne Parillaud, Jason Scott Lee, John Cusack, Jeanne Moreau

'What we learn about the human heart remains a matter of guesswork, but as a map the film certainly offers some eye-catching perspectives.' – *Philip Strick, Sight and Sound*

'A true one-off, this is a poignant, thoughtfully drawn map of love, death and life.' – *Angie Errigo, Empire*

† The film was cut from 126m after it was shown at the Cannes Film Festival, and had an extra day's shooting in London to add scenes with Lee and Parillaud. The ending was also recut to give it a more upbeat feeling.

Mapantsula *

South Africa   1988   104m   Agfacolor
Electric/One Look Productions/David Hannay Productions/Haverbeam (Max Montocchio)
V

A petty criminal in Soweto stands firm against police oppression.

Lively look at the underside of life in a black township, but lacking in depth.

w Oliver Schmitz, Thomas Mogotlane   *d* Oliver Schmitz   *ph* Rod Stewart   *m* The Ouens
ad Robin Hofmeyr   *ed* Mike Baard

Thomas Mogotlane, Thembi Mtshali, Peter Sephuma, Marcel Van Heerden, Eugene Majola, Dolly Rathebe, Darlington Michaels

Mara Maru

US   1952   98m   bw
Warner (David Weisbart)

A Manila salvage expert locates a sunken treasure and defeats crooks who are also in pursuit of it.

Lethargic but pleasant-looking star vehicle with a plot borrowed from *The Maltese Falcon*.

w N. Richard Nash, Philip Yordan, Sidney Harmon, Hollister Noble   d Gordon Douglas   ph *Robert Burks*   m Max Steiner

Errol Flynn, Ruth Roman, Raymond Burr, Paul Picerni, Richard Webb

Maracaibo

US   1958   88m   Technicolor   Vistavision
Paramount/Theodora (Cornel Wilde)

A Texan oil fire expert finds himself unexpectedly busy when on holiday in Venezuela.

Meandering action melodrama with too much local colour.

w Ted Sherdeman   novel Stirling Silliphant   d Cornel Wilde   ph Ellsworth Fredericks   m Laurindo Almeida

Cornel Wilde, Jean Wallace, Abbe Lane, Francis Lederer, Joe E. Ross, Michael Landon

The Marat/Sade *

GB   1966   116m   DeLuxe
UA/Marat Sade (Michael Birkett)
V*, L
aka: *The Persecution and Assassination of Jean-Paul Marat as performed by the inmates of the Asylum of Charenton under the direction of the Marquis de Sade*

The title tells all, except that at the end the inmates go berserk.

Fairly plain filming of an Old Vic *succès d'estime* which it became fashionable to announce that one had seen and understood. The film makes no effort to attract the unbeliever.

w Adrian Mitchell   play Peter Weiss   d Peter Brook   ph David Watkin   m Richard Peaslee

Glenda Jackson, Patrick Magee, Ian Richardson, Michael Williams, Robert Lloyd, Clifford Rose, Freddie Jones

'I loathed and detested doing the play. I couldn't wait for it to end. Then we all did the film and it was a shattering experience. People twitching, slobber running down their chins, everyone screaming from nerves and exhaustion.' – *Glenda Jackson*

Marathon Man **

US   1976   126m   Metrocolor
Paramount (Robert Evans, Sidney Beckerman)
V*, L

A vicious Nazi returns from Uruguay to New York in search of diamonds which had been kept for him by his now-dead brother, and is outwitted by the young brother of an American agent he has killed.

Complex mystery thriller which seems to have things to mutter about freedom and McCarthyism and Nazism, but finally settles down to being a simple shocker with a nick-of-time climax. The presentation is dazzling.

w William Goldman   novel William Goldman   d *John Schlesinger*   ph *Conrad Hall*   m Michael Small   pd Richard MacDonald

Dustin Hoffman, *Laurence Olivier*, Roy Scheider, William Devane, Marthe Keller, Fritz Weaver, Marc Lawrence

'A film of such rich texture and density in its construction, so fascinatingly complex in its unfolding, so engrossing in its personalities, and so powerful in its performance and pace that the seduction of the senses has physical force.' – *Judith Crist, Saturday Review*

'Fashionably violent . . . distinctly self-conscious . . . conventionally moralistic . . . and absolutely devoid of resonance.' – *Tom Milne, MFB*

'If at the film's end, you have followed the series of double and triple crosses, braved the torture scenes, and still don't know what it was about, you're bound to have company.' – *Paul Coleman, Film Information*

'A Jewish revenge fantasy.' – *Pauline Kael*

'He has made a most elegant, bizarre, rococo melodrama out of material which, when you think about it, makes hardly any sense at all.' – *Vincent Canby, New York Times*

AAN: Laurence Olivier

The Marauders

US   1955   81m   Eastmancolor
MGM (Arthur M. Loew Jnr)

A rancher hires gunmen to drive away squatters, but the gunmen kill him and take over.

Slightly sinister Western with a plot probably worth trying again.

w Jack Leonard, Earl Fenton   novel Alan Marcus   d Gerald Mayer   ph Harold Marzorati   m Paul Sawtell

Dan Duryea, Jeff Richards, Keenan Wynn, Jarma Lewis, Harry Shannon

March of the Wooden Soldiers: see *Babes in Toyland*

March or Die

GB   1977   107m   Technicolor
ITC/Associated General (Dick Richards, Jerry Bruckheimer)
V*

In 1918, tensions rise at a Foreign Legion outpost threatened by Arabs.

Incredibly old-hat romantic melodrama of the kind that was being spoofed forty years ago. The considerable talent involved seems unfortunately under instruction to take it seriously.

w David Zelag Goodman   d Dick Richards   ph John Alcott   m Maurice Jarre

Gene Hackman, Terence Hill, Catherine Deneuve, Max von Sydow, Ian Holm, Marcel Bozzuffi

† The writer and director more successfully revived a different set of clichés in *Farewell My Lovely*.

Marching Along: see *Stars and Stripes Forever*

Marco the Magnificent: see *The Fabulous Adventures of Marco Polo*

Mardi Gras

US   1958   107m   DeLuxe   Cinemascope
TCF (Jerry Wald)

In New Orleans at holiday time, a film star falls for a cadet.

Mindless musical using up available talent.

w Winston Miller, Hal Kanter   d Edmund Goulding   ph Wilfrid M. Cline   md Lionel Newman

Pat Boone, Christine Carere, Sheree North, Tommy Sands, Gary Crosby, Fred Clark, Richard Sargent, Barrie Chase

AAN: Lionel Newman

Mare Nostrum *

US   1925   approx 110m   bw   silent
MGM

A Spanish captain loves a German spy.

Tragic romantic melodrama, a major attraction of its time.

w Willis Goldbeck   novel Vicente Blasco Ibanez   d Rex Ingram   ph John Seitz

Antonio Moreno, Alice Terry

'The girl of the moment in the picture of America's hey! hey! day!'

Margie ***

US   1946   94m   Technicolor
TCF (Walter Morosco)

A married woman reminisces about her college days, when she married the French teacher despite her tendency to lose her bloomers at the most embarrassing moments.

Wholly pleasing nostalgia, very smartly and brightly handled.

w F. Hugh Herbert   stories Ruth McKinney, Richard Bransten   d Henry King   ph Charles Clarke   md Alfred Newman

Jeanne Crain, Glenn Langan, *Alan Young*, Lynn Bari, Barbara Lawrence, Conrad Janis, Esther Dale

'Direction, script and settings skilfully interpret the fashions and crazes of the twenties.' – *MFB*

Margin for Error *

US   1943   74m   bw
TCF (Ralph Dietrich)

Just before World War II, the Nazi consul in New York is murdered in his own office.

Mildly intriguing whodunnit with the case solved by a Jewish cop.

w Lillie Hayward   play Clare Boothe Luce   d Otto Preminger   ph Edward Cronjager   m Leigh Harline

Milton Berle, Joan Bennett, Otto Preminger, Carl Esmond, Howard Freeman, Poldy Dur, Hans von Twardowski

Marguerite de la Nuit *

France/Italy   1955   126m   Technicolor
SNEG/Gaumont Actualités/Cino del Duca (Léon Carré)

An octogenarian signs a pact with the devil in return for his lost youth; but when he has it he causes the death of the woman he loves.

Expensive, sporadically interesting, but unpersuasive updating of Faust.

w Ghislaine Autant-Lara, Gabriel Arout   d Claude Autant-Lara   ph Jacques Natteau   m René Cloërc

Michèle Morgan, Yves Montand, Jean-François Calvé, Massimo Girotti

Le Mari de la coiffeuse: see *The Hairdresser's Husband*

Maria Chapdelaine *

France   1935   73m   bw
Société Nouvelle

In a hard Quebec winter Maria loses her mother and her lover, but resists temptation by a man from the city.

Artistically telling drama, later flatly remade as *The Naked Heart*.   novel Louis Hémon   d Julien Duvivier

Madeleine Renaud, Jean Gabin, Suzanne Despres, Jean-Pierre Aumont

'A fine achievement, it gives the feeling of a sort of epic poem.' – *Variety*

Maria Marten, or The Murder in the Red Barn

GB   1935   67m   bw
George King

A wicked Victorian squire kills his pregnant mistress and is haunted.

Stilted melodrama, ripely played, from a real-life case. (The villain's scalp is still exhibited in a museum at Bury St Edmunds.)

w Randall Faye   d George King   ph George Stretton

Tod Slaughter, Sophie Stewart, Eric Portman, Clare Greet

† Several versions had been made in silent days.

El Mariachi: see under E

Marie
US   1985   112m   Technicolor   Dunton vision
Dino de Laurentiis
V*

A battered wife leaves her husband and becomes chairman of the Tennessee parole board.

An edifying biopic to which the only answer is, so what?

w John Briley   book Peter Maas   d Roger Donaldson

Sissy Spacek, Jeff Daniels, Morgan Freeman

'Blessed are the pure in heart but also deadly dull.' – *Time Out*

Marie Antoinette *
US   1938   160m   bw
MGM (Hunt Stromberg)
V*, L

The last days of the French court before the revolution.

Too slow by half, and so glamorized and fictionalized as to lack all interest, this long delayed production stands only as an example of MGM's expensive prestige movies of the thirties.

w Claudine West, Donald Ogden Stewart, Ernest Vajda   d W. S. Van Dyke   ph William Daniels   montage Slavko Vorkapich   m Herbert Stothart   ad Cedric Gibbons

Norma Shearer, Tyrone Power, John Barrymore, Robert Morley, Gladys George, Anita Louise, Joseph Schildkraut, Henry Stephenson, Reginald Gardiner, Peter Bull, Albert Dekker, Cora Witherspoon, Barnett Parker, Joseph Calleia, Henry Kolker, George Zucco, Henry Daniell, Harry Davenport, Barry Fitzgerald, Mae Busch, Robert Barrat

'Produced on a scale of incomparable splendour and extravagance, it approaches real greatness as cinematic historical literature.' – *Variety*

'A resplendent bore.' – *New Yorker, 1977*

AAN: Herbert Stothart; Norma Shearer; Robert Morley

La Marie du Port
France   1949   95m   bw
Sacha Gordine

A Cherbourg restaurateur takes his mistress home for her father's funeral, and falls in love with her younger sister.

Slight romantic drama, well enough put over but not very memorable except for its slightly cynical mood.

w Louis Chavance, Marcel Carné   novel Georges Simenon   d Marcel Carné   ph Henri Alekan   m Joseph Kosma

Jean Gabin, Blanchette Brunoy, Nicole Courcel, Claude Romain, Louis Seigner, Jeanne Marken, Carette

Marie Galante
US   1934   90m   bw
Fox
V*

A French girl stranded in the Canal Zone becomes involved in international intrigue.

Slightly unusual spy romance.

w Reginald Berkeley   novel Jacques Deval   d Henry King

Spencer Tracy, Ketti Gallian, Ned Sparks, Helen Morgan, Sig Rumann, Leslie Fenton, Stepin Fetchit

'Production and handling should carry it to moderate grosses.' – *Variety*

Marie Octobre
France   1958   102m   bw
Orex/SF/Abbey/Doxa (Lucien Viard)
US title: *Secret Meeting*

At a reunion dinner of a wartime resistance group, a traitor is exposed and killed.

Stultifying one-set talkfest employing Hitchcock's long-discarded ten-minute take.

w Julien Duvivier, Jacques Robert   novel Jacques Robert   d Julien Duvivier   ph Robert Le Fèbvre   m Jean Yatove   ad Georges Wakhevitch

Danielle Darrieux, Serge Reggiani, Bernard Blier, Paul Meurisse, Noel Roquevert, Lino Ventura, Paul Guers, Paul Frankeur

Marie Walewska: see *Conquest*

La Mariée Etait en Noir: see *The Bride Wore Black*

Marine Raiders
US   1944   90m   bw
Robert Fellows/RKO
V*

The marines do battle in Guadalcanal.

Standard romantic flagwaver.

w Warren Duff   d Harold Schuster

Pat O'Brien, Robert Ryan, Ruth Hussey, Frank McHugh, Barton MacLane

The Marines Fly High
US   1940   68m   bw
Robert Sisk/RKO

Two leathernecks combat a mysterious South American villain.

Formula action fare, intended as a Flagg and Quirt adventure but made with a second team.

w Jerry Cady and A. J. Bolton   d George Nicholls Jnr and Ben Stoloff

Richard Dix, Chester Morris, Lucille Ball, John Eldredge, Steffi Duna

'Up to their necks in fights and loving!'
Marines Let's Go
US   1961   103m   DeLuxe   Cinemascope
TCF (Raoul Walsh)

Marines fighting in Korea are granted leave in Japan.

Brawling tragi-farce with predictable characters, a long way after *What Price Glory*.

w John Twist   story Raoul Walsh   d Raoul Walsh   ph Lucien Ballard   m Irving Gertz

Tom Tryon, David Hedison, Tom Reese, Linda Hutchins, William Tyler

'A typically noisy, insensitive and maudlin tribute to the American Marines.' – *MFB*

Marius **
France   1931   125m   bw
Marcel Pagnol/Paramount
V

The son of a Marseilles waterfront café owner gives up his sweetheart to go to sea.

Celebrated character drama which succeeds through the realism and vitality of its people and their dialogue.

w Marcel Pagnol,   play Marcel Pagnol   d Alexander Korda   ph Ted Pahle   m Francis Grammon

Raimu, Pierre Fresnay, Charpin, Orane Demazis

† Two sequels with the same players and from the same pen made this a famous trilogy: *Fanny* (qv) and *César* (qv).
†† *Port of Seven Seas* (MGM 1938) was a hammy and stagey Hollywood compression of the trilogy. See also *Fanny* (1960), a dull version of the stage musical, with the songs removed.

Marjorie Morningstar
US   1958   123m   Warnercolor
(Warner) United States Pictures (Milton Sperling)

A New York Jewish girl has great ambitions for herself but ends up a suburban housewife.

Stodgy 'woman's picture' with all talents somewhat uneasy in their assignments, mainly because the Jewish quality is imperfectly conveyed.

w Everett Freeman   novel Herman Wouk   d Irving Rapper   ph Harry Stradling   m Max Steiner

Natalie Wood, Gene Kelly, Claire Trevor, Everett Sloane, Ed Wynn, Martin Milner, Carolyn Jones, George Tobias, Jesse White, Martin Balsam

† The first film in which perfume was credited.

AAN: song 'A Very Precious Love' (m Sammy Fain, ly Francis Webster)

'Lock me up! Please lock me up!'
The Mark *
GB   1961   127m   bw   Cinemascope
TCF/Raymond Stross/Sidney Buchman
V*

A sexual psychopath finds on emerging from prison that his past still haunts him despite the help of his psychiatrist.

Worthy but evasive social drama which outstays its welcome but provides good performances.

w Sidney Buchman, Stanley Mann   d Guy Green   ph Douglas Slocombe   m Richard Rodney Bennett

Stuart Whitman, Maria Schell, *Rod Steiger,* Brenda de Banzie, Maurice Denham, Donald Wolfit, Paul Rogers, Donald Houston

'There is seriousness and care, but neither boldness nor passion . . . no hint of the truly sordid is allowed to seep through.' – *MFB*

AAN: Stuart Whitman

The Mark of Cain
GB   1947   88m   bw
GFD/Two Cities (W. P. Lipscomb)

The attractive housekeeper of a Manchester businessman is blamed when his brother accidentally poisons him.

Turgid period melodrama in which few opportunities are offered and none taken.

w Francis Crowdy, Christianna Brand, W. P. Lipscomb   novel *Airing in a Closed Carriage* by Joseph Shearing   d Brian Desmond Hurst   ph Erwin Hillier   m Bernard Stevens

Sally Gray, Eric Portman, Patrick Holt, Dermot Walsh, Denis O'Dea, Edward Lexy, Miles Malleson

'Positively The Most Horrifying Film Ever Made.'
'Likely to upset your stomach.'
Mark of the Devil (dubbed)
West Germany   1969   97m   colour
Atlas/Hi-Fi Stereo 70 (Adrian Hoven)
V, V*
original title: *Hexen geschändet und zu Tode gequält;* aka: *Austria 1700*

A bloodthirsty and lecherous witch-finder's activities are usurped by an even more sadistic aristocrat, acting in the name of the Church.

A nasty, garish horror that lingers over scenes of torture and brutality. The movie claims to be based on cases 'taken from authentic documents', but the result is the same old exploitative rubbish as usual.

w Sergio Casstner (Michael Armstrong), Percy Parker (Adrian Hoven)   d Michael Armstrong   ph Ernst W. Kulinke   m Michael Holm   ad Max Mellin   ed Siegrun Jager

Herbert Lom, Olivera Vuco, Udo Kier, Reggie Nalder, Herbert Fux, Michael Maien, Ingeborg Schoener, Johannes Buzalski, Gaby Fuchs

† The film was refused a certificate and never shown in British cinemas. It was released on video in the 1980s and quickly withdrawn before being given a British video release in 1993 with an 18 certificate. When it first opened in America, audiences were supplied with sick-bags as they went in.

The Mark of the Hawk

US 1958 84m Technicolor Superscope
Universal-International

An educated African fights for the emergence of his people by peaceful means.

Well-intentioned but muddled topical drama.

w H. Kenn Carmichael *d* Michael Audley

Sidney Poitier, Juano Hernandez, Eartha Kitt, John McIntire, Marne Maitland, Patrick Allen

Mark of the Renegade

US 1951 81m Technicolor
Jack Gross/Universal-International

In 1824, a Mexican agent in California pretends to be a rotter in order to unmask villains.

Shakily constructed action piece which quickly wears out its welcome.

w Louis Solomon and Robert Hardy Andrews *story* Johnston McCulley *d* Hugo Fregonese

Ricardo Montalban, Gilbert Roland, Cyd Charisse, J. Carrol Naish, Andrea King, George Tobias, Antonio Moreno

Mark of the Vampire *

US 1935 61m bw
MGM (E. J. Mannix)
V*

A policeman tries to solve an old murder in an eerie house by hiring vaudeville performers to pose as vampires.

Semi-spoof horror which is flawed by lack of pace and a patchy script, but contains splendid visual moments. A remake of the Lon Chaney silent, *London After Midnight*.

w Guy Endore, Bernard Schubert *d* Tod Browning *ph* James Wong Howe

Lionel Barrymore, Jean Hersholt, Elizabeth Allan, Bela Lugosi, Carol Borland, Lionel Atwill, Henry Wadsworth, Donald Meek, Jessie Ralph, Ivan Simpson, Holmes Herbert

'Deftly combines murder mystery, chiller and novelty elements for pretty good entertainment results.' – *Variety*.

'Even the adults in the audience may feel a bit skittery at the sight of two or three vampires, a bevy of bats, a drove of rodents, a herd of spiders and a cluster of cobwebs, not forgetting the swarm of fog.' – *New York Times*

The Mark of Zorro *

US 1920 90m (24 fps) bw silent
Douglas Fairbanks
V*, L

A Mexican Robin Hood carves his initial wherever he turns up to harass the Spanish invaders.

A little faded now, but this swashbuckler opened up a whole new career for its star; the 1940 version clearly has more style.

novel The Curse of Capistrano by Johnston McCulley *d* Fred Niblo *ph* William McGann *m* William Perry

Douglas Fairbanks, Marguerite de la Motte, Noah Beery

The Mark of Zorro ***

US 1940 94m bw
TCF (Raymond Griffith)
V*, L

After being educated in Spain, Diego de Vega returns to California and finds the country enslaved and his father half-corrupted by tyrants. Disguising himself as a masked bandit, he leads the country to expel the usurpers.

Splendid adventure stuff for boys of all ages, an amalgam of *The Scarlet Pimpernel* and *Robin Hood* to which in this version the director adds an overwhelming pictorial sense which makes it stand out as the finest of all.

w John Taintor Foote, Garrett Fort, Bess Meredyth *d* Rouben Mamoulian *ph* Arthur Miller *m* Alfred Newman *ad* Richard Day, Joseph C. Wright

Tyrone Power, Basil Rathbone, J. Edward Bromberg, Linda Darnell, Eugene Pallette, Montagu Love, Janet Beecher, Robert Lowery

AAN: Alfred Newman

Marked for Death

US 1990 93m DeLuxe
TCF/Steamroller (Michael Grais, Mark Victor, Steven Seagal)
V, V*, L, S

A former agent takes action against a Jamaican drug dealer and his gang.

Familiar scenario offering the usual mix of grunts and orchestrated violence.

w Michael Grais, Mark Victor *d* Dwight H. Little *ph* Ric Waite *m* James Newton Howard *pd* Robb Wilson King *ed* O. Nicholas Brown

Steven Seagal, Basil Wallace, Keith David, Tom Wright, Joanna Pacula, Elizabeth Gracen, Bette Ford, Danielle Harris

Marked Woman *

US 1937 96m bw
Warner (Lou Edelman)
V*, L

A night-club girl is persuaded to testify against an underworld boss.

A twist on the usual run of gangster melodramas, performed with the star's accustomed intensity and presented with the studio's usual panache.

w Robert Rossen, Abem Finkel *d* Lloyd Bacon *ph* George Barnes *md* Leo F. Forbstein *m* Heinz Roemheld

Bette Davis, Humphrey Bogart, Jane Bryan, Eduardo Ciannelli, Isabel Jewell, Allen Jenkins, Mayo Methot, Lola Lane, Henry O'Neill

'Spotty draw depending on feminine reaction . . . there is nothing that is light, and very little that is funny.' – *Variety*

† Remade as *Lady Gangster*.
†† Humphrey Bogart's character was based on Thomas E. Dewey, and Eduardo Ciannelli's on Lucky Luciano.

Marlowe *

US 1969 95m Metrocolor
MGM/Katzka-Berne-Cherokee/Beckerman (Sergei Petchnikoff)

Private eye Philip Marlowe is hired by a nervous girl to find her missing brother.

The authentic Chandler atmosphere is caught by this busy thriller, but there seems to be a deliberate attempt to make a confusing plot even more obscure, so that the end result is more tiresome than amusing.

w Stirling Silliphant *novel* The Little Sister by Raymond Chandler *d* Paul Bogart *ph* William H. Daniels *m* Peter Matz

James Garner, Rita Moreno, Sharon Farrell, Bruce Lee, Gayle Hunnicutt, Carroll O'Connor, William Daniels, Jackie Coogan

'One does wonder whether the simple human squalor of the Bogart-Chandler era can ever be recaptured by an increasingly meretricious Hollywood.' – *MFB*

Marnie *

US 1964 130m Technicolor
Universal/Geoffrey Stanley Inc (Alfred Hitchcock)
V*, L

A rich man marries a kleptomaniac and cures her, but a nightmare in her past makes her still sexually frigid.

Psychodrama with background crime and suspense, lethargically handled by the old master, who alone knows what he saw in it in the first place, as this heroine does not even have fire under her ice. The production is curiously artificial in many ways, from dummy horses to backcloths to back projection.

w Jay Presson Allen *novel* Winston Graham *d* Alfred Hitchcock *ph* Robert Burks *m* Bernard Herrmann *pd* Robert Boyle

Tippi Hedren, Sean Connery, Martin Gabel, Diane Baker, Louise Latham

Maroc 7

GB 1967 91m Eastmancolor Panavision
Cyclone/Rank

The lady editor of a top fashion magazine doubles as a jewel thief and becomes involved in Moroccan intrigue.

Complex sub-Bond tale of cross and double cross; hardly worth following, really.

w David Osborn *d* Gerry O'Hara

Gene Barry, Elsa Martinelli, Cyd Charisse, Leslie Phillips, Denholm Elliott, Alexandra Stewart, Eric Barker, Angela Douglas

Marooned *

US 1969 134m Technicolor Panavision 70
Columbia/Frankovich-Sturges (Frank Capra Jnr)
V*, L

Three astronauts are stranded in space, and a rescue mission gets under way.

Very heavy-going space suspenser with all possible technical accomplishment but little life of its own.

w Mayo Simon *novel* Martin Caidin *d* John Sturges *ph* Daniel Fapp *pd* Lyle R. Wheeler

Gregory Peck, Richard Crenna, David Janssen, James Franciscus, Gene Hackman, Lee Grant, Nancy Kovack, Mariette Hartley, Scott Brady

'In something like the plight of Ironman One, Sturges' work seems on the point of slowing to a standstill as it drifts further into projects of ever-increasing, self-effacing size and anonymous technical dexterity.' – *Richard Combs*

'It has all the zip, zest and zing of a moon walk, and I suspect a computer fed a dictionary could come up with better dialogue.' – *Judith Crist, 1973*

'A space epic with a horse-and-buggy script.' – *Pauline Kael*

AA: special visual effects (Robbie Robertson)

AAN: Daniel Fapp

'The Marquis de Sade at his most bestial.'
Marquis
Belgium/France 1989 83m colour
ICA/Y. C. Aligator/Constellation/Tchin Tchin
V

Imprisoned in the Bastille in the 1780s, Marquis, an aristocratic spaniel, who passes the time by writing pornography and talking to his chatty penis, Colin, is accused of raping another prisoner, a cow impregnated by the king.

Bizarre, erotic fantasy about the Marquis de Sade by an iconoclastic French cartoonist in which all the characters are played by actors wearing animal masks. Its point remains obscure, though there are a few good jokes, as well as some unpleasant moments, along the way.

w Roland Topor, Henri Xhonneux   *d* Henri Xhonneux   *ph* Etienne Fauduet   *m* Reinhardt Wagner   *ad* Roland Topor   *ed* Chantal Hymans

Philippe Bizot, Bien de Moor, Gabrielle Van Damme, Olivier Duchaveau, Bernard Cogneux, Pierre Decuypere

The Marquise of O *
West Germany/France   1976   107m   Eastmancolor
Janus/Films du Losange
V

At the end of the 18th century, during the Russian invasion of an Italian town, a noblewoman finds herself pregnant . . .

Careful novella with many ambiguities, more concerned with what might have happened than with what did. Interesting but exasperating.

wd Eric Rohmer   *story* Heinrich von Kleist
ph Nestor Almendros   *m* Roger Delmotte

Edith Clever, Bruno Ganz, Peter Luhr, Edda Seippel

'Some may find it slow, sentimental, naïve and old-fashioned; others leisurely, beautiful, controlled and illuminating. I found it both, often at the same time.' – *Alan Brien, Sunday Times*

'A bold, funny story becomes a formal, tame film, like a historical work recreated for educational TV.' – *New Yorker, 1980*

The Marriage Circle **
US   1924   78m (24 fps)   bw   silent
Warner
V*

A bachelor on the loose becomes amorously involved in two marriages.

Feather-light comedy of manners which began a whole new American school, heavily influenced by various European masters.

w Paul Bern   *play* Only a Dream by Lothar Schmidt
d Ernst Lubitsch   *ph* Charles Van Enger

Monte Blue, Florence Vidor, Marie Prevost, Adolphe Menjou, Creighton Hale

'A vanished world of roses, kisses and embraces, of whispers and sighs, of a woman's shadowed arm encased in georgette beckoning across a moonlit garden . . . and hand-kissing all over the place.' – *Herman G. Weinberg*

'At once perfect cinematography and perfect conventional drama.' – *Iris Barry, The Spectator*

'So slim a plot, so hackneyed if you will, is told with gaiety and a wit that lift it into the very first rank of screen comedy.' – *National Board of Review*

† Remade as *One Hour with You*, also by Lubitsch.

'It's the most hilarious proposition a wife ever had!'
The Marriage Go Round
US   1961   98m   DeLuxe   Cinemascope
TCF (Leslie Stevens)

A Swedish girl suggests to a married American professor that she borrow his body for mating purposes, believing they would produce the perfect child.

Silly, unfunny sex comedy.

w Leslie Stevens   *play* Leslie Stevens   *d* Walter Lang   *ph* Leo Tover   *m* Dominic Frontière

James Mason, Susan Hayward, Julie Newmar, Robert Paige, June Clayworth

'As tedious as it is tasteless.' – *Evening Standard*

'It offers James Mason, an actor who couldn't crack a joke if it was a lichee nut, and Susan Hayward, a bargain basement Bette Davis whose lightest touch as a comedienne would stun a horse.' – *Time*

Marriage Is a Private Affair
US   1944   116m   bw
MGM (Pandro S. Berman)

A spoilt rich girl becomes a petulant wife.

Abysmally slow, uninvolving and poorly acted star fodder.

w David Hertz, Lenore Coffee   *novel* Judith Kelly
d Robert Z. Leonard   *ph* Ray June   *m* Bronislau Kaper

Lana Turner, James Craig, John Hodiak, Frances Gifford, Keenan Wynn, Natalie Schafer, Hugh Marlowe, Paul Cavanagh

The Marriage of a Young Stockbroker **
US   1971   95m   DeLuxe
TCF/Lawrence Turman
V*

A stockbroker who finds his life and his marriage dull tries voyeurism and extramarital sex.

Sardonic adult comedy of the battle between the sexes, pretty lively from start to finish.

w Lorenzo Semple Jnr   *novel* Charles Webb
d Lawrence Turman   *ph* Laszlo Kovacs   *m* Fred Karlin

Richard Benjamin, Joanna Shimkus, Elizabeth Ashley, Adam West, Patricia Barry

The Marriage of Corbal
GB   1936   93m   bw
Capitol
US title: *Prisoner of Corbal*

Before the French revolution, an aristocratic lady tries to escape disaster by the right marriage.

Stilted adventure story with too much talk.

w S. Fullman   *novel* The Nuptials of Corbal by Rafael Sabatini   *d* Karl Grune

Nils Asther, Hugh Sinclair, Hazel Terry, Noah Beery, Davy Burnaby

The Marriage of Maria Braun *
West Germany   1978   119m   Fujicolor
Albatros/Trio/WDR/FdA (Michael Fengler)
V*
original title: *Die Ehe der Maria Braun*

Vicissitudes of a post-war bride who is eventually blown up in a gas explosion.

A mixture of solemnity and irony which keeps its basic points well concealed but, despite a sometimes flagging pace, more or less consistently entertains the eye.

w Peter Märthesheimer, Pea Fröhloch   *d* Rainer Werner Fassbinder   *ph* Michael Ballhaus   *m* Peer Raben

Hanna Schygulla, Klaus Löwitsch, Ivan Desny, Gottfried John

Marriage on the Rocks
US   1965   109m   Technicolor   Panavision
Warner/A-C/Sinatra (William H. Daniels)

An ad man and his wife decide to go to Mexico for a divorce but once there change their minds; she ends up accidentally married to his best friend.

All this talent retreats fearfully from a witless, tasteless script and slow handling. A dismal comedy.

w Cy Howard   *d* Jack Donohue   *ph* William H. Daniels   *m* Nelson Riddle

Frank Sinatra, Dean Martin, Deborah Kerr, Cesar Romero, Hermione Baddeley, Tony Bill, Nancy Sinatra, John McGiver

'A long, coarse, and nearly always unfunny comedy, hammered together for no apparent reason except to make money.' – *New Yorker*

The Marriage Playground
US   1929   70m   bw
Paramount

Children of divorced rich parents wander round Europe in a group.

Slightly unusual drama of its day; sound technique very thin.

w J. Walter Rubin, Doris Anderson   *novel* The Children by Edith Wharton   *d* Lothar Mendes
ph Victor Milner

Fredric March, Kay Francis, Mary Brian, Lilyan Tashman, Huntley Gordon, Anita Louise

Married Before Breakfast
US   1937   70m   bw
MGM

An impecunious inventor has a razorless shaving cream.

Scatty comedy which seldom amuses.

w George Oppenheimer, Everett Freeman, Harry Ruskin   *d* Edwin L. Marin

Robert Young, Florence Rice, June Clayworth, Barnett Parker, Warren Hymer

'It has practically nothing in its favour.' – *Variety*

Married but Single: see *This Thing Called Love*

Married to the Mob **
US   1988   103m   DuArt
Rank/Orion/Mysterious Arts (Kenneth Utt, Edward Saxon)
V, V*, L

The wife of a murdered gangster tries to live an honest life after her husband's death.

Effervescent comedy-thriller that bubbles merrily along.

w Barry Strugatz, Mark R. Burns   *d* Jonathan Demme   *ph* Tak Fujimoto   *m* David Byrne
pd Kristi Zea   *ed* Craig McKay

Michelle Pfeiffer, Matthew Modine, Dean Stockwell, Mercedes Ruehl, Alec Baldwin, Trey Wilson, Joan Cusack

AAN: Dean Stockwell

A Married Woman *
France   1964   98m   bw
Anouchka/Orsay (Philippe Dusart)
V*
original title: *Une Femme Mariée*

A pilot's wife has an actor lover.

Fragments of character observation, in various cinematic techniques, build up into an intense personal study if not a plot.

wd Jean-Luc Godard   *ph* Raoul Coutard   *m* Claude Nougaro

Macha Meril, Bernard Noel, Roger Leenhardt

'A minefield of paradoxes . . . the essence of cinema 1965.' – *Peter John Dyer, MFB*

Marry Me
GB   1949   97m   bw
GFD/Gainsborough (Betty Box)

Four stories of a marriage bureau.

A styleless portmanteau of anecdotes put over by a clear second team.

w Lewis Gilbert, Denis Waldock   *d* Terence Fisher
ph Ray Elton   *m* Clifton Parker

Derek Bond, Susan Shaw, Patrick Holt, Carol Marsh, David Tomlinson, Zena Marshall, Guy Middleton, Nora Swinburne, Jean Cadell, Mary Jerrold

Marry Me Again
US   1953   73m   bw
RKO (Alex Gottlieb)

A man returns from war to find that his fiancée has inherited a million dollars.

Zany comedy with tilts at psychiatry: not too bad.

wd Frank Tashlin

Robert Cummings, Marie Wilson, Ray Walker, Mary Costa, Jess Barker

Marry the Girl

US 1937 66m bw
Warner

A crazy family owns a newspaper syndicate.

Fashionable comedy which goes far too far.

w Sig Herzig, Pat C. Flick, Tom Reed novel Edward Hope d William McGann

Mary Boland, Frank McHugh, Hugh Herbert, Mischa Auer, Carol Hughes, Allen Jenkins, Alan Mowbray, Hugh O'Connell

'Pic will probably get by on duals in the nabes and should be a panic with juve audiences. But it will probably lay an egg in first runs.' – *Variety*

The Marrying Kind *

US 1952 93m bw
Columbia (Bert Granet)

A couple seeking divorce tell their troubles to a judge, and change their minds.

Smart, New Yorkish, tragi-comic star vehicle which works pretty well.

w Ruth Gordon, Garson Kanin d George Cukor ph Joseph Walker m Hugo Friedhofer

Judy Holliday, Aldo Ray, Madge Kennedy, Mickey Shaughnessy

The Marrying Man

US 1991 116m Technicolor
Warner/Hollywood Pictures/Silver Screen Partners IV/Odyssey (David Permut)
V, V*, L, S
GB title: *Too Hot To Handle*

A playboy, forced to marry a gangster's girlfriend, finds himself repeating the experience several times.

A misfiring romantic comedy, both involved and uninvolving.

w Neil Simon d Jerry Rees ph Donald E. Thorin m David Newman pd William F. Matthews ed Michael Jablow

Kim Basinger, Alec Baldwin, Elisabeth Shue, Armand Assante, Paul Reiser, Fisher Stevens, Peter Dobson, Steve Hytner

'A still-born romantic comedy of staggering ineptitude. Industry bad-mouthing of the stars during production was just a preview of the terrible picture.' – *Variety*

'A comedy that bounces skittishly down a lane that memory has not travelled in a while. Maybe it's silly. But it does awaken a nostalgic fondness for an era when celebrity dreaming was goofier, giddier and less consequential than it is now.' – *Richard Schickel, Time*

La Marseillaise *

France 1938 145m bw
Films La Marseillaise (André Zwoboda)

The story of the French revolution of 1789.

A rather disconnected epic which, despite a few splendid scenes, never moved its audiences to enthusiasm.

wd Jean Renoir ph Jean Bourgoin and others md Joseph Kosma

Pierre Renoir, Lise Delemare, Louis Jouvet, Léon Larive, Georges Spanelly, Elisa Ruis, William Aguet

'France's super-super film production is a near flopperoo.' – *Variety*

The Marseille Contract

GB/France 1974 89m Eastmancolor
Warner/AIP/Kettledrum/PECF (Judd Bernard)
V*
US title: *The Destructors*

An American narcotics agent in Paris hires an assassin to dispose of a drug smuggler.

Routine action melodrama with a jokey atmosphere not sustained by a downbeat script.

w Judd Bernard d Robert Parrish ph Douglas Slocombe m Roy Budd

Michael Caine, Anthony Quinn, James Mason, Alexandra Stewart, Marcel Bozzuffi, Maurice Ronet

Marseilles trilogy: see *Marius; Fanny; César*

Marshmallow Moon: see *Aaron Slick from Punkin Crick*

Martin *

US 1978 95m colour
Laurel (Richard Rubinstein)
V*, L

A disturbed youth may be a vampire or just a boy with sexual hangups and an appetite for blood.

Gory thriller with a sense of irony, making fun of the superstitions surrounding vampires yet utilizing them for its shocking climax. wd George A. Romero ph Michael Gornick m Donald Rubinstein

John Amplas, Lincoln Maazel, Christine Forrest, Elyane Nadeau, Tom Savine, Sarah Venable, Fran Middleton, Al Lavistsky

Martin Luther *

US/Germany 1953 114m bw
Louis de Rochemont/Lutheran Church Productions (Lothar Wolff)

The career and doubts of Martin Luther.

Frequently vivid, occasionally boring, small-scale account of the first Protestant.

w Allan Sloane, Lothar Wolff, others d Irving Pichel ph Joseph C. Brun m Mark Lothar ad Fritz Maurischat, Paul Markwitz

Niall MacGinnis, John Ruddock, Pierre Lefèvre, Guy Verney, David Horne, Philip Leaver, Irving Pichel, Alexander Gauge

AAN: Joseph C. Brun; art direction

Martin Roumagnac

France 1946 99m bw
Alcina (Marc Le Pelletier)

The trial, with flashbacks, of a small-town businessman who has murdered his mistress.

Wholly unabsorbing and ordinary story of a *crime passionnel*, totally wasting its stars. wd Georges Lacombe ph Roger Hubert m Marcel Mirouze

Jean Gabin, Marlene Dietrich, Margo Lion, Marcel Hérrand

Martin's Day

Canada 1985 98m Medallion colour
World Film Services/MGM-UA
V*

An escaped convict and the young boy he kidnaps become friends.

Predictable melodrama which gets nowhere.

w Allan Scott, Chris Bryant d Alan Gibson

Richard Harris, Lindsay Wagner, James Coburn, Justin Henry, Karen Black, John Ireland

Marty ****

US 1955 91m bw
UA/Hecht-Hill-Lancaster (Harold Hecht)
V*, L

A 34-year-old Bronx butcher fears he will never get a girl because he is unattractive, but at a Saturday night dance he meets a girl with similar fears. Unfortunately she is not Italian . . .

The first of the filmed teleplays which in the mid-fifties seemed like a breath of spring to Hollywood (they were cheap) and also brought in a new wave of talent. This is one of the best, its new naturalistic dialogue falling happily on the ear; but it has been so frequently imitated since that its revolutionary appearance is hard to imagine.

w Paddy Chayevsky play Paddy Chayevsky d Delbert Mann ph Joseph LaShelle m Roy Webb ad Edward S. Howarth, Walter Simonds

Ernest Borgnine, Betsy Blair, Esther Minciotti, Joe Mantell, Karen Steele, Jerry Paris

'Something rare in the American cinema today: a subtle, ironic and compassionate study of ordinary human relationships.' – *Gavin Lambert*

AA: best picture; Paddy Chayevsky; Delbert Mann; Ernest Borgnine

AAN: Joseph LaShelle; Betsy Blair; Joe Mantell; art direction

Marusa no onna: see *A Taxing Woman*

The Marx Brothers at the Circus: see *At The Circus*

Mary Burns Fugitive *

US 1935 84m bw
Paramount (Walter Wanger)

The innocent girlfriend of a gangster is convicted through circumstantial evidence, escapes from prison and finds true love.

Competent meshing of well-tried thirties elements, a good typical wish-fulfilment melodrama of its time.

w Gene Towne, Graham Baker, Louis Stevens d William K. Howard ph Leon Shamroy

Sylvia Sidney, Melvyn Douglas, Alan Baxter, Pert Kelton, Wallace Ford, Brian Donlevy, Esther Dale

'As a piece of synthetic studio slickness it has enough on the ball to qualify.' – *Variety*

Mary Jane's Pa

US 1935 70m bw
Warner
GB title: *Wanderlust*

A husband goes wandering for ten years. On his return, his wife has magnified what he left into a newspaper empire.

Adequate stagey comedy, well acted.

w Tom Reed, Peter Milne play Edith Ellis Furness novel Norman Way d William Keighley

Aline MacMahon, Guy Kibbee, Tom Brown, Robert McWade, Minor Watson, Nan Grey

'Okay for secondary bills.' – *Variety*

Mary Mary

US 1963 126m Technicolor
Warner (Mervyn Le Roy)

A publisher falls in love again with his ex-wife but finds she is being pursued by a film star.

Feeble film version of a lighter-than-air Broadway success, with the actors paralysed behind the footlights and the camera asleep in the stalls.

w Richard L. Breen play Jean Kerr d Mervyn Le Roy ph Harry Stradling m Frank Perkins

Debbie Reynolds, Barry Nelson, Michael Rennie, Diane McBain

Mary of Scotland *

US 1936 123m bw
RKO (Pandro S. Berman)
V*, L

Mary Stuart refuses to give up her claim to the English throne, and is eventually executed.

Sombre historical charade with splendid sets and atmosphere but suffering from script and performances that don't quite make it despite effort all round.

w Dudley Nichols   *play* Maxwell Anderson
d John Ford   *ph* *Joseph H. August*   *m* Nathaniel
Shilkret   *ad* *Van Nest Polglase, Carroll Clark*

Katharine Hepburn, Fredric March, Donald Crisp,
Florence Eldridge, Douglas Walton, John Carradine,
Robert Barrat, Monte Blue, Moroni Olsen, Frieda
Inescort, Alan Mowbray

'An unpromising and stagey play is fleshed out into a
rich and confident exercise in filmcraft.' – *John Baxter,
1968*

'Events are walked through as though they were
rooms in a museum, and closing time at three.' – *Otis
Ferguson*

Mary Poppins ***
US   1964   139m   Technicolor
Walt Disney (Bill Walsh)
V, V*, L, S

In Edwardian London a magical nanny teaches two
slightly naughty children to make life enjoyable for
themselves and others.

Sporadically a very pleasant and effective
entertainment for children of all ages, with plenty of
brightness and charm including magic tricks, the
mixing of live with cartoon adventures, and just plain
fun. It suffers, however, from a wandering narrative
in the second half (when Miss Poppins scarcely
appears) and from Mr Van Dyke's really lamentable
attempt at Cockney.

w Bill Walsh, Don da Gradi   *novel* P. L. Travers
d Robert Stevenson   *ph* Edward Colman
md Irwin Kostal   *pd* Tony Walton   *m/ly* Richard M.
and Robert B. Sherman   *ad* Carroll Clark, William H.
Tuntke   *sp* Eustace Lycett, *Peter Ellenshaw, Robert A.
Mattey*   *ed* Cotton Warburton

Julie Andrews, David Tomlinson, Glynis Johns, Dick
Van Dyke, Reginald Owen, Ed Wynn, Matthew
Garber, Karen Dotrice, Hermione Baddeley, Elsa
Lanchester, Arthur Treacher, Jane Darwell

'A charming, imaginative and technically superb
movie musical, sparkling with originality, melody
and magical performances.' – *Judith Crist*

AA: Richard M. and Robert B. Sherman; Julie
Andrews; song 'Chim Chim Cheree'; special visual
effects; editing

AAN: best picture; script; Robert Stevenson; Edward
Colman; Irwin Kostal; art direction

'They used every passion in their incredible duel, and every
man in their savage games of intrigue!'

Mary Queen of Scots
GB   1971   128m   Technicolor   Panavision
Universal/Hal B. Wallis

The story of Mary Stuart's opposition to Elizabeth I,
her imprisonment and execution.

Schoolbook history in which none of the characters
comes to life; dramatic movement is almost entirely
lacking despite the liberties taken with fact.

w John Hale   *d* Charles Jarrott   *ph* Christopher
Challis   *m* John Barry

Vanessa Redgrave, Glenda Jackson, Trevor Howard,
Patrick McGoohan, Nigel Davenport

'Without a better script, Hercules couldn't lift this
story off the ground.' – *Pauline Kael, New Yorker*

AAN: John Barry; Vanessa Redgrave

Mary Stevens M.D.
US   1933   71m   bw
Warner

A lady doctor decides to have a baby before getting
married.

Saucy drama which engrossed audiences in its day.

w Rian James   *novel* Virginia Kellogg   *d* Lloyd
Bacon

Kay Francis, Lyle Talbot, Glenda Farrell, Thelma
Todd, Una O'Connor, Hobart Cavanaugh, Harold
Huber

'Exceptionally good adult entertainment, with a
pronounced feminine appeal.' – *Variety*

Masala *
Canada   1991   106m   colour
Metro/Divani/Telefilm Canada/Ontario Film Development/
   Ontario Arts Council (Srinivas Krishna, Camelia Freiberg)

The Hindu god Krishna grants a miracle to a Sikh
family living in Toronto.

An irreverent small-scale movie that provides
pleasure.

wd Srinivas Krishna   *ph* Paul Sarossy   *m* The West
India Company, Leslie Winston   *pd* Tamara Deverell
ed Michael Munn

Srinivas Krishna, Sakina Jaffrey, Zohra Segal, Saeed
Jaffrey, Heri Johal, Madhuri Bhatia, Ronica Sajnani,
Les Porter

'A highly entertaining work.' – *Sight and Sound*

La Maschera
Italy   1988   90m   Eastmancolor
RAIDVE/Istituto Luce/Best International (Lilia Smecchia, Ettore
   Rosboch)
aka: The Mask

In the 18th century a young actress rejects the
advances of a dissolute aristocrat and then falls in love
with a mysterious masked stranger.

Lugubrious romance, concentrating on glossy
surfaces.

w Adriano Apra, Fiorella Infascelli, Enzo Ungari,
Ennio de Concini   *d* Fiorella Infascelli   *ph* Acacio
de Almeida   *m* Luis Bacalov   *ad* Antonello Geleng
ed Francisco Malvestito

Helena Bonham Carter, Michael Maloney, Feodor
Chaliapin Jnr, Roberto Herlitzka, Michele de Marchi,
Alberto Cracco

La Maschera del Demonio: see *Mask of Satan*

Masculin Féminin **
France/Sweden   1966   110m   bw
Gala/Anouchka/Argos/Svensk/Sandrews (Philippe Dussart)
V, V*

A young, romantic revolutionary imagines that he is
in love with a would-be singer.

An exploration of pop culture and politics, in a
sequence of episodes intercut with arbitrary
happenings, and as much concerned with form as
content, moving cinema away from straightforward
narrative to something more abstract and less
interesting.

wd Jean-Luc Godard   *story* La Femme de Paul *and* Le
Signe *by* Guy de Maupassant   *ph* Willy Kurant
m Francis Lai   *ed* Agnès Guillemot

Jean-Pierre Léaud, Chantal Goya, Catherine-Isabelle
Duport, Marlène Jobert, Michel Debord, Birger-
Malmsten, Eva Britt Strandberg, Brigitte Bardot,
Françoise Hardy

'Godard's exercise in self-indulgence.' – *John Simon*

'That rare movie achievement: a work of grace and
beauty in a contemporary setting.' – *Pauline Kael*

'By this defiantly unrealistic system of narrative,
Godard manages to present us with all the problems
facing his hero and facing boys of his generation.' –
Richard Roud

'Mainly it seems to be a movie happening, in which
Mr Godard can play whimsical and sometimes
comical stunts, not leading to any clear conclusion as
to the stability of youth. He himself, as a motion-
picture maker, seems to have little more
concentration-span than his saucy, good-looking

youngsters, who evidently have none at all.' – *Bosley
Crowther*

† For its American release, it was cut to 103m.

M*A*S*H ****
US   1970   116m   DeLuxe   Panavision
TCF/Aspen (Ingo Preminger, Leon Ericksen)
V, V*, L

Surgeons at a mobile hospital in Korea spend what
spare time they have chasing women and bucking
authority.

Savage comedy of man's rebellion in the face of death,
alternating sex farce with gory operation scenes;
hailed as the great anti-everything film, and certainly
very funny for those who can take it. It led to a
television series which for once did not disgrace its
original.

w Ring Lardner Jnr   *novel* Richard Hooker   *d* Robert
Altman   *ph* Harold E. Stine   *m* Johnny Mandel

Donald Sutherland, Elliott Gould, Tom Skerritt, Sally
Kellerman, Robert Duvall, Jo Ann Pflug, René
Auberjonois, Gary Burghof

'Bloody funny. A hyper-acute wiretap on mankind's
death wish.' – *Joseph Morgenstern*

'The laughter is blood-soaked and the comedy cloaks
a bitter and terrible truth.' – *Judith Crist*

'A foul-mouthed, raucous, anti-establishment
comedy, combining gallows humour, sexual slapstick
and outrageous satire.' – *Les Keyser, Hollywood in the
Seventies*

AA: Ring Lardner Jnr

AAN: best picture; Robert Altman; Sally Kellerman

Mask **
US   1985   120m   Technicolor
Universal/Martin Starger
V, V*, L

A boy of 16 has a rare and disfiguring bone disease,
but his mother fights for his rights.

More of a character study than a movie, this also has
the problem of being emotionally hard to take; but
one ends up respecting it.

w Anna Hamilton Phelan, from her true story of
Rocky Dennis   *d* Peter Bogdanovich   *ph* Laszlo
Kovacs   *m* Dennis Ricotta   *ed* Barbara Ford

Cher, Sam Elliott, Eric Stoltz, Estelle Getty

'Anyone looking for a good uplifting cry should be
well satisfied.' – *Variety*

The Mask: see *La Maschera*

The Mask of Dijon
US   1946   73m   bw
PRC

A conjuror becomes obsessed by hypnotism and takes
to murder to prove his superiority.

Heavy-going thriller with little discernible point.

w Arthur St Claire and Griffin Jay   *d* Lew Landers

Erich von Stroheim, Jeanne Bates, William Wright

The Mask of Dimitrios **
US   1944   99m   bw
Warner (Henry Blanke)

A timid Dutch novelist is drawn into a Middle-
Eastern intrigue with money at the centre of it.

Generally successful international intriguer, moodily
shot in evocative sets, and remarkable for its time in
that the story is not distorted to fit romantic stars:
character actors bear the entire burden.

w Frank Gruber,   *novel* Eric Ambler   *d* Jean Negulesco
ph Arthur Edeson   *m* Adolph Deutsch

Peter Lorre, Sidney Greenstreet, Zachary Scott, Faye
Emerson, *Victor Francen, Steven Geray, Florence Bates,
Eduardo Ciannelli, Kurt Katch, John Abbott, Monte Blue*

'The picture has more mood than excitement.' – *Pauline Kael, 70s*

The Mask of Fu Manchu **
US   1932   70m   bw
MGM

Nayland Smith and his party are caught and threatened with torture by the yellow terror.

Highly satisfactory episode in the nefarious adventures of the master criminal, fast moving, humorous and very good to look at.

w John Willard, Edgar Woolf, Irene Kuhn   *stories* Sax Rohmer   *d* Charles Brabin, Charles Vidor   *ph* Tony Gaudio

Boris Karloff, Myrna Loy, Lewis Stone, Karen Morley, Charles Starrett, Jean Hersholt, Lawrence Grant

'The diabolical stuff is piled on so thick at the finish, audiences are liable to laugh where they oughtn't.' – *Variety*

'A tolerable, campy entertainment.' – *Pauline Kael, 70s*

Mask of Satan *
Italy   1960   84m   bw
Galatea/Jolly (Massimo de Rita)
V
original title: *La Maschera del Demonio*; aka: *Black Sunday; Revenge of the Vampire*

A princess who was executed for witchcraft by her brother returns 200 years later to wreak vengeance on his descendants.

A stylish, though gruesome, horror movie.

w Mario Bava, Ennio de Concini, Marcello Coscia, Mario Serandrei   *d* Mario Bava   *ph* Mario Bava, Ubaldo Terzano   *sp* Mario Bava

Barbara Steele, John Richardson, Ivo Garrani, Andrea Cecchi, Arturo Doninici, Enrico Olivieri, Clara Bindi

'The greatest gothic horror movie ever made in Italy.' – *Empire*

Mask of the Avenger
US   1951   83m   Technicolor
Hunt Stromberg/Columbia

During the Austro-Italian War, a count's son avenges his father's death and exposes a traitor.

Very moderate swashbuckler on the lines of *The Mark of Zorro*.

w Jesse Lasky Jnr   *d* Phil Karlson

John Derek, Anthony Quinn, Jody Lawrence, Arnold Moss, Eugene Iglesias

The Masked Marvel
US   1943   bw   serial: 12 eps
Republic

An insurance company hires The Masked Marvel to prove that Japanese agents are sabotaging war industries.

Highly derivative serial adventures.   *d* Spencer Bennet

David Bacon, William Forrest, Louise Currie, Johnny Arthur

Maskerade *
Austria   1935   87m   bw
Tobis/Sascha

An inveterate ladies' man finds himself trapped.

Charming romantic comedy.

wd Willi Forst

Anton Walbrook, Paula Wessely, Olga Tscheshowa

'Not a real masterpiece like *Liebelei*, but it has the same b.o. elements.' – *Variety*

The Masque of the Red Death **
GB   1964   89m   Pathecolor   'Scope
AIP/Alta Vista (George Willoughby)
V*, L

A medieval Italian prince practises devil worship while the plague rages outside, but when he holds a ball, death is an uninvited guest.

Languorous, overstretched, often visually striking horror piece with some extremely effective touches among its longueurs.

w Charles Beaumont, R. Wright Campbell   *story* Edgar Allan Poe   *d* Roger Corman   *ph* Nicolas Roeg   *m* David Lee   *ad* Robert Jones   *costumes* Laura Nightingale

Vincent Price, Hazel Court, Jane Asher, Patrick Magee, John Westbrook

Masquerade *
GB   1965   101m   Eastmancolor
UA/Novus (Michael Relph)

To avert friction between Arab states the young heir to one of them is abducted by a British secret service agent; but one of the plotters has other fish to fry.

Quite a lively spy romp with a spectacular action climax, but the plot is simply too complicated.

w Michael Relph, William Goldman   *novel Castle Minerva* by Victor Canning   *d* Basil Dearden   *ph* Otto Heller   *m* Philip Green   *pd* Don Ashton

Cliff Robertson, Jack Hawkins, Charles Gray, Bill Fraser, Marisa Mell, Michel Piccoli, John Le Mesurier

Masquerade
US   1988   91m   colour
UIP/MGM (Michael I. Levy)
V*, L

A gigolo marries a wealthy woman with the intention of murdering her for her money.

Dull thriller that fails to maintain interest.

w Dick Wolf   *d* Bob Swaim   *ph* David Watkin   *m* John Barry   *pd* John Kasarda   *ed* Scott Conrad

Rob Lowe, Meg Tilly, Kim Cattrall, Doug Savant, John Glover, Dana Delany, Erik Holland, Brian Davies, Barton Heyman

'A tranquil, sophisticated thriller.' – *Pauline Kael, New Yorker*

'A gay and gorgeous whirl of romance, adventure and rhythm ... in the billion-dollar pan-American postwar playground!'

Masquerade in Mexico
US   1945   96m   bw
Paramount (Karl Tunberg)

A stranded showgirl is hired by a Mexican banker to entice a gigolo away from his wife.

Talent-starved remake of *Midnight* (qv), which seems second-hand even if you don't know why.

w Karl Tunberg   *d* Mitchell Leisen   *ph* Lionel Lindon   *m* Victor Young

Dorothy Lamour, Arturo de Cordova, Patric Knowles, Ann Dvorak, George Rigaud, Natalie Schafer, Mikhail Rasumny, Billy Daniels

The Masquerader *
US   1933   75m   bw
Samuel Goldwyn

A drug-addicted politician is replaced by his lookalike cousin.

Pleasing dual role star vehicle with good production and support. Very much of its period.

w Howard Estabrook, Moss Hart   *play* John Hunter Booth   *novel* Katherine Cecil Thurston   *d* Richard Wallace   *ph* Gregg Toland   *m* Alfred Newman

Ronald Colman, Elissa Landi, *Halliwell Hobbes*, Juliette Compton, David Torrence

'A fine production with too much story handicap ... Colman's best is not enough.' – *Variety*

'The first amusing and believable tale of English politics and society ... made of all places in Hollywood.' – *Newsweek*

Masques *
France   1987   100m   colour
Cannon/MK2 Productions/A2 (Marin Karmitz)

A thriller writer inveigles his way into the home of a TV game-show host to solve the mysterious disappearance of his sister.

Glossy, well-made thriller that promises more than it delivers, but is enjoyable for Noiret's performance as a hypocritically hearty television celebrity.

w Odile Barski, Claude Chabrol   *d* Claude Chabrol   *ph* Jean Rabier   *m* Matthieu Chabrol   *ad* Françoise Benoit-Fresco   *ed* Monique Fardoulis

Philippe Noiret, Robin Renucci, Bernadette Lafont, Monique Chaumette, Anne Brochet, Roger Dumas, Pierre-François Dumeniaud

Mass Appeal *
US   1984   100m   Technicolor
Universal/Turman-Foster

An idealistic student matches wits with a compromising priest.

Amusing, opened-out version of a two-character play: good for minority audiences.

w Bill C. David   *play* Bill C. David   *d* Glenn Jordan   *ph* Don Peterman   *m* Bill Conti   *pd* Philip Jefferies

Jack Lemmon, Zeljko Ivanek, Charles Durning, Louise Latham

'Saved from damnation by the originality of its central theme and by the excellence of its acting.' – *Quentin Crisp*

Massacre Hill: see *Eureka Stockade*

Massacre in Rome
Italy   1973   103m   Technicolor
Compagnia Cinematografica Champion (Carlo Ponti)
V*, S

In 1944, after partisans blow up a detachment of SS troops in a Rome street, a German colonel makes an ineffectual attempt to resist an order to shoot 330 Italians in retaliation.

Moderately effective drama, based on a true story.

w Robert Katz, George Pan Cosmatos   *book* Death in Rome by Robert Katz   *d* George Pan Cosmatos   *ph* Marcello Gatti   *m* Ennio Morricone   *pd* Morton Haack   *ed* Françoise Bonnot, Roberto Silvi

Richard Burton, Marcello Mastroianni, Leo McKern, John Steiner, Anthony Steel, Robert Harris, Peter Vaughan, Delia Boccardo

The Master Gunfighter
US   1975   120m   Metrocolor   Panavision
Avondale/Warner

In gold rush California, a mysterious avenger rights a variety of wrongs.

Pretentious Western which failed to advance the career of its somewhat over-confident creator.

w Harold Lapland   *d* Tom Laughlin

Tom Laughlin, Ron O'Neal, Lincoln Kilpatrick, Barbara Carrera

† From a Japanese film *Goyokin* written by Kei Tasaka and Hideo Gosha

The Master Key
US   1945   bw   serial: 13 eps
Universal

Nazi agents led by The Master Key plan to spread panic in the US.

Wartime serial with the usual cliffhangers. *d* Ray Taylor and Lewis D. Collins

Milburn Stone, Jan Wiley, Dennis Moore, Addison Richards

The Master of Ballantrae
GB   1953   89m   Technicolor
Warner
V, V*, L

Two brothers toss to decide which shall join Bonnie Prince Charlie's 1745 rebellion.

Half-hearted version of a classic adventure novel.

w Herb Meadow   *novel* R. L. Stevenson   *d* William Keighley   *ph* Jack Cardiff   *m* William Alwyn

Errol Flynn, Anthony Steel, Roger Livesey, Beatrice Campbell, Felix Aylmer, Mervyn Johns, Jacques Berthier, Yvonne Furneaux, Ralph Truman

'All that can be salvaged from this rather unforgivable Anglo-American junket are some pleasant exteriors.' – *Gavin Lambert*

Master of Bankdam *
GB   1947   105m   bw
GFD/Holbein (Nat Bronsten, Walter Forde, Edward Dryhurst)

19th-century chronicles of a mill-owning Yorkshire family.

Archetypal 'trouble at t'mill' saga with moderate production, good acting and undeniably compulsive story.

w Edward Dryhurst, Moie Charles   *novel The Crowthers of Bankdam* by Thomas Armstrong   *d* Walter Forde   *ph* Basil Emmott

Tom Walls, Anne Crawford, Dennis Price, Stephen Murray, Linden Travers, Jimmy Hanley, Nancy Price, David Tomlinson, Herbert Lomas

Master of Lassie: see *The Hills of Home*

Master of the Islands: see *The Hawaiians*

Master of the World
US   1961   104m   Magnacolor
AIP/Alta Vista (James H. Nicholson, Anthony Carras)
V*

In 1848 a mad inventor takes to the air in his magnificent flying machine in the hope of persuading men to stop war.

Aerial version of *Twenty Thousand Leagues under the Sea*, with cheap sets and much use of stock footage; some scenes however have a certain vigour.

w Richard Matheson   *novel* Jules Verne   *d* William Witney   *ph* Gil Warrenton   *m* Les Baxter

Vincent Price, Charles Bronson, Henry Hull, Mary Webster, David Frankham

The Master Plan
GB   1954   78m   bw
Gibraltar

An American agent, concealing the fact that he suffers from blackouts, is sent to investigate information leakages in England.

Quite lively second feature spylarks.   *wd* Hugh Raker (i.e. Cy Endfield)

Wayne Morris, Tilda Thamar, Norman Wooland, Mary Mackenzie, Arnold Bell

The Master Race
US   1944   96m   bw
Edward A. Golden/RKO
V*

German generals realize that the war is lost, and plan counter-measures.

Timely propaganda melodrama warning against premature rejoicing, from the producer of *Hitler's Children*.   *wd* Herbert J. Biberman.

George Coulouris, Osa Massen, Stanley Ridges, Nancy Gates, Carl Esmond, Morris Carnovsky, Lloyd Bridges

The Masters
Italy   1975   100m   Technospes
Campagnia Cinematografica Champion (Carlo Ponti)
original title: *Gente di rispetto*

A new and naïve schoolteacher in a small Sicilian town becomes involved in corrupt local politics after a man who insulted her is murdered by the Mafia.

Glossy thriller that fails to carry any conviction.

w Leo Benevenuti, Piero de Bernardi, Luigi Zampa   *story* Giuseppe Fava   *d* Luigi Zampa   *ph* Ennio Guarnieri   *m* Ennio Morricone   *ad* Luigi Scaccianoce   *ed* Franco Fraticelli

James Mason, Jennifer O'Neill, Franco Nero, Orazio Orlando, Claudio Gora, Franco Fabrizi, Aldo Giuffré

Masters of the Universe
US   1987   106m   Metrocolor
Edward R. Pressman/Cannon
V*

He-Man defends the planet Eternia from the evil Skeletor.

Live action version of the TV cartoons of the toys of the comic strip. Pretty weak stuff, even for five-year-olds.

w David Odell   *d* Gary Goddard

Dolph Lundgren, Frank Langella, Meg Foster, Billy Barty

Masterson of Kansas
US   1955   73m   Technicolor
Sam Katzman/Columbia

The sheriff of Dodge City prevents an Indian uprising by saving an innocent man from the gallows.

Unhistorical two-bit Western.

w Douglas Heyes   *d* William Castle

George Montgomery, Nancy Gates, James Griffith, Jean Willes

Mat: see *Mother*

'Men worshipped her like a goddess, only to be betrayed by a kiss!'
Mata Hari **
US   1931   92m   bw
MGM
V*, L

The career of the famous lady spy of World War I.

Elaborate melodrama, pictorially satisfying and generally more entertaining than might be supposed, with both star and supporting cast in rich thespian form.

w Benjamin Glazer, Leo Birinski, Doris Anderson, Gilbert Emery   *d George Fitzmaurice*   *ph* William Daniels

Greta Garbo, Ramon Novarro, Lionel Barrymore, Lewis Stone, C. Henry Gordon, Karen Morley, Blanche Frederici

'Picture's strength is all in the players; an important grosser on that account.' – *Variety*

Mata Hari
US   1985   108m   Eastmancolor
Rony Yacov/Cannon
V*

The career of the famous lady spy of World War I.

Absurd melodrama which in places seems to be spoofing itself.

w Joel Ziskin   *d* Curtis Harrington

Sylvia Kristel, Christopher Cazenove, Oliver Tobias, Gaye Brown, William Fox

Mata Hari, Agent H21 *
France/Italy   1964   99m   bw
Filmel/Les Films du Carrosse/Simar/Fida Cinematografica (Eugene Lepicier)

A rather unnecessary revamp of the same story, with interesting details but not much resonance.

w Jean-Louis Richard, François Truffaut   *d* Jean-Louis Richard   *ph* Michel Kelber   *m* Georges Delerue   *ad* Claude Pignot

Jeanne Moreau, Jean-Louis Trintignant, Claude Rich, Frank Villard

'All that we are left with is a generous dollop of period charm, and the fascinating spontaneity of an actress.' – *Peter John Dyer, MFB*

Matador *
Spain   1988   106m   colour
Iberoamericana de TV/Televisión Española (Andrés Vicente Gómez)
V, V*, L

A lame, death-obsessed matador is smitten by a sex-and death-obsessed woman, the defending lawyer of a psychic, guilt-obsessed, would-be bullfighter who has confessed to a series of murders he did not commit.

An intense though unerotic treatment of decadent passions; it is comparatively restrained by its director's usual standards, avoiding camp, though it manages to encompass scenes of attempted rape, violent death, and masturbation to images of mutilation.

w Jesus Ferrero, Pedro Almodóvar   *d* Pedro Almodóvar   *ph* Angel Luis Fernández   *m* Bernardo Bonezzi   *ad* Roman Arango, José Morales, José Rosell   *ed* Pepe Salcedo

Assumpta Serna, Antonio Banderas, Bibi Andersen, Nacho Martinez, Eva Cobo, Julieta Serrano, Chus Lampreave, Carmen Maura, Eusebio Poncela

'Chips away at the surface elegance of the bourgeoisie to expose its private vices.' – *Sight and Sound*

'A piece of voluptuous tom-foolery.' – *Pauline Kael, New Yorker*

The Match Factory Girl **
Finland/Sweden   1990   70m   Eastmancolor
Electric Pictures/Swedish Film Institute/ Viillealfa/Aki Kaurismäki
V*
original title: *Tulitikkutehtaan Tytto*

A downtrodden factory girl takes her revenge on those who have taken her for granted.

Quietly savage comedy, filmed in a minimalist style.

wd Aki Kaurismäki   *ph* Timo Salminen   *pd* Risto Karhula   *ed* Aki Kaurismäki

Kati Outinen, Elina Salo, Esko Nikkari, Vesa Vierikko, Reijo Taipale, Silu Seppälä

The Match King
US   1932   80m   bw
Warner

A world-famous match manufacturer gets into spectacular money difficulties.

Thinly veiled biopic of Ivar Kreuger; not at all bad.

w Houston Branch and Sidney Sutherland   *d* Howard Bretherton

Warren William, Lili Damita, Glenda Farrell, Harold Huber

'Good entertainment, uncommonly well acted . . . in Swedish-populated sections should be top moneymaker.' – *Variety*

The Matchmaker *

US 1958 101m bw Vistavision
Paramount (Don Hartman)
V*, L

In New York at the turn of the century, a rich merchant decides to marry again but the matchmaker he consults has her own eye on him.

Cold and lifeless version of an amusing play which also served as the basis for the musical *Hello Dolly* (qv).

w John Michael Hayes   play Thornton Wilder
d Joseph Anthony   ph Charles Lang   m Adolph Deutsch

Shirley Booth, Paul Ford, Anthony Perkins, Shirley Maclaine, Wallace Ford, Robert Morse, Perry Wilson

DOLLY LEVI (Shirley Booth) to the audience:
'Life's never quite interesting enough, somehow. You people who come to the movies know that.'

'Long static dialogue exchanges are further extended by frequent confidences expressed directly to the audience . . . but in spite of the general lack of pace, lightness and dimension there is still a great deal to enjoy.' – *Peter John Dyer*

La Maternelle *

France 1932 89m bw
Photosonor

A maid in a nursery school becomes devoted to the children and in particular to one who causes trouble when her friend decides to marry.

A touching drama of its day which now seems rather primitive.

w Jean Benoit-Lévy   d Jean Benoit-Lévy, Marie Epstein   ph Georges Asselin   m Edouard Flament

Madeleine Renaud, Paulette Elambert, Alice Tissot, Mady Berry

'By any standard the finest foreign-language talker shown in the US in a couple of years.' – *Variety*

Matewan **

US 1987 133m DuArt
Enterprise/Cinecom Entertainment/Film Gallery/Red Dog (Peggy Rajski, Maggie Renzi)
V*, L

Striking miners battle against brutal owners determined to break the strike.

Engaging hard-edged political drama.   wd John Sayles   ph Haskell Wexler   pd Nora Chavooshian   ed Sonya Polonsky

Chris Cooper, Mary McDonnell, Will Oldham, David Strathairn, Ken Jenkins, Kevin Tighe, Gordon Clapp, James Earl Jones, Bob Gunton, Jace Alexander

AAN: Haskell Wexler

Matilda

US 1978 105m Movielab
AIP/Albert S. Ruddy

A down-at-heel theatrical agent finds success with a boxing kangaroo.

Damon Runyon meets Walt Disney in an old-fashioned family audience picture for which there may no longer be an audience.

w Albert S. Ruddy, Timothy Galfas   novel Paul Gallico   d Daniel Mann   ph Jack Woolf   m Jerrold Immel   pd Boris Leven

Elliott Gould, Robert Mitchum, Harry Guardino, Clive Revill, Karen Carlson, Lionel Stander, Art Metrano, Roy Clark

'Lawrence Woolsey presents the end of civilisation as we know it. Make that . . . Proudly Presents!

Matinee *

US 1993 99m DeLuxe
Guild/Universal
V, V*, S

At the time of the Cuban missile crisis, a B-movie-maker arrives at a US naval base to stage the premiere of his new horror film about a half-man, half-ant, incorporating the cinema-seat-shaking Rumblerama.

An enjoyable celebration of the nuclear-inspired, gimmicky horror movies of the 50s, brilliantly parodied; but it is hampered by a teen romance, presented without apparent irony, which might have been lifted from any drive-in movie of the period.

w Charlie Haas   story Jerico   d Joe Dante
ph John Hora   m Jerry Goldsmith   pd Steven Legler   ed Marshall Harvey

John Goodman, Cathy Moriarty, Simon Fenton, Omri Katz, Lisa Jakub, Kellie Martin, Jesse Lee, Dick Miller, John Sayles

'Even when the film gets bogged down in romantic drivel, there are enough clever in-jokes and well-remembered period details to keep buffs happy.' – *Variety*

† The character played by Goodman is based on the showman-producer-director William Castle.

The Mating Game

US 1959 96m Metrocolor Cinemascope
MGM (Philip Barry Jnr)

An income-tax inspector becomes involved in the affairs of an unorthodox farming family.

Dismally unfunny adaptation for Americans of a very English novel; everyone works hard to no avail.

w William Roberts   novel *The Darling Buds of May* by H. E. Bates   d George Marshall   ph Robert Bronner   m Jeff Alexander

Debbie Reynolds, Tony Randall, Paul Douglas, Fred Clark, Una Merkel, Philip Ober, Charles Lane, Philip Coolidge

'Every joke is driven past the point of exhaustion.' – *MFB*

The Mating of Millie

US 1948 87m bw
Columbia

A self-confident young woman wants to adopt a small boy and tries to propel a bus driver into a marriage of convenience.

Amiable if protracted romantic comedy with dashes of sentiment and an obvious outcome.

w Louella MacFarlane, St Clair McKelway   d Henry Levin

Glenn Ford, Evelyn Keyes, Willard Parker, Jimmy Hunt, Ron Randell

The Mating Season

US 1951 101m bw
Paramount (Charles Brackett)

A factory draughtsman marries an ambassador's daughter; his mother loses her job and comes incognito to work for them as a cook.

Uninteresting mechanical domestic comedy in which the young folk are dull and the older ones overplay.

w Walter Reisch, Charles Brackett, Richard Breen   d Mitchell Leisen   ph Charles Lang

Gene Tierney, John Lund, Miriam Hopkins, Thelma Ritter, Jan Sterling

AAN: Thelma Ritter

Matka Joanna od Aniolow: see *The Devil and the Nun*

A Matter of Dignity *

Greece 1957 104m bw
Finos (Anis Nohra)
original title: *To Telefteo Psemma*

The daughter of a bankrupt family reluctantly agrees to marry a millionaire, and the family's false values lead to tragedy.

Rather offbeat melodrama with the director in good form.

wd Michael Cacoyannis   ph Walter Lassally
m Manos Hadjidakis

Ellie Lambetti, Georges Pappas, Athena Michaelidou

A Matter of Innocence: see *Pretty Polly*

A Matter of Life and Death ****

GB 1946 104m Technicolor
GFD/Archers (Michael Powell, Emeric Pressburger)
US title: *Stairway to Heaven*

A pilot with brain damage after bailing out is torn between this world and the next, but an operation puts things to rights.

Outrageous fantasy which seemed more in keeping after the huge death toll of a world war, and in any case learned the Hollywood lesson of eating its cake and still having it, the supernatural elements being capable of explanation. A mammoth technical job in the heavenly sequences, it deserves full marks for its sheer arrogance, wit, style and film flair.

wd Michael Powell, Emeric Pressburger   ph Jack Cardiff   m Allan Gray   pd Hein Heckroth

David Niven, Roger Livesey, Kim Hunter, Marius Goring, Raymond Massey, Abraham Sofaer

'Powell and Pressburger seem to have reached their heaven at last . . . an illimitable Wembley stadium, surrounded by tinkly music and mists, from which all men of insight, if they were ever careless enough to get there, would quickly blaspheme their way out.' – *Richard Winnington*

'A dazzling mesh of visionary satire, postwar politics and the mystical side of English romanticism.' – *Tony Rayns, Time Out, 1979*

'Beautifully written, beautifully acted, beautifully executed . . . you would think such formidable merits would add up to quite a film – and darned if they don't.' – *Time Out*

'This film, whether or not you find its philosophy half-baked, is downright good cinema, doing things that couldn't be done in any other medium' – *Tribune*

'It compelled attention and created emotion.' – *Basil Wright, 1972*

'Some women are born to have a glorious affair with life . . . !'

A Matter of Time

US/Italy 1976 97m (originally 165m) Technicolor
(AIP) Jack H. Skirball, J. Edmund Grainger
V*

An Italian country chambermaid is taught about life by a faded countess.

Interminable even in its abbreviated form, this woebegone fantasy is a tribute to his miscast daughter by a director who never had much sense of plot to begin with. It has to be seen to be believed.

w John Gay   novel *The Film of Memory* by Maurice Druon   d Vincente Minnelli   ph Geoffrey Unsworth   m Nino Oliviero

Liza Minnelli, Ingrid Bergman, Charles Boyer, Tina Aumont, Gabriele Ferzetti, Spiros Andros

'So hackneyed, inept and stupid as to be almost amusing.' – *John Simon, New York*

'So spectacularly crazy that if Minnelli could only persuade Mel Brooks to put his name on it, *A Matter of Time* might yet be the comedy sleeper of the year.' – *Frank Rich, New York Post*

A Matter of Who

GB 1961 92m bw
MGM/Foray (Walter Shenson, Milton Holmes)
V*

The World Health Organization tracks down a smallpox outbreak.

Curious blend of semi-documentary with suspense and comedy; not really a starter.

w Milton Holmes d Don Chaffey ph Erwin Hillier m Edwin Astley

Terry-Thomas, Sonja Ziemann, Alex Nicol, Guy Deghy, Richard Briers, Clive Morton, Geoffrey Keen, Martin Benson, Honor Blackman, Carol White

Les Maudits
France 1947 103m bw
Speva/Discina
UK title: *The Damned*

A U-boat with an assorted human cargo escapes the allied blockade as the war ends.

Striking but aimless melodrama which plays like an early *Ship of Fools*.

w J. Companeez, V. Alexandrov d René Clément

Dalio, Henri Vidal, Michel Auclair, Florence Marly, Paul Bernard

Maurice *
GB 1987 140m Technicolor
Cinecom/Merchant Ivory (Ismail Merchant)
V*, L, S

The life of a Cambridge homosexual.

Hothouse study of E. M. Forster's posthumously published and semi-autobiographical novel. An acquired taste, but many scenes have general appeal.

w Kit Hesketh-Harvey, James Ivory d *James Ivory* ph Pierre Lhomme m Richard Robbins pd Brian Ackland-Snow ed Katherine Wenning

James Wilby, Hugh Grant, Rupert Graves, Denholm Elliott, Simon Callow, Billie Whitelaw, Ben Kingsley, Judy Parfitt

AAN: costume design (Jenny Beavan, John Bright)

Mauvais Sang: see *The Night Is Young*

The Maverick Queen
US 1955 90m Trucolor Naturama
Republic

A lady rustler falls for a Pinkerton detective sent to arrest her.

Tedious Western in bilious colour.

w Kenneth Gamet, De Vallon Scott *novel* Zane Grey d Joe Kane

Barbara Stanwyck, Barry Sullivan, Scott Brady, Mary Murphy, Wallace Ford, Jim Davis

Max Dugan Returns **
US 1983 98m colour
TCF (Herbert Ross, Neil Simon)
V*, L

A hard-up widow with a 15-year-old son is visited by her dying father who abandoned her when she was a child.

Slight, sentimental but gently amusing comedy.

w Neil Simon d Herbert Ross ph David M. Walsh m David Shire ad Albert Brenner ed Richard Marks

Marsha Mason, Jason Robards, Donald Sutherland, Matthew Broderick

'A consistently happy comedic fable.' – *Variety*

Max Mon Amour
France/US 1986 97m colour
Electric/Greenwich Film/A2 (Serge Silberman)

The wife of a British diplomat in Paris falls in love with a chimpanzee.

Odd tale that strives for, but fails to achieve, an air of unease.

w Nagisa Oshima, Jean-Claude Carrière d Nagisa Oshima ph Raoul Coutard m Michel Portal pd Pierre Guffroy ed Hélène Plemiannikov

Charlotte Rampling, Anthony Higgins, Bernard-Pierre Donnadieu, Victoria Abril, Anne-Marie Besse, Nicole Clafan, Pierre Etaix, Bernard Haller, Sabine Haudepin

Maxie
US 1985 98m DeLuxe
Carter de Haven/Ellsboy/Aurora/Orion
V*, L

The ghost of a twenties starlet revisits her old apartment and takes over the body of the wife of the tenant.

Heavenly comedy which would have been funnier in the forties.

w Patricia Resnick *novel* Marion's Wall by Jack Finney d Paul Aaron

Glenn Close, Mandy Patinkin, Ruth Gordon, Barnard Hughes, Valerie Curtin

Maximum Overdrive
US 1986 97m Technicolor
Martha Schumacher/Dino de Laurentiis
V, V*, L, S

In a corner of North Carolina, all mechanical devices go haywire, and trucks menace a group of humans caught in a filling station.

Idiotic premise for sensational action sequences, which are well staged but go on too long.

wd Stephen King

Emilio Estevez, Pat Hingle, Laura Harrington, Yeardley Smith

Maya
US 1966 91m Technicolor Panavision
MGM/King Brothers (Mary P. Murray, Herman King)

A teenage American boy arrives in India to visit his disillusioned father, who finally comes to understand him only after he has run away.

Good-looking but otherwise uninteresting animal drama which served as the pilot for a TV series.

w John Fante d John Berry ph Gunter Senftleben m Riz Ortolani

Clint Walker, Jay North, I. S. Johar, Sajid Khan

Maybe Baby
US 1988 98m colour
Columbia/Tri-Star (Jerry Belson, Walter Coblenz)
US title: *For Keeps*

Two teenagers, who marry when pregnancy looms, face up to adult responsibilities.

Tiresome and sentimental account of young motherhood.

w Tim Kazurinsky, Denise DeClue d John G. Avildsen ph James Crabe m Bill Conti pd William J. Cassidy ed John G. Avildsen

Molly Ringwald, Randall Batinkoff, Kenneth Mars, Miriam Flynn, Conchata Ferrell, Sharon Brown

Mayerling **
France 1935 90m bw
Seymour Nebenzal/Nero Film
V*

In 1889, imperial lovers are found dead in a country house.

Classic French version of a somewhat chilly subject.

w Joseph Kessel, V. Cube *novel* Claude Anet d Anatole Litvak

Charles Boyer, Danielle Darrieux, Marthe Regnier, Yolande Laffon, Suzy Prim

'As good a picture as Hollywood could produce, plus some local touches that are inaccessible to Hollywood.' – *Variety*

Mayerling
France/GB 1968 141m Eastmancolor Panavision
Corona/Winchester (Robert Dorfmann)
V

In 1889 the heir to the Habsburg Empire is forced into a suicide pact with his mistress.

Tedious dramatization of historical events which in 1935 had made a delicate French film but in these hands seems an endless and boring manipulation of doubtful events into turgid romance.

wd Terence Young *novel* Claude Anet ph Henri Alekan m Francis Lai pd Georges Wakhevitch

Omar Sharif, Catherine Deneuve, James Mason, Ava Gardner, James Robertson Justice, Genevieve Page, Ivan Desny, Maurice Teynac

The Mayor of 44th Street
US 1942 86m bw
RKO (Cliff Reid)

Dance bands are threatened by hooligans demanding protection money.

Boring melodrama with music.

w Lewis R. Foster d Alfred E. Green ph Robert de Grasse *songs* Mort Greene, Harry Revel

George Murphy, Anne Shirley, Richard Barthelmess, William Gargan, Joan Merrill, Millard Mitchell, Mary Wickes, Freddy Martin and band

AAN: song 'There's a Breeze on Lake Louise'

The Mayor of Hell *
US 1933 90m bw
Warner

A racketeer becomes superintendent of a reform school, and it changes his life.

Moderate star vehicle with a plot that did yeoman service thereafter in Dead End Kids films.

w Edward Chodorov d Archie Mayo ph Barney McGill m Leo F. Forbstein

James Cagney, Madge Evans, Allen Jenkins, Dudley Digges, Frankie Darro

'Has the outline of a junior Big House. Offers exploitation easily.' – *Variety*

'Propaganda for nothing: like most of what comes out of Hollywood, it is entertaining trash.' – *Time*

† Remade in 1938 as *Crime School* with Humphrey Bogart, 1939 as *Hell's Kitchen* with Ronald Reagan.

Maytime **
US 1937 132m bw (sepia sequence)
MGM (Hunt Stromberg)
V*, L

An opera star falls in love with a penniless singer but her jealous impresario shoots him.

Lush romantic musical which turns gradually into melodrama and ends in a ghostly reunion for the lovers. If that's what you like, it could scarcely be better done.

w Noel Langley *operetta* Rida Johnson Young d Robert Z. Leonard ph Oliver T. Marsh md Herbert Stothart m Sigmund Romberg

Jeanette MacDonald, Nelson Eddy, John Barrymore, Herman Bing, Lynne Carver, Rafaela Ottiano, Paul Porcasi, Sig Rumann

'Click operetta . . . cinch for the foreign market also.' – *Variety*

'Enjoyable for more than camp reasons . . . the atmosphere of thwarted passion is compelling.' – *Pauline Kael, 70s*

† Shooting had begun in colour with Frank Morgan in Bing's part and Paul Lukas in Barrymore's; this footage, directed Edmund Goulding, was abandoned on Irving Thalberg's death.

AAN: Herbert Stothart

Maytime in Mayfair

GB 1949 95m Technicolor
British Lion/Imperadio (Herbert Wilcox)
V*

A playboy inherits a dress salon and falls for the lady manager.

Witless comedy fit to set one's teeth on edge, with over-acting and poor musical numbers. Not in the same street as its predecessor *Spring in Park Lane*.

w Nicholas Phipps d Herbert Wilcox ph Max Greene md Robert Farnon

Anna Neagle, Michael Wilding, Nicholas Phipps, Peter Graves, Tom Walls

'Painstakingly refined.' – *MFB*

The Maze

US 1953 81m bw 3-D
Allied Artists (Richard Heermance)

The heir to a title also inherits a family curse and turns into a giant frog.

Rather splendidly idiotic horror film which raises plenty of laughs but no *frissons*.

w Dan Ullman story Maurice Sandoz d William Cameron Menzies ph Harry Neumann m Marlin Skiles

Richard Carlson, Veronica Hurst, Katherine Emery, Michael Pate, Lillian Bond, Hillary Brooke, Owen McGiveney

Me and Him

US 1988 90m colour
Columbia/Egmont/Neue Constantin (Bernd Eichinger)
V, V*, L

A New Yorker's penis begins to talk back to him.

A comedy about male chauvinism that fails to raise a smile.

w Warren D. Leight, Michael Junker, Doris Dörrie novel Io e Lui by Alberto Moravia d Doris Dörrie ph Helge Weindler ed Raimund Barthelmes

Griffin Dunne, Ellen Greene, Steven Marcus, Craig T. Nelson, Kelly Bishop, Carey Lowell, Kara Glover, Kim Flowers

Me and Marlborough *

GB 1935 84m bw
GFD/Gainsborough (Michael Balcon)

In Marlborough's army, a woman takes the place of her soldier husband to prove his innocence of spying.

Curious period service farce, not quite a success but an interesting attempt at something different.

w Ian Hay, Marjorie Gaffney story W. P. Lipscomb, Reginald Pound d Victor Saville ph Charles Van Enger

Cicely Courtneidge, Tom Walls, Barry McKay, Alfred Drayton

'In most cases the comedy is totally uncalled for and destroys the period atmosphere.' – *Variety*

Me and My Gal *

US 1932 79m bw
Fox
GB title: Pier 13

A cop on the beat romances a hashslinger and catches a crook.

Pleasant little programmer, very evocative of its period.

w Arthur Kober d Raoul Walsh ph Arthur Miller

Spencer Tracy, Joan Bennett, George Walsh, Marion Burns, J. Farrell MacDonald, Noel Madison, Henry B. Walthall

'Lacking in nearly everything that makes box office.' – *Variety*

† Remade in 1949 as *Pier 13*.

Me and My Pal *

US 1933 20m bw
Hal Roach

Ollie becomes engrossed in a jigsaw puzzle and forgets to get married.

Oddball star comedy which nearly comes off but simply doesn't provide enough jokes.

w Stan Laurel d Charles Rogers, Lloyd French

Laurel and Hardy, James Finlayson, Eddie Dunn

Me and the Colonel

US 1958 110m bw
Columbia/Court-Goetz (William Goetz)

In 1940 an anti-semitic Polish colonel is obliged to flee from France in the company of a Jewish refugee.

Rather obvious war comedy with predictable but not very entertaining situations, sentiment, action and pathos. The stars cope well enough but the picture never picks up steam.

w S. N. Behrman, George Froeschel play Franz Werfel d Peter Glenville ph Burnett Guffey m George Duning

Danny Kaye, Curt Jurgens, Nicole Maurey, Françoise Rosay, Akim Tamiroff, Martita Hunt, Alexander Scourby, Liliane Montevecchi, Ludwig Stossel

Me, Natalie *

US 1969 111m DeLuxe
Cinema Center (Stanley Shapiro)

An unattractive 18-year-old girl moves into Greenwich Village and learns to accept herself as she is.

Basically very predictable but rather well done character study with excellent detail.

w A. Martin Zweiback d Fred Coe ph Arthur J. Ornitz m Henry Mancini

Patty Duke, James Farentino, Martin Balsam, Elsa Lanchester, Salome Jens, Nancy Marchand, Al Pacino

The Mean Machine: see *The Longest Yard*

The Mean Season

US 1985 103m DeLuxe Panavision
Orion/Turman-Foster
V*, L

A Miami police reporter becomes the personal spokesman for a murderous psychopath.

Tolerable murder thriller with asides on politics and the media.

w Leon Piedmont novel In the Heat of the Summer by John Katzenbach d Philip Borsos ph Frank Tidy m Lalo Schifrin pd Philip Jefferies

Kurt Russell, Mariel Hemingway, Richard Jordan, Richard Masur, Richard Bradford, Joe Pantoliano

Mean Streets ****

US 1973 110m Technicolor
Taplin-Perry-Scorsese (Jonathan T. Taplin)
V, V*, L

Four young Italian-Americans use Tony's Bar as a base for drinking, brawling and hustling.

Relentlessly sordid melodrama with a good eye for realistic detail. The first film in which Scorsese announced himself as a major talent and discovered the subject matter that has served him so well.

w Martin Scorsese, Mardik Martin d Martin Scorsese ph Norman Gerard

Harvey Keitel, Robert de Niro, David Proval, Amy Robinson, Richard Romanus

'Lacks a sense of story and structure . . . unless a film-maker respects the needs of his audience, he can't complain if that audience fails to show up.' – *Variety*

'A thicker-textured rot than we have ever had in an American movie, and a deeper sense of evil.' – *New Yorker*

'Extraordinarily rich and distinguished on many levels.' – *Joseph Gelmis*

The Meanest Man in the World

US 1943 57m bw
TCF

An easy-going small-town lawyer finds that business picks up when he becomes tough and mean.

Very minor star comedy with a muddled opening followed by strictly rationed laughs.

w George Seaton, Allan House play George M. Cohan d Sidney Lanfield

Jack Benny, Priscilla Lane, Rochester, Edmund Gwenn, Anne Revere

Meatballs

Canada 1979 92m Sonolab Color
Paramount
V*, L

Adventures at an ineptly run summer camp.

Adolescent fun and games for the easily pleased adolescent. (By 1987, *Meatballs 3* had been reached.)

w Len Blum, Dan Goldberg, Harold Ramis, Janis Allen d Ivan Reitman

Bill Murray, Harvey Atkin, Russ Banham, Ron Barry

'The Mechanic must be dead sure . . . or dead!'

The Mechanic

US 1972 100m Technicolor
UA/Chartoff/Winkler/Carlino
V*
reissue title: Killer of Killers

A professional assassin under contract to the Mafia makes his missions look like accidents.

Violent thriller with a few pretensions, but too flashily made to be taken seriously.

w Lewis John Carlino d Michael Winner ph Richard Kline, Robert Paynter m Jerry Fielding

Charles Bronson, Jan-Michael Vincent, Keenan Wynn, Jill Ireland

'A hymn to technological violence, efficiently and convincingly made.' – *George Melly, Observer*

Med Kaerlig Hilsen: see *Love Me Darling*

A Medal for Benny *

US 1945 77m bw
Paramount (Paul Jones)

An old rustic is the centre of small town celebrations in honour of his dead war hero son.

Satirical-sentimental location drama, effective but not memorable.

w Frank Butler original story John Steinbeck, Jack Wagner d Irving Pichel ph Lionel Lindon m Victor Young

Dorothy Lamour, Arturo de Cordova, J. Carrol Naish, Mikhail Rasumny, Charles Dingle, Frank McHugh, Grant Mitchell

AAN: original story; J. Carrol Naish

Medal for the General

GB 1944 99m bw
British National

An old general takes in evacuees and finds a new interest in life.

Uneventful character drama which seemed mildly pleasing at the time.

w Elizabeth Baron novel James Ronald d Maurice Elvey

Godfrey Tearle, Jeanne de Casalis, Morland Graham, Mabel Constanduros, John Laurie, Petula Clark

Medals: see *Seven Days Leave* (1929)

Medea *
Italy/France/West Germany   1970   118m
Eastmancolor
San Marco/Number One/Janus (Franco Rossellini, Marina Cicogna)
V

Jason brings back as his wife the high priestess of the Golden Fleece, but her adjustment is to say the least uncomfortable.

In modern terms the case history of a psychopath, this weird production plays like an opera without music, and seems to have been designed as a vehicle for its charismatic star.

wd Pier Paolo Pasolini   *play* Euripides   *ph* Ennio Guarnieri

Maria Callas, Giuseppe Gentile, Laurent Terzieff, Massimo Girotti

'He turned his back on civilization. Only to discover he had the power to save it.'
Medicine Man
US   1992   105m   Technicolor   Panavision
Guild/Cinergi (Andrew G. Vajna, Donna Dubrow)
V, V*, L, S

A scientist, who has discovered a cure for cancer while working in the South American rain forest, is upset to find that his new research assistant is a woman.

Unpalatable mix of ecology and romance, with a long-delayed outcome that is predictable from the opening minutes.

w Tom Schulman, Sally Robinson   *d* John McTiernan   *ph* Donald McAlpine   *m* Jerry Goldsmith

Sean Connery, Lorraine Bracco, José Wilker, Rodolfo de Alexandre, Angelo Barra Moreira

'This jumbo-budget two-character piece suffers from a very weak script and a lethal job of miscasting.' – *Variety*

† Tom Schulman was reportedly paid $3 million for his script, with another $1 million being spent on rewrites. And still they got it wrong.

'A film dedicated to all those who are running away.'
Mediterraneo *
Italy   1991   90m   Technicolor
Mayfair/Penta/AMA/Berlusconi (Gianni Minervini)
V, V*, L, S

During the Second World War, eight Italian soldiers find themselves forgotten and stranded on an idyllic Aegean island.

Based on a true story, this is a pleasant, bitter-sweet, nostalgic comedy that prefers the past to the present.

w Vincenzo Monteleone   *d* Gabriele Salvatores
ph Italo Pettriccione   *m* Giancarlo Bigazzi, Marco Falagiani   *ad* Thalia Istikopoulos   *ed* Nino Baragali

Diego Abatantuono, Claudio Bigagli, Giuseppe Cederna, Claudio Bisio, Gigio Alberti, Ugo Conti, Memo Dini, Vasco Mirondola, Vanna Barba

'An ironic, gently amusing charmer, even though its anti-war elements jostle clumsily with its not entirely persuasive case for running away from real life's disappointments.' – *Angie Errigo, Empire*

AA: best foreign film

The Medium *
Italy   1951   80m   bw
Transfilm (Walter Lowendahl)

A fake medium feels a genuine manifestation, shoots at it and kills her assistant, but is still not sure whether he was responsible.

A filmic but not entirely satisfactory treatment of a modest but popular modern opera.

wd/m Gian-Carlo Menotti, his opera   *co-d* Alexander Hammid   *ph* Enzo Serafin

Marie Powers, Anna Maria Alberghetti, Leo Coleman

AAN: Gian-Carlo Menotti (for music)

Medium Cool **
US   1969   111m   Technicolor
Paramount/H & J Pictures (Tully Friedman)
V*

A TV news cameraman is made apathetic by the events around him.

Stimulating if overlong comment on the quality of life in the sixties, immaculately made and with a rather effective though obvious twist ending.

wd/ph Haskell Wexler   *m* Mike Bloomfield   *ad* Leon Ericksen

Robert Forster, Verna Bloom, Peter Bonerz, Marianna Hill, Sid McCoy

'A deeply moving questioning of America's violence and voyeurism.' – *Jan Dawson*

'I can't think of any film that tells one more about the texture of American life today.' – *Michael Billington, Illustrated London News*

'By the time he was eleven he had killed nine people!'
The Medusa Touch *
GB/France   1978   109m   Technicolor
ITC/Bulldog/Citeca (Arnon Milchan, Elliott Kastner)
V*

A novelist is haunted by the belief that he can cause disaster.

And he does, very predictably, while any intellectual excitement in the script is rapidly replaced by mere mayhem. Different, but not exciting.

w John Briley   *novel* Peter Van Greenway   *d* Jack Gold   *ph* Arthur Ibbetson   *m* Michael J. Lewis   *sp* Doug Ferris

Richard Burton, Lee Remick, Lino Ventura, Harry Andrews, Alan Badel, Jeremy Brett, Michael Hordern, Gordon Jackson

Meet Danny Wilson
US   1951   83m   bw
U-I (Leonard Goldstein)

An overbearing crooner gets to the top with the help of gangsters.

Fairly abrasive star vehicle, almost amounting to self-parody.

w Don McGuire   *d* Joseph Pevney   *ph* Maury Gertsman   *md* Joseph Gershenson

Frank Sinatra, Shelley Winters, Alex Nicol, Raymond Burr

Meet Dr Christian
US   1939   68m   bw
William Stephens/RKO

A dedicated small-town doctor has no concern for financial reward.

Adequate pot-boiler based on a radio character, and following Hersholt's popularity as Dr Dafoe.

w Ian McLellan Hunter, Harvey Gates, Ring Lardner Jnr   *d* Bernard Vorhaus

Jean Hersholt, Dorothy Lovett, Robert Baldwin, Enid Bennett, Paul Harvey, Marcia Mae Jones

'First of a series . . . profitable programme material for the family trade.' – *Variety*

Meet John Doe ***
US   1941   123m   bw
Liberty Films (Frank Capra)
V, V*, L

A tramp is hired to embody the common man in a phony political drive, and almost commits suicide.

Vividly staged but over-sentimental Capra extravaganza with high spots outnumbering low.

w Robert Riskin   *d* Frank Capra   *ph* George Barnes   *m* Dimitri Tiomkin

Gary Cooper, *Barbara Stanwyck*, Edward Arnold, Walter Brennan, James Gleason, Spring Byington, Gene Lockhart, Rod la Rocque, Irving Bacon, Regis Toomey, Ann Doran, Warren Hymer, Andrew Tombes

'For the sake of a happy ending that would keep Gary Cooper alive, the meanings were so distorted that the original authors sued.' – *New Yorker, 1978*

'Capra is as skilled as ever in keeping things moving along briskly and dramatically.' – *National Board of Review*

'The meanings were so distorted that the original authors sued . . . It starts out in the confident Capra manner, but with a darker tone; by the end, you feel puzzled and cheated.' – *Pauline Kael, 70s*

AAN: original story (Richard Connell, Robert Presnell)

Meet Me after the Show *
US   1951   88m   Technicolor
TCF (George Jessel)

A musical star thinks she has discovered an affair between her husband and his glamorous backer.

Surprisingly bright routine musical.

w Mary Loos, Richard Sale   *d* Richard Sale
ph Arthur E. Arling   *md* Lionel Newman   *songs* Jule Styne, Leo Robin

Betty Grable, Macdonald Carey, Rory Calhoun, Eddie Albert, Irene Ryan

Meet Me at Dawn
GB   1946   99m   bw
Excelsior/Marcel Hellman
US title: *The Gay Duellist*

A professional duellist is commissioned to provoke a duel with a senator, but unwittingly hires the senator's daughter to play the injured party.

A totally laborious and artificial period comedy which never seems even to aspire to the style required.

w Lesley Storm, James Seymour, Maurice Cowan
story Le Tueur by Anatole Litvak, Marcel Achard
d Thornton Freeland   *ph* Gunther Krampf
m Mischa Spoliansky

Hazel Court, William Eythe, Stanley Holloway, Margaret Rutherford, Basil Sydney, Irene Browne

Meet Me at the Fair
US   1952   87m   Technicolor
U-I (Albert J. Cohen)

In 1900, an orphan joins a travelling medicine show.

Mildly pleasing open-air comedy drama.

w Irving Wallace   *novel* The Great Companions by Gene Markey   *d* Douglas Sirk   *ph* Maury Gertsman   *md* Joseph Gershenson

Diana Lynn, Dan Dailey, Hugh O'Brian, Chet Allen, Rhys Williams

Meet Me in Las Vegas
US   1956   112m   Eastmancolor   Cinemascope
MGM (Joe Pasternak)
V*
GB title: *Viva Las Vegas!*

A gambler's luck changes when he grabs the hand of a passing ballerina.

Listless song-and-dance extravaganza which wastes a great deal of talent.

w Isobel Lennart   *d* Roy Rowland   *ph* Robert Bronner   *m* Georgie Stoll, Johnny Green
ly Sammy Cahn   *ch* Eugène Loring, Hermes Pan

Dan Dailey, Cyd Charisse, Agnes Moorehead, Lili Darvas, Paul Henreid, Oscar Karlweis, Lena Horne, Jerry Colonna, Frankie Laine

'A large-scale musical of almost stupefying banality.' – *MFB*

AAN: Georgie Stoll, Johnny Green

Meet Me in St Louis ***
US 1944 113m Technicolor
MGM (Arthur Freed)
V, V*, L

Scenes in the life of an affectionate family at the turn of the century.

Patchy but generally highly agreeable musical nostalgia with an effective sense of the passing years and seasons.

w Irving Brecher, Fred F. Finklehoffe *novel* Sally Benson *d* Vincente Minnelli *ph* George Folsey *md* Georgie Stoll

Judy Garland, Margaret O'Brien, Tom Drake, Leon Ames, Mary Astor, Lucille Bremer, June Lockhart, *Harry Davenport,* Marjorie Main, Joan Carroll, Hugh Marlowe, Robert Sully, Chill Wills

'A family group framed in velvet and tinsel . . . it has everything a romantic musical should have.' – *Dilys Powell, 1955*

'A charming picture. There is much more in it than meets the ear.' – *C. A. Lejeune*

AAN: script; George Folsey; Georgie Stoll; song 'The Trolley Song' (*m/ly* Ralph Blane, Hugh Martin)

Meet Me on Broadway
US 1946 77m bw
Burt Kelly/Columbia

A young musical director determines to hit Broadway.

Mild revue with a skimpy plot.

w George Bricker, Jack Henley *d* Leigh Jason

Marjorie Reynolds, Fred Brady, Jinx Falkenburg, Spring Byington, Gene Lockhart, Allen Jenkins

Meet Me Tonight
GB 1952 85m Technicolor
British Film Makers/Anthony Havelock Allan

Three short Noël Coward plays: *Red Peppers, Fumed Oak, Ways and Means.*

Regrettably bald treatment of three playlets which have not lasted well. A thoroughly artificial evening.

w/m Noël Coward *d* Anthony Pelissier *ph* Desmond Dickinson

Ted Ray, Kay Walsh, Stanley Holloway, Betty Ann Davies, Nigel Patrick, Valerie Hobson

Meet Mr Callaghan
GB 1954 88m bw
Pinnacle

A private detective unmasks a rich man's killer.

Routine thick ear on American lines; moderately popular at the time, it spawned no sequels.

w Brock Williams *play* Gerald Verner based on Peter Cheyney's novel *The Urgent Hangman* *d* Charles Saunders

Derrick de Marney, Harriet Johns, Peter Neil, Adrienne Corri, Delphi Lawrence, Belinda Lee

Meet Mr Lucifer *
GB 1953 81m bw
Ealing (Monja Danischewsky)

The Demon King in a tatty provincial pantomime dreams he is the devil preventing people from wasting time watching television.

Clean and occasionally amusing piece of topical satire on tellymania; but the prologue is funnier than the sketches.

w Monja Danischewsky *play Beggar My Neighbour* by Arnold Ridley *d* Anthony Pelissier *ph* Desmond Dickinson *m* Eric Rogers

Stanley Holloway, Peggy Cummins, Jack Watling, Barbara Murray, Joseph Tomelty, Gordon Jackson, Jean Cadell, Kay Kendall, Ian Carmichael, Gilbert Harding, Charles Victor, Humphrey Lestocq

Meet Mr Penny
GB 1938 70m bw
British National

A meek clerk leads a revolt against a speculator who wants to build on allotments.

Early Ealing-style social comedy based on a radio character; of no abiding interest.

w Victor Kendall, Doreen Montgomery, from the character created by Maurice Moisiewicz *d* David MacDonald

Richard Goolden, Vic Oliver, Fabia Drake, Kay Walsh, Patrick Barr, Hermione Gingold, Wilfrid Hyde-White

Meet Nero Wolfe *
US 1936 73m bw
Columbia

A corpulent stay-at-home sleuth solves a disappearance and a murder.

The film début of an engaging crime character, who oddly never made it to a series.

w Howard J. Green, Bruce Manning, Joseph Anthony *play Fer de Lance* by Rex Stout *d* Herbert Biberman *ph* Henry Freulich

Edward Arnold, Lionel Stander, Joan Perry, Rita Hayworth, Victor Jory, Nana Bryant, Walter Kingsford, John Qualen

Meet Simon Cherry
GB 1949 67m bw
Hammer

A clergyman on holiday proves that a rich recluse was not murdered.

Elementary programme filler from a radio series.

w Gale Pedrick, A. R. Rawlinson, Godfrey Grayson *radio series Meet the Rev* by Gale Pedrick *d* Godfrey Grayson

Hugh Moxey, Zena Marshall, John Bailey, Anthony Forwood, Ernest Butcher, Courtney Hope

'The human race is about to be destroyed by people who wouldn't hurt a fly'

Meet the Applegates
US 1990 82m DuArt
Castle Premier/New World (Denise Di Novi)
V, V*, L
US title: *The Applegates*

Giant insects, whose habitat in the Brazilian rain forests has been destroyed, disguise themselves as humans and go to America to wreck a nuclear power plant.

Ineffectual slapstick satire aimed at suburban lifestyles.

w Redbeard Simmons, Michael Lehmann *d* Michael Lehmann *ph* Mitchell Dubin *m* David Newman *pd* John Hutman *ad* Kara Lindstrom, Adam Lustig *ed* Norman Hollyn

Ed Begley Jnr, Stockard Channing, Dabney Coleman, Bobby Jacoby, Cami Cooper, Glenn Shadix, Susan Barnes, Adam Bieski

'This wayward movie has a great deal of charm.' – *MFB*

Meet the Baron
US 1933 79m bw
MGM

A nincompoop is fêted as the real Baron Münchhausen.

An incoherent script provides an opportunity for several comics to do their stuff.

w Herman J. Mankiewicz, Norman Krasna, Allen Rivkin, P. J. Wolfson, Arthur Kober, William K. Wells *d* Walter Lang

Jack Pearl, Jimmy Durante, ZaSu Pitts, Ted Healy and his Stooges, Edna May Oliver, Henry Kolker

'Not so forte in the material division, but saved by its capable crew of comics.' – *Variety*

Meet the Feebles
New Zealand 1989 97m colour
Arrow/Wingnut (Jim Booth, Peter Jackson)
V, S

A troupe of puppets indulge in sex, drugs, violence and general vulgarity.

A semi-pornographic horror with Muppet-like creatures that is determined to offend.

w Danny Mulheron, Frances Walsh, Stephen Sinclair, Peter Jackson *d* Peter Jackson *ph* Murray Milne *m* Peter Dasent *pd* Mike Kane *sp* Steve Ingram *ed* Jamie Selkirk

Danny Mulheron; voices of: Donna Akersten, Stuart Devenie, Mark Hadlow, Ross Jolly, Brian Sergent, Peter Vere Jones, Mark Wright

'No excuse for spurting bodily secretions – blood, pus, vomit, or whatever – is passed up.' – *Sight and Sound*

Meet the Mayor
US 1938 63m bw
Frank Fay/Times

A veteran small-town elevator operator becomes involved in politics.

Curious semi-comedy in which the star uses up most of his old vaudeville routines.

w Walter DeLeon, Charles Belden, Frank Fay *d* Ralph Ceder

Frank Fay, Ruth Hall, Hale Hamilton, George Meeker, Berton Churchill, Franklin Pangborn

'Flimsy meller for secondary duallers.' – *Variety*

Meet the Missus
US 1937 55m bw
Albert Lewis/RKO

A worm turns when his wife constantly involves him in newspaper contests.

Very slight farce for the rurals.

w Jack Townley, Bert Granet, Joel Sayre *story Lady Average* by Jack Goodman and Albert Rice *d* Joseph Santley

Victor Moore, Helen Broderick, Anne Shirley, Alan Bruce, Willie Best

'Destined for the lower half of duals.' – *Variety*

Meet the Navy
GB 1946 85m bw (Technicolor sequence)
British National

The story of a revue featuring amateurs from the allied navies.

Patchy but generally good-natured wartime entertainment.

w Lester Cooper, James Seymour *d* Alfred Travers

Lionel Murton, John Pratt, Oscar Naske, Alan Lund

Meet the People
US 1944 100m bw
MGM (E. Y. Harburg)

A Broadway musical star proves she isn't snooty by taking a job in a shipyard.

Thin propaganda musical which wastes a fair amount of talent.

w S. M. Herzig, Fred Saidy *play* Louis Lantz, Sol and Ben Barzman *d* Charles Reisner *ph* Robert Surtees *songs* various

Lucille Ball, Dick Powell, Virginia O'Brien, Bert Lahr, Rags Ragland, June Allyson, Steve Geray, Phil Regan, Spike Jones and his City Slickers, Vaughn Monroe and his Orchestra

Meet the Stewarts
US 1942 74m bw
Columbia

Newlyweds have trouble when he's poor and she's used to rich living.

Modest marital comedy with young talent.

w Elizabeth Dunn, Karen de Wolf *d* Alfred E. Green

William Holden, Frances Dee, Grant Mitchell

Meet Whiplash Willie: see *The Fortune Cookie*

'Love. Lust. Betrayal. Chaos. And the overture hasn't even begun.'

Meeting Venus *
GB 1990 120m colour
Warner/Enigma/BSB/County NatWest (David Puttnam)
V, V*, L, S

A married Hungarian conductor, having problems over a performance of *Tannhäuser* to an international audience, has an affair with the principal singer.

Bold attempt at a European film, but one that works only fitfully.

w Istvan Szabo, Michael Hirst *d* Istvan Szabo *ph* Lajos Koltai *md* Marek Janowski *m* Richard Wagner *pd* Attila Kovacs *ed* Jim Clark

Glenn Close, Niels Arestrup, Moscu Alcallay, Macha Meril, Johanna Ter Steege, Maite Nahyr, Victor Poletti, Marian Labuda

'A comedy with something to say, and the audacity to mix its laughs with a decent seriousness of purpose.' – *Derek Malcolm, Guardian*

Mein Kampf *
Sweden 1961 118m bw
Töre Sjöberg/Minerva International
V*, L
original title: *Den Blodiga Tiden*

A newsreel compilation tracing the rise and fall of Nazi Germany.

A simple but highly effective and reliable selection of actualities leaves conclusions to the viewer, letting the events speak for themselves. A powerful documentary.

wd Erwin Leiser *ed* Erwin Leiser

Het Meisje Met Het Rode Haar: see *The Girl with the Red Hair*

Melancholia
GB 1989 87m colour
BFI/Lichtblik Filmproduktion/Channel 4/Norddeutscher Rundfunk/Film Fons Hamburg/Hamburger Filmbüro (Colin MacCabe, Helga Bahr)
V, S

A German art critic, a former radical, is asked to take part in a political assassination in London.

Downbeat thriller built around an enigmatic protagonist.

w Andi Engel, Lewis Rodia *d* Andi Engel *ph* Denis Crossan *m* Simon Fisher Turner *pd* Jock Scott *ed* Christopher Roth

Jeroen Krabbé, Susannah York, Ulrich Wildgruber, Jane Gurnett, Kate Hardie, Saul Reichlin, John Sparkes

Melba
GB 1953 113m Technicolor
Horizon (Sam Spiegel)
V

The life of the internationally famous Australian opera singer of Victorian days.

Moderately interesting recreation of a woman and an era, though dramatically rather stodgy.

w Harry Kurnitz *d* Lewis Milestone *ph* Ted Scaife *md* Muir Mathieson *ad* Andrei Andreiev

Patrice Munsel, Robert Morley, Alec Clunes, Martita Hunt, Sybil Thorndike, John McCallum

O Melissokomos: see *The Beekeeper*

Mélo **
France 1986 112m colour
Artificial Eye/MK2/Films A2/CNC (Marin Karmitz)

A wife, tormented by her affair with another man, kills herself.

Deliberately theatrical treatment of a once-potent play of the 1920s that gives its principals a chance to revel in their roles.

wd Alain Resnais *play* Henry Bernstein *ph* Charlie Van Damme *m* Philippe Gérard *pd* Jacques Saulnier *ed* Albert Jurgenson, Jean-Pierre Besnard

Sabine Azéma, Fanny Ardant, Pierre Aditi, André Dussollier, Jacques Dacqmine

† The same play was filmed as *Dreaming Lips* in 1936.

Melody
GB 1971 106m Eastmancolor
Hemdale/Sagittarius/Goodtimes (David Puttnam)
V*
aka: *S.W.A.L.K.*

Calf love at school causes jealousy between two boys.

Tough-sentimental teenage comedy-drama of little interest to adults.

w Alan Parker *d* Waris Hussein *ph* Peter Suschitsky *m* Richard Hewson

Jack Wild, Mark Lester, Tracy Hyde

Melody Cruise
US 1933 74m bw
Merian C. Cooper/RKO

A lady killer gets his come-uppance on board ship, but wins the girl he really wants.

Very messy mixture of comedy, romance and music.

w Mark Sandrich, Ben Holmes *d* Mark Sandrich

Phil Harris, Charles Ruggles, Greta Nissen, Helen Mack, Chick Chandler

'Ought to be a moderate grosser . . . the meat just isn't there for the principals, and they seem to feel it in their work.' – *Variety*

Melody for Two
US 1937 60m bw
Warner

A singing bandleader argues with his team and picks up with an all-girl crew.

Simple-minded peg for a few songs; rather a yawn.

w George Bricker, Luci Ward, Joseph K. Watson *d* Louis King

James Melton, Patricia Ellis, Wini Shaw, Marie Wilson, Fred Keating, Dick Purcell

'Okay twin-bill fodder.' – *Variety*

Melody in Spring
US 1934 75m bw
Douglas MacLean/Paramount

An ambitious radio singer follows the sponsor's daughter on a European holiday.

Mild vehicle for a tenor who didn't sustain.

w Benn W. Levy *d* Norman Z. McLeod

Lanny Ross, Charles Ruggles, Mary Boland, Ann Sothern, George Meeker, Herman Bing

'Farfetched, somewhat boresome, and generally airy.' – *Variety*

Melody Inn: see *Riding High*

The Melody Lingers On
US 1935 65m bw
Edward Small

During World War I, an Italian soldier is killed after fathering an illegitimate baby, which grows up with no knowledge of mother, who watches from afar.

Old-fashioned tearjerker with musical background.

w Ralph Spence, Philip Dunne *novel* Lowell Brentano *d* David Burton

Josephine Hutchinson, George Houston, John Halliday, Mona Barrie, Helen Westley, Laura Hope Crews

'Will probably wind up topping the duals.' – *Variety*

Melody of Life: see *Symphony of Six Million*

Melody of Youth: see *They Shall Have Music*

Melody Time *
US 1948 75m Technicolor
Walt Disney (Ben Sharpsteen)

An unlinked variety show of cartoon segments.

A mainly mediocre selection with the usual moments of high style: *Once upon a Wintertime, Bumble Boogie, Johnny Appleseed, Little Toot, Trees, Blame it on the Samba, Pecos Bill.*

wd various

'There seems to be an obvious connection between the Disney artists' increasing insipidity and their increasing talent for fright, but I will leave it to accredited sado-masochists to make the discovery.' – *James Agee*

Melvin and Howard *
US 1980 95m Technicolor
Universal (Terry Nelson)
V*

The life of a factory worker is changed when a man he picks up in the Nevada desert claims to be Howard Hughes.

Eccentric comedy which has been compared to the work of Preston Sturges, but has an agreeable style of its own.

w Bo Goldman *d* Jonathan Demme *ph* Tak Fujimoto *m* Bruce Langhorne

Paul Le Mat, Jason Robards Jnr, Mary Steenburgen, Elizabeth Cheshire, Michael J. Pollard, Gloria Grahame

'An almost flawless act of sympathetic imagination . . . it's what might have happened if Jean Renoir had directed a comedy script by Preston Sturges.' – *New Yorker*

AA: Bo Goldman; Mary Steenburgen
AAN: Jason Robards Jnr (supporting actor)

The Member of the Wedding *
US 1952 91m bw
Columbia/Stanley Kramer
V*

A 12-year-old girl learns something about life when her sister gets married and a young boy dies.

Boringly contained in a kitchen set, this filmed play has interesting characters but is really not good enough for the talent involved.

w Edna and Edward Anhalt *play and novel* Carson McCullers *d* Fred Zinnemann *ph* Hal Mohr *m* Alex North

Julie Harris, *Ethel Waters*, Brandon de Wilde, Arthur Franz, Nancy Gates, James Edwards

AAN: Julie Harris

Memed My Hawk

GB 1984 110m colour
Fuad Kavur/Peter Ustinov Productions

In 1923 Turkey, an inept tyrant chases one of his young villagers, who flees to the rebels.

Weird but not wonderful mix of comedy and melodrama in an unfamiliar and unattractive setting.

wd Peter Ustinov *novel* Yashar Kemal *ph* Freddie Francis *m* Manos Hadjidakis *ad* Veljko Despotovic *ed* Peter Honess

Peter Ustinov, Herbert Lom, Denis Quilley, Michael Elphick, Simon Dutton

Memoirs of a Survivor

GB 1981 115m Technicolor
EMI/Memorial (Michael Medwin, Penny Clark)

In the future, a single woman finds that urban civilization has decayed, and after many horrors finds refuge in an old Victorian house.

Unappetizing mixture of *1984* and *Alice in Wonderland*, too despairing and plotless to find many takers.

w Kerry Crabbe, David Gladwell *novel* Doris Lessing *d* David Gladwell *ph* Walter Lassally *m* Mike Thorn *pd* Keith Wilson *ed* William Shapter

Julie Christie, Christopher Guard, Debbie Hutchings, Leonie Mellinger, Nigel Hawthorne, Pat Keen

'A film of wild ambition, sadly and hopelessly bungled.' – *Geoff Brown, MFB*

'Women want him for his wit. The C.I.A. wants him for his body. All Nick wants is his molecules back.'
'An adventure like you've never seen.'

Memoirs of an Invisible Man *

US 1992 99m Technicolor Panavision
Warner/Le Studio Canal Plus/Regency Enterprises/Alcor (Bruce Bodner, Dan Kolsrud)
V, V*, L

A CIA agent pursues a stock analyst who has turned invisible after an accident.

Clever special effects fail to compensate for the lacklustre script and uninspired performances.

w Robert Collector, Dana Olsen, William Goldman *novel* H. F. Saint *d* John Carpenter *ph* William A. Fraker *m* Shirley Walker *pd* Lawrence G. Paull *sp* Industrial Light and Magic *ed* Marion Rothman

Chevy Chase, Daryl Hannah, Sam Neill, Michael McKean, Stephen Tobolowsky, Jim Norton

'Where's the wit? It fades into invisibility while you're watching it.' – *Los Angeles Times*

The Memory Expert: see *The Man on the Flying Trapeze*

The Memphis Belle *

US/GB 1943 43m Technicolor
War Activities Commission

The last mission over Germany of a Flying Fortress.

Impressive on-the-spot documentary which provided a lot of library footage for later movies.

d William Wyler

Memphis Belle **

GB 1990 106m colour
Warner/Enigma (David Puttnam, Catherine Wyler)
V, V*, L, S

In the Second World War, the crew of an American B-17 bomber fly their final mission over Germany.

Sentimental drama that is a throwback to war films of an earlier era.

w Monte Merrick *d* Michael Caton-Jones *ph* David Watkin *m* George Fenton *pd* Stuart Craig *ed* Jim Clark

Matthew Modine, Eric Stolz, Tate Donovan, D. B. Sweeney, Billy Zane, Sean Astin, Harry Connick Jnr, Reed Edward Diamond, Courtney Gains, Neil Giuntoli

'Another chapter in David Puttnam's peculiar cinema of history lessons without cinematic depth or sound dramatic portfolio.' – *Richard Combs, MFB*

'A completely new experience between men and women!'
'I was afraid I was gonna die … now I'm afraid I'm gonna live!'

The Men ***

US 1950 85m bw
Stanley Kramer
V*, L
reissue title: *Battle Stripe*

Paraplegic war veterans are prepared for civilian life; the fiancée of one of them helps overcome his problems.

Vivid semi-documentary melodrama, at the time rather shocking in its no-holds-barred treatment of sexual problems.

w Carl Foreman *d* Fred Zinnemann *ph* Robert de Grasse *m* Dimitri Tiomkin

Marlon Brando, Teresa Wright, Everett Sloane, Jack Webb, Howard St John

'Don't be misled into feeling that to see this film is merely a duty; it is, simply, an experience worth having.' – *Richard Mallett, Punch*

'As a bold, brave motion picture, *The Men* is to be applauded; but it would be a mistake to imagine that noble intentions and the courage to speak in hitherto unmentionable medical jargon necessarily make great films.' – *Margaret Hinxman*

AAN: Carl Foreman

Men . . . **

West Germany 1985 99m colour
Artificial Eye/Olga Film/ZDF (Harald Kugler)
V*
original title: *Männer . . .*

A bourgeois husband turns his wife's lover, a hippy artist, into a carbon copy of himself

Light-hearted indictment of men as overgrown children

wd Doris Dörrie *ph* Helge Weindler *m* Claus Bantzer *ed* Raimund Barthelmes, Jeanette Magerl

Heiner Lauterbach, Uwe Ochsenknecht, Ulrike Kriener, Janna Marangosoff

'Dörrie's deadpan giddiness is likeable enough. The picture is insignificant, though – a piece of fluff without the wit that you might hope for.' – *Pauline Kael, New Yorker*

Men Against the Sky

US 1940 73m bw
Howard Benedict/RKO

A stunt pilot advises on a new plane design instrumental to the war effort.

Routine heroics mixed with romance.

w Nathanael West *d* Leslie Goodwins

Richard Dix, Kent Taylor, Edmund Lowe, Wendy Barrie, Grant Withers

Men Are Not Gods

GB 1936 92m bw
UA/London (Alexander Korda)

An actor playing Othello nearly strangles his wife.

Tepid melodramatic attempt at a theme later used in *A Double Life*.

w G. B. Stern, Iris Wright *d* Walter Reisch *ph* Charles Rosher *m* Geoffrey Toye *ad* Vincent Korda *ed* Henry Cornelius

Miriam Hopkins, Sebastian Shaw, Rex Harrison, Gertrude Lawrence, A. E. Matthews, Val Gielgud, Laura Smithson

'A nearer approximation to box office quality than some recent London productions.' – *Variety*

Men Are Such Fools

US 1938 69m bw
Warner

The worm turns when his wife threatens to leave him for a singing career.

Mediocre is the word for this threadbare drama.

w Norman Reilly Raine, Horace Jackson *d* Busby Berkeley

Wayne Morris, Humphrey Bogart, Priscilla Lane, Hugh Herbert, Penny Singleton

Men at Work

US 1990 98m DeLuxe
Entertainment/Epic Productions/Euphoria Films/Sarlui/Diamant (Cassian Elwes)
V, V*, L, S

Two garbage men find a corpse and set out to discover its killer.

Clumsily directed, witless rubbish. *wd* Emilio Estevez *ph* Tim Suhrstedt *m* Stewart Copeland, Greg DeBelles *pd* Dins Danielsen *ed* Craig Bassett

Charlie Sheen, Emilio Estevez, Leslie Hope, Keith David, Dean Cameron, John Getz, Hawk Wolinski, John Lavachielli, Geoffrey Blake

'This still manages to be an ordeal thanks to its endless procession of excrement jokes, kindergarten-level sex-jokes, contrived and pointless wandering around, and collection of arbitrary and oft-forgotten MacGuffins.' – *Kim Newman, MFB*

Men Behind Bars: see *Duffy of San Quentin*

Men Don't Leave

US 1990 115m CFI
Warner (Jon Avnet)
V, V*, L

Following the death of her husband in an accident, a widow with two sons strives to keep the family together.

Just about rises above the level of an average soap opera.

w Barbara Benedek, Paul Brickman *d* Paul Brickman *ph* Bruce Surtees *m* Thomas Newman *pd* Barbara Ling *ed* Richard Chew

Jessica Lange, Arliss Howard, Joan Cusack, Kathy Bates, Tom Mason, Chris O'Donnell, Charlie Korsmo, Belita Moreno, Jim Haynie, Cory Carrier, Shannon Moffett

Men in Her Diary

US 1945 73m bw
Universal

A jealous woman tries to hire an unattractive girl as her husband's secretary.

Very mild lower-berth comedy.

w F. Hugh Herbert and Elwood Ullman *story* Kerry Shaw *d* Charles Barton

Peggy Ryan, Jon Hall, Louise Allbritton, William Terry, Virginia Grey, Ernest Truex, Alan Mowbray, Eric Blore, Sig Rumann

The Men in Her Life

US 1941 90m bw
Columbia (Gregory Ratoff)

A former circus rider becomes a ballerina.

Well-worn rags-to-riches romance of little interest.

w Frederick Kohner, Michael Wilson, Paul Trivers novel *Ballerina* by Lady Eleanor Smith d Gregory Ratoff ph Harry Stradling, Arthur Miller md David Raksin

Loretta Young, Conrad Veidt, Dean Jagger, Eugenie Leontovich, Shepperd Strudwick, Otto Kruger, Paul Baratoff

Men in War
US 1957 104m bw
Security (Sidney Harmon)
V*

Korea 1950: an infantry platoon is cut off from HQ and tries to take an enemy-occupied hill.

Stereotyped small-scale war heroics; the film makes its points but fails to entertain.

w Philip Yordan d Anthony Mann ph Ernest Haller m Elmer Bernstein

Robert Ryan, Robert Keith, Aldo Ray, Vic Morrow, James Edwards, Sen Yung

Men in White *
US 1934 80m bw
MGM (Monta Bell)

An ambitious intern is in love with an attractive socialite who resents his devotion to duty.

Popular but obvious star drama.

w Waldemar Young play Sidney Kingsley d Richard Boleslawski ph George Folsey

Clark Gable, Myrna Loy, Jean Hersholt, Elizabeth Allan, Otto Kruger, C. Henry Gordon, Wallace Ford

'Belongs in the strictly adult class of pictures . . . show spells money from plenty of angles.' – *Variety*

Men Must Fight
US 1933 73m bw
MGM

War comes to New York in 1940.

A forgotten pacifist tract which trod the same paths as did H. G. Wells; of historical interest only apart from a spectacular air raid climax.

w S. K. Lauren, Reginald Lawrence, C. Gardner Sullivan d Edgar Selwyn

Robert Young, Diana Wynyard, Mary Robson, Phillips Holmes, Lewis Stone

Men of Boys' Town
US 1941 106m bw
MGM (John W. Considine Jnr)
V*

Further adventures of Father Flanagan.

Mushy sequel to *Boys' Town* (qv).

w James Kevin McGuinness d Norman Taurog ph Harold Rosson m Herbert Stothart

Spencer Tracy, Mickey Rooney, Bobs Watson, Larry Nunn, Lee J. Cobb, Mary Nash, Henry O'Neill, Darryl Hickman, Anne Revere

Men of Respect
US 1990 113m colour
Central City/Arthur Goldblatt (Ephraim Horowitz)
V, V*, L

Told by a fortune-teller that he will become the next Mafia Godfather, a gangster is urged by his wife to make sure the prediction comes true.

Shakespeare's *Macbeth* is the inspiration for this odd little thriller, with the plot sticking close to the original and some of the dialogue being repeated virtually word for word. But guilt over a murder seems an unlikely emotion for a hitman to feel.

wd William Reilly ph Bobby Bukowski m Misha Segal ad William Barclay ed Elizabeth Kling

John Turturro, Katherine Borowitz, Dennis Farina, Peter Boyle, Rod Steiger

'One has the feeling of watching an end-of-the-term show at Yale Drama School.' – *Philip French, Observer*

† An earlier thriller, *Joe Macbeth* (qv), also borrowed its plot from Shakespeare's play.

Men of Sherwood Forest
GB 1954 77m Eastmancolor
Hammer (Michael Carreras)

Robin Hood frees King Richard from bondage.

Fairly lively adventure romp on a low level.

w Allan MacKinnon d Val Guest ph Jimmy Harvey m Doreen Corwithen

Don Taylor, Reginald Beckwith, Eileen Moore, David King-Wood, Patrick Holt, John Van Eyssen

Men of Texas
US 1942 71m bw
Universal
GB title: *Men of Destiny*

After the Civil War, a Yankee reporter is sent to investigate rumours of a further uprising.

Routine Western, not unentertaining in its modest way.

w Harold Shumate d Ray Enright

Robert Stack, Anne Gwynne, Broderick Crawford, Jackie Cooper, Ralph Bellamy, Jane Darwell, Leo Carrillo, John Litel

Men of the Fighting Lady
US 1954 80m Anscocolor
MGM (Henry Berman)

Adventures of an aircraft carrier during the Korean War.

Tepid war actioner with a few effective semi-documentary sequences of naval tactics.

w Art Cohn d Andrew Marton ph George Folsey m Miklos Rozsa

Van Johnson, Walter Pidgeon, Louis Calhern, Dewey Martin, Keenan Wynn, Frank Lovejoy, Robert Horton

Men of the Sea: see *Midshipman Easy*

Men of Tomorrow
GB 1932 88m bw
Paramount/London Films (Alexander Korda)

Oxford students have more than academic work on their minds.

Dim comedy-drama with an interesting cast.

w Arthur Wimperis, Anthony Gibbs play *Young Apollo* by Anthony Gibbs d Leontine Sagan, Zoltan Korda ph Bernard Browne ad Vincent Korda ed Leontine Sagan

Maurice Braddell, Joan Gardner, Emlyn Williams, Merle Oberon, Robert Donat

Men of Two Worlds
GB 1946 109m Technicolor
GFD/Two Cities (John Sutro)
V*, S
US title: *Witch Doctor*, aka: *Kisenga, Man of Africa*

In Tanganyika, an educated native helps white men to counter the force of witch doctors and persuade tribes to leave an infected area.

Earnest but totally unpersuasive semi-documentary shot in unconvincing sets and garish colour.

w Thorold Dickinson, Joyce Cary, E. Arnot Robertson, Herbert Victor d Thorold Dickinson ph Geoffrey Unsworth, Desmond Dickinson m Arthur Bliss

Eric Portman, Phyllis Calvert, Robert Adams, Orlando Martins, Arnold Marle, Cathleen Nesbitt, David Horne, Cyril Raymond

Men o' War *
US 1929 20m bw
Hal Roach
V

Two sailors and two girls have adventures in a park.

Simple-minded early talkie star comedy featuring their famous soda fountain routine.

w H. M. Walker d Lewis R. Foster

Laurel and Hardy, James Finlayson

Men of Yesterday
GB 1936 82m bw
UK Films

Old army rivalries die down at a reunion.

Dated but interesting drama with interpolated variety talent.

w Gerald Elliott, Jack Francis d John Baxter

Stewart Rome, Sam Livesey, Hay Petrie, Cecil Parker, with George Robey, Ella Shields, Will Fyffe, Dick Henderson

Men on Her Mind: see *The Girl from Tenth Avenue*

Men with Wings
US 1938 106m Technicolor
Paramount (William Wellman)

Civil aviation pioneers fall out over a girl.

Disappointing epic from the maker of *Wings*, with highly predictable story line, modest acting and ho-hum spectacle.

w Robert Carson d William Wellman ph W. Howard Greene m W. Franke Harling, Gerard Carbonara

Fred MacMurray, Ray Milland, Louise Campbell, Andy Devine, Lynne Overman, Porter Hall, Walter Abel, Virginia Weidler, Donald O'Connor

'To all women who love and admire the fearless heroes of the air, and who, with brave hearts, encourage them, hope, and pray for them.' – *director's dedication*

'Lavish air spectacle in Technicolor that means big business . . . it will triumph through rain, sleet or snow.' – *Variety*

'Give the rats a taste of their own medicine!'
Men without Names
US 1935 67m bw
Paramount

Bank robbers are cornered in a small town and picked off by the FBI.

Routine crime feature, less exciting than it sounds.

w Marguerite Roberts, Kubec Glasmon, Dale Van Every d Ralph Murphy

Fred MacMurray, Madge Evans, Lynne Overman, David Holt, John Wray, Dean Jagger

'Another of the new gangster films, and too flimsy. Grooved for the pops.' – *Variety*

Men without Women
US 1930 77m bw
Fox

Men in a submarine are trapped on the ocean bed.

Early talkie action drama noted more for its credits than its accomplishment.

w Dudley Nichols d John Ford ph Joseph H. August

Kenneth MacKenna, Frank Albertson, Paul Page, Pat Somerset, Stuart Erwin, Warren Hymer, John Wayne

'Stunning, realistic picture that will make talk.' – *Variety*

The Menace

US 1932 64m bw
Columbia

A convict escapes, gets a new face through plastic surgery, and plans his revenge.

Muddled melodrama.

w Dorothy Howell, Charles Logue, Roy Chanslor
d Roy William Neill

Walter Byron, H. B. Warner, Bette Davis, Natalie Moorhead, William Davidson, Halliwell Hobbes

'A halting and frequently clumsy development leads to a weak climax.' – Variety

Menace

US 1934 58m bw
Paramount

Murders follow the suicide of a mining engineer.

Compact little dark house thriller with good stagey performances.

w Chandler Sprague and Anthony Veiller
story Philip MacDonald d Ralph Murphy

Gertrude Michael, Paul Cavanagh, Henrietta Crosman, John Lodge, Ray Milland, Berton Churchill, Halliwell Hobbes

'A pat specimen of the mystery film, expertly manipulated.' – Variety

'This is the truth. This is what's real.'
Menace II Society *

US 1993 97m Foto-Kem colour
First Independent/New Line (Darin Scott)
V, V*, L, S

In the Watts district of Los Angeles, young blacks become involved in robbery and murder.

A harsh and violent movie that sticks close to the expectations of gangster films while claiming to be dealing with reality; its young directors show promise.

w Tyger Williams, Allen Hughes, Albert Hughes
d Allen Hughes, Albert Hughes ph Lisa Rinzler
m QD III pd Penny Barrett ed Christopher Koefoed

Tyrin Turner, Jada Pinkett, Larenz Tate, Arnold Johnson, MC Eiht, Marilyn Coleman, Vonte Sweet, Clifton Powell, Samuel L. Jackson

'The clichés of racial stereotyping lie piled as high as the bodies . . . It's a dreadfully inflammatory film to bring to our society. Hollywood is exporting too many of America's menaces.' – Alexander Walker, London Evening Standard

'A grim, nihilistic trip to the inner city . . . Fierce, violent and searing in its observation, the film makes all previous excursions seem like a walk in the park.' – Variety

Menilmontant *

France 1924 50m (24 fps) bw silent
Dimitri Kirsanov (for his own company)

Respected but fairly impenetrable piece of avant-garde which appears to be about two sisters haunted by memories of the murder of their parents, for which they may or may not have been responsible.

wd Dimitri Kirsanov ed Dimitri Kirsanov

'A flurry of hand-held camera shots, incisive montages and elliptical progressions.' – Geoff Brown, MFB, 1981

The Men's Club

US 1986 100m colour
Atlantic Releasing/Howard Gottfried
V*, L

Friends nearing forty get together and bemoan their lot.

Curious, talky, rather dreary piece which gets almost nowhere.

w Leonard Michaels novel Leonard Michaels
d Peter Medak ph John Fleckenstein m Lee Holdridge pd Ken Davis ed Cynthia Scheider, David Dresser, Bill Butler

Roy Scheider, Frank Langella, Harvey Keitel, Treat Williams, Richard Jordan, David Dukes, Craig Wasson, Stockard Channing, Jennifer Jason Leigh

'A club few will want to join . . . a distasteful piece of work that displays the worst in men.' – Variety

Menschen am Sonntag: see People on Sunday

Mensonge *

France 1993 89m colour
Gala/Cuel Lavalette/France-3/Alain Sarde
V
aka: The Lie

A faithful wife discovers that she is both pregnant and HIV positive.

Interesting, though too easily resolved, exploration of relationships and the effect of AIDS on those innocently involved.

w Denis Saada, François Margolin d François Margolin ph Caroline Champetier pd Julie Sfez, Arnaud de Moleron ed Martine Giordano

Nathalie Baye, Didier Sandre, Hélène Lapiower, Marc Citti, Dominique Besnehard, Christophe Bourseiller, Louis Ducreux, Adrien Beau

'Rather than flagging the disease as a metaphor of sanctification-through-degradation, it rolls it into a disease-of-the-week movie and uses it as a trigger for tears, lots of talk, pat ironies and soapy symbolism. And on that level, it's actually quite accomplished.' – Steve Beard, Empire

Mephisto ****

Hungary 1981 144m Eastmancolor
Mafilm/Manfred Durniok
V, V*

In Germany in the twenties, an actor committed to the idea of a workers' theatre becomes a puppet of the Nazis.

Chilling and fiercely compelling melodrama of moral corruption, with a bravura performance from Brandauer as a man who willingly sells his soul.

w Peter Dobai, Istvan Szabo novel Klaus Mann
d Istvan Szabo ph Lajos Koltai m Zdenko Tamassy

Klaus Maria Brandauer, Ildikó Bánsági, Krystyna Janda

AA: best foreign film

The Mephisto Waltz *

US 1971 109m DeLuxe
TCF/QM Productions
V*

A satanic concert pianist on the point of death wills his soul into the body of a journalist.

Complex diabolical mumbo-jumbo with plenty of style.

w Ben Maddow novel Fred Mustard Stewart
d Paul Wendkos ph William W. Spencer m Jerry Goldsmith

Alan Alda, Jacqueline Bisset, Curt Jurgens, Barbara Parkins

La Mer Cruelle

Kuwait 1983 107m bw
Sakr Films (Abbas Redha, Hassan Redha)
original title: Bas Ya Bahar, aka: Sea of Silence

In Kuwait before the discovery of oil, a youth becomes a pearl diver against his father's wishes.

Competent, but slow-moving and of interest mainly for its documentary content.

w Rahman Saleh d Khalid Al Siddiq ph Tanfig Al Amir m Abu Tariq ed Hassanof

Saad Al Faraj, Mohammed Al Mansour, Hayat Al Fahd

The Mercenaries

GB 1968 100m Metrocolor Panavision
MGM/George Englund
US title: Dark of the Sun

In the Belgian Congo in 1960 a mercenary officer is ordered to bring back a fortune in diamonds by armoured train.

Basically an old-fashioned thriller about the hazards of a journey beset by brutish villains and damsels in distress, this unpleasant film is notable for the amount of sadistic action it crams into its running time.

w Quentin Werty, Adrian Spies novel Dark of the Sun by Wilbur Smith d Jack Cardiff ph Edward Scaife m Jacques Loussier

Rod Taylor, Yvette Mimieux, Kenneth More, Jim Brown, Peter Carsten, André Morell, Guy Deghy, Calvin Lockhart, Alan Gifford

'The violence done to the human body is matched by violence done to the intelligence by a stock adventure story given a gloss of topicality and social insult.' – Judith Crist

Merci La Vie **

France 1991 119m Eastmancolor/bw
Cine Valse/Film par Film/Orly/DD/SEDIF/A2 (Barnard Marescot)
V

A bored teenager befriends a girl with a venereal disease, who has been persuaded by a doctor to infect as many men as she can in order to provide him with patients.

Inventive, playful film which mixes the present day and the Nazi occupation of France, switching between reality, day-dreams and movies in which the girls appear – though the final effect may be more exhausting than invigorating.

wd Bernard Blier ph Philippe Rousselot
pd Theobald Meurisse ed Claudine Merlin

Charlotte Gainsbourg, Anouk Grinberg, Gérard Depardieu, Michael Blanc, Jean Carmet, Catherine Jacob, Annie Girardot, Jean-Louis Trintignant, Thierry Frémont

'A bold, often exciting, sometimes frustrating but always challenging pic.' – Variety

'The art-house equivalent of a Hollywood rollercoaster where sensation is all and decorous values – logic, good taste, some ultimate meaning – get trampled in the rush to amaze.' – Geoff Brown, The Times

Merely Mary Ann

US 1931 74m bw
Fox

The maid of all work falls for the gentleman lodger.

Cinderella stuff redesigned for two popular stars, but of no lasting appeal.

w Jules Furthman story Israel Zangwill d Henry King

Janet Gaynor, Charles Farrell, Beryl Mercer, J. M. Kerrigan, G. P. Huntley Jnr

'Bound to pull after a summer of gang violence, mystery shockers, and much sex urge study.' – Variety

Mermaids

US 1990 110m colour
Rank/Orion (Lauren Lloyd, Wallis Nichita, Patrick Palmer)
V, V*, L, S

A daughter, torn between becoming a nun and her feelings for a handsome boy, resolves her difficulties with her flirtatious mother.

A romantic comedy uncertain whether it is trying for laughs or tears; it attempts, unsuccessfully, to settle for both.

w June Roberts *novel* Patty Dann *d* Richard Benjamin *ph* Howard Atherton *m* Jack Nitzsche *pd* Stuart Wurtzel *ed* Jacqueline Cambas

Cher, Bob Hoskins, Winona Ryder, Michael Schoeffling, Christina Ricci, Caroline McWilliams, Jan Miner, Betsey Townsend

'It wavers between arch comedy and hollow melodrama, each desperately over-pitched.' – *Sight and Sound*

† Lasse Halstrom was replaced by Frank Oz as director before filming began. Two weeks after filming started, Richard Benjamin replaced Frank Oz. Winona Ryder's role as Cher's daughter was to have been played by Emily Lloyd until Cher objected that Lloyd did not look like her.

Merrill's Marauders *
US 1962 98m Technicolor Cinemascope
Warner/US Pictures (Milton Sperling)
V*

Adventures of a crack US army unit in 1942 Burma.

Physically exhausting war adventure with emphasis on hand-to-hand fighting and much bloodshed.

w Samuel Fuller, Milton Sperling *d* Samuel Fuller *ph* William Clothier *m* Howard Jackson *ed* Folmar Blangsted

Jeff Chandler, Ty Hardin, Andrew Duggan, Peter Brown, Will Hutchins, Claude Akins

Merrily We Go to Hell
US 1932 78m bw
Paramount
GB title: *Merrily We Go to —*

A socialite marries a dipsomaniac journalist.

Glum problem drama.

w Edwin Justin Mayer *novel I Jerry Take Thee Joan* by Cleo Lucas *d* Dorothy Arzner *ph* David Abel

Sylvia Sidney, Fredric March, Adrienne Allen, Richard Gallagher, Florence Burton, Esther Howard, Kent Taylor

Merrily We Live *
US 1938 90m bw
Hal Roach

A zany family hires a chauffeur who is actually a famous writer posing as a tramp.

Quite likeable compound of *My Man Godfrey* and *You Can't Take It with You.*

w Eddie Moran, Jack Jevne *d* Norman Z. McLeod *ph* Norbert Brodine *md* Marvin Hatley *ad* Charles D. Hall

Constance Bennett, Brian Aherne, Billie Burke, Alan Mowbray, Patsy Kelly, Ann Dvorak, Tom Brown, Bonita Granville, Marjorie Rambeau, Clarence Kolb

'In the high cost bracket and rates top billing when dualled, with a chance it is strong enough to carry first runs as a single.' – *Variety*

AAN: Norbert Brodine; Billie Burke; title song (*m* Phil Craig, *ly* Arthur Quenzer); Charles D. Hall

Merry Andrew
US 1958 103m Metrocolor Cinemascope
MGM/Sol C. Siegel

A stuffy teacher in search of an ancient statue joins a travelling circus.

Deliberately charming star comedy which plumps too firmly for whimsy and, despite its professionalism, provokes barely a smile, let alone a laugh.

w Isobel Lennart, I. A. L. Diamond *story* Paul Gallico *d/ch* Michael Kidd *ph* Robert Surtees *m* Saul Chaplin *ly* Johnny Mercer

Danny Kaye, Pier Angeli, Baccaloni, Noel Purcell, Robert Coote, Patricia Cutts, Rex Evans, Walter Kingsford, Tommy Rall, Rhys Williams

Merry Christmas, Mr Lawrence *
GB 1982 124m Eastmancolor
V*, S

In a Japanese prisoner-of-war camp in Java in 1942, an English captive strikes up a strange relationship with the commandant.

Uncomfortably titled and unavoidably downbeat character drama with some unpleasant moments; despite good work all round it seems to head straight for every cliché perpetuated by *The Bridge on the River Kwai.*

w Nagisa Oshima with Paul Mayersberg *novel The Seed and the Sower* by Laurens van der Post *d* Nagisa Oshima *ph* Toichiro Narushima *m* Ryuichi Sakamoto

David Bowie, Tom Conti, Ryuichi Sakamoto, Takeshi, Jack Thompson, Johnny Okura, Alistair Browning

'It always seems like a cocktail of saleable ingredients rather than genuine cinema.' – *Sunday Times*

Merry Comes to Town
GB 1937 79m bw
Embassy/Sound City
US title: *Merry Comes to Stay*

A professor's family is disappointed when a relative visiting from America turns out to be as poor as they are.

Thin, predictable comedy with the visitor finally hailed as a saviour.

w Evadne Price *d* George King

ZaSu Pitts, Guy Newall, Betty Ann Davies, Muriel George, Basil Langton

'A pleasant comedy which will improve with cutting.' – *Variety*

The Merry Frinks
US 1934 68m bw
First National
GB title: *Happy Family*

A sportswriter down on his luck has a crazy family.

And didn't everybody in the mid-thirties? But this one is crazy without being very funny.

w Gene Markey, Kathryn Scola *d* Alfred E. Green

Aline MacMahon, Guy Kibbee, Allen Jenkins, Hugh Herbert, Frankie Darro

'The most disagreeable family group since Three Cornered Moon. Poor comedy and lacks names.' – *Variety.*

Merry Go Round of 1938
US 1937 87m bw
Universal

Four vaudevillians adopt a small girl, and later head for Hollywood.

Sentimental farce with zany moments and an encouraging cast.

w Monte Brice, A. Dorian Otvos *d* Irving Cummings

Jimmy Savo, Bert Lahr, Mischa Auer, Billy House, Alice Brady, Louise Fazenda

'First rate filmusical packed with laughs.' – *Variety*

The Merry Monahans
US 1944 90m bw
Universal (Michael Fessier, Ernest Pagano)

Adventures of a family of vaudeville performers.

Acceptable backstage comedy drama with good atmosphere.

w Michael Fessier, Ernest Pagano *d* Charles Lamont *ph* Charles Van Enger *m* Hans Salter

Donald O'Connor, Jack Oakie, Rosemary de Camp, Peggy Ryan, Ann Blyth, Isabel Jewell, John Miljan

AAN: Hans Salter

The Merry Widow *
US 1925 111m (24 fps) bw silent
MGM (Irving Thalberg)

A bankrupt king orders a nobleman to woo a wealthy American widow.

An operetta without music (or dialogue) is usually a poor thing, but the director added a few unpredictable touches.

w Erich von Stroheim, Benjamin Glazer *operetta* Victor Leon, Leo Stein *d* Erich von Stroheim *ph* Oliver Marsh, Ben Reynolds, William Daniels *m* William Axt, D. Mendoza

Mae Murray, John Gilbert, Roy D'Arcy, Tully Marshall

† The story goes that when reproved by Thalberg for wasting film stock on, for instance, endless shots of a wardrobe full of shoes, von Stroheim remarked: 'The character has a foot fetish.' 'And you,' said Thalberg, 'have a footage fetish!'

'Surrender to the happy seduction of Ernst Lubitsch's most glorious picture holiday!'

The Merry Widow **
US 1934 99m bw
MGM
V*, L

Patchy, but sometimes sparkling version.

w Samson Raphaelson, Ernest Vajda *d* Ernst Lubitsch *ph* Oliver T. Marsh *m* Franz Lehar *ad* Cedric Gibbons, Frederic Hope

Maurice Chevalier, Jeanette MacDonald, Edward Everett Horton, Una Merkel, George Barbier, Donald Meek, Sterling Holloway, Shirley Ross

'Fine all-around job and an entertainment natural.' – *Variety*

'It is Lubitsch; it is also Hollywood; it is the cream of the American bourgeois film. It is a charlotte russe.' – *Peter Ellis, New Masses*

AA: art direction

The Merry Widow
US 1952 105m Technicolor
MGM (Joe Pasternak)
V*

Chill, empty remake.

w Sonya Levien, William Ludwig *d* Curtis Bernhardt *ph* Robert Surtees

Fernando Lamas, Lana Turner, Richard Haydn, Una Merkel, Thomas Gomez, John Abbott

'Nothing has been omitted (except the spirit of the original).' – *MFB*

The Merry Wives of Reno *
US 1934 61m bw
Warner

Three couples go to a Reno hotel to get a divorce.

Amusing but scrappy comedy in the vein of the successful *Convention City.*

w Robert Lord *d* H. Bruce Humberstone

Margaret Lindsay, Donald Woods, Guy Kibbee, Glenda Farrell, Ruth Donnelly, Hugh Herbert, Frank McHugh, Roscoe Ates, Hobart Cavanaugh

'Stylized farce with excellent cast and considerable humour.' – *Variety*

Merton of the Movies *
US 1947 82m bw
MGM

An innocent young man in Hollywood becomes a star.

The plot and characterizations of this old chestnut are resistible, but the Hollywood background is well managed and convincing.

w George Wells, Lou Breslow   *novel* Harry Leon Wilson   *d* Robert Alton   *ph* Paul C. Vogel   *m* David Snell

Red Skelton, Virginia O'Brien, Alan Mowbray, Gloria Grahame, Leon Ames

† There were previous versions in 1924 and (as *Make Me a Star*) in 1932.

Mery per sempre
Italy   1988   106m   Telecolor
BFI/Numero Uno (Claudio Bonivento)

In Sicily, a new liberal teacher at a reform school tries to win over the tough and suspicious pupils.

Downbeat documentary-style movie that substitutes earnestness for art.

w Sandro Petraglia, Stefano Rulli   *novel* Aurello Grimaldi   *d* Marco Risi   *ph* Mauro Marchetti   *m* Giancarlo Bigazzi   *ad* Massimo Spano   *ed* Claudio Di Mauro

Michele Placido, Claudio Amendola, Francesco Benigno, Alessandro Di Sanzo

Mes Petites Amoureuses
France   1975   123m   Eastmancolor
Gala/Elite (Pierre Cottrell)

A sex-obsessed schoolboy finds life full of frustrations when he goes to live with his mother and her Spanish lover.

A long-winded exploration of adolescence, which offers no fresh insights.

wd Jean Eustache   *ph* Nestor Almendros   *ed* Françoise Belleville, Alberto Yacelini, Vincent Cottrell

Martin Loeb, Ingrid Caven, Jacqueline Dufranne, Dionys Mascolo, Henri Martinez, Pierre Edelman, Maurice Pialat

Mesa of Lost Women
US   1952   70m   bw
Wade Williams Productions/Howco (G. William Perkins, Melvin Gordon)

A scientist experiments in the Mexican desert to combine the qualities of beautiful women and spiders.

Bizarre B-movie, ineptly directed, with portentous voice-over, a score played by piano and guitar, and two mad scientists, one of them one-eyed, as well as scantily clad female assistants and dwarfs, operating from a laboratory carved into a mountainside. It also has what may be the least erotic would-be seductive dance on film.

w Herbert Tevos   *d* Herbert Tevos, Ron Ormond   *ph* Karl Strauss, Gil Warrenton   *m* Hoyt S. Curtin   *ed* W. Donn Hayes, Hugh Winn, Ray H. Lockert

Jackie Coogan, Allan Nixon, Richard Travis, Mary Hill, Robert Knapp, Tandra Quinn

The Message: see *Mohammed, Messenger of God*

A Message to Garcia *
US   1936   86m   bw
TCF (Raymond Griffith)

During the Spanish-American war a Cuban girl helps an American agent get through to the rebel leader with a diplomatic message.

Agreeable embroidery of a historical incident: good production values and entertaining star performances.

w W. P. Lipscomb, Gene Fowler   *book* Andrew S. Rohan   *d* George Marshall   *ph* Rudolph Maté   *m* Louis Silvers

Wallace Beery, Barbara Stanwyck, John Boles, Alan Hale, Herbert Mundin, Mona Barrie

'It's five miles wide ... It's coming at 30,000 mph ... and there's no place on Earth to hide!'

Meteor
US   1979   107m   Movielab   Panavision
Palladium (Sandy Howard, Gabriel Katzka)
V*

A huge meteor, preceded by dangerous fragments, heads relentlessly towards Earth . . .

Talkative disaster movie with occasional moments of interest.

w Stanley Mann, Edmund H. North   *d* Ronald Neame   *ph* Paul Lohmann   *m* Laurence Rosenthal   *visual effects* Margo Anderson, William Cruse

Sean Connery, Natalie Wood, Karl Malden, Brian Keith, Martin Landau, Trevor Howard, Henry Fonda, Joseph Campanella

'There are moments that make Godzilla look like a masterpiece.' – *Boxoffice*

The Meteor Man
US   1993   99m   DeLuxe
MGM/Tinsel Townsend (Loretha C. Jones)

A schoolteacher hit by a meteor acquires super-human powers and begins to clean up his gang-ridden neighbourhood.

Mild morality tale for our times, pleasant enough, but it lacks impact.

wd Robert Townsend   *ph* John A. Alonzo   *m* Cliff Eidelman   *pd* Toby Corbett   *sp* Industrial Light and Magic   *ed* Adam Bernardi

Robert Townsend, Marla Gibbs, Eddie Griffin, Robert Guillaume, James Earl Jones, Bill Cosby, Frank Gorshin

'A cute skit expanded out of all proportion for the big screen.' – *Variety*

'Townsend's good nature will win most audiences over.' – *Adam Mars-Jones*

Metropolis ***
Germany   1926   120m approx (24 fps) · bw   silent
UFA (Erich Pommer)
V, V*, L

In the year 2000, the workers in a modernistic city live underground and unrest is quelled by the persuasion of a saintly girl, Maria; but a mad inventor creates an evil Maria to incite them to revolt.

Always somewhat overlong, and certainly heavy-going in places, this futuristic fantasy not only has many brilliant sequences which created genuine excitement and terror, but it inspired a great many Hollywood clichés to come, notably the Frankenstein theme. The BBC's version of the seventies, with an electronic music sound track, is the most satisfactory.

w Thea von Harbou   *d* Fritz Lang   *ph* Karl Freund, Günther Rittau   *ad* Otto Hunte, Erich Kettelhut, Karl Volbrecht   *sp* Eugene Schufftan

Brigitte Helm, Alfred Abel, Gustav Fröhlich, Rudolf Klein-Rogge, Fritz Rasp

'It goes too far and always gets away with it.' – *New Yorker, 1978*

'A wonderful, stupefying folly.' – *New Yorker, 1982*

† In 1984 Giorgio Moroder put out his own new version, with tinted sequences and a re-edited running time of 83 minutes. It was received with a mixture of distaste, respect and caution. The latest version on video is 139m long.

Metropolitan *
US   1935   79m   bw
TCF (Darryl F. Zanuck)

A capricious prima donna walks out of the Metropolitan Opera and forms her own company.

Earnest and well-made melodrama with song; it earned critical plaudits but was a disappointment at the box-office.

w Bess Meredyth, George Marion Jnr   *d* Richard Boleslawski   *ph* Rudolph Maté   *md* Alfred Newman

Lawrence Tibbett, Alice Brady, Virginia Bruce, Cesar Romero, Thurston Hall, Luis Alberni

'Tibbett and exploitation should carry so-so operatic story into fair money.' – *Variety*

Metropolitan ***
US   1989   98m   DuArt
Mainline/Westerly Film-Video/Allagash Films (Whit Stillman)
V, V*, L, S

A left-wing student becomes a member of a group of rich young people intent on having a good time.

A conversation piece with wit and style to recommend it.

wd Whit Stillman   *ph* John Thomas   *m* Mark Suozzo, Tom Judson   *ed* Christopher Tellefsen

Carolyn Farina, Edward Clements, Christopher Eigeman, Taylor Nichols, Allison Rutledge-Parisi, Dylan Hundley, Isabel Gillies, Bryan Leder, Will Kempe

'A cast of attractive young newcomers plays out this ironic, arch, gently mocking and refreshingly original comedy with confident style.' – *David Robinson, The Times*

AAN: best original screenplay

Meurtres *
France   1950   91m   bw
Cité Film/Fides

A doctor's wife suffering from an incurable illness begs him to give her an overdose of morphia; he does so and proposes to give himself up for murder; his family, afraid of scandal, try to have him certified.

A distinct change of pace for a star comedian, and not an unsuccessful one, though the satire is rather crudely handled.

w Charles Plisnier and Maurice Barry   *d* Richard Pottier

Fernandel, Raymond Souplex, Jacques Varennes, Jeanne Moreau

Mexican Hayride
US   1948   77m   bw
Universal (Robert Arthur)
V*

Various swindlers come together at a Mexican bullfight.

A Cole Porter Broadway musical without the music makes an odd sort of vehicle for Abbott and Costello, but they inject a few good vaudeville gags.

w Oscar Brodney, John Grant   *play* Herbert and Dorothy Fields   *d* Charles Barton   *ph* Charles Van Enger

Bud Abbott, Lou Costello, Virginia Grey, John Hubbard, Pedro de Cordoba, Fritz Feld, Luba Malina

Mexican Manhunt
US   1953   73m   bw
Lindsley Parsons/AA

A detective helps solve an old crime.

Routine support which coasts along on the strength of its star.

w George Bricker   *d* Rex Bailey

George Brent, Hillary Brooke, Morris Ankrum, Karen Sharpe, Marjorie Lord

Mexican Spitfire

A series of second feature comedies nominally about a young businessman and his temperamental Mexican wife (Donald Woods and Lupe Velez), whose interest shifted firmly to the young man's accident-prone uncle Matt and his aristocratic boss Lord Epping, both of whom were played by the rubber-legged Ziegfeld comic Leon Errol at something near the top of his form. The plots made little sense, but the hectic situations provoked hearty roars of laughter. The films were all made by RKO, and all directed by Leslie Goodwins.

1939: THE GIRL FROM MEXICO, MEXICAN
    SPITFIRE
1940: MEXICAN SPITFIRE OUT WEST
1941: MEXICAN SPITFIRE'S BABY, MEXICAN
    SPITFIRE AT SEA
1942: MEXICAN SPITFIRE SEES A GHOST,
    MEXICAN SPITFIRE'S ELEPHANT
1943: MEXICAN SPITFIRE'S BLESSED EVENT

Mexicana
US   1945   83m   bw
Republic (Alfred Santell)

The Frank Sinatra of Mexico is beset by bobbysoxers.

Thin excuse for a moderate musical.

w Frank Gill Jnr   d Alfred Santell

Tito Guizar, Constance Moore, Leo Carrillo, Howard Freeman, Steve Geray, Estelita Rodriguez

MGM's Big Parade of Comedy: see *The Big Parade of Comedy*

Miami Blues **
US   1990   97m
Rank/Orion/Tristes Tropiques (Jonathan Demme, Gary Goetzman)
V, V*, L

A dogged policeman follows the trail of a murderous criminal who pretends to be an undercover cop.

Slick thriller with an undercurrent of lugubrious black humour.

wd George Armitage   novel Charles Willeford
ph Tak Fujimoto   m Gary Chang   pd Maher Ahmad   ed Craig McKay, Bill Johnson

Fred Ward, Jennifer Jason Leigh, Alec Baldwin, Cecilia Perez-Cervera, Georgie Cranford, Edward Saxon, Jose Perez, Obba Babatunde

'America's playground becomes gang war battleground!'
Miami Exposé
US   1956   74m   bw
Sam Katzman/Columbia

An undercover policeman cracks down on a vice operation.

Routine thick ear with more suspense than sense.

w James B. Gordon   d Fred F. Sears

Lee J. Cobb, Patricia Medina, Edward Arnold

The Miami Story
US   1954   75m   bw
Sam Katzman/Columbia

The syndicate is cracked by a reformed gangster.

Routine gangster alarms and excursions, like an extended Crime Does Not Pay.

w Robert E. Kent   d Fred F. Sears

Barry Sullivan, Luther Adler, John Baer, Adele Jergens, Beverly Garland

Michael and Mary
GB   1931   85m   bw
Gaumont

A husband thought dead for many years returns to disturb his wife's second marriage.

Acceptable comedy from a popular stage play; it headed its stars towards Hollywood.

w Angus MacPhail, Robert Stevenson and Lajos Biro play A. A. Milne   d Victor Saville

Herbert Marshall, Edna Best, Elizabeth Allan, Frank Lawton, D. A. Clarke-Smith

Michael Shayne

The private eye created by Brett Halliday was featured in several second features starring Lloyd Nolan, mostly Eugene Forde for Fox. They were adequate time-passers without too much sparkle.

1940: MICHAEL SHAYNE PRIVATE DETECTIVE
1941: DRESSED TO KILL, JUST OFF BROADWAY,
    THE MAN WHO WOULDN'T DIE
1942: TIME TO KILL (a version of Chandler's
    FAREWELL MY LOVELY), BLUE WHITE AND
    PERFECT

Michael Strogoff: see *The Soldier and the Lady*

The Michigan Kid
US   1947   70m   Cinecolor
Universal
V*

Several people hunt for treasure stolen from a stagecoach.

Lower-berth Western.

w Roy Chanslor   novel Rex Beach   d Ray Taylor

Jon Hall, Victor McLaglen, Rita Johnson, Andy Devine, Byron Foulger, Milburn Stone

Mickey One *
US   1965   93m   bw
Columbia/Florin/Tatira (Arthur Penn, Harrison Starr)
V*

A night-club entertainer runs away after an orgy to find some meaning in his life.

Obscure symbolic melodrama whose flashes of talent and interest needed firmer control.

w Alan Surgal   d Arthur Penn   ph Ghislain Cloquet   m Eddie Sauter   pd George Jenkins

Warren Beatty, Hurd Hatfield, Alexandra Stewart, Franchot Tone, Teddy Hart, Jeff Corey

'Arresting at first, it becomes more and more bogged down by its own pretensions, until one's main interest is simply in seeing it through.' – *MFB*

Mickey's Christmas Carol ***
US   1983   26m   Technicolor
Disney
V, V*, L

A cartoon version of Dickens with the parts played by familiar Disney characters; and a supreme re-establishment of the old Disney production values.

d Burney Mattinson

'For anyone over 35, this little jewel of a film is truly the Ghost of Christmas Past.' – *Gilbert Adair, MFB*

AAN: animated film

Micki and Maude *
US   1984   118m   Metrocolor   Panavision
Columbia/Delphi III/B.E.E. (Tony Adams)
V*, L

A TV show host accidentally gets his wife and his mistress pregnant at the same time.

Wild and overlong farce with some undeniably funnier scenes than have been noted in the participants' work for some years.

w Jonathan Reynolds   d Blake Edwards   ph Harry Stradling Jnr   m Lee Holdridge   pd Roger Maus   ed Ralph E. Winters

Dudley Moore, Amy Irving, Ann Reinking, Richard Mulligan, George Gaynes, Wallace Shawn, John Pleshette

Midas Run
US   1969   104m   Technicolor
Raymond Stross/MPI (Leon Chooluck)
GB title: *A Run on Gold*

An ageing secret service chief plans to hi-jack a bullion shipment.

Incompetently handled caper story with interest unwisely shifted for romantic purposes to the plotter's recruits.

w James D. Buchanan, Ronald Austin, Berne Giler   d Alf Kjellin   ph Ken Higgins   m Elmer Bernstein

Fred Astaire, Richard Crenna, Anne Heywood, Ralph Richardson, Roddy McDowall, Adolfo Celi, Maurice Denham, Cesar Romero

Middle Age Crazy
Canada   1980   91m   DeLuxe
Barber International/Sid & Marty Krofft/Robert Cooper & Ronald Cohen
V*

A 40-year-old husband begins to feel his age.

Mildly satirical sex comedy, all too easily forgotten among the rest.

w Carl Kleinschmitt   d John Trent   ph Reginald Morris   m Matthew McCauley   ad Jill Scott   ed John Kelly

Bruce Dern, Ann-Margret, Graham Jarvis, Eric Christmas

The Middle Man **
India   1975   131m   bw
Connoisseur/Indus (Subir Guha)
original title: *Jana-Aranya*

Unable to find a job in overcrowded Calcutta, a young graduate has no option but to set up as a small 'middle man', buying goods cheaply and selling them at a profit, and slips into acting as a pimp for his customers.

Satirical, cutting portrait of the moral corruption of an innocent, which produces some fine ensemble acting from its cast.

wd Satyajit Ray   novel Shankar   ph Soumendu Roy   m Satyajit Ray   ad Ashoke Bose   ed Dulal Dutt

Pradip Mukherji, Satya Bannerji, Dipankar Dey, Lily Chakravarti, Aparna Sen, Goutam Chakravarti, Sudeshna Das, Utpal Dutt

'Nothing can detract from the film's overall success and its penetrating charm.' – *MFB*

Middle of Nowhere: see *The Webster Boy*

Middle of the Night **
US   1959   118m   bw
Columbia (George Justin)

An elderly garment manufacturer falls in love with a young girl.

Serious and moving examination of a human predicament, shot against beautifully observed New York backgrounds.

w Paddy Chayevsky, from his TV play   d Delbert Mann   ph Joseph Brun   m George Bassman

Fredric March, Kim Novak, Glenda Farrell, Jan Norris, Lee Grant

'A work of greater cogency than his New York play script and of deeper maturity than his Marty.' – *Time*

'The best of the TV transformations into film.' – *Stanley Kauffmann*

The Middle Watch
GB   1930   112m   bw
BIP

Female guests on board ship have to be hidden from the captain.

Naval froth in primitive talkie form; absurdly long but popular.

w Norman Walker and Frank Launder   play Ian Hay and Stephen King-Hall   d Norman Walker

Owen Nares, Jacqueline Logan, Jack Raine, Dodo Watts, Reginald Purdell

† In 1940 ABPC made a smoother version with Jack Buchanan, Greta Gynt, David Hutcheson, Kay Walsh, Fred Emney and Reginald Purdell (in the same role); directed by Thomas Bentley.

Midnight

US   1934   80m   bw
Universal/All Star (Chester Erskine)
aka: *Call It Murder*

A jury foreman in a murder trial tips the scales in favour of guilty, but is haunted when his own daughter kills her lover.

Tepid family melodrama, very stagebound.

wd Chester Erskine   *play* Paul and Claire Sifton   *ph* William Steiner

Sidney Fox, O. P. Heggie, Henry Hull, Humphrey Bogart, Margaret Wycherly, Lynne Overman, Richard Whorf, Cora Witherspoon

'It's pretty strong stuff and will hold audiences once they're in . . . but it's not a good adaptation and is badly dialogued.' – *Variety*

Midnight ***

US   1939   95m   bw
Paramount (Arthur Hornblow Jnr)

A girl stranded in Paris is hired by an aristocrat to seduce the gigolo paying unwelcome attention to his wife.

Sparkling sophisticated comedy which barely flags until a slightly disappointing ending; all the talents involved are in excellent form.

w Billy Wilder, Charles Brackett   *story* Edwin Justus Mayer, Franz Schultz   *d Mitchell Leisen*   *ph* Charles Lang   *m* Frederick Hollander

Claudette Colbert, Don Ameche, John Barrymore, Francis Lederer, Mary Astor, Elaine Barrie, Hedda Hopper, Rex O'Malley

'Leisen's masterpiece, one of the best comedies of the thirties.' – *John Baxter, 1968*

'One of the authentic delights of the thirties.' – *New Yorker, 1976*

'It has the elements of an American *La Règle du Jeu.*' – *John Gillett*

'Just about the best light comedy ever caught by the camera.' – *Motion Picture Daily*

Midnight

US   1989   86m   colour
SVS/Kuys Entertainment/Gomillion (Norman Thaddeus Vane, Gloria J. Morrison)
V*, L

The hostess of a horror movie show on TV is targeted by a murderer.

Occasionally amusing spoof of horror films, though too stately to create any tension on its own account.

wd Norman Thaddeus Vane   *ph* David Golia   *m* Michael Weatherwax   *ad* Mark Simon   *ed* Sam Adelman

Lynn Redgrave, Tony Curtis, Steve Parrish, Rita Gam, Gustav Vintas, Karen Witter, Frank Gorshin

Midnight at Madame Tussauds

GB   1936   74m   bw
Premier

For a bet, an explorer spends the night in a waxworks Chamber of Horrors.

Tepid thriller, done in a stilted manner.

w Kim Peacock   *story* James S. Edwards, Roger MacDougall   *d* George Pearson   *ph* Jimmy Berger   *ad* Donald Russell   *ed* E. D. G. Pilkington

James Carew, Charles Oliver, Lucille Lisle, Kim Peacock, Patrick Barr, Billy Hartnell, Lydia Sherwood, Bernard Miles

'At the frontlines of life, near the end of innocence, came the beginning of manhood.'

A Midnight Clear **

US   1992   107m   CFI colour
Sovereign/Beacon/A&M (Dale Pollock, Bill Borden)
V, V*, L

In the Ardennes Forest in 1944, a reconnaissance patrol composed of young and reluctant American soldiers goes disastrously wrong.

Effectively low-key, quietly ironic tale of the idiocies of war.

wd Keith Gordon   *novel* William Wharton   *ph* Tom Richmond   *m* Mark Isham   *pd* David Nichols   *ed* Don Brochu

Peter Berg, Kevin Dillon, Arye Gross, Ethan Hawke, Gary Sinise, Frank Whaley, John C. McGinley

'An extremely well-crafted and entirely absorbing movie.' – *Philip Thomas, Empire*

Midnight Club

US   1933   65m   bw
Paramount

An American detective in London nabs a jewel gang.

Very tolerable smart-set crime melodrama.

w Seton I. Miller, Leslie Charteris   *story* E. Phillips Oppenheim   *d* Alexander Hall

Clive Brook, George Raft, Helen Vinson, Alison Skipworth, Sir Guy Standing, Alan Mowbray

'Its London manners and locale lend it a polish which should renew interest in this school of celluloid melodramatics.' – *Variety*

'To tell you the truth, I ain't a real cowboy. But I'm one helluva stud!'

Midnight Cowboy ****

US   1969   113m   DeLuxe
UA/Jerome Hellman
V, V*, L, S

A slightly dim-witted Texan comes to New York to offer his services as a stud for rich ladies, but spends a hard winter helping a tubercular con man.

Life in the New York gutter, brilliantly if not too accurately observed by a master showman with no heart.

w Waldo Salt   *novel* James Leo Herlihy   *d* John Schlesinger   *ph* Adam Holender   *md* John Barry   *pd* John Robert Lloyd

Jon Voight, Dustin Hoffman, Brenda Vaccaro, Sylvia Miles, John McGiver

'If only Schlesinger's directorial self-discipline had matched his luminous sense of scene and his extraordinary skill in handling actors, this would have been a far more considerable film.' – *Arthur Schlesinger Jnr (no relation)*

'A great deal besides cleverness, a great deal of good feeling and perception and purposeful dexterity.' – *Stanley Kauffmann*

AA: best picture; Waldo Salt; John Schlesinger

AAN: Dustin Hoffman; Jon Voight; Sylvia Miles

Midnight Crossing

US   1987   104m   Technicolor
Vestron/Team Effort/Limelite Studios (Mathew Hayden)
V*, L

An insurance agent returns to a small Caribbean island to retrieve stolen treasure.

Glossily empty, often hysterical thriller that never rises above the ordinary.

w Roger Holzberg, Doug Weiser   *d* Roger Holzberg   *ph* Henry Vargas   *m* Paul Buckmaster, Al Gorgoni   *pd* José Duarte   *ed* Earl Watson

Faye Dunaway, Daniel J. Travanti, Kim Cattrall, Ned Beatty, John Laughlin

Midnight Episode

GB   1950   78m   bw
Columbia/Triangle (Thomas Lageard)

An old busker stumbles over a dead body and a lot of money.

Tame British version of Raimu's French success *Monsieur La Souris,* saved only by its star performance.

w Rita Barisse, Reeve Taylor, Paul Vincent Carroll, David Evans, William Templeton   *d* Gordon Parry   *ph* Hone Glendinning

Stanley Holloway, Natasha Parry, Leslie Dwyer, Reginald Tate, Meredith Edwards, Wilfrid Hyde-White, Joy Shelton

Midnight Express **

GB   1978   121m   Eastmancolor
Columbia/Casablanca (Alan Marshall, David Puttnam)
V, V*, L, S

Tribulations of an American student arrested in Turkey for carrying hashish.

Misleadingly-tilted wallow in prison atrocities, extremely well made but certainly not entertaining and with little discernible point.

w Oliver Stone   *memoir* Billy Hayes   *d* Alan Parker   *ph* Michael Seresin   *m* Giorgio Moroder

Brad Davis, Randy Quaid, John Hurt, Irene Miracle, Bo Hopkins

'One of the ugliest sado-masochistic trips, with heavy homosexual overtones, that our thoroughly nasty movie age has yet produced.' – *Richard Schickel, Time*

'The film details all [the horrors] so relentlessly on one screaming note that it is rather like being hit in the gut until you no longer feel a thing.' – *Derek Malcolm, Guardian*

'Muted squalor with a disco beat in the background, all packaged as social protest.' – *New Yorker, 1982*

AA: script; music

AAN: best picture; Alan Parker; John Hurt

Midnight Lace *

US   1960   108m   Eastmancolor
Universal (Ross Hunter, Martin Melcher)

The wife of a rich Londoner is terrorized by threatening phone calls and voices in the fog.

Thoroughly silly rehash of *Gaslight* and *The Boy Who Cried Wolf;* its glamorous accoutrements can't fight a lack of humour or predictable plot development.

w Ivan Goff, Ben Roberts   *play Matilda Shouted Fire* by Janet Green   *d* David Miller   *ph* Russell Metty   *m* Frank Skinner

Doris Day, Rex Harrison, John Gavin, Myrna Loy, Roddy McDowall, Herbert Marshall, Natasha Parry, John Williams, Anthony Dawson, Hermione Baddeley, Richard Ney, Rhys Williams, Doris Lloyd

Midnight Madonna

US   1937   56m   bw
Paramount

There is a legal fight for custody of a child who has inherited a fortune.

Efficient programmer built around a new child actress, Kitty Clancy, who didn't take.

w Doris Malloy, Gladys Lehman   *d* James Flood

Warren William, Mady Correll, Edward Ellis, Robert Baldwin, Jonathan Hale

'It will be found fairly entertaining by the family trade.' – *Variety*

The Midnight Man

US   1974   117m   Technicolor
Universal/Norlan (Roland Kibbee, Burt Lancaster)

An ex-cop, paroled after killing his wife's lover, takes a job as security guard and runs into a murder case.

Muddled mystery with pretentious characterization and bouts of violence.

wd Roland Kibbee, Burt Lancaster novel The Midnight Lady and the Mourning Man by David Anthony ph Jack Priestley m Dave Grusin

Burt Lancaster, Susan Clark, Cameron Mitchell, Morgan Woodward, Harris Yulin, Robert Quarry, Joan Lorring, Lawrence Dobkin, Ed Lauter

'A thriller that has the impenetrability of Chandler but none of the flavour.' – Tom Milne

'Efficient enough but lifeless, and burdened with portentous sentiments about solitude, violence and the nature of the beast.' – Sight and Sound

Midnight Mary
US   1933   76m   bw
MGM

A gangster's moll on trial for her life thinks back to her past.

Intolerable now, but a hit of its year despite star miscasting.

w Gene Markey and Anita Loos   d William Wellman

Loretta Young, Ricardo Cortez, Franchot Tone, Una Merkel, Andy Devine, Harold Huber

Midnight Melody: see Murder in the Music Hall

Midnight Patrol *
US   1933   20m   bw
Hal Roach
V

Incompetent policemen arrest their own chief as a burglar.

Good standard star slapstick.

w uncredited   d Lloyd French

Laurel and Hardy, Charlie Hall, Walter Plinge

Midnight Run **
US   1988   126m   colour
UIP/Universal (Martin Brest)
V, V*, L

A bounty hunter tries to bring in an embezzler, despite attempts by rivals, gangsters and the FBI to stop him.

Fast-paced action comedy, full of quick-fire wit and graced by some excellent performances.

w George Gallo   d Martin Brest   ph Donald Thorin   m Danny Elfman   pd Angelo Graham   ed Billy Weber, Chris Lebenzon, Michael Tronick

Robert de Niro, Charles Grodin, Yaphet Kotto, John Ashton, Dennis Farina, Joe Pantoliano

Midnight Sting: see Diggstown

Midnight Taxi
US   1937   73m   bw
TCF

A G-man becomes a taxi driver to rout a gang of counterfeiters.

Competent, predictable crime programmer.

w Lou Breslow, John Patrick   d Eugene Forde

Brian Donlevy, Frances Drake, Alan Dinehart, Sig Rumann, Gilbert Roland, Harold Huber, Lon Chaney Jnr

The Midshipmaid
GB   1932   84m   bw
Gaumont
US title: Midshipmaid Gob

A naval commander loves the daughter of a politician out to effect navy cuts.

Very modest comedy with music, a key step in the star's success story.

w Ian Hay and Stephen King-Hall   play Ian Hay and Stephen King-Hall   d Albert de Courville

Jessie Matthews, Frederick Kerr, Basil Sydney, Nigel Bruce, Claud Allister, John Mills, George Zucco

Midshipman Easy
GB   1935   77m   bw
ATP (Basil Dean, Thorold Dickinson)
US title: Men of the Sea

In 1790, young naval officers rescue a girl from Spanish bandits.

Stilted adventure story with interesting credits.

w Anthony Kimmins   novel Frederick Marryat   d Carol Reed   ph John W. Boyle

Hughie Green, Margaret Lockwood, Harry Tate, Robert Adams, Roger Livesey, Lewis Casson

'Three centuries in the making!'
A Midsummer Night's Dream ***
US   1935   133m   bw
Warner (Max Reinhardt)
V*, L

Two pairs of lovers sort out their problems with fairy help at midnight in the woods of Athens.

Shakespeare's play is treated with remarkable respect in this super-glamorous Hollywood adaptation based on the Broadway production by Max Reinhardt. Much of it comes off, and visually it's a treat.

w Charles Kenyon, Mary McCall Jnr   play William Shakespeare   d Max Reinhardt, William Dieterle   ph Hal Mohr, Fred Jackman, Byron Haskin, H. F. Koenekamp   md Erich Wolfgang Korngold   ch Bronislawa Nijinska   m Mendelssohn   ad Anton Grot   ed Ralph Dawson

James Cagney, Dick Powell, Jean Muir, Ross Alexander, Olivia de Havilland, Joe E. Brown, Hugh Herbert, Arthur Treacher, Frank McHugh, Otis Harlan, Dewey Robinson, Victor Jory, Verree Teasdale, Mickey Rooney, Anita Louise, Grant Mitchell, Ian Hunter, Hobart Cavanaugh

'General b.o. chances could be improved by judicious pruning and appreciative selling . . . a fine prestige picture not only for Warners but for the industry as a whole.' – Variety

'You must see it if you want to be in a position to argue about the future of the film!' – Picturegoer

'The publicity push behind the film is tremendous – it is going to be a success or everyone at Warner Brothers is going to get fired.' – Robert Forsythe

'Its assurance as a work of film technique is undoubted.' – John Baxter, 1968

'Its worst contradiction lies in the way Warners first ordered up a whole batch of foreign and high-sounding names to handle music, dances, general production – and then turned around and handed them empty vessels for actors.' – Otis Ferguson

AA: photography; editing

AAN: best picture

A Midsummer Night's Sex Comedy *
US   1982   88m   Technicolor
Warner/Orion/Rollins-Joffe (Robert Greenhut)
V, V*

Around the turn of the century, a Wall Street broker expects various weekend guests at his country retreat.

Subdued, melancholy and rather uninventive Woody Allen variation on Smiles of a Summer Night.

wd Woody Allen   ph Gordon Willis   m from Mendelssohn   pd Mel Bourne   ed Susan E. Morse

Woody Allen, Mia Farrow, José Ferrer, Julie Hagerty, Tony Roberts, Mary Steenburgen

Midway *
US   1976   131m   Technicolor   Panavision   Sensurround
Universal/Mirisch Corporation (Walter Mirisch)
V, V*, L
GB title: The Battle of Midway

The tide turns for the Americans when the Japanese attack the Pacific island of Midway in 1942.

Noisy flagwaver with confused strategy and too many stars in small parts.

w Donald S. Sanford   d Jack Smight   ph Harry Stradling Jnr   m John Williams

Charlton Heston, Henry Fonda, Robert Mitchum, Glenn Ford, Edward Albert, James Coburn, Hal Holbrook, Toshiro Mifune, Robert Wagner, Robert Webber, Ed Nelson, James Shigeta, Monte Markham, Christopher George, Glenn Corbett

'We are over-informed about the movements of every ship and plane, under-informed about how the battle was finally won, and positively swamped with tedious human interest.' – Sight and Sound

The Mighty Barnum *
US   1934   87m   bw
Twentieth Century (Darryl F. Zanuck)

A fictionalized biopic of the great showman of the 1890s.

Lively without being very memorable.

w Gene Fowler, Bess Meredyth   play Gene Fowler, Bess Meredyth   d Walter Lang   ph Peverell Marley   m Alfred Newman

Wallace Beery, Virginia Bruce, Adolphe Menjou, Janet Beecher, Rochelle Hudson

The Mighty Ducks
US   1992   101m   Technicolor   Panavision
Buena Vista/Walt Disney (Jordan Kerner, Jon Avnet)
V, V*
GB title: Champions; video title: The Mighty Ducks Are Champions

A lawyer doing community service for drunk driving turns a group of drop-out kids into a winning hockey team.

Simple-minded and sentimental movie hymning the joys of team spirit.

w Steven Brill   d Stephen Herek   ph Thomas Del Ruth   m David Newman   pd Randy Ser   ed Larry Bock, John F. Link

Emilio Estevez, Joss Ackland, Lane Smith, Heidi King, Josef Sommer, Joshua Jackson

'A formulaic pic meant for children but actually focusing on a yuppie's struggle for redemption. Mildly entertaining but unexciting.' – Variety

'The ten most terrific thrills ever pictured!'
Mighty Joe Young *
US   1949   94m   bw
RKO (Merian C. Cooper)
V*, L

A little girl brings back from Africa a pet gorilla which grows to enormous size and causes a city to panic.

Rather tired comic-sentimental follow-up to King Kong, with a tedious plot and variable animation but a few endearing highlights.

w Ruth Rose   d Ernest Schoedsack   ph J. Roy Hunt   m Roy Webb   sp Willis O'Brien, Ray Harryhausen

Terry Moore, Ben Johnson, Robert Armstrong, Frank McHugh, Douglas Fowley

The Mighty McGurk
US   1946   83m   bw
Nat Perrin/MGM

In the Bowery in the 1890s, a bragging ex-fighter takes in a small boy.

Sentimental melodrama which unspools like a joint remake of *The Champ* and *The Bowery*.

w William H. Lipman, Grant Garrett, Harry Clork d John Waters

Wallace Beery, Dean Stockwell, Edward Arnold, Aline MacMahon, Cameron Mitchell, Aubrey Mather

The Mighty Quinn
US 1989 98m colour
UIP/MGM/Star partners II/A & M Films (Sandy Lieberson, Marion Hunt, Ed Elbert)
V*, L

On a Caribbean island, the police chief investigates the murder of an American.

Routine thriller offering little in the way of suspense or excitement.

w Hampton Fancher novel *Finding Maubee* by A. H. Z. Carr d Carl Shenkel ph Jacques Steyn m Anne Dudley pd Roger Murray-Leach ed John Jympson

Denzel Washington, James Fox, Mimi Rogers, M. Emmet Walsh, Sheryl Lee Ralph, Art Evans, Esther Rolle, Norman Beaton, Alex Colon

'A spy thriller, a buddy movie, a musical, a comedy, and a picture that is wise about human nature. And yet with all of those qualities, it never seems to strain. This is a graceful, almost charmed, entertainment.' – *Roger Ebert*

Mighty Ursus: see *Ursus*

The Mighty Warrior: see *The Vengeance of Ursus*

Mignon Has Left **
Italy/France 1988 90m Eastmancolor
Metro/Ellepi Film/Chrysalide Film/RAI/RAITRE (Leo Pescarolo, Guido de Laurentiis)
original title: *Mignon è Partita*

Adolescent traumas come to a head in a Rome household when their French cousin comes to stay.

A slight but charming study of children in the transition to adulthood, much admired by Continental audiences.

w Francesca Archibugi, Gloria Malatesta, Claudia Sbarigia d Francesca Archibugi ph Luigi Verga m Roberto Gatto, Battista Lena ad Massimo Spano ed Alfredo Muschietti

Stefania Sandelli, Jean-Pierre Duriez, Leonardo Ruta, Celine Beauvallet, Francesca Antonelli, Lorenzo de Pasqua, Eleonora Sambiagio, Daniele Zaccaria

The Mikado *
GB 1939 91m Technicolor
GFD/G and S (Geoffrey Toye, Joseph Somlo)

In Japan, a timid official is appointed Lord High Executioner and finds that his first intended victim is the Emperor's son, travelling incognito.

Agreeable film version of the classic Gilbert and Sullivan comic opera, with some of the D'Oyly Carte Company's most celebrated members in excellent form.

w Geoffrey Toye opera W. S. Gilbert d Victor Schertzinger ph Bernard Knowles m Arthur Sullivan

Martyn Green, John Barclay, Sydney Granville, Kenny Baker, Jean Colin, Constance Willis

'An odd film that pulls this way and that way and never quite gets anywhere. On the credit side must be put down the colour and the music.' – *C. A. Lejeune*

† The 1966 version by British Home Entertainment featured a later D'Oyly Carte company including John Reed but suffered from a frozen camera and flat lighting, so that little of the original vivacity and charm came over

Mike's Murder
US 1984 97m Technicolor
Warner/Ladd Company/Skyeway
V, V*

A bank teller decides to investigate the killing of the man she loved, an unstable, bisexual drug-dealer and tennis coach.

A turn-off: a combination of an unlikely narrative, a mediocre script, sleazy characters and indifferent performances.

wd James Bridges ph Reynaldo Villalobos m John Barry, Joe Jackson pd Peter Jamison ed Jeff Gourson, Dede Allen

Debra Winger, Mark Keyloun, Darrell Larson, Brooke Alderson, Paul Winfield, Daniel Shor

Mikey and Nicky
US 1976 118m colour
Paramount (Michael Hausman)
V*

Two crooks are old friends, but one has been hired to kill the other . . .

Intolerable improvisatory sentimental melodrama. Who on earth shells out the money for pictures like this?

wd Elaine May ph Victor Kemper m John Strauss

Peter Falk, John Cassavetes, Ned Beatty, Sanford Meisner, Rose Arrick, Joyce Van Patten

'An impenetrable, ugly and almost unendurable mess.' – *Frank Rich, New York Post*

'A pretext for Falk and Cassavetes to indulge in one of those long, lugubrious Actors' Studio exercises that wore out its welcome with the last frame of *Husbands* and the first frame of *The Killing of a Chinese Bookie*.' – *Molly Haskell, Village Voice*

The Milagro Beanfield War
US 1988 118m MGM color
Universal (Robert Redford)
V, V*, L

Impoverished farmers in New Mexico defy developers who try to take over their land.

Serious issues treated with quirky humour and visual lyricism.

w David Ward, John Nichols book John Nichols d Robert Redford ph Robbie Greenberg m Dave Grusin ad Joe Aubel

Ruben Blades, Richard Bradford, Sonia Braga, Julie Carmen, James Gammon, John Heard, M. Emmet Walsh

'A very peculiar mixture of warmed-over movie conventions.' – *MFB*

AA: Dave Grusin

'The kind of woman most men want . . . and shouldn't have!'
Mildred Pierce **
US 1945 113m bw
Warner (Jerry Wald)
V*, L

A dowdy housewife breaks with her husband, becomes the owner (through hard work) of a restaurant chain, and survives a murder case before true love comes her way.

A woman's picture *par excellence*, glossily and moodily photographed, with a star suffering in luxury on behalf of the most ungrateful daughter of all time.

w Ranald MacDougall, Catherine Turney novel James M. Cain d Michael Curtiz ph Ernest Haller m Max Steiner ad Anton Grot

Joan Crawford, Jack Carson, Zachary Scott, *Eve Arden*, Ann Blyth, Bruce Bennett, George Tobias, Lee Patrick, Moroni Olsen

'Constant, lambent, virulent attention to money and its effects, and more authentic suggestions of sex than one hopes to see in American films.' – *James Agee*

AA: Joan Crawford

AAN: best picture; script; Ernest Haller; Eve Arden; Ann Blyth

Miles from Home *
US 1988 108m DeLuxe
Fox/Braveworld/Cinemcom/J & M Entertainment (Frederick Zollo, Paul Kurta)
V, V*, L

Facing hard times, two brothers burn down their farm and take to the road.

Unconventional road movie with some interesting moments.

w Chris Gerolmo d Gary Sinise ph Elliot Davis m Robert Folk pd David Gropman ed Jane Schwartz Jaffe

Richard Gere, Kevin Anderson, Brian Dennehy, Jason Campbell, Austin Bamgarner, Larry Poling, Terry Kinney, Penelope Ann Miller, Helen Hunt, John Malkovich

Military Policeman: see *Off Limits*

Milk and Honey
Canada 1988 95m colour
Zenith/JA Film (Peter O'Brian)

In an attempt to improve her life, a Jamaican woman leaves her home and young son to work in Canada as a nanny.

Moderate domestic drama, given a little fillip by the novelty of its subject matter.

w Glen Salzman, Trevor Rhone d Rebecca Yates, Glen Salzman ph Guy Dufaux m Mickey Erbe, Maribeth Solomon ad François Seguin ed Bruce Nyznik

Josette Simon, Lyman Ward, Djanet Sears, Fiona Reid, Leonie Forbes, Richard Mills

The Milkman
US 1950 87m bw
Universal-International (Ted Richmond)

Two milkmen tangle with gangsters.

Odd little comedy which gets the benefit of the doubt more by bringing its stars together than by giving them anything to do.

w Albert Beich, James O'Hanlon, Martin Ragaway, Leonard Stern d Charles Barton ph Clifford Stine m Milton Rosen

Donald O'Connor, Jimmy Durante, Joyce Holden, Piper Laurie, William Conrad, Paul Harvey, Henry O'Neill

The Milky Way *
US 1936 88m bw
Paramount/Harold Lloyd (Edward Sheldon)
V*, L

A milkman becomes a prizefighter and overcomes a gang of crooks.

Modest Harold Lloyd comedy towards the end of his career; remade as *The Kid from Brooklyn* (qv).

w Grover Jones, Frank Butler, Richard Connell play Lynn Root, Harry Clork d Leo McCarey ph Alfred Gilks

Harold Lloyd, Adolphe Menjou, Verree Teasdale, Helen Mack, William Gargan, George Barbier, Lionel Stander

'The work of many hands, all laid on expertly.' – *Otis Ferguson*

'One is more amazed than ever at the good fortune of this youngish man whose chief talent is not to act at all, to do nothing, to serve as a blank wall for other people to scrawl their ideas on.' – *Graham Greene*

The Milky Way *

France/Italy 1968 102m Eastmancolor
Greenwich/Medusa (Serge Silberman)
V, V*, L
original title: *La Voie Lactée*

Two tramps set off on pilgrimage from Paris to a
Spanish shrine, and have various surprising
encounters.

A picaresque examination of Catholic doctrine, full of
surface interest but requiring special knowledge for
full appreciation.

w Luis Buñuel, Jean-Claude Carrière *d* Luis Buñuel
ph Christian Matras *m* Luis Buñuel

Laurent Terzieff, Paul Frankeur, Delphine Seyrig,
Edith Scon

'A mere trifle wrapped in a triple cloak of befuddling
obscurantism.' – *John Simon*

The Mill on the Floss

GB 1937 94m bw
Morgan/National Provincial
V*

A Victorian mill owner and the lord of the manor start
a family feud which ends in tragedy.

Romeo and Juliet in crinolines; a stilted and
unpersuasive film of the book.

w John Drinkwater, Garnett Weston, Austin Melford,
Tim Whelan *novel* George Eliot *d* Tim Whelan

Geraldine Fitzgerald, Frank Lawton, James Mason,
Victoria Hopper, Fay Compton, Griffith Jones, Mary
Clare, Athene Seyler, Felix Aylmer

'A series of stiff little sequences, decorously posed.' –
New York Times.

Millennium

US 1989 105m DeLuxe
Rank/First Millennium Partnership/Gladden Entertainment
   (Douglas Leiterman, Robert Vince)
V, V*, L

The investigator of a mid-air collision of two planes
discovers that people from the future are involved.

Implausible time travel story that never holds
together or keeps an audience's interest.

w John Varley *story* Air Raid by John Varley
d Michael Anderson *ph* Rene Ohashi *pd* Gene
Rudolf *ed* Ron Wisman

Kris Kristofferson, Cheryl Ladd, Daniel J. Travanti,
Robert Joy, Lloyd Bochner, Brent Carver, David
McIlwraith, Maury Chaykin, Al Waxman

Miller's Crossing **

US 1990 115m DuArt
Fox/Circle Films/Ted and Jim Pedas/Ben Barenholtz/Bill Durkin
   (Ethan Coen)
V, V*, L, S

The duplicitous aide to a corrupt and powerful
politician is caught in the crossfire between two rival
gangsters.

Sombre, solidly made thriller, directed with a
macabre skill.

w Joel Coen, Ethan Coen *d* Joel Coen *ph* Barry
Sonnenfeld *m* Carter Burwell *pd* Dennis Gassner
ed Michael Miller

Gabriel Byrne, Marcia Gay Harden, John Turturro,
Jon Polito, J. E. Freeman, Albert Finney, Mike Starr,
Al Mancini, Richard Woods

Le Million ****

France 1931 89m bw
Tobis (Frank Clifford)

An artist and an ingratiating crook search Paris for a
lost lottery ticket.

With its delicate touch, perfect sense of comedy
timing and infectious use of recitative and song, this is

superb screen entertainment using most of the
medium's resources.

wd René Clair *musical comedy* Georges Berr, M.
Guillemaud *ph* Georges Périnal *m* Georges Van
Parys, Armand Bernard, Philippe Parès *ad* Lazare
Meerson

Annabella, René Lefèvre, *Paul Olivier*, Louis Allibert,
Vanda Gréville, Raymond Cordy

'A good musical farce that ought to do well
everywhere . . . it has speed, laughs, splendid
photography and a good cast.' – *Variety*

'René Clair at his exquisite best; no one else has ever
been able to make a comedy move with such delicate
inevitability.' – *New Yorker, 1978*

'I wanted an atmosphere of foolishness . . . we put
gauze between the actors and the sets, which created
an illusion of unreality.' – *René Clair*

† The style of this film was developed and expanded
in Hollywood by Lubitsch in *One Hour with You* and by
Mamoulian in *Love Me Tonight*.

Million Dollar Baby

US 1941 100m bw
Warner (Hal B. Wallis, David Lewis)

A girl inherits a fortune and a lot of problems.

Very predictable but sometimes sprightly comedy
with a hard-working cast.

w Richard Macaulay, Jerry Wald, Casey Robinson
story Miss Wheelwright Discovers America by Leonard
Spigelgass *d* Curtis Bernhardt *ph* Charles Rosher
m Max Steiner

Priscilla Lane, Jeffrey Lynn, Ronald Reagan, May
Robson, Lee Patrick, Helen Westley, George Barbier,
John Qualen, Walter Catlett, Nan Wynn

Million Dollar Duck

US 1971 92m Technicolor
Walt Disney (Bill Anderson)

A duck lays eggs with solid gold yolks, which
provoke interest from gangsters as well as the
government.

Minor Disney fantasy borrowed without permission
from *Mr Drake's Duck* (qv).

w Roswell Rogers *d* Vincent McEveety
ph William Snyder *m* Buddy Baker

Dean Jones, Sandy Duncan, Joe Flynn, Tony Roberts

'Roaring laughs in a story built of goofer dust and frog fur!'

Million Dollar Legs *

US 1932 64m bw
Paramount

A mythical sport-ridden country decides to enter the
Olympic Games.

The good gags in this film are weighted down by
plodding treatment, and the general effect is more
doleful than funny.

w Harry Myers, Nick Barrows, Joseph L. Mankiewicz
d Edward Cline *ph* Arthur Todd

W. C. Fields, Jack Oakie, Andy Clyde, Lyda Roberti,
Ben Turpin, Hugh Herbert, Billy Gilbert, George
Barbier, Susan Fleming

'One of the silliest and funniest pictures ever made.' –
New Yorker, 1977

Million Dollar Legs

US 1939 59m bw
Paramount

College students back a favourite horse.

Very modest collegiate comedy.

w Lewis Foster, Richard English *d* Nick Grinde
ph Harry Fischbeck

Betty Grable, John Hartley, Donald O'Connor, Jackie
Coogan, Buster Crabbe, Thurston Hall

Million Dollar Mermaid *

US 1952 115m Technicolor
MGM (Arthur Hornblow Jnr)
V*
GB title: *The One Piece Bathing Suit*

The story of Australian swimmer Annette Kellerman.

Inaccurate biopic with a *raison d'être* in its spectacular
aquashow scenes, but nothing at all new in its script.

w Everett Freeman *d* Mervyn Le Roy *ph* George
J. Folsey *md* Adolph Deutsch *ch* Busby Berkeley

Esther Williams, Victor Mature, Walter Pidgeon, David
Brian, Jesse White, Maria Tallchief, Howard Freeman

AAN: George J. Folsey

Million Dollar Mystery: see *Money Mania*

Million Dollar Ransom

US 1934 67m bw
Universal

A racketeer consolidates his family affairs before
being bumped off by his gang.

Slightly odd underworld melodrama, interesting but
not very satisfying.

w William R. Lipman, Ben Ryan *story* Damon
Runyon *d* Murray Roth

Edward Arnold, Phillips Holmes, Mary Carlisle, Wini
Shaw, Andy Devine

'Lacks names but offers fair possibilities.' – *Variety*

The Million Pound Note *

GB 1954 91m Technicolor
GFD/Group Films (John Bryan)
US title: *Man with a Million*

A man is given a million pounds in the form of a
single banknote and finds it difficult to spend.

Fairly pleasing period comedy which wears its one
joke pretty thin but is nicely decorated and acted.

w Jill Craigie *story* Mark Twain *d* Ronald Neame
ph Geoffrey Unsworth *m* William Alwyn

Gregory Peck, Jane Griffiths, Ronald Squire, Joyce
Grenfell, A. E. Matthews, Reginald Beckwith, Hartley
Power, Wilfrid Hyde-White

The Millionaire *

US 1931 80m bw
Warner

A bored millionaire retires and secretly buys a garage.

Fairly deft star comedy which well satisfied
Depression audiences.

w Julien Josephson and Booth Tarkington
story Earl Derr Biggers *d* John Adolfi

George Arliss, Florence Arliss, Evalyn Knapp, David
Manners, Noah Beery, J. Farrell MacDonald, James
Cagney

'Should bring Arliss within mental reach of all
theatres . . . Should enjoy a substantial career.' –
Variety

† Remade in 1947 as *That Way with Women* (qv)

A Millionaire for Christy

US 1951 91m bw
TCF (Bert Friedlob)

A lawyer's secretary is sent to Los Angeles to inform
an heir of his good fortune, and decides to marry him.

Modest romantic comedy with plenty to be modest
about.

w Ken Englund *d* George Marshall *ph* Harry
Stradling *m* Victor Young

Eleanor Parker, Fred MacMurray, Richard Carlson,
Douglass Dumbrille

Millionaire Merry Go Round: see *Kicking the
Moon Around*

'From naughty, notorious George Bernard Shaw, the sultry story of the beautiful babe in the Balmain gowns who pants for romance . . . !'

The Millionairess *

GB   1960   90m   DeLuxe   Cinemascope
TCF/Dimitri de Grunwald (Pierre Rouve)
V*

The richest woman in the world falls for a poor Indian doctor.

Messy travesty of a Shavian comedy that was never more than a star vehicle to begin with. Hardly any of it works despite the star cast, who are mostly miscast.

w Wolf Mankowitz   play Bernard Shaw
d Anthony Asquith   ph Jack Hildyard   m Georges Van Parys

Sophia Loren, Peter Sellers, Alastair Sim, Vittorio de Sica, Dennis Price, Gary Raymond, Alfie Bass, Miriam Karlin, Noel Purcell

'The result, lacking any sort of dramatic cohesion or continuity and seemingly planned less as a film than as a series of haphazard effects, is merely tiring.' – Peter John Dyer

Millions

GB   1936   70m   bw
Herbert Wilcox

A struggling composer is really the son of a millionaire.

Fairly lively comedy of rival self-made men.

w Michael Barringer   d Leslie Hiscott

Gordon Harker, Frank Pettingell, Richard Hearne, Jane Carr

Millions in the Air

US   1935   72m   bw
Harold Hurley/Paramount

Complications of a radio amateur contest.

Scrappy comedy with more historical interest than entertainment value.

w Sig Herzig, Jane Storm   d Ray McCarey

Willie Howard, John Howard, Robert Cummings, Inez Courtney, Benny Baker, Dave Chasen, Wendy Barrie, Samuel S. Hinds

'Without a substantial monicker in the cast, it hasn't much to offer at the box office.' – Variety

Millions like Us **

GB   1943   103m   bw
GFD/Gainsborough (Edward Black)

The tribulations of a family in wartime, especially of the meek daughter who goes into war work and marries an airman, who is killed.

Fragmentary but reasonably accurate picture of the Home Front during World War II; a little more humour would not have been out of place, but as propaganda it proved an effective weapon.

wd Frank Launder, Sidney Gilliat   ph Jack Cox
md Louis Levy

Patricia Roc, Gordon Jackson, Moore Marriott, Eric Portman, Anne Crawford, Basil Radford, Naunton Wayne, Joy Shelton, Megs Jenkins

'There is an unsentimental warmheartedness which I hope we shall cling to and extend in filmed representations of the British scene.' – Richard Winnington

† The only picture Launder and Gilliat directed side by side on the floor.

Mills of the Gods

US   1934   66m   bw
Columbia

An elderly businesswoman, unimpressed by her family, turns her business over to a committee of executives.

Interesting plot which would have justified better production.

w Garrett Fort, John S. Kirkland, Melville Baker
d Roy William Neill

May Robson, Fay Wray, Victor Jory, Raymond Walburn, Mayo Methot

'Stilted story with some good trouping. A double-upper.' – Variety

Milou in May ***

France/Italy   1989   108m   colour
Gala/Nouvelles Éditions de Films/TFI/Ellepi Film (Jean-Yves Asselin)
V, S

Following the death of his mother, a 60-year-old man invites her relatives to the funeral.

Gentle, well-observed study of family relationships.

w Louis Malle, Jean-Claude Carrière   d Louis Malle
ph Renato Berta   m Stéphane Grappelli
ed Emmanuelle Castro

Michel Piccoli, Miou-Miou, Michel Duchaussoy, Dominique Blanc, Harriet Walter, Bruno Carette, François Berléand, Martine Gautier, Paulette Dubost

'A film of Chekhovian generosity that never strays into sentimentality or cynicism.' – Philip French, Observer

Mimi

GB   1935   94m   bw
BIP
V*

In a Paris garret, a poor girl dies after encouraging a playwright.

La Bohème without the music; not a good idea.

w Clifford Grey, Paul Merzbach, Jack Davies, Denis Waldock   novel La Vie Bohème by Henri Murger
d Paul Stein

Douglas Fairbanks Jnr, Gertrude Lawrence, Diana Napier, Harold Warrender, Carol Goodner, Richard Bird

'A cyclone of human emotion roars across the screen!'

Min and Bill **

US   1930   69m   bw
MGM
V*

A boozy old waterfront character and his wife try to keep their daughter from being placed in care.

Well-remembered and much-loved character comedy which led to the even more successful Tugboat Annie with the same team.

w Frances Marion, Marion Jackson   play Dark Star by Lorna Moon   d George Hill   ph Harold Wenstrom

Marie Dressler, Wallace Beery, Dorothy Jordan, Marjorie Rambeau, Donald Dillaway, Russell Hopton

'Comedy-drama of distinction. All ingredients for all theatres, from keys down.' – Variety

AA: Marie Dressler

The Mind Benders *

GB   1963   113m   bw
Anglo-Amalgamated/Novus (Michael Relph)

A scientist undergoes an experiment aimed at depriving him of all sensation. It works too well; he becomes a sadist; and his colleagues can't reverse the process.

Matter-of-factly played hocus-pocus with spy asides; quite gripping while it's on, but in no way memorable.

w James Kennaway   d Basil Dearden   ph Denys Coop   m Georges Auric

Dirk Bogarde, John Clements, Mary Ure, Michael Bryant

The Mind of Mr Reeder *

GB   1939   75m   bw
Jack Raymond

An elderly government employee unmasks a forger and murderer.

Entertaining crime comedy-drama which never quite realizes its potential.

w Bryan Edgar Wallace, Marjorie Gaffney, Michael Hogan   novel Edgar Wallace   d Jack Raymond

Will Fyffe, Kay Walsh, George Curzon, Chili Bouchier, John Warwick

The Mind of Mr Soames

GB   1970   98m   Technicolor
Columbia/Amicus (Teresa Bolland)

A man who has lived in a coma for thirty years is cured but faces the world as a new-born infant.

Ill-advised attempt at science fiction with meaning; its earnestness becomes a bore.

w John Hale, Edward Simpson   novel Charles Eric Maine   d Alan Cooke   ph Billy Williams
m Michael Dress

Terence Stamp, Robert Vaughn, Nigel Davenport, Donal Donnelly, Christian Roberts, Vickery Turner, Scott Forbes

The Mind Reader *

US   1933   69m   bw
Warner

A phoney mind reader tries to go straight for his wife's sake, and ends up in jail.

Reasonably mordant satirical drama with good performances.

w Wilson Mizner, Robert Lord   play Vivian Cosby
d Roy del Ruth

Warren William, Constance Cummings, Allen Jenkins, Donald Dillaway, Mayo Methot, Clarence Muse

'Star performance plus laugh dialogue enough to send this into okay programmer class.' – Variety

Mind Your Own Business

US   1937   75m   bw
Emmanuel Cohen/Paramount

Boy scouts help to capture gangsters.

Slightly rocky comedy which finally comes across as unsatisfactory.

w Dore Schary   story John Francis Larkin
d Norman Z. McLeod

Charles Ruggles, Alice Brady, Lyle Talbot, Benny Baker, Jack La Rue, William Demarest, Frankie Darro

'It will have a tough time standing alone.' – Variety

Mine Own Executioner ***

GB   1947   108m   bw
London Films (Anthony Kimmins, Jack Kitchin)
V*

A lay psychiatrist undertakes the care of a mentally disturbed war veteran, but fails to prevent him from murdering his wife.

When this film first appeared it seemed like the first adult drama featuring sophisticated people to emerge from a British studio. Time and television have blunted its impact, but it remains a well told suspense melodrama with memorable characters.

w Nigel Balchin,   novel Nigel Balchin   d Anthony Kimmins   ph Wilkie Cooper   m Benjamin Frankel
ad William C. Andrews   ed Richard Best

Burgess Meredith, Kieron Moore, Dulcie Gray, Barbara White, Christine Norden

'The first psychoanalytical film that a grown-up can sit through without squirming.' – Richard Winnington

'One feels invigorated by having seen and understood other people's lives.' – Daily Worker

'His secret meant death to one man if he didn't talk . . . to countless thousands if he did!'

Ministry of Fear **
US   1944   85m   bw
Paramount (Seton I. Miller)

During World War II in England, a man just out of a mental hospital wins a cake at a village fair and finds himself caught up in bewildering intrigues.

Little to do with the novel, but a watchable, well-detailed little thriller on Hitchcock lines, once you forgive the usual phoney Hollywood England.

w Seton I. Miller   novel Graham Greene   d Fritz Lang   ph Henry Sharp   m Victor Young

Ray Milland, Marjorie Reynolds, Carl Esmond, Hillary Brooke, Dan Duryea, Percy Waram, Alan Napier, Erskine Sanford

'A crisp and efficiently made thriller with no pretension to intellectual content.' – Paul Jensen

The Miniver Story
GB   1950   104m   bw
MGM (Sidney Franklin)
V*

Mrs Miniver faces the tribulations of post-war Britain.

Glum sequel to Mrs Miniver, with the dauntless heroine finally succumbing to a glossy but fatal disease. Well enough made, but very hard to take.

w Ronald Millar, George Froeschel   d H. C. Potter   ph Joseph Ruttenberg   m Miklos Rozsa

Greer Garson, Walter Pidgeon, Cathy O'Donnell, John Hodiak, Leo Genn, Reginald Owen, Henry Wilcoxon, William Fox, Anthony Bushell

Minnie and Moskowitz *
US   1971   115m   Technicolor
Universal (Al Rubin)

Two lonely Los Angeles misfits have a bumpy courtship.

Enjoyably aimless character comedy.

wd John Cassavetes   ph Arthur J. Ornitz   m Bob Harwood

Gena Rowlands, Seymour Cassel

Minstrel Man *
US   1944   70m   bw
PRC

A minstrel star seeks his long-lost daughter.

Interesting sidelights on old-time minstrel shows in a production somewhat less tatty than is usual from this company.

w Irwin Franklin, Pierre Gendron   d Joseph H. Lewis   m Leo Erdody, Ferdie Grofe

Benny Fields, Gladys George, Roscoe Karns

AAN: song, 'Remember Me to Carolina' (m Harry Revel, ly Paul Webster); music

A Minute to Pray, a Second to Die: see Dead or Alive

The Miracle
Italy   1948   40m   bw
Tania Film (Roberto Rossellini)

A simple-minded peasant woman is seduced by a shepherd but believes her baby has been immaculately conceived.

Curious, rather unsatisfactory parable originally intended as part of a two-item tribute to the power of a star actress. (The other section, Cocteau's The Human Voice, was withdrawn for copyright reasons.)

w Tullio Pinelli, Roberto Rossellini, Federico Fellini   d Roberto Rossellini   ph Aldo Tonti   m Renzo Rossellini

Anna Magnani, Federico Fellini

'Acting on a plane scarcely known to the cinema.' – Sunday Times

'The mightiest story of fame and the flesh known to our time!'

The Miracle
US   1959   121m   Technirama
Warner (Henry Blanke)

In Spain during the Peninsular War, a nun breaks her vows in order to follow a British soldier, and a statue of the Virgin Mary steps down to take her place.

And that's only the beginning in this very tall tale, full of heavy breathing, violent action and religiosity, from the old Max Reinhardt pageant. Quite incredible, and sloppily done.

w Frank Butler   play Karl Vollmoeller   d Irving Rapper   ph Ernest Haller   m Elmer Bernstein

Carroll Baker, Roger Moore, Walter Slezak, Vittorio Gassman, Katina Paxinou, Dennis King, Isobel Elsom, Torin Thatcher

The Miracle
GB   1990   97m   colour
Palace/Promenade/British Screen/Film Four (Stephen Woolley, Redmond Morris)
V, V*

An actress becomes the focus of the romantic attentions of an adolescent saxophonist.

Desultory tale of incipient incest with a few striking moments.

wd Neil Jordan   ph Philippe Rousselot   m Anne Dudley   pd Gemma Jackson   ed Joke Van Wijk

Beverly D'Angelo, Donal McCann, Nial Byrne, Lorraine Pilkington, J. G. Devlin, Cathleen Delaney, Tom Hickey, Shane Connaughton

'Insubstantial fare, with predictable situations and plotting.' – Variety

A Miracle Can Happen: see On Our Merry Way

Miracle in Milan **
Italy   1951   101m   bw
PDS/ENIC (Vittorio de Sica)
V*, L

A foundling goes to live with the poor on the outskirts of Milan, and his erstwhile guardian returns from heaven to help them repel capitalists and fly away on broomsticks to a better land.

An unlikely fable which manages to avoid all the obvious pitfalls and sends one out of the cinema in a warm glow.

w Cesare Zavattini, Vittorio de Sica   novel Toto il Buono by Cesare Zavattini   d Vittorio de Sica   ph G. R. Aldo   m Alessandro Cicognini

Francesco Golisano, Brunella Bovo, Emma Gramatica, Paolo Stoppa

Miracle in Soho
GB   1957   93m   Eastmancolor
Rank (Emeric Pressburger)

A Soho roadworker falls for a barmaid.

Rudimentary romantic whimsy in an unconvincing street set, with characters either too voluble or just plain dull.

w Emeric Pressburger   d Julian Amyes   ph Christopher Challis   m Brian Easdale

John Gregson, Belinda Lee, Cyril Cusack

'A street corner pick-up that worked a miracle of love! A picture of very special greatness!'

Miracle in the Rain **
US   1954   107m   bw
Warner (Frank P. Rosenberg)

A plain New York girl falls for a soldier; when he is killed in action, he keeps their appointment on the church steps as a ghost.

Archetypal Hollywood schmaltz, half acute observation of amusing types, half sentimental whimsy, with a final supernatural touch of eating your cake and having it.

w Ben Hecht   d Rudolph Maté   ph Russell Metty   m Franz Waxman

Jane Wyman, Van Johnson, Fred Clark, Eileen Heckart, William Gargan

The Miracle Man
US   1932   85m   bw
Paramount

A gang of crooks is reformed by a faith healer they have exploited.

Adequate remake of the silent Lon Chaney vehicle; no sparks this time.

w Waldemar Young, Samuel Hoffenstein   play Frank L. Packard, George M. Cohan   d Norman Z. McLeod   ph David Abel   m W. Franke Harling

Sylvia Sidney, Chester Morris, Irving Pichel, John Wray, Robert Coogan, Hobart Bosworth, Boris Karloff, Ned Sparks, Virginia Bruce

'50 minutes and counting . . .'

Miracle Mile *
US   1989   88m   CFI
Hemdale (John Daly, Derek Gibson)
V*, L, S

A town panics as it learns that a nuclear strike is on the way.

Suspense and black humour are maintained to the final moments in an engagingly odd little movie.

wd Steve DeJarnatt   ph Theo Van de Sande   m Tangerine Dream   pd Christopher Horner   ed Stephen Semel, Kathie Weaver

Anthony Edwards, Mare Winningham, John Agar, Lou Hancock, Mykel T. Williamson, Kelly Minter, Kurt Fuller, Denise Crosby

The Miracle of Fatima: see The Miracle of Our Lady of Fatima

The Miracle of Morgan's Creek ***
US   1943   99m   bw
Paramount (Preston Sturges)
V*

Chaos results when a stuttering hayseed tries to help a girl accidentally pregnant by a soldier she met hazily at a dance.

Weird and wonderful one-man assault on the Hays Office and sundry other American institutions such as motherhood and politics; an indescribable, tasteless, roaringly funny mêlée, as unexpected at the time as it was effective, like a kick in the pants to all other film comedies.

wd Preston Sturges   ph John Seitz   m Leo Shuken, Charles Bradshaw

Betty Hutton, Eddie Bracken, William Demarest, Diana Lynn, Porter Hall, Akim Tamiroff, Brian Donlevy, Alan Bridge

OFFICER KOCKENLOCKER (William Demarest): 'Daughters. They're a mess no matter how you look at 'em. A headache till they get married – if they get married – and after that they get worse . . . Either they leave their husbands and come back with four kids and move into your guest room or the husband loses his job and the whole caboodle comes back. Or else they're so homely that you can't get rid of them at all and they sit around like Spanish moss and shame you into an early grave.'

EMILY KOCKENLOCKER (Diana Lynn): 'If you don't mind my mentioning it, father, I think you have a mind like a swamp.'

'Like taking a nun on a roller coaster.' – James Agee

'This film moves in a fantastic and irreverent whirl of slapstick, nonsense, farce, sentiment, satire, romance, melodrama – is there any ingredient of dramatic entertainment except maybe tragedy and grand opera that hasn't been tossed into it?' – *National Board of Review*

'Bad taste, or no bad taste, I thoroughly enjoyed it.' – *Richard Mallett, Punch*

AAN: Preston Sturges (as writer)

The Miracle of Our Lady of Fatima

US   1952   102m   Warnercolor
Warner (Bryan Foy)
V*, L
GB title: *The Miracle of Fatima*

An account of the 1917 appearance of the Virgin Mary to three Portuguese peasant children.

Poorly staged religious film which manages to be less pro-Catholic than anti-communist, and was clearly seen by Jack L. Warner as a means of atoning for *Mission to Moscow*. A real cold war piece.

w Crane Wilbur, James O'Hanlon   d John Brahm   ph Edwin DuPar   m Max Steiner   ad Edward Carrere

Gilbert Roland, Frank Silvera, Angela Clarke, Jay Novello

AAN: Max Steiner

The Miracle of the Bells

US   1948   120m   bw
Jesse L. Lasky
V*

The death of a glamorous film star causes a small-town miracle and a nationwide publicity stunt.

One hopes that this oddity was intended as a satire; as a straight entertainment it's more than a little icky, and good production values scarcely help.

w Ben Hecht   novel Russell Janney   d Irving Pichel   ph Robert de Grasse   m Leigh Harline

Fred MacMurray, Alida Valli, Frank Sinatra, Lee J. Cobb

'An offensive exhibition of vulgar insensitivity.' – *MFB*

'I hereby declare myself the founding father of the Society for the Prevention of Cruelty to God.' – *James Agee*

The Miracle of the White Stallions *

US   1963   118m   Technicolor
Walt Disney (Peter V. Herald)
V*
GB title: *The Flight of the White Stallions*

During World War II the Nazis occupy Vienna and the owner of the Spanish Riding School guides his stallions to safety.

Adequate family adventure fare with a dull hero but interesting backgrounds.

w A. J. Carothers   d Arthur Hiller   ph Gunther Anders   m Paul Smith

Robert Taylor, Lilli Palmer, Eddie Albert, Curt Jurgens

Miracle on Main Street *

US   1940   76m   bw
RKO/Jack Skirball

A cabaret dancer finds an abandoned baby but her plans are thwarted by the return of her husband.

Odd, interesting but flatly handled melodrama.

w Sam Ornitz, Boris Ingster   story Felix Jackson   d Steve Sekely   ph Charles Van Enger   m Walter Jurmann, Hans Salter

Walter Abel, Margo, William Collier, Jane Darwell, Lyle Talbot, Wynne Gibson

Miracle on 34th Street ***

US   1947   94m   bw
TCF (William Perlberg)
V, V*, L
GB title: *The Big Heart*

A department store Santa Claus claims to be the real thing.

Mainly charming comedy fantasy which quickly became an American classic but does suffer from a few dull romantic stretches.

wd George Seaton   story Valentine Davies   ph Charles Clarke, Lloyd Ahern   m Cyril Mockridge

Edmund Gwenn, Maureen O'Hara, John Payne, Natalie Wood, Gene Lockhart, Porter Hall, William Frawley, Jerome Cowan, Thelma Ritter

'Altogether wholesome, stimulating and enjoyable.' – *Motion Picture Herald*

AA: George Seaton (as writer); Valentine Davies; Edmund Gwenn

AAN: best picture

The Miracle Rider

US   1935   bw   serial: 15 eps
Mascot

A captain in the Texas Rangers is made a blood brother of the Ravenhead tribe, but the activities of a villain named Zaroff strain the friendship.

Unpretentious serial exploits.

d Armand Schaefer, B. Reeves Eason

Tom Mix, Charles Middleton, Jean Gale, Jason Robards

'Never give away what you can sell!'
The Miracle Woman *

US   1932   90m   bw
Columbia (Harry Cohn)

A lady evangelist turns confidence trickster.

Mild satirical drama inspired by the career of Aimée Semple Macpherson.

w Jo Swerling   play *Bless You Sister* by Robert Riskin, John Meehan   d Frank Capra   ph Joseph Walker

Barbara Stanwyck, Sam Hardy, David Manners, Beryl Mercer, Russell Hopton

'Splendid programme leader, a big and strong film opening up numerous channels of publicity.' – *Variety*

'Such a beauty, well staged and handsomely lighted.' – *New Yorker, 1977*

The Miracle Worker *

US   1962   106m   bw
UA/Playfilms (Fred Coe)
V*, L

The childhood of Helen Keller, taught by Annie Sullivan after being left blind, deaf and dumb in an illness.

A moving real-life story is given hysterical treatment and the good scenes have a hard task winning through; in any case a documentary might have been more persuasive.

w William Gibson   play William Gibson   d Arthur Penn   ph Ernest Caparros   m Laurence Rosenthal   ad George Jenkins

Anne Bancroft, Patty Duke, Victor Jory, Inga Swenson, Andrew Prine, Beah Richards

AA: Anne Bancroft; Patty Duke

AAN: William Gibson; Arthur Penn

Miracles

US   1985   87m   Technicolor   Super Technicope
Orion/Steve Roth, Bernard Williams
V*, L

A chase begins when bank robbers kidnap an innocent couple.

Exhausting action comedy with no real finesse.

wd Jim Kouf   ph John Alcott   m Peter Bernstein   pd Terence Marsh

Tom Conti, Teri Garr, Paul Rodriguez, Christopher Lloyd

Miracles for Sale

US   1939   71m   bw
MGM

An illusionist catches a murderer.

What could have been a smart mystery piece is sabotaged by stilted writing and direction, a muddled narrative style, and illusions which are patently faked by the camera.

w James Edward Grant, Marion Parsonnet, Harry Ruskin   novel *Death in a Top Hat* by Clayton Rawson   d Tod Browning

Robert Young, Florence Rice, Henry Hull, Frank Craven, Lee Bowman, William Demarest

'Unexciting whodunit . . . the plot stumbles over itself most of the time.' – *Variety*

Mirage **

US   1965   109m   bw
U-I (Harry Keller)
V*

During a New York power blackout, an executive falls to his death from a skyscraper and a cost accountant loses his memory.

Striking puzzler, rather slowly developed but generally effective and with a strong sense of place and timing.

w Peter Stone,   novel Walter Ericson   d Edward Dmytryk   ph Joe MacDonald   m Quincy Jones

Gregory Peck, Diane Baker, Walter Abel, Walter Matthau, Leif Erickson, Kevin McCarthy

'Worthy of Hitchcock at his vintage best.' – *Daily Express*

Miranda *

GB   1947   80m   bw
GFD/Gainsborough/Sydney Box (Betty Box)

A doctor on holiday in Cornwall catches a mermaid and takes her to London disguised as an invalid.

Simple-minded comedy which scores a few easy laughs on obvious targets.

w Peter Blackmore   play Peter Blackmore   d Ken Annakin   ph Ray Elton   m Temple Abady

Glynis Johns, Griffith Jones, Googie Withers, Margaret Rutherford, David Tomlinson, Sonia Holm, John McCallum

† Sequel 1949, *Mad about Men*.

Mirror **

USSR   1974   106m   bw/colour
Artificial Eye/Mosfilm Unit 4 (E. Waisberg)
V, V*
original title: *Zerkalo*

An artist considers his relationships with his parents and with his wife and young son.

Intensely personal meditation, with the director's father reading his own poems and his mother playing the narrator's mother, which may baffle audiences, despite its assurance and visual beauty.

w Andrei Tarkovsky, Aleksandr Misharin   d Andrei Tarkovsky   ph Georgy Rerberg   m Eduard Artemyev   ad Nikolai Dvigubsky   ed L. Feiginova

Innokenti Smoktunovsky, Margarita Terekhova, L. Tarkovskaya, Philip Yankovsky, Ignat Daniltsev, Anatoli Solonitsin

'Tarkovsky's autobiographical essay in the interaction of private and collective memories, via a multi-layered structure of flashbacks, dream sequences and newsreel footage, is chillingly impressive even at its most hermetic.' – *Sight and Sound*

† Tarkovsky said of the film, 'We wanted to make a simple film which would signify only what was shown'. It was given a very restricted release in the USSR.

The Mirror

West Germany/Turkey   1984   94m   colour
Von Vietinghoff Filmproduction/ZDF/Channel 4 (Joachim von Vietinghoff)
original title: *Der Spiegel Ayna*

A Turkish peasant reacts violently on discovering that the son of the local landowner is in love with his wife.

Ponderously told folk tale, full of stolid symbolism.

wd Erden Kiral   *novel* *The White Ox* by Osman Sahin
ph Kenan Ormanler   *m* Brymor Jones

Nur Surer, Suavi Eren, Hikmet Celik

'Mirror, mirror, on the wall, who's the killer among them all?'

The Mirror Crack'd

GB   1980   105m   Technicolor
EMI/John Brabourne, Richard Goodwin
V, V*, L

Murders result from the making of an all-star film in an English village.

After adventures on the Orient Express and the Nile, this follow-up in the Agatha Christie stakes seems woefully restricted with stilted dialogue and playing.

w Jonathan Hales, Barry Sandler   *novel* Agatha Christie   *d* Guy Hamilton   *ph* Christopher Challis
m John Cameron   *pd* Michael Stringer

Angela Lansbury, Geraldine Chaplin, Elizabeth Taylor, Rock Hudson, Tony Curtis, Edward Fox, Kim Novak, Marella Oppenheim, Charles Gray

Mischief *

US   1985   93m   DeLuxe
Jere Henshaw-Michael Nolin/TCF
V, V*, L

Teenage anxieties in smalltown America in 1956

Clearly not for export, but a smooth piece of its kind.

w Noel Black   *d* Mel Damski   *ph* Donald E. Thorin   *pd* Paul Peters   *ed* Nick Brown

Doug McKeon, Catherine Mary Stewart, Kelly Preston, Chris Nash

Les Misérables ****

US   1935   109m   bw
Twentieth Century (Darryl F. Zanuck)
V*, L

Unjustly convicted and sentenced to years in the galleys, Jean Valjean emerges to build up his life again but is hounded by a cruel and relentless police officer.

Solid, telling, intelligent version of a much-filmed classic novel; in adaptation and performance it is hard to see how this film could be bettered.

w W. P. Lipscomb   *novel* Victor Hugo   *d* Richard Boleslawski   *ph* Gregg Toland   *m* Alfred Newman
ed Barbara McLean

Fredric March, Charles Laughton, Cedric Hardwicke, Rochelle Hudson, Frances Drake, John Beal, Jessie Ralph, Florence Eldridge

'Brilliant filmization, sure fire for heavy money.' – *Variety*

'Unbelievably thrilling in all the departments of its manufacture . . . a memorable experience in the cinema.' – *New York Times*

'A superlative effort, a thrilling, powerful, poignant picture.' – *New York Evening Post*

'Deserving of rank among the cinema's finest achievements.' – *New York World Telegram*

† Other versions of the story: 1909, 1913 (French); 1917 (William Farnum); 1923 (French: Gabriel Gabrio); 1929 as *The Bishop's Candlesticks* (Walter Huston); 1934 (French: Harry Baur); 1946 (Italian: Gino Cervi); 1952 (see below); 1956 (French: Jean Gabin; see below); 1978 (British: Richard Jordan)

AAN: best picture; Gregg Toland; editing

Les Misérables **

US   1952   106m   bw
TCF (Fred Kohlmar)

Solemn remake, well done but lacking the spark of inspiration.

w Richard Murphy   *d* Lewis Milestone   *ph* Joseph LaShelle   *m* Alex North

Michael Rennie, Robert Newton, Edmund Gwenn, Debra Paget, Cameron Mitchell, Sylvia Sidney, Elsa Lanchester, James Robertson Justice, Joseph Wiseman, Rhys Williams

Les Misérables de Victor Hugo *

France/Italy   1958   210m   Technicolor
                              Technirama
Pathé/P.A.C./Serena (Paul Cadeac)
V*

Jean Valjean escapes from prison and makes a new life for himself, but his old one catches up with him.

Stolid version of Hugo's classic, gaining what distinction it has from Gabin's performance.

w René Barjavel, Jean-Paul Le Chanois   *d* Jean-Paul Le Chanois   *ph* Jacques Natteau   *m* Georges Van Parys   *ad* Serge Pimenoff, Karl Schneider
ed Emma Le Chanois

Jean Gabin (as Jean Valjean), Bernard Blier (as Javert), Danièle Delorme, Serge Reggiani, Bourvil, Giani Esposito, Martine Havet, Béatrice Altariba, Elfriede Florin, Jimmy Urbain, Jean Murat, Lucien Baroux, Silvia Monfort

† The film is sometimes shown in two parts. The best French version is that of Raymond Bernard, who made a three-part adaptation of the novel in 1933 starring Harry Baur under the titles *Tempête sous un Crane* (120m), *Les Thénardiers* (90m), and *Liberté, Liberté Chérie* (95m). He later cut it to a two-part film: *Jean Valjean* (109m) and *Cosette* (100m).

'Paul Sheldon used to write for a living. Now he's writing to stay alive.'

Misery **

US   1990   107m   CFI colour
Medusa/Castle Rock/Nelson (Andrew Scheinman, Rob Reiner)
V, V*, L, S

A disturbed fan kidnaps an injured novelist and forces him to write a novel featuring her favourite heroine.

Impeccably directed, tense thriller.

w William Goldman   *novel* Stephen King   *d* Rob Reiner   *ph* Barry Sonnenfeld   *m* Marc Shaiman
pd Norman Garwood   *ed* Robert Leighton

James Caan, Kathy Bates, Richard Farnsworth, Frances Sternhagen, Lauren Bacall, Graham Jarvis, Jerry Potter

'This astonishing film is a taut, darkly comic thriller and a post-modernist examination of the relationship between writer and reader, detached producer and vulnerable consumer, artist and critic.' – *Philip French, Observer*

AA: Kathy Bates

The Misfits *

US   1961   124m   bw
United Artists/Seven Arts (Frank E. Taylor)
V, V*, L

Cowboys gather in the Nevada desert to rope wild mustangs, and a divorcee becomes involved with one of them.

Ill-fated melodrama whose stars both died shortly afterwards; a solemn, unattractive, pretentious film which seldom stops wallowing in self-pity.

w Arthur Miller   *d* John Huston   *ph* Russell Metty
m Alex North

Clark Gable, Marilyn Monroe, Montgomery Clift, Eli Wallach, Thelma Ritter, James Barton, Estelle Winwood, Kevin McCarthy

'The theme with its implications of an essentially male savagery suits Mr Huston, and he has drawn extraordinary qualities from all his chief players.' – *Dilys Powell*

Mishima *

US   1985   120m   Technicolor   Panavision
Coppola-Lucas/Warner
V, V*, S

Fragments of autobiography by the self-destructing Japanese writer.

A complete switch-off for all but the initiated, this indulgent, delicate, violent kaleidoscope is half a work of art and half an utter waste of other people's money.

w Paul and Leonard Schrader   *d* Paul Schrader

Ken Ogata, Kanji Sawada, Yasosuke Bando

The Misleading Lady

US   1932   75m   bw
Paramount

A social butterfly aspires to be an actress.

Ho-hum romantic comedy, quite unmemorable.

w Adelaide Heilbron, Caroline Francke
play Charles W. Goddard and Paul Dickey   *d* Stuart Walker

Claudette Colbert, Edmund Lowe, Stuart Erwin, Robert Strange, George Meeker

'Lightweight stuff of conventional pattern.' – *Variety*

Miss Annie Rooney

US   1942   86m   bw
Edward Small

Poor Irish girl loves rich boy.

A totally routine offering for a teenage star; no wonder she didn't make it.

w George Bruce   *d* Edwin L. Marin   *ph* Lester White   *md* Edward Paul

Shirley Temple, William Gargan, Guy Kibbee, Dickie Moore, Peggy Ryan, Gloria Holden, Jonathan Hale, Mary Field

Miss Fane's Baby Is Stolen

US   1933   67m   bw
Paramount
GB title: *Kidnapped*

A film star's baby is kidnapped.

Fairly straightforward crime yarn with comic asides.

w Adela Rogers St John, Rupert Hughes
d Alexander Hall

Dorothea Wieck, Alice Brady, Baby LeRoy, William Frawley, George Barbier, Alan Hale, Jack La Rue

'Box office as well as entertainment . . . the first picture of its kind since the Lindbergh kidnapping.' – *Variety*

Miss Firecracker

US   1989   103m   DuArt
Rank/Firecracker Company/Corsair (Fred Berner)
V, V*, L

An orphaned girl enters her home-town beauty contest.

Unconvincing in its portrayal of a young woman discovering her individuality.

w Beth Hanley   *play The Miss Firecracker Contest* by Beth Hanley   *d* Thomas Schlamme   *ph* Arthur Albert   *m* David Mansfield, Homer Denison   *pd* Maher Ahmad   *ed* Peter C. Frank

Holly Hunter, Mary Steenburgen, Tim Robbins, Alfre Woodard, Scott Glenn, Veanne Cox, Ann Wedgeworth, Trey Wilson, Amy Wright, Kathleen Chalfant

Miss Grant Takes Richmond *
US   1949   87m   bw
Columbia (S. Sylvan Simon)
GB title: *Innocence Is Bliss*

A dumb secretary helps defeat crooks and improve the local housing situation.

Mildly amusing star comedy.

w Nat Perrin, Devery Freeman, Frank Tashlin   *d* Lloyd Bacon   *ph* Charles Lawton Jnr   *md* Morris Stoloff   *m* Heinz Roemheld

Lucille Ball, William Holden, Janis Carter, James Gleason, Gloria Henry, Frank McHugh, George Cleveland

'One of the more delightful comedies of the season.' – *Lawrence J. Quirk*

Miss Julie *
Sweden   1950   87m   bw
Sandrew (Rune Waldekranz)
V*

In a lonely house, the count's daughter kills herself after being seduced by a valet.

Intense melodramatic fragment, just a little long for comfort.

wd Alf Sjöberg   play August Strindberg   *ph* Göran Strindberg   *m* Dag Wirén

Anita Björk, Ulf Palme, Anders Henrikson

'The outstanding achievement of the Swedish cinema in recent years.' – *Gavin Lambert, Sight and Sound*

Miss London Ltd
GB   1943   99m   bw
GFD/Gainsborough (Edward Black)

An escort agency is formed to assist soldiers on leave.

Flagwaving light entertainment with popular performers of the time.

w Val Guest, Marriott Edgar   *d* Val Guest   *ph* Basil Emmott   *md* Louis Levy   *songs* Manning Sherwin (*m*), Val Guest (*ly*)

Arthur Askey, Anne Shelton, Evelyn Dall, Richard Hearne, Max Bacon, Jack Train, Peter Graves, Jean Kent

Miss Marple

Agatha Christie's inquisitive spinster detective was brought to the screen by director George Pollock and star Margaret Rutherford in four increasingly disappointing films for MGM.

1962: MURDER SHE SAID (qv)
1963: MURDER AT THE GALLOP (V)
1964: MURDER MOST FOUL, MURDER AHOY (V)
See also *The Mirror Crack'd.*

Miss Pacific Fleet
US   1935   76m   bw
Warner

Two stranded show girls enter a popularity contest to win the fare back home.

A comedy with little to laugh at.

w Lucille Newmark, Peter Milne, Patsy Flick   *d* Ray Enright

Glenda Farrell, Joan Blondell, Hugh Herbert, Allen Jenkins, Warren Hull, Guinn Williams

'Maybe OK for double feature bills, but that's the best it can hope for.' – *Variety*

Miss Pilgrim's Progress
GB   1949   82m   bw
Daniel M. Angel

An American working girl in Britain helps to save a village from development.

Wholly artificial and unendearing comedy.

wd Val Guest

Yolande Donlan, Michael Rennie, Garry Marsh, Emrys Jones, Reginald Beckwith, Helena Pickard, Jon Pertwee

Miss Pinkerton *
US   1932   66m   bw
Warner

A private nurse helps a police detective to solve a murder case.

Pleasing little mystery comedy.

w Lilyan Hayward, Niven Busch   *story* Mary Roberts Rinehart   *d* Lloyd Bacon   *ph* Barney McGill

Joan Blondell, George Brent, Mae Madison, John Wray, Ruth Hall, C. Henry Gordon, Elizabeth Patterson

'Formula mystery story . . . picture is outdated and has nothing to draw.' – *Variety*

† Remade as *The Nurse's Secret* (1946).

Miss Robin Hood
GB   1952   78m   bw
Group 3

A lady author pits her wits against crooks and saves an old lady's fortune.

Disappointing star comedy with no build-up.

w Val Valentine, Patrick Campbell, Geoffrey Orme   *d* John Guillermin

Margaret Rutherford, Richard Hearne, Michael Medwin, Peter Jones, James Robertson Justice, Sidney James, Dora Bryan

Miss Sadie Thompson *
US   1953   91m   Technicolor   3-D
Columbia (Lewis J. Rachmil)

Vigorous semi-musical remake of *Rain* (qv); a good star vehicle, but not otherwise notable.

w Harry Kleiner   *d* Curtis Bernhardt   *ph* Charles Lawton   *md* George Duning

Rita Hayworth, José Ferrer, Aldo Ray, Russell Collins, Harry Bellaver

AAN: song 'Blue Pacific Blues' (*m* Lester Lee, *ly* Ned Washington)

'A story for lovers . . . past, present and perfect!'
Miss Susie Slagle's
US   1946   88m   bw
Paramount (John Houseman)

Romances of nursing students in 1910 Baltimore.

Modest melodramatic potboiler.

w Anne Froelich, Hugo Butler   *novel* Augusta Tucker   *d* John Berry   *ph* Charles Lang Jnr   *m* Daniele Amfitheatrof

Veronica Lake, Joan Caulfield, Sonny Tufts, Lillian Gish, Ray Collins, Billy de Wolfe, Bill Edwards, Roman Bohnen, Morris Carnovsky, Lloyd Bridges

Miss Tatlock's Millions *
US   1948   101m   bw
Paramount (Charles Brackett)

A stunt man impersonates the idiot heir to a fortune.

Tasteless but quite funny comedy with a cast of eccentrics indulging in enjoyable fooling.

w Charles Brackett, Richard L. Breen   *d* Richard Haydn   *ph* Charles Lang Jnr   *m* Victor Young

John Lund, Wanda Hendrix, Monty Woolley, Barry Fitzgerald, Robert Stack, Ilka Chase, Dorothy Stickney

Miss V from Moscow
US   1943   70m   bw
PRC

A Russian spy impersonates a German spy in Paris.

Hilariously inept propaganda piece; since the Cold War it has been retitled *Intrigue in Paris*.

w Arthur St Claire and Sherman Lowe   *d* Albert Herman

Lola Lane, Noel Madison, Howard Banks

Missiles from Hell: see *The Battle of the V1*

Missing *
US   1982   122m   Technicolor
Universal/Polygram/Peter Guber, Jon Peters (Edward and Mildred Lewis)
V*, L

An American seeks his young son who has disappeared in Chile.

A further link in the chain of political thrillers from this director; well-wrought and compulsive but finally disappointing in its mixture of fact and fiction.

w Costa-Gavras, Donald Stewart   *book* Thomas Hauser   *d* Costa-Gavras   *ph* Ricardo Aronovich   *m* Vangelis   *pd* Peter Jamieson   *ed* Françoise Bonnot

Jack Lemmon, Sissy Spacek, Melanie Mayron, John Shea, Charles Cioffi, Richard Bradford

'Provocation and entertainment prove to be uneasy allies.' – *Tom Milne, MFB*

AA: screenplay (adaptation)
AAN: Jack Lemmon; best picture; Sissy Spacek

The Missing Corpse
US   1945   54m   bw
Leon Fromkess/PRC

A publisher tries to hide a corpse he is suspected of murdering.

Adequate filler for indulgent audiences.

w Ray Schrock   *d* Albert Herman

J. Edward Bromberg, Ben Welden, Frank Jenks, Isabel Randolph

Missing in Action
US   1984   101m   Metrocolor
Cannon (Menahem Golan, Yoram Globus)
V, V*, L, S

An American colonel, having been taken prisoner and escaped, returns to Vietnam to find other 'missing' men.

Naïve, violent, jingoistic romp which caused quite a lot of box-office business around the world.

w James Bruner   *d* Joseph Zito   *ph* Joao Fernandes   *m* Jay Chattaway   *ad* Ladi Wilheim, Toto Castillo   *ed* Joel Goodman

Chuck Norris, M. Emmet Walsh, Lenore Kasdorf, James Hong

Missing in Action 2 – The Beginning
US   1985   95m   TVC colour
Cannon (Menahem Golan, Yoram Globus)
V*, L, S

A prequel to the above, showing the colonel's first escape.

More cheaply made, it runs like a series of offcuts, with emphasis on unpleasant violence.

w Arthur Silver, Larry Levinson, Steve Bing   *d* Lance Hool   *ph* Jorge Stahl Jnr   *m* Brian May   *pd* Michael Baugh   *ed* Mark Conte, Marcus Nanton

Chuck Norris, Soon Teck-Oh, Cosie Costa, Steven Williams

The Missing Juror

US 1944 71m bw
Columbia

Members of a murder jury are killed off one by one.

Minor puzzle piece from the *I Love a Mystery* series.

w Charles O'Neal d Budd Boetticher

Jim Bannon, Janis Carter, George Macready

Missing Pieces

US 1991 92m colour
Rank/Aaron Russo Entertainment
V*

An out-of-work writer and an unemployed musician are pursued by crooks as they try to solve a riddle that will net them a fortune.

A chase comedy that rounds up the usual clichés and then recycles them.

wd Leonard Stern ph Peter Stein m Marvin Hamlisch pd Michael Z. Hanan ed Evan Lottman

Eric Idle, Robert Wuhl, Lauren Hutton, Bob Gunton, Richard Belzer, Bernie Kopell, Kim Lankford, Don Gibb

The Missing Rembrandt

GB 1932 82m bw
Twickenham

Sherlock Holmes saves a lady's honour and nails a blackmailer.

Not the best of this particular series, but Wontner is a Holmes to relish.

w Cyril Twyford, H. Fowler Mear story Charles Augustus Milverton by Arthur Conan Doyle d Leslie Hiscott

Arthur Wontner, Ian Fleming, Jane Welsh, Miles Mander, Francis L. Sullivan

Missing Ten Days: see *Ten Days in Paris*

The Mission **

GB 1986 128m Rank colour JDC wide screen
Goldcrest/Kingsmere/Enigma/Fernando Ghia (David Puttnam)
V, V*, L, S

In mid-18th-century South America, Jesuit priests fall foul of avaricious colonialists.

Sincere to the point of boredom, this 22-million-dollar would-be epic is short on plot development, long on superb photography of remote actualities.

w Robert Bolt d Roland Joffe ph Chris Menges m Ennio Morricone pd Norma Dorme, Francesco Broznik, George Richardson, John King ed Jim Clark

Robert de Niro, Jeremy Irons, Ray McAnally, Liam Neeson, Aidan Quinn, Ronald Pickup, Cherie Lunghi

AA: Chris Menges

AAN: best picture; Roland Joffe; Ennio Morricone; Jim Clark; art direction (Stuart Craig); sound (Jack Stephens); costumes (Enrico Sabbatini)

Mission to Moscow **

US 1943 112m bw
Warner (Robert Buckner)

The Russian career of US Ambassador Joseph E. Davies.

Stodgy but fascinating wartime propaganda piece viewing the Russians as warm-hearted allies; in the later days of the McCarthy witch hunt, Jack L. Warner regretted he had ever allowed it to be made.

w Howard Koch book Joseph E. Davies d Michael Curtiz ph Bert Glennon m Max Steiner ad Carl Weyl

Walter Huston, Ann Harding, Oscar Homolka, George Tobias, Gene Lockhart, Eleanor Parker, Richard Travis, Helmut Dantine, Victor Francen, Henry Daniell, Barbara Everest, Dudley Field Malone, Roman Bohnen, Maria Palmer, Moroni Olsen, Minor Watson

'A mishmash: of Stalinism with New Dealism with Hollywoodism with opportunism with shaky experimentalism with mesmerism with onanism, all mosaicked into a remarkable portrait of what the makers of the film think the Soviet Union is like – a great glad two-million-dollar bowl of canned borscht, eminently approvable by the Institute of Good Housekeeping.' – *James Agee*

AAN: Carl Weyl

The Missionary *

GB 1983 86m colour Panavision
HandMade Films (Michael Palin)
V*

In 1906, a clergyman returns from darkest Africa and sets up a Mission to Fallen Women in the East End of London.

Sporadically amusing comedy of a reformer being tempted; the decoration is funnier than the central theme.

w Michael Palin d Richard Loncraine ph Peter Hannan m Mike Moran ad Norman Garwood

Michael Palin, Maggie Smith, Michael Hordern, Trevor Howard, Denholm Elliott, Graham Crowden, Phoebe Nichols, Roland Culver

'It leaves one with a half-frozen smile, in anticipation of a comic fulfilment which never quite happens.' – *Nick Roddick, MFB*

'A deliciously straight-faced acceptance of the palpably absurd.' – *Daily Mail*

Mississippi *

US 1935 75m bw
Paramount (Arthur Hornblow Jnr)

A showboat singer has a cloud on his reputation.

Mild period musical with occasional stops for comedy.

w Herbert Fields, Claude Binyon story Booth Tarkington d A. Edward Sutherland ph Charles Lang m/ly Rodgers and Hart

Bing Crosby, W. C. Fields, Joan Bennett, Gail Patrick, Claude Gillingwater, John Miljan, Queenie Smith

'A dull film, rambling and hokey.' – *Variety*

Mississippi Burning **

US 1988 127m DeLuxe
Rank/Orion (Frederick Zollo, Robert F. Colesberry)
V, V*, L

In Mississippi in the mid-1960s, FBI agents investigate the murder of three civil rights workers.

Melodramatic and sensational account of racism in action that caused controversy on its release because of its concentration on white activists; but it has a power that sweeps its audience along with it.

w Chris Gerolmo d Alan Parker ph Peter Biziou m Trevor Jones pd Philip Harrison, Geoffrey Kirkland ed Gerry Hambling

Gene Hackman, Willem Dafoe, Frances McDormand, Brad Dourif, R. Lee Ermey, Gailard Sartain, Stephen Tobolowsky, Michael Rooker, Pruitt Taylor Vince

AA: Peter Biziou

AAN: best picture; Alan Parker; Gene Hackman; Frances McDormand; Gerry Hambling; best sound

Mississippi Gambler

US 1953 98m Technicolor
U-I (Ted Richmond)

A showboat gambler has trouble with a bad loser, but finally marries his sister.

Picturesque star melodrama with period settings and not much meat in the story.

w Seton I. Miller d Rudolph Maté ph Irving Glassberg m Frank Skinner

Tyrone Power, Piper Laurie, John McIntire, Julia Adams, Dennis Weaver

'Romeo And Juliet Had It Easy.'
Mississippi Masala *

US 1991 113m colour
SCS/Odyssey/Cinecom/Film Four/Mirabai/Movieworks/Black River (Michael Nozick, Mira Nair)
V, V*, L, S

A young Asian woman living in Mississippi falls in love with a black American, to the distress of both their families.

Uninvolving treatment of romance and racism.

w Sooni Taraporevala d Mira Nair ph Ed Lachman m L. Subramaniam pd Mitch Epstein ed Roberto Silvi

Denzel Washington, Roshan Seth, Sarita Choudhury, Charles S. Dutton, Joe Seneca, Sharmila Tagore, Ranjit Chowdhry

'A film about racial issues which manages to avoid hatred and this leaves a joyously hopeful, if occasionally naive, aftertaste.' – *Empire*

The Mississippi Mermaid *

France/Italy 1969 123m Eastmancolor Dyaliscope
Films du Carrosse/PAA/Delphos (Marcel Berbert)
V*, S
original title: *La Sirène du Mississippi*

After a courtship by mail, a factory owner on a remote African island finds that the girl who arrives by steamer does not fit his preconceptions . . .

Oddly obsessive romantic murder mystery: the hero continues to love the girl who tries to kill him, and at the end they are still together. Interesting when it is not uncomfortable.

wd François Truffaut novel Waltz into Darkness by William Irish ph Denys Clerval m Antoine Duhamel ad Claude Pignot ed Agnès Guillemot

Jean-Paul Belmondo, Catherine Deneuve, Michel Bouquet, Nelly Borgeaud, Marcel Berbert

'One Steals. One Kills. One Dies.'
The Missouri Breaks

US 1976 126m DeLuxe
UA/Elliott Kastner/Robert B. Sherman
V, V*

Montana ranchers and rustlers fight over land and livestock, and a hired killer shoots it out with a horse thief.

Savage, dislikeable Western with both stars over the top.

w Thomas McGuane d Arthur Penn ph Michael Butler m John Williams

Marlon Brando, Jack Nicholson, Randy Quaid, Kathleen Lloyd, Frederic Forrest, Harry Dean Stanton

'It is typical of the film's richness and ambiguity that the title has about five possible punning meanings.' – *Michael Billington, Illustrated London News*

'Although listed as the director, Mr Penn finds himself perched on Brando's knee and manipulated as shamelessly as Edgar Bergen used to waggle Charlie McCarthy.' – *Benny Green, Punch*

'Nothing more than the self-conscious cleverness of some merry prankster with a blanket of scorn for all who don't share his flippancy.' – *William S. Pechter*

'A pair of million dollar babies in a five and ten cent flick.' – *Charles Champlin, Los Angeles Times*

'A picture of which it might be said they shouldn't make 'em like that any more . . . a picture that explains very little, including why anyone thought it a work that demanded to be made.' – *Robert Hatch, Nation*

Mr Ace

US   1946   84m   bw
Benedict Bogeaus

A rich, spoiled congresswoman is backed by a gangster but gets religion.

Odd star drama, perfunctorily made.

w Fred Finklehoffe   *d* Edwin L. Marin   *ph* Karl Struss   *m* Heinz Roemheld

Sylvia Sidney, George Raft, Stanley Ridges, Sara Haden, Jerome Cowan

Mr & Mrs Bridge **

US   1990   124m   Technicolor
Palace/Cineplex Odeon/Merchant Ivory/Robert Halmi (Ismail Merchant)
V, V*, L, S

An inhibited lawyer snuffs out his wife's individuality during a long and apparently happy marriage.

Intriguing portrait of two self-limiting lives, made more effective by being played by a real-life husband and wife.

w Ruth Prawer Jhabvala   *novel* Evan S. Connell   *d* James Ivory   *ph* Tony Pierce-Roberts   *m* Richard Robbins   *pd* David Gropman   *ed* Humphrey Dixon

Paul Newman, Joanne Woodward, Robert Sean Leonard, Margaret Walsh, Kyra Sedgwick, Blythe Danner, Simon Callow, Saundra McClain

'Brilliantly written and acted, and immensely watchable.' – *MFB*

AAN: Joanne Woodward

Mr and Mrs North

US   1941   68m   bw
Irving Asher/MGM

Mr and Mrs find a corpse in their closet.

Reasonably lively transcription of a Broadway success.

w S. K. Lauren   *play* Owen Davis   *d* Robert B. Sinclair

Gracie Allen, William Post Jnr, Paul Kelly, Rose Hobart, Virginia Grey, Tom Conway, Felix Bressart, Porter Hall, Millard Mitchell, Keye Luke, Jerome Cowan

Mr and Mrs Smith *

US   1941   95m   bw
RKO (Harry E. Edington)
V*, L

A much-married couple discover that their marriage wasn't legal.

Smartish matrimonial comedy, surprisingly but not obviously by the master of suspense.

w Norman Krasna   *d* Alfred Hitchcock   *ph* Harry Stradling   *m* Edward Ward

Carole Lombard, Robert Montgomery, Gene Raymond, Jack Carson, Philip Merivale, Lucile Watson, William Tracy

'I doubt that your interest or amusement will last as long as the picture.' – *Otis Ferguson*

Mr Arkadin: see *Confidential Report*

Mr Ashton Was Indiscreet: see *The Senator Was Indiscreet*

Mr Belvedere Goes to College *

US   1949   88m   bw
TCF (Samuel G. Engel)

A self-styled genius goes back to school and helps a college widow.

Flat follow up to *Sitting Pretty* (qv), with only a few laughs.

w Richard Sale, Mary Loos, Mary McCall Jnr   *d* Elliott Nugent   *ph* Lloyd Ahern   *m* Alfred Newman

Clifton Webb, Shirley Temple, Alan Young, Tom Drake, Jessie Royce Landis, Kathleen Hughes, Taylor Holmes

Mr Belvedere Rings the Bell *

US   1951   87m   bw
TCF (André Hakim)

Imperturbable Mr Belvedere enters an old folk's home under false pretences to test his theories of ageing.

A not unagreeable star vehicle for those who can stand the sentiment.

w Ranald MacDougall   *play The Silver Whistle* by Robert E. McEnroe   *d* Henry Koster   *ph* Joseph LaShelle   *m* Cyril Mockridge

Clifton Webb, Joanne Dru, Hugh Marlowe, Zero Mostel, Doro Merande

Mr Big

US   1943   73m   bw
Ken Goldsmith/Universal

Drama school students concoct a musical show.

Tolerable minor showcase for a new young star.

w Jack Pollexfen, Dorothy Bennett   *d* Charles Lamont

Donald O'Connor, Gloria Jean, Peggy Ryan, Robert Paige, Elyse Knox, Samuel S. Hinds, Florence Bates

Mr Billion *

US   1977   93m   DeLuxe
TCF/Pantheon (Gabriel Katzka, Steve Bach, Ken Friedman)
V*

An Italian garage mechanic becomes heir to a vast estate, providing he can get to San Francisco in time for the signing ceremony and outwit the villains trying to stop him.

Moderately engaging old-fashioned comedy-adventure.

w Ken Friedman, Jonathan Kaplan   *d* Jonathan Kaplan   *ph* Matthew F. Leonetti   *m* Dave Grusin

Terence Hill, Valerie Perrine, Jackie Gleason, Slim Pickens, William Redfield, Chill Wills

Mr Blandings Builds His Dream House ***

US   1948   84m   bw
RKO (Norman Panama, Melvin Frank)
V*, L

A New York advertising man longs to live in the Connecticut countryside, but finds the way to rural satisfaction is hard.

It hasn't the lightness and brightness of the book, but this is a fun film for the middle-aged who like to watch three agreeable stars doing their thing.

w Norman Panama, Melvin Frank   *novel* Eric Hodgins   *d* H. C. Potter   *ph* James Wong Howe   *md* Constantin Bakaleinikoff   *m* Leigh Harline

Cary Grant, Myrna Loy, Melvyn Douglas, Reginald Denny, Louise Beavers, Ian Wolfe, Harry Shannon, Nestor Paiva, Jason Robards

'A bulls-eye for middle-class middlebrows.' – *James Agee*

'I loved it. That was really a pleasure to make.' – *H. C. Potter, 1973*

Mister Buddwing

US   1966   99m   bw
MGM/DDD/Cherokee (Douglas Laurence, Delbert Mann)
GB title: *Woman without a Face*

An amnesiac wakes up in Central Park and goes in search of his identity.

Rather muddled melodrama in which the characters are so dull that by the time the flashbacks fall into place we scarcely care.

w Dale Wassermann   *novel Buddwing* by Evan Hunter   *d* Delbert Mann   *ph* Ellsworth Fredericks   *m* Kenyon Hopkins

James Garner, Jean Simmons, Angela Lansbury, Suzanne Pleshette, Katharine Ross, George Voskovec, Jack Gilford, Joe Mantell, Raymond St Jacques

'Its distinction is its pretension, its banality and its complete success in making all the authentic New York backgrounds look like the studio's cheaper backdrops.' – *Judith Crist*

Mr Bug Goes to Town *

US   1941   78m   Technicolor
Max Fleischer
V*
aka: *Hoppity Goes to Town*

An urban community of insects is in danger from developers.

A cartoon feature which failed to make its mark despite clever detail; perhaps because insects make poor heroes, or because there simply wasn't enough plot.

d Dave Fleischer   *m* Leigh Harline

Mr Chedworth Steps Out

Australia   1939   92m   bw
Cinesound

In a period of redundancy a clerk has to take a job as a caretaker, but discovers a cache of counterfeit money.

Mild comedy-drama.

w Frank Harvey   *d* Ken G. Hall

Cecil Kellaway, Jean Hatton, James Raglan, Rita Pauncefort, Peter Finch

Mister Cinderella

US   1936   75m   bw
Hal Roach/MGM

A meek-and-mild youth aspires to crash high society.

Milk-and-water comedy with insufficient get-up-and-go.

w Arthur Vernon Jones, Richard Flournoy, Jack Jevne   *d* Edward Sedgwick

Jack Haley, Betty Furness, Arthur Treacher, Raymond Walburn, Rosina Lawrence, Monroe Owsley

'Too crammed with slaptrap hokum to stand alone.' – *Variety*

Mister Cory

US   1957   92m   Eastmancolor   Cinemascope
U-I (Robert Arthur)

A small-time gangster leaves the Chicago slums to seek fame and fortune among the country-club set.

Modest star comedy drama.

wd Blake Edwards   *ph* Russell Metty   *m* Joseph Gershenson

Tony Curtis, Martha Hyer, Charles Bickford, Kathryn Grant

Mr Deeds Goes to Town ***

US   1936   118m   bw
Columbia (Frank Capra)
V, V*, L

A small-town poet inherits a vast fortune and sets New York on its heels by his honesty.

What once was fresh and charming now seems rather laboured in spots, and the production is parsimonious indeed, but the courtroom scene still works, and the good intentions conquer all.

w Robert Riskin   *story Opera Hat* by Clarence Budington Kelland   *d Frank Capra*   *ph* Joseph Walker   *md* Howard Jackson   *m* Adolph Deutsch

Gary Cooper, Jean Arthur, Raymond Walburn, Lionel Stander, Walter Catlett, George Bancroft, Douglass Dumbrille, H. B. Warner, Ruth Donnelly, *Margaret Seddon, Margaret McWade*

'I have an uneasy feeling he's on his way out. He's started to make pictures about themes instead of people.' – *Alistair Cooke*

'Everywhere the picture goes, from the endearing to the absurd, the accompanying business is carried through with perfect zip and relish.' – *Otis Ferguson*

'A comedy quite unmatched on the screen.' – *Graham Greene*

'The film culminates in a courtroom sequence that introduced the word "pixilated" to just about every American home, and set people to examining each other's casual scribbles or sketches – their "doddles".' – *Pauline Kael, 70s*

AA: Frank Capra

AAN: best picture; Robert Riskin; Gary Cooper

Mr Denning Drives North
GB 1951 93m bw
London Films (Anthony Kimmins, Stephen Mitchell)

A wealthy man accidentally kills a criminal in love with his daughter; he hides the body, which then disappears.

Initially suspenseful but finally disappointing melodrama which seems to lack a twist or two.

w Alec Coppel *d* Anthony Kimmins *ph* John Wilcox *m* Benjamin Frankel

John Mills, Phyllis Calvert, Sam Wanamaker, Freda Jackson

Mr Destiny
US 1990 105m colour
Buena Vista/Touchstone/Silver Screen Partners IV (James Orr, Jim Cruikshank)
V*, L, S

A 35-year-old failure is given the chance to re-live his life as a success.

Dim comedy with the dimmer moral that everyone gets the life they deserve.

w James Orr, Jim Cruikshank *d* James Orr *ph* Alex Thomson *m* David Newman *pd* Michael Seymour *ed* Michael R. Miller

James Belushi, Linda Hamilton, Michael Caine, Jon Lovitz, Hart Bochner, Bill McCutcheon, René Russo

'A heavy-handed by-the-numbers fantasy.' – *Variety*

Mr District Attorney
US 1941 69m bw
Leonard Fields/Republic

A lady reporter helps a young assistant DA to ferret out crooks.

Dim movie version of a radio series.

w Karl Brown, Malcolm Stuart Boylan *d* William Morgan

Dennis O'Keefe, Florence Rice, Peter Lorre, Stanley Ridges, Minor Watson

Mr Dodd Takes the Air
US 1937 78m bw
Warner (Mervyn Le Roy)

A country cousin becomes a hit as a crooner.

Modest comedy for small towns.

w William Wister Haines, Elaine Ryan *story* Clarence Budington Kelland *d* Alfred E. Green *ph* Arthur Edeson *songs* Al Dubin, Harry Warren *md* Adolph Deutsch

Kenny Baker, Jane Wyman, Alice Brady, Gertrude Michael, Frank McHugh, Luis Alberni, Henry O'Neill, Harry Davenport

AAN: Al Dubin and Harry Warren for 'Remember Me'

Mr Drake's Duck **
GB 1950 85m bw
Daniel M. Angel/Douglas Fairbanks

A duck lays a uranium egg, and a gentleman farmer finds himself at the centre of international military disagreement.

Brisk and amusing minor comedy deploying British comic types to good purpose.

wd Val Guest radio play Ian Messiter *ph* Jack Cox *m* Philip Martell

Douglas Fairbanks Jnr, Yolande Donlan, Wilfrid Hyde-White, A. E. Matthews, Jon Pertwee, Reginald Beckwith, Howard Marion-Crawford, Peter Butterworth, Tom Gill

'One of the funniest films I have ever seen.' – *News of the World*

Mr Dynamite
US 1935 75m bw
Universal

An unconventional private detective outsmarts the police.

Amusing, wisecracking crime caper.

w Doris Malloy, Harry Clork *story* Dashiell Hammett *d* Alan Crosland

Edmund Lowe, Jean Dixon, Esther Ralston, Victor Varconi, Minor Watson, Robert Gleckler

'Nice entertainment.' – *Variety*

Mister 880 **
US 1950 90m bw
TCF (Julian Blaustein)

An elderly counterfeiter perplexes the US Secret Service.

Whimsical star comedy which moves along cheerfully enough to be a good example of the Hollywood programmer at its prime.

w Robert Riskin *d* Edmund Goulding *ph* Joseph LaShelle *m* Sol Kaplan

Edmund Gwenn, Burt Lancaster, Dorothy McGuire, Millard Mitchell

AAN: Edmund Gwenn

Mr Emmanuel *
GB 1944 97m bw
Two Cities (William Sistrom)

In 1936 an elderly Jew visits Germany in search of the mother of an orphan boy.

Simply made but quite effective and unusual story giving Aylmer his only star part.

w Gordon Wellesley, Norman Ginsburg *novel* Louis Golding *d* Harold French *ph* Otto Heller

Felix Aylmer, Greta Gynt, Walter Rilla, Peter Mullins, Ursula Jeans, Elspeth March, Meier Tzelniker

Mr Forbush and the Penguins *
GB 1971 101m Technicolor
EMI/PGI/Henry Trettin

A biologist is sent to the Antarctic to study penguins, and gets a new understanding of life.

Rather broken-backed animal film with a moral; pleasant enough, its two halves don't fit together.

w Anthony Shaffer *novel* Graham Billey *d* Roy Boulting, *Arne Sucksdorff ph* Harry Waxman, Ted Scaife *m* John Addison

John Hurt, Hayley Mills, Tony Britton, Thorley Walters, Judy Campbell, Joss Ackland, Sally Geeson, Cyril Luckham

Mister Frost
France/UK 1990 104m colour
Blue Dolphin/AAA/Hugo Films/Overseas Multi Media (Xavier Gelin)
V, V*, L

The devil incarnate tempts a hospital doctor.

Nonsensical and incomprehensible, a lurid mess from start to finish.

w Philippe Setbon, Brad Lynch *d* Philippe Setbon *ph* Dominique Brenguier *m* Steve Levine *ad* Max Berto *m* Ray Lovejoy

Jeff Goldblum, Alan Bates, Kathy Baker, Roland Giraud, Jean-Pierre Cassell, Daniel Gelin, François Negret, Maxime Leroux, Boris Bergman

'Staggeringly bad.' – *Philip French, Observer*

Mr Griggs Returns: see The Cockeyed Miracle

Mr Hobbs Takes a Vacation *
US 1962 116m DeLuxe Cinemascope
TCF (Jerry Wald)

A city dweller takes a seaside house for a family holiday, but it turns out to be a crumbling ruin.

Overlong, sloppy comedy which devotes too much time to teenage romance but manages occasional smiles.

w Nunnally Johnson *novel* Edward Streeter *d* Henry Koster *ph* W. C. Mellor *m* Henry Mancini

James Stewart, Maureen O'Hara, Fabian, John Saxon, Marie Wilson, Reginald Gardiner, *John McGiver*

Mr Hobo: see The Guvnor

Mr Imperium
US 1951 87m Technicolor
MGM (Edwin H. Knopf)
GB title: *You Belong to My Heart*

An exiled king in Hollywood meets a famous film star with whom he once had a romance.

Minor romantic drama with songs.

w Edwin Knopf, Don Hartman *d* Don Hartman *ph* George J. Folsey *songs* Harold Arlen (*m*), Dorothy Fields (*ly*) *m* Bronislau Kaper

Lana Turner, Ezio Pinza, Marjorie Main, Barry Sullivan, Cedric Hardwicke, Debbie Reynolds

'He's a proper Englishman in his heart. But Africa is in his soul'

Mr Johnson **
US 1990 101m Eastmancolor Panavision
TCF/Avenue Pictures (Michael Fitzgerald)
V, V*

In West Africa in the 1920s a naïve and feckless clerk, who attempts to be more English than the English, destroys himself by seeking the easy way out of his problems.

Deftly acted and directed tragi-comedy of human fallibility and colonial attitudes.

w William Boyd *novel* Joyce Cary *d* Bruce Beresford *m* Georges Delerue *pd* Herbert Pinter *ed* Humphrey Dixon

Pierce Brosnan, Edward Woodward, *Maynard Eziashi*, Beatie Edney, Denis Quilley, Bella Enahoro, Kwabena Manso, Nick Reding, Femi Fatoba

'Suffers the same fate as its title character, never coming close to being as important as it desperately wants to be.' – *Variety*

'A very generous, thoughtful and affecting movie.' – *Philip French, Observer*

Mr Klein *
France/Italy 1976 123m Eastmancolor
Lira/Adel/Nova/Mondial Te-Fi (Raymond Danon, Alain Delon)
V*, S

In 1942 Paris, a prosperous antique dealer is mistaken for a mysterious Jew of the same name, and despite the danger gradually assumes his identity.

Complex Kafkaesque character study: occasionally arresting but generally rather glum.

w Franco Solinas d Joseph Losey ph Gerry Fisher m Egisto Macchi, Pierre Porte

Alain Delon, Jeanne Moreau, Suzanne Flon, Michael Lonsdale, Louis Seigner, Juliet Berto

Mr Lord Says No: see The Happy Family

Mr Love
GB 1986 91m colour
Warner/Goldcrest/Enigma (Susan Richards, Robin Douet)

A mild-mannered cinema projectionist develops an erroneous reputation as a Don Juan.

Ineffective character comedy with too few laughs and a minimum of accurate observation.

w Kenneth Eastaugh d Roy Battersby ph Clive Tickner m Willy Russell

Barry Jackson, Maurice Denham, Margaret Tyzack, Linda Marlowe, Cristina Collier

'It renders would-be regional fantasy into something merely parochial.' – Tim Pulleine, MFB

Mr Lucky *
US 1943 98m bw
RKO (David Hempstead)
V

During World War II a gambling ship owner goes straight and instigates Bundles for Britain.

Unconvincing mixture of comedy and drama with the actors looking somewhat bewildered.

w Milton Holmes, Adrian Scott d H. C. Potter ph George Barnes m Roy Webb

Cary Grant, Laraine Day, Charles Bickford, Gladys Cooper, Alan Carney, Henry Stephenson, Paul Stewart, Walter Kingsford

'If it weren't for Cary Grant's persuasive personality the whole thing would melt away to nothing at all.' – Philip G. Hartung

† Remade 1950 as Gambling House.

Mr Majestyk *
US 1974 103m DeLuxe
UA/Mirisch (Walter Mirisch)

A Colorado melon grower crosses swords with the local Mafia.

Violent but unexpectedly enjoyable action melodrama.

w Elmore Leonard d Richard Fleischer ph Richard Kline m Charles Bernstein

Charles Bronson, Al Lettieri, Linda Cristal, Lee Purcell, Paul Keslo

'What I liked best about this trash is that Bronson begins each action sequence like Nureyev beginning a difficult solo.' – Stanley Kauffmann

Mr Mom
US 1983 91m Metrocolor
Fox/Sherwood (Lynn Loring)
V, V*, L
GB title: Mr Mum

Dad loses his executive job and stays home to mind the kids while his wife works.

Obvious farce with too much messy slapstick and no real development.

w John Hughes d Stan Dragoti ph Victor J. Kemper m Lee Holdridge pd Alfred Sweeney ed Patrick Kennedy

Michael Keaton, Teri Garr, Frederick Koehler, Martin Mull, Ann Jillian

'The jokes almost sink without trace in a hazy domestic setting straight from the hoariest sitcom.' – Geoff Brown, MFB

Mister Moses *
GB 1965 103m Technicolor Panavision
UA/Frank Ross/Talbot

A quack doctor is the only person who can persuade an African tribe to move before their land is flooded, and he leads them to their promised land.

Adventure spectacle with naïve biblical parallels; quite agreeable.

w Charles Beaumont, Monja Danischewsky novel Max Catto d Ronald Neame ph Oswald Morris m John Barry

Robert Mitchum, Carroll Baker, Ian Bannen, Alexander Knox, Reginald Beckwith, Raymond St Jacques

Mr Moto
The Japanese detective created by John P. Marquand and played by Peter Lorre figured in several above-average second features of the late thirties, but the outbreak of war caused him to vanish.

The casts were interesting, the TCF production excellent, and the director usually Norman Foster. The 1965 attempt to revive the character with Henry Silva was painfully boring.

1937: THINK FAST MR MOTO (with Virginia Field, Sig Rumann), THANK YOU MR MOTO (with Pauline Frederick, Sidney Blackmer)
1938: MR MOTO'S GAMBLE (with Keye Luke, Lynn Bari), MR MOTO TAKES A CHANCE (with Rochelle Hudson, J. Edward Bromberg), MYSTERIOUS MR MOTO (with Henry Wilcoxon, Erik Rhodes)
1939: MR MOTO'S LAST WARNING (with Ricardo Cortez, George Sanders, Robert Coote, John Carradine), MR MOTO IN DANGER ISLAND (with Jean Hersholt, Warren Hymer), MR MOTO TAKES A VACATION (with Joseph Schildkraut, Lionel Atwill)
1965: THE RETURN OF MR MOTO

Mr Moto's Gamble
US 1938 71m bw
TCF

Mr Moto investigates the murder of a boxer in the ring.

An enjoyable, if silly, B feature; it is a more conventional mystery than most of the Moto series, owing to its origins as a movie intended to feature Charlie Chan.

w Charles Belden, Jerry Cady d James Tinling ph Lucien Andriot ad Bernard Herzbrun, Haldane Douglas ed Nick DeMaggio

Peter Lorre, Keye Luke, Dick Baldwin, Lynn Bari, Douglas Fowley, Jayne Regan, Harold Huber, Maxie Rosenbloom, Ward Bond, Lon Chaney Jnr

† The script was originally intended as a Charlie Chan mystery, but was changed following the death of the star of that series, Warner Oland. It explains the appearance here of Key Luke as Chan's Number One son.

Mr Mum: see Mr Mom

Mr Music *
US 1950 113m bw
Paramount (Robert L. Welch)
V*

A college girl is employed to keep an idle middle-aged songwriter's nose to the grindstone.

Bland musical remake of Accent on Youth (qv); pleasant performances, moments of comedy, guest stars.

w Arthur Sheekman d Richard Haydn ph George Barnes songs Johnny Burke, James Van Heusen ad Hans Dreier, Earl Hedrick

Bing Crosby, Nancy Olson, Charles Coburn, Ruth Hussey, Marge and Gower Champion, Peggy Lee, Groucho Marx

Mr Nanny
US 1992 84m colour
Entertainment (Bob Engelman)
V, V*

A child-hating wrestler acts as a bodyguard to the two small and mischievous children of an inventor.

Wearying comedy that might amuse the very young, in which Hulk Hogan can be seen trying, and failing, to find a suitable role for himself in the movies.

w Edward Rugoff, Michael Gottlieb d Michael Gottlieb ph Peter Stein m David Johansen, Brian Koonin pd Don de Fina ed Earl Ghaffari, Michael Ripps

Terry 'Hulk' Hogan, Sherman Hemsley, Austin Pendelton, Robert Gorman, Madeline Zima, Raymond O'Connor, David Johansen

'A banal exercise in low-budget comedy.' – Sight and Sound

Mr North *
US 1988 93m Metrocolor
Columbia TriStar/Heritage Entertainment/Showcase Productions (Steven Haft, Skip Steloff)
V*, L

In the wealthy society of Newport in the 1920s, a young man angers the local doctor by gaining a reputation as a miracle healer.

Gentle, amusing fable, peopled by some engaging eccentrics.

w Joanet Roach, John Huston, James Costigan novel Theophilus North by Thornton Wilder d Danny Huston ph Robin Vidgeon m David McHugh pd Eugene Lee ed Roberto Silvi

Anthony Edwards, Robert Mitchum, Lauren Bacall, Harry Dean Stanton, Anjelica Huston, Mary Stuart Masterson, Virginia Madsen, Tammy Grimes, David Warner

Mr Peabody and the Mermaid
US 1948 89m bw
U-I (Nunnally Johnson)
V*

A middle-aged husband imagines an affair with a mermaid.

Bone-headed quick-cash-in on Miranda (qv); it never begins to work.

w Nunnally Johnson novel Guy and Constance Jones d Irving Pichel ph Russell Metty m Robert Emmett Dolan

William Powell, Ann Blyth, Irene Hervey, Andrea King, Clinton Sundberg

Mr Perrin and Mr Traill *
GB 1948 92m bw
GFD/Two Cities (Alexander Galperson)

A handsome young master at a boys' school incurs the jealousy of an embittered colleague.

Flat, over-acted but mildly watchable picturization of a well-known story.

w L. A. G. Strong novel Hugh Walpole d Lawrence Huntington ph Erwin Hillier m Alan Gray

Marius Goring, David Farrar, Greta Gynt, Edward Chapman, Raymond Huntley, Mary Jerrold, Finlay Currie, Ralph Truman

Mr Potts Goes to Moscow: see Top Secret

Mister Quilp

GB 1975 119m Technicolor Panavision
Reader's Digest (Helen M. Straus)
aka: The Old Curiosity Shop

In 1840 London, an antique-shop owner is in debt to a hunchback moneylender who has designs on his business.

The novel, with its villainous lead, is a curious choice for musicalizing, and in this treatment falls desperately flat, with no sparkle of imagination visible anywhere.

w Louis Kamp, Irene Kamp novel The Old Curiosity Shop by Charles Dickens d Michael Tuchner ph Christopher Challis md Elmer Bernstein m Anthony Newley pd Elliot Gould ch: Gillian Lynne

Anthony Newley, Michael Hordern, David Hemmings, Sarah-Jane Varley, David Warner, Paul Rogers, Jill Bennett

'Another soggy piece of family entertainment from Reader's Digest, who produced the toothless screen musicals of Tom Sawyer and Huckleberry Finn.' – Philip French

'Dickens shorn of sentiment, melodrama or love . . . Mr Newley's Quilp, a galvanized Quasimodo on a permanent high, is something of a strain to watch.' – Michael Billington, Illustrated London News

Mr Ricco

US 1975 98m colour Panavision
MGM (Douglas Netter)

A defence counsel risks his life to prove his black client innocent.

Complex urban action thriller with a tired, ageing hero and impenetrable plot.

w Robert Hoban d Paul Bogart ph Frank Stanley m Chico Hamilton

Dean Martin, Eugene Roche, Thalmus Rasulala, Denise Nicholas, Cindy Williams, Geraldine Brooks, Frank Puglia

Mister Roberts **

US 1955 123m Warnercolor Cinemascope
Warner/Leland Hayward
V*

Life aboard a World War II cargo ship yearning for action.

A mixture of comedy and sentimentality which has become an American minor classic as a play; this film version is a shambling affair but gets most of the effects over.

w Frank Nugent, Joshua Logan play Thomas Heggen and Joshua Logan novel Thomas Heggen d John Ford, Mervyn Le Roy ph Winton Hoch m Franz Waxman

Henry Fonda, James Cagney, William Powell, Jack Lemmon, Betsy Palmer, Ward Bond, Phil Carey, Ken Curtis, Harry Carey Jnr

AA: Jack Lemmon

AAN: best picture

Mr Robinson Crusoe

US 1932 76m bw
Douglas Fairbanks
V*, L

A playboy takes a bet that he could live alone on a desert island . . . but a girl turns up.

Mild adventure comedy with the star in subdued form.

w Douglas Fairbanks d Edward Sutherland ph Max Dupont m Alfred Newman

Douglas Fairbanks, William Farnum, Earle Browne, Maria Alba

'A man so evil – his face could stop a heart!'
Mr Sardonicus

US 1961 90m bw
Columbia/William Castle

A surgeon is lured to an ex-girlfriend's remote home to cure her sadistic husband's crippled face.

Flatly handled, boring semi-horror.

w Robb White d William Castle ph Burnett Guffey m Von Dexter

Ronald Lewis, Guy Rolfe, Audrey Dalton, Oscar Homolka

'It's lonely at the middle.'
Mr Saturday Night *

US 1992 119m colour
Columbia/Castle Rock/New Line (Billy Crystal)
V, V*, L, S

In his dotage, a successful comedian looks back over his long career.

Intermittently amusing comedy, not helped by over-generous dollops of sentimentality.

w Billy Crystal, Lowell Ganz, Babaloo Mandel d Billy Crystal ph Don Peterman m Marc Shaiman pd Albert Brenner ed Kent Beyda

Billy Crystal, David Paymer, Julie Warner, Helen Hunt, Ron Silver

'What's so special about this movie is that the funny parts are so funny, with gags coming too fast and too good to be assimilated on first hearing. At such moments, the main reaction is exhausted gratitude. It's as if you hired a painter to do your bathroom and he gave you the Sistine Chapel at no extra cost.' – Richard Corliss, Time

AAN: David Paymer

Mr Scoutmaster

US 1953 87m bw
TCF

A TV personality wants to understand children and is persuaded to take over a scout troop.

A star vehicle which starts promisingly enough in the Sitting Pretty vein but quickly falls headlong into an abyss of sentimentality.

w Leonard Praskins, Barney Slater d Henry Levin ph Joseph LaShelle md Lionel Newman m Cyril Mockridge

Clifton Webb, Edmund Gwenn, George Winslow, Frances Dee, Veda Ann Borg

Mr Skeffington ***

US 1944 127m bw
Warner (Julius J. and Philip G. Epstein)
V*, L

A selfish beauty finally turns to her discarded dull husband; when he is blind, he doesn't mind her faded looks.

Long, patchily made, but thoroughly enjoyable star melodrama.

w Julius J. and Philip G. Epstein novel Elizabeth d Vincent Sherman ph Ernest Haller m Franz Waxman

Bette Davis, Claude Rains, Walter Abel, Richard Waring, George Coulouris, John Alexander, Jerome Cowan

'An endless woman's page dissertation on What To Do When Beauty Fades.' – James Agee

'To call the film a good one would be to exaggerate; but entertaining and interesting, I insist, it is.' – Richard Mallett, Punch

AAN: Bette Davis; Claude Rains

Mr Skitch

US 1933 70m bw
Fox

A Missouri family heads for California.

Very passable star family entertainment.

w Anne Cameron novel Green Dice by Anne Cameron d James Cruze

Will Rogers, ZaSu Pitts, Florence Desmond, Rochelle Hudson

'Enough laughs to please in general.' – Variety

'Stirring – in the seeing! Precious – in the remembering!
Mr Smith Goes to Washington ****

US 1939 130m bw
Columbia (Frank Capra)
V, V*, L

Washington's youngest senator exposes corruption in high places, almost at the cost of his own career.

Archetypal high-flying Capra vehicle, with the little man coming out top as he seldom does in life. Supreme gloss hides the corn, helter-skelter direction keeps one watching, and all concerned give memorable performances. A cinema classic.

w Sidney Buchman, story Lewis R. Foster d Frank Capra ph Joseph Walker montage Slavko Vorkapich m Dimitri Tiomkin ad Lionel Banks

James Stewart, Claude Rains, Jean Arthur, Thomas Mitchell, Edward Arnold, Guy Kibbee, Eugene Pallette, Beulah Bondi, Harry Carey, H. B. Warner, Astrid Allwyn, Ruth Donnelly, Charles Lane, Porter Hall

SMITH (James Stewart): 'I wouldn't give you two cents for all your fancy rules if, behind them, they didn't have a little bit of plain, ordinary kindness – and a little looking out for the other fella, too.'

'Timely and absorbing drama presented in best Capra craftsmanship.' – Variety

'More fun, even, than the Senate itself . . . not merely a brilliant jest, but a stirring and even inspiring testament to liberty and freedom.' – Frank S. Nugent, New York Times

'It says all the things about America that have been crying out to be said again – and says them beautifully.' – Los Angeles Times

'The great American picture.' – Billboard

'I feel that to show this film in foreign countries will do inestimable harm to American prestige all over the world.' – Joseph P. Kennedy, then American ambassador to Great Britain

'A totally compelling piece of movie-making, upholding the virtues of traditional American ideals.' – NFT, 1973

'Very good, beautifully done and extremely entertaining; long, but worth the time it takes.' – Richard Mallett, Punch

'More of the heartfelt than is good for the stomach.' – New Yorker, 1977

AA: Lewis R. Foster

AAN: best picture; Sidney Buchman; Frank Capra; Dimitri Tiomkin; James Stewart; Claude Rains; Harry Carey; Lionel Banks

Mr Soft Touch

US 1949 93m bw
Columbia
GB title: House of Settlement

A gangster is reformed at Christmas by a social worker.

Dewy-eyed romance with Damon Runyonish asides; only for soft touches.

w Orin Jannings d Henry Levin and Gordon Douglas

Glenn Ford, Evelyn Keyes, John Ireland, Beulah Bondi, Percy Kilbride, Roman Bohnen

Mr Topaze

GB 1961 84m Eastmancolor Cinemascope
TCF/Dimitri de Grunwald (Pierre Rouve)
US title: I Like Money

An honest ex-schoolmaster becomes prosperous when he joins some shady businessmen.

Predictable, sluggish character comedy, with a good actor unable to make it as a star. Or as a director.

w Pierre Rouve play Topaze by Marcel Pagnol
d Peter Sellers ph John Wilcox m Georges Van Parys

Peter Sellers, Herbert Lom, Leo McKern, Nadia Gray, Martita Hunt, John Neville, Billie Whitelaw, Michael Gough, Joan Sims, John Le Mesurier, Michael Sellers

'A film of minor pleasures and major inadequacies.' – Penelope Houston, MFB

† See also Topaze (1933).

Mr Universe
US 1951 79m bw
Laurel/Eagle Lion

Con men promote a new wrestler.

Fair low-class comedy with some laughs.

w Earle Kramer d Joseph Lerner

Bert Lahr, Jack Carson, Vincent Edwards, Janis Paige, Robert Alda

Mister V: see Pimpernel Smith

Mr Winkle Goes to War
US 1944 80m bw
Columbia (Jack Moss)
GB title: Arms and the Woman

A middle-aged bank clerk joins the army and becomes a hero.

Agreeable, forgettable propaganda comedy-drama.

w Waldo Salt, George Corey, Louis Solomon
novel Theodore Pratt d Alfred E. Green ph Joseph Walker m Carmen Dragon, Paul Sawtell

Edward G. Robinson, Ruth Warrick, Ted Donaldson, Bob Haymes, Richard Lane, Robert Armstrong, Walter Baldwin

'Sometimes the wrong person is the only right person for you.'

Mr Wonderful
US 1992 97m Technicolor
Buena Vista/Samuel Goldwyn (Marianne Moloney)

A divorced couple decide to get together again.

A romantic comedy about star-crossed lovers becoming uncrossed that lacks force or passion.

wd Anthony Minghella from original screenplay by Amy Schor, Vicki Polon ph Geoffrey Simpson
m Michael Gore pd Doug Kraner ed John Tintori

Matt Dillon, Annabella Sciorra, Mary-Louise Parker, William Hurt, Vincent D'Onfronio, David Barry Gray, Dan Hedaya

'Makes a good shot at the difficult assignment of making romantic comedy for a modern audience.' – Adam Mars-Jones, Independent

Mr Wong

A cheeseparing set of second features from Monogram, based on stories by Hugh Wiley.

Boris Karloff was unsuitably cast as a Chinese detective, and in the last film he was replaced by Keye Luke. The films were directed by William Nigh.

1938: MR WONG DETECTIVE
1939: THE MYSTERY OF MR WONG, MR WONG IN CHINATOWN
1940: THE FATAL HOUR, DOOMED TO DIE (GB title: THE MYSTERY OF THE WENTWORTH CASTLE)
1941: PHANTOM OF CHINATOWN

Mr Wu *
US 1927 80m approx (24 fps) bw silent
MGM

A Chinese villain kills his daughter when she wants to marry an Englishman.

Turgid outmoded melodrama from a stage success: purely a star vehicle.

w Lorna Moon play Maurice Vernon, Harold Owen
d William Nigh ph John Arnold

Lon Chaney, Louise Dresser, Anna May Wong, Ralph Forbes, Renee Adoree, Holmes Herbert

Il Mistero di Oberwald: see The Oberwald Mystery

'Everybody's trying to get their girlfriend into the movies . . .'

Mistress *
US 1992 110m CFI colour
Tribeca (Meir Teper, Robert de Niro)
V, V*

A writer-director discovers that all those approached to finance his movie have girlfriends who want a leading part in it, providing he changes the script to suit them.

Enjoyable satire on the dangers of integrity among minor players in a movie-making industry.

w Barry Primus, Jonathan L. Lawton d Barry Primus ph Sven Kirsten m Galt MacDermot
pd Phil Peters ed Steve Weisberg

Robert Wuhl, Martin Landau, Robert de Niro, Jace Alexander, Laurie Metcalf, Danny Aiello, Christopher Walken, Eli Wallach, Tuesday Weld, Sheryl Lee Ralph, Ernest Borgnine

'Can't seem to decide if it's supposed to be a comedy about Hollywood small-timers trying to get an indie pic off the ground, or a somber drama in which greed and lust overwhelm art.' – Variety

Mrs Brown, You've Got a Lovely Daughter
GB 1968 95m Metrocolor Panavision
MGM/Allen Klein
V*

A young singer inherits a prize greyhound.

Inoffensive comedy musical with a swinging London background.

w Thaddeus Vane d Saul Swimmer

Peter Noone and Herman's Hermits, Stanley Holloway, Mona Washbourne, Lance Percival, Marjorie Rhodes

'She makes dinner. She does windows. She reads bedtime stories. She's a blessing . . . in disguise.'

Mrs Doubtfire *
US 1993 125m DeLuxe Panavision
TCF/Blue Wolf (Marcia Garces Williams, Robin Williams, Mark Radcliffe)
S

An unemployed actor, allowed only weekly visits to his two children, disguises himself as a nanny so that he can spend more time with them.

If you can accept Williams as an Englishwoman – he looks like a truck driver in drag and sounds like Miss Jean Brodie long past her prime – there is occasional slapstick amusement to be found in this over-long and sickly sweet comedy.

w Randi Mayem Singer, Leslie Dixon novel Alias Madam Doubtfire by Anne Fine d Chris Columbus
ph Donald McAlpine m Howard Shore
pd Angelo Graham sp Grag Cannom ed Raja Gosnell

Robin Williams, Sally Field, Pierce Brosnan, Harvey Fierstein, Polly Holiday, Lisa Jakub, Matthew Lawrence, Mara Wilson, Robert Prosky

'Lessons are learned, loved ones are hugged, and personal growth is achieved – as usual, at the expense of the comedy. Some, apparently, including Williams, like it warm and cuddly, too. Nobody's perfect.' – Terrence Rafferty, New Yorker

'A really wholesome movie about a man in a bra; it's like watching a John Waters movie rewritten by John Hughes.' – Libby Gelman-Waxner, Premiere

'This Robin Williams-in-drag vehicle provides the comic with a slick surface for doing his shtick, within a story possessing broad family appeal.' – Variety

† The film was a success in America, taking more than $200m at the box-office.

AAN: make-up

Mrs Fitzherbert
GB 1947 99m bw
British National (Louis H. Jackson)

The Prince Regent secretly marries a Catholic widow.

Stilted, ill-cast historical charade.

wd Montgomery Tully novel Winifred Carter
ph James Wilson m Hans May

Peter Graves, Joyce Howard, Leslie Banks, Margaretta Scott

Mrs Gibbons' Boys
GB 1962 82m bw Byronscope
Byron/British Lion

A widow plans to marry respectably for the sake of her three convict sons.

Unattractive farce with clodhopping characters and too much slapstick.

w Peter Blackmore, Max Varnel play Joseph Stein, Will Glickman d Max Varnel

Kathleen Harrison, Lionel Jeffries, Diana Dors, John Le Mesurier, Frederick Bartman, David Lodge, Dick Emery, Eric Pohlmann, Milo O'Shea

Mrs Loring's Secret: see The Imperfect Lady

Mrs Mike
US 1949 99m bw
Nassour/Huntingdon Hartford (Edward Gross)

A Mountie takes his new wife to live in the frozen northwest.

Predictable sentimental drama, well enough done to keep interest, but only just.

w Lewis Levitt, De Witt Bodeen d Louis King
ph Joseph Biroc m Max Steiner

Dick Powell, Evelyn Keyes, J. M. Kerrigan, Angela Clarke

Mrs Miniver **
US 1942 134m bw
MGM (Sidney Franklin)
V, V*, L

An English housewife survives World War II.

This is the rose-strewn English village, Hollywood variety, but when released it proved a beacon of morale despite its false sentiment, absurd rural types and melodramatic situations. It is therefore beyond criticism, except that some of the people involved should have known better.

w Arthur Wimperis, George Froeschel, James Hilton, Claudine West novel Jan Struther d William Wyler ph Joseph Ruttenberg m Herbert Stothart
ed Harold F. Kress

Greer Garson, Walter Pidgeon, Teresa Wright, Richard Ney, Dame May Whitty, Henry Travers, Reginald Owen, Henry Wilcoxon, Helmut Dantine, Rhys Williams, Aubrey Mather

VICAR (Henry Wilcoxon) preaching final sermon in bombed church: 'This is not only a war of soldiers in uniforms. It is a war of the people – of all the people – and it must be fought not only on the battlefield but in the cities and in the villages, in the factories and on the farms, in the home and in the heart of every man, woman and child who loves freedom. Well, we have buried our dead, but we shall not forget them. Instead, they will inspire us with an unbreakable determination to free ourselves and those who come after us from the tyranny and terror that threaten to strike us down. This is the people's war. It is our war. We are the fighters. Fight it, then. Fight it with all that is in us. And may God defend the right.'

'That almost impossible feat, a war picture that photographs the inner meaning, instead of the outward realism of World War II.' – *Time*

AA: best picture; script; William Wyler; Joseph Ruttenberg; Greer Garson; Teresa Wright

AAN: Walter Pidgeon; Dame May Whitty; Henry Travers; Harold F. Kress

Mrs O'Malley and Mr Malone *
US   1950   69m   bw
MGM (William H. Wright)

On a train to New York, a radio contest winner and a lawyer help solve a murder.

Lively second feature farce.

w William Bowers   *d* Norman Taurog   *m* Adolph Deutsch

Marjorie Main, James Whitmore, Ann Dvorak, Fred Clark, Dorothy Malone, Phyllis Kirk

Mrs Parkington
US   1944   124m   bw
MGM (Leon Gordon)
V*

A lady's maid marries a miner who becomes wealthy, and pushes her way into society.

Thoroughly unconvincing three-generation drama, with a bewigged and powdered star giving the boot to her conniving relations. It has production values and nothing else.

w Robert Thoeren, Polly James   *novel* Louis Bromfield   *d* Tay Garnett   *ph* Joseph Ruttenberg   *m* Bronislau Kaper

Greer Garson, Walter Pidgeon, Edward Arnold, Agnes Moorehead, Cecil Kellaway, Gladys Cooper, Frances Rafferty, Tom Drake, Peter Lawford, Dan Duryea, Hugh Marlowe, Selena Royle

† The heroine is shown having a romance with Edward VII when Prince of Wales; special scenes were shot for the European version substituting Cecil Kellaway, who played Edward, by Hugo Haas who played a European king of indeterminate origin.

AAN: Greer Garson; Agnes Moorehead

Mrs Pollifax – Spy
US   1970   110m   DeLuxe
UA/Mellor (Frederick Brisson)

A respectable American matron offers her services to the CIA and sees active service in Albania.

Incredible comedy-dramatic vehicle for a star who won't give up. An obvious failure from the word go.

w C. A. McKnight   *novel* Dorothy Gilman   *d* Leslie Martinson   *ph* Joseph Biroc   *m* Lalo Schifrin

Rosalind Russell, Darren McGavin

† C. A. McKnight was Rosalind Russell.

Mrs Pym of Scotland Yard
GB   1939   65m   bw
Hurley/Grand National

A lady detective exposes a fake spiritualist.

A would-be series character bites the dust through plot malnutrition.

w Fred Elles, Peggy Barwell and Nigel Morland   *novel* Nigel Morland   *d* Fred Elles

Mary Clare, Edward Lexy, Nigel Patrick, Anthony Ireland, Irene Handl

Mrs Soffel
US   1984   110m   Metrocolor
MGM-UA/Edgar Scherick/Scott Rudin
V, V*, L

In 1901 Pittsburgh, a warder's wife falls for a prisoner and helps him escape.

A basis in truth does not prevent this from being both glum and dull from beginning to end, and pretentious treatment doesn't help.

w Ron Nyswaner   *d* Gillian Armstrong   *ph* Russell Boyd   *m* Mark Isham   *pd* Luciana Arrighi   *ed* Nicholas Beauman

Diane Keaton, Mel Gibson, Matthew Modine, Edward Herrmann

Mrs Wiggs of the Cabbage Patch *
US   1934   80m   bw
Paramount (Douglas MacLean)

Adventures of a poor family who live on the wrong side of the tracks in a broken down old shack.

A Depression fantasy of respectability and optimism, almost incredible to see now, although it plumbed the same never-never milieu as did Chaplin. Moments of comedy still please, but one does long for Mr Fields's delayed entry.

w William Slavens McNutt, Jane Storm   *novel* Alice Hegan Rice   *d* Norman Taurog   *ph* Charles Lang

Pauline Lord, ZaSu Pitts, W. C. Fields, Evelyn Venable, Kent Taylor, Charles Middleton, Donald Meek, Edith Fellows, Virginia Weidler, George Breakston

'A nasty all's-right-with-the-world burlesque of poverty, with emotions to tug at such heartstrings as are worn dangling from the mouth.' – *Otis Ferguson*

Mrs Wiggs of the Cabbage Patch
US   1942   80m   bw
Paramount

Curiously quick remake, almost word for word, but without the moments of inspiration.

w Doris Anderson, Jane Storm, William Slavens McNutt   *d* Ralph Murphy   *ph* Leo Tover

Fay Bainter, Hugh Herbert, Vera Vague, Barbara Britton, Carl Switzer, Moroni Olsen, Billy Lee

Mix Me a Person
GB   1961   116m   bw
Wessex (Sergei Nolbandov)

A barrister's psychiatrist wife takes on one of his failures, a client condemned to death for murder.

Once it gets started, a routine suspense thriller with the wrong man convicted and an espresso bar background. Not a very good one, though.

w Ian Dalrymple   *novel* Jack Trevor Story   *d* Leslie Norman   *ph* Ted Moore   *songs* Johnny Worth   *md* Muir Mathieson

Anne Baxter, Donald Sinden, Adam Faith, Walter Brown, Glyn Houston

Mixed Company
US   1974   109m   DeLuxe
UA/Cornell (Melville Shavelson)

A basketball coach and his wife adopt several children of different races.

Room for One More and then some, but not very interesting.

w Melville Shavelson, Mort Lachman   *d* Melville Shavelson   *ph* Stan Lazan   *m* Fred Karlin   *pd* Stan Jolley

Barbara Harris, Joseph Bologna, Lisa Gerritson, Arianne Heller

M'liss
US   1936   66m   bw
RKO

A drunkard's daughter washes dishes in a Western saloon.

Laundered and fairly inept family version of a roistering tale.

w Dorothy Yost   *story* Bret Harte   *d* George Nicholls Jnr

Anne Shirley, Guy Kibbee, John Beal, Douglass Dumbrille, Moroni Olsen, Arthur Hoyt

Mo' Better Blues *
US   1990   127m   DeLuxe
UIP/40 Acres and a Mule Filmworks/Spike Lee
V, V*, L, S

A jazz trumpeter redeems himself as a person, but loses out as a musician.

An unfocused narrative, caused by trying to say too much about too many things, results in an unsatisfactory film, though it has its moments.

wd Spike Lee   *ph* Ernest Dickerson   *m* Bill Lee   *pd* Wynn Thomas   *ed* Sam Pollard

Denzel Washington, Spike Lee, Wesley Snipe, Joie Lee, Cynda Williams, Giancarlo Esposito, Robin Harris, Bill Nunn

The film's movement is fitful and arbitrary – all mood swings and unpersuasive melodrama.' – *Richard Schickel, Time*

Mo' Money
US   1992   90m   colour
Columbia TriStar/Columbia/A Wife N'Kids (Michael Rachmil)
V, V*, L

After trying and failing to go straight, a hustler and his brother make money with a stolen credit card but also expose a big-time crook.

A vehicle of dubious morality, with some street-wise comedy, expertly delivered, from its star.

w Damon Wayans   *d* Peter Macdonald   *ph* Don Burgess   *m* Jay Gruska   *pd* William Arnold   *ed* Hubert C. de La Bouillerie

Damon Wayans, Stacey Dash, Joe Santos, John Diehl, Harry J. Lennix, Marlon Wayans, Mark Beltzman

'The comedy is, in truth, pretty feeble – rancid without the redeeming virtue of wit.' – *Sheila Johnston, Independent*

'If this is grown-up cinema, give me Peter Rabbit.' – *Geoff Brown, The Times*

The Mob *
US   1951   87m   bw
Columbia (Jerry Bresler)
GB title: *Remember That Face*

A policeman works undercover to catch a dockside racketeer.

Tough, lively thriller with effectively sustained mystery and a serial-like finale.

w William Bowers   *d* Robert Parrish   *ph* Joseph Walker   *m* George Duning

Broderick Crawford, Richard Kiley, Ernest Borgnine, Neville Brand, Charles Bronson

Mob Town
US   1941   61m   bw
Universal

A policeman tries to rehabilitate the young brother of an executed gangster.

Another spin-off from the Dead End Kids, quite unremarkable.

w Brenda Weisberg   *d* William Nigh

Dick Foran, Anne Gwynne, Billy Halop, Huntz Hall, Bernard Punsley, Gabriel Dell, Samuel S. Hinds

Mobsters

US 1991 104m DeLuxe
Universal (Steve Roth)
V, V*, L, S
GB title: Mobsters – The Evil Empire

Four youths grow up to become gangsters Lucky
Luciano, Meyer Lansky, Bugsy Siegel and Frank
Costello.

Bungled attempt, full of gratuitous violence, to create
an adolescent Godfather.

w Michael Mahern, Nicholas Kazan d Michael
Karbelnikoff ph Lajos Koltai m Michael Small
pd Richard Sylbert ed Scott Smith, Joe D'Augustine

Christian Slater, Patrick Dempsey, Richard Grieco,
Costas Mandylor, F. Murray Abraham, Lara Flynn
Boyle, Michael Gambon, Christopher Penn, Anthony
Quinn

'Armed with teen appeal thanks to its leads, this
hollow pic may mow down strong boxoffice early but
will start hemorrhaging quickly as mixed-to-poor
word-of-mouth cuts off its legs.' – Variety

'America's greatest actor – as you like him!'
Moby Dick *

US 1930 75m bw
Warner

Captain Ahab returns minus a leg from fighting the
white whale, and finds that his fiancée is too shocked
to love him.

Mangled remake of a fine novel filmed in silent form
as The Sea Beast.

w J. Grubb Alexander novel Herman Melville
d Lloyd Bacon ph Robert Kurrle

John Barrymore, Joan Bennett, Lloyd Hughes, May
Boley, Walter Long

'Money picture, guaranteed by its action and by
Barrymore.' – Variety

'In All The World – In All The Seas – In All Adventure
There Is No Might Like The Might of Moby Dick.'
Moby Dick **

GB 1956 116m Technicolor
Warner/Moulin (John Huston)
V*, L

A whaling skipper is determined to harpoon the
white whale which robbed him of a leg.

Pretentious period adventure, rather too slowly
developed, but full of interesting detail which almost
outweighs the central miscasting.

w Ray Bradbury, John Huston novel Herman
Melville d John Huston ph Oswald Morris
m Philip Stainton

Gregory Peck, Richard Basehart, Friedrich Ledebur,
Leo Genn, Orson Welles, James Robertson Justice,
Harry Andrews, Bernard Miles, Noel Purcell, Edric
Connor, Joseph Tomelty, Mervyn Johns

'Interesting more often than exciting.' – Variety

Mockery

US 1927 75m approx at 24 fps bw silent
MGM

A noble peasant saves a countess from the Russian
revolution.

Overly serious vehicle for a star more at ease in
melodrama.

wd Benjamin Christensen

Lon Chaney, Barbara Bedford, Ricardo Cortez, Emily
Fitzroy

The Model and the Marriage Broker

US 1951 103m bw
TCF (Charles Brackett)

A broker conceals her profession from a friend but
gets the friend fixed up.

Moderate, unsurprising comedy somewhat
overweighted by talent which can't express itself.

w Charles Brackett, Walter Reisch, Richard Breen
d George Cukor ph Milton Krasner m Cyril
Mockridge

Thelma Ritter, Jeanne Crain, Scott Brady, Zero
Mostel, Michael O'Shea, Nancy Kulp

The Model Murder Case: see The Girl in the
Headlines

Model Wife

US 1941 78m bw
Universal

Young marrieds must pretend to be single in order to
keep their jobs.

Tedious comedy.

w Charles Kaufman, Horace Jackson, Grant Garrett
d Leigh Jason

Joan Blondell, Dick Powell, Charles Ruggles, Lee
Bowman, Lucile Watson

A Modern Hero *

US 1934 70m bw
Warner

A young circus rider becomes an automobile tycoon
but overreaches himself.

Unconvincing moral tale, performed and presented
with nice touches.

w Gene Markey, Kathryn Scola novel Louis
Bromfield d G. W. Pabst

Richard Barthelmess, Jean Muir, Marjorie Ranbeau,
Verree Teasdale, Florence Eldredge

'Essentially weak on plot and characterization.' –
Variety

A Modern Hero (1940): see Knute Rockne, All
American

The Modern Miracle: see The Story of Alexander
Graham Bell

'You'll never laugh as long and as loud again as long as you
live! The laughs come so fast and so furious you'll wish it
would end before you collapse!'
Modern Times ***

US 1936 87m bw
Charles Chaplin
V, V*, L

An assembly-line worker goes berserk but can't get
another job.

Silent star comedy produced in the middle of the
sound period; flashes of genius alternate with
sentimental sequences and jokes without punch.

wd Charles Chaplin ph Rollie Totheroh, Ira
Morgan m Charles Chaplin

Charles Chaplin, Paulette Goddard, Henry Bergman,
Chester Conklin, Tiny Sandford

'A natural for the world market . . . box office with a
capital B.' – Variety

'A feature picture made out of several one- and two-
reel shorts, proposed titles being The Shop, The Jailbird,
The Singing Waiter.' – Otis Ferguson

El Moderno Barba Azul: see Boom in the Moon

The Moderns **

US 1988 126m colour
Rank/Alive Films/Nelson (Carolyn Pfeiffer, David Blocker)
V, V*, L, S

In Paris in the 1920s a struggling American expatriate
artist agrees to fake some modern masterpieces.

Witty recreation of the past and an enjoyable
dissection of the aspirations of the second-rate.

w Alan Rudolph, Jon Bradshaw d Alan Rudolph
ph Toyomichoi Kurita m Mark Isham pd Steven
Legler ed Debra T. Smith, Scott Brock

Keith Carradine, Linda Fiorentino, Geneviève Bujold,
Geraldine Chaplin, Wallace Shawn, John Lone, Kevin
O'Connor, Elsa Raven, Ali Giron

'Beautifully shot and impeccably acted all the way
down the cast list, weaving an astonishingly complex
path through the ''seems'' and ''is'' of countless
varieties of relationship, The Moderns is undoubtedly
Rudolph's best film to date.' – Tom Milne, MFB

Modesty Blaise

GB 1966 119m Technicolor
TCF/Modesty Blaise Ltd (Joseph Janni)

Female arch-agent Modesty Blaise defends a shipload
of diamonds against a sadistic master criminal.

Comic-strip adventures made by people with no
sense of humour; Fu Manchu was much more fun.

w Evan Jones comic strip Peter O'Donnell, Jim
Holdaway d Joseph Losey ph Jack Hildyard
m Johnny Dankworth

Monica Vitti, Dirk Bogarde, Terence Stamp, Harry
Andrews, Michael Craig, Scilla Gabel, Clive Revill,
Rossella Falk, Joe Melia

'Demonstrated that Joseph Losey is completely
without a sense of humour when dealing with
comedy.' – Judith Crist

Modigliani of Montparnasse: see The Lovers of
Montparnasse

'Flaming love found in the savage heart of the jungle!'
Mogambo *

GB 1953 116m Technicolor
MGM (Sam Zimbalist)
V*, L

The headquarters of a Kenyan white hunter is
invaded by an American showgirl and a British
archaeologist and his wife, and they all go off on a
gorilla hunt.

Amiable, flabby remake of Red Dust, with direction
scarcely in evidence and the gorillas out-acting a
genial cast.

w John Lee Mahin d John Ford ph Robert
Surtees, F. A. Young m A. N. Watkins

Clark Gable, Ava Gardner, Grace Kelly, Donald
Sinden, Laurence Naismith, Philip Stainton

† The story was also made as Congo Maisie in 1940.

AAN: Ava Gardner; Grace Kelly

La Moglie del Prete: see The Priest's Wife

Mohammed, Messenger of God

Lebanon 1976 182m Eastmancolor Panavision
Filmco International (Moustapha Akkad)
V, V*, S
aka: The Message

The life of the seventh-century religious leader.

Predictably reverential and exceedingly tedious
religious epic, rather like a lesser de Mille item and
fatally handicapped by the decision never to show
Mohammed at all.

w H. A. L. Craig (with Arab advice) d Moustapha
Akkad ph Jack Hildyard m Maurice Jarre
pd Tambi Larsen, Maurice Fowler

Anthony Quinn, Irene Papas, Michael Ansara,
Johnny Sekka, Michael Forest, André Morell

'For well over three hours this film stumbles, staggers,
lurches and bumbles ahead, without any true rhythm,
construction, vision, or even bare minimum of craft.' –
John Simon, New York

AAN: Maurice Jarre

Moi Drug Ivan Lapshin: see *My Friend Ivan Lapshin*

Le Moine: see *The Monk (1972)*

'Horror crawls from the depths of the earth!'
The Mole People
US   1956   78m   bw
Universal-International
V*

Archaeologists fall down a shaft and find themselves in a subterranean civilization where mole people are ruled by albinos.

Thoroughly boring nonsense which would insult a Saturday matinée.

w Lazlo Gorog   *d* Virgil Vogel

John Agar, Cynthia Patrick, Hugh Beaumont, Alan Napier

Molly
Australia   1983   82m   colour
NSW Film Corp./Greater Union/M&L (Hilary Linstead)

A little girl, with the help of some circus children, looks after a singing dog when its owner is taken ill.

Amusing, although slow-moving, family film that will appeal most to soft-hearted sub-teens.

w Phillip Roope, Mark Thomas, Hilary Linstead, Ned Lander   *d* Ned Lander   *ph* Vincent Monton   *md* Graeme Isaac   *ad* Robert Dein   *ed* Stewart Young

Claudia Karvan, Garry McDonald, Reg Lye, Melissa Jaffer, Ruth Cracknell

Molly and Me
US   1945   76m   bw
TCF

A cantankerous old man is tamed by his new housekeeper.

Sentimental little star vehicle.

w Leonard Praskins   *d* Lewis Seiler   *ph* Charles G. Clarke   *m* Cyril Mockridge

Gracie Fields, Monty Woolley, Reginald Gardiner, Roddy McDowall, Natalie Schafer, Edith Barrett

† This followed the more successful teaming of the stars in *Holy Matrimony*.

The Molly Maguires
US   1970   123m   Technicolor   Panavision
Paramount/Tamm (Martin Ritt, Walter Bernstein)
V*, S

In the Pennsylvania coalmining district in the 1870s, an undercover detective exposes the leaders of a secret society.

Sober-sided and slow-moving account of actual events which also formed the basis for Conan Doyle's rather more entertaining *The Valley of Fear*. Expensive, nicely photographed, but unpersuasive and empty.

w Walter Bernstein   *d* Martin Ritt   *ph* James Wong Howe   *m* Henry Mancini

Richard Harris, Sean Connery, Samantha Eggar, Frank Finlay, Anthony Zerbe, Bethel Leslie, Art Lund

'The film's vague sense of grievance and harrowing circumstances hangs in the air like the smoky pall cast up by the anthracite workings.' – *Richard Combs*

'A cold, dry and rather perfunctory film.' – *Arthur Schlesinger Jnr*

Mom and Dad Save the World
US   1992   88m   Foto-Kem color
Warner/HBO/Cinema Plus/Douglas (Michael Phillips)
V, V*, S

A Californian couple are transported to an alien planet ruled by a mad dictator who has imprisoned the king.

A dim comedy for easily pleased children.

w Chris Matheson, Ed Solomon   *d* Greg Beeman   *ph* Jacques Haitkin   *m* Jerry Goldsmith   *pd* Craig Stearns   *sp* Alterian Studios; Perpetual Motion Pictures   *ed* W. O. Garret

Teri Garr, Jeffrey Jones, Jon Lovitz, Thalmus Rasulala, Wallace Shawn, Eric Idle, Dwier Brown, Kathy Ireland

'With garish color, goofy-looking creatures in rubbery costumes and sets parodying old Flash Gordon serials, pic flaunts its modest budget with engaging candor.' – *Variety*

Moment by Moment
US   1979   105m   Technicolor   Panavision
Universal (Robert Stigwood)

A bored Beverly Hills wife has an affair with a young drifter.

Tedious proof that even the biggest new stars of the seventies can't carry a no-good picture.

wd Jane Wagner   *ph* Philip Lathrop   *m* Lee Holdridge   *pd* Harry Horner

John Travolta, Lily Tomlin, Andra Akers, Bert Kramer, Debra Feuer

'Little more than an animated snapshot of its leading man, baring body and soul to various effect . . . truly terrible.' – *Gilbert Adair, MFB*

Un Moment d'Egarement: see *A Summer Affair*

Moment of Danger
GB   1960   87m   bw
ABPC/Douglas Fairbanks Jnr
US title: *Malaga*

Thieves fall out and pursue each other to Malaga.

Falling between the stools of thriller and character drama, this is a poor effort in either category.

w David Osborn and Donald Ogden Stewart   *novel* Donald MacKenzie   *d* Laslo Benedek

Trevor Howard, Dorothy Dandridge, Edmund Purdom, Michael Hordern, Paul Stassino

Moment to Moment
US   1966   108m   Technicolor
Universal (Mervyn Le Roy)

A housewife finds herself with a body on her hands.

Incredibly old-fashioned romantic/melodramatic malarkey set on the French Riviera but scarcely moving a step out of Hollywood. Lush settings made it marketable to women.

w John Lee Mahin, Alec Coppel   *d* Mervyn Le Roy   *ph* Harry Stradling   *m* Henry Mancini

Jean Seberg, *Honor Blackman*, Sean Garrison, Arthur Hill, Grégoire Aslan

Mommie Dearest
US   1981   129m   Metrocolor
Paramount/Frank Yablans
V*, L

An account of the private life of Joan Crawford, from the biography by her adopted daughter Christina, who claimed spectacular ill-treatment.

On the screen it all seemed too silly for words, and nobody cared anyway.

w Frank Yablans, Frank Perry, Tracy Hotchner, Robert Getchell   *d* Frank Perry   *ph* Paul Lohmann   *m* Henry Mancini   *pd* Bill Malley

Faye Dunaway, Diana Scarwid, Steve Forrest, Howard da Silva (as Louis B. Mayer)

'The only thing that is not transparent about this film is why it was ever made.' – *Jo Imeson, MFB*

Mon Oncle *
France   1956   116m   Eastmancolor
Specta/Gray/Alterdel-Centaure (Louis Dolivet)
V, V*, L

A small boy has less affection for his parents than for his vague, clumsy uncle.

Tiresomely long star vehicle, with Tati harping on his theory of detachment, i.e. keeping his comic character on the fringes of the action. It really doesn't work in a film of this length, and the jokes are thin.

w *Jacques Tati, Jacques Lagrange*   *d* Jacques Tati   *ph* Jean Bourgoin   *m* Alain Romains, Franck Barcellini

Jacques Tati, Jean-Pierre Zola, Adrienne Servatie, Alain Becourt, Yvonne Arnaud

'Deft, elusive, full of heart.' – *Brenda Davies, MFB*

'Cinema humour at its brilliant best.' – *Daily Worker*

AA: best foreign film

Mon Oncle Américain: see *My American Uncle*

Mon Oncle Benjamin: see *Uncle Benjamin*

Mon Père, Ce Héros
France   1991   104m   colour
Gala/Film Par Film/DD/Orly/TF1/Paravision/Canal+ (Jean-Louis Livi)
V

A teenage girl on holiday tells a boy she fancies that her father is a spy and her lover.

A dull and sentimental comedy that sanitizes incest.

wd Gérard Lauzier   *ph* Patrick Blossier   *m* François Bernheim   *ad* Christian Marti   *ed* Georges Klotz

Gérard Depardieu, Marie Gillain, Patrick Mille, Catherine Jacob, Charlotte de Turckheim, Jean-François Rangasamy, Koomaren Chetty

'This syrupy teen romance would be all but unwatchable were it not for the presence of Depardieu.' – *Empire*

† The film was remade in America in 1994 as *My Father, the Hero*, again starring Gèrard Depardieu.

Mona Lisa **
GB   1986   104m   Technicolor
HandMade/Palace (Stephen Woolley, Patrick Cassavetti)
V, V*, L

An ex-con becomes chauffeur for a prostitute and becomes involved in the kinkier areas of the vice trade.

Only this actor could make a hit of this unsavoury yarn, with its highlights of sex and violence. But he did.

w Neil Jordan, David Leland   *d* Neil Jordan   *ph* Roger Pratt   *m* Michael Kamen   *pd* Jamie Leonard   *ed* Lesley Walker

Bob Hoskins, Cathy Tyson, Michael Caine

'A film to see again, with the certainty that each viewing will add something new.' – *MFB*

Un Monde sans Pitié: see *A World without Pity*

Mondo Cane *
Italy   1961   105m   Technicolor
Cineriz
V*, L
aka: *A Dog's Life*

A documentary of thirty sequences of violently eccentric human behaviour, including cannibalism, pig killing, a dog meal restaurant, etc.

Emetic exploitation piece, quite glibly assembled. Its huge commercial success made one worry for the world.

wd Gualtiero Jacopetti   *ph* Antonio Climati, Benito Frattari

AAN: song 'More' (*m* Riz Ortolani, Nino Oliviero, *ly* Norman Newell)

Money and the Woman
US 1940 80m bw
First National/Warner

A bank executive falls for the wife of a thieving teller.

Muddled drama which never gets its storyline straight.

w Robert Presnell story James M. Cain d William K. Howard

Jeffrey Lynn, Brenda Marshall, John Litel, Lee Patrick, Henry O'Neill, Roger Pryor, Henry Kolker

Money for Jam: see It Ain't Hay

Money from Home
US 1954 100m Technicolor 3-D
Paramount/Hal Wallis

A racing tipster and an assistant veterinary surgeon find themselves in charge of a horse.

A comedy with two strokes against it: the stars, and that never-never gangster land which was already a terrible cliché in the early fifties.

w Hal Kanter story Damon Runyon d George Marshall ph Daniel L. Fapp m Leigh Harline

Dean Martin, Jerry Lewis, Marjie Millar, Pat Crowley, Richard Haydn, Robert Strauss, Gerald Mohr, Sheldon Leonard

Money Mania
US 1987 95m Technicolor
De Laurentiis (Stephen F. Kesten)
V, V*, L
aka: Million Dollar Mystery

A dying man tells a group of people at a wayside diner that he has hidden four million dollars in four hiding places.

A vigorous reworking of It's a Mad Mad Mad Mad World, even broader and cruder than the original.

w Tim Metcalfe, Miguel Tejada-Flores, Rudy de Luca d Richard Fleischer ph Jack Cardiff m Al Gorgoni pd Jack G. Taylor Jnr ed John W. Wheeler

Jamie Alcroft, Royce D. Applegate, Penny Baker, Eddie Deezen, Mack Dryden, Douglas Emerson, Tawny Ferée, H. B. Haggerty, Rich Hall, Tom Bosley

Money Movers
Australia 1978 90m colour
South Australian Film Corp (Matt Carroll)

A supervisor of a security firm plans a $20-million robbery.

An engaging, though occasionally violent, tale of crooked cops and double-crossing robbers.

wd Bruce Beresford novel The Money Movers by Devon Minchin ph Don McAlpine ed William Anderson, Jeanine Chialvo

Terence Donovan, Tony Bonner, Ed Devereaux, Charles 'Bud' Tingwell, Candy Raymond, Jeanie Drynan, Bryan Brown, Lucky Grills

The Money Pit
US 1986 91m DuArt Color
Universal/Steven Spielberg (Frank Marshall, Kathleen Kennedy, Art Levinson)
V, V*, L

New Yorkers take on an old suburban house, and find it was no bargain.

Witless semi-remake of Mr Blandings Builds His Dream House, with screams instead of subtlety and no real humour at all.

w David Giler d Richard Benjamin ph Gordon Willis m Michel Colombier pd Patrizia von Brandenstein ed Jacqueline Cambas

Tom Hanks, Shelley Long, Alexander Godunov, Maureen Stapleton, Joe Mantegna, Philip Bosco, Josh Mostel

'It begins unpromisingly and slides irrevocably downward from there.' – Variety

The Money Trap
US 1966 92m bw Panavision
MGM (Max E. Youngstein, David Karr)

A hard-up policeman turns to crime.

A cheap thriller decorated with waning stars; competent at the lowest level.

w Walter Bernstein novel Lionel White d Burt Kennedy ph Paul C. Vogel m Hal Schaefer

Glenn Ford, Rita Hayworth, Elke Sommer, Ricardo Montalban, Joseph Cotten, Tom Reese, James Mitchum

Money, Women and Guns
US 1959 80m Eastmancolor Cinemascope
Universal-International

A murdered prospector scrawls a will before dying; a detective investigates the beneficiaries.

What could have been an effective Western whodunnit is jinxed by erratic writing and direction.

w Montgomery Pittman d Richard H. Bartlett

Jock Mahoney, Kim Hunter, Tim Hovey, Gene Evans, William Campbell, Lon Chaney Jnr, Tom Drake, James Gleason

The Monk (dubbed)
France/Italy/West Germany 1972 90m
Eastmancolor
Rank/Maya/Comacico/Peri/Tritone/Studio Films (Henry Lange)
original title: Le Moine

An abbot, seduced by a woman disguised as a monk, sinks into a life of debauchery and escapes punishment by selling his soul to the devil.

Ineptly directed, poorly dubbed version of the classic Gothic novel which makes one regret that Buñuel did not direct as well as writing the script.

w Luis Buñuel, Jean-Claude Carrière novel M. G. Lewis d Ado Kyrou ph Sacha Vierny m Piero Piccione ad Max Douy ed Eric Pluet

Franco Nero, Nathalie Delon, Nicol Williamson, Nadja Tiller, Elizabeth Wiener, Denis Manuel

'A near disaster . . . Kyrou's treatment, in fact, reduces the whole thing to the level of a kinky charade.' – MFB

The Monk
GB/Spain 1990 106m colour
Arrow/Celtic/Mediterraneo Cine-TV (Muir Sutherland, Paco Lara)
V

A priest is corrupted by a woman who enters his monastery disguised as a boy.

Highly coloured version of a Gothic classic, although it adds a touch of morality and repentance missing from the original.

wd Paco Lara novel M. G. Lewis ph Angel Luis Fernandez m Anton Garcia Abril pd Gumersindo Andres sp Alberto Nombela ed José Luis Matesanz

Paul McGann, Sophie Ward, Isla Blair, Freda Dowie, Aitana Sanchez-Gijon, Laura Davenport, Suzanne Bertish, Mark Elstob

'The 1931 nut crop is ready!'
Monkey Business ***
US 1931 81m bw
Paramount (Herman J. Mankiewicz)
V, V*, L

Four ship's stowaways crash a society party and catch a few crooks.

The shipboard part of this extravaganza is one of the best stretches of Marxian lunacy, but after the Chevalier impersonations it runs out of steam. Who's grumbling?

w S. J. Perelman, Will B. Johnstone, Arthur Sheekman d Norman Z. McLeod. ph Arthur L. Todd

Groucho, Chico, Harpo, Zeppo, Thelma Todd, Rockcliffe Fellowes, Ruth Hall, Harry Woods

'Surefire for laughs despite working along familiar lines . . . picture has started off by doing sweeping business all over, and no reason why it shouldn't continue to tickle wherever it plays.' – Variety

Monkey Business *
US 1952 97m bw
TCF (Sol C. Siegel)
V*, L
original title: Darling I Am Growing Younger

A chimpanzee in a research lab accidentally concocts an elixir of youth.

Remarkably laboured comedy by and with top people; it can't fail to have funny moments, but they are few and far between.

w Ben Hecht, Charles Lederer, I.A.L. Diamond d Howard Hawks ph Milton Krasner m Leigh Harline

Cary Grant, Ginger Rogers, Charles Coburn, Marilyn Monroe, Hugh Marlowe

CHARLES COBURN to Marilyn Monroe (playing his secretary): 'Find someone to type this.'

Monkey Grip
Australia 1983 102m Eastmancolor
Mainline/Pavilion/Cinecom (Patricia Lovell)
V*

A single mother begins an affair with a drug-addict.

Sprawling, downbeat story of suburban desolation and shiftless lives in Melbourne.

w Ken Cameron, Helen Graham novel Helen Graham d Ken Cameron ph David Gribble m Bruce Smeaton pd Clark Munro ed David Huggett

Noni Hazelhurst, Colin Friels, Alice Garner, Harold Hopkins, Candy Raymond, Michael Caton, Tim Burns, Christina Amphlett

A Monkey in Winter *
France 1962 103m bw Totalvision
CIPRA/Cité (Jacques Bar)
aka: Une Singe en Hiver; It's Hot in Hell

In a small Normandy resort, a hotel owner and a literary guest get drunk together and plan great fantasies, but finally return to their responsibilities.

Amiable, meandering star character comedy.

w François Boyer novel Antoine Blondin d Henri Verneuil ph Louis Page m Michel Magne

Jean Gabin, Jean-Paul Belmondo, Suzanne Flon, Noël Roquevert, Paul Frankeur, Gabrielle Dorziat

Monkey on My Back
US 1957 93m bw
UA/Imperial/Edward Small

A Guadalcanal hero is given morphine to relieve malaria and becomes addicted.

Dreary case history sold as exploitation.

w Crane Wilbur, Anthony Veiller, Peter Dudley, from the experiences of Barney Ross d André de Toth ph Maury Gertsman m Paul Sawtell, Bert Shefter

Cameron Mitchell, Dianne Foster, Jack Albertson, Paul Richards

Monkey Shines *
US 1988 109m DeLuxe
Rank/Orion (Charles Evans)
V, V*, L

A student, paralysed in an accident, forms a deadly symbiotic relationship with a monkey trained to help him.

Deft psychological thriller, spoilt by its ending, which was forced on its director.

wd George A. Romero   novel Michael Stewart ph James A. Contner   m David Shire   pd Cletus Anderson   ed Pasquale Buba

Jason Beghe, John Pankow, Kate McNeil, Joyce Van Patten, Christine Forrest

Monkeys Go Home
US   1966   101m   Technicolor
Walt Disney (Ron Miller)
V*

An American inherits a French olive farm and trains chimpanzees to harvest the crop.

Footling comedy with not much of an idea, let alone a plot.

w Maurice Tombragel   novel The Monkeys by G. K. Wilkinson   d Andrew V. McLaglen   ph William Snyder   m Robert F. Brunner

Maurice Chevalier, Dean Jones, Yvette Mimieux, Bernard Woringer, Jules Munshin, Alan Carney

'Innocuous, extrovertly cheerful and good-humoured – and very dull.' – MFB

El Mono Loco: see The Mad Monkey

The Monolith Monsters
US   1957   77m   bw
U-I (Howard Christie)

A meteorite lands in the desert and causes rocks to rise and expand, becoming toppling pillars which threaten a local community.

Dully-written science fiction with moderate special effects.

w Norman Jolley, Robert M. Fresco   d John Sherwood   ph Ellis Carter   md Joseph Gershenson

Lola Albright, Grant Williams, Les Tremayne, Phil Harvey

Monsieur Beaucaire *
US   1946   93m   bw
Paramount (Paul Jones)

King Louis XV's bumbling barber impersonates a court dandy.

What seemed a lively period burlesque has faded somewhat with age, but it still has its moments. Any relation between this and the silent Valentino film is quite accidental.

w Melvin Frank, Norman Panama   d George Marshall   ph Lionel Lindon   md Robert Emmett Dolan

Bob Hope, Joan Caulfield, Patric Knowles, Marjorie Reynolds, Cecil Kellaway, Joseph Schildkraut, Reginald Owen, Constance Collier, Hillary Brooke, Douglass Dumbrille, Mary Nash

'Whether you yawn or rather wearily laugh depends chiefly on your chance state of mind.' – James Agee

Monsieur Hire **
France   1989   82m   colour   Panavision
Palace/Cinea/Hachette Premiere/FR3
V, V*, L

A middle-aged voyeur, disliked by his neighbours and suspected by the police of murder, becomes involved with a young girl on whom he spies.

Meticulously stylish study of sexual obsession.

w Patrice Leconte, Patrick Dewolf   novel Les Fiançailles de M. Hire by Georges Simenon   d Patrice Leconte   ph Denis Lenoir   m Michael Nyman   pd Ivan Mausson   ed Joelle Hache

Michel Blanc, Sandrine Bonnaire, André Wilms, Luc Thuillier

'Brilliantly conceived, admirably acted, and staged with stunning confidence.' – Tom Milne, MFB

'A classic pyschological thriller made with all the subtlety, elegance and skill which have placed the French at the head of the field in this genre.' – Daily Telegraph

Monsieur Hulot's Holiday ****
France   1953   91m   bw
Cady/Discina (Fred Orain)
V, V*, L
original title: Les Vacances de Monsieur Hulot

An accident-prone bachelor arrives at a seaside resort and unwittingly causes havoc for himself and everyone else.

Despite lame endings to some of the jokes, this is a film to set the whole world laughing, Hulot himself being an unforgettable character and some of the timing magnificent. One feels that it could very nearly happen.

w Jacques Tati, Henri Marquet   d Jacques Tati ph Jacques Mercanton, Jean Mouselle   m Alain Romans

Jacques Tati, Nathalie Pascaud, Michèle Rolla, Valentine Camax

'The casual, amateurish air of his films clearly adds to their appeal: it also appears to explain their defects.' – Penelope Houston, MFB

'It had me laughing out loud with more enjoyment than any other comedy film this year.' – Daily Express

AAN: script

Monsieur Ripois et Son Némésis: see Knave of Hearts

Monsieur Verdoux **
US   1947   125m   bw
Charles Chaplin
V, V*

A bank cashier marries and murders rich women to support his real wife.

Interesting but unsatisfactory redrafting of the Landru case; the star is more dapper than funny, the moral is unconvincing, and the slapstick sequences too often raise yawns.

wd Charles Chaplin   ph Rollie Totheroh m Charles Chaplin

Charles Chaplin, Martha Raye, Isobel Elsom

'The cleverest and most brilliant film I have yet made.' – Charles Chaplin

'The result is pure Chaplin; and his genius alone has perfected the astonishing central portrait, among the few which, owing nothing to stage or fiction, belong entirely to the cinema.' – Dilys Powell

'Even today it will seem a failure to anyone who has taken half a dozen lessons in film technique.' – Andrew Sarris, 1970

AAN: Charles Chaplin (as writer)

Monsieur Vincent *
France   1947   113m   bw
EDIC/UGC

The life of 17th-century St Vincent de Paul, who gave up all worldly goods to devote his life to the poor.

Earnest, realistic Catholic biopic.

w Jean-Bernard Luc, Jean Anouilh   d Maurice Cloche   ph Claude Renoir   m J. J. Grunenwald

Pierre Fresnay, Aimé Clairiond, Jean Debucourt, Lise Delemare

'In the sum of things writers and director, players, composer and technicians, have laboured together to make a film with a humanity which makes one forget the narrow criteria of cinema.' – Dilys Powell

AA: best foreign film

Monsignor
US   1982   121m   DeLuxe
TCF/Frank Yablans (Kurt Neumann)
V*

An Irish cardinal supports the Vatican by doubtful financial means.

A largely boring roman à clef, with a sluggish story and uninspired performances.

w Abraham Polonsky, Wendell Mayes   novel Jack Alain Leger   d Frank Perry   ph Billy Williams m John Williams   pd John DeCuir

Christopher Reeve, Geneviève Bujold, Fernando Rey, Jason Miller, Joe Cortese, Adolfo Celi, Leonardo Cimino

'Irrevocably grounded in a hash of breast-beating and pious platitudes.' – Sight and Sound

The Monster
US   1925   70m approx at 24 fps   bw   silent
MGM
V*

A scientist abducts passing motorists and uses them in his experiments at bringing the dead back to life.

Typical star grotesquerie without much flair.

w Willard Mack and Albert Kenyon   play Crane Wilbur   d Roland West

Lon Chaney, Gertrude Olmstead, Hallam Cooley, Walter James

Monster (1980): see Humanoids of the Deep

The Monster and the Ape
US   1946   bw   serial: 15 eps
Columbia

The Matelogen Man is coveted by enemy agents, who set a trained ape loose on it.

Archetypal 'horror' serial.

d Howard Bretherton

Robert Lowery, George Macready, Ralph Morgan, Carole Mathews, Willie Best

The Monster and the Girl
US   1940   64m   bw
Paramount (Jack Moss)

A man is wrongfully executed and his brain is implanted in a gorilla, which goes on the rampage.

Curiously ineffectual considering its plot and cast, this little horror thriller seems to have been the first to use this particular situation, which became very well worn later.

w Stuart Anthony   d Stuart Heisler   ph Victor Milner   m Sigmund Krumgold

Paul Lukas, Ellen Drew, Joseph Calleia, George Zucco, Robert Paige, Rod Cameron, Phillip Terry, Onslow Stevens, Gerald Mohr

'The ape steals the picture.' – Variety

The Monster Club
GB   1980   97m   colour
ITC/Chips (Milton Subotsky)
V*, L

A vampire introduces his victim to a club for ghouls and witches, who tell their stories.

A spoofy but not very entertaining variation on a too-familiar formula.

w Edward and Valerie Abraham   stories R. Chetwynd-Hayes   d Roy Ward Baker   ph Peter Jessop   md Graham Walker

Vincent Price, John Carradine, Anthony Steel, Simon Ward, James Laurenson, Geoffrey Bayldon, Donald Pleasence, Richard Johnson, Britt Ekland, Anthony Valentine, Stuart Whitman, Patrick Magee

Monster from Green Hell

US 1956 71m bw/colour
Grosse-Krasne (Al Zimbalist)
V*

Wasps sent into space and exposed to cosmic radiation in an experiment return to Earth as huge killer mutants with tiny wings.

Silly low-budget science fiction, with risible monsters, which has an underlying theme of the fear of a nuclear holocaust.

w Louis Vittes, Endre Bohem d Kenneth G. Crane
ph Ray Flin m Albert Glasser pd Ernst Fegte
sp Jack Rabin, Louis DeWitt ed Kenneth G. Crane

Jim Davis, Robert E. Griffin, Barbara Turner, Joel Fluellen, Eduardo Ciannelli, Vladimir Sokoloff

Monster in a Box *

GB 1991 88m Eastmancolor
ICA/Jon Blair Film Co.
V*

A monologue by actor Spalding Gray about his 'monster' of an autobiographical novel.

Engaging encounter with a master of the casual anecdote.

w Spalding Gray play Spalding Gray d Nick Broomfield ph Michael Coulter m Laurie Anderson ed Graham Hutchings

Spalding Gray

The Monster Maker

US 1944 64m bw
Sigmund Neufeld/PRC
V*

A doctor frustrated in love turns his girlfriend's father into a monster by injecting him with acromegaly, a distorting disease.

Ludicrous tinpot shocker.

w Pierre Gendron, Martin Mooney, Lawrence Williams d Sam Newfield

Ralph Morgan, J. Carrol Naish, Tala Birell, Wanda McKay, Glenn Strange

'Horror that waited 100 million years becomes a terrifying reality!'

Monster on the Campus

US 1958 76m bw
Joseph Gershenson/Universal

A college professor studies a prehistoric fossilized fish, which turns everything that touches it into monsters.

Silly horror stuff with little to take the attention.

w David Duncan d Jack Arnold

Arthur Franz, Whit Bissell, Joanna Moore

The Monster Squad *

Canada 1987 81m Metrocolor Panavision
Keith Barish/Taft/Tri-Star
V, V*, L

Dracula, Frankenstein's monster, the Wolf Man, the Gill Man and the Mummy take refuge in a small American town.

Mildly amusing spoof for the teenage audience.

w Shane Black, Fred Dekker d Fred Dekker

Stephen Macht, Duncan Regehr, Andre Gower, Robby Kiger, Tom Noonan

'Crawling Up From The Depths ... To Terrify And Torture!'
'A New Kind Of Terror To Numb The Nerves!'

The Monster that Challenged the World

US 1957 83m bw
Levy-Gardner-Laven/United Artists

A giant caterpillar lays eggs in California's Salton Sea: one hatches ...

Overlong shocker for kids.

w Pat Fielder d Arnold Laven

Tim Holt, Audrey Dalton, Hans Conried, Milton Parsons

The Monster Walks

US 1932 57m bw
Like/Action
V*

A supposed paralytic plans the death of his rich niece.

Spooky house murder mystery, too hammy by half.

w Robert Ellis d Frank Strayer

Sheldon Lewis, Mischa Auer, Martha Mattox, Vera Reynolds, Willie Best

'Not badly done, but lacking utterly in novelty.' – Variety

Monster Zero: see Invasion of the Astro-Monsters

Monsters from an Unknown Planet (dubbed)

Japan 1975 80m colour
Miracle/Toho (Tomoyuki Tanaka)
original title: Mekagojira No Gyakushu; aka: The Escape of Mechagodzilla; Terror of Mechagodzilla

Godzilla is outclassed when aliens reanimate Mechagodzilla and loose Titanosaurus on Tokyo with the help of a renegade scientist and his cyborg daughter.

The usual nonsense from one of the later Godzilla movies, with the monsters inactive for much of the time.

w Yukiko Takayama d Ishiro Honda

Katsuhiko Sasaki, Tomoko Ai, Akihiko Mirata, Tadao Nakamura, Katsumasu Uchida

Montana

US 1950 76m Technicolor
Warner (William Jacobs)
L

An Australian sheepman fights the cattle barons of Montana.

Modest Western from the star's declining years at Warner.

w James R. Webb, Borden Chase, Charles O'Neal story Ernest Haycox d Ray Enright ph Karl Freund m David Buttolph

Errol Flynn, Alexis Smith, S. Z. Sakall, Douglas Kennedy, James Brown, Ian MacDonald

Montana Belle

US 1952 82m Trucolor
RKO (Howard Welsch)
V*

The Daltons rescue Belle Starr and insist that she works with them on a dangerous raid.

Warmed-over Western melodramatics, quite unmemorable.

w Horace McCoy, Norman S. Hall d Allan Dwan ph Jack Marta m Nathan Scott

Jane Russell, George Brent, Scott Brady, Forrest Tucker, Andy Devine, Jack Lambert, John Litel, Ray Teal

† The film was completed in 1948, but held over.

Montana Moon

US 1930 88m bw
MGM

A wealthy rancher's spoiled daughter is about to leave for New York when she falls for a handsome cowboy.

A long string of nothings with bursts of song; incompetent early talkie.

w Sylvia Thalberg, Frank Butler d Malcolm St Clair

Joan Crawford, Johnny Mack Brown, Ricardo Cortez, Lloyd Ingraham, Cliff Edwards

Monte Carlo *

US 1930 94m bw
Paramount (Ernst Lubitsch)

A count passes himself off as a hairdresser to win a gambling lady.

Faded but charming romantic comedy with music, the first to show its director's sound style in full throttle, notably in the final 'Beyond the Blue Horizon' sequence.

w Ernest Vajda play The Blue Coast by Hans Muller novel Monsieur Beaucaire by Booth Tarkington d Ernst Lubitsch ph Victor Milner m W. Franke Harling songs Leo Robin, Richard Whiting ad Hans Dreier

Jack Buchanan, Jeanette MacDonald, ZaSu Pitts, Tyler Brooke, Claud Allister, Lionel Belmore

'Nothing extra beyond usual par programmer.' – Variety

'Very stylish and sly, not to be missed.' – New Yorker, 1978

Monte Carlo or Bust: see Those Daring Young Men in Their Jaunty Jalopies

The Monte Carlo Story

Italy/US 1956 101m Technirama
Tatanus (Marcello Girosi)

A gambler looks for a rich wife, and finds instead a glamorous woman as penniless as himself: they become confidence tricksters but suffer a change of heart.

Lubitsch might have made something of it, but this is a flavourless pudding of a film and the stars can do nothing with it.

wd Samuel Taylor story Marcello Girosi, Dino Risi ph Giuseppe Rotunno m Renzo Rossellini

Marlene Dietrich, Vittorio de Sica, Arthur O'Connell, Mischa Auer, Natalie Trundy, Jane Rose, Renato Rascel

'He's a cowboy. She's a woman. He's the best at what he does. And so is she.'

Monte Walsh *

US 1970 108m Technicolor
Cinema Center (Hal Landers, Bobby Roberts)
V*

Two ageing cowboys find life increasingly hard and hopeless; an old acquaintance kills one and is shot by the other.

'Realistic' Western developed in leisurely style with the emphasis on character and on the real drudgery of frontier life.

w David Z. Goodman, Lukas Heller novel Jack Schaefer d William A. Fraker ph David M. Walsh m John Barry

Lee Marvin, Jack Palance, Jeanne Moreau, Mitch Ryan, Jim Davis

'As boring a western as ever involved a bronco-busting scene that alone cost almost half a million dollars.' – Judith Crist

Montenegro *

Sweden/GB 1981 96m Eastmancolor
Viking/Europa/Smart Egg (Bo Jonsson)
V*

A housewife driven mad by boredom takes a lover and murders him.

Another case history in which the creator finds more symbolic meaning than the audience is likely to see. On the surface, a mildly entertaining piece of near-pornography.

wd Dusan Makavejev ph Tomislav Pinter m Kornell Kovach

Susan Anspach, Erland Josephson, Bora Todorovic, Per Oscarsson

A Month in the Country *
GB 1987 96m colour
Euston Films (Kenith Trodd)
V, V*, L

In the English countryside, two men recover from the horrors of World War I.

Traditional British teledrama with much going for it despite a final lack of direction.

w Simon Gray novel J. L. Carr d Pat O'Connor
ph Kenneth MacMillan m Howard Blake pd Leo
Austin ed John Victor

Colin Firth, Kenneth Branagh, Natasha Richardson, Patrick Malahide, Tony Haygarth, Richard Vernon

'Makes Ben-Hur look like an epic!'
Monty Python and the Holy Grail **
GB 1975 90m Technicolor
EMI/Python (Monty) Pictures/Michael White (Mark Forstater)
V, V*, L, S

King Arthur and his knights seek the Holy Grail.

Hellzapoppin-like series of linked sketches on a medieval theme; some slow bits, but often uproariously funny and with a remarkable visual sense of the Middle Ages.

w Graham Chapman, John Cleese, Terry Gilliam, Eric
Idle, Michael Palin d Terry Gilliam, Terry Jones
ph Terry Bedford animation Terry Gilliam m Neil
Innes pd Roy Smith

Graham Chapman, John Cleese, Terry Gilliam, Eric Idle, Michael Palin

'The team's visual buffooneries and verbal rigmaroles are piled on top of each other with no attention to judicious timing or structure, and a form which began as a jaunty assault on the well-made revue sketch and an ingenious misuse of television's fragmented style of presentation, threatens to become as unyielding and unfruitful as the conventions it originally attacked.' – Geoff Brown

Monty Python's Life of Brian **
GB 1979 93m Eastmancolor
Hand Made Films (John Goldstone)
V, V*, L

A contemporary of Jesus is mistaken for him and crucified.

Controversial middle-eastern romp which left its creators battered but extremely wealthy. In the face of such an onslaught of bad taste, criticism seems irrelevant.

w and starring John Cleese, Graham Chapman, Eric
Idle, Michael Palin, Terry Gilliam, Terry Jones
d Terry Jones ph Peter Biziou m Geoffrey Burgon
ad Roger Christian ed Julian Doyle

Monty Python's The Meaning of Life
GB 1983 90m Technicolor
Universal/Celandine/The Monty Python Partnership (John Goldstone)
V, V*, L

A series of sketches in questionable taste.

Subjects include organ transplants, sex, death and the results of overeating.

w and starring Graham Chapman, John Cleese, Terry
Gilliam, Eric Idle, Michael Palin, Terry Jones
d Terry Jones ph Peter Hannan m various
pd Harry Lange

The Moon and Sixpence ***
US 1943 85m bw (colour sequence)
Albert Lewin/David L. Loew (Stanley Kramer)
V*

A stockbroker leaves his wife and family, spends some selfish years painting in Paris and finally dies of leprosy on a South Sea island.

Pleasantly literary adaptation of an elegant novel based on the life of Gauguin; a little stodgy in presentation now, but much of it still pleases.

w Albert Lewin novel W. Somerset Maugham
d Albert Lewin ph John Seitz m Dimitri Tiomkin

George Sanders, Herbert Marshall (as Maugham), Steve Geray, Doris Dudley, Elena Verdugo, Florence Bates, Heather Thatcher, Eric Blore, Albert Basserman

'An admirable film until the end, when it lapses into Technicolor and techni-pathos.' – James Agate

AAN: Dimitri Tiomkin

Moon 44
West Germany 1989 99m colour
Medusa/Centropolis Filmproduktion (Dean Heyde, Roland Emmerich)
V, V*, L, S

In the future, an undercover agent is sent to a far-away planet to unearth a saboteur.

Science fiction melodrama that borrows from most other recent films in the genre to little effect.

w Dean Heyde, Oliver Eberle story Roland
Emmerich, Dean Heyde, Oliver Eberle, P. J. Mitchell
d Roland Emmerich ph Karl Walter Undenlaub
m Joel Goldsmith pd Oliver Scholl ed Tony
Wigand

Michael Pare, Lisa Eichhorn, Malcolm McDowell, Dean Devlin, Brian Thompson, Stephen Geoffreys, Leon Rippy, Jochen Nickel, Mechmed Yilmez

The Moon in the Gutter
French/Italian 1983 130m Eastmancolor
Panavision
Palace/Gaumont/TF1 Films/SFPC/Opera Film Produzione (Lise Fayolle)
V, V*, L, S
original title: La Lune dans le Caniveau

A stevedore, haunting the docks to find the man who raped his sister, becomes involved with a rich woman.

Relentlessly fashionable, now dated, low-life mystery that gets nowhere slowly.

w Jean-Jacques Beineix, Olivier Mergault
novel David Goodis d Jean-Jacques Beineix
ph Philippe Rousselot m Gabriel Yared ad Hilton
McConnico ed Monique Prim, Yves Deschamps

Gérard Depardieu, Natassia Kinski, Victoria Abril, Beatrice Reading, Gabriel Monnet, Dominique Pinon, Milena Vukotic, Vittorio Mezzogiorno

The Moon Is Blue *
US 1953 99m bw
Otto Preminger
V*, L

A spry young girl balances the attractions of a middle-aged lover against her young one.

Paper-thin comedy partly set on top of the Empire State Building (and thereafter in a dowdy set); mildly amusing in spots, it gained notoriety, and a Production Code ban, by its use of such naughty words as 'virgin' and 'mistress'.

w F. Hugh Herbert play F. Hugh Herbert d Otto
Preminger ph Ernest Laszlo m Herschel Burke
Gilbert ed Otto Ludwig

Maggie McNamara, David Niven, William Holden, Tom Tully, Dawn Addams

PATTY (Maggie McNamara): 'Men are usually bored with virgins. I'm so glad you're not . . . Have you a mistress?'
DONALD: 'Don't you think it's better for a girl to be preoccupied with sex than occupied with it?'

'It adds nothing to the art of cinema and certainly does not deserve the attention it will get for flouting the Production Code.' – Philip T. Hartung

† The film was made simultaneously in German, as Die Jungfrau auf dem Dach, with Hardy Kruger, Johanna Matz and Johannes Heesters.

AAN: Maggie McNamara; title song (m Herschel Burke Gilbert, ly Sylvia Fine); editing

The Moon Is Down **
US 1943 90m bw
TCF (Nunnally Johnson)

A Norwegian village resists the Nazis.

Sombre, talkative, intelligent little drama, the best of the resistance films, shot on the set of How Green Was My Valley (with snow covering).

w Nunnally Johnson, novel John Steinbeck
d Irving Pichel ph Arthur Miller m Alfred
Newman

Henry Travers, Cedric Hardwicke, Lee J. Cobb, Dorris Bowden, Margaret Wycherly, Peter Van Eyck, John Banner

'This may well be a true picture of Norway and its people. But it fails to strike fire, to generate passion. It leaves one feeling rather proud but also sad.' – Bosley Crowther

'Jungle love tease! It's hot!'
Moon over Burma
US 1940 76m bw
Paramount

Jungle lumbermen fight over a stranded American entertainer.

Routine adventure romance climaxing in a forest fire.

w Frank Wead, W. P. Lipscomb, Harry Clork
d Louis King ph William Mellor m Victor Young

Dorothy Lamour, Robert Preston, Preston Foster, Doris Nolan, Albert Basserman, Frederick Worlock, Addison Richards

Moon over Miami *
US 1941 92m Technicolor
TCF (Harry Joe Brown)
V

Two sisters seek rich husbands in Florida.

Musical remake of Three Blind Mice, which was suspiciously similar to Golddiggers of Broadway, The Greeks Had a Word for Them, etc., and the later How to Marry a Millionaire and Three Little Girls in Blue. In short, a Hollywood standard, not too badly done.

w Vincent Lawrence, Brown Holmes d Walter Lang
ph Peverell Marley, Leon Shamroy md Alfred
Newman songs Leo Robin, Ralph Rainger

Don Ameche, Betty Grable, Carole Landis, Robert Cummings, Charlotte Greenwood, Jack Haley, Cobina Wright Jnr, Robert Greig

Moon over Parador
US 1988 104m DeLuxe
UIP/Universal (Paul Mazursky)
V, V*, L, S

An actor is kidnapped and forced to impersonate the president of a Caribbean country.

Occasionally amusing, but the joke is too thin to bear much watching.

w Leon Capetanos, Paul Mazursky story Charles G.
Booth d Paul Mazursky ph Donald McAlpine
m Maurice Jarre pd Pato Guzman ed Stuart
Pappe

Richard Dreyfuss, Raul Julia, Sonia Bragg, Jonathan Winters, Fernando Rey, Sammy Davis Jnr, Michael Greene, Polly Holliday, Milton Goncalves, Charo, Marianne Sagebrecht

Moon Pilot **
US 1961 98m Technicolor
Walt Disney (Ron Miller)
V*

A reluctant astronaut falls in love with a girl from outer space, who finally accompanies him on his mission.

Engaging science-fiction spoof with good performances.

w Maurice Tombragel   serial Robert Buckner d James Neilson   ph William Snyder   m Peter Smith   sp Eustace Lycett

Edmond O'Brien, Tom Tryon, Brian Keith

The Moon Spinners *
GB   1964   119m   Technicolor
Walt Disney (Bill Anderson)
V*

A young girl holidaying in Crete becomes involved with jewel robbers.

Teenage adventure against attractive locations; quite agreeable but overlong.

w Michael Dyne   novel Mary Stewart   d James Neilson   ph Paul Beeson   m Ron Grainer

Hayley Mills, Peter McEnery, Eli Wallach, Joan Greenwood, John Le Mesurier, Pola Negri

'The number one space western!'
Moon Zero Two
GB   1969   100m   Technicolor
Hammer (Michael Carreras)
V*

In 2021, the moon is being colonized and crooks are trying to get control of an asteroid.

A self-acknowledged 'space western' which has a few bright ideas but suffers from a childish script.

w Michael Carreras   story Gavin Lyall, Frank Hardman, Martin Davidson   d Roy Ward Baker ph Paul Beeson   m Don Ellis

James Olson, Catharina von Schell, Warren Mitchell, Ori Levy, Adrienne Corri, Dudley Foster, Bernard Bresslaw, Neil McCallum

'It's all just about bad enough to fill older audiences with nostalgia for the inspired innocence of Flash Gordon, or even the good old days of Abbott and Costello in outer space.' – MFB

Moonfleet *
US   1955   87m   Eastmancolor   Cinemascope
MGM (John Houseman)
V*, L

In Dorset in 1770 an orphan boy finds that his elegant guardian leads a gang of smugglers.

Period gothic melodrama which nearly, but not quite, comes off; the script simply doesn't build to the right climax, and too many characters come to nothing. But there are splendid moments.

w Margaret Fitts, Jan Lustig   novel J. Meade Faulkner   d Fritz Lang   ph Robert Planck m Miklos Rozsa

Stewart Granger, Jon Whiteley, George Sanders, Joan Greenwood, Viveca Lindfors, Liliane Montevecchi, Melville Cooper, Sean McClory, John Hoyt, Alan Napier

Moonlight in Havana
US   1942   63m   bw
Bernard W. Burton/Universal

A baseball catcher goes to Havana for spring training.

Another in the long line of lightweight musical supports from this studio.

w Oscar Brodney   d Anthony Mann

Allan Jones, Jane Frazee, Marjorie Lord, William Frawley, the Jiving Jacks and Jills

Moonlight Sonata *
GB   1937   90m   bw
Pall Mall (Lothar Mendes)
V*

Stranded victims of a plane crash are affected by the art of a famous pianist.

Curious, slight, unexpected play-on-film designed to showcase the talent of Paderewski.

w Edward Knoblock, E. M. Delafield   d Lothar Mendes   ph Jan Stallich

Ignace Paderewski, Eric Portman, Marie Tempest, Charles Farrell, Barbara Greene, Binkie Stuart

'Should make good with class audiences.' – Variety

'Dame Marie is a sparking line-tosser who keeps the script alive when Paderewski (then 77) is not putting it to music.' – New York Times

The Moonlighter
US   1953   77m   bw   3-D
Warner (Joseph Bernhard)

A cattle rustler moves towards reforming.

Ho-hum Western which offers its stars little to work with and was not even very exciting in 3-D.

w Niven Busch   d Roy Rowland   ph Bert Glennon m Heinz Roemheld

Fred MacMurray, Barbara Stanwyck, Ward Bond, William Ching, John Dierkes, Morris Ankrum

Moonlighting **
GB   1982   97m   colour
Michael White/Channel 4 (Mark Shivas, Jerzy Skolimowski)
V, V*, L

In 1981 four Polish building workers arrive in London to renovate a house for their boss and make a quick profit. The scheme is somewhat upset by the news of martial law at home . . .

Very interesting and well-acted anecdote, virtually constructed out of the headlines.

wd Jerzy Skolimowski   ph Tony Pierce Roberts m Stanley Myers   pd Tony Woollard   ed Barrie Vince

Jeremy Irons, Eugene Lipinski, Jiri Stanislaw, Eugeniusz Haczkiewicz

The Moonraker *
GB   1958   82m   Technicolor
ABPC (Hamilton Inglis)

During the English Civil War, a noble highwayman smuggles the king's son into France.

Likeable swashbuckler which confines its second half to suspense at an inn, a who-is-it rather than a whodunnit. Good fun.

w Robert Hall, Wilfred Eades, Alistair Bell play Arthur Watkyn   d David MacDonald   ph Max Greene   m Laurie Johnson

George Baker, Sylvia Syms, Marius Goring, Peter Arne, Richard Leech, Clive Morton, Paul Whitsun-Jones, Gary Raymond, John Le Mesurier (as Cromwell), Patrick Troughton, Michael Anderson Jnr

Moonraker
GB   1979   126m   Technicolor   Panavision
UA/Eon (Albert S. Broccoli)
V, V*, L, S

James Bond investigates the disappearance of a space shuttle during a test flight.

Adventures in Venice, Rio and the upper Amazon; all very repetitive and no longer more than faintly amusing.

w Christopher Wood   novel Ian Fleming   d Lewis Gilbert   ph Jean Tournier   m John Barry   pd Ken Adam

Roger Moore, Lois Chiles, Michael Lonsdale, Richard Kiel, Geoffrey Keen, Lois Maxwell, Bernard Lee

'Conspicuously expensive production values but an unmistakably cut price plot.' – Sight and Sound

Moonrise *
US   1948   90m   bw
Republic/Frank Borzage Productions (Charles F. Haas)
V*, L

A murderer's son is driven into violence by memories and fears of his childhood.

Broody melodrama set against a remote village and swamp background; not a very interesting story, but memorable detail.

w Charles Haas   d Frank Borzage   ph John L. Russell   m William Lava   ed Harry Keller

Gail Russell, Dane Clark, Ethel Barrymore, Allyn Joslyn, Rex Ingram

'The story is told with a unity of mood, sombre and poignant, set by some impressionistic opening passages and sustained by the slow yet firmly compressed style and the strong, low-toned images.' – Gavin Lambert

'If the world is sane – then they're completely mad!'
The Moon's Our Home *
US   1936   80m   bw
Paramount (Walter Wanger)
V*

A headstrong actress marries an adventurer on impulse, and they both try to work it out.

Light, bright romantic comedy with the zany tinge then in fashion.

w Isabel Dawn, Boyce DeGaw   novel Faith Baldwin d William A. Seiter   ph Joseph Valentine m Gerard Carbonara

Margaret Sullavan, Henry Fonda, Beulah Bondi, Charles Butterworth, Margaret Hamilton, Dorothy Stickney, Lucien Littlefield

'It isn't, of course, as good as all that; nothing is as good as all that in the cinema, but the great commercial wheels don't grind here quite so effortlessly; a little satire, a little imagination, a little feeling for human inconsistency, has got into the works.' – Graham Greene, The Spectator

The Moonshine War
US   1970   100m   Metrocolor   Panavision
MGM/Filmways (James C. Pratt, Leonard Blair)

In Kentucky just before the repeal of prohibition, a corruptible revenue agent regrets bringing in a sadistic crook to help confiscate illegal whisky.

Downright peculiar hillbilly melodrama, neither straight nor satirical; interesting only in fits and starts.

w Elmore Leonard   novel Elmore Leonard d Richard Quine   ph Richard H. Kline   m Fred Karger

Patrick McGoohan, Richard Widmark, Alan Alda, Melodie Johnson, Will Geer

The Moonspinners: see The Moon Spinners

Moonstruck *
US   1987   102m   Technicolor
Patrick Palmer/Norman Jewison
V, V*, L, S

Young widow falls for the estranged brother of her husband-to-be.

Noisy, sometimes heavy-handed romantic comedy of Italian-American manners.

w John Patrick Shanley   d Norman Jewison ph David Watkin   m Dick Hyman   pd Philip Rosenberg

Cher, Nicolas Cage, Vincent Gardenia, Olympia Dukakis, Danny Aiello

AA: Cher; John Patrick Shanley; Olympia Dukakis

AAN: best picture; Norman Jewison; Vincent Gardenia

Moontide *
US   1942   94m   bw
TCF (Mark Hellinger)

A seaman cares for an unhappy waif.

A Hollywood attempt at romantic melodrama in the
French manner. It looks good, and the cast is fine, but
everything is just a bit too glum.

w John O'Hara   novel Willard Robertson   d Archie
Mayo   ph Charles G. Clarke   m Cyril Mockridge,
David Buttolph

Jean Gabin, Ida Lupino, Claude Rains, Thomas
Mitchell, Jerome Cowan, Sen Yung, Tully Marshall,
Helen Reynolds

AAN: Charles G. Clarke

Moonwalker
US   1988   93m
Warner/Ultimate Productions
V, V*, L

Episodic look at the life and performances of Michael
Jackson, culminating in a fantasy in which he stops a
gangster turning children into junkies.

Strictly for fans.

w David Newman   story Michael Jackson   d Colin
Chilvers, Jerry Kramer   ph John Hora, Tom
Ackerman, Bob Collins, Fred Elmes, Crescenzo
Notarile   m Bruce Broughton   pd Michael Ploog
ed David E. Blewitt, Mitchell Sinoway, Dale Beldin

Michael Jackson, Joe Pesci, Sean Lennon, Kellie
Parker, Brandon Adams

The Morals of Marcus
GB   1936   75m   bw
Real Art (W. J. Locke)

A girl escapes from a Middle Eastern harem by
stowing away with a British aristocrat.

Feeble 'naughty' comedy, killed by lack of wit and
pace.

w Guy Bolton, Miles Mander   play W. J. Locke
d Miles Mander   ph John W. Boyle

Lupe Velez, Ian Hunter, Adrienne Allen, Noel
Madison, J. H. Roberts, H. F. Maltby

'Acceptable feature for general consumption.' – Variety

Die Mörder Sind Unter Uns: see The Murderers
Are Among Us

More American Graffiti
US   1979   111m   Technicolor
Universal/Lucasfilm (Howard Kazanjian)
V*, L

In 1964, American small-town teenagers quarrel over
drugs and drag racing.

Tedious sequel to a movie which was more than
enough.

wd B. W. L. Norton   ph Caleb Deschanel
m various

Candy Clark, Bo Hopkins, Ron Howard, Paul Le Mat,
Mackenzie Phillips, Richard Bradford

'What once was a crate of dynamite has been
cosmetically giftwrapped à la Happy Days.' – Cynthia
Rose, MFB

More Dead Than Alive
US   1968   99m   DeLuxe
United Artists/Aubrey Schenck

Revenge erupts some years after a violent jail break.

Eccentric and pretentious Western with a complex
story which might have intrigued if handled better.

w George Schenck   d Robert Sparr   ph Jack
Marquette   m Philip Springer

Clint Walker, Vincent Price, Anne Francis, Paul
Hampton, Mike Henry, Craig Littler

More than a Secretary
US   1936   80m   bw
Columbia

A dowdy secretary loses her glasses and wins her
boss.

That old story, and the treatment isn't anything to get
excited about either.

w Dale Van Every, Lynn Starling   d Alfred E. Green

Jean Arthur, George Brent, Lionel Stander, Ruth
Donnelly, Reginald Denny, Dorothea Kent, Charles
Halton

'Fair b.o. possibilities, but the story doesn't belong on
the same block as the production afforded to it.' –
Variety

The More the Merrier ***
US   1943   104m   bw
Columbia (George Stevens)
V*, L

In crowded Washington during World War II, a girl
allows two men to share her apartment and falls in
love with the younger one.

Thoroughly amusing romantic comedy with bright
lines and situations; remade less effectively as Walk
Don't Run (qv).

w Robert Russell, Frank Ross, Richard Flournoy,
Lewis R. Foster   d George Stevens   ph Ted Tetzlaff
md Morris Stoloff   m Leigh Harline

Jean Arthur, Joel McCrea, Charles Coburn, Richard Gaines,
Bruce Bennett

'The gayest comedy that has come from Hollywood in
a long time. It has no more substance than a
watermelon, but is equally delectable.' – Howard
Barnes

'Farce, like melodrama, offers very special chances for
accurate observation, but here accuracy is avoided ten
times to one in favour of the easy burlesque or the
easier idealization which drops the bottom out of
farce. Every good moment frazzles or drowns.' – James
Agee

† Garson Kanin has claimed to have written virtually
all the script.

AA: Charles Coburn

AAN: best picture; script; original story (Frank Ross,
Robert Russell); George Stevens; Jean Arthur

Morgan – A Suitable Case for Treatment ***
GB   1966   97m   bw
British Lion/Quintra (Leon Clore)
V, V*, L
US title: Morgan!

A young woman determines to leave her talented but
half-mad artist husband, who has a fixation on
gorillas and behaves in a generally uncivilized
manner.

Archetypal sixties marital fantasy, an extension of
Look Back in Anger in the mood of swinging London.
As tiresome as it is funny – but it is funny.

w David Mercer,   play David Mercer   d Karel Reisz
ph Larry Pizer, Gerry Turpin   m Johnny Dankworth

Vanessa Redgrave, David Warner, Robert Stephens,
Irene Handl, Newton Blick, Nan Munro

'Poor Morgan: victim of a satire that doesn't bite, lost
in a technical confusion of means and ends, and
emerging like an identikit photograph, all bits and
pieces and no recognizable face.' – Penelope Houston

'The first underground movie made above ground.' –
John Simon

'I think Morgan is so appealing to college students
because it shares their self-view: they accept this mess
of cute infantilism and obsessions and aberrations
without expecting the writer and director to resolve it
and without themselves feeling a necessity to sort it
out.' – Pauline Kael

AAN: Vanessa Redgrave

Morituri: The Saboteur: see The Saboteur, Code
Name Morituri

The Morning After
US   1986   103m   DeLuxe
TCF/Lorimar/American Filmworks (Bruce Gilbert)
V, V*, L

A drunken actress wakes up one morning next to a
man with a dagger in his heart.

A mystery which starts as intriguing but is
insufficiently developed and peters out into a series of
casual encounters between unattractive people.

w James Hicks   d Sidney Lumet   ph Andrzej
Bartkowiak   m Paul Chihara   pd Albert Brenner
ed Joel Goodman

Jane Fonda, Jeff Bridges, Raul Julia, Diane Salinger

AAN: Jane Fonda

Morning Departure *
GB   1950   102m   bw
Rank/Jay Lewis (Leslie Parkyn)
US title: Operation Disaster

Twelve men are caught in a trapped submarine, and
only eight can escape.

Archetypal stiff-upper-lip service tragedy, which
moves from briskness to a slow funereal ending.

w William Fairchild   play Kenneth Woolard
d Roy Baker   ph Desmond Dickinson

John Mills, Richard Attenborough, Nigel Patrick,
Lana Morris, Peter Hammond, Helen Cherry, James
Hayter, Andrew Crawford, George Cole, Michael
Brennan, Wylie Watson, Bernard Lee, Kenneth More

Morning Glory **
US   1933   74m   bw
RKO (Pandro S. Berman)
V*, L

A young actress comes to New York determined to
succeed.

Marvellously evocative theatrical drama which
provided a strong star part for a fresh young actress
and surrounded her with accomplished thespians.
Remade to much less effect as Stage Struck (qv).

w Howard J. Green   play Zoe Akins   d Lowell
Sherman   ph Bert Glennon   m Max Steiner

Katharine Hepburn, Douglas Fairbanks Jnr, Adolphe
Menjou, Mary Duncan, C. Aubrey Smith, Don
Alvarado

'Star vastly superior to this sometimes misdirected
arty story.' – Variety

AA: Katharine Hepburn

'Revealing the amazing things a woman will do for love!'
Morocco ***
US   1930   97m   bw
Paramount (Louis D. Lighton)
V*, L

A cabaret singer arrives in Morocco and continues her
wicked career by enslaving all the men in sight; but
true love reaches her at last.

The star's first American film reveals her
quintessence, and although wildly dated in subject
matter remains a perversely enjoyable entertainment.

w Jules Furthman   novel Amy Jolly by Benno Vigny
d Josef von Sternberg   ph Lee Garmes   m Karl Hajos
ad Hans Dreier

Marlene Dietrich, Gary Cooper, Adolphe Menjou,
Ullrich Haupt, Juliette Compton, Francis McDonald

'Lightweight story with good direction . . . needs
plenty of exploitation to do over average.' – Variety

'A definite step forward in the art of motion pictures.'
– National Board of Review

'A cinematic pattern, brilliant, profuse, subtle, and at almost every turn inventive.' – *Wilton A. Barrett*

'Enchantingly silly, full of soulful grand passions, drifting cigarette smoke, and perhaps a few too many pictorial shots of the Foreign Legion marching this way and that.' – *New Yorker, 1979*

AAN: Josef von Sternberg; Lee Garmes; Marlene Dietrich; Hans Dreier

Morons from Outer Space
GB 1985 91m colour
Thorn EMI (Barry Hanson)
V, V*

Dopey space travellers arrive on Earth.

Spoofy comedy which, apart from staging a spectacular motorway landing and mocking various popular film genres, never decides where to go.

w Griff Rhys Jones, Mel Smith   d Michael Hodges
ph Phil Meheux   m Peter Brewis

Mel Smith, Griff Rhys Jones, Paul Bown, Joanne Pearce, Jimmy Nail, Dinsdale Landen, James B. Sikking

'It remains stuck on the launch pad.' – *Variety*

'The love story of today with the popular stars of The Shop Around the Corner!'

The Mortal Storm **
US 1940 100m bw
MGM (Sidney Franklin)

A German family in the thirties is split by Nazism.

Solid anti-Nazi melodrama typical of the period before America entered the war; good performances outweigh unconvincing studio sets.

w Claudine West, George Froeschel, Anderson Ellis
novel Phyllis Bottome   d Frank Borzage   ph William Daniels   m Edward Kane

Margaret Sullavan, Robert Young, James Stewart, Frank Morgan, Robert Stack, Bonita Granville, Irene Rich, Maria Ouspenskaya

† The film caused Goebbels to ban the showing of MGM pictures in all German territories.

'Murder is a secret that should never be shared.'

Mortal Thoughts *
US 1991 103m DeLuxe
Columbia TriStar/New Visions/Polar/Rufglen (John Fiedler, Mark Tarlov)
V, V*, L

Two women, who are best friends, are questioned about the murder of the husband of one of them.

Entertaining thriller which sustains its mystery to the end.

w William Reilly, Claude Kerven   d Alan Rudolph
ph Elliot Davis   m Mark Isham   pd Howard Cummings   ed Tom Walls

Demi Moore, Glenne Headly, Bruce Willis, John Pankow, Harvey Keitel, Billie Neal, Frank Vincent

'A bravely downbeat movie.' – *Empire*

Morte a Venezia: see *Death in Venice*

La Morte Vivante: see *The Living Dead Girl*

Moscow Distrusts Tears *
USSR 1979 148m Sovcolor
Mosfilm (V. Kuchinsky)
original title: *Moskva Slezam Ne Verit*; US title: *Moscow Does Not Believe In Tears*

In Moscow in 1958, three working girls have love affairs. Twenty years later they compare notes.

Odd portmanteau drama, most interesting for its picture of life in Russia.

w Valentin Chernykh   d Vladimir Menshov
ph Igor Slabnevich   m Sergei Nikitin

AA: best foreign film

Moscow Nights
GB 1936 75m bw
London Films/Capitol Films (Alexis Granowsky, Max Schach)
V*
US title: *I Stand Condemned*

A Russian girl sacrifices her virtue to save her lover from execution.

Cardboard melodrama of pre-revolutionary Moscow; not by any means a classic.

w Erich Seipmann   novel Pierre Benoît   d Anthony Asquith   ph Phil Tannura   md Muir Mathieson
ad Vincent Korda   ed Francis Lyon

Laurence Olivier, Penelope Dudley Ward, Harry Baur, Robert Cochran, Morton Selten, Athene Seyler

'Completely bogus . . . The direction is puerile.' – *Graham Greene, The Spectator*

† This was based directly on a 1934 French film, *Nuits Moscovites*, with Annabella, Pierre-Richard Willm, and Harry Baur.

Moscow on the Hudson *
US 1984 117m Metrocolor
Columbia/Delphi (Paul Mazursky)
V, V*, L

A Soviet circus artiste defects in New York but has second thoughts.

Not so much a political comedy as an immigrant one, with the Big Apple shown at its worst. As such, occasionally funny in a desperate way, but overlong.

w Paul Mazursky, Leon Capetanos   d Paul Mazursky   ph Donald McAlpine   m David McHugh   pd Pato Guzman

Robin Williams, Maria Conchita Alonso, Cleavant Derricks, Alejandro Rey, Savely Kramarov

The Mosquito Coast *
US 1986 117m Technicolor
Saul Zaentz/Jerome Hellman
V, V*, L, S

A frustrated visionary packs up and moves his family to a remote Caribbean island, where he fails to notice the seeds of downfall.

An antidote to *Robinson Crusoe* which is often wryly amusing, but the leading character is too hysterical and his fall too complete to make good drama.

w Paul Schrader   novel Paul Theroux   d Peter Weir
ph John Seale   m Maurice Jarre   pd John Stoddart
ed Thom Noble

Harrison Ford, Helen Mirren, River Phoenix, Jadrien Steele, André Gregory

'In the end there is barely a thread of hope to take home, other than some strikingly beautiful and sad images of a man grasping for something just beyond his reach.' – *Variety*

Mosquito Squadron
GB 1968 90m DeLuxe
Lewis J. Rachmil/UA

In 1944, the RAF tries out bouncing bombs in a French offensive.

Very minor and belated war heroics for double-billing.

w Donald Sanford, Joyce Perry   d Boris Sagal

David McCallum, Suzanne Neve, David Buck, Dinsdale Landen, Charles Gray

Moss Rose
US 1947 82m bw
TCF (Gene Markey)

A Victorian chorus girl suspects her aristocratic admirer of being a murderer.

Absurd, stilted mystery melodrama with a better-looking production than it deserves.

w Jules Furthman, Tom Reed   d Gregory Ratoff
ph Joe MacDonald   m David Buttolph

Peggy Cummins, Victor Mature, Ethel Barrymore, Vincent Price

The Most Dangerous Game ***
US 1932 63m bw
(RKO) Merian C. Cooper
V*
GB title: *The Hounds of Zaroff*

A mad hunter lures guests on to his island so that he can hunt them down like animals.

Dated but splendidly shivery melodrama with moments of horror and mystery and a splendidly photographed chase sequence. Much imitated in curious ways, and not only by direct remakes such as *A Game of Death* and *Run for the Sun* (qv).

w James Creelman   story Richard Connell   d Ernest B. Schoedsack, Irving Pichel   ph Henry Gerrard   m Max Steiner

Leslie Banks, Joel McCrea, Fay Wray, Robert Armstrong, Noble Johnson

'Futile stab at horror film classification, ineffective as entertainment and minus cast names to compensate.' – *Variety*

The Most Dangerous Man in the World
GB 1969 99m DeLuxe Panavision
TCF/APJAC (Mort Abrahams)
US title: *The Chairman*

A top scientist is sent by western intelligence on a mission into Red China, with a transmitter and a detonator implanted in his skull.

Wild Boys' Own Paper adventure which regrettably slows down in the middle for political philosophizing.

w Ben Maddow   novel *The Chairman* by Jay Richard Kennedy   d J. Lee-Thompson   ph Ted Moore
m Jerry Goldsmith

Gregory Peck, Anne Heywood, Arthur Hill, Conrad Yama, Francisca Tu, Keye Luke, Alan Dobie, Ori Levy

The Most Precious Thing
US 1934 67m bw
Columbia

A college boy marries a waitress; his mother eases the girl out but keeps the baby.

Unconvincing domestic drama, rather drab.

w Ethel Hill, Dore Schary   story Travis Ingham
d Lambert Hillyer

Anita Louise, Mary Forbes, Jane Darwell, Ben Alexander, John Wray, Ward Bond

'Not enough strength for the more important spots.' – *Variety*

'It takes all kinds of critters to make Farmer Vincent's fritters!'

Motel Hell
US 1980 106m Technicolor
United Artists/Camp Hill (Herb Jaffe)
V*, L

Benign motel owners are famous for their spiced meat, which is in fact made from their human guests.

Horror comic intended to amuse, but too repulsive to do so.

w Robert Jaffe, Steven-Charles Jaffe   d Kevin Connor   ph Thomas Del Ruth   m Lance Rubin

Rory Calhoun, Paul Linke, Nancy Parsons, Nina Axelrod, Wolfman Jack

Mother ***
USSR 1926 90m approx (24 fps) bw silent
Mezhrabpom-Russ
V
original title: *Mat*

A mother incriminates her strike-breaking son, but realizes her error.

Propagandist social melodrama which is also brilliantly conceived and edited, with sequences matching those of Eisenstein.

w N. Zarkhi, V. I. Pudovkin   *novel* Maxim Gorky
d V. I. Pudovkin   *ph* A. Golovnia

Vera Baranovskaya, Nikolai Batalov

† Other versions appeared in 1920 and (*d* Mark Donskoi) 1955

The Mother and the Whore **
France   1973   219m   bw
Gala/Films du Losange/Elite/Cine Qua Non/Simar/V.M. (Pierre Cottrell)
original title: *La Maman et la Putain*

A charming but idle man, who lives with his older mistress, dates a young nurse who moves in with them.

A long, sometimes desultory, but often engrossing debate on love, fidelity, sex, marriage and the comedy of human affairs.

wd Jean Eustache   *ph* Pierre Lhomme, Jacques Renard, Michel Cenet   *m* Mozart, Offenbach and others   *ed* Jean Eustache, Denise de Casabianca

Jean-Pierre Léaud, Françoise Lebrun, Bernadette Lafont, Isabelle Weingarten, Jacques Renard, Jean Eustache

'What is extraordinary is that Eustache mesmerises us into caring about each emotional quaver, creating suspense from seemingly inert surfaces, a tension between elusive sensibility and indisputable presence.' – *Jan Dawson, MFB*

Mother Carey's Chickens
US   1938   82m   bw
RKO (Pandro S. Berman)

The tribulations of a small-town family in the 1890s.

Modest domestic drama, not totally unpleasing.

w S. K. Lauren, Gertrude Purcell   *novel* Kate Douglas Wiggin   *d* Rowland V. Lee   *ph* Roy Hunt   *m* Frank Tours

Anne Shirley, Ruby Keeler, Fay Bainter, James Ellison, Walter Brennan, Donnie Dunagan, Frank Albertson, Alma Kruger, Jackie Moran, Virginia Weidler, Margaret Hamilton

† Remade 1963 as *Summer Magic*.

Mother Didn't Tell Me
US   1950   88m   bw
TCF (Fred Kohlmar)

A working girl marries a doctor and their off duty hours don't coincide.

Thin comedy.

wd Claude Binyon   *novel* The Doctor Wears Three Faces by Mary Baird   *ph* Joseph LaShelle   *m* Cyril Mockridge

Dorothy McGuire, William Lundigan, June Havoc, Gary Merrill, Jessie Royce Landis

Mother Is a Freshman
US   1948   80m   Technicolor
TCF
GB title: *Mother Knows Best*

A mother goes to college and falls for the teacher with whom her daughter is infatuated.

Thin romantic comedy lacking the piquancy at which it aims.

w Mary Loos, Richard Sale   *d* Lloyd Bacon

Loretta Young, Van Johnson, Rudy Vallee, Barbara Lawrence, Betty Lynn, Robert Arthur

Mother Joan of the Angels: see *The Devil and the Nun*

Mother, Jugs and Speed
US   1976   98m   DeLuxe   Panavision
TCF (Joseph R. Barbera)
V, V*

Comic and tragic events in the lives of Los Angeles drivers of private commercial ambulances.

Black comedy of incidents ranging from farcical to sentimental, sometimes funny but basically unacceptable in either vein.

w Tom Mankiewicz   *d* Peter Yates   *ph* Ralph Woolsey   *md* Joel Sill   *m* various

Bill Cosby, Raquel Welch, Harvey Keitel, *Allen Garfield*, Bruce Davison, Larry Hagman

'The writer has found a way to get into the underbelly of a city, to survey the twilight territory where tragedy and comedy trip over each other and make an unsightly mess.' – *Time*

Mother Knows Best: see *Mother Is A Freshman*

'The lure of gold can make a man do anything!'
Mother Lode
US   1982   101m   colour
Agamemnon/Martin Shafter, Andrew Scheinman (Fraser Clarke Heston, Andrew Snell)
V*

A villainous miner stops at nothing to protect his goldfield.

More-or-less old-fashioned Western with a change of pace for the star. No world beater, but not bad.

w Fraser Clarke Heston, Peter Snell   *d* Charlton Heston   *ph* Richard Leiterman   *m* Ken Wannberg   *pd* Douglas Higgins

Charlton Heston, Nick Mancuso, Kim Basinger, John Marley

Mother Riley Meets the Vampire
GB   1952   74m   bw
Renown (John Gilling)
US title: *My Son the Vampire*

An old washerwoman accidentally catches a robot-wielding crook called The Vampire.

Childish farce notable for Lucan's last appearance in his dame role, and Lugosi's last substantial appearance of any kind – two pros at the end of their tether.

w Val Valentine   *d* John Gilling   *ph* Stan Pavey   *m* Linda Southworth

Arthur Lucan, Bela Lugosi, Dora Bryan, Richard Wattis

'Stupid, humourless and repulsive.' – *MFB*

Mother, Sir!: see *Navy Wife*

Mother Wore Tights *
US   1947   109m   Technicolor
TCF (Lamar Trotti)

Recollections of a vaudeville team and their growing family.

Well-mounted, reasonably charming family musical, one of the best of the many TCF examples of this genre.

w Lamar Trotti   *book* Miriam Young   *d* Walter Lang   *ph* Harry Jackson   *md* Alfred Newman, Charles Henderson

Betty Grable, Dan Dailey, Mona Freeman, Connie Marshall, Vanessa Brown, Robert Arthur, Sara Allgood, William Frawley, Ruth Nelson

AA: Alfred Newman, Charles Henderson

AAN: Harry Jackson; song 'You Do' (*m* Josef Myrow, *ly* Mack Gordon)

La Motocyclette: see *Girl on a Motorcycle*

Moulin Rouge
US   1934   69m   bw
Twentieth Century (Darryl F. Zanuck)

The wife of a songwriter impersonates her own sister in order to revitalize her marriage and her stage career.

Predictable minor star vehicle, quite competently done.

w Nunnally Johnson, Henry Lehrman   *play* Lyon de Bri   *d* Sidney Lanfield   *ph* Charles Rosher   *md* Alfred Newman   *songs* Harry Warren, Al Dubin

Constance Bennett, Franchot Tone, Tulio Carminati, Helen Westley, Andrew Tombes, Hobart Cavanaugh

Moulin Rouge **
GB   1952   119m   Technicolor
Romulus (Jack Clayton)
V*, L

Fictional biopic of Toulouse Lautrec.

The dramatic emphasis is on the love affairs of the dwarfish artist, but the film's real interest is in its evocation of 19th-century Montmartre, and especially in the first twenty-minute can-can sequence. Nothing later can stand up to the exhilaration of this, and the film slowly slides into boredom.

w John Huston, Anthony Veiller   *novel* Pierre La Mure   *d* John Huston   *ph* Oswald Morris   *m* Georges Auric   *ad* Paul Sheriff   *ed* Ralph Kemplen

José Ferrer, Zsa Zsa Gabor, Katherine Kath, Colette Marchand, Suzanne Flon

AA: art direction

AAN: best picture; John Huston (as director); José Ferrer; Colette Marchand; editing

The Mountain *
US   1956   105m   Technicolor   Vistavision
Paramount (Edward Dmytryk)
V*

After an airplane crash the wreck is difficult to reach. A young man sets off alone to loot it, and his elder brother follows to stop him.

An indeterminate production in which one believes neither the setting, the plot nor the characters, especially not with Vistavision making everything sharply unreal and the brothers seeming two generations apart.

w Ranald MacDougall   *novel* Henri Troyat   *d* Edward Dmytryk   *ph* Franz Planer   *m* Daniele Amfitheatrof

Spencer Tracy, Robert Wagner, Claire Trevor, William Demarest, E. G. Marshall

The Mountain Eagle
GB   1926   72m approx (24 fps)   bw   silent
Gainsborough/Emelka (Michael Balcon)
US title: *Fear o' God*

A young schoolmistress resists the attentions of a businessman, escapes to the mountains, and marries a recluse.

Unremarkable romantic drama; one of the lost Hitchcock films.

w Eliot Stannard   *d* Alfred Hitchcock   *ph* Baron Ventimiglia

Nita Naldi, Bernard Goetzke, Malcolm Keen

Mountain Justice
US   1937   82m   bw
Warner

A frightened hillbilly girl kills her brutal father and is protected by a lawyer.

Involved backwoods melodrama, not really worth the trouble.

w Norman Reilly Raine, Luci Ward   *d* Michael Curtiz

Josephine Hutchinson, George Brent, Robert Barrat, Guy Kibbee, Mona Barrie, Margaret Hamilton, Robert McWade

'Too much plot, but okay for duals.' – *Variety*

The Mountain Men
US 1980 102m Metrocolor Panavision
Columbia (Martin Ransohoff)

Two 19th-century trappers have adventures with Indians.

Rumbustious, foul-mouthed and lethargic Western of the primitive kind; no possible interest.

w Frazer Clarke Heston   d Richard Lang

Charlton Heston, Brian Keith, Victoria Racimo, Stephen Macht, John Glover

'It plays like a Sunn Classic four-waller uncomfortably spiced up with violence and profanity.' – *Variety*

Mountain Music
US 1937 76m bw
Paramount

A hillbilly runs from a marriage and loses his memory.

Tiresome comedy with music.

w J. C. Moffitt, Duke Atteberry, Russel Crouse, Charles Lederer   story Mackinlay Kantor   d Robert Florey

Martha Raye, Bob Burns, John Howard, George Hayes, Rufe Davis, Fuzzy Knight

'Burns and Raye have trouble topping a cast. Mild and minor.' – *Variety*

The Mountain Road
US 1960 102m bw
Columbia/William Goetz

In 1944 China, an American officer helps peasants against the Japanese.

Confused and rather dreary war adventure with pretensions.

w Alfred Hayes   novel Theodore White   d Daniel Mann   ph Burnett Guffey   md Morris Stoloff   m Jerome Moross

James Stewart, Lisa Lu, Glenn Corbett, Henry Morgan, Frank Silvera, James Best, Mike Kellin, Frank Maxwell, Alan Baxter

Mountains of the Moon **
US 1989 136m Technicolor
Guild/Carolco/IndieProd (Daniel Melnick)
V, V*, L

Explorers Richard Burton and John Hanning Speke go in search of the source of the Nile.

Exuberant and engrossing epic that catches the mood of the times.

w William Harrison, Bob Rafelson   story Burton and Speke by William Harrison   d Bob Rafelson   ph Dick Pope   m Michael Small   pd Norman Reynolds   ed Thom Noble

Patrick Bergin, Iain Glen, Richard E. Grant, Fiona Shaw, John Savident, James Villiers, Adrian Rawlins, Peter Vaughan, Delroy Lindo, Bernard Hill

'Somehow it conveys, as few movies ever have, the miserable realities that underlay the 19th century's heroic age of exploration.' – *Richard Schickel, Time*

'Worth seeing principally because it is a real film, by a director who understands the true nature of cinema as a visual medium.' – *Derek Malcolm, Guardian*

'Mother and daughter! Rivals in love!'
Mourning Becomes Electra *
US 1947 170m bw
RKO/Theatre Guild (Dudley Nichols)
V*, L

Murder, doom and guilt affect a New England family at the end of the Civil War.

A mark for trying is all. This is a clearly fated attempt to film the unfilmable, a long and lugubrious updating of Sophocles with more than its share of risible moments.

wd Dudley Nichols   play Eugene O'Neill
ph George Barnes   m Richard Hagemann   ad Albert D'Agostino

Michael Redgrave, Rosalind Russell, Katina Paxinou, Kirk Douglas, Raymond Massey, Nancy Coleman, Leo Genn

'A star cast fumbles with helpless and sometimes touching ineptitude.' – *Gavin Lambert*

'Within its own terms of mistaken reverence, a good, straight, deliberately unimaginative production.' – *James Agee*

'It is apparent from their accents that they have only recently become a family.' – *Pauline Kael, 70s*

AAN: Michael Redgrave; Rosalind Russell

The Mouse on the Moon
GB 1963 85m Eastmancolor
UA/Walter Shenson

The tiny duchy of Grand Fenwick discovers that its home-made wine makes excellent rocket fuel.

Piddling sequel to *The Mouse that Roared*, suffering from a hesitant script, too few jokes, and overacting.

w Michael Pertwee   d Richard Lester   ph Wilkie Cooper   m Ron Grainer

Margaret Rutherford, Ron Moody, Bernard Cribbins, David Kossoff, Terry-Thomas, Michael Crawford

The Mouse that Roared **
GB 1959 85m Technicolor
Columbia/Open Road (Carl Foreman)
V, V*

The tiny duchy of Grand Fenwick is bankrupt, and its minister decides to declare war on the United States, be defeated, and receive Marshall Aid.

Lively comedy which sounds rather better than it plays, but has bright moments.

w Roger Macdougall, Stanley Mann   novel Leonard Wibberley   d Jack Arnold   ph John Wilcox   m Edwin Astley

Peter Sellers (playing three parts), Jean Seberg, David Kossoff, William Hartnell, Leo McKern, Macdonald Parke, Harold Kasket

'The kind of irrepressible topical satire whose artistic flaws become increasingly apparent but whose merits outlast them.' – *Peter John Dyer*

The Mouthpiece **
US 1932 90m bw
Warner (Lucien Hubbard)

A prosecuting counsel successfully turns to defence but becomes corrupt.

A hard-hitting and entertaining melodrama allegedly based on the career of William Fallon, a New York lawyer.

w Joseph Jackson, Earl Baldwin   d James Flood, Elliott Nugent   ph Barney McGill

Warren William, Sidney Fox, Aline MacMahon, John Wray, Ralph Ince, Guy Kibbee

'First-grade melodrama, a bet for all grades of houses.' – *Variety*

Le Mouton a Cinq Pattes: see *The Sheep Has Five Legs*

Move
US 1970 88m DeLuxe Panavision
TCF

A frustrated playwright writes pornography to make

money; he moves to a larger apartment but his mind is full of fantasies.

None of which are of much interest to the paying customers, the movie being drenched with self-pity.

w Joel Lieber, Stanley Hart   novel Joel Lieber   d Stuart Rosenberg

Elliott Gould, Paula Prentiss, Genevieve Waite, John Larch, Joe Silver

Move Over Darling **
US 1963 103m DeLuxe Cinemascope
TCF/Arcola/Arwin (Aaron Rosenberg, Marty Melcher)
V

A wife who has spent five years shipwrecked on a desert island returns to find that her husband has just remarried.

Thin but fitfully amusing remake of *My Favorite Wife;* sheer professionalism gets it by.

w Hal Kanter, Jack Sher   d Michael Gordon   ph Daniel L. Fapp   m Lionel Newman

Doris Day, James Garner, Polly Bergen, Thelma Ritter, Chuck Connors, Fred Clark

Movers and Shakers
US 1985 79m Metrocolor
MGM-UA/BHC (Charles Grodin, William Asher)
V*

A Hollywood writer tries to cope with a difficult project while having personal problems with his wife.

Mishmash of unrealized anecdotes with pauses for studio in-jokes. Despite the talent, it could never have worked, not even under the previously announced title *Dreamers*.

w Charles Grodin   d William Asher   ph Robbie Greenberg   m Ken and Mitzie Welch

Walter Matthau, Charles Grodin, Vincent Gardenia, Tyne Daly, Bill Macy, Gilda Radner, Steve Martin, Nita Talbot

'Only occasionally amusing: faces a bleak box-office future.' – *Variety*

Movie Crazy **
US 1932 82m bw
Harold Lloyd

A filmstruck young man is mistakenly invited to Hollywood for a film test.

The silent comedian is not quite at his best in this early sound comedy, but it contains his last really superb sequences and its picture of Hollywood is both amusing and nostalgic.

w Harold Lloyd and others   d Clyde Bruckman   ph Walter Lundin

Harold Lloyd, Constance Cummings

'A corking comedy, replete with wow belly laughs. Sure-fire.' – *Variety*

Movie Movie **
US 1978 106m part colour
ITC (Stanley Donen)
V, V*

A pastiche of a thirties double bill, including a boxing yarn (*Dynamite Hands*) and a Busby-Berkeley style girlie show (*Baxter's Beauties of 1933*).

Unfortunately there weren't enough paying customers to appreciate the spoofs, which are pretty patchy anyway; but golden moments stay in the mind.

w Larry Gelbart, Sheldon Keller   d Stanley Donen   ph Chuck Rosher Jnr, Bruce Surtees   m Ralph Burns   ch Michael Kidd

George C. Scott, Trish Van Devere, Red Buttons, Eli Wallach, Michael Kidd, Barbara Harris, Barry Bostwick, Art Carney, Jocelyn Brando

'Camp, which has to do with a switch of vision from one era to another, cannot be created, and where it is, as this and previous attempts testify, it is immediately swallowed in its own idiocy.' – *Richard Combs, MFB*

Movietone Follies of 1930
US   1930   70m   bw
Fox

A rich boy courts a chorus girl, and her friends give a show on his estate.

Thin, fumbling drama which doesn't remember to become a musical till it's halfway through, and even then has little spark.

w William K. Wells   d Ben Stoloff

El Brendel, Marjorie White, William Collier Jnr, Miriam Seegar, Frank Richardson

Moving
US   1988   89m   Technicolor
Warner (Stuart Cornfeld)
V*, L

A traffic engineer runs into all kinds of trouble when he decides to move his family from New Jersey to Idaho.

Disappointingly predictable comedy, making all the obvious jokes in a leaden way.

w Andy Breckman   d Alan Metter   ph Donald McAlpine   m Howard Shore   pd David L. Snyder   ed Alan Balsam

Richard Pryor, Beverly Todd, Randy Quaid, Dave Thomas, Dana Carvey, Stacey Dash, Gordon Jump, Morris Day

The Moving Target: see *Harper*

Moving Violation *
US   1976   91m   DeLuxe
TCF/Roger Corman
V, V*, L

Small-town teenagers are pursued by the sheriff because they saw him commit a murder.

Old hat suspenser with a smart new line in thrills.

w David R. Osterhout, William Norton   d Charles S. Dubin   ph Charles Correll   m Don Leake

Stephen McHattie, Kay Lenz, Eddie Albert, Lonnie Chapman, Will Geer

'Probably the most hair-raising pursuit sequences in the history of film.' – *Cleveland Amory*

Moving Violations
US   1985   90m   DeLuxe
Ufland-Roth-IPI-James G. Robinson/TCF
V, L

Misadventures of trainee traffic school cops.

Wasn't *Police Academy* bad enough?

w Neal Israel, Pat Proft   d Neal Israel

John Murray, Jennifer Tilly, James Keach, Brian Backer

'A Romantic Comedy For Anyone Who's Ever Been In Love.'
Much Ado about Nothing **
GB   1993   111m   Technicolor
Samuel Goldwyn/Renaissance (Steven Evans, David Parfitt, Kenneth Branagh)
V, V*, L, S

A man and a woman who have sworn never to marry are tricked into falling in love with each other.

A lively version of Shakespeare's witty romantic comedy, but suffering from some miscasting, plodding direction and rather too much forced jollity to be entirely successful.

wd Kenneth Branagh   play William Shakespeare   ph Roger Lanser   m Patrick Doyle   pd Tim Harvey   ed Andrew Marcus

Kenneth Branagh, *Richard Briers*, Michael Keaton, Denzel Washington, Robert Sean Leonard, Keanu

Reeves, Emma Thompson, Kate Beckinsale, Brian Blessed, Patrick Doyle, Imelda Staunton, Phyllida Law, Ben Elton

'This isn't the best Shakespeare on film . . . but it may be the best movie Shakespeare.' – *Richard Corliss, Time*

'Triumphantly romantic, comic and emotionally alive.' – *Vincent Canby, New York Times*

'One of the few movies of recent years that could leave audiences weeping for joy.' – *David Denby, New York*

Much Too Shy
GB   1942   92m   bw
Columbia (Ben Henry)

A gormless handyman gets into trouble when the portraits of his lady clients are sold to an advertising agency with nude bodies added to them.

A slightly vulgar and talkative farce which restricts the star.

w Ronald Frankau   d Marcel Varnel   ph Arthur Crabtree

George Formby, Kathleen Harrison, Hylda Bayley, Eileen Bennett, Joss Ambler, Jimmy Clitheroe

Muddy River *
Japan   1981   105m   bw
Unifilm/Contemporary/Kimura Productions (Motoyasu Kimura)
original title: *Doro No Kawa*

Two nine-year-old boys become friends and try to make sense of the adult world around them.

A small and charming story, sharply observed and photographed.

w Takaki Shigemori   novel Teru Miyamoto   d Kohei Oguri   ph Shohei Ando   m Kuroudo Mori   ad Akira Naito   ed Nobuo Ogawa

Nobutaka Asahara, Takahiro Tamura, Yumiko Fujita, Masako Yagi, Minoru Sakurai, Makiko Shibata, Mariko Kaga

AAN: best foreign film

Der Müde Tod: see *Destiny*

The Mudlark **
GB   1950   98m   bw
TCF (Nunnally Johnson)

A scruffy boy from the docks breaks into Windsor Castle to see Queen Victoria and ends her fifteen years of seclusion.

A pleasant whimsical legend which could have done without the romantic interest, but which despite an air of unreality provides warm-hearted, well upholstered entertainment for family audiences.

w Nunnally Johnson,   novel Theodore Bonnet   d Jean Negulesco   ph Georges Périnal   m William Alwyn   ad C. P. Norman

Alec Guinness, Irene Dunne, *Andrew Ray*, Anthony Steel, Constance Smith, *Finlay Currie, Edward Rigby*

Muerte de un Ciclista: see *Death of a Cyclist*

Mug Town
US   1943   60m   bw
Universal

The Little Tough Guys get mixed up with hi-jackers.

A failing entry in this series: the ageing teenagers shortly decided to play for laughs.

w Brenda Weisberg, Harold Tarshis, Harry Sucher and Lewis Amster   d Ray Taylor

Billy Halop, Huntz Hall, Bernard Punsley, Gabriel Dell, Grace McDonald, Edward Norris, Jed Prouty

Mùi Du Du Xanh: see *The Scent of the Green Papaya*

Mujeres al Borde de un Ataque de Nervios: see *Women on the Verge of a Nervous Breakdown*

'It comes to life!'
'A love story that lived for three thousand years!'
The Mummy **
US   1932   72m   bw
Universal (Stanley Bergerman)
V*, L

An Egyptian mummy comes back to life and covets a young girl.

Strange dreamlike horror film with only fleeting *frissons* but plenty of narrative interest despite the silliest of stories and some fairly stilted acting.

w John I. Balderston   d Karl Freund   ph Charles Stumar   m Tchaikovsky   ad Willy Pogany

Boris Karloff, Zita Johann, David Manners, Arthur Byron, Edward Van Sloan

'Should show profit despite fairy tale theme.' – *Variety*

'It beggars description . . . one of the most unusual talkies ever produced.' – *New York Times*

'Editing very much in the Germanic style, magnificent lighting and a superb performance from Karloff make this a fantasy almost without equal.' – *John Baxter, 1968*

† The star was billed simply as 'Karloff the uncanny'.

The Mummy *
GB   1959   88m   Technicolor
Hammer (Michael Carreras)
V*, L

A mummy brought back to England by archaeologists wakes up and goes on the rampage.

Typical Hammer vulgarization of a Hollywood legend; starts slowly and unpleasantly, but picks up speed and resource in the last half hour.

w Jimmy Sangster   d Terence Fisher   ph Jack Asher   m Frank Reizenstein

Peter Cushing, Christopher Lee, Yvonne Furneaux, Eddie Byrne, Felix Aylmer, Raymond Huntley, John Stuart

† Hammer sequels, of little interest, were *Curse of the Mummy's Tomb* (1964), *The Mummy's Shroud* (1966) and *Blood from the Mummy's Tomb* (1971).

Mummy's Boys
US   1936   68m   bw
RKO (Lee Marcus)

Two ditch diggers in Egypt encounter some dirty work by a mad archaeologist.

Ho-hum comedy with tired old gags.

w Jack Townley, Philip G. Epstein, Charles Roberts   d Fred Guiol

Bert Wheeler, Robert Woolsey, Barbara Pepper, Moroni Olsen, Willie Best

'Poorly acted, raggedly written . . . net result of the dialogue is about four snickers.' – *Variety*

'Egypt's ancient loves live again in evil!'
The Mummy's Curse
US   1945   62m   bw
Universal (Oliver Drake)

Sequel to *The Mummy's Ghost* (qv), notable for many loose ends of narrative.

Last of the Universal mummy films (until Abbott and Costello met him).

w Bernard Schubert   d Leslie Goodwins

Peter Coe, Martin Kosleck, Kay Harding, Kurt Katch, Virginia Christine, Lon Chaney Jnr

'This film contains the most nauseous horror imaginable and is not for the squeamish.' – *MFB*

† See also *Abbott and Costello Meet the Mummy*.

'Nameless! Fleshless! Deathless!'
The Mummy's Ghost
US   1944   60m   bw
Universal (Ben Pivar)

The slow but unstoppable Kharis is now on the trail of his long-lost princess.

A slight improvement on its predecessor, *The Mummy's Tomb*.

w Griffin Jay, Henry Sucher, Brenda Weisberg *d* Reginald LeBorg

John Carradine, George Zucco, Ramsay Ames, Robert Lowery, Barton MacLane, Lon Chaney Jnr

'Tomb of a thousand terrors!'
The Mummy's Hand **
US   1940   67m   bw
Universal (Ben Pivar)
V*

The high priest of an evil sect revivifies an Egyptian mummy and uses it to kill off members of an archaeological expedition.

Semi-sequel to 1932's *The Mummy*, economically using the same flashback. It starts off in comedy vein, but the last half hour is among the most scary in horror film history.

w Griffin Jay, Maxwell Shane   *d* Christy Cabanne
ph Elwood Bredell

Dick Foran, Wallace Ford, *George Zucco*, Cecil Kellaway, Peggy Moran, *Tom Tyler*, *Eduardo Ciannelli*

† Sequels, of decreasing merit, were *The Mummy's Tomb* (1942) (in which the heroes of *The Mummy's Hand* are killed off), *The Mummy's Ghost* (1944) and *The Mummy's Curse* (1944). See also *Abbott and Costello Meet the Mummy*.

'Buried alive for 3700 years! Brought back to live, love and kill!'
'Beware the beat of the cloth-wrapped feet!'
The Mummy's Shroud
GB   1966   84m   Technicolor
Hammer (Anthony Nelson-Keys)

In the twenties, an exhumed mummy brought to the city museum is restored to life and slaughters those who disturbed his rest.

Uninventive rehash of every other mummy movie; too hackneyed to be saved even by a good cast and production values.

wd John Gilling   *ph* Arthur Grant   *m* Don Banks

John Phillips, André Morell, David Buck, Elizabeth Sellars, Catherine Lacey, Maggie Kimberley, Michael Ripper, Tim Barrett, Roger Delgado, Dickie Owen

The Mummy's Tomb
US   1942   61m   bw
Ben Pivar/Universal
V*

The aged high priest sends a young disciple to America, where Kharis dutifully kills off those who violated his tomb.

Shoddily made sequel to *The Mummy's Hand*, with much re-used footage; astonishingly, it broke box-office records for its year, and provoked two more episodes.

w Griffin Jay, Henry Sucher   *d* Harold Young

Turhan Bey, George Zucco, Dick Foran, Wallace Ford, Elyse Knox, Lon Chaney Jnr

Mumsy, Nanny, Sonny and Girly
GB   1959   102m   Eastmancolor
CIRO/Brigitte (Ronald J. Kahn)
V*
aka: *Girly*

Two adolescents bring home lonely people as playthings for a homicidal family.

Revolting black comedy for masochists, representing the British cinema at its lowest ebb.

w Brian Comport   *play* Maisie Mosco   *d* Freddie Francis   *ph* David Muir   *m* Bernard Ebbinghouse

Michael Bryant, Ursula Howells, Pat Heywood, Howard Trevor, Vanessa Howard

Münchausen **
Germany   1943   134m   Agfacolor
UFA (Eberhard Schmidt)
aka: *The Adventures of Baron Münchausen*

In the 1940s Baron Münchausen tells stories of his fabulous ancestor who, it is soon clear, is himself, having been given immortality by a magician.

Lavish but somewhat stilted spectacle, produced on the orders of Nazi propagandist Joseph Goebbels to mark the studio's twenty-fifth anniversary. His influence is evident in the way that all other nationalities are shown as comic.

w Berthold Bürger (Erich Kästner)   *d* Josef von Baky   *ph* Werner Krien   *m* Georg Haentzschel
ad Emil Hasler, Otto Gulstorff

Hans Albers, Wilhelm Bendow, Michael Bohnen, Marina von Ditmar, Hans Brausewetter, Brigitte Horney, Käthe Haack

† Kästner used a pseudonym because his writings had been banned since 1933. After the film was released, Hitler ordered that he should receive no further commissions.

The Muppet Christmas Carol *
US   1992   86m   colour
Buena Vista/Walt Disney/Jim Henson (Brian Henson, Martin G. Baker)
V, V*, L, S

A Christmas-hating miser is reformed by the visitations of five ghosts.

Cheerful adaptation of the perennial story, in a version that should appeal to the young.

w Jerry Juhl   *story* A Christmas Carol by Charles Dickens   *d* Brian Henson   *ph* John Fenner
m Miles Goodman   *pd* Val Strazovec   *m/y* Paul Williams   *sp* The Computer Film Company
ed Michael Jablow

Michael Caine, Steven MacKintosh, Meredith Brown, Robin Weaver, Kermit the Frog, Miss Piggy, The Great Gonzo, Fozzie Bear

'The film sinks into a quagmire of sentimentality; the Muppets withdraw discreetly during Scrooge's ghostly visitations and the dominant flavour is more saccharine than humbug. Nice try, though.' – *Sheila Johnston, Independent*

'More entertainment than humanly possible!'
The Muppet Movie **
GB   1979   97m   Eastmancolor
ITC (Jim Henson)
V*, L, S

Kermit the Frog and friends travel across America to Hollywood and are offered a film contract by Lew Lord, the famous impresario.

Technically an adroit transfer of the celebrated puppets from their TV backstage milieu to a wider canvas; but the latter tends to dwarf them, the material is very variable, the guest stars look embarrassed and the show goes on too long.

w Jerry Juhl, Jack Burns   *d* James Frawley
ph Isidore Mankofsky   *m* Paul Williams, Kenny Ascher   *pd* Joel Schiller

Charles Durning, Edgar Bergen, Bob Hope, Milton Berle, Mel Brooks, James Coburn, Dom DeLuise, Elliott Gould, Cloris Leachman, Telly Savalas, Orson Welles

AAN: Paul Williams, Kenny Ascher; song 'The Rainbow Connection'

The Muppets Take Manhattan *
US   1984   94m   Technicolor
Tri-Star (David Lazer)
V*, L

The Muppets' varsity show is promised a New York opening.

Probably the best of the Muppet features, but by the time of its arrival the early brilliance had been forgotten and even Miss Piggy had worn out her welcome.

w Frank Oz, Tom Patchett, Jay Tarses   *d* Frank Oz

AAN: Jeffrey Moss (music)

Le Mur: see *The Wall*

La Mura de Malapaga: see *Au delà des Grilles*

Murder **
GB   1930   92m   bw
British International (John Maxwell)
V*

A girl is convicted of murder, but one of the jurors sets out to prove her innocent.

Interesting early Hitchcock, a rare whodunnit for him.

w Alma Reville   *novel* Enter Sir John by Clemence Dane, Helen Simpson   *d* Alfred Hitchcock   *ph* Jack Cox

Herbert Marshall, Norah Baring, Phyllis Konstam, Edward Chapman, Miles Mander, Esmé Percy, Donald Calthrop

'If Hitchcock produced in Hollywood and was wise enough to keep his films to six or seven reels, he might be a rave anywhere.' – *Variety*

Murder Ahoy
GB   1964   74m   bw
MGM (Lawrence P. Bachmann)
V*

Miss Marple investigates murders on a naval cadet training ship.

Weakest of the Marple mysteries: all chat and no interest.

w David Pursall, Jack Seddon   *d* George Pollock
ph Desmond Dickinson   *m* Ron Goodwin

Margaret Rutherford, Lionel Jeffries, Stringer Davis, Charles Tingwell, William Mervyn, Joan Benham, Nicholas Parsons, Miles Malleson, Henry Oscar, Derek Nimmo, Francis Matthews, Gerald Cross

Murder among Friends
US   1941   61m   bw
Ralph Dietrich-Walter Morosco/TCF

Subscribers to a 200,000-dollar insurance policy die one by one.

Pleasingly efficient supporting mystery.

w John Larkin   *d* Ray McCarey

John Hubbard, Marjorie Weaver, Cobina Wright Jnr, Mona Barrie, Douglass Dumbrille, Sidney Blackmer, Lucien Littlefield, Milton Parsons

Murder at Monte Carlo
GB   1934   70m   bw
Warner (Irving Asher)

A professor is murdered for his roulette system.

Modest second feature notable only as a springboard for the career of its star.

w John Hastings Turner, Michael Barringer
novel Tom Van Dyke   *d* Ralph Ince   *ph* Basil Emmott

Errol Flynn, Eve Gray, Paul Graetz, Molly Lamont, Ellis Irving

Murder at the Baskervilles: see *Silver Blaze*

'By the first lady of mystery – with the last word in detectives!'

Murder at the Gallop *

GB   1963   81m   bw
MGM (Lawrence P. Bachmann)
V*

Miss Marple investigates when an old man is apparently frightened to death by a cat.

Probably the best of the Marples, with a good sense of place and lively performances.

w James P. Cavanagh   *novel* *After the Funeral* by Agatha Christie   *d* George Pollock   *ph* Arthur Ibbetson   *m* Ron Goodwin

Margaret Rutherford, Flora Robson, Robert Morley, Stringer Davis, Charles Tingwell, Duncan Lamont, James Villiers, Robert Urquhart, Katya Douglas

Murder at the Vanities *

US   1934   95m   bw
Paramount (E. Lloyd Sheldon)
V*

Murder backstage at the first night of Earl Carroll's Vanities.

Curious, stylish mixture of musical numbers, broad comedy and mystery. Dated, but fun.

w Carey Wilson, Joseph Gollomb, Sam Hellman   *d* Mitchell Leisen   *ph* Leo Tover   *songs* Arthur Johnston, Sam Coslow   *md* Rudolph Kopp

Jack Oakie, Victor McLaglen, Carl Brisson, Kitty Carlisle, Dorothy Stickney, Gertrude Michael, Jessie Ralph, Gail Patrick

'Above average and for the masses . . . long but does not drag.' – *Variety*

'It can boast lavish staging, tuneful melodies, and a host of attractive girls.' – *New York Times*

Murder at the Windmill

GB   1949   70m   bw
Daniel Angel and Nat Cohen
US title: *Murder at the Burlesque*

At London's famous girlie show, a front row patron is murdered.

Rather rushed-looking whodunnit with interesting detail.

wd Val Guest

Garry Marsh, Jack Livesey, Jon Pertwee, Diana Decker, Jimmy Edwards, Eliot Makeham

Murder by Contract *

US   1958   81m   bw
Columbia/Orbin (Leon Chooluck)

A professional killer makes a fatal mistake and is shot down by police.

Low-budgeter which seemed stark and original at the time, but television has familiarized its contents. Moody, contrasty photography and restrained style give it a minor distinction.

w Ben Simcoe   *d* Irving Lerner   *ph* Lucien Ballard   *m* Perry Borkin

Vince Edwards, Philip Pine, Herschel Bernardi, Caprice Toriel

'Ice cold and completely unsentimental.' – *John Gillett*

'A bloody funny movie!'

Murder by Death *

US   1976   94m   Metrocolor
Columbia/Ray Stark
V, V*, L

Several (fictional) detectives are invited to stay at the home of a wealthy recluse, and mystery and murder follow.

Sometimes thin but generally likeable spoof of a longstanding genre; the stars seize their opportunities avidly, and the film does not outstay its welcome.

w Neil Simon   *d* Robert Moore   *ph* David M. Walsh   *m* Dave Grusin   *pd* Stephen Grimes

Peter Falk, Alec Guinness, Peter Sellers, Truman Capote, Estelle Winwood, Elsa Lanchester, Eileen Brennan, James Coco, David Niven, Maggie Smith, Nancy Walker

'Plenty of scene-stealing actors but not many scenes worth stealing.' – *Michael Billington, Illustrated London News*

'Polished performances fail to compensate for a vacuous and frustratingly tortuous plot.' – *Sight and Sound*

'It seems to me that if you haven't watched the real Thin Man and the real Bogie in the real *Maltese Falcon* you won't see the joke; and if you have watched them, the joke is not good enough.' – *Dilys Powell, Sunday Times*

Murder by Decree

GB/Canada   1978   112m   Metrocolor
Avco/Decree Productions/Saucy Jack (Robert A. Goldstone)
V*, L

Sherlock Holmes investigates the matter of Jack the Ripper and comes upon a Masonic conspiracy.

Interminably long and unpardonably muddled variation on this over-familiar theme, with halts for the performances of guest artists and no clear grip on narrative or character.

w John Hopkins   *d* Bob Clark   *ph* Reginald H. Morris   *m* Carl Zittrer, Paul Zaza   *pd* Harry Pottle

Christopher Plummer, James Mason, Anthony Quayle, David Hemmings, Susan Clark, John Gielgud, Donald Sutherland, Frank Finlay, Geneviève Bujold

Murder by Illusion: see *F/X*

Murder by the Clock

US   1931   76m   bw
Paramount

Creepy goings on in an old house after the death of a dowager who has built herself a tomb from which she can escape if buried alive.

Tasteless chiller which had the distinction of being withdrawn from British circulation after public protests.

w Henry Myers, Rufus King, Charles Beahan   *play* Charles Beahan   *novel* Rufus King   *d* Edward Sloman   *ph* Karl Struss

Lilyan Tashman, William 'Stage' Boyd, Regis Toomey, Irving Pichel, Blanche Frederici, Walter McGrail

'Lacking in punch as a strongie for first runs. Below that should do oke.' – *Variety*

Murder by Television

US   1935   60m   bw
Edward M. Spitz/Imperial

The inventor of a television process is murdered.

Static whodunnit with the star as twin brothers. Only a curio.

w Joseph O'Donnell   *d* Clifford Sanforth

Bela Lugosi, June Collyer, Huntley Gordon, George Meeker

Murder Goes to College

US   1937   77m   bw
Paramount

A reporter on vacation helps solve a campus killing.

Reasonably lively comedy mystery which might have started a series, but didn't.

w Brian Marlow, Eddie Welch, Robert Wyler   *novel* Kurt Steele   *d* Charles Reisner

Roscoe Karns, Lynne Overman, Marsha Hunt, Astrid Allwyn, Harvey Stephens, Larry Crabbe

'Dialogue crackles with humour . . . this whodunit will be welcome material on many programmes.' – *Variety*

'You'll die laughing!'

Murder He Says **

US   1945   91m   bw
Paramount (E. D. Leshin)

An insurance salesman stays with a homicidal family of hillbillies.

A curious black farce which seems to be compounded of *Cold Comfort Farm* and *The Red Inn*. Very funny, and ahead of its time.

w Lou Breslow   *d* George Marshall   *ph* Theodor Sparkuhl

Fred MacMurray, Marjorie Main, Helen Walker, Peter Whitney, Jean Heather, Porter Hall, Mabel Paige

Murder in Reverse

GB   1945   88m   bw
British National

After long imprisonment for a supposed murder, a convict comes out and hunts down the victim, who isn't really dead.

A reasonable crime entertainment of its day which seemed to introduce a new star; but it hasn't worn well.

wd Montgomery Tully   *novel* 'Seamark'

William Hartnell, Jimmy Hanley, Chili Bouchier, John Slater, Dinah Sheridan, Wylie Watson

Murder in the Big House

US   1942   67m   bw
Warner

Two reporters uncover a murder ring in a prison.

Acceptable second feature which catapulted its star to fame – at another studio.

w Raymond Schrock   *d* B. Reeves Eason

Van Johnson, George Meeker, Faye Emerson, Frank Wilcox

† A previous 1936 version was called *Jailbreak* and starred Craig Reynolds. *Murder in the Big House* was reissued in 1945 as *Born for Trouble*.

Murder in the Blue Room

US   1944   61m   bw
Frank Gross/Universal

Volunteering to sleep in a room where a murder was committed, a guest is found dead.

Tepid remake of *The Secret of the Blue Room*.

w I. A. L. Diamond, Stanley Davis   *d* Leslie Goodwins

Anne Gwynne, Donald Cook, John Litel, Grace McDonald, June Preisser, Regis Toomey

Murder in the Cathedral

GB   1951   136m   bw
Film Traders/George Hoellering

The 12th-century struggle between Henry II and his archbishop culminates in the assassination of Becket in Canterbury Cathedral.

Plainly filmed, slightly amateur version of the celebrated verse play; scarcely a rewarding cinematic experience.

wd George Hoellering   *play* T. S. Eliot   *ph* David Kosky   *m* Laszlo Lajtha   *ad* Peter Pendrey

Father John Grosner, Alexander Gauge, David Ward, George Woodbridge, Basil Burton, Paul Rogers, Niall MacGinnis, Mark Dignam, Leo McKern

'A curious ordeal for the audience . . . a no-man's-land between cinema and drama has been discovered, rather than any extension of either.' – *Gavin Lambert*

Murder in the Family

GB 1938 75m bw
TCF

Who killed rich Aunt Octavia?

Mild whodunnit with interesting cast.

w David Evans   novel James Ronald   d Al Parker

Barry Jones, Jessica Tandy, Evelyn Ankers, Donald Gray, David Markham, Glynis Johns, Roddy McDowall

Murder in the Fleet

US 1935 70m bw
MGM (Lucien Hubbard)

Sabotage on a navy cruiser turns out to be the work of a mad inventor.

Weak and confused mixture of melodrama and comedy.

wd Edward Sedgwick   ph Milton Krasner

Robert Taylor, Jean Parker, Jean Hersholt, Ted Healy, Una Merkel, Nat Pendleton, Raymond Hatton, Donald Cook, Mischa Auer

Murder in the Music Hall

US 1946 84m bw
Republic (Herman Millakowsky)
reissue title: Midnight Melody

A former criminal, now Broadway producer, is murdered on opening night.

Humdrum extravaganza built round its star, whose last skating appearance this was.

w Frances Hyland, Laszlo Gorog   d John English
ph John Alton   md Walter Scharf

Vera Hruba Ralston, William Marshall, Helen Walker, Nancy Kelly, William Gargan, Ann Rutherford, Julie Bishop, Jerome Cowan, Edward Norris, Paul Hurst, Jack La Rue

Murder in the Private Car *

US 1934 60m bw
Lucien Hubbard/MGM
GB title: Murder on the Runaway Train

Mysteries proliferate aboard a fast-moving train.

Adequate second feature which builds up to a remarkably well-staged climax in a runaway carriage.

w Ralph Spence, Edgar Allen Woolf, Al Boasberg, Harvey Thew   d Harry Beaumont

Russell Hardie, Charles Ruggles, Mary Carlisle, Una Merkel, Porter Hall

'About the swiftest 61 minutes of entertainment you are ever likely to see.' – Picturegoer

The Murder in Thornton Square: see Gaslight (1944)

Murder in Times Square

US 1943 72m bw
Columbia

An actor-playwright is suspected of four theatrical murders.

Standard detection work with some slight claim to sophistication.

w Stuart Palmer, Paul Gangelin   d Lew Landers

Edmund Lowe, Sidney Blackmer, Marguerite Chapman, John Litel

Murder in Trinidad

US 1934 74m bw
Fox

A quiet detective solves a murder in the tropics.

Modest whodunnit with Nigel Bruce for once playing the sleuth instead of Watson.

w Seton I. Miller   novel John W. Vandercook
d Louis King

Nigel Bruce, Heather Angel, Victor Jory, Murray Kinnell, Douglas Walton, J. Carrol Naish

'Amusing, but not particularly intriguing.' – Variety

Murder Inc: see The Enforcer

Murder, Incorporated

US 1960 103m bw Cinemascope
TCF (Burt Balaban)

In the thirties, Anastasia and Lepke build up their crime syndicate which spreads terror through New York.

Tedious and poorly made gangster thriller, unforgivable faults considering the many admirable models it has to follow.

w Irv Tunick, Mel Barr   d Burt Balaban, Stuart Rosenberg   ph Gayne Rescher   m Frank de Vol

Stuart Whitman, Mai Britt, Henry Morgan, Peter Falk, David J. Stewart, Simon Oakland, Morey Amsterdam

AAN: Peter Falk

Murder Is News: see The Delavine Affair

The Murder Man *

US 1935 84m bw
MGM (Harry Rapf)

A reporter investigating a murder becomes one of the suspects.

Good low-key melodrama with an interesting cast.

w Tim Whelan, John C. Higgins   d Tim Whelan
ph Lester White   m William Axt

Spencer Tracy, Virginia Bruce, Lionel Atwill, James Stewart, Harvey Stephens, William Collier Snr

'It will please in the lesser houses.' – Variety

Murder Most Foul

GB 1964 91m bw
MGM/Lawrence P. Bachmann (Ben Arbeid)

Refusing to return a guilty verdict, juror Miss Marple makes her own murder investigation backstage at a third-rate repertory company.

Moderate Marple mystery which hasn't quite found the light touch it seeks.

w David Pursall, Jack Seddon   novel Mrs McGinty's Dead by Agatha Christie   d George Pollock
ph Desmond Dickinson   m Ron Goodwin

Margaret Rutherford, Ron Moody, Charles Tingwell, Andrew Cruickshank, Megs Jenkins, Ralph Michael, James Bolam, Stringer Davis, Francesca Annis, Dennis Price, Terry Scott

Murder My Sweet: see Farewell My Lovely (1944)

The Murder of Dr Harrigan

US 1935 67m bw
Warner

A hospital founder disappears while on his way to the operating room.

Formula murder mystery without much special interest.

w Peter Milne, Sy Bartlett   novel Mignon G. Eberhart   d Frank McDonald

Kay Linaker, Ricardo Cortez, Mary Astor, John Eldredge, Joseph Crehan, Frank Reicher

'Will probably do no better than mildly.' – Variety

Murder on Diamond Row: see The Squeaker

Murder on Monday: see Home at Seven

Murder on the Blackboard

US 1934 71m bw
RKO

Hildegarde Withers solves a murder in school.

Modest mystery with popular leads; it satisfied.

w Willis Goldbeck, Stuart Palmer   d George Archainbaud

Edna May Oliver, James Gleason, Bruce Cabot, Gertrude Michael, Regis Toomey, Edgar Kennedy

'Moderate entertainment in its class.' – Variety

Murder on the Orient Express **

GB 1974 131m Technicolor
EMI/GW Films (John Brabourne, Richard Goodwin)
V*, L, S

In the early thirties, Hercule Poirot solves a murder on a snowbound train.

Reasonably elegant but disappointingly slackly-handled version of a classic mystery novel. Finney overacts and his all-star support is distracting, while as soon as the train chugs into its snowdrift the film stops moving too, without even a dramatic 'curtain'.

w Paul Dehn   novel Agatha Christie   d Sidney Lumet   ph Geoffrey Unsworth   m Richard Rodney Bennett   pd Tony Walton

Albert Finney, Ingrid Bergman, Lauren Bacall, Wendy Hiller, Sean Connery, Vanessa Redgrave, Michael York, Martin Balsam, Richard Widmark, Jacqueline Bisset, Jean-Pierre Cassel, Rachel Roberts, George Coulouris, John Gielgud, Anthony Perkins, Colin Blakely, Jeremy Lloyd, Denis Quilley

'Audiences appear to be so hungry for this type of entertainment that maybe it hardly matters that it isn't very good.' – Judith Crist

AA: Ingrid Bergman

AAN: Paul Dehn; Geoffrey Unsworth; Richard Rodney Bennett; Albert Finney

Murder She Said *

GB 1961 87m bw
MGM (George H. Brown)
V, V*

An elderly spinster investigates after seeing a woman strangled in a passing train.

Frightfully British and disappointingly tame adaptation of an Agatha Christie character, with only the star (who is somewhat miscast) holding one's attention.

w David Pursall, Jack Seddon   novel 4.50 from Paddington by Agatha Christie   d George Pollock
ph Geoffrey Faithfull   m Ron Goodwin

Margaret Rutherford, Charles Tingwell, Muriel Pavlow, Arthur Kennedy, James Robertson Justice, Thorley Walters, Gerald Cross, Conrad Phillips

† Thanks to Miss Rutherford's popularity, three increasingly poor sequels were made: Murder at the Gallop (1963), Murder Most Foul (1964), Murder Ahoy (1964).

Murder Will Out: see The Voice of Merrill

Murder without Crime

GB 1950 76m bw
ABPC

A blackmailer extracts money for a crime not yet committed.

Thin four-hander from a rather mysterious West End success.

wd J. Lee-Thompson   play Double Error by J. Lee-Thompson

Dennis Price, Derek Farr, Joan Dowling, Patricia Plunkett

The Murderer Lives at 21: see L'Assassin habite au 21

The Murderers Are Among Us *
Germany   1947   87m   bw
Defa
original title: *Die Mörder Sind Unter Uns*

In the ruins of Berlin several post-war characters indulge in gloomy self-examination.

Almost a caricature of what one would expect from a defeated people, this now-curious item has a certain power of its own. wd Wolfgang Staudte ph Friedl Behn-Grund, Eugen Klagemann m Ernst Roters

Hildegard Knef, Ernst Fischer, Arno Paulsen

Murderer's Row
US   1966   108m   Technicolor
Columbia/Meadway-Claude/Euan Lloyd
V*

Matt Helm tracks down an international villain who has kidnapped an inventor.

Witless and uninventive spy spoof which drags itself wearily along but never attempts an explanation of its own title.

w Herbert Baker novel Donald Hamilton d Henry Levin ph Sam Leavitt m Lalo Schifrin

Dean Martin, Ann-Margret, Karl Malden, Camilla Sparv, James Gregory, Beverly Adams, Tom Reese

'The blood will run cold in your veins!'
Murders in the Rue Morgue *
US   1932   62m   bw
Universal (Carl Laemmle Jnr)
V*

A series of grisly murders prove to be the work of a trained ape.

A distant relation of the original story, mildly interesting for its obvious Caligari influences, but not very good in any way.

w Tom Reed, Dale Van Every, John Huston story Edgar Allan Poe d Robert Florey ph Karl Freund

Bela Lugosi, Sidney Fox, Leon Ames, Bert Roach, Brandon Hurst

'Synthetic studio rewrite . . . Poe wouldn't recognize his story.' – *Variety*

'Where sights of passion end in screams of terror!'
Murders in the Rue Morgue *
US   1971   86m   Foto Film Color
AIP (Louis M. Heyward)
V*

Poe's story is being presented at a Grand Guignol theatre in Paris, and when murders happen within the company Inspector Vidocq comes to investigate.

Playfully plotted chiller which has more to do with *The Phantom of the Opera* than with Poe. A good time-waster for addicts.

w Charles Wicking, Henry Slesar d Gordon Hessler ph Manuel Berengier m Waldo de Los Rios

Jason Robards Jnr, Herbert Lom, Lilli Palmer, Adolfo Celi, Michael Dunn, Christine Kaufmann

Murders in the Zoo
US   1933   64m   bw
Paramount

A jealous zoologist finds interesting ways to murder any man who shows interest in his wife.

Modest time-passer with a rampant star.

w Philip Wylie, Seton I. Miller d Edward Sutherland

Lionel Atwill, Charles Ruggles, Kathleen Burke, John Lodge, Randolph Scott, Gail Patrick

'Has what it takes to chill and entertain.' – *Variety*

Muriel *
France/Italy   1963   116m   Eastmancolor
Argos/Alpha/Eclair/Films de la Pléiade/Dear Films (Anatole Dauman)
V*
aka: *Muriel, ou le Temps d'un Retour*

A widow and her stepson are both misled by memories of past loves.

Elusive character drama which, though over-generous in length, fails to satisfy.

w Jean Cayrol d Alain Resnais ph Sacha Vierny m Hans Werner Henze

Delphine Seyrig, Jean-Pierre Kérien, Nita Klein, Jean-Baptiste Thierrée

'One has to watch and listen with every nerve alert.' – *Tom Milne, MFB*

Muriel, ou le Temps d'un Retour: see *Muriel*

Murmur of the Heart: see *Le Souffle au Coeur*

Murph the Surf: see *Live a Little, Steal a Lot*

Murphy's Law
US   1986   100m   TVC colour
Cannon (Pancho Kohner)
V, V*, L

A tough LA cop with a drink problem is arrested for his ex-wife's murder.

Unattractively violent and foul-mouthed urban thriller in the wake of *Dirty Harry*.

w Gail Morgan Hickman d J. Lee Thompson ph Alex Phillips m Marc Donahue, Valentine McCallum

Charles Bronson, Carrie Snodgress, Kathleen Wilhoite, Robert F. Lyons, Richard Romanus

Murphy's Romance
US   1985   107m   Metrocolor   Panavision
Columbia/Martin Ritt-Fogwood (Laura Ziskin)
V*, L

A divorcée determined to make a living as a horse trainer in rural Arizona falls for the ageing local chemist.

Well-meaning but somewhat yawnworthy romantic comedy-drama which might almost have strayed from the days of the Hardy family.

w Harriet Frank Jnr, Irving Ravetch d Martin Ritt ph William A. Fraker m Carole King pd Joel Schiller

Sally Field, James Garner, Brian Kerwin, Corey Haim

'Sweet and homey, but falls far short of compelling film-making.' – *Variety*

AAN: James Garner; photography

Murphy's War *
GB   1971   108m   Eastmancolor   Panavision
Hemdale/Yates-Deeley (Michael Deeley)
V*

A torpedoed British merchantman in Venezuela devotes himself to bombing a U-boat from a home-made plane.

Modest adventure story with the star in better form than the script.

w Stirling Silliphant novel Max Catto d Peter Yates ph Douglas Slocombe m John Barry

Peter O'Toole, Sian Phillips, Philippe Noiret, Horst Janson

The Music Box ****
US   1932   30m   bw
Hal Roach
V

Two delivery men take a piano to a house at the top of a flight of steps.

Quintessential Laurel and Hardy, involving almost all their aspects including a slight song and dance. With Billy Gilbert.

w H. M. Walker d James Parrott

AA: best short

'As a lawyer all she wanted was the truth. As a daughter all she wanted was his innocence. How well do you really know your father?'
Music Box *
US   1989   126m   colour   Cinemascope
Guild/Carolco (Irwin Winkler)
V, V*, L, S

A lawyer defends her father against charges that he was a war criminal.

An effectively melodramatic courtroom drama, but no more than that, despite winning the Golden Bear at the Berlin Film Festival in 1990.

w Joe Eszterhas d Costa-Gavras ph Patrick Blossier m Philippe Sarde pd Jeannine Claudia Oppewall ed Joelle Van Effenterre

Jessica Lange, Armin Mueller-Stahl, Frederic Forrest, Donald Moffat, Lukas Haas, Cheryl Lynne Bruce, Mari Torocsik, J. S. Block, Sol Frieder

AAN: Jessica Lange

Music for Madame
US   1937   81m   bw
RKO (Jesse L. Lasky)

An opera singer goes to Hollywood and becomes the dupe of jewel thieves.

Tolerable star musical with rather stale comedy elements.

w Gertrude Purcell, Robert Harari d John G. Blystone

Nino Martini, Joan Fontaine, Alan Mowbray, Erik Rhodes, Alan Hale, Billy Gilbert, Grant Mitchell, Lee Patrick

'Seems that Nino just can't make the grade as a film star.' – *Variety*

Music for Millions *
US   1944   117m   bw
MGM (Joe Pasternak)

A small girl helps her pregnant sister who is a member of José Iturbi's orchestra.

Dewy-eyed wartime musical, full of popular classics, sentimentality and child interest, all smoothly packaged. As an example of what the public wanted in 1944, quite an eye-opener.

w Myles Connelly d Henry Koster ph Robert Surtees md George Stoll

Margaret O'Brien, June Allyson, José Iturbi, Jimmy Durante, Marsha Hunt, Hugh Herbert, Harry Davenport, Connie Gilchrist

AAN: Myles Connelly

Music Hath Charms *
GB   1935   70m   bw
BIP (Walter C. Mycroft)

A dance band's broadcast has various effects on listeners.

Pleasing, modest portmanteau of sketches with music.

w Jack Davies, Courtney Territt, L. Du Garde Peach d Thomas Bentley, Alexander Esway, Walter Summers, Arthur Woods ph Jack Cox, Claude Friese-Greene, Ronald Neame

Henry Hall and his Orchestra, Carol Goodner, W. H. Berry, Arthur Margetson, Antoinette Cellier, Billy Milton

Music in Darkness: see *Music is My Future*

Music in My Heart
US 1940 70m bw
Columbia
V*

An alien singer wins the lead in a Broadway musical, which prevents him from being deported.

Forgettable second feature which was its leading lady's last stepping stone before stardom.

w James Edward Grant d Joseph Santley

Rita Hayworth, Tony Martin, Edith Fellows, Alan Mowbray, George Tobias, Eric Blore, André Kostelanetz and his orchestra

AAN: song 'It's a Blue World' (m/y Chet Forrest, Bob Wright)

Music in the Air
US 1934 85m bw
Fox (Erich Pommer)

An opera singer is torn between two men.

Heavy-going light entertainment.

w Howard Young, Billy Wilder play Oscar Hammerstein II, Jerome Kern d Joe May
ph Ernest Palmer

Gloria Swanson, John Boles, Douglass Montgomery, June Lang, Al Shean, Reginald Owen, Joseph Cawthorn, Hobart Bosworth

'Mild operetta of class appeal, which limits its b.o. sturdiness.' – Variety

Music Is Magic
US 1935 67m bw
TCF

By a series of unexpected events, a young girl becomes a Hollywood star.

Unpretentious and fairly snappy musical which still provides moments to enjoy.

w Edward Eliscu, Lou Breslow d George Marshall

Alice Faye, Bebe Daniels, Ray Walker, Frank Mitchell, Jack Durant, Hattie McDaniel

'One of those flighty affairs that will have trouble getting past the dual barricade.' – Variety

Music Is My Future *
Sweden 1948 85m bw
Terrafilm (Lorens Marmstedt)
original title: Musik i Mörker, aka: Music In Darkness, Night is My Future

Blinded in an accident, a young pianist forms a relationship with a poor girl.

Saved from its persistent sentimentality by occasional stringency, it survives as an early example of a developing talent.

w Dagmar Edquist novel Dagmar Edquist
d Ingmar Bergman ph Göran Strindberg
m Erland von Koch ad P. A. Lundgren
ed Lennart Wallén

Mai Zetterling, Birger Malmsten, Olaf Winnerstrand, Naima Wifstrand, Bibi Skoglund, Hilda Borgström, Douglas Hage, Gunnar Björnstrand, Bengt Eklund

'My fourth film became a modest success, thanks to Lorens Marmstedt's wisdom, thoughtfulness and patience . . . It was he who taught me how to make films.' – Ingmar Bergman, The Magic Lantern

'The story of a homosexual who married a nymphomaniac!'

The Music Lovers *
GB 1970 123m Eastmancolor Panavision
UA/Rossfilms (Roy Baird)
V, V*

Homosexual composer Tchaikovsky is impelled to marry, loses his sponsor, drives his wife into an asylum and dies of cholera.

Absurd fantasia on the life of a great composer, produced in a manner reminiscent of MGM's sillier musicals; up to a point hysterically (and unintentionally) funny, then rather sickening.

w Melvyn Bragg book Beloved Friend by C. D. Bowen, Barbara von Meck d Ken Russell
ph Douglas Slocombe md André Previn

Richard Chamberlain, Glenda Jackson, Christopher Gable, Max Adrian, Isabella Telezynska, Maureen Pryor, Andrew Faulds

'Tchaikovsky has been made the excuse for a crude melodrama about sex.' – Konstantin Bazarov

'Libellous not only to the composer but to his music.' – Roger Ebert

The Music Man ***
US 1962 151m Technirama
Warner (Morton da Costa)
V, V*, L, S

A confidence trickster persuades a small-town council to start a boys' band, with himself as the agent for all the expenses.

Reasonably cinematic, thoroughly invigorating transference to the screen of a hit Broadway musical. Splendid period 'feel', standout performances, slight sag in second half.

w Marion Hargrove book Meredith Willson
d Morton da Costa ph Robert Burks md Ray Heindorf ch Onna White songs Meredith Willson

Robert Preston, Shirley Jones, Buddy Hackett, Hermione Gingold, Pert Kelton, Paul Ford

'This is one of those triumphs that only a veteran performer can have; Preston's years of experience and his love of performing come together joyously.' – Pauline Kael

AA: Ray Heindorf

AAN: best picture

The Music of Chance *
US 1993 97m Foto-Kem colour
Feature film/I.R.S. Media/American Playhouse (Frederick Zollo, Dylan Sellers)

Two millionaires force two poker players, who lose all their money in a game, to work off the debt by remaining on their estate and building a wall.

A good-looking, well-acted, minimalist, lightweight drama of men trapped by their own greed.

w Philip Haas, Belinda Haas novel Paul Auster
d Philip Haas m Philip Johnston pd Hugo Luczyc-Wyhowski ed Belinda Haas

James Spader, Mandy Patinkin, M. Emmet Walsh, Charles Durning, Joel Grey, Samantha Mathis, Christopher Penn

'A lean, convincing fable in the tradition of Kafka, Borges and Pinter.' – Philip French, Observer

The Music Room **
India 1958 100m bw
Satyajit Ray Productions
original title: Jalsaghar

An elderly and reclusive aristocratic connoisseur of music stages a magnificent musical evening in his crumbling palace as a gesture of defiance at the modern world.

Elegant, small-scale work of a man destroying himself through his obsessive pride.

wd Satyajit Ray story Tarasankar Banerjee
ph Subrata Mitra m Vilayat Khan ad Bansi Chandragupta ed Dulal Dutta

Chhabi Biswas, Padman Devi, Pinaki Sen Gupta, Gangapada Bose

'A deeply felt, extremely tedious film. On the one hand its western derivations are patent (the Greek-revival mansion no more than the Chekhovian theme). On the other hand its chief indigenous

element, the Indian music, is simply uncongenial and tiresome to our ears. No doubt these are excellent musical performances for those who understand them, but they make us start counting the bulbs in the theater chandelier.' – Stanley Kauffman

'A great, flawed, maddening film – hard to take but probably impossible to forget. It's often crude and it's poorly constructed, but it's a great experience.' – Pauline Kael

† The film was hampered by casting an unmusical actor in the leading role.

The Music Teacher *
Belgium 1988 98m Fujicolor
Mainline/RTBF/K2-One (Alexandre Pletser)
V, V*, L
original title: Le Maître de Musique

Protégées of two rival singing teachers engage in a contest.

Resolutely old-fashioned drama, done with a certain style.

w Gérard Corbiau, André Corbiau story Luc Jabon, Gérard Corbiau d Gérard Corbiau ph Walther Van Den Ende m Ronald Zollman ad Zouc Lanc
ed Denise Vindevogel

José Van Dam, Anne Roussel, Philippe Volter, Sylvie Fennec, Patrick Bauchau, Johan Leysen, Marc Schreiber

'Verbal and visual clichés provide the setting for a selection of popular operatic gems. Culture of this kind makes gun-reaching Goerings of us all.' – Philip French, Observer

AAN: best foreign film

Musik I Mörker: see Music Is My Future

Muss 'em Up
US 1936 70m bw
Pandro S. Berman/RKO

A cop with a Philo Vance complex routs out gangsters.

Competent crime programmer.

w Erwin Gelsey, James Edward Grant d Charles Vidor

Preston Foster, Margaret Callahan, Alan Mowbray, Ralph Morgan, Guinn Williams, Maxie Rosenbloom

'Enough comedy and other values to make it fairly passable fare.' – Variety

Mustang Country
US 1976 79m Technicolor
Universal (John Champion)

In 1925 Montana, a rancher comes out of retirement to help to round up a wild stallion.

Mild outdoor yarn for family audiences.

wd John Champion ph J. Barry Herron m Lee Holdridge

Joel McCrea, Nika Mina, Robert Fuller, Patrick Wayne

The Mutations
GB 1974 92m Eastmancolor
Columbia/Getty (Robert D. Weinbach)
V*

A bio-chemist uses circus freaks in his experiments to find the perfect synthesis of plant and animal.

Tasteless horror film with little style of any kind.

w Robert D. Weinbach, Edward Mann d Jack Cardiff ph Paul Beeson m Basil Kirchin

Donald Pleasence, Tom Baker, Brad Harris, Julie Ege, Michael Dunn, Scott Antony, Jill Haworth, Lisa Collings

Mutiny

US   1952   77m   Technicolor
King Brothers/United Artists
V*

During the war of 1812, an American ship runs the English blockade to collect gold bullion from France.

Fairly lively swashbuckler.

w Philip Yordan and Sydney Harmon   d Edward Dmytryk

Mark Stevens, Angela Lansbury, Patric Knowles, Gene Evans, Rhys Williams

Mutiny in the Big House

US   1939   83m   bw
Monogram

A chaplain is at the centre of a prison break, and tries to calm the mob.

Archetypal cellblock movie, and not the worst of them.

w Robert D. Andrews and Martin Mooney
d William Nigh

Charles Bickford, Barton MacLane

'Will edge toward the profit side of the ledger for the pop-pricers.' – Variety

The Mutiny of the Elsinore

GB   1937   79m   bw
Argyle British

A reporter on a sailing ship for a story finds himself in the middle of a mutiny.

Very studio-bound seafaring adventure.

w Walter Summers and Beaufoy Milton   novel Jack London   d Roy Lockwood

Paul Lukas, Lyn Harding, Kathleen Kelly, Clifford Evans

'They'll take this town by storm ... fighting, laughing, loving, breaking every law of the seven seas!'

Mutiny on the Bounty ***

US   1935   135m   bw
MGM (Irving Thalberg, Albert Lewin)
V*, L

An 18th-century British naval vessel sets off for South America but during a mutiny the captain is cast adrift and the mutineers settle in the Pitcairn Islands.

A still-entertaining adventure film which seemed at the time like the pinnacle of Hollywood's achievement but can now be seen to be slackly told, with wholesale pre-release editing very evident. Individual scenes and performances are however refreshingly well-handled.

w Talbot Jennings, Jules Furthman, Carey Wilson
book Charles Nordhoff, James Hall   d Frank Lloyd
ph Arthur Edeson   m Herbert Stothart
ed Margaret Booth

Charles Laughton, Clark Gable, Franchot Tone, Movita, Dudley Digges, Henry Stephenson, Donald Crisp, Eddie Quillan, Francis Lister, Spring Byington, Ian Wolfe

BLIGH (Charles Laughton): 'Casting me adrift 3,500 miles from a port of call! You're sending me to my doom, eh? Well, you're wrong, Christian. I'll take this boat, as she floats, to England if I must. I'll live to see you – all of you – hanging from the highest yardarm in the British fleet . . .'

'Nothing to stand in the way of a box office dynamite rating.' – Variety

'Incidents are made vivid in terms of the medium – the swish and pistol crack of the lash, the sweating lean bodies, the terrible labour, and the ominous judgment from the quarterdeck.' – Otis Ferguson

AA: best picture

AAN: script; Frank Lloyd; Herbert Stothart; Charles Laughton; Clark Gable; Franchot Tone (whose role was originally to have been played by Robert Montgomery); Margaret Booth

Mutiny on the Bounty

US   1962   185m   Technicolor   Ultra Panavision 70
MGM/Arcola (Aaron Rosenberg)
V, V*, L

Overlong and unattractive remake marred principally by Brando's English accent and various production follies, not to mention his overlong and bloody death scene.

The shipboard sadism still works pretty well, but after the landing in Tahiti boredom takes over.

w Charles Lederer   d Lewis Milestone   ph Robert Surtees   m Bronislau Kaper

Trevor Howard, Marlon Brando, Richard Harris, Hugh Griffith, Tarita, Richard Haydn, Percy Herbert, Duncan Lamont, Gordon Jackson, Chips Rafferty, Noel Purcell

AAN: best picture; Robert Surtees; Bronislau Kaper; Song 'Follow Me' (m Bronislau Kaper, ly Paul Francis Webster)

My Ain Folk **

GB   1973   55m   bw
Connoisseur/BFI (Nick Nascht)
V

Following the death of his maternal grandmother, a boy is reluctantly taken in by his father's mother until he goes away to an orphanage.

Stark account of narrow and damaged lives, told with an intense sympathy.

wd Bill Douglas   ph Gale Tattersall   ed Peter West

Stephen Archibald, Hughie Restorick, Jean Taylor Smith, Bernard McKenna, Mr Munro, Paul Kermack, Helena Gloag, Jessie Combe

'A very considerable work of art, more profound, more terrible and ultimately more inspiring than My Childhood, all of whose virtues it shares.' – Elizabeth Sussex, MFB

† The second part of an autobiographical trilogy that began with My Childhood and was completed by My Way Home (qqv).

My American Uncle *

France   1980   126m   Eastmancolor
Andrea Films/TF1 (Philippe Dussart)
original title: Mon Oncle Américain

Professor Henri Laborit explains the lives of two men and a woman in terms of animal behaviour.

Fascinatingly assembled but basically pessimistic dissection of human life, in the director's most meticulous style. The American uncle is the piece of good luck which may be just around the corner (but probably isn't).

w Jean Gruault   books Henri Laborit   d Alain Resnais   ph Sacha Vierny   m Arié Dzierlatka

Gérard Depardieu, Nicole Garcia, Roger Pierre, Henri Laborit

AAN: screenplay

My Beautiful Laundrette *

GB   1985   97m   colour
Working Title/SAF/Channel 4 (Sarah Radclyffe, Tim Bevan)
V, V*, L

A young south London Asian manages his uncle's launderette and falls for a white racist boy.

Made for TV, but fashionable enough to get critical acclaim and cinema distribution, this soft-centred anecdote was a bit of a puzzle to those neither Asian nor homosexual.

w Hanif Kureishi   d Stephen Frears   ph Oliver Stapleton   m Ludus Tonalis

Saeed Jaffrey, Roshan Seth, Daniel Day-Lewis, Gordon Warnecke, Shirley Anne Field, Rita Wolf

AAN: best original screenplay

My Best Friend's Girl

France   1983   100m   Eastmancolor
Cannon/Renn Productions/Sara Films (Alain Sarde)
V*
original title: La Femme de Mon Pote

A day worker asks his friend, a night worker, to look after his girlfriend.

Mildly amusing comedy.

w Bertrand Blier, Gérard Brach   d Bertrand Blier
ph Jean Penzer, Yves Agostini, Michel Coteret, Eric Vallée   m J. J. Cale   ed Claudine Merline, Sylvie Quester, Annick Menier, Jeanne Kef

Coluche, Isabelle Huppert, Thierry Lhermitte, Farid Chopel, François Perrot, Daniel Colas, Frédérique Michot

My Best Girl *

US   1927   84m (24 fps)   bw   silent
Mary Pickford Corporation

A shopgirl falls for a co-worker, unaware that he is the son of the owner.

The star's last silent film is a charming comedy which tends to fade in the memory.

w Allen McNeil, Tim Whelan   d Sam Taylor
ph Charles Roshner   m Gaylord Carter

Mary Pickford, Charles 'Buddy' Rogers, Sunshine Hart, Lucien Littlefield, Hobart Bosworth

AAN: Charles Rosher

'Perhaps it is not for the living to know the truth about reincarnation!'
'If you give away the ending, may your blood run cold forever!'

My Blood Runs Cold

US   1965   108m   bw   Panavision
Warner (William Conrad)

A spoilt heiress meets a strange young man who claims she is the reincarnation of a long dead charmer; he turns out to be a madman who has come across an old diary.

Initially intriguing but eventually exhausting melodrama with a weak solution.

w John Mantley   d William Conrad   ph Sam Leavitt   m George Duning

Troy Donahue, Joey Heatherton, Barry Sullivan, Jeanette Nolan

'Not all that bad, but not worth missing I Love Lucy for either.' – Leonard Maltin

My Blue Heaven

US   1950   96m   Technicolor
TCF (Sol C. Siegel)

A pair of troupers want a family, by adoption if not otherwise.

Routine musical drenched in sentimentality.

w Lamar Trotti, Claude Binyon   d Henry Koster
ph Alfred E. Arling   m Alfred Newman
songs Harold Arlen (m), Ralph Blane (ly)

Betty Grable, Dan Dailey, Mitzi Gaynor, David Wayne, Jane Wyatt, Una Merkel

My Blue Heaven

US   1990   95m   Technicolor
Warner (Herbert Ross, Anthea Sylbert)
V, V*, L

Relocated in a small town, a gangster who has turned state's evidence decides not to go straight.

Dull comedy, broadly acted and directed.

w Nora Ephron *d* Herbert Ross *ph* John Bailey
m Ira Newborn *pd* Charles Rosen *ed* Stephen A. Rotter, Robert Reitano

Steve Martin, Rick Moranis, Joan Cusack, Melanie Mayron, William Irwin, Carol Kane, William Hickey, Deborah Rush, Daniel Stern, Jesse Bradford

My Bodyguard

US 1980 96m CFI Color
Market Street/Melvin Simon
V*

A 15-year-old Chicago boy has trouble at school.

Oddly titled, uncommercial but quite watchable drama of adolescence. Not surprisingly, it failed to find an audience.

w Alan Ormsby *d* Tony Bill *ph* Michael D. Margulies *m* Dave Grusin *pd* Jackson de Givia

Chris Makepeace, Adam Baldwin, Ruth Gordon, Matt Dillon, Martin Mull, John Houseman

My Boyfriend's Back

US 1993 84m DeLuxe
Buena Vista/Touchstone (Sean S. Cunningham)

A high-school student, killed in a bungled robbery planned to impress a girl, returns as a zombie to demonstrate his undying love.

Ghoulish and unedifying horror.

w Dean Lorey *d* Bob Balaban *ph* Mac Ahlberg
m Harry Manfredini *pd* Michael Hanan
ed Michael Jablow

Andrew Lowery, Traci Lind, Danny Zorn, Edward Herrmann, Mary Beth Hurt, Austin Pendelton, Cloris Leachman, Paxton Whitehead

'Lacking any redeeming quality, it's a matter of days before this tasteless pic is buried without trace in the sands of Hollywood.' – *Variety*

My Brilliant Career **

Australia 1979 100m Eastmancolor
NSW Film Corporation/Margaret Fink
V*

The daughter of an Australian bush farmer at the turn of the century dreams of the world beyond and writes a memoir.

Pleasing but very slow picture of a world gone by.

w Eleanor Witcombe *novel* Miles Franklin
d Gillian Armstrong *ph* Don McAlpine
m Nathan Waks

Judy Davis, Sam Neill, Wendy Hughes, Robert Grubb, Max Cullen

BFA: Judy Davis

My Brother Jonathan

GB 1947 108m bw
ABP (Warwick Ward)

The life of a small-town doctor who wanted to be a great surgeon.

Unobjectionable, unexciting novel-on-film with the typically British artificial studio look of the time.

w Leslie Landau, Adrian Arlington *novel* Francis Brett Young *d* Harold French *ph* Derick Williams *m* Hans May

Michael Denison, Dulcie Gray, Ronald Howard, Stephen Murray

My Brother Talks to Horses

US 1946 93m bw
MGM (Samuel Marx)

A boy who can talk to horses finds himself in demand by racetrack gamblers.

Well-mounted but uninspired whimsy with a fatal lack of pace.

w Morton Thompson *novel* Joe the Wounded Tennis Player by Morton Thompson *d* Fred Zinnemann
ph Joseph Ruttenberg *m* Rudolph Kopp

Butch Jenkins, Peter Lawford, Charlie Ruggles, Edward Arnold, Beverly Tyler, Spring Byington

My Brother's Keeper

GB 1948 91m bw
GFD/Gainsborough (Anthony Damborough)

Two convicts escape, handcuffed together; one is violent, the other innocent.

Pre-Defiant Ones social melodrama, quite well made but suffering from miscasting.

w Frank Harvey *story* Maurice Wiltshire *d* Alfred Roome, Roy Rich *ph* Gordon Lang *m* Clifton Parker

Jack Warner, George Cole, Jane Hylton, David Tomlinson, Bill Owen, Raymond Lovell, Yvonne Owen, Beatrice Varley

My Buddy *

US 1944 67m bw
Eddy White/Republic

A World War I veteran is forced into crime.

Not a new message, but a second feature with sincerity and conviction. A better title would have helped.

w Arnold Manoff, Prescott Chaplin *d* Steve Sekely

Don Barry, Alexander Granach, Ruth Terry, Lynne Roberts, Emma Dunn, John Litel, George E. Stone

My Childhood **

GB 1972 48m bw
Connoisseur/BFI (Geoffrey Evans)
V

An eight-year-old boy lives with his half-brother and ailing grandmother in dire poverty in a Scottish mining village.

Passionate, autobiographical account of a life of almost total bleakness observed with scrupulous honesty.

wd Bill Douglas *ph* Mick Campbell *ed* Brand Thumim

Stephen Archibald, Hughie Restorick, Jean Taylor Smith, Karl Fieseler, Paul Kermack, Helena Gloag

'The story unfolds with pathos, tension and considerable humour.' – *MFB*

† The first part of an autobiographical trilogy that was followed by *My Ain Folk* and *My Way Home* (qqv).

My Cousin Rachel *

US 1952 98m bw
TCF (Nunnally Johnson)

A Cornish gentleman dies in Italy after marrying a mysterious lady; when she comes to England she arouses the hostility, and love, of her husband's foster son.

Well-wrought but dramatically unsatisfactory Victorian melodrama from a bestseller; plenty of suspicion but no solution makes Rachel a dull girl.

w Nunnally Johnson *novel* Daphne du Maurier
d Henry Koster *ph* Joseph LaShelle *m* Franz Waxman *ad* Lyle Wheeler, John DeCuir

Olivia de Havilland, Richard Burton, John Sutton, Audrey Dalton, Ronald Squire

AAN: Joseph LaShelle; Richard Burton; art direction

My Cousin Vinny *

US 1992 119m DeLuxe
TCF/Peter V. Miller Investment Corp. (Dale Launer, Paul Schiff)
V, V*, L, S

An inexperienced New York lawyer goes to Alabama to defend his cousin who is charged with murder.

Ramshackle comedy that raises an occasional smile and one or two laughs.

w Dale Launer *d* Jonathan Lynn *ph* Peter Deming *m* Randy Edelman *pd* Victoria Paul
ed Tony Lombardo

Joe Pesci, Ralph Macchio, Marisa Tomei, Mitchell Whitfield, Fred Gwynne, Lane Smith, Austin Pendleton, Bruce McGill, Maury Chaykin

'The bits and pieces never quite add up. Somewhere during this film's making I suspect that half the script was mysteriously lost down a street grating.' – *Nigel Andrews, Financial Times*

AA: Marisa Tomei

My Crasy Life

US 1992 98m colour
BBC/FR3 (Daniel Marks, Cameron Allan)

American-Samoan members of a Californian street-gang talk about their violent lives.

Unilluminating mix of documentary and fiction about the inarticulate young being assimilated into a ghetto culture.

w Jean-Pierre Gorin, Howard Rodman *d* Jean-Pierre Gorin *ph* Babette Mangolte *m* Joyi Yuasa *ed* Brad Thumin

'An aggravatingly tedious docu-drama.' – *Variety*

'She was everything the west was – young, fiery, exciting!'
My Darling Clementine ***

US 1946 98m bw
TCF (Samuel G. Engel)
V*, L

Wyatt Earp cleans up Tombstone and wipes out the Clanton gang at the OK corral.

Archetypal Western mood piece, full of nostalgia for times gone by and crackling with memorable scenes and characterizations.

w Samuel G. Engel, Winston Miller *book* Wyatt Earp, Frontier Marshal by Stuart N. Lake *d* John Ford *ph* Joe MacDonald *m* Cyril Mockridge

Henry Fonda, Victor Mature, Walter Brennan, Linda Darnell, Cathy Downs, Tim Holt, Ward Bond, *Alan Mowbray*, John Ireland, Jane Darwell

'Every scene, every shot is the product of a keen and sensitive eye.' – *Bosley Crowther*

'Considerable care has gone to its period reconstruction, but the view is a poetic one.' – *Lindsay Anderson*

My Daughter Joy

GB 1950 81m bw
London Films/Gregory Ratoff
US title: *Operation X*

In order to cement a new trade pact, an international financier plans to marry his daughter to the son of an African sultan.

Turgid melodrama swamping some good actors.

w Robert Thoeren, William Rose *novel* David Golder by Irene Neirowsky *d* Gregory Ratoff *ph* Georges Périnal *m* Raymond Gallois-Montbrun

Edward G. Robinson, Peggy Cummins, Nora Swinburne, Richard Greene, Finlay Currie, Gregory Ratoff, Ronald Adam, Walter Rilla, James Robertson Justice, David Hutcheson

My Dear Miss Aldrich

US 1937 73m bw
MGM

The glamorous new owner of a newspaper never agrees with its editor.

Skilful light comedy with good work all round.

w Herman Mankiewicz *d* George B. Seitz

Maureen O'Sullivan, Walter Pidgeon, Edna May Oliver, Rita Johnson, Janet Beecher

My Dear Secretary

US   1948   96m   bw
Cardinal/UA

A secretary marries her boss and becomes jealous of his new secretary.

Slow-paced, frivolous romantic comedy.

wd Charles Martin

Kirk Douglas, Laraine Day, Keenan Wynn, Rudy Vallee, Helen Walker, Florence Bates, Alan Mowbray

My Dinner with André *

US   1981   111m   Movielab
André Company/George W. George/Michael White
V*, L

Two men start a dinner table conversation which becomes a philosophical argument.

Curious two-hander which can please the right audience when it's in the mood; for selling tickets, forget it.

w Wallace Shawn, André Gregory   *d* Louis Malle
ph Jeri Sopanen   *m* Allen Shawn

Wallace Shawn, André Gregory, Jean Lenauer, Roy Butler

'A magical mystery tour of thoughts, dreams, fantasies and emotions.' – *Time Out*

'An adventure through a magically cracked looking glass.' – *San Francisco Chronicle*

'A dazzling cerebral comedy of ideas.' – *Los Angeles Times*

My Dream Is Yours

US   1949   101m   Technicolor
Warner (Michael Curtiz)

A Hollywood talent scout discovers a new singer.

Competent, forgettable musical.

w Harry Kurnitz, Dane Lussier   *d* Michael Curtiz
ph Ernest Haller   *m* Harry Warren   *ly* Ralph Blane
ch: Le Roy Prinz

Doris Day, Jack Carson, Lee Bowman, Adolphe Menjou, Eve Arden, S. Z. Sakall

† A remake of *Twenty Million Sweethearts.*

My Fair Lady ***

US   1964   175m   Technicolor   Super Panavision
70
CBS/Warner (Jack L. Warner)
V, V*, L, S

Musical version of *Pygmalion*, about a flower girl trained by an arrogant elocutionist to pass as a lady.

Careful, cold transcription of a stage success; cinematically quite uninventive when compared with *Pygmalion* itself, but a pretty good entertainment.

w Alan Jay Lerner   *play Pygmalion* by Bernard Shaw
d George Cukor   *ph* Harry Stradling   *m* André
Previn   *m* Frederick Loewe   *ch* Hermes Pan
ad Gene Allen   *costumes* Cecil Beaton   *ed* William
Ziegler

Rex Harrison, Audrey Hepburn, Stanley Holloway, Wilfrid Hyde-White, Gladys Cooper, Jeremy Brett, Theodore Bikel, Isobel Elsom, Mona Washbourne, Walter Burke

'The property has been not so much adapted as elegantly embalmed.' – *Andrew Sarris*

AA: best picture; George Cukor; Harry Stradling; Rex Harrison; André Previn (scoring of music); costumes; sound

AAN: Alan Jay Lerner; Stanley Holloway; Gladys Cooper; editing

My Father Is Coming

Germany/US   1991   81m   TVC color
Out on a Limb/Hyane/Hyena (Monika Treut)
V*

A German would-be actress in New York auditions

for a sex movie, makes friends with a transsexual and goes to bed with a Puerto Rican woman.

A movie without a redeeming feature, other than its short running time.

w Monika Treut, Bruce Benderson, Sarah Schulman
d Monika Treut   *ph* Elfi Mikesch   *m* David Van
Tieghem   *pd* Robin Ford   *ed* Steve Brown

Alfred Edel, Shelley Kästner, Annie Sprinkle, Mery Lou Graulau, David Bronstein, Michael Massee

'A scrappy little film, ill-scripted, photographed and, in particular, directed, and the weird, but very likeable cast is the only reason to see it.' – *Sheila Johnston, Independent*

'Treut's film seems to condemn rather than celebrate the effects of implementing consumerist notions of choice within the field of sexuality.' – *Verina Glaessner, Sight and Sound*

My Father's Glory: see *La Gloire de mon père*

My Father, the Hero

US   1994   90m   Technicolor
Buena Vista/Touchstone/Cité (Jacques Bar, Jean-Louis Livi)

A young girl on holiday in the Caribbean pretends that her father is actually her lover.

Dull and corny comedy, with little appeal to any age group.

w Francis Veber, Charlie Peters   *d* Steve Miner
ph Daryn Okada   *m* David Newman
pd Christopher Nowak   *ed* Marshall Harvey

Gérard Depardieu, Katherine Heigl, Emma Thompson, Dalton James, Lauren Hutton, Faith Prince, Stephen Tobolowsky, Ann Hearn

'You don't have to be a black-polo-neck-wearing francophile to see that hardly a single remake of a French movie has been any good. Let us hope that the flopping of this latest atrocity augurs the cessation of this insidious Hollywood habit.' – *Leslie Felperin Sharman, Sight and Sound*

† The film is a remake of *Mon Père, Ce Héros*, which also starred Gérard Depardieu.

My Favorite Blonde ***

US   1942   78m   bw
Paramount (Paul Jones)

A burlesque comic travelling by train helps a lady in distress and lives to regret it.

Smartly paced spy comedy thriller, one of its star's best vehicles.

w Don Hartman, Frank Butler, Melvin Frank, Norman
Panama   *d* Sidney Lanfield   *ph* William Mellor
m David Buttolph

Bob Hope, Madeleine Carroll, Gale Sondergaard, George Zucco, Lionel Royce, Walter Kingsford, Victor Varconi

My Favorite Brunette *

US   1947   87m   bw
Paramount/Hope Enterprises (Daniel Dare)
V*, L

A photographer gets mixed up with mobsters.

Pretty fair star vehicle which half-heartedly spoofs *Farewell My Lovely.*

w Edmund Beloin, Jack Rose   *d* Elliott Nugent
ph Lionel Lindon   *m* Robert Emmett Dolan

Bob Hope, Dorothy Lamour, Peter Lorre, Lon Chaney Jnr, John Hoyt, Charles Dingle, Reginald Denny

My Favorite Spy

US   1942   86m   bw
RKO

The bandleader Kay Kyser has to postpone his honeymoon when he is called up and set to spy-catching.

Fairly slick nonsense featuring a band popular at the time.

w Sig Herzig, William Bowers   *d* Tay Garnett

Kay Kyser, Ginny Simms, Ish Kabibble, Ellen Drew, Jane Wyman

My Favorite Spy *

US   1951   93m   bw
Paramount (Paul Jones)

A burlesque comic is asked by the US government to pose as an international spy who happens to be his double.

Moderately funny star vehicle with more willing hands than good ideas. The chase finale however is worth waiting for.

w Edmund Hartmann, Jack Sher   *d* Norman Z.
McLeod   *ph* Victor Milner   *m* Victor Young

Bob Hope, Hedy Lamarr, Francis L. Sullivan, Arnold Moss, Mike Mazurki, Luis Van Rooten

'The funniest, fastest honeymoon ever screened!'

My Favorite Wife ***

US   1940   88m   bw
RKO (Leo McCarey)
V*, L

A lady explorer returns after several shipwrecked years to find that her husband has married again.

A well-worn situation gets its brightest treatment in this light star vehicle.

w Sam and Bella Spewack, Leo McCarey   *d* Garson Kanin
ph Rudolph Maté   *m* Roy Webb   *ad* Van Nest
Polglase, Mark-Lee Kirk

Cary Grant, Irene Dunne, Randolph Scott, Gail Patrick, Ann Shoemaker, Donald MacBride

'One of those comedies with a glow on it.' – *Otis Ferguson*

† Other variations (qv): *Too Many Husbands, Our Wife, Three for the Show, Move Over Darling.*

AAN: story; Roy Webb; art direction

'I can't go on *live*! I'm a movie star, not an actor!'

My Favorite Year **

US   1982   92m   Metrocolor
MGM-UA/Brooksfilms/Michael Gruskoff
V, V*, L

In 1954, a legendary Hollywood star noted for wine and women is unwisely invited to star in a television series.

A good-humoured and well-researched romp with a central character not too far removed from Errol Flynn.

w Norman Steinberg, Dennis Palumbo   *d* Richard
Benjamin   *ph* Gerald Hirschfeld   *m* Ralph Burns
pd Charles Rosen   *ed* Richard Chew

Peter O'Toole, Mark Linn-Baker, Jessica Harper, Joseph Bologna, Bill Macy, Lainie Kazan, Lou Jacobi, Cameron Mitchell

'A field day for a wonderful bunch of actors.' – *Variety*

AAN: Peter O'Toole

My First 40 Years

Italy   1989   107m (dubbed)   Technicolor
Columbia TriStar/CG Silver Film/Reteitalia (Mario Cecchi Gori,
Vittorio Cecchi Gori)

A fashion designer recalls her numerous affairs on her fortieth birthday.

Charmless romantic drama, not helped by some inept dubbing.

w Enrico Vanzina, Carlo Vanzina   *novel I Miei Primi
40 Anni* by Marina Ripa Di Meana   *d* Carlo Vanzina
ph Luigi Kuveiller   *m* Umberto Smaila   *ad* Mario
Chiari   *ed* Ruggero Mastroianni

Carol Alt, Elliott Gould, Jean Rochefort, Pierre Cosso, Massimo Venturiello, Isabel Russinova, Paolo Quattrini, Riccardo Garrone, Capucine

My First Wife *

Australia 1984 98m colour
Artificial Eye/Dofine Productions/Film Victoria/Spectrafilm (Jane
Ballantyne; Paul Cox)
V*

A composer is heart-stricken when his wife decides to
leave him.

Passionate, emotionally painful study of relationships
over two generations that comes to the somewhat pat
conclusion that the family is everything.

w Paul Cox, Bob Ellis d Paul Cox ph Yuri Sokol
m Gluck, Orff, Haydn and others pd Asher Bilu
ed Tim Lewis

John Hargreaves, Wendy Hughes, Lucy Angwin,
David Cameron, Anna Jemison, Charles Tingwell,
Betty Lucas, Robin Lovejoy

'I was a good girl – wasn't I?'

My Foolish Heart *

US 1949 98m bw
Samuel Goldwyn

A woman deceives her husband into thinking her
forthcoming child is his.

A 'woman's picture' par excellence, and among the first
to benefit from commercial plugging of a schmaltzy
theme tune.

w Julius J. and Philip G. Epstein story J. D.
Salinger d Mark Robson ph Lee Garmes
m Victor Young

Susan Hayward, Dana Andrews, Kent Smith, Robert
Keith, Gigi Perreau, Lois Wheeler, Jessie Royce
Landis

'Obviously designed to pull the plugs out of the tear
glands and cause the ducts to overflow.' – Bosley
Crowther, New York Times

'In its dry-eyed moments, this damp fable is
brightened by some well-written patches of wryly
amusing dialogue.' – Time

AAN: Susan Hayward; title song (m Victor Young, ly
Ned Washington)

My Forbidden Past

US 1951 81m bw
RKO (Polan Banks)
V*

A New Orleans beauty seeks vengeance when her
cousin prevents her marriage.

Stuffy period melodrama with vigorous performances.

w Marion Parsonnet novel Polan Banks d Robert
Stevenson ph Harry J. Wild m Frederick
Hollander ad Albert S. D'Agostino

Ava Gardner, Melvyn Douglas, Robert Mitchum,
Janis Carter, Lucile Watson

My Friend Flicka *

US 1943 89m Technicolor
TCF
V*

Adventures of a young boy and his pet colt.

Winsome boy-and-horse story, one of the most
popular family films of the forties. Sequel 1945 with
virtually the same cast: Thunderhead Son of Flicka.

w Mary O'Hara novel Mary O'Hara d Harold
Schuster m Alfred Newman

Roddy McDowall, Preston Foster, Rita Johnson,
James Bell, Jeff Corey

My Friend Irma *

US 1949 103m bw
Paramount/Hal B. Wallis
V*

Dumb blonde Irma's con man boyfriend lends her
apartment to two soda jerks.

Comic strip humour responsible for the screen début
of Martin and Lewis. Sequel 1950: My Friend Irma Goes
West.

w Cy Howard, Parke Levy radio show Cy Howard.
d George Marshall ph Leo Tover m Roy Webb

Marie Wilson, John Lund, Diana Lynn, Dean Martin,
Jerry Lewis, Don Defore, Hans Conried, Kathryn
Givney

My Friend Irma Goes West

US 1950 90m bw
Paramount/Hal Wallis

Irma's friends Steve and Seymour are offered a
Hollywood contract and have adventures on the train.

Witless farce of mild historical interest.

w Cy Howard, Parke Levy d Hal Walker ph Lee
Garmes m Leigh Harline

John Lund, Marie Wilson, Dean Martin, Jerry Lewis,
Diana Lynn, Corinne Calvet, Lloyd Corrigan

'The general mental level can be judged from the fact
that the performance of the chimpanzee seems the
most natural thing in the film.' – MFB

My Friend Ivan Lapshin **

USSR 1986 99m bw/colour
Metro/Lenfilm

Memories of life in a provincial Russian town in the
1930s, where a harassed policeman pursues a criminal
gang.

Made in 1982, but not shown for four years, this is a
well-observed, well-directed and acted slice-of-
Soviet-life.

w Eduard Volodarski d Alexei Gherman
ph Valeri Fedosov m Arkadi Gagulachvili
ad Yuri Pougatch ed L. Semionovi

Andrei Boltnev, Nina Rousianova, Andrei Mironov,
Alexei Zharkov, Z. Adamovich, A. Filippenko

'It takes a girl like Rita to play a gal like Sal!'

My Gal Sal *

US 1942 103m Technicolor
TCF (Robert Bassler)

The career and romances of songwriter Paul Dresser.

Conventional 1890s musical biopic, more vigorous
and likeable than most.

w Seton I. Miller, Darrell Ware, Karl Tunberg
book My Brother Paul by Theodore Dreiser d Irving
Cummings ph Ernest Palmer md Alfred Newman
ad Richard Day, Joseph Wright

Rita Hayworth, Victor Mature, John Sutton, Carole
Landis, James Gleason, Phil Silvers, Walter Catlett,
Mona Maris, Frank Orth

† The title role was intended for Alice Faye, but she
was pregnant. Irene Dunne was too busy, Mae West
refused, and Betty Grable didn't test well.

AA: Richard Day, Joseph Wright

AAN: Alfred Newman

My Geisha

US 1962 120m Technirama
Paramount/Steve Parker
V*

A director makes a film in Japan; his wife disguises
herself as a geisha and gets the leading role.

Silly, overstretched comedy with pretty locations.

w Norman Krasna d Jack Cardiff ph Shunichuro
Nakao m Franz Waxman

Shirley Maclaine, Yves Montand, Robert Cummings,
Edward G. Robinson, Yoko Tani

'Mac's back and he's not alone ...'

My Girl

US 1991 102m Technicolor
Columbia TriStar/Imagine (Brian Grazer)
V, V*, L, S

In the 1970s, the 11-year-old daughter of an
undertaker comes to terms with her widowed father's
romance and the death of a friend.

Slick, over-sentimental account of growing up, part of
Hollywood's early 90s cycle of films centred on
children. It provided the first screen kiss for Culkin.

w Laurice Elehwany d Howard Zieff ph Paul
Elliott m James Newton Howard pd Joseph T.
Garrity ed Wendy Green Bricmont

Dan Aykroyd, Jamie Lee Curtis, Macaulay Culkin,
Anna Chlumsky, Richard Masur, Griffin Dunne, Ann
Nelson

'As pleasant as a warm summer day and as
ephemeral.' – Variety

'A hilarious mix of schmaltz, angst and shlock. In
other words a joy to watch. One asks hopefully, it
can't get worse, surely, can it? But it does.' – Alexander
Walker, London Evening Standard

My Girl Tisa ***

US 1948 95m bw
United States Pictures (Milton Sperling)

An immigrant girl in New York in the 1890s falls for
an aspiring politician, is threatened with deportation
but saved by the intervention of Theodore Roosevelt.

Charming period fairy tale with excellent background
detail and attractive performances.

w Allen Boretz play Lucille S. Prumbs, Sara B.
Smith d Elliott Nugent ph Ernest Haller m Max
Steiner

Lilli Palmer, Sam Wanamaker, Alan Hale, Stella Adler,
Akim Tamiroff

My Girlfriend's Boyfriend *

France 1987 102m colour
Artificial Eye/AAA/Les Films Du Losange (Margaret Menegoz)
V, V*

original title: L'Ami de Mon Amie

Two young couples find themselves attracted to each
other's partner.

Charming conversation piece, the sixth in Rohmer's
series of Comedies and Proverbs.

wd Eric Rohmer ph Bernard Lutic, Sabine
Lanceline m Jean-Louis Valero ed Luisa Garcia

Emmanuelle Chaulet, Sophie Renoir, Anne-Laure
Meury, Eric Vieillard, François-Eric Gendron

My Gun Is Quick

US 1957 90m bw
United Artists/Victor Saville

Mike Hammer investigates the murder of a bar girl
and is led to rival gangs of jewel thieves.

Impenetrably plotted but quite violent brew of typical
Spillane ingredients.

w Richard Collins, Richard Powell novel Mickey
Spillane d George A. White, Phil Victor ph Harry
Neumann m Marlin Skiles

Robert Bray, Whitney Blake, Pat Donahue, Pamela
Duncan, Booth Colman

My Heart Belongs to Daddy

US 1942 73m bw
Sol C. Siegel/Paramount

A cabby helps a pregnant widow to find shelter in the
home of a professor.

Unsparkling B romance with a totally unrelated title.

w F. Hugh Herbert d Robert Siodmak

Richard Carlson, Martha O'Driscoll, Cecil Kellaway, Frances Gifford, Florence Bates

My Heart Goes Crazy: see *London Town*

My Heart Is Calling
GB 1935 91m bw
Cine-Allianz

An opera singer falls for a stowaway to Monte Carlo.

Musical trifle with little to be said for or against it.

w Sidney Gilliat story Ernst Marischka
d Carmine Gallone

Jan Kiepura, Marta Eggerth, Sonnie Hale, Hugh Wakefield, Ernest Thesiger, Marie Lohr

My Hero: see *A Southern Yankee*

My Hustler *
US 1965 70m bw
Vaughan/Factory Films (Andy Warhol)

Two men and two women compete for the sexual attentions of a blond hustler.

An apparently unedited two reels of film that, for all its apparent casualness and spontaneity, maintains its interest.

w Chuck Wein d Andy Warhol ph Andy Warhol

Paul America, Ed Hood, Joseph Campbell, John McDermott, Genevieve Charbon, Dorothy Dean

'A complex and unified whole, in which the form and the content relate in new and surprising ways. The film is the clearest guide we have to the innovations which are uniquely Warhol's.' – *Tony Rayns, MFB*

'The downer, and it is a major one, is that these shallow, one-dimensional people are worth examining at all. They, and their situation, like their existence, are not really worth a second look, let alone seventy minutes of film.' – *Peter Buckley, Films and Filming*

My Kingdom for a Cook
US 1943 81m bw
P. J. Wolfson/Columbia

An English author on a US lecture tour steals his hostess's cook.

Curious comedy with the star seeming to play an unsympathetic Alexander Woolcott type.

w Harold Goldman, Andrew Solt, Joseph Hoffman, Jack Henley d Richard Wallace

Charles Coburn, Marguerite Chapman, Bill Carter, Isobel Elsom, Ed Gargan

My Learned Friend ***
GB 1943 76m bw
Ealing (Robert Hamer)

A shady lawyer is last on a mad ex-convict's murder list of those who helped get him convicted.

Madcap black farce, pluck-packed and generally hilarious; the star's last vehicle, but one of his best, with superbly timed sequences during a pantomime and on the face of Big Ben.

w John Dighton, Angus Macphail d Basil Dearden, Will Hay ph Wilkie Cooper m Ernest Irving

Will Hay, Claude Hulbert, Mervyn Johns, Ernest Thesiger, Charles Victor, Lloyd Pearson, Maudie Edwards, G. H. Mulcaster, Gibb McLaughlin

My Left Foot **
GB 1989 103m Technicolor
Palace/Ferndale Films/Granada TV International/Radio Telefis Eireann (Noel Pearson)
V, V*, L, S

Biopic of the Irish writer and painter Christy Brown, crippled from birth by cerebral palsy.

Pedestrian narrative, relying on cinematic clichés, but enlivened by the intensity of Day-Lewis's performance and some good ensemble acting.

w Shane Connaughton, Jim Sheridan book Christy Brown d Jim Sheridan ph Jack Conroy m Elmer Bernstein pd Austen Spriggs ed J. Patrick Duffner

Daniel Day-Lewis, Ray McAnally, Brenda Fricker, Ruth McCabe, Fiona Shaw, Eanna MacLiam, Alison Whelan, Declan Croghan, Hugh O'Conor, Cyril Cusack

AA: Daniel Day-Lewis; Brenda Fricker

AAN: best picture; best director; best adapted screenplay

My Life
US 1993 116m Technicolor
Guild/Zucker Brothers (Jerry Zucker, Bruce Joel Rubin, Hunt Lowry)
S

A man dying of cancer decides to make a videotape explaining himself to his unborn son.

A film that is interesting as a social document, in articulating American attitudes to life and its championing of childish attitudes, but which is much less successful as a movie, content to evoke easy tears.

wd Bruce Joel Rubin ph Peter James m John Barry pd Neil Spisak ed Richard Chew

Michael Keaton, Nicole Kidman, Bradley Whitford, Queen Latifah, Michael Constantine, Rebecca Schull, Mark Lowenthal, Haing S. Ngor

'The sincere, often touching story tugs shamelessly at the heart strings.' – *Variety*

'This bravely sentimental Hollywood film misses the mark.' – *Derek Malcolm, Guardian*

'The sort of New Age film that believes in everything and nothing at the same time, and turns every emotion into a therapy-wallow.' – *Adam Mars-Jones, Independent*

My Life as a Dog **
Sweden 1985 101m Fujicolor
Svensk Filmindustri/Film-Teknik
V, V*, L, S

12-year-old Ingemar learns to cope with his mother's illness and death, and his own propensity for getting into trouble, while staying with his aunt and uncle in the country.

By turns painful and funny, the film manages to achieve genuine charm while steering clear of sentimentality.

w Lasse Hallström, Reidar Jonsson, Brasse Brännström, Per Berglund novel Reidar Jonsson d Lasse Hallström ph Jörgen Persson, Rolf Lindström m Björn Isfält

Anton Glanzelius, Manfred Serner, Anki Lidén, Tomas von Bromssen, Melinda Kinnaman, Ing-Marie Carlsson

AAN: best director; best adapted screenplay

My Life with Caroline *
US 1941 81m bw
RKO (Lewis Milestone)

An understanding husband thinks his high-spirited wife may be having an affair.

Very minor romantic comedy with an agreeable air but no substance whatever.

w John Van Druten, Arnold Belgard d Lewis Milestone ph Victor Milner m Werner Heymann

Ronald Colman, Anna Lee, Reginald Gardiner, Charles Winninger, Gilbert Roland

My Little Chickadee *
US 1939 83m bw
Universal (Lester Cowan)
V*, L

A shady lady and an incompetent cardsharp unmask a villain in the old West.

A clash of comedy personalities which is affectionately remembered but in truth does not play very well apart from the odd line.

w Mae West, W. C. Fields d Edward Cline ph Joseph Valentine md Charles Previn m Frank Skinner

Mae West, W. C. Fields, Joseph Calleia, Dick Foran, Margaret Hamilton

'It obstinately refuses to gather momentum.' – *The Times*

'A classic among bad movies . . . the satire never really gets off the ground. But the ground is such an honest mixture of dirt, manure and corn that at times it is fairly aromatic.' – *Pauline Kael, 1968*

My Little Girl *
US 1986 117m colour
Hemdale (Ismail Merchant)
V*, L

A privileged teenager encounters problems when she goes to work at a centre for children in care.

Well-acted, moderately engaging drama of innocence and experience.

w Connie Kaiserman, Nan Mason d Connie Kaiserman ph Pierre Lhomme m Richard Robbins pd Dan Leigh ed Katherine Wenning

James Earl Jones, Geraldine Page, Mary Stuart Masterson, Anne Meara, Pamela Payton Wright, Peter Michael Goetz, Peter Gallagher, Erika Alexander, Traci Lin

My Little Pony
US 1986 100m Technicolor
Sunbow/Hasbro
V*

The inhabitants of Ponyland fear the wicked witch Hydia.

Immensely distended cartoon meant to plug a fashionable line of children's dolls.

w George Arthur Bloom d Michael Jones

† Animated in Japan.

My Love Came Back
US 1940 85m bw
Warner
V*

A millionaire helps the career of a pretty young violinist.

Palatable comedy of its day, promptly forgotten.

w Robert Buckner, Ivan Goff, Earl Baldwin d Curtis Bernhardt

Olivia de Havilland, Jeffrey Lynn, Charles Winninger, Eddie Albert, Spring Byington, S. Z. Sakall, Jane Wyman

My Lucky Star *
US 1938 84m bw
TCF (Harry Joe Brown)

A shopgirl is innocently caught in a compromising situation with the owner's son.

Fluffy comedy, acceptable as a background for skating sequences.

w Harry Tugend, Jack Yellen d Roy del Ruth ph John Mescall songs Mack Gordon, Harry Revel m Louis Silvers

Sonja Henie, Richard Greene, Joan Davis, Buddy Ebsen, Cesar Romero, Arthur Treacher, George Barbier, Louise Hovick, Billy Gilbert

'The characters act and talk like living people!'
My Man
US 1928 85m approx bw part talkie
Warner

A poor girl becomes a Broadway star.

Lachrymose and technically primitive début for the ebullient Fanny Brice.

w Joe Jackson story Robert Lord, Darryl F. Zanuck d Archie Mayo

Fanny Brice, Guinn Williams, André de Segurola, Edna Murphy

My Man and I
US 1952 99m bw
MGM (Stephen Ames)

A Mexican farm labourer, proud of his American citizenship, is drawn into trouble.

Eccentric melodrama in which all the native Americans are whores, cheats or murderers; well enough made but not very interesting.

w John Fante, Jack Leonard d William Wellman ph William Mellor m David Buttolph

Ricardo Montalban, Shelley Winters, Claire Trevor, Wendell Corey

My Man Godfrey ***
US 1936 90m bw
Universal (Gregory La Cava)
V*

A zany millionaire family invite a tramp to be their butler and find he is richer than they are.

Archetypal Depression concept which is also one of the best of the thirties crazy sophisticated comedies, though its pacing today seems somewhat unsure.

w Morrie Ryskind, Eric Hatch, Gregory La Cava d Gregory La Cava ph Ted Tetzlaff m Charles Previn

Carole Lombard, William Powell, Alice Brady, Mischa Auer, Eugene Pallette, Gail Patrick, Alan Mowbray, Jean Dixon

AAN: script; Gregory La Cava (as director); Carole Lombard; William Powell; Alice Brady; Mischa Auer

'The butler did it! He made every lady in the house oh so very happy!'
My Man Godfrey
US 1957 92m Technicolor Cinemascope
U-I (Ross Hunter)

Tepid remake which without the period background, and in unsuitable wide screen, raises very few laughs.

w Everett Freeman, Peter Berneis, William Bowers d Henry Koster ph William Daniels m Frank Skinner

June Allyson, David Niven, Jessie Royce Landis, Jay Robinson, Robert Keith, Martha Hyer, Eva Gabor

My Marriage
US 1936 68m bw
TCF

A girl finds that her marriage is not accepted by her high society in-laws.

Satisfactory woman's picture.

w Frances Hyland d George Archainbaud

Claire Trevor, Kent Taylor, Pauline Frederick, Paul Kelly, Thomas Beck, Beryl Mercer

'Will get by with family audiences.' – Variety

My Mother's Castle: see Le Château de ma Mère

My Name Is Julia Ross **
US 1945 65m bw
Columbia

A girl is kidnapped and forced to impersonate an heiress.

A very good second feature which has been culted into a reputation beyond its worth, though it is undeniably slick and entertaining.

w Muriel Roy Bolton novel The Woman in Red by Anthony Gilbert d Joseph H. Lewis ph Burnett Guffey md Mischa Bakaleinikoff

Nina Foch, Dame May Whitty, George Macready, Roland Varno, Doris Lloyd

'A superior, well-knit thriller.' – Don Miller

'A likeable, unpretentious, generally successful attempt to turn good trash into decently artful entertainment.' – James Agee

My Name Is Nobody *
Italy/France/West Germany 1973 116m
Technicolor Panavision
Gala/Rafran/Jacques Leitienne/Alcinter/Société Imp. Ex. Ci./
Rialto (Claudio Mancini)
V*, S
original title: Il mio nome è Nessuno

A young admirer persuades an ageing gunfighter to end his career in an explosive fashion.

This is less a conventional Western and more a comic horse opera, complete with a tombstone bearing the name of Sam Peckinpah and with Wagner's Ride of the Valkyrie, scored country and western style, accompanying the 150-strong Wild Bunch as they thunder by. Along the way it makes the occasional interesting comment about the reality and the mythology of the West.

w Ernesto Gastaldi story Fulvio Morsella, Ernesto Gastaldi, from an idea by Sergio Leone d Tonino Valerii ph Giuseppe Ruzzolini, Armando Nannuzzi m Ennio Morricone ad Gianni Polidori ed Nino Baragli

Henry Fonda, Terence Hill (Mario Girotti), Jean Martin, Piero Lulli, Leo Gordon, Neil Summers, R. K. Armstrong, Steve Kanaly, Geoffrey Lewis

'Constitutes an explicit, thoroughgoing critique of Sam Peckinpah's work up to 1970, and if its own whimsical/elegiac tone is closer to the romantic comedy of Cable Hogue than to the romantic tragedies of Major Dundee and The Wild Bunch, then that signifies the warmth of its engagement with its subject rather than any reluctance to face up to Peckinpah's capacity for nihilism.' – Tony Rayns, MFB

My Night with Maud: see Ma Nuit chez Maud

My Old Dutch
GB 1934 82m bw
Gainsborough

Ageing cockney parents see their son die a hero.

Historically interesting sentimental wallow, built around a popular song; very primitive by most standards.

w Bryan Wallace, Marjorie Gaffney, Mary Murillo, Michael Hogan d Sinclair Hill

Gordon Harker, Betty Balfour, Michael Hogan, Florrie Forde

† A 1915 version had starred the original singer, Albert Chevalier, with Florence Turner and Henry Edwards.

My Old Man's a Fireman: see The Chief

My Outlaw Brother
US 1951 78m bw
Eagle Lion
V*

A young man is shocked to find that his elder brother is a notorious bandit.

Glum little semi-Western, unpersuasively cast.

w Gene Fowler Jnr d Elliott Nugent

Mickey Rooney, Robert Preston, Robert Stack, Wanda Hendrix

'Wherever, Whatever, Have a nice day.'
My Own Private Idaho *
US 1991 102m Alpha Cine colour
New Line (Laurie Parker)
V, V*, L

A narcoleptic male prostitute makes friends with a slumming rich youth.

A variation on Shakespeare's Henry IV, complete with a seductive but dangerous Falstaffian figure, which becomes a distracting device, lessening the film's impact.

wd Gus Van Sant ph Eric Alan Edwards, John Campbell pd David Brisbin ed Curtiss Clayton

River Phoenix, Keanu Reeves, James Russo, William Richert, Rodney Harvey, Michael Parker, Udo Kier

'One of those ambitious, over-reaching disappointments that is more interesting than some conservative successes.' – Variety

'It's a beautiful disaster, like a bomb test in the middle of nowhere.' – New Yorker

'Desperately loved by two men – father and son!'
My Own True Love
US 1948 84m bw
Paramount (Val Lewton)

A lonely man home from the war quarrels with his son over a girl twenty years younger than himself.

Minor romantic drama, competently but coldly presented.

w Arthur Kober novel Yolanda Foldes d Compton Bennett ph Charles Lang m Robert Emmett Dolan

Phyllis Calvert, Melvyn Douglas, Philip Friend, Wanda Hendrix, Binnie Barnes

My Pal Gus
US 1952 84m bw
TCF (Stanley Rubin)

A business man has a five-year-old problem son and in sorting him out falls in love with his schoolteacher.

Unrewarding domestic drama with actors who look as though they would rather be somewhere else.

w Fay and Michael Kanin d Robert Parrish ph Leo Tover m Leigh Harline

Richard Widmark, Joanne Dru, Audrey Totter, George Winslow, Joan Banks, Regis Toomey, Ludwig Donath

My Pal Trigger
US 1946 79m bw
Armand Schaefer/Republic

A cowboy tracks down the man who killed his horse's sire.

Folksy Western drama, a cut above the usual Rogers episode.

w Jack Townley, John K. Butler d Frank McDonald

Roy Rogers, Dale Evans, Jack Holt, George 'Gabby' Hayes, Roy Barcroft

My Reputation
US 1946 96m bw
Warner (Henry Blanke)

A widow is talked about for dispensing too soon with her weeds.

Dim drama, hastily shot on familiar sets with a reach-me-down script.

w Catherine Turney novel Instruct My Sorrows by Clare Jaynes d Curtis Bernhardt ph James Wong Howe m Max Steiner

Barbara Stanwyck, George Brent, Warner Anderson, Lucile Watson, John Ridgely, Eve Arden, Jerome Cowan, Esther Dale, Scotty Beckett

My Science Project

US   1985   91m   Technicolor
Touchstone/Silver Screen Partners
V*, L

A high school student investigates an old UFO and finds an energy-absorbing machine which can materialize objects from the past and future.

Disney-style fare with teenage sex: the mixture may not be for many.

wd Jonathan R. Betuel

John Stockwell, Danielle von Zerneck, Fisher Stevens, Raphael Sbarge, Richard Masur, Dennis Hopper

My Sin

US   1931   79m   bw
Paramount

A drunken lawyer helps a woman who has shot her husband.

Turgid melodrama which failed to make a screen idol of its star.

w Owen David, Adelaide Heilbron   *story* Frederick Jackson   *d* George Abbott

Tallulah Bankhead, Fredric March, Harry Davenport, Scott Kolk, Ann Sutherland

'Fair returns will be top.' – *Variety*

My Sister Eileen *

US   1942   96m   bw
Columbia (Max Gordon)
V*, L

Two Ohio girls come to New York and live with some zany friends in a Greenwich Village basement apartment.

Rather strained high jinks which were, not surprisingly, later musicalized.

w Ruth McKinney, Joseph Fields, Jerome Chodorov   *book* Ruth McKinney   *d* Alexander Hall   *ph* Joseph Walker   *md* Morris Stoloff

Rosalind Russell, Janet Blair, Brian Aherne, Allyn Joslyn, George Tobias, Elizabeth Patterson, June Havoc

AAN: Rosalind Russell

My Sister Eileen *

US   1955   108m   Technicolor   Cinemascope
Columbia (Fred Kohlmar)
V*, L

Musical version of the above, via a Broadway show.

Watchable but hardly stimulating.

w Blake Edwards, Richard Quine   *play* Joseph Fields, Jerome Chodorov   *d* Richard Quine   *ph* Charles Lawton Jnr   *md* Morris Stoloff   *ch* Bob Fosse,   *songs* Jule Styne, Leo Robin   *m* George Duning

Betty Garrett, Janet Leigh, Jack Lemmon, Bob Fosse, Kurt Kasznar, Horace MacMahon, Dick York

My Six Convicts *

US   1952   104m   bw
Columbia/Stanley Kramer

A psychologist joins the staff of an American prison and gains the trust of six inmates.

Moderately interesting semi-documentary melodrama marred by a conventional prison break climax.

w Michael Blankfort   *book* Donald Powell Wilson   *d* Hugo Fregonese   *ph* Guy Roe   *m* Dmitri Tiomkin

John Beal, *Millard Mitchell, Gilbert Roland*, Marshall Thompson, Regis Toomey

My Six Loves

US   1963   101m   Technicolor
Paramount/Gant Gaither

A musical comedy star goes to the country for a rest and with the help of the local minister adopts six scruffy children.

Icky sentimental comedy for the easily pleased.

w John Fante, Joseph Calvelli, William Wood   *d* Gower Champion   *ph* Arthur E. Arling   *m* Walter Scharf   *songs* Jimmy Van Heusen, Sammy Cahn

Debbie Reynolds, David Janssen, Cliff Robertson, Eileen Heckart

'Enough to make you settle for cyclamates – or cyanide.' – *Judith Crist, 1973*

My Son Alone: see *American Empire*

My Son John

US   1952   122m   bw
Paramount/Rainbow (Leo McCarey)

An American Catholic family is horrified when its eldest son is revealed as a communist.

The lower depths of Hollywood's witch hunt cycle are marked by this Goldwynesque family saga, all sweetness and light, in which the commie son is treated as though he had rabies. Purely as entertainment the plot is pretty choppy and defeats all attempts at acting.

w Myles Connelly, Leo McCarey   *d* Leo McCarey   *ph* Harry Stradling   *m* Robert Emmett Dolan

Helen Hayes, Robert Walker, Dean Jagger, Van Heflin, Minor Watson, Frank McHugh, Richard Jaeckel

AAN: Leo McCarey (original story)

'Their tangled loves wove a web of hate!'

My Son, My Son *

US   1940   117m   bw
Edward Small

A man who becomes rich spoils his son and lives to regret it.

Solid narrative from a bestseller.

w Lenore Coffee   *novel* Howard Spring   *d* Charles Vidor   *ph* Harry Stradling   *m* Edward Ward   *ad* John DuCasse Schulze

Brian Aherne, Madeleine Carroll, Louis Hayward, Laraine Day, Henry Hull

AAN: art direction

My Song for You

GB   1934   90m   bw
Gaumont-British

A grand opera tenor tries to help a young girl and falls for her.

The story is an excuse for the songs, and looks it.

w Austin Melford, Robert Edmunds, Richard Benson from a German original, *Ein Lied für Dich*, by Ernst Marischka, Irmgard von Cube   *d* Maurice Elvey

Jan Kiepura, Aileen Marson, Sonnie Hale, Emlyn Williams, Gina Malo

My Son the Vampire: see *Mother Riley Meets the Vampire*

My Stepmother Is an Alien

US   1988   108m   The Film House
Columbia TriStar/Weintraub Entertainment (Ronald Parker, Franklin R. Levy)
V, V*, L, S

A scientist marries a beautiful woman from another planet.

Feeble comedy with little point and no taste.

w Jerico, Herschel Weingrod, Timothy Harris, Jonathan Reynolds   *d* Richard Benjamin   *ph* Richard H. Kline   *m* Alan Silvestri   *pd* Charles Rosen   *ed* Jacqueline Cambas, Brian Chambers

Dan Aykroyd, Kim Basinger, Jon Lovitz, Alyson Hannigan, Joseph Maher, Seth Green, Ann Prentiss, Wesley Mann, Tony Jay, Peter Bromilow

My Sweet Little Village **

Czechoslovakia   1985   100m   colour
Cannon/Barrandov Film Studio '85 (Jan Suster)

Life in a small village, where a mentally-retarded worker is forced to move to Prague.

Charming, good-hearted film of a small community where individuality flourishes.

w Zdenek Sverak   *d* Jiri Menzel   *ph* Jaromir Sofr   *m* Jiri Sust   *pd* Zbyner Hoch   *ed* Jiri Brozeck

Janos Ban, Marian Labuda, Rudolf Hrusinsky, Milena Dvorska, Ladislav Zupanic, Petr Cepek

AAN: best foreign film

My Teenage Daughter **

GB   1956   100m   bw
British Lion/Everest (Herbert Wilcox)
US title: *Teenage Bad Girl*

A widow's seventeen-year-old daughter meets an aggressive young man and ends up in court.

Predictable domestic drama, a tame British version of *Rebel without a Cause*.

w Felicity Douglas   *d* Herbert Wilcox   *ph* Max Greene

Anna Neagle, Sylvia Syms, Kenneth Haigh, Norman Wooland, Wilfrid Hyde-White, Julia Lockwood, Helen Haye

My Tutor

US   1982   97m   DeLuxe
Crown
V*, L

Two teenage boys try to lose their virginity.

As woeful as it sounds.

w Joe Roberts   *d* George Bowers

Matt Lattanzi, Caren Kaye, Kevin McCarthy, Arlene Golonka

My Two Husbands: see *Too Many Husbands*

My Uncle Antoine

Canada   1971   110m   Eastmancolor
National Film Board of Canada
V*

In a Quebec village a young boy reluctantly helps his undertaker uncle to deliver a coffin.

French-speaking comedy drama with a sour edge, as thoughts of death mar a family Christmas.

w Clément Perron   *d* Claude Jutra

Jacques Gagnon, Lyne Champagne, Jean Duceppe, Olivette Thibault

My Way Home **

GB   1979   72m   bw
BFI (Judy Cottam, Richard Craven)
V

Leaving a children's home to become a miner and then a tramp, a young man's miserable life changes for the better when he is called up for National Service and goes to Egypt.

The poverty of the lives depicted is mirrored by the directorial style – austere, spare, non-committal – to create a Calvinist masterpiece illumined by a little hope.

wd Bill Douglas   *ph* Ray Orton   *ad* Oliver Bouchier, Elsie Restorick   *ed* Mick Audsley

Stephen Archibald, Paul Kermack, Jessie Combe, William Carrol, Morag McNee, Lennox Milne, Gerald James

† The third of a trilogy of autobiographical films that began with *My Childhood* and *My Ain Folk* (qqv).

My Weakness *
US 1933 74m bw
Fox

As part of a joke, a hotel slavey is disguised as a grand lady, and warms to the part.

Tolerable comedy with songs, using some ingenuity of presentation to ingratiate its German star with American audiences.

w B. G. de Sylva   d David Butler

Lilian Harvey, Lew Ayres, Charles Butterworth, Harry Langdon, Sid Silvers, Henry Travers

'A highly favourable début.' – Variety

My Wife's Best Friend
US 1952 87m bw
TCF

A wife learns of her husband's infidelity, and imagines how Cleopatra, Joan of Arc and other historical figures might handle the situation.

A sharp little comedy rather similar to Unfaithfully Yours.

w Isobel Lennart   d Richard Sale

Anne Baxter, Macdonald Carey, Cecil Kellaway, Casey Adams, Catherine McLeod

My Wife's Family
GB 1931 80m bw
BIP

A wife thinks her husband has an illegitimate child. Archetypal British farce.

This may be the best version; it was also made with Charlie Clapham in 1941 and with Ronald Shiner in 1956.

w Fred Duprez and Val Valentine   play Fred Duprez, Hal Stephens and Harry B. Linton   d Monty Banks

Gene Gerrard, Muriel Angelus, Jimmy Godden, Amy Veness

My Wild Irish Rose
US 1947 101m Technicolor
Warner (William Jacobs)

The ups and downs of Irish tenor Chauncey Olcott and his encounters with Lillian Russell.

Inoffensive but not very exciting period musical, rather lacking in humour.

w Peter Milne   book Rita Ilcott   d David Butler   ph Arthur Edeson   m Ray Heindorf, Max Steiner   ch Le Roy Prinz

Dennis Morgan, Arlene Dahl, Andrea King, Alan Hale, George Tobias

AAN: Ray Heindorf, Max Steiner

My World Dies Screaming: see Terror in the Haunted House

'At last, the book that couldn't be written is now the motion picture that couldn't be made!'
Myra Breckinridge
US 1970 94m DeLuxe Panavision
TCF (Robert Fryer)
V, V*

After a sex-change operation a film critic goes to Hollywood to accomplish the deflation of the American male.

A sharply satirical novel has been turned into a sleazy and aimless picture which became a watershed of permissiveness; after international outcry it was shunned even by its own studio. A few good laughs do emerge from the morass, but even the old clips are misused.

w Mike Sarne, David Giler   novel Gore Vidal   d Mike Sarne   ph Richard Moore   md Lionel Newman   m John Philips

Mae West, Raquel Welch, John Huston, Rex Reed, Jim Backus, John Carradine, Andy Devine

'Whatever the novel may be like, it surely cannot be this sort of witless, lip-smacking, continuously inept cop-out.' – John Simon

'About as funny as a child molester.' – Time

'A disjointed patchwork of leers, vulgarity and general ineptness.' – Cue

'An incompetent attempt at exploitation by an industry that knew once, at the very least, how to make a dishonest buck.' – Newsweek

'I don't want subtlety. I want vulgarity.' – Michael Sarne

The Mysterious Doctor
US 1942 57m bw
Warner

Nazis strike at an English village by staging a headless ghost.

Risible propaganda hokum which somehow earned an 'H' certificate.

w Richard Weil   d Ben Stoloff

John Loder, Eleanor Parker, Bruce Lester, Lester Matthews, Forrester Harvey

The Mysterious Dr Fu Manchu
US 1929 80m bw
Paramount

After the Boxer rebellion an evil Chinese seeks the death of British officers.

First but not the worst of the yellow peril's sinister adventures; to be taken for what it is, however.

w Florence Ryerson, Lloyd Corrigan   d Rowland V. Lee

Warner Oland, Jean Arthur, Neil Hamilton, O. P. Heggie, William Austin

The Mysterious Dr Satan
US 1940 bw serial: 15 eps
Republic

A master criminal invents a mechanical man.

Rousing serial stuff with most of the regular elements.

d William Witney, John English

Eduardo Ciannelli, Robert Wilcox, William Newell, C. Montague Shaw

Mysterious Intruder
US 1946 62m bw
Columbia

A private detective seeks a missing heiress.

Intriguing minor thriller, part of the Whistler series.

w Eric Taylor   d William Castle

Richard Dix, Barton MacLane, Nina Vale, Regis Toomey

Mysterious Invader: see The Astounding She-Monster

Mysterious Island
US 1951 bw serial: 15 eps
Columbia

A serialization of the Jules Verne book, with Captain Nemo and a final volcano.

d Spencer Bennet

Richard Crane, Marshall Reed, Karen Randle, Gene Roth, Leonard Penn

Mysterious Island *
GB 1961 101m Technicolor
Columbia/Ameran (Charles Schneer)
V*, L, S

Confederate officers escape by balloon and join shipwrecked English ladies on a strange island where they are menaced by prehistoric monsters and helped by Captain Nemo.

Rambling, lively juvenile adventure with good moments and excellent monsters.

w John Prebble, Dan Ullman, Crane Wilbur   novel Jules Verne   d Cy Endfield   ph Wilkie Cooper   m Bernard Herrmann   sp Ray Harryhausen

Joan Greenwood, Michael Craig, Herbert Lom, Michael Callan, Gary Merrill

† An early sound version was made by MGM in 1929, directed by Lucien Hubbard. Despite Technicolor and a cast which included Lionel Barrymore it was judged unsatisfactory, and concentrated less on stop-frame monsters than on the submarine elements ignored in the above but remade in Captain Nemo and the Underwater City (qv).

The Mysterious Lady
US 1928 84m (24 fps) bw silent
MGM
V*

A glamorous Russian spy has to save her lover from execution as a traitor.

Threadbare star melodrama.

w Bess Meredyth   d Fred Niblo   ph William Daniels

Greta Garbo, Conrad Nagel, Gustav von Seyffertitz

The Mysterious Mr M
US 1946 bw serial: 13 eps
Universal

A submarine inventor is kidnapped and murdered by a master criminal.

Predictable serial adventures.

d Lewis D. Collins and Vernon Keays

Richard Martin, Pamela Blake, Dennis Moore, Jane Randolph, Byron Foulger, Edmund MacDonald

Mysterious Mr Wong
US 1935 60m bw
Monogram
V*

A mandarin in New York's Chinatown will stop at nothing to collect the twelve coins of Confucius.

Tolerable programme filler with old-fashioned thrills.

w Nina Howatt   story Stephen Keeler   d William Nigh

Bela Lugosi, Wallace Ford, Arline Judge, Fred Warren

'Passably exciting.' – Variety

The Mysterious Pilot
US 1937 bw serial: 15 eps
Columbia

A villainous executive tries to kill his fiancée when she learns that he has murdered a man; but the Mounties help.

Open-air serial adventures: one long chase.

d Spencer Gordon Bennet

Frank Hawks, Dorothy Sebastian, Rex Lease, Guy Bates Post, Kenneth Harlan

Mystery Broadcast
US 1943 63m bw
Republic

A radio crime writer tackles a real case.

Acceptable lower-case mystery.

w Dane Lussier   d George Sherman

Frank Albertson, Ruth Terry, Nils Asther, Wynne Gibson, Addison Richards

Mystery in Mexico
US   1948   65m   bw
RKO

An insurance detective disappears in Mexico; another
is sent to find him and uncovers a complex plot.

Fairly effective time-passer shot on location.

w Lawrence Kimble   *d* Robert Wise

William Lundigan, Ricardo Cortez, Jacqueline White,
Tony Barrett

Mystery Junction
GB   1951   67m   bw
Merton Park

Passengers stranded in a snowbound railway station
solve a mystery.

One of the better second features of its type.

wd Michael McCarthy

Sidney Tafler, Barbara Murray, Pat Owens, Martin
Benson

Mystery Liner
US   1934   62m   bw
Monogram

Several murders take place at sea on a passenger liner.

Reputedly above-average whodunnit.

w Wellyn Totman   *novel* The Ghost of John Holling by
Edgar Wallace   *d* William Nigh

Noah Beery, Astrid Allwyn, Cornelius Keefe, Gustav
von Seyffertitz, Edwin Maxwell

'Too good for the lesser grinds: exceptional indie
entertainment.' – *Variety*

Mystery Mountain
US   1934   bw   serial: 12 eps
Mascot

A master criminal named The Rattler has a mountain
lair from which he directs attacks on a new Western
railroad.

Modest serial hair-raiser.

d Otto Brower, B. Reeves Eason

Ken Maynard, Eddie Cobb, Verna Hillie, Edward
Earle

The Mystery of Alexina
France   1985   90m   colour
Electric Pictures/Les Cinéastes Associés/TF1
original title: *Mystère Alexina*

A convent-educated girl discovers that in reality she is
masculine.

Although based on the diary of a 19th-century
hermaphrodite, it fails to explore the subject in any
depth, preferring a glossy romanticism instead.

w Jean Gruault, René Feret   *d* René Feret
ph Bernard Zitzermann   *m* Anne-Marie Deschamps
ed Ariane Boeglin

Philippe Vuillemin, Valerie Stroh, Véronique Silver,
Bernard Freyd, Marianne Basler, Pierre Vial

'A thing to bewitch your senses for days and days!
    Charming in the thrills! Gripping in the suspense!'
The Mystery of Edwin Drood *
US   1935   85m   bw
Universal

In a cathedral town, a drug-addicted choirmaster is
his nephew's rival for the hand of Rosa Bud.

Fairly creditable attempt to deal with a famous
unfinished novel. Slightly stilted, but good visuals
and performances.

w John L. Balderston, Gladys Unger, Bradley King,
Leopold Atlas   *novel* Charles Dickens   *d* Stuart
Walker   *ph* George Robinson   *m* Edward Ward

Claude Rains, Douglass Montgomery, Heather Angel,
David Manners, E. E. Clive, Valerie Hobson

The Mystery of Edwin Drood
GB   1993   112m   Metrocolor
Mayfair/First Standard Media (Keith Hayley)

An opium-addicted choirmaster becomes obsessed
with the fiancée of his nephew and plots to marry her.

A low-budget thriller that fails to match Dickens's
lurid imaginings and makes a poor job of completing
the novel satisfactorily.

wd Timothy Forder   *novel* Charles Dickens
ph Martin McGrath   *m* Kick Production
pd Edward Thomas   *ed* Sue Alhadeff

Robert Powell, Nanette Newman, Gemma Craven,
Jonathan Phillips, Rupert Rainsford, Michelle Evans,
Rosemary Leach, Finty Williams, Ronald Fraser, Glyn
Huston, Andrew Sachs, Freddie Jones, Barry Evans

'The only mystery about this Edwin Drood is why
anyone bothered to make it.' – *Philip Kemp, Sight and
Sound*

The Mystery of Kaspar Hauser: see The Enigma
of Kaspar Hauser

The Mystery of Marie Roget
US   1942   61m   bw
Universal (Paul Malvern)

A Parisian music hall star plots to kill her sister but
herself disappears.

Ham-fisted, stilted mystery drama relying hardly at all
on its original.

w Michael Jacoby   *story* Edgar Allan Poe   *d* Phil
Rosen   *ph* Elwood Bredell   *m* Hans Salter

Maria Montez, Patric Knowles, *Maria Ouspenskaya*,
Lloyd Corrigan, John Litel, Edward Norris, Frank
Reicher

The Mystery of Mr X *
US   1934   84m   bw
MGM (Lawrence Weingarten)

In foggy London, a jewel thief protects himself by
finding the murderer of several policemen.

Passable mystery, later remade as *The Hour of Thirteen*.

w Howard Emmett Rogers, Philip MacDonald,
Monckton Hoffe   *novel* X vs Rex by Philip MacDonald
d Edgar Selwyn   *ph* Oliver T. Marsh

Robert Montgomery, Elizabeth Allan, Lewis Stone,
Ralph Forbes, Henry Stephenson, Forrester Harvey

'One of the best-made mystery mellers yet.' – *Variety*

The Mystery of the Mary Celeste
GB   1935   80m   bw
Hammer
V*
US title: *Phantom Ship*

A mad sailor kills his fellow crew members and
jumps overboard.

Unpersuasive solution to an unsolved mystery in a
production which sounds more interesting than it is.

wd Denison Clift

Bela Lugosi, Shirley Grey, Arthur Margetson,
Edmund Willard, Dennis Hoey

'Very strong stuff for those who like tragic
entertainment.' – *Variety*

Mystery of the River Boat
US   1944   bw   serial: 13 eps
Universal

Three old Louisiana families control swampland
containing valuable oil deposits, which a villain is
after.

Rather complicated basis for a serial, but the usual
thrills evolve.

d Ray Taylor, Lewis D. Collins

Robert Lowery, Eddie Quillan, Marion Martin, Lyle
Talbot, Arthur Hohl, Mantan Moreland

The Mystery of the 13th Guest
US   1943   60m   bw
Lindsley Parsons/Monogram

A girl beneficiary under her uncle's will is menaced
when she goes to visit.

Ham-fisted remake of *The Thirteenth Guest*, which was a
mite too complex in the first place. This version makes
no sense at all and is cheaply produced.

w Charles Marion, Tim Ryan   *play* Armitage Trail
d William Beaudine

Helen Parrish, Dick Purcell, Tim Ryan, Frank Faylen

'Images of wax that throbbed with human passion. Almost
    woman! What did they lack?'
Mystery of the Wax Museum ***
US   1933   77m   Technicolor
Warner (Henry Blanke)
V*, L

A sculptor disfigured in a fire builds a wax museum
by covering live victims in wax.

Archetypal horror material is augmented by a sub-
plot about drug-running and an authoritative example
of the wisecracking reporter school of the early
thirties. The film is also notable for its highly
satisfactory use of two-colour Technicolor and for its
splendid art direction. Remade 1953 as *House of Wax*
(qv).

w Don Mullaly, Carl Erickson,   *play* Charles S. Belden
d Michael Curtiz   *ph* Ray Rennahan   *ad* Anton Grot

Lionel Atwill, Fay Wray, *Glenda Farrell, Frank McHugh*,
Gavin Gordon, Allen Vincent, Edwin Maxwell

ATWILL: 'I offer you immortality, my child. Think
of it: in a thousand years you shall be as lovely as you
are now!'

'Would have been certain of better gate support a year
ago. Recognizing this, the Technicolor and hyper-
weirdness were apparently mandatory studio
precautions to offset the element of belated arrival.' –
Variety

'Marvellously grisly chiller.' – *Judith Crist, 1977*

'Its most telling details are its horrific ones. The fire at
the beginning, with lifelike figures melting into grisly
ooze; night time in the city morgue, with a dead body
suddenly popping up as a side effect of embalming
fluid; chases through shadows as the ghoulish
sculptor collects bodies for his exhibit; and the shock
when Atwill's homemade wax face crumbles to the
floor and exposes the hidden demon.' – *Tom Shales, The
American Film Heritage, 1972*

The Mystery of the Wentworth Castle: see Mr
Wong

The Mystery of the Yellow Room *
France   1931   96m   bw
Osso

An attempt is made on the life of a scientist's
daughter.

Complex mystery which has maintained some
reputation.

wd Marcel L'Herbier   *novel* Gaston Leroux   *ph* L.
H. Burel   *m* Edouard Flament

Hugette Ex-Duclos, Roland Toutain, Maxime
Desjardins

Mystery Sea Raider
US   1940   76m   bw
Eugene J. Zukor/Paramount

A ship is hijacked and converted into a German raider
in the Caribbean.

Standard propaganda potboiler with little
imagination.

w Edward E. Paramore Jnr   *d* Edward Dmytryk

Carole Landis, Henry Wilcoxon, Onslow Stevens,
Kathleen Howard, Henry Victor

Mystery Squadron

US 1933 bw serial: 12 eps
Mascot

Mysterious airplane raids threaten destruction to a power dam: they are the work of The Black Ace.

Pot-boiling serial.

d Colbert Clark and David Howard

Bob Steele, Big Boy Williams, Lucile Browne, Jack Mulhall

Mystery Street *

US 1950 93m bw
MGM (Frank E. Taylor)

Harvard medical scientists help solve a murder by examining the victim's bones.

Standard semi-documentary police thriller; well paced and quite entertaining.

w Sidney Boehm, Richard Brooks d John Sturges
ph John Alton *m* Rudolph Kopp

Ricardo Montalban, Sally Forrest, Elsa Lanchester, Bruce Bennett, Marshall Thompson, Jan Sterling

AAN: Leonard Spigelgass (original story)

Mystery Submarine

GB 1962 92m bw
British Lion/Britannia/Bertram Ostrer
US title: *Decoy*

A Nazi submarine is captured and sent out again with a British crew.

Routine war adventure.

w Hugh Woodhouse, Bertram Ostrer, Jon Manchip White *d* C. M. Pennington-Richards *ph* Stan Pavey *m* Clifton Parker

Edward Judd, James Robertson Justice, Laurence Payne, Albert Lieven

Mystery Train **

US 1989 110m DuArt
Palace/JVC (Jim Stark)
V, V*, L, S

Episodic film involving two Elvis Presley fans in Memphis, an Italian woman who sees Elvis's ghost and a Presley look-alike, all of whom converge on a seedy hotel for the night.

Rambling, leisurely film that contains a multitude of small pleasures.

wd Jim Jarmusch *ph* Robby Müller *m* John Lurie *pd* Dan Bishop *ed* Melody London

Masotoshi Nagase, Youki Kudoh, Screamin' Jay Hawkins, Cinque Lee, Rufus Thomas, Nicoletta Braschi, Elizabeth Bracco, Joe Strummer, Rick Aviles, Steve Buscemi

Mystery Woman

US 1934 69m bw
Fox

Recovery of a secret document will mean freedom for a soldier sent to Devil's Island.

Tolerable time-passer, with action mostly on a liner.

w Philip MacDonald, Dudley Nichols, E. E. Paramore Jnr *d* Eugene Forde

Mona Barrie, Gilbert Roland, John Halliday, Rod La Rocque, Mischa Auer, Billy Bevan

'Entertainment of a just passable sort.' – *Variety*

Mystic Pizza

US 1988 104m colour
Virgin/Samuel Goldwyn Company (Mark Levinson, Scott Rosenfelt)
V, V*, L

Three young women experience love and affairs for the first time.

Likely to appeal to a young female audience and offering little of interest to anyone else.

w Amy Jones, Perry Howze, Randy Howze, Alfred Uhry *story* Amy Jones *d* Donald Petrie *ph* Tim Suhrstedt *m* David McHugh *pd* David Chapman *ed* Marion Rothman, Don Brochu

Vincent Phillip D'Onofrio, Annabeth Gish, William R. Moses, Julia Roberts, Adam Storke, Lili Taylor, Conchata Ferrell, Porscha Radcliffe

Nada **

France/Italy   1974   134m   Eastmancolor
Academy/Connoisseur/Verona/Films La Boétie (André
Génovès)

A tough policeman tracks down a group of anarchists
who kidnap the American Ambassador in Paris.

Bleak and violent film, expertly made, in which it is
difficult to tell the good guys from the bad.

w Jean-Patrick Manchette   novel Jean-Patrick
Manchette   d Claude Chabrol   ph Jean Rabier
m Pierre Jansen   ad Guy Littaye   ed Jacques
Gaillard

Fabio Testi, Michel Duchaussoy, Maurice Garrel,
Michel Aumont, Lou Castel, Didier Kaminka, Lyle
Joyce, Viviane Romance

'Chabrol's most profoundly cynical film to date . . . he
lays bare the cause-and-effect mechanism of
terrorism.' – Jan Dawson, MFB

Nadine

US   1987   88m   Metrocolor
Columbia TriStar/ML Delphi (Arlene Donovan)
V, V*, L

Husband and wife on the brink of divorce are drawn
together by a suspicious killing.

Unresolvedly old-fashioned comedy which seems to
need the Cary Grant touch.

wd Robert Benton   ph Nestor Almendros
m Howard Shore   pd Paul Sylbert   ed Sam
O'Steen

Jeff Bridges, Kim Basinger, Rip Torn, Gwen Verdon,
Glenne Headly, Jerry Stiller

Nagana

US   1933   73m   bw
Universal

Doctors in Africa try to cure sleeping sickness.

Dreary drama with cut-in animal footage.

w James Light, Dale Van Every, Don Ryan, Lester
Cohen   d Ernst L. Frank

Tala Birell, Melvyn Douglas, M. Morita, Onslow
Stevens

Naked *

GB   1993   131m   Metrocolor
First Independent/Thin Man/Film Four (Simon Channing-
Williams)
V

Running away from Manchester, where he rapes a
woman, an unemployed, compulsively talkative
misogynist comes to London and moves in with a
former girlfriend.

A saga of an unlovely man out to destroy himself and
others, which is bleak and despairing at its best, but
more often is embittered overstatement and caricature.

wd Mike Leigh   ph Dick Pope   m Andrew
Dickson   pd Alison Chitty   ed Jon Gregory

David Thewlis, Lesley Sharp, Katrin Cartlidge, Greg
Cruttwell, Claire Skinner, Peter Wight, Ewen
Bremner, Susan Vidler

'It would be hard to imagine a film much sourer than
Naked, but sourness is not a fault, merely a
characteristic. Hollowness, now, self-indulgence, a

sort of gloating emotional ugliness – those are faults.'
– Adam Mars-Jones, Independent

'This is a neorealist monster movie, and the monster
won't lie down and die – he just keeps coming.' –
Gavin Smith, Film Comment

'A startling leap from the petty comic viciousness of
Mike Leigh's domestic satires into darker, more
complex philosophical territory.' – Claire Monk, Sight
and Sound

David Thewlis won the award for best actor, and
Mike Leigh for best director, at the Cannes Film
Festival in 1993.

Naked Alibi

US   1954   85m   bw
U-I (Ross Hunter)

The police track a homicidal baker to a Mexican
border town.

Modest police thriller which sags after it crosses the
border.

w Lawrence Roman   d Jerry Hopper   ph Russell
Metty   m Hans Salter

Sterling Hayden, Gene Barry, Gloria Grahame, Marcia
Henderson, Casey Adams, Chuck Connors

The Naked and the Dead

US   1958   131m   Technicolor   RKOscope
RKO Teleradio/Gregjac (Paul Gregory)
V

Adventures of an army platoon in the Pacific war.

Shorn of the four letter words which made the novel
notorious, this is a routine war film, neither very good
nor very bad.

w Denis and Terry Sanders   novel Norman Mailer
d Raoul Walsh   ph Joseph LaShelle   m Bernard
Herrmann

Aldo Ray, Cliff Robertson, Raymond Massey, William
Campbell, Richard Jaeckel, James Best, Joey Bishop,
Robert Gist, Jerry Paris, L. Q. Jones

The Naked City ****

US   1948   96m   bw
Universal (Mark Hellinger)
V*

New York police track down a killer.

Highly influential documentary thriller which, shot
on location in New York's teeming streets, claimed to
be giving an impression of city life; actually its real
mission was to tell an ordinary murder tale with an
impressive accumulation of detail and humour. The
narrator's last words became a cliché: 'There are eight
million stories in the naked city. This has been one of
them.'

w Malvin Wald, Albert Maltz   d Jules Dassin
ph William Daniels   md Milton Schwarzwald
m Frank Skinner, Miklos Rozsa   ed Paul Weatherwax

Barry Fitzgerald, Don Taylor, Howard Duff, Dorothy
Hart, Ted de Corsia, Adelaide Klein

AA: William Daniels; Paul Weatherwax

AAN: original story (Malvin Wald)

The Naked Dawn

US   1956   82m   Technicolor
Universal-International

A hired robber finds that his boss is not to be trusted.

Heavy-going Mexican Western.

w Nina and Herman Schneider   d Edgar G. Ulmer

Arthur Kennedy, Eugene Iglesias, Betta St John

Naked Earth

GB   1958   96m   bw   Cinemascope
TCF/Foray Films (Adrian Worker)

In 1895 a young Irish farmer goes to Africa to grow
tobacco, but moves on to crocodile hunting.

Predictable and uninteresting epic of endurance; not
very convincing either.

w Milton Holmes   d Vincent Sherman   ph Erwin
Hillier

Richard Todd, Juliette Greco, John Kitzmiller, Finlay
Currie, Laurence Naismith, Christopher Rhodes,
Orlando Martins

The Naked Edge

GB   1961   100m   bw
UA/Pennebaker/Baroda (Walter Seltzer, George Glass)
V*

A successful executive is suspected by his wife of an
old murder in which he testified against the man who
was convicted.

Dreary thriller which piles up red herrings in shoals,
then abandons them all for a razor-and-bathroom
finale.

w Joseph Stefano   novel First Train to Babylon by Max
Ehrlich   d Michael Anderson   ph Erwin Hillier
m William Alwyn

Gary Cooper, Deborah Kerr, Peter Cushing, Eric
Portman, Diane Cilento, Hermione Gingold, Michael
Wilding, Ronald Howard

The Naked Face

US   1984   106m   Metrocolor
Cannon (Rony Yacov)
V*

A Chicago psychiatrist finds himself a potential victim
of the Mafia.

Muddled and violent mystery with a rather boring
solution.

wd Bryan Forbes   novel Sidney Sheldon   ph David
Gurfinkel   m Michael J. Lewis   pd William Fosser

Roger Moore, Rod Steiger, Elliott Gould, Anne
Archer, David Hedison, Art Carney, Ron Parady

**The Naked Gun: From the Files of Police
Squad** *

US   1988   85m   Technicolor
UIP/Paramount (Robert K. Weiss)
V, V*, CD, L

A bungling detective foils attempts to assassinate the
Queen in Los Angeles.

A barrage of gags, some good, some dreadful, is
harnessed to a limp narrative. Not as funny as it
should be.

w Jerry Zucker, Jim Abrahams, David Zucker, Pat
Profit   d David Zucker   ph Robert Stevens   m Ira
Newborn   pd John J. Lloyd   ed Michael Jablow

Leslie Nielsen, Priscilla Presley, Ricardo Montalban, George Kennedy, O. J. Simpson, Susan Beaubian, Nancy Marchand, Raye Birk, Jeannette Charles

'Quickly and efficiently establishes its pattern of wildly escalating absurdity within each scene, combined with a series of gags related to each character throughout the film.' – *Philip Strick, MFB*

Naked Gun 2½: The Smell of Fear

US   1991   85m   Technicolor
UIP/Paramount/Zucker/Abrahams/Zucker (Robert K. Weiss)
V, V*, L, CD, S

A clumsy police lieutenant investigates an attempt to kill a solar energy expert.

The mixture as before, although this time around the slapstick comedy is enlivened with fewer good jokes.

w David Zucker, Pat Proft   *d* David Zucker
ph Robert Stevens   *m* Ira Newborn   *pd* John J. Lloyd   *ed* James Symons, Chris Greenbury

Leslie Nielsen, Priscilla Presley, George Kennedy, O.J. Simpson, Robert Goulet, Richard Griffiths, Jacqueline Brookes, Anthony James, Lloyd Bochner

'At least two-and-a-half times less funny than its hilarious progenitor.' – *Variety*

'An appealing rag-bag of the ribald and the ridiculous, showing only the slightest signs of running out of steam.' – *Philip Strick, Sight and Sound*

Naked Gun 33⅓: The Final Insult *

US.   1994   82m   DeLuxe
Paramount (Robert K. Weiss, David Zucker)

Detective Frank Drebin retires from the force and is persuaded to return as an undercover cop.

With some new jokes this time around, and deft parodies, this is the funniest of the series so far.

w Pat Proft, David Zucker, Robert LoCash   *d* Peter Segal   *ph* Robert Stevens   *m* Ira Newborn
pd Lawrence G. Paull   *ed* Jim Symons

Leslie Nielsen, Priscilla Presley, George Kennedy, O. J. Simpson, Fred Ward, Kathleen Freeman, Anna Nicole Smith, Ellen Greene, Ed Williams

'Loaded with the usual barrage of irreverent, politically incorrect and virtually non-stop gags.' – *Variety*

The Naked Hills

US   1955   73m   Pathecolor
Allied Artists/La Salle (Josef Shaftel)
V*

Starting in 1849, a young prospector spends his life looking for gold.

Curious, mildly interesting saga with an obsession instead of a plot.

wd Josef Shaftel   *ph* Frederick Gately   *m* Herschel Burke Gilbert

David Wayne, Marcia Henderson, Keenan Wynn, James Barton, Jim Backus, Denver Pyle

The Naked Jungle *

US   1954   95m   Technicolor
Paramount/George Pal (Frank Freeman Jnr)
V*, L

In 1901 a young woman is married by proxy to a South American cocoa planter, and when she arrives at his jungle home she has to conquer not only him but an army of soldier ants.

Mixture of *Rebecca* elements with a more unusual kind of thrill; all quite watchable, and the ant scenes very effective.

w Philip Yordan, Ranald MacDougall
story Leiningen Versus the Ants by Carl Stephenson
d Byron Haskin   *ph* Ernest Laszlo   *m* Daniele Amfitheatrof

Charlton Heston, Eleanor Parker, William Conrad, Abraham Sofaer, John Dierkes, Douglas Fowley

The Naked Kiss *

US   1964   92m   bw
Allied Artists/F and F/AA (Samuel Fuller)
V, V*, L

A prostitute tries to enter mainstream society.

Tough early work by a director who never compromised but seldom hit the public fancy.

wd Samuel Fuller   *ph* Stanley Cortez   *m* Paul Dunlap   *ad* Eugene Lourie   *ed* Jerome Thomas

Constance Towers, Anthony Eisley, Michael Dante, Virginia Grey, Patsy Kelly, Betty Bronson

'Exterminate all rational thought.'

Naked Lunch *

Canada/GB   1991   115m   Film House colour
First Independent (Jeremy Thomas)
V, V*, L, S

In the 1950s, a drug-addicted writer kills his wife while trying to emulate William Tell and flees to Interzone, an exotic place of paranoid fantasy.

Instead of the savagery and rampant homosexuality of the original, the film concerns the act of the book's creation, through the hallucinatory experiences of a writer, based on Burroughs, among the expatriate artistic community of Tangier. All that is carried over from the novel is the title and lack of narrative coherence.

wd David Cronenberg   *novel* William S. Burroughs
ph Peter Suschitzky   *m* Howard Shore, Ornette Coleman (alto sax solos)   *pd* Carol Spier
sp creature effects: Chris Walas Inc.   *ed* Ronald Sanders

Peter Weller, Judy Davis, Ian Holm, Julian Sands, Roy Scheider, Monique Mercure, Nicholas Campbell, Michael Zelinker, Robert A. Silverman, Joseph Scorsiani

'A fascinating, demanding, mordantly funny picture that echoes many of the book's chief concerns, but also stands as a distinctively personal creation in its own right.' – *Variety*

'It's impossible to make a movie out of *Naked Lunch*. A literal translation just wouldn't work. It would cost $400 million to make and would be banned in every country of the world.' – *David Cronenberg*

The Naked Maja

Italy/US   1959   112m   Technirama
MGM/Titanus (Goffredo Lombardo)

Peasant Francisco Goya becomes a famous painter through the influence of the Duchess of Alba.

Boring and unconvincing biopic.

w Giorgio Prosperi, Norman Corwin, Albert Lewin, Oscar Saul   *d* Henry Koster   *ph* Giuseppe Rotunno   *m* Francesco Lavagnino

Anthony Franciosa, Ava Gardner, Amedeo Nazzari, Gino Cervi, Lea Padovani, Massimo Serrato

'This travesty of Goya's life, country and period adds up to nothing more entertaining than a perfunctory, heavy-handed pageant.' – *MFB*

The Naked Night: see *Sawdust and Tinsel*

The Naked Prey *

US   1966   94m   Technicolor   Panavision
Paramount/Theodora/Sven Persson (Cornel Wilde)
V*, L

In 1840, a white hunter becomes brutalized when a tribe hunts him down as though he were a lion.

Savage adventure story with bloodthirsty detail; unusual and certainly effective.

w Clint Johnston, Don Peters   *d* Cornel Wilde   *ph* I. A. R. Thompson   *md* Andrew Tracy, from African folk music

Cornel Wilde, Gert Van Den Berg, Ken Gampu

'Overtones pretentious, but it tries.' – *Sight and Sound*

AAN: script

The Naked Runner

GB   1967   104m   Techniscope
Warner/Artanis (Brad Dexter)

British intelligence conceive a plan to turn an innocent businessman into a spy killer.

Silly espionage thriller further marred by its director's penchant for making a zany composition of every frame.

w Stanley Mann   *novel* Francis Clifford   *d* Sidney J. Furie   *ph* Otto Heller   *m* Harry Sukman

Frank Sinatra, Peter Vaughan, Derren Nesbitt, Nadia Gray, Toby Robins, Cyril Luckham, Edward Fox, Inger Stratton

'It might be a good movie to read by if there were light in the theatre.' – *Pauline Kael*

The Naked Spur *

US   1953   91m   Technicolor
MGM (William H. Wright)
V*

A bounty hunter has trouble getting his quarry back to base.

Standard big-studio Western shot in Colorado, with all characters motivated by greed.

w Sam Rolfe, Harold Jack Bloom   *d* Anthony Mann   *ph* William Mellor   *m* Bronislau Kaper

James Stewart, Robert Ryan, Janet Leigh, Millard Mitchell

AAN: script

The Naked Street

US   1955   83m   bw
Edward Small

A racketeer's daughter marries a worthless crook: her father saves him from the electric chair but he murders again.

Semi-documentary exposé melodrama about unpleasant people; reasonably proficient on its level.

w Maxwell Shane, Leo Katcher   *d* Maxwell Shane   *ph* Floyd Crosby   *md* Emil Newman   *m* Ernest Gold

Anthony Quinn, Anne Bancroft, Farley Granger, Peter Graves

Naked Tango

US   1990   92m   DeLuxe
Blue Dolphin/Sugarloaf/Gotan/Towa/Praesens/Grupo Baires (David Weisman)
V

In the 1920s a bored wife assumes the identity of a suicide, marries a dubious night-club owner in Buenos Aires, and falls in love with a tango-dancing gangster.

Luridly directed and acted, over-the-top romance that fails to convince, particularly in its attempt at a period setting.

wd Leonard Schrader   *story* inspired by the work of Manuel Puig   *ph* Juan Ruiz-Anchia   *m* Thomas Newman   *pd* Anthony Pratt   *ed* Lee Percy, Debra McDermott

Vincent D'Onofrio, Mathilda May, Esai Morales, Fernando Rey, Cipe Lincovsky, Josh Mostel, Patricio Bisso, Constance McCashin

'Too morbid and narrowly conceived to interest mainstream audiences.' – *Variety*

The Naked Truth *

GB   1957   92m   bw
Rank/Mario Zampi
V*
US title: *Your Past is Showing*

Celebrities band together to kill a blackmailer who threatens to expose unsavoury aspects of their lives.

Frenzied black farce, quite a lot of which comes off.

w Michael Pertwee d Mario Zampi ph Stan Pavey m Stanley Black

Peter Sellers, Terry-Thomas, Peggy Mount, Dennis Price, Shirley Eaton, Georgina Cookson

Naked under Leather: see *Girl on a Motorcycle*

The Naked Vampire: see *La Vampire Nue*

Naked Warriors: see *The Arena*

'Even men of God can trade with the Devil'
The Name of the Rose *
US   1986   130m   colour
TCF/Bernd Eichinger/Bernd-Schaefers/Cristaldi/Ariane/ZDF
V, V*, L, S

In the 14th century, an English monk's visit to an Italian abbey is soured by a series of murders.

Curious, remote, randomly developed and edited, this can never have been an obvious candidate for box-office success: yet it did pretty well.

w Andrew Birkin, Gerard Brach, Howard Franklin, Alain Godard novel Umberto Eco d Jean-Jacques Annaud ph Tonio Delli Colli m James Horner pd Dante Ferretti ed Jane Seitz

Sean Connery, F. Murray Abraham, Christian Slater, Michael Lonsdale, Elya Baskin

'A plodding misfire . . . sorrowfully mediocre.' – *Variety*

Nana *
US   1934   89m   bw
Samuel Goldwyn
V
GB title: *Lady of the Boulevards*

The high life and subsequent degradation of a Parisian demi-mondaine in the 1890s.

Stylish yet stolid slice of *le beau monde,* intended to create a new star.

w Willard Mack, Harry Wagstaff Gribble novel Emile Zola d Dorothy Arzner ph Gregg Toland m Alfred Newman

Anna Sten, Lionel Atwill, Phillips Holmes, Richard Bennett, Mae Clarke, Muriel Kirkland, Reginald Owen, Jessie Ralph

'The star's resources should be sufficient to offset some of the lesser script deficiencies.' – *Variety*

Nana
France/Italy   1955   100m
Cygno Films/FLF (Jacques Roitfeld)

A courtesan and actress comes to grief.

Glossily unconvincing version, with a performance in the title role in the style of Lucille Ball.

w Henri Jeanson, Albert Valentin d Christian-Jaque ph Christian Matras m Georges Van Parys ad Robert Gys ed Jacques Desagneaux

Charles Boyer, Martine Carol, Walter Chiari, Marguerite Pierry, Paul Frankeur, Elisa Cegani, Dora Doll, Jacques Castlelot, Noel Roquevert

Nancy Drew

This series of second features starring Bonita Granville as a teenage small-town detective was moderately well received but quickly forgotten. The character was created in novels by Edward Stratemeyer and his daughter Harriet Evans; the films were all directed by William Clemens for Warner.

1938: NANCY DREW, DETECTIVE
1939: NANCY DREW, REPORTER; NANCY DREW, TROUBLE SHOOTER; NANCY DREW AND THE HIDDEN STAIRCASE

Nancy Goes to Rio
US   1950   99m   Technicolor
MGM (Joe Pasternak)

Two actresses, mother and daughter, are both after the same part.

Mild shipboard musical.

w Sidney Sheldon d Robert Z. Leonard ph Ray June m George Stoll

Jane Powell, Ann Sothern, Carmen Miranda, Barry Sullivan, Louis Calhern, Fortunio Bonanova, Hans Conried

Nancy Steele is Missing *
US   1937   85m   bw
TCF (Nunnally Johnson)

Crooks try to pass off a girl as the long lost heir to a fortune.

Slightly unusual, well cast melodrama.

w Gene Fowler, Hal Long novel C. F. Coe d George Marshall ph Barney McGill m David Buttolph

Victor McLaglen, Peter Lorre, June Lang, Jane Darwell, John Carradine, Walter Connolly

The Nanny *
GB   1965   93m   bw
ABP/Hammer (Jimmy Sangster)
V

A 10-year-old boy hates his nanny, and with good reason, for she is a neurotic murderess.

Muted Hammer experiment in psycho- pathology, with too much equivocation before the dénouement; the star's role allows few fireworks, and the plot is rather unpleasant.

w Jimmy Sangster novel Evelyn Piper d Seth Holt ph Harry Waxman m Richard Rodney Bennett

Bette Davis, Jill Bennett, William Dix, James Villiers, Wendy Craig, Pamela Franklin, Maurice Denham

Nanook of the North *
US   1921   57m (1947 sound version)   bw   silent
Revillon Frères
V*

The life of an Eskimo and his family.

Primitive but trail-blazing documentary, hard to sit through for modern audiences.

wd/ph/ed Robert Flaherty

'In a day of emotional and artistic deliquescence on the screen, a picture with the fresh strength and pictorial promise of *Nanook of the North* is in the nature of a revolution.' – *Frances Taylor Patterson*

† Nanook himself died of hunger on the ice shortly after the film was released.

Nanou
UK/France   1986   110m   Eastmancolor
Umbrella-Caulfield/Arion

A young English girl, travelling through France, has an affair with a political activist.

Unsatisfactory film of an unsatisfactory romance.

wd Conny Templeman ph Martin Fuhrer m John Keane pd Andrew Mollo ed Tom Priestley

Imogen Stubbs, Jean-Philippe Ecoffey, Daniel Day-Lewis, Lou Castel, Valentine Pelka, Anne-Marie Jabraud, Dominique Rousseau, Michel Robin, Roger Ibanez

Napló Gyermekeimnek: see *Diary for My Children*

Napoleon **
France   1927   378m approx (24 fps)   bw (some colour)   silent
WESTI/Société Générale de Films
V*, L

The early life of Napoleon.

A cinematic epic which, although brilliant in most particulars, owes its greatest interest to its narrative sweep, its flair for composition and its use of triptych screens which at the end combine to show one giant picture, the clear precursor of Cinerama. In 1934 Gance revised his film and added stereophonic sound.

wd/ed Abel Gance ph various m Arthur Honegger

Albert Dieudonné, Antonin Artaud, Pierre Batcheff

† The 1934 version ran 140m and included three-dimensional sound.

Napoleon and Samantha
US   1972   91m   Technicolor
Walt Disney (Winston Hibler)
V*

When his old guardian dies, a small boy and his girl friend run away with their pet lion.

Patchy, episodic action drama for older children, with a very sleepy lion.

w Stewart Raffil d Bernard McEveety ph Monroe Askins m Buddy Baker

Michael Douglas, Will Geer

AAN: Buddy Baker

Narayama Bushi-Ko: see *The Ballad of Narayama*

The Narrow Corner
US   1933   71m   bw
Warner

On an eastern island, a man on the run for murder finds he can't escape his fate.

Mediocre adaptation of a Somerset Maugham novel in which very little happens; the added love interest doesn't help.

w Robert Presnell d Alfred E. Green

Douglas Fairbanks Jnr, Ralph Bellamy, Dudley Digges, Arthur Hohl, Patricia Ellis

'Considerably better than fair.' – *Variety*

† Remade three years later as *Isle of Fury* (qv).

The Narrow Margin **
US   1952   70m   bw
RKO (Stanley Rubin)
V*, L

Police try to guard a prosecution witness on a train from Chicago to Los Angeles.

Tight little thriller which takes every advantage of its train setting. What the trade used to call a sleeper, it gave more satisfaction than many a top feature.

w Earl Fenton d Richard Fleischer ph George E. Diskant

Charles McGraw, Marie Windsor, Jacqueline White, Queenie Leonard

'A taut, breathlessly fast and highly suspenseful "sleeper" par excellence.' – *Time Out, 1986*

AAN: original story (Martin Goldsmith, Jack Leonard)

'They Want Her Dead. He Needs Her Alive.'
Narrow Margin
US   1990   97m   Technicolor   Panavision
Guild/Carolco (Jonathan A. Zimbert)
V, V*, L

A district attorney and a key witness in a trial take refuge on a train from pursuing gangsters.

Inferior remake of the 1952 film, with little sense of suspense.

w Earl Fenton Jnr story Martin Goldsmith, Jack Leonard d/ph Peter Hyams m Bruce Broughton pd Joel Schiller ad Kim Mooney ed James Mitchell

Gene Hackman, Anne Archer, James B. Sikking, J. T. Walsh, M. Emmet Walsh, Susan Hogan, Nigel Bennett, J. A. Preston

† *Variety* reported that while the original film cost $230,000 to make, the remake was nearly a hundred times more expensive, at $21 million.

The Narrowing Circle
GB   1955   66m   bw
Fortress Films/Eros

Murder on the staff of a magazine.

Very tolerable mystery which wastes no time and plays fair.

w Doreen Montgomery   *novel* Julian Symons
d Charles Saunders

Paul Carpenter, Hazel Court, Ferdy Mayne, Russell Napier, Trevor Reid

'The damnedest thing you ever saw!'
Nashville ***
US   1975   161m   Metrocolor   Panavision
Paramount/ABC (Robert Altman)
V*, L

A political campaign in Nashville organizes a mammoth pop concert to gain support.

Kaleidoscopic, fragmented, multi-storied musical melodrama, a mammoth movie which can be a bore or an inspiration according to taste. Certainly many exciting moments pass by, but the length is self-defeating.

w Joan Tewkesbury   d Robert Altman   ph Paul Lohmann   md Richard Baskin

Geraldine Chaplin, David Arkin, Barbara Baxley, Ned Beatty, Karen Black, Keith Carradine, Henry Gibson, Keenan Wynn, Lily Tomlin, Ronee Blakley

'A gigantic parody . . . crammed with samples taken from every level of Nashville society, revealed in affectionate detail bordering on caricature in a manner that would surely delight Norman Rockwell.' – *Philip Strick*

'Wildly over-praised Altman, with all the defects we once looked on as marks of healthy ambitiousness: terrible construction, messy editing, leering jokes at its own characters, unending pomposity.' – *Time Out, 1980*

AA: song 'I'm Easy' (*m/y* Keith Carradine)

AAN: best picture; Robert Altman; Lily Tomlin; Ronee Blakley

The Nasty Girl ***
West Germany   1990   92m   Eastmancolor
Mainline/Sentana/ZDF
V, V*, L
original title: *Das Schreckliche Mädchen*

Despite local hostility, a girl researches into events in her home town during the Nazi regime.

A witty and exuberant social satire, using very effectively a documentary approach to the subject.

wd Michael Verhoeven   ph Axel de Roche   m Mike Hertung, Elmar Schloter, Billy Gorlt, Lydie Auvray   ad Hubert Popp   ed Barbara Hennings

Lena Stolze, Monika Baumgartner, Michael Gahr, Fred Stillkrauth, Elisabeth Bertram, Robert Giggenbach, Karin Thaler, Hans-Reinhard Muller

AAN: best foreign film

Nasty Habits *
GB   1976   92m   Technicolor
Brut/Bowden (Robert Enders)
V*

An abbess dies and the nuns vie for succession.

Satirical comedy rather obviously based on the Watergate scandals; initially amusing, but very tiresome by the end.

w Robert Enders   *novel The Abbess of Crewe* by Muriel Spark   d Michael Lindsay-Hogg   ph Douglas Slocombe   m John Cameron

Glenda Jackson, Melina Mercouri, Geraldine Page, Sandy Dennis, Anne Jackson, Anne Meara, Edith Evans, Susan Penhaligon, Rip Torn, Eli Wallach, Jerry Stiller

'The sort of material just about fit for a half-hour TV sketch.' – *Richard Combs, MFB*

The National Health *
GB   1973   97m   Eastmancolor
Columbia (Ned Sherrin, Terry Glinwood)

Life in the general men's ward of a large antiquated hospital.

Acerbic comedy from a National Theatre play which mixes tragedy and farce into a kind of *Carry on Dying*.

w Peter Nichols,   play Peter Nichols   d Jack Gold   ph John Coquillon   m Carl Davis   pd Ray Simm

Jim Dale, Lynn Redgrave, Eleanor Bron, Sheila Scott-Wilkinson, Donald Sinden, Colin Blakely, Clive Swift

National Lampoon Goes to the Movies: see
National Lampoon's Movie Madness

National Lampoon's Animal House *
US   1978   109m   Technicolor
Universal (Matty Simmons, Ivan Reitman)
V, V*, L, S

On an American campus around 1962, scruffy newcomers challenge the elegant élite.

A ragbag of college gags, of interest only to those who have had the experience; but its success caused much imitation, especially in American television.

w Harold Ramis, Douglas Kenney, Chris Miller   d John Landis   ph Charles Correll   m Elmer Bernstein

John Belushi, Tim Matheson, John Vernon, Donald Sutherland, Verna Bloom, Cesare Danova, Mary Louise Weller

National Lampoon's Christmas Vacation
US   1989   97m   colour
Warner/Hughes Entertainment (John Hughes, Tom Jacobson)
V, V*, L

A father decides to give the family an old-fashioned Christmas at home.

Unsubtle comedy that always goes for the easy laugh.

w John Hughes   d Jeremiah S. Chechik   ph Thomas Ackerman   m Angelo Badalamenti   pd Stephen Marsh   ed Jerry Greenberg

Chevy Chase, Beverly D'Angelo, Randy Quaid, Diane Ladd, E. G. Marshall, Doris Roberts, Julia Louis-Dreyfus, Mae Questel, William Hickey

National Lampoon's Class Reunion
US   1982   85m   Metrocolor
Fox/ABC Productions (Matty Simmons)
V*, L

The class of '72 foregathers at Lizzie Borden High, where a murderer is lurking.

An entertainment in which the presentation is better than the material, which is a vague spoof of high school and horror films.

w John Hughes   d Michael Miller   ph Phil Lathrop   m Peter Bernstein, Mark Goldenberg   pd Dean Edward Mitzner   ed Richard C. Meyer, Ann Mills

Gerrit Graham, Michael Lerner, Fred McCarren, Miriam Flynn, Stephen Furst

National Lampoon's European Vacation
US   1985   94m   Technicolor
Warner (Matty Simmons)
V, V*, L

An American family determines to see Europe.

Hopelessly unfunny and simple-minded comedy, lacking even the usual schoolboy smut.

w John Hughes, Robert Klane   d Amy Heckerling   ph Bob Paynter   m Charles Fox   pd Bob Cartwright   ed Paul Herring

Chevy Chase, Beverly D'Angelo, Jason Lively, Dana Hill, Eric Idle

'See it before they make the sequel!'
National Lampoon's Loaded Weapon 1
US   1993   83m   DeLuxe
Guild/New Line (Suzanne Todd, David Willis)
V, V*

Two cops investigate a cocaine-cookie smuggling ring.

A lacklustre parody of the *Lethal Weapon* movies; it not only has no style, it does not even have any jokes.

w Don Holley, Gene Quintano   d Gene Quintano   ph Peter Dening   m Robert Folk   pd Jaymes Hinkle   ed Christopher Greenbury

Emilio Estevez, Samuel L. Jackson, Jon Lovitz, Tim Curry, Kathy Ireland, Frank McRae, William Shatner, James Doohan, F. Murray Abraham

'This would-be comedy is very short on laughs and virtually all are given away in its trailer.' – *Variety*

National Lampoon's Movie Madness
US   1981   89m   Technicolor   Panavision
UA (Matty Simmons)
V*
aka: *National Lampoon Goes to the Movies*

Three parodies of movie genres: an insurance salesman seeks personal growth; a stripper becomes First Lady in three days; a young cop learns how to be tough.

Cinema audiences were spared this inept and witless display, though it turns up on late-night TV to bore the unwary.

w Tod Carroll, Shary Flenniken, Pat Mephitis, Gerald Sussman, Ellis Weiner   d Bob Giraldi, Henry Jaglom   ph Charles Correll, Tak Fujimoto   m Andy Stein   ad Alexander A. Mayer   ed James Coblentz, Bud S. Isaacs

Robby Benson, Richard Widmark, Diane Lane, Candy Clark, Christopher Lloyd, Peter Riegert, Ann Dusenberry, Elisha Cook, Robert Culp

National Lampoon's Vacation
US   1983   98m   Technicolor
Warner (Matty Simmons)
V, V*, L

An inventor drives his family on a holiday starting in Chicago and ending in California, but the journey is fraught with disaster.

Episodic, more or less straight black comedy, with detail more often boring or repellent than funny.

w John Hughes   d Harold Ramis   ph Victor J. Kemper   m Ralph Burns   pd Jack Collis   ed Paul Herring

Chevy Chase, Imogene Coca, Beverly D'Angelo, Randy Quaid, Eddie Bracken

National Velvet *
US   1945   125m   Technicolor
MGM (Pandro S. Berman)
V, V*, L

Children train a horse to win the Grand National.

A big bestseller from another era; its flaws of conception and production quickly became evident.

w Theodore Reeves, Helen Deutsch   *novel* Enid Bagnold   d Clarence Brown   ph Leonard Smith   m Herbert Stothart   ed Robert J. Kern

Mickey Rooney, Elizabeth Taylor, *Anne Revere*, Donald Crisp, Angela Lansbury, Jackie Jenkins, Reginald

Owen, Terry Kilburn, Norma Varden, Alec Craig,
Arthur Shields, Dennis Hoey

† Sequel 1978: *International Velvet*.

AA: Anne Revere; Robert J. Kern

AAN: Clarence Brown; Leonard Smith

Native Son
US   1986   112m   colour
Cinecom/Diane Silver/American Playhouse/Cinetudes
V*

A poor black teenager commits murder.

Heavy-going adaptation of a novel seen in some
American quarters as a symbol of classic guilt.

w Richard Wesley   *novel* Richard Wright
d Jerrold Freedman   *ph* Thomas Burstyn   *m* James
Mtume

Carroll Baker, Akousuwa Busia, Matt Dillon, Art
Evans, Elizabeth McGovern, John McMartin,
Geraldine Page

† A low-budget Argentine version had been filmed in
1950 by Pierre Chenal, with the author in the leading
role

Nattlek: see *Night Games*

Nattvardsgästerna: see *Winter Light*

The Natural *
US   1984   137m   Technicolor
Tri-Star/Delphi II (Mark Johnson)
V, V*, L, S

The life of a baseball star who reaches the heights and
can only fall.

Curious attempt to modernize the King Arthur legend,
with a baseball bat substituting for Excalibur and
hints of magic everywhere. A generally mystifying if
occasionally an attractive experience.

w Roger Towne, Phil Dusenberry   *d* Barry Levinson
ph Caleb Deschanel   *m* Randy Newman

Robert Redford, Robert Duvall, Glenn Close, Kim
Basinger, Wilford Brimley, Barbara Hershey, Robert
Prosky, Joe Don Baker, Richard Farnsworth

AAN: Glenn Close (supporting actress);
photography; music; art direction

A Natural Born Salesman: see *Earthworm
Tractors*

The Nature of the Beast *
UK   1988   95m   colour
Cannon/Film Four International/British Screen (Joanna Smith)

In a small industrial town, where unemployment is
rife, a young boy and his friend stalk a mysterious
beast that is killing animals.

An unsuccessful allegory of social disintegration that
stays in the shadow of *Kes*.

w Janni Howker   *novel* Janni Howker   *d* Franco
Rosso   *ph* Nat Crosby   *m* Stanley Myers, Hans
Zimmer   *pd* Jamie Leonard   *ed* George Akers

Lynton Dearden, Paul Simpson, Tony Melody,
Freddie Fletcher, Dave Hill, Roberta Kerr, David
Fleeshman

Naughty Arlette: see *The Romantic Age*

Naughty but Nice
US   1939   90m   bw
Warner (Sam Bischoff)

A professor of classical music accidentally writes a
popular song.

Mildly amusing comedy musical with all the tunes
adapted from the classics (cf *That Night with You*).

w Jerry Wald, Richard Macaulay   *d* Ray Enright
ph Arthur L. Todd   *songs* Harry Warren, Johnny
Mercer

Dick Powell, Ann Sheridan, Ronald Reagan, Gale
Page, ZaSu Pitts, Jerry Colonna

Naughty Marietta **
US   1935   106m   bw
MGM (Hunt Stromberg)
V*, L

A French princess goes to America and falls in love
with an Indian scout.

Period operetta which set the seal of success on the
MacDonald-Eddy team. In itself, dated but quite
pleasing for those who like the genre.

w John Lee Mahin, Frances Goodrich, Albert Hackett
operetta Rida Johnson Young   *d* W. S. Van Dyke
ph William Daniels   *m* Victor Herbert   *ad* Cedric
Gibbons

Jeanette MacDonald, Nelson Eddy, Frank Morgan, Elsa
Lanchester, Douglass Dumbrille, Joseph Cawthorn,
Cecelia Parker, Walter Kingsford

'Slow-moving operetta which singing must sustain.' –
Variety

'When these two profiles come together to sing Ah
Sweet Mystery of Life, it's beyond camp, it's in a
realm of its own.' – *Judith Crist, 1977*

AAN: best picture

The Naughty Nineties
US   1945   72m   bw
Universal (Edward L. Hartmann, John Grant)
V*, L

Two incompetents help an old showboat owner.

Dim star comedy apart from the team's rendition of
their most famous routine, 'Who's On First'.

w Edmund L. Hartmann, John Grant, Edmund
Joseph, Hal Fimburg   *d* Jean Yarborough
ph George Robinson

Bud Abbott, Lou Costello, Henry Travers, Alan Curtis,
Rita Johnson, Joe Sawyer

The Navigator ***
US   1924   63m approx (24 fps)   bw   silent
Metro-Goldwyn/Buster Keaton (Joseph M. Schenck)
V, V*

A millionaire and his girl are the only people on a
transatlantic liner marooned in mid-ocean.

A succession of hilarious sight gags: the star in top
form.

w Jean Havez, Clyde Bruckman, J. A. Mitchell
d Buster Keaton, Donald Crisp   *ph* Elgin Lessley,
Byron Houck

Buster Keaton, Kathryn McGuire

'Studded with hilarious moments and a hundred and
one adroit gags.' – *Photoplay*

The Navigator: A Medieval Odyssey **
Australia   1988   91m   colour/bw
Recorded Releasing/Arenafilm (John Maynard, Gary Hannam)
V, V*

Medieval villagers, fearful of the Black Death, go on a
pilgrimage through a mine and emerge in the modern
world.

Oddly disturbing fable, imaginatively presented.

w Vincent Ward, Kely Lyons, Geoff Chapple
d Vincent Ward   *ph* Geoffrey Simpson   *m* Davood
A. Tabrizi   *pd* Sally Campbell   *ed* John Scott

Bruce Lyons, Chris Haywood, Hamish McFarlane,
Marshall Napier, Noel Appleby, Paul Livingstone,
Sarah Pierse, Mark Wheatley, Tony Herbert

'It is not the victory that is important, it is how the game is
played!'
Navy Blue and Gold
US   1937   93m   bw
Sam Zimbalist/MGM

An unpopular naval cadet makes good.

Ingenuous flagwaver, like a wrap-up of umpteen
others but with better production.

w George Bruce   *d* Sam Wood

Robert Young, James Stewart, Florence Rice, Billie
Burke, Lionel Barrymore, Tom Brown, Samuel
S. Hinds, Paul Kelly

'Expertly made and sure box office.' – *Variety*

Navy Blues
US   1941   109m   bw
Warner (Jerry Wald)

Naval ratings get into trouble in Honolulu.

Undernourished musical comedy with not too much
of either commodity.

w Jerry Wald, Richard Macaulay, Arthur T. Horman
d Lloyd Bacon   *ph* Tony Gaudio   *ch* Seymour Felix
songs Arthur Schwartz, Johnny Mercer

Ann Sheridan, Jack Oakie, Martha Raye, Jack Haley,
Herbert Anderson, Jack Carson, Richard Lane, Jackie
Gleason, Howard da Silva

The Navy Comes Through
US   1942   81m   bw
RKO
V*

The story of a merchant marine ship.

Propaganda potboiler with a reasonably efficient cast
and production.

w Roy Chanslor, Aeneas Mackenzie   *story* Borden
Chase   *d* A. Edward Sutherland

Pat O'Brien, George Murphy, Jane Wyatt, Jackie
Cooper, Carl Esmond, Max Baer, Desi Arnaz, Ray
Collins

Navy SEALS
US   1990   114m   Technicolor
Rank/Orion (Brenda Feigen, Bernard Williams)
V, V*, L, S

Naval commandos attempt to kidnap an Arab terrorist
and destroy a missile store in Lebanon.

Flaccid action picture, peopled by comic-strip
stereotypes and full of nothing but sound and fury.

w Chuck Pfarrer, Gary Goldman   *d* Lewis Teague
ph John A. Alonzo   *m* Sylvester Levay   *pd* Guy J.
Comtois, Veronica Hadfield   *ed* Don Zimmerman

Charlie Sheen, Michael Biehn, Joanne Whalley-
Kilmer, Rick Rossovich, Cyril O'Reilly, Bill Paxton,
Dennis Haysbert, Paul Sanchez

'Quite what this balefully predictable action-
adventure is trying to prove totally escapes me. Unless
it is that there is nothing much these days that the
American public won't take in the way of flag-waving
juvenilia.' – *Derek Malcolm, Guardian*

The Navy Steps Out: see *A Girl, a Guy and a Gob*

Navy Wife
US   1935   72m   bw
Fox

A girl who marries a navy doctor is unhappy with the
life.

Routine domestic drama with a propaganda angle.

w Sonya Levien   *novel* *Beauty's Daughter* by Kathleen
Norris   *d* Allan Dwan

Claire Trevor, Ralph Bellamy, Jane Darwell, Ben
Lyon, Warren Hymer, Kathleen Burke

'Problem play for the duals.' – *Variety*

Navy Wife
US   1956   83m   bw
Allied Artists
GB title: *Mother, Sir!*

A commander's wife visits her husband in Japan and
learns about Japanese attitudes.

Silly hands-across-the-sea comedy which takes a long time to get nowhere.

w Kay Lenard *d* Edward Bernds

Joan Bennett, Gary Merrill, Shirley Yagamuchi, Judy Nugent

Nazarin *
Mexico 1958 94m bw
Barbachano Ponce
V*, L

A Catholic priest tries to take the teachings of Christ literally, but is drastically misunderstood.

A black atheistic satire pretty typical of its director, but not among his most enjoyable works.

w Julio Alejandro, Luis Buñuel *novel* Benito Perez Galdos *d* Luis Buñuel *ph* Gabriel Figueroa

Francisco Rabal, Marga Lopez, Rita Macedo, Ignacio Lopez Tarso

Nazi Agent *
US 1942 84m bw
MGM (Irving Asher)

A German-American is forced by his Nazi twin to help a group of German spies.

Modest suspenser with a plot twist similar to *The Great Impersonation* and *Dead Ringer*.

w Paul Gangelin, John Meehan Jnr *d* Jules Dassin
ph Harry Stradling *m* Lennie Hayton

Conrad Veidt, Ann Ayars, Frank Reicher, Dorothy Tree, Martin Kosleck

The Neanderthal Man
US 1953 75m bw
United Artists/Global

A scientist transforms a cat into a sabre-toothed tiger and himself into a neanderthal man; he is then eaten by the tiger.

By no means as amusing as it sounds.

w Aubrey Wisberg, Jack Pollexfen *d* E. A. Dupont
ph Stanley Cortez

Robert Shayne, Richard Crane, Doris Merrick, Joyce Terry

Near Dark
US 1987 94m colour
Entertainment/Scotti Brothers/International Video Entertainment (Steven-Charles Jaffe)
V, V*, L, S

A cowboy is seduced into joining a roving gang of vampires.

Fast moving, moderately successful attempt to bring the vampire movie screaming into the 20th century.

w Eric Red, Kathryn Bigelow *d* Kathryn Bigelow
ph Adam Greenberg *m* Tangerine Dream
pd Stephen Altman *ed* Howard Smith

Adrian Pasdar, Jenny Wright, Lance Henriksen, Bill Paxton, Jenette Goldstein, Tim Thomerson, Joshua Miller

'Projects a truly upsetting image of revulsion and horror, and its scenes of blood-letting – especially a long spectacular set piece featuring the killing of the clientele of a lowlife tavern – are not merely gross, but genuinely disturbing.' – *Henry Sheehan, L.A. Reader*

Nearly a Nasty Accident
GB 1961 91m bw
British Lion/Britannia/Marlow (Bertram Ostrer)

A mild-mannered aircraftman causes disaster wherever he goes.

Familiar faces just about save from disaster this underscripted comedy for indulgent audiences.

w Jack Davies, Hugh Woodruff *play* Touch Wood by David Stringer, David Carr *d* Don Chaffey
ph Paul Beeson *m* Ken Jones

Kenneth Connor, Jimmy Edwards, Shirley Eaton, Richard Wattis, Ronnie Stevens, Jon Pertwee, Eric Barker, Peter Jones, Jack Watling, Joyce Carey, Terry Scott

'Three men and a woman face death beside a man they want to kill!'
The Nebraskan
US 1953 66m Technicolor 3D
Columbia

An army scout proves the innocence of an Indian supposed to have murdered a Sioux chief.

Two-bit Western which looked even worse in three dimensions.

w David Lang and Martin Berkeley *d* Fred F. Sears

Phil Carey, Roberta Haynes, Wallace Ford, Richard Webb, Lee Van Cleef

Necessary Roughness
US 1991 104m Technicolor
UIP/Paramount (Mace Neufeld, Robert Rehme)
V, V*

After a college football team has been dismissed for corruption, a coach attempts to create a new squad from unathletic students.

Drear movie that is never less than predictable and never more than tedious.

w Rick Natkin, David Fuller *d* Stan Dragoti
ph Peter Stein *m* Bill Conti *pd* Paul Peters
ed John Wright, Steve Mirkovich, Wayne Wahrman

Scott Bakula, Robert Loggia, Hector Elizondo, Harley Jane Kozack, Larry Miller, Sinbad, Fred Dalton Thompson

'All the expected clichés of the losers-make-a-comeback plot.' – *Variety*

'As phoney as the Astroturf on which most of it takes place.' – *Philip French, Observer*

Necromancy
US 1973 83m colour
Cinerama (Bert I. Gordon)
V*

Two young people become involved in small-town witchcraft.

Low-key, low-talent thriller overbalanced by its star.

wd Bert I. Gordon *ph* Winton C. Hoch *m* Fred Karger

Orson Welles, Pamela Franklin, Michael Ontkean, Lee Purcell

Necronomicon – Geträumte Sünden: see
Succubus

Ned Kelly
GB 1970 103m Technicolor
UA/Woodfall (Neil Hartley)
V*

The career of a 19th-century Australian outlaw.

Obstinately unlikeable action picture with some kind of message which never becomes clear amid all the cleverness.

w Tony Richardson, Ian Jones *d* Tony Richardson
ph Gerry Fisher *m* Shel Silverstein *pd* Jocelyn Herbert

Mick Jagger, Allen Bickford, Geoff Gilmour, Mark McManus

Negatives *
GB 1968 98m Eastmancolor
Crispin/Kettledrum (Judd Bernard)
V*

Three people indulge in sexual fantasies involving Dr Crippen and Baron von Richthofen.

Smoothly done but impenetrable psychological poppycock: what is fact and what is fancy, only the author knows.

w Peter Everett, Roger Lowry *novel* Peter Everett
d Peter Medak *ph* Ken Hodges *m* Basil Kirchin

Glenda Jackson, Peter McEnery, Diane Cilento, Maurice Denham, Steven Lewis, Norman Rossington

Neighbors *
US 1981 94m Technicolor
Columbia/Zanuck-Brown
V*, L

A staid suburbanite is first irritated, then taken over by his splashy neighbours.

Hit-or-miss but generally quite funny comedy in a style familiar to viewers of American late night television.

w Larry Gelbart *novel* Thomas Berger *d* John G. Avildsen *ph* Gerald Hirschfeld *m* Bill Conti
pd Peter Larkin *ed* Jan Kurson

John Belushi, Dan Aykroyd, Kathryn Walker, Cathy Moriarty, Igors Gavon, Dru-Ann Chukron

Neither the Sea nor the Sand
GB 1972 94m Eastmancolor
LMG/Portland (Jack Smith, Peter Fetterman)

Holidaying in Jersey, a married woman begins a love-affair with a local man which survives his sudden death.

An attempt at a Gothic romance ruined by half-hearted acting and direction; all that remains is a dull zombie movie and an unpleasant exercise in necrophilia.

w Gordon Honeycombe, Rosemary Davies
novel Gordon Honeycombe *d* Fred Burnley
ph David Muir *m* Nachum Heiman *ad* Michael Bastow *ed* Norman Wanstall

Susan Hampshire, Frank Finlay, Michael Petrovitch, Michael Craze, Jack Lambert, Betty Duncan, David Garth, Tony Booth

'To depict the macabre in the midst of the everyday requires a greater degree of artifice than is displayed here.' – *MFB*

'Hampshire and Petrovitch are no Heathcliff and Cathy, and the director's "realistic" style which stops short at the genuinely macabre makes a mockery of the story's metaphysical overtones.' – *Films and Filming*

Nel Segno di Roma: see *Sign of the Gladiator*

Nell Gwyn **
GB 1934 85m bw
B and D (Herbert Wilcox)

The affair of Charles II and an orange seller.

Naïve, vivid account of a famous couple; physically cheap and rather faded, but the best film on the subject and one of the best covering this period.

w Miles Malleson *d* Herbert Wilcox *ph* F. A. Young

Anna Neagle, Cedric Hardwicke, Jeanne de Casalis, Muriel George, Miles Malleson, Esmé Percy, Moore Marriott

'Slow costumer, also lacking marquee value.' – *Variety*

The Nelson Affair: see *Bequest to the Nation*

The Nelson Touch: see *Corvette K 225*

'In The Future … It Pays To Be More Than Human.'
Nemesis
US 1993 95m colour
Imperial (Ash R. Shah, Eric Karson, Tom Karnowski)
V, V*

In Los Angeles in 2027, where most people speak with thick foreign accents, a cop shot to pieces is reassembled as an android for a special assignment and uncovers a plot to take over the world.

Derivative and violent action film, strictly for those whose idea of a good time is bimbos with big guns.

w Rebecca Charles   d Albert Pyun   ph George Mooradian   m Michel Rubini   pd E. Colleen Saro   sp Gene Warren Jnr, Fantasy II Film Effects   ed David Kern, Mark Conte

Olivier Gruner, Tim Thomerson, Cary-Hiroyuki Tagawa, Merle Kennedy, Yuji Okumoto, Marjorie Monaghan, Brion James, Deborah Shelton

'Fails in almost every respect.' – *Variety*

The Neptune Disaster: see *The Neptune Factor*

'Wherever you've been – this is where you've never been before!'

The Neptune Factor
Canada   1972   98m   DeLuxe   Panavision
TCF/Quadrant/Bellevue-Pathé (Sanford Howard)
V*

later retitled: *The Neptune Disaster*

American oceanologists conduct an experiment in underwater living.

Wet 'actioner' in which very little happens except a few porthole views of magnified fish.

w Jack de Witt   d Daniel Petrie   ph Harry Makin   m Lalo Schifrin

Ben Gazzara, Walter Pidgeon, Yvette Mimieux, Ernest Borgnine, Chris Wiggins

Neptune's Daughter *
US   1949   93m   Technicolor
MGM (Jack Cummings)
V*

A lady bathing suit designer has a South American romance.

Generally thought one of the better aquatic musicals, and certainly very typical of them and its studio at this time.

w Dorothy Kingsley   d Edward Buzzell   ph Charles Rosher   m George Stoll   songs Frank Loesser

Esther Williams, Red Skelton, Ricardo Montalban, Betty Garrett, Keenan Wynn, Xavier Cugat and his Orchestra, Mike Mazurki, Ted de Corsia, Mel Blanc

AA: song 'Baby, It's Cold Outside'

Neskolko Intervyu Po Lichnyam Voprosam:
see *Several Interviews On Personal Problems*

The Net
GB   1953   86m   bw
Rank/Two Cities (Anthony Darnborough)
US title: *Project M7*

Tension among boffins in an aviation research station leads to murder and the discovery of a spy.

Low-key suspenser, quite adequately presented.

w William Fairchild   novel John Pudney   d Anthony Asquith   ph Desmond Dickinson   m Benjamin Frankel

Phyllis Calvert, Noel Willman, Herbert Lom, James Donald, Robert Beatty, Muriel Pavlow, Walter Fitzgerald, Maurice Denham

'Television will never be the same!'
'Prepare yourself for a perfectly outrageous motion picture!'
Network ****
US   1976   121m   Metrocolor   Panavision
MGM/UA (Howard Gottfried, Fred Caruso)
V, V*, L

A network news commentator begins to say what he thinks about the world and becomes a new messiah to the people and an embarrassment to his sponsors.

A deliberately melodramatic satire on media corruption, it is passionate and compulsively watchable in its attack on demagoguery and in its

depiction of the dangerous madness exploited by the mass media. What once seemed overheated satire has come, with time, to resemble accurate reporting. Its very existence in a commercial system is as remarkable as its box-office success.

w Paddy Chayevsky   d Sidney Lumet   ph Owen Roizman   m Elliot Lawrence

Peter Finch, William Holden, Faye Dunaway, Robert Duvall, Wesley Addy, Ned Beatty, Beatrice Straight, John Carpenter

HOWARD BEALE (Peter Finch) on live television: 'I don't know what to do about the depression and the inflation and the Russians and the crime in the streets. All I know is that first you've got to get mad. You've got to say: "I'm a human being, god damn it, my life has some value!" So I want you to get up now. I want all of you to get up out of your chairs. I want you to get up right now and go to the window, open it and stick your head out and yell "I'm mad as hell, and I'm not going to take this any more!"'
Ditto: 'Ladies and gentlemen, I would like at this moment to announce that I will be retiring from this programme in two weeks' time because of poor ratings. Since this show was the only thing I had going for me in my life, I have decided to kill myself. I'm going to blow my brains out right on this programme a week from today.'
MAX SCHUMACHER (William Holden): 'You're television incarnate, Diana, indifferent to suffering, insensitive to joy. All of life is reduced to the common rubble of banality. War, murder, death – all the same to you as bottles of beer, and the daily business of life is a corrupt comedy. You even shatter the sensations of time and space into split seconds and instant replays. You're madness, Diana.'

'The cast of this messianic farce take turns yelling at us soulless masses.' – *New Yorker*

'Too much of this film has the hectoring stridency of tabloid headlines.' – *Michael Billington, Illustrated London News*

† The theme was taken up a year later in the shortlived TV series *W.E.B.*

AA: Paddy Chayevsky; Peter Finch; Faye Dunaway; Beatrice Straight
AAN: best picture; Sidney Lumet; Owen Roizman; William Holden; Ned Beatty

Neutral Port
GB   1940   92m   bw
Gainsborough

A merchant navy captain avenges the loss of his ship by sabotaging a German U-boat.

Unconvincing propaganda, rather stagily presented.

w J. B. Williams, T. J. Morrison   d Marcel Varnel

Will Fyffe, Phyllis Calvert, Leslie Banks, Yvonne Arnaud, Hugh McDermott, Frederick Valk

Nevada Smith *
US   1966   131m   Eastmancolor   Panavision
Avco/Solar (Joe Levine, Henry Hathaway)
V, V*, L

A cowboy takes a long revenge on the outlaws who murdered his parents.

Violent, sour, occasionally lively but frequently boring Western melodrama on a well worn theme.

w John Michael Hayes, from the 'early life' of a character in *The Carpetbaggers* by Harold Robbins   d Henry Hathaway   ph Lucien Ballard   m Alfred Newman

Steve McQueen, Karl Malden, Brian Keith, Suzanne Pleshette, Arthur Kennedy, Janet Margolin, Howard da Silva, Raf Vallone, Pat Hingle

The Nevadan
US   1950   81m   Cinecolor
Harry Joe Brown/Columbia
GB title: *The Man from Nevada*

A marshal recovers stolen gold.

Solid Western programmer, compromised by poor colour.

w George W. George, George F. Slavin   d Gordon Douglas

Randolph Scott, Dorothy Malone, Forrest Tucker, Frank Faylen, George Macready

Never a Dull Moment
US   1943   60m   bw
Universal

Three comedians prevent a night-club owner from carrying out a robbery.

The last thin vehicle for a famous comedy trio; even here they have their moments.

w Mel Ronson, Stanley Roberts   d Edward Lilley

The Ritz Brothers, Frances Langford, Mary Beth Hughes, George Zucco, Franklin Pangborn

Never a Dull Moment
US   1950   89m   bw
RKO (Harriet Parsons)
V*, L

A lady music critic marries a rodeo cowboy and finds life hard down on the ranch.

Very mild star programmer.

w Lou Breslow, Doris Anderson   novel Who Could Ask for Anything More? by Kay Swift   d George Marshall   ph Joseph Walker   md Constantin Bakaleinikoff   m Frederick Hollander

Irene Dunne, Fred MacMurray, William Demarest, Andy Devine, Gigi Perreau, Natalie Wood, Philip Ober, Jack Kirkwood

Never a Dull Moment
US   1967   100m   Technicolor
Walt Disney (Ron Miller)
V*, L

An unsuccessful actor is mistaken for a notorious gangster.

Slapstick romp with vigour but not much flair.

w A. J. Carothers   novel John Godey   d Jerry Paris   ph William Snyder   m Robert F. Brunner

Dick Van Dyke, Edward G. Robinson, Dorothy Provine, Henry Silva, Joanna Moore, Tony Bill, Slim Pickens, Jack Elam

'They thought he couldn't do the job: that's why they chose him!'
Never Cry Wolf
US   1983   105m   Technicolor
Walt Disney
V*, L

A scientist is dumped alone in the Arctic to collect evidence against wolves.

Weird fable whose comic asides diminish its serious intent, and whose leading characterization is so eccentric as to bewilder any audience.

w Curtis Hanson, Sam Hamm, Richard Kletter   book Farley Mowat   d Carroll Ballard

Charles Martin Smith, Brian Dennehy, Samson Jorah

'There are sequences in this movie that make your jaw drop open out of genuine amazement. To put it simply, he shows you sights you've never seen before . . . It's no mere environmentalist film, but a meditation on survival and the story of its hero's inner rebirth.' – *David Ansen, Newsweek*

Never Give a Sucker an Even Break *
US   1941   70m   bw
Universal
V*, L
GB title: *What a Man*

W. C. Fields dives off an aeroplane into the lap of a

young woman who has never seen a man; she falls in love with him.

Stupefyingly inept in its scripting and pacing, this comedy is often irresistibly funny because of the anti-everything personality of its writer-star. No one else could have got away with it, or would have been likely to try.

w John T. Neville, Prescott Chaplin   story Otis Criblecoblis (W. C. Fields)   d Edward Cline
ph Charles Van Enger   m Frank Skinner

W. C. Fields, Gloria Jean, Leon Errol, Butch and Buddy, Franklin Pangborn, Anne Nagel, Mona Barrie, Susan Miller, Margaret Dumont

'A beautifully timed exhibition of mock pomposity, puzzled ineffectualness, subtle understatement and true-blue nonchalance.' – *James Agee*

Never Give an Inch: see *Sometimes a Great Notion*

Never Let Go
GB   1960   91m   bw
Rank/Julian Wintle-Leslie Parkin (Peter de Sarigny)
V*

A travelling salesman has his car stolen and stands up to the sadistic gang boss responsible.

Brutishly unattractive thriller, apparently designed for the sole purpose of giving Peter Sellers a villainous part.

w Alun Falconer   d John Guillermin
ph Christopher Challis   m John Barry

Richard Todd, Peter Sellers, Elizabeth Sellars, Adam Faith, Carol White, Mervyn Johns, Noel Willman

Never Let Me Go
GB   1953   94m   bw
MGM (Clarence Brown)

After World War II an American correspondent marries a Russian ballerina but is later deported by the authorities.

Ho-hum romantic melodrama, quite interestingly cast.

w Ronald Millar, George Froeschel   novel *Came the Dawn* by Roger Bax   d Delmer Daves   ph Robert Krasker   m Hans May

Clark Gable, Gene Tierney, Richard Haydn, Belita, Bernard Miles, Kenneth More, Karel Stepanek, Theodore Bikel, Frederick Valk

Never Look Back
GB   1952   73m   bw
Michael Carreras/Hammer

A lady barrister finds she must defend an old boyfriend on a murder charge.

Plausible drama which never quite comes to the boil.

w John Hunter, Guy Morgan, Francis Searle
d Francis Searle

Rosamund John, Hugh Sinclair, Guy Middleton, Henry Edwards, Terence Longdon

Never Love a Stranger
US   1958   93m   bw
Harold Robbins/Allied Artists (Peter Gettlinger)
V*

A Catholic boy who has become a gangster helps his Jewish friend who has become assistant district attorney to trap a vicious hoodlum.

The old *Manhattan Melodrama* theme is dusted off once again, this time to very little effect.

w Harold Robbins, Richard Day   novel Harold Robbins   d Robert Stevens   ph Lee Garmes
m Raymond Scott

John Drew Barrymore, Steve McQueen, Robert Bray, Lita Milan, R. G. Armstrong, Salem Ludwig

Never on Sunday *
Greece   1959   97m   bw
Lopert/Melinafilm (Jules Dassin)
V*
original title: *Pote tin Kyriaki*

An American scholar in Greece is infatuated by a prostitute and sets about improving her.

Amiable if rather shoddy variation on *Pygmalion*: the star performance and the music carried it, along with its own naughtiness, to success.

wd Jules Dassin   ph Jacques Natteau   m Manos Hadjidakis

Melina Mercouri, Jules Dassin, Georges Foundas, Titos Vandis, Despo Diamantidou

'It barely stands scrutiny, but it communicates cheerfulness, and this in itself is no mean achievement.' – *Penelope Houston, MFB*

AA: title song (Manos Hadjidakis)

AAN: direction; script; Melina Mercouri

Never Put It in Writing *
GB   1963   93m   bw
MGM/Andrew Stone

A young executive tries to recover from the mail an indiscreet letter he has written to his boss.

Frantic hit-or-miss farcical comedy distinguished by Dublin locations and cast.

wd Andrew Stone   ph Martin Curtis   m Frank Cordell

Pat Boone, Fidelma Murphy, Reginald Beckwith, John Le Mesurier, Colin Blakely, Milo O'Shea

Never Say Die *
US   1939   80m   bw
Paramount (Paul Jones)

A millionaire hypochondriac is convinced he is dying.

Thin farce with Hope on the very brink of stardom; some bright moments.

w Don Hartman, Frank Butler, Preston Sturges
d Elliott Nugent   ph Leo Tover   md Boris Morros

Martha Raye, Bob Hope, Andy Devine, Alan Mowbray, Gale Sondergaard, Sig Rumann, Ernest Cossart, Monty Woolley, Christian Rub

'Needs strong support for top dual spots.' – *Variety*

'The most enjoyable film for weeks . . . consistently absurd . . . no dignity, no passion, and a magnificent cast.' – *Graham Greene*

Never Say Goodbye
US   1946   97m   bw
Warner (William Jacobs)

A seven-year-old girl draws her divorced parents back together.

Highly derivative romantic comedy mishmash which did its star's career no good at all.

w James V. Kern, I. A. L. Diamond, Lewis R. Foster, Ben and Norma Barzman   d James V. Kern
ph Arthur Edeson   m Frederick Hollander

Errol Flynn, Eleanor Parker, Lucile Watson, S. Z. Sakall, Donald Woods, Patti Brady, Forrest Tucker, Hattie McDaniel

Never Say Goodbye
US   1955   96m   Technicolor
U-I (Albert J. Cohen)

In 1945 Berlin an American army doctor marries a pianist who is later trapped in the Russian zone; they meet years later in America.

Romantic drama aimed at a female audience, remade from *This Love of Ours* (qv).

w Charles Hoffman   d Jerry Hopper   ph Maury Gertsman   m Frank Skinner

Rock Hudson, George Sanders, Cornell Borchers, Ray Collins, David Janssen

Never Say Never Again *
GB   1983   134m   Technicolor   Panavision
Warner/Woodcote/Taliafilm (Jack Schwartzman)
V, V*, L, S

James Bond foils a world domination attempt by Blofeld.

Reasonably enjoyable mishmash of Bondery; the plot is technically a remake of *Thunderball*, not that it matters much until the end, when the underwater stuff becomes tiresome because one hardly knows who is under the masks.

w Lorenzo Semple Jnr   d Irvin Kershner
ph Douglas Slocombe   m Michel Legrand
pd Philip Harrison, Stephen Grimes

Sean Connery, Klaus Maria Brandauer, Max von Sydow, Barbara Carrera, Kim Basinger, Bernie Casey, Alec McCowen, Edward Fox, Rowan Atkinson

'Q' (Alec McCowen): 'Good to see you again, Mr Bond. Let's get back to some gratuitous sex and violence, I say.'

Never So Few
US   1959   124m   Metrocolor   Cinemascope
MGM/Canterbury (Edmund Grainger)
V*, L

Adventures of World War II Americans commanding Burmese guerrillas.

Jungle actioner with pauses for philosophizing; well enough made but not very interesting.

w Millard Kaufman   novel Tom Chamales   d John Sturges   ph William H. Daniels   m Hugo Friedhofer

Frank Sinatra, Gina Lollobrigida, Peter Lawford, Steve McQueen, Paul Henreid, Richard Johnson, Brian Donlevy, Charles Bronson, Dean Jones

Never Steal Anything Small
US   1958   94m   Eastmancolor   Cinemascope
U-I (Aaron Rosenberg)
V*

The reformation of a corrupt but sympathetic dockers' union boss.

Curious semi-musical which doesn't come off at all despite excellent credentials.

wd Charles Lederer   play The Devil's Hornpipe by Rouben Mamoulian, Maxwell Anderson   ph Harold Lipstein   m Allie Wrubel   ly Maxwell Anderson
ch Hermes Pan

James Cagney, Shirley Jones, Roger Smith, Cara Williams, Nehemiah Persoff, Royal Dano, Anthony Caruso

'The closest thing to it, I'd say, is *The Threepenny Opera*. It's witty, and it has some good radical lyrics. Films must have some comment to make.' – *James Cagney*

Never Take No for an Answer *
GB   1951   82m   bw
Constellation (Anthony Havelock-Allan)

A small boy goes to Rome to get permission from the Pope to take his sick donkey to be blessed in the church.

Slight, easy-going whimsy with attractive sunlit locations.

w Paul and Pauline Gallico   novel *The Small Miracle* by Paul Gallico   d Maurice Cloche, Ralph Smart
ph Otto Heller   m Nino Rota

Vittorio Manunta, Denis O'Dea, Guido Cellano, Nerio Bernardi

'The main pleasures of this slender film are visual ones.' – *MFB*

† Remade as a TV movie *Small Miracle*.

Never Take Sweets from a Stranger
GB   1960   81m   bw   Megascope
Hammer/Columbia

In a Canadian town, a respected elderly man is accused of improper sexual advances to a child.

In the awful warning category, and rather predictable.

w John Hunter   play The Pony Cart by Roger Garis
d Cyril Frankel

Gwen Watford, Patrick Allen, Felix Aylmer, Niall MacGinnis, Bill Nagy, Janina Faye, Michael Gwynn

Never the Twain Shall Meet
US   1931   89m   bw
MGM

A young lawyer goes native when he falls for a South Sea island girl.

Stilted misalliance melodrama, previously made in 1925 as a silent with Bert Lytell and Anita Stewart; its faded notions simply didn't survive sound.

w Ruth Cummings and Edwin Justus Mayer
novel Peter B. Kyne   d W. S. Van Dyke

Leslie Howard, Conchita Montenegro, Karen Morley, C. Aubrey Smith

Never to Love: see A Bill of Divorcement (1940)

Never Too Late
US   1965   104m   Technicolor   Panavision
Warner/Lear-Yorkin (Norman Lear)

A well-to-do middle-aged housewife discovers she is pregnant.

Predictable, rather hysterical domestic comedy, flatly developed from a successful play which offered two star parts for old stagers.

w Sumner Arthur Long   play Sumner Arthur Long
d Bud Yorkin   ph Philip Lathrop   m David Rose

Paul Ford, Maureen O'Sullivan, Connie Stevens, Jim Hutton, Lloyd Nolan, Henry Jones, Jane Wyatt

Never Wave at a WAC
US   1952   87m   bw
Independent Artists (Frederick Brisson)
V*
GB title: The Private Wore Skirts

A Washington hostess joins the WACs and finds she can't get beyond the rank of private.

Pattern comedy, unconvincing in all respects but with a smattering of funny moments. Flagwaving takes over towards the end.

w Ken Englund   d Norman Z. McLeod
ph William Daniels   m Elmer Bernstein

Rosalind Russell, Paul Douglas, Marie Wilson, William Ching, Leif Erickson, Arleen Whelan, Charles Dingle

'A boy who needs a friend finds a world that needs a hero in a land beyond imagination!'
The Neverending Story *
West Germany   1984   94m   Technicolor
Technovision
Warner/Bavaria Studios/WDR/Neue Constantin Filmproduktion (Bernd Eichinger, Dieter Geissler)
V, V*, L, S

A reluctant student reads a book instead: dealing with mystical monsters and make-believe, it takes him back into their world.

Slow-starting fantasy with agreeable enough creations but not a lot of humour despite its intended stimulus to the imagination.

wd Wolfgang Petersen   novel Michael Ende
ph Jost Vacano   m Klaus Doldinger, Giorgio Moroder   pd Rolf Zehetbauer   ed Jane Seitz

Barret Oliver, Gerald McRaney, Moses Gunn, Patricia Hayes

The Neverending Story II: The Next Chapter
Germany   1990   89m   Eastmancolor   Panavision
Warner/Soriba & Dehle (Dieter Geissler)
V, V*, L

A boy and his fantasy alter-ego search for an imprisoned empress in a fairy-tale land of dreams.

Sequel that does little to expand the imagination.

w Karin Howard   novel Michael Ende   d George Miller   ph Dave Connell   m Robert Folk   pd Bob Laing, Götz Weidner   sp creature effects Colin Arthur   ed Peter Hollywood, Chris Blunden

Jonathan Brandis, Kenny Morrison, Clarissa Burt, Alexandra Johnes, Martin Umbach, John Wesley Shiff, Helena Michell, Chris Burton, Thomas Hill

The New Adventures of Don Juan: see The Adventures of Don Juan

The New Adventures of Get-Rich-Quick Wallingford
US   1931   76m   bw
MGM

Exploits of an attractive go-getter.

Reliable comedy of its day.

w Charles MacArthur   novel G. R. Chester   d Sam Wood

William Haines, Jimmy Durante, Leila Hyams, Guy Kibbee

The New Adventures of Tarzan
US   1935   bw   serial: 12 eps
Dearholt-Stout and Cohen
V*

Tarzan goes to Guatemala to find a friend captured by Mayans.

Modestly intriguing serial which was also released as two features: the first under the above title and the second as Tarzan and the Green Goddess.

w Chas F. Royal   d Edward Krull, W. F. McGaugh
ph Edward Krull, Ernest E. Smith   ad Chas Clague

Herman Brix (aka Bruce Bennett), Ula Holt, Frank Baker, Dale Walsh

The New Babylon *
USSR   1929   80m approx (24 fps)   bw   silent
Sovkino
original title: Novyi Vavilon

The rise and fall of the 1871 French commune, seen through the eyes of a girl department store worker.

Propagandist socio-historical melodrama, most interesting now for its sub-Eisenstein technique.

wd Leonid Trauberg, Grigori Kozintsev   ph Andrei Moskvin, Yevgeni Mikhailov   m Dmitri Shostakovich   ad Yevgeni Enei

Yelena Kuzmina, Pyotr Sobelevsky, Sophie Magarill

The New Barbarians
Italy   1983   91m   Telecolor
Entertainment/Deaf International (Fabrizi de Angelis)
original title: I Nuovi Barbari

In a post-holocaust future, two wandering warriors destroy a vicious gang of murdering homosexuals.

Mad Max, Italian-style, in an untalented low-budget rip-off.

w Tito Carpi, Enzo Girolami   d Enzo G. Catellari
ph Fausto Amicucci   m Claudio Simonetti
pd Antonio Visune   ed Gianfranco Amicucci

Fred Williamson, Timothy Brent, George Eastman, Anna Kanakis, Thomas Moore

The New Centurions *
US   1972   103m   Eastmancolor   Panavision
Columbia/Chartoff-Winkler
V*, L
GB title: Precinct 45: Los Angeles Police

An old cop teaches a new one.

'Realistic' crime prevention saga which spawned the TV series Police Story and Police Woman. Well done within its limits.

w Stirling Silliphant   novel Joseph Wambaugh
d Richard Fleischer   ph Ralph Woolsey   m Quincy Jones

George C. Scott, Stacy Keach, Jane Alexander, Rosalind Cash, Scott Wilson

New Face in Hell: see P.J.

New Faces *
US   1954   99m   Eastmancolor   Cinemascope
Edward L. Alperson (Leonard Sillman)
V*

A revue goes on despite money problems.

Five minutes of plot, ninety-five minutes of revue from the Broadway stage; mostly quite amusing, and chiefly notable for introducing Eartha Kitt with all her standards.

w various   d Harry Horner   ph Lucien Ballard
m Raoul Kraushaar   revue deviser John Murray Anderson

Eartha Kitt, Ronny Graham, Alice Ghostley, Robert Clary, Paul Lynde

New Faces of 1937
US   1937   105m   bw
RKO
L

Talent auditions for a Broadway show.

Shapeless agglomeration of variety acts with a wisp of story; the level of talent is not outstandingly high.

w Nat Perrin, P. G. Epstein, Irving Brecher, Harold Russell, Harry Clork, Howard J. Green
story Shoestring by George Bradshaw   d Leigh Jason

Joe Penner, Milton Berle, Parkyakarkus, Harriet Hilliard, Jerome Cowan, Bert Gordon, Ann Miller, Richard Lane

'A hodgepodge of vaudeville, night club and radio talent, unskilfully blended and rather inanely promulgated.' – Variety

The New Gulliver *
USSR   1933   85m approx   bw

Gulliver's Travels is retold in puppet form, but the plot has become a satire against capitalism.

Interesting both as animation and as propaganda.

w A. Ptoushko, B. Roshal   d Alexander Ptoushko, A. Vanitchkin

'The invention is often delightful (one wonders how such humour in detail can exist with so humourless a philosophy), and the marvellous ingenuity of the puppets is beyond praise.' – Graham Greene, The Spectator

The New Interns
US   1964   123m   bw
Columbia (Robert Cohn)

Young doctors at a city hospital have trouble saving a rapist and his victim.

Unnecessary sequel to The Interns, its 'realism' requiring large pinches of salt.

w Wilton Schiller   d John Rich   ph Lucien Ballard
m Earle Hagen

George Segal, Telly Savalas, Michael Callan, Dean Jones, Inger Stevens, Stefanie Powers, Lee Patrick

New Jack City **
US   1991   100m   Technicolor
Warner (Doug McHenry, George Jackson)
V, V*, L, S

Undercover cops go after a successful gangster dealing drugs in Harlem.

Fast-moving, street-wise thriller with an anti-drugs stance.

w Thomas Lee Wright, Barry Michael Cooper d Mario Van Peebles ph Francis Kenny m Michael Colombier pd Charles C. Bennett ed Steven Kemper, Kevin Stitt

Wesley Snipes, Ice T, Allen Payne, Chris Rock, Mario Van Peebles, Michael Michele, Bill Nunn, Russell Wong, Bill Cobbs

'A provocative, pulsating update on gangster pics.' – Variety

A New Kind of Love

US 1963 110m Technicolor
Paramount/Llenroc (Melville Shavelson)

An American dress designer in Paris is softened by a boorish newspaper columnist.

Very thin sex comedy, dressed to kill but with nowhere to go.

wd Melville Shavelson ph Daniel Fapp m Leith Stevens

Paul Newman, Joanne Woodward, Maurice Chevalier, Thelma Ritter, George Tobias

AAN: Leith Stevens

The New Land: see The Emigrants

A New Leaf *

US 1970 102m Movielab
Paramount/Aries/Elkins (Joe Manduke)
V*

A middle-aged playboy, close to bankruptcy, thinks of acquiring a wealthy wife.

Agreeably mordant comedy which sparkles in patches rather than as a whole.

wd Elaine May, story The Green Heart by Jack Ritchie ph Gayne Rescher m John Mandel, Neal Hefti pd Richard Fried

Walter Matthau, Elaine May, Jack Weston, George Rose, William Redfield, James Coco

'Unashamedly a thirties fairy tale in modern, but not fashionable, dress.' – Jan Dawson

A New Life

US 1988 104m Technicolor Panavision
Paramount (Martin Bregman)
V*, L

A middle-aged couple divorce and find new partners and problems.

Occasionally wry, but more often sentimental, romantic comedy.

wd Alan Alda ph Kelvin Pike m Joseph Turrin pd Barbara Dunphy ed William Reynolds

Alan Alda, Ann-Margret, Hal Linden, Veronica Hamel, John Shea, Mary Kay Place

New Mexico

US 1952 78m Anscocolor
Irving Allen/United Artists

A cavalry officer tries to make peace with the Indians, but when an Indian child is accidentally killed a savage war breaks out.

Standard Western, not badly made.

w Max Trell d Irving Reis

Lew Ayres, Marilyn Maxwell, Robert Hutton, Andy Devine, Raymond Burr, Jeff Corey

New Moon *

US 1940 105m bw
MGM (Robert Z. Leonard)
V*

Romance in old French Louisiana.

Stalwart adaptation of an operetta previously filmed in 1930 with Lawrence Tibbett and Grace Moore.

w Jacques Deval, Robert Arthur d Robert Z. Leonard ph William Daniels m/y Sigmund Romberg, Oscar Hammerstein

Jeanette MacDonald, Nelson Eddy, Mary Boland, George Zucco, H. B. Warner, Stanley Fields, Grant Mitchell

New Morals for Old

US 1932 77m bw
MGM

John Van Druten's play After All, about the generation gap in the London aristocracy, was here rather unwisely translated to the American middle class and emerged as a decided curiosity.

w Zelda Sears, Wanda Tuchock d Charles Brabin

Robert Young, Myrna Loy, Jean Hersholt, Lewis Stone, Laura Hope Crews, Elizabeth Patterson

'A weak sister, swathed in gloom, muddled, and without names that will draw.' – Variety

New Orleans *

US 1947 89m bw
Jules Levey

How jazz was born, according to the movies.

Routine low-budgeter enlivened by a splendid array of guest musicians.

w Elliot Paul, Dick Irving Hyland d Arthur Lubin ph Lucien Andriot md Nathaniel Finston

Louis Armstrong and his All Stars, Arturo de Cordova, Dorothy Patrick, Billie Holiday, Meade Lux Lewis, Woody Herman and his Orchestra

New Wine

US 1941 89m bw
Gloria/UA
GB title: The Great Awakening

Franz Schubert seeks the patronage of Beethoven and sacrifices his love life to music.

Weirdly cast romantic drama, rather fumbling in all departments.

w Howard Estabrook and Nicholas Jory d Reinhold Schunzel

Alan Curtis (as Schubert!), Ilona Massey, Albert Basserman, Binnie Barnes, Sterling Holloway

New Year's Day *

US 1989 92m Technicolor
Contemporary/International Rainbow/Jagfilm (Judith Wolinsky)
V*

A writer moves back from Los Angeles to his New York apartment and becomes involved in the lives of three young women, his previous tenants, and their friends.

A conversation piece, in which a varied group sound off about their lives and loves in a manner ranging from the engaging to the uninteresting; worth a listen for the most part.

wd Henry Jaglom ph Joey Forsyte ad Barbara Flood ed Ruth Zucker Ward

Maggie Jakobson, Gwen Welles, Henry Jaglom, Devid Duchovny, Milos Forman, Michael Emil, Donna Germain, Tracy Reiner, Harvey Miller, Irene Moore

'Warm, perceptive, wryly comic.' – Philip French, Observer

New York Confidential

US 1955 87m bw
Warner/Russel Rouse, Clarence Greene

The head of a crime syndicate is assassinated by his own hired killer.

Unexciting 'realistic' thriller with the gangsters presented as family and businessmen; seventeen years later The Godfather did it rather better.

w Clarence Greene, Russel Rouse d Russel Rouse ph Edward Fitzgerald m Joseph Mullendore pd Fernando Carrere

Broderick Crawford, Richard Conte, Anne Bancroft, Marilyn Maxwell, Onslow Stevens, J. Carrol Naish, Barry Kelley, Mike Mazurki, Celia Lovsky

The New York Hat *

US 1912 10m approx (24 fps) bw silent
D. W. Griffith

A small-town minister is gossiped about when he buys a hat for a young girl.

Influential early short story film with good local backgrounds.

w Anita Loos d D. W. Griffith ph Billy Bitzer

Mary Pickford, Lionel Barrymore, Lillian Gish, Dorothy Gish, Robert Harron, Mack Sennett, Mae Marsh

New York, New York *

US 1977 153m Technicolor Panavision
UA/Chartoff-Winkler (Gene Kirkwood)
V, V*, L

In the late forties in New York, a single-minded saxophonist fails to do right by his girlfriend, who becomes a Hollywood star.

A clever recreation of the big band era, hampered by gross overlength, unattractive characters and a pessimistic plot.

w Earl Mac Rauch, Mardik Martin d Martin Scorsese ph Laszlo Kovacs md Ralph Burns pd Boris Leven

Liza Minnelli, Robert de Niro, Lionel Stander, Barry Primus

New York Nights

US 1929 81m bw
UA/Talmadge

A musical comedy star has a husband who drinks, and she accepts help from a gangster.

The star's sound début was a hit-and-miss affair composed of familiar elements.

w Jules Furthman play Tin Pan Alley by Hugh Stanislaus Stange d Lewis Milestone

Norma Talmadge, Gilbert Roland, John Wray, Lilyan Tashman, Roscoe Karns

'Good performance, fair picture.' – Variety

New York Stories **

US 1989 124m Technicolor
Warner/Touchstone (Robert Greenhut)
V*, L, S

Anthology of three stories: 'Life Lessons', dealing with a painter's attitude to life and art; 'Life Without Zoë', in which a 12-year-old girl brings her parents back together; and 'Oedipus Wrecks', in which a son is tyrannized by his mother materializing in the sky over New York.

Worth watching for Scorsese's sharp look at the art world and Allen's ultimate Jewish mother joke. Sandwiched between them is Coppola at his most disastrously winsome.

w Richard Price, Francis Coppola, Sofia Coppola, Woody Allen d Martin Scorsese, Francis Coppola, Woody Allen ph Nestor Almedros, Vittorio Storaro, Sven Nykvist m Carmine Coppola, Kid Creole and the Coconuts pd Kristi Zea, Dean Tavoularis, Santo Loquasto ed Thelma Schoonmaker, Barry Malkin, Susan E. Morse

Nick Nolte, Patrick O'Neal, Rosanna Arquette, Heather McComb, Talia Shire, Gia Coppola, Giancarlo Giannini, Woody Allen, Marvin Chatinover, Mae Questel, Mia Farrow

New York Town

US 1941 94m bw
Paramount (Anthony Veiller)

A girl new to the Big Apple befriends a sidewalk photographer.

Flat romantic comedy, a soufflé which doesn't rise despite the talents involved.

w Lewis Seltzer (and, uncredited, Preston Sturges) d Charles Vidor (and Sturges) ph Charles Schoenbaum m Leo Shuken

Fred MacMurray, Mary Martin, Robert Preston, Akim Tamiroff, Lynne Overman, Eric Blore, Cecil Kellaway, Fuzzy Knight

Newman's Law
US 1974 99m Technicolor
Universal (Richard Irving)

A cop uses unconventional methods to trap drug smugglers.

Very routine police actioner, just above TV movie level.

w Anthony Wilson d Richard Heffron ph Vilis Lapenieks m Robert Prince

George Peppard, Roger Robinson, Eugene Roche, Gordon Pinsent, Abe Vigoda

The News Boys: see Newsies

News Is Made at Night
US 1939 72m bw
TCF

To boost circulation, a news editor pins a string of murders on a well-known gangster, and soon regrets it.

Pacy crime comedy-drama, very acceptable as the lower half of a double bill.

w John Larkin d Alfred Werker

Preston Foster, Lynn Bari, Eddie Collins, Russell Gleason, George Barbier, Charles Halton

'Above average B; should do all right where properly placed.' – Variety

Newsboys' Home
US 1939 73m bw
Universal

A girl inherits a newspaper which sponsors a home for boys.

Modest debut for the East Side Kids, a spin-off group from the Dead End Kids.

w Gordon Kahn d Harold Young

Jackie Cooper, Edmund Lowe, Wendy Barrie, Edward Norris, Samuel S. Hinds; and Elisha Cook Jnr, Hally Chester, Harris Berger, David Gorcey, Billy Benedict, Charles Duncan

'Another in the tough kid cycle. Will easily handle its end of dual depots.' – Variety

Newsfront **
Australia 1978 110m colour/bw
Palm Beach Productions (David Elfick)
V*, L

In the fifties, rival news teams battle to get the best shots for cinema newsreels.

Lively nostalgic feature with slick modern technique.

wd Phillip Noyce, from a concept by David Elfick ph Vincent Monton pd Lissa Coote ed John Scott

Bill Hunter, Wendy Hughes, Gerald Kennedy, Chris Haywood

Newsies
US 1992 121m Technicolor Panavision
Warner/Walt Disney/Touchwood Pacific Partners I (Michael Finnell)
V*, L, S

In the 1890s news boys in New York call a strike when a newspaper publisher charges them more for his papers.

Unsuccessful attempt to create a youthful musical – the model seems to be Oliver! but it lacks any Dickensian dimension despite its subplot of the exploitation of child labour.

w Bob Tzudiker, Noni White d Kenny Ortega ph Andrew Laszlo m Alan Menken pd William Sandell ch Kenny Ortega, Peggy Holmes ed William Reynolds

Christian Bale, Bill Pullman, Ann-Margret, Robert Duvall, David Moscow, Ele Keats, Kevin Tighe, Luke Edwards

'With many catchy if forgettable ditties littered throughout, one is led to the inevitable conclusion that nine-year-old girls will just love it.' – Angie Errigo, Empire

The Next Man
US 1976 107m Technicolor
Artists Entertainment Complex (Martin Bregman)

A female assassin is hired to kill the Saudi Arabian Minister of State at the United Nations.

Fractured and uninteresting thriller in which all manner of cinematic styles obscure the storyline but point up the lack of narrative skill.

w Mort Fine, Alan R. Trustman, David M. Wolf, Michael Chapman d Richard C. Sarafian ph Michael Chapman m Michael Kamen pd Gene Callahan

Sean Connery, Cornelia Sharpe, Albert Paulsen, Adolfo Celi, Charles Cioffi

'The director takes forever to set up the film's premise, and then he lingers over interminable street festivals and lush scenery.' – Dave Pomeroy, Film Information

The Next of Kin ***
GB 1942 102m bw
Ealing (S. C. Balcon)

Careless talk causes loss of life in a commando raid.

A propaganda instructional film which was made so entertainingly that it achieved commercial success and remains an excellent example of how to make a bitter pill palatable.

w Thorold Dickinson, Basil Bartlett, Angus Macphail, John Dighton d Thorold Dickinson ph Ernest Palmer m William Walton

Mervyn Johns, Nova Pilbeam, Stephen Murray, Reginald Tate, Basil Radford, Naunton Wayne, Geoffrey Hibbert, Philip Friend, Mary Clare, Basil Sydney

'The detail everywhere is curious and surprising, with something of the fascination of a Simenon crime being unravelled.' – William Whitebait

Next of Kin
Australia 1982 86m Eastmancolor
Miracle/SIS Productions/Filmco (Robert Le Tet)

A young girl teacher inherits an old people's home, and finds murder lurking.

Slow-starting but finally over-the-top melodrama, with elements borrowed from Psycho, Taste of Fear and a score of other creepies.

w Michael Heath, Tony Williams d Tony Williams ph Gary Hansen m Klaus Schulze ad Richard Francis, Nick Hepworth ed Max Lemon

Jackie Kerin, John Jarratt, Alex Scott, Gerda Nicolson

'Genre awareness is one thing; a dreary sense of déjà vu is another matter entirely.' – Paul Taylor, MFB

Next of Kin
US 1989 108m Metrocolor
Warner/Lorimar (Les Alexander, Don Enright)
V, V*, L

Two brothers, one a cop, the other a hillbilly, take their revenge when another brother is killed by gangsters.

Dreary action movie of no originality.

w Michael Jenning, Jeb Stuart d John Irvin ph Steven Poster m Jack Nitzsche, Gary Chang, Todd Hayen pd Jack T. Collis ed Peter Honess

Patrick Swayze, Liam Neeson, Adan Baldwin, Helen Hunt, Andreas Katsulas, Bill Paxton, Ben Stiller, Michael J. Pollard, Ted Levine

The Next One
US 1984 105m colour
Allstar Productions (Constantine Vlachakis)
V*

An American widow, living on a Greek island, becomes involved with a mysterious stranger she finds washed up on the beach.

Glossy, dull fantasy about a man from the future with a Christ complex, made in 1981.

wd Nico Mastorakis ph Ari Stavrou m Stanley Myers pd Paul Acciari ed George Rosenberg

Keir Dullea, Adrienne Barbeau, Peter Hobbs, Phaedon Georgitsis, Betty Arvanitis, Jeremy Licht

Next Stop Greenwich Village *
US 1975 111m Movielab
TCF (Paul Mazursky, Tony Ray)
V*

In 1953 in a poor quarter of New York, a young Jew tries to stretch his wings.

A bumper bundle of Jewish clichés dressed up as autobiography, and switching abruptly from comedy to tragedy and back. Vivid, but not exactly entertaining.

wd Paul Mazursky ph Arthur Ornitz m Bill Conti

Lenny Baker, Shelley Winters, Ellen Greene, Lois Smith, Dori Brenner

'Some tartly comic observation, but the fragmented structure keeps the mixture inert.' – Sight and Sound

The Next Time I Marry
US 1938 64m bw
RKO

In order to become the richest girl in America, an heiress must marry in haste.

Tedious comedy which falls apart halfway.

w John Twist and Helen Meinardi d Garson Kanin

Lucille Ball, James Ellison, Lee Bowman, Granville Bates, Mantan Moreland

'A very poor entry. The story is banal, production values poor, direction sloppy and most of the performances bad.' – Variety

Next Time We Live: see Next Time We Love

Next Time We Love
US 1936 87m bw
Universal (Paul Kohner)
GB title: Next Time We Live

The wife of a war correspondent has plenty of time for romance.

Romantic drama which badly needs an injection of comedy.

w Melville Baker stories Ursula Parrott d Edward H. Griffith ph Joseph Valentine m Franz Waxman

Margaret Sullavan, Ray Milland, James Stewart, Grant Mitchell, Robert McWade

'Draggy, complex tale . . . will have to be sold on the star's past performances.' – Variety

Next to No Time
GB 1958 93m Eastmancolor
British Lion/Montpelier (Albert Fennell)

A meek-and-mild engineer crossing the Atlantic gains confidence when told that anything is possible during the hour 'lost' every day.

Whimsical comedy which never gains momentum.

wd Henry Cornelius story The Enchanted Hour by Paul Gallico ph Freddie Francis m Georges Auric

Kenneth More, Betsy Drake, Bessie Love, Harry Green, Roland Culver, Reginald Beckwith, John Welsh, John Laurie, Howard Marion-Crawford

The Next Voice You Hear *
US 1950 83m bw
MGM (Dore Schary)
V*

God speaks to mankind on the radio, and the life of Joe Smith American is changed.

Soppy parable, the archetypal instance of Schary's reign of do-goodery at MGM. (He wrote a book about it, Case History of a Movie.) The idea is handled with deadly reverence, and falls quite flat, while the depiction of the inhabitants of American suburbia is depressing.

w Charles Schnee d William Wellman ph William Mellor m David Raksin

James Whitmore, Nancy Davis, Lillian Bronson, Jeff Corey

'The sins of the American working man are singularly uninteresting and their obliteration seems scarcely to require the very voice of God.' – Henry Hart

Ni ju-seiki Shonen Dokuhon: see Circus Boys

'A raging torrent of emotion that even nature can't control!'
Niagara ***
US 1952 89m Technicolor
TCF (Charles Brackett)
V, V*, L

While visiting Niagara Falls, a faithless wife is plotting to murder her husband, but he turns the tables.

Excellent suspenser with breathtaking locations; in the best Hitchcock class though slightly marred by the emphasis on Monroe's wiggly walk (it was her first big part).

w Charles Brackett, Walter Reisch, Richard Breen d Henry Hathaway ph Joe MacDonald m Sol Kaplan

Joseph Cotten, Jean Peters, Marilyn Monroe, Don Wilson, Casey Adams

'The story is most imaginatively treated, the production values are excellent.' – CEA Film Report

'Seen from any angle, the Falls and Miss Monroe leave little to be desired.' – New York Times

'A masterly example of fluid screen narrative.' – Charles Higham

'It would have turned out a much better picture if James Mason had played the husband as I wanted. He has that intensity, that neurotic edge. He was all set to do it, but his daughter Portland said she was sick of seeing him die in his pictures.' – Henry Hathaway

'This isn't a good movie but it's compellingly tawdry and nasty . . . the only movie that explored the mean, unsavoury potential of Marilyn Monroe's cuddly, infantile perversity.' – Pauline Kael, 70s

Niagara Falls
US 1941 43m bw
Hal Roach

Confusion reigns in a hotel overlooking the falls.

Potted farce in the producer's season of 'shorties'; not the worst, but far from brilliant.

w Paul Gerard Smith, Hal Yates, Eugene Conrad d Gordon Douglas

ZaSu Pitts, Slim Summerville, Tom Brown, Marjorie Woodworth, Chester Clute

Nice Girl? *
US 1941 95m bw
Universal (Joe Pasternak)

A teenager finds herself in demand by two older men.

Amusing romantic trifle supposed to mark the growing up of Universal's great teenage star.

w Richard Connell, Gladys Lehman d William A. Seiter ph Joseph Valentine md Charles Previn

Deanna Durbin, Franchot Tone, Robert Stack, Walter Brennan, Robert Benchley, Helen Broderick, Ann Gillis

A Nice Girl Like Me
GB 1969 91m Eastmancolor
Anglo Embassy/Partisan (Roy Millichip)

A sheltered young lady sets out to see life but keeps getting pregnant.

Insufferable romantic whimsy, made to look like a marathon TV commercial but never so interesting.

w Anne Piper, Desmond Davis d Desmond Davis ph Gil Taylor, Manny Wynn m Pat Williams

Barbara Ferris, Harry Andrews, Gladys Cooper, Joyce Carey, Bill Hinnant, James Villiers, Christopher Guinee, Fabia Drake

'High-toned woman's magazine nostalgia.' – MFB

A Nice Little Bank That Should Be Robbed
US 1958 87m bw Cinemascope
TCF (Anthony Muto)
GB title: How to Rob a Bank

Two incompetent crooks rob a bank and buy a racehorse.

Feeble comedy, a sad waste of its stars.

w Sidney Boehm d Henry Levin ph Leo Tover m Lionel Newman

Mickey Rooney, Tom Ewell, Mickey Shaughnessy, Dina Merrill

Nicholas and Alexandra *
GB 1971 189m Eastmancolor Panavision
Columbia/Horizon (Sam Spiegel)
V, V*, L

The life of Tsar Nicholas II from 1904 to the execution of the family in 1918.

Inflated epic of occasional interest, mainly for its sets; generally heavy going.

w James Goldman book Robert K. Massie d Franklin Schaffner ph Frederick A. Young m Richard Rodney Bennett pd John Box

Michael Jayston, Janet Suzman, Laurence Olivier, Jack Hawkins, Tom Baker, Harry Andrews, Michael Redgrave, Alexander Knox

† Original preferred casting: Rex Harrison, Vanessa Redgrave

AA: art direction; costumes (Yvonne Blake, Antonio Castillo)

AAN: best picture; Frederick A. Young; Richard Rodney Bennett; Janet Suzman

Nicholas Nickleby **
GB 1947 108m bw
Ealing (John Croydon)
V, V*

The adventures of a Victorian schoolmaster, deprived of his rightful fortune, who joins a band of travelling entertainers.

Quite tasteful and expert but too light-handed potted version of Dickens, which suffered by comparison with the David Lean versions.

w John Dighton novel Charles Dickens d Alberto Cavalcanti ph Gordon Dines m Lord Berners

Derek Bond, Cedric Hardwicke, Alfred Drayton, Sybil Thorndike, Stanley Holloway, James Hayter, Sally Ann Howes, Jill Balcon, Cyril Fletcher, Fay Compton

'Here's richness! Not all the novel, perhaps, but enough to make a film full of the Dickens spirit.' – Star

Nick Carter, Master Detective
US 1939 57m bw
MGM (Lucien Hubbard)

Carter uncovers a spy ring in a plane factory.

Dull, devitalized version of the old dime novel adventures; generally characterless and unmemorable.

w Bertram Millhauser d Jacques Tourneur

Walter Pidgeon, Rita Johnson, Henry Hull, Stanley Ridges, Donald Meek, Addison Richards, Milburn Stone, Martin Kosleck

'Just another screen sleuth.' – Variety

The Nickel Queen
Australia 1971 89m colour
Fox/Rank/Woomera (Bob Austin, Lee Robinson)

A back country barmaid becomes a rich woman with a nickel share in the mineral boom; but she is swindled by con men.

Mild comedy-drama.

w Henry C. James, John McCallum, Joy Cavill d John McCallum

Googie Withers, John McCallum, John Laws, Ed Devereaux

The Nickel Ride
US 1975 110m DeLuxe
TCF
V*

A wheeler dealer in downtown Los Angeles learns that he is marked for elimination.

Unpleasant and entirely uninteresting low-life crime melodrama.

w Eric Roth d Robert Mulligan

Jason Miller, Linda Haynes, Victor French, John Hillerman, Bo Hopkins

Nickelodeon *
US/GB 1976 122m Metrocolor
Columbia/EMI/Chartoff-Winkler (Frank Marshall)
V

In 1910, various characters come together to make movies, finally attending the 1915 opening in Hollywood of The Birth of a Nation.

What should have been a hugely entertaining chunk of comic nostalgia is killed stone dead by embarrassed acting, poor timing, and a general lack of funny ideas, despite having so much to borrow from.

w W. D. Richter, Peter Bogdanovich d Peter Bogdanovich ph Laszlo Kovacs md Richard Hazard

Ryan O'Neal, Burt Reynolds, Tatum O'Neal, Brian Keith, Stella Stevens, John Ritter, Jane Hitchcock

'Ponderous slapstick and a pathetic parody of Harold Lloyd.' – Sight and Sound

'Another collection of scenes from other people's films.' – Howard Kissel, Women's Wear Daily

'The slightest familiarity with the early works of Hal Roach – not to mention D. W. Griffith, here pretentiously quoted – reveals how little Bogdanovich understands his vastly superior predecessors.' – Robert Asahina, New Leader

'The crudest, stupidest, unfunniest farce of this or any other year.' – John Simon, New York

Nick's Movie: see Lightning Over Water

Nicky and Gino
US   1988   109m   DeLuxe
Rank/Orion (Marvin Minoff, Mike Farrell)
V*, L, S
aka: *Dominick and Eugene*

A hospital doctor tries to keep his brain-damaged twin brother out of trouble.

Sentimental drama of no particular distinction.

w Alvin Sargent, Corey Blechman   *story* Danny Porfirio   *d* Robert M. Young   *ph* Curtis Clark   *pd* Doug Kraner   *ed* Arthur Coburn – Trevor Jones

Tom Hulce, Ray Liotta, Jamie Lee Curtis, Todd Graff, Bill Cobbs, David Strathairn, Mimi Cecchini, Robert Levine

Nico: see *Above the Law*

The Niebelungen ***
Germany   1924   bw   silent
Decla-Bioscop (Erich Pommer)
Part One: 'Siegfried': 115m approx (24 fps)
Part Two: 'Kriemheld's Revenge': 125m approx (24 fps)

Siegfried kills a dragon and marries a princess of Burgundy but the fierce queen Brunhilde arranges his death. His widow marries Attila the Hun and they massacre the Burgundians.

Stately, warlike legends are transformed into a slow, chilling, awe-inspiring sequence of films, the décor being of special interest. The films were conceived as a tribute to the German nation, and were among Hitler's favourites.

w Thea von Harbou   *d* Fritz Lang   *ph* Carl Hoffman, Günther Rittau   *ad* Otto Hunte, Karl Vollbrecht, Erich Kettelhut

Paul Richter, Marguerite Schön, Theodor Loos, Hannah Ralph, Rudolph Klein-Rogge

'They all loved him – a schoolteacher, a night club hostess, and a luscious society bud!'

Night After Night *
US   1932   76m   bw
Paramount

An ex-boxer seeking refinement buys a night-club and falls for a socialite.

Dim little drama which is remembered for introducing Mae West to the screen with her famous line, 'Goodness had nothing to do with it'.

w Vincent Laurence   *novel* *Single Night* by Louis Bromfield   *d* Archie Mayo   *ph* Ernest Haller

George Raft, Constance Cummings, Wynne Gibson, *Mae West*, Alison Skipworth, Roscoe Karns, Louis Calhern

'Mae West stole everything but the cameras. I never made another picture with her. I knew she had me licked.' – *George Raft*

Night Ambush: see *Ill Met by Moonlight*

Night and Day *
US   1946   132m   Technicolor
Warner (Arthur Schwarz)
V, V*

The life of Cole Porter.

Or rather, a fictitious story about a composer who happens to be called Cole Porter. A careful but undistinguished musical with pleasant moments.

w Charles Hoffman, Leo Townsend, William Bowers   *d* Michael Curtiz   *ph* Peverell Marley, William V. Skall   *md* Max Steiner, Ray Heindorf   *m/ly* Cole Porter   *ch* Le Roy Prinz

Cary Grant, Alexis Smith, Monty Woolley, Mary Martin, Ginny Simms, Jane Wyman, Eve Arden, Victor Francen, Alan Hale, Dorothy Malone

AAN: Max Steiner, Ray Heindorf

Night and Day *
France   1991   100m   colour
Artificial Eye/Pierre Grise Productions (Martine Marignac, Maurice Tinchant)
original title: *Nuit et Jour*

A woman has simultaneous and passionate affairs with two men.

A celebration of guilt-free sex, rather than love, with men depicted as adjuncts to a strong woman.

wd Chantal Akerman   *ph* Jean-Claude Neckelbrouck   *m* Marc Herouet   *ad* Michel Vandestein, Dominique Douret   *ed* Francine Sandberg, Camille Bordes-Resnais

Guillaine Londez, Thomas Langmann, François Negret, Nicole Colchat, Pierre Laroche

Night and Fog *
France   1955   31m   Eastmancolor
Argos/Como
V
original title: *Nuit et Brouillard*

An account of the concentration camp at Auschwitz, contrasted with the peaceful surroundings ten years after its disbandment.

An official film of great dignity.

d/ed Alain Resnais   *ph* Ghislain Cloquet, Sacha Vierny

Night and the City
GB   1950   101m   bw
TCF (Samuel G. Engel)
V*

A crooked wrestling promoter is tracked down by an underworld gang.

A fated attempt to extend the success of *Naked City* in a London setting; the surface is accomplished enough, but the plot and characters are just plain dull, especially as little is seen of the police.

w Jo Eisinger   *novel* Gerald Kersh   *d* Jules Dassin   *ph* Max Greene   *m* Benjamin Frankel

Richard Widmark, Gene Tierney, Googie Withers, Hugh Marlow, Herbert Lom

'Brilliantly photographed, it is an example of neo-expressionist techniques at their most potent.' – *Richard Roud, 1964*

'When you're down to your last dream, you either live it or lose it.'

Night and the City
US   1992   104m   colour
First Independent/Penta/Tribeca (Jane Rosenthal, Irwin Winkler)
V, V*, L, S

A small-time lawyer talks himself into trouble when he sets up as a boxing promoter and has an affair with the wife of one of his backers.

Dully directed, the movie comes to life only spasmodically; for the most part, it just lies there, completely inert.

w Richard Price   *novel* Gerald Kersh   *d* Irwin Winkler   *ph* Tak Fujimoto   *m* James Newton Howard   *pd* Peter Larkin   *ed* David Brenner

Robert de Niro, Jessica Lange, Cliff Gorman, Jack Warden, Alan King, Eli Wallach, Barry Primus

'It resembles a cigarette lighter with a worn flint and a dry wick that never ignites, leaving everyone with bruised thumbs from vainly flicking the spiked wheel.' – *Philip French, Observer*

'A useless film.' – *Rupert Murdoch*

† A remake of Jules Dassin's 1950 film.

The Night Angel
US   1931   75m   bw
Paramount

A Prague lawyer falls for the daughter of the brothel

keeper he has sent to prison, and after killing a jealous suitor is himself accused of murder.

Would-be Dietrichean high-style melodrama which did its stars no good at all and virtually ended Miss Carroll's career.   *wd* Edmund Goulding

Fredric March, Nancy Carroll, Alan Hale, Alison Skipworth, Katherine Emmett

'Mild and frequently boring entertainment of the kind that can just about last a week in most of the de luxers.' – *Variety*

A Night at Earl Carroll's
US   1940   63m   bw
Paramount

When gangsters kidnap stars of Earl Carroll's night-club, the restaurant staff put on their own show.

Tinseltown time-passer which served a very small purpose.

w Lynn Starling   *d* Kurt Neumann

Ken Murray, J. Carrol Naish, Lilian Cornell, Blanche Stewart

A Night at the Opera ****
US   1935   96m   bw
MGM (Irving Thalberg)
V, V*, L

Three zanies first wreck, then help an opera company.

Certainly among the best of the Marxian extravaganzas, and the first to give them a big production to play with as well as musical interludes by other than themselves for a change of pace. The mix plays beautifully.

w George S. Kaufman, Morrie Ryskind   *d* Sam Wood   *ph* Merritt Gerstad   *md* Herbert Stothart

Groucho, Chico, Harpo (Zeppo absented himself from here on), *Margaret Dumont*, Kitty Carlisle, Allan Jones, Walter Woolf King, *Sig Rumann*

'Corking comedy with the brothers at par and biz chances excellent . . . songs in a Marx picture are generally at a disadvantage because they're more or less interruptions, the customers awaiting the next laugh.' – *Variety*

Night Beat
GB   1948   91m   bw
BLPA (Harold Huth)

Demobbed, a commando becomes a policeman and his friend becomes a crook.

Manhattan Melodrama, British style; no more than an adequate offering of its type.

w T. J. Morrison, Roland Pertwee, Robert Westerby   *d* Harold Huth   *ph* Vaclav Vich   *m* Benjamin Frankel   *ed* Grace Garland

Anne Crawford, Maxwell Reed, Ronald Howard, Christine Norden, Hector Ross, Sidney James

Night Boat to Dublin
GB   1945   99m   bw
ABP (Hamilton Inglis)

An MI5 man saves an atom scientist from kidnapping.

Generally watchable low key thriller with familiar British ingredients.

w Lawrence Huntington, Robert Hall   *d* Lawrence Huntington   *ph* Otto Heller

Robert Newton, Raymond Lovell, Muriel Pavlow, Guy Middleton, Herbert Lom, Martin Miller, Marius Goring

The Night Caller *
GB   1965   84m   bw
New Art/Armitage
US title: *Blood Beast from Outer Space*

An alien being arrives on Earth to abduct girls for genetic purposes.

Reasonably well made science fiction thriller.

w Jim O'Connelly   *novel* Frank Crisp   *d* John Gilling

John Saxon, Maurice Denham, Patricia Haines, Alfred Burke, John Carson, Jack Watson, Warren Mitchell

Night Caller (dubbed)

France/Italy   1975   125m   Eastmancolor
Columbia-Warner/Cerito/Mondial (Henri Verneuil)
original title: *Peur sur la Ville*

A moody inspector, obsessed with his personal vendetta against a crook, pays little attention to tracking down a serial killer who is murdering women.

Slight but enjoyable thriller, with some fancy stunts to enliven a familiar story.

w Henri Verneuil, Francis Veber   *d* Henri Verneuil   *ph* Jean Penzer   *m* Ennio Morricone   *ad* Jean André   *ed* Pierre Gillette, Henri Lanoë

Jean-Paul Belmondo, Charles Denner, Catherine Morin, Adalberto-Maria Merli, Lea Massari, Giovanni Cianfriglia, Rosy Varte, Henri-Jacques Huet

'A routine policier, which seems to have one eye on the American tough cop series.' – *John Gillett, MFB*

Night Club Hostess: see *Unmarried*

Night Club Lady

US   1932   66m   bw
Columbia

A police commissioner solves the murder of a night-club hostess.

Straightforward cops and killers melodrama with the star in his first non-romantic role.

w Robert Riskin   *novel* Anthony Abbott   *d* Irving Cummings

Adolphe Menjou, Mayo Methot, Skeets Gallagher, Blanche Friderici, Nat Pendleton

Night Club Scandal

US   1937   74m   bw
Paramount

A society doctor murders his wife and incriminates her lover.

Smooth second feature remake of *Guilty as Hell*, chiefly notable for its star's last controlled performance.

w Lillie Hayward   *play* Riddle Me This by Daniel Rubin   *d* Ralph Murphy   *ph* Leo Tover

John Barrymore, Lynne Overman, Charles Bickford, Elizabeth Patterson, Evelyn Brent, Louise Campbell, J. Carrol Naish

Night Court

US   1932   90m   bw
MGM
GB title: *Justice for Sale*

A corrupt judge frames a girl on a prostitution charge.

Tough star melodrama.

w Mark Hellinger, Bayard Veiller, Charles Beehan, Lenore Coffee   *d* W. S. Van Dyke

Walter Huston, Lewis Stone, Anita Page, Phillips Holmes, Jean Hersholt

'Political frame-up of women is made the subject of a vigorous melodrama, though it comes after the New York scandal on the subject is largely forgotten.' – *Variety*

Night Creatures: see *Captain Clegg*

Night Crossing

US   1982   106m   Technicolor
Walt Disney (Tom Leetch)
V*, S

East Germans escape to the west via air balloon.

Well-meaning melodrama which sadly lacks plot development and suspense, and is also rather miserable to look at.

w John McGreevey   *d* Delbert Mann   *ph* Tony Imi   *m* Jerry Goldsmith

John Hurt, Jane Alexander, Doug McKeon, Frank McKeon, Beau Bridges, Glynnis O'Connor, Ian Bannen

The Night Digger

GB   1971   100m   colour
MGM

A frustrated spinster protects a handyman clearly guilty of murder, and runs away with him.

How this came to be made at all when the Finney version of *Night Must Fall* had recently flopped is a mystery; it had so little box-office appeal that it was barely released.

w Roald Dahl   *story* Joy Cowley   *d* Alastair Reid

Patricia Neal, Nicholas Clay, Pamela Browne, Jean Sanderson, Yootha Joyce, Peter Sallis, Graham Crowden

Night Fighters: see *A Terrible Beauty*

Night Flight *

US   1933   84m   bw
MGM (David O. Selznick)

The president of a civil airline insists that dangerous night flights must continue as a mark of progress.

Spurious, unsatisfactory, multi-star air melodrama lacking both narrative flow and the common touch.

w Oliver H. P. Garrett   *stories* Antoine de St Exupéry   *d* Clarence Brown   *ph* Oliver T. Marsh, Elmer Dyer, Charles Marshall

John Barrymore, Helen Hayes, Lionel Barrymore, Clark Gable, Robert Montgomery, Myrna Loy, William Gargan, C. Henry Gordon

'Punch aviation film with a flock of potent marquee names.' – *Variety*

'It is in the sense it conveys of human beings caught in the swift machinery of modern living that *Night Flight* soars above other pictures of its kind.' – *James Shelley Hamilton*

Night Games *

Sweden   1966   105m   bw
Sandrews (Lena Malmsjö)
original title: *Nattlek*

A 35-year-old man is sexually inhibited by memories of his dead mother's passions and perversions.

Curious Freudian parable apparently intended as a comment on the state of Europe. Audiences found it merely peculiar.

wd Mai Zetterling   *novel* Mai Zetterling   *ph* Rune Ericson   *m* Jan Johansson, George Riedel

Ingrid Thulin, Keve Hjelm, Lena Brundin, Naima Wifstrand

'The best one can say is that it never lets up for a moment.' – *David Wilson, MFB*

Night Games

US   1980   100m   Technicolor
Golden Harvest/Avco
V*

A neurotic Beverly Hills housewife is terrified of men.

Crazy mix of case history, eroticism and suspense with insufficient of any to satisfy fans.

w Anton Diether, Clarke Reynolds   *d* Roger Vadim

Cindy Pickett, Joanna Cassidy, Barry Primus

Night Hair Child

GB   1971   89m   Movielab
Leander/Harry Alan Towers (Graham Harris)

A 12-year-old boy makes sexual advances to his stepmother.

Corrupt voyeuristic weirdie which has to be seen to be believed.

w Trevor Preston   *d* James Kelly   *ph* Harry Waxman   *m* Stelvio Cipriani

Mark Lester, Britt Ekland, Hardy Kruger, Harry Andrews, Lilli Palmer

'Was his strange power a blessing or a curse? He was a refugee from love – because he could foretell that their marriage and their kisses would dissolve in a tragedy of tears!'

Night Has a Thousand Eyes

US   1948   80m   bw
Paramount (André Boehm)

A vaudeville mentalist finds that he really does have the power to predict the future.

Predictable supernatural melodrama closely modelled on *The Clairvoyant* (qv); quite nicely made but simply not exciting.

w Barre Lyndon, Jonathan Latimer   *novel* Cornell Woolrich   *d* John Farrow   *ph* John F. Seitz   *m* Victor Young

Edward G. Robinson, Gail Russell, John Lund, Virginia Bruce, William Demarest, Richard Webb, Jerome Cowan

'For those who like sweet hocus-pocus and Edward G. Robinson.' – *Sunday Express*

The Night Has Eyes *

GB   1942   79m   bw
ABP (John Argyle)
V*
US title: *Terror House*

A young teacher disappears on the Yorkshire moors; her friend goes in search, and comes under the influence of a strange young man and his sinister housekeeper.

Stagey but effective little thriller, with oodles of fog and bog to help the suspense.

w Alan Kennington   *d* Leslie Arliss   *ph* Günther Krampf   *m* Charles Williams

James Mason, Joyce Howard, *Wilfrid Lawson, Mary Clare*, Tucker McGuire, John Fernald

'Some ingenuity and not a little style.' – *The Times*

The Night Holds Terror *

US   1955   86m   bw
Columbia (Andrew Stone)

Three gunmen on the run kidnap a factory worker and hold him to ransom.

Effective, detailed, low-budget police melodrama; its plot may be over familiar now, but at the time it was refreshing and the whole film an intelligent exercise in suspense.

wd Andrew Stone   *ph* Fred Jackman Jnr   *m* Lucien Cailliet

Jack Kelly, Hildy Parks, John Cassavetes, David Cross, Edward Marr, Jack Kruschen

A Night in Cairo: see *The Barbarian*

A Night in Casablanca **

US   1946   85m   bw
David L. Loew

Three zanies rout Nazi refugees in a North African hotel.

The last authentic Marxian extravaganza; it starts uncertainly, builds to a fine sustained frenzy, then peters out in some overstretched airplane acrobatics.

w Joseph Fields, Roland Kibbee, Frank Tashlin   *d* Archie Mayo   *ph* James Van Trees   *m* Werner Janssen   *pd* Duncan Cramer

Groucho, Chico, Harpo, Sig Rumann, Lisette Verea, Charles Drake, Lois Collier, Dan Seymour

KORNBLOW (Groucho Marx): 'I don't mind being killed, but I resent hearing it from a character whose head comes to a point.'

KORNBLOW: 'From now on the essence of this hotel will be speed. If a customer asks you for a three-minute egg, give it to him in two minutes. If he asks you for a two-minute egg, give it to him in one minute. If he asks you for a one-minute egg, give him the chicken and let him work it out for himself.'

BEATRICE (Lisette Verea): 'My name's Beatrice Ryner. I stop at the hotel.'

KORNBLOW: 'My name's Ronald Kornblow. I stop at nothing.'

'It is beside the main point to add that it isn't one of their best movies; for the worst they might ever make would be better worth seeing than most other things I can think of.' – *James Agee*

A Night in Havana: see *The Big Boodle*

'It's a swell night for kissing or killing – or both!'
A Night in New Orleans
US   1942   75m   bw
Paramount

A policeman goes after gamblers and finds one of them murdered.

Routine mystery, competently made.

w Jonathan Latimer   *d* William C. Clemens

Preston Foster, Albert Dekker, Patricia Morison, Charles Butterworth, Dooley Wilson

A Night in Paradise
US   1946   84m   Technicolor
(Universal) Walter Wanger

Aesop falls in love at the court of King Croesus.

Deadly boring, unintentionally funny Arabian Nights farrago without the saving grace of action.

w Ernest Pascal, Emmet Lavery   *novel Peacock's Feather* by George S. Hellman   *d* Arthur Lubin   *ph* Hal Mohr   *m* Frank Skinner

Merle Oberon, Turhan Bey, Thomas Gomez, Gale Sondergaard, Ray Collins, George Dolenz, John Litel, Ernest Truex, Jerome Cowan, Douglass Dumbrille

A Night in the Life of Jimmy Reardon: see
Jimmy Reardon

Night into Morning
US   1951   86m   bw
MGM (Edwin H. Knopf)

A college professor loses his wife and son in an accident; despair drives him to drink and attempted suicide.

Well-made and well-meaning melodrama whose virtual absence of plot makes it seem by the end merely maudlin.

w Karl Tunberg, Leonard Spigelgass   *d* Fletcher Markle   *ph* George Folsey   *m* Carmen Dragon

Ray Milland, Nancy Davis, John Hodiak, Lewis Stone, Jean Hagen, Rosemary de Camp

'Tediously uneventful, as sincere and futile as a note of condolence.' – *Time*

The Night Invader
GB   1942   81m   bw
Warner

A Britisher in an occupied country is helped to capture a Nazi count.

Propaganda potboiler for double billing.

w Brock Williams, Edward Dryhurst, Roland Pertwee *novel Rendezvous with Death* by John Bentley   *d* Herbert Mason

Anne Crawford, David Farrar, Carl Jaffe, Sybilla Binder, Marius Goring

The Night Is Ending: see *Paris After Dark*

Night Is My Future: see *Music Is My Future*

The Night Is Young
US   1934   82m   bw
MGM

A European archduke loves a ballerina.

High-class musical which failed despite an intriguing cast and a Romberg and Hammerstein score.

w Vicki Baum   *d* Dudley Murphy

Evelyn Laye, Ramon Novarro, Una Merkel, Edward Everett Horton, Rosalind Russell, Charles Butterworth, Herman Bing, Henry Stephenson, Donald Cook

'Disappointing entertainment . . . feeble in plot, with a cast struggling to carry assignments and failing to ignite any real romantic fire, film also seems to lack a single strong musical number.' – *Variety*

The Night Is Young
France   1986   119m   colour
Artificial Eye/Les Films Plain Chant/Soporfilms/FR3 (Philippe Diaz)
V
original title: *Mauvais Sang*

In the future, a gang of criminals set out to steal an antidote to a disease which kills those who indulge in sex without love.

Chic, slight tale, influenced for the bad by Godard.

wd Leos Carax   *ph* Jean-Yves Escoffier   *pd* Michel Vandestien   *ed* Nelly Quettier

Michel Piccoli, Juliette Binoche, Denis Lavant, Hans Meyer, Julie Delphy, Carroll Brooks, Hugo Pratty

Night Key
US   1937   67m   bw
Universal (Robert Presnell)

An inventor's idea is stolen by his former partner, and he takes an appropriate revenge.

Low-key star melodrama: competent, but no great shakes.

w Tristram Tupper, John C. Moffitt   *d* Lloyd Corrigan   *ph* George Robinson   *m* Louis Forbes *make up* Jack Pierce

Boris Karloff, Jean Rogers, Warren Hull, Samuel S. Hinds, Alan Baxter, Ward Bond, Edwin Maxwell

'Mildly entertaining dualler . . . one of those impossible gadget yarns with liberal injections of cops and robbers stuff.' – *Variety*

The Night Life of the Gods
US   1935   75m   bw
Universal

An inventor turns statues into people, and vice versa.

Fantasy comedy from a well-known comic novel; interesting despite low level of invention.

w Barry Trivers   *novel* Thorne Smith   *d* Lowell Sherman

Alan Mowbray, Florine McKinney, Richard Carle, Peggy Shannon

'Universal has managed to keep in the fun and restrain it from getting too rough.' – *Variety*

A Night Like This
GB   1932   74m   bw
British and Dominions

An Irish policeman breaks up a crooked gambling club.

Minor Aldwych farce which hasn't worn well.

w Ben Travers   *play* Ben Travers   *d* Tom Walls

Tom Walls, Ralph Lynn, Robertson Hare, Winifred Shotter, Mary Brough, Claude Hulbert

Night Mail ***
GB   1936   24m   bw
GPO Film Unit (John Grierson)

A 'film poem' showing the journey of the mail train from London to Glasgow.

One of the best and most influential of British documentaries: despite a few absurdities, it remains a pleasure to watch.

wd Basil Wright, Harry Watt   *ph* J. Jones, H. E. Fowle *m* Benjamin Britten, *poem* W. H. Auden   *sound arrangements* Alberto Cavalcanti

'The final sequences as the train drives at dawn through the northern moors, the sheep-dog racing the train and the rabbits scurrying to cover, set to the simple visual verses of Mr Auden, are extraordinarily exciting.' – *Graham Greene, The Spectator*

Night Mayor
US   1932   65m   bw
Columbia

The Mayor of New York pays too much attention to night life and not enough to his desk.

Thinly veiled account of the Jimmy Walker affair, released after Walker had been discredited. As entertainment, punchy, but in the end only fair.

w Gertrude Purcell, Sam Marx   *d* Ben Stoloff

Lee Tracy, Evalyn Knapp, Eugene Pallette, Warren Hymer, Donald Dillaway, Astrid Allwyn

'It is a safe general statement that the screen ought never to exploit a public character who is the center of debate.' – *Variety*

Night Monster
US   1942   73m   bw
Universal (Ford Beebe)
GB title: *House of Mystery*

Murders are committed in a spooky house by a cripple who produces synthetic legs by self-hypnotism.

Stilted, creaky would-be thriller with a good cast and an impertinent plot.

w Clarence Upson Young   *d* Ford Beebe   *ph* Charles Van Enger

Ralph Morgan, Don Porter, Irene Hervey, Bela Lugosi, Lionel Atwill, Nils Asther, Leif Erickson, Frank Reicher

'Night, Mother
US   1986   96m   DeLuxe
Universal/Aaron Spelling, Alan Greisman
V*, L

A mother gets to grips with the problems of her suicidal daughter.

Rueful drama which pares down the nerve ends but was clearly not designed for box-office, and remains a play rather than a film.

w Marsha Norman   *play* Marsha Norman   *d* Tom Moore   *ph* Stephen M. Katz   *m* David Shire

Anne Bancroft, Sissy Spacek, Ed Berke, Carol Robbins

'Maybe he would find the girl – maybe he would find himself!'
Night Moves *
US   1975   99m   Technicolor
Warner/Hiller/Layton (Robert M. Sherman)
V*, L

A private eye is engaged to find a runaway teenager.

Apparently a Chandlerish mystery, this is really a Pinterish audience-teaser with obsessions about communication and the meaning of life. A smart-ass entertainment for eager trendies.

w Alan Sharp   *d* Arthur Penn   *ph* Bruce Surtees
m Michael Small   *pd* George Jenkins

Gene Hackman, Jennifer Warren, Edward Binns, Harris Yulin, Kenneth Mars

'Beneath the complicated unravelling of a mystery, an anti-mystery, with the hero's detection registering as an evasion of his own problems; beneath a densely charted intrigue of betrayals and cross purposes, a cryptic void . . .' – *Jonathan Rosenbaum*

'A suspenseless suspenser . . . there's very little rhyme or reason for the plot's progression.' – *Variety*

'Rich and dense enough to set up reverberations long after one has left the cinema.' – *Michael Billington, Illustrated London News*

Night Must Fall **
US   1937   117m   bw
MGM (Hunt Stromberg)

A bland young bellboy who is really a psychopathic murderer attaches himself to the household of a rich old lady.

Unconvincing but memorable Hollywood expansion of an effective British chiller.

w John Van Druten   *play* Emlyn Williams
d Richard Thorpe   *ph* Ray June   *m* Edward Ward

Robert Montgomery, Rosalind Russell, *May Whitty*, Alan Marshal, Merle Tottenham, Kathleen Harrison, Matthew Boulton, E. E. Clive

'Too long and not box office . . . tedious, slow, and even dull in spots.' – *Variety*

'A pretty little murder play has made a long dim film.' – *Graham Greene*

'The most exhilarating shrouds of horror hang over it. It represents a provocative imagination, a skilled adapter, a sensitive director, a splendid acting job.' – *Bland Johaneson, New York Daily Mirror*

† Louis B. Mayer so disliked this film that at the New York première he ordered the distribution of leaflets disowning it on behalf of MGM.

AAN: Robert Montgomery; May Whitty

Night Must Fall
GB   1964   105m   bw
MGM (Albert Finney, Karel Reisz)

Dreary remake with a mannered star performance and the emphasis on axe murders. A mistake from beginning to end.

w Clive Exton   *d* Karel Reisz   *ph* Freddie Francis
m Ron Grainer

Albert Finney, Susan Hampshire, Mona Washbourne, Sheila Hancock, Michael Medwin, Joe Gladwin, Martin Wyldeck

'Not so much a thriller as a typically humourless example of that overworked genre known as psychological drama . . . [Finney] constantly recalls a ventriloquist's dummy.' – *MFB*

The Night My Number Came Up *
GB   1954   94m   bw
Ealing (Tom Morahan)
V*

A man dreams that his plane will crash, and the dream begins to come true.

Intriguing little melodrama which badly lacks a twist ending and foxes itself by a flashback construction which leaves very little open to doubt. Production generally good.

w R. C. Sherriff   *d* Leslie Norman   *ph* Lionel Banes   *m* Malcolm Arnold

Michael Redgrave, Alexander Knox, Sheila Sim, Denholm Elliott, Ursula Jeans, George Rose, Nigel Stock, Michael Hordern, Ralph Truman, Victor Maddern, Bill Kerr, Alfie Bass

'A story which, in its delicately measured suspenses and reliefs, has been beautifully built.' – *Times Educational Supplement*

'The idea of destiny as predestiny is an old psychological trump, but it still takes tricks.' – *Time*

† The story was taken from a personal account by Sir Victor Goddard.

Night Nurse *
US   1931   72m   bw
Warner
V*, L

A nurse uncovers a plot by other members of the household against her patient's children.

Fast-moving melodrama with solid star performances; just what the public wanted in 1931.

w Oliver H. P. Garrett   *novel* Dora Macy
d William Wellman   *ph* Chick McGill

Barbara Stanwyck, Ben Lyon, Joan Blondell, Clark Gable, Charles Winninger, Vera Lewis, Blanche Frederici, Charlotte Merriam

'A conglomeration of exaggerations, often bordering on serial dramatics.' – *Hollywood Reporter*

Night of Counting the Years **
Egypt   1969   102m   colour
Egyptian Cinema General Organization
original title: *El Mumia*

Horrified to discover that his tribe has grown rich by robbing the tombs of the Pharaohs, a young leader faces the dilemma of what to do about it.

Engrossing, if rather stately, account of a moral choice against the magnificent background of Egypt's past. The film was sponsored by Italian director Roberto Rossellini.

wd Shadi Abdelsalam   *ph* Abdel Aziz Fahmy
m Mario Nascimbene

Ahmed Marel, Zouzou El Hakim, Ahmad Hegazi, Nadia Loutfy, Gaby Karraz

Night of Dark Shadows
US   1971   97m   Metrocolor   Panavision
MGM (Dan Curtis)
V*
aka: *Curse of Dark Shadows*

After moving to his ancestral home, an artist begins to experience strange and violent visions of the past.

Tame tale of the supernatural that fails to hold one's interest.

w Sam Hall   *story* Sam Hall, Dan Curtis   *d* Dan Curtis   *ph* Richard Shore   *m* Robert Cobert
pd Trevor Williams   *ed* Charles Goldsmith

David Selby, Grayson Hall, Lara Parker, John Karlen, Nancy Barrett, James Storm, Thayer David, Christopher Pennock, Diana Millay, Kate Jackson

† The film was an unsuccessful follow-up to Curtis's 1970 film *House of Dark Shadows* (qv).

The Night of January 16th
US   1941   79m   bw
Paramount

A secretary is arrested for her boss's murder; but is he really dead?

A stage thriller full of theatrical trickery becomes a very mundane film.

w Delmer Daves, Robert Pirosh, Eve Greene
play Ayn Rand   *d* William Clemens

Robert Preston, Ellen Drew, Nils Asther, Margaret Hayes

The Night of June 13th
US   1932   76m   bw
Paramount

A suburban street is transformed when one of its residents goes on trial for murder.

Combination courtroom and slice-of-life drama which satisfied most audiences.

w Agnes Brand Leahy, Brian Marlow, William Slavens McNutt   *story* Vera Caspary   *d* Stephen Roberts

Clive Brook, Lila Lee, Mary Boland, Adrienne Allen, Gene Raymond, Frances Dee, Charley Grapewin

'Absorbingly worked out with fascinating character study and a touch of satire.' – *Variety*

'What happens after they turn the lights out on Broadway?'

The Night of Nights
US   1939   86m   bw
Paramount

A once-famous Broadway writer, now a drunk, tries to ensure his daughter's fame.

Curious downbeat melodrama without the courage of its convictions, or the actors to give the right bravura performances.

w Donald Ogden Stewart   *d* Lewis Milestone

Pat O'Brien, Olympe Bradna, Reginald Gardiner, Roland Young

'Backstage drama lightened by direction and cast performances. Nominal supporter for key duals.' – *Variety*

The Night of San Lorenzo **
Italy   1981   107m   Agfacolor
UA/Premier/RAI/Ager Cinematografica (Giuliani G. de Negri)
S

original title: *La Notte Di San Lorenzo*; aka: *Night of the Shooting Stars*

In the Second World War a six-year-old girl watches events in her town as American forces advance to liberate it.

Touching, powerfully nostalgic study of a community in ferment.

wd Paolo Taviani, Vittorio Taviani   *ph* Franco Di Giacomo   *m* Nicola Piovani   *ad* Gianni Sbarra
ed Roberto Perpignani

Omero Antonutti, Margarita Lozano, Claudio Bigagli, Massimo Bonetti, Norma Martelli, Enrica Maria Modugno, Sabina Vannucchi

Night of the Big Heat
GB   1967   94m   Eastmancolor
Tom Blakeley/Planet
US title: *Island of the Burning Damned*

Invaders from outer space take over a remote Scottish island and make it unbearably hot so that they can survive.

Sloppily made and over-prolonged science fiction with far too much irrelevant talk.

w Ronald Liles   *novel* John Lymington   *d* Terence Fisher

Christopher Lee, Peter Cushing, Patrick Allen, Sarah Lawson, Jane Merrow, William Lucas, Kenneth Cope

Night of the Bloody Apes (dubbed)
Mexico   1970   82m   Eastmancolor
Grand National/Unistar (Alfredo Salazar)
V, V*
original title: *Horriplante Bestia Humana*; aka: *Gomar the Human Gorilla*

In an attempt to save his son's life, a doctor gives him the heart of a gorilla, causing him to change into a murderous ape.

Bizarre horror that may appeal to lovers of terrible movies; it borrows from every major film of the genre, from *Jekyll and Hyde* and *Frankenstein* to *King Kong* and *The Murders of the Rue Morgue*.

w René Cardona, René Cardona Jnr   *d* René Cardona   *ph* Raúl Martinez Solares   *m* Antonio Diaz Conde   *ad* Carlos Arjona   *sp* Javier Torres Torija   *ed* Jorge Bustos

José Elias Moreno, Carlos López Moctezuma, Armando Silvestre, Norma Lazareno, Agustin Martinez Solares, Noelia Noel

'Patience is severely tried by the stately pace, the endless expressions of paternal devotion, and the script's risible attempts to offer medical explanations and justifications.' – *Tom Milne, MFB*

Night of the Comet
US   1984   98m   colour
Atlantic/Thomas Coleman-Michael Rosenblatt (Andrew Lane, Wayne Crawford)
V, V*

In Los Angeles two sisters are the only survivors of a cosmic storm that kills the population or turns them into zombies.

Low-budget science-fiction thriller, done with humour and some imagination.

wd Tom Eberhardt   *ph* Arthur Albert   *m* David Richard Campbell   *pd* John Muto   *ed* Fred Stafford

Robert Beltran, Catharine Mary Stewart, Kelli Maroney, Sharon Farrell, Mary Woronov, Geoffrey Lewis

Night of the Demon ***
GB   1957   87m   bw
Columbia/Sabre (Frank Bevis)
V*, L
US title: *Curse of the Demon*

An occultist despatches his enemies by raising a giant medieval devil.

Despite dim work from the leads, this supernatural thriller is intelligently scripted and achieves several frightening and memorable sequences in the best Hitchcock manner.

w Charles Bennett, Hal E. Chester,   story *Casting the Runes* by M. R. James   *d* Jacques Tourneur   *ph* Ted Scaife   *m* Clifton Parker   *ad* Ken Adam

Dana Andrews, Peggy Cummins, *Niall MacGinnis, Athene Seyler*, Brian Wilde, Maurice Denham, Ewan Roberts, Liam Redmond, Reginald Beckwith

Night of the Eagle **
GB   1961   87m   bw
Independent Artists (Albert Fennell)
US title: *Burn, Witch, Burn*

At a medical school, a jealous witch sets an evil force on her rival.

Pretty good supernatural thriller, let down by leading performances and sustained by character roles and solid production values in creepy sequences.

w Charles Beaumont, Richard Matheson, George Baxt   *novel Conjure Wife* by Fritz Leiber Jnr   *d* Sidney Hayers   *ph* Reg Wyer   *m* William Alwyn

Margaret Johnston, Janet Blair, Peter Wyngarde, Anthony Nicholls, Reginald Beckwith, Kathleen Byron

The Night of the Following Day *
US   1969   100m   Technicolor
Universal/Gina (Hubert Comfield)
V, V*

A young girl arriving in Paris to stay with her father is kidnapped and held to ransom by an eccentric gang.

Straightforward suspense thriller with delusions of grandeur; the second half bogs down in pretentious talk and the end suggests that the whole thing was a dream.

w Hubert Cornfield, Robert Phippeny   *novel The Snatchers* by Lionel White   *d* Hubert Cornfield   *ph* Willy Kurant   *m* Stanley Myers

Marlon Brando, Richard Boone, Rita Moreno, Pamela Franklin, Jess Hahn

Night of the Garter
GB   1933   86m   bw
British and Dominions (Herbert Wilcox)

A newly married man tries to retrieve an intimate gift from an old flame.

One of the best-remembered comedies of Sydney Howard.

w Austin Melford, Marjorie Gaffney   *play Getting Gertie's Garter* by Avery Hopwood, Wilson Collison   *d* Jack Raymond

Sydney Howard, Winifred Shotter, Elsie Randolph, Austin Melford

The Night of the Generals **
GB   1967   148m   Technicolor   Panavision
Columbia/Horizon/Filmsonor (Sam Spiegel)
V, V*, L, S

A German intelligence agent tracks down a psychopathic Nazi general who started killing prostitutes in Warsaw during World War II.

A curiously bumpy narrative which is neither mystery nor character study but does provide a few effective sequences and impressive performances. The big budget seems well spent.

w Joseph Kessel, Paul Dehn   *novel* Hans Helmut Kirst   *d* Anatole Litvak   *ph* Henri Decaë   *m* Maurice Jarre   *pd* Alexander Trauner

Peter O'Toole, *Omar Sharif, Tom Courtenay*, Donald Pleasence, Joanna Pettet, *Philippe Noiret*, Charles Gray, Coral Browne, John Gregson, Harry Andrews, Nigel Stock, Christopher Plummer, Juliette Greco

'The "who" is obvious from the first and the "dunnit" interminable.' – *Judith Crist, 1973*

'Lurid and vivid, if nothing else.' – *Robert Windeler*

Night of the Ghouls
US   1958   75m   bw
Wade Williams (Edward D. Wood Jnr)
V*
aka: *Revenge of the Dead*

Dr Acula, a fake medium, takes up residence in a haunted house where he manages to raise the dead.

Aficionados of the work of the totally inept Wood may enjoy this, since it has all the hallmarks of his movies: bad acting, irrelevant voice-over and hopeless direction, although it lacks the delirium of *Plan 9 from Outer Space*.

wd Edward D. Wood Jnr   *ph* William C. Thompson   *md* Gordon Zahler   *ad* Kathleen O'Hara Everett

Criswell, Kenne Duncan, 'Duke' Moore, Valda Hansen, Tor Johnson, John Carpenter, Paul Marco

The Night of the Grizzly
US   1966   102m   Techniscope
Paramount (Burt Dunne)
V*

A Wyoming ex-sheriff kills a marauding bear and earns the respect of his son.

Stout-hearted family film, rather sluggishly made.

w Warren Douglas   *d* Joseph Pevney   *ph* Harold Lipstein, Loyal Griggs   *m* Leith Stevens

Clint Walker, Martha Hyer, Keenan Wynn, Leo Gordon, Kevin Brodie, Nancy Kulp, Ellen Corby, Jack Elam, Ron Ely

'The scenes! The story! The stars! But above all – the suspense!'
The Night of the Hunter ***
US   1955   93m   bw
UA/Paul Gregory
V*, L

A psychopathic preacher goes on the trail of hidden money, the secret of which is held by two children.

Weird, manic fantasy in which evil finally comes to grief against the forces of sweetness and light (the children, an old lady, water, animals). Although the narrative does not flow smoothly there are splendidly imaginative moments, and no other film has ever quite achieved its texture.

w James Agee,   *novel* Davis Grubb   *d* Charles Laughton   *ph* Stanley Cortez   *m* Walter Schumann

Robert Mitchum, Shelley Winters, Lillian Gish, Don Beddoe, Evelyn Varden, Peter Graves, James Gleason

   PREACHER (Robert Mitchum): 'Lord, you sure knew what you was doing when you brung me to this very cell at this very time. A man with ten thousand dollars hid somewhere, and a widder in the makin'.'

'One of the most frightening movies ever made.' – *Pauline Kael, 1968*

'A genuinely sinister work, full of shocks and over-emphatic sound effects, camera angles and shadowy lighting.' – *NFT, 1973*

'One of the most daring, eloquent and personal films to have come from America in a long time.' – *Derek Prouse*

'One man … three women … one night!'
The Night of the Iguana ***
US   1964   125m   bw
MGM/Seven Arts (Ray Stark)
V*

A disbarred clergyman becomes a travel courier in Mexico and is sexually desired by a teenage nymphomaniac, a middle-aged hotel owner and a frustrated itinerant artist.

The author is most tolerable when poking fun at his own types, and this is a sharp, funny picture with a touch of poetry.

w Anthony Veiller   *play Tennessee Williams*   *d* John Huston   *ph* Gabriel Figueroa   *m* Benjamin Frankel   *ad* Stephen Grimes

Richard Burton, Deborah Kerr, Ava Gardner, Sue Lyon, *Grayson Hall, Cyril Delevanti*

'Whatever poetry it had seems to have leaked out.' – *New Yorker, 1982*

AAN: Gabriel Figueroa; Grayson Hall

Night of the Juggler
US   1980   100m   Technicolor
Columbia
V*

A New Yorker relentlessly pursues the kidnapper of his daughter.

Average chase thriller with good location staging of car crashes.

w Bill Norton Snr and Rick Natkin   *d* Robert Butler

James Brolin, Cliff Gorman, Richard Castellano, Abby Bluestone

'There's a herd of killer rabbits heading this way!'
Night of the Lepus
US   1972   88m   Metrocolor
MGM (A. C. Lyles)

A serum meant to control a surplus of rabbits instead produces monster varieties four feet tall.

Tolerable sci-fi tailored to a very tired formula.

w Don Holiday, Gene R. Kearney   *novel The Year of the Angry Rabbit* by Russell Braddon   *d* William F. Claxton   *ph* Ted Voigtlander   *m* Jimmie Haskell

Stuart Whitman, Rory Calhoun, Janet Leigh, Paul Fix, De Forrest Kelley

'For insomniacs with lax standards.' – *Judith Crist*

The Night of The Living Dead ***
US 1968 98m bw
Image Ten
V, V*, L

Flesh-eating zombies, activated by radiation from a space rocket, ravage the countryside.

Gruesome horror comic with effective moments; the director was still doing the same schtick ten years later. One of the most influential, and most imitated, of modern horror movies.

w John A. Russo   d George A. Romero

Judith O'Dea, Duane Jones, Karl Hardman, Keith Wayne

'The best film ever made in Pittsburgh.' – *Anon.*

'Casts serious aspersions on the integrity of its makers . . . the film industry as a whole and exhibs who book the pic, as well as raising doubts about the future of the regional cinema movement and the moral health of filmgoers who cheerfully opt for unrelieved sadism.' – *Variety*

Night of The Living Dead
US 1990 89m TVC
Columbia/21st Century/George A. Romero/Menaham Golan
(John A. Russo, Russ Steiner)
V, V*, L

Cannibalistic corpses rise from their graves to terrorize people trapped in a farmhouse.

Remake lacking the relentless intensity of the original.

w George A. Romero   d Tom Savani   ph Frank Prinzi   m Paul McCollough   ad James Feng   ed Tom Dubensky

Tony Wood, Patricia Tallman, Tom Towles, McKee Anderson, William Butler, Katie Finnerman, Bill Mosley, Heather Mazur

'A crass bit of cinematic grave-robbing.' – *Variety*

Night of the Party
GB 1934 60m bw
Gaumont-British (Jerome Jackson)

A game of murder at a dinner party leads to a real one.

Solid supporting thriller with interesting credits.

w Ralph Smart   play Roland Pertwee, John Hastings Turner   d Michael Powell   ph Glen MacWilliams   ad Alfred Junge

Leslie Banks, Jane Baxter, Viola Keats, Ian Hunter, Ernest Thesiger, Malcolm Keen

'Nothing original, but good entertainment.' – *Variety*

Night of the Prowler
GB 1962 60m bw
Butcher's Film Distributors (John I. Phillips)

Partners in an engineering firm receive death threats.

Dim and implausible second-feature thriller that is mediocre in every respect.

w Paul Erickson   d Francis A. Searle   ph Walter J. Harvey   m Johnny Gregory   ad George Provis   ed Jim Connock

Patrick Holt, Colette Wilde, Bill Nagy, Mitzi Rogers, John Horsley, Benny Lee

Night of the Shooting Stars: see *The Night of San Lorenzo*

Night on Earth **
US 1992 129m colour
Electric/Locus Solus/Victor/Victor Musical Industries/Pyramide/Canal+/Pandora/Channel 4 (Jim Jarmusch)
V, V*, S

Five individuals take simultaneous taxi rides in five cities: Los Angeles, New York, Paris, Rome and Helsinki.

Engaging series of shaggy dog stories, expertly told.

wd Jim Jarmusch   ph Frederick Elmes   m Tom Waits   ed Jay Ribinowitz

Winona Ryder, Gena Rowlands, Giancarlo Esposito, Armin Mueller-Stahl, Rosie Perez, Isaach de Bankolé, Béatrice Dalle, Roberto Benigni, Paolo Bonacelli, Matti Pellonpää

'For the most part, the movie induces in the viewer an eerie, suspended feeling that mimics the time-stands-still monotony of a long airplane journey. It tries for a chipper, lighthearted tone, but it gives the audience a gruelling flight – a red-eye to nowhere.' – *Terrence Rafferty, New Yorker*

Night on the Town
US 1987 99m DeLuxe
Touchstone/Silver Screen Partners III/Debra Hill/Linda Obst
V, V*, L
US title: *Adventures in Babysitting*

Babysitting young children, a girl takes them for a ride in her car and unwittingly becomes a target for gangsters.

A sequence of tepid chases aimed at an undemanding audience.

w David Simkins   d Chris Columbus   ph Ric Waite   m Michael Kamen   pd Todd Hallowell   ad Gregory Keen   ed Frederic Steinkamp

Elisabeth Shue, Maia Brewton, Keith Coogan, Anthony Rapp, Calvin Levels

Night Owls *
US 1930 20m bw
Hal Roach
V

A policeman wanting to record an arrest bribes two tramps to burgle a house.

The stars at their most hilariously incompetent, unable even to get through a doorway efficiently.

w Leo McCarey, H. M. Walker   d James Parrott

Laurel and Hardy, Edgar Kennedy, James Finlayson

Night Passage *
US 1957 90m Technirama
U-I (Aaron Rosenberg)

A railroad worker entrusted with a payroll finds that the bandits trying to rob it are led by his own brother.

Obscurely titled and rather empty Western providing standard excitements.

w Borden Chase   d James Neilson   ph William Daniels   m Dimitri Tiomkin

James Stewart, Audie Murphy, Dan Duryea, Brandon de Wilde, Dianne Foster, Elaine Stewart

'You have never really seen Gregory Peck until you see him in CinemaScope!'
'We didn't say nice people, we said *night people!*'
Night People *
US 1954 93m Technicolor Cinemascope
TCF (Nunnally Johnson)

When a US corporal stationed in Berlin is kidnapped by the Russians, his influential father flies into action.

Curiously titled cold war suspenser which would have been more memorable if not in Cinemascope; the pace and talent are visible, but the wide screen and poor colour dissipate them.

wd Nunnally Johnson   ph Charles G. Clarke   m Cyril Mockridge

Gregory Peck, Broderick Crawford, Anita Bjork, Walter Abel, Rita Gam, Buddy Ebsen, Jill Esmond, Peter Van Eyck

AAN: original story (Jed Harris, Tom Reed)

'Seven in the skies over China – and one of them a dangerous Axis spy!'
Night Plane from Chungking
US 1942 69m bw
Paramount

Assorted international passengers are flown from Chungking to India, but one of their number is a German spy who will kill to get his hands on vital information.

A lower-case 'who is it' based on *Shanghai Express*. Not bad according to its lights.

w Earl Felton, Theodore Reeves, Lester Cole   d Ralph Murphy   ph Theodor Sparkuhl   m Gerard Carbonara

Ellen Drew, Robert Preston, Otto Kruger, Steve Geray, Ernest Dorian, Tamara Geva, Sen Yung

'The most controversial film of our time!'
The Night Porter
Italy 1973 118m Technicolor
Lotar Films (Robert Gordon Edwards, Esa de Simone)
V, V*, L

The wife of an opera conductor recognizes a hotel porter as the sadistic SS commandant of a concentration camp in which she spent the war years; they now resume a sado-masochistic love affair.

A downright deplorable film, with no cinematic skill or grace to excuse it; the visuals are as loathsome as the sound is indecipherable, and the sheer pointlessness of it is insulting.

w Liliana Cavani, Italo Moscati   d Liliana Cavani   ph Alfio Contini   m Daniele Paris

Dirk Bogarde, Charlotte Rampling, Philippe Leroy, Gabriele Ferzetti, Isa Miranda

'Its claim to be saying something important is offensive, but the picture is too crudely trumped up to be a serious insult.' – *New Yorker*

Night Ride
GB 1937 70m bw
Paramount

Unemployed lorry drivers start an independent co-operative.

Brisk action programmer.

w Ralph Bettinson   d John Paddy Carstairs

Julian Vedey, Wally Patch, Jimmy Hanley, Joan Ponsford

Night Shift
US 1982 106m Technicolor
Warner/Ladd (Brian Grazer)
V*, L

A weary financial analyst becomes a morgue attendant and finds himself involved with gangsters and pimps.

Unattractive comedy that outstays its welcome, which wasn't very enthusiastic in the first place.

w Lowell Ganz, Babaloo Mandel   d Ron Howard   ph James Crabe   m Burt Bacharach   pd Jack Collis

Henry Winkler, Michael Keaton, Shelley Long, Gina Hecht

Night Song
US 1947 101m bw
RKO (Harriet Parsons)

A wealthy socialite falls for a blind pianist and pretends to be blind also, and poor to boot.

Silly, pretentious soaper, moodily photographed.

w Frank Fenton, Irving Hyland, De Witt Bodeen   d John Cromwell   ph *Lucien Ballard*   m Leith Stevens

Dana Andrews, Merle Oberon, Hoagy Carmichael, Ethel Barrymore, Artur Rubenstein, Eugene Ormandy

Night Sun *
Italy/France/Germany   1990   113m   Eastmancolor
Artificial Eye/Filmtre/Raiuno/Capoul/Interpool/Sara/Direkt
   (Giuliani G. de Negri)
V
original title: Il sole anche di notte

In 18th-century Italy, a nobleman, upset to discover
that he is expected to marry the king's mistress,
becomes a hermit credited with miraculous powers.

Austere fable of a search for salvation that is likely to
tire most audiences before the end.

w Paolo and Vittorio Taviani, Tonino Guerra
story Father Sergius by Leo Tolstoy   d Paolo and
Vittorio Taviani   ph Giuseppe Lanci   m Nicola
Piovani   ad Gianni Sbarra   ed Roberto Perpignani

Julian Sands, Charlotte Gainsbourg, Nastassja Kinski,
Massimo Bonetti, Margarita Lozano, Patricia
Millardet, Rudiger Vogler, Pamela Villoresi

'A hauntingly spiritual film which is never afraid to
explore the unfashionable themes of longing, solitude
and meditation.' – Sight and Sound

The Night the Lights Went Out in Georgia
US   1981   120m   Technicolor
Avco Embassy/Viacom (Elliot Geisinger, Howard Kuperman,
   Ronald Saland, Howard Smith)
V*

A young girl tries to guide her rambunctious brother
to success as a country and western singer.

A poorly constructed narrative ensures that the level
of interest remains low.

w Bob Bonney   song Bobby Russell   d Ronald F.
Maxwell   ph Bill Butler   m David Shire   pd Gene
Rudolf   ed Anne Goursand

Kristy McNichol, Dennis Quaid, Don Stroud, Mark
Hamill, Arlen Dean Snyder

The Night They Invented Striptease: see The
Night They Raided Minsky's

The Night They Raided Minsky's **
US   1968   99m   DeLuxe
UA/Tandem (Norman Lear)
V*
GB title: The Night They Invented Striptease

Various human problems are posed and solved during
a night at a burlesque theatre.

Marvellous kaleidoscopic ragbag of brilliant
fragments which unfortunately don't cohere in the
mind into a really memorable film, though it gives
detailed pleasure on every viewing.

w Arnold Schulman, Sidney Michaels, Norman Lear
book Rowland Barber   d William Friedkin
ph Andrew Laszlo   m Charles Strouse   pd William
Eckart, Jean Eckar   ch Danny Daniels   narrator Rudy
Vallee

Jason Robards, Britt Ekland, Norman Wisdom, Forrest
Tucker, Joseph Wiseman, Bert Lahr, Harry Andrews,
Denholm Elliott, Elliott Gould, Jack Burns

'The Fanny Brice country stunningly brought to life –
every face a snapshot of yesterday.' – Alexander Walker

'It's lightweight and disorganized; it's a shambles; yet
a lot of it is charming, and it has a wonderful seedy
chorus line – a row of pudgy girls with faces like
slipped discs.' – Pauline Kael, New Yorker

'A brilliant pastiche of classic American burlesque on
the lower east side in the twenties.' – Time

'An entire way of life is encapsulated' – Morning Star

Night Tide
US   1961   84m   bw
Virgo Films
V*

A sailor falls in love with a fairground freak show girl
who may be a real mermaid.

Cheaply made and very derivative romantic fantasy
which seemed to hold a promise never fulfilled.

wd Curtis Harrington

Dennis Hopper, Linda Lawson, Gavin Muir, Luana
Anders

A Night to Remember *
US   1943   91m   bw
Columbia (Samuel Bischoff)
V*, L

A Greenwich Village mystery-writing couple try to
solve a murder.

Reasonably sparkling comedy whodunnit with a zany
tinge.

w Richard Flournoy, Jack Henley   d Richard
Wallace   ph Joseph Walker   md Morris Stoloff
m Werner Heymann

Loretta Young, Brian Aherne, Jeff Donnell, William
Wright, Sidney Toler, Gale Sondergaard, Donald
MacBride, Lee Patrick, Blanche Yurka

'A first-rate gloom chaser.' – Picture Show

A Night to Remember ***
GB   1958   123m   bw
Rank (William Macquitty)
V, V*, L

The story of the 1912 sea disaster when the Titanic
struck an iceberg.

A major film enterprise featuring hundreds of cameos,
none discernibly more important than the other. On
this account the film seems alternately stiff and flabby
as narrative, but there is much to enjoy and admire
along the way, though the sense of awe is dissipated
by the final model shots.

w Eric Ambler, book Walter Lord   d Roy Baker
ph Geoffrey Unsworth   m William Alwyn

Kenneth More, Honor Blackman, Michael Goodliffe,
David McCallum, George Rose, Anthony Bushell,
Ralph Michael, John Cairney, Kenneth Griffith, Frank
Lawton, Michael Bryant

'A worthy, long-drawn-out documentary, with
noticeably more honesty about human nature than
most films, but little shape or style.' – Kenneth Cavender

Night Train: see Night Train to Munich

Night Train to Munich ***
GB   1940   93m   bw
TCF (Edward Black)
V*
aka: Gestapo; Night Train

A British agent poses as a Nazi in order to rescue a
Czech inventor.

First-rate comedy suspenser obviously inspired by the
success of The Lady Vanishes and providing much the
same measure of thrills and laughs.

w Frank Launder, Sidney Gilliat,   novel Report on a
Fugitive by Gordon Wellesley   d Carol Reed   ph Otto
Kanturek   md Louis Levy   m Charles Williams

Margaret Lockwood, Rex Harrison, Basil Radford,
Naunton Wayne, Paul Henreid, Keneth Kent, Felix
Aylmer, Roland Culver, Eliot Makeham, Raymond
Huntley, Wyndham Goldie

'A very nice triumph of skill and maturity in films,
and thus a pleasure to have.' – Otis Ferguson

AAN: Gordon Wellesley

Night unto Night *
US   1949   85m   bw
Warner (Owen Crump)

An epileptic scientist falls for a girl hallucinated by
the ghost of her dead husband.

Cheerless nuthouse melodrama, one of the well-
meant aberrations which Hollywood studios used to
produce as a sop to conscience.

w Kathryn Scola   novel Philip Wylie   d Don Siegel
ph Peverell Marley   m Franz Waxman

Ronald Reagan, Viveca Lindfors, Rosemary de Camp,
Broderick Crawford, Osa Massen, Craig Stevens,
Erskine Sanford

'Locked in the cold asylum of the mind – a sane man stalks
his prey!'
The Night Visitor
Sweden/US   1970   102m   Eastmancolor
Hemisphere/UMC
V*

Imprisoned for an axe murder he didn't commit, a
man escapes and takes revenge.

Overdone Grand Guignol which simply doesn't come
off.

w Guy Elmes   story Salem Came to Supper by Samuel
Roecca   d Laslo Benedek

Max von Sydow, Trevor Howard, Liv Ullmann,
Rupert Davies, Per Oscarsson, Andrew Keir

'Do you know that a dream can kill you?'
The Night Walker *
US   1965   86m   bw
U-I/William Castle
V*

The widow of a tough executive, killed and disfigured
in an explosion, is haunted in her dreams not only by
him but by a mysterious lover who turns up in reality.

Stiff and unconvincing but still fairly frightening low-
budget shocker with a plot twist or two.

w Robert Bloch   d William Castle   ph Harold Stine
m Vic Mizzy

Robert Taylor, Barbara Stanwyck, Lloyd Bochner,
Rochelle Hudson, Judi Meredith, Hayden Rorke

Night Watch
GB   1973   98m   Technicolor
Avco/Brut (David White)
V*

A widow recovering from a nervous breakdown
keeps seeing bodies in the night. Her friends try to
help, but things are not quite what they seem.

Predictable coiled-spring shocker which goes
curiously flat despite a star cast and lashings of blood.
Perhaps we have all been here once too often.

w Tony Williamson   play Lucille Fletcher   d Brian
G. Hutton   ph Billie Williams   m John Cameron

Elizabeth Taylor, Laurence Harvey, Billie Whitelaw,
Robert Lang, Tony Britton, Bill Dean

'It has all the trappings of a Joan Crawford vehicle of
the forties, with numerous elegant dresses for Miss
Taylor, an appropriately unbecoming wardrobe for
Miss Whitelaw, and a set which is an art director's
dream.' – Brenda Davies

'Elizabeth Taylor's gowns are by Valentino, her
jewellery is by Van Cleef and Arpels, even her
kitchen is by Westinghouse. And she is still going out
of her mind.' – Alexander Walker

The Night We Dropped a Clanger
GB   1959   86m   bw
Sidney Box/Four Star/Rank
US title: Make Mine a Double

During World War II, a wing commander's double is
accidentally sent to the front line in his place.

Feeble take-off on I Was Monty's Double; a few bright
gags survive.

w John Chapman   d Darcy Conyers

Brian Rix, Cecil Parker, William Hartnell, Leslie
Phillips, Leo Franklyn, John Welsh, Liz Fraser

The Night We Got the Bird
GB   1960   82m   bw
Rix-Conyers/British Lion

A husband is driven bonkers by a talking parrot which he believes to be the reincarnation of his predecessor.

Pretty awful farce with the sole virtue of a frantic pace.

w Ray Cooney, Tony Hilton, Darcy Conyers *d* Darcy Conyers

Brian Rix, Dora Bryan, Ronald Shiner, Leo Franklyn, Irene Handl, John Slater, Liz Fraser, Reginald Beckwith, Robertson Hare, John Le Mesurier, Terry Scott

The Night We Never Met

US 1993 99m DuArt color
Guild/Miramax (Michael Peyser)
V, V*

Three young New Yorkers organize a time-share on a Greenwich Village apartment, but the days on which each uses the place become confused.

Brash and not very likeable farce that will mean little outside the city in which it is set.

wd Warren Leight *ph* John A. Thomas *m* Evan Lurie *pd* Lester Cohen *ed* Camilla Toniolo

Matthew Broderick, Annabella Sciorra, Kevin Anderson, Jeanne Tripplehorn, Justine Bateman, Michael Mantell, Christine Baranski

'If you're in the mood to indulge in some light cultural snobbery, you'll enjoy this film . . . a rickety structure with trendy interior design, an old-fashioned sex comedy for the nouveau hip.' – *Leslie Felperin Sharman, Sight and Sound*

Night without Sleep

US 1952 77m bw
TCF (Robert Bassler)

A man reconstructs his drunken actions the night before, and fears he has committed a murder.

Dreary melodrama, all frayed tempers, drunkenness and cigarette smoke.

w Frank Partos, Elick Moll *d* Roy Baker *ph* Lucien Ballard *m* Cyril Mockridge

Gary Merrill, Linda Darnell, Hildegarde Neff, Hugh Beaumont, Mae Marsh

Night Without Stars

GB 1951 86m bw
Hugh Stewart/GFD

A blind lawyer solves the death of a traitor.

Enervated romantic melodrama.

w Winston Graham *novel* Winston Graham *d* Anthony Pelissier

David Farrar, Nadia Gray, Maurice Teynac, Gilles Queyant

Night World

US 1932 58m bw
Universal

Characters with an assortment of problems congregate in a night-club.

Tolerable slice-of-life drama with interesting cast.

w Richard Schayer *story* P.J. Wolfson and Allen Rivkin *d* Hobart Henley

Lew Ayres, Boris Karloff, Mae Clarke, Russell Hopton, George Raft, Dorothy Revier, Bert Roach, Hedda Hopper

'Sum total is an impression that this was a two-reeler blown up into five.' – *Variety*

Night Zoo

Canada 1987 115m colour
Hendring/Oz Productions/National Film Board Of Canada (Roger Frappier, Pierre Gendron)
V, V*, L
original title: *Un Zoo la Nuit*

A drug dealer, out of prison on parole, is reconciled with his father and outwits his former bosses, who include a sadistic homosexual cop.

Lurid thriller which, inexplicably, was much honoured in its home country.

wd Jean-Claude Lauzon *ph* Guy Dufaux *m* Jean Corriveau *ad* Jean-Baptiste Tard *ed* Michel Arcand

Roger Le Bel, Gilles Maheu, Lorne Brass, Germain Houde, Jerry Snell, Corrado Mastropasqua, Lynne Adams, Amulette Garneau, Anna-Maria Giannotti

Nightbreed

US 1990 102m Technicolor
Fox/Morgan Creek (Gariella Martinelli)
V, V*, L, S

A teenager discovers Midian, a world of shape-shifting monsters.

Novel horror movie, in which the monsters are nicer than the humans, but without much narrative drive.

wd Clive Barker *novel* Cabal by Clive Barker *ph* Robin Vidgeon *pd* Steve Hardie, Mark Haskins *sp* Image Animation *ed* Richard Marden, Mark Goldblatt

Craig Sheffer, Anne Bobby, David Cronenberg, Charles Haid, Hugh Quarshie, Hugh Ross, Doug Bradley, Catherine Chevalier, Malcolm Sith, Bob Sessions, Oliver Parker

The Nightcomers *

GB 1971 96m Technicolor
Scimitar/Kastner-Kanter-Ladd (Michael Winner)
V*, L

How the ghost-ridden children in *The Turn of the Screw* became evil; they became involved in aberrant sexual activities between the gardener and the housekeeper, and finally murdered the former.

Despite its unexpected literariness this is unpleasant and unconvincing nonsense with a boring script punctuated by shock cuts and very little period feel.

w Michael Hastings *d* Michael Winner *ph* Robert Paynter *m* Jerry Fielding

Stephanie Beacham, Marlon Brando, Thora Hird, Harry Andrews, Verna Harvey, Christopher Ellis

'It leaves the viewer cold – perhaps even repelled. How could anybody think this movie would be entertaining?' – *Pauline Kael, New Yorker*

Nightfall *

US 1956 78m bw
Columbia (Ted Richmond)

The police and two bank robbers chase an innocent artist who happens to know that the loot is hidden in a Wisconsin snowdrift.

Occasionally stylish but obscurely narrated suspenser.

w Stirling Silliphant *novel* David Goodis *d* Jacques Tourneur *ph* Burnett Guffey *m* George Duning

Anne Bancroft, Aldo Ray, Brian Keith, James Gregory, Jocelyn Brando, Frank Albertson

Nighthawks

GB 1978 113m Eastmancolor
Cinegate/Nashburgh/Four Corner Films (Ron Peck, Paul Hallam)
V

The life of an actively homosexual schoolteacher.

Painful low-life drama with many signs of its amateur status.

wd Ron Peck, Paul Hallam *ph* Joanna Davis, Patrick Duval, Sebastian Dewsbery, Ian Owles, Steve Shaw *m* David Graham Ellis *ad* Jan Sender

ed Richard Taylor, Mary Pat Leece, Debra Daley, Tim Horrocks

Ken Robertson and non-professionals

Nighthawks

US 1981 99m Technicolor
Universal/Herb Nanas (Martin Poll)
V*, L

New York cops track an international terrorist.

Kojak-style thriller with a rather glum attitude to its subject.

w David Shaber *d* Bruce Malmuth *ph* James A. Contner *m* Keith Emerson

Sylvester Stallone, Billy Dee Williams, Rutger Hauer, Lindsay Wagner, Persis Khambatta, Nigel Davenport

Nighthawks 2: Strip Jack Naked

GB 1991 94m bw/colour
BFI/Channel 4 (Ron Peck)
V

An autobiographical documentary on the background to the making of *Nighthawks*, including material cut from the original film.

An amateurish and boring film, on the level of a home movie, and a demonstration that earnestness can be trying.

w Ron Peck, Paul Hallam *d* Ron Peck *ph* Ron Peck, Christopher Hughes *m* Adrian James Carbutt *ed* Ron Peck, Adrian James Carbutt

John Brown, John Daimon, Nick Bolton

Nightmare

US 1942 81m bw
Universal (Dwight Taylor)

A gambler in wartime London helps a beautiful girl escape from Nazi spies.

Thin espionage thriller with a good sequence or two and a smooth villain.

w Dwight Taylor *novel* Escape by Philip MacDonald *d* Tim Whelan *ph* George Barnes *m* Frank Skinner

Brian Donlevy, Diana Barrymore, *Gavin Muir*, Henry Daniell, Hans Conried, Arthur Shields

Nightmare *

US 1956 89m bw
UA/Pine-Thomas/Shane (Maxwell Shane)

A young musician is hypnotized into committing a murder, and reconstructs his actions with the help of his policeman brother-in-law.

Lethargic remake of the ingenious *Fear in the Night* (qv). Watchable.

wd Maxwell Shane *novel* Cornell Woolrich *ph* Joseph Biroc *m* Herschel Burke Gilbert

Edward G. Robinson, Kevin McCarthy, Virginia Christine, Connie Russell

'A chilling, highly suspenseful little item.' – *Motion Picture Herald*

'Three shocking murders . . . did she dream them? . . . or do them?'

Nightmare *

GB 1964 82m bw Hammerscope
U-I/Hammer (Jimmy Sangster)

18-year-old Janet still has nightmares after seeing her mad mother kill her father six years ago; brought home, even more frightening visions afflict her.

Genuinely scary *Diabolique*-type mystery with the usual Hammer borrowings put to good use.

w Jimmy Sangster *d* Freddie Francis *ph* John Wilcox *m* Don Banks

Moira Redmond, David Knight, Brenda Bruce, John Welsh, *Jennie Linden*

Nightmare Alley **

US   1947   112m   bw
TCF (George Jessel)

A fairground barker becomes a successful confidence trickster dealing with the supernatural, but finally sinks to the depths.

Unusual road to ruin melodrama, a striking oddity from Hollywood at the time, and still quite interesting and well done.

w *Jules Furthman,*   *novel* William Lindsay Gresham
d *Edmund Goulding*   ph *Lee Garmes*   m Cyril Mockridge

Tyrone Power, Coleen Gray, Joan Blondell, *Taylor Holmes,* Helen Walker, Mike Mazurki, Ian Keith

'The picture goes just short of all that might have made it very interesting . . . even so, two or three sharply comic and cynical scenes make it worth seeing.' – *James Agee*

The Nightmare before Christmas ***

US   1993   75m   Technicolor
Buena Vista/Touchstone (Tim Burton, Denise Di Novi)
V*, L, S
aka: *Tim Burton's The Nightmare before Christmas*

Jack Skellington, Pumpkin King of Halloween Town, tries to take over Christmas as well.

Imaginative, superbly animated (using stop-motion techniques with figures) musical, although children may not warm to its quirky humour.

w Caroline Thompson, Michael McDowell
story Tim Burton   m/ly *Danny Elfman*   sp Pete Kozachik, Eric Leighton, Ariel Velasco Shaw, Gordon Baker   ed Stan Webb

voices of Danny Elfman, Chris Sarandon, Catherine O'Hara, William Hickey, Glenn Shadix, Paul Reubens

'The dazzling techniques employed here create a striking look that has never been seen in such a sustained form before, making this a unique curio that will appeal to kids and film enthusiasts alike.' – *Variety*

'An animated fun-house for eeek freaks of all ages.' – *Peter Travers, Rolling Stone*

'It displays more inventiveness than some studios can manage in an entire year.' – *Kenneth Turan, Los Angeles Times*

AAN: visual effects

Nightmare in the Sun *

US   1963   81m   DeLuxe
Afilmco (Marc Lawrence, John Derek)
V*

A rich man kills his wife and blames a hitch-hiker who has had a brief affair with her.

Modest independent melodrama, quite interestingly made though not entirely effective.

w Ted Thomas   d Marc Lawrence   ph Stanley Cortez   m Paul Glass

John Derek, Ursula Andress, Arthur O'Connell, Aldo Ray

'See Freddy – before he sees you!'
A Nightmare on Elm Street

US   1984   91m   DeLuxe
New Line/Media/Smart Egg/Elm Street Venture/Robert Shaye
V, V*, L

Suburban teenagers find their communal dreams becoming reality when they are menaced by a creepy figure with knives for fingernails.

Unpleasant semi-splatter movie which was well enough made to take a lot of money.

wd Wes Craven   ph Jacques Haitkin   m Charles Bernstein   pd Greg Fonseca

John Saxon, Ronee Blakley, Heather Langenkamp, Amanda Wyss, Nick Corri, Robert Englund (as Freddy)

A Nightmare on Elm Street Part Two: Freddy's Revenge

US   1985   84m   DeLuxe
Heron/Smart Egg/New Line/Robert Shaye
V, V*, L

Freddy comes back and tries to take over the mind and body of a young boy.

More horror nonsense in the same mould as the above.

w David Chaskin   d Jack Sholder   ph Jacques Haitkin   m Christopher Young   ed Bob Brady

Mark Patton, Kim Myers, Hope Lange, Clu Gulager, Robert Englund

'Much as one loves watching unpleasant American teenagers ripped to death, the slasher formula has worn thin of late.' – *Time Out*

A Nightmare on Elm Street Part Three: Dream Warriors

US   1987   96m   DeLuxe
Heron/Smart Egg/New Line/Robert Shaye
V, V*, L, S

Freddy now invades the minds of teenagers under group hypnosis for nightmares.

Diminishing returns set in as this tedious bloodbath (all in the mind) gets under way.

w Wes Craven, Bruce Wagner   d Chuck Russell
ph Roy H. Wagner   m Angelo Badalamenti, Don Dokken   ad Mick Strawn, C. J. Strawn   ed Terry Stokes

Heather Langenkamp, Patricia Arquette, Larry Fishburne, Robert Englund, Priscilla Pointer, Craig Wasson

A Nightmare on Elm Street Part Four: The Dream Master

US   1988   93m   Metrocolor
Palace/New Line Cinema/Heron Communications/Smart Egg Pictures (Robert Shaye, Rachel Talalay)
V, V*, L, S

As Freddy goes on his usual killing spree, a teenager discovers that she can destroy him.

A mixture, as before, of spectacularly unpleasant special effects and grotesque humour, except that Freddy is now firmly established as the star.

w Brian Helgeland, Scott Pierce   story Brian Helgeland, William Kotzwinkle   d Renny Harlin
ph Steven Fierberg   m Craig Safan   pd Mick Strawn, C. J. Strawn   ed Michael N. Knue, Chuck Weiss, Jack Tucker, Charley Coleman

Robert Englund, Rodney Eastman, Danny Hassel, Andras Jones, Tuesday Knight, Toy Newkirk, Ken Sagoes

'The fact remains that the child-killer of Elm Street has simply run out of things to do and say.' – *MFB*

A Nightmare on Elm Street: The Dream Child

US   1989   89m   Metrocolor
Enterprise/New Line Cinema/Heron Communications/Smart Egg Pictures (Robert Shaye, Rupert Harvey)
V, V*, L, S

Freddy attempts to possess a girl's unborn child.

The murderer of the young continues in an incoherent sequel with some clever special effects. It is time that Freddy was laid to rest.

w Leslie Bohem   story John Skipp, Craig Spector, Leslie Bohem   d Stephen Hopkins   ph Peter Levy
m Jay Ferguson   pd C. J. Strawn   ed Chuck Weiss, Brent Schoenfeld

Robert Englund, Lisa Wilcox, Kelly Jo Minter, Danny Hassel, Erika Anderson, Nick Mele, Whitby Hertford, Joe Seely

'The scariest idea in the film, underlined by yet another open ending, is the possibility that this nightmare will never end, the non-existent story spinning out forever.' – *Kim Newman, MFB*

Nights of Cabiria: see *Cabiria*

Nightwing

Netherlands   1979   105m   Metrocolor
Columbia/Polyc/Martin Ransohoff
V*, L

In Arizona, mysterious deaths turn out to be caused by plague-bearing vampire bats.

Tedious shocker in the vein of *Them* but with 'modern' unpleasantness of detail.

w Steve Shagan, Bud Shrake   novel Martin Cruz Smith   d Arthur Hiller   ph Charles Rosher
m Henry Mancini

David Warner, Kathryn Harrold, Stephen Macht, Strother Martin, Nick Mancuso, Ben Piazza

'Genius. Madman. Animal. God.'
Nijinsky *

US   1980   125m   Metrocolor
Paramount/Hera (Harry Saltzman)
V*

The rise and fall of a great dancer groomed for stardom in the Ballets Russes by the impresario Diaghilev.

Rather boringly scripted with the emphasis on homosexual love, this film finally survives through its electrifying personalities and its strong sense of period.

w Hugh Wheeler   d Herbert Ross   ph Douglas Slocombe   md John Lanchbery   pd John Blezard

Alan Bates, George de la Pena, Leslie Browne, *Alan Badel,* Colin Blakely, Ronald Pickup, Ronald Lacey, Jeremy Irons, Anton Dolin, Janet Suzman, Sian Phillips, members of the London Festival Ballet

'The impression is left of a fascinating subject which proved too challenging for its makers, who settle eventually for what is uncomfortably near *All About Eve* with Bette Davis in a dinner jacket and Anne Baxter in a jock strap.' – *Alan Brien, Sunday Times*

Nikita *

France/Italy   1990   117m   Eastmancolor Technovision
Palace/Gaumont/Cecci/Tiger (Jérôme Chalou)
V, V*, L, S
aka: *La Femme Nikita*

A young criminal turns assassin for the intelligence services.

Implausible, though stylish and very watchable, thriller. wd Luc Besson   ph Thierry Arbogast
m Eric Serra   pd Dan Weil   ed Olivier Mauffroy

Anne Parillaud, Jean-Hugues Anglade, Tcheky Karyo, Jeanne Moreau, Jean Reno, Roland Blanche, Marc Duret

'An absurd, shrill, ultraviolent but soft-centered urban thriller.' – *Variety*

Nikki, Wild Dog of the North *

US   1961   74m   Technicolor
Walt Disney (Winston Hibler)
V*

The life of a Canadian trapper's wolf dog.

Pleasing 'true life fiction' which didn't quite reach top feature status.

w Ralph Wright, Winston Hibler   novel James Oliver Curwood   d Jack Couffer   m Oliver Wallace

Emile Genest, Jean Coutu

Nilouhe, Nuer: see *Daughter of the Nile*

Nine and a Half Weeks

US   1986   113m   colour
MGM/UA/PSO/Sidney Kimmel/Keith Barish/Jonesfilm/Galactic Films/Triple Ajaxx (Anthony Rufus Isaacs, Zalman King)
V, V*, L

A Wall Street executive and an art gallery employee embark upon a passionate affair.

Crash course in hot sex for those who wish to major in such studies; of no other interest despite its aspirations to being some sort of art.

w Patricia Knop, Zalman King, Sarah Kernochan novel Elizabeth McNeill d Adrian Lyne ph Peter Biziou m Jack Nitzsche pd Ken Davis

Mickey Rourke, Kim Basinger, Margaret Whitton, David Margulies, Christine Baranski

'The virtual absence of anything happening between them – like plausible attraction, amazing sex or, God forbid, good dialogue – leaves one great hole on the screen for two hours.' – Variety

Nine Days a Queen: see Tudor Rose

9 Deaths of the Ninja

US   1985   94m   colour
Crown International (Ashok Amritraj)

An anti-terrorist outfit rescues hostages captured by a mad German drug dealer.

Bungled attempt at a comic martial arts movie.
wd Emmett Alston ph Roy H. Wagner m Cecile Colayco pd Rodell Cruz ed Emmett Alston, Robert E. Waters

Sho Kosugi, Brent Huff, Emilia Lesniak, Regina Richardson, Vijay Amritraj, Blackie Dammett

Nine Girls

US   1944   78m   bw
Columbia (Burt Kelly)

College girls are murdered in a sorority house.

Cheapjack whodunnit with a cardboard look and feel.

w Karen de Wolff, Connie Lee play Wilfred H. Pettit d Leigh Jason ph James Van Trees m John Leopold

Ann Harding, Evelyn Keyes, Jinx Falkenburg, Anita Louise, Leslie Brooks, Lynn Merrick, Jeff Donnell, Nina Foch, Marcia Mae Jones, William Demarest

Nine Hours to Rama

GB   1962   125m   DeLuxe   Cinemascope
TCF/Red Lion (Mark Robson)

Events leading to the assassination of Mahatma Gandhi.

Fictionalized, sensationalized and very dull, this multi-character drama holds interest only for snatches of acting and location backgrounds.

w Nelson Gidding novel Stanley Wolpert d Mark Robson ph Arthur Ibbetson m Malcolm Arnold

José Ferrer, Diane Baker, Robert Morley, J. S. Casshyap, Horst Buchholz, Harry Andrews

'The only interesting line in the movie is the thick brown one visible on the inside of every white collar.' – John Simon

976-Evil

US   1988   100m   colour
Medusa/Cinetel/Horrorscope (Lisa M. Hansen)
V, V*, L

A teenager gains evil powers after summoning a demon by telephone.

Directed by the star of A Nightmare on Elm Street and its sequels, it resembles those films in its mixture of grotesque humour and gruesome special effects.

w Rhet Topham, Brian Helgeland d Robert Englund ph Paul Elliot m Thomas Chase, Steve Rucker ad David Brian Miller ed Stephen Myers

Stephen Geoffreys, Patrick O'Bryan, Sandy Dennis, Jim Metzler, Maria Rubell, Robert Picardo, Lezlie Deane, J. J. Cohen, Paul Wilson

Nine Lives Are Not Enough

US   1941   63m   bw
Warner

A reporter solves a multi-murder in a boarding house.

Lively second feature which moves at a commendable pace.

w Fred Niblo Jnr d A. Edward Sutherland

Ronald Reagan, Howard da Silva, James Gleason, Ed Brophy, Faye Emerson, Peter Whitney, Charles Drake

Nine Men *

GB   1943   68m   bw
Ealing

A sergeant and a handful of men in an old fort hold off the Italians in the Libyan desert.

Sharp semi-documentary of the war which paled against the mightier epics to follow. wd Harry Watt

Jack Lambert, Gordon Jackson, Frederick Piper, Grant Sutherland, Bill Blewett

9/30/55 *

US   1977   101m   colour
Columbia (Jerry Weintraub)

The death of James Dean on 9 September 1955 has a devastating effect on a teenager at an Arkansas college who identifies with him.

Effective story of adolescent feelings and frustrations.

wd James Bridges ph Gordon Willis m Leonard Rosenman ad Robert Luthardt ed Jeff Gourson

Richard Thomas, Susan Tyrrell, Deborah Benson, Lisa Blount, Thomas Hulce, Dennis Quaid, Dennis Christopher

'This is the sort of low-budget, personal moviemaking that Hollywood is presumed to shy away from, and it would be a shame if it got overlooked.' – David Ansen, Newsweek

† Leonard Rosenman wrote the music for two films starring James Dean, East of Eden and Rebel without a Cause.

Nine to Five *

US   1980   110m   DeLuxe
TCF/IPC (Bruce Gilbert)
V*, L

Three office women plot to get rid of their boss, and nearly make it.

Sporadically agreeable comedy somewhat reminiscent of Sturges's Unfaithfully Yours.

w Colin Higgins, Patricia Resnick d Colin Higgins ph Reynaldo Villalobos m Charles Fox pd Dean Mitzner

Jane Fonda, Dolly Parton, Lily Tomlin, Dabney Coleman, Sterling Hayden, Elizabeth Wilson, Henry Jones

'An effective escapist feast with lotsa funny physical schtick.' – Variety

AAN: title song (Dolly Parton)

1984 *

GB   1955   91m   bw
Holiday (N. Peter Rathvon)

Europe has become the fascist state of Oceania, ruled by Big Brother; Winston Smith yearns for the old days, and is brainwashed.

The famous prophecy of a dehumanized future is followed with reasonable fidelity apart from the defiant ending, but the novel is too literary for cinematic success and the result is too often both downbeat and boring.

w William P. Templeton, Ralph Bettinson novel George Orwell d Michael Anderson ph C. Pennington Richards m Malcolm Arnold

Michael Redgrave, Edmond O'Brien, Jan Sterling, David Kossoff, Mervyn Johns, Donald Pleasence

'Will ecstasy be a crime – in the terrifying world of the future?'

1984 *

GB   1984   110m   Eastmancolor
Umbrella/Rosenblum/Virgin (Simon Perry)
V*, L

Winston Smith comes to love Big Brother after being brainwashed and taught Doublethink.

Pointless, perhaps, to make a prophetic film in the year it was supposed to be prophesying, but this version adds a few twists to Orwell's nightmarish original and is well if sometimes confusingly made.

wd Michael Radford novel George Orwell d/ph Roger Deakins m Dominic Muldowney pd Allan Cameron ed Tom Priestley

John Hurt, Richard Burton, Suzanna Hamilton, Cyril Cusack, Gregor Fisher, James Walker

'A tale of unrelieved bleakness is told with relentless accuracy to Mr Orwell's novel, to which it is a kind of homage.' – Quentin Crisp

1941 *

US   1979   118m   Metrocolor   Panavision
Columbia/Universal/A-Team (John Milius)
V, V*, L

Just after Pearl Harbor, a stray Japanese submarine terrorizes Hollywood.

Absurdly over-budgeted manic farce which substitutes noise for wit and slapstick for comedy; it fails on every level.

w Robert Zemeckis, Bob Gale d Steven Spielberg ph William A. Fraker m John Williams pd Dean Edward Mitzner

Dan Aykroyd, Ned Beatty, John Belushi, Lorraine Gary, Murray Hamilton, Christopher Lee, Tim Matheson, Toshiro Mifune, Warren Oates, Robert Stack, Elisha Cook Jnr

'So overloaded with visual humour of rather monstrous nature that the feeling emerges that once you've seen ten explosions, you've seen them all.' – Variety

'Aimed at young audiences, who deserve better fun.' – New Yorker

'Its sheer relentless physicality, its elaborately orchestrated pointlessness on every other level, make it probably the purest demonstration of what it means to have two of the all-time commercial blockbusters to one's record and one's hands firmly on the fantasy machine.' – Richard Combs, MFB

'Spielberg intended it as "a stupidly outrageous celebration of paranoia" . . . audiences found it curiously unfunny and elephantine.' – Les Keyser, Hollywood in the Seventies

AAN: William A. Fraker

1900 *

Italy/France/West Germany   1976   320m   Technicolor
TCF/PEA/Artistes Associés/Artemis (Alberto Grimaldi)
V, V*, S
original title: Novecento

The political and personal vicissitudes of a noble Italian family between 1900 and 1945

Immensely long and heavy-going study of the rise of fascism in the form of a family saga. For specialists only.

w Bernardo Bertolucci, Franco Arcalli, Giuseppe Bertolucci d Bernardo Bertolucci ph Vittorio Storaro m Ennio Morricone ad Enzo Frigiero

Burt Lancaster, Robert de Niro, Gérard Depardieu, Dominique Sanda, Donald Sutherland, Sterling Hayden

'Exasperatingly uneven, but its most powerful moments can't be matched by any movie since Godfather Two.' – *Time*

'Bertolucci tried to write a 19th-century novel on film: the result is appalling, yet it has the grandeur of a classic visionary folly.' – *New Yorker*

† The film was normally shown in two separate parts.

1969
US 1988 96m colour
Entertainment/Atlantic (Daniel Grodnick, Bill Badalato)
V, V*, L

As the Vietnam War gets under way, two small-town youths protest for peace.

A nostalgic wallow that never rises above cliché.

wd Ernest Thompson *ph* Jules Brenner *m* Michael Small *pd* Marcia Hinds *ed* William Anderson

Robert Downey Jnr, Kiefer Sutherland, Bruce Dern, Mariette Hartley, Winona Ryder, Joanna Cassidy, Christopher Wynne

92 in the Shade *
US 1975 88m colour
United Artists (George Pappas)
V*

A drifter who becomes a fishing guide in Florida's Key West finds himself in competition with the captain of another fishing boat.

For the most part, an engaging and atmospheric study of coolly observed eccentricity, though lacking any narrative thrust.

wd Thomas McGuane *novel* Thomas McGuane *ph* Michael C. Butler *m* Michael J. Lewis *ed* Ed Rothkowitz

Peter Fonda, Warren Oates, Margot Kidder, Elizabeth Ashley, Burgess Meredith, Harry Dean Stanton, Sylvia Miles, William Hickey, Louise Latham

† The film was recut and re-released in 1981.

99 and 44/100 Per Cent Dead
US 1974 98m DeLuxe Panavision
TCF/Joe Wizan/Vashon
V*
aka: *Call Harry Crown*

A losing gang boss hires a trouble shooter.

Violent gangster melodrama apparently intended as a black comedy; if so, as clumsy as its title.

w Robert Dillon *d* John Frankenheimer *ph* Ralph Woolsey *m* Henry Mancini

Richard Harris, Edmond O'Brien, Bradford Dillman, Ann Turkel, Chuck Connors, Constance Ford

'Esthetically, commercially and morally, a quintessential fiasco.' – *Variety*

† The title in fact spoofs an ad familiar to Americans for a soap which was said to be '99 and 44/100 per cent pure'.

99 River Street *
US 1953 83m bw
UA/Edward Small

A taxi driver becomes involved in a diamond robbery.

Adequate thick ear with quite good detection and action sequences.

w Robert Smith *d* Phil Karlson *ph* Franz Planer

John Payne, Evelyn Keyes, Frank Faylen, Brad Dexter, Peggie Castle

19/19
GB 1984 99m colour/bw
BFI/Channel 4 (Nita Amy)

Two former patients of Sigmund Freud meet in old age to recall their past treatment.

Interminable and unilluminating conversation piece, intercut with documentary footage and flashbacks that illustrate what has just been said.

w Hugh Brody, Michael Ignatieff *d* Hugh Brody *ph* Ivan Strasburg *m* Brian Gascoigne *ad* Caroline Amies *ed* David Gladwell

Paul Scofield, Maria Schell, Frank Finlay, Diana Quick, Clare Higgins, Colin Firth

'He has the Power. He can stop the killings. He is the …'
Ninja Dragon (dubbed)
Hong Kong 1986 87m colour
IFD Films and Arts (Joseph Lai, Betty Chan)
V

The daughter of a murdered gang-leader returns to take over his territory and precipitates a power struggle between rival gangsters on the streets of Shanghai.

Ludicrous thriller, with unconvincing martial arts interludes, notable for its high body-count and for having not one redeeming character in its large cast; with its hooded avenger, wearing a great deal of eye-liner, and cackling black-hatted hoodlums, its overwrought style can best be described as high camp.

wd Godfrey Ho *story* Frank Hor, AAV Creative Unit *d* Joseph Lai *ph* Raymond Chang *m* Stephen Tsang *pd* Hiram Lai *sp* Simon Chu *ed* Nicky Au

Richard Harrison, Bruce Stallion, Melvin Pitcher, Konrad Chang, Lily Lan, Freya Patrick

'The picture that kids the commissars!'
'Garbo laughs!'
'Don't pronounce it – see it!'
Ninotchka ***
US 1939 110m bw
MGM (Ernst Lubitsch)
V, V*, L

A Paris playboy falls for a communist emissary sent to sell some crown jewels.

Sparkling comedy on a theme which has been frequently explored; delicate pointing and hilarious character comedy sustain this version perfectly until the last half hour, when it certainly sags; but it remains a favourite Hollywood example of this genre.

w Charles Brackett, Billy Wilder, Walter Reisch, *story* Melchior Lengyel *d* Ernst Lubitsch *ph* William Daniels *m* Werner Heymann

Greta Garbo, Melvyn Douglas, Sig Rumann, Alexander Granach, Felix Bressart, Ina Claire, Bela Lugosi

PROLOGUE: This picture takes place in Paris in those wonderful days when a siren was a brunette and not an alarm – and if a Frenchman turned out the light it was not on account of an air raid!
NINOTCHKA (Greta Garbo): 'I must have a complete report of your negotiations and a detailed expense account.'
BULJANOFF (Felix Bressart): 'No, non, Ninotchka. Don't ask for it. There is an old Turkish proverb that says, if something smells bad, why put your nose in it?'
NINOTCHKA: 'And there is an old Russian saying, the cat who has cream on his whiskers had better find good excuses.'
NINOTCHKA: 'The last mass trials were a great success. There are going to be fewer but better Russians.'

'High calibre entertainment for adult audiences, and a top attraction for the key de-luxers.' – *Variety*

'The Lubitsch style, in which much was made of subtleties – glances, finger movements, raised eyebrows – has disappeared. Instead we have a hard, brightly lit, cynical comedy with the wisecrack completely in control.' – *John Baxter, 1968*

† William Powell and Robert Montgomery were formerly considered for the Melvyn Douglas role.

AAN: best picture; script; story; Greta Garbo

The Ninth Configuration
US 1980 105m Metrocolor
ITC/Lorimar (William Peter Blatty)
V*, L

A new psychiatrist in a compound of military misfits becomes the victim of a terror campaign.

Weirdly obscure would-be thriller which only mystifies and annoys.

wd William Peter Blatty *ph* Gerry Fisher *m* Barry DeVorzon *pd* Bill Malley, J. Dennis Washington *ed* Peter Taylor

Stacy Keach, Scott Wilson, Jason Miller, Ed Flanders, Neville Brand, Moses Gunn

'Quite astonishingly garbled, trailing yards of portentous religious allegory.' – *Observer*

'The pretensions are enough to raise the *Titanic* – and sink it again.' – *Guardian*

The Ninth Guest
US 1934 65m bw
Columbia

Eight people are trapped by a murderer in a penthouse suite.

Whodunnit which must have been seen by Agatha Christie before she wrote *And Then There Were None*. This version however is flatly scripted and characterized, with no real interest in the (unlikely) outcome.

w Garnett Weston *stage play* Owen Davis *novel* Gwen Bristow *d* Roy William Neill

Donald Cook, Genevieve Tobin, Hardie Albright, Edward Ellis, Edwin Maxwell, Vince Barnett, Samuel S. Hinds

'It ought to get a neat return in most spots.' – *Variety*

The Nitwits
US 1935 81m bw
RKO
L

Two cigar-stand assistants solve the murder of a music publisher.

Overlong crime comedy with a good finale.

w Fred Guiol, Al Boasberg, Stuart Palmer *d* George Stevens

Bert Wheeler, Robert Woolsey, Fred Keating, Betty Grable, Evelyn Brent

'Fair.' – *Variety*

Niu-Peng **
China/France 1989 100m colour
Titane/Flach Film/La Sept (Jean-Luc Ormieres)
aka: *China, My Sorrow*

A 13-year-old boy is sent to Niu-Peng, a detention centre for 'the re-education of enemies of the people', for listening to love songs on his record-player.

Moving and compassionate account of a community of independent spirits surviving in the face of intransigence.

w Dai Sijie, Shan Yuan Zhu *d* Dai Sijie *ph* Jean-Michel Humeau *m* Chen Qi Gang *ad* Christian Marti *ed* Chantal Delattre

Guo Liang Yi, Tien Quan Nghieu, Vuong Han Lai, Sam Chi-Vy, Truong Loi

No Blade of Grass
GB 1970 97m Metrocolor Panavision
MGM (Cornel Wilde)

Industrial pollution sets a destructive virus ruining the crops of the world; anarchy spreads through

Britain and one family takes refuge in the Lake District.

Apocalyptic sci-fi, moderately well done though so humourless as to be almost funny.

w Sean Forestal, Jefferson Pascal *novel The Death of Grass* by John Christopher *d* Cornel Wilde *ph* H. A. R. Thompson *m* Burnell Whibley

Nigel Davenport, Jean Wallace, Patrick Holt, John Hamill

No Deposit, No Return
US   1976   112m   Technicolor
Walt Disney (Ron Miller)
V*

Airport confusion causes crooks to abduct (unwittingly) a millionaire's grandchildren; the millionaire gives chase.

Overlong and tedious action comedy which makes little sense.

w Arthur Alsberg, Don Nelson   *d* Norman Tokar
ph Frank Phillips   *m* Buddy Baker

David Niven, Darren McGavin, Don Knotts, Herschel Bernardi, Barbara Feldon, John Williams, Vic Tayback, Kim Richards

'Once again one is left wondering why there should be such an unbridgeable gulf between the brilliant professionalism and sometimes innovative genius of the Disney animated films, and the dull artlessness of the majority of their live-action pictures.' – *Philip French, The Times*

'You can't throw so many young couples together and not expect explosions!'
No Down Payment **
US   1957   105m   bw   Cinemascope
TCF (Jerry Wald)

Tension among smart suburban couples in a Los Angeles housing development.

Lively domestic melodrama, very useful to sociologists as a mirror of its times.

w Philip Yordan,   *novel* John McPartland   *d Martin Ritt*   *ph* Joseph LaShelle   *m* Leigh Harline

Joanne Woodward, Tony Randall, Sheree North, Jeffrey Hunter, Cameron Mitchell, Patricia Owens, Barbara Rush, Pat Hingle

No End *
Poland   1984   107m   colour
Artificial Eye/Zespoly Filmowe (Ryszard Chutkowski)
original title: *Bez Konca*

The ghost of a radical lawyer watches over his wife and son and an elderly lawyer who has taken over his final case, defending the leader of a strike.

Intense domestic and political drama, set against a background of the imposition of martial law.

w Krzysztof Kieslowski, Krzysztof Piesiewicz
d Krzysztof Kieslowski   *ph* Jacek Petrycki
m Zbigniew Preisner   *ad* Allan Starski
ed Krystyna Rutowska

Grazyna Szapolowska, Maria Pakulnis, Aleksander Bardini, Jerzy Radziwilowicz, Artur Barcis, Michel Bajor, Marek Kondrat

No Escape
GB   1936   85m   bw
Pathé Welwyn

A man pretends to be dead as a hoax, and when he is found so, his accomplice is suspected.

Twisty thriller from a popular play.

w George Goodchild, Frank Witty   *play No Exit* by George Goodchild, Frank Witty   *d* Norman Lee

Valerie Hobson, Leslie Perrins, Robert Cochran, Billy Milton, Henry Oscar

'Good programme picture for almost anywhere.' – *Variety*

No Funny Business
GB   1933   75m   bw
John Stafford

Two professional co-respondents are sent to the Riviera; each mistakes the other as his client.

Stagey farce, notable for its unlikely star teaming and its hilariously dated style.

w Victor Hanbury, Frank Vosper, Dorothy Hope
d John Stafford, Victor Hanbury

Gertrude Lawrence, Laurence Olivier, Jill Esmond, Edmund Breon, Gibb McLaughlin, Muriel Aked

No Greater Glory
US   1934   78m   bw
Columbia

Boys learn through their play that there is no greater glory than to die for one's country.

Glum parable which probably worked better in the original German.

w Jo Swerling   *film script The Paul Street Boys* by Ferenc Molnar   *d* Frank Borzage

George Breakston, Jimmy Butler, Jackie Searl, Frankie Darro, Ralph Morgan, Christian Rub

'Not for the general trade, but a prospective hit in the arties.' – *Variety*

No Habra Mas Penas Ni Olvido: see *A Funny Dirty Little War*

No Hands on the Clock
US   1941   76m   bw
Pine-Thomas/Paramount

A private eye on honeymoon steps right into a kidnapping.

Rather flat time-passer with too many loose ends.

w Maxwell Shane   *novel* Geoffrey Homes   *d* Frank McDonald

Chester Morris, Jean Parker, Rose Hobart, Dick Purcell, Astrid Allwyn, Rod Cameron

'Turn back, I tell you! Any minute may be too late!'
No Highway **
GB   1951   98m   bw
TCF (Louis D. Lighton)
US title: *No Highway in the Sky*

During a transatlantic flight, a boffin works out that the plane's tail is about to fall off from metal fatigue.

The central premise of this adaptation from a popular novel is fascinating, but the romantic asides are a distraction and the characters cardboard; the film still entertains through sheer professionalism.

w R. C. Sherriff, Oscar Millard, Alec Coppel
novel Nevil Shute   *d* Henry Koster   *ph* Georges Périnal

James Stewart, Marlene Dietrich, Glynis Johns, Jack Hawkins, Janette Scott, Elizabeth Allan, Kenneth More, Niall MacGinnis, Ronald Squire

No Highway in the Sky: see *No Highway*

No Kidding
GB   1960   86m   bw
Peter Rogers/GHW/Anglo Amalgamated
US title: *Beware of Children*

An old house is turned into a holiday home for deprived rich children.

Strained comedy with agreeable cast.

w Norman Hudis, Robin Estridge   *novel* Verity Anderson   *d* Gerald Thomas

Leslie Phillips, Geraldine McEwan, Julia Lockwood, Noel Purcell, Irene Handl, Joan Hickson, Cyril Raymond

No Leave, No Love
US   1946   118m   bw
MGM (Joe Pasternak)

Sailors on leave meet an English girl.

Witless, overlong musical extravaganza.

w Charles Martin, Leslie Karkos   *d* Charles Martin
ph Harold Rosson, Robert Surtees   *md* Georgie Stoll

Van Johnson, Pat Kirkwood, Keenan Wynn, Guy Lombardo and his Orchestra, Edward Arnold, Marie Wilson, Leon Ames

No Limit *
GB   1935   79m   bw
ATP (Basil Dean)
V

A motor mechanic enters for the TT Races.

Lively star comedy with Isle of Man locations.

w Tom Geraghty, Fred Thompson   *story* Walter Greenwood   *d* Monty Banks   *ph* Bob Martin

George Formby, Florence Desmond, Edward Rigby, Jack Hobbs, Peter Gawthorne, Alf Goddard

No Love for Johnnie *
GB   1960   111m   bw   Cinemascope
Rank/Five Star (Betty E. Box)
V*

The personal and political problems of a Labour MP.

Predictable but quite lively study of ambition and frustration, with good cameos; Cinemascope all but ruins its impact.

w Nicholas Phipps, Mordecai Richler   *novel* Wilfred Fienburgh   *d* Ralph Thomas   *ph* Ernest Steward
m Malcolm Arnold

Peter Finch, Mary Peach, *Stanley Holloway*, Donald Pleasence, Billie Whitelaw, Hugh Burden, Rosalie Crutchley, Michael Goodliffe, Mervyn Johns, Geoffrey Keen, Paul Rogers, Dennis Price, Peter Barkworth, Fenella Fielding, Gladys Henson

No Man Is an Island
US   1962   114m   Eastmancolor
U-I/Gold Coast (John Monks Jnr, Richard Goldstone)
GB title: *Island Escape*

After the Japanese attack on Guam, a radioman finds refuge in a leper colony and sets up his own resistance unit.

Unexceptional war adventure in the jungle.

wd John Monks Jnr, Richard Goldstone   *ph* Carl Kayser   *m* Restie Umali

Jeffrey Hunter, Marshall Thompson, Barbara Perez, Ronald Remy

'Good clean fun for right-minded teenagers.' – *MFB*

'He was a hit and run lover ... personally, he preferred a cigarette to any dame!'
No Man of Her Own *
US   1932   98m   bw
Paramount
V*, L

A big-time gambler marries a local girl on a bet and tries to keep her innocent of his activities.

Star romantic comedy drama, quite professionally assembled and played.

w Maurine Watkins, Milton H. Gropper   *d* Wesley Ruggles   *ph* Leo Tover

Clark Gable, Carole Lombard, Dorothy Mackaill, Grant Mitchell, George Barbier, Elizabeth Patterson, J. Farrell MacDonald

'Entertaining film with national appeal.' – *Variety*

'Just about everything that the ordinary picture fan looks for: drama, romance, comedy, strong build-ups, exciting climaxes, a fine line of human interest.' – *Film Daily*

No Man of Her Own *
US   1949   98m   bw
Paramount (Richard Maibaum)

A pregnant wanderer is involved in a train crash and
assumes the identity of the wife of a dead passenger.

Glossy star melodrama, very watchable.

w Catherine Turney, Sally Benson, Mitchell Leisen
d *Mitchell Leisen*   ph Daniel L. Fapp   m Hugo
Friedhofer

Barbara Stanwyck, John Lund, Lyle Bettger, *Jane Cowl*,
Phyllis Thaxter, Henry O'Neill, Richard Denning

No Man's Land *
France/Switzerland   1985   110m   colour
Filmograph/MK2 (Alain Tanner, Marin Karmitz)

A group of smugglers, each wanting a better way of
life, operate on the borders of France and Switzerland.

Coolly detached account of people on the point of
breakdown.

wd Alain Tanner   ph Bernard Zitzermann   m Terry
Riley   pd Alain Nicolet   ed Laurent Uhler

Jean-Philippe Ecoffey, Betty Berr, Marie-Luce Felber,
Hugues Quester, Myriam Mézières

No Man's Land
1987   105m   colour
Rank/Orion (Joseph Stern, Dick Wolf)
V*, L

A young undercover cop falls in love with the sister of
the car thief he is trying to bring to justice.

Moderate low-key thriller with lacklustre
performances.

w Dick Wolf   d Peter Werner   ph Hiro Narita
m Basil Poledouris   pd Paul Peters   ed Steve
Cohen

D. B. Sweeney, Charlie Sheen, Lara Harris, Randy
Quaid, Bill Duke, R. D. Call, Arlen Dean Snyder, M.
Emmett Walsh, Al Shannon

No Mercy
US   1986   105m   Metrocolor
Tri-Star/Delphi IV (D. Constantine Conte)
V, V*, L

Policemen pretend to be hit men in an attempt to
infiltrate a murder-by-contract organization.

Fashionable violence, slick production, nothing new.

w Jim Carabatsos   d Richard Pearce   ph Michael
Brault   m Alan Silvestri

Richard Gere, Kim Basinger, Jeroen Krabbe, George
Dzundza, Gary Basaraba, William Atherton

No Mercy, No Future
West Germany   1981   100m   colour
Mainline/Halma Sanders-Brahms
original title: *Die Berührte*

A suicidal schizophrenic wanders through Berlin
looking for Christ and indulging in casual affairs.

Uncompromisingly downbeat study of madness that
provides a succession of shocking images which
become hard to bear.

wd Halma Sanders-Brahms   ph Thomas Mauch
m Manfred Opitz, Harald Grosskopf   ed Ursula
West, Hanni Lewerenz

Elisabeth Stepanek, Hubertus von Weyrauch, Irmgard
Mellinger, Nguyen Chi Canh

No Minor Vices
US   1948   96m   bw
(MGM) Enterprise (Lewis Milestone)

A doctor brings home an artist friend who proceeds to
wreck his household.

Interminable thin comedy which gives no clue as to
what the talent involved thought it was doing.

w Arnold Manoff   d Lewis Milestone   ph George
Barnes   m Franz Waxman

Dana Andrews, Lilli Palmer, Louis Jourdan, Jane
Wyatt, Norman Lloyd

No More Ladies
US   1935   79m   bw
MGM

A society girl thinks that by marrying a rake she can
reform him.

Breezy sophisticated comedy which doesn't quite
maintain its impetus.

w Donald Ogden Stewart, Horace Jackson   play A.
E. Thomas   d Edward H. Griffith, George Cukor
ph Oliver T. Marsh   m Edward Ward

Joan Crawford, Robert Montgomery, Franchot Tone,
Charles Ruggles, Edna May Oliver, Gail Patrick,
Reginald Denny, Arthur Treacher

'Sophistication plus in society setting and probably
too much on the ultra side for sock appreciation. But
okay.' – *Variety*

No More Women
US   1934   73m   bw
Paramount

Deep-sea divers compete for jobs and a woman.

Flagg and Quirt in all but name, with action
melodrama largely substituted for skirt-chasing.

w Delmer Daves, Lou Breslow   story John M. Strong
d Al Rogell

Edmund Lowe, Victor McLaglen, Sally Blane, Minna
Gombell, Harold Huber

'Quirt and Flagg under the Hays morality code, and
they can't take it.' – *Variety*

No, My Darling Daughter
GB   1961   96m   bw
Rank/Five Star/Betty E. Box-Ralph Thomas

Chaos ensues when a tycoon's daughter is thought to
be eloping with an American boyfriend.

Clumsy comedy with moments of brightness
provided by the actors.

w Frank Harvey   play *A Handful of Tansy* by Harold
Brooke, Kay Bannerman   d Ralph Thomas
ph Ernest Steward   m Norrie Paramor

Michael Redgrave, Michael Craig, Roger Livesey, Rad
Fulton, Juliet Mills, Renee Houston, Joan Sims, Peter
Butterworth

No Name on the Bullet
US   1958   77m   Eastmancolor   Cinemascope
Universal (Howard Christie, Jack Arnold)

A hired gunman books into the hotel of a small
Western town, and everybody wonders who he is
after.

Tolerable Western programmer with more emphasis
than usual on characterization.

w Gene L. Coon   d Jack Arnold   ph Harold
Lipstein   m Herman Stein

Audie Murphy, Charles Drake, Joan Evans, R. G.
Armstrong, Willis Bouchey, Karl Swenson

No No Nanette
US   1930   90m approx   bw with Technicolor
     sequences
Warner

A married bible publisher secretly helps three girls,
who all visit him on the same day.

Early talkie version of the rather naïve musical hit,
with a priceless moment or two among the dross.

w Howard Emmett Rogers   play Otto Harbach and
Frank Mandel   d Clarence Badger

Bernice Claire, Lucien Littlefield, Lilyan Tashman,
Bert Roach, ZaSu Pitts

No No Nanette
US   1940   90m   bw
RKO/Suffolk (Herbert Wilcox)

Slightly altered remake with too little attention to the
musical numbers.

w Ken Englund   d Herbert Wilcox   md Anthony
Collins

Anna Neagle, Richard Carlson, Victor Mature, Helen
Broderick, Roland Young, ZaSu Pitts, Eve Arden,
Billy Gilbert

'It's overboard on inaction, with most of the dead
wood up front.' – *Variety*

No Orchids for Miss Blandish
GB   1948   102m   bw
Alliance/Tudor (A. R. Shipman, Oswald Mitchell)

An heiress is kidnapped by gangsters and falls for
their psychopathic leader.

Hilariously awful gangster movie from a bestselling
shocker. Everyone concerned is all at sea, and the
result is one of the worst films ever made.

wd St John L. Clowes   novel James Hadley Chase
ph Gerald Gibbs

Jack La Rue, Linden Travers, Hugh McDermott,
Walter Crisham, Lily Molnar, Zoe Gail

'This must be the most sickening exhibition of
brutality, perversion, sex and sadism ever to be
shown on a cinema screen . . . with pseudo-American
accents the actors literally battle their way through a
script laden with suggestive dialogue.' – *MFB*

'A most vicious display of sadism, brutality and
suggestiveness.' – *Milton Shulman, Evening Standard*

'The morals are about level with those of a scavenger
dog.' – *Daily Express*

'It has all the morals of an alley cat and all the
sweetness of a sewer.' – *Observer*

'The worst film I have ever seen.' – *Sunday Express*

† Remade as *The Grissom Gang* (qv).

No Parking
GB   1938   72m   bw
Herbert Wilcox

A car park attendant is mistaken for an American
killer.

Modest, entertaining star comedy.

w Gerald Elliott   story Carol Reed   d Jack
Raymond   ph Francis Carver

Gordon Harker, Leslie Perrins, Irene Ware, Cyril
Smith

No Peace among the Olives
Italy   1950   99m   bw
Lux (Domenico Davanzati)

A young shepherd goes home after the war and finds
himself at war again – against a local racketeer.

A rather crude melodrama comparable with the
American *Thieves' Highway* and other *films noirs* of the
time.

w Giuseppe de Santis and others   d Giuseppe de
Santis   ph Pietro Portalupi   m Goffredo Petrassi

Lucia Bose, Raf Vallone, Folco Lulli, Dante Maggio

No Place for Jennifer
GB   1949   90m   bw
ABPC

Divorcing parents think again when their twelve-
year-old daughter runs away.

Very predictable tearjerker which kept box offices
busy in its day.

w J. Lee-Thompson   novel *No Difference to Me* by
Phyllis Hambledon   d Henry Cass

Leo Genn, Rosamund John, Janette Scott, Beatrice Campbell, Guy Middleton, Anthony Nicholls, Jean Cadell

No Problem! (dubbed) *
France   1975   100m   Eastmancolor
Gaumont International 2000 (Alain Poiré)
original title: *Pas de Problème*

Enlisting the aid of a medical student in ridding her flat of a dead man, a young woman triggers a series of mishaps.

A hectic farce that, despite some unsympathetic dubbing, manages to raise a few smiles.

w Jean-Marie Poiré   *d* Georges Lautner *ph* Maurice Fellous   *m* Philippe Sarde *ed* Michelle David

Miou-Miou, Bernard Menez, Jean Lefebvre, Anny Duperey, Henri Guybet, Renée Saint-Cyr, Patrick Dewaere (cameo)

No Questions Asked
US   1951   80m   bw
MGM (Nicholas Nayfack)

A young lawyer undertakes shady business and finds himself framed for murder.

Well made second feature on conventional lines.

w Sidney Sheldon   *d* Harold Kress   *ph* Harold Lipstein   *m* Leith Stevens

Barry Sullivan, George Murphy, Arlene Dahl, Jean Hagen, William Reynolds, Mari Blanchard

No Resting Place
GB   1951   77m   bw
Colin Lesslie

A wandering Irish tinker accidentally kills a man and is hounded by a Civil Guard.

Interesting attempt at realistic location drama, suffering from a dejected plot and unsympathetic characters.

w Paul Rotha, Colin Lesslie, Michael Orrom *novel* Ian Niall   *d* Paul Rotha   *ph* Wolfgang Suschitzky   *m* William Alwyn

Michael Gough, Noel Purcell, Jack McGowran

No Room at the Inn
GB   1948   82m   bw
British National (Ivan Foxwell)

A monstrous woman half-starves evacuees and turns her house into a brothel.

Absurd melodrama from a play which was popular because it offered a full-blooded star performance. The film is less convincing but works pretty well on its level.

w Ivan Foxwell, Dylan Thomas   *play* Joan Temple *d* Dan Birt   *ph* James Wilson

Freda Jackson, Joy Shelton, Hermione Baddeley, Joan Dowling, Harcourt Williams, Sydney Tafler, Frank Pettingell, Niall MacGinnis

No Room for the Groom *
US   1952   82m   bw
Universal-International (Ted Richmond)

An army veteran returns to his wife, who has moved in with her family without telling them of her marriage.

Amiable comedy which rises to a fair pitch of frenzy.

w Joseph Hoffman   *story* Darwin H. Teilhet *d* Douglas Sirk   *ph* Clifford Stine   *m* Frank Skinner

Tony Curtis, Piper Laurie, Don Defore, *Spring Byington,* Lee Aaker, Jack Kelly, Lillian Bronson

No Sad Songs for Me
US   1950   89m   bw
Columbia (Buddy Adler)

A young wife discovers she has only eight months to live, and spends it planning her husband's future.

Well-meant but rather icky melodrama featuring one of those beautiful illnesses that appear to have no physical effect.

w Howard Koch   *novel* Ruth Southard   *d* Rudolph Maté   *ph* Joseph Walker   *m* George Duning

Margaret Sullavan, Wendell Corey, Viveca Lindfors, Natalie Wood, John McIntire

AAN: George Duning

No Sex Please, We're British
GB   1973   91m   Technicolor
Columbia/BHP (John R. Sloan)
V

Confusion ensues when a wrongly addressed parcel of dirty postcards arrives at a bank.

Fairly lively farce with everything from mistaken identity to falling trousers.

w Anthony Marriott, Johnnie Mortimer, Brian Cooke *play* Anthony Marriott, Alistair Foot   *d* Cliff Owen *ph* Ken Hodges   *m* Eric Rogers

Ronnie Corbett, Arthur Lowe, Beryl Reid, Ian Ogilvy, Susan Penhaligon, David Swift, Michael Bates

No Sleep Till Dawn: see *Bombers B52*

No Smoking
GB   1955   72m   bw
Tempean (Robert S. Baker, Monty Berman)

Tobacco companies take action when a simple-minded village chemist invents a no-smoking pill that works.

Dreary B-feature comedy with a ludicrous plot that failed to make an amiable radio comedian funny on the screen.

w Kenneth Hayles, Phil Park   *play* George Moresby-White, Rex Rientis   *d* Henry Cass   *ph* Monty Berman   *md* Stanley Black   *m* Ivor Slaney *ad* Wilfred Arnold   *ed* Jack Slade

Reg Dixon, Belinda Lee, Lionel Jeffries, Ruth Trouncer, Alexander Gauge, Myrtle Rowe, Arthur Young, Hal Osmond, Tom Gill, Ronnie Stevens

No Surrender *
GB   1985   104m   colour
Dumbarton/NFFC/Lauron/Film Four International (Mamoun Hassan)
V, V*

Irish factions collide in a Liverpool club.

Black comedy typical of the author of *Boys from the Black Stuff.*

w Alan Bleasdale   *d* Peter Smith   *ph* Mick Coulter *m* Daryl Runswick

Michael Angelis, Avis Bunnage, James Ellis, Ray McAnally, Tom Georgeson, Bernard Hill, J. G. Devlin

'Monstrous and marvellous, it combines the disturbing, the disorienting and the downright daft.' – *Paul Taylor, MFB*

No Time for Comedy *
US   1940   93m   bw
Warner (Robert Lord)

A playwright is depressed by the times and has lost the knack of making people laugh.

Smooth film version of a thoughtful romantic comedy play.

w Julius J. and Philip G. Epstein   *play* S. N. Behrman *d* William Keighley   *ph* Ernest Haller   *m* Heinz Roemheld

James Stewart, Rosalind Russell, Charles Ruggles, Genevieve Tobin, Allyn Joslyn, Clarence Kolb, Louise Beavers

'Claudette loves the men with muscles!'
No Time for Love *
US   1943   83m   bw
Paramount (Mitchell Leisen)

A lady photographer falls for the foreman of a crew digging a tunnel under the Hudson.

Agreeable romantic slapstick farce.

w Claude Binyon   *d* Mitchell Leisen   *ph* Charles Lang Jnr   *m* Victor Young   *ad* Hans Dreier, Robert Usher

Claudette Colbert, Fred MacMurray, Ilka Chase, Richard Haydn, June Havoc, Marjorie Gateson, Bill Goodwin

AAN: art direction

No Time for Sergeants
US   1958   111m   bw
Warner (Mervyn Le Roy)
V*, L

Adventures of a hillbilly army conscript.

Heavy-handed adaptation of the stage success, a real piece of filmed theatre with not much sparkle to it.

w John Lee Mahin   *play* Ira Levin   *novel* Mac Hyman   *d* Mervyn Le Roy   *ph* Harold Rosson *m* Ray Heindorf

Andy Griffith, William Fawcett, Murray Hamilton, Nick Adams, Myron McCormick, Bartlett Robinson

No Time for Tears
GB   1957   86m   Eastmancolor   Cinemascope
ABPC (W. A. Whittaker)

Problems of a children's hospital.

Totally predictable British tearjerker with a happy ending.

w Anne Burnaby   *d* Cyril Frankel   *ph* Gilbert Taylor   *m* Francis Chagrin

Anna Neagle, Anthony Quayle, Sylvia Syms, Flora Robson, George Baker, Alan White, Daphne Anderson, Michael Hordern, Joan Hickson, Sophie Stewart, Rosalie Crutchley

No Trees in the Street
GB   1958   96m   bw
ABP/Allegro (Frank Godwin)

Problems of a London slum family in the thirties.

Artificial and unconvincing attempt at a London *Love on the Dole,* dragged up and redigested in a later era when 'realism' was thought to be fashionable.

w Ted Willis   *play* Ted Willis   *d* J. Lee-Thompson *ph* Gilbert Taylor   *m* Laurie Johnson

Sylvia Syms, Herbert Lom, Joan Miller, Melvyn Hayes, Stanley Holloway, Liam Redmond, Ronald Howard, Carole Lesley, Lana Morris, Lily Kann

'Nothing remains but crude sensationalism and several moments of unconscious humour.' – *MFB*

No Way Out *
US   1950   106m   bw
TCF (Darryl F. Zanuck)

A crook stirs up racial feeling against a black doctor in whose hands his brother has died.

Vivid, hard-hitting melodrama with a hospital background and a strong sociological flavour.

w Joseph L. Mankiewicz, Lesser Samuels   *d* Joseph L. Mankiewicz   *ph* Milton Krasner   *m* Alfred Newman

Richard Widmark, Sidney Poitier, Linda Darnell, Stephen McNally, Harry Bellaver, Stanley Ridges, Ossie Davis, Ruby Dee

'A production designed solely for purposes of agitation and propaganda, unworthy of literary or cinematic consideration.' – *Henry Hart, Films in Review*

AAN: script

No Way Out *
US 1987 116m Metrocolor
Orion/Neufeld/Ziskin/Garland (Laura Ziskin, Robert Garland)
V, V*, L, S

A Pentagon officer is convinced his boss is guilty of murder, but the evidence points to himself.

Fast-paced remake of *The Big Clock* (qv) which does not efface the memory of the original.

w Robert Garland *novel* Kenneth Fearing
d Roger Donaldson ph John Alcott m Maurice Jarre pd Dennis Washington

Kevin Costner, Gene Hackman, Sean Young, Will Patton, Howard Duff, George Dzundza

No Way to Treat a Lady *
US 1968 108m Technicolor
Paramount/Sol C. Siegel
V*

A mass murderer of women who is also a master of disguise has a running battle with a police detective.

Curious mixture of star show-off piece, murder mystery, black farce, suspense melodrama and Jewish comedy. Bits of it come off very well, but it's a bumpy ride.

w John Gay *novel* William Goldman d Jack Smight ph Jack Priestley m Stanley Myers

Rod Steiger, George Segal, Lee Remick, Eileen Heckart, Murray Hamilton, Michael Dunn

'The sweetest love story ever told! The epic drama of the age! Drama with a world sweep, colossal and sublime!'

Noah's Ark **
US 1929 135m bw
Warner

The biblical story of Noah is paralleled, rather loosely, with a tragedy of World War I.

Naïve but fascinating Hollywood epic which in patches triumphantly overcomes the problems of the part-talkie period and is always fascinating to look at.

w Anthony Coldeway, Darryl F. Zanuck d Michael Curtiz ph Hal Mohr, Barney McGill pd Anton Grot

Dolores Costello, Noah Beery, Louise Fazenda, Guinn Williams, Paul McAllister, Myrna Loy, George O'Brien

'The biggest and best edited picture of the industry . . . mobs, Niagaras, train wrecks, war aplenty, crashes, deluges and everything that goes to give the picture fan a thrill.' – *Variety*

'Staggering . . . the greatest thing the screen has done.' – *The Film Spectator*

† On première it was Warner's longest film, but the release version was cut by nearly half.

Nob Hill *
US 1945 95m Technicolor
TCF (André Daven)

In the gay 1890s, a San Francisco saloon owner tries to step into society and win one of its most eligible young ladies.

Engaging period musical drama with all talents working well.

w Wanda Tuchock, Norman Reilly Raine d Henry Hathaway ph Edward Cronjager md Emil Newman, Charles Henderson m David Buttolph

George Raft, Joan Bennett, Peggy Ann Garner, Vivian Blaine, Alan Reed, B. S. Pully, Edgar Barrier

Nobi: see *Fires on the Plain*

Nobody Lives Forever
US 1946 100m bw
Warner (Robert Buckner)

A con man fleeces a rich widow, then falls in love with her.

Forgettable romantic melodrama.

w W. R. Burnett d Jean Negulesco ph Arthur Edeson m Adolph Deutsch

John Garfield, Geraldine Fitzgerald, Walter Brennan, Faye Emerson, George Coulouris, George Tobias

Nobody Runs Forever *
GB 1968 101m Eastmancolor
Rank/Selmur (Betty E. Box)
US title: *The High Commissioner*

An Australian detective is sent to arrest the high commissioner in London on a charge of murdering his first wife.

Sub-Hitchcock thriller which comes to life in patches but has a plot and dialogue which obviously embarrass the actors.

w Wilfred Greatorex *novel* *The High Commissioner* by Jon Cleary d Ralph Thomas ph Ernest Steward m Georges Delerue

Rod Taylor, Christopher Plummer, Lilli Palmer, Camilla Sparv, Daliah Lavi, Clive Revill, Lee Montague, Calvin Lockhart, Derren Nesbitt, Leo McKern, Franchot Tone

Nobody's Baby
US 1937 67m bw
MGM (Hal Roach)

Girls at a training school for nurses find themselves looking after a baby.

Lightweight comedy filler.

w Harold Law, Hal Yates, Pat C. Flick d Gus Meins

Lyda Roberti, Patsy Kelly, Lynne Overman, Robert Armstrong, Rosina Lawrence, Don Alvarado, Tom Dugan

'Agreeable enough number two feature for duals.' – *Variety*

Nobody's Fool
US 1986 107m CFI colour
Enterprise/Island (James C. Katz, Jon S. Denny)

A small-town girl with a mild past falls for a lighting technician with a visiting theatrical troupe.

Much ado about nothing; good observant touches don't stifle the yawns.

w Beth Henley d Evelyn Purcell ph Mikhail Suslov m James Newton pd Jackson DeGovia ed Dennis Virkler

Rosanna Arquette, Eric Roberts, Mare Winningham, Jim Youngs, Louise Fletcher, Gwen Welles

Nobody's Perfect
US 1968 103m Techniscope
Universal (Howard Christie)
V*, L

An ex-naval officer returns to Japan to make amends for stealing a buddha.

Flatfooted comedy adventure.

w John D. F. Black *novel* *The Crows of Edwina Hill* by Allan R. Bosworth d Alan Rafkin ph Robert H. Wyckoff m Irving Gertz

Doug McClure, Nancy Kwan, Steve Carlson, James Whitmore, David Hartman, Gary Vinson, James Shigeta

Noce Blanche
France 1989 92m colour
Gala/Les films du Losange/La Sept/La Sorcière Rouge/Sofia/Investimage 2 (Margaret Menégoz)
V

A middle-aged teacher has a stormy affair with his seventeen-year-old pupil.

Cliché-ridden account of mid-life fantasies and adolescent problems, from drugs to prostitution, that offers little in the way of enlightenment.

wd Jean-Claude Brisseau ph Romain Winding ad Maria-Luisa Garcia ed Maria-Luisa Garcia

Vanessa Paradis, Bruno Cremer, Ludmila Mikael, François Negret, Jean Deste, Véronique Silver, Philippe Tuin

La Noche del Terror Ciego: see *Tombs of the Blind Dead*

Nocturne *
US 1946 87m bw
RKO (Joan Harrison)
V*, L

A police detective investigates the death of a composer.

Amusingly self-mocking crime thriller, quite smoothly done in all departments.

w Jonathan Latimer d Edwin L. Marin ph Harry J. Wild m Leigh Harline

George Raft, Lynn Bari, Virginia Huston, Joseph Pevney, Myrna Dell, Edward Ashley, Walter Sande, Mabel Paige

'As for the plot, I confess I could not follow it, nor did I care.' – *Paul Holt, Daily Express*

Noi Tre
Italy 1984 96m colour
Instituto Luce/Duea Film/RAI (Paolo Bacchi, Francesco Guerrieri)
V
aka: *The Three of Us*

On a summer visit to the estate of an Italian count, the young Mozart falls in love.

Pleasant but inconsequential pastoral idyll which treats the composer as an exceptionally innocent adolescent.

w Pupi Avati, Antonio Avati, Cesare Bornazzini d Pupi Avati ph Pasquale Rachini m Riz Ortolani pd Giancarlo Basili, Leonardo Scarpa ed Amedeo Salfa

Lino Capolicchio, Gianni Cavina, Carlo Delle Piane, Ida Di Benedetto, Giulio Pizzirani

La Noia: see *The Empty Canvas*

Noir et Blanc
France 1986 80m bw
Electric/Les Films Du Volcan

A timid accountant forms a sado-masochistic relationship with a black masseur.

Claustrophobic study of sexual obsession which eschews sensationalism.

wd Claire Devers *story* *Desire and the Black Masseur* by Tennessee Williams ph Daniel Desbois, Christopher Doyle, Alain Lasfargues, Jean-Paul de Costa pd Claire Devers ed Fabienne Alvarez, Yves Sarda

Francis Frappat, Jacques Martial, Joséphine Fresson, Marc Berman, Claire Rigollier

Noises Off
US 1992 104m Technicolor
Warner/Touchstone/Touchstone Pacific Partners I/Amblin (Frank Marshall)
V, V*, L

The American cast of a British sex comedy suffer a series of disasters, on-stage and off, during a pre-Broadway tour.

Brave though misguided attempt to transfer to the screen an intensely theatrical work, depending on live performance for its effect. It begins well but soon ceases to amuse.

w Marty Kaplan *play* Michael Frayn d Peter Bogdanovich ph Tim Suhrstedt m Phil Marshall pd Norman Newberry ed Lisa Day

Carol Burnett, Michael Caine, Denholm Elliott, Julie Hagerty, Marilu Henner, Mark Linn-Baker, Christopher Reeve, John Ritter, Nicollette Sheridan

'Serves up plenty of laughs, and in many ways it stands as a model transfer of a play to the screen.' – *Variety*

'If I say that I laughed till I cried, I have a dreadful fear the words will be ripped out and stuck on the poster. But I did.' – *Nigel Andrews, Financial Times*

'On screen, *Noises Off* fails in the only way that films can fail – bit by bit. But utterly.' – *Adam Mars-Jones, Independent*

Nomads

US 1985 100m Eastmancolor
PSO/Elliott Kastner/Cinema 7 (George Pappas, Cassian Elwes)
V, V*, L

An anthropologist settling in Los Angeles is haunted by vengeful spirits of remote tribes he had investigated.

Stylish nonsense, but nonsense none the less: it would have seemed more striking if it hadn't been five-hundredth in line.

wd John McTiernan *ph* Stephen Ramsey *m* Bill Conti *pd* Marcia Hinds

Pierce Brosnan, Lesley-Anne Down, Anna Maria Monticelli, Adam Ant, Hector Mercado

Non Stop New York

GB 1937 71m bw
GFD/Gaumont (Michael Balcon)

In 1940, gangsters on a transatlantic airliner try to kill a key witness.

Slightly futuristic thriller of its time, now hilariously dated but quite entertaining as well as giving a rare picture of air travel in the thirties.

w Curt Siodmak, Roland Pertwee, J. O. C. Orton, Derek Twist *novel* Sky Steward by Ken Attiwill *d* Robert Stevenson

John Loder, Anna Lee, Francis L. Sullivan, Frank Cellier, Desmond Tester, Athene Seyler, Jerry Verno

None but the Brave (1960): see For the Love of Mike

None but the Brave

US 1965 105m Technicolor Panavision
Warner/Eiga/Toho/Artanis (Frank Sinatra)
V*, L

During World War II a plane carrying US Marines to the Pacific front crashlands on an island held by Japanese.

Anti-war melodrama in which the action scenes are more memorable than the admirable sentiments.

w John Twist, Katsuya Susaki *d* Frank Sinatra *ph* Harold Lipstein *m* Johnny Williams

Frank Sinatra, Clint Walker, Tommy Sands, Tony Bill, Brad Dexter

'When is the world coming out of its midnight? When is the human race going to get off its knees?'

None but the Lonely Heart *

US 1944 113m bw
RKO (David Hempstead)
V*, L

In the thirties, a cockney drifter finds himself when he learns that his mother is dying.

Wildly astonishing moodpiece to come from Hollywood during World War II; its picture of East End low life is as rocky as its star performance, but it started Miss Barrymore on the west coast career which sustained her old age.

wd Clifford Odets *novel* Richard Llewellyn *ph* George Barnes *md* Constantin Bakaleinikoff *m* Hanns Eisler *ed* Roland Gross

Cary Grant, *Ethel Barrymore*, June Duprez, Barry Fitzgerald, Jane Wyatt, George Coulouris, Dan Duryea, Konstantin Shayne, Morton Lowry, Helene Thimig

'A perplexing mixture of good and bad, authentic and phony.' – *Hermione Rich Isaacs, Theatre Arts*

AA: Ethel Barrymore

AAN: Hanns Eisler; Cary Grant; Roland Gross

None Shall Escape *

US 1944 85m bw
Columbia (Sam Bischoff)

The career of a Nazi officer shown as flashbacks from his trial as a war criminal.

Taut topical melodrama reflecting the mood of the time.

w Lester Cole *d* André de Toth *ph* Lee Garmes *m* Ernst Toch

Alexander Knox, Marsha Hunt, Henry Travers, Dorothy Morris, Richard Crane

AAN: original story (Alfred Neumann, Joseph Than)

De Noorderlingen: see The Northerners

Noose

GB 1948 98m bw
ABPC/Edward Dryhurst
V*

A Soho black market gang is exposed.

Vivid though rather tatty film version of a West End play success.

w Richard Llewellyn *play* Richard Llewellyn *d* Edmond T. Greville *ph* Hone Glendinning *m* Charles Williams

Nigel Patrick, Carole Landis, Derek Farr, Joseph Calleia, Stanley Holloway, Hay Petrie, John Slater

The Noose Hangs High

US 1948 77m bw
Eagle-Lion

Two window washers are hired by a crooked bookie who finds their incompetence hard to tolerate when they lose his winnings.

Thin star comedy filled with the team's cornier routines, not too cleverly revived.

w John Grant and Howard Harris *d* Charles Barton

Bud Abbott, Lou Costello, Leon Errol, Joseph Calleia, Murray Leonard, Cathy Downs, Mike Mazurki, Fritz Feld

† A previous film of the same story was made in 1939 under the title *For Love or Money*, with June Lang, Robert Kent and Ed Brophy.

Nor the Moon By Night

GB 1958 92m Eastmancolor
Rank (John Stafford)
US title: *Elephant Gun*

An African game warden marries a longtime penfriend who finds that Africa presents unexpected problems.

Paperback romance with pleasant backgrounds.

w Guy Elmes *novel* Joy Packer *d* Ken Annakin *ph* Harry Waxman *m* James Bernard

Belinda Lee, Michael Craig, Patrick McGoohan, Anna Gaylor, Eric Pohlmann

'Neither character nor incident nor theme has any coherence or interest.' – *MFB*

'A mouth like hers is just for kissing . . . not for telling!'

Nora Prentiss *

US 1946 117m bw
Warner (William Jacobs)

A doctor falls for a café singer who ruins his life.

Standard star melodrama aimed at women, and appreciated by them.

w N. Richard Nash *story* Paul Webster, Jack Sobell *d* Vincent Sherman *ph* James Wong Howe *m* Franz Waxman

Ann Sheridan, Kent Smith, Bruce Bennett, Robert Alda, Rosemary de Camp, John Ridgely, Wanda Hendrix

Norma Rae *

US 1979 114m DeLuxe Panavision
TCF/Martin Ritt/Rose and Asseyev
V*, L

A Southern girl becomes an angry union organizer.

Well-intentioned and well-acted pamphlet of political enlightenment with an inevitably ambivalent attitude.

w Irving Ravetch, Harriet Frank Jnr *d* Martin Ritt *ph* John A. Alonzo *m* David Shire *pd* Walter Scott Herndon

Sally Field, Beau Bridges, Ron Leibman, Pat Hingle, Barbara Baxley

AA: Sally Field; song 'It Goes Like It Goes' (*m* David Shire, *ly* Norman Gimbel)

AAN: best picture; best script

Norman, Is That You?

US 1976 92m Metrocolor
MGM (George Schlatter)

Adulterous parents find that their son is a homosexual.

Unattractive comedy roughly filmed and given a black ambience. Not worth buying a ticket.

w Ron Clark, Sam Bobrick *play* Ron Clark, Sam Bobrick *d* George Schlatter

Redd Foxx, Pearl Bailey, Dennis Dugan, Michael Warren, Tamara Dobson

The Norseman

US 1978 90m Movielab
AIP/Charles B. Pierce/Fawcett Majors
V*

A Viking heads across the sea to America in search of his long lost father.

Low grade hokum for the easily pleased.

wd Charles B. Pierce *ph* Robert Bethard *m* Jaime Mendoza-Nava

Lee Majors, Cornel Wilde, Mel Ferrer, Jack Elam, Chris Connelly

El Norte **

GB/US 1983 139m
Independent Productions/American Playhouse Theatre/Channel 4 (Anna Thomas)

Fleeing from a murderous army in Guatemala, a brother and sister travel north to try to make a new life in the United States.

Conceived on a grand scale and often moving, it is nevertheless too long to bear its fragile narrative.

w Gregory Nava, Anna Thomas *d* Gregory Nava *ph* James Glennon *ed* Betsy Blankett

Zaide Silvia Gutierrez, David Villalpando, Ernest Gomez Cruz, Alicia del Lago, Eraclio Zepeda

The North Avenue Irregulars

US 1978 99m Technicolor
Disney
V*
GB title: *Hill's Angels*

A Presbyterian minister becomes an undercover agent for the FBI, helping to expose a crooked gambling syndicate.

Very heavy comedy which seems to find itself much funnier than the audience does.

w Don Tait *novel* the Rev. Albert Fay Hill *d* Bruce Bilson

Edward Herrmann, Barbara Harris, Susan Clark, Karen Valentine, Michael Constantine, Cloris Leachman, Patsy Kelly, Douglas Fowley, Alan Hale Jnr

North by Northwest ****
US   1959   136m   Technicolor   Vistavision
MGM (Alfred Hitchcock)
V, V*, L, S

A businessman is mistaken for a spy, and enemy agents then try to kill him because he knows too much.

Delightful chase comedy-thriller with a touch of sex, a kind of compendium of its director's best work, with memories of *The 39 Steps, Saboteur* and *Foreign Correspondent* among others.

w *Ernest Lehman*   d *Alfred Hitchcock*   ph *Robert Burks*   m *Bernard Herrmann*   ad *William A. Horning, Robert Boyle, Merrill Pye*   ed *George Tomasini*

Cary Grant, Eva Marie Saint, James Mason, Leo G. Carroll, Martin Landau, Jessie Royce Landis, Adam Williams

'It is only when you adopt the basic premise that Cary Grant could not possibly come to harm that the tongue in Hitchcock's cheek becomes plainly visible.' – *Hollis Alpert, Saturday Review*

'North by Northwest is never brutal. Mr Grant calls it a comedy; I would agree that it is consistently entertaining, its excitement pointed by but never interrupted by the jokes.' – *Dilys Powell*

'You get a lot of entertainment for your money. You get a couple of clever, sophisticated screen actors and an elegant actress with a fine-drawn, exciting face. You get one scene that will be talked about as long as people talk about films at all.' – *C. A. Lejeune*

AAN: Ernest Lehman; art direction; editing

North Dallas Forty
US   1979   118m   Metrocolor
Paramount (Frank Yablans)
V*, L

The gruelling life of a professional football player, laced with drugs, sex and alcohol.

Well made but generally unattractive, the kind of movie for which one wouldn't expect to find an audience.

w *Frank Yablans, Ted Kotcheff, Peter Gent*   *novel* Peter Gent   d *Ted Kotcheff*   ph *Paul Lohmann*   m *John Scott*   pd *Alfred Sweeney*

Nick Nolte, Mac Davis, Charles Durning, Dayle Haddon, Bo Swenson

North Sea Hijack
GB   1979   100m   Technicolor
Universal/Cinema Seven (Mo Rothman)
V*
US title: *ffoulkes*

A British oil rig in the North Sea is held for ransom.

Asinine *Boys' Own Paper* adventure story with the very minimum of thrills and a totally miscast hero.

w *Jack Davis*   *novel* Esther, Ruth and Jennifer *by* Jack Davis   d *Andrew V. McLaglen*   ph *Tony Imi*   m *Michael J. Lewis*   pd *Maurice Carter*

Roger Moore, Anthony Perkins, James Mason, Michael Parks, David Hedison, Jack Watson, George Baker, Faith Brook

North Star *
US   1943   105m   bw
Samuel Goldwyn (William Cameron Menzies)
V*
aka: *Armored Attack*

A Russian village defends itself against the Nazi onslaught.

Highly artificial propaganda piece later disowned by its makers and retitled. Good acting can't make its

mark when the Russian steppes become a never-never land.

w *Lillian Hellman*   d *Lewis Milestone*   ph *James Wong Howe*   m *Aaron Copland*   ad *Perry Ferguson*

Anne Baxter, Farley Granger, Jane Withers, Dana Andrews, Walter Brennan, Erich von Stroheim, Dean Jagger, Ann Harding, Carl Benton Reid, Walter Huston

'Putting American villagers into Russian costumes and calling them by Russian names is never going to deceive this old bird.' – *James Agate*

'Its failure is the case history of every Hollywood film that steps out of its scope.' – *Richard Winnington*

'Something to be seen more in sorrow than in anger and more in the attitude of the diagnostician in any emotion at all.' – *James Agee*

AAN: Lillian Hellman; James Wong Howe; Aaron Copland; Perry Ferguson

North to Alaska *
US   1960   122m   DeLuxe   Cinemascope
TCF (Henry Hathaway)
V, V*, L

In 1900, two successful gold prospectors have woman trouble.

Good-natured brawling adventure story which could do with cutting but is certainly the type of action movie they don't make 'em like any more.

w *John Lee Mahin, Martin Rackin, Claude Binyon*   *play* Birthday Gift *by* Ladislas Fodor   d *Henry Hathaway*   ph *Leon Shamroy*   m *Lionel Newman*

John Wayne, Stewart Granger, Fabian, Capucine, Ernie Kovacs, Mickey Shaughnessy, Karl Swenson, Joe Sawyer, John Qualen

North to the Klondike
US   1942   60m   bw
Universal

Gold hunters protect the rights of a girl who has made a strike.

Typical economy size programme filler with a studio look and a stalwart cast.

w *Clarence Upson Young, Lew Sarecky, George Bricker, William Castle*   d *Erle C. Kenton*

Broderick Crawford, Lon Chaney Jnr, Andy Devine, Evelyn Ankers, Keye Luke

Northern Pursuit *
US   1943   94m   bw
Warner (Jack Chertok)

A Mountie tracks a stranded Nazi pilot through the Canadian wastes.

Rather unusual star actioner, not badly done.

w *Frank Gruber, Alvah Bessie*   d *Raoul Walsh*   ph *Sid Hickox*   m *Adolph Deutsch*

Errol Flynn, Helmut Dantine, Julie Bishop, John Ridgely, Gene Lockhart, Tom Tully, Bernard Nedell

The Northerners *
Holland   1993   105m   colour
Mayfair/First Floor (Laurens Geels, Dick Maas)
original title: *De Noorderlingen*

In the only occupied street on a half-built housing estate at the edge of nowhere, everyone is acting rather strangely.

A cool and bizarre comedy of frustrated lives and eccentric behaviour.

w *Alex Van Warmerdam, Aat Ceelen*   d *Alex Van Warmerdam*   ph *Marc Felperlaan*   m *Vincent Van Warmerdam*   pd *Rikke Jelier*   ed *René Wiegmans*

Leonard Lucieer, Jack Wouterse, Rudolf Lucieer, Alex Van Warmerdam, Annet Malherbe, Loes Wouterson, Veerle Dobbelaere

'Witty and original comedy . . . Showcases a vision and style reminiscent of both Jacques Tati and Aki Kaurismäki.' – *Variety*

'Mean-spirited in its emphasis on the characters' physical indignity, this is a cold, unwelcoming movie whose studied weirdness soon becomes wearisome in the extreme.' – *Kim Newman*

Northwest Frontier ***
GB   1959   129m   Eastmancolor   Cinemascope
Rank/Marcel Hellman
V*
US title: *Flame Over India*

In 1905 an English officer during a rebellion escorts a young Hindu prince on a dangerous train journey.

Thoroughly enjoyable *Boys' Own Paper* adventure story with excellent set-pieces and a spot-the-villain mystery.

w *Robin Estridge*   d *J. Lee-Thompson*   ph *Geoffrey Unsworth*   m *Mischa Spoliansky*

Kenneth More, Lauren Bacall, Herbert Lom, Ursula Jeans, Wilfrid Hyde-White, I. S. Johar, Eugene Deckers, Ian Hunter

'*Northwest Frontier* seems to have borrowed its eccentric engine from *The General*, its hazardous expedition from *Stagecoach* and its background of tribal violence from *The Drum*.' – *Penelope Houston*

'Ten stars! Two love stories! One thousand thrills!'
Northwest Mounted Police *
US   1940   125m   Technicolor
Paramount (Cecil B. de Mille)

A Texas Ranger seeks a fugitive in Canada.

Typical big-scale action concoction by de Mille, but in this case none of it's very memorable and the detail is poor.

w *Alan Le May, Jesse Lasky Jnr, C. Gardner Sullivan*   d *Cecil B. de Mille*   ph *Victor Milner, Howard Greene*   m *Victor Young*   ad *Hans Dreier, Roland Anderson*   ed *Anne Bauchens*

Gary Cooper, Paulette Goddard, Madeleine Carroll, Preston Foster, Robert Preston, George Bancroft, Lynne Overman, Akim Tamiroff, Walter Hampden, Lon Chaney Jnr, Montagu Love, George E. Stone

'Two hours of colour, killing, kindness and magnificent country.' – *Otis Ferguson*

'A movie in the grand style. God's own biggest trees and mountains for prop and backdrop; staunch courage and lofty aims among the good people; cunning and treachery lurking within the sinister forces; the ominous note of doom finally stifled by the fortitude of noble men.' – *Time*

AA: Anne Bauchens

AAN: Victor Milner, Howard Greene; Victor Young; art direction

Northwest Outpost
US   1947   91m   bw
Republic (Allan Dwan)
GB title: *End of the Rainbow*

Adventures of California cavalrymen.

Milk-and-water adventures in a forgettable operetta.

w *Elizabeth Meehan, Richard Sale*   d *Allan Dwan*   ph *Reggie Lanning*   m *Rudolf Friml*

Nelson Eddy, Ilona Massey, Hugo Haas, Elsa Lanchester

'Half men, half demons, warriors such as the world has never known . . . they lived with death and danger for the women who hungered for their love!'

Northwest Passage (Part One, Rogers' Rangers) ***
US   1940   126m   Technicolor
MGM (Hunt Stromberg)
V*, L

Colonial rangers fight it out with hostile Indians.

Part Two was never made, but no one seemed to mind that the characters in Part One never got round to seeking the titular sea route. The adventures depicted had the feel of historical actuality, and the star was well cast.

w Laurence Stallings, Talbot Jennings novel Kenneth Roberts d King Vidor ph Sidney Wagner, William V. Skall m Herbert Stothart

Spencer Tracy, Robert Young, Ruth Hussey, Walter Brennan, Nat Pendleton, Robert Barrat, Lumsden Hare, Donald MacBride

AAN: Sidney Wagner, William V. Skall

Norwood
US 1969 95m Technicolor
Paramount/Hal B. Wallis

A Vietnam veteran returns to his Texas home but feels restless and decides to become a radio singer.

A rather ordinary film about an innocent abroad, neither very funny nor very moving.

w Marguerite Roberts d Jack Haley Jnr ph Robert B. Hauser m Al de Lory

Glen Campbell, Kim Darby, Joe Namath, Carol Lynley, Pat Hingle, Tisha Sterling, Dom de Luise, Jack Haley, Cass Daley, Gil Lamb

Nosferatu ***
Germany 1921 72m approx (24 fps) bw
Prana
V, V*, L

Count Dracula goes to Bremen and is destroyed by sunlight.

An unofficial treatment of the Bram Stoker novel, with a terrifying count and several splendid moments. It took its director to Hollywood.

w Henrik Galeen d F. W. Murnau ph Fritz Arno Wagner ad Albin Grau

Max Schreck, Gustav von Wangenheim, Greta Schröder, Alexander Granach

Nosferatu a Venezia: see Vampires in Venice

Nosferatu, Phantom der Nacht: see Nosferatu the Vampyre

Nosferatu the Vampyre *
West Germany/France 1979 107m Eastmancolor
Gaumont/Werner Herzog Filmproduktion
V
original title: Nosferatu, Phantom der Nacht

Excruciatingly slow retread of the German silent film.

Despite the star's splendidly loathsome appearance, the overall is no improvement, and the colour in the English prints is quite dreadful.

wd Werner Herzog

Klaus Kinski, Isabelle Adjani, Bruno Ganz, Walter Ladengast

'Like a dream from which you keep waking with indigestion.' – *Guardian*

Nostalgia *
Italy 1983 126m Eastmancolor
Artificial Eye/Opera Film/Sovin Film/RAI (Francesco Casati)
V

A Russian writer in Italy meets a social outcast who is expecting the end of the world.

Indescribably doomladen, occasionally beautiful, stylistically interesting and for the most part very boring parable of a kind unique to this director.

w Andrei Tarkovsky, Tonino Guerra d Andrei Tarkovsky ph Giuseppe Lanci ad Andrea Crisanti ed Erminia Marani, Amedeo Salfa

Oleg Jankovsky, Erland Josephson, Domiziana Giordano

Not as a Stranger **
US 1955 135m bw
UA/Stanley Kramer
V*

A medical student has professional and personal struggles.

Earnest filming of a bestseller, with all the actors too old for their parts.

w Edna and Edward Anhalt novel Morton Thompson d Stanley Kramer ph Franz Planer m George Antheil pd Rudolph Sternad

Robert Mitchum, Olivia de Havilland, Broderick Crawford, Frank Sinatra, Gloria Grahame, Charles Bickford, Myron McCormick, Lon Chaney Jnr, Jesse White, Henry Morgan, Lee Marvin, Virginia Christine

Not Now, Darling
GB 1972 97m Eastmancolor
LMG/Sedgemoor/Not Now Films
V

A furrier gets into a complicated situation when he arranges for his mistress to have a cheap mink coat.

Interminable film version (in Multivista, a shoot-and-edit equivalent to TV taping which gives a dingy look and can only work in a single set) of a West End farce which wasn't marvellous to begin with.

w John Chapman play Ray Cooney d Ray Cooney and David Croft

Leslie Phillips, Ray Cooney, Moira Lister, Julie Ege, Joan Sims, Derren Nesbitt, Barbara Windsor, Jack Hulbert, Cicely Courtneidge, Bill Fraser

Not of This Earth **
US 1957 72m bw
AA (Roger Corman)

An alien comes to Earth in human form in search of blood which may save his planet.

Modestly budgeted minor sci-fi; ruthless, original and competent.

w Charles Griffith, Mark Hanna d Roger Corman ph John Mescall m Ronald Stein

Paul Birch, Beverly Garland, Morgan Jones

Not Quite Jerusalem
GB 1985 114m colour
Rank/Acorn/Lewis Gilbert
V*

An Israeli girl and an American volunteer fall in love on the kibbutz.

A curious misfire. Interest in the subject is cancelled out by unattractive, slangy or caricatured people and by a muddled approach suggesting that a fairer title might have been *Carry on Terrorist.*

w Paul Kember play Paul Kember d Lewis Gilbert ph Tony Imi m Rondo Veneziano

Joanna Pacula, Sam Robards, Kevin McNally, Todd Graff, Selina Cadell

Not So Dumb
US 1929 80m bw
MGM

A naïve girl throws a big party in the hope of advancing her boyfriend's career.

Popular comedy of its time.

w Wanda Tuchock, Edwin Justus Mayer play Dulcy by George S. Kaufman and Marc Connolly d King Vidor

Marion Davies, Elliott Nugent, Raymond Hackett, Franklin Pangborn, Julia Faye

† Previously made as *Dulcy* by Warner in 1923, directed by Sidney Franklin, with Constance Talmadge.

Not Wanted on Voyage
GB 1957 82m bw
Renown

A necklace is stolen on an ocean liner.

Feeble fun from an old play.

w Michael and Roland Pertwee and others play Evadne Price, Ken Attiwill d Maclean Rogers

Ronald Shiner, Brian Rix, Griffith Jones, Katie Boyle, Fabia Drake, Michael Brennan

Not with My Wife You Don't
US 1966 119m Technicolor
Warner/Fernwood/Reynard (Norman Panama, Joel Freeman)

A Korean war veteran is furious when an old rival turns up in London and again makes eyes at his wife.

Extraordinarily flat star comedy of cross and double cross among friends.

w Norman Panama, Larry Gelbart, Peter Barnes d Norman Panama ph Charles Lang, Paul Beeson m Johnny Williams

Tony Curtis, George C. Scott, Virna Lisi, Carroll O'Connor, Richard Eastham

'About as frothy as a tin of dehydrated milk.' – *MFB*

'It has all the verve, subtlety and sophistication of its title.' – *Judith Crist*

Not without My Daughter
US 1991 114m colour
UIP/MGM/Pathé (Harry J. and Mary Jane Ufland)
V, V*, L, S

Accompanying her Iranian husband to his homeland for a holiday, an American-born wife discovers that she and her young daughter will not be permitted by him to return to America.

A plodding account of a true story, told with little imagination or flair.

w David W. Rintels book Betty Mahmoody, William Hoffer d Brian Gilbert ph Peter Hannan m Jerry Goldsmith pd Anthony Pratt ed Terry Rawlings

Sally Field, Alfred Molina, Sheila Rosenthal, Roshan Seth, Sarah Badel, Soudabeh Farrokhnia

'It is certainly as propaganda that the film is most successful, for its artlessness in all other respects will be noticeable even to those who may be convulsed by the central dilemma.' – *Variety*

'Fits with eerie precision into the cycle of paranoid and xenophobic Hollywood films familiar from the Cold War era.' – *Verina Glaessner, Sight and Sound*

Nothing Barred
GB 1961 83m bw
British Lion (Brian Rix, Darcy Conyers)

A burglar helps a noble lord steal one of his own paintings.

Leaden-footed farce.

w John Chapman d Darcy Conyers

Brian Rix, Leo Franklyn, Naunton Wayne, Charles Heslop, John Slater, Vera Pearce

Nothing but a Man *
US 1964 95m bw
Roemer-Young/DuArt (Robert Young, Michael Roemer, Robert Rubin)
V*

In a small Southern town, a black railroad worker, who decides to marry and settle down, runs into trouble with the locals when he asserts his independence.

One of the first movies to treat the subject of racial discrimination without condescension, it is effective and engaging for the most part with its documentary-style approach, even though Abbey Lincoln's wife is too good to be true.

w Michael Roemer, Robert Young   *d* Michael Roemer   *ph* Robert Young   *ed* Luke Bennett

Ivan Dixon, Abbey Lincoln, Julius Harris, Gloria Foster, Martin Priest, Leonard Parker, Yaphet Kotto, Stanley Greene

'A fine film – a first one that sets a towering standard for its makers.' – *Judith Crist*

Nothing but the Best **
GB   1964   99m   Eastmancolor
Anglo Amalgamated/Domino (David Deutsch)

An ambitious clerk learns to fight his way to the top by cheek and one-upmanship.

Hard, skilful, rather unattractive comedy with interesting social comments on its time.

w Frederic Raphael   *d* Clive Donner   *ph* Nicolas Roeg   *m* Ron Grainer   *ad* Reece Pemberton

Alan Bates, Denholm Elliott, Harry Andrews, Millicent Martin, Pauline Delany

'It is a film with a smooth, smiling elegant fun, witty but never concentrating on wit to the detriment of tension; it makes a logical step-by-step progression towards a climax which is hilarious in a Stygian way without resort to the usual bangabout.' – *Dilys Powell*

'The nightmare has already killed five people. Now it's yours to live!'
Nothing but the Night *
GB   1972   90m   Eastmancolor
Rank/Charlemagne (Anthony Nelson Keys)
V*

The trustees of an orphanage die off mysteriously, and it seems that the orphans themselves are responsible.

Convoluted murder mystery with horror elements and a twist hardly worth waiting for; earnest performances help.

w Brian Hayles   *novel* John Blackburn   *d* Peter Sasdy   *ph* Ken Talbot   *m* Malcolm Williamson

Christopher Lee, Peter Cushing, Diana Dors, Georgia Brown, Keith Barron, John Robinson

Nothing but the Truth
US   1941   90m   bw
Paramount (Arthur Hornlow Jnr)

A stockbroker takes a bet that he can tell the absolute truth for twenty-four hours.

Rather unsurprising version of a stage comedy previously filmed as a silent. It lacks the style one might expect from the team which made *The Cat and the Canary*.

w Don Hartman, Ken Englund   *play* James Montgomery   *novel* Frederic S. Isham   *d* Elliott Nugent   *ph* Charles Lang

Bob Hope, Paulette Goddard, Edward Arnold, Leif Erickson, Glenn Anders, Helen Vinson, Grant Mitchell, Willie Best

Nothing but Trouble
US   1944   70m   bw
MGM (B. F. Ziedman)
V, V*

A chef and butler accidentally prevent a poison plot against a young king.

Feebly-devised star comedy, their last for a big studio.

w Russel Rouse, Ray Golden   *d* Sam Taylor   *ph* Charles Salerno Jnr   *m* Nathaniel Shilkret

Stan Laurel, Oliver Hardy, Mary Boland, Henry O'Neill, David Leland

Nothing but Trouble
US   1991   94m   Technicolor
Warner/Applied Action (Robert K. Weiss)
V, V*, L, S

A New York couple find themselves stranded in a village where a centenarian judge has absolute rule.

Exceedingly dismal comedy, in which a group of self-indulgent comedians, having been given a great deal of rope, proceed to hang themselves; it is not a pretty sight.

wd Dan Aykroyd   *story* Peter Aykroyd   *ph* Dean Cundey   *m* Michael Kamen   *pd* William Sandell   *ed* Malcolm Campbell, James Symons

Chevy Chase, Dan Aykroyd, John Candy, Demi Moore, Valri Bromfield, Taylor Negron, Bertila Damas, Raymond J. Barry, Brian Doyle-Murray, Peter Aykroyd

'Astonishingly poor effort . . . one of the longest 94 minutes on record.' – *Variety*

'Combines absolute failure as a comedy with a surprisingly interesting and disgusting vision of grotesque America.' – *Kim Newman, Sight and Sound*

Nothing in Common
US   1986   118m   Metrocolor
Tri-Star/Rastar (Alexandra Rose)
V, V*, L

Problems of an eccentric family when mum decides to walk out after 36 years.

Edgy comedy which misfires in all directions.

w Rick Podell, Michael Preminger   *d* Garry Marshall   *ph* John A. Alonzo   *m* Patrick Leonard

Jackie Gleason, Eva Marie Saint, Tom Hanks, Hector Elizondo, Barry Corbin, Bess Armstrong

Nothing Personal
US   1980   97m   Movielab
AIP (David M. Perlmutter)
V*

A professor and a lady lawyer try to stop seal hunting.

The subject is an unsuitable starting point for a thin and zany comedy which gets nowhere and stays there.

w Robert Kaufman   *d* George Bloomfield

Donald Sutherland, Suzanne Somers, Laurence Dane, Roscoe Lee Browne

Nothing Sacred ***
US   1937   77m   Technicolor
David O. Selznick
V*, L

A girl thought to be dying of a rare disease is built up by the press into a national heroine; but the diagnosis was wrong.

Hollywood's most bitter and hilarious satire, with crazy comedy elements and superb wisecracks; a historical monument of screen comedy, though its freshness at the time can't now be recaptured.

w Ben Hecht,   *story* Letter to the Editor *by* James H. Street   *d* William Wellman   *ph* W. Howard Greene   *m* Oscar Levant

Carole Lombard, Fredric March, Walter Connolly, Charles Winninger, Sig Rumann, Frank Fay, Maxie Rosenbloom, Margaret Hamilton, Hedda Hopper, Monty Woolley, Hattie McDaniel, Olin Howland, John Qualen

DOCTOR (Charles Winninger): 'I'll tell you briefly what I think of newspapermen. The hand of God, reaching down into the mire, couldn't elevate one of them to the depths of degradation.'
EDITOR (Walter Connolly): 'I am sitting here, Mr Cook, toying with the idea of cutting out your heart and stuffing it – like an olive!'

'Hit comedy . . . will be one of the big grossers of the year.' – *Variety*

'Because it does hold up a mirror, even though a distorting mirror, to a very real world of ballyhoo and cheap sensationalism, the pleasure to be obtained from it is something more than the usual mulish guffaw.' – *Spectator*

† Refashioned in 1953 as a stage musical, *Hazel Flagg*, with Jule Styne; this in turn became a Martin and

Lewis comedy *Living It Up* (Jerry Lewis in the Carole Lombard part).

'Fateful Fascination! Electric Tension!'
'The screen's top romantic stars in a melodramatic masterpiece!'
Notorious ***
US   1946   101m   bw
RKO (Alfred Hitchcock)
V*, L

In Rio, a notorious lady marries a Nazi renegade to help the US government but finds herself falling in love with her contact.

Superb romantic suspenser containing some of Hitchcock's best work.

w Ben Hecht   *d* Alfred Hitchcock   *ph* Ted Tetzlaff   *m* Roy Webb

Cary Grant, Ingrid Bergman, Claude Rains, Louis Calhern, Leopoldine Konstantin, Reinhold Schünzel

'Velvet smooth in dramatic action, sharp and sure in its characters, and heavily charged with the intensity of warm emotional appeal.' – *Bosley Crowther*

'The suspense is terrific.' – *New Yorker, 1976*

'A film in the supercharged American idiom which made *Casablanca* popular.' – *Hermione Rich Isaacs, Theatre Arts*

AAN: Ben Hecht; Claude Rains

A Notorious Gentleman
US   1935   73m   bw
Universal

A man plans murder and incriminates the victim's fiancée.

Basically intriguing crime yarn spoiled by over-enthusiastic direction.

w Leopold Atlas, Robert Trasker   *d* Edward Laemmle

Charles Bickford, Helen Vinson, Sidney Blackmer, Onslow Stevens, Dudley Digges

'Too heavily handled for first consideration.' – *Variety*

Notorious Gentleman (1945): see *The Rake's Progress*

The Notorious Landlady
GB   1962   127m   bw
Columbia/Kohlmar/Quine (Fred Kohlmar)

An American diplomat in London takes rooms with a murder suspect; after many mysterious happenings he helps to clear her.

Flatly whimsical goings on in comical old London, complete with fog and eccentrics. The actors all try hard but are deflated by the script.

w Larry Gelbart, Richard Quine   *d* Richard Quine   *ph* Arthur E. Arling   *m* George Duning

Kim Novak, Jack Lemmon, Fred Astaire, Lionel Jeffries, Estelle Winwood, Maxwell Reed

The Notorious Sophie Lang
US   1934   60m   bw
Paramount

A lady jewel thief matches wits with a rival from abroad.

Frothy crime comedy which isn't quite smart enough to avoid boredom.

w Anthony Veiller   *d* Ralph Murphy

Gertrude Michael, Paul Cavanagh, Arthur Byron, Alison Skipworth, Leon Errol

'No marquee strength, but nice pace and some genuine amusement.' – *Variety*

† There was a sequel in 1937, *Sophie Goes West*, also starring Gertrude Michael, directed by Charles Reisner.

Notre Histoire: see *Our Story*

La Notte *
Italy/France   1960   121m   bw
Nepi/Sofitedip/Silver

A moderately successful novelist and his wife begin to question their marriage and their life.

Slow but engaging character drama set during one night in Milan.

w Michelangelo Antonioni, Ennio Flaiano, Antonio Guerra   *d* Michelangelo Antonioni   *ph* Gianni di Venanzo   *m* Giorgio Gaslini

Marcello Mastroianni, Jeanne Moreau, Monica Vitti, Bernhard Wicki

'A film of supreme, of ferocious elegance: a film belonging in its rejection of the traditional forms of narrative to the new worlds of fiction.' – *Dilys Powell*

La Notte di San Lorenzo: see *The Night of San Lorenzo*

Le Notti di Cabiria: see *Cabiria*

Nous Sommes Tous les Assassins *
France   1952   108m   bw
UGC
aka: *Are We All Murderers?*

An illiterate youth is taught to kill during the war; afterwards he kills again for money and is sent for execution.

A solemn sermon on capital punishment, and a powerful though rather glib one.

w André Cayatte, Charles Spaak   *d* André Cayatte   *ph* Jean Bourgoin

Marcel Mouloudji, Raymond Pellégrin, Antoine Balpêtre, Claude Laydu

Les Nouveaux Messieurs *
France   1928   135m approx (24 fps)   bw   silent
Albatros/Séquance

A glamorous dancer forsakes a count for a rising trade union official.

Lengthy political satire which caused a few headlines when first released.

w Charles Spaak, Jacques Feyder   *play* Robert de Flers, Francis de Grosset   *d* Jacques Feyder   *ph* Georges Périnal, Maurice Defassiaux   *ad* Lazare Meerson

Albert Préjean, Gaby Morlay, Henri Roussel

Novecento: see *1900*

A Novel Affair: see *The Passionate Stranger*

Novembermond
West Germany   1984   106m   colour
ICA/Ottokar Runze Film/Sun 7

A Jewish refugee fleeing from Nazi Germany has a lesbian love affair in Germany.

Slight, anecdotal film with little insight into the period.

wd Alexandra von Grote   *ph* Bernard Zitzermann   *ad* Helger Gross, Jean-Pierre Balzerolla   *ed* Susan Lahaye

Gabrile Osburg, Christine Millet, Danièle Delorme, Bruno Pradal, Stéphane Garcin, Louise Martini

The Novices (dubbed)
France/Italy   1970   95m   Eastmancolor
Scotia-Barber/Les Films La Boétie/Rizzoli (André Génovès)
original title: *Les Novices*

After trying to become a prostitute in Paris, a nun decides that convent life is best.

Occasionally amusing comedy, sabotaged by its unsympathetic and out-of-sync dubbing.

wd Guy Casaril   *ph* Claude Lecomte   *m* François de Roubaix   *ed* Nicole Gauduchon

Brigitte Bardot, Annie Girardot, Lucien Barjon, Angelo Bardi, Jean Carmet, Jess Hahn

The film was cut to 90m on its British release.

Novyi Vavilon: see *The New Babylon*

Now About These Women . . . *
Sweden   1964   80m   Eastmancolor
Svensk Filmindustri
aka: *All These Women*

A critic comes to stay with a famous cellist whose biography he is writing, but his efforts are hampered by all the women in the house.

Virtually indescribable black farce comedy which doesn't really work, yet, as always with this director, is continually of interest.

w Erland Josephson, Ingmar Bergman   *d* Ingmar Bergman   *ph* Sven Nykvist   *m* Erik Nordgren

Jarl Kulle, Georg Funkquist, Eva Dahlbeck, Karen Kavli, Harriet Andersson, Bibi Andersson, Gertrud Fridh

Now and Forever *
US   1934   82m   bw
Paramount (Louis D. Lighton)

A jewel thief and his mistress are taught a thing or two by his small daughter.

Odd mixture of comedy and drama which was box-office at the time but seems pretty dated after nearly fifty years, though technically very smooth.

w Vincent Lawrence, Sylvia Thalberg   *d* Henry Hathaway   *ph* Harry Fischbeck

Gary Cooper, Carole Lombard, Shirley Temple, Guy Standing, Charlotte Granville, Gilbert Emery, Henry Kolker

'Cinch b.o. entertainment.' – *Variety*

'Expertly contrived to furnish first-rate entertainment.' – *Thornton Delehanty, New York Post*

Now and Forever
GB   1955   91m   Technicolor
ABPC/Mario Zampi

A lonely schoolgirl plans an elopement and is chased across England by two sets of parents.

Teenage romance with elements of both farce and melodrama. It seemed to please at the time.

w R. F. Delderfield, Michael Pertwee   *play The Orchard Walls* by R. F. Delderfield   *d* Mario Zampi   *ph* Erwin Hillier   *m* Stanley Black

Janette Scott, Vernon Gray, Kay Walsh, Jack Warner, Pamela Brown, Charles Victor, Wilfrid Lawson, Marjorie Rhodes, Sonia Dresdel, Ronald Squire, David Kossoff

Now Barabbas . . .
GB   1949   87m   bw
Warner/Anatole de Grunwald
aka: *Now Barabbas Was a Robber*

Stories of men in prison.

Thinly intercut dramas; from a stage success.

w Anatole de Grunwald   *play* William Douglas Home   *d* Gordon Parry   *ph* Otto Heller

Richard Greene, Cedric Hardwicke, William Hartnell, Kathleen Harrison, Leslie Dwyer, Richard Burton, Kenneth More, Ronald Howard, Stephen Murray, Beatrice Campbell, Betty Ann Davies, Alec Clunes

Now Barabbas Was a Robber: see *Now Barabbas . . .*

Now I'll Tell
US   1934   72m   bw
Fox (Winfield Sheehan)
GB title: *When New York Sleeps*

The story of Arnold Rothstein, gambler-racketeer of the twenties, as told by his widow.

Competent crime/domestic programmer.   *wd* Edwin Burke   *ph* Ernest Palmer   *m* Hugo Friedhofer

Spencer Tracy, Helen Twelvetrees, Hobart Cavanaugh, Alice Faye, G. P. Huntley Jnr, Shirley Temple, Leon Ames

'In spite of the breezy sequences with which it starts, it quickly gets improbable and goes from bad to maudlin.' – *Otis Ferguson*

Now Voyager ***
US   1942   117m   bw
Warner (Hal B. Wallis)
V, V*, L

A dowdy frustrated spinster takes the psychiatric cure and embarks on a doomed love affair.

A basically soggy script still gets by, and how, through the romantic magic of its stars, who were all at their best; and suffering in mink went over very big in wartime.

w Casey Robinson   *novel* Olive Higgins Prouty   *d* Irving Rapper   *ph* Sol Polito   *m* Max Steiner

Bette Davis, Claude Rains, Paul Henreid, Gladys Cooper, John Loder, Bonita Granville, Ilka Chase, Lee Patrick, Charles Drake, Franklin Pangborn, Janis Wilson

CHARLOTTE (Bette Davis): 'Oh, Jerry, don't let's ask for the moon. We have the stars!'

'If it were better, it might not work at all. This way, it's a crummy classic.' – *New Yorker, 1977*

AA: Max Steiner

AAN: Bette Davis; Gladys Cooper

Now You See Him Now You Don't
US   1972   88m   Technicolor
Walt Disney

Two students discover an elixir of invisibility and help prevent a gangster from taking over the college.

Flat Disney frolic with fair trick effects.

w Joseph L. McEveety   *d* Robert Butler   *ph* Frank Phillips   *m* Robert F. Brunner   *sp* Eustace Lycett, Danny Lee

Kurt Russell, Cesar Romero, Joe Flynn, Jim Backus, William Windom, Edward Andrews, Richard Bakalyan

Nowhere to Go
GB   1958   87m   bw
Ealing (Eric Williams)

A thief escapes from prison but can get no help from the underworld and is accidentally shot after being sheltered by a socialite.

Glum character melodrama which fails to sustain interest despite the best intentions.

w Seth Holt, Ken Tynan   *book* Donald MacKenzie   *d* Seth Holt   *ph* Paul Beeson   *m* Dizzy Reece

George Nader, Maggie Smith, Bernard Lee, Geoffrey Keen, Andree Melly, Bessie Love, Howard Marion Crawford

'When the law can't protect the innocent . . . it takes an outlaw to deliver justice.'

Nowhere to Run
US   1992   94m   Technicolor
Columbia (Craig Baumgarten, Gary Adelson)

An escaped prisoner helps a widow and her two young sons who are being threatened by an evil property developer.

Tedious action movie with a little added sentimentality, intended, but failing, to give its star a wider appeal.

w Joe Eszterhas, Leslie Bohem, Randy Feldman d Robert Harmon ph David Gribble m Mark Isham pd Dennis Washington ed Zack Staenberg, Mark Helfrich

Jean-Claude Van Damme, Rosanna Arquette, Kieran Culkin, Ted Levine, Tiffany Taubman, Edward Blatchford, Anthony Starke, Joss Ackland

'A relentlessly corny and shamelessly derivative vehicle.' – *Variety*

Noz w Wodzie: see *Knife in the Water*

The Nude Bomb
US   1980   94m   Technicolor
Universal/Time-Life Films (Jennings Lang)
V*, L
aka: *The Return of Maxwell Smart*

An incompetent secret agent chases a missile launching villain.

Curious and unsatisfactory attempt to revive a twenty-year-old TV situation comedy minus half its personnel.

w Arne Sultan, Bill Dana, Leonard B. Stern d Clive Donner ph Harry L. Wolf m Lalo Schifrin pd William Tuntke ed Walter Hannemann

Don Adams, Sylvia Kristel, Dana Elcar, Rhonda Fleming, Andrea Howard, Norman Lloyd

'Fans of the vidshow will derive much more enjoyment by crowding round their television sets with a bowl of popcorn watching *Get Smart* reruns.' – *Variety*.

La Nuit Américaine: see *Day for Night*

La Nuit de Varennes *
France/Italy   1982   165m   Eastmancolor
    Technovision
Electric/Contemporary/Gaumont-FR3/Opera Film (Renzo Rossellini)

In the early days of the French Revolution, a mixed coachload of travellers, including Restif de la Bretonne, Tom Paine and Casanova, make their way to Varennes, where King Louis is held captive.

Moderately engaging historical tale that does not take itself, or the times, too seriously.

w Sergio Amidei, Ettore Scola d Ettore Scola ph Armando Nannuzzi m Armando Trovajoli pd Dante Ferretti ed Raimondo Crociani

Jean-Louis Barrault, Marcello Mastrioanni, Hanna Schygulla, Harvey Keitel, Jean-Claude Brialy, Daniel Gelin, Andrea Ferreol, Michael Vitold, Laura Betti

Nuit et Brouillard: see *Night and Fog*

Les Nuits de la Pleine Lune: see *Full Moon in Paris*

Les Nuits Fauves: see *Savage Nights*

Number One
GB   1984   106m   Technicolor
Videoform (Mark Forstater, Raymond Day)

Adventures of a snooker hall hustler.

Unappetizingly foul-mouthed low-life saga.

w G. F. Newman d Les Blair ph Bahram Manocheri m David Mackay pd Martin Johnson ed Jon Gregory

Bob Geldof, Mel Smith, Alison Steadman, P. H. Moriarty, Phil Daniels, Alfred Molina

Number One with a Bullet
US   1987   101m   colour
Cannon
V*

An LA detective is obsessed with busting a big drug dealer who is also a pillar of the community.

Ho-hum *policier* with routine violence.

w Gail Morgan Hickman and others d Jack Smight

Robert Carradine, Billy Dee Williams, Valerie Bertinelli, Peter Graves, Doris Roberts

Number Seventeen *
GB   1932   63m   bw
BIP (John Maxwell)

A girl jewel thief reforms and helps the police track down her former gang.

Minor Hitchcock thriller largely confined to a single interior until the final train chase, which despite obvious models remains exhilarating.

w Alfred Hitchcock, Alma Reville, Rodney Ackland play J. Jefferson Farjeon d Alfred Hitchcock ph Jack Cox

Leon M. Lion, Anne Grey, John Stuart, Donald Calthrop, Barry Jones, Garry Marsh

'Only spasmodically good photography and usual slow tempo British direction. Wonder why they can't speed up a picture? Maybe it's the tea.' – *Variety*

† The same play had been filmed as a silent in 1928 by Geza Bolvary, with Guy Newall; it was shot in Germany.

The Nun and the Sergeant
US   1962   74m   bw
UA/Springfield

In Korea, a tough sergeant commanding a 'dirty dozen' mission is joined by a schoolgirl and a nun.

Minor war adventure, moderately well done but highly unconvincing.

w Don Cerveris d Franklin Adreon ph Paul Ivano m Jerry Fielding

Anna Sten, Robert Webber, Leo Gordon, Hari Rhodes

Nuns on the Run
GB   1990   92m   Technicolor
Palace/Handmade Films (Michael White)
V, V*, L, S

Two petty criminals disguise themselves as nuns to escape capture.

Broad, slapstick comedy that provides scant amusement, although it went down well in America.

wd Jonathan Lynn ph Michael Garfath m Hidden Faces pd Simon Holland ed David Martin

Eric Idle, Robbie Coltrane, Camille Coduri, Janet Suzman, Doris Hare, Lila Kaye, Robert Patterson, Robert Morgan, Winston Dennis, Tom Hickey

'Filmed in Belgium, Italy, Africa . . . and mostly in the conscience of a beautiful young girl!'

The Nun's Story ***
US   1959   151m   Technicolor
Warner (Henry Blanke)
V, V*, L

A Belgian girl joins a strict order, endures hardship in the Congo, and finally returns to ordinary life.

The fascinating early sequences of convent routine are more interesting than the African adventures, but this is a careful, composed and impressive film with little Hollywood exaggeration.

w Robert Anderson, book Kathryn C. Hulme d Fred Zinnemann ph Franz Planer m Franz Waxman ed Walter Thompson

Audrey Hepburn, Peter Finch, Edith Evans, Peggy Ashcroft, Dean Jagger, Mildred Dunnock, Patricia Collinge, Beatrice Straight

'A major directorial achievement . . . the best study of the religious life ever made in the American cinema.' – *Albert Johnson, Film Quarterly*

AAN: best picture; Robert Anderson; Fred Zinnemann; Franz Planer; Franz Waxman; Audrey Hepburn; editing

I Nuovi Barbari: see *The New Barbarians*

Nuovo Cinema Paradiso: see *Cinema Paradiso*

Nurse Edith Cavell
US   1939   98m   bw
Imperator/RKO
V*

The story of a British nurse executed as a spy during World War I; previously filmed in 1930 as *Dawn* with Sybil Thorndike.

This is a moderately touching but uninspired treatment.

w Michael Hogan novel Dawn by Reginald Berkeley d Herbert Wilcox m Anthony Collins

Anna Neagle, George Sanders, May Robson, Edna May Oliver, Alan Marshal

'Excellently produced documentary film, but not for general audience appeal . . . no light moments to relieve the tragic aspects.' – *Variety*

'Miss Neagle looked nice as Queen Victoria, she looks just as nice as Nurse Cavell: she moves rigidly on to the set, as if wheels were concealed under the stately skirt: she says her piece with flat dignity and trolleys out again – rather like a mechanical marvel from the World's Fair.' – *Graham Greene, The Spectator*

AAN: Anthony Collins

Nurse on Wheels
GB   1963   86m   bw
Anglo Amalgamated/GHW (Peter Rogers)

Adventures of a young District Nurse.

Part sentimental, part Carry On; watchable of its curious kind.

w Norman Hudis novel Nurse Is a Neighbour by Joanna Jones d Gerald Thomas ph Alan Hume m Eric Rogers

Juliet Mills, Ronald Lewis, Joan Sims, Raymond Huntley, Athene Seyler

The Nursemaid Who Disappeared
GB   1939   86m   bw
Warner

A domestic agency hides a gang of kidnappers.

Fairly pleasing mystery of the old school.

w Paul Gangelin and Connery Chappell novel Philip MacDonald d Arthur Woods

Arthur Margetson, Peter Coke, Lesley Brook, Edward Chapman, Coral Browne, Martita Hunt

The Nurse's Secret
US   1941   56m   bw
First National/Warner

A hired nurse solves her patient's murder.

Potboiling remake of *Miss Pinkerton*, rather better written than the original.

w Anthony Coldeway d Noel M. Smith

Lee Patrick, Regis Toomey, Julie Bishop, Charles D. Waldron, Charles Trowbridge, Leonard Mudie

Nutcracker
GB   1982   101m   Eastmancolor
Rank/Ezshaw (Panos Nicolaou)

A Russian ballerina defects in London but finds that she is being used for business/political purposes.

Weird, dated and utterly mediocre melodrama with pauses for sexual revels. Not a goer.

w Raymond Christodoulou d Anwar Kawadri ph Peter Jessop m Simon Park

Joan Collins, Carol White, Paul Nicholas, Finola Hughes, William Franklyn, Murray Melvin

Nutcracker – The Motion Picture *
US   1986   85m   colour
Entertainment/Hyperion/Kushner/Locke
V, V*

A movie based on the Pacific Northwest Ballet company's version of the classic ballet.

The restless and moody direction does not always do justice to the dancing, although it effectively conjures a slightly sinister atmosphere.

d Carroll Ballard   *ph* Stephen M. Burum
m Tchaikovsky   *pd* Maurice Sendak   *ed* John Nutt, Michael Silvers

Hugh Bigney, Vanessa Sharp, Patricia Barker, Wade Walthall

Nuts
US   1987   116m   Technicolor
Warner (Barbra Streisand)
V, V*, L

Classy prostitute kills a client; at her trial she battles against attempts to find her mentally unstable.

Star vehicle, strictly for fans.

w Tom Topor and others   *play* Tom Topor
d Martin Ritt   *ph* Andrzej Bartkowiak   *m* Barbra Streisand   *pd* Joel Schiller

Barbra Streisand, Richard Dreyfuss, Maureen Stapleton, Karl Malden, Eli Wallach

The Nutty Professor
US   1963   107m   Technicolor
Paramount/Jerry Lewis (Ernest D. Glucksman)
V*, L

An eccentric chemistry professor discovers an elixir which turns him into a pop idol.

Long dreary comedy which contains patches of its star at somewhere near his best; but even *Dr Jekyll and Mr Hyde* is funnier.

w Jerry Lewis, Bill Richmond   *d* Jerry Lewis
ph W. Wallace Kelley   *m* Walter Scharf

Jerry Lewis, Stella Stevens, Howard Morris, Kathleen Freeman

O. C. and Stiggs

US 1987 109m Metrocolor
MGM (Robert Altman, Peter Newman)

Two teenagers spend their summer playing practical
jokes, particularly on their obnoxious neighbour.

Tedious comedy with an air of desperate
improvisation about it.

w Donald Cantrell, Ted Mann story Tod Carroll,
Ted Mann d Robert Altman ph Pierre Mignot
m King Sunny Ade and his African Beats pd Scott
Bushnell ed Elizabeth Kling

Daniel H. Jenkins, Neill Barry, Paul Dooley, Jane
Curtin, Jon Cryer, Ray Walston, Louis Nye, Tina
Louise, Dennis Hopper, Melvin Van Peebles

O Dragao da Maldade contra o Santo
Guerreiro: see *Antonio das Mortes*

O. Henry's Full House **

US 1952 117m bw
TCF (André Hakim)
GB title: *Full House*

John Steinbeck introduces five stories by O. Henry.

Modelled on the success of *Quartet* (qv), this
compendium was less successful because these turn-
of-the-century tales of New York depend less on
character than on the sting in the tail; but the cast and
production were lavish.

m Alfred Newman

THE COP AND THE ANTHEM

w Lamar Trotti d Henry Koster ph Lloyd Ahern

Charles Laughton, David Wayne, Marilyn Monroe

THE CLARION CALL

w Richard Breen d Henry Hathaway ph Lucien
Ballard

Dale Robertson, Richard Widmark

THE LAST LEAF

w Ivan Goff, Ben Roberts d Jean Negulesco
ph Joe MacDonald

Anne Baxter, Jean Peters, Gregory Ratoff

THE RANSOM OF RED CHIEF

w Nunnally Johnson d Howard Hawks
ph Milton Krasner

Fred Allen, Oscar Levant

THE GIFT OF THE MAGI

w Walter Bullock d Henry King ph Joe
MacDonald

Jeanne Crain, Farley Granger

O.H.M.S.

GB 1936 86m bw
Gaumont (Geoffrey Barkas)
US title: *You're in the Army Now*

British forces fighting in China are joined by an
American gangster on the run, who dies a hero.

Stiff-upper-lip adventure of no particular interest.

w Bryan Edgar Wallace, Austin Melford, A.
R. Rawlinson story Lesser Samuels, Ralph
Bettinson d Raoul Walsh ph Roy Kellino

John Mills, Wallace Ford, Anna Lee, Frank Cellier,
Grace Bradley, Frederick Leister

'As near 100% entertainment value as can reasonably
be hoped for without the employment of a superstar,
super-cast, super-director and super-production.' –
Variety

'Smile while you're makin' it   Laugh while you're takin'
it   Even though you're fakin' it   Nobody's gonna know

O Lucky Man **

GB 1973 174m Eastmancolor
Warner/Memorial/Sam (Michael Medwin, Lindsay Anderson)
V

The odyssey of a trainee salesman who after a while
as an international financier settles down to be a do-
gooder.

Modern revue-style version of *Candide/Decline and Fall*;
very hit or miss in style and effect, and hellishly
overlong, but with good things along the way.

w David Sherwin d Lindsay Anderson
ph Miroslav Ondricek m Alan Price pd Jocelyn
Herbert

Malcolm McDowell, Arthur Lowe, Ralph Richardson, Rachel
Roberts, Helen Mirren, Mona Washbourne, Dandy
Nichols

'A sort of mod Pilgrim's Progress.' – *New Yorker*

O Mary This London

GB 1994 90m colour
BBC (Helen Greaves)

Two Irish teenagers and their girlfriend come to
London in search of adventure and an abortion.

A desultory, episodic road movie that manages to
caricature the English and the Irish without creating
any identity of its own.

w Shane Connaughton d Suri Krishnamma
ph Sean Van Hales m Stephen Warbeck ed Sue
Wyatt

Jason Barry, Oba Seagrave, Dylan Tighe, Ram John
Holder, Leslie Manville, John Otway

'The writer of this dismal, overlong farrago did his
research in three London hostels; which suggests that
the young Irish people he talked to must enjoy
playing up all the most damaging stereotypes of their
nation.' – *Hugh Hebert, Guardian*

'An implausible production, full of cultural clichés
and based on a plot which threw in a dollop of
mindless violence whenever things began to pall. The
fact that much of the dialogue sounded like a
preliminary read-through by an amateur dramatic
society might be taken as a clever way of symbolising
the inarticulateness of the characters, but somehow I
don't think it was that smart.' – *John Naughton, Observer*

† Seen first in BBC-TV's *Screen Two* series, it was
shown in cinemas in the United States.

'He's deep in danger, deeper in love!'

O.S.S. *

US 1946 107m bw
Paramount (Richard Maibaum)

American spies are parachuted into France in 1943.

Espionage heroics with an unhappy ending and a
slight documentary flavour. Not bad of its kind.

w Richard Maibaum d Irving Pichel ph Lionel
Lindon m Daniele Amfitheatrof, Heinz Roemheld

Alan Ladd, Geraldine Fitzgerald, Patric Knowles,
John Hoyt, Don Beddoe

Oasis

France/Germany 1956 100m approx Eastmancolor
  Cinemascope
TCF/Roxy/Criterion (Gerd Oswald, Luggi Waldleitner)

An ex-pilot gets involved with two attractive women
who are smuggling gold across the Sahara.

Glum romantic adventure.

w Joseph and Georges Kessel d Yves Allégret
ph Roger Hubert m Paul Misraki

Pierre Brasseur, Michèle Morgan, Cornell Borchers,
Grégoire Aslan

Obchod na Korze: see *The Shop on Main Street*

Oberst Redl: see *Colonel Redl*

The Oberwald Mystery

Italy 1980 129m colour
Artificial Eye/Polytel International/RAI (Sergio Benevenuti,
  Alessandro von Norman)
original title: *Il Mistero di Oberwald*

The queen of a Middle European country falls in love
with an assassin who looks like her dead husband.

Shot on videotape and transferred to film, it is in
unpleasing colour and takes an understated approach
to a melodramatic work.

w Michelangelo Antonioni, Tonino Guerra
play *L'Aigle A Deux Têtes* by Jean Cocteau
d Michelangelo Antonioni ph Luciano Tovoli
m Strauss, Schoenberg, Brahms ad Mischa
Scandella ed Michelangelo Antonioni, Francesco
Grandoni

Monica Vitti, Franco Branciaroli, Luigi Diberti,
Elisabetta Pozzi, Amad Saha Alan, Paolo Bonacelli

Object of Beauty

US/GB 1991 103m colour
Samuel Goldwyn/Winston/Avenue/BBC (Jon S. Denny, Alex
  Gohar)
V, V*

In a luxurious London hotel, a deaf-mute maid steals
a Henry Moore bronze from the bedroom of an
adulterous American couple.

Dull and muted romantic comedy with obnoxious
protagonists.

wd Michael Lindsay-Hogg ph David Watkin
m Tom Bahler pd Derek Dodd ed Ruth Foster

John Malkovich, Andie MacDowell, Lolita
Davidovich, Rudi Davies, Joss Ackland, Bill Paterson,
Ricci Harnett, Peter Riegert, Jack Shepherd

'A mildly diverting but empty picture.' – *Variety*

Objective Burma *

US 1945 142m bw
Warner (Jerry Wald)
V, V*

Exploits of an American platoon in the Burma
campaign.

Overlong but vivid war actioner which caused a diplomatic incident by failing to mention the British contribution.

w Ranald MacDougall, Lester Cole, Alvah Bessie *d* Raoul Walsh *ph* James Wong Howe *m* Franz Waxman *ed* George Amy

Errol Flynn, James Brown, William Prince, George Tobias, Henry Hull, Warner Anderson, John Alvin

'At the rate Errol Flynn and co. knock off the Japanese, it may make you wonder why the war need outlast next weekend.' – *Time*

'I am amazed that Warner Brothers ever made it, or having made it failed to think again and smother it.' – *Reynolds News*

† The film was not released in Britain until 1952, and then with an apologetic prologue.

AAN: original story (Alvah Bessie); Franz Waxman; George Amy

The Obliging Young Lady
US 1941 80m bw
RKO

A secretary escorts a wealthy child out of town while her parents wrangle over custody.

Tedious comedy with interest occasionally provided by the supporting cast.

w Frank Ryan, Bert Granet *d* Richard Wallace

Joan Carroll, Ruth Warrick, Edmond O'Brien, Eve Arden, Franklin Pangborn, Marjorie Gateson, John Miljan, George Cleveland, Luis Alberni, Charles Lane

The Oblong Box
GB 1969 95m Eastmancolor
AIP (Gordon Hessler)
V*, L

One of two 19th-century brothers is mysteriously disfigured and buried alive; he recovers and runs amok.

Nastily effective horror film with a frail story but good background detail.

w Lawrence Huntington *d* Gordon Hessler *ph* John Coquillon *m* Harry Robinson

Vincent Price, Christopher Lee, Alastair Williamson, Hilary Dwyer, Peter Arne, Maxwell Shaw, Rupert Davies

'A pervasive aura of evil.' – *MFB*

Obsessed: see *The Late Edwina Black*

Obsession *
GB 1948 98m bw
GFD/Independent Sovereign (Nat Bronsten)
V*
US title: *The Hidden Room*

A doctor decides to kill his wife's lover by imprisoning him in a lonely cellar while he accumulates enough acid to destroy all traces of his body.

Implausible, overstretched thriller, carefully enough done to be bearable.

w Alec Coppel *play* A Man About a Dog by Alec Coppel *d* Edward Dmytryk *ph* C. Pennington Richards *m* Nino Rota

Robert Newton, Sally Gray, Phil Brown, Naunton Wayne

Obsession *
US 1976 98m Technicolor Panavision
Columbia (Robert S. Bremson)
V*, L

A widower with guilt feelings meets the double of his dead wife and is drawn into a strange plot.

Hitchcockian adventure with a few unwise attempts at seriousness, à la *Don't Look Now*. Generally entertaining, skilled and quite rewarding.

w Paul Schrader *d* Brian de Palma *ph* Vilmos Zsigmond *m* Bernard Herrmann

Cliff Robertson, Geneviève Bujold, John Lithgow, Sylvia Williams, Wanda Blackman, Patrick McNamara

'An unholy mess. Intended as an *hommage* to Hitchcock . . . it attitudinizes [also] towards the old-fashioned tearjerker and towards the sophisticated European film, with cultural references strewn like breadcrumbs along the way of Hansel and Gretel . . .' – *John Simon, New York*

'Merely a mannered cerebral exercise without any emotional underpinning or unconscious feeling of its own.' – *Andrew Sarris, Village Voice*

AAN: Bernard Herrmann

Occupe-Toi d'Amélie ***
France 1949 95m bw
Lux (Louis Wipf)
aka: *Keep an Eye on Amelia*

A Parisian cocotte agrees to go through a mock marriage ceremony with her lover's best friend to fool his uncle: but the ceremony turns out to be real.

Hilarious and superbly stylized adaptation of a period boulevard farce: the play starts in a theatre, showing the audience, but gradually cinema technique takes over. Acting, timing and editing are all impeccable, and the production stands as a model of how such things should be done.

w Jean Aurenche, Pierre Bost, *play* Georges Feydeau *d* Claude Autant-Lara *ph* André Bac *m* René Cloërc

Danielle Darrieux, Jean Desailly, Bourvil, Carette, Grégoire Aslan

'Even those who do not respond to the artificialities of French vaudeville will admire the ingenuity and elegance of treatment.' – *Gavin Lambert, MFB*

'Most people, I think, could see it with considerable enjoyment even twice on the same evening.' – *Richard Mallett, Punch*

Ocean's Eleven *
US 1960 128m Technicolor Panavision
Warner/Dorchester (Lewis Milestone)
V*, L

A gang of friends plan to rob a Las Vegas casino.

Self-indulgent and overlong caper comedy which marked Hollywood's entry into a subsequently much overworked field. In this case the plot stops all too frequently for guest spots and in-jokes.

w Harry Brown, Charles Lederer *d* Lewis Milestone *ph* William H. Daniels *m* Nelson Riddle

Frank Sinatra, Peter Lawford, Sammy Davis Jnr, Richard Conte, Dean Martin, Angie Dickinson, Cesar Romero, Joey Bishop, Patrice Wymore, Akim Tamiroff, Henry Silva, Ilka Chase

October ****
USSR 1927 95m approx bw silent
Sovkino
V, V*, L

In 1917, the Kerensky regime is overthrown by the Bolsheviks.

A propaganda masterpiece whose images have all too often been mistaken and used for genuine newsreel. Cinematically, an undoubted masterpiece.

w Sergei M. Eisenstein, Grigory Alexandrov *d* Sergei M. Eisenstein *ph* Edouard Tissé, V. Popov

The October Man **
GB 1947 98m bw
GFD/Two Cities (Eric Ambler)
V*

After an accident which causes a head injury and subsequent depression, a lonely man staying at a small hotel is suspected of a local murder.

Nice blend of character study, mystery and suspense, with excellent attention to suburban detail.

w Eric Ambler *d* Roy Baker *ph* Erwin Hillier

John Mills, Joan Greenwood, Edward Chapman, Kay Walsh, Catherine Lacey, Joyce Carey, Adrianne Allen, Felix Aylmer

'This film of psychological suspense tells its complicated story with complete clarity, but it is mainly to be noted for its settings.' – *Basil Wright, 1972*

'A new type of thriller in which tension is heightened by the vivid realism of its setting and the complete credibility of its characters.' – *Reynolds News*

October Moth
GB 1959 54m bw
Independent Artists

A mentally retarded farmhand goes berserk after causing a fatal car crash.

Unattractive and singularly pointless little melodrama which neither edifies nor entertains.

wd John Kruse

Lana Morris, Lee Patterson, Peter Dynely, Robert Cawdron

Octopussy
GB 1983 131m Technicolor Panavision
Eon/Danjaq (Albert R. Broccoli)
V, V*, L

James Bond takes on an evil Afghan prince and a glamorous woman who plan between them to plunder Tsarist treasures.

Bond at the end of his tether: such far-stretched adventures have become merely a tedious way of passing the time.

w George MacDonald Fraser, Richard Maibaum, Michael G. Wilson *d* John Glen *ph* Alan Hume *m* John Barry *pd* Peter Lamont

Roger Moore, Maud Adams, Louis Jourdan, Kristina Wayborn, Kabir Bedi, Desmond Llewellyn, Lois Maxwell

'As the films drift further and further into self-parody, no one seems to notice and no one (at any rate in box office terms) seems to mind.' – *Nick Roddick, MFB*

The Odd Couple **
US 1968 105m Technicolor Panavision
Paramount (Howard W. Koch)
V*, L

A fussy divorce-shocked newswriter moves in with his sloppy sportscaster friend, and they get on each other's nerves.

Straight filming of a funny play which sometimes seems lost on the wide screen, but the performances are fine.

w Neil Simon, *play* Neil Simon *d* Gene Saks *ph* Robert B. Hauser *m* Neal Hefti

Jack Lemmon, Walter Matthau, John Fiedler, Herb Edelman, David Sheiner, Larry Haines, Monica Evans, Carole Sheely, Iris Adrian

OSCAR (Walter Matthau): 'I can't take it anymore, Felix. I'm crackin' up. Everything you do irritates me. And when you're not here, the things I know you're gonna do when you come in irritate me. You leave me little notes on my pillow. I told you 158 times I cannot stand little notes on my pillow. "We are all out of cornflakes, F.U." It took me three hours to figure out that F.U. was Felix Ungar. It's not your fault, Felix. It's a rotten combination, that's all.'

AAN: Neil Simon

The Odd Job
GB 1978 86m colour
Charisma/Steve O'Rourke (Mark Forstater, Graham Chapman)
V, V*

A husband, upset because his wife has left him, hires an odd-job man to kill him; then his wife returns . . .

Listless comedy that lacks the necessary invention or style to be funny.

w Bernard McKenna, Graham Chapman   d Peter Medak   ph Ken Hodges   m Howard Blake
ad Tony Curtis   ed Barrie Vince

Graham Chapman, David Jason, Simon Williams, Diana Quick, Edward Hardwicke, Bill Paterson, Michael Elphick, Joe Melia, Carolyn Seymour, Richard O'Brien

Odd Man Out ***
GB   1946   115m   bw
GFD/Two Cities (Carol Reed)
V*, L
US title: *Gang War*

An IRA gunman, wounded and on the run in Belfast, is helped and hindered by a variety of people.

Superbly crafted but rather empty dramatic charade, visually and emotionally memorable but with nothing whatever to say.

w F. L. Green, R. C. Sherriff   novel F. L. Green
d Carol Reed   ph Robert Krasker   m William Alwyn
ed Fergus McDonnell

James Mason, Robert Newton, Kathleen Ryan, F. J. McCormick, Cyril Cusack, Robert Beatty, Fay Compton, Dan O'Herlihy, Denis O'Dea, Maureen Delany, Joseph Tomelty, William Hartnell

'The story seems to ramify too much, to go on too long, and at its unluckiest to go arty. Yet detail by detail *Odd Man Out* is made with great skill and imaginativeness and with a depth of ardour that is very rare.' – *James Agee*

'Quite simply the most imaginative film yet produced in England, comparable with *Quai des Brumes* and *Le Jour se Lève*.' – *William Whitebait, New Statesman*

AAN: Fergus McDonnell

Odds against Tomorrow *
US   1959   96m   bw
UA/Harbel (Robert Wise)
S

Three crooks plan to rob a bank, but two of them cause the enterprise to fail because of their own racist hatreds.

Sour, glossy crime thriller with elementary social significance.

w John O. Killens, Nelson Gidding   novel William P. McGivern   d Robert Wise   ph Joseph Brun
m John Lewis

Robert Ryan, Harry Belafonte, *Ed Begley*, Shelley Winters, Gloria Grahame, Will Kuluva, Kim Hamilton

'An efficient but unnecessarily portentous thriller.' – *Penelope Houston*

† The writer was actually Abraham Polonsky, who was blacklisted at the time.

Ode to Billy Joe *
US   1976   106m   CFI colour
Columbia-Warner/Max Baer Productions (Max Baer, Roger Camras)
V*

In Mississippi in the early 1950s a 17-year-old youth, who is in love with a 15-year-old girl, is driven to kill himself.

Based on the hit song of the 1960s by Bobbie Gentry, a melodramatic account of the frustrations of growing up in a small town.

w Herman Raucher   d Max Baer   ph Michael Hugo   m Michel Legrand   ad Philip Jefferies
ed Frank E. Morriss

Robby Benson, Glynnis O'Connor, Joan Hotchkiss, Sandy McPeak, James Best, Terence Goodman, Becky Brown

'The ultimate tribute earned by the film is that it retrospectively makes Bobbie Gentry's song sound still better – the distillation of a complex experience charted by the film rather than just an isolated epigram and postscript framing it.' – *Jonathan Rosenbam, MFB*

'Unusually refreshing and moving' – *Films and Filming*

The Odessa File **
GB   1974   129m   Eastmancolor   Panavision
Columbia/Domino/Oceanic (John Woolf)
V, V*, L

In 1963, a young German reporter tracks down a gang of neo-Nazis.

Elaborate but uninvolving suspenser with several excellent cliffhanging sequences and a let-down climax.

w Kenneth Ross, George Markstein   novel Frederick Forsyth   d Ronald Neame   ph Oswald Morris
m Andrew Lloyd Webber   pd Rolf Zehetbauer

Jon Voight, Maria Schell, Maximilian Schell, Mary Tamm, Derek Jacobi, Peter Jeffrey, *Noel Willman*

'As resistible a parcel of sedative entertainment as ever induced narcolepsy in a healthy man.' – *Benny Green, Punch*

Odette *
GB   1950   123m   bw
Herbert Wilcox

A Frenchwoman with an English husband spies for the French resistance, is caught and tortured.

Deglamorized true life spy story with emotional moments let down by generally uninspired handling, also by the too well-known image of its star, who however gives a remarkable performance.

w Warren Chetham Strode   book Jerrard Tickell
d Herbert Wilcox   ph Max Greene   m Anthony Collins

Anna Neagle, Trevor Howard, Peter Ustinov, Marius Goring

'As a work of art, pretty flat . . . though innumerable people will find it moving and impressive, they will have done the work themselves.' – *Richard Mallett, Punch*

Odongo
GB   1956   85m   Technicolor   Cinemascope
Warwick/Columbia

A collector of animals for zoos runs into various kinds of trouble during an African safari.

Elementary jungle adventure centring on a small Sabu-like jungle boy. For the now extinct family audience.

wd John Gilling

Macdonald Carey, Rhonda Fleming, Juma, Eleanor Summerfield, Francis de Wolff, Earl Cameron

Oedipus Rex **
Italy/Morocco   1967   110m   Technicolor   Panoramica
Arco/Somafis
V*, L
original title: *Edipo Re*

Oedipus, returning to his home of Thebes, suffers through unwittingly killing his father and marrying his mother.

Austerely involving adaptation of the Greek tragedy, sandwiched between scenes set in modern Italy.

wd Pier Paolo Pasolini   play Sophocles
ph Giuseppe Ruzzolini   ad Luigi Scaccianoce
ed Nino Baragli

Franco Citti, Silvana Mangano, Carmelo Bene, Julian Beck, Pier Paolo Pasolini, Alida Valli, Ninetto Davoli

Of Human Bondage **
US   1934   83m   bw
(RKO) Pandro S. Berman
V*, L

A well-to-do Englishman is brought down by his infatuation with a sluttish waitress.

This version of the famous novel brought Bette Davis to prominence but is not otherwise any better than the others.

w Lester Cohen   novel W. Somerset Maugham
d John Cromwell   ph Henry W. Gerrard   m Max Steiner

Leslie Howard, Bette Davis, Frances Dee, Reginald Owen, Reginald Denny, Kay Johnson, Alan Hale

'Stars and the novel rep will have to carry a lethargic romance.' – *Variety*

'A totally obtuse concoction, serving only to demonstrate how untalented an actress Bette Davis was before she perfected those camp mannerisms.' – *John Simon, 1967*

Of Human Bondage *
US   1946   105m   bw
Warner (Henry Blanke)

Good-looking but thoroughly dull remake.

w Catherine Turney   d Edmund Goulding
ph Peverell Marley   m Erich Wolfgang Korngold

Paul Henreid, Eleanor Parker, Alexis Smith, Edmund Gwenn, Patric Knowles, Janis Paige, Henry Stephenson

Of Human Bondage
GB   1964   99m   bw
MGM/Seven Arts (James Woolf)
V*

Disastrous remake with both star roles miscast.

w Bryan Forbes   d Henry Hathaway, Ken Hughes
ph Oswald Morris   m Ron Goodwin   pd John Box

Laurence Harvey, Kim Novak, Nanette Newman, Roger Livesey, Jack Hedley, Robert Morley, Siobhan McKenna, Ronald Lacey

Of Human Hearts *
US   1938   100m   bw
MGM (John Considine Jnr)

A 19th-century idyll of middle America and especially of a preacher and his wayward son.

Curious all-American moral fable, splendidly made and acted.

w Bradbury Foote   novel *Benefits Forgot* by Honoré Morrow   d Clarence Brown   ph Clyde de Vinna
m Herbert Stothart

Walter Huston, James Stewart, Beulah Bondi, Gene Reynolds, Charles Coburn, Guy Kibbee, John Carradine, Gene Lockhart, Ann Rutherford

'Long on narrative and short on romance . . . the box office reaction is likely to dampen the enthusiasm of those who believe the film possesses any wide public appeal.' – *Variety*

† The title was chosen via a radio contest, the winner being a high-school student.

AAN: Beulah Bondi

Of Love and Desire
US   1963   97m   DeLuxe
New World (Victor Stoloff)

An engineer in Mexico takes up with the boss's nymphomaniac sister.

Unwise sensationalist vehicle for an ageing leading lady who is past such carryings on.

w Laslo Gorag, Richard Rush   d Richard Rush
ph Alex Phillips   m Ronald Stein

Merle Oberon, Steve Cochran, John Agar, Curt Jurgens

'I'm decent, I tell ya! Nobody's got the right to call me names!'
'The picture Hollywood said could never be made!'
Of Mice and Men ***
US 1939 107m bw
Hal Roach (Lewis Milestone)
V*

An itinerant worker looks after his mentally retarded cousin, a giant who doesn't know his own strength.

A strange and unexpected tragedy which has strength and is very persuasively made but seems somehow unnecessary.

w Eugene Solow   novel John Steinbeck   d Lewis Milestone   ph Norbert Brodine   m Aaron Copland

Burgess Meredith, Lon Chaney Jnr, Betty Field, Charles Bickford, Roman Bohnen, Bob Steele, Noah Beery Jnr

'The film is excellently acted by everyone . . . there are, mercifully, no stars to intrude their tedious flat personalities into this picture of life. It is a picture which, for all its grief, is not depressing; and if it should be said that this is no time for adding to one's own melancholy, let me reply that it is sometimes well not to lose from sight the individual pity of the lives of men.' – Dilys Powell

AAN: best picture; Aaron Copland

'We have a dream. Someday we'll have a little house and a couple of acres. A place to call home.'
Of Mice and Men *
US 1992 111m DeLuxe
UIP/MGM (Russ Smith, Gary Sinise)
V, V*, S

While dreaming of better times, an itinerant farm worker tries to keep his companion, a dim but well-meaning giant, out of trouble.

Despite the good intentions of those involved, a strangely unemotional and inert remake.

w Horton Foote   novel John Steinbeck   d Gary Sinise   ph Kenneth MacMillan   m Mark Isham   pd David Gropman   ed Robert L. Sinise

John Malkovich, Gary Sinise, Ray Walston, Casey Siemaszko, Sherilyn Fenn, John Terry

'Little more than a lacklustre ramble through an old favourite.' – Geoffrey Macnab, Sight and Sound

Ofelas: see Pathfinder

Off and Running
US 1991 90m colour
Rank/Aaron Russo Entertainment (Aaron Russo, William C. Carraro)

An actress flees from the killer of her fiancé while she tries to discover why he was murdered.

Misfiring romantic comedy with some violent action thrown in for bad measure.

w Mitch Glazer   d Edward Bianchi   ph Andrzrej Bartkowiak   m Mason Daring   ad Norman E. Weber   ed Rick Shaine

Cyndi Lauper, David Keith, Johnny Pinto, David Thornton, Richard Belzer, José Perez, Anita Morris, Hazen Gifford

Off Limits
US 1953 89m bw
Paramount (Harry Tugend)
GB title: Military Policemen

A boxing manager trains a young fighter in the military police.

Flat star comedy.

w Hal Kanter, Jack Sher   d George Marshall   ph Peverell Marley   m Van Cleave

Bob Hope, Mickey Rooney, Marilyn Maxwell, Marvin Miller

Off Limits: see Saigon

Off the Beaten Track: see Behind the Eight Ball

Off the Dole
GB 1935 89m bw
Mancunian

An amateur detective catches burglars.

Artless comedy shot on a minuscule budget; it helped to make George Formby a star.

wd Arthur Mertz

George Formby, Beryl Formby, Constance Shotter, Dan Young

Off the Record
US 1939 71m bw
Warner

A star reporter exposes the mob's use of youngsters as spotters in the gambling racket.

Predictable crime support.

w Niven Busch, Lawrence Kimble, Earl Baldwin   d James Flood

Pat O'Brien, Joan Blondell, Bobby Jordan, Alan Baxter, Morgan Conway

'Stereotype dualler.' – Variety

Offbeat *
GB 1960 72m bw
British Lion/Northiam (M. Smedley Aston)

An MI5 undercover man finds himself sympathizing with a gang of robbers and falling in love with one of them.

Sharply observed thriller which gets a bit glum in dealing with its rather contrived 'switch'.

w Peter Barnes   d Cliff Owen   ph Geoffrey Faithfull   m Ken Jones

William Sylvester, Mai Zetterling, Anthony Dawson, John Meillon, John Phillips, Victor Brooks, Joseph Furst, Neil McCarthy, Harry Baird

The Offence *
GB 1972 113m DeLuxe
United Artists/Tantallon (Denis O'Dell)

A tough police inspector bullies a suspected child molester.

Tortuous psychological study on the fringe of hysteria; good performances.

w John Hopkins   play This Story of Yours by John Hopkins   d Sidney Lumet   ph Gerry Fisher   m Harrison Birtwistle

Sean Connery, Trevor Howard, Ian Bannen, Vivien Merchant

An Officer and a Gentleman *
US 1982 126m Metrocolor
Paramount/Lorimar (Martin Elfand)
V, V*, L

A potential officer suffers thirteen weeks of agony at the Naval Aviation Officer Candidate School.

Old-hat stuff given a fresh look and some smart acting.

w Douglas Day Stewart   d Taylor Hackford   ph Donald Thorin   m Jack Nitzsche   pd Philip M. Jefferies

Richard Gere, Debra Winger, Louis Gossett Jnr, David Keith, Lisa Blount, Lisa Eilbacher

'Shamelessly manipulative, but whether the manipulations are funny, dramatic or tear-jerking, it knows exactly what and how to deliver.' – Sunday Telegraph

AA: Louis Gossett Jnr (as supporting actor); song 'Up Where We Belong' by Jack Nitzsche, Buffy Sainte-Marie (m), Will Jennings (ly)

AAN: Debra Winger; original screenplay; editing (Peter Zinner); music

The Official Version **
Argentina 1985 115m Eastmancolor
Virgin/Almi/HistoriasCinematograficas/Progress Communications (Marcelo Pineyro)
original title: La Historia Official, aka: The Official Story

A teacher begins to realize that her adopted daughter was probably the child of parents murdered by the regime under which she lives.

Strong and moving drama of the stirrings of a political conscience.

w Aida Bortnik, Luis Puenzo   d Luis Puenzo   ph Felix Monti   m Atilio Stampone   ad Abel Facello   ed Juan Carlos Macias

Hector Alterio, Norma Aleandro, Chela Ruiz, Chunchuna Villafane, Hugo Arana, Patricio Contreras

AA: best foreign film

Offret: see The Sacrifice

Ad Ogni Costo: see Grand Slam

Oh Dad, Poor Dad, Mamma's Hung You in the Closet and I'm Feelin' So Sad
US 1966 86m Technicolor
Paramount/Seven Arts (Ray Stark, Stanley Rubin)
V*

A dead father helps his son to get married despite his mother's influence to the contrary.

Zany black comedy which never really worked on the stage, let alone the screen.

w Ian Bernard   play Arthur Kopit   d Richard Quine   ph Geoffrey Unsworth   m Neal Hefti

Rosalind Russell, Jonathan Winters, Robert Morse, Hugh Griffith, Barbara Harris, Lionel Jeffries, Cyril Delevanti, Hiram Sherman

Oh Doctor
US 1937 67m bw
Universal

A rich hypochondriac is the target of confidence tricksters.

Moderate star comedy.   d Edmund Grainger

Edward Everett Horton, Donrue Leighton, Eve Arden, Thurston Hall, William Demarest

'Smooth dialogue keeps this hokey picture from going completely corkscrew.' – Variety

Oh! For a Man!: see Will Success Spoil Rock Hunter?

'It's an almighty laugh!'
Oh, God *
US 1977 104m Technicolor
Warner (Jerry Weintraub)
V, V*, L

A bewildered supermarket manager is enlisted by God to prove to the world that it can only work if people try.

Overlong but generally amiable reversion to the supernatural farces of the forties: its success seems to show that people again need this kind of comfort.

w Larry Gelbart   novel Avery Corman   d Carl Reiner   ph Victor Kemper   m Jack Elliott

George Burns, John Denver, Ralph Bellamy, Donald Pleasence, Teri Garr, William Daniels, Barnard Hughes, Paul Sorvino, Barry Sullivan, Dinah Shore, Jeff Corey, David Ogden Stiers

'Undeniably funny and almost impossible to dislike.' – Tom Milne, MFB

'Basically a single-joke movie: George Burns is God in a football cap.' – Pauline Kael, New Yorker

AAN: Larry Gelbart

Oh God Book Two

US 1980 94m Technicolor
Warner (Gilbert Cates)
V, V*

God enlists a child to remind people that he is still around.

Crass sequel with sentiment replacing jokes.

w Josh Greenfeld, Hal Goldman, Fred S. Fox, Seaman Jacobs, Melissa Miller d Gilbert Cates ph Ralph Woolsey m Charles Fox pd Preston Ames ed Peter E. Bergher

George Burns, Suzanne Pleshette, David Birney, Louanne, Howard Duff, Hans Conried, Wilfrid Hyde-White

Oh God, You Devil

US 1984 96m Technicolor
Warner (Robert M. Sherman)
V, V*, L

A struggling musician sells his soul to the devil in exchange for success.

A comic version of Faust, appended to the two films in which George Burns played God; he now puts on the other hat to fairly, but not very, comic effect.

w Andrew Bergman d Paul Bogart ph King Baggot m David Shire pd Peter Wooley ed Andy Zall

George Burns, Ted Wass, Ron Silver, Roxanne Hart, Eugene Roche

Oh Heavenly Dog

US 1980 103m DeLuxe
Mulberry Square/TCF
V*

A private eye is reincarnated as a dog and solves his own murder.

Witless fantasy comedy, an uncredited remake of *You Never Can Tell* which also rates as a Benji movie with curious additions of sex and profanity. A total muddle.

w Rod Browning, Joe Camp d Joe Camp

Chevy Chase, Jane Seymour, Omar Sharif, Robert Morley, Alan Sues

Oh Men! Oh Women!

US 1957 90m Eastmancolor Cinemascope
TCF (Nunnally Johnson)

A psychoanalyst discovers that his wife is involved with two of his patients.

Scatty Broadway comedy which strains the patience.
wd Nunnally Johnson play Edward Chodorov ph Charles G. Clarke m Cyril Mockridge

David Niven, Ginger Rogers, Dan Dailey, Barbara Rush, Tony Randall

'The ugliest sort of fun.' – *Observer*

'Cinemascope discovers a solution to the problem of filling its wide screen; the characters spend most of their time full length on the psychoanalyst's couch.' – *Sunday Times*

Oh Mr Porter ****

GB 1937 84m bw
GFD/Gainsborough (Edward Black)

The stationmaster of an Irish halt catches gun-runners posing as ghosts.

Marvellous star comedy showing this trio of comedians at their best, and especially Hay as the seedy incompetent. The plot is borrowed from *The Ghost Train*, but each line and gag brings its own inventiveness. A delight of character comedy and cinematic narrative.

w Marriott Edgar, Val Guest, J. O. C. Orton, story Frank Launder d Marcel Varnel ph Arthur Crabtree md Louis Levy

Will Hay, Moore Marriott, Graham Moffatt, Dave O'Toole, Dennis Wyndham

'That rare phenomenon: a film comedy without a dud scene.' – *Peter Barnes, 1964*

'Behind it lie the gusty uplands of the British music hall tradition, whose rich soil the British film industry is at last beginning to exploit.' – *Basil Wright*

Oh Rosalinda!

GB 1955 105m Technicolor Cinemascope
ABP/Powell and Pressburger

A playboy in four-power Vienna plays a practical joke on four officers and the flirtatious wife of one of them.

Lumbering attempt to modernize *Die Fledermaus*, unsuitably wide-screened and totally lacking the desired Lubitsch touch. A monumental step in the decline of these producers, and a sad stranding of a brilliant cast.

wd Michael Powell, Emeric Pressburger ph Christopher Challis m Johann Strauss ad Hein Heckroth

Anton Walbrook, Michael Redgrave, Anthony Quayle, Mel Ferrer, Dennis Price, Ludmilla Tcherina

Oh What a Lovely War **

GB 1969 144m Technicolor Panavision
Paramount/Accord (Brian Duffy, Richard Attenborough)

A fantasia with music on World War I.

A brave all-star attempt which comes off only in patches; the pier apparatus from the stage show really doesn't translate, the piece only works well when it becomes cinematic, as in the recruiting song and the final track-back from the graves. But there are many pleasures, as well as yawns, along the way.

w Len Deighton stage show Joan Littlewood, Charles Chilton d Richard Attenborough ph Gerry Turpin md Alfred Ralston m various pd Don Ashton

Ralph Richardson, Meriel Forbes, John Gielgud, Kenneth More, John Clements, Paul Daneman, Joe Melia, Jack Hawkins, John Mills, Maggie Smith, Michael Redgrave, Laurence Olivier, Susannah York, Dirk Bogarde, Phyllis Calvert, Vanessa Redgrave

'This musical lampoon is meant to stir your sentiments, evoke nostalgia, and make you react to the obscenity of battles and bloodshed, and apparently it does all that for some people.' – *New Yorker, 1977*

'A naïve, sentimental, populist affair, using many (too many) clever devices yet making the same old simplistic statements.' – *John Simon*

'An overlong and rarely cinematic musical satire that ladles its anti-war message on by the bucketload.' – *Time Out, 1984*

Oh You Beautiful Doll *

US 1949 93m Technicolor
TCF (George Jessel)

Fred Fisher wants to write opera but is more successful with pop songs.

Standard turn-of-the-century biopic, very pleasantly handled and performed.

w Albert and George Lewis d John M. Stahl ph Harry Jackson md Alfred Newman

S. Z. Sakall, Mark Stevens, June Haver, *Charlotte Greenwood*, Jay C. Flippen, Gale Robbins

O'Hara's Wife

US 1983 87m DeLuxe
David-Panzer
V*

A widower is helped by his wife's ghost.

Rather icky sentimental comedy.

w James Nasella and William S. Bartman d William S. Bartman

Ed Asner, Mariette Hartley, Jodie Foster, Perry Lang, Tom Bosley, Ray Walston

Oil for the Lamps of China *

US 1935 98m bw
Warner (Robert Lord)

The career in China of an American oil company representative.

Adequate general audience picture from a bestseller.

w Laird Doyle novel Alice Tisdale Hobart d Mervyn Le Roy ph Tony Gaudio md Leo F. Forbstein m Heinz Roemheld

Pat O'Brien, Josephine Hutchinson, Jean Muir, Lyle Talbot, Arthur Byron, John Eldredge, Henry O'Neill, Donald Crisp

'Long and choppy version of a best-seller novel. Little marquee strength will probably mean light returns.' – *Variety*

'Far above average in performance, direction and content.' – *John Baxter, 1968*

† Remade 1941 as *Law of the Tropics*.

OK Connery: see *Operation Kid Brother*

Okay America

US 1932 80m bw
Universal
GB title: *Penalty of Fame*

A brash reporter saves a politician's daughter from kidnapping.

Okay melodrama remade in 1939 as *Risky Business*.

w William Anthony McGuire d Tay Garnett

Lew Ayres, Maureen O'Sullivan, Louis Calhern, Walter Catlett, Edward Arnold

Okay for Sound *

GB 1937 85m bw
GFD/Gainsborough (Edward Black)

The Crazy Gang runs amok in a film studio.

Patchy farce with music hall talents of the time.

w Marriott Edgar, Val Guest, R. P. Weston, Bert Lee d Marcel Varnel ph Jack Cox md Louis Levy

Bud Flanagan, Chesney Allen, Jimmy Nervo, Teddy Knox, Charlie Naughton, Jimmy Gold, Fred Duprez, Enid Stamp-Taylor, Graham Moffatt, Meinhart Maur, H. F. Maltby, Peter Dawson, The Radio Three, The Sherman Fisher Girls

Okinawa

US 1952 67m bw
Columbia

Adventures of the gun crew of a Pacific destroyer.

Routine war actioner with much newsreel padding.

w Jameson Bewer, Arthur Ross, Leonard Stern d Leigh Jason

Pat O'Brien, Richard Denning, Cameron Mitchell, Rhys Williams

'A picture straight from the heart of America!'
Oklahoma! **

US 1955 143m Technicolor Todd-AO
Magna/Rodgers and Hammerstein (Arthur Hornblow Jnr)
V, V (W), V*, L

A cowboy wins his girl despite the intervention of a sinister hired hand.

Much of the appeal of the musical was in its simple timeworn story and stylized sets; the film makes the first merely boring and the latter are replaced by standard scenery, not even of Oklahoma. The result is efficient rather than startling or memorable.

w Sonya Levien, William Ludwig book Oscar Hammerstein play Green Grow the Rushes by Lynn Riggs d Fred Zinnemann ph Robert Surtees songs Richard Rodgers, Oscar Hammerstein II *m* Robert Russell Bennett, Jay Blackton, Adolph Deutsch *pd* Oliver Smith *ed* Gene Ruggiero, George Boemler

Gordon Macrae, Shirley Jones, Rod Steiger, Gloria Grahame, Charlotte Greenwood, Gene Nelson, Eddie Albert

AA: music score

AAN: Robert Surtees; editing

'A story of wooden derricks, iron men, and a defiant woman!'

Oklahoma Crude *

US   1973   111m   Technicolor
Columbia/Stanley Kramer
V*

In 1913, a drifting oil man stops to help a girl develop her rig.

Dour, downbeat melodrama with restricted action and much bad language; within its lights quite entertaining, but odd.

w Marc Norman   *d* Stanley Kramer   *ph* Robert Surtees   *m* Henry Mancini   *pd* Alfred Sweeney

Faye Dunaway, George C. Scott, John Mills, Jack Palance, Woodrow Parfrey

The Oklahoma Kid **

US   1939   80m   bw
Warner (Samuel Bischoff)
V*

During the settlement of the Cherokee Strip a cowboy avenges the unjust lynching of his father.

Competent but slightly disappointing star Western memorable for the clash in this guise of its protagonists, more usually seen as gangsters.

w Warren Duff, Robert Buckner, Edward E. Paramore   *d* Lloyd Bacon   *ph* James Wong Howe   *m* Max Steiner

James Cagney, Humphrey Bogart, Rosemary Lane, Donald Crisp, Harvey Stephens, Charles Middleton, Edward Pawley, Ward Bond

'Its b.o. potency will depend on Cagney's name and draw, rather than story or production, neither of which is commendable.' – *Variety*

'There's something entirely disarming about the way he has tackled horse opera, not pretending for a minute to be anything but New York's Jimmy Cagney all dressed up as a Robin Hood of the old west.' – *Frank Nugent*

The Oklahoman

US   1956   78m   DeLuxe   Cinemascope
Walter Mirisch/Allied Artists
V*

A widowed doctor becomes the subject of gossip when he takes an Indian girl for his housekeeper.

Rather curious domestic Western which erupts into action sequences but devotes too much time to talk and romance.

w Daniel B. Ullman   *d* Francis D. Lyon

Joel McCrea, Barbara Hale, Brad Dexter, Gloria Talbott, Michael Pate

Old Acquaintance **

US   1943   110m   bw
Warner (Henry Blanke)

Two jealous lady novelists interfere in each other's love lives.

A dated but rather splendid battle of the wild cats, with two stars fighting their way through a plush production and a rather overlong script.

w John Van Druten, Lenore Coffee   *play* John Van Druten   *d* Vincent Sherman   *ph* Sol Polito   *m* Franz Waxman

Bette Davis, Miriam Hopkins, Gig Young, John Loder, Dolores Moran, Philip Reed, Roscoe Karns, Anne Revere

'The odd thing is that the two ladies and the director can make the whole business look fairly intelligent, detailed and plausible; and that on the screen such trash can seem, even, mature and adventurous.' – *James Agee*

'Trashy fun, on an unusually literate level.' – *New Yorker, 1978*

Old and New: see *The General Line*

Old Bill and Son

GB   1941   96m   bw
GFD/Legeran Films/London Films (Josef Somlo, Harold Boxall)

Too old for active duty, a veteran follows his son to Flanders.

Ineffective screen version of a popular newspaper strip.

w Bruce Bairnsfather, Ian Dalrymple   *cartoons* Bruce Bairnsfather   *d* Ian Dalrymple   *ph* Georges Périnal   *md* Muir Mathieson   *ed* Charles Crichton

Morland Graham, John Mills, Mary Clare, Renée Houston, Rene Ray, Roland Culver

Old Bones of the River *

GB   1938   90m   bw
GFD/Gainsborough (Edward Black)

A teacher in Africa accidentally quells a native rising.

Tediously funny star comedy; enough said.

w Marriott Edgar, Val Guest, J. O. C. Orton   *character* Edgar Wallace   *d* Marcel Varnel   *ph* Arthur Crabtree   *m* Louis Levy   *ad* Vetchinsky

Will Hay, Moore Marriott, Graham Moffatt, Robert Adams, Jack Livesey

Old Boyfriends *

US   1978   103m   Technicolor
Edward R. Pressman Productions (Paul Schrader)
V*, L

A divorcee survives a nervous breakdown and goes on a journey of her past life to find out where she went wrong.

Low-key and somehow rather flat romantic odyssey, with interesting sequences and characters muted by the director's jaundiced eye.

w Paul and Leonard Schrader   *d* Joan Tewkesbury   *ph* William A. Fraker   *m* David Shire

Talia Shire, Richard Jordan, John Belushi, Keith Carradine, John Houseman, Buck Henry, Bethel Leslie

The Old Curiosity Shop *

GB   1934   95m   bw
BIP (Walter C. Mycroft)

The lives of a gambler and his granddaughter are affected by a miserly dwarf.

Heavy-going Dickens novel given reasonably rich production and well enough acted; sentimentality prevented a remake until the unsuccessful *Mister Quilp* (qv) in 1975.

w Margaret Kennedy, Ralph Neale   *novel* Charles Dickens   *d* Thomas Bentley   *ph* Claude Friese-Greene

Hay Petrie, Ben Webster, Elaine Benson, Beatrice Thompson, Gibb McLaughlin, Reginald Purdell, Polly Ward

The Old Curiosity Shop (1975): see
Mister Quilp

The Old Dark House ****

US   1932   71m   bw
Universal (Carl Laemmle Jnr)
V*

Stranded travellers take refuge in the house of a family of eccentrics.

Marvellous horror comedy filled with superb grotesques and memorable lines, closely based on a Priestley novel but omitting the more thoughtful moments. A stylist's and connoisseur's treat.

w Benn W. Levy, R. C. Sherriff,   *novel Benighted* by J. B. Priestley   *d* James Whale   *ph* Arthur Edeson   *ad* Charles D. Hall

Melvyn Douglas, Charles Laughton, Raymond Massey, Boris Karloff, Ernest Thesiger, Eva Moore, Gloria Stuart, Lilian Bond, Brember Wills, John Dudgeon (Elspeth Dudgeon)

'Somewhat inane, it's a cinch for trick ballyhooing. Better for the nabes than the big keys.' – *Variety*

'An unbridled camp fantasy directed with great wit.' – *Charles Higham*

'Each threat as it appears is revealed to be burlap and poster paint . . . despite storm, attempted rape and a remarkable final chase, the film is basically a confidence trick worked with cynical humour by a brilliant technician.' – *John Baxter, 1968*

'Basically a *jeu d'esprit* in which comedy of manners is edged into tragedy of horrors, the film never puts a foot wrong.' – *Tom Milne, MFB, 1978*

'The ghost doesn't walk in this family – it runs riot!'

The Old Dark House

GB   1962   86m   Eastmancolor
Columbia/Hammer/William Castle

An American accepts an invitation to visit Femm Manor and finds the inhabitants either mad or homicidal.

A travesty which has nothing to do with the 1932 film and possesses no merit of its own. The cast is left floundering.

w Robert Dillon   *d* William Castle   *ph* Arthur Grant   *m* Benjamin Frankel

Tom Poston, Janette Scott, Robert Morley, Joyce Grenfell, Mervyn Johns, Fenella Fielding, Peter Bull

Old Dracula: see *Vampira*

'Come and meet a grand old sinner!'

Old English

US   1930   87m   bw
Warner

In order to provide for his grandchildren, a financier makes certain illegal arrangements which involve his prearranged death.

Satisfying pattern play arranged for its star.

w Walter Anthony, Maude Howell   *play* John Galsworthy   *d* Alfred E. Green

George Arliss, Leon Janney, Doris Lloyd, Betty Lawford, Ivan Simpson

'Will call for most careful placement by chains and indies to draw the class trade it will only appeal to.' – *Variety*

Old Enough

US   1984   91m   colour
Silverfilm (Dina Silver)
V*

During one summer, a rich girl learns about life from a poor girl.

A dull movie about the first slow stirrings of adolescence.

wd Marisa Silver   *ph* Michael Ballhaus   *m* Julian Marshall   *pd* Jeffrey Townsend   *ed* Mark Burns

Sarah Boyd, Rainbow Harvest, Neill Barry, Danny Aiello, Fran Brill

'You dastard! Get thee hence or I shall smite thee in the puss!'

The Old-Fashioned Way *

US   1934   74m   bw
Paramount/(William Le Baron)

Adventures of The Great McGonigle and his troupe of travelling players.

Period comedy tailored for its star and incorporating fragments of *The Drunkard*. Not so funny as it might be, but essential for students.

w Garnett Weston, Jack Cunningham, Charles Bogle (W. C. Fields)   *d* William Beaudine   *ph* Benjamin Reynolds   *m* Harry Revel

W. C. Fields, Joe Morrison, Judith Allen, Jan Duggan, Jack Mulhall, Baby Leroy

Old Gringo

US   1989   120m   DeLuxe
Columbia TriStar (Lois Bonfiglio)
V, V*, L, S

The writer Ambrose Bierce and an American schoolteacher become involved in the Mexican revolution of Pancho Villa.

Confused romantic drama that attempts large gestures and bungles even small ones.

w Aida Bortnik, Luis Puenzo   *novel* *Gringo Viejo* by Carlos Fuentes   *d* Luis Puenzo   *ph* Felix Monti   *m* Lee Holdridge   *pd* Stuart Wurzel, Bruno Rubeo   *ed* Juan Carlos Macias, William Anderson, Glenn Farr

Jane Fonda, Gregory Peck, Jimmy Smits, Patricio Contreras, Jenny Gago, Gabriela Roel, Sergio Calderon

Old Hutch

US   1936   80m   bw
MGM

An idler finds a fortune but can't spend it because everybody knows he hasn't worked for years.

Satisfactory star comedy.

w George Kelly   *d* J. Walter Ruben

Wallace Beery, Elizabeth Patterson, Eric Linden, Cecilia Parker, Donald Meek, Virginia Grey

'Hasn't the backbone usually associated with Wallace Beery's vehicles. A nice light comedy which will doubtless garner fair box office.' – *Variety*

Old Iron

GB   1938   80m   bw
TW Productions/British Lion

A shipping magnate disowns his son for marrying against his will, but a car accident reconciles them.

Very boring drama, an odd choice for this star, who can't cope with it.

w Ben Travers   *d* Tom Walls

Tom Walls, Eva Moore, Cecil Parker, Richard Ainley, David Tree, Enid Stamp-Taylor

The Old Lady Who Walked in the Sea

France   1991   94m   colour
Gala/Blue Dahlia/SFC/A2/Little Bear/JM Productions (Gérard Jourd'hui)
original title: *La vieille qui marchait dans la mer*

Two aged confidence tricksters fall out after they take on a young apprentice in crime.

A defiantly tasteless and foul-mouthed comedy that somehow manages to charm as well, mainly due to Moreau's imperious performance.

w Dominique Roulet, Laurent Heynemann   *novel* San Antonio   *d* Laurent Heynemann   *ph* Robert Alazraki   *m* Philippe Sarde   *pd* Valérie Grall   *ed* Jacques Comets

Jeanne Moreau, Michel Serrault, Luc Thuillier, Geraldine Danon, Jean Bouchaud, Marie-Dominique Aumont, Hester Wilcox

'A film to test the audience's patience.' – *Geoff Brown, The Times*

'Tasteless, vulgar and even badly shot.' – *Derek Malcolm, Guardian*

The Old Maid **

US   1939   95m   bw
Warner (Henry Blanke)
V*, L

When her suitor is killed in the Civil War, an unmarried mother lets her childless cousin bring up her daughter as her own.

A 'woman's picture' *par excellence*, given no-holds-barred treatment by all concerned but a little lacking in surprise.

w Casey Robinson   *play* Zoe Akins   *novel* Edith Wharton   *d* Edmund Goulding   *ph* Tony Gaudio   *md* Leo F. Forbstein   *m* Max Steiner

Bette Davis, Miriam Hopkins, George Brent, Jane Bryan, Donald Crisp, Louise Fazenda, Henry Stephenson, Jerome Cowan, William Lundigan, Rand Brooks

'Stagey, sombre and generally confusing fare. Must aim for the femme trade chiefly.' – *Variety*

'It is better than average and sticks heroically to its problem, forsaking all delights and filling a whole laundry bag with wet and twisted handkerchiefs.' – *Otis Ferguson*

'The picture isn't bad, but it trudges along and never becomes exciting.' – *New Yorker, 1977*

The Old Man and the Sea *

US   1958   89m   Technicolor
Warner/Leland Hayward
S

An old fisherman dreams of hooking a great fish.

Expensive but poor-looking and stultifyingly dull one-character drama with variable production effects, a low key *Moby Dick*. Interesting but not effective.

w Peter Viertel   *novella* Ernest Hemingway   *d* John Sturges   *ph* James Wong Howe, Floyd Crosby, Tom Tutweiler, Larna Boren   *m* Dimitri Tiomkin

Spencer Tracy, Felipe Pazos, Harry Bellaver

'A literary property about as suited for the movie medium as *The Love Song of J. Alfred Prufrock*.' – *Time*

'A strange amalgam of practically unassisted acting, good camerawork and editing, and a lot of special effects.' – *Ernest Callenbach, Film Quarterly*

'Tracy struggles valiantly with the endless monologues . . . misguided in the extreme.' – *Time Out, 1984*

'This is not a picture audiences are going to tear down the doors to see.' – *Motion Picture Herald*

AA: Dimitri Tiomkin

AAN: James Wong Howe; Spencer Tracy

Old Mother Riley

This Irish washerwoman with flailing arms and a nice line in invective was a music hall creation of Arthur Lucan, a variation of a pantomime dame. His wife Kitty Macshane played Mother Riley's daughter, and despite personal difficulties they were top of the bill for nearly 30 years. Their first film was *Stars on Parade*, a collection of music-hall acts, in 1935.

The films were very cheaply made and the padding is difficult to sit through, but Lucan at his best is a superb comedian: they were made for small independent companies such as Butcher's and usually directed by Maclean Rogers.

1937: OLD MOTHER RILEY
1938: OLD MOTHER RILEY IN PARIS
1939: OLD MOTHER RILEY MP, OLD MOTHER
   RILEY JOINS UP

1940: OLD MOTHER RILEY IN BUSINESS, OLD
   MOTHER RILEY'S GHOSTS
1941: OLD MOTHER RILEY'S CIRCUS
1942: OLD MOTHER RILEY IN SOCIETY
1943: OLD MOTHER RILEY DETECTIVE
1943: OLD MOTHER RILEY OVERSEAS
1944: OLD MOTHER RILEY AT HOME
1945: OLD MOTHER RILEY HEADMISTRESS
1947: OLD MOTHER RILEY'S NEW VENTURE
1949: OLD MOTHER RILEY'S JUNGLE TREASURE
1952: MOTHER RILEY MEETS THE VAMPIRE

Old Yeller *

US   1957   83m   Technicolor
Walt Disney
V*, L

The love of a boy for his dog.

Archetypal family movie set in a remote rural area.

w Fred Gipson, William Tunberg   *novel* Fred Gipson   *d* Robert Stevenson   *ph* Charles P. Boyle   *m* Oliver Wallace

Dorothy McGuire, Fess Parker, Tommy Kirk, Kevin Corcoran, Jeff York, Chuck Connors

The Oldest Profession

France/West Germany/Italy   1967   115m
   Eastmancolor
Gibe/Francoriz/Rialto/Rizzoli

Six sketches about prostitution.

Very variable portmanteau, with moments of interest towards the end.

w Ennio Flaiano, Daniel Boulanger, Georges and André Tabet, Jean Aurenche, Jean-Luc Godard   *d* Franco Indovina, Mauro Bolognini, Philippe de Broca, Michel Pfleghar, Claude Autant-Lara, Jean-Luc Godard

Michele Mercier, Elsa Martinelli, Jeanne Moreau, Jean-Claude Brialy, Raquel Welch, Nadia Gray, Anna Karina

'Much much more than a musical!'

Oliver! ***

GB   1968   146m   Technicolor   Panavision 70
Columbia/Warwick/Romulus (John Woolf)
V, V*, L, S

A musical version of *Oliver Twist*.

The last, perhaps, of the splendid film musicals which have priced themselves out of existence; it drags a little in spots but on the whole it does credit both to the show and the original novel, though eclipsed in style by David Lean's straight version.

w Vernon Harris   *play* Lionel Bart   *novel* *Charles Dickens*   *d* Carol Reed   *ph* Oswald Morris   *md* John Green   *m* Lionel Bart   *pd* *John Box*   *ch* *Onna White*   *ed* Ralph Kemplen

Ron Moody, Oliver Reed, Harry Secombe, Mark Lester, Shani Wallis, *Jack Wild*, Hugh Griffith, Joseph O'Conor, Leonard Rossiter, Hylda Baker, Peggy Mount, Megs Jenkins

'Only time will tell if it is a great film but it is certainly a great experience.' – *Joseph Morgenstern*

'There is a heightened discrepancy between the romping jollity with which everyone goes about his business and the actual business being gone about . . . such narrative elements as the exploitation of child labour, pimping, abduction, prostitution and murder combine to make Oliver! the most non-U subject ever to receive a U certificate.' – *Jan Dawson*

AA: best picture; Carol Reed; John Green; Onna White; sound

AAN: Vernon Harris; Oswald Morris; Ron Moody; Jack Wild; costumes (Phyllis Dalton); editing

Oliver and Company *

US   1988   74m   Metrocolor
Warner/Walt Disney/Silver Screen Partners III

A kitten becomes friends with a gang of criminal dogs and their human master.

Episodic film, short on charm, that only now and then provides glimpses of stylish animation.

w Jim Cox, Timothy J. Disney, James Mangold novel *Oliver Twist* by Charles Dickens d George Scribner m J. A. C. Redford ad Dan Hansen ed Jim Melton, Mark Hester

voices of Joey Lawrence, Bill Joel, Cheech Marin, Richard Mulligan, Roscoe Lee Browne, Sheryl Lee Ralph, Dom DeLuise, Taurean Blacque, Carl Weintraub, Robert Loggia, Natalie Gregory, William Glover, Bette Midler

Oliver the Eighth

US 1933 20m bw
Hal Roach

Ollie goes on a blind date, and the lady turns out to be homicidal.

Star farce which never quite rises to the occasion; pleasant fooling but no more.

w anon d Lloyd French

Laurel and Hardy, Mae Busch, Jack Barty

Oliver Twist ****

GB 1948 116m bw
GFD/Cineguild (Ronald Neame)
V, V*, L, S

A foundling falls among thieves but is rescued by a benevolent old gentleman.

Simplified, brilliantly cinematic version of a voluminous Victorian novel, beautiful to look at and memorably played, with every scene achieving the perfect maximum impact.

w David Lean, Stanley Haynes, novel Charles Dickens d David Lean ph Guy Green m Arnold Bax pd John Bryan

Alec Guinness, Robert Newton, Francis L. Sullivan, John Howard Davies, Kay Walsh, Anthony Newley, Henry Stephenson, Mary Clare, Gibb McLaughlin, Diana Dors

'A thoroughly expert piece of movie entertainment.' – *Richard Winnington*

'A brilliant, fascinating movie, no less a classic than the Dickens novel which it brings to life.' – *Time*

Oliver's Story

US 1978 92m Technicolor
Paramount (David V. Picker)
V*

A sequel to *Love Story*, showing how Oliver succumbed to depression but finally found another girlfriend.

Love means never having to watch this trendy rubbish.

w Erich Segal, John Korty d John Korty ph Arthur Ornitz m Francis Lai, Lee Holdridge

Ryan O'Neal, Candice Bergen, Nicola Pagett, Edward Binns, Ray Milland

Olivier, Olivier **

France 1992 109m Eastmancolor
Gala/Oliane/A2 (Marie-Laure Reyre)
V, V*, L

A middle-class family is thrown into confusion when a 15-year-old male prostitute claims to be the son who vanished six years earlier.

Engrossing examination of identity, credulity and family harmony.

w Agnieszka Holland, Yves Lapointe, Régis Debray d Agnieszka Holland ph Bernard Zitzermann m Zbigniew Preisner pd Helene Bourgy ed Isabelle Lorente

Françoise Cluzet, Brigitte Roüan, Jean-Françoise Stévenin, Grégoire Colin, Marina Golovine, Frédéric Quiring

'What could have been a deadly mysterious tale becomes modestly intriguing, almost prosaic.' – *Geoff Brown, The Times*

'A seemingly simple but intriguing and ultimately powerful film.' – *Variety*

Olly Olly Oxen Free

US 1978 93m Metrocolor
Rico Lion (Richard A. Colla)

A junkyard proprietress helps two young children to launch a decrepit hot-air balloon.

Simpleminded children's adventure with a surprising star.

w Eugene Poinc d Richard A. Colla ph Gayne Rescher m Bob Alcivar pd Peter Wooley

Katharine Hepburn, Kevin McKenzie, Dennis Dimster

Los Olvidados *

Mexico 1951 88m bw
Utramar/Oscar Dancigers
V*
aka: *The Young and the Damned*

A good boy is contaminated by the young thugs in Mexico City's slums, and both he and his tormentor die violently.

Sober but penetrating analysis of social conditions leading to violence. The film was widely acclaimed, yet its very proficiency and excellent photography tend to glamorize its subject. Compare, however, the Hollywood resolutions of *Dead End*, on a similar subject.

w Luis Buñuel, Luis Alcoriza, Oscar Dancigers d Luis Buñuel ph Gabriel Figueroa m Gustavo Pitaluga

Alfonso Mejia, Miguel Inclan, Estela Inda, Roberto Cobo

'I shall not put *Los Olvidados* among the films I have most enjoyed; but I am far from sure that it should not go among the monuments of the cinema.' – *Dilys Powell*

Olympische Spiele ***

Germany 1936 Part 1, 118m; Part 2, 107m bw
Leni Riefenstahl
V*

An account of the Berlin Olympic Games.

This magnificent film is in no sense a mere reporting of an event. Camera movement, photography and editing combine with music to make it an experience truly olympian, especially in the introductory symbolic sequence suggesting the birth of the games. It was also, dangerously, a hymn to Nazi strength.

d/ed Leni Riefenstahl, assistant Walter Ruttman ph Hans Ertl, Walter Franz and 42 others m Herbert Windt

'Here is the camera doing superbly what only the camera can do: refashioning the rhythms of the visible; of the moment seen.' – *Dilys Powell*

The Omaha Trail

US 1942 62m bw
MGM

The laying of train track across the west causes Indian wars.

Brisk second-feature Western with good production values.

w Jesse Lasky Jnr, Hugo Butler d Edward Buzzell

James Craig, Dean Jagger, Edward Ellis, Chill Wills, Donald Meek, Pamela Blake, Howard da Silva

'One thousand years ago, Omar Khayyam was a poet, a scientist and military leader so great that an army of Assassins dedicated to world domination fell before his genius!'

Omar Khayyam

US 1956 101m Technicolor Vistavision
Paramount (Frank Freeman Jnr)

The Persian poet and philosopher defends his Shah against the Assassins.

Clean but dull Arabian Nights fantasy with pantomime sets and no humour.

w Barre Lyndon d William Dieterle ph Ernest Laszlo m Victor Young

Cornel Wilde, Michael Rennie, Raymond Massey, John Derek, Yma Sumac, Sebastian Cabot, Debra Paget

The Omega Man *

US 1971 98m Technicolor Panavision
Warner/Walter Seltzer
V, V*

In 1977 a plague resulting from germ warfare has decimated the world's population; in Los Angeles, one man wages war against loathsome carriers of the disease.

'Realistic' version of a novel which was about vampires taking over, and was previously filmed unsatisfactorily as *The Last Man on Earth*. This nasty version rises to a few good action sequences but is bogged down by talk in between.

w John William Corrington, Joyce M. Corrington novel *I am Legend* by Richard Matheson d Boris Sagal ph Russell Metty m Ron Grainer

Charlton Heston, Rosalind Cash, Anthony Zerbe

'Good morning. You are one day closer to the end of the world!'

The Omen **

US 1976 111m DeLuxe Panavision
TCF (Harvey Bernhard)
V, V*, L, S

The adopted child of an ambassador to Great Britain shows unnerving signs of being diabolically inspired.

Commercially successful variation on *The Exorcist*, quite professionally assembled and more enjoyable as entertainment than its predecessor.

w David Seltzer d Richard Donner ph Gil Taylor m Jerry Goldsmith

Gregory Peck, Lee Remick, David Warner, Billie Whitelaw, Leo McKern, Harvey Stevens, Patrick Troughton, Anthony Nicholls, Martin Benson

'A cut above the rest in that it has an ingenious premise, a teasingly labyrinthine development, a neat sting in its tail, and enough confidence in its own absurdities to carry them off.' – *David Robinson, The Times*

'Dreadfully silly . . . its horrors are not horrible, its terrors are not terrifying, its violence is ludicrous.' – *New York Times*

'More laughs than an average comedy.' – *Judith Crist*

'I did it strictly for the money.' – *David Seltzer*

† See *Damien: Omen II* and *The Final Conflict*.
†† Gregory Peck inherited his role from Charlton Heston, who turned it down.

AA: Jerry Goldsmith

AAN: song 'Ave Satani'

Omen IV: The Awakening

US 1991 97m colour
TCF/FNM (Harvey Bernhard)
V*, L, S

A wealthy couple adopt a young girl who turns out to be the daughter of the Anti-Christ.

An American TV movie, virtually rehashing *The Omen*, that was given a cinema release elsewhere, it has all the sins of a film made for the small screen, looking cheap and clearly intended for audiences with brief attention spans.

w Brian Taggert d Jorge Montesi, Dominique Othenin-Gérard ph Martin Fuhrer m Jonathan Sheffer pd Richard Wilcox ed Frank Irvine

Faye Grant, Michael Woods, Michael Lerner, Madison Mason, Asia Vieira

'This mainly serves to remind you that, silly though they were, the earlier films were at least quality entertainment. Further sequels would be as welcome as a plague of locusts.' – *Kim Newman, Empire*

'While pic offers a few creepy moments, its structure is so convoluted that it's sheer hell to follow.' – *Variety*

On a Clear Day You Can See For Ever *
US 1970 129m Technicolor Panavision
Paramount (Howard Koch)
V, V*, L, S

A psychiatric hypnotist helps a girl to stop smoking, and finds that in trances she remembers previous incarnations.

Romantic musical which tries, and fails, to substitute wispy charm for its original Broadway vitality. There are compensations.

w Alan Jay Lerner play Alan Jay Lerner
d Vincente Minnelli ph Harry Stradling
m Burton Lane

Barbra Streisand, Yves Montand, Bob Newhart, Larry Blyden, Jack Nicholson, Simon Oakland

On an Island with You
US 1948 104m Technicolor
MGM (Joe Pasternak)

A film actress on location in the South Seas is chased by a naval officer.

Below par musical which far outstays its welcome.

w Dorothy Kingsley, Dorothy Cooper, Charles Martin, Hans Wilhelm d Richard Thorpe
ph Charles Rosher md George Stoll

Esther Williams, Peter Lawford, Jimmy Durante, Ricardo Montalban, Cyd Charisse, Xavier Cugat and his Orchestra

On Approval ***
GB 1943 80m bw
(GFD) Clive Brook
V*

An Edwardian duke and an American heiress plan a chaperoned trial marriage in a remote Scottish castle.

Sparkling comedy of manners made even more piquant by careful casting and mounting; a minor delight.

w Clive Brook, Terence Young, play Frederick Lonsdale
d Clive Brook ph C. Friese-Greene m William Alwyn

Clive Brook, Beatrice Lillie, Googie Withers, Roland Culver, O. B. Clarence, Lawrence Hanray, Hay Petrie

'Totally diverting, highly cinematic.' – *NFT, 1974*

'There has probably never been a richer, funnier anthology of late-Victorian mannerisms.' – *Time*

'I enjoyed it so thoroughly that I have to fight off superlatives.' – *James Agee*

† Also filmed in 1930 by Tom Walls for Herbert Wilcox, with Walls, Yvonne Arnaud, Winifred Shotter and Edmund Breon.

On Borrowed Time *
US 1939 98m bw
MGM (Sidney Franklin)

An old man refuses to die and chases Death up the apple tree.

Amiable, very American fantasy with much sentiment and several effective moments.

w Alice Duer Miller, Frank O'Neill, Claudine West
novel Lawrence Edward Watkin d Harold
S. Bucquet ph Joseph Ruttenberg m Franz Waxman

Lionel Barrymore, Bobs Watson, Beulah Bondi, *Cedric Hardwicke* (as Mr Brink), Una Merkel, Ian Wolfe, Philip Terry, Eily Malyon

'General audiences may cotton to the novelty . . . artistically fine prestige production.' – *Variety*

'A weird, wild, totally unpredictable fantasy with dream sequences more like Buñuel than anything in the cinema.' – *John Russell Taylor, 1965*

On Dangerous Ground
US 1951 82m bw
RKO (John Houseman)
V*, L

A tough cop falls in love with the blind sister of a mentally defective murderer.

Pretentious Hollywood *film noir* in the Gabin manner, partly redeemed by its glossy surface.

w A. I. Bezzerides, novel George Butler d Nicholas Ray ph George E. Diskant m Bernard Herrmann

Robert Ryan, Ida Lupino, Ward Bond, Ed Begley, Cleo Moore, Charles Kemper

'His battle to save the Alaskan wilderness and protect its people can only be won . . .'

On Deadly Ground
US 1994 101m Technicolor
Warner/Seagal/Nasso (Steven Seagal, Julius R. Nasso, A. Kitman Ho)
S

A former CIA agent protects the Alaskan environment against a wicked oil mogul.

Risible action movie in which the pollution-count is high, particularly since Seagal's notion of saving the environment is to destroy it and everyone who stands in his way.

w Ed Horowitz, Robin U. Russin d Steven Seagal
ph Ric Waite m Basil Poledouris pd William Ladd Skinner ed Robert Ferreti, Don Brochu

Steven Seagal, Michael Caine, Joan Chen, John C. McGinley, R. Lee Ermey, Shari Shattuck, Billy Bob Thornton, Richard Hamilton, Chief Irvin Brink

'A vanity production parading as a social statement. It nonetheless has enough sound, fury and flash to satisfy the action crowd who have propped up Seagal's career.' – *Variety*

'Seagal, of course, remains exactly himself – a human bullet winging its way towards the flabby guts of the baddies. But he seems to be getting a little older now, and the martial arts are not as spectacular.' – *Derek Malcolm*

On Dress Parade
US 1939 62m bw
Warner

The Dead End Kids go to military school.

Cleaned-up comedy-drama, the last for the Kids before they split up.

w Tom Reed, Charles Belden d William Clemens

Billy Halop, Leo Gorcey, Huntz Hall, Bobby Jordan, Gabriel Dell, Bernard Punsley, John Litel, Frankie Thomas

'It just doesn't ring true. Dualler.' – *Variety*

On Friday at Eleven
West Germany/France/Italy 1960 93m bw
Corona/Criterion/Erredi (Alexander Gruter)
aka: *The World in My Pocket*

A cold-hearted gang plans to rob a heavily armoured American army truck.

Unsurprising but vaguely unpleasant thriller with nary a character left alive at the end.

w Frank Harvey novel James Hadley Chase
d Alvin Rakoff ph Vaclav Vich m Claude Bolling

Rod Steiger, Nadja Tiller, Peter Van Eyck, Jean Servais, Ian Bannen

'Growing up isn't easy at any age'
On Golden Pond ***
US 1981 109m colour Panavision
ITC/IPC (Bruce Gilbert)
V, V*, L

An 80-year-old, his wife and his daughter spend a holiday at their New England lakeside cottage.

A film remarkable not so much for what it is – a well-acted, decent screen presentation of a rather waffling and sentimental play – as for the fact that in the sophisticated eighties enough people paid to see it to make it a box-office record-breaker. This was mainly due to affection for its star, whose last film it was, but also to an American desire for a reversion to the old values of warmth and humanity after the sex and violence which the screen had lately been offering.

w Ernest Thompson play Ernest Thompson
d Mark Rydell ph Billy Williams m Dave Grusin

Henry Fonda, Katharine Hepburn, Jane Fonda, Doug McKeon, Dabney Coleman

'Moments of truth survive some cloying contrivance; Rydell directs on bended knees.' – *Sight and Sound*

'Two of Hollywood's best-loved veterans deserve a far better swansong than this sticky confection.' – *Time Out*

'The kind of uplifting twaddle that traffics heavily in rather basic symbols: the gold light on the pond stands for the sunset of life, and so on.' – *Pauline Kael, New Yorker*

AA: Ernest Thompson; Henry Fonda; Katharine Hepburn

AAN: best film; Mark Rydell; editing (Robert L. Wolfe); Dave Grusin; Jane Fonda; Billy Williams; best actress (Katharine Hepburn)

On Her Majesty's Secret Service **
GB 1969 140m Technicolor Panavision
UA/Eon/Danilaq (Harry Saltzman, Albert R. Broccoli)
V, V*, L, S

James Bond tracks down master criminal Blofeld in Switzerland.

Perhaps to compensate for no Sean Connery and a tragic ending, the producers of this sixth Bond opus shower largesse upon us in the shape of no fewer than four protracted and spectacular climaxes. Splendid stuff, but too much of it, and the lack of a happy centre does show.

w Richard Maibaum novel Ian Fleming d Peter Hunt ph Michael Reed, Egil Woxholt, Roy Ford, John Jordan m John Barry pd Syd Cain

George Lazenby, Diana Rigg, Telly Savalas, Ilse Steppat, Gabriele Ferzetti, Yuri Borienko, Bernard Lee, Lois Maxwell

On Moonlight Bay **
US 1951 95m Technicolor
Warner (William Jacobs)
V*, L

Family crises, to do with growing up and young love, in a 1917 Indiana town.

Pleasant musical, competently made, from the Penrod stories, with the emphasis switched to big sister.

w Melville Shavelson, Jack Rose stories Booth Tarkington d Roy del Ruth ph Ernest Haller
md Ray Heindorf

Doris Day, Gordon Macrae, Leon Ames, Rosemary de Camp, Billy Gray

† See also *By the Light of the Silvery Moon*, a companion piece.

On My Way to the Crusades I Met a Girl Who
. . .: see *The Chastity Belt*

On Our Merry Way *

US   1948   107m   bw
Miracle Productions (Benedict Bogeaus, Burgess Meredith)
aka: *A Miracle Can Happen*

A reporter is urged by his wife to dig up some human interest stories.

Frail compendium of anecdotes which barely work.

w Laurence Stallings   *story* Arch Oboler   *d* King Vidor, Leslie Fenton (also John Huston, George Stevens, uncredited)   *ph* Joseph August, Gordon Avil, John Seitz, Edward Cronjager   *md* David Chudnow, Skitch Henderson   *m* Heinz Roemheld

Burgess Meredith, Paulette Goddard, Fred MacMurray, Hugh Herbert, James Stewart, Dorothy Lamour, Victor Moore, Henry Fonda, William Demarest

On Our Selection

Australia   1932   99m   bw
Australasian Films

The life of the Rudd family in rural Queensland.

Predictable plot complications and loveable characters.

w Bert Bailey, Ken G. Hall   *d* Ken G. Hall

Bert Bailey, Fred McDonald, Alfreda Bevan, Jack McGowan

† Subsequent Rudd adventures included *Dad and Dave Come to Town* (1938) and *Dad Rudd M.P.* (1940).

On Stage Everybody

US   1945   65m   bw
Universal

A vaudevillian helps youngsters put on a radio show.

Tired musical support.

w Warren Wilson, Oscar Brodney   *d* Jean Yarbrough

Jack Oakie, Peggy Ryan, Johnny Coy, Julie London, Otto Kruger

On Such a Night

US   1937   71m   bw
Emmanuel Cohen/Paramount

Gangsters get caught in a Mississippi flood.

Confusing action yarn which fizzles out before it gets going.

w Doris Malloy, William Lipman, and various hands   *d* E. A. Dupont

Grant Richards, Roscoe Karns, Karen Morley, Eduardo Ciannelli, Alan Mowbray, Robert McWade

'So many baffling twists that the thread of the narrative is soon lost.' – *Variety*

On Such a Night *

GB   1955   37m   Eastmancolor
Screen Audiences/Rank

An American is initiated into the splendours of Glyndebourne Opera.

Modestly pleasing documentary with fictionalized bookends.

w Paul Dehn   *d* Anthony Asquith

David Knight, Josephine Griffin, Marie Lohr

On the Avenue **

US   1937   89m   bw
TCF (Gene Markey)

An heiress rages because she is being satirized in a revue, but later falls in love with the star.

Bright musical which keeps moving and uses its talents wisely.

w Gene Markey, William Conselman   *d* Roy del Ruth   *ph* Lucien Andriot   *m/ly* Irving Berlin   *ch* Seymour Felix

Dick Powell, Madeleine Carroll, *The Ritz Brothers*, George Barbier, Alice Faye, Walter Catlett, Joan Davis, E. E. Clive

songs: 'He Ain't Got Rhythm'; 'The Girl on the Police Gazette'; 'This Year's Kisses'; 'I've Got My Love to Keep Me Warm'. The title song was dropped before release.

'An amusing revue, with a pleasant score and a disarming informality in its production to lure us into liking it.' – *New York Times*

† Revamped as *Let's Make Love* (qv).

On the Beach **

US   1959   134m   bw
United Artists/Stanley Kramer
V*, L

When most of the world has been devastated by atomic waste, an American atomic submarine sets out to investigate.

Gloomy prophecy which works well in spasms but is generally too content to chat rather than imagine. A solid prestige job nevertheless.

w John Paxton, James Lee Barrett   *novel* Nevil Shute   *d* Stanley Kramer   *ph* Giuseppe Rotunno, Daniel Fapp   *m* Ernest Gold   *pd* Rudolph Sternad   *ed* Frederic Knudtson

Gregory Peck, Ava Gardner, *Fred Astaire*, Anthony Perkins, Donna Anderson, John Tate, Lola Brooks

'Its humanism is clearly of the order that seeks the support of a clamorous music score. The characters remain little more than spokesmen for timid ideas and Salvation Army slogans, their emotions hired from a Hollywood prop room; which is all pretty disturbing in a film about nothing less than the end of the world.' – *Robert Vas*

AAN: Ernest Gold; editing

On the Beat

GB   1962   105m   bw
Rank (Hugh Stewart)
V

A Scotland Yard car park attendant manages to capture some crooks and become a policeman.

Busy but flat comedy vehicle, never very likeable.

w Jack Davies   *d* Robert Asher   *ph* Geoffrey Faithfull   *m* Philip Green

Norman Wisdom, Jennifer Jayne, Raymond Huntley, David Lodge

On the Black Hill *

GB   1988   117m   colour
BFI/Channel 4/British Screen
V

Twin brothers grow up on a Welsh hill farm.

Unsentimental and episodic narrative of limited lives, but not without its longueurs.

wd Andrew Grieve   *novel* Bruce Chatwin   *ph* Thaddeus O'Sullivan   *m* Robert Lockhart   *ad* Jocelyn James   *ed* Scott Thomas

Mike Gwilym, Robert Gwilym, Bob Peck, Gemma Jones, Jack Walters, Nesta Harris, Huw Toghill, Gareth Toghill

On the Buses

GB   1971   88m   Technicolor
EMI/Hammer (Ronald Woolfe, Ronald Chesney)
V

Women drivers cause trouble at a bus depot.

Grotesque, ham-handed farce from a TV series which was sometimes funny; this is merely vulgar.

w Ronald Woolfe, Ronald Chesney   *d* Harry Booth   *ph* Mark MacDonald   *m* Max Harris

Reg Varney, Doris Hare, Anna Karen, Michael Robbins, Stephen Lewis

† *Mutiny on the Buses* followed in 1972 and *Holiday on the Buses* in 1973. Both were deplorably witless.

On the Carpet: see *Little Giant*

On the Double *

US   1961   92m   Technicolor   Panavision
Paramount/Dena-Capri (Jack Rose)

During World War II, an American private is asked to impersonate a British intelligence officer.

From the plot and the talents it seems one might start laughing at this while still in the queue, but in fact most of it goes sadly awry and it never quite comes to the boil.

w Jack Rose, Melville Shavelson   *d* Melville Shavelson   *ph* Harry Stradling, Geoffrey Unsworth   *m* Leith Stevens

Danny Kaye, Dana Wynter, Wilfrid Hyde-White, Diana Dors, Margaret Rutherford, Allan Cuthbertson, Jesse White

On the Fiddle *

GB   1961   97m   bw
Anglo-Amalgamated/S. Benjamin Fisz
US title: *Operation Snafu*

A wide boy and a slow-witted gypsy have comic and other adventures in the RAF.

Curious mixture of farce and action, more on American lines than British, but quite entertainingly presented.

w Harold Buchman   *novel* Stop at a Winner by R. F. Delderfield   *d* Cyril Frankel   *ph* Ted Scaife   *m* Malcolm Arnold

Alfred Lynch, Sean Connery, Cecil Parker, Wilfrid Hyde-White, Kathleen Harrison, Alan King, Eleanor Summerfield, Eric Barker, Terence Longdon, John Le Mesurier, Harry Locke

On the Night of the Fire *

GB   1939   94m   bw
GFD/G & S (Josef Somlo)
US title: *The Fugitive*

A barber kills the blackmailer of his wife.

Dour little drama, rather unusual for pre-war British studios.

w Brian Desmond Hurst, Terence Young   *novel* F. L. Green   *d* Brian Desmond Hurst   *ph* Gunther Krampf

Ralph Richardson, Diana Wynyard, Romney Brent, Mary Clare, Henry Oscar, Frederick Leister

'The kind of film either liked very much or very little . . . absorbingly entertaining, and b.o. should profit considerably by word of mouth.' – *Variety*

On the Riviera **

US   1951   90m   Technicolor
TCF (Sol C. Siegel)

A cabaret artist is persuaded to pose as a philandering businessman.

Remake of *Folies Bergère* and *That Night in Rio* (see also *On the Double*); disliked at the time and accused of tastelessness, it now seems smarter and funnier than comparable films of its era.

w Valentine Davies, Phoebe and Henry Ephron   *d* Walter Lang   *ph* Leon Shamroy   *m* Alfred Newman   *ad* Lyle Wheeler, Leland Fuller

Danny Kaye, Corinne Calvet, Gene Tierney, Marcel Dalio, Jean Murat

AAN: Alfred Newman; art direction

On the Threshold of Space

US   1956   96m   Eastmancolor   Cinemascope
TCF (William Bloom)

The USAF medical corps explores human reactions at high altitudes.

Semi-documentary flagwaver with dreary domestic asides; very dated now, and of no particular nostalgic interest.

w Simon Wincelberg, Francis Cockrill   *d* Robert D. Webb   *ph* Joe MacDonald   *m* Lyn Murray

Guy Madison, Virginia Leith, John Hodiak, Dean Jagger, Warren Stevens

On the Town ****
US   1949   98m   Technicolor
MGM (Arthur Freed)
V, V*, L

Three sailors enjoy 24 hours' leave in New York.

Most of this brash location musical counts as among the best things ever to come out of Hollywood; the serious ballet towards the end tends to kill it, but it contains much to be grateful for.

w Betty Comden, Adolph Green,   *ballet Fancy Free* by Leonard Bernstein   *d/ch* Gene Kelly, Stanley Donen   *ph* Harold Rosson   *md* Lennie Hayton, Roger Edens   *songs* various

Gene Kelly, Frank Sinatra, Jules Munshin, Vera-Ellen, Betty Garrett, Ann Miller, Tom Dugan, Florence Bates, Alice Pearce

'A film that will be enjoyed more than twice.' – *Lindsay Anderson*

'So exuberant that it threatens at moments to bounce right off the screen.' – *Time*

'The speed, the vitality, the flashing colour and design, the tricks of timing by which motion is fitted to music, the wit and invention and superlative technical accomplishment make it a really exhilarating experience.' – *Richard Mallett, Punch*

AA: Lennie Hayton, Roger Edens

On the Twelfth Day *
GB   1956   23m   Eastmancolor
George K. Arthur/Bahamian

A balletic presentation of the song about the 12 days of Christmas, with plenty of maids a'milking and lords a'leaping.

A refreshing and extravagant novelty.

w James Matthews, Val Valentine   *d* Wendy Toye

Wendy Toye, Franklin Bennett, David O'Brien

On the Waterfront ****
US   1954   108m   bw
Columbia/Sam Spiegel
V, V*, L

After the death of his brother, a young stevedore breaks the hold of a waterfront gang boss.

Intense, broody dockside thriller with 'method' performances; very powerful of its kind, and much imitated.

w Budd Schulberg   *novel* Budd Schulberg   *d* Elia Kazan   *ph* Boris Kaufman   *m* Leonard Bernstein   *ad* Richard Day   *ed* Gene Milford

Marlon Brando, Eva Marie Saint, Lee J. Cobb, Rod Steiger, Karl Malden, Pat Henning, Leif Erickson, James Westerfield, John Hamilton

'An uncommonly powerful, exciting and imaginative use of the screen by gifted professionals.' – *New York Times*

'A medley of items from the Warner gangland pictures of the thirties, brought up to date.' – *Steven Sondheim, Films in Review*

† Sample dialogue: 'Charlie, oh Charlie, you don't understand. I coulda had class. I coulda been a contender.'

AA: best picture; Budd Schulberg; Elia Kazan; Boris Kaufman; Richard Day; Marlon Brando; Eva Marie Saint; editing

AAN: Leonard Bernstein; Lee J. Cobb; Rod Steiger; Karl Malden

On Trial
US   1939   60m   bw
Warner

A man kills his wife's lover and is put on trial for murder.

Dozy film version of a once sensational play.

w Don Ryan   *play* Elmer Rice   *d* Terry Morse

John Litel, Margaret Lindsay, Edward Norris, James Stephenson

'Strictly dual fodder, talking along for an hour without going anywhere.' – *Variety*

On Wings of Song: see *Love Me Forever*

On with the Show
US   1929   98m   Technicolor (two-colour)
Warner

Crude early talkie musical revue with historical interest.

w Robert Lord   *play Shoestring* by Humphrey Pearson   *d* Alan Crosland   *ph* Tony Gaudio   *ch* Larry Ceballos   *songs* Grant Clarke, Harry Akst

Betty Compson, Louise Fazenda, Sally O'Neil, Joe E. Brown, Ethel Waters, Arthur Lake

On Your Toes *
US   1939   94m   bw
Warner (Robert Lord)

Backstage jealousies at the ballet.

Smooth film version of a top Broadway show of its time.

w Jerry Wald, Richard Macaulay   *play* George Abbott   *d* Ray Enright   *ph* James Wong Howe, Sol Polito   *m/ly* Richard Rodgers, Lorenz Hart

Vera Zorina, Eddie Albert, Alan Hale, Frank McHugh, James Gleason, Donald O'Connor, Gloria Dickson

'Box office prospects appear to be pretty good, but more than the average campaigning should be indulged.' – *Variety*

Once a Crook
GB   1941   81m   bw
TCF

A publican with a shady past helps his son who is in trouble with the law.

Low-key character comedy for two stars who would benefit from a greater tendency to farce.

w Roger Burford   *play* Evadne Price, Ken Attiwill   *d* Herbert Mason

Gordon Harker, Sydney Howard, Frank Pettingell, Carla Lehmann, Bernard Lee, Kathleen Harrison, Cyril Cusack

Once a Jolly Swagman *
GB   1948   100m   bw
GFD/Wessex (Ian Dalrymple)
US title: *Maniacs on Wheels*

A factory worker becomes a speedway rider.

Competent sporting drama of no particular interest.

w William Rose, Jack Lee   *d* Jack Lee   *ph* H. E. Fowle   *m* Bernard Stevens

Dirk Bogarde, Renée Asherson, Bonar Colleano, Bill Owen

Once a Lady
US   1931   65m   bw
Paramount

An illegitimate baby grows up to meet her mother without recognizing her.

A plot that was often tried out during the early thirties, seldom more boringly than on this occasion.

w Zoe Akins, Samuel Hoffenstein   *play The Second Life* by Rudolf Bernauer, Rudolf Oesterreicher   *d* Guthrie McClintic

Ruth Chatterton, Ivor Novello, Jill Esmond, Geoffrey Kerr, Doris Lloyd

'Another crying towel special.' – *Variety*

Once a Sinner
US   1930   71m   bw

A girl criminal reforms but almost loses the love of her new boyfriend when he finds out about her past.

Transparent melodrama, strictly for indulgent ladies.

Dorothy Mackaill, Joel McCrea, John Halliday, C. Henry Gordon, Ilka Chase, Clara Blandick, George Brent

'Slow drama that needs plenty of support.' – *Variety*

Once a Sinner
GB   1950   80m   bw
John Argyle/Butcher

A girl with a shady past finds her husband is being threatened by her ex-partner.

Uninteresting character melodrama which defeats its lightweight stars.

w David Evans   *novel Irene* by Ronald Marsh   *d* Lewis Gilbert

Pat Kirkwood, Jack Watling, Joy Shelton, Sidney Tafler, Thora Hird

Once a Thief
US   1965   107m   bw   Panavision
MGM/Cipra/RN/Fred Engel (Jacques Bar)

An ex-convict is hounded by a vengeful cop.

Glum crime melodrama gleamingly photographed but otherwise quite routine.

w Zekial Marko   *d* Ralph Nelson   *ph* Robert Burks   *m* Lalo Schifrin

Alain Delon, Ann-Margret, Van Heflin, Jack Palance, John Davis Chandler

Once Around **
US   1991   114m   colour
Universal/Cinecom (Amy Robinson, Griffin Dunne)
V, V*, L, S

Urged by her loving family to marry, a thirtyish woman chooses as a husband a brash and vulgar salesman who does not win their approval.

Perceptive drama of the swings and roundabouts of marital and family life.

w Malia Scotch Marmo   *d* Lasse Hallstrom   *ph* Theo Van de Sande   *m* James Horner   *ad* David Gropman   *ed* Andrew Monsheim

Richard Dreyfuss, Holly Hunter, Danny Aiello, Laura San Giacomo, Gena Rowlands, Roxanne Hart, Griffin Dunne

'An intelligently engaging domestic comedy-drama.' – *Variety*

Once Before I Die
US   1966   97m   Eastmancolor
F.8 Productions (John Derek)

In the Philippines, after a Jap aerial attack, a cavalry major's girlfriend causes complications in her bids to escape.

Mildly hilarious action melodrama in which the star's superstructure is made the focus of the action.

w Vance Skarstedt   *d* John Derek   *ph* Arthur Arling   *m* Emmanuel Vardi

Ursula Andress, John Derek, Richard Jaeckel, Rod Lauren

'Mark Kendell just found out that his one-night stand has been around for centuries.'

Once Bitten

US   1985   93m   Metrocolor
Villard-Wald-Hilderbrand
V*, L

Teenage sex problems are complicated by a visiting vampiress who needs the blood of a virgin three times before Hallowe'en.

Dispiriting attempt to mix genres without even a tinge of talent or sophistication.

w David Hines, Jeffrey Hause, Jonathan Roberts
d Howard Storm

Lauren Hutton, Jim Carrey, Karen Kopins, Cleavon Little

'Mr Storm might have found his ideas for the tone of this movie written on high school locker walls.' – *People*

Once in a Blue Moon

US   1936 (produced 1934)   65m   bw
Paramount

Adventures of an innocent abroad in contemporary Russia.

Would-be satire which was seen by very few people indeed.

wd Ben Hecht, Charles MacArthur

Jimmy Savo, Nikita Balieff, Whitney Bourne, Cecilia Loftus

'A dud. The exhibitors who are kidded into playing it won't be very happy afterwards.' – *Variety*

Once in a Lifetime *

US   1933   80m approx   bw
Universal (Carl Laemmle Jnr)

How a script was sold in old-time Hollywood.

Half good-humoured, half-scathing satire on Hollywood; technique dated, content still amusing.

w Seton I. Miller   play Moss Hart, George S. Kaufman   d Russell Mack   ph George Robinson

Jack Oakie, Sidney Fox, Aline MacMahon, Russell Hopton, ZaSu Pitts, Louise Fazenda, Gregory Ratoff, Onslow Stevens

'Idol-smashing satire, strictly for the initiated.' – *Variety*

Once in Paris

US   1978   100m   TVC color
Frank D. Gilroy

A naïve American writer is introduced to the delights of Paris by a worldly chauffeur and an amorous British noblewoman.

A movie that adds up to very little, but pleases along the way.

wd Frank D. Gilroy

Wayne Rogers, Gayle Hunnicutt, Jack Lenoir, Philippe Hart, Tanya Lopert

'The darkest alleys of love among the international set!'

Once Is Not Enough

US   1975   122m   Movielab   Panavision
Paramount/Sujac/Aries (Howard W. Koch)
V*
aka: *Jacqueline Susann's Once Is Not Enough*

The daughter of a movie producer is corrupted by his circle.

Old-fashioned jet-set melodrama with new-fashioned sexual novelties.

w Julius J. Epstein   novel Jacqueline Susann
d Guy Green   ph John A. Alonzo   m Henry Mancini   pd John DeCuir

Kirk Douglas, Alexis Smith, David Janssen, George Hamilton, Melina Mercouri, Gary Conway, Brenda Vaccaro, Deborah Raffin

AAN: Brenda Vaccaro

Once More My Darling

US   1949   92m   bw
Universal (Joan Harrison)

A young girl is romantically pursued by an older man.

Tame comedy.

w Robert Carson   d Robert Montgomery   ph Franz Planer   m Elizabeth Firestone

Robert Montgomery, Ann Blyth, Jane Cowl, Taylor Holmes, Charles McGraw

Once More with Feeling

GB   1960   92m   Technicolor
Columbia/Stanley Donen

The volatile private life of an orchestral conductor.

Thin comedy from a West End play, something between a shouting match and a fashion show.

w Harry Kurnitz   play Harry Kurnitz   d Stanley Donen   ph Georges Périnal   md Muir Mathieson   pd Alexander Trauner

Yul Brynner, Kay Kendall, Geoffrey Toone, Maxwell Shaw, Mervyn Johns, Martin Benson, Gregory Ratoff

Once to Every Woman

US   1934   70m   bw
Columbia

A young doctor saves a patient's life by pushing his ailing chief aside during an operation.

Tedious, routine hospital stuff.

w Jo Swerling   story A. J. Cronin   d Lambert Hillyer

Walter Connolly, Ralph Bellamy, Fay Wray, Mary Carlisle, Walter Byron

'A programmer which won't make the grade in key houses.' – *Variety*

Once Upon a Crime

US   1992   94m   Technicolor
Entertainment/Troublemakers/Dino de Laurentiis
V, V*, L

Two Americans in Europe, hoping to collect a reward for finding a valuable dog, are suspected of murdering the animal's owner.

Hysterically unamusing comedy, performed in a frantic style.

w Charles Shyer, Nancy Myers, Steve Kluger
story Rodolfo Sonego   d Eugene Levy
ph Giuseppe Rotunno   m Richard Gibbs   pd Pier Luigi Basile   ed Patrick Kennedy

John Candy, James Belushi, Cybill Shepherd, Sean Young, Richard Lewis, Ornella Muti, Giancarlo Giannini, George Hamilton, Joss Ackland

'An overacted, unfunny, unexciting comedy-thriller.' – *Philip French, Observer*

'The film gives the impression of having been assembled, at great haste and in a state of panic, from bits and pieces left over from several other "international comedies".' – *Philip Kemp, Sight and Sound*

'Abysmal comedy.' – *Variety*

† A remake of *Crimen*, directed by Mario Camerini in 1960.

Once Upon a Dream

GB   1948   84m   bw
Triton/Rank

An officer's wife has a romantic dream about her husband's batman, and comes to believe it true.

Very wispy comedy which does none of its principals any good.

w Patrick Kirwan, Victor Katona   d Ralph Thomas

Googie Withers, Griffith Jones, Guy Middleton, Raymond Lovell, Hubert Gregg

Once Upon a Forest

US   1992   71m   CFI colour
TCF/Hanna-Barbera/HTV (David Kirschner, Jerry Mills)

After toxic waste destroys their environment, a mouse, a mole and a hedgehog have two days to find herbs that will save the life of their friend, a badger.

Dull and unimaginative animated movie that is unlikely to engage anyone's attention.

w Mark Young, Kelly Ward   story Rae Lambert
d Charles Grosvenor   m James Horner   pd Carol Holman Grosvenor, Bill Proctor   ed Pat A. Foley

voices of Michael Crawford, Ben Vereen, Ellen Blain, Ben Gregory, Paige Gosney, Elizabeth Moss, Paul Elding, Janet Waldo

'It might, just, be of mild interest to the very young. But most kids, you suspect, are unregenerate sadists who will run a mile from something so earnestly improving.' – *Sheila Johnston, Independent*

'One long yawn.' – *Geoff Brown, The Times*

Once Upon a Honeymoon *

US   1942   116m   bw
RKO (Leo McCarey)
V*, L

An American radio correspondent and an ex-burlesque queen cheat the Nazis – and her husband – in Europe during World War II.

Smooth but curious mixture of comedy and drama, a satisfactory but unmemorable star vehicle.

w Sheridan Gibney, Leo McCarey   d Leo McCarey
ph George Barnes   m Robert Emmett Dolan

Cary Grant, Ginger Rogers, Walter Slezak, Albert Dekker, Albert Bassermann, Ferike Boros, Harry Shannon

'The attempt to play for both laughs and significance against a terrifying background of Nazi aggression is on the whole a little disappointing.' – *Newsweek*

Once Upon a Horse

US   1958   85m   bw   Cinemascope
Universal (Hal Kanter)

Two cowboys steal a herd of cattle but can't afford to feed them.

Unprepossessing comedy vehicle for a team which found success only on television.   wd Hal Kanter

Dan Rowan, Dick Martin, Martha Hyer, Leif Erickson, Nita Talbot, James Gleason

Once Upon A Thursday: see *The Affairs Of Martha*

Once Upon a Time *

US   1944   89m   bw
Columbia (Louis Edelman)

A luckless producer makes a sensation out of a boy and his dancing caterpillar.

Thin whimsical comedy, too slight to come off given such standard treatment, but with nice touches along the way.

w Lewis Meltzer, Oscar Saul   radio play My Client Curley by Norman Corwin, Lucille F. Herrmann
d Alexander Hall   ph Franz Planer   m Frederick Hollander

Cary Grant, Janet Blair, James Gleason, Ted Donaldson, Howard Freeman, William Demarest, Art Baker, John Abbott

'There just isn't enough material here for a full-length feature.' – *Philip T. Hartung*

'It would be nice to see some screen fantasy if it were done by anyone with half a heart, mind and hand for it. But when the studios try to make it, duck and stay hid till the mood has passed.' – *James Agee*

'As boys they said they would die for each other. As men, they did.'

Once Upon a Time in America ****
US   1984   228m (also in 147m version)   Technicolor
Warner/Embassy/Ladd/PSO (Arnon Milchan)
V, V*, L, S

The lives of four gangsters between 1922 and 1968.

Vast, sprawling, violent crime saga that is both the epitome and summation of gangster movies, a powerful, almost operatic drama of waste and despair.

w Leonardo Benvenuti, Piero de Bernardi, Enrico Medioli, Franco Arcalli, Franco Ferrini, Sergio Leone novel *The Hoods* by David Aaronson ('Harry Grey') d *Sergio Leone*   ph Tonino Delli Colli   m Ennio Morricone   ed Nino Baragli

Robert de Niro, James Woods, Elizabeth McGovern, Treat Williams, Tuesday Weld, Burt Young, Danny Aiello, William Forsythe

'It is, finally, a heart-breaking story of mutual need. By matching that need with his own need to come to terms with his own cultural memories, Leone has made his most oneiric and extraordinary film.' – *Tony Rayns, MFB*

BFA: music

Once Upon a Time in the West ***
Italy/US   1969   165m   Techniscope
Paramount/Rafran/San Marco (Fulvio Morsella)
V*, L, S

A lonely woman in the old west is in danger from a band of gunmen.

Immensely long and convoluted epic Western marking its director's collaboration with an American studio and his desire to make serious statements about something or other. Beautifully made, empty, and very violent.

w Sergio Leone, Sergio Donati   d Sergio Leone ph Tonino Delli Colli   m Ennio Morricone

Henry Fonda, Claudia Cardinale, Jason Robards, Charles Bronson, Gabriele Ferzetti, Keenan Wynn, Paolo Stoppa, Lionel Stander, Jack Elam, Woody Strode

† This film has the longest credits of all: they sprawl through the first twelve minutes.

One Against Seven: see *Counterattack*

The One and Only
US   1978   98m   Movielab
Paramount/First Artists (Steve Gordon, David V. Picker)
V*

A stage-struck egomaniac finds success at the expense of happiness with his wife.

Uneasy mixture of farce and sentiment intended as a star vehicle, but not a very successful one.

w Steve Gordon   d Carl Reiner   ph Victor J. Kemper   m Patrick Williams

Henry Winkler, Kim Darby, Gene Saks, William Daniels, Polly Holiday, Herve Villechaize, Harold Gould, Richard Lane

The One and Only Genuine Original Family Band
US   1968   110m   Technicolor
Disney
V*, L

Adventures of a Republican family at the 1888 convention.

Long and rather muddled family comedy with politics and music; not a winner anywhere.

w Lowell S. Hawley   book Laura Bower Van Nuys d Michael O'Herlihy

Walter Brennan, Buddy Ebsen, John Davidson, Lesley Ann Warren, Janet Blair, Kurt Russell, Richard Deacon

One Armed Boxer
Hong Kong   1972   97m   Eastmancolor
Cathay/Champion (Raymond Chow)
V

original title: *Dop Bey Kuan Wan*

A young boxer seeks revenge after he loses an arm in a fight against a gang leader and his assorted thugs, each expert in a different martial art.

Little more than a series of fight sequences, which are well choreographed and will no doubt appeal to fans of the genre.

wd Wang Yu   ph Mo Shen Ku   m Wang Fu Ling, Wang Ping   ed Cheng Hung Min

Wang Yu, Tang Shin, Tien Yeh, Lung Fei, Wu Tung Choo, Pan Chun Lin, San Mao

'The photography and cutting of the fights is, as usual, highly expert, with a splendid sense of movement.' – *MFB*

† The film was cut to 92m for its British release.

One Body Too Many
US   1944   74m   bw
Pine-Thomas/Paramount
V*

An insurance salesman arrives at a spooky house to find his prospect murdered.

Comedy melodrama which could have been a lot funnier and more melodramatic; once more, the butler didn't do it.

w Winston Miller, Maxwell Shane   d Frank McDonald

Jack Haley, Bela Lugosi, Jean Parker, Bernard Nedell, Blanche Yurka, Douglas Fowley, Lyle Talbot

One Born Every Minute: see *The Flim Flam Man*

One Brief Summer
GB   1969   86m   Eastmancolor
TCF/Twickenham (Guido Coen)

A wealthy man loses interest in his mistress and begins courting his daughter's friend.

Odd, downbeat melodrama with hints of incest; a sophisticated time-passer.

w Wendy Marshall   play *Valkyrie's Armour* by Harry Tierney   d John Mackenzie   ph David MacDonald m Roger Webb

Clifford Evans, Felicity Gibson, Jennifer Hilary, Jan Holden, Peter Egan, Fanny Carby, Richard Vernon, Brian Wilde

One Day in the Life of Ivan Denisovich *
GB   1971   105m   Eastmancolor
Group W/Leontes/Norsk (Caspar Wrede)
V*, L

Life in a Siberian labour camp in 1950.

A fairly successful book adaptation, as far as mere pictures can cope with the harrowing detail.

w Ronald Harwood   novel Alexander Solzhenitsyn d Caspar Wrede   ph Sven Nykvist   m Arne Nordheim

Tom Courtenay, Espen Skjonberg, James Maxwell, Alfred Burke, Eric Thompson, Matthew Guinness

'The film's general air of earnestness deflects rather than stimulates involvement.' – *David Wilson*

One Deadly Summer *
France   1983   133m   Eastmancolor
Premier/SNC/CAPAC/TFI (Christine Beytout)
V*

original title: *L'Été Meurtrier*

A nineteen-year-old girl seduces a villager into marrying her as the first step in a long-delayed act of revenge.

Moody psychological thriller, an award-winner in France, that grows more engrossing as it continues.

w Sebastien Japrisot   novel Sebastien Japrisot d Jean Becker   ph Etienne Becker   m Georges Delerue   ad Jean-Claude Gallouin   ed Jacques Witta

Isabelle Adjani, Alain Souchon, Suzanne Flon, Jenny Clève, Michel Galabru, François Cluzet

One Desire
US   1955   94m   Technicolor
U-I (Ross Hunter)

The romantic career of the lady owner of a gambling saloon.

Tawdry 1890s drama which never really gets going.

w Lawrence Roman, Robert Blees   novel *Tacey Cromwell* by Conrad Richter   d Jerry Hopper ph Maury Gertsman   md Joseph Gershenson m Frank Skinner

Anne Baxter, Rock Hudson, Julia Adams, Natalie Wood, Barry Curtis, William Hopper, Carl Benton Reid

'The standards of writing and characterization belong to a Victorian servant girl's paper-covered romance.' – *MFB*

One Exciting Night
GB   1944   89m   bw
Columbia British

A singing welfare worker averts a plan to steal a Rembrandt.

Very ho-hum stuff for a very popular but histrionically untried star.

w Howard Irving Young, Peter Fraser, Margaret Kennedy and Emery Bonnet   d Walter Forde

Vera Lynn, Donald Stewart, Mary Clare, Frederick Leister, Richard Murdoch

One Eyed Jacks
US   1961   141m   Technicolor   Vistavision
Paramount/Pennebaker (Frank P. Rosenberg)
V, V*, L

An outlaw has a running battle with an old friend.

Grossly self-indulgent Western controlled (unwisely) by its star, full of solemn pauses and bouts of violence.

w Guy Trosper, Calder Willingham   novel *The Authentic Death of Hendry Jones* by Charles Neider d Marlon Brando   ph Charles Lang Jnr   m Hugo Friedhofer

Marlon Brando, Karl Malden, Pina Pellicer, Katy Jurado, Slim Pickens, Ben Johnson, Timothy Carey, Elisha Cook Jnr

'This is not the ordinary Western; not the ordinary good Western; not even the ordinary extraordinary Western . . . The figures and the background, the colour and the movement repeatedly unite in compositions of mesmerizing beauty.' – *Dilys Powell*

'The picture is of variable quality: it has some visual grandeur; it also has some bizarrely brutal scenes. It isn't clear why Brando made this peculiarly masochistic revenge fantasy, or whether he hoped for something quite different from what he finished with.' – *Pauline Kael*

AAN: Charles Lang Jnr

One False Move ***
US 1992 105m colour
Metro/I.R.S. Media (Jesse Beaton, Ben Myron)
V, V*

Two killers on the run with their black girlfriend head for a small town in Alabama where the local police chief and two big city detectives are waiting for them.

A tough, complex, suspenseful thriller-cum-road movie that also finds room to concern itself with relationships and racism.

w Billy Bob Thornton, Tom Epperson d Carl Franklin ph James L. Carter m Peter Haycock, Derek Holt pd Gary T. New ed Carole Kravetz

Bill Paxton, Cynda Williams, Billy Bob Thornton, Michael Beach, Jim Metzler, Earl Billings, Natalie Canerday

'Gives film buffs that special jolt they're always looking for.' – Jami Bernard, New York Post

'A crime film that lifts you up and carries you along in an ominously rising tide of tension, building to an emotional pay-off of amazing power.' – Roger Ebert

One Flew over the Cuckoo's Nest ****
US 1975 134m DeLuxe
UA/Fantasy Films (Saul Zaentz, Michael Douglas)
V, V*, L

A cheerful immoralist imprisoned for rape is transferred for observation to a state mental hospital.

Wildly and unexpectedly commercial film of a project which had lain dormant for fourteen years, this amusing and horrifying film conveniently sums up anti-government attitudes as well as make love not war and all that. It's certainly impossible to ignore.

w Laurence Hauben, Bo Goldman novel Ken Kesey d Milos Forman ph Haskell Wexler m Jack Nitzsche pd Paul Sylbert

Jack Nicholson, Louise Fletcher, William Redfield, Will Sampson, Brad Dourif, Christopher Lloyd

'Lacks the excitement of movie art, but the story and the acting make the film emotionally powerful.' – New Yorker

† Kirk Douglas bought the rights to the book and starred in a Broadway adaptation of it, but he was unable to obtain backing for a film version. When Michael Douglas obtained finance from outside the movie industry, his father was too old to play the lead role. James Caan turned down the role. Louise Fletcher's role was turned down by Anne Bancroft, Angela Lansbury and Ellen Burstyn.

AA: best picture; script; Milos Forman; Jack Nicholson; Louise Fletcher

AAN: Haskell Wexler; Jack Nitzsche; Brad Dourif

One Foot in Heaven *
US 1941 108m bw
Warner (Robert Lord, Irving Rapper)

The small-town doings of a methodist minister.

Slow but pleasing chronicle, nicely assembled.

w Casey Robinson biography (of his father) Hartzell Spence d Irving Rapper ph Charles Rosher m Max Steiner

Fredric March, Martha Scott, Beulah Bondi, Gene Lockhart, Elisabeth Fraser, Harry Davenport, Laura Hope Crews, Grant Mitchell, Moroni Olsen, Ernest Cossart, Jerome Cowan

'A clean, sweet, decent picture.' – Cecilia Ager

AAN: best picture

One Foot in Hell
US 1960 89m DeLuxe Cinemascope
TCF (Sydney Boehm)

The sheriff of a small Western town is secretly plotting revenge on the townfolk for their long-ago treatment of his wife.

Unusual Western suspenser with plenty of violent action and an extremely equivocal hero.

w Aaron Spelling, Sydney Boehm d James B. Clark ph William C. Mellor m Dominic Frontière

Alan Ladd, Dan O'Herlihy, Don Murray, Dolores Michaels, Barry Coe, Larry Gates, John Alexander

One for the Book: see The Voice of the Turtle

One Frightened Night
US 1935 67m bw
Mascot
V*

Relatives assemble in a spooky house in the hope of inheriting an old man's wealth.

Low-budget thriller that sometimes seems like a spoof of The Cat and the Canary.

w Wellyn Totman d Christy Cabanne

Charles Grapewin, Mary Carlisle, Arthur Hohl, Evalyn Knapp, Wallace Ford, Hedda Hopper, Lucien Littlefield, Regis Toomey, Rafaela Ottiano

One from the Heart *
US 1982 101m Metrocolor
Zoetrope Studios (Gray Frederickson, Fred Roos, Armyan Bernstein)
V, V*, L, S

On Independence Day in Las Vegas, a pair of lovers quarrel and make up.

Extraordinarily slim (for its cost) romantic fantasy which makes one wonder why, of all stories in the world, its creator chose this one. It does however boast attractive visuals.

w Armyan Bernstein, Francis Coppola d Francis Coppola ph Vittorio Storaro m Tom Waits pd Dean Tavoularis

Frederic Forrest, Teri Garr, Raul Julia, Nastassja Kinski, Lainie Kazan, Harry Dean Stanton

'Giddy heights of visual imagination and technical brilliance are lavished on a wafer-thin story.' – Variety

'If this is the essence of cinema, then Salvador Dali is the essence of painting.' – Sunday Times

'A very beautiful film, the background of which totally drowns a wafer-thin plot. A musical non-musical, a spectacular nonspectacular, a fantasy with realist aspirations.' – Guardian

'Escapism running away with itself.' – Standard

AAN: original song score

One Good Cop
US 1991 105m colour
Hollywood/Silver Screen Partners IV (Laurence Mark)
V, V*, L

A policeman and his wife run into problems when they try to adopt the three young girls of his murdered partner.

Mundane and manipulative drama that is never arresting.

Heywood Gould d Ralf Bode m David Foster, William Ross ad Sandy Veneziano ed Richard Marks

Michael Keaton, René Russo, Anthony LaPaglia, Kevin Conway, Rachel Ticotin, Tony Plana, Benjamin Bratt

'Excruciating dialogue, stagnant ideas and acting more wooden than Sherwood Forest.' – Sight and Sound

One Good Turn
US 1931 20m bw
Hal Roach
V (C)

Two odd-job men see their benefactress rehearsing a play, and think she is really being evicted.

Moderate star comedy with nice moments.

w H. M. Walker d James W. Horne

Laurel and Hardy, Mary Carr, Billy Gilbert

One Good Turn
GB 1954 90m bw
GFD/Two Cities (Maurice Cowan)
V

An orphan stays on to become an odd job man, and tries to raise money to buy an old car.

The star's second comedy is an almost unmitigated disaster, disjointed and depending too much on pathos.

w Maurice Cowan, John Paddy Carstairs, Ted Willis d John Paddy Carstairs ph Jack Cox m John Addison

Norman Wisdom, Joan Rice, Shirley Abicair, Thora Hird, William Russell, Richard Caldicot

One Heavenly Night
US 1930 82m bw
Samuel Goldwyn

A flower girl in a Budapest music hall finds herself imitating the absent star.

Would-be-Lubitsch-like musical comedy which doesn't quite succeed in its pleasant aims.

w Sidney Howard story Louis Bromfield d George Fitzmaurice

Evelyn Laye, John Boles, Leon Errol, Lilyan Tashman, Hugh Cameron, Lionel Belmore

'It will satisfy the customers, but lacks the intrinsic quality that makes 'em talk and recommends it as an entertainment for big grosses.' – Variety

One Hour with You (1924): see The Marriage Circle

'Gayest screen event of the year!'
One Hour with You ***
US 1932 84m bw
Paramount (Ernst Lubitsch)

The affairs of a philandering Parisian doctor.

Superbly handled comedy of manners in Lubitsch's most inventive form, handled by a most capable cast. Unique entertainment of a kind which is, alas, no more.

w Samson Raphaelson, play Only a Dream by Lothar Schmidt d George Cukor, Ernst Lubitsch ph Victor Milner m Oscar Straus, Richard Whiting ly Leo Robin ad Hans Dreier

Maurice Chevalier, Jeanette MacDonald, Genevieve Tobin, Roland Young, Charles Ruggles, George Barbier

'Sure fire if frothy screen fare, cinch b.o. at all times.' – Variety

'A brand new form of musical entertainment . . . he has mixed verse, spoken and sung, a smart and satiric musical background, asides to the audience, and sophisticated dialogue, as well as lilting and delightful songs . . . The result is something so delightful that it places the circle of golden leaves jauntily upon the knowing head of Hollywood's most original director.' – Philadelphia Inquirer

† A remake of Lubitsch's silent success The Marriage Circle.

AAN: best picture

One Hundred and One Dalmatians ***
US 1961 79m Technicolor
Walt Disney
V*

The dogs of London help save puppies which are being stolen for their skins by a cruel villainess.

Disney's last really splendid feature cartoon, with the old flexible style cleverly modernized and plenty of invention and detail in the story line. The London backgrounds are especially nicely judged.

w Bill Peet *novel* Dodie Smith *d* Wolfgang Reitherman, Hamilton S. Luske, Clyde Geronimi *m* George Bruns

voices of Rod Taylor, Cate Bauer, Betty Lou Gerson, J. Pat O'Malley

'It has the freshness of the early short colour-cartoons without the savagery which has often disfigured the later feature-length stories.' – *Dilys Powell*

120 Days of Sodom
Italy/France 1975 117m Technicolor
PEA/PAA

After the Italian campaign of 1944, four local dignitaries marry each other's daughters, withdraw with a bevy of nubile girls to a mountain retreat, and tell each other sado-masochistic sexual adventures.

Thoroughly revolting and much banned piece with no perceptible point but a good deal of emetic detail.

wd Pier Paolo Pasolini *novel* Marquis de Sade

Paolo Bonacelli, Giorgio Cataldi, Uberto P. Quintavalle, Aldo Valetti

One Hundred Men and a Girl ***
US 1937 84m bw
Universal (Joe Pasternak)

A young girl persuades a great conductor to form an orchestra of unemployed musicians.

Delightful and funny musical fable, an instance of the Pasternak formula of sweetness and light at its richest and best.

w Bruce Manning, Charles Kenyon, Hans Kraly *d* Henry Koster *ph* Joseph Valentine *m* Charles Previn *songs* various *ed* Bernard W. Burton

Deanna Durbin, Adolphe Menjou, Leopold Stokowski, Alice Brady, Mischa Auer, Eugene Pallette, Billy Gilbert, Alma Kruger, Jed Prouty, Frank Jenks, Christian Rub

'Smash hit for all the family . . . something new in entertainment.' – *Variety*

'Apart from its value as entertainment, which is considerable, it reveals the cinema at its sunny-sided best.' – *New York Times.*

'An original story put over with considerable skill.' – *MFB*

AA: Charles Previn

AAN: best picture; original story (Hans Kraly); editing

One Hundred Per Cent Pure: see *The Girl from Missouri*

100 Rifles *
US 1969 109m DeLuxe
TCF/Marvin Schwartz
V*

In war-torn Mexico, a black American sheriff and his prisoner become involved in a girl's fight for vengeance after her father's death.

Blood-soaked adventure with plenty of tough action and tight pace. A little too purposeful in its unpleasantness to be very entertaining.

w Clair Huffaker, Tom Gries *novel* Robert MacLeod *d* Tom Gries *ph* Cecilio Paniagua *m* Jerry Goldsmith

Jim Brown, Raquel Welch, Burt Reynolds, Fernando Lamas, Dan O'Herlihy, Hans Gudegast

One in a Million **
US 1936 94m bw
TCF (Raymond Griffith)

The daughter of a Swiss innkeeper becomes an Olympic ice-skating champion.

Sonja Henie's film debut shows Hollywood at its most professional, making entertainment out of the purest moonshine with considerable injections of novelty talent.

w Leonard Praskins, Mark Kelly *d* Sidney Lanfield *ph* Edward Cronjager *md* Louis Silvers *songs* Sidney Mitchell, Lew Pollack *ch* Jack Haskell

Sonja Henie, Don Ameche, *The Ritz Brothers*, Jean Hersholt, Ned Sparks, Arline Judge, Dixie Dunbar, Borrah Minnevitch and his Rascals, Montagu Love

'A very entertaining, adroitly mixed concoction of romance, music, comedy and skating . . . Miss Henie is a screen find.' – *Variety*

AAN: Jack Haskell

One Is a Lonely Number *
US 1972 97m Metrocolor
MGM (Stan Margulies)

When her husband leaves her, a woman tries to develop new interests.

Satirical sentimental view of American divorce, with interesting moments.

w David Seltzer *novel* Rebecca Morris *d* Mel Stuart *ph* Michel Hugo *m* Michel Legrand

Trish Van Devere, Monte Markham, Melvyn Douglas, Janet Leigh

One Little Indian
US 1973 91m Technicolor
Walt Disney (Winston Hibler)
V*

A cavalry corporal escapes from jail and falls in with a ten-year-old Indian.

Sentimental semi-Western, a bit dull for Disney apart from a camel.

w Harry Spalding *d* Bernard McEveety *ph* Charles F. Wheeler *m* Jerry Goldsmith

James Garner, Vera Miles, Pat Hingle, Morgan Woodward, John Doucette

One Magic Christmas
Canada 1985 88m DeLuxe
Silver Screen/Telefilm Canada/Walt Disney (Peter O'Brian, Fred Roos)
V*, L

An angel interferes in the lives of a family with problems.

Decidedly downbeat Christmas fantasy: daddy gets drowned, mother is a nut, and the angel looks like a tramp. Santa Claus puts in an appearance for a happy finale, but *It's a Wonderful Life* should sue for plagiarism.

w Thomas Meecham *d* Philip Borsos *ph* Frank Tidy *m* Michael Conway *pd* Bill Brodie *ed* Sidney Wolinksy

Mary Steenburgen, Gary Basaraba, Harry Dean Stanton, Arthur Hill

One Man Mutiny: see *The Court Martial of Billy Mitchell*

One Man's Journey
US 1933 72m bw
RKO

The career of a rural doctor for whom fame arrives too late.

Pleasant, predictable, rather downbeat small-town drama.

w Lester Cohen, Sam Ornitz *story* Failure by Katharine Haviland Taylor *d* John Robertson

Lionel Barrymore, May Robson, Dorothy Jordan, Joel McCrea, Frances Dee, David Landau, Samuel S. Hinds

'Carries sympathetic interest and appeal.' – *Variety*

One Man's Way
US 1964 105m bw
UA

A crime reporter becomes a priest.

Rather self-conscious biography of Norman Vincent Peale, adequately assembled but containing no surprises.

w Eleanore Griffin, John W. Bloch *book* Minister to Millions by Arthur Gordon *d* Denis Sanders

Don Murray, Diana Hyland, William Windom, Virginia Christine, Carol Ohmart

One Mile from Heaven
US 1937 68m bw
TCF

A girl reporter makes hay with the story of a black woman who is raising a white child.

Curious mixture of melodrama and wisecracking farce, with tap dancing from Bill Robinson thrown in.

w Lou Breslow, John Patrick *d* Allan Dwan

Claire Trevor, Sally Blane, Douglas Fowley, Fredi Washington, Ralf Harolde

'Whether the theme fits into the popular groove is something to think about.' – *Variety*

'The most exciting adventure in a million years!'
One Million BC *
US 1940 80m bw
Hal Roach
V*, L
GB title: *Man and His Mate*
aka: *The Cave Dwellers*

Life between warring tribes of primitive man in the stone age.

Impressive-looking but slow-moving grunt-and-groan epic originally based on D. W. Griffith's *Man's Genesis* and on which Griffith did some work. The totally unhistoric dinosaurs (which had disappeared long before man arrived) are impressively concocted by magnifying lizards.

w Mickell Novak, George Baker, Joseph Frickert *d* Hal Roach, Hal Roach Jnr, D. W. Griffith *ph* Norbert Brodine *m* Werner R. Heymann

Victor Mature, Carole Landis, Lon Chaney Jnr, John Hubbard, Nigel de Brulier, Conrad Nagel

AAN: Werner R. Heymann

'This is the way it was!'
One Million Years BC *
GB 1966 100m Technicolor
Hammer (Michael Carreras)
V

A vague remake of the above, with animated monsters.

Not badly done, with some lively action.

w Michael Carreras *d* Don Chaffey *ph* Wilkie Cooper *m* Mario Nascimbene

John Richardson, Raquel Welch, Robert Brown, Percy Herbert, Martine Beswick

'Very easy to dismiss the film as a silly spectacle; but Hammer production finesse is much in evidence and Don Chaffey has done a competent job of direction. And it is all hugely enjoyable.' – *David Wilson*

One Minute to Zero
US 1952 105m bw
RKO (Edmund Grainger)
V*

In Korea a US colonel is evacuating American civilians but is forced to bomb refugees.

Flat war film with Something To Say and the star at his most humourless.

w Milton Krims, William Haines   *d* Tay Garnett
ph William E. Snyder   *md* Constantin Bakaleinikoff
m Victor Young

Robert Mitchum, Ann Blyth, William Talman, Charles
McGraw, Richard Egan

One More River *
US   1934   88m   bw
Universal (James Whale)
GB title: *Over the River*

A wife runs away from her husband, and he sets
detectives on her and her lover.

Old-fashioned, well made picturization of a novel.

w R. C. Sherriff   *novel* John Galsworthy   *d* James
Whale   *ph* John Mescall   *m* W. Franke Harling

Colin Clive, Diana Wynyard, C. Aubrey Smith, Jane
Wyatt, Lionel Atwill, Mrs Patrick Campbell, Frank
Lawton, Reginald Denny, Henry Stephenson, Alan
Mowbray, E. E. Clive

'Galsworthy beautifully transmuted to the screen . . .
Very British and ultra, but should prove nice enough
b.o.' – *Variety*

'Taste, elegance, narrative drive and a deliberate
nostalgia for the Galsworthy period.' – *Peter John Dyer,
1966*

'One of the finest courtroom episodes ever projected
on a screen.' – *Motion Picture Herald*

One More Spring *
US   1935   87m   bw
Fox (Winfield Sheehan)

Three strangers, in reduced circumstances due to the
Depression, meet in Central Park and pool their
resources.

Topical serio-comedy which looks pretty dated but
still serves as a summation of American mid-thirties
attitudes.

w Edwin Burke,   *novel* Robert Nathan   *d* Henry
King   *ph* John Seitz   *md* Arthur Lange

Janet Gaynor, Warner Baxter, Walter Woolf King,
Grant Mitchell, Jane Darwell, Roger Imhof, John
Qualen, Dick Foran, Stepin Fetchit

'Whimsical comedy with plenty of laughs. Should do
well.' – *Variety*

One More Time
GB   1969   93m   DeLuxe
UA/Chrislaw-Tracemark (Milton Ebbins)

Two London club owners become involved with
spies, gangsters and jewel-thieves.

The stars of the tedious *Salt and Pepper* are reunited for
an even less amusing film.

w Michael Pertwee   *d* Jerry Lewis   *ph* Ernest
Steward   *m* Les Reed

Peter Lawford, Sammy Davis Jnr, Esther Anderson,
Maggie Wright

One More Tomorrow *
US   1946   89m   bw
Warner (Henry Blanke)

A wealthy playboy marries a left-wing photographer
and buys up her magazine.

An interesting but dated play fails to come to life
because neither cast nor director seem to understand
what it's about.

w Charles Hoffman, Catherine Turney, Julius J. and
Philip G. Epstein   *play* The Animal Kingdom by Philip
Barry   *d* Peter Godfrey   *ph* Bert Glennon   *m* Max
Steiner

Ann Sheridan, Dennis Morgan, Jack Carson, Alexis
Smith, Jane Wyman, Reginald Gardiner, John Loder,
Marjorie Gateson

One More Train to Rob
US   1971   108m   Technicolor
Universal (Robert Arthur)

A train robber comes out of prison and warily takes
up with his old partners.

Undistinguished Western which tries to be funny and
serious at the same time.

w Don Tait, Dick Nelson   *d* Andrew V. McLaglen
ph Alric Edens   *m* David Shire

George Peppard, Diana Muldaur, John Vernon,
France Nuyen, Steve Sandor

One New York Night *
US   1935   80m   bw
MGM (Bernard Hyman)
GB title: *The Trunk Mystery*

A young farmer in Manhattan on a visit finds a body
in the hotel room next to his.

Slick comedy thriller very typical of its date and
studio.

w Frank Davis   *play* Edward Childs Carpenter
d Jack Conway

Franchot Tone, Una Merkel, Steffi Duna, Conrad
Nagel, Charles Starrett, Harold Huber

'Sprightly devised murder mystery accounting for
plenty of laughs . . . studded with multiple touches of
production value.' – *Variety*

'A comedy of astonishing intelligence and finish . . . it
ought to take its place immediately with the classics.'
– *Graham Greene*

One Night in Lisbon
US   1941   97m   bw
Paramount (Edward H. Griffith)

During World War II an American flyer falls for a
British socialite who is being used by the government
as a decoy for spies.

Flabby romantic comedy-drama which mostly wastes
a good cast.

w Virginia Van Upp   *play* There's Always Juliet by
John Van Druten   *d* Edward H. Griffith   *ph* Bert
Glennon   *m* Sigmund Krumgold

Madeleine Carroll, Fred MacMurray, Edmund
Gwenn, Patricia Morison, Billie Burke, John Loder,
Dame May Whitty, Reginald Denny, Billy Gilbert

One Night in the Tropics
US   1940   69m   bw
Universal (Leonard Spigelgass)

Holidays on a Caribbean island lead to a double
wedding.

Very lightweight comedy-musical notable only for
introducing Abbott and Costello.

w Gertrude Purcell, Charles Grayson   *play* Love
Insurance by Earl Derr Biggers   *d* A. Edward
Sutherland   *ph* Joseph Valentine   *md* Charles
Previn   *songs* Oscar Hammerstein II, Jerome Kern,
Otto Harbach, Dorothy Fields

Allan Jones, Nancy Kelly, Bud Abbott, Lou Costello,
Robert Cummings, Leo Carillo, Peggy Moran, Mary
Boland

One Night of Love **
US   1934   95m   bw
Columbia (Harry Cohn)
V*, L

An opera star rebels against her demanding teacher.

Light classical musical which was a surprising box-
office success and brought Hollywood careers for Lily
Pons, Gladys Swarthout, Miliza Korjus, etc.

w Dorothy Speare, Charles Beahan, S. K. Lauren,
James Gow, Edmund North   *d* Victor Schertzinger
ph Joseph Walker   *md* Pietro Cimini   *m* Victor
Schezinger, Gus Kahn   *ed* Gene Milford

Grace Moore, Tullio Carminati, Lyle Talbot, Mona Barrie,
Nydia Westman, Jessie Ralph, Luis Alberni, Jane
Darwell

AA: score

AAN: best picture; direction; Grace Moore; editing

One Night With You
GB   1948   92m   bw
Two Cities/Rank

An English girl and an Italian tenor, stranded by a
train failure, are taken for forgers.

Rather frantic but occasionally amusing Italian-set
comedy.

w Caryl Brahms, S. J. Simon   *d* Terence Young

Nino Martini, Patricia Roc, Hugh Wakefield, Bonar
Colleano, Guy Middleton, Stanley Holloway, Irene
Worth, Charles Goldner

One of Our Aircraft Is Missing *
GB   1941   102m   bw
British National (Michael Powell, Emeric Pressburger)
V*

A bomber is grounded after a raid and its crew is
helped by the Dutch resistance.

Efficient propaganda piece which starts vigorously
but gets bogged down in talk.

wd Michael Powell, Emeric Pressburger   *ph* Ronald
Neame

Godfrey Tearle, Eric Portman, Hugh Williams,
Bernard Miles, Hugh Burden, Emrys Jones, Googie
Withers, Pamela Brown, Peter Ustinov, Joyce
Redman, Hay Petrie, Robert Helpmann, Alec Clunes

AAN: script

One of Our Dinosaurs Is Missing *
US   1975   94m   Technicolor
Walt Disney (Bill Walsh)
V*

In the 1920s a strip of secret microfilm is smuggled
out of China and hidden in a dinosaur's skeleton in
the Natural History Museum.

Unexceptional family comedy with everyone trying
hard; somehow it just misses, perhaps because it is
told through talk rather than cinematic narrative.

w Bill Walsh   *novel* The Great Dinosaur Robbery by
David Forrest   *d* Robert Stevenson   *ph* Paul
Beeson   *m* Ron Goodwin

Helen Hayes, Peter Ustinov, Derek Nimmo, Clive
Revill, Joan Sims, Bernard Bresslaw, Roy Kinnear,
Deryck Guyler, Richard Pearson

One on One
US   1977   98m   colour
Warner (Martin Hornstein)
V*

An idealistic young basketball star finds life hard after
he wins a scholarship to university.

Dull teen drama of a misfit making good.

w Robby Benson, Jerry Segal   *d* Lamont Johnson
ph Donald M. Morgan   *m* Charles Fox
ad Sherman Laudermilk   *ed* Robbe Roberts

Robby Benson, Annette O'Toole, G. D. Spradlin, Gail
Strickland, Melanie Griffith

The One Piece Bathing Suit: see *Million Dollar
Mermaid*

One Plus One
GB   1968   104m   Eastmancolor
Connoisseur/Cupid (Michael Pearson, Iain Quarrier)
V*
aka: *Sympathy for the Devil*

As the Rolling Stones rehearse their song 'Sympathy
for the Devil', the film cuts between black militants, a
television interview about revolution and its

relationship with culture, and a bookshop where someone recites excerpts from *Mein Kampf*.

A confused revolutionary statement, with Godard trying to annex rock 'n' roll for his own impenetrable purposes. The last words in the film are the director's, stating that he is fed up and wants to go home; his audience is likely to have left earlier.

wd Jean-Luc Godard *ph* Tony Richmond *m* The Rolling Stones *ed* Ken Rowles

Jean-Luc Godard (voice), Sean Lynch (voice), Mick Jagger, Keith Richard, Brian Jones, Charlie Watts, Bill Wyman, Anne Wiazemsky, Iain Quarrier, Frankie Dymon Jnr, Nike Arrighi

'Regardless of the effectiveness of certain scenes and sequences, one is left with the feeling that the film as a whole doesn't add up. But this is falling into the trap Godard has set for us: it is not meant to add up, and it won't.' – *Richard Roud, MFB*

† The producers increased Godard's cut by five minutes to 109m to include a full version of the Stones' song 'Sympathy for the Devil' at the end of the film.

One Rainy Afternoon *
US 1935 79m bw
Pickford-Lasky
V*

In a cinema one afternoon, a gigolo kisses the wrong girl.

Rather heavy-handed light comedy with interesting credentials.

w Stephen Morehouse Avery, Maurice Hanline *play* Emeric Pressburger and René Pujal *d* Rowland V. Lee

Francis Lederer, Ida Lupino, Roland Young, Hugh Herbert, Erik Rhodes, Mischa Auer

'Mr Lee has given a useful demonstration of how not to direct this kind of story: he has been remorselessly logical when he should have been crazy; his only idea of humour is speed and noise, not speed of thought or situation, but just literal speed of walking and talking.' – *Graham Greene, The Spectator*

One Spy Too Many
US 1966 102m Metrocolor
MGM/Arena (David Victor)

A modern-day Alexander the Great is foiled in his attempt to conquer the world.

Trivial spy caper, edited from episodes of the television series *The Man from U.N.C.L.E.*

w Dean Hargrove *d* Joseph Sargent *ph* Fred Koenekamp *m* Gerald Fried *ad* George W. Davis, Merrill Pye *ed* Henry Berman

Robert Vaughn, David McCallum, Rip Torn, Dorothy Provine, Leo G. Carroll, David Opatoshu, David Sheiner

One Summer Love
US 1976 97m colour Panavision
AIP
aka: *Dragonfly*

A young man leaves mental hospital for his Connecticut home, only to find everyone there nuttier than he is.

Over-the-top melodrama.

w N. Richard Nash *d* Gilbert Cates

Beau Bridges, Susan Sarandon, Mildred Dunnock, Michael B. Miller

One Sunday Afternoon **
US 1933 82m bw
Paramount (Louis D. Lighton)

In 1910, a Brooklyn dentist feels he has married the wrong girl, but discovers that his choice was the right one.

Pleasant period comedy drama which was twice remade: as *The Strawberry Blonde* (qv) and see below.

w William Slavens McNutt, Grover Jones *play* James Hagan *d* Stephen Roberts *ph* Victor Milner

Gary Cooper, Frances Fuller, Fay Wray, Neil Hamilton, Roscoe Karns

'Still pitched in stage tempo and unfolds haltingly.' – *Variety*

One Sunday Afternoon
US 1948 90m Technicolor
Warner (Jerry Wald)

Pleasant but undistinguished musical remake of the above.

w Robert L. Richards *d* Raoul Walsh *ph* Sid Hickox, Wilfrid M. Cline *md* Ray Heindorf *ad* Anton Grot

Dennis Morgan, Dorothy Malone, Janis Paige, Don Defore, Ben Blue

'A lackadaisical and uninspired jaunt down memory lane.' – *New Yorker, 1978*

The One that Got Away **
GB 1957 111m bw
Rank (Julian Wintle)
V*

A German flyer, Franz von Werra, is captured and sent to various British prisoner-of-war camps, from all of which he escapes.

True-life biopic, developed in a number of suspense and action sequences, all very well done.

w Howard Clewes *book* Kendal Burt, James Leasor *d* Roy Baker *ph* Eric Cross *m* Hubert Clifford

Hardy Kruger, Michael Goodliffe, Colin Gordon, *Alec McCowen*

One Third of a Nation *
US 1939 79m bw
Federal Theatre (Dudley Murphy)
V*

A shopgirl persuades a landlord to tear down his dangerous slums and put up good buildings.

Naïve do-goodery, not too persuasively managed.

w Dudley Murphy, Oliver H. P. Garrett *play* Arthur Arent *d* Dudley Murphy *ph* William Mellor *m* Nathaniel Shilkret

Sylvia Sidney, Leif Erickson, Myron McCormick, Hiram Sherman, Sidney Lumet, Percy Waram

'No worse and rather better than a commensurate modest-budgeter essayed on the coast . . . the cinematic transition however seems to have almost wholly ditched the Federal Housing "living newspaper" purpose of the stage version, emphasizing the boy-meets-girl premise against the shocking slum background.' – *Variety*

The One Thousand Plane Raid
US 1969 94m DeLuxe
Oakwood/UA

An American colonel persuades top brass of the need for daylight bombing of Germany.

Reasonable routine war action drama.

w Donald S. Sanford *d* Boris Sagal

Christopher George, Laraine Stephens, J. D. Cannon, Gary Marshall, Michael Evans, Ben Murphy

One Touch of Venus *
US 1948 82m bw
Universal/Lester Cowan
V*, L

In a fashionable department store, a statue of Venus comes to life and falls for a window dresser.

Pleasant satirical comedy, watered down from the Broadway original.

w Harry Kurnitz, Frank Tashlin *play* S. J. Perelman, Ogden Nash *d* William A. Seiter *ph* Franz Planer *songs* Kurt Weill *ad* Bernard Herzbrun, Emrich Nicholson

Ava Gardner, Robert Walker, Eve Arden, Dick Haymes, Olga San Juan, Tom Conway

One, Two, Three **
US 1961 115m bw Panavision
United Artists/Mirisch/Pyramid (Billy Wilder)
V*, L

An executive in West Berlin is trying to sell Coca Cola to the Russians while preventing his boss's daughter from marrying a communist.

Back to *Ninotchka* territory, but this time the tone is that of a wild farce which achieves fine momentum in stretches but also flags a lot in between, teetering the while on the edge of taste.

w Billy Wilder, I. A. L. Diamond *play* Ferenc Molnar *d* Billy Wilder *ph* Daniel Fapp *m* André Previn

James Cagney, Horst Buchholz, Arlene Francis, Pamela Tiffin, Lilo Pulver, Howard St John, Leon Askin

'A sometimes bewildered, often wonderfully funny exercise in nonstop nuttiness.' – *Time*

'This first-class featherweight farce is a serious achievement.' – *Stanley Kauffmann*

AAN: Daniel Fapp

One Way Out
GB 1955 80m bw
Rank/Major (John Temple-Smith)

A detective on the point of retirement is forced to cover up a crime to protect his daughter.

Pedestrian thriller that never rises above the commonplace.

w Jonathan Roche *story* John Temple-Smith, Jean Scott Rogers *d* Francis Searle *ph* Walter Harvey *ad* William Kellner *ed* Maurice Rootes

Jill Adams, Eddie Byrne, Lyndon Brook, John Chandos, Olive Milbourne, Arthur Howard, Arthur Lowe

One Way Passage *
US 1932 69m bw
Warner (Robert Lord)

On an ocean voyage, a dying girl falls in love with a crook going home to face a life sentence.

Pattern melodrama which stood Hollywood in good stead.

w Wilson Mizner, Joseph Jackson, Robert Lord *d* Tay Garnett *ph* Robert Kurrie *m* W. Franke Harling

William Powell, Kay Francis, Frank McHugh, Aline MacMahon, Warren Hymer, Herbert Mundin, Roscoe Karns, Stanley Fields

'Will reach house averages for this time of year.' – *Variety*

† Remade as *'Til We Meet Again* (qv).

AA: original story (Robert Lord)

One Way Pendulum
GB 1964 85m bw
UA/Woodfall (Michael Deeley)

A suburban clerk leads a dream existence; his son teaches speak-your-weight machines to sing, while he sets an imaginary murder trial in motion.

A nonsense play (which has many adherents) resists the literalness of the camera eye.

w N. F. Simpson *play* N. F. Simpson *d* Peter Yates *ph* Denys Coop *m* Richard Rodney Bennett

Eric Sykes, George Cole, Julia Foster, Jonathan Miller, Peggy Mount, Alison Leggatt, Mona Washbourne

One Way Street
US 1950 79m bw
U-I/Leonard Goldstein (Sam Goldwyn Jnr)

A disillusioned doctor steals a fortune and hides out in a Mexican village, where he regains his self-respect.

Thin and pointless melodrama.

w Lawrence Kimble d Hugo Fregonese
ph Maury Gertsman m Frank Skinner

James Mason, Marta Toren, Dan Duryea, William Conrad, King Donovan, Jack Elam

'It is reported that James Mason chooses his own parts, and if this is true I have to report that he is a glutton for punishment.' – Daily Herald

'One of the dullest, most stupid films of the year.' – Sunday Pictorial

One-Way Ticket
US 1935 66m bw
Columbia

A convicted bank robber falls in love with the warden's daughter.

Prison break drama which seems to be trying to make a point but is not sure what.

w Vincent Lawrence, Joseph Anthony, Oliver H. P. Garrett, Grover Jones novel Ethel Turner
d Herbert Biberman

Lloyd Nolan, Walter Connolly, Peggy Conklin, Edith Fellows, Nana Bryant, Thurston Hall

'It is "different" at the cost of credulity.' – Variety

A One-Way Ticket: see Un Pasaje de Ida

One Way to Love
US 1945 83m bw
Burt Kelly/Columbia

A Chicago radio writer gets a chance in Hollywood.

Hit-and-miss romantic comedy which takes place largely on a westbound train.

w Joseph Hoffman, Jack Henley, Lester Lee, Larry Marks d Ray Enright

Willard Parker, Marguerite Chapman, Hugh Herbert, Chester Morris, Jerome Cowan, Janis Carter

One Wild Moment: see A Summer Affair

One Wild Night
US 1938 63m bw
John Stone/TCF

Four small-town citizens anxious for vacations away from their wives plot their own kidnapping.

Tolerable second feature comedy, but the plot might have been better developed.

w Charles Belden, Jerry Cady d Eugene Forde

June Lang, Dick Baldwin, Lyle Talbot, J. Edward Bromberg, Sidney Toler, William Demarest, Andrew Tombes, Spencer Charters

One Wild Oat
GB 1951 78m bw
Coronet/Eros

An old flame tries to blackmail a highly respectable solicitor.

Modest film version of a popular West End farce.

w Vernon Sylvaine, Lawrence Huntington
play Vernon Sylvaine d Charles Saunders

Robertson Hare, Stanley Holloway, Sam Costa, Andrew Crawford, Vera Pearce, Robert Moreton, Irene Handl

One Woman or Two: see Une Femme ou Deux

One Woman's Story: see The Passionate Friends

Onibaba *
Japan 1964 104m bw Tohoscope
Kindai Eiga Kyokai/Tokyo Eiga
aka: The Hole

In medieval times on a remote marshy plain, mother and daughter live by killing stray soldiers and selling their armour, until daughter takes one for a lover and mother becomes jealous.

A kind of original horror legend is told by this strange, compelling piece with its frequent moments of nastiness. It remains, perhaps mercifully, unique.

wd Kaneto Shindo ph Kiyomi Juroda m Hikaru Hayashi

Nobuko Otowa, Jitsuko Yoshimura, Kei Sato

'What happened is true ... but the real crime is what happened after!'
The Onion Field
US 1979 126m Eastmancolor
Black Marble (Walter Coblenz)
V, V*, L

Two policemen are shot at by a manic killer, and the one who survives finds that he is suspected of cowardice and has to resign from the force.

Well meaning but lumbering case history. The author must carry the blame, as for once the picture was made exactly on his terms.

w Joseph Wambaugh novel Joseph Wambaugh
d Harold Becker ph Charles Rosher m Eumir Deptado pd Brian Eatwell

John Savage, James Woods, Franklyn Seales, Ted Danson, Ronny Cox, David Huffman

Onionhead
US 1958 110m bw
Warner (Jules Schermer)

Adventures of a ship's cook in the US Coastguard.

Service comedy that must have seemed funnier in the US than in Britain.

w Nelson Gidding novel Weldon Hill d Norman Taurog ph Harold Rosson md Ray Heindorf

Andy Griffith, Felicia Farr, Walter Matthau, Erin O'Brien, Joe Mantell, Ray Danton, Roscoe Karns, James Gregory, Tige Andrews

† An attempt to cash in on the success of No Time for Sergeants.

'Romance as glorious as the towering Andes!'
Only Angels Have Wings **
US 1939 121m bw
Columbia (Howard Hawks)
V, V*

Tension creeps into the relationships of the men who fly cargo planes over the Andes when a stranded showgirl sets her cap at the boss.

For an action film this is really too restricted by talk and cramped studio sets, and its theme was more entertainingly explored in Red Dust. Still, it couldn't be more typical of the Howard Hawks film world, where men are men and women have to be as tough as they are.

w Jules Furthman story Howard Hawks
d Howard Hawks ph Joseph Walker, Elmer Dyer
md Morris Stoloff m Dimitri Tiomkin

Cary Grant, Jean Arthur, Rita Hayworth, Richard Barthelmess, Thomas Mitchell, Sig Rumann, Victor Kilian, John Carroll, Allyn Joslyn

'All these people did the best they could with what they were given – but look at it.' – Otis Ferguson

The Only Game in Town
US 1969 113m DeLuxe
TCF (Fred Kohlmar)
V*

A Las Vegas chorus girl and a piano player have an unhappy life because of his gambling fever.

Uninteresting two-header from a play that didn't make it; no light relief, no action, and not even very good acting.

w Frank D. Gilroy play Frank D. Gilroy d George Stevens ph Henri Decaë m Maurice Jarre

Elizabeth Taylor, Warren Beatty, Charles Braswell, Hank Henry

'It epitomizes the disaster the studio and star systems foist on films . . . the only two-character tale around to cost $11 million.' – Judith Crist

† Frank Sinatra was originally cast but walked out after production started; Warren Beatty astonishingly chose to do this rather than Butch Cassidy and the Sundance Kid.

Only the Best: see I Can Get It for You Wholesale

'A comedy for anyone who's ever had a mother.'
Only the Lonely
US 1991 104m DeLuxe
TCF/Hughes Entertainment (John Hughes, Hunt Lowry)
V, V*, L, S

A mother-dominated cop falls in love with a shy beautician at his neighbourhood undertakers.

Soft-centred, sentimental drama that lacks the courage to be convincing.

wd Chris Columbus ph Julio Macat m Maurice Jarre pd John Muto ch Monica Devereux
ed Raja Gosnell

John Candy, Maureen O'Hara, Ally Sheedy, Anthony Quinn, James Belushi, Kevin Dunn, Milo O'Shea, Bert Remsen, Macaulay Culkin

† It was Maureen O'Hara's first film for 20 years.

'They were six and they fought like six hundred!'
Only the Valiant
US 1950 105m bw
(Warner) William Cagney
V, V*, L

A tough cavalry officer in a lonely fort wins a battle against Indians.

Standard top-of-the-bill Western; competent but not very gripping.

w Edmund H. North, Harry Brown d Gordon Douglas ph Lionel Lindon m Franz Waxman

Gregory Peck, Ward Bond, Gig Young, Lon Chaney Jnr, Barbara Payton, Neville Brand

Only Two Can Play ***
GB 1962 106m bw
British Lion/Vale (Launder and Gilliat)
V, V*

A much married assistant librarian in a Welsh town has an abortive affair with a councillor's wife.

Well characterized and generally diverting 'realistic' comedy which slows up a bit towards the end but contains many memorable sequences and provides its star's last good character performance.

w Bryan Forbes novel That Uncertain Feeling by Kingsley Amis d Sidney Gilliat ph John Wilcox
m Richard Rodney Bennett ad Albert Witherick

Peter Sellers, Mai Zetterling, Virginia Maskell, Richard Attenborough, Raymond Huntley, John Le Mesurier, Kenneth Griffith

'It has a kind of near-truth which is at once hilarious and faintly macabre.' – Dilys Powell

Only When I Larf *

GB   1968   103m   Eastmancolor
Paramount/Beecord (Len Deighton, Brian Duffy, Hugh
    Attwooll)

The adventures of three confidence tricksters.

Quite likeable but unmemorable 'with it' comedy of
the sixties; the tricks are more amusing than the
characterization.

w John Salmon   novel Len Deighton   d Basil
Dearden   ph Anthony Richmond   m Ron Grainer

Richard Attenborough, David Hemmings, Alexandra
Stewart, Nicholas Pennell, Melissa Stribling, Terence
Alexander, Edric Connor, Calvin Lockhart, Clifton
Jones

Only When I Laugh

US   1981   120m   Metrocolor
Columbia (Roger M. Rothstein, Neil Simon)
V, V*, L
GB title: *It Hurts Only When I Laugh*

An alcoholic actress tries to rebuild her life.

Last desperate fling (one hopes) of the Neil Simon
industry, dispensing in this case more bitter tears than
laughs, and generally failing to stay the course.

w Neil Simon   play The Gingerbread Lady by Neil
Simon   d Glenn Jordan   ph David M. Walsh
m David Shire

Marsha Mason, Kristy McNichol, James Coco, Joan
Hackett, David Dukes, John Bennett Perry

'One can almost hear the click of typewriter keys.' –
Geoff Brown, MFB

AAN: Marsha Mason; James Coco (supporting actor);
Joan Hackett (supporting actress)

Only Yesterday *

US   1933   105m   bw
Universal

An unmarried mother is seduced twice by the same
man.

One that Ross Hunter didn't get around to remaking
. . . and a good job too.

w William Hurlbut, George O'Neill, Arthur Richman
d John M. Stahl

Margaret Sullavan, John Boles, Billie Burke, Reginald
Denny, Edna May Oliver, Benita Hume

'The film needs little more praise than that it warrants
its unusual length.' – *Variety*

† The original intention seems to have been to mirror
recent history as in Frederick Lewis Allen's book of
the same title.

Ooh, You Are Awful *

GB   1972   97m   Eastmancolor
British Lion/Quintain (E. M. Smedley Aston)
V
US title: *Get Charlie Tully*

A London con man seeks a fortune, the clue to which
is tattooed on the behind of one of several girls.

Amusing star vehicle with plenty of room for
impersonations and outrageous jokes.

w John Warren, John Singer   d Cliff Owen
ph Ernest Stewart   m Christopher Gunning

Dick Emery, Derren Nesbitt, Ronald Fraser, Pat
Coombs, William Franklyn, Brian Oulton, Norman
Bird

Open City **

Italy   1945   101m   bw
Minerva
V, V*
original title: *Roma, Città Aperta*

Italian underground workers defy the Nazis in Rome
towards the end of the war.

A vivid newsreel quality is achieved by this nerve-
stretching melodrama in which all the background
detail is as real as care could make it.

w Sergio Amidei, Federico Fellini   d Roberto
Rossellini   ph Ubaldo Arata   m Renzo Rossellini

Aldo Fabrizzi, *Anna Magnani*, Marcello Pagliero, Maria
Michi

AAN: script

Open Season

US/Spain/Switzerland   1974   104m   Eastmancolor
    Panavision
Impala/Arpa (George H. Brown, Jose S. Vicuna)

Three young criminals hunt human prey, but one of
their victims takes his own revenge.

Rough, flashy, violent melodrama which pretends to
have something to say but in fact is merely
sensationalist.

w David Osborn, Liz Charles Williams   d Peter
Collinson   ph Fernando Arribas   m Ruggero Cini

Peter Fonda, Cornelia Sharpe, John Phillip Law,
Richard Lynch, Albert Mendoza, William Holden

'An offensive, gamy potboiler.' – *Variety*

'Both patience and the plot line are severely strained
by the artiness Collinson frequently indulges, with
frozen shots to mark the moments of truth and a
meaningless punctuation throughout of long shots,
angles and flashes.' – *Tom Milne*

Opening Night

US   1978   144m   Metrocolor
Faces Distribution (Al Ruban)
V, V*

A Broadway actress is on the point of a nervous
breakdown.

Interminable addition to the director's list of
unwatchable personal films.

wd John Cassavetes   ph Al Ruban   m Bo Horwood

Gena Rowlands, Ben Gazzara, John Cassavetes, Joan
Blondell, Paul Stewart, Zohra Lampert, Laura
Johnson

'Shrill, puzzling, depressing and overlong.' – *Variety*

L'Opéra de Quat' Sous: see *Die Dreigroschenoper*

Opera do Malandro

Brazil   1986   105m   colour
Goldwyn/MK2/Austra/TF1 (Marin Karmitz, Ruy Guerra)

A pro-American pimp in pro-Nazi Brazil becomes
involved with the daughter of his enemy, a corrupt
night-club owner.

A South American treatment of Brecht's *Threepenny
Opera* without Kurt Weill's music or much to
recommend it.

w Chico Buarque, Orlando Senna, Ruy Guerra
d Ruy Guerra   ph Antonio Luis Mendes   m Chico
Buarque   ed Mair Tavares, Ide Lacreta, Kenout
Peltier

Edson Celulari, Claudia Ohana, Elba Ramalho, Ney
Latorraca, Fabio Sabag, J. C. Violla, Wilson Grey

Operation Amsterdam *

GB   1958   104m   bw
Rank/Maurice Cowan
V*

In 1940 spies are sent into Holland to prevent the
invading Germans from finding Amsterdam's stock of
industrial diamonds.

Semi-documentary war adventure, well mounted and
played.

w Michael McCarthy, John Eldridge   book Adventure
in Diamonds by David Walker   d Michael McCarthy
ph Reg Wyer   m Philip Green

Peter Finch, Tony Britton, Eva Bartok, Alexander
Knox, Malcolm Keen, Tim Turner, John Horsley,
Melvyn Hayes, Christopher Rhodes

Operation Bullshine

GB   1959   84m   Technicolor
ABPC

In 1942, complications ensue when an ATS private
suspects her husband of infidelity.

Flabby army comedy with a few laughs.

w Anne Burnaby, Rupert Lang, Gilbert Gunn
d Gilbert Gunn

Donald Sinden, Barbara Murray, Carole Lesley,
Ronald Shiner, Naunton Wayne, Daniel Massey, Dora
Bryan

Operation CIA

US   1965   90m   bw
Allied Artists
V*

An agent is rushed to Saigon to find a secret message
which was never delivered.

Crude thick ear with a few suspenseful moments.

w Bill S. Ballinger, Peer J. Oppenheimer
d Christian Nyby

Burt Reynolds, John Hoyt, Daniele Aubry, Kieu
Chinh, Cyril Collick

Operation Condor

Hong Kong   1991   103m   colour
Golden Harvest/Golden Way (Raymond Chow)
original title: *Feiying Gaiwak*; aka: *The Armor of God II*

A Chinese explorer is hired by a Spanish aristocrat to
find a hoard of Nazi gold buried in the Sahara Desert.

Genial and energetic martial arts movie, less effective
than usual because the action is removed from its
normal Hong Kong context, though no doubt its
desert setting seemed exotic to its home audience.

w Jackie Chan, Edward Tang, Ma Mei-ping
d Jackie Chan   ph Arthur Wong   m Peter Pau
ad Oliver Wong, Eddie Ma, Lou Ka-yiu   ed Peter
Cheung

Jackie Chan, Carol Cheng, Eva Cobo de Garcia,
Shoko Ikeda

'A breezy actioneer that's always watchable.' – *Variety*

† The film was the most expensive so far made in
Hong Kong, at a cost of $15 million ($HK115).

Operation Crossbow *

GB   1965   116m   Metrocolor   Panavision
MGM/Carlo Ponti
V*, L
aka: *The Great Spy Mission*

In World War II, trained scientists are parachuted into
Europe to destroy the Nazi rocket-making plant at
Peenemunde.

Unlikely, star-packed war yarn with more passing
tragedy than most, all obliterated by a shoot-em-up
James Bond finale.

w Robert Imrie (Emeric Pressburger), Derry Quinn,
Ray Rigby   d Michael Anderson   ph Erwin Hillier
m Ron Goodwin

George Peppard, Tom Courtenay, John Mills, Sophia
Loren, Lilli Palmer, Anthony Quayle, Patrick
Wymark, Jeremy Kemp, Paul Henreid, Trevor
Howard, Sylvia Sims, Richard Todd, Richard Johnson

Operation Daybreak

US   1975   119m   Technicolor
Warner/Howard R. Schuster/American Allied (Carter de
Haven)

In 1941, Czech patriots kill the hated Nazi Heydrich
and are hunted down.

Curiously-timed evocation of wartime resistance
adventures, too realistic for the squeamish and

certainly not very entertaining despite a fair level of professionalism.

w Ronald Harwood   *novel Seven Men at Daybreak* by Alan Burgess   *d* Lewis Gilbert   *ph* Henri Decaë   *m* David Hentschel

Timothy Bottoms, Martin Shaw, Joss Ackland, Nicola Pagett, Anthony Andrews, Anton Diffring, Carl Duering, Diana Coupland

Operation Disaster: see *Morning Departure*

Operation Eichmann
US   1961   94m   bw
Allied Artists
V*

After the war, the Nazi who exterminated six million Jews escapes from Europe but is eventually recaptured.

Crude exploitation item designed to cash in on Eichmann's trial, a documentary on which would have been much more interesting.

w Lewis Copley   *d* R. G. Springsteen

Werner Klemperer (as Eichmann), Ruta Lee, Donald Buka, John Banner

Operation Kid Brother
Italy   1967   105m   Techniscope
Dario Sabatello
V*
aka: *OK Connery*

007's brother defeats an international mastermind with the help of a Scottish archery team.

Very elementary James Bond spoof, with a confusing array of old and new elements but less than the required minimum of style.

w Paolo Levi, Vincenzo Mannino, Carlo Tritto   *d* Alberto de Martino

Neil Connery (Sean's kid brother), Daniela Bianchi, Adolfo Celi, Bernard Lee, Lois Maxwell, Agata Flori

'A grotesque parody of a parody . . . bad enough to be hysterically funny.' – *MFB*

Operation Mad Ball *
US   1957   105m   bw
Columbia (Jed Harris)

American troops in Normandy are forbidden to fraternize with nurses, but a clandestine dance is arranged.

Madcap army farce which keeps promising to be funnier than it is.

w Arthur Carter, Jed Harris, Blake Edwards   *play* Arthur Carter   *d Richard Quine*   *ph* Charles Lawton Jnr   *m* George Duning

Jack Lemmon, Ernie Kovacs, Kathryn Grant, Mickey Rooney, James Darren, Arthur O'Connell

Operation Pacific
US   1950   109m   bw
Warner (Louis F. Edelman)
V*, L

Adventures of a submarine commander in the Pacific war.

Routine war heroics, tolerably done but overstretched.   *wd* George Waggner   *ph* Bert Glennon   *m* Max Steiner

John Wayne, Patricia Neal, Ward Bond, Scott Forbes, Phil Carey, Paul Picerni, William Campbell, Martin Milner

Operation Petticoat *
US   1959   124m   Eastmancolor
Universal/Granart (Robert Arthur)
V*, L

During World War II, a crippled submarine is

refloated by fair means and foul, and a party of nurses is taken aboard.

Flabby comedy with good moments, but not many.

w Stanley Shapiro, Maurice Richlin   *story* Paul King, Joseph Stone   *d* Blake Edwards   *ph* Russell Harlan   *m* David Rose

Cary Grant, Tony Curtis, Joan O'Brien, Dina Merrill, Gene Evans, Arthur O'Connell, Richard Sargent

'Grant is a living lesson in getting laughs without lines.' – *Variety*

AAN: story and screenplay

Operation St Peter's
Italy   1968   100m   colour
Turi Vasile/Paramount

Three thieves steal Michelangelo's *Pietà* and sell it for forty dollars to an American gangster.

Rather surprisingly watchable comedy chase, with the star parodying his past roles.

w Ennio de Concini, Adriano Baracco, Roberto Gianviti, Lucio Fulci   *d* Lucio Fulci

Edward G. Robinson, Lando Buzzanca, Heinz Ruhmann, Jean-Claude Brialy

Operation Secret
US   1952   108m   bw
Warner (Henry Blanke)

A traitor in the French resistance movement shoots a colleague, and the wrong man is accused.

Belated World War II adventure which gives the impression of having been discarded by Errol Flynn.

w James R. Webb, Harold Medford   *d* Lewis Seiler   *ph* Ted McCord   *m* Roy Webb

Cornel Wilde, Steve Cochran, Paul Picerni, Karl Malden

Operation Snafu: see *On the Fiddle*

Operation Thunderbolt *
Israel   1977   117m   Eastmancolor   Panavision
GS Films (Menahem Golan, Yoram Globus)
V*
aka: *Entebbe: Operation Thunderbolt*

An account of the rescue of Israeli hostages from terrorists who have hijacked their plane to Entebbe.

Victory at Entebbe and *Raid on Entebbe* were made with all-star casts for American television. This home-grown account of a famous deed is more modest yet more authoritative.

w Clark Reynolds   *d* Menahem Golan   *ph* Adam Greenberg   *m* Dov Seltzer

Klaus Kinski, Assaf Dayan, Ori Levy, Yehoram Geon, Mark Heath

AAN: best foreign film

Operation Undercover: see *Report to the Commissioner*

Operation X: see *My Daughter Joy*

Operator 13
US   1934   86m   bw
MGM/Cosmopolitan (Lucien Hubbard)
GB title: *Spy 13*

During the Civil War an actress becomes a Union spy.

Elaborate period romance with action highlights.

w Harry Thew, Zelda Sears, Eve Greene   *d* Richard Boleslawski   *ph* George Folsey   *m* William Axt

Marion Davies, Gary Cooper, Jean Parker, Katherine Alexander, Ted Healy, Russell Hardie, Henry Wadsworth, Douglass Dumbrille

'Will please generally . . . one of Davies' best.' – *Variety*

AAN: George Folsey

The Opposite Sex
US   1956   116m   Metrocolor   Cinemascope
MGM (Joe Pasternak)

A New York socialite divorces her unfaithful husband but finally takes him back.

Softened, musicalized version of *The Women* (qv); very patchy, shapeless, and not nearly sharp enough.

w Fay and Michael Kanin   *play* Clare Boothe   *d* David Miller   *ph* Robert Bronner   *m* Nicholas Brodszky   *songs* Nicholas Brodszky, Sammy Cahn

June Allyson, Dolores Gray, Joan Collins, Ann Sheridan, Agnes Moorehead, Joan Blondell, Barbara Jo Allen, Charlotte Greenwood

The Optimists of Nine Elms *
GB   1973   110m   Eastmancolor
Cheetah/Sagittarius (Adrian Gaye, Victor Lyndon)

Children of a London slum make friends with an old busker.

Gentle, sentimental, quite well-observed piece of wistful melancholia, falsified by its star performance.

wd Anthony Simmons,   *co-w* Tudor Gates   *novel* Anthony Simmons   *ph* Larry Pizer   *m* George Martin

Peter Sellers, Donna Mullane, John Chaffey, David Daker, Marjorie Yates

The Oracle
GB   1952   83m   bw
Group Three (Colin Lesslie)
US title: *The Horse's Mouth*

A reporter discovers that a village well in Ireland contains an oracle which can predict the future.

Weak sub-Ealing comedy which aims to please and gets a few laughs. All very British.

w Patrick Campbell   *d* C. M. Pennington-Richards   *ph* Wolfgang Suschitzky   *m* Temple Abady

Robert Beatty, Virginia McKenna, Mervyn Johns, Gilbert Harding

Orca – Killer Whale
US   1977   92m   Technicolor   Panavision
Famous Films/Dino de Laurentiis (Luciano Vincenzoni)
V, V*, L, S

Off Newfoundland, a killer whale takes revenge for its mate's death.

A rather unpleasant attempt to mix horror and thrills with ecology: not very entertaining, and not for the squeamish.

w Luciano Vincenzoni, Sergio Donati   *d* Michael Anderson   *ph* Ted Moore, J. Barry Herron   *m* Ennio Morricone

Richard Harris, Charlotte Rampling, Will Sampson, Keenan Wynn

'The biggest load of cod imaginable.' – *Philip Bergson, Sunday Times*

'There are more thrills to be had in the average dolphinarium.' – *Sight and Sound*

Orchestra Wives **
US   1942   97m   bw
TCF (William Le Baron)
V*, L

A small town girl marries the trumpet player of a travelling swing band.

Fresh and lively musical of its period, full of first-class music and amusing backstage backbiting.

w Karl Tunberg, Darrell Ware   *d* Archie Mayo   *ph* Lucien Ballard   *md* Alfred Newman

Ann Rutherford, George Montgomery, Lynn Bari, *Glenn Miller and his Orchestra*, Carole Landis, Jackie Gleason, Cesar Romero

'A natural for any theatre that hasn't got an ironclad rule against jive.' – *Hollywood Reporter*

AAN: song 'I've Got a Girl in Kalamazoo' (*m* Harry Warren, *ly* Mack Gordon)

Orchids to You *
US   1935   74m   bw
Robert T. Kane/Fox

A florist pulls several strokes to prevent an attorney from taking over her lease.

Amusing comedy drama which failed through lack of strong names.

w William Hurlbut, Bartlett Cormack, Glenn Tryon, Howard Estabrook   *d* William A. Seiter

John Boles, Jean Muir, Charles Butterworth, Ruthelma Stevens, Arthur Lake, Spring Byington

'One of those productions that just misses the top rung.' – *Variety*

Ordeal by Innocence
US   1985   88m   Eastmancolor
Cannon (Jenny Craven)
V*, L

An explorer returning from an Antarctic trip discovers that an acquaintance has been two years in prison for murder, and he might have saved him.

Rather dim Agatha Christie adaptation (though set in her favourite Devon from her favourite book), with workaday actors and a most unsuitable music score. By the time the end comes, nobody could possibly care who done it.

w Alexander Stuart   *d* Desmond Davis   *ph* Billy Williams   *m* Dave Brubeck

Donald Sutherland, Christopher Plummer, Faye Dunaway, Sarah Miles, Ian MacShane, Diana Quick, Annette Crosbie, Michael Elphick, Phoebe Nichols

Order of Death
Italian   1983   101m   colour
New Line/Virgin/RAI (Elda Ferri)

A corrupt cop and a cop-killer form a sado-masochistic relationship.

Confused personalities battle it out in an exaggerated, bombastic psychological thriller.

w Ennio de Concini, Hugh Fleetwood   *novel* Hugh Fleetwood   *d* Roberto Faenza   *ph* Giuseppe Pinori   *m* Ennio Morricone   *ad* Giantito Burchiellaro   *ed* Nini Baragli

Harvey Keitel, John Lydon, Nicole Garcia, Leonard Mann, Sylvia Sidney, Carlo Romanelli, Bob Kelly, Tony Mayer

Orders Are Orders
GB   1954   78m   bw
Group 3 (Donald Taylor)

Flabby update of *Orders Is Orders* with an interesting cast below par.

w Donald Taylor, Geoffrey Orme   *d* David Paltenghi   *ph* Arthur Grant   *m* Stanley Black

Peter Sellers, Brian Reece, Sid James, Tony Hancock, Margot Grahame, Raymond Huntley, Maureen Johnson, June Thorburn, Bill Fraser

Orders Is Orders *
GB   1933   88m   bw
Gaumont British (Michael Balcon)

An army barracks is disrupted when an American film company gets permission to work there.

Breezy farce which pleased at the time.

w Leslie Arliss, Sidney Gilliat   *play* Ian Hay, Anthony Armstrong   *d* Walter Forde   *ph* Glen MacWilliams

Charlotte Greenwood, James Gleason, Cedric Hardwicke, Cyril Maude, Ian Hunter, Ray Milland, Jane Carr, Donald Calthrop, Eliot Makeham, Wally Patch, Finlay Currie

'A wow from start to finish.' – *Variety*

'They made this boy a cold-blooded killer!'
Orders to Kill *
GB   1958   111m   bw
British Lion/Lynx (Anthony Asquith, Anthony Havelock-Allan)

During World War II a bomber pilot undertakes a mission to parachute into occupied France and kill a double agent, who turns out afterwards to have been innocent.

Strong, hard-to-take but well made war story about the effect of war on conscience.

w Paul Dehn   *d* Anthony Asquith   *ph* Desmond Dickinson   *m* Benjamin Frankel

Paul Massie, Irene Worth, James Robertson Justice, *Leslie French*, Eddie Albert, Lillian Gish, John Crawford, Jacques Brunius, Lionel Jeffries

Ordet *
Denmark   1957   126m   bw
Palladium (Carl Theodor Dreyer)

In a God-fearing village, a father and his three sons have various religious experiences.

Hard-to-take intellectual drama of the faith, very slow and austere but strangely compelling.

wd Carl Theodor Dreyer   *ph* Henning Bendtsen   *m* Poul Schierbeck

Henrik Malberg, Emil Hass Christensen, Preben Lerdorff-Rye, Caj Kristensen

'Everything is in its proper place – except the past!'
Ordinary People **
US   1980   124m   Technicolor
Paramount/Wildwood (Ronald L. Schwary)
V, V*, L

The eldest son of a well-heeled American family is drowned, and the survivors take stock and indulge in recriminations.

An actor's piece which on that level succeeds very well, and accurately pins down a certain species of modern American family.

w Alvin Sargent,   *novel* Judith Guest   *d* Robert Redford   *ph* John Bailey   *m* Marvin Hamlisch

Donald Sutherland, *Mary Tyler Moore, Timothy Hutton*, Judd Hirsch, Elizabeth McGovern, M. Emmet Walsh

'This is an academic exercise in catharsis: it's earnest, it means to improve people, and it lasts a lifetime.' – *New Yorker*

AA: best film; Alvin Sargent; Robert Redford; Timothy Hutton

AAN: Mary Tyler Moore; Judd Hirsch (supporting actor)

The Oregon Trail
US   1939   bw   serial: 15 eps
Universal

Outlaws and Indians harass pioneer wagon trains.

Well-mounted serial.   *d* Ford Beebe, Saul A. Goodkind

Johnny Mack Brown, Louise Stanley, Bill Cody Jnr, Fuzzy Knight, Roy Barcroft

The Oregon Trail
US   1959   86m   DeLuxe   Cinemascope
TCF

A New York reporter in 1846 is sent to cover a westward trek.

Prototype settlers vs Indians Western with all the expected incident.

w Louis Vittes, Gene Fowler Jnr   *d* Gene Fowler Jnr

Fred MacMurray, William Bishop, Nina Shipman, Gloria Talbott, Henry Hull, John Carradine, Elizabeth Patterson

Orfeu Negro: see *Black Orpheus*

The Organization
US   1971   108m   DeLuxe
UA/Mirisch (Walter Mirisch)
V*

San Francisco policemen combat an international drug smuggling organization.

The third and weakest adventure of Virgil Tibbs, black policeman of *In the Heat of the Night*. Absolutely routine.

w James R. Webb   *d* Don Medford   *ph* Joseph Biroc   *m* Gil Melle

Sidney Poitier, Barbara McNair, Sheree North, Gerald S. O'Loughlin

Orient Express *
US   1934   71m   bw
Fox

Various stories conflict on the Orient Express.

Moderately successful multi-drama in the wake of *Grand Hotel*.

w Paul Martin, Carl Hovey, Oscar Levant, William Conselman   *novel* Graham Greene   *d* Paul Martin

Heather Angel, Ralph Morgan, Norman Foster, Herbert Mundin, Una O'Connor, Irene Ware, Dorothy Burgess

'Rather too much story all of a sudden; auditors may be lulled to quiet by the easy, non-exciting early action.' – *Variety*

Oriental Dream: see *Kismet* (1944)

Orion's Belt
Norway   1985   103m   Eastmancolor
Enterprise/Filmeffekt (Dag Alveberg, Petter Borgli)
original title: *Orions Belte*

Three sailors discover a Soviet spy station.

Plodding Cold War thriller.

w Richard Harris   *novel* Jon Michelet   *d* Ola Solum   *ph* Harald Paalgard   *m* Geir Bohren, Bent Aserud   *ad* Harald Egede-Nissen   *ed* Bjorn Breigutu, Yngve Refseth

Helge Jordal, Sverre Anker Ousdal, Hans Ola Sorlie, Kjersti Holmen, Vidar Sandem, Nils Johnson

Orlando **
GB/Russia/France/Italy/Netherlands   1992   93m   Eastmancolor
Electric/Adventure Pictures/Lenfilm/Mikado/Sigma/British Screen (Christopher Sheppard)
V, S

In a life that lasts for 400 years, a male favourite of Queen Elizabeth I undergoes a sex change and becomes a 20th-century woman.

A divertingly different romp, amusing and occasionally provocative in its examination of identity and gender.

wd Sally Potter   *novel* Virginia Woolf   *ph* Alexsei Rodionov   *m* David Motion, Sally Potter   *pd* Ben Van Os, Jan Roelfs   *ed* Herve Schneid

Tilda Swinton, Billy Zane, Lothaire Bluteau, John Wood, Charlotte Valandrey, Heathcote Williams, Quentin Crisp, Peter Eyre, Thom Hoffman, Jimmy Somerville, Dudley Sutton, Anna Healy

'Exciting, wonderfully witty entertainment for discriminating auds.' – *Variety*

AAN: Ben Van Os, Jan Roelfs; costume design (Sally Potter)

L'Oro di Napoli: see *Gold of Naples*

O'Rourke of the Royal Mounted: see *Saskatchewan*

Orphans

US 1987 120m colour
Lorimar
V*, L

Two outcast brothers have their lives transformed by a gangster.

Photographed talk-piece which could hope for few takers among the general audience: one for actor-fanciers.

w Lyle Kessler play Lyle Kessler d Alan J. Pakula

Albert Finney, Matthew Modine, Kevin Anderson, John Kellogg

'Can a woman love more than one man?'
Orphans of the Storm *

US 1921 124m (24 fps) bw silent
D. W. Griffith
V*, L

Two sisters are caught up in the French revolution of 1789.

Half melodrama, half epic, this celebrated film survives chiefly by its careful attention to historical detail and by the excitement of its crowd scenes.

w D. W. Griffith play Adolph Ennery d D. W. Griffith ph Henrick Sartov

Lillian Gish, Dorothy Gish, Joseph Schildkraut, Lucille La Verne, Morgan Wallace, Frank Puglia, Creighton Hale

'There is scarcely a scene or an effect in the entire production that is not beautiful to look upon, and there is scarcely a moment that is not charged with intense dramatic power.' – *Robert E. Sherwood, Life*

Orphée ***

France 1949 112m bw
André Paulvé I/Films du Palais Royal
V, V*

Death, represented by a princess, falls in love with Orpheus, a poet, and helps him when he goes into hell in pursuit of his dead love.

Fascinating poetic fantasy which may have been finally unintelligible but was filled to overflowing with memorable scenes and cinematic tricks, from the entry to the hereafter through a mirror to intercepted code messages such as 'L'oiseau compte avec ses doigts'. The closest the cinema has got to poetry.

wd Jean Cocteau, play Jean Cocteau ph Nicolas Hayer m Georges Auric ad Jean d'Eaubonne

Jean Marais, François Périer, Maria Casarès, Marie Déa, Edouard Dermithe, Juliette Greco

'It is a drama of the visible and the invisible . . . I interwove many myths. Death condemns herself in order to help the man she is duty bound to destroy. The man is saved but Death dies: it is the myth of immortality.' – *Jean Cocteau*

† See the sequel *Le Testament d'Orphée*.

† The film was dedicated to its designer Christian Bérard (1902–49).

The Oscar *

US 1966 118m Pathecolor
Paramount/Greene-Rouse (Russel Rouse)
V*

On the night of the Academy Awards his friend recalls a heel's rise to stardom.

Squalid, sensationalist account of Hollywood mores; one hopes it isn't quite true.

w Harlan Ellison, Russel Rouse, Clarence Greene novel Richard Sale d Russel Rouse ph Joseph Ruttenberg m Percy Faith

Stephen Boyd, Elke Sommer, Tony Bennett, Eleanor Parker, Milton Berle, Joseph Cotten, Jill St John, Edie Adams, Ernest Borgnine, Ed Begley, Walter Brennan, Broderick Crawford, James Dunn, Peter Lawford, Edith Head, Hedda Hopper, Merle Oberon, Bob Hope, Frank Sinatra

'This is the sort of film that only Hollywood could make, and on that level it is preposterously enjoyable.' – *David Wilson*

'That true movie rarity – a picture that attains a perfection of ineptitude quite beyond the power of words to describe.' – *Richard Schickel*

Oscar

US 1991 109m Technicolor
Warner/Touchstone/Silver Screen Partners IV (Leslie Belzberg)
V, V*, L, S

A gangster who is trying to reform attempts to sort out the marital problems of his daughters.

Leaden attempt at a screwball comedy, and one that sinks under its own witlessness.

w Michael Barrie, Jim Mulholland play Claude Magnier d John Landis ph Mac Ahlberg m Elmer Bernstein pd Bill Kenney ed Dale Beldin, Michael R. Miller

Sylvester Stallone, Ornella Muti, Kirk Douglas, Peter Riegert, Chazz Palminteri, Vincent Spano, Marisa Tomei, Tim Curry, Don Ameche, Yvonne DeCarlo, Linda Gray

'Zany farce generates a fair share of laughs but still probably remains too creaky a conceit for modern audiences to go for in a big way.' – *Variety*

† Magnier's play was first filmed in France in 1967, directed by Eduardo Molinaro and starring Louis de Funes.

Oscar Wilde **

GB 1959 96m bw
Vantage (William Kirby)

Scandal strikes Oscar Wilde through his involvement with Lord Alfred Douglas.

Competent, well acted version of well-known events of the 1890s, with Morley in his original stage role; generally more satisfactory than *The Trials of Oscar Wilde* which was shot simultaneously.

w Jo Eisinger d Gregory Ratoff ph Georges Périnal m Kenneth V. Jones

Robert Morley, John Neville, Phyllis Calvert, *Ralph Richardson*, Dennis Price, Alexander Knox, Edward Chapman, Martin Benson, Robert Harris, Henry Oscar, William Devlin

O'Shaughnessy's Boy

US 1935 88m bw
MGM

A circus performer is reunited with the son his wife took away in childhood.

Shameless sentiment which failed to repeat for its stars the success of *The Champ*.

w Leonard Praskins, Otis Garrett d Richard Boleslawski

Wallace Beery, Jackie Cooper, Leona Maricle, Sara Haden, Henry Stephenson, Spanky MacFarland

'Far too much crying. Good production will help.' – *Variety*

Ososhiki: see *Death Japanese Style*

Ossessione **

Italy 1942 135m bw
ICI
V, V*

A wanderer falls for the wife of an innkeeper and they murder him, but fate takes a hand.

Unofficial remake of *The Postman Always Rings Twice*, barely released outside Italy. A powerful melodrama credited with starting the neo-realist school.

w Antonio Pietrangeli, Giuseppe de Santis, Gianni Puccini, Luchino Visconti, Mario Alicata d Luchino Visconti ph Aldo Tonti, Domenico Scala m Giuseppe Rosati

Massimo Girotti, Clara Calamai, Elio Marcuzzo

† Other versions: *Le Dernier Tournant* (France 1939); *The Postman Always Rings Twice* (US 1945); *The Postman Always Rings Twice* (US 1981).

Ostatni Etap: see *The Last Stage*

The Osterman Weekend

US 1983 102m DeLuxe
Davis-Panzer/Fox
V, V*, L

A CIA chief tries to convince a powerful TV journalist that several of his trusted informants are Soviet agents.

Convoluted bloodbath with absolutely nothing new in its locker.

w Alan Sharp, Ian Masters novel Robert Ludlum d Sam Peckinpah

Rutger Hauer, John Hurt, Burt Lancaster, Craig T. Nelson, Dennis Hopper, Chris Sarandon, Meg Foster, Helen Shaver

'A competent, professional, but thoroughly impersonal meller.' – *Variety*

Otac Na Sluǎbenom Putu: see *When Father Was Away On Business*

Otello *

US/Italy 1986 120m Eastmancolor
Cannon/RAI (John Thompson, Fulvio Lucisano)
V*, L

An adaptation of Verdi's opera, based on Shakespeare's play.

A visually splendid transcription, which however did not hit the mark with audiences.

wd Franco Zeffirelli ph Ennio Guarnieri m Giuseppe Verdi ed Peter Taylor, Franca Silvi

Placido Domingo, Katia Ricciarelli, Justino Diaz, Petra Malakova

AA: costumes (Anna Anni, Maurizio Millenotti)

Othello *

US/France 1951 91m bw
Mercury/Films Marceau (Orson Welles)
V*, L, S

Shakespeare's play as rearranged by Orson Welles at the start of his European wanderings; modest budget, flashes of brilliance, poor technical quality, variable acting.

Not really the best way to film Shakespeare.

wd Orson Welles play William Shakespeare ph Anchise Brizzi, George Fanto, Obadan Troania, Roberto Fusi, G. Araldo m Francesco Lavagnino, Alberto Barberis ad Alexander Trauner

Orson Welles, Michael MacLiammoir, Fay Compton, Robert Cook, Suzanne Cloutier, Michael Laurence, Hilton Edwards, Doris Dowling

Othello *

GB 1965 166m Technicolor Panavision
BHE (Richard Godwin)
V

A record of the National Theatre production, disappointing in terms of cinema but a valuable record of a famous performance.

d Stuart Burge *ph* Geoffrey Unsworth
md Richard Hampton

Laurence Olivier, Frank Finlay, Joyce Redman, Maggie Smith, Derek Jacobi, Robert Lang, Anthony Nicholls

'What the director does is keep the camera moving among the actors with the most intelligent precision.' – *Observer*

AAN: Laurence Olivier; Frank Finlay; Joyce Redman; Maggie Smith

The Other *
US 1972 100m DeLuxe
TCF/Rex-Benchmark (Tom Tryon)
V*

A boy insists that his dead twin is responsible for several unexplained deaths.

Subtle family ghost story for intellectuals; a bit pretentious and restrained for popular success.

w Tom Tryon *novel* Tom Tryon *d* Robert Mulligan *ph* Robert Surtees *m* Jerry Goldsmith
pd Albert Brenner

Uta Hagen, Diana Muldaur, Chris Connelly, Victor French

Other Halves
New Zealand 1984 95m Eastmancolor
Oringham/Galatea (Tom Finlayson, Dean Hill)

A middle-class woman, recovering from a breakdown and the end of her marriage, falls for a homeless and delinquent 16-year-old Maori youth.

Confused melodrama of racial intolerance and an unlikely love affair, unconvincing for the most part.

w Sue McCauley *novel* Sue McCauley *d* John Laing *ph* Leon Narbey *m* Don McGlashan
pd Robert Gillies *ed* Harley Oliver

Lisa Harrow, Mark Pilisi, Clare Clifford, Bruce Purchase, Emma Piper, Paul Gittins, John Bach

'Her every exciting moment was an unforgettable experience!'
The Other Love
US 1947 96m bw
Enterprise (David Lewis)

At a Swiss sanatorium, a lady concert pianist who is dying falls in love with her doctor.

Fairly icky 'woman's picture' with uncomfortable performances.

w Ladislas Fodor, Harry Brown *story* Erich Maria Remarque *d* André de Toth *ph* Victor Milner
m Miklos Rozsa

Barbara Stanwyck, David Niven, Richard Conte, Gilbert Roland, Joan Lorring, Lenore Aubert

Other Men's Women
US 1931 70m bw
Warner

A train driver falls for his partner's wife.

Stilted heavy-breathing melodrama.

w William K. Wells *d* William A. Wellman

Grant Withers, James Cagney, Mary Astor, Joan Blondell, Regis Toomey

'Good railroad melo for the lesser run theatres.' – *Variety*

'Meet Larry the Liquidator. Arrogant. Greedy. Self-centered. Ruthless. You gotta love the guy.'
Other People's Money *
US 1991 101m Technicolor
Warner/Yorktown (Norman Jewison, Ric Kidney)
V, V*, L

A selfish asset-stripper attempts to take over an old-established company and its attractive young lawyer.

Entertaining comedy of the conflict between big-city and small-town values in the modern manner: that is, greed wins.

w Alvin Sargent *play* Jerry Sterner *d* Norman Jewison *ph* Haskell Wexler *m* David Newman
pd Philip Rosenberg *ed* Lou Lombardo, Michael Pacek, Hubert de la Bouillerie

Danny DeVito, Gregory Peck, Penelope Ann Miller, Piper Laurie, Dean Jones, R. D. Call, Mo Gaffney, Bette Henritze

'The romance of passion and power!'
The Other Side of Midnight
US 1977 166m DeLuxe Panavision
TCF/Frank Yablans, Martin Ransohoff (Howard W. Koch Jnr)
V, V*

Before and after World War II a young Parisienne courts an American flyer, but her tycoon husband eventually exacts a grim revenge on both of them.

Turgid and interminable adaptation of a best-seller, with no likeable characters and several unpleasant sequences.

w Herman Raucher, Daniel Taradash *novel* Sidney Sheldon *d* Charles Jarrott *ph* Fred J. Koenekamp
m Michel Legrand *pd* John DeCuir

Marie-France Pisier, John Beck, Susan Sarandon, Raf Vallone, Clu Gulager, Christian Marquand

'After 166 minutes the feeling that one has actually lived through it all is a little too real for comfort.' – *David Badder, MFB*

'A fatuous, money-spinning film from the fatuous, money-spinning book.' – *New Yorker*

'Right down to the nonsense title, this epic of schlock restores the era of *Now Voyager* . . . the movie equivalent of a good bad read.' – *Time Out*

'Once in your life – may someone love you like this!'
The Other Side of the Mountain
US 1975 102m Technicolor
Universal/Filmways/Larry Peerce (Edward S. Feldman)
V*
GB title: *A Window to the Sky*

A girl skiing champion is paralysed by polio.

Maudlin tearjerker based on a real case; altogether too much of a good thing.

w David Seltzer *book* A Long Way Up by E. G. Valens *d* Larry Peerce *ph* David M. Walsh
m Charles Fox

Marilyn Hassett, Beau Bridges, Belinda Montgomery, Nan Martin, William Bryant, Dabney Coleman

AAN: song 'Richard's Window' (*m* Charles Fox, *ly* Norman Gimbel)

'For everyone who believes in happy endings!'
The Other Side of the Mountain Part Two
US 1977 99m Technicolor
Universal/Filmways (Edward S. Feldman)
V*

Crippled skier Jill Kinmont becomes a teacher and falls in love again.

More true-life weepie material spun out from the first successful film; the sequel is quickly forgettable.

w Douglas Day Stewart *d* Larry Peerce *ph* Ric Waite *m* Lee Holdridge

Marilyn Hassett, Timothy Bottoms, Nan Martin, Belinda J. Montgomery

Otley **
GB 1968 91m Technicolor
Columbia/Open Road (Bruce Cohn Curtis)

An inoffensive Londoner falls in with spies and murderers.

Semi-spoof comedy thriller taking in James Bondery and the swinging London set. Generally pretty funny, but not entirely certain of its own motives.

w Ian La Frenais, Dick Clement *novel* Martin Waddell *d* Dick Clement *ph* Austin Dempster
m Stanley Myers

Tom Courtenay, Romy Schneider, Alan Badel, James Villiers, Leonard Rossiter, Freddie Jones, James Bolam, Fiona Lewis

Otto e Mezzo: see *Eight and a Half*

Our Betters *
US 1933 83m bw
RKO (David O. Selznick)

An American woman in London finds her titled husband is unfaithful and sets about causing society scandals.

Dimly adapted West End success makes an interesting but unamusing film.

w Jane Murfin, Harry Wagstaff Gribble *play* W. Somerset Maugham *d* George Cukor *ph* Charles Rosher *md* Max Steiner

Constance Bennett, Violet Kemble Cooper, Alan Mowbray, Gilbert Roland, Phoebe Foster, Charles Starrett, Grant Mitchell, Anita Louise, Minor Watson, Hugh Sinclair

'It's all very English and so sophisticated . . . they will really have to go for Constance Bennett to go for this picture.' – *Variety*

'One of those familiar dreams of high life in which we are asked to admire even while we condemn the superb immorality of our almost godlike betters.' – *The Times*

Our Blushing Brides: see *Our Dancing Daughters*

Our Daily Bread *
US 1934 80m bw
(UA) Viking/King Vidor
V*, L

A young couple in the Depression inherit a broken-down farm and make it work.

A rather drab sequel to *The Crowd*, with an irrigation ditch finale in clear imitation of Eisenstein.

w Elizabeth Hill *story* King Vidor *d* King Vidor
ph Robert Planck *m* Alfred Newman

Karen Morley, Tom Keene, John Qualen, Barbara Pepper, Addison Richards

'Regardless of the scepticism on the matter of box office, and its chances seem thin, it ranks as a fine effort.' – *Variety*

'With the arrival of the ditchdigging sequence, all that has gone before seems but buildup for this compelling climax.' – *Eileen Bowser, Film Notes, 1969*

† Vidor so desperately wanted to make the film that, discovering its theme to be unpopular with sponsors, he pawned everything he owned to finance it.

Our Dancing Daughters *
US 1928 86m approx (24 fps) bw silent
MGM/Cosmopolitan (Hunt Stromberg)
V*

A wild young socialite knows when to stop, and makes a good marriage; her friend doesn't and falls to her death while drunk.

Mild exploitation piece of its time which swept Joan Crawford to stardom after her dance in her underwear.

w Josephine Lovett *d* Harry Beaumont
ph George Barnes

Joan Crawford, John Mack Brown, Dorothy Sebastian, Anita Page, Nils Asther

† Sequels: *Our Modern Maidens* (silent, 1929) with JC, Rod La Rocque, Douglas Fairbanks Jnr, Anita Page, *w* Josephine Lovett; *Our Blushing Brides* (sound, 1930) with JC, Robert Montgomery, Anita Page, Dorothy

Sebastian, Raymond Hackett, w Bess Meredyth and John Howard Lawson. Neither was remarkable.

AAN: Josephine Lovett; George Barnes

Our Fighting Navy
GB 1937 75m bw
Herbert Wilcox
US title: *Torpedoed*

In South America, a British naval captain saves the consul's daughter from a revolutionary.

Tuppenny blood heroics, unconvincingly staged.

w 'Bartimeus', Guy Pollock, H. T. Bishop, Gerald Elliott, Harrison Owens   d Norman Walker

Robert Douglas, H. B. Warner, Noah Beery, Richard Cromwell, Hazel Terry, Esme Percy

Our Girl Friday
GB 1953 87m Eastmancolor
Renown
V*
US title: *The Adventures of Sadie*

Four shipwrecked survivors are washed up on a desert island.

Coy sex comedy for the family; pretty unbearable.

wd Noel Langley

Kenneth More, Joan Collins, George Cole, Robertson Hare, Hermione Gingold, Walter Fitzgerald

Our Hearts Were Young and Gay *
US 1944 81m bw
Paramount (Sheridan Gibney)

Two well-to-do flappers of the twenties find fun and romance in Paris.

A pleasant, undemanding piece of nostalgia based on a popular biography.

w Sheridan Gibney   book Cornelia Otis Skinner, Emily Kimbrough   d Lewis Allen   ph Theodor Sparkuhl   m Werner Heymann

Gail Russell, Diana Lynn, Charles Ruggles, Dorothy Gish, Beulah Bondi, James Brown, Bill Edwards, Jean Heather

Our Hearts Were Growing Up
US 1946 83m bw
Daniel Dare/Paramount

Our two heroines experience their college days during the roaring twenties.

Rather stiffly made but fitfully amusing sequel to the above.

w Norman Panama, Melvin Frank   d William D. Russell

Gail Russell, Diana Lynn, Brian Donlevy, James Brown, William Demarest, Bill Edwards, Billy DeWolfe, Sara Haden

Our Hospitality ***
US 1923 70m approx (24 fps) bw silent
Metro/Buster Keaton (Joseph M. Schenck)
V, V*, L

Around 1850, a Southerner returns home to claim his bride and finds himself in the middle of a blood feud.

Charming rather than hilarious star comedy with a splendid ancient train and at least one incredible stunt by the star.

w Jean Havez, Joseph Mitchell, Clyde Bruckman   d Buster Keaton, Jack Blystone   ph Elgin Lessley, Gordon Jennings

Buster Keaton, Natalie Talmadge, Joe Keaton, Buster Keaton Jnr

'A novelty mélange of dramatics, low comedy, laughs and thrills . . . one of the best comedies ever produced.' – *Variety*

Our Leading Citizen
US 1939 87m bw
George Arthur/Paramount

A philosophical lawman tries to deal with labour unrest in his community.

Another attempt to make a star out of a character who appealed only in rural districts.

w John C. Moffitt   stories Irvin S. Cobb   d Alfred Santell

Bob Burns, Susan Hayward, Joseph Allen, Charles Bickford, Elizabeth Patterson, Clarence Kolb, Paul Guilfoyle

'Confusing and burdensome script . . . programme supporter.' – *Variety*

Our Little Girl
US 1935 63m bw
Fox (Edward Butcher)

A doctor's daughter brings her parents together.

One of the child star's thinner and more sentimental vehicles.

w Stephen Morehouse Avery, Allen Rivkin, Jack Yellen   story *Heaven's Gate* by Florence Leighton Pfalzgraf   d John Robertson   ph John Seitz   md Oscar Bradley

Shirley Temple, Joel McCrea, Rosemary Ames, Lyle Talbot, Erin O'Brien-Moore

'She should easily satisfy her following and assure business.' – *Variety*

Our Man Flint *
US 1965 108m DeLuxe Cinemascope
TCF (Saul David)
V*, L

An American secret agent and super stud fights an organization bent on controlling the world through its weather.

Comic strip imitation of James Bond; in its wild way the first instalment scored a good many laughs, but the sequel, *In Like Flint* (qv), quickly ended the series.

w Hal Fimberg, Ben Starr   d Daniel Mann   ph Daniel L. Fapp   m Jerry Goldsmith

James Coburn, Lee J. Cobb, Gila Golan, Edward Mulhare, Benson Fong, Sigrid Valdis

'Despite the fact that everyone from designers to actors seems to be having a ball, the film somehow goes over the edge of parody – ultimately it looks suspiciously like a case of wish-fulfilment.' – *John Gillett*

Our Man in Havana *
GB 1959 112m bw Cinemascope
Columbia/Kingsmead (Carol Reed)

A British vacuum cleaner salesman in Havana allows himself to be recruited as a spy, and wishes he hadn't.

The wry flavour of the novel does not really translate to the screen, and especially not to the wide screen, but a few lines and characters offer compensation.

w Graham Greene   novel Graham Greene   d Carol Reed   ph Oswald Morris   m Hermanos Deniz Cuban Rhythm Band

Alec Guinness, *Noël Coward*, Burl Ives, Maureen O'Hara, Ernie Kovacs, *Ralph Richardson*, Jo Morrow, Paul Rogers, Grégoire Aslan, Duncan Macrae

'The main weakness is the absence of economic, expressive cutting and visual flow. As a result . . . stretches of dialogue become tedious to watch; and the essential awareness of the writer's shifting tensions yields disappointingly to the easier mannerisms of any conventional comedy-thriller.' – *Peter John Dyer*

Our Man in Marrakesh
GB 1966 92m Technicolor
Harry Alan Towers
US title: *Bang Bang, You're Dead*

A tourist becomes involved with gangsters.

Thin comedy-thriller with exotic locations.

w Peter Yeldham   d Don Sharp

Tony Randall, Senta Berger, Terry-Thomas, Herbert Lom, Wilfrid Hyde-White, Grégoire Aslan, Klaus Kinski

Our Miss Brooks
US 1955 85m bw
Warner
V*

A lady teacher finds that the professor to whom she is engaged is tied to mother's apron strings.

Verbose comedy considerably less funny than the TV series from which it was spun off.

w Al Lewis, Joseph Quillan   d Al Lewis

Eve Arden, Gale Gordon, Robert Rockwell, Don Porter, Jane Morgan, Richard Crenna, Nick Adams

Our Miss Fred *
GB 1972 96m Technicolor
EMI/Willis World Wide (Josephine Douglas)

In World War II France, an actor escapes in women's clothes when his troupe is captured by the Nazis.

A carefully nurtured vehicle for Britain's top female impersonator somehow doesn't come off; celluloid both constrains his range and reveals his inadequacies.

w Hugh Leonard   d Bob Kellett   ph Dick Bush   m Peter Greenwell

Danny La Rue, Alfred Marks, Lance Percival, Lally Bowers, Frances de la Tour, Walter Gotell

Our Modern Maidens: see *Our Dancing Daughters*

Our Mother's House
GB 1967 105m Metrocolor
MGM/Filmways (Jack Clayton)

When mother dies, seven children, who don't want to go to an orphanage, bury her in the garden. Then their ne'er-do-well father turns up.

Unpleasant and rather boring melodrama, too silly to have much dramatic impact.

w Jeremy Brooks, Haya Harareet   novel Julian Gloag   d Jack Clayton   ph Larry Pizer   m Georges Delerue

Dirk Bogarde, Margaret Brooks, Pamela Franklin, Mark Lester, Yootha Joyce, Anthony Nicholls

'The children begin to display an alarming variety of accents . . . and when Dirk Bogarde enters, doing a rich Bill Sykes act as the long lost wicked father to a predominantly genteel family, the whole structure collapses.' – *Tom Milne*

'Clayton succeeds where upstarts have failed in capturing the essence of the horror-suspense film – and that is the realization that the monsters among us are human.' – *Judith Crist*

Our Neighbours the Carters
US 1939 85m bw
Paramount

A small-town pharmacist is so poor that he considers an offer from a wealthy friend to adopt one of his children.

A small-town saga of smiles and tears, much appreciated at the time.

w S. K. Lauren, Renaud Hoffman   d Ralph Murphy

Fay Bainter, Frank Craven, Genevieve Tobin, Edmund Lowe

'Neatly set up as a programmer for the family trade.' – *Variety*

Our Relations ***
US   1936   65m   bw
Hal Roach/Stan Laurel Productions
V, V (C), V*, L

Two sailors entrusted with a diamond ring get mixed up with their long lost and happily married twin brothers.

A fast-moving comedy which contains some of Laurel and Hardy's most polished work as well as being their most satisfying production.

w Richard Connell, Felix Adler, Charles Rogers, Jack Jevne   story The Money Box by W. W. Jacobs   d Harry Lachman   ph Rudolph Maté

Stan Laurel, Oliver Hardy, James Finlayson, Alan Hale, Sidney Toler, Daphne Pollard, Iris Adrian, Noel Madison, Ralf Harolde, Arthur Housman

Our Story
France   1984   111m   Eastmancolor
Artificial Eye/Adel Productions/Sara Films-A2 (Alain Sarde)
original title: Notre Histoire

A boozy traveller falls for a beautiful woman he meets on a train.

Sub-Buñuel surrealism that is an irritant rather than a pleasure.

wd Bertrand Blier   ph Jean Penzer   m Martinu, Beethoven, Schubert and others   ad Bernard Evien   ed Claudine Merlin

Alain Delon, Nathalie Baye, Michel Galabru, Geneviève Fontanel, Jean-Pierre Darroussin, Gérard Darmon

'The story of a love affair that lasted a lifetime!'
Our Town **
US   1940   90m   bw
Principal Artists/Sol Lesser
V*

Birth, life and death in a small New Hampshire community.

One of the main points of the play, the absence of scenery, is abandoned in this screen version, and the graveyard scene has to be presented as a dream, but the film retains the narrator and manages to make points of its own while absorbing the endearing qualities which made the play a classic.

w Thornton Wilder, Frank Craven, Harry Chantlee   play Thornton Wilder   d Sam Wood   ph Bert Glennon   m Aaron Copland   pd William Cameron Menzies

Frank Craven, William Holden, Martha Scott, Thomas Mitchell, Fay Bainter, Guy Kibbee, Beulah Bondi, Stuart Erwin

'You can nearly smell things cooking, and feel the night air.' – Otis Ferguson

AAN: best picture; Aaron Copland; Martha Scott; art direction

Our Very Own
US   1950   93m   bw
Samuel Goldwyn

A girl is shocked to discover that she is adopted.

Another Goldwyn foray into chintzy, middle-class, small-town America, but not a winning example.

w F. Hugh Herbert   d David Miller   ph Lee Garmes   m Victor Young   sp Richard Day

Ann Blyth, Farley Granger, Joan Evans, Jane Wyatt, Ann Dvorak, Donald Cook, Natalie Wood, Gus Schilling, Phyllis Kirk

Our Vines Have Tender Grapes *
US   1945   105m   bw
MGM (Robert Sisk)
V*

Life in a Norwegian farm community in southern Wisconsin.

Unexceptionable family picture produced in MGM's best manner.

w Dalton Trumbo   novel George Victor Martin   d Roy Rowland   ph Robert Surtees   m Bronislau Kaper

Edward G. Robinson, Margaret O'Brien, James Craig, Agnes Moorehead, Jackie 'Butch' Jenkins, Morris Carnovsky, Frances Gifford, Sara Haden

Our Wife *
US   1931   20m   bw
Hal Roach

Stan helps Ollie to elope.

Good standard star comedy with a rather disappointing third sequence as three people try to get into a car designed for one.

w H. M. Walker   d James W. Horne

Laurel and Hardy, James Finlayson, Jean London

Our Wife
US   1941   95m   bw
Columbia (John M. Stahl)

A composer is romantically torn between a lady scientist and his own ex-wife.

Middling romantic comedy of a kind very familiar at the time.

w P. J. Wolfson   play Lillian Day by Lyon Mearson   d John M. Stahl   ph Franz Planer   m Leo Shuken

Melvyn Douglas, Ruth Hussey, Ellen Drew, Charles Coburn, John Hubbard, Harvey Stephens

Ourselves Alone
GB   1936   87m   bw
British International

An Irish colleen has a brother in the IRA and a lover in the British Army.

Rather tired hawking of a theme already treated in Beloved Enemy.

w Dudley Leslie, Marjorie Jeans, Dennis Johnstone   play Dudley Sturrock, Noel Scott   d Brian Desmond Hurst, Walter Summers

Antoinette Cellier, Niall MacGinnis, John Lodge, John Loder, Clifford Evans

'Will find tough sledding because of the subject matter.' – Variety

'One of the silliest pictures which even an English studio has yet managed to turn out.' – Graham Greene, The Spectator

Out Cold
US   1989   92m   CFI
Hemdale (George G. Braunstein, Ron Hamady)
V, V*, L

Believing that he has inadvertently killed his partner, a butcher covers up the crime with the help of the widow, who is the real murderer.

Limp comedy that quickly runs out of ideas.

w Leonard Glasser, George Malko   d Malcolm Mowbray   ph Tony Pierce-Roberts   m Michel Colombier   pd Linda Pearl   ed Dennis M. Hill

John Lithgow, Teri Garr, Randy Quaid, Bruce McGill, Lisa Blount, Alan Blumenfeld, Morgan Paull, Barbara Rhoades

Out for Justice
US   1991   91m   Technicolor   Panavision
Warner (Steven Seagal, Arnold Kopelson)
V, V*, S

In Brooklyn, a cop hunts down the drug-crazed killer who murdered his best friend.

Despite the title, our hero is out for revenge, and the bloodier the better. The familiar theme is played out with the maximum amount of violence.

w David Lee Henry   d John Flynn   ph Ric Waite   m David Michael Frank   pd Gene Rudolf   ed Robert A. Ferretti, Donald Brochu

Steven Seagal, William Forsythe, Jerry Orbach, Jo Champa, Shareen Mitchell, Sal Richards, Gina Gershon, Jay Acovone

'Steven Seagal should snap off another hefty chunk of box-office with this latest lame-brained excuse to showcase his bone-breaking talents.' – Variety

Out of Africa **
US/GB   1985   150m   Rank colour   Technovision
Mirage/Sydney Pollack
V, V*, L, S

In 1914 Karen Blixen arrives in Africa for a marriage of convenience with a German baron who ignores her; a white hunter remedies the situation.

Heavy going but critically lauded transcription of a semi-classic which ambles along for an extremely long time without really getting anywhere.

w Kurt Luedtke, from writings of 'Isak Dinesen' (Karen Blixen)   d Sydney Pollack   ph David Watkin   m John Barry   pd Stephen Grimes   ed Frederic Steinkamp, William Steinkamp

Meryl Streep, Robert Redford, Klaus Maria Brandauer, Michael Kitchen, Michael Gough

'It's a long way to go for a downbeat ending.' – Variety

'The film purrs pleasantly along like one of its own big cats.' – Sight and Sound

AA: best picture; direction; photography; music; art direction; adapted screenplay; sound

AAN: Meryl Streep; Klaus Maria Brandauer (supporting actor); editing

Out of Order *
West Germany   1984   88m   colour
Virgin/Sandstar/Laura Film (Thomas Schuhly, Mathias Deyle)
original title: Abwärts

Four people in a high-rise office block are trapped in a lift that may crash to the ground at any moment.

Effective, claustrophobic thriller that maintains its suspense.

wd Carl Schenkel   novel Wilhelm Heyne   ph Jacques Steyn   m Jacques Zwart   ad Tony Ludi   ed Norbert Herzner

Götz George, Renée Soutendijk, Wolfgang Kieling, Hannes Jaenicke, Klaus Wennemann, Ralph Richter, Kurt Raab, Jan Groth

Out of Rosenheim: see Bagdad Café

Out of Season *
GB   1975   90m   Technicolor
EMI/Lorimar (Robert Enders, Merv Adelson)
V*

One winter in an English seaside resort, an old love is rekindled.

Restrained sexual fireworks in the old French manner, well enough done with excellent atmosphere but a shade overlong and marred by the need to indulge in modern tricks such as a deliberately ambiguous ending.

w Reuben Bercovitch, Eric Bercovici   d Alan Bridges   ph Arthur Ibbetson   m John Cameron

Cliff Robertson, Vanessa Redgrave, Susan George, Edward Evans

Out of the Blue
GB   1931   88m   bw
BIP

An aristocrat's daughter loves the radio singer who is engaged to her sister.

Dated frou-frou with interesting talent.

w R. P. Weston, Frank Miller, Bert Lee   *play Little Tommy Tucker* by Caswell Garth and Desmond Carter   *d* Gene Gerrard and John Orton

Jessie Matthews, Gene Gerrard, Kay Hammond, Kenneth Kove, Binnie Barnes

Out of the Blue
US   1947   86m   bw
Eagle Lion

A Greenwich village artist thinks a girl who has passed out in his apartment is dead, and tries to hide the body.

Tasteless and very unfunny farce.

w Vera Caspary, Walter Bullock, Edward Eliscu   *d* Leigh Jason

George Brent, Carole Landis, Ann Dvorak, Turhan Bey, Virginia Mayo, Elizabeth Patterson, Julia Dean, Richard Lane

Out of the Blue
Canada   1980   94m   colour
(Leonard Yakir, Gary Jules Jouvenat)
V, V*

A wayward teenage punk, with a drug-addicted mother and a drunken, sexually abusive ex-convict for a father, finds her life unendurable.

At least she can count herself fortunate that she didn't have to sit through this film.

w Leonard Yakir, Brenda Nelson   *d* Dennis Hopper   *ph* Marc Champion   *m* Tom Lavin, Neil Young   *ad* David Hiscox   *ed* Doris Dyck

Linda Manz, Dennis Hopper, Sharon Farrell, Don Gordon, Raymond Burr

Out of the Clouds
GB   1954   88m   Eastmancolor
Ealing (Michael Relph, Basil Dearden)

Several personal stories mesh against a background of London airport during a fog.

A dull compendium of stories with a background of documentary detail which is now fascinating because it's so dated.

w John Eldridge, Michael Relph   *d* Michael Relph, Basil Dearden   *ph* Paul Beeson   *m* Richard Addinsell

Anthony Steel, Robert Beatty, David Knight, Margo Lorenz, James Robertson Justice, Eunice Gayson, Isabel Dean, Gordon Harker, Bernard Lee, Michael Howard, Marie Lohr, Esme Cannon, Abraham Sofaer

'The film relies considerably on small-time players and marginal incidents; the detail, however, never looks like adding up to a satisfactory whole.' – *Penelope Houston*

Out of the Dark
US   1988   89m   colour
Medusa/Zel Films (Zane W. Levitt)
V*, L

Cops investigate a series of sex-related murders by a man dressed as a clown.

Camp horror film, full of sniggers at its own nastiness.

w J. Gregory de Felice, Zane W. Levitt   *d* Michael Schroeder   *ph* Julio Macat   *m* Paul F. Antonelli, David Wheatley   *pd* Robert Schulenberg   *ed* Mark Manos

Cameron Dye, Karen Black, Lynn Danielson, Karen Witter, Tracey Walter, Silvana Gallardo, Bud Cort, Geoffrey Lewis, Divine, Paul Bartel, Tab Hunter

Out of the Fog *
US   1941   86m   bw
Warner (Henry Blanke)

Gangsters move in to terrorize an innocent Brooklyn family.

Standard exploration of a situation which became routine.

w Robert Rossen, Jerry Wald, Richard Macaulay   *play The Gentle People* by Irwin Shaw   *d* Anatole Litvak   *ph* James Wong Howe

Ida Lupino, John Garfield, Thomas Mitchell, Eddie Albert, George Tobias, Aline MacMahon, Jerome Cowan, John Qualen, Leo Gorcey

'You're no good and neither am I. We deserve each other!'
Out of the Past **
US   1947   97m   bw
RKO (Warren Duff)
V*, L
GB title: *Build My Gallows High*

A private detective is hired by a hoodlum to find his homicidal girlfriend; he does, and falls in love with her.

Moody *film noir* with Hollywood imitating French models; plenty of snarling and a death-strewn climax.

w Geoffrey Homes   *novel Build My Gallows High* by Geoffrey Homes   *d* Jacques Tourneur   *ph* Nicholas Musuraca   *m* Roy Webb

Robert Mitchum, Jane Greer, Kirk Douglas, Rhonda Fleming, Richard Webb, Steve Brodie, Virginia Houston, Dickie Moore

'Is this not an outcrop of the national masochism induced by a quite aimless, newly industrialized society proceeding rapidly on its way to nowhere?' – *Richard Winnington*

'Mitchum is so sleepily self-confident with the women that when he slopes into clinches you expect him to snore in their faces.' – *James Agee*

'The laugh-a-minute lowdown on the birth of swoon!'
Out of this World
US   1945   96m   bw
Paramount (Sam Coslow)

A Western Union messenger becomes a hit crooner and a national phenomenon.

Very mild comedy with the gimmick that Bing Crosby dubbed the singing.

w Walter de Leon, Arthur Phillips   *d* Hal Walker   *ph* Stuart Thompson   *m* Victor Young

Eddie Bracken, Veronica Lake, Diana Lynn, Cass Daley, Parkyakarkus, Donald MacBride, Florence Bates, Carmen Cavallero

The Out of Towners *
US   1970   98m   Movielab
Paramount/Jalem (Paul Nathan)
V*, L

An executive and his wife fly into New York for an interview, but their encounter with the city is a mounting series of traumatic disasters.

A love-hate relationship with a city demonstrated by a resident is something of an in-joke and becomes increasingly hysterical and unsympathetic, but there are bright moments in this company.

w Neil Simon   *d* Arthur Hiller   *ph* Andrew Laszlo   *m* Quincy Jones

Jack Lemmon, Sandy Dennis

Outback *
Australia   1970   109m   Technicolor
NIT/Group W (George Willoughby)

A young teacher becomes involved in the rougher side of life in a remote Australian village.

A convincingly brutal picture of a community whose interests range from homosexuality to a bloody kangaroo hunt.

w Evan Jones   *novel Wake in Fright* by Kenneth Cook   *d* Ted Kotcheff   *ph* Brian West   *m* John Scott

Gary Bond, Donald Pleasence, Chips Rafferty

The Outcast: see *Man in the Saddle*

Outcast
US   1954   87m   Trucolor
Republic (Herbert J. Yates)
V*

A cowboy returns home to claim the ranch his uncle stole from him.

Fast-paced Western that relies on non-stop action to distract attention from its clichéd narrative.

w John K. Butler, Richard Wormser   *story* Todhunter Ballard   *d* William Witney   *ph* Reggie Lanning   *m* R. Dale Butts   *ad* Frank Arrigo   *ed* Tony Martinelli

John Derek, Joan Evans, Jim Davis, Slim Pickens, Harry Carey Jnr

Outcast Lady
US   1934   79m   bw
MGM
GB title: *A Woman of the World*

A spoilt rich girl goes from man to man but helps her drunken brother.

Modest remake of the Garbo vehicle *A Woman of Affairs*.

w Zoe Akins   *novel The Green Hat* by Michael Arlen   *d* Robert Z. Leonard

Constance Bennett, Hugh Williams, Mrs Patrick Campbell, Elizabeth Allan, Henry Stephenson, Leo G. Carroll

'Even her love was primitive!'
An Outcast of the Islands **
GB   1951   102m   bw
London Films (Carol Reed)

A shiftless trader finds a secret Far Eastern trading post where he can be happy – but even here he becomes an outcast.

An interesting but not wholly successful attempt to dramatize a complex character study. It looks great and is well acted.

w William Fairchild   *novel* Joseph Conrad   *d* Carol Reed   *ph* John Wilcox   *m* Brian Easdale

Trevor Howard, Ralph Richardson, Kerima, Robert Morley, Wendy Hiller, George Coulouris, Frederick Valk, Wilfrid Hyde-White, Betty Ann Davies

'The script is so overwhelmed by the narrative itself that the characters and relationships fail to crystallize . . . while the handling is often intelligent, ingenious, and has its effective moments, no real conception emerges.' – *Gavin Lambert*

'Its sordidness is not veneered by the usual lyricism of Hollywood.' – *London Evening News*

'The most powerful film ever made in this country.' – *Observer*

The Outcasts of Poker Flat
US   1937   68m   bw
RKO (Robert Sisk)

Four undesirables are run out of town and stuck in a mountain cabin during a snowstorm.

Overstretched anecdote with a predictably downbeat finale and not much action.

w John Twist, Harry Segall   *story* Bret Harte   *d* Christy Cabanne   *ph* Robert de Grasse

Preston Foster, Jean Muir, Van Heflin

The Outcasts of Poker Flat
US   1952   80m   bw
TCF (Julian Blaustein)

Good-looking but equally undramatic remake of the above.

w Edmund H. North   *d* Joseph M. Newman
ph Joseph LaShelle   *m* Hugo Friedhofer

Dale Robertson, Anne Baxter, Cameron Mitchell,
Miriam Hopkins

'Fails badly either as dramatic or as western fare . . .
best where two features prevail.' – *Variety*

The Outfit
US   1973   103m   Metrocolor
MGM (Carter de Haven)

A criminal just out of prison finds himself in danger
from the Syndicate.

Unattractive rehash of *Point Blank* with much
gratuitous violence.

wd John Flynn   *novel* Richard Stark   *ph* Bruce
Surtees   *m* Jerry Fielding

Robert Duvall, Karen Black, Robert Ryan, Joe Don
Baker, Timothy Carey, Richard Jaeckel, Sheree North,
Marie Windsor, Jane Greer, Elisha Cook Jnr

'A nice profusion of Hollywood character actors
makes up for the overall lack of drive.' – *Sight and
Sound*

'Even in space, the ultimate enemy is man!'
'On Jupiter's moon, something deadly is happening!'
Outland
GB   1981   109m   Technicolor   Panavision
Warner/Ladd (Richard A. Roth)
V, V*, L

The marshal of a mining base on the third moon of
Jupiter waits for hired killers to arrive from Earth and
try to assassinate him.

Ludicrous, over-plotted outer-space version of *High
Noon*, in such thick colour that the action is hard to
follow.

wd Peter Hyams   *ph* Stephen Goldblatt   *m* Jerry
Goldsmith   *pd* Philip Harrison

Sean Connery, Peter Boyle, Francis Sternhagen,
James B. Sikking, Kika Markham, Clarke Peters

'Acres of footage are expended on the same old dreary
electronic gadgetry and the same old hollowly
echoing metalwork sets.' – *Tom Milne, MFB*

'Action! Thrills! Sensations! Primitive Love!'
The Outlaw *
US   1943   126m   bw
Howard Hughes
V, V*, L

Billy the Kid, Doc Holliday and Pat Garrett meet up at
a way station and quarrel over a half-breed girl.

Half-baked Western with much pretentious chat and
the main interest squarely focused on the bosom of
the producer's new discovery. This aspect kept
censorship ballyhoo going for six years before the film
was finally released in truncated form, and audiences
found it not worth the wait, though it does look good.

w Jules Furthman   *d* Howard Hughes   *ph* Gregg
Toland   *md* Victor Young

Jack Beutel, Jane Russell, Thomas Mitchell, Walter
Huston

'A Western employing every ingredient ever used in
this brand of production, but in such a naive fashion
that you will laugh – not with the picture but at it.' –
Ewart Hodgson, News of the World

† Despite the controversy, the British Board of Film
Censors gave the film a 'U' certificate, which meant
that children could see it.

Outlaw Blues
US   1977   101m   Technicolor
Warner/Fred Weintraub–Paul Heller (Steve Tisch)
V*

An ex-con finds that a singing star has stolen his song.

Fashionable comedy-melodrama with no great
entertainment value despite action scenes towards the
end.

w B. W. L. Norton   *d* Richard T. Heffron   *ph* Jules
Brenner   *m* Charles Bernstein

Peter Fonda, Susan Saint James, John Crawford,
James Callahan, Michael Lerner

The Outlaw Josey Wales *
US   1976   135m   DeLuxe   Panavision
Warner/Malpaso (Robert Daley)
V, V*, L, S

A Westerner gradually avenges the death of his wife
at the hands of bandits.

Bloodthirsty actioner in the star's usual mould; likely
to prove unintentionally funny for hardened addicts.

w Phil Kaufman, Sonia Chernus   *novel* Gone to Texas
by Forrest Carter   *d* Clint Eastwood   *ph* Bruce
Surtees   *m* Jerry Fielding

Clint Eastwood, Chief Dan George, Sondra Locke,
John Vernon, Bill McKinney

'If only the actors hadn't got in the way of the scenery,
it would have been a very beautiful film indeed.' –
Benny Green, Punch

AAN: Jerry Fielding

Outpost in Malaya: see *The Planter's Wife*

Outpost in Morocco
US   1949   92m   bw
Joseph N. Ermolieff

A romantic Foreign Legion officer falls for the
daughter of an enemy Arab.

Despite authentic locations and the cooperation of the
Legion this is a stolid piece of work, too dull even for
children's matinees.

w Charles Grayson, Paul de St Columbe   *d* Robert
Florey   *ph* Lucien Andriot

George Raft, Akim Tamiroff, Marie Windsor, John
Litel, Eduard Franz

Outrage
US   1950   75m   bw
Filmmakers (Collier Young)

A girl who has been raped is almost unhinged by the
experience.

Well-meaning low-budgeter, thin in entertainment
value.

w Ida Lupino, Collier Young, Malvin Wald   *d* Ida
Lupino   *ph* Archie Stout   *md* Constantin
Bakaleinikoff   *m* Paul Sawtell   *pd* Harry Horner

Mala Powers, Tod Andrews, Robert Clarke, Raymond
Bond, Lilian Hamilton

'An unconvincing mixture of sensationalism,
sentiment and half-baked sociology.' – *MFB*

The Outrage *
US   1964   97m   bw   Panavision
MGM/Harvest/February/Ritt/Kayos (A. Ronald Lubin)
V*

Conflicting views of a Western murder.

Wildly ineffective remake of *Rashomon*, with everyone
strangely overacting and little sense of the West as it
is normally depicted.

w Michael Kanin   *d* Martin Ritt   *ph* James Wong
Howe   *m* Alex North

Paul Newman, Edward G. Robinson, Laurence
Harvey, Claire Bloom, William Shatner, Albert Salmi

Outrageous Fortune *
US   1987   100m   DeLuxe
Touchstone/Interscope (Ted Field, Robert Cort)
V, V*, L

Two disparate women are in love with the same man,
who is wanted by the CIA and the KGB.

Chase comedy with sex elements and plenty going on:
old-fashioned jokes wrapped up in a modern
package.

w Leslie Dixon   *d* Arthur Hiller   *ph* David M.
Walsh   *m* Alan Silvestri   *pd* James D. Vance

Shelley Long, Bette Midler, Peter Coyote, Robert
Prosky, John Schuck

'Really a risqué film for a conservative audience.' –
Daily Variety

The Outriders
US   1950   93m   Technicolor
MGM (Richard Goldstone)

Three Confederate soldiers escape from a yankee
prison camp.

Competent star Western with solid production values.

w Irving Ravetch   *d* Roy Rowland   *ph* Charles
Schoenbaum   *m* André Previn

Joel McCrea, Arlene Dahl, Barry Sullivan, Claude
Jarman Jnr, Ramon Novarro

The Outside Man **
France/Italy   1972   104m   DeLuxe
United Artists/Cité Films/Mondial TE.FI (Jacques Bar)
V*
original title: *Un Homme est Mort*

After he has killed a Mafia boss in Los Angeles to pay
off his debts, a Frenchman discovers that he is to be
killed and goes on the run from his assassin.

Well-made thriller full of unexpected twists and
turns, with some intriguing set-pieces, including a
shoot-out at a funeral.

w Jean-Claude Carrière, Jacques Deray, Ian McLellan
Hunter   *d* Jacques Deray   *ph* Terry K. Meade,
Silvano Ippoliti   *m* Michel Legrand   *pd* Marvin
March   *ed* Henri Lanoe, William K. Chulack

Jean-Louis Trintignant, Ann-Margret, Roy Scheider,
Angie Dickinson, Georgia Engel, Felice Orlandi, Talia
Shire

'A neat, intriguing thriller which never gets ambitions
above its station.' – *Tom Milne, MFB*

The Outside Man
US/France   1973   104m   colour
Jacques Bar/UA

A French hit man comes to Los Angeles on a mission.

Tough gangster movie which will satisfy fans.

w Jacques Deray, Ian McLellan Hunter, Jean-Claude
Carrière   *d* Jacques Deray

Jean-Louis Trintignant, Roy Scheider, Ann-Margret,
Angie Dickinson, Georgia Engel

Outside the Law
US   1930   76m   bw
Universal

A girl becomes involved between two crooks
planning a bank robbery.

Incompetent early talkie with some familiar talents all
at sea.

w Tod Browning, Garrett Fort   *d* Tod Browning

Mary Nolan, Edward G. Robinson, Owen Moore,
Edwin Sturgis

'One of the worst examples of claptrap since sound
came in . . . no continuity and the director lets the cast
run wild.' – *Variety*

The Outsider
GB   1931   93m   bw
Cinema House/MGM

A 'quack' osteopath is finally able to make a surgeon's
crippled daughter walk.

Cast-iron theatre and a fairly successful quota quickie which was also released in America.

w Harry Lachman, Alma Reville   play Dorothy Brandon   d Harry Lachman

Harold Huth, Joan Barry, Norman McKinnel, Frank Lawton, Mary Clare

The Outsider
GB   1939   90m   bw
ABPC

Sturdy remake of the above.

w Dudley Leslie   d Paul Stein

George Sanders, Mary Maguire, Frederick Leister, Peter Murray Hill, Kathleen Harrison

'Up-to-date and should appeal to popular-priced audiences.' – Variety

The Outsider (US 1948): see The Guinea Pig

The Outsider
US   1961   108m   bw
U-I (Sy Bartlett)

Ira Hayes, a simple Red Indian, becomes a war hero but cannot reconcile himself to living in a white society.

Prolonged biopic which proves a shade too much for an eager star; it's all earnest and mildly interesting but not cinematically compulsive.

w Stewart Stern   d Delbert Mann   ph Joseph LaShelle   m Leonard Rosenman

Tony Curtis, James Franciscus, Bruce Bennett, Gregory Walcott, Vivian Nathan, Edmund Hashim, Stanley Adams

The Outsiders (1964): see Bande à Part

The Outsiders
US   1983   91m   Technicolor   Panavision
Zoetrope/Warner
V, V*, L, S

A young punk leads a high school gang against another higher in the social scale.

Oddball youth melodrama, a curious choice for a director with big successes behind him.

w Katherine Knutsen Rowell   novel S. E. Hinton   d Francis Ford Coppola

Matt Dillon, Ralph Macchio, C. Thomas Howell, Patrick Swayze, Rob Lowe, Emilio Estevez, Tom Cruise

'No more than a well-acted teen film.' – Motion Picture Guide

Outward Bound *
US   1930   82m   bw
Warner

Passengers on a strange liner discover that they are all dead and heading for purgatory.

Early sound version of a popular twenties play which does not translate too well to cinematic forms and now seems very dated apart from a couple of performances; remade as Between Two Worlds (qv).

w J. Grubb Alexander   play Sutton Vane   d Robert Milton   ph Hal Mohr

Leslie Howard, Douglas Fairbanks Jnr, Alec B. Francis, Helen Chandler, Beryl Mercer, Alison Skipworth, Montagu Love, Dudley Digges

'Intelligentsia subject that must be spotted carefully . . . seems to lack the essentials of mass entertainment.' – Variety

Over Her Dead Body: see Enid Is Sleeping

Over My Dead Body
US   1942   67m   bw
Walter Morosco/TCF

A writer plans commercial success by pleading guilty to an imaginary crime, but truth is stranger than fiction.

Over-talkative crime comedy.

w Edward James   novel James O'Hanlon   d Mal St Clair

Milton Berle, Mary Beth Hughes, Reginald Denny, Frank Orth, J. Pat O'Malley

Over She Goes *
GB   1937   74m   bw
ABPC

An old friend helps a nobleman to thwart a blackmailer.

Lively comedy vehicle for a forgotten star.

w Elizabeth Meehan, Hugh Brooke   play Stanley Lupino   d Graham Cutts

Stanley Lupino, Laddie Cliff, Gina Malo, Clare Luce, Max Baer, Sally Gray, Syd Walker

Over the Brooklyn Bridge
US   1983   106m   Metrocolor
Golan-Globus
V*

Misadventures of a family-ridden Jewish restaurant owner in New York.

Frantic ethnic comedy with an unsympathetic hero.

w Arnold Somkin   d Menahem Golan

Elliott Gould, Margaux Hemingway, Sid Caesar, Shelley Winters, Burt Young, Carol Kane

'The film's lip service to liberalism is offset by a blatantly sexist storyline.' – Ruth Baumgarten, MFB

Over the Hill
US   1931   87m   bw
Fox

An ageing mother is sent to the poorhouse by her hard-hearted older son, but rescued by her ne'er-do-well younger one.

Sound remake of a silent success which in 1920 made a star of Mary Carr, who thereafter specialized in playing dear old ladies.

w Tom Barry, Jules Furthman   poems Will Carleton   d Henry King

James Dunn, Sally Eilers, Mae Marsh, Edward Crandall, James Kirkwood

'There isn't a single overacted scene and there isn't a sequence that doesn't reach straight to the heart.' – Variety

Over the Moon
GB   1940 (made in 1937—8, but not released)   78m
   Technicolor   London Films (Alexander Korda)

A poor girl comes into a fortune but this does not help her romance with a proud young doctor.

Insubstantial comedy which turns itself into a European travelogue before petering out.

w Anthony Pelissier, Arthur Wimperis, Alec Coppel   d Thornton Freeland   ph Harry Stradling   m Mischa Spoliansky

Merle Oberon, Rex Harrison, Ursula Jeans, Robert Douglas, Louis Borell, Zena Dare, Peter Haddon, David Tree

Over the River: see One More River

Over the Top
US   1987   93m   Metrocolor   Panavision
Cannon (Menahem Golan, Yoram Globus)
V, V*, L, S

An arm wrestler tries to win the love of his son.

Mundane melodrama which its star couldn't carry.

w Stirling Silliphant, Sylvester Stallone   d Menahem Golan   ph David Gurfinkel   m Giorgio Moroder   pd James Schoppe   ed Don Zimmerman, James Symons

Sylvester Stallone, Robert Loggia, Susan Blakely, Rick Zumwalt, David Mendenhall

'Routinely made in every respect.' – Daily Variety

Over the Wall
US   1938   72m   bw
Warner

A man wrongly convicted of murder fights the prison system.

Predictable semi-documentary thriller from the prolific pen of Warden Lewis E. Lawes; just an efficient second feature.

w Crane Wilbur, George Bricker   d Frank MacDonald

Dick Foran, John Litel, June Travis, Dick Purcell, Veda Ann Borg, George E. Stone

'Authentic melodrama, headed for nice biz.' – Variety

Over Twenty-One
US   1945   102m   bw
Columbia (Sidney Buchman)

A famous lady screenwriter copes with wartime domestic problems while her husband is off at the war.

Thin star comedy based on Ruth Gordon's play about her own predicament; not for the wider audience, and not very good anyway.

w Sidney Buchman   play Ruth Gordon   d Alexander Hall   ph Rudolph Maté   m Marlin Skiles

Irene Dunne, Alexander Knox, Charles Coburn, Jeff Donnell, Lee Patrick, Phil Brown, Cora Witherspoon

Overboard
US   1987   112m   colour
UIP/MGM (Alexandra Rose, Anthea Sylbert)
V, V*, L

An heiress suffering from amnesia is claimed as a wife by a carpenter with three kids.

Mild amusement is provided by a predictable comedy.

w Leslie Dixon   d Garry Marshall   ph John A. Alonzo   m Alan Silvestri   ad James Shanahan, Jim Dultz   ed Dov Hoenig, Sonny Baskin

Goldie Hawn, Kurt Russell, Edward Herrmann, Katherine Helmond, Roddy McDowall, Michael Hagerty, Jeffrey Wiseman

Overland Mail
US   1942   bw   serial: 15 eps
Universal

A Western frontiersman investigates mail thefts.

Strongly cast but otherwise ordinary serial.   d Ford Beebe, John Rawlins

Lon Chaney Jnr, Noah Beery, Noah Beery Jnr, Helen Parrish, Don Terry

Overland with Kit Carson
US   1939   bw   serial: 15 eps
Columbia

West of the Mississippi, a mysterious outlaw named Pegleg builds a corrupt empire.

Rather yawnworthy adventures.

d Sam Nelson, Norman Denning

Bill Elliott, Iris Meredith, Richard Fiske, Trevor Bardette

The Overlanders **
Australia   1946   91m   bw
Ealing (Ralph Smart)
V*

In 1943 a drover saves a thousand head of cattle from the Japanese by taking them two thousand miles across country.

Attractive, easy-going semi-Western, the first and best of several films made by Ealing Studios in Australia.

wd Harry Watt   *ph* Osmond Borradaile   *m* John Ireland

Chips Rafferty, John Heyward, Daphne Campbell

Overlord *
GB   1975   83m   bw
EMI/Jowsend (James Quinn)

An eighteen-year-old is called up in early 1944 and killed in the D-Day landings.

Semi-documentary recreating a time in history (with much aid from newsreels) but making no discernible point. Interesting, though.

w Stuart Cooper, Christopher Hudson   *d* Stuart Cooper   *ph* John Alcott   *m* Paul Glass

Brian Stirner, Davyd Harries, Nicholas Ball, Julie Neesam

Owd Bob *
GB   1938   78m   bw
GFD/Gainsborough (Edward Black)
US title: *To the Victor*

A Cumberland farmer's faithful dog is accused of killing sheep.

Sentimental yarn with good location backgrounds; the plot was later reused as *Thunder in the Valley*.

w Michael Hogan, J. B. Williams   *novel* Alfred Olivant   *d* Robert Stevenson   *ph* Jack Cox   *md* Louis Levy

Will Fyffe, John Loder, Margaret Lockwood, Moore Marriott, Graham Moffatt, Wilfred Walter, Elliot Mason

'When she starts mixing business with pleasure, she goes out of business'

The Owl and the Pussycat *
US   1970   96m   Eastmancolor   Panavision
Columbia/Rastar (Ray Stark)
V, V*, L

A bookstore assistant reports a fellow tenant for prostitution, and when she is evicted she moves in with him.

Wacky, bawdy double act which starts promisingly but outstays its welcome. A solid step forward in permissiveness, with kinky behaviour as well as four-letter words.

w Buck Henry   *play* Bill Manhoff   *d* Herbert Ross   *ph* Harry Stradling, Andrew Laszlo   *m* Richard Halligan

Barbra Streisand, George Segal, Robert Klein, Allen Garfield

'If computers ever turn out romantic comedies, the results will look like this.' – *Stanley Kauffmann*

The Ox **
Sweden/Norway/Denmark   1992   92m   Eastmancolor
Artificial Eye/Sweetland (Jean Doumanian)
V
original title: *Oxen*

In a time of famine, a man kills his employer's ox in order to feed his starving family and is condemned to hard labour in prison for life.

A harrowing and humane story of hardship and forgiveness, much in the Bergman manner and as visually striking as you'd expect from a great cinematographer in his directorial debut.

w Sven Nykvist, Lasse Summanen   *d* Sven Nykvist   *ph* Sven Nykvist   *m* Greig and others   *pd* Peter Høimark   *ed* Lasse Summanen

Max von Sydow, Stellan Skarsgård, Ewa Fröling, Erland Josephson, Liv Ullmann

'Much more than just another snowy Scandinavian tale, this infuses its bleakness with tenderness and

compassion while remaining a million miles away from sentimentality.' – *Empire*

AAN: best foreign film

The Ox-Bow Incident **
US   1943   75m   bw
TCF (Lamar Trotti)
V*, L
GB title: *Strange Incident*

A cowboy is unable to prevent three wandering travellers being unjustly lynched for murder.

Stark lynch law parable, beautifully made but very depressing.

w Lamar Trotti   *novel* Walter Van Tilburg Clark   *d* William Wellman   *ph* Arthur Miller   *m* Cyril Mockridge

Henry Fonda, Henry Morgan, Jane Darwell, Anthony Quinn, Dana Andrews, Mary Beth Hughes, William Eythe, Harry Davenport, *Frank Conroy*

'Realism that is as sharp and cold as a knife.' – *Frank S. Nugent, New York Times*

'Very firm, respectable, and sympathetic; but I still think it suffers from rigor artis.' – *James Agee*

AAN: best picture

Oxen: see *The Ox*

Oxford Blues
US   1984   97m   colour
Winkast/Baltic Industrial (Peter Kohn, David Wimbury)
V*, L

A Los Angeles casino worker wins enough to finance an Oxford education.

Sexed-up version of *A Yank at Oxford*; only tolerable when the tone gets close to the original.

wd Robert Boris   *ph* John Stanier   *m* John Du Prez

Rob Lowe, Ally Sheedy, Alan Howard, Amanda Pays, Julian Sands, Julian Firth, Michael Gough, Aubrey Morris

P

'Gun in one hand – woman in the other!'

P.J.
US   1967   109m   Techniscope
Universal (Edward J. Montagne)
GB title: New Face in Hell

A down-at-heel private eye takes a job as bodyguard to a boorish businessman.

Routine thick ear with a predictable turnabout plot.

w Philip Reisman Jnr   d John Guillermin
ph Loyal Griggs   m Neal Hefti

George Peppard, Gayle Hunnicutt, Raymond Burr, Susan St James, Coleen Gray, Jason Evers, Wilfrid Hyde-White, Severn Darden

'Enough action to keep you from noticing that the plot doesn't make any sense.' – Judith Crist

P.K. and the Kid
US   1982   89m   CFI colour
Sunn Classic (Joe Roth)

A teenager, running away from her brutal step-father, goes on the road with a contestant heading for the world arm-wrestling championships in Los Angeles.

Mundane teen pic with too much concentration on the world's least photogenic sport.

w Neal Barbera   d Lou Lombardo   ph Ed Koons
m James Horner   pd Chet Allen   ed Tony Lombardo

Paul Le Mat, Molly Ringwald, Alex Rocco, Charles Hallahan, John Di Santi, Fionnula Flanagan, Bert Remsen, Leigh Hamilton, Esther Rolle

'A killer and a girl – trapped in America's first air raid!'

Pacific Blackout
US   1942   76m   bw
Paramount (Sol C. Siegel)

An inventor escapes from jail and proves his innocence during a practice air raid blackout.

Minor melo which proved profitably topical, being released shortly after the Japanese attack on Pearl Harbor.

w Lester Cole, W. P. Lipscomb   d Ralph Murphy
ph Theodor Sparkuhl

Robert Preston, Martha O'Driscoll, Philip Merivale, Eva Gabor, Louis Jean Heydt, Thurston Hall

Pacific Destiny
GB   1956   97m   Eastmancolor   Cinemascope
James Lawrie

Experiences of a British colonial servant in the South Seas.

Pleasant episodic drama which needed a firmer hand all round.

w Richard Mason   autobiography A Pattern of Islands
by Sir Arthur Grimble   d Wolf Rilla   ph Martin Curtis   m James Bernard

Denholm Elliott, Susan Stephen, Michael Hordern

Pacific Heights *
US   1990   104m   DeLuxe
Fox/Morgan Creek (James G. Robinson, Joe Roth)
V, V*, L, S

A young couple let part of their house to a dangerously unbalanced tenant.

A suburban horror that rapidly goes over the top into unconvincing melodrama.

w Daniel Pyne   d John Schlesinger   ph Amir Mokri   m Hans Zimmer   pd Neil Spisak   ed Mark Warner, Steven Ramirez

Melanie Griffith, Matthew Modine, Michael Keaton, Mako, Nobu McCarthy, Laurie Metcalf, Carl Lumbly, Dorian Harewood, Luca Bercovici, Tippi Hedren

Pacific Liner
US   1938   73m   bw
RKO

Cholera breaks out on a ship bound from Shanghai to San Francisco.

Rather a depressing melodrama with all the action below decks, and very slow at that.

w John Twist, Anthony Coldeway, Henry Roberts Symonds   d Lew Landers

Victor McLaglen, Chester Morris, Wendy Barrie, Alan Hale, Barry Fitzgerald, Halliwell Hobbes, Cy Kendall

'Drab melodrama with little of interest to hold attention.' – Variety

AAN: music (Robert Russell Bennett)

Pacific Rendezvous
US   1942   76m   bw
MGM

A coding expert breaks up an enemy spy ring.

Competent propaganda potboiler, rehashed from the rather smarter Rendezvous, which was set one war earlier.

w Harry Kurnitz, P. J. Wolfson, George Oppenheimer
d George Sidney

Lee Bowman, Jean Rogers, Mona Maris, Carl Esmond, Paul Cavanagh, Blanche Yurka

Paciorki Jednego Rózańca: see The Beads of One Rosary

The Pack
US   1977   99m   colour
Warner (Fred Weintraub, Paul Heller)
V*

Abandoned dogs on a remote island turn on holidaymakers.

The Birds becomes The Dogs; competently made but unsurprising thriller.

wd Robert Clouse   novel Dave Fisher   ph Ralph Woolsey   m Lee Holdridge   sp Milton Rice
ed Peter Berger

Joe Don Baker, Hope Alexander Willis, Richard B. Shull, R. G. Armstrong

Pack Up Your Troubles *
US   1931   68m   bw
Hal Roach
V, V*

Two World War I veterans try to look after their late pal's orphan daughter.

Patchy comedy vehicle in which too many gags are not fully thought out or timed.

w H. M. Walker   d George Marshall, Ray McCarey
ph Art Lloyd

Stan Laurel, Oliver Hardy, Donald Dillaway, Mary Carr, Charles Middleton, Dick Cramer, James Finlayson, Tom Kennedy, Billy Gilbert

Pack Up Your Troubles *
US   1939   75m   bw
TCF
GB title: We're in the Army Now

Exploits in Flanders of three zany soldiers.

Good slapstick antics in an unfamiliar venue.

w Lou Breslow, Owen Francis   d H. Bruce Humberstone

The Ritz Brothers, Jane Withers, Joseph Schildkraut, Lynn Bari, Stanley Fields

'A pretty good programmer in the B division.' – Variety

The Package
US   1989   108m   DeLuxe
Rank/Orion (Beverly J. Camhe, Tobie Haggerty)
V, V*, L

An army sergeant discovers an assassination plot after the escape of a prisoner he is escorting.

Unconvincing and melodramatic thriller that rarely grips the attention.

w John Bishop   d Andrew Davis   ph Frank Tidy
m James Newton Howard   pd Michael Levesque
ed Don Zimmerman, Billy Weber

Gene Hackman, Joanna Cassidy, Tommy Lee Jones, Dennis Franz, Reni Santoni, Pam Grier, Chelcie Ross, Ron Dean, Kevin Crowley

The Pad, and How to Use It *
US   1966   86m   Technicolor
Universal (Ross Hunter)

A shy young man has his first date.

Pleasant, odd little comedy apparently made in emulation of The Knack.

w Thomas C. Ryan, Benn Starr   play The Private Ear
by Peter Shaffer   d Brian C. Hutton   ph Ellsworth Fredericks   m Russ Garcia

Brian Bedford, James Farentino, Julie Sommars, Edy Williams, Nick Navarro

Paddy O'Day
US   1935   73m   bw
TCF

An Irish child emigrates to America to find that her mother has died.

One of the more satisfactory vehicles for a child star maintained by the studio as an antidote to the cuter antics of Shirley Temple.

w Lou Breslow, Edward Eliscu   d Lewis Seiler

Jane Withers, Pinky Tomlin, Rita Hayworth, Jane Darwell, Francis Ford

Paddy the Next Best Thing
US   1933   75m   bw
Fox

Adventures of an Irish tomboy in New York.

Modest star comedy from a popular play.

w Edwin Burke   play Gertrude Page   d Harry Lachman   ph John Seitz

Janet Gaynor, Warner Baxter, Walter Connolly, Harvey Stephens, Margaret Lindsay

'Easy entertainment: excellent, wholesome and amusing.' – *Variety*

Padre Padrone **
Italy   1977   113m   Eastmancolor
Radiotelevisione Italia (Tonino Paoletti)
V, V*
aka: *Father and Master*

The author recounts how he grew up with a violent and tyrannical father.

A vivid chunk of autobiography with food for thought on several levels, and a clever piece of film-making to boot.

wd Paolo Taviani, Vittorio Taviani,   *book* Gavino Ledda
ph Mario Masini   *md* Egisto Macchi

Omero Antonutti, Saverio Marconi, Marcella Michelangeli

The Pagan
US   1929   85m approx   bw
MGM

A South Sea islander falls for the daughter of a white trader.

Highly commercial star vehicle apparently made as an afterthought to *White Shadows in the South Seas.*

w Dorothy Farnum   *d* W. S. Van Dyke

Ramon Novarro, Renee Adoree, Dorothy Janis, Donald Crisp

Pagan Lady
US   1931   70m   bw
Columbia

A nice American boy in Havana falls for a girl who is no better than she should be.

Sultry melodrama reminiscent of *Rain* but of no intrinsic merit.

w Ben Glazer   *play* William Dubois   *d* John Francis Dillon

Evelyn Brent, Conrad Nagel, Charles Bickford, Roland Young, William Farnum

'Something of a lightweight; the storm is quite the best thing in the picture.' – *Variety*

Pagan Love Song
US   1950   76m   Technicolor
MGM (Arthur Freed)
V*

An American schoolteacher marries a Tahitian girl.

Very mild musical potboiler using familiar talents.

w Robert Nathan, Jerry Davis   *d* Robert Alton
ph Charles Rosher   *m* Harry Warren   *ly* Arthur Freed

Esther Williams, Howard Keel, Rita Moreno, Minna Gombell

Page Miss Glory *
US   1935   90m   bw
Warner/Cosmopolitan

A con man wins a beauty contest with a composite photograph of a non-existent girl.

Amusing comedy-musical, unjustly forgotten.

w Delmer Daves, Robert Lord   *play* Joseph Schrank, Philip Dunning   *d* Mervyn Le Roy   *ph* George Folsey   *m/ly* Harry Warren, Al Dubin

Dick Powell, Marion Davies, Frank McHugh, Pat O'Brien, Mary Astor, Lyle Talbot, Patsy Kelly, Allen Jenkins, Barton MacLane

Pagliacci *
GB   1936   92m   colour
Trafalgar
US title: *A Clown Must Laugh*

A jealous clown kills his wife and her lover.

A surprising British enterprise of the time which did fairly well at the box-office, presumably because of the colour.

w Monckton Hoffe, John Drinkwater, Roger Burford, Ernest Betts   *opera* Ruggiero Leoncavallo   *d* Karl Grune

Richard Tauber, Steffi Duna, Diana Napier, Arthur Margetson, Esmond Knight, Jerry Verno

Paid *
US   1930   80m   bw
MGM
GB title: *Within the Law*

A woman sent to prison unjustly plots revenge on those responsible.

Reliable melodrama with the heroine eventually forgiving and forgetting.

w Charles MacArthur, Lucien Hubbard   *play Within the Law* by Bayard Veiller   *d* Sam Wood
ph Charles Rosher

Joan Crawford, Kent Douglass, Robert Armstrong, Marie Prévost, John Miljan, Polly Moran

Paid in Full
US   1949   105m   bw
Paramount/Hal B. Wallis

A woman is responsible for the death of her sister's child, and becomes pregnant herself in the knowledge that giving birth will be fatal to her.

Stolid, contrived tearjerker.

w Robert Blees, Charles Schnee   *d* William Dieterle   *ph* Leo Tover   *m* Victor Young

Lizabeth Scott, Diana Lynn, Robert Cummings, Eve Arden, Ray Collins, Frank McHugh, Stanley Ridges, Louis Jean Heydt

'Aimed straight at the lachrymal glands, if it can be said to be aimed at anything. The dialogue is appalling.' – *C. A. Lejeune*

A Pain in the A—: see *L'Emmerdeur*

'Ben and pardner shared everything – even their wife!'

Paint Your Wagon *
US   1969   164m   Technicolor   Panavision 70
Paramount/Alan Jay Lerner (Tom Shaw)
V, V (W), V*, L

During the California Gold Rush, two prospectors set up a Mormon menage with the same wife.

Good-looking but uncinematic and monumentally long version of an old musical with a new plot and not much dancing. There are minor pleasures, but it really shouldn't have been allowed.

w Paddy Chayevsky   *musical play* Alan Jay Lerner, Frederick Loewe   *d* Joshua Logan   *ph* William A. Fraker   *md* Nelson Riddle   *pd* John Truscott

Lee Marvin, Clint Eastwood, Jean Seberg, Harve Presnell, Ray Walston

'One of those big movies in which the themes are undersized and the elements are juggled around until nothing fits together right and even the good bits of the original show you started with are shot to hell.' – *Pauline Kael*

AAN: Nelson Riddle

Painted Boats
GB   1945   63m   bw
Ealing
US title: *The Girl on the Canal*

Romance among the bargees.

Excessively thin location drama, which nevertheless has an early place in the Ealing tradition.

w Louis MacNeice, Michael McCarthy   *d* Charles Crichton

Jenny Laird, Bill Blewett, Robert Griffith, May Hallatt

Painted Desert
US   1938   59m   bw
RKO (Bert Gilroy)
V*

A rancher becomes a miner for romantic reasons but has to overcome a crooked banker and his followers.

A B-Western with B-picture acting and direction. A remake of a 1931 movie starring William Boyd, it contains footage from the earlier film.

w John Rathmell, Oliver Drake   *story* Jack Cunningham   *d* David Howard   *ph* Harry Wild
md Roy Webb   *ad* Van Nest Polglase   *ed* Frederick Knudtson

George O'Brien, Laraine Day, Ray Whitley, Fred Kohler Snr, Stanley Fields, William V. Mong, Maude Allen

The Painted Stallion
US   1937   bw   serial: 12 eps
Republic

Jim Bowie and Kit Carson lead the first wagon train to Santa Fe, and are helped by a mysterious girl rider.

Adequate serial Western.

d William Witney and Ray Taylor

Ray Corrigan, Hoot Gibson, Sammy McKim, Leroy Mason, Duncan Renaldo

The Painted Veil *
US   1934   84m   bw
MGM (Hunt Stromberg)
V*

In China, a doctor's wife gives up her lover to join her husband fighting an epidemic.

Soulful melodrama which seemed much more acceptable in this version than in the summer stock style remake *The Seventh Sin.*

w John Meehan, Salka Viertel, Edith Fitzgerald
novel W. Somerset Maugham   *d* Richard Boleslawski   *ph* William Daniels   *m* Herbert Stothart

Greta Garbo, George Brent, Herbert Marshall, Warner Oland, Jean Hersholt

'Confused and slow, but extra heavy name cast should get it by.' – *Variety*

Painted Woman
US   1932   73m   bw
Fox

A floozie stranded on a South Sea island resists offers of help from several men.

Another variation on *Rain,* and not the best.

w Guy Bolton, Leon Gordon   *novel After the Rain* by A. C. Kennedy   *d* John Blystone

Spencer Tracy, Peggy Shannon, William Stage Boyd, Irving Pichel, Raul Roulien

'It's hard to see how the studio figured a good picture would result from the material at hand.' – *Variety*

Painting the Clouds with Sunshine
US   1951   86m   Technicolor
Warner (William Jacobs)

Three singing sisters go to Las Vegas in search of rich husbands.

Yet another revamp of the original *Gold Diggers* (qv), and not a very lively one.

w Harry Clork, Roland Kibbee, Peter Milne
d David Butler   *ph* Wilfred Cline

Virginia Mayo, Gene Nelson, Dennis Morgan, S. Z. Sakall, Lucille Norman, Tom Conway

A Pair of Briefs
GB   1961   90m   bw
Rank/Betty E. Box-Ralph Thomas

Barristers Tony and Frances fall in love while opposing each other in court.

Adam's Rib need have no fears; this is the palest of imitations.

w Nicholas Phipps   *play How Say You* by Harold Brooke, Kay Bannerman   d Ralph Thomas   ph Ernest Steward   m Norrie Paramor

Michael Craig, Mary Peach, Brenda de Banzie, James Robertson Justice, Roland Culver, Liz Fraser, Ron Moody, Jameson Clark, Charles Heslop

Paisà *
Italy   1946   115m   bw
Foreign Film Productions/OFI
V

Six episodes in the Battle of Italy between 1943 and 1945.

More important historically than dramatically, *Paisà* was always a somewhat disappointing experience, especially as the earlier episodes are stronger than the later ones. Like *Open City*, it was partly improvised and had a gritty documentary quality.

w Federico Fellini, Roberto Rossellini   d Roberto Rossellini   ph Otello Martelli   m Renzo Rossellini

William Tubbs, Gar Moore, Maria Michi and non-professionals

'It brings to the picture of war a pity at once savage and tender which is quite foreign to the studio-made film – or, come to that, the contemporary documentary film.' – *Dilys Powell*

AAN: script

The Pajama Game ***
US   1957   101m   Warnercolor
Warner/George Abbott
V, V*, L

Workers in a pajama factory demand a pay rise, but their lady negotiator falls for the new boss.

Brilliantly conceived musical on an unlikely subject, effectively concealing its Broadway origins and becoming an expert, fast-moving, hard-hitting piece of modern musical cinema.

w *George Abbott, Richard Bissell   book Seven and a Half Cents* by Richard Bissell   d *Stanley Donen,* ph Harry Stradling   *songs Richard Adler, Jerry Ross   ch Bob Fosse*

Doris Day, John Raitt, *Eddie Foy Jnr,* Reta Shaw, Carol Haney

Pal Joey **
US   1957   109m   Technicolor
Columbia/Essex-Sidney (Fred Kohlmar)
V, V*, L

The rise of a night-club entertainer who is also a heel.

Smart musical which begins very brightly indeed but slides off alarmingly into conventional sentiment.

w Dorothy Kingsley   *play* John O'Hara   *stories* John O'Hara   d George Sidney   ph Harold Lipstein   *songs Richard Rodgers, Lorenz Hart*   ad Walter Holscher   ed Viola Lawrence, Jerome Thomas

Frank Sinatra, Rita Hayworth, Kim Novak, Bobby Sherwood, Hank Henry, Elizabeth Patterson, Barbara Nichols

AAN: Walter Holscher; editing

Pale Rider
US   1985   115m   Technicolor   Panavision
Warner/Malpaso (Clint Eastwood)
V, V*, L

Harassed gold prospecting families are helped by a mysterious avenger.

Unreeling like a supernatural *Shane,* this is a violent and pretentious Western with nothing to be pretentious about.

w Michael Butler, Dennis Shryack   d Clint Eastwood   ph Bruce Surtees   m Lennie Niehaus   pd Edward Carfagno   ed Joel Cox

Clint Eastwood, Michael Moriarty, Carrie Snodgress, Christopher Penn, Richard Dysart, Richard Kiel

The Paleface ***
US   1948   91m   Technicolor
Paramount (Robert L. Welch)
V*, L

Calamity Jane undertakes an undercover mission against desperadoes, and marries a timid dentist as a cover.

Splendid wagon train comedy Western with the stars in excellent form.

w *Edmund Hartman, Frank Tashlin*   d Norman Z. McLeod   ph Ray Rennahan   m Victor Young

Bob Hope, Jane Russell, Robert Armstrong, Iris Adrian, Robert Watson, Jack Searle, Joe Vitale, Clem Bevans, Charles Trowbridge

† Sequel: *Son of Paleface* (qv); remake, *The Shakiest Gun in the West* (1968).

AA: song 'Buttons and Bows' (*m* Jay Livingston, *ly* Ray Evans)

The Palm Beach Story ***
US   1942   88m   bw
Paramount (Paul Jones)
V*, L

The wife of a penurious engineer takes off for Florida to set her sights on a millionaire.

Flighty comedy, inconsequential in itself, but decorated with scenes, characters and zany touches typical of its creator, here at his most brilliant if uncontrolled.

wd Preston Sturges   ph Victor Milner   m Victor Young

Claudette Colbert, Joel McCrea, Rudy Vallee, Mary Astor, Sig Arno, Robert Warwick, Torben Meyer, Jimmy Conlin, William Demarest, Jack Norton, Robert Greig, Roscoe Ates, Chester Conklin, Franklin Pangborn, Alan Bridge, *Robert Dudley*

HACKENSACKER (Rudy Vallee): 'That's one of the tragedies of this life, that the men most in need of a beating up are always enormous.'

WEENIE KING (Robert Dudley): 'Anyway, I'd be too old for you. Cold are the hands of time that creep along relentlessly, destroying slowly but without pity that which yesterday was young. Alone, our memories resist this disintegration and grow more lovely with the passing years. That's hard to say with false teeth.'

'Surprises and delights as though nothing of the kind had been known before . . . farce and tenderness are combined without a fault.' – *William Whitebait*

'Minus even a hint of the war . . . packed with delightful absurdities.' – *Variety*

Palm Springs
US   1936   74m   bw
Paramount
GB title: *Palm Springs Affair*

An elderly Englishman becomes a gambler in order to give his daughter the appropriate upbringing.

Slight romantic comedy which gave a young Englishman a foothold in Hollywood.

w Joseph Fields   d Aubrey Scotto

David Niven, Sir Guy Standing, Frances Langford, Ernest Cossart, Spring Byington

Palm Springs Affair: see *Palm Springs*

Palm Springs Weekend
US   1963   100m   Technicolor
Warner (Michael Hoey)
V*, L

Various holidaymakers at Palm Springs get romantically involved.

Youth-oriented farce, better produced than most but basically a depressing experience.

w Earl Hamner Jnr   d Norman Taurog   ph Harold Lipstein   m Frank Perkins

Troy Donahue, Ty Hardin, Connie Stevens, Stefanie Powers, Robert Conrad, Jack Weston, Andrew Duggan

Palmy Days
US   1932   77m   bw
Samuel Goldwyn

Shady fortune tellers find a willing stooge.

Dated star comedy.

w Eddie Cantor, Morrie Ryskind, David Freedman, Keene Thompson   d A. Edward Sutherland   ph Gregg Toland   ch Busby Berkeley

Eddie Cantor, Charlotte Greenwood, Charles Middleton, George Raft, Walter Catlett

'Heavily hoked but funny throughout.' – *Variety*

Palooka
US   1934   80m   bw
Reliance (Edward Small)
V*
GB title: *The Great Schnozzle*

An eccentric manager makes a prizefighter of a country cousin.

Fairly amusing first-feature version of the strip cartoon hero Joe Palooka.

w Jack Jevne, Arthur Kober, Gertrude Purcell   *strip* Ham Fisher   d Ben Stoloff

Jimmy Durante (as Knobby Walsh), Stuart Erwin, Lupe Velez, Marjorie Rambeau, Robert Armstrong, Mary Carlisle, William Cagney, Thelma Todd

'A laugh riot, the nearest approach to a Marx picture that's been around.' – *Variety*

Paltoquet
France   1986   92m   colour
Artificial Eye/Elefilm/Erato/Soprofilm/TF1/Sofia/Sofima (Rosalinde Damamme)

A detective tries to discover which habitué of a seedy bar, with its shiftless waiter, is a killer.

Intellectual thriller in which film theory takes precedence over practice, resulting in tedium.

wd Michel Deville   *novel On A Tué Pendant L'Escale* by Franz-Rudolf Falk   ph André Diot   m Dvořák, Janáček   pd Thierry Leproust   ed Raymonde Guyot

Jeanne Moreau, Michel Piccoli, Fanny Ardant, Daniel Auteuil, Richard Bohringer, Philippe Léotard, Claude Piéplu, Jean Yanne

Pan-Americana *
US   1945   85m   bw
RKO (Sid Rogell)

A New York magazine sends editors around South America to choose the prettiest girl of each nation.

Slick, mindless musical with good numbers.

w Lawrence Kimble   d John H. Auer   ph Frank Redman   md Constantin Bakaleinikoff   ch Charles O'Curran

Audrey Long, Phillip Terry, Robert Benchley, Eve Arden, Ernest Truex, Marc Cramer

Panama Hattie
US   1942   79m   bw
MGM (Arthur Freed)
V*

A showgirl in Panama helps to capture Nazis.

Dim film version of a Broadway musical, stripped of most of its music and more like a *Maisie* comedy.

w Jack McGowan, Wilkie Mahoney   *musical play* Herbert Fields, B. G. de Sylva, Cole Porter   *d* Norman Z. McLeod   *ph* George Folsey   *md* George Stoll

Ann Sothern, Dan Dailey, Red Skelton, Marsha Hunt, Rags Ragland, Virginia O'Brien, Alan Mowbray, Ben Blue, Carl Esmond

Pancho Villa
Spain   1972   93m   Technicolor
Granada Films (Bernard Gordon)
V*

In 1916 Villa is rescued from execution and starts a reign of terror.

Mexican banditry played half for laughs and half for real; not a successful compromise.

w Julian Halevy   *d* Eugenio Martin   *ph* Allejandro Ulloa   *m* Anton Garcia-Abril

Telly Savalas, Clint Walker, Chuck Connors

Pandora and the Flying Dutchman *
GB   1950   122m   Technicolor
Romulus (Albert Lewin)

A cold but beautiful American woman in Spain falls for a mystery man who turns out to be a ghostly sea captain; she dies so as to be with him.

Pretentious, humourless, totally unpersuasive fantasy of the kind much better done in *Portrait of Jennie*. The writer-director wears Omar Khayyam's moving finger to the bone, and the actors look thoroughly unhappy; even the colour is a bit thick.

wd Albert Lewin   *ph* Jack Cardiff   *m* Alan Rawsthorne   *ad* John Bryan

James Mason, Ava Gardner, Harold Warrender, Nigel Patrick, Sheila Sim, Mario Cabre, John Laurie, Pamela Kellino, Marius Goring

'Conspicuous in its confident assumption of scholarship and its utter poverty of imagination and taste.' – *C. A. Lejeune*

'It might have been enjoyably silly but for Lewin's striving to be classy and an air of third-rate decadence that hangs about it. This is an Anglo-American co-production and one of the occasions, I think, when we might be generous and let Hollywood have all the credit.' – *Richard Winnington*

Pandora's Box *
Germany   1929   97m approx (24 fps)   bw   silent
Nero Film
V, V*
original title: *Die Büchse der Pandora*
aka: *Lulu*

A woman murders her lover, becomes a prostitute, and is murdered in London by Jack the Ripper.

Oddball fantasy on a few favourite German themes: very watchable, and benefiting from its star performance.

w G. W. Pabst, Laszlo Wajda   *plays Erdgeist* and *Pandora's Box* by Franz Wedekind   *d* G. W. Pabst   *ph* Günther Krampf

Louise Brooks, Fritz Kortner, Franz Lederer, Gustav Diessl

'A disconnected melodramatic effusion.' – *Mordaunt Hall, New York Times*

† Remade in Austria in 1962 as *No Orchids for Lulu*, with Nadja Tiller.

Panhandle
US   1948   84m   bw
Champion-Edwards/Allied Artists

A reformed gunman avenges the murder of his brother.

Solid co-feature Western.

w Blake Edwards, John C. Champion   *d* Lesley Selander

Rod Cameron, Cathy Downs, Reed Hadley, Anne Gwynne, Blake Edwards

Panic Button
US   1963   98m   bw
Gorton Associates

A has-been film star is hired by gangsters to star in a film which must lose money; but it wins the Venice Festival award.

Artless and padded comedy with good moments provided by an intriguing cast.

w Hal Biller   *d* George Sherman

Maurice Chevalier, Akim Tamiroff, Jayne Mansfield, Eleanor Parker, Michael Connors

The Panic in Needle Park
US   1971   110m   DeLuxe
Gadd Productions (Dominick Dunne)
V, V*

Drug addiction problems in a New York ghetto.

Vivid, intimate but overlong and unsympathetic account of a junkie and his mistress.

w Joan Didion, John Gregory Dunne   *novel* James Mills   *d* Jerry Schatzberg   *ph* Adam Holender   *m* none

Al Pacino, Kitty Winn, Adam Vint, Richard Bright, Kiel Martin

Panic in the Parlor: see *Sailor Beware* (1956)

Panic in the Streets ***
US   1950   96m   bw
TCF (Sol C. Siegel)
V*, L

On the New Orleans waterfront, public health officials seek a carrier of bubonic plague.

Semi-documentary suspenser in the *Naked City* manner; location Hollywood at its best.

w Richard Murphy, Edward and Edna Anhalt   *d* Elia Kazan   *ph* Joe MacDonald   *m* Alfred Newman

Richard Widmark, Jack Palance, Paul Douglas, Barbara Bel Geddes, Zero Mostel

'Elia Kazan directs this tough and unique story with the speed, imagination and ruthlessness that it needs.' – *Milton Shulman*

'A model of what an action story should be . . . every department is admirably handled.' – *Richard Mallett, Punch*

AA: original story (Edward and Edna Anhalt)

Panic in Year Zero *
US   1962   93m   bw   Cinemascope
AIP (Lou Rusoff, Arnold Houghland)

Adventures of a family on a fishing trip in the mountains when Los Angeles is blasted by a nuclear attack.

Mildly interesting catalogue of predictable events – thugs, looting, fear of fall-out – in a simple-minded script finishing with a hopeful meeting of the UN.

w Jay Simms, John Morton   *d* Ray Milland   *ph* Gil Warrenton   *m* Les Baxter

Ray Milland, Jean Hagen, Frankie Avalon, Joan Freeman

Pánico en el Transiberiano: see *Horror Express*

Panique *
France   1946   98m   bw
Filmsonor

A respectable man knows who committed a murder, and the murderer cunningly swings the blame onto him.

Careful suspenser with a twist ending.

w Charles Spaak, Julien Duvivier   *novel* Georges Simenon   *d* Julien Duvivier   *ph* Nicolas Hayer

Michel Simon, Viviane Romance, Paul Bernard

'Whether you like it or not, you may be forced to agree that it's a near-perfect movie.' – *Pauline Kael, 1972*

The Panther's Claw
US   1942   73m   bw
PRC

Thatcher Colt solves a blackmail case which ends in murder.

Unassuming but efficient second-feature mystery.

w Martin Mooney, Anthony Abbott   *d* William Beaudine

Sidney Blackmer, Byron Foulger, Rick Vallin

Panther Girl of the Congo
US   1955   bw   serial: 12 eps
Republic

A villainous chemist grows monster crawfish which frighten natives away from an African diamond mine.

One of the last half-dozen serials made, and a silly one.   *d* Franklin Adreon

Phyllis Coates, Myron Healey, Arthur Space, Roy Glenn Snr

Panther's Moon: see *Spy Hunt*

Papa's Delicate Condition
US   1963   98m   Technicolor
Paramount/Amro (Jack Rose)
V*

At the turn of the century in a small Texas town an amiable family man gets into scrapes when he drinks too much.

Basically pleasing period comedy which suffers from slow, stiff treatment.

w Jack Rose   *book* Corinne Griffith   *d* George Marshall   *ph* Loyal Griggs   *m* Joseph J. Lilley

Jackie Gleason, Glynis Johns, Charles Ruggles, Charles Lane, Laurel Goodwin, Juanita Moore, Elisha Cook Jnr, Murray Hamilton

AA: song 'Call Me Irresponsible' (*m* James Van Heusen, *ly* Sammy Cahn)

Paper Bullets
US   1941   69m   bw
King Brothers/PRC
V*

Three orphanage pals grow up to be involved in crime.

Fast-moving second feature.

w Martin Mooney   *d* Phil Rosen

Joan Woodbury, Jack La Rue, Alan Ladd, Linda Ware, Vince Barnett, Gavin Gordon, John Archer

The Paper Chase **
US   1973   111m   DeLuxe   Panavision
TCF (Robert C. Thompson, Rodrick Paul)
V*, L

A Harvard law graduate falls in love with the divorced daughter of his tetchiest professor.

A thoughtful analysis of attitudes to learning turns into just another youth movie.

wd James Bridges   *novel* John Jay Osborn Jnr   *ph* Gordon Willis   *m* John Williams

Timothy Bottoms, Lindsay Wagner, *John Houseman*, Graham Bickel

'A slightly unfocused account of conformism and milk-mild rebellion on the campus.' – *Sight and Sound*

'A worthy film which engages the eye and the brain.' – *Benny Green, Punch*

AA: John Houseman

AAN: James Bridges (as writer)

Paper Lion
US 1968 105m colour
Stuart Millar/United Artist

The training of a professional football player.

Rather single-minded sporting biography from a book by George Plimpton.

w Lawrence Roman *d* Alex March

Alan Alda, Lauren Hutton, David Doyle, Sugar Ray Robinson

'Trust me. I'm a doctor.'
Paper Mask **
GB 1990 105m colour
Enterprise/Film Four International (Christopher Morahan)
V, V*

A hospital porter pretends to be a doctor.

Chilling and enjoyable small-scale thriller.

w John Collee *d* Christopher Morahan *ph* Nat Crosby *m* Richard Harvey *pd* Caroline Hanania *ed* Peter Coulson

Paul McGann, Amanda Donohoe, Frederick Treves, Tom Wilkinson, Barbara Leigh-Hunt, Jimmy Yuill, Mark Lewis Jones, John Warnaby, Alexandra Mathie

'As P. T. Barnum put it, "There's a sucker born every minute".'
Paper Moon **
US 1973 103m bw
Paramount/Saticoy (Peter Bogdanovich)
V*, L

In the American midwest in the thirties, a bible salesman and a plain little girl make a great con team.

Unusual but overrated comedy, imperfectly adapted from a very funny book, with careful but disappointing period sense and photography. A lot more style and gloss was required.

w Alvin Sargent *novel* Addie Pray by *Joe David Brown* *d* Peter Bogdanovich *ph* Laszlo Kovacs *m* popular songs and recordings

Ryan O'Neal, Tatum O'Neal, Madeline Kahn, John Hillerman

'I've rarely seen a film that looked so unlike what it was about.' – *Stanley Kauffmann*

'At its best the film is only mildly amusing, and I'm not sure I could recall a few undeniable highlights if pressed on the point.' – *Gary Arnold*

'Bogdanovich once again deploys the armoury of nostalgia with relentless cunning to evoke the threadbare side of American life forty years ago . . . one of those rare movies which engages at least two of the senses.' – *Benny Green, Punch*

'It is so enjoyable, so funny, so touching that I couldn't care less about its morals.' – *Daily Telegraph*

AA: Tatum O'Neal

AAN: Alvin Sargent; Madeline Kahn

Paper Orchid
GB 1949 86m bw
Ganesh/Columbia

A girl reporter is suspected of murdering an actor.

Mystery programmer which did not displease.

w Val Guest *novel* Arthur La Bern *d* Roy Baker

Hugh Williams, Hy Hazell, Sidney James, Garry Marsh, Andrew Cruickshank, Ivor Barnard, Walter Hudd

Paper Tiger
GB 1975 99m Technicolor
Maclean and Co (Euan Lloyd)
V, V*

An ageing Englishman becomes tutor to the son of the

Japanese ambassador in a Pacific state, and finds he has to live his heroic fantasies in reality.

Uneasy adventure comedy drama which might, given more skilled handling, have been much better than it is.

w Jack Davies *d* Ken Annakin *ph* John Cabrera *m* Roy Budd

David Niven, Toshiro Mifune, Hardy Kruger, Ando, Ivan Desny, Irene Tsu, Miiko Taka, Ronald Fraser, Jeff Corey

'Makes no demands, except on 99 minutes of our time.' – *Michael Billington, Illustrated London News*

Paperhouse
GB 1988 92m Technicolor
Vestron/Working Title (Tim Bevan, Sarah Radcliffe)
V, V*, L, S

An 11-year-old girl has fainting fits which take her into a dangerous fantasy world that resembles her drawings.

Slow-moving, shallow fantasy.

w Matthew Jacobs *novel* Marianne's Dream by Catherine Storr *d* Bernard Rose *ph* Mike Southon *m* Hans Zimmer, Stanley Myers *pd* Gemma Jackson *ed* Dan Rae

Charlotte Burke, Ben Cross, Glenne Headley, Elliott Spiers, Gemma Jones

Papillon *
US 1973 150m Technicolor Panavision
Papillon Partnership/Corona/General Production Co (Robert Dorfmann)
V, V*, L, S

Filmed autobiography of life on Devil's Island.

Overlong and rather dreary film of a bestseller; it determinedly rubs the audience's nose in ordure from the start, and the final successful escape is one try too many.

w Dalton Trumbo, Lorenzo Semple Jnr *book* Henri Charrière *d* Franklin Schaffner *ph* Fred Koenekamp *m* Jerry Goldsmith

Steve McQueen, Dustin Hoffman, Victor Jory, Don Gordon, Anthony Zerbe, George Couldouris, Woodrow Parfrey

'A 2 1/2-hour epic trampling the corn growing round the theme of man's inhumanity to man.' – *Sight and Sound*

'Papillon offers torture as entertainment but winds up making entertainment a form of torture . . . a tournament of brutality unrelieved by imagination.' – *Paul D. Zimmermann*

'So overloaded with details that the stars are almost lost in exposition, repetition and unfocused drama.' – *Judith Crist, 1977*

'So solemn one would think it the story of a pope at the very least.' – *New Yorker, 1980*

AAN: Jerry Goldsmith

Parachute Battalion
US 1941 75m bw
Howard Benedict/RKO

Three boys go through parachute training school.

Propaganda quickie.

w John Twist and Major Hugh Fite *d* Leslie Goodwins

Robert Preston, Nancy Kelly, Edmond O'Brien, Harry Carey, Buddy Ebsen, Paul Kelly, Richard Cromwell, Robert Barrat

'It would make a nice educational short, but as feature material it rates in the secondary dual category.' – *Variety*

Parachute Jumper
US 1932 70m bw
Warner

Ex-flying Marines out of a job fall in with gangsters.

Easy-going adventure yarn with agreeable players.

w Rian James, John Francis Larkin *d* Alfred E. Green

Douglas Fairbanks Jnr, Bette Davis, Leo Carrillo, Claire Dodd, Frank McHugh, Harold Huber

'Breezy treatment of a not very brilliant yarn.' – *Variety*

Parade *
France/Sweden 1974 85m Technicolor
Gray Film/Sveriges Radio

Jacques Tati introduces a series of acts in a small-scale circus.

Pleasant, sometimes boring variety show, to be included in the Tati canon for completeness; it does include some of his unique pieces of mime.

wd Jacques Tati

'A curious, unresolved envoi.' – *John Pym, MFB*

'Moments of great good humour and flashes of incomparable magic.' – *Sight and Sound*

The Paradine Case **
US 1947 115m bw
Selznick
V, V*, L

A barrister falls in love with his client, who is suspected of murder.

A stodgy and old-fashioned script is given gleaming treatment; this and the acting make it seem better thirty years later than it did on release.

w David O. Selznick *novel* Robert Hichens *d* Alfred Hitchcock *ph* Lee Garmes *m* Franz Waxman

Gregory Peck, *Alida Valli*, Ann Todd, Louis Jourdan, *Charles Laughton*, Charles Coburn, Ethel Barrymore, Leo G. Carroll

'This is the wordiest script since the death of Edmund Burke.' – *James Agee*

'The characters and their problems don't make much imprint on a viewer; if you can't remember whether you've seen the picture or not, chances are you did and forgot it.' – *New Yorker, 1976*

† Original choices were Olivier instead of Peck, Garbo instead of Valli, and Robert Newton instead of Jourdan.

AAN: Ethel Barrymore

Paradise *
US 1991 110m Technicolor
Buena Vista/Touchstone/Touchwood Pacific Partners I/ Interscope/Jean-François Lepetit (Scott Kroopf, Patrick Palmer)
V, V*

A ten-year-old boy makes friends with a young girl when he goes to spend the summer with a childless couple.

Sentimentality is kept at bay for the most part and charm predominates in a gently effective narrative.

wd Mary Agnes Donoghue *ph* Jerzy Zielinksi *m* David Newman *pd* Evelyn Sakash, Marcia Hinds *ed* Eva Gardos, Debra McDermott

Melanie Griffith, Don Johnson, Elijah Wood, Thora Birch, Sheila McCarthy, Eve Gordon, Louis Latham, Greg Travis, Sarah Trigger, Richard K. Olsen

'Excellent ensemble acting and a feel-good payoff to this bittersweet tale could produce a sleeper hit.' – *Variety*

† A remake of *Le Grand Chemin* (qv), directed in 1987 by Jean-Loup Hubert.

Paradise Alley
US 1978 107m Technicolor
Universal/Force Ten (John F. Roach, Ronald A. Suppa)
V*, L

The adventures of three wrestling brothers in New York's Hell's Kitchen during the forties.

Fashionable update of the *City for Conquest* school, not in itself very interesting despite amusing bits.

wd Sylvester Stallone   ph Laszlo Kovacs   m Bill Conti   pd John W. Corso

Sylvester Stallone, Kevin Conway, Anne Archer, Joe Spinell, Armand Assante, Lee Canalito

Paradise Canyon

US   1935   52m   bw
Monogram/Lone Star (Paul Malvern)

An undercover federal agent tracks down a gang of counterfeiters.

Lamentable Western with sub-standard acting, predictable plot and uninspired direction.

w Robert Emmett   story Lindsley Parsons   d Carl L. Pierson   ph Archie Stout   ed Jerry Roberts

John Wayne, Marion Burns, Reed Howes, Earle Hodgins, Gino Corrado, Yakima Canutt

Paradise for Three

US   1937   78m   bw
MGM
GB title: *Romance for Three*

A businessman goes to Germany to find out how the workers live.

An interesting premise leads inevitably into a flimsy romantic comedy.

w George Oppenheimer, Harry Ruskin   d Edward Buzzell

Robert Young, Frank Morgan, Mary Astor, Edna May Oliver, Florence Rice, Reginald Owen, Henry Hull, Sig Rumann, Herman Bing

Paradise for Two

GB   1937   77m   bw
Günther Stapenhorst/Denham
US title: *Gaiety Girls*

A millionaire posing as a reporter is asked to pose as a millionaire.

Cheerful comedy-romance.

w Robert Stevenson, Arthur Macrae   d Thornton Freeland   ph Gunther Krampf   m Mischa Spoliansky   ad Vincent Korda, Shamoon Nadir   ed E. B. Jarvis

Jack Hulbert, Patricia Ellis, Arthur Riscoe, Googie Withers, Sidney Fairbrother, Wylie Watson, David Tree

Paradise Hawaiian Style

US   1965   91m   Technicolor
Paramount/Hal Wallis/Joseph H. Hazen
V*

An amorous airline pilot returns to Hawaii and sets up a helicopter service.

Mindless musical vehicle for an increasingly resistible star.

w Allan Weiss, Anthony Lawrence   d Michael Moore   ph W. Wallace Kelley   md Joseph J. Lilley

Elvis Presley, Suzanna Leigh, James Shigeta, Irene Tsu

Paradise Lagoon: see *The Admirable Crichton*

The Parallax View *

US   1974   102m   Technicolor   Panavision
Paramount/Gus/Harbour/Doubleday (Alan J. Pakula)
V*

Witnesses to a political assassination are systematically killed, despite the efforts of a crusading journalist.

Stylish, persuasive political thriller with a downbeat ending; the villains win.

w David Giler, Lorenzo Semple Jnr   novel Loren Singer   d Alan J. Pakula   ph Gordon Willis   m Michael Small

Warren Beatty, Paula Prentiss, William Daniels, Hume Cronyn, Walter McGinn

'Pakula at his best . . . the test sequence is one of the most celebrated, manipulating the audience as it bombards Beatty's psyche.' – *Les Keyser, Hollywood in the Seventies*

'It is terribly important to give an audience a lot of things they may not get as well as those they will, so that finally the film does take on a texture and is not just simplistic communication.' – *Alan J. Pakula*

Paramount on Parade *

US   1930   102m   bw   (Technicolor sequence)
Paramount (Elsie Janis)
V*

A revue featuring Paramount contract stars.

A ragged affair by any standard, but worth a look for a couple of Chevalier's numbers.

w various   d Dorothy Arzner, Otto Brower, Edmund Goulding, Victor Heerman, Edwin H. Knopf, Rowland V. Lee, Ernst Lubitsch, Lothar Mendes, Victor Schertzinger, Edward Sutherland, Frank Tuttle   ph Harry Fischbeck, Victor Milner   m various

Richard Arlen, Jean Arthur, George Bancroft, Clara Bow, Nancy Carroll, Ruth Chatterton, Maurice Chevalier, Gary Cooper, Leon Errol, Kay Francis, Harry Green, Mitzi Green, Dennis King, Fredric March, Nino Martini, Jack Oakie, Charles 'Buddy' Rogers, Lillian Roth, Fay Wray, Clive Brook, Warner Oland, Eugene Pallette, William Powell

'Pip revue packed with laughs and talent.' – *Variety*

Paranoia

Italy/Spain   1969   88m   Technicolor   Techniscope
Eagle/Tritone/Medusa/D.I.A.
aka: *A Quiet Place to Kill*

A jealous wife plots to murder her philandering husband with the help of his former wife.

Lacklustre thriller that seemingly failed to engage the interest of director or cast.

w Rafael Romero Marchent, Marcello Coscia, Bruno di Geronimo   d Umberto Lenzi   ph Guglie Imo Mancori   m Gregorio Garcia Segura   ad Wolfgang Burmann   ed Antonio Ramirez, Enzo Alabiso

Carroll Baker, Jean Sorel, Marina Coffa, Anna Proclemer, Alberto Dalbes

'A sun-struck little thriller so listlessly plotted – between Majorca beach and luxury poolside – that not even the occasional homicide can shake its mildly enervated holiday air.' – *Richard Combs, MFB*

† The film was cut to 77m on its British release.

'Suddenly, she knew the lips burning on hers did not belong to any normal man!'

Paranoiac *

GB   1963   80m   bw   Cinemascope
U-I/Hammer (Anthony Hinds)

An heiress is saved from a suicide attempt by a young man claiming to be her dead brother.

A complex maze of disguise, mistaken identity, family curses and revelations of something nasty in the woodshed, out of *Psycho* by *Taste of Fear*. Not very good in itself, but interesting in its borrowings.

w Jimmy Sangster   d Freddie Francis   ph Arthur Grant   m Elisabeth Lutyens

Oliver Reed, Janette Scott, Alexander Davion, Sheila Burrell, Liliane Brousse, Maurice Denham, John Bonney

Les Parapluies de Cherbourg **

France/West Germany   1964   92m   Eastmancolor
Parc/Madeleine/Beta
aka: *The Umbrellas of Cherbourg*

A shopgirl loves a gas station attendant. He goes on military service; she finds she is pregnant and marries for security. Years later they meet briefly by accident.

Unexpected, charming, pretty successful screen operetta with only sung dialogue. Careful acting and exquisite use of colour and camera movement paste over the thinner sections of the plot.

wd Jacques Demy   ph Jean Rabier   m Michel Legrand, Jacques Demy   ad Bernard Evein

Catherine Deneuve, *Anne Vernon,* Nino Castelnuovo

'Poetic neo-realism.' – *Georges Sadoul*

'We are told that in Paris the opening night audience wept and the critics were ecstatic. It would have made a little more sense the other way round.' – *John Simon*

AAN: best foreign film; script; Michel Legrand, Jacques Demy; song 'I Will Wait for You'; scoring

The Parasite Murders

Canada   1974   87m   colour
Target/Cinepix/Canadian Film Development Corp. (Ivan Reitman)
V, V*
aka: *Shivers*; US title: *They Came from Within*

Parasites that turn people into diseased sex maniacs infect the inhabitants of a luxury hotel.

Bloody and violent horror movie, the first to explore its director's obsession with the alteration of the human body from one form to another.

wd David Cronenberg   ph Robert Saad   ad Erla Gliserman   sp Joe Blasco   ed Patrick Dodd

Paul Hampton, Joe Silver, Lynn Lowry, Allan Migicovsky, Susan Petrie, Barbara Steele, Ronald Mlodzik

'A fresh and diverting variation of a hoary entertainment formula.' – *Richard Combs, MFB*

'I was saying "I love sex, but I love sex as a venereal disease. I am syphilis. I am enthusiastic about it, but in a very different way from you".' – *David Cronenberg*

Paratrooper: see *The Red Beret*

Pardners

US   1956   88m   Technicolor   Vistavision
Paramount (Paul Jones)

An incompetent idiot goes west and accidentally cleans up the town.

Stiff Western star burlesque, a remake of *Rhythm on the Range.*

w Sidney Sheldon   d Norman Taurog   ph Daniel Fapp   songs Sammy Cahn, Jimmy Van Heusen

Dean Martin, Jerry Lewis, Agnes Moorehead, Lori Nelson, John Baragrey, Jeff Morrow, Lon Chaney Jnr

Pardon Mon Affaire *

France   1977   108m   Eastmancolor
Gaumont/La Guéville (Daniel Deschamps)
V*, L
aka: *Un Eléphant Ça Trompe Enormément*

A middle-aged married man discovers that he is a very unsuccessful adulterer.

Unsubtle comedy that was successful in France, though it does not travel well.

w Jean-Loup Dabadie, Yves Robert   d Yves Robert   ph René Mathelin   m Vladimir Cosma   ad Jean-Pierre Kohut-Svelko   ed Gérard Pollicand

Jean Rochefort, Claude Brasseur, Guy Bedos, Victor Lanoux, Danielle Delorme, Anny Duperey

† The film was remade by Hollywood as *The Woman In Red* (qv), directed by Gene Wilder.

Pardon My Past *

US   1945   88m   bw
Columbia

A man unwittingly takes on the problems of his double, a shady playboy.

Amusing mistaken identity comedy.

w Earl Felton, Karl Kamb   d Leslie Fenton
ph Russell Metty   m Dimitri Tiomkin

Fred MacMurray, Marguerite Chapman, Akim
Tamiroff, Rita Johnson, William Demarest, Harry
Davenport

Pardon My Rhythm
US   1944   61m   bw
Bernard W. Burton/Universal

A kid orchestra participates in a national radio
contest.

We have all been here before.

w Val Burton, Eugene Conrad   d Felix Feist

Gloria Jean, Mel Tormé, Patric Knowles, Evelyn
Ankers, Marjorie Weaver, Walter Catlett, Bob Crosby
and his orchestra

Pardon Us *
US   1931   55m   bw
Hal Roach
V, V (C), V*, L
aka: Jailbirds

Two zany bootleggers find themselves in and out of
prison.

Patchy star comedy which finds the boys on the whole
not in quite their best form.

w H. M. Walker   d James Parrott   ph Jack Stevens

Stan Laurel, Oliver Hardy, Wilfred Lucas, Walter
Long, James Finlayson

'Their first full-length, with not over two reels of
value.' – Variety

The Parent Trap *
US   1961   129m   Technicolor
Walt Disney (George Golitzen)
V*, L

Twin daughters of separated parents determine to
bring the family together again.

Quite bright but awesomely extended juvenile romp.

wd David Swift   novel Das Doppelte Lottchen by Erich
Kästner   ph Lucien Ballard   m Paul Smith

Hayley Mills, Maureen O'Hara, Brian Keith, Charles
Ruggles, Leo G. Carroll, Una Merkel, Joanna Barnes,
Cathleen Nesbitt, Ruth McDevitt, Nancy Kulp

Parenthood **
US   1989   99m   DeLuxe   Panavision
UIP/Imagine Entertainment (Brian Grazer)
V, V*, L, S

Three generations of fathers and sons try to come to
terms with each other.

Expertly packaged, frequently funny, sometimes
accurate, but more often sentimental, study of paternal
relationships (maternal relationships are defined in
terms of the absence of a father).

w Lowell Ganz, Babaloo Mandel   d Ron Howard
ph Donald McAlpine   m Randy Newman
pd Todd Hallowell   ed Michael Hill, Daniel Hanley

Steve Martin, Tom Hulce, Rick Moranis, Martha
Plimpton, Keanu Reeves, Jason Robards, Mary
Steenburgen, Dianne Wiest

AAN: Dianne Wiest

Parents
US   1988   82m   colour
Vestron/Parents Productions (Bonnie Palef-Woolf)
V*, L

A child in small-town America of the 1950s discovers
that his parents are cannibals.

Black comedy all the more unsettling because of its
resolutely suburban setting.

w Christopher Hawthorne   d Bob Balaban
ph Ernest Day, Robin Vidgeon   m Angelo

Badalamenti, Jonathan Elias   ad Andris Hausmanis
ed Bill Pankow

Randy Quaid, Mary Beth Hurt, Sandy Dennis, Bryan
Madorsky, Juno Mills-Cockell, Kathryn Grody,
Deborah Rush, Graham Jarvis

'The most interesting and exciting directorial debut
that I have encountered in some time – a "failure" that
makes most recent successes seem like cold mush.' –
Jonathan Rosenbaum, Chicago Reader

Les Parents Terribles **
France   1948   98m   bw
Sirius

Life with a family in which the children are as
neurotic as the parents.

Alternately hilarious and tragic, this is a fascinating
two-set piece of filmed theatre, with every
performance a pleasure.

wd Jean Cocteau   play Jean Cocteau   ph Michel
Kelber   m Georges Auric   ad Christian Bérard,
Guy de Gastyne

Jean Marais, Yvonne de Bray, Gabrielle Dorziat, Marcel
André, Josette Day

† In 1953 a curious and unsatisfactory British version
was made by Charles Frank under the title Intimate
Relations, with Marian Spencer, Russell Enoch, Ruth
Dunning, Harold Warrender and Elsy Albiin.

Paris
US   1929   88m   part colour
Warner

An American stage star, her fiancé, her partner and
her mother-in-law-to-be converge on the Champs
Elysées.

Shaky musical with interesting talent, but bereft of its
original Cole Porter score.

w Hope Loring   d Clarence Badger

Irene Bordoni, Jack Buchanan, Louise Closser Hale,
Jason Robards

Paris after Dark
US   1943   85m   bw
TCF
GB title: The Night Is Ending

In wartime Paris a doctor leads the resistance forces.

Propaganda potboiler, quite neatly made and cast.

w Howard Buchman   d Leonide Moguy

George Sanders, Philip Dorn, Brenda Marshall,
Marcel Dalio, Madeleine LeBeau

Paris Belongs to Us
France   1961   140m   bw
AJYM/Films du Carrosse (Roland Nonia)
original title: Paris Nous Appartient

A student becomes involved with a group
unsuccessfully rehearsing a Shakespearean play who
fear a conspiracy to take over the world.

Overlong, often pretentious and frequently
amateurish, Rivette's first feature reflects an
adolescent despair of the future.

w Jacques Rivette, Jean Gruault   d Jacques Rivette
ph Charles Bitsch   m Philippe Arthuys   ed Denise
de Casablanca

Betty Schneider, Gianni Esposito, Françoise Prévost,
Daniel Crohem, François Maistre, Jean-Marie Robain,
Hans Lucas, Jean-Claude Brialy

Paris Blues *
US   1961   98m   Technicolor
UA/Pennebaker/Diane/Jason/Monica/Monmouth (Sam Shaw)
V*

Two jazz musicians have romantic problems in Paris.

Semi-serious mini-drama with emphasis on the
music; one is not quite sure what the actors thought
they were up to.

w Jack Sher, Irene Kamp, Walter Bernstein
novel Harold Flender   d Martin Ritt   ph Christian
Matras   m Duke Ellington

Paul Newman, Joanne Woodward, Sidney Poitier,
Louis Armstrong, Diahann Carroll, Serge Reggiani,
Barbara Laage

AAN: Duke Ellington

Paris by Night
GB   1988   103m   Eastmancolor
Virgin/British Screen/Film Four International/Zenith

Harassed by personal problems, a Conservative MP in
the European Parliament is driven to extreme actions.

Unsatisfactory political drama, intended to expose
social and moral hypocrisies but rarely rising above
melodrama.

wd David Hare   ph Roger Pratt   m Georges
Delerue   pd Anthony Pratt   ed George Akers

Charlotte Rampling, Michael Gambon, Robert Hardy,
Iain Glen, Jane Asher, Andrew Ray, Niamh Cusack,
Jonathan White, Linda Bassett, Robert Flemyng,
Robert David MacDonald

Paris Calling
US   1941   95m   bw
Universal/Charles K. Feldman

When the Nazis invade Paris, a woman discovers that
her husband is a traitor.

Totally predictable flagwaver.

w Benjamin Glazer, Charles Kaufman   d Edwin L.
Marin   ph Milton Krasner   m Richard Hageman

Elisabeth Bergner, Basil Rathbone, Randolph Scott,
Gale Sondergaard, Lee J. Cobb, Eduardo Ciannelli,
Charles Arnt

Paris Express: see The Man Who Watched Trains Go
By

Paris Holiday *
US   1957   101m   Technirama
UA/Tolda (Bob Hope)
V*

An American comedian meets a French one in Paris,
and both have narrow escapes because their script
contains the clue to a gang of counterfeiters.

Amiable location romp with the stars in pretty good
form.

w Edmund Beloin, Dean Riesner   d Gerd Oswald
ph Roger Hubert   m Joseph J. Lilley

Bob Hope, Fernandel, Anita Ekberg, Martha Hyer,
André Morell, Maurice Teynac, Jean Murat, Preston
Sturges

Paris Honeymoon
US   1938   85m   bw
Paramount

An American in Paris persuades his fiancée to forget a
French nobleman.

Candy floss musical for star fans.

w Frank Butler, Don Hartman   d Frank Tuttle

Bing Crosby, Franciska Gaal, Akim Tamiroff

'Entertaining offering that will click substantially at
the box office.' – Variety

Paris in Spring
US   1935   81m   bw
Paramount
GB title: Paris Love Song

Four visitors change partners in the romantic city.

Predictable romance with good ingredients.

w Samuel Hoffenstein, Franz Schulz, Keene
Thompson   play Dwight Taylor   d Lewis
Milestone

Mary Ellis, Tullio Carminati, Lynne Overman, Ida Lupino

'In everything except the unhappy choice of narrative it comes close to being an ideal production.' – *Variety*

Paris Interlude
US   1934   72m   bw
MGM

American newspapermen hang out in a Paris bar.

Aimless comedy-drama which fails to achieve the intended mood of world-weariness.

w Wells Root   *play All Good Americans* by S. J. and Laura Perelman   *d* Edwin L. Marin

Madge Evans, Otto Kruger, Robert Young, Una Merkel, Ted Healy, Louise Henry, Edward Brophy

'60 minutes instead of 72 would still have left something to be desired – further cutting.' – *Variety*

Paris Is Burning **
US   1990   78m   colour
ICA/OffWhite (Jennie Livingston)
V

Documentary about gay black men who compete for prizes at drag balls.

Fascinating glimpse of an enclosed world, reported with insight and sensitivity.

d Jennie Livingston   *ph* Paul Gibson   *ed* Jonathan Oppenheim

Paris Dupree, Andre Christian, Dorian Corey, Pepper Labeija, Willi Ninja

'A masterpiece of underworld reportage.' – *Sight and Sound*

Paris Love Song: see *Paris in Spring*

Paris Model
US   1953   88m   bw
Albert Zugsmith/Columbia

Stories involving four copies of the same Paris gown.

Depressing dramatic package with production values at a low ebb and some pleasant talents going awry.

w Robert Smith   *d* Alfred E. Green

Paulette Goddard, Eva Gabor, Marilyn Maxwell, Barbara Lawrence, Tom Conway, Leif Erickson, Florence Bates, Cecil Kellaway, Robert Hutton

Paris Nous Appartient: see *Paris Belongs to Us*

Paris Qui Dort *
France   1923   40m approx (24 fps)   bw   silent
Films Diamant (Maurice Diamant-Berger)
aka: *The Crazy Ray*

A mad scientist invents a ray which brings everyone but six people in Paris to a halt.

Mildly entertaining semi-professional comedy showing several of its director's most engaging traits.

wd/ed René Clair   *ph* Maurice Défassiaux, Paul Guichard

Henri Rollan, Albert Préjean, Marcel Vallée, Madeleine Rodrigue

Paris, Texas **
West Germany/France   1984   148m   colour
Road Movies/Argos (Don Guest, Anatole Dauman)
V, V*, L

After separating from his wife a man goes missing and is later found in the small town where he was born.

Long, enigmatic but generally fascinating puzzle-without-a-solution, about people who never find what they want.

w Sam Shepard   *d* Wim Wenders   *ph* Robby Müller
m Ry Cooder

Harry Dean Stanton, Dean Stockwell, Aurore Clement, Hunter Carson, Nastassja Kinski, Bernhard Wicki

† Filmed in English.

BFA: best director

Paris Trout **
US   1991   99m   CFI color   Panavision
Palace/Viacom (Frank Konigsberg, Larry Sanitsky)
V, V*, L

In the 1940s, in a small town in Georgia, a bigoted white store-owner is amazed to be tried for shooting a black girl and wounding her mother in a dispute over a car.

Powerful if predictable drama of racial hatred and a disintegrating marriage, though not helped by a portentous voice-over narration.

w Pete Dexter   *novel* Pete Dexter   *d* Stephen Gyllenhaal   *ph* Robert Elswit   *m* David Shire
pd Richard Sherman   *ed* Harvey Rosenstock

Dennis Hopper, Barbara Hershey, Ed Harris, Ray McKinnon, Tina Lifford, Darnita Henry, Eric Ware, Ronreaco Lee, Gary Bullock

Paris Underground
US   1945   97m   bw
(UA) Constance Bennett
GB title: *Madame Pimpernel*

Two women caught in Paris when the Nazis invade continue their resistance activities.

Artificial and not very exciting flagwaver.

w Boris Ingster, Gertrude Purcell   *novel* Etta Shiber
d Gregory Ratoff   *ph* Lee Garmes   *m* Alexander Tansman

Constance Bennett, Gracie Fields, George Rigaud, Kurt Kreuger, Leslie Vincent

'Mainly trash, involving enough handsome young men, in various poses of gallant gratitude, to satisfy Mae West in her prime.' – *James Agee*

AAN: Alexander Tansman

Paris Vu Par . . . **
France   1965   98m   colour
Films du Losange/Les Films du Cyprès/Barbet Schroeder
V, V*
aka: *Six in Paris*

Six short stories set in different parts of Paris: in Douchet's 'Saint Germain-des-Prés', an American girl is seduced by appearances. In Rouch's 'Gard du Nord', a discontented wife is offered the freedom that she thinks she desires. In Pollet's 'Rue St Denis', a dull dishwasher takes a prostitute back to his dingy flat. In Rohmer's 'Place de l'Étoile', a fastidious shirt-salesman thinks he has killed someone in a roadside brawl. In Godard's 'Montparnasse et Levallois', a girl believes she has mixed up telegrams sent to her two lovers. In Chabrol's 'La Muette Chabrol', a young boy buys ear-plugs to avoid listening to his parents' quarrel and so misses a vital cry for help.

Enjoyable, ironic anecdotes by six French 'New Wave' directors, originally shot in 16mm using hand-held cameras and natural lighting to achieve an appropriately offhand style.

wd Jean Douchet; Jean Rouch; Jean-Daniel Pollet; Eric Rohmer; Jean-Luc Godard; Claude Chabrol
ph Nestor Almendros; Etienne Becker; Alain Levent; Albert Maysles; Jean Rabier   *ed* Jacqueline Raynal

Barbara Wilkind, Jean-François Chappey, Jean-Pierre Andréani; Nadine Ballot, Barbet Schroeder, Gilles Quéant; Micheline Dax, Claude Melki; Jean-Michel Rouzière, Marcel Gallon; Joanna Shimkus, Philippe Hiquily, Serge Davri; Stéphane Audran, Gilles Chusseau, Claude Chabrol

Paris When It Sizzles
US   1963   110m   Technicolor
Paramount (Richard Quine, George Axelrod)
V*

A film writer tries out several script ideas with his secretary as heroine and himself as hero or villain.

As a French film called *La Fête à Henriette* this was a charming whimsy, but Hollywood made it heavy-handed and boring, especially as no one in it seems to

be having much fun.

w George Axelrod   *screenplay* Julien Duvivier, Henri Jeanson   *d* Richard Quine   *ph* Charles Lang Jnr
m Nelson Riddle

William Holden, Audrey Hepburn, Grégoire Aslan, Noël Coward, Raymond Bussières

'The new script embalms the original instead of reviving it.' – *Stanley Kauffmann, New Republic*

Park Row *
US   1952   83m   bw
UA/Samuel Fuller

Conflict breaks out between two newspapers in 1886 New York.

Earnest but flat low-budgeter of a rather unusual kind.

wd Samuel Fuller   *ph* Jack Russell   *m* Paul Dunlap   *ad* Theobold Holsopple

Gene Evans, Mary Welch, Bela Kovacs, Herbert Heyes, Forrest Taylor

Parker
GB   1984   97m   colour
Moving Picture Company (Nigel Stafford-Clark)

A British businessman turns up after claiming to have been kidnapped in Munich, but the police don't necessarily believe him.

Suspense thriller hampered by overblown bits of ambivalence which prevent sympathy from lodging in any quarter.

w Trevor Preston   *d* Jim Goddard   *ph* Peter Jessop
m Richard Hartley

Bryan Brown, Cherie Lunghi, Kurt Raab, Bob Peck, Beate Finkh

Parlor, Bedroom and Bath
US   1931   72m   bw
MGM
V*
GB title: *Romeo in Pyjamas*

A mild-mannered husband has trouble when he becomes a landlord.

Rather flatfooted farce, on a par with the star's other talkies.

w Richard Schayer, Robert Hopkins   *play* Charles W. Bell, Mark Swan   *d* Edward Sedgwick

Buster Keaton, Charlotte Greenwood, Reginald Denny, Cliff Edwards

'Funny, clean enough for kids, and generally well made.' – *Variety*

† The film was largely shot on location in Keaton's own house.

'As though torn from life's pages!'
Parnell *
US   1937   115m   bw
MGM (John M. Stahl)

A 19th-century Irish politician comes to grief through his love for a married woman.

Well made but miscast biopic, a resounding thud at the box-office.

w John Van Druten, S. N. Behrman   *play* Elsie T. Schauffler   *d* John M. Stahl   *ph* Karl Freund
m William Axt

Clark Gable, Myrna Loy, Edmund Gwenn, Edna May Oliver, Alan Marshal, Donald Crisp, Billie Burke, Berton Churchill, Donald Meek, Montagu Love, George Zucco

'Dull and overlong historical drama . . . word of mouth is likely to be poor.' – *Variety*

'A singularly pallid, tedious and unconvincing drama.' – *Frank Nugent*

'Poor though the picture may be, it is pleasing to think how clean a film magnate's wish-fulfilments are, how virginal and high-minded the tawdry pathetic human past becomes when the Mayers and Goldwyns turn the magic ring.' – *Graham Greene*

Parole, Inc

US   1948   71m   bw
Orbit/Eagle Lion
V*

A racketeer arranges to spring hardened criminals from the state prison.

Routine crime stuff, quite efficiently handled.

w Sherman T. Lowe   d Alfred Zeisler

Michael O'Shea, Turhan Bey, Evelyn Ankers, Virginia Lee, Lyle Talbot

Parrish

US   1961   137m   Technicolor
Warner (Delmer Daves)

A young tobacco plantation worker has an ample sex life and the luck to become boss.

Predictable trudge through scenes from a bestselling novel, less offensive than most such adaptations.

wd Delmer Daves   novel Mildred Savage   ph Harry Stradling   m Max Steiner

Troy Donahue, Claudette Colbert, Karl Malden, Dean Jagger, Connie Stevens, Diane McBain, Sharon Hugueny

Parsifal **

West Germany   1982   255m   colour
Artificial Eye/Gaumont/TMS
V

Cinematic version of Wagner's opera of the knights of the Holy Grail.

Imaginative treatment, set around the composer's death mask, with a youth and a girl playing Parsifal; its actors are dubbed by singers.

d Hans Jürgen Syberberg   ph Igor Luther
md Armin Jordan   m Richard Wagner   ed Jutta Brandstaedter, Marianne Fehrenberg

Michael Kutter, Karin Krick, Edith Clever, Armin Jordan, Robert Lloyd, Aage Haugland, Martin Sperr, with the voices of Rainer Goldberg, Yvonne Minton and Wolfgang Schöne

The Parson of Panamint

US   1941   84m   bw
Paramount (Harry Sherman)

A gold-rush mountain town is corrupted by success until a two-fisted parson puts things right.

Middling Western morality play.

w Harold Shumate, Adrian Scott   novel Peter B. Kyne   d William McGann   ph Russell Harlan   m Irvin Talbot

Charles Ruggles, Ellen Drew, Phillip Terry, Joseph Schildkraut, Henry Kolker, Janet Beecher, Paul Hurst

Une Partie de Campagne ***

France   1936   40m   bw
Pantheon/Pierre Braunberger
aka: *A Day in the Country*

Around 1880, a Parisian tradesman and his family picnic one Sunday in the country, and one of the daughters falls in love.

An unfinished film which was much admired for its local colour, like an impressionist picture come to life.

wd Jean Renoir,   story Guy de Maupassant
ph Claude Renoir, Jean Bourgoin   m Joseph Kosma

Sylvie Bataille, Georges Darnoul, Jane Marken, Paul Temps

Une Partie de Plaisir *

France   1975   100m   colour
La Boétie/Sunchild/Gerico (André Genoves)

The analysis of a divorce.

Bitter comedy drama, with the director's usual scriptwriter playing out his own life story. A little too incestuous for its own good, but with striking moments.

w Paul Gegauff   d Claude Chabrol   ph Jean Rabier

Paul Gegauff, Danielle Gegauff, Paula Moore, Michel Valette

Partners

US   1982   98m   Movielab
Titan (Aaron Russo)
V, V*

Two Los Angeles police officers, one straight and one gay, investigate the murder of a homosexual.

Uneasy comedy-melodrama of somewhat mysterious purpose.

w Francis Veber   d James Burrows   ph Victor J. Kemper   m Georges Delerue

John Hurt, Ryan O'Neal, Kenneth McMillan, Robyn Douglass, Jay Robinson

Partners in Crime

US   1937   66m   bw
Paramount

A private eye stumbles on a plot to victimize the reform candidate in a local election.

Reliable second feature with few surprises.

w Garnett Weston   novel Kurt Steel   d Ralph Murphy

Lynne Overman, Roscoe Karns, Muriel Hutchinson, Anthony Quinn, Inez Courtney, Charles Halton, Lucien Littlefield

'A cockeyed affair, perforated with surprises.' – *Variety*

The Party *

US   1968   98m   DeLuxe   Panavision
UA/Mirisch/Geoffrey (Blake Edwards)
V*, V

An accident-prone Indian actor is accidentally invited to a swank Hollywood party and wrecks it.

Would-be Tatiesque comedy of disaster, occasionally well-timed but far too long for all its gloss.

w Blake Edwards, Tom and Frank Waldman
d Blake Edwards   ph Lucien Ballard   m Henry Mancini   pd Fernando Carrere

Peter Sellers, Claudine Longet, Marge Champion, Fay McKenzie, Steve Franken, Buddy Lester

'One thing the old movie makers did know is that two reels is more than enough of this stuff.' – *Wilfred Sheed*

'It is only rarely that one laughs or even smiles; mostly one just chalks up another point for ingenuity.' – *Tom Milne*

The Party and the Guests *

Czechoslovakia   1966   71m   bw
Barrandov Studio
original title: *O Slavnosti A Hostech*

A reluctant guest at an outdoor birthday and wedding party refuses to join in the celebrations.

Biting political allegory on the nature of tyranny.

w Ester Krumbachová, Jan Němec   d Jan Němec
ph Jaromir Šofr   m Karel Mares

Helena Pejsková, Jana Pracharova, Zdena Skvorecká, Pavel Bosek, Karel Mares, Ewald Schorm, Jan Klusak, Jiří Němec, Wan Vyskocil

Party Girl

US   1958   98m   Metrocolor   Cinemascope
MGM/Euterpe (Joe Pasternak)
V*

In twenties Chicago, a lawyer wins a girl from a gangster.

Heavy-handed Scarface-style saga which at one time won a curious reputation for being a satire.

w George Wells   d Nicholas Ray   ph Robert Bronner   m Jeff Alexander

Robert Taylor, Cyd Charisse, Lee J. Cobb, John Ireland, Kent Smith, Claire Kelly, Corey Allen

Party, Party

GB   1983   98m   colour
A & M Records

A teenager throws a drunken party while his parents are out.

Ghastly British rubbish: no plot and nothing to laugh at at all, just young people making asses of themselves.

w Daniel Peacock, Terry Winsor   d Terry Winsor

Daniel Peacock, Karl Howman, Perry Fenwick, Sean Chapman, Phoebe Nicholls, Caroline Quentin

Party Wire

US   1935   70m   bw
Columbia

Small-town gossipers listen in on party wires and draw the wrong conclusions.

Multi-stranded comedy-drama; not important but quite pleasant.

w Ethel Hill, John Howard Lawson, Bruce Manning
d Erle C. Kenton

Jean Arthur, Victor Jory, Helen Lowell, Charley Grapewin, Clara Blandick, Maude Eburne

'Entertaining for the family trade.' – *Variety*

The Party's Over

GB   1963   94m   bw
Tricastle (Anthony Perry)

An American girl joins a group of Chelsea beatniks and dies in a fall from a balcony; her father investigates.

Tasteless and boring swinging London trash which became notorious when its producers (Rank) disowned it because it features a party at which a man makes love to a dead girl. An unattractive display of moral squalor.

w Marc Behm   d Guy Hamilton   ph Larry Pizer
m John Barry

Oliver Reed, Eddie Albert, Ann Lynn, Louise Sorel

Pas de Problème: see *No Problem!*

Un Pasaje de Ida

Dominican Republic   1988   90m   colour
Producciones Testimonio (Agliberto Melendez)
aka: *A One-Way Ticket*

A ship's captain, who is smuggling 40 men to America, panics when police come aboard to search the vessel.

A competent exposé of high-level corruption and low-level greed which gains some resonance from its harrowing climax, based as it is on a true story.

w Agliberto Melendez, Adelso Cass, Danilo Taveras
d Agliberto Melendez   ph Pedro Guzman Cordero
m Rafael Solano   pd Orlando Menicucci
ed Pericles Mejia

Horacio Veloz, Miguel Buccarelli, Victor Checo, Felix
German, Pepito Guerra, Nini German, Giovanni Cruz,
Delta Soto

Pasazerka: see *Passenger*

Pascali's Island *
GB   1988   104m   Metrocolor
Virgin/Avenue Pictures/Initial/Film Four International
V, V*, L, S

On an Aegean island, a Turkish spy and an English
con man attempt to double-cross one another.

Elegant period drama full of an understated sexual
tension.

wd James Dearden   *novel* Barry Unsworth
ph Roger Deakins   *m* Loek Dikker   *pd* Andrew
Mollo   *ed* Edward Marnier

Ben Kingsley, Charles Dance, Helen Mirren, Stefan Gryff,
George Murcell, Nadim Sawalha, T. P. McKenna,
Sheila Allan

Pasqualino Settebellezze: see *Seven Beauties*

The Passage
GB   1978   98m   Eastmancolor   Technovision
Hemdale/Passage/Lester Goldsmith-Maurice Binder (John
   Quested)

A Basque shepherd guides a scientist and his family
from occupied France over the mountains into Spain.

Routine war suspenser given an unnecessary taint of
sadism. Only those addicted to unpleasant detail will
enjoy it.

w Bruce Micolaysen   *novel The Perilous Passage* by
Bruce Micolaysen   *d* J. Lee Thompson   *ph* Michael
Reed   *m* Michael J. Lewis

Anthony Quinn, James Mason, Malcolm McDowell,
Patricia Neal, Kay Lenz, Paul Clemens, Christopher
Lee

Le Passage du Rhin: see *The Crossing of the Rhine*

Passage Home
GB   1955   102m   bw
GFD/Group Films (Julian Wintle)

In 1931, tensions run high on a merchant ship when
the captain accepts an attractive girl as passenger from
South America.

Obvious melodrama complete with drunken captain
and storm at sea; not badly done if it must be done at
all.

w William Fairchild   *novel* Richard Armstrong
d Roy Baker   *ph* Geoffrey Unsworth   *m* Clifton
Parker

Peter Finch, Anthony Steel, Diane Cilento, Cyril
Cusack, Geoffrey Keen, Hugh Griffith, Duncan
Lamont, Bryan Forbes, Gordon Jackson, Michael
Craig

A Passage to India **
GB   1984   163m   Technicolor
EMI/John Brabourne-Richard Goodwin/HBO/John Heyman/
   Edward Sands
V, V*, L

An English girl in India accuses an Indian doctor of
rape.

Another film about India under the Raj seems
somewhat redundant after *The Jewel in the Crown,
Gandhi* and *The Far Pavilions,* but at least under David
Lean's direction this is intelligent and good to look at.

wd/ed David Lean,   novel E. M. Forster   *ph* Ernest
Day   *m* Maurice Jarre   *pd* John Box

Judy Davis, Alec Guinness, Victor Bannerjee, Peggy
Ashcroft, James Fox, Nigel Havers, Richard Wilson,
Antonia Pemberton, Michael Culver, Art Malik

AA: Peggy Ashcroft (supporting actress); music

AAN: best picture; direction; Judy Davis; adapted
screenplay; photography; editing; art direction

BFA: Peggy Ashcroft

Passage to Marseilles *
US   1944   110m   bw
Warner (Hal B. Wallis)
V, V*, L

Convicts escape from Devil's Island and join the Free
French.

A rare example of a film boasting flashbacks within
flashbacks within flashbacks, this confusing if
sometimes entertaining all-star saga is done to death
by its unconvincing flagwaving endpapers which
prevent it from being at all comparable with
Casablanca, as was clearly intended.

w Casey Robinson, Jack Moffitt   *story* Charles
Nordhoff, James Hall   *d* Michael Curtiz   *ph* James
Wong Howe   *m* Max Steiner

Humphrey Bogart, Michèle Morgan, Claude Rains,
Philip Dorn, Sidney Greenstreet, Peter Lorre, Helmut
Dantine, George Tobias, John Loder, Victor Francen,
Eduardo Ciannelli

'Invincibly second rate.' – *Richard Mallet, Punch*

Passage West
US   1951   81m   Technicolor
Pine-Thomas/Paramount

Religious pioneers headed west are menaced by
escaped convicts.

Entertaining minor Western.

w Lewis R. Foster, Nedrick Young   *d* Lewis
R. Foster

John Payne, Dennis O'Keefe, Arleen Whelan, Peter
Hanson

Passager de la Pluie: see *Rider on the Rain*

Passenger *
Poland   1963   63m   bw   Dyaliscope
Kadr
original title: *Pasazerka*

A German woman on a liner sees a woman she thinks
she recognizes, and realizes that it is one of her
charges when she was an official in a concentration
camp.

Minor but effective character drama, in essence an
investigation of guilt. The director died during its
making, so some scenes are replaced by still
photographs.

wd Andrzej Munk,   play Zofia Posmysz-Piasecka
ph Krzysztof Winiewicz

Aleksandra Slaska, Anna Ciepielewska

'I used to be somebody else; but I traded myself in ...'
The Passenger *
Italy/France/Spain   1975   119m   Metrocolor
MGM/CCC/Concordia/CIPI (Carlo Ponti)
V*
aka: *Profession: Reporter*

A TV reporter in a desert hotel changes identities with
a dead man and finds he is now an African gun
runner being drawn irresistibly towards his own
death.

Pretty much in the style of *Blow Up,* but this time with
no frills of fashion or nudity to bring the public in.
After this, Antonioni was given up by the commercial
cinema.

w Mark Peploe, Peter Wollen, Michelangelo
Antonioni   *d* Michelangelo Antonioni   *ph* Luciano
Tovoli   *md* Ivan Vandor

Jack Nicholson, Maria Schneider, Jenny Runacre, Ian
Hendry

'A film of real romance, depth and power ... the very
quintessence of cinema.' – *Michael Billington, Illustrated
London News*

'He's an ex-cop with a bad mouth, a bad attitude, and a
   bad seat. For the terrorists on flight 163 ... he's very bad
   news.'
Passenger 57
US   1992   84m   Technicolor
Warner (Lee Rich, Dan Paulson, Dylan Sellers)
V, V*, L, S

An ex-cop goes into action when terrorists hijack his
plane.

A *Die Hard*-style thriller, entertaining enough
although inevitably predictable.

w David Loughery, Dan Gordon, Stewart Raffill
d Kevin Hooks   *ph* Mark Irwin   *m* Stanley Clarke
pd Jaymes Hinkle   *ed* Richard Nord

Wesley Snipes, Bruce Payne, Tom Sizemore, Alex
Datcher, Bruce Greenwood, Robert Hooks, Elizabeth
Hurley, Michael Horse

'About as fresh as an in-flight meal. Even so, it has a
certain appetizing quality about it.' – *Guardian*

Passing Clouds: see *Spellbound*

The Passing of the Third Floor Back *
GB   1935   90m   bw
Gaumont (Ivor Montagu)

A Christ-like visitor stays at a London boarding house
and changes the lives of the inmates.

Competent film version of a famous, sentimental,
dated play.

w Michael Hogan, Alma Reville   *play* Jerome K.
Jerome   *d* Berthold Viertel   *ph* Curt Courant
m Hubert Bath

Conrad Veidt, René Ray, Anna Lee, Frank Cellier, Mary
Clare, Beatrix Lehmann, Cathleen Nesbitt, Sara
Allgood

'Drawing power of the book, the play, the
picturization and the star should, on form, be
invincible.' – *Variety*

'The pious note has been toned down, the milk of
human kindness has been agreeably watered, and the
types in the small London private hotel are observed
with malicious realism.' – *Graham Greene*

Passion (1919): see *Madame Dubarry*

Passion
US   1954   84m   Technicolor
Benedict Bogeaus/RKO
V*

Jealousy erupts between ranchers in Spanish
California.

Peculiarly titled Western of no merit whatsoever.

w Beatrice A. Dresher, Joseph Leytes   *d* Allan
Dwan

Yvonne de Carlo, Cornel Wilde, Raymond Burr, Lon
Chaney Jnr, Rodolfo Acosta, John Qualen

Passion *
France   1982   88m   Eastmancolor
Artificial Eye/Sonimage/Sara Films/A2/Film et Video Productions
   (Alain Sarde)
V

A Polish film director has an affair with the wife of a
factory owner who is trying to cope with a threatened
strike.

Visually complex examination of film-making, work,
love and betrayal.

wd Jean-Luc Godard   ph Raoul Coutard   *m* Ravel,
Mozart and others   *ad* Serge Marzolff

Isabelle Huppert, Hanna Schygulla, Michel Piccoli,
Jerzy Radziwilowicz, Lázló Szabó, Jean-François
Stevenin, Patrick Bonnel, Sophie Loucachevsky

Passion Fish

US   1992   134m   DuArt
Atchafalaya (Sarah Green, Maggie Renzi)
V, V*, L

A new nurse with problems of her own gives a crippled TV actress a reason to live.

A well-acted but constricting domestic drama.

wd John Sayles   *ph* Roger Deakins   *m* Mason Daring   *pd* Dan Bishop, Dianna Freas   *ed* John Sayles

Mary McDonnell, Alfre Woodard, David Strathairn, Vondie Curtis-Hall, Nora Dunn, Sheila Kelley, Angela Bassett, Leo Burmester

'Pic has a measure of charm, plenty of validity and some fine scenes, but lacks the intensity that would have made it galvanizing or transcendent.' – *Variety*

AAN: Mary McDonnell; John Sayles

Passion Flower

US   1930   78m   bw
MGM
V*

Two rich girls marry beneath them.

Tedious romantic drama about class and true love.

w Martin Flavin, L. E. Johnson, Edith Fitzgerald   *novel* Kathleen Norris   *d* William de Mille

Kay Francis, Kay Johnson, Charles Bickford, Lewis Stone, ZaSu Pitts, Dickie Moore, Winter Hall

'A flock of talent, but talent doesn't always count on a marquee.' – *Variety*

The Passion of Joan of Arc ****

France   1928   110m   bw   silent
Société Générale des Films
original title: *La Passion de Jeanne d'Arc*

On her last day on Earth, Joan of Arc is subjected to five increasingly threatening interrogations before being burned at the stake.

Austerely moving drama, using close-ups to give intense scrutiny to Joan and her accusers, drawing in the audience to become involved in the action.

w Carl Dreyer, Joseph Delteil   *d Carl Dreyer*
ph Rudolph Maté   *ad* Hermann Warm, Jean Hugo
ed Carl Dreyer

Renée Falconetti, Eugène Silvain, Maurice Schutz, Michel Simon, Antonin Artaud, Louis Ravet, André Berley, Jean d'Yid

'One of the greatest of all movies . . . Falconetti's Joan may be the finest performance ever recorded on film.' – *Pauline Kael*

'Isn't worth a dollar to any commercial regular picture theatre in the US.' – *Variety*

† Lilian Gish was first considered for the role of Joan. Falconetti never made another film. After its first showing the film was cut by the French authorities and was banned by the British until 1930.

The Passionate Friends **

GB   1948   91m   bw
GFD/Cineguild (Eric Ambler)
US title: *One Woman's Story*

A woman marries an older man, then meets again her young lover.

A simple and obvious dramatic situation is tricked out with flashbacks and the inimitable high style of its director to make a satisfying entertainment.

w Eric Ambler   *novel* H. G. Wells   *d* David Lean
ph Guy Green   *m* Richard Addinsell

Ann Todd, Trevor Howard, Claude Rains, Betty Ann Davies, Isabel Dean, Arthur Howard, Wilfrid Hyde-White

'Mr Lean plants his clues with the certainty of a master of the detective story, and heightens their

effect with a sure handling of camera and sound track.' – *The Times*

The Passionate Plumber

US   1932   73m   bw
MGM

A woman hires a professional lover to fend off the man she really loves but thinks she shouldn't have.

Much revamped farce version of a comedy made straight in 1927 and 1942. All flopped, but this is the worst.

w Laurence E. Johnson   *play Her Cardboard Lover* by Frederick Lonsdale   *d* Edward Sedgwick

Buster Keaton, Jimmy Durante, Irene Purcell, Polly Moran, Gilbert Roland, Mona Maris, Maude Eburne

'Another lay-me-down-to-sleeper for box offices.' – *Variety*

The Passionate Sentry: see *Who Goes There?*

The Passionate Stranger

GB   1956   97m   part bw, part Eastmancolor
British Lion/Beaconsfield (Peter Rogers, Gerald Thomas)
US title: *A Novel Affair*

A lady novelist bases a character on her virile chauffeur; he reads the book and thinks she fancies him.

Feeble comedy, half of it consisting of a dramatization of the heroine's very dull novel.

w Muriel and Sydney Box   *d* Muriel Box   *ph* Otto Heller   *m* Humphrey Searle

Ralph Richardson, Margaret Leighton, Carlo Justini, Patricia Dainton, Marjorie Rhodes, Thorley Walters, Frederick Piper

Passionate Summer

GB   1958   104m   Eastmancolor
Briar/Kenneth Harper

A divorced headmaster at a Jamaican school is loved by three women.

Silly melodrama with splendid backgrounds ruined by poor colour.

w Joan Henry   *novel The Shadow and the Peak* by Richard Mason   *d* Rudolph Cartier   *ph* Ernest Steward   *m* Angelo Lavagnino

Virginia McKenna, Bill Travers, Yvonne Mitchell, Alexander Knox, Ellen Barrie, Carl Mohner

'The climactic hurricane does little to dispel the overall feeling of emotional suffocation.' – *MFB*

Passione d'Amore

Italy/France   1982   119m (dubbed)   Eastmancolor
Connoisseur/Rizzoli Films/Massfilm/Marceau Cocinor (Franco Committou, Gino Santarelli)
V*

A neurotic and unattractive woman becomes infatuated with a handsome young army captain.

Turgid 19th-century melodrama.

w Ruggero Maccari, Ettore Scola   *novel Fosca* by Ignio Ugo Tarchetti   *d* Ettore Scola   *ph* Claudio Ragona   *m* Armando Trovagoli   *ad* Fiorenzo Senese   *ed* Raimondo Crociani

Valeria D'Obici, Bernard Giraudeau, Jean-Louis Trintignant, Massimo Girotti, Bernard Blier, Laura Antonelli

Passport to Fame: see *The Whole Town's Talking*

Passport to Hell

US   1932   72m   bw
Fox

A woman tainted by scandal moves from country to country and marries a German commandant in the Cameroons to avoid internment.

Reasonably lively drama which ends less well than it began.

w Bradley King, Leon Gordon, Harry Hervey
d Frank Lloyd

Elissa Landi, Paul Lukas, Warner Oland, Alexander Kirkland, Donald Crisp

'Not a de luxer; Broadway spotted because of the product shortage.' – *Variety*

Passport to Pimlico ****

GB   1949   84m   bw
Ealing (E. V. H. Emmett)
V*

Part of a London district is discovered to belong to Burgundy, and the inhabitants find themselves free of rationing restrictions.

A cleverly detailed little comedy which inaugurated the best period of Ealing, its preoccupation with suburban man and his foibles. Not exactly satire, but great fun, and kindly with it.

w T. E. B. Clarke   *d* Henry Cornelius   *ph* Lionel Banes   *m* Georges Auric

Stanley Holloway, *Margaret Rutherford*, Basil Radford, Naunton Wayne, Hermione Baddeley, John Slater, Paul Dupuis, Jane Hylton, Raymond Huntley, Betty Warren, Barbara Murray, Sidney Tafler

'One of the most felicitous and funny films since the age of the René Clair comedies.' – *C. A. Lejeune*

† The film was based on a genuine news item. The Canadian government presented to the Netherlands the room in which Princess Juliana was to bear a child.

AAN: T. E. B. Clarke

Passport to Shame

GB   1959   88m   bw
United/Cory/Eros
US title: *Room 43*

A taxi driver rescues his girl from the white slave business.

Would-be seamy melodrama which just about serves its purpose.

w Patrick Alexander   *d* Alvin Rakoff

Eddie Constantine, Diana Dors, Odile Versois, Herbert Lom, Brenda de Banzie, Robert Brown

Passport to Treason

GB   1956   80m   bw
Mid Century/Eros

A detective traces the death of his colleague to fascists working within an alleged peace group.

Stock melodramatic situations straightforwardly presented make this a watchable support.

w Kenneth Hales, Norman Hudis   *d* Robert S. Baker

Rod Cameron, Lois Maxwell, Clifford Evans, John Colicos, Ballard Berkeley

The Password Is Courage *

GB   1962   116m   bw
MGM/Andrew and Virginia Stone

In Europe during World War II, Sgt-Major Charles Coward has a career of escapes and audacious anti-Nazi exploits.

Lively, slightly over-humorous account of one man's war, well mounted and shot entirely on location.

wd Andrew L. Stone   *biography* John Castle
ph David Boulton

Dirk Bogarde, Maria Perschy, Alfred Lynch, Nigel Stock, Reginald Beckwith

'The experiences are, it seems, mainly true but they do not seem so.' – *Guardian*

Past Midnight *

US   1991   96m   Fotokem colour
Cinetel (Lisa M. Hansen)
V, V*

A social worker begins an affair with a paroled prisoner, convicted of murdering his pregnant wife.

Utterly predictable thriller, taken at a slow pace that does nothing to disguise its deficiencies.

w Frank Norwood   d Jan Eliasberg   ph Robert Yeoman   m Steve Barteck   pd Sharon Seymour   ed Christopher Rouse

Rutger Hauer, Natasha Richardson, Clancy Brown, Guy Bond, Ernie Lively, Tom Wright

Pastor Hall *

GB   1940   97m   bw
Charter (John Boulting)

The story of German village pastor Niemöller, who in 1934 was shot for denouncing the Nazis.

A courageous film of its time, not very interesting dramatically or cinematically.

w Leslie Arliss, Haworth Bromley, Anna Reiner   play Ernst Toller   d Roy Boulting   ph Max Greene

Wilfrid Lawson, Nova Pilbeam, Seymour Hicks, Marius Goring, Percy Walsh, Brian Worth, Peter Cotes, Hay Petrie

'Not much meat on her, but what there is is cherce!'
Pat and Mike **

US   1952   95m   bw
MGM (Lawrence Weingarten)
V*, L

A small-time sports promoter takes on a female intellectual multi-champion.

A comedy which amuses because of its star playing, but doesn't really develop. All very easy going, with guest appearances from sporting personalities.

w Ruth Gordon, Garson Kanin   d George Cukor   ph William Daniels   m David Raksin

Spencer Tracy, Katharine Hepburn, Aldo Ray, William Ching, Sammy White, Jim Backus, Phyllis Povah

'They do not, like the Lunts, give the impression of a rigid calculated effect; rather, they complement and stimulate each other.' – MFB

AAN: script

Pat Garrett and Billy the Kid

US   1973   106m   Metrocolor   Panavision
MGM (Gordon Carroll)
V, V*

Blood-spattered version of a Western legend, with violence always to the fore, accentuated by the impossibility of listening to the dialogue because of poor direction and recording.

w Rudolph Wurlitzer   d Sam Peckinpah   ph John Coquillon   m Bob Dylan

James Coburn, Kris Kristofferson, Bob Dylan, Richard Jaeckel, Katy Jurado, Slim Pickens, Chill Wills, Jason Robards Jnr

'A sombre, intense, downbeat essay on the truth behind the legend and the legend behind the truth.' – Sight and Sound

'Shows what Peckinpah can do when he doesn't put his mind to it.' – Stanley Kauffmann

'A rash adventure in inadvertent self-parody.' – William S. Pechter

'Ambitious, erotic, peculiarly unrealized . . .' – Pauline Kael, New Yorker

A Patch of Blue *

US   1965   105m   bw   Panavision
MGM/Pandro S. Berman
V*, S

A blind girl who lives in a slum is helped by a Negro

with whom she falls in love without realizing his colour.

Polished tearjerker with racial overtones; nicely done for those who can take it.

novel Be Ready with Bells and Drums by Elizabeth Kata   d Guy Green   ph Robert Burks   m Jerry Goldsmith

Sidney Poitier, Elizabeth Hartman, Shelley Winters, Wallace Ford, Ivan Dixon, Elisabeth Fraser, John Qualen

AA: Shelley Winters

AAN: Robert Burks; Jerry Goldsmith; Elizabeth Hartman

'He wants YOU to have his baby!'
Paternity

US   1981   93m   Movielab
Paramount (Jerry Tokofsky)
V, V*, L

A middle-aged bachelor decides to father a son via a hired mother, who will then return the child to him.

Tastelessly up-dated Hollywood romance with predictable complications. Not worth sitting through.

w Charlie Peters   d David Steinberg   ph Bobby Byrne   m David Shire

Burt Reynolds, Beverly D'Angelo, Norman Fell, Paul Dooley, Elizabeth Ashley, Lauren Hutton, Juanita Moore

Pather Panchali ****

India   1955   115m   bw
Government of West Bengal
V, V*

In a small Bengal village, the son of a would-be writer grows up in poverty and tragedy before setting off with what remains of the family to seek a living in Benares.

A remarkable first film of a director now famous, showing that people are much the same though the details of their daily lives may be different. The pace may be slow but the content is mainly absorbing.

wd Satyajit Ray,   novels Bhibuti Bashan Bannerjee   ph Subrata Mitra   m Ravi Shankar

Kanu Bannerjee, Karuna Bannerjee, Uma Das Gupta, Subir Bannerjee, Chunibala

'It has been left to the Indian cinema to give us a picture of a childhood which preserves under the shadow of experience not only its innocence but its gaiety.' – Dilys Powell

† The film was the first part of a trilogy and was followed by Aparajito (1956) and The World of Apu (1959).

Pathfinder **

Norway   1987   86m   colour
Guild/Filmkameratene/Norsk Film (John M. Jacobson)
V, V*, L
original title: Ofelas

A gang of ruthless raiders capture a 16-year-old boy and force him to lead them to his village so that they may plunder it.

Based on an ancient Lapp folk-tale, this is a simple, direct, marvellously exciting adventure shot in a snow- and ice-bound landscape.

wd Nils Gaup   ph Erling Thurmann-Andersen   m Nils-Aslak Valkeapaa   pd Harald Egede-Nissen   ed Niels Pagh Andersen

Mikkel Gaup, Nils Utsi, Svein Scharffenberg, Helgi Skulason, Sverre Porsanger, Svein Birger Olsen

AAN: best foreign film

Paths of Glory ****

US   1957   86m   bw
UA/Bryna (James B. Harris)
V*, L

In 1916 in the French trenches, three soldiers are courtmartialled for cowardice.

Incisive melodrama chiefly depicting the corruption and incompetence of the high command; the plight of the soldiers is less interesting. The trench scenes are the most vivid ever made, and the rest is shot in genuine castles, with resultant difficulties of lighting and recording; the overall result is an overpowering piece of cinema.

w Stanley Kubrick, Calder Willingham, Jim Thompson   novel Humphrey Cobb   d Stanley Kubrick   ph Georg Krause   m Gerald Fried

Kirk Douglas, Adolphe Menjou, George Macready, Wayne Morris, Richard Anderson, Ralph Meeker, Timothy Carey

'A bitter and biting tale, told with stunning point and nerve-racking intensity.' – Judith Crist

'Beautifully performed, staged, photographed, cut and scored.' – Colin Young

The Patient Vanishes: see This Man Is Dangerous

Patrick the Great *

US   1944   88m   bw
Universal (Howard Benedict)

An actor whose career is waning is jealous of his young son.

Slick teenage family comedy, virtually a one-man show for O'Connor.

w Jane Hall, Bertram Millhauser, Dorothy Bennett, Frederick Kohner, Ralph Block   d Frank Ryan   ph Frank Redman   m Hans Salter

Donald O'Connor, Donald Cook, Peggy Ryan, Frances Dee, Eve Arden, Thomas Gomez, Gavin Muir, Andrew Tombes

The Patriot **

US   1928   110m approx (24 fps)   bw   silent
Paramount (Ernst Lubitsch)

Mad Czar Paul I is assassinated by his chief adviser for the good of the state.

Historical melodrama with a good many comedy touches: the director makes the most of both aspects, but they don't in the end hang together despite bravura acting.

w Hans Kraly,   novel Alfred Neumann   d Ernst Lubitsch   ph Bert Glennon   ad Hans Dreier

Emil Jannings, Lewis Stone, Florence Vidor, Neil Hamilton

'I believe this picture the most suggestive we ever ran. Just another reason why we need censorship. Small-town exhibitors need clean pictures.' – Ohio exhibitor's report in Motion Picture Herald

AA: Hans Kraly

AAN: best picture; Ernst Lubitsch; Lewis Stone; Hans Dreier

The Patriot

West Germany   1979   120m   bw/colour
The Other Cinema/Kairos Film/ZDF (Alexander Kluge)
original title: Die Patriotin

A schoolteacher looks for new ways of presenting the history of Germany.

Intellectually austere examination of Germany's past and future, using newsreels, commentary and documentary footage; as cinema it is inert and condescending.

wd Alexander Kluge   ph Thomas Mauch, Jörg Schmidt-Reitwein, Werner Lring, Gunther Hörmann ed Beate Mainka-Jellinghaus

Hannelore Hoger, Alfred Edel, Alexander von Eschwege, Hans Heckel, Beate Holle, Kurt Jürgens, Dieter Mainka, Willi Münch

'Not for honour. Not for country. For his wife and child.'
Patriot Games
US 1992 117m Technicolor Panavision
UIP/Paramount (Mace Neufeld, Robert Rehme)
V, V*, L, CD, S

In London, a former CIA agent shoots an IRA terrorist in a street battle and becomes a target for the organization's revenge on his return to the States.

Muddled and melodramatic, it relies on nationalistic clichés and violent set-pieces rather than narrative coherence; it is certainly not for posterity.

w W. Peter Iliff, Donald Stewart, Steven Zaillian *novel* Tom Clancy *d* Phillip Noyce *ph* Donald McAlpine *m* James Horner *pd* Joseph Nemec III *ed* Neil Travis, William Hoy

Harrison Ford, Anne Archer, Patrick Bergin, Sean Bean, Thora Birch, James Fox, Samuel L. Jackson, Polly Walker, J. E. Freeman, James Earl Jones, Richard Harris, Hugh Fraser, David Threlfall, Alun Armstrong

'A star turn and smart action sequences enliven an otherwise abstract film.' – *Time*

'It flounders from one absurdity to another, with results that are hilarious when they aren't insulting.' – *Adam Mars-Jones, Independent*

'Mindless, morally repugnant and ineptly directed to boot.' – *Variety*

The Patsy *
US 1927 80m approx (24 fps) bw silent
MGM (Irving Thalberg)
GB title: *The Politic Flapper*

Tired of being taken for granted, a girl puts on a surprising show for her family.

Amusing comedy which, in sound, might have made Miss Davies a bigger star than she ever became.

w Agnes Christine Johnston *play* Barry Connors *d* King Vidor

Marion Davies, Marie Dressler, Lawrence Gray, Del Henderson, Jane Winton

'Marion Davies is in my opinion Filmland's Funniest Female, the only one I would mention in the same breath as Charlie Chaplin.' – *A. P. Herbert, Punch*

The Patsy
US 1964 101m Technicolor
Paramount/Jerry Lewis (E. J. Glucksman)
V, V*, L

Hollywood executives try to mould a bellboy to replace a deceased comedian.

A few mildly funny scenes scarcely atone for a long raucous comedy in which the star upstages his betters.

wd Jerry Lewis *ph* Wallace Kelley *m* David Raksin

Jerry Lewis, Everett Sloane, Peter Lorre, John Carradine, Phil Harris, Hans Conried, Ina Balin

'Inside the skyscraper jungle! Ruthless men and ambitious women clawing for control of a billion-dollar empire!'
Patterns ***
US 1956 88m bw
UA/Jed Harris, Michael Myerberg
V*
GB title: *Patterns of Power*

The tough boss of a New York corporation forces a showdown between a young executive and the older ineffectual man who he hopes will resign.

Tense little boardroom melodrama with domestic asides, one of the best of the filmed TV plays of the mid-fifties.

w *Rod Serling,* *play* Rod Serling *d* *Fielder Cook* *ph* Boris Kaufman

Van Heflin, Everett Sloane, Ed Begley, Beatrice Straight, Elizabeth Wilson

Patterns of Power: see *Patterns*

Patti Rocks *
US 1987 87m colour
Premier/FilmDallas (Gwen Field, Gregory M. Cummins)

A married man takes an old, but estranged, friend on a long car ride to the home of his pregnant girlfriend.

Low-budget movie concentrating on character development, though the likelihood of the slobbish male and the sensitive woman ever being attracted to one another seems remote.

w David Burton Morris, Chris Mulkey, John Jenkins, Karen Landry *d* David Burton Morris *ph* Gregory M. Cummins *m* Doug Maynard *ad* Charlotte Whitaker *ed* Gregory M. Cummins

Chris Mulkey, John Jenkins, Karen Landry, David L. Turk, Stephen Yoakam

'Nobody ever won a war by dying for his country. He won it by making the other poor dumb bastard die for his country!'
Patton ***
US 1970 171m DeLuxe Dimension 150
TCF (Frank McCarthy)
V, V*, L
GB title: *Patton – Lust for Glory*

World War II adventures of an aggressive American general.

Brilliantly handled wartime character study which is also a spectacle and tries too hard to have it both ways, but as a piece of film-making is hard to beat.

w Francis Ford Coppola, Edmund H. North *d* *Franklin Schaffner* *ph* Fred Koenekamp *m* *Jerry Goldsmith* *ad* Urie McCleary, Gil Parrondo *ed* Hugh S. Fowler

George C. Scott, Karl Malden, Michael Bates, Stephen Young, Michael Strong, Frank Latimore

'Here is an actor so totally immersed in his part that he almost makes you believe he is the man himself.' – *John Gillett*

AA: best picture; script; Franklin Schaffner; George C. Scott; art direction; editing; sound (Douglas Williams, Don Bassman)

AAN: Fred Koenekamp; Jerry Goldsmith; special visual effects

Patton – Lust for Glory: see *Patton*

Patty Hearst *
US/GB 1988 104m DeLuxe
Entertainment/Atlantic Entertainment/Zenith (Marvin Worth)
V*, L

After being kidnapped and imprisoned by a revolutionary group, a wealthy, privileged teenager joins in their terrorist activities.

Based on fact, though impressionistic in approach, it concerns itself, not always successfully, with questions of identity and personal responsibility.

w Nicholas Kazan *book* *Every Secret Thing* by Patricia Campbell Hearst with Alvin Moscow *d* Paul Schrader *ph* Bojan Bazelli, Stuart Barbee *m* Scott Johnson *pd* Jane Musky *ed* Michael R. Miller

Natasha Richardson, William Forsythe, Ving Rhames, Frances Fisher, Jodi Long, Olivia Barash, Dana Delany, Marek Johnson, Kitty Swink, Peter Kowanko

Paula (1947): see *Framed*

Paula
US 1952 80m bw
Columbia (Buddy Adler)
GB title: *The Silent Voice*

A barren wife causes a boy's deafness in an accident; she cures and adopts him.

Adequate woman's picture, a vehicle for a star and a luxuriant wardrobe.

w James Poe, William Sackheim *d* Rudolph Maté *ph* Charles Lawton Jnr *m* George Duning

Loretta Young, Kent Smith, Alexander Knox, Tommy Rettig

Pauline at the Beach **
France 1983 94m colour
Gala/Les Films Du Losange/Les Films Ariane (Margaret Menegoz)
V, V*, L
original title: *Pauline à la Plage*

A young girl observes her older cousin's disastrous holiday romances.

Delicately witty, eminently civilized entertainment.

wd Eric Rohmer *ph* Nestor Almendros *m* Jean-Louis Valero *ed* Cécile Decugis

Arielle Dombasle, Amanda Langlet, Pascal Greggory, Féodor Atkine, Simon de la Brosse, Rosette

Paura E Amore: see *Three Sisters*

Paura nella Città dei Morti Viventi: see *City of The Living Dead*

The Pawnbroker **
US 1965 114m bw
Landau-Unger (Worthington Miner)
V*, L

A Jew in slummy New York is haunted by his experiences in Nazi prison camps.

Engrossing, somewhat over-melodramatic character study, generally well done.

w David Friedkin, Morton Fine *novel* Edward Lewis Wallant *d* Sidney Lumet *ph* Boris Kaufman *m* Quincy Jones

Rod Steiger, Brock Peters, Geraldine Fitzgerald, Jaime Sanchez, Thelma Oliver, Juano Hernandez

'Might have been a great film had the director been able to restrain his dual tendency towards artiness and towards slickness.' – *Judith Crist*

'The film is trite, and you can see the big pushes for powerful effects, yet it isn't negligible.' – *Pauline Kael*

AAN: Rod Steiger

Pay or Die! *
US 1960 109m bw
Allied Artists (Richard Wilson)
V*

In 1906, a New York Italian police detective forms a special squad to combat the Black Hand.

Tough, convincing period melodrama.

w Richard Wilson, Bertram Millhauser *d* Richard Wilson *ph* Lucien Ballard *m* David Raksin *ad* Fernando Carrere

Ernest Borgnine, Alan Austin, Zohra Lampert, Robert F. Simon, Renata Vanni

Payday
US 1972 103m colour
Cinerama/Pumice/Fantasy (Ralph J. Gleason)
V*

An over-age pop singer has personal problems which erupt into violence.

Well made, dislikeable melodrama.

w Don Carpenter *d* Daryl Duke *ph* Richard C. Glouner *md* Ed Bogas

Rip Torn, Ahna Capri, Elayne Heilveil, Michael C. Gwynn

'Explores the Nashville-centered world of country with an easy authenticity which makes this nothing like a repetition of what has been before.' – *Charles Champlin*

Paydirt: see *There Goes the Neighborhood*

Paying the Penalty: see *Underworld*

Payment Deferred *
US   1932   75m   bw
MGM (Irving Thalberg)

A man desperate for money poisons his wealthy nephew.

Watchable photographed play.

w Ernest Vajda, Claudine West   *play* Jeffrey Dell
d Lothar Mendes   *ph* Merritt Gerstad

Charles Laughton, Maureen O'Sullivan, Ray Milland, Dorothy Peterson, Verree Teasdale, Billy Bevan, Halliwell Hobbes

'In spite of its excellence, it will probably prove indifferent box office.' – *Variety*

Payment on Demand *
US   1951   90m   bw
RKO/Jack H. Skirball

A happy wife and mother is appalled when her husband asks for a divorce.

A star suffers her way through luxury to a happy ending; good enough stuff for its intended audience.

w Bruce Manning, Curtis Bernhardt   *d* Curtis Bernhardt   *ph* Leo Tover   *m* Victor Young

Bette Davis, Barry Sullivan, Jane Cowl, Kent Taylor, Betty Lynn, John Sutton, Frances Dee, Otto Kruger

'An absolutely typical Joan Crawford picture except that Bette Davis happens to be in the Joan Crawford part.' – *Richard Mallett, Punch*

The Payoff
US   1943   74m   bw
Jack Schwarz/PRC

A star reporter nabs the killer of a prosecuting attorney.

A fading star in a role he had played several times before.

w Edward Dein   *d* Arthur Dreifuss

Lee Tracy, Tom Brown, Tina Thayer, Evelyn Brent, Jack La Rue

Payroll *
GB   1961   105m   bw
Anglo Amalgamated/Lynx (Norman Priggen)

Small-time crooks snatch £100,000, but after the getaway things begin to go wrong.

Tense, vivid, thoroughly predictable *Rififi*-style thriller, handled with solid professionalism.

w George Baxt   *novel* Derek Bickerton   *d* Sidney Hayers   *ph* Ernest Steward   *m* Reg Owen

Michael Craig, Billie Whitelaw, Françoise Prévost, Kenneth Griffith, William Lucas, Tom Bell, Barry Keegan, Joan Rice, Glyn Houston

Peach O'Reno
US   1931   66m   bw
RKO-Pathé

Two incompetent lawyers work on a divorce case.

Burlesque-style comedy with cabaret asides. Thin stuff.

w Ralph Spence, Tim Whelan   *d* William Seiter

Bert Wheeler, Robert Woolsey, Dorothy Lee, Joseph Cawthorn, Cora Witherspoon, Zelma O'Neal

'Less than average; low comedy laughs for the minor spots.' – *Variety*

The Pearl *
US/Mexico   1948   72m   bw
RKO/Oscar Dancigers
V*

In a remote Mexican village, a simple shell diver finds

a pearl of great price, but finds his life complicated as a result.

A fable which at the time seemed to have considerable quality, being the first Mexican film to receive international distribution.

w John Steinbeck, Emilio Fernandez, Kack Wagner   *d* Emilio Fernandez   *ph* Gabriel Figueroa   *m* Antonio Diaz Conde

Pedro Armendariz, Maria Elena Marques, Alfonso Bedoya

The Pearl of Death **
US   1944   67m   bw
Universal (Howard S. Benedict)
V*

When a valuable pearl is stolen, Sherlock Holmes has only his own cleverness to blame; but he redeems himself by trapping 'The Creeper'.

An amusing picturization of Doyle's *The Six Napoleons*, with the addition of a horror figure; it plays very well and is certainly among the best of this series.

w Bertram Millhauser   *d* Roy William Neill   *ph* Virgil Miller   *m* Paul Sawtell

Basil Rathbone, Nigel Bruce, Dennis Hoey, Miles Mander, Rondo Hatton, Evelyn Ankers

Peau d'Espion: see *To Commit A Murder*

La Peau Douce: see *Silken Skin*

Peck's Bad Boy
US   1934   70m   bw
Sol Lesser/Fox
V*

Adventures of a well-intentioned but accident-prone boy in a midwestern town.

Old-fashioned American juvenile classic, modestly well done.

w Bernard Schubert, Marguerite Roberts   *story* G. W. Peck   *d* Edward Cline

Jackie Cooper, Jackie Searle, Dorothy Peterson, Thomas Meighan

† Previously made in 1921 with Jackie Coogan. Cline also directed a sequel, *Peck's Bad Boy with the Circus* starring Tommy Kelly, in 1938.

Peeper
US   1975   87m   DeLuxe   Panavision
TCF/Chartoff-Winkler (Ron Buck)

In 1947 Los Angeles, a poor British private eye gets into trouble when he seeks a man's lost daughter.

Semi-spoofing Chandleresque caper which is never quite funny or quite thrilling enough.

w W. D. Richter   *novel Deadfall* by Keith Laumer   *d* Peter Hyams   *ph* Earl Rath   *m* Richard Clements

Michael Caine, Natalie Wood, Kitty Winn, Thayer David, Liam Dunn

'Flimsy whimsy.' – *Variety*

'More horrible than horror! More terrible than terror!'
Peeping Tom *
GB   1959   109m   Eastmancolor
Anglo Amalgamated/Michael Powell
V, V*

A film studio focus puller is obsessed by the lust to murder beautiful women and photograph the fear on their faces.

Thoroughly disagreeable suspenser, a kind of compendium of the bad taste the director showed in flashes during his career.

w Leo Marks   *d* Michael Powell   *ph* Otto Heller   *m* Brian Easdale

Carl Boehm, Moira Shearer, Anna Massey, Maxine Audley, Esmond Knight, Michael Goodliffe, Shirley Ann Field, Jack Watson

'Perhaps one would not be so disagreeably affected by this exercise in the lower regions of the psychopathic were it handled in a more bluntly debased fashion.' – *Dilys Powell*

'Of enormous and deserved reputation.' – *Time Out, 1982*

Pee-wee's Big Adventure *
US   1985   92m   colour
Mainline/Aspen Film Society/Robert Shapiro
V, V*, L, S

Pee-wee Herman loses his red bicycle and goes looking for it.

Starring an American TV comedian who acts like a small child, this offbeat, episodic comedy has some amusing moments.

w Phil Hartman, Paul Reubens, Michael Varhol   *d* Tim Burton   *ph* Victor J. Kemper   *m* Danny Elfman   *pd* David L. Snyder   *ed* Billy Weber

Paul Reubens, Elizabeth Daily, Mark Holton, Diane Salinger, Judd Omen, Jon Harris, Carmen Filpi, Tony Bill, James Brolin, Morgan Fairchild

'This slapstick fantasy has the bouncing-along inventiveness of a good cartoon.' – *Pauline Kael, New Yorker*

Peg of Old Drury *
GB   1935   76m   bw
British and Dominions/Herbert Wilcox

The romance of 18th-century actress Peg Woffington with David Garrick.

Primitive but vivacious historical romp with adequate star performances.

w Miles Malleson   *play Masks and Faces* by Charles Reade, Tom Taylor   *d* Herbert Wilcox   *ph* F. A. Young

Anna Neagle, Cedric Hardwicke, Jack Hawkins, Margaretta Scott, Hay Petrie

'I never tired of Miss Neagle's physical appearance, which was as pretty as a Chelsea figure. The whole film indeed is very pretty, with the sentiment neatly handled. But prettiness is a quality one wants, if at all, in small quantities.' – *Graham Greene, The Spectator*

Peg o' My Heart
US   1933   86m   bw
MGM

To the concern of his family, an English nobleman falls for an Irish colleen.

Half-hearted version of a famous lavender-tinted stage hit previously filmed in the twenties with its original star Laurette Taylor; but by 1933 its time was past.

w Frances Marion   *play* J. Hartley Manners   *d* Robert Z. Leonard

Marion Davies, Onslow Stevens, Alan Mowbray, Robert Greig, Irene Browne, J. Farrell MacDonald, Juliette Compton

'Just an 86-minute Irish monologue . . . undeservedly flattered by an almost perfect production.' – *Variety*

Peggy Sue Got Married **
US   1986   104m   DeLuxe
Tri-Star/Rastar (Paul R. Gurian)
V, V*, L

A disillusioned woman goes to her 25th high school reunion and finds herself reliving her young life.

It plays like an extended *Twilight Zone*, but with plenty of interesting details to back up an excellent leading performance.

w Jerry Leichtling, Arlene Sarner   *d Francis Coppola   ph* Jordan Cronenweth   *m* John Barry   *pd* Dean Tavoularis   *ed* Barry Malkin

Kathleen Turner, Nicolas Cage, Barry Miller, Catherine Hicks, Maureen O'Sullivan, Leon Ames, Helen Hunt, Don Murray, Barbara Harris, Kevin J. O'Connor

'Provocative, well acted, stylish and uneven.' – *Variety*

AAN: Jordan Cronenweth; Theodora Van Runkle (costumes); Kathleen Turner

Peking Express

US 1951 90m bw
Paramount/Hal B. Wallis

In communist China, an assortment of people are aboard a train which is diverted by outlaws.

Pot-boiling remake of *Shanghai Express* (qv); an adequate time-passer.

w John Meredyth Lucas d William Dieterle
ph Charles Lang m Dimitri Tiomkin

Joseph Cotten, Corinne Calvet, Edmund Gwenn, Marvin Miller

'Lacks flavour or distinction.' – *Leonard Maltin*

'Two Supreme Court Justices have been assassinated. One lone law student has stumbled upon the truth. An investigative journalist wants her story. Everyone else wants her dead.'

The Pelican Brief

US 1993 141m Technicolor
Warner (Alan J. Pakula, Pieter Jan Brugge)
S

A law student is stalked by hitmen after she speculates on the reasons behind the killings of two leading judges.

Mundane chase movie, a paranoid thriller that rarely rings true and mainly consists of Julia Roberts being chased but not caught. Her fans may enjoy it.

wd Alan J. Pakula novel John Grisham
ph Stephen Goldblatt m James Horner pd Philip Rosenberg ed Tom Rolf, Trudy Ship

Julia Roberts, Denzel Washington, Sam Shepard, John Heard, Tony Goldwyn, James B. Sikking, William Atherton, Robert Culp, Stanley Tucci, Hume Cronyn, John Lithgow

'This crackling thriller will have a long, prosperous box-office flight.' – *Variety*

'Pakula allows everyone to be briefly implicated, with menace poured on by the gallon, but fails to raise a spark of interest.' – *Lizzie Francke, Sight and Sound*

Pelle the Conqueror ****

Denmark/Sweden 1987 150m colour
Curzon/Danish Film Institute/Swedish Film Institute/Svensk Filmindustri/Per Holst
V, V*, L, S
original title: *Pelle Erobreren*

In the early 1900s, the young son of a Swedish immigrant worker enduring hardship on a Danish farm learns to be self-sufficient.

Winner of the Palme D'Or at the Cannes Film Festival in 1988, it matches an epic scope with domestic detail in a finely acted, beautifully photographed movie.

wd Bille August novel Martin Andersen Nexö
ph Jörgen Persson m Stefan Nilsson pd Anna Asp
ed Janus Billeskov Jansen

Max von Sydow, Pelle Hvenegaard, Erik Paaske, Kristina Tornqvist, Morten Jørgensen, Alex Strøbye, Astrid Villaume, Björn Granath

† It was released on video in two versions, one subtitled, one dubbed by American actors.

AA: best foreign film
AAN: Max von Sydow

Pelle Erobreren: see *Pelle the Conqueror*

The Penalty

US 1941 81m bw
MGM (Jack Chertok)

The son of a gangster is regenerated by farm life and turns against his father.

Antediluvian sweetness and light which wastes a good cast.

w Harry Ruskin, John C. Higgins d Harold S. Bucquet ph Harold Rosson m David Snell

Edward Arnold, Lionel Barrymore, Marsha Hunt, Robert Sterling, Gene Reynolds

Penalty of Fame: see *Okay America*

Pendulum *

US 1969 102m Technicolor
Columbia/Pendulum (Stanley Niss)
V*, L

A convicted murderer and rapist is freed on appeal and kills the wife of the detective who arrested him.

Heavy-going police melodrama, efficient but not very interesting.

w Stanley Niss d George Schaefer ph Lionel Lindon m Walter Scharf

George Peppard, Jean Seberg, Richard Kiley, Charles McGraw, Robert F. Lyons, Madeleine Sherwood

Penelope

US 1966 98m Metrocolor Panavision
MGM/Euterpe (Joe Pasternak, Arthur Loew Jnr)

The wife of a bank vice-president is a bank robber and kleptomaniac.

Would-be cute comedy which only sickens one for wasting its talent.

w George Wells novel E. V. Cunningham
d Arthur Hiller ph Harry Stradling m Johnny Williams

Natalie Wood, Ian Bannen, Dick Shawn, Peter Falk, Jonathan Winters, Lila Kedrova, Lou Jacobi, Norma Crane, Arthur Malet, Jerome Cowan

The Penguin Pool Murder *

US 1932 69m bw
RKO
L

Inspector Piper on a murder case is outsmarted by schoolmarm Hildegarde Withers.

Mystery comedy which started a short series: plot smothered by wisecracks.

w Willis Goldbeck novel Stuart Palmer d George Archainbaud

Edna May Oliver, James Gleason, Mae Clarke, Robert Armstrong, Donald Cook, Edgar Kennedy

'An odd blend of illogical happenings, but basically broad comedy.' – *Variety*

Penitentiary

US 1938 78m bw
Columbia
V*

A district attorney becomes prison warden, and his daughter falls for a convict.

Scene-for-scene remake of *The Criminal Code* (qv) but considerably less dynamic.

w Fred Niblo Jnr, Seton I. Miller play Martin Flavin d John Brahm

Walter Connolly, John Howard, Jean Parker, Robert Barrat, Marc Lawrence, Arthur Hohl, Paul Fix

Penn of Pennsylvania

GB 1941 79m bw
British National (Richard Vernon)
V*
US title: *The Courageous Mr Penn*

Persecuted Quakers leave England for America.

Stodgily fictionalized history.

w Anatole de Grunwald book William Penn by C. E. Vulliamy d Lance Comfort ph Ernest Palmer

Clifford Evans, Deborah Kerr, Denis Arundell, Aubrey Mallalieu, Henry Oscar, Max Adrian

Pennies from Heaven

US 1936 81m bw
Columbia
V*

A wanderer protects a homeless little girl from the truant officer.

Mild star musical, lucky enough to have a hit title song.

w Katherine Leslie Moore, William Rankin, Jo Swerling d Norman Z. McLeod

Bing Crosby, Edith Fellows, Madge Evans, Louis Armstrong and his band

AAN: song 'Pennies from Heaven' (m Arthur Johnson, ly Sidney Mitchell)

Pennies from Heaven *

US 1981 108m Metrocolor
MGM/Hera (Nora Kaye, Herbert Ross)
V, V*, L

In 1934 Chicago, a sheet music salesman consoles himself for his drab and tragic life by fantasies induced by his songs.

The essence of Dennis Potter's British TV serial was hard enough to get at; transposed to America it becomes unattractive nonsense, and the song sequences are not even well staged despite the enormous expense.

w Dennis Potter d Herbert Ross ph Gordon Willis md Marvin Hamlisch, Billy May pd Ken Adam

Steve Martin, Bernadette Peters, Christopher Walken, Jessica Harper, John McMartin

'All flash and style and no heart.' – *Roger Ebert*

AAN: Dennis Potter

Penny Paradise

GB 1938 72m bw
ATP

A tugboat captain thinks he has won the football pools; but the coupon wasn't posted.

An old, old story, put over with modest effectiveness.

w Tommy Thompson, W. L. Meade, Thomas Browne d Carol Reed

Edmund Gwenn, Betty Driver, Jimmy O'Dea, Maire O'Neill, Jack Livesey

Penny Points to Paradise

GB 1951 77m bw
Advance/Adelphi

A pools winner takes cash but nearly loses it to a forger.

Abysmally made comedy, only interesting as an early teaming of the Goons.

w John Ormonde d Tony Young

Harry Secombe, Peter Sellers, Spike Milligan, Alfred Marks, Bill Kerr, Freddie Frinton, Paddy O'Neil

Penny Princess

GB 1952 94m Technicolor
Rank/Conquest (Frank Godwin)

A New York shopgirl inherits a tiny European state and boosts its economy by marketing a mixture of cheese and schnapps.

Thin, spoofy comedy with mild moments of fun.

wd Val Guest ph Geoffrey Unsworth m Ronald Hammer

Dirk Bogarde, Yolande Donlan, A. E. Matthews, Anthony Oliver, Edwin Styles, Reginald Beckwith, Kynaston Reeves, Peter Butterworth, Laurence Naismith, Mary Clare, Desmond Walter-Ellis

Penny Serenade *
US   1941   120m   bw
Columbia (Fred Guiol)
V*, L

Courtship, marriage and the death of two children are recollected by a woman contemplating divorce.

Well-played but uneasy film which veers suddenly and disconcertingly from light comedy into tragedy.

w Morrie Ryskind   d George Stevens   ph Joseph Walker   m W. Franke Harling

Cary Grant, Irene Dunne, Beulah Bondi, Edgar Buchanan, Ann Doran

'To make something out of very little, and that so near at hand, is one of the tests of artistry.' – Otis Ferguson

'A tear compeller showing how Cary Grant and Irene Dunne lose first their own baby and then the one they adopt. Which, as Lady Bracknell would certainly have observed, looks like carelessness.' – James Agate

AAN: Cary Grant

Penrod and Sam
US   1937   68m   bw
Warner

Exploits of a club for juvenile sleuths.

Start of a second feature series which had little to do with the original period characters but was generally well received. Later the same year came Penrod and his Twin Brother, and in 1938 Penrod's Double Trouble.

w Lillie Hayward, Hugh Cummings from the characters created by Booth Tarkington   d William McGann

Billy Mauch, Frank Craven, Spring Byington, Craig Reynolds, Charles Halton

'Should serve as a nucleus for swell exploitation tie-ups.' – Variety

† There had been an earlier version in 1931, starring Leon Janney; and the family turned up again in the Doris Day musicals On Moonlight Bay and By the Light of the Silvery Moon.

Penthouse *
US   1933   90m   bw
Hunt Stromberg/MGM
V*, L
GB title: Crooks in Clover

When he outlives his usefulness to the underworld, a lawyer is framed for murder.

Sprightly murder comedy-drama which plays like a try-out for The Thin Man.

w Frances Goodrich, Albert Hackett   d W. S. Van Dyke

Warner Baxter, Myrna Loy, C. Henry Gordon, Nat Pendleton, Charles Butterworth, George E. Stone

'Well-sustained crime solution with smashing climax and arresting title.' – Variety

The Penthouse
GB   1967   96m   Eastmancolor
Paramount/Tahiti (Harry Fine)

Illicit lovers in an unfinished block of flats are terrorized by intruders.

Thoroughly objectionable and unpleasant melodrama with no attractive characters and no attempt to explain itself.

wd Peter Collinson   play The Meter Man by J. Scott Forbes   ph Arthur Lavis   m John Hawkesworth

Suzy Kendall, Terence Morgan, Tony Beckley, Norman Rodway, Martine Beswick

'Pornography in Pinter's clothing.' – MFB

The People against O'Hara *
US   1951   102m   bw
MGM (William H. Wright)

An ex-alcoholic defence lawyer sacrifices himself to prove his client's innocence.

Formula drama, well made and entertainingly performed, with snatches of bright dialogue.

w John Monks Jnr   novel Eleazar Lipsky   d John Sturges   ph John Alton   m Carmen Dragon

Spencer Tracy, Diana Lynn, Pat O'Brien, John Hodiak, James Arness, Arthur Shields, Eduardo Ciannelli, Louise Lorimer

The People Next Door
US   1970   93m   DeLuxe
Avco Embassy (Herb Brodkin)
V*

Suburban parents have trouble with their drug-addicted teenage daughter.

Hysterical melodrama with good credentials.

w J. P. Miller   TV play J. P. Miller   d David Greene   ph Gordon Willis   m Don Sebesky

Eli Wallach, Julie Harris, Hal Holbrook, Cloris Leachman, Stephen McHattie, Nehemiah Persoff

'As unlovely a picture of suburban living as one is likely to see.' – Judith Crist

People on Sunday *
Germany   1929   72m approx (24 fps)   bw   silent
Filmstudio 1929
original title: Menschen am Sonntag

Two couples spend a day in Berlin's countryside.

Influential semi-documentary with fascinating credits.

w Billy Wilder, Curt Siodmak   d Robert Siodmak, Fred Zinnemann, Edgar G. Ulmer   ph Eugen Schüfftan

Brigitte Borchert, Christl Ehlers, Annie Schreyer

The People that Time Forgot
GB   1977   90m   Technicolor
AIP/Amicus (John Dark)
V*

Major McBride tries to rescue his old friend from a prehistoric island on which he disappeared in 1916.

Tepid sequel to The Land that Time Forgot: even the dinosaurs don't rise to the occasion.

w Patrick Tilley   d Kevin Connor   ph Alan Hume   m John Scott   pd Maurice Carter

Patrick Wayne, Sarah Douglas, Dana Gillespie, Doug McClure, Thorley Walters, Shane Rimmer, Tony Britton

'They'll devour everything but your screams.'

The People under the Stairs *
US   1991   102m   DeLuxe
UIP/Universal/Alive (Marianne Maddalena, Stuart M. Besser)
V, V*, L, S

A 13-year-old boy discovers that the wealthy couple he attempts to rob have imprisoned in their cellar kidnapped youths who have become damaged mutants.

An effective horror film, or possibly a less effective allegory about the exploitation of the urban poor.

wd Wes Craven   ph Sandi Sissel   m Don Peake   pd Bryan Jones   sp Image Engineering Inc.   ed James Coblentz, Tom Walls

Brandon Adams, Everett McGill, Wendy Robie, A. J. Langer, Ving Rhames, Sean Whalen, Bill Cobbs, Kelly Jo Minter, Jeremy Roberts

'This revival of the plot-driven, exhausting, funny-pointed, suspense-horror picture is a welcome change.' – Kim Newman, Sight and Sound

People Will Talk
US   1935   60m   bw
Paramount

Mr and Mrs Wilton try to patch up their daughter's failing marriage.

Slight domestic comedy with popular leads.

w Herbert Fields, Sophie Kerr, F. Hugh Herbert   d Al Santell

Charles Ruggles, Mary Boland, Leila Hyams, Dean Jagger, Edward Brophy

'Strictly light summer fare and not solid enough to stand alone.' – Variety

People Will Talk **
US   1951   110m   bw
TCF (Darryl F. Zanuck)
V*

A surgeon's unorthodox psychological methods cause jealousy among his colleagues, especially when he falls in love with a pregnant patient.

Oddly entertaining jumble of melodrama, comedy, romance, speeches and a little mystery, all quite typical of its director.

wd Joseph L. Mankiewicz,   play Dr Praetorius by Curt Goetz   ph Milton Krasner   md Alfred Newman

Cary Grant, Jeanne Crain, Finlay Currie, Hume Cronyn, Walter Slezak, Sidney Blackmer, Basil Ruysdael

'A picture so mature and refreshingly frank as to hold that an erring young woman might be rewarded with a wise and loving mate is most certainly a significant milestone in the moral emancipation of American films.' – New York Times

Pepe
US   1960   195m   Eastmancolor   Cinemascope
Columbia/George Sidney (Jacques Gelman)

A Mexican peasant in Hollywood gets help from the stars.

Feeble and seemingly endless extravaganza in which the boring stretches far outnumber the rest, and few of the guests have anything worthwhile to do.

w Dorothy Kingsley, Claude Binyon   d George Sidney   ph Joe MacDonald   md Johnny Green   ed Viola Lawrence, Al Clark

Cantinflas, Dan Dailey, Shirley Jones, Ernie Kovacs, Jay North, William Demarest, Michael Callan, Maurice Chevalier, Bing Crosby, Richard Conte, Bobby Darin, Sammy Davis Jnr, Jimmy Durante, Zsa Zsa Gabor, Judy Garland, Hedda Hopper, Joey Bishop, Peter Lawford, Janet Leigh, Jack Lemmon, Kim Novak, André Previn, Donna Reed, Debbie Reynolds, Greer Garson, Edward G. Robinson, Cesar Romero, Frank Sinatra, Billie Burke, Tony Curtis, Dean Martin, Charles Coburn

AAN: Joe MacDonald; Johnny Green; song 'Faraway Part of Town' (m André Previn, ly Dory Langdon); editing

Pépé le Moko **
France   1936   90m   bw
Paris Film
V, V*

A Parisian gangster lives in the Algerian casbah where the police can't get at him; but love causes him to emerge and be shot.

Romantic melodrama modelled on the American gangster film but with a decided poetic quality of its own: the Americans promptly paid it the compliment of remaking it as the not-too-bad Algiers.

w Henri Jeanson, Roger d'Ashelbe   novel Roger d'Ashelbe (Henri La Barthe)   d Julien Duvivier   ph Jules Kruger   m Vincent Scotto   ad Jacques Krauss

Jean Gabin, Mireille Ballin, Gabriel Gabrio, Lucas Gridoux

'One of the most compelling of all French films.' – New Yorker, 1977

'Perhaps there have been pictures as exciting on the thriller level . . . but I cannot remember one which has succeeded so admirably in raising the thriller to a poetic level.' – *Graham Greene*

Pepi, Luci, Bom

Spain   1980   80m   colour
Metro/Figaro (Pepon Corominas)
V, V*
original title: *Pepi, Luci, Bom y otras chicas del montón*

A woman raped by a policeman takes her revenge by encouraging his wife to form a lesbian relationship with a sadistic singer.

Almodóvar's first full-length feature attempts to shock and surprise with a kitsch mix of sex, cruelty and eccentricity.

wd Pedro Almodóvar   *ph* Paco Femenia*ed* Pepe Salcedo

Carmen Maura, Félix Rotaeta, Olvido 'Alaska' Gara, Eva Siva, Diego Alvarez, Pedro Almodóvar

'The roots of Almodóvar's down-and-dirty, intentionally amoral and often disgusting films are abundant in *Pepi, Luci, Bom*.' – *Variety*

Perceval Le Gallois

France   1978   140m   colour   Panavision
Les Films du Losange/Barbet Schroeder/FR3/ARD/SSR/RAI/
    Gaumont (Margaret Menegoz)
V

A naïve Welsh youth becomes a knight at the court of King Arthur and meets the Fisher King.

This is less a film than an interesting, though not engrossing, illustrated accompaniment, against stylized backgrounds, to a long medieval poem.

wd Eric Rohmer   *poem* Chrétien de Troyes
ph Nestor Almendros   *m* Guy Robert   *ad* Jean-Pierre Kohut-Svelko   *ed* Cecile Decugis

Fabrice Luchini, André Dussollier, Solange Boulanger, Catherine Schroeder, Francisco Orozco, Deborah Nathan, Pascal Ogier

'Combines real people and real horses with toy castles and small, stylized trees, and the effect is just the opposite of what Rohmer could have wanted: it's cute. And it's cute for only a short time because nothing can be cute for a long time.' – *Stanley Kauffmann*

Percy

GB   1971   103m   Eastmancolor
Anglo EMI/Welbeck (Betty E. Box)
V

After an unfortunate accident, a young man undergoes a successful penis transplant, and sets out to discover who the donor was.

Barrage of phallic jokes, some quite funny, but mostly as witless as the whole idea.

w Hugh Leonard   *novel* Raymond Hitchcock
d Ralph Thomas   *ph* Ernest Steward   *m* Ray Davies

Hywel Bennett, Elke Sommer, *Denholm Elliott*, Britt Ekland, Cyd Hayman

Percy's Progress

GB   1974   101m   Eastmancolor
EMI (Betty E. Box)
V, V*

A chemical causes impotence in all males except the owner of the first transplanted penis.

Percy dug deep, but this is really the bottom of the barrel.

w Sid Colin   *d* Ralph Thomas   *ph* Tony Imi
m Tony Macauley

Leigh Lawson, Elke Sommer, Denholm Elliott, Judy Geeson, Harry H. Corbett, Vincent Price, Adrienne Posta, Julie Ege, James Booth

'Health clubs – more sex than sweat?'
Perfect

US   1985   115m   Technicolor
V, V*, L

An aerobics instructor (female) meets a reporter (male) doing a story on health clubs, but it isn't love at first sight.

Nervy, unattractive drama which didn't find an audience.

w Aaron Latham, James Bridges   *d* James Bridges
ph Gordon Willis   *m* Ralph Burns

John Travolta, Jamie Lee Curtis, Anne de Salvo, Marilu Henner, Laraine Newman

'Guilty of the sins it condemns – superficiality, manipulation and smugness.' – *Variety*

A Perfect Couple *

US   1979   112m   DeLuxe
TCF/Lions Gate (Robert Altman)

A middle-aged Greek much dependent on his family meets a jazz singer through a dating service.

A free-speaking update of *Marty*, featuring the Altman repertory company; intelligent sequences are muffled by the familiar Altman messiness of approach.

w Robert Altman, Allan Nicholls   *d* Robert Altman
ph Edmond L. Koons   *md* Tom Pierson, Tony Berg

Paul Dooley, Marta Heflin, Titos Vandis, Belita Moreno, Henry Gibson, Dimitra Arliss

'Has the usual Altman assets: technical deftness, idiosyncrasy, unexpected subject. But the deftness rattles around in a vacuum, the idiosyncrasy – because unsupported in theme or dynamics – degenerates quickly into egotism, and the unexpected subject is so poorly developed that it quickly becomes sterile.' – *Stanley Kauffmann*

Perfect Day *

US   1929   20m   bw
Hal Roach
V

Various problems delay a family's departure for a picnic.

Technically a most adept star comedy but its repetition can annoy.

w Hal Roach, Leo McCarey, H. M. Walker   *d* James Parrott

Laurel and Hardy, Edgar Kennedy

† The picnic was originally to have occupied the second reel, but the departure gags swelled to occupy the entire footage.

Perfect Friday *

GB   1970   95m   Eastmancolor
London Screenplays/Sunnymede (Dimitri de Grunwald)

A bank manager engages aristocratic help to rob his own bank.

Middling comedy caper.

w Anthony Greville-Bell, J. Scott Forbes   *d* Peter Hall   *ph* Alan Hume   *m* Johnny Dankworth
pd Terence Marsh

Stanley Baker, Ursula Andress, David Warner, Patience Collier, T. P. McKenna, David Waller, Joan Benham, Julian Orchard

The Perfect Furlough

US   1958   93m   Eastmancolor   Cinemascope
U-I (Robert Arthur)
V*
GB title: *Strictly for Pleasure*

To help morale at a remote Arctic army unit, one of the men is selected to enjoy the perfect leave in Paris on behalf of the others.

Amiable farce which entertains while it's on but is quickly forgotten.

w Stanley Shapiro   *d* Blake Edwards   *ph* Philip Lathrop   *m* Frank Skinner

Tony Curtis, Janet Leigh, Elaine Stritch, Keenan Wynn, Troy Donahue, King Donovan, Linda Cristal

The Perfect Gentleman

US   1935   73m   bw
MGM
GB title: *The Imperfect Lady*

A retired officer helps an actress make a comeback.

Genial comedy which didn't quite work well enough to make an English variety star popular on both sides of the Atlantic.

w Edward Childs Carpenter   *d* Tim Whelan

Cicely Courtneidge, Frank Morgan, Heather Angel, Herbert Mundin, Henry Stephenson

The Perfect Marriage

US   1946   88m   bw
Paramount/Hal B. Wallis

On their tenth wedding anniversary, a happy couple have a row and start divorce proceedings.

Wispy comedy, unmemorable and rather tiresome.

w Leonard Spigelgass   *play* Samson Raphaelson
d Lewis Allen   *ph* Russell Metty   *m* Frederick Hollander

David Niven, Loretta Young, Eddie Albert, Nona Griffith, Virginia Field, Jerome Cowan, Rita Johnson, Charles Ruggles, Nana Bryant, ZaSu Pitts

'Another film about disillusionment and reconciliation in a mansion with constant evening dress.' – *Sunday Times*

The Perfect Murder

India   1988   95m   colour
Enterprise/Merchant Ivory (Wahid Chowhan)

A Bombay detective investigates an attempted murder, with a little diamond smuggling on the side.

Keating's fictional Inspector Ghote transfers poorly to the screen in a film that is more slapstick than thriller.

w Zafar Hai, H. R. F. Keating   *novel* H. R. F. Keating
d Zafar Hai   *ph* Walter Lassally   *m* Richard Robbins   *pd* Kiran Patki, Sartaj Noorani
ed Charles Rees

Naseeruddin Shah, Stellen Skarsgard, Dalip Tahil, Madhur Jaffrey, Sakeena Jaffrey, Dinshaw Daji

The Perfect Snob

US   1941   63m   bw
Walter Morosco/TCF

A woman tosses her daughter at millionaires. The girl settles on a poor boy . . . who turns out to be a millionaire after all.

Predictable comedy with competent cast.

w Lee Loeb, Harold Buchman   *d* Ray McCarey

Charles Ruggles, Charlotte Greenwood, Lynn Bari, Cornel Wilde, Anthony Quinn, Alan Mowbray

'. . . They Thought He Was A "Mamma's Boy" . . . But When He Broke Loose! . . . Wow!'
The Perfect Specimen

US   1937   82m   bw
Warner (Harry Joe Brown)

The grandmother of a rich young man brings him up uncontaminated by the world, but when a girl crashes her car into his fence he proves fitted to deal with the situation.

Fantasticated comedy a long way after *Mr Deeds* and too slow by half.

w Norman Reilly Raine, Lawrence Riley, Brewster Morse, Fritz Falkenstein, Samuel Hopkins Adams
d Michael Curtiz   *ph* Charles Rosher

Errol Flynn, Joan Blondell, Hugh Herbert, Edward Everett Horton, May Robson, Dick Foran, Beverly Roberts, Allen Jenkins

'Upper bracket comedy for the family trade.' – *Variety*

Perfect Strangers **
GB   1945   102m   bw
MGM/London Films (Alexander Korda)
US title: *Vacation from Marriage*

A downtrodden clerk and his dowdy wife go to war, and come back unrecognizably improved.

Pleasant comedy with good actors; but the turnabout of two such caricatures really strains credibility.

w Clemence Dane, Anthony Pelissier   *d* Alexander Korda   *ph* Georges Périnal   *m* Clifton Parker

Robert Donat, Deborah Kerr, Glynis Johns, Ann Todd, Roland Culver, Elliot Mason, Eliot Makeham, Brefni O'Rourke, Edward Rigby

'War is supposed to be the catalyst, the sportsman's bracer; and the film's chief weakness is its failure to show the briefly exalted couple sinking back, uncontrollably, under their peacetime stone.' – *James Agee*

'It glows with laughter and honest sentiment.' – *New York Times*

AA: original story (Clemence Dane)

'They met by chance, and once they kissed, they knew they never should have!'
Perfect Strangers
US   1950   87m   bw
Warner (Jerry Wald)
GB title: *Too Dangerous to Love*

Two jurors on a murder case fall in love.

Talkative, unlikely, and rather boring potboiler.

w Edith Sommer   *play Ladies and Gentlemen* by Charles MacArthur, Ben Hecht   *d* Bretaigne Windust   *ph* Peverell Marley   *m* Leigh Harline

Ginger Rogers, Dennis Morgan, Thelma Ritter, Margalo Gillmore, Howard Freeman, Alan Reed, Paul Ford, George Chandler

Perfect Strangers (1984): see Blind Alley

Perfect Understanding *
GB   1933   80m   bw
Gloria Swanson British Pictures Ltd

A couple agree to marry on condition that they will never disagree with each other.

Silly comedy with a unique star combination looking acutely uncomfortable.

w Miles Malleson, Michael Powell   *d* Cyril Gardner   *ph* Curt Courant

Gloria Swanson, Laurence Olivier, John Halliday, Nigel Playfair, Michael Farmer, Genevieve Tobin, Nora Swinburne

'Dull and talky picture, done in the uninspiring British style.' – *Variety*

A Perfect Weekend: see The St Louis Kid

The Perfect Woman *
GB   1949   89m   bw
GFD/Two Cities (George and Alfred Black)

A girl changes places with her inventor uncle's robot woman.

Described as a romp, this is in fact a pretty good farce, very fast moving and well played after the usual expository start.

w George Black, Bernard Knowles, J. B. Boothroyd   *play* Wallace Geoffrey, Basil Mitchell   *d* Bernard Knowles   *ph* Jack Hildyard   *m* Arthur Wilkinson

Patricia Roc, Nigel Patrick, Stanley Holloway, David Hurst, Miles Malleson, Irene Handl

A Perfect World *
US   1993   138m   Technicolor   Panavision
Warner/Malpaso (Mark Johnson, David Valdes)
S

A father–son relationship develops between an escaped convict and the seven-year-old boy he takes as a hostage.

A very American mix of male bonding, road movie and thriller that every now and then reveals a few signs of originality.

w John Lee Hancock   *d* Clint Eastwood   *ph* Jack N. Green   *m* Lennie Niehaus   *pd* Henry Bumstead   *ed* Joel Cox, Ron Spang

Kevin Costner, Clint Eastwood, Laura Dern, T. J. Lowther, Keith Szarabajka, Leo Burmester, Paul Hewitt, Bradley Whitford

'A somber, subtly nuanced study of an escaped con's complex relationship with an abducted boy that carries a bit too much narrative flab for its own good.' – *Variety*

'As jarring and fundamentally goofy as the movie is, it never feels like an ordinary, generic Hollywood product: at every moment, there's something to gape at – sometimes in admiration, often in disbelief.' – *Terrence Rafferty, New Yorker*

Perfectly Normal *
Canada   1990   105m   colour
Palace/Bialystock & Bloom/Téléfilm Canada/BSB/Skyhost/British Screen (Michael Burns)
V, V*, L

An ice hockey-playing brewery worker teams up with a dubious chef to open an operatic restaurant.

Bizarre comedy of eccentric lives in a small-town setting.

w Eugene Lipinski, Paul Quarrington   *d* Yves Simoneau   *ph* Alain Dostie   *m* Richard Gregoire   *pd* Anne Pritchard   *ed* Ronald Sanders

Robbie Coltrane, Michael Riley, Deborah Duchene, Eugene Lipinski, Jack Nichols, Elizabeth Harpur, Patricia Gage, Kenneth Welsh

'The movie is too eager to be loved, but has its moments.' – *Philip French, Observer*

Performance ***
GB   1970   105m   Technicolor
Warner/Goodtimes (Donald Cammell)
V, V*, L, S

A vicious gangster moves in with an ex-pop star.

Dense, Pinterish melodrama about alter egos.

w Donald Cammell   *d* Nicolas Roeg, Donald Cammell   *ph* Nicolas Roeg   *md* Randy Newman   *m* Jack Nitzsche

James Fox, Mick Jagger, Anita Pallenberg, Michèle Breton, Stanley Meadows, Allan Cuthbertson

'A humourless, messy mixture of crime and decadence and drug-induced hallucination.' – *New Yorker, 1980*

'You don't have to be a drug addict, pederast, sado-masochist or nitwit to enjoy it, but being one or more of these things would help.' – *John Simon*

Péril: see Death in a French Garden

Péril en la Demeure: see Death in a French Garden

Perilous Holiday
US   1946   89m   bw
Columbia

A newly acquainted couple become involved with counterfeiters in Mexico City.

Passable comedy-crime programme filler.

w Robert Carson, Roy Chanslor   *d* Edward H. Griffith

Pat O'Brien, Ruth Warrick, Alan Hale, Minna Gombell

A Perilous Journey
US   1953   87m   bw
Republic (W. J. O'Sullivan)

A party of women sail to the California goldfields to sell themselves into marriage.

Reasonably lively action drama.

w Richard Wormser   *novel The Golden Tide* by Virgie Roe   *d* R. G. Springsteen   *ph* Jack Marta   *m* Victor Young

Vera Ralston, David Brian, Charles Winninger, Scott Brady, Virginia Grey, Ben Cooper

Perils of Nyoka
US   1942   bw   serial: 15 eps
Republic

Archaeologists seek the long lost Tablets of Hippocrates, and are helped by a girl explorer seeking her lost father.

Wildly plotted serial; incidents routine.

d William Witney

Kay Aldridge, Clayton Moore, William Benedict, Charles Middleton

The Perils of Pauline
US   1934   bw   serial: 12 eps
Universal

The daughter of a noted scientist seeks a deadly gas formula in Indo-China.

Semi-remake of the famous silent serial.

d Ray Taylor

Evalyn Knapp, Robert Allan, James Durkin, Sonny Ray, Frank Lackteen

The Perils of Pauline *
US   1947   96m   Technicolor
Paramount (Sol C. Siegel)

The career of silent serial queen Pearl White.

An agreeable recreation of old time Hollywood, with plenty of slapstick chases but a shade too much sentiment also.

w P. J. Wolfson   *d* George Marshall   *ph* Ray Rennahan   *md* Robert Emmett Dolan

Betty Hutton, John Lund, Billy de Wolfe, William Demarest, Constance Collier, Frank Faylen, William Farnum, Paul Panzer, Snub Pollard, Creighton Hale, Chester Conklin, James Finlayson, Hank Mann, Bert Roach, Francis McDonald, Chester Clute

'People who can accept such stuff as solid gold have either forgotten a lot, or never knew first-rate slapstick when they saw it, twenty or thirty years ago, when it was one of the wonders of the world.' – *James Agee*

AAN: song 'I Wish I Didn't Love You So' (*m/y* Frank Loesser)

Perils of the Royal Mounted
US   1942   bw   serial: 15 eps
Columbia

Indians accused of massacring settlers turn out to have been white outlaws in disguise.

The Mounties get their man once more.   *d* James W. Horne

Robert Stevens, Kenneth MacDonald, Herbert Rawlinson, Nell O'Day

Perils of the Wilderness
US   1956   bw   serial: 15 eps
Columbia

The Mounties pursue a ruthless crime lord in the Canadian northwest.

Unsurprising serial, one of the last to be made.

d Spencer Bennet

Dennis Moore, Richard Emory, Eve Anderson, Kenneth MacDonald

Period of Adjustment

US   1962   122m   bw   Panavision
MGM/Marton (Lawrence Weingarten)

A Korean War veteran has the shakes and his sexual adequacy is affected, as his wife furiously discovers.

Comedy of maladjustment, tolerably witty but unsuitably widescreened.

w Isobel Lennart   play Tennessee Williams
d George Roy Hill   ph Paul C. Vogel   m Lyn Murray

Tony Franciosa, Jane Fonda, Jim Hutton, Lois Nettleton

Les Perles de la Couronne *

France   1937   118m   bw
Serge Sandburg/Tobis

The history over four centuries of seven pearls given by Pope Clement VII to Catherine de Medici.

Generally amusing series of historical sketches in Guitry's inimitable style.

w Sacha Guitry   d Sacha Guitry, Christian-Jaque

Sacha Guitry, Renée Saint-Cyr, Lyn Harding, Percy Marmont, Arletty, Claude Dauphin, Raimu, Jean-Louis Barrault, Jacqueline Delubac

'Headed to bring in returns both at home and abroad.' – Variety

† The picture tried, but failed, to be intelligible without sub-titles to all language-speakers.

Permanent Record

US   1988   91m   Technicolor
Paramount (Frank Mancuso Jnr)
V, V*, L

The unexpected suicide of a popular high school student has a traumatic effect on his friends.

Well-meaning but dull drama of teenage angst.

w Jarre Fees, Alice Liddle, Larry Ketron   d Marisa Silver   ph Frederick Elmes   m Joe Strummer
pd Michel Levesque   ed Robert Brown

Keanu Reeves, Alan Boyce, Michelle Meyrink, Jennifer Rubin, Barry Corbin, Kathy Baker, Pamela Gidley, Richard Bradford

Permission to Kill

US/Austria   1975   97m   Technicolor   Panavision
Warner/Sascha (Paul Mills)
V*

British agents try to stop a communist returning home from the west.

Prolonged, confusing and boring spy melodrama in which everyone looks understandably glum.

w Robin Estridge   novel Robin Estridge   d Cyril Frankel   ph Freddie Young   m Richard Rodney Bennett

Bekim Fehmiu, Dirk Bogarde, Ava Gardner, Timothy Dalton, Frederic Forrest

'Pretentious political mishmash.' – MFB

Perri **

US   1957   75m   Technicolor
Walt Disney (Winston Hibler)

The life of a squirrel.

Disney's first True Life Fantasy, in which live footage of animals is manipulated against artificial backgrounds to produce an effect as charming and unreal as a cartoon.

w Ralph Wright, Winston Hibler   novel Felix Salten
d Ralph Wright   ph various   m Paul Smith

AAN: Paul Smith

Persecution

GB   1974   96m   Eastmancolor
Fanfare/Tyburn (Kevin Francis)
V*

A rich American woman in England is hated by her son and fearful that her murky past will be revealed.

Rich but not engrossing nonsense, somewhat à la Baby Jane, with hazy script and stolid production.

w Robert B. Hutton, Rosemary Wootten   d Don Chaffey   ph Ken Talbot   m Paul Ferris

Lana Turner, Ralph Bates, Olga Georges-Picot, Trevor Howard, Suzan Farmer, Ronald Howard, Patrick Allen

'Gives off the unmistakable odour of damp mothballs.' – Michael Billington, Illustrated London News

The Persecution and Assassination of Jean-Paul Marat: see The Marat/Sade

Persona ****

Sweden   1966   81m   bw
Svensk Filmindustri (Lars-Owe Carlberg)
V*

A nurse begins to identify with her mentally ill patient, and herself has a nervous breakdown.

Intense clinical study presented in a very complex cinematic manner which tends to obscure the main theme while providing endless fascination for cinéastes.

wd Ingmar Bergman   ph Sven Nykvist   m Lars Johan Werle   ad Bibi Lindström

Liv Ullmann, Bibi Andersson, Margaretha Krook, Gunnar Björnstrand

'Reactions have ranged from incomprehension to irritation with what is dismissed as a characteristic piece of self-indulgence on Bergman's part – Bergman talking to himself again.' – David Wilson, MFB

'A puzzling, obsessive film that Bergman seems not so much to have worked out as to have torn from himself.' – New Yorker, 1977

Personal Affair

GB   1953   83m   bw
Rank/Two Cities (Anthony Darnborough)

A schoolmaster and his neurotic wife run into trouble when a girl pupil develops a crush on him.

Preposterous domestic drama making much ado about nothing.

w Lesley Storm   play Lesley Storm   d Anthony Pelissier   ph Reg Wyer   m William Alwyn

Leo Genn, Gene Tierney, Glynis Johns, Pamela Brown

Personal Best

US   1982   122m   Technicolor
Warner (Robert Towne)
V*

A female Olympic track star has a lesbian relationship.

So what, is the response to two numbing hours of tedium.

wd Robert Towne   ph Michael Chapman   m Jack Nitzsche

Mariel Hemingway, Scott Glenn, Patrice Donnelly, Kenny Moore, Jim Moody

'There's an undercurrent of flabbergasted awe in this celebration of women's bodies, and everything in the movie is physically charged.' – Pauline Kael, New Yorker

Personal Choice: see Beyond the Stars

Personal Column (1939): see Pièges

Personal Column: see Lured

Personal Maid's Secret

US   1935   60m   bw
Bryan Foy/Warner

A maid's financial tips keep her master and mistress solvent.

Modest comedy which was well liked at the time.

w F. Hugh Herbert, Lillie Hayward   story Lillian Day   d Arthur Greville Collins

Ruth Donnelly, Anita Louise, Warren Hull, Margaret Lindsay, Frank Albertson, Arthur Treacher

Personal Property *

US   1937   84m   bw
MGM (John W. Considine Jnr)
V*
GB title: The Man in Possession

An American widow in England, in financial straits, falls for the bailiff sent to keep an eye on her.

Moderate star comedy which still amuses.

w Hugh Mills, Ernest Vajda   play The Man in Possession by H. M. Harwood   d W. S. Van Dyke II   ph William Daniels   m Franz Waxman

Jean Harlow, Robert Taylor, Reginald Owen, Una O'Connor, Henrietta Crosman, E. E. Clive, Cora Witherspoon, Barnett Parker

'Harmless boudoir farce, for the undergraduates.' – Variety

Personal Services *

GB   1987   105m   Eastmancolor
Zenith (Tim Bevan)
V, V*, L

Adventures of a London madam.

Rather astonishing study of British attitudes to sex; not for Aunt Edna, but with a fair measure of interest for many.

w David Leland   d Terry Jones   ph Roger Deakins
ed George Akers

Julie Walters, Alec McCowen, Shirley Stelfox, Danny Schiller, Victoria Hardcastle

The Personality Kid

US   1934   70m   bw
Warner

A prizefighter becomes intoxicated by his own success and ignores his faithful wife.

Mediocre filler wasting reliable stars.

w F. Hugh Herbert, Erwin Gelsey, Gene Towne, Graham Baker   d Alan Crosland

Pat O'Brien, Glenda Farrell, Claire Dodd, Henry O'Neill, Robert Gleckler, Thomas Jackson

'Rates poorly: strictly cuffo yarn.' – Variety

'She's the woman behind the killer behind the gun!'
Persons in Hiding *

US   1939   71m   bw
Paramount

A bored girl absconds with gangsters and becomes a public enemy.

Interesting programmer which led to several sequels using the same book as source; this one was vaguely inspired by the story of Bonnie and Clyde.

w William R. Lipman, Horace McCoy   book J. Edgar Hoover   d Louis King   ph Harry Fischbeck   m Boris Morros

Patricia Morison, J. Carrol Naish, Lynne Overman, William Henry, Helen Twelvetrees, William Frawley

'Strong supporter for the duals . . . will depend entirely on rep of J. Edgar Hoover to attract.' – Variety

'A little on the tame side, but distinguished by the presence of a crooked and merciless heroine.' – Graham Greene

Persons Unknown *

Italy   1958   105m   bw
Lux/Vides/Cinecittà (Franco Cristaldi)
original title: *I Soliti Ignoti*; US title: *Big Deal on Madonna Street*

Adventures of a gang of incompetent thieves, who get arrested more often than they get away, and finally, elaborately drill through a wall into the bank . . . only to find it's the wrong wall and they are in another room of the same flat.

Spoof black comedy working up to an elaborate take-off of *Rififi*; a great success in Italy and the USA, mildly received elsewhere.

w Age Scarpelli, Suso Cecchi d'Amico, Mario Monicelli   d Mario Monicelli   ph Gianni di Venanzo   m Piero Umiliani

Vittorio Gassman, Renato Salvatori, Toto, Marcello Mastroianni, Memmo Carotenuto, Carla Gravina, Rosanna Rory

Pet Sematary

US   1989   103m   Technicolor   Panavision
UIP/Paramount (Richard P. Rubinstein)
V, V*, L S

A doctor and his family move into a house near a burial ground where the dead can be brought back to life.

Turgid horror, lacking in suspense and excitement.

w Stephen King   novel Stephen King   d Mary Lambert   ph Peter Stein   m Elliot Goldenthal
pd Michael Z. Hanan   ed Michael Hill, Daniel Hanley

Dale Midkiff, Fred Gwynne, Denise Crosby, Brad Greenquist, Michael Lombard, Miko Hughes, Blaze Berdahl

'If all the usual excesses of the genre are well exercised, King's old-dark-house clichés have come up with far more edge and shine than he deserved.' – *Philip Strick, MFB*

'Raise some hell.'
Pet Sematary Two

US   1992   102m   DuArt
Paramount (Ralph S. Singleton)
V, V*

A father and son move to a new house, next to a cemetery where the dead can be resurrected.

Nasty little shocker, with no redeeming features.

w Richard Outten   novel Stephen King   d Mary Lambert   ph Russell Carpenter   m Mark Governor
pd Michelle Minch   sp Peter Chesney, Steve Johnson   ed Tom Finan

Edward Furlong, Anthony Edwards, Clancy Brown, Jared Rushton, Darlanne Fluegel, Jason McGuire, Sarah Trigger, Lisa Waltz

'About 50% better than its predecessor, which is to say it's not very good at all.' – *Variety*

'A complete waste of time.' – *Nigel Floyd, The Dark Side*

Pétain

France   1992   133m   colour
Gala/Mod/France 2 (Jacques Kirsner)

In 1940, the ageing Marshall Pétain becomes the leader of France; in Vichy, he makes peace with the invading German army and, under the influence of Laval, collaborates with the Nazis.

Mundane biopic that plods through the facts without making them seem particularly relevant.

w Jean-Pierre Marchand   book Marc Ferro   d Jean Marboeuf   ph Dominique Bouilleret   m Georges Garvarentz   pd Jerome Clément   ed Anne-France Lebrun

Jacques Dufilho, Jean Yanne, Jean-Pierre Cassel, Jean-Claude Dreyfus, Antoinette Moya, Julie Marboeuf, Ludwig Haas (as Hitler)

'A major accomplishment. Taboo-breaking and ideologically irreproachable pic about Vichy and its legacy is a clear and nuanced – and long overdue – view of crucial French history. Unfailingly cinematic, intelligently structured and beautifully cast, pic is essential viewing for Gallic auds and deserves to be shown everywhere.' – *Variety*

'The film plods along, serenely untroubled by anything that would justify its 133 minutes. Quiet days in Vichy indeed.' – *Sheila Johnston, Independent*

'Honeymoon's over – time to get married!'
Pete 'n Tillie *

US   1972   100m   Technicolor   Panavision
Universal (Julius J. Epstein)

The tragi-comic marriage of two eccentrics.

Curious: plain drama treated as comedy, with surprisingly satisfactory results, but not an example to be followed.

w Julius J. Epstein   novel *Witch's Milk* by Peter de Vries   d Martin Ritt   ph John Alonzo   m John T. Williams

Walter Matthau, Carol Burnett, Geraldine Page, René Auberjonois, Barry Nelson, Henry Jones

'For the most part an amusing, moving, sentimental comedy. The wisecracks stay on this side of human possibility – that is, we don't feel, as we do so often with Neil Simon, that the characters have private gag writers in their homes.' – *Stanley Kauffmann*

AAN: Julius J. Epstein; Geraldine Page

'The story of a jazz-man of the wide-open 20s . . . caught in the crossfire of its blazing .38s!'
Pete Kelly's Blues *

US   1955   95m   Warnercolor   Cinemascope
(Warner) Mark VII Ltd (Jack Webb)
V (W), V*, L

Jazz musicians in the twenties get involved with gangsters.

Minor cult film, mainly for the score; dramatically it is not exactly compelling.

w Richard L. Breen   d Jack Webb   ph Hal Rosson
ph Harper Goff   m Sammy Cahn, Ray Heindorf, Arthur Hamilton, Matty Matlock

Jack Webb, Edmond O'Brien, Janet Leigh, Peggy Lee, Andy Devine, *Ella Fitzgerald*, Lee Marvin, Martin Milner

'Concerned with striking attitudes and establishing an atmosphere rather than developing anything very coherent in the way of narrative . . . one remains aware of an over-deliberate straining after effect.' – *Penelope Houston*

AAN: Peggy Lee

'The most beautiful romance in all modern literature!'
Peter Ibbetson *

US   1935   85m   bw
Paramount (Louis D. Lighton)

Childhood sweethearts meet again as adults, are separated when he is imprisoned for her husband's murder, but are reunited in heaven.

Downright peculiar romantic fantasy, even more oddly cast, but extremely well produced.

w Vincent Lawrence, Waldemar Young, Constance Collier   novel George du Maurier   d Henry Hathaway   ph Charles Lang   m Ernst Toch

Gary Cooper, Ann Harding, Ida Lupino, John Halliday, Douglass Dumbrille, Virginia Weidler, Dickie Moore, Doris Lloyd

'In a day and a world hard-boiled and realistic Paramount hopes to sell a picture about dreams and beauty and love. It just isn't in the cards.' – *Variety*

'A triumph of surrealist thought.' – *André Breton*

'One of the world's ten best films.' – *Luis Buñuel*

AAN: Ernst Toch

Peter Pan ***

US   1953   76m   Technicolor
Walt Disney
V, V*, L

Three London children are taken into fairyland by a magic flying boy who cannot grow up.

Solidly crafted cartoon version of a famous children's play; not Disney's best work, but still miles ahead of the competition.

supervisor Ben Sharpsteen   d Wilfred Jackson, Clyde Geronimi, Hamilton Luske   m Oliver Wallace

voices of Bobbie Driscoll, Kathryn Beaumont, Hans Conried, Bill Thompson, Heather Angel

'A painful travesty.' – *C. A. Lejeune*

Peter Rabbit and the Tales of Beatrix Potter:
see *Tales of Beatrix Potter*

Peter the Great *

USSR   1937   96m   bw
Lenfilm

The rise to power of the famous autocrat.

Standard Russian first feature with plenty of action and striking composition, but not really memorable.

w Alexei Tolstoy, Vladimir Petrov   d Vladimir Petrov

Nikolai Simonov, Nikolai Cherkassov, Alla Tarasova, M. Zharov

'Surprisingly strong: a cinch in Russian-languagers.' – *Variety*

'A comedy about love, friendship and other natural disasters.'
Peter's Friends **

GB   1992   101m   Technicolor
Entertainment/Renaissance/SamuelGoldwyn/Channel 4
(Kenneth Branagh)
V, V*, L

A decade after they left university, a group of former friends get together for a New Year's reunion at a country mansion.

A British variation on *The Big Chill* that is a good deal chillier, with a cast too familiar from innumerable television comedies to be entirely convincing in their roles.

w Martin Bergman, Rita Rudner   d Kenneth Branagh   ph Roger Lanser   m Gavin Greenaway
pd Tim Harvey   ed Andrew Marcus

Kenneth Branagh, Alphonsia Emmanuel, Stephen Fry, Hugh Laurie, Phyllida Law, Alex Lowe, Rita Rudner, Tony Slattery, Imelda Staunton, Emma Thompson, Richard Briers

'Well written, beautifully performed and highly entertaining.' – *Derek Malcolm, Guardian*

'A lot more work is called for all round before these likeable people produce something worthy to be called disposable film entertainment.' – *Adam Mars-Jones, Independent*

'Awful, with glimpses of wit. The script is hopelessly schematic: one long, drawing-room chat in which people dish each other, then leave the room so they can be talked about.' – *Richard Corliss, Time*

The Peterville Diamond

GB   1942   85m   bw
Warner (A. H. Salomon)

A bored wife revives her husband's interest by cultivating the advances of a jewel thief.

Modest comedy-drama, smoothly presented: the same play formed the basis of Dieterle's *Jewel Robbery*.

w Brock Williams, Gordon Wellesley   play *Jewel Robbery* by Ladislas Fodor   d Walter Forde
ph Basil Emmott   md Jack Beaver

Anne Crawford, Donald Stewart, Renee Houston, Oliver Wakefield, Charles Heslop, William Hartnell, Felix Aylmer, Charles Victor

Pete's Dragon

US 1977 127m Technicolor
Walt Disney (Ron Miller, Jerome Courtland)
V, V*, L

In Maine in 1900, a nine-year-old boy escapes from grasping foster-parents with his pet dragon, which no one but himself can see.

A kind of juvenile rewrite of *Harvey*. The dragon is drawn (rather poorly) and the human characters are not exactly three-dimensional. A long way from *Mary Poppins*.

w Malcolm Marmorstein *story* Seton I. Miller, S. S. Field *d* Don Chaffey *ph* Frank Phillips *animation* Ken Anderson *md* Irwin Kostal *songs* Al Kasha, Joel Hirschhorn *ch* Onna White

Sean Marshall, Mickey Rooney, Jim Dale, Helen Reddy, Red Buttons, Shelley Winters, Jim Backus, Joe E. Ross, Ben Wrigley

'For a Disney film it's terribly badly made, in parts so clumsy that it looks like the work of the Burbank Amateur Camera Club.' – *Barry Took, Punch*

AAN: music; song 'Candle on the Water'

La Petite Bande **

France 1983 91m colour
Squirrel/Gaumont-Stand'Art/FR3/Hamster Productions (Denis Mermet)

A gang of English children stow away to France where they cause mayhem and save the world from a gang of wicked adults before ending up on a desert island.

Lively and subversive entertainment intended for children.

w Gilles Perrault, Michel Deville, Yan Appas, Joan Népami *d* Michel Deville *ph* Claude Lecompte *m* Edgar Cosma *pd* Michel Guyot, Régis Des Plas *ed* Raymonde Guyot

Andrew Chandler, Hélène Dassule, Nicole Palmer, Hamish Scrimgeour, Katherine Scrimgeour, Nicolas Sireau, Rémi Usquin, Valérie Gauthier

La Petite Voleuse *

France 1988 109m Fujicolor
Pathé/Orly Films/Renn Productions/Ciné Cinq/Les Films du Carrosse/Sedif (Jean-José Richer)

A young girl becomes the lover and accomplice of a thief.

Moderately engaging account of a defiant, amoral outlaw determined to make her own way in the world.

w François Truffaut, Claude de Givray *d* Claude Miller *ph* Dominique Chapuis *ad* Jean-Pierre Kohut Svelko *ed* Albert Jurgenson

Charlotte Gainsbourg, Didier Bazace, Simon de la Brosse, Raoul Billerey, Chantal Banlier, Nathalie Cardone, Clotilde de Bayser

The Petrified Forest **

US 1936 83m bw
Warner (Henry Blanke)
V*, L

Travellers at a way station in the Arizona desert are held up by gangsters.

Rather faded melodrama (it always was), which is important to Hollywood for introducing such well used figures as the poet idealist hero and the gangster anti-hero, and for giving Bogart his first meaty role. Otherwise, the settings are artificial, the acting theatrical, the development predictable and the dialogue pretentious.

w Charles Kenyon, Delmer Daves *play* Robert E. Sherwood *d* Archie Mayo *ph* Sol Polito *md* Leo F. Forbstein

Leslie Howard, Bette Davis, *Humphrey Bogart*, Genevieve Tobin, Dick Foran, Joe Sawyer, Porter Hall, Charley Grapewin

ALAN SQUIER (Leslie Howard): 'Let there be killing. All this evening I've had a feeling of destiny closing in.'
JACKIE (Joe Sawyer): 'Now, just behave yourself and nobody'll get hurt. This is Duke Mantee, the world-famous killer, and he's hungry.'

'Marquee draft should offset the philosophic meanderings which minimize appeal.' – *Variety*

'Drama slackens under the weight of Mr Sherwood's rather half-baked philosophy.' – *Alistair Cooke*

'There is good dramatic material here, but Mr Sherwood doesn't see his play as certain things happening, but as ideas being expressed, "significant" cosmic ideas. . . .. Life itself, which crept in during the opening scene, embarrassed perhaps at hearing itself so explicitly discussed, crept out again, leaving us only with the symbols, the too pasteboard desert, the stunted cardboard studio trees.' – *Graham Greene*

† Remade as *Escape in the Desert* (qv).

Petticoat Fever

US 1936 80m bw
MGM (Frank Davis)

A girl and her stuffy fiancé crash land their plane in sub-Arctic Labrador and are helped by a wireless operator who has not seen a woman for two years.

Pert, slightly unusual comedy which comes off pretty well.

w Harold Goldman *play* Mark Reed *d* George Fitzmaurice *ph* Ernest Haller *m* William Axt

Robert Montgomery, Myrna Loy, Reginald Owen, Winifred Shotter

Petticoat Pirates

GB 1961 87m Technicolor CinemaScope
Gordon L. T. Scott/ABPC
V

Women naval officers mutiny and take a nervous male stoker with them.

Uncertain comedy fantasy.

w Lew Schwarz, Charlie Drake *d* David MacDonald

Charlie Drake, Cecil Parker, Anne Heywood, John Turner, Maxine Audley, Thorley Walters

The Petty Girl

US 1950 88m Technicolor
Columbia (Nat Perrin)
GB title: *Girl of the Year*

A calendar artist takes a staid college professor as his model, and causes a scandal.

Witless comedy musical which barely lingers in the memory.

w Nat Perrin *story* Mary McCarthy *d* Henry Levin *ph* William Snyder *m* George Duning *songs* Harold Arlen, Johnny Mercer

Robert Cummings, Joan Caulfield, Melville Cooper, Elsa Lanchester, Audrey Long, Mary Wickes, Frank Orth

Petulia *

US 1968 105m Technicolor
Warner/Petersham (Raymond Wagner)
V, V*

A doctor's life is disrupted by his meeting and loving a kooky girl who has family problems.

Swinging London melodrama which happens to be set in San Francisco. All very flashy, and occasionally arresting or well acted, but adding up to nothing.

w Lawrence B. Marcus *novel Me and the Arch Kook Petulia* by John Haase *d* Richard Lester *ph* Nicolas Roeg *m* John Barry

George C. Scott, Julie Christie, Richard Chamberlain, Joseph Cotten, Arthur Hill, Shirley Knight, Kathleen Widdoes, Pippa Scott

'A sad and savage comment on the ways we waste our time and ourselves in upper-middle-class America.' – *Richard Schickel*

'A soulless, arbitrary, attitudinizing piece of claptrap.' – *John Simon*

Peur sur la Ville: see *Night Caller*

'Everybody in this town hides behind plain wrappers!'
Peyton Place **

US 1957 157m DeLuxe Cinemascope
TCF (Jerry Wald)
V, V*

Sex, frustration and violence ferment under the placid surface of a small New England town.

Well-made film of what was at the time a scandalous bestseller, one of the first to reveal those nasty secrets of 'ordinary people'.

w John Michael Hayes *novel* Grace Metalious *d* Mark Robson *ph* William Mellor *m* Franz Waxman

Lana Turner, Arthur Kennedy, Hope Lange, Lee Philips, Lloyd Nolan, Diane Varsi, Russ Tamblyn, Terry Moore, Barry Coe, David Nelson, Betty Field, Mildred Dunnock, Leon Ames, Lorne Greene

AAN: best picture; John Michael Hayes; Mark Robson; William Mellor; Lana Turner; Arthur Kennedy; Hope Lange; Diane Varsi; Russ Tamblyn

Phaedra *

US/Greece 1961 116m bw
UA/Melinafilm (Jules Dassin)

A tycoon's wife falls in love with her stepson.

Ludicrous, awesomely folly-filled attempt to modernize and sex up Greek tragedy.

wd Jules Dassin *ph* Jacques Natteau *m* Mikis Theodorakis

Melina Mercouri, Anthony Perkins, Raf Vallone, Elizabeth Ercy

'Unfortunately unforgettable.' – *John Simon*

'If this one doesn't scare you . . . you're already dead!'
Phantasm

US 1979 90m Technicolor
Avco Embassy
V, V*, L, S

A 16-year-old has nightmares which seem to come true.

Cleverly assembled horror comic with many nasty moments. Not for the squeamish, and with no real merit except the power to frighten.

wd Don Coscarelli (who was 20 at the time) *ph* Don Coscarelli *ed* Don Coscarelli

Michael Baldwin, Bill Thornbury, Reggie Bannister, Angus Scrimm

Phantasm II

US 1988 97m colour
Guild/Starway International (Roberto A. Quezada)
V, V*, L, S

A creature from another dimension who brings corpses back to life is thwarted by a teenager and his old adversary.

In the nine years separating this sequel from the original, its director has retained his ability to shock but still cannot tell a story convincingly.

wd Don Coscarelli *ph* Dayn Okada *m* Fred Myrow, Christopher L. Stone *pd* Philip J. C. Duffin *ed* Peter Teschner

James Le Gros, Reggie Bannister, Angus Scrimm, Paula Irvine, Samantha Phillips, Kenneth Tigar, Ruth C. Engel, Mark Anthony Major, Rubin Kushner

'A slick-looking but uninvolving, uncertain picture.' – *MFB*

The Phantom
US   1943   bw   serial: 15 eps
Columbia

Various factions seek the lost city of Zoloz.

Fantasy serial with Ace the Wonder Dog and everything but the kitchen sink.   *d* B. Reeves Eason

Tom Tyler, Kenneth MacDonald, Frank Shannon, Jeanne Bates

The Phantom Baron: see *Le Baron Fantôme*

The Phantom Carriage: see *Thy Soul Shall Bear Witness*

The Phantom Creeps
US   1939   bw   serial: 12 eps
Universal

Dr Alex Zorka has invented a giant robot and can also turn whole armies into zombies.

Silly serial which was also cut into an indecipherable feature.

d Ford Beebe, Saul Goodkind

Bela Lugosi, Robert Kent, Regis Toomey, Dorothy Arnold, Edward Van Sloan

Phantom Empire
US   1935   bw   serial: 12 eps
Mascot

Western crooks covet radium-covered land.

Elementary serial adventures.

d Otto Brewer, B. Reeves Eason

Gene Autry, Frankie Darro, Betsy King Ross, Dorothy Christy, Smiley Burnette

The Phantom Fiend: see *The Lodger*

Phantom Killer
US   1942   57m   bw
A. W. Hackel/Monogram

A young district attorney uncovers an ingenious criminal ruse by twin brothers.

Better-than-average crime filler.

w Karl Brown   *d* William Beaudine

Dick Purcell, Joan Woodbury, John Hamilton, Warren Hymer, J. Farrell MacDonald, Mantan Moreland

Phantom Lady **
US   1944   87m   bw
Universal (Joan Harrison)

A man is accused of murder and his only alibi is a mysterious lady he met in a bar.

Odd little thriller which doesn't really hold together but is made for the most part with great style.

w Bernard C. Schoenfeld   *novel* William Irish   *d* Robert Siodmak   *ph* Woody Bredell   *m* Hans Salter

Franchot Tone, Alan Curtis, Ella Raines, Elisha Cook Jnr, Fay Helm, Andrew Tombes

The Phantom Light
GB   1935   76m   bw
Gaumont British/Gainsborough (Jerome Jackson)

A new keeper takes over at a remote Welsh lighthouse which is reputed to be haunted.

An old-fashioned and stagey melodrama, a sort of seafaring *Ghost Train*, which defeats the director's best efforts to create something more realistic.

w Ralph Smart, J. Jefferson Farjeon, Austin Melford *play* *The Haunted Light* by Evadne Price, Joan Roy Byford   *d* Michael Powell   *ph* Roy Kellino *md* Louis Levy   *ad* A. Vetchinsky   *ed* D. N. Twist

Binnie Hale, Gordon Harker, Donald Calthrop, Milton Rosmer, Ian Hunter, Herbert Lomas

Phantom of Crestwood *
US   1932   77m   bw
RKO (David O. Selznick)
L

Murder strikes when a blackmailer assembles her victims.

Lively mystery with spoof elements.

w Bartlett Cormack, J. Walter Ruben   *d* J. Walter Ruben   *ph* Henry Gerrard   *m* Max Steiner

Ricardo Cortez, H. B. Warner, Anita Louise, Karen Morley, Pauline Frederick, Robert McWade, Skeets Gallagher

'Below the deluxe classification it should give a good account of itself.' – *Variety*

Phantom of 42nd Street
US   1945   58m   bw
Mooney-Herman/PRC

A young Broadway star is suspected when her uncle is murdered backstage.

Lightweight but amiable mystery.

w Milton Ralson   *d* Albert Herman

Dave O'Brien, Kay Aldredge, Alan Mowbray, Frank Jenks, Jack Mulhall

The Phantom of Liberty **
France   1974   104m   Eastmancolor
Fox-Rank/Greenwich (Serge Silberman)
V, V*, L
original title: *Le Fantôme de la Liberté*

Surrealist episodes in the lives of various loosely linked individuals that range from a firing squad in 1808 to modern-day Paris where a dead woman phones her brother to offer him consolation and the police prepare to suppress a revolt.

A hit and miss affair in its treatment of middle-class hypocrisies, often funny, but sometimes no more than bizarre, although you keep watching, just to see what happens next.

w Luis Buñuel, Jean-Claude Carrière   *d* Luis Buñuel   *ph* Edmond Richard   *ad* Pierre Guffroy *ed* Hélène Plemiannikov

Monica Vitti, Jean-Claude Brialy, Michel Piccoli, Jean Rochefort, Adolfo Celli, Michel Lonsdale, Adriana Asti, Bernard Verley, Maxence Mailfort, Muni, Philippe Brigaud

'A magnificent film . . . one of Buñuel's masterpieces.' – *Tom Milne, Sight and Sound*

'Buñuel has a great spare, tonic style, but the domesticated surrealism of this picture has no sting and no after-effect. The film drifts out of your head before it's over.' – *Pauline Kael, New Yorker*

Phantom of Paris
US   1931   73m   bw
MGM

A magician proves by a complex plan that he did not kill his fiancée's father.

Unusual but tortuous thriller which fails to thrill.

w Bess Meredyth, John Meehan, Edwin Justus Mayer   *d* John S. Robertson

John Gilbert, Leila Hyams, Ian Keith, C. Aubrey Smith, Lewis Stone, Jean Hersholt

'It isn't Gilbert that makes the picture, it makes itself. Merits above-average gross.' – *Variety*

The Phantom of the Air
US   1933   bw   serial: 12 eps
Universal

Various criminals covet a new airplane which can defy gravity.

Standard serial exploits.

d Ray Taylor

Tom Tyler, Gloria Shea, LeRoy Mason, William Desmond

Phantom of the Opera ***
US   1925   94m (24 fps)   bw (Technicolor sequence)
    silent
Universal
V*, L

A disfigured man in a mask abducts the prima donna of the Paris Opera House to his lair in the sewers below.

Patchy but often splendid piece of Grand Guignol which not only provided its star with a famous role but was notable for its magnificent visual style.

w Raymond Shrock, Elliot Clawson   *novel* Gaston Leroux   *d* Rupert Julian   *ph* Charles Van Enger, Virgil Miller   *ad* Dan Hall

Lon Chaney, Mary Philbin, Norman Kerry, Gibson Gowland

'The greatest inducement to nightmare that has yet been screened.' – *Variety*

† The chase was directed by Edward Sedgwick.
†† In 1930 an 89m talkie version was issued (L), with approximately 35% dialogue which had been recorded by the surviving actors, and some new footage.

The Phantom of the Opera *
US   1943   92m   Technicolor
Universal (George Waggner)
V, V*, L

This version is more decorous and gentlemanly, with much attention paid to the music, but it certainly has its moments.

w Erich Taylor, Samuel Hoffenstein   *d* Arthur Lubin *ph* Hal Mohr, W. Howard Greene   *m* Edward Ward *ad* John B. Goodman, Alexander Golitzen

Claude Rains, Nelson Eddy, Susanna Foster, Edgar Barrier, Leo Carrillo, J. Edward Bromberg, Jane Farrar, Hume Cronyn

'A grand and gaudy entertainment.' – *Manchester Guardian*

AA: Hal Mohr, W. Howard Greene; John B. Goodman, Alexander Golitzen; Edward Ward

Phantom of the Opera
GB   1962   90m   Technicolor
U-I/Hammer (Anthony Hinds)
V

Stodgy remake with the accent on shock.

w John Elder   *d* Terence Fisher   *ph* Arthur Grant *m* Edwin Astley

Herbert Lom, Edward de Souza, Heather Sears, Thorley Walters, Michael Gough, Ian Wilson, Martin Miller, John Harvey, Miriam Karlin

'The only shock is that the British, who could have had a field day with this antique, have simply wafted it back with a lick and a promise.' – *New York Times*

Phantom of the Opera
US   1989   93m   colour
Castle Premier/21st Century/Breton Film (Harry Alan Towers)
V*, L, S

Struck on the head, a singer finds herself back in Victorian England, where she falls under the influence of a disfigured musical genius who has sold his soul to the devil.

Undistinguished variation on a familiar story, cashing in on the popularity of the actor who plays 'Freddy' in the *Nightmare On Elm Street* series.

w Duke Sandefur, Gerry O'Hara   *d* Dwight H. Little
ph Elemer Ragalyi   *m* Misha Segal   *ad* Tivadar
Bertalan   *ed* Charles Bornstein

Robert Englund, Jill Schoelen, Alex Hyde-White, Bill
Nighy, Terence Harvey, Stephanie Lawrence, Nathan
Lewis, Peter Clapham

Phantom of the Paradise *
US   1974   91m   Movielab
TCF/Pressman Williams (Edward R. Pressman)
V*, L

A modern satirical remake of *Phantom of the Opera* in
rock opera terms, set in a pop music palace.

Not bad in spots, but it doesn't really know where it's
going.

wd Brian de Palma   *ph* Larry Pizer   *m* Paul Williams
pd Jack Fisk

Paul Williams, William Finley, Jessica Harper, George
Memmoli, Gerrit Graham

'Too broad in its effects and too bloated in style to cut
very deeply as a parody . . . closer to the anything goes
mode of a *Mad* magazine lampoon.' – *Richard Combs*

AAN: Paul Williams

Phantom of the Rue Morgue
US   1954   84m   Warnercolor   3-D
Warner (Henry Blanke)

In old Paris, a killer of pretty girls turns out to be an
ape.

Dull revamping of a rather dull story, with boring
characters and little horror.

w Harold Medford, James R. Webb   *story Murders in
the Rue Morgue* by Edgar Allan Poe   *d* Roy del Ruth
ph Peverell Marley   *m* David Buttolph

Karl Malden, Claude Dauphin, Steve Forrest, Patricia
Medina, Allyn McLerie, Dolores Dorn

The Phantom of the West
US   1931   bw   serial: 10 eps
Mascot

A mysterious Phantom haunts a Western town where
one of the townsmen is a murderer.

A serial somewhat more straightforward than usual in
its plotting.

d Ross Lederman

Tom Tyler, Dorothy Gulliver, William Desmond, Tom
Santschi, Tom Dugan

The Phantom President *
US   1932   78m   bw
Paramount

A fast-talking quack doubles for a lacklustre
presidential candidate.

A likely but in fact unsuccessful film début for a
famous Broadway star: many points of interest.

w Walter de Leon, Harlan Thompson   *d* Norman
Taurog   *ph* David Abel   *songs* Richard Rodgers,
Lorenz Hart

George M. Cohan, Claudette Colbert, Jimmy Durante,
George Barbier, Sidney Toler, Jameson Thomas, Paul
Hurst, Alan Mowbray

'A lot of smart stuff is packed into the footage . . .
should do well without threatening to rate itself a
smash.' – *Variety*

'For anyone who cares about American theatrical
history, it's an indispensable record of Cohan's style.'
– *New Yorker, 1978*

The Phantom Rider
US   1936   bw   serial: 15 eps
Universal

The state governor sends Buck Grant on a secret
mission to investigate outlaw activity in Maverick.

Serial chapters with a stalwart hero.

d Ray Taylor

Buck Jones, Maria Shelton, Diana Gibson, Joey Ray

The Phantom Rider
US   1946   bw   serial: 12 eps
Republic

Dr Jim Sterling poses as a phantom rider to deal with
Western outlaws. Or, Zorro Rides Again.

Formula stuff.

d Spencer Bennet, Fred Brannon

Robert Kent, Peggy Stewart, LeRoy Mason, George J.
Lewis

Phantom Ship: see *The Mystery of the Marie Celeste*

The Phantom Strikes: see *The Gaunt Stranger*

The Phantom Tollbooth **
US   1969   90m   Metrocolor
MGM/Animation Visual Arts
V*

A bored boy goes through a magic tollbooth to a land
beyond his wildest imagination, rescues Rhyme and
Reason, and defeats the Demons of Ignorance.

Ambitious and well-devised, though rather slow-
starting, cartoon feature which falls in style
somewhere between *Alice in Wonderland* and *The
Wizard of Oz* but is more intellectual than either and
would be beyond the reach of most children.
Discerning adults may have a ball.

w Chuck Jones, Sam Rosen   *novel* Norton Juster
d Chuck Jones, Abe Levitow   *ph* Maurice Noble

Butch Patrick

Phar Lap
Australia   1983   118m   colour   Panavision
TCF/Michael Edgley International (John Sexton)
V, V*
GB title: *Phar Lap – Heart of a Nation*

The story of a crack racehorse which was the talk of
the world in the early thirties but died of a mysterious
disease.

The film, though adequately textured, won't win any
races.

w David Williamson   *d* Simon Wincer   *ph* Russell
Boyd   *m* Bruce Rowland

Tom Burlinson, Martin Vaughan, Judy Morris, Celia
de Burgh, Ron Liebman, Vincent Ball

'The day the earth was turned into a cemetery!'

Phase IV *
GB   1973   84m   Technicolor
Paramount/Alced (Paul B. Radin)
V*, L

In the Arizona desert, ants attack a scientific
installation.

Oddly effective if repulsive science fiction; the ants
are all the more unpleasant because they stay the
normal size.

w Mayo Simon   *d* Saul Bass   *ph* Dick Bush
m Brian Gascoyne

Nigel Davenport, Lynne Frederick, Michael Murphy,
Alan Gifford

'Sin City of Alabama!'

The Phenix City Story *
US   1955   100m   bw
Allied Artists (Sam Bischoff, David Diamond)

A young lawyer fights the racketeers who control his
town.

Goodish example of the semi-documentary
melodramas of small-town corruption which

swarmed out of Hollywood following the Kefauver
investigations.

w Crane Wilbur, Dan Mainwaring   *d* Phil Karlson
ph Harry Neumann   *m* Harry Sukman

Richard Kiley, *Edward Andrews,* John McIntire,
Kathryn Grant

Phfft
US   1954   91m   bw
Columbia (Fred Kohlmar)
V*

The title refers to the sound of an expiring match; the
story tells of a couple who get divorced and try to find
out what they have been missing.

Champagne comedy with no bubbles.

w George Axelrod   *d* Mark Robson   *ph* Charles
Lang   *m* Frederick Hollander

Jack Lemmon, Judy Holliday, Kim Novak, Jack
Carson, Luella Gear, Donald Randolph, Donald
Curtis, Merry Anders

'No One Would Take On His Case . . . Until One Man
Was Willing To Take On The System.'

Philadelphia **
US   1993   125m   Technicolor
TriStar/Clinca Estetico (Edward Saxon, Jonathan Demme)
S

A successful homosexual lawyer with AIDS sues his
firm for unfair dismissal after he is sacked for 'an
attitude problem'.

A feel-good film about AIDS, set within a standard
Hollywood courtroom drama; it is well made and
absorbing, given its limits.

w Ron Nyswaner   *d* Jonathan Demme   *ph* Tak
Fujimoto   *m* Howard Shore   *pd* Kristi Zea
ed Craig McKay

Tom Hanks, Denzel Washington, Jason Robards,
Mary Steenburgen, Antonio Banderas, Ron Vawter,
Robert Ridgely, Charles Napier, Joanne Woodward

'An ideal film for people who have never known
anyone with AIDS . . . extremely well-made message
picture.' – *Variety*

'The film ultimately becomes a documentary on the
ravages of AIDS – and on the masochistic machismo
of Method acting.' – *Richard Corliss, Time*

'A heartbreakingly mediocre film. It's dishonest, it's
often legally, medically and politically inaccurate, and
it breaks my heart that I must say it's simply not good
enough and I'd rather people not see it at all.' – *Larry
Kramer*

AA: Tom Hanks; song 'Streets of Philadelphia' (*m/y*
Bruce Springsteen)

AAN: Ron Nyswaner; song 'Philadelphia' (*m/y* Neil
Young); make-up

The Philadelphia Experiment *
US   1984   101m   CFI colour
New World/Cinema Group (Joel B. Michaels, Douglas Curtis)
V*, L, S

Seamen on a 1943 destroyer fall through a time warp
into 1984, and have one hell of a job getting back.

Science fiction, *Outer Limits/Final Countdown* style; quite
watchable, and technically proficient, but the claim
that it was based on an actual incident seems a bit tall.

w William Gray, Michael Janover   *book* William I.
Moore, Charles Berlitz   *d* Stewart Raffill   *ph* Dick
Bush   *m* Ken Wannberg   *ad* Chris Campbell
ed Neil Travis, William Hoy

Michael Paré, Nancy Allen, Eric Christmas, Bobby Di
Cicco, Louise Latham

The Philadelphia Experiment 2
US   1993   97m   colour
Trimark (Mark Levinson, Doug Curtis)
V, V*

An experiment goes wrong and a modern bomber-plane goes through the space-time continuum into a place of dictatorship and concentration camps.

Undemanding action fare that does little with its science-fiction elements.

w Kevin Rock, Nick Paine   *d* Stephen Cornwell
ph Ronn Schmidt   *m* Gerald Couriet   *pd* Armin Ganz   *sp* Frank Ceglia   *ed* Nina Gilberti

Brad Johnson, Marjean Holden, Gerrit Graham, James Greene, Geoffrey Blake, Cyril O'Reilly, John Christian Grass

'An old idea, passably reworked.' – *Sight and Sound*

† The film was released direct to video in Britain.

'Uncle Leo's bedtime story for you older tots! The things they do among the playful rich – oh, boy!'

The Philadelphia Story ****
US   1940   112m   bw
MGM (Joseph L. Mankiewicz)
V*, L

A stuffy heiress, about to be married for the second time, turns human and returns gratefully to number one.

Hollywood's most wise and sparkling comedy, with a script which is even an improvement on the original play. Cukor's direction is so discreet you can hardly sense it, and all the performances are just perfect.

w Donald Ogden Stewart,   *play* Philip Barry   *d* George Cukor   *ph* Joseph Ruttenberg   *m* Franz Waxman   *ad* Cedric Gibbons

Katharine Hepburn, Cary Grant, James Stewart, Ruth Hussey, Roland Young, John Halliday, Mary Nash, Virginia Weidler, John Howard, Henry Daniell

'There are just not enough superlatives sufficiently to appreciate this show.' – *Hollywood Reporter*

'An exceptionally bright job of screenplay writing . . . though films like this do little to advance the art of motion pictures, they may help to convince some of the more discerning among cultural slugabeds that when movies want to turn their hand to anything, they can turn it.' – *Otis Ferguson*

† Cary Grant donated his salary to war relief.

AA: Donald Ogden Stewart; James Stewart

AAN: best picture; George Cukor; Katharine Hepburn; Ruth Hussey

Philo Vance

The smooth sleuth created by S. S. Van Dine was a popular film hero of the thirties, for several different companies and with several different actors. As a series it was very variable indeed.

1929: THE CANARY MURDER CASE (Paramount: William Powell); THE GREENE MURDER CASE (Paramount: William Powell)
1930: THE BISHOP MURDER CASE (MGM: Basil Rathbone); THE BENSON MURDER CASE (Paramount: William Powell)
1933: THE KENNEL MURDER CASE (qv) (Warner: William Powell)
1934: THE DRAGON MURDER CASE (Warner: Warren William)
1935: THE CASINO MURDER CASE (MGM: Paul Lukas)
1936: THE GARDEN MURDER CASE (MGM: Edmund Lowe)
1937: NIGHT OF MYSTERY (Paramount: Grant Richards)
1937: THE SCARAB MURDER CASE (British: Wilfrid Hyde-White)
1939: THE GRACIE ALLEN MURDER CASE (Paramount: Warren William); CALLING PHILO VANCE (Warner: James Stephenson)
1947: PHILO VANCE RETURNS (PRC: William Wright); PHILO VANCE'S GAMBLE (PRC: Alan Curtis); PHILO VANCE'S SECRET MISSION (PRC: Alan Curtis)

Der Philosoph
West Germany   1988   83m   colour
Mainline/Moana Film Produktion (Rudolf Thome)
aka: *Three Women in Love*

A writer finds three women to love and look after him.

Updating of Greek myth to male fantasy.

wd Rudolf Thome   *ph* Reinhold Vorschneider   *m* Hanno Rinne   *ad* Eve Schaenen   *ed* Dörte Völz-Mannarell

Johannes Herrschmann, Adriana Altaras, Friederike Tiefenbacher, Claudia Matschulla, Jürgen Wink, Werner Gerber, Anton Rey

Phobia
Canada   1980   90m   colour
Borough Park (Zale Magder)
V*

Five volunteer phobics, released from jail for experiments, are killed one by one.

Unprepossessing whodunnit with horror touches but none of the style one might expect from its director.

w Lew Lehman, Jimmy Sangster, Peter Bellwood   *d* John Huston   *ph* Reginald H. Morris   *m* Andre Gagnon

Paul Michael Glaser, John Colicos, Susan Hogan, Alexandra Stewart, David Bolt

Phone Call from a Stranger
US   1952   96m   bw
TCF (Nunnally Johnson)
V*

Of four airplane acquaintances, only one survives a crash; he visits the families of the others.

Four stories with an unlikely link. (The compendium craze, which had started in 1948 with *Quartet*, was now straining itself.) Nothing to remember except Miss Davis.

w Nunnally Johnson   *d* Jean Negulesco   *ph* Milton Krasner   *m* Franz Waxman

Bette Davis, Gary Merrill, Michael Rennie, Shelley Winters, Keenan Wynn, Evelyn Varden, Warren Stevens, Craig Stevens

'A cinematic party line on which several conversations are going at once, none of them coming across very distinctly.' – *Time*

The Photograph *
Greece/France   1986   120m   colour

Two expatriate Greeks living in Paris encourage each other's hopes for the future with tragic results.

Dour, skilfully made film of people unable to alter the trajectory of their lives.

wd Nicos Papatakis   *ph* Aris Stavrou   *m* Christodoulos Chalaris

Aris Retsos, Christos Tsangas

Physical Evidence
US   1988   99m   colour
Rank/Columbia (Martin Ransohoff)
V, V*, L

An ex-cop, accused of murder, begins to have doubts about the female lawyer hired to defend him.

Dull thriller with an unnecessarily convoluted plot.

w Bill Phillips   *story* Steve Ransohoff, Bill Phillips   *d* Michael Crichton   *ph* John A. Alonzo   *m* Henry Mancini   *pd* Dan Yarhi   *ed* Glenn Farr

Burt Reynolds, Theresa Russell, Ned Beatty, Kay Lenz, Ted McGinley, Tom O'Brien, Kenneth Welsh, Ray Baker, Ken James, Michael P. Moran

'The whole exercise, while never quite collapsing, contrives to look and sound peculiarly futile.' – *Philip Strick, MFB*

The Piano ****
Australia   1993   120m   Eastmancolor
Entertainment/CIBY 2000/Jan Chapman
S

A mute Scottish widow travels with her young daughter for an arranged marriage to a landowner in New Zealand, where she is forced to leave her most-treasured possession, her piano, on a beach.

A complex drama of lust, love and a woman emerging from an emotional silence in a repressive community into a self-determined and fulfilled life; beautifully photographed and impeccably acted, it is powerful and moving.

wd Jane Campion   *ph* Stuart Dryburgh   *m* Michael Nyman   *pd* Andrew McAlpine   *ed* Veronika Jenet

Holly Hunter, Harvey Keitel, Sam Neill, *Anna Paquin*, Kerry Walker, Genevieve Lemon, Tungla Baker, Ian Mune

'A riveting excursion into 19th-century sexuality, a movie that takes the conventions of the Gothic romance and refracts them through a dark contemporary lens.' – *David Ansen, Newsweek*

'Not since the early days of cinema, when audiences trampled over each other towards the exit to avoid the train emerging from the screen, could I imagine the medium of film to be so powerful.' – *Lizzie Francke, Sight and Sound*

'An emotionally devastating tour de force, both heart-rending and heart-warming.' – *Film Review*

The film shared the *Palme d'Or* as best film, and Holly Hunter won the award as best actress, at the Cannes Film Festival in 1993.

AA: Holly Hunter; Anna Paquin; Jane Campion (as writer)

AAN: best picture; Jane Campion (as director); Stuart Dryburgh; Veronika Jenet; costume design (Janet Patterson)

Piatka z Ulicy Barskiej: see *Five Boys from Barska Street*

Piccadilly *
GB   1929   105m (24 fps)   bw   silent
BIP (E. A. Dupont)

A club owner's fiancée is accused of killing his Chinese mistress.

Sub-Edgar Wallace melodrama, no longer watchable with a straight face.

w Arnold Bennett   *d* E. A. Dupont   *ph* Werner Brandes

Gilda Gray, Anna May Wong, Jameson Thomas, Cyril Ritchard, Ellen Pollock, Charles Laughton, Debroy Somers and his Band

† Sound added in 1930.

Piccadilly Incident *
GB   1946   102m   bw
ABP (Herbert Wilcox)

During World War II, a girl believed drowned returns from the front to find her husband remarried.

The Enoch Arden theme again, and the first of the Wilcox-Neagle 'London' films, though untypically a melodrama with a sad ending. Efficient enough for its chosen audience.

w Nicholas Phipps   *d* Herbert Wilcox   *ph* Max Greene   *m* Anthony Collins

Anna Neagle, Michael Wilding, Michael Laurence, Frances Mercer, Coral Browne, A. E. Matthews, Edward Rigby, Brenda Bruce

† Michael Wilding was cast only after Rex Harrison and John Mills had proved unavailable.

Piccadilly Jim *
US   1936   100m   bw
MGM (Harry Rapf)

A cartoonist helps his father to marry by making the bride's stuffy family objects of ridicule.

Amiable comedy with a diverting London setting.

w Charles Brackett, Edwin Knopf   novel P. G. Wodehouse   d Robert Z. Leonard   ph Joseph Ruttenberg   m William Axt

Robert Montgomery, Madge Evans, Frank Morgan, Billie Burke, Eric Blore, Robert Benchley, Ralph Forbes, Cora Witherspoon, E. E. Clive

Piccadilly Third Stop

GB   1960   90m   bw
Rank/Sydney Box/Ethiro (Norman Williams)

A smooth crook seduces the daughter of an eastern ambassador in London to gain entry to the embassy and rob it.

Boring and rather unpleasant thriller partly redeemed by a final chase through the Underground.

w Leigh Vance   d Wolf Rilla   ph Ernest Steward   m Philip Green

Terence Morgan, Yoko Tani, John Crawford, William Hartnell, Mai Zetterling, Dennis Price, Ann Lynn

Pick a Star

US   1937   76m   bw
MGM/Hal Roach
V*, L

An innocent girl in Hollywood achieves stardom with the help of a publicity man.

Perfectly awful Cinderella story with interesting glimpses behind the studio scenes and (if you can wait that long) a couple of good Laurel and Hardy sequences.

w Richard Flournoy, Arthur Vernon Jones, Thomas J. Dugan   d Edward Sedgwick   ph Norbert Brodine   m Marvin Hatley, Arthur Morton

Rosina Lawrence, Jack Haley, Patsy Kelly, Mischa Auer, *Stan Laurel, Oliver Hardy,* Charles Halton, Lyda Roberti

'Part farce, part comedy, part musical and three parts dull.' – *Variety*

Pick Up

US   1933   80m   bw
B. P. Schulberg/Paramount

A girl released from jail picks up with a truck driver, but her crooked husband reappears.

Sob story of the *Peg's Paper* type; a yawn.

w S. K. Lauren, Agnes Leahy, Vina Delmar   d Marion Gering

Sylvia Sidney, George Raft, William Harrigan, Lillian Bond

'Good title and cast, weakish film.' – *Variety*

Pick Up

US   1951   78m   bw
Columbia (Hugo Haas)

A lonely middle-aged man falls for a tart who is interested only in his money.

Modest variation on *The Blue Angel,* the first of several second features made by Haas to feature himself as a second Emil Jannings. They got progressively more maudlin.

wd *Hugo Haas*   ph Paul Ivano

Hugo Haas, Beverly Michaels, Allan Nixon, Howard Chamberlin

Pickpocket **

France   1959   80m   bw
Lux

A lonely, compulsive pickpocket is redeemed through love.

Based on the themes of Dostoevsky's *Crime and Punishment,* an austere but moving and complex drama, notable for its scenes of thievery.

wd Robert Bresson   ph Léonce-Henry Burel   m Jean-Baptiste Lully   ed Raymond Lamy

Martin Lassalle, Marika Green, Pierre Leymarie, Jean Pelegri, Pierre Etaix, Kassagi, Dolly Scal, César Gattegno   'The style of the film is characteristic of the director. It is one of persistent concentration: the camera will not be deflected from its close stare at the silent face, the tense figure in the foreground. But this time the method defeats itself. In rejecting every irrelevant action, in ruthlessly refining away every decoration, Bresson has thrown away the motives as well.' – Dilys Powell

Pickup Alley: see *Interpol*

'Anybody's back seat will do – as long as he's going her way!'

Pickup on 101

US   1972   93m   Movielab
AIP
V*

A lady hitchhiker picks up with an old hobo and an unemployed rock 'n' roller.

Sentimental rather than sensational is this small drama which starts slowly and goes nowhere.

w Anthony Blake   d John Florea

Lesley Warren, Jack Albertson, Martin Sheen, Michael Ontkean

Pickup on South Street **

US   1953   80m   bw
TCF (Jules Schermer)
V*

A pickpocket steals a girl's wallet and finds himself up to his neck in espionage.

Over-rich mixture of crime, violence and anti-communism, smartly made without being very interesting.

wd *Samuel Fuller*   story Dwight Taylor   ph Joe MacDonald   m Leigh Harline   ad Lyle R. Wheeler, George Patrick   ed Nick de Maggio

Richard Widmark, Jean Peters, *Thelma Ritter,* Richard Kiley

† Remade 1968 as *Capetown Affair.*

AAN: Thelma Ritter

The Pickwick Papers *

GB   1952   115m   bw
George Minter (Bob McNaught)
V, V*

Various adventures of the Pickwick Club culminate in Mrs Bardell's suit for breach of promise.

Flatly conceived and loosely constructed Dickensian comedy; good humour and lots of well-known faces do not entirely atone for lack of artifice.

wd Noel Langley   ph Wilkie Cooper   m Antony Hopkins   ad Fred Pusey

James Hayter, James Donald, Donald Wolfit, Hermione Baddeley, Hermione Gingold, Kathleen Harrison, *Nigel Patrick,* Alexander Gauge, Lionel Murton

'As welcome as the sun in the morning and as British as a cup of tea.' – *Daily Mirror*

'A town – a stranger – and the things he does to its people! Especially its women!'

Picnic ***

US   1955   113m   Technicolor   Cinemascope
Columbia (Fred Kohlmar)
V*, L, S

A brawny wanderer causes sexual havoc one summer in a small American town.

Seminal melodrama setting new directions for Hollywood and illustrating the side of life the Hardy

family never showed. Generally quite compulsive despite some overacting.

w Daniel Taradash   play William Inge   d Joshua Logan   ph James Wong Howe   m George Duning   pd Jo Mielziner   ad William Flannery   ed Charles Nelson, William A. Lyon

William Holden, Kim Novak, Rosalind Russell, *Susan Strasberg,* Arthur O'Connell, Cliff Robertson, Betty Field, Verna Felton, Reta Shaw

'Mr Logan's idea of an outing in the corn country includes a choir of at least a hundred voices, a camera so alert that it can pick up the significance of the reflection of a Japanese lantern in a pool (futility, wistfulness, the general transience of life, as I get it) and a sound track let loose in the most formidable music I've heard in my time at the movies.' – *New Yorker*

AA: art direction; editing

AAN: best picture; Joshua Logan; George Duning; Arthur O'Connell

'A recollection of evil . . .'

Picnic at Hanging Rock ****

Australia   1975   115m   Eastmancolor
Picnic Productions/Australia Film Corporation (Hal and Jim McElroy)
V, V*

In 1900, schoolgirls set out for a picnic; some disappear and are never found.

A film that ventures successfully into the mystic and bravely offers no answer to its central puzzle, just a question that continues to haunt the mind. Whether you want to regard it as a parable of sexual awakening or of colonial repression, it successfully retains its own mystery.

w Cliff Green   novel Joan Lindsay   d Peter Weir   ph Russell Boyd   m Bruce Smeaton

Rachel Roberts, Dominic Guard, Helen Morse, Jacki Weaver, Vivean Gray, Kirsty Child

'Atmospherically vivid, beautifully shot, and palpably haunting.' – *Michael Billington, Illustrated London News*

'If this film had a rational and tidy conclusion, it would be a good deal less interesting. But as a tantalizing puzzle, a tease, a suggestion of forbidden answer just out of earshot, it works hypnotically and very nicely indeed.' – *Roger Ebert*

Picture Mommy Dead

US   1966   88m   Pathecolor
Embassy/Berkeley (Bert I. Gordon)
V*

A girl who has been hospitalized following the death of her mother in a fire returns home to find, apparently, that her father's new wife is trying to kill her.

Twist-ending shocker with tired stars, from the tag end of the *Baby Jane* cycle.

w Robert Sherman   d Bert I. Gordon   ph Ellsworth Fredericks   m Robert Drasnin

Don Ameche, Martha Hyer, Zsa Zsa Gabor, Susan Gordon, Maxwell Reed, Signe Hasso, Wendell Corey

The Picture of Dorian Gray ***

US   1945   110m   bw   (Technicolor inserts)
MGM (Pandro S. Berman)
V*, L

A Victorian gentleman keeps in the attic a picture of himself, which shows his age and depravity while he stays eternally young.

Elegant variation on *Dr Jekyll and Mr Hyde,* presented in portentous style which suits the subject admirably.

wd *Albert Lewin,* novel Oscar Wilde   ph Harry Stradling   m Herbert Stothart   ad Cedric Gibbons, Hans Peters

George Sanders, Hurd Hatfield, Donna Reed, Angela Lansbury, Peter Lawford

SIR HENRY (George Sanders): 'If I could get back my youth, I'd do anything in the world – except get up early, take exercise or be respectable.'

SIR HENRY: 'I apologize for the intelligence of my remarks, Sir Thomas, I had forgotten that you were a Member of Parliament.'

DORIAN (Hurd Hatfield): 'If only the picture could change and I could be always what I am now. For that, I would give anything. Yes, there's nothing in the whole world I wouldn't give. I'd give my soul for that.'

'Respectful, earnest, and, I'm afraid, dead.' – *James Agee*

'Loving and practised hands have really improved Wilde's original, cutting down the epigrammatic flow . . . and rooting out all the preciousness which gets in the way of the melodrama.' – *Richard Winnington*

AA: Harry Stradling

AAN: Angela Lansbury; art direction

The Picture Show Man *
Australia   1977   98m   Eastmancolor
Limelight (Joan Long)

Adventures of a travelling picture show troupe in the 1920s.

Agreeably nostalgic incidents, not very dramatically connected.

w Joan Long   d John Power   ph Geoffrey Burton
m Peter Best

Rod Taylor, John Meillon, John Ewart, Harold Hopkins, Judy Morris, Patrick Cargill

The Picture Snatcher *
US   1933   77m   bw
Warner

An ex-racketeer just out of prison becomes a scandal photographer.

Lively star vehicle, interesting for period detail.

w Allen Rivkin, P. J. Wolfson   d Lloyd Bacon
ph Sol Polito   md Leo F. Forbstein

James Cagney, Ralph Bellamy, Patricia Ellis, Alice White, Ralf Harolde, Robert Emmett O'Connor, Robert Barrat

'A vulgar but generally funny collection of blackouts.' – *Time*

'Fast, snappy, tough and packed with action.' – *New York Herald Tribune*

† Remade 1947 as *Escape from Crime*, with Richard Travis.

A Piece of the Action
US   1977   135m   Metrocolor
Warner/First Artists/Verdon (Melville Tucker)
V*

Crooks are blackmailed into helping rebellious adolescents.

A black version, at immense length, of the hoodlum comedies in which the Dead End Kids so often featured. Not badly made, but out of date without being nostalgic.

w Charles Blackwell   story Timothy March
d Sidney Poitier   ph Don Morgan   m Curtis Mayfield

Sidney Poitier, James Earl Jones, Bill Cosby, Denise Nicholas, Hope Clarke, Tracy Reed, Jason Evers, Marc Lawrence

The Pied Piper **
US   1942   86m   bw
TCF (Nunnally Johnson)

An elderly man who hates children finds himself smuggling several of them out of occupied France.

Smart, sentimental, occasionally funny war adventure.

w Nunnally Johnson   novel Nevil Shute   d Irving Pichel   ph Edward Cronjager   m Alfred Newman

Monty Woolley, Anne Baxter, Roddy McDowall, Otto Preminger, J. Carrol Naish, Lester Matthews, Jill Eastmond, Peggy Ann Garner

AAN: best picture; Edward Cronjager; Monty Woolley

The Pied Piper
GB   1971   90m   Eastmancolor   Panavision
Sagittarius/Goodtimes (David Puttnam, Sanford Lieberson)

In 1349 a strolling minstrel rids Hamelin of a plague of rats.

Paceless, slightly too horrific, and generally disappointing fantasy, especially from this director; poor sets and restricted action.

w Jacques Demy, Mark Peploe, Andrew Birkin
d Jacques Demy   ph Peter Suschitsky   m Donovan
pd Assheton Gorton

Donovan, Donald Pleasence, Michael Hordern, Jack Wild, Diana Dors, John Hurt

Pièges
France   1939   120m   bw
Speva (Michel Safra)
US title: *Personal Column*; aka: *Snares*

A dancer acts as a decoy to trap a serial killer murdering women who answer lonely hearts advertisements.

A thriller that finds it hard to accommodate murders and leave room for its debonair singing star.

w Jacques Companeea, Ernest Neuville, Simon Gantillon   d Robert Siodmak   m Michelet   ad G. Wakhevitch   ed Yvonne Martin

Maurice Chevalier, Pierre Renoir, Marie Déa, Erich von Stroheim, Jean Temerson, André Brunot

† This was Siodmak's last French film before he left for Hollywood. It was remade in Hollywood in 1947 as *Lured* (qv), directed by Douglas Sirk.

Pier 13 (1932): see *Me and My Gal*

Pierre of the Plains
US   1942   66m   bw
MGM

Adventures of a cheerful trapper in Canada's northwest territory.

Unashamed second-feature version of a play which its producer, Edgar Selwyn, had written in 1907 and which had been filmed in 1918 (as *Hearts of the Wild*) and in 1922 (as *Over the Border*). (Selwyn was the man who once merged with Goldfish to form Goldwyn, a name which Goldfish then kept.)

w Bertram Millhauser, Laurence Kimble   d George B. Seitz

John Carroll, Ruth Hussey, Bruce Cabot, Reginald Owen, Henry Travers, Evelyn Ankers

Pierrot Le Fou **
France/Italy   1968   110m   Eastmancolor
    Techniscope
Rome/Paris/SNC (Reneé Pigneres, Gerard Beytout)
V (W), V*, L, S

Bored by his marriage, a Frenchman leaves his wife at a party and takes off with an old flame, now involved in gun-running and crime.

A pulp thriller re-told in terms of farce and artifice, and a playful and enjoyably intellectual romp through pop culture, though it is difficult to take it as seriously as its maker intended.

wd Jean-Luc Godard   novel *Obsession* by Lionel White   ph Raoul Coutard   m Antoine Duhamel
ad Pierre Guffroy   ed Françoise Colin

Jean-Paul Belmondo, Anna Karina, Dirk Sanders, Raymond Devos, Graziella Galvani

'Godard has reached a stage at which self-confidence and self-indulgence join hands to lead him into a disaster area.' – *Dilys Powell*

'Purports to be against a world of advertising and conspicuous consumption; yet what it offers as an alternative, the mindless, feckless, and finally feelingless relationship of its hero and heroine, is at least as repugnant.' – *John Simon*

The Pigeon that Took Rome
US   1962   101m   bw   Panavision
Paramount/Llenroc (Melville Shavelson)

American undercover agents are smuggled into Rome during the German occupation.

Heavy-going war comedy-drama with bright sequences countered by too little wit and too many voluble Italians.

wd Melville Shavelson   novel *The Easter Dinner* by Donald Downes   ph Daniel Fapp   m Alessandro Cicognini

Charlton Heston, Elsa Martinelli, Brian Donlevy, Harry Guardino, Baccaloni

Pigskin Parade
US   1936   93m   bw
TCF (Bogart Rogers)
GB title: *Harmony Parade*

A country farmer becomes a college football hero.

Livelier-than-average college comedy.

w Harry Tugend, Jack Yellen, William Conselman
d David Butler   ph Arthur Miller   md David Buttolph   songs Sidney Mitchell, Lew Pollack

Stuart Erwin, Patsy Kelly, Jack Haley, Johnny Downs, Betty Grable, Arline Judge, Dixie Dunbar, Judy Garland, Tony Martin, Elisha Cook Jnr

AAN: Stuart Erwin

The Pilgrim *
US   1923   38m approx (24 fps)   bw   silent
First National/Charles Chaplin

An escaped convict disguises himself as a minister and does a few good deeds.

Star comedy with more sentiment than laughter.

wd Charles Chaplin   ph Rollie Totheroh

Charles Chaplin, Edna Purviance, Kitty Bradbury, Mack Swain

Pilgrimage *
US   1933   95m   bw
Fox

A selfish mother sees the error of her ways when she makes a post-war journey to her son's grave.

Strong character study, put across with style.

w Dudley Nichols, Philip Klein, Barry Conners
story I. A. R. Wylie   d John Ford

Henrietta Crosman, Heather Angel, Norman Foster, Marian Nixon, Maurice Murphy, Charley Grapewin, Hedda Hopper

'A natural for residential clienteles: mother love from a new angle.' – *Variety*

Pillars of the Sky
US   1956   95m   Technicolor   Cinemascope
U-I (Robert Arthur)
GB title: *The Tomahawk and the Cross*

An Indian scout and a missionary help bring peace between cavalry and Indians.

Modest Western, adequately done.

w Sam Rolfe   d George Marshall   ph Harold Lipstein   m Joseph Gershenson

Jeff Chandler, Dorothy Malone, Ward Bond, Keith Andes, Lee Marvin, Sydney Chaplin, Michael Ansara, Willis Bouchey

Pillow of Death

US   1945   66m   bw
Universal

A lawyer is suspected when his wife is murdered.

First fumbling story in the Inner Sanctum series, of which the title sequence was always the most entertaining portion.

w George Bricker   d Wallace Fox

Lon Chaney Jnr, Brenda Joyce, J. Edward Bromberg, Rosalind Ivan, Clara Blandick

Pillow Talk **

US   1959   110m   Eastmancolor   Cinemascope
Universal/Arwin (Ross Hunter, Martin Melcher)
V*, L

Two people who can't stand each other fall in love via a party line.

Slightly elephantine romantic comedy which nevertheless contains a number of funny scenes and was notable for starting off the Hudson-Day partnership and a run of similar comedies which survived the sixties.

w Stanley Shapiro, Maurice Richlin, Russell Rouse, Clarence Greene   d Michael Gordon   ph Arthur E. Arling   m Frank de Vol   ad Richard H. Riedel

Doris Day, Rock Hudson, Tony Randall, Thelma Ritter, Nick Adams, Julia Meade, Allen Jenkins, Marcel Dalio, Lee Patrick

AA: Stanley Shapiro, Maurice Richlin, Russell Rouse, Clarence Greene

AAN: Frank de Vol; Doris Day; Thelma Ritter; art direction

Pillow to Post

US   1945   96m   bw
Warner (Alex Gottlieb)

A girl poses as a soldier's wife to get a hotel room.

World War II comedy on a familiar theme (The More the Merrier, Standing Room Only, The Doughgirls, etc). Uninspired.

w Charles Hoffman   play Pillar to Post by Rose Simon Kohn   d Vincent Sherman   ph Wesley Anderson   m Frederick Hollander

Ida Lupino, Sidney Greenstreet, William Prince, Stuart Erwin, Ruth Donnelly, Barbara Brown, Frank Orth

The Pilot *

US   1979   92m   colour
Summit/New Line

A once great pilot insists on working despite an alcohol problem.

Not enough meat on the story bones is enough to ground this dismal drama, but the air scenes look terrific and the actors seem to believe in what they're doing.

wd Cliff Robertson   novel Robert P. Davis   ph Walter Lassally   m John Addison

Cliff Robertson, Frank Converse, Diane Baker, Gordon MacRae, Dana Andrews, Milo O'Shea

Pilot Number Five

US   1943   71m   bw
MGM (B. P. Fineman)

A pilot in the South Pacific volunteers for a desperate mission because – we learn in flashback – he hates fascists.

Rather unpalatable propaganda encased in dim drama.

w David Hertz   d George Sidney   ph Paul C. Vogel   m Lennie Hayton

Franchot Tone, Gene Kelly, Marsha Hunt, Van Johnson, Alan Baxter, Dick Simmons, Steve Geray

Pimpernel Smith **

GB   1941   121m   bw
British National (Leslie Howard)
V*
US titles: Mister V; The Fighting Pimpernel

A professor of archaeology goes into war-torn Europe to rescue refugees.

The Scarlet Pimpernel unassumingly and quite effectively brought up to date, with memorable scenes after a slow start.

w Anatole de Grunwald, Roland Pertwee, Ian Dalrymple   d Leslie Howard   ph Max Greene   m John Greenwood

Leslie Howard, Mary Morris, Francis L. Sullivan, Hugh McDermott, Raymond Huntley, Manning Whiley, Peter Gawthorne, David Tomlinson

'Funny, touching, imaginative, and enormously exciting.' – C. A. Lejeune

'Just an amusing piece of hokum.' – Leslie Howard

Pin Up Girl

US   1944   83m   Technicolor
TCF (William Le Baron)
V*, L

A Washington secretary becomes a national celebrity when she meets a navy hero.

Adequate star flagwaver, mildly interesting for its new streamlined set designs.

w Robert Ells, Helen Logan, Earl Baldwin   d Bruce Humberstone   ph Ernest Palmer   md Emil Newman, Charles Henderson   songs James V. Monaco, Mack Gordon   ch Hermes Pan   ad James Basevi, Joseph C. Wright

Betty Grable, John Harvey, Martha Raye, Joe E. Brown, Eugene Pallette, Dave Willcock, Charles Spivak and his Orchestra

'A spiritless blob of a musical, and a desecration of a most inviting theme.' – Bosley Crowther

Pink Cadillac *

US   1989   122m   Technicolor
Warner/Malpaso (David Valdes)
V, V*, L

A bounty hunter goes in search of a mother who has disappeared with her baby and a pink Cadillac containing $250,000 belonging to a bunch of neo-Nazis.

Amiable, if somewhat aimless, comedy with unsubtle performances.

w John Eskow   d Buddy Van Horn   ph Jack N. Green   m Steve Dorff   pd Edward C. Carfagno   ed Joel Cox

Clint Eastwood, Bernadette Peters, Timothy Carhart, John Dennis Johnston, Michael Des Barres, Geoffrey Lewis

Pink Floyd The Wall *

GB   1982   95m   Metrocolor
MGM/Tin Blue/Goldcrest (Alan Marshall)
V, V*, L

A washed-up pop star finds his life a mixture of fact and fiction, of reality and animation.

Dislikeable self-pitying dirge, accompanied by animation which will not be to everybody's taste but is sometimes brilliantly arranged.

w Roger Waters   d Alan Parker   ph Peter Biziou   m Roger Waters   animation designer Gerald Scarfe

Bob Geldof, Christine Hargreaves, James Laurenson, Eleanor David, Kevin McKeon, Bob Hoskins

'A vacuous, bombastic and humourless piece of self-indulgence.' – Steve Jenkins, MFB

'Roger Waters flounders in woman-hating self-pity; Gerald Scarfe turns up particularly weedy examples of his animated savagery; and Alan Parker revels in

the chance to make a feature-length TV commercial.' – Sight and Sound

The Pink Jungle

US   1968   104m   Technicope
Universal/Cherokee (Stan Margulies)

A photographer and his model are stranded in a South American village and become involved in a diamond hunt.

Curious mixture of adventure and light comedy that works only in patches.

w Charles Williams   novel Snake Water by Alan Williams   d Delbert Mann   ph Russell Metty   m Ernie Freeman

James Garner, Eva Renzi, George Kennedy, Nigel Green, Michael Ansara, George Rose

'Another backlot cheapie.' – Robert Windeler

'A unique experience in visual fantasy.'

Pink Narcissus

US   1971   102m   colour
Smerpix/Les Folies des Hommes
V

A young hustler, trying to escape the sordid reality of his life, imagines a series of mainly masturbatory homosexual encounters: as a matador, a Roman slave, a harem boy in the tent of a sheik, a wood nymph, and as his own, ageing client.

A once-notorious gaudily coloured exploitation film aimed at gay audiences which is very much of its time, being almost a definitive example of camp and kitsch. It received its first large-scale British showing in a grainy video release in 1993.

w Anonymous   d Anonymous   ph Anonymous   md Martin Jay Sadoff, Gary Goch   ed Martin Jay Sadoff

Bobby Kendall

'We are expected to be drooling, aroused, captivated – and weak enough to approve this celebration of the bottomless Narcissistic pit – instead of damning it as the oafish indulgence it really is. One would care less if it were content to be pornography, but instead it operates smugly within the "decadent" underground style of Anger et al.' – Shock Xpress

† Although the film and the video release list the producer, director and writer as anonymous, some prints credit 'Jim Bidgood' as director.

The Pink Panther **

US   1963   113m   Technirama
UA/Mirisch (Martin Jurow)
V, V*, L, S

An incompetent Sûreté inspector is in Switzerland on the trail of a jewel thief called The Phantom.

Sporadically engaging mixture of pratfalls, Raffles, and Monsieur Hulot, all dressed to kill and quite palatable for the uncritical.

w Maurice Richlin, Blake Edwards   d Blake Edwards   ph Philip Lathrop   m Henry Mancini   ad Fernando Carrere   animation De Patie-Freleng

David Niven, Peter Sellers, Capucine, Claudia Cardinale, Robert Wagner, Brenda de Banzie, Colin Gordon

† Inspector Clouseau later became a cartoon character and also provoked five sequels: A Shot in the Dark, Inspector Clouseau, The Return of the Pink Panther, The Pink Panther Strikes Again and The Revenge of the Pink Panther.

AAN: Henry Mancini

The Pink Panther Strikes Again *

GB   1976   103m   DeLuxe   Panavision
United Artists/Amjo (Blake Edwards)
V, V*, L

After a nervous breakdown, Chief Inspector Dreyfus builds up a vast criminal organization devoted to the extermination of Inspector Clouseau.

Zany pratfall farce with signs of over-confidence since the success of *The Return of the Pink Panther*. But some gags are funny, despite a rather boring star.

w Frank Waldman, Blake Edwards d Blake Edwards ph Harry Waxman m Henry Mancini

Peter Sellers, Herbert Lom, Colin Blakely, Leonard Rossiter, Lesley-Anne Down, Burt Kwouk

AAN: song 'Come To Me' (m Henry Mancini, ly Don Black)

Pink String and Sealing Wax *
GB   1945   89m   bw
Ealing (S. C. Balcon)

In 1880 Brighton, a publican's wife plans to have her husband poisoned.

Unusual, carefully handled period crime melodrama which needed a slightly firmer grip.

w Diana Morgan, Robert Hamer play Roland Pertwee d Robert Hamer ph Stanley Pavey m Norman Demuth

Googie Withers, Mervyn Johns, Gordon Jackson, Sally Ann Howes, Mary Merrall, John Carol, Catherine Lacey, Gary Marsh

The Pink Telephone
France   1975   93m   colour
Gaumont International/Les Productions 2000 (Alain Poire)
aka: Le Téléphone Rose

An old-fashioned, provincial businessman becomes involved with an expensive Parisian call-girl.

Satire on big business, sexual politics and middle-aged angst that runs out of steam before the end.

w Francis Véber d Edouard Molinaro ph Gérard Hameline m Vladimir Cosma pd Robert Sussfeld, Michel Choquet ed Robert and Monique Isnardon

Mireille Darc, Pierre Mondy, Michel Lonsdale, Daniel Ceccaldi, Françoise Prevost, Gérard Hérold

'She passed for white!'
Pinky **
US   1949   102m   bw
TCF (Darryl F. Zanuck)
V*

In the American South, a Negro girl who passes for white has romantic problems.

Rather blah problem picture which seemed brave at the time; a highly professional piece of work nevertheless.

w Philip Dunne, Dudley Nichols novel Quality by Cid Ricketts Summer d Elia Kazan ph Joe MacDonald m Alfred Newman

Jeanne Crain, Ethel Barrymore, Ethel Waters, William Lundigan, Basil Ruysdael, Nina Mae McKinney, Frederick O'Neal, Evelyn Varden

'It has about as much daring as a cheese-mite. It is careful to affront no particular section of the public, to draw no particular conclusion, to outrage no particular code of cinema ethics, to challenge no particular box-office convention.' – C. A. Lejeune

AAN: Jeanne Crain; Ethel Barrymore; Ethel Waters

'Out of a dream world into yours!'
Pinocchio ****
US   1940   77m   Technicolor
Walt Disney
V, V*, L, S

The blue fairy breathes life into a puppet, which has to prove itself before it can turn into a real boy.

Charming, fascinating, superbly organized and streamlined cartoon feature without a single second of boredom.

supervisors Ben Sharpsteen, Hamilton Luske m/ly Leigh Harline, Ned Washington, Paul J. Smith

voices of Dickie Jones, Christian Rub, Cliff Edwards, Evelyn Venable, Walter Catlett, Frankie Darro

'A film of amazing detail and brilliant conception.' – Leonard Maltin

'A work that gives you almost every possible kind of pleasure to be got from a motion picture.' – Richard Mallett, Punch

'The limits of the animated cartoon have been blown so wide open that some of the original wonder of pictures has been restored.' – Otis Ferguson

AA: Leigh Harline, Ned Washington, Paul J. Smith (m); song 'When You Wish Upon a Star' (m Leigh Harline, ly Ned Washington)

Pinocchio and the Emperor of the Night
US   1987   90m   colour
Palace/Filmation (Lou Scheimer)
V*, L

Pinocchio continues his adventures as a real boy.

Sugary confection that cannot stand comparison with Disney's classic.

w Robby London d Hal Sutherland m Anthony Marinelli, Brian Banks songs Will Jennings, Barry Mann, Steve Tyrell

voices of Ed Asner, Lana Beeson, Tom Bosley, Linda Gary, Scott Grimes, James Earl Jones, Rickie Lee Jones, Don Knotts

Pioneer Builders: see *The Conquerors*

Pippi in the South Seas (dubbed)
Sweden/Germany   1974   100m   Movielab colour
Beta/Iduna/K B Nordart (Olle Nordemar)

Pippi, a girl with superhuman strength, sets off with two friends to rescue her father who has been captured by pirates.

An atrocious children's film, cheap and shoddy and so badly dubbed as to be unwatchable.

novel Astrid Lindgren d Olle Hellbom ph Kalle Bergholm m George Riedel ed Jan Persson, Jutte Schweden

Inger Nilsson, Maria Persson, Par Sundberg, Alfred Schieske, Wolfgang Volz, Nikolaus Schilling

'Lost River Lake was a thriving resort – until they discovered . . .'
Piranha *
US   1978   92m   Metrocolor
New World (Roger Corman, Jeff Schechtman, Jon Davison)
V*

A mad doctor's stock of man-eating fish is accidentally released into the local rivers.

Slightly spoofy thriller with a high death rate and a better than usual script. On the whole, an improvement on *Jaws*.

w John Sayles d Joe Dante ph Jamie Anderson m Pino Danaggio sp Jon Berg

Bradford Dillman, Heather Menzies, Kevin McCarthy, Bruce Gordon, Barbara Steele, Keenan Wynn, Dick Miller

'They bred the ultimate killing machine. . .Now you're not safe OUT of the water!'
Piranha II: The Spawning
Italy/US   1982   94m   Technicolor
Columbia/Chako (Chako van Leevwew, Jeff Schechtman)
V*, L
aka: Piranha II: Flying Killers

Holiday-makers are attacked by mutant flying fish.

Feeble low-budget sequel, the first feature of a director who went on to make more successful action movies, including *Terminator* and *Terminator 2*.

w H. A. Milton d James Cameron ph Roberto D'Ettore m Steve Powder ed Robert Silvi

Tricia O'Neil, Steve Marachuk, Lance Henriksen, Ricky G. Paull, Ted Richert, Leslie Graves

The Pirate **
US   1948   102m   Technicolor
MGM (Arthur Freed)
V, V*, L

In a West Indian port, a girl imagines that a wandering player is a famous pirate, who in fact is her despised and elderly suitor.

Minor MGM musical with vivid moments and some intimation of the greatness shortly to come; all very set-bound, but the star quality is infectious.

w Albert Hackett, Frances Goodrich play S. N. Behrman d Vincente Minnelli ph Harry Stradling md Lennie Hayton m/ly Cole Porter

Gene Kelly, Judy Garland, Walter Slezak, Gladys Cooper, Reginald Owen, George Zucco, the Nicholas Brothers

AAN: Lennie Hayton

The Pirate Movie
Australia   1982   105m   Colorfilm
Fox/Joseph Hamilton International
V*

A girl dreams herself back into *The Pirates of Penzance* but changes some of the details.

Galumphing fantasy which suggests that Australian film-makers had better stick to *Botany Bay*, *Gallipoli* and sheep shearing.

w Trevor Farrant d Ken Annakin ph Robin Copping pd Tony Woollard ed Kenneth W. Zemke

Kristy McNichol, Christopher Atkins, Ted Hamilton, Bill Kerr, Maggie Kirkpatrick, Garry Macdonald

'The slapstick and the swordplay are as ineptly choreographed as the production numbers.' – Kim Newman, MFB

Pirate Treasure
US   1934   bw   serial: 12 eps
Universal

An adventurer finds a treasure map and heads for a tropical island, but is followed by a criminal lawyer with ideas of his own.

A serial which plays like a modernized *Treasure Island*.

d Ray Taylor

Richard Talmadge, Lucile Lund, Walter Miller, Pat O'Malley

Pirates
France/Tunisia   1986   124m   Eclaircolor
    Panavision
Cannon/Carthago/Accent Dominco (Tarak Ben Ammar)
V*, S

A British buccaneer, cast adrift on a raft, is taken aboard a Spanish galleon and causes mayhem.

A disaster from a director who should never be allowed to attempt comedy. This one is revolting when it is not a crashing bore.

w Gerard Brach, Roman Polanski d Roman Polanski ph Witold Sobocinski m Philippe Sarde

Walter Matthau, Damien Thomas, Richard Pearson, Roy Kinnear, Ferdy Mayne, Charlotte Lewis

† The galleon, which cost 8 million dollars, was not wasted. It was given to the municipality of Cannes and became a tourist attraction.

AAN: costumes (Anthony Powell)

Pirates of Blood River *
GB   1961   84m   Technicolor   Hammerscope
Hammer (Anthony Nelson Keys)

Pirates in search of gold terrorize a Huguenot settlement.

Land-locked blood and thunder for tough schoolboys.

w John Hunter, John Gilling d John Gilling ph Arthur Grant

Christopher Lee, Andrew Keir, Kerwin Mathews, Glenn Corbett, Peter Arne, Oliver Reed, Marla Landi, Michael Ripper

Pirates of Monterey

US   1947   72m   Technicolor
Paul Malvern/Universal-International

A Spanish girl goes to California to marry a soldier but is romanced by an outlaw.

Predictable action hokum.

w Sam Hellman, Margaret Buell Wilder   d Alfred Werker

Maria Montez, Rod Cameron, Mikhail Rasumny, Philip Reed, Gilbert Roland, Gale Sondergaard, Tamara Shayne, Robert Warwick

The Pirates of Penzance

GB   1982   112m   Technicolor   Panavision
Universal (Joseph Papp, Timothy Burrill)
V*, L

An adaptation of the Gilbert and Sullivan operetta in the form of the Joseph Papp Broadway revival.

What was tolerably pretty and witty on the stage is a great bore on wide film.

wd Wilford Leach   ph Douglas Slocombe
m Gilbert and Sullivan   pd Elliott Scott   ed Anne V. Coates

Kevin Kline, Angela Lansbury, Linda Ronstadt, George Rose, Tony Azito, Rex Smith

'Not the slightest trace of imagination.' – MFB

'Anyone who thinks Gilbert and Sullivan indestructible should see this.' – Observer

Pirates of the High Seas

US   1950   bw   serial: 15 eps
Columbia

A one-ship Pacific freight line is under constant attack from a pirate cruiser; an adventurer buddy comes to help.

A serial for its times: the villain turns out to be an escaped war criminal.

d Spencer Bennet, Thomas Carr

Buster Crabbe, Lois Hall, Tommy Farrell, Gene Roth, Tristram Coffin

Pirates of Tortuga

US   1961   97m   DeLuxe   Cinemascope
Sam Katzman/TCF

In the 17th-century Caribbean, a privateer is ordered by the king to go undercover and rout Sir Henry Morgan.

Listless swashbuckler with inferior talent.

w Melvin Levy, Jesse L. Lasky Jnr, Pat Silver
d Robert D. Webb

Ken Scott, Dave King, Letitia Roman, John Richardson, Robert Stephens, Edgar Barrier

Pirates of Tripoli

US   1955   72m   Technicolor
Sam Katzman/Columbia

A pirate captain comes to the aid of an oriental princess.

More akin to the Arabian Knights than Blackbeard, but not bad for a double-biller.

w Allen March   d Felix Feist

Paul Henreid, Patricia Medina, Paul Newland, John Miljan, Lillian Bond

Pisma Myortovovo Cheloveka: see Letters from a Dead Man

A Pistol for Ringo *

Italy/Spain   1965   99m   colour
PCM/Balcàzar (Alberto Pugliese, Luciano Ercoli)
original title: Una Pistola per Ringo

A wandering gunman goes to the aid of a Texan family whose ranch has been taken over by Mexican bandits.

Above-average spaghetti Western, much influenced by the work of John Ford and Howard Hawks.

wd Duccio Tessari   ph Francisco Marin   m Ennio Morricone   ad Juan Alberto Soler   ed Lucia Quaglia

Giuliano Gemma, Fernando Sancho, Hally Hammond (Lorella de Luca), Nieves Navarro, Antonio Casas, Jorge Martin

† It was followed by a sequel, The Return of Ringo (qv).

The Pit and the Pendulum *

US   1961   85m   Pathecolor   Panavision
AIP/Alta Vista (Roger Corman)
V, V*

Lovers plan to drive her brother mad; he responds by locking them in his torture chamber.

The centrepiece only is borrowed from Poe; the rest is lurid but mostly ineffective. Still, its commercial success started the Poe cycle of the sixties.

w Richard Matheson   d Roger Corman   ph Floyd Crosby   m Les Baxter

Vincent Price, Barbara Steele, John Kerr

'As in House of Usher, the quality of the film is its full-blooded feeling for Gothic horror – storms and lightning, mouldering castles and cobwebbed torture chambers, bleeding brides trying to tear the lids from their untimely tombs.' – David Robinson

Pitfall

US   1948   85m   bw
Samuel Bischoff
V*, L

An insurance investigator proves easy prey for a grasping woman.

Modest suspenser, quite efficiently made.

w Jay Dratler   novel Jay Dratler   d André de Toth
ph Harry Wild   md Louis Forbes

Dick Powell, Lizabeth Scott, Jane Wyatt, Raymond Burr, John Litel, Byron Barr, Ann Doran

Pittsburgh

US   1942   91m   bw
Universal (Charles K. Feldman)

A coal miner's daughter has two loves, all of them trying to improve their social status as Pittsburgh becomes a world centre of steel production.

Routine melodrama ending as a flagwaver, and allowing none of its stars any opportunity.

w Kenneth Gamet, Tom Reed   d Lewis Seiler
ph Robert de Grasse   m Hans Salter

Marlene Dietrich, Randolph Scott, John Wayne, Frank Craven, Louise Allbritton, Shemp Howard, Ludwig Stossel, Thomas Gomez

Pixote **

Brazil   1981   127m   colour
Palace/Embrafilme
V, V*

A 10-year-old living on the streets of São Paulo tries to survive by pimping, drug-dealing and murder.

Grim and sensational exposé of a social problem, using actual homeless children to add to its reality.

w Hector Babenco, Jorge Duran   novel Infancia dos Mortos by José Louzeiro   d Hector Babenco
ph Rodolfo Sanches   m John Neschling   ad Clovis Bueno   ed Luiz Elias

Fernando Ramos da Silva, Jorge Julião, Gilberto Moura, Edilson Lino, Zenildo Oliveira Santos, Claudio Bernardo, Marilia Pera, José Nilson Dos Santos

The Pizza Triangle: see Jealousy Italian Style

'They do it in the name of love!'

A Place for Lovers

US   1969   102m   colour
MGM

A dying American fashion designer retires to her Italian villa and has a high old time with an Italian engineer.

Incomparably crass tearjerker which seems eager to offer too many morals about life and love and art.

w Peter Baldwin, Ennio de Concini, Tonino Guerra, Julian Halevy, Cesare Zavattini   d Vittorio de Sica

Faye Dunaway, Marcello Mastroianni, Caroline Mortimer, Karin Engh

'The most God-awful piece of pseudo-romantic slop I've ever seen.' – Roger Ebert, Chicago Sun Times

'The worst movie I have seen all year and possibly since 1926.' – Charles Champlin, L.A. Times

'The five scriptwriters who supposedly worked on the film must have spent time enough at the watercooler to flood a camel.' – Time

'Seldom has the screen so captured the fire and fever of today's youth! Seldom has a film boasted three such exciting star performances!'

A Place in the Sun **

US   1951   122m   bw
Paramount/George Stevens
V*, L

A poor young man, offered the chance of a rich wife, allows himself to be convicted and executed for the accidental death of his former fiancée.

Overblown, overlong and over-praised melodrama from a monumental novel of social guilt; sometimes visually striking, this version alters the stresses of the plot and leaves no time for sociological detail. A film so clearly intended as a masterpiece could hardly fail to be boring.

w Michael Wilson, Harry Brown   novel An American Tragedy by Theodore Dreiser   d George Stevens
ph William C. Mellor   m Franz Waxman   ad Hans Dreier, Walter Tyler   ed William Hornbeck

Montgomery Clift, Elizabeth Taylor, Shelley Winters, Anne Revere, Keefe Brasselle, Fred Clark, Raymond Burr, Frieda Inescort, Shepperd Strudwick, Kathryn Givney, Walter Sande   'An almost incredibly painstaking work . . . mannered enough for a very fancy Gothic murder mystery. This version gives the story a modern setting, but the town is an arrangement of symbols of wealth, glamour and power versus symbols of poor, drab helplessness – an arrangement far more suitable to the thirties than to the fifties.' – Pauline Kael

AA: script; George Stevens; William C. Mellor; Franz Waxman; editing

AAN: best picture; Montgomery Clift; Shelley Winters

A Place of One's Own **

GB   1944   92m   bw
GFD/Gainsborough (R. J. Minney)

In Edwardian times, an old house is taken over by an elderly couple, and their young companion is possessed by the spirit of a murdered girl.

Charming little ghost story, not quite detailed enough to be totally effective.

w Brock Williams   novel Osbert Sitwell   d Bernard Knowles   ph Stephen Dade   md Louis Levy
m Hubert Bath

James Mason, Barbara Mullen, Margaret Lockwood, Dennis Price, Helen Haye, Michael Shepley, Dulcie Gray, Moore Marriott

'A fine piece of work . . . gripping, marvellous, outstanding, eerie, perky, beautiful, lovely and different.' – C. A. Lejeune

'One comes away with an impression of elegance which has not so far been frequent in the British cinema.' – *Dilys Powell*

A Place to Go
GB   1963   86m   bw
British Lion/Excalibur (Michael Relph, Basil Dearden)

A young man depressed by his urban environment turns to crime.

Panorama of London low life, efficiently varied and well made but not in any way memorable. *It Always Rains on Sunday,* fifteen years earlier, wears better.

w Michael Relph, Clive Exton   *novel Bethnal Green by* Michael Fisher   *d* Basil Dearden   *ph* Reg Wyer   *m* Charles Blackwell

Rita Tushingham, Mike Sarne, Doris Hare, John Slater, Bernard Lee, Barbara Ferris, Roy Kinnear

Places in the Heart
US   1984   111m   Technicolor
Tri-Star/Delphi (Arlene Donovan)
V, V*, L

In 1935 Texas, the sheriff's widow struggles to maintain the family farm.

All-American saga with asides including the Ku Klux Klan; though based on the author's recollections of childhood, it all seems predictable.

wd Robert Benton   *ph* Nestor Almendros   *m* John Kander   *pd* Gene Callahan

Sally Field, Lindsay Crouse, Ed Harris, Amy Madigan, John Malkovich, Danny Glover

'Basically just another calculated tug at the heartstrings.' – *Tom Milne, MFB*

AA: Sally Field; original screenplay

AAN: best picture; John Malkovich (supporting actor); Lindsay Crouse (supporting actress); direction

Plaff! Or Too Afraid of Life *
Cuba   1988   92m   colour
Metro/ICAIC (Ricardo Avila)
original title: *Desmasiado Miedo A La Vida, O Plaff*

A superstitious mother tries to get rid of her scientific daughter-in-law.

Deliberately ramshackle political comedy – the beginning of the film is kept to the end – which is not without a certain surrealist charm.

w Daniel Chavarría, Juan Carlos Tabío   *d* Juan Carlos Tabío   *ph* Julio Valdés   *ad* Raúl Oliva   *ed* Roberto Bravo, Osvaldo M. Donatien

Daysi Granados, Thais Valdés, Luis Alberto Garcia, Raúl Pamares, Alicia Bustamente, Jorge Cao

'A wittily cynical exercise in alienation which oozes awkwardness and provokes uncomfortable laughter.' – *MFB*

La Plage des Enfants Perdus: see *The Beach of Lost Children*

The Plague Dogs
GB/US   1982   103m   Technicolor
Nepenthe Productions
V*

Two dogs escape from a research laboratory and are in danger of infecting the country with a deadly virus.

Misguided and woefully overlong attempt to preach a message through a cartoon. Like *Watership Down,* it needs the printed word and is deflected by the inevitably cuddly look of the animated animals.

wd Martin Rosen   *novel* Richard Adams

voices of John Hurt, James Bolam, Christopher Benjamin, Judy Geeson, Barbara Leigh-Hunt

The Plague of the Zombies *
GB   1965   91m   Technicolor
Hammer (Anthony Nelson Keys)

A voodoo-practising Cornish squire raises zombies from the dead and uses them to work his tin mine.

They don't explain why he didn't simply hire the living; apart from that this is Hammer on its better side, with a charming elderly hero and good suspense sequences.

w Peter Bryan   *d* John Gilling   *ph* Arthur Grant   *m* James Bernard

André Morell, John Carson, Diane Clare, Brook Williams, Jacqueline Pearce, Alex Davion, Michael Ripper

'Visually the film is splendid . . . the script manages several offbeat strokes.' – *MFB*

'Grandest love story ever told!'
The Plainsman **
US   1936   113m   bw
Paramount/Cecil B. de Mille
V*, L

The life of Wild Bill Hickok and his friends Buffalo Bill and Calamity Jane.

Standard big-scale 30s Western; narrative lumpy, characters idealized, spectacle impressive, technical credits high.

w Waldemar Young, Lynn Riggs, Harold Lamb   *d Cecil B. de Mille   ph* Victor Milner, George Robinson   *md* Boris Morros   *m* George Antheil

Gary Cooper, James Ellison, Jean Arthur, Charles Bickford, Helen Burgess, Porter Hall, Paul Harvey, Victor Varconi

'It should do all right for business, ranging from big to good, possibly irregular in spots.' – *Variety*

'Certainly the finest western since *The Virginian;* perhaps the finest western in the history of the film.' – *Graham Greene*

† The story was remade as a TV movie in 1966, with Don Murray.

The Plainsman and the Lady
US   1946   84m   bw
Republic

In 1847, the Pony Express is threatened by stagecoach owners.

Moderate Western for family consumption.

w Richard Wormser   *d* Joseph Kane

William Elliott, Gail Patrick, Vera Ralston, Joseph Schildkraut

Le Plaisir *
France   1952   97m   bw
Stera/CCFC

Three stories by Guy de Maupassant, about the search for pleasure: 'Le Masque', 'La Maison Tellier', 'Le Modèle'.

Stylish but rather subdued compendium, with no highlights to stay in the memory.

w Jacques Natanson, Max Ophuls   *d* Max Ophuls   *ph* Christian Matras, Philippe Agostini   *m* Joe Hajos   *ad* Max Ophuls

Claude Dauphin, Gaby Morlay; Madeleine Renaud, Danielle Darrieux, Ginette Leclerc, Jean Gabin, Pierre Brasseur; Simone Simon, Daniel Gélin

'An attractive theme tune, good performances, and the pleasure itself of virtuosity.' – *Gavin Lambert, MFB*

AAN: art direction

'There comes a time in every man's life when he just can't believe his eyes!'
Plan 9 from Outer Space
US   1958   79m   bw
Wade Williams Productions (Edward D. Wood Jnr)
V*, L
aka: *Grave Robbers from Outer Space*

Space people try to resurrect the Earth's dead and turn them against the world.

Inept mini-budgeter often hailed as the worst film ever made. It is certainly among the most boring.

wd Edward D. Wood Jnr   *ph* William C. Thompson   *md* Gordon Zahler   *ad* Tom Kemp   *sp* Charles Duncan

Bela Lugosi (who died after four days of shooting and is mostly represented by a double), Tor Johnson, Gregory Walcott, Mona McKinnon, Vampira, Lyle Talbot

SAMPLE DIALOGUE: 'One thing's sure, Inspector Clay's dead. Murdered. And somebody's responsible.'

Planes, Trains and Automobiles *
US   1987   93m   colour
UIP/Paramount (John Hughes)
V, V*, L

An advertising executive, trying to get home for Thanksgiving, finds many obstacles hampering his progress, including an insufferable companion.

Cheerful farce that allows some room for characterization.

wd John Hughes   *ph* Don Peterman   *m* Ira Newborn   *pd* John W. Corso   *ed* Paul Hirsch

Steve Martin, John Candy, Michael McKean, Kevin Bacon, Dylan Baker, Carol Bruce, Olivia Burnette, Diana Douglas, William Windom

'Somewhere in the universe, there must be something better than man!'
Planet of the Apes ***
US   1968   119m   DeLuxe   Panavision
TCF/Apjac (Mort Abrahams)
V, V*, L, S

Astronauts caught in a time warp land on a planet which turns out to be Earth in the distant future, when men have become beasts and the apes have taken over.

Stylish, thoughtful science fiction which starts and finishes splendidly but suffers from a sag in the middle. The ape make-up is great.

w Michael Wilson, Rod Serling,   novel Monkey Planet by Pierre Boulle   *d Franklin Schaffner   ph* Leon Shamroy   *m* Jerry Goldsmith

Charlton Heston, Roddy McDowall, *Kim Hunter,* Maurice Evans, James Whitmore, James Daly, Linda Harrison

'One of the most telling science fiction films to date.' – *Tom Milne*

† Sequels, in roughly descending order of interest, were BENEATH THE PLANET OF THE APES (1969), ESCAPE FROM THE PLANET OF THE APES (1970), CONQUEST OF THE PLANET OF THE APES (1972) and BATTLE FOR THE PLANET OF THE APES (1973). A TV series followed in 1974, and a cartoon series in 1975.

AA: make-up (John Chambers)

AAN: Jerry Goldsmith; costumes (Morton Haack)

The Planter's Wife
GB   1952   91m   bw
Rank/Pinnacle (John Stafford)
US title: *Outpost in Malaya;* original title: *White Blood*

Malaya under the terrorists. A wife is planning to leave but changes her mind after she and her husband defend their home in a siege.

Superficial studio-bound melodrama unworthy of its subject but a good star vehicle.

w Peter Proud, Guy Elmes   *d* Ken Annakin   *ph* Geoffrey Unsworth   *m* Allan Gray

Claudette Colbert, Jack Hawkins, Ram Gopal, Jeremy Spenser, Tom Macauley, Helen Goss

Platinum Blonde *
US   1931   92m   bw
Columbia
V*

A newspaper reporter falls for an heiress.

Limp romantic comedy with interesting performances: the film which established Jean Harlow.

w Robert Riskin, Jo Swerling story Harry E. Chandler, Doug Churchill d Frank Capra ph Joseph Walker

Robert Williams, Loretta Young, Jean Harlow, Halliwell Hobbes, Reginald Owen

'A programmer that fully entertains, is laughy and represents what cast, dialogue and direction can do with a lean story.' – *Variety*

Platinum High School

US 1960 96m bw
Albert Zugsmith/MGM
GB title: *Rich, Young and Deadly*

A father investigates his son's death at a military academy for rich juvenile delinquents.

Hilarious serial-like melodrama with the worm turning to some effect.

w Robert Smith d Charles Haas

Mickey Rooney, Dan Duryea, Terry Moore, Warren Berlinger, Yvette Mimieux, Conway Twitty, Elisha Cook Jnr, Richard Jaeckel

Platoon **

US 1986 120m CFI colour
Hemdale/Arnold Kopelson
V (W), V*, L, S

Experiences of infantrymen during the Vietnam war.

Not badly done in the style of *Bataan* (plus brutality and gore). One would have thought it too late to do it at all, but the American public made it a box-office hit.

wd Oliver Stone ph Robert Richardson m Georges Delerue ed Claire Simpson

Tom Berenger, William DaFoe, Charlie Sheen, Forest Whitaker, Francesco Quinn

AA: best picture; Oliver Stone as director; Claire Simpson

AAN: Tom Berenger, William DaFoe; Oliver Stone for original screenplay; Robert Richardson

Play Dirty *

GB 1969 118m Technicolor Panavision
UA/Lowndes (Harry Saltzman)

During World War II, a squad of ex-criminals is given the job of destroying an enemy oil depot in North Africa.

Small-scale *Dirty Dozen* with would-be ironic twists; well made entertainment for the stout-hearted.

w Lotte Colin, Melvyn Bragg d André de Toth ph Edward Scaife m Michel Legrand

Michael Caine, Nigel Davenport, Nigel Green, Harry Andrews, Bernard Archard, Daniel Pilon

Play It Again Sam *

US 1972 86m Technicolor Panavision
Paramount/APJAC/Rollins-Joffe (Arthur P. Jacobs)
V, V*, L

A neurotic film critic is abandoned by his wife and seeks fresh companionship, with help from the shade of Humphrey Bogart.

Random comedy for star fans, mainly quite lively and painless.

w Woody Allen play Woody Allen d Herbert Ross ph Owen Roizman m Billy Goldenberg

Woody Allen, Diane Keaton, Jerry Lacy, Susan Anspach

Play It as It Lays

US 1972 94m Technicolor Panavision
Universal

An unsuccessful actress takes stock of her wrecked life.

With-it melodrama which audiences preferred to be without.

w Joan Didion, John Gregory Dunne novel Joan Didion d Frank Perry

Anthony Perkins, Tuesday Weld, Tammy Grimes, Adam Roarke, Ruth Ford

Play Me Something

GB 1989 72m bw/colour
BFI/Film Four International/Scottish Film Production Fund/ Grampian TV (Kate Swan)

On a small Scottish island, a group of passengers waiting for a plane listen to a story about an Italian peasant leaving his village to go to Venice.

An intellectual endeavour that never quite comes alive on the screen.

w John Berger, Timothy Neat story *Once in Europe* by John Berger d Timothy Neat ph Chris Cox m Jim Sutherland ad Annette Gillies ed Russell Fenton

Lucia Lanzarini, Charlie Barron, John Berger, Hamish Henderson, Tilda Swinton, Stewart Ennis, Robert Carr, Liz Lochhead

'The scream you hear may be your own!'

Play Misty for Me *

US 1971 102m Technicolor
Universal/Malpaso (Robert Daley)
V, V*, L

A radio disc jockey is pestered by a girl who turns out to be homicidally jealous.

Smartly made if over-extended psycho melodrama with good suspense sequences and a fair quota of shocks.

w Jo Heims, Dean Reisner d Clint Eastwood ph Bruce Surtees m Dee Barton

Clint Eastwood, Jessica Walter, Donna Mills, John Larch

The Playboy: see *Kicking the Moon Around*

'Maurice brings a new kind of love to you!'

Playboy of Paris

US 1930 82m bw
Paramount

A waiter inherits a million but finds he can't leave his job, so he becomes a playboy by night only.

Rather rickety star vehicle which demands attention only when he is on screen.

w Percy Heath play *The Little Café* by Tristan Bernard d Ludwig Berger

Maurice Chevalier, Frances Dee, O. P. Heggie, Stuart Erwin, Eugene Pallette

'Light, amusing farce story doesn't help and may hurt ... Chevalier's the only draw.' – *Variety*

'In a small community, love is never a private affair.'

The Playboys *

GB 1992 109m Technicolor
Samuel Goldwyn/Green Umbrella (William P. Cartlidge, Simon Perry)
V, V*, L

In an Irish village in the 1950s, the alcoholic local policeman and a strolling player both fall in love with an unmarried mother.

A soap opera-style narrative of thwarted love, of interest mainly for its performances.

w Shane Connaughton, Kerry Crabbe d Gillies MacKinnon ph Jack Conroy m Jean-Claude Petit pd Andy Harris ed Humphrey Dixon

Albert Finney, Aidan Quinn, Robin Wright, Milo O'Shea, Alan Devlin, Niamh Cusack, Niall Buggy, Adrian Dunbar

'A heartbreak tragedy wrapped up inside an ingratiating comedy.' – *Alexander Walker, London Evening Standard*

The Player ****

US 1992 124m DeLuxe
Guild/Avenue (David Brown, Michael Tolkin, Nick Wechsler)
V, V*, L, S

A Hollywood studio executive gets away with murder.

A deft and dazzling satire on the film industry – witty, surprising and intelligent.

w Michael Tolkin novel Michael Tolkin d Robert Altman ph Jean Lepine m Thomas Newman pd Stephen Altman ed Geraldine Peroni

Tim Robbins, Greta Scacchi, Fred Ward, Whoopi Goldberg, Peter Gallagher, Brion James, Cynthia Stevenson, Vincent D'Onofrio, Dean Stockwell, Richard E. Grant, Sydney Pollack

'The movie has the exhilarating nonchalance of the director's seventies classics, and its tone is volatile, elusive: with breathtaking assurance, it veers from psychological-thriller suspense to goofball comedy to icy satire.' – *Terrence Rafferty, New Yorker*

† The film featured more than 60 stars playing themselves, including Harry Belafonte, James Coburn, Peter Falk, Teri Garr, Angelica Huston, Jack Lemmon, Nick Nolte, Burt Reynolds, Julia Roberts, Susan Sarandon, Rod Steiger and Bruce Willis.

AAN: Robert Altman; Michael Tolkin; Geraldine Peroni

Players

US 1979 120m Metrocolor
Paramount (Robert Evans)
V*

A pro tennis player is trained for top stardom by a sculptress with a mysterious past.

Entirely uninvolving romantic drama stretched around a Wimbledon match; slickness does not compensate for a gaping hole at the centre.

w Arnold Schulman d Anthony Harvey ph James Crabe m Jerry Goldsmith pd Richard Sylbert

Ali MacGraw, Dean-Paul Martin, Maximilian Schell, Pancho Gonzalez

Players: see *The Club*

Playgirl

US 1954 85m bw
Universal-International

A small-town girl becomes a good-time girl in the big city.

Totally unsurprising melodrama.

w Robert Blees d Joseph Pevney

Shelley Winters, Barry Sullivan, Colleen Miller, Gregg Palmer, Richard Long, Kent Taylor

The Playgirl and the War Minister: see *The Amorous Prawn*

Playmates *

US 1941 96m bw
RKO (Cliff Reid)
V*

For the sake of a lucrative radio contract, John Barrymore agrees to turn bandleader Kay Kyser into a Shakespearian actor.

Barrymore's last film is a weird comedy concoction, awesome in its waste of his talents but fairly funny in a high school kind of way.

w James V. Kern d David Butler ph Frank Redman songs James Van Heusen, Johnny Burke

Kay Kyser and his Band, *John Barrymore,* Ginny Simms, Lupe Velez, May Robson, Patsy Kelly, Peter Lind Hayes, George Cleveland

Playtime *
France   1968   152m   Eastmancolor   70mm
Specta Films (René Silvera)
V, V*

Hulot and a group of American tourists are bewildered by life in an airport, a business block and a restaurant.

Incredibly extended series of sketches, none of which is devastatingly funny. The irritation is that the talent is clearly there but needs control.

w Jacques Tati, Jacques Lagrange   d Jacques Tati   ph Jean Badal, Andreas Winding   m Francis Lemarque   pd Eugène Roman

Jacques Tati, Barbara Dennek, Jacqueline Lecomte, Henri Piccoli

'Tati still seems the wrong distance from his audience: not so far that we cannot see his gifts, not close enough so that they really touch.' – *Stanley Kauffmann*

'How sad that the result of all this, though it includes a great deal of intermittent pleasure, comes at times so dangerously close to boredom.' – *Brenda Davies, MFB*

'A series of brilliant doodles by an artist who has earned the right to indulge himself on such a scale.' – *Alexander Walker*

Plaza Suite *
US   1971   114m   Technicolor
Paramount (Howard B. Koch)
V*, L

Three sketches set in the same suite at New York's Plaza Hotel, with Walter Matthau appearing in all three but in different character.

A highly theatrical entertainment which was bound to seem flattened on the screen, but emerges with at least some of its laughs intact.

w Neil Simon   play Neil Simon   d Arthur Hiller   ph Jack Marta   m Maurice Jarre

Walter Matthau, Maureen Stapleton, Barbara Harris, Lee Grant, Louise Sorel

† In the play, Maureen Stapleton played all three female roles.

Please Believe Me
US   1950   87m   bw
MGM (Val Lewton)

An English girl inherits an American ranch and is chased by a millionaire, a con man and a lawyer.

Dullsville comedy which failed to establish its star in America.

w Nathaniel Curtis   d Norman Taurog   ph Robert Planck   m Hans Salter

Deborah Kerr, Robert Walker, Mark Stevens, Peter Lawford, James Whitmore, Spring Byington

Please Don't Eat the Daisies
US   1960   111m   Metrocolor   Panavision
MGM (Joe Pasternak)
V*

The family of a drama critic move to the country.

Thin, obvious comedy, all dressed up but with nowhere to go.

w Isobel Lennart   book Jean Kerr   d Charles Walters   ph Robert Bronner   m David Rose

Doris Day, David Niven, Janis Paige, Spring Byington, Patsy Kelly, Richard Haydn, Jack Weston, John Harding, Margaret Lindsay

Please Murder Me
US   1956   78m   bw
DCA (Donald Hyde)

An attorney defends an accused murderess, at great cost to himself.

Adequate Poverty Row suspenser with a foreseeable trick ending.

w Al C. Ward, Donald Hyde   d Peter Godfrey   ph Allen Stensvold

Angela Lansbury, Raymond Burr, Dick Foran, John Dehner, Lamont Johnson, Denver Pyle

Please Sir
GB   1971   101m   Eastmancolor
Rank/LWI/Leslie Grade (Andrew Mitchell)

The masters and pupils of Fenn Street school go on an annual camp.

Grossly inflated, occasionally funny big-screen version of the TV series.

w John Esmonde, Bob Larbey   d Mark Stuart   ph Wilkie Cooper   m Mike Vickers

John Alderton, Deryck Guyler, Joan Sanderson, Noel Howlett, Eric Chitty, Richard Davies

Please Teacher
GB   1937   75m   bw
Associated British

An heir tries to find his bequest in the country house he has sold as a girls' school.

Cheerful star farce with songs.   wd Stafford Dickens   *musical* K. R. G. Browne and R. P. Weston

Bobby Howes, René Ray, Vera Pearce, Wylie Watson, Bertha Belmore, Lyn Harding

'Plenty of laughs.' – *Variety*

Please Turn Over
GB   1959   87m   bw
Beaconsfield/Anglo Amalgamated

A teenager writes a sexy best-seller clearly featuring her family and friends.

Acceptable but uninspired comedy from a West End success.

w Norman Hudis   play Book of the Month by Basil Thomas   d Gerald Thomas

Ted Ray, Jean Kent, Leslie Phillips, Joan Sims, Julia Lockwood, Charles Hawtrey, Lionel Jeffries

The Pleasure Garden
GB/Germany   1925   74m approx (24 fps)   bw   silent
Gainsborough/Emelka (Michael Balcon, Erich Pommer)

A chorus girl marries a rich colonial who goes native.

Boring melodrama with a few touches typical of its director, whose first film it is.

w Eliot Stannard   novel Oliver Sandys   d Alfred Hitchcock   ph Baron Ventigmilia

Virginia Valli, John Stuart, Miles Mander, Carmelita Gerghty

The Pleasure Girls
GB   1965   88m   bw
Compton Tekli (Harry Fine)

Girl flatmates in London have trouble with their boyfriends.

The road to ruin sixties style, hackneyed but quite well observed.

wd Gerry O'Hara   ph Michael Reed   m Malcolm Lockyer

Ian McShane, Francesca Annis, Tony Tanner, Klaus Kinski, Mark Eden, Suzanna Leigh

The Pleasure of His Company
US   1961   114m   Technicolor
Paramount/Perlberg-Seaton

An ageing playboy arrives unexpectedly in San Francisco for his daughter's wedding.

Tame family comedy, very flatly adapted from the stage; dressed to kill, but with no narrative or cinematic drive.

w Samuel Taylor   play Samuel Taylor, Cornelia Otis Skinner   d George Seaton   ph Robert Burks   m Alfred Newman

Fred Astaire, Lilli Palmer, Debbie Reynolds, Charles Ruggles, Tab Hunter, Gary Merrill, Harold Fong

'Smart comedy in its most diluted form.' – *MFB*

'Do Men Deserve Everything They Get?'
The Pleasure Principle
GB   1991   100m   Metrocolor
Palace/Psychology News (David Cohen)
V

A medical journalist, divorced from his lesbian wife, tries to keep three affairs on the go at once.

Flaccid farce of sexual misadventures, performed with perfunctory interest.

wd David Cohen   ph Andrew Spellar   m Sonny Southon   pd Cecilia Brereton   ed Joe McAllister

Peter Firth, Lynsey Baxter, Haydn Gwynne, Lysette Anthony, Sara Mair-Thomas, Ian Hogg, Francesca Folan, Liam McDermott

'A refreshing light comedy that simply asks its audience to lie back and enjoy.' – *Variety*

'It does not stimulate as it simulates and is essentially a throwback to those sleazy British soft-core comedies of the mid-Seventies.' – *Philip French, Observer*

† The film was made for £200,000, which its producer-director borrowed from his bank.

The Pleasure Seekers
US   1964   107m   DeLuxe   Cinemascope
TCF (David Weisbart)

Three girls in Madrid find boyfriends.

Dim remake of *Three Coins in the Fountain,* adequate but unstimulating on all levels.

w Edith Sommer   d Jean Negulesco   ph Daniel L. Fapp   m Lionel Newman, Alexander Courage

Ann-Margret, Tony Franciosa, Carol Lynley, Gene Tierney, Brian Keith, Gardner McKay, Isobel Elsom

AAN: Lionel Newman, Alexander Courage

Plenty *
US   1985   124m   Technicolor   Panavision
TCF/RKO/Edward R. Pressman
V, V*, L

After World War II, the career of a neurotic society woman has parallels with the problems of western Europe.

Heavy-going allegory which should have stayed on the stage.

w David Hare   play David Hare   d Fred Schepisi   ph Ian Baker   m Bruce Smeaton   pd Richard MacDonald   ed Peter Honess

Meryl Streep, Charles Dance, Tracey Ullman, John Gielgud, Sting, Ian McKellen, Sam Neill

'The press tell us that this film is an allegory of the fall of the British Empire. No wonder it is dreary!' – *Quentin Crisp*

The Plot Against Harry
US   1969   81m   bw
Electric/Contemporary/King Screen (Robert Young, Michael Roemer)
V*

Out of jail on parole, a gangster finds that business and his family are not what they were.

Put on the shelf for twenty years before its eventual release and hailed by some as a comic masterpiece, it turns out to be a moderately amusing movie that shows its age.

wd Michael Roemer   *ph* Robert Young   *m* Frank Lewin   *ad* Howard Mandel   *ed* Maurice Schell

Martin Priest, Ben Lang, Maxine Woods, Henry Nemo, Jacques Taylor, Jean Leslie, Ellen Herbert, Sandra Kazan

'Harry's wit looks less deadpan than stone dead.' – *Kevin Jackson, Independent*

The Plot Thickens
US   1936   69m   bw
William Sistrom/RKO

A murder proves to be connected with an art swindle.

Another minor case for Hildegarde Withers.

w Clarence Upson Young, Jack Townley
novel Stuart Palmer   *d* Ben Holmes

James Gleason, ZaSu Pitts, Owen Davis Jnr, Louise Latimer

The Plot to Kill Roosevelt: see *Teheran*

The Plough and the Stars *
US   1936   72m   bw
RKO (Cliff Reid, Robert Sisk)

In 1916, a Dublin marriage is threatened by the husband's appointment as commander of the citizen army.

Rather elementary film version of the play about the Troubles; interesting for effort rather than performance, and for the talent involved.

w Dudley Nichols   *play* Sean O'Casey   *d* John Ford   *ph* Joseph August   *m* Roy Webb

Barbara Stanwyck, Preston Foster, Barry Fitzgerald, Denis O'Dea, Eileen Crowe, F. J. McCormick, Arthur Shields, Una O'Connor, Moroni Olsen, J. M. Kerrigan, Bonita Granville

'Skilfully made but not impressive as a money entry.' – *Variety*

The Ploughman's Lunch ***
GB   1983   107m   colour
Goldcrest/Greenpoint/AC & D (Simon Relph, Ann Scott)
V*

Media people find their cynicism deepened after the Falklands War.

Tough and intelligent, with nice observation and twists of detail.

w Ian McEwan   *d* Richard Eyre   *ph* Clive Tickner   *m* Dominic Muldowney

Jonathan Pryce, Tim Curry, Rosemary Harris, Frank Finlay, Charlie Dore, David de Keyser, Nat Jackley

'You don't have to agree with it, but you can't ignore it.' – *Daily Mail*

'It quietly and persuasively suggests that we get precisely the media we deserve.' – *Guardian*

Plovec: see *The Swimmer*

The Plow that Broke the Plains **
US   1936   28m   bw
Resettlement Administration Film Unit
S

The story of how overcultivation of America's Great Plains resulted in the Dust Bowl.

Classic documentary which inevitably means less now than it did at the time but is still an impressive counterpoint to *The Grapes of Wrath*.

wd Pare Lorenz   *m* Virgil Thomson

Pluck of the Irish: see *Great Guy*

Plunder *
GB   1930   98m   bw
Herbert Wilcox/British and Dominions

Two society friends turn jewel thieves to help an heiress.

Primitive talkie version of a Ben Travers farce which veered towards melodrama but had a successful stage revival at the National Theatre in 1978; valuable as a record of the original performances.

w W. P. Lipscomb   *d* Tom Walls

Tom Walls, Ralph Lynn, Robertson Hare, Winifred Shotter, Sydney Lynn, Ethel Coleridge

'Just a photographic record of the stage success.' – *Variety*

Plunder of the Sun *
US   1953   81m   bw
Warner (Robert Fellows)

Various criminal elements seek buried treasure among the Mexican Aztec ruins.

Interestingly located, well made, unconvincingly scripted melodrama, yet another borrowing from *The Maltese Falcon*.

w Jonathan Latimer   *novel* David Dodge   *d* John Farrow   *ph* Jack Draper   *m* Antonio D. Conde

Glenn Ford, Diana Lynn, Francis L. Sullivan, Patricia Medina, Sean McClory, Douglass Dumbrille, Eduardo Noriega

The Plunderers
US   1947   87m   bw
Republic

An undercover cavalry officer becomes friends with an outlaw who saves his life.

Routine Western, just about watchable.

w Gerald Geraghty and Gerald Drayson Adams
d Joseph Kane

Rod Cameron, Ilona Massey, Adrian Booth

The Plunderers
US   1960   94m   bw
Allied Artists/August (Joseph Pevney)

In the old west, four juvenile delinquents take over a town.

The Wild One in period dress. Nothing in particular.

w Bob Barbash   *d* Joseph Pevney   *ph* Eugene Polito   *m* Leonard Rosenman

Jeff Chandler, John Saxon, Ray Stricklyn, Roger Torrey, Dee Pollock, Marsha Hunt, Dolores Hart, Jay C. Flippen, James Westerfield

Plymouth Adventure *
US   1952   105m   Technicolor
MGM (Dore Schary)

The Pilgrim Fathers sail from Plymouth on the *Mayflower* and spend their first months ashore on the coast of America.

Well-meaning schoolbook history, totally unconvincing and very dull despite obvious effort all round. One or two of the actors have their moments.

w Helen Deutsch   *novel* Ernest Gebler   *d* Clarence Brown   *ph* William Daniels   *m* Miklos Rozsa

Spencer Tracy, Gene Tierney, Van Johnson, Leo Genn, Dawn Addams

'It demonstrates how Hollywood can dull down as well as jazz up history.' – *Judith Crist, 1973*

Pocket Money
US   1972   100m   Technicolor
First Artists/Coleytown (John Foreman)
V, V*

Two slow-thinking Arizona cowboys try to make money herding cattle.

Peculiar modern Western comedy drama which doesn't work.

w Terry Malick   *novel* Jim Kane by J. K. S. Brown
d Stuart Rosenberg   *ph* Laszlo Kovacs   *m* Alex North

Paul Newman, Lee Marvin, Strother Martin, Kelly Jean Peters, Wayne Rogers

Pocketful of Miracles
US   1961   136m   Technicolor   Panavision
UA/Franton (Frank Capra)
V*, L

Kindly gangsters help an old apple seller to persuade her long lost daughter that she is a lady of means.

Boring, overlong remake of *Lady for a Day*, showing that Capra's touch simply doesn't work on the wide screen, that his themes are dated anyway, and that all the fine character actors in Hollywood are a liability unless you find them something to do.

w Hal Kanter, Harry Tugend   *scenario* Robert Riskin
story Damon Runyon   *d* Frank Capra   *ph* Robert Bronner   *m* Walter Scharf

Bette Davis, Glenn Ford, Hope Lange, Arthur O'Connell, Peter Falk, Thomas Mitchell, Edward Everett Horton, Sheldon Leonard, Barton MacLane, Jerome Cowan, Fritz Feld, Snub Pollard, David Brian, Ann-Margret, John Litel, Jay Novello, Willis Bouchey, George E. Stone, Mike Mazurki, Jack Elam, Mickey Shaughnessy, Peter Mann, Frank Ferguson

'The effect is less one of whimsy than of being bludgeoned to death with a toffee apple.' – *Peter John Dyer*

'The story has enough cracks in it for the syrup to leak through.' – *Playboy*

AAN: title song (*m* James Van Heusen, *ly* Sammy Cahn); Peter Falk

Poet's Pub
GB   1949   79m   bw
GFD/Aquila (Donald B. Wilson)

A rowing blue takes over a Tudor inn and discovers a priceless jewelled gauntlet, the wearer of which is kidnapped during the performance of a pageant.

Very thin, naïve treatment of a whimsical novel. The last film to use the Independent Frame process.

w Diana Morgan   *novel* Eric Linklater   *d* Frederick Wilson   *ph* George Stretton   *m* Clifton Parker

Derek Bond, Rona Anderson, Barbara Murray, Leslie Dwyer, Joyce Grenfell

Poil de Carotte ***
France   1932   94m   bw
Legrand Majestic/Marcel Vandal-Charles Delac
aka: *The Redhead*

A red-haired boy, neglected by his father and tormented by his mother, attempts suicide.

A moving and unsentimental account of childhood, notable for the performances of Baur and Lynen as father and son.

wd Julien Duvivier   *story* Jules Renard   *ph* Armand Thirard   *m* Alexandre Tansman   *ed* Marthe Poncin

Harry Baur, Robert Lynen, Catherine Fonteney, Louis Gouthier, Simone Aubry, Maxime Fromiot, Colette Segall, Christiane Dor

† The British censors banned the film for a time and in America it was restricted to adult audiences. Duvivier had made a silent version of the story in 1925. There were less successful remakes by Paul Mesnier in 1951 and Henri Graziani in 1973.

Point Blank *
US   1967   92m   Metrocolor   Panavision
MGM/Judd Bernard, Irwin Winkler
V, V*

A gangster takes an elaborate revenge on his cheating partner.

Extremely violent gangster thriller, well shot on location and something of a cult, but with irritating pretentiousness and obscure plot points.

w Alexander Jacobs, David Newhouse, Rafe Newhouse   *novel* The Hunter by Richard Stark *d* John Boorman   *ph* Philip Lathrop   *m* Johnny Mandel

Lee Marvin, Angie Dickinson, Keenan Wynn, Carroll O'Connor, Lloyd Bochner, Michael Strong, John Vernon, Sharon Acker

'The fragmentation was necessary to give the characters and the situation ambiguity, to suggest another meaning beyond the immediate plot.' – *John Boorman*

† *The Outfit* (qv) is a kind of sequel/reprise.

'Every Friendship Has Its Limits. Every Man Has His Breaking Point. Together They Take Adventure Past The Point Of No Return.'
Point Break
US   1991   122m   DeLuxe
TCF/Largo/Tapestry (Peter Abrams, Robert L. Levy)
V, V (W), V*, L, S

An FBI agent goes undercover among Californian surfers and skydivers to investigate a series of bank robberies.

Ridiculous thriller, with convoluted and unbelievable plot and a great deal of masculine posturing.

w W. Peter Iliff   *d* Kathryn Bigelow   *ph* Donald Peterman   *m* Mark Isham   *pd* Peter Jamison   *ed* Howard Smith, Scott Conrad, Burt Lovitt

Patrick Swayze, Keanu Reeves, Gary Busey, Lori Petty, John McGinley, James Le Gros, John Philbin, Bojesse Christopher, Julian Reyes

'Acts like a huge, nasty wave, picking up viewers for a few major thrills but ultimately grinding them into the sand via overkill and absurdity.' – *Variety*

'The Government Gave Her A Choice. Death. Or Life As An Assassin. Now, There's No Turning Back.'
Point of No Return
US   1993   108m   Technicolor   Panavision
Warner (Art Linson)
V, V*, L
GB title: *The Assassin*

A drug addict captured by the police during a robbery is given a choice between dying or becoming a government assassin.

A remake of the French movie *Nikita* which apes the original in virtually every respect, yet fails to match it in interest; it says much about Hollywood, and American attitudes to subtitles, that such a pointless exercise should ever have been carried out.

w Robert Getchell, Alexandra Seros   *d* John Badham   *ph* Michael Watkins   *m* Hans Zimmer, Nick Glennie-Smith   *pd* Philip Harrison   *ed* Frank Morris

Bridget Fonda, Gabriel Byrne, Dermot Mulroney, Miguel Ferrer, Harvey Keitel, Olivia D'Abo, Richard Romanus, Geoffrey Lewis

'A soulless, efficiently slavish remake.' – *Variety*

Pointed Heels
US   1929   61m   bw (colour sequence)
Paramount

A theatrical producer loves a musical comedy star but loses her to a young composer.

Predictable backstage drama.

w Florence Ryerson, John V. A. Weaver   *story* Charles Brackett   *d* A. Edward Sutherland

William Powell, Fay Wray, Helen Kane, Phillips Holmes, Richard 'Skeets' Gallagher, Eugene Pallette

'Moderate business likely for a light comedy that choked on too big a mouthful.' – *Variety*

'The Film That Shocked America! Denounced As "Obscene" and "Pornographic" by the Moral Majority.'
Poison *
US   1990   85m   colour/bw
Mainline/Bronze Eye (Christine Vachon)
V, V*

Three stories are interwoven: 'Hero', in which a seven-year-old boy kills his father and flies away; 'Homo', in which a jealous prisoner rapes another; 'Horror', in which a doctor creates a serum containing the sex drive, drinks it and becomes a monster.

Cleverly dealing with deviance, sexual and social, and inspired by the work of Jean Genet, it ranges in style from the risible to the repugnant.

wd Todd Haynes   *ph* Maryse Alberti   *m* James Bennett   *pd* Sarah Stollman   *ed* James Lyons, Todd Haynes

'Hero': Edith Meeks, Millie White, Buck Smith, Anne Giotta. 'Homo': Scott Renderer, James Lyons, John R. Lombardi, Tony Pemberton, Andrew Harpending, Tony Gigante. 'Horror': Larry Maxwell, Susan Norman, Al Quagliata, Michelle Sullivan.

'A provocative look at societal outcasts and twisted behavior that can be read in ways both artistic and political.' – *Variety*

'A whole that is often uneven but, in less than 90 minutes, says more about desire and transgression than most more straightforward movies on that theme.' – *Derek Malcolm, Guardian*

Poison Ivy
US   1992   89m   colour
New Line (Andy Ruben)
V, V*

A teenage schoolgirl decides she wants the father of her best friend, which means getting rid of his invalid wife.

A heady brew of incest, lesbianism, drunkenness and death which quickly goes flat.

w Katt Shea Ruben, Andy Ruben   *d* Katt Shea Ruben   *ph* Phedon Papamichael   *m* Aaron Davies   *pd* Virginia Lee   *ed* Gina Mittleman

Drew Barrymore, Sara Gilbert, Tom Skerritt, Cheryl Ladd

'Will make audiences itch to get out of the theater and into the open.' – *Variety*

'The film, distinguished by a complete absence of thrills, is too turgid even to qualify as camp.' – *Stephen Farber, Movieline*

Poison Pen *
GB   1939   79m   bw
ABP (Walter C. Mycroft)

A village community is set at odds by a writer of vindictive anonymous letters.

Effective minor drama, with good location atmosphere.

w Doreen Montgomery, William Freshman, N. C. Hunter, Esther McCracken   *play* Richard Llewellyn   *d* Paul Stein

Flora Robson, Reginald Tate, Robert Newton, Ann Todd, Geoffrey Toone, Belle Chrystal, Edward Chapman, Edward Rigby

'Sordid theme makes it doubtful film fare.' – *Variety*

'A lamentably artificial piece.' – *Richard Mallett, Punch*

Pokolenie: see *Generation*

Police *
France   1985   113m   colour   Panavision
Artificial Eye/Gaumont/TF1
V, V*

A tough and bigoted cop, investigating Tunisian drug-dealers, falls for a suspect.

Well-directed thriller, filmed in documentary style, that was a box-office hit in France, though it offers nothing that has not been seen before.

w Catherine Breillat, Sylvie Danton, Jacques Fieschi, Maurice Pialat   *d* Maurice Pialat   *ph* Luciano Tovoli   *m* Henryk Mikolaj Gorecki   *ad* Constantin Mejinksy   *ed* Yann Dedet, Helene Viard, Nathalie Letrosne

Gérard Depardieu, Sophie Marceau, Richard Ancanina, Pascale Rocard, Sandrine Bonnaire, Franck Karoul, Jonathan Leina

'Call them what you like. Just don't call them when you're in trouble!'
Police Academy
US   1984   96m   Technicolor
Paul Maslansky/Ladd Company/Warner Brothers
V, V*, L

The mayor of an American city lifts all restrictions on entry to the police force.

Appallingly unfunny series of snippets about police training, like an American Carry On with few jokes leading to a punch line and occasional resorting to dirty bits.

w Neal Israel, Pat Proft, Hugh Wilson   *d* Hugh Wilson

Steve Guttenberg, Kim Cattrall, G. W. Bailey, Bubba Smith, Donovan Scott, George Gaynes

'Hit or miss comic juvenilia . . . pure popcorn fantasy fodder.' – *Paul Taylor, MFB*

Police Academy 2: Their First Assignment
US   1985   87m   Technicolor
Warner/Ladd (Paul Maslansky)
V, V*, L

The new recruits foil attempts from an ambitious lieutenant to take over command.

An unambitious and dull sequel.

w Barry Blaustein, David Sheffield   *d* Jerry Paris   *ph* James Crabe   *m* Robert Folk   *pd* Trevor Williams   *ed* Bob Wyman

Steve Guttenberg, Bubba Smith, David Graf, Michael Winslow, Art Metrano, Marion Ramsey, George Gaynes

Police Academy 3: Back in Training
US   1986   82m   colour
Warner (Paul Maslansky)
V, V*, L

Rival police academies vie for survival.

Plodding comedy that recycles a few familiar, unfunny routines.

w Gene Quintano   *d* Jerry Paris   *ph* Robert Saad   *m* Robert Folk   *pd* Trevor Williams   *ed* Bud Malin

Steve Guttenberg, Bubba Smith, David Graf, Michael Winslow, Marion Ramsey, Leslie Easterbrook, George Gaynes, Bobcat Goldthwait, Art Metrano

Police Academy 4: Citizens on Patrol
US   1987   87m   colour
Warner (Paul Maslansky)
V, V*, L

A police commandant attempts to involve ordinary people in law enforcement.

A feeble comedy that makes it impossible to understand the apparent popularity of this turgid series.

w Gene Quintano   *d* Jim Drake   *ph* Robert Saad   *m* Robert Folk   *pd* Trevor Williams   *ed* David Rawlins

Steve Guttenberg, Bubba Smith, David Graf, Michael Winslow, Sharon Stone, Leslie Easterbrook, Bobcat Goldthwait, George Gaynes

'Carries the banner of tasteless humor . . . to new heights of insipidness.' – *Variety*

Police Academy 5: Assignment: Miami Beach
US   1988   90m   colour
Warner (Paul Maslansky)
V, V*, L

Cops on holiday in Miami help foil a gang of jewel thieves.

Witlessness reaches a new low in a comedy devoid of laughs.

w Stephen J. Curwick *d* Alan Myerson *ph* Jim Pergola *m* Robert Folk *pd* Trevor Williams *ed* Hubert de la Bouillerie

Matt McCoy, Janet Jones, George Gaynes, G. W. Bailey, Rene Auberjonois, Bubba Smith, David Graf, Michael Winslow, Leslie Easterbook

Police Academy 6: City Under Siege
US 1989 84m Technicolor
Warner (Paul Maslansky)
V, V*, L

The police squad track down a criminal mastermind responsible for a massive crime wave.

Farcical, broadly acted comedy that does raise an occasional smile.

w Stephen J. Curwick *d* Peter Bonerz *ph* Charles Rosher Jnr *m* Robert Folk *pd* Tho E. Azzari *ed* Hubert de la Bouillerie

Bubba Smith, David Graf, Michael Winslow, Leslie Easterbrook, Marion Ramsey, Lance Kinsey, Matt McCoy, Bruce Mahler, G. W. Bailey, George Gaynes, Kenneth Mars

Police Force: see *Police Story* (1985)

Police Story (dubbed) *
Hong Kong 1985 85m colour
Golden Harvest/Paragon (Leonard Ho)
V, V*
original title: *Jingcha Gushi*; US title: *Police Force*

A cop is given the task of guarding a witness who is the girlfriend of a drug-dealing gangster.

Standard cops and robbers martial arts mayhem, enlivened by some spectacular stunts and chases.

w Edward Tang *d* Jackie Chan *ph* Cheung Yiu Joe *m* Kevin Bassingson *ad* Oliver Wong *ed* Peter Cheung

Jackie Chan, Brigette Lin, Maggie Cheung, Cho Yuen, Bill Tung, Kenneth Tong

† The film was cut by 15 minutes for its release on video cassette.

Police Story II (dubbed)
Hong Kong 1988 92m colour
Golden Harvest/Paragon (Leonard Ho)
V, V*

Demoted to traffic cop, a former detective is re-instated to combat a gang extorting money from big business.

The mixture as before: elaborately choreographed fights and broad comedy, but lacking the set-pieces of the first film.

w Jackie Chan, Edward Tang *d* Jackie Chan *ph* Cheung Yiu Joe, Lee Yau Tong *m* Michael Lai *pd* Oliver Wong *ed* Peter Cheung

Jackie Chan, Maggie Cheung, Bill Tung, Lam Kwok Hung, Charles Chao, Cho Yuen

The Politic Flapper: see *The Patsy*

Politics
US 1931 71m bw
MGM

Two small-town women get into politics to fight racketeers.

Scrappy star comedy which probably seemed funnier at the time.

w Robert E. Hopkins, Wells Root, Zelda Sears, Malcolm Stuart Boylan *d* Charles F. Reisner

Marie Dressler, Polly Moran, Roscoe Ates, Karen Morley, William Bakewell, John Miljan

'Loaded with technical faults, but it has too many laugh moments to fail to sock the b.o.' – *Variety*

Polly Fulton: see *BF's Daughter*

Polly of the Circus
US 1932 72m bw
MGM (Paul Bern)

A trapeze artiste falls for the local minister, but incurs disapproval from his bishop.

Elementary romance reminiscent of silent drama.

w Carey Wilson *play* Margaret Mayo *d* Alfred Santell *ph* George Barnes *m* William Axt

Marion Davies, Clark Gable, C. Aubrey Smith, Raymond Hatton, David Landau, Maude Eburne, Guinn Williams, Ray Milland

'Frail entertainment with both leads miscast.' – *Variety*

Pollyanna *
US 1960 134m Technicolor
Walt Disney (George Golitzen)
V*, L

A 12-year-old orphan girl cheers up the grumps of the small town where she comes to live.

Well cast but overlong and rather humourless remake of a children's classic from an earlier age.

wd David Swift *novel* Eleanor Porter *ph* Russell Harlan *m* Paul Smith *ad* Carroll Clark, Robert Clatworthy

Hayley Mills, Jane Wyman, Karl Malden, Nancy Olson, Adolphe Menjou, Donald Crisp, Agnes Moorehead, Richard Egan, Kevin Corcoran, James Drury, Reta Shaw, Leora Dana

'Even Hayley Mills can neither prevent one from sympathizing with the crusty aunts, hermits, vicars and hypochondriacs who get so forcibly cheered up, nor from feverishly speculating whether films like this don't run the risk of inciting normally kind and gentle people into certain excesses of violent crime – child murder, for instance.' – *MFB*

AA: special award to Hayley Mills for 'the most outstanding juvenile performance'

'It knows what scares you!'
Poltergeist **
US 1982 114m Metrocolor Panavision
MGM/SLM (Steven Spielberg)
V, V*, L

Suburban life is disrupted when through her TV set a young girl releases unpleasant forces from the cemetery over which the modern estate was built.

Skilful but dramatically thin and sometimes rather nasty horror movie in which the producer's hand seems often to have controlled the director's. Misjudgment must be the reason that it was not the huge success intended.

w Steven Spielberg, Michael Grais, Mark Victor *d* Tobe Hooper *ph* Matthew F. Leonetti *m* Jerry Goldsmith *ed* Michael Kahn

Jobeth Williams, Craig T. Nelson, Beatrice Straight, Dominique Dunne, Oliver Robbins

AAN: music, visual effects (Richard Edlund, Michael Wood, Bruce Nicholson)

Poltergeist II
US 1986 90m Metrocolor Panavision
MGM-UA/Freddie Fields/Victor-Grais
V, V*, L, S

The family from *Poltergeist* is in for more trouble when Grandma dies and they begin receiving phone messages from the other side.

More pointless spine-shivering: good technical effects but no message of any kind, not even entertainment.

w Mark Victor, Michael Grais *d* Brian Gibson *ph* Andrew Laszlo *pd* Ted Haworth

Jobeth Williams, Craig T. Nelson, Heather O'Rourke, Oliver Robins, Julian Beck

Poltergeist III
US 1988 98m AstroColor
UIP/MGM-UA (Barry Bernardi)
V*, L

A young child living in Chicago is haunted by an evil ghost who takes her and others into another dimension.

Lacklustre sequel, with only the occasional effective shock to recommend it.

w Gary Shearman, Brian Taggert *d* Gary Shearman *ph* Alex Nepomniaschy *m* Joe Renzetti *pd* Paul Eads *ed* Ross Albert

Tom Skerritt, Nancy Allen, Heather O'Rourke, Zelda Rubinstein, Lara Flynn Boyle, Kip Wentz, Richard Fire

Pontius Pilate
Italy/France 1961 100m Technicolor
Glomer Film/Lux (Enzo Merolle)
original title: *Ponzio Pilato*

Pontius Pilate runs into political and personal problems while trying to govern Israel.

Pilate's love-life is given prominence over Jesus's trial and crucifixion, although both receive standard Italian sword-and-sandals treatment to reduce them to banality. Barrymore doubles as Judas and Jesus (who is seen only from the back).

w Gino de Santis, Ivo Perilli, Oreste Biancoli, Gian Paolo Callegari, Guglielmo Santangelo, Josette France, Guy Elmes *d* Irving Rapper *ph* Massimo Dallamano *m* A. Francesco Lavagnino

Jean Marais, Jeanne Crain, Basil Rathbone, Leticia Roman, John Drew Barrymore, Massimo Serato

Pony Express *
US 1953 101m Technicolor
Paramount (Nat Holt)
V*

In 1860 Buffalo Bill Cody and Wild Bill Hickok are sent to establish pony express stations across California.

Standard Western which tells a factual tale adequately if rather slowly.

w Charles Marquis Warren *d* Jerry Hopper *ph* Ray Rennahan *m* Paul Sawtell

Charlton Heston, Forrest Tucker, Rhonda Fleming, Jan Sterling

Pony Soldier
US 1952 82m Technicolor
TCF (Samuel G. Engel)
GB title: *MacDonald of the Canadian Mounties*

The Mounties settle the hash of Canadian Indian renegades who have been causing trouble on the American border.

Mediocre outdoor adventure.

w John C. Higgins *d* Joseph M. Newman *ph* Harry Jackson *m* Alex North

Tyrone Power, Cameron Mitchell, Robert Horton, Thomas Gomez, Penny Edwards, *Adeline de Walt Reynolds*

Ponzio Pilato: see *Pontius Pilate*

Pookie: see *The Sterile Cuckoo*

Pool of London
GB 1950 85m bw
Ealing (Michael Relph)

A smuggling sailor gets involved in murder.

Routine semi-documentary police thriller with locations in London docks decorating a standard piece of thick ear.

w Jack Whittingham, John Eldridge   *d* Basil Dearden   *ph* Gordon Dines   *m* John Addison

Bonar Colleano, Susan Shaw, Earl Cameron, Renée Asherson, Moira Lister, Max Adrian, James Robertson Justice, Joan Dowling

'Done with such imagination, humour and visual attractiveness as to hold the pleased attention of all who like to use their eyes and their ears.' – *Richard Mallett, Punch*

Poor Cow *
GB   1967   101m   Eastmancolor
Anglo Amalgamated/Vic/Fenchurch (Joe Janni)
V

The dismal life of a young London mother who lives in squalor with her criminal husband.

Television-style fictional documentary determined to rub one's nose in the mire. Innovative and occasionally striking but not very likeable.

w Nell Dunn, Ken Loach   *novel* Nell Dunn   *d* Ken Loach   *ph* Brian Probyn   *m* Donovan

Carol White, Terence Stamp, John Bindon, Kate Williams, Queenie Watts

'A superficial, slightly patronizing excursion into the nether realms of social realism.' – *Jan Dawson*

Poor Little Rich Girl *
US   1936   79m   bw
TCF (Darryl F. Zanuck)

A child is separated from her father and joins a radio singing act.

Pleasing star vehicle with all the expected elements, adapted from a Mary Pickford vehicle of 1917.

w Sam Hellman, Gladys Lehman, Harry Tugend   *d* Irving Cummings   *ph* John Seitz   *songs* Mack Gordon, Harry Revel

Shirley Temple, Jack Haley, Alice Faye, Gloria Stuart, Michael Whalen, Sara Haden, Jane Darwell, Claude Gillingwater, Henry Armetta

Pop Always Pays
US   1940   65m   bw
Bert Gilroy/RKO

Pop promises to match his future son-in-law's savings, but runs into a business slump.

Minor comedy which accelerates into frantic farce, but the star was always funnier at two-reel length.

w Charles E. Roberts   *d* Leslie Goodwins

Leon Errol, Dennis O'Keefe, Adele Pearce, Walter Catlett, Marjorie Gateson, Tom Kennedy

Pope Joan
GB   1972   132m   Eastmancolor   Panavision
Big City Productions/Kurt Unger
aka: *The Devil's Imposter*

The legend of a ninth-century German semi-prostitute who discovered a vocation to preach and was made Pope.

Uninspiring pageant, brutish and rather silly, full of would-be medieval sensationalism.

w John Briley   *d* Michael Anderson   *ph* Billy Williams   *m* Maurice Jarre   *pd* Elliott Scott

Liv Ullmann, Trevor Howard, Olivia de Havilland, Maximilian Schell, Keir Dullea, Robert Beatty, Franco Nero, Patrick Magee

'In the tradition of the great religious epics, *Ben Hur, The Greatest Story Ever Told* and *9½ Weeks*, comes a film that breaks all Ten Commandments and a few laws of nature.'

The Pope Must Die
GB   1991   99m   colour
Palace/Michael White/Miramax/British Film/Film Four (Stephen Woolley)
V, V*
US title: *The Pope Must Diet*

Through an error, a former car mechanic, rock singer and inept priest becomes Pope and tries to clean up a Vatican infiltrated by the Mafia.

Farcical and misfiring comedy, a poor attempt at a parody of gangster films.

w Peter Richardson, Pete Richens   *d* Peter Richardson   *ph* Frank Gell   *m* Anne Dudley, Jeff Beck   *pd* John Ebden   *ed* Katharine Wenning

Robbie Coltrane, Beverly D'Angelo, Herbert Lom, Alex Rocco, Paul Bartel, Balthazar Getty, William Hootkins, Robert Stephens, Annette Crosbie, Steve O'Donnell, John Sessions

The Pope of Greenwich Village
US   1984   120m   Metrocolor
MGM-UA/Koch-Kirkwood (Benjy Rosenberg)
V, V*, L

In New York, Charlie and his cousin Paulie become thieves and fall foul of the Mafia.

Back again to the mean streets of the east side, but with nothing at all new to add to the scores of indistinguishable real-life melodramas of this kind.

w Vincent Patrick   *novel* Vincent Patrick   *d* Stuart Rosenberg   *ph* John Bailey   *m* Dave Grusin   *pd* Paul Sylbert

Eric Roberts, Mickey Rourke, Daryl Hannah, Geraldine Page, Kenneth McMillan, Tony Musante, M. Emmet Walsh, Burt Young

AAN: Geraldine Page (supporting actress)

Popeye
US   1980   114m   colour
Paramount/Disney (Robert Evans)
V*, L

Popeye returns to Sweethaven in search of the father who abandoned him.

Lamentable attempt by an ill-chosen director to humanize and sentimentalize a celebrated cartoon character who doesn't get into the expected physical action until the film is nearly over.

w Jules Feiffer, from characters created by E. C. Segar   *d* Robert Altman   *ph* Giuseppe Rotunno   *pd* Wolf Kroeger   *m/ly* Harry Nilsson

Robin Williams, Shelley Duvall, Ray Walston, Paul Dooley

'The picture doesn't come together, and much of it is cluttered, squawky, and eerily unfunny.' – *Pauline Kael, New Yorker*

Popi *
US   1969   113m   DeLuxe
UA/Leonard Films (Herbert B. Leonard)
V*

Adventures of a cheerful inhabitant of New York's Puerto Rican ghetto.

Ethnic comedy-drama of the kind that has since found its way in abundance into American TV series. Very competently done for those who like it, e.g. Puerto Ricans.

w Tina and Lester Pine   *d* Arthur Hiller   *ph* Ross Lowell   *m* Dominic Frontière

Alan Arkin, Rita Moreno, Miguel Alejandro, Ruben Figuero

'An appropriately disenchanted view of an immigrant's struggling ambitions in the Promised Land.' – *Richard Combs*

Popiol y Diament: see *Ashes and Diamonds*

Poppy *
US   1936   74m   bw
Paramount (Paul Jones)

An itinerant medicine-seller sets up his stall in a small town where his daughter falls in love with the mayor's son.

Clumsily but heavily plotted vehicle for W. C. Fields, who as usual has great moments but seems to rob the show of its proper pace.

w Waldemar Young, Virginia Van Upp   *play* Dorothy Donnelly   *d* A. Edward Sutherland   *ph* William Mellor   *m* Frederick Hollander

W. C. Fields, Rochelle Hudson, Richard Cromwell, Granville Bates, Catherine Doucet, Lynne Overman, Maude Eburne

'Antique hokum trussed up for a Fields vehicle.' – *Literary Digest*

'To watch Mr Fields, as Dickensian as anything Dickens ever wrote, is a form of escape for poor human creatures: we who are haunted by pity, by fear, by our sense of right and wrong, who are tongue-tied by conscience, watch with envious love this free spirit robbing the gardener of ten dollars, cheating the country yokels by his own variant of the three-card trick, faking a marriage certificate, and keeping up all the time, in the least worthy and the most embarrassing circumstances, his amazing flow of inflated sentiments.' – *Graham Greene, The Spectator*

Porgy and Bess *
US   1959   138m   Technicolor   Todd-AO
Columbia/Samuel Goldwyn

A slum girl falls in love with a crippled beggar.

Negro opera about the inhabitants of Catfish Row; full of interest for music lovers, but not lending itself very readily to screen treatment.

w N. Richard Nash   *libretto* DuBose Heyward   *play* Porgy by DuBose and Dorothy Heyward   *d* Otto Preminger   *ph* Leon Shamroy   *md* André Previn, Ken Darby   *ph* Hermes Pan   *m* George Gershwin   *ly* DuBose Heyward, Ira Gershwin

Sidney Poitier, Dorothy Dandridge, Sammy Davis Jnr, Pearl Bailey, Brock Peters, Diahann Carroll, Clarence Muse

AA: André Previn, Ken Darby

AAN: Leon Shamroy

'Bold! blunt! blustering! the battle picture without equal!'
Pork Chop Hill *
US   1959   97m   bw
United Artists/Melville/Lewis Milestone
V*, L

The Americans in Korea take a vital hill but the colonel in command finds it difficult to hold.

Ironic war film with vivid spectacle separated by much talk.

w James R. Webb   *d* Lewis Milestone   *ph* Sam Leavitt   *m* Leonard Rosenman   *pd* Nicolai Remisoff

Gregory Peck, Harry Guardino, George Shibata, Woody Strode, James Edwards, Rip Torn, George Peppard, Barry Atwater, Robert Blake

Porky's
Canada   1982   98m   colour
Melvin Simon/Astral Bellevue Pathé/Porky's Productions/(Don Carmody, Bob Clark)
V, V*, L

In Florida in the early fifties, high school boys try to get into a local brothel.

Ghastly teenage goings-on taking cinema bad taste just about as far as it will get.

wd Bob Clark   *ph* Reginald H. Morris   *m* Carl Zittrer, Paul Zaza   *pd* Reuben Freed

Dan Monahan, Mark Herrier, Wyatt Knight, Roger Wilson, Kim Cattrall, Art Hindle, Wayne Maunder, Alex Karras, Nancy Parsons

'It is difficult to say which is the more depressing: the technical expertise with which this mind-numbing tripe has been put together, or its great success at the US box office.' – *Jo Imeson, MFB*

'One of those movies that makes you weep for the state of the contemporary commercial cinema – and, even more, for the gullibility of the public that pays to see it.' – *Margaret Hinxman, Daily Mail*

† *Porky's 2* followed in 1983 and was even worse. 1985 brought *Porky's Revenge*, about which there is nothing to be said.

Porridge *
GB 1979 93m Eastmancolor
Black Lion/Witzend
V

Old lags at Slade Prison try to arrange an escape for a first offender.

Genial expansion of a successful TV series to the big screen; alas, as usual the material is stretched to snapping point, and the welcome irony of the original becomes sentimentality. Still, the film is a valuable record of memorable characters.

w Dick Clement, Ian La Frenais *d* Dick Clement *ph* Bob Huke *md* Terry Oates

Ronnie Barker, Richard Beckinsale, Fulton Mackay, Brian Wilde, Peter Vaughan, Geoffrey Bayldon, Julian Holloway

Port Afrique
GB 1956 92m Technicolor
David E. Rose/Columbia

In Morocco, an American pilot solves the shooting of his wife.

Tropical variation on *The Maltese Falcon* and *The Blue Dahlia;* not much cop on its own account.

w Frank Partos and John Cresswell *novel* Bernard Victor Dyer *d* Rudolph Maté

Phil Carey, Pier Angeli, Dennis Price, Eugene Deckers, James Hayter, Rachel Gurney, Anthony Newley

Port of Call *
Sweden 1948 99m bw
Svensk Filmindustri
original title: *Hamnstad*

A sailor who quits the sea begins an affair with a lonely and unhappy girl recently released from reform school.

A tough and perceptive drama of class, conventions and relationships, particularly a destructive one between mother and daughter, shot in a documentary style against a background of docks.

wd Ingmar Bergman *story* Olle Länsberg *ph* Gunnar Fischer *m* Erland von Koch *ad* Nils Svenwall *ed* Oscar Rosander

Nine Christine Jönsson, Bengt Eklund, Berta Hall, Mimi Nelson, Birgitta Valberg, Sif Ruud, Else Merete Heiberg

Port of New York *
US 1949 82m bw
Eagle Lion (Aubrey Schenck)
V*

A woman narcotics smuggler determines to betray her colleagues to the authorities.

Good routine semi-documentary thick ear, notable for an early appearance by Yul Brynner as villain-in-chief.

w Eugene Ling *d* Laslo Benedek *ph* George E. Diskant *m* Sol Kaplan

Scott Brady, Richard Rober, K. T. Stevens, Yul Brynner

Port of Seven Seas *
US 1938 81m bw
MGM (Henry Henigson)

Love on the Marseilles waterfront.

Stagey Hollywoodization of Pagnol's *Marius* trilogy: some vigour shows through.

---

w Preston Sturges *d* James Whale *ph* Karl Freund *m* Franz Waxman

Wallace Beery, Frank Morgan, Maureen O'Sullivan, John Beal, Jessie Ralph, Cora Witherspoon

'Genuine and touching drama . . . strong solo biller.' – *Variety*

Port of Shadows: see *Quai des Brumes*

Porte des Lilas *
France/Italy 1957 95m bw
Filmsonor/Rizzoli (Jacques Plante)
aka: *Gate of Lilacs*

A gangster on the run shelters in a poor quarter of Paris, but his treachery is his undoing.

Atmospheric comedy-drama put across with the expected style but providing very little to smile at.

w René Clair, Jean Aurel *novel* La Grande Ceinture by René Fallet *d* René Clair *ph* Robert Le Fèbvre *m* Georges Brassens

Pierre Brasseur, Georges Brassens, Henri Vidal, Dany Carrel, Raymond Bussières, Amedée, Alain Bouvette

Les Portes de la Nuit *
France 1946 106m bw
Pathé Cinema
aka: *Gates of Night*

Various people in post-war Paris are drawn into a pattern woven by Destiny – who appears as a melancholy tramp.

A polished piece of post-war gloom, and the archetype of all *films noirs* of the period. The beginning, also, of its director's decline.

w Jacques Prévert *d* Marcel Carné *ph* Philippe Agostini *m* Joseph Kosma *ad* Alexander Trauner

Pierre Brasseur, Yves Montand, Nathalie Nattier, Serge Reggiani, Jean Vilar, Saturnin Fabre, Mady Berry, Dany Robin

† One of the few films to have been based on a ballet – *Le Rendezvous* by Prévert. Oddly enough its realistic scenes of daily life are among its most successful elements.

Les Portes Tournantes: see *The Revolving Doors*

Portia on Trial *
US 1937 83m bw
Republic
GB title: *The Trial of Portia Merriman*

A lady lawyer uses her skills in the courtroom to right the personal wrongs done to her years before.

Efficient tearjerker, *Madame X* style, and one of the comparatively big productions Republic occasionally tried.

w Sam Ornitz, E. E. Paramore Jnr *novel* Faith Baldwin *d* George Nicholls Jnr *m* Alberto Colombo

Frieda Inescort, Walter Abel, Neil Hamilton, Heather Angel, Ruth Donnelly, Barbara Pepper, Clarence Kolb

'A distinguished production: exploitation required to overcome title and no-name handicap.' – *Variety*

AAN: Alberto Colombo

Portnoy's Complaint
US 1972 101m Technicolor Panavision
Warner/Chenault (Ernest Lehman)
V*

A young New York Jewish boy has mother and masturbation problems.

Foolhardy attempt to film a fashionably sensational literary exercise; one of Hollywood's last attempts – thank goodness – to be 'with it'.

wd Ernest Lehman *novel* Philip Roth *ph* Philip Lathrop *m* Michel Legrand

---

Richard Benjamin, Karen Black, Lee Black, Jack Somack, Jill Clayburgh, Jeannie Berlin

'The spectator is forced into the doubly uncomfortable position of a voyeur who can't actually see anything.' – *Jan Dawson*

Portrait from Life
GB 1948 90m bw
GFD/Gainsborough (Antony Damborough)
US title: *The Girl in the Painting*

In an art gallery, a German professor recognizes a portrait as that of his daughter, lost during the war in Germany, and after a search discovers her to have been an amnesiac under the protection of a leading Nazi.

Tolerable melodrama with similarities to *The Seventh Veil* (the girl has to choose between four men).

w Frank Harvey Jnr, Muriel and Sydney Box *d* Terence Fisher *ph* Jack Asher *m* Benjamin Frankel

Mai Zetterling, Robert Beatty, Guy Rolfe, Herbert Lom, Patrick Holt

Portrait in Black *
US 1960 113m Eastmancolor
U-I/Ross Hunter

An elderly shipping tycoon is murdered by his wife and doctor, but they are blackmailed.

Absurd old-fashioned melodrama of dark doings among the idle rich. Quite entertaining for addicts.

w Ivan Goff, Ben Roberts *d* Michael Gordon *ph* Russell Metty *m* Frank Skinner

Lana Turner, Anthony Quinn, Richard Basehart, Anna May Wong, Lloyd Nolan, Sandra Dee, John Saxon, Ray Walston, Virginia Grey

'Connoisseurs of the higher tosh should find it irresistible.' – *Penelope Houston*

Portrait in Smoke: see *Wicked as They Come*

Portrait of a Mobster
US 1961 108m bw
Warner

The career of twenties gangster Dutch Schultz.

Over-familiar, warmed over racketeering stuff with no particular edge or style.

w Howard Browne *d* Joseph Pevney *ph* Eugene Polito *m* Max Steiner

Vic Morrow, Leslie Parrish, Peter Breck, Ray Danton (repeating as Legs Diamond), Norman Alden, Ken Lynch

Portrait of a Sinner: see *The Rough and the Smooth*

Portrait of Alison *
GB 1955 84m bw
Anglo-Amalgamated/Insignia (Frank Godwin)
aka: *Postmark for Danger*

A journalist dies while investigating an international smuggling ring, and his brother takes up the case.

Solidly carpentered mystery with all the twists expected from this source.

w Guy Green, Ken Hughes *radio serial* Francis Durbridge *d* Guy Green *ph* Wilkie Cooper *m* John Veale

Robert Beatty, Terry Moore, William Sylvester, Josephine Griffin, Geoffrey Keen, Allan Cuthbertson, Henry Oscar

Portrait of Clare
GB 1950 98m bw
ABPC (Leslie Landau)

In 1900, a woman looks back on her three marriages.

High school novelette for easily pleased female audiences.

w Leslie Landau, Adrian Arlington   *novel* Francis
Brett Young   *d* Lance Comfort   *ph* Günther Krampf
ad Don Ashton

Margaret Johnston, Richard Todd, Robin Bailey,
Ronald Howard, Mary Clare, Marjorie Fielding,
Anthony Nicholls, Lloyd Pearson

Portrait of Jennie ***
US   1948   86m   bw (tinted sequence)
David O. Selznick
V, V*, L
GB title: *Jennie*

A penniless artist meets a strange girl who seems to
age each time he sees her; they fall in love and he
discovers that she has long been dead, though she
finally comes to life once more during a sea storm like
the one in which she perished.

A splendid example of the higher Hollywood lunacy:
a silly story with pretensions about life and death and
time and art, presented with superb persuasiveness
by a first-class team of actors and technicians.

w Peter Berneis, Paul Osborn, Leonard Bernovici
novel Robert Nathan   *d* William Dieterle   *ph* Joseph
August   *m* Dimitri Tiomkin, after Debussy   *ad* J.
McMillan Johnson   *ed* William Morgan, Gerald
Wilson

Jennifer Jones, Joseph Cotten, Ethel Barrymore, David
Wayne, Lillian Gish, Henry Hull, Florence Bates

PROLOGUE: Since time began man has looked into
the awesome reaches of infinity and asked the eternal
questions: What is time? What is life? What is space?
What is death? Through a hundred civilizations,
philosophers and scientists have come together with
answers, but the bewilderment remains. . . . Science
tells us that nothing ever dies but only changes, that
time itself does not pass but curves around us, and
that the past and the future are together at our side for
ever. Out of the shadows of knowledge, and out of a
painting that hung on a museum wall, comes our
story, the truth of which lies not on our screen but in
your hearts.

JENNIE'S SONG: 'Where I come from, nobody
knows . . . And where I'm going, everything goes
. . . The wind blows The sea flows . . . And nobody
knows . . .'

EBEN (Joseph Cotten): 'I want you, not dreams of
you.'

JENNIE (Jennifer Jones): 'There is no life, my
darling, until you love and have been loved. And then
there is no death.'

'Easily the Selznick masterpiece, rich in superb
performances, tasteful direction and superb
photography.' – *Motion Picture Herald*

'One of the most exquisite fantasy films ever made . . .
a milieu rich in visual and aural imagery . . . a
sensuous evocation of time and timelessness.' –
Cinefantastique

'Though the story may not make sense, the
pyrotechnics, joined to the dumbfounded silliness,
keep one watching.' – *New Yorker, 1976*

AA: special effects

AAN: Joseph August

The Poseidon Adventure **
US   1972   117m   DeLuxe   Panavision
TCF/Kent (Irwin Allen)
V, V*, L

A luxury liner is capsized, and trapped passengers
have to find their way to freedom via an upside down
world.

Tedious disaster movie which caught the public fancy
and started a cycle. Spectacular moments, cardboard
characters, flashes of imagination.

w Stirling Silliphant, Wendell Mayes   *novel* Paul
Gallico   *d* Ronald Neame   *ph* Harold Stine
m John Williams   *pd* William Creber

Gene Hackman, Ernest Borgnine, Shelley Winters,
Red Buttons, Carol Lynley, Leslie Nielson, Arthur
O'Connell, Pamela Sue Martin, Roddy McDowall,
Eric Shea, Jack Albertson, Stella Stevens

'The script is the only cataclysm in this waterlogged
Grand Hotel.' – *New Yorker*

† See also: *Beyond the Poseidon Adventure*.

AA: song 'The Morning After' (*m/ly* Al Kasha, Joel
Hirschhorn)

AAN: Harold Stine; John Williams; Shelley Winters

Posse **
US   1975   93m   Technicolor   Panavision
Paramount/Bryna (Kirk Douglas)
V*, L

A US marshal seeking higher office vows to capture a
railroad bandit, but the tables are smartly turned.

Unusual minor Western, quite pleasing in all
departments and neither mindless nor violent.

w William Roberts, Christopher Knopf   *d* Kirk Douglas
ph Fred Koenekamp   *m* Maurice Jarre

Kirk Douglas, Bruce Dern, Bo Hopkins, James Stacy,
Luke Askey, David Canary

Posse
GB/US   1993   111m   Technicolor
Rank/Polygram/Working Title (Preston Holmes, Jim Steel)
V, V*

In the 1890s, a group of black cowboys defeat the Ku
Klux Klan and other dastardly whites.

An undistinguished Western in the Italian manner,
but lacking style and substance.

w Sy Richardson, Dario Scardapane   *d* Mario Van
Peebles   *ph* Peter Menzies Jnr   *m* Michel
Colombier   *pd* Catherine Hardwicke   *ed* Mark
Conte, Seth Flaum

Mario Van Peebles, Stephen Baldwin, Charles Lane,
Tiny Lister, Big Daddy Kane, Billy Zane, Blair
Underwood, Melvin Van Peebles, Tone Loc, Isaac
Hayes

'Races through its paces with little attention to nuance
or characterization, but its action, hip attitude, and
cool cast should score with youthful general auds as
well as blacks.' – *Variety*

Posse from Hell
US   1961   89m   Technicolor
Universal-International

Four killers escape from jail and take over a town.

Moderate Western programmer with more violence
than usual.

w Clair Huffaker   *d* Herbert Coleman

Audie Murphy, John Saxon, Zohra Lampert, Vic
Morrow, Robert Keith

Possessed *
US   1931   76m   bw
MGM
V*

A factory girl goes to New York in search of riches.

Reasonably gutsy Depression melodrama which
moves at a fair pace.

w Lenore Coffee   *play* The Mirage by Edgar Selwyn
d Clarence Brown   *ph* Oliver T. Marsh

Joan Crawford, Clark Gable, Wallace Ford, Skeets
Gallagher, Frank Conroy, Marjorie White, John
Miljan

'Lots of luxury; lots of charm; lots of smooth talk
about courage and marriage and what women want.'
– *James R. Quirk*

'You'll be possessed by its love madness!'

Possessed *
US   1947   108m   bw
Warner (Jerry Wald)
V*, L

An emotionally unstable nurse marries her employer
but retains a passionate love for an engineer whom
she kills when he does not respond.

Extremely heavy, almost Germanic, flashback
melodrama with everyone tearing hammer and tongs
at the rather ailing script. Fun if you're in that mood,
and an interesting example of the American *film noir*
of the forties.

w Silvia Richards, Ranald MacDougall   *novel* One
Man's Secret by Rita Weiman   *d* Curtis Bernhardt
ph Joseph Valentine   *m* Franz Waxman

Joan Crawford, Raymond Massey, Van Heflin,
Geraldine Brooks, Stanley Ridges, John Ridgely,
Moroni Olsen

'Acting with bells on.' – *Richard Winnington*

'Miss Crawford performs with the passion and
intelligence of an actress who is not content with just
one Oscar.' – *James Agee*

AAN: Joan Crawford

The Possession of Joel Delaney
US   1971   108m   Eastmancolor
ITC/Haworth (George Justin)
V*

A wealthy New York divorcee tries to save her brother
from death at the hands of a Puerto Rican occult group
who believe in ritual murder and demonic
possession.

Unpleasant, frightening and overlong horror film with
some kind of message struggling to get out but
precious little entertainment value.

w Matt Robinson, Grimes Grice   *novel* Ramona
Stewart   *d* Waris Hussein   *ph* Arthur J. Ornitz
m Joe Ragoso

Shirley Maclaine, Perry King, Lisa Kohane, David
Ellacott

'Some see the film as a political allegory; I see it as a
piece of political tosh.' – *Michael Billington, Illustrated
London News*

Postcards from the Edge *
US   1990   101m   Technicolor
Columbia (Mike Nichols, John Calley)
V, V*, L

A drug-addicted actress is forced to live with her
unstable mother, an ageing film star.

Entertaining parade of Hollywood egos, enjoyable
providing you do not take it seriously.

w Carrie Fisher   *novel* Carrie Fisher   *d* Mike
Nichols   *ph* Michael Ballhaus   *m* Carly Simon
pd Patrizia von Brandenstein   *ed* Sam O'Steen

Meryl Streep, Shirley Maclaine, Dennis Quaid, Gene
Hackman, Richard Dreyfuss, Rob Reiner, Mary
Wickes, Conrad Bain, Annette Bening, Simon Callow

'Packs a fair amount of emotional wallop in its dark-
hued comic take on a chemically dependent
Hollywood mother and daughter.' – *Variety*

AAN: Meryl Streep; original song 'I'm Checkin' Out'
(*m/ly* Shel Silverstein)

The Postman Always Rings Twice *
US   1946   113m   bw
MGM (Carey Wilson)
V*, L

A guilty couple murder her husband but get their
come-uppance.

Pale shadow of *Double Indemnity*, efficient but not
interesting or very suspenseful.

w Harry Ruskin, Niven Busch   *novel* James M. Cain
d Tay Garnett   *ph* Sidney Wagner   *m* George
Bassman

Lana Turner, John Garfield, Cecil Kellaway, Hume
Cronyn, Leon Ames, Audrey Totter, Alan Reed

'It was a real chore to do *Postman* under the Hays
Office, but I think I managed to get the sex across.' –
Tay Garnett

'You will feel the heat!'
'Their love was a war that destroyed!'
The Postman Always Rings Twice *
US   1981   121m   Metrocolor
Lorimar/Northstar International (Charles Mulvehill, Bob
Rafelson)
V*, L

A remake of the above with more heavy breathing
and some table-ending.

Not otherwise any better, but an interesting measure
of the times.

w David Mamet   *novel* James M. Cain   d Bob
Rafelson   *ph* Sven Nykvist   *m* Michael Small
pd George Jenkins   *ed* Graeme Clifford

Jack Nicholson, Jessica Lange, John Colicos, Michael
Lerner, John P. Ryan, Anjelica Huston

'Too cheerless to be erotic, too charmless to be
titillating.' – *Margaret Hinxman, Daily Mail*

Postman's Knock *
GB   1961   88m   bw
MGM (Ronald Kinnoch)

A village postman is transferred to London, finds life
and work bewildering, but captures some crooks and
ends up a hero.

Mildly amusing star vehicle rising to good comic
climaxes.

w John Briley, Jack Trevor Story   d Robert Lynn
ph Gerald Moss   *m* Ron Goodwin

Spike Milligan, Barbara Shelley, Wilfrid Lawson

Postmark for Danger: see *Portrait of Alison*

Il Posto: see *The Job*

The Pot Carriers
GB   1962   84m   bw
Associated British

A sensitive young man is debased by prison routine.

Odd little comedy-drama with comedy moments
seeming to set the mood.

w T. J. Morrison, Mike Watts   *play* Mike Watts
d Peter Graham Scott

Paul Massie, Ronald Fraser, Carole Lesley, Dennis
Price, Paul Rogers, Davy Kaye, Eddie Byrne

Pot Luck *
GB   1936   71m   bw
Gainsborough

A Scotland Yard inspector enlists the aid of
department store staff to recover a stolen Chinese
vase.

Surprisingly not from a stage original, this action farce
gets better as it goes along and finds time for a quick
spoof of *The Old Dark House*.

w Ben Travers   d Tom Walls

Tom Walls, Ralph Lynn, Robertson Hare, Diana
Churchill, Gordon James, Martita Hunt

Pot o' Gold
US   1941   87m   bw
Globe/James Roosevelt
V*, L
GB title: *The Golden Hour*

A radio giveaway show finds work for idle musicians.

Thin Capraesque comedy which needed more
determined handling.

w Walter de Leon   d George Marshall   *ph* Hal
Mohr   *md* Lou Forbes

James Stewart, Paulette Goddard, Horace Heidt,
Charles Winninger, Mary Gordon, Frank Melton, Jed
Prouty

Pote tin Kyriaki: see *Never on Sunday*

Potemkin: see *The Battleship Potemkin*

Potomok Chingis-Khana: see *Storm over Asia*

Poulet au Vinaigre: see *Cop au Vin*

Powaqqatsi *
US   1988   97m   colour
Cannon/Golan-Globus (Mel Lawrence, Godfrey Reggio,
Lawrence Taub)
V, V*, S

Montage of images of back-breaking labour in the
Third World.

A sequel to *Koyaanisqatsi*, silent apart from the
hypnotic score, its beautifully composed images
detract from the undignified labour it shows.

w Geoffrey Reggio, Ken Richards   d Geoffrey
Reggio   *ph* Graham Berry, Leonidas Zourdoumis
m Philip Glass   *ed* Iris Cahn, Alton Walpole

Powder River
US   1953   77m   Technicolor
TCF

A marshal finds that an embittered doctor is the killer
he is seeking.

Satisfactory programmer, more of a suspense drama
than a Western.

w Geoffrey Holmes   *novel* Stuart Lake   d Louis
King

Rory Calhoun, Cameron Mitchell, Corinne Calvet,
Penny Edwards, Carl Betz, John Dehner

Powder Town
US   1942   79m   bw
RKO

A scientist in a munitions plant comes into conflict
with a tough foreman.

Propaganda action programmer.

w David Boehm and Vicki Baum   *novel* Max Brand
d Rowland V. Lee

Victor Mclaglen, Edmond O'Brien, June Havoc

Power: see *Jew Suss* (1934)

The Power *
US   1967   109m   Metrocolor   Cinemascope
MGM/George Pal

Scientists researching into human endurance are
menaced by one of their number who has developed
the ability to kill by will power.

Interesting but finally unexciting and exasperating
science fiction which badly lacks a gimmick one can
actually see.

w John Gay   *novel* Frank M. Robinson   d Byron
Haskin   *ph* Ellsworth Fredericks   *m* Miklos Rozsa

Michael Rennie, George Hamilton, Suzanne Pleshette,
Nehemiah Persoff, Earl Holliman, Arthur O'Connell,
Aldo Ray, Barbara Nichols, Yvonne de Carlo, Richard
Carlson, Gary Merrill, Ken Murray, Miiko Taka, Celia
Lovsky

'The movie takes itself very seriously. We don't have
to.' – *Robert Windeler*

Power
US   1985   111m   Technicolor
TCF/Lorimar/Polar (Reene Schisgal, Mark Tarlov)
V*, L

A political PR man takes on an industrialist of
dubious background.

Slick and punchy but somewhat unnecessary
investigation of corruption in the media, an American
version of *The Ploughman's Lunch*.

w David Himmelstein   d Sidney Lumet
ph Andrzej Bartkowiak   *m* Cy Coleman   *pd* Peter
Larkin   *ed* Andrew Mondsheim

Richard Gere, Julie Christie, Gene Hackman, Kate
Capshaw, Denzel Washington, E. G. Marshall,
Beatrice Straight, Fritz Weaver, Michael Learned

The Power and the Glory *
US   1933   76m   bw
Fox (Jesse L. Lasky)

The flashback story of a tycoon who rose from nothing
and was corrupted by power.

Often noted as a forerunner of *Citizen Kane*, this is in
fact a disappointing film with a very thin script and a
general sense of aimlessness. 'Presented in narratage'
meant that the characters voice their unspoken
thoughts. Most interesting for its credits.

w Preston Sturges   d William K. Howard
ph James Wong Howe

Spencer Tracy, Colleen Moore, Ralph Morgan, Helen
Vinson

'Débuting at two dollars on Broadway. Not two
dollars but decidedly above-average film fare. Packs
plenty of appeal, even with a not too punch marquee
cast.' – *Variety*

The Power and the Prize *
US   1956   98m   bw   Cinemascope
MGM (Nicholas Nayfack)

An ambitious company executive is criticized by his
president for wanting to marry a European refugee,
but the other executives support him.

Unconvincing big business fairy tale which passes the
time competently enough, though Taylor is a
humourless hero.

w Robert Ardrey   *novel* Howard Swiggett   d Henry
Koster   *ph* George Folsey   *m* Bronislau Kaper

Robert Taylor, Elizabeth Mueller, Mary Astor, Burl
Ives, Charles Coburn, Cedric Hardwicke

'He's had to fight all his life. Now he's fighting for theirs.'
The Power of One
US   1991   127m   Technicolor
Warner (Amon Milchan)
V, V*, L, S

In South Africa in the 1930s, an English boy, who
witnesses the brutality of the Afrikaners and is taught
boxing by a black prisoner, decides to dedicate his life
to the cause of racial equality.

Sentimental and unconvincing account of an African
childhood, with *Rocky*-like moments thrown in for
good measure.

w Robert Mark Kamen   *novel* Bryce Courtenay
d John G. Avildsen   *ph* Dean Semler   *m* Hans
Zimmer, Lebo M   *pd* Roger Hall   *ed* John G.
Avildsen

Stephen Dorff, John Gielgud, Armin Mueller-Stahl,
Morgan Freeman, Guy Witcher, Simon Fenton

'Crude, patronising and mawkish, sure, but rescued
by excellent performances, beautiful landscape
photography, and hard-to-argue-with themes of
natural justice, delivered with a punch.' – *Angie Errigo,
Empire*

Power of the Press
US   1943   63m   bw
Columbia

The owner of a New York paper kills to maintain its isolationist line.

Hard-hitting melodrama which overdoes the propaganda.

w Samuel Fuller, Robert D. Andrews   d Lew Landers

Lee Tracy, Guy Kibbee, Otto Kruger, Gloria Dickson

Power Play
GB/Canada   1978   109m   colour
Robert Cooper/Canada United Kingdom (Christopher Dalton)
V*

In a mythical country, a tank commander joins the leaders of a coup d'état only to doublecross them.

Uninteresting mixture of violent action and verbosity.
wd Martyn Burke   ph Ousama Rawi   m Ken Thorne

Peter O'Toole, David Hemmings, Donald Pleasence, Barry Morse

The Powers Girl
US   1942   92m   bw
UA/Charles R. Rogers
GB title: Hello Beautiful

Girls come to New York to become models for John Robert Powers.

Extremely thin and forgettable musical.

w Edwin Moran, Harry Segall   book John Robert Powers   d Norman Z. McLeod   ph Stanley Cortez md Louis Silvers

George Murphy, Anne Shirley, Carole Landis, Alan Mowbray (as Powers), Dennis Day, Benny Goodman and his Orchestra, Mary Treen

Powwow Highway
UK   1988   91m   Technicolor
Handmade (Jan Wieringa)
V, V*

A militant American Indian leaves the reservation with his simple friend to make a long journey to rescue his sister, imprisoned on a trumped-up drugs charge.

Rambling road movie that comes to the conclusion that it is morally justifiable for the exploited to lie, cheat and steal.

w Janet Heaney, Jean Stawarz   novel David Seals d Jonathan Wacks   ph Toyomichi Kurita   m Barry Goldberg   pd Cynthia Sowder   ed Hilarie Roope

A. Martinez, Gary Farmer, Joanelle Nadine Romero, Geoff Rivas, Roscoe Born, Wayne Waterman, Margo Kane, Amanda Wyss, Sam Vlanos

'Settles for the affirmations of the buddy movie, without achieving either a consistently manic tone or a convincing balance between character, humour and suspense.' – Farrah Anwar, MFB

Practically Yours
US   1944   89m   bw
Paramount (Mitchell Leisen)

A war hero comes back after being supposed dead, and finds himself with a fiancée he never met.

Silly romantic comedy which never gets going.

w Norman Krasna   d Mitchell Leisen   ph Charles Lang Jnr   m Victor Young

Claudette Colbert, Fred MacMurray, Gil Lamb, Cecil Kellaway, Robert Benchley, Rosemary de Camp, Tom Powers, Jane Frazee

'It Started With A Kiss.'
Prague *
GB/France   1991   89m   Eastmancolor
Winstone/BBC/Constellation/UGC Hachette-Premiere/British
  Screen/Canal+ (Christopher Young)

A Scot goes to Prague in search of a wartime newsreel

that will reveal information about his mother and her family.

Moderately interesting account of a shared European past that illumines the present, but lacking narrative drive.

wd Ian Sellar   ph Darius Khondji   m Jonathan Dove   pd Jiri Matolin   ed John Bloom

Alan Cumming, Sandrine Bonnaire, Bruno Ganz, Raphael Meiss, Henri Meiss, Hana Gregorova

'A decent Euro-movie that makes good use of the idea of film as collective memory.' – Philip French, Observer

'Comes across like a collection of ideas for a Euro co-production to be lensed in a photogenic city rather than an accomplished vital picture.' – Variety

A Prayer for the Dying
GB   1987   107m   Metrocolor
Peter Snell/Samuel Goldwyn Co
V, V*, L

An ex-IRA gunman feels unable to silence a priest witness of a killing, and confesses his sins instead.

Convoluted melodrama which kills its chances as a thriller by striving to say something meaningful.

w Edmund Ward, Martin Lynch   novel Jack Higgins d Mike Hodges (who disowned the version released) m Bill Conti

Mickey Rourke, Bob Hoskins, Alan Bates, Sammi Davis, Christopher Fulford

Prayer of the Rollerboys
US   1990   94m   colour
First Independent/Gaga/Fox Lorber/Academy/JVC/TV Tokyo
  (Robert Mickelson)
V, V*, L

In a future bankrupt America, a youth, working undercover for the police, infiltrates a vicious gang of young, skating drug dealers.

Dull, paranoid science fiction aimed at a teenage audience.

w W. Peter Iliff   d Rick King   ph Phedon Papamichael   m Stacy Widelitz   pd Thomas A. Walsh   ed Daniel Loewenthal

Corey Haim, Patricia Arquette, Christopher Collet, J. C. Quinn, Julius Harris, Devin Clark, Mark Pellegrino, Morgan Weisser

'Offers blood-pumping entertainment in a pulpy, cartoonish mode.' – Variety

Precinct 45: Los Angeles Police: see The New Centurions

Predator
US   1987   107m   DeLuxe
TCF/Lawrence Gordon/Joel Silver/John Davis
V, V*, L

An allied military rescue team gets into trouble in South America.

Lethargic action thriller with unpleasant moments.

w Jim and John Thomas   d John McTiernan ph Donald McAlpine, Leon Sanchez   m Alan Silvestri   pd John Vallone   ed John F. Link, Mark Helfrich

Arnold Schwarzenegger, Carl Weathers, Bill Duke, Elpidia Carrillo, Jesse Ventura

Predator 2
US   1990   108m   DeLuxe
Fox/Lawrence Gordon/Joel Silver/John Davis
V, V*, L, S

A heavily armed alien killer visits Earth.

Violent and gore-filled, filmed in a frenetic style that soon wearies.

w Jim Thomas, John Thomas   d Stephen Hopkins ph Peter Levy   m Alan Silvestri   pd Lawrence G. Paull   ed Mark Goldblatt

Danny Glover, Gary Busey, Ruben Blades, Maria Conchita Alonso, Bill Paxton, Kevin Peter Hall

'In terms of overall excitement, it outdoes its first safari in start-to-finish hysteria.' – Variety

Prehistoric Women: see Slave Girls

Prelude to Fame
GB   1950   88m   bw
Rank/Two Cities (Donald B. Wilson)

The health of a child musical prodigy is endangered by an ambitious woman who pushes him to the top.

Banal drama with classical music, generally overacted by the adults.

w Robert Westerby   story Young Archimedes by Aldous Huxley   d Fergus McDonell   ph George Stretton

Jeremy Spenser, Guy Rolfe, Kathleen Ryan, Kathleen Byron, James Robertson Justice, Henry Oscar, Rosalie Crutchley

Prelude to War ***
US   1943   53m   bw
US Signal Corps (Frank Capra)

First in the Why We Fight series.

A brilliant assemblage of newsreel, diagrams, and March of Time techniques which pointed a new way for documentary.

'There isn't a dull second.' – Variety

The Premature Burial
US   1961   81m   Eastmancolor   Panavision
AIP (Roger Corman)
V*, L

A man afraid of being buried alive suffers just that fate, but later comes to and wreaks revenge on his tormentors.

Gloomy Gothic horror based vaguely on Edgar Allan Poe: the ultimate in graveyard ghoulishness.

w Charles Beaumont, Ray Russell   d Roger Corman ph Floyd Crosby   m Ronald Stein   ad Daniel Haller

Ray Milland, Heather Angel, Hazel Court, Richard Ney, Alan Napier, John Dierkes

Premiere
GB   1938   71m   bw
ABPC

The principal backer of a stage show is shot during the first performance.

Slightly unusual mystery drama.

w F. McGrew Willis   d Walter Summers

John Lodge, Judy Kelly, Joan Marion, Hugh Williams, Edmund Breon, Steven Geray, Edward Chapman

Préparez Vos Mouchoirs: see Get Out Your Handkerchiefs

Present Arms: see Leathernecking

Presenting Lily Mars *
US   1943   104m   bw
MGM (Joe Pasternak)

A girl from the sticks hits it big on Broadway.

No, the plot wasn't new, but some of the numbers were nice.

w Richard Connell, Gladys Lehman   novel Booth Tarkington   d Norman Taurog   ph Joseph Ruttenberg   md George Stoll

Judy Garland, Van Heflin, Fay Bainter, Richard Carlson, Martha Eggerth, Spring Byington, Bob Crosby and his band, Tommy Dorsey and his band

The President Vanishes
US   1934   80m   bw
Walter Wanger (Paramount)
GB title: *Strange Conspiracy*

The president of the US agrees to drop out of sight for a few days, pretending to have been kidnapped, so that his country will not be drawn into a European war.

Reasonably intriguing political fantasy with good production and performances.

w Lynn Starling, Carey Wilson, Cedric Worth novel anonymous   d William A. Wellman

Arthur Byron, Janet Beecher, Paul Kelly, Peggy Conklin, Rosalind Russell, Sidney Blackmer, Walter Kingsford, Charley Grapewin, Edward Arnold

'Provocative topical meller, but likely to be spotty.' – *Variety*

The President's Analyst *
US   1967   104m   Technicolor   Panavision
Paramount/Panpiper (Stanley Rubin)
V*

A psychiatrist who has been asked to treat the president is pursued by spies of every nationality.

Wild political satirical farce which finally unmasks as its chief villain the telephone company. Laughs along the way, but it's all rather too much.

wd *Theodore J. Flicker*   ph William A. Fraker
m *Lalo Schifrin*   pd Pato Guzman

James Coburn, Godfrey Cambridge, Severn Darden, Joan Delaney, Pat Harrington, Eduard Franz, Will Geer

'Free-wheeling, outrageous and very funny, laced with a sophisticated zaniness that is sheer delight.' – *Judith Crist*

The President's Lady *
US   1953   96m   bw
TCF (Sol C. Siegel)

An account of the early career of Andrew Jackson, a lawyer whose frail wife died shortly after he became president.

Well-produced political historical romance.

w John Patrick   novel Irving Stone   d Henry Levin
ph *Leo Tover*   m Alfred Newman   ad Lyle Wheeler, Leland Fuller

Charlton Heston, Susan Hayward, John McIntire, Fay Bainter, Carl Betz

'History plays a curious second fiddle to love's old sweet song.' – *New York Times*

AAN: art direction

The Presidio
US   1988   98m   Technicolor   Panavision
UIP/Paramount (D. Constantine Conte)
V, V*, L

An army officer and a former cop, who are old adversaries, investigate a murder at an army base.

Tame and uninvolving action movie.

w Larry Ferguson   d Peter Hyams   ph Peter Hyams
m Bruce Broughton   pd Albert Brenner   ed James Mitchell, Diane Adler, Beau Barthel-Blair

Sean Connery, Mark Harmon, Meg Ryan, Jack Warden, Mark Blum, Dana Gladstone, Jenette Goldstein, Marvin J. McIntyre, Dan Calfa, John DiSanti

Press for Time
GB   1966   102m   Eastmancolor
Rank/Ivy/Titan (Robert Hartford Davis, Peter Newbrook)
V

The prime minister's grandson is a newspaper seller, and is quietly promoted to be a journalist in a seaside town where it is thought he can do no harm.

The star's last comedy in his original style; competent but nothing special.

w Norman Wisdom, Eddie Leslie   novel Yea Yea Yea by Angus McGill   d Robert Asher   ph Peter Newbrook   m Mike Vickers

Norman Wisdom, Derek Bond, Angela Browne, Derek Francis, Noel Dyson, Peter Jones, David Lodge

Pressure Point *
US   1962   89m   bw
UA/Larcas/Stanley Kramer
V*

A black prison psychiatrist has longstanding trouble with a violent racist inmate.

Curious, quite compelling case history, told in pointless and confusing flashback; sharply made and photographed, melodramatically acted.

w Hubert Cornfield, S. Lee Pogostin   d Hubert Cornfield   ph Ernest Haller   m Ernest Gold

Sidney Poitier, Bobby Darin, Peter Falk, Carl Benton Reid

Prestige
US   1932   71m   bw
RKO

A woman follows her fiancé to a Malayan prison colony where he is on the staff, and finds he has become an alcoholic.

Tediously stilted romantic melodrama which seems at least twice as long as its actual running time.

w Francis Edwards Faragoh   novel Lips of Steel by Harry Hervey   d Tay Garnett

Ann Harding, Melvyn Douglas, Adolphe Menjou, Guy Bates Post, Clarence Muse

'Attraction. Desire. Deception. Murder. No one is ever completely innocent.'

Presumed Innocent **
US   1990   127m   DuArt
Warner/Mirage (Sydney Pollack, Mark Rosenberg)
V, V*, L, S

A public prosecutor is accused of murdering a colleague.

Gripping courtroom drama in which very little is what it seems.

w Frank Pierson, Alan J. Pakula   novel Scott Turow   d Alan J. Pakula   ph Gordon Willis   m John Williams   pd George Jenkins   ed Evan Lottman

Harrison Ford, Brian Dennehy, Raul Julia, Bonnie Bedelia, Paul Winfield, Greta Scacchi, John Spencer, Joe Grifasi, Sab Shimono, Jesse Bradford

'A demanding, disturbing javelin of a courtroom murder mystery.' – *Variety*

Pretty Baby *
US   1950   92m   bw
Warner (Harry Kurnitz)

A girl finds it easier to get a seat on the subway if she is carrying a (dummy) baby, but gets into complications when she meets a baby food king.

Silly but quite pleasant comedy variation on *Bachelor Mother*.

w Everett Freeman, Harry Kurnitz   d Bretaigne Windust   ph Peverell Marley   m David Buttolph

Betsy Drake, Edmund Gwenn, Dennis Morgan, Zachary Scott, William Frawley

Pretty Baby **
US   1978   109m   Metrocolor
Paramount (Louis Malle)
V*, L

A 12-year-old girl grows up in a New Orleans brothel in the 1910s.

A teasing exploration of adult hypocrisies as seen through the eyes of a child, beautifully composed in the manner of French paintings of the period.

w Polly Platt, Louis Malle   d Louis Malle   ph Sven Nykvist   md Jerry Wexler

Keith Carradine, Susan Sarandon, Brooke Shields, Francis Faye, Antonio Fargas

'The picture is too rotten to be worth much of a fuss; it's worth just enough attention to show why it's rotten.' – *Stanley Kauffmann*

AAN: Jerry Wexler

Pretty in Pink
US   1986   96m   Technicolor
Lauren Shuler/Paramount
V, V*, L, S

A pretty girl from the wrong side of the tracks begins to find herself when she goes to a classy high school.

Slick but not very interesting look at the insecurities of American adolescents.

w John Hughes   d Howard Deutch

Molly Ringwald, Harry Dean Stanton, Jon Cryer, Andrew McCarthy, Annie Potts

Pretty Ladies
US   1925   70m at 24 fps   bw   silent
MGM

The husband of a Broadway actress leaves her for a chorus girl.

Heavy-going melodrama with a star who later turned comedienne and a couple of stars-to-be playing bits.

w Adela Rogers St John   d Monta Bell

ZaSu Pitts, Tom Moore, Norma Shearer, Lilyan Tashman, Conrad Nagel, George K. Arthur, Myrna Loy, Joan Crawford

Pretty Maids All in a Row
US   1971   95m   Metrocolor
MGM (Gene Roddenberry)

High school girl students are being murdered by their guidance counsellor.

Uneasy murder comedy with few laughs, casting its star as a most unlikely villain. An interesting if unsuccessful attempt to be different.

w Gene Roddenberry   novel Francis Pollini
d Roger Vadim   ph Charles Rosher   m Lalo Schifrin

Rock Hudson, Angie Dickinson, Telly Savalas, Roddy McDowall, Keenan Wynn

Pretty Poison *
US   1968   89m   DeLuxe
TCF/Lawrence Turman/Mollino (Marshal Backlar, Noel Black)
V*

A psychotic arsonist enlists the aid of a teenager but soon discovers she is kinkier than he and has murder in mind.

Bizarre black comedy-melodrama, quite successfully mixed and served.

w Lorenzo Semple Jnr   novel She Let Him Continue by Stephen Geller   d Noel Black   ph David Quaid   m Johnny Mandel

Anthony Perkins, Tuesday Weld, Beverly Garland, John Randolph, Dick O'Neill, Clarice Blackburn

Pretty Polly
GB   1967   102m   Techniscope
Universal/George W. George, Frank Granat
US title: *A Matter of Innocence*

On a world tour with her vulgar aunt, a timid maiden finds romance in Singapore.

Slight romantic fable decked out with travel guide backgrounds and at odds with the cynicism of the short story from which it originates.

w Keith Waterhouse, Willis Hall   story Noël Coward   d Guy Green   ph Arthur Ibbetson   m Michel Legrand

Hayley Mills, Trevor Howard, Shashi Kapoor, Brenda de Banzie, Dick Patterson, Peter Bayliss, Patricia Routledge, Dorothy Alison

'It came and went this winter, leaving a slight trace of camphor and old knitting needles.' – *Wilfrid Sheed*

Pretty Woman *
US   1990   119m   Technicolor
Buena Vista/Touchstone (Arnon Milchan, Steven Reuther)
V, V*, L, S

A wealthy workaholic asset stripper picks up a hooker and invites her to spend a week with him.

Shameless Hollywood concoction of romance and glossy fantasy that was an immense popular success in 1990, proving that there remains an insatiable demand for escapist fairy tales.

w J. F. Lawton   *d* Garry Marshall   *ph* Charles Minsky   *m* James Newton Howard   *pd* Albert Brenner   *ed* Priscilla Nedd

Richard Gere, Julia Roberts, Ralph Bellamy, Jason Alexander, Laura San Giacomo, Hector Elizondo

'Despite its obvious flaws, Garry Marshall's sentimental pic hits the right emotional targets to shape up as a monster hit.' – *Variety*

AAN: Julia Roberts

The Price of Fear
US   1956   79m   bw
Universal-International (Howard Christie)

A lady hit-and-run driver falls for a man on the run from racketeers but plans to give him away in order to save herself.

Vaguely unpleasing programmer in which nobody is sympathetic.

w Robert Tallman   *d* Abner Biberman   *ph* Irving Glassberg   *md* Joseph Gershenson

Merle Oberon, Lex Barker, Charles Drake, Gia Scala, Warren Stevens

Prick up Your Ears **
GB   1987   108m   Eastmancolor
Zenith/Civilhand (Andrew Brown)
V, L

The life and violent death of Joe Orton, playwright.

Raunchy homosexual saga of a writer who became a cult figure with the sophisticated; treatment full of vigour for those who can take the pace.

w Alan Bennett   *biography* John Lahr   *d* Stephen Frears   *ph* Oliver Stapleton   *m* Stanley Myers   *pd* Hugo Luczyc-Wyhowski

Gary Oldman, Alfred Molina, Vanessa Redgrave, Wallace Shawn, Julie Walters, James Grant

'Five charming sisters on the gayest, merriest manhunt that ever snared a bewildered bachelor! Girls! take a lesson from these husband hunters!'
Pride and Prejudice ***
US   1940   116m   bw
MGM (Hunt Stromberg)
V, V*, L

An opinionated young lady of the early 19th century wins herself a rich husband she had at first despised for his pride.

A pretty respectable version of Jane Austen's splendid romantic comedy, with a generally excellent cast; full of pleasurable moments.

w Aldous Huxley, Jane Murfin   *play* Helen Jerome   *novel* Jane Austen   *d* Robert Z. Leonard   *ph* Karl Freund   *m* Herbert Stothart   *ad* Cedric Gibbons, Paul Groesse

Laurence Olivier, Greer Garson, Edmund Gwenn, Mary Boland, Melville Cooper, Edna May Oliver, Karen Morley, Frieda Inescort, Bruce Lester, Edward Ashley, Ann Rutherford, Maureen O'Sullivan, E. E. Clive, Heather Angel, Marsha Hunt

'The most deliciously pert comedy of old manners, the most crisp and crackling satire in costume that we can remember ever having seen on the screen.' – *Bosley Crowther*

'Animated and bouncing, the movie is more Dickens than Austen; once one adjusts to this, it's a happy and carefree viewing experience.' – *New Yorker, 1980*

AA: art direction

The Pride and the Passion *
US   1957   131m   Technicolor   Vistavision
UA/Stanley Kramer
V*

In 1810 Spain a British naval officer helps Spanish guerrillas, by reactivating an old cannon, to win their fight against Napoleon.

Stolid, miscast adventure spectacle, its main interest being the deployment of the gun across country by surging throngs of peasants.

w Edna and Edward Anhalt   *novel* The Gun by C. S. Forester   *d* Stanley Kramer   *ph* Franz Planer   *m* Georges Antheil

Cary Grant, Sophia Loren, Frank Sinatra, Theodore Bikel, John Wengraf, Jay Novello, Philip Van Zandt

'The whirr of the cameras often seems as loud as the thunderous cannonades. It evidently takes more than dedication, cooperative multitudes and four million dollars to shoot history in the face.' – *Time*

Pride of Kentucky: see *The Story of Seabiscuit*

The Pride of St Louis
US   1952   93m   bw
TCF (Jules Schermer)
V*

The life of baseball star Dizzy Dean, who injured himself and became a commentator.

Sporting biopic of clearly restricted interest; modestly well done.

w Herman J. Mankiewicz   *d* Harmon Jones   *ph* Leo Tover   *m* Arthur Lange

Dan Dailey, Joanne Dru, Richard Haydn, Richard Crenna, Hugh Sanders

AAN: original story (Guy Trosper)

Pride of the Marines *
US   1945   120m   bw
Warner (Jerry Wald)
GB title: *Forever in Love*

The story of Marine Al Schmid, blinded while fighting the Japanese.

Over-dramatic, sudsy biopic which is well enough mounted to carry quite an impact in the flagwaving Hollywood style.

w Albert Maltz   *d* Delmer Daves   *ph* Peverell Marley   *m* Franz Waxman

John Garfield, Eleanor Parker, Dane Clark, John Ridgely, Rosemary de Camp, Ann Doran, Warren Douglas, Tom D'Andrea

'Long drawn out and never inspired, but very respectably honest and dogged.' – *James Agee*

AAN: Albert Maltz

'The most wonderful story America ever took to its heart!'
The Pride of the Yankees *
US   1942   128m   bw
Samuel Goldwyn
V*, L

The story of baseball star Lou Gehrig, who died of amytropic lateral sclerosis at the height of his powers.

Standard sporting biopic ending on Gehrig's famous speech to the crowd; emotion covers the film's other deficiencies.

w Jo Swerling, Herman J. Mankiewicz   *story* Paul Gallico   *d* Sam Wood   *ph* Rudolph Maté

m Leigh Harline   *pd* William Cameron Menzies   *ed* Daniel Mandell

Gary Cooper, Teresa Wright, Babe Ruth, Walter Brennan, Dan Duryea, Elsa Janssen, Ludwig Stossel, Virginia Gilmore

'A simple, tender, meticulous and explicitly narrative film . . . a real saga of American life, homey, humorous, sentimental, and composed in patient detail.' – *New York Times*

AA: Daniel Mandell

AAN: best picture; script; Paul Gallico; Rudolph Maté; Leigh Harline; Gary Cooper; Teresa Wright

'Their extravagant romance was more tempestuous than anything he wrote!'
Priest of Love
GB   1981   125m   colour
Ronceval/Milesian (Stanley J. Seeger)
V, V*

The last years of D. H. Lawrence, when his books were banned and he was seeking warmer climes to help his TB.

An extremely disappointing film, seeming to consist of aimless travelling by fractious people who never have anything interesting to say. Stilted in all departments.

w Alan Plater   *d* Christopher Miles   *ph* Ted Moore   *m* Joseph James

Ian McKellen, Janet Suzman, Helen Mirren, Penelope Keith, Jorge Rivero, John Gielgud

'Miles has assigned himself a missionary role but he is just not up to the task.' – *Jill Forbes, MFB*

The Priest's Wife (dubbed)
Italy/France   1970   106m   Technicolor
Warner/Champion/ECF (Carlo Ponti)
original title: *La Moglie del Prete*

A pop singer seduces a priest who attempts to save her from suicide.

Dreary treatment of the topical theme of celibacy.

w Ruggero Maccari, Bernardino Zapponi   *d* Dino Risi   *ph* Alfio Contini   *m* Armando Trovaioli   *ad* Gianni Polidori   *ed* Alberto Gallitti

Sophia Loren, Marcello Mastroianni, Venantino Venantini, Jacques Stany, Pippo Starnazza

'Vulgar, fence-sitting charade.' – *John Gillett, MFB*

† The film was cut to 103m on its British release.

Prima della Rivoluzione: see *Before the Revolution*

Prime Cut
US   1972   91m   Technicolor   Panavision
Cinema Center (Joe Wizan)
V*

A Kansas gangster incurs the wrath of his Chicago bosses, and a hired killer is sent to eliminate him.

Gory cat-and-mouse chase melodrama with no interest save its excesses.

w Robert Dillon   *d* Michael Ritchie   *ph* Gene Polito   *m* Lalo Schifrin

Gene Hackman, Lee Marvin, Angel Tompkins, Sissy Spacek

The Prime Minister *
GB   1940   109m   bw
Warner (Max Milder)

Episodes in the life of Disraeli.

Modestly budgeted historical pageant notable only for performances.

w Brock Williams, Michael Hogan   *d* Thorold Dickinson   *ph* Basil Emmott

John Gielgud, Diana Wynyard, Will Fyffe, Stephen Murray, Owen Nares, Fay Compton (as Queen Victoria), Lyn Harding, Leslie Perrins

The Prime of Miss Jean Brodie *

GB . 1969 116m DeLuxe
TCF (Robert Fryer)
V, V*

A sharp-minded Edinburgh schoolmistress of the thirties is a bad influence on her more easily-swayed pupils.

Interesting but slackly handled and maddeningly played character drama.

w Jay Presson Allen novel Muriel Spark
d Ronald Neame ph Ted Moore pd John Howell
m/y Rod McKuen

Maggie Smith, Robert Stephens, Pamela Franklin, Celia Johnson, Gordon Jackson, Jane Carr

'The novel lost a good deal in its stage simplification, and loses still more in its movie reduction of that stage version.' – John Simon

AA: Maggie Smith

AAN: song 'Jean' (m/y Rod McKuen)

The Primrose Path

US 1940 92m bw
RKO (Gregory La Cava)
V*

The youngest of a family of shanty-town prostitutes falls in love with an honest hamburger stand proprietor.

Downright peculiar melodrama for its day and age, and not very entertaining either, spending most of its time being evasive.

w Allan Scott, Gregory La Cava play Robert Buckner, Walter Hart novel February Hill by Victoria Lincoln d Gregory La Cava ph Joseph H. August
m Werner Heymann

Ginger Rogers, Joel McCrea, Marjorie Rambeau, Henry Travers, Miles Mander, Queenie Vassar, Joan Carroll

'The story isn't good enough, the direction isn't sincere enough, to give any pain to the lumps in the throat which its designers obviously had in mind.' – Richard Mallett, Punch

AAN: Marjorie Rambeau

The Prince and the Pauper *

US 1937 118m bw
Warner (Robert Lord)
V*

In Tudor London, young Edward VI changes places with a street urchin who happens to be his double.

Well-produced version of a famous story; it never quite seems to hit the right style or pace, but is satisfying in patches.

w Laird Doyle novel Mark Twain d William Keighley ph Sol Polito m Erich Wolfgang Korngold

Errol Flynn, Claude Rains, Billy and Bobby Mauch, Henry Stephenson, Barton MacLane, Alan Hale, Eric Portman, Montagu Love (as Henry VIII), Lionel Pape, Halliwell Hobbes, Fritz Leiber

'Lavish but not convincing. Doubtful box office: the commercial aspect seems wholly concerned in the timeliness of a Coronation sequence and the name of Errol Flynn. It is not enough.' – Variety

The Prince and the Pauper *

Panama 1977 121m Technicolor Panavision
International Film Production/Ilya and Alexander Salkind (Pierre Spengler)
V, V*
US title: Crossed Swords

Young Edward VI changes place with a beggar, who helps to expose a traitor.

Moderately well-made swashbuckler with an old-fashioned air, not really helped by stars in cameo roles or by the poor playing of the title roles.

w George MacDonald Fraser novel Mark Twain
d Richard Fleischer ph Jack Cardiff m Maurice Jarre pd Anthony Pratt

Mark Lester, Oliver Reed, Raquel Welch, Ernest Borgnine, George C. Scott, Rex Harrison, David Hemmings, Charlton Heston (as Henry VIII), Harry Andrews, Murray Melvin, Julian Orchard

The Prince and the Showgirl *

GB 1957 117m Technicolor
Warner/Marilyn Monroe Productions (Laurence Olivier)
V, V*, L

In London for the 1911 coronation, a Ruritanian prince picks up a chorus girl and they come to understand and respect each other.

Heavy-going comedy, rich in production values but weak in dramatic style and impact.

w Terence Rattigan play The Sleeping Prince by Terence Rattigan d Laurence Olivier ph Jack Cardiff m Richard Addinsell pd Roger Furse
ad Carmen Dillon

Laurence Olivier, Marilyn Monroe, Sybil Thorndike, Richard Wattis, Jeremy Spenser, Esmond Knight, Rosamund Greenwood, Maxine Audley

Prince of Darkness

US 1987 101m colour
Guild/Alive (Larry Franco)
V*, L, S

Scientists are called in by a priest to deal with a canister containing the spirit of Satan.

Risible horror that never arouses any interest.

w Martin Quatermass d John Carpenter ph Gary B. Kibbe m John Carpenter, Alan Howarth
pd Daniel Lomino ed Steve Mirkovich

Donald Pleasence, Victor Wong, Lisa Blount, Dennis Dun, Jameson Parker, Susan Blanchard, Ann Howard, Ann Yen, Ken Wright

'A saga of scoundrels in a century of infamy!'

Prince of Foxes *

US 1949 107m bw
TCF (Sol. C. Siegel)

A wandering adventurer in medieval Italy gets mixed up with the Borgias.

Good-looking historical fiction with a slight edge to it.

w Milton Krims novel Samuel Shellabarger
d Henry King ph Leon Shamroy m Alfred Newman

Tyrone Power, Orson Welles, Wanda Hendrix, Felix Aylmer, Everett Sloane, Katina Paxinou, Marina Berti

'Plot, counterplot, action and vengeance.' – MFB

'This pretentious chapter of pseudo-history never rises above the merely spectacular, hovers mostly around the conventionally banal, and descends once to the unpardonably crude.' – Richard Mallett, Punch

AAN: Leon Shamroy

The Prince of Pennsylvania *

US 1988 93m Technicolor
Palace/New Line Cinema (Joan Fishman)
V, V*, L

A rebellious teenager has problems with his father.

Sensitive, downbeat tale of a boy's alienation from his family that avoids easy conclusions.

wd Ron Nyswaner ph Frank Prinzi m Thomas Newman pd Tony Corbett ed William Scharf

Fred Ward, Keanu Reeves, Bonnie Bedelia, Amy Madigan, Jeff Hayenga, Tracey Ellis, Joseph de Lisi, Jay O. Sanders, Kari Keegan

Prince of Pirates

US 1953 80m Technicolor
Columbia

A young prince of the Netherlands turns pirate when his brother allies with the Spanish invader.

Fast-moving costume potboiler with lavish use of action scenes from Joan of Arc.

w John O'Dea, Samuel Newman d Sidney Salkow

John Derek, Barbara Rush, Carla Balenda, Whitfield Connor, Edgar Barrier

Prince of Players *

US 1955 102m DeLuxe Cinemascope
TCF (Philip Dunne)

Episodes in the life of actor Edwin Booth, brother of the man who killed Abraham Lincoln.

Earnest but ham-fisted biopic more notable, as a Hollywood entertainment, for its dollops of straight Shakespeare than for any dramatic interest.

w Moss Hart book Eleanor Ruggles d Philip Dunne ph Charles G. Clarke m Bernard Herrmann

Richard Burton, Eva Le Gallienne, Maggie McNamara, John Derek, Raymond Massey, Charles Bickford, Elizabeth Sellars, Ian Keith

Prince of the City *

US 1981 167m Technicolor
Warner/Orion (Jay Presson Allen)
V, V*, L

A New York policeman on the drug beat is induced to inform on his corrupt colleagues.

Punishingly long police semi-documentary based on real events and apparently filmed with a political motive. Excellent acting and production detail do not prevent the enterprise from seeming like a half-speed version of Serpico.

w Jay Presson Allen, Sidney Lumet book Robert Daley d Sidney Lumet

Treat Williams, Jerry Orbach, Don Billett, Richard Foronjy, Carmine Caridi, Kenny Marino

AAN: screenplay

Prince of Thieves

US 1948 72m bw
Sam Katzman/Columbia

Robin Hood saves a nobleman's intended from Baron Tristram.

Tatty second-feature version of a legendary figure.

w Maurice Tombragel d Howard Bretherton

Jon Hall, Patricia Morison, Alan Mowbray, Michael Duane, Adele Jergens

'A story about the memories that haunt us, and the truth that sets us free.'

The Prince of Tides **

US 1991 132m Technicolor
Columbia/Barwood/Longfellow (Barbra Streisand, Andrew Karsch)
V, V*, L, S

A married psychiatrist falls in love with the unhappy brother of her catatonic patient.

Excellent performances enliven a lushly romantic melodrama.

w Pat Conroy, Becky Johnston novel Pat Conroy
d Barbra Streisand ph Stephen Goldblatt
m James Newton Howard pd Paul Sylbert
ed Don Zimmerman

Barbra Streisand, Nick Nolte, Blythe Danner, Kate Nelligan, Jeroen Krabbé, Melinda Dillon, George Carlin, Jason Gould, Brad Sullivan

'Has a passion seldom found in contempo US films and a quality not usually associated with Barbra Streisand – self-effacement.' – Variety

'This phoney overblown movie. . . is the king of soaps.' – Philip French, Observer

AAN: film; Nick Nolte; Kate Nelligan; Pat Conroy, Becky Johnston; Stephen Goldblatt; James Newton Howard; Paul Sylbert

Prince Valiant *
US   1954   100m   Technicolor   Cinemascope
TCF (Robert L. Jacks)

The son of the exiled king of Scandia seeks King Arthur's help against the usurper, and becomes involved in a court plot.

Agreeable historical nonsense for teenagers, admittedly and sometimes hilariously from a comic strip.

w Dudley Nichols   *comic strip* Harold Foster
d Henry Hathaway   ph Lucien Ballard   m Franz Waxman

Robert Wagner, James Mason, Debra Paget, Janet Leigh, Sterling Hayden, Victor McLaglen, Donald Crisp, Brian Aherne, Barry Jones, Primo Carnera

The Prince Who Was a Thief
US   1951   88m   Technicolor
U-I (Leonard Goldstein)

An Arabian Nights prince is lost as a baby and brought up by thieves, but finally fights back to his rightful throne.

Given the synopsis, any viewer can write the script himself. Standard eastern Western romp.

w Gerald Drayson Adams, Aeneas Mackenzie   *story* Theodore Dreiser   d Rudolph Maté   ph Irving Glassberg   m Hans Salter

Tony Curtis, Piper Laurie, Everett Sloane, Jeff Corey

The Princess *
Hungary   1982   113m   bw
Cinegate/Tarsulas Studio/Mafilm (Pal Erdoss)
original title: *Adj Király Katonát!*

A 15-year-old girl moves to Budapest to discover that life is tougher than she expected.

Downbeat, documentary-style examination of a teenager facing a succession of disappointments; the film, though, manages to suggest that there is hope for the future.

w Istvan Kardos   d Pál Erdöss   ph Ferenc Pap, Lajos Koltai, Gabor Szabo   pd Andras Gyurki   ed Klara Majoros

Erika Ozda, Andrea Szendrei, Denes Diczhazi, Arpad Toth, Juli Nyako, Lajos Soltis

The Princess and the Goblin
GB/Hungary   1992   111m   colour
Entertainment/Siriol/Pannonia/SC4/NHK Enterprises (Robin Lyons)
V

A miner's son saves a princess from being kidnapped by goblins.

Uninteresting animated feature, with a dull fairy-tale plot dully executed.

w Robin Lyons   *novel* George MacDonald   d József Gémes   ph Arpad Lessecry, Gyergy Verga, Ede Pagner, Nick Smith, Pete Turner, Steve Turner, Andreas Klawsz   m István Lerch   ed Magda Hap

voices of: Joss Ackland, Claire Bloom, Roy Kinnear, Sally Ann Marsh, Rik Mayall, Peggy Mount, Peter Murray, Victor Spinetti, Mollie Sugden

'A potentially charming medieval cartoon let down by so-so technique and unimaginative plotting.' – *Variety*

The Princess and the Pirate *
US   1944   94m   Technicolor
Samuel Goldwyn (Don Hartman)
V*, L

An impostor is on the run from a vicious pirate.

Typical star costume extravaganza with fewer laughs than you'd expect.

w Don Hartman, Melville Shavelson, Everett Freeman   d David Butler   ph William Snyder, Victor Milner   m David Rose   ad Ernst Fegte

Bob Hope, Virginia Mayo, Victor McLaglen, Walter Slezak, Walter Brennan, Marc Lawrence, Hugo Haas, Maude Eburne

'From start to finish, Hope dominates the action with well-timed colloquial nifties.' – *Variety*

AAN: David Rose; Ernst Fegte

The Princess Bride *
US   1987   98m   DeLuxe
Act III (Andrew Scheinmann, Rob Reiner)
V, V*, L, S

Grandfather tells a fairy tale of good and evil.

Rather strained fantasy with occasional bright moments.

w William Goldman   *novel* William Goldman   d Rob Reiner   ph Adrian Biddle   m Mark Knopfler   pd Norman Garwood

Cary Elwes, Mandy Patinkin, Chris Sarandon, Christopher Guest, Peter Falk, Wallace Shawn

AAN: song 'Storybook Love'

Princess Charming
GB   1934   78m   bw
Gainsborough

A Ruritanian revolution forces a princess to escape in disguise.

Light operetta with an intriguing cast.

w L. DuGarde Peach, Arthur Wimperis, Lauri Wylie   *play* Alexandra by F. Martos   d Maurice Elvey

Evelyn Laye, Yvonne Arnaud, George Grossmith, Max Miller, Henry Wilcoxon, Ivor Barnard, Francis L. Sullivan

'Still just below the peak of excellence for which Hollywood is noted.' – *Variety*

The Princess Comes Across *
US   1936   76m   bw
Paramount (Arthur Hornblow Jnr)

A starstruck Brooklyn girl makes a transatlantic liner voyage disguised as a princess, and finds herself involved in a murder mystery.

Zany comedy thriller with plenty of jokes.

w Walter de Leon, Frances Martin, Frank Butler, Don Hartman, Philip MacDonald   *novel* Louis Lucien Rogger   d William K. Howard   ph Ted Tetzlaff   m Phil Boutelje

Carole Lombard, Fred MacMurray, Alison Skipworth, Douglass Dumbrille, William Frawley, Porter Hall, George Barbier, Lumsden Hare, Sig Rumann, Mischa Auer, Tetsu Komai

Princess of the Nile
US   1954   71m   Technicolor
TCF

An Egyptian princess of the middle ages leads her country against the invasion of a bedouin prince.

Lethargic costume piece with hopelessly miscast actors.

w Gerald Drayson Adams   d Harmon Jones

Debra Paget, Michael Rennie, Jeffrey Hunter, Dona Drake, Edgar Barrier, Jack Elam, Lee Van Cleef

Princess O'Hara
US   1935   79m   bw
Universal

In her father's memory a girl steals the racehorse he loved.

Sentimental comedy from Damon Runyon, later remade for Abbott and Costello as *It Ain't Hay*. Not up to much in either version.

w Doris Malloy, Harry Clork   d David Burton

Jean Parker, Chester Morris, Leon Errol, Vince Barnett, Henry Armetta, Ralph Remley, Clara Blandick

'Poor construction limits this one's chances . . . not likely to go above average grosses.' – *Variety*

Princess O'Rourke
US   1943   94m   bw
Warner (Hal B. Wallis)

An ace pilot falls for a princess and causes diplomatic complications.

Very thin wartime comedy with a propaganda ending involving Franklin Roosevelt.

wd Norman Krasna   ph Ernest Haller   m Frederick Hollander

Olivia de Havilland, Robert Cummings, Charles Coburn, Jack Carson, Jane Wyman, Harry Davenport, Gladys Cooper, Minor Watson, Curt Bois

AA: Norman Krasna (as writer)

Priorities on Parade
US   1942   79m   bw
Sol C. Siegel/Paramount

Members of a swing band get jobs in a munitions factory.

Inept propaganda musical.

w Art Arthur, Frank Loesser   d Albert S. Rogell

Ann Miller, Johnnie Johnston, Jerry Colonna, Betty Jane Rhodes, Vera Vague, Eddie Quillan, The Debonaires

'Manifestly just another of the misfortunes of war.' – *Variety*

La Prise de Pouvoir par Louis XIV: see *The Rise of Louis XIV*

Prison
US   1988   103m   colour
Entertainment/Empire (Irwin Yablans)
V*, L

The spirit of a long-dead prisoner returns for revenge against the prison's new governor.

Energetic horror movie, re-animating all the clichés of prison dramas.

w C. Courtney Joyner   *story* Irwin Yablans   d Renny Harlin   ph Michael Ballhaus   m Richard Band, Christopher Stone   pd Phillip Duffin   ed Ray Lovejoy

Viggo Mortensen, Chelsea Field, Lane Smith, Lincoln Kilpatrick, Tom Everett, Ivan Kane

Prison: see *The Devil's Wanton*

Prison Farm
US   1938   69m   bw
Paramount

A girl denounces her boyfriend when he is wanted for robbery and murder.

Good example of this studio's tour of criminals and penal institutions.

w Eddie Welch, Robert Yost, Stuart Anthony   d Louis King

Lloyd Nolan, Shirley Ross, John Howard, J. Carrol Naish, Porter Hall, Anna Q. Nilsson, Esther Dale, May Boley

'First-rate entertainment despite lightweight star names.' – *Variety*

Prison without Bars
GB   1938   80m   bw
Columbia/London Films (Arnold Pressburger)

The newest inmate of a reform school for girls vies with the superintendent for the love of the doctor.

Basically paperback trash, this film of a notorious original was shot in three languages, but the English version at least omitted the lesbianism, except by implication. Cinematically it was without style.

w Hans Wilhelm, Margaret Kennedy, Arthur Wimperis   play Prison sans Barreau by Gina Kaus, E. and O. Eis, Hilde Koveloff   d Brian Desmond Hurst   ph Georges Périnal   m John Greenwood   ad Vincent Korda   ed Charles Crichton

Edna Best, Corinne Luchaire, Barry K. Barnes, Mary Morris, Lorraine Clewes, Martita Hunt, Glynis Johns

The Prisoner *
GB   1955   91m   bw
(Columbia) Facet/London Independent Producers (Vivian A. Cox)
V*

In a European totalitarian state, a Cardinal is tortured and brainwashed.

Virtually a two-character talkpiece from an offbeat play which should have stayed in the theatre.

w Bridget Boland   play Bridget Boland   d Peter Glenville   ph Reg Wyer   m Benjamin Frankel

Alec Guinness, Jack Hawkins, Wilfrid Lawson, Kenneth Griffith, Ronald Lewis, Raymond Huntley

'An undercover cop. An investigation. A mistake . . . he's dead meat.'

The Prisoner (dubbed) *
Hong Kong   1991   91m   colour
Golden Harvest/Blaine & Blake (Jimmy Wang Yu)
V

An episodic film set in a tough prison ruled by thuggish warders, where an undercover cop is sent to discover the assassin of his elderly mentor, a prisoner keeps escaping to see his young son, and a gangster arrives to murder the man who accidentally killed his brother.

Interlocking plots give this downbeat martial arts movie a greater narrative appeal than most of its kind, though its morality is hardly endearing and Jackie Chan fans may be disappointed that he plays only a minor role, despite his star billing.

w Fu Li, Yeh Yuen Chin   d Chu Yen Ping   m Fu Lap   ad Cheung Sau Ping   ed Chow Tak Yeung

Jackie Chan, Andy Lau, Samo Hung, Tony Leung, Jimmy Wang Yu, Ko Chuen Hsiung, Tao Chung Hwa

'Surprisingly good entertainment.' – Impact

'Unsurprising but enjoyable chop-sockey fodder.' – Sight and Sound

Prisoner of Rio
Brazil   1988   105m   colour
Palace/Doisirmaos Producioes (Klaus Pagh, Michael Lunderskoff)

A British policeman goes to Brazil to bring back to justice one of the Great Train Robbers.

Special pleading on behalf of Ronald Biggs, one of the thieves involved in the robbery in 1963, which even he may find embarrassing to watch.

w Lech Majewski, Ronald Biggs, Julia Frankel   d Lech Majewski   ph George Mooradian   m Luis Bonfa, Hans Zimmer, Luciano Perrone   ad Oscar Ramos   ed Darren Kloomok

Steven Berkoff, Paul Freeman, Peter Firth, Florinda Bolkan, Jose Wilker, Zeze Mota, Desmond Llewellyn, Breno Mello

'And you think you've got problems?'

The Prisoner of Second Avenue *
US   1975   98m   Technicolor   Panavision
Warner (Melvin Frank)
V*, L

A New York clerk and his wife are driven to distraction by the problems of urban living.

Gloomier-than-usual (from this author) collection of one-liners which almost turns into a psychopathic

melodrama and causes its amiable leading players to overact horrendously.

w Neil Simon   play Neil Simon   d Melvin Frank   ph Philip Lathrop   m Marvin Hamlisch

Jack Lemmon, Anne Bancroft, Gene Saks, Elizabeth Wilson

The Prisoner of Shark Island **
US   1936   95m   bw
TCF (Darryl F. Zanuck)

The story of the doctor who treated the assassin of President Lincoln.

Well-mounted historical semi-fiction with excellent detail.

w Nunnally Johnson   d John Ford   ph Bert Glennon   md Louis Silvers

Warner Baxter, Gloria Stuart, Joyce Kay, Claude Gillingwater, Douglas Wood, Harry Carey, Paul Fix, John Carradine

'Strong film fare for men; will have to be sold for femme appeal.' – Variety

'A powerful film, rarely false or slow, maintaining the relentless cumulative pressure, the logical falling of one thing into another, until the audience is included in the movement and carried along with it in some definite emotional life that is peculiar to the art of motion pictures at its best.' – Otis Ferguson

Prisoner of War
US   1954   81m   bw
MGM (Henry Berman)

Life in a communist prison camp in Korea.

Sensational propaganda, reduced to comic strip level.

w Allen Rivkin   d Andrew Marton   ph Robert Planck   m Jeff Alexander

Ronald Reagan, Steve Forrest, Dewey Martin, Oscar Homolka, Robert Horton, Paul Stewart, Henry Morgan, Stephen Bekassy

'It presents its catalogue of horrors in a manner unworthy of the cause it attempts to uphold.' – John Gillett

The Prisoner of Zenda ****
US   1937   101m   bw
David O. Selznick
V*, L

An Englishman on holiday in Ruritania finds himself helping to defeat a rebel plot by impersonating the kidnapped king at his coronation.

A splendid schoolboy adventure story is perfectly transferred to the screen in this exhilarating swashbuckler, one of the most entertaining films to come out of Hollywood.

w John Balderston, Wills Root, Donald Ogden Stewart, novel Anthony Hope   d John Cromwell   ph James Wong Howe   m Alfred Newman   ad Lyle Wheeler

Ronald Colman, Douglas Fairbanks Jnr, Madeleine Carroll, David Niven, Raymond Massey, Mary Astor, C. Aubrey Smith, Byron Foulger, Montagu Love

'The most pleasing film that has come along in ages.' – New York Times

'One of those rare movies that seem, by some magic trick, to become more fascinating and beguiling with each passing year.' – John Cutts, 1971

† Previously filmed in 1913 and 1922.

AAN: Alfred Newman; Lyle Wheeler

The Prisoner of Zenda *
US   1952   100m   Technicolor
MGM (Pandro S. Berman)
V, V*, L

A costly scene-for-scene remake which only goes to show that care and discretion are no match for the happy inspiration of the original.

w John Balderston, Noel Langley   d Richard Thorpe   ph Joseph Ruttenberg   m Alfred Newman

Stewart Granger, James Mason, Deborah Kerr, Robert Coote, Robert Douglas, Jane Greer, Louis Calhern, Francis Pierlot, Lewis Stone

The Prisoner of Zenda
US   1979   108m   Technicolor
Universal (Walter Mirisch)
V*

Palpably uneasy version of the above which teeters between comedy and straight romance, with barely a moment of real zest creeping in. The star is way off form in both roles.

w Dick Clement, Ian La Frenais   d Richard Quine   ph Arthur Ibbetson   m Henry Mancini   pd John J. Lloyd

Peter Sellers, Lynne Frederick, Lionel Jeffries, Elke Sommer, Gregory Sierra, Stuart Wilson, Jeremy Kemp, Catherine Schell, Simon Williams, Norman Rossington, John Laurie

'Flatly directed, leadenly unfunny.' – Paul Taylor, MFB

Prisoners of the Casbah
US   1953   78m   Technicolor
Sam Katzman/Columbia

An Eastern princess and her lover take refuge from the evil Grand Vizier in the Casbah, a haven for outcasts.

Inept sword and sandal actioner; you can almost smell the Turkish delight.

w DeVallon Scott   d Richard Bare

Gloria Grahame, Cesar Romero, Turhan Bey, Nestor Paiva

Private Affairs
US   1940   74m   bw
Universal

A girl with problems seeks out the father she has never met.

Thin comedy with a pleasant cast.

w Charles Grayson, Leonard Spigelgass, Peter Milne   story Walter Green   d Albert S. Rogell

Nancy Kelly, Robert Cummings, Roland Young, Hugh Herbert, Montagu Love, Jonathan Hale

'All women take to men who have the appearance of wickedness!'

The Private Affairs of Bel Ami *
US   1947   119m   bw
UA/David L. Loew (Ray Heinz)
V*

In 1890s Paris, a career journalist climbs to fame over the ruined lives of his friends.

Tame and stuffy adaptation of an incisive novel, rather poorly produced.

wd Albert Lewin   novel Guy de Maupassant   ph Russell Metty   m Darius Milhaud

George Sanders, Angela Lansbury, Ann Dvorak, Frances Dee, John Carradine, Hugo Haas, Marie Wilson, Albert Basserman, Warren William

Private Angelo
GB   1949   106m   bw
Pilgrim (Peter Ustinov)

An Italian soldier hates war and spends World War II on the run from both sides.

Listless satirical comedy that just isn't funny enough.

w Peter Ustinov, Michael Anderson   novel Eric Linklater   d Peter Ustinov   ph Erwin Hillier

Peter Ustinov, Godfrey Tearle, Robin Bailey, Maria Denis, Marjorie Rhodes, James Robertson Justice, Moyna McGill

Private Benjamin

US   1980   110m   Technicolor
Warner/Hawn-Myers-Shyer-Miller
V, V*, L

A well-heeled Jewish widow, at a crossroads in her life, joins the army.

Half-assed attempt at combining slapstick, character study, sentiment, sex and a recruiting poster. Some funny moments don't really make it worth sitting through.

w Nancy Meyers, Charles Shyer, Harvey Miller
d Howard Zieff   ph David M. Walsh   m Bill Conti

Goldie Hawn, Eileen Brennan, Armand Assante, Robert Webber, Sam Wanamaker, Barbara Barrie, Harry Dean Stanton

AAN: screenplay; Goldie Hawn; Eileen Brennan (supporting actress)

Private Buckaroo

US   1942   68m   bw
Universal
V*

The difficulties of putting on shows for soldiers.

Slaphappy second feature worth preserving for the talent.

w Edmund Kelso, Edmund James   d Edward Cline

The Andrews Sisters, Harry James and his Orchestra, Joe E. Lewis, Donald O'Connor, Peggy Ryan, Huntz Hall, Ernest Truex, Shemp Howard

A Private Conversation ***

USSR   1983   96m   colour
Contemporary/Mosfilm
original title: Bez Svidetelei; aka: Without Witnesses

A party hack visits his ex-wife for an evening of recrimination and raking over the past.

A two-character movie in the limited setting of a small flat, but one that succeeds in its searing portrait of a failed marriage and a wasted life.

w Nikita Mikhalov, Sofia Prokofieva, Ramiz Fataliev
play Sofia Prokofieva   d Nikita Mikhalov
ph Pavel Lebeshev   m Eduard Artemiev
ad Alexander Adabashian, Igor Makarov, Alexander Samulekin

Mikhail Ulyanov, Irina Kupchenko

The Private Files of J. Edgar Hoover *

US   1978   112m   Movielab
AIP/Larco (Larry Cohen)
V*, S

The supposedly true facts of the career of the longtime head of the FBI.

Unreliable exposé with some interesting bits.

wd Larry Cohen   ph Paul Glickman   m Miklos Rozsa

Broderick Crawford, José Ferrer, Michael Parks, Ronee Blakely, Rip Torn, Celeste Holm, Dan Dailey, Raymond St Jacques, Howard Da Silva, June Havoc, John Marley, Andrew Duggan, Lloyd Nolan

A Private Function **

GB   1984   94m   colour
Handmade (Mark Shivas)
V*

In 1947 Yorkshire, a doctor and his family secretly fatten an unlicensed pig.

Sharply-detailed comedy typical of its author, but less likeable than many.

w Alan Bennett   d Malcolm Mowbray   ph Tony Pierce-Roberts   m John Du Prez   pd Stuart Walker
ed Barrie Vince

Michael Palin, Maggie Smith, Denholm Elliott, Richard Griffiths, Tony Haygarth, Liz Smith, John Normington

BFA: Maggie Smith; Liz Smith (supporting actress); Denholm Elliott (supporting actor)

Private Hell 36 *

US   1954   81m   bw
Filmakers
V*, L

Two cops on a robbery trail find the loot and keep it for themselves.

Predictable but stylish film noir, still moderately watchable.

w Collier Young, Ida Lupino   d Don Siegel

Ida Lupino, Steve Cochran, Howard Duff, Dean Jagger, Dorothy Malone

Private Izzy Murphy

US   1926   80m approx at 24 fps   bw   silent
Warner

A Jewish boy loves a Catholic girl.

Dreary variant on Abie's Irish Rose, popular enough for a 1927 sequel called Sailor Izzy Murphy.

w Philip Lonergan   d Lloyd Bacon

George Jessel, Patsy Ruth Miller, Vera Gordon

Private Life *

USSR   1982   104m   colour
Contemporary/Mosfilm
original title: Chastnaya Zhizn

A businessman, retiring in his fifties, discovers that he has drifted away from his wife and children.

Perceptive, occasionally ponderous, study of a man in crisis.

w Anatoly Grebnyev, Yuli Raizman   d Yuli Raizman
ph Nikolai Olonovsky   ad Tatyana Lapshina

Mikhail Ulyanov, Iya Savvina, Irina Gubanova, Tatyana Dogileva, Aleksei Blokhin, Elena Sanayeva, Liliya Gritsenko

AAN: best foreign film

The Private Life of Don Juan

GB   1934   90m   bw
London Films (Alexander Korda)
V*

In 17th-century Spain, the famous lover fakes death and makes a comeback in disguise.

Lacklustre frolic by an overage star through dismal sets. The production was meant to extend the success of The Private Life of Henry VIII, but totally failed to do so.

w Lajos Biro, Frederick Lonsdale   play Henri Bataille   d Alexander Korda   ph Georges Périnal
m Ernst Toch

Douglas Fairbanks, Merle Oberon, Binnie Barnes, Benita Hume, Joan Gardner, Melville Cooper, Athene Seyler, Owen Nares

'Technically it has so much in its favour that it's too bad it doesn't promise solid b.o. attraction.' – Variety

'One of those ideas that never really take off.' – New Yorker, 1977

'The things I do for England!'

The Private Life of Henry VIII ***

GB   1933   97m   bw
London Films (Alexander Korda)
V, V*, L

How Henry beheaded his second wife and acquired four more.

This never was a perfect film, but certain scenes are very funny and its sheer sauciness established the possibility of British films making money abroad, as well as starting several star careers. It now looks very dated and even amateurish in parts.

w Lajos Biro, Arthur Wimperis   d Alexander Korda
ph Georges Périnal   m Kurt Schroeder

Charles Laughton, Elsa Lanchester, Robert Donat, Merle Oberon, Binnie Barnes, Franklin Dyall, Miles Mander, Wendy Barrie, Claud Allister, Everly Gregg

'Among the best anywhere and by far the top British picture . . . figures a sock entry, especially for the best houses.' – Variety

AA: Charles Laughton

AAN: best picture

The Private Life of Sherlock Holmes ***

GB   1970   125m   DeLuxe   Panavision
UA/Phalanx/Mirisch/Sir Nigel (Billy Wilder)
V, V*

A secret Watson manuscript reveals cases in which Sherlock Holmes became involved with women.

What started as four stories is reduced to two, one brightly satirical and the other no more than a careful and discreet recreation, with the occasional jocular aside, of the flavour of the stories themselves. A very civilized and pleasing entertainment except for the hurried rounding-off which is a let-down.

w Billy Wilder, I. A. L. Diamond   d Billy Wilder
ph Christopher Challis   m Miklos Rozsa
ad Alexander Trauner

Robert Stephens, Colin Blakely, Genevieve Page, Clive Revill, Christopher Lee, Catherine Lacey, Stanley Holloway

'Affectionately conceived and flawlessly executed.' – NFT, 1974

'Wilder's least embittered film, and by far his most moving. Great.' – Time Out, 1984

Private Lives *

US   1931   82m   bw
MGM (Albert Lewin)
V*

Ex-marrieds desert their intended new spouses to try each other again.

An essentially theatrical comedy, and a great one, seems somewhat slow-witted on film.

w Hans Kraly, Richard Schayer   play Noël Coward
d Sidney Franklin   ph Ray Binger

Norma Shearer, Robert Montgomery, Reginald Denny, Una Merkel, Jean Hersholt

'Stars are a big asset to this parlour comedy which will amuse the women more than the men.' – Variety

'For polish, few comedies of the thirties can equal this early alliance of cinema and stage.' – John Baxter, 1968

The Private Lives of Elizabeth and Essex **

US   1939   106m   Technicolor
Warner (Robert Lord)
V, V*
reissue title: Elizabeth the Queen

Elizabeth I falls in love with the Earl of Essex, but events turn him into a rebel and she has to order his execution.

Unhistorical history given the grand treatment; a Hollywood picture book, not quite satisfying dramatically despite all the effort.

w Norman Reilly Raine, Aeneas Mackenzie
play Elizabeth the Queen by Maxwell Anderson
d Michael Curtiz   ph Sol Polito, W. Howard Greene
m Erich Wolfgang Korngold   ad Anton Grot

Bette Davis, Errol Flynn, Olivia de Havilland, Donald Crisp, Vincent Price, Alan Hale, Henry Stephenson, Henry Daniell, Leo G. Carroll, Nanette Fabray, Robert Warwick, John Sutton

'Solid box office material, with fine grosses and holdovers indicated . . . in all technical departments, picture has received topnotch investiture.' – Variety

'A rather stately, rigorously posed and artistically technicolored production.' – Frank S. Nugent

AAN: Sol Polito, W. Howard Greene; Erich Wolfgang Korngold; Anton Grot

The Private Navy of Sergeant O'Farrell
US 1968 92m Technicolor
Hope Enterprises (John Beck)

After World War II, military personnel congregate on an island which has been by-passed by hostilities.

Nothing much wrong with the plot, but at this time in his career Hope seemed unable to do anything right, and the film was barely released.

wd Frank Tashlin *ph* Alan Stensvold *m* Harry Stikman

Bob Hope, Gina Lollobrigida, Phyllis Diller, Jeffrey Hunter, Mylene Demongeot, Henry Wilcoxon

Private Number
US 1936 80m bw
TCF (Raymond Griffith)
GB title: *Secret Interlude*

A wealthy young man keeps a secret of his marriage to a housemaid.

Warmed-over class melodrama previously filmed in 1930 as *Common Clay*. Adequate within its lights.

w Gene Markey, William Conselman *play Common Clay* by Cleves Kinkead *d* Roy del Ruth *ph* Peverell Marley *m* Louis Silvers

Loretta Young, Robert Taylor, Basil Rathbone, Patsy Kelly, Marjorie Gateson, Paul Harvey, Monroe Owsley, John Miljan

Private Potter
GB 1962 89m bw
MGM/Ben Arbeid

A young soldier is court-martialled for cowardice but claims he had a vision of God.

Stilted morality play, unpersuasively made and acted.

w Ronald Harwood *TV play* Ronald Harwood *d* Caspar Wrede *ph* Arthur Lavis *m* George Hall

Tom Courtenay, Mogens Wieth, Ronald Fraser, James Maxwell, Ralph Michael, Brewster Mason

The Private Secretary
GB 1935 70m bw
Twickenham

A clerical gentleman is duped into protecting a rich young idler from his creditors.

Moderately effective filming of a popular stage farce from a German original.

w Arthur Macrae, George Broadhurst, H. Fowler Mear *play* Van Moser *d* Henry Edwards

Edward Everett Horton, Barry Mackay, Judy Gunn, Oscar Asche, Sydney Fairbrother, Alastair Sim, Michael Shepley

The Private War of Major Benson
US 1955 105m Technicolor Cinemascope
U-I (Howard Pine)

A soldier with outspoken views is sent to cool off as commander of a military academy run by an order of nuns.

Cute and sentimental nonsense with unlikely situations, a martinet becoming soft-centred and a happy-ever-after finale.

w William Roberts, Richard Alan Simmons *d* Jerry Hopper *ph* Harold Lipstein *m* Henry Mancini, Herman Stein

Charlton Heston, Julie Adams, Tim Hovey, William Demarest, Tim Considine, Sal Mineo, Nana Bryant, Milburn Stone, Mary Field

AAN: original story (Bob Mosher, Joe Connelly)

The Private Wore Skirts: see *Never Wave at a WAC*

'She loved a man who did not exist – except in her own private world!'

Private Worlds *
US 1935 84m bw
Paramount (Walter Wanger)

Romance among the doctors at a mental hospital.

Melodrama treated with what was at the time unexpected seriousness.

w Lynn Starling *novel* Phyllis Bottome *d* Gregory La Cava *ph* Leon Shamroy *m* Heinz Roemheld

Claudette Colbert, Charles Boyer, Joel McCrea, Joan Bennett, Helen Vinson, Esther Dale, Samuel S. Hinds

'Fine but not too artistic production . . . woman's picture of fair b.o. potentialities.' – *Variety*

AAN: Claudette Colbert

A Private's Affair
US 1959 92m DeLuxe Cinemascope
TCF (David Weisbart)

Three army recruits form a close harmony trio and get into various scrapes.

Thin service comedy for the 'new' youth audience.

w Winston Miller *d* Raoul Walsh *ph* Charles G. Clarke *m* Cyril Mockridge

Sal Mineo, Christine Carere, Barry Coe, Barbara Eden, Gary Crosby, Terry Moore, Jim Backus, Jessie Royce Landis

Privates on Parade *
GB 1982 113m colour
Handmade (Simon Relph)
V*

Farcical and serious incidents in the lives of an army concert party in 1948 Singapore.

Rather heavy-going comedy with much bad language and an overdose of effeminacy; on the whole no funnier than *It Ain't Half Hot, Mum*.

w Peter Nichols *play* Peter Nichols *d* Michael Blakemore *ph* Ian Wilson *m* Denis King

John Cleese, Denis Quilley, Michael Elphick, Nicola Pagett, Bruce Payne, Joe Melia

Private's Progress ***
GB 1956 97m bw
British Lion/Charter (Roy Boulting)
V

An extremely innocent young national serviceman is taught a few army dodges and becomes a dupe for jewel thieves.

Celebrated army farce with satirical pretensions; when released it had something to make everyone in Britain laugh.

w Frank Harvey, John Boulting *novel* Alan Hackney *d* John Boulting *ph* Eric Cross *m* John Addison

Ian Carmichael, Terry-Thomas, Richard Attenborough, *Dennis Price*, Peter Jones, William Hartnell, Thorley Walters, Ian Bannen, Jill Adams, Victor Maddern, Kenneth Griffith, Miles Malleson, *John Le Mesurier*

Prividenie, Kotoroe ne Vozvrashchaetsya: see
The Ghost That Never Returns

Privilege *
GB 1967 103m Technicolor
Universal/Worldfilm/Memorial (John Heyman)

The publicity campaign for a pop star turns him into a religious messiah.

Rather hysterical fable for our time, undeniably forceful in spots and yawnful in others.

w Norman Bogner *story* Johnny Speight *d* Peter Watkins *ph* Peter Suschitzky *m* Mike Leander

Paul Jones, Jean Shrimpton, Mark London, Max Bacon, Jeremy Child, James Cossins, Victor Henry

'Everything in it goes wrong, and one can do little but catalogue the failures.' – *MFB*

Privileged *
GB 1982 96m Technicolor
ITC/The Oxford Film Company (Richard Stevenson)

Oxford undergraduates rehearsing *The Duchess of Malfi* become involved in sexual intrigues which result in suicide.

Highly unusual because made and funded by the students themselves, this melodrama has vivid patches but generally lacks a professional eye.

w Michael Hoffman, David Woollcombe, Rupert Walters *d* Michael Hoffman *ph* Fiona Cunningham Reid *m* Rachel Portman *ad* Peter Schwabach *ed* Derek Goldman

Robert Woolley, Diana Katis, Hughie Grant, Victoria Studd, James Wilby

Le Prix du Danger: see *The Prize of Peril*

The Prize ***
US 1963 135m Metrocolor Panavision
MGM/Roxbury (Pandro S. Berman)
V*

In Stockholm during the Nobel Prize awards, a drunken American author stumbles on a spy plot.

Whatever the original novel is like, the film is a Hitchcock pastiche which works better than most Hitchcocks: suspenseful, well characterized, fast moving and funny from beginning to end.

w Ernest Lehman, *novel* Irving Wallace *d* Mark Robson *ph* William Daniels *m* Jerry Goldsmith

Paul Newman, Elke Sommer, *Edward G. Robinson*, Diane Baker, Kevin McCarthy, *Leo G. Carroll*, Micheline Presle

A Prize of Arms
GB 1961 105m bw
British Lion/Interstate (George Maynard)

An ex-army officer and an explosives expert plan to steal an army payroll.

Standard, pacy caper melodrama offering nothing at all new.

w Paul Ryder *d* Cliff Owen *ph* Gilbert Taylor *m* Robert Sharples

Stanley Baker, Tom Bell, Helmut Schmid, John Phillips

A Prize of Gold
GB 1955 100m Technicolor
Columbia/Warwick (Phil C. Samuel)

An American army sergeant in Berlin decides to steal a cargo of Nazi loot.

Routine caper thriller with sentimental leanings.

w Robert Buckner, John Paxton *novel* Max Catto *d* Mark Robson *ph* Ted Moore *m* Malcolm Arnold

Richard Widmark, Mai Zetterling, Nigel Patrick, George Cole, Donald Wolfit, Andrew Ray, Joseph Tomelty, Karel Stepanek

The Prize of Peril
France/Yugoslavia 1983 88m Eastmancolor
Brent Walker/Swanie Productions/ TF1/UGC/Top 1/Avala (Norbert Saada)
original title: *Le Prix du Danger*

A man volunteers to enter a TV contest, where the prize goes to the person who can survive being hunted across Paris by armed killers.

An interesting idea, badly executed.

w Yves Boisset, Jean Curtelin *story* Robert Sheckley *d* Yves Boisset *ph* Pierre-William Glenn *m* Vladimir Cosmo *ad* Aleksandar Milovic *ed* Michelle David

Gérard Lanvin, Michel Piccoli, Marie-France Pisier, Bruno Cremer, Andréa Ferréol, Jean Rougerie, Jean-Claude Dreyfus

The Prizefighter and the Lady

US   1933   102m   bw
MGM (Hunt Stromberg)
GB title: *Every Woman's Man*

A boxer falls for a high-class gangster's girl.

Plodding romantic melodrama, popular because it starred a real boxer.

w John Meehan, John Lee Mahin   *d* W. S. Van Dyke   *ph* Lester White   *m* David Snell

Myrna Loy, Max Baer, Otto Kruger, Walter Huston, Jack Dempsey, Primo Carnera

'Freak Max Baer starrer, a picture that entertains in high-pressure manner.' – *Variety*

AAN: original story (Frances Marion)

Prizzi's Honor *

US   1985   129m   DeLuxe
ABC/John Foreman
V, V*, L

Male and female hired killers for Mafia families fall in love but are assigned to 'hit' each other.

Critically lauded but puzzling and unsatisfactory black comedy which takes far too long to get going, is muddled in narrative, and leaves an unpleasant taste.

w Richard Condon, Janet Roach   *novel* Richard Condon   *d* John Huston   *ph* Andrzej Bartkowiak   *m* Alex North   *pd* Dennis Washington   *ed* Rudi and Kaja Fehr

Jack Nicholson, Kathleen Turner, Robert Loggia, William Hickey, John Randolph, *Anjelica Huston*

'Certainly one of the most curious films to kick off the summer season by an American major.' – *Variety*

AA: Anjelica Huston (supporting actress)

AAN: best picture; direction; Jack Nicholson; William Hickey; adapted screenplay; editing

BFA: adapted screenplay

Problem Child

US   1990   81m   DeLuxe
UIP/Universal/Imagine Entertainment (Robert Simonds)
V, V*, L

A badly behaved boy is adopted by a small-town couple.

Broadly played, predictable comedy of mayhem and misunderstandings.

w Scott Alexander, Larry Karaszewski   *d* Dennis Dugan   *ph* Peter Lyons Collister   *m* Miles Goodman   *pd* George Costello   *ed* Daniel Hanley, Michael Hill

John Ritter, Jack Warden, Michael Oliver, Gilbert Gottfried, Amy Yasbeck, Michael Richards, Peter Jurasik, Charlotte Akin

'Universal took a step in the right direction by whittling it down to just 81 minutes but didn't go far enough. The studio should have excised another 75 minutes and released this unbelievable mess as a short.' – *Variety*

'Now, Junior has a brand new friend. He's bad. She's worse.'

Problem Child 2

US   1991   91m   DeLuxe
UIP/Universal/Imagine (Robert Simonds)
V, V*, L

An ill-behaved boy decides that his father should marry the mother of his friend, a badly behaved girl.

Nasty-minded, witless slapstick with an anal fixation.

w Scott Alexander, Larry Karaszewski   *d* Brian Levant   *ph* Peter Smokler   *m* David Kitay   *pd* Maria Caso   *ed* Lois Freeman-Fox, Robert P. Seppey

John Ritter, Michael Oliver, Jack Warden, Laraine Newman, Amy Yasbeck, Ivyann Schwan, Gilbert Gottfried, Paul Wilson

'No seam of bad taste is left unmined as the screenwriters sink to impossibly low depths in pursuit of anything vaguely resembling a laugh.' – *Mark Salisbury, Empire*

Le Procès: see *The Trial*

The Prodigal

US   1931   76m   bw
MGM

The scion of a Southern plantation becomes a tramp.

Pleasant minor musical with a star who never really caught on.

w Bess Meredyth, Wells Root   *d* Harry Pollard

Lawrence Tibbett, Esther Ralston, Roland Young, Cliff Edwards, Purnell Pratt, Hedda Hopper, Stepin Fetchit

'Between average and good . . . should top the normal gross.' – *Variety*

'The story of woman's beauty and man's temptation!'

The Prodigal

US   1955   115m   Eastmancolor   Cinemascope
MGM (Charles Schnee)
V*, L

The son of a Hebrew farmer falls for the high priestess of a pagan cult.

Wildly apocryphal 'biblical' story of obvious expensiveness but no merit.

w Maurice Zimm   *d* Richard Thorpe   *ph* Joseph Ruttenberg   *m* Bronislau Kaper

Lana Turner, Edmund Purdom, Louis Calhern, James Mitchell, Walter Hampden, Francis L. Sullivan, Joseph Wiseman, Audrey Dalton, Taina Elg, Neville Brand, Cecil Kellaway

'A few lines of dialogue derive from the Bible; the rest is pure Hollywood, but Hollywood in its mood of sham solemnity when even the unintentional jokes are not funny.' – *MFB*

'A costume stinker . . . it should have played Disneyland!' – *Lana Turner*

The Producers *

US   1968   88m   Pathecolor
Avco /Springtime/Crossbow (Sidney Glazier)
V*, L

A Broadway producer seduces elderly widows to obtain finance for his new play, sells 25,000 per cent in the expectation that it will flop, and is horrified when it succeeds.

Dismally unfunny satire except for the play itself, *Springtime for Hitler*, which is neatly put down. This has, however, become a cult film, so that criticism is pointless.

wd Mel Brooks   *ph* Joseph Coffey   *m* John Morris

Zero Mostel, Gene Wilder, Kenneth Mars, Estelle Winwood, Renee Taylor, Dick Shawn

'Over and over again promising ideas are killed off, either by over-exposure or bad timing.' – *Tom Milne*

'An almost flawless triumph of bad taste, unredeemed by wit or style.' – *Arthur Schlesinger Jnr*

AA: Mel Brooks (as writer)

AAN: Gene Wilder

Profession: Reporter: see *The Passenger*

Professional Soldier

US   1936   75m   bw
TCF (Darryl F. Zanuck)

A kidnapper befriends the young prince who is his victim.

Predictable, polished family film.

w Gene Fowler, Howard Willis Smith   *story* Damon Runyon   *d* Tay Garnett   *ph* Rudolph Maté   *m* Louis Silvers

Victor McLaglen, Freddie Bartholomew, Constance Collier, Gloria Stuart, Michael Whalen

'Some of the sequences are amusing; some of the action is very fast. But fundamentally the story is not believable.' – *Variety*

Professional Sweetheart

US   1933   70m   bw
RKO (Merian C. Cooper)
GB title: *Imaginary Sweetheart*

A radio 'purity girl' seeks some real life romance.

Modestly smart comedy of no lasting merit.

w Maurine Watkins   *d* William Seiter   *ph* Edward Cronjager   *m* Max Steiner

Ginger Rogers, Betty Furness, Gregory Ratoff, Sterling Holloway, Frank McHugh, ZaSu Pitts, Allen Jenkins, Norman Foster, Edgar Kennedy, Franklin Pangborn

'After a fast start this radio satire loses a lot of ground . . . but comedy's there all the way.' – *Variety*

The Professionals **

US   1966   123m   Technicolor   Panavision
Columbia/Pax (Richard Brooks)
V*, L, S

Skilled soldiers of fortune are hired by a millionaire rancher to get back his kidnapped wife.

Strong-flavoured star Western with good suspense sequences.

wd Richard Brooks   *novel* A Mule for the Marquesa by Frank O'Rourke   *ph* Conrad Hall   *m* Maurice Jarre

Burt Lancaster, Lee Marvin, Robert Ryan, Jack Palance, Ralph Bellamy, Claudia Cardinale, Woody Strode

'After the *Lord Jim* excursion, it is good to see Brooks back on his own professional form, filming the tight, laconic sort of adventure which usually seems to bring out the best in Hollywood veterans.' – *Penelope Houston*

'It has the expertise of a cold old whore with practised hands and no thoughts of love.' – *Pauline Kael, 1968*

AAN: Richard Brooks (as writer and as director); Conrad Hall

Professor Beware *

US   1938   93m   bw
Paramount

A staid professor finds himself on the run across America in pursuit of an Egyptian artefact.

Slow-starting comedy with only moments of the comedian at his best.

w Delmer Daves, Jack Cunningham   *story* Crampton Harris, Francis M. and Marian B. Cockrell   *d* Elliott Nugent   *ph* Archie Stout

Harold Lloyd, Phyllis Welch, Raymond Walburn, Lionel Stander, William Frawley, Thurston Hall, Cora Witherspoon, Sterling Holloway

'Both Lloyd and the audience are out of breath after 3000 miles cross country, but most of it is exhaustion from laughing.' – *Variety*

Professor Mamlock **

USSR   1938   100m   bw
Lenfilm

The leading surgeon of a Berlin hospital is driven to attempt suicide because he is a Jew.

Ironic in all kinds of ways, this quite devastating film was a unique attack by one government on a neighbouring one.

w Friedrich Wolf, Adolph Minkin, Herbert Rappaport   *d* Adolph Minkin, Herbert Rappaport

Sergei Mezhinski, E. Nikitina, Oleg Zhakov, Nina Shaternikova, Vasili Merkuriev

'An arresting picture which is sure to arouse strenuous comment.' – *Variety*

'The theme of a story should never be expressed so plainly; argument is valueless in fiction unless it is dramatic and individualized.' – *Graham Greene, The Spectator*

Profondo Rosso: see *Deep Red*

Il Proiezionista: see *The Inner Circle*

Project A *
Hong Kong   1984   108m   colour
Golden Harvest (Leonard K. C. Ho)
V

In 1903 a Chinese coastguard quits the force in order to track down pirates that his superiors tolerate.

One of the better kung-fu movies, mixing humour with spectacular stunts and frenetically choreographed fights.

wd Jackie Chan

Jackie Chan, Samo Hung, Li Hai Sheng, Yuan Baio

Project A-Ko (dubbed)
Japan   1986   120m   colour
Soeishinsha/APPP (Kazufumu Nomura)
V

While aliens try to kidnap her, a 16-year-old girl with superhuman powers fights a rival for the friendship of another girl.

Bizarre animated parody of high-tech science fantasy and high-school romance.

w Yuji Moriyama, Katsuhiko Nishijima, Tomoko Kawasaki   *d* Katsuhiko Nishijima   *ph* Takafumi Arai   *m* Richie Zito, Joey Carbone, Toji Akasaka   *ad* Shinji Kimura

voices of: Stacey Gregg, Denica Fairman, Julia Brahms, Marc Smith, Jay Benedict, Lisa Ross

Project M 7: see *The Net*

Project X *
US   1968   97m   Technicolor
Paramount/William Castle
V, V*, L

In the year 2118, a man is scientifically induced to think he lives in the 1960s so that he can recover a lost secret.

Fearsomely complex science fiction, cheaply made but on the whole intriguingly imagined.

w Edmund Morris   *novel* Leslie P. Davies   *d* William Castle   *ph* Harold Stine   *m* Van Cleave

Christopher George, Greta Baldwin, Henry Jones, Monte Markham, Harold Gould

The Promise
GB   1969   98m   Eastmancolor
Commonwealth United/Howard and Wyndham

Two young men and a girl share a flat after the 1942 siege of Leningrad; thirteen years later, their dreams of life considerably modified, they meet again and change partners.

Talky and too carefully budgeted screen version of a somewhat pretentious play.

w Michael Hayes   *play* Aleksei Arbuzov   *d* Michael Hayes   *ph* Brendan Stafford   *m* Iwan Williams   *pd* William McCrow

Ian McKellen, John Castle, Susan Macready, Mary Jones, David Mettheim

The Promise
US   1979   97m   Technicolor   Panavision
Universal (Fred Weintraub, Paul Heller)
V*
GB TV title: *Face of a Stranger*

A young man fails to recognize his lost love when her face has been rebuilt after an accident.

Rambling teenage variation on *Random Harvest,* not very well done and about forty years behind its proper times.

w Garry Michael White   *d* Gilbert Cates   *ph* Ralph Woolsey   *m* David Shire

Kathleen Quinlan, Stephen Collins, Beatrice Straight, Larry Luckinbill, William Prince

'Appalling romantic tushery by any standards.' – *Tom Milne, MFB*

AAN: song 'I'll Never Say Goodbye' (*m* David Shire, *ly* Alan and Marilyn Bergman)

Promise at Dawn
US/France   1970   102m   DeLuxe
Avco/Nathalie (Jules Dassin)
V*

The boyhood of novelist Romain Gary and the last years of his fearsome Russian Jewish actress mother with whom he traipses around Europe.

Scrappy star vehicle and unnecessary biopic in a variety of indulgent styles.

w Jules Dassin   *play* First Love by Samuel Taylor   *d* Jules Dassin   *ph* Jean Badal   *m* Georges Delerue

Melina Mercouri, Assef Dayan

Promise Her Anything
GB   1966   97m   Technicolor
Seven Arts (Stanley Rubin)

A mail order movie maker falls for a young French widow in the next flat.

Scatty comedy set in Greenwich Village and aiming in vain for a kind of frantic bohemian charm, with a baby as deus ex machina.

w William Peter Blatty   *d* Arthur Hiller   *ph* Douglas Slocombe   *m* Lynn Murray

Warren Beatty, Leslie Caron, Hermione Gingold, Lionel Stander, Robert Cummings, Keenan Wynn, Cathleen Nesbitt

Promised Land
US   1988   103m   colour
Vestron/Wildwood/Oxford Film Company
V, V*, L, S

Two high-school friends meet a couple of years later, when one is a cop and the other a robber.

Atmospheric, downbeat tale of thwarted hopes.

wd Michael Hoffman   *ph* Ueli Steiger, Alexander Gruszynski   *m* James Newton Howard   *pd* Eugenion Zanetti   *ed* David Spiers

Kiefer Sutherland, Meg Ryan, Jason Gedrick, Tracy Pollan, Googy Gress, Deborah Richter

Promises in the Dark
US   1979   115m   Metrocolor
Warner/Orion (Jerome Hellman)

A young girl dies of cancer.

Depressing and not particularly well done case history, a curious enterprise in view of the hundreds of television movies relentlessly exploring the same field.

w Loring Mandel   *d* Jerome Hellman   *ph* Adam Holender   *m* Leonard Rosenman

Marsha Mason, Ned Beatty, Susan Clark, Michael Brandon, Kathleen Beller, Paul Clemens

The Promoter: see *The Card*

'Before Love Comes Trust. Before Trust Comes...'
Proof **
Australia   1991   90m   colour
Artificial Eye/House & Moorhouse Films/Australian Film Commission/Film Victoria (Lynda House)
V, V*, S

A blind photographer spurns the love of his housekeeper and forms a friendship with a restaurant worker who describes his photographs to him.

A complex story of betrayal that was a notable debut for its director.

wd Jocelyn Moorhouse   *ph* Martin McGrath   *m* Not Drowning, Waving   *pd* Patrick Reardon   *ed* Ken Sallows

Hugo Weaving, Genevieve Picot, Heather Mitchell, Jeffrey Walker, Daniel Pollock, Frankie J. Holden, Frank Gallacher, Saskia Post

'An imaginative ethical and psychological drama that is as gripping as a thriller.' – *Philip French, Observer*

'One of this or any year's most confident and original writer-director debuts. . . a breakthrough in concept and technique.' – *Alexander Walker, London Evening Standard*

'It lives. Don't move. Don't breathe. There's nowhere to run. It will find you.'
Prophecy
US   1979   102m   Movielab   Panavision
Paramount (Robert L. Rosen)
V*

In rural Maine, mercury poisoning produces huge animal mutants.

Unpleasant ecological shocker with no particular talent in evidence.

w David Seltzer   *d* John Frankenheimer   *ph* Harry Stradling Jnr   *m* Leonard Rosenman   *pd* William Craig Smith

Talia Shire, Robert Foxworth, Armand Assante, Richard Dysart

Proshchanie: see *Farewell*

Prosperity
US   1932   90m   bw
MGM

Mothers-in-law disagree about the marriage of their children.

Reliable comedy of the Depression, marking the last teaming of its popular stars.

w Eve Greene, Zelda Sears   *d* Sam Wood

Marie Dressler, Polly Moran, Anita Page, Norman Foster, Henry Armetta

'Sure-fire money picture . . . could stand a little cutting but on the whole it's a workmanlike production.' – *Variety*

Prospero's Books **
Netherlands/France/Italy   1991   120m   colour
Palace/Allarts/Cinea/Camera One/Penta/Elsevier Vendex/Film Four/VPRO/Canal Plus/NHK (Kees Kasander, Denis Wigman)
V, V*, L, S

Abandoned with his daughter on an island, the former Duke of Milan invokes a storm to wreck the ship carrying those who betrayed him and so regain his dukedom.

A free and exuberant adaptation of Shakespeare, using the techniques of High Definition Television and computer technology to create dense, rich, bookish images and with Gielgud speaking virtually all of the verse. It may be best watched on video, where you can rewind the film or freeze-frame images to take it all in.   *wd* Peter Greenaway   *play The Tempest* by William Shakespeare   *ph* Sacha Vierny   *m* Michael Nyman   *pd* Ben van Os, Jan Roelfs   *ed* Marina Bodbyl

John Gielgud, Michael Clark, Michel Blanc, Erland Josephson, Isabelle Pasco, Tom Bell, Kenneth Cranham, Mark Rylance, Gérard Thoolen, Pierre Bokma, Michiel Romeyn

'An intellectually and erotically rampaging meditation on the arrogance and value of the artistic process.' – *Variety*

'A remarkable feast, taking in the video revolution at one level and a highly literate interpretation of Shakespeare at another. Nothing quite like it has been seen before, let alone from a British director.' – *Derek Malcolm, Guardian*

Prostitute
GB   1980   96m   colour
Kestrel (Tony Garnett)

A provincial tart moves into the West End.

Downbeat, supposedly realistic documentary drama which ends up being depressing but not in the least titillating.

wd Tony Garnett   *ph* Charles Stewart   *m* The Gangsters

Eleanor Forsythe, Kate Crutchley, Kim Lockett, Nancy Samuels

'There's something funny going on in the world of diplomacy!'
Protocol
US   1984   96m   Technicolor
Warner (Anthea Sylbert)
V, V*, L

A cocktail waitress thwarts an assassination and becomes a career diplomat.

Star comedy with Something to Say and not much to laugh at; a step down even from *Private Benjamin*.

w Buck Henry   *d* Herbert Ross   *ph* William A. Fraker   *m* Basil Poledouris   *pd* Bill Malley   *ed* Paul Hirsch

Goldie Hawn, Chris Sarandon, Gail Strickland, Richard Romanus, André Gregory, Cliff de Young

Prototype
US   1992   94m   colour
Filmtown (Gian-Carlo Scandiuzzi, Phillip Roth)
V, V*

In Los Angeles in the 21st century, a cripple is transformed into an indestructible cybernetic robot in order to eliminate the last of the Omegas, human beings altered to become the new leaders of civilization.

Post-apocalyptic science fiction, cheap in every respect, indifferently acted and where the future looks much like the present, only dirtier and with no-smoking rules relaxed.

wd Phillip Roth   *ph* Mark W. Gray   *m* Emilio Kauderer   *ed* Daniel Lawrence

Lane Lenhart, Robert Tossberg, Brenda Swanson, Paul Coulj, Mitchell Cox, Sebastien Scandiuzzi

'Dingy visuals, murky scripting, vague characters and a lack of actual action render the whole thing remarkably unexciting.' – *Empire*

The Proud and Profane
US   1956   112m   bw   Vistavision
Paramount (William Perlberg)

In the Pacific War a Roman Catholic widow falls for a tough lieutenant colonel. ('My pleasure is physical; my men call me The Beast.')

Unlikely romantic melodrama with a certain amount of plain speaking, otherwise routine.

wd George Seaton   *novel* The Magnificent Bastards by Lucy Herndon Crockett   *ph* John F. Warren   *m* Victor Young   *ad* Hal Pereira, A. Earl Hedrick

William Holden, Deborah Kerr, Thelma Ritter, Dewey Martin, William Redfield

AAN: art direction

The Proud and the Beautiful
France   1953   90m   bw
C.I.C.C./Chrysaor/Iena/Reforma (Louis Wipf, Felipe Suberville)
V*
original title: *Les Orgueilleux*; aka: *The Proud Ones*

In a small Mexican town, a drunken doctor is redeemed by the love of a tourist unexpectedly detained by the sudden death of her husband from a contagious disease.

Ineffably silly, poorly acted and unconvincing romance.

w Jean Aurenche, Yves Allegret   *novel L'Amour Rédempteur* by Jean-Paul Sartre   *d* Yves Allegret   *ph* Alex Phillips   *m* Paul Misraki   *ad* Gunther Gerszo   *ed* Claude Nicole

Michele Morgan, Gérard Philipe, Victor Manuel Mendoza, Carlos Lopez Moctezuma, Michele Cordoue, Andre Toffel, Arturo Soto Rangel

The Proud Ones (1953): see The Proud and the Beautiful

The Proud Ones
US   1956   94m   Eastmancolor   Cinemascope
TCF (Robert L. Jacks)

A marshal cleans up a crooked town despite the hazards of his own physical disability and a deputy who hates him.

Entertaining though rather foolishly scripted Western.

w Edmund North, Joseph Patracca   *d* Robert D. Webb   *ph* Lucien Ballard   *m* Lionel Newman

Robert Ryan, Jeffrey Hunter, Virginia Mayo, Robert Middleton

'One has only to look at a first-rate Western to recognise the makeshift quality of *The Proud Ones*.' – *Dilys Powell*

The Proud Ones *
France   1980   118m   Eastmancolor
Gala/Production Bela/TF1 (Georges de Beauregard)
V*
original title: *Le Cheval d'Orgueil*

In the early years of the century, a young boy grows up in a peasant community in Brittany.

Lovingly observed and glossy exercise in nostalgia, ravishing to look at, but somewhat stilted.

w Daniel Boulanger, Claude Chabrol   *book* Pierre-Jakez Helias   *d* Claude Chabrol   *ph* Jean Rabier   *m* Pierre Jansen   *ad* Hilton McConnico   *ed* Monique Fardoulis

Jacques Dufilho, Bernadette Lesache, François Cluzet, Ronan Hubert, Paul Leperson, Pierre Le Rumeur, Michel Blanc

The Proud Rebel
US   1958   103m   Technicolor
MGM/Sam Goldwyn Jnr
V*

After the Civil War, a Southerner wanders the Yankee states in search of a doctor to cure his mute son; he falls for a lady farmer and his son finds his voice at a crucial moment.

Pretty dim family Western for pretty dim families; everything happens precisely according to plan.

w Joseph Patracca, Lillie Hayward   *d* Michael Curtiz   *ph* Ted McCord   *m* Jerome Moross

Alan Ladd, Olivia de Havilland, David Ladd, Dean Jagger, Cecil Kellaway, Dean Stanton, Henry Hull, John Carradine, James Westerfield

The Proud Valley *
GB   1939   76m   bw
Ealing (Sergei Nolbandov)

A black stoker helps unemployed Welsh miners reopen their pits.

Neat little propaganda drama.

w Roland Pertwee, Louis Golding, Jack Jones   *d* Pen Tennyson   *ph* Roy Kellino, Glen MacWilliams   *m* Ernest Irving

Paul Robeson, Edward Chapman, Edward Rigby, *Rachel Thomas*, Simon Lack, Clifford Evans, Allan Jeayes

'The direction of the quiet documentary scenes is good, but Mr Pen Tennyson, who may have been handicapped by an undistinguished cast and a wobbly script, seems ill at ease with drama.' – *Graham Greene, The Spectator*

Providence *
France/Switzerland   1977   107m   Eastmancolor
Action Film/Société Française de Production/FR3/Citel (Philippe Dussart)
V*, S

A famous writer, dying, spends a painful night in unpleasant and sometimes fantastic recollections of his sons and their women; but the reality, when they come to lunch next day, is somewhat different.

Despite its cast and other credits, this is a repellent and not too well acted study in the lack of communication, told at undue length and in turgid colour.

w David Mercer   *d* Alain Resnais   *ph* Ricardo Aronovitch   *m* Miklos Rozsa   *ad* Jacques Saulnier

John Gielgud, Dirk Bogarde, Ellen Burstyn, David Warner, Elaine Stritch

'The movie is peculiarly fastidious and static: you feel as if it were going to dry up and blow away.' – *New Yorker*

La Provinciale: see A Girl from Lorraine

The Prowler *
US   1951   92m   bw
Horizon (Sam Spiegel)

A discontented wife thinks she sees a prowler and calls a cop; they have an affair and murder her husband.

Another variant on *Double Indemnity* and *The Postman Always Rings Twice*; the script is terse and the actors well-handled.

w Hugo Butler   *d* Joseph Losey   *ph* Arthur Miller   *m* Lyn Murray

Van Heflin, Evelyn Keyes, John Maxwell, Katharine Warren

'A film in which the spectator is repelled by the characters, finds in them no curiosity of nature to overcome his repugnance, and is therefore indifferent to their fate; and I call that a nauseating film.' – *Dilys Powell*

'A rivetingly cool, clean thriller.' – *NFT, 1973*

Prudence and the Pill *
GB   1968   92m   DeLuxe
TCF/Kenneth Harper, Ronald Kahn

A girl borrows her mother's contraceptive pills and replaces them with aspirin, causing no end of complications.

Self-consciously naughty sex comedy with a long dénouement and some stiff patches to affect one's enjoyment of the brighter moments.

w Hugh Mills   *play* Hugh Mills   *d* Fielder Cook   *ph* Ted Moore   *m* Bernard Ebbinghouse

David Niven, Deborah Kerr, Edith Evans, Keith Michell, Robert Coote, Irina Demick, Joyce Redman, Judy Geeson

'Everybody winds up pregnant to clutter the earth, apparently, with people as obnoxious as their progenitors.' – *Judith Crist*

Przesluchnie: see Interrogation

Psyche 59

GB   1964   94m   bw
Columbia/Troy/Schenck (Philip Hazelton)

A wife recovers from blindness after realizing that her husband is in love with her sister.

Pretentious melodrama with stuffy dialogue, pompous direction and irritating characters.

w Julian Halevy   novel Françoise de Ligneris
d Alexander Singer   ph Walter Lassally
m Kenneth V. Jones

Patricia Neal, Curt Jurgens, Samantha Eggar, Ian Bannen, Beatrix Lehmann

Psychic Killer

US   1975   90m
Avco Embassy (Mardi Rustam)
V*

A man released from an asylum kills those who put him there by the power of his mind.

Low-budget exploitation movie that draws heavily on Hitchcock, even if it substitutes heavy-handedness for his teasing style.

w Mike Angel, Greydon Clark, Raymond Danton
d Raymond Danton   ph Herb Pearl   m William Kraft   ad Joel Leonard   ed Mike Brown

Jim Hutton, Paul Burke, Julie Adams, Nehemiah Persoff, Neville Brand, Aldo Ray, Della Reese, Rod Cameron

'The screen's master of suspense moves his camera into the icy blackness of the unexplained!'
'Don't give away the ending – it's the only one we have!'

Psycho ****

US   1960   109m   bw
Shamley/Alfred Hitchcock
V, V*, L

At a lonely motel vicious murders take place and are attributed to the manic mother of the young owner.

Curious shocker devised by Hitchcock as a tease and received by most critics as an unpleasant horror piece in which the main scene, the shower stabbing, was allegedly directed not by Hitchcock but by Saul Bass. After enormous commercial success it achieved classic status over the years; despite effective moments of fright, it has a childish plot and script, and its interest is that of a tremendously successful confidence trick, made for very little money by a TV crew.

w Joseph Stefano   novel Robert Bloch   d Alfred Hitchcock (and Saul Bass)   ph John L. Russell
m Bernard Herrmann   ad Joseph Hurley, Robert Clatworthy

Anthony Perkins, Vera Miles, John Gavin, Janet Leigh, John McIntire, Martin Balsam, Simon Oakland

'Probably the most visual, most cinematic picture he has ever made.' – Peter Bogdanovich

'I think the film is a reflection of a most unpleasant mind, a mean, sly, sadistic little mind.' – Dwight MacDonald

† When asked by the press what he used for the blood in the bath, Mr Hitchcock said: 'Chocolate sauce.'
†† This is the whole text of Hitchcock's trailer, in which he audaciously wandered round the sets and practically gave away the entire plot: Here we have a quiet little motel, tucked away off the main highway, and as you see perfectly harmless looking, whereas it has now become known as the scene of a crime. . . . This motel also has an adjunct, an old house which is, if I may say so, a little more sinister looking. And in this house the most dire, horrible events took place. I think we can go inside because the place is up for sale – though I don't know who would buy it now.In that window in the second floor, the one in front, that's where the woman was first seen. Let's go inside. You see, even in daylight this place looks a bit sinister. It was at the top of these stairs that the second murder took place. She came out of that door there and met the victim at the top. Of course in a flash there was the

knife, and in no time the victim tumbled and fell with a horrible crash. . . . I think the back broke immediately it hit the floor. It's difficult to describe the way . . . the twisting of the . . . I won't dwell on it.Come upstairs. Of course the victim, or should I say victims, hadn't any idea of the kind of people they'd be confronted with in this house. Especially the woman. She was the weirdest and the most . . . well, let's go into her bedroom.Here's the woman's room, still beautifully preserved. And the imprint of her body on the bed where she used to lie. I think some of her clothes are still in the wardrobe. (He looks, and shakes his head.) Bathroom.This was the son's room but we won't go in there because his favourite spot was the little parlour behind the office in the motel. Let's go down there. This young man . . . you have to feel sorry for him. After all, being dominated by an almost maniacal woman was enough to . . . well, let's go in. I suppose you'd call this his hideaway. His hobby was taxidermy. A crow here, an owl there. An important scene took place in this room. There was a private supper here. By the way, this picture has great significance because . . . let's go along into cabin number one. I want to show you something there.All tidied up. The bathroom. Oh, they've cleaned all this up now. Big difference. You should have seen the blood. The whole place was . . . well, it's too horrible to describe. Dreadful. And I tell you, a very important clue was found here. (Shows toilet.) Down there. Well, the murderer, you see, crept in here very slowly – of course, the shower was on, there was no sound, and . . . MUSIC WELLS UP FIERCELY, SHOWER CURTAIN SWISHES ACROSS, BLACKOUT.
Voice: THE PICTURE YOU MUST SEE FROM THE BEGINNING – OR NOT AT ALL.

AAN: Alfred Hitchcock; John L. Russell; Janet Leigh; art direction

'It's 22 years later and Norman Bates is coming home!'

Psycho 2 *

US   1983   113m   Technicolor
Universal/Oak (Hilton A. Green)
V*, L, S

Despite protests from the sister of one of his victims, Norman Bates is released after 22 years in a mental institution . . . and the murders begin again.

A reasonably inventive sequel, if on the gory side. It probably holds the record for the longest delayed follow-up.

w Tom Holland   d Richard Franklin   ph Dean Cundey   m Jerry Goldsmith   pd John W. Corso

Anthony Perkins, Vera Miles, Meg Tilly, Robert Loggia, Dennis Franz

'It's all very well having your tongue in your cheek, but it helps to have a brain in your head.' – Sunday Times

Psycho 3

US   1986   93m   colour
Universal/Hilton A. Green
V*, L

A suicidal novice flees after unwittingly causing the death of another nun, and takes refuge at the Bates Motel.

More variations on the original Psycho murders, with invention wearing a bit thin by now.

w Charles Edward Pogue   d Anthony Perkins
ph Bruce Surtees   m Carter Burwell   pd Henry Bumstead   ed David Blewitt

Anthony Perkins, Diana Scarwid, Jeff Fahey, Roberta Maxwell

Psycho Sex Fiend: see Scream . . . and Die!

Psychomania

GB   1972   91m   Technicolor
Benmar (Andrew Donally)
V*

A Hells Angels motor cyclist commits suicide and returns from the dead an invulnerable monster.

Arrant nonsense of the macabre sort, sometimes irresistibly amusing.

w Armand d'Usseau   d Don Sharp   ph Ted Moore
m David Whitaker

George Sanders, Nicky Henson, Beryl Reid, Robert Hardy

The Psychopath

GB   1966   83m   Techniscope
Paramount/Amicus (Milton Subotsky)

Men are found dead in London, each with a doll beside him.

Complicated horror thriller in which the actors go further over the top the more the plot winds down.

w Robert Bloch   d Freddie Francis   ph John Wilcox   m Philip Martell

Patrick Wymark, Margaret Johnston, John Standing, Alexander Knox, Judy Huxtable, Don Borisenko, Thorley Walters, Colin Gordon

PT 109

US   1963   140m   Technicolor   Panavision
Warner (Brian Foy)
V*, L

Adventures of president-to-be John F. Kennedy when he was a naval lieutenant in the Pacific during World War II.

Extraordinarily protracted and very dull action story which seems to have been overawed by its subject.

w Richard L. Breen   d Leslie H. Martinson
ph Robert Surtees   m William Lava, David Buttolph

Cliff Robertson, Ty Hardin, James Gregory, Robert Blake

Puberty Blues

Australia   1982   81m   Eastmancolor   Panavision
Limelight
V*

Teenage girls aim to become beach groupies.

Both repellent and boring, this mindless sex movie has little more to offer than the beach extravaganzas of the sixties.

w Margaret Kelly   novel Kathy Lette and Gabrielle Carey   d Bruce Beresford

Nell Schofield, Jad Capelja, Geoff Rhoe, Tony Hughes, Sandy Paul

Public Deb Number One

US   1940   80m   bw
TCF

A waiter spanks a spoiled society girl at a communist rally, and accepts a job which makes him a capitalist.

Lively comedy packed with familiar faces.

w Karl Tunberg, Darrell Ware   d Gregory Ratoff

Brenda Joyce, George Murphy, Ralph Bellamy, Elsa Maxwell, Mischa Auer, Charles Ruggles, Maxie Rosenbloom, Berton Churchill, Franklin Pangborn, Hobart Cavanaugh, Lloyd Corrigan, Elisha Cook Jnr

'Drama that hurls a mighty challenge to all humanity!'

The Public Enemy ***

US   1931   84m   bw
Warner
V, V*, L, S
GB title: Enemies of the Public

Two slum boys begin as bootleggers, get too big for their boots, and wind up dead.

Although it doesn't flow as a narrative, this early gangster film still has vivid and startling scenes and was most influential in the development of the urban American crime film.

w Harvey Thew   *story* Kubec Glasmon, John Bright
d *William Wellman*   *ph* *Dev Jennings*   *m* David
Mendoza

James Cagney, Edward Woods, Jean Harlow, Joan
Blondell, Beryl Mercer, Donald Cook, Mae Clarke,
Leslie Fenton

'Roughest, most powerful and best gang picture to
date. So strong as to be repulsive in some aspects,
plus a revolting climax. No strong cast names but a lot
of merit.' – *Variety*

'The real power of The Public Enemy lies in its
vigorous and brutal assault on the nerves and in the
stunning acting of James Cagney.' – *James Shelley
Hamilton*

'A postscript said that the producers wanted to
"depict honestly an environment that exists today in
certain strata of American life, rather than glorify the
hoodlum or the criminal". The film had a different
effect: Cagney was playful and dynamic, and so much
more appealing than the characters opposed to him
that audiences rooted for him in spite of themselves.' –
Martin Quigley Jnr, 1970

'What not many people know is that right up to two
days before shooting started, I was going to play the
good guy, the pal. Edward Woods played it in the
end.' – *James Cagney*

AAN: Kubec Glasmon, John Bright

Public Enemy's Wife

US   1936   78m   bw
Warner (Sam Bischoff)
GB title: *G-Man's Wife*

A girl agrees to marry an escaped convict so that the
FBI can track him down.

Lower-berth gangster thrills culminating in a chase
climax; neatly enough done.

w Abem Finkel, Harold Buckley   *story* David O.
Selznick, P. J. Wolfson   *d* Nick Grinde   *ph* Ernest
Haller

Pat O'Brien, Margaret Lindsay, Robert Armstrong,
Cesar Romero, Dick Foran, Dick Purcell

† Remade as *Bullets for O'Hara* (1942).

The Public Eye: see *Follow Me*

'Murder. Scandal. Crime. No matter what he was shooting,
   Bernzy never took sides he only took pictures …
   Except once.'
The Public Eye
US   1992   99m   colour
UIP/Universal (Sue Baden-Powell)
V, V*, L

A tabloid newspaper photographer becomes involved
with a beautiful woman who runs a night-club and is
in trouble with the Mafia.

A modern attempt at a *film noir* set in the 1940s that
works only intermittently.

wd Howard Franklin   *ph* Peter Suschitzky
m Mark Isham   *pd* Marcia Hinds-Johnson
sp Industrial Light and Magic   *ed* Evan Lottman

John Pesci, Barbara Hershey, Stanley Tucci, Jerry
Adler, Jared Harris, Richard Riehle, Bryan Travis
Smith

'Never quite takes off, either as romantic melodrama
or as a consideration of one very eccentric man's
means of self-expression.' – *Vincent Canby, New York
Times*

† The film was based in part on the New York
photographer Weegee, whose book of photographs of
the seamier side of life inspired the movie *The Naked
City* (qv).

Public Hero Number One

US   1935   89m   bw
MGM (Lucien Hubbard)

A G-man goes undercover to track down the Purple
Gang.

Moderate thick ear dating from the time when studios
tried to smother public outcry against gangster films
by presenting the cop as the hero.

w Wells Root   *d* J. Walter Ruben   *ph* Gregg
Toland

Chester Morris, Jean Arthur, Joseph Calleia, Lionel
Barrymore, Paul Kelly, Lewis Stone, Paul Hurst

'Rates with the best of the G-men pictures.' – *Variety*

'The best picture on criminal life I've seen.' – *Otis
Ferguson*

Puerto Escondido

Italy   1993   125m   colour
Mayfair/Pentafilm/Colorado (Maurizio Totti, Mario and Vittorio
  Cecchi Gori)

A Milanese bank manager drops out and goes to
Mexico after seeing a policeman murder a colleague
and then try to kill him, but his troubles follow him.

Amiable comedy, but one that never comes close to
making any point, other than a vague approval of
escapism.

w Enzo Monteleone, Diego Abatantuono, Gabriele
Salvatores   *d* Gabriele Salvatores   *ph* Italo
Petriccione   *m* Mauro Pagani, Federico de Robertis
ad Marco Belluzzu, Alejandro Olmas   *ed* Nino
Baragli

Diego Abatantuono, Valeria Golino, Claudio Bisio,
Renato Carpentieri, Antonio Catania

'So drawn out it will take a very mellow-minded
viewer not to lose patience with the cartoonish
characters and their unconnected adventures.' – *Variety*

Pufnstuf

US   1970   98m   Technicolor
Universal/Krofft Enterprises

A dejected boy is led by his talking flute on a talking
boat to Living Island, full of strange but friendly
animals in fear of an incompetent witch.

Amalgam of a TV series using life-size puppets to
project a mildly pleasing variation on *The Wizard of Oz*,
without quite achieving the right blend of wit and
charm.

w John Fenton Murray, Si Rose   *d* Hollingsworth
Morse   *ph* Kenneth Peach   *m* Charles Fox
ad Alexander Golitzen

Jack Wild, Billie Hayes, Martha Raye, Mama Cass

I Pugni in Tasca: see *Fists in the Pocket*

Pulp *

GB   1972   95m   colour
UA/Klinger-Caine-Hodges (Michael Klinger)
V*

An ex-funeral director now living in the
Mediterranean as a successful pulp fiction writer gets
involved with gangsters and weirdos.

Occasionally funny pastiche which sorely lacks shape
and is sustained by guest appearances and zany ideas.

wd Mike Hodges   *ph* Ousama Rawi   *m* George
Martin

Michael Caine, *Mickey Rooney*, Lizabeth Scott, Lionel
Stander, Nadia Cassini, Al Lettieri, Dennis Price

'Various eccentrics act out their "turns", but never
quite lift a light comedy-thriller through the more
playful and productive inversions of parody.' – *Richard
Combs*

Pulse

US   1988   95m   DeLuxe
Columbia/Aspen (Patricia A. Stallone)
V*, L

Visiting his father, a small boy discovers that there is

a malevolent force affecting the electrical equipment
in the home.

Tepid thriller, a tame variation on *Poltergeist*.

wd Paul Golding   *ph* Peter Lyons Collister   *m* Jay
Ferguson   *pd* Holger Gross   *ed* Gib Jaffe

Joey Lawrence, Cliff de Young, Roxanne Hart,
Charles Tyner, Myron Healey

Pump Up the Volume *

US   1990   105m
New Line/SC Entertainment (Rupert Harvey, Sandy Stern)
V, V*, L, S

A discontented student starts his own pirate radio
station.

Loud and raucous and aimed at an audience that
reveres rebellion and rock music.

wd Allan Moyle   *ph* Walt Lloyd   *md* Nicole
Freegard   *pd* Bruce Bolander   *ed* Wendy Bricmont,
Ric Keeley, Kurt Hathaway

'It could appeal not only to '90s teens, but to
sympathetic young adults who remember the stormy
passage through adolescence.' – *Variety*

Pumping Iron **

US   1976   81m   colour
White Mountain Films (George Butler, Jerome Gary)
V*, L

Documentary on body-builders' contest for the title of
Mr Olympia.

Well-observed study in competitiveness and
obsession that first brought Arnold Schwarzenegger
to the general attention.

book Pumping Iron by Charles Gaines, George Butler
d George Butler, Robert Fiore   *ph* Robert Fiore
m Michael Small   *ed* Larry Silk, Geof Bartz

Arnold Schwarzenegger, Louis Ferrigno, Natty and
Victoria Ferrigno, Mike Katz, Franco Columbu

Pumping Iron II: The Women *

US   1984   107m   colour
Blue Dolphin/Cinecom (George Butler)
V*, L

Documentary on a 1983 contest and its preliminaries
in Las Vegas, with the male judges trying to decide at
what point musculation ceases to be feminine.

Enjoyable and sometimes witty, though it has an air
of contrivance about it.

w Charles Gaines, George Butler   *book* Pumping Iron
II: The Unprecedented Women by Charles Gains, George
Butler   *d* George Butler   *ph* Dyanna Taylor
m David McHugh, Michael Montes   *ed* Paul Barnes,
Susan Crutcher, Jane Kurson

Lori Bowen, Carla Dunlop, Bev Francis, Rachel
McLish, Kris Alexander, Lydia Cheng

The Pumpkin Eater ***

GB   1964   118m   bw
Columbia/Romulus (James Woolf)

A compulsive mother (of eight children) finds her
third marriage rocking when she gets evidence of her
husband's affairs.

Brilliantly made if basically rather irritating
kaleidoscope of vivid scenes about silly people, all
quite recognizable as sixties Londoners; very well
acted.

w Harold Pinter   *novel* Penelope Mortimer   *d* Jack
Clayton   *ph* Oswald Morris   *m* Georges Delerue

Anne Bancroft, Peter Finch, James Mason, Maggie Smith,
Cedric Hardwicke, Richard Johnson, Eric Porter

'There never was a film so rawly memorable.' –
Evening Standard

'It is solid, serious, intelligent, stylish. It is also, for
the most part, quite dead.' – *The Times*

'It plays like a house afire.' – *Time*

AAN: Anne Bancroft

The Punch and Judy Man *
GB 1962 96m bw
(ABP) Macconkey (Gordon L. T. Scott)
V

A seashore children's entertainer tries and fails to establish himself as an important citizen.

Melancholy comedy of failure which did not please its star's adherents and indeed just missed the style it was seeking.

w Philip Oakes, Tony Hancock   d Jeremy Summers
ph Gilbert Taylor   m Derek Scott, Don Banks

Tony Hancock, Sylvia Syms, Ronald Fraser, Barbara Murray, John Le Mesurier, Hugh Lloyd

'Dying's easy. Comedy's hard'
Punchline *
US 1988 122m DeLuxe
Columbia TriStar (Daniel Melnick, Michael Rachmil)
V*, L

A housewife and aspiring stand-up comedienne is helped by another comedian with personality problems.

A serious look at the business of being funny.

wd David Seltzer   ph Reynaldo Villalobos
m Charles Gross   pd Jack Degovia   ed Bruce Green

Sally Field, Tom Hanks, John Goodman, Mark Rydell, Kim Greist, Paul Mazursky, Pam Matteson

'Is there a limit to revenge?'
The Punisher
Australia 1989 90m Eastmancolor
Castle Premier/New World International/Marvel Entertainment
   (Robert Mark Kamen)
V, V*, L

A former policeman, who lives in the sewers, takes revenge on the gangsters who killed his family.

Undistinguished, excessively violent action movie based on a comic-book character.

w Robert Mark Kamen, Boaz Yakin   d Mark Goldblatt   ph Ian Baker   m Dennis Dreith
pd Norma Moriceau   ed Tim Wellburn

Dolph Lundgren, Louis Gossett Jnr, Jeroen Krabbe, Kim Miyori, Bryan Marshall, Nancy Everhard, Barry Otto, Brian Rooney, Zoshka Mizak, Todd Boyce

Puppet Master
US 1990 90m colour
Full Moon (Hope Perello)
V, V*, S

Four psychics who go to investigate strange happenings at an isolated hotel find themselves being attacked by living puppets.

A twist on the Frankenstein story, with some clever special effects adding a little interest to the usual slasher narrative.

w Joseph G. Collodi   story Charles Band, Kenneth J. Hall   d David Schmoeller   ph Sergio Salvati
m Richard Band   pd John Myhre   sp David Allen Productions   ed Tom Meshelski

Paul Le Mat, Irene Miracle, Matt Roe, Kathryn O'Reilly, Robert Frates, Merrya Small, William Hickey

Puppet Master II
US 1991 88m DeLuxe
Full Moon (David DeCoteau, John Schouweiler)
V, V*, S

Puppets who have been brought to life, each with their own special weapon, stalk and slay a group of psychic researchers staying in a supposedly haunted hotel.

All that distinguishes this sequel from the original is the addition of some new puppets with different and gory ways of killing. They, unlike the remainder of the cast, are effectively animated.

w David Pabian   story Charles Band   d David Allen   ph Thomas F. DeNove   m Richard Band
pd Kathleen Coates   sp David Allen, David Barton, Steve Neill   ed Peter Teschner, Bert Glatstein

Elizabeth MacClellan, Collin Bernsen, Gregory Webb, Charlie Spradling, Steve Welles, Jeff Weston, Nita Talbot

'Gruesome thrills.' – *Variety*

Puppet on a Chain *
GB 1970 98m Technicolor
Big City (Kurt Unger)
V*

An American Interpol agent hunts down drug smugglers in Amsterdam.

Sadistic adventure thriller, a toughened version of James Bond, climaxing in a splendid boat chase through Amsterdam.

w Alistair MacLean, Don Sharp, Paul Wheeler
novel Alistair MacLean   d Geoffrey Reeve, *Don Sharp*   ph Jack Hildyard, Skeets Kelly   m Piero Piccioni

Sven Bertil Taube, Barbara Parkins, Patrick Allen, Alexander Knox, Vladek Sheybal

'One suspects that a marionette also sat in for Alistair MacLean.' – *Judith Crist*

The Pure Hell of St Trinian's *
GB 1960 94m bw
Hallmark/Tudor (Frank Launder, Sidney Gilliat)

After the girls burn down St Trinian's, a dubious headmaster offers to create a new school for them.

Bright comedy performances from some of the best of character actors add a gloss to familiar material.

w Frank Launder, Sidney Gilliat, Val Valentine
d Frank Launder   ph Gerald Gibbs   m Malcolm Arnold   ed Thelma Connell

Cecil Parker, Joyce Grenfell, George Cole, Thorley Walters, Irene Handl, Eric Barker, Dennis Price, Raymond Huntley, Julie Alexander

The Purple Gang
US 1960 85m bw
Allied Artists

In Detroit during prohibition a gang of juvenile delinquents become as powerful as the gangsters.

Unpleasant detail mars this cops-and-robbers subject; twenty years later it would have been even more of a shocker, but it's bad enough as it is.

w Jack DeWitt   d Frank McDonald

Robert Blake, Barry Sullivan, Elaine Edwards, Marc Cavell, Jody Lawrance, Susie Marquette, Paul Dubov

'The "Inside Japan" Story Of Yanks Bombing Tokyo … Taken Jap Prisoners … Put On Trial For "Murder"!'
The Purple Heart *
US 1944 99m bw
TCF (Darryl F. Zanuck)
V*

American prisoners of war in Japan are tried and executed.

Relentlessly sombre flagwaver, extremely persuasively presented.

w Jerome Cady, Darryl F. Zanuck   d Lewis Milestone
ph Arthur Miller   m Alfred Newman

Dana Andrews, Richard Conte, Farley Granger, Kevin O'Shea, Sam Levene, Don Barry, Richard Loo

'It is unusually edged, well organized and solidly acted. But I feel extremely queasy watching fiction – especially persuasive fiction – which pretends to clarify facts that are not clear, and may never become so.' – *James Agee*

Purple Heart Diary
US 1951 73m bw
Sam Katzman/Columbia
GB title: *No Time for Tears*

Entertainers tour war zones and bring various comforts.

Sentimental piece which the USO picked up as useful propaganda.

w William Sackheim   d Richard Quine

Frances Langford, Ben Lessy, Tony Romano, Judd Holdren

The Purple Mask
US 1955 82m Technicolor Cinemascope
U-I (Howard Christie)

In 1802 Paris the Royalist resistance to Napoleon is led by the mysterious Purple Mask, who also disguises himself as a foppish dandy.

Cheeky rewrite of *The Scarlet Pimpernel*, with plenty of gusto but not much style.

w Oscar Brodney   d Bruce Humberstone
ph Irving Glassberg   m Joseph Gershenson

Tony Curtis, Dan O'Herlihy, Colleen Miller, Gene Barry, Angela Lansbury, George Dolenz, John Hoyt

'Sir Percy, one feels, would have personally conducted this lot to the guillotine.' – *MFB*

The Purple Monster Strikes
US 1945 bw serial: 15 eps
Republic
V*

A Martian kills a great scientist and enters his body.

Early example of unpleasant aliens, a precursor of *It Came from Outer Space* and *Invasion of the Body Snatchers*.

d Spencer Bennet and Fred Brannon

Dennis Moore, Linda Stirling, Roy Barcroft

The Purple Plain *
GB 1954 100m Technicolor
GFD/Two Cities (John Bryan)

During the Burma campaign, a Canadian squadron leader regains his shattered nerves during an arduous trek across country.

Psychological study and eastern adventure combined; not the best of either, but a potent crowd-puller.

w Eric Ambler   novel H. E. Bates   d Robert Parrish
ph Geoffrey Unsworth   m John Veale

Gregory Peck, Maurice Denham, Win Min Than, Lyndon Brook, Brenda de Banzie, Bernard Lee, Anthony Bushell, Ram Gopal

The Purple Rose of Cairo *
US 1984 82m DeLuxe
Orion/Jack Rollins-Charles H. Joffe (Robert Greenhut)
V, V*, L

In the thirties, a film-struck woman is confronted in reality by the hero of her dreams.

Amusing but slight comedy: several good jokes, but in sum no more than an elongated sketch.

wd Woody Allen   ph Gordon Willis   m Dick Hyman   pd Stuart Wurtzel   ed Susan E. Morse

Mia Farrow, Jeff Daniels, Danny Aiello, Dianne Wiest, Van Johnson, Zoe Caldwell, John Wood, Milo O'Shea

BFA: best picture, original screenplay

Pursued *
US 1947 101m bw
(Warner) United States (Milton Sperling)
V*, L

A revenge-seeking cowboy accidentally causes a tragedy in his adopted family.

Glum, good-looking revenge Western.

w Niven Busch *d* Raoul Walsh *ph* *James Wong Howe* *m* Max Steiner

Robert Mitchum, Teresa Wright, Judith Anderson, Dean Jagger, Alan Hale, Harry Carey Jnr

Pursuit
US 1935 73m bw
Lucien Hubbard-Ned Marin/MGM

A child is kidnapped, and several people want the reward for restoring him.

Rather frantic chase thriller with insufficient variety.

w Wells Root, Lawrence G. Blochman *d* Edwin L. Marin

Chester Morris, Sally Eilers, Scotty Beckett, Henry Travers, C. Henry Gordon, Dorothy Peterson, Harold Huber

The Pursuit of D. B. Cooper
US 1981 100m Metrocolor
Polygram (Daniel Wigutow, Michael Taylor)
V*, L

A skyjacker bails out with his loot and is chased by various people after the reward.

Fantasy variation on a real case which was never solved; of no interest whatever despite the talent involved.

w Jeffrey Alan Fiskin *book* *Free Fall* by J. D. Reed *d* Roger Spottiswoode (also John Frankenheimer, Buzz Kulik) *ph* Harry Stradling *m* James Horner *pd* Preston Ames

Robert Duvall, Treat Williams, Kathryn Harrod, Ed Flanders, Paul Gleason, R. G. Armstrong

'Doubtless a law-enforcement ploy to lure the skyjacker out of hiding: surely after seeing this mess he will want to surface and sue somebody.' – *Variety*

The Pursuit of Happiness
US 1934 75m bw
Paramount (Arthur Hornblow Jnr)

In 1776 Connecticut a Puritan maid falls for a Hessian soldier.

Mildly pleasing romantic comedy centring on the ancient practice of 'bundling' in which betrothed couples might sleep together fully clothed.

w Stephen Morehouse Avery, Jack Cunningham, J. P. McEvoy, Virginia Van Upp *play* Lawrence Langner, Armina Marshall *d* Alexander Hall *ph* Karl Struss

Francis Lederer, Joan Bennett, Charles Ruggles, Mary Boland, Walter Kingsford, Minor Watson

'A comedy that will entertain and merits business.' – *Variety*

The Pursuit of Happiness *
US 1970 98m Eastmancolor
Columbia/TA Films/Norton-Simon (David Susskind)
V*

A New York college dropout is sent to prison after a hit and run accident.

Smooth, watchable but empty youth movie.

w Sidney Carroll, George L. Sherman *d* Robert Mulligan *ph* Dick Kratina *m* Dave Grusin

Michael Sarrazin, Barbara Hershey, Robert Klein, Ruth White, E. G. Marshall, Arthur Hill

Pursuit of the Graf Spee: see *The Battle of the River Plate*

Pursuit to Algiers
US 1945 65m bw
Universal (Roy William Neill)

Sherlock Holmes guards the young king of Ruritania on a sea voyage.

After an amiably lunatic first reel, this settles down as one of the dullest of the series, but it never entirely taxes the patience.

w Leonard Lee *d* Roy William Neill *ph* Paul Ivano *md* Edgar Fairchild *m* Hans Salter

Basil Rathbone, Nigel Bruce, Martin Kosleck, Marjorie Riordan, Rosalind Ivan, John Abbott, Frederic Worlock, Morton Lowry

Pushover *
US 1954 91m bw
Columbia (Jules Schermer)
V*

An honest policeman involves himself in murder for loot.

Another variation on *Double Indemnity*, smoothly carpentered as the first appearance of newly-groomed star Kim Novak. The events of a night were familiar and watchable.

w Roy Huggins *novels* *The Night Watch* by Thomas Walsh, *Rafferty* by William S. Ballinger *d* Richard Quine *ph* Lester B. White *m* Arthur Morton

Fred MacMurray, Kim Novak, Phil Carey, Dorothy Malone, E. G. Marshall

Puss och Kram: see *Hugs and Kisses*

Pussycat Alley: see *The World Ten Times Over*

Pussycat, Pussycat, I Love You
US 1970 100m DeLuxe
UA/Three Pictures (Jerry Bresler)

A sex-mad writer tells a doctor how he lost his wife to a film-star.

Tedious chase comedy that goes nowhere in particular.

wd Rod Amateau *ph* Tonino Delli Colli *m* Lalo Schifrin *ad* Toni Sarzi-Braga *ed* Larry Heath

Ian McShane, Anna Calder-Marshall, Severn Darden, Joyce Van Patten, John Gavin, Beba Loncar

'The gags, both visual and verbal, strain and creak, giving the impression of being made up on the spur of the moment.' – *David McGillivray, MFB*

Putney Swope *
US 1969 85m bw/Eastmancolor
Contemporary/Herald
V*

A black adman takes over an agency, renaming it Truth and Soul Inc. and staffing it with black militants.

Anarchic, intermittently funny comedy, stuffed with jokes at the expense of most institutions.

wd Robert Downey *ph* Gerald Cotts *m* Charley Cuva *ad* Gary Weist *ed* Bud Smith

Arnold Johnson, Antonio Fargas, Laura Greene, Eric Krupnik, Pepi Hermine, Ruth Hermine

'Visual graffiti of this order don't merit public exposure.' – *David Wilson, MFB*

Puttin' on the Ritz
US 1930 88m bw (colour sequence)
UA/Joseph M. Schenck (John W. Considine Jnr)

A has-been vaudevillian gets a second chance but succumbs to the demon rum.

Primitive early musical melodrama valuable only as an example of the work of its star.

w John W. Considine Jnr *d* Edward Sloman *ph* Ray June *ad* William Cameron Menzies

Harry Richman, Joan Bennett, James Gleason, Aileen Pringle, Lilyan Tashman, Purnell Pratt

'Entertaining backstage story with ultra production values.' – *Variety*

Putting Pants on Philip *
US 1927 20m bw silent
Hal Roach

A respectable man meets his randy Scottish nephew who wears nothing under his kilt.

Early star comedy, allegedly their first as a team but before their more recognizable characteristics had developed. Not at all bad in its way, though developing into one long chase.

w H. M. Walker *d* Clyde Bruckman

Laurel and Hardy, Sam Lufkin, Harvey Clark

Puzzle of a Downfall Child
US 1970 104m Technicolor
Universal/Newman-Foreman

Fantasy reminiscences of a top fashion model.

Pretentious, fashionable, seemingly interminable collage of sex and high living.

w Adrien Joyce (Carol Eastman) *d* Jerry Schatzberg *ph* Adam Holender *m* Michael Small

Faye Dunaway, Barry Primus, Viveca Lindfors, Barry Morse, Roy Scheider

Pygmalion ****
GB 1938 96m bw
Gabriel Pascal
V*, L

A professor of phonetics takes a bet that he can turn a cockney flower seller in six months into a lady who can pass as a duchess.

Perfectly splendid Shavian comedy of bad manners, extremely well filmed and containing memorable lines and performances; subsequently turned into the musical *My Fair Lady* (qv). One of the most heartening and adult British films of the thirties.

w Anatole de Grunwald, W. P. Lipscomb, Cecil Lewis, Ian Dalrymple *play* Bernard Shaw *d* Anthony Asquith, Leslie Howard *ph* Harry Stradling *m* Arthur Honegger

Leslie Howard, Wendy Hiller, Wilfrid Lawson, Scott Sunderland, Marie Lohr, David Tree, Esmé Percy, Everley Gregg, Jean Cadell

HIGGINS (Leslie Howard): 'Yes, you squashed cabbage leaf, you disgrace to the noble architecture of these columns, you incarnate insult to the English language, I can pass you off as the Queen of Sheba.'

HIGGINS: 'Where the devil are my slippers, Eliza?'

'Ought to have big potentialities in the US, with some cutting. . .. An introductory title briefly gives the source of the play, which was Shakespeare's Pygmalion.' (!) – *Variety*

'An exhibition of real movie-making – of a sound score woven in and out of tense scenes, creating mood and tempo and characterization.' – *Pare Lorentz*

'Every possible care has been taken in the presentation of what may well prove to have a significant effect on future British film production, for it is live, human entertainment, flawlessly presented and making an obvious appeal to all kinds of audiences.' – *The Cinema*

AA: Bernard Shaw; Ian Dalrymple, Cecil Lewis, W. P. Lipscomb

AAN: best picture; Leslie Howard; Wendy Hiller

Q

Q & A *
US 1990 132m Technicolor
Virgin/Regency/Odyssey (Arnon Milchan, Burtt Harris)
V, V*, L

An inexperienced assistant D.A. investigates the killing of a Puerto Rican crook by a veteran policeman and uncovers widespread corruption.

Increasingly ponderous and predictable drama of an innocent struggling in a moral quicksand.

wd Sidney Lumet *novel* Judge Edwin Torres *ph* Andrezej Bartkowiak *m* Ruben Blades *pd* Philip Rosenberg *ed* Richard Cirincione

Nick Nolte, Timothy Hutton, Armand Assante, Patrick O'Neal, Lee Richardson, Luis Guzman, Charles Dutton, Jenny Lumet, Paul Calderon

'One is left reflecting sadly on the miscalculations . . . that make a film which opens with the bang of a superb first half gradually tail away to a whimper.' – *Tom Milne, MFB*

Q Planes **
GB 1939 82m bw
Harefield/London Films (Irving Asher, Alexander Korda)
US title: *Clouds over Europe*

A secret ray helps spies to steal test aircraft during proving flights.

Lively comedy thriller distinguished by a droll leading performance.

w Ian Dalrymple, Brock Williams, Jack Whittingham, Arthur Wimperis *d* Tim Whelan *ph* Harry Stradling *md* Muir Mathieson

Ralph Richardson, Laurence Olivier, Valerie Hobson, George Merritt, George Curzon, Gus McNaughton, David Tree

'A bright vigorous little picture, and Mr Richardson's Major is the brightest thing in it. You should see it. You'll like it. It has savour.' – *C. A. Lejeune*

Q – The Winged Serpent **
US 1982 93m colour Panavision
Larco/Larry Cohen
V*
aka: *The Winged Serpent*

An ex-con on the run finds a monstrous Aztec god, a flying serpent, nesting in the spire of the Chrysler building.

Quirky, above-average horror film with flashes of brightness.

wd Larry Cohen *ph* Fred Murphy *m* Robert O. Ragland *ed* Armand Lebowitz

Michael Moriarty, Candy Clark, David Carradine, Richard Roundtree, James Dixon

Qiu Ju Da Guansi: see *The Story of Qiu Ju*

Quackser Fortune Has a Cousin in the Bronx *
US 1970 90m Eastmancolor
UMC (John H. Cushingham)
V*, L

An Irish layabout strikes up an acquaintance with an American student.

Likeable if plotless Dublin comedy, pleasantly photographed.

w Gabriel Walsh *d* Waris Hussein *ph* Gil Taylor *m* Michael Dress

Gene Wilder, Margot Kidder, Eileen Colgen, Seamus Ford

Quadrophenia
GB 1979 120m Eastmancolor
Brent-Walker/Polytel (Roy Baird, Bill Curbishley)
V, V*, L

A drama of bitter rivalry between Mods and Rockers on the Brighton beaches in 1964.

What passes for a successful musical at the end of the seventies is typified by this violent, screaming and wholly unattractive amalgam of noise, violence, sex and profanity.

w Dave Humphries, Martin Stellman, Franc Roddam *d* Franc Roddam *ph* Brian Tufano *md* John Entwistle, Pete Townshend *m* The Who *pd* Simon Holland *ed* Mike Taylor

Phil Daniels, Mark Wingett, Philip Davis, Leslie Ash, Garry Cooper, Toyah Wilcox, Sting

Quai des Brumes ***
France 1938 89m bw
Rabinovitch
V
US title: *Port of Shadows*

An army deserter rescues a girl from crooks but is killed before they can escape.

Artificial, set-bound, but at the time wholly persuasive melodrama which became one of the archetypal French films of the thirties, its doomed lovers syndrome not being picked up by Hollywood until after World War II.

w Jacques Prévert, *novel* Pierre MacOrlan *d* Marcel Carné *ph* Eugen Schüfftan *m* Maurice Jaubert *ad* Alexander Trauner

Jean Gabin, Michèle Morgan, Michel Simon, Pierre Brasseur

'Unity of space, time and action give the film a classical finish.' – *Georges Sadoul*

'The sort of powerful and joyless film that the French do so well – a study in foetid atmosphere, in which the one beauty is its uncompromising honesty.' – *C. A. Lejeune*

† The plot was in fact almost identical with that of *Pépé le Moko*. The romantic pessimism of these films, plus *Le Jour Se Lève*, so suited the mood of France that Vichy officials later said: 'If we have lost the war it is because of *Quai des Brumes*.'

Quai des Orfèvres *
France 1947 105m bw
Majestic

A music hall artiste is accused of murdering the man he took to be seducing his mistress.

The equivalent of many a British Scotland Yard thriller, but a good one, with excellent acting, atmosphere and suspense.

w Henri-Georges Clouzot, Jean Ferry *novel Légitime Défense* by Stanislas-André Steeman *d* Henri-Georges Clouzot *ph* Armand Thirard *m* Francis Lopez

Louis Jouvet, Bernard Blier, Suzy Delair, Pierre Larquey, Simone Rennant

'The wonder of *Quai des Orfèvres* is the way Clouzot has pricked it with life.' – *Guardian*

'A stunningly well made entertainment.' – *New Yorker, 1982*

'Two love experts in a daring game of hearts!'
Quality Street *
US 1937 84m bw
RKO (Pandro S. Berman)
V*, L

When an officer returns from the Napoleonic wars, he does not recognize his sweetheart, whose beauty has faded, so she masquerades as her own capricious niece.

Fairly successful attempt to capture on screen the essence of Barrie whimsy; everyone tries hard, anyway.

w Mortimer Offner, Allan Scott *play* J. M. Barrie *d* George Stevens *ph* Robert de Grasse *m* Roy Webb

Katharine Hepburn, Franchot Tone, Fay Bainter, Eric Blore, Cora Witherspoon, Estelle Winwood, Florence Lake, Joan Fontaine

'Hepburn and Tone unable to instil any life, and little entertainment, into this old-timer from legit . . . one for the bonnet and shawl trade.' – *Variety*

'It is strictly a self-propelled picture, tearing breathlessly, even hysterically, through Barrie's quizzical account of a man-hunt. . . . But we were exhausted by the intensity of Miss Hepburn's concentration on it. Her Phoebe needs a neurologist far more than a husband. Such flutterings and jitterings and twitchings, such hand-wringings and mouth-quiverings, such runnings-about and eyebrow-raisings have not been on the screen in many a moon.' – *Frank Nugent, New York Times*

† Previously made by MGM in 1927 (silent), with Marion Davies and Conrad Nagel; directed by Sidney Franklin

AAN: Roy Webb

Quantez
US 1957 80m Eastmancolor Cinemascope
Universal-International

Robbers hiding for the night in a frontier town become involved in an Indian attack.

Curious, slow-paced attempt to redo *The Gunfight* with inferior materials; not a profitable experience.

w R. Wright Campbell *d* Harry Keller

Fred MacMurray, Dorothy Malone, James Barton, Sydney Chaplin, John Gavin, John Larch, Michael Ansara

The Quare Fellow
GB 1962 90m bw
BLC/Bryanston (Anthony Havelock-Allan)
V

Life in a Dublin prison when two men are to be hanged, as experienced by a new young warder.

Watered-down version of a rumbustious stage tragi-comedy, with not much but the gloom left.

wd Arthur Dreifuss *play* Brendan Behan *ph* Peter Hennessey *m* Alexander Faris

Patrick McGoohan, Sylvia Syms, Walter Macken, Dermot Kelly, Hilton Edwards

Quartet ***
GB   1948   120m   bw
GFD/Gainsborough (Anthony Darnborough)
V*

Four stories introduced by the author.

This entertaining production began the compendium fashion (*Full House, Phone Call from a Stranger*, etc) and is fondly remembered, though all the stories had softened endings and the middle two did not work very well as drama. Subsequent Maugham compilations were *Trio* and *Encore* (both qv).

w R. C. Sherriff,   *stories* W. Somerset Maugham
m John Greenwood

THE FACTS OF LIFE

d Ralph Smart   *ph* Ray Elton

Basil Radford, Naunton Wayne, Mai Zetterling, Jack Watling, James Robertson Justice

THE ALIEN CORN

d Harold French   *ph* Ray Elton

Dirk Bogarde, Françoise Rosay, Raymond Lovell, Honor Blackman, Irene Browne

THE KITE

d Arthur Crabtree   *ph* Ray Elton

George Cole, Hermione Baddeley, Susan Shaw, Mervyn Johns, Bernard Lee

THE COLONEL'S LADY

d Ken Annakin   *ph* Reg Wyer

Cecil Parker, Linden Travers, Nora Swinburne, Ernest Thesiger, Felix Aylmer, Henry Edwards, Wilfrid Hyde-White

Quartet *
GB/France   1981   101m   GTC colour
TCF/Merchant Ivory (Ismail Merchant, Jean Pierre Mahot de la Querantonnais)
V*

In 1927 Paris, a convict's wife finds herself part of a *ménage à trois.*

Slow-moving, good-looking study of characters in a milieu; as usual with films from this stable, it has nothing to please the majority.

w Ruth Prawer Jhabvala   *novel* Jean Rhys
d James Ivory   *ph* Pierre Lhomme   *m* Richard Robbins

Isabelle Adjani, Maggie Smith, Alan Bates, Anthony Higgins

'See women defiled by monsters from outer space! Men turned killers by mysterious power more incredible than anything today's science or fiction ever imagined!'
Quatermass and the Pit **
GB   1967   97m   Technicolor
Hammer/Anthony Nelson Keys
V
US title: *Five Million Years to Earth*

Prehistoric skulls are unearthed during London Underground excavations, and a weird and deadly force makes itself felt.

The third film of a Quatermass serial is the most ambitious, and in many ways inventive and enjoyable, yet spoiled by the very fertility of the author's imagination: the concepts are simply too intellectual to be easily followed in what should be a visual thriller. The climax, in which the devil rears over London and is 'earthed', is satisfactorily harrowing.

w Nigel Kneale,   *TV serial* Nigel Kneale   *d* Roy Ward Baker   *ph* Arthur Grant   *m* Tristam Cary

Andrew Keir, James Donald, Barbara Shelley, Julian Glover, Duncan Lamont, Edwin Richfield, Peter Copley

'You Can't Escape It! Nothing Can Destroy It! It's Coming For You From Space To Wipe All Living Things From The Face Of The Earth! Can It Be Stopped?'
The Quatermass Experiment **
GB   1955   82m   bw
Exclusive/Hammer (Anthony Hinds)
US title: *The Creeping Unknown*

When a rocketship returns from space, two of its three crew members have disappeared and the third is slowly taken over by a fungus which thrives on blood.

Intelligent science fiction based on a highly successful BBC TV serial; the film version is generally workmanlike despite its obvious low budget.

w Richard Landau, Val Guest   *serial* Nigel Kneale
d Val Guest   *ph* Jimmy Harvey

Brian Donlevy, Jack Warner, Margia Dean, *Richard Wordsworth*, David King Wood, Thora Hird, Gordon Jackson

Quatermass II **
GB   1957   85m   bw
Hammer (Anthony Hinds)
V*, L
US title: *Enemy from Space*

A research station operating under military secrecy is supposed to be making synthetic foods, but is in fact an acclimatization centre for invaders from outer space.

Simplified version of a TV serial, a bit stodgy in the talk scenes, but building into sequences of genuine alarm and based on an idea of lingering persuasiveness.

w Nigel Kneale, Val Guest   *serial Nigel Kneale*   *d* Val Guest   *ph* Gerald Gibbs   *m* James Bernard

Brian Donlevy, John Longden, Sidney James, Bryan Forbes, William Franklyn, Charles Lloyd Pack, Percy Herbert, Tom Chatto

Quatre Aventures de Reinette et Mirabelle:
see *Four Adventures of Reinette and Mirabelle*

Les Quatre Cents Coups: see *The Four Hundred Blows*

I Quattro dell'Ave Maria: see *Ace High*

Quattro Passi fra le Nuvole: see *Four Steps in the Clouds*

¿Que He Hecho Yo Para Merecer Esto?: see *What Have I Done to Deserve This?*

Quebec
US   1951   85m   Technicolor
Paramount
V*

The wife of the loyalist governor of Quebec is in love with the leader of the rebels.

Ho-hum period actioner with some pretty backgrounds and not much personality.

w Alan Le May   *d* George Templeton

Corinne Calvet, John Barrymore Jnr, Barbara Rush, Patric Knowles, John Hoyt, Arnold Moss

'She's so excitingly good when she's so wonderfully bad!'
Queen Bee *
US   1955   95m   bw
Columbia (Jerry Wald)
V

A wealthy woman has a compulsion to dominate everyone around her.

Claustrophobic Southern-set melodrama obviously created for its star.

wd Ranald MacDougall   *novel* Edna Lee
ph Charles Lang   *md* Morris Stoloff   *m* George Duning

Joan Crawford, Barry Sullivan, Betsy Palmer, John Ireland, Lucy Marlow, William Leslie, Fay Wray

AAN: Charles Lang

Queen Christina ***
US   1933   101m   bw
MGM (Walter Wanger)
V, V*, L

The queen of 17th-century Sweden, distressed at the thought of a political marriage, goes wandering through her country in men's clothes and falls in love with the new Spanish ambassador.

The star vehicle *par excellence*, superb to look at and one of its star's most fondly remembered films. Historically it's nonsense, but put across with great style.

w Salka Viertel, H. M. Harwood, S. N. Behrman
d Rouben Mamoulian   *ph* William Daniels   *m* Herbert Stothart

Greta Garbo, John Gilbert, Ian Keith, Lewis Stone, C. Aubrey Smith, Reginald Owen, Elizabeth Young

ANTONIO (John Gilbert): 'It's all a question of climate. You cannot serenade a woman in a snowstorm. All the graces in the art of love – elaborate approaches that will make the game of love amusing – can only be practised in those countries that quiver in the heat of the sun.'
CHRISTINA (Greta Garbo): 'I have been memorizing this room. In the future, in my memory, I shall live a great deal in this room.'

'The shortcomings, such as they are, are so far overshadowed by the potency of the premier satellite, the sterling support, the Mamoulian montage and the Behrman crisp dialogue that they're relatively unimportant; for Christina is cinch b.o.' – *Variety*

'Garbo, as enchanting as ever, is still enveloped by her unfathomable mystery.' – *Photoplay*

'An unending series of exceptional scenes.' – *Modern Screen*

† The leading male role was announced in turn for Leslie Howard, Franchot Tone, Nils Asther, Bruce Cabot and Laurence Olivier: Garbo turned them all down.

Queen Elizabeth *
France   1912   35m approx (24 fps)   bw   silent
Histrionic Film
original title: *Les Amours de la Reine Elisabeth*

Scenes from the life of the queen.

Abysmally boring now, this film is important in several ways. It is our best record of Sarah Bernhardt. It was immensely successful throughout the world. It made cinema interesting to all classes, not just the hoi polloi. It made the fortunes of Adolph Zukor, who bought it cheaply and went on to found Paramount Pictures. (Bernhardt is said to have remarked to him: 'You have put me in pickle for all time!')

w Eugène Moreau   *d* Henri Desfontaines, Louis Mercanton

Sarah Bernhardt, Lou Tellegen

Queen Kelly **
US   1928   100m approx (24 fps) (unfinished version)   bw   silent
United Artists/Gloria Productions/Joseph Kennedy
V, V*, L

A convent girl goes to the bad, is ill-used by a prince, becomes a white slave in Africa but finally inherits a fortune.

Sexually-oriented extravaganza, the last great folly of its director but never finished by him. Various versions exist: in all of them individual scenes are more entertaining than the whole. Extracts were shown in *Sunset Boulevard*.

wd Erich von Stroheim   *ph* Gordon Pollock, Paul Ivano, Ben Reynolds.   *m* Adolf Tandler   *ad* Harry Miles

Gloria Swanson, Walter Byron, Seena Owen

† The version released on video in 1994 is the European version of 1931, which runs for 115m.

Queen of Atlantis: see *L'Atlantide*

Queen of Destiny: see *Sixty Glorious Years*

Queen of Hearts *
GB   1936   80m   bw
ATP (Basil Dean)

A working girl poses as a socialite and wins a matinée idol.

Stalwart romantic comedy with its star slightly more glamorized than usual.

w Clifford Grey, H. F. Maltby, Douglas Furber, Anthony Kimmins, Gordon Wellesley   *d* Monty Banks

Gracie Fields, John Loder, Enid Stamp Taylor, Fred Duprez, Edward Rigby, Hal Gordon

Queen of Hearts *
GB   1989   112m   colour
Enterprise/TVS Films/Nelson Entertainment/Film Four International/Telso International (John Hardy)
V*, L

A ten-year-old, part of a large and happy Italian family living in London, watches while his father risks everything by gambling.

Odd and ultimately unsatisfactory mix of fantasy and reality, contrasting Italian warmth and British cool to the detriment of both.

w Tony Grisoni   *d* Jon Amiel   *ph* Mike Southon   *m* Michael Convertino   *pd* Jim Clay   *ed* Peter Boyle

Vittorio Duse, Joseph Long, Anita Zagaria, Eileen Way, Vittorio Amandola, Roberto Scateni, Stefano Spagnoli, Alec Bregonzi

The Queen of Spades **
GB   1948   96m   bw
ABP/World Screen Plays (Anatole de Grunwald)
V*

A Russian officer tries to wrest from an ancient countess the secret of winning at cards, in return for which he has sold his soul to the devil; but she dies of fright and haunts him.

Disappointingly slow-moving but splendidly atmospheric recreation of an old Russian story with all the decorative stops out; the chills when they come are quite frightening, the style is impressionist and the acting suitably extravagant.

w Rodney Ackland, Arthur Boys   *novel* Alexander Pushkin   *d* Thorold Dickinson   *ph* Otto Heller   *m* Georges Auric   *ad* Oliver Messel

Anton Walbrook, Edith Evans, Ronald Howard, Yvonne Mitchell, Mary Jerrold

'The photography is adventurous, the cutting imaginative and the sets startling.' – *Evening Standard*

'It is fine to come across such distinguished filmcraft.' – *Evening News*

The Queen of Spies: see *Joan of Ozark*

Queen of the Mob *
US   1940   61m   bw
Paramount

A murderess and her three sons are captured by the FBI.

Pacy crime melodrama from the *Persons in Hiding* series, based on the exploits of Ma Barker.

w Horace McCoy, William R. Lippmann   *d* James Hogan   *ph* Theodor Sparkuhl

Blanche Yurka, Ralph Bellamy, Jack Carson, Richard Denning, Paul Kelly, J. Carrol Naish, Jeanne Cagney, William Henry, James Seay, Hedda Hopper

Queen of the Road
Australia   1984   96m   colour
JNP (James Davern)

A daughter inherits trouble when she takes over her father's truck haulage business.

A dull comedy of mishap and misadventure, interspersed with country and western songs and relying for the most part on the old joke (though it may be new to Australia) that women are poor drivers.

w Tom Mitchell   *d* Bruce Best   *ph* Joseph Pickering   *m* Mike Perjanik   *ad* Michael Ralph   *ed* Zsolt Kollanyi

Joanne Samuel, Amanda Muggleton, Shane Worthington, Jonathan Sweet, Chris Hession

The Queen's Guards
GB   1960   112m   Technicolor   Cinemascope
TCF/Imperial (Michael Powell)

Reminiscences during trooping the colour of father and son guardsmen.

Incredibly old-fashioned family melodrama complete with skeleton in family closet; despite its date it has a decidedly pre-war air, except that it might have been more smartly done then.

w Roger Milner   *d* Michael Powell   *ph* Gerald Turpin   *m* Brian Easdale

Raymond Massey, Daniel Massey, Robert Stephens, Ursula Jeans, Judith Stott, Elizabeth Shepherd, Duncan Lamont, Ian Hunter, Jack Watling

'This flagwaving museum piece would be distressing if it weren't so inept . . . [the actors] battle manfully with dialogue and characters as dated as a Crimean cavalry charge. The film could scarcely be taken as a tribute to the Guards except, just possibly, by elderly aunts in Cheltenham.' – *MFB*

The Queen's Husband: see *The Royal Bed*

Queens Logic *
US   1991   116m   DeLuxe
New Visions (Stuart Oken, Russ Smith)
V, V*, L

Friends from boyhood offer each other support and succour at a moment of marital crisis.

Energetically acted domestic drama that covers familiar ground but does so in an enjoyably high-spirited manner.

w Tony Spiridakis   *story* Tony Spiridakis, Joseph W. Savino   *d* Steve Rash   *ph* Amir Mokri   *m* Joe Jackson   *pd* Edward Pisoni   *ed* Patrick Kennedy

Kevin Bacon, Linda Fiorentino, John Malkovich, Joe Mantegna, Ken Olin, Tony Spiridakis, Tom Waits, Chloe Webb, Jamie Lee Curtis

'This deadpan midlife crisis comedy-drama is undeniably compulsive in its simplified TV fashion, thanks to a cleverly worked script and some heartening acting.' – *John Lyttle, Independent*

Queimada!
France/Italy   1968   132m   DeLuxe
PEA/PPA (Alberto Grimaldi)
V*
aka: *Burn!*

A diplomat is sent to a Caribbean island to break the Portuguese sugar monopoly and becomes involved with revolutionaries.

An indigestible attempt to combine adventure with the film of ideas; very tedious.

w Franco Solinas, Giorgio Arlorio   *d* Gillo Pontecorvo   *ph* Marcello Gatti   *m* Ennio Morricone

Marlon Brando, Renato Salvatori, Norman Hill, Evaristo Marquez

'Theirs was a time of love and violence!'
Quentin Durward *
GB   1955   101m   Eastmancolor   Cinemascope
MGM (Pandro S. Berman)
aka: *The Adventures of Quentin Durward*

An elderly English lord sends his nephew to woo a French lady on his behalf; but the boy falls in love with her himself.

Haphazardly constructed and produced, but quite enjoyable, period romp, with a bold black villain and several rousing set-pieces including a final set-to on bell ropes.

w Robert Ardrey   *novel* Sir Walter Scott   *d* Richard Thorpe   *ph* Christopher Challis   *m* Bronislau Kaper

Robert Taylor, Kay Kendall, Robert Morley, Alec Clunes, Marius Goring, Wilfrid Hyde-White, Ernest Thesiger, Duncan Lamont, Harcourt Williams, Laya Raki, George Cole

Querelle
West Germany/France   1982   108m   Eastmancolor
Planet/Albatross/Gaumont
V, V*

A homosexual sailor has a mystical quest which involves murder.

Overheated fantasy which may have something to say to gays, but not much to other audiences.

wd Rainer Werner Fassbinder   *book* Jean Genet   *ph* Xaver Schwarzenberger   *m* Peer Raben

Brad Davis, Franco Nero, Jeanne Moreau, Laurent Malet

Quest for Fire
Canada/France   1981   100m   Bellevue-Pathecolor Panavision
ICC/Cine Trail/Belstar/Stephan (Michael Gruskoff)
V*, L, S

Eighty thousand years ago, a primitive tribe uses the discovery of fire to defeat its enemies.

Scientifically cosseted but sometimes unintentionally funny attempt to make us care about the problems of primitive man. Lively sequences are separated by longueurs.

w Gérard Brach   *novel* La Guerre du Feu by J. H. Rosny   *d* Jean-Jacques Annaud   *ph* Claude Agostini   *m* Philippe Sarde   *pd* Guy Comtois, Brian Morris   *special language* Anthony Burgess   *body movement* Desmond Morris

Everett McGill, Ron Perlman, Rae Dawn, Nameer El-Kadi

'He had seen her, felt her touch, knew she existed . . .'
Quest for Love *
GB   1971   90m   Eastmancolor
Rank/Peter Rogers Productions (Peter Eton)
V*

After an explosion during an experiment, a young physicist finds himself living a different life, in love with a dying girl; returning to normal, he finds the girl and saves her.

Pleasing variation on *Berkeley Square*, quite well staged and played.

w Terence Feely   *story* Random Quest by John Wyndham   *d* Ralph Thomas   *ph* Ernest Steward   *m* Eric Rogers

Tom Bell, Joan Collins, Denholm Elliott, Laurence Naismith, Lyn Ashley

A Question of Adultery
GB   1958   84m   bw
Eros/Connaught Place/Raymond Stross

When a husband is discovered to be sterile, his wife suggests artificial insemination, but when she seems to have a lover he institutes divorce proceedings.

Opportunist melodrama from the headlines. Not even interesting *then*.

w Anne Edwards   *play Breach of Marriage* by Dan Sutherland   *d* Don Chaffey   *ph* Stephen Dale   *m* Philip Green

Julie London, Anthony Steel, Basil Sidney, Donald Houston, Anton Diffring, Andrew Cruickshank, Conrad Philips, Kynaston Reeves

A Question of Silence *
Netherlands   1982   96m   colour
C.O.W./Sigma Films (Matthijs van Heijningen)
original title: *De Stilte Rond Christine M*

A lawyer, defending three women who commit a gratuitous act of murder of a male boutique owner, claims that their action is the result of masculine oppression.

Stylish feminist thriller that skilfully wraps its propagandist message.

wd Marleen Gorris   *ph* Frans Bromet   *m* Lodewijk de Boer, Martijn Hasebos   *ad* Harry Ammerlaan   *ed* Hans van Dongen

Edda Barends, Nelly Frijda, Henriette Tol, Cox Habbema, Eddy Brugman, Hans Croiset, Eric Plooyer

Quick Before It Melts
US   1964   97m   Metrocolor   Panavision
MGM/Biography (Douglas Lawrence, Delbert Mann)

A journalist is sent to cover a naval enterprise in the Antarctic, and gets a scoop despite his shyness.

Noisy service comedy with precious little plot.

w Dale Wasserman   *novel* Philip Benjamin   *d* Delbert Mann   *ph* Russell Harlan   *m* David Rose

George Maharis, Robert Morse, Anjanette Comer, James Gregory, Howard St John, Janine Gray, Michael Constantine

'The combination of romantic dalliance, service high jinks and hectic journalism remains uniformly flat all through.' – *MFB*

Quick Change
US   1990   88m   DuArt   Panavision
Warner/Devoted (Robert Greenhut, Bill Murray)
V, V*, L

Two men and a woman stage a flawless bank robbery and then have trouble making their getaway from New York.

Farcical comedy taken at a decorous pace and with the joke of an escalating series of disasters too often mistimed to produce any amusement.

w Howard Franklin   *novel* Jay Cronley   *d* Howard Franklin, Bill Murray   *ph* Michael Chapman   *m* Randy Edelman   *ad* Speed Hopkins   *ed* Alan Heim

Bill Murray, Geena Davis, Randy Quaid, Jason Robards, Bob Elliott, Kimberleigh Aarn, Ron Ryan, Brian McConnachie, Jack Gilpin

The Quick Gun
US   1964   88m   Techniscope
Admiral/Columbia

A gunfighter gets an icy welcome when he returns home to claim his father's farm.

Standard Western with the hero redeemed and elected sheriff at the end.

w Robert E. Kent   *d* Sidney Salkow

Audie Murphy, Merry Anders, James Best, Ted de Corsia, Walter Sande, Frank Ferguson

Quick Let's Get Married
US   1965   100m   colour
Golden Eagle (William Marshall)
aka: *The Confession, Seven Different Ways*

The voice of a sneak thief in a ruined church is taken by an unwed mother as a miracle.

Downright peculiar mishmash wasting interesting stars; an independent production by Rogers and husband in Jamaica.

w Allen Scott   *d* William Dieterle   *ph* Robert Bronner   *m* Michael Colicchio

Ginger Rogers, Ray Milland, Barbara Eden, Walter Abel, Cecil Kellaway, Elliott Gould, Michael Ansara, David Hurst

Quick Millions **
US   1931   69m   bw
Fox

An ambitious truck driver becomes a ruthless racketeer.

Fast-moving, otherwise naïve early gangster melodrama notable for Tracy's first star performance.

w Courtney Terrett, Rowland Brown, John Wray   *d* Rowland Brown   *ph* Joseph August

Spencer Tracy, Marguerite Churchill, Sally Eilers, Robert Burns, John Wray, George Raft

'This film is in the money. Ranks with the best of the gangster items.' – *Variety*

Quicksand
US   1950   79m   bw
Mort Briskin/UA

A garage mechanic gets involved in crime for the sake of an unworthy girl.

Lower-case melodrama of no notable merit.

w Robert Smith   *d* Irving Pichel

Mickey Rooney, Jeanne Cagney, Barbara Bates, Peter Lorre

The Quiet American **
US   1957   122m   bw
UA/Figaro (Joseph L. Mankiewicz)

An American in Saigon has naïve ideas for ending the war; he saves the life of a journalist who for various reasons becomes jealous and is duped into betraying the American to the communists.

Semi-successful excursion into the territory of Graham Greene, who as in *Brighton Rock* has allowed his ironic ending to be totally re-emphasized, here making the film anti-communist instead of anti-American.

wd Joseph L. Mankiewicz   *novel* Graham Greene   *ph* Robert Krasker   *m* Mario Nascimbene

Michael Redgrave, Audie Murphy, Claude Dauphin, Giorgia Moll, Bruce Cabot, Fred Sadoff, Richard Loo

The Quiet Earth **
New Zealand   1985   94m   colour
Cinepro/Pillsbury Films (Sam Pillsbury, Don Reynolds)
V, V*, L

After an experiment goes disastrously wrong, a suicidal scientist wakes to discover that he appears to be the only person left alive in the world.

An intriguing and often witty exercise in apocalyptic science fiction, with an unconventional approach.

w Bill Baer, Bruno Lawrence, Sam Pillsbury   *novel* Craig Harrison   *d* Geoff Murphy   *ph* James Bartle   *m* John Charles   *pd* Josephine Ford   *ed* Michael Horton

Bruno Lawrence, Alison Routledge, Peter Smith

The Quiet Man ***
US   1952   129m   Technicolor
Republic/Argosy (John Ford, Merian C. Cooper)
V, V*, L

An Irish village version of *The Taming of the Shrew*, the tamer being an ex-boxer retired to the land of his fathers and in need of a wife. Archetypal John Ford comedy, as Irish as can be, with everything but leprechauns and the Blarney Stone on hand.

Despite some poor sets the film has a gay swing to it, much brawling vigour and broad comedy, while the actors all give their roistering best.

w Frank Nugent,   *story* Maurice Walsh   *d* John Ford   *ph* Winton C. Hoch, Archie Stout   *m* Victor Young

John Wayne, Maureen O'Hara, Barry Fitzgerald, Victor McLaglen, Ward Bond, Mildred Natwick, Francis Ford, Arthur Shields, Eileen Crowe, Sean McClory, Jack McGowran

'Ford's art and artifice . . . are employed to reveal a way of life – stable, rooted, honourable, purposeful in nature's way, and thereby rhythmic. Everyone is an individual, yet everyone and everything has a place.' – *Henry Hart, Films in Review*

AA: John Ford; Winton C. Hoch, Archie Stout

AAN: best picture; Frank Nugent; Victor McLaglen

A Quiet Place to Kill: see *Paranoia*

Quiet Please, Murder *
US   1943   70m   bw
TCF (Ralph Dietrich)

Nazis and art thieves cause a high death rate in a public library.

Unusual, stylish second feature.

wd John Larkin   *ph* Joe MacDonald   *md* Emil Newman   *m* Arthur Lange

George Sanders, Kurt Katch, Gail Patrick, Richard Denning, Lynne Roberts, Sidney Blackmer, Byron FoulgerSamples of quirky dialogue:

PATRICK TO SANDERS: 'How many butterflies did you torture since lunch, hoping one would turn on you?'

SANDERS: 'I am a punishment in your life. Your conscience demands it. The unconscious instinct to punish ourselves sometimes becomes self-destructive. The way we live is a constant threat to our own security. We love it. Giving and taking pain.'

PATRICK: 'You hate because you fear love – and the thought of desiring.'

Quiet Wedding ***
GB   1940   80m   bw
Paramount/Conqueror (Paul Soskin)

Middle-class wedding preparations are complicated by family guests.

A semi-classic British stage comedy is admirably filmed with a splendid cast.

w Terence Rattigan, Anatole de Grunwald,   *play Esther McCracken*   *d* Anthony Asquith

Margaret Lockwood, Derek Farr, A. E. Matthews, *Marjorie Fielding, Athene Seyler, Peggy Ashcroft,* Margaretta Scott, Frank Cellier, Roland Culver, Jean Cadell, David Tomlinson, Bernard Miles

'A completely unpretentious and charming film, the components of which are as delicately balanced as the mechanism of a watch.' – *New York Times*

'No subtlety of glance, movement or dialogue has been missed, no possible highlight omitted.' – *MFB*

† Production was halted five times when bombs fell on the studio.
†† Remade as *Happy is the Bride* (qv).

Quiet Weekend
GB   1946   92m   bw
Associated British (Warwick Ward)

The Royds spend a weekend at their country cottage and get involved with poachers.

Trivial and poorly-made sequel, not up to the standard of *Quiet Wedding* as a comic study of British types.

w Victor Skuzetsky *play* Esther McCracken *d* Harold French *ph* Eric Cross

Derek Farr, Marjorie Fielding, George Thorpe, Frank Cellier

Quigley Down Under

US 1990 120m colour Panavision
UIP/Pathé (Stanley O'Toole, Alexandra Rose)
V, V*, L, S

In 1860s Australia, an American hired gun is outlawed after quarrelling with his employer, a violent British cattle rancher.

Apart from its outback setting, a conventional and unoriginal Western, given perfunctory treatment.

w John Hill *d* Simon Wincer *ph* David Egby *m* Basil Poledouris *pd* Ross Major *ed* Peter Burgess

Tom Selleck, Laura San Giacomo, Alan Rickman, Chris Haywood, Ron Hadrick, Tony Bonner, Jerome Ehlers, Conor McDermottroe, Roger Ward, Ben Mendelsohn, Steve Dodd

'Potters along for two hours juggling cardboard figures and contrived situations that might have strayed in from some Hollywood potboiler of the 50s.' – *Geoff Brown, MFB*

† The script was originally written in the 1970s for Steve McQueen.

The Quiller Memorandum *

GB 1966 105m Eastmancolor Panavision
Rank/Ivan Foxwell/Carthay
V*

A British secret service man is sent to Berlin to combat a neo-Nazi organization.

Disappointingly thin but smooth and watchable spy story.

w Harold Pinter *novel* The Berlin Memorandum by Adam Hall (Elleston Trevor) *d* Michael Anderson *ph* Erwin Hillier *m* John Barry

George Segal, Max von Sydow, Alec Guinness, Senta Berger, George Sanders, Robert Helpmann, Robert Flemyng

'In disposing of most of the storyline Pinter has virtually thrown out the baby with the bathwater; all that remains is a skeleton plot which barely makes sense and is totally lacking in excitement.' – *Brenda Davies*

'Harold Pinter wrote the screenplay and for each word of dialogue there has to be a separate scene involving several different camera angles, which is perhaps why they asked him to do it as the story is pretty thin.' – *J. A., Illustrated London News*

The Quince Tree Sun **

Spain 1992 137m Eastmancolor
Artificial Eye/Maria Moreno
V
original title: *El Sol del Membrillo*

Painter Antonio López meticulously prepares a canvas and his subject: a tree of yellow, ripening quinces in the morning sun. The documentary then follows his progress through ten weeks, struggling against the fading light and unsympathetic weather, reminiscing and talking to friends, eventually abandoning his original oil painting and making a drawing instead.

A slow but absorbing examination of the process of artistic creation.

d Victor Erice *ph* Javier Aguirresarobe, Angel Luis Fernéndez *m* Pascal Gaigne *ed* Juan Ignacio San Mateo

'What might have proven a poignant statement on life and art unfortunately runs so long impact is diluted.' – *Variety*

Quingchun Ji: see *Sacrificed Youth*

Quintet

US 1979 118m DeLuxe
TCF/Lions Gate (Robert Altman)
V*

In an icebound city of the future, citizens play a death game and a survivor hunts down a killer who plays for real.

Dismayingly pretentious claptrap which did its star's career no good at all.

w Frank Barhydt, Robert Altman, Patricia Resnick *d* Robert Altman *ph* Jean Boffety *m* Tom Pierson *pd* Leon Ericksen

Paul Newman, Vittorio Gassman, Fernando Rey, Bibi Andersson, Brigitte Fossey, Nina Van Pallandt

'I find it mysterious, exciting, tenacious.' – *Dilys Powell, Punch*

'Paralyzingly stupid.' – *Stanley Kauffmann*

'In making this film, MGM feel privileged to add something of permanent value to the cultural treasure house of mankind . . .'
'Ancient Rome is going to the dogs, Robert Taylor is going to the lions, and Peter Ustinov is going crazy!'

Quo Vadis **

US 1951 171m Technicolor
MGM (Sam Zimbalist)
V, V*, L

A Roman commander under Nero falls in love with a Christian girl and jealous Poppea has them both thrown to the lions.

Spectacular but stagey and heavy-handed Hollywood version of a much-filmed colossus which shares much of its plot line with *The Sign of the Cross*. Three hours of solemn tedium with flashes of vigorous acting and a few set-pieces to take the eye; but the sermonizing does not take away the bad taste of the emphasis on physical brutality.

w John Lee Mahin, S. N. Behrman, Sonya Levien *d* Mervyn Le Roy *ph* Robert Surtees, William V. Skall *m* Miklos Rozsa *ad* Cedric Gibbons, Edward Carfagno, William Horning *ed* Ralph E. Winters

Robert Taylor, Deborah Kerr, *Peter Ustinov, Leo Genn, Patricia Laffan,* Finlay Currie, Abraham Sofaer, Marina Berti, Buddy Baer, Felix Aylmer, Nora Swinburne, Ralph Truman, Norman Wooland

AAN: best picture; Robert Surtees, William V. Skall; Miklos Rozsa; Peter Ustinov; Leo Genn; art direction; editing

RPM (Revolutions Per Minute)

US 1970 97m colour
Columbia/Stanley Kramer
V*

At an American college, a middle-aged professor teaches liberal ideas.

Dim, thankfully forgotten addition to the *Strawberry Statement* cycle.

w Erich Segal *d* Stanley Kramer *ph* Michel Hugo, Perry Botkin Jnr *m* Barry de Vorzon

Anthony Quinn, Ann-Margret, Gary Lockwood, Paul Winfield, Alan Hewitt

'Three years ago Rabbit Angstrom ran out to buy his wife cigarettes. He hasn't come back yet ...'

Rabbit, Run

US 1970 94m Technicolor Panavision
Warner (Howard Kreitsek)

A man leaves his pregnant wife for a prostitute.

Uninteresting sex melodrama without any of the wit which distinguishes the book; hard to sit through.

w Howard B. Kreitsek *novel* John Updike *d* Jack Smight *ph* Philip Lathrop *m* Ray Burton, Brian King

James Caan, Anjanette Comer, Arthur Hill, Jack Albertson, Carrie Snodgress

Rabbit Test

US 1978 84m colour
Avco Embassy (Edgar Rosenberg)
V*, L

A man becomes pregnant.

Dreary and tasteless film, the nadir of comedy.

w Jay Redack, Joan Rivers *d* Joan Rivers *ph* Lucien Ballard *m* Peter Carpenter, Mike Post *ad* Robert Kinoshita *ed* Stanford C. Allen

Billy Crystal, Joan Prather, Alex Rocco, Doris Roberts, Edward Ansara, Imogene Coca, Jane Connell, Keene Curtis, Roddy McDowall, Sheree North, Joan Rivers

The Rabbit Trap *

US 1959 76m bw
UA/Canon (Harry Kleiner)

A hardworking draughtsman finally defies his boss and completes his holiday with his family.

Watchable minor drama just about marking the end of Hollywood's infatuation with TV plays which had begun with *Marty*; the moral and family problems of ordinary people were beginning to prove a shade lacking in excitement.

w J. P. Miller *TV play* J. P. Miller *d* Philip Leacock *ph* Irving Glassberg *m* Jack Marshall

Ernest Borgnine, Bethel Leslie, David Brian, Kevin Corcoran

Rabid

Canada 1976 91m colour
Alpha/Cinepix/Dibar/Famous Players (Dan Goldberg)
V, V*
aka: *Rage*

After extensive intestinal surgery, a woman develops a taste for human blood, infecting her victims with a form of rabies.

Gory though stylish horror about predatory sexuality that features a star of pornographic movies and has gained a cult following.

wd David Cronenberg *ph* René Verzier *m* Ivan Reitman *ad* Claude Marchand *sp* Art Griswold *ed* Jean Lafleur

Marilyn Chambers, Frank Moore, Joe Silver, Howard Ryshpan, Patricia Gage, Susan Roman

Rabid Grannies

Belgium/US 1988 88m (dubbed) colour
Troma/Star Pictures Nr 1 (James Desert, Jonathan Rambert)
V

Two elderly aunts (there is not a granny to be seen) invite their family to a birthday celebration and, under demonic influence, proceed to murder them.

Exceptionally silly and unpleasant, gore-filled horror.

wd Emmanuel Kervyn *ph* Hugo Labye *m* Pierre-Damien Castelain, Jean-Bruno Castelain *pd* Luc Bertrand *ed* Philippe Ravoet

Elie Lison, Catherine Aymerie, Jacques Mayar, Françoise Moens, Robert du Bois, Florine Elslande, Guy Van Riet, Françoise Lamoureux

Race for the Yankee Zephyr

New Zealand/Australia 1981 108m Eastmancolor
Panavision
V*, S

Adventurers discover an American aircraft wrecked in 1944, and argue over the loot without knowing that it contains a 50-million-dollar payroll.

Very moderate adventure story distinguished only by good locations.

w Everett de Roche *d* David Hemmings *ph* Vincent Monton *m* Brian May

Kan Wahl, Lesley Ann Warren, Donald Pleasence, George Peppard, Bruno Lawrence, Robert Bruce

Race Gang: see The Green Cockatoo

Race Street

US 1948 79m bw
RKO (Nat Holt)
L

A bookie vows revenge when his pal is killed by an extortionist gang, but discovers that his girlfriend is married to the leader.

Routine thick ear, quite adequately handled.

w Martin Rackin *story* Maurice Davis *d* Edwin L. Marin *ph* J. Roy Hunt *m* Roy Webb

George Raft, Marilyn Maxwell, William Bendix, Frank Faylen, Henry Morgan, Gale Robbins

Race with the Devil

US 1975 88m DeLuxe
TCF/Saber/Maslansky (Wes Bishop)
V*

Holidaymakers witness a black mass and are pursued by the diabolists.

Silly melodrama which resolves into a wild car chase and much violence.

w Lee Frost, Wes Bishop *d* Jack Starrett *ph* Robert Jessup *m* Leonard Rosenman

Peter Fonda, Warren Oates, Loretta Swit, Lara Parker, R. G. Armstrong

'Why do you need a woman when death is your mistress every afternoon?'

'A love story that hurtles full speed across the barriers of convention!'

The Racers

US 1955 112m DeLuxe Cinemascope
TCF (Julian Blaustein)
GB title: *Such Men Are Dangerous*

A Monte Carlo Rally contestant is financed by an attractive lady gambler.

Routine racing car melodrama, totally unmemorable but impersonally efficient.

w Charles Kaufman *novel* Hans Ruesch *d* Henry Hathaway *ph* Joe MacDonald *m* Alex North

Kirk Douglas, Bella Darvi, Gilbert Roland, Cesar Romero, Lee J. Cobb, Katy Jurado, Charles Goldner, George Dolenz

Rachel and the Stranger *

US 1948 92m bw
RKO (Richard H. Berger)

A Western farmer feels real love for his wife for the first time when an attractive stranger seems likely to take her away from him.

Modestly appealing romantic drama in a Western setting.

w Martin Rackin *novel* Howard Fast *d* Norman Foster *ph* Maury Gertsman *md* Constantin Bakaleinikoff *m* Roy Webb

Loretta Young, Robert Mitchum, William Holden, Gary Gray, Tom Tully, Sara Haden, Frank Ferguson

The Rachel Papers

GB 1989 95m colour
Virgin/Initial Film and Television/Longfellow Pictures (Andrew S. Karsch)
V, V*

A would-be Oxford University student has an on-and-off affair with an American girl.

Bungled attempt at a contemporary comedy of manners.

wd Damian Harris *novel* Martin Amis *ph* Alex Thomson *m* Chaz Jankel, David Storrs *pd* Andrew McAlpine *ed* David Martin

Dexter Fletcher, Ione Skye, Jonathan Pryce, James Spader, Bill Paterson, Shirley Anne Field, Michael Gambon, Lesley Sharp, Jared Harris, Aubrey Morris

Rachel, Rachel **

US 1968 101m Eastmancolor
Warner/Kayos (Paul Newman)
V*

Events in the life of a middle-aged schoolmistress in a small New England town.

Appealing and freshly observed study of a limited personality in a small community.

w Stewart Stern, *novel* A Jest of God *by* Margaret Laurence *d* Paul Newman *ph* Gayne Rescher *m* Jerome Moross

Joanne Woodward, Estelle Parsons, James Olson, Kate Harrington, Donald Moffat, Geraldine Fitzgerald, Bernard Barrow

'It could all very easily degenerate into a woman's weepy; and the fact that it doesn't is due largely to Newman's refusal to treat Manawaka as another Peyton Place.' – *Jan Dawson*

'It tends to verge on dullness, but something always saves it.' – *John Simon*

AAN: best picture; Stewart Stern; Joanne Woodward; Estelle Parsons

Racing with the Moon

US 1984 108m Movielab
Paramount/Jaffe-Lansing (Alain Bernheim, John Kohn)
V*, L

In 1942 California, two young men await induction into the Marines and say goodbye to their girlfriends.

Disappointing flashback by people who fail to capture the spirit of the time, and replace it by conventional boy—girl teenage antics.

w Steven Kloves d Richard Benjamin ph John Bailey m Dave Grusin pd David L. Snyder

Sean Penn, Elizabeth McGovern, Nicolas Cage, John Karlen, Max Showalter

The Rack

US 1956 100m bw
MGM (Arthur M. Loew Jnr)

A veteran of the Korean War is courtmartialled for collaborating with the enemy under torture.

Dullish courtroom melodrama overstretched from a TV play.

w Stewart Stern play Rod Serling d Arnold Laven ph Paul Vogel m Adolph Deutsch

Paul Newman, Walter Pidgeon, Edmond O'Brien, Lee Marvin, Cloris Leachman, Wendell Corey

The Racket *

US 1951 88m bw
RKO/Edmund Grainger
V*, L

Police break up the empire of a powerful gangster.

Oddly timed and rather weak remake of the 1928 film; glossy but very old-fashioned in treatment.

w William Wister Haines play Bartlett Cormack
d John Cromwell ph George E. Diskant
m Constantin Bakaleinikoff

Robert Ryan, Robert Mitchum, Ray Collins, Lizabeth Scott, William Talman

Racket Busters

US 1938 71m bw
Warner (Samuel Bischoff)

A gangster aiming to take over a trucking enterprise is opposed by the special prosecutor's office.

Routine cops and robbers, still very watchable but also forgettable.

w Robert Rossen, Leonardo Bercovici d Lloyd Bacon ph Arthur Edeson m Adolph Deutsch

George Brent, Humphrey Bogart, Gloria Dickson, Allen Jenkins, Walter Abel, Penny Singleton, Henry O'Neill

Rackety Rax

US 1932 65m bw
Fox

Gangster methods are applied to college football.

Stiff burlesque which didn't transfer well from the printed page.

w Ben Markson, Lou Breslow novel Joel Sayre
d Alfred Werker

Victor McLaglen, Greta Nissen, Nell O'Day, Alan Dinehart, Allen Jenkins

Radar Men from the Moon

US 1952 bw serial: 12 eps
Republic

Commander Cody, Sky Marshal of the Universe, settles the hash of moonmen who plan to conquer the Earth.

Hilarious comic strip stuff played with straight faces.

d Fred Brannon

George Wallace, Aline Towne, Roy Barcroft, William Blakewell, Clayton Moore

Radar Patrol vs Spy King

US 1950 bw serial: 12 eps
Republic

International saboteurs threaten America's defence system.

Lively thick ear on formula serial lines.

d Fred C. Brannon

Kirk Alyn, Jean Dean, Anthony Warde, George J. Lewis, Tristram Coffin

Radio City Revels

US 1938 90m bw
RKO

A songwriter can work only in his sleep.

A wisp of plot is the peg for a very moderate revue.

w Matt Brooks, Eddie Davis, Anthony Veiller, Mortimer Offner d Ben Stoloff

Bob Burns, Jack Oakie, Kenny Baker, Victor Moore, Ann Miller, Milton Berle, Helen Broderick, Jane Froman, Buster West, Richard Lane

'Should do well at b.o., but no smash.' – *Variety*

Radio Days **

US 1987 85m DuArt
Orion (Robert Greenhut)
V, V*, L, S

At the beginning of World War II, families near New York are affected by what they hear on the radio.

Shapeless montage of funny bits, best appreciated by those who lived through the time at somewhere near the place.

wd Woody Allen ph Carlo Di Palma m/ed Dick Hyman pd Santo Loquasto ed Susan E. Morse

Mia Farrow, Dianne Wiest, Seth Green, Julie Kavner, Josh Mostel, Michael Tucker, Wallace Shawn

'One of his most purely entertaining pictures.' – *Daily Variety*

AAN: best original screenplay; art direction (Speed Hopkins)

'Powered By Imagination.'
Radio Flyer

US 1992 113m Technicolor Panavision
Columbia/Stonebridge Entertainment (Lauren Shuler-Donner)
V, V*, L, S

A father tells his sons how, when he was young, he and his small brother decided to build a flying machine in an attempt to escape from their increasingly violent stepfather.

An uneasy mix of fantasy and reality that remains stolidly earthbound.

w David Mickey Evans d Richard Donner
ph Laszlo Kovacs m Hans Zimmer ad J. Michael Riva ed Stuart Baird, Dallas Puett

Lorraine Bracco, John Heard, Elijah Wood, Joseph Mazello, Adam Baldwin, Ben Johnson, Tom Hanks (uncredited)

'A film one would like to like more.' – *Variety*

† Originally, David Mickey Evans was assigned to direct with Rosanna Arquette playing the mother, but that production was abandoned. The film was released direct to video in Britain.

Radio On

GB 1979 101m bw
BFI/Road Movies (Keith Griffiths)

A disc-jockey in a biscuit factory makes a haphazard journey from London to Bristol to discover the circumstances of his brother's death.

Inconsequential road movie that can barely summon up any interest in its characters; it is much influenced by the films of Wim Wenders, who was its associate producer.

wd Chris Petit ph Martin Schafer ad Susannah Buxton ed Anthony Sloman

David Beames, Lisa Kreuzer, Sandy Ratcliff, Andrew Byatt, Sue Jones, Sting

'For all its German and American antecedents, however, *Radio On* remains peculiarly English in its concerns and atmosphere. It is in fact one of the most distinguished attempts by a native film-maker to contain all those influences and emerge with a firm sense of its own identity.' – *Richard Combs*

Radio Parade of 1935

GB 1934 96m bw with colour sequence
BIP
US title: *Radio Follies*

Amateur talent makes it big for a radio station.

Historically interesting revue which unfortunately requires its comic lead to play straight.

w Jack Davies, Paul Perez, Arthur Woods, James Bunting d Arthur Woods

Will Hay, Helen Chandler, Clifford Mollison, Davy Burnaby, The Western Brothers, Alfred Drayton, Lily Morris, Nellie Wallace, Clapham and Dwyer, Claude Dampier, Ronald Frankau, Ted Ray, Beryl Orde, Stanelli

Radio Patrol

US 1937 bw serial: 12 eps
Universal

Radio cops foil international crooks who seek a formula for flexible bulletproof steel.

Average serial chapters.

d Ford Beebe, Cliff Smith

Grant Withers, Catherine Hughes, Adrian Morris, Frank Lackteen

Radio Stars on Parade

US 1945 69m bw
Ben Stoloff/RKO

Agents fix up a show despite threats from gangsters.

Slim excuse for a revue including talent popular at the time.

w Robert E. Kent, Monty Brice d Leslie Goodwins

Wally Brown, Alan Carney, Frances Langford, Don Wilson, Tony Romano, Rufe Davis, Sheldon Leonard, Ralph Edwards, Skinnay Ennis and his band

Rafferty and the Gold Dust Twins

US 1975 92m Technicolor Panavision
Warner/Gruskoff-Venture-Linson
V*

A drifter encounters two female vagrants who force him at gunpoint to drive them to New Orleans and get him into various adventures.

Indulgent and unattractive 'road' movie which despite occasional amusing incident gets nowhere very slowly.

w John Kaye d Dick Richards ph Ralph Woolsey
m Artie Butler

Alan Arkin, Sally Kellerman, MacKenzie Phillips, Alex Rocco, Charlie Martin Smith, Harry Dean Stanton, John McLiam

Raffles *

US   1939   72m   bw
Samuel Goldwyn

Raffles the famous cricketer is also a compulsive and daring amateur thief.

Slight, modernized version of the turn-of-the-century stories; very palatable, but it could have been better.

w John Van Druten, Sydney Howard   novel Raffles the Amateur Cracksman by E. W. Hornung   d Sam Wood   ph Gregg Toland   m Victor Young

David Niven, Olivia de Havilland, Dudley Digges, May Whitty, Douglas Walton, Lionel Pape, E. E. Clive, Peter Godfrey

'Fair remake . . . moderate b.o. potential.' – Variety

† This was virtually a scene-for-scene remake of the 1930 Goldwyn version starring Ronald Colman, Kay Francis and Alison Skipworth. It was written by Sidney Howard and George Fitzmaurice.

Rage

US   1966   103m   Technicolor
Columbia/Joseph M. Schenck/Cinematografico Jalisco (Gilberto Gazcon)

A drunken doctor finds a new will to live during a difficult journey to avert a rabies epidemic.

Pattern melodrama with no surprises, but gripping most of the way.

w Teddi Sherman, Gilberto Gazcon, Fernando Mendez   d Gilberto Gazcon   ph Rosalio Solano   m Gustavo Cesar Carreon

Glenn Ford, Stella Stevens, David Reynoso, Armando Silvestre

Rage

US   1972   99m   DeLuxe   Panavision
Warner (Fred Weintraub)
V*

A father takes revenge when his son dies after a chemical warfare accident.

Well-meaning but turgid and boring melodrama.

w Philip Friedman, Dan Kleinman   d George C. Scott   ph Fred Koenekamp   m Lalo Schifrin

George C. Scott, Richard Basehart, Martin Sheen, Barnard Hughes, Stephen Young

'Sluggish, tired and tiring.' – Variety

Rage at Dawn

US   1955   86m   Technicolor
Nat Holt/RKO
V*

Detectives stage a fake train robbery to attract the evil Reno brothers.

Very moderate Western programmer.

w Horace McCoy   d Tim Whelan

Randolph Scott, Forrest Tucker, J. Carrol Naish, Mala Powers, Edgar Buchanan, Ray Teal

A Rage in Harlem **

GB   1991   108m   DeLuxe
Palace/Miramax (Stephen Woolley, Kerry Boyle)
V, V*, L, S

In 1950s Harlem, a gullible undertaker's assistant gives refuge to a gangster's mistress with a trunkful of gold.

Lively, entertaining, fast-paced tongue-in-cheek thriller.

w John Toles-Bey, Bobby Crawford   novel Chester Himes   d Bill Duke   ph Toyomichi Kurita   m Elmer Bernstein   pd Steven Legler   ed Curtis Clayton

Forest Whitaker, Gregory Hines, Robin Givens, Zakes Mokae, Danny Glover, Badja Djola, John Toles-Bey, Ron Taylor, Samm-Art Williams

'Many will be turned off by the excessive bloodshed, but the fine cast keeps the pic watchable.' – Variety

'Enjoyable though it is, Bill Duke's mix of brisk action, sexy innuendo and cameo-studded comedy takes considerable liberties with the spirit of Himes' Harlem.' – Jonathan Romney, Sight and Sound

Rage in Heaven

US   1941   82m   bw
MGM (Gottfried Reinhardt)

An unstable millionaire becomes jealous of his wife and arranges his own death so that her supposed lover will be suspected.

Stilted melodrama with the stars more or less at sea.

w Christopher Isherwood, Robert Thoeren   novel James Hilton   d W. S. Van Dyke II   ph Oliver T. Marsh   m Bronislau Kaper

Robert Montgomery, Ingrid Bergman, George Sanders, Lucile Watson, Oscar Homolka, Philip Merivale, Matthew Boulton, Aubrey Mather

'Nothing happens but the obvious, and that only after a long and confused struggle.' – Otis Ferguson

The Rage of Paris *

US   1938   78m   bw
Universal (B. G. de Sylva)
V*

Confidence tricksters invest their money in a French girl who is out to nail a millionaire.

If memory serves right, an amusingly amoral trifle in the best style of its year.

w Bruce Manning, Felix Jackson   d Henry Koster

Danielle Darrieux, Douglas Fairbanks Jnr, Louis Hayward, Mischa Auer, Helen Broderick, Harry Davenport, Samuel S. Hinds, Mary Martin (in a bit part)

'Smart comedy of first-run calibre . . . a finished and polished job.' – Variety

'The names and the places didn't matter – only when!'

A Rage to Live

US   1965   101m   bw   Panavision
UA/Mirisch (Lewis J. Rachmil)

The unhappy college and married life of a nymphomaniac.

Well made but deliberately 'daring' case history which becomes too obvious and silly.

w John T. Kelley   novel John O'Hara   d Walter Grauman   ph Charles Lawton   m Nelson Riddle

Suzanne Pleshette, Bradford Dillman, Ben Gazzara, Peter Graves, Bethel Leslie, James Gregory, Ruth White

'Stuff like this needs the exuberance of grand opera; sadly, all it gets here is a blue note.' – MFB

Raggedy Ann and Andy *

US   1977   85m   Movielab   Panavision
Lester Osterman (Richard Horner)

Toys come to life and have their own adventures while their owner is absent.

Attractive fully animated cartoon feature in which only the central story is lacking in pace and humour.

w Patricia Thackray, Max Wilk   stories Johnny Gruelle   d Richard Williams   m Joe Raposo

Raggedy Man

US   1981   94m   Technicolor
Universal/William D. Wittliff, Burt Weissbourd
V*, L

In 1944, a small-town switchboard operator and her two children are protected by a mysterious stranger.

Curious and quite unnecessary melodrama of some skill but very dubious appeal.

w William D. Wittliff   d Jack Fisk   ph Ralf Bode   m Jerry Goldsmith   ed Edward Warschilka

Sissy Spacek, Eric Roberts, Sam Shepard, William Sanderson, Tracey Walter, R. G. Armstrong

'Despite the casual, unhurried pace of the film, it doesn't seem to observe much.' – Richard Combs, MFB

The Raggedy Rawney *

GB   1987   103m   Technicolor
Virgin/HandMade (Bob Weis)
V, S

An army deserter disguises himself as a woman and joins a group of wandering gypsies.

Downbeat rural tale, providing cold comfort.

w Bob Hoskins, Nicole de Wilde   d Bob Hoskins   ph Frank Tidy   m Michael Kamen   pd Jiri Matolin   ed Alan Jones

Bob Hoskins, Dexter Fletcher, Zoe Nathenson, Zoe Wanamaker, David Hill, Ian Dury, Ian McNiece, Veronica Clifford, Gawn Grainger, Jim Carter

Raging Bull ****

US   1980   119m   colour
UA/Chartoff-Winkler
V, V*

The rise to fame of an unlikeable middle-weight boxer, based on the autobiography of Jake La Motta.

Tough, compelling, powerfully made ringside melodrama. A poll of American critics voted it the best movie of the 1980s.

w Paul Schrader, Mardik Martin   d Martin Scorsese   ph Michael Chapman   m from library sources   pd Gene Rudolf

Robert de Niro, Cathy Moriarty, Joe Pesci, Frank Vincent, Nicholas Colasanto

'Scorsese makes pictures about the kind of people you wouldn't want to know.' – Variety

'A bravura display of cinematic skill.' – Daily Mail

AA: editing (Thelma Schoonmaker); Robert de Niro

AAN: best film; best direction; Cathy Moriarty; Joe Pesci; Michael Chapman

BFA: editing

The Raging Moon *

GB   1970   111m   Technicolor
EMI (Bruce Cohn Curtis)
V, V*
aka: Long Ago Tomorrow

A love affair develops between two inmates of a home for the physically handicapped.

Appealing romantic drama which nearly became a big commercial success.

wd Bryan Forbes   novel Peter Marshall   ph Tony Imi   m Stanley Myers

Malcolm McDowell, Nanette Newman, Georgia Brown, Bernard Lee, Gerald Sim, Michael Flanders

The Raging Tide

US   1951   93m   bw
U-I (Aaron Rosenberg)

A San Francisco gangster stows away on a fishing trawler and redeems himself when he perishes saving the life of a fisherman.

Fearfully old-fashioned seafaring melodrama, rather well made.

w Ernest K. Gann   novel Fiddler's Green by Ernest K. Gann   d George Sherman   ph Russell Metty   m Frank Skinner

Richard Conte, Charles Bickford, Shelley Winters, Stephen McNally, Alex Nicol, Jesse White, John McIntire

Raging Waters: see Green Promise

Una Ragione per Vivere e Una per Morire: see
A Reason to Live, a Reason to Die

The Ragman's Daughter
GB   1972   94m   Technicolor
TCF/Penelope (Harold Becker)

A Nottingham layabout falls in love with an exciting
middle-class girl; they fail to overcome parental
opposition and she is killed in a road accident.

Wispy drama framed in pointless flashbacks; done on
the cheap, it never seems to get anywhere and even
fails to use its locations to advantage.

w Alan Sillitoe   *story* Alan Sillitoe   *d* Harold
Becker   *ph* Michael Seresin   *m* Kenny Clayton

Simon Rouse, Victoria Tennant, Patrick O'Connell,
Leslie Sands

'What a time it was, an incredible time, a good time, a bad
time ...'

Ragtime *
US   1981   155m   Technicolor   Todd-AO
Ragtime/Sunley (Dino de Laurentiis)
V*, L

Just before World War I, various Americans are
affected by world events, and a chapter of accidents
turns a placid Negro into a revolutionary.

The fascinating patchwork of the novel has been
virtually abandoned in favour of its least interesting
episode, which is even further drawn out by the
decision to bring on the aged James Cagney as a
comic turn not in the novel. The early sequences show
what might have been.

w Michael Weller   *novel* E. L. Doctorow   *d* Milos
Forman   *ph* Miroslav Ondricek   *m* Randy Newman
ad John Graysmark, Patrizia von Brandenstein,
Anthony Reading

James Olson, Mary Steenburgen, James Cagney, Pat
O'Brien, Elizabeth McGovern, *Howard E. Rollins Jnr,*
Brad Dourif, Moses Gunn, Kenneth McMillan,
Donald O'Connor

'It's limp . . . it always seems to be aiming about
halfway toward the effects that Doctorow achieved in
his literary extravaganza.' – *New Yorker*

'The book, despite its defects, was funny, radical and
angry. The film, despite its virtues, is solemn, liberal
and passive.' – *Sunday Times*

† The film cost 32 million dollars and took eleven.

AAN: screenplay; Miroslav Ondricek; Randy
Newman; Elizabeth McGovern (supporting actress);
Howard E. Rollins Jnr; art direction; song 'One More
Hour'

The Raid *
US   1954   83m   Technicolor
TCF (Robert L. Jacks)

In 1864 six confederate soldiers escape from a union
prison, and from a Canadian refuge carry out a
revenge raid on a small Vermont town.

Interesting little action drama, crisply characterized
and plotted, and based on a historical incident.

w Sidney Boehm,   *story* Affair at St Albans by Herbert
Ravenal Sass   *d* Hugo Fregonese   *ph* Lucien Ballard
m Roy Webb

Van Heflin, Anne Bancroft, Richard Boone, Lee
Marvin, Tommy Rettig, Peter Graves, Douglas
Spencer, Will Wright, John Dierkes

Raid on Rommel
US   1971   99m   Technicolor
Universal (Harry Tatelman)
V (W), V*

In North Africa during World War II, a British officer
releases prisoners of war and leads them in an assault
on Tobruk.

Dispirited low-budget actioner apparently first
intended for television.

w Richard Bluel   *d* Henry Hathaway   *ph* Earl Rath
m Hal Mooney

Richard Burton, John Colicos, Clinton Greyn,
Wolfgang Preiss

The Raiders (1952): see *Riders of Vengeance*

The Raiders
US   1964   75m   Technicolor
Revue/Universal

Cattle drovers enlist the aid of famous Western
characters to persuade the railroad company to extend
its line through dangerous country.

Slightly oddball Western with endearing moments
amid the miscalculations.

w Gene L. Coon   *d* Herschel Daugherty

Robert Culp (as Wild Bill Hickok), Judi Meredith (as
Calamity Jane), James McMullan (as Buffalo Bill
Cody), Brian Keith, Alfred Ryder, Simon Oakland

Raiders of Ghost City
US   1944   bw   serial: 13 eps
Universal

During the Civil War, fake confederates steal bullion
shipments, and a Union secret service agent is sent to
investigate.

Solid Western adventures.

d Ray Taylor, Lewis D. Collins

Dennis Moore, Wanda McKay, Lionel Atwill, Joe
Sawyer, Regis Toomey

Raiders of the Lost Ark **
US   1981   115m   Metrocolor   Panavision
Paramount/Lucasfilm (Frank Marshall)
V, V*, L, S

In the thirties, an American archaeologist and
explorer beats the Nazis to a priceless artefact, the
magical box containing fragments of the stones on
which God wrote his laws.

Commercially very successful, this attempted wrap-
up of the Saturday morning serials of two generations
ago spends a great deal of money and expertise on
frightening us rather than exciting us; in Dolby sound
the experience is horrendous. Second time round, one
can better enjoy the ingenious detail of the hero's
exploits and ignore the insistence on unpleasantness;
still, there are boring bits in between, and the story
doesn't make a lot of sense.

w Lawrence Kasdan   *d* Steven Spielberg   *ph* Douglas
Slocombe   *m* John Williams   *pd* Norman Reynolds

Harrison Ford, Karen Allen, Ronald Lacey, Paul
Freeman, John Rhys-Davies, Denholm Elliott

'Both de trop and not enough.' – *Sight and Sound*

'Children may well enjoy its simple-mindedness,
untroubled by the fact that it looks so shoddy and so
uninventive.' – *Observer*

'Kinesthetically, the film gets to you, but there's no
exhilaration, and no surge of feeling at the end.' –
Pauline Kael, New Yorker

'An out of body experience, a movie of glorious
imagination and breakneck speed that grabs you in
the first shot, hurtles you through a series of
incredible adventures, and deposits you back in
reality two hours later – breathless, dizzy, wrung-out,
and with a silly grin on your face.' – *Roger Ebert*

† Tom Selleck was the first choice for the lead, but
was tied up with his TV series *Magnum.*
†† It was followed by two sequels: *Indiana Jones and
the Temple of Doom* and *Indiana Jones and the Last Crusade*
(qqv).

AA: editing (Michael Kahn); visual effects

AAN: best picture; Steven Spielberg; Douglas
Slocombe; John Williams

BFA: Norman Reynolds

Railroaded *
US   1947   72m   bw
Charles F. Reisner/Eagle Lion

A detective is on the trail of a ruthless mobster.

A new post-war toughness was evident in this
sharply made second feature.

w John C. Higgins, Gertrude Walker   *d* Anthony
Mann

John Ireland, Sheila Ryan, Hugh Beaumont, Jane
Randolph, Ed Kelly, Charles D. Brown

Rails into Laramie
US   1954   81m   Technicolor
Universal-International

Railway construction is hampered in Laramie by a
salon keeper who keeps the workers too happy.

Solid co-feature Western, quite enjoyable.

w D. D. Beauchamp, Joseph Hoffman   *d* Jesse
Hibbs

John Payne, Dan Duryea, Mari Blanchard, Barton
MacLane, Harry Shannon, Lee Van Cleef

'A film for adults to take their children, too!'
The Railway Children ***
GB   1970   108m   Technicolor
EMI (Robert Lynn)
V*

Three Edwardian children and their mother move into
Yorkshire when their father is imprisoned as a spy,
and have adventures on the railway line while
helping to prove his innocence.

Fresh and agreeable family film with many pleasing
touches to compensate for its meandering plot.

wd Lionel Jeffries,   *novel* E. Nesbit   *ph* Arthur Ibbetson
m Johnny Douglas

Dinah Sheridan, William Mervyn, Jenny Agutter,
Bernard Cribbins, Iain Cuthbertson, Gary Warren,
Sally Thomsett

'There are passages in Mr Jeffries' deliberately
nostalgic film which may appeal more to sensitive
parents than to their bloodthirsty offspring. But
everybody, I hope, will enjoy the playing.' – *Dilys
Powell*

Rain *
US   1932   92m   bw
UA/Art Cinema Corporation (Joseph Schenck)
V*

Stranded passengers in Pago Pago during an epidemic
include a prostitute and a missionary who lusts after
her.

Early talkie version of a much filmed story; interesting
but not very entertaining now that the sensational
aspects have worn off.

w Maxwell Anderson   *play* John Colton, Clemence
Randolph   *story* W. Somerset Maugham   *ph* Lewis
Milestone   *ph* Oliver T. Marsh   *m* Alfred Newman

Joan Crawford, Walter Huston, William Gargan,
Beulah Bondi, Matt Moore, Guy Kibbee, Walter
Catlett

'A b.o. disappointer. Only the play's rep and Joan
Crawford's personal pull will save it.' – *Variety*

† Other versions: *Sadie Thompson* (1928) with Gloria
Swanson; *Miss Sadie Thompson* (1953) (qv).

Rain Man **
US   1988   133m   DeLuxe
UIP/United Artists/Guber-Peters (Mark Johnson)
V, V*, L, S

A fast-talking salesman discovers, on his father's
death, that he has an autistic elder brother.

An intelligent road movie, but one that does not move
far enough from more conventional buddy-buddy
movies.

w Ronald Bass, Barry Morrow   *d Barry Levinson*
ph John Seale   *m* Hans Zimmer   *pd* Ida Random
ed Stu Linder, Thomas R. Moore

Dustin Hoffman, Tom Cruise, Valeria Golino, Jerry
Molen, Jack Murdock, Michael D. Roberts, Ralph
Seymour, Lucinda Jenney, Bonnie Hunt

AA: best picture; best director; best original
screenplay; Dustin Hoffman

AAN: best original score; best cinematography; best
film editing; best art direction

Rain or Shine *
US   1930   90m   bw
Columbia (Harry Cohn)

A circus performer puts on a one-man show in an
attempt to stop it from closing.

A musical comedy translated to the screen without its
songs as a showcase for the acrobatic, slack-wire and
juggling talents of its star, a Broadway comedian
famous for his wide smile and nonsense patter.

w Jo Swerling, Dorothy Howell   *musical comedy:*
James Gleason, Maurice Marks   *d* Frank Capra
ph Joe Walker   *md* Bakaleinikoff   *ed* Maurice
Wright

Joe Cook, Louise Fazenda, Joan Peers, William
Collier Jnr, Tom Howard

The Rain People
US   1969   101m   Technicolor
Warner/American Zoetrope (Bart Patton, Ronald Colby)
V*

A depressed housewife leaves home, drives across
country, and picks up a mentally retarded hitch-hiker
who tries to protect her.

Slow, pretentious character drama which strains after
art but only presents an unedifying study of failure.

wd Francis Ford Coppola   *ph* Wilmer Butler
m Ronald Stein

Shirley Knight, James Caan, Robert Duvall, Tom
Aldredge, Marya Zimmet

'The rain people are people made of rain and when
they cry they disappear because they cry themselves
away.' – *sample dialogue*

The Rainbow *
GB   1988   111m   Technicolor
Vestron (Ken Russell)
V, V*, L, S

Determined to be independent, a farmer's daughter
rejects her lover to go to university.

Over-simplified version of the novel, but watchable
enough.

w Ken Russell, Vivian Russell   *novel* D. H.
Lawrence   *d* Ken Russell   *ph* Billy Williams
m Carl Davis   *pd* Luciana Arrighi   *ed* Peter Davies

Sammi Davis, Paul McGann, Amanda Donohue,
Christopher Gable, David Hemmings, Glenda
Jackson, Dudley Sutton, Jim Carter, Judith Paris, Ken
Colley

'The siren of the sarongs is calling you!'
Rainbow Island
US   1944   95m   Technicolor
Paramount (I. D. Leshin)

A white girl brought up by her doctor father on a
Pacific island is pursued by three sailors escaping
from the Japanese.

Cheerful spoof of the sarong cycle with the star seeing
the joke; otherwise a silly service farce with South Sea
trimmings.

w Walter de Leon, Seena Owen, Arthur Phillips
d Ralph Murphy   *ph* Karl Struss   *m* Roy Webb
songs Burton Lane, Ted Koehler

Dorothy Lamour, Eddie Bracken, Gil Lamb, Barry
Sullivan, Forrest Orr, Anne Revere, Reed Hadley,
Marc Lawrence

The Rainbow Jacket
GB   1954   99m   Technicolor
Ealing (Michael Relph)

A boy jockey is blackmailed into losing a big race.

Disappointing racecourse drama which packs in all
the expected ingredients.

w T. E. B. Clarke   *d* Basil Dearden   *ph* Otto Heller
m William Alwyn

Kay Walsh, Bill Owen, Edward Underdown, Robert
Morley, Wilfrid Hyde-White, Charles Victor, Honor
Blackman, Sidney James

'Probably the best racing film ever made.' – *C. A.
Lejeune*

Rainbow on the River
US   1936   83m   bw
Sol Lesser (RKO)

After the Civil War, an orphan is brought up by a
Black mammy and later discovered to be rich.

Sentimental drama with songs from its boy star; not
much, but popular.

w Earle Snell, William Hurlbut   *story* Mrs C. V.
Jamison   *d* Kurt Neumann

Bobby Breen, May Robson, Charles Butterworth,
Louise Beavers, Alan Mowbray, Benita Hume, Henry
O'Neill

'Phoney and over-sugared sentimentality.' – *Variety*

Rainbow round My Shoulder
US   1952   78m   Technicolor
Columbia

A society girl breaks into show business.

Agreeable light musical for the easily pleased.

w Blake Edwards, Richard Quine   *d* Richard Quine

Frankie Laine, Billy Daniels, Charlotte Austin, Arthur
Franz, Ida Moore, Lloyd Corrigan

Raining Stones **
GB   1993   91m   colour
First Independent/Parallax/Channel 4 (Sally Hibbin)
V

An unemployed Catholic father tries to raise the
money to buy a communion dress for his seven-year-
old daughter.

A realistic drama about working-class lives,
absorbing, richly detailed and welcome as one of the
few British films of recent years to concern itself with
contemporary, everyday life and its problems.

w Jim Allen   *d* Ken Loach   *ph* Barry Ackroyd
m Stewart Copeland   *pd* Martin Johnson
ed Jonathan Morris

Bruce Jones, Julie Brown, Gemma Phoenix, Ricky
Tomlinson, Tom Hickey, Mike Fallon, Ronnie Ravey,
Lee Brennan

'The film contains more truth and humor than many a
large-screen picture, and is sure to captivate audiences
who seek it out.' – *Variety*

The Rainmaker
US   1956   121m   Technicolor   Vistavision
Paramount/Hal B. Wallis (Paul Nathan)
V*, L

In 1913 Kansas, a fake rainmaker has more success
melting the heart of a confirmed spinster.

Such a whimsical play is too talky to make a good
movie, especially as the actors are over-age, their
performances are mannered, the dialogue seems
interminable and the production is too stagey.

w N. Richard Nash   *play* N. Richard Nash
d Joseph Anthony   *ph* Charles Lang Jnr   *m* Alex
North

Katharine Hepburn, Burt Lancaster, Wendell Corey,
Lloyd Bridges, Earl Holliman, Cameron Prud'homme,
Wallace Ford

AAN: Alex North; Katharine Hepburn

The Rainmakers
US   1935   79m   bw
RKO

Fake rainmakers are chased by midwestern farmers to
California, where they get involved in an irrigation
scheme.

Slow-paced comedy with a train chase finale which
comes too late.

w Grant Garrett, Leslie Goodwins   *d* Fred Guiol

Bert Wheeler, Robert Woolsey, Dorothy Lee, Berton
Churchill, George Meeker

'May appeal mildly to their fans, but won't make new
business.' – *Variety*

The Rains Came ***
US   1939   103m   bw
TCF (Harry Joe Brown)

High-class parasites in India during the Raj redeem
themselves when a flood disaster strikes.

Wholly absorbing disaster spectacular in which the
characterization and personal plot development are at
least as interesting as the spectacle, and all are
encased in a glowingly professional production.

w Philip Dunne, Julien Josephson,   *novel* Louis
Bromfield   *d* Clarence Brown   *ph* Arthur Miller
m Alfred Newman   *sp* Fred Sersen   *ed* Barbara McLean

Myrna Loy, *George Brent,* Tyrone Power, Brenda Joyce,
Maria Ouspenskaya, Joseph Schildkraut, H. B. Warner,
Nigel Bruce, Mary Nash, Jane Darwell, Marjorie
Rambeau, Henry Travers

'A big box-office picture with the advantage of a new
locale.' – *Variety*

'It would be difficult to improve on the direction,
the outbreak of the monsoon, a curtain billowing
in the breeze, a lamp casting the shadow of lattice
work against white silk, servants scattering for
cover . . .' – *Charles Higham, 1972*

'Slick Hollywood film-making at its professional
best.' – *Channel 4, 1982*

† Myrna Loy was third choice after Dietrich and
Lamarr; Brent second choice after Ronald Colman.

AAN: Alfred Newman; editing

The Rains of Ranchipur
US   1955   104m   Eastmancolor   Cinemascope
TCF (Frank Ross)

Dismal remake of *The Rains Came,* with bored actors
and inferior production, all the character of the
original being wiped out by badly processed widescreen spectacle.

w Merle Miller   *d* Jean Negulesco   *ph* Milton
Krasner   *m* Hugo Friedhofer

Lana Turner, Fred MacMurray, Richard Burton, Joan
Caulfield, Eugenie Leontovich, Michael Rennie

Raintree County
US   1957   166m   Technicolor   Panavision
(Camera 65)
MGM (David Lewis)
V*

During the Civil War a Southern belle gets the man
she thinks she wants, but subsequently finds life as a
schoolmaster's wife boring.

Dreary attempt by MGM to out-do *Gone with the Wind,*
with neither characters nor plot one third as
interesting and the production values merely
expensive.

w Millard Kaufman   *novel* Ross Lockridge
d Edward Dmytryk   *ph* Robert Surtees   *m* Johnny
Green   *ad* William A. Horning, Urie McCleary

Montgomery Clift, Elizabeth Taylor, Eva Marie Saint,
Nigel Patrick, Lee Marvin, Rod Taylor, Agnes
Moorehead, Walter Abel, Jarma Lewis, Tom Drake,
Gardner McKay, Rhys Williams

AAN: Johnny Green; Elizabeth Taylor; art direction

'China. 1920's. One master, four wives . . . One fate.'
Raise the Red Lantern **
Hong Kong   1991   125m   Eastmancolor
Palace/Era/China Film (Chiu Fu-Sheng)
V, V*, L
original title: *Dahong Denglong Gaogao Gua*

A young woman, who has become the fourth wife of a
rich merchant, finds herself in competition with his
other wives for her husband's favour.

Cool study of sexual politics and the subjugation of
women.

w Ni Zhen   *story* Su Tong   *d* Zhang Yimou
ph Zhao Fei   *m* Zhao Jiping   *ad* Cao Jiuping,
Dong Huamiao   *ed* Du Yuan

Gong Li, Ma Jingwu, He Caifei, Cao Cuifeng, Jin
Shuyuan, Kong Li, Ding Weimin, Cui Zhigang, Chu
Xiao

AAN: best foreign film

Raise the Roof
GB   1930   77m   bw
BIP

An actress is bribed to sabotage a touring show.

Early talkie which retains surprising freshness.

w Walter Summers, Philip MacDonald   *d* Walter
Summers

Betty Balfour, Maurice Evans, Jack Raine, Sam
Livesey, Ellis Jeffreys

† Credited as the first British musical.

Raise the Titanic!
US   1980   122m   DeLuxe
Lord Grade/Martin Starger (William Frye)
V*, L

Assorted Americans try to recover rare minerals from
the wreck of the ship which sank in the North
Atlantic in 1912.

Heavy-going exploiter with little action and even less
plot.

w Adam Kennedy, Eric Hughes   *novel* Clive Cussler
d Jerry Jameson   *ph* Matthew F. Leonetti   *second
unit ph* Rex Metz   *underwater ph* Bob Steadman
m John Barry   *pd* John F. DeCuir

Jason Robards, Richard Jordan, Alec Guinness, David
Selby, Anne Archer, J. D. Cannon

'Hits new depths hitherto unexplored by the worst of
Lew Grade's overloaded ark melodramas. This one
wastes a potentially intriguing premise with dull
scripting, a lacklustre cast, laughably phony trick
work and clunky direction that makes *Voyage of the
Damned* seem inspired by comparison.' – *Variety*

'The longer it all goes on, the more one hopes that, if
they ever do raise the *Titanic*, they'll heave the film
overboard to replace it.' – *Guardian*

† The film cost 40 million dollars and took 7 million.

A Raisin in the Sun *
US   1961   128m   bw
Columbia/Paman – Doris (David Susskind, Philip Rose)
V*, L

The life of a struggling black family in a cramped
Chicago flat.

Earnest but claustrophobic play-on-film which long
outstays its welcome but contains good performances.

w *Lorraine Hansberry*,   *play* Lorraine Hansberry
d Daniel Petrie   *ph* Charles Lawton Jnr
m Laurence Rosenthal

Sidney Poitier, Ruby Dee, Claudia McNeil, Diana
Sands, Ivan Dixon, John Fielder, Lou Gossett

Raising a Riot
GB   1955   90m   Technicolor
British Lion/Wessex (Ian Dalrymple, Hugh Perceval)

With his wife away, a naval officer tries to cope with
his three lively children while staying with his
elderly father in a derelict windmill.

Sentimental domestic comedy that goes for easy
laughs and misses most of them.

w Ian Dalrymple, Hugh Perceval   *novel* Alfred
Toombs   *d* Wendy Toye   *ph* Christopher Challis
md Muir Mathieson   *m* Bruce Montgomery
ad Joseph Bato   *ed* Albert Rule

Kenneth More, Shelagh Fraser, Ronald Squire, Olga
Lindo, Jan Miller, Nora Nicholson, Lionel Murton,
Mandy, Gary Billings, Fusty Bentine, Robin Brown

Raising Arizona *
US   1987   94m   DuArt
Circle Films/TCF
V, V*, L

In the American heartlands, a petty crook falls for the
lady cop who regularly checks him into jail.

Zany collection of incidents which scarcely welds
itself into a story but offers a few laughs along the
way.

w Ethan and Joel Coen   *d* Joel Coen

Nicolas Cage, Holly Hunter, Trey Wilson, John
Goodman, William Forsythe

'When Jenny cheated on her husband, he didn't just leave
. . . he split.'
Raising Cain
US   1992   92m   colour
UIP/Universal (Gale Anne Hurd)
V, V*, L, S

A psychologist develops multiple personalities,
including that of a murderous twin brother.

Risible thriller, stuffed full of shock moments that
hamper the narrative flow, and growing increasingly
ridiculous throughout; it fails to repay its huge debt to
Peeping Tom and to Hitchcock.

wd Brian de Palma   *ph* Stephen H. Burum   *m* Pino
Donaggio   *pd* Doug Kraner   *ed* Paul Hirsch, Bonnie
Koehler, Robert Dalva

John Lithgow, Lolita Davidovich, Steven Bauer,
Frances Sternhagen, Gregg Henry, Tom Bower, Mel
Harris, Teri Austin, Gabrielle Carteris

'Scandalously prodigal with its loose ends and red
herrings, and scandalously unfair with its narrative
let-outs.' – *Sight and Sound*

'A superficial, often risible, exercise in pure aesthetics
that's likely to turn off mainstream audiences,
spelling a fast flop.' – *Variety*

Raising the Wind
GB   1961   91m   colour
GHW/Anglo Amalgamated
V
US title: *Roommates*

Misadventures of students at a music academy.

A Carry On in all but name, from the same stable;
good moments among the dross.

w Bruce Montgomery   *d* Gerald Thomas

James Robertson Justice, Leslie Phillips, Kenneth
Williams, Sidney James, Paul Massie, Liz Fraser, Eric
Barker, Jennifer Jayne, Geoffrey Keen, Esma Cannon

The Rake's Progress *
GB   1945   123m   bw
GFD/Individual (Frank Launder, Sidney Gilliat)
US title: *Notorious Gentleman*

The career of a cheerful ne'er-do-well playboy of the
thirties.

The road to ruin played for light comedy, with silly
endpapers in which, quite out of character, the rake
becomes a war hero. Generally good production,
witty script.

w Frank Launder, Sidney Gilliat   *story* Val
Valentine   *d* Sidney Gilliat   *ph* Wilkie Cooper
m William Alwyn   *pd* David Rawnsley

Rex Harrison, Lilli Palmer, Margaret Johnston,
Godfrey Tearle, Griffith Jones, Guy Middleton, Jean
Kent, Marie Lohr, Garry Marsh, David Horne, Alan
Wheatley

† In the American version Harrison crowned the
Martyrs' Memorial not with a chamber pot but with a
top hat.

Rally Round the Flag Boys
US   1958   106m   DeLuxe   Cinemascope
TCF (Leo McCarey)
V

A small community protests at the siting nearby of a
missile base.

Raucous service and sex comedy which becomes
frenetic without ever being very funny.

w Claude Binyon, Leo McCarey   *novel* Max
Shulman   *d* Leo McCarey   *ph* Leon Shamroy
m Cyril Mockridge

Paul Newman, Joanne Woodward, Joan Collins, Jack
Carson, Dwayne Hickman, Tuesday Weld, Gale
Gordon, Murvyn Vye

'She has been quite promiscuous since early childhood.
She has absolutely no control over her sexual impulses.
Miss Rosebud has arrived!'
Rambling Rose **
US   1991   112m   DuArt/DeLuxe
Guild/Carolco (Renny Harlin)
V, V*, L, S

During the Depression, a boy becomes infatuated
with a sexually-free young woman who comes to
work at his home.

Gripping domestic drama that gains from its period
setting.

w Calder Willingham   *novel* Calder Willingham
d Martha Coolidge   *ph* Johnny E. Jensen
m Elmer Bernstein   *pd* John Vallone   *ed* Steven
Cohen

Laura Dern, Robert Duvall, Diane Ladd, Lukas Haas,
John Heard, Kevin Conway, Robert Burke, Lisa
Jakub, Evan Lockwood, Matt Sutherland

'A quiet, unassertive picture, very literary in the
memories it evokes, full of universal insights into
family life, and performed with delicacy by all
concerned.' – *Philip French, Guardian*

AAN: Laura Dern; Diane Ladd

Rambo: First Blood Part Two
US   1985   92m   Technicolor   Panavision
Anabasis Investments NV/Buzz Feitshans
V, V*, L

A special ops veteran is sent to spring POWs in
Vietnam.

Absurdly overwrought comic strip action which
shamefully caught the mood of America at the time of
its release.

w Sylvester Stallone, James Cameron   *d* George Pan
Cosmatos   *ph* Jack Cardiff   *m* Jerry Goldsmith

Sylvester Stallone, Richard Crenna, Charles Napier,
Julia Nickson, Steven Berkoff

'One mounting fireball . . . risible production, comic book heroics.' – *Variety*

Rambo III

US 1988 101m Technicolor
Columbia TriStar/Carolco (Buzz Feitshans)
V, V*, L, S

Rambo invades Afghanistan to rescue a friend captured by the Soviet forces.

More ludicrously melodramatic heroics, with Stallone as a one-man army defeating the massed forces of the enemy.

w Sylvester Stallone, Sheldon Lettich *d* Peter MacDonald *ph* John Stanier *m* Jerry Goldsmith *pd* Bill Kenney *ed* James Symons, Andrew London, O. Nicholas Brown, Edward Warschilka

Sylvester Stallone, Richard Crenna, Marc de Jonge, Kurtwood Smith, Spiros Focas, Sasson Gabai

† Russel Mulcahy began directing the film but left after a few days. It was the most expensive film made to that date, costing in excess of $60 million.

Ramona

US 1936 90m Technicolor
TCF (Sol M. Wurtzel)

A half-breed girl and an Indian chief's son combat the greed of white pioneers.

Old-fashioned, stuffy adventure romance, much filmed in silent days.

w Lamar Trotti *novel* Helen Hunt Jackson *d* Henry King *ph* William Skall, Chester Lyons *m* Alfred Newman

Loretta Young, Don Ameche, Kent Taylor, Pauline Frederick, Jane Darwell, Katherine de Mille, Victor Kilian, John Carradine

Rampage

US 1963 98m Technicolor
Warner Seven Arts/Talbot (William Fadiman)
V

Two white hunters love the same girl; one releases a tiger to harm the other, but it escapes.

Silly, unconvincing, old-style melodrama in which even the animals seem to overact.

w Robert Holt, Marguerite Roberts *novel* Alan Caillou *d* Phil Karlson *ph* Harold Lipstein *m* Elmer Bernstein

Robert Mitchum, Jack Hawkins, Elsa Martinelli, Sabu, Emile Genest

The Ramparts We Watch *

US 1940 87m bw
RKO/Louis de Rochemont

A typical American family exemplifies the need for military preparedness.

A feature acted by amateurs, produced by the March of Time unit; interesting rather than influential, as it still took Pearl Harbor to bring the Americans into the war.

w Robert Richards, Cedric B. Worth *d* Louis de Rochemont

'It enters the fray with frankness in its favour.' – *Variety*

'A woman is soft and warm . . . and deadlier than steel!'
Ramrod

US 1947 94m bw
(MGM) Enterprise
V*

A predatory lady ranch owner hires a tough foreman and her ruthlessness causes several deaths and a stampede.

Ho-hum minor Western with fading stars.

w Jack Moffit, Graham Baker, Cecile Kramer *story* Luke Short *d* André de Toth *ph* Russell Harlan *m* Adolph Deutsch

Veronica Lake, Joel McCrea, Preston Foster, Charles Ruggles, Donald Crisp, Arleen Whelan, Lloyd Bridges

Ran ****

Japan 1985 161m colour
Herald-Ace/Nippon-Herald/Greenwich (Masato Hara, Serge Silberman)
V, V*, L, S

A Japanese version of *King Lear*, with three sons instead of three daughters.

Predictable bloodshed and tremendous style are evident in this oriental epic from a master hand at the age of 75.

w Akira Kurosawa, Hideo Oguni, Masato Ide *d* *Akira Kurosawa* *ph* *Takao Saito* *m* Toru Takemitsu

Tatsuya Nakadai, Satoshi Terao, Jinpachi Nezu, Daisuke Ryu

'Prepare to be astonished . . . a towering achievement in any language.' – *People*

AA: costumes (Emi Wada)

AAN: direction, photography, art direction

Rancho De Luxe

US 1974 95m DeLuxe
UA/EK (Anthony Ray)
V*

Cheerful cattle rustlers go on a binge and end up in prison.

Modern anti-everything Western; it's anti-entertainment as well.

w Thomas McGuane *d* Frank Perry *ph* William A. Fraker *m* Jimmy Buffett

Sam Waterston, Jeff Bridges, Elizabeth Ashley, Charlene Dallas, Clifton James, Slim Pickens

'Where anything goes . . . for a price!'
Rancho Notorious

US 1952 89m Technicolor
RKO/Fidelity (Howard Welsch)
V*, L

A cowboy seeking revenge for his girlfriend's murder follows a clue to a lonely ranch run by a saloon singer.

Curious Western which seems to have been intended as another *Destry Rides Again* but is made in a hard inflexible style which prevents it from appealing.

w Daniel Taradash *d* Fritz Lang *ph* Hal Mohr *md* Emil Newman *m* Hugo Friedhofer

Marlene Dietrich, Arthur Kennedy, Mel Ferrer, Gloria Henry, William Frawley, Jack Elam

'Every quality you might ask of a western is in lavish supply – except entertainment value.' – *Alton Cook*

The Randolph Family: see *Dear Octopus*

Random Harvest ***

US 1942 126m bw
MGM (Sidney Franklin)
V*, L

A shell-shocked officer in the 1914—18 war escapes from an asylum, marries a music hall singer and is idyllically happy until a shock makes him remember that he is the head of a noble family. His wife, whom he does not now remember, dutifully becomes his secretary and years later another shock brings memory and happiness back.

A silly enough story works remarkably well in this rather splendid, no holds barred, roses round the door romance in Hollywood's best style with incomparable stars. A triumph of the Peg's Paper syndrome, and hugely enjoyable because it is done so enthusiastically.

w Claudine West, George Froeschel, Arthur Wimperis *novel* James Hilton *d* Mervyn Le Roy *ph* Joseph Ruttenberg *m* Herbert Stothart *ad* Cedric Gibbons, Randall Duell

Ronald Colman, Greer Garson, Susan Peters, Philip Dorn, Reginald Owen, Henry Travers, Margaret Wycherly, Bramwell Fletcher, Arthur Margetson

'I would like to recommend this film to those who can stay interested in Ronald Colman's amnesia for two hours and who could with pleasure eat a bowl of Yardley's shaving soap for breakfast.' – *James Agee*

'A strangely empty film . . . its characters are creatures of fortune, not partisans in determining their own fates.' – *Bosley Crowther, New York Times*

'It is cast with pearly players in every part. Its pedigreed plot is savoured with just the right mixture of ups and downs, ecstasy and well-bred anguish, implausibility and psyche. And it moves towards its climax with the measured tread and nicely timed emotional bumps of a Hearst Cosmopolitan serial. It is perhaps the clearest example of the year of how a studio possessing lion's shares of movie-making capital and ingratiating talent can mate these two to synthesize a magnificent neuter, which will predictably bring in vast box office returns with which to produce more neuters.' – *John McManus, PM*

AAN: best picture; script; Mervyn Le Roy; Herbert Stothart; Ronald Colman; Susan Peters; art direction

Randy Rides Alone

US 1934 53m bw
Monogram/Lone Star (Paul Malvern)
V*

An undercover agent unmasks a murdering outlaw, who is disguised as a dumb storekeeper, Matt the Mute. He also gets the girl.

Quickie Western with some of the trappings of a detective story, including secret hiding places and a portrait whose eyes move.

w Lindsley Parsons *d* Harry Fraser *ph* Archie Stout *ed* Carl Pierson

John Wayne, Alberta Vaughn, George Hayes, Yakima Canutt, Earl Dwire

Rangers of Fortune

US 1940 79m bw
Dale Van Every/Paramount

Three amiable gun-runners clean up a south-west town.

Good reliable Western with star appeal.

w Frank Butler *d* Sam Wood

Fred MacMurray, Albert Dekker, Gilbert Roland, Patricia Morison, Joseph Schildkraut, Dick Foran, Betty Brewer

Rango

US 1931 70m bw
Paramount

An old man and a boy in Sumatra go about their business of killing tigers.

Faded semi-documentary by the man who was about to direct *King Kong*.

wd Ernest B. Schoedsack

Claude King, Douglas Scott

'He faced a decision that someday may be yours to make!'
Ransom *

US 1955 104m bw
MGM (Nicholas Nayfack)

A rich man takes desperate measures to rescue his son from a kidnapper.

Solid but overlong suspenser, virtually a vehicle for a star at his twitchiest and most dogged.

w Cyril Hume, Richard Maibaum *d* Alex Segal *ph* Arthur E. Arling *m* Jeff Alexander

Glenn Ford, Donna Reed, Leslie Nielsen, Juano Hernandez, Robert Keith

Ransom *
GB   1975   98m   Eastmancolor
Lion International (Peter Rawley)
S
aka: *The Terrorists*

A British ambassador to Scandinavia is kidnapped by terrorists and a Norwegian security chief gives chase.

Topical but unconvincing action thriller with unfamiliar detail; builds up to exciting sequences but is quickly forgotten.

w Paul Wheeler   *d* Caspar Wrede   *ph* Sven Nykvist   *m* Jerry Goldsmith

Sean Connery, Ian McShane, Norman Bristow, John Cording, Isabel Dean, William Fox, Robert Harris

The Rape of Malaya: see *A Town Like Alice*

Rapid Fire
US   1992   95m   DeLuxe
TCF (Robert Lawrence)
V*, S

After a Chinese college student is witness to a mob murder he has no alternative but to help the FBI bust two international drugs rings.

Cliché-ridden action movie whose only point of interest is that it stars Bruce Lee's son, although he has yet to acquire his father's charisma.

w Alan McElroy   *story* Cindy Cirile, Alan McElroy   *d* Dwight H. Little   *ph* Ric Waite   *m* Christopher Young   *pd* Ron Foreman   *ed* Gib Jaffe

Brandon Lee, Powers Boothe, Nick Mancuso, Raymond J. Barry, Kate Hodge, Tzi Ma, Tony Longo, Michael Paul Chan, Dustin Nguyen

'A clumsily plotted, clumsily choreographed and clumsily acted attempt at combining a hard-nosed cop thriller with an old-fashioned martial arts fable.' – *Geoffrey Macnab, Sight and Sound*

Rapture
US/France   1965   104m   bw
International Classics/TCF (Christian Ferry)

A mentally unstable girl has a tragic romance with a fugitive murderer.

Gloomy all the way, and if it's art it needs explaining.

w Stanley Mann   *novel Rapture in My Rags* by Phyllis Hastings   *d* John Guillermin   *ph* Marcel Grignon

Patricia Gozzi, Dean Stockwell, Melvyn Douglas, Gunnel Lindblom

The Rapture **
US   1991   100m   DeLuxe
Electric/New Line/Wechsler/Tenenbaum/Parker
V, V*, L

Tiring of her empty and promiscuous life, a telephone operator turns to fundamentalist religion and, claiming she has received a message from God, heads for the desert with her young daughter to await the Second Coming.

A clever and thought-provoking movie which overturns expectations – the apparently mad and neurotic turn out to be right in their predictions – but finally seems to side with an individual's right to justice at all costs.

wd Michael Tolkin   *ph* Bojan Bazelli   *m* Thomas Newman   *pd* Robert Standefer   *ed* Suzanne Fenn

Mimi Rogers, David Duchovny, Patrick Bauchau, Kimberly Cullum, Terri Hanauer, Dick Anthony Williams, James Le Gros

'The film is long on empathy, short on insight.' – *Philip French, Observer*

'A complex and intellectual horror story tackling a thorny subject in a manner simply guaranteed to offend almost everyone at some point.' – *Kim Newman, Empire*

The Rare Breed
US   1966   97m   Technicolor   Panavision
Universal (William Alland)
V*

An English bull is taken by its woman owner to St Louis to breed with American longhorns, and various frictions are caused among the ranchers.

Amusing Western idea which misses fire by not coming down firmly as either drama or comedy; it does however pass the time amiably enough.

w Ric Hardman   *d* Andrew V. McLaglen   *ph* William H. Clothier   *m* Johnny Williams

James Stewart, Maureen O'Hara, Brian Keith, Juliet Mills, Don Galloway, David Brian, Jack Elam, Ben Johnson

Rascals
US   1938   77m   bw
TCF

A rich young man and a girl suffering from amnesia join a gypsy troupe.

Absurdly cast and plotted semi-musical with a certain liveliness to keep it going.

w Robert Ellis, Helen Logan   *d* H. Bruce Humberstone

Jane Withers, Borrah Minevitch and his Rascals, Robert Wilcox, Rochelle Hudson, Steffi Duna

'In the main amusing and entertaining.' – *Variety*

Rashomon ****
Japan   1951   83m   bw
Daiei (Jingo Minoura)
V*, L, S
aka: *In the Woods*

In medieval Japan, four people have different versions of a violent incident when a bandit attacks a nobleman in the forest.

Indescribably vivid in itself, and genuinely strange (one of the versions is told by a ghost), *Rashomon* reintroduced Japanese films to the world market and was remade (badly) in Hollywood as *The Outrage*.

wd Akira Kurosawa   *story Inside a Bush* by Ryunosuke Akutagawa   *ph* Kazuo Matsuyama   *m* Takashi Matsuyama   *ad* H. Motsumoto

Toshiro Mifune, Machiko Kyo, Masayuki Mori, Takashi Shimura

'A masterpiece, and a revelation.' – *Gavin Lambert, MFB*

AA: best foreign film

AAN: art direction

Raskolnikov *
Germany   1923   80m approx (at 24 fps)   bw
    silent
Neumann (Robert Wiene)

A student kills a pawnbroker and is hounded by a police inspector until he confesses.

Interesting adaptation of *Crime and Punishment* with some of the expressionist aspects of the same director's *The Cabinet of Dr Caligari*.

wd Robert Wiene   *ph* Willy Godberger   *ad* Andre Andreyev

Gregory Khmara, Michael Tarkhanov, Pavel Pavlov, Vera Toma

Rasputin: see *Agony*

Rasputin and the Empress *
US   1932   133m   bw
MGM (Irving Thalberg)
V*
GB title: *Rasputin the Mad Monk*

The story of the last years of the Russian court, when a sinister monk gained influence over the empress.

An unhappy film which was besieged by lawsuits and never generated much drama of its own despite starring the three Barrymores, who all seemed to be acting in separate rooms. Production values are the most impressive thing about it.

w Charles MacArthur   *d* Richard Boleslawski   *ph* William Daniels   *m* Herbert Stothart

John Barrymore, Ethel Barrymore, Lionel Barrymore, Diana Wynyard, Ralph Morgan, C. Henry Gordon, Edward Arnold, Jean Parker, Gustav von Seyffertitz, Anne Shirley (Dawn O'Day)

† The lawsuit was by Prince Youssoupoff (portrayed as Chegodieff), who claimed that although he did kill Rasputin his wife was never raped. He was awarded one million dollars.

AAN: Charles MacArthur

Rasputin the Mad Monk (1932): see *Rasputin and the Empress*

Rasputin the Mad Monk
GB   1966   92m   DeLuxe   CinemaScope
Warner-Pathé/Hammer/7 Arts (Anthony Nelson-Keys)

A recapitulation of well-known events with fictional trimmings.

Dreary excuse for its star to go berserk.

w John Elder   *d* Don Sharp   *ph* Michael Reed   *m* Don Banks   *pd* Bernard Robinson   *ed* James Needs, Roy Hyde

Christopher Lee, Barbara Shelley, Richard Pasco, Francis Matthews, Renee Asherson

The Rat *
GB   1937   72m   bw
Herbert Wilcox/Imperator

A Parisian thief takes the blame for murder, but is saved by the socialite who loves him.

Rather smart talkie version of a well-worn theatrical hit, previously filmed in 1925 as a silent, with Ivor Novello as star.

w Hans Rameau, Marjorie Gaffney, Miles Malleson and Romney Brent   *play* Ivor Novello, Constance Collier   *d* Jack Raymond

Anton Walbrook, Ruth Chatterton, Rene Ray, Beatrix Lehmann, Felix Aylmer, Mary Clare

The Rat Race *
US   1960   105m   Technicolor
Paramount/Perlberg-Seaton

A young jazz musician and a dance hall hostess share a flat and face the adversities of New York.

A kind of sour fairy tale of the big city which has neither enough jokes nor enough incident but purveys the kind of charm that grows on one despite oneself.

w Garson Kanin   *play* Garson Kanin   *d* Robert Mulligan   *ph* Robert Burks   *m* Elmer Bernstein

Tony Curtis, Debbie Reynolds, Jack Oakie, Kay Medford, Don Rickles

'The New Yorkers of *The Rat Race* – noisy soft-hearted landlady, philosophical bartender, backchatting taxi driver – are as familiar as the settings of shabby apartment house and quiet little bar across the street. Film makers no longer need to invent here – they simply move in for a few weeks.' – *Penelope Houston*

Ratboy
US   1986   104m   Technicolor
Malpaso/Warner
V*

A half-rodent alien gets the anticipated rough treatment when he visits Earth.

Clint Eastwood's favourite co-star was given leave to make the film of her choice, but the choice is inexplicable in the wake of so many other *E.T.* imitations.

w Rob Thompson *d* Sondra Locke

Sondra Locke, Robert Townsend, Christopher Hewett, Larry Hankin

Rationing
US 1943 93m bw
MGM

A small-town shopkeeper is frustrated by wartime restrictions.

Amiable comedy for established stars.

w William Lipman, Grant Garrett and Harry Ruskin *d* Willis Goldbeck

Wallace Beery, Marjorie Main, Donald Meek, Howard Freeman, Connie Gilchrist

Raton Pass
US 1951 84m bw
Warner
GB title: *Canyon Pass*

A greedy wife swindles her husband out of his share in their ranch.

Unusual Western melodrama; quite entertaining.

w Tom Blackburn, James Webb *d* Edwin L. Marin

Dennis Morgan, Patricia Neal, Steve Cochran, Scott Forbes, Dorothy Hart

Rattle of a Simple Man
GB 1964 95m bw
Sydney Box (William Gell)
V, V*

A shy football supporter in London spends the night with a tart for a bet.

Archetypal farcical situation with sentiment added to string it out to twice its proper length. Production values modest but adequate.

w Charles Dyer *play* Charles Dyer *d* Muriel Box *ph* Reg Wyer *m* Stanley Black

Harry H. Corbett, *Diane Cilento*, Thora Hird, Charles Dyer

The Raven *
US 1935 61m bw
Universal
V*, L

A doctor obsessed by Poe-inspired torture devices transforms a gangster on the run into a hideous mutant.

Silly but quite effective horror film with memorable sequences.

w David Boehm *d* Lew Landers *ph* Charles Stumar *md* Gilbert Kurland

Bela Lugosi, Boris Karloff, Samuel S. Hinds, Irene Ware, Lester Matthews

'Maintains Universal's high batting average with the shockers . . . should come through with nice grosses.' – *Variety*

The Raven (1943): see *Le Corbeau*

The Raven *
US 1963 86m Pathecolor Panavision
AIP/Alta Vista (Roger Corman)
V*, L

Two 15th-century conjurors fight a deadly duel of magic.

The rather splendid duel is a long time coming; the preliminaries are largely confined to chat in a single set, and the random jokes do not quite atone for the boredom.

w Richard Matheson *d* Roger Corman *ph* Floyd Crosby *m* Les Baxter

Vincent Price, Peter Lorre, Boris Karloff, Hazel Court, Jack Nicholson

Raw Courage
US 1984 90m colour
Adams Apple/Sandy Howard (Ronny Cox, Robert L. Rosen)
aka: *Courage*

Three long-distance runners are attacked by a fanatical group of would-be soldiers in the New Mexican desert.

A land-locked, brain-dead variation on *Deliverance,* notably short on thrills.

w Ronny Cox, Mary Cox *d* Robert L. Rosen *ph* F. Pershing Flynn *m* Johnny Harris *pd* Don Nunley *ed* Steven Polivka

Ronny Cox, Art Hindle, M. Emmet Walsh, Tim Maier, Lois Chiles, William Russ, Lisa Sutton

Raw Deal
US 1948 78m bw
Reliance/Eagle Lion

A convict is helped by his girlfriend to escape, and the police chase them across country.

Fairly violent crime melodrama which holds the attention.

w Leopold Atlas, John C. Higgins *d* Anthony Mann

Dennis O'Keefe, Claire Trevor, Marsha Hunt, John Ireland, Raymond Burr

Raw Deal
US 1986 106m Technicolor JDC Wide Screen
De Laurentiis/International (Martha Schumacher)
V, V*, L

An ex-FBI man is recruited to infiltrate Chicago's biggest mob.

Violent crime hokum with momentary amusements.

w Gary M. DeVore, Norman Wexler *d* John Irvin *ph* Alex Thomson *m* Cinemascore

Arnold Schwarzenegger, Kathryn Harrold, Sam Wanamaker, Paul Shenar, Ed Lauter, Darren McGavin, Joe Regalbuto

'Comic book crime meller suffers from an irredeemable script' – *Variety*

Raw Edge
US 1956 76m Technicolor
Universal-International

A rancher's workers plan to kill him.

Tense, fairly adult Western.

w Harry Essex, Robert Hill *d* John Sherwood

Rory Calhoun, Yvonne de Carlo, Mara Corday, Rex Reason, Neville Brand

Raw Meat: see *Death Line*

Raw Wind in Eden
US 1958 93m Eastmancolor Cinemascope
U-I (William Alland)

A model is stranded on a Sardinian island, and falls in love with a mysterious American who turns out to be a disillusioned millionaire.

Wish-fulfilment woman's picture with the occasional relief of a smart line.

w Elizabeth and Richard Wilson *d* Richard Wilson *ph* Enzo Serafin *m* Hans Salter

Esther Williams, Jeff Chandler, Carlos Thompson, Rossana Podesta, Eduardo de Filippo, Rik Battaglia

Rawhead Rex
US 1987 86m colour
Empire/Alpine/Paradise/Green Man (Kevin Attew, Don Hawkins)
V, L

In Ireland a farmer unwittingly releases a primitive demon, which immediately goes on the rampage.

Ineffectual, low-budget horror.

w Clive Barker *d* George Pavlou *ph* John Metcalfe *ad* Lee Huntingford *ed* Andy Horvitch

David Dukes, Kelly Piper, Ronan Wilmot, Niall Toibin, Heinrich von Schellendoft, Niall O'Brian

Rawhide **
US 1950 86m bw
TCF (Samuel G. Engel)
V*
TV title: *Desperate Siege*

Four escaped convicts terrorize a stagecoach stop.

Good suspense Western with excellent technical credits.

w Dudley Nichols *d* Henry Hathaway *ph* Milton Krasner *m* Sol Kaplan

Tyrone Power, Susan Hayward, Hugh Marlowe, Jack Elam, Dean Jagger, George Tobias, Edgar Buchanan, Jeff Corey

Le Rayon Vert: see *The Green Ray*

Razorback
Australia 1984 95m colour Panavision
UAA/Western (Hal McElroy)
V, V*

In a small outback town a man is tried for the murder of his grandson, actually carried off by a wild boar.

Grim images of Australian life pepper this cross between *Jaws* and the dingo baby case. Not, as they say, for the squeamish.

w Everett de Roche *novel* Peter Brennan *d* Russell Mulcahy *ph* Dean Semler *m* Iva Davies *pd* Bryce Walmsley *ed* William Anderson

Gregory Harrison, Arkie Whiteley, Bill Kerr, Chris Haywood

'Between love and hatred there is a line as sharp as a razor's edge!'
The Razor's Edge *
US 1946 146m bw
TCF (Darryl F. Zanuck)
V*, L, S

A well-to-do young man spends the years between the wars first idling, then looking for essential truth.

The novel was an empty parable with amusing trimmings. In the film the trimmings seem amusing, but the presentation is glossy.

w Lamar Trotti *novel* W. Somerset Maugham *d* Edmund Goulding *ph* Arthur Miller *m* Alfred Newman *ad* Richard Day, Nathan Juran

Tyrone Power, Gene Tierney, *Clifton Webb, Herbert Marshall,* John Payne, Anne Baxter, Lucile Watson, Frank Latimore, Elsa Lanchester, Fritz Kortner

'I like Somerset Maugham when he's looking through keyholes or down cracks, not at vistas.' – *Richard Winnington*

'Almost as irresistibly funny and terrible as *The Fountainhead.*' – *Pauline Kael, 70s*

† Maugham has a different source for his title, in the shape of an Oriental proverb, probably invented: 'The sharp edge of a razor is difficult to pass over; thus the wise say that the path to salvation is hard.'

AA: Anne Baxter

AAN: best picture; Clifton Webb; art direction

The Razor's Edge

US 1984 128m colour
Columbia (Robert P. Marucci, Harry Benn)
V*, L

An unlikely remake which came into being because the star persuaded the studio to do it, then failed in his attempt to convey the necessary spirituality. As for the rest, the time is out of joint (except for Denholm Elliott).

w John Byrum, Bill Murray d John Byrum
ph Peter Hannan m Jack Nietzche pd Philip Harrison ed Peter Boyle

Bill Murray, Denholm Elliott, Theresa Russel, Catherine Hicks, James Keach, Peter Vaughan, Faith Brook

Reach for Glory *

GB 1962 86m bw
Columbia/Blazer (John Kohn, Jud Kinberg)

During World War II, evacuee boys play war games and a German refugee is accidentally killed.

Grim and unpalatable parable, competently rather than excitingly made.

w John Rae novel The Custard Boys by John Rae d Philip Leacock ph Bob Huke m Bob Russell

Kay Walsh, Harry Andrews, Michael Anderson Jnr, Oliver Grimm, Alexis Kanner, Martin Tomlinson, Richard Vernon

Reach for the Sky *

GB 1956 135m bw
Rank/Pinnacle (Daniel M. Angel)
V, V*

Douglas Bader loses both legs in a 1931 air crash, learns to walk on artificial limbs and flies again in World War II.

Box-office exploitation of one man's personal heroism, adequately but not inspiringly put together with many stiff upper lips and much jocular humour.

wd Lewis Gilbert book Paul Brickhill ph Jack Asher m John Addison

Kenneth More, Muriel Pavlow, Lyndon Brook, Lee Patterson, Alexander Knox, Dorothy Alison, Sydney Tafler, Howard Marion Crawford

'It is least successful in what should be exciting action.' – Dilys Powell

Reaching for the Moon

US 1931 90m bw
United Artists (Douglas Fairbanks)
V*

On a transatlantic liner, a new cocktail has a sensational effect on a mild-mannered hero.

Very flimsy comedy with songs and some athletic stunts for its hero.

wd Edmund Goulding ph Ray June song Irving Berlin

Douglas Fairbanks, Bebe Daniels, Edward Everett Horton, Claud Allister, Jack Mulhall, Bing Crosby

'Not a smash entry, but should do moderately and perhaps a little better than that.' – Variety

'You'll love them as much as they love each other!'
Reaching for the Sun

US 1941 90m bw
Paramount

A clam digger who needs an outboard motor goes to work in a Detroit car plant.

Easygoing comedy, too muted to recommend itself widely.

w W. L. River novel Wessel Smitter d William Wellman

Joel McCrea, Ellen Drew, Eddie Bracken, Albert Dekker

Ready Willing and Able

US 1937 93m bw
Warner (Samuel Bischoff)

Two songwriters import an English leading lady for their new show.

Lightweight star musical with no outstanding qualities except a number in which girls dance on the keys of a huge typewriter.

w Sig Herzig, Jerry Wald, Warren Duff d Ray Enright ph Sol Polito ch Bobby Connolly songs Johnny Mercer, Richard Whiting

Ruby Keeler, Ross Alexander, Lee Dixon, Wini Shaw, Jane Wyman, Allen Jenkins

'Too many numbers and a slow script.' – Variety

AAN: Bobby Connolly

Real Genius

US 1985 104m Metrocolor Panavision
TriStar/Delphi III (Brian Grazer)
V*, L

A 15-year-old scientific prodigy joins a think-tank of whizz kids who are being unwittingly exploited by the military.

Slickly directed youth movie that abandons any seriousness in favour of anarchic slapstick comedy; its message appears to be that too much intelligence is bad for you.

w Neil Israel, Pat Proft, Peter Torokvei d Martha Coolidge ph Vilmos Zsigmond m Thomas Newman pd Josan F. Russo ed Richard Chew

Val Kilmer, Gabe Jarret, Michelle Meyrink, William Atherton, Patti D'Arbanville, Robert Prescott

'Always outnumbered! Never outfought!'
'One of the most stunning dramas of love and courage ever brought to the screen!'
The Real Glory *

US 1939 96m bw
Samuel Goldwyn
V*

Soldiers of fortune help the American Army to quell a terrorist uprising in the Philippines just after the Spanish-American War.

Well made Gunga Dinnery.

w Jo Swerling, Robert R. Presnell d Henry Hathaway ph Rudolph Maté m Alfred Newman ad James Basevi

Gary Cooper, David Niven, Broderick Crawford, Andrea Leeds, Reginald Owen, Kay Johnson, Russell Hicks, Vladimir Sokoloff

'Moro uprisings, guerrilla warfare, cholera epidemics, and fancy exhibitions of inhuman cruelty are the frame against which an innocuous melodramatic yarn is told.' – Variety

'The same sort of picture as Gunga Din.' – Richard Mallett, Punch

'Recommended to adolescents of all ages.' – New Statesman

'In times like these, we question the wisdom of rattling the bones in Yankee imperialism's closet.' – Daily Worker

Real Life *

US 1979 99m colour
Paramount (Penelope Spheeris)
V*

A self-centred film-maker moves in with an average family in order to make a documentary about them.

Clever satire on a certain style of television programme, but the joke is over-stretched.

w Albert Brooks, Monica Johnson, Harry Shearer d Albert Brooks ph Eric Saarinen m Mort Lindsay ad Linda Marder, Linda Spheeris ed David Finfer

Albert Brooks, Charles Grodin, Frances Lee McCain, J. A. Preston, Matthew Tobin, Jennings Lang

Real Life

GB 1983 92m colour
Entertainment/The Real Life Partnership (Mike Dinseen)

An estate agent's assistant with a vivid imagination becomes involved in thefts.

Clumsy, witless comedy which quickly bores.

w Francis Megahy, Bernie Cooper d Francis Megahy ph Peter Jessop m David Mindel pd John White ed Peter Delfgou

Rupert Everett, Cristina Raines, Norman Beaton, Warren Clarke, Isla Blair, James Faulkner

'Try as one may to look sympathetically on this brand of independent British venture, the resolute lack of wit or style wipes the indulgent smile from one's lips early on, and it never returns.' – Guardian

'She's the only one who can break into a bank that holds $18m, but it's not for the money.'
The Real McCoy

US 1993 101m Technicolor
Capella (Martin Bregman, Willi Baer, Michael S. Bregman)
V, V*, L, S

A reluctant cat burglar is forced to rob a bank by a gangster who kidnaps her young son.

There is nothing original here, merely a competent director and cast going through familiar routines with moderate enthusiasm.

w William Davies, William Osborne d Russell Mulcahy ph Denis Crossan m Brad Fiedel pd Kim Colefax ed Peter Honess

Kim Basinger, Val Kilmer, Terence Stamp, Gailard Sartain, Zach English, Raynor Scheine

'Provides scant suspense, and the final bank job doesn't blaze any trails for anyone who's seen caper movies. Similarly, the payoff may satisfy the undemanding, but most viewers will have seen it coming a mile off.' – Variety

Real Men

US 1987 96m Metrocolor
United Artists (Martin Bregman)
V*, L

An unpredictable CIA agent recruits a timid insurance clerk to deliver a message to friendly aliens while rival agents attempt to kill them both.

Dim though frenetic comedy that provides nothing but tedium.

wd Dennis Feldman ph John A. Alonzo m Miles Goodman ad William J. Cassidy, James Allen ed Malcolm Campbell, Glenn Farr

James Belushi, John Ritter, Barbara Barrie, Bill Morey, Isa Andersen, Gale Barle, Mark Herrier

'Death is just the beginning!'
Re-Animator

US 1985 86m DeLuxe
Entertainment/Empire International (Brian Yuzna)
V, V*, L, S

When a crazy scientist brings people back to life, they come back violent.

Gross and grisly horror comic which amused some critics.

w Dennis Paoli, William J. Norris, Stuart Gordon story Herbert West – Re-animator by H. P. Lovecraft d Stuart Gordon ph Mac Ahlberg, Stephen Sealy m Richard Band ad R. A. Burns, Charles Nixon ed Lee Percy

Jeffrey Combs, Bruce Abbott, Barbara Crampton, David Gale

'For those with a strong sense of humour, and a stomach stronger still.' – Sunday Times

'A cheap smell of excess.' – Observer

Re-Animator 2

US   1989   96m   colour
Medusa/Wildstreet (Paul White, Keith Walley, Hidetaka
   Konno)
V, V*, L, S
aka: *Bride of Re-Animator*

A scientist, building himself a woman from spare
parts, is attacked by the re-animated remnants of his
previous experiments.

The mixture much as before, and gaining nothing
from the repetition.

w Woody Keith, Rick Fry   *story* H. P. Lovecraft
d Brian Yuzna   *ph* Rick Fichter   *m* Richard Band
pd Philip J. C. Duffin   *ed* Peter Teschner

Bruce Abbott, Claude Earl Jones, Fabiana Udenio,
David Gale, Kathleen Kinmont, Jeffrey Combs, Mel
Stewart, Michael Strasser, Irene Forrest

'Yet another example of a sequel that is content to
rehash all the ingredients of the first film without ever
gelling in the way that made the original work.' –
MFB

Reap the Wild Wind **

'Man against terrifying monster – in the most spectacular
   underwater scenes ever filmed!'

US   1942   124m   Technicolor
Paramount/Cecil B. de Mille
V*

Seafaring salvage engineers fight over a Southern
belle.

Georgia-set period adventure; intended as another
Gone with the Wind, it simply doesn't have the
necessary, but on its level it entertains solidly,
climaxing with the famous giant squid fight.

w Alan le May, Jesse Lasky Jnr   *d* Cecil B. de Mille
ph Victor Milner, Dewey Wrigley, William V. Skall
m Victor Young   *ad* Hans Dreier, Roland Anderson

Ray Milland, John Wayne, *Paulette Goddard*, Raymond
Massey, Robert Preston, Lynne Overman, Susan
Hayward, Charles Bickford, Walter Hampden, Louise
Beavers, Martha O'Driscoll, Hedda Hopper

'The essence of all his experience, the apogee of all his
art, and as jamfull a motion picture as has ever played
two hours upon a screen.' – *Howard Barnes, New York
Herald Tribune*

† The underwater scenes were filmed in the Santa
Monica Pan Pacific Marine Museum, which had a
pool 100 feet long and 50 feet wide. The 50-foot giant
squid was operated by a 24-button electronic
keyboard

AAN: photography; art direction

Rear Window ****

US   1954   112m   Technicolor
Alfred Hitchcock
V, V*, L

A news photographer, confined to his room by a
broken leg, sees a murder committed in a room on the
other side of the court.

Artificial but gripping suspenser of an unusual kind;
with such restricted settings, all depends on the script
and the acting, and they generally come up trumps.

w John Michael Hayes   *novel* Cornell Woolrich
d Alfred Hitchcock   *ph* Robert Burks   *m* Franz
Waxman

James Stewart, Grace Kelly, Raymond Burr, Judith
Evelyn, Wendell Corey, Thelma Ritter

AAN: John Michael Hayes; Alfred Hitchcock; Robert
Burks

A Reason to Live, a Reason to Die (dubbed)

Italy/France/Spain   1972   96m   colour   Scope
K-Tel/Sancrosiap-Terza/Europrodis/Atlantida/Corona (Michael
   Billingsley)
V*
original title: *Una Ragione per Vivere e Una per Morire*

In the American Civil War, a Union colonel recruits
seven desperadoes, all due to be executed, for a daring
raid to recapture a Confederate fort.

An unexciting cut-rate variation on *The Dirty Dozen*.

w Tonino Valerii, Ernesto Gastaldi   *d* Tonino
Valerii   *ph* Alejandro Ulloa   *m* Riz Ortolani
ed Franklin Boll

James Coburn, Telly Savalas, Bud Spencer, Ralph
Goodwin, Joseph Mitchell, Robert Burton, William
Spofford

'A colourless, perfunctory gloss on a text that the
director and scriptwriters might assume their
audiences to know by heart.' – *MFB*

† The film was cut to 91m on its British release.

Rebecca ****

US   1940   130m   bw
David O. Selznick
V, V*, L

The naïve young second wife of a Cornish landowner
is haunted by the image of his glamorous first wife
Rebecca.

The supreme Hollywood entertainment package, set
in Monte Carlo and Cornwall, with generous
helpings of romance, comedy, suspense, melodrama
and mystery, all indulged in by strongly-drawn
characters, and directed by the new English wizard
for the glossiest producer in town, from a novel which
sold millions of copies. It really couldn't miss, and it
didn't.

w Robert E. Sherwood, Joan Harrison,   *novel* Daphne du
Maurier   *d* Alfred Hitchcock   *ph* George Barnes
m Franz Waxman   *ad* Lyle Wheeler   *ed* Hal C. Kern

*Laurence Olivier, Joan Fontaine, George Sanders, Judith
Anderson, Nigel Bruce, Gladys Cooper, Florence Bates,
Reginald Denny, C. Aubrey Smith, Melville Cooper, Leo
G. Carroll, Leonard Carey*

  NARRATOR: 'Last night I dreamed I went to
Manderley again . . .'
  FAVELL (George Sanders) to Mrs de Winter: 'I say,
marriage with Max is not exactly a bed of roses, is it?'
  MRS DANVERS (Judith Anderson): 'You're
overwrought, madam. I've opened a window for you.
A little air will do you good. Why don't you go? Why
don't you leave Manderley? He doesn't need you.
He's got his memories. He doesn't love you – he wants
to be alone again with *her*. You've nothing to stay for.
You've nothing to live for, have you, really? Look
down there. It's easy, isn't it? Why don't you? Go on,
go on. Don't be afraid . . .'
  MAXIM (Laurence Olivier): 'You thought I loved
Rebecca? You thought that? I hated her. Oh, I was
carried away by her – enchanted by her, as everyone
was – and when I was married, I was told I was the
luckiest man in the world. She was so lovely, so
accomplished, so amusing. "She's got the three things
that really matter in a wife," everyone said,
"breeding, brains and beauty." And I believed them
completely. But I never had a moment's happiness
with her. She was incapable of love, or tenderness, or
decency.'

'A carefully considered trying out of the superior
technical resources now at Hitchcock's disposal.' –
George Perry, 1965

'Hitchcock fans will have to put up with a surprising
lack of the characteristic Hitchcock improvisations in
the way of salty minor personages and humorous
interludes, and satisfy themselves with a masterly
exhibition of the Hitchcock skill in creating suspense
and shock with his action and his camera.' – *National
Board of Review*

'Riveting and painful – a tale of fear and guilt, class
and power.' – *Time Out, 1988*

'Hitch kept me off balance, much to his own delight
. . . he would constantly tell me that no one thought I
was very good except himself.' – *Joan Fontaine*

† Original casting thoughts, all rejected, were Ronald
Colman, William Powell and Leslie Howard for
Maxim; Anne Baxter, Margaret Sullavan, Loretta
Young, Vivien Leigh and Olivia de Havilland (for the
second Mrs de Winter).

AA: best picture; George Barnes

AAN: script; Alfred Hitchcock; Franz Waxman;
Laurence Olivier; Joan Fontaine; Judith Anderson;
Lyle Wheeler; Hal C. Kern

Rebecca of Sunnybrook Farm

US   1932   75m   bw
Fox

A rural glad girl wins over her dour aunt and reforms
an atheist.

Routine sound remake of the children's classic in a
1921 silent version in which Mary Pickford starred.

w S. N. Behrman, Sonya Levien   *novel* Kate Douglas
Wiggin and Charlotte Thompson   *d* Alfred Santell

Marian Nixon, Ralph Bellamy, Mae Marsh, Louise
Closser Hale, Alan Hale, Charlotte Henry

Rebecca of Sunnybrook Farm

US   1938   80m   bw
TCF (Raymond Griffith)
V*, L

A child performer becomes a pawn in the fight to
exploit her talents on radio.

Unrecognizable revamping of a famous story makes a
very thin star vehicle.

w Karl Tunberg, Don Ettlinger   *novel* Kate Douglas
Wiggin and Charlotte Thompson   *d* Allan Dwan
ph Arthur Miller   *m* Arthur Lange   *songs* various

Shirley Temple, Randolph Scott, Jack Haley, Gloria
Stuart, Phyllis Brooks, Helen Westley, Slim
Summerville, Bill Robinson

'More fitting title would be *Rebecca of Radio City* . . . a
weak story, indifferently directed and acted.' – *Variety*

Rebecca's Daughters *

GB/Germany   1991   97m   colour
Mayfair/Palace/Rebecca's Daughters/Astralma Erste
   Filmproduktions/Delta/BBC Wales/British Screen (Chris
   Sievernich)
V

In the 19th century, Welsh farmers form gangs
dressed in women's clothes to protest against unfair
toll-gate charges imposed by the local aristocracy.

Ramshackle caper, ripely performed and occasionally
amusing.

w Guy Jenkin, Karl Francis   *story* based on a
screenplay by Dylan Thomas   *d* Karl Francis
ph Russ Walker   *m* Rachel Portman   *pd* Ray Price
ed Roy Sharman

Peter O'Toole, Paul Rhys, Joely Richardson, Keith
Allen, Simon Dormandy, Dafydd Hywel, Sue
Roderick

'An irresistible period romp.' – *Variety*

The Rebel *

GB   1960   105m   Technicolor
Associated British (W. A. Whitaker)
V
US title: *Call Me Genius*

A suburban businessman goes to Paris to become an
artist.

A kind of farcical *The Moon and Sixpence*, insufficiently
well tailored to the requirements of a very specialized
comic, but occasionally diverting none the less.

w Alan Simpson, Ray Galton   *d* Robert Day
ph Gilbert Taylor   *m* Frank Cordell

Tony Hancock, George Sanders, Paul Massie, Margit
Saad, Grégoire Aslan, Dennis Price, Irene Handl,
Mervyn Johns, Peter Bull, John Le Mesurier, Nanette
Newman, Oliver Reed, John Wood

'The more prosaic the setting, the funnier Hancock seems; transplanted into a conventionally silly screen art world, he is submerged among the other grotesques.' – *Penelope Houston*

Rebel

Australia 1985 89m colour
Village Roadshow (Phillip Emanuel)
V, V*, L

In wartime Sydney, a singer shelters a deserter from the US Marines.

Dim romance, punctuated by some dull song and dance routines.

w Michael Jenkins, Bob Herbert *play No Names, No Pack Drill* by Bob Herbert *d* Michael Jenkins *ph* Peter James *m* Chris Neal *pd* Brian Thomson *m/ly* Peter Best *ed* Michael Honey

Matt Dillon, Debbie Byrne, Bryan Brown, Bill Hunter, Ray Barrett, Julie Nihill

Rebel in Town

US 1956 78m bw
Bel Air/UA

A bank robber accidentally kills a small boy and is hunted down by the father.

Surprisingly stark Western with no particular merit.

w Danny Arnold *d* Alfred Werker

John Payne, John Smith, Ruth Roman, J. Carrol Naish, Ben Cooper

The Rebel Nun: see *Flavia the Heretic*

Rebel Rousers

US 1969 78m colour
Paragon International (Martin B. Cohen)
V*

An architect and his pregnant lover are terrorized by a gang of bikers in a small Arizona town.

Typical low-budget biker movie, lacking any originality but peopled by actors who went on to better films later.

w Abe Polsky, Michael Kars, Martin B. Cohen *d* Martin B. Cohen *ph* Leslie Kouvacs, Glen Smith *m* William Loose *ed* Thor Brooks

Cameron Mitchell, Diane Ladd, Bruce Dern, Jack Nicholson, Harry Dean Stanton, Neil Burstyn, Lou Procopo, Earl Finn, Phil Carey

The Rebel Son

GB 1939 90m bw
London Films Omnia (E. C. Molinier, Charles David)

A Tartar leader's son falls in love with the daughter of the opposing leader.

Resistible grafting of the Romeo and Juliet story into the barbarians of the Steppes, with much carousing and threatened violence surrounding a good central performance. It includes much footage from a 1936 French film, *Taras Bulba*, directed by Alexis Granowsky.

w Adrian Brunel *story* Gogol *d* Alexis Granowsky, Adrian Brunel *ph* Franz Planer and Bernard Browne

Harry Baur, Patricia Roc, Roger Livesey, Anthony Bushell, Joan Gardner

'After half an hour the joke had gone on long enough and I left. A man in the audience was remarking slowly, with some of Dr Johnson's weight, "I am still wondering what the reason for the existence of this film can be".' – *Graham Greene, The Spectator*

'The bad boy from a good family!'
Rebel without a Cause **

US 1955 111m Warnercolor Cinemascope
Warner (David Weisbart)
V, V*, L, S

The adolescent son of a well-to-do family gets into trouble with other kids and the police.

The first film to suggest that juvenile violence is not necessarily bred in the slums, this somewhat dreary melodrama also catapulted James Dean to stardom as the prototype fifties rebel.

w Stewart Stern *d* Nicholas Ray *ph* Ernest Haller *m* Leonard Rosenman

James Dean, Natalie Wood, Jim Backus, Sal Mineo, Ann Doran, Dennis Hopper

AAN: original story (Nicholas Ray); Natalie Wood; Sal Mineo

Rebound

US 1931 88m bw
RKO-Pathé

A woman tries to forgive her husband when he is jilted by a girlfriend.

A sophisticated stage comedy presented with the minimum of alteration.

w Horace Jackson *play* Donald Ogden Stuart *d* E. H. Griffith

Ina Claire, Robert Williams, Robert Ames, Myrna Loy, Hedda Hopper, Louise Closser Hale

'A splendidly made picture which will delight smart audiences.' – *Variety*

'The biggest musical show of the century, with a throbbing love story as exciting as its title!'
Reckless

US 1935 96m bw
MGM (David O. Selznick)
V, V*, L

A theatrical agent loves the glamorous star he represents, but she marries a drunken millionaire.

Remarkably flat backstage melodrama with music, based on the life of Libby Holman.

w P. J. Wolfson *d* Victor Fleming *ph* George Folsey *songs* various *md* Edward Ward

Jean Harlow, William Powell, Franchot Tone, May Robson, Ted Healy, Nat Pendleton, Rosalind Russell, Henry Stephenson

'Several sets of dramatic premises are established and then permitted to wander aimlessly, making the 93 minutes seem much longer than that.' – *Variety*

The Reckless Moment *

US 1949 82m bw
Columbia (Walter Wanger)
V*

A woman accidentally kills her daughter's would-be seducer, and is then trailed by a blackmailer.

Uninteresting melodrama electrified by Ophuls's direction, which might have been applied to something more worthwhile.

w Henry Garson, R. W. Soderborg *novel The Blank Wall* by Elizabeth Sanxay Holding *d* Max Ophuls *ph* Burnett Guffey *md* Morris Stoloff *m* Hans Salter

Joan Bennett, James Mason, Geraldine Brooks, Henry O'Neill, Shepperd Strudwick

'Swift, sure narrative and solidly pleasurable detail.' – *Richard Winnington*

The Reckoning **

GB 1969 108m Technicolor
Columbia/Ronald Shedlo (Hugh Perceval)

A tough London executive with a Liverpool-Irish background has a brutal streak and a self-destructive urge, but goes on narrowly averting misfortune.

Interesting melodrama of a man disgusted with both bourgeois and working-class values; slickly made and fast-moving.

w John McGrath, *novel The Harp That Once* by Patrick Hall *d* Jack Gold *ph* Geoffrey Unsworth *m* Malcolm Arnold

Nicol Williamson, Rachel Roberts, Paul Rogers, Zena Walker, Ann Bell, Gwen Nelson, J. G. Devlin

Recollections of the Yellow House

Portugal 1989 119m colour
Invicta (João Pedro Bénard, Joaquim Pinto)

original title: *Recordacões da Casa Amarela*

Life in a Lisbon boarding house, where a middle-aged voyeur and fetishist goes slowly mad.

Despite its billing as 'a Portugeuse comedy', a drawn-out, downbeat movie that strives too hard for significance.

wd João César Monteiro *ph* José Antonio Loureiro *m* Schubert, Vivaldi *ad* Luis Monteiro *ed* Helena Alvez, Claudio Martinez

Manuela de Freitas, João César Monteiro, Sabina Sacchi, Teresa Calado, Ruy Furtado, Henrique Viana, Luis Miguel Cintra

Recordacões da Casa Amarela: see *Recollections of the Yellow House*

The Red Badge of Courage **

US 1951 69m bw
MGM (Gottfried Reinhardt)
V, V*

A youth called up during the Civil War gets his first taste of battle.

Fresh, poetic, but dramatically unsatisfactory filming of a classic American novel. The story of its production is fascinatingly told in *Picture*, a book by Lillian Ross.

wd John Huston, *novel* Stephen Crane *ph* Harold Rosson *m* Bronislau Kaper

Audie Murphy, Bill Mauldin, Douglas Dick, Royal Dano, John Dierkes, Andy Devine, Arthur Hunnicutt

Red Ball Express

US 1952 83m bw
U-I (Aaron Rosenberg)

A supply column runs from the Normandy beachhead to Patton's army on the outskirts of Paris.

Standard war adventure, not too convincingly mounted but providing the usual excitements.

w John Michael Hayes *d* Budd Boetticher *ph* Maury Gertsman

Jeff Chandler, Sidney Poitier, Alex Nicol, Judith Braun, Hugh O'Brian, Jack Kelly, Jack Warden

The Red Balloon ****

France 1955 34m Technicolor
Films Montsouris
V

A lonely boy finds a balloon which becomes his constant companion and finally lifts him to the skies.

Absorbing and quite perfectly timed fantasy, one of the great film shorts.

wd Albert Lamorisse *ph* Edmond Sechan *m* Maurice Le Roux

Pascal Lamorisse

AA: best original screenplay

The Red Baron: see *Von Richthofen and Brown*

Red Barry

US 1938 bw serial: 13 eps
Universal

A famous detective chases villains named Natacha and Chong Lee.

Acceptable serial thick ear.

d Ford Beebe, Alan James

Buster Crabbe, Frances Robinson, Edna Sedgwick, Cyril Delevanti, Frank Lackteen

The Red Beret

GB   1953   88m   Technicolor
Warwick (Irving Allen, Albert R. Broccoli)
US title: *Paratrooper*

In 1940, an American with a guilt complex joins the British paratroopers.

Routine war action flagwaver; good battle scenes, rubbish in between.

w Richard Maibaum, Frank Nugent   *book* Hilary St George Saunders   *d* Terence Young   *ph* John Wilcox   *m* John Addison

Alan Ladd, Susan Stephen, Leo Genn, Harry Andrews, Donald Houston, Anthony Bushell, Patric Doonan, Stanley Baker, Lana Morris

Red Canyon

US   1949   82m   Technicolor
Leonard Goldstein/Universal

A cowboy drifter sets out to corral a famous wild stallion.

Old-fashioned family Western.

w Maurice Geraghty   *novel* Zane Grey   *d* George Sherman

Howard Duff, George Brent, Ann Blyth, Edgar Buchanan, John McIntire, Chill Wills, Jane Darwell, Lloyd Bridges

The Red Circle (dubbed) *

France/Italy   1970   102m   colour
Corona (Robert Dorfmann)
original title: *Le Cercle Rouge*

An ex-convict teams up with a criminal on the run and a former police marksman to steal jewels from a shop equipped with a high-tech security system.

Dark, grim thriller with downbeat ending, enlivened by the central set-piece of the robbery itself.

wd Jean-Pierre Melville   *ph* Henri Decae   *m* Eric de Marsan   *ad* Theo Meurisse

Alain Delon, André Bourvil, Gian-Maria Volonte, Yves Montand, Paul Crauchet, François Périer

The Red Danube

US   1950   119m   bw
MGM (Carey Wilson)

In occupied Vienna, citizens are being returned to Russia against their will.

Tedious and silly Red-baiting cold war charade.

w Gina Kaus, Arthur Wimperis   *novel Vespers in Vienna* by Bryan Marshall   *d* George Sidney
ph Charles Rosher   *m* Miklos Rozsa   *ad* Cedric Gibbons, Hans Peters

Ethel Barrymore, Walter Pidgeon, Janet Leigh, Peter Lawford, Francis L. Sullivan, Angela Lansbury, Louis Calhern, Melville Cooper

AAN: art direction

Red Dawn

US   1984   114m   Metrocolor
MGM-UA/Valkyrie (Buzz Feitshans, Barry Beckerman)
V, V*, L, S

Russians lead a violent invasion into Colorado and are wiped out by the locals.

Ludicrous and somewhat dangerous Cold War throwback with little entertainment value to commend it. Violent teenage nonsense.

w Kevin Reynolds, John Milius   *d* John Milius
ph Ric Waite   *m* Basil Poledouris   *pd* Jackson de Govia   *ed* Thom Noble

Patrick Swayze, C. Thomas Howell, Lea Thompson, Charlie Sheen, Darren Dalton, Jennifer Grey, Ben Johnson, Harry Dean Stanton, Ron O'Neal, Vladek Sheybal, Powers Boothe

The Red Desert *

Italy/France   1964   116m   Eastmancolor
Duemila/Federiz (Angelo Rizzoli)
V*, L, S
original title: *Il Deserto Rosso*

A wife suffers from depression, and a brief affair with her husband's friend doesn't help.

Elongated character study, very talkative but rather decoratively designed with the same subtle use of colour in an urban landscape as was seen later in *Blow Up*.

w Michelangelo Antonioni, Tonino Guerra
d Michelangelo Antonioni   *ph* Carlo di Palma
m Giovanni Chionetti

Monica Vitti, Richard Harris, Carlos Chionetti

'The beauty is stationary, painterly; and the arresting image precisely arrests and retards the already moribund thrust of the film.' – *John Simon*

'Boredom in Ravenna, and it seeps into the viewer's bones.' – *Pauline Kael, New Yorker, 1984*

'He treated her rough – and she loved it!'
Red Dust ***

US   1932   86m   bw
MGM (Hunt Stromberg)
V, V*, L

On a rubber plantation in Indo-China, the overseer is pursued by his engineer's bride but himself falls for a stranded prostitute.

Vigorous romantic melodrama with echoes of *Rain*; remade as *Congo Maisie* (1940) and *Mogambo* (1954).

w John Lee Mahin   *play* Wilson Collison   *d* Victor Fleming   *ph* Harold Rosson

Clark Gable, Jean Harlow, Mary Astor, Gene Raymond, Donald Crisp, Tully Marshall, Forrester Harvey

'Lots of pash, sex and undress . . . an exhib's delight and a cinch for fancy takings. Done so expertly it almost overcomes the basic script shortcomings.' – *Variety*

'Gable and Harlow have full play for their curiously similar sort of good-natured toughness.' – *Time*

† The Gable role was first announced for John Gilbert.
†† Scenes showing the shooting of *Red Dust* are included in *Bombshell*.

Red Garters **

US   1954   91m   Technicolor
Paramount (Pat Duggan)
V*

Various familiar types congregate in the Western town of Paradise Lost, and settle matters by the Code of the West.

Amusing Western musical spoof slightly deadened by its pretty but finally boring theatrically stylized scenery. Songs are catchy, performances good natured.

w *Michael Fessier*   *d* George Marshall   *ph* Arthur E. Arling   *m* Joseph J. Lilley   *songs* Jay Livingston, Ray Evans   *ad* Hal Pereira, Roland Anderson

Rosemary Clooney, Guy Mitchell, Gene Barry, Jack Carson, Pat Crowley, Cass Daley, Frank Faylen, Reginald Owen

'A musical of considerable freshness and gaiety.' – *MFB*

AAN: art direction

Red Headed Woman *

US   1932   74m   bw
MGM (Albert Lewin)
V*

A shopgirl marries the boss but is rejected in his social circles.

Unconvincing but occasionally entertaining melodrama.

w Anita Loos   *novel* Katharine Brush   *d* Jack Conway   *ph* Harold Rosson

Jean Harlow, Chester Morris, Lewis Stone, Leila Hyams, Una Merkel, Henry Stephenson, Charles Boyer, May Robson

'Gingery treatment of a controversial subject that is bound to engage femme interest.' – *Variety*

Red Heat *

US   1988   104m   Technicolor
Columbia TriStar/Carolco/Lone Wolf/Oak (Walter Hill, Gordon Carroll)
V, V*, L, S

A Russian and a Chicago cop team up against an international gang of drug smugglers.

Fast-moving action movie, but one that offers only a minor variation on the standard plot of ill-assorted partners.

w Harry Kleiner, Walter Hill, Troy Kennedy Martin   *d* Walter Hill   *ph* Matthew F. Leonetti   *pd* John Vallone   *ed* Freeman Davies, Carmel Davies, Donn Aron

Arnold Schwarzenegger, James Belushi, Peter Boyle, Ed O'Ross, Larry Fishburne, Gina Gershon, Richard Bright, J. W. Smith, Brent Jennings

The Red House *

US   1947   100m   bw
(UA) Thalia (Sol Lesser)
V*

A moody farmer's guilty obsession with an old house in the woods is that he murdered his parents in it.

Psycho-like suspense melodrama, too extended for comfort and too restricting for the actors, but effective in spurts.

wd Delmer Daves   *novel* George Agnew Chamberlain   *ph* Bert Glennon   *m* Miklos Rozsa

Edward G. Robinson, Judith Anderson, Lon McCallister, Allene Roberts, Rory Calhoun, Julie London, Ona Munson

The Red Inn *

France   1951   95m   bw
Memnon
original title: *L'Auberge Rouge*

In 1833, stagecoach travellers stay at a remote inn, where the owners intend to rob and murder them.

Extreme black farce which manages to be pretty funny for those who can take this kind of thing: even the survivors of the night's massacre fall down a ravine.

w *Jean Aurenche, Pierre Bost*   *d* Claude Autant-Lara   *ph* André Bac   *m* René Cloërc   *ad* Max Douy

Fernandel, Françoise Rosay, Carette, Grégoire Aslan

The Red Light

US   1949   83m   bw
UA/Pioneer (Roy Del Ruth)

An industrialist tracks down his brother's murderer.

Competent routine detection piece with engaging clues.

w George Callahan   *d* Roy Del Ruth   *ph* Bert Glennon   *m* Dimitri Tiomkin

George Raft, Virginia Mayo, Raymond Burr, Gene Lockhart, Henry Morgan, Arthur Franz

Red Line 7000

US   1965   110m   Technicolor
Paramount/Laurel (Howard Hawks)

The career and loves of a stock car racer.

Very routine romantic actioner full of the director's favourite situations but failing to find any fresh slant.

w George Kirgo   *d* Howard Hawks   *ph* Milton Krasner   *m* Nelson Riddle

James Caan, Laura Devon, Gail Hire, Charlene Holt, John Robert Crawford

The Red Menace

US 1949 87m bw
Republic
V*, L
GB title: *The Enemy Within*

A discontented war veteran is preyed on by communists.

An odd piece of anti-Red propaganda to come from an action studio, but it had some effect on thinking at the time.

w Albert DeMond, Gerald Geraghty d R. G. Springsteen

Robert Rockwell, Hanne Axman, Shepard Menken. (Cast deliberately chosen from unknowns.)

'It waves the flag at the proper times and is an okay melodrama on other points.' – *Variety*

Red Mountain

US 1951 84m Technicolor
Paramount/Hal B. Wallis

A Confederate captain joins Quantrell's Raiders but is horrified by their brutality.

Fast-moving action Western.

w John Meredyth Lucas, George W. George, George F. Slavin d William Dieterle ph Charles Lang Jnr m Franz Waxman

Alan Ladd, Lizabeth Scott, Arthur Kennedy, John Ireland, Jeff Corey, James Bell

'The World Torn Asunder By A Threat From Outer Space!'

Red Planet Mars

US 1952 87m bw
UA/Donald Hyde, Anthony Veiller

Americans and Russians both tune in to Mars and learn that it is a powerful Christian planet; the news causes first panic, then a religious revival and a determination to live more harmoniously on Earth.

Lunatic farrago that has to be seen to be believed.

w Anthony Veiller, John L. Balderston d Harry Horner ph Joseph Biroc md David Chudnow m Mahlon Merrick ad Charles D. Hall

Herbert Berghof, Peter Graves, Andrea King, Marvin Miller

The Red Pony

US 1949 88m Technicolor
Republic (Lewis Milestone)
V*, L

When his pet pony dies after an illness, a farmer's son loses faith in his father.

Sincere but rather obvious little fable which although capably made does not make inspiring film drama.

w John Steinbeck d Lewis Milestone ph Tony Gaudio m Aaron Copland pd Nicolai Remisoff

Myrna Loy, Robert Mitchum, Peter Miles, Louis Calhern, Shepperd Strudwick, Margaret Hamilton

The Red Rider

US 1934 bw serial: 15 eps
Universal

A Western sheriff saves his best pal from the noose and proves him innocent.

Adequate Western serial.

d Louis Friedlander

Buck Jones, Grant Withers, Marion Shilling, Walter Miller, Richard Cramer

Red River **

US 1948 133m bw
UA/Monterey (Howard Hawks)
V, V*, L

How the Chisholm Trail was developed as a cattle drive.

Brawling Western, a bit serious and long drawn out but with splendid action sequences.

w Borden Chase, Charles Schnee d Howard Hawks ph Russell Harlan m Dimitri Tiomkin ed Christian Nyby

John Wayne, *Montgomery Clift*, Joanne Dru, Walter Brennan, Colleen Gray, John Ireland, Noah Beery Jnr, Harry Carey Jnr

AAN: original story (Borden Chase); editing

'Death is a $10,000 Bullet.'
Red Rock West *

US 1992 98m DeLuxe
Rank/Red Rock (Sigurjon Sighvatsson, Steve Golin)
V, V*

A drifter who arrives in a small town is mistaken for a hitman and hired by both a husband and a wife to kill the other.

Enjoyable, blackly comic thriller with plenty of twists and turns.

w John Dahl, Rick Dahl d John Dahl ph Marc Reshovsky m William Olvis pd Robert Pearson ed Scott Chestnut

Nicolas Cage, Lara Flynn Boyle, Dennis Hopper, J. T. Walsh, Craig Reay, Vance Johnson, Robert Apel

'Though it vaguely resembles a droll Buñuel construction, it owes more to the hard-boiled thrillers of the 1940s, albeit with a very large tongue-in-cheek quotient.' – *Variety*

'Very entertaining, doesn't detain you long, and has total confidence in its cinematic convictions.' – *Derek Malcolm, Guardian*

Red Salute *

US 1935 78m bw
Edward Small
aka: *Runaway Daughter*;
GB title: *Arms and the Girl*

A college girl with communist leanings takes a cross country trip with an American soldier.

Odd little romantic comedy modelled on *It Happened One Night*; it was picketed for its inconsequential attitude to politics.

w Humphrey Pearson, Manuel Seff d Sidney Lanfield ph Robert Planck

Barbara Stanwyck, Robert Young, Hardie Albright, Cliff Edwards, Ruth Donnelly, Gordon Jones, Henry Kolker

'Tepid comedy romance wrapped up in a preachment against campus agitators who oppose militarism.' – *Variety*

Red Scorpion

US 1989 102m DeLuxe
Shapiro Glickenhaus (Jack Abramoff)
V, V*, S

A Russian agent's assignment is to assassinate the leader of a group of African terrorists.

Incompetent action movie that staggers from one dull moment to another with a complete lack of conviction.

w Arne Olsen d Joseph Zito ph João Fernandes m Jay Chattaway pd Ladislav Wilheim sp John Evans; make-up: Tom Savini ed Daniel Loewenthal

Dolph Lundgren, M. Emmet Walsh, Al White, T. P. McKenna, Carmen Argenziano, Alex Cohen, Brion James

The Red Shoes ****

GB 1948 136m Technicolor
GFD/The Archers (Michael Powell, Emeric Pressburger)
V, V*, L

A girl student becomes a great ballet star but commits suicide when torn between love and her career.

Never was a better film made from such a penny plain story so unpersuasively written and performed; the splendour of the production is in the intimate view it gives of life backstage in the ballet world with its larger-than-life characters. The ballet excerpts are very fine, and the colour discreet; the whole film is charged with excitement.

wd Michael Powell, Emeric Pressburger ph Jack Cardiff m Brian Easdale pd Hein Heckroth ed Reginald Mills

Anton Walbrook, Moira Shearer, Marius Goring, Robert Helpmann, Albert Basserman, Frederick Ashton, Leonide Massine, Ludmilla Tcherina, Esmond Knight

'In texture, like nothing the British cinema has ever seen.' – *Time Out, 1981*

AA: Brian Easdale

AAN: best picture; original story (Michael Powell, Emeric Pressburger); art direction; editing

Red Skies of Montana

US 1952 99m Technicolor
TCF (Samuel G. Engel)
aka: *Smoke Jumpers*

Tension among firefighting crews in the mountains of Montana.

Adequate, routine action melodrama with semi-documentary touches.

w Harry Kleiner d Joseph M. Newman ph Charles G. Clarke m Sol Kaplan

Richard Widmark, Jeffrey Hunter, Constance Smith, Richard Boone, Richard Crenna

'A man's desperation – a woman's passion – a boy's awakening – a girl's desire!'
Red Sky at Morning

US 1970 113m Technicolor
Universal/Hal Wallis

During World War II the family of an officer on active service find life in New Mexico not what they've been used to.

Peyton Place by any other name, well produced but of little real interest.

w Marguerite Roberts novel Richard Bradford d James Goldstone ph Vilmos Zsigismond m Billy Goldenberg

Claire Bloom, Richard Thomas, Richard Crenna, Catherine Burns, Desi Arnaz Jnr, John Colicos, Harry Guardino

Red Sonja

US 1985 89m Metrocolor
MGM-UA/Thorn EMI (Christian Ferry)
V, V*, L

In the times of sword and sorcery, Sonja avenges her sister's death and deposes an evil queen.

Absolute comic strip nonsense: even the monsters look mechanical.

w Clive Exton, George MacDonald Fraser stories Robert E. Howard d Richard Fleischer ph Giuseppe Rotunno m Ennio Morricone pd Danilo Donati ed Frank J. Urioste

Brigitte Nielsen, Arnold Schwarzenegger, Sandahl Bergman, Paul Smith, Ronald Lacey

Red Sorghum ***

China 1987 92m Eastmancolor
Palace/Xi'an Film Studio (Li Changqing)
V, V*
original title: *Hong Gaoliang*

A man recalls his grandparents' love affair and violent times.

Exuberant tragi-comic folk tale, told with immense panache.

w Chen Jianyu, Zhu Wei, Mo Yan d Zhang Yimou ph Gu Changwei m Zhao Jiping ad Yang Gang ed Du Yuan

Gong Li, Jiang Wen, Teng Rujun, Liu Ji, Qian Ming, Ji Chunhua, Zhai Chunhua

'A rough, proletarian belch of a film, a gleeful assertion of peasant vitality, founded on amoral (but fully justified) acts of transgression' – *Tony Rayns, MFB*

Red Sun
France/Italy/Spain   1971   108m   Eastmancolor
Corona/Oceania/Balcazar (Robert Dorfman)
V*

In 1870 Arizona, an outlaw is forced to accompany a Japanese samurai to recover a ceremonial sword which his partner has stolen.

Unusual but generally ineffective Western with a fashionable international cast.

w Lair Koenig, D. B. Petitclerc, W. Roberts, L. Roman   d Terence Young   ph Henri Alekan   m Maurice Jarre

Charles Bronson, Toshiro Mifune, Alain Delon, Ursula Andress, Capucine

'A nice exotic item ruined by suburban direction.' – *Sight and Sound*

Red Sundown
US   1956   81m   Technicolor
Universal-International

A gunslinger becomes a deputy and tames a lawless town.

Elementary Western action piece, not unentertaining.

w Martin Berkeley   d Jack Arnold

Rory Calhoun, Martha Hyer, Dean Jagger, Robert Middleton, James Millican, Grant Williams

The Red Tent *
Italy/USSR   1970   121m   Technicolor
Paramount/Vides/Mosfilm (Franco Cristaldi)
V*, L

The story of General Nobile's ill-fated 1928 expedition by dirigible to the Arctic.

Stiffly-conceived international spectacular with one striking sequence but not much good cheer.

w Ennio de Concini, Richard Adams   d Mikhail Kalatozov   ph Leonid Kalashnikov   m Ennio Morricone

Peter Finch, Sean Connery, Hardy Kruger, Claudia Cardinale, Mario Adorf, Massimo Girotti

Red Tomahawk
US   1967   80m   Technicolor
A. C. Lyles/Paramount

The small town of Deadwood is caught up in the aftermath of Little Big Horn.

Talkative Western filled with old faces, as is this producer's wont.

w Steve Fisher   d R. G. Springsteen

Howard Keel, Joan Caulfield, Broderick Crawford, Scott Brady, Wendell Corey, Richard Arlen, Tom Drake

Red Wagon
GB   1933   107m   bw
BIP

Passions mount in a travelling circus. Gypsies and jealousies are the ingredients of a melodrama aimed at the international market.

It failed.

w Roger Burford, Edward Knoblock, Arthur Woods   novel Lady Eleanor Smith   d Paul Stein

Charles Bickford, Raquel Torres, Greta Nissen, Don Alvarado, Anthony Bushell, Paul Graetz, Jimmy Hanley, Frank Pettingell

Redbeard *
Japan   1965   165m   bw   Tohoscope
Toho-Kurosawa
V*, L
original title: *Akahige*

Problems of a 19th-century doctor. Almost a Japanese version of *The Citadel*: Kurosawa himself called it 'a monument to goodness in man'.

Rather heavy-going, but sporadically compelling.

w Masato Ide, Hideo Oguni, Akira Kurosawa   novel Shugoro Yamamoto   d Akira Kurosawa   ph A. Nakai, T. Saito   m M. Sato

Toshiro Mifune, Yuzo Kayama

'A three-hour excursion into nineteenth-century hospital soap opera; a mediocre enough script, but beautifully directed and flawlessly acted.' – *John Simon*

Redemption
US   1930   82m   bw
MGM

A man thought dead commits suicide rather than interrupt his wife's new life.

Elaborate but unsuccessful talkie début of a waning star; very hard going.

w Dorothy Farnum, Edwin Justus Mayer   novel The Living Corpse by Leo Tolstoy   d Fred Niblo

John Gilbert, Renee Adoree, Eleanor Boardman, Conrad Nagel

The Redhead: see *Poil de Carotte*

Redneck
Italy/GB   1972   87m   colour
Crawford/CIAC/Sterle (Michael Lester, Silvio Narizzano)
original title: *Senza Ragione*

Two crooks on the run steal a car and discover that it contains a teenage boy.

Dull chase film that wanders around the Italian countryside to little effect.

w Win Wells, Masolino D'Amico   story Rafael Sanchez Campoy   d Silvio Narizzano   ph Giorgio Tonti   m Maurizio Catalano   ad Arrigo Equini   ed Thom Noble

Franco Nero, Telly Savalas, Mark Lester, Ely Galleani, Duilio Del Prete, Maria Michi

'Not since *Gone with the Wind* has there been a great romantic epic like it!'

Reds **
US   1981   196m   Technicolor
Paramount (Warren Beatty)
V, V*, L

The last years of John Reed, an American writer who after stormy romantic vicissitudes goes with his wife to Russia and writes *Ten Days That Shook the World*.

Interminably long but full of quality, this immensely detailed work was a most unlikely project to succeed in the eighties, but its very strangeness enabled it to break even.

w Warren Beatty, Trevor Griffiths   d Warren Beatty   ph Vittorio Storaro   m Stephen Sondheim   pd Richard Sylbert

Warren Beatty, Diane Keaton, Edward Herrman, Jerzy Kosincki, Jack Nicholson, Maureen Stapleton, Paul Sorvino

AA: Warren Beatty (as director); Vittorio Storaro; Maureen Stapleton (supporting actress)

AAN: best picture; screenplay; editing (Dede Allen, Craig McKay); Warren Beatty (as actor); Diane Keaton; Jack Nicholson

BFA: best supporting actor (Jack Nicholson); best supporting actress (Maureen Stapleton)

Reducing
US   1931   73m   bw
MGM

The proprietress of a beauty parlour sends for an old family servant to help her.

Loosely plotted comedy consisting largely of slapstick in a Turkish bath.

w Willard Mack, Beatrice Banyard   d Charles F. Reisner

Marie Dressler, Polly Moran, Anita Page, Lucien Littlefield, Sally Eilers

'Rough and tumble hoke comedy addressed to the banana peel sense of humour.' – *Variety*

Reed – México Insurgente **
Mexico   1971   106m   bw
Salvador Lopez/Ollin y Asociados

Reporting the Mexican revolution in 1913, American journalist John Reed learns to identify with the oppressed.

A low-key documentary-style account of Reed's conversion to political action, eschewing mock-heroics and enhanced by sepia photography.

wd Paul Leduc

Claudio Obregón, Ernesto Gómez Cruz, Eduardo López Rojas, Juan Angel Martinez, Carlos Castañón

Reefer and the Model *
Ireland   1988   93m   Technicolor
Metro/Berber Films (Lelia Doolan)
V

A former IRA man, his trawler-owning friends, and a pregnant girl he picks up, attempt a bank robbery to raise money.

Raffishly enjoyable thriller, though its attempt to explain the political context of modern Ireland lacks resonance.

wd Joe Comerford   ph Breffni Byrne   m Johnny Duhan   pd John Lucas   ed Sé Merry

Ian McElhinney, Eve Watkinson, Carol Scanlan, Birdy Sweeney, Sean Lawlor, Ray McBride

'It's all part of the American Dream.'
The Reflecting Skin
GB   1990   95m   Technicolor
Virgin/Fugitive Features/BBC Films/British Screen/Zenith (Dominic Anciano, Ray Burdis)
V, V*, L

A young boy suspects a strange woman of having killed his friends.

Grotesque, death-obsessed movie, directed at a somnambulistic pace, though it found admirers at several film festivals.

wd Philip Ridley   ph Dick Pope   m Nick Bicat   ad Rick Roberts   ed Scott Thomas

Viggo Mortensen, Lindsay Duncan, Jeremy Cooper, Sheila Moore, Duncan Fraser, David Longworth, Robert Koons, David Bloom

'The film strains for poetic resonance: a puffed-up frog trying to pass as a prince.' – *Independent*

'This is American Grand Guignol orchestrated by a foreigner with a frightening idea of how the mysteries of the adult world seem to the highly imaginative but still relatively innocent young.' – *Guardian*

Reflection of Fear
US   1971   90m   Eastmancolor
Columbia (Howard B. Jaffe)
V*

A retarded teenage girl kills her mother and her grandmother.

Psycho thriller of little interest or suspense.

w Edward Hume, Lewis John Carlino *novel Go to Thy Deathbed* by Stanton Forbes *d* William A. Fraker *ph* Laszlo Kovacs *m* Fred Myrow

Robert Shaw, Mary Ure, Signe Hasso, Sondra Locke, Mitch Ryan

Reflections in a Golden Eye *
US 1967 108m Technicolor
Warner Seven Arts (Ray Stark)
V, V*

Repressions at a peacetime army camp in Georgia. A private soldier rides nude on horseback, a major has the hots for him, the major's wife has an affair with their neighbour, whose wife has cut off her nipples with garden shears.

A film as idiotic as its story line, but smoothly marshalled so that at least it's more amusing than boring.

w Chapman Mortimer, Gladys Hill *novel* Carson McCullers *d John Huston ph* Aldo Tonti *m* Toshiro Mayuzumi *pd* Stephen Grimes

Marlon Brando, Elizabeth Taylor, Brian Keith, Julie Harris, Robert Forster, Zorro David

'One feels trapped in a huge overheated hothouse containing nothing but common snapdragons. Pedestrian, crass, and uninvolving to the point of repellence.' – *John Simon*

'Nothing more than nutty people and pseudo porn.' – *Judith Crist*

The Reformer and the Redhead *
US 1950 90m bw
MGM (Norman Panama, Melvin Frank)

A small-town reform candidate abandons his crooked protector and wins under his own steam, helped by the daughter of the zoo superintendent.

Scatty sub-Capra comedy with a lightweight script but good production and playing.

wd Norman Panama, Melvin Frank *ph* Ray June *m* David Raksin

Dick Powell, June Allyson, Cecil Kellaway, David Wayne, Ray Collins, Robert Keith, Marvin Kaplan

Regain: see *Harvest*

Regarding Henry
US 1991 108m Technicolor
UIP/Paramount (Scott Rudin, Mike Nichols)
V, V*, L

A tough lawyer, who loses most of his faculties in a shooting, becomes a much nicer person as he recovers.

Sentimental fable that fails to convince.

w Jeffrey Abrams *d* Mike Nichols *ph* Giuseppe Rotunno *m* Hans Zimmer *pd* Tony Walton *ed* Sam O'Steen

Harrison Ford, Annette Bening, Bill Nunn, Mikki Allen, Donald Moffat, Aida Linares, Elizabeth Wilson, Robin Bartlett, Bruce Altman, Rebecca Miller

La Règle du Jeu ***
France 1939 113m bw
La Nouvelle Edition Française (Claude Renoir)
V, V*, L
aka: *The Rules of the Game*

A count organizes a weekend shooting party which results in complex love intrigues among servants as well as masters.

Celebrated satirical comedy with a uniquely bleak outlook.

w Jean Renoir, Carl Koch *d* Jean Renoir *ph* Jean Bachelet, Alain Renoir *m* Joseph Kosma, Roger Desormières *ad* Eugène Lourié, Max Douy *ed* Marguerite Renoir, Marthe Huguet

Marcel Dalio, Nora Gregor, Jean Renoir, Mila Parély, Julien Carette, Gaston Modot, Roland Toutain

'It is a question of panache, of preserving a casual indifference to the workings of fate.' – *The Times*

'How brilliantly Renoir focuses the confusion! The rather fusty luxury of the chateau, the constant mindless slaughter of wild animals, the minuets of adultery and seduction, the gavottes of mutual hatred or mistrust . . .' – *Basil Wright, 1972*

† The film was originally banned as indicting the corruption of France, and during the war the negative was destroyed during an air raid; but eventually a full version was pieced together from various materials.

Det Regnar Pa Var Kärlek: see *It Rains on Our Love*

Reign of Terror: see *The Black Book*

The Reincarnation of Peter Proud
US 1974 104m Technicolor
Avco Embassy/Bing Crosby (Frank P. Rosenberg)
V*, L

A history professor is troubled by recurring dreams of his former existence.

Hysterical psychic melodrama which pretty well ruins its own chances by failing to explain its plot.

w Max Ehrlich *novel* Max Ehrlich *d* J. Lee-Thompson *ph* Victor J. Kemper *m* Jerry Goldsmith

Michael Sarrazin, Jennifer O'Neill, Margot Kidder, Cornelia Sharpe, Paul Hecht

'It may well be the silliest approach to the subject in any medium . . . all flashbacks trampling the action with the finesse of a rogue elephant.' – *Tom Milne*

Reise der Hoffnung: see *Journey of Hope*

The Reivers *
US 1969 111m Technicolor Panavision
Cinema Center/Duo/Solar (Irving Ravetch)
V*

In Mississippi at the turn of the century a hired hand borrows the new family auto for a trip into Memphis with the grandson of the family and a black stablehand.

Pleasant but insubstantial yarn of more gracious days; most attractive to look at, it entertains gently without ever reaching a point.

w Irving Ravetch, Harriet Frank Jnr *novel* William Faulkner *d* Mark Rydell *ph* Richard Moore *m* John Williams

Steve McQueen, Sharon Farrell, Will Geer, Rupert Crosse, Mitch Vogel, Michael Constantine, Juano Hernandez, Clifton James

AAN: John Williams; Rupert Crosse

Relentless
US 1948 93m Technicolor
Columbia

A cowboy framed for murder must clear himself before the posse catches up with him.

Brisk Western copy of *The 39 Steps*.

w Winston Miller *d* George Sherman

Robert Young, Marguerite Chapman, Willard Parker, Barton MacLane, Will Wright

The Reluctant Astronaut
US 1967 101m Technicolor
Universal

By a series of accidents a man with vertigo becomes an astronaut.

Feeble vehicle for a comedian briefly popular.

w Jim Fritzell, Everett Greenbaum *d* Edward J. Montagne

Don Knotts, Leslie Nielsen, Joan Freeman, Jesse White, Jeanette Nolan, Arthur O'Connell

The Reluctant Débutante *
US 1958 96m Metrocolor Cinemascope
MGM/Avon (Pandro S. Berman)
V*

A noble couple have difficulty in steering their American-educated daughter through the intricacies of the London season.

A slight but pleasing British comedy has become a rather strident example of lend-lease, but still affords minor pleasures.

w William Douglas Home *play* William Douglas Home *d* Vincente Minnelli *ph* Joseph Ruttenberg *md* Eddie Warner *ad* Jean d'Aubonne

Rex Harrison, Kay Kendall, Sandra Dee, Peter Myers, Angela Lansbury, John Saxon, Diane Clare

The Reluctant Dragon **
US 1941 72m Technicolor
Walt Disney
V, V*

A tour of the Disney Studios affords some glimpses of how cartoons are made.

Amiable pot-pourri of cartoon shorts (*Baby Weems, How to Ride a Horse* and the title story) linked by a studio tour of absorbing interest.

w various *d* Alfred Werker (live action), various

Robert Benchley, Frances Gifford, Nana Bryant

Reluctant Heroes *
GB 1951 80m bw
Byron (Henry Halstead)
V

Comedy of national servicemen and their misdemeanours.

Simple-minded army farce which was popular for years as play and film.

w Colin Morris *play* Colin Morris *d* Jack Raymond *ph* James Wilson

Brian Rix, Ronald Shiner, Derek Farr, Christine Norden, Larry Noble

The Reluctant Widow
GB 1950 91m bw
Rank/Two Cities (Gordon Wellesley)

During the Napoleonic wars a governess is co-opted as a spy.

Thin romantic drama which despite nice art direction never really sparks into life.

w Gordon Wellesley, J. B. Boothroyd *novel* Georgette Heyer *d* Bernard Knowles *ph* Jack Hildyard *ad* Carmen Dillon

Jean Kent, Guy Rolfe, Kathleen Byron, Paul Dupuis, Lana Morris, Julian Dallas, Peter Hammond, Andrew Cruickshank

The Remains of the Day **
GB/US 1993 134m Technicolor
Columbia/Merchant Ivory (Ishmail Merchant, Mike Nichols, John Calley)
S

A butler comes to realize that his lifelong respect for, and loyalty to, his aristocratic master was misplaced.

An artful, nicely composed study in repressed emotions, stiff upper lips and class attitudes; in the final analysis, though, it seems no more than P. G. Wodehouse re-played as tragedy.

w Ruth Prawer Jhabvala *novel* Kazuo Ishiguro *d* James Ivory *ph* Tony Pierce-Roberts *m* Richard Robbins *pd* Luciana Arrighi *ed* Andrew Marcus

Anthony Hopkins, Emma Thompson, James Fox, Christopher Reeve, Peter Vaughan, Hugh Grant, Michel Lonsdale, Tim Piggot-Smith, Patrick Godfrey

'Continuously absorbing, but lacks the emotional resonance that would have made it completely satisfying.' – *Variety*

'This luxuriously mounted and often brilliantly engineered adaptation . . . could well be the producer and director team Merchant Ivory's most comprehensive success. It unquestionably deserves to be.' – *Derek Malcolm, Guardian*

AAN: Anthony Hopkins; Emma Thompson; James Ivory; best picture; Ruth Prawer Jhabvala; Richard Robbins; Luciana Arrighi; costume design (Jenny Beaven, John Bright)

Remains to Be Seen
US   1953   88m   bw
MGM (Arthur Hornblow Jnr)

The manager of an apartment house finds a dead body, and before the police arrive someone sticks a knife into it.

Flabby comedy-thriller giving the cast little to work on.

w Sidney Sheldon   *play* Howard Lindsay, Russel Crouse   d Don Weis   ph Robert Planck   md Jeff Alexander

June Allyson, Van Johnson, Angela Lansbury, Louis Calhern, John Beal, Dorothy Dandridge

'By thunderation, I'll show America how to get tough!'
The Remarkable Andrew *
US   1942   80m   bw
Paramount (Richard Blumenthal)

A young municipal bookkeeper is framed by local politicians but helped by the ghost of Andrew Jackson and friends.

Pleasant, rather faded, whimsical comedy which also managed to be propaganda for the war effort.

w Dalton Trumbo   d Stuart Heisler   ph Theodor Sparkuhl   m Victor Young

William Holden, Ellen Drew, Brian Donlevy, Rod Cameron, Richard Webb, Porter Hall, Frances Gifford, Nydia Westman, Montagu Love

'About all that comes through in the juxtaposition of these lithograph characters over modern Shale City is Franklin's delight over the electric light and Jackson's alarm over the radio.' – *John McManus, PM*

The Remarkable Mr Kipps: see *Kipps*

The Remarkable Mr Pennypacker
US   1958   87m   Technicolor   Cinemascope
TCF (Charles Brackett)

A Pennsylvania businessman leads two lives with two separate families.

Feeble and obvious period comedy of bigamy; very few laughs.

w Walter Reisch   *play* Liam O'Brien   d Henry Levin   ph Milton Krasner   m Leigh Harline

Clifton Webb, Dorothy McGuire, Charles Coburn, Ray Stricklyn, Jill St John, Ron Ely, David Nelson

Rembrandt ****
GB   1936   85m   bw
London Films (Alexander Korda)
V*

Episodes in the life of the 17th-century painter.

Austerely comic, gently tragic character piece, superbly staged and photographed, with a great performance at its centre.

w *Lajos Biro, June Head, Carl Zuckmayer*   d *Alexander Korda*   ph *Georges Perinal, Richard Angst*   m Geoffrey Toye

Charles Laughton, Elsa Lanchester, Gertrude Lawrence, Edward Chapman, Walter Hudd, Roger Livesey, Herbert Lomas, Allan Jeayes, Sam Livesey, Raymond Huntley, John Clements

'Never exciting, and only partly believable . . . a feature film without a story plot.' – *Variety*

'Amazingly full of that light which the great master of painting subdued to his supreme purpose.' – *James Agate*

'The film is ruined by lack of story and continuity: it has no drive. Like *The Private Life of Henry the Eighth* it is a series of unrelated tableaux.' – *Graham Greene*

Remember?
US   1939   83m   bw
MGM (Milton Bren)

A newly married couple do not get on, so a friend gives them a potion which makes them lose their memories and fall in love all over again.

Silly, witless comedy which did no good for anyone concerned.

w Corey Ford, Norman Z. McLeod   d Norman Z. McLeod   ph George Folsey   m Edward Ward

Robert Taylor, Greer Garson, Lew Ayres, Billie Burke, Reginald Owen, George Barbier, Henry Travers, Richard Carle, Laura Hope Crews, Halliwell Hobbes, Sig Rumann

'Many bright episodes contrast with some bumpy and over-dialogued stretches.' – *Variety*

Remember Last Night? **
US   1936   80m   bw
Universal

Socialites with hangovers find that murder was committed during their party.

Ingenious but overlong mixture of styles: farce, *Thin Man* comedy, murder mystery, satire, fantasy. Very well worth looking at.

w Harry Clork, Dan Totheroh, Doris Malloy   *novel* The Hangover Murders by Adam Hobhouse   d James Whale   ph Joseph Valentine   m Franz Waxman

Robert Young, Edward Arnold, Arthur Treacher, Constance Cummings, Robert Armstrong, Sally Eilers, Reginald Denny, Ed Brophy, Jack La Rue, Gustav von Seyffertitz, Gregory Ratoff

'It will be hard to sell because it is hard to understand . . . the basic story can scarcely be followed, while the superficial gloss of phoney sophistication neither fits a narrative in which four murders and two suicides are recorded, nor carries conviction of itself.' – *Variety*

'Parodying the detective thriller in a dazzling cascade of gags, this brilliant divertissement eventually takes off into pure surrealism.' – *Tom Milne, MFB, 1974*

Remember My Name *
US   1978   94m   DeLuxe
Columbia/Lion's Gate (Robert Altman)

After twelve years in prison, a woman takes calm revenge on the man who allowed her to take the blame for his crime.

Basically reminiscent of a Barbara Stanwyck vehicle of the forties, this interesting film is finally too concerned to strike on all levels, including satire, social awareness and fashionable pessimism.

wd Alan Rudolph   ph Tak Fujimoto   *songs* Alberta Hunter   ed Thomas Walls, William A. Sawyer

Geraldine Chaplin, Anthony Perkins, Moses Gunn, Berry Berenson, Jeff Goldblum

Remember That Face: see *The Mob*

Remember the Day *
US   1941   86m   bw
TCF (William Perlberg)

An elderly schoolteacher recollects her past life.

Pleasant sentimental drama, very well mounted.

w Tess Schlesinger, Frank Davis, Allan Scott   *play* Philo Higley   d Henry King   ph George Barnes   m Alfred Newman

Claudette Colbert, John Payne, Shepperd Strudwick, Jane Seymour, Anne Revere, Frieda Inescort

Remember the Night *
US   1940   94m   bw
Paramount (Mitchell Leisen)

An assistant district attorney takes a lady shoplifter home with him for Christmas.

Eccentric but winning blend of comedy, romance and drama, deftly mixed by master chefs.

w Preston Sturges   d Mitchell Leisen   ph Ted Tetzlaff   m Frederick Hollander

Barbara Stanwyck, Fred MacMurray, Beulah Bondi, Elizabeth Patterson, Sterling Holloway, Paul Guilfoyle, Willard Robertson

'Rarely has such a theme been so smoothly advanced and so pleasantly played out to so sensible and credible a conclusion.' – *New York Times*

Remembrance
GB   1982   117m   Eastmancolor
Channel 4/Colin Gregg

Young sailors in Plymouth enjoy a last night's leave before a six-month tour of duty with the NATO forces.

A few slices of what in the eyes of film-makers passes for realism these days: boozing, violence and bad language. The film seems to make no point and certainly doesn't entertain, though the components are slickly enough assembled.

w Hugh Stoddart   d Colin Gregg   ph John Metcalfe   m various pop performances   ed Peter Delfgou

John Altman, Al Ashton, Martin Barrass, Nick Dunning, Sally Jane Jackson, David John, Peter Lee-Wilson, Kenneth Griffith

'A clear and disheartening case of ambition exceeding grasp.' – *Geoff Brown, MFB*

Remo Williams: The Adventure Begins
US   1985   121m   DeLuxe
Orion/Dick Clark, Larry Spiegel, Mel Bergman
V, V*, L
GB title: *Remo: Unarmed and Dangerous*

A New York cop is recruited by the CIA to learn martial arts which will help him to fight an evil arms manufacturer.

Po-faced and oddly unlikeable, this elaborate adventure movie never really finds a style, and is dislocated by a middle section in which our hero is taught by an elderly Korean.

w Christopher Wood   *novels Destroyer* series by Richard Sapir, Warren Murphy   d Guy Hamilton   ph Andrew Laszlo   m Craig Safan   pd Jackson de Govia

Fred Ward, Joel Grey, Wilford Brimley, J. A. Preston, Charles Cioffi, Kate Mulgrew, George Coe

Remorques *
France   1941   80m   bw
MAIC
US title: *Stormy Waters*

A tugboat captain falls in love with a mysterious woman but remains faithful to his invalid wife.

Effective, minor, romantic melodrama.

w Jacques Prévert, André Cayatte   *novel* Roger Vercel   d Jean Grémillon   ph Armand Thirard, Louis Née   m Roland Manuel

Jean Gabin, Michèle Morgan, Madeleine Renaud, Fernand Ledoux

Rendezvous
US   1935   106m   bw
MGM (Lawrence Weingarten)

A decoding expert breaks an enemy spy ring.

Agreeable light romantic comedy drama with an espionage plot.

w Bella and Samuel Spewack *novel Black Chamber* by Herbert Yardley d William K. Howard ph William Daniels m William Axt

William Powell, Rosalind Russell, Binnie Barnes, Lionel Atwill, Cesar Romero, Samuel S. Hinds, Henry Stephenson, Frank Reicher

'Another chill-and-chuckle play aiming at the *Thin Man* trade and scoring a bull's-eye.' – *Variety*

Rendezvous (1951): see *Darling How Could You?*

Rendez-Vous **
France   1985   83m   colour
Cannon/T Films/A2 (Alain Terzian)
V*, L

A provincial actress, trying for success in Paris, becomes involved with a self-destructive actor.

Stylish drama of young hopefuls that won the best director award at the Cannes Film Festival in 1985.

w André Téchiné, Olivier Assayas d André Téchiné ph Renato Berta m Philippe Sarde pd Jean-Pierre Kohut Svelko ed Martine Giordano

Juliette Binoche, Lambert Wilson, Wadeck Stanczak, Jean-Louis Trintignant, Dominique Lavanant

Rendezvous at Midnight
US   1935   60m   bw
Universal

A police commissioner investigates the murder of his predecessor.

Modest mystery co-feature which wastes time up front on a fashion show.

w Gladys Unger *play The Silver Fox* by Gaetano Sazlo d Christy Cabanne

Ralph Bellamy, Valerie Hobson, Catherine Doucet, Irene Ware, Helen Jerome Eddy

'The woeful lack of action drags it down.' – *Variety*

Rendezvous de Juillet **
France   1949   110m   bw
UGC-SNEG (René G. Vuattoux)

A group of young people in post-war St Germain-des-Prés plan an expedition to the Congo.

Highly likeable series of impressions of interesting people, a little indeterminate and possibly dated now, but in its time extremely fresh and vital.

wd *Jacques Becker* ph Claude Renoir m Jean Wiener, Mezz Mezzrow

Daniel Gelin, Maurice Ronet, Brigitte Auber, Pierre Trabaud, Nicole Courcel

Les Rendezvous du Diable **
France   1958   80m   colour
Union Générale Cinématographique/Jacques Constant/Haroun Tazieff
aka: *Volcano*

Adventures of a Belgian volcanologist.

Daring exploits on the rims of the world's most active volcanoes, including Etna and Stromboli in eruption. Fascinating footage is urbanely presented.

wd/ph *Haroun Tazieff* m Marius-François Gaillard

'Beauty blends with horror, romantic grandeur with fear.' – *MFB*

Rendezvous 24
US   1946   70m   bw
Sol M. Wurtzel/TCF

American secret agents track down post-war Nazis who are working on atomic explosions from a remote base in the Harz mountains.

Routine thick ear despite claims of timeliness; as such, quite tolerable.

w Aubrey Wisberg d James Tinling

William Gargan, Maria Palmer, Pat O'Moore, David Leonard, Kurt Katch, Herman Bing

Rendezvous with Annie
US   1946   89m   bw
Republic

An American soldier in England goes absent without leave to see his wife in New York, an exploit which later nearly loses him a fortune.

An engaging comedy idea filmed with insufficient wit, this gets by on charm.

w Mary Loos, Richard Sale d Allan Dwan

Eddie Albert, Faye Marlowe, C. Aubrey Smith

Réne La Canne *
France/Italy   1977   98m   Telecolor
Président/Rizzoli (Jacques-Eric Strauss)
V

During the Second World War a French policeman and a thief defy the Germans; after it, they find themselves in friendly rivalry.

Broad and sometimes blackish farce which amuses mainly by the expert and stylized comedy performances of the two male leads.

w Jacques Rouffio, Francis Girod *novel* Roger Borniche d Francis Girod ph Aldo Tonti m Ennio Morricone ad Jean-Jacques Caziot ed Eva Zora

Gérard Depardieu, Sylvia Kristel, Michel Piccoli, Stefano Patrizi, Ricardo Garrone, Jacques Jouanneau, Jean Rigaux, Orchidea de Santis, Venantino Venantini, Valerie Mairesse, Jean Carmet

Renegade
US   1993   95m   Foto-Kem colour
Cannell Entertainment
V, V*

An ex-cop turned bounty hunter joins an organization that stages fights to the death in order to discover what happened to his brother, who disappeared 17 years earlier.

Risible action adventure with muscle-bound acting and dialogue, and padded out with some irrelevant scenes of love-making between extras.

w Stephen J. Cannell, Nick Corea d Ralph Hemecker, R. Marvin ph Kenneth L. Gibb m Roger Neill ad Michel Levesque ed John W. Carr, Skip Robinson

Lorenzo Lamas, Branscombe Mond, Kathleen Kinmont, Charles Napier, Madison Mason, Stephen J. Cannell, Marjean Holden, Danny Wells, Mitchell Ryan, Martin Kove

Renegade Girls: see *Caged Heat*

Renegades
US   1930   84m   bw
Fox

A disgraced French officer becomes a hero of the Foreign Legion.

Satisfying romantic melodrama of its period.

w Jules Furthman *novel* André Armandy d Victor Fleming

Warner Baxter, Myrna Loy, Bela Lugosi, Noah Beery, C. Henry Gordon, Gregory Gaye

'Everyone in the picture dies in the last few feet.' – *Variety*

Renegades
US   1946   88m   Technicolor
Columbia

An outlaw's son tries in vain to go straight.

Unsurprising but efficient bill-topping Western of its day.

w Melvin Levey, Francis Faragoh d George Sherman

Evelyn Keyes, Larry Parks, Willard Parker, Edgar Buchanan

Renegades
US   1989   105m   colour
Virgin/Morgan Creek/Interscope Communications (David Madden)
V, V*, L

A cop and an Indian team up to recover a stolen sacred lance.

Run-of-the-mill action movie in which nothing memorable occurs.

w David Rich d Jack Sholder ph Phil Meheux m Michael Kamen pd Carol Spier ed Caroline Biggerstaff

Kiefer Sutherland, Lou Diamond Phillips, Jami Gertz, Rob Knepper, Bill Smitrovich, Peter MacNeill

Reno
US   1939   72m   bw
RKO

As Reno becomes a great city for gambling and divorce, a lawyer becomes a gambling hall proprietor.

Mildly interesting romantic drama in a flashback format.

w John Twist, Ellis St Joseph d John Farrow

Richard Dix, Gail Patrick, Anita Louise, Paul Cavanagh, Laura Hope Crews, Louis Jean Heydt, Hobart Cavanaugh, Charles Halton

'Capable handling of an interesting story against a colourful background.' – *Variety*

Rentadick
GB   1972   94m   Eastmancolor
Rank/Paradine/Virgin (Ned Sherrin)
V*

Incompetent private eyes become involved in the battle for a deadly nerve gas.

Ineffective crazy comedy which never takes shape, preferring to aim barbs of satire in all directions.

w John Wells, John Fortune d Jim Clark ph John Coquillon m Carl Davis

James Booth, Richard Briers, Julie Ege, Donald Sinden

Repeat Performance *
US   1947   93m   bw
Eagle Lion/Aubrey Schenck

People in trouble find they can repeat the previous year.

Adequate flashback fantasy, very dated now.

w Walter Bullock d Alfred L. Werker ph Lew O'Connell m George Antheil

Louis Hayward, Joan Leslie, Tom Conway, Richard Basehart, Virginia Field

Repo Man *
US   1984   92m   DeLuxe
Universal/Edge City (Peter McCarthy, Jonathan Wacks)
V, V*, L, S

A repossessor of cars finds himself on the run from all manner of dangers.

Nightmarish *film noir* with nods to many predecessors and some elements of black fantasy.

wd Alex Cox ph Robby Müller m Tito Larriva, Steven Hufsteter

Harry Dean Stanton, Emilio Estevez, Tracey Walter, Olivia Barash, Sy Richardson, Susan Barnes

'The saltiest, sweetest, most sublimely sleazy tickle in the Los Angeles ribs. If it doesn't convulse you with belly laughs, then you're a stiff.' – *Carrie Rickey, Boston Herald*

Report from the Aleutians **
US 1943 45m colour
US Signal Corps

American forces live under tough conditions on a group of Arctic islands from which they raid Japanese bases.

Simple and somewhat overlong, but still one of the better US documentaries to come out of World War II.

wd and narrated by John Huston; additional narration by Walter Huston

Report to the Commissioner
US 1974 112m Metrocolor
UA/M. J. Frankovich
V*
GB title: Operation Undercover

A policeman's son follows in father's footsteps but finds life around Times Square dismaying.

Realistic, concerned crime melodrama with nothing very new to say.

w Abby Mann, Ernest Tidyman novel James Mills d Milton Katselas ph Mario Tosi m Elmer Bernstein

Michael Moriarty, Yaphet Kotto, Susan Blakely, Hector Elizondo, Tony King, Michael McGuire

'A clear also-ran in the police thriller stakes.' – Verina Glaessner

'A bit too full of sweat and frenzy.' – Michael Billington, Illustrated London News

Repossessed
US 1990 84m CFI
Guild/First Class films (Steve Wizan)
V, V*, L

Attempting an exorcism on television, a priest struggles to control a demon intent on possessing the entire viewing audience.

Raucous parody of The Exorcist, crammed with jokes, most of them juvenile.

wd Bob Logan ph Michael D. Margulies m Charles Fox pd Shay Austin ed Jeff Freeman

Linda Blair, Ned Beatty, Leslie Nielsen, Anthony Starke, Thom J. Sharp, Lana Schwab

'Clunking, but the jokes are just about numerous enough to stifle the groans.' – Sight and Sound

Reprieve: see Convicts Four

The Reptile *
GB 1966 90m Technicolor
Warner-Pathé/Hammer (Anthony Nelson-Keys)
V

A Cornish village is terrified by several mysterious and unpleasant deaths; it turns out that the daughter of the local doctor, victim of a Malayan sect, periodically turns into a deadly snake.

Silly horror story most effectively filmed as a mixture of chills, detection and good characterization.

w John Elder d John Gilling ph Arthur Grant m Don Banks pd Bernard Robinson ed James Needs, Roy Hyde

Noel Willman, Jennifer Daniel, Ray Barrett, Jaqueline Pearce, Michael Ripper, John Laurie, Marne Maitland

Repulsion **
GB 1965 105m bw
Compton/Tekli (Gene Gutowski)
V, V*

A Belgian manicurist in London is driven by pressures into neurotic withdrawal; terrified above all by sex, she locks herself up in her gloomy flat and murders her boyfriend and landlord when they try to approach her.

Weird, unmotivated but undeniably effective Grand Guignol in the form of a case history; little dialogue,

which is just as well as the director at that time clearly had no ear for the language.

w Roman Polanski, Gerard Brach d Roman Polanski ph Gilbert Taylor m Chico Hamilton

Catherine Deneuve, Ian Hendry, John Fraser, Patrick Wymark, Yvonne Furneaux

'An unashamedly ugly film, but as a lynx-eyed view of a crumbling mind it is a masterpiece of the macabre.' – Daily Mail

Reputation: see Lady with a Past

Requiem for a Heavyweight *
US 1962 87m bw
Columbia (David Susskind)
GB title: Blood Money

The last bouts of a prizefighter who will not realize his career is over.

Tough, effective melodrama, extremely well acted.

w Rod Serling TV play Rod Serling d Ralph Nelson ph Arthur J. Ornitz m Laurence Rosenthal

Anthony Quinn, Jackie Gleason, Mickey Rooney, Julie Harris, Stan Adams, Madame Spivy, Jack Dempsey, Cassius Clay

Requiem for a Vampire (dubbed)
France 1971 95m colour
Les Films A.B.C. (Jean Rollin)
V
original title: Requiem pour un Vampire; aka: Virgins and Vampires

Two young gun-toting girls on the run from killers take refuge in a ruined chateau where vampires live.

Stylish, dreamlike fantasy, with little dialogue, intermingled with scenes of sex and sadism that have no connection to the main narrative; the music is unpleasantly obtrusive.

wd Jean Rollin ph Renan Polles m Pierre Raph ed Michel Patient

Marie-Pierre Castel, Mireille D'Argent, Philippe Gasté, Dominique, Louise Dhour, Paul Bisciglia
'You will get more out of this if you abandon all foolish misconceptions of discovering a coherent plotline and any form of characterisation. Rollin makes these things up as he goes along and to enjoy them you have to get into the same "anything goes" spirit. I always find a stiff drink helps fortify the critical faculties.' – The Dark Side

† The British video release runs for 78m.

Requiem for Dominic: see Requiem für Dominic

Requiem für Dominic **
Austria 1990 90m
Terra Film/OFF/ORF (Norbert Blecha)
V*
aka: Requiem for Dominic

An exiled Romanian scientist returns to his home town of Timişoara to investigate the death of a friend accused of mass murder.

Based on a true story and filmed where the events happened, the documentary style thriller achieves a horrific truth by incorporating actual footage of the accused man as he lay dying.

w Michael Kohlmeier, Felix Mitterer d Robert Dorhelm ph Hans Selikovsky m Harald Kloser ed Ingrid Koller

Felix Mitterer, Viktoria Schubert, August Schmolzer, Angelica Schutz, Antonia Rados, Nikolas Vogel, Georg Hoffman-Ostenhorf, Werner Prinz, Georg Metzenrad

'The most remarkable political thriller since Z . . . nail-biting cinema' – Variety

Requiescant: see Kill and Pray

La Resa dei Conti: see The Big Gundown

The Rescue
US 1988 98m colour
Touchstone/Silver Screen Partners III (Laura Ziskin)
V*, L

A group of American teenagers in South Korea set out to rescue their fathers, imprisoned in North Korea as spies.

Ludicrous film, of a quite stupifying banality, which even its intended audience of gung-ho 13-year-olds are likely to treat with the derision it deserves.

w Jim Thomas, John Thomas d Ferdinand Fairfax ph Russell Boyd m Bruce Broughton pd Maurice Cain ed David Holden, Carroll Timothy O'Meara

Kevin Dillon, Christina Harnos, Marc Price, Ned Vaughn, Ian Giatti, Charles Haid, Edward Albert, Mel Wong

The Rescuers *
US 1977 77m Technicolor
Walt Disney (Ron Miller)
V, V*, L

The Mouse Rescue Aid Society volunteer to bring back a girl lost in a swamp.

Feature-length cartoon which, while by no means as bad as some of Disney's very routine seventies product, still seems light years away from his classics of the thirties.

w Larry Clemmons, Ken Anderson stories Margery Sharp d Wolfgang Reitherman, John Lounsbery, Art Stevens m Artie Butler

voices of Bob Newhart, Eva Gabor, Geraldine Page, Joe Flynn, Jim Jordan, John McIntire

'The people who really need rescuing are the Disney animators and cameramen.' – Time Out

'It's no Snow White but there are long moments when its inventiveness and skill are entirely captivating. I have only this one lingering doubt: if you are going to put this amount of effort into a movie shouldn't you have more at the end than a snappy collection of 330,000 drawings and a bill for six million dollars?' – Barry Took, Punch

AAN: song 'Someone's Waiting for You' (m Sammy Fain, ly Carol Conners, Ayn Robbins)

The Rescuers Down Under **
US 1990 77m Technicolor
Warner/Walt Disney/Silver Screen Partners IV (Thomas Schumacher)
V, V*, L, S

The mouse Rescue Aid Society goes to help a trapped eagle and a boy in Australia.

Slick, lively and enjoyable animated feature, an improvement on the original.

w Jim Cox, Karey Kirkpatrick, Byron Simpson, Joe Ranft d Hendel Butoy, Mike Gabriel m Bruce Broughton ad Maurice Hunt ed Michael Kelly, Mark Hester

voices of Bob Newhart, Eva Gabor, John Candy, Tristan Rogers, Adam Ryen, George C. Scott, Wayne Robson, Douglas Seale, Frank Walker, Peter Firth, Bill Barty

'Comes on like an Indiana Jones movie which has been reconceived as animation and then proceeded to push back that medium's technical boundaries.' – Sight and Sound

Reserved for Ladies: see Service for Ladies

'Let's go to work.'
Reservoir Dogs ***
US 1991 99m colour
Rank/Live America/Dog Eat Dog (Lawrence Bender)
V*, L, S

While one of their number bleeds to death after a bungled robbery, the rest of the gang, hiding out in a warehouse, try to discover what went wrong.

Brilliant, if sometimes repellent, gangster movie; notably violent, it is also a tense and exciting examination of male egos on a collision course.

wd Quentin Tarantino   *ph* Andrzej Sekula   *pd* David Wasco   *ed* Sally Menks

Harvey Keitel, Tim Roth, Michael Madsen, Chris Penn, Steve Buscemi, Lawrence Tierney, Randy Brooks, Kirk Baltz, Eddie Bunker, Quentin Tarantino

'An astute mix of wit and cynicism which washes down its melodramatic excesses with sly satire on the blood-and-guts elements of the crime movie, this is a film of considerable acuity and power.' – *Kim Newman, Sight and Sound*

'Undeniably juicy, with its salty talk and gunplay, film is nihilistic but not resonantly so, giving it no meaning outside the immediate story and characters. Pic is impressive, but impossible to love.' – *Variety*

'No one should go to see *Reservoir Dogs* without prior thought. But what they will see is a riveting treatment on the theme of betrayal set in an urban wasteland that murders hope and makes redemption virtually impossible.' – *Derek Malcolm, Guardian*

'Torn from the blazing pages of Texas history!'
The Restless Breed
US   1957   81m   Eastmancolor by Pathé
Edward L. Alperson
V*, L

The son of a secret service agent arrives in a frontier town to avenge his father's death.

Standard star Western full of expected elements.

w Steve Fisher   *d* Allan Dwan

Scott Brady, Anne Bancroft, Jay C. Flippen, Jim Davis, Rhys Williams

Restless Natives
GB   1985   89m   Technicolor
Thorn EMI/Oxford Film Company (Rick Stevenson)
V

Two young idlers set up as modern highwaymen, robbing American visitors on coach tours; to their surprise, they become a tourist attraction.

Irritatingly patchy and amoral comedy which wastes a potentially interesting idea.

w Ninian Dunnett   *d* Michael Hoffman   *ph* Oliver Stapleton   *m* Stuart Adamson   *pd* Adrienne Atkinson   *ed* Sean Barton

Vincent Friell, Joe Mullaney, Teri Lally, Ned Beatty, Robert Urquhart

The Restless Years
US   1959   86m   bw   Cinemascope
Universal-International

A small-town dressmaker tries to prevent her daughter from discovering that she is illegitimate.

Antediluvian sudser with second-string talent.

w Edward Anhalt   *play* Teach Me How to Cry by Patricia Joudry   *d* Helmut Kautner

John Saxon, Sandra Dee, Margaret Lindsay, Luana Patten, Virginia Grey

Resurrected *
GB   1989   92m   colour
Hobo/St Pancras Films/Film Four International/British Screen (Tara Prem, Adrian Hughes)

A soldier believed killed in the Falklands War turns up alive after the fighting is over and is accused of being a deserter.

Effective and dramatic examination of patriotism and the aftermath of battle.

w Martin Allen   *d* Paul Greengrass   *ph* Ivan Strasburg   *m* John Keane   *pd* Chris Burke   *ed* Dan Rae

David Thewlis, Tom Bell, Rita Tushingham, Michael Pollitt, Rudi Davies, William Hoyland, Evan Stewart, Christopher Fulford, David Lonsdale

Resurrection
US   1931   81m   bw
Universal

In 1870s Russia, a peasant girl is seduced by a prince and bears his child.

Unremarkable version of a much-filmed melodrama.

w Finis Fox   *novel* Leo Tolstoy   *d* Edwin Carewe   *ph* Robert B. Kurrle, Al Green   *m* Dimitri Tiomkin

Lupe Velez, John Boles, Nance O'Neil, William Keighley, Rose Tapley

† See also: *We Live Again.*

Resurrection
US   1980   103m   Technicolor
Universal (Renee Missel, Howard Rosenman)
V*

A woman who has escaped death in a car crash finds herself miraculously able to heal others.

Curious modern parable with nowhere to go; even religious reactionaries may find it rather boring.

w Lewis John Carlino   *d* Daniel Petrie   *ph* Mario Tosi   *m* Maurice Jarre

Ellen Burstyn, Sam Shepard, Richard Farnsworth, Eva LeGallienne, Roberts Blossom, Clifford David

AAN: Ellen Burstyn; Eva LeGallienne (supporting actress)

Le Retour de Martin Guerre: see *The Return of Martin Guerre*

Le Retour du Grand Blond: see *Return of the Tall Blond*

Retreat, Hell!
US   1952   95m   bw
(Warner) United States (Milton Sperling)

Adventures of a Marine unit in the Korean War.

Standard war film.

w Milton Sperling, Ted Sherdeman   *d* Joseph H. Lewis   *ph* Warren Lynch   *m* William Lava

Frank Lovejoy, Richard Carlson, Anita Louise, Russ Tamblyn

Retribution
US   1988   108m   colour
Medusa/Unicorn/Renegade (Guy Magar)
V*, L

A shy artist is possessed by the vengeful spirit of a murderer.

Gory, predictable and fussily frenetic horror movie.

w Guy Magar, Lee Wasserman   *d* Guy Magar   *ph* Gary Thieltges   *m* Alan Howarth   *pd* Robb Wilson King   *ed* Guy Magar

Dennis Lipscomb, Leslie Wing, Suzanne Snyder, Jeff Pomerantz, George Murdock, Pamela Dunlap, Susan Peretz

Return from the Ashes *
GB   1965   104m   bw   Panavision
UA/Mirisch (J. Lee-Thompson)

A woman returns from Dachau to find that her husband is living with her step-daughter and that they plan to murder her.

Broken-backed thriller melodrama, the first half of which is quite irrelevant to the second. The whole is modestly inventive for those who don't mind a mixture of *Enoch Arden*, *Psycho* and *Dial M for Murder*

with a touch of the concentration camps and a background of post-war misery.

w Julius J. Epstein   *novel* Hubert Monteilhet   *d* J. Lee-Thompson   *ph* Christopher Challis   *m* Johnny Dankworth

Ingrid Thulin, Maximilian Schell, Samantha Eggar, Herbert Lom

Return from the River Kwai
GB   1988   101m   colour
Rank/Screenlife Establishment (Kurt Unger)
V

An American pilot teams up with a British officer to try to prevent the Japanese taking prisoners of war back to Japan.

Rambling adventure movie that has no connection, other than its title, with *The Bridge on the River Kwai*.

w Sargon Tamini, Paul Mayersberg   *book* Joan Blair, Clay Blair Jnr   *d* Andrew V. McLaglen   *ph* Arthur Wooster   *m* Lalo Schifrin   *pd* Michael Stringer   *ed* Alan Strachan

Edward Fox, Denholm Elliott, Christopher Penn, Tatsuya Nakadai, George Takei, Nick Tate, Timothy Bottoms, Michael Dante, Richard Graham

Return from Witch Mountain
US   1978   93m   Technicolor
Walt Disney (Ron Miller, Jerome Courtland)
V*

A brother and sister from outer space come back to Earth for a vacation and are used by crooks for their own purposes.

Acceptable sequel to *Escape from Witch Mountain*, with improved special effects.

w Malcolm Marmorstein   *d* John Hough   *ph* Frank Phillips   *m* Lalo Schifrin   *sp* Eustace Lycett, Art Cruickshank, Danny Lee

Bette Davis, Christopher Lee, Ike Eisenmann, Kim Richards, Jack Soo

Return Home
Australia   1989   90m   colour
Musical Films/Film Victoria/Australian Film Commission (Cristina Pozzan)

Unhappy with his life, a successful insurance broker returns to his home town to visit his brother who runs a garage.

Amiable domestic drama that comes to few conclusions slowly..

wd Ray Argall   *ph* Mandy Walker   *ad* Kerith Holmes   *ed* Ken Sallows

Dennis Coard, Frankie J. Holden, Ben Mendelsohn, Micki Camilleri

The Return of a Man Called Horse *
US   1976   125m   DeLuxe   Panavision
UA/Sandy Howard/Richard Harris
V*

The English nobleman of *A Man Called Horse* goes back to the West to save his adopted Indian tribe from extinction.

Another 'realistic' action adventure with torture highlights; nicely made, but not for the squeamish.

w Jack de Witt   *d* Irvin Kershner   *ph* Owen Roizman   *m* Laurence Rosenthal

Richard Harris, Gale Sondergaard, Geoffrey Lewis, Bill Lucking, Jorge Luke

'Maintains a tidy balance between nausea and boredom.' – *Judith Crist*

† At 17 minutes, this pre-title sequence must be the longest so far.

The Return of Bulldog Drummond
GB   1934   71m   bw
BIP

Drummond forms a society to oust crooked foreigners from Britain.

Thin Drummond exploit with traces of the original Fascism.

wd Walter Summers   novel The Black Gang by 'Sapper'

Ralph Richardson, Ann Todd, Francis L. Sullivan, Claud Allister, Joyce Kennedy

The Return of Captain Invincible
Australia   1982   91m   Eastmancolor   Panavision
Seven Keys/Willarra
V*, L

An American superhero is discovered in the back streets of Sydney, a down-and-out drunk; but his skills are needed for the fight against Mr Midnight.

Occasionally agreeable spoof which for most of its length is too frantic.

w Steven E. de Souza, Andrew Gaty   d Philippe Mora

Alan Arkin, Christopher Lee, Kate Fitzpatrick, Bill Hunter, Michael Pate, John Bluthal

The Return of Chandu
US   1934   bw   serial: 12 eps
Principal

A supernatural magician rescues a princess from the Black Magic Cult of Ubasti.

Lively nonsense emanating from the feature film Chandu the Magician.

d Ray Taylor

Bela Lugosi, Maria Alba, Clara Kimball Young, Luvien Prival, Phyllis Ludwig

The Return of Dr X *
US   1939   62m   bw
Warner (Bryan Foy)

A modern vampire terrorizes the city.

Minor thriller which doesn't get going till the last reel; only notable for Bogart's appearance as the monster. Nothing to do with Dr X.

w Lee Katz   novel The Doctor's Secret by William J. Makin   d Vincent Sherman   ph Sid Hickox   m Bernhard Kaun

Dennis Morgan, Rosemary Lane, Wayne Morris, Humphrey Bogart, Olin Howland, John Litel

The Return of Dracula *
US   1958   77m   bw
UA/Gramercy (Jules V. Levy, Arthur Gardner)
GB title: The Fantastic Disappearing Man

A European vampire makes his way to an American small town in the guise of a refugee Iron Curtain painter.

Quite nicely made low-budget horror film with a good balance of the supernatural and the ordinary.

w Pat Fielder   d Paul Landres   ph Jack McKenzie   m Gerald Fried

Francis Lederer, Norma Eberhardt, Ray Stricklyn, Jimmie Baird, John Wengraf

The Return of Frank James *
US   1940   92m   Technicolor
TCF (Darryl F. Zanuck)
V*, L

A sequel to Jesse James (qv).

Moody, nicely photographed Western in which Jesse's brother avenges his murder.

w Sam Hellman   d Fritz Lang   ph George Barnes, William V. Skall   m David Buttolph

Henry Fonda, Gene Tierney, Jackie Cooper, Henry Hull, John Carradine, J. Edward Bromberg, Donald Meek, Eddie Collins, George Barbier

'I doubt if any character was ever as lily white as that of Frank James here, but that is a present from the Hays Office to you, and anyway the part is played by Henry Fonda. Durn if I don't like that boy.' – Otis Ferguson

The Return of Martin Guerre *
France   1982   123m   Fujicolor
Palace/Marcel Dassault/SFP
V, V*, L
original title: Le Retour de Martin Guerre

In the 16th century, a man comes to a French village claiming to be the one who left his wife and child eight years before. Complaints are laid that he is an impostor . . .

Mildly intriguing story which falls apart because one is never sure where the film's sympathies lie.

w Jean-Claude Carrière, Daniel Vigne   d Daniel Vigne   ph André Neau   m Michel Portal   ad Alain Negre   ed Denise de Casabianca

Gérard Depardieu, Nathalie Baye, Sylvie Meda, Maurice Barrier

'By far the most enigmatic film seen in London this year.' – Sunday Times

'A plodding, confusing narrative that neither does proper justice to the story nor really teases out the complex historical, moral and psychological issues which it raises.' – Observer

The Return of Monte Cristo *
US   1946   92m   bw
Columbia/Edward Small-Grant Whytock
GB title: Monte Cristo's Revenge

The grandson of the original count is framed and sent to Devil's Island, but escapes.

Very tolerable action romp of its time, with a fair troupe of actors enjoying themselves.

w George Bruce, Alfred Neumann, Kurt Siodmak   d Henry Levin   ph Charles Lawton Jnr   m Lucien Moraweck

Louis Hayward, Barbara Britton, George Macready, Una O'Connor, Henry Stephenson, Steve Geray, Ray Collins, Ludwig Donath, Ivan Triesault

The Return of October
US   1948   89m   Technicolor
Columbia
GB title: A Date with Destiny

A girl's inheritance is contested on the grounds that she thinks a horse is the reincarnation of her Uncle Willie.

Thin whimsy which leaves its stars with egg on their faces.

w Norman Panama, Melvin Frank   d Joseph H. Lewis

Glenn Ford, Terry Moore, Dame May Whitty, James Gleason, Albert Sharpe

The Return of Peter Grimm
US   1935   82m   bw
RKO
V*

A strong-minded family man returns as a ghost to see how his family is getting on without him.

Fairly satisfying fantasy with good performances.

w Francis Edwards Faragoh   play David Belasco   d George Nicholls Jnr

Lionel Barrymore, Helen Mack, Edward Ellis, Donald Meek

'Sombre fantasy . . . pretty dull and boresome.' – Variety

† Previously filmed in 1925 with Alec B. Francis and Janet Gaynor.

The Return of Ringo (dubbed) **
Italy/Spain   1965   96m   Eastmancolor
Golden Era/Mediterranee/Rizzoli/Balcàzar (Alberto Pugliese, Luciano Ercoli)
original title: Il Ritorno di Ringo

Returning home after the Civil War, a man discovers that the town, including his family and home, have been taken over by a Mexican bandit.

Superior spaghetti Western that allows room for character development among the usual baroque touches.

w Duccio Tessari, Fernando Di Leo   d Duccio Tessari   ph Francisco Marin   m Ennio Morricone   ad Juan Alberto Soler   ed Lucia Quaglia

Giuliano Gemma, Fernando Sancho, Hally Hammond (Lorella de Luca), Nieves Navarro, Antonio Casas, Pajarito, Jorge Martin

† The movie was a sequel to A Pistol for Ringo (qv).

Return of Sabata (dubbed)
Italy/France/West Germany   1971   88m   Technicolor   Techniscope
UA/PEA/Artistes Associés/Artemis (Alberto Grimaldi)
original title: E Tornato Sabata . . . Hai Chiuso un'Altra Volta

The gunfighter Sabata is double-crossed by an old friend in his search for gold but emerges victorious as usual.

Almost a repeat of the original film, except that it now lacks the element of surprise and has little else to offer.

w Renato Izzo, Gianfranco Parolini   d Frank Kramer (Gianfranco Parolini)   ph Sandro Mancori   m Marcello Giombini   ad Luciano Puccini   ed Gianfranco Parolini, Salvatore Aventario

Lee Van Cleef, Reiner Schöne, Annabella Incontrera, Gianni Rizzo, Gianpiero Albertini, Pedro Sanchez (Ignazio Spalla)

'Fairly run-of-the-mill Spaghetti Western, with the usual quota of menacing close-ups and modish camera angles.' – Alistair Whyte, MFB

† The film was a sequel to Sabata (qv). It was originally released in Italy at 107m.

Return of Superfly
US   1990   95m   colour
Crash Pictures (Sig Shore, Anthony Wisdom)
V*, S

A former drug-dealer decides to destroy his old gang.

Dull and violent sequel that hits a new low.

w Anthony Wisdom   d Sig Shore   ph Anghel Decca   m Curtis Mayfield   pd Jeremie Frank   ed John Mullen

Nathan Purdee, Margaret Avery, Leonard Thomas, Christopher Curry

'Shore brings no style or humor to a routine portrayal of New York's drug underground.' – Variety

Return of the Ape Man: see The Ape Man

The Return of the Bad Men
US   1948   90m   bw
RKO (Nat Holt)

A farmer tries to reform the female leader of a terrorist outlaw gang, but she is killed in a bank raid.

Standard, well-shot Western which contrives to introduce a number of well-known historical bandits.

w Charles O'Neal, Jack Netteford, Luci Ward   d Ray Enright   ph J. Roy Hunt   md Constantin Bakaleinikoff   m Roy Webb

Randolph Scott, Robert Ryan, Anne Jeffreys, Jacqueline White, Steve Brodie

'Riding to greater glory as the gay O. Henry hero!'
The Return of the Cisco Kid
US   1939   70m   bw
TCF (Kenneth MacGowan)

The Kid escapes a Mexican firing squad into Arizona and defeats swindlers.

Modest Western with plenty of zip.

w Milton Sperling   d Herbert I. Leeds

Warner Baxter, Lynn Bari, Cesar Romero, Henry Hull, Kane Richmond, C. Henry Gordon, Robert Barrat

'Substantial fare for adventure audiences.' – *Variety*

The Return of the Corsican Brothers: see
Bandits of Corsica

The Return of The Evil Dead
Spain   1973   91m   Eastmancolor
London International/Ancla Century (Roman Plana)
original title: *El Ataque de los Muertos sin Ojos*

Devil-worshipping Knights Templar, blinded and killed by villagers in the Middle Ages, rise from their graves to slaughter the locals and a visiting American.

Gruesome but dull horror movie, one of a series featuring the dead Knights.

wd Amando de Ossorio   ph Miguel F. Mila
m Tony Abril   ed Joseph Anthony

Tony Kendal, Fernando Sancha, Esther Rey, Lone Fleming, Frank Blake

'Blood-Curdling Giant Fly-Creature Runs Amok!'
'Scream At The Human Terror Created By Atoms Gone Wild!'
'Scream At Ghastly Fly Monster As He Keeps A Love Tryst!'
'Scream At The Desperate Search For The Fly With A Heart Of A Man!'
Return of the Fly
US   1959   80m   bw
Bernard Glasser/TCF
V, V*, L

The son of the original fly man meets the same fate as his father.

Cheerless follow-up.

wd Edward Bernds

Vincent Price, Brett Halsey, John Sutton, David Frankham, Dan Seymour

Return of the Frontiersman
US   1950   74m   Technicolor
Warner

A man escapes from prison to prove himself innocent of the bank robbery for which he was convicted.

Goodish double-bill Western with no surprises.

w Edna Anhalt   d Richard Bare

Gordon Macrae, Julie London, Rory Calhoun, Fred Clark, Edwin Rand

Return of the Jedi *
US   1983   132m   DeLuxe   Panavision
TCF/Lucasfilm (Howard Kazanjian)
V, V (W), V*, L, S

'Episode 6' of the *Star Wars* serial: our heroes combat Darth Vader and Jabba the Hutt.

More expensive fantasy for the world's children of all ages, especially the undemanding ones.

w Lawrence Kasdan, George Lucas   d Richard Marquand   ph Alan Hume   m John Williams
pd Norman Reynolds

Mark Hamill, Harrison Ford, Carrie Fisher, Billy Dee Williams, Anthony Daniels, Peter Mayhew, Kenny Baker

'I admire the exquisite skill and talent which have been poured into these films, while finding the

concepts behind these gigantic video games in the sky mindlessly tedious.' – *Margaret Hinxman, Daily Mail*

'An impersonal and rather junky piece of moviemaking.' – *Pauline Kael, New Yorker*

'Only the effects are special.' – *Sight and Sound*

AAN: John Williams; art direction

'They're back – and they're hungry!'
The Return of The Living Dead
US   1985   90m   DeLuxe
Tom Fox/Hemdale/Orion
V, V (W), V*, L, S

The army is called in to repel a zombie onslaught.

Cult horror movie hailed by some as a black comedy, but likely to repel most audiences.

wd Dan O'Bannon   story Rudy Ricci, John Russo, Russell Streiner   ph Jules Brenner   m Matt Clifford   pd William Stout   ed Robert Gordon

Clu Gulager, James Karen, Don Calfa, Thom Matthews

Return of The Living Dead Part II
US   1987   89m   Photolab
Guild/Lorimar/Greenfox (Tom Fox)
V, V*, L

Brain-eating zombies attack a small town.

Dismal horror movie, unable to raise chills or laughs.

wd Ken Widerhorn   ph Robert Elswit   m J. Peter Robinson, Vladimir Horunzhy   ad Dale Allan Pelton
ed Charles Bornstein

James Karen, Thom Matthews, Dana Ashbrook, Marsha Dietlein, Suzanne Snyder, Philip Bruns, Michael Kenworthy, Thor Van Lingen, Jason Hogan

'The film is typical of the juvenile, enervating would-be comic approach adopted by too many horror movies in the late 80s.' – *Kim Newman, MFB*

'Back From The Dead And Hungry For More.'
Return of The Living Dead III
US   1993   105m   Foto-Kem colour
Trimark/Bandai Visual/Ozla (Gary Schmoeller, Brian Yuzna)
V, V*

A youth who spies on an experiment to revive the dead decides to bring his girlfriend back to life when she is killed in a motorcycle accident.

A Romeo and Juliet for the splatter generation: an extremely gory movie of flesh-eating zombies, aimed unerringly at the teens and twenties with its narrative of young love gone awry; it is slickly done, though its scenes with blood-spattered, mutilated bodies and decaying corpses are not for the squeamish.

w John Penney   d Brian Yuzna   ph Gerry Lively
m Barry Goldberg   pd Anthony Tremblay   sp Steve Johnson, Tim Ralston, Kevin Brennan, Christopher Nelson, Wayne Toth   ed Christopher Roth

Mindy Clarke, J. Trevor Edmond, Kent McCord, Sarah Douglas, James T. Callahan, Mike Moroff, Sal Lopez, Basil Wallace

'A pedestrian and gruesome, but never really scary, story.' – *Variety*

'The best of the series so far, with a back-to-basics scenario that goes for solid scares rather than splatter spoofery . . . one of the best zombie movies since the glory days of George Romero.' – *The Dark Side*

† The film was released direct to video in Britain in an uncut version. For the American cinema release, which runs for 97m, some of the bloodier scenes were removed.

The Return of the Musketeers
GB/France/Spain   1989   101m   colour
Entertainment/Timoth Burrill Productions/Fildebroc-Cine 5/Iberoamericana (Pierre Spengler)
V, S

The daughter of Milady de Winter vows vengeance on

the Musketeers who were responsible for her mother's execution.

A sequel to *The Four Musketeers*, it is a lacklustre affair of four middle-aged failures attempting to redeem themselves.

w George MacDonald Fraser   novel *Vingt Ans Après* by Alexandre Dumas   d Richard Lester
ph Bernard Lutic   m Jean-Claude Petit   pd Gil Parrondo   ed John Victor Smith

Michael York, Oliver Reed, Frank Finlay, C. Thomas Howell, Kim Cattrall, Geraldine Chaplin, Roy Kinnear, Christopher Lee, Philippe Noiret, Richard Chamberlain, Eusebio Lazaro, Alan Howard, Jean-Pierre Cassel

The Return of the Pink Panther *
GB   1974   113m   DeLuxe   Panavision
UA/Jewel/Pimlico/Mirisch/Geoffrey (Blake Edwards)
V, V*, L, S

When the Pink Panther diamond – national treasure of the Eastern state of Lugash – is once again stolen, bungling Inspector Clouseau is called in.

Rehash of jokes from *The Pink Panther* (qv), not bad in parts but a rather tedious whole.

w Frank Waldman, Blake Edwards   d Blake Edwards   ph Geoffrey Unsworth   m Henry Mancini

Peter Sellers, Christopher Plummer, Herbert Lom, Catherine Schell, Peter Arne, Peter Jeffrey, Grégoire Aslan, David Lodge, Graham Stark

'The film never comes fully to the boil, but simmers in a series of self-contained, self-destructing little set pieces.' – *Richard Combs*

'The first film in history to be upstaged by its own credit titles.' – *Benny Green, Punch*

The Return of the Scarlet Pimpernel *
GB   1937   94m   bw
London Films (Alexander Korda, Arnold Pressburger)

Sir Percy Blakeney saves his wife and other French aristos from the guillotine.

Predictable, stylish revolutionary romance, much thinner in plot and performance than its predecessor.

w Lajos Biro, Arthur Wimperis, Adrian Brunel
d Hans Schwarz   ph Mutz Greenbaum   m Arthur Benjamin

Barry K. Barnes, Sophie Stewart, Margaretta Scott, James Mason, *Henry Oscar,* Francis Lister, Anthony Bushell

The Return of the Seven
US   1966   95m   Technicolor   Panavision
UA/Mirisch/CB (Ted Richmond)
V*

The seven gunmen, slightly reconstituted, fight again to rescue some kidnapped farmers.

The mixture as before (see *The Magnificent Seven*); adequate but scarcely inspired.

w Larry Cohen   d Burt Kennedy   ph Paul Vogel
m Elmer Bernstein

Yul Brynner, Robert Fuller, Julian Mateos, Warren Oates, Claude Akins, Virgilio Texeira, Emilio Fernandez, Jordan Christopher

AAN: Elmer Bernstein

The Return of the Soldier *
GB   1982   102m   Technicolor
Brent Walker/Barry R. Cooper (Ann Skinner, Simon Relph)
V*

In 1916, a shellshocked soldier returns home, able to remember his old sweetheart but not his wife.

Overcast and heavy-handed treatment of a classy novella.

w Hugh Whitemore   novel Rebecca West   d Alan Bridges   ph Stephen Goldblatt   m Richard Rodney Bennett   pd Luciana Arrighi

Alan Bates, Ann-Margret, Julie Christie, Glenda Jackson, Jeremy Kemp, Edward de Souza, Frank Finlay, Jack May, Ian Holm

'The film has nowhere to go except into rhetorical bluster about class distinctions.' – *Tom Milne, MFB*

Return of the Swamp Thing
US   1989   85m   DeLuxe
Medusa/Lightyear Entertainment/J & M Entertainment (Benjamin Melniker, Michael E. Uslan)
V, V*, L

A mad scientist is thwarted from using his step-daughter in genetic experiments by a vegetable monster.

Ineffectual and relentlessly jokey approach to a comic-book hero.

w Derek Spencer, Grant Morris   *d* Jim Wynorski *ph* Zoran Hochstatter   *m* Chuck Cirino   *pd* Robb Wilson King   *ed* Leslie Rosenthal

Louis Jourdan, Heather Locklear, Sarah Douglas, Dick Durock, Joey Sagal, Ace Mask, Chris Doyle, Daniel Taylor

Return of the Tall Blond *
France   1974   89m   colour
Fox-Rank/Gaumont/De la Gueville (Alain Poiré, Yves Robert)
V*
original title: *Le Retour du Grand Blond*

A violinist is once again caught up in rivalry between the police and the secret service.

Enjoyable, gently humorous sequel that lives up to the original.

w Francis Veber, Yves Robert   *d* Yves Robert *ph* René Mathelin   *m* Vladimir Cosma   *pd* Guy Blanc   *ed* Ghislaine Desjonquières, Françoise London

Pierre Richard, Mireille Darc, Jean Carmet, Jean Rochefort, Michel Duchaussoy, Paul Le Person, Colette Castel

'The film never loses its light-hearted humour.' – *MFB*

† A sequel to *Le Grand Blond avec une Chaussure Noire*.

The Return of the Terror
US   1934   65m   bw
Warner

A scientist feigns insanity to avoid prosecution for murder, and escapes to his old sanatorium, where murder strikes again.

Barnstorming murder mystery borrowing its title and nothing else from Edgar Wallace.

w Eugene Solow, Peter Milne   *d* Howard Bretherton

John Halliday, Mary Astor, Lyle Talbot, Frank McHugh, Irving Pichel, J. Carrol Naish

'Formula mystery, but speedy.' – *Variety*

'Terrifying! Paralysing! Horrifying!'
The Return of the Vampire *
US   1943   69m   bw
Columbia (Sam White)
V*, L

Dracula reappears amid the London blitz.

Surprisingly well made and complexly plotted horror film; it looks good and only lacks humour. The wolf man, however, is a regrettable intrusion.

w Griffin Jay   *d* Lew Landers   *ph* John Stumar, L. J. O'Connell   *md* Morris Stoloff   *m* Mario Castelnuovo-Tedesco

Bela Lugosi, Nina Foch, Frieda Inescort, Miles Mander, Matt Willis, Roland Varno, Ottola Nesmith

Return to Glennascaul *
Eire   1951   23m   bw
Dublin Gate Theatre

Orson Welles gives a man a lift and is told a gentle ghost story.

Neither very satisfying nor very well done, this little film deserves a niche in history because of the talents involved. It was apparently made during one of the many intervals in the filming of *Othello*.

wd Hilton Edwards   *narrator* Orson Welles

Return to Macon County
US   1975   89m   Movielab
AIP/Macon Service Company (Eliot Schick)

In the fifties, two wandering youths pick up a waitress and have serious trouble with a manic policeman in America's unfriendliest area.

Slam-bang sequel to *Macon County Line*, rather unintentionally comic.

wd Richard Compton   *ph* Jacques Marquette *m* Robert O. Ragland

Nick Nolte, Don Johnson, Robin Mattson, Robert Viharo

Return to Oz
US   1985   110m   Technicolor
Walt Disney/Silver Screen Partners (Paul Maslansky)
V*, L, S

Dorothy has traumas because of her Oz experiences, and suffers further nightmares under shock treatment.

A weird way to treat a children's classic, the result being a movie which appealed strongly to nobody except, possibly, the producer. The Disney people should have known better.

w Walter Murch, Gill Dennis   *d* Walter Murch *ph* David Watkin   *m* David Shire

Fairuza Balk, Jean Marsh, Nicol Williamson, Piper Laurie, Matt Clark, Emma Ridley

'Astonishingly sombre, melancholy, and sadly unengaging.' – *Variety*

'Without musical numbers this narrative seems a perilously thin journey with no particular purpose.' – *Time Out*

Return to Paradise *
US   1953   109m   Technicolor
UA/Aspen (Theron Warth)

A peace seeker settles on a tiny South Sea island and leaves when his wife dies; he returns after World War II with his daughter.

Curious idyll, slow but not displeasing.

w Charles Kaufman   *novel* James Michener *d* Mark Robson   *ph* Winton Hoch   *m* Dimitri Tiomkin

Gary Cooper, Barry Jones, Roberta Haynes, Moira MacDonald

Return to Peyton Place *
US   1961   122m   DeLuxe   Cinemascope
TCF/API (Jerry Wald)
V*

Constance Mackenzie's daughter writes a novel about Peyton Place and falls in love with the publisher.

More closets are unlocked, more skeletons fall out; for addicts, the sequel does not disappoint, and it's all very glossy.

w Ronald Alexander   *d* José Ferrer   *ph* Charles G. Clarke   *m* Franz Waxman

Jeff Chandler, Carol Lynley, Eleanor Parker, Mary Astor, Robert Sterling, Luciana Paluzzi, Brett Halsey, Tuesday Weld

'Enough soap suds to pollute the Mississippi along with the mind.' – *Judith Crist, 1973*

Return to the Blue Lagoon
US   1991   98m   Technicolor
Columbia TriStar/Price (William A. Graham)
V, V*, L

A mother, her daughter and an orphaned boy are washed up on a desert island; the girl and boy grow to adulthood and fall in love.

A sequel that, once it has disposed of the adult, is virtually a remake of the 1980 version and no better the second time around.

w Leslie Stevens   *novel* The Garden of God by Henry de Vere Stacpoole   *d* William A. Graham *ph* Robert Steadman   *m* Basil Poledouris   *pd* Jon Dowding   *ed* Ronald J. Fagan

Milla Jovovich, Brian Krause, Lisa Pelikan, Courtney Phillips

Return to Yesterday
GB   1940   68m   bw
Ealing

A bored Hollywood star seeks anonymity in a seaside repertory company.

Mild comedy, not without interest.

w Robert Stevenson, Margaret Kennedy, Roland Pertwee, Angus MacPhail   *play* Goodness How Sad by Robert Morley   *d* Robert Stevenson

Clive Brook, Anna Lee, Dame May Whitty, Hartley Power, Milton Rosmer, David Tree, Olga Lindo

Reuben, Reuben *
US   1982   101m   CFI colour
Saltair/Taft (Walter Shenson)
V*

A drunken British poet upsets a New England community.

Oddball comedy at which one laughs without much enthusiasm.

w Julius J. Epstein   *play* Spofford by Herman Shumlin   *novel* Peter de Vries   *d* Robert Ellis Miller   *ph* Peter Stein   *m* Billy Goldenberg *pd* Peter Larkin

Tom Conti, Kelly McGillis, Roberts Blossom, Cynthia Harris, Joel Fabiani

AAN: Tom Conti; adaptation

Reunion
US   1936   83m   bw
Darryl Zanuck/TCF
GB title: *Hearts in Reunion*

When a doctor retires, the townsfolk reunite him with many of the children he has brought into the world.

Tiresome second attempt to cash in on the Dionne Quintuplets, who make several appearances.

w Sam Hellman, Gladys Lehman, Sonya Levien *d* Norman Taurog

Jean Hersholt, Rochelle Hudson, Helen Vinson, Slim Summerville, J. Edward Bromberg, Sara Haden

'Too episodic to command interest or supply suspense.' – *Variety*

† A sequel to *The Country Doctor*.

Reunion
France/West Germany/GB   1989   110m   colour
Rank/Les Films Ariane/FR3/NEF/CLG/TAC (Anne Françoise)
V, V*
original title: *L'Ami Retrouvé*

Returning to Germany as an old man, a Jewish lawyer recalls a schoolboy friendship destroyed by the Nazis' anti-Semitism.

Minimally scripted, ploddingly directed and lacking in emotional weight.

w Harold Pinter   *novel* Reunion by Fred Uhlman *d* Jerry Schatzberg   *ph* Bruno de Keyzer *m* Philippe Sarde   *pd* Alexandre Trauner *ed* Martine Barraque

Jason Robards, Christien Anholt, Samuel West, Françoise Fabian, Maureen Kerwin, Barbara Jefford, Dorothea Alexander, Frank Baker, Tim Barker

'A tedious re-exploration of already over-charted territory.' – *Tom Milne, MFB*

Reunion in France
US   1943   104m   bw
MGM (Joseph L. Mankiewicz)
V*
GB title: *Mademoiselle France*

A selfish Parisian dress designer gradually realizes that her world has changed when the Nazis invade and she is asked to help an American flyer.

Action flagwaver which tries also to be a woman's picture and goes pretty soppily about it.

w Jan Lustig, Marvin Borowsky, Marc Connelly *story* Ladislas Bus-Fekete   *d* Jules Dassin *ph* Robert Planck   *m* Franz Waxman

Joan Crawford, John Wayne, Philip Dorn, Reginald Owen, Albert Basserman, John Carradine, Ann Ayars, J. Edward Bromberg, Henry Daniell, Moroni Olsen, Howard da Silva

'Miss Crawford isn't making all the sacrifices implied in the script . . . Dressing like a refugee is certainly not in her contract.' – *New York Herald Tribune*

Reunion in Vienna *
US   1933   100m   bw
MGM

A long-exiled nobleman tries to take up an old romance even though the lady is married.

Lacklustre adaptation of a play which must have style; the performances remain interesting.

w Ernest Vajda, Claudine West   *play* Robert E. Sherwood   *d* Sidney Franklin   *ph* George Folsey *m* William Axt

John Barrymore, Diana Wynyard, Frank Morgan, May Robson, Eduardo Ciannelli, Una Merkel, Henry Travers

'Unlikely money film outside a few of the larger cities.' – *Variety*

AAN: George Folsey

Reveille With Beverly *
US   1943   78m   bw
Columbia (Sam White)

A girl disc jockey runs a programme for soldiers.

Thin excuse for a musical, but the result was pretty popular.

w Howard J. Green, Jack Henley, Albert Duffy *d* Charles Barton

Ann Miller, William Wright, Dick Purcell, Franklin Pangborn, Tim Ryan, Larry Parks

Revenge
GB   1971   89m   Eastmancolor
Rank/Peter Rogers Productions (George H. Brown)

When children are raped and murdered in a north country town, two men take the law into their own hands.

Crude melodrama set in *Cold Comfort Farm* country; efficient but unrewarding.

w John Kruse   *d* Sidney Hayers   *ph* Ken Hodges *m* Eric Rodgers

Joan Collins, Sinead Cusack, James Booth, Ray Barrett, Kenneth Griffith

Revenge (1979): see *Blood Feud*

Revenge
US   1989   124m   DeLuxe   Panavision
Columbia TriStar/Raster (Hunt Lowry, Stanley Rubin)
V, V*, L, S

Left for dead by a jealous husband, a former pilot seeks revenge and reunion with his lover.

Brutal, shallow thriller that is too predictable to be enjoyable.

w Jim Harrison, Jeffrey Fiskin   *novel* Jim Harrison *d* Tony Scott   *ph* Jeffrey Kimball   *m* Jack Nitzsche *pd* Michael Seymour, Benjamin Fernandez   *ed* Chris Lebenzon, Michael Tronick

Kevin Costner, Anthony Quinn, Madeleine Stowe, Tom Milian, Joaquin Martinez, James Gammon, Jesse Corti, Sally Kirkland, Miguel Ferrer

Revenge at El Paso: see *Ace High*

Revenge of Billy the Kid
GB   1992   87m   Colour
Powerhouse Pictures/Montage (Tim Dennison)
V

A carnivorous monster, the offspring of a goat and a farmer, kills off his father's family.

Grotesque and disgusting low-budget horror comedy, obsessed with rape, bestiality and the nastier bodily functions. A credit for 'Flatulence Artists' sets the tone.

w Tim Dennison, Jim Groom, Richard Matthews *d* Jim Groom   *ph* David Read   *m* Tony Flynn

Michael Balfour, Samantha Perkins, Jackie D. Broad, Trevor Peake, Bryan Heeley, Norman Mitchell, Dean Williamson, Michael Ripper

'Amateurish horror spoof made on a tiny budget and with even less wit or intelligence.' – *Sight and Sound*

'If you go alone – you'll find yourself running all the way home!'
The Revenge of Frankenstein
GB   1958   89m   Technicolor
Columbia/Hammer (Anthony Hinds)

Baron Frankenstein evades the guillotine and makes a new creature with the brain of a homicidal dwarf.

Dullish horror farrago with a few indications of quirkish humour.

w Jimmy Sangster, Hurford Janes   *d* Terence Fisher *ph* Jack Asher   *m* Leonard Salzedo   *pd* Bernard Robinson   *ed* James Needs, Alfred Cox

Peter Cushing, Michael Gwynn, Oscar Quitak, Francis Matthews, Eunice Gayson, John Welsh, Lionel Jeffries, Richard Wordsworth, Charles Lloyd Pack, John Stuart, Arnold Diamond

† This second Hammer Frankenstein set the tone for the rest; see *The Curse of Frankenstein*.

Revenge of the Dead: see *Night of the Ghouls*

Revenge of the Gladiators: see *Fire over Rome*

The Revenge of the Pink Panther
US   1978   98m   Technicolor   Panavision
UA/Blake Edwards
V, V*, L

Inspector Clouseau tracks down a drug-smuggling industrialist.

Feeble addition to a series which was always too pleased with itself.

w Frank Waldman, Ron Clarke, Blake Edwards *d* Blake Edwards   *ph* Ernie Day   *m* Henry Mancini

Peter Sellers, Herbert Lom, Robert Webber, Dyan Cannon, Burt Kwouk, Paul Stewart, Robert Loggia, Graham Stark

Revenge of the Vampire: see *Mask of Satan*

Revenge of the Zombies
US   1943   61m   bw
Lindsley Parsons/Monogram

A Nazi scientist in Mexico tries to convert an army of the dead for Hitler's use.

Unpersuasive horror cheapie.

w Edmund Kelso, Van Norcross   *d* Steve Sekely

John Carradine, Robert Lowery, Gale Storm, Veda Ann Borg, Mantan Moreland

The Revengers
US   1972   108m   DeLuxe   Panavision
Cinema Center/Martin Rackin

A rancher gathers a posse to hunt down the Indians who have allegedly murdered his wife and family.

Standard major Western with a dismal script which echoes *The Dirty Dozen* and *The Wild Bunch:* sometimes repulsive, seldom exciting.

w Wendell Mayes   *d* Daniel Mann   *ph* Gabriel Torres   *m* Pino Calvi

William Holden, Ernest Borgnine, Susan Hayward, Woody Strode, Roger Hanin

Reversal of Fortune **
US   1990   111m   Technicolor
Warner/Shochiku Fuji/Sovereign Pictures/Edward R. Pressman, Oliver Stone
V, V*, L, S

A European aristocrat, found guilty of attempting to murder his wealthy American wife, hires a brilliant lawyer to mount an appeal against the sentence.

Based on a true story, it combines the appeal of courtroom drama with a prurient curiosity about the lives of the very rich.

w Nicholas Kazan   *book* Alan Dershowitz *d* Barbet Schroeder   *ph* Luciano Tovoli   *m* Mark Isham   *pd* Mel Bourne   *ed* Lee Percy

Glenn Close, Jeremy Irons, Ron Silver, Anabella Sciorra, Uta Hagen, Fisher Stevens, Christine Baranski, Jack Gilpin, Stephen Mailer

'A classy piece of filmmaking.' – *Variety*

AA: Jeremy Irons

AAN: Barbet Schroeder

The Revolt of Job **
Hungary   1983   98m   colour
Mafilm Tarsulas Filmstudio/Hungarian TV/ZDF
V*
original title: *Jób Lázadása*

A young Christian orphan is adopted by a Jewish farmer and his wife, who fear the coming of the Nazis.

Touching, understated film, told from the perspective of the child, which gives a freshness and poignancy to a familiar theme.

w Katalin Petényi, Imre Gyöngyössi, Barna Kabay *d* Imre Gyöngyössi, Barna Kabay   *ph* Gábor Szabó *m* Zoltán Jeney

Ference Zenthe, Hédi Temessy, Gábor Fehér, Péter Rudolf, Leticia Cano, Gregor Henry

AAN: best foreign-language film

The Revolt of Mamie Stover
US   1956   93m   Eastmancolor   Cinemascope
TCF (Buddy Adler)

A dance hall girl leaves San Francisco for Honolulu, makes money there but reforms for love of a rich novelist.

Absurdly bowdlerized and boring film version of a novel about a sleazy prostitute; hardly worth making at all in this form, especially as the cast seems well capable of a raunchier version.

w Sidney Boehm   *novel* William Bradford Huie *d* Raoul Walsh   *ph* Leo Tover   *m* Hugo Friedhofer

Jane Russell, Agnes Moorehead, Richard Egan, Joan Leslie

Revolution
US   1985   125m   Technicolor
Warner/Goldcrest/Viking (Irwin Winkler)

A trapper becomes involved in the American War of Independence and with the aristocratic daughter of a loyalist.

A mouse of a movie, despite its epic pretensions; the narrative has been swallowed by incoherent set-pieces and the period setting falters under the Method acting of its star.

w Robert Dillon *d* Hugh Hudson *ph* Bernard Lutic *m* John Corigliano *pd* Assheton Gorton *ed* Stuart Baird

Al Pacino, Donald Sutherland, Nastassja Kinski, Joan Plowright, Dave King, Steven Berkoff, John Wells, Annie Lennox, Dexter Fletcher, Richard O'Brien

'Hudson has thrown what doubtless started as a perfectly straightforward script to the winds and marched off in search of images that would somehow galvanise the whole show into life. But as his camera stumbles through the smoke, fire, and mobs of expensively costumed extras it's clear he's not going to find them.' – *David Ehrenstein*

The Revolutionary
US 1970 101m Technicolor
(UA) Pressman-Williams (Edward R. Pressman)
V*

Episodes in the life of a revolutionary, from distributing leaflets to attempted assassination.

A rather casual study of one man's radicalism, in no particular time or place; no doubt of great interest to other revolutionaries.

w Hans Königsberger *d* Paul Williams *ph* Brian Probyn *m* Michael Small

Jon Voight, Jennifer Salt, Robert Duvall

The Revolving Doors
France/Canada 1988 102m colour
Gala/Malofilm/Canal Plus (René Malo, Francyne Morin)
original title: *Les Portes Tournantes*

A dying woman recalls her earlier life, marriage and musical ambitions.

Slight but quite enjoyable bout of nostalgia, heavy on period charm.

w Jacques Savoie, Francis Mankiewicz *d* Francis Mankiewicz *ph* Thomas Vamos *m* François Dompierre *ad* Anne Pritchard *ed* André Corriveau

Monique Spaziani, Gabriel Arcand, Miou-Miou, François Methe, Jacques Penot, Françoise Faucher, Jean-Louis Roux, Remy Girard, Charles Reiner

'This lumbering tale of thwarted mother-love seems even more bereft of sense than sensibility.' – *Derek Malcolm, Guardian*

The Reward
US 1965 92m DeLuxe Cinemascope
TCF/Aaron Rosenberg

A mixed group of adventurers set out across the desert to capture a murderer; but thieves fall out.

Pretentious and talky melodrama which quickly scuttled its director's chances in Hollywood. Little action, obvious outcome, attractive Death Valley locations.

w Serge Bourguignon, Oscar Mullard *novel* Michael Barrett *d* Serge Bourguignon *ph* Joe MacDonald *m* Elmer Bernstein

Max von Sydow, Efrem Zimbalist Jnr, Yvette Mimieux, Gilbert Roland, Emilio Fernandez, Henry Silva

'Emotions clash in a crescendo of drama!'

Rhapsody
US 1954 116m Technicolor
MGM (Lawrence Weingarten)
V*

A wealthy woman affects the lives of two quite different musicians, each of whom has his weakness.

Tedious romantic drama which vainly attempted a smart veneer but boasted a splendid musical soundtrack.

w Fay and Michael Kanin *novel Maurice Guest* by Henry Handel Richardson *d* Charles Vidor *ph* Robert Planck *md* Johnny Green, Bronislau Kaper *piano* Claudio Arrau *violin* Michael Rabin

Elizabeth Taylor, Vittorio Gassman, John Ericson, Louis Calhern, Michael Chekhov, Barbara Bates, Celia Lovsky, Richard Hageman

Rhapsody in August *
Japan 1990 97m colour
Palace/Shochiku/Akira Kurosawa
S
original title: *Hachigatsu-no-Kyoshikyoku*

A grandmother, prompted by her grandchildren and a visit from her Japanese-American nephew, recalls the death of her husband when the atomic bomb was dropped on Nagasaki.

A small-scale but ponderous plea for an understanding of the past. *wd* Akira Kurosawa *novel Nabe-no-Naka* by Kiyoko Murata *ph* Takao Saito, Masaharu Ueda *m* Shinichiro Ikebe *ad* Yoshiro Muraki *ed* Akira Kurosawa

Richard Gere, Sachiko Murasé, Hisashi Igawa, Narumi Kayashima, Tomoko Ohtakara, Mitsunori Isaki, Toshié Negishi, Choichiro Kawarasaki, Hidetaka Yoshioka, Mié Suzuki

Rhapsody in Blue **
US 1945 139m bw
Warner (Jesse L. Lasky)
V*, L

The life story of composer George Gershwin.

No more trustworthy on factual matters than other Hollywood biopics of its era, this rather glum saga at least presented the music and the performers to excellent advantage.

w Howard Koch, Elliot Paul *d* Irving Rapper *ph* Sol Polito *md* Ray Heindorf, Max Steiner *ch* Le Roy Prinz *ad* Anton Grot, John Hughes

Robert Alda, Joan Leslie, Alexis Smith, Charles Coburn, Julie Bishop, *Albert Basserman, Oscar Levant, Herbert Rudley*, Rosemary de Camp, Morris Carnovsky, *Al Jolson, Paul Whiteman*, George White, Hazel Scott

'With no story at all, this two-hour concert of Gershwin music would be well worth the price of admission' – *Daily Mail*

AAN: Ray Heindorf, Max Steiner

Rhinestone
US 1984 111m DeLuxe
TCF/Howard Smith, Marvin Worth
V*, L

A night-club singer bets her obnoxious employer that she can turn a cab driver into a star.

Crude and witless *Pygmalion* variation with unsympathetic leads.

w Phil Alden Robinson, Sylvester Stallone *d* Bob Clark *ph* Timothy Galfas *m* Dolly Parton

Dolly Parton, Sylvester Stallone, Richard Farnsworth, Ron Leibman, Tim Thomerson

Rhino
US 1964 91m Metrocolor
MGM/Ivan Tors (Ben Chapman)

A scientist working with white rhinos is joined by an unscrupulous big game hunter.

Inoffensive African adventure.

w Art Arthur, Arthur Weiss *d* Ivan Tors *ph* Sven Persson, Lamar Boren *m* Lalo Schifrin

Harry Guardino, Robert Culp, Shirley Eaton

Rhodes: see *Rhodes of Africa*

Rhodes of Africa *
GB 1936 91m bw
Gaumont (Geoffrey Barkas)
V*
US title: *Rhodes*

A rough-hewn diamond miner becomes Prime Minister of Cape Colony.

Heavy-going but generally interesting historical drama shot on location.

w Michael Barringer, Leslie Arliss, Miles Malleson *book* Sarah Millin *d* Berthold Viertel *ph* Bernard Knowles *m* Hubert Bath

Walter Huston, Oscar Homolka, Basil Sydney, Peggy Ashcroft, Frank Cellier, Bernard Lee, Lewis Casson

'One of the better English-made pictures . . . should do all right even if it doesn't get the women.' – *Variety*

'Solid, worthy, humourless, it unrolls its eleven well-bred reels with all the technical advantages of 1936.' – *Graham Greene*

Rhubarb
US 1951 94m bw
Paramount (Perlberg-Seaton)

A millionaire leaves his fortune, including a baseball team, to a wild ginger cat, which means problems for his publicity agent.

Typical scatty farce of the early fifties, held together by the splendid performance of the disdainful feline in the title role rather than by any special merit in the handling.

w Dorothy Reid, Francis Cockrill *novel* H. Allen Smith *d* Arthur Lubin *ph* Lionel Lindon *m* Van Cleave

Ray Milland, Jan Sterling, Gene Lockhart, William Frawley

Rhubarb
GB 1969 37m Technicolor
ABPC/Avalon

Various village notables congregate on the golf course.

Virtually silent comedy (nobody says anything but 'rhubarb') which could have been very funny with better jokes. A TV remake in 1979 was however much worse.

wd Eric Sykes

Harry Secombe, Eric Sykes, Jimmy Edwards, Hattie Jacques, Gordon Rollins, Graham Stark, Kenneth Connor

Rhythm of the Islands
US 1943 60m bw
Bernard Burton/Universal

A rather dull South Sea island sets itself up to attract tourists.

Moderate musical programmer, one of many from this studio during the war.

w Oscar Brodney, M. M. Musselman *d* Roy William Neill

Allan Jones, Jane Frazee, Andy Devine, Ernest Truex, Marjorie Gateson, Mary Wickes

'Acceptably fulfils its purpose of providing an hour's diverting footage for dual support in the general runs.' – *Variety*

Rhythm on the Range *
US 1936 87m bw
Paramount (Benjamin Glazer)

A hired hand saves the boss's daughter when she is kidnapped by local badmen.

Easy-going musical comedy with a Western background, later remade as *Pardners* (qv).

w John C. Moffett, Sidney Salkow, Walter de Leon, Francis Martin *d* Norman Taurog *ph* Karl Struss *songs* various

Bing Crosby, Martha Raye, Frances Farmer, Bob Burns, Lucile Watson, Samuel S. Hinds, George E. Stone, Warren Hymer

'Bing Crosby as a cowboy; Bing Crosby crooning a prize bull to sleep on a freight car; Bing Crosby more than ever like Walt Disney's Cock Robin; it needs some stamina to be a film reviewer.' – *Graham Greene*

Rhythm on the River *

US 1940 92m bw
Paramount (William Le Baron)

A song writer employs 'ghosts' to produce his music and lyrics; they discover this fact and go into business for themselves.

Cheerful musical with strong billing.

w Dwight Taylor, Billy Wilder, Jacques Théry *d* Victor Schertzinger *ph* Ted Tetzlaff *m* Johnny Burke, James V. Monaco

Bing Crosby, Mary Martin, Basil Rathbone, Oscar Levant, Oscar Shaw, Charley Grapewin, William Frawley

AAN: song 'Only Forever'

Rhythm Romance: see *Some Like It Hot*

Rhythm Serenade

GB 1943 87m bw
Columbia British (Ben Henry)

During the Second World War, a teacher who starts a day nursery so that mothers can work in a munitions factory falls in love with a commando recovering from a breakdown.

Sentimental little flag-waver with a few songs thrown in.

w Basil Woon, Marjorie Deans *d* Gordon Wellesley *ph* Erwin Hillier, Geoffrey Faithfull *md* Harry Bidgood *ad* George Provis *ed* Alan Jaggs

Vera Lynn, Peter Murray-Hill, Julien Mitchell, Charles Victor, Jimmie Jewel, Ben Warris, Irene Handl, Jimmy Clitheroe, Joan Kemp Welch

'From the very beginning, they knew they'd be friends to the end. What they didn't count on was everything in between!'

Rich and Famous

US 1981 117m Metrocolor
MGM/Jaquet/William Allyn
V*, L

Two girlfriends meet again years after college; one has become a famous highbrow novelist, and with her help the other becomes a lowbrow one.

Unattractively sexed-up remake of *Old Acquaintance*, with even more talk than the original, and much less style.

w Gerald Ayres *d* George Cukor *ph* Don Peterman, Peter Eco *m* Georges Delerue *pd* Jan Scott *ed* John F. Burnett

Candice Bergen, Jacqueline Bisset, David Selby, Hart Bochner, Steven Hill, Meg Ryan

'A sadly dispiriting occasion . . . a jumbled conflation of *The Group* and a female version of *Carnal Knowledge*.' – *Tim Pulleine, MFB*

† The director was 82 when the film was shot, which must be some kind of record.

Rich and Strange *

GB 1931 83m bw
BIP (John Maxwell)
V*, L
US title: *East of Shanghai*

A young couple come into money and take a trip around the world.

Slight, agreeable early talkie with a few Hitchcock touches.

w Alma Reville, Val Valentine, Alfred Hitchcock *novel* Dale Collins *d* Alfred Hitchcock *ph* Jack Cox, Charles Martin *m* Hal Dolphe

Henry Kendall, Joan Barry, Percy Marmont, Betty Amann, Elsie Randolph

'Hitchcock, being Britain's D. W. Griffith, according to the press agents around here, usually gets a rave as his pictures take the screen. Here's one where the admirers will have difficulty knowing what to say.' – *Variety*

'Perhaps his bravest failure.' – *George Perry, 1965*

The Rich Are Always with Us

US 1932 73m bw
Warner (Sam Bischoff)

A socialite determines on a divorce but her new love is annoyed by her concern for her ex-husband.

Cocktail drama of a kind which totally disappeared from the screen.

w Austin Parker *novel* E. Pettit *d* Alfred E. Green *ph* Ernest Haller *m* W. Franke Harling

Ruth Chatterton, George Brent, John Miljan, Bette Davis, Adrienne Dore, Mae Madison, Robert Warwick

'Chiefly a femme picture . . . the title's appropriateness is as obscure as the wisdom of so metaphoric a label for a flicker.' – *Variety*

The Rich Full Life: see *Cynthia*

Rich in Love

US 1992 105m DeLuxe Panavision
UPI/MGM (Richard D. Zanuck/Lili Fini Zanuck)
V, V*, S

A teenage schoolgirl tries to keep the family together as her father begins to disintegrate after her mother leaves home suddenly, and her pregnant sister arrives with her new husband.

Meandering domestic drama, an attempt at a character study which fails because its participants distinctly lack character, cleaving only to the obvious and expected.

w Alfred Uhry *novel* Josephine Humphreys *d* Bruce Beresford *ph* Peter James *m* Georges Delerue *pd* John Stoddart *ed* Mark Warner

Albert Finney, Jill Clayburgh, Kathryn Erbe, Kyle MacLachlan, Piper Laurie, Ethan Hawke, Suzy Amis, Alfre Woodward

'It could play on television tomorrow, and no-one would find anything amiss, save perhaps the ratings dropping precipitously as the audience drifted away in search of something more than genteel good taste.' – *John Harkness, Sight and Sound*

Rich Kids

US 1979 96m Technicolor
Robert Altman/Lion's Gate/UA
V*

An adolescent boy and girl are mildly corrupted by the behaviour of their parents.

Spasmodically interesting comedy-drama which seems ill at ease among the rich and alternates between exploitation, satire and whimsy.

w Judith Ross *d* Robert M. Young

Trini Alvarado, Jeremy Levy, Kathryn Walker, John Lithgow, Terry Kiser, David Selby

Rich Man, Poor Girl

US 1938 72m bw
MGM

Consternation takes a white-collar family when a millionaire takes a fancy to one of its daughters.

Unexciting comedy-drama vaguely modelled on *You Can't Take It With You*.

w Joseph Fields, Jerome Chodorov *play* Edith Ellis *d* Reinhold Schünzel

Lew Ayres, Ruth Hussey, Robert Young, Don Castle, Guy Kibbee, Lana Turner, Rita Johnson

'Lightweight in marquee strength but should build through word of mouth.' – *Variety*

Rich Man's Folly

US 1931 80m bw
Paramount

A rich man has no time for his children.

Curious updating of Dickens's *Dombey and Son*; not really a success.

w Grover Jones, Edward Paramore Jnr *d* John Cromwell *ph* David Abel

George Bancroft, Frances Dee, Robert Ames, Juliette Compton, Dorothy Peterson

'Splendid cast and serviceable product anywhere.' – *Variety*

Rich, Young and Deadly: see *Platinum High School*

Rich, Young and Pretty

US 1951 95m Technicolor
MGM (Joe Pasternak)
V*, L

A Texas rancher takes his young daughter to Paris, where she meets her real mother.

Moderate musical.

w Dorothy Cooper, Sidney Sheldon *d* Norman Taurog *ph* Robert Planck *m* Nicholas Brodszky *ly* Sammy Cahn *ch* Nick Castle

Danielle Darrieux, Wendell Corey, Jane Powell, Fernando Lamas, Vic Damone

AAN: song 'Wonder Why'(*m* Nicholas Brodszky, *ly* Sammy Cahn)

Richard III ***

GB 1955 161m Technicolor Vistavision
London Films (Laurence Olivier)
V, V*

Shakespeare's play about Richard Crookback, his seizure of the throne and his defeat at Bosworth.

Theatrical but highly satisfying filming of a splendidly melodramatic view of history. Interesting but not fussy camera movement, delightful sets (followed by a disappointingly 'realistic' battle) and superb performances.

w William Shakespeare (adapted by Laurence Olivier, Alan Dent, with additions) *d* Laurence Olivier *ph* Otto Heller *m* William Walton *pd* Roger Furse *ad* Carmen Dillon

Laurence Olivier, Claire Bloom, Ralph Richardson, Cedric Hardwicke, Stanley Baker, Alec Clunes, John Gielgud, Mary Kerridge, Pamela Brown, Michael Gough, Norman Wooland, Helen Haye, Patrick Troughton, Clive Morton, Andrew Cruickshank

'Wherever the play was loose-jointed or ill-fitting, Sir Laurence has been its tinker and its tailor, but never once its butcher.' – *Paul Dehn, News Chronicle*

AAN: Laurence Olivier

Richer than the Earth: see *The Whistle at Eaton Falls*

The Richest Girl in the World

US 1934 80m bw
RKO

A millionairess changes places with her secretary to find a man who will love her for herself.

Rose-coloured romance, remade in 1944 as *Bride by Mistake*.

w Norman Krasna *d* William A. Seiter

Miriam Hopkins, Joel McCrea, Fay Wray, Henry Stephenson, Reginald Denny, Beryl Mercer

'Eighty minutes of unerring entertainment . . . a pip picture for Miriam Hopkins.' – *Variety*

AAN: Norman Krasna

The Richest Man in Town
US 1941 70m bw
Jack Fier/Columbia

A small-town newspaper publisher feuds with an old friend over his prepared obituary of the latter.

A fragment of Americana with an unfinished feel.

w Farnya Foss, Jerry Sackheim d Charles Barton

Frank Craven, Edgar Buchanan, Eileen O'Hearn, Roger Pryor, Tom Dugan

'He's a cop accused of murder. The only person who
  knows he's innocent is the psycho who wants him
  dead.'
'This is one case that's going to be settled out of court.'
Ricochet
US 1991 102m colour
First Independent/Summit/Silver (Joel Silver, Michael Levy)
V, V*, L, S

Seeking revenge, a murderer sets out to frame the one-time cop, now an assistant district attorney, who put him inside.

Depressingly violent and unpleasant thriller.

w Steven E. de Souza story Fred Dekker, Menno Meyjes d Russell Mulcahy ph Peter Levy
m Alan Silvestri pd Jay Hinkle ed Peter Honess

Denzel Washington, John Lithgow, Ice T, Kevin Pollak, Lindsay Wagner, Mary Ellen Trainor, Josh Evans, Victoria Dillard

'If you don't flinch when power tools are being abused and can swallow ridiculous plot points if more dynamite action is only a minute away, then this is a good bet for an entertaining night out.' – *Kim Newman, Empire*

Ricochet Romance
US 1954 80m bw
Universal

The new cook transforms a dude ranch which had been allowed to run down.

Modest programme filler on well-established lines.

w Kay Lennard d Charles Lamont

Marjorie Main, Chill Wills, Rudy Vallee, Pedro Gonzales-Gonzales, Alfonso Bedoya, Ruth Hampton

The Riddle of the Sands *
GB 1978 102m Eastmancolor Panavision
Rank/Worldmark (Drummond Challis)
V*

In 1901 a British yachtsman in the North Sea hits upon a German trial invasion.

Rather too placid adaptation of a semi-classic adventure story in which too little happens to make a rousing action film; points of interest along the way, though.

w Tony Maylam, John Bailey novel Erskine Childers d Tony Maylam ph Christopher Challis
ph Hazel Peiser m Howard Blake

Michael York, Simon MacCorkindale, Jenny Agutter, Alan Badel, Jurgen Andersen

The Riddle of the Stinson *
Australia 1988 95m colour
Kennedy Miller (Terry Hayes, George Miller, Doug Mitchell)

In 1937, a farmer goes to the rescue of survivors of a plane crash in inaccessible country.

A pleasant period picture, based on fact and told in direct and simple manner.

w Tony Morphett d Chris Noonan ph Geoffrey Simpson m Jim Conway, Colin Watson pd Owen Paterson ed Frans Vandenburgh

Norman Kaye, Richard Roxburgh, Helen O'Connor, Esben Storm, Huw Williams, Susan Lyons

Ride a Crooked Mile *
US 1938 70m bw
Jeff Lazarus/Paramount

An ex-Cossack cattle hijacker is disappointed when jailed to find that his son will not help him escape.

Lively crime melodrama with an unusual twist.

w Ferdinand Reyher, John C. Moffitt d Alfred E. Green

Akim Tamiroff, Leif Erickson, Frances Farmer, Lynne Overman, John Miljan, Vladimir Sokoloff

'Fine melodrama, handicapped by lack of cast strength and so-so title.' – *Variety*

Ride a Crooked Trail
US 1958 88m Eastmancolor Cinemascope
Universal-International

A crook takes refuge in a small town and becomes its honest marshal.

One we've heard before, and seen better done.

w Borden Chase d Jesse Hibbs

Audie Murphy, Walter Matthau, Gia Scala, Henry Silva

The Ride Back *
US 1957 79m bw
UA/Associates and Aldrich (William Conrad)

A lawman arrests an outlaw wanted for murder, but has the problem of getting him back to base.

Slightly offbeat low-budget Western, well enough done if it had to be done at all.

w Anthony Ellis d Allen H. Miner ph Joseph Biroc m Frank de Vol

Anthony Quinn, William Conrad, George Trevino, Lita Milan

Ride Beyond Vengeance
US 1966 100m Technicolor
Columbia/Tiger/Goodson/Todman/Sentinel/Fenady

A young Westerner, accused of cattle rustling and branded, vows revenge.

Dourly brutal but studio-bound and very padded Western; if there is any entertainment value it doesn't emerge for more than a few moments.

w Andrew J. Fenady novel The Night of the Tiger by Al Dewlen d Bernard McEveety ph Lester Shorr
m Richard Markowitz

Chuck Connors, Michael Rennie, Kathryn Hays, Claude Akins, Bill Bixby, Paul Fix, Gary Merrill, Joan Blondell, Gloria Grahame, Ruth Warrick, Arthur O'Connell, Frank Gorshin, James MacArthur

† Probably intended as a TV movie and found too violent.

Ride Clear of Diablo
US 1954 80m Technicolor
Universal-International

A young man seeking vengeance on his father's murderer becomes deputy to a sheriff hired to kill him too.

Lively enough star Western.

w George Zuckerman d Jesse Hibbs

Audie Murphy, Dan Duryea, Susan Cabot, Abbe Lane, Russell Johnson, Paul Birch, Jack Elam

Ride 'Em Cowboy
US 1941 82m bw
Universal (Alex Gottlieb)
V*

Two hot dog vendors find themselves working on an Arizona dude ranch.

Slick but routine comedy star vehicle with no outstanding sequences.

w True Boardman, John Grant d Arthur Lubin
ph John W. Boyle m Frank Skinner songs Don Raye, Gene de Paul

Bud Abbott, Lou Costello, Dick Foran, Anne Gwynne, Samuel S. Hinds, Richard Lane, Johnny Mack Brown, Ella Fitzgerald

Ride in the Whirlwind *
US 1965 82m colour
Jack H. Harris/Proteus (Jack Nicholson, Monte Hellman)
V*, L

Three cowhands are mistaken for outlaws by a vengeful posse.

Grim and talkative Western about lives trapped by circumstance.

w Jack Nicholson d Monte Hellman ph Gregory Sandor m Robert Drasnin ad James Campbell

Cameron Mitchell, Millie Perkins, Jack Nicholson, Katherine Squire, George Mitchell, Rupert Crosse, Harry Dean Stanton

Ride Lonesome *
US 1959 73m Eastmancolor Cinemascope
Columbia

A bounty hunter catches a killer as bait to trap the criminal's brother against whom he plots vengeance.

Mildly suspenseful Western, rather lost on the wide screen.

w Burt Kennedy d Budd Boetticher

Randolph Scott, Karen Steele, Pernell Roberts, James Best, James Coburn, Lee Van Cleef

Ride Out for Revenge
US 1957 79m bw
Bryna/UA (Norman Retchin)

Gold is discovered on land to which the army is moving Indians, and this causes second thoughts.

Low-key, rather brooding Western which aims to be different.

w Norman Retchin d Bernard Girard

Rory Calhoun, Lloyd Bridges, Gloria Grahame, Joanne Gilbert, Vince Edwards

Ride the High Country **
US 1962 94m Metrocolor Cinemascope
MGM (Richard E. Lyons)
GB title: Guns in the Afternoon

Two retired lawmen help transport gold from a mining camp to the bank, but one has ideas of his own.

Thoughtful Western graced by ageing star presences; generally well done.

w N. B. Stone Jnr d Sam Peckinpah ph Lucien Ballard m George Bassman

Joel McCrea, Randolph Scott, Edgar Buchanan, Mariette Hartley, James Drury

'A nice little conventional unconventional Western.' – *Stanley Kauffmann*

'The movie that rocked the debutantes – down to their last martini!'
Ride the High Iron
US 1957 74m bw
Columbia
V*, L

A war veteran gets into the seamier side of public relations.

Curious little urban melodrama with a high moral tone, like a cut-price *Sweet Smell of Success*.

w Milton Gelman d Don Weis

Don Taylor, Raymond Burr, Sally Forrest

† Originally made for TV.

Ride the Man Down

US 1952 90m Trucolor
Republic

The death of a rancher sets off a bitter fight for his lands.

Flat and uninteresting Western melodrama.

w Mary McCall Jnr d Joe Kane

Brian Donlevy, Ella Raines, Rod Cameron, Forrest Tucker, Barbara Britton, James Bell, Chill Wills, J. Carrol Naish, Jim Davis

Ride the Pink Horse *

US 1947 101m bw
U-I (Joan Harrison)

An ex-serviceman visits a New Mexican town in search of the gangster who killed his buddy.

Dour, complex melodrama with a certain amount of style but not enough substance.

w Charles Lederer novel Dorothy B. Hughes
d Robert Montgomery ph Russell Metty m Frank Skinner

Robert Montgomery, Wanda Hendrix, Andrea King, Thomas Gomez, Fred Clark, Art Smith

'One of a kind: no one in his right mind would imitate it.' – Pauline Kael, 70s

AAN: Thomas Gomez

Ride the Wild Surf

US 1964 101m Eastmancolor
Columbia/Jana (Jo and Art Napoleon)

Surf riders go to Hawaii and find romance.

Pleasant, overlong, open air fun and games.

w Jo and Art Napoleon d Don Taylor ph Joseph Biroc m Stu Phillips

Fabian, Shelley Fabares, Tab Hunter, Barbara Eden

The Ride to Hangman's Tree

US 1967 90m Technicolor
Universal

Three bandits never quite manage to reform.

Easy-going Western, played on the light side in a vein later developed in Butch Cassidy and the Sundance Kid.

w Luci Ward, Jack Natteford, William Bowers
d Alan Rafkin

Jack Lord, James Farentino, Don Galloway, Melody Johnson, Richard Anderson

Ride, Vaquero

US 1953 90m Anscocolor
MGM (Stephen Ames)

Ranchers settling in New Mexico after the Civil War cause some natives to turn bandit; one of them has a mysterious American associate called Rio.

Very mildly interesting Western with the stars rather swamping a humourless script.

w Frank Fenton d John Farrow ph Robert Surtees m Bronislau Kaper

Robert Taylor, Ava Gardner, Howard Keel, Anthony Quinn, Charlita

Le Rideau Cramoisi: see The Crimson Curtain

Rider on a Dead Horse

US 1962 72m bw
Allied Artists

A prospector murders one partner for his gold and tries to pin the blame on the other.

Watchable minor Western with good use of location.

w Stephen Longstreet d Herbert L. Strock

John Vyvyan, Bruce Gordon, Kevin Hagen, Lisa Lu

Rider on the Rain

France/Italy 1969 119m colour
Joseph E. Levine, Serge Silberman
V*, S
original title: Passager de la Pluie

A woman shoots her rapist and then tries to conceal the crime.

Routine, fairly implausible thriller that owes much to Hitchcock.

w Sebastian Japrisot d René Clément
ph Andreas Winding m Francis Lai ad Pierre Guffroy

Charles Bronson, Marlène Jobert, Annie Cordy, Jill Ireland, Gabriele Tinti, Jean Gaven, Jean Piat, Corinne Marchand

Riders of Death Valley

US 1941 bw serial: 15 eps
Universal

During the California gold rush, vigilantes protect the mines against raiders.

Fairly vigorous serial action with good locations.

d Ford Beebe, Ray Taylor

Dick Foran, Leo Carrillo, Buck Jones, Charles Bickford, Lon Chaney Jnr, Noah Beery Jnr, Guinn 'Big Boy' Williams, Monte Blue, Glenn Strange

Riders of the Purple Sage

US 1931 58m bw
Fox

A rootin', tootin' cowboy traps a villain and weathers a stampede and an avalanche.

Good standard Western previously filmed in 1918 with William Farnum and in 1925 with Tom Mix. This version was premièred on the wide screens of the period.

novel Zane Grey d Hamilton McFadden

George O'Brien, Marguerite Churchill, Noah Beery, Yvonne Pelletier, Stanley Fields

'Still a good Western and okay outside the de luxers.' – Variety

Riders of Vengeance

US 1952 80m Technicolor
Universal-International
GB title: The Raiders

During the California gold rush, a prospector takes revenge on a local dictator.

Standard Western themes against a colourful background.

w Polly James, Lillie Hayward d Lesley Selander

Richard Conte, Barbara Britton, Viveca Lindfors, Hugh O'Brian, Morris Ankrum, William Reynolds, Dennis Weaver

Riders to the Stars *

US 1954 81m Color Corporation
UA/Ivan Tors

Rocket scientists investigate the problems of cosmic bombardment.

Enjoyably straightforward science fiction with no monsters or political problems; it has decided historic interest as a record of what scientists in 1954 thought rocket travel would be like.

w Curt Siodmak d Richard Carlson ph Stanley Cortez m Harry Sukman

Richard Carlson, Herbert Marshall, William Lundigan, Dawn Addams, Martha Hyer, Robert Karnes, Lawrence Dobkin

'It's a rootin', tootin', six-gun shootin' musicalallapalooza!'

Riding High

US 1943 88m Technicolor
Paramount (Fred Kohlmar)
GB title: Melody Inn

A burlesque queen goes home to Arizona and helps ranchers by performing at a dude ranch.

Dim formula musical with exuberance but neither wit nor style.

w Walter de Leon, Arthur Phillips, Art Arthur
play Ready Money by James Montgomery d George Marshall ph Karl Struss, Harry Hallenberger
md Victor Young

Dorothy Lamour, Dick Powell, Victor Moore, Gil Lamb, Cass Daley, Bill Goodwin, Rod Cameron, Glenn Langan, Andrew Tombes, Tim Ryan, Douglas Fowley, Milt Britton and his Band

Riding High *

US 1950 112m bw
Paramount (Frank Capra)

An easygoing racing man forsakes the chance of wealth to train his beloved horse for the Imperial Derby.

The director's familiar ingredients – farce, sentimentality, fast cutting, nice people and a lot of noise – seem a shade too tried and tested in this remake of his 1934 success Broadway Bill. Despite the cast, the result is only moderately entertaining.

w Robert Riskin d Frank Capra ph George Barnes, Ernest Laszlo m James Van Heusen
ly Johnny Burke

Bing Crosby, Coleen Gray, Charles Bickford, Raymond Walburn, James Gleason, Oliver Hardy, Frances Gifford, William Demarest, Ward Bond, Clarence Muse, Percy Kilbride, Harry Davenport, Margaret Hamilton, Douglass Dumbrille, Gene Lockhart

Riding Shotgun

US 1954 75m Warnercolor
Warner

A shotgun stagecoach guard carries on a long vendetta against an outlaw.

Routine Western excitements, played mainly indoors.

w Tom Blackburn d André de Toth

Randolph Scott, Wayne Morris, Joan Weldon, Joe Sawyer, James Millican, Charles Bronson, James Bell

Riding with Buffalo Bill

US 1954 bw serial: 15 eps
Columbia

The famous Indian scout helps a miner against outlaws.

Unremarkable Western serial.

d Spencer Bennet

Marshall Reed, Rick Vallin, Joanne Rio, Shirley Whitney

Riff Raff *

US 1935 90m bw
MGM (Irving Thalberg)

A con man and his wife end up on the wrong side of the law.

Modest comedy drama that never quite sparks.

w Frances Marion, H. W. Haneman, Anita Loos d J. Walter Ruben m Edward Ward

Jean Harlow, Spencer Tracy, Joseph Calleia, Una Merkel, Mickey Rooney, Victor Kilian, J. Farrell MacDonald

'It ain't art, but it's box office.' – Variety

Riff Raff *
US   1947   80m   bw
RKO (Nat Holt)
V*, L

A dying man hands a Panama City con man a map to valuable oil deposits, and various shady people are after it.

Rather heavy but well made comedy-drama with some striking scenes.

w Martin Rackin   d Ted Tetzlaff   ph George E. Diskant   m Roy Webb

Pat O'Brien, Walter Slezak, Anne Jeffreys, Percy Kilbride, Jerome Cowan

'Those that live on the edge sometimes fall.'

Riff-Raff **
GB   1990   95m   colour
BFI/Parallax (Sally Hibbin)
V, V*, L

Labourers on a building site take revenge on their employers when one of them is killed in an accident.

Successful blend of wit and naturalism, although the overlapping dialogue in many regional accents can be hard to follow at times.

w Bill Jesse   d Ken Loach   ph Barry Ackroyd   m Stewart Copeland   pd Martin Johnson   ed Jonathan Morris

Robert Carlyle, Emer McCourt, Jimmy Coleman, George Moss, Ricky Tomlinson, David Finch, Richard Belgrave, Ade Sapara, Derek Young, Bill Moores

'A wonderfully entertaining account of life on the margins in London that combines laughter and tears, delivering its message in an intimate and subtle way.' – Screen International

† The film was turned down by Britain's major distributors. It received a limited release after winning an award as the best European film of the year and receiving the International Critics Prize at the Cannes Film Festival.

Rififi **
France   1955   116m   bw
Indus/Pathé/Prima
V*
original title: Du Rififi chez les Hommes

After an elaborate raid on a jewellery store, thieves fall out and the caper ends in bloodshed.

A film with much to answer for, in the form of hundreds of imitations showing either detailed accounts of robberies (Topkapi, Gambit) or gloomy looks at the private lives of criminals. At the time it seemed crisp and exciting, and the 25-minute silent robbery sequence is quite something.

w René Wheeler, Jules Dassin, Auguste le Breton   novel Auguste le Breton   d Jules Dassin   ph Philippe Agostini   m Georges Auric

Jean Servais, Carl Mohner, Robert Manuel, Marie Sabouret, Perlo Vita (Jules Dassin)

'I sometimes ask myself whether so much of the film is silent because of my own lack of French.' – Jules Dassin

† Several 'sequels' were made using the word rififi (criminal argot for 'trouble') in the title, but in plot terms they were entirely unrelated.

The Rift: see La Grieta

The Right Approach
US   1961   92m   bw   Cinemascope
TCF (Oscar Brodney)

A Hollywood opportunist tries to make it as a star.

A potentially witty Hollywood story is sabotaged by a style which is as naïve as it is dismal; and Mr Vaughan's hopes of stardom unfairly ended right here.

w Fay and Michael Kanin   play Garson Kanin   d David Butler   ph Sam Leavitt   m Dominic Frontière

Frankie Vaughan, Martha Hyer, Juliet Prowse, Gary Crosby, David MacLean, Jesse White, Jane Withers

Right Cross
US   1950   90m   bw
MGM (Armand Deutsch)

A boxing champion injures his hand and has to abandon his career.

Rather dull sporting melodrama with a Mexican background, saved by good production values.

w Charles Schnee   d John Sturges   ph Norbert Brodine   m David Raksin

Dick Powell, June Allyson, Lionel Barrymore, Ricardo Montalban

The Right Stuff *
US   1983   193m   Technicolor
Warner/Ladd (Irwin Winkler, Robert Chartoff)
V, V*, L

Test pilots are recruited and trained as astronauts.

A reasonably factual account of the Mercury programme: extremely well made but somehow too brash and inhuman to provide much entertainment. An unexpected commercial flop.

wd Philip Kaufman   book Tom Wolfe   ph Caleb Deschanel   m Bill Conti   pd Geoffrey Kirkland   ed Glenn Farr, Lisa Fruchtman, Stephen A. Rotter, Douglas Stewart, Tom Rolf

Sam Shepard, Scott Glenn, Ed Harris, Dennis Quaid, Fred Ward, Barbara Hershey, Kim Stanley, Veronica Cartwright

AA: Bill Conti; editing; sound; sound editing

AAN: best picture; Sam Shepard; Caleb Deschanel

The Right to Live
US   1935   75m   bw
Warner
GB title: The Sacred Flame

Someone in the family mercifully kills a crippled war hero.

Uninspired rendering of Somerset Maugham's play The Sacred Flame, previously filmed under its own title in 1929 (with Pauline Frederick, Henrietta Crosman).

w Ralph Block   d William Keighley

George Brent, Colin Clive, Josephine Hutchinson, Peggy Wood, C. Aubrey Smith, Leo G. Carroll, Halliwell Hobbes

The Right to Love *
US   1930   79m   bw
Paramount

A mother has a strong affinity with her illegitimate daughter who is a missionary on the other side of the world.

Curious mystic melodrama which adds a twist to the popular mother-love devices. Technically it introduced the Bell light valve which improved sound reproduction, and also the Dunning process which improved the presentation of dual roles. (The star played mother and daughter.)

w Zoe Akins   novel Brook Adams by Susan Glaspell   d Richard Wallace   ph Charles Lang

Ruth Chatterton, Paul Lukas, David Manners, Irving Pichel, George Baxter

'A profound and thoughtful romantic drama treated with utmost refinement of sophistication and still possessing elements which will appeal to the broadest kind of screen audience.' – Variety

AAN: Charles Lang

The Right to Love (1972): see Brainwashed

The Ring *
GB   1927   approx 116m (8454 feet)   bw
BIP (John Maxwell)
V*

Two boxers vie for the love of a woman.

Early Hitchcock that shows his already developed skill for deft story-telling; it was the first of his films to reveal his individuality as a director.

w Alfred Hitchcock, Alma Reville, Eliot Stannard   d Alfred Hitchcock   ph John J. Cox   ad C. Wilfred Arnold

Carl Brisson, Lilian Hall Davis, Ian Hunter, Forrester Harvey, Harry Terry, Gordon Harker, Billy Wells

'Succeeds in that very rare accomplishment of being the purest film art and a fine popular entertainment.' – Evening News

† The version released on video runs for 73m.

The Ring
US   1952   79m   bw
King Brothers
V*

A young Mexican becomes a prizefighter in the hope of winning greater respect for Mexican-Americans.

Well-meant low-budget programmer.

w Irving Shulman   d Kurt Neumann   ph Russell Harlan   m Herschel Burke Gilbert

Gerald Mohr, Lalo Rios, Rita Moreno, Robert Arthur

Ring of Bright Water *
GB   1969   107m   Technicolor
Palomar/Brightwater (Joseph Strick)
V, V*

A civil servant buys a pet otter and moves to a remote cottage in the western Highlands.

Disneyesque fable for animal lovers, from a bestselling book.

w Jack Couffer, Bill Travers   book Gavin Maxwell   d Jack Couffer   ph Wolfgang Suschitsky   m Frank Cordell

Bill Travers, Virginia McKenna, Peter Jeffrey, Roddy McMillan, Jameson Clark

Ring of Fear
US   1954   88m   Warnercolor   Cinemascope
Warner/Wayne-Fellows (Robert M. Fellows)

A homicidal maniac returns to the circus where he used to work and causes various 'accidents.'

Tediously predictable circus melodrama with a curious but not very likeable cast.

w Paul Fix, Philip MacDonald, James Edward Grant   d James Edward Grant   ph Edwin DuPar   m Emil Newman, Arthur Lange

Clyde Beatty, Pat O'Brien, Mickey Spillane, Sean McClory, Marion Carr, John Bromfield, Pedro Gonzalez Gonzalez, Emett Lynn

Ring of Fire
US   1961   90m   Metrocolor
MGM/Andrew and Virginia Stone

An Oregon sheriff is kidnapped by teenage delinquents but manages to lead them into both a police trap and a forest fire.

Outdoor action thriller with a plot which is ludicrously unconvincing in detail, though the fire scenes impress.

wd Andrew L. Stone   ph William H. Clothier   m Duane Eddy

David Janssen, Joyce Taylor, Frank Gorshin, Joel Marston

Ring of Spies *

GB 1963 90m bw
British Lion (Leslie Gilliatt)
US title: Ring of Treason

How the Portland spy ring was tracked down.

Documentary drama, rather less intriguing, somehow, than the actual facts; but the sheer thought of spies in the suburbs keeps interest going.

w Frank Launder, Peter Barnes   d Robert Tronson
ph Arthur Lavis

Bernard Lee, Margaret Tyzack, David Kossoff, Nancy Nevinson, William Sylvester

Ring of Treason: see *Ring of Spies*

Ring Up the Curtain: see *Broadway to Hollywood*

The Ringer *

GB 1952 78m bw
BL/London (Hugh Perceval)

A dangerous criminal known only as The Ringer threatens to kill the crooked lawyer responsible for his sister's death.

Artful old-fashioned mystery, quite well restaged, and in fact the best extant example of filmed Wallace.

w Val Valentine   play and novel Edgar Wallace
d Guy Hamilton   ph Ted Scaife   m Malcolm Arnold

Donald Wolfit, Mai Zetterling, Herbert Lom, Greta Gynt, William Hartnell, Norman Wooland

† The play was also filmed in 1931 with Patrick Curwen, Franklin Dyall and Gordon Harker; and in 1938 as *The Gaunt Stranger* (qv).

Rings on Her Fingers *

US 1942 85m bw
TCF (Milton Sperling)

The front girl for a couple of confidence tricksters falls in love with their first victim.

Lively comedy which drags into drama in its second half.

w Ken Englund   d Rouben Mamoulian
ph George Barnes   m Cyril Mockridge

Gene Tierney, Henry Fonda, Laird Cregar, Spring Byington, Shepperd Strudwick, Frank Orth, Henry Stephenson, Marjorie Gateson

Rio

US 1939 78m bw
Universal

A crooked financier escapes from Devil's Island to join his wife in Rio, only to find she has been unfaithful.

Modest but well made melodrama.

w Stephen Morehouse Avery, Frank Partos, Edwin Justus Mayer, Abem Kandel, Jean Negulesco
d John Brahm   ph Hal Mohr   md Charles Previn
m Frank Skinner

Basil Rathbone, Victor McLaglen, Sigrid Gurie, Robert Cummings, Leo Carrillo, Billy Gilbert, Irving Bacon, Irving Pichel

'A fair programmer with a blend of romance and adventure . . . should stand up satisfactorily as a top dualler in most situations.' – *Variety*

Rio Bravo **

US 1959 141m Technicolor
Warner/Armada (Howard Hawks)
V, V*, L

A wandering cowboy and a drunken sheriff hold a town against outlaws.

Cheerfully overlong and slow-moving Western in which everybody, including the director, does his thing. All very watchable for those with time to spare, but more a series of revue sketches than an epic.

w Jules Furthman, Leigh Brackett   d Howard Hawks
ph Russell Harlan   m Dimitri Tiomkin

John Wayne, Dean Martin, Ricky Nelson, Angie Dickinson, Walter Brennan, Ward Bond, John Russell, Pedro Gonzalez Gonzalez, Claude Akins, Harry Carey Jnr, Bob Steele

'After we finished we found we could have done it a lot better . . . and that's why we went ahead and made *El Dorado*.' – *Howard Hawks*

† More or less remade in 1966 as *El Dorado* and in 1970 as *Rio Lobo*.

Rio Conchos *

US 1964 107m DeLuxe Cinemascope
TCF (David Weisbart)
V*

Two thousand rifles are stolen from an army command post and traced to the hide-out of a former Confederate colonel who wants to continue the Civil War.

Good standard Western which shares much of its story line with *The Comancheros*.

w Clair Huffaker, Joseph Landon   d Gordon Douglas   ph Joe MacDonald   m Jerry Goldsmith

Richard Boone, Edmond O'Brien, Stuart Whitman, Tony Franciosa

Rio Grande *

US 1950 105m bw
Republic/Argosy (John Ford, Merian C. Cooper)
V, V*, L, S

A Cavalry unit on the Mexican border in the 1880s conducts a vain campaign against marauding Indians.

Thin Ford Western on his favourite theme, with too many pauses for song, too many studio sets, and too little plot. Aficionados, however, will find much to admire.

w James Kevin McGuinness   story James Warner Bellah   d John Ford   ph Bert Glennon, Archie Stout   m Victor Young

John Wayne, Maureen O'Hara, Ben Johnson, Claude Jarman Jnr, Harry Carey Jnr, Chill Wills, J. Carrol Naish, Victor McLaglen

Rio Lobo *

US 1970 114m Technicolor
Cinema Center (Howard Hawks)
V, V*, L

A Union colonel near the end of the Civil War recovers a gold shipment and exposes a traitor.

Rambling Western with traces of former glory, enjoyable at least for its sense of humour.

w Leigh Brackett, Burton Wohl   d Howard Hawks
ph William Clothier   m Jerry Goldsmith

John Wayne, Jorge Rivero, Jennifer O'Neill, *Jack Elam*, Victor French, Chris Mitchum, Mike Henry

Rio Rita

US 1929 135m bw and Technicolor
RKO (William Le Baron)

Romance on a ranch near the Mexican border.

Very early talkie version of a popular Broadway operetta of the twenties; historical interest only.

w Luther Reed, Russell Mack   book Guy Bolton, Fred Thomson, as produced by Florenz Ziegfeld   d Luther Reed   ph Robert Kurle, Lloyd Knetchel   md Victor Baravalle   songs Harry Tierney, Joe McCarthy

Bebe Daniels, John Boles, Bert Wheeler, Robert Woolsey, Dorothy Lee, Don Alvarado, George Renavent

Rio Rita

US 1942 91m bw
MGM (Pandro S. Berman)
V*

Flat-footed remake bringing in Nazi spies.

Poor comedy even by Abbott and Costello standards.

w Richard Connell, Gladys Lehman   d S. Sylvan Simon   ph George J. Folsey   m Herbert Stothart

Bud Abbott, Lou Costello, John Carroll, Kathryn Grayson, Tom Conway, Barry Nelson

Riot

US 1968 98m Technicolor
Paramount/William Castle
V*

While the warden is away, thirty-five convicts take over a state penitentiary and are violently subdued.

Strikingly bloody melodrama set in an actual prison in Arizona; well made, but less entertaining than Cagney and Raft used to be.

w James Poe   novel Frank Elli   d Buzz Kulik
ph Robert B. Hauser   m Christopher Komeda

Gene Hackman, Jim Brown, Ben Carruthers, Mike Kellin, Gerald O'Loughlin, Clifford David

Riot in Cell Block Eleven *

US 1954 80m bw
Allied Artists/Walter Wanger
V*

In a big American prison three convicts seize their guards, free the other prisoners and barricade themselves in their block.

Socially concerned low-budgeter, quite nicely made and persuasive of the need for prison reform.

w Richard Collins   d Don Siegel   ph Russell Harlan   m Herschel Burke Gilbert

Neville Brand, *Emile Meyer*, Frank Faylen, Leo Gordon, Robert Osterloh, Paul Frees, Don Keefer

'As a compassionate, angry, unsensational account of an episode of violence it makes considerably more impact than many of the overblown melodramas currently in fashion.' – *Penelope Houston*

Ripoux contre ripoux: see *Le Cop 2*

Riptide *

US 1934 90m bw
MGM (Irving Thalberg)

A British diplomat weds a Manhattan chorus girl, but she later falls for an old flame.

Elegantly set, star-packed drawing-room drama which somehow didn't click.

wd Edmund Goulding   ph Ray June   m Herbert Stothart

Norma Shearer, Robert Montgomery, Herbert Marshall, Mrs Patrick Campbell, Skeets Gallagher, Ralph Forbes, Lilyan Tashman, Helen Jerome Eddy, George K. Arthur, Halliwell Hobbes

'Has all the earmarks of box office . . . a commendable job all round.' – *Variety*

The Rise and Fall of Legs Diamond

US 1960 101m bw
Warner/United States (Milton Sperling)
V*, L

The career of a New York hoodlum of the twenties.

Inspired, like *King of the Roaring Twenties,* by the TV success of *The Untouchables,* this was part of a brief attempt by Warner to recapture its pre-war gangster image. Alas, stars and style were equally lacking.

w Joseph Landon   d Budd Boetticher   ph Lucien Ballard   m Leonard Rosenman

Ray Danton, Karen Steele, Elaine Stewart, Jesse White, Simon Oakland, Robert Lowery, Warren Oates, Judson Pratt

The Rise and Rise of Michael Rimmer
GB   1970   101m   Technicolor
Warner/David Frost (Harry Fine)

An efficiency expert takes over an advertising agency and is soon an MP, a cabinet minister, and PM.

Satirical comedy which quickly goes overboard and is only occasionally funny; it does, however, mark the final death throes of the swinging sixties, and the changeover to *Monty Python*.

w Peter Cook, John Cleese, Kevin Billington, Graham Chapman   d Kevin Billington   ph Alex Thompson   m John Cameron

Peter Cook, John Cleese, Arthur Lowe, Denholm Elliott, Ronald Fraser, Vanessa Howard, George A. Cooper, Harold Pinter, James Cossins, Roland Culver, Dudley Foster, Julian Glover, Dennis Price, Ronnie Corbett

Rise and Shine
US   1941   93m   bw
TCF (Mark Hellinger)

A dumb but brilliant football player is kidnapped by the other side.

Drab collegiate comedy, disappointing considering the credits.

w Herman J. Mankiewicz   novel My Life and Hard Times by James Thurber   d Allan Dwan   ph Edward Cronjager   m Emil Newman   songs Leo Robin, Ralph Rainger

Linda Darnell, Jack Oakie, George Murphy, Walter Brennan, Milton Berle, Sheldon Leonard, Donald Meek, Ruth Donnelly, Donald MacBride, Raymond Walburn, Emma Dunn

The Rise of Helga: see Susan Lenox, Her Fall and Rise

The Rise of Louis XIV **
France   1966   100m   Eastmancolor
ORTF (Pierre Gout)
V*
original title: La Prise de Pouvoir par Louis XIV

The young King of France asserts his power through the use of fashion, style and spectacle.

A complex study of power, shot in a direct, semi-documentary manner, with much use of a zoom lens.

w Jean Gruault   story Philippe Erlanger   d Roberto Rossellini   ph Georges Leclerc, Jean-Louis Picavet   ad Maurice Valay   ed Armand Ridel

Jean-Michel Patte, Raymond Jourdan, Silvagni, Katharine Renn, Dominique Vincent, Pierre Barrat

'Even the fact that it was made as a spectacular for French television does not quite justify its singular vapidity and pointlessness.' – *John Simon*

† The film was first shown on French TV before being given a cinema release.

Rising Damp
GB   1980   98m   colour
ITC/Black Lion (Roy Skeggs)
V

The amorous and conniving landlord of a slum boarding house develops a passion for one of his tenants.

A useful reminder of a TV sitcom worth remembering, but handicapped by restriction of action, paucity of plot and the overlength usual in film versions of such things, not to mention the premature death of its original co-star Richard Beckinsale.

w Eric Chappell   d Joe McGrath   ph Frank Watts   m David Lindup

Leonard Rossiter, Frances de la Tour, Don Warrington, Denholm Elliott, Christopher Strauli

'Unforgettably John Ford's finest film!'
The Rising of the Moon
Eire   1957   81m   bw
Warner/Four Provinces (Lord Killanin)

Three Irish short stories.

Curiously dull John Ford portmanteau with the Abbey players.

w Frank Nugent   stories Frank O'Connor, Malcolm J. McHugh, Lady Gregory   d John Ford   ph Robert Krasker   m Eamonn O'Gallagher   narrator Tyrone Power

Maureen Connell, Eileen Crowe, Cyril Cusack, Maureen Delany, Donald Donelly, Frank Lawton, Edward Lexy, Jack MacGowran, Denis O'Dea, Jimmy O'Dea, Noel Purcell

'A collision of East and West. A conspiracy of seduction and murder. A battle between tradition and power. Business is war.'
Rising Sun
US   1993   129m   DeLuxe
TCF (Peter Kaufman)
V, V*, L, S

Two cops, one an expert in Japanese culture, investigate the murder of a prostitute in the boardroom of a Japanese corporation's new Los Angeles headquarters.

Turgid thriller, revealing paranoid feelings about the Japanese in America but not much else to engage the interest.

w Philip Kaufman, Michael Crichton, Michael Backes   novel Michael Crichton   d Philip Kaufman   ph Michael Chapman   m Toru Takemitsu, Richard Marriott   pd Dean Tavoularis   ed Stephen A. Rotter, William S. Scharf

Sean Connery, Wesley Snipes, Harvey Keitel, Cary-Hiroyuki Tagawa, Kevin Anderson, Mako, Ray Wise, Stan Egi, Stan Shaw, Tia Carrere, Steve Buscemi

'The myth in *Rising Sun* is that found in most late 20th-century boysy genre films – the battle to prove white (or sometimes these days, black) male superiority in a world in which extreme male violence is constant, natural, and inevitable . . . one sits in the cinema feeling spattered by something false and degrading' – *Marilyn French*

'Even if the director was keen on doing a thriller exercise, his creative instincts don't seem to have been fully ignited.' – *Variety*

Risky Business
US   1939   67m   bw
Universal

A crusading radio columnist tracks down a kidnapper.

Tolerable crime programmer.

w Charles Grayson from a previous script by William Anthony McGuire   d Arthur Lubin

George Murphy, Dorothea Kent, Eduardo Ciannelli, Leon Ames, El Brendel, John Wray

'It will garner nice business in city spots, where they like their melodrama realistic.' – *Variety*

'Joel was a perfectly ordinary high-school virgin with two perfectly ordinary obsessions: SEX and MONEY'
Risky Business
US   1983   99m   Technicolor
Tisch-Avnet/Geffen
V, V*, L, S

A 17-year-old is left in charge of his parents' house and fills it with pimps and prostitutes . . . a lucrative business.

Would-be outrageous teenage comedy which is pretty well made but soon wears out its welcome.

wd Paul Brickman   ph Reynaldo Villalobos, Bruce Surtees   m Tangerine Dream   pd William J. Cassidy   ed Richard Chew

Tom Cruise, Rebecca de Mornay, Joe Pantoliano, Richard Masur, Bronson Pinchot, Curtis Armstrong, Nicholas Pryor

Riso Amaro: see Bitter Rice

Rita, Sue and Bob Too *
GB   1987   95m   Eastmancolor
Mainline/Umbrella/British Screen/Film Four (Sandy Lieberson)
V*, L

Schoolgirl babysitters are introduced to sex by their employer on the way home.

Raunchy yet appealing study of British attitudes to sex, in the tradition of *Letter to Brezhnev*.

w Andrea Dunbar   plays The Arbour and Rita, Sue And Bob Too by Andrea Dunbar   d Alan Clarke   ph Ivan Strasburg   m Michael Kamen   pd Len Huntingford   ed Stephen Singleton

Michelle Holmes, Siobhan Finneran, George Costigan, Lesley Sharp

Il Ritorno di Ringo: see The Return of Ringo

The Ritz *
US   1976   90m   Technicolor
Warner/Courtyard (Denis O'Dell)
V, V*, L

A comedy of mistaken identities in a gay New York turkish bath.

An adaptation of a stage success which doesn't seem nearly as funny as it thinks it is; but some of it does work.

w Terrance McNally   play Terrance McNally   d Richard Lester   ph Paul Wilson   m Ken Thorne   pd Phillip Harrison

Jack Weston, Rita Moreno, Jerry Stiller, Kaye Ballard, Bessie Love, George Coulouris, F. Murray Abraham, Treat Williams

The River *
India   1951   87m   Technicolor
Oriental/International/Theatre Guild (Kenneth McEldowney)
V*, L

Episodes in the life of a small English community living on the banks of the Ganges.

A slight and surprising work from this director, superbly observed and a pleasure to watch but dramatically very thin.

w Rumer Godden, Jean Renoir   novel Rumer Godden   d Jean Renoir   ph Claude Renoir   m M. A. Partha Sarathy   pd Eugene Lourié

Nora Swinburne, Esmond Knight, Arthur Shields, Adrienne Corri

† Renoir's assistant was Satyajit Ray.

The River
US   1984   122m   Technicolor
Universal/Edward Lewis
V*, L, S

The Garveys battle flood waters to save the family farm.

Old-fashioned rural drama, at times reminiscent of *Way Down East* plus a dash of symbolism. A surprise in 1984, and not a very pleasant one, despite or because of its political awareness.

w Robert Dillon, Julian Barry   d Mark Rydell   ph Vilmos Zsigmond   m John Williams   pd Charles Rosen   ed Sidney Levin

Mel Gibson, Sissy Spacek, Shane Bailey, Becky Jo Lynch, Scott Glenn, Billy Green Bush

AAN: Sissy Spacek; photography; music

River Lady

US 1948 78m Technicolor
Universal-International

The beautiful owner of a Mississippi gambling boat tries to buy up all her rivals.

Routine romantic drama.

w D. D. Beauchamp, William Bowers d George Sherman

Yvonne de Carlo, Rod Cameron, Dan Duryea, Helena Carter, Lloyd Gough, Florence Bates, John McIntire

River of No Return *

US 1954 91m Technicolor Cinemascope
TCF (Stanley Rubin)
V, V*, L

During the California gold rush a widower and his 10-year-old son encounter a saloon singer with a gold claim.

Cheerful, clichéd star Western designed to exploit the splendours of early Cinemascope, and very adequate for this purpose.

w Frank Fenton d Otto Preminger ph Joseph LaShelle md Lionel Newman m Cyril Mockridge

Robert Mitchum, Marilyn Monroe, Tommy Rettig, Rory Calhoun, Murvyn Vye

The River Rat

US 1984 93m Technicolor
Paramount/Sundance/Larson Rickman (Bob Larson)
V*, L

During a river journey on a raft to escape from a dishonest parole officer, a just-released convict tries to form a relationship with the young daughter he has never known.

A domestic drama that is never more than moderately effective.

wd Tom Rickman ph Jan Kiesser m Mike Post pd John J. Lloyd ed Dennis Virkler

Tommy Lee Jones, Nancy Lea Owen, Brian Dennehy, Martha Plimpton

A River Runs through It *

US 1992 123m Technicolor
Guild/Allied Filmmaker/Columbia (Robert Redford, Patrick Markey)
V, V*, L

Two brothers, whose relationship with each other is often troubled, find shared pleasure in fly-fishing.

A soothingly nostalgic movie, often graceful but more often sluggish.

w Richard Friedenberg story Norman Maclean d Robert Redford ph Philippe Rousselot m Mark Isham pd Jon Hutman ed Lynzee Klingman, Robert Estrin

Craig Sheffer, Brad Pitt, Tom Skerritt, Brenda Blethyn, Emily Lloyd, Edie McClurg, Stephen Shellen, Nicole Burdette, Susan Traylor

'Old-fashioned, literary and restrained . . . but its concerns are too refined, gentle and, finally, unexciting to stir the masses.' – Variety

'Cool, allusive and, in the best sense, poetic movie, rich in unforced metaphors and feelings.' – Richard Schickel, Time

'As a film, it has all the virtues except tension, which is unfortunately like saying that a watch would be a good timekeeper if the mainspring wasn't bust.' – Adam Mars-Jones, Independent

AAN: Philipe Rousselot; Richard Friedenberg; Mark Isham

Riverboat Rhythm

US 1946 65m bw
RKO

A Mississippi riverboat captain is financially embarrassed.

Very mild comedy with the star in dual roles.

w Robert Faber, Charles Roberts d Leslie Goodwins

Leon Errol, Walter Catlett, Glenn Vernon, Marc Cramer, Jonathan Hale, Joan Newton

The River's Edge

US 1956 87m Eastmancolor Cinemascope
TCF (Benedict Bogeaus)

A fugitive bank robber forces a farmer to guide him over the mountains into Mexico.

Sluggish open-air character melodrama.

w Harold J. Smith d Allan Dwan ph Harold Lipstein m Lou Forbes

Ray Milland, Anthony Quinn, Debra Paget, Byron Foulger

River's Edge **

US 1986 99m Metrocolor
Palace/Hemdale (Sarah Pillsbury, Midge Sanford)
V, V*, L

After a teenager murders his girlfriend, his friends wonder what action they should take.

A gripping drama of teenage alienation.

w Neal Jiminez d Tim Hunter ph Frederick Elmes m Jurgen Knieper pd John Muto ed Howard Smith, Sonya Sones

Crispin Glover, Keanu Reeves, Ione Skye, David Roebuck, Dennis Hopper, Joshua Miller

'An unusually downbeat and depressing youth pic.' – Variety

'This brilliant, messy little picture, another triumph for the independent film movement, should cause people to argue and celebrate for years – argue over how it could have been done better, celebrate that it was done at all.' – David Denby, New York

River's End

US 1930 74m bw
Warner

A Mountie dies chasing his man, who then impersonates him.

Popular, contrived, outdoor thriller, previously filmed in 1922 with Lewis Stone, and subsequently in 1940 with Dennis Morgan (this version became known as Double Identity).

w Charles Kenyon story James Oliver Curwood d Michael Curtiz

Charles Bickford, Evalyn Knapp, J. Farrell MacDonald, ZaSu Pitts, David Torrence

La Rivière du Hibou: see Incident at Owl Creek

The Road: see La Strada

The Road Back **

US 1937 105m bw
Universal (James Whale)

After World War I, German soldiers go home to problems and disillusion.

A major work, intended as a sequel to All Quiet on the Western Front. Despite impressive sequences, it doesn't quite reach inspiring heights.

w R. C. Sherriff, Charles Kenyon novel Erich Maria Remarque d James Whale ph John Mescall, George Robinson m Dimitri Tiomkin ad Charles D. Hall

Richard Cromwell, John King, Slim Summerville, Andy Devine, Barbara Read, Louise Fazenda, Noah Beery Jnr, Lionel Atwill, John Emery, Etienne Girardot, Spring Byington, Laura Hope Crews

'Big and frequently effective, but a let-down in toto . . . does not compare with All Quiet in quality or power.' – Variety

'They call it an all-star cast and that means there isn't a single player of any distinction to be picked out of the herd. . . . It might be funny if it wasn't horrifying. This is America seeing the world in its own image.' – Graham Greene

† The film is said to have been extensively reshot after protests from the German consul in Los Angeles. No 35mm negative now exists, as it reverted to Remarque and was lost.

Road Games

Australia 1981 110m colour
Avco Embassy/Barber International/Quest (Richard Franklin)
V*, S

A long-distance truck-driver unwittingly picks up a murderer on the run.

Tolerable but overlong road thriller.

w Everett de Roche d Richard Franklin ph Vincent Monton m Brian May pd John Dowding ed Edward McQueen-Mason

Stacy Keach, Jamie Lee Curtis, Marion Edwards, Grant Page

Road Gang

US 1936 60m bw
First National
GB title: Injustice

Penal corruption and brutality in a Southern state is exposed by the Chicago Sun.

A rough ride over familiar ground.

w Abem Finkel, Dalton Trumbo, Harold Buckley d Louis King

Donald Woods, Carlyle Moore Jnr, Kay Linaker, Harry Cording, Marc Lawrence

The Road Home

US 1989 116m colour
Rank/Orion (Howard Rosenman, Thomas Baer)
V
aka: Lost Angels

A rebellious youth is sent to a private institution for the problem children of the wealthy.

Confused and unconvincing picture of teenage traumas.

w Michael Weller d Hugh Hudson ph Juan Ruiz-Anchia m Philippe Sarde pd Assheton Gorton ed David Gladwell

Donald Sutherland, Adam Horovitz, Amy Locane, Don Bloomfield, Celia Weston, Graham Beckel, Patricia Richardson, Ron Frazier, Joseph d'Angerio

'What is wrong with it, apart from a rather overblown style which is never hard-edged enough, is the depiction of the rebellion itself which seems too predicated on adult perfidy to be entirely true.' – Derek Malcolm, Guardian

Road House

GB 1934 76m bw
Michael Balcon/Gaumont

A barmaid helps to track down a murderer.

Mild comedy melodrama with music.

w Austin Melford, Leslie Arliss play Walter Hackett d Maurice Elvey

Violet Loraine, Gordon Harker, Emlyn Williams, Aileen Marson, Hartley Power, Stanley Holloway, Marie Lohr

Road House *

US 1948 95m bw
TCF (Edward Chodorov)

A road house owner is jealous of his manager and frames him for murder.

Dated but watchable film noir of its era, with all characters cynical or homicidal.

w Edward Chodorov   *d* Jean Negulesco
ph Joseph LaShelle   *m* Cyril Mockridge

Richard Widmark, Ida Lupino, Cornel Wilde, Celeste Holm

Road House *
US   1989   114m   DeLuxe   Panavision
UIP/United Artists/Star Partners II/Silver Pictures (Joel Silver)
V, V*, L, S

A kung fu expert, who is hired to clean up a saloon, incurs the enmity of a local racketeer.

Rowdy action movie that provides unthinking enjoyment.

w David Lee Henry, Hilary Henkin   *d* Rowdy Herrington   *ph* Dean Cundey   *ad* William J. Durrell Jnr   *ed* Frank J. Urioste, John F. Link

Patrick Swayze, Kelly Lynch, Sam Elliott, Ben Gazzara, Marshall Teague, Julie Michaels, Red West, Sunshine Parker, Jeff Healey

'Very nearly a perfect exploitation movie.' – *MFB*

Road Show *
US   1941   86m   bw
Hal Roach
V*

A young man wrongly committed to an insane asylum escapes with another inmate and joins a travelling circus.

Engaging scatty comedy on familiar Roach lines which suffers from lame pacing but manages some likeable moments.

w Arnold Beldard, Harry Langdon, Mickell Novak *novel* Eric Hatch   *d* Gordon Douglas   *ph* Norbert Brodine   *m* George Stoll

John Hubbard, Adolphe Menjou, Carole Landis, Patsy Kelly, George E. Stone

Road to Denver
US   1955   90m   Trucolor
Republic

An honest ranch hand gets into trouble when he tries to help his lawless brother.

Uninspired Western which just about passes the time.

w Horace McCoy, Allen Rivkin   *d* Joe Kane

John Payne, Lee J. Cobb, Skip Homeier, Mona Freeman, Ray Middleton, Andy Clyde, Lee Van Cleef

The Road to Frisco: see *They Drive by Night*

The Road to Glory *
US   1936   103m   bw
TCF (Darryl F. Zanuck)

Adventures of a French regiment in World War I.

Meticulously produced war movie which bears comparison with *All Quiet on the Western Front*.

w Joel Sayre, William Faulkner   *d* Howard Hawks
ph Gregg Toland   *m* Louis Silvers

Fredric March, Warner Baxter, Lionel Barrymore, June Lang, Gregory Ratoff, Victor Kilian, John Qualen, Julius Tannen, Leonid Kinskey

The Road to Hope: see *Il Cammino della Speranza*

The Road to Life *
USSR   1930   100m   bw
Mejrabpom

Moscow street children are rounded up and reformed.

A kind of Russian prequel to the *Dead End Kids*, presented with much style.

wd Nikolai Ekk

Mikhail Zharov, Maria Gonfa, Tsifan Kyrla

'Judged purely as entertainment the film recedes quickly, as do most Russian films.' – *Variety*

'Where the human wreckage of the seven seas foregather, this powerful tale of love and intrigue is told!'

Road to Mandalay
US   1926   77m at 24 fps   bw   silent
MGM

Two eastern planters quarrel over a girl.

Potboiling star vehicle.

w Elliott Clawson, Herman Mankiewicz   *d* Tod Browning

Lon Chaney, Lois Moran, Owen Moore, Henry B. Walthall

The Road to Reno
US   1938   69m   bw
Universal

A rancher won't give his wife the divorce she thinks she wants.

Combination comedy, drama, romance and horse opera which doesn't gel.

w Roy Chanslor, Adele Comandini, Brian Marlowe *novel* I. A. R. Wylie   *d* S. Sylvan Simon

Randolph Scott, Hope Hampton, Glenda Farrell, Helen Broderick, Alan Marshal, Samuel S. Hinds

The Road to Salina
France/Italy   1971   96m   colour   Panavision
Robert Dorfmann
V*

original title: *Quando il Sola Scotta*

The proprietress of a roadside café recognizes a drifter as her long-lost son.

Boring emotional drama stymied by the multi-language problem.

w Georges Lautner, Pascal Jardin, Jack Miller
d Georges Lautner

Rita Hayworth, Mimsy Farmer, Robert Walker Jnr, Ed Begley, Sophie Hardy

Road to Singapore
US   1931   70m   bw
Warner

A doctor's wife is caught with her lover, and her life falls to pieces.

Tensions among the oriental upper crust: very dated and not very convincing.

w J. Grubb Alexander   *play* Roland Pertwee
d Alfred E. Green

William Powell, Louis Calhern, Doris Kenyon, Marian Marsh, Alison Skipworth

THE 'ROAD' SERIES:
Road to Singapore *
US   1940   84m   bw
Paramount (Harlan Thompson)
V*, L

Two rich playboys swear off women until they quarrel over a Singapore maiden.

The first Hope-Crosby-Lamour 'road' picture is basically a light romantic comedy and quite forgettable; the series got zanier as it progressed.

w Don Hartman, Frank Butler   *story* Harry Hervey
d Victor Schertzinger   *ph* William C. Mellor
m Victor Young

Bing Crosby, Bob Hope, Dorothy Lamour, Charles Coburn, Judith Barrett, Anthony Quinn, Jerry Colonna

'A deft blend of romance and comedy, songs and fisticuffs.' – *Picture Show*

'Two of the most congenially harmonized performances caught by the camera in recent years.' – *Motion Picture Herald*

† The script was originally designed for Fred MacMurray and Jack Oakie, who weren't available; then for Burns and Allen, who turned it down.

Road to Zanzibar **
US   1941   92m   bw
Paramount (Paul Jones)
V*, L

The trio on safari in Africa, with *Hellzapoppin* gags breaking in and an anything-goes atmosphere.

w Frank Butler, Don Hartman   *d* Victor Schertzinger
ph Ted Tetzlaff   *m* Victor Young   *songs* Johnny Burke, Jimmy Van Heusen

Hope, Crosby, Lamour, Una Merkel, Eric Blore, Luis Alberni, Douglass Dumbrille

'The funniest thing I've seen on the screen in years. Years.' – *Otis Ferguson*

Road to Morocco **
US   1942   83m   bw
Paramount (Paul Jones)
V*, L

Hollywood Arab palaces, a captive princess, topical gags and talking camels.

w Frank Butler, Don Hartman   *d* David Butler
ph William C. Mellor   *md* Victor Young
songs Johnny Burke, Jimmy Van Heusen

Hope, Crosby, Lamour, Anthony Quinn, Dona Drake

'A bubbly spontaneous entertainment without a semblance of sanity.' – *Variety*

'It would be difficult to find a screen pantomime with better wartime credentials.' – *Kine Weekly*

'This is the screwiest picture I've ever been in.' – *Camel*

AAN: script

Road to Utopia **
US   1945   89m   bw
Paramount (Paul Jones)
V, V*, L

The Klondike gold rush, with all the previous gag styles in good order, capped by a cheeky epilogue and constant explanatory narration by Robert Benchley.

w Norman Panama, Melvin Frank   *d* Hal Walker
ph Lionel Lindon   *m* Leigh Harline   *songs* Johnny Burke, Jimmy Van Heusen

Hope, Crosby, Lamour, Douglass Dumbrille, Hillary Brooke, Jack La Rue

AAN: script

Road to Rio **
US   1947   100m   bw
Paramount (Daniel Dare)
V*

Guest stars are given their head, plot intrudes again in the shape of a hypnotized heiress, and the style is more constrained (but still funny).

w Edmund Beloin, Jack Rose   *d* Norman Z. McLeod
ph Ernest Laszlo   *md* Robert Emmett Dolan
songs Johnny Burke, Jimmy Van Heusen

Hope, Crosby, Lamour, Gale Sondergaard, Frank Faylen, the Wiere Brothers, the Andrews Sisters

'Enough laughs to pass the time easily and to remind you how completely, since sound came in, the American genius for movie comedy has disintegrated.' – *James Agee*

AAN: Robert Emmett Dolan

Road to Bali *
US   1952   91m   Technicolor
Paramount (Harry Tugend)
V*

In and around the South Seas, with colour making the sets obvious and the gags only tediously funny.

The team's zest was also flagging.

w Frank Butler, Hal Kanter, William Morrow   *d* Hal Walker   *ph* George Barnes   *md* Joseph J. Lilley   *songs* Johnny Burke, Jimmy Van Heusen

Hope, Crosby, Lamour, Murvyn Vye, Peter Coe

Road to Hong Kong
GB   1962   91m   bw
UA/Melnor (Melvin Frank)
V*

Curious, slightly dismal-looking attempt to continue the series in a British studio and on a low budget.

A few good gags, but it's all very tired by now, and the space fiction plot makes it seem more so.

w Norman Panama, Melvin Frank   *d* Norman Panama   *ph* Jack Hildyard   *m* Robert Farnon   *pd* Roger Furse

Hope, Crosby, Lamour, Joan Collins, Robert Morley, Walter Gotell, Felix Aylmer and guests Peter Sellers, David Niven, Frank Sinatra, Dean Martin, Jerry Colonna

The Road Warrior: see *Mad Max 2*

Roadhouse Nights *
US   1930   71m   bw
Paramount

A reporter exposes a gangster operating from a country night-club.

Experimental mingling of elements which later become very familiar.

w Garrett Fort   *story* Ben Hecht   *d* Hobart Henley   *ph* William Steiner

Helen Morgan, Charles Ruggles, Fred Kohler, Jimmy Durante, Fuller Mellish Jnr

Roadside Prophets
US   1992   96m   CFI colour
Electric/New Line (Peter McCarthy, David Swinson)

A biker sets off across country to scatter the ashes of his friend in a place where he had been happy.

A punkish road movie, mainly peopled by the sort of eccentrics you would take back-roads to avoid; an *Easy Rider* for the 90s it isn't.

wd Abbe Wool   *story* David Swinson   *ph* Tom Richmond   *m* Pray For Rain, John Doe   *pd* J. Rae Fox   *ed* Nancy Richardson

John Doe, David Anthony Marshall, Adam Horovitz, Barton Heyman, John Cusack, Jennifer Balgobin, Ellie Raab, David Carradine, Timothy Leary, Arlo Guthrie

'With its unfashionable adherence to the idealism of 60s drop-out cinema and occasional deadpan belly laughs, this is well worth travelling along with for an hour and a half.' – *Kim Newman, Empire*

Roar *
US   1981   102m   colour   Panavision
Noel Marshall/Banjiro Uemura

A research biologist lives in the African bush with assorted wild animals. He is expecting his family, but they arrive a day early when he is out . . .

A rather silly story takes in some of the most remarkable animal photography on record, and there is a sub-plot involving villainous game hunters.

wd Noel Marshall   *ph* Jan de Bont   *m* Dominic Frontière

Noel Marshall, Tippi Hedren, and family

† The Marshalls live with their 150 lions and other wild animals in a ranch near Los Angeles. During production the film, which eventually cost 17 million dollars, was halted by flood, fire, epidemic and injury.

Roar of the Dragon
US   1932   70m   bw
Radio

Passengers in a Chinese river boat are menaced by bandits.

Curious water-set version of *Shanghai Express,* with a good cast its best recommendation.

w Howard Estabrook   *story* George Kibbee Turner, Merian C. Cooper, Jane Bigelow   *d* Wesley Ruggles

Richard Dix, Edward Everett Horton, Gwili Andre, ZaSu Pitts, Arline Judge, Dudley Digges, C. Henry Gordon

Roar of the Iron Horse
US   1951   bw   serial: 15 eps
Columbia

A railroad engineer goes out west to find why the new line is subject to so many accidents.

Tolerable iron horse serial saga.

d Spencer G. Bennett, Thomas Carr

Jock O'Mahoney, Virginia Herrick, William Fawcett, Hal Landon

'The land of the free gone wild! The heyday of the hotcha! The shock-crammed days G-men took ten whole years to lick!'

The Roaring Twenties ***
US   1939   106m   bw
Warner (Hal B. Wallis)
V, V*, L

A World War I veteran returns to New York, innocently becomes involved in bootlegging, builds up an empire and dies in a gang war.

Among the last of the Warner gangster cycle, this was perhaps the best production of them all, despite the familiar plot line: stars and studio were in cracking form.

w Jerry Wald, Richard Macaulay, Robert Rossen   *story* Mark Hellinger   *d* Raoul Walsh, Anatole Litvak   *ph* Ernest Haller   *m* Heinz Roemheld

James Cagney, Humphrey Bogart, Priscilla Lane, Jeffrey Lynn, Gladys George, Frank McHugh, Paul Kelly, Elizabeth Risdon

† The James Cagney character was based on Larry Fay, who was Texas Guinan's partner, and Gladys George is clearly Guinan herself.

The Roaring West
US   1935   bw   serial: 15 eps
Universal

Cowboys participating in a land rush hope that a map will lead them to the most valuable sites.

Routine star Western serial.

d Ray Taylor

Buck Jones, Muriel Evans, Walter Miller, Frank McGlynn Snr, William Desmond

Rob Roy the Highland Rogue
GB   1953   81m   Technicolor
Walt Disney (Perce Pearce)
V*

After the defeat of the clans in the 1715 rebellion, their leader escapes and after several adventures is granted a royal pardon.

A kind of Scottish Robin Hood, so stiffly acted and made that it might as well – or better – be a cartoon.

w Lawrence E. Watkin   *d* Harold French   *ph* Guy Green   *m* Cedric Thorpe Davie

Richard Todd, Glynis Johns, James Robertson Justice, Michael Gough, Finlay Currie, Geoffrey Keen, Archie Duncan

Robbers' Roost
US   1955   82m   DeLuxe
UA (Leonard Goldstein)

An honest cowboy is employed by cattle rustlers and strives to clear his name.

Fair Western programmer.

w John O'Dea, Sidney Salkow, Maurice Geraghty   *novel* Zane Grey   *d* Sidney Salkow

George Montgomery, Richard Boone, Sylvia Findley, Bruce Bennett, Peter Graves, Warren Stevens, William Hopper

Robbery *
GB   1967   113m   Eastmancolor
Joseph E. Levine/Oakhurst (Michael Deeley, Stanley Baker)
V*

Criminals conspire to rob the night mail train from Glasgow.

Heavy-going fictionalized account of the famous train robbery of 1963; best seen as standard cops and robbers, with some good chase sequences.

w Edward Boyd, Peter Yates, George Markstein   *d* Peter Yates   *ph* Douglas Slocombe   *m* Johnny Keating

Stanley Baker, James Booth, Frank Finlay, Joanna Pettet, Barry Foster, William Marlowe, Clinton Greyn, George Sewell

Robbery under Arms
GB   1957   99m   Eastmancolor
Rank (Joe Janni)
V*

In 19th-century Australia, two farming brothers join the notorious outlaw Captain Starlight.

Howlingly dull film version of a semi-classic adventure novel; a rambling story with no unity of viewpoint is saved only by excellent photography.

w Alexander Baron, W. P. Lipscomb   *novel* Rolf Boldrewood   *d* Jack Lee   *ph* Harry Waxman   *m* Matyas Seiber

Peter Finch, David McCallum, Ronald Lewis, Maureen Swanson, Jill Ireland, Laurence Naismith, Jean Anderson

Robbery under Arms
Australia   1985   141m   colour
Jock Blair/South Australia Film Corporation

Adventures of two young followers of the highwayman Captain Starlight.

Uninteresting cut-down of a TV mini-series; earlier versions were made in 1907, 1911, 1920 and 1957 (above).

w Graeme Koestveld, Tony Morphett   *novel* Rolf Boldrewood   *d* Ken Hannam, Donald Crombie

Sam Neill, Steven Vidler, Christopher Cummins, Liz Newman, Ed Devereux

'The miracle story of all time!'
The Robe **
US   1953   135m   Technicolor   Cinemascope
TCF (Frank Ross)
V, V*, L, S

Followers and opponents of Jesus are affected by the robe handed down by him at his crucifixion.

The first film in Cinemascope was, surprisingly, a biblical bestseller, but the crowded Roman sets hid most of the flaws in the process. The film itself was competent and unsurprising in the well-tried *Sign of the Cross* manner.

w Philip Dunne   *novel* Lloyd C. Douglas   *d* Henry Koster   *ph* Leon Shamroy   *m* Alfred Newman   *ad* Lyle Wheeler, George W. Davis

Richard Burton, Jean Simmons, Michael Rennie, *Victor Mature,* Jay Robinson, Torin Thatcher, Dean Jagger, Richard Boone, Betta St John, Jeff Morrow, Ernest Thesiger, Dawn Addams

'The film, then, is the usual vulgarising stuff; and to judge CinemaScope on this evidence would be unfair. The weaknesses of the system are obvious.' – *Dilys Powell*

† Power was originally cast in the Burton role, and Burt Lancaster in Mature's.

AA: art direction

AAN: best picture; Leon Shamroy; Richard Burton

Roberta *
US   1935   105m   bw (Technicolor sequence)
RKO (Pandro S. Berman)
V*, L

An American inherits a Parisian fashion house.

Thin and remarkably flatly-handled musical romance of the old school, charged only by the occasional appearances in supporting roles of Astaire and Rogers, then on the brink of stardom.

w Jane Murfin, Sam Mintz, Allan Scott play Otto Harbach book Gowns by Roberta by Alice Duer Miller d William A. Seiter ph Edward Cronjager md Max Steiner ch Fred Astaire m Jerome Kern ad Van Nest Polglase

Irene Dunne, Fred Astaire, Ginger Rogers, Randolph Scott, Helen Westley, Claire Dodd, Victor Varconi, Torben Meyer

'Musical picture-making at its best – fast, smart, good-looking and tuneful.' – Variety

† Remade as Lovely to Look At (qv).

AAN: song 'Lovely to Look At' (m Jerome Kern, ly Dorothy Fields, Jimmy McHugh)

Robin and Marian *
US   1976   107m   Technicolor
Columbia/Rastar (Dennis O'Dell)
V, V*, L

Robin Hood returns from the Crusades and finds conditions in Britain depressing; he finally conquers the evil Sheriff but dies in the attempt.

A kind of serious parody of medieval life, after the fashion of The Lion in Winter but much glummer; in fact, nothing to laugh at at all.

w James Goldman d Richard Lester ph David Watkin m John Barry pd Michael Stringer

Sean Connery, Audrey Hepburn, Robert Shaw, Ronnie Barker, Nicol Williamson, Richard Harris, Denholm Elliott, Kenneth Haigh, Ian Holm, Bill Maynard, Esmond Knight, Peter Butterworth

'Surface realism only hides a core of mush, suddenly revealed when the hero and heroine settle down for love-making in a field of corn.' – Geoff Brown

'Whimsical jokiness is a bit hard to reconcile with the final plunge into sacrificial romance.' – Michael Billington, Illustrated London News

Robin and the Seven Hoods *
US   1964   123m   Technicolor   Panavision
Warner/PC (Howard W. Koch, William H. Daniels)
V, V*, L

A spoof of the Robin Hood legend set in gangland Chicago of the twenties.

Too flabby by far to be as funny as it thinks it is, this farrago of cheerful jokes has effective moments and lively routines, but most of them are nearly swamped by flat treatment and the wide screen.

w David Schwartz d Gordon Douglas ph William H. Daniels m Nelson Riddle songs Sammy Cahn, James Van Heusen

Frank Sinatra, Dean Martin, Bing Crosby, Sammy Davis Jnr, Peter Falk, Barbara Rush, Edward G. Robinson, Victor Buono, Barry Kelley, Jack La Rue, Allen Jenkins, Sig Rumann, Hans Conried

AAN: Nelson Riddle; song 'My Kind of Town' (m James Van Heusen, ly Sammy Cahn)

Robin Hood **
US   1922   127m approx (24 fps)   bw   silent
Douglas Fairbanks

Robin Hood combats Prince John and the Sheriff of Nottingham.

An elaborate version of the legend which featured some of Hollywood's most celebrated sets and allowed the star to perform a selection of exhilarating stunts.

w Douglas Fairbanks d Allan Dwan ph Arthur Edeson ad Wilfrid Buckland, Irvin J. Martin

Douglas Fairbanks, Wallace Beery, Alan Hale, Enid Bennett

'The high water mark of film production. It did not grow from the bankroll, it grew from the mind.' – R. E. Sherwood

'A story book picture, as gorgeous and glamorous a thing in innumerable scenes as the screen has yet shown . . . thrilling entertainment for the whole family group.' – National Board of Review

† See also The Adventures of Robin Hood and The Story of Robin Hood and his Merrie Men.

Robin Hood
US   1973   83m   Technicolor
Walt Disney (Wolfgang Reitherman)
V, V*, L

Alarmingly poor cartoon feature with all the characters 'played' by animals; songs especially dim and treatment quite lifeless.

w Larry Clemmons, Ken Anderson, others d Wolfgang Reitherman

voices of Brian Bedford, Peter Ustinov, Terry-Thomas, Phil Harris, Andy Devine, Pat Buttram

AAN: song 'Love' (m George Bruns ly Floyd Huddleston)

Robin Hood
US   1990   104m   colour
TCF/Working Title (Sarah Radclyffe, Tim Bevan)
V, V*, L

Condemned for saving a poacher, a Saxon nobleman, Robert Hode, becomes the outlaw Robin Hood.

Dully facetious re-telling of a familiar tale.

w Mark Allen Smith, John McGrath d John Irvin ph Jason Lehel m Geoffrey Burgon pd Austen Spriggs ed Peter Tanner

Patrick Bergin, Uma Thurman, Jurgen Prochnow, Edward Fox, Jeroen Krabbé, Owen Teale, David Morrissey, Alex North, Gabrielle Reidy

'The film increasingly comes to resemble a 1960s Hammer cheapie.' – Sight and Sound

Robin Hood: Men in Tights
US   1993   102m   DeLuxe
TCF/Brooksfilms/Gaumont (Mel Brooks)
V, V*, L, S

Robin Hood escapes from prison in the Holy Land to return to England and fight against the tyranny of the Sheriff of Rottingham with the help of his merry men, including Will Scarlett O'Hara and Rabbi Tuckman.

An uninventive parody of Kevin Costner's commercially successful outing as the outlaw of Sherwood Forest; the Costner version is the funnier.

w Mel Brooks, J. David Shapiro, Evan Chandler d Mel Brooks ph Michael D. O'Shea m Hummie Mann pd Roy Forge Smith ed Steven E. Rivkin

Cary Elwes, Richard Lewis, Roger Rees, Amy Yasbeck, Tracy Ullman, Mel Brooks, Dom DeLuise, Dick Van Patten, Isaac Hayes, Patrick Stewart

'A return to the wild anarchic scatological comedies that made Mel Brooks a marquee name around the world.' – Variety

'Doesn't so much lampoon Prince of Thieves as try to rise on its jerkin-tails – what is it that he thinks he is adding when he takes off a film?' – Adam Mars-Jones

'To say it's feeble would be to give it the benefit of quite a few doubts. It's very feeble indeed.' – Derek Malcolm

Robin Hood of El Dorado *
US   1936   86m   bw
MGM

Joaquin Murieta turns bandit to avenge himself on the men who killed his wife.

Whitewashed biopic of a notorious Western desperado, played mainly for action and light relief.

w William Wellman, Melvin Levy, Joseph Calleia d William Wellman

Warner Baxter, Bruce Cabot, Margo, Eric Linden, J. Carrol Naish, Ann Loring

Robin Hood: Prince of Thieves *
US   1991   143m   Technicolor
Warner/Morgan Creek (John Watson, Pen Densham, Richard B. Lewis)
V, V*, L, S

Returning from the Crusades to discover that his father has been killed by the Sheriff of Nottingham, Robin of Locksley becomes an outlaw to get his revenge.

A glum version, with little sense of community among the outlaws and an odd mix of acting styles. But it found great favour with the public, becoming one of the most commercially successful films of the year.

w Pen Densham, John Watson d Kevin Reynolds ph Douglas Milsome m John Blakeley pd John Graysmark ed Peter Boyle

Kevin Costner, Morgan Freeman, Mary Elizabeth Mastrantonio, Christian Slater, Alan Rickman, Sean Connery (uncredited), Geraldine McEwan, Michael McShane, Brian Blessed, Michael Wincott, Nick Brimble

AAN: song '(Everything I Do) I Do For You' (m Michael Kamen, ly Bryan Adams, Robert John Lange)

Robinson Crusoe: see The Adventures of Robinson Crusoe

Robinson Crusoe and the Tiger
Mexico   1969   110m   Eastmancolor
Avant/Avco Embassy

Simple but extremely handsome version of the famous story, with the addition of a tiger which Crusoe takes as a pet.

w Mario Marzac, Rene Cardona Jnr novel Daniel Defoe d Rene Cardona Jnr

Hugo Stieglitz, Ahui

Robinson Crusoe of Clipper Island
US   1936   bw   serial: 14 eps
Republic

A search for an international spy group which has wrecked a giant dirigible.

Lively serial with animal interest.

d Mack V. Wright, Ray Taylor

Mala (a Polynesian), Rex (a horse), Buck (a dog), Mamo Clark, Herbert Rawlinson, William Newell

Robinson Crusoe on Mars **
US   1964   110m   Techniscope
Paramount/Devonshire (Aubrey Schenck)

An astronaut lands on Mars and learns to survive until rescue comes.

Remarkably close to Defoe (Man Friday being a refugee in an interplanetary war) this is an absorbing, entertaining and well-staged piece of science fiction, strikingly shot in Death Valley.

w Ib Melchior, John C. Higgins   *d* Byron Haskin
ph Winton C. Hoch   *m* Van Cleave   *ad* Hal Pereira,
Arthur Lonergan   *sp* Lawrence Butler

Paul Mantee, Adam West, Vic Lundin

'Here comes a pleasant surprise, a piece of science
fiction based on valid speculation . . . modest yet
provocative.' – *Time*

Robinson Crusoeland
France/Italy   1950   98m   bw
Sirius/Franco-London/Fortezza
V
aka: *Atoll K; Escapade; Utopia*

Stan and Ollie inherit an island in the Pacific, but
uranium is discovered on it.

Laurel and Hardy's last film is a dispiriting mess, and
the less said about it the better.

w unknown   *d* Leo Joannon, John Berry
ph Armand Thirard, Louis Née   *m* Paul Misraki

Stan Laurel, Oliver Hardy, Suzy Delair

'Part man. Part machine. All cop.'
Robocop ***
US   1987   103m   DuArt
Rank/Orion (Arne Schmidt)
V, V*, L, S

Detroit in the future: a badly injured cop is
reconstructed by science, and defeats the forces of evil.

Gleefully dark vision of the future, directed with flair,
although the violence goes over the top towards the
end. It gained a best director award at the Sitges Film
Festival and a special award for excellence at the 16th
Fantasy Film Festival at Avoriaz.

w Edward Neumeier, Michael Miner   *d* Paul
Verhoeven   *ph* Jost Vacano   *m* Basil Poledouris
pd William Sandell   *ed* Frank J. Urioste

Peter Weller, Nancy Allen, Ronny Cox, Kurtwood
Smith, Dan O'Herlihy, Miguel Ferrer

'The greatest science-fiction film since Metropolis' –
Ken Russell

'A comic book film that's definitely not for kids.' –
Daily Variety

'Very violent and very funny.' – *Time Out*

'Essentially, it's just a hipper, more bam-bam version
of the law-and-order hits of the seventies . . . The
picture keeps telling you that its brutishness is a
terrific turn-on, and maybe it is if you're hooked on
Wagnerian sci-fi comic books.' – *Pauline Kael, New
Yorker*

AAN: editing (Frank J. Urioste)

Robocop 2
US   1990   118m   DuArt
Rank/Orion (Jon Davison)
V, V*, L, S

Robocop goes into battle against Robocop 2, a vicious
cyborg with the brain of a criminal drug-addict.

Stupefyingly frenetic sequel with none of the panache
or wit of the original.

w Frank Miller, Walon Green   *d* Irvin Kershner
ph Mark Irwin   *m* Leonard Rosenman   *pd* Peter
Jamison   *ad* Pam Marcotte   *ed* William Anderson

Peter Weller, Nancy Allen, Dan O'Herlihy, Belinda
Bauer, Tom Noonan, Gabriel Damon, Felton Perry,
Willard Pugh

'The level of constant violence, with noisy sound
effects, explosions and hundreds of thousands of
rounds fired by automatic weaponry, is at first
arresting but ultimately numbing and boring.' –
Variety

'If you like to stagger away from a film feeling numb
and slightly sick, this one's for you.' – *Empire*

Robocop 3
US   1993   104m   DuArt color
Orion (Patrick Crowley)
S

Robocop is caught in a fight between a controlling
Japanese corporation and the poor it is trying to evict
to build a new city.

Inspiration is sadly lacking here in a film aimed at an
audience of early teens; all that can be said in its
favour is that it contains less violence than its
predecessor.

w Frank Miller, Fred Dekker   *d* Fred Dekker
ph Gary B. Kibbe   *m* Basil Poledouris   *pd* Hilda
Stark   *sp* Jeff Jarvis   *ed* Bert Lovitt

Robert John Burke, Nancy Allen, Rip Torn, John
Castle, Jill Hennessy, Mako, Robert DoQui

'A cluttered, nasty exercise that seems principally
intent on selling action figures.' – *Variety*

† A *Robocop* television series followed in 1994.

Rocco and His Brothers **
Italy/France   1960   180m   bw
Titanus/Les Films Marceau (Goffredo Lombardo)
V, V*, L, S

A peasant family moves into Milan, and each of its
five brothers has his problems.

Massive portmanteau of realistic stories, a bit hard to
take despite its undoubted brilliance.

w Luchino Visconti, Suso Cecchi d'Amico, Vasco
Pratolini   *d* Luchino Visconti   *ph* Giuseppe Rotunno
m Nino Rota

Alain Delon, Renato Salvatori, Annie Girardot, Katina
Paxinou, Roger Hanin, Paolo Stoppa, Suzy Delair,
Claudia Cardinale

'Joins the band of films which, these last months,
have given one new hope for the cinema.' – *Dilys
Powell*

Rock a Bye Baby
US   1958   107m   Technicolor   Vistavision
Paramount (Jerry Lewis)

A film star asks her devoted schoolday admirer to
look after her triplets by a secret marriage.

Tasteless jazzing-up of *The Miracle of Morgan's Creek* by
talents distinctly unsympathetic.

wd Frank Tashlin   *ph* Haskell Boggs   *m* Walter
Scharf

Jerry Lewis, Marilyn Maxwell, Reginald Gardiner,
Salvatore Baccaloni, Hans Conried, Isobel Elsom,
James Gleason, Isa Moore, Connie Stevens

Rock-a-Doodle
GB   1990   74m   Technicolor
Rank/Goldcrest/Sullivan Bluth (Don Bluth, Gary Goldman, John
   Pomeroy, Robert Enrietto)
V, V*, L, S

A farmboy, transformed into a cat by a wicked owl,
travels to the big city to persuade a rock-singing
rooster to return home and make the sun shine again.

Excellent animation is rendered pointless by a poor
and confusing narrative.

w David N. Weiss   *story* Don Bluth, David N. Weiss,
John Pomeroy, T. J. Kuenster, David Steinberg, Gary
Goldman   *d* Don Bluth   *m* Robert Folk, T. J.
Kuenster   *pd* David Goetz   *ed* Bernard Caputo,
Fiona Trayler, Lisa Dorney, Joe Gall

voices of Phil Harris, Glen Campbell, Eddie Deezen,
Kathryn Holcomb, Toby Scott Ganger, Stan Ivar,
Christian Hoff, Jason Marin, Christopher Plummer,
Sandy Duncan

Rock around the Clock *
US   1956   74m   bw
Columbia (Sam Katzman)
V*

A band playing a new form of jive – rock 'n' roll –
becomes a nationwide sensation.

A cheap second feature with guest artists, this
cheerful little movie deserved at least a footnote in the
histories because it spotlights the origins and the
leading purveyors of rock 'n' roll. It also caused
serious riots in several countries. A sequel in 1957,
Don't Knock the Rock, was merely cheap.

w Robert E. Kent, James B. Gordon   *d* Fred F. Sears
ph Benjamin H. Kline

Bill Haley and the Comets, the Platters, Little Richard,
Tony Martinez and his Band, Freddie Bell and the
Bellboys, Johnny Johnson, Alan Freed, Lisa Gaye,
Alix Talton

Rock Hudson's Home Movies **
US   1992   63m   video
Mark Rappaport

A semi-documentary, in which an actor playing the
role of Rock Hudson comments on film clips of the
real Hudson, looking at his performances from a gay
perspective.

A witty deconstruction of Hudson's masculine and
heterosexual screen image and the constraints and
evasions of Hollywood movies in the 1950s and 60s.

wd Mark Rappaport   *ph* Mark Daniels   *ed* Mark
Rappaport

Eric Farr (as Rock Hudson)

'Shatters the false image of the movies so completely
that you wonder how it ever lasted so long.' – *Premiere*

Rock 'n' Roll High School *
US   1979   93m   colour
New World (Michael Finnell)

High-school students rebel against an oppressive
principal.

A tongue-in-cheek, sometimes self-conscious update
of a 1950s rock movie, retaining and enjoying every
cliché.

w Russ Dvonch, Joseph McBride, Richard Whitley
story Allan Arkush, Joe Dante   *d* Allan Arkush
ph Dean Cundey   *m* The Ramones   *ad* Marie
Kordus   *ed* Larry Bock, Gail Werbin

P. J. Soles, Vincent Van Patten, Clint Howard, Dey
Young, Mary Woronov, Paul Bartel, Dick Miller,
Grady Sutton

Rock Rock Rock
US   1957   83m   bw
Vanguard (Max J. Rosenberg, Milton Subotsky)
V*

Two girls are rivals for the love of a high-school rock
singer.

Poorly written and ineptly acted low-budget movie
exploiting the popularity of rock 'n' roll. It consists
mainly of a series of performances that have nothing
to do with the narrative, which are either by second-
string performers – the appalling Ivy Schulman,
Cirino and The Bowties, Jimmy Cavallo and His
House Rockers, The Three Chuckles, The Moonglows
– or better ones such as Chuck Berry, The Flamingos,
Frankie Lymon and LaVern Baker performing second-
rate material.

w Milton Subotsky   *d* Will Price   *ph* Morris
Hartzband   *md* Milton Subotsky   *ad* Paul M.
Heller   *ed* Blandine Hafela

Tuesday Weld, Teddy Randazzo, Jacqueline Kerr, Ivy
Schulman, Alan Freed, Fran Manfred, Jack Collins,
Carol Moss   Rock singer Johnny Burnette (1934—
64) is featured in his only screen performance.

† Connie Francis dubbed Tuesday Weld's two songs.

Rockabye
US   1932   70m   bw
Radio

A great actress who has scratched her way up is unhappy because of frustrated mother love.

One of many tearjerkers of its type produced in the first three years of the thirties: it doesn't travel well across the decades.

w Jane Murfin, Kubec Glasmon   *play* Lucia Bronder *d* George Cukor

Constance Bennett, Joel McCrea, Paul Lukas, Walter Pidgeon, Jobyna Howland, Walter Catlett

'Moderate grosser, best for the neighbourhood mats.' – *Variety*

The Rocket Man

US   1954   79m   bw
TCF

A visitor from outer space gives a magic ray gun to an orphan boy and tells him to use it only for good.

Elementary fantasy with amusing moments.

w Lenny Bruce, Jack Henley   *d* Oscar Rudolph

Charles Coburn, George 'Foghorn' Winslow, Spring Byington, Anne Francis, John Agar

Rocket to the Moon: see *Cat Women of the Moon*

The Rocketeer

US   1991   108m   Technicolor   Panavision
Walt Disney/Silver Screen Partners IV (Lawrence Gordon, Charles Gordon, Lloyd Levin)
V, V*, L

In 1938 a racing pilot finds a one-man rocket pack which he uses to foil a Nazi's attempt at world domination.

Tame attempt at a period adventure that never gets off the ground.

w Danny Bilson, Paul de Meo   *graphic novel* Dave Stevens   *d* Joe Johnston   *ph* Hiro Narita *m* James Horner   *pd* Jim Bissell   *sp* Jon G. Belyeu *ed* Arthur Schmidt

Bill Campbell, Jennifer Connelly, Alan Arkin, Timothy Dalton, Paul Sorvino, Terry O'Quinn, Ed Lauter, James Handy

'This high-octane, high-flying, live-action comic strip has been machine-tooled into agreeable lightweight summer fare.' – *Variety*

Rockets Galore

GB   1958   94m   Technicolor
Rank/Relph and Dearden
US title: *Mad Little Island*

The Scottish island of Todday resists the installation of a rocket-launching site.

Amiable but disappointingly listless sequel to *Whisky Galore.*

w Monja Danischewsky   *d* Michael Relph   *ph* Reg Wyer   *m* Cedric Thorpe Davie

Jeannie Carson, Donald Sinden, Roland Culver, Noel Purcell, Ian Hunter, Duncan Macrae, Jean Cadell, Carl Jaffe, Gordon Jackson, Catherine Lacey

Rocketship XM *

US   1950   79m   bw
Lippert (Kurt Neumann)

An expedition to the moon lands by accident on Mars.

The first post-war space adventure is sheer hokum, quite likeable for its cheek though not for its cheap sets.

wd Kurt Neumann   *ph* Karl Struss   *m* Ferde Grofe

Lloyd Bridges, Osa Massen, John Emery, Hugh O'Brian

'The message of *Rocketship X-M* is clear: never take a lady as your fuel expert on a trip into interstellar space.' – *C. A. Lejeune*

The Rocking Horse Winner *

GB   1949   90m   bw
Rank/Two Cities (John Mills)
V*

A boy discovers he can predict winners while riding an old rocking horse; his mother's greed has fatal results.

A very short story is fatally over-extended and becomes bathetic; but the production is solid and the film deserves a mark for trying.

wd Anthony Pelissier   *story* D. H. Lawrence *ph* Desmond Dickinson   *m* William Alwyn *ad* Carmen Dillon

John Mills, Valerie Hobson, John Howard Davies, Ronald Squire, Hugh Sinclair, Cyril Smith

'Fails as an interpretation of D. H. Lawrence. But as a skilful piece of narrative with excellent technical qualities it is well worth a visit.' – *Dilys Powell, Britain Today*

'His whole life was a million-to-one shot!'

Rocky **

US   1976   119m   Technicolor
UA/Chartoff-Winkler (Gene Kirkwood)
V, V*, L, S

A slightly dimwitted Philadelphia boxer makes good.

Pleasantly old-fashioned comedy-drama with rather unattractive characters in the modern manner. Despite the freshness, on the whole *Marty* is still preferable.

w Sylvester Stallone   *d* John G. Avildsen   *ph* James Crabe   *m* Bill Conti

Sylvester Stallone, Burgess Meredith, Talia Shire, Burt Young, Carl Weathers, Thayer David

AA: best picture; John G. Avildsen

AAN: Sylvester Stallone (as writer); song 'Gonna Fly Now' (*m* Bill Conti, *ly* Carol Connors, Ayn Robbins); Sylvester Stallone (as actor); Burgess Meredith; Talia Shire; Burt Young

Rocky II

US   1979   119m   Technicolor
UA/Irwin Winkler, Robert Chartoff
V, V*, L, S

After success comes failure; then Rocky marries his sweetheart and works for another big fight.

Over-inflated but under-nourished sequel with absolutely nothing new to offer.

wd Sylvester Stallone   *ph* Bill Butler   *m* Bill Conti

Sylvester Stallone, Talia Shire, Burt Young, Carl Weathers, Burgess Meredith

'A Fighter. A Lover. A Legend. The Greatest Challenge.'

Rocky III

US   1982   99m   Technicolor
United Artists/Chartoff-Winkler (James D. Brubaker)
V, V*, L, S

Rocky is challenged by a brutal slugger who beats him at the first match . . .

Unnecessary regurgitation of bits and pieces from the first two Rocky movies.

wd Sylvester Stallone   *ph* Bill Butler   *m* Bill Conti *pd* William J. Cassidy   *ed* Don Zimmerman, Mark Warner

Sylvester Stallone, Talia Shire, Burt Young, Burgess Meredith, Carl Weathers, Tony Burton, Mr T, Hulk Hogan

'The time has surely come for Rocky Balboa to take the final count.' – *Tom Milne, MFB*

'The first Rocky was primitive in a relatively innocent way. This picture is primitive too, but it's also shrewd and empty and inept.' – *New Yorker*

AAN: original song 'Eye of the Tiger' by Jim Peterik and Frankie Sullivan III

Rocky IV

US   1985   91m   Metrocolor
MGM/UA/Winkler-Chartoff
V, V*, L, S

Rocky takes on a Russian champion.

Hilarious, hysterical, would-be allegorical, this is the pits; but it took a lot of money.

wd Sylvester Stallone   *ph* Bill Butler   *m* Vince DiCola, Bill Conti   *pd* Bill Kenney   *ed* Don Zimmerman, John W. Wheeler

Sylvester Stallone, Dolph Lundren, Carl Weathers, Talia Shire, Burt Young, Brigitte Nielsen

'Ludicrous rubbish, but efficient with it.' – *Shaun Usher, Daily Mail*

'Where does a champion go when he takes off the gloves?'

Rocky V

US   1990   104m   DeLuxe
UIP/United Artists/Star Partners III (Robert Chartoff, Irwin Winkler)
V, V*, L, S

Rocky, suffering, unsurprisingly, from brain-damage, takes on a young protégé.

The series continues its steep, downward spiral into insipid nonsense.

w Sylvester Stallone   *d* John G. Avildsen *ph* Steven Poster   *m* Bill Conti   *pd* William J. Cassidy   *ed* John G. Avildsen, Michael N. Knue

Sylvester Stallone, Talia Shire, Burt Young, Sage Stallone, Burgess Meredith, Tommy Morrison, Richard Gant, Tony Burton

† Stallone's original ending had Rocky dying in his moment of final triumph.

The Rocky Horror Picture Show **

GB   1975   100m   Eastmancolor
TCF (Michael White)
V, V*, S

A couple, whose car breaks down on a dark and stormy night, take refuge in an old, dark mansion where a mad scientist is trying to make the perfect man.

A spoof of horror and science-fiction movies, based on a hit musical, and notable mainly for the high-energy performance of Tim Curry, repeating his stage success as a transvestite transsexual from Transylvania.

w Richard O'Brien, Jim Sharman   *play The Rocky Horror Show* by Richard O'Brien   *d* Jim Sharman *ph* Peter Suschitzky   *m* Richard O'Brien   *pd* Brian Thomson   *ed* Graeme Clifford

Tim Curry, Susan Sarandon, Barry Bostwick, Richard O'Brien, Patricia Quinn, Little Nell, Jonathan Adams, Peter Hinwood, Meatloaf, Charles Gray

'A self-consciously slick rendition of the original material, shorn of the song reprises, staged and performed with evident delight in having larger and more lavish sets to move around in.' – *Tony Rayns, MFB*

'A quite wonderful mixture of spoof horror and sci-fi.' – *Empire*

† The film was a failure on its first release but later became a cult phenomenon at midnight screenings, with audiences dressed as the characters and chanting their dialogue.

Rocky Mountain

US   1950   83m   bw
Warner (William Jacobs)

A Confederate horseman gets involved in an Indian war.

Routine star Western with unusual tragic ending.

w Winston Miller, Alan le May   *d* William Keighley *ph* Ted McCord   *m* Max Steiner

Errol Flynn, Patrice Wymore, Scott Forbes, Guinn Williams, Slim Pickens

Rocky Mountain Mystery

US   1935   64m   bw
Paramount

An engineer solves a number of murders at a radium mine.

Routine whodunnit in an unfamiliar setting.

w Edward E. Paramore Jnr   novel Golden Dreams by Zane Grey   d Charles Barton

Randolph Scott, Charles Chic Sale, Mrs Leslie Carter (a rare screen appearance, and just as well to judge from her performance), Kathleen Burke, Ann Sheridan

'Good entertainment in spite of minor shortcomings.' – Variety

Roger & Me **

US   1989   90m   DuArt
Warner/Dog Eat Dog Films/Michael Moore
V, V*, L

A journalist attempts to interview the chairman of General Motors about his decision to close its factory in the town where the company began and so put thousands of people out of work.

Entertaining, blackly comic (though not always accurate) documentary on the human cost of big business.

wd Michael Moore   ph Christopher Beaver, John Prusak, Kevin Rafferty, Bruce Schermer   ed Wendy Stanzler, Jennifer Beman

'A fascinating account of blue collar life unable to come to terms with the clouding of the American Dream they are perpetually adjured to believe in.' – Derek Malcolm, Guardian

Roger Touhy, Gangster

US   1944   73m   bw
TCF
GB title: The Last Gangster

An associate of Al Capone is finally cornered by the FBI.

Unsurprising, competent cops-and-robbers melodrama, based more or less on fact.

w Crane Wilbur, Jerry Cady   d Robert Florey

Preston Foster, Victor McLaglen, Lois Andrews, Kent Taylor, Anthony Quinn, Henry Morgan

Rogue Cop

US   1954   92m   bw
MGM (Nicholas Nayfack)

A police detective is on the payroll of a crime syndicate.

Uncompelling star melodrama.

w Sidney Boehm   novel William P. McGivern   d Roy Rowland   ph John Seitz   m Jeff Alexander

Robert Taylor, George Raft, Janet Leigh, Steve Forrest, Anne Francis

'Another of the sour, disillusioned crime stories which have recently been coming into fashion.' – Penelope Houston

AAN: John Seitz

The Rogue Song *

US   1930   115m   Technicolor
MGM (Lionel Barrymore)

A bandit wins the hand of a Russian princess.

Primitive early sound operetta, not salvaged by a few Laurel and Hardy scenes added as an afterthought.

w Frances Marion, John Colton   operetta Gypsy Love by Franz Lehàr, Robert Bodansky   d Lionel Barrymore, Hal Roach   ph Percy Hilburn, C. Edgar Schoenbaum   m Dimitri Tiomkin

Lawrence Tibbett, Catherine Dale Owen, Florence Lake, Judith Voselli, Nance O'Neill, Stan Laurel, Oliver Hardy

'Slow unto dullness outside of Tibbett's singing; Laurel and Hardy names draw but their comedy is very weak.' – Variety

† No print is known to exist, but in 1980 the sound track was issued on record.

AAN: Lawrence Tibbett

Rogue's March

US   1953   84m   bw
MGM (Leon Gordon)

A British army officer is unjustly accused of espionage but becomes a hero in India.

Victorian comedy adventure set on a never-never frontier. Not much.

w Leon Gordon   d Allan Davis   ph Paul C. Vogel   m Alberto Columbo

Peter Lawford, Richard Greene, Janice Rule, Leo G. Carroll, John Abbott, Patrick Aherne

Rogues of Sherwood Forest *

US   1950   80m   Technicolor
Columbia (Fred M. Packard)

Robin Hood's son helps the barons to force the signing of Magna Carta.

Satisfactory action adventure.

w George Bruce   d Gordon Douglas   ph Charles Lawton Jnr   m Heinz Roemheld, Arthur Morton

John Derek, Diana Lynn, George Macready, Alan Hale, Paul Cavanagh, Lowell Gilmore, Billy House

Rogues' Regiment

US   1948   86m   bw
Universal-International (Robert Buckner)

An intelligence man joins the French Foreign Legion in Saigon to track down an ex-Nazi.

Keen but rather muddled actioner.

w Robert Buckner   d Robert Florey   ph Maury Gertsman   m Daniele Amfitheatrof

Dick Powell, Marta Toren, Vincent Price, Stephen McNally

Le Roi de Coeur: see King of Hearts

Rollerball *

US   1975   129m   Technicolor   Scope
UA/Norman Jewison
V, V*, L

In the 21st century an ultra-violent game is used to release the anti-social feelings of the masses.

A one-point parable, and an obvious point at that, is stretched out over more than two hours of violence in which the rules of the game are not even explained. A distinctly unlikeable film.

w William Harrison   d Norman Jewison   ph Douglas Slocombe   md André Previn   pd John Box

James Caan, John Houseman, Ralph Richardson, Maud Adams, John Beck, Moses Gunn

'A classic demonstration of how several millions of dollars can be unenjoyably wasted.' – Jonathan Rosenbaum

Rollercoaster

US   1977   118m   Technicolor   Panavision
Sensurround
Universal (Jennings Lang)
V*, L

A saboteur blows up rollercoasters if his blackmail demands are not met.

Limp, unsuspenseful, would-be spectacular in which a stalwart cast struggles with inane dialogue and situations.

w Richard Levinson, William Link   d James Goldstone   ph David M. Walsh   m Lalo Schifrin

George Segal, Timothy Bottoms, Richard Widmark, Susan Strasberg, Harry Guardino, Henry Fonda

Rolling Thunder

US   1977   94m   DeLuxe
AIP (Norman T. Herman)
V*, L

A former prisoner of war in Vietnam seeks revenge on the killers of his wife and son.

Moderate action thriller, although its use of the Vietnam War seems opportunistic rather than apposite.

w Heywood Gould, Paul Schrader   d John Flynn   ph Jordan Cronenweth   m Barry DeVorzon   ad Steve Burger   ed Frank P. Keller

William Devane, Tommy Lee Jones, Linda Haynes, Lisa Richards, Dabney Coleman, James Best

Rollover

US   1981   115m   Technicolor   Panavision
Orion/IPC (Bruce Gilbert)
V*

The widow of a murdered bank president exposes various kinds of financial chicanery on an international scale.

So complexly plotted as to be virtually unintelligible, this slick romantic melodrama was caviare to the general despite its stars.

w David Shaber   d Alan J. Pakula   ph Giuseppe Rotunno, William Garroni   m Michael Small

Jane Fonda, Kris Kristofferson, Hume Cronyn, Josef Sommer, Bob Gunton

Roma, Città Aperta: see Open City

Le Roman de Renard: see The Tale of the Fox

Le Roman d'un Tricheur *

France   1936   83m   bw
Cinéas
aka: The Story of a Cheat

A reformed elderly cardsharp writes his memoirs.

First person singular comedy, a tour de force in which only the narrator speaks, the rest use pantomime only.

wd Sacha Guitry   ph Marcel Lucien

Sacha Guitry, Marguerite Moreno, Serge Grave

Roman Holiday **

US   1953   118m   bw
Paramount (William Wyler)
V, V*, L

A princess on an official visit to Rome slips away incognito and falls in love with a newspaperman.

Wispy, charming, old-fashioned romantic comedy shot in Rome and a little obsessed by the locations; one feels that a studio base would have resulted in firmer control of the elements. The stars, however, made it memorable.

w Ian McLellan Hunter, John Dighton   d William Wyler   ph Franz Planer, Henri Alekan   m Georges Auric   ad Hal Pereira, Walter Tyler   ed Robert Swink

Gregory Peck, Audrey Hepburn, Eddie Albert, Hartley Power, Harcourt Williams

'While Capra, or in a different way Lubitsch, could have made something wholly enjoyable from it, it would seem that Wyler's technique is now too ponderously inflexible for such lightweight material.' – MFB

† Dalton Trumbo, then a blacklisted writer, was the actual author of the original story, although Ian McLellan Hunter received the credit for it.

AA: original story (Ian McLellan Hunter); Audrey Hepburn; costumes (Edith Head)

AAN: best picture; script; William Wyler; photography; Eddie Albert; art direction; editing

Roman Scandals **
US   1933   93m   bw
Samuel Goldwyn
V*

A troubled young man dreams himself back in ancient Rome.

Musical farce which is not only pretty entertaining on its own account but remains interesting for a number of reasons; as its star's best vehicle, for its Depression bookends, as a spoof on *The Sign of the Cross* and the inspiration of scores of other comedies in which the heroes dreamed themselves back into other times. Note also the musical numbers, the chariot race finale, and the rare appearance of Ruth Etting.

w William Anthony McGuire, George Oppenheimer, Arthur Sheekman, Nat Perrin *story* George S. Kaufman, Robert E. Sherwood *d* Frank Tuttle *chariot sequence* Ralph Cedar *ph* Gregg Toland *m* Alfred Newman *ch* Busby Berkeley *songs* Harry Warren (*m*), Al Dubin, L. Wolfe Gilbert (*ly*)

Eddie Cantor, Gloria Stuart, Ruth Etting, Edward Arnold, Alan Mowbray, Verree Teasdale

'An extraordinary rigmarole containing everything from chariot races to a torch song.' – *Time*

The Roman Spring of Mrs Stone *
GB   1961   104m   Technicolor
Warner Seven Arts/AA (Louis de Rochemont)
V*

A widowed American actress in Rome begins to drift into lassitude and moral decline.

Vivien Leigh gets degraded again in this rambling novella complete with mysterious dark stranger waiting at the end. Nice to look at, and occasionally compelling, but unsuccessful as a whole.

w Gavin Lambert *novel* Tennessee Williams *d* José Quintero *ph* Harry Waxman *m* Richard Addinsell *pd* Roger Furse *ad* Herbert Smith

Vivien Leigh, Warren Beatty, Lotte Lenya, Jeremy Spenser, Coral Browne, Ernest Thesiger

AAN: Lotte Lenya

Romance *
US   1930   76m   bw
MGM
V*

A clergyman falls in love with the opera singer mistress of an industrialist.

Simple-minded romantic drama with the star not at her best; but an interesting example of 'high class' romance of the time.

w Bess Meredyth, Edwin Justus Mayer *play* Edward Sheldon *d* Clarence Brown *ph* William Daniels

Greta Garbo, Lewis Stone, Gavin Gordon, Elliott Nugent, Clara Blandick, Florence Lake, Henry Armetta

'A first-run hit of the sort that won't miss.' – *Variety*

AAN: Clarence Brown; Greta Garbo

Romance and Riches: see *The Amazing Quest of Ernest Bliss*

Romance for Three: see *Paradise for Three*

Romance in Flanders
GB   1937   73m   bw
Franco-London/British Lion
US title: *Romance on the Western Front*

Two sergeants fall for a Belgian farmer's daughter; she marries the one she doesn't love, thinking the other is dead.

Rose-coloured romantic hokum, of no sustaining interest.

w Harold Simpson *book* Mario Fort, Ralph E. Vanloc *d* Maurice Elvey

Paul Cavanagh, Marcelle Chantal, Garry Marsh, Olga Lindo, Alastair Sim

Romance in Manhattan
US   1934   78m   bw
RKO
V*

A New York girl helps a Czech immigrant to find work in the metropolis.

Slim, sentimental movie novelette without a touch of sophistication.

w Jane Murfin, Edward Kaufmann *d* Stephen Roberts

Ginger Rogers, Francis Lederer, Arthur Hohl, J. Farrell MacDonald, Eily Malyon, Donald Meek

Romance in the Dark
US   1938   78m   bw
Paramount

A famous baritone helps a singing servant to get famous.

Musical romance for the carriage trade, with apparently more comedy asides than were originally intended.

w Frank Partos, Anne Morrison Chapin *d* H. C. Potter

Gladys Swarthout, John Boles, John Barrymore, Claire Dodd, Fritz Field, Curt Bois

'Biz will be good, if no wow. Boles and Barrymore will give some tug to the tide against the turnstiles.' – *Variety*

Romance in the Rain
US   1934   74m   bw
Universal

A girl from the slums wins a Cinderella contest and falls for the press agent.

Lightweight romantic concoction which pleased at the time.

w Barry Trivers, Gladys Unger, John V. A. Weaver, Sig Herzig, Jay Gorney *d* Stuart Walker

Roger Pryor, Heather Angel, Victor Moore, Esther Ralston, Ruth Donnelly, Christian Rub

Romance is Sacred: see *The King and the Chorus Girl*

Romance of a Horse Thief
US/Yugoslavia   1971   100m   Technicolor
Allied Artists/Jadran/Emmanuel L. Wolf (Gene Gutowski)
V*

In a Polish village in 1904 there is dismay when horses are commandeered by Cossacks for service in the Russo-Japanese war.

Nostalgic Jewish drama which ends up rather like *Fiddler on the Roof* without the music.

w David Opatoshu, based on his father's novel *d* Abraham Polonsky *ph* Piero Portalupsisic *m* Mort Shuman

Yul Brynner, Eli Wallach, Jane Birkin, Oliver Tobias, Lainie Kazan, David Opatoshu

The Romance of Rosy Ridge
US   1947   103m   bw
MGM (Jack Cummings)

After the Civil War, farmers make their own peace.

Mild period romance with everything settled by a betrothal.

w Lester Cole *novel* Mackinlay Kantor *d* Roy Rowland *ph* Sidney Wagner *m* George Bassman

Van Johnson, Thomas Mitchell, Janet Leigh, Selena Royle, Marshall Thompson, Dean Stockwell

'Rustic charm spread through it like molasses.' – *Douglas Eames*

Romance on the High Seas *
US   1948   99m   Technicolor
Warner (Alex Gottleib, George Amy)
V*, L
GB title: *It's Magic*

Various romances mesh on an ocean voyage.

Lightweight musical which introduces Doris Day and generally manages to keep afloat.

w Julius J. and Philip G. Epstein, I. A. L. Diamond *d* Michael Curtiz *ph* Elwood Bredell *m* Ray Heindorf *songs* Jule Styne, Sammy Cahn

Jack Carson, Janis Paige, Don Defore, Doris Day, Oscar Levant, S. Z. Sakall, Eric Blore, Franklin Pangborn, Fortunio Bonanova

AAN: Ray Heindorf; song 'It's Magic' (*m* Jule Styne, *ly* Sammy Cahn)

Romancing the Stone *
US   1984   106m   DeLuxe   Panavision
TCF/El Corazon (Michael Douglas)
V, V*, L

A best-selling lady romance novelist gets more than she bargained for when she tries to find her kidnapped sister in Colombia.

Spoof adventure thriller which takes too long to get going and then finds it has nowhere to go. But commercial . . .

w Diane Thomas *d* Robert Zemeckis *ph* Dean Cundey *m* Alan Silvestri *pd* Lawrence G. Paull

Michael Douglas, Kathleen Turner, Danny DeVito, Zack Norman, Alfonso Arau

'The picture has a bravura opening and a jolly kind of movement, but it becomes too slambang.' – *Pauline Kael, New Yorker*

Romanoff and Juliet *
US   1961   103m   Technicolor
U-I/Pavla (Peter Ustinov)

Both Americans and Russians woo the tiny country of Concordia, and war threatens while the ambassadors' children fall in love.

Despite the author's wit this pattern comedy became something of a bore as a stylized stage piece, and the film is not smartly enough handled to be anything but a yawn; the humour never becomes cinematic.

wd Peter Ustinov *play* Peter Ustinov *ph* Robert Krasker *m* Mario Nascimbene *ad* Alexander Trauner

Peter Ustinov, Sandra Dee, John Gavin, Akim Tamiroff, Tamara Shayne, John Phillips, Alix Talton, Peter Jones

The Romantic Age
GB   1949   86m   bw
Pinnacle – Rank
US title: *Naughty Arlette*

A precocious French student sets her cap at the art teacher.

Fluffy farce in which all the adults behave like children; not well regarded.

w Edward Dryhurst, Peggy Barwell *novel* Serge Weber *d* Edmond T. Greville

Mai Zetterling, Hugh Williams, Margot Grahame, Petula Clark, Carol Marsh, Raymond Lovell, Paul Dupuis

Romantic Comedy

US   1983   102m   Metrocolor
MGM-UA/Taft Entertainment/The Mirisch Corporation (Walter Mirisch, Morton Gottlieb)
V*

A Broadway playwright and a New England schoolteacher have a creative partnership that is more personal than professional.

Tedious film version of a play which wallows in autobiography.

w Bernard Slade   play Bernard Slade   d Arthur Hiller   ph David M. Walsh   m Marvin Hamlisch   pd Alfred Sweeney

Dudley Moore, Mary Steenburgen, Frances Sternhagen, Janet Eilber, Robyn Douglass, Ron Leibman

'When a movie's production notes wax lyrical about the pile of the living room carpet, one senses that they're in trouble.' – Nick Roddick, MFB

The Romantic Englishwoman *

GB   1975   116m   Eastmancolor
Dial/Meric-Matalon (Daniel M. Angel)
V, V*

A discontented woman, holidaying at Baden Baden, falls in love with a stranger while her husband completes a novel on the same theme.

Almost as ambiguous as Last Year in Marienbad, this annoying film wastes good actors in a script which hovers uncertainly between fantasy, melodrama and reality, intending one supposes to make humourless and obvious comparisons between romance and life.

w Tom Stoppard, Thomas Wiseman   novel Thomas Wiseman   d Joseph Losey   ph Gerry Fisher   m Richard Hartley

Glenda Jackson, Michael Caine, Helmut Berger, Marcus Richardson, Kate Nelligan, René Kolldehoff, Michel Lonsdale

'The central trio bite off their lines, play deviously with hypocrisies and humiliations, and seem slightly aware that they're creations by artifice out of artificiality.' – Penelope Houston

'An itsy-bitsy, fragmented film that seems less than the sum of its parts.' – Michael Billington, Illustrated London News

Rome Adventure

US   1962   119m   Warnercolor
Warner
V*, L
GB title: Lovers Must Learn

A pretty American librarian goes to Rome to learn about love, and does.

Sluggish and overstretched travelogue with dollops of arch romance; hard to take.

wd Delmer Daves

Suzanne Pleshette, Troy Donahue, Angie Dickinson, Rossano Brazzi, Constance Ford, Chad Everett

Rome Express ***

GB   1932   94m   bw
Gaumont (Michael Balcon)

Thieves and blackmail victims are among the passengers on an express train.

Just a little faded now as sheer entertainment, this remains the prototype train thriller from which The Lady Vanishes, Murder on the Orient Express and a hundred others are all borrowed; it also spawned a myriad movies in which strangers are thrown together in dangerous situations. Technically it still works very well, though the script needs modernizing.

w Clifford Grey, Sidney Gilliat, Frank Vosper, Ralph Stock   d Walter Forde   ph Gunther Krampf

Conrad Veidt, Gordon Harker, Esther Ralston, Joan Barry, Harold Huth, Cedric Hardwicke, Donald Calthrop, Hugh Williams, Finlay Currie, Frank Vosper, Muriel Aked, Eliot Makeham

'A first class craftsman's job.' – Basil Wright

'Technically, and in a sense intellectually speaking, this film puts Forde into Class A1.' – Cinema Quarterly

HARKER: 'Discretion is the better part of Wagons Lits.'

† Remade 1948 as Sleeping Car to Trieste (qv).

Romeo and Juliet *

US   1936   127m   bw
MGM (Irving Thalberg)
V*

Hollywood Shakespeare with a super production and a rather elderly cast.

Not entertaining in the strict sense, but full of interest.

w Talbot Jennings   d George Cukor   ph William Daniels   m Herbert Stothart   ad Cedric Gibbons, Frederic Hope, Edwin B. Willis

Leslie Howard, Norma Shearer, John Barrymore, Basil Rathbone, Edna May Oliver, Henry Kolker, C. Aubrey Smith, Violet Kemble-Cooper, Robert Warwick, Virginia Hammond, Reginald Denny, Ralph Forbes, Andy Devine, Conway Tearle

'Unimaginative, coarse-grained, a little banal, it is frequently saved – by Shakespeare – from being a bad film.' – Graham Greene

'It is impossible to realize how bad this film was unless you reflect on how good it might have been.' – Alberto Cavalcanti

† Fredric March, Robert Donat and Robert Montgomery all refused the lead before Leslie Howard accepted.

AAN: best picture; Norma Shearer; Basil Rathbone; art direction

Romeo and Juliet

GB   1954   138m   Technicolor
Rank/Verona (Joe Janni, Sandro Ghenzi)
V*

Good-looking but extremely boring version shot on Italian locations with quite unacceptable leads.

wd Renato Castellani   ph Robert Krasker   m Roman Vlad

Laurence Harvey, Susan Shentall, Aldo Zollo, Enzo Fiermonte, Flora Robson, Mervyn Johns, Sebastian Cabot, Lydia Sherwood, Giulio Garbinetti, Nietta Zocchi, Bill Travers, Norman Wooland, John Gielgud as prologue speaker

Romeo and Juliet *

GB   1968   152m   Technicolor
Paramount/BHE/Verona/Dino de Laurentiis (Anthony Havelock-Allan, John Brabourne, Richard Goodwin)
V, V*, L, S

The with-it version for modern youngsters.

Unfortunately the admirably rapid style does not suit the verse, and long before the much-deferred end the thing becomes just as tiresome as the other versions.

w Franco Brusati, Masolino D'Amico   d Franco Zeffirelli   ph Pasquale de Santis   m Nino Rota

Leonard Whiting, Olivia Hussey, John McEnery, Michael York, Pat Heywood, Milo O'Shea, Paul Hardwick, Natasha Parry, Antonio Pierfederici, Esmeralda Ruspoli, Bruce Robinson, Roberto Bisacco, Laurence Olivier as prologue speaker

'A large gold watch should be tossed to Zeffirelli for his part in reversing the movies' reputation for emasculating the classics.' – Newsweek

AA: Pasquale de Santis; costumes (Danilo Donati)

AAN: best picture; Franco Zeffirelli

Romeo in Pajamas: see Parlor, Bedroom and Bath

Romeo Is Bleeding

US   1993   108m   DeLuxe
Rank/Polygram/Working Title (Hilary Henkin)

A cop, who takes bribes from the crooks he investigates while trying to keep his wife and his mistress happy, is assigned to protect a sexy hitwoman on the run from her gangster friends; it proves to be a recipe for mayhem.

Hectic, delirious thriller in which violence takes precedence over character and plot.

w Hilary Henkin   d Peter Medak   ph Dariusz Wolski   m Mark Isham   pd Stuart Wurtzel   ed Walter Murch

Gary Oldman, Lena Olin, Annabella Sciorra, Juliette Lewis, Roy Scheider, David Proval, Will Patton

'This heavy dose of ultra-violent neo-noir gives Gary Oldman a face-first trip through the gutter that would make Mickey Rourke drool, but the far-fetched plotting eventually goes so far over the top that pic flirts with inventing a new genre of film noir camp.' – Variety

Romero

US   1989   105m   DeLuxe
Warner/Paulist Pictures (Ellwood E. Kieser)
V*, L

An apolitical priest is transformed by events into an archbishop who vigorously opposes El Salvador's government-sanctioned death squads.

Low-key biopic that tends to pussyfoot around its subject.

w John Sacret Young   d John Duigan   ph Geoff Burton   m Gabriel Yared   ad Francisco Magallon   ed Frans Vandenburg

Raul Julia, Richard Jordan, Ana Alicia, Eddie Velez, Alejandro Bracho, Tony Plana, Harold Gould, Lucy Reina

Rommel, Desert Fox: see The Desert Fox

Romper Stomper *

Australia   1992   92m   Eastmancolor
Seon/Australian Film Commission/Film Victoria (Daniel Scharf, Ian Pringle)
V, V*, L

In Melbourne, Nazi-loving skinheads battle with a Vietnamese gang.

A violent excursion into Australian low-life and one that refrains from any implied comment on the anti-social action it presents.

wd Geoffrey Wright   ph Ron Hagen   m John Clifford White   pd Steven Jones-Evans   ed Bill Murphy

Russell Crowe, Daniel Pollock, Jacqueline McKenzie, Alex Scott, Leigh Russell

'Swiftly turns into another from the seemingly endless conveyor belt of debut moviemakers who use street violence as their calling card and a hand-held camera to conceal their other deficiencies of talent, imagination or personal vision.' – Alexander Walker, London Evening Standard

'Art house patrons are likely to be turned off by the brutally depicted violence and dominant antisocial behaviour . . . Pic is well acted and directed with a certain slickness, but rarely has there been such a disturbing, essentially misconceived pic.' – Variety

Romuald et Juliette *

France   1989   112m   colour
Gala/Cinéa/Eniloc/FR3 (Jean-Louis Piel, Philippe Carcassonne)
V

A managing director, whose business is being sabotaged by disgruntled colleagues, is saved by his cleaner.

Amusing comedy of ineffectual men and strong women.

wd Coline Serreau   *ph* Jean-Noël Ferragut
ad Jean-Marc Stehle   *ed* Catherine Renault

Daniel Auteuil, Firmine Richard, Pierre Vernier, Maxime Leroux, Gilles Privat, Muriel Combeau, Catherine Salviat

La Ronde ***
France   1950   100m   bw
Sacha Gordine
V

In 1900 Vienna, an elegant compère shows that love is a merry-go-round: prostitute meets soldier meets housemaid meets master meets married woman meets husband meets midinette meets poet meets actress meets officer meets prostitute meets soldier . . .

Superb stylized comedy with a fine cast, subtle jokes, rich decor and fluent direction; not to mention a haunting theme tune.

w Jacques Natanson, Max Ophuls   *novel* Arthur Schnitzler   *d* Max Ophuls   *ph* Christian Matras
m Oscar Straus

Anton Walbrook, Simone Signoret, Serge Reggiani, Simone Simon, Daniel Gélin, Danielle Darrieux, Fernand Gravey, Odette Joyeux, Jean-Louis Barrault, Isa Miranda, Gérard Philipe

'One of the most civilized films to have come from Europe in a long time.' – *Gavin Lambert, MFB*

'A film that drags on and on by what seems like geometric progression.' – *John Simon, 1968*

AAN: script

La Ronde
France   1964   110m   Eastmancolor   Franscope
Robert and Raymond Hakim

Vulgarization of the above, reset in Paris in 1913.

The lack of a compère vastly reduces the number of jokes.

w Jean Anouilh   *d* Roger Vadim   *ph* Henri Decaë
m Michel Magne

Marie Dubois, Claude Giraud, Anna Karina, Jean-Claude Brialy, Jane Fonda, Maurice Ronet, Catherine Spaak, Bernard Noel, Francine Bergé, Jean Sorel

Rooftops
US   1989   95m   DeLuxe
Fox/New Vision/Koch Company (Howard W. Koch)
V*, L

Teenagers living on the roofs of an old tenement building combine to fight a vicious drug dealer.

Uninteresting teen movie, involving unlikeable characters.

w Terence Brennan   *story* Allan Goldstein
d Robert Wise   *ph* Theo Van de Sande   *m* Michael Kamen   *pd* Jeannine C. Oppewall   *ed* William Reynolds

Jason Gedrick, Troy Beyer, Eddie Velez, Tisha Campbell, Alexis Cruz, Allen Payne, Steve Love, Rafael Baez, Jaime Tirelli

'Words fail me where this absurd piece of tuppence-coloured fantasy is concerned.' – *Derek Malcolm, Guardian*

Rookery Nook **
GB   1930   107m   bw
British and Dominions (Herbert Wilcox)

A nervous husband on holiday tries to hide a runaway girl who has asked for protection against her stepfather.

Primitive talkie technique cannot entirely conceal the brilliance of the original Aldwych farce team in their most enduring vehicle.

w Ben Travers,   *play* Ben Travers   *d* Tom Walls
ph Dave Kessan

Ralph Lynn, Tom Walls, Robertson Hare, Winifred Shotter, Mary Brough, Ethel Coleridge, Griffith Humphreys, Margot Grahame

'As a talker it is the best specimen so far made on this side.' – *Variety*

'He took a new kid and made a hero out of him.'

The Rookie
US   1990   121m   Technicolor
Warner/Malpaso (Howard Kazanjian, Steven Siebert, David Valdes)
V, V*, L

Ageing cop teaches his new young partner how to act tough.

Dreary, amoral and cliché-ridden slog through all-too-familiar territory.

w Boaz Yakin, Scott Spiegel   *d* Clint Eastwood
ph Jack N. Green   *m* Lennie Niehaus   *ed* Joel Cox

Clint Eastwood, Charlie Sheen, Raul Julia, Sonia Braga, Tom Skerrit, Lara Flynn Boyle, Pepe Serna, Marco Rodriguez, Pete Randall

'Overlong, sadistic and stale even by the conventions of the buddy pic genre.' – *Variety*

'Clint Eastwood has forgotten how to make popular entertainment.' – *Philip French, Observer*

Rookies
US   1927   75m at 24 fps   bw   silent
MGM

Army adventures of a tough sergeant and a bumbling recruit.

Popular comedy of its day which established the new team of Karl Dane and George K. Arthur.

w Byron Morgan   *d* Sam Wood

also with Marceline Day, Louise Lorraine, Tom O'Brien

Rookies (1941): see *Buck Privates*

Rookies Come Home: see *Buck Privates Come Home*

Room at the Top ***
GB   1958   117m   bw
Remus (John and James Woolf)
V*

An ambitious young clerk causes the death of his real love but manages to marry into a rich family.

Claimed as the first British film to take sex seriously, and the first to show the industrial north as it really was, this melodrama actually cheats on both counts but scene for scene is vivid and entertaining despite a weak central performance.

w Neil Paterson,   *novel* John Braine   *d* Jack Clayton
ph Freddie Francis   *m* Mario Nascimbene

Laurence Harvey, *Simone Signoret*, Heather Sears, Donald Wolfit, Ambrosine Philpotts, Donald Houston, Raymond Huntley, John Westbrook, Allan Cuthbertson, Hermione Baddeley, Mary Peach

'A drama of human drives and torments told with maturity and precision.' – *Stanley Kauffmann*

AA: Neil Paterson; Simone Signoret

AAN: best picture; Jack Clayton; Laurence Harvey; Hermione Baddeley

Room for One More
US   1952   95m   bw
Warner (Henry Blanke)

A married couple adopt several underprivileged children.

Slightly mawkish family movie redeemed by star performances.

w Jack Rose, Melville Shavelson   *d* Norman Taurog
ph Robert Burks   *m* Max Steiner

Cary Grant, Betsy Drake, Lurene Tuttle, Randy Stuart, George Winslow

The Room of Words
Italy   1989   97m   Kodak Color
Filmirage/Wind Film
V

Anaïs Nin falls in love with writer Henry Miller and his wife June.

Inept on every level, lacking any sense of period or place (despite a streetcar named Desire) and concentrating on artfully shot lesbian love scenes. It is also saddled with an obtrusive and unsympathetic score and the near incomprehensible English of Martine Brochard as Anaïs Nin.

w Franco Molè   *play* Franco Molè   *d* Joe D'Amato
ph Giancarlo Ferrando   *m* Gianni Silano
ed Kathleen Stratton

Martine Brochard, David Brandon, Linda Carol, Ron Gural, Colette de La Croix

Room Service *
US   1938   78m   bw
RKO (Pandro S. Berman)
V, V*, L

Penniless theatricals find ways of staying in a hotel until they can find a backer.

Claustrophobic Broadway farce unsuitably adapted for the Marx Brothers, who are constrained by having to play characters with a passing resemblance to human beings.

w Morrie Ryskind   *play* John Murray, Allen Boretz
d William A. Seiter   *ph* Russell Metty   *m* Roy Webb

Groucho, Chico, Harpo, Lucille Ball, *Donald MacBride*, Frank Albertson, Ann Miller, Philip Loeb

'A natural for the box office . . . the change of pace is a good idea.' – *Variety*

'It should also be noted . . . that there is a scene in which a turkey is chased around a room. Not everybody will care for this.' – *MFB*

† Remade as *Step Lively* (qv).

A Room with a View ***
GB   1985   115m   colour
Merchant Ivory/Goldcrest (Ismail Merchant)
V, V*, L, S

An innocent Edwardian girl travelling in Italy has her eyes opened to real life and romance.

Competent, unexciting equivalent of a television classic mini-series which so perfectly filled a need as to become a runaway commercial success.

w Ruth Prawer Jhabvala   *novel* E. M. Forster
d James Ivory   *ph* Tony Pierce-Roberts   *m* Richard Robbins   *pd* Gianna Quaranta, Brian Ackland-Snow
ed Humphrey Dixon

Maggie Smith, Denholm Elliot, Helena Bonham Carter, Julian Sands, Daniel Day Lewis, Simon Callow, Judi Dench, Rosemary Leach, Rupert Graves

'Quality-starved filmgoers will welcome it.' – *Variety*

AA: art direction; adapted screenplay; costumes (Jenny Beavan, John Bright)

AAN: James Ivory as director; Tony Pierce-Roberts; best picture; Maggie Smith; Denholm Elliott

Rooney *
GB   1958   88m   bw
Rank (George H. Brown)

Adventures of a bachelor Irish dustman.

Moderately charming, though unconvincing, Dublin comedy.

w Patrick Kirwan   *novel* Catherine Cookson
d George Pollock   *ph* Christopher Challis
m Philip Green

John Gregson, Barry Fitzgerald, Muriel Pavlow, June Thorburn, Noel Purcell, Marie Kean, Liam Redmond, Jack MacGowan, Eddie Byrne

Rooster Cogburn *
US   1975   108m   Technicolor   Panavision
Universal (Paul Nathan)
V, V*, L

An elderly marshal after a gang of outlaws is helped by the Bible-thumping daughter of a priest.

Disappointing Western too obviously patterned after *True Grit* and *The African Queen*. Having had the idea for outrageous star casting, the producers obviously decided erroneously that the film would make itself.

w Martin Julien   d Stuart Millar   ph Harry Stradling Jnr   m Laurence Rosenthal

John Wayne, Katharine Hepburn, Anthony Zerbe, Richard Jordan, John McIntyre, Strother Martin

'Like one of those infuriating exhibition bouts in which two resilient old pros bob, weave and spar without ever landing any punches.' – *Michael Billington, Illustrated London News*

† 'Martin Julien' allegedly covers the writing talents of Hal Wallis, his wife Martha Hyer, and some friends.

The Root of All Evil
GB   1946   110m   bw
Gainsborough

A jilted woman becomes unscrupulous in business in order to get even with her ex-boyfriend.

Incredible farrago with a star ill at ease.

wd Brock Williams   novel J. S. Fletcher

Phyllis Calvert, Michael Rennie, John McCallum, Moore Marriott, Brefni O'Rourke, Hazel Court, Edward Rigby

The Roots of Heaven *
US   1958   125m   Eastmancolor   Cinemascope
TCF/Darryl F. Zanuck

A white man in central Africa dedicates himself to prevent the slaughtering of elephants.

Curiously patchy version of a novel which was a strange choice for filming; so many side issues are introduced that at times it takes on the look of another jolly safari adventure.

w Romain Gary, Patrick Leigh-Fermor   novel Romain Gary   d John Huston   ph Oswald Morris   m Malcolm Arnold

Trevor Howard, Juliette Greco, Errol Flynn, Eddie Albert, Orson Welles, Paul Lukas, Herbert Lom, Grégoire Aslan, Friedrich Ledebur, Edric Connor

'The Huston who did *Sierra Madre* would have lighted his cigar with this script.' – *Stanley Kauffmann*

Rope **
US   1948   80m   Technicolor
Transatlantic (Sidney Bernstein, Alfred Hitchcock)
V, V*, L

Two homosexuals murder a friend for the thrill of it and conceal his body in a trunk from which they serve cocktails to a party including his father and girlfriend.

An effective piece of Grand Guignol on the stage, this seemed rather tasteless when set in a New York skyscraper, especially when the leading role of the investigator was miscast and Hitch had saddled himself with the ten-minute take, a short-lived technique which made the entire action (set in one room) cinematically continuous (and dizzy-making). Of considerable historic interest, nevertheless.

w Arthur Laurents   play Patrick Hamilton   d Alfred Hitchcock   ph Joseph Valentine, William V. Skall   md Leo F. Forbstein   theme Francis Poulenc

James Stewart, John Dall, Farley Granger, Joan Chandler, Cedric Hardwicke, Constance Collier, Edith Evanson, Douglas Dick

'It was a limiting use of the medium, and parts of the film are unbearably tedious.' – *George Perry, 1965*

'A mighty story of savage greed and sultry love!'
Rope of Sand *
US   1949   105m   bw
Paramount (Hal B. Wallis)

Various factions seek hidden diamonds in a prohibited South African area.

Ham-fisted adventure story which suggests at times that a violent parody of *Casablanca* was intended. The stars carry it through.

w Walter Doniger   d William Dieterle   ph Charles Lang   m Franz Waxman

Burt Lancaster, Paul Henreid, Claude Rains, Peter Lorre, Corinne Calvet, Sam Jaffe

Rosa Luxemburg *
West Germany   1986   124m   colour
Artificial Eye/Bioskop (Eberhard Junkersdorf)

Biopic of the Polish-born German left-wing revolutionary who was murdered in Berlin in 1919.

Moderately effective look at a radical martyr, enhanced by Sukowa's performance in the title role.

wd Margarethe von Trotta   ph Franz Rath   m Nicolas Economou   ed Dagmar Hirtz

Barbara Sukowa, Daniel Olbrychski, Otto Sander, Adelheid Arndt, Jürgen Holtz, Doris Schade, Hannes Jaenicke

'The entertainment world is ablaze!'
Rosalie *
US   1937   118m   bw
MGM (William Anthony McGuire)
V*

A college football hero falls for an incognito Balkan princess.

Ambitious light musical with a wispy plot but satisfying numbers.

w William Anthony McGuire   play William Anthony McGuire, Guy Bolton   d W. S. Van Dyke   ph Oliver T. Marsh   m Herbert Stothart   songs Cole Porter

Nelson Eddy, Eleanor Powell, Frank Morgan, Ray Bolger, Ilona Massey, Reginald Owen, Edna May Oliver, Jerry Colonna

'The most lavish, ornate, tinselled and glittering production which has come from Hollywood.' – *Variety*

Rosalie Goes Shopping
West Germany   1989   93m   colour
Mainline/Pelemele (Percy Adlon, Eleonore Adlon)
V, V*

A German housewife, living in Arizona with her large family, uses credit card frauds to keep them supplied with the good things of life.

Slight comedy of consumerism that relies too heavily on the charm of its performers.

w Percy Adlon, Eleonore Adlon, Christopher Doherty   d Percy Adlon   ph Bernd Heinl   ad Stephen Lineweaver   ed Heiko Hinders

Marianne Sägebrecht, Brad Davis, Judge Reinhold, William Harlander, Erika Blumberger, Patricia Zehentmayr, John Hawkes, Alex Winter, Courtney Kraus

The Rosary Murders
US   1987   105m   colour
Laurel-Mihalich/Samuel Goldwyn
V*, L

In Detroit, murders are committed by someone with a grudge against the Catholic Church.

Lax thriller with a priest detective.

w Elmore Leonard, Fred Walton   d Fred Walton

Donald Sutherland, Charles Durning, Josef Sommer, Belinda Bauer

'She gave . . . and gave . . . and gave . . . until there was nothing left to give!'
The Rose
US   1979   134m   DeLuxe
TCF (Tony Ray)
V, V*, L

Drink and drugs cause the decline and death of a famous rock singer.

An unattractive, hysterical, foul-mouthed show business biopic roughly based on Janis Joplin, this does afford an undisciplined night-club talent a role to get her teeth into.

w Bill Kerby, Bo Goodman   d Mark Rydell   ph Vilmos Zsigmond   md Paul A. Rothchild   pd Richard MacDonald

Bette Midler, Alan Bates, Frederic Forrest, Harry Dean Stanton, Barry Primus

AAN: Frederic Forrest; Bette Midler

The Rose and the Sword: see *Flesh and Blood* (1985)

Rose Marie *
US   1936   113m   bw
MGM (Hunt Stromberg)
V*, L

A Canadian Mountie gets his man – and a lady.

Backwoods romance from a stage success, filmed mostly on location and quite successfully.

w Frances Goodrich, Albert Hackett, Alice Duer Miller   play Otto Harbach, Oscar Hammerstein II   d W. S. Van Dyke   ph William Daniels   md Herbert Stothart   songs various   m Rudolf Friml

Nelson Eddy, Jeanette MacDonald, James Stewart, Reginald Owen, Allan Jones, Gilda Gray, George Regas, Alan Mowbray, Robert Greig, Una O'Connor, David Niven, Herman Bing

'An operatic honey with MacDonald and Eddy for the tungstens.' – *Variety*

† Previously filmed in 1928 – and see below.

Rose Marie
US   1954   115m   Technicolor   Cinemascope
MGM (Mervyn Le Roy)
V, V*, L

Dull remake with stodgy handling and poor sets.

w Ronald Millar   d Mervyn Le Roy   ph Paul C. Vogel   md Georgie Stoll   ch Busby Berkeley

Howard Keel, Ann Blyth, Fernando Lamas, Bert Lahr, Marjorie Main, Ray Collins

'The wildcat of the west has the outlaws in her gunsights!'
Rose of Cimarron
US   1952   72m   Natural Color
Edward L. Alperson/TCF

A girl tracks down the killers of her Indian foster-parents.

Routine lower-berth Western.

w Maurice Geraghty   d Harry Keller

Mala Powers, Jack Buetel, Bill Williams, Jim Davis

Rose of the Rancho
US   1935   83m   bw
William LeBaron/Paramount

Spanish settlers in California fight landgrabbers.

Romantic musical with interesting if seldom-used talent.

w Frank Partos, Charles Brackett, Arthur Sheekman, Nat Perrin, Harlan Thompson, Brian Hooker play Richard Walton Tully, David Belasco d Marion Gering

John Boles, Gladys Swarthout, Willie Howard, Charles Bickford, Herb Williams, H. B. Warner

'A fandango mustang meller . . . a tango version of a bronc opera.' – *Variety*

'Song by song . . . scene by scene . . . the thrill grows greater!'

Rose of Washington Square **
US   1939   86m   bw
TCF (Nunnally Johnson)

Tribulations of a Broadway singer in love with a worthless husband.

Revamping of the Fanny Brice story; smartly done, but the material interpolated for Jolson is what makes the film notable.

w Nunnally Johnson   d Gregory Ratoff   ph Karl Freund   m Louis Silvers   songs various

Alice Faye, Tyrone Power, *Al Jolson, Hobart Cavanaugh,* William Frawley, Joyce Compton, Louis Prima and his band

'This is Jolson's picture . . . the rest is also-ran.' – *Variety*

'Jolson's singing is something for the memory book.' – *New York Times*

† Fanny Brice sued TCF for 75,000 dollars for invasion of privacy; the defendants settled.

'The boldest story of love you have ever been permitted to see!'

The Rose Tattoo
US   1955   117m   bw   Vistavision
Paramount/Hal B. Wallis
V*, L

A Sicilian woman on the gulf coast is tormented by the infidelity of her dead husband, but a brawny truckdriver makes her forget him.

Heavily theatrical material, unsuited to the big screen for all the powerful acting (or perhaps because of it).

w John Michael Hayes   play Tennessee Williams d Daniel Mann   ph James Wong Howe   m Alex North   ad Hal Pereira, Tambi Larsen   ed Warren Low

Anna Magnani, Burt Lancaster, Marisa Pavan, Ben Cooper, Virginia Grey, Jo Van Fleet

AA: James Wong Howe; Anna Magnani; art direction

AAN: best picture; Alex North; Marisa Pavan; editing

Roseanna McCoy
US   1949   89m   bw
Samuel Goldwyn
V

In old Virginia the Hatfields and the McCoys continue their feud with tragic results.

Hillbilly Romeo and Juliet saga, a shade too cornfed despite the credits.

w John Collier   d Irving Reis   ph Lee Garmes m David Buttolph

Joan Evans, Farley Granger, Charles Bickford, Raymond Massey, Richard Basehart, Aline MacMahon

Rosebud
US   1975   126m   Eastmancolor   Panavision
UA/Otto Preminger

Five girls of wealthy families are kidnapped by the Palestine Liberation Army.

Overlong topical suspenser which goes awry by not being very suspenseful, and by packing in too many irrelevant satirical jibes.

w Erik Lee Preminger   novel Joan Hemingway, Paul Bonnecarrere   d Otto Preminger   ph Denys Coop m Laurent Petitgerard   titles Saul Bass

Peter O'Toole, Richard Attenborough, Cliff Gorman, Claude Dauphin, John V. Lindsay, Peter Lawford, Raf Vallone, Adrienne Corri

Roseland *
US   1977   103m   color
Cinema Shares/Merchant Ivory (Ismail Merchant)
V*

Generation after generation, the lonely and the loving come to a New York ballroom.

Pleasantly intentioned slice-of-life drama which is rather slackly written and handled, with unprofessionalism showing through at several points.

w Ruth Prawer Jhabvala   d James Ivory ph Ernest Vincze   m Michael Gibson

Geraldine Chaplin, Teresa Wright, Lou Jacobi, Don de Natale, Louise Kirkland, Helen Gallagher, Joan Copeland, Conrad Janis, Lilia Skala, Christopher Walken

'Typically discreet and dull film from Merchant-Ivory . . . what one might call over-decorous.' – *Time Out, 1984*

Roselyne and the Lions **
France   1989   137m   colour
Palace/Cargo Films/Gaumont (Jean-Jacques Beineix)
V

original title: *Roselyne et les Lions*

Two trainee lion tamers fall in love and run away to join a circus.

Charming, dreamlike boy-meets-girl romance.

w Jean-Jacques Beineix, Jacques Forgeas, Thierry Le Portier   d Jean-Jacques Beineix   ph Jean-François Robin   m Reinhardt Wagner   ad Carlos Conti ed Marie Castro-Brechignac, Annick Baly, Danielle Fillios, Oswald Bargero

Isabelle Pasco, Gérard Sandoz, Philippe Clevenot, Gunter Meisner, Wolf Harnisch, Gabriel Monnet, Jacques Le Carpentier, Dimitro Furdui

Rosemary's Baby **
US   1968   137m   Technicolor
Paramount/William Castle
V*, L

After unwittingly becoming friendly with diabolists, an actor's wife is impregnated by the Devil.

Seminal gothic melodrama which led in due course to the excesses of *The Exorcist;* in itself well done in a heavy-handed way, the book being much more subtle.

wd Roman Polanski   novel Ira Levin   ph William Fraker   m Krzysztof Komeda   pd Richard Sylbert

Mia Farrow, John Cassavetes, Ruth Gordon, Sidney Blackmer, Patsy Kelly, Ralph Bellamy, Maurice Evans, Angela Dorian, Elisha Cook, Charles Grodin

'It may not be for the very young, and perhaps pregnant women should see it at their own risk.' – *Motion Picture Herald*

'Tension is sustained to a degree surpassing Alfred Hitchcock at his best.' – *Daily Telegraph*

† William Castle, the producer, is glimpsed outside a phone booth.
†† A TV sequel followed: *Look What Happened to Rosemary's Baby.*

AA: Ruth Gordon

AAN: Roman Polanski (as writer)

Rosencrantz and Guildenstern Are Dead *
US   1990   118m   Technicolor
Hobo/Brandenburg (Michael Brandman, Emanuel Azenburg)
V, V*, L

Two courtiers are summoned to Elsinore by the King of Denmark to discover why Prince Hamlet is behaving so strangely.

A celebrated stage play, and gloss on Shakespeare, transfers awkwardly to the screen.

wd Tom Stoppard   play Tom Stoppard   ph Peter Biziou   m Stanley Myers   pd Vaughan Edwards ed Nicolas Gaster

Gary Oldman, Tim Roth, Richard Dreyfuss, Joanna Roth, Iain Glen, Donald Sumpter, Joanna Miles, Ljubo Zecevic, Ian Richardson, Sven Medvesck

'Stoppard's adaptation, at a shade under two hours, is too long, too slow, and ponderous when it is trying to be humorous.' – *Sight and Sound*

Rosie
US   1967   98m   Techniscope
Universal/Ross Hunter (Jacque Mapes)

A rich woman spends wildly and her daughters try to have her committed to safeguard their inheritance.

Hopelessly muddled comedy drama which flits from one mood to the other without making a success of either.

w Samuel Taylor   play Ruth Gordon   French original Les Joies de la Famille by Philippe Heriat d David Lowell Rich   ph Clifford Stine   m Lyn Murray

Rosalind Russell, Brian Aherne, Sandra Dee, Vanessa Brown, Audrey Meadows, James Farentino, Leslie Nielsen, Margaret Hamilton, Reginald Owen, Juanita Moore, Virginia Grey

'A mawkish mixture of *Auntie Mame* and *King Lear.'* – *MFB*

Rosie the Riveter
US   1944   75m   bw
Armand Schaefer/Republic
V*

GB title:*In Rosie's Room*

Warplant workers have to share rooms in a boarding house.

Easy-going wartime comedy.

w Jack Townley, Aileen Leslie   story Dorothy Curnow Handley   d Joseph Santley

Jane Frazee, Frank Albertson, Vera Vague, Frank Jenks, Lloyd Corrigan, Frank Fenton, Maude Eburne, Carl 'Alfalfa' Switzer

Rotten to the Core
GB   1965   88m   bw   Panavision
BL-Tudor (The Boulting Brothers)

Ex-convicts plan an army payroll robbery.

Routine caper comedy, unsuitably widescreened, with a few good jokes along the way.

w Jeffrey Dell, Roy Boulting, John Warren, Len Heath   d John Boulting   ph Freddie Young m Michael Dress

Anton Rodgers, *Thorley Walters,* Eric Sykes, Kenneth Griffith, Charlotte Rampling, Ian Bannen, Avis Bunnage, Raymond Huntley

† The original title, *Rotten to the Corps,* was more apt but plainly seemed too subtle.

Rouge *
Hong Kong   1987   96m   colour
ICA/Golden Way/Golden Harvest (Jackie Chan)
original title: *Yanzhi Kou*

Fifty years after killing herself in a suicide pact, a courtesan returns from the netherworld to find her lost lover.

Slow-moving, bitter-sweet love story that contrasts the sexual attitudes of the 1930s and 1980s.

w Lee Bik-Wah, Chui-Dai An-Ping   novel Lee Bik-Wah   d Stanley Kwan   ph Bill Wong   m Michael Lai   pd Pan Lai, Ma Kwong-Wing   ed Cheung Yu-Chung

Anita Mui, Leslie Chueng, Alex Man, Emily Chu, Irene Wan

'Seems assured of its status as a classic.' – *Tony Rayns, MFB*

Le Rouge et le Noir *
France/Italy   1954   170m approx   Eastmancolor
Franco London/Documento
aka: *Scarlet and Black*

A carpenter's son becomes a private tutor, seduces his master's wife and is sent to study for the priesthood . . .

Massive attempt to conquer an unfilmable novel. Some enjoyable scenes and décor are the best it can offer.

w Jean Aurenche, Pierre Bost, Claude Autant-Lara   novel Stendhal   d Claude Autant-Lara   ph Michael Kelber   m René Cloërc   ad Max Douy

Gérard Philipe, Danielle Darrieux, Antonella Lualdi, Jean Martinelli

The Rough and the Smooth
GB   1959   99m   bw
Renown (George Minter)
US title: *Portrait of a Sinner*

An archaeologist about to marry the niece of a press lord falls for a mysterious nymphomaniac.

Preposterous melodrama about unreal people; its very excesses become enjoyable for those who can stay the course.

w Audrey Erskin-Lindop, Dudley Leslie   novel Robin Maugham   d Robert Siodmak   ph Otto Heller   md Muir Mathieson   m Douglas Gamley

Tony Britton, Nadja Tiller, William Bendix, Natasha Parry, Norman Wooland, Donald Wolfit, Tony Wright, Adrienne Corri, Joyce Carey

'The script is never even on nodding terms with life, and tries to make up for this deficiency by a candidly explosive vocabulary which gives the production a weirdly old-fashioned air.' – *MFB*

Rough Company: see *The Violent Men*

Rough Cut
US   1980   112m   Movielab
Paramount/David Merrick
V*, L

A retiring Scotland Yard inspector spars with a jewel thief and finally changes sides.

Dated comedy which required a much lighter touch in all departments.

w Francis Burns   novel *Touch the Lion's Paw* by Derek Lambert   d Don Siegel   ph Frederick Young   m Nelson Riddle, from Duke Ellington themes   pd Ted Haworth

Burt Reynolds, Lesley Anne Down, David Niven, Timothy West, Patrick Magee, Joss Ackland

'All surface smartness without a single structural idea.' – *Richard Combs, MFB*

Rough Night in Jericho
US   1967   97m   Techniscope
Universal (Martin Rackin)

A stagecoach man rids a cattle town of a villain.

Totally uninteresting star Western with glum performances.

w Sidney Boehm, Marvin H. Albert   novel *The Man in Black* by Marvin H. Albert   d Arnold Laven   ph Russell Metty   m Don Costa

George Peppard, Dean Martin, Jean Simmons, John McIntire, Slim Pickens, Don Galloway, Brad Weston

Rough Shoot *
GB   1952   86m   bw
Raymond Stross
US title: *Shoot First*

A retired US officer in Dorset thinks he has shot a poacher – but the dead man is a spy, and someone else shot him.

Minor Hitchcock-style thriller with a climax in Madame Tussaud's. Generally efficient and entertaining.

w Eric Ambler,   novel Geoffrey Household   d Robert Parrish   ph Stan Pavey   md Hans May

Joel McCrea, Evelyn Keyes, Marius Goring, Roland Culver, Frank Lawton, Herbert Lom

Rough, Tough and Ready
US   1945   64m   bw
Alexis Thurn-Taxis/Columbia

Two members of the Army engineers' port repair service fall out over a girl.

A faint echo of the old Flagg and Quirt comedies.

w Edward T. Lowe   d Del Lord

Victor McLaglen, Chester Morris, Veda Ann Borg, Jean Rogers

Roughly Speaking *
US   1945   117m   bw
Warner (Henry Blanke)

Oddball, overlong domestic drama about father's wild and impractical schemes.

w Louise Randall Pierson   book Louise Randall Pierson   d Michael Curtiz   ph Joseph Walker   m Max Steiner

Rosalind Russell, Jack Carson, Robert Hutton, Jean Sullivan, Alan Hale, Donald Woods, Andrea King, Ray Collins, Kathleen Lockhart

Roughshod
US   1949   88m   bw
RKO (Richard H. Berger)

Two cowboys journeying to California with a herd of horses come up against villains intent on revenge.

Likeable old-fashioned Western.

w Geoffrey Homes, Hugo Butler   d Mark Robson   ph Joseph F. Biroc   m Roy Webb

Robert Sterling, Gloria Grahame, Claude Jarman Jnr, John Ireland, Jeff Donnell, Martha Hyer

Round Midnight **
France   1986   133m   Eastmancolor
Warner/Little Bear/PECF (Irwin Winkler)
V, V*, L, S

A black American jazz musician spends his last days in Paris.

A jazz buff's tribute to Bud Powell and Lester Young; acclaimed by the critics but essentially a film for minorities.

w Bertrand Tavernier, David Rayfiel   d Bertrand Tavernier   ph Bruno de Keyzer   md Herbie Hancock   m Herbie Hancock   pd Alexandre Trauner

Dexter Gordon, François Cluzet, Gabrielle Haker, John Berry, Martin Scorsese

AA: Herbie Hancock

AAN: Dexter Gordon

The Rounders
US   1965   85m   Metrocolor   Panavision
MGM (Richard E. Lyons)

Two modern cowboys mean to settle down but never get around to it.

Pale comedy Western which never gets going.

wd Burt Kennedy   novel Max Evans   ph Paul C. Vogel   m Jeff Alexander

Henry Fonda, Glenn Ford, Chill Wills, Sue Ann Langdon, Edgar Buchanan

'One of those utterly relaxed comedies that make ideal entertainment because there's tender loving care every step of the way and no sweat.' – *Judith Crist*

Roustabout
US   1964   101m   Techniscope
Hal B. Wallis
V, V*

A wandering tough guy joins a travelling carnival.

Dreary star vehicle momentarily salvaged by its co-star.

w Allan Weiss, Anthony Lawrence   d John Rich   ph Lucien Ballard   m Joseph L. Lilley

Elvis Presley, Barbara Stanwyck, Sue Ann Langdon, Joan Freeman, Leif Erickson

Rowing with the Wind *
Spain/Norway   1987   94m   colour
Ditirambo (Andres Vincente Gomez)

Mary Shelley recalls her elopement with Shelley, their meeting with Byron and her creation of Frankenstein.

A glossy death-haunted romantic melodrama, with Frankenstein's monster popping up throughout as a reminder of mortality; a few startling images, such as a meeting between a giraffe and a cardinal in a Venetian palace, spice the familiar story.

wd Gonzalo Suarez   ph Carlos Suarez   m Alejandro Masso   ad Wolfgang Burman   ed José Salcedo

Hugh Grant, Lizzy McInnerny, Valentine Pelka, Elizabeth Hurley, José Luis Gomez, Virginia Mataix, Ronan Vibert, José Carlos Rivas, Bibi Andersen

† Other films on a similar theme include *Gothic, Haunted Summer* and *Frankenstein Unbound* (qqv).

Roxanne *
US   1987   107m   DeLuxe
Columbia/Michael Rachmil, Daniel Melnick
V, V*, L

An ugly man writes love letters for his friend . . . but true love will find a way.

Zany modernization of Rostand's *Cyrano de Bergerac,* funny in spots but way overlong.

w Steve Martin   d Fred Schepisi   ph Ian Baker   m Bruce Smeaton   pd Jack DeGovia

Steve Martin, Daryl Hannah, Rick Rossovich, Shelley Duvall, John Kapelos, Fred Willard, Michael J. Pollard

'The low down story of a high class gal!'
Roxie Hart **
US   1942   72m   bw
TCF (Nunnally Johnson)

A twenties showgirl confesses for the sake of publicity to a murder of which she is innocent.

Crowded Chicago burlesque which now seems less funny than it did but is full of smart moments.

w *Nunnally Johnson,*   play *Chicago* by Maurine Watkins   d *William Wellman*   ph Leon Shamroy   m Alfred Newman

Ginger Rogers, George Montgomery, *Adolphe Menjou,* Lynne Overman, Nigel Bruce, Spring Byington, Sara Allgood, William Fawley

DEDICATION: To all the beautiful women in the world who have shot their husbands full of holes out of pique.

'A masterpiece of form, of ensemble acting, of powerhouse comedy and scripting.' – *NFT, 1974*

'Why then, am I not in the aisles all the time? Is it possible that Ginger Rogers, by overplaying the brainless little creature, destroys some of the plausibility and therefore some of the fun? Maybe; I can offer no other explanation of my moments of repose, straight-faced and in my stall.' – *Dilys Powell*

† The play was also filmed in 1927 under its original title, with Phyllis Haver.

Royal African Rifles
US   1954   75m   Cinecolor
Allied Artists
GB title: *Storm over Africa*

In British East Africa in 1914, a lieutenant tracks down a consignment of stolen guns.

Mini-budgeted *Boy's Own Paper* heroics; quite enjoyable on its level.

w Dan Ullman   d Lesley Selander

Louis Hayward, Veronica Hurst, Michael Pate, Angela Greene, Steve Geray, Bruce Lester

The Royal Bed
US   1931   74m   bw
RKO
GB title: *The Queen's Husband*

The king and queen of a European country lead their own private lives.

Insufficient wit graces this would-be daring romantic drama from a Broadway hit.

w J. Walter Ruben   play *The Queen's Husband* by Robert E. Sherwood   d Lowell Sherman

Mary Astor, Lowell Sherman, Nance O'Neill, Anthony Bushell, Robert Warwick

Royal Cavalcade
GB   1935   104m   bw
BIP

A chronicle of the events of the reign of King George V.

Thoroughly embarrassing jubilee tribute, of historical interest only.

w Majorie Deans   d Marcel Varnel, Thomas Bentley, Herbert Brenon, Norman Lee, Walter Summers and Will Kellino

Marie Lohr, Hermione Baddeley, Esme Percy, John Mills, Reginald Gardiner, Syd Walker, Seymour Hicks, Owen Nares, Matheson Lang, George Robey, Florrie Forde, many others

A Royal Divorce
GB   1938   85m   bw
Herbert Wilcox/Imperator

Napoleon Bonaparte in 1809 marries a widow whose reputation isn't exactly spotless.

Heavy comedy or light drama, take your pick; not exactly riveting as either.

w Miles Malleson   novel *Josephine* by Jacques Thery   d Jack Raymond

Pierre Blanchar, Ruth Chatterton, Frank Cellier, Carol Goodner, George Curzon, John Laurie, Jack Hawkins

The Royal Family of Broadway *
US   1930   82m   bw
Paramount
GB title: *Theatre Royal*

The off-stage escapades of a famous family of actors.

Fairly funny lampoon of the Barrymores, primitively staged and very talky but still entertaining for those in the joke.

w Herman J. Mankiewicz, Gertrude Purcell play George S. Kaufman, Edna Ferber   d George Cukor, Cyril Gardner   ph George Folsey

Fredric March, Henrietta Crosman, Ina Claire, Mary Brian, Charles Starrett, Frank Conroy

'Lionel does not come into the burlesque at all, and I can quite believe that he is the most damaged of the entire family.' – *James Agate*

'Stagebound and awkward, but great fun anyway.' – *New Yorker, 1977*

AAN: Fredric March

Royal Flash
GB   1975   118m   Technicolor
TCF/Two Roads (David V. Picker, Denis O'Dell)
V*

A Victorian bully and braggart has various adventures in Europe and Ruritania.

A rather unsatisfactory romp which takes pot shots at every 19th-century person and object in the encyclopaedia, but is never as funny as it intends to be.

w George Macdonald Fraser   novel George Macdonald Fraser   d Richard Lester   ph Geoffrey Unsworth   m Ken Thorpe   pd Terence Marsh

Malcolm McDowell, Oliver Reed, Alan Bates, Florinda Bolkan, Britt Ekland, Lionel Jeffries, Tom Bell, Joss Ackland, Leon Greene, Richard Hurndall, Alastair Sim, Michael Hordern

Royal Flush: see *Two Guys from Milwaukee*

The Royal Hunt of the Sun
GB   1969   121m   Technicolor
Security Pictures (Eugene Frenke, Philip Yordan)

How the Spanish soldier Pizarro on his South American trek overcame the Inca god-king Atahualpa.

Deadly literal rendering with nothing to replace the play's theatrical splendour, resembling nothing so much as an opera without the music.

w Philip Yordan   play Peter Shaffer   d Irving Lerner   ph Roger Barlow   m Marc Wilkinson

Robert Shaw, Christopher Plummer, Nigel Davenport, Michael Craig, Leonard Whiting, Andrew Keir, James Donald, Percy Herbert, Alexander Davion

The Royal Mounted Rides Again
US   1945   bw   serial: 13 eps
Universal

Captain Decker of the Mounties seeks the true culprit of a murder for which his father is prime suspect.

Adequate chapter play with location settings.

d Ray Taylor, Lewis D. Collins

George Dolenz, Bill Kennedy, Addison Richards, Daun Kennedy

A Royal Scandal
US   1945   94m   bw
TCF (Ernst Lubitsch)
GB title: *Czarina*

The illicit loves of Catherine the Great.

Censored romps around some chilly court sets; very few moments of interest, and none of the style of the silent version *Forbidden Paradise*.

w Edwin Justus Mayer   play Lajos Biro, Melchior Lengyel   d Otto Preminger   ph Arthur Miller   m Alfred Newman

Tallulah Bankhead, Charles Coburn, Anne Baxter, William Eythe, Vincent Price, Mischa Auer, Sig Rumann, Vladimir Sokoloff

'Nothing is one-tenth well enough done, and all the laughs are played for at their cheapest, far down the ramp.' – *James Agee*

Royal Wedding
US   1951   93m   Technicolor
MGM (Arthur Freed)
V, V*, L
GB title: *Wedding Bells*

Journalists congregate in London for the royal wedding.

Thin musical with acceptable numbers.

w Alan Jay Lerner   d Stanley Donen   ph Robert Planck   md Johnny Green   songs Alan Jay Lerner, Burton Lane

Fred Astaire, Jane Powell, Sarah Churchill, Peter Lawford, Keenan Wynn

AAN: song 'Too Late Now' (m Burton Lane, ly Alan Jay Lerner)

Ruba al Prossimo Tua: see *A Fine Pair*

Ruby
US   1992   DeLuxe
Rank/Propaganda (Sigurjon Sighvatsson, Steve Golin)
V, V*

A shady night-club owner kills Lee Harvey Oswald, assassin of President Kennedy, in order to expose a plot by the Mafia and the CIA to murder the President.

Muddled, small-scale, mainly fictional conspiracy movie that confuses the issues it attempts to explain.

w Stephen Davis   play *Love Field* by Stephen Davis   d John MacKenzie   ph Phil Meheux   m John Scott   pd David Brisbin   ed Richard Trevor

Danny Aiello, Sherilyn Fenn, Frank Orsatti, Jeffrey Nordling, Jane Hamilton, Maurice Bernard, Joe Viterelli, Robert S. Telford

Ruby Cairo
US   1992   111m   Technicolor
Entertainment/Majestic (Lloyd Phillips)
S

After her husband is reported killed in a car crash, his hard-up wife discovers that he has a fortune hidden in bank accounts across the world.

Dull thriller, which doubles as an attractive travelogue.

w Robert Dillon, Michael Thomas   d Graeme Clifford   ph Laszlo Kovacs   m John Barry   pd Richard Sylbert   ed Caroline Biggerstaff

Andie MacDowell, Liam Neeson, Viggo Mortensen, Jack Thompson, Paul Spencer, Chad Power, Monica Mikala

'An old-fashioned Yank-in-Europe mystery-adventure that squanders an interesting cast.' – *Variety*

'Nothing but a plot and the plot nothing but predictable.' – *Sight and Sound*

'Dangerous … destructive … deadly to love!'
Ruby Gentry
US   1952   82m   bw
Joseph Bernhard/King Vidor
V, V*

A tempestuous girl, brought up as a boy in the Carolina swamps, has a love-hate relationship with a local aristocrat, revenges herself on the people who scorn her, loses her lover in a swamp shooting, and becomes a sea captain.

Richly absurd sex melodrama typical of its director and star yet not very entertaining.

w Sylvia Richards   d King Vidor   ph Russell Harlan   m Heinz Roemheld   ad Dan Hall

Jennifer Jones, Charlton Heston, Karl Malden, Josephine Hutchinson

Ruby in Paradise
US   1993   114m   DuArt color
Mainline/Ruby in Paradise/A Full Crew/Say Yea

A young woman leaves home to seek life and love and ends up in an out-of-season holiday resort.

A deliberately small-scale movie, focussing its attention on minor matters and the frequently dull intricacies of everyday living.

wd Victor Nuñez *ph* Alex Vlacos *m* Charles Engstrom *pd* John Iacovelli *ed* Victor Nuñez

Ashley Judd, Todd Field, Bentley Mitchum, Allison Dean, Dorothy Lyman, Betsy Douds, Felicia Hernandez, Sharon Lewis

'Very well played, very well set and directed with a sharp eye for detail.' – *Derek Malcolm, Guardian*

'Two hippies come back from 1969 to get the bad news...'

Rude Awakening
US 1989 101m Technicolor
Rank (Aaron Russo)
V, V*, L

Two hippies return to New York after twenty years in Central America.

Weak ecological and political farce.

w Neil Levy, Richard LaGravenese *d* Aaron Russo, David Greenwalt *ph* Tim Sigel *m* Jonathan Elias *pd* Mel Bourne *ed* Paul Fried

Cheech Marin, Eric Roberts, Julie Hagerty, Robert Carradine, Buck Henry, Louise Lasser, Cindy Williams

Rudyard Kipling's Jungle Book: see *The Jungle Book*

Rue Cases Nègres **
France 1983 106m Fujicolor
Artificial Eye/Orion Classics/Su Ma Fa/Orca/NEF Diffusion (Jean-Luc Ormieres)
V, V*, L
US title: *Sugar Cane Alley*; aka: *Black Shack Alley*

In Martinique in the 1930s, a woman sacrifices herself so that her grandson can escape from poverty through education.

Moving and evocative account of colonial life, tinged with nostalgia but marked by some full-blooded performances.

wd Euzhan Palcy *novel* Joseph Zobel *ph* Dominique Chapuis *m* Groupe Malavoi *ad* Hoang Thanh At, Romul Eloise *ed* Marie-Joseph Yoyotte

Garry Cadenat, Darling Legitimus, Douta Seck, Joby Bernabe, Francisco Charles, Marie-Jo Descas, Marie-Ange Farot

Rue de l'Estrapade *
France 1953 95m bw
Cinephonic/SGGC/Filmsonor
aka: *Françoise Steps Out*

A young Parisienne suspects her husband of having an affair.

Lightly likeable domestic comedy in the vein of *Edouard et Caroline*, but not quite up to its standard.

w Annette Wademant *d* Jacques Becker *ph* Marcel Grignon *m* Georges Van Parys, Marguerite Monnot

Louis Jourdan, Anne Vernon, Daniel Gelin, Jean Servais, Micheline Dax

'Five comedy stars in a five-star comedy!'

Ruggles of Red Gap **
US 1935 90m bw
Paramount (Arthur Hornblow Jnr)
V*

A British butler has a startling effect on the family of an American rancher who takes him out west.

A famous comedy which seemed hilarious at the time but can now be seen as mostly composed of flat spots; the performances however are worth remembering.

w Walter de Leon, Harlan Thompson, Humphrey Pearson *novel* Harry Leon Wilson *d* Leo McCarey *ph* Alfred Gilks

Charles Laughton, Mary Boland, Charles Ruggles, ZaSu Pitts, Roland Young, Leila Hyams, James Burke, Maude Eburne, Lucien Littlefield

'Plenty of marquee strength, and dynamite on the inside. An A1 comedy.' – *Variety*

'A sane, witty, moving and quite unusual picture of Anglo-American relations.' – *C. A. Lejeune*

'The most heart-warming comedy of the season . . . there is about it a sympathetic and even a patriotic quality which is touching.' – *Literary Digest*

'The archetypal film they don't make any more, partly because comedy has now grown too raucous to favour the quiet drollery of players like Charlie Ruggles and Mary Boland, partly because even McCarey himself had trouble after the thirties separating sentiment from sentimentality.' – *Time Out, 1980*

† Remade as *Fancy Pants* (qv).

AAN: best picture

Rulers of the Sea *
US 1939 96m bw
Paramount (Frank Lloyd)

Problems surround the first steamship voyage across the Atlantic.

Well-made period action drama.

w Talbot Jennings, Frank Cavett, Richard Collins *d* Frank Lloyd *ph* Theodor Sparkuhl, Archie Stout *m* Richard Hageman

Douglas Fairbanks Jnr, Margaret Lockwood, Will Fyffe, Montagu Love, George Bancroft, Mary Gordon, Alan Ladd

'Timely in content and grand for exploitation. In the British Empire it will be greeted as inspirational entertainment.' – *Variety*

The Rules of the Game: see *La Règle du Jeu*

The Ruling Class *
GB 1972 155m DeLuxe
Keep Films (Jules Buck, Jack Hawkins)
V*, L

The fetishistic Earl of Gurney is succeeded by his mad son Jack who believes he is God.

An overlong satirical play with brilliant patches is hamfistedly filmed but boasts some bright performances. The hits are as random as the misses, however.

w Peter Barnes *play* Peter Barnes *d* Peter Medak *ph* Ken Hodges *m* John Cameron

Peter O'Toole, Harry Andrews, *Arthur Lowe, Alastair Sim*, Coral Browne, Michael Bryant

'This irritating and unsatisfying film is worth being irritated and unsatisfied by.' – *Stanley Kauffmann*

AAN: Peter O'Toole

'This is the dance of love!'

Rumba *
US 1935 71m bw
Paramount (William Le Baron)

A society girl has a yen for a Broadway hoofer.

Streamlined star vehicle which attempts to recapture the success of *Bolero* (qv).

w Howard J. Green *d* Marion Gering *ph* Ted Tetzlaff

Carole Lombard, George Raft, Margo, Lynne Overman, Monroe Owsley, Iris Adrian, Gail Patrick, Samuel S. Hinds, Jameson Thomas

Rumble Fish
US 1983 94m bw (with colour inserts)
Universal/Zoetrope (Fred Roos, Douglas Claybourne)
V, V*, S

A Tulsa teenager survives local gang violence and while working in a petshop sees himself in the rumble fish, which fights even its own image in a glass.

Glum piece of self-absorption by a director going rapidly downhill.

wd Francis Ford Coppola *novel* S. E. Hinton *ph* Stephen H. Burum *m* Stewart Copeland *pd* Dean Tavoularis *ed* Barry Malkin

Matt Dillon, Mickey Rourke, Diane Lane, Dennis Hopper, Diana Scarwid

Run for Cover *
US 1955 92m Technicolor Vistavision
Paramount (William H. Pine)

An ex-convict becomes innocently involved in a train robbery.

Adequate star Western.

w William C. Thomas *story* Harriet Frank Jnr, Irving Ravetch *d* Nicholas Ray *ph* Daniel Fapp *md* Howard Jackson

James Cagney, Viveca Lindfors, John Derek, Jean Hersholt, Grant Withers, Ernest Borgnine, Jack Lambert

Run for the Sun
US 1956 99m Technicolor Superscope
UA/Russ-Field (Harry Tatelman)

Crashlanding in the Mexican jungle, a disillusioned author and a lady journalist find themselves at the mercy of renegade Nazis.

Tame remake of *The Most Dangerous Game* with Count Zaroff replaced by Lord Haw-Haw. Sluggish plot development mars the action.

w Dudley Nichols, Roy Boulting *d* Roy Boulting *ph* Joseph LaShelle *m* Fred Steiner

Richard Widmark, Jane Greer, Trevor Howard, Peter Van Eyck

A Run for Your Money *
GB 1949 83m bw
Ealing (Leslie Norman)

Welsh Rugby supporters have various adventures on their one day in London.

Slight, bright, British chase comedy with characterizations as excellent as they are expected.

w Richard Hughes, Charles Frend, Leslie Norman *d* Charles Frend *ph* Douglas Slocombe *m* Ernest Irving

Alec Guinness, Meredith Edwards, Moira Lister, Donald Houston, Hugh Griffith, Clive Morton, Joyce Grenfell

Run of the Arrow *
US 1956 85m Technicolor RKOscope
Global (Samuel Fuller)
V*

An ex-Civil War soldier is captured by Indians and accepted by them, but sickened by their violence.

Bloody little Western in the accustomed Fuller vein.

wd Samuel Fuller *ph* Joseph Biroc *m* Victor Young

Rod Steiger, Sarita Montiel, Charles Bronson, Tim McCoy, Ralph Meeker

A Run on Gold: see *Midas Run*

Run Silent Run Deep *
US 1958 93m bw
UA/Hecht-Hill-Lancaster (William Schorr)
V, V*

Antagonisms flare up between the officers of a US submarine in Tokyo Bay during World War II

Competent, unsurprising war actioner trading on its stars.

w John Gay *d* Robert Wise *ph* Russell Harlan *m* Franz Waxman

Clark Gable, Burt Lancaster, Jack Warden, Brad Dexter, Nick Cravat, Joe Maross, H. M. Wynant

'Mostly good sea fights. Otherwise it's damn the torpedoes, half speed ahead.' – *Time*

Run Wild, Run Free *
GB   1969   98m   Technicolor
Columbia/Irving Allen (John Danischewsky)
V

A mute boy living on Dartmoor gains self-confidence through the love of animals.

Rather vaguely developed family film with agreeable sequences.

w David Rook   *novel* The White Colt by David Rook
d Richard C. Sarafian   *ph* Wilkie Cooper   *m* David Whitaker

John Mills, Sylvia Syms, Mark Lester, Bernard Miles, Gordon Jackson, Fiona Fullerton

The Runaround *
US   1946   100m   bw
Universal (Joseph Gershenson)

Two rival detectives are hired to find a missing heiress.

Peripatetic comedy on the lines of *It Happened One Night*; unexpectedly enjoyable.

w Arthur T. Horman, Sam Hellman   *d* Charles Lamont   *ph* George Robinson   *m* Frank Skinner

Rod Cameron, Broderick Crawford, Ella Raines, Samuel S. Hinds, Frank McHugh, George Cleveland

Runaway
US   1984   100m   Metrocolor   Panavision
Tri-Star/Michael Crichton (Michael Rachmil)

An electronics wizard sets a half-perfected robot on the rampage.

Simple-minded comedy-melodrama which feels as though it ought to have been played entirely for laughs.

wd Michael Crichton   *ph* John A. Alonzo   *m* Jerry Goldsmith   *pd* Douglas Higgins   *ed* Glenn Farr

Tom Selleck, Cynthia Rhodes, Gene L. Simmons, Kirstie Alley, Stan Shaw

The Runaway Bus *
GB   1954   78m   bw
Eros/Conquest-Guest (Val Guest)

Passengers at London Airport are fogbound, and a relief bus driver takes some of them to Blackbushe. Incognito among them are robbers and detectives . . .

Vaguely plotted variation on *The Ghost Train*, with fair production, a good smattering of jokes, and a hilarious view of a great airport in its earlier days.

wd Val Guest   *ph* Stan Pavey   *m* Ronald Binge

Frankie Howerd, Margaret Rutherford, George Coulouris, Petula Clark, Terence Alexander, Toke Townley, Belinda Lee

Runaway Daughter: see Red Salute

'Once it starts, nothing can stop it!'
Runaway Train *
US   1985   111m   Rank colour
Cannon/Northbrook (Menahem Golan, Yoram Globus)
V, V*, L, S

Prison breakers escape into the Alaskan wilderness and commandeer a train which can't stop.

Violent, foul-mouthed melodrama with no interest beyond breathtaking photography of the speeding train. Its general pretentiousness, perhaps, is also something to experience.

w Djordje Milicevic, Paul Zindel, Edward Bunker, from screenplay by Akira Kurosawa   *d* Andrei Konchalovsky   *ph* Alan Hume   *m* Trevor Jones   *pd* Stephen Marsh

Jon Voight, Eric Roberts, Rebecca DeMornay, Kyle T. Heffner

'The most exciting epic since *The Road Warrior*.' – *Variety*

'Nervy, exciting violence; immaculate, metallic camerawork; unstoppable pace.' – *Sight and Sound*

AAN: Jon Voight; Eric Roberts (supporting actor); editing

The Runner
Iran   1984   94m   colour
Electric/Studio of the Voice and Portrait of the Islamic Revolution of Iran (Fatholah Dalili)
original title: *Dawandeh*

A 13-year-old orphan makes his living on the streets of a Gulf port while learning to outdistance his peers.

Unsparing but repetitive account of childhood poverty.

w Amir Naderi, Behruz Gharibpur   *d* Amir Naderi
ph Firuz Malekzadeh   *pd* Gholam Reza Ramezani
ed Bahram Beyza'i

Majid Nirumand, Musa Torkizadeh, A. Gholamzadeh, Reza Ramezani

The Runner Stumbles
US   1979   110m   CFI color
Melvin Simon Productions (Stanley Kramer)
V*

In the mid-twenties, a Catholic priest is accused of the murder of a nun for whom he had felt a strong romantic attraction.

Musty exhumation of a genuine case which has little dramatic interest and even less wider significance. Good acting does not atone.

w Milan Stiff   *play* Milan Stiff   *d* Stanley Kramer
ph Laszlo Kovacs   *m* Ernest Gold   *pd* Alfred Sweeney Jnr

Dick Van Dyke, Kathleen Quinlan, Maureen Stapleton, Ray Bolger, Tammy Grimes, Beau Bridges

'The reanimated corpse of middlebrow Hollywood pretension . . . funereal pacing, portentous low angles and symbolic overkill.' – *Paul Taylor, MFB*

Runners
GB   1983   106m   colour
Goldcrest (Barry Hanson)
V

Distraught parents try to trace their missing children in London.

Heavy-going realistic drama with apparent inner meanings which are not brought to the surface.

w Stephen Poliakoff   *d* Charles Sturridge
ph Howard Atherton   *m* George Fenton
pd Arnold Chapkis

James Fox, Kate Hardie, Jane Asher, Eileen O'Brien, Ruti Simon

Running Brave
US   1983   106m   colour
ITC/Englander Productions
V*, L

A young Sioux from the reservation faces the pressures of the white world and becomes an Olympic runner.

The terrible punning title is the best thing in this very predictable piece of do-goodery, which would just about have passed muster as a TV movie.

w Henry Bean, Shirl Hendryx   *d* D. S. Everett
ph François Protat   *m* Mike Post   *pd* Carol Spier
ed Tony Lower, Earle Herden

Robby Benson, Pat Hingle, Claudia Cron, Jeff McCracken

'This is in essence a propaganda film for the American way, masked as a piece of liberal sentiment, and I distrust it thoroughly.' – *Observer*

'Time is running out for him!'
The Running Man *
GB   1963   103m   Technicolor   Panavision
Columbia/Peet (Carol Reed, John R. Sloan)

A private airline pilot fakes an accident and disappears, leaving his wife to collect the insurance and meet him in Spain.

Flabby, expensive suspenser; both plot and character take a back seat to scenic views.

w John Mortimer   *novel* The Ballad of the Running Man by Shelley Smith   *d* Carol Reed   *ph* Robert Krasker   *m* William Alwyn

Laurence Harvey, Alan Bates, Lee Remick, Felix Aylmer, Eleanor Summerfield, Allan Cuthbertson

'There seems to be something about the panoramic screen that seduces film-makers into filling it with irrelevant local colour and drawing the whole proceedings out to a length that matches its width.' – *Brenda Davies*

The Running Man
US   1987   101m   colour
Rank/Braveworld (Tim Zinnemann, George Linder)
V, V*, L, S

In the future, a convict, framed on a murder charge, takes part in a TV game show in which he is hunted through Los Angeles by expert killers.

Fast-moving action movie, full of violence and some dubious jokes.

w Steven E. de Souza   *novel* Stephen King   *d* Paul Michael Glaser   *ph* Thomas Del Ruth   *m* Harold Faltermeyer   *pd* Jack T. Collis   *ed* Mark Roy Warner, Edward A. Warschilka, John Wright

Arnold Schwarzenegger, Maria Conchita Alonso, Yaphet Kotto, Jim Brown, Jesse Ventura, Erland Van Lidth, Marvin J. McIntyre, Mick Fleetwood, Richard Dawson

Running on Empty
US   1988   116m   Technicolor
Warner/Lorimar/Double Play (Amy Robinson, Griffin Dunne)
V, V*, L

A teenager, whose parents are long-time political activists on the run from the FBI, tries to live his own life as a budding musician.

Mundane family drama that fails to illuminate the problems it describes.

w Naomi Foner   *d* Sidney Lumet   *ph* Gerry Fisher
m Tony Mottola   *pd* Philip Rosenberg   *ed* Andre Mondshein

Christine Lahti, River Phoenix, Judd Hirsch, Jonas Abry, Martha Plimpton, Ed Crowley, L. M. Kit Carson, Steven Hill, Augusta Dabney, David Margulies

AAN: best original screenplay; River Phoenix

Running Scared
GB   1972   98m   Technicolor   Panavision
Paramount/Wigan/Hemmings/O'Toole (Gareth Wigan)

A university student is generally condemned for allowing his friend to commit suicide; eventually he takes his own life.

Depressing and rather pointless exercise in death wish complicated by a doomed love affair.

w Clive Exton, David Hemmings   *novel* Gregory MacDonald   *d* David Hemmings   *ph* Ernest Day
m Michael J. Lewis

Robert Powell, Gayle Hunnicutt, Barry Morse, Stephanie Bidmead, Edward Underdown, Maxine Audley, Georgia Brown

Running Scared
US   1986   106m   Metrocolor   Panavision
MGM-UA/Turman-Foster (Peter Hyams)
V, V*, L

Accident-prone Chicago cops nevertheless succeed in getting their man.

Crime comedy-melodrama of a type seen far too often before.

w Guy Devore, Jimmy Huston d Peter Hyams ph Peter Hyams m Rod Temperton pd Albert Brenner

Gregory Hines, Billy Crystal, Steven Bauer, Joe Pantoliano, Tracy Reed, Darlanne Fluegel

La Rupture *
Belgium/France/Italy 1970 125m Eastmancolor
Contemporary/Films de la Boetie (André Genoves)
aka: The Breakup

A mother who wants custody of her young son after she divorces her drug-addicted husband finds herself in conflict with her ruthless and powerful father-in-law.

Enjoyable thriller in which innocence triumphs over experience.

wd Claude Chabrol novel Charlotte Armstrong ph Jean Rabier m Pierre Jansen

Stéphane Audran, Jean-Pierre Cassel, Michel Bouquet, Jean-Claude Drouot, Annie Cordy, Jean Carmet, Michel Duchaussoy, Catherine Rouvel

'The director, who can indubitably be very subtle if he chooses, is pleased this time to wallow in the obvious, but to do so with a fine cinematic judgement.' – Gordon Gow, Films and Filming

'How far do they go before they've gone too far?'
Rush *
US 1992 120m DeLuxe Panavision
MGM/Zanuck (Richard D. Zanuck)
V, V*, L, S

In the 1970s two undercover narcotics cops become drug addicts.

Unrelenting, though skilfully made, tale of degradation and despair.

w Pete Dexter book Kim Wozencraft d Lili Fini Zanuck ph Kenneth MacMillan m Eric Clapton pd Paul Sylbert ed Mark Warner

Jason Patrick, Jennifer Jason Leigh, Sam Elliott, Max Perlich, Gregg Allman, Tony Frank

'Downbeat nature of this addiction saga may be too intense and draining for general audiences, but resounding implications of the subject are bound to touch a nerve.' – Variety

The Russia House *
US 1990 123m Technicolor
UIP/Pathé Entertainment (Paul Maslansky, Fred Schepisi)
V, V*, L, S

A publisher, acting as a go-between for western intelligence and a Soviet scientist, finds life complicated by love.

Intelligent but sluggish thriller with few surprises.

w Tom Stoppard novel John Le Carré d Fred Schepisi ph Ian Baker m Jerry Goldsmith pd Richard MacDonald ad Roger Cain ed Peter Honess

Sean Connery, Michelle Pfeiffer, Roy Scheider, James Fox, John Mahoney, Michael Kitchen, J. T. Walsh, Ken Russell, David Threlfall, Klaus Maria Brandauer

'An absorbing but muted yarn of romance and political intrigue.' – Variety

Russian Roulette
US 1975 90m Eastmancolor
ITC/Elliott Kastner/Bulldog

Real and fake secret agents shoot it out when the Russian premier is about to visit Vancouver.

Fast-moving but impossible to follow location thriller which resolves itself into a series of chases.

w Tom Ardies, Stanley Mann, Arnold Margolin novel Kosygin is Coming by Tom Ardies d Lou Lombardo ph Brian West m Michael J. Lewis

George Segal, Gordon Jackson, Denholm Elliott, Cristina Raines, Richard Romanus, Louise Fletcher, Nigel Stock

'A stale, mechanical espionage caper that wastes its star.' – Kevin Thomas

'Why the crazy title? If we told you, you'd only laugh!'
The Russians Are Coming, The Russians Are Coming *
US 1966 126m DeLuxe Panavision
UA/Mirisch (Norman Jewison)
V*, L

Russian submariners make a forced landing on a Connecticut holiday island and cause panic.

'Daring' cold war comedy which turns out to be of the most elementary and protracted nature, saved from boredom only by a few cameos.

w William Rose novel The Off-Islanders by Nathaniel Benchley d Norman Jewison ph Joseph Biroc m Johnny Mandel

Carl Reiner, Eva Marie Saint, Alan Arkin, John Philip Law, Paul Ford, Tessie O'Shea, Brian Keith, Jonathan Winters, Theodore Bikel, Ben Blue

'Rather amiable, though the film, like its title, seems to repeat most things twice.' – Sight and Sound

AAN: best picture; William Rose; Alan Arkin

Russicum
Italy 1987 112m colour Cinemascope
Columbia TriStar/TigerCinematographica/RAI/Mario Cecchi Gori, Vittorio Cecchi Gori
V*

Investigating the death of an American nun in Rome, a diplomat discovers a plot to prevent the Pope visiting Russia.

Dull, lifeless thriller in which it becomes difficult to discover who is doing what to whom.

w Valerio Riva, Robert Balchus, Pasquale Squitieri novel I Mertedi del Diavolo by Enzo Russo d Pasquale Squitieri ph Giuseppe Tinelli m Renato Serio ad Emilio Baldelli ed Mauro Bonanni

F. Murray Abraham, Treat Williams, Danny Aiello, Rita Rusic, Luigi Montini, Robert Balchus, Nigel Court, Leopoldo Mastelloni, Rossano Brazzi

'Clearly destined to drop straight into the dustiest oubliette in film history.' – Tom Milne, MFB

Rustlers of Red Dog
US 1935 bw serial: 12 eps
Universal

Three musketeers of the old west find plenty of action with rustlers and renegade Indians.

Western serial with all the expected elements.

d Louis Friedlander

Johnny Mack Brown, Joyce Compton, Walter Miller, Raymond Hatton, H. L. Woods

Rustler's Rhapsody *
US 1985 88m Metrocolor Panavision
Paramount/Impala/Tesauro (David Giler, Walter Hill)
V*, L

A 'B' Western hero of 1940s movies copes with a more modern and colourful world where life is no longer a matter of simple black and white.

An affectionate parody of cowboy clichés, though the joke begins to wear thin before the final shoot-out.
wd Hugh Wilson ph José Luis Alcaine m Steve Dorff pd Gil Parrondo ed John Victor Smith

Tom Berenger, G. W. Bailey, Marilu Henner, Fernando Rey, Andy Griffith, Sela Ward

'Love betrayed them – power destroyed them!'
Ruthless *
US 1948 104m bw
Eagle Lion/Arthur S. Lyons

A conniver breaks several lives on his way to the top.

Rich melodrama with some entertaining moments.

w S. K. Lauren, Gordon Kahn novel Prelude to Night by Dayton Stoddert d Edgar G. Ulmer ph Bert Glennon m Werner Janssen

Zachary Scott, Sidney Greenstreet, Diana Lynn, Louis Hayward, Martha Vickers, Lucille Bremer, Edith Barrett, Raymond Burr, Dennis Hoey

'Beginning pictures at the end
Is, I'm afraid, the modern trend.
But I'd find Ruthless much more winning
If it could end at the beginning.' – C. A. Lejeune

Ruthless People *
US 1986 93m DeLuxe
Touchstone/Silver Screen Partners/Wagner-Lancaster
V, V*, L, S

Comic kidnappers find they have on their hands a troublesome woman whose husband won't pay for her return.

Raucous comedy which packs a few good laughs before wearing out its welcome.

w Dane Launer d Jim Abrahams, David and Jerry Zucker ph Jan DeBont m Michel Colombier

Danny DeVito, Bette Midler, Judge Reinhold, Helen Slater, Anita Morris, Bill Pulman

RX Murder
GB 1958 85m bw Cinemascope
TCF
aka: Family Doctor

The doctor of a small seaside resort has had four wives die on him. Could it be murder?

Modest mystery with an obvious outcome.

wd Derek Twist novel The Deeds of Dr Deadcert by Joan Fleming

Marius Goring, Rick Jason, Lisa Gastoni, Mary Merrall, Vida Hope, Phyllis Neilson-Terry, Frederick Leister, Nicholas Hannen

Ryan's Daughter **
GB 1970 206m Metrocolor Panavision 70
MGM/Faraway (Anthony Havelock-Allan)
V, V*, L, S

1916 Ireland: a village schoolmaster's wife falls for a British officer.

A modestly effective pastoral romantic melodrama, stretched on the rack of its director's meticulous film-making technique and unnecessarily big budget. A beautiful, impressive, well-staged and well-acted film but not really four hours' worth of drama.

w Robert Bolt d David Lean ph Frederick A. Young m Maurice Jarre pd Stephen Grimes (who created an entire village)

Sarah Miles, Robert Mitchum, Chris Jones, John Mills, Trevor Howard, Leo McKern

'Instead of looking like the money it cost to make, the film feels like the time it took to shoot.' – Alexander Walker

'Gush made repectable by millions of dollars tastefully wasted.' – Pauline Kael

AA: Frederick A. Young; John Mills

AAN: Sarah Miles

S.O.B.
US 1981 121m Metrocolor Panavision
Lorimar/Geoffrey (Blake Edwards, Tony Adams)
V*, L

A Hollywood director goes bananas when his much-touted epic is a fiasco, and decides to remake it as a sex picture.

Tasteless, vulgar and unfunny comedy, with everybody shouting at once and most of the jokes about vomiting, farting and funerals. Julie Andrews, who is made to bare her breasts, could surely use it as grounds for divorce.

wd Blake Edwards   *ph* Harry Stradling   *m* Henry Mancini

Julie Andrews, Richard Mulligan, *Robert Preston,* William Holden, Robert Vaughn, Robert Webber, Larry Hagman, Shelley Winters, Marisa Berenson, Loretta Swit, Craig Stevens, Robert Loggia

'One feels that this in-house comedy was in some way intended as a purge and not an entertainment.' – *John Pym, MFB*

'At best the humour is cheap and at worst unnecessarily vulgar.' – *Margaret Hinxman, Daily Mail*

† S.O.B., it seems, stands no longer for Son Of a Bitch but for Standard Operational Bullshit.

SOS Coast Guard
US 1937 bw serial: 12 eps
Republic

The coast guards combat a half-mad inventor who is prepared to sell to all comers his deadly disintegrating gas.

Hilarious thick ear, one of the more revivable serials.

d William Witney, Alan James

Ralph Byrd, Bela Lugosi, Maxine Doyle, Herbert Rawlinson, Lawrence Grant

SOS Iceberg *
US 1933 117m (at first showings) bw
Universal

A young scientist seeks to recover the records of the lost Wegener expedition to the Arctic.

At the time this was a spectacular semi-documentary, but it did no business.

w Tom Reed, Edwin H. Knopf   *d* Tay Garnett

Rod la Rocque, Leni Riefenstahl, Sepp Rist, Gibson Gowland

† The production was begun in Berlin and taken over by Universal when the producers ran out of money.

SOS Pacific *
GB 1959 91m bw
Rank/Sydney Box (John Nasht, Patrick Filmer-Sankey)

Survivors of a Pacific plane crash await rescue on a small island which is the site of an imminent H-bomb test.

Satisfactory open-air thick ear with strongly deployed types and a suspense climax.

w Robert Westerby   *d* Guy Green   *ph* Wilkie Cooper   *m* Georges Auric

Eddie Constantine, Pier Angeli, John Gregson, Richard Attenborough, Eva Bartok, Clifford Evans, Jean Anderson, Cec Linder

Saadia
US 1953 87m Technicolor
MGM (Albert Lewin)

A young French doctor in the Sahara has trouble with the local witch doctor.

Pretentious and ill-considered multi-national romance from the champion of Omar's Rubaiyat.

wd Albert Lewin   *novel Echec au Destin* by Francis D'Autheville   *ph* Christopher Challis   *m* Bronislau Kaper

Cornel Wilde, Mel Ferrer, Rita Gam, Michel Simon, Wanda Rotha, Cyril Cusack, Marcel Poncin, Peter Bull

Sabata (dubbed) *
Italy 1969 106m Technicolor Techniscope
UA/PEA/Delphos (Alberto Grimaldi)
original title: *Ehi, Amico ... C'è Sabata, Hai Chiuso*

An inventive bounty hunter attempts to find the brains behind a bank robbery.

Stylish over-the-top spaghetti Western.

w Gianfranco Parolini, Renato Izzo   *d* Frank Kramer (Gianfranco Parolini)   *ph* Sandro Mancori   *m* Marcello Giombini   *ad* Carlo Simi   *ed* Edmondo Lozzi

Lee Van Cleef, William Berger, Franco Ressel, Linda Veras, Pedro Sanchez (Ignazio Spalla), Gianni Rizzo

'A certain cold-blooded ingenuity provides a substitute for inspiration in this colourful but extended anthology of Italian Western clichés.' – *Richard Combs, MFB*

† The film was followed by two sequels, *The Bounty Hunters* and *Return of Sabata* (qqv).

Sabotage ***
GB 1936 76m bw
Gaumont British (Michael Balcon, Ivor Montagu)
V*, L
US title: *A Woman Alone*

The proprietor of a small London cinema is a dangerous foreign agent.

Unattractively plotted but fascinatingly detailed Hitchcock suspenser with famous sequences and a splendidly brooding melodramatic atmosphere.

w Charles Bennett, Ian Hay, Helen Simpson, E. V. H. Emmett   *novel The Secret Agent* by Joseph Conrad   *d* Alfred Hitchcock   *ph* Bernard Knowles   *md* Louis Levy

Oscar Homolka, Sylvia Sidney, John Loder, Desmond Tester, Joyce Barbour, Matthew Boulton

'Tightly packed, economical, full of invention and detail.' – *NFT, 1961*

'The cleverest picture Alfred Hitchcock has made since the arrival of the talkies. It is also, to me, the least likeable of them all . . . Discreet directors don't kill schoolboys and dogs in omnibuses. Believe me, it isn't done.' – *C. A. Lejeune*

Saboteur ***
US 1942 108m bw
Universal (Frank Lloyd, Jack H. Skirball)
V*, L

A war worker unjustly suspected of sabotage flees across the country and unmasks a spy ring.

Flawed Hitchcock action thriller, generally unsatisfactory in plot and pace but with splendid sequences at a ball, in Radio City Music Hall, and atop the Statue of Liberty.

w Peter Viertel, Joan Harrison, Dorothy Parker   *story* Alfred Hitchcock   *d* Alfred Hitchcock   *ph* Joseph Valentine   *md* Charles Previn   *m* Frank Skinner

Robert Cummings, Priscilla Lane, Otto Kruger, Alan Baxter, Alma Kruger, *Norman Lloyd*

'It throws itself forward so rapidly that it allows slight opportunity for looking back.' – *New York Times*

'The drama of a nation stirred to action, of a people's growing realization of themselves and their responsibilities.' – *Motion Picture Herald*

† Hitchcock wanted for the three leading roles Gary Cooper, Barbara Stanwyck and Harry Carey, but all refused or were unavailable.

'World War II espionage adventure and human lives have never before been combined so explosively!'

The Saboteur, Code Name Morituri *
US 1965 122m bw
TCF/Arcola/Colony (Aaron Rosenberg)
V*
aka: *Morituri; The Saboteur*

In 1942 a German pacifist working for the allies is actually a German spy.

Dreary as a whole, suspenseful in snatches, this shipboard melodrama is full of irrelevancies and is in any case played much more seriously than the matter demands.

w Daniel Taradash   *novel* Werner Jeorg Kosa   *d* Bernhard Wicki   *ph* Conrad Hall   *m* Jerry Goldsmith

Yul Brynner, Marlon Brando, Trevor Howard, Janet Margolin

AAN: Conrad Hall

The Sabre and the Arrow: see *Last of the Comanches*

Sabre Jet
US 1953 96m Cinecolor
Krueger Productions/UA

A US Air Force colonel in Korea has trouble with his career-hunting wife as well as with the enemy.

Propaganda cheapie with a few stirring aerial moments.

w Dale Eunson, Katherine Albert   *d* Louis King

Robert Stack, Coleen Gray, Richard Arlen, Julie Bishop, Leon Ames, Amanda Blake

Sabrina *
US 1954 113m bw
Paramount (Billy Wilder)
V, V*, L
GB title: *Sabrina Fair*

The chauffeur's daughter is wooed by both her brother employers.

Superior comedy, rather uneasily cast.

w Billy Wilder   *play* Samuel Taylor   *d* Billy Wilder   *ph* Charles Lang Jnr   *m* Frederick Hollander   *ad* Hal Pereira, Walter Tyler

Humphrey Bogart, William Holden, Audrey Hepburn, Walter Hampden, John Williams, Martha Hyer, Joan Vohs, Marcel Dalio

'This is never less than a glittering entertainment, but somehow a certain measure of lead has found its way into the formula.' – *Time*

† Cary Grant was sought for the role played by Bogart.

AAN: Billy Wilder (as writer and director); Charles Lang Jnr; Audrey Hepburn; art direction

Sabrina Fair: see *Sabrina*

The Sacred Flame: see *The Right to Live*

The Sacrifice *
Sweden 1986 149m Eastmancolor/bw
Swedish Film Institute/SVT2/Film Four/Argos/Sandrew/
Josephson & Nykvist (Katinka Farago)
V, V*, L
original title: *Offret*

A writer, who dreams that a nuclear war has begun, promises God that he will renounce his home, his family and speech if the world can return to normal.

A brilliantly filmed but obscure and confusing parable that does not easily yield its meaning.

wd Andrei Tarkovsky *ph* Sven Nykvist *m* J. S. Bach, folk music *ad* Anna Asp *ed* Andrei Tarkovsky, Michel Leszczlylowski

Erland Josephson, Susan Fleetwood, Valerie Mairesse, Allan Edwall, Gudrün Gísladóttir, Sven Wollter, Filippa Franzén

Sacrificed Youth *
China 1985 96m colour
Artificial Eye/Peking Youth Studio (Zhao Yamin)
original title: *Quingchun Ji*

During the Cultural Revolution, a young student is sent from her family in the city to work on a remote farm.

Touching, quietly elegant account of a girl growing to adulthood.

wd Zhang Nuanxin *story* There Was That Beautiful *Place* by Zhang Manling *ph* My Deyuan, Deng Wei *m* Liu Suola, Qu Xiaosong *pd* Li Yonxin, Wang Yanjin *ed* Zhao Qihua

Li Fengxu, Feng Yuanzheng, Song Tao, Guo Jianguo, Yu Da

The Sad Sack
US 1957 98m bw Vistavision
Paramount (Paul Nathan)
V*

Adventures of an army misfit.

Resistible star comedy.

w Edmund Beloin, Nate Monaster *cartoon* George Baker *d* George Marshall *ph* Loyal Griggs *m* Walter Scharf

Jerry Lewis, David Wayne, Phyllis Kirk, Peter Lorre, Joe Mantell, Gene Evans, George Dolenz, Liliane Montevecchi, Shepperd Strudwick

Saddle the Wind *
US 1958 84m Metrocolor Cinemascope
MGM (Armand Deutsch)

A reformed gunman's young brother gets into bad company.

Modestly effective, humourless Western drama.

w Rod Serling *d* Robert Parrish *ph* George J. Folsey *m* Jeff Alexander

Robert Taylor, John Cassavetes, Julie London, Donald Crisp, Charles McGraw, Royal Dano, Richard Erdman

Saddle Tramp
US 1950 76m Technicolor
Universal-International

A wandering cowboy adopts four orphan children and after various adventures marries the eldest of them.

Mild family Western for star-fanciers.

w Harold Shumate *d* Hugo Fregonese

Joel McCrea, Wanda Hendrix, John Russell, John McIntire, Jeanette Nolan, Russell Simpson

Sadie McKee *
US 1934 88m bw
MGM (Lawrence Weingarten)

A maid at various times loves her master, a young ne'er-do-well, and a middle-aged millionaire.

Solidly carpentered millgirl's romance of the period.

w John Meehan *story* Vina Delmar *d* Clarence Brown *ph* Oliver T. Marsh *m* William Axt

Joan Crawford, Franchot Tone, Gene Raymond, Edward Arnold, Esther Ralston, Jean Dixon, Leo Carrillo, Akim Tamiroff

'The stuff the fans cry for.' – *Hollywood Reporter*

Sadie Thompson *
US 1928 95m (24 fps) bw silent
Gloria Swanson
V*, L

In the South Seas, a fire-and-brimstone missionary is attracted to a prostitute.

Steamy, much-filmed melodrama (see *Rain, Miss Sadie Thompson*). This version has long been unavailable for revaluation.

w G. Gardner Sullivan *story* Rain *by W. Somerset Maugham *d* Raoul Walsh *ph* George Barnes, Robert Kurrle *ad* William Cameron Menzies

Gloria Swanson, Lionel Barrymore, Blanche Frederici, Charles Lane, Florence Midgley, Raoul Walsh

'It's stirring and ironic and funny. You couldn't ask more.' – *Photoplay*

AAN: George Barnes; Gloria Swanson

'Her hungry heart beat to tom-tom rhythm!'
Safari
US 1940 82m bw
Paramount (Anthony Veiller)

A disillusioned girl goes to Africa with her sportsman fiancé, but falls for the hired white hunter.

We had heard that before, even in 1940. Moderate time-passer.

w Delmer Daves *story* Paul Hervey Fox *d* Edward H. Griffith

Douglas Fairbanks Jnr, Madeleine Carroll, Tullio Carminati, Billy Gilbert, Muriel Angelus, Lynne Overman

Safari
GB 1956 91m Technicolor Cinemascope
Warwick (Adrian Worker)

A white hunter falls in love with the wife of his employer and luckily the latter is killed by the Mau Mau.

Feeble adventure story exploiting political tensions.

w Anthony Veiller *d* Terence Young *ph* John Wilcox, Fred Ford, Ted Moore *m* William Alwyn

Victor Mature, Janet Leigh, Roland Culver, John Justin, Earl Cameron, Liam Redmond, Orlando Martins

The Safecracker
GB 1958 96m bw
MGM/Coronado (David E. Rose)

A safecracker is released to help in a commando raid during World War II.

One-twelfth of a dirty dozen, with a long indecisive lead-up and not much pull as drama or comedy.

w Paul Monash *story* Rhys Davies *d* Ray Milland *ph* Gerald Gibbs *m* Richard Rodney Bennett

Ray Milland, Barry Jones, Jeanette Sterke, Victor Maddern, Ernest Clark, Cyril Raymond, Melissa Stribling

Safety Last **
US 1923 70m (24 fps) bw silent
Harold Lloyd
V, V*

A small-town boy goes to the big city and to impress his girlfriend enters a contest to climb a skyscraper.

Marvellous star comedy which set a new standard not only in sight gags but in the comedy-thrill stunts which became Lloyd's stock-in-trade.

w Harold Lloyd, Sam Taylor, Tim Whelan, Hal Roach *d* Sam Taylor, Fred Newmeyer *ph* Walter Lundin

Harold Lloyd, Mildred Davis, Noah Young

The Saga of Anatahan
Japan 1953 90m bw
Daiwa

During the Pacific war, castaways on a remote island kill each other for the sake of one woman.

A curious footnote to its director's career, this mannered film is entirely in Japanese with English commentary, and does not recommend itself to western audiences.

wd Josef von Sternberg

Sagebrush Trail
US 1933 58m bw
Monogram/Lone Star (Paul Malvern)
V*, L

Falsely imprisoned for murder, a cowboy escapes from jail to discover the real killer.

Routine Western with the occasional spectacular stunt.

w Lindsley Parsons *d* Armand Schaefer *ph* Archie Stout *ed* Carl Pierson

John Wayne, Nancy Shubert, Lane Chandler, Yakima Canutt, Henry Hall, Wally Wales, Bob Burns

Sahara **
US 1943 97m bw
Columbia (Harry Joe Brown)
V, V*, S

During the retreat from Tobruk a group of men of mixed nationality find water for themselves and harass the Nazis.

Good, simple war actioner with a realistic feel and strong characters deployed in melodramatic situations.

w John Howard Lawson, Zoltan Korda *d* Zoltan Korda *ph* Rudolph Maté *m* Miklos Rozsa

Humphrey Bogart, Bruce Bennett, Lloyd Bridges, Rex Ingram, J. Carrol Naish, Dan Duryea, Kurt Kreuger

'It borrows, chiefly from the English, a sort of light-alloy modification of realism which makes the traditional Hollywood idiom seem as obsolete as a minuet.' – *James Agee*

'The tank keeps rolling, picking up strays along the way until it has a full Hollywood ethnic complement.' – *Pauline Kael, 70s*

AAN: Rudolph Maté; J. Carrol Naish

Sahara
US 1984 111m Metrocolor
MGM-UA/Cannon (Menahem Golan, Yoram Globus)
V, V*, S

In the 1920s, an heiress who competes in a trans-Sahara rally in a car made by her father's company is kidnapped by a lecherous Arab sheik.

Laughably bad and unoriginal romantic adventure, given a perfunctory treatment by all concerned.

w James R. Silke d Andrew V. McLaglen
ph David Gurfinkel, Armando Nunnuzzi m Ennio Morricone ad Luciano Spadoni ed Michael Duthie

Brooke Shields, Lambert Wilson, Horst Buchholz, John Rhys-Davies, Ronald Lacey, John Mills, Steve Forrest

'Lamentably low on excitement, laughs and passion.' – Variety

Said O'Reilly to McNab

GB   1937   83m   bw
Gainsborough
US title: Sez O'Reilly to McNab

A rich Scot is afflicted by an Irish con man.

Lively ethnic comedy, a good vehicle for two stars.

w Leslie Arliss, Howard Irving Young d William Beaudine

Will Mahoney, Will Fyffe, Ellis Drake, Sandy McDougal

'Most hinterland exhibs have the quakes and headaches when it comes time on their sked to play a British film, but here's one, if sold along American lines, which may be found acceptable to the patrons in most places.' – Variety

'It's dynamite – when these two come together in the powderkeg city of the Far East!'

Saigon

US   1947   93m   bw
Paramount (P. J. Wolfson)

Veteran airmen in Saigon are offered half a million to help in a robbery.

Tired studio-set star actioner.

w P. J. Wolfson, Arthur Sheekman d Leslie Fenton
ph John Seitz m Robert Emmett Dolan

Alan Ladd, Veronica Lake, Douglas Dick, Wally Cassell, Luther Adler, Morris Carnovsky, Mikhail Rasumny

Saigon

US   1988   102m   colour
Fox (Alan Barnette)
V, V*, L
aka: Off Limits

Two cops in Saigon track down a mass murderer of Vietnamese prostitutes.

Violent thriller for those with a boredom threshold as high as the body count.

w Christopher Crowe, Jack Thibeau d Christopher Crowe ph David Gribble m James Newton Howard pd Dennis Washington ed Douglas Ibold

Willem Dafoe, Gregory Hines, Fred Ward, Amanda Pays, Scott Glenn, Kay Tong Lim, David Alan Grier

Saikaku Ichidai Onna: see The Life of Oharu

Sail a Crooked Ship

US   1961   88m   bw
Columbia/Philip Barry Jnr
V*

A shipowner unwittingly takes on a crew of crooks intending to use the boat as a getaway after a bank robbery.

Flimsy comedy sustained by a star comedian.

w Ruth Brooks Flippen, Bruce Geller
novel Nathaniel Benchley d Irving Brecher
ph Joseph Biroc m George Duning

Robert Wagner, Ernie Kovacs, Dolores Hart, Carolyn Jones, Frank Gorshin

Sailing Along

GB   1938   90m   bw
Gaumont-British (Michael Balcon)

A girl barge hand meets an impresario and becomes a dancing star.

Rather deadly British musical romance with the star not at her best, the supporting talents wasted, and a generally heavy hand in evidence.

wd Sonnie Hale ph Glen MacWilliams
m/ly Arthur Johnston, Maurice Sigler ad Alfred Junge

Jessie Matthews, Roland Young, Barry Mackay, Jack Whiting, Noel Madison, Alastair Sim, Athene Seyler, Frank Pettingell

Sailor Beware

US   1952   103m   bw
Paramount/Hal B. Wallis

Martin and Lewis in the navy.

Unlovable star antics.

w James Allardice, Martin Rackin play Kenyon Nicholson, Charles Robinson d Hal Walker
ph Daniel L. Fapp m Joseph J. Lilley

Dean Martin, Jerry Lewis, Corinne Calvet, Marion Marshall, Robert Strauss, Leif Erickson

Sailor Beware *

GB   1956   80m   bw
Romulus (Jack Clayton)
US title: Panic in the Parlor

A young sailor has trouble with his mother-in-law-to-be.

Plain but adequate film version of a successful lowbrow stage farce about an archetypal female dragon.

w Philip King, Falkland L. Cary play Philip King, Falkland L. Cary d Gordon Parry ph Douglas Slocombe m Peter Akister

Peggy Mount, Esma Cannon, Cyril Smith, Shirley Eaton, Ronald Lewis

'It's the music-hall mother-in-law joke inflated to gigantic proportions.' – The Times

The Sailor from Gibraltar

GB   1967   89m   bw
Lopert (Oscar Lewenstein, Neil Hartley)

A mysterious woman searching for her lost lover meets a man determined to abandon his mistress.

A dry and unimaginative movie, with a good cast seemingly all at sea.

w Christopher Isherwood, Don Magner, Tony Richardson novel Marguerite Duras d Tony Richardson ph Raoul Coutard m Antoine Duhamel ad Marilena Aravantinou ed Anthony Gibbs

Jeanne Moreau, Ian Bannen, Vanessa Redgrave, Zia Moyheddin, Hugh Griffith, Orson Welles, Eleanor Bron, John Hurt

The Sailor Takes a Wife

US   1945   91m   bw
MGM

A sailor on leave gets married and finds he has acquired a few problems.

Rather self-consciously cute sentimental comedy, proficiently staged.

w Anne Chapin, Whitfield Cook play Chester Erskine d Richard Whorf

June Allyson, Robert Walker, Reginald Owen, Hume Cronyn, Eddie Anderson, Audrey Totter, Gerald Oliver Smith

'He gave his soul to the sea and his heart to a woman! Their love will arouse you – their story will disturb you – the ending will startle you!'
'Like the act of love, this film must be experienced from beginning to end!'

The Sailor Who Fell from Grace with the Sea

GB   1976   105m   Technicolor
AVCO/Sailor Company (Martin Poll)
V*

A precocious boy interferes with his widowed mother's affair with a sailor by castrating the latter.

Weird and unattractive sex fantasy set in Dartmouth of all places and not helped by tiresome sex scenes.

wd Lewis John Carlino novel Gogo No Eiko by Yukio Mishima ph Douglas Slocombe m John Mandel

Sarah Miles, Kris Kristofferson, Jonathan Kahn, Margo Cunningham, Earl Rhodes

'This everyday tale of torture, scopophilia, copulation, masturbation, dismemberment and antique dealing deserves to be traded back to the Japs and made required viewing for timorous kamikaze pilots.' – Benny Green, Punch

The Sailor's Return

GB   1978   100m   colour
Euston Films

A Victorian seaman returns to his native village with a black bride, and opens a pub.

Lame-paced and highly predictable yarn of prejudice and doomed love, assembled with almost no cinematic flair.

w James Saunders novel David Garnett d Jack Gold

Tom Bell, Shope Sodeinde, Elton Charles, Mick Ford, Clive Swift

† As a theatrical film it found no takers, and in GB was first shown on television in 1980.

Sailors Three **

GB   1940   86m   bw
Ealing (Culley Forde)
US title: Three Cockeyed Sailors

Drunken sailors capture a German battleship by mistake.

Low service comedy which keeps moving, is brightly played and reaches a good standard. Sequel: Fiddlers Three (qv).

w Angus Macphail, John Dighton, Austin Melford
d Walter Forde ph Gunther Krampf md Ernest Irving

Tommy Trinder, Claude Hulbert, Michael Wilding, Carla Lehmann, Jeanne de Casalis, James Hayter, John Laurie

The Saint

Leslie Charteris's famous character, the reformed British gentleman crook who becomes a Robin Hood of crime, has been most popular in the long-running sixties TV series starring Roger Moore.

The films which featured him never seemed to hit quite the right note, and now seem slow. All were made for RKO, who later switched allegiance to THE FALCON (qv).

1938: THE SAINT IN NEW YORK
1939: THE SAINT STRIKES BACK, THE SAINT IN LONDON
1940: THE SAINT'S DOUBLE TROUBLE, THE SAINT TAKES OVER
1941: THE SAINT IN PALM SPRINGS, THE SAINT'S VACATION, THE SAINT MEETS THE TIGER
1953: THE SAINT'S RETURN (US: THE SAINT'S GIRL FRIDAY)

Louis Hayward played the role in the first and last; Hugh Sinclair in VACATION and TIGER; George Sanders in the rest.

St Benny the Dip

US 1951 79m bw
Danzigers
GB title: *Escape If You Can*

Gamblers learn to escape the law by dressing as priests, but circumstance converts them to good works.

Unfunny comedy notable only for its cast.

w John Roeburt   d Edgar G. Ulmer   ph Don Malkames   m Robert Stringer

Freddie Bartholomew, Roland Young, Dick Haymes, Lionel Stander, Nina Foch

'The passion burns deep!'
St Elmo's Fire

US 1985 108m Metrocolor
Columbia/Lauren Shuler
V, V*, L, S

A group of college graduates drift apart as realities impinge on their lives.

Nobody explained why audiences should want to interest themselves in such a group of objectionable people; and they didn't.

w Joel Schumacher, Carl Kurlander   d Joel Schumacher   ph Stephen H. Burum   m David Foster

Rob Lowe, Demi Moore, Andrew McCarthy, Judd Nelson, Ally Sheedy, Emilio Estevez, Mare Winningham, Martin Balsam

'He's clean! He's mean! He's the go-between!'
St Ives

US 1976 93m Technicolor
Warner (Pancho Kohner, Stanley Kanter)
V*

An ex-police reporter gets involved in a complex murder puzzle.

Soporific suspenser with every tired situation in the book.

w Barry Beckerman   novel *The Procane Chronicle* by Oliver Bleeck   d J. Lee- Thompson   ph Lucien Ballard   m Lalo Schifrin

Charles Bronson, Harry Guardino, John Houseman, Jacqueline Bisset, Maximilian Schell, Harris Yulin, Dana Elcar, Elisha Cook Jnr

'Much cross-cutting of the sort where the only events you care less about than the ones you cut from are the ones you cut to.' – *John Simon*

'People make love for so many crazy reasons – why shouldn't money be one of them?'
Saint Jack

US 1979 115m colour
New World/Shoals Creek/Playboy/Copa de Oro (Roger Corman)
V*

An American wanderer in Singapore finds his metier as a pimp.

Whimsical, loquacious black comedy which failed to set its wavering director back on the firm ground he needed.

w Peter Bogdanovich, Howard Sackler, Paul Theroux   novel Paul Theroux   d Peter Bogdanovich   ph Robby Muller   m various

Ben Gazzara, Denholm Elliott, James Villiers, Joss Ackland, Rodney Bewes, Mark Kingston, Lisa Lu, George Lazenby, Peter Bogdanovich

Saint Joan

GB 1957 110m bw
Wheel (Otto Preminger)
V*

Glumly assembled screen version of the brilliantly argumentative play about the Maid of Orleans.

Plenty of talent, but neither wit nor style.

w Graham Greene   play Bernard Shaw   d Otto Preminger   ph Georges Périnal   m Mischa Spoliansky   pd Roger Furse

Jean Seberg, Anton Walbrook, Richard Widmark, John Gielgud, Felix Aylmer, Harry Andrews, Richard Todd

St Louis Blues *

US 1939 92m bw
Paramount (Jeff Lazarus)

A Broadway musical star finds new fame down south.

Moderate star entertainment with good guest artists.

w John C. Moffitt, Malcolm Stuart Boylan, Frederick Hazlitt Brennan   d Raoul Walsh   ph Theodor Sparkuhl   songs Frank Loesser, Burton Lane

Dorothy Lamour, Lloyd Nolan, Tito Guizar, Jerome Cowan, Jessie Ralph, William Frawley, the King's Men, Matty Melneck and his Orchestra

'It doesn't quite jell but will suffice as passable divertissement.' – *Variety*

St Louis Blues

US 1958 93m bw VistaVision
Paramount (Robert Smith)

W. C. Handy, son of a black Memphis preacher, becomes a blues composer.

Unsurprising biopic with some good music and the usual strained plot about father's disapproval of the new music.

w Robert Smith, Ted Sherdeman   d Allen Reisner   ph Haskell Boggs   md Nelson Riddle

Nat King Cole, Eartha Kitt, Pearl Bailey, Cab Calloway, Mahalia Jackson, Ruby Dee, Juano Hernandez, Ella Fitzgerald

The St Louis Kid

US 1934 67m bw
Warner (Sam Bischoff)
GB title: *A Perfect Weekend*

A hot-headed truck driver takes the side of milk farmers in a trade dispute.

Modest star action comedy with a fair amount to amuse.

w Seton I. Miller, Warren Duff   d Ray Enright   ph Sid Hickox

James Cagney, Patricia Ellis, Hobart Cavanaugh, Spencer Charters, Addison Richards

'Jimmy in another slugger role, with results this time not so satisfactory.' – *Variety*

St Martin's Lane *

GB 1938 85m bw
Mayflower (Erich Pommer)
V*
US title: *Sidewalks of London*

A middle-aged busker falls in love with a brilliant girl dancer who becomes a star.

Well-made romantic drama with star performances and interesting theatrical background.

w Clemence Dane   d Tim Whelan   ph Jules Kruger   m Arthur Johnson

Charles Laughton, Vivien Leigh, Rex Harrison, Tyrone Guthrie, Larry Adler, Gus MacNaughton

'In its choice of subject, its overwhelming interest in character and its introspective, uncompromising treatment, it is experimental in a courageous fashion.' – *Film Weekly*

The St Valentine's Day Massacre

US 1967 99m DeLuxe Panavision
TCF/Los Altos (Roger Corman)
V*

The twenties gang war between Al Capone and Bugs Moran.

The director's first big studio film is disappointing; stagey, poorly developed, unconvincing-looking and overacted.

w Howard Browne   d Roger Corman   ph Milton Krasner   md Lionel Newman   m Fred Steiner

Jason Robards Jnr, George Segal, Ralph Meeker, Jean Hale, Clint Ritchie, Joseph Campanella, Richard Bakalyan, David Canary, Bruce Dern, Harold J. Stone, Kurt Kreuger, John Agar, Alex D'Arcy

'You'll love every illegal inch of 'em!'
The Sainted Sisters

US 1948 89m bw
Paramount (Richard Maibaum)

Two New York con girls find themselves taken in by the inhabitants of the small town in which they are hiding out.

Unfunny period comedy which misses on all cylinders.

w Harry Clork   d William D. Russell   ph Lionel Lindon   m Van Cleave

Veronica Lake, Joan Caulfield, Barry Fitzgerald, William Demarest, George Reeves, Beulah Bondi, Chill Wills, Darryl Hickman

'Lake, Caulfield, and a swarm of clichés, pleasantly kidded in a manner derived from Preston Sturges.' – *James Agee*

Saints and Sinners

GB 1948 85m bw
London Films/BLPA (Leslie Arliss)

An ex-convict comes back to his home town to prove that those who condemned him were fools or knaves.

Curious slice of Irish whimsy mixed with Ealing comedy; not very satisfactory.

w Paul Vincent Carroll, Leslie Arliss   d Leslie Arliss   ph Osmond Borradaile   m Philip Green   ad Wilfred Shingleton   ed David Newhouse

Kieron Moore, Christine Norden, Sheila Manahan, Michael Dolan, Maire O'Neill, Noel Purcell

Saiyu-ki: see *Alakazam the Great*

Salaam Bombay! **

India/France/GB 1988 114m colour
Mainline/Mirabai Films/NFDC/Cadrage/La SEPT/Channel 4 (Mira Nair)
V, V*, L, S

Street life in an Indian city among pimps, prostitutes, drug peddlers and addicts, as seen by a tea-boy abandoned by his mother.

Poignant, well-observed narrative of small treacheries and smaller hope, acted by a mainly amateur cast.

w Sooni Taraporevala   d Mira Nair   ph Sandi Sissel   m L. Subramaniam   pd Mitch Epstein   ed Barry Alexander Brown

Shafiq Syed, Raghubir Yadav, Nana Patekar, Irshad Hasni, Aneeta Kanwar, Hansa Vithal

'A notable debut.' – *MFB*

Le Salaire de la Peur: see *The Wages of Fear*

The Salamander

US/GB/Italy 1981 101m colour
Grade/William R. Foreman (Paul Maslansky)
V*

A colonel in army intelligence thwarts a fascist takeover of Italy.

Lurid melodrama with an inane script.

w Robert Katz, Rod Serling   novel Morris West   d Peter Zinner   ph Marcello Gatti   m Jerry Goldsmith   pd Giantito Burchiellaro   ed Claudio Cutry

Franco Nero, Anthony Quinn, Martin Balsam, Sybil Danning, Christopher Lee, Cleavon Little, Paul Smith, John Steiner, Claudia Cardinale, Eli Wallach

Salem's Lot: The Movie *

US   1979   112m   colour   Panavision
Warner/Serendipity Productions (Richard Kobritz)
V, V*, L

A writer returns to his small hometown to discover that it is being taken over by vampires.

Effective horror movie, cut from a 200 minute two-part TV mini-series.

w Paul Monash novel Stephen King d Tobe Hooper ph Jules Brenner m Harry Sukman pd Mort Rabinowitz ed Carol Sax, Tom Pryor

David Soul, *James Mason*, Lance Kerwin, Bonnie Bedelia, Lew Ayres, Julie Cobb, Elisha Cook, George Dzundra, Ed Flanders, Kenneth McMillan

Salesman **

US   1969   95m   bw
Maysles Films

A team of salesmen, urged on by their aggressive manager, sell Bibles door to door to Catholics mostly reluctant to buy.

Fascinating cinema-verité documentary, especially in the contrast between the sales convention, with its sanctimonious hyperbole, and the actual experiences on the road.

d Albert and David Maysles, Charlotte Zwerin ph Albert Maysles ed David Maysles, Charlotte Zwerin

'The film tries to be at once tough and sentimental, mocking and sympathetic . . . They have stumbled onto something much bigger than they realize: a condemnation – however fragmented, fortuitous, and even inept – of the human condition, of man himself; but also of a society plagued by superstition, idiotic competitiveness, and stultifying materialism.' – *John Simon*

Sally

US   1930   c. 90m   Technicolor
Warner

A waitress makes it to the lights of Broadway.

Lightweight musical play, previously filmed in 1925 with Colleen Moore and Leon Errol, here the basis of an elaborate colour production with its original star, who however did not take too kindly to the camera.

w Waldemar Young play Guy Bolton and Jerome Kern d John Francis Dillon ph Dev Jennings, E. E. Schoenbaum ch Larry Ceballos ad Jack Okey

Marilyn Miller, Joe E. Brown, Alexander Grey, T. Roy Barnes, Pert Kelton, Ford Sterling

AAN: Jack Okey

Sally and St Anne

US   1952   90m   bw
U-I (Leonard Goldstein)

When an Irish-American family is threatened with eviction, the daughter appeals to St Anne for help.

Whimsical comedy, quite nimbly performed.

w James O'Hanlon, Herb Meadow d Rudolph Maté ph Irving Glassberg m Frank Skinner

Ann Blyth, Edmund Gwenn, Hugh O'Brian, John McIntire, Jack Kelly

Sally in Our Alley *

GB   1931   77m   bw
ATP/Basil Dean

Poor girl loves wounded soldier.

Early talkie drama with music which made Gracie Fields a star and gave her a theme song.

w Miles Malleson, Archie Pitt, Alma Reville play The Likes of 'Er by Charles McEvoy d Maurice Elvey ph Robert G. Martin, Alex Bryce

Gracie Fields, Ian Hunter, Florence Desmond, Ivor Barnard

'The songs are just numbers, the general standard nothing to shout about.' – *Variety*

Sally, Irene and Mary

US   1938   86m   bw
TCF (Gene Markey)

Three girls try to break into show business.

Simple-minded romantic comedy-musical, well enough done.

w Harry Tugend, Jack Yellen d William A. Seiter ph Peverell Marley md Arthur Lange

Alice Faye, Tony Martin, Fred Allen, Jimmy Durante, Gregory Ratoff, Joan Davis, Marjorie Weaver, Gypsy Rose Lee

'Palatable light entertainment that is no Pulitzer prizer but prize b.o.' – *Variety*

Sally of the Sawdust

US   1925   78m at 24 fps   bw   silent
Paramount/United Artists
V*

A circus juggler and faker tries to prevent his daughter from discovering that she is adopted.

Silent version of the stage hit *Poppy*, remade under its own title in 1936 (qv). In both versions W. C. Fields takes over the whole show (not to one's entire satisfaction) and the director's name in this case should not lead one to expect a film of significance, as he seems to have been glad of the work.

w Forrest Halsey play Dorothy Donnelly d D. W. Griffith

W. C. Fields, Carol Dempster, Alfred Lunt, Effie Shannon, Erville Anderson

Salmonberries

Germany   1991   95m   DeLuxe
Electric/PeleMele (Eleonore Adlon)
V

A mysterious and parentless young woman is attracted to a middle-aged German woman, working as a librarian in a small Alaskan mining town.

A somewhat glum and claustrophobic account of thwarted lives.

w Percy Adlon, Felix O. Adlon d Percy Adlon ph Tom Sigel m Bob Telson pd Amadeus Capra ed Conrad Gonzalez

k. d. lang, Rosel Zech, Chuck Connors, Jane Lind, Oscar Kawagley, Wolfgang Steinberg, Christel Merian

'An exhaustingly slow-moving tale which makes for trying viewing.' – *Empire*

Salome

US   1923   80m at 24 fps   bw   silent
Nazimova

Almost unendurable as an entertainment, this stylized silent provided a famous role for its star against backgrounds in Aubrey Beardsley style, and is much illustrated in film histories. The *New Yorker* commented on a 1980 revival: 'The movie looks better in stills than when one actually sees it, but a folly like this should probably be experienced.'

d Charles Bryant drawings Aubrey Beardsley play Oscar Wilde sets and costumes Natacha Rambova

Nazimova, Mitchell Lewis, Nigel de Brulier

'The supreme screen achievement of our time!'
Salome

US   1953   103m   Technicolor
Columbia/Beckworth (Buddy Adler)
V*

Princess Salome of Galilee eludes her licentious stepfather, falls in love with a secret Christian, and leaves home when her dancing fails to save the life of John the Baptist.

Distorted biblical hokum with an interesting cast frozen into unconvincing attitudes.

w Harry Kleiner, Jesse Lasky Jnr d William Dieterle ph Charles Lang md Daniele Amfitheatrof m George Duning ad John Meehan

Rita Hayworth, Charles Laughton, Stewart Granger, Judith Anderson, Cedric Hardwicke, Alan Badel, Basil Sydney, Maurice Schwartz, Rex Reason, Arnold Moss

'Pomp and splendour are paraded across the screen as a background to the story's combination of sex and religion.' – *Variety*

Salome Where She Danced *

US   1945   90m   Technicolor
Universal (Walter Wanger, Alexander Golitzen)
V*

During the Austro-Prussian war a dancer is suspected of being a spy and flees to Arizona, where she affects the lives of the citizenry.

Absurdly plotted and stiffly played romantic actioner whose sheer creakiness made it a minor cult film.

w Laurence Stallings story Michael J. Phillips d Charles Lamont ph Hal Mohr, W. Howard Green m Edward Ward

Yvonne de Carlo, Rod Cameron, Albert Dekker, David Bruce, Walter Slezak, Marjorie Rambeau, J. Edward Bromberg, Abner Biberman, John Litel, Kurt Katch

'I gratefully salute it as the funniest dead-pan parody I have ever seen.' – *James Agee*

Salome's Last Dance

GB   1987   90m   Technicolor
Vestron/Jolly Russell Productions (Penny Corke)
V, V*, L

Oscar Wilde watches a production of his banned play, *Salome*, acted by prostitutes in a brothel.

Coarse and clumsy treatment, all excess and no moderation, though some found it entertaining.

wd Ken Russell play Salome by Oscar Wilde ph Harvey Harrison md Richard Cooke, Ray Beckett ad Michael Buchanan ed Timothy Gee

Glenda Jackson, Stratford Johns, Nickolas Grace, Douglas Hodge, Imogen Millais-Scott, Dennis Ull, Ken Russell

'An outstanding film marking a new career bent for film-maker Russell.' – *Variety*

Salon Kitty

France/Germany/Italy   1978   127m   colour
TCF/Coralta/S.R.L./Cinema Seven (Giulio Barigia, Ermanno Donati)
V

In 1939, a Nazi army officer takes over a Berlin brothel and installs spying devices and prostitutes loyal to the party to report on their clients.

A voyeuristic movie with a gloating nastiness about it that is thoroughly dislikeable.

w Ennio de Concini, Maria Pia Fusco, Tinto Brass d Tinto Brass ph Silvano Ippoliti m Fiorenzo Caspi pd Ken Adam ed Luciana di Russo, Fiorenza Muller

Helmut Berger, Ingrid Thulin, Teresa Ann Savoy, Bekim Fehmiu, John Ireland, Tina Aumont

Saloon Bar *

GB   1940   76m   bw
Ealing (Michael Balcon)

A murder is solved during an evening in a pub.

Amusing, well-made little suspenser from a West End success.

w Angus MacPhail, John Dighton   play Frank Harvey   d Walter Forde   ph Ronald Neame   md Ernest Irving

Gordon Harker, Elizabeth Allen, Mervyn Johns, Joyce Barbour, Anna Konstam, Judy Campbell, Norman Pierce, Alec Clunes, Felix Aylmer, Mavis Villiers, Torin Thatcher, O. B. Clarence

'The detail has been sought lovingly and with exactitude . . . this is a modest and endearing film.' – *New Statesman*

Salsa

US   1988   99m   TVC
Cannon/Menahem Golan, Yoram Globus
V*, L

A motor mechanic is determined to become the best salsa dancer.

A few energetic dance routines break up a weak narrative and some sub-standard acting.

w Boaz Davidson, Tomas Benitez, Shepherd Goldman   story Boaz Davidson, Eli Tabor   d Boaz Davidson   ph David Gurfinkel   pd Mark Hastings   ed Alain Jakubowicz

Robby Rosa, Rodney Harvey, Magali Alvarado, Miranda Garrison, Moon Orona, Angela Alvarado, Loyda Ramos, Valente Rodriguez

Salt and Pepper

GB   1968   101m   DeLuxe
UA/Chrislaw/Tracemark (Milton Ebbins)

Soho night-club proprietors solve a murder.

Infuriating throwaway star vehicle set in the dregs of swinging London. The two stars teamed up again in an even worse film, *One More Time* (1970).

w Michael Pertwee   d Richard Donner   ph Ken Higgins   m Johnny Dankworth

Sammy Davis Jnr, Peter Lawford, Michael Bates, Ilona Rodgers, John Le Mesurier, Graham Stark, Ernest Clark

Salt on Our Skin

Germany/France/Canada   1992   106m   colour
Warner/Neue Constantin/Torii/Telescene/RTL Plus/Canal+
   (Bernd Eichinger, Martin Moszkowicz)
V

A sophisticated half-French woman remembers a youthful love affair in Scotland with the son of a local farmer, which she resumed a decade later.

A dull romantic drama of minimal interest and credibility.

w Andrew Birkin, Bee Gilbert   novel *Les Vaisseaux du Coeur* by Benoîte Groult   d Andrew Birkin   ph Dietrich Lohmann   m Klaus Doldinger   pd Jean-Baptiste Tard, Robert Laing   ed Dagmar Hirtz

Greta Scacchi, Vincent D'Onofrio, Anais Jeanneret, Hanns Zischler, Barbara Jones, Rolf Illic, Petra Berndt, László Kish, Claudine Auger

'An old-fashioned weepie.' – *Variety*

Salt to the Devil: see *Give Us This Day*

Salty O'Rourke

US   1945   100m   bw
Paramount/E. D. Leshin

A racetrack con man is reformed by a schoolteacher.

Very moderate and overlong star vehicle.

w Milton Holmes   d Raoul Walsh   ph Theodor Sparkuhl   m Robert Emmett Dolan

Alan Ladd, Gail Russell, William Demarest, Bruce Cabot, Spring Byington, Stanley Clements

AAN: Milton Holmes

Saludos Amigos *

US   1943   43m   Technicolor
Walt Disney

Donald Duck has various South American adventures with a parrot named Joe Carioca.

Basically a naïve implementation of the good neighbour policy, but with flashes of brilliant animation and some mingling of live-action with cartoon.

production supervisor Norman Ferguson

'Self-interested, belated ingratiation embarrasses me, and Disney's famous cuteness, however richly it may mirror national infantilism, is hard on my stomach.' – *James Agee*

AAN: music (Edward H. Plumb, Paul J. Smith, Charles Wolcott); title song (m Charles Wolcott, ly Ned Washington)

Salut l'Artiste (dubbed) **

France/Italy   1973   97m   Eastmancolor
Gaumont/De La Guéville/Euro-Internazionale (Alain Poiré, Yves Robert)
V*
GB title: *The Bit Player*

After his mistress walks out, an unsuccessful actor tries to return to his wife and children but finds life too complicated.

Adroit and witty comedy, performed with insouciant skill.

w Jean-Loup Dabadie, Yves Robert   d Yves Robert   ph Jean Penzer   m Vladimir Cosma   ad Theo Meurisse   ed Ghislaine Desjonquières

Marcello Mastroianni, Françoise Fabian, Jean Rochefort, Carla Gravina, Xavier Gelin, Evelyne Buyle

Salute for Three

US   1943   75m   bw
Paramount

An all-girl orchestra opens a canteen for servicemen.

Modest, middling propaganda musical with minimum talents.

w Davis Anderson, Curtis Kenyon, Hugh Wedlock Jnr and Howard Snyder   d Ralph Murphy

Betty Jane Rhodes, Macdonald Carey, Dona Drake and her orchestra, Marty May, Lorraine and Rognan

Salute John Citizen

GB   1942   98m   bw
British National (Wallace Orton)

A clerk and his family suffer cheerfully through the blitz.

Modest, competent propaganda piece.

w Clemence Dane, Elizabeth Baron   novel *Mr Bunting at War* by Robert Greenwood   d Maurice Elvey   ph James Wilson

Edward Rigby, Stanley Holloway, George Robey, Mabel Constanduros, Jimmy Hanley, Dinah Sheridan, Peggy Cummins, Stewart Rome

The Salute of the Jugger

Australia   1989   91m   Technicolor
Virgin/Handistrom/Kamisha Corporation/Kings Road
   Entertainment
V, V*, L

In the future, a group of outcasts challenges a big city team to a violent sports contest.

Derivative and pallid low-budget science fiction movie of little interest.

wd David Peoples   ph David Eggby   m Todd Boekelheide   pd John Stoddart   ed Richard Francis-Bruce

Rutger Hauer, Delroy Lindo, Anna Katarina, Vincent Phillip D'Onofrio, Gandhi McIntyre, Justin Monju, Aaron Martin, Joan Chen

Salute to the Marines

US   1943   101m   Technicolor
MGM (John Considine Jnr)

A sergeant-major struggles to get his family out of the Philippines when the Japs attack.

Recruiting poster heroics with comedy interludes.

w Wells Root, George Bruce   story Robert Andrews   d S. Sylvan Simon   ph Charles Schoenbaum, W. Howard Green   m Lennie Hayton

Wallace Beery, Fay Bainter, Marilyn Maxwell, William Lundigan, Keye Luke, Reginald Owen, Ray Collins, Noah Beery, Russell Gleason

Salvador *

US   1986   123m   colour
Hemdale/Gerald Green, Oliver Stone
V, V*, S

Adventures of an American photo-journalist in Central America.

Drama torn from the headlines; it should perhaps have stayed there, as few people proved to be interested in paying to see it. One cannot, however, deny its brilliant if superficial technical command.

w Oliver Stone, Richard Boyle   d Oliver Stone   ph Robert Richardson   m Georges Delerue

James Woods, James Belushi, Michael Murphy, John Savage

'As raw, difficult, compelling, unreasonable, reckless and vivid as its protagonist.' – *Variety*

AAN: best original screenplay; James Woods

The Salvation Hunters **

US   1925   65m (24 fps)   bw   silent
Academy Photoplays (Josef von Sternberg, George K. Arthur)

Among the mud flats of San Pedro, a boy wins his girl from a brute.

Mini-budgeted minor classic whose very artiness and pretentiousness were keys to its director's later development.

wd *Josef von Sternberg*   ph Josef von Sternberg, Edward Gheller

George K. Arthur, Georgia Hale, Bruce Guerin

'Audience reaction was: even our lives are not so drab as this, and if they are we don't want to know about it. Asked to comment on the failure of a film he had praised so highly, Chaplin said, "Well, you know I was only kidding. They all take everything I say so seriously. I thought I'd praise a bad picture and see what happened."' – *Richard Griffith and Arthur Mayer, The Movies*

Salvation Nell

US   1931   83m   bw
Tiffany

A wronged girl sinks lower and lower until she joins the Salvation Army.

One thinks it must have been meant as a spoof, but apparently not.

w Selma Stein, Walter Woods   play Edward Sheldon   d James Cruze

Helen Chandler, Ralph Graves, Sally O'Neill, Jason Robards, Dewitt Jennings

'It probably will be livelier in the States, where the Mme Cloquette scene is not cut out.' – *Variety*

Salvatore Giuliano *

Italy   1961   125m   bw
Lux/Vides/Galatea (Franco Cristaldi)

The bullet-ridden body of key Sicilian Mafia leader Giuliano triggers flashbacks to his complex and brutal career.

Vivid, sometimes obscure, politically oriented melodrama based on fact. Undoubtedly a local classic, but not an easy film to appreciate.

w Francesco Rosi, Suso Cecchi d'Amico, Enzo Provenzale, Franco Solinas   *d* Francesco Rosi   *ph* Gianni di Venanzo   *m* Piero Piccioni

Frank Wolff, Salvo Randone, Federico Zardi

'Epic reportage in the twentieth-century manner of a society reminiscent of some backward corner of the nineteenth century.' – *Peter John Dyer, MFB*

The Salzburg Connection
US   1972   93m   DeLuxe   Panavision
TCF (Ingo Preminger)
V*

An American lawyer on holiday in Salzburg finds himself suspected by spies of both sides.

Turgid, routine action thriller with attractive locations.

w Oscar Millard   *novel* Helen MacInnes   *d* Lee H. Katzin   *ph* Wolfgang Treu   *md* Lionel Newman

Barry Newman, Anna Karina, Maria Brandauer, Karen Jensen, Wolfgang Preiss

'So dull you can't tell the CIA agents from the neo-Nazis or double agents – or the inept actors from the blocks and stones in the handsome Austrian locales.' – *Judith Crist*

Sam Whiskey
US   1969   96m   DeLuxe
UA/Brighton (Jules Levy, Arthur Gardner, Arnold Laven)

An itinerant gambler is paid to recover a fortune in gold bars from the bottom of a Colorado river.

Easy-going but rather slackly handled Western.

w William W. Norton   *d* Arnold Laven   *ph* Robert Moreno   *m* Herschel Burke Gilbert

Burt Reynolds, Clint Walker, Ossie Davis, Angie Dickinson, Rick Davis, William Schallert

'The story of the longest-run date in the history of non-marriage!'
Same Time, Next Year *
US   1978   119m   colour
Universal/Walter Mirisch, Robert Mulligan
V*, L

An illicit affair is carried on for twenty-five years, the couple confining themselves to one annual meeting in a hotel.

Careful film version of a smash Broadway comedy; the flimsiness of the premise is well concealed, but it remains a one-set play.

w Bernard Slade   *play* Bernard Slade   *d* Robert Mulligan   *ph* Robert Surtees   *m* Marvin Hamlisch   *pd* Henry Bumstead

Ellen Burstyn, Alan Alda

AAN: Bernard Slade; Robert Surtees; Ellen Burstyn; song 'The Last Time I Felt Like This' (*m* Marvin Hamlisch, *ly* Alan and Marilyn Bergman)

Sammy and Rosie Get Laid *
GB   1987   100m   colour
Cinecom/Film Four (Tim Bevan, Sarah Radclyffe)
V*, L, S

A young Pakistani accountant in London is confused by the return of his long-lost father, and vice versa.

Those who liked the harsh conflicts of *My Beautiful Laundrette* will get similar *frissons* from this; others will be as confused as the characters.

w Hanif Kureishi   *d* Stephen Frears   *ph* Oliver Stapleton   *m* Stanley Myers   *ed* Mick Audsley

Shashi Kapoor, Claire Bloom, Ayub Khan Din, Frances Barber, Roland Gift

Sammy Going South *
GB   1963   128m   Eastmancolor   Cinemascope
Bryanston (Hal Mason)
US title: *A Boy Ten Feet Tall*

A 10-year-old boy is orphaned in Port Said and hitch-hikes to his aunt in Durban.

Disappointing family-fodder epic in which the mini-adventures follow each other too predictably.

w Denis Cannan   *novel* W. H. Canaway   *d* Alexander Mackendrick   *ph* Erwin Hillier   *m* Tristam Cary

Fergus McClelland, Edward G. Robinson, Constance Cummings, Harry H. Corbett

'A story as timeless and tumultuous as the violent age it spreads before you!'
Samson and Delilah
US   1949   128m   Technicolor
Paramount/Cecil B. de Mille
V, V*, L

Delilah, rejected by religious strong man Samson, cuts his hair and delivers him to his enemies.

Absurd biblical hokum, stodgily narrated and directed, monotonously photographed and edited, and notable only for the 30-second destruction of the temple at the end.

w Jesse L. Lasky Jnr, Fredric M. Frank   *d* Cecil B. de Mille   *ph* George Barnes   *m* Victor Young   *ad* Hans Dreier, Walter Tyler

Hedy Lamarr, Victor Mature, Angela Lansbury, George Sanders, Henry Wilcoxon, Olive Deering, Fay Holden, Russ Tamblyn

'To ignore so enormous, over-coloured, over-stuffed, flamboyant an "epic" would be almost as absurd as taking it seriously.' – *Richard Mallett, Punch*

'Perhaps de Mille's survival is due to the fact that he decided in his movie nonage to ally himself with God as his co-maker and get his major scripts from the Bible, which he has always handled with the proprietary air of a gentleman fondling old love letters.' – *New Yorker*

AA: art direction

AAN: George Barnes; Victor Young

The Samurai ***
France   1967   95m   colour
Filmel/CICC/Fida (Raymond Borderie, Eugene Lepicier)
V
original title: *Le Samourai*; US title: *The Godson*

A hired assassin who lives by a code of self-sufficiency betrays himself by falling in love with the woman who witnessed his murder of a night-club owner.

Moodily atmospheric, engrossing, low-key thriller with minimal dialogue, shot in tones of greys and blues.

wd Jean-Pierre Melville   *ph* Henri Decaë   *m* François de Roubaix   *pd* Georges Casati   *ad* François de Lamothe   *ed* Monique Bonnot, Yo Maurette

Alain Delon, François Périer, Nathalie Delon, Caty Rosier, Jacques Le Roy, Michel Boisrond, Robert Favart

† A dubbed version released in Britain in 1971 ran for 86m.

San Antone
US   1952   90m   bw
Republic

During the Civil War a Texas rancher antagonizes an army lieutenant.

Very routine, competent Western without any moment of inspiration.

w Steve Fisher   *novel* *Golden Herd* by Curt Carroll   *d* Joe Kane

Rod Cameron, Forrest Tucker, Arleen Whelan, Katy Jurado, Rodolfo Acosta

San Antonio *
US   1945   109m   Technicolor
Warner (Robert Buckner)
V, V*

A cowboy incurs the jealousy of a saloon owner.

Typically thinly plotted Warner star Western which works well enough sequence by sequence, climaxing with a fight in the deserted Alamo.

w Alan le May, W. R. Burnett   *d* David Butler   *ph* Bert Glennon   *m* Max Steiner   *ad* Ted Smith

Errol Flynn, Alexis Smith, Paul Kelly, Victor Francen, S. Z. Sakall, John Litel, Florence Bates, Robert Shayne, Monte Blue, Robert Barrat

AAN: song 'Some Sunday Morning' (*m* Ray Heindorf, M. K. Jerome, *ly* Ted Koehler); Ted Smith

San Demetrio London *
GB   1943   105m   bw
Ealing (Robert Hamer)

In 1940, the survivors of a crippled tanker bring it back home.

Rather flat and dated propaganda piece which seemed much more vivid at the time.

w Robert Hamer, Charles Frend   *story* F. Tennyson Jesse   *d* Charles Frend   *ph* Ernest Palmer, Roy Kellino   *m* John Greenwood

Walter Fitzgerald, Mervyn Johns, Ralph Michael, Robert Beatty, Charles Victor, Frederick Piper, Gordon Jackson

'In many ways a model for war films.' – *Dilys Powell*

San Diego I Love You *
US   1944   83m   bw
Universal (Michael Fessier, Ernest Pagano)

A family travels to San Diego to promote father's inventions.

Pleasing, easy-come-easy-go comedy full of memorable incident and characterization.

w Michael Fessier, Ernest Pagano   *d* Reginald Le Borg   *ph* Hal Mohr   *m* Hans Salter

Louise Allbritton, Edward Everett Horton, Jon Hall, Eric Blore, *Buster Keaton,* Irene Ryan

'She fell in love with the toughest guy on the toughest street in the world!'
San Francisco ****
US   1936   117m   bw
MGM (John Emerson, Bernard Hyman)
V*, L

The loves and career problems of a Barbary Coast saloon proprietor climax in the 1906 earthquake.

Incisive, star-packed, superbly-handled melodrama which weaves in every kind of appeal and for a finale has some of the best special effects ever conceived.

w Anita Loos,   *story* Robert Hopkins   *d* W. S. Van Dyke   *ph* Oliver T. Marsh   *md* Herbert Stothart   *montage* John Hoffman   *title song* Bronislau Kaper   *m* Edward Ward

Clark Gable, Spencer Tracy, Jeanette MacDonald, Jack Holt, Jessie Ralph, Ted Healy, Shirley Ross, Al Shean, Harold Huber

'Prodigally generous and completely satisfying.' – *Frank S. Nugent*

AAN: best picture; Robert Hopkins; W. S. Van Dyke; Spencer Tracy

San Francisco Docks

US   1940   64m   bw
Marshall Grant/Universal

A man accused of killing a crooked politician proves he didn't do it.

Curiously pretentious melodrama with suggestions of Group Theater style; not for the action buffs, or anybody else.

w Stanley Crea Rubin, Edmund L. Hartmann
d Arthur Lubin

Burgess Meredith, Irene Hervey, Raymond Walburn, Barry Fitzgerald, Robert Armstrong, Lewis Howard

'Between the sea and the Sierras stood the brawling gateway to gold!'

The San Francisco Story *

US   1952   90m   bw
Warner/Fidelity-Vogue (Howard Welsch)

In 1856, a wanderer bound for China stops in San Francisco to get involved in politics.

Lively melodrama with good period feel.

w D. D. Beauchamp   novel Richard Summers
d Robert Parrish   ph John Seitz   md Emil Newman   m Paul Dunlap

Joel McCrea, Yvonne de Carlo, Sidney Blackmer, Florence Bates

San Quentin *

US   1937   70m   bw
Warner (Sam Bischoff)

A convict's sister loves the warden.

Standard tough prison melodrama, competently done.

w Peter Milne, Humphrey Cobb   story John Bright, Robert Tasker   d Lloyd Bacon   ph Sid Hickox   m Heinz Roemheld, David Raksin

Pat O'Brien, Ann Sheridan, Humphrey Bogart, Barton MacLane, Joseph Sawyer, Veda Ann Borg

'Fairly good appeal but will need pushing.' – Variety

San Quentin

US   1946   66m   bw
RKO

A convict starts a movement for the rehabilitation of prisoners after release, but despite himself is caught up in a prison break.

Tolerable support of a familiar kind.

w Lawrence Kimble, Arthur A. Ross and Howard J. Green   d Gordon Douglas

Lawrence Tierney, Barton MacLane, Marian Carr, Raymond Burr, Joe Devlin

Sanctuary

US   1960   90m   bw   Cinemascope
TCF (Richard D. Zanuck)

The governor's daughter is seduced by a bootlegger, and her life goes from one tragedy to another.

Confused adaptation of unadaptable material, full of pussyfoot daring but little sense.

w James Poe   novel William Faulkner   d Tony Richardson   ph Ellsworth Fredericks   m Alex North

Lee Remick, Bradford Dillman, Yves Montand, Odetta, Harry Townes, Howard St John, Reta Shaw, Strother Martin

'This is the story of the men on the USS San Pablo who disturbed the sleeping dragon of China as the world watched in breathless terror.'

The Sand Pebbles *

US   1966   193m   DeLuxe   Panavision
TCF/Argyle/Solar (Robert Wise)
V*, L

In 1926 an American gunboat patrolling the Yangtze river gets involved with Chinese warlords.

Confused action blockbuster with Vietnam parallels for those who care to pick them up; pretty thinly stretched entertainment despite the tons of explosive.

w Robert Anderson   novel Richard McKenna
d Robert Wise   ph Joseph MacDonald   m Jerry Goldsmith

Steve McQueen, Candice Bergen, Richard Attenborough, Richard Crenna, Marayat Andriane, Mako, Larry Gates, Simon Oakland

'If it had been done twenty years ago, it would have been fast and unpretentious, with some ingeniously faked background shots . . . and we would never have asked for larger historical meanings.' – Pauline Kael

AAN: best picture; Joseph MacDonald; Jerry Goldsmith; Steve McQueen; Mako

Sanders: see Death Drums along the River

Sanders of the River *

GB   1935   98m   bw
London (Alexander Korda)
V*
US title: Bosambo

Problems of a British colonial servant in keeping peace among the tribes.

Much-caricatured African adventure of the very old school, helped by Robeson's personality.

w Lajos Biro, Jeffrey Dell, Arthur Wimperis   stories Edgar Wallace   d Zoltan Korda   ph Georges Perinal   m Mischa Spoliansky

Leslie Banks, Paul Robeson, Nina Mae McKinney, Robert Cochran

'It will interest those who are sincerely interested in the cinema as an art form, but it will suffer the hazards of all pioneers.' – Variety

Sandokan against the Leopard of Sarawak

Italy   1964   94m   Eastmancolor   Totalscope
Liber (Ottavio Poggi)

Three years after recovering his kingdom of Sarawak, Sandokan rescues his bride-to-be after she is kidnapped by the ambitious son of the former ruler.

A gaudy, plodding, low-brow adventure, short on thrills and likely to irritate many with its insistence that men have stronger wills than women.

w Deriso Arpad, Luigi Capuano   novel Emilio Salgari   d Luigi Capuano   ph Adalberto Albertini   m Carlo Rustichelli   ad Giancarlo Bartolini Salimbeni, Ernest Kronberg   ed Antonietta Zita

Ray Danton, Guy Madison, Franca Bettoja, Mario Petri, Alberto Farnese, Mino Doro, Giulio Marchetti, Aldo Bufi-Landi

† It was a sequel to Sandokan Fights Back (qv).

Sandokan Fights Back

Italy/West Germany   1964   96m   colour
Liber/Eichberg (Ottavio Poggi)

A Malaysian pirate discovers that he is the rightful Rajah of Sarawak and decides to regain his kingdom.

Inept and trivial adventure, devoid of thrills.

w Arpad de Riso, Luigi Capuano   novel Emilio Salgari   d Luigi Capuano   ph Adalberto Albertini   ed Antonietta Zita

Ray Danton, Guy Madison, Franca Bettoja, Mino Doro

† It was followed by a sequel, Sandokan against the Leopard of Sarawak (qv).

Sandokan the Great

Italy/France/Spain   1963   114m   Techniscope
Filmes/CCF/Ocean
V*

The son of the Sultan of Borneo wages jungle war against the oppressive British.

A curious mixture of Tarzan and Robin Hood, this character appeared in several adventures before expiring; the first chapter is the best, or least worst.

w Fulvio Gicca, Umberto Lenzi   novel Emilio Salgari
d Umberto Lenzi

Steve Reeves, Genevieve Grad, Rik Battaglia, Andrea Bosic

The Sandpiper

US   1965   116m   Metrocolor   Panavision
MGM/Filmways (John Calley)
V

An artist lives with her illegitimate son in a Monterey beach shack; when she is forced to send the boy to school he attracts the attention of the minister in charge.

Absurd novelettish love story basically copied from The Garden of Allah; pretty seascapes are the most rewarding aspect.

w Dalton Trumbo, Michael Wilson   d Vincente Minnelli   ph Milton Krasner   m Johnny Mandel

Elizabeth Taylor, Richard Burton, Eva Marie Saint, Charles Bronson, Robert Webber

'Straight Louisa May Alcott interlarded with discreet pornographic allusions.' – John Simon

'Sex-on-the-sand soap opera.' – Robert Windeler

AA: song 'The Shadow of Your Smile' (m Johnny Mandel, ly Paul Francis Webster)

'My name is Stryker. Sgt John M. Stryker. You're gonna be my squad!'

Sands of Iwo Jima *

US   1949   109m   bw
Republic (Edmund Grainger)
V, V*, L

During World War II in the Pacific, a tough sergeant of marines moulds raw recruits into fighting men but is himself shot by a sniper.

Celebrated star war comic, still quite hypnotic in its flagwaving way.

w Harry Brown, James Edward Grant   d Allan Dwan   ph Reggie Lanning   m Victor Young   ed Richard L. Van Enger

John Wayne, John Agar, Adele Mara, Forrest Tucker, Arthur Franz, Julie Bishop, Richard Jaeckel

'The battle sequences are terrifyingly real . . . but the personal dramatics make up a compendium of war-picture clichés.' – Variety

'Say what you like about the sentimental flavour of war pictures such as this, there's no denying they keep you in your seat.' – Richard Mallett, Punch

AAN: Harry Brown (original story); John Wayne; editing

Sands of the Desert

GB   1960   92m   Technicolor
Associated British
V

A diminutive travel agent goes out to investigate a desert holiday camp which has suffered from sabotage.

Limp star comedy with poor studio work and meandering script.

wd John Paddy Carstairs

Charlie Drake, Peter Arne, Sarah Branch, Raymond Huntley, Peter Illing, Harold Kasket

Sands of the Kalahari

GB   1965   119m   Technicolor   Panavision
Pendennis (Cy Endfield, Stanley Baker)

Survivors of a plane crash trek across the desert and are menaced by baboons and each other.

Hysterical melodrama with predictable heebie-jeebies by all concerned and the baddie finally left to the mercy of the monkeys. For hardened sensationalists.

wd Cy Endfield novel William Mulvihill
ph Erwin Hillier m Johnny Dankworth

Stanley Baker, Stuart Whitman, Harry Andrews, Susannah York, Theodore Bikel, Nigel Davenport, Barry Lowe

The Sandwich Man *
GB 1966 95m Eastmancolor
Rank/Titan (Peter Newbrook)

In the course of a walking day around London a sandwich man encounters many of his eccentric acquaintances.

Spurned when it was first released, this comedy variety show, mostly in mime, can now be seen to be of a kind popularized by TV, and may have been simply ahead of its time. It certainly seems funnier than it did.

w Michael Bentine, Robert Hartford-Davis
d Robert Hartford-Davis ph Peter Newbrook
m Mike Vickers

Michael Bentine, Dora Bryan, Suzy Kendall, Norman Wisdom, Harry H. Corbett, Bernard Cribbins, Ian Hendry, Stanley Holloway, Alfie Bass, Diana Dors, Ron Moody, Wilfrid Hyde-White, Donald Wolfit, Max Bacon, Fred Emney, Frank Finlay, Peter Jones, Michael Medwin, Ronnie Stevens, John Le Mesurier, Sidney Tafler, John Junkin, Warren Mitchell

Sandy Gets Her Man
US 1940 65m bw
Burt Kelly/Universal

A councilman's baby gets involved in the rival claims of police and fire departments for the best funding.

Rather complex excuse for a slight family comedy.

w Sy Bartlett, Jane Storm d Otis Garrett and Paul Gerard Smith

Baby Sandy, Stuart Erwin, Edgar Kennedy, Una Merkel, William Frawley, Edward Brophy

Sandy Is a Lady
US 1940 62m bw
Burt Kelly/Universal

A baby is responsible for her father's promotion.

Third of a series featuring the gurgling infant introduced in East Side of Heaven. (The others: Little Accident, Unexpected Father, Sandy Gets Her Man.) This one is an excuse for slapstick comedy situations.

w Charles Grayson d Charles Lamont

Baby Sandy, Butch and Buddy, Eugene Pallette, Nan Grey, Tom Brown, Mischa Auer, Billy Gilbert, Edgar Kennedy

Sandy Takes a Bow: see Unexpected Father

Le Sang d'un Poète: see The Blood of a Poet

Sangaree
US 1953 95m Technicolor 3-D
Paramount/Pine-Thomas

Trouble ensues when a plantation owner wills his wealth to the son of a slave.

Period skullduggery rather hammily presented.

w David Duncan novel Frank G. Slaughter
d Edward Ludwig ph Lionel Lindon, W. Wallace Kelley m Lucien Caillet

Fernando Lamas, Arlene Dahl, Patricia Medina, Francis L. Sullivan, Charles Korvin, Tom Drake, John Sutton, Willard Parker, Lester Matthews

Sango Malo *
Cameroon/Burkina Faso 1991 93m colour
Les Films Terre Africaine/Cameroun Radio and TV/FODIC/ DIPROCI (Emmanuel Toko)

An idealistic schoolteacher in his first job angers village leaders and his punitive and conservative headmaster by ignoring traditional ways and putting the emphasis on practical education.

A tough and complex view of Cameroonian village life, in which there are no heroes.

wd Bassek Ba Kobhio novel Sango Malo – Le Maître du Canton by Bassek Ba Kobhio ph Joseph Guerin m Francis Bebey ad François Bollo ed Marie-Jeanne Kanyala

Jérome Bolo, Marcel Mvondo II, Edwige Ntongon è Zock, Jean Minguele, Jimmy Biyong, Henriette Fenda

'Offers a valuable look at the harsh realities of life in this little-seen land. But despite a relatively lively script, pic is unable to sustain its initially fast pace.' – Variety

Sanjuro **
Japan 1962 96m bw Tohoscope
Toho/Kurosawa (Tomoyuki Tanaka, Ryuzo Kikushima)
V*, L
original title: Tsubaki Sanjuro

A ronin, or wandering samurai, inspires some young and rebellious warriors to fight against corruption.

Deftly enjoyable drama, spiced with wit and humanity, and tinged with sadness for its lone and homeless hero.

w Ryuzo Kikushima, Hideo Oguni, Akira Kurosawa novel Shugoro Yamamoto d Akira Kurosawa ph Fukuzo Koizumi m Masaru Sato ad Yoshio Muraki

Toshiro Mifune, Tatsuya Nakadai, Yuzo Kayama, Akihiko Hirata, Kunie Tanaka

'The most autumnal of Kurosawa's Japanese Westerns.' – Nigel Andrews

† Despite the change in name, the ronin played by Mifune is the same character who appeared in the earlier Yojimbo (qv).

Sans Lendemain *
France 1940 83m bw
Gregor Rabinovitch/Cine Alliance

A night-club hostess with a mysterious past is troubled when an old lover turns up.

Moody melodrama in the Quai des Brumes tradition.

w Jean Wilhelm, Max Colpet d Max Ophuls

Edwige Feuillère, Georges Rigaud, Georges Lannes, Paul Azais

Sans Toit ni Loi: see Vagabonde

Santa Claus
GB 1985 112m Rank colour Panavision
Alexander Salkind (Ilya Salkind, Pierre Spengler)
V, V*, L

An old woodcutter is given immortality by the elves and turned into Santa Claus; in modern times, he goes to New York to rescue a discontented elf from the clutches of a demon toymaker.

Utterly charmless treatment of an extremely vague legend, with the two halves entirely failing to coalesce and the level of invention low throughout.

w David Newman d Jeannot Szwarc ph Arthur Ibbetson m Henry Mancini pd Anthony Pratt ed Peter Hollywood

David Huddleston, Dudley Moore, John Lithgow, Judy Cornwell, Christian Fitzpatrick, Burgess Meredith

'For children of all ages, but it skews best towards infancy or senility.' – Variety

Santa Fe
US 1951 89m Technicolor
Columbia (Harry Joe Brown)

After the Civil War, the eldest of four westbound

brothers tries to prevent the others from becoming outlaws.

Regulation star Western, with action sequences a little under par.

w Kenneth Gamet d Irving Pichel

Randolph Scott, Jerome Courtland, Janis Carter, Peter Thompson, John Archer, Warner Anderson, Roy Roberts

Santa Fe Passage
US 1954 89m Trucolor
Republic

An Indian-hating scout with a bad record is hired to transport arms to Santa Fe.

Rough-and-ready brawling Western with very little going for it.

w Lillie Hayward d William Witney

John Payne, Rod Cameron, Faith Domergue, Slim Pickens, Leo Gordon

'The thundering story that challenges all filmdom to match its excitement!'

Santa Fe Trail **
US 1940 110m bw
Warner (Robert Fellows)
V, V*, L

A cavalry officer is responsible for the final capture of John Brown.

The most solemn Western from star or studio has impressive patches amid routine excitements.

w Robert Buckner d Michael Curtiz ph Sol Polito m Max Steiner

Errol Flynn, Olivia de Havilland, Raymond Massey, Ronald Reagan, Alan Hale, Van Heflin, Gene Reynolds, Henry O'Neill

'Forget everything you have ever seen!'

Santa Sangre
Italy 1989 123m colour
Mainline/Produzioni Intersound (Claudio Argento)
V, V*, L

An armless, but far from harmless, mother forces her demented son to use his arms and hands as substitutes for her own, severed by her jealous husband.

Phantasmagoria of images of death and mutilation that, despite their occasional visual flamboyance, signify very little.

w Robert Leoni, Alejandro Jodorowsky, Claudio Argento d Alejandro Jodorowsky ph Daniele Nannuzzi m Simon Boswell pd Alejandro Luna ed Mauro Bonanni

Axel Jodorowsky, Blanca Guerra, Guy Stockwell, Thelma Tixou, Sabrina Dennison, Adan Jodorowski, Faviola Elenka Tapia, Teo Jodorowsky

Santee
US 1972 93m colour
Vagabond (Deno Paoli, Edward Platt)
V*

A boy goes west to find his father and befriends the bounty hunter who has killed him.

Personable, violent Western with adequate style and performances.

w Brand Bell d Gary Nelson ph Donald Morgan m Don Randi

Glenn Ford, Michael Burns, Dana Wynter, Jay Silverheels, Harry Townes, John Larch

Santiago
US 1956 92m Warnercolor Cinemascope
Warner (Martin Rackin)
GB title: The Gun Runner

A Mississippi paddle-boat sets out for Cuba with a consignment of guns for the rebels.

Stiff period actioner of no particular merit.

w Martin Rackin, John Twist   d Gordon Douglas
ph John Seitz   m David Buttolph

Alan Ladd, Rossana Podesta, Lloyd Nolan, Chill
Wills, Paul Fix, L. Q. Jones, Frank de Kova

The Saphead *
US   1920   70m (24 fps)   bw   silent
Metro/Buster Keaton

A shy young man reads a manual on how to win the
modern girl.

Interesting early star comedy: quite winning in its
way, but without the spectacular moments which
were a feature of his later films.

w June Mathis   play The New Henrietta by Winchell
Smith, Victor Mapes   d Herbert Blache   ph Harold
Wenstrom

Buster Keaton, Beula Booker, William H. Crane,
Irving Cummings

Sapphire **
GB   1959   92m   Eastmancolor
Rank/Artna (Michael Relph)
V*

Scotland Yard solves the murder of a black music
student.

Efficient police thriller with a strong race angle.

w Janet Green   d Basil Dearden   ph Harry
Waxman   m Philip Green

Nigel Patrick, Michael Craig, Yvonne Mitchell, Paul
Massie, Bernard Miles, Olga Lindo, Earl Cameron,
Gordon Heath, Robert Adams

'A dandy murder mystery – taut, tantalizing and
beautifully done.' – Judith Crist, 1980

Saps at Sea
US   1940   60m   bw
Hal Roach
V, V (C), V*, L

Ollie needs a rest after working in a horn factory, so
he and Stan take a boating holiday but are kidnapped
by a gangster.

Disappointing star comedy with gags too few and too
long drawn out.

w Charles Rogers, Harry Langdon, Gil Pratt, Felix
Adler   d Gordon Douglas   ph Art Lloyd
m Marvin Hatley

Stan Laurel, Oliver Hardy, James Finlayson, Dick
Cramer, Ben Turpin

Saraband: see Saraband for Dead Lovers

Saraband for Dead Lovers *
GB   1948   96m   Technicolor
Ealing (Michael Relph)
V, V*
US title: Saraband

The tragic love affair of Konigsmark and Sophie
Dorothea, wife of the Elector of Hanover who later
became George I of England.

Gloomy but superb-looking historical love story; it
just misses being a memorable film.

w John Dighton, Alexander Mackendrick
novel Helen Simpson   d Basil Dearden, Michael
Relph   ph Douglas Slocombe   m Alan Rawsthorne
ad Jim Morahan, William Kellner, Michael Relph

Stewart Granger, Joan Greenwood, Françoise Rosay,
Flora Robson, Peter Bull

'Suspense, romance, interest and excitement in full
measure.' – MFB

AAN: art direction

The Saracen Blade
US   1954   76m   Technicolor
Columbia (Sam Katzman)

In the 13th century a young Italian crusader devotes
himself to avenging the murder of his father.

Cut-price swashbuckler full of unintentional laughs
and therefore quite watchable.

w DeVallon Scott, Worthing Yates   novel Frank
Yerby   d William Castle

Ricardo Montalban, Betta St John, Rick Jason,
Carolyn Jones, Michael Ansara

'The Sound of Freedom.'
'Her story will move you. Her struggle will change you.
Her spirit will inspire you.'
Sarafina!
South Africa   1992   116m   Agfacolor
Warner/Ideal/Distant Horizon/Videovision/Ariane/VPI/BBC
(Anant Singh, David M. Thompson)
V, V*, L, S

A South African schoolgirl in Soweto realizes she has
to fight for freedom, following the example of her
history teacher and her mother – and learning from
her own experiences when she is imprisoned and
tortured.

An odd mix of musical and near-documentary realism
that obstinately fails to comes to life on the screen.

w William Nicholson, Mbongeni Ngema
musical Mbongeni Ngema   d Darrell James Roodt
ph Mark Vincente   m Stanley Myers   ch Michael
Peters, Mbongeni Ngema   ed Peter Hollywood,
Sarah Thomas

Leleti Khumalo, Whoopi Goldberg, Miriam Makeba,
John Kani, Dumisani Diamini, Mbongeni Ngema,
Sipho Kunene

'If one is prepared to forgive it its large measure of
amateurishness and naivety, and is braced for the
distress inherent in the subject matter, this can be
cautiously recommended as a vivid testament to the
unacceptable circumstances in which too many
children grow up.' – Angie Errigo, Empire

Sarah and Son
US   1930   85m   bw
Paramount (David O. Selznick)

A widow seeks the baby her husband took away from
her.

Mother love saga; soppy but with good credits.

w Zoe Akins   novel Timothy Shea   d Dorothy
Arzner   ph Charles Lang

Ruth Chatterton, Fredric March, Fuller Mellish Jnr,
Gilbert Emery, Doris Lloyd

'Madame X with a slightly varied theme. Photography
and recording par.' – Variety

AAN: Ruth Chatterton

Saratoga *
US   1937   102m   bw
MGM (Bernard H. Hyman)
V*, L

A bookmaker helps the daughter of a horse breeder.

Forgettable racetrack drama notable chiefly as the last
film of Jean Harlow who died before it was
completed.

w Anita Loos, Robert Hopkins   d Jack Conway
ph Ray June   m Edward Ward

Clark Gable, Jean Harlow, Lionel Barrymore, Frank
Morgan, Walter Pidgeon, Una Merkel, Cliff Edwards,
George Zucco, Jonathan Hale

'Glib, forthright, knowing and adroit.' – Time

'Surefire box office, and tastefully produced.' – Variety

'Their times were violent – and so was their love!'
Saratoga Trunk *
US   1943   135m   bw
Warner (Hal B. Wallis)

A notorious woman comes back to New Orleans and

falls for a cowboy helping a railroad combine against
their rivals.

Curious, unsatisfactory, miscast and overlong film
version of a bestseller; there are enjoyable sequences,
but it simply fails to come alive.

w Casey Robinson   novel Edna Ferber   d Sam
Wood   ph Ernest Haller   ph Joseph St Amaad
m Max Steiner

Ingrid Bergman, Gary Cooper, Flora Robson, Jerry
Austin, Florence Bates, John Warburton, John
Abbott, Curt Bois, Ethel Griffies

'It lacks a logical pattern of drama and character . . . a
piece of baggage labelled solely for the stars.' – Bosley
Crowther

AAN: Flora Robson

Sarraounia *
Burkina Faso   1986   121m   Fujicolour
Technovision
Les Films Soleil (Med Hondo)

An African warrior queen resists white colonization of
her country.

Based on actual events in the 1890s in what is now
Nigeria, an ambitious, if flawed, attempt at an epic of
repression and power politics.

w Med Hondo, Abdoulaye Mamani, Abdoul War
book Abdoulaye Mamani   d Med Hondo   ph Guy
Famechon   m Pierre Akendengue   pd Jacques
D'Ovidio   ed Marie-Therese Boiché

Ai Keïta, Jean-Roger Milo, Feodor Atkine, Didier
Sauvegrain, Roger Mirmont, Luc-Antoine Diquaro,
Jean-Pierre Castaldi, Tidjani Ouedraogo

Saskatchewan
US   1954   87m   Technicolor
U-I (Aaron Rosenberg)
GB title: O'Rourke of the Royal Mounted

A mountie helps the lady survivor of an Indian attack.

Standard star actioner.

w Gil Doud   d Raoul Walsh   ph John Seitz
m Hans Salter

Alan Ladd, Shelley Winters, J. Carrol Naish, Hugh
O'Brian, Robert Douglas, Richard Long, Jay
Silverheels

The Satan Bug *
US   1965   114m   DeLuxe   Panavision
UA/Mirisch/Kappa (John Sturges)

At a top-secret desert research station, one scientist is
a traitor, and a deadly virus has been stolen for use by
a mad millionaire.

Slow-moving, portentous, gadget-filled actioner
which looks good but seldom stimulates.

w James Clavell, Edward Anhalt   novel Alistair
MacLean   d John Sturges   ph Robert Surtees
m Jerry Goldsmith

George Maharis, Richard Basehart, Anne Francis,
Dana Andrews, Ed Asner

Satan Met a Lady *
US   1936   74m   bw
Warner (Henry Blanke)

Various crooks and a private detective pursue a rare
artifact.

Perversely rewritten version of The Maltese Falcon (qv).
Fascinating but not really successful.

w Brown Holmes   d William Dieterle   ph Arthur
Edeson   m Leo F. Forbstein

Bette Davis, Warren William, Alison Skipworth,
Arthur Treacher, Wini Shaw, Marie Wilson, Porter
Hall

'One lives through it in constant expectation of seeing
a group of uniformed individuals appear suddenly

from behind the furniture and take the entire cast into protective custody.' – *Bosley Crowther*

Satan Never Sleeps

US/GB 1962 126m DeLuxe Cinemascope
TCF/Leo McCarey
GB title: *The Devil Never Sleeps*

In the late forties in China, Catholic missionaries defy the communists.

Failed anti-Red imitation of *Inn of the Sixth Happiness* with the priests from *Going My Way*. Has to be seen to be believed.

w Claude Binyon, Leo McCarey   *d* Leo McCarey *ph* Oswald Morris   *m* Richard Rodney Bennett

Clifton Webb, William Holden, France Nuyen, Weaver Lee, Athene Seyler, Martin Benson

'For all its superficial smirk of piety, this is just a prurient, soft-soapy and holy water version of the spicy story about the lonely missionary and the beautiful native girl.' – *Time*

The Satanic Rites of Dracula

GB 1973 88m Technicolor
Hammer (Roy Skeggs)
V, V*
US title: *Count Dracula and His Vampire Bride*

When vampires infest London, a property speculator proves to be Dracula himself.

Intriguingly plotted screamer with more mystery than horror.

w Don Houghton   *d* Alan Gibson   *ph* Brian Probyn   *m* John Cacavas   *ad* Lionel Couch *sp* Les Bowie   *ed* Chris Barnes

Peter Cushing, Christopher Lee, Michael Coles, William Franklyn, Freddie Jones, Richard Vernon, Patrick Barr

'Shot with the kind of flashy anonymity that one expects of a TV series.' – *David Pirie, MFB*

Satan's Skin: see *Blood on Satan's Claw*

'Never told till now! The world's most guarded secret!'
Satellite in the Sky

GB 1956 85m Warnercolor Cinemascope
Warner/Tridelta/Danziger

A rocketship is ordered to lose a tritonium bomb in space, but the device attaches itself to the side of the ship.

Boringly talkative low-budget science fiction with ideas beyond its station but not enough talent to put them over.

w John Mather, J. T. McIntosh, Edith Dell   *d* Paul Dickson   *ph* Georges Périnal   *m* Albert Elms

Kieron Moore, Lois Maxwell, Donald Wolfit, Bryan Forbes, Jimmy Hanley, Alan Gifford

Satisfaction

US 1988 96m DeLuxe
TCF/NBC (Aaron Spelling, Alan Greisman)
V*, L
aka: *The Girls of Summer*

A rock band – three women, one man – win a summer residency and find romance, or sex, at a smart club.

Inconsequential teen drama providing no entertainment and sub-standard rock.

w Charles Purpura   *d* Joan Freeman   *ph* Thomas Del Ruth   *m* Michel Colombier   *ed* Joel Goodman

Justine Bateman, Liam Neeson, Trini Alvarado, Scott Coffey, Britta Phillips, Julia Roberts, Debbie Harry

Saturday Island

GB 1951 102m Technicolor
Coronado (David E. Rose)
US title: *Island of Desire*

In 1943 a supply boat is torpedoed and a Canadian

nurse finds romance on a desert island with a US marine and a one-armed RAF pilot.

Unlikely, conversational, old-fashioned love story.

wd Stuart Heisler   *novel* Hugh Brooke   *ph* Oswald Morris   *m* William Alwyn

Linda Darnell, Tab Hunter, Donald Gray

Saturday Night and Sunday Morning ****

GB 1960 89m bw
Bryanston/Woodfall (Harry Salzman, Tony Richardson)
V

A Nottingham factory worker is dissatisfied with his lot, gets into trouble through an affair with a married woman, but finally settles for convention.

Startling when it emerged, this raw working-class melodrama, with its sharp detail and strong comedy asides, delighted the mass audience chiefly because of its strong central character thumbing his nose at authority. Matching the mood of the times, and displaying a new attitude to sex, it transformed British cinema and was much imitated.

w Alan Sillitoe, *novel* Alan Sillitoe   *d* Karel Reisz *ph* Freddie Francis   *m* Johnny Dankworth

*A*lbert Finney, Shirley Anne Field, *Rachel Roberts*, Bryan Pringle, Norman Rossington, Hylda Baker

'Here is a chance for our own new wave.' – *Evening Standard*

† Warwickshire never showed the film because the producers refused to delete two love scenes. David Kingsley of British Lion said: 'We are not prepared to agree that a film of outstanding importance and merit should be re-edited by the Mrs Grundys of the Warwickshire County Council. It is fortunate for the world that Warwickshire's greatest and often bawdy son, William Shakespeare, was not subject in his day to the restrictions of prim and petty officialdom.'

Saturday Night at the Palace *

South Africa 1987 90m colour
Intertrade (Robert Davies)

An embittered, unemployed white vents his anger on the black manager of an all-night diner.

Tough drama of racial antagonism, based on a true story, with a slow start and a rousing, if overly theatrical, conclusion.

w Paul Slabolepszy, Bill Flynn   *play* Paul Slabolepszy   *d* Robert Davies   *ph* Robert Davies *ad* Wayne and Sandy Attrill   *ed* Lena Farugia, Carla Sandrock

Bill Flynn, John Kani, Paul Slabolepszy

Saturday Night Fever *

US 1977 119m Movielab
Paramount/Robert Stigwood (Milt Felsen)
V, V*, L, S

Italian roughnecks in Brooklyn live for their Saturday night disco dancing, and one of them falls in love with a girl who makes him realize there are better things in life.

Foul-mouthed, fast-paced slice of life which plays like an updated version of *Marty* except that all the characters seem to have crawled from under stones. The slick direction, fast editing and exciting dance numbers do something to take away the sour taste.

w Norman Wexler   *story* Nik Cohn   *d* John Badham *ph* Ralf D. Bode   *m* David Shire   *songs* Barry, Robin and Maurice Gibb (and others), performed by the Bee Gees   *pd* Charles Bailey   *ed* David Rawlins

John Travolta, Karen Lynn Gorney, Barry Miller, Joseph Cali, Paul Pape, Bruce Ornstein

'A stylish piece of contemporary anthropology, an urban safari into darkest America, a field study of the mystery cults among the young braves and squaws

growing up in North Brooklyn.' – *Alan Brien, Sunday Times*

AAN: John Travolta

Saturday Night Out

GB 1963 96m bw
Compton-Tekli

Five sailors spend an overnight leave in London.

Portmanteau drama in which all elements are equally uninteresting.

w Donald and Derek Ford   *d* Robert Hartford-Davis

Bernard Lee, Heather Sears, John Bonney, Francesca Annis, Erika Remberg, Colin Campbell, David Lodge

Saturday's Children

US 1940 101m bw
Warner (Henry Blanke)

An impractical young inventor marries an ambitious young woman, but depressed finances lead to discord.

Glum, dated rehash of a 1929 silent; watchable but not compelling.

w Julius J. and Philip G. Epstein   *play* Maxwell Anderson   *d* Vincent Sherman   *ph* James Wong Howe

John Garfield, Claude Rains, Anne Shirley, Lee Patrick, George Tobias, Roscoe Karns, Elizabeth Risdon, Berton Churchill

† The story was also made in 1935 as *Maybe It's Love*, with Ross Alexander, Henry Travers and Gloria Stuart; William McGann directed without flair.

Saturday's Hero

US 1951 110m bw
Columbia (Sidney Buchman)
GB title: *Idols in the Dust*

A poor boy wins a football scholarship but finds his value to the college is purely commercial and he isn't given time to learn anything.

A spirited attack on the American sporting system, but a dull and overlong film.

w Millard Lampell, Sidney Buchman   *novel The Hero* by Millard Lampell   *d* David Miller   *ph* Lee Garmes   *m* Elmer Bernstein

John Derek, Donna Reed, Sidney Blackmer, Alexander Knox, Elliott Lewis, Howard St John

Saturn Three

GB 1980 87m colour
ITC/Transcontinental (Stanley Donen)
V, V*, L

A maniac builds a robot on a remote space station, and they both go berserk.

Rather unpleasant blend of space fiction, horror and suspense, with some nasty detail and a general feeling that the actors wish they were elsewhere.

w Martin Amis   *story* John Barry   *d* Stanley Donen *ph* Billy Williams   *m* Elmer Bernstein   *pd* Stuart Craig

Kirk Douglas, Farrah Fawcett, Harvey Keitel, Ed Bishop

Satyricon *

Italy/France 1969 129m DeLuxe Panavision
UA/PAA/PEA (Alberto Grimaldi)
V, V*, L
aka: *Fellini Satyricon*

Sexual adventures of a Roman student.

Garish, sporadically enjoyable sketches on a very thin thread of plot: a more benevolent version of the usual Fellini nightmare.

w Federico Fellini, Bernardino Zapponi   *d* Federico Fellini   *ph* Giuseppe Rotunno   *m* Nino Rota, Ilhan Mimaroglu, Tod Dockstader, Andrew Rudin *pd* Danilo Donati

Martin Potter, Hiram Keller, Salvo Randone, Max Born

'A picaresque satire in fragments . . . a series of tableaux which carry the poetry visually at the price of coherence.' – *Mike Wallington, MFB*

'Part of the gradual decomposition of what once was one of the greatest talents in film history . . . a gimcrack, shopworn nightmare.' – *John Simon*

AAN: Federico Fellini (as director)

Le Sauvage

France/Italy 1978 107m Eastmancolor
Lira/PAI (Raymond Danon)

A business executive has opted out of life to be alone on a desert island, but on his last night in the city accidentally helps a runaway heiress who follows him.

A promising and amusing start is squandered in the tedious island sequences of this patchy romantic comedy, which does however leave one with a sense of freshness and optimism rare in the cinema of the seventies.

w Jean-Paul Rappeneau, Elizabeth Rappeneau, Jean-Loup Dabadie d Jean-Paul Rappeneau ph Pierre Lhomme m Michel Legrand

Yves Montand, Catherine Deneuve, Luigi Vannucchi, Dana Wynter

Sauve Qui Peut (La Vie) *

France/Switzerland 1980 87m colour
Sara/MK2/Saga/Sonimage/CDIC/ZDF/SSR/ORF
aka: *Slow Motion*; US title: *Every Man for Himself*

The lives of three people cross: a country girl who becomes a prostitute in the city, a woman leaving the city for a rural life, and her lover, who is not sure where he wants to be.

Godard's return to more commercial cinema is intermittently interesting, but lacks the challenge and playfulness of his best work.

w Anne-Marie Miéville, Jean-Claude Carrière d Jean-Luc Godard ph William Lubchansky, Renato Berta, Jean-Bernard Menoud m Gabriel Yared ad Romain Goupil ed Anne-Marie Miéville, Jean-Luc Godard

Isabelle Huppert, Jacques Dutronc, Nathalie Baye, Roland Amstutz, Anna Baldaccini, Fred Personne

The Savage

US 1952 95m Technicolor
Paramount (Mel Epstein)

A white boy grows up with Indians and later suffers from divided loyalties.

Solemn, rather tedious but well produced Western.

w Sidney Boehm novel L. L. Foreman d George Marshall ph John F. Seitz m Paul Sawtell

Charlton Heston, Susan Morrow, Peter Hanson, Joan Taylor, Richard Rober, Don Porter

The Savage Eye *

US 1959 68m bw
City Film Corporation (Ben Maddow, Joseph Strick, Sidney Meyers)

An unhappily married young woman takes a jaundiced view of life around her in Los Angeles.

The wisp of plot is merely an excuse to present a documentary exposé of the seamier side of life in America's most eccentric city, with its faith healers and revellers. Much of it is fascinating, though the film is not a cohesive whole and the would-be poetic commentary falls on its face.

wd/ed Ben Maddow, Joseph Strick, Sidney Meyers ph Jack Couffer, Haskell Wexler, Helen Levitt m Leonard Rosenman

Barbara Baxley, Gary Merrill, Herschel Bernardi

'The picture is funny, pathetic, cruel, terrible; and it is worth going miles to see.' – *Dilys Powell, Sunday Times*

The Savage Guns

US/Spain 1961 83m Metrocolor Cinemascope
Capricorn/Tecisa/MGM

After the Civil War, an American rancher settles in Mexico but finds his pacifist principles tested by bandits.

Unappealing, stodgy Western with the Hammer horror team rather curiously cast as co-producers.

w Edmund Morris (?Jimmy Sangster) d Michael Carreras

Richard Basehart, Don Taylor, Alex Nicol, Jose Nieto, Fernando Rey

The Savage Innocents

GB/France/Italy 1960 107m SuperTechnirama 70
Joseph Janni/Magic Film/Playart/Gray Films (Maleno Malenotti)
aka: *Ombre Bianchi*

Trials of an Eskimo and his wife in Canada's frozen north.

Conscientious, determined and very boring account of Eskimo life played by actors talking pidgin English. Not a success despite the magnificent photography.

w Nicholas Ray novel Top of the World by Hans Ruesch d Nicholas Ray, Baccio Bandini ph Aldo Tonti, Peter Hennessy m Angelo Lavagnino

Anthony Quinn, Yoko Tani, Marie Yang, Peter O'Toole, Carlo Justini, Anna May Wong, Lee Montague, Ed Devereaux

† The Anna May Wong in the cast is not the famous silent star.

'Don't Bother To Hide . . . He's Already Inside.'
The Savage Intruder

US 1973 90m Movielab colour
Congdon Films (Donald Wolfe)
V

A former Hollywood star hires as a nurse a psychopathic killer who dismembers middle-aged women.

Gruesome thriller, which borrows from *Night Must Fall* and *Sunset Boulevard* and is inept when it is not unpleasant.

wd Donald Wolfe ph John A. Morrill m Stu Phillips pd Norman Houlé ed Hatwig Deeb

Miriam Hopkins, John David Garfield, Gale Sondergaard, Florence Lake, Lester Mathews, Riza Royce, Joe Besser, Minta Durfee, Virginia Wing

† The film was cut to 85m for its British video release.

Savage Islands

New Zealand 1983 94m colour
Paramount (Lloyd Phillips, Rob Whitehouse)

On the morning of his execution, a pirate recalls rescuing a beautiful Englishwoman from a rival brigand.

Standard adventure fare, given a slight novelty by being set in the era of steam warships.

w John Hughes, David Odell story Lloyd Phillips d Ferdinand Fairfax ph Tony Imi m Trevor Jones pd Maurice Cain ed John Shirley

Tommy Lee Jones, Michael O'Keefe, Max Phipps, Jenny Seagrove, Bruce Allpress, Grant Tilley

Savage Messiah *

GB 1972 103m Metrocolor
MGM/Russ-Arts (Ken Russell)

The life together (1910–14) of the 18-year-old painter Gaudier and 38-year-old Sophie Brzeska.

Intense, fragmentary art film about two eccentrics; would have better suited TV.

w Christopher Logue book H. S. Ede d Ken Russell ph Dick Bush m Michael Garrett pd Derek Jarman

Dorothy Tutin, Scott Anthony, Helen Mirren, Lindsay Kemp, Michael Gough, John Justin

'1986. Passion, Rage, Liberty and Love.'
Savage Nights *

France 1992 126m colour
Banfilm Ter/La Sept/Erre/Canal+/Sofinergie II/CNC (Nella Banfi)
V, S
original title: *Les Nuits Fauves*

A bisexual cameraman begins an affair with a 17-year-old girl without telling her he is HIV positive; she finds it impossible to share him with others.

A rawly emotional film about sex, love and death and rootless, excitement-seeking young people, often hysterical in tone and curiously uninvolving.

wd Cyril Collard novel Les Nuits Fauves by Cyril Collard ph Manuel Téran m Cyril Collard and others ed Lise Beaulieu

Cyril Collard, Romane Bohringer, Carlos Lopez, Corine Blue, Claude Winter, René-Marc Bini, Maria Schneider, Clémentine Célarié

'The movie finally confounds everyone's best intentions, including the audience's. It is both sensational and sentimentalized. It ricochets from one lurid fresco to another.' – *Richard Corliss, Time*

† Cyril Collard died of AIDS in 1993, four days before his film won French César awards for best film, best first film, best female newcomer (Romane Bohringer) and best editing.

Savage Pampas

Spain/Argentina/US 1967 108m Eastmancolor
Superpanorama
Jaime Prados-Dasa-Sam Bronston

In 19th-century Argentina the commander of an isolated fort finds that a bandit is bribing his men to desert.

Densely plotted semi-Western, sometimes good to look at but slow and lugubrious.

w Hugo Fregonese, John Melson d Hugo Fregonese ph Marcel Berenguer m Waldo de los Rios

Robert Taylor, Ron Randell, Ty Hardin, Rosenda Monteros, Marc Lawrence

Savage Princess: see Aan

Savage Sam *

US 1962 104m Technicolor
Walt Disney (Bill Anderson)

The youngest son of a homesteading family has a troublesome dog which redeems itself by tracking down Apaches.

Folksy boy-and-dog Western, good of its kind, with adequate suspense and scenery.

w Fred Gipson, William Tunberg d Norman Tokar ph Edward Colman m Oliver Wallace

Brian Keith, Tommy Kirk, Kevin Corcoran, Dewey Martin, Jeff York

'A cadet edition of the best of Ford.' – *MFB*

Savage Wilderness

US 1956 98m Technicolor Cinemascope
Columbia (William Fadiman)
GB title: *The Last Frontier*

An Indian-hating fort commander puts himself and his charges in jeopardy.

Standard Western with good performances and excellent action scenes.

w Philip Yordan, Russell S. Hughes *novel The Gilded Rooster* by Richard Emery Roberts *d* Anthony Mann *ph* William Mellor *m* Leigh Harline

Victor Mature, *Robert Preston*, Guy Madison, Anne Bancroft, James Whitmore, Peter Whitney

Savages

US 1972 106m colour
Angelika/Merchant-Ivory (Joseph Saleh)

Forest wanderers take over a deserted mansion and begin to feel its civilizing influence.

Mild fable which needed a Buñuel to do it justice; a few lively moments.

w George Swift Trow, Michael O'Donoghue *d* James Ivory *ph* Walter Lassally *m* Joe Raposo

Louis Stadlen, Anne Francine, Thayer David, Salome Jens, Neil Fitzgerald

Save the Tiger *

US 1973 100m Movielab
Paramount/Jalem/Filmways/Cirandinha (Steve Shagan)
V*, L

A middle-aged businessman regrets the slack morality of modern America.

Self-adulatory drama which really has little point but gets a few marks for meaning well and for vivid scenes.

w Steve Shagan *d* John G. Avildsen *ph* Jim Crabe *m* Marvin Hamlisch

Jack Lemmon, Jack Gilford, Laurie Heineman, Norman Burton, Thayer David

'A scathing indictment of the US, of materialism, war, marriage – the works. Wordy, literate and deeply felt.' – *NFT, 1974*

AA: Jack Lemmon

AAN: Steve Shagan; Jack Gilford

Saving Grace

US 1986 112m Technicolor Technovision
Columbia/Embassy (Herbert F. Solow)
V*, L

A Pope escapes from office to meet the real people.

The trouble with this movie is, he learns nothing by doing so.

w Joaquin Montana *novel* Celia Gittelson *d* Robert M. Young *ph* Reynaldo Villalobos

Tom Conti, Fernando Rey, Erland Josephson, Giancarlo Giannini, Donald Hewlett

'More sleeping draught than balm for the spirits.' – *Sight and Sound*

Sawdust and Tinsel *

Sweden 1953 95m bw
Svensk Filmindustri
V*, L
aka: *The Naked Night*; original title: *Gycklarnas Afton*

The owner of a travelling circus leaves his mistress for his separated wife, and is challenged to fight by the mistress's new lover.

Powerfully-made yet rather pointless melodrama about unpleasant people.

wd Ingmar Bergman *ph* Sven Nykvist *m* Karl-Birger Blomdahl

Harriet Andersson, Ake Grönberg, Hasse Ekman, Annika Tretow

'One of the extremely rare instances of a film's elements all blending perfectly.' – *John Simon*

The Saxon Charm

US 1948 88m bw
Universal (Joseph Sistrom)

A Broadway impresario dominates the lives of those around him.

Rather heavy-going comedy drama which could have done with more malicious wit; allegedly based on Jed Harris.

wd Claude Binyon *novel* Frederick Wakeman *ph* Milton Krasner *m* Walter Scharf

Robert Montgomery, Susan Hayward, John Payne, Audrey Totter, Henry Morgan, Harry von Zell, Cara Williams, Chill Wills, Heather Angel

Say Anything . . . *

US 1989 100m DeLuxe
TCF (Polly Platt)
V, V*, L, S

A student whose ambition it is to become a kick-boxer dates a beautiful and brainy girl, to the distress of her father.

Better than average teenage romance, deft and sometimes witty.

wd Cameron Crowe *ph* Laszlo Kovacs *m* Richard Gibbs, Anne Dudley, Nancy Wilson *pd* Mark Mansbridge *ed* Richard Marks

John Cusack, Ione Skye, John Mahoney, Lili Taylor, Amy Brooks, Pamela Segall, Jason Gould, Joan Cusack, Lois Chiles

'One of the best films of 1989 – a film that is really about something, that cares deeply about the issues it contains – and yet it also works wonderfully as a funny, warmhearted romantic comedy.' – *Roger Ebert*

'My husband has a memory that you can never share – he can remember me when I was nineteen'

Say Hello to Yesterday

GB 1970 92m Eastmancolor
Josef Shaftel (William Hill)
V*

A middle-aged married woman goes to London for shopping and is pursued by a strange young man whom she allows to seduce her.

Unattractive 'with it' romantic drama with a swinging London setting, a long way after *Brief Encounter*.

w Alvin Rakoff, Peter King *d* Alvin Rakoff *ph* Geoffrey Unsworth *m* Riz Ortolani

Jean Simmons, Leonard Whiting, *Evelyn Laye*, John Lee, Jack Woolgar

Say It in French

US 1938 67m bw
Paramount

A golf champion marries a French girl, but on his return, in order to help his father's finances, has to pretend to be marrying a rich girl, so his wife pretends to be a maid.

Thin comedy which has a job to sustain its short running time.

w Frederick Jackson *play* Jacques Deval *d* Andrew L. Stone

Ray Milland, Olympe Bradna, Irene Hervey, Janet Beecher, Mary Carlisle, Holmes Herbert, Erik Rhodes

'The harder it strives for hare-brained badinage, the more laboured it becomes.' – *Variety*

Say It with Flowers (A Human Story) *

GB 1934 bw
Real Art (Julius Hagen)

Traders in a London street market rally round when a flower-seller becomes too ill to work.

A mix of music-hall jokes and a documentary on cockney life which, for all its caricatures, reveals more about the everyday life of its time than many more ambitious films. It has not only acquired the fascination of a social document but also gives a rare glimpse of several music-hall performers: Charles Coburn (singing 'The Man Who Broke the Bank at Monte Carlo'), Marie Kendall (singing 'Did Your First Wife Ever Do That?' and 'Just Like the Ivy'), and Florrie Forde (reprising her hits 'Lassie from

Lancashire', 'Has Anybody Here Seen Kelly?', 'Hold Your Hand Out Naughty Boy', 'Oh, Oh Antonio' and 'Down at the Old Bull and Bush').

w H. Fowler Mear *story* William Orton *d* John Baxter *ph* Sydney Blythe *md* Colin Wark *ad* James A. Carter *ed* Michael C. Chorlton

Mary Clare, Ben Field, George Carney, Mark Daly, Edgar Driver, Freddie Watts, Edwin Ellis, Wilson Coleman

Say It with Songs

US 1929 89m bw
Warner

A radio singer accidentally kills a man and is jailed for manslaughter.

Miscalculated star vehicle with a few good moments among the sentiment and melodrama.

w Darryl F. Zanuck, Joseph Jackson, Harvey Gates *d* Lloyd Bacon *ph* Lee Garmes

Al Jolson, Davey Lee, Marian Nixon, Fred Kohler, Holmes Herbert

† Though Jolson was paid half a million dollars to do it, the film was a tremendous flop. The songs were again by De Sylva, Brown and Henderson, but 'Little Pal' was not another 'Sonny Boy'.

Say One for Me

US 1959 117m DeLuxe Cinemascope
TCF/Bing Crosby (Frank Tashlin)

Adventures of a parish priest in New York's theatrical quarter.

Unconvincing, unattractive imitation of *Going My Way* which counters bad taste with religiosity.

w Robert O'Brien *d* Frank Tashlin *ph* Leo Tover *songs* Sammy Cahn, James Van Heusen *md* Lionel Newman

Bing Crosby, Robert Wagner, Debbie Reynolds, Ray Walston, Les Tremayne, Connie Gilchrist, Frank McHugh, Joe Besser, Sebastian Cabot

'Tasteless and disturbing.' – *Variety*

AAN: Lionel Newman

'I am not allowed to love. But I will love you if that is your desire!'

Sayonara **

US 1957 147m Technirama
Goetz Pictures-Pennebaker (William Goetz)
V, V*, L

An American air force major in Tokyo after the war falls in love with a Japanese actress.

A lush travelogue interrupted by two romances, one tragic and one happy. A great success at the time, though mainly of interest to Americans; now vaguely dated.

w Paul Osborn *novel* James A. Michener *d* Joshua Logan *ph* Ellsworth Fredericks *m* Franz Waxman *ad* Ted Haworth *ed* Arthur P. Schmidt, Philip W. Anderson

Marlon Brando, Miyoshi Umeki, Miiko Taka, Red Buttons, Ricardo Montalban, Patricia Owens, Kent Smith, Martha Scott, James Garner

AA: Miyoshi Umeki; Red Buttons; art direction

AAN: best picture; Paul Osborn; Joshua Logan; Ellsworth Fredericks; Marlon Brando; editing

Scalawag

US/Italy 1973 93m Technicolor
Bryna/Inex-Oceania (Anne Douglas)

Mexico 1840: a one-legged pirate and a boy try to trace a hidden treasure.

Flagrant reworking of *Treasure Island*, heavily overdone by stars and rhubarbing extras alike.

w Albert Maltz, Sid Fleischman *d* Kirk Douglas *ph* Jack Cardiff *m* John Cameron

Kirk Douglas, Mark Lester, Neville Brand, David Stroud, Lesley-Anne Down, Phil Brown

The Scalphunters *

US 1968 102m DeLuxe Panavision
UA/Bristol/Norlan (Levy-Gardner-Laven)
V

An old cowboy and a black ex-slave track down a gang who kill Indians for their scalps.

Vigorous, aimless, likeable comedy Western with the emphasis on brawling.

w William Norton d Sydney Pollack ph Duke Callaghan, Richard Moore m Elmer Bernstein

Burt Lancaster, Ossie Davis, Telly Savalas, Shelley Winters, Nick Cravat, Paul Picerni

'It is the sort of frolic where bodies litter the ground, but you know they'll get up and draw their pay. And where even a villain can crack a joke without losing face.' – Robert Ottaway

Scandal *

GB 1988 115m Fujicolor
Palace/Miramax/British Screen (Stephen Woolley)
V, V*, L

A showgirl's sexual relationships with a leading British politician and a Russian diplomat cause a major upset.

Leaden account of the British scandal of the 1960s involving Christine Keeler, osteopath Stephen Ward and John Profumo, a Conservative Minister.

w Michael Thomas d Michael Caton-Jones
ph Mike Molloy m Carl Davis pd Simon Holland
ed Angus Newton

John Hurt, Joanne Whalley-Kilmer, Ian McKellen, Bridget Fonda, Leslie Phillips, Britt Ekland, Daniel Massey, Roland Gift, Jeroen Krabbé

Scandal at Scourie

US 1953 90m Metrocolor
MGM (Edwin H. Knopf)

The wife of the Protestant reeve of a Scottish-Canadian Protestant community adopts a Catholic child.

Sentimental whimsy with no holds barred, but with rather jaded acting and production.

w Norman Corwin, Leonard Spigelgass, Karl Tunberg d Jean Negulesco ph Robert Planck
m Daniele Amfitheatrof

Greer Garson, Walter Pidgeon, Agnes Moorehead, Arthur Shields, Philip Ober, Donna Corcoran

A Scandal in Paris *

US 1946 100m bw
UA/Arnold Pressburger
aka: Thieves' Holiday

Adventures of Vidocq, a 19th-century rogue who became Paris chief of police.

The actors look uneasy in their costumes, and the sets are cardboard, but there is fun to be had from this light comedy-drama.

w Ellis St Joseph d Douglas Sirk ph Guy Roe
m Hanns Eisler

George Sanders, Signe Hasso, Carole Landis, Akim Tamiroff, Gene Lockhart

Scandal Sheet

US 1931 77m bw
Paramount

A newspaper editor with principles prints scandal involving his wife.

Dated star drama.

w Vincent Lawrence, Max Marcin d John Cromwell

George Bancroft, Kay Francis, Regis Toomey, Clive Brook

Scandal Sheet

US 1939 67m bw
Columbia

A ruthless publisher sacrifices himself to save his son.

Uninteresting star quickie.

w Joseph Carole d Nick Grinde

Otto Kruger, Ona Munson, Edward Norris

Scandal Sheet

US 1952 81m bw
Columbia (Edward Small)
GB title: The Dark Page

An editor has to allow his star reporter to expose a murderer – himself.

Obvious, reasonably holding melodrama with familiar characters.

w Ted Sherdeman, Eugene Ling, James Poe
novel Samuel Fuller d Phil Karlson ph Burnett Guffey m George Duning

Broderick Crawford, John Derek, Donna Reed, Rosemary de Camp, Henry O'Neill, Henry Morgan

Scandal Street

US 1937 63m bw
Paramount

The arrival in a small town of an innocent young girl causes gossip which leads to murder.

Satisfactory mini-drama for the easily pleased.

w Bertram Millhauser, Eddie Welch story Vera Caspary d James Hogan

Lew Ayres, Louise Campbell, Roscoe Karns, Porter Hall, Virginia Weidler, Edgar Kennedy, Elizabeth Patterson

'A curiously beguiling little hodge-podge.' – Variety

Le Scandale: see The Champagne Murders

Scandalous!

GB 1984 92m Technicolor
Hemdale/Raleigh/Angeles Cinema Investors (Arlene Sellers, Alex Winitsky)

A TV reporter becomes involved with two con artists, who seem to have some connection with the murder of his wife.

Frantic black comedy which never even begins to be funny.

w Rob Cohen, John Byrum d Rob Cohen ph Jack Cardiff m Dave Grusin pd Peter Mullins

Robert Hays, John Gielgud, Pamela Stephenson, M. Emmet Walsh, Nancy Wood, Jim Dale

Scandalous John

US 1971 117m Technicolor
Walt Disney (Bill Walsh)
V*

The elderly owner of a derelict ranch resists all efforts to close him up.

Unsatisfactory Disney attempt to capture a more adult audience than usual; overlong, repetitious and dreary.

w Bill Walsh, Don da Gradi novel Richard Gardner
d Robert Butler ph Frank Phillips m Rod McKuen

Brian Keith, Alfonso Arau, Michele Carey, Rick Lenz, Henry Morgan, Simon Oakland

'Their thoughts can kill!'
Scanners

Canada 1980 103m Eastmancolor
Filmplan International (Claude Heroux)
V, V*, L, S

Certain people are found to be telepathic 'scanners' able to lock at will into other people's nervous systems. This has the occasional result of blowing apart the other people's heads.

Overlong science fiction which concentrates on the nastier elements.

wd David Cronenberg ph Mark Irwin m Howard Shore

Jennifer O'Neill, Patrick McGoohan, Stephen Lack, Lawrence Dane, Michael Ironside

Scanners II: The New Order

Canada 1991 104m colour
Malofilm (René Malo)
V, V*

A corrupt police chief attempts to use people with frightening telepathic powers for his own ends.

Effective sequel with several exploding heads.

w B. J. Nelson d Christian Duguay ph Rodney Gibbons m Marty Simon pd Richard Tassé
sp Michael Smithson ed Yves Langlois

David Hewlett, Yvan Ponton, Deborah Raffin, Isabelle Majias, Raoul Trujillo, Tom Bulter, Vlasta Vrana

'A first class imitation of the mind-blowing original.' – Variety

Scanners III: The Takeover

Canada 1992 101m colour
Republic/Malofilm (Rene Malo)
V*

An experimental drug turns a female scanner into a power-hungry killer.

The intriguing notion of the first film has now become an excuse for a horror movie indistinguishable from, and no more distinguished than, a hundred others.

w B. J. Nelson, Julie Richard, David Preston, Christian Duguay d Christian Duguay ph Hughes de Haeck m Marty Simon pd Michael Joy
sp Mike Maddi ed Yves Langlois

Liliana Komorowska, Valerie Valois, Steve Parrish, Collin Fox, Daniel Pilon, Michel Perron, Harry Hill

'A technically slick, relatively mindless thriller.' – Variety

The Scapegoat *

GB 1959 92m bw
MGM/Du Maurier-Guinness (Dennis Van Thal)

A quiet bachelor on a French holiday is tricked into assuming the identity of a lookalike aristocrat who wants to commit a murder.

Disappointing adaptation of a good story, with much evidence of re-cutting and an especially slack middle section.

w Gore Vidal, Robert Hamer novel Daphne du Maurier d Robert Hamer ph Paul Beeson
m Bronislau Kaper

Alec Guinness, Bette Davis, Irene Worth, Nicole Maurey, Pamela Brown, Geoffrey Keen

The Scar

US 1948 83m bw
Eagle-Lion (Bryan Foy, Paul Henreid)
V*
aka: Hollow Triumph

A fugitive kills his psychoanalyst double and takes his place, but is caught for the double's crimes.

Cheap suspense thriller with no suspense and no surprises.

w Daniel Fuchs novel Murray Forbes d Steve Sekely ph John Alton m Sol Kaplan

Joan Bennett, Paul Henreid, Eduard Franz, Leslie Brooks, John Qualen, Mabel Paige, Herbert Rudley

Scaramouche **

US 1952 115m Technicolor
MGM (Carey Wilson)
V*, L

A young man disguises himself as an actor to avenge

the death of his friend at the hands of a wicked marquis.

Cheerful swashbuckler set in French revolutionary times, first filmed in the twenties with Ramon Novarro. MGM costume production at somewhere near its best.

w Ronald Millar, George Froeschel   *novel* Rafael Sabatini   *d* George Sidney   *ph* Charles Rosher   *m* Victor Young   *ad* Cedric Gibbons, Hans Peters

Stewart Granger, Mel Ferrer, Eleanor Parker, Janet Leigh, Henry Wilcoxon, Nina Foch, Lewis Stone, Robert Coote, Richard Anderson

† The sword fight, at 6½ minutes, is credited with being the longest in cinema history.

Scarecrow *
US   1973   112m   Technicolor   Panavision
Warner (Robert M. Sherman)

Two of the world's losers hitch-hike across America.

Well-shot but eventually dreary parable of friendship, a pedestrian *Easy Rider.*

w Garry Michael White   *d* Jerry Schatzberg   *ph* Vilmos Zsigmond   *m* Fred Myrow

Gene Hackman, Al Pacino

'Here's a picture that manages to abuse two American myths at once – the Road and the Male Pair.' – *Stanley Kauffmann*

The Scarecrow *
New Zealand   1981   88m   colour
Oasis/New Zealand National Film Unit (Rob Whitehouse)
V, V*

In a small town in the early fifties, a strange chain of events is set in motion by the disappearance of six chickens.

A curious mix of sinister atmosphere which seems mystical and sinister events which are all too real. Interesting but unsatisfying, both as a murder mystery and as a study in evil.

w Michael Heath, Sam Pilsbury   *novel* Ronald Hugh Morrieson   *d* Sam Pilsbury   *ph* James Bartle   *m* Schtung

John Carradine, Tracy Mann, Jonathan Smith, Daniel McLaren, Denise O'Connell, Anne Flannery

Scared Stiff
US   1945   65m   bw
Pine-Thomas/Paramount
V*

A timid reporter stumbles over a murder on a bus and finds the culprit before the sheriff arrives.

Tedious comedy mystery.

w Geoffrey Homes and Maxwell Shane   *d* Frank McDonald

Jack Haley, Ann Savage, Barton MacLane, Veda Ann Borg, George E. Stone, Lucien Littlefield

'They're making a spook-tacle of themselves!'
Scared Stiff
US   1953   108m   bw
Paramount (Hal B. Wallis)
V*

Night-club entertainers get involved with a girl who has inherited a spooky castle off the Cuban coast.

Stretched-out remake of *The Ghost Breakers;* the last half hour, being closest to the original, is the most nearly funny.

w Herbert Baker, Walter de Leon   *d* George Marshall, Ed Simmons, Norman Lear   *ph* Ernest Laszlo   *md* Joseph J. Lilley

Dean Martin, Jerry Lewis, Lizabeth Scott, Carmen Miranda, George Dolenz, Dorothy Malone, William Ching, Jack Lambert

The Scarf
US   1951   86m   bw
UA/Gloria (I. G. Goldsmith)

A man escapes from a lunatic asylum and proves himself innocent of the crime for which he was committed.

Glum and pretentious murder mystery with a pictorial style to match its flowery dialogue.

wd E. A. Dupont   *ph* Franz Planer   *m* Herschel Burke Gilbert

John Ireland, Mercedes McCambridge, Emlyn Williams, James Barton, Lloyd Gough, Basil Ruysdael

'I'm going to run the whole works. There's only one law: do it first, do it yourself, and keep doing it!'
Scarface ****
US   1932   99m   bw
Howard Hughes
V, V*, L
aka: *The Shame of a Nation*

The life and death of a Chicago gangster of the twenties.

Obviously modelled on Al Capone, with an incestuous sister thrown in, this was perhaps the most vivid film of the gangster cycle, and its revelling in its own sins was not obscured by the subtitle, *The Shame of a Nation.*

w Ben Hecht, Seton I. Miller, John Lee Mahin, W. R. Burnett, Fred Pasley   *novel* Armitage Traill   *d* Howard Hawks   *ph* Lee Garmes, L. W. O'Connell   *m* Adolph Tandler, Gus Arnheim

Paul Muni, Ann Dvorak, George Raft, Boris Karloff, Osgood Perkins, Karen Morley, C. Henry Gordon, Vince Barnett, Henry Armetta, Edwin Maxwell

'Presumably the last of the gangster films, on a promise, it is going to make people sorry that there won't be any more. Should draw wherever it can play.' – *Variety*

'More brutal, more cruel, more wholesale than any of its predecessors.' – *James Shelley Hamilton*

'Because it was so close to the actual events, it possesses a kind of newsreel quality which cannot be recaptured or imitated. It vibrates with the impact of things that were real and deeply felt.' – *National Film Theatre programme, 1961*

† On original release added scenes showed Tony tried, convicted and hanged, though since Muni is never seen, it appears that they were an afterthought made when he was not available.

Scarface
US   1983   170m   Technicolor   Panavision
Universal (Martin Bregman)
V, V*, L

Absurdly brutalized version of the above, with detailed violence and a superabundance of foul language. Scarface has now become an emigré Cuban, and the film seems to want to make a political statement.

w Oliver Stone   *d* Brian de Palma   *ph* John A. Alonzo   *m* Giorgio Moroder

Al Pacino, Steven Bauer, Michelle Pfeiffer, Mary Elizabeth Mastrantonio, Robert Loggia, Paul Shenar, Harris Yulin

The Scarface Mob *
US   1958   96m   bw
Desilu (Quinn Martin)
V*

Al Capone's empire thrives while he is in Alcatraz, and prohibition agent Eliot Ness recruits a tough squad to fight the gangsters.

Though released theatrically, this was in effect a pilot film for the successful TV series *The Untouchables,* well enough done within its limits.

w Paul Monash   *novel* *The Untouchables* by Eliot Ness   *d* Phil Karlson   *ph* Charles Straumer   *m* Wilbur Hatch

Robert Stack, Neville Brand, Keenan Wynn, Barbara Nichols, Joe Mantell, Pat Crowley, Bruce Gordon, Paul Picerni, Abel Fernandez

Scarlet and Black: see *Le Rouge et le Noir*

Scarlet Angel
US   1952   81m   Technicolor
U-I (Leonard Goldstein)

A saloon hostess presents herself to a wealthy family as their dead son's wife.

Modest, satisfactorily plotted picture with action interludes.

w Oscar Brodney   *d* Sidney Salkow   *ph* Russell Metty   *m* Joseph Gershenson

Yvonne de Carlo, Rock Hudson, Richard Denning, Henry O'Neill, Amanda Blake

The Scarlet Blade *
GB   1963   82m   Technicolor   Hammerscope
Hammer (Anthony Nelson-Keys)
US title: *The Crimson Blade*

In 1648, a Cromwellian colonel plans to hang every royalist rebel.

Adequate swashbuckler.

wd John Gilling   *ph* Jack Asher   *m* Gary Hughes   *pd* Bernard Robinson   *ed* John Dunsford

Lionel Jeffries, Oliver Reed, Jack Hedley, June Thorburn, Duncan Lamont

The Scarlet Buccaneer: see *Swashbuckler*

The Scarlet Claw **
US   1944   74m   bw
Universal (Roy William Neill)
V, V*

Grisly revenge murders take place in the fog-bound Canadian village of Le Mort Rouge.

Possibly the best of the modernized Sherlock Holmes series, with a plot hastily borrowed from *The Hound of the Baskervilles.*

w Edmund L. Hartmann, Roy William Neill   *d* Roy William Neill   *ph* George Robinson   *md* Paul Sawtell   *m* Hans Salter

Basil Rathbone, Nigel Bruce, Miles Mander, Gerald Hamer, Paul Cavanagh, Kay Harding, Arthur Hohl

The Scarlet Coat
US   1955   99m   Eastmancolor   Cinemascope
MGM (Nicholas Nayfack)

During the American War of Independence, an American officer deserts to the British in order to unmask a traitor.

Rather talky historical actioner with too much time spent on friendship and romance.

w Karl Tunberg   *d* John Sturges   *ph* Paul C. Vogel   *m* Conrad Salinger

Cornel Wilde, Michael Wilding, George Sanders, Anne Francis, Robert Douglas, Bobby Driscoll, John McIntire

Scarlet Dawn *
US   1932   76m   bw
Warner (Hal Wallis)

During the Russian revolution, an exiled aristocrat loves a serving maid.

Heavy-going romantic drama distinguished by stylish direction and sets.

w Niven Busch, Erwin Gelsey, Douglas Fairbanks Jnr   *novel* *Revolt* by Mary McCall Jnr   *d* William Dieterle   *ph* Ernest Haller   *ad* Anton Grot

Douglas Fairbanks Jnr, Nancy Carroll, Lilyan
Tashman, Guy Kibbee, Sheila Terry, Frank Reicher

'The story starts off to get somewhere but fails to
arrive.' – *Variety*

'Based on a private diary of Catherine the Great!'
'The screen's reigning beauty in a wild pageant of barbaric
splendour!'
'A cavalcade of fury led by a woman of fire!'

The Scarlet Empress ***
US   1934   109m   bw
Paramount

A fantasia on the love life of Catherine the Great.

A marvellous, overwhelming, dramatically
insubstantial but pictorially brilliant homage to a star;
not to everyone's taste, but a film to remember.

w Manuel Komroff   d Josef von Sternberg   ph Bert
Glennon   md W. Franke Harling, John M. Leipold,
Milan Roder   ad Hans Dreier, Peter Ballbusch, Richard
Kollorsz   costumes Travis Banton

Marlene Dietrich, John Lodge, Sam Jaffe, Louise Dresser,
C. Aubrey Smith, Gavin Gordon, Jameson Thomas

'She's photographed behind veils and fishnets, while
dwarfs slither about and bells ring and everybody
tries to look degenerate.' – *New Yorker, 1975*

'A ponderous, strangely beautiful, lengthy and
frequently wearying production.' – *Mordaunt Hall, New
York Times*

The Scarlet Horseman
US   1946   bw   serial: 13 eps
Universal

An undercover agent assumes the identity of The
Scarlet Horseman in order to identify gun smugglers.

Adequate Western serial.

d Ray Taylor, Lewis Collins

Peter Cookson, Paul Guilfoyle, Virginia Christine,
Victoria Horne

The Scarlet Hour
US   1955   93m   bw   Vistavision
Paramount (Michael Curtiz)

A bored wife persuades her lover to turn thief; her
husband misconstrues the situation and is
accidentally killed.

Complex suspenser designed to introduce new talent;
rather too smooth, and pretty boring.

w Rip van Ronkel, Frank Tashlin, Meredyth Lucas
d Michael Curtiz   ph Lionel Lindon   m Leith
Stevens

Carol Ohmart, Tom Tryon, James Gregory, Jody
Lawrance, E. G. Marshall, Elaine Stritch

The Scarlet Letter *
US   1926   90m (24 fps)   bw   silent
MGM/Jury

In Puritan New England, the mother of an illegitimate
child wears the scarlet A (for adulteress) for years
rather than reveal that her lover was the village priest.

Celebrated 17th-century melodrama, quite powerfully
made in the best silent tradition, but of little intrinsic
interest for modern audiences.

w Frances Marion   novel Nathaniel Hawthorne
d Victor Sjostrom   ph Henrik Sartov   ad Cedric
Gibbons

Lillian Gish, Lars Hanson, Karl Dane, Henry B.
Walthall

† Other versions include the following: US 1910, US
1911, US 1913, US 1917, US 1920, GB 1922, US 1934,
Germany 1971, US (TV) 1979.

The Scarlet Letter
US   1934   70m   bw
Darmour/Majestic
V*

A lightened version with an attempt at comedy relief.
Not in any way remarkable.

w Leonard Fields, David Silverstein   d Robert G.
Vignola

Colleen Moore, Hardie Albright, Henry B. Walthall,
William Farnum, Alan Hale

The Scarlet Pimpernel ***
GB   1934   98m   bw
London Films (Alexander Korda)
V*, L

In the early days of the French revolution, an
apparently foppish Englishman leads a daring band
in rescuing aristocrats from the guillotine.

First-class period adventure with a splendid and
much imitated plot, strong characters, humour and a
richly detailed historical background.

w Robert E. Sherwood, Sam Berman, Arthur
Wimperis, Lajos Biro   novel Baroness Orczy
d Harold Young   ph Harold Rosson   m Arthur
Benjamin

Leslie Howard, Merle Oberon, Raymond Massey, Nigel
Bruce, Bramwell Fletcher, Anthony Bushell, Joan
Gardner, Walter Rilla

'Excellent British import that will do business.' –
Variety

'One of the most romantic and durable of all
swashbucklers.' – *New Yorker, 1976*

'A triumph for the British film world.' – *Sunday Times*

† Some scenes were directed by Alexander Korda,
others by Rowland Brown.
†† The story was remade as *The Elusive Pimpernel* (qv)
and in 1982 in a TV version starring Anthony
Andrews. See also *The Return of the Scarlet Pimpernel.*

'I've been wanting to laugh in your face ever since I met
you. You're old and ugly and I'm sick of you – sick, sick,
sick!'

Scarlet Street **
US   1945   103m   bw
(Universal) Walter Wanger (Fritz Lang)
V*

A prostitute is murdered by her client and her pimp is
executed for the crime.

Daring but rather gloomy Hollywood melodrama, the
first in which a crime went unpunished (though the
culprit was shown suffering remorse). Interesting and
heavily Teutonic, but as entertainment not a patch on
the similar but lighter *The Woman in the Window*, which
the same team had made a year previously.

w Dudley Nichols   play La Chienne by George de la
Fouchardière (filmed by Jean Renoir in 1932)
d Fritz Lang   ph Milton Krasner   m Hans Salter
ad Alexander Golitzen

Edward G. Robinson, Joan Bennett, Dan Duryea, Jess
Barker, Margaret Lindsay, Rosalind Ivan, Samuel
S. Hinds, Arthur Loft

'The director unerringly chooses the right sound and
image to assault the spectator's sensibilities.' – *C. A.
Lejeune*

The Scarlet Thread
GB   1950   84m   bw
Nettlefold/Butcher

Jewel thieves take refuge in a Cambridge college.

Flabby melodrama featuring emergent young talent.

w A. R. Rawlinson   play A. R. Rawlinson and Moie
Charles   d Lewis Gilbert

Kathleen Byron, Laurence Harvey, Sidney Tafler,
Arthur Hill, Dora Bryan

Scars of Dracula
GB   1970   96m   Technicolor
Hammer/EMI (Aida Young)
V*, L

A young man on the run finds himself an unwitting
guest of Count Dracula.

Overpadded vampire saga, its few effective moments
stemming directly from the original novel.

w John Elder   d Roy Ward Baker   ph Moray Grant
m James Bernard   ad Scott MacGregor   ed James
Needs

Christopher Lee, Dennis Waterman, Christopher
Matthews, Jenny Hanley, Patrick Troughton, Michael
Gwynn, Bob Todd

Scattergood Baines
US   1941   69m   bw
RKO

The new owner of a small-town hardware store takes
an interest in his fellow men.

First of several second features featuring the exploits
of a likeable busybody.

w Michael L. Simmons, Edward T. Lowe
stories Clarence Budington Kelland   d Christy
Cabanne

Guy Kibbee, Carol Hughes, John Archer, Emma Dunn

† The succeeding episodes were as follows: *Scattergood
Pulls the Strings*, 1941; *Scattergood Meets Broadway*, 1941;
Scattergood Rides High, 1942; *Scattergood Survives a Murder*,
1942; *Cinderella Swings It*, 1943.

Scavenger Hunt
US   1979   116m   DeLuxe
TCF/Melvin Simon
V*

A rich man leaves a fortune to the member of his
family who can collect most of the useless objects in a
list provided.

Depressing cheapjack imitation of Kramer's *It's a Mad
Mad Mad Mad World*, which itself was not free from
fault.

w Steven A. Vail, Henry Harper   d Michael Schultz
ph Ken Lamkin   m Billy Goldenberg

Richard Benjamin, James Coco, Scatman Crothers,
Cloris Leachman, Cleavon Little, Roddy McDowall,
Robert Morley, Richard Mulligan, Tony Randall, Dirk
Benedict, Vincent Price

'Loud, obnoxious, and above all unfunny.' – *Variety*

Lo Sceicco Bianco: see The White Sheik

Scenes from a Mall
US   1990   87m   DuArt   Panavision
Warner/Touchstone/Silver Screen Partners IV (Paul Mazursky)
V, V*, L

Preparing to celebrate their sixteenth wedding
anniversary, a Los Angeles couple confess their recent
affairs while on a shopping spree.

An unsuccessful comic teaming in a wordy
celebration of conspicuous consumption.

w Roger L. Simon, Paul Mazursky   d Paul
Mazursky   ph Fred Murphy   m Marc Shaiman
pd Pato Guzman   ed Stuart Pappé

Bette Midler, Woody Allen, Bill Irwin, Daren
Firestone, Rebecca Nickels, Paul Mazursky

Scenes from the Class Struggle in Beverly
Hills
US   1989   103m   CFI
Rank/North Street Films/Cinecom Entertainment (Amir J. Malin,
Ira Deutchman)
V, V*, L

Two servants bet that they can seduce the other's
mistress, both of whom have sexual problems of their
own.

Bed-hopping black-tinged comedy that never goes
quite far enough to be funny.

w Bruce Wagner *story* Paul Bartel, Bruce Wagner *d* Paul Bartel *ph* Steven Fierberg *m* Stanley Myers *pd* Alex Tavoularis *ed* Alan Toomayan

Jacqueline Bisset, Ray Sharkey, Mary Woronov, Robert Beltran, Ed Begley Jnr, Wallace Shawn, Arnetia Walker, Paul Bartel, Paul Mazursky, Rebecca Schaeffer

'Col. Frank Slade has a very special plan for the weekend. It involves travel, women, good food, fine wine, the tango, chauffeured limousines and a loaded forty-five. And he's bringing Charlie along for the ride.'

Scent of a Woman *
US   1992   157m   DeLuxe
UIP/Universal/City Lights (Martin Brest)
V, V*, L, S

A blind former soldier shows a high-school student how to enjoy life.

Sentimental drama showcasing a flamboyant over-the-top performance from Pacino.

w Bo Goldman   *d* Martin Brest   *ph* Donald E. Thorin   *m* Thomas Newman   *pd* Angelo Graham   *ed* William Steinkamp

Al Pacino, Chris O'Donnell, James Rebhorn, Gabrielle Anwar, Philip S. Hoffman, Richard Venture

'Essentially a two-character piece that goes on nearly an hour too long, Martin Brest's latest boasts good writing, filmmaking and performances; but far too much of each.' – *Variety*

† The film was suggested by the Italian movie *Profumo di Donna*, directed in 1974 by Dino Risi from the novel *Il Buio e il Miele* by Giovanni Arpino.

AA: Al Pacino

AAN: Best picture; Martin Brest; Bo Goldman

'First they moved (1895)! Then they talked (1927)! Now they smell!'
Scent of Mystery *
US   1959   125m   Technicolor   Cinerama (70mm)
Cinerama/Mike Todd Jnr
aka: *Holiday in Spain*

An Englishman on holiday in Spain protects a mysterious girl.

More of a travelogue than a thriller, but worth a note as the cinema's first 'smellie'. A process called Smell-o-Vision released appropriate odours throughout the auditorium . . .

w William Rose   *d* Jack Cardiff   *ph* John von Kotze   *m* Mario Nascimbene

Denholm Elliott, Peter Lorre, Beverly Bentley, Paul Lukas, Liam Redmond, Leo McKern, Peter Arne, Mary Laura Wood, Elizabeth Taylor

† The first film to credit its providers of shoe polish.

The Scent of the Green Papaya **
France   1993   104m   colour
Artificial Eye/Lazennec/La Sept/Canal+
original title: *Mùi Du Du Xanh*

In Saigon in the 50s, a young village girl grows up as she works as a maid for a family where the mother struggles to bring up her sons in the absence of their father.

Gentle, well-observed domestic drama, crafted with care and visual style.

wd Tran Anh Hung   *ph* Benoît Delhomme   *m* Tiêt Ton-That   *ad* Alain Nègre   *ed* Nicole Dedieu, Jean-Pierre Roques

Yên-Khê Tran Nu, Man San Lu, Thi Lôc Truong, Anh Hoa Nguyen, Hoa Hôi Vuong, Ngoc Trung Tran

'Although visually more rigorous, Hung's movie in some ways recalls the early works of Indian helmer Satyajit Ray in its portrayal of childhood dreams and the invisible walls between kids and adults.' – *Variety*

'Marries nature and artifice, taking the graceful shape of an Oriental character that grows, like a cherry tree,

into ever larger meaning as pen-strokes are slowly added.' – *Kathleen Murphy, Film Comment*

AAN: best foreign film

Die Schaukel: see *The Swing*

'The List Is Life. The Man Was Real. The Story Is True.'
Schindler's List ****
US   1993   195m   bw/colour
Universal/Amblin (Steven Spielberg, Gerald R. Molen, Branko Lustig)
V, V*, L, S

During the Second World War, an Austrian businessman persuades the Nazis to let him use Jewish slave labour in his factory; and then, with the money he earns, bribes a brutal SS commandant to save 1,100 Jews from the concentration camps.

A brilliantly realized, fiercely controlled and restrained treatment of a true story, using monochrome photography for the most part to achieve a documentary feel; harsh and compassionate, it avoids sentimentality until the end. It marks not only a notable achievement, but Spielberg's coming of age as an adult film-maker.

w Steven Zaillian   *novel* Thomas Keneally   *d* Steven Spielberg   *ph* Janusz Kaminski   *m* John Williams   *pd* Allan Starski   *ed* Michael Kahn

Liam Neeson, Ben Kingsley, Ralph Fiennes, Caroline Goodall, Jonathan Sagalle, Embeth Davidtz, Malgosha Gebel, Shmulik Levy, Mark Ivanir

'Evinces an artistic rigor and unsentimental intelligence unlike anything the world's most successful filmmaker has demonstrated before.' – *Variety*

'The elevated downer of the decade.' – *Richard Corliss, Time*

'He captures images of experience that most of us thought we would never see represented adequately on the screen. This is by far the finest, fullest dramatic (i.e. nondocumentary) film ever made about the Holocaust.' – *Terrence Rafferty, New Yorker*

'Indiana Jones in the Cracow Ghetto.' – *Will Tremper, Die Welt*

AA: best film; Steven Spielberg; Steven Zaillian; Janusz Kaminski; Michael Kahn; John Williams; Allan Starski

AAN: Liam Neeson; Ralph Fiennes; costume design (Anna Biedrzycka-Sheppard); make-up

Schizo
GB   1976   109m   Technicolor
Columbia-Warner/Pete Walker
V, V*
aka: *Amok; Blood of the Undead*

A series of bloody murders result when a famous ice-skater announces that she is to be married.

An unsuccessful attempt at a slick and surprising thriller; the twist in the plot is obvious from the beginning.

w David McGillivray   *d* Pete Walker   *ph* Peter Jessop   *m* Stanley Myers   *ad* Chris Burke   *ed* Alan Brett

Lynne Frederick, John Leyton, Stephanie Beacham, John Fraser, Jack Watson, Queenie Watts, John McEnery, Colin Jeavons

'Deprived of any support from the script this time, Pete Walker's direction, all thump, scream and cut as shadows lurk and doorknobs turn – with each cliché heralded by a triumphant tremolo or bass boom from the score – reduces the whole thing to risible absurdity.' – *Tom Milne, MFB*

Die Schlangengrube und das Pendel: see *The Blood Demon*

School for Husbands
GB   1937   71m   bw
Wainwright (Richard Wainwright)

A romantic novelist annoys the husbands of his adoring fans.

Would-be champagne comedy which bubbles pretty well for most of its length.

w Frederick Jackson, Gordon Aherry, Austin Melford *play* Frederick Jackson   *d* Andrew Marton   *ph* Phil Tannura

Rex Harrison, Henry Kendall, Romney Brent, Diana Churchill, June Clyde

The School for Scandal
GB   1930   73m   Raycol Colour
Albion Film Syndicate

Two brothers have characters opposite to their appearances.

Doomed attempt to film the famous 18th-century comedy of manners.

w Jean Jay   *play* Richard Brinsley Sheridan   *d* Maurice Elvey

Madeleine Carroll, Basil Gill, Henry Hewitt, Ian Fleming

'Its value in the States looks like exactly nothing.' – *Variety*

School for Scoundrels *
GB   1960   94m   bw
ABP/Guardsman (Hal E. Chester)
V

A failure reports to the College of One-Upmanship and his life is transformed.

Amusing trifle, basically a series of sketches by familiar comic actors.

w Patricia Mayes, Hal E. Chester   *books* Stephen Potter   *d* Robert Hamer   *ph* Erwin Hillier   *m* John Addison

Ian Carmichael, Alastair Sim, Terry-Thomas, Janette Scott, Dennis Price, Peter Jones, Edward Chapman, John Le Mesurier

School for Secrets
GB   1946   108m   bw
Rank/Two Cities (George H. Brown, Peter Ustinov)
US title: *Secret Flight*

The boffins who invented radar find themselves in a little war action of their own.

An unsatisfactory entertainment which, with the best intentions, shuffles between arch comedy, character drama, war action and documentary, doing less than justice to any of these aspects.

wd Peter Ustinov   *ph* Jack Hildyard

Ralph Richardson, Raymond Huntley, Richard Attenborough, Marjorie Rhodes, John Laurie, Ernest Jay, David Tomlinson, Finlay Currie

School Ties *
US   1992   107m   DeLuxe
Paramount (Stanley R. Jaffe, Sherry Lansing)
V*, L, S

In the mid-1950s a Jewish boy conceals his religion when he wins a scholarship to an exclusive school rife with anti-Semitism.

A slickly directed, well-acted, moderately gripping drama.

w Dick Wolf, Darryl Ponicsan   *d* Robert Mandel   *ph* Freddie Francis   *m* Maurice Jarre   *pd* Jeannine Claudia Oppewall   *ed* Jerry Greenberg, Jacqueline Cambas

Brendan Fraser, Matt Damon, Chris O'Donnell, Randall Batinkoff, Andrew Lowery, Amy Locane, Ed Lauter

'Gives a multifaceted, nuanced look at the roots of prejudice and self-denial.' – *Variety*

Das Schreckliche Mädchen: see *The Nasty Girl*

Schtonk!
Germany 1992 111m colour
Artificial Eye/Bavarian Film/WDR (Gunter Rohrbach, Helmut Dietl)
V

A forger decides to fake Hitler's diaries to sell to a collector of Nazi memorabilia and enlists the aid of a journalist.

The heavy-handed farcical treatment of an hilarious true story provides little amusement, although it was a great success in its home country.

w Helmut Dietl, Ulrich Limmer   *d* Helmut Dietl
ph Xaver Schwarzenberger   *m* Konstantin Wecker
ad Götz Weidner, Benedikt Herforth   *ed* Tanja Schmidbauer

Götz George, Uwe Ochsenknecht, Christiane Hörbiger, Rolf Hoppe, Dagmar Manzel, Veronica Ferres, Rosemarie Fendel

'This crude, overacted account of the Hitler diaries scandal is largely of sociological interest, an occasion for sporadic chuckles rather than sustained laughter.' – *Philip French, Observer*

AAN: Foreign language film

Schweik's New Adventures
GB 1943 84m bw
Eden Films

An unassuming Czechoslovakian writer gently kids the Nazi occupiers and manages to save some of his friends from the concentration camp.

Curious English attempt to film a popular Czechoslovakian character; it made mildly effective wartime propaganda, though few went to see it.

w Karel Lamac and Con West   *novel* Jaroslav Hasek
d Karel Lamac

Lloyd Pearson, George Carney, Julien Mitchell, Richard Attenborough, Margaret McGrath

Schwestern oder die Balance des Glücks: see *Sisters or the Balance of Happiness*

Sciuscià: see *Shoeshine*

Scorchers
US 1991 82m colour
Rank/Goldcrest/FilmWorks (Morrie Eisenman, Richard Hellman)
V

In a sleazy bar, a prostitute sorts out a wife's marital problems while nearby a newly-wed couple have troubles of their own.

Risibly decadent movie, set in a town of misfits.

wd David Beaird   *play* David Beaird   *ph* Peter Deming   *m* Carter Burwell   *pd* Bill Eigenbrodt
ed David Garfield

Faye Dunaway, Denholm Elliott, James Earl Jones, Emily Lloyd, Jennifer Tilly, James Wilder, Anthony Geary, Leland Crooke, Luke Perry

'An uncomfortable mix of melodrama, sentimentality and failed farce.' – *Empire*

'When Scorpio wants you, there is nowhere to hide!'
Scorpio
US 1972 114m Technicolor
UA/Scimitar (Walter Mirisch)
V*

CIA agents doublecross each other.

Incredibly complex spy thriller in which it's difficult to know, or care, who's following whom. The brutalities, however, are capably staged.

w David W. Rintels, Gerald Wilson   *d* Michael Winner   *ph* Robert Paynter   *m* Jerry Fielding

Burt Lancaster, Alain Delon, Paul Scofield, John Colicos, Gayle Hunnicutt, J. D. Cannon

'Strictly zoom and thump.' – *Sight and Sound*

'Relying on moments of violence for effect, Winner directs with typically crass abandon.' – *Time Out, 1984*

Scorsese x 4: see *The Big Shave, ItalianAmerican, It's Not Just You Murray!, What's A Nice Girl Like You Doing in a Place Like This?*

Scotch on the Rocks: see *Laxdale Hall*

Scotland Yard
US 1941 68m bw
TCF (Sol M. Wurtzel)

The Nazis capture a London banker and use his double to turn funds over to them.

Outlandish spy melodrama which certainly keeps the interest.

w Samuel G. Engel, John Balderston   *play* Deniston Clift   *d* Norman Foster   *ph* Virgil Miller   *m* Emil Newman

Nancy Kelly, Edmund Gwenn, Henry Wilcoxon, John Loder, Melville Cooper, Gilbert Emery, Norma Varden

Scotland Yard Investigator
US 1945 68m bw
Republic (George Blair)

Frenchmen attempt to steal the Mona Lisa from its wartime home in the National Gallery.

Very passable programme filler with stalwart actors enjoying themselves.

w Randall Faye   *d* George Blair

Sir Aubrey Smith, Erich von Stroheim, Stephanie Bachelor, Forrester Harvey, Richard Fraser, Frederick Worlock

Scott of the Antarctic **
GB 1948 111m Technicolor
Ealing (Sidney Cole)
V, V*

After long preparation, Captain Scott sets off on his ill-fated 1912 expedition to the South Pole.

The stiff-upper-lip saga *par excellence*; inevitable knowledge of the end makes it pretty downbeat, and the actors can only be sincere; but the snowscapes, most of them artificial, are fine.

w Ivor Montagu, Walter Meade, Mary Hayley Bell
d Charles Frend   *ph* Geoffrey Unsworth, Jack Cardiff, Osmond Borradaile   *m* Ralph Vaughan Williams

John Mills, James Robertson Justice, Derek Bond, Harold Warrender, Reginald Beckwith, Kenneth More, James McKechnie, John Gregson

The Scoundrel **
US 1935 74m bw
Paramount (Ben Hecht, Charles MacArthur)

A famous writer dies; his ghost comes back to find the meaning of love.

Unique thirties supernatural melodrama with barbs of dated wit despatched by a splendid cast. Nonsense, but great nonsense.

wd Ben Hecht, Charles MacArthur   *ph* Lee Garmes
m George Antheil

Noël Coward, Alexander Woolcott, Julie Haydon, Stanley Ridges, Eduardo Ciannelli

'Good Hotel Algonquin literati stuff, but not for the Automat trade.' – *Variety*

'An unmistakable whiff from a gossip column world which tries hard to split the difference between an epigram and a wisecrack.' – *William Whitebait*

'Practically flawless drama. It's arty, but if this is art, let us have more of it.' – *Photoplay*

'An impudent work . . . but there are brains in it, and observation, and even a kind of stunted poetry.' – *Observer*

† Helen Hayes and Edna Ferber made cameo appearances.

AA: original story

Scouts to the Rescue
US 1939 bw serial: 12 eps
Universal

Eagle Scouts find buried treasure in a ghost town.

Juvenile serial.

d Ray Taylor and Alan James

Jackie Cooper, Frank Coghlan Jnr, Bill Cody Jnr, Vondell Darr, Edwin Stanley

Scram! *
US 1932 20m bw
Hal Roach
V

Two vagrants are ordered out of town but by a series of misadventures are found drunk with the judge's wife.

Generally sprightly star comedy culminating in a marathon laughing session.

w H. M. Walker   *d* Ray McCarey

Laurel and Hardy, Arthur Housman, Rychard Cramer, Vivien Oakland

Scream . . . and Die!
GB 1973 99m Eastmancolor
Variety/Blackwater (Diana Daubeney)
aka: *Psycho Sex Fiend*

A model fears that she may be murdered after witnessing an unidentifiable man in black stab a girl to death in a remote country mansion.

Trivial thriller that sets out to titillate, but fails miserably.

w Derek Ford   *d* Joseph Larraz (José Larraz)
ph Trevor Wrenn   *m* Terry Warr   *ad* John Hoesli
ed Roy Deverell

Andrea Allan, Karl Lanchbury, Maggie Walker, Peter Forbes-Robertson, Judy Matheson, Annabella Wood, Alex Leppard

'At heart just another sexploitation film posing as a thriller.' – *Tom Milne, MFB*

'Triple distilled horror . . . as powerful as a vat of boiling acid!'
Scream and Scream Again *
GB 1969 94m Eastmancolor
AIP/Amicus (Milton Subotsky)
V, V*

Murders are traced to superhuman composite beings created by a mad scientist.

Energetic and well-staged though rather humourless shocker.

w Christopher Wicking   *novel The Disorientated Man* by Peter Saxon   *d* Gordon Hessler   *ph* John Coquillon   *m* David Whittaker   *ad* Don Mingaye

Vincent Price, Christopher Lee, Peter Cushing, Alfred Marks, Anthony Newlands, David Lodge

Scream for Help
US 1984 90m colour
Miracle/Lorimar/Videoform (Michael Winner)

A teenager becomes convinced that her stepfather is trying to murder her mother.

Crude splatter movie which the director presumably undertook as a joke.

w Tom Holland   *d* Michael Winner   *ph* Robert Paynter, Dick Kratina   *m* Howard Blake   *ad* Tony Reading   *ed* Christopher Barnes

Rachael Kelly, David Brooks, Marie Masters, Rocco Sisto, Lolita Lorre

'Over the moronic characterization, daft dialogue, inept performances and opportunistic camerawork, music has been poured like a constant stream of cold gravy, making a sound that on occasion resembles, not inappropriately, a growling stomach.' – *Philip Strick, MFB*

A Scream in the Dark
US   1943   53m   bw
Republic (George Sherman)

A private eye tracks down a constant widow with a trail of dead husbands.

Lightweight mystery which might have been better.

w Gerald Schnitzer, Anthony Coldeway   *novel The Morgue Is Always Open* by Jerome Odlum   *d* George Sherman

Robert Lowery, Marie McDonald, Edward S. Brophy, Wally Vernon, Hobart Cavanaugh, Jack La Rue, Elizabeth Russell

Scream of Fear: see *Taste of Fear*

Scream of Stone *
Germany/France/Canada   1991   105m   colour
SERA/A2/Les Films Stock/ZDF/Canal Plus/Telefilm Canada/
   Lucky Red/RAI2 (Walter Saxer)

A young climber challenges an older one to tackle the most difficult mountain in the world in Patagonia.

Spectacular photography compensates for a muddled narrative about obsessive people.

w Hans-Ulrich Klenner, Walter Saxer   *story* Reinhold Messner   *d* Werner Herzog   *ph* Rainer Klausmann, Herbert Raditschnig   *m* Ingram Marshall, Alan Lamb   *pd* Juan Santiago   *ed* Suzanne Baron

Vittorio Mezzogiorno, Mathilda May, Stefan Glowacz, Brad Dourif, Donald Sutherland

'While it does feature some spectacular mountain photography in an area of the world few will ever see first-hand, the dramatic and psychological aspects remain so obscure as to become silly.' – *Variety*

The Screaming Dead: see *Dracula – Prisoner of Frankenstein*

Screaming Mimi
US   1958   79m   bw
Sage/Columbia

After being sexually assaulted a dancer comes to believe she has committed murder . . . and later we learn that she has.

Sub-Freudian melodrama on the comic strip level.

w Robert Blees   *book* Frederic Brown   *d* Gerd Oswald

Anita Ekberg, Phil Carey, Harry Townes, Gypsy Rose Lee, Romney Brent, Alan Gifford

Scrooge *
GB   1935   78m   bw
Twickenham (Julius Hagen, John Brahm)
V*

A miser reforms after ghosts haunt him on Christmas Eve.

Acceptable unambitious version with interesting performances.

w Seymour Hicks, H. Fowler Mear   *novel* Charles Dickens   *d* Henry Edwards   *ph* Sidney Blythe, William Luff

Seymour Hicks, Donald Calthrop (Cratchit), Athene Seyler, Oscar Asche, Barbara Everest, Maurice Evans, C. V. France, Marie Ney

Scrooge ***
GB   1951   86m   bw
Renown (Brian Desmond Hurst)
V, V*, L
US title: *A Christmas Carol*

By far the best available version of the classic parable; casting, art direction, pace and general handling are as good as can be.

w Noel Langley   *d* Brian Desmond Hurst   *ph* C. Pennington-Richards   *m* Richard Addinsell

Alastair Sim, Mervyn Johns, Kathleen Harrison, Jack Warner, Michael Hordern, Hermione Baddeley, George Cole, Miles Malleson

Scrooge *
GB   1970   113m   Technicolor   Panavision
Cinema Center/Waterbury (Robert H. Solo)
V, V*, L

Dim musical version, darkly coloured and quite lost on the wide screen; but it has its macabre moments of trick photography.

w/m/ly Leslie Bricusse   *d* Ronald Neame   *ph* Oswald Morris   *pd* Terry Marsh

Albert Finney, Michael Medwin, Alec Guinness, Edith Evans, Kenneth More, David Collings, Laurence Naismith, Kay Walsh

† Richard Harris and Rex Harrison were both sought before Finney was signed.

AAN: song 'Thank You Very Much' (*m/ly* Leslie Bricusse)

Scrooged *
US   1988   101m   Technicolor
Paramount/Mirage (Richard Donner, Art Linson)
V, V*, L

Updated version of Dickens's *A Christmas Carol*, centring on the president of a New York television company.

Energetic and sometimes genuinely scary seasonal entertainment for modern kids.

w Mitch Glazer, Michael O'Donoghue   *d* Richard Donner   *ph* Michael Chapman   *m* Danny Elfman   *pd* J. Michael Riva

Bill Murray, Karen Allen, John Forsythe, Robert Mitchum, John Housman, Lee Majors

Scrubbers
GB   1982   93m   Eastmancolor
Handmade (Don Boyd)
V*

Sensational events in a girls' borstal.

Wild-eyed melodrama which seems to serve no sort of purpose and is certainly not entertaining.

w Roy Minton, Jeremy Watt, Mai Zetterling   *d* Mai Zetterling   *ph* Ernest Vincze   *m* Michael Hurd

Amanda York, Chrissie Cotterill, Elizabeth Edmonds, Kate Ingram, Honey Bane, Eva Motley

Scudda Hoo, Scudda Hay
US   1948   98m   Technicolor
TCF (Walter Morosco)
GB title: *Summer Lightning*

A farmer's son is less interested in girls than in the welfare of his two mules.

Antediluvian rural romance for the simple-minded.

wd F. Hugh Herbert   *novel* George Agnew Chamberlain   *ph* Ernest Palmer   *m* Cyril Mockridge

June Haver, Lon McCallister, Walter Brennan, Anne Revere, Natalie Wood, Robert Karnes, Henry Hull, Tom Tully, Marilyn Monroe

Scum *
GB   1979   97m   Eastmancolor
GTO/Berwick Street Films (Clive Parsons, Davina Belling)
V, V*

Injustices in a Borstal institution lead to a riot.

Gorily overstated view of boys' prison life from the inside, with the camera gloating over each violent close-up. (The original TV play had been made, then banned, by the BBC.)

w Roy Minton   *d* Alan Clarke   *ph* Phil Meheux   *ad* Judith Lang   *ed* Mike Bradsell

Ray Winstone, Mick Ford, Julian Firth, John Blundell

The Sea Bat
US   1930   69m   bw
MGM

Mexican fishermen compete to kill a deadly sting-ray.

The *Jaws* of its time; box-office hokum.

w Bess Meredyth and John Howard Lawson   *d* Wesley Ruggles

Charles Bickford, Raquel Torres, Nils Asther, John Miljan, Gibson Gowland, Boris Karloff

The Sea Beast *
US   1926   125m approx   bw   silent
Warner

In this version of *Moby Dick*, Ahab gets to settle down at the end with his lady love.

Memorable sea scenes and a star performance.

w Bess Meredyth   *d* Millard Webb

John Barrymore, Dolores Costello, George O'Hara, Mike Donlin, Sam Baker

The Sea Chase *
US   1955   117m   Warnercolor   Cinemascope
Warner (John Farrow)
V*, L

In 1939 a German freighter tries to make it from Sydney harbour back to Germany.

Unusual but not very compelling naval melodrama, chiefly because the leads are miscast.

w James Warner Bellah, John Twist   *novel* Andrew Geer   *d* John Farrow   *ph* William Clothier   *m* Roy Webb

John Wayne, Lana Turner, David Farrar, Lyle Bettger, Tab Hunter, James Arness, Dick Davalos, John Qualen

'A film compounded of monotonously familiar ingredients.' – *Penelope Houston*

Sea Devils
US   1937   88m   bw
RKO
V*

Exploits of the ice patrols of the US Coast Guard.

Flagwaving action hokum for popular stars.

w Frank Wead, John Twist and P. J. Wolfson   *d* Ben Stoloff

Victor McLaglen, Preston Foster, Ida Lupino, Donald Woods

Sea Devils
GB   1953   90m   Technicolor
Coronado (David E. Rose)
V*

Spies prevent Napoleon's invasion of England.

Cheerful, forgettable swashbuckler.

w Borden Chase   *d* Raoul Walsh   *ph* Wilkie Cooper   *m* Richard Addinsell

Yvonne de Carlo, Rock Hudson, Maxwell Reed, Denis O'Dea, Michael Goodliffe, Bryan Forbes, Ivor Barnard, Arthur Wontner

Sea Fury

GB 1958 97m bw
Rank (Benjamin Fisz)

Rivalry strikes up between an old and a young sailor on tugboats plying between Spain and England.

Shapeless, leery melodrama with strong performances and an exciting storm-at-sea climax.

w John Kruse, Cy Endfield   d Cy Endfield   ph Reg Wyer   m Philip Green

Stanley Baker, Victor McLaglen, Luciana Paluzzi, Grégoire Aslan, Francis de Wolff, David Oxley, Rupert Davies, Robert Shaw

'They stand side by side. Young and old. Rich and poor. They gather together for a single purpose. Survival.'

The Sea Gull *

GB 1968 141m Technicolor
Warner/Sidney Lumet

Loves and hates on a 19th-century Russian estate.

Rather heavily star-studded, but certainly proficient film version of a Chekhov favourite.

w Moura Budberg   play Anton Chekhov   d Sidney Lumet   ph Gerry Fisher   m none   pd Tony Walton

James Mason, Simone Signoret, Vanessa Redgrave, David Warner, Harry Andrews, Ronald Radd, Eileen Herlie, Kathleen Widdoes, Denholm Elliott, Alfred Lynch

'The camera cannot capture the hollowness of space, the oppressive immovableness of a seemingly harmless enclosure, stasis settling on everything like a fine, corrosive dust.' – John Simon

'If you miss it, you will owe yourself an apology!'

The Sea Hawk ***

US 1940 122m bw
Warner (Hal B. Wallis, Henry Blanke)
V, V*, L, S

Elizabeth I encourages one of her most able captains to acts of piracy against the Spanish.

Wobbly-plotted but stirring and exciting seafaring actioner, with splendid battle and duel scenes.

w Seton I. Miller, Howard Koch   d Michael Curtiz   ph Sol Polito   m Erich Wolfgang Korngold   ad Anton Grot

Errol Flynn, Flora Robson, Brenda Marshall, Henry Daniell, Claude Rains, Donald Crisp, Alan Hale, Una O'Connor, James Stephenson, Gilbert Roland, William Lundigan

'Endless episodes of court intrigue tend to diminish the effect of the epic sweep of the high seas dramatics.' – Variety

AAN: Erich Wolfgang Korngold; Anton Grot

The Sea Hound

US 1947 bw serial: 15 eps
Columbia

The owner of a private schooner tracks down modern pirates in search of Spanish gold.

Tolerable adventure serial.

d Walter B. Eason, Mack Wright

Buster Crabbe, Jimmy Lloyd, Pamela Blake, Rick Vallin

'A man who loved as ruthlessly as he ruled. A woman whose indiscretions cost a lifetime of happiness!'

The Sea of Grass

US 1947 131m bw
MGM (Pandro S. Berman)

A cattle tycoon is so obsessed by his work that he alienates his family.

Brooding, overlong semi-Western with an unexpected cast.

w Marguerite Roberts, Vincent Lawrence   novel Conrad Richter   d Elia Kazan   ph Harry Stradling   m Herbert Stothart

Spencer Tracy, Katharine Hepburn, Melvyn Douglas, Phyllis Thaxter, Robert Walker, Edgar Buchanan, Harry Carey, Ruth Nelson, James Bell

'In spite of all the sincerity and talent involved, an epically dreary film.' – Time

Sea of Lost Ships

US 1953 85m bw
Republic

The US Coast Guard saves a passenger ship from an iceberg.

Scrappy, semi-documentary account punctuated by rough action highlights.

w Steve Fisher   d Joe Kane

Walter Brennan, John Derek, Wanda Hendrix, Richard Jaeckel, Barton MacLane, Darryl Hickman

Sea of Love **

US 1989 112m DeLuxe Panavision
Universal (Martin Bregman, Louis A. Stroller)
V, V*, L, S

A New York cop, suffering a mid-life crisis, falls in love with the chief suspect of a series of murders of men advertising in lonely hearts columns.

Effective urban thriller, though the emphasis is more on the romance than in discovering whodunnit.

w Richard Price   d Harold Becker   ph Ronnie Taylor   m Trevor Jones   pd John Jay Moore   ed David Bretherton

Al Pacino, Ellen Barkin, John Goodman, William Hickey, Michael Rooker, Richard Jenkins

Sea of Sand *

GB 1958 98m bw
Rank/Tempean (Robert Baker, Monty Berman)
V*
US title: Desert Patrol

Just before Alamein an Eighth Army desert group plans to destroy one of Rommel's last petrol dumps.

Good standard war suspenser.

w Robert Westerby   d Guy Green   ph Wilkie Cooper   m Clifton Parker

Richard Attenborough, John Gregson, Vincent Ball, Percy Herbert, Michael Craig, Barry Foster, Andrew Faulds, Dermot Walsh

Sea of Silence: see La Mer Cruelle

The Sea Shall Not Have Them

GB 1954 93m bw
Eros/Daniel M. Angel
V*

Survivors of a seaplane crash await rescue in a dinghy.

Rather dim computerized compendium of flashback mini-dramas.

w Lewis Gilbert, Vernon Harris   d Lewis Gilbert   ph Stephen Dade   m Malcolm Arnold

Dirk Bogarde, Michael Redgrave, Bonar Colleano, Jack Watling, Anthony Steel, Nigel Patrick, James Kenney, Sidney Tafler, George Rose

The Sea Wall: see This Angry Age

'One of the most challenging stories of faith ever told! What happened out there . . . in the surging vastness of the Indian Ocean?'

Sea Wife

GB 1957 82m DeLuxe Cinemascope
TCF/Sumar (André Hakim)
V, V*

Survivors of a shipwreck near Singapore in 1942 are rescued, not before the bosun has fallen in love with the only lady, not knowing she is a nun.

Flashbacked, uncertain, intermittently effective film of a popular minor novel.

w George K. Burke   novel Sea Wyf by J. M. Scott   d Bob McNaught   ph Ted Scaife   m Kenneth V. Jones, Leonard Salzedo

Richard Burton, Joan Collins, Basil Sydney, Cy Grant

The Sea Wolf **

US 1941 90m bw
Warner (Henry Blanke)
V, V*

Survivors of a ferry crash in San Francisco Bay are picked up by a psychopathic freighter captain who keeps them captive.

Much filmed action suspenser which in this version looks great but overdoes the talk.

w Robert Rossen   novel Jack London   d Michael Curtiz   ph Sol Polito   m Erich Wolfgang Korngold

Edward G. Robinson, Alexander Knox, Ida Lupino, John Garfield, Gene Lockhart, Barry Fitzgerald, Stanley Ridges, David Bruce, Howard da Silva

'A Germanic, powerful work almost devoid of compromise.' – Charles Higham, 1972

† Other versions appeared in 1913, with Hobart Bosworth; in 1920, with Noah Beery; in 1925, with Ralph Ince; in 1930, with Milton Sills; in 1950 (as Barricade, turned into a Western), with Raymond Massey; in 1958 (as Wolf Larsen), with Barry Sullivan; and in 1975 (Italian), as Wolf of the Seven Seas, with Chuck Connors.

The Sea Wolves *

GB/US/Switzerland 1980 122m Eastmancolor
Richmond-Lorimar-Varius (Euan Lloyd)
V, V*

In 1943, elderly British territorials living in India dispose of a Nazi transmitter in neutral Goa.

Mildly larkish Boy's Own Paper adventure with a somewhat geriatric air; an interesting 1980 throwback to the films of 1950.

w Reginald Rose   novel Boarding Party by James Leasor   d Andrew McLaglen   ph Tony Imi   m Roy Budd

Gregory Peck, Roger Moore, Trevor Howard, David Niven, Barbara Kellerman, Patrick MacNee, Patrick Allen, Bernard Archard, Faith Brook, Martin Benson, Allan Cuthbertson, Kenneth Griffith, Donald Houston, Glyn Houston, Percy Herbert, Patrick Holt, Terence Longdon, John Standing, Michael Medwin

'As a genre – the arterio-sclerotic war movie – it'll never catch on.' – Time Out

† The film was dedicated to Earl Mountbatten after his assassination.

Seagulls over Sorrento

GB 1954 92m bw
MGM (John Boulting)
US title: Crest of the Wave

Life on a naval research station on a small Scottish island.

A long-running British service comedy has been Americanized to little effect, but it remains just about watchable.

w Frank Harvey, Roy Boulting   play Hugh Hastings   d Roy Boulting   ph Gilbert Taylor   m Miklos Rozsa

Gene Kelly, John Justin, Bernard Lee, Sidney James, Jeff Richards, Patric Doonan, Patrick Barr

Seal Island: see The Living Desert

Sealed Lips: see After Tonight

'What is the truth about fraternization?'
Sealed Verdict
US   1948   83m   bw
Paramount (Robert Fellows)

An American officer in Germany falls in love with the ex-girlfriend of a Nazi war criminal.

Routine melodrama, as boring as it sounds.

w Jonathan Latimer   novel Lionel Shapiro
d Lewis Allen   ph Leo Tover   m Hugo Friedhofer

Ray Milland, Florence Marly, Broderick Crawford, John Hoyt, John Ridgely, Ludwig Donath

Seance on a Wet Afternoon *
GB   1964   121m   bw
Rank/Allied Film Makers (Richard Attenborough, Bryan Forbes, Jack Rix)
V*

A fake medium persuades her husband to kidnap a child so that she can become famous by revealing its whereabouts in a trance.

Overlong character melodrama in which the suspense is better than the psychopathology. A mannered performance from the lady, a false nose from the gentleman, and a general air of gloom.

wd Bryan Forbes   ph Gerry Turpin   m John Barry

Kim Stanley, Richard Attenborough, Nanette Newman, Patrick Magee

'Not only a psychological suspense thriller but also a top-notch crime-and-detection tale and, above all, a horror film.' – Judith Crist

AAN: Kim Stanley

The Search *
US/Switzerland   1948   105m   bw
MGM/Praesens Film (Lazar Wechsler)
V*

An American soldier in Germany cares for a war orphan.

Vivid semi-documentary post-war drama which falls down in its elementary dramatics but sent audiences home wiping away tears.

w Richard Schweizer, David Wechsler, Paul Jarrico
d Fred Zinnemann   ph Emil Berna   m Robert Blum

Montgomery Clift, Aline MacMahon, Ivan Jandl, Wendell Corey

'Far and away the most touching film we have seen for years.' – C. A. Lejeune

AA: original story (Richard Schweizer, David Wechsler); Ivan Jandl (special award for outstanding juvenile performance)

AAN: script; Fred Zinnemann; Montgomery Clift

'You never saw so many skins you'd like to touch!'
Search for Beauty
US   1934   77m   bw
Paramount

A physical culture magazine sponsors an international contest for beauties of both sexes.

Mildly amusing extravaganza staking its popularity on girls in bathing dress.

w Claude Binyon, Sam Hellman, Frank Butler and others   play Schuyler E. Gray and Paul R. Milton
d Erle C. Kenton

Larry Buster Crabbe, Ida Lupino, Toby Wing, James Gleason, Robert Armstrong, Gertrude Michael, Roscoe Karns

'A couple of years ago so many girls in abbreviated dress would have been enough for one picture . . . but they've seen massed pulchritude quite often lately, so the girls here are just trimmings.' – Variety

The Search for Bridey Murphy *
US   1956   84m   bw   Vistavision
Paramount (Pat Duggan)
V*

A Colorado businessman and amateur hypnotist finds a lady neighbour so good a subject that he is able to delve into her previous incarnation as a long-dead Irish peasant.

Adequately presented with alienation effects, but mainly consisting of two-shots and fuzzy flashbacks, this treatment of an actual case (subsequently discredited) works up to a fine pitch of frenzy when the subject seems unable to come back from her previous life.

wd Noel Langley,   book Morey Bernstein   ph John F. Warren   m Irving Talbot

Teresa Wright, Louis Hayward, Kenneth Tobey, Nancy Gates, Richard Anderson

'He had to find her . . . he had to find her . . .'
The Searchers ****
US   1956   119m   Technicolor   Vistavision
Warner/C. V. Whitney (Merian C. Cooper)
V, V (W), V*, L

A Confederate war veteran tracks down the Indians who have slaughtered his brother and sister-in-law and carried off their daughter.

Disturbing Western of obsession and racism which has become Ford's most influential film, in which Wayne gives his most ambiguous performance, being no longer a simple gung-ho hero, but a tormented loner out of step with his society. Its themes of loss and reconciliation are echoed in many films that followed.

w Frank S. Nugent   novel Alan le May   d John Ford
ph Winton C. Hoch   m Max Steiner

John Wayne, Jeffrey Hunter, Natalie Wood, Vera Miles, Ward Bond, John Qualen, Henry Brandon, Antonio Moreno

'You can read a lot into it, but it isn't very enjoyable.' – Pauline Kael, 70s

Searching for Bobby Fischer
US   1993   110m   DeLuxe
Paramount/Mirage (Scott Rudin, William Horberg)
GB title: Innocent Moves

A father discovers that his seven-year-old son is a chess prodigy.

An off-beat film that concentrates on the father–son relationship, although it does attempt the impossible of making chess games visually exciting and accessible to non-players.

wd Steven Zaillian   book Fred Waitzkin
ph Conrad L. Hall   m James Horner   pd David Gropman   ed Wayne Wahrman

Joe Mantegna, Max Pomeranc, Ben Kingsley, Joan Allen, Laurence Fishburne, Michael Nirenberg, Robert Stephens, David Paymer

'Earnest and well-acted.' – Variety

AAN: Conrad L. Hall

'What strange power could drive this man from the lips of the woman he married to the arms of the woman he loved?'
The Searching Wind *
US   1946   107m   bw
Paramount (Hal B. Wallis)

Affairs of an American diplomat in Europe during the thirties.

Earnest melodrama which would have been better timed six years earlier. Excellent production, though.

w Lillian Hellman   play Lillian Hellman
d William Dieterle   ph Lee Garmes   m Victor Young   ad Hans Drier, Franz Bachelin

Robert Young, Sylvia Sidney, Ann Richards, Douglas Dick, Dudley Digges, Albert Basserman, Dan Seymour

The Seashell and the Clergyman *
France   1928   30m approx (24 fps)   bw   silent
(Producer unknown)

A clergyman is afflicted by sexual torments.

Celebrated surrealist short with memorable images and a great deal of confusion.

w Antonin Artaud   d Germaine Dulac   ph Paul Guichard

Alix Allin

† In GB the film was banned by the censor with the famous comment: 'It is so cryptic as to have no apparent meaning. If there is a meaning, it is doubtless objectionable.'

Season of Passion: see Summer of the Seventeenth Doll

The Seaweed Children: see Malachi's Cove

Sebastian
GB   1968   100m   Eastmancolor
Paramount/Maccius (Herb Brodkin, Michael Powell)
V*

An Oxford professor and code expert is appointed to the secret service.

Mildly spoofy spy yarn: style but not much substance.

w Gerald Vaughan-Hughes   d David Greene
ph Gerry Fisher   m Jerry Goldsmith   pd Wilfred Shingleton

Dirk Bogarde, John Gielgud, Lilli Palmer, Susannah York, Janet Munro, Margaret Johnston, Nigel Davenport, Ronald Fraser

'One of the problems with this kind of movie is the enormous pressure put on the audience to have a good time over practically nothing.' – Renata Adler

Sebastiane *
GB   1976   86m   colour
Megalovision/Cinegate/Disctac (James Waley, Howard Malin)

Sebastian, a soldier and former favourite banished to a remote outpost by the Emperor Diocletian, is executed by his commander when he refuses his sexual advances.

Unusual semi-improvised feature in which the dialogue is in Latin with English subtitles. It was the first British film to deal openly with homosexual desire.

w Derek Jarman, James Waley   d Derek Jarman
Paul Humfress   ph Peter Middleton   m Brian Eno
pd Derek Jarman   ed Paul Humfress

Leonardo Treviglio, Barney James, Neil Kennedy, Richard Warwick, Donald Dunham, Ken Hicks, Lindsay Kemp

'The most promising sign of new film life in independent narrative cinema in this country in many, many years.' – Tony Rayns, MFB

Second Best Bed
GB   1938   74m   bw
Capitol

A magistrate is suspected of adultery.

Cheerful star comedy with a touch of sophistication.

w Ben Travers   d Tom Walls

Tom Walls, Jane Baxter, Veronica Rose, Carl Jaffe, Greta Gynt

The Second Best Secret Agent in the Whole Wide World: see Licensed to Kill

Second Chance

US 1953 82m Technicolor 3-D
RKO (Edmund Grainger)
V*, L

In South America, a professional killer stalks a gangster's moll.

Comic strip antics with a climax on a stalled cable car.

w Oscar Millard, Sidney Boehm story D. M. Marshman Jnr d Rudolph Maté ph William Snyder m Roy Webb

Robert Mitchum, Linda Darnell, Jack Palance, Reginald Sheffield, Roy Roberts

Second Chorus

US 1940 84m bw
Paramount (Boris Morros)
V, V*, L

Two trumpeters and their lady manager hit Broadway.

Mild musical.

w Elaine Ryan, Ian McClellan Hunter, Frank Cavett d H. C. Potter ph Theodor Sparkuhl songs various m Artie Shaw

Fred Astaire, Burgess Meredith, Paulette Goddard, Charles Butterworth, Artie Shaw and his Band, Frank Melton, Jimmy Conlon

AAN: Artie Shaw; song 'Love of my Life' (m Artie Shaw, ly Johnny Mercer)

Second Fiddle

US 1939 86m bw
TCF (Gene Markey)
V*

A Minnesota skating schoolteacher goes to Hollywood and becomes a star.

Routine star vehicle.

w Harry Tugend d Sidney Lanfield ph Leon Shamroy md Louis Silvers songs Irving Berlin

Sonja Henie, Tyrone Power, Edna May Oliver, Rudy Vallee, Mary Healy, Lyle Talbot, Alan Dinehart

AAN: song 'I Poured My Heart into a Song' (m/y Irving Berlin)

The Second-Floor Mystery

US 1930 56m bw
Warner

Correspondents through an agony column find themselves enmeshed in mystery and murder.

Burlesque whodunnit which seemed a smart trick at the time.

w Joseph Jackson novel The Agony Column by Earl Derr Biggers d Roy del Ruth

Loretta Young, Grant Withers, H. B. Warner, Clare McDowell, John Loder

The Second Greatest Sex

US 1955 87m Technicolor Cinemascope
U-I (Albert J. Cohen)

Western women emulate Lysistrata to stop their men from feuding.

Flat attempt to cash in on Seven Brides for Seven Brothers; some good acrobatic dancing but no style.

w Charles Hoffman d George Marshall ph Wilfrid M. Cline md Joseph Gershenson ch Lee Scott

Jeanne Crain, George Nader, Bert Lahr, Kitty Kallen, Paul Gilbert, Keith Andes, Mamie Van Doren, Tommy Rall

Second Honeymoon

US 1937 79m bw
TCF (Raymond Griffith)

A man tries to win back his ex-wife.

Moderate star romantic comedy.

w Kathryn Scola, Darrell Ware story Philip Wylie d Walter Lang ph Ernest Palmer m David Buttolph

Tyrone Power, Loretta Young, Stuart Erwin, Claire Trevor, Marjorie Weaver, Lyle Talbot, J. Edward Bromberg

The Second Mrs Tanqueray

GB 1952 75m bw
Vandyke (Roger Proudlock)

A Victorian society widower marries a notorious lady.

Stiff-backed penny-pinching version of an interestingly antiquated play.

play Arthur Wing Pinero d Dallas Bower

Pamela Brown, Hugh Sinclair, Ronald Ward, Virginia McKenna, Andrew Osborn

Second Thoughts

US 1982 98m Movielab
Turman-Foster/EMI
V*

A lady lawyer gets into complex trouble when she bails out her inconsiderate lover from a Santa Fe jail.

An absurd series of situations is played for drama rather than comedy, and the feminist flag is frequently waved. The result is an unlikeable muddle.

w Steve Brown d Lawrence Turman

Lucie Arnaz, Craig Wasson, Ken Howard, Anne Schedeen

'Alternately dull and risible.' – Chris Auty, MFB

The Second Time Around

US 1961 99m DeLuxe Cinemascope
TCF/Cummings/Harman (Jack Cummings)

In 1912 Arizona, a widow stands for sheriff and has plenty of choice for a husband.

Light-hearted Western fun mixed with family sentimentality.

w Oscar Saul, Cecil Van Heusen novel Richard Emery Roberts d Vincent Sherman ph Ellis W. Carter m Gerald Fried

Debbie Reynolds, Steve Forrest, Andy Griffith, Juliet Prowse, Thelma Ritter, Ken Scott, Isobel Elsom

'Keep a lemon handy for sucking to ward off an attack of the terminal cutesies.' – Judith Crist, 1973

The Second Victory

GB 1986 112m Rank colour
Lelaleuka/J and M (Gerald Thomas)

In Austria after World War II, British occupation forces try to keep order in face of unrest following the murder of a sergeant.

Curiously timed return to the Third Man era, with a plotline unlikely to appeal to modern filmgoers; technical resources adequate rather than inspired.

w Morris West novel Morris West d Gerald Thomas

Anthony Andrews, Helmut Griem, Max von Sydow, Mario Adorf, Birgit Doll

The Second Woman

US 1950 91m bw
United Artists/Cardinal (Mort Briskin)
V*
GB title: Ellen

An architect, apparently paranoic, is proved to be the victim of a revenge plot.

Tolerable semi-star melodrama with a deliberate film noir look.

w Robert Smith d James V. Kern ph Hal Mohr md Nat Finston

Robert Young, Betsy Drake, John Sutton, Florence Bates, Morris Carnovsky, Henry O'Neill

Seconds **

US 1966 106m bw
Paramount/Joel/Gibraltar (Edward Lewis)

A secret organization sells a special service to the jaded rich; apparent death followed by physical rejuvenation.

An intriguing half-hour is followed by a glum new life for our hero, capped by a horrifying finale in which, dissatisfied, he learns he is to become one of the corpses necessary to the organization's continuance.

w Lewis John Carlino novel David Ely d John Frankenheimer ph James Wong Howe m Jerry Goldsmith titles Saul Bass

Rock Hudson, John Randolph, Will Geer, Salome Jens, Jeff Corey, Richard Anderson, Murray Hamilton, Wesley Addy

'A really horrifying piece of science fiction that burns its way into your mind like a gnawing headache.' – Sunday Express

'An ending that is one of the most terrifying episodes I have ever seen on the screen.' – Daily Express

AAN: James Wong Howe

'A nursery crime of epic proportions…'
The Secret Adventures of Tom Thumb **

GB 1993 60m colour
Bolex Brothers/BBC Bristol/La Sept/Manga/Lumen (Richard 'Hutch' Hutchison)
V

A freakish tiny child, taken from his parents to a laboratory full of mutants, escapes into a rubbish dump inhabited by small people much like himself.

A squalid, predatory and unlovely universe is brilliantly created using a mix of live action, pixilation and stop-motion animation. The images are of decay and dissolution and disturbing in their detail (a laboratory technician's rubber gloves covered in bristles, a crucified Father Christmas, a man catching and eating a moth). The overall effect is of a wayward originality.

wd Dave Borthwick ph Dave Borthwick, Frank Passingham m John Paul Jones, Startled Insects pd Dave Borthwick ed Dave Borthwick

Nick Upton, Deborah Collard, Frank Passingham, John Schofield, Mike Gifford, Robert Heath, George Brandt

'Brilliantly achieved but not one for the delectation of the feelgood brigade.' – Derek Malcolm, Guardian

The Secret Agent **

GB 1936 83m bw
Gaumont British (Michael Balcon, Ivor Montagu)
V*, L

A reluctantly recruited spy is ordered to kill a man.

Unsatisfactory in casting and writing, this Hitchcock suspenser nevertheless has many typically amusing moments.

w Charles Bennett play Campbell Dixon story Ashenden by Somerset Maugham d Alfred Hitchcock ph Bernard Knowles md Louis Levy

John Gielgud, Robert Young, Peter Lorre, Madeleine Carroll, Percy Marmont, Lilli Palmer, Florence Kahn

'As uncommon as it is unsentimentally cruel.' – Peter John Dyer, 1964

'Many sequences which show Hitchcock at his very best: the fake funeral, the murder on the mountainside, the riverside café, and the climax in a chocolate factory.' – NFT, 1961

'How unfortunate it is that Mr Hitchcock, a clever director, is allowed to produce and even to write his own films, though as a producer he has no sense of continuity and as a writer he has no sense of life. His films consist of a series of small "amusing" melodramatic situations: the murderer's button dropped on the baccarat board; the strangled organist's hands prolonging the notes in the empty church; the fugitives hiding in the bell tower when the bell begins to swing. Very perfunctorily he builds up to these tricky situations . . . and then drops them.' – *Graham Greene*

'Hitch said he was offering me Hamlet in modern dress. But when we came to make it, all the psychological interest was dissipated.' – *John Gielgud*

Secret Agent of Japan

US   1942   72m   bw
TCF

A female British agent tangles with Japanese in the Shanghai international settlement.

Standard propaganda filler with caricature Japs.

w John Larkin   *d* Irving Pichel

Preston Foster, Lynn Bari, Noel Madison, Sen Yung, Janis Carter, Steve Geray, Kurt Katch

Secret Agent X9

US   1937   bw   serial: 12 eps
Universal

A G-man goes undercover to track down the Belgravian crown jewels.

Mildly amusing adventures.

d Ford Beebe, Cliff Smith

Scott Kolk, Jean Rogers, Henry Hunter, Henry Brandon, Monte Blue

Secret Agent X9

US   1945   bw   serial: 13 eps
Universal

More adventures of the G-man, this time sent to the China coast to destroy the Black Dragon Intelligence service.

Predictable propaganda serial.

d Ray Taylor, Lewis Collins

Lloyd Bridges, Keye Luke, Jan Wiley, Victoria Horne, Samuel S. Hinds, Cy Kendall

'Behind a locked door – the relentless evil of his past!'
The Secret beyond the Door

US   1948   98m   bw
Universal/Walter Wanger (Fritz Lang)
V*

An heiress marries a moody millionaire with a death fixation, and comes to think of herself as his next potential victim.

Silly melodrama with much chat and little suspense.

w Sylvia Richards   *story* Rufus King   *d* Fritz Lang
ph Stanley Cortez   *m* Miklos Rozsa

Joan Bennett, Michael Redgrave, Anne Revere, Barbara O'Neil, Natalie Schaefer, Paul Cavanagh

'A dog-wagon *Rebecca* with a seasoning of psychiatrics.' – *Otis L. Guernsey Jnr*

'Lang gets a few wood-silky highlights out of this sow's ear, but it is a hopeless job and a worthless movie.' – *James Agee*

The Secret Bride

US   1935   63m   bw
Warner
GB title: *Concealment*

A District Attorney is secretly married to the daughter of the politician he is trying to convict.

Dismal melodrama, tritely scripted.

w Tom Buckingham, F. Hugh Herbert, Mary McCall Jnr   *play Concealment* by Leonard Ide   *d* William Dieterle   *ph* Ernest Haller

Barbara Stanwyck, Warren William, Glenda Farrell, Grant Mitchell, Arthur Byron, Henry O'Neill, Douglass Dumbrille

'Fast moving melodrama, well above average.' – *Variety*

Secret Ceremony

GB   1969   109m   Eastmancolor
Universal/World Films/Paul M. Heller (John Heyman, Norman Priggen)
V*

A prostitute mothers a young girl with a strange past.

Nuthouse melodrama for devotees of the director.

w George Tabori   *short story* Marco Denevi
d Joseph Losey   *ph* Gerry Fisher   *m* Richard Rodney Bennett

Elizabeth Taylor, Robert Mitchum, Mia Farrow, Pamela Brown, Peggy Ashcroft

'This piece of garbage is so totally ridiculous that I can't imagine why anyone would want to be in it, let alone see it.' – *Rex Reed*

The Secret Code

US   1942   bw   serial: 15 eps
Columbia

A police lieutenant arranges to be thrown off the force in disgrace so that he can infiltrate an enemy sabotage ring.

Standard wartime thick ear.

d Spencer G. Bennet

Paul Kelly, Anne Nagel, Clancy Cooper, Trevor Bardette

Secret Command

US   1944   92m   bw
Columbia (Phil L. Ryan)

An ex-foreign correspondent goes undercover at a shipyard to track down saboteurs.

Routine wartime thick ear.

w Roy Chanslor   *story The Saboteurs* by John and Ward Hawkins   *d* Eddie Sutherland   *ph* Franz Planer   *m* Paul Sawtell

Pat O'Brien, Carole Landis, Chester Morris, Ruth Warrick, Barton MacLane, Tom Tully, Wallace Ford, Howard Freeman

Secret Flight: see *School for Secrets*

The Secret Four: see *The Four Just Men* (1939)

The Secret Four: see *Kansas City Confidential* (1952)

Secret Friends

GB   1991   97m   Metrocolor
Feature/Whistling Gypsy/Film Four (Rosemarie Whitman)

On a train journey an artist hovers between dreams and reality as he imagines that his wife is a killer and that he has murdered his mistress.

Confusing account of a mid-life crisis in which it is difficult to separate fantasy from real life and hardly worth the effort of working out which is which.

wd Dennis Potter   *novel Ticket to Ride* by Dennis Potter   *ph* Sue Gibson   *m* Nicholas Russell-Pavier   *pd* Gary Williamson   *ed* Clare Douglas

Alan Bates, Gina Bellman, Frances Barber, Tony Doyle, Joanna David, Colin Jeavons, Rowena Cooper

'A tough ride for a very small return: the cramped and narcissistic anguish of a middle-aged male as seen in Potter passim.' – *Sheila Johnston, Independent*

'It is time that Potter pulled the communication cord on this particular train of thought.' – *Jonathan Romney, Sight and Sound*

The Secret Fury

US   1950   86m   bw
RKO (Jack H. Skirball, Bruce Manning)

A successful pianist is deliberately driven insane by her fiancé.

Derivative melodrama of no great interest.

w Lionel House   *d* Mel Ferrer   *ph* Leo Tover
md Constantin Bakaleinikoff   *m* Roy Webb

Claudette Colbert, Robert Ryan, Jane Cowl, Paul Kelly, Philip Ober, Elizabeth Risdon, Doris Dudley

The Secret Game: see *Les Jeux Interdits*

The Secret Garden *

US   1949   92m   bw   (Technicolor sequence)
MGM (Clarence Brown)
V, V*

An orphan girl goes to stay with her moody uncle and brightens up the lives of those around her.

Subdued, richly produced, rather likeable Victorian fable with the same moral as *The Bluebird* and *The Wizard of Oz*: happiness is in your own back yard.

w Robert Ardrey   *novel* Frances Hodgson Burnett
d Fred M. Wilcox   *ph* Ray June   *m* Bronislau Kaper

Margaret O'Brien, Herbert Marshall, Gladys Cooper, Elsa Lanchester, Dean Stockwell, Brian Roper

'Uneven, but oddly and unexpectedly interesting.' – *Richard Mallett, Punch*

'Let's have more pictures in this kindly vein.' – *Picturegoer*

'The timeless tale of a special place where magic, hope and love grow.'
The Secret Garden **

US   1993   101m   Technicolor
Warner/American Zoetrope (Fred Fuchs, Fred Roos, Tom Luddy)
V, V*, L, S

A young, lonely, orphaned girl, sent to live with her aristocratic uncle, helps her invalid cousin back to life.

A charming version of the classic children's story, deftly made, though its appeal may be too tame for today's audiences.

w Caroline Thompson   *novel* Frances Hodgson Burnett   *d* Agnieszka Holland   *ph* Roger Deakins   *m* Zbigniew Preisner   *pd* Stuart Craig   *ed* Isabelle Lorente

Maggie Smith, Kate Maberly, Heydon Prowse, Andrew Knott, Laura Crossley, John Lynch, Walter Sparrow, Irene Jacob

'Executed to near perfection in all artistic departments, this superior adaptation of the perennial favorite novel will find its core public among girls but should prove satisfying enough to a range of audiences.' – *Variety*

The Secret Heart

US   1946   97m   bw
MGM (Edwin H. Knopf)

A widow has problems with her emotionally disturbed daughter.

Old-fashioned woman's picture.

w Whitfield, Cook, Anne M. Chapin   *story* Rose Franken, William Brown Meloney   *d* Robert Z. Leonard   *ph* George Folsey   *m* Bronislau Kaper

Claudette Colbert, Walter Pidgeon, June Allyson, Robert Sterling, Marshall Thompson, Elizabeth Patterson, Richard Derr, Patricia Medina

'"There are three things you can't hide," says Walter Pidgeon in one of his bantering moments; "love, smoke, and a man riding a camel." I would add a fourth – that old MGM touch.' – *Richard Winnington*

Secret Interlude: see *The View From Pompey's Head* (1955)

Secret Interlude (1936): see *Private Number*

'The daring plan – the staggering odds – the incredible five!'
The Secret Invasion
US   1964   98m   DeLuxe   Panavision
UA/San Carlos (Gene Corman)
V

During World War II five convicted criminals become commandos.

Cut price *Dirty Dozen*, quite well made and exciting.

w R. Wright Campbell   d Roger Corman
ph Arthur E. Arling   m Hugo Friedhofer

Stewart Granger, Raf Vallone, Henry Silva, Mickey Rooney, Edd Byrnes, William Campbell, Peter Coe

The Secret Life of an American Wife **
US   1968   92m   DeLuxe
TCF/Charlton (George Axelrod)
V*

A bored suburban housewife sets out to seduce a movie star.

Sympathetic comedy of sixties suburban manners.

wd *George Axelrod*   ph Leon Shamroy   m Billy May

Walter Matthau, Anne Jackson, Patrick O'Neal, Edy Williams

'Both a first-class satire on American mores and a compassionate study of wish-fulfilment.' – *NFT, 1970*

The Secret Life of Walter Mitty **
US   1947   110m   Technicolor
Samuel Goldwyn
V, V*, L

A mother's boy dreams of derring-do, and eventually life catches up with fiction.

This pleasantly remembered star comedy, though it never had much to do with Thurber, can now be seen to have missed most of its opportunities, though the nice moments do tend to compensate.

w Ken Englund, Everett Freeman   story James Thurber   d Norman Z. McLeod   ph Lee Garmes   m David Raksin

Danny Kaye, Virginia Mayo, Boris Karloff, Florence Bates, Fay Bainter, *Thurston Hall*, Ann Rutherford, Gordon Jones, Reginald Denny

Secret Meeting: see *Marie Octobre*

Secret Mission
GB   1942   94m   bw
GFD/Marcel Hellman/Excelsior

During World War II four British Intelligence officers are landed in occupied France to discover the truth about German defences.

Stilted war suspenser.

w Anatole de Grunwald, Basil Bartlett, Terence Young   d Harold French   ph Bernard Knowles   m Mischa Spoliansky

Hugh Williams, Carla Lehmann, James Mason, Roland Culver, Nancy Price, Michael Wilding, Percy Walsh

Secret Motive: see *The London Blackout Murders*

The Secret of Blood Island
GB   1964   84m   Technicolor
U-I/Hammer (Anthony Nelson Keys)
V*

A girl parachutist secret agent is smuggled into a Japanese POW camp and out again.

Absurd blood and thunder, almost perversely enjoyable – but not quite.

w John Gilling   d Quentin Lawrence   ph Jack Asher   m James Bernard

Barbara Shelley, Jack Hedley, Charles Tingwell, Bill Owen, Lee Montague

The Secret of Convict Lake *
US   1951   83m   bw
TCF (Frank P. Rosenberg)

In the 1870s, escaped convicts take over a California town.

Brooding, snowy, set-bound Western melodrama; predictable but watchable.

w Oscar Saul   d Michael Gordon   ph Leo Tover
md Lionel Newman   m Sol Kaplan

Glenn Ford, Gene Tierney, Ann Dvorak, Ethel Barrymore, Zachary Scott, Barbara Bates, Cyril Cusack, Jeanette Nolan, Ruth Donnelly

The Secret of Madame Blanche
US   1933   85m   bw
MGM

The woman who takes the blame for murder committed by a young man is the mother he never knew.

Or, *Madame X* unofficially revisited: all-stops-out melodrama very typical of its time.

w Frances Goodrich and Albert Hackett   d Charles Brabin

Irene Dunne, Phillips Holmes, Lionel Atwill, Douglas Walton, Jean Parker, Una Merkel

The Secret of My Success
GB   1965   105m   Metrocolor   Panavision
MGM/Andrew and Virginia Stone

A village policeman follows his mother's dictum that he should not think ill of others, and accidentally goes from success to success.

Flabby portmanteau comedy full of in-jokes and flat-footed farce; satire is not evident.

wd Andrew L. Stone   ph David Boulton
md Roland Shaw   m Lucien Caillet and others

James Booth, Lionel Jeffries, *Amy Dalby*, Stella Stevens, Honor Blackman, Shirley Jones, Joan Hickson

The Secret of My Success *
US   1987   110m   DeLuxe
Universal/Rastar (Herbert Ross)
V, V*, L, S

A country cousin in New York is determined to hit the big time.

An amiable melange of familiar situations with just a touch of *Midnight Cowboy* and a sharp edge to some of the writing; but not enough to keep its star at the top.

w Jim Cash, Jack Epps, A. J. Carothers   d Herbert Ross   ph Carlo Di Palma   m David Foster

Michael J. Fox, Helen Slater, Richard Jordan, Margaret Whitton, John Pankow, Christopher Murney

'A bedroom farce with a leaden touch, a corporate comedy without teeth.' – *Daily Variety*

The Secret of Nimh *
US   1982   82m   Technicolor
Aurora/Don Bluth
V*, L, S

Forced out of her cosy field, a widowed mouse seeks the help of Nicodemus, king of the rat pack.

Animated cartoon by Disney artists who rejected that company's declining standards and set up their own factory. Alas, though they have the skills, the narrative they have chosen needed refining.

w Don Bluth, John Pomeroy, Gary Foldman, Will Finn   novel Mrs Frisby and the Rats of Nimh by Robert C. O'Brien   d Don Bluth   m Jerry Goldsmith

'Vintage techniques are proudly invoked, but the story desperately needs loving care.' – *Sight and Sound*

The Secret of St Ives
US   1949   76m   bw
Columbia

During the Napoleonic War, a French prisoner-of-war escapes from Edinburgh Castle, only to be accused of murder.

Modest swashbuckler with a somewhat lacklustre atmosphere.

w Eric Taylor   story Robert Louis Stevenson
d Phil Rosen

Richard Ney, Vanessa Brown, Henry Daniell, Aubrey Mather

The Secret of Santa Vittoria *
US   1969   140m   Technicolor   Panavision
UA/Stanley Kramer

In 1945 an Italian village hides its wine from the occupying Germans.

Expected, exhausting epic comedy with everyone talking at once.

w William Rose, Ben Maddow   novel Robert Crichton   d Stanley Kramer   ph Giuseppe Rotunno   m Ernest Gold

Anthony Quinn, Anna Magnani, Virna Lisi, Hardy Kruger, Sergio Franchi, Renato Rascel

'A brainless farrago of flying rolling pins and rotten vegetables, filled with the kind of screaming, belching, eye-rolling fictional Italians only Stanley Kramer could invent.' – *Rex Reed*

AAN: Ernest Gold

The Secret of Stamboul
GB   1936   93m   bw
Wainwright
reissue title: *The Spy in White*

An English adventurer foils a Turkish revolution.

Pale rendering of a full-blooded best-seller.

w Richard Wainwright, Howard Irving Young, Noel Langley   novel The Eunuch of Stamboul by Dennis Wheatley   d Andrew Marton

Valerie Hobson, Frank Vosper, James Mason, Kay Walsh, Peter Haddon

The Secret of the Blue Room
US   1933   66m   bw
Universal

An heiress's three suitors all volunteer to spend the night in the haunted room of her mansion.

Murderous malarkey without the courage of its convictions.

w William Hurlbut   d Kurt Neumann

Lionel Atwill, Gloria Stuart, Paul Lukas, Edward Arnold, Onslow Stevens, Robert Barrat, Elizabeth Patterson

'Americanization of a German mystery yarn which ought to do well in the smaller spots.' – *Variety*

† Remade in 1938 as *The Missing Guest* and in 1944 as *Murder in the Blue Room*.

The Secret of the Incas
US   1954   101m   Technicolor
Paramount (Mel Epstein)

Various adventurers seek a priceless Inca jewel.

Boys' Own Paper yarn which sounds a good deal more exciting than it is: too much talk and a few choice studio backcloths drop the tension alarmingly, and the script lacks humour and conciseness.

w Ranald MacDougall, Sidney Boehm   d Jerry Hopper   ph Lionel Lindon   m David Buttolph

Charlton Heston, Robert Young, Thomas Mitchell, Nicole Maurey, Yma Sumac, Glenda Farrell, Michael Pate

The Secret of the Loch

GB 1934 80m bw
ABFD/Bray Wyndham

A diver thinks he finds a prehistoric monster in Loch Ness.

Mildly amusing exploitation item following the 1934 rebirth of interest in the old legend.

w Charles Bennett, Billie Bristow d Milton Rosmer

Seymour Hicks, Nancy O'Neil, Gibson Gowland, Frederick Peisley, Rosamund John, Ben Field

The Secret of Treasure Island

US 1938 bw serial: 15 eps
Columbia

A reporter investigates a friend's disappearance in the Caribbean.

Juvenile serial with plenty of action involving a sinister Doctor X and some skull-faced pirates.

d Elmer Clifton

Don Terry, Gwen Gaze, Grant Withers, Hobart Bosworth, William Farnum, Dave O'Brien

'Run for your life! You must find the secret before it finds you!'
The Secret Partner *

GB 1961 91m bw
MGM (Michael Relph)

A blackmailing dentist is visited by a mysterious hooded stranger who forces him to rob one of his businessman victims.

Complex puzzle thriller, neatly made in sub-Hitchcock style.

w David Pursall, Jack Seddon d Basil Dearden
ph Harry Waxman m Philip Green

Stewart Granger, Haya Harareet, Bernard Lee, Hugh Burden, Melissa Stribling, Norman Bird, Conrad Philips

The Secret People *

GB 1951 96m bw
Ealing (Sidney Cole)

European refugees in London during the thirties become members of a ring of anarchists.

Downbeat political melodrama which pleased neither the masses nor the highbrows, despite plaudits for sensitive direction and performances.

w Thorold Dickinson, Wolfgang Wilhelm d Thorold Dickinson ph Gordon Dines m Roberto Gerhard

Valentina Cortese, Serge Reggiani, Audrey Hepburn, Charles Goldner, Megs Jenkins, Irene Worth, Athene Seyler, Reginald Tate

'The tension and power of the film make it one of the most remarkable British productions for some time.' – Penelope Houston

'That Secret People, despite the creative agonies recorded by Mr Lindsay Anderson [in a book on the making of the film] should turn out to be a confused, unco-ordinated spy thriller concealing a tentative message deep down below some strained effects of style is another tragedy of British film hopes.' – Richard Winnington

Secret Places

GB 1984 98m Eastmancolor
Rank/Skreba/Virgin (Simon Relph, Ann Skinner)
V*

At the beginning of the Second World War an English schoolgirl forms a close relationship with another boarder, a refugee from Germany.

Psychological drama that is too sensitive for its own good, so that it seems more attenuated than intense.

wd Zelda Barron novel Janice Elliott ph Peter MacDonald m Michel Legrand ed Laurence Mery-Clark

Marie-Therese Relin, Tara MacGowran, Claudine Auger, Jenny Agutter, Cassie Stuart, Anne-Marie Gwatkin, Klaus Barner, Sylvia Coleridge

Secret Service

US 1931 67m bw
RKO

During the Civil War a Yankee officer goes behind enemy lines and falls in love with a Southern girl.

Sluggish romantic adventure.

w Bernard Schubert play William Gillette
d J. Walter Ruben

Richard Dix, Shirley Grey, William Post Jnr, Gavin Gordon

'Dix does a good character. It's all the picture has.' – Variety

Secret Service in Darkest Africa

US 1943 bw serial: 15 eps
Republic

An American undercover agent posing as a member of the Gestapo in Berlin learns of a plan to convert the Arabs to the Nazi cause by means of a forged scroll and the dagger of Solomon.

Lively cliffhanging adventures.

d Spencer G. Bennet

Rod Cameron, Joan Marsh, Duncan Renaldo, Lionel Royce, Kurt Kreuger, Kurt Katch

Secret Service of the Air

US 1939 61m bw
Warner

A government agent tracks down smugglers.

Serial-like thrills and comedy, adequately presented.

w Raymond Shrock d Noel Smith

Ronald Reagan, Eddie Foy Jnr, John Litel, Ila Rhodes, James Stephenson

'No marquee names, but a better than average story of its kind.' – Variety

The Secret Six *

US 1931 83m bw
MGM

A syndicate of businessmen finance two reporters to get evidence against a gang of bootleggers.

Solidly carpentered gangster thriller.

w Frances Marion d George Hill ph Harold Wenstrom

Wallace Beery, Lewis Stone, Clark Gable, John Mack Brown, Jean Harlow, Marjorie Rambeau, Paul Hurst, Ralph Bellamy, John Miljan

'A gangster talker too rough, crude and familiar. In big cities it may pull the roughneck trade . . . but the vocalized expression for it will be adverse.' – Variety

'It's not who you con – it's how you do it!'
The Secret War of Harry Frigg

US 1967 109m Techniscope
Universal/Albion (Hal E. Chester)

In 1943 a private engineers the escape of five captured generals.

Unattractive war comedy; slow, uninventive and overlong.

w Peter Stone, Frank Tarloff d Jack Smight
ph Russell Metty m Carlo Rustichelli

Paul Newman, John Williams, Sylva Koscina, Andrew Duggan, Tom Bosley, Charles D. Gray, Vito Scotti, James Gregory

The Secret Ways *

US 1961 112m bw
U-I/Heath (Richard Widmark)

An American reporter is recruited to rescue a scholar from communist Hungary.

Pretentious Iron Curtain melodrama, quite good to look at but overlong and no Third Man.

w Jean Hazelwood novel Alistair MacLean d Phil Karlson ph Max Greene m Johnny Williams

Richard Widmark, Sonja Ziemann, Charles Regnier, Walter Rilla, Howard Vernon, Senta Berger

Secret Wedding **

Argentina/Netherlands 1989 95m colour
Allarts/Cogurccio/Cinéphile (Lujan Pflaum)
original title: Boda Secreta

Returning home after 13 years unjustly imprisoned in Buenos Aires, a man discovers that no one is prepared to recognize him, not even the woman he loves.

A gripping tale of political persecution, underscored by an unhappy romance.

wd Alejandro Agresti ph Ricardo Rodriguez
m Paul Michael Van Brugge pd Juan Collini
ed Rene Wiegmans

Tito Haas, Mirtha Busnelli, Sergio Poves Campos, Nathan Pinzon, Flora Bloise, Elio Marchi

Secrets *

US 1933 85m bw
Mary Pickford/UA

A pioneering couple stick together despite the husband's infidelities.

Curiously mixed-up star vehicle, part romantic comedy, part Western, part sob-stuff. Interesting rather than entertaining.

w Frances Marion play Rudolf Besier, May Edgington d Frank Borzage

Mary Pickford, Leslie Howard, C. Aubrey Smith, Blanche Friderici, Doris Lloyd, Ned Sparks

'Singularly uneven . . . but at least the story is given fine production and interesting playing.' – Variety.

'You can be sure you won't make any mistake by taking the family to see it.' – Photoplay

† Norma Talmadge starred in a 1923 silent version.

Secrets of a Secretary

US 1931 76m bw
Paramount

A social secretary discovers that her ex-husband is blackmailing her employer's daughter.

Peg's Paper romance of a heroine who rises above her many problems.

w Dwight Taylor, Charles Brackett d George Abbott

Claudette Colbert, Herbert Marshall, George Metaxas, Mary Boland, Berton Churchill

Secrets of a Soul **

Germany 1926 95m (24 fps) bw silent
UFA/Hans Neumann

A chemist develops a knife phobia, has hallucinations, and tries to cut his wife's throat.

A lesson in elementary psychology which was innovatory at the time and survives as cinema for its stylish and impressionist use of visual techniques.

w Colin Ross, Hans Neumann, G. W. Pabst d G. W. Pabst ph Guido Seeber, Curt Oertel, Robert Lach

Werner Krauss, Jack Trevor, Ruth Weyher, Pawel Pawlow

Secrets of an Actress

US 1938 70m bw
Warner

A star actress falls for one of her backers, a married architect.

High-life suffering of a familiar kind: it satisfied the *Peg's Paper* audience.

w Milton Krims, Rowland Leigh, Julius J. Epstein d William Keighley

Kay Francis, George Brent, Ian Hunter, Gloria Dickson, Isabel Jeans, Peggy Singleton

'Miss Francis may be able to live up to all requirements except an acrobatic dance on the toes, but it's no use hitching race horses to milk wagons.' – *Variety*

Secrets of G32: see *Fly By Night*

Secrets of Scotland Yard
US   1944   68m   bw
Republic (George Blair)

A British secret service man is impersonated by his Nazi twin brother.

Likeable absurdities with a strong cast.

w Denison Clift   *novel Room 40, O.B.* by Denison Clift d George Blair

C. Aubrey Smith, Edgar Barrier, Stephanie Bachelor, Lionel Atwill, Henry Stephenson, John Abbott, Walter Kingsford, Martin Kosleck

Secrets of the French Police
US   1932   55m   bw
RKO

The Sûreté tracks down a hypnotist and murderer.

Rather wildly-imagined suspenser with points of interest.

w Samuel Ornitz, Robert Tasker   d Edward Sutherland

Gwili André, Frank Morgan, Gregory Ratoff, Murray Kinnell, John Warburton

'Hodge-podge of melodramatics . . . hardly enough for the de luxers.' – *Variety*

Secrets of the Phantom Caverns
GB   1984   90m   colour
Adams Apple (Sandy Howard, Robert D. Bailey)

Anthropologists and soldiers exploring a cave system in Latin America discover a lost albino tribe living underground.

Totally inept fantasy from beginning to end.

w Christy Marx, Robert Vincent O'Neil   *story* Ken Barnett   d Don Sharp   ph Virgil Harper m Michael Rubini, Denny Jaeger   ad Stephen Marsh   ed John R. Bowey

Robert Powell, Lisa Blount, Richard Johnson, Anne Heywood, A. C. Weary, Timothy Bottoms

Secrets of the Underground
US   1943   70m   bw
Republic

The proprietor of a fashionable gown shop is a Nazi agent.

Nifty second feature on predictable wartime lines.

w Robert Tasker, Geoffrey Homes   d William Morgan

John Hubbard, Virginia Grey, Lloyd Corrigan, Miles Mander, Ben Welden

Sedmikrasky: see *Daisies*

'There are many ways to be seduced. Fame . . . power . . . love!'
The Seduction of Joe Tynan *
US   1979   107m   Technicolor
Universal (Martin Bregman)
V*, L

A young senator alienates his wife when he sacrifices his principles for advancement.

Fairly arresting political character drama with strong narrative and acting.

w *Alan Alda*   d Jerry Schatzberg   ph Adam Holender   m Bill Conti

Alan Alda, Barbara Harris, Meryl Streep, *Melvyn Douglas*, Rip Torn, Carrie Nye, Charles Kimbrough

The Seduction of Julia: see *Adorable Julia*

See America Thirst
US   1930   71m   bw
Universal

Two hoboes become involved with rum runners.

Poorly constructed talkie début for a silent comedian who never made it.

w Edward Luddy, Vin Moore, C. J. Horwin   d W. J. Craft

Harry Langdon, Slim Summerville, Bessie Love, Mitchell Lewis, Stanley Fields

'Direction shows silent technique throughout, and is unmindful of the talkie advent. Rub is that this system got reversed in the important sequences.' – *Variety*

See Here Private Hargrove *
US   1944   102m   bw
MGM (George Haight)

Adventures of a raw recruit in the US army.

Standard transcription of a humorous bestseller which did its best to make the war painless for Americans.

w Harry Kurnitz   *book* Marion Hargrove   d Wesley Ruggles   ph Charles Lawton   m David Snell

Robert Walker, Donna Reed, Robert Benchley, Keenan Wynn, Bob Crosby, Ray Collins, Chill Wills, Grant Mitchell

† Sequel 1945: *What Next, Corporal Hargrove?*

See How They Run
GB   1955   84m   bw
Winwell (BL)

A country vicarage gets lively when several miscreants pretend to be the vicar.

Reliable stage farce which doesn't get the laughs on screen.

w Leslie Arliss, Philip King, Val Valentine *play* Philip King   d Leslie Arlis

Ronald Shiner, Greta Gynt, James Hayter, Wilfrid Hyde-White, Dora Bryan, Richard Wattis, Viola Lyel

See My Lawyer
US   1945   67m   bw
Universal

Comedians try to get out of a night-club commitment by insulting the customers.

Thin vehicle for a team that wasn't going anywhere: too many variety acts got in their way.

w Edmund L. Hartmann, Stanley Davis   d Edward Cline

Ole Olsen, Chic Johnson, Grace McDonald, Franklin Pangborn, Alan Curtis, Noah Beery Jnr, Ed Brophy

See No Evil: see *Blind Terror*

See No Evil, Hear No Evil
US   1989   102m   Technicolor
Columbia TriStar (Marvin Worth)
V, V*, L

Suspected of murder, two friends, one deaf and the other blind, go in pursuit of the real killer.

Halting comedy that is not worth watching.

w Earl Barret, Arne Sultan, Eliot Wald, Andrew Kurtzman, Gene Wilder   *story* Earl Barret, Arne Sullivan, Marvin Worth   d Arthur Hiller   ph Victor J. Kemper   m Stewart Copeland   pd Robert Gundlach   ed Robert C. Jones

Richard Pryor, Gene Wilder, Joan Severance, Kevin Spacey, Alan North, Anthony Zerbe, Louis Giambalvo, Kirsten Childs

See You in Hell Darling: see *An American Dream*

See You in the Morning
US   1988   119m   Metrocolor
Warner/Lorimar (Alan J. Pakula)
V, V*, L

A divorced psychiatrist begins an affair with an insecure widow with two young children.

Enjoyable, though hardly memorable, study of confused relationships.

wd Alan J. Pakula   ph Donald McAlpine m Michael Small   pd George Jenkins   ed Evan Lottman

Jeff Bridges, Alice Krige, Farrah Fawcett, Drew Barrymore, Lukas Haas, David Dukes, Frances Sternhagen, George Hearn, Theodore Bikel, Macaulay Culkin

Seed
US   1931   96m   bw
Universal

A husband leaves his family to become a novelist, but returns ten years later.

Long-drawn-out domestic drama whose few virtues have not weathered the years.

w Gladys Lehman   *novel* Charles G. Norris   d John Stahl

John Boles, Genevieve Tobin, Lois Wilson, Raymond Hackett, Bette Davis, ZaSu Pitts

'Good woman's picture that will strike generous b.o. anywhere.' – *Variety*

The Seekers
GB   1954   90m   Eastmancolor
GFD/Fanfare (George H. Brown)
V*
US title: *Land of Fury*

In 1820 a British sailor and his family emigrate to New Zealand.

Stilted epic which never gains the viewer's sympathy or interest.

w William Fairchild   d Ken Annakin   ph Geoffrey Unsworth   m William Alwyn

Jack Hawkins, Glynis Johns, Inia Te Wiata, Noel Purcell, Kenneth Williams, Laya Raki

Seemabadha: see *Company Limited*

Seems Like Old Times *
US   1980   102m   Metrocolor
Columbia/Ray Stark
V, V*, L

An innocently involved bank robber takes refuge with his ex-wife, a lady lawyer married to the district attorney.

Nostalgic farce which doesn't quite live up to the old skills and often bogs down in talk. Funny moments, though.

w Neil Simon   d Jay Sandrich   ph David M. Walsh   m Marvin Hamlisch   pd Gene Callahan

Goldie Hawn, Chevy Chase, Charles Grodin, Robert Guillaume, Harold Gould, George Grizzard

Sei Donne per l'Assassino: see *Blood and Black Lace*

Seize the Day *
US 1986 93m colour
Learning in Focus (Chiz Schultz)

In the mid-50s a salesman who quits his job meets rejection and disillusion at every turn.

A movie faithful to the book, but its relentless portrait of a man's disintegration and humiliation is much less easy to bear on the screen than it was on the page.

w Ronald Ribman novel Saul Bellow d Fiedler Cook ph Eric Van Haren Noman m Elizabeth Swados pd John Robert Lloyd ed Sidney Katz, Rachel Igel

Robin Williams, Joseph Wiseman, Jerry Stiller, Glenne Headly, William Hickey, Tony Roberts, Tom Aldredge

† The film was made for TV. Saul Bellow has a walk-on role as a man in a hotel corridor.

The Selling of America: see Beer

The Sellout
US 1951 82m bw
MGM (Nicholas Nayfack)

A newspaper exposes a corrupt administration.

Competent melodrama with no surprises.

w Charles Palmer d Gerald Mayer ph Paul Vogel m David Buttolph

Walter Pidgeon, John Hodiak, Audrey Totter, Thomas Gomez, Everett Sloane, Cameron Mitchell, Karl Malden, Paula Raymond

The Sellout
GB/Italy 1975 102m colour
Warner/Oceanglade/Amerifilm (Josef Shaftel)

Russians and Americans lure a double agent to Jerusalem in order to eliminate him.

Unsmiling spy melodrama with a complex plot, a bagful of clichés and some unnecessarily unpleasant violence.

w Judson Kinberg, Murray Smith d Peter Collinson ph Arthur Ibbetson m Mike Green, Colin Frechter

Richard Widmark, Oliver Reed, Gayle Hunnicutt, Sam Wanamaker, Vladek Sheybal, Ori Levy, Assef Dayan

La Semana del Asesino: see Cannibal Man

Seminole
US 1953 86m Technicolor
Universal-International

A West Point graduate goes to Florida to make peace with the Indians.

Slightly unusual but not very interesting semi-Western with the usual clichés.

w Charles K. Peck Jnr d Budd Boetticher

Rock Hudson, Anthony Quinn, Barbara Hale, Richard Carlson, Hugh O'Brian, Russell Johnson, Lee Marvin, James Best

Semi-Tough *
US 1977 107m DeLuxe
UA/David Merrick
V, V*, L

The manager's daughter decides between two star members of a football team.

Rambling satiric comedy which takes jabs at various states of mind in America today, notably the fashionable forms of self-help therapy. Much of it comes off quite well.

w Walter Bernstein novel Dan Jenkins d Michael Ritchie ph Charles Rosher Jnr m Jerry Fielding

Burt Reynolds, Kris Kristofferson, Jill Clayburgh, Bert Convy, Robert Preston, Lotte Lenya, Roger E. Mosley

The Senator Was Indiscreet *
US 1947 95m bw
U-I (Nunnally Johnson)
V*
GB title: Mr Ashton Was Indiscreet

A foolish politician determines to become president and hires a press agent.

Satirical political farce which hurls its shafts wide and doesn't seem to mind how few of them hit.

w Charles MacArthur story Edwin Lanham d George S. Kaufman ph William Mellor m Daniele Amfitheatrof

William Powell, Ella Raines, Peter Lind Hayes, Ray Collins, Arleen Whelan, Allen Jenkins, Hans Conried, Charles D. Brown

Send Me No Flowers *
US 1964 100m Technicolor
U-I/Martin Melcher (Harry Keller)
V*

A hypochondriac mistakenly thinks he is dying and tries to provide another spouse for his wife.

A timeworn farcical situation is handled in the glossy Doris Day manner; it all starts quite brightly but gradually fizzles out.

w Julius Epstein play Norman Barrasch, Carroll Moore d Norman Jewison ph Daniel Fapp m Frank de Vol ad Alexander Golitzen, Robert Clatworthy

Doris Day, Rock Hudson, Tony Randall, Paul Lynde, Clint Walker, Hal March, Edward Andrews

The Seniors
US 1977 87m Metrocolor
CSI (Stanley Shapiro, Carter de Haven)
V*

Four college students discover a way to become rich by making prostitution respectable.

Exploitative comedy, mixing teenage wish-fulfilment with black but unfunny farce.

w Stanley Shapiro d Rod Amateau ph Robert Jessup ed Guy Scarpitta

Jeffrey Byron, Gary Imhoff, Dennis Quaid, Lou Richards, Rocky Flintermann, Priscilla Barnes, Alan Reed

Sensation
GB 1936 67m bw
BIP

A village barmaid is murdered and only our reporter hero sees the wider implications.

Presentable murder mystery.

w Dudley Leslie, Marjorie Deans, William Freshman play Murder Gang by Basil Dean and George Munro d Brian Desmond Hurst

John Lodge, Diana Churchill, Francis Lister, Joan Marion, Margaret Vyner, Athene Seyler, Richard Bird

'The genuine situation is lost in false trials, in an absurd love story, in humour based on American films, and in the complete unreality of the "murder gang".' – Graham Greene.

Sensations of 1945
US 1944 87m bw
Andrew L. Stone

Father and son disagree over the handling of their publicity agency.

Slim plot holds together a ragbag of variety acts, some quite choice.

w Dorothy Bennett d Andrew L. Stone ph Peverell Marley, John Mescall md Mahlon Merrick

Eleanor Powell, W. C. Fields, Sophie Tucker, Dennis O'Keefe, Eugene Pallette, C. Aubrey Smith, Lyle

Talbot, Dorothy Donegan, Cab Calloway and his band, Woody Herman and his band

AAN: Mahlon Merrick

Senso *
Italy 1953 115m Technicolor
Lux
V*
aka: The Wanton Countess (cut version)

In 1866 Venice a noblewoman falls in love with an officer of the invading Austrian army, but finally denounces him.

The melodramatic plot is less important than the portrait of a period, for this is an expensive film in the grand style, often breathtaking to look at.

w Luchino Visconti, Suso Cecchi d'Amico and others story Camilla Botto d Luchino Visconti ph G. R. Aldo, Robert Krasker m Anton Bruckner ad Ottavio Scotti

Alida Valli, Farley Granger, Massimo Girotti, Christian Marquand

The Sensualist
Japan 1992 54m colour
Ren Usami, Tsunemasa Hatano, Zuza Hagiwara
V

A merchant, whose life is dedicated to lust, aids a tailor who has wagered his manhood on bedding a courtesan at their first meeting.

A rarity: an animated film intended for an adult audience. The images, based on traditional Japanese woodcuts, are attractive; the inconsequential narrative less so.

w Eiichi Yamamoto novel Saikaku Ihara d Yukio Abe ph Minoru Fujita m Keiju Ishikawa ad Yukio Abe ed Kenichi Takashima

Sentimental Journey
US 1946 94m bw
TCF (Walter Morosco)

An actress who knows she is dying arranges for a little orphan girl to take her place in her husband's affections.

Hollywood's most incredible three-handkerchief picture; nicely made, but who dared to write it?

w Samuel Hoffenstein, Elizabeth Reinhardt story Nelia Gardner White d Walter Lang ph Norbert Brodine m Cyril Mockridge

Maureen O'Hara, John Payne, William Bendix, Cedric Hardwicke, Glenn Langan, Mischa Auer, Connie Marshall, Kurt Kreuger

'In twenty years of filmgoing I can't remember being so slobbered at: the apotheosis of the weepie.' – Richard Winnington

'It may not be for the critics, but who are critics? Just a lot of Joes, with passes.' – Variety

† Remade as The Gift of Love (qv).

'Doomed to guard the gates of Hell forever!'
The Sentinel
US 1976 92m Technicolor
Universal/Jeffrey Konvitz
V*

A disturbed girl in an old apartment house is haunted by walking corpses: the house turns out to be the gateway to hell and she its appointed sentinel.

Vulgarly modish rip-off of several fashionable themes, notably Rosemary's Baby and The Exorcist.

w Michael Winner, Jeffrey Konvitz novel Jeffrey Konvitz d Michael Winner ph Dick Kratina m Gil Melle

Chris Sarandon, Cristina Raines, Martin Balsam, John Carradine, José Ferrer, Ava Gardner, Arthur

Kennedy, Burgess Meredith, Sylvia Miles, Deborah Raffin, Eli Wallach, Jerry Orbach

'Moral or ironic points are hard to discern in the eye-wrenching flux of a Michael Winner movie, which drifts and zooms across its polished people and places in a continual caressing motion, as crudely excitatory as any sex movie when the climaxes are approaching.' – *Richard Combs, MFB*

'A man with a face that looks like chicken giblets, a naked whore with a mouse on her thigh, a cat devouring a canary and Sylvia Miles in a tight leotard – these are some of the highlights of *The Sentinel*, a perfect film for those who like to slow down and look at traffic accidents.' – *Janet Maslin, Newsweek*

La Senyora *
Spain 1987 103m colour
ICA/Virgin (Jonni Bassiner)

Sexually frustrated by a loveless marriage, an aristocratic woman finds temporary happiness with her gardener.

Moderately engrossing melodrama of sex and class.

w Jordi Cadena, Silvia Tortosa *novel* Antoni Mus *d* Jordi Cadena *ph* Jose G. Galisteo *m* J. M. Pagana *pd* Joseph Maria Espada *ed* Amat Carreras

Silvia Tortosa, Hermann Bonnin, Luis Merlo, Fernando Guillén-Cuervo, Jeannine Mestre, Alfonso Guirao

Senza Ragione: see *Redneck*

Separate Beds: see *The Wheeler Dealers*

Separate Tables **
US 1958 98m bw
UA/Hecht-Hill-Lancaster (Harold Hecht)
V, V*

Emotional tensions among the boarders at a British seaside guest house.

The genteel melodramas seem less convincing on the Hollywood screen than they did on the London stage, but the handling is thoroughly professional.

w Terence Rattigan, John Gay *play* Terence Rattigan *d* Delbert Mann *ph* Charles Lang *m* David Raksin

Burt Lancaster, Rita Hayworth, *David Niven*, Deborah Kerr, *Wendy Hiller, Gladys Cooper, Cathleen Nesbitt, Felix Aylmer*, Rod Taylor, Audrey Dalton, *May Hallatt*

AA: David Niven; Wendy Hiller

AAN: best picture; script; Charles Lang; David Raksin; Deborah Kerr

Seppuku: see *Hara Kiri*

September
US 1987 83m DuArt/DeLuxe
Orion (Jack Rollins, Charles H. Joffe)
V, V*, L

Enclosed family drama: Allen in his melancholy Bergman mode.

wd Woody Allen *ph* Carlo Di Palma *m* various *ad* Speed Hopkins *ed* Susan E. Morse

Denholm Elliott, Dianne Wiest, Mia Farrow, Elaine Stritch, Sam Waterston

'The debts to Chekhov are everywhere.' – *Variety*

September Affair
US 1950 104m bw
Paramount (Hal B. Wallis)
V*, L

Two married people fall in love and a plane crash in which they are reported dead gives them their chance.

Turgid romantic melodrama, not very well made despite the background tour of Capri; what made it a

hit was the playing of the old Walter Huston record of the title song.

w Robert Thoeren *d* William Dieterle *ph* Charles B. Lang *m* Victor Young

Joseph Cotten, Joan Fontaine, Françoise Rosay, Jessica Tandy, Robert Arthur, Jimmy Lydon

'A smooth surface mirrors the film's essential superficiality.' – *Penelope Houston*

September Storm
US 1960 110m DeLuxe Cinemascope 3-D
TCF/Alco (Edward L. Alperson)

A New York model and two adventurers search for sunken treasure off an uncharted Mediterranean island.

Thin actioner originally intended to marry 3-D and Cinemascope, but failed to do so.

w W. R. Burnett *novel The Girl in the Red Bikini* by Steve Fisher *d* Byron Haskin *ph* Jorge Stahl Jnr, Lamar Boren *m* Edward L. Alperson Jnr

Joanne Dru, Mark Stevens, Robert Strauss

Sequestro di Persona: see *Island of Crime*

Sequoia
US 1934 73m bw
MGM

A girl living in the High Sierras defends wild animals from hunters.

Refreshingly unusual outdoor drama with good location photography.

w Ann Cunningham, Sam Arnstrong, Carey Wilson *d* Chester Franklin *ph* Chester Lyons

Jean Parker, Russell Hardie, Samuel S. Hinds, Paul Hurst

'It was unlikely that either Miss Parker or the deer would eat the puma, but I hung on hoping that the puma would eat the deer or Miss Parker.' – *James Agate*

SER *
USSR 1989 75m colour
Artificial Eye/Mosfilm (Victor Trakhtenberg)
aka: *Freedom is Paradise*

A boy escapes from reform school to find his father who is also a prisoner.

Simple, understated and gripping account of the dispossessed.

wd Sergei Bodrov *ph* Yuri Skirtladze *m* Alexander Raskatov *pd* Velery Kostrin *ed* Valentina Kulagina

Volodya Kozyrev, Alexander Bureyev, Svetlana Gaitan, Vitautas Tomkus

'It may not be too great a hope to see in its spare approach a hitherto under-explored way forward for Russian, or even Soviet, cinema.' – *Verina Glaessner, MFB*

Serenade (1939): see *Broadway Serenade*

Serenade
US 1956 121m Warnercolor
Warner (Henry Blanke)

A vineyard worker becomes a successful opera singer and is desired by two women.

Cliché success story with plot taking second place to singing.

w Ivan Goff, Ben Roberts, John Twist *novel* James M. Cain *d* Anthony Mann *ph* Peverell Marley *md* Ray Heindorf *songs* Nicholas Brodszky (*m*), Sammy Cahn (*ly*)

Mario Lanza, Joan Fontaine, Sarita Montiel, Vincent Price, Joseph Calleia, Harry Bellaver, Vince Edwards, Silvio Minciotti

The Sergeant
US 1968 108m Technicolor
Warner/Robert Wise (Richard Goldstone)

France, 1952. In a dreary army camp, a tough army sergeant with a guilt complex is brought face to face with his own homosexuality.

Well-made but very ponderous and limited melodrama which could have been told in half the time.

w Dennis Murphy *play* Dennis Murphy *d* John Flynn *ph* Henri Persin *m* Michel Mayne

Rod Steiger, John Philip Law, Frank Latimore, Ludmila Mikael

'The funniest foul-up of the space age!'
Sergeant Deadhead
US 1965 89m CFI colour
AIP

An army sergeant is accidentally sent into orbit and undergoes a personality change.

Clumsy comedy partially redeemed by its supporting players.

w Louis M. Heyward *d* Norman Taurog

Frankie Avalon, Deborah Walley, Fred Clark, Cesar Romero, Eve Arden, Gale Gordon, Buster Keaton, Harvey Lembeck, John Ashley

Sergeant Madden
US 1939 78m bw
MGM (J. Walter Ruben)

A policeman's son becomes a gangster.

Routine crime melodrama with sentimental trimmings, quite untypical of its director.

w Wells Root *story A Gun in His Hand* by William A. Ulman *d* Josef von Sternberg *ph* John Seitz *m* William Axt

Wallace Beery, Tom Brown, Alan Curtis, Laraine Day, Fay Holden, Marc Lawrence, Marion Martin

'Good programme drama, geared to supply strong support in the key duals.' – *Variety*

Sgt Pepper's Lonely Hearts Club Band
US 1978 111m Technicolor Panavision
Universal/Robert Stigwood (Dee Anthony)
V*, L

A family band finds a new sound despite the activities of villains.

Oddball hotch-potch of middle-aged comedy and youth nostalgia with an American small-town setting. Some moments please, but most of it simply doesn't gell.

w Henry Edwards *d* Michael Schultz *ph* Owen Roizman *m* various (mostly the Beatles) *pd* Brian Eatwell

Peter Frampton, Barry Gibb, Robin Gibb, Maurice Gibb, George Burns, Frankie Howerd, Donald Pleasence, Paul Nicholas, Sandy Farina, Alice Cooper, Steve Martin, Earth Wind and Fire

'Another of those films which serve as feature-length screen advertising for an album.' – *Variety*

Sergeant Rutledge *
US 1960 111m Technicolor
Warner/John Ford (Willis Goldbeck, Patrick Ford)
V*

In 1881 a black army sergeant is on trial for rape and murder, but his defence counsel reveals the real culprit.

Flashback Western; not the director's best, but generally of some interest.

w James Warner Bellah, Willis Goldbeck *d* John Ford *ph* Bert Glennon *m* Howard Jackson

Woody Strode, Jeffrey Hunter, Constance Towers, Willis Bouchey, Billie Burke, Carleton Young, Juano Hernandez, Mae Marsh

Sergeant Steiner

West Germany   1979   115m   Eastmancolor
  Panavision
Palladium/Rapidfilm (Arlene Sellers, Alex Winitsky)
V*

The German sergeant hero of *Cross of Iron* survives the Western Front and involvement in an anti-Hitler conspiracy.

Somewhat bloodless though interesting sequel to an exceptionally nasty war film, with an international cast aiming at better box-office.

w Tony Williamson   *d* Andrew McLaglen
ph Tony Imi   *m* Peter Thomas

Richard Burton, Robert Mitchum, Curt Jurgens, Rod Steiger, Helmut Griem, Michael Parks

Sergeant York **

US   1941   134m   bw
Warner (Jesse L. Lasky)
V, V*, L

The story of a gentle hillbilly farmer who became a hero of World War I.

Standard real-life fiction given the big treatment; a key Hollywood film of its time in several ways.

w Abem Finkel, Harry Chandler, Howard Koch, John Huston   *d* Howard Hawks   *ph* Sol Polito   *m* Max Steiner   *ad* John Hughes   *ed* William Holmes

Gary Cooper, Joan Leslie, Walter Brennan, George Tobias, David Bruce, Stanley Ridges, Margaret Wycherly, Dickie Moore, Ward Bond

'I hardly think the effect is any different from that of a parade, with colours and a band; it is stirring and it is too long; there are too many holdups and too many people out of step, and your residue of opinion on the matter is that it will be nice to get home and get your shoes off.' – *Otis Ferguson*

'It has all the flavour of true Americana, the blunt and homely humour of backwoodsmen and the raw integrity peculiar to simple folk.' – *Bosley Crowther, New York Times*

AA: Gary Cooper

AAN: best picture; script; Howard Hawks; Sol Polito; Max Steiner; Walter Brennan; Margaret Wycherly; John Hughes; William Holmes

Sergeants Three

US   1961   112m   Technicolor   Panavision
(UA) Essex-Claude (Frank Sinatra)

Just after the Civil War three cavalry sergeants, with the help of an ex-slave bugler, dispose of some hostile Indians.

High-spirited but exhausting parody of *Gunga Din*, with bouts of unfunny bloodthirstiness separated by tedious slabs of dialogue.

w W. R. Burnett   *d* John Sturges   *ph* Winton Hoch, Carl Guthrie   *m* Billy May

Frank Sinatra, Dean Martin, Peter Lawford, Sammy Davis Jnr, Joey Bishop, Henry Silva, Ruta Lee

'The participants have a better time than the onlookers.' – *Judith Crist, 1973*

Serial *

US   1980   91m   Movielab
Paramount/Sidney Beckerman
V*, L

Well-heeled Californians in a high suburban community go in for various cults and fashions.

Amusing satire on everything from *Peyton Place* to *Bob and Carol and Ted and Alice*. Just a little late in coming, that's all.

---

w Rich Eustis, Michael Elias   *novel* Cyra McFadden
d Bill Persky   *ph* Rexford Metz   *m* Lalo Schifrin

Martin Mull, Tuesday Weld, Jennifer McAllister, Sam Chew Jnr, Sally Kellerman, Nita Talbot, Bill Macy, Christopher Lee, Pamela Bellwood, Peter Bonerz, Tom Smothers

Serious Charge

GB   1959   99m   bw
Alva (Mickey Delamar)

A small-town troublemaker, accused by his priest of being responsible for the death of a young girl, amuses himself by accusing the priest of making homosexual advances.

A sensational play of its time makes a dull film despite earnest performances.

w Guy Elmes, Mickey Delamar   *play* Philip King
d Terence Young   *ph* Georges Périnal   *m* Leighton Lucas

Anthony Quayle, Andrew Ray, Sarah Churchill, Irene Browne, Percy Herbert, Cliff Richard

The Serpent

France/Italy/Germany   1974   124m   colour
Films La Boetie (Henri Verneuil)
V*

A top KGB official defects to the West.

Complicated, humourless, multi-lingual spy capers.

w Henri Verneuil, Gilles Perrault   *novel* Pierre Nord
d Henri Verneuil   *ph* Claude Renoir   *m* Ennio Morricone

Yul Brynner, Henry Fonda, Dirk Bogarde, Philippe Noiret, Farley Granger, Virna Lisi

The Serpent and the Rainbow

US   1987   98m   DuArt
UIP/Universal (David Ladd, Doug Claybourne)
V, V*, L

A scientist travels to Haiti to investigate zombies.

Standard horror film, designed to shock, in which it succeeds.

w Richard Maxwell, A. R. Simoun   *book* Wade Davis   *d* Wes Craven   *ph* John Lindley   *m* Brad Fiedel   *pd* David Nichols   *ed* Glenn Farr

Bill Pullman, Cathy Tyson, Zakes Mokae, Paul Winfield, Brent Jennings, Conrad Roberts, Badja Djola, Theresa Merritt, Michael Gough

The Serpent's Egg *

West Germany/US   1977   120m   Eastmancolor
Rialto-Dino de Laurentiis
V*

An American trapeze artist has a hard time in Berlin at the time of Hitler's rise to power.

More of a curate's egg, really, with a poor leading performance and too many lapses into nastiness, but much incidental interest of the kind one associates with the director.

wd Ingmar Bergman   *ph* Sven Nykvist   *m* Rolf Wilhelm   *pd* Rolf Zehetbauer

David Carradine, Liv Ullmann, Gert Frobe, James Whitmore, Heinz Bennent

'A crackpot tragedy: everything is strained, insufficient, underfelt.' – *New Yorker*

Serpico *

US   1973   130m   Technicolor
Paramount/Artists Entertainment Complex/Dino de Laurentiis
  (Martin Bregman)
V*, L, S

A New York cop reveals police corruption and is eventually forced to leave the country.

A harrowing true story played with authentic gloom and violence.

---

w Waldo Salt, Norman Wexler   *book* Peter Maas
d Sidney Lumet   *ph* Arthur J. Ornitz   *m* Mikis Theodorakis

Al Pacino, John Randolph, Jack Kehoe, Biff McGuire

'There's nothing seriously wrong with *Serpico* except that it's unmemorable, and not even terribly interesting while it's going on.' – *Stanley Kauffmann*

AAN: script; Al Pacino

The Servant **

GB   1963   116m   bw
Elstree/Springbok (Joseph Losey, Norman Priggen)
V, V*

A rich, ineffectual young man is gradually debased and overruled by his sinister manservant and his sexy 'sister'.

Acclaimed in many quarters on its first release, this downbeat melodrama now seems rather naïve and long drawn out; its surface gloss is undeniable, but the final orgy is more risible than satanic.

w Harold Pinter   *novel* Robin Maugham   *d* Joseph Losey   *ph* Douglas Slocombe   *m* Johnny Dankworth

Dirk Bogarde, James Fox, Sarah Miles, Wendy Craig, Catherine Lacey, Richard Vernon

'Moodily suggestive, well acted, but petering out into a trickle of repetitious unmeaningful nastiness.' – *John Simon*

Servants' Entrance

US   1934   88m   bw
Fox

A maid falls in love with a chauffeur.

Upstairs downstairs style comedy drama; passable.

w Samson Raphaelson   *novel* Sigrid Boo   *d* Frank Lloyd   *ph* Hal Mohr   *m* Arthur Lange

Janet Gaynor, Lew Ayres, Walter Connolly, G. P. Huntley Jnr, Sig Rumann, Louise Dresser, Astrid Allwyn, Ned Sparks

'Capable production, directing and casting manages to make it fair entertainment.' – *Variety*

Service De Luxe *

US   1938   85m   bw
Universal

Adventures of the members of a super-secretarial agency.

Very tolerable but uninspired comedy which doesn't really allow its acting talent full rein.

w Gertrude Purcell, Leonard Spigelgass   *d* Rowland V Lee

Constance Bennett, Vincent Price, Charles Ruggles, Helen Broderick, Mischa Auer, Halliwell Hobbes

'A speedy comedy-drama . . . will hold its own as a leadoff attraction in the keys.' – *Variety*

Service for Ladies

GB   1932   93m   bw
Paramount (Alexander Korda)
US title: *Reserved for Ladies*

A waiter has a way with his rich lady clients.

Tenuous satirical comedy, a variation on the American silent *The Grand Duchess and the Waiter*.

w Eliot Crawshay-Williams, Lajos Biro   *novel The Head Waiter* by Ernst Vajda   *d* Alexander Korda   *m* Percival Mackey   *ad* Alfred Junge   *ed* Harold Young

Leslie Howard, George Grossmith, Benita Hume, Elizabeth Allan, Morton Selten, Cyril Ritchard, Martita Hunt, Merle Oberon

'Too talky and English for general American consumption.' – *Variety*

The Set Up ***

US 1949 72m bw
RKO (Richard Goldstone)
V*, L

An ageing boxer refuses to pull his last fight, and is beaten up by gangsters.

One of the most brilliant little *films noirs* of the late forties; thoroughly studio-bound, yet evoking a brilliant feeling for time and place. Photography, direction, editing, acting are all of a piece.

w Art Cohn *poem* Joseph Moncure March *d* Robert Wise *ph* Milton Krasner *md* Constantin Bakaleinikoff

Robert Ryan, Audrey Totter, George Tobias, Alan Baxter, Wallace Ford

The Settlement

Australia 1983 100m colour
Queensland Film Corporation/Robert Bruning

In Queensland in the 1950s, two drifters outrage locals when they set up house with a prostitute.

Small, enjoyable movie, with the accent on character and humour.

w Ted Roberts *d* Howard Rubie *ph* Ernest Clark *m* Sven Libaek *ad* John Watson *ed* Henry Dangar

Bill Kerr, John Jarratt, Lorna Lesley, Tony Barry, Katy Wild, David Downer, Elaine Cusick, Alan Cassell

Seven Angry Men *

US 1954 90m bw
Allied Artists (Vincent M. Fennelly)

In Kansas, John Brown determines to abolish slavery by violence.

Low-budget, intensely felt little biopic of the celebrated 19th-century fanatic and his sons.

w Daniel B. Ullman *d* Charles Marquis Warren *ph* Ellsworth Fredericks *m* Carl Brandt

Raymond Massey, Jeffrey Hunter, Larry Pennell, Debra Paget, Leo Gordon, John Smith, James Best, Dennis Weaver

Seven Beauties *

Italy 1975 115m Technicolor
Medusa (Lina Wertmuller, Giancarlo Giannini, Arrigo Colombo)
V*, L
original title: *Pasqualino Settebellezze*

An incorrigible survivor manages to get through the rigours of World War II and scarcely notices the damage to his honour.

Candide-like mixture of farce and satire with the addition of a good deal of unpleasantness. Less meaningful abroad than on its home ground.

wd Lina Wertmuller *ph* Tonino delli Colli *m* Enzo Jannacci

Giancarlo Giannini, Fernando Rey, Shirley Stoler, Piero di Iorio

'A stunning piece of work. Wertmuller proves here more brilliantly than before she is a somewhat erratic but individual, strong, fierce talent.' – *Stanley Kauffmann*

AAN: Lina Wertmuller (as writer and as director); best foreign film; Giancarlo Giannini

'I now pronounce you – men and wives!'
Seven Brides for Seven Brothers **

US 1954 104m Anscocolor Cinemascope
MGM (Jack Cummings)
V, V*, L, S

In the Old West, seven hard-working brothers decide they need wives, and carry off young women from the villages around.

Disappointingly studio-bound Western musical, distinguished by an excellent score and some brilliant dancing, notably the barn-raising sequence.

w Frances Goodrich, Albert Hackett *story Sobbin' Women* by Stephen Vincent Benet *d* Stanley Donen *ph* George Folsey *ch* Michael Kidd *songs* Johnny Mercer, Gene de Paul *m* Adolph Deutsch, Saul Chaplin *ed* Ralph E. Winters

Howard Keel, Jane Powell, Jeff Richards, Russ Tamblyn, Tommy Rall, Howard Petrie, Marc Platt, Jacques d'Amboise, Matt Mattox

'It does have a plot, it does have imagination, it fairly explodes into life, and many discerning people will find the dance arrangements – exact, insidious, acrobatic, graceful, slipped in as if they were a natural development of the story – wildly exciting.' – *C. A. Lejeune*

AA: Adolph Deutsch, Saul Chaplin

AAN: best picture; script; George Folsey; editing

Seven Chances **

US 1925 69m (24 fps) bw silent
Buster Keaton/Joseph M. Schenck

A meek young man finds that he is to inherit seven million dollars if he is married within a few hours.

Slim and rather slow comedy which builds to a fine climax as the hero is pursued first by hordes of women and then by rolling boulders.

w Clyde Bruckman, Jean Havez, Joseph A. Mitchell *play* Roi Cooper Megrue *d* Buster Keaton *ph* Elgin Lessley, Byron Houck

Buster Keaton, Ruth Dwyer, Ray Barnes, Snitz Edwards

† The rocks sequence, which makes the film, was added only after a disappointing sneak preview.

'The sword and the cross battle for California's soul!'
Seven Cities of Gold *

US 1955 103m DeLuxe Cinemascope
TCF (Robert D. Webb, Barbara McLean)
V*

In 1796, a Spanish expedition sets out from Mexico to annex California, but with it goes Father Junipero Serra . . .

A semi-historical, semi-religious Western which ends up not being much of anything but has interesting sequences.

w Richard L. Breen, John C. Higgins *novel* Isabelle Gibson Ziegler *d* Robert D. Webb *ph* Lucien Ballard *m* Hugo Friedhofer

Michael Rennie, Richard Egan, Anthony Quinn, Rita Moreno, Jeffrey Hunter, Eduardo Noriega, John Doucette

Seven Days in May ***

US 1964 120m bw
Seven Arts/Joel/John Frankenheimer (Edward Lewis)
V*, L

An American general's aide discovers that his boss intends a military takeover because he considers the President's pacifism traitorous.

Absorbing political mystery drama marred only by the unnecessary introduction of a female character. Stimulating entertainment.

w Rod Serling, *novel* Fletcher Knebel, Charles W. Bailey II *d* John Frankenheimer *ph* Ellsworth Fredericks *m* Jerry Goldsmith

Kirk Douglas, Burt Lancaster, Fredric March, Ava Gardner, Martin Balsam, Edmond O'Brien, George Macready, John Houseman

'A political thriller which grips from start to finish.' – *Penelope Houston*

'It is to be enjoyed without feelings of guilt, there should be more movies like it, and there is nothing first class about it.' – *John Simon*

'In the best tradition of the suspense thriller, with the ultimate thrill our awareness of its actual potential.' – *Judith Crist*

'An entertainment, in Graham Greene's sense of the word, and an intelligent one.' – *MFB*

AAN: Edmond O'Brien

Seven Days Leave

US 1929 83m bw
Paramount (Louis D. Lighton)
GB title: *Medals*

A London charlady 'adopts' a soldier, and both their lives are changed.

Sentimental melodrama which suited the times and confirmed Cooper's stardom.

w John Farrow, Dan Totheroh *play The Old Lady Shows Her Medals* by J. M. Barrie *d* Richard Wallace *ph* Charles Lang

Gary Cooper, Beryl Mercer, Daisy Belmore, Nora Cecil, Tempe Piggott, Arthur Hoyt, Basil Radford

Seven Days Leave

US 1942 87m bw
RKO (Tim Whelan)
V*

In order to inherit a hundred thousand dollars, a soldier must marry within a week.

Cheerful frivolity featuring radio stars of the time.

w William Bowers, Ralph Spence, Curtis Kenyon, Kenneth Earl *d* Tim Whelan *ph* Robert de Grasse *md* Roy Webb *songs* Frank Loesser, Jimmy McHugh

Lucille Ball, Victor Mature, Harold Peary, Mary Cortes, Ginny Simms, Ralph Edwards, Peter Lind Hayes, Marcy McGuire, Wallace Ford

Seven Days to Noon **

GB 1950 94m bw
London Films (Roy Boulting)

A professor engaged on atomic research threatens to blow up London unless his work is brought to an end.

Persuasively understated suspense piece which was subsequently much copied, so that it now seems rather obvious.

w Frank Harvey, Roy Boulting, Paul Dehn, James Bernard *d* John Boulting *ph* Gilbert Taylor *m* John Addison

Barry Jones, Olive Sloane, André Morell, Joan Hickson, Sheila Manahan, Hugh Cross, Ronald Adam, Marie Ney

'A first rate thriller that does not pretend to a serious message, but yet will leave a query in the mind.' – *Richard Winnington*

'A film of great tension and excitement with a climax that is reached after breathless suspense.' – *Star*

AA: Paul Dehn, James Bernard (motion picture story)

The Seven Deadly Sins *

France/Italy 1952 150m bw
Franco London/Costellazione
V*

The master of ceremonies introduces seven stories and an epilogue.

Among the most successful compendiums of its kind, partly because of cast and credits and partly because it came when French naughtiness was appealing to a wide international audience.

w Jean Aurenche, Pierre Bost, Roberto Rossellini, Leo Joannon, Carlo Rim, Diego Fabbri, Liana Ferri, Eduardo de Filippo, Charles Spaak, Turi Vaselle, René Wheeler *d* Eduardo de Filippo, Jean Dréville, Yves Allégret, Roberto Rossellini, Carlo Rim, Claude Autant-Lara, Georges Lacombe

Gérard Philipe, Isa Miranda, Eduardo de Filippo, Noel-Noel, Louis de Funès, Viviane Romance, Frank

Villard, Henri Vidal, Michèle Morgan, Françoise Rosay

Seven Different Ways: see *Quick Let's Get Married*

Seven Doors to Death
US   1944   60m   bw
Alfred Stern/PRC

The owners of six exclusive shops and an apartment house are all murder suspects.

Flabby little bottom-biller which never gets going.

wd Elmer Clifton

Chick Chandler, June Clyde, George Meeker, Gregory Gay, Edgar Dearing

711 Ocean Drive *
US   1950   102m   bw
Columbia (Frank N. Seltzer)

A wireless expert is drawn into the bookie racket.

Overlong but vigorous crime exposé melodrama with excellent location sequences, notably a climax on Hoover Dam.

w Richard English, Francis Swann   *d* Joseph H. Newman   *ph* Franz Planer   *m* Sol Kaplan

Edmond O'Brien, Joanne Dru, Otto Kruger, Don Porter, Sammy White, Dorothy Patrick, Barry Kelley, Howard St John

Seven Faces of Dr Lao *
US   1964   100m   Metrocolor
MGM/George Pal
V*, L

An elderly Chinaman with a penchant for spectacular disguise solves the problems of a Western desert town.

A pleasant idea and excellent production are submerged in a sloppily sentimental and verbose script.

w Charles Beaumont   *novel* The Circus of Dr Lao by Charles G. Finney   *d* George Pal   *ph* Robert Bronner   *m* Leigh Harline   *make-up* William Tuttle

Tony Randall, Arthur O'Connell, John Ericson, Barbara Eden, Noah Beery Jnr, Lee Patrick, Minerva Urecal, John Qualen

Seven Footsteps to Satan
US   1929   70m   bw
Warner

A rich recluse plays an elaborate and macabre joke on his niece and nephew.

Richly-designed but dramatically disappointing haunted house spoof.

w Richard Bee   *d* Benjamin Christensen

Thelma Todd, Creighton Hale, Sheldon Lewis, Ivan Christie, Sojin

Seven Golden Men *
Italy/France/Spain   1965   91m   Eastmancolor
Atlantica/PUF/Asfilm/Warner

Seven master criminals plot to rob a bank of its gold.

Simple-minded but slickly handled caper story with many visual pleasures.

wd Marco Vicario

Rossana Podesta, Philippe Leroy, Gastone Moschin, Gabriele Tinti

† A sequel, *Seven Golden Men Strike Again*, was less successful.

Seven Hills of Rome
US/Italy   1957   104m   Technirama
MGM/Titanus (Lester Welch)

An American singer in Italy is pursued by the fiancée with whom he has quarrelled.

Thin travelogue with several halts for the star to sing; production very patchy.

w Art Cohn, Giorgio Prosperi   *d* Roy Rowland   *ph* Tonino Delli Colli   *md* George Stoll

Mario Lanza, Renato Rascel, Marisa Allasio, Peggie Castle

Seven Keys to Baldpate *
US   1935   69m   bw
RKO

A novelist retiring to a lonely inn for inspiration finds it full of criminals and damsels in distress.

An old theatrical warhorse with a trick ending, also filmed in 1929 (with Richard Dix; *Variety* said 'it all happens like a synopsis of what might have occurred') and in 1947 with Philip Terry. There was also a horror variation in 1982, *House of the Long Shadows* (qv). None was as satisfying as a good stage production.

play George M. Cohan   *story* Earl Derr Biggers   *d* William Hamilton, Edward Killy   *ph* Robert de Grasse

Gene Raymond, Margaret Callahan, Eric Blore, Grant Mitchell, Moroni Olsen, Henry Travers

'Too much conversation and too little action.' – *Variety*

† The 1935 version at least will be found to have lost its trick ending, without which it ends lamely. A curious executive decision.

The Seven Little Foys *
US   1955   95m   Technicolor   Vistavision
Paramount (Jack Rose)
V*

The story of a family vaudeville act.

Routine showbiz biopic, a little heavy on the syrup.

w Melville Shavelson, Jack Rose   *d* Melville Shavelson   *ph* John F. Warren   *md* Joseph J. Lilley

Bob Hope, Milly Vitale, George Tobias, Angela Clarke, Herbert Heyes, *James Cagney* as George M. Cohan

AAN: script

Seven Men from Now
US   1956   78m   Warnercolor
Batjac (Andrew V. McLaglen, Robert E. Morrison)

A sheriff seeks revenge when his wife is killed by bandits.

Good Western programmer.

w Burt Kennedy   *d* Budd Boetticher   *ph* William H. Clothier   *m* Henry Vars

Randolph Scott, Gail Russell, Lee Marvin, Walter Reed, Don Barry, John Larch

Seven Miles from Alcatraz
US   1942   62m   bw
RKO (Herman Schlom)
V*

Prison escapees take over an offshore lighthouse.

Compact melodrama with the lifers heroically catching spies.

w Joseph Krumgold, John D. Klorer   *d* Edward Dmytryk

James Craig, Bonita Granville, Frank Jenks, Cliff Edwards, George Cleveland, Tala Birell, John Banner

The Seven Minutes
US   1971   102m   DeLuxe
TCF (Russ Meyer)

A bookseller is arrested for distributing an obscene novel, and many people are unexpectedly involved in the court case.

A fascinating piece of old-fashioned hokum, full of 'daring' words and cameo performances.

w Richard Warren Lewis   *novel* Irving Wallace   *d* Russ Meyer   *ph* Fred Mandl   *m* Stu Philips

Wayne Maunder, Marianne MacAndrew, Yvonne de Carlo, Phil Carey, Jay C. Flippen, Edy Williams, Lyle Bettger, Ron Randell, David Brian, Charles Drake, John Carradine, Harold J. Stone

Seven Nights in Japan
GB/France   1976   104m   Eastmancolor
EMI-Marianne (Lewis Gilbert)

The heir to the British throne has shore leave in Tokyo and falls in love with a geisha.

Tediously daring romance with a banal script which seems over impressed by its own barely-existent controversial qualities.

w Christopher Wood   *d* Lewis Gilbert   *ph* Henri Decaë   *m* David Hentschel

Michael York, Hidemi Aoki, James Villiers, Peter Jones, Charles Gray

The Seven Per Cent Solution
US   1976   114m   Technicolor
Universal (Herbert Ross)
V*, L

Dr Watson lures Sherlock Holmes to Vienna so that Professor Freud can cure him of persecution complex and cocaine addiction.

Drearily serious spoof with only a glimmer of the required style and a totally miscast Holmes.

w Nicholas Meyer   *novel* Nicholas Meyer   *d* Herbert Ross   *ph* Oswald Morris   *m* John Addison   *pd* Ken Adam

Nicol Williamson, Robert Duvall, Alan Arkin, Vanessa Redgrave, Laurence Olivier, Jeremy Kemp, Samantha Eggar, Joel Grey, Charles Gray, Georgia Brown, Regine

'Sorrily botched all-star extravaganza.' – *Sight and Sound*

'Comes into the category of hit and myth . . . A heavyweight spoof in which Sherlock Holmes is placed under hypnosis by Sigmund Freud. The audience is then placed under hypnosis by director Herbert Ross.' – *Michael Billington, Illustrated London News*

AAN: script

The Seven Samurai ****
Japan   1954   155m   bw
Toho (Shojiro Motoki)
V, V*, L, S
original title: *Shichi-nin no Samurai*

16th-century villagers hire samurai to defend their property against an annual raid by bandits.

Superbly strange, vivid and violent medieval adventure which later served as the basis for the Western *The Magnificent Seven* and the science-fiction film *Battle Beyond the Stars*.

w Akira Kurosawa, Shinobu Hashimoto, Hideo Oguni   *d* Akira Kurosawa   *ph* Asaichi Nakai   *m* Fumio Hayasaka   *ad* Takashi Matsuyama

Toshiro Mifune, Takashi Shimura, Kuninori Kodo

'It is as sheer narrative, rich in imagery, incisiveness and sharp observation, that it makes its strongest impact . . . It provides a fascinating display of talent, and places its director in the forefront of creative film-makers of his generation.' – *Gavin Lambert, Sight and Sound*

'This, on the surface, is a work of relentless, unmitigated action, as epic as any film ever made, and, again on the surface, sheer entertainment. Yet it is also an unquestionable triumph of art.' – *John Simon*

AAN: art direction

Seven Seas to Calais

US/Italy 1962 103m Eastmancolor
Cinemascope
MGM/Adelphia (Paolo Moffa)

In 1577, Sir Francis Drake follows the Spanish treasure route.

Ho-hum swashbuckler with a background of schoolboy history.

w Filippo Sanjust d Rudolph Maté ph Giulio Gianini m Franco Mannino

Rod Taylor, Keith Michell, Irene Worth, Anthony Dawson, Basil Dignam

Seven Sinners *

GB 1936 70m bw
Gaumont (Michael Balcon)
US title: Doomed Cargo

Gunrunners wreck trains to cover traces of murder.

Fascinatingly dated comedy suspenser with excellent sub-Hitchcock sequences, the whole thing having a strong flavour of The 39 Steps.

w Frank Launder, Sidney Gilliat, L. DuGarde Peach, Austin Melford play The Wrecker by Arnold Ridley, Bernard Merivale d Albert de Courville ph Mutz Greenbaum (Max Greene)

Edmund Lowe, Constance Cummings, Thomy Bourdelle, Henry Oscar, Felix Aylmer, Allan Jeayes, O. B. Clarence

Seven Sinners *

US 1940 86m bw
Universal (Joe Pasternak)
V*
GB title: Café of Seven Sinners

A cabaret singer is deported from several South Sea islands for causing too many fights among the naval officers.

Ho-hum hokum with an amiable cast and a good-natured final free-for-all.

w John Meehan, Harry Tugend d Tay Garnett ph Rudolph Maté m Frank Skinner

Marlene Dietrich, John Wayne, Albert Dekker, Broderick Crawford, Mischa Auer, Billy Gilbert, Oscar Homolka, Anne Lee, Samuel S. Hinds

'Nothing to worry about, unless you happen to be in the theatre, watching it go from fairly good to worse than worse.' – Otis Ferguson

Seven Sweethearts

US 1942 98m bw
MGM (Joe Pasternak)

Seven daughters must marry in sequence, eldest first.

Period musical frou-frou inspired by Pride and Prejudice. So light it almost floats.

w Walter Reisch, Leo Townsend d Frank Borzage ph George Folsey m Franz Waxman

Kathryn Grayson, Marsha Hunt, Van Heflin, Cecelia Parker, S. Z. Sakall, Peggy Moran, Isobel Elsom, Diana Lewis, Donald Meek, Louise Beavers

Seven Thieves *

US 1960 102m bw Cinemascope
TCF (Sidney Boehm)
V*

An elderly crook conceives a last plan to rob the Monte Carlo casino.

Routine caper story, efficiently presented with some humour.

w Sidney Boehm novel Lions at the Kill by Max Catto d Henry Hathaway ph Sam Leavitt m Dominic Frontière

Edward G. Robinson, Rod Steiger, Joan Collins, Eli Wallach, Michael Dante, Alexander Scourby, Berry Kroeger, Sebastian Cabot

'Christ, it was supposed to be a fun film, and Steiger is far, far from having a sense of humour.' – Henry Hathaway

Seven Thunders

GB 1957 100m bw
Daniel M. Angel/Rank
US title: The Beasts of Marseilles

In wartime Marseilles, escaped POWs are helped by a doctor who turns out to have sinister intent.

Slow chiller which telegraphs its surprises but gets by on good production values.

w John Baines novel Rupert Croft-Cooke d Hugo Fregonese

James Robertson Justice, Stephen Boyd, Kathleen Harrison, Anna Gaylor, Tony Wright, Eugene Deckers, Rosalie Crutchley

'They take the third degree one step further!'

The Seven-Ups

US 1973 103m DeLuxe
TCF/Philip D'Antoni

Gangsters are hunted down by a secret force of the New York police.

Formulary realistic rough stuff in the wake of The French Connection.

w Albert Ruben, Alexander Jacobs d Philip D'Antoni ph Urs Furrer m Don Ellis

Roy Scheider, Victor Arnold, Jerry Leon, Tony Lo Bianco, Richard Lynch

Seven Waves Away

GB 1956 95m bw
Columbia/Copa (John R. Sloan)
US title: Abandon Ship

After the sinking of a luxury liner, the officer in charge of a lifeboat has to make life or death decisions.

Initially gripping but finally depressing open sea melodrama derived from Souls at Sea and later remade for TV as The Last Survivors.

wd Richard Sale ph Wilkie Cooper m Arthur Bliss

Tyrone Power, Mai Zetterling, Lloyd Nolan, Stephen Boyd, Moira Lister, James Hayter, Marie Lohr, Moultrie Kelsall, Noel Willman, Gordon Jackson, Clive Morton, John Stratton

'Eventually one is bludgeoned into a grudging admiration for the film's staying power.' – Peter John Dyer

'It jabs at your entrails with a cold unrelenting spear.' – New York Times

Seven Ways from Sundown

US 1960 87m Eastmancolor
Universal-International

A Texas Ranger befriends an outlaw, but has twinges of conscience.

Straightforward character Western with the inevitable shootout finale.

w Clair Huffaker d Harry Keller

Audie Murphy, Barry Sullivan, Venetia Stevenson, John McIntire, Kenneth Tobey

'Love, lust, courage and cowardice! Faith, fury and sacrifice!'

Seven Women *

US 1966 100m Metrocolor Panavision
MGM/John Ford/Bernard Smith
L

In 1935, an isolated Chinese mission staffed by American women is overrun by bandits.

Dusty melodrama which might have appealed in the thirties but was quite out of tune with the sixties. Well enough made and acted, but a strange choice for Ford's last film.

w Janet Green, John McCormick story Chinese Finale by Norah Lofts d John Ford ph Joseph LaShelle m Elmer Bernstein

Anne Bancroft, Flora Robson, Margaret Leighton, Sue Lyon, Mildred Dunnock, Betty Field, Anna Lee, Eddie Albert, Mike Mazurki, Woody Strode, Irene Tsu

The Seven Year Itch *

US 1955 105m DeLuxe Cinemascope
TCF (Charles K. Feldman, Billy Wilder)
V, V*, L

A married man has a fling with the girl upstairs.

An amusing theatrical joke, with dream sequences like revue sketches, is really all at sea on the big screen, especially as the affair remains unconsummated, but direction and performances keep the party going more or less.

w Billy Wilder, George Axelrod play George Axelrod d Billy Wilder ph Milton Krasner m Alfred Newman

Tom Ewell, Marilyn Monroe, Sonny Tufts, Evelyn Keyes, Robert Strauss, Oscar Homolka, Marguerite Chapman, Victor Moore

Seventeen

US 1940 76m bw
Stuart Walker/Paramount

Adolescent problems of a midwestern small-town boy.

Old-fashioned family entertainment, smartly cast and filmed.

w Agnes Christine Johnston, Stuart Palmer novel Booth Tarkington d Louis King

Jackie Cooper, Betty Field, Otto Kruger, Ann Shoemaker, Norma Nelson

1776 *

US 1972 141m Eastmancolor Panavision
Columbia/Jack L. Warner
V*, L

The thirteen American colonies prepare to declare their independence of Great Britain.

Plain, low-key filming of the successful Broadway musical showing the domestic lives of the historical figures concerned. Splendid moments alternate with stretches of tedium.

w Peter Stone play Peter Stone d Peter Hunt ph Harry Stradling Jnr md Ray Heindorf m/ly Sherman Edwards ad George Jenkins

William Daniels, Howard da Silva, Ken Howard, Donald Madden, Blythe Danner

AAN: Harry Stradling Jnr

Seventh Cavalry

US 1956 75m Technicolor
Columbia/Scott-Brown

An officer accused of cowardice volunteers to bring back General Custer's body after Little Big Horn.

Lively co-feature with a good traditional action climax.

w Peter Packer d Joseph H. Lewis ph Ray Rennahan m Mischa Bakaleinikoff

Randolph Scott, Barbara Hale, Jay C. Flippen, Jeanette Nolan, Frank Faylen

The Seventh Cross **

US 1944 112m bw
MGM (Pandro S. Berman)
V*

Seven Germans escape from a concentration camp, and the Nazis threaten to execute them all. Just one escapes.

Impressive melodrama, brilliantly limiting its escape/suspense story to studio sets. Old style Hollywood production at its best; but a rather obviously contrived story.

w Helen Deutsch　*novel* Anna Seghers　*d* Fred Zinnemann　*ph* Karl Freund　*m* Roy Webb　*ad* Cedric Gibbons, Leonid Vasian

Spencer Tracy, Signe Hasso, Hume Cronyn, Jessica Tandy, Agnes Moorehead, Felix Bressart, George Macready, George Zucco

AAN: Hume Cronyn

The Seventh Dawn
GB　1964　123m　Technicolor
UA/Holden/Charles K. Feldman (Karl Tunberg)

In the early fifties a Malayan rubber planter finds that his best friend is a leading terrorist.

Doom-laden romantic adventure drama with a lot of suffering and too little entertainment value.

w Karl Tunberg　*novel* The Durian Tree by Michael Keon　*d* Lewis Gilbert　*ph* Freddie Young　*m* Riz Ortolani

William Holden, Tetsuro Tamba, Capucine, Susannah York, Michael Goodliffe, Allan Cuthbertson, Maurice Denham

'Echoes of The Ugly American, Love Is a Many-Splendored Thing, and many another adventure East of Sumatra, with every character running absolutely true to form.' – MFB

'An interminable melange of political, racial and romantic clichés, with performances and dialogue as overripe as the jungle setting.' – Judith Crist, 1973

Seventh Day, Eighth Night **
Czechoslovakia　1969　108m　bw
Filmowe Studio Barrandov (Vera Kadlecova)
original title: Den Sedmy – Osma Noc

Following the disappearance of the station master, a village is panicked into believing that it is facing danger from an unknown enemy.

Savage, black political farce of intimidation and betrayal that was withheld for several years by the Czech authorities.

w Zdenek Mahler, Evald Schorm　*d* Evald Schorm　*ph* Vaclav Hanus　*m* Jan Klusak　*pd* Karel Lier

Jaroslav Wagner-Kleuka, Jan Kacer, Jana Markova, Kveta Fialova, Ljuba Skorepova, Josef Bek

Seventh Heaven **
US　1927　93m approx (24 fps)　bw　silent
Fox (William Fox)

A Paris sewer worker shelters a street waif, marries her and after idyllic happiness goes off to war, returning blinded.

All softness, sweetness and light, a very typical – and attractive – film of its director and a big influence on Hollywood's European period.

w Benjamin Glazer　*play* Austin Strong　*d* Frank Borzage　*ph* Ernest Palmer, J. A. Valentine　*ad* Harry Oliver

Janet Gaynor, Charles Farrell, Gladys Brockwell, David Butler

AA: Benjamin Glazer; Frank Borzage; Janet Gaynor

AAN: best picture; Harry Oliver

Seventh Heaven *
US　1937　102m　bw
TCF (Raymond Griffith)

Dewy-eyed remake; the mood is antediluvian but the production impresses.

w Melville Baker　*d* Henry King　*ph* Merritt Gerstad　*md* Louis Silvers　*ad* William Darling

James Stewart, Simone Simon, Jean Hersholt, Gale Sondergaard, J. Edward Bromberg, Gregory Ratoff, John Qualen, Victor Kilian, Sig Rumann, Mady Christians

---

'A romance that can stand another telling . . . the older element will join in making it a bracer for the box office.' – Variety

The Seventh Seal ****
Sweden　1957　95m　bw
Svensk Filmindustri (Allan Ekelund)
V, V*, L
original title: Det Sjunde Inseglet

Death comes for a knight, who challenges him to a game of chess while he tries to show illustrations of goodness in mankind: but Death takes them all away in the end.

A modestly budgeted minor classic which, because of its international success and its famous shots, is seldom analysed in detail. It is kept going by its splendid cinematic feel and its atmosphere is that of a dark world irrationally sustained by religion.

wd Ingmar Bergman　*ph* Gunnar Fischer　*m* Erik Nordgren

Max von Sydow, Bengt Ekerot, Gunnar Bjornstrand, Nils Poppe, Bibi Andersson, Gunnel Lindblom

'The most extraordinary mixture of beauty and lust and cruelty, Odin-worship and Christian faith, darkness and light.' – Alan Dent, Illustrated London News

'You know where they dance along the horizon? We'd packed up for the evening and were about to go home. Suddenly I saw a cloud, and Fischer swung his camera up. Some actors had gone, so grips had to stand in. The whole scene was improvised in ten minutes flat.' – Ingmar Bergman

The Seventh Sign
US　1988　95m　colour
Columbia Tri-Star/Interscope (Ted Field, Robert Cort)
V, V*, L, S

A pregnant mother fears that the birth of her baby will signal the end of the world.

Apocalyptic thriller that is too silly to be enjoyable on any level.

w Clifford Green, Ellen Green　*d* Carl Schultz　*ph* Juan Ruiz-Anchia　*m* Jack Nitzsche　*pd* Stephen Marsh　*ed* Caroline Biggerstaff

Jürgen Prochnow, Demi Moore, Michael Biehn, Peter Friedman, John Taylor, John Heard

The Seventh Sin
US　1957　94m　bw　Cinemascope
MGM (David Lewis)

A faithless wife accompanies her bacteriologist husband to fight a Chinese cholera epidemic, and regains her self-respect.

Tatty remake of a Garbo vehicle which was dated even in 1934. (See The Painted Veil.)

w Karl Tunberg　*novel* The Painted Veil by Somerset Maugham　*d* Ronald Neame　*ph* Ray June　*m* Miklos Rozsa

Eleanor Parker, Bill Travers, George Sanders, Jean-Pierre Aumont, Françoise Rosay

The Seventh Survivor
GB　1941　75m　bw
British National

Survivors of a shipwreck gather in a lighthouse and discover that one of them is a Nazi agent.

Adequate mystery potboiler, comparable with Hitchcock's talkier Lifeboat.

w Michael Barringer　*d* Leslie Hiscott

Linden Travers, Austin Trevor, John Stuart, Martita Hunt, Frank Pettingell, Jane Carr, Felix Aylmer, Wally Patch, Henry Oscar

The Seventh Veil **
GB　1945　94m　bw
Theatrecraft/Sydney Box/Ortus
V, V*

A concert pianist is romantically torn between her psychiatrist, her guardian, and two other fellows.

A splendid modern melodrama in the tradition of Jane Eyre and Rebecca; it set the seal of moviegoing approval on psychiatry, classical music, and James Mason, and it is the most utter tosh.

w Muriel and Sydney Box　*d* Compton Bennett　*ph* Reg Wyer　*m* Benjamin Frankel

James Mason, Ann Todd, Herbert Lom, Albert Lieven, Hugh McDermott, Yvonne Owen, David Horne, Manning Whiley

'An example of the intelligent, medium-priced picture made with great technical polish which has represented for Hollywood the middle path between the vulgar and the highbrow.' – Spectator

'A popular film that does not discard taste and atmosphere.' – Daily Mail

'A rich, portentous mixture of Beethoven, Chopin, Kitsch and Freud.' – Pauline Kael, 1968

'An odd, artificial, best sellerish kind of story, with reminiscences of Trilby and Jane Eyre and all their imitations down to Rebecca.' – Richard Mallett, Punch

'Maybe, with a few veils stripped away, all of us have a fantasist inside who gobbles up this sadomasochistic sundae.' – Pauline Kael, 70s

AA: script

The Seventh Victim *
US　1943　71m　bw
RKO (Val Lewton)
V*, L

A girl goes to New York in search of her sister, who is under the influence of Satanists.

Much praised but in effect rather boring little thriller, with rather stately acting and ponderous direction and dialogue. Censorship made the plot so obscure that it's difficult to follow.

w Charles O'Neal, De Witt Bodeen　*d* Mark Robson　*ph* Nicholas Musuraca　*m* Constantin Bakaleinikoff

Kim Hunter, Tom Conway, Jean Brooks, Hugh Beaumont, Erford Gage, Isabel Jewell, Evelyn Brent

'It is the almost oppressive mood, the romantic obsession with death-in-life, which dominates the film.' – NFT, 1973

† Note the use in the first scene of the staircase from The Magnificent Ambersons.

The Seventh Voyage of Sinbad *
US　1958　89m　Technicolor
Columbia/Morningside (Charles Schneer)
V, V*, L

Sinbad seeks a roc's egg which will restore his fiancée from the midget size to which an evil magician has reduced her.

Lively fantasy with narrative drive and excellent effects.

w Kenneth Kolb　*d* Nathan Juran　*ph* Wilkie Cooper　*m* Bernard Herrmann　*sp* Ray Harryhausen

Kerwin Mathews, Kathryn Grant, Torin Thatcher, Richard Eyer, Alec Mango

70,000 Witnesses
US　1932　69m　bw
Harry Joe Brown/Paramount

A football star is murdered in the middle of a game.

Okay for sports fans, but not much of a murder mystery.

w Garrett Fort, P. J. Wolfson, Allen Rivkin　*novel* Cortland Fitzsimmons　*d* Ralph Murphy

Phillips Holmes, Johnny Mack Brown, Charles Ruggles, Dorothy Jordan, J. Farrell MacDonald, Lew Cody

'Will make money and please . . . enough comedy interwoven to satisfy on laughs alone.' – *Variety*

Several Interviews on Personal Problems **
USSR   1979   94m   colour
Gruziafilm
original title: *Neskolko Intervyu Po Lichnyam Voprosam*

A busy journalist spends her time sorting out other people's problems while failing to solve her own domestic difficulties.

Interspersed with interviews with Soviet women on their lives, it provides a compassionate, witty look at the situation of women in Russia.

w Zaira Arsenishvili, Erlom Akhviediani, Lana Gogoberidze   *d* Lana Gogoberidze   *ph* Nugzar Erkomaishvili   *m* Gia Kanchell

Sofiko Chiaureli, Gia Badrize, Ketevan Orakhelashvili, Janri Lolashvili, Salome Kancheli, Ketevan Bochorishvili, Noutsa Alexi-Meskhshvili

A Severed Head *
GB   1970   98m   Technicolor
Columbia/Winkast (Alan Ladd Jnr)

A wine merchant has a long-standing affair which he thinks is secret, but is annoyed when his wife tries the same game.

Unwisely boisterous screen version of a slyly academic novel; tolerably sophisticated for those who don't know the original.

w Frederic Raphael   *novel* Iris Murdoch   *d* Dick Clement   *ph* Austin Dempster   *m* Stanley Myers   *pd* Richard Macdonald

Lee Remick, Richard Attenborough, Ian Holm, Claire Bloom, Jennie Linden, Clive Revill

Severed Ties
US   1991   90m   colour
Fangoria Films (Christopher Webster)
V

A mad, mother-dominated scientist grows himself a new arm from plasma taken from a serial killer and a lizard, with predictable results.

Unbelievably cheap, would-be comic horror, by far the worst film its two stars have ever made (and they have appeared in some appalling ones), devoid of style or invention, and taking its plot from half a dozen better movies.

w John Nystrom, Henry Dominic   *story* Damon Santostefano, David A. Casci   *d* Damon Santostefano   *ph* Geza Sincovics   *m* Daniel Licht   *pd* Don Day   *sp* KNB Effects   *ed* Richard Roberts

Oliver Reed, Elke Sommer, Garrett Morris, Johnny Legend, Denise Wallace, Roger Perkovich, Bekki Vallin, Billy Morrisette

'Combo of grotesque gore effects and over-the-top acting is a winning one.' – *Variety*

Sex and the Single Girl
US   1964   114m   Technicolor
Warner/Richard Quine/Reynard (William T. Orr)
V*, L

A journalist worms his way into the life of a lady sexologist in order to unmask her – but guess what.

Coy sex comedy with noise substituting for wit and style, all pretence being abandoned in a wild chase climax.

w Joseph Heller, David R. Schwarz   *book* Helen Gurley Brown   *d* Richard Quine   *ph* Charles Lang Jnr   *m* Neal Hefti

Natalie Wood, Tony Curtis, Henry Fonda, Lauren Bacall, Mel Ferrer, Fran Jeffries, Edward Everett Horton, Otto Kruger

'For those willing to devote two hours of their lives to a consideration of Natalie Wood's virginity.' – *Judith Crist, 1973*

Sex and the Vampire: see Le Frisson des Vampires

sex, lies and videotape **
US   1989   100m   CFI
Virgin/Outlaw Productions (Robert Newmyer, John Hardy)
V, V*, L, S

An old college friend, who likes to videotape interviews with women about their sexual experiences, visits a couple whose marriage is in difficulties.

Witty, intelligent conversation piece that won the Palme D'Or for best film at the Cannes Film Festival.

wd Steve Soderbergh   *ph* Walt Lloyd   *m* Cliff Martinez   *ad* Joanne Schmidt   *ed* Steve Soderbergh

James Spader, Andie MacDowell, Peter Gallagher, Laura San Giacomo, Ron Vawter

AAN: best original screenplay

The Sex Life of a Female Private Eye: see Big Zapper

Sextette *
US   1978   91m   Metrocolor
Briggs and Sullivan (Warren G. Toub)
V*

The honeymoon of a Hollywood film star is interrupted by her previous husbands.

An amazing last stab at her old métier by an 86-year-old ex-star. It doesn't work, of course, and most of it is embarrassing, but the attempt is in itself remarkable.

w Herbert Baker   *play* Mae West   *d* Ken Hughes   *ph* James Crabe   *m* Artie Butler

Mae West, Tony Curtis, Ringo Starr, Dom de Luise, Timothy Dalton, George Hamilton, Alice Cooper, Rona Barrett, Walter Pidgeon, George Raft

Sexton Blake and the Hooded Terror
GB   1938   70m   bw
George King

A millionaire is unmasked as the head of a criminal gang.

Rather unyielding series melodrama, chiefly interesting for the casting of Tod Slaughter as Blake's Moriarty.

w A. R. Rawlinson   *d* George King

George Curzon, Tod Slaughter, Greta Gynt, Charles Oliver, David Farrar

TERROR: 'You little fool! Don't you realise that the game is up? The Black Quorum has seen through your treacheries. I alone can save you from their revenge!'
GIRL: 'I'd rather die.'

† Other Sexton Blake movies, all cheaply made by British independents, include six 1928 two-reelers starring Langhorne Burton: *Sexton Blake and the Bearded Doctor* and *Sexton Blake and the Mademoiselle*, both 1935, both with Curzon; *Meet Sexton Blake* and *The Echo Murders*, both 1943, both with David Farrar; and *Murder on Site Three*, 1963 with Geoffrey Toone.

Sh! The Octopus
US   1937   54m   bw
First National

Lamebrain detectives fight a giant octopus in a lighthouse.

Footling remake of *The Gorilla* (qv).

w George Bricker   *d* William McGann

Hugh Herbert, Allen Jenkins, Marcia Ralston, John Eldredge, George Rosener

'This bit of grist for the double-feature mills is so feeble even the actors seem embarrassed.' – *Variety*

Shack Out on 101 *
US   1955   80m   bw
AA/William F. Broidy
V*

A waitress at a café near a research establishment unmasks two spies.

Modest suspenser which seemed at the time to have some fresh and realistic attitudes.

w Ed and Mildred Dein   *d* Ed Dein   *ph* Floyd Crosby   *m* Paul Dunlap

Frank Lovejoy, Lee Marvin, Keenan Wynn, Terry Moore, Whit Bissell

Shadey
GB   1985   106m   colour
Larkspur/Otto Plashkes

A bankrupt car mechanic will do almost anything to finance his sex change operation.

Weird, utterly unprovoked and unmotivated black comedy which confounded all comers.

w Snoo Wilson   *d* Philip Saville   *ph* Roger Deakins   *m* Colin Towns

Anthony Sher, Billie Whitelaw, Patrick MacNee, Leslie Ash, Bernard Hepton, Larry Lamb, Katherine Helmond

The Shadow
GB   1933   74m   bw
UA/Real Art (Julius Hagen)

A police hunt for a murderous blackmailer leads to the Chief Commissioner's house.

Old-fashioned whodunnit that looks like a stage production transferred intact to the screen.

w H. Fowler Mear, Terence Egan   Donald Stuart   *d* George A. Cooper   *ph* Sydney Blythe   *ad* James A. Carter   *ed* Jack Harris

Henry Kendall, Elizabeth Allan, Felix Aylmer, John Turnbull, Cyril Raymond

The Shadow
US   1940   bw   serial: 15 eps
Columbia

A scientist and criminologist assumes the guise of The Shadow in order to combat The Black Tiger.

Archetypal silly season serial.

d James W. Horne

Victor Jory, Veda Ann Borg, Robert Moore, Robert Fiske, J. Paul Jones

Shadow in the Sky
US   1951   78m   bw
MGM (William H. Wright)

A shell-shocked marine moves from a psychiatric hospital to live with his sister.

Low-key drama, plainly but quite well done, though of little continuing interest.

w Ben Maddow   *d* Fred M. Wilcox   *ph* George Folsey   *m* Bronislau Kaper

Ralph Meeker, Nancy Davis, James Whitmore, Jean Hagen

Shadow Makers
US   1989   127m   Technicolor
UIP/Paramount (Tony Garnett)
V, V*, L

The army and scientists clash when working on a project to develop the first atom bomb.

A significant moment in history is rendered mundane in a damp squib of a film.

w Bruce Robinson, Roland Joffe   *d* Roland Joffe   *ph* Vilmos Zsigmond   *m* Ennio Morricone   *pd* Gregg Fonseca   *ed* Françoise Bonnot

Paul Newman, Dwight Schultz, Bonnie Bedelia, John Cusack, Laura Dern, Ron Frazier, John C. McGinley, Natasha Richardson, Ron Vawter

Shadow of a Doubt ***
US 1943 108m bw
Universal (Jack H. Skirball)
V*, L

A favourite uncle comes to visit his family in a small Californian town. He is actually on the run from police, who know him as the Merry Widow murderer.

Hitchcock's quietest film is memorable chiefly for its depiction of small-town life; but the script is well written and keeps the suspense moving slowly but surely.

w *Thornton Wilder, Sally Benson, Alma Reville,* story Gordon McDonell d *Alfred Hitchcock* ph Joe Valentine m Dimitri Tiomkin

Joseph Cotten, Teresa Wright, Hume Cronyn, Macdonald Carey, Patricia Collinge, Henry Travers, Wallace Ford

'Some clever observation of rabbity white-collar life which, in spite of a specious sweetness, is the best since *It's a Gift.*' – *James Agee*

† Remade in 1959 as *Step Down to Terror,* with Charles Drake.

AAN: original story

Shadow of a Woman
US 1946 78m bw
Warner

A woman suspects her husband of trying to murder his son by a former marriage.

Poor melodrama on *Love from a Stranger* lines.

w Whitman Chambers, C. Graham Baker d Joseph Santley

Andrea King, Helmut Dantine, Don McGuire, Richard Erdman, William Prince

Shadow of Chinatown
US 1936 bw serial: 15 eps
Victory

A master villain is employed by international businessmen to close down the trade of Chinatown.

Inept but action-packed serial with unintentional laughs.

d Bob Hill

Bela Lugosi, Joan Barclay, Herman Brix, Luana Walters

Shadow of Doubt
US 1935 71m bw
MGM

An actress suspected of murder is cleared by the efforts of her fiancé's aunt.

Routine mystery with a strong part for a new character actress from England.

w Wells Root, Arthur Somers Roche d George B. Seitz

Ricardo Cortez, Virginia Bruce, *Constance Collier,* Arthur Byron, Isabel Jewell, Regis Toomey, Edward Brophy

'Passable murder mystery.' – *Variety*

Shadow of Fear
GB 1963 60m bw
Butcher's (John I. Phillips)

An American oilman, returning to London from Baghdad, is caught up in espionage.

Mundane and stupid programmer, ploddingly directed.

w Ronald Liles, James O'Connolly story *Decoy, Be Damned* by T. F. Fotherby d Ernest Morris ph Walter J. Harvey m Martin Slavin ad Wilfred Arnold ed Henry Richardson

Paul Maxwell, Clare Owen, Anita West, John Sutton, John Arnatt, Eric Pohlmann, Alan Tilvern, Reginald Marsh

Shadow of the Cat
GB 1961 79m bw
U-I/BHP (Jon Penington)

A cat appears to wreak vengeance on those who murdered its mistress.

Tolerable old dark house shocker with an amusing theme not too well sustained.

w George Baxt d John Gilling ph Alec Grant m Mikis Theodorakis

André Morell, William Lucas, Barbara Shelley, Conrad Phillips, Alan Wheatley, Vanda Godsell, Richard Warner, Freda Jackson

The Shadow of the Eagle
US 1932 bw serial: 12 eps
Mascot

An airborne criminal sends his threats by skywriting.

Silly adventure serial.

d Ford Beebe

John Wayne, Dorothy Gulliver, Walter Miller, Kenneth Harlan, Yakima Canutt

Shadow of the Eagle
GB 1950 92m bw
Valiant (Anthony Havelock-Allan)

In 1770, a Russian envoy to Venice falls for the princess he is supposed to kidnap.

Limp swashbuckler based on a deservedly shadowy corner of European history.

w Doreen Montgomery, Hagar Wilde d Sidney Salkow

Richard Greene, Valentina Cortese, Greta Gynt, Binnie Barnes, Charles Goldner, Walter Rilla

Shadow of the Wolf
Canada/France 1993 112m Sonlab colour
Cinemascope
Vision/Transfilm/Eiffel/Canal+ (Claude Leger)
V, V*
aka: *Agaguk*

In the 1930s, an Eskimo, banished for his hatred of white men, becomes an outcast who has to learn to fend for himself.

Simple-minded rites-of-passage drama of a man pitted against the elements.

w Rudy Wurlitzer, Evan Jones, David Milhaud novel Yves Theriault d Jacques Dorfmann ph Billy Williams m Maurice Jarre pd Wolf Kroeger ed Françoise Bonnot

Lou Diamond Phillips, Toshiro Mifune, Jennifer Tilly, Bernard-Pierre Donnadieu, Donald Sutherland

'Pic is too simple-minded and clichéd for adults, but probably too rough for kids.' – *Variety*

† The film, which cost around $30 million, was the most expensive Canadian production so far. It was released direct to video in Britain.

Shadow on the Wall
US 1949 84m bw
MGM (Robert Sisk)

A child is traumatized by the accidental witnessing of the murder of her unpleasant stepmother.

Forgettable melodramatic suspenser.

w William Ludwig d Pat Jackson ph Ray June m André Previn

Ann Sothern, Zachary Scott, Gigi Perreau, Nancy Davis, Kristine Miller, John McIntire

The Shadow on the Window
US 1957 73m bw
Columbia (Jonie Taps)

Three teenage thugs break into a lonely house, murder its owner and hold a girl hostage.

Routine crime programmer, rather boringly unravelled.

w Leo Townsend, David Harmon d William Asher ph Kit Carson m George Duning

Betty Garrett, Phil Carey, John Barrymore Jnr, Corey Allen, Gerald Saracini

Shadow Warrior: see *Kagemusha*

'He thought that magic only existed in books, and then he met her.'

Shadowlands ***
GB 1993 131m colour Scope
UIP/Showlands/Spelling/Pirce/Savoy (Richard Attenborough, Brian Eastman)
S

The emotionally repressed C. S. Lewis, Oxford don and famous writer of children's books and works of popular theology, enters into a marriage of convenience with an American woman, whom he grows to love, only to learn that she has terminal cancer.

Impeccably acted and directed drama of emotional risk and the pain and joy it can bring.

w William Nicholson play William Nicholson d *Richard Attenborough* ph Roger Pratt m George Fenton pd Stuart Craig ed Lesley Walker

Anthony Hopkins, Debra Winger, John Wood, Edward Hardwicke, Joseph Mazzello, Julian Fellowes, Roddy Maude-Roxby, Michael Denison, Peter Firth

'A mature film for grown-ups.' – *Variety*

'Reticent is the word for Richard Attenborough's film version. But that's a virtue, not a defect, when the setting is English academia (no one has more persuasively captured its manners) and your subject is mortality.' – *Richard Corliss, Time*

'The picture isn't actually very good; it's just a tearjerker with clumsy interpolations of theology.' – *Terrence Rafferty, New Yorker*

'A beautifully crafted movie that gleams like a newly-made antique.' – *Philip French, Observer*

† William Nicholson first wrote the story as a play for BBC TV and then adapted it for the stage before it became a film. Despite Hopkins's Welsh accent, Lewis was an Ulsterman, born in Belfast.

AAN: Debra Winger; William Nicholson

Shadows *
US 1959 81m bw
Cassavetes/Cassel/Maurice McEndree
V, V*

Two blacks and their sister find their identities in Manhattan.

16mm realistic drama which began a new and essentially dreary trend of grainily true-life pictures with improvised dialogue and little dramatic compression.

w the cast d John Cassavetes ph Erich Kollmar m Charles Mingus

Ben Carruthers, Leila Goldoni, Hugh Hurd, Rupert Crosse, Anthony Ray

'I don't so much object to its mindlessness as to its formlessness, regardless of the practical excuses that may be advanced for its rambling incoherence.' – *William S. Pechter*

'A picture of startling immediacy and shocking power.' – *Robert Hatch, Nation*

'We were improvising . . . every scene was very simple. They were predicated on people having problems that were overcome with other problems. At the end of the scene another problem would come in and overlap.' – *John Cassavetes*

Shadows and Fog *
US 1991 86m bw
Columbia TriStar/Orion (Jack Rollins, Charles Joffe)
V, V*, L

In a town where a circus has come to visit, a timid individual is forced by his neighbours to join vigilantes trying to trap a murderer.

An occasionally witty excursion into the world of German expressionist movies of the 20s.

wd Woody Allen *ph* Carlo Di Palma *m* Kurt Weill *pd* Santo Loquasto *ed* Susan E. Morse

Woody Allen, Mia Farrow, John Malkovich, Madonna, Donald Pleasence, Lily Tomlin, Jodie Foster, Kathy Bates, John Cusack, Kate Nelligan, Julie Kavner, Fred Gwynne

'Is Allen confronting his inability to treat history, or anything else, as tragedy rather than farce? The film is a serious joke, possibly reflecting on German re-unification, and it has an unpleasant aftertaste.' – *Philip French, Observer*

Shadows of our Forgotten Ancestors *
USSR 1964 100m bw/colour
Dovzhenko Film Studios
original title: *Teni Zabytykh Predkov*

A youth falls in love with the daughter of the rich landowner who killed his father.

A story of a doomed love, told in the form of a folk-tale, episodic and highly coloured.

w Sergo Paradjanov, Ivan Chendei *d* Sergo Paradjanov *ph* Y. Ilyenko *m* M. Sorik

Ivan Nikolaichuk, Larisa Kadochnikova, Tatiana Bestayeva, Spartak Bagashvili

Shadows of the Peacock
Australia 1987 94m colour
Laughing Kookaburra (Jane Scott)
V*

After discovering her husband's infidelity, a politician's wife asserts her independence by going to Thailand and falling for a Balinese dancer.

Slight, bitter-sweet romance, acted and directed at a somnambulistic pace.

w Jan Sharp, Anne Brooksbank *d* Philip Noyce *ph* Peter James *m* William Motzing *pd* Judith Russell *ed* Frans Vandenburg

Wendy Hughes, John Lone, Rod Mullinar, Peta Toppano, Steven Jacobs, Gillian Jones

Shady Lady
US 1945 90m bw
Universal

An elderly cardsharp is persuaded to help the district attorney nab others of his kind.

Poorish comedy which offers its star little support.

w Curt Siodmak, Gerald Geraghty and M. M. Musselman *d* George Waggner

Charles Coburn, Ginny Simms, Robert Paige, Martha O'Driscoll, Alan Curtis

Shaft *
US 1971 100m Metrocolor
MGM/Shaft Productions (Joel Freeman)
V, V*, S

A black private eye finds himself at odds with a powerful racketeer.

Violent, commercial action thriller which spawned two sequels and a tele-series as well as stimulating innumerable even more violent imitations.

w Ernest Tidyman, John D. F. Black *d* Gordon Parks *ph* Urs Furrer *m* Isaac Hayes

Richard Roundtree, Moses Gunn, Charles Cioffi, Christopher St John

'Relentlessly supercool dialogue, all throwaway colloquialisms and tough Chandlerian wisecracks.' – *MFB*

AA: title song (*m/ly* Isaac Hayes)

AAN: Isaac Hayes (musical score)

Shaft in Africa
US 1973 112m Metrocolor Panavision
MGM/Shaft Productions (Roger Lewis)

Shaft is kidnapped by an Ethiopian emir who wants him to track down a gang of slavers.

More miscellaneous violence, rather shoddily assembled, with a few good jokes.

w Stirling Silliphant *d* John Guillermin *ph* Marcel Grignon *m* Johnny Pate

Richard Roundtree, Frank Finlay, Vonetta McGee

Shaft's Big Score
US 1972 105m Metrocolor Panavision
MGM/Shaft Productions (Richard Lewis, Ernest Tidyman)
V*

Shaft avenges the death of a friend and comes up against the numbers racket.

Violent footage and an incomprehensible plot.

w Ernest Tidyman *d* Gordon Parks *ph* Urs Furrer *m* Gordon Parks

Richard Roundtree, Moses Gunn, Drew Bundini Brown, Joseph Mascolo

Shag
GB 1988 100m colour
Palace/Hemdale (Stephen Woolley, Julia Chasman)
V, V*, L, S

Four girls go to the beach for fun and boys.

Set in the 1960s, it is an attempt, successful enough in its inane way, to revive the style of the teen movies of the time.

w Robin Swicord, Lanier Laney, Terry Sweeney *d* Zelda Barron *ph* Peter MacDonald *pd* Buddy Cone *ed* Laurence Mery Clark

Phoebe Cates, Scott Coffey, Bridget Fonda, Annabeth Gish, Page Hannah, Robert Rusler, Tyrone Power III, Jeff Yagher

The Shaggy DA
US 1976 92m Technicolor
Walt Disney (Ron Miller)
V*

A magic ring enables a young lawyer to become a talking dog and thus expose corruption.

Rather feeble sequel to *The Shaggy Dog*, with overtones of Watergate.

w Don Tait *d* Robert Stevenson *ph* Frank Phillips *m* Buddy Baker *sp* Eustace Lycett, Art Cruickshank, Danne Lee

Dean Jones, Tim Conway, Suzanne Pleshette, Jo Anne Worley, Vic Tayback, Keenan Wynn, Dick Van Patten

The Shaggy Dog *
US 1959 101m bw
Walt Disney (Bill Walsh)
V*, L

A small boy turns into a big shaggy dog and catches some crooks.

Simple-minded, overlong Disney comedy for kids and their indulgent parents; good laughs in the chase scenes.

w Bill Walsh, Lillie Hayward *novel The Hound of Florence* by Felix Salten *d* Charles Barton *ph* Edward Colman *m* Paul Sawtell

Fred MacMurray, Jean Hagen, Tommy Kirk, Cecil Kellaway, Annette Funicello, Tim Considine, Kevin Corcoran, Alexander Scourby

Shake Hands with Murder
US 1944 61m bw
American Productions/PRC

Bailbondsmen get involved in murder.

Tolerable little mystery for the bottom of the bill.

w John T. Neville, Martin Mooney *d* Albert Herman

Frank Jenks, Iris Adrian, Douglas Fowley, Jack Raymond

Shake Hands with the Devil *
Eire 1959 110m bw
UA/Troy/Pennebaker (Michael Anderson)
V*

In 1921 Dublin a surgeon is the secret leader of the IRA, and comes to cherish violence as an end rather than a means.

Downbeat action melodrama, politically very questionable but well made.

w Ivan Goff, Ben Roberts *novel* Rearden Connor *d* Michael Anderson *ph* Erwin Hillier *m* William Alwyn

James Cagney, Glynis Johns, Don Murray, Dana Wynter, Michael Redgrave, Sybil Thorndike, Cyril Cusack, Niall MacGinnis, Richard Harris, Ray McAnally, Noel Purcell

Shakedown
US 1950 80m bw
U-I (Ted Richmond)

A ruthless press photographer becomes a blackmailer.

Routine crime melodrama, adequately done.

w Alfred Lewis, Martin Goldsmith *d* Joseph Pevney *ph* Irving Glassberg *m* Joseph Gershenson

Howard Duff, Brian Donlevy, Anne Vernon, Peggy Dow, Lawrence Tierney, Bruce Bennett

The Shakedown
GB 1959 92m bw
Rank/Alliance/Ethiro (Norman Williams)

A Soho vice boss photographs prominent people in compromising situations and blackmails them.

A semi-remake set in the squalid London so beloved of film makers at the time, before it became 'swinging'. Of no interest or entertainment value.

w Leigh Vance *d* John Lemont *ph* Brendan J. Stafford *m* Philip Green

Terence Morgan, Hazel Court, Donald Pleasence, Bill Owen, Robert Beatty, Harry H. Corbett, Gene Anderson, Eddie Byrne

Shakedown (1988): see *Blue Jean Cop*

Shaker Run
New Zealand 1985 90m colour
Laurelwood/Aviscom/Mirage
V*, L

Two American stunt car drivers help a girl who for the best political reasons has stolen a deadly virus.

Harebrained excuse for car chases against beautiful scenery; quite exhausting.

w James Kouf Jnr, Henry Fownes, Bruce Morrison *d* Bruce Morrison

Cliff Robertson, Leif Garrett, Lisa Harrow, Shane Briant

Shakespeare Wallah *
India 1965 125m bw
Merchant Ivory (Ismail Merchant)
V*

A troupe of English actors find their Indian tour interrupted by romance.

Interesting but sluggish drama on an unusual subject. Not by any means a classic, but it set off this partnership on an enduring wave of critical acclaim and public indifference.

w Ruth Prawer Jhabvala, James Ivory　d James Ivory　ph Subrata Mitra　m Satyajit Ray

Felicity Kendal, Shashi Kapoor, Laura Liddell, Geoffrey Kendal, Madhur Jaffrey, Utpal Dutt

'Touched by brilliance, marked throughout by grace, it is a quiet film that allows one to perceive the ironies and the poignancy of a time of transition.' – *Judith Crist*

Shakha Proshakha: see *Branches of the Tree*

The Shakiest Gun in the West
US　1967　101m　Techniscope
Universal (Edward J. Montagne)
V*, L

A cowardly dentist becomes a Western hero.

Dreary farce, an unsubtle remake of *The Paleface*.

w Jim Fritzell, Everett Greenbaum　d Alan Rafkin ph Andrew Jackson　m Vic Mizzy

Don Knotts, Barbara Rhoades, Jackie Coogan, Don Barry

'Sex. Love. Marriage. Infidelity. Happiness. Success. Friendship. Trust. Babies. Work. Deadlines. Parents. Dreams. Money. Hopes. Fears. Secrets. Growing Up. Hanging Out. Hanging In.'

Shaking the Tree
US　1990　107m　Astor Color
Hobo/Reality (Robert J. Wilson)
V, V*

The lives of a group of old schoolfriends go through changes as they gather for a Christmas reunion.

Tedium sets in early in this examination of the dull lives of uninteresting people.

w Duane Clark, Steven Wilde　d Duane Clark ph Ronn Schmidt　m David E. Russo　ed Martin L. Bernstein

Arye Gross, Gale Hansen, Doug Savant, Steven Wilde, Courteney Cox, Christina Haag

'Lackluster tale of four childhood buddies generates little interest despite competent technical credits all-around and some nice acting turns. The who-cares factor is simply too high.' – *Variety*

Shalako
GB　1968　118m　Technicolor　Franscope
Kingston/Dimitri de Grunwald (Euan Lloyd)
V, V*

New Mexico, 1880: a cowboy acts as guide to European aristocratic big game hunters, but the Indians become annoyed and attack.

A cute idea is given routine treatment; though packed with stars, the action never becomes very exciting despite incidental brutalities.

w J. J. Griffith, Hal Hopper, Scot Finch　novel Louis L'Amour　d Edward Dmytryk　ph Ted Moore m Robert Farnon

Sean Connery, Brigitte Bardot, Jack Hawkins, Stephen Boyd, Peter Van Eyck, Honor Blackman, Eric Sykes, Alexander Knox, Woody Strode, Valerie French

Shall We Dance? **
US　1937　116m　bw
RKO (Pandro S. Berman)
V, V*, L

Dancing partners pretend to be married but are not; until they both get the same idea.

A light musical which was full of good things but nevertheless began the decline of Astaire-Rogers

films; repetition was obvious, as was ostentation for its own sake, and the audience was expecting too much.

w Allan Scott, Ernest Pagano　d Mark Sandrich ph David Abel　md Nathaniel Shilkret　m/ly George and Ira Gershwin　ad Van Nest Polglase

Fred Astaire, Ginger Rogers, Edward Everett Horton, Eric Blore, Harriet Hoctor, Jerome Cowan, Ketti Gallian, Ann Shoemaker

'Another holdover musical in the Astaire-Rogers string . . . it has everything it needs on production.' – *Variety*

AAN: song 'They Can't Take That Away From Me'

Shame **
Australia　1987　94m　Eastmancolor
Metro/Barron Films/UAA Films (Damien Parer, Paul D. Barron)
V*, L

A female lawyer uncovers a series of rapes in a small town.

Powerful indictment of male bonding and aggression.

w Beverly Blankenship, Michael Brindley　d Steve Jodrell　ph Joseph Pickering　m Mario Millo pd Phil Peters　ed Kerry Regan

Deborra-Lee Furness, Tony Barry, Simone Buchanan, Gillian Jones, Peter Aanensen, Margaret Ford, David Franklin, Bill McClusky

The Shame of a Nation: see *Scarface*

Shampoo *
US　1975　110m　Technicolor
Columbia/Persky-Bright/Vista (Warren Beatty)
V, V*, L

A Beverly Hills hairdresser seduces his most glamorous clients.

Ugly little sex farce with few laughs but much dashing about and bad language. Its setting on election eve 1968 has made some people think it a political satire.

w Robert Towne, Warren Beatty　d Hal Ashby ph Laszlo Kovacs　m Paul Simon

Warren Beatty, Julie Christie, Lee Grant, Goldie Hawn, Jack Warden, Tony Bill, Jay Robinson

'It has the bursting-with-talent but fuzziness-of-effect aspect of a movie made by a group of friends for their own amusement.' – *Richard Combs*

AA: Lee Grant

AAN: script; Jack Warden

Shamus
US　1972　98m　Eastmancolor
Columbia/Robert M. Weitman
V, V*, L

A private eye is hired by a wealthy man to recover stolen jewels and find a murderer.

A forties retread with seventies violence; junky stuff, with a few laughs for buffs who can spot the in-jokes.

w Barry Beckerman　d Buzz Kulik　ph Victor J. Kemper　m Jerry Goldsmith

Burt Reynolds, Dyan Cannon, John Ryan, Joe Santos, Giorgio Tozzi, Ron Weyland

'Very hectic, very vividly New York and as idiotic as Reynolds' physical resiliency.' – *Judith Crist*

Shane ***
US　1953　118m　Technicolor
Paramount (George Stevens, Ivan Moffat)
V, V*, L

A mysterious stranger helps a family of homesteaders.

Archetypal family Western, but much slower and statelier than most, as though to emphasize its own quality, which is evident anyway.

w A. B. Guthrie Jnr　novel Jack Schaefer　d George Stevens　ph Loyal Griggs　m Victor Young

Alan Ladd, Jean Arthur, Van Heflin, Jack Palance, Brandon de Wilde, Ben Johnson, Edgar Buchanan, Emile Meyer, Elisha Cook Jnr, John Dierkes

'A kind of dramatic documentary of the pioneer days of the west.' – *MFB*

'Westerns are better when they're not too self-importantly self-conscious.' – *New Yorker, 1975*

'Stevens managed to infuse a new vitality, a new sense of realism into the time-worn story through the strength and freshness of his visuals.' – *Arthur Knight*

AA: Loyal Griggs

AAN: best picture; A. B. Guthrie Jnr; George Stevens; Jack Palance; Brandon de Wilde

Shanghai
US　1935　77m　bw
(Paramount) Walter Wanger

A visiting American lady falls in love with a half caste.

Romantic drama programmer.

w Gene Towne, Graham Baker, Lynn Starling d James Flood　ph James Van Trees

Loretta Young, Charles Boyer, Warner Oland, Alison Skipworth, Fred Keating, Charles Grapewin, Walter Kingsford

Shanghai Express ***
US　1932　84m　bw
Paramount

A British officer and his old flame meet on a train which is waylaid by Chinese bandits.

Superbly pictorial melodrama which set the pattern for innumerable train movies to come, though none matched its deft visual quality and few sketched in their characters so neatly. Plot and dialogue are silent style, but refreshingly so.

w Jules Furthman　d Josef von Sternberg　ph Lee Garmes m W. Franke Harling　ad Hans Dreier

Marlene Dietrich, Clive Brook, Warner Oland, Anna May Wong, Eugene Pallette, Lawrence Grant, Louise Closser Hale, Gustav von Seyffertitz

LILY (Marlene Dietrich): 'It took more than one man to change my name to Shanghai Lily.'

'Good programme picture bolstered by the Dietrich name . . . Excellent camerawork overcomes really hoke melodramatic story.' – *Variety*

'A limited number of characters, all meticulously etched, highly atmospheric sets and innumerable striking photographic compositions.' – *Curtis Harrington, 1964*

AA: Lee Garmes

AAN: best picture; Josef von Sternberg

'Shanghai. Where Almost Anything Can Happen . . . And Does!'

The Shanghai Gesture *
US　1941　90m　bw
Arnold Pressburger (Albert de Courville)
V*, L

The proprietress of a Shanghai gambling casino taunts her ex-husband by showing him his daughter in a state of degradation; but he proves that the girl is her daughter also.

An ancient theatrical shocker was completely bowdlerized and chopped into nonsense for the screen; but the director's hand showed in the handling of the vast casino set.

w Josef von Sternberg, Geza Herczeg, Karl Vollmoeller, Jules Furthman　play John Colton d Josef von Sternberg　ph Paul Ivano　m Richard Hageman　ad Boris Leven

Ona Munson, Victor Mature, Walter Huston, Gene Tierney, Albert Basserman, Phyllis Brooks, Maria Ouspenskaya, Eric Blore, Ivan Lebedeff, Mike Mazurki

'The effect of a descent into a maelstrom of iniquity.' – *Curtis Harrington, 1962*

'In spite of all the changes necessitated by the Hays Office, seldom have decadence and sexual depravity been better suggested on the screen.' – *Richard Roud, 1966*

'Hilariously, awesomely terrible.' – *New Yorker, 1977*

AAN: Richard Hageman; Boris Leven

Shanghai Madness
US   1933   63m   bw
Fox

A naval officer is cashiered in Shanghai and gets mixed up with Communists.

Weakish melodrama which goes the long way round to a happy ending.

w Frederick Hazlitt Brennan, Austin Parker, Gordon Wellesley   d John G. Blystone

Spencer Tracy, Fay Wray, Ralph Morgan, Eugene Pallette, Herbert Mundin

'Okay generally but in big spots will need stage support.' – *Variety*

Shanghai Surprise
GB   1986   97m   Technicolor
HandMade/Vista/John Kohn
V*, L

A lady missionary hires an adventurer to track down a stack of opium before it falls into the wrong hands.

Astonishingly abysmal adventure romance set rather uncertainly in the 1937 Orient. Nothing matches the so-called talents involved.

w John Kohn, Robert Bentley   *novel Faraday's Flowers* by Tony Kenrick   d Jim Goddard   ph Ernest Vincze   m George Harrison, Michael Kamen

Madonna, Sean Penn, Paul Freeman, Richard Griffiths

'A silly little trifle which wouldn't even have passed muster as a 1930s programmer.' – *Variety*

Shark
US/Mexico   1969   88m   Eastmancolor
Heritage/Cinematografica Calderon
V, V*

A gunrunner in the Sudan becomes involved with unscrupulous divers after wrecks.

Tepid adventure yarn allegedly damaged by recutting but showing very little sign of original talent.

w Samuel Fuller, John Kingsbridge   *novel His Bones Are Coral* by Victor Canning   d Samuel Fuller   ph Raul Martinez Solares   m Rafael Moroyoqui

Burt Reynolds, Arthur Kennedy, Barry Sullivan, Silvia Pinal, Enrique Lucero

The Sharkfighters
US   1956   72m   Technicolor   Cinemascope
(UA) Formosa (Samuel Goldwyn Jnr)

To save the lives of flyers forced down into the sea, navy scientists experiment with a shark repellent.

Straightforward semi-documentary with suspenseful action sequences.

w Lawrence Roman, John Robinson   d Jerry Hopper   ph Lee Garmes   m Jerome Moross

Victor Mature, Karen Steele, James Olson, Claude Akins

Shark's Treasure *
US   1974   95m   DeLuxe
UA/Symbol (Cornel Wilde)

Treasure hunters seek buried gold in the Caribbean where sharks abound.

Fairly thrilling action hokum.

wd Cornel Wilde   ph Jack Atcheler, Al Giddings   m Robert O. Ragland

Cornel Wilde, Yaphet Kotto, John Neilson, David Canary, Cliff Osmond

'Wilde maintains his reputation for making the most likeable bad movies around.' – *Tom Milne*

'Some cops are good at opening a case. Sharky knows how to finish one.'
Sharky's Machine
US   1981   120m   Technicolor
Warner/Orion/Deliverance (Hank Moonjean)
V, V*, L

A vice squad policeman builds up a new team.

Exceptionally violent cop thriller on the lines of *Dirty Harry.*

w Gerald Di Pego   *novel* William Diehl   d Burt Reynolds   ph William A. Fraker   md Al Capps

Burt Reynolds, Vittorio Gassman, Brian Keith, Charles Durning, Earl Holliman, Bernie Casey, Henry Silva

Sharpshooters
US   1938   63m   bw
TCF

Adventures of a newsreel cameraman who saves a young prince from kidnapping.

Serial-like action and comedy very palatably blended: the first of a short series.

w Robert Ellis, Helen Logan   d James Tinling

Brian Donlevy, Lynn Bari, Wally Vernon, John King, Douglass Dumbrille, C. Henry Gordon, Sidney Blackmer

'A standard programmer to entertain, and a natural for the juve trade.' – *Variety*

Shatter
GB   1974   90m   colour
Hammer (Michael Carreras, Vee King Shaw)
V*
US title: *Call Him Mr Shatter*

A professional assassin is marked for death by his former employer in Hong Kong.

Botched attempt to combine a thriller with the style of a kung fu movie.

w Don Houghton   d Michael Carreras   ph Brian Probyn, John Wilcox, Roy Ford   m David Lindup   ed Eric Boyd-Perkins

Stuart Whitman, Ti Lung, Peter Cushing, Anton Diffring, Lily Li

'Murder Is Never An Accident.'
Shattered *
US   1991   98m   Technicolor
Palace/Capella/Davis Entertainment (Wolfgang Petersen, John Davis, David Korda)
V, V*, L

Recovering from a car crash that left him with no memory and facial injuries that required plastic surgery, a property developer hires a private eye to discover more about his past.

Clever, unsettling mystery that keeps an audience guessing until the end.

wd Wolfgang Petersen   *novel The Plastic Nightmare* by Richard Neely   ph Laszlo Kovacs   m Angelo Badalamenti   pd Gregg Fonseca   ed Hannes Nikel, Glenn Farr

Tom Berenger, Greta Scacchi, Bob Hoskins, Joanne Whalley-Kilmer, Corbin Bernsen, Debi A. Monahan, Bert Robario, Scott Getlin, Kellye Nakahara

'A solidly entertaining plot-driven thriller which, although it requires an initial act of faith from its

audience, rewards them with an intelligent, satisfying mystery.' – *Nigel Floyd, Sight and Sound*

'Young and beautiful for 500 years – and wicked every one of them!'
She *
US   1935   89m   bw
RKO (Merian C. Cooper)

Ancient papers lead a Cambridge professor and his friends to the lost city where dwells a queen who cannot die – until she falls in love.

The producers have the right spirit for this Victorian fantasy, but tried too hard to emulate the mood of their own *King Kong,* and it was a mistake to transfer the setting from Africa to the Arctic. One for connoisseurs, though.

w Ruth Rose, Dudley Nichols   *novel* H. Rider Haggard   d Irving Pichel, Lansing G. Holden   ph J. Roy Hunt   m Max Steiner   ch Benjamin Zemach

Randolph Scott, Nigel Bruce, Helen Gahagan

'Beautiful production, but story dubious for discriminating adults.' – *Variety*

'To an unrepentant Haggard fan it does sometimes seem to catch the thrill as well as the childishness of his invention.' – *Graham Greene*

'A spectacle of magnificent proportions with the decadent effluvium of the tomb period.' – *Photoplay*

'The stagey décor of Kor is in the art deco style of Radio City Music Hall, and you keep expecting the Rockettes to turn up.' – *Pauline Kael, 70s*

AAN: Benjamin Zemach

She
GB   1965   105m   Technicolor   Hammerscope
ABP/Hammer (Michael Carreras, Aida Young)
V

Flat, uninventive and tedious remake which reverts to Africa but does nothing else right; it ignores the essential Cambridge prologue and ignores all suggestions of fantasy.

w David T. Chantler   *novel* H. Rider Haggard   d Robert Day   ph Harry Waxman   m James Bernard   ad Robert Jones, Don Mingaye   ed James Needs, Eric Boyd-Perkins

Peter Cushing, Ursula Andress, Christopher Lee, John Richardson, Bernard Cribbins, André Morell, Rosenda Monteros

She Couldn't Say No
US   1952   89m   bw
RKO (Robert Sparks)
V*
GB title: *Beautiful But Dangerous*

An heiress returns to the town of her childhood to distribute anonymous gifts to those who had helped her.

Moderate Capraesque comedy which doesn't quite come off.

w D. D. Beauchamp, William Bowers, Richard Flournoy   d Lloyd Bacon   ph Harold J. Wild   m Roy Webb

Jean Simmons, Robert Mitchum, Arthur Hunnicutt, Edgar Buchanan, Wallace Ford, Raymond Walburn

She Couldn't Take It *
US   1935   89m   bw
Columbia (B. P. Schulberg)

A rich old reprobate meets a gangster in prison and puts him in charge of his rebellious family.

Little-known crazy comedy with touches of melodrama; not a success, but with interesting elements.

w Gene Towne, Oliver H. P. Garrett   *story* Graham Baker   d Tay Garnett   ph Leon Shamroy

George Raft, Joan Bennett, Walter Connelly, Billie Burke, Lloyd Nolan, Wallace Ford, Alan Mowbray, Donald Meek

The She Creature
US   1956   77m   bw
AIP/Golden State (Alex Gordon)

An evil hypnotist regresses his subject back through time to summon up a murderous prehistoric monster from the sea.

Unusual B movie that concentrates less on the monster and more on its exploitation by a corrupt businessman.

w Lou Rusoff   story Jerry Zigmond   d Edward L. Cahn   ph Frederick E. West   m Ronald Stein   ad Don Ament   ed Ronald Sinclair

Chester Morris, Tom Conway, Cathy Downs, Lance Fuller, Ron Randell, Freda Inescort, Marla English

She Didn't Say No!
GB   1958   97m   Technicolor
GW Films (Sergei Nolbandov)

A young Irish widow has five illegitimate children, each by a different father.

Coyly daring comedy full of stage Oirishisms and obvious jokes, a few of which work.

w T. J. Morison, Una Troy   novel We Are Seven by Una Troy   d Cyril Frankel   ph Gilbert Taylor   m Tristam Cary

Eileen Herlie, Jack MacGowran, Perlita Neilson, Niall MacGinnis, Ian Bannen

She Done Him Wrong ***
US   1933   68m   bw
Paramount (William Le Baron)
V*, L

A lady saloon keeper of the Gay Nineties falls for the undercover cop who is after her.

As near undiluted Mae West as Hollywood ever came: fast, funny, melodramatic and pretty sexy; also a very atmospheric and well-made movie.

w Mae West   play Diamond Lil by Mae West (with help on the scenario from Harry Thew, John Bright)   d Lowell Sherman   ph Charles Lang   songs Ralph Rainger (m), Leo Robin (ly)

Mae West, Cary Grant, Owen Moore, Gilbert Roland, Noah Beery, David Landau, Rafaela Ottiano, Rochelle Hudson, Dewey Robinson

'Only alternative to a strong drawing cast, nowadays if a picture wants business, is strong entertainment. This one has neither.' – Variety

AAN: best picture

She Gets Her Man *
US   1945   73m   bw
Universal (Warren Wilson)

A country girl in New York tracks down a blowgun murderer.

Disarming mystery farce which tries every slapstick situation known to gag writers, and gets away with it.

w Warren Wilson, Clyde Bruckman   d Erle C. Kenton   ph Jerry Ash

Joan Davis, William Gargan, Leon Errol, Milburn Stone, Russell Hicks

She Got Her Man: see Maisie (Maisie Gets Her Man)

She Has What It Takes
US   1943   66m   bw
Colbert Clark/Columbia

A small-time singer masquerades as the long-lost daughter of a famous stage star.

An excuse for musical padding, for indulgent audiences.

w Paul Yawitz   d Charles Barton

Jinx Falkenberg, Tom Neal, Constance Worth, Joe King, The Radio Rogues, The Vagabonds

She Knew All the Answers
US   1941   84m   bw
Charles R. Rogers/Columbia

Prevented by his uncle from marrying a playboy, a chorine falls for the uncle.

Mildly merry comedy which came and went without being noticed.

w Harry Segall, Kenneth Earl, Curtis Kenyon   story Jane Allen   d Richard Wallace

Joan Bennett, Franchot Tone, John Hubbard, Eve Arden, William Tracy

She Learned about Sailors
US   1934   82m   bw
Fox

In Shanghai, a couple get married so that they will be permitted to leave; back home, they're not sure they want an annulment.

Mild comedy with music.

w William Conselman, Henry Johnson   story Randall H. Faye   d George Marshall

Alice Faye, Lew Ayres, Harry Green, Mitchell and Durant

'The hi-de-hi of higher education!'
She Loves Me Not *
US   1934   85m   bw
Paramount (Benjamin Glazer)

A showgirl murder witness takes refuge in a men's college.

Larky musical farce later remade as True to the Army and How to be Very Very Popular; this first version is perhaps the most nearly amusing.

w Ben Glazer   play Howard Lindsay   novel Edward Hope   d Elliott Nugent   ph Charles Lang   songs various

Bing Crosby, Miriam Hopkins, Kitty Carlisle, Edward Nugent, Lynne Overman, Henry Stephenson, Warren Hymer, George Barbier

AAN: song 'Love in Bloom' (m Ralph Rainger, ly Leo Robin)

She Married an Artist
US   1938   78m   bw
Columbia

A wife becomes jealous of her husband's models.

Very mild romantic comedy.

w Avery Strakosch, Delmer Daves, Gladys Lehman   d Marion Gering

John Boles, Francis Drake, Albert Dekker

She Married Her Boss
US   1935   90m   bw
Columbia

A secretary marries her boss and finds herself taken for granted.

Pleasant but rather thin romantic comedy with amiable stars.

w Sidney Buchman   d Gregory La Cava

Claudette Colbert, Melvyn Douglas, Raymond Walburn, Edith Fellows, Jean Dixon, Katherine Alexander

She Played with Fire: see Fortune is a Woman

She Shall Have Murder
GB   1950   90m   bw
Concanen/IFD

A law clerk helps to solve the murder of an elderly client.

Old-fashioned light comedy whodunnit, the equivalent of reading a Crime Club thriller.

w Allan Mackinnon   novel Delano Ames   d Daniel Birt

Rosamund John, Derrick de Marney, Mary Jerrold, Felix Aylmer, Joyce Heron, Beatrice Varley

She Shall Have Music
GB   1935   91m   bw
Twickenham (Julius Hagen)

A band leader helps prevent dirty doings at sea.

A story that is no more than an excuse for a series of dull production numbers by Jack Hylton's Band and assorted singers.

w H. Fowler Mear, Arthur Macrae   story Paul England   d Leslie Hiscott   ph Sydney Blythe, William Luff   ad James Carter

Claude Dampier, June Clyde, Jack Hylton

She Wanted a Millionaire
US   1932   74m   bw
Fox

A girl spurns her childhood sweetheart for a rich man who turns out to be dangerous.

Curious comedy-melodrama which confuses its watchers.

w Sonja Levien   story William Anthony McGuire   d John G. Blystone

Joan Bennett, Spencer Tracy, James Kirkwood, Una Merkel, Dorothy Peterson

The She-Wolf
US   1931   90m   bw
Universal

A woman gets rich but neglects her children.

Talkative filmed play, almost redeemed by its star performance.

w Winfred Dunn   play Mother's Millions by Winfred Dunn   d James Flood

May Robson, James Hall, Lawrence Gray, Frances Dade

'Beauty or beast? Woman or monster?'
She Wolf of London
US   1946   61m   bw
Universal
GB title: The Curse of the Allenbys

A girl thinks she must be the family werewolf.

Risibly inept semi-horror melodrama with a highly implausible solution and poor production.

w George Bricker   d Jean Yarbrough

June Lockhart, Don Porter, Sara Haden, Lloyd Corrigan, Dennis Hoey, Martin Kosleck

She Wore a Yellow Ribbon **
US   1949   103m   Technicolor
RKO/Argosy (John Ford, Merian C. Cooper)
V, V*, L

Problems of a cavalry officer about to retire.

Fragmentary but very enjoyable Western with all Ford ingredients served piping hot.

w Frank Nugent, Laurence Stallings   story James Warner Bellah   d John Ford   ph Winton C. Hoch   m Richard Hageman

John Wayne, Joanne Dru, John Agar, Ben Johnson, Harry Carey Jnr, Victor McLaglen, Mildred Natwick, George O'Brien, Arthur Shields

AA: Winton C. Hoch

She Wouldn't Say Yes
US   1945   87m   bw
Columbia

A lady psychiatrist falls for the subject of an experiment.

Star comedy vehicle which falls rather flat.

w Laslo Gorog, William Thiele, Virginia Van Upp, John Jacoby, Sarett Tobias   d Alexander Hall

Rosalind Russell, Lee Bowman, Charles Winninger, Adele Jergens

She Wrote the Book
US   1946   72m   bw
Universal

A lady professor imagines herself to be the glamorous femme fatale heroine of a lurid novel.

Adventures of a female Walter Mitty; one of the star's better comedies.

w Warren Wilson, Oscar Brodney   d Charles Lamont

Joan Davis, Mischa Auer, Jack Oakie, Kirby Grant, John Litel, Gloria Stuart, Thurston Hall

She-Devil
US   1989   99m   DuArt
Rank/Orion (Jonathan Brett, Susan Seidelman)
V, V*, L

An unattractive housewife takes her revenge when her husband leaves her for a glamorous romantic novelist.

Unsuccessful and bland adaptation of the sour comedy of the original.

w Barry Strugatz, Mark R. Burns   novel The Life and Loves of a She-Devil by Fay Weldon   d Susan Seidelman   ph Oliver Stapleton   m Howard Shore   pd Santo Loquasto   ed Craig McKay

Meryl Streep, Roseanne Barr, Ed Begley Jnr, Sylvia Miles, Linda Hunt, Elisebeth Peters, Bryan Larkin, A. Martinez

She-Devils On Wheels
US   1968   83m   colour
Mayflower Pictures/Herschell Gordon Lewis
V

A gang of female bikers indulge in sex and violence, including the decapitation of a rival male biker.

Ineptly written, poorly acted, photographed and directed – a sort of inferior home movie – it reveals that a cult reputation is not necessarily an indication of talent.

w Louise Downe   d Herschell Gordon Lewis   ph Roy Collodi   m Larry Wellington   pd Robert Enrietto   ed Richard Brinkman

Betty Connell, Nancy Lee Noble, Christie Wagner, Rodney Bedell

'When paradise became a battleground, she led the fight for survival!'
Sheena, Queen of the Jungle
US   1984   115m   Metrocolor   Panavision
Columbia/Delphi II (Paul Aratow)

Orphaned when her explorer parents are killed, a white girl is raised by an African tribe.

Female Tarzan stuff from a comic strip, smoothly made but too rough and slightly too sexy for the family audience which must have been intended.

w David Newman, Lorenzo Semple Jnr   d John Guillermin   ph Pasqualino de Santis   m Richard Hartley

Tanya Roberts, Ted Wass, Donovan Scott

The Sheep Has Five Legs *
France   1954   96m   bw
Raoul Ploquin
V*

original title: Le Mouton a Cinq Pattes

A town seeking publicity tries to bring together the five quintuplet grandsons of its oldest inhabitant.

Mildly saucy star vehicle which was in fact most notable for introducing Fernandel to an international audience.

w Albert Valentin   d Henri Verneuil   ph Armand Thirard   m Georges Van Parys

Fernandel, Françoise Arnoul, Delmont, Paulette Dubost, Louis de Funès

AAN: original story

The Sheepman *
US   1958   91m   Metrocolor   Cinemascope
MGM (Edmund Grainger)

A tough sheep farmer determines to settle in a cattle town.

Easy-going Western with humorous moments.

w William Bowers, James Edward Grant   d George Marshall   ph Robert Bronner   m Jeff Alexander

Glenn Ford, Shirley Maclaine, Leslie Nielsen, Mickey Shaughnessy, Edgar Buchanan

AAN: script

'When an Arab sees a woman he wants, he takes her!' – ancient Arabian proverb
'A photoplay of tempestuous love between a madcap English beauty and a bronzed Arab chief!'
The Sheik *
US   1921   73m (24 fps)   bw   silent
Famous Players-Lasky/George Melford
V*

An English heiress falls for a desert chieftain.

Archetypal romantic tosh which set the seal on Valentino's superstardom.

w Monte M. Katterjohn   novel E. M. Hull   d George Melford   ph William Marshall

Rudolph Valentino, Agnes Ayres, Adolphe Menjou, Walter Long, Lucien Littlefield

† Son of the Sheik, released in 1926, was even more popular.

The Sheik Steps Out
US   1937   68m   bw
Republic (Herman Schlom)

A modern sheik has a riotous time in the big city.

Uninventive spoof of the Valentino myth.

w Adele Buffington, Gordon Kahn   d Irving Pichel   ph Jack Marta   md Alberto Columbo

Ramon Novarro, Lola Lane, Gene Lockhart, Kathleen Burke, Stanley Fields

'Novarro in a comeback start. An action picture of the desert for the lower half of the duals.' – Variety

She'll Be Wearing Pink Pajamas
GB   1985   90m   Eastmancolor
Virgin/Pink Pajamas/Film Four International (Tara Prem, John Goldschmidt)

Women go on an outdoor survival course.

Basically an excuse for a lot of female nattering; it might have seemed more appealing under a more sensible title.

w Eva Hardy   d John Goldschmidt   ph Clive Tickner   m John Du Prez   pd Colin Pocock   ed Richard Key

Julie Walters, Anthony Higgins, Jane Evers, Janet Henfrey, Paula Jacobs

'A woman's dangerous and erotic journey beneath . . .'
The Sheltering Sky **
GB/Italy   1990   138m   Technicolor   Technovision
Palace/Sahara Company/TAO Film/Recorded Picture Company/Aldrich Group (Jeremy Thomas)
V, V (W), V*, L, S

An American couple wander through North Africa in search of themselves.

Austere, stunningly photographed movie that yields rewards if approached on its own terms.

w Mark Peploe, Bernardo Bertolucci   novel Paul Bowles   d Bernardo Bertolucci   ph Vittorio Storaro   m Ryuichi Sakamoto, Richard Horowitz   pd Gianni Silvestri   ed Gabriella Cristiani

Debra Winger, John Malkovich, Campbell Scott, Jill Bennett, Timothy Spall, Eric Vu-An, Amina Annabi, Philippe Morier-Genoud, Paul Bowles

'It refuses to indulge those who believe movies should be easy and edifying, with characters worth snuggling up to.' – Richard Corliss, Time

Shenandoah **
US   1965   105m   Technicolor
Universal (Robert Arthur)
V*, L

How the American Civil War affected the lives of a Virginia family.

Surprisingly hard-centred and moving semi-Western for the family; excellent performances and well-controlled mood.

w James Lee Barrett   d Andrew V. McLaglen   ph William Clothier   md Joseph Gershenson   m Frank Skinner

James Stewart, Rosemary Forsyth, Doug McClure, Glenn Corbett, Katharine Ross, Philip Alford

Shepherd of the Hills *
US   1941   98m   Technicolor
Paramount/Jack Moss

Ozarkian backwoodsmen enjoy their lifestyle except for the intrusions of the revenue men and a mysterious stranger.

Early colour adaptation of a long-favourite American story, deliberately styled for rural audiences.

w Grover Jones, Stuart Anthony   novel Harold Bell Wright Jnr   d Henry Hathaway   ph Charles Lang Jnr, W. Howard Greene   m Gerard Carbonara

John Wayne, Betty Field, Harry Carey, Beulah Bondi, James Barton, Samuel S. Hinds, Marjorie Main, Ward Bond, Marc Lawrence, John Qualen, Fuzzy Knight

The Sheriff of Fractured Jaw
GB   1958   103m   Eastmancolor   Cinemascope
TCF/Daniel M. Angel
V*

A London gunsmith in the old west accidentally becomes a hero.

Tame, predictable comedy with a clear lack of invention.

w Arthur Dales   d Raoul Walsh   ph Otto Heller   m Robert Farnon

Kenneth More, Jayne Mansfield, Robert Morley, Ronald Squire, David Horne, Henry Hull, Eynon Evans, Bruce Cabot, William Campbell

Sherlock Holmes

The innumerable Sherlock Holmes films are noted in Filmgoer's Companion, and in this volume the appropriate films are listed under their own titles including the modernized dozen made in the forties by Universal, starring Basil Rathbone as Holmes and Nigel Bruce as Watson. These followed on from Fox's two period pieces, THE HOUND OF THE BASKERVILLES and THE ADVENTURES OF SHERLOCK HOLMES (qv). The series started and ended somewhat lamely but several of the episodes remain highly enjoyable, for performances and dialogue rather than plot or pacing. All but the first were directed by Roy William Neill.

1942: SHERLOCK HOLMES AND THE VOICE OF TERROR (d John Rawlins, with Reginald Denny, Thomas Gomez); SHERLOCK HOLMES AND THE SECRET WEAPON (L)* (with Lionel Atwill as Moriarty)

1943: SHERLOCK HOLMES IN WASHINGTON (V)*
(with Henry Daniell, George Zucco);
SHERLOCK HOLMES FACES DEATH (V, L)**
(with Halliwell Hobbes, Dennis Hoey)

1944: SHERLOCK HOLMES AND THE SPIDER
WOMAN (V)** (with Gale Sondergaard,
Dennis Hoey); THE SCARLET CLAW** (with
Gerald Hamer); THE PEARL OF DEATH**
(with Miles Mander, Dennis Hoey, Rondo
Hatton)

1945: THE HOUSE OF FEAR* (with Aubrey Mather,
Dennis Hoey); THE WOMAN IN GREEN (L)*
(with Henry Daniell as Moriarty); PURSUIT TO
ALGIERS (with Martin Kosleck)

1946: TERROR BY NIGHT (V)* (with Alan
Mowbray), DRESSED TO KILL (GB title:
SHERLOCK HOLMES AND THE SECRET
CODE (V); with Patricia Morison)

Sherlock Holmes *

US   1932   68m   bw
Fox

Moriarty brings Chicago gangsters into London.

Interesting but rather unsatisfactory Holmes
adventure.

w Bertram Milhauser   d William K. Howard
ph George Barnes

Clive Brook, Reginald Owen, Ernest Torrence,
Miriam Jordan, Alan Mowbray, Herbert Mundin

'Old-fashioned artificial stage play with modern
trimmings that only muddle it. The interpolated
modern gangster angle will mystify the mugs who go
for underworld and it's a late day to offer the Conan
Doyle thing straight to educated clienteles.' – Variety

Sherlock Holmes (1939): see The Adventures of
Sherlock Holmes

Sherlock Holmes and the Secret Code: see
Dressed to Kill (1946)

Sherlock Holmes and the Secret Weapon *

US   1942   68m   bw
Universal (Howard Benedict)
V, V*, L

Sherlock Holmes saves a stolen bombsight from Nazi
agents.

Slightly stiff modernized Holmes story with amusing
ingredients.

w Edward T. Lowe, W. Scott Darling, Edmund L.
Hartmann, vaguely based on The Dancing Men by Sir
Arthur Conan Doyle   d Roy William Neill   ph Les
White   m Frank Skinner

Basil Rathbone, Nigel Bruce, Lionel Atwill (as
Moriarty), Dennis Hoey, Karen Verne, William Post
Jnr, Mary Gordon

Sherlock Holmes and the Spider Woman: see
Spider Woman

Sherlock Holmes and the Voice of Terror

US   1942   65m   bw
Universal (Howard Benedict)
V*, L

Sherlock Holmes unmasks a Lord Haw Haw in the
war cabinet.

Fairly risible first entry in the modernized series, with
a Hollywood view of London and a singular haircut
for the star.

w Lynn Riggs   story His Last Bow by Sir Arthur
Conan Doyle   d John Rawlins   ph Woody Bredell
m Frank Skinner

Basil Rathbone, Nigel Bruce, Hillary Brooke, Reginald
Denny, Evelyn Ankers, Montagu Love, Thomas
Gomez, Mary Gordon

Sherlock Holmes Faces Death **

US   1943   68m   bw
Universal (Roy William Neill)
V*, L

Weird murders occur in a convalescent home for
retired officers.

One of the better entries in this rather likeable
modernized series; fairly close to the original story
except that the events don't make a lot of sense.

w Bertram Millhauser   story The Musgrave Ritual by
Sir Arthur Conan Doyle   d Roy William Niell
ph Charles Van Enger   m Hans Salter

Basil Rathbone, Nigel Bruce, Hillary Brooke, Milburn
Stone, Halliwell Hobbes, Arthur Margetson, Dennis
Hoey, Gavin Muir, Frederic Worlock, Olaf Hytten,
Gerald Hamer, Mary Gordon, Vernon Downing

Sherlock Holmes in Washington *

US   1943   70m   bw
Universal (Howard Benedict)
V*

Sherlock Holmes flies west and prevents Nazi spies
from grabbing a microfilmed document concealed in a
match folder.

Moderate adventure in the modernized series, with a
good beginning and end but a sag in the middle.

w Bertram Millhauser, Lynn Riggs   d Roy William
Niell   ph Lester White   m Frank Skinner

Basil Rathbone, Nigel Bruce, Henry Daniell, George
Zucco, Marjorie Lord, John Archer, Gavin Muir

Sherlock Junior **

US   1924   45m (24 fps)   bw   silent
Metro/Buster Keaton (Joseph M. Schenck)
V

A film projectionist, unjustly accused of stealing a
watch, has dreams of being a great detective.

Fast-moving, gag-filled comedy which ranks among
its star's best.

w Clyde Bruckman, Jean Havez, Joseph Mitchell
d/ed Buster Keaton   ph Elgin Lessley, Byron Houck

Buster Keaton, Kathryn McGuire, Ward Crane, Joseph
Keaton

She's Got Everything

US   1937   70m   bw
RKO

A young woman in debt meets a stuffed shirt coffee
planter.

Mild comedy which never seems to jell despite the
talent assembled.

w Harry Segal, Maxwell Shane   d Joseph Santley

Ann Sothern, Gene Raymond, Victor Moore, Helen
Broderick, Parkyakarkus, Billy Gilbert

She's Gotta Have It

US   1986   84m   bw/colour
40 Acres And A Mule Filmworks (Shelton J. Lee)
V, V*, S

Three men woo the same woman.

Smart, but ultimately tiresome, comedy as the men
explain one-by-one and then together why each
would make the perfect lover.

wd Spike Lee   ph Ernest Dickerson   m Bill Lee
pd Wynn Thomas   ed Spike Lee

Tracy Camilla Jones, Tommy Redmon Hicks, John
Canada Terrell, Raye Dowell, Joie Lee, Spike Lee

She's My Lovely: see Get Hep to Love

She's Out of Control

US   1989   95m   CFI
Columbia TriStar/Weintraub Entertainment (Stephen Deutsch)
V, V*, L

A widower follows the advice of a psychiatrist in
trying to control the sex life of his teenage daughter.

Lifeless and singularly witless comedy.

w Seth Winston, Michael J. Nathanson   d Stan
Dragoti   ph Donald Peterman   m Alan Silvestri
pd David L. Snyder   ed Dov Hoenig

Tony Danza, Catherine Hicks, Wallace Shawn, Dick
O'Neill, Ami Dolenz, Laura Mooney, Derek McGrath,
Dana Ashbrook

'The movie begins shakily and ends feebly, but, in
between, is often sharp and funny.' – Philip French,
Observer

'She shakes the student body like it's never been shook
before!'

She's Working Her Way through College

US   1952   101m   Technicolor
Warner (William Jacobs)

A burlesque queen goes to college and brings out the
beast in an English professor.

Limp and vulgar musical remake of a well-liked play
and film; just about gets by as a lowbrow timekiller.

w Peter Milne   play The Male Animal by James
Thurber, Elliott Nugent   d Bruce Humberstone
ph Wilfrid Cline   md Ray Heindorf   ch Le Roy
Prinz   songs Sammy Cahn, Vernon Duke

Virginia Mayo, Ronald Reagan, Don Defore, Gene
Nelson, Phyllis Thaxter, Patrice Wymore

† Sequel 1953: She's Back on Broadway.

Shichi-nin no Samurai: see Seven Samurai

Shine on Harvest Moon *

US   1944   112m   bw   (Technicolor sequence)
Warner (William Jacobs)

The life and times of vaudeville singer Nora Bayes.

Standard ragtime biopic, very adequately made.

w Sam Hellman, Richard Weil, Francis Swan, James
Kern   d David Butler   ph Arthur Edeson
md Heinz Roemheld

Ann Sheridan, Dennis Morgan, Jack Carson, Irene
Manning, S. Z. Sakall, Marie Wilson, Robert Shayne

The Shining *

GB   1980   119m (general release; cut from première
length of 146m)   colour
Warner/Stanley Kubrick
V, V*, L

Under the influence of a desolate hotel where murders
had occurred, a caretaker goes berserk and threatens
his family.

Uninteresting ghost story sparked by meticulous
detail and sets but finally vitiated by overlength and
an absurdly over-the-top star performance.

w Stanley Kubrick, Diane Johnson   novel Stephen
King   d Stanley Kubrick   ph John Alcott   m Bela
Bartok (on record)   pd Roy Walker

Jack Nicholson, Shelley Duvall, Danny Lloyd, Barry
Nelson, Scatman Crothers, Philip Stone

'The truly amazing question is why a director of
Kubrick's stature would spend his time and effort on
a novel that he changes so much it's barely
recognizable, taking away whatever originality it
possessed while emphasizing its banality. The answer
presumably is that Kubrick was looking for a
"commercial" property he could impose his own
vision on, and Warners, not having learned its lesson
with Barry Lyndon, was silly enough to let him do it.'
– Variety

'A grandiose horror tale which consumes itself,
snake-like, swallowing its own tail in a series of
narrowing spirals.' – Sunday Times

The Shining Hour
US   1938   76m   bw
MGM
V*

A night-club dancer marries a gentleman farmer, but has trouble with his family.

Overcast melodrama with insufficient basic interest in the characters.

w Ogden Nash, Jane Murfin   play Keith Winter
d Frank Borzage

Joan Crawford, Melvyn Douglas, Margaret Sullavan, Robert Young, Fay Bainter, Allyn Joslyn, Hattie McDaniel

'A confused jumble of cross-purpose motivations and situations that fail entirely to arouse interest.' – *Variety*

'He needed to trust her with his secret. She had to trust him with her life.'

Shining Through
US   1992   132m   Panavision
TCF/Peter V. Miller Investment Corp/Sandollar (Howard Rosenman, Carol Baum)
V, V*, L, S

A secretary recalls how she fell in love with a lawyer and became an American spy in wartime Berlin.

Glossily romantic thriller, not only soft-centred but also coated in marshmallow.   wd David Seltzer
novel Susan Isaacs   ph Jan de Bont   m Michael Kamen   pd Anthony Pratt   ed Craig McKay

Michael Douglas, Melanie Griffith, Liam Neeson, Joely Richardson, John Gielgud

'Little more than a big, brassy Hallmark card with a World War II backdrop.' – *Variety*

'Fun, in an extravagant, hopelessly retrograde fashion.' – *Janet Maslin, New York Times*

Shining Victory
US   1941   80m   bw
Warner (Robert Lord)

A psychiatrist is torn between love and duty.

Adequate romantic programmer.

w Howard Koch, Ann Froelick   play *Jupiter Laughs* by A. J. Cronin   d Irving Rapper   ph James Wong Howe   m Max Steiner

James Stephenson, Geraldine Fitzgerald, Donald Crisp, Barbara O'Neil, Montagu Love, Sig Rumann

Shinjuku Dorobo Nikki: see *Diary of a Shinjuku Thief*

Ship Ahoy
US   1942   95m   bw
MGM (Jack Cummings)
V*, L

On a trip to Puerto Rico, a tap dancer is enlisted as a spy.

Tepid musi-comedy.

w Harry Clork   d Eddie Buzzell   ph Leonard Smith   md George Stoll   ad Merrill Pye

Eleanor Powell, Red Skelton, Bert Lahr, Virginia O'Brien, William Post Jnr, James Cross

Ship Café
US   1935   65m   bw
Harold Hurley/Paramount

A singing stoker wins a rich girl.

Musical star vehicle of the lower class.

w Harlan Thompson, Herbert Fields   d Robert Florey

Carl Brisson, Arline Judge, Mady Christians, William Frawley, Eddie Davis

Ship of Fools ***
US   1965   150m   bw
Columbia/Stanley Kramer
V*, L

In 1933 a German liner leaves Vera Cruz for Bremerhaven with a mixed bag of passengers.

Ambitious, serious, quite fascinating slice-of-life shipboard multi-melodrama. Capable mounting, memorable performances and a bravura finale erase memories of padding and symbolic pretensions.

w Abby Mann,   novel Katherine Anne Porter
d Stanley Kramer   ph Ernest Laszlo   m Ernest Gold

Vivien Leigh, Simone Signoret, Oskar Werner, Heinz Ruhmann, José Ferrer, Lee Marvin, Elizabeth Ashley, Michael Dunn, George Segal, Jose Greco, Charles Korvin, Alf Kjellin, Werner Klemperer, John Wengraf, Lilia Skala, Karen Verne

GLOCKEN (Michael Dunn): 'My name is Karl Glocken, and this is a ship of fools. I'm a fool. You'll meet more fools as we go along. This tub is packed with them. Emancipated ladies and ballplayers. Lovers. Dog lovers. Ladies of joy. Tolerant Jews, Dwarfs. All kinds. And who knows – if you look closely enough, you may even find yourself on board!'

'When you're not being hit over the head with the symbolism, you're being punched in the stomach by would-be inventive camera work while the music score unremittingly fills your nostrils with acrid exhalations.' – *John Simon*

'There is such wealth of reflection upon the human condition, so subtle an orchestration of the elements of love and hate, that it is not fair to tag this with the label of any other film.' – *New York Times*

AA: Ernest Laszlo

AAN: best picture; Abby Mann; Simone Signoret; Oskar Werner; Michael Dunn

The Ship that Died of Shame
GB   1955   91m   bw
Ealing (Michael Relph)
V

The wartime crew of a motor gunboat buy the vessel and go into postwar business as smugglers.

Thin and rather obvious melodramatic fable.

w John Whiting, Michael Relph, Basil Dearden
novel Nicholas Monsarrat   d Basil Dearden
ph Gordon Dines   m William Alwyn

Richard Attenborough, George Baker, Bill Owen, Virginia McKenna, Roland Culver, Bernard Lee, Ralph Truman, John Chandos

'A sentimental fantasy tacked on to a basically conventional thriller.' – *Penelope Houston*

A Ship to India *
Sweden   1947   102m   bw
Sveriges Folkbiografer (Lorens Marmstedt)
original title: *Skepp Till Indialand*; aka: *The Land of Desire*

A hunchbacked sailor, returning after seven years at sea and searching for the woman he loved, recalls how the affair began after his father, a bullying tugboat captain, brought her aboard.

Despite the movie's low-budget origins, a sombre, claustrophobic and complex study of relationships and damaged lives which builds to a hopeful ending.

wd Ingmar Bergman   play Martin Soederhjelm
ph Goran Strindberg   m Erland von Koch   ad O. A. Lundgren   ed Tage Holmberg

Holger Lowenadler, Anna Lindahl, Birger Malmsten, Getrud Fridh, Naemi Brise, Hjordis Pettersson

Shipbuilders
GB   1943   89m   bw
British National

A cavalcade of the problems of a Clydeside tycoon in the thirties.

Plodding propaganda piece ending with masters and unions working for Britain.

w Gordon Wellesley, Stephen Potter, Reginald Pound
d John Baxter

Clive Brook, Morland Graham, Finlay Currie, Maudie Edwards

Shipmates Forever
US   1935   124m   bw
Warner

An admiral's son disappoints his dad by preferring song and dance to the navy.

Very stretched light musical without any overpowering talents.

w Delmer Daves   d Frank Borzage

Dick Powell, Ruby Keeler, Lewis Stone, Ross Alexander, Eddie Acuff, Dick Foran

Ships with Wings *
GB   1941   103m   bw
Ealing (S. C. Balcon)
V*

Aircraft carriers prepare for World War II.

Historically interesting, dramatically insubstantial flagwaver.

w Sergei Nolbandov, Patrick Kirwan, Austin Melford, Diana Morgan   d Sergei Nolbandov
ph Max Greene, Eric Cross, Roy Kellino, Wilkie Cooper   m Geoffrey Wright

John Clements, Leslie Banks, Jane Baxter, Ann Todd, Basil Sydney, Edward Chapman, Hugh Williams, Frank Pettingell, Michael Wilding

Shipyard Sally
GB   1939   79m   bw
TCF

A barmaid persuades a shipyard owner to reopen.

Sub-Ealing style comedy with music which manages to bring in management and man as well as waving a flag or two.

w Karl Tunberg, Don Ettlinger   d Monty Banks

Gracie Fields, Sydney Howard, Morton Selten, Norma Varden, Oliver Wakefield

The Shiralee *
GB   1957   99m   bw
Ealing (Jack Rix)

An Australian swagman leaves his wife and takes to the road with his small daughter.

Episodic character comedy-drama throwing a fairly sharp light on the Australian scene.

w Neil Paterson, Leslie Norman   novel D'Arcy Niland   d Leslie Norman   ph Paul Beeson   m John Addison

Peter Finch, Dana Wilson, Elizabeth Sellars, George Rose, Russell Napier, Niall MacGinnis, Tessie O'Shea

Shirley Valentine **
US   1989   108m   Technicolor
UIP/Paramount (Lewis Gilbert)
V, V*, L, S

A bored housewife abandons her husband to enjoy a holiday romance in Greece.

Enjoyably old-fashioned movie, with some entertaining monologues on her narrow existence from its heroine.

w Willy Russell   play Willy Russell   d Lewis Gilbert   ph Alan Hune   m Willy Russell, George Hatzinassios   pd John Stoll   ed Lesley Walker

Pauline Collins, Tom Conti, Julia McKenzie, Alison Steadman, Joanna Lumley, Sylvia Sims, Bernard Hill

AAN: Pauline Collins

Shivers: see *The Parasite Murders*

Shoah

France   1985   Part I 274m/Part 2 292m   colour
Aleph/Historia

Massive documentary history of the Holocaust, using survivors' testimony and some reenactment but no historical footage.

d Claude Lanzmann

Shock

US   1946   70m   bw
TCF
V*

A girl in a hotel sees a murder committed, and an elaborate plan is concocted to silence her.

Flat treatment ruins a good suspense situation.

w Eugene Ling   *d* Alfred Werker   *ph* Glen MacWilliams, Joe MacDonald   *m* David Buttolph

Vincent Price, Lynn Bari, Frank Latimore, Annabel Shaw

'Extreme improbabilities and a general lack of finish.' – *MFB*

The Shock *

France   1982   95m   colour   Panavision
Sara Films/T. Films (Charlotte Fraisse)
original title: *Le Choc*

A professional killer finds himself in trouble with his boss when he decides to retire.

Slick, glossy romantic thriller that is enjoyable providing you can stomach its amorality or believe that Catherine Deneuve could be the wife of a turkey farmer.

w Alain Delon, Dominique Robelet, Claude Veillot, Robin Davis   *novel* La Position du Tireur Couché by Jean-Patrick Manchette   *d* Robin Davis   *ph* Pierre-William Glenn   *m* Philippe Sarde   *ad* Serge Douy   *ed* Thierry Derocles

Alain Delon, Catherine Deneuve, Philippe Leotard, Etienne Chicot, Jean-Louis Richard, Catherine Leprince, François Perrot

Shock Corridor **

US   1963   101m   bw   (colour sequence)
Leon Fromkess/Sam Firks (Samuel Fuller)
V, V*, L

A journalist gets himself admitted to a mental asylum to solve the murder of an inmate.

Sensational melodrama, a cinematic equivalent of the yellow press, and on that level quite lively.

wd Samuel Fuller   *ph* Stanley Cortez   *m* Paul Dunlap

Peter Breck, Constance Towers, Gene Evans, James Best, Hari Rhodes, Philip Ahn

'A minor masterpiece' – *Derek Malcolm, Guardian*

'Killing is easy. Getting away with it is murder'
A Shock to the System

US   1990   87m   DuArt
Medusa/Corsair (Patrick McCormick)
V, V*, L

Passed over for promotion and bored by his wife, a marketing executive turns to murder to resolve his difficulties.

Lacklustre black comedy.

w Andrew Klavan   *novel* Simon Brett   *d* Jan Egleson   *ph* Paul Goldsmith   *m* Gary Chang   *pd* Howard Cummings   *ed* Peter C. Frank, William A. Anderson

Michael Caine, Elizabeth McGovern, Peter Riegart, Swoosie Kurtz, Will Patton, Jenny Wright, John McMartin, Barbara Baxley, Haviland Morris, Philip Moon

'A study of personal psychosis and corporate ruthlessness that is at once mordantly comic and chillingly controlled.' – *Nigel Floyd, MFB*

Shock Treatment

US   1964   94m   bw
Warner (Aaron Rosenberg)

Murders are committed in a mental institution.

Tasteless thriller, not even very arresting as a yarn.

w Sidney Boehm   *d* Denis Sanders   *ph* Sam Leavitt   *m* Jerry Goldsmith

Lauren Bacall, Roddy McDowall, Carol Lynley, Ossie Davis, Stuart Whitman, Douglass Dumbrille

'Trust me, I'm a doctor.'
Shock Treatment

GB   1982   95m   Technicolor
TCF (John Goldstone)
V*

An innocent young couple are trapped on a bizarre TV game show.

A sort of sequel to *The Rocky Horror Show* (qv), featuring the same hapless hero and heroine, but lacking any spark of originality. It also failed to attract its predecessor's cult following.

w Richard O'Brien, Jim Sharman   *d* Jim Sharman   *ph* Mike Molloy   *m* Richard Hartley, Richard O'Brien   *pd* Brian Thomson   *ed* Richard Bedford

Jessica Harper, Cliff de Young, Richard O'Brien, Patricia Quinn, Charles Gray, Nell Campbell, Ruby Wax, Barry Humphries, Rik Mayall

Shocker

US   1989   110m   Foto-Kem
Guild/Alive Films/Carolco International (Marianne Maddalena, Barin Kumar)
V, V*, L, S

The spirit of a mass murderer survives his execution.

Mundane horror, lacking any spark of originality and obviously patterned on the director's *Nightmare On Elm Street.*

wd Wes Craven   *ph* Jacques Haitkin   *m* William Goldstein   *ad* Randy Moore   *ed* Andy Blumenthal

Michael Murphy, Peter Berg, Cami Cooper, Mitch Pileggi, John Tesh, Heather Langenkamp, Jessica Craven, Richard Brooks

The Shocking Miss Pilgrim

US   1946   85m   Technicolor
TCF (William Perlberg)

In 1894 Boston, a lady typist (stenographer) fights for women's rights.

Period comedy with music; not nearly as sharp as it thinks it is.

wd George Seaton   *ph* Leon Shamroy   *md* David Raksin   *ad* James Basevi, Boris Leven   *songs* George and Ira Gershwin

Betty Grable, Dick Haymes, Anne Revere, Allyn Joslyn, Gene Lockhart, Elizabeth Patterson, Arthur Shields, Elizabeth Risdon

Shockproof

US   1949   79m   bw
Columbia (S. Sylvan Simon)

A parole officer falls in love with his protégée and becomes corrupted.

Predictable programmer with a few pleasant touches.

w Helen Deutsch, Samuel Fuller   *d* Douglas Sirk   *ph* Charles Lawton Jnr   *m* George Duning

Cornel Wilde, Patricia Knight, John Baragrey, Esther Minciotti, Howard St John, Russell Collins

The Shoes of the Fisherman **

US   1968   157m   Metrocolor   Panavision
MGM (George Englund)
V*

After twenty years as a political prisoner, a Russian bishop becomes Pope.

Predigested but heavy-going picturization of a bestseller; big budget, big stars, big hopes. In fact a commercial dud, with plenty of superficial interest but more dramatic contrivance than religious feeling.

w John Patrick, James Kennaway   *novel* Morris West   *d* Michael Anderson   *ph* Erwin Hillier   *m* Alex North   *ad* Edward Carfagno, George W. Davis

Anthony Quinn, David Janssen, Laurence Olivier, Oskar Werner, John Gielgud, Barbara Jefford, Leo McKern, Vittorio de Sica, Clive Revill, Paul Rogers

'A splendidly decorated curate's egg.' – *MFB*

AAN: Alex North

Shoeshine **

Italy   1946   90m   bw
Alfa (Paolo W. Tamburella)
V*
original title: *Sciuscià*

In Nazi-occupied Rome two shoeshine boys become involved in black marketeering, with tragic consequences.

Not especially rewarding to watch now, this was a key film in the development of Italian neo-realism.

w Cesare Zavattini, Sergio Amidei, Adolfo Franci, C. G. Viola   *d* Vittorio de Sica   *ph* Anchise Brizzi, Elio Paccara

Franco Interlenghi, Rinaldo Smordoni

'It is filled in every scene with an awareness of the painful complexity of even simple evil.' – *James Agee*

AA: special award
AAN: script

Shogun Assassin *

Japan/US   1980   86m (dubbed)   Fujicolor   Tohoscope
Facelift/Katsu (Shintaro Katsu, Hisaharu Matsubara, David Weisman)
V, V*

A disgraced shogun executioner seeks revenge for the murder of his wife.

Dubbed and edited for American consumption from the first two films in a Japanese series featuring Lone Wolf, a comic-book character and the hero of the goriest martial arts films so far made, it concentrates on the violence.

w Kazuo Koike, Robert Houston, David Weisman   *d* Kenji Misumi, Robert Houston   *ph* Chishi Makiura   *m* Hideakira Sakurai, Mark Lindsay, W. Michael Lewis   *ad* Akira Naito   *ed* Toshio Taniguchi, Lee Percy

Tomisaburo Wakayama, Masahiro Tomikawa, Kayo Matsuo, Minoru Ohki, Shoji Kobayashi, Shia Kishida, Akhiro Tomikawa

'No one bleeds like this unless they have garden hoses for veins.' – *Roger Ebert*

Shokutaku No Nai Ie: see *The Empty Table*

Shoot First: see *Rough Shoot*

Shoot the Moon *

US   1981   123m   Metrocolor
MGM (Alan Marshall)
V*, L

The family is affected when well-heeled parents decide to split up.

A halfway decent actors' piece which doesn't really justify its time or leave affectionate memories behind. In essence it adds nothing except noise to what was being done in this field forty years ago.

w Bo Goldman   *d* Alan Parker   *ph* Michael Seresin   *m* no credit   *pd* Geoffrey Kirkland

Albert Finney, Diane Keaton, Karen Allen, Peter Weller, Dana Hill, Leora Dana

'Despite their superficial sophistication, these are immature creatures playing grown-up games which would be thought childish in Bugsy Malone.' – *Sunday Times*

Shoot the Pianist *
France 1960 80m bw Dyaliscope
Films de la Pléiade (Pierre Braunberger)
V, V*, L
original title: *Tirez sur le Pianiste*

A bar-room piano player becomes involved with gangsters and his girlfriend is killed.

Fair copy of an American *film noir*, not especially interesting except for its sharp observation.

w Marcel Moussy, François Truffaut *novel Down There* by David Goodis *d* François Truffaut *ph* Raoul Coutard *m* Jean Constantin, Georges Delerue

Charles Aznavour, Nicole Berger, Marie Dubois, Michèle Mercier, Albert Rémy

'Pictorially it is magnificent, revealing Truffaut's brilliant control over his images; emotionally, it is all a little jejeune.' – *John Gillett, MFB*

Shoot the Works
US 1934 82m bw
Albert Lewis/Paramount

A band leader and a gossip columnist stage a fake feud.

Anaemic Hollywood version of a rather sharp Broadway play which in this form means less than nothing.

w Howard J. Green, Claude Binyon *play The Great Magoo* by Ben Hecht, Gene Fowler *d* Wesley Ruggles

Jack Oakie, Ben Bernie, Dorothy Dell, Arline Judge, Alison Skipworth, Roscoe Karns, William Frawley, Paul Cavanaugh, Lew Cody

Shoot to Kill
US 1988 110m colour
Touchstone/Silver Screen Partners III (Ron Silverman, Daniel Petrie Jnr)
V*, L

An FBI agent and a guide track down a killer who is hiding in the mountains.

Moderately suspenseful, though unmemorable, thriller.

w Harv Zimmell, Michael Burton, Daniel Petrie Jnr *d* Roger Spottiswoode *ph* Michael Chapman *m* John Scott *pd* Richard Sylbert *ed* Garth Craven, George Bowers

Sidney Poitier, Tom Berenger, Kirstie Alley, Clancy Brown, Frederick Coffin, Richard Masur, Andrew Robinson, Kevin Scannell

The Shooting
US 1966 82m DeLuxe
Santa Clara (Jack Nicholson, Monte Hellman)
V*, L

An ex-bounty hunter is trailed by a hired killer.

Simplistic semi-professional Western which achieves some power despite poor technical quality and a deliberately obscure ending.

w Adrien Joyce *d* Monte Hellman *ph* Gregory Sandor *m* Richard Markowitz

Warren Oates, Will Hutchins, Jack Nicholson, Millie Perkins

The Shooting Party *
GB 1984 96m Technicolor
Edenflow/Geoff Reeve (Peter Dolman)
V*, S

In 1913 Sir Randolph Nettleby invites guests for a weekend at his country estate, but the coming war is foretold in their behaviour.

Mild little symbolic play which provides the expected minor pleasures.

w Julian Bond *novel* Isabel Colegate *d* Alan Bridges *ph* Fred Tammes *m* John Scott

James Mason, Edward Fox, Dorothy Tutin, John Gielgud, Gordon Jackson, Cheryl Campbell, Robert Hardy

Shooting Stars *
GB 1928 80m (24 fps) bw silent
British Instructional (H. Bruce Woolf)

The wife of a film star puts real bullets in a prop gun but her lover is killed by mistake.

Late silent drama with comedy touches: its main interest lies in its behind-the-scenes background and in the emergence of a new director.

w John Orton, Anthony Asquith *d* Anthony Asquith, A. V. Bramble

Annette Benson, Brian Aherne, Donald Calthrop, Wally Patch, Chili Bouchier

The Shootist **
US 1976 100m Technicolor Panavision
Paramount/Frankovich-Self
V, V*, L

In 1901, a dying ex-gunfighter arrives in a small town to set his affairs in order.

Impressive semi-Western melodrama, very well written and acted all round; the kind of solidly entertaining and thoughtful movie one imagined they didn't make any more.

w Miles Hood Swarthout, Scott Hale, *novel* Glendon Swarthout *d* Don Siegel *ph* Bruce Surtees *m* Elmer Bernstein

John Wayne, Lauren Bacall, James Stewart, Ron Howard, Bill McKinney, Richard Boone, John Carradine, Scatman Crothers, Harry Morgan, Hugh O'Brian, Sheree North

'Just when it seemed that the western was an endangered species, due for extinction because it had repeated itself too many times, Wayne and Siegel have managed to validate it once more.' – *Arthur Knight*

'Watching this film is like taking a tour of Hollywood legends.' – *Frank Rich*

'Three fast guns against one determined man!'
Shootout
US 1971 94m Technicolor
Universal (Hal B. Wallis)

After seven years in prison, a bank robber seeks out his betrayer.

Routine, flatly-handled revenge Western.

w Marguerite Roberts *novel The Lone Cowboy* by Will James *d* Henry Hathaway *ph* Earl Rath *m* Dave Grusin

Gregory Peck, Pat Quinn, Robert F. Lyons, Susan Tyrell, Jeff Corey, James Gregory, Rita Gam

Shootout at Medicine Bend
US 1957 87m bw
Warner

Three ex-soldiers clean up a corrupt community.

Entertaining Western programmer.

w John Tucker Battle, D. D. Beauchamp *d* Richard Bare

Randolph Scott, James Craig, Angie Dickinson, James Garner, Gordon Jones

The Shop around the Corner **
US 1940 97m bw
MGM (Ernst Lubitsch)
V*, L

In a Budapest shop, the new floorwalker and a girl who dislikes him find they are pen pals.

Pleasant period romantic comedy which holds no surprises but is presented with great style.

w Samson Raphaelson, *play* Nikolaus Laszlo *d* Ernst Lubitsch *ph* William Daniels *m* Werner Heymann

James Stewart, Margaret Sullavan, *Frank Morgan*, Joseph Schildkraut, Sara Haden, *Felix Bressart*, William Tracy

'It's not pretentious but it's a beautiful job of picture-making, and the people who did it seem to have enjoyed doing it just as much as their audiences will enjoy seeing it.' – *James Shelley Hamilton*

'An agreeably bittersweet example of light entertainment.' – *Charles Higham, 1972*

'One of the most beautifully acted and paced romantic comedies ever made in this country.' – *New Yorker, 1978*

† Remade as *In the Good Old Summertime* (qv).

The Shop at Sly Corner
GB 1946 92m bw
Pennant (George King)
US title: *Code of Scotland Yard*

An antique dealer who is also a fence kills a blackmailer in order to shield his daughter.

Competent but stagey version of a West End success, giving full rein to a bravura star performance.

w Katherine Strueby *play* Edward Percy *d* George King *ph* Hone Glendinning *m* George Melachrino

Oscar Homolka, Muriel Pavlow, Derek Farr, Manning Whiley, Kenneth Griffith, Kathleen Harrison, Garry Marsh, Irene Handl

The Shop on Main Street *
Czechoslovakia 1965 128m bw
Ceskoslovensky Film
V, V*, L
original title: *Obchod na Korze*; aka: *The Shop on the High Street*

During the German invasion of Czechoslovakia, a well-meaning carpenter tries to shield an old Jewish lady, but his own rough treatment kills her.

A rather obvious sentimental fable, developed at too great length, but with bravura acting.

w Ladislav Grosman, Jan Kadar, Einar Klos *d* Jan Kadar, Einar Klos *ph* Vladimir Novotny *m* Zdenek Liska

Ida Kaminska, Jozef Kroner, Hana Slivkova, Martin Holly

'Overlong, derivative, ploddingly directed.' – *John Simon*

AA: best foreign film
AAN: Ida Kaminska

The Shop on the High Street: see The Shop on Main Street

Shopworn Angel *
US 1928 90m approx bw part-talkie
Paramount (Louis D. Lighton)

A showgirl meets a naïve young soldier off to war and forsakes her man about town.

Hard-boiled, soft-centred romantic drama remade as below and later as *That Kind of Woman* (qv).

w Howard Estabrook, Albert Shelby Le Vino *play Private Pettigrew's Girl* by Dana Burnet *d* Richard Wallace *ph* Charles Lang

Nancy Carroll, Gary Cooper, Paul Lukas, Emmett King

Shopworn Angel *
US 1938 85m bw
MGM (Joseph L. Mankiewicz)

Smooth, close remake of the above.

w Waldo Salt *d* H. C. Potter *ph* Joseph Ruttenberg *m* Edward Ward *montage* Slavko Vorkapich

Margaret Sullavan, James Stewart, Walter Pidgeon, Hattie McDaniel, Sam Levene

Short Circuit *

US 1986 98m Metrocolor Panavision
Rank/PSO (David Foster, Lawrence Turman)
V, V*, L

An electric shock transforms a military robot into a creature with a mind of its own.

Amusing, if predictable comedy that owes much to *E.T.*

w S. S. Wilson, Brent Maddock *d* John Badham *ph* Nick McLean *m* David Shire *ad* Dianne Wager *ed* Frank Morriss

Ally Sheedy, Steve Guttenberg, Fisher Stevens, Austin Pendleton, G. W. Bailey, Brian McNamara, Tim Blaney

Short Circuit 2

US 1988 110m Technicolor
Columbia TriStar (David Foster, Lawrence Turman, Gary Foster)
V, V*, L

At large in the big city, a robot with human sensibilities is fooled into helping jewel thieves.

Ineffectual sequel, lacking in laughs and bungling the action.

w S. S. Wilson, Brent Maddock *d* Kenneth Johnson *ph* John McPherson *m* Charles Fox *pd* Bill Brodie *ed* Conrad Buff

Fisher Stevens, Michael McKean, Cynthia Gibb, Jack Weston, Dee McCafferty, David Hemblen, Tim Blaney

Short Cut to Hell

US 1957 89m bw Vistavision
Paramount (A. C. Lyles)

A racketeer hires a gunman to commit a double murder, then double-crosses him.

Rough and ready remake of *This Gun for Hire* (qv), less arresting than the original.

w Ted Berkeman, Raphael Blau, W. R. Burnett *novel A Gun for Sale* by Graham Greene *d* James Cagney *ph* Haskell Boggs *md* Irvin Talbot

Robert Ivers, Georgeann Johnson, William Bishop, Murvyn Vye

Short Cuts ***

US 1993 188m colour Panavision
Artificial Eye/Spelling/Fine Line/Avenue (Cary Brokaw)

In Los Angeles, the lives of nine dysfunctional, suburban couples interwine.

An excellent, continually fascinating examination of people living on the edge, cut off from the truth of their emotions. The complexity of the cross-cutting between one scene and another is brilliantly achieved; what mars the film is its tendency to melodrama, particularly in its treatment of an alcoholic jazz singer and her equally disturbed cello-playing daughter.

w Robert Altman, Frank Barhydt *story* Raymond Carver *d* Robert Altman *ph* Walt Lloyd *m* Mark Isham *pd* Stephen Altman *ed* Geraldine Peroni

Andie MacDowell, Bruce Davison, Jack Lemmon, Zane Cassidy, Julianne Moore, Matthew Modine, Anne Archer, Fred Ward, Jennifer Jason Lee, Chris Penn, Joseph C. Hopkins, Josette Macario, Robert Downey Jnr, Madeleine Stowe, Tim Robbins, Lily Tomlin, Tom Waits, Frances McDormand, Peter Gallagher, Annie Ross, Lori Singer, Lyle Lovett, Buck Henry

'Altman has used Carver's stories as a vehicle for presenting a vast panorama of life problems that are humorous, grim and absurd in equal measure. Viewer

interest in the goings-on is generated not by artificial melodrama or hyped-up filmmaking technique, but by the recognition factor of the human foibles on display.' – *Todd McCarthy, Variety*

'A victory both as a summation of Altman's unflattering, but not unloving, view of American society, and an epic piece of cinema of innate daring and imagination.' – *Derek Malcolm, Guardian*

'A film with no dud line, flawed performance or slick piece of editing in all its 188 minutes . . . Only at a second viewing can one fully appreciate the magnificence of the film's grand design, which is the presentation of life as a mutually shared tragi-comedy.' – *Philip French, Observer*

AAN: Robert Altman (as director)

Short Encounters *

USSR 1967 95m bw
Odessa Feature Film Studio
original title: *Korotkie Vstrechi*

Two women, one a bureaucrat, the other a young country girl, recall their love for the same man, a footloose geologist.

An innocuous love story, it was banned for 20 years by the Soviet authorities because of the attitudes it displays towards sex and social misdemeanours.

w Kira Muratova, Leonid Zhukhovitsky *d* Kira Muratova *ph* G. Kariuk *m* Oleg Karavaichuk

Nina Ruslanova, Vladimir Vysotsky, Kira Muratova

A Short Film about Killing ****

Poland 1988 84m colour
Gala/Film Unit 'Tor'/Zespoly Filmowe (Ryszard Chutkowski)
V
original title: *Krótki Film O Zabijaniu*

A disenchanted youth who commits a bungled and motiveless murder is defended by an idealistic lawyer opposed to capital punishment.

Powerful and unremittingly bleak, but unforgettable in its condemnation of killing, whether criminal or judicial. It is one of the Decalogues, a series of films on the ten commandments made for television.

w Krzysztof Piesiewicz, Krzysztof Kieslowski *d* Krzysztof Kieslowski *ph* Slawomir Idziak *m* Zbigniew Preisner *ad* Halina Dobrowolska *ed* Ewa Small

Miroslaw Baka, Krzysztof Globisz, Jan Tesarz, Zbigniew Zapasiewicz

A Short Film about Love **

Poland 1988 87m colour
Gala/Polish Film Producers' Corporation (Ryszard Chutkowski)
V
original title: *Krótki Film O Milosci*

A teenager spies on the sexual activities of a woman who lives opposite his flat.

Grim but gripping film on the impossibility of love.

w Krzysztof Piesiewicz, Krzysztof Kieslowski *d* Krzysztof Kieslowski *ph* Witold Adamek *m* Zbigniew Preisner *pd* Halina Dobrowolska *ed* Ewa Smal

Grazyna Szapolowska, Olaf Lubaszenko, Stefania Iwinska, Piotr Machalica, Artur Barcis

'Getting killed isn't as easy as it looks'
Short Time

US 1987 102m colour
Rank/Gladden Entertainment/Touchstone (Todd Black)
V, V*, L

Discovering he has a fatal disease and wanting to die on active service so his family can collect on his insurance policy, an ageing cop volunteers for dangerous assignments.

A comedy suffering from a terminal lack of laughs.

w John Blumenthal, Michael Berry *d* Gregg Champion *ph* John Connor *m* Ira Newborn *pd* Michael Bolton *ed* Frank Morriss

Dabney Coleman, Matt Frewer, Teri Garr, Barry Corbin, Joe Pantoliano, Xander Berkeley, Rob Roy

Shot in the Dark

GB 1933 53m bw
Real Art (Julius Hagen)

A golfing rector solves the murder of an eccentric who was hated by his relatives.

A country-house melodrama of a very old-fashioned kind, moderately enjoyable as an example of English acting styles of the time.

w George Pearson, Terence Egan *novel* Gerard Fairlie *d* George Pearson *ph* Ernest Palmer *ad* James A. Carter *ed* Lister Laurance

Jack Hawkins, Michael Shepley, Dorothy Boyd, O. B. Clarence, Dave Burnaby, Russell Thorndike, Margaret Yarde, A. Bromley Davenport

A Shot in the Dark *

US 1964 101m DeLuxe Panavision
UA/Mirisch/Geoffrey (Blake Edwards)
V, V*, L

A woman is accused of shooting her lover; accident-prone Inspector Clouseau investigates.

Further adventures of the oafish, Tatiesque clodhopper from *The Pink Panther;* mildly funny for those in the mood for pratfalls.

w Blake Edwards, William Peter Blatty *d* Blake Edwards *ph* Christopher Challis *m* Henry Mancini *pd* Michael Stringer

Peter Sellers, Elke Sommer, George Sanders, Herbert Lom, Tracy Reed, Graham Stark

Shotgun

US 1954 81m Technicolor print
Allied Artists
V*

A deputy marshal avenges the death of his boss.

Rather violent Western with a few unusual angles.

w Clark E. Reynolds, Rory Calhoun *d* Lesley Selander

Sterling Hayden, Zachary Scott, Yvonne de Carlo, Guy Prescott, Robert Wilke

Should Ladies Behave?

US 1933 90m bw
MGM

A young girl falls for her aunt's lover.

Brittle comedy of manners which transferred poorly from Broadway with a star well over the top.

w Sam and Bella Spewack *play The Vinegar Tree* by Paul Osborn *d* Harry Beaumont

Alice Brady, Lionel Barrymore, Conway Tearle, Katherine Alexander, Halliwell Hobbes, Mary Carlisle

Should Married Men Go Home?

US 1928 20m bw silent
Hal Roach

Tribulations on the golf course end in a mud-slinging contest.

Goodish star slapstick, but the preliminary domestic scene is the funniest.

w Leo McCarey, James Parrott, H. M. Walker *d* James Parrott

Laurel and Hardy, Edgar Kennedy

Shoulder Arms *

US 1918 24m (24 fps) bw silent
Charles Chaplin/First National

A soldier in the trenches dreams of winning the war single-handedly.

A comedy which meant a great deal at the time of its release but now provides precious little to laugh at.

wd Charles Chaplin   *ph* Rollie Totheroh

Charles Chaplin, Edna Purviance, Sydney Chaplin, Henry Bergman, Albert Austin

The Shout *
GB   1978   87m   colour
Rank/Recorded Picture (Jeremy Thomas)
V*

A man who may be mad claims that, like the old aborigine magicians, he can kill by shouting.

Curiously gripping but ultimately pointless fable, very well done to little purpose.

w Michael Austin, Jerzy Skolimowsky   *story* Robert Graves & Jerzy Skolimowsky   *ph* Mike Molloy   *m* Rupert Hine, Anthony Banks, Michael Rutherford

Alan Bates, Susannah York, John Hurt, Robert Stephens, Tim Curry

'Poorly acted, incoherent and unendurably loud.' – *Pauline Kael, New Yorker*

Shout at the Devil *
GB   1976   147m   Technicolor   Panavision
Tonav (Michael Klinger)
V*, L

In 1913 Zanzibar, a hard-drinking American and an old Etonian Englishman join forces to rout a brutal German commissioner who resents their poaching ivory in his territory.

The main characters are respectively repellent, effete, and just plain nasty, but the action scenes are vivid and the production is mainly notable as an expensive old-fashioned British film made at a time when there were few British films of any kind.

w Wilbur Smith, Stanley Price, Alastair Reid   *novel* Wilbur Smith   *d* Peter Hunt   *ph* Mike Reed   *m* Maurice Jarre

Lee Marvin, Roger Moore, Barbara Parkins, René Kolldehoff, Ian Holm, Karl Michael Vogler, Maurice Denham, Jean Kent, Robert Lang, Murray Melvin, George Coulouris

'Elephantine plod through the action highlights of a best seller.' – *Sight and Sound*

Show Business ***
US   1944   92m   bw
RKO (Eddie Cantor)
V*, L

The careers of four friends in vaudeville.

Lively low-budget period musical which probably presents the best picture of what old-time vaudeville was really like; a lot of fun when the plot doesn't get in the way.

w Joseph Quillan, Dorothy Bennett   *d* Edwin L. Marin   *ph* Robert de Grasse, Vernon L. Walker   *md* Constantin Bakaleinikoff   *m* George Duning   *ch* Nick Castle

Eddie Cantor, Joan Davis, George Murphy, Constance Moore, Don Douglas, Nancy Kelly

'Bits of archaic vaudeville which give off a moderately pleasant smell of peanuts and cigar smoke.' – *James Agee*

Show Girl in Hollywood
US   1930   77m   bw (colour sequence)
First National

Adventures of a New York girl on the west coast.

Comedy with music; it seems content to wallow in supposed Hollywood glamour without contributing much by way of wit or storyline.

w Harvey Thew, James A. Starr, J. P. McEvoy   *d* Mervyn Le Roy

Alice White, Jack Mulhall, Blanche Sweet, Ford Sterling, John Miljan, Herman Bing

The Show Goes On
GB   1937   93m   bw
ATP (Basil Dean)

A mill girl becomes a star singer with the help of a dying composer.

An attempt to turn Gracie Fields into a serious performer, this was not much enjoyed by her fans.

w Austin Melford, Anthony Kimmins, E. G. Valentine   *d* Basil Dean   *ph* Jan Stallich

Gracie Fields, Owen Nares, Edward Rigby, John Stuart, Horace Hodges, Amy Veness, Cyril Rutchard

The Show-Off
US   1934   80m   bw
MGM

A girl's blundering new husband alienates his in-laws and nearly wrecks his brother-in-law's career.

Surefire satirical comedy-drama from a Broadway staple, this low-budget item gave MGM a new star.

w Herman Mankiewicz   *play* George Kelly   *d* Charles Riesner

Spencer Tracy, Madge Evans, Clara Blandick, Henry Wadsworth, Grant Mitchell, Lois Wilson

† The play had been filmed twice in silent days by Paramount, and turned up again in 1946 as a Red Skelton vehicle.

'In Vitaphone, it eclipses the sun in splendour!'
Show of Shows **
US   1929   128m   Technicolor
Warner (Darryl F. Zanuck)

A big musical show put on by Warner contract artists.

Primitive early talkie, of vital historical interest but mostly photographed from a seat in the stalls.

w/m various   *d* John G. Adolfi   *ph* Barney McGill

Frank Fay, H. B. Warner, Monte Blue, Lupino Lane, Ben Turpin, Chester Morris, Ted Lewis and his band, Georges Carpentier, Patsy Ruth Miller, Beatrice Lillie, Winnie Lightner, Irene Bordoni, Myrna Loy, Douglas Fairbanks Jnr, John Barrymore, Betty Compson

'Colour photography of the crudest, most garish kind, the resulting impression being that a child of seven has been let loose with a shilling box of paints.' – *James Agate*

Show People
US   1928   80m at 24 fps   bw   silent
MGM
V*

A naïve young actress makes it in Hollywood.

Historically important comedy with cameo appearances by many stars of the time.

w Wanda Tuchock, Agnes Christine Johnston, Lawrence Stallings   *d* King Vidor

Marion Davies, William Haines

Show Them No Mercy *
US   1935   76m   bw
TCF (Raymond Griffith)
V*
GB title: *Tainted Money*

Kidnappers are rounded up by G-men.

Lively crime thriller typical of its time.

w Kubec Glasmon, Henry Lehrman   *d* George Marshall   *ph* Bert Glennon   *m* David Buttolph

Rochelle Hudson, Cesar Romero, Bruce Cabot, Edward Norris, Edward Brophy, Warren Hymer

'Direct, surely dramatic, inevitable and full of terror.' – *Otis Ferguson*

Showboat ***
US   1936   110m   bw
Universal (Carl Laemmle Jnr)
V*, L

Lives and loves of the personnel on an old-time Mississippi showboat.

Great style and excellent performances mark this version, which still suffers from longueurs in the middle followed by the rapid passage of many years to provide a happy ending.

w Oscar Hammerstein II   *book* Oscar Hammerstein II for the Broadway musical   *novel* Edna Ferber   *d* James Whale   *ph* John Mescall   *m* Jerome Kern   *ly* Oscar Hammerstein II

Irene Dunne, Allan Jones, Helen Morgan, Paul Robeson, Charles Winninger, Hattie McDaniel, Donald Cook, Sammy White

'For three quarters of its length good entertainment: sentimental, literary, but oddly appealing.' – *Graham Greene*

† A primitive talkie version of *Showboat*, now lost, was made in 1929.
†† Before Allan Jones was cast, Walter Pidgeon, Robert Taylor, John Boles, Fredric March and Nelson Eddy were all considered.

Showboat **
US   1951   108m   Technicolor
MGM (Arthur Freed)
V, V*, L, S

Vigorous remake with good ensemble dancing; otherwise inferior to the 1936 version.

w John Lee Mahin   *d* George Sidney   *ph* Charles Rosher   *md* Conrad Salinger, Adolph Deutsch   *ch* Robert Alton

Kathryn Grayson, *Howard Keel,* Ava Gardner, William Warfield, *Joe E. Brown,* Robert Sterling, Marge and Gower Champion, Agnes Moorehead

† Ava Gardner's singing was dubbed by Annette Warren.

AAN: Charles Rosher; Conrad Salinger, Adolph Deutsch

The Showdown
US   1950   86m   bw
Republic

A trail boss seeks revenge on his brother's killer.

Routine Western with a touch of mystery.

w Richard Wormser and Dan Gordon   *d* Darrell and Stuart McGowan

Wild Bill Elliott, Marie Windsor, Walter Brennan, Henry Morgan, William Ching, Rhys Williams

Showdown
US   1963   79m   Technicolor
Universal
V*

Two wandering cowboys become involved with a criminal.

Below-par Western with little action and rather boring characters.

w Bronson Howitzer   *d* R. G. Springsteen

Audie Murphy, Charles Drake, Harold J. Stone, Kathleen Crowley, Skip Homeier, L. Q. Jones, Strother Martin

Showdown
US   1972   99m   Technicolor   Todd-AO 35
Universal (George Seaton)
V*

A sheriff finds that his old friend is leader of an outlaw gang.

Routine star Western adequately done.

w Theodore Taylor   *d* George Seaton   *ph* Ernest Laszlo   *m* David Shire

Rock Hudson, Dean Martin, Susan Clark, Donald Moffat, Don McLiam

Showdown at Abilene
US   1956   80m   Technicolor
Universal-International

A shellshocked Civil War veteran, returning home to find his girl married, reluctantly takes a job as sheriff.

Fairly lively Western remade eleven years later as *Gunfight in Abilene*.

w Bernie Giler   *novel* Gun Shy by Clarence Upson Young   *d* Charles Haas

Jock Mahoney, David Janssen, Martha Hyer, Lyle Bettger, Grant Williams

Showgirl in Hollywood
US   1930   80m   bw and Technicolor
Warner

A girl singer is spotted and trained for movie stardom.

Naïve look behind the studio scenes, historically fascinating but dramatically dull.

w Harvey Thew, James A. Starr   *novel* Hollywood Girl by J. P. McEvoy   *d* Mervyn LeRoy

Alice White, Jack Mulhall, Blanche Sweet, Ford Sterling, John Miljan, Herman Bing

Showtime: see Gaiety George

The Shrike
US   1955   88m   bw
U-I (Aaron Rosenberg)

A brilliant theatre man has a nervous breakdown because his wife is a vindictive harpy.

Theatrical two-hander, aridly filmed, of little interest except to show that both stars are capable of sustained emotional acting.

w Ketti Frings   *play* Joseph Kramm   *d* José Ferrer   *ph* William Daniels   *m* Frank Skinner   *titles* Saul Bass

José Ferrer, June Allyson, Joy Page, Jacqueline de Wit, Kendall Clark

'The film is unvaryingly paced, the result, one feels, of a respectable but far from invigorating honesty of purpose.' – *MFB*

The Shuttered Room
GB   1967   110m   Technicolor
Warner/Troy-Schenck (Philip Hazelton)
V*

Returning to her childhood home on an island off the New England coast, a girl and her husband are subjected to terror and violence.

Stretched out suspenser which looks good and is carefully made but fails in its effort to combine the menace of teenage yobboes with that of the monster lurking upstairs.

w D. B. Ledrov, Nathaniel Tanchuck   *story* H. P. Lovecraft, August Derleth   *d David Greene*   *ph* Ken Hodges   *m* Basil Kirchin

Gig Young, Carol Lynley, Flora Robson, Oliver Reed, William Devlin

Shy People *
US   1987   120m   colour
Cannon/Menahem Golan, Yoram Globus
V*, L, S

A glamorous journalist, who researches into her family, traces some isolated relatives to the bayous of Louisiana.

Off-beat melodrama that has a queasy fascination.

w Gérard Brach, Marjorie David, Andrei Konchalovsky   *d* Andrei Konchalovsky   *ph* Chris

Menges   *m* Tangerine Dream   *pd* Stephen Marsh   *ed* Alain Jakubowicz

Jill Clayburgh, Barbara Hershey, Martha Plimpton, Merritt Butrick, John Philbin, Don Swayze, Pruitt Taylor Vince

Une Si Jolie Petite Plage *
France   1948   91m   bw
CICC (Emile Darbon)
aka: Such a Pretty Little Beach

A murderer returns to the small seaside town where he spent his childhood, befriends the maid at the hotel, and after a few days kills himself.

A melancholy anecdote which works both as a character study and pictorially.

w Jacques Sigurd   *d* Yves Allégret   *ph* Henri Alekan   *m* Maurice Thiriet

Gérard Philipe, Jean Servais, *Madeleine Robinson*, Jane Marken, Carette

'Shows fine craftsmanship and is beautifully sensitive to place and atmosphere.' – *Gavin Lambert, MFB*

Si Può Fare . . . Amigo: see The Big and the Bad

Si Tous les Gars du Monde . . . *
France   1956   108m   bw
Ariane/Filmsonor/Francinex (Alexandre Mnouchkine)
aka: Race for Life

When members of a French trawler crew fall ill in mid-Atlantic, amateur radio operators around the world arrange rescue.

Well-meaning realistic melodrama with a hands-across-the-sea message.

w Jacques Remy   *d* Christian-Jaque   *ph* Armand Thiraud   *m* Georges Van Parys

Andre Valmy, Jean Gaven, Doudou-Babet, Jean-Louis Trintignant

Si Tutte le Donne del Mondo: see Kiss the Girls and Make Them Cry

'It was not sex it was good!'
Sibling Rivalry
US   1990   88m   colour
First Independent/Castle Rock/Nelson
V, V*, L

Complications ensue after an unhappy wife, advised by her sister to have an affair, goes to bed with her sister's husband.

Broad farce of marital upset that causes an occasional smile.

w Martha Goldhirsh   *d* Carl Reiner   *ph* Reynaldo Villalobos   *m* Jack Elliott   *pd* Jeannine C. Oppewall   *ed* Bud Molin

Kirstie Alley, Bill Pullman, Carrie Fisher, Jami Gertz, Scott Bakula, Frances Sternhagen, John Randolph, Sam Elliott, Ed O'Neill, Paul Benedict

'In opting for romantic comedy rather than the black variety, the picture has grave problems of mood which are never resolved.' – *Philip French, Observer*

The Sicilian
US   1987   146m   Technicolor
Fox/Gladden Entertainment (Michael Cimino, Joann Carelli)
V, V*, L

The Sicilian bandit Salvatore Giuliano, who robs the rich in order to give to the poor, is betrayed by his own men.

Over-long and with a cast that lack authenticity as Sicilians, the movie rarely rises above incoherence.

w Steve Shagan   *novel* Mario Puzo   *d* Michael Cimino   *ph* Alex Thomson   *m* David Mansfield   *pd* Wolf Kroeger   *ed* Françoise Bonnot

Christophe Lambert, Terence Stamp, Joss Ackland, John Turturro, Richard Bauer, Barbara Sukowa, Ray McAnally, Aldo Ray

The Sicilian Cross
Italy   1976   92m   colour
Aetos (Manolo Bolognini, Luigi Borghese)
US title: Street People; original title: Gli Esecutori

A Mafia investigator and his racing-driver buddy set out to discover the person responsible for double-crossing a gang leader by hiding heroin in a crucifix sent from Sicily to the United States.

Conventional thriller, composed of shoot-outs and car chases, in which it is difficult to remember, or care, who is doing what to whom.

w Ernest Tidyman, Randall Kleiser, Gianfranco Bucceri, Roberto Leoni, Gian Franco Bucceri, Nicola Badalucco, Maurizio Lucidi   *story* Gianfranco Bucceri, Roberto Leoni   *d* Maurizio Lucidi   *ph* Aiace Parolin   *m* Luis Enriquez   *ad* Gastone Carsetti   *ed* Renzo Lucidi

Roger Moore, Stacy Keach, Ivo Garrani, Fausto Tozzi, Ennio Balbo, Rosemarie Lindt, Ettore Manni

'The uneasy pairing of Moore and Stacy Keach suggests, however, that Maurizio Lucidi intended to enter his picture in the even less inspired Starsky and Hutch stakes.' – *MFB*

Sid and Nancy
GB   1986   111m   colour
Zenith/Initial (Eric Feliner)
V, V*, L, S

An account of the self-destruction of the leader of a punk rock group and his American girlfriend.

Some have said stimulating, most have preferred revolting. Consensus, an example of the dregs to which cinema has been reduced.

w Alex Cox, Abbe Wool   *d* Alex Cox   *ph* Roger Deakins   *m* The Pogues

Gary Oldman, Chloe Webb, David Hayman

'The dialogue is extremely rough, the settings sordid, the theme of wasted lives depressing.' – *Variety*

'Relentlessly whingeing performances and a lengthy slide into drugs, degradation and death make this a solemnly off-putting moral tract.' – *Sight and Sound*

Siddharta
US   1972   94m   Eastmancolor   Panavision
Columbia-Warner/Lotus (Conrad Rooks)

A young Brahmin leaves his comfortable home to join a band of itinerant holy men.

Despite its visual charm, a dull, though faithful, version of the book.

wd Conrad Rooks   *novel* Hermann Hesse   *ph* Sven Nykvist   *m* Hemanta Kuma   *ad* Malcolm Golding   *ed* Willy Kemplen

Shashi Kapoor, Simi Garewal, Rommesh Sharma, Pincho Kapoor, Amrik Singh, Zul Vellani, Shanti Hiranand, Kunal Kapoor

Side Street
US   1950   83m   bw
MGM (Sam Zimbalist)

A petty thief finds himself involved with big-time crooks.

Well-made but rather boring crime melodrama with an excellent car chase finale.

w Sidney Boehm   *d* Anthony Mann   *ph* Joseph Ruttenberg   *m* Lennie Hayton

Farley Granger, Cathy O'Donnell, James Craig, Paul Kelly, Jean Hagen, Edmond Ryan, Paul Harvey

Side Streets

US 1934 63m bw
First National
GB title: A Woman in Her Thirties

A lady furrier takes pity on a sailor, and finally marries him, only to find that he has a past.

Strange, rather tedious, and quite unconvincing character drama.

w Manuel Seff story Ann Garrick, Ethel Hill
d Alfred E. Green

Aline MacMahon, Paul Kelly, Ann Dvorak, Helen Lowell, Henry O'Neill, Marjorie Gateson

Sidekicks

US 1993 100m colour
Gallery (Don Carmody)

An asthmatic teenager escapes his unhappiness by day-dreams of heroic acts at the side of his hero, Chuck Norris.

A movie for young audiences, who may be able to share the fantasies on offer.

w Don Thompson, Lou Illar d Aaron Norris
ph João Fernandes m Alan Silvestri pd Reuben Freed ed David Rawlins, Bernard Weiser

Chuck Norris, Beau Bridges, Jonathan Brandis, Mako, Julia Nickson-Soul, Joe Piscopo, Danica McKellar

Sidewalks of London: see St Martin's Lane

Sidewalks of New York *

US 1931 73m bw
MGM (Lawrence Weingarten)

The playboy owner of some tenement apartments falls in love with the daughter of one of the tenants.

Interesting rather than wholly successful early sound comedy which marked the beginning of Keaton's decline; he was not allowed full control and the comedy scenes are thinly spaced.

w George Landy, Paul Gerard Smith, Eric Hatch, Robert E. Hopkins d Jules White, Zion Myers
ph Leonard Smith

Buster Keaton, Anita Page, Cliff Edwards, Frank Rowan

The Siege at Red River

US 1954 86m Technicolor
TCF/Panoramic (Leonard Goldstein)

During the American Civil War a Confederate agent behind northern lines defeats a treacherous helper and escapes to the South.

Modest, generally watchable, and quite forgettable Western.

w Sidney Boehm d Rudolph Maté ph Edward Cronjager m Lionel Newman

Van Johnson, Joanne Dru, Richard Boone, Milburn Stone, Jeff Morrow, Craig Hill

The Siege of Pinchgut

GB 1959 104m bw
Ealing (Eric Williams)
US title: Four Desperate Men

Escaped convicts take over a small island in Sydney harbour.

Disappointingly obvious location melodrama with routine excitements.

w Harry Watt, Jon Cleary d Harry Watt
ph Gordon Dines m Kenneth V. Jones

Aldo Ray, Heather Sears, Neil McCallum, Victor Maddern, Carlo Justini

The Siege of Sidney Street *

GB 1960 92m bw Dyaliscope
Midcentury (Robert S. Baker, Monty Berman)

An account of the anarchists who infiltrated London in 1912.

Detailed but not dramatically absorbing historical reconstruction with unsatisfactory fictional trimmings.

w Jimmy Sangster, Alexander Baron d/ph Robert S. Baker, Monty Berman m Stanley Black

Peter Wyngarde, Donald Sinden, Nicole Berger, Kieron Moore, Leonard Sachs, Tutte Lemkow

The Siege of the Saxons

GB 1963 85m Technicolor
Columbia/Ameran (Jud Kinberg)

When King Arthur is ill, the Saxons plot his overthrow but are foiled by a handsome outlaw.

Comic strip adventure with action highlights borrowed from older and better films.

w John Kohn, Jud Kinberg d Nathan Juran
ph Wilkie Cooper, Jack Willis m Laurie Johnson

Ronald Lewis, Janette Scott, Ronald Howard, Mark Dignam, John Laurie, Richard Clarke, Jerome Willis

Siesta

US 1987 100m colour
Palace/Lorimar (Gary Kurfirst)
V, V*, L, S

An amnesiac skydiver, visiting her former lover in Spain, is implicated in a murder.

Pretentious, deliberately obscure movie where there is little reward for working out what is happening.

w Patricia Louisiana Knop novel Patrice Chaplin
d Mary Lambert ph Bryan Loftus m Miles Davis
pd John Beard ed Glen Morgan

Ellen Barkin, Gabriel Byrne, Julian Sands, Isabella Rossellini, Martin Sheen, Alexei Sayle, Grace Jones, Jodie Foster

The Sign of Four

GB 1932 75m bw
ATP

Sherlock Holmes clears up a mystery including a hidden fortune, a secret pact, revenge from the east, and a pygmy who blows poison darts through a pipe.

Very acceptable version of the famous story, previously filmed as a silent.

w W. P. Lipscomb novel Sir Arthur Conan Doyle
d Rowland V. Lee and Graham Cutts

Arthur Wontner, Ian Hunter, Isla Bevan, Miles Malleson, Herbert Lomas, Roy Emerton

'A picture which will proudly lead all the entertainments the world has ever seen!'
'Like a shining light – the simple faith that was mightier than a pagan empire!'

The Sign of the Cross ***

US 1932 123m bw
Paramount (Cecil B. de Mille)

In the days of Nero, a Roman officer is converted to Christianity.

A heavily theatrical play becomes one of de Mille's most impressive films, the genuine horror of the arena mingling with the debauched humour of the court. A wartime prologue added in 1943 prolongs the film without improving it.

w Waldemar Young, Sidney Buchman play Wilson Barrett d Cecil B. de Mille ph Karl Struss
m Rudolph Kopp

Fredric March, Elissa Landi, Charles Laughton, Claudette Colbert, Ian Keith, Harry Beresford, Arthur Hohl, Nat Pendleton

'A beautiful film to watch . . . a triumph of popular art.' – Charles Higham, 1972

'However contemptible one may find de Mille's moralizing, it is impossible not to be impressed by The Sign of the Cross.' – John Baxter, 1968

'De Mille's bang-them-on-the-head-with-wild-orgies-and-imperilled-virginity style is at its ripest.' – New Yorker, 1976

'Preposterous, but the laughter dies on the lips.' – NFT, 1974

'This slice of "history" has it all: Laughton's implicitly gay Nero fiddling away while an impressive miniature set burns, Colbert bathing up to her nipples in asses' milk, Christians and other unfortunates thrown to a fearsome menagerie, much suggestive slinking about in Mitchell Leisen's costumes, much general debauchery teetering between the sadistic and the erotic. Not for people with scruples.' – Geoff Brown, Time Out, 1980

AAN: Karl Struss

Sign of the Gladiator

Italy/France/West Germany 1959 84m
Eastmancolor Dyaliscope
Glomer Film/Lyre-Lux/Tele Film (Rino Merolle)
original title: Nel Segno di Roma

Zenobia, Queen of Syria, revolts against Roman rule but falls in love with the consul sent to destroy her.

An early, dull example of Italy's 'sword and sandal' cycle, lacking the genre's saving spectacle

w F. Thellung, F. de Feo, Sergio Leone, G. Mangione, Guido Brignone d Guido Brignone, Riccardo Freda (battle scenes) ph Luciano Trasatti m A. Francesco Lavagnino ad Ottavio Scotti ed Nino Baragli

Anita Ekberg, George Marchal, Folco Lulli, Jacques Sernas, Lorella de Luca, Alberto Farnese, Chelo Alonso

'Against his ruthless pagan lusts – the power of a woman's love!'

The Sign of the Pagan

US 1954 92m Technicolor Cinemascope
U-I (Albert J. Cohen)

Attila the Hun is defeated by the Romans.

Historic horse opera, rather cheaply done.

w Oscar Brodney, Barre Lyndon d Douglas Sirk
ph Russell Metty m Frank Skinner, Hans Salter

Jeff Chandler, Jack Palance, Rita Gam, Ludmilla Tcherina, Jeff Morrow, George Dolenz, Eduard Franz, Alexander Scourby

The Sign of the Ram

US 1948 84m bw
Columbia (Irving Cummings Jnr)

A selfish invalid interferes in her family's affairs.

Stultifying melodrama in the wake of Guest in the House, devised for the unfortunate Miss Peters who was crippled after an accident. Poor production values don't help.

w Charles Bennett d John Sturges ph Burnett Guffey m Hans Salter

Susan Peters, Alexander Knox, Peggy Ann Garner, May Whitty

Le Signe du Lion *

France 1959 90m bw
AJYM Films/Claude Chabrol (Jean Cotet)
V
aka: The Sign of Leo

An American composer living in Paris mistakenly believes he has inherited a fortune and is reduced to penury as a result.

Rohmer's first feature, a lively slice-of-life among French bohemians, but spoiled by its unlikely ending.

w Eric Rohmer, Paul Gegauff d Eric Rohmer
ph Nicolas Hayer m Louis Saguer ed Anne-Marie Cotret

Jess Hahn, Michèle Girardon, Van Doude, Paul Bisciglia, Gilbert Edard, Stéphane Audran, Jean Le Poulain

Signore e Signori: see *The Birds, the Bees and the Italians*

Signpost to Murder
US   1964   74m   bw   Panavision
MGM/Martin (Lawrence Weingarten)

A convicted murderer escapes after ten years and a lonely wife promises to help him.

Tricksy mystery set in a never-never English village.

w Sally Benson   play Monte Doyle   d George Englund   ph Paul C. Vogel   m Lyn Murray

Joanne Woodward, Stuart Whitman, Edward Mulhare, Alan Napier, Murray Matheson

Signs of Life *
West Germany   1968   90m   bw
Werner Herzog
original title: *Lebenszeichen*

During the Second World War, a German soldier, sent to a small Greek island to guard a fortress while he recovers from a wound, is maddened by the peace and boredom of the place.

A coolly dispassionate account of an individual's breakdown when faced with the apparent meaningless of existence.

wd Werner Herzog   story Der tolle Invalide auf dem Fort Ratonneau by Achim von Arnim   ph Thomas Mauch   m Stavros Xarchakos   ed Beate Mainke-Jellinghaus, Maxi Mainke

Peter Brogle, Wolfgang Reichmann, Julio Pinheiro, Athina Zacharopoulou, Wolfgang von Ungern-Sternberg, Wolfgang Stumpf

'A limpidly clear meditation on life shrivelling under a self-imposed oppression.' – *Richard Combs, MFB*

The Silence *
Sweden   1963   96m   bw
Svensk Filmindustri
V, V*, L
original title: *Tystnaden*

Of two women in a large hotel in a foreign city where the military are dominant, one masturbates while the other sleeps with a barman.

Bergman may know what this was all about, but it's a certainty that no one else did: so everyone thought it must be very clever and went to see it. Superficially, as usual, it is careful and fascinating.

wd Ingmar Bergman   ph Sven Nykvist   m from Bach

Ingrid Thulin, Gunnel Lindblom

'There is not enough forward thrust, not enough momentum to unite the specific points, the complementary but discrete images. The pearls are there, but the string is too weak to hold them.' – *John Simon*

Le Silence est d'Or *
France   1947   99m   bw
Pathé/RKO Radio (René Clair)

In 1906 a comedian becomes a film producer and as a result falls into an affair with a young girl.

Somehow not an important film, but quite a delightful one, especially for its local colour and for the combination of Clair and Chevalier up to their old tricks.

wd René Clair   ph Armand Thirard   m Georges Van Parys

Maurice Chevalier, François Périer, Marcelle Derrien

The Silence of Dean Maitland
Australia   1934   97m   bw
Cinesound (Ken G. Hall)

A clergyman sires an illegitimate baby, kills the girl's father and allows another man to be convicted.

Once sensational stuff which almost caused an Australian scandal.

w Gayne Dexter, Edmund Barclay   d Ken G. Hall

John Longden, Charlotte Francis, Jocelyn Howarth, Patricia Minchin

Silence of the Lambs ***
US   1990   118m   Technicolor   Panavision
Rank/Orion/Strong Heart/Demme (Edward Saxon, Kenneth Utt, Ron Bozman)
V, V*, L, S

A young female FBI agent seeks the aid of an imprisoned serial killer and psychiatrist, Hannibal 'The Cannibal' Lecter, to track down another mass murderer.

Tense, exciting and sometimes gruesome thriller, suspenseful enough to make you overlook its essential absurdities. Hopkins plays the role of the devious Lecter with lip-smacking relish.

w Ted Tally   novel Thomas Harris   d Jonathan Demme   ph Tak Fujimoto   m Howard Shore   pd Kristi Zea   ed Craig McKay

Jodie Foster, Anthony Hopkins, Scott Glenn, Ted Levine, Anthony Heald, Lawrence A. Bonney, Kasi Lemmons, Lawrence J. Wrentz, Frankie Faison, Roger Corman

'A mesmerizing thriller that will grip audiences from first scene to last.' – *Variety*

'A sombre masterpiece' – Sight and Sound   'An exceptionally good film, perhaps this fine director's best, in which the horror genre is elevated into the kind of cinema that can at least be argued about as a treatise for its unsettling times.' – *Derek Malcolm, Guardian*

HANNIBAL LECTER: 'I do wish we could chat longer, but I'm having an old friend for dinner.'

AA: film; Jonathan Demme; Anthony Hopkins; Jodie Foster; Ted Tally

AAN: editing; sound

Silence of the North
Canada   1981   94m   colour
Universal (Canada) (Murray Shostak)
V*

In 1919 a city girl is courted by a trapper and joins him in the north country.

Nicely filmed but utterly predictable romantic melodrama, based on a biography but not carrying much conviction. D. W. Griffith would have liked it.

w Patricia Louisiana Knop   book Olive Fredrickson, Ben East   d Allan Winton King   ph Richard Leiterman   m Allan MacMillan

Ellen Burstyn, Tom Skerritt, Gordon Pinsent, Jennifer McKinney

'Follow his secret from bedroom to bedlam, with guns, girls and dynamite!'
The Silencers *
US   1966   103m   Technicolor
Columbia/Irving Allen (Jim Schmerer)

Adventures of a sexy secret agent.

Or, James Bond sent up rotten. Plenty of fun along the way, with in-jokes and characters like Lovey Kravezit, but the plot could have done with more attention, and the sequels (*Murderers Row, The Ambushers, Wrecking Crew*) were uncontrolled disaster areas.

w Oscar Saul   novel Donald Hamilton   d Phil Karlson   ph Burnett Guffey   m Elmer Bernstein

Dean Martin, Stella Stevens, Victor Buono, Daliah Lavi, Cyd Charisse, Robert Webber, James Gregory, Nancy Kovack

'The dullest, dirtiest thud excreted by the sex-and-sadism spoofs of Bondism.' – *Judith Crist*

The Silent Battle
GB   1939   84m   bw
Pinebrook (Anthony Havelock-Allan)

A French agent battles revolutionaries in the Balkans.

Unconvincing spy stuff with an uncertain tone.

w Wolfgang Wilhelm, Rodney Ackland   novel Jean Bommart   d Herbert Mason

Rex Harrison, Valerie Hobson, John Loder, Muriel Aked, John Salew, George Devine

Silent Dust *
GB   1948   82m   bw
ABP/Independent Sovereign (Nat Bronsten)

A baronet builds a memorial to his son who has apparently been killed in action, but the son turns up and proves to be an absolute bounder.

Effective stage melodrama, quite neatly filmed.

w Michael Pertwee   play The Paragon by Roland and Michael Pertwee   d Lance Comfort   ph Wilkie Cooper   m Georges Auric

Sally Gray, Derek Farr, Stephen Murray, Nigel Patrick, Seymour Hicks

The Silent Enemy
GB   1958   112m   bw
Romulus (Bertram Ostrer)
V*

The World War II exploits of a naval frogman in the Mediterranean.

Stereotyped naval underwater adventures, adequately presented.   wd William Fairchild   ph Egil Woxholt, Otto Heller   m William Alwyn

Laurence Harvey, John Clements, Michael Craig, Dawn Addams, Sidney James, Alec McCowen, Nigel Stock

The Silent Flute
US   1978   95m   colour
Volare (Richard St Johns)

In a martial arts tournament, a hero is chosen to challenge the wizard Zetan.

Curiously mystical adventure allegory with an unhelpful title. Not too bad for those in the mood.

w Stirling Silliphant, Stanley Mann   d Richard Moore   ph Ronnie Taylor   m Bruce Smeaton

Jeff Cooper, David Carradine, Roddy McDowall, Christopher Lee, Eli Wallach

Silent Movie *
US   1976   87m   DeLuxe
TCF/Crossbow (Michael Hertzberg)
V, V*, L

An alcoholic producer gets the idea that a silent movie would be a great novelty, and tries to get stars to take part.

Fairly lively spoof with the talents concerned in variable form. The shortage of laughter made it a hit in the seventies, but at no time does it approach the Keaton or Laurel and Hardy level.

w Mel Brooks, Ron Clark, Rudy de Luca, Barry Levinson   d Mel Brooks   ph Paul Lohmann   m John Morris

Mel Brooks, Marty Feldman, Dom de Luise, Bernardette Peters, Sid Caesar, Harold Gould, Fritz Feld, Harry Ritz, Henny Youngman

guest stars Anne Bancroft, Paul Newman, Burt Reynolds, James Caan, Liza Minnelli, Marcel Marceau

† Marcel Marceau utters the only word in the movie, which is 'Non'.

Silent Night, Evil Night: see *Black Christmas*

The Silent Partner
Canada   1978   105m   colour
Carolco (Garth H. Drabinsky)
V*, L

A bank teller foils an attempted raid and steals the money himself.

A suspense thriller of a familiar kind; it might have been entertaining but elects instead to be unpleasant.

w Curtis Hanson *novel Think of a Number* by Anders Bodelson *d* Daryl Duke *ph* Stephen Katz *m* Oscar Peterson

Christopher Plummer, Elliott Gould, Susannah York, Celine Lomez, Michael Kirby

The Silent Passenger

GB 1935 75m bw
Phoenix

Lord Peter Wimsey clears a man of a murder charge.

Not an unappealing presentation of Dorothy Sayers's famous detective, though he is presented as too much the silly ass and the story is weak.

w Basil Mason *d* Reginald Denham

Peter Haddon, John Loder, Mary Newland, Austin Trevor, Donald Wolfit, Leslie Perrins, Robb Wilton

Silent Running *

US 1971 90m Technicolor
Universal/Michel Gruskoff/Douglas Trumbull
V*, L

Members of a space station crew in 2001 are space gardening to replenish nuclear-devastated Earth.

Sombre futuristic fantasy, well made but slow and muddled in development.

w Deric Washburn, Mike Cimino, Steve Bocho *d* Douglas Trumbull *ph* Charles F. Wheeler *m* Peter Schickele

Bruce Dern, Cliff Potts, Ron Rifkin, Jesse Vint

Silent Scream *

GB 1989 85m
BFI/Film Four International (Paddy Higson)

Jailed for the murder of a bartender, a depressive prisoner, dying from an overdose of drugs, recalls his past life.

Based on the writings and life of Larry Winters, who was transferred to a prison where he was encouraged to be creative, the film's hallucinatory style too often obscures its intentions.

w Bill Beech, Jane Beech *d* David Hayman *ph* Denis Crossan *m* Callum McNair *pd* Andy Harris *ed* Justin Krish

Iain Glenn, Paul Samson, Andrew Barr, Kenneth Glenaan, Steve Hotchkiss, John Murtagh, Bobby Carlyle, Tom Watson, Julie Graham

'I felt as if someone had handed me a bag of jumbled jigsaw pieces and told me to make up my own picture.' – *Philip French, Observer*

The Silent Stranger: see *Step Down to Terror*

The Silent Touch

GB/Poland/Denmark 1992 96m colour
Mayfair/Tor/Mark Forstater

A Polish music student goes to Denmark to encourage a composer who has not written a note for 40 years to complete his work.

A curious fable about creativity, which precisely lacks that quality.

w Peter Morgan, Mark Wadlow *story* Krzysztof Zanussi, Edward Zebrowski *d* Krzysztof Zanussi *ph* Jaroslaw Zamojda *m* Wojciech Kilar *pd* Ewa Braun *ed* Mark Denys

Max von Sydow, Luthar Bluteau, Sarah Miles, Sofie Grabol, Aleksander Bardini, Peter Hesse Overgaard, Lars Lunoe

'A great score, von Sydow's performance and a number of delightful moments do not compensate for the ludicrous plot which fails to fully engage the imagination.' – *Empire*

The Silent Village **

GB 1943 35m bw
Humphrey Jennings/Ministry of Information

Harrowing depiction, by the members of a Welsh village, of what happened to the Czech population of Lidice after the assassination of Heydrich.

A chilling documentary at the time, this little classic has kept its kick.

wd Humphrey Jennings *ed* Stewart McAllister

Silent Voice: see *Amazing Grace and Chuck*

The Silent Voice (1932): see *The Man Who Played God*

The Silent Voice (1952): see *Paula*

The Silent Witness

US 1932 73m bw
Fox

A man confesses to murder in order to protect his son.

Solid courtroom stuff of its day, built for a new star who never quite made it.

play Jack de Leon and Jack Celestin *d* Marcel Varnel, R. L. Hough

Lionel Atwill, Helen Mack, Greta Nissen, Bramwell Fletcher, Alan Mowbray

'A gripping talker that rates well above most of the creep releases.' – *Variety*

The Silk Hat Kid

US 1935 70m bw
Fox (Joseph Engel)

A settlement housekeeper accepts help from a racketeer.

Thin little drama, perfunctorily played.

w Edward Eliscu, Lou Breslow, Dore Schary *story* Gerald Beaumont *d* H. Bruce Humberstone

Lew Ayres, Mae Clarke, Paul Kelly, Ralf Harolde, William Harrigan

'It hasn't the story nor the entertainment weight to lift it out of the double feature classification.' – *Variety*

Silk Stockings *

US 1957 116m Metrocolor Cinemascope
MGM (Arthur Freed)
V, V*, L

A Russian composer in Paris agrees to write music for a Hollywood film; a lady commissar is sent to get him back.

Musical rewrite of *Ninotchka* via a Broadway show; good moments but generally very stretched.

w Leonard Gershe, Leonard Spigelgass *play* George S. Kaufman, Leueen McGrath, Abe Burrows *original play* Melchior Lengyel *d* Rouben Mamoulian *ph* Robert Bronner *md* André Previn *m/ly* Cole Porter

Fred Astaire, Cyd Charisse, Peter Lorre, Janis Paige, George Tobias, Jules Munshin, Joseph Buloff

The Silken Affair

GB 1956 96m bw
Dragon (Fred Feldkamp)

An accountant decides to live it up, and finds himself on trial for manipulating the firm's books.

Unsatisfactory mix of comedy and fantasy, with a dim plot and virtually no comic ideas.

w Robert Lewis Taylor *d* Roy Kellino *ph* Gilbert Taylor *m* Peggy Stuart

David Niven, Genevieve Page, Wilfrid Hyde-White, Ronald Squire, Beatrice Straight, Howard Marion Crawford, Dorothy Alison

Silken Skin **

France 1964 118m bw
Films du Carrosse/SEDIF
V
original title: *La Peau Douce*

A middle-aged married man leaves his wife for an attractive young girl, but the latter leaves him and his wife shoots him.

Carefully balanced mixture of comedy and melodrama which rings almost every possible change on the theme of adultery and does so with wit.

w François Truffaut, Jean-Louis Richard *d* François Truffaut *ph* Raoul Coutard *m* Georges Delerue

Jean Desailly, François Dorléac, Nelly Benedetti

'Very funny, very touching, very wise about human beings.' – *New York Herald Tribune*

Silkwood *

US 1983 131m Technicolor
ABC (Mike Nichols, Michael Hausman)
V, V*, L

The true story, more or less, of a girl worker in a nuclear processing plant who mysteriously dies in an accident just before she is going to talk to a reporter about a safety problem.

Despite the historical interest of the case, it is too simple to merit a film of this length, which is filled with pregnant pauses and romantic asides. Nor are the actors quite so charismatic as they think they are.

w Nora Ephron, Alice Arlen *d* Mike Nichols *ph* Miroslav Ondricek *m* Georges Delerue *pd* Patrizia von Brandenstein

Meryl Streep, Cher, Kurt Russell, Craig T. Nelson, Diana Scarwid, Fred Ward

'A movie with a preordained conclusion but nowhere to go . . . it submerges what could have been its most telling points in a kind of concentrated soap opera.' – *Richard Combs, MFB*

AAN: Meryl Streep; Cher; direction; screenplay; editing (Sam O'Steen)

Silver Bears

GB 1977 113m Technicolor
EMI/Raleigh (Martin Schute)
V*

A Las Vegas money man invests money in various European outlets and makes a killing.

Extraordinarily complex financial jape which tries the patience of all but financiers.

w Peter Stone *novel* Paul Erdman *d* Ivan Passer *ph* Anthony Richmond *m* Claude Bolling

Michael Caine, Louis Jourdan, Cybill Shepherd, Stephane Audran, David Warner, Tom Smothers, Martin Balsam, Charles Gray

Silver Blaze

GB 1937 70m bw
Twickenham
V*
US title: *Murder at the Baskervilles*

Sherlock Holmes clears a racehorse of having killed its trainer.

Not the best of the Holmes series, but this is a very satisfying Holmes.

w Arthur Macrae, H. Fowler Mear *story* Sir Arthur Conan Doyle *d* Thomas Bentley

Arthur Wontner, Ian Fleming, Lyn Harding, Judy Gunn, Lawrence Grossmith, Arthur Macrae

Silver Bullet

US 1985 95m Technicolor
Paramount/Dino de Laurentiis (Martha Schumacher)
V, V*, L

Murders at Tarker's Mill turn out to be the work of a werewolf.

Dreary, unimaginative rendition of a theme that was more entertaining in 1941.

w Stephen King novelette Cycle of the Werewolf by Stephen King d Daniel Attias ph Armando Nannuzzi m Jay Chataway

Corey Haim, Gary Busey, Megan Follows, Everett McGill

'It's a Stephen King filmette from his novelette which may sell some tickettes but not without regrettes.' – Variety

'I bid you seek the lost silver cup … for sin is rising like the swollen rivers!'
'Against the broad canvas of history's mad era of splendour and seduction – here is the story of the sacred cup of silver that challenged the iron sword of tyranny – the mighty struggle to possess it – and the loves and the faith that triumphed in humanity's darkest hour!'

The Silver Chalice

US   1954   142m   Warnercolor   Cinemascope
Warner (Victor Saville)
V*

Adventures of a slave freed by Luke the apostle to fashion a chalice to hold the cup used at the Last Supper.

Po-faced biblical hokum, slower and deadlier than most, with howlingly bad casting and direction. On reflection, interesting things are being attempted with limbo set design, but in this sea of boredom the attempt only raises an eyebrow.

w Lesser Samuels novel Thomas B. Costain
d Victor Saville ph William V. Skall m Franz Waxman pd Rolf Gerard

Paul Newman, Pier Angeli, Jack Palance, Virginia Mayo, Walter Hampden, Joseph Wiseman, Alexander Scourby, Lorne Greene, Michael Pate, E. G. Marshall

AAN: William V. Skall; Franz Waxman

Silver City

US   1951   90m   Technicolor
Nat Holt/Paramount
GB title: High Vermilion

A mining assayer helps a farmer and his daughter protect the ore found on their land.

Standard Western programmer with plenty of action

w Frank Gruber story Luke Short d Byron Haskin

Yvonne de Carlo, Edmond O'Brien, Barry Fitzgerald, Richard Arlen, Gladys George, Laura Elliot, Edgar Buchanan, John Dierkes

Silver City *

Australia   1984   102m   Eastmancolor
Artificial Eye/Limelight Productions (Joan Long)
V*

Arriving in Australia in 1949, a Polish woman is sent to a camp where she has an affair with another, married immigrant.

Sharp study of bigotry and hostility undercut by a limp romance.

w Sophia Turkiewicz, Thomas Keneally d Sophia Turkiewicz ph John Seale m William Motzing ad Igot Nay ed Don Saunders

Gosia Dobrowolska, Ivar Kants, Anna Jemison, Steve Bisley, Debra Lawrance, Ewa Brok, Joel Cohen, Tim McKenzie, Dennis Miller, Annie Byron

'Works best as a sociological study of cultural clash.' – Brian McFarlane, Australian Cinema 1970–1985

The Silver Cord

US   1933   74m   bw
RKO (Pandro S. Berman)

A young wife threatens to leave her husband because of his excessive devotion to his mother.

Stilted version of an old theatrical warhorse.

w Jane Murfin play Sidney Howard d John Cromwell ph Charles Rosher

Irene Dunne, Joel McCrea, Laura Hope Crews, Frances Dee, Eric Linden, Helen Cromwell

The Silver Darlings

GB   1947   84m   bw
Holyrood

Hebridean islanders take to herring fishing as a last chance to avoid emigration.

Uneventful island mood piece which lacks the poetic quality which might have made it memorable.

w Clarence Elder novel Neil Gunn d Clarence Elder and Clifford Evans

Clifford Evans, Helen Shingler, Carl Bernard, Norman Shelley, Simon Lack, Hugh Griffith

Silver Dollar *

US   1932   84m   bw
Warner

A poor farmer goes to Colorado for the gold rush, strikes it rich, and learns that money doesn't bring happiness.

Packed biopic of one H. A. W. Tabor, an excellent star vehicle.

w Carl Erickson, Harvey Thew d Alfred E. Green
ph James Van Trees m Milan Roder

Edward G. Robinson, Bebe Daniels, Aline MacMahon, Jobyna Howland, Robert Warwick, Russell Simpson

'Historical subject admirably done as to its variety but not so strong on its commercial side.' – Variety

Silver Dream Racer

GB   1980   111m   Eastmancolor   Panavision
Rank/David Wickes (Rene Dupont)
V, V*

A garage mechanic becomes a racing motorcyclist and is killed at the peak of success.

One wonders who can have thought there was any box-office appeal in this cliché-ridden, derivative, flashily made update of the Road to Ruin.

wd David Wickes ph Paul Beeson m David Essex

David Essex, Beau Bridges, Cristina Raines, Harry H. Corbett, Lee Montague, Clark Peters

'Watching this grotesque hotch-potch of implausible characters being shunted through improbable situations is uncannily akin to being assaulted by a non-stop stream of TV commercials.' – Tom Milne, MFB

The Silver Fleet *

GB   1943   87m   bw
GFD/Archers (Michael Powell, Emeric Pressburger, Ralph Richardson)
V

In occupied Holland, a shipping magnate destroys his new U-boat and himself and his Nazi mentors with it.

Slow-starting, rather stilted melodrama which when it gets into its stride provides good acting and gripping propaganda.

wd Vernon Sewell, Gordon Wellesley ph Erwin Hillier

Ralph Richardson, Esmond Knight, Googie Withers, Beresford Egan, Frederick Burtwell, Kathleen Byron

Silver Lode

US   1954   80m   Technicolor print
Benedict Bogeaus/RKO

A respected citizen of Silver Lode proves that the marshal who rides into town on his wedding day to accuse him of murder is a civilian bent on revenge.

Broody little Western melodrama, not half bad.

w Karen de Wolf d Allan Dwan

John Payne, Dan Duryea, Lizabeth Scott, Dolores Moran, Emile Meyer, Robert Warwick

Silver Queen

US   1942   80m   bw
UA/Harry Sherman
V*

A chivalrous Western gambler rescues a girl from the wiles of a villain.

Standard romantic melodrama mainly set in saloons.

w Bernard Schubert, Cecile Kramer d Lloyd Bacon
ph Russell Harlan m Victor Young ad Ralph Berger

George Brent, Priscilla Lane, Bruce Cabot, Lynne Overman, Eugene Pallette, Janet Beecher, Guinn Williams, Roy Barcroft

AAN: Victor Young; Ralph Berger

Silver River

US   1948   110m   bw
Warner (Owen Crump)
V*

A ruthless gambler becomes powerful but loses everything because of his character defects.

Meandering Western drama with a few good highlights dissipated by long chunks of character building and a rehash of the David and Bathsheba story.

w Stephen Longstreet, Harriet Frank Jnr d Raoul Walsh ph Sid Hickox m Max Steiner

Errol Flynn, Ann Sheridan, Thomas Mitchell, Bruce Bennett, Tom D'Andrea, Barton MacLane, Monte Blue, Alan Bridge

Silver Skates

US   1942   73m   bw
Monogram (Lindsley Parsons)

A touring ice revue is lapsing into debt.

Novelties on ice occupy more screen time than the story, which is just as well. Competent small-scale musical filler.

w Jerry Cady d Leslie Goodwins

Kenny Baker, Patricia Morison, Belita, Frick and Frack

The Silver Streak *

US   1934   85m   bw
RKO
V*

A streamlined train makes its first run from Chicago to Boulder Dam, where a victim of infantile paralysis must be got into an iron lung.

Historically interesting melodrama which seldom pauses for breath.

w H. W. Hanemann, Jack O'Donnell, Roger Whately d Tommy Atkins

Sally Blane, Charles Starrett, Hardie Albright, William Farnum, Irving Pichel, Arthur Lake, Edgar Kennedy

'Pretty absurd, yet exciting and fast . . . there's scarcely a stunt known to the railroad picture formula that hasn't been employed.' – Variety

Silver Streak *

US   1976   113m   DeLuxe
TCF/Martin Ransohoff, Frank Yablans
V, V*, L

On a trans-continental train, a young publisher discovers a murder and is at the mercy of the culprits.

Rather like an update of a Bob Hope comedy-thriller with a whiff of sex, this amiable spoof goes on too long, brings in a second comic too late, and ends with fashionable but irrelevant violence.

w Colin Higgins d Arthur Hiller ph David M. Walsh m Henry Mancini pd Alfred Sweeney

Gene Wilder, Jill Clayburgh, Richard Pryor, Patrick McGoohan, Ned Beatty, Clifton James, Ray Walston, Richard Kiel

'Nineteen-seventies performers are trapped in this fake thirties mystery comedy, which is so inept you can't even get angry.' – *New Yorker*

Silverado *
US 1985 132m Technicolor Super Techniscope
Lawrence Kasdan
V, V*, L, S

In the 1880s, various pioneers try to establish a future in the west.

Interesting but not wholly successful attempt to revive in one movie various Western myths and legends; a little more conscious humour might have helped.

w Lawrence and Mark Kasdan *d* Lawrence Kasdan *ph* John Bailey *m* Bruce Broughton *pd* Ida Random *ed* Carol Littleton

Kevin Kline, Scott Glenn, Kevin Costner, Danny Glover, John Cleese, Rosanna Arquette, Brian Dennehy, Linda Hunt, Jeff Goldblum

'Less like the film westerns of imagination and more like something more common. Maybe it was that way in real life.' – *Variety*

AAN: music

Simba
GB 1955 99m Eastmancolor
GFD/Group Film (Peter de Sarigny)
V*

An English farmer in Kenya fights the Mau Mau.

Savagely topical melodrama which tends to cheapen a tragic situation.

w John Baines *d* Brian Desmond Hurst *ph* Geoffrey Unsworth *m* Francis Chagrin

Dirk Bogarde, Donald Sinden, Virginia McKenna, Basil Sydney, Marie Ney, Joseph Tomelty, Earl Cameron, Orlando Martins

Simon *
US 1980 97m Technicolor
Warner/Orion (Louis A. Stroller, Martin Bregman)
V*

Corrupt scientists brainwash a psychology professor into thinking he's from another planet.

Solemn comic fantasy which doesn't seem to make much of a point and only superficially entertains, but is well made and well acted.

wd Marshall Brickman *ph* Adam Holender *m* Stanley Silverman *pd* Stuart Wurtzel

Alan Arkin, Madeline Kahn, Austin Pendleton, Judy Graubert, William Finley, Fred Gwynne

Simon and Laura *
GB 1955 91m Technicolor Vistavision
GFD/Group Films (Teddy Baird)

The actors who play husband and wife in a TV series are married in reality and hate each other, a fact that shows in the live Christmas episode.

Adequate film of a reasonably sophisticated West End comedy; good lines and performances.

w Peter Blackmore *play* Alan Melville *d* Muriel Box *ph* Ernest Steward *m* Benjamin Frankel

Peter Finch, Kay Kendall, Ian Carmichael, Alan Wheatley, Richard Wattis, Muriel Pavlow, Maurice Denham, Hubert Gregg

Simon the Swiss: see *Le Voyou*

'There is no such thing as adventure and romance. There's only trouble and desire.'

Simple Men *
GB/US 1992 105m Technicolor
Metro/Zenith/American Playhouse/Fine Line/Film Four/BIM (Ted Hope, Hal Hartley)
V, V*, L

A petty crook and his brother search for their father, a former radical baseball star who has been on the run since the 60s.

Off-beat, occasionally amusing road movie that goes nowhere very interesting. It is too determinedly eccentric to be effective, but incidental pleasures include a fight between a nun and a policeman and a sheriff desperately searching for the meaning of life.

wd Hal Hartley *ph* Michael Spiller *m* Ned Rifle *pd* Daniel Ouellette *ed* Steve Hamilton

Robert Burke, William Sage, Karen Sillas, Elina Löwensohn, Martin Donovan, Mark Chandler Bailey, Chris Cooke

'Effortlessly manages to encompass social comment and satire as it oscillates between the comic and the absurd with a stylish self-confidence.' – *Mark Salisbury, Empire*

The Sin of Madelon Claudet
US 1931 74m bw
MGM (Harry Rapf)
GB title: *The Lullaby*

A mother is separated from her illegitimate baby.

Sob stuff for a rising star: hilarious now.

w Charles MacArthur *play* Edward Knoblock *d* Edgar Selwyn

Helen Hayes, Robert Young, Neil Hamilton, Lewis Stone, Marie Prevost, Cliff Edwards, Jean Hersholt, Karen Morley

'Natural sobber for women and grosses . . . but you don't have to go back as far as *Madame X* to find a parallel for the plot.' – *Variety*

AA: Helen Hayes

Sin Town
US 1942 74m bw
Universal (George Waggner)

Two confidence tricksters arrive in a Western town and solve a murder.

Members of the studio repertory company in a passable Western discarded by Marlene Dietrich.

w Gerald Geraghty, W. Scott Darling, Richard Brooks *d* Ray Enright *m* Hans Salter

Constance Bennett, Broderick Crawford, Leo Carrillo, Anne Gwynne, Patric Knowles, Andy Devine, Ward Bond, Ralf Harolde

Sinbad and the Eye of the Tiger
GB 1977 113m Metrocolor
Columbia/Andor (Charles H. Schneer, Ray Harryhausen)
V, L

Sinbad frees a city from a wicked woman's spell.

Lumpish sequel to a sequel: even the animated monsters raise a yawn this time.

w Beverly Cross *d* Sam Wanamaker *ph* Ted Moore *m* Roy Budd *sp* Ray Harryhausen

Patrick Wayne, Taryn Power, Jane Seymour, Margaret Whiting, Patrick Troughton

Sinbad the Sailor
US 1947 117m Technicolor
RKO (Stephen Ames)
L

Sinbad sets off on his eighth voyage to find the lost treasure of Alexander.

Well-staged but humourless Arabian Nights swashbuckler.

w John Twist *d* Richard Wallace *ph* George Barnes *m* Roy Webb

Douglas Fairbanks Jnr, Walter Slezak, Maureen O'Hara, Anthony Quinn, George Tobias, Jane Greer, Mike Mazurki, Sheldon Leonard

'Is there a public for this twopence-coloured rubbish. For me, it belongs to the Christmas theatre, with a principal boy in tights.' – *Stephen Watts, Sunday Express*

Since You Went Away ***
US 1944 172m bw
David O. Selznick

When hubby is away at the war, his wife and family adopt stiff upper lips.

Elaborate flagwaving investigation of the well-heeled American home front in World War II, with everyone brimming with goodwill and not a dry eye in the place. Absolutely superbly done, if it must be done at all, and a symposium of Hollywood values and techniques of the time.

w David O. Selznick *book* Margaret Buell Wilder *d* John Cromwell *ph* Stanley Cortez, Lee Garmes *m* Max Steiner *pd* William L. Pereira *ad* Mark-Lee Kirk *ed* Hal C. Kern, James E. Newcom

Claudette Colbert, Joseph Cotten, Jennifer Jones, Shirley Temple, Agnes Moorehead, Monty Woolley, Lionel Barrymore, Guy Madison, Robert Walker, Hattie McDaniel, Craig Stevens, Keenan Wynn, Albert Basserman, Nazimova, Lloyd Corrigan

PREFACE: 'This is the story of the unconquerable fortress – the American home, 1943.'

'A deft, valid blend of showmanship, humour, and yard-wide Americanism.' – *James Agee*

'The whole litany of that middle-class synthetic emotionalism, meticulously annotated over a decade by tough and sentimental experts, has been procured for us.' – *Richard Winnington*

'A rather large dose of choking sentiment.' – *Bosley Crowther*

'It is not an average US reality. It is an average US dream.' – *Time*

'Selznick wrote the script himself, intending his story to be moving and simple, along epic lines; the result is pedestrian in a peculiarly grandiose manner.' – *Pauline Kael, 70s*

AA: Max Steiner

AAN: best picture; Stanley Cortez; Claudette Colbert; Jennifer Jones; Monty Woolley; art direction; editing

Sincerely Yours
US 1955 115m Warnercolor
Warner (Henry Blanke)

A concert pianist goes deaf and retires to his penthouse, but with the help of binoculars lipreads the humble folk below. Helping them anonymously gives him courage to have an operation.

Absurd updating for a modern non-star of a creaky old George Arliss vehicle *The Man Who Played God*.

w Irving Wallace *d* Gordon Douglas *ph* William H. Clothier *musical advisor* George Liberace

Liberace, Joanne Dru, Dorothy Malone, Alex Nicol, William Demarest

'Drenched in coy bathos to the point of embarrassment.' – *Films and Filming*

'Given sufficient intoxication, you could find this movie amusing.' – *Saturday Review*

Sinful Davey
GB 1968 95m Eastmancolor Panavision
UA/Mirisch/Webb (William N. Graf)

In 1821 a young Scotsman determines to become a criminal like his father, but falls in love.

Thin imitation of *Tom Jones*, highly implausible but played with some zest.

w James R. Webb   *autobiography* David Haggart
d John Huston   *ph* Ted Scaife, Freddie Young
m Ken Thorne   *pd* Stephen Grimes

John Hurt, Pamela Franklin, Nigel Davenport, Ronald Fraser, Robert Morley, Maxine Audley, Noel Purcell

Sing
US   1988   98m   Technicolor
Columbia TriStar (Craig Zadan)

Students at a school faced with closure organise a singing and dancing competition.

Dim, cliché-ridden movie that offers little, even for its target audience of the young and undemanding.

w Dean Pitchford   *d* Richard Baskin   *ph* Peter Sova   *m* Jay Gruska   *pd* Carol Spier   *ed* Bud Smith, Jere Huggins, Scott Smith

Lorraine Bracco, Peter Dobson, Jessica Steen, Louise Lasser, Goerge DiCenzo, Patti LaBelle, Susan Peretz

'Remarkably old-fashioned.' – *MFB*

Sing and Be Happy
US   1937   67m   bw
TCF (Milton H. Feld)

A young man is too irresponsible to work in his father's advertising agency.

A wisp of a plot with some wisps of music attached; nothing to remember next day.

w Ben Markson, Lou Breslow, John Patrick
d James Tinling

Tony Martin, Leah Ray, Joan Davis, Chick Chandler, Helen Westley, Allan Lane, Berton Churchill

'This musical will require plenty of exploitative pressure by exhibs.' – *Variety*

Sing As We Go ***
GB   1934   80m   bw
ATP (Basil Dean)

An unemployed millgirl gets various holiday jobs in Blackpool.

A splendid, pawky star vehicle which is also the best picture we have of industrial Lancashire in the thirties. Great fun.

w J. B. Priestley, Gordon Wellesley   *d* Basil Dean
ph Robert G. Martin

Gracie Fields, John Loder, *Frank Pettingell*, Dorothy Hyson, Stanley Holloway

'We have an industrial north that is bigger than Gracie Fields running around a Blackpool fun fair.' – *C. A. Lejeune*

Sing Baby Sing *
US   1936   87m   bw
TCF (Darryl F. Zanuck)

A drunken Shakespearian actor sets his sights on a night-club singer.

Reasonably hilarious take-off on the John Barrymore-Elaine Barrie affair, with several Fox contractees fooling to the top of their bent with the help of good musical numbers.

w Milton Sperling, Jack Yellen, Harry Tugend
d Sidney Lanfield   *ph* Peverell Marley
songs various   *md* Louis Silvers

Alice Faye, Adolphe Menjou, Gregory Ratoff, Patsy Kelly, Ted Healy, The Ritz Brothers, Montagu Love, Dixie Dunbar

AAN: song 'When Did You Leave Heaven?' (*m* Richard Whiting, *ly* Walter Bullock)

Sing, Boy, Sing
US   1958   91m   bw   Cinemascope
TCF (Henry Ephron)

A rock and roll star comes close to a nervous breakdown because of an unscrupulous manager and a revivalist grandfather.

Fairly painless vehicle for a singing star.

w Claude Binyon   *d* Henry Ephron   *ph* William C. Mellor   *m* Lionel Newman

Tommy Sands, Edmond O'Brien, John McIntire, Lili Gentle, Nick Adams, Josephine Hutchinson

Sing Me a Love Song
US   1936   78m   bw
Cosmopolitan/First National

A reformed playboy starts at the bottom as a clerk in his father's department store.

Thin but mildly pleasing musical with good comedy support.

w Sig Herzig, Jerry Wald, Harry Sauber   *d* Ray Enright

James Melton, Patricia Ellis, *Hugh Herbert*, ZaSu Pitts, Allen Jenkins, Nat Pendleton, Ann Sheridan, Walter Catlett, Hobart Cavanaugh, Charles Halton

'Story isn't much and the dialogue fails to sparkle, yet there's a constant stream of laughs.' – *Variety*

'The god-damedest family in the whole USA!'
Sing You Sinners **
US   1938   88m   bw
Paramount (Wesley Ruggles)

The adventures of a happy-go-lucky family and their racehorse.

Cheerful family musical with amiable cast and good tunes.

w Claude Binyon   *d* Wesley Ruggles   *ph* Karl Struss   *md* Boris Morros   *songs* James V. Monaco, Johnny Burke

Bing Crosby, Donald O'Connor, Fred MacMurray, Elizabeth Patterson, Ellen Drew, John Gallaudet

'Homespun, down to earth, and as natural as eggs for breakfast.' – *Variety*

Sing Your Worries Away
US   1941   71m   bw
Cliff Reid/RKO
V*

A debt-ridden songwriter has a girlfriend unaware of a huge pending inheritance.

Rather ribby comedy material which adds up to very little.

w Monte Brice   *d* Edward Sutherland

Bert Lahr, Buddy Ebsen, June Havoc, Patsy Kelly, Sam Levene, Margaret Dumont

Singapore Woman
US   1941   65m   bw
Warner (Harlan Thompson)

A slightly fallen woman is redeemed by a plantation owner.

Hasty and uninteresting remake of the Bette Davis vehicle *Dangerous*.

w Laird Doyle   *d* Jean Negulesco

Brenda Marshall, David Bruce, Virginia Field, Jerome Cowan, Rose Hobart, Heather Angel

Un Singe en Hiver: see *A Monkey in Winter*

The Singer Not the Song
GB   1960   132m   colour   Cinemascope
Rank (Roy Baker)
V*

In an isolated Mexican town a priest defies an outlaw who oddly respects him.

Lengthy character drama with little action or humour but a great deal of moody introspection and a suggestion of homosexuality.

w Nigel Balchin   *novel* Audrey Erskine Lindop
d Roy Baker   *ph* Otto Heller   *m* Philip Green

John Mills, Dirk Bogarde, Mylene Demongeot, John Bentley, Laurence Naismith, Eric Pohlmann

'A rewarding film, as startling as a muffled scream from the subconscious.' – *Peter John Dyer*

The Singing Fool **
US   1928   110m   bw
Warner
L

A successful singer goes on the skids when his small son dies.

Early talkie musical, a sensation because of its star's personality, but a pretty maudlin piece of drama.

w C. Graham Baker   *play* Leslie S. Barrows
d Lloyd Bacon   *ph* Byron Haskin   *songs* Lew Brown, Ray Henderson, B. G. de Sylva

Al Jolson, Davey Lee, Betty Bronson, Josephine Dunn, Arthur Housman

'Obvious and tedious as the climax is, when the black-faced comedian stands before the camera and sings "Sonny Boy" you know the man is greater, somehow, than the situation, the story or the movie.' – *Pare Lorentz*

Singin' in the Rain ****
US   1952   102m   Technicolor
MGM (Arthur Freed)
V, V*, L, S

When talkies are invented, the reputation of one female star shrivels while another grows.

Brilliant comic musical, the best picture by far of Hollywood in transition, with the catchiest tunes, the liveliest choreography, the most engaging performances and the most hilarious jokes of any musical.

w Adolph Green, Betty Comden   *d/ch* Gene Kelly, Stanley Donen   *ph* Harold Rosson   *md* Lennie Hayton   *m* Nacio Herb Brown   *ly* Arthur Freed

Gene Kelly, Donald O'Connor, Debbie Reynolds, Millard Mitchell, Jean Hagen, Rita Moreno, Cyd Charisse, Douglas Fowley

'Perhaps the most enjoyable of all movie musicals.' – *New Yorker, 1975*

AAN: Lennie Hayton; Jean Hagen

The Singing Kid
US   1936   83m   bw
Warner (Robert Lord)
L

A cocky night-club singer takes a talented juvenile under his wing.

Routine star vehicle most notable for a string of standards sung by him right after the credits.

w Warren Duff, Pat C. Flick   *d* William Keighley
ph George Barnes   *md* Leo F. Forbstein   *songs* E. Y. Harburg, Harold Arlen

Al Jolson, Sybil Jason, Allen Jenkins, Lyle Talbot, Edward Everett Horton, Beverly Roberts, Claire Dodd

The Singing Marine
US   1937   107m   bw
Warner

A marine singer wins a talent contest and success goes to his head.

Light musical of very little interest save two dance sequences by Busby Berkeley.

w Delmer Daves   *d* Ray Enright

Dick Powell, Doris Weston, Jane Darwell, Hugh Herbert, Lee Dixon, Dick Wesson, Allen Jenkins, Jane Wyman, Larry Adler

The Singing Musketeer: see *The Three Musketeers* (1939)

The Singing Nun

US   1966   98m   Metrocolor   Panavision
MGM (Jon Beck)
V*

Adventures of a nun who takes her music to the outside world.

Icky musical drama based on a true character.

w Sally Benson, John Furia   d Henry Koster
ph Milton Krasner   md Harry Sukman
songs Soeur Sourire

Debbie Reynolds, Greer Garson, Ricardo Montalban, Agnes Moorehead, Chad Everett, Katharine Ross, Ed Sullivan, Juanita Moore

AAN: Harry Sukman

A Single Life

Australia   1985   108m   colour
AFT (Hugh Rule)

Desperate to have a child, an unmarried woman begins an affair with her married boss.

Unsatisfactory domestic drama in which the characters' actions seem dictated solely by the whims of the authors.

w Mark Poole, John Power   d John Power
ph Vladimir Osherov   m Brett Goldsmith
pd Chris Kennedy   ed Ian Lang

Tina Bursill, Steven Jacobs, Jane Clifton, Pamela Rabe, Tony Rickards, Esben Storm

'Allie's new roommate is about to borrow a few things without asking. Her clothes. Her boyfriend. Her life.'
'Living with a roommate can be murder.'

Single White Female *

US   1992   108m   Technicolor
Columbia TriStar/Columbia (Barbet Shroeder)
V, V*, L

A young Manhattan businesswoman finds that her new flatmate is taking over her life.

Well-done thriller, but its subject-matter is too familiar from too many recent films to cause much in the way of a frisson.

w Don Roos   novel SWF Seeks Same by John Lutz
d Barbet Shroeder   ph Luciano Tovoli   m Howard Shore   pd Milena Canonero   ed Lee Percy

Bridget Fonda, Jennifer Jason Leigh, Steven Weber, Peter Friedman, Stephen Tobolowsky

'It is saddening to see a fine filmmaker courting the crowds by trashing his talent.' – Geoff Brown, The Times

Singles *

US   1992   99m   Technicolor
Warner/Atkinson/Knickerbocker (Cameron Crowe, Richard Hashimoto)
V, V*, L, S

The young occupants of an apartment block in Seattle fall in and out of love.

A meandering movie of singles attempting to become couples in order to occupy their empty lives; it is slight, but perceptive.

wd Cameron Crowe   ph Ueli Steiger   m Paul Westerberg   pd Stephen Lineweaver

Bridget Fonda, Campbell Scott, Kyra Sedgwick, Sheila Kelley, Jim True, Matt Dillon, Ally Walker, Eric Stoltz, Tom Skerritt

'The movie gets nowhere in particular, but the leading performances are immensely attractive.' – Philip French, Observer

'Superbly scripted, cast and scored, pic is a natural for the partner-hunting twentysomething crowd and should easily cross over to thirtysomething singles or couples primed to laugh at the dating syndrome.' – Variety

The Sinister Man *

GB   1961   60m   bw
Anglo Amalgamated/Merton Park (Jack Greenwood)

The murder of an Oxford scholar is linked to archaeological relics which are coveted for political purposes.

Very tolerable minor thriller in the Edgar Wallace series: short, sharp and snappy.

w Robert Banks Stewart   d Clive Donner   ph Bert Mason   m Charles Blackwell

Patrick Allen, John Bentley, Jacqueline Ellis, Eric Young, Arnold Lee, John Glyn-Jones, William Gaunt, Wilfrid Brambell

'Personal! Powerful! Human! Heroic!'

Sink the Bismarck **

GB   1960   97m   bw   Cinemascope
TCF/John Brabourne
V, V*, L

In 1941, Britain's director of naval operations arranges the trapping and sinking of Germany's greatest battleship.

Tight little personal drama which would have been better on a standard screen, as its ships are plainly models and much of the footage stretched-out newsreel. Nevertheless, a good example of the stiff-upper-lip school.

w Edmund H. North   d Lewis Gilbert
ph Christopher Challis   md Muir Mathieson
m Clifton Parker

Kenneth More, Dana Wynter, Karel Stepanek, Carl Mohner, Laurence Naismith, Geoffrey Keen, Michael Hordern, Maurice Denham, Esmond Knight

Sinner Take All

US   1937   74m   bw
Lucien Hubbard/Sam Marx/MGM

Members of a family are murdered one by one.

Moderate puzzler with a reporter sharing solving honours with the police.

w Leonard Lee, Walter Wise   novel Murder of a Wanton by Whitman Chambers   d Errol Taggart

Bruce Cabot, Margaret Lindsay, Joseph Calleia, Stanley Ridges, Vivienne Osborne, Charley Grapewin, Edward Pawley, George Zucco

'Above the usual whodunit average . . . able to make its way alone in the less exacting spots.' – Variety

Sinner's Holiday

US   1930   55m   bw
Warner

A fairground barker loves the daughter of a penny arcade owner, but is framed by her brother.

Early talkie quickie using Broadway talent, and introducing James Cagney to the screen. It still has vigour if little else.

w Harvey Thew, George Rosener   play Penny Arcade by Marie Baumer   d John G. Adolfi   ph Ira Morgan

Grant Withers, Evalyn Knapp, James Cagney, Joan Blondell, Lucille La Verne, Warren Hymer, Noel Madison

Sinners' Holiday (1947): see Christmas Eve

Sinners in Paradise

US   1938   65m   bw
Universal (Ken Goldsmith)
V*

Air travellers are wrecked on a South Sea island.

Much ado about very little, and a grave disappointment from its director.

w Lester Cole, Harold Buckley, Louis Stevens
d James Whale

Madge Evans, John Boles, Bruce Cabot, Marion Martin, Gene Lockhart, Charlotte Wynters, Nana Bryant

'Melodrama sufficiently lurid to be cut into several parts and released as a serial.' – Variety

Sinners in the Sun

US   1932   69m   bw
Paramount

A young couple break up; each has romantic adventures, but eventually they come together again.

Blah comedy-drama with the defects of its period.

w Vincent Lawrence, Waldemar Young, Samuel Hoffenstein, Mildred Cram   d Alexander Hall

Carole Lombard, Chester Morris, Adrienne Allen, Alison Skipworth, Walter Byron, Cary Grant

'Only high-powered selling will aid a dull and poorly-handled story.' – Variety

The Sins of Rachel Cade

US   1960   123m   Technicolor
Warner (Henry Blanke)

An American missionary nurse in the Belgian Congo falls in love with a crashed flyer and has a baby.

Romantic melodrama which starts like The Nun's Story and ends like Peg's Paper; competent on its level.

w Edward Anhalt   novel Charles Mercer
d Gordon Douglas   ph Peverell Marley   m Max Steiner

Angie Dickinson, Roger Moore, Peter Finch, Errol John, Woody Strode, Juano Hernandez, Frederick O'Neal, Mary Wickes

Sir Henry at Rawlinson End

GB   1980   71m   bw
Charisma (Tony Stratton Smith)
V

A grossly eccentric English aristocrat lays a family ghost.

Weirdly isolated, semi-professional comedy with elements of everything from Ealing to Monty Python.

w Vivien Stanshall, Steve Roberts   radio play Vivien Stanshall   d Steve Roberts   ph Martin Bell
m Vivian Stanshall   pd Alistair Bowtell   ed Chris Rose

Trevor Howard, Patrick Magee, Denise Coffey, J. G. Devlin, Vivian Stanshall

Siren of Atlantis: see L'Atlantide

Siren of Bagdad

US   1953   72m   Technicolor
Sam Katzman/Columbia

A travelling magician helps reinstate a deposed sultan.

Flippant oriental extravaganza aiming at the Hope-Crosby style but falling sadly short of it.

w Robert E. Kent   d Richard Quine

Paul Henreid, Patricia Medina, Hans Conried, Charlie Lung

La Sirène du Mississippi: see The Mississippi Mermaid

Sirocco

US   1951   98m   bw
Columbia/Santana (Robert Lord)
L

In 1925 Damascus, an American runs guns for the rebels.

Tedious romantic drama in the Casablanca vein but with none of the magic.

w A. I. Bezzerides, Hans Jacoby   novel Coup de Grâce by Joseph Kessel   d Curtis Bernhardt   ph Burnett Guffey   m George Antheil

Humphrey Bogart, Marta Toren, Lee J. Cobb, Everett Sloane, Gerald Mohr, Zero Mostel, Onslow Stevens

'No Sex. No Booze. No Men. No Way.'
Sister Act *
US   1992   100m   Technicolor
Buena Vista/Touchstone/Touchwood Pacific Partners (Teri Schwartz)
V, V*, L, S

A singer on the run from the Mafia takes refuge in a convent and transforms its choir.

Cheerful and modest comedy, though lacking in wit and with a plot that makes little sense. It was the surprise hit of 1992, ranking fourth at the box-office.

w Joseph Howard   d Emile Ardolino   ph Adam Greenberg   m Marc Shaiman   pd Jackson DeGovia   ed Richard Halsey

Whoopi Goldberg, Maggie Smith, Kathy Najimy, Wendy Makkena, Mary Wickes, Harvey Keitel, Bill Nunn, Robert Miranda, Richard Portnow

'The film isn't a divine comedy, and it's not satisfyingly profane either. But it generates a few laughs. It's got a good beat, and you can dance to it.' – *Michael Sragow, New Yorker*

'Offers the kind of cute, synthetic uplift usually found in television commercials and casts its nun characters as walking sight gags rather than real people.' – *Janet Maslin, New York Times*

'A truly awful film, pretending to be audacious but in fact pandering to every facile assumption in the book.' – *Derek Malcolm, Guardian*

Sister Act 2: Back in the Habit
US   1993   106m   Technicolor   Cinemascope
Buena Vista/Touchstone (Scott Rudin, Dawn Steel)
S

A Las Vegas singer agrees to dress as a nun to teach singing at a ghetto school that is in trouble.

Distressingly dire comedy, sickly and silly; it is smug and patronizing in its attitudes to the problems of inner-city life and not at all amusing.

w James Orr, Jim Cruickshank, Judi Ann Mason   d Bill Duke   ph Oliver Wood   m Miles Goodman   pd John DeCuir Jnr   ed John Carter, Pem Herring, Stuart Pappé

Whoopi Goldberg, Kathy Najimy, Barnard Hughes, Mary Wickes, James Coburn, Maggie Smith, Wendy Makkena, Lauryn Hill, Sheryl Lee Ralph

'Two trips to the convent is one too many.' – *Variety*

'If *Sister Act 2* is how Hollywood rewards success, how does it punish failure?' – *Adam Mars-Jones, Independent*

† Kathy Najimy's singing was dubbed by Andrea Robinson.

Sister Kenny *
US   1946   116m   bw
RKO (Dudley Nichols)
V*, L

The career of a nurse who instigated treatment for polio.

Standard, well-done biopic.

w Dudley Nichols, Alexander Knox, Mary McCarthy   d Dudley Nichols   ph George Barnes   m Alexander Tansman

Rosalind Russell, Alexander Knox, Dean Jagger, Philip Merivale, Beulah Bondi, Dorothy Peterson

† From the autobiography of Australian nurse Mary Kenny: *And They Shall Walk*.

AAN: Rosalind Russell

The Sisters *
US   1938   98m   bw
Warner (Hal B. Wallis)
V*

The marriages of three sisters from a small Montana town.

Well-made potboiler for women; it even brings in the San Francisco earthquake, and the star teaming is piquant to say the least.

w Milton Krims   novel Myron Brinig   d Anatole Litvak   ph Tony Gaudio   m Max Steiner

Bette Davis, Errol Flynn, Anita Louise, Ian Hunter, Donald Crisp, Beulah Bondi, Jane Bryan, Alan Hale, Dick Foran, Henry Travers, Patrick Knowles, Lee Patrick, Harry Davenport

Sisters *
US   1973   92m   colour
British Lion/Pressman-Williams Enterprises (Edward R. Pressman)
V*, S
GB title: *Blood Sisters*

A Siamese twin takes on the personality of her deranged and dead sister.

The plots of Alfred Hitchcock's *Psycho* and *Rear Window* are both raided for this effective, if derivative, shocker.

w Brian de Palma, Louisa Rose   d Brian de Palma   ph Gregory Sandor   m Bernard Herrmann   pd Gary Weist   ed Paul Hirsch

Margot Kidder, Jennifer Salt, Charles Durning, Bill Finley, Lisle Wilson, Barnard Hughes

'A long way from being the brilliant thriller the ads say it is, but its limp technique doesn't seem to matter to the people who want their gratuitous gore. The movie supplies it, but why is there so much gratuitous dumbness, too?' – *Pauline Kael, New Yorker*

'A distinctly uneasy blend of that brand of unprincipled exploitation that makes horror out of madness and birth abnormality.' – *MFB*

Sisters *
US   1988   93m   colour
UIP/MGM/Oxford Film Company (Andy Paterson, Mark Bentley)
US title: *Some Girls*

An American student who goes to spend Christmas with the Catholic family of his girlfriend in Quebec finds himself looking after her dying grandmother.

Mildly amusing comedy of cultural misunderstandings.

w Rupert Walters   d Michael Hoffman   ph Ueli Steiger   m James Newton Horner   pd Eugenio Zanetti   ed David Spiers

Patrick Dempsey, Jennifer Connelly, Sheila Kelley, Lance Edwards, Lila Kedrova, Florinda Balkan, Andre Gregory, Ashley Greenfield

Sisters or The Balance of Happiness *
West Germany   1979   95m   colour
Blue Dolphin/Bioskop Film/WDR (Eberhard Junkersdorf)
original title: *Schwestern Oder Die Balance Des Glücks*

Two sisters, one an executive secretary, the other a biology student whom she supports and stifles, grow ever more dependent upon each other.

Troubling, claustrophobic study of damaging family relationships.

wd Margarethe von Trotta   ph Franz Rath, Thomas Schwan   m Konstantin Wecker   ad Winifred Hennig   ed Annette Dorn

Jutta Lampe, Gudrun Gabriel, Jessica Fruh, Konstantin Wecker, Heinz Bennet

Sisters under the Skin
US   1934   65m   bw
Columbia

An older man loses his mistress to a bohemian composer.

Surprise, surprise: and the screenplay does not enliven the situation.

w Jo Swerling, S. K. Lauren   d David Burton

Frank Morgan, Elissa Landi, Joseph Schildkraut, Doris Lloyd, Clara Blandick, Samuel S. Hinds

'Mild flicker of obvious triangle story texture.' – *Variety*

Sitting Bull
US   1954   106m   Eastmancolor   Cinemascope
United Artists/W. R. Frank/Televoz of Mexico
V*

Despite the massacre of Custer's men, a cavalry officer strives to establish a relationship with Sitting Bull.

Sloppy and undernourished Western epic in abysmal colour, not helped by Mexicans pretending to be Indians.

w Jack de Witt, Sidney Salkow   d Sidney Salkow   ph Charles Van Enger, Victor Herrara   m Raoul Kraushaar

Dale Robertson, Mary Murphy, J. Carrol Naish, Iron Eyes Cody, John Litel, William Hopper, Douglas Kennedy (as Custer)

Sitting Ducks
US   1978   88m   DeLuxe
Sunny Side Up (Meira Atta Dor)
V*

Two men steal a fortune and abscond to Miami with two women who turn out to have a contract on them.

Endlessly talkative sex comedy from a practitioner who scorns built-up gags. The kind of movie that puts people off movies.

wd Henry Jaglom   ph Paul Glickman   m Richard Romanus

Michael E. Jaglom, Zack Norman, Patrice Townsend, Irene Forrest, Richard Romanus, Henry Jaglom

Sitting Pretty
US   1933   85m   bw
Paramount (Charles R. Rogers)

Two songwriters strike it rich in Hollywood.

Cheerful comedy musical, interesting for its backgrounds.

w Jack McGowan, S. J. Perelman, Lou Breslow   d Harry Joe Brown   ph Milton Krasner   songs Mack Gordon, Harry Revel

Jack Oakie, Jack Haley, Ginger Rogers, Thelma Todd, Gregory Ratoff, Lew Cody, Harry Revel, Mack Gordon

'Should please all over.' – *Variety*

Sitting Pretty ***
US   1948   84m   bw
TCF (Samuel G. Engel)

A young couple acquire a most unusual male baby sitter, a self-styled genius who sets the neighbourhood on its ears by writing a novel about it.

Out of the blue, a very funny comedy which entrenched Clifton Webb as one of Hollywood's great characters and led to two sequels, *Mr Belvedere Goes to College* and *Mr Belvedere Rings the Bell* (qv).

w F. Hugh Herbert,   novel *Belvedere* by Gwen Davenport   d Walter Lang   ph Norbert Brodine   m Alfred Newman

Clifton Webb, Robert Young, Maureen O'Hara, *Richard Haydn*, Louise Allbritton, Ed Begley, Randy Stuart, Larry Olsen

AAN: Clifton Webb

Sitting Target
GB   1972   92m   Metrocolor
MGM (Barry Kulick)

A violent killer escapes from jail and seeks revenge on those who 'shopped' him.

Rough, tough action thriller; passes the time for hardened addicts.

w Alexander Jacobs novel Lawrence Henderson d Douglas Hickox ph Ted Scaife m Stanley Myers pd Jonathan Barry

Oliver Reed, Jill St John, Edward Woodward, Frank Finlay, Ian McShane, Freddie Jones, Robert Beatty

Situation Hopeless But Not Serious
US 1965 97m bw
Paramount/Castle (Gottfried Reinhardt)

In 1944, two American flyers are captured by a friendly, lonely mild-mannered German, who keeps them in his cellar and hasn't the heart to tell them when the war is over . . .

Flat little comedy which leaves a talented cast no room for manoeuvre.

w Silvia Reinhardt novel The Hiding Place by Robert Shaw d Gottfried Reinhardt ph Kurt Hasse m Harold Byrne

Alec Guinness, Robert Redford, Mike Connors, Anita Hoefer

Six Black Horses
US 1962 80m Eastmancolor
Universal-International

A girl hires a gunslinger and a horse thief to escort her across Indian territory.

Rather glum Western programmer.

w Burt Kennedy d Harry Keller

Audie Murphy, Dan Duryea, Joan O'Brien, George Wallace, Roy Barcroft

Six Bridges to Cross
US 1955 96m bw
U-I (Aaron Rosenberg)

The criminal career of a young hoodlum in Boston in the thirties.

Public Enemy reprise with a sentimental veneer, smooth but uninteresting.

w Sidney Boehm novel They Stole Two and a Half Million Dollars and Got Away with It by Joseph F. Dineen d Joseph Pevney ph William Daniels m Joseph Gershenson

Tony Curtis, George Nader, Julie Adams, Jay C. Flippen, Sal Mineo, Jan Merlin

Six Day Bike Rider
US 1934 69m bw
Warner (Sam Bischoff)

One of life's failures impresses his girl by entering a cycling contest.

One of the star's stronger comedy vehicles.

w Earl Baldwin d Lloyd Bacon ph Warren Lynch

Joe E. Brown, Maxine Doyle, Frank McHugh, Gordon Westcott

Six Hours to Live *
US 1932 78m bw
Fox

A scientist revives a diplomat for six hours so that his murderer can be traced.

Fanciful hokum set at a Geneva peace conference.

story Gordon Morris, Morton Barteaux d William Dieterle

Warner Baxter, John Boles, Miriam Jordan, Irene Ware, George Marion

'A strong box office title which together with an aggressive sales campaign should bring picture into the money.' – Variety

Six in Paris: see Paris Vu Par . . .

Six Inches Tall: see Attack of the Puppet People

Six Lessons from Madame La Zonga
US 1941 62m bw
Universal

A Cuban night-club proprietress causes mix-ups on a pleasure boat.

Witless vehicle for two stars popular at another studio in the Mexican Spitfire series.

w Stanley Rubin, Marion Orth, Larry Rhine, Ben Chapman d John Rawlins

Lupe Velez, Leon Errol, William Frawley, Helen Parrish, Charles Lang, Eddie Quillan, Quinn Williams

'Their first honeymoon was so much fun They're off to have another one!'

Six of a Kind *
US 1934 69m bw
Paramount

Comic adventures of six people driving across America.

Minor comedy which doesn't come off as a whole but adequately displays the talents of its stars.

w Walter de Leon, Harry Ruskin d Leo McCarey ph Henry Sharp m Ralph Rainger

Charles Ruggles, Mary Boland, W. C. Fields, Alison Skipworth, George Burns, Gracie Allen

'Another pleasing film . . . it reminds the Englishman of Three Men in a Boat.' – E. V. Lucas, Punch

'Old-fashioned farce that gets a lot of laughs. Better for duals than de luxers.' – Variety

Six Pack
US 1982 110m DeLuxe
TCF/Lion Share (Michael Trikilis)
V*

A loner stock car driver finds himself fathering six orphan kids.

Old-fashioned family picture built around a country singer.

w Mike Marvin, Alex Matter d Daniel Petrie ph Mario Tosi m Charles Fox

Kenny Rogers, Diane Lane, Erin Gray, Barry Corbin

6,000 Enemies
US 1939 61m bw
Lucien Hubbard/MGM

A district attorney is framed for a prison stretch and finds himself hated by every convict inside.

Formula support climaxing in a prison break: well enough done.

w Bertram Millhauser d George B. Seitz

Walter Pidgeon, Rita Johnson, Paul Kelly, Nat Pendleton, Harold Huber, Grant Mitchell

'Prison meller with action aplenty.' – Variety

633 Squadron *
GB 1964 94m Technicolor Panavision
UA/Mirisch (Cecil F. Ford)
V, V*

In 1944 Mosquito aircraft try to collapse a cliff overhanging a munitions factory in a Norwegian fjord.

Standard war heroics with enough noise and disorder to keep most audiences hypnotized.

w James Clavell, Howard Koch novel Frederick E. Smith d Walter Grauman ph Ted Scaife, John Wilcox m Ron Goodwin

Cliff Robertson, George Chakiris, Maria Perschy, Harry Andrews, Donald Houston, Michael Goodliffe

Six Weeks
US 1982 107m Metrocolor
Polygram (Peter Guber, Jon Peters)

A lady cosmetics tycoon whose ten-year-old daughter

is dying of leukaemia enlists the aid of a politician to make what's left of her life a triumph.

Icky tearjerker on the lines of The Christmas Tree. Everything is done to make it palatable, but it won't be many people's cup of bromide.

w David Seltzer novel Fred Mustard Stewart d Tony Bill ph Michael D. Margulies m Dudley Moore ad Hilyard Brown ed Stu Linder

Dudley Moore, Mary Tyler Moore, Katherine Healy, Shannon Wilcox, Bill Calvert

'Very sleek and very sickmaking.' – Observer

'68
US 1988 98m colour
Entertainment/New World (Dale Djerassi, Isabel Maxwell, Steven Kovacs)
V*, L

A Hungarian immigrant experiences problems with his children as he opens a restaurant in San Francisco in the mid-1960s.

The movie's background, with its emphasis on the political events of the time, overwhelms its insufficiently developed characters.

wd Steven Kovacs ph Daniel Lacambre ad Joshua Koral ed Cari Coughlin

Eric Larsen, Robert Locke, Sandor Tecsi, Anna Dukasz, Neil Young

Sixty Glorious Years **
GB 1938 95m Technicolor
Imperator (Herbert Wilcox)
US title: Queen of Destiny

Scenes from the life of Queen Victoria.

A stately pageant apparently composed of material which couldn't be fitted into the previous year's black-and-white success Victoria the Great. Fascinating, though the camerawork is not very nimble.

w Robert Vansittart, Miles Malleson, Charles de Grandcourt d Herbert Wilcox ph Frederick A. Young

Anna Neagle, Anton Walbrook, C. Aubrey Smith, Walter Rilla, Charles Carson, Felix Aylmer, Lewis Casson

'One of the most artistic and expensive films made in England.' – Variety

† The two films were edited together in 1943 to make a new selection called Queen Victoria, and in the process the original negatives were accidentally destroyed, so that both films now have to be printed from unattractive dupes.

Det Sjunde Inseglet: see The Seventh Seal

Skateboard
US 1977 95m Technicolor
Universal
V*

A small-time theatrical agent in trouble builds up a professional skateboard team.

Unsatisfactory exploitation item which devotes more time to its plot than to its sport.

w Richard A. Wolf, George Gage d George Gage

Allen Garfield, Kathleen Lloyd, Leif Garrett, Richard Van Der Wyk

Skepp Till Indialand: see A Ship to India

Sketch Artist
US 1992 86m Foto-Kem colour
Motion Picture Corp of America (Brad Krevoy, Steve Stabler)
V, V*

A police artist sketching a witness's description of a murderer finds that he has produced a drawing of his wife.

A slick little thriller, enjoyable enough on its own limited terms.

w Michael Angeli   d Phedon Papamichael
ph Wally Pfister   m Mark Isham   pd Phedon Papamichael Snr   ed Carole Kravetz

Jeff Fahey, Sean Young, Frank McRae, Tcheky Karyo, James Tolkan, Charlotte Lewis, Drew Barrymore

'Pray they never have to rescue YOU . . .!'
Ski Patrol
US   1989   92m   DeLuxe
Entertainment/Epic/Sarlui/Diamant/Paul Maslansky (Phillip B. Goldfine, Donald L. West)
V, V*, L

A developer attempts to sabotage the safety record of a ski resort.

Broad farce in the style of the *Police Academy* series and no funnier.

w Steven Long Mitchell, Craig W. Van Sickle
d Richard Correll   ph John Stephens   m Bruce Miller   pd Fred Weiler   ed Scott Wallace

Roger Rose, Yvette Nipar, T. K. Carter, Leslie Jordan, Paul Feig, Sean Gregory Sullivan, Tess, George Lopez, Ray Walston

The Ski Raiders
US   1972   90m   Technicolor   Panavision
Warner (Edward L. Rissien)
aka: *Snow Job*

An alpine ski instructor devises a scheme to rob a bank.

Very medium caper thriller with a breathtaking opening sequence.

w Ken Kolb, Jeffrey Bloom   d George Englund
ph Gabor Pogany, Willy Bogner   m Jacques Loussier

Jean Claude Killy, Cliff Potts, Vittorio de Sica, Daniele Gaubert

Ski School
Canada   1991   88m   colour
Movie Store Entertainment/Rose & Ruby (Damian Lee)

Rival groups of skiers try to sabotage each other.

Crass comedy that is mainly an excuse for ski stunts and the cavortings of skimpily clad bimbos.

w David Mitchell   d Damian Lee   ph Curtis Petersen, Roxanne Di Santo   m Steven Hunter
ad Craig MacMillan   ed Robert Gordon

Dean Cameron, Tom Breznahan, Patrick Laborteaux, Mark Thomas Miller, Darlene Vogel, Charlie Spradling

Skidoo
US   1968   98m   Technicolor   Panavision
Paramount/Sigma (Otto Preminger)

Active and reformed gangsters get involved with hippies and preach universal love.

Abysmal mishmash with top talent abused; clearly intended as satirical farce, but in fact one of the most woebegone movies ever made.

w Doran William Cannon   d Otto Preminger
ph Leon Shamroy   m Harry Nilsson

Jackie Gleason, Carol Channing, Groucho Marx, Frankie Avalon, Fred Clark, Michael Constantine, Frank Gorshin, John Philip Law, Peter Lawford, Burgess Meredith, George Raft, Cesar Romero, Mickey Rooney

'Unspeakable.' – *Michael Billington, Illustrated London News*

Skin Deep
US   1989   101m   Technicolor   Panavision
Braveworld/Fox/Morgan Creek/BECO (Tony Adams)
V, V*, L

A best-selling author devotes his time to booze and women.

Shallow comedy too much in love with its unprepossessing hero.

wd Blake Edwards   ph Isidore Mankofsky
pd Rodger Maus   ed Robert Pergament

John Ritter, Vincent Gardenia, Alyson Reed, Joel Brooks, Julianne Phillips, Chelsea Field, Peter Donat, Don Gordon, Nina Foch

'Edwards' undeniable personal obsessions are winding up as bland, uniform, nothing-in-particular films like this.' – *Kim Newman, MFB*

The Skin Game
GB   1932   85m   bw
BIP (John Maxwell)
V*

A landowner hates his self-made neighbour.

Stiff picturization of a well-known stage play.

w Alfred Hitchcock, Alma Reville   play John Galsworthy   d Alfred Hitchcock   ph Jack Cox

Edmund Gwenn, John Longden, Jill Esmond, C. V. France, Helen Haye, Phyllis Konstam, Frank Lawton

The Skin Game *
US   1971   102m   Technicolor   Panavision
Warner/Cherokee (Harry Keller)
V*

A white and a black con man have near escapes in many a Western town.

Amusing comedy Western with good pace and a few shafts of wit.

w Peter Stone, Richard Alan Simmons   d Paul Bogart   ph Fred Koenekamp   m David Shire

James Garner, Lou Gossett, Susan Clark, Brenda Sykes, Ed Asner, Andrew Duggan, Henry Jones, Neva Patterson

Skinheads
US   1988   93m   colour
Greydon Clark
V, V*
aka: *Skinheads: The Second Coming of Hate*

A gang of neo-Nazis hunt down a couple who witnessed their slaughter of a café owner and her customers.

Unpleasant low-budget shocker, badly written, hammily acted and dully directed. Despite his star billing, Connors sensibly makes a brief appearance.

w David Reskin, Greydon Clark   d Greydon Clark
ph Nicholas von Sternberg   m Dan Slider
ad Doug Abrahamson   ed Travis Clark

Chuck Connors, Barbara Bain, Brian Brophy, Jason Culp, Elizabeth Sagal

Skippy *
US   1931   88m   bw
Paramount

The young son of a local health inspector makes friends in the slums.

Standard, blameless family entertainment.

w Joseph L. Mankiewicz, Norman McLeod   comic strip Percy Crosby   d Norman Taurog   ph Karl Struss

Jackie Cooper, Robert Coogan, Mitzi Green, Jackie Searl, Willard Robertson

'A great kid talker, but not for kids only . . . if there is such a thing as being 100% inhuman, only then is it possible for anyone to dislike *Skippy* as entertainment.' – *Variety*

AA: Norman Taurog
AAN: best picture; script; Jackie Cooper

Skirts Ahoy
US   1952   105m   Technicolor
MGM (Joe Pasternak)
V*

Three girls join the navy and get their men.

Musical recruiting poster, quite devoid of interest.

w Isobel Lennart   d Sidney Lanfield   ph William Mellor   m Harry Warren   ly Ralph Blane   ch Nick Castle

Esther Williams, Vivian Blaine, Joan Evans, Barry Sullivan, Keefe Brasselle, Dean Miller, Debbie Reynolds, Bobby Van, Billy Eckstine

The Skull
GB   1965   83m   Techniscope
Paramount/Amicus (Milton Subotsky)
V*

The skull of the Marquis de Sade haunts two antiquarians.

Clodhopping horror with very visible wires.

w Milton Subotsky   story Robert Bloch   d Freddie Francis   ph John Wilcox   m Elisabeth Lutyens

Peter Cushing, Christopher Lee, Patrick Wymark, Jill Bennett, Nigel Green, Michael Gough, George Coulouris

Skullduggery
US   1969   105m   Technicolor   Panavision
Universal (Saul David)
V*

Archaeologists and adventurers clash on a trek in New Guinea.

Fashionable oddball adventure about the discovery of an unspoiled primitive tribe; the elements don't jell.

w Nelson Gidding   d Gordon Douglas   ph Robert Moreno   m Oliver Nelson

Burt Reynolds, Susan Clark, Roger C. Carmel, Paul Hubschmid, Chips Rafferty, Alexander Knox, Edward Fox, Wilfrid Hyde-White, Rhys Williams

Sky Bandits
GB   1986   93m   Rank colour
London Front Ltd (Richard Herland)

Adventures of World War I flyers.

An attempt at a light-hearted *Hell's Angels*. It misfires on all cylinders.

w Thom Keyes   d Zoran Perisic   ph David Watkin
m Alfie Kabilje   pd Tony Woollard   ed Peter Tanner

Scott McGinnis, Jeff Osterhage, Ronald Lacey, Miles Anderson, Valerie Steffen, Ingrid Held

Sky Bride
US   1932   75m   bw
Paramount

An aerial barnstormer loses his nerve after an accident.

Formula melodrama with aerobatics.

w Joseph L. Mankiewicz, Agnes Brand Leahy, Grover Jones   d Stephen Roberts

Richard Arlen, Jack Oakie, Virginia Bruce, Robert Coogan, Charles Starrett

'Lack of romantic interest is somewhat of a handicap to a conventional air plot with a suspensive finish.' – *Variety*

Sky Devils
US   1931   89m   bw
Caddo/Howard Hughes

Two draft dodgers find themselves heroes of the Army Air Corps in World War I France.

Little-seen but unremarkable adventure comedy in the Flagg and Quirt tradition.

w Joseph Moncure March, Edward Sutherland *d* Edward Sutherland *ph* Tony Gaudio *md* Alfred Newman *ch* Busby Berkeley

Spencer Tracy, William Boyd, Ann Dvorak, George Cooper, Billy Bevan, Forrester Harvey

'A hodge-podge of all the laugh war stuff . . . and how they want something to laugh about right now. Psychologically and in a material way, it should do nicely.' – *Variety*

Sky Full of Moon
US   1952   73m   bw
MGM (Sidney Franklin Jnr)

A rodeo cowboy wins money and a showgirl in Las Vegas.

Ambling comedy with an agreeable air of innocence.

wd Norman Foster   *ph* Ray June   *m* Paul Sawtell

Carleton Carpenter, Jan Sterling, Keenan Wynn

Sky Giant
US   1938   80m   bw
RKO (Robert Sisk)

Romance and adventure at a flying school.

Unremarkable melodrama with expected heroics.

w Lionel Houser   *d* Ken Landers

Richard Dix, Joan Fontaine, Chester Morris, Harry Carey, Paul Guilfoyle

'Good for the lighter weight first run houses and the upper berth of double deckers.' – *Variety*

Sky Pirates
Australia   1986   89m   Colorfilm   Panavision
John Lamond Motion Pictures (John Lamond, Michael Hirsh)
V, V*

A pilot foils a crazed squadron leader attempting to obtain the three parts of an ancient stone that will provide him with unlimited power.

Silly and thrill-free adventure with an over-complicated narrative which amounts to no more than a feeble imitation of the Indiana Jones movies.

w John Lamond   *d* Colin Eggleston   *ph* Garry Wapshott   *m* Brian May   *pd* Kristian Fredrickson *sp* Dennis Nicholson   *ed* John Lamond, Michael Hirsh

John Hargreaves, Meredith Phillips, Max Phipps, Bill Hunter, Simon Chilvers, Alex Scott

Sky Raiders
US   1941   bw   serial: 12 eps
Universal

Airplane manufacturers combat enemy agents.

Routine thick ear with a better than average cast.

d Ford Beebe, Ray Taylor

Donald Woods, Billy Halop, Robert Armstrong, Eduardo Ciannelli, Kathryn Adams, Reed Hadley

'He'll try anything once . . . even if it's impossible!'
Sky Riders *
US   1976   91m   DeLuxe   Todd-AO 35
TCF (Terry Morse Jnr)
V*

In Athens, the family of an American businessman is kidnapped by terrorists and rescued by hang-gliders led by a soldier of fortune.

Old-fashioned actioner with new-fashioned political concern.

w Jack de Witt, Stanley Mann, Gary Michael White, Hall T. Sprague, Bill McGaw   *d* Douglas Hickox *ph* Ousama Rawi   *m* Lalo Schifrin

James Coburn, Susannah York, Robert Culp, Charles Aznavour, Werner Pochath, Kenneth Griffith, Harry Andrews

Sky West and Crooked
GB   1965   102m   Eastmancolor
Rank/John Mills (Jack Hanbury)
US title: *Gypsy Girl*

A mentally retarded girl falls in love with a gypsy.

Eccentric rural melodrama with echoes of *Cold Comfort Farm* and *Les Jeux Interdits*. Interesting, but scarcely a runaway success.

w Mary Hayley Bell, John Prebble   *d* John Mills *ph* Arthur Ibbetson   *m* Malcolm Arnold

Hayley Mills, Ian McShane, Laurence Naismith, *Geoffrey Bayldon*, Annette Crosbie, Norman Bird

'Behind the overwhelming feyness of it all lurk assumptions which in cold blood look almost sinister.' – *MFB*

Skyjacked *
US   1972   101m   Metrocolor   Panavision
MGM/Walter Seltzer

A Boeing 707 on a flight from Los Angeles to Minneapolis is forced by a mad bomber to fly to Moscow.

Shamelessly hackneyed aeroplane adventure with quite enjoyable elements.

w Stanley R. Greenberg   *novel* *Hijacked* by David Harper   *d* John Guillermin   *ph* Harry Stradling Jnr *m* Perry Botkin Jnr

Charlton Heston, Yvette Mimieux, James Brolin, Claude Akins, Jeanne Crain, Rosey Grier, Walter Pidgeon, Leslie Uggams

Skylark
US   1941   94m   bw
Paramount (Mark Sandrich)

A wife decides on her fifth anniversary that she is tired of being secondary to her husband's career, and needs a fling.

Formula matrimonial comedy; plenty of talent but no sparkle.

w Z. Myers   *play* Samson Raphaelson   *d* Mark Sandrich   *ph* Charles Lang   *m* Victor Young

Claudette Colbert, Ray Milland, Brian Aherne, Binnie Barnes, Walter Abel, Grant Mitchell, Mona Barrie, Ernest Cossart

Skyliner
US   1949   61m   bw
Lippert/William Stephens

The FBI nabs a spy on a transcontinental plane.

Second feature chiefly interesting for its setting.

w Maurice Tombragel   *d* William Berke

Richard Travis, Pamela Blake, Rochelle Hudson, Steve Geray, Greg McClure

The Sky's the Limit
GB   1937   79m   bw
Jack Buchanan

A sacked aircraft designer suddenly finds himself in demand.

Amiable star musical.

w Jack Buchanan, Douglas Furber   *d* Lee Garmes and Jack Buchanan

Jack Buchanan, Mara Loseff, William Kendall, David Hutcheson, H. F. Maltby, Athene Seyler, Sara Allgood

The Sky's the Limit *
US   1943   89m   bw
RKO (David Hempstead)
V*, L

A flyer on leave meets and falls for a news photographer.

Thin musical with incidental compensations.

w Frank Fenton, Lynn Root   *d* Edward H. Griffith *ph* Russell Metty   *md* Leo F. Forbstein   *m* Leigh Harline

Fred Astaire, Joan Leslie, *Robert Benchley*, Robert Ryan, Elizabeth Patterson

AAN: Leigh Harline; song 'My Shining Hour' (*m* Harold Arlen, *ly* Johnny Mercer)

Skyscraper Souls
US   1932   100m   bw
MGM
V*

In an office building, several personal dilemmas interlock.

Portmanteau drama in the *Grand Hotel* mould, and quite comparable.

w C. G. Sullivan, Elmer Harris   *book* Faith Baldwin *d* Edgar Selwyn

Warren William, Maureen O'Sullivan, Verree Teasdale, Gregory Ratoff, Jean Hersholt, Norman Foster, Anita Page, George Barbier, Wallace Ford, Hedda Hopper

Slacker **
US   1991   97m   colour
Feature/Detour (Richard Linklater)
V, V*

In Austin, Texas, young people wandering the streets confide to the camera their odd beliefs and attitudes, including the avoidance of careers.

Leisurely, lackadaisical feature of oddballs that exerts a certain bemused fascination.

wd Richard Linklater   *ph* Lee Daniel   *m* Buffalo Gals, Triangle Mallet Apron, The Texas Instruments *ad* Debbie Pastor   *ed* Scott Rhodes

Richard Linklater, Rudy Basquez, Jean Caffeine, Jan Hockey, Stephan Hockey, Mark James

'A film of quirky, unpredictable and oddly poetic charm.' – *Philip Kemp, Sight and Sound*

'One of the freshest independent films to come along in some time, but because of its non-narrative, non-characterization approach, film won't be to all tastes.' – *Variety*

Slade: see *Jack Slade*

Slamdance
US   1987   99m   colour
Zenith Productions/Island Pictures (Rupert Harvey, Barty Opper)
V, V*

A newspaper cartoonist is framed for a murder by a corrupt cop.

Silly, convoluted mish-mash of a thriller.

w Don Opper   *d* Wayne Wang   *ph* Amie Mokri *m* Mitchell Froom   *pd* Eugenio Zanetti   *ed* Lee Percy

Tom Hulce, Mary Elizabeth Mastrantonio, Virginia Madsen, Millie Perkins, Don Opper, Adam Ant, John Doe, Robert Beltran, Judith Barsi, Harry Dean Stanton

Slander
US   1956   81m   bw
MGM (Armand Deutsch)

Revelations about a film star in a scandal magazine lead to blackmail and murder.

Unlikely melodrama, routinely assembled, based on the Confidential Magazine lawsuits.

w Jerome Weidman   *d* Roy Rowland   *ph* Harold J. Marzerati   *m* Jeff Alexander

Van Johnson, Ann Blyth, Steve Cochran, *Marjorie Rambeau*, Harold J. Stone

Slap Shot *

US　1977　124m　Technicolor
Universal/Robert J. Wunsch, Stephen Friedman
V, V*, L

The wily player-coach of a fading ice hockey team finds ways, including dirty play, of keeping it going.

Violent, foul-mouthed comedy which works as it goes but leaves a bad taste in the mouth.

w Nancy Dowd　d George Roy Hill　ph Victor Kemper, Wallace Worsley　md Elmer Bernstein

Paul Newman, Michael Ontkean, Lindsay Crouse, Jennifer Warren, Strother Martin

'Fast, noisy, profane . . . gets you laughing, all right, but you don't necessarily enjoy yourself.' – New Yorker
'Both indulgent and moralizing, the self-consciously racy script ends up looking merely opportunistic.' – Time Out

Slattery's Hurricane

US　1949　87m　bw
TCF (William Perlberg)

Loves of a storm-spotting pilot with the US Weather Bureau in Florida.

Forgettable programmer with good storm sequences.

w Herman Wouk, Richard Murphy　novel Herman Wouk　d André de Toth　ph Charles G. Clarke　m Cyril Mockridge

Richard Widmark, Linda Darnell, Veronica Lake, John Russell, Gary Merrill, Walter Kingsford

Slaughter

US　1972　90m　DeLuxe　Todd-AO 35
AIP/Slaughter United (Monroe Sachson)

A black Vietnam veteran hunts down the underworld syndicate which killed his mother and father.

Hectic crime yarn with a pitilessly violent hero and not enough style to relieve the unappetizing monotony.

w Mark Hanna, Don Williams　d Jack Starrett　ph Rosanio Solano　m Luchi de Jesus

Jim Brown, Rip Torn, Don Gordon, Cameron Mitchell

'The cast perform their trigger-happy tasks with all the passionate conviction of a team of well-oiled robots.' – Jan Dawson

Slaughter on Tenth Avenue

US　1957　103m　bw
U-I (Albert Zugsmith)

The New York DA's office investigates union murders on the docks.

Uninteresting imitation of On the Waterfront.

w Lawrence Roman　novel The Man Who Rocked the Boat by William J. Keating, Richard Carter　d Arnold Laven　ph Fred Jackman　m Richard Rodgers

Richard Egan, Jan Sterling, Dan Duryea, Julie Adams, Walter Matthau, Charles McGraw, Sam Levene, Mickey Shaughnessy, Harry Bellaver

Slaughter Trail

US　1952　78m　Cinecolor
RKO (Irving Allen)
V*

Three outlaws cause trouble between white man and Indian.

Rough-hewn Western strung together by verses of a ballad.

w Sid Kuller　d Irving Allen　ph Jack Greenhalgh　ad George Van Marter　ed Fred Allen

Brian Donlevy, Gig Young, Virginia Grey, Andy Devine, Robert Hutton

Slaughterhouse Five *

US　1972　104m　Technicolor
Universal/Vanadas (Paul Monash)
V*, L

A suburban optometrist has nightmare space/time fantasies involving Nazi POW camps and a strange futuristic planet.

Interesting but infuriating anti-war fantasy for intellectuals.

w Stephen Geller　novel Kurt Vonnegut Jnr　d George Roy Hill　ph Miroslav Ondricek　m J. S. Bach, performed by Glen Gould　pd Henry Bumstead

Michael Sacks, Ron Leibman, Eugène Roche, Sharon Gans, Valerie Perrine, Sorrell Booke, John Dehner

'A lot of good makings in this picture; but very little is made.' – Stanley Kauffmann

Slaughter's Big Rip-Off

US　1973　93m　Movielab　Todd-AO 35
AIP (Monroe Sachson)
V*

Still on the run from gangsters who have killed his best friend, Slaughter violently disposes of a number of adversaries.

More routine black violence, a rampage of senseless brutality against sunny Los Angeles backgrounds.

w Charles Johnson　d Gordon Douglas　ph Charles Wheeler　m Jim Brown, Fred Wesley

Jim Brown, Ed MacMahon, Brock Peters, Don Stroud

Slave Girl

US　1947　79m　Technicolor
U-I (Michael Fessier, Ernest Pagano)

In the early 1800s, a diplomat is sent to Tripoli to ransom sailors held by the power-mad potentate.

Criticism would be superfluous; when the film was finished it was obviously so bad that executives ordered the addition of a talking camel and other Hellzapoppin-type jokes in order to turn it into a comedy.

w Michael Fessier, Ernest Pagano　d Charles Lamont　ph George Robinson, W. Howard Greene　m Milton Rosen

George Brent, Yvonne de Carlo, Albert Dekker, Broderick Crawford, Lois Collier, Andy Devine, Carl Esmond, Arthur Treacher

Slave Girls

GB　1968　74m (GB), 95m (US)　Technicolor　Cinemascope
Hammer (Aida Young)
V*
US title: Prehistoric Women

A hunter seeking white rhinoceros finds himself in a lost valley ruled by a tribe of women.

Feebly preposterous comic strip farrago without the saving grace of humour.

w Henry Younger (Michael Carreras)　d Michael Carreras　ph Michael Reed　m Carlo Mantelli　ad Robert Jones　ed Jim Needs, Roy Hyde

Michael Latimer, Martine Beswick, Edina Ronay, Carol White

Slave Ship **

US　1937　100m　bw
TCF (Darryl F. Zanuck)

An American slave captain decides to become respectable but finds a mutiny on his hands.

Well-made adventure movie in the old tradition, a model of studio production.

w Sam Hellman, Lamar Trotti, Gladys Lehman　novel George S. King　story William Faulkner　d Tay Garnett　ph Ernest Palmer　m Alfred Newman

Wallace Beery, Warner Baxter, Elizabeth Allen, Mickey Rooney, George Sanders, Jane Darwell, Joseph Schildkraut, Arthur Hohl, Minna Gombell, Billy Bevan, Francis Ford, Edwin Maxwell, J. Farrell MacDonald, Paul Hurst, Holmes Herbert

'Plenty of action and de luxe scenic trimmings . . . good box office blood and thunder.' – Variety

Slave Women of Corinth: see Aphrodite, Goddess of Love

Slaves

US　1969　110m　Eastmancolor
Slaves Company/Theatre Guild/Walter Reade (Philip Langner)

In 1850 Kentucky a slave stands up for his rights and plans escape.

Well-meaning but muddled and old-fashioned melodrama, hardly well enough done to raise comparison with Gone with the Wind.

wd Herbert J. Biberman　ph Joseph Brun　m Bobby Scott

Stephen Boyd, Ossie Davis, Dionne Warwick, Shepperd Strudwick, Nancy Coleman, David Huddleston, Gale Sondergaard

Slaves of New York

US　1989　125m　Technicolor
Columbia TriStar/Hendler-Merchant Ivory/Ismail Merchant, Gary Hendler
V*, L

Trendy young artists and fashion designers in New York fall in and out of love.

Inconsequential movie that is unable to get to grips with its insubstantial characters.

w Tama Janowitz　stories Tama Janowitz　d James Ivory　ph Tony Pierce-Roberts　m Richard Robbins　pd David Gropman　ed Katherine Wenning

Bernadette Peters, Madeleine Potter, Adam Coleman Howard, Nick Corri, Charles McCaughan, Jonas Abry, Tama Janowitz

Slayground

GB　1983　89m　Technicolor
EMI/Jennie and Co. (John Dark, Gower Frost)
V, V*

A rich man hires an assassin to track down a criminal who accidentally killed his daughter.

One of those tedious and violent films in which the criminal wins out; slickness seems to make it worse.

w Trevor Preston　novel Richard Stark　d Terry Bedford　ph Stephen Smith, Herb Wagreich　m Colin Towns　pd Keith Wilson

Peter Coyote, Mel Smith, Billie Whitelaw, Philip Sayer, Bill Luhrs

'A disappointingly lame front runner for the new EMI stable.' – Philip Strick, MFB

Sleep My Love *

US　1948　96m　bw
UA/Mary Pickford (Charles 'Buddy' Rogers)

A man plots to murder his wife, but is foiled.

Thin suspenser, rather splendidly photographed in the expressionist manner.

w St Clair McKelway　novel Leo Rosten　d Douglas Sirk　ph Joseph Valentine　m Rudy Schrager

Claudette Colbert, Don Ameche, Robert Cummings, Rita Johnson, George Coulouris, Hazel Brooks, Keye Luke

'A love story about two people who hate each other!'

Sleeper **

US　1973　88m　DeLuxe
UA/Jack Rollins, Charles Joffe (Jack Grossberg)
V, V*, L

A health food store owner is deep frozen after an operation and wakes two hundred years in the future.

Predictable star vehicle with an agreeable string of bright gags.

w *Woody Allen, Marshall Brickman* d *Woody Allen* ph *David M. Walsh* m *Woody Allen* pd *Dale Hennesy*

Woody Allen, Diane Keaton, John Beck, Mary Gregory

'Verbal and visual gags rain down like hailstones.' – *Michael Billington, Illustrated London News*

The Sleeping Beauty *

US 1959 75m Technirama 70
Walt Disney (Ken Peterson)
V, V*, L

Rather stodgy, unwisely Cinemascoped feature cartoon of the old legend; very fashionable and detailed, but somehow lifeless.

d *Clyde Geronimi* md *George Bruns* pd *Don da Gradi, Ken Anderson*

voices of Mary Costa, Bill Shirley, Eleanor Audley, Verna Felton, Barbara Jo Allen, Barbara Luddy

AAN: George Bruns

Sleeping Car

GB 1933 82m bw
Gaumont

A woman on the run pretends to marry a sleeping car attendant, then finds they really are married.

Artificial comedy with interesting cast from London stage.

w *Franz Schultz* d *Anatole Litvak*

Madeleine Carroll, Ivor Novello, Laddie Cliff, Kay Hammond, Claud Allister, Stanley Holloway

The Sleeping Car Murders *

France 1965 95m bw Cinemascope
PECF (Julien Derode)
original title: *Compartiment Tueurs*

When the overnight express from Marseilles reaches Paris, a girl is found dead in the sleeping car.

Rather long-winded whodunnit with an unlikely solution: a good pace helps, however, as do skilful borrowings from American police films of the forties.

wd *Costa-Gavras* novel *Sebastien Japrisot* ph *Jean Tournier* m *Michel Magne*

Yves Montand, Simone Signoret, Pierre Mondy, Catherine Allégret, Jacques Pérrin, Jean-Louis Trintignant, Michel Piccoli

Sleeping Car to Trieste *

GB 1948 95m bw
GFD/Two Cities (George H. Brown)
V*

Spy melodrama, a slow-starting but generally entertaining remake of *Rome Express* (qv).

w *Allan Mackinnon* d *John Paddy Carstairs* ph *Jack Hildyard* m *Benjamin Frankel*

Albert Lieven, Jean Kent, David Tomlinson, David Hutcheson, Rona Anderson, Paul Dupuis, Finlay Currie, *Alan Wheatley*, Derrick de Marney, Grégoire Aslan, Hugh Burden

The Sleeping Cardinal

GB 1931 84m bw
Twickenham

Sherlock Holmes exposes a smuggling ring.

Slow-paced but interesting adaptation, vaguely based on *The Empty House*.

w *Cyril Twyford, H. Fowler Mear* stories *Sir Arthur Conan Doyle* d *Leslie Hiscott*

Arthur Wontner, Ian Fleming, Norman McKinnel, Jane Welsh, Louis Goodrich

The Sleeping City **

US 1950 85m bw
U-I (Leonard Goldstein)

A policeman disguises himself as a medical student to learn more about a murder in a general hospital.

A location melodrama of modest excellence.

w *Jo Eisinger* d *George Sherman* ph *William Miller* m *Frank Skinner*

Richard Conte, Richard Taber, Coleen Gray, John Alexander, Peggy Dow, Alex Nicol

The Sleeping Tiger

GB 1954 89m bw
Anglo-Amalgamated/Insignia (Victor Hanbury)
V*

A psychiatrist overpowers a criminal and takes him home as a guinea pig; the criminal then falls in love with the psychiatrist's wife.

Turgid and unconvincing melodrama, a thoroughgoing bore.

w *Harold Buchman, Carl Foreman* novel *Maurice Moiseiwitch* d *Joseph Losey* ph *Harry Waxman* m *Malcolm Arnold*

Dirk Bogarde, Alexander Knox, Alexis Smith, Hugh Griffith, Maxine Audley, Glyn Houston, Billie Whitelaw

'There is a splendour about this film, which has one of the most absurdly extravagant plots on record, and never flinches from it.' – *Gavin Lambert*

'She changed her name. Her looks. Her life. All to escape the most dangerous man she's ever met. Her husband.'
Sleeping with the Enemy

US 1990 99m DeLuxe
TCF (Leonard Goldberg)
V, V*, L, S

In order to leave her violent husband, a wife fakes her own death and takes a new identity.

Uninvolving thriller that is never original enough to overcome its predictability.

w *Ronald Bass* novel *Nancy Price* d *Joseph Ruben* ph *John W. Lindley* m *Jerry Goldsmith* pd *Doug Kraner* ed *George Bowers*

Julia Roberts, Patrick Bergin, Kevin Anderson, Elizabeth Lawrence, Kyle Secor, Claudette Nevins, Tony Abatemarco, Marita Geraghty, Harley Venton

'A glossy combination of secondhand showing-off-Julia scenes from Pretty Woman and secondhand scares from The Stepfather.' – *Pauline Kael, New Yorker*

'What if someone you never met, someone you never saw, someone you never knew was the only someone for you?'
Sleepless in Seattle *

US 1993 105m Technicolor
TriStar (Gary Foster)
S

After his mother dies, an eight-year-old boy confides to a radio phone-in that he wants to find someone for his father to marry; the call is heard by an intrigued journalist, worried about her engagement to a dull man.

Enjoyable romantic comedy, although its overall tone is excessively sweet.

w *Norah Ephron, David S. Ward, Jeff Arch* d *Nora Ephron* ph *Sven Nykvist* m *Marc Shaiman* pd *Jeffrey Townsend* ed *Robert Reitano*

Tom Hanks, Meg Ryan, Ross Malinger, Rita Wilson, Victor Garber, Tom Riis Farrell, Carey Lowell, Bill Pullman

'This shamelessly romantic comedy . . . delivers ample warmth and some explosively funny moments.' – *Variety*

AAN: Nora Ephron, David S. Ward, Jeff Arch; song 'A Wink and a Smile' (m *Marc Shaiman*, ly *Ramsey McLean*)

Sleepwalkers

US 1992 89m Technicolor
Columbia TriStar/Columbia/ION (Mark Victor, Michael Grais, Nabeel Zahid)
V, V*, L, S

A mother and son, shape-shifting monsters, move into a new community.

Ridiculous horror, lacking suspense, sense or the slightest ability to shock or scare.

w *Stephen King* d *Mick Garris* ph *Rodney Charters* m *Nicholas Pike* pd *John DeCuir Jnr* sp *Apogee Productions* ed *O. Nicholas Brown*

Brian Krause, Mädchen Amick, Alice Krige, Jim Haynie, Cindy Pickett, Ron Perlman, Lyman Ward, Dan Martin, John Landis, Joe Dante, Stephen King, Clive Barker, Tobe Hooper

'Piffle.' – *Sheila Johnston, Independent*

'This technically proficient, surprisingly gory but utterly nonsensical movie is billed as the first screenplay written by horror novelist Stephen King expressly for the screen. Unfortunately, this hardly rates as a recommendation.' – *Nigel Floyd, Sight and Sound*

The Slender Thread *

US 1965 98m bw
Paramount/Athene (Stephen Alexander)
V*

A volunteer social worker tries to prevent a woman from committing suicide while police track her down from their phone conversations.

Acceptable star melodrama, curiously artificially styled.

w *Stirling Silliphant* d *Sydney Pollack* ph *Loyal Griggs* m *Quincy Jones*

Anne Bancroft, Sidney Poitier, Steven Hill, Telly Savalas

'Think of the crime . . . then go one step further . . . If it was murder, where's the body? If it was for a woman, which woman? If it's only a game, why the blood?'
Sleuth **

GB 1972 139m colour
Palomar (Morton Gottlieb)
V*, L

A successful thriller writer invents a murder plot which rebounds on himself.

Well-acted version of a highly successful piece of stage trickery; despite hard work all round it seems much less clever and arresting on the screen, and the tricks do show.

w *Anthony Shaffer*, play *Anthony Shaffer* d *Joseph L. Mankiewicz* ph *Oswald Morris* m *John Addison*

Laurence Olivier, Michael Caine

AAN: Joseph L. Mankiewicz; John Addison; Laurence Olivier; Michael Caine

A Slight Case of Larceny

US 1952 71m bw
MGM

Garage proprietors find a way of tapping their rivals' supply of petrol.

Laboured comedy for two rather tiresome stars.

w *Jerry Davis* d *Don Weis*

Mickey Rooney, Eddie Bracken, Elaine Stewart, Marilyn Erskine, Douglas Fowley

A Slight Case of Murder ***

US 1938 85m bw
Warner (Sam Bischoff)

When a beer baron tries to go legitimate his

colleagues attempt to kill him, but end up shooting each other.

Amusing black farce, remade to less effect as *Stop, You're Killing Me* (qv).

w Earl Baldwin, Joseph Schrank   *play* Damon Runyon, Howard Lindsay   d *Lloyd Bacon*   ph Sid Hickox   m M. K. Jerome, Jack Scholl

Edward G. Robinson, Jane Bryan, Willard Parker, *Ruth Donnelly*, Allen Jenkins, John Litel, Harold Huber, Edward Brophy, Bobby Jordan

'Nothing funnier has been produced by Hollywood for a long time . . . a mirthful and hilarious whimsy.' – *Variety*

'The complications crazily mount, sentiment never raises its ugly head, a long nose is made at violence and death.' – *Graham Greene*

Slightly Dangerous
US   1943   94m   bw
Pandro S. Berman/MGM

A small-town girl goes to New York and establishes herself by fraudulent impersonation; meanwhile a boy back home is suspected of being involved in her disappearance.

Unsatisfactory comedy-drama.

w Charles Lederer, George Oppenheimer, Ian McLellan Hunter, Aileen Hamilton   d Wesley Ruggles

Lana Turner, Robert Young, Dame May Whitty, Walter Brennan, Eugene Pallette, Alan Mowbray, Florence Bates

Slightly French
US   1948   81m   bw
Columbia

A film director in trouble passes off a Bowery-born carnival dancer as an exotic French star.

Rather tedious comedy which lively performances can't sustain.

w Karen de Wolf   d Douglas Sirk

Dorothy Lamour, Don Ameche, Janis Carter, Jeanne Manet, Willard Parker

'Her heart belongs to daddy, and she calls everybody daddy!'
Slightly Honorable
US   1940   85m   bw
UA/Walter Wanger (Tay Garnett)
V*

Lawyer partners set out to break a crime syndicate.

Fair crime thriller which can't decide whether it's comedy or drama.

w John Hunter Lay, Robert Tallman, Ken Englund   *novel Send Another Coffin* by F. G. Presnell   d Tay Garnett   ph Merritt Gerstad   m Werner Janssen

Pat O'Brien, Broderick Crawford, Edward Arnold, Eve Arden, Claire Dodd, Ruth Terry, Bernard Nedell, Alan Dinehart, Douglass Dumbrille, Ernest Truex

'The story skips along without deftness between serious drama and comedy, and winds up in the aggregate as a whatisit.' – *Variety*

Slightly Scarlet
US   1930   72m   bw
Paramount

Two jewel thieves outwit a malicious mastermind.

Somewhat effete comedy-drama in a long bygone style.

w Howard Estabrook, Joseph L. Mankiewicz, Percy Heath   d Louis Gasnier, Edwin H. Knopf

Clive Brook, Evelyn Brent, Paul Lukas, Eugene Pallette, Helen Ware, Virginia Bruce, Henry Wadsworth, Claud Allister

'Fair general programme feature.' – *Variety*

Slightly Scarlet
US   1956   92m   Technicolor   Superscope
(RKO) Benedict Bogeaus
V*

The mayor's secretary loves the leader of a criminal gang.

Competent but uninteresting crime romance.

w Robert Blees   *novel* James A. Cain   d Allan Dwan   ph John Alton   m Louis Forbes

Arlene Dahl, John Payne, Rhonda Fleming, Kent Taylor, Ted de Corsia

'So complicated that it is difficult to sort out which characters are supposed to be sympathetic.' – *MFB*

Slim
US   1937   85m   bw
Warner

Electric linesmen argue about their work and their women.

A reworking of *Tiger Shark* which itself later became *Manpower*; competent action stuff.

w William Wister Haines   d Ray Enright

Pat O'Brien, Margaret Lindsay, Henry Fonda, Stuart Erwin, J. Farrell MacDonald, Jane Wyman

'A comedy drama which will do all right without setting off fireworks.' – *Variety*

Slim Carter
US   1957   82m   Eastmancolor
Universal-International

A playboy is signed up by a Hollywood studio and required to change his image.

Curious sentimental comedy which might have worked with stronger casting.

w Montgomery Pitman   d Richard H. Bartlett

Jock Mahoney, Julie Adams, Tim Hovey, William Hopper, Ben Johnson, Barbara Hale

'You'll forget every love story you ever saw – or sang to!'
The Slipper and the Rose *
GB   1976   146m   Technicolor   Panavision
Paradine Co-Productions (David Frost, Stuart Lyons)
V

The story of Cinderella.

The elements are charming, but the treatment is fussy yet uninventive and the film is immensely overlong and lacking in magic and wit. Alas, not the renaissance of the family film that was hoped for.

w Bryan Forbes, Robert and Richard Sherman   d Bryan Forbes   ph Tony Imi   *songs* Robert and Richard Sherman   pd Ray Simm

Richard Chamberlain, Gemma Craven, Kenneth More, Michael Hordern, Edith Evans, Annette Crosbie, Margaret Lockwood, *Christopher Gable*, Julian Orchard, Lally Bowers, John Turner

'The tunes, I'm afraid, go in one ear and out the other; and, as Dr Johnson said of *Paradise Lost*, no man wished it a minute longer.' – *Michael Billington, Illustrated London News*

AAN: music; song 'He Danced with Me'

Slipstream
GB   1989   102m   Eastmancolor
Entertainment/Entertainment Film Productions (Gary Kurtz)
V, V*, L

In a post-holocaust future, an android learns human feelings while being hunted by a policeman and woman.

Futuristic chase movie, a little lacking in imagination.

w Tony Kayden   *story* Bill Bauer   d Steven M. Listberger   ph Frank Tidy   m Elmer Bernstein   pd Andrew McAlpine   ed Terry Rawlings

Mark Hamill, Bob Peck, Bill Paxton, Kitty Aldridge, Eleanor David, Ben Kingsley, F. Murray Abraham, Robbie Coltrane

Slither *
US   1972   96m   Metrocolor
MGM/Talent Associates/Jack Sher
V*

An ex-con, some gangsters, and a few mobile homes are involved in a chase across California for some hidden loot.

Wackily with-it comedy-thriller ranging from violence to slapstick, the former always undercut into the latter. Pretty funny, once you get the idea.

w W. D. Richter   d Howard Zieff   ph Laszlo Kovacs   m Tom McIntosh

James Caan, Peter Boyle, Sally Kellerman, Louise Lasser

'You Like To Watch *Don't You*.'
Sliver
US   1993   108m   DeLuxe
Paramount (Robert Evans)
V, V*, L, CD, S

A woman moves into an apartment block where the tenants are being murdered and discovers that its owner maintains a video surveillance of every room in the building.

A voyeuristic thriller, no doubt intended to be erotic but only succeeding in being dull.

w Joe Eszterhas   *novel* Ira Levin   d Phillip Noyce   ph Vilmos Zsigmond   m Howard Shire   pd Paul Sylbert   ed Richard Francis-Bruce, William Hoy

Sharon Stone, William Baldwin, Tom Berenger, Polly Walker, Collen Camp, Amanda Foreman, Martin Landau, C. C. H. Pounder

'All flash and no sizzle.' – *Variety*

Slow Dancing in the Big City
US   1978   110m   Technicolor
UA/CIP (Michael Levee, John G. Avildsen)

A New York newspaper columnist is affected by a dying eight-year-old drug addict and an ailing girl ballet dancer.

Warner in the 30s might have got away with this corn, but in 1978, played against a realistic backdrop, it seems merely silly and indigestible, its title as pretentious as its use of four-letter words.

w Barra Grant   d John G. Avildsen   ph Ralf D. Bode   m Bill Conti

Paul Sorvino, Anne Ditchburn, Nicholas Coster, Anita Dangler

'The earnestness and shamelessness of the director are so awesome that if the picture fails as romance, it succeeds as camp.' – *New Yorker*

Slow Motion: see *Sauve Qui Peut (La Vie)*

Smack and Thistle *
GB   1990   90m   Technicolor
Channel 4/Working Title (Sarah Cellan Jones, Alison Jackson)

A former convict, chased by police and gangsters after he gains possession of an MP's stolen briefcase containing details of shady deals, falls in love with an upper-class heroin addict.

A fast-paced thriller, with a little romance thrown in, acted and directed with verve.

wd Tunde Ikoli   ph Peter Sinclair   m Colin Towns   pd Hugo Luczyc-Wyhowski   ed Angus Newton

Charlie Cain, Rosalind Bennett, Patrick Malahide, Connie Booth, Rudolph Walker, John Elmes, James Saxon, Geoffrey Palmer, Trevor Laird, Thomas Craig

The Small Back Room **

GB 1949 106m bw
London Films/The Archers
V*
US title: *Hour of Glory*

A bomb expert with a lame foot and a drink problem risks his life dismantling a booby bomb and returns to his long-suffering girlfriend.

Rather gloomy suspense thriller with ineffective personal aspects but well-made location sequences and a fascinating background of boffins at work in post-war London.

wd Michael Powell, Emeric Pressburger *novel* Nigel Balchin *ph* Christopher Challis *m* Brian Easdale

David Farrar, Kathleen Byron, Jack Hawkins, Leslie Banks, Robert Morley, Cyril Cusack

'The film as a whole can be recommended as unusually adult entertainment, notable for some admirable writing and acting.' – *Campbell Dixon*

'An exceptionally well-told story.' – *Dilys Powell*

Small Change *

France 1976 105m Eastmancolor
Films du Carosse/Artistes Associés (Marcel Berbert, Roland Thenot)
V*, L
original title: *L'Argent de Poche*

Linked incidents affecting a class of small boys in provincial France.

Competent if rather ordinary little portmanteau which one can't imagine adults actually paying to see.

w François Truffaut, Susan Schiffman *d* François Truffaut *ph* Pierre-William Glenn *m* Maurice Jaubert

Geory Desmouceaux, Philippe Goldman, Claudio Deluca

'Aside from the arrant sentimentality of much of Truffaut's text, the picture is depressed by the self-imitation of his film-making: the opening iris-in, the wipes. His eye for color has never been worse.' – *Stanley Kauffmann*

A Small Circle of Friends

US 1980 112m Technicolor
United Artists
V*

Adventures of Harvard men at the end of the sixties.

Comedy, sex, politics and melodrama are all ploughed into this tiresome and predictable mixture.

w Ezra Sacks *d* Rob Cohen

Brad Davis, Karen Allen, Jameson Parker, Shelley Long, John Friedrich

'Sacks' recreation of his college days relies on a mistaken belief that an audience will love his characters as much as they love each other.' – *John Pym, MFB*

Small Town Girl *

US 1936 90m bw
MGM (Hunt Stromberg)

A girl traps a handsome stranger into offering marriage when he's drunk, then sets out to win him when he's sober.

Thin but adequate romantic comedy, a good example of MGM's production line of the mid-thirties, with established star and character players helping upcoming talents.

w John Lee Mahin, Edith Fitzgerald *novel* Ben Ames Williams *d* William A. Wellman *ph* Oliver Marsh, Charles Rosher *m* Edward Ward

Janet Gaynor, Robert Taylor, James Stewart, Binnie Barnes, Frank Craven, Elizabeth Patterson, Lewis Stone, Andy Devine, Isabel Jewell, Charley Grapewin, Robert Greig, Agnes Ayres

Small Town Girl *

US 1953 93m Technicolor
MGM (Joe Pasternak)
V*, L

Musical remake of the above.

Willing hands make the most of it, but the songs are not the best.

w Dorothy Cooper, Dorothy Kingsley *d* Leslie Kardos *ph* Joseph Ruttenberg *songs* Leo Robin, Nicholas Brodszky *md* André Previn *ch* Busby Berkeley

Jane Powell, Farley Granger, *Bobby Van*, Ann Miller, Robert Keith, Billie Burke, S. Z. Sakall, Fay Wray, Nat King Cole

AAN: song 'My Flaming Heart'

A Small Town in Texas

US 1976 96m colour
AIP
V*

An ex-convict returns to his home town seeking revenge on those who framed him.

Unpleasant shock thriller with much violence.

w William Norton *d* Jack Starrett

Susan George, Timothy Bottoms, Bo Hopkins, Art Hindle

The Small Voice *

GB 1948 83m bw
British Lion/Constellation (Anthony Havelock-Allan)
US title: *Hideout*

Escaped convicts hold up a playwright and his wife in their country cottage.

Gripping, well-characterized version of a very well worn plot.

w Derek Neame, Julian Orde *novel* Robert Westerby *d* Fergus McDonell *ph* Stan Pavey

James Donald, Valerie Hobson, Howard Keel, David Greene, Michael Balfour, Joan Young

The Small World of Sammy Lee

GB 1962 107m bw
Bryanston/Seven Arts/Ken Hughes (Frank Godwin)

A small-time Soho crook tries desperately to raise money to pay off threatening bookies.

Overlong 'realist' comedy-melodrama based on a TV play and filled with low-life 'characters'; vivid but cursed with a tedious hero.

wd Ken Hughes *TV play* Ken Hughes *ph* Wolfgang Suschitzky *m* Kenny Graham *ad* Seamus Flannery

Anthony Newley, Julia Foster, Robert Stephens, Wilfrid Brambell, Warren Mitchell, Miriam Karlin, Kenneth J. Warren

The Smallest Show on Earth *

GB 1957 81m bw
British Lion/Launder and Gilliat (Michael Relph)
US title: *Big Time Operators*

Two young marrieds inherit a decayed cinema and make it pay.

Amiable caricature comedy with plenty of obvious jokes and a sentimental attachment to old cinemas but absolutely no conviction, little plot, and a very muddled sense of the line between farce and reality.

w William Rose, John Eldridge *d* Basil Dearden *ph* Douglas Slocombe *m* William Alwyn

Bill Travers, Virginia McKenna, Margaret Rutherford, Bernard Miles, Peter Sellers, Leslie Phillips, Francis de Wolff

Smart Blonde *

US 1936 57m bw
Warner

A female reporter beats the cops to the solution of a murder.

Slick second feature, first in the Torchy Blane series.

w Don Ryan, Kenneth Gamet, Frederick Nebel *d* Frank McDonald

Glenda Farrell, Barton MacLane, Wini Shaw, Craig Reynolds, Addison Richards, Jane Wyman

'Fairly well paced with gunplay, an amount of smart talk, but no mountings to mention.' – *Variety*

Smart Girl

US 1935 78m bw
Paramount (Walter Wanger)

Girls left orphaned and penniless get their men – each other's.

Very mild comedy.

w Frances Hyland, Wilson Collison *d* Aubrey Scotto

Ida Lupino, Kent Taylor, Gail Patrick, Joseph Cawthorn, Sidney Blackmer, Pinky Tomlin

Smart Girls Don't Talk

US 1948 81m bw
Warner

A society girl rats on her gangster boyfriend after her brother has been killed.

Flatly handled underworld melodrama, as uninteresting as its cast.

w William Sackheim *d* Richard Bare

Virginia Mayo, Bruce Bennett, Robert Hutton, Richard Rober, Tom D'Andrea

'A fool in love! A sap for women!'

Smart Money

US 1931 67m bw
Warner

A gambler hits the big time but finally goes to jail.

Rather ordinary crime drama, a distinct letdown for its star after *Little Caesar*.

w Kubec Glasmon, John Bright *story* Lucien Hubbard, Joseph Jackson *d* Alfred E. Green *ph* Robert Kurrie

Edward G. Robinson, James Cagney, Evalyn Knapp, Ralf Harolde, Noel Francis, Margaret Livingstone, Boris Karloff, Billy House

'It will have no trouble upholding its title at the box office.' – *Variety*

† This film marks the only teaming of Robinson and Cagney.

AAN: Lucien Hubbard, Joseph Jackson

Smart Woman

US 1948 93m bw
Monogram (Hal E. Chester)

A crafty lady lawyer becomes romantically involved with a crusading district attorney.

What to Monogram was a high-class production would have been a very routine programmer from anyone else.

w Alvah Bessie, Louise Morheim, Herbert Margolis *d* Edward A. Blatt *ph* Stanley Cortez *md* Constantin Bakaleinikoff *m* Louis Gruenberg

Constance Bennett, Brian Aherne, Barry Sullivan, Michael O'Shea, James Gleason, Otto Kruger, Isobel Elsom, Taylor Holmes, John Litel

Smash and Grab

GB 1937 76m bw
GFD/Jack Buchanan
US title: *Larceny Street*

A detective's wife helps him track down a criminal mastermind.

Agreeable star comedy.

w Ralph Spence   *d* Tim Whelan

Jack Buchanan, Elsie Randolph, Arthur Margetson, Antony Holles, Zoe Wynn, Edmund Willard, David Burns

Smash Palace *
New Zealand   1981   108m   colour
Aardvark Films
V*, L

The owner of a car-wrecking business goes to pieces when his wife leaves him.

Downbeat character study of the kind of psychopath who doesn't arouse much sympathy; but the film is well mounted.

wd Roger Donaldson

Bruno Lawrence, Anna Jemison, Keith Aberdein, Greer Robson

'May be the most melodramatic but also the most acutely motivated film yet about divorce.' – *Richard Schickel, Time*

Smash-up, The Story of a Woman
US   1947   113m   bw
Universal-International (Walter Wanger)
V*
GB title: *A Woman Destroyed*

The story of a lady alcoholic.

Tedious distaff side of *The Lost Weekend*.

w John Howard Lawson   *d* Stuart Heisler   *ph* Stanley Cortez   *m* Daniele Amfitheatrof

Susan Hayward, Lee Bowman, Eddie Albert, Marsha Hunt, Carl Esmond, Carleton Young, Charles D. Brown

AAN: original story (Dorothy Parker, Frank Cavett); Susan Hayward

Smashing the Money Ring
US   1939   57m   bw
Bryan Foy/First National/Warner

The Secret Service investigates gambling ships.

Fast-moving serial-like action.

w Anthony Coldeway, Raymond Shrock   *d* Terry Morse

Ronald Reagan, Eddie Foy Jnr, Margot Stevenson, Charles D. Brown

Smashing Time
GB   1967   96m   Eastmancolor
Paramount/Partisan/Carlo Ponti (Ray Millichip)

Two north country girls have farcical adventures in swinging London, including paint squirting and pie throwing.

Horrendous attempt to turn two unsuitable actresses into a female Laurel and Hardy; plenty of coarse vigour but no style or sympathy.

w George Melly   *d* Desmond Davis   *ph* Manny Wynn   *m* John Addison

Rita Tushingham, Lynn Redgrave, Ian Carmichael, Anna Quayle, Michael York, Irene Handl, Jeremy Lloyd

Smile *
US   1975   113m   DeLuxe
UA (Michael Ritchie)
V*, L

A bird's eye view of the Young Miss America pageant in a small California town.

A witty series of sketches in the form of a drama-documentary or satirical mosaic. Highly polished fun for those who can stay the course.

w Jerry Belson   *d* Michael Ritchie   *ph* Conrad Hall   *m* various

Bruce Dern, Barbara Feldon, Michael Kidd, Geoffrey Lewis, Nicholas Pryor

'A beady, precise, technically skilful movie.' – *Michael Billington, Illustrated London News*

Smiles of a Summer Night ***
Sweden   1955   105m   bw
Svensk Filmindustri
V*, L
original title: *Sommarnattens Leende*

A country lawyer meets again a touring actress who was once his mistress, and accepts an invitation for him and his young wife to stay at her mother's country home for a weekend.

Comedy of high period manners with an admirable detached viewpoint and elegant trappings. It later formed the basis of Stephen Sondheim's *A Little Night Music*, a stage musical which was later filmed.

wd Ingmar Bergman   *ph* Gunnar Fischer   *m* Erik Nordgren

Gunnar Bjornstrand, Eva Dahlbeck, Ulla Jacobsson, Harriet Andersson, Margit Carlquist, Naima Wifstrand, Jarl Kulle

Smiley *
GB   1956   97m   Technicolor   Cinemascope
TCF/London Films (Anthony Kimmins)

An adventurous Australian boy has various adventures and finally gets the bicycle he wants.

An open-air 'William'-type story for children, quite nicely done and generally refreshing. *Smiley Gets a Gun* was a less effective sequel.

w Moore Raymond, Anthony Kimmins   *novel* Moore Raymond   *d* Anthony Kimmins   *ph* Ted Scaife, Russ Wood   *m* William Alwyn

Colin Petersen, Ralph Richardson, Chips Rafferty, John McCallum

Smiley Gets a Gun
Australia   1958   90m   Technicolor   Cinemascope
Canberra Films

Smiley is promised a rifle if he can keep out of trouble.

Unexceptional sequel.

w Anthony Kimmins, Rex Rienits   *d* Anthony Kimmins

Keith Calvert, Bruce Archer, Sybil Thorndike, Chips Rafferty

Smilin' Through *
US   1932   97m   bw
MGM (Irving Thalberg)

Three generations of complications follow when a Victorian lady is accidentally killed by a jealous lover on her wedding day.

Archetypal sentimental romantic drama, wholly absorbing to the mass audience and extremely well done; originally a 1922 Norma Talmadge vehicle.

w Ernest Vajda, Claudine West, Donald Ogden Stewart, J. B. Fagan   *play* Jane Cowl, Jane Murfin   *d* Sidney Franklin   *ph* Lee Garmes   *m* William Axt

Norma Shearer, Leslie Howard, Fredric March, O. P. Heggie, Ralph Forbes, Beryl Mercer

'A big women's picture of tear-drawing power, done with satisfying sincerity by a cast which spells money.' – *Variety*

'A sensitive and beautiful production distinguished by excellent settings and rich photography.' – *New York Mirror*

AAN: best picture

Smilin' Through *
US   1941   100m   Technicolor
MGM (Victor Saville)
V*

Flat but adequate remake of the above.

w Donald Ogden Stewart, John Balderston   *d* Frank Borzage   *ph* Leonard Smith   *m* Herbert Stothart

Jeanette MacDonald, Gene Raymond, Brian Aherne, Ian Hunter, Frances Robinson, Patrick O'Moore

Smiling Along: see *Keep Smiling*

The Smiling Ghost
US   1941   71m   bw
Warner

A girl reporter solves a haunted house mystery.

Moderate comedy chiller with plenty going on.

w Kenneth Gamet   *d* Lewis Seiler

Alexis Smith, Wayne Morris, Brenda Marshall, Alan Hale, Willie Best, David Bruce, Helen Westley, Richard Ainley

'His intimate and roguish romance will break your heart – with love and laughter!'

The Smiling Lieutenant **
US   1931   88m   bw
Paramount (Ernst Lubitsch)

A Viennese guards officer leaves his mistress to become consort to a visiting princess.

A sophisticated soufflé in Lubitsch's best style, naughty but quite nice, with visual effects largely replacing dialogue.

w Ernest Vajda, Samson Raphaelson   *operetta* A Waltz Dream   *d* Ernst Lubitsch   *ph* George Folsey   *md* Adolph Deutsch   *m* Oscar Straus

Maurice Chevalier, Miriam Hopkins, Claudette Colbert, Charles Ruggles, George Barbier, Elizabeth Patterson

'Will delight smart audiences and figures to be liked well enough by the average fan. A good but not a smash picture.' – *Variety*

'All the shrewd delights that were promised in *The Love Parade* all realized with an economy and sureness that give it a luster which no other American-made comedy satire has achieved. One must look to *Le Million* to find its peer.' – *Richard Watts, New York Post*

AAN: best picture

Smithereens *
US   1982   90m   colour
Susan Seidelman
V*, L

Obsessed with becoming manager of a punk rock band, a young girl in New York drifts through a series of unsatisfactory encounters.

Unblinking account of empty lives, well done but ultimately depressing.

w Susan Seidelman, Ron Nyswaner, Peter Askin   *d* Susan Seidelman   *ph* Chirine El Khadem   *m* Glenn Mercer, Bill Million   *pd* Franz Harland   *ed* Susan Seidelman

Susan Berman, Brad Rinn, Richard Hell, Roger Jet

Smoke Jumpers: see *Red Skies of Montana*

Smokey and the Bandit *
US   1977   97m   Technicolor
Universal/Rastar (Robert L. Levy)
V, V*, L

A Georgia bootlegger on a mission picks up a girl in distress and is chased by her irate sheriff fiancé.

Frantic chase comedy full of car crashes and low lines: a surprise box-office smash.

w James Lee Barrett, Charles Shyer, Alan Mandel   *d* Hal Needham   *ph* Bobby Byrne   *m* Bill Justis, Jerry Reed, Art Feller

Burt Reynolds, Jackie Gleason, Sally Field, Jerry Reed, Mike Henry, Pat McCormick, Paul Williams

Smokey and the Bandit Ride Again: see *Smokey and the Bandit II*

Smokey and the Bandit II

US 1980 101m Technicolor
Universal/Rastar/Mort Engelberg
V*, L
GB title: Smokey and the Bandit Ride Again

A trucker is hired to take a pregnant elephant to the Republican convention.

More mindless chasing and crashing, with even less wit than before and rather more wholesale destruction.

w Jerry Belson, Brock Yates   d Hal Needham
ph Michael Butler   md Snuff Garrett

Burt Reynolds, Jackie Gleason, Sally Field, Jerry Reed, Dom DeLuise, Paul Williams

Smokey and the Bandit III

US 1983 88m Technicolor
Mort Engelberg/Universal
V*, L

Sheriff Justice mistakes an innocent driver for his old enemy.

A rather random car chase movie, obviously the last of a short line.

w Stuart Birnbaum, David Dashev   d Dick Lowry
ph James Pergola   m Larry Cansler   ad Ron Hobbs
ed Byron Brandt, David Blewitt, Christopher Greenbury

Jackie Gleason, Jerry Reed, Mike Henry, Pat McCormick, Burt Reynolds (for a cameo)

'A patchwork of arbitrary mayhem.' – Variety

Smoky

US 1946 87m Technicolor
TCF (Robert Bassler)

An especially independent horse virtually runs the ranch on which he lives.

Family saga of the great outdoors, well enough assembled.

w Dwight Cummings, Lillie Hayward, Dorothy Yost
novel Will James   d Louis King   ph Charles Clarke
md Emil Newman   m David Raksin

Fred MacMurray, Anne Baxter, Burl Ives, Bruce Cabot, Esther Dale

† The story was also made by Fox in 1933 with Victor Jory, and in 1966 with Fess Parker.

Smooth as Silk

US 1946 64m bw
Jack Bernhard/Universal

When his girlfriend jilts him, a criminal lawyer plans to murder her new sweetheart.

Watchable supporting feature.

w Dane Lussier, Kerry Shaw   d Charles Barton

Kent Taylor, Virginia Grey, Jane Adams, Milburn Stone, John Litel

Smooth Talk

US 1985 92m colour
Nepenthe/American Playhouse/Goldcrest (Martin Rosen)
V, V*, L

A mixed-up 15-year-old girl has a dangerous encounter with a mildly psychopathic male.

Unattractive scenario about thoroughly dislikeable people.

w Tom Cole   story Joyce Carol Oates   d Joyce Chopra   ph James Glennon   md James Taylor
m Bill Payne, Russ Kunkel, George Massenburg
pd David Wasco   ed Patrick Dodd

Treat Williams, Laura Dern, Mary Kay Place, Levon Helm

The Smugglers: see The Man Within

Smultronstället: see Wild Strawberries

SNAFU

US 1945 85m bw
Columbia
GB title: Welcome Home

Middle-class parents rescue their difficult 15-year-old son from the army, then wish they hadn't.

Predictable, well-greased comedy of a rebellious teenager.

w Louis Solomon, Harold Buchman   play Louis Solomon, Harold Buchman   d Jack Moss   ph Franz Planer   m Paul Sawtell

Robert Benchley, Vera Vague, Conrad Janis, Nanetta Parks

† The title can be bowdlerized as 'Situation Normal, All Fouled Up'.

The Snake Pit **

US 1948 108m bw
TCF (Anatole Litvak, Robert Bassler)
V*

A girl becomes mentally deranged and has horrifying experiences in an institution.

A headline-hitting film which made a stirring plea for more sympathetic treatment of mental illness. Very well made, and arrestingly acted, but somehow nobody's favourite movie.

w Frank Partos, Millen Brand   novel Mary Jane Ward   d Anatole Litvak   ph Leo Tover   m Alfred Newman

Olivia de Havilland, Leo Genn, Mark Stevens, Celeste Holm, Glenn Langan, Leif Erickson, Beulah Bondi, Lee Patrick, Natalie Schaefer

'A film of superficial veracity that requires a bigger man than Litvak; a good film with bad things.' – Herman G. Weinberg

† The British censor insisted on a foreword explaining that everyone in the film was an actor and that conditions in British mental hospitals were unlike those depicted.

AAN: best picture; script; Anatole Litvak; Alfred Newman; Olivia de Havilland

Snares: see Pièges

'We could tell you what it's about. But then, of course, we would have to kill you.'

Sneakers **

US 1992 125m DeLuxe
UIP/Universal (Walter F. Parkes, Lawrence Lasker)
V, V*, L, S

A group of oddball experts is hired to recover from a criminal mastermind an electronic device that can penetrate the government's most secure computer systems.

Enjoyable caper that pleasantly passes a couple of hours.

w Phil Alden Robinson, Lawrence Lasker, Walter F. Parkes   d Phil Alden Robinson   ph John Lindley
m James Horner   pd Patrizia von Brandenstein
ed Tom Rolf

Robert Redford, Dan Aykroyd, Ben Kingsley, Mary McDonnell, River Phoenix, Sidney Poitier, David Strathairn, James Earl Jones, Stephen Tobolowsky

'The mainstream pleasures it affords should appeal to just about all audience segments, save perhaps ultra-sophisticates and low-brow teens.' – Variety

'This isn't really a serious film. It's over-stretched and under-characterised, but watchable for all that if you don't find the techno aspects too depressing.' – Derek Malcolm, Guardian

The Sniper **

US 1952 87m bw
Columbia/Stanley Kramer (Edna and Edward Anhalt)

A psychopath kills a succession of blondes with a high-powered rifle.

Semi-documentary police drama which was quite startling and influential when released but seems quite routine now.

w Harry Brown   d Edward Dmytryk   ph Burnett Guffey   m George Antheil

Adolphe Menjou, Arthur Franz, Gerald Mohr, Richard Kiley, Frank Faylen, Marie Windsor

AAN: original story (Edna and Edward Anhalt)

Sniper *

US 1993 98m colour
Columbia TriStar/Baltimore (Robert L. Rosen)
V, V*, L

An experienced Marine sniper is joined by a novice on a dangerous assignment in Panama.

Familiar ingredients are expertly mixed to create a tense action picture.

w Michael Frost Beckner, Crash Leyland   d Luis Llosa   ph Bill Butler   m Gary Chang   pd Herbert Pinter   ed Scott Smith

Tom Berenger, Bill Zane, J. T. Walsh, Aden Young, Ken Radley, Reinaldo Arenas, Carlos Alvarez, Roy Edmonds

'An expertly directed, yet ultimately unsatisfying psychological thriller.' – Variety

The Snorkel

GB 1958 90m (GB), 74m (US) bw
Columbia/Hammer (Michael Carreras)

A man murders his wife and is given away by his observant young stepdaughter.

Tenuous suspenser which outstays its welcome.

w Peter Myers, Jimmy Sangster, Anthony Dawson
d Guy Green   ph Jack Asher   ad John Stoll
ed James Needs, Bill Lenney

Peter Van Eyck, Betta St John, Mandy Miller, William Franklyn, Grégoire Aslan

Snow Job: see The Ski Raiders

Snow Treasure

US 1968 95m Eastmancolor
Sagittarius (Irving Jacoby)

In Nazi-occupied Norway a teenage boy finds gold hidden in the snow; an underground agent helps him get it to safety.

Curiously undernourished but attractively made adventure film.

w Irving Jacoby, Peter Hansen   novel Marie McSwigan   d Irving Jacoby   ph Sverre Bergli
m Egil Monn-Iversen

James Franciscus, Paul Anstad, Paoul Oyen, Randi Borch

Snow White and the Seven Dwarfs ****

US 1937 82m Technicolor
Walt Disney
S

Disney's first feature cartoon, a mammoth enterprise which no one in the business thought would work. The romantic leads were wishy-washy but the splendid songs and the marvellous comic and villainous characters turned the film into a worldwide box-office bombshell which is almost as fresh today as when it was made.

w Ted Sears, Otto Englander, Earl Hurd, Dorothy Ann Blank, Richard Creedon, Dick Richard, Merrill de Maris, Webb Smith, from the fairy tale by the brothers Grimm   supervising director David Hand
m Frank Churchill, Leigh Harline, Paul Smith
songs Larry Morey, Frank Churchill

voices of Adriana Caselotti, Harry Stockwell, Lucille La Verne, Billy Gilbert

'The first full-length animated feature, the turning point in Disney's career, a milestone in film history, and a great film.' – *Leonard Maltin*

'Sustained fantasy, the animated cartoon grown up.' – *Otis Ferguson*

'The sort of film that happens once in a generation. It is as necessary a part of our film upbringing as *The Birth of a Nation* or *The Jazz Singer*. Crude, tentative, and born of compromise it may be, but it is still history in the making.' – *C. A. Lejeune*

AA: Special Award to Walt Disney for 'a significant screen innovation'. He was given one Oscar and seven miniature statuettes.

AAN: Frank Churchill, Leigh Harline, Paul Smith

Snow White and the Three Clowns: see *Snow White and the Three Stooges*

Snow White and the Three Stooges *
US   1961   107m   DeLuxe   Cinemascope
(TCF) Chanford (Charles Wick)
V*
GB title: *Snow White and the Three Clowns*

The old story retold as a vehicle for a champion skater and three veteran clowns.

Surprisingly tolerable as a holiday attraction, once you get over the shock.

w Noel Langley, Elwood Ullman   d Walter Lang
ph Leon Shamroy   m Lyn Murray   ad Jack Martin Smith, Maurice Ransford

Carol Heiss, Moe Howard, Larry Fine, Joe de Rita, Edson Stroll, Patricia Medina, Guy Rolfe, Buddy Baer, Edgar Barrier

Snowball Express
US   1972   99m   Technicolor
Walt Disney (Ron Miller)
V*

An insurance accountant inherits a dilapidated skiing hotel in the Colorado Rockies.

Uninspired family comedy with slapstick on the snow slopes.

w Don Tait, Jim Parker, Arnold Margolin
novel *Château Bon Vivant* by Frankie and John O'Rear
d Norman Tokar   ph Frank Phillips   m Robert F. Brunner

Dean Jones, Nancy Olson, Henry Morgan, Keenan Wynn, Mary Wickes, Johnny Whittaker

'As wholesome and bland as that old American favourite the peanut butter and jelly sandwich.' – *MFB*

Snowbound
GB   1948   87m   bw
GFD/Gainsborough

Various people congregate at a ski hut in the Swiss Alps; all are after buried Nazi loot.

A rather foolish story which provides little in the way of action but at least assembles a fine crop of character actors.

w David Evans, Keith Campbell   novel *The Lonely Skier* by Hammond Innes   d David MacDonald
ph Stephen Dade

Robert Newton, Dennis Price, Herbert Lom, Stanley Holloway, Marcel Dalio, Mila Parely, Guy Middleton

'Out of one masterpiece, another has been created!'
The Snows of Kilimanjaro **
US   1952   117m   Technicolor
TCF (Darryl F. Zanuck)
V, V*

A hunter lies wounded in Africa and while waiting for help looks back over his life and loves.

Hollywood version of a portable Hemingway, with reminiscences of several novels stirred into a lush and sprawling mix of action and romance, open spaces

and smart salons. A big popular star film of its time, despite constricted and unconvincing characters.

w Casey Robinson   story Ernest Hemingway
d Henry King   ph Leon Shamroy   m Bernard Herrmann   ad Lyle Wheeler, John DeCuir

Gregory Peck, Susan Hayward, Ava Gardner, Hildegard Neff, Leo G. Carroll, Torin Thatcher, Marcel Dalio

'A naïve kind of success story with a conventional boy-meets-lots-of-girls plot.' – *Karel Reisz*

'The succinct and vivid qualities associated with Hemingway are rarely evoked, and what has been substituted is for the most part meandering, pretentious and more or less maudlin romance.' – *Newsweek*

AAN: Leon Shamroy; art direction

So Big *
US   1932   80m   bw
Warner (Lucien Hubbard)

A schoolteacher marries a farmer, has trouble with her son, falls in love with a sculptor.

Watchable, superficial, top-talented adaptation of a best-seller, first filmed in 1925 with Colleen Moore.

w J. Grubb Alexander, Robert Lord   novel Edna Ferber   d William Wellman   ph Sid Hickox
m W. Franke Harling

Barbara Stanwyck, George Brent, Dickie Moore, Guy Kibbee, Bette Davis, Hardie Albright

'Too long getting started, and only has moments towards the end . . . somewhat of a bore for the major part of its footage.' – *Variety*

So Big
US   1953   101m   bw
Warner (Henry Blanke)

By the time this inflated remake came along, the story was just too corny despite careful production.

w John Twist   d Robert Wise   ph Ellsworth Fredericks   m Max Steiner

Jane Wyman, Sterling Hayden, Richard Beymer, Nancy Olson, Steve Forrest, Elizabeth Fraser, Martha Hyer

So Bright the Flame: see *The Girl in White*

So Dark the Night *
US   1946   71m   bw
Columbia

A detective tracks down a murderer whom he finds to be himself.

Smart second feature with a likeable leading performance.

w Aubrey Wisberg, Martin Berkeley, Dwight Babcock   d Joseph H. Lewis   m Hugo Friedhofer

Steven Geray, Ann Codee, Micheleine Cheirel

So Dear to My Heart *
US   1948   84m   Technicolor
Walt Disney
V*, L

Life on a country farm in 1903

Live action nostalgia with a few cartoon segments; well enough done, but mainly appealing to well brought up children.

w John Tucker Battle   novel *Midnight and Jeremiah* by Sterling North   d Harold Schuster   ph Winton C. Hoch   m Paul Smith

Burl Ives, Beulah Bondi, Harry Carey, Luana Patten, Bobby Driscoll

AAN: song 'Lavender Blue' (m Eliot Daniel, ly Larry Morey)

So Ends Our Night *
US   1941   120m   bw
UA (David L. Loew, Albert Lewin)

Refugees from Nazi Germany are driven from country to country and meet persecution everywhere.

Worthy but rather drab and unfocused melodrama from the headlines.

w Talbot Jennings   novel *Flotsam* by Erich Maria Remarque   d John Cromwell   ph William Daniels
m Louis Gruenberg

Fredric March, Margaret Sullavan, Glenn Ford, Frances Dee, Anna Sten, Erich von Stroheim, Joseph Cawthorn, Leonid Kinskey, Alexander Granach, Sig Rumann

'It ought to be a great picture but it isn't.' – *Archer Winsten, New York Post*

AAN: Louis Gruenberg

So Evil My Love *
GB   1948   100m   bw
Paramount (Hal B. Wallis)

A missionary's widow is enticed into a life of crime and immorality by a scoundrelly artist.

Curious Victorian melodrama with a Wildean flavour; doesn't quite come off.

w Leonard Spigelgass, Ronald Miller   novel Joseph Shearing   d Lewis Allen   ph Max Greene
m Victor Young, William Alwyn

Ray Milland, Ann Todd, Geraldine Fitzgerald, Leo G. Carroll, Raymond Huntley, Martita Hunt, Moira Lister, Raymond Lovell, Muriel Aked, Finlay Currie, Hugh Griffith

'There's only one thing that can keep them apart – the seven-foot thing she's married to!'
So Fine
US   1981   91m   Technicolor
Warner/Lobell – Bergman (Mike Lobell)
V*

A professor of literature trying to save his father from gangsters becomes involved in strange adventures.

Weirdly titled action comedy which tries to be far too clever for its own good.

wd Andrew Bergman   ph James A. Contner
m Ennio Morricone

Ryan O'Neal, Jack Warden, Mariangela Melato, Richard Kiel, Fred Gwynne, Mike Kellin

'A visual insult, crudely lighted and framed, and jumping out at you.' – *Pauline Kael, New Yorker*

So Goes My Love
US   1946   88m   bw
U-I (Jack H. Skirball, Bruce Manning)
GB title: *A Genius in the Family*

The domestic life of inventor Hiram Maxim.

Formula period family film with pleasant moments.

w Bruce Manning, James Clifden   d Frank Ryan
ph Joseph Valentine   m Hans Salter

Myrna Loy, Don Ameche, Rhys Williams, Bobby Driscoll, Richard Gaines

'For Harriet, the honeymoon was her best yet. For Charles, it was a pain in the neck.'
So I Married an Axe Murderer
US   1993   92m   Technicolor
TriStar/Fried/Woods Films
S

A poet suspects that his newly married wife, a butcher, is a serial killer of husbands.

Slight and slightly amusing comedy, parodying Hitchcock with some sophistication and moderate success.

w Robbie Fox *d* Thomas Schlamme *ph* Julio Macat *m* Bruce Broughton *pd* John Graysmark *ed* Richard Halsey, Colleen Halsey

Mike Myers, Nancy Travis, Anthony LaPaglia, Amanda Plummer, Brenda Fricker, Matt Doherty, Charles Grodin, Phil Hartman

'A hip slice of life about the dilemma of marital commitment with just a pinch of Hitchcock providing a cutting edge. Fueled by an anarchic style and a winning cast, it looks like an appealing commercial prospect.' – *Variety*

'An inconsequential, light-hearted black comedy populated by San Francisco eccentrics.' – *Philip French, Observer*

So Little Time

GB   1952   88m   bw
ABP/Mayflower (Aubrey Baring, Maxwell Setton)

In occupied Belgium an aristocratic lady falls in love with a Nazi colonel.

Doomed love story with musical accompaniment; tolerable but slow.

w John Cresswell *d* Compton Bennett *ph* Oswald Morris *m* Robert Gill

Marius Goring, Maria Schell, Gabrielle Dorziat, Barbara Mullen

So Long at the Fair *

GB   1950   86m   bw
Rank/Gainsborough/Sydney Box (Betty E. Box)

During the 1889 Paris Exposition a girl books into a hotel with her brother, and next day finds that he has totally disappeared and his existence is denied by all concerned.

Straightforward version of an old yarn which has turned up in such varied forms as *The Lady Vanishes* and *Bunny Lake is Missing*. This modest production is pleasant enough but badly lacks drive.

w Hugh Mills, Anthony Thorne *d* Terence Fisher, Anthony Darnborough *ph* Reginald Wyer *m* Benjamin Frankel *ad* Cedric Dawe

Jean Simmons, Dirk Bogarde, David Tomlinson, Marcel Poncin, Cathleen Nesbitt, Honor Blackman, Betty Warren, Felix Aylmer, André Morell

'A foxhole was her honeymoon hotel!'
'The first great story of our women at the fighting front!'
So Proudly We Hail *

US   1943   125m   bw
Paramount (Mark Sandrich)

The self-sacrifice of war nurses in the Pacific.

Fairly harrowing and well-meant but studio-bound and unconvincing flagwaver.

w Allan Scott *d* Mark Sandrich *ph* Charles Lang *m* Miklos Rozsa

Claudette Colbert, Paulette Goddard, Veronica Lake, George Reeves, Barbara Britton, Walter Abel, Sonny Tufts, John Litel

'Probably the most deadly accurate picture ever made of what war looks like through the lenses of a housewives' magazine romance.' – *James Agee*

'The stars are devotedly, almost gallantly, deglamorized and dishevelled but they cannot escape the smell of studio varnish.' – *Richard Winnington*

AAN: Allan Scott; Charles Lang; Paulette Goddard

'The flower of southern chivalry dewed with the shining glory of a woman's tears!'
So Red the Rose *

US   1935   82m   bw
Paramount (Douglas MacLean)

The life of a Southern family during the Civil War.

Quiet, pleasing historical romance.

w Laurence Stallings, Maxwell Anderson, Edwin Justus Mayer *novel* Stark Young *d* King Vidor *ph* Victor Milner *m* W. Franke Harling

Margaret Sullavan, Randolph Scott, Walter Connolly, Elizabeth Patterson, Janet Beecher, Robert Cummings

'Certain to go better in the Dixie belt than north, but okay on average.' – *Variety*

So This Is London

GB   1939   89m   bw
TCF

An American magnate visits his English rival, and romance springs up between their children.

Brightish comedy with a fair scattering of funny lines.

w William Conselman, Ben Travers, Tom Phipps, Douglas Furber *d* Thornton Freeland

Robertson Hare, Alfred Drayton, George Sanders, Berton Churchill, Fay Compton, Carla Lehmann, Stewart Granger, Ethel Revnell, Gracie West

So This Is Love

US   1953   101m   Technicolor
Warner (Henry Blanke)
GB title: *The Grace Moore Story*

Events leading up to Grace Moore's debut at the Metropolitan Opera in 1928.

Acceptable musical biopic full of the usual Hollywood contrivances.

w John Monks Jnr *autobiography* Grace Moore *d* Gordon Douglas *ph* Robert Burks *md* Ray Heindorf, Max Steiner *ch* Le Roy Prinz *ad* Edward Carrere

Kathryn Grayson, Merv Griffin, Joan Weldon, Walter Abel, Rosemary de Camp, Jeff Donnell, Douglas Dick, Mabel Albertson, Fortunio Bonanova

So This Is New York *

US   1948   78m   bw
Enterprise/Stanley Kramer

In 1919 some country cousins who have come into money have a big time in the gay city.

Curious, sporadically effective, silent-style comedy which doesn't quite come off.

w Carl Foreman, Herbert Baker *novel* *The Big Town* by Ring Lardner *d* Richard Fleischer *ph* Jack Russell *m* Dimitri Tiomkin

Henry Morgan, Rudy Vallee, Hugh Herbert, Bill Goodwin, Virginia Grey, Dona Drake, Leo Gorcey

So This Is Paris

US   1954   96m   Technicolor
U-I (Albert J. Cohen)
V*

Three American sailors on leave in Paris meet girls and help war orphans.

Very thin imitation of *On the Town*, bogged down by sentimentality and lack of sparkle. The musical numbers, however, are not bad.

w Charles Hoffman *d* Richard Quine *ph* Maury Gertsman *md* Joseph Gershenson *ch* Gene Nelson, Lee Scott

Tony Curtis, Gloria de Haven, Gene Nelson, *Corinne Calvet*, Paul Gilbert, Mara Corday, Allison Hayes

So Well Remembered *

GB   1947   114m   bw
RKO/Alliance (Adrian Scott)
L

The ambitious daughter of a mill-owner marries a rising politician but almost ruins his life.

Rather routine treatment of a three-decker north country novel; humdrum incident and unsympathetic characters, but full of minor British virtues.

w John Paxton *novel* James Hilton *d* Edward Dmytryk *ph* Frederick A. Young

John Mills, Martha Scott, Trevor Howard, Patricia Roc, Richard Carlson

'The occasional slackness of narrative is atoned for by a strongly communicated sense of place: the mean streets shining with rain, the sullen suffocated houses.' – *Dilys Powell, Sunday Times*

Soak the Rich *

US   1935   74m   bw
Paramount (Ben Hecht, Charles MacArthur)

A rebellious rich girl is cured when she is rescued from kidnapping.

Smartly written social comedy-melodrama.

wd Ben Hecht, Charles MacArthur *ph* Leon Shamroy

Walter Connolly, John Howard, Mary Taylor, Lionel Stander, Ilka Chase

'Hecht and MacArthur have not been very successful in their attempts to gauge public opinion . . . inadequate entertainment.' – *Variety*

Soapdish *

US   1991   97m   Technicolor
UIP/Paramount (Aaron Spelling, Alan Greisman)
V, V*, L, S

A jealous co-star tries to sabotage the popularity of America's most popular star of a daily soap-opera.

Fitfully amusing parody of a TV soap, but one that failed to find much of an audience.

w Robert Harling, Andrew Bergman *d* Michael Hoffman *ph* Ueli Steiger *m* Alan Silvestri *pd* Eugenio Zanetti *ed* Garth Craven

Sally Field, Kevin Kline, Robert Downey Jnr, Whoopi Goldberg, Carrie Fisher, Cathy Moriarty, Teri Hatcher, Paul Johansson, Elisabeth Shue, Garry Marshall

'An amiable comedy with enough one-liners to keep the chuckles coming regularly.' – *Sight and Sound*

Social Register

US   1934   71m   bw
Columbia (William de Mille)

A chorus girl fights the prejudices of her in-laws to be.

Dull and obvious romantic drama mainly notable for its cast, and for the star who failed to make a comeback.

w Clara Beranger, Anita Loos, John Emerson *d* Marshall Neilan

Colleen Moore, Charles Winninger, Pauline Frederick, Alexander Kirkland, Robert Benchley, Ross Alexander

'Good players lost in a trite story.' – *Variety*

Society

US   1989   99m   colour
Medusa/Society Productions/Wild Street Pictures (Keith Walley)
V

A student discovers that his wealthy parents and friends are shape-shifting monsters who devour the poor.

Weird allegory of class warfare that contains stomach-turning special effects.

w Woody Keith, Rick Fry *d* Brian Yuzna *ph* Rick Fichter *m* Mark Ryder, Phil Davies *pd* Mathew C. Jacobs *sp* Screaming Mad George *ed* Peter Teschner

Bill Warlock, Devin DeVasquez, Evan Richards, Ben Meyerson, Charles Lucia, Connie Danese, Patrice Jennings

'One of the most extraordinary genre debuts of the 80s.' – *MFB*

Society Doctor
US   1935   63m   bw
MGM (Lucien Hubbard)
GB title: *After Eight Hours*

A doctor's modern ideas incur hostility: he goes into
private practice, but returning to the hospital is
wounded by a gangster and supervises his own
operation under spinal anaesthetic.

Melodramatic hokum with most attention going to the
second male lead, the young and rising Robert Taylor.

w Sam Marx, Michael Fessier   *novel The Harbor* by
Theodore Reeves   *d* George B. Seitz   *ph* Lester
White   *m* Oscar Radin

Chester Morris, Virginia Bruce, Robert Taylor, Billie
Burke, Raymond Walburn, Henry Kolker, William
Henry

Society Girl
US   1932   72m   bw
Fox

A prizefighter falls for a society girl.

Weak melodrama whose best scenes are in the ring.

w Charles Benhan, Elmer Harris   *play* John Larkin
Jnr   *d* Sidney Lanfield

James Dunn, Spencer Tracy, Peggy Shannon, Walter
Byron, Marjorie Gateson

'Falls short of first-rate classification.' – *Variety*

Society Lawyer
US   1939   77m   bw
MGM (John W. Considine Jnr)

A lawyer is embarrassed by the gratitude of a
racketeer.

Tolerable co-feature with class production.

w Frances Goodrich, Albert Hackett, Leon Gordon,
Hugo Butler   *d* Edwin L. Marin

Walter Pidgeon, Virginia Bruce, Leo Carrillo, Eduardo
Ciannelli, Lee Bowman, Herbert Mundin

'Fairish murder mystery with sophisticated
background. For duals.' – *Variety*

Sodom and Gomorrah
Italy/France   1962   154m   colour
Titanus/S. N. Pathé (Gottfredo Lombardo)
S

Lot and the Hebrews become involved in a Helamite
plan to take over the rich sinful cities of Sodom and
Gomorrah.

Dreary biblical blood-and-thunder; an international
muddle, tedious in the extreme outside a few
hilariously misjudged moments.

w Hugo Butler, Giorgio Prosperi   *d* Robert Aldrich
ph Silvano Ippoliti, Cyril Knowles   *m* Miklos Rozsa
ad Ken Adam

Stewart Granger, Stanley Baker, Pier Angeli, Anouk
Aimée, Rossana Podesta

Sofie *
Denmark/Norway/Sweden   1992   152m   colour
Arrow/Nordisk/Norsk/Svensk Filmindustri (Lars Kolvig)
V

In Copenhagen in the 1890s, a Jewish woman is
forced by her family to reject her non-Jewish admirer
and move away from the city to marry a cousin who
goes slowly mad.

A well-acted, long domestic saga that follows
changing attitudes across three generations, from
Sofie's parents, anxious to be anonymous in a larger
society while preserving their own way of life, to
Sofie, wanting to break away but unable to do so, to
her son, who rejects the old traditions; it is
nevertheless at its most affecting when depicting the
pleasures of Sofie's parents rather than the miseries of
her own mismatch.

w Liv Ullman, Peter Poulsen   *novel Mendel Philipsen
and Son* by Henri Nathansen   *d* Liv Ullman
ph Jörgen Persson   *pd* Peter Hoimark   *ed* Grete
Moldrup

Karen-Lise Mynster, Ghita Norby, Erland Josephson,
Jesper Christensen, Torben Zeller, Henning Moritzen,
Stig Hoffmeyer, Kirsten Rolffes

'Lurches regrettably towards the gratuitous
miserablism of Bergmanesque stereotype.' – *Sight and
Sound*

Soft Beds, Hard Battles
GB   1973   107m   colour
Rank/Charter (John Boulting)
US title: *Undercovers Hero*

Inhabitants of a Paris brothel help to win World War
II.

Ragbag of poor sketches and dirty jokes, with the star
in several ineffective roles including Hitler.

w Leo Marks, Roy Boulting   *d* Roy Boulting
ph Gil Taylor   *m* Neil Rhoden

Peter Sellers, Lila Kedrova, Curt Jurgens, Gabriella
Licudi, Jenny Hanley

'A Motorvated Comedy.'
'They're going to make it. Nothing will stop them now …'

Soft Top, Hard Shoulder *
GB   1992   95m   colour
Feature/Road Movie Productions (Richard Holmes)

An unsuccessful Scottish artist living in London has
36 hours to drive to Glasgow in his ancient car so that
he can share in the family fortune; on the way he
picks up a female hitch-hiker.

Amiable, soft-centred road movie with an affection for
eccentricity.

w Peter Capaldi   *d* Stefan Schwartz   *ph* Henry
Braham   *m* Chris Rea   *pd* Sonja Klaus   *ed* Derek
Trigg

Peter Capaldi, Frances Barber, Catherine Russell,
Jeremy Northam, Richard Wilson, Peter Ferninando,
Simon Callow, Phyllis Logan

'The initial novelty of this particular roadshow
ultimately pales.' – *Empire*

Soigne Ton Gauche *
France   1937   12m   bw
Cady (Fred Orain)
V

A boxing training session in a village ends in chaos.

A gentle short comedy from Tati, revealing his
pleasure in the eccentric details of life.

w Jean Marie Huard   *d* René Clément   *m* Jean
Yatove

Jacques Tati, Max Martell, Robur Cliville

† It was released on video together with *L'École des
Facteurs* and *Cours du Soir* under the title *Tati Shorts*.

Sol Madrid
US   1968   90m   Metrocolor   Panavision
MGM/Gershwin-Kastner (Hall Bartlett)
GB title: *The Heroin Gang*

An undercover narcotics agent is assigned to track
down an elusive Mafia executive.

Humdrum, predictable, brutishly violent international
crime caper.

w David Karp   *novel Fruit of the Poppy* by Robert
Wilder   *d* Brian G. Hutton   *ph* Fred Koenekamp
m Lalo Schifrin

David McCallum, Telly Savalas, Stella Stevens,
Ricardo Montalban, Rip Torn, Pat Hingle, Paul Lukas,
Perry Lopez, Michael Ansara

Solange Du da bist: see *As Long as You're Near Me*

Solar Crisis
US/Japan   1992   107m   DeLuxe
Trimark/Gakken/NHK (Richard Edlund, James Nelson, Morris
Morishima)
V, V*

A power-crazed industrialist plans to sabotage Earth's
last hope: a spaceship carrying an anti-matter bomb to
the sun in order to prevent a massive flare from
burning up the planet.

Dire science-fiction extravaganza; the banality of the
plot is exceeded only by the stupidity of the dialogue.

w Joe Gannon, Crispan Bolt   *novel* Takeshi Kawata
d Alan Smithee (Richard Sarafian)   *ph* Russ
Carpenter   *m* Maurice Jarre, Michael Boddicker
pd George Jenson   *sp* Neil Krepela   *ed* Richard
Trevor

Tim Matheson, Charlton Heston, Peter Boyle,
Annabel Schofield, Corin 'Corky' Nemec, Tetsuya
Bessho, Jack Palance, David Ursin, Brenda Bakke,
Paul Williams (voice)

† The movie cost $35 million. It was released direct to
video in Britain.

Solar Warriors
US   1986   94m   colour
MBM/Brooksfilms (Irene Walzer, Jack Frost Sanders)
V*, L
US title: *Solarbabies*

In a future world where water is scarce, a gang of
roller-skating teenagers rebel against authority with
the aid of a mystic ball.

Ludicrous science fiction adventure that lacks
invention, style and plausibility.

w Walon Green, Douglas Anthony Metrov   *d* Alan
Johnson   *ph* Peter MacDonald   *m* Maurice Jarre
pd Anthony Pratt   *ed* Conrad Buff

Richard Jordan, Jami Gertz, Jason Patric, Lukas Haas,
James Le Gros, Claude Brooks, Peter DeLuise, Sarah
Douglas, Charles Durning

Solarbabies: see *Solar Warriors*

'The planet where nightmares come true …'
Solaris **
USSR   1972   165m   Sovcolor   'Scope
Mosfilm
V, V*, L

A psychologist is sent to investigate the many deaths
in a space station orbiting a remote planet.

Heavy-going but highly imaginative space fiction in
which the menaces are ghosts materialized from the
subjects' guilty pasts. The technology is superbly
managed, but the whole thing is rather humourless.

w Andrei Tarkovsky, Friedrich Gorenstein
novel Stanislaw Lem   *d* Andrei Tarkovsky
ph Vadim Yusov   *m* Eduard Artemyev

Natalya Bondarchuk, Donatas Banionis, Yuri Yarvet

The Soldier and the Lady *
US   1937   85m   bw
RKO (Pandro S. Berman)
GB title: *Michael Strogoff*

In Napoleonic times, a messenger from the Czar sees
more trouble than he expected.

Mildly ambitious swashbuckler from a story much
remade in Europe; the elements jelled quite well in
the Hollywood fashion.

w Mortimer Offner, Anthony Veiller and Anne
Morrison Chapin   *novel* Jules Verne   *d* George
Nicholls Jnr   *ph* Joseph H. August

Anton Walbrook, Elizabeth Allan, Akim Tamiroff

'Spectacle film lacking strength and names. Will have
its troubles.' – *Variety*

† Exteriors were taken from a German/French film of
1936, *Courier to the Star*.

'Stained with the blood of the innocent!'

Soldier Blue *

US   1970   114m   Technicolor   Panavision
Avco (Gabriel Katzka, Harold Loeb)
V, V*, S

A paymaster's detachment of the US cavalry is attacked by Indians seeking gold, and two white survivors trek through the desert.

Extremely violent 'anti-violence' Western with a particularly nauseating climax following clichés all the way. From a director with pretensions.

w John Gay   novel Arrow in the Sun by Theodore V. Olsen   d Ralph Nelson   ph Robert Hauser   m Roy Budd

Candice Bergen, Peter Strauss, Donald Pleasence

'One is more likely to be sickened by the film itself than by the wrongs it tries to right.' – Tom Milne

Soldier in the Rain

US   1963   87m   bw
AA/Cedar/Solar (Martin Jurow)
V*

Two army sergeants have wild plans for their demob, but one dies.

Curious sentimental tragi-comedy which misfires on all cylinders.

w Blake Edwards, Maurice Richlin   novel William Goldman   d Ralph Nelson   ph Philip Lathrop   m Henry Mancini

Steve McQueen, Jackie Gleason, Tuesday Weld, Tony Bill, Tom Poston, Ed Nelson, John Hubbard

Soldier of Fortune *

US   1955   96m   DeLuxe   Cinemascope
TCF (Buddy Adler)
V*

When a photographer disappears in Red China, his wife comes to Hong Kong to institute a search, enlists the aid of an amiable smuggler.

Cheerful Boy's Own Paper adventure romance with attractive locations and some silly anti-Red dialogue.

w Ernest K. Gann   novel Ernest K. Gann   d Edward Dmytryk   ph Leo Tover   m Hugo Friedhofer

Clark Gable, Susan Hayward, Gene Barry, Alex D'Arcy, Michael Rennie, Tom Tully, Anna Sten, Russell Collins, Leo Gordon

'A very good adventure film but not one of the Gable smashes.' – Hollywood Reporter

Soldiers of the King

GB   1933   80m   bw
Gainsborough

A guards lieutenant causes trouble when he wants to marry a music hall star.

Sprightly star vehicle with all talents in good form.

w J. O. C. Orton, Jack Hulbert, W. P. Lipscomb   d Maurice Elvey

Cicely Courtneidge, Edward Everett Horton, Anthony Bushell, Frank Cellier, Dorothy Hyson, Leslie Sarony

A Soldier's Story *

US   1984   101m   Metrocolor
Columbia/Delphi (Norman Jewison, Patrick Palmer)
V, V*, L

In 1944 Louisiana, a hated sergeant at a small army post is shot dead.

Investigative melodrama on the old lines of Boomerang; quite watchable and well acted.

w Charles Fuller   play Charles Fuller   d Norman Jewison   ph Russell Boyd   m Herbie Hancock

Howard E. Rollins Jnr, Adolph Caesar, Art Evans, David Alan Grier, David Harris, Denzel Washington

AAN: best picture; Adolph Caesar (supporting actor); adapted screenplay

Soldiers Three

US   1951   87m   bw
MGM (Pandro S. Berman)

Adventures of three roistering British officers on the North-West Frontier.

A kind of unofficial remake of Gunga Din without the title character; one suspects it was meant seriously and found to be so bad that the only way out was strenuously to play it for laughs.

w Marguerite Roberts, Tom Reed, Malcolm Stuart Boylan   d Tay Garnett   ph William Mellor   m Adolph Deutsch

Stewart Granger, David Niven, Robert Newton, Walter Pidgeon, Cyril Cusack, Greta Gynt, Frank Allenby, Robert Coote, Dan O'Herlihy

'Kipling fans will probably have a fit but my guess is that it will have most people in fits of laughter.' – Daily Mail

Il sole anche di notte: see Night Sun

The Solid Gold Cadillac **

US   1956   99m   bw
Columbia (Fred Kohlmar)
V

A very minor stockholder upsets the crooked board of a large corporation.

Vaguely Capraesque comedy which begins brightly but peters out; performances sustain passing interest.

w Abe Burrows   play George S. Kaufman, Howard Teichmann   d Richard Quine   ph Charles Lang   m Cyril Mockridge   ad Ross Bellah

Judy Holliday, Paul Douglas, John Williams, Fred Clark, Hiram Sherman, Neva Patterson, Ralph Dumke, Ray Collins, Arthur O'Connell

AAN: art direction

The Solitaire Man *

US   1933   68m   bw
MGM

Crooks doublecross each other on a Paris-London aeroplane.

Smart little comedy with top talent.

w James Kevin McGuinness   play Bella and Samuel Spewack   d Jack Conway

Herbert Marshall, Elizabeth Allan, Mary Boland, Lionel Atwill, May Robson, Ralph Forbes

'Diverting crook melodrama in the drawing room manner . . . a lot better than the grosses it will probably get.' – Variety

I Soliti Ignoti: see Persons Unknown

'Only once in 3000 years – anything like it!'

Solomon and Sheba

US   1959   142m   Super Technirama 70
UA/Edward Small (Ted Richmond)
V*, L, S

When David names his younger son as heir, his older son plots revenge.

Dullish biblical spectacle, alternating between pretentiousness and cowboys and Indians.

w Anthony Veiller, Paul Dudley, George Bruce   d King Vidor   ph Frederick A. Young   m Mario Nascimbene   ad Richard Day, Alfred Sweeney

Yul Brynner, Gina Lollobrigida, George Sanders, Marisa Pavan, David Farrar, John Crawford, Laurence Naismith, Alejandro Rey, Harry Andrews

'Penance is due.' – Hollis Alpert

'Watch out it doesn't put you to sleep.' – New York Times

Sombrero

US   1953   103m   Technicolor
MGM (Jack Cummings)

Two Mexican villages feud over the burial place of a famous poet.

Rather self-consciously unusual musical which never catches fire but certainly keeps one watching its incredible mixture of music and melodrama.

w Norman Foster, Josefina Niggli   novel A Mexican Village by Josefina Niggli   d Norman Foster   ph Ray June   m Leo Arnaud

Ricardo Montalban, Pier Angeli, Yvonne de Carlo, Nina Foch, Cyd Charisse, Rick Jason, Jose Greco, Thomas Gomez, Kurt Kasznar, Walter Hampden, John Abbott

'Staggering is the only word for the hokum of this extraordinary film.' – Gavin Lambert

Some Call It Loving

US   1973   103m   Technicolor
Pleasant Pastures/James B. Harris
V*

A young man buys a 'sleeping beauty' at a fair but is sorry when he wakes her up.

Fashionable fantasy, amplified from a slender, winning short story.

wd James B. Harris   story Sleeping Beauty by John Collier   ph Mario Tosi   m Richard Hazard

Zalman King, Carol White, Tisa Farrow, Richard Pryor, Veronica Anderson

Some Came Running

US   1958   136m   Metrocolor   Cinemascope
MGM/Sol C. Siegel
V*, L, S

A disillusioned writer returns after service to his home town and takes up with a gambler and a prostitute.

Strident and rather pointless melodrama with solid acting and production values.

w John Patrick, Arthur Sheekman   novel James Jones   d Vincente Minnelli   ph William H. Daniels   m Elmer Bernstein

Frank Sinatra, Dean Martin, Shirley Maclaine, Martha Hyer, Arthur Kennedy, Nancy Gates, Leora Dana

AAN: song 'To Love and Be Loved' (m James Van Heusen, ly Sammy Cahn); Shirley Maclaine; Martha Hyer; Arthur Kennedy

Some Girls: see Sisters

Some Girls Do

GB   1969   93m   Eastmancolor
Rank/Ashdown (Betty E. Box)

Bulldog Drummond traces the sabotage of a supersonic airliner to a gang of murderous women.

Abysmal spoof melodrama in the swinging sixties mould; a travesty of a famous character.

w David Osborn, Liz Charles-Williams   d Ralph Thomas   ph Ernest Steward   m Charles Blackwell

Richard Johnson, Daliah Lavi, Bebi Loncar, James Villiers, Sydne Rome, Robert Morley, Maurice Denham, Florence Desmond, Ronnie Stevens

Some Kind of a Nut

US   1969   89m   DeLuxe
UA/Mirisch/TFT/DFI (Walter Mirisch)

When a bank teller grows a beard because of an unsightly bee sting, he is thought to be flouting authority and his whole life changes.

Laboured, cliché-ridden anti-establishment comedy, a waste of the talent involved.

wd Garson Kanin   ph Burnett Guffey, Gerald Hirschfeld   m Johnny Mandel

Dick Van Dyke, Angie Dickinson, Rosemary Forsyth, Zohra Lampert, Elliot Reid, Dennis King

Some Kind of Hero

US   1981   97m   Movielab
Paramount (Howard W. Koch)
V, V*, L

After six years as a prisoner of the Vietcong, an army veteran returns home to find his life no bed of roses.

Weird mixture of comedy and melodrama which simply doesn't jell, especially when it tries to get earnest.

d James Kirkwood, Robert Boris   *novel* James Kirkwood   *d* Michael Pressman   *ph* King Baggot   *m* Patrick Williams   *ad* James L. Schoppe   *ed* Christopher Greenbury

Richard Pryor, Margot Kidder, Ray Sharkey, Ronny Cox, Lynne Moody, Olivia Cole

Some Kind of Wonderful

US   1987   95m   Technicolor   Panavision
Paramount (John Hughes)
V, V*, L, S

Girl meets boy, boy meets another girl, boy loses girl, boy gets first girl.

Teen romance pandering to its target audience: all adults are stupid and repressive and maturity and wisdom are to be found among the young. Its appeal will be limited to the immature.

w John Hughes   *d* Howard Deutch   *ph* Jan Kiesser   *m* Stephen Hague, John Musser   *pd* Josan Russo   *ed* Bud Smith, Scott Smith

Eric Stoltz, Mary Stuart Masterson, Craig Sheffer, John Ashton, Lea Thompson, Elias Koteas, Maddie Corman

'The killer-diller of all swing shows!'

Some Like It Hot

US   1939   65m   bw
Paramount (William C. Thomas)
TV reissue title: *Rhythm Romance*

A sideshow owner runs out of money.

Very mild comedy, one of several which helped to establish Hope's star potential.

w Lewis R. Foster   *play* Wilkie C. Mahoney, Ben Hecht, Gene Fowler   *d* George Archainbaud   *ph* Karl Struss

Bob Hope, Shirley Ross, Una Merkel, Gene Krupa, Richard Denning

'Turned out deliberately to catch the jitterbug devotees . . . will satisfy moderately.' – *Variety*

† The play, *The Great Magoo*, was previously filmed in 1934 as *Shoot the Works*.

Some Like It Hot ****

US   1959   122m   bw
UA/Mirisch (Billy Wilder)
V, V*, L, S

Two unemployed musicians accidentally witness the St Valentine's Day Massacre and flee to Miami disguised as girl musicians.

A milestone of film comedy which keeps its central situation alive with constant and fresh invention; its wit, combined with a sense of danger, has rarely been duplicated and never equalled.

w Billy Wilder, I. A. L. Diamond   *d* Billy Wilder   *ph* Charles Lang Jnr   *m* Adolph Deutsch   *ad* Ted Howarth

Jack Lemmon, Tony Curtis, Marilyn Monroe, Joe E. Brown, George Raft, Pat O'Brien, Nehemiah Persoff, George E. Stone, Joan Shawlee

'A comedy set in the Prohibition era, with transvestism, impotence, role confusion, and borderline inversion – and all hilariously innocent,

though always on the brink of really disastrous double-entendre.' – *Pauline Kael*

'Most of the time Billy Wilder's new piece – a farce blacker than is common on the American screen – whistles along at a smart, murderous pace.' – *Dilys Powell*

'Hectic slapstick, smartass movie pardies, sexist stereotyping, crass one-liners, and bad taste galore.' – *Time Out, 1984*

AAN: script; Billy Wilder (as director); Charles Lang Jnr; Jack Lemmon; art direction

Some People

GB   1962   93m   Eastmancolor
Vic Films (James Archibald)

Troublesome teenage factory workers are helped by a church organist and become model citizens.

Bland propaganda for the Duke of Edinburgh's Award scheme for young people, quite acceptably presented, with pop music ad lib.

w John Eldridge   *d* Clive Donner   *ph* John Wilcox   *m* Ron Grainer

Kenneth More, Ray Brooks, Annika Wells, David Andrews, Angela Douglas, David Hemmings, Harry H. Corbett

Some Will, Some Won't

GB   1969   90m   Technicolor
ABP/Transocean (Giulio Zampi)
V

In order to inherit under an eccentric will, four people have to perform tasks out of character.

Thin remake of *Laughter in Paradise* (qv); funny moments extremely few.

w Lew Schwarz   *d* Duncan Wood   *ph* Harry Waxman   *m* Howard Blake

Ronnie Corbett, Thora Hird, Michael Hordern, Leslie Phillips, Barbara Murray, James Robertson Justice, Dennis Price, Wilfrid Brambell, Eleanor Summerfield, Arthur Lowe

Somebody Killed Her Husband

US   1978   96m   Movielab
Columbia/Melvin Simon (Martin Poll)

The title tells what happened when an unhappily married young mother falls in love.

Very thin suspense comedy which starts as it ends, uncertainly.

w Reginald Rose   *d* Lamont Johnson   *ph* Andrew Laszlo, Ralf D. Bode   *m* Alex North   *pd* Ted Haworth

Farrah Fawcett-Majors, Jeff Bridges, John Wood, Tammy Grimes, John Glover, Patricia Elliott

Somebody Loves Me

US   1952   97m   Technicolor
Paramount/Perlberg-Seaton

First successful in San Francisco at earthquake time, Blossom Seeley climbs to Broadway success with her partner Benny Fields, then retires to become his wife.

Adequate, unsurprising star musical of the second or third rank.

wd Irving Brecher   *ph* George Barnes   *songs* Jay Livingston, Ray Evans

Betty Hutton, Ralph Meeker, Robert Keith, Adele Jergens, Billie Bird, Sid Tomack, Ludwig Stossel

Somebody Up There Likes Me *

US   1956   112m   bw
MGM (Charles Schnee)
V*

An East Side kid with reform school experience becomes middleweight boxing champion of the world.

A sentimental fantasia on the life of Rocky Graziano, expertly blending violence, depression, prizefight sequences and fake uplift.

w Ernest Lehman   *d* Robert Wise   *ph* Joseph Ruttenberg   *m* Bronislau Kaper   *ad* Cedric Gibbons, Malcolm F. Brown   *ed* Albert Akst

Paul Newman, Pier Angeli, Everett Sloane, Eileen Heckart, Sal Mineo, Joseph Buloff, Harold J. Stone, Robert Loggia

AA: Joseph Ruttenberg; art direction

AAN: editing

Someone at the Door

GB   1936   74m   bw
BIP

The new owner of a spooky house invents a murder which seems to come true.

Derivative but quite amusing comedy thriller.

w Jack Davies and Marjorie Deans   *play* Dorothy and Campbell Christie   *d* Herbert Brenon

Billy Milton, Aileen Marson, Noah Beery, Edward Chapman, Hermione Gingold, John Irwin

† Remade in 1950 with Michael Medwin, Yvonne Owen and Garry Marsh; directed by Francis Searle; for Hammer.

Someone Behind the Door

France   1971   97m   colour
Miracle/Lira Film/Comaccio/SNC (Raymond Danon)
V*, L
original title: *Quelqu'un derrière la Porte*; aka: *Two Minds for Murder*

A brain surgeon takes a psychopathic patient home and tries to make him commit murder.

Adequate but somehow unexciting suspenser.

w Mark Boehm, Jacques Robert   *novel* Jacques Robert   *d* Nicolas Gessner

Charles Bronson, Anthony Perkins, Jill Ireland, Henri Garcia

Someone to Love *

US   1987   105m   DeLuxe
ICA/International Rainbow/Jagfilm (M. H. Simonsons)
V*, L

On Valentine's Day, a director throws a party for his single and divorced friends and questions them on camera about their attitudes to love and relationships.

Little more than a succession of turns by various actors and actresses, but intermittently interesting and notable for Welles's final appearance on film, bringing it to an end with a shout of 'Cut!'

wd Henry Jaglom   *ph* Hanania Baer   *ed* Henry Jaglom

Orson Welles, Henry Jaglom, Andrea Marcovicci, Michael Emil, Sally Kellerman, Oja Kodar, Stephen Bishop, Dave Frishberg

Someone to Watch Over Me *

US   1987   106m   DeLuxe
Columbia/Thierry de Ganay
V, V*, L

A New York cop falls for the witness he must protect from a vicious killer.

Lively thriller with slick technicalities.

w Howard Franklin   *d* Ridley Scott   *ph* Steven Poster   *m* Michael Kamen   *pd* Jim Bissell

Tom Berenger, Mimi Rogers, Lorraine Bracco, Jerry Orbach, John Rubinstein, Andreas Katsulas

'Stylish and romantic . . . manages to triumph over several hard-to-swallow plot developments.' – *Daily Variety*

Something Big

US   1971   108m   Technicolor
Cinema Center/Stanmore and Penbar (Andrew V. McLaglen)

A retiring cavalry colonel has a last battle with his old enemy.

Wry serio-comic Western in the Ford tradition.

w James Lee Barrett   d Andrew V. McLaglen
ph Harry Stradling Jnr   m Marvin Hamlisch

Dean Martin, Brian Keith, Honor Blackman, Carol White, Ben Johnson, Albert Salmi, Denver Pyle

Something for Everyone *

US   1970   110m   colour
National General (John Flaxman)
V*
GB title: Black Flowers for the Bride

A young con man insinuates himself into the household of a widowed Austrian countess.

Unusual black comedy which doesn't quite come off.

w Hugh Wheeler   novel The Cook by Harry Kressing
d Harold Prince   ph Walter Lassally   m John Kander

Angela Lansbury, Michael York, Anthony Corlan, Heidelinde Weis

'Nothing much for anyone, actually.' – New Yorker

Something for the Birds

US   1952   81m   bw
TCF (Samuel G. Engel)

An elderly fraud is of help to a Washington girl trying to save a bird sanctuary.

Derivative, competent but slightly boring political whimsy on Capra lines.

w I. A. L. Diamond, Boris Ingster   d Robert Wise
ph Joseph LaShelle   m Sol Kaplan

Edmund Gwenn, Victor Mature, Patricia Neal, Larry Keating, Christian Rub

Something for the Boys

US   1944   87m   Technicolor
TCF (Irving Starr)

A Southern plantation is turned into a retreat for army wives.

Modest musical, vaguely based on a Broadway success.

w Robert Ellis, Helen Logan, Frank Gabrielson
musical comedy Cole Porter, Herbert and Dorothy Fields   d Lewis Seiler   ph Ernest Palmer   title song Cole Porter   other songs Harold Adamson, Jimmy McHugh   m Cyril Mockridge

Carmen Miranda, Michael O'Shea, Vivian Blaine, Phil Silvers, Sheila Ryan, Perry Como, Glenn Langan, Cara Williams

Something in the Wind

US   1947   89m   bw
U-I (Joseph Sistrom)

A lady disc jockey is mistaken for her aunt, who has been seeing too much for the heirs' liking of a wealthy old man.

Poorish star musical comedy.

w Harry Kurnitz, William Bowers   d Irving Pichel

Deanna Durbin, Donald O'Connor, John Dall, Charles Winninger, Helena Carter

Something Money Can't Buy

GB   1952   82m   bw
Rank/Vic (Joe Janni)

After World War II a young couple find civilian life difficult and dreary, but finally start a catering and secretarial business.

Weakly contrived comedy which makes nothing of its possibilities and is limply handled all round.

---

w Pat Jackson, James Landsdale Hodson   d Pat Jackson   ph C. Pennington-Richards   m Nino Rota

Patricia Roc, Anthony Steel, A. E. Matthews, Moira Lister, David Hutcheson, Michael Trubshawe, Diane Hart, Charles Victor, Henry Edwards

Something of Value

US   1957   113m   bw
MGM (Pandro S. Berman)
V*

A young African with many English friends is initiated into the Kikuyu.

An attempt to see all sides in the case of the African ritual murders of the fifties; bloodthirsty and unconvincing as well as dull.

wd Richard Brooks   novel Robert Ruark
ph Russell Harlan   m Miklos Rozsa

Rock Hudson, Sidney Poitier, Dana Wynter, Wendy Hiller, Robert Beatty, Juano Hernandez, William Marshall, Walter Fitzgerald, Michael Pate

Something to Hide

GB   1971   99m   Eastmancolor
Avton (Michael Klinger)
V*

A civil servant has a row with his wife, kills her and buries her body on the Isle of Wight.

Unpleasant and uninteresting melodrama demanding a hysterical performance from its star. Pleasant photography is its only asset.

wd Alastair Reid   novel Nicholas Monsarrat
ph Wolfgang Suschitzky   m Roy Budd, Jack Fishman

Peter Finch, Colin Blakely, John Stride, Shelley Winters, Linda Hayden, Harold Goldblatt

Something to Live For

US   1952 (completed 1950)   89m   bw
Paramount (George Stevens)

A commercial artist member of Alcoholics Anonymous falls for a dipsomaniac actress but refuses to break up his marriage.

Glossy romantic melodrama with some style but no depth; the casting makes it seem like a sequel to The Lost Weekend.

w Dwight Taylor   d George Stevens   ph George Barnes   m Victor Young

Ray Milland, Joan Fontaine, Teresa Wright, Richard Derr, Douglas Dick

'The victory over alcohol becomes a somewhat woebegone business.' – Penelope Houston

Something to Shout About

US   1943   93m   bw
Columbia (Gregory Ratoff)

A press agent tries to get rid of an untalented star.

Tolerable musical comedy.

w Fred Shiller, Lou Breslow, Edward Eliscu, George Owen   d Gregory Ratoff   md Morris Stoloff
songs Cole Porter

Don Ameche, Janet Blair, William Gaxton, Perry Como

AAN: Morris Stoloff; song 'You'd Be So Nice to Come Home To'

Something to Sing About *

US   1937   90m   bw
Grand National (Zion Myers)
V*, L

A New York bandleader decides to take a fling at Hollywood.

Lightweight but reasonably pleasing musical, made by the star as an independent during a rift with his studio, Warner.

---

w Austin Parker   d/songs Victor Schertzinger
ph John Stumar   md Constantin Bakaleinikoff

James Cagney, Evelyn Daw, Mona Barrie, William Frawley, Gene Lockhart

'A first-class comedy with music; will please everywhere.' – Variety

AAN: Victor Schertzinger

Something Wicked This Way Comes *

US   1983   95m   Technicolor
Walt Disney/Bryna (Peter Vincent Douglas)
V*, L

A sinister carnival with a power over time and age visits a small town in Illinois.

A curious departure for the Disney studio is this grim fairy tale from a novel which was probably intractable. In the cinema, this is the sort of film very lucky to find an audience despite its good qualities.

w Ray Bradbury   novel Ray Bradbury   d Jack Clayton   ph Stephen H. Burum   m James Horner
pd Richard MacDonald

Jason Robards, Jonathan Pryce, Diane Ladd, Pam Grier, Royal Dano, Vidal Peterson, Shawn Carson

Something Wild

US   1961   112m   bw
(UA) Prometheus (George Justin)

A girl's life and attitudes change after she is raped, and she moves in with a garage mechanic.

A bit of a wallow, with much method acting but no clear analysis of the central relationship.

w Jack Garfein, Alex Karmel   novel Mary Ann by Alex Karmel   d Jack Garfein   ph Eugene Schufftan
m Aaron Copland   ad Richard Day

Carroll Baker, Ralph Meeker, Mildred Dunnock, Charles Watts, Martin Kosleck, Jean Stapleton

Something Wild

US   1986   113m   colour
Orion/Religioso Primitiva Du Art (Jonathan Demme, Kenneth Utt)
V, V*, L, S

Two irresponsible young people find themselves on the run from police and criminals.

Unremarkable melodrama with trendy musical trappings.

w E. Max Frye   d Jonathan Demme   ph Tak Fujimoto   m John Cale, Laurie Anderson

Jeff Daniels, Melanie Griffith, Ray Liotta, Margaret Colin

Sometimes a Great Notion *

US   1971   114m   Technicolor   Panavision
Universal/Newman-Foreman
V*
GB title: Never Give an Inch

In a small Oregon township, trouble is caused by an independent family of lumberjacks.

Freewheeling but unsatisfactorily eccentric comedy-melodrama which never quite jells but has flashes of individuality.

w John Gay   novel Ken Kesey   d Paul Newman
ph Richard Moore   m Henry Mancini

Paul Newman, Henry Fonda, Lee Remick, Michael Sarrazin, Richard Jaeckel, Linda Lawson, Cliff Potts

AAN: song 'All His Children' (m Henry Mancini, ly Alan and Marilyn Bergman); Richard Jaeckel

Somewhere I'll Find You *

US   1942   108m   bw
MGM (Pandro S. Berman)

Brother war correspondents quarrel over a girl and later find her in Indo-China smuggling Chinese babies to safety.

Absurd but satisfactory star vehicle of the second
rank, with the theme designed to prepare America for
war.

w Marguerite Roberts   story Charles Hoffman
d Wesley Ruggles   ph Harold Rosson
m Bronislau Kaper

Clark Gable, Lana Turner, Robert Sterling, Patricia
Dane, Reginald Owen, Lee Patrick, Charles Dingle,
Rags Ragland, William Henry

Somewhere in England
GB 1940 79m bw
Mancunian (John E. Blakeley)

High jinks among army recruits staging a show.

One of a series of misshapen and badly made regional
comedies which afflicted British cinemas in the forties
and should be mentioned for their immense
popularity, their new-style vulgarity (later to be
refined by the Carry On series) and their highly
popular stars.

w Arthur Mertz, Rodney Parsons   d John E.
Blakeley   ph Geoffrey Faithfull

Frank Randle, Harry Korris, Robbie Vincent, Winki
Turner, Dan Young

† Subsequently released, or allowed to escape,
between 1941 and 1949 were Somewhere in Camp,
Somewhere on Leave, Somewhere in Civvies and Somewhere
in Politics.

Somewhere in France: see The Foreman Went to
France

Somewhere in the Night *
US 1946 111m bw
TCF (Anderson Lawler)

An amnesiac war veteran tries to discover his true
identity and discovers he is a crook with much-
wanted information.

Overlong suspenser with a tentative film noir
atmosphere. A few nice touches partly atone for a
tediously conversational plot.

w Howard Dimsdale, Joseph L. Mankiewicz
story The Lonely Journey by Marvin Borowsky
d Joseph L. Mankiewicz   ph Norbert Brodine
m David Buttolph

John Hodiak, Nancy Guild, Lloyd Nolan, Richard
Conte, Josephine Hutchinson, Fritz Kortner

Somewhere in Time *
US 1980 104m Technicolor
Universal/Rastar (Stephen Deutsch)
V, V*, L, S

A playwright finds a way back in time for another
encounter with the girl he loved and lost in a previous
incarnation.

Rather a charming variation on Berkeley Square, but
hardly a theme to do well in the hardnosed eighties.

w Richard Matheson,   novel Bid Time Return by Richard
Matheson   d Jeannot Szwarc   ph Isidore
Mankofsky   m John Barry

Christopher Reeve, Christopher Plummer, Jane
Seymour, Teresa Wright, Bill Erwin, George Voskovec

Somewhere Tomorrow
US 1983 87m colour
Blue Marble (Robert Wiemer, Glenn Kershaw)
V*

After watching Topper on TV, a girl falls in love with
the ghost of a boy killed in a plane crash.

Forgettable teenage romance, over-sentimental for all
but the very sweet-toothed.

wd Robert Wiemer   ph Glenn Kershaw   m Paul
Baillargeon   ad Richard Hoover, Ruth Ammon
ed Peter Hammer

Sarah Jessica Parker, Nancy Addison, Tom Shea, Rick
Weber, Paul Bates

Sommarlek: see Summer Interlude

Sommarnattens Leende: see Smiles of a Summer
Night

Sommersby
US/France 1993 113m Technicolor
Warner/Regency/Canal+ (Arnon Milchan, Steven Reuther)
S

After the American Civil War, a man who returns
home after a gap of seven years is suspected of being
an imposter.

Lush costume piece that never comes to terms with
the ambiguity of its story.

w Nicholas Meyer, Sarah Kernochan   d Jon Amiel
ph Philippe Rousselot   m Danny Elfman
pd Bruno Rubeo   ed Peter Boyle

Richard Gere, Jodie Foster, Bill Pullman, James Earl
Jones, Lanny Flaherty, William Windom, Wendell
Wellman, Brett Kelley

'Fails to generate any sense of tragedy or passion,
preferring to remain at a distance to the story,
mistaking seriousness for profundity and aloofness
for sophistication.' – Jason Drake, Sight and Sound

† It is a remake of the French film The Return of Martin
Guerre (qv).

The Son-Daughter
US 1932 79m bw
MGM

True love among the San Francisco Chinese is affected
by warring Tongs.

Ill-advised oriental romance which failed to please.

w Claudine West, Leon Gordon, John Goodrich
play David Belasco, George Scarborough
d Clarence Brown

Ramon Novarro, Helen Hayes, Lewis Stone, Warner
Oland, Ralph Morgan, H. B. Warner, Louise Closser
Hale

'Old-time stuff, moving slowly and laboriously
towards a sad climax.' – Variety

Son-in-Law
US 1993 95m Technicolor
Buena Vista/Hollywood Pictures (Michael Rotenberg, Peter M.
Lenkov)
V, V*

A girl takes her Californian boyfriend home to the
family farm for Thanksgiving.

A sickly, oversweet comedy featuring an antic,
unfunny comedian caught in direly predictable
situations.

w Fax Bahr, Adam Small, Shawn Schepps
story Patrick J. Clifton, Susan McMartin, Peter
Lenkov   d Steve Rash   ph Peter Deming
m Richard Gibbs   pd Joseph T. Garrity   ed Dennis
M. Hill

Pauly Shore, Carla Gugino, Lane Smith, Cindy
Pickett, Mason Adams, Patrick Renna, Dennis
Burkley

'You'd have to dig way back to the likes of Sleep 'n'
Eat and the Bowery Boys' Huntz Hall to find a moron-
funnyman persona as irksome as Pauly Shore's.' –
Variety

Son of a Gunfighter
US/Spain 1964 90m Metrocolor Cinemascope
Lester Welch/Zurbano/MGM

A young Westerner stalks the outlaw responsible for
his mother's death.

Tolerable international Western.

w Clarke Reynolds   d Paul Landres

Russ Tamblyn, Kieron Moore, James Philbrook,
Fernando Rey

Son of Ali Baba
US 1952 75m Technicolor
U-I (Leonard Goldstein)

A cadet of the military academy outwits a wicked
caliph.

Routine Arabian Nights hokum.

w Gerald Drayson Adams   d Kurt Neumann
ph Maury Gertsman   m Joseph Gershenson

Tony Curtis, Piper Laurie, Susan Cabot, Victor Jory

Son of Blob: see Beware! The Blob

Son of Captain Blood
Italy/Spain 1962 95m Eastmancolor Dyaliscope
CCM/BP/Harry Joe Brown
V*

Captain Blood's son routs his father's enemies.

Lively swashbuckler with the original star's son
rather unhappily cast.

w Mario Caiano   d Tullio Demichelli

Sean Flynn, Ann Todd, Jose Nieto, John Kitzmiller

Son of Dr Jekyll
US 1951 77m bw
Columbia

Dr Jekyll's son worries about developing a split
personality, but discovers that his father's supposed
friend Dr Lanyon is the spanner in the works.

Irresistibly silly elaboration of a famous story; no
thrills but several good unintentional laughs.

w Mortimer Braus, Jack Pollexfen   d Seymour
Friedman

Louis Hayward, Alexander Knox, Jody Lawrance,
Lester Matthews, Paul Cavanagh, Gavin Muir, Rhys
Williams

'Searing the screen with new terror!'

Son of Dracula *
US 1943 80m bw
Universal (Ford Beebe)
V*, L

A mysterious stranger named Alucard, with a
penchant for disappearing in puffs of smoke, turns up
on a Southern plantation.

Stolid series entry with a miscast lead; nicely handled
moments.

w Eric Taylor   d Robert Siodmak   ph George Robinson
m Hans Salter

Lon Chaney Jnr, Louise Allbritton, Robert Paige,
Samuel S. Hinds, Evelyn Ankers, Frank Craven, J.
Edward Bromberg

† The title cheats: he isn't the son of, but the old man
himself . . .

'The black shadows of the past bred this half-man, half-
demon!'

Son of Frankenstein ***
US 1939 99m bw
Universal (Rowland V. Lee)
V*, L

The old baron's son comes home and starts to dabble,
with the help of a broken-necked and vindictive
shepherd.

Handsomely mounted sequel to Bride of Frankenstein
and the last of the classic trio. The monster is less
interesting, but there are plenty of other diversions,
including the splendid if impractical sets.

w Willis Cooper   d Rowland V. Lee   ph George Robinson
m Frank Skinner   ad Jack Otterson

Basil Rathbone, Boris Karloff, Bela Lugosi, Lionel Atwill,
Josephine Hutchinson, Donnie Dunagan, Emma
Dunn, Edgar Norton, Lawrence Grant

'Rather strong material for the top keys, picture will still garner plenty of bookings in the secondary first runs along the main stem.' – *Variety*

'The slickness of production gives a kind of refinement to the horrific moments and a subtlety to the suspense.' – *Film Weekly*

Son of Fury *
US 1942 102m bw
TCF (William Perlberg)

An 18th-century Englishman is deprived of his inheritance, flees to a South Sea island but comes back seeking restitution.

Elaborate costumer which suffers from loss of suspense during the central idyll. Much to enjoy along the way.

w Philip Dunne *novel Benjamin Blake* by Edison Marshall *d* John Cromwell *ph* Arthur Miller *m* Alfred Newman

Tyrone Power, Gene Tierney, George Sanders, Frances Farmer, Roddy McDowall, John Carradine, Elsa Lanchester, *Dudley Digges*, Harry Davenport, Halliwell Hobbes

† Remade as *Treasure of the Golden Condor* (qv).

Son of Geronimo
US 1952 bw serial: 15 eps
Columbia

Jim Scott seeks to end the bloodshed between whites and Indians.

Rather solemn Western serial.

d Spencer Bennet

Clayton Moore, Bud Osborne, Tommy Farrell, Rodd Redwing

Son of Godzilla
Japan 1967 86m (dubbed) colour
Toho Company (Tomoyuki Tanaka)
V*

Intrepid scientists, experimenting with the weather on a remote island, battle against back projections of spiders and a giant mantis as a motherless son is born to Godzilla.

Standard monster hokum, with actors in rubber suits trampling on model buildings.

w Shinichi Sekizawa, Kazue Shiba *d* Jun Fukuda *ph* Kazuo Yamada *m* Masaru Sato *ad* Takeo Kita *ed* Ryohei Fujii

Tadeo Takashima, Bibari Maeda, Akira Kubo, Akihiko Hirata, Kenji Sahara, Yoshio Tsuchiya

Son of Kong *
US 1933 69m bw
RKO (Merian C. Cooper)
V*, L

After Kong has wrecked New York, producer Carl Denham flees from his creditors and finds more monsters on the old island.

Hasty sequel to the splendid *King Kong;* the results were so tame and unconvincing that the film was sold as a comedy, but it does have a few lively moments after four reels of padding.

w Ruth Rose *d* Ernest B. Schoedsack *ph* Eddie Linden, Vernon Walker, J. O. Taylor *m* Max Steiner *sp* Willis O'Brien

Robert Armstrong, Helen Mack, Frank Reicher, John Marston, Victor Wong

'The sequel to and wash-up of the King Kong theme, consisting of salvaged remnants from the original production . . . the punch is no longer there.' – *Variety*

Son of Lassie
US 1945 100m Technicolor
MGM (Samuel Marx)
V*

A dog follows its young master to the war and helps settle the hash of a few Nazis.

Silly dog story, the first sequel to *Lassie Come Home;* far too slow to start with, then packed with serial-like action.

w Jeanne Bartlett *d* S. Sylvan Simon *ph* Charles Schoenbaum *m* Herbert Stothart

Peter Lawford, Donald Crisp, June Lockhart, Nigel Bruce, Leon Ames, Nils Asther

'Good old sentimental hokum.' – *Variety*

Son of Monte Cristo *
US 1940 102m bw
(UA) Edward Small
V*, L

The masked avenger who quashes a dictatorship in 1865 Lichtenstein is none other than the son of Edmond Dantes.

Cheerful swashbuckler of the second class.

w George Bruce *d* Rowland V. Lee *ph* George Robinson *m* Edward Ward *ad* John DuCasse Schulze

Louis Hayward, Joan Bennett, George Sanders, Florence Bates, Lionel Royce, Montagu Love, Clayton Moore, Ralph Byrd

AAN: art direction

Son of Paleface *
US 1952 95m Technicolor
(Paramount) Bob Hope (Robert L. Welch)
V*, L

A tenderfoot and a government agent compete for the attentions of a lady bandit.

Gagged-up sequel to *The Paleface;* much of the humour now seems self-conscious and dated in the *Road* tradition which it apes, but there are still moments of delight.

w Frank Tashlin, Joseph Quillan, Robert L. Welch *d* Frank Tashlin *ph* Harry J. Wild *m* Lyn Murray

Bob Hope, Roy Rogers, Jane Russell, Trigger, Douglass Dumbrille, Harry von Zell, Bill Williams, Lloyd Corrigan

AAN: song 'Am I in Love' (*m/y* Jack Brooks)

Son of Robin Hood
GB 1958 77m Eastmancolor Cinemascope
TCF/Argo (George Sherman)

Robin's daughter joins with the Regent's brother to overthrow the Black Duke.

Empty-headed romp, more or less in the accepted tradition.

w George George, George Slavin *d* George Sherman *ph* Arthur Grant *m* Leighton Lucas

David Hedison, June Laverick, David Farrar, Marius Goring, Philip Friend, Delphi Lawrence, George Coulouris, George Woodbridge

Son of Sinbad *
US 1955 88m Technicolor Superscope
RKO (Robert Sparks)
V*

Sinbad and Omar Khayyam are imprisoned by the Caliph but escape with the secret of green fire.

Arabian Nights burlesque, mainly quite bright, with the forty thieves played by harem girls.

w Aubrey Wisberg, Jack Pollexfen *d* Ted Tetzlaff *ph* William Snyder *m* Victor Young

Dale Robertson, Vincent Price, Sally Forrest, Lili St Cyr, Mari Blanchard, Leon Askin, Jay Novello

Son of the Gods
US 1930 90m bw
First National

A Chinaman falls in love with a white girl . . . but turns out not to be a Chinaman after all.

Antediluvian miscegenation melodrama with an unconvincing twist.

w Bradley King *novel* Rex Beach *d* Frank Lloyd

Richard Barthelmess, Constance Bennett, Geneva Mitchell, E. Alyn Warren

'High-class general programme release.' – *Variety*

Son of the Guardsman
US 1946 bw serial: 15 eps
Columbia

In medieval England, David Trent turns against his thieving uncle and joins a band of outlaws.

Muddled serial antics in the style of Robin Hood.

d Derwin Abrahams

Robert Shaw, Daun Kennedy, Robert 'Buzz' Henry, Jim Diehl

'An eye feast of virile action, colourful settings and glowing climaxes!'

The Son of the Sheik *
US 1926 74m at 24 fps bw silent
(UA) J. M. Schenck
V, V*, L

Ahmed protects a dancing girl from a band of renegades.

Tongue-in-cheek desert romp which was probably its star's best film. He plays a dual role of father and son.

w Frances Marion, George Marion Jnr, Frederick Gresac *d* George Fitzmaurice *m* (1934 sound version) Jack Ward

Rudolph Valentino, Vilma Banky, Agnes Ayres

'The very picture for which the world's wife, mother and daughter have been waiting!' – *Louella Parsons*

'We expect every fan in the country to be saying: It is Rudy's best. We can never forget him.' – *Photoplay*

Son of Zorro
US 1947 bw serial: 13 eps
Republic

After the Civil War, a Southern officer takes on a ring of crooked politicians who are bleeding his home town dry.

Reasonably lively treading on familiar waters.

d Spencer Bennet, Fred Brannon

George Turner, Peggy Stewart, Roy Barcroft

Sonatine
Canada 1983 92m colour
Corporation Image/M & M (Pierre Gendron)

Two teenage girls form tentative relationships with older men before joining in a public suicide pact.

Trite tale of teenagers unable to make contact with a wider world than themselves.

wd Micheline Lanctôt *ph* Guy Dufaux *m* François Lanctôt *ed* Louise Surprenant

Pascale Bussieres, Marcia Pilote, Pierre Fauteux, Kliment Dentchev

Sonatine *
Japan 1993 93m colour
ICA/Bandai/Shochiku Dai-ichi Kogyo (Masayuki Mori, Hisao Nabeshima, Takio Yoshida)

A violent Tokyo gangster, sent to intervene in a gang war in Okinawa, realizes that he has made a mistake and, after relaxing at the seaside with his gang, faces a final showdown.

An odd gangster movie, violent and downbeat, but also veering away from the genre into casual moments of fun and games.

wd Takeshi Kitano   *ph* Katsumi Yanagishima
m Joe Hisaishi   *ad* Osamu Sasaki   *ed* Takeshi
Kitano

'Beat' Takeshi (Takeshi Kitano), Aya Kokumai, Tetsu
Watanabe, Masanobu Katsumura, Susumu
Terashima, Ren Ohsugi, Tonbo Zushi, Kenichi Yajima

'Pic's combo of dry humor, sudden bursts of violence,
and world-weary romanticism will take a while to
build for first-time viewers of Kitano's movies, and
the jigsaw of plot and characters only takes
recognisable shape about halfway in.' – *Variety*

The Song and Dance Man
US   1936   72m   bw
TCF

A vaudeville dancer goes on the skids but turns up
when his former partner needs him.

Hokey backstage drama with interesting detail.

w Maude Fulton   *play* George M. Cohan   *d* Allan
Dwan

Paul Kelly, Claire Trevor, Michael Whalen, Ruth
Donelly, James Burke

A Song Is Born *
US   1948   113m   Technicolor
Samuel Goldwyn
V*

Flat remake of *Ball of Fire* (qv), graced by an array of
top-flight musical talent.

w Harry Tugend   *d* Howard Hawks   *ph* Gregg
Toland   *md* Emil Newman   *songs* Don Raye, Gene
de Paul   *m* Hugo Friedhofer

Danny Kaye, Virginia Mayo, Hugh Herbert, Steve
Cochran, Felix Bressart, J. Edward Bromberg, Mary
Field, Ludwig Stossel, Louis Armstrong, Charlie
Barnet, Benny Goodman, Lionel Hampton, Tommy
Dorsey, Mel Powell

Song o' My Heart
US   1930   85m   bw
Fox

A professional singer looks after the orphaned
children of his former love.

A thin story is the excuse for a great tenor to sing
eleven songs.

w Tom Barry, J. J. McCarthy   *d* Frank Borzage

John McCormack, Maureen O'Sullivan, John Garrick, J.
M. Kerrigan, Alice Joyce

'A simple tale charmingly told . . . sitting through it is
no hardship.' – *Variety*

'We're going to see Jennifer Jones again in . . .'
The Song of Bernadette **
US   1943   156m   bw
TCF (William Perlberg)
V, V*, L

A peasant girl has a vision of the Virgin Mary at what
becomes the shrine of Lourdes.

Hollywood religiosity at its most commercial; but
behind the lapses of taste and truth is an excellent
production which was phenomenally popular and
created a new star.

w George Seaton   *novel* Franz Werfel   *d* Henry King
ph Arthur Miller   *m* Alfred Newman   *ad* James Basevi,
William Darling   *ed* Barbara McLean

Jennifer Jones, William Eythe, Charles Bickford,
Vincent Price, Lee J. Cobb, Gladys Cooper, Anne
Revere, Roman Bohnen, Patricia Morison, Aubrey
Mather, Charles Dingle, Mary Anderson, Edith
Barrett, Sig Rumann

  PROLOGUE: 'For those who believe in God, no
explanation is necessary. For those who do not
believe in God, no explanation is possible.'

'A tamed and pretty image, highly varnished,
sensitively lighted, and exhibited behind immaculate

glass, the window at once of a shrine and of a box
office.' – *James Agee*

'It contains much to conciliate even the crustiest and
most prejudiced objector.' – *Richard Mallett, Punch*

AA: Arthur Miller; Alfred Newman; Jennifer Jones;
James Basevi, William Darling

AAN: best picture; George Seaton; Henry King;
Charles Bickford; Gladys Cooper; Anne Revere;
Barbara McLean

Song of Ceylon **
GB   1934   40m   bw
Ceylon Tea Board (John Grierson)

A pictorial, almost sensuous, but not very informative
documentary in four sections: 'The Buddha', 'The
Virgin Island', 'The Voices of Commerce', 'The
Apparel of a God'. Its influence was immense.

wd/ph Basil Wright   *m* Walter Leigh

Song of Freedom *
GB   1936   80m   bw
Hammer (J. Fraser Passmore)
V*

A black London docker becomes an opera singer, then
goes to Africa to free the tribe of which he has
discovered himself to be the head.

A weird fable but a good star vehicle and a
surprisingly smart production for the time.

w Fenn Sherie, Ingram d'Abbes, Michael Barringer,
Philip Lindsay   *d* J. Elder Wills   *ph* Eric Cross

Paul Robeson, Elizabeth Welch, George Mosart, Esmé
Percy

Song of India
US   1949   77m   bw
Columbia (Albert S. Rogell)

An Indian prince protects his land against a big game
hunter.

Not much singing, but lots of animals and a fight with
knives: tolerable programme filler.

w Art Arthur, Kenneth Perkins   *d* Albert S. Rogell

Sabu, Gail Russell, Turhan Bey, Anthony Caruso,
Aminta Dyne, Fritz Leiber

Song of Love *
US   1947   118m   bw
MGM (Clarence Brown)
V*

The story of Clara and Robert Schumann and their
friend Johannes Brahms.

Dignified musical biopic which unfortunately falls
into most of the pitfall clichés of the genre. Dull it may
be, but it looks good and the music is fine.

w Ivan Tors, Irmgard von Cube, Allen Vincent,
Robert Ardrey   *d* Clarence Brown   *ph* Harry
Stradling   *md* Bronislau Kaper   *ad* Cedric Gibbons
piano Artur Rubenstein

Katharine Hepburn, Paul Henreid, Robert Walker,
Henry Daniell, Leo G. Carroll, Else Janssen, Gigi
Perreau

'This is how Brahms and the Schumanns might very
possibly have acted if they had realized that later on
they would break into the movies.' – *Time*

Song of Norway *
US   1970   141m   DeLuxe   Super Panavision 70
ABC/Andrew and Virginia Stone
V*

A fantasia on the life of Grieg.

Multinational hodgepodge, mostly in the *Sound of
Music* style but with everything from cartoons to
Christmas cracker backgrounds. Quite watchable, and
the landscapes are certainly splendid.

wd Andrew Stone   *ph* Davis Boulton   *stage
musical* Milton Lazarus (*book*), Robert Wright, George
Forrest (*m/ly*)

Toralv Maurstad, Florence Henderson, Christina
Schollin, Frank Poretta, Harry Secombe, Edward G.
Robinson, Robert Morley, Elizabeth Larner, Bernard
Archard, Oscar Homolka, Richard Wordsworth

Song of Russia
US   1944   107m   bw
MGM (Joe Pasternak)

An American symphony conductor is in Russia when
hostilities begin, and watches the citizens' war effort
with admiration.

A terrible big-budget film which followed the
wartime propaganda line but five years later was
heavily criticized by the Unamerican Activities
Committee (for the wrong reasons).

w Paul Jarrico, Richard Collins   *d* Gregory Ratoff
ph Harry Stradling   *m* Herbert Stothart

Robert Taylor, Susan Peters, John Hodiak, Robert
Benchley, Felix Bressart, Michael Chekhov, Darryl
Hickman

'Film makers have evolved a new tongue – the broken
accent deriving from no known language to be used
by foreigners on all occasions.' – *Richard Winnington*

'MGM performs the neatest trick of the week by
leaning over backward in Russia's favour without
once swaying from right to left.' – *Newsweek*

Song of Scheherezade
US   1947   107m   Technicolor
Universal (Edward Kaufman)

In 1865 naval cadet Rimsky-Korsakov falls in love
with a dancer.

Yet another composer takes a drubbing in this dull
and unconvincing hodgepodge.

wd Walter Reisch   *ph* Hal Mohr, William V. Skall
md Miklos Rozsa   *ch* Tilly Losch   *ad* Jack Otterson

Yvonne de Carlo, Jean-Pierre Aumont, Brian
Donlevy, Eve Arden, Charles Kullman, John Qualen,
Richard Lane, Terry Kilburn

'One of the world's great love stories comes to the star
  who can make it live!'
Song of Songs *
US   1933   89m   bw
Paramount (Rouben Mamoulian)

A German peasant girl falls for a sculptor but marries
a lecherous baron.

Pretentious romantic nonsense, made fairly palatable
by the director's steady hand.

w Leo Birinsky, Samuel Hoffenstein   *play* Edward
Sheldon   *novel* Das hohe Lied by Herman Sudermann
d Rouben Mamoulian   *ph* Victor Milner   *m* Karl
Hajos, Milien Rodern   *ad* Hans Dreier

Marlene Dietrich, Brian Aherne, Lionel Atwill, Alison
Skipworth, Hardie Albright

'An ornate and irresistible slice of outright hokum.' –
Peter John Dyer, 1966

'From the moment she heard this strange, compelling
  music of love – she was lost!'
Song of Surrender
US   1949   93m   bw
Paramount (Richard Maibaum)

In turn-of-the-century New England, a sophisticated
visitor from New York falls for the wife of the
museum curator.

Ho-hum romantic drama, well enough presented.

w Richard Maibaum   *d* Mitchell Leisen   *ph* Daniel
L. Fapp   *m* Victor Young

Wanda Hendrix, Claude Rains, Macdonald Carey,
Andrea King, Henry Hull, Elizabeth Patterson, Art
Smith

Song of the City

US 1937 73m bw
MGM (Lucien Hubbard)

Italian fisherfolk in San Francisco pull a socialite out of the bay and make a man of him.

Unlikely and unlovable moral tale, full of warm-hearted simple people.

w Michael Fessier d Errol Taggart

Margaret Lindsay, Jeffrey Dean, J. Carrol Naish, Nat Pendleton, Stanley Morner, Edward Norris

'Elemental stuff with some nice photography but needs bolstering for b.o. allure.' – Variety

Song of the Eagle

US 1933 65m bw
Paramount (Charles R. Rogers)

Racketeers try to control the supply of beer both after and during prohibition.

Tolerable crime/family saga which becomes sentimental.

w Casey Robinson, Willard Mack, Gene Towne, Graham Baker d Ralph Murphy

Charles Bickford, Richard Arlen, Jean Hersholt, Mary Brian, Louise Dresser, George E. Stone, Andy Devine

'Fairly good programmer and timely. What hurts is the title. Remember Animal Kingdom.' – Variety

Song of the Islands *

US 1942 75m Technicolor
TCF (William Le Baron)
V*, L

On a South Sea island, the daughter of an Irish beachcomber falls for the son of an American cattle king.

Wispy musical with agreeable settings and lively songs.

w Joseph Schrank, Robert Pirosh, Robert Ellis, Helen Logan d Walter Lang ph Ernest Palmer md Alfred Newman songs various

Betty Grable, Victor Mature, Jack Oakie, Thomas Mitchell, Hilo Hattie, Billy Gilbert, George Barbier

Song of the Open Road

US 1944 93m bw
UA (Charles R. Rogers)

A dissatisfied child movie star goes off to help volunteers to save a tomato crop.

Thin youth drama enlivened by a putting-on-a-show finale.

w Albert Mannheimer d S. Sylvan Simon

Jane Powell, Bonita Granville, Jackie Moran, W. C. Fields, Edgar Bergen and Charlie McCarthy, Sammy Kaye and his orchestra

AAN: Charles Previn (music direction); song 'Too Much in Love' (m Walter Kent, ly Kim Gannon)

Song of the South *

US 1946 94m Technicolor
Walt Disney (Perce Pearce)
V, L

On a long-ago Southern plantation, small boys listen to the Brer Rabbit stories from an elderly black servant.

Too much Uncle Remus and not enough Brer Rabbit, we fear, but children liked it. The cartoons were actually very good.

w Dalton Raymond d Harve Foster ph Gregg Toland m Daniele Amfitheatrof, Paul J. Smith, Charles Wolcott cartoon credits various

Ruth Warrick, Bobby Driscoll, James Baskett, Luana Patten, Lucile Watson, Hattie McDaniel

'The ratio of live to cartoon action is approximately two to one, and that is the ratio of the film's mediocrity to its charm.' – Bosley Crowther

AA: song 'Zip-a-Dee-Do-Dah' (m Allie Wrubel, ly Ray Gilbert); James Baskett (special award)

AAN: Daniele Amfitheatrof, Paul J. Smith, Charles Wolcott

A Song to Remember **

US 1944 113m Technicolor
Columbia (Louis F. Edelman)
V, V*, L

The life and death of Chopin and his liaison with George Sand.

Hilarious classical musical biopic which was unexpectedly popular and provoked a flood of similar pieces. As a production, not at all bad, but the script . . .

w Sidney Buchman d Charles Vidor ph Tony Gaudio, Allan M. Davey md Miklos Rozsa, Morris Stoloff piano José Iturbi ad Lionel Banks, Van Nest Polglase ed Charles Nelson

Cornel Wilde, Merle Oberon, Paul Muni, Stephen Bekassy, Nina Foch, George Coulouris, Sig Arno, Howard Freeman, George Macready

'It is the business of Hollywood to shape the truth into box-office contours.' – Richard Winnington

'This glorious picture is a major event in film history.' – Hollywood Reporter

'As infuriating and funny a misrepresentation of an artist's life and work as I have seen.' – James Agee

AAN: original story (Ernst Marischka); Tony Gaudio, Allen M. Davey; Miklos Rozsa, Morris Stoloff; Cornel Wilde; Charles Nelson

Song without End

US 1960 142m Eastmancolor Cinemascope
Columbia (William Goetz)
V*

The life and loves of Franz Liszt.

What worked at the box-office for Chopin failed disastrously for Liszt; famous people are turned into papier mâché dullards. Again, the production is elegance itself.

w Oscar Millard d Charles Vidor, George Cukor ph James Wong Howe md Morris Stoloff, Henry Sukman piano Jorge Bolet ad Walter Holscher

Dirk Bogarde, Capucine, Genevieve Page, Patricia Morison, Ivan Desny, Martita Hunt, Lyndon Brook, Alex Davion (as Chopin)

AA: Morris Stoloff, Henry Sukman

Songwriter

US 1984 94m Metrocolor
Tri-Star (Sydney Pollack)
V*, L

Adventures of a country-music duo.

Very moderate entertainment which gives the impression of stars doing their own thing.

w Bud Shrake d Alan Rudolph ph Matthew Leonetti m Kris Kristofferson pd Joel Schiller ed Stuart Pappe

Willie Nelson, Kris Kristofferson, Melinda Dillon, Rip Torn, Lesley Ann Warren, Richard C. Sarafian

AAN: Kris Kristofferson (for music)

Sono Otoko Kyobo ni Tsuki: see Violent Cop

'The first experiences of a young man in the mysteries of woman!'

Sons and Lovers ***

GB 1960 103m bw Cinemascope
TCF/Company of Artists/Jerry Wald

A Nottingham miner's son learns about life and love.

Well-produced and generally absorbing, if unsurprising, treatment of a famous novel.

w Gavin Lambert, T. E. B. Clarke, novel D. H. Lawrence d Jack Cardiff ph Freddie Francis m Mario Nascimbene ad Tom Morahan

Dean Stockwell, Trevor Howard, Wendy Hiller, Mary Ure, Heather Sears, William Lucas, Donald Pleasence, Ernest Thesiger

'An album of decent Edwardian snapshots.' – Peter John Dyer

'A rare, remarkable and courageous film.' – Daily Herald

AA: Freddie Francis

AAN: best picture; script; Jack Cardiff; Trevor Howard; Mary Ure; art direction

Sons o' Guns

US 1936 79m bw
Warner

A Broadway dancer in uniform finds himself accidentally enlisted and sent to France.

Among the better comedies of this star.

w Julius J. Epstein, Jerry Wald d Lloyd Bacon

Joe E. Brown, Joan Blondell, Eric Blore, Wini Shaw, Robert Barrat

The Sons of Katie Elder *

US 1965 122m Technicolor Panavision
Paramount/Hal B. Wallis (Paul Nathan)
V*, L

At Katie Elder's funeral, her four troublesome wandering sons find themselves on the verge of further trouble.

Sluggish all-star Western with predictable highlights.

w Allan Weiss, William H. Wright, Harry Essex d Henry Hathaway ph Lucien Ballard m Elmer Bernstein

John Wayne, Dean Martin, Michael Anderson Jnr, Earl Holliman, Martha Hyer, Jeremy Slate, James Gregory, George Kennedy, Paul Fix

Sons of the Desert ****

US 1934 68m bw
Hal Roach
V, V*, L
GB title: Fraternally Yours

Stan and Ollie want to go to a Chicago convention, but kid their wives that they are going on a cruise for health reasons.

Archetypal Laurel and Hardy comedy, unsurpassed for gags, pacing and sympathetic characterization.

w Frank Craven, Byron Morgan d William A. Seiter ph Kenneth Peach

Stan Laurel, Oliver Hardy, Charlie Chase, Mae Busch, Dorothy Christie

Sons of the Musketeers: see At Sword's Point

Sons of the Sea

GB 1939 82m Dufaycolor
British Consolidated

Life at the Royal Naval College in Dartmouth.

Simple-minded recruiter with a top dressing of spy stuff: naïve but well liked at the time.

w Gerald Elliott, Maurice Elvey, D. William Woolf, George Barraud d Maurice Elvey

Leslie Banks, Mackenzie Ward, Kay Walsh, Simon Lack, Cecil Parker, Ellen Pollock, Nigel Stock

Sons of the Sea (1941): see Atlantic Ferry

Sophie's Choice *
US 1982 157m Technicolor
Universal/AFD/ITC/Keith Barish
V, V*, L, S

In 1947, a Polish girl who has been in a concentration camp finds that her past still haunts her in New York.

Glum romantic drama about guilt and retribution, long and uncinematic as well as rather poorly done; but its intentions are doubtless honourable.

wd Alan J. Pakula novel William Styron
ph Nestor Almendros m Marvin Hamlisch
pd George Jenkins ed Evan Lottman

Meryl Streep, Kevin Kline, Peter MacNicol, Rita Karin, Stephen D. Newman, Josh Mostel

'Handsome, doggedly faithful and astoundingly tedious.' – Variety

'Not boring, simply unilluminating. By the end, only one question remains: why did Pakula have to make this movie?' – Sight and Sound

AA: Meryl Streep

AAN: screenplay (adaptation); cinematography; costume design; music

Sophie's Place: see Crooks and Coronets

Sorcerer
US 1977 121m Technicolor
Universal/Film Properties International (William Friedkin)
V*, L, S
GB title: Wages of Fear

Volunteers are needed to drive nitro-glycerine to an outpost in the South American jungle.

Why anyone should have wanted to spend twenty million dollars on a remake of The Wages of Fear, do it badly, and give it a misleading title is anybody's guess. The result is dire.

w Walon Green novel Georges Arnaud (and the film by Henri-Georges Clouzot) d William Friedkin
ph John M. Stephens, Dick Bush m Tangerine Dream, Keith Jarrett, Charlie Parker pd John Box

Roy Scheider, Bruno Cremer, Francisco Rabal, Amidou, Ramon Bieri

AAN: sound

The Sorcerers
GB 1967 85m Eastmancolor
Tigon/Curtwel/Global (Patrick Curtis, Tony Tenser)
V*

An old couple find a way of regaining their youth through hypnotizing a young man to do their bidding.

Rather slight but oddly memorable horror film, with an elegant old lady becoming the real monster.

w Michael Reeves, Tom Baker, John Burke
d Michael Reeves ph Stanley Long m Paul Ferris

Boris Karloff, Catherine Lacey, Ian Ogilvy, Elizabeth Ercy, Victor Henry, Susan George, Meier Tzelniker

Les Sorcières de Salem: see The Witches of Salem

Sorok Pervyi: see The Forty First

Sorority Girl
US 1957 61m bw
AIP/Sunset (Roger Corman)
V*

A poor little rich college girl feels alienated from her mother and her contemporaries.

Corman's campus exploitation movie is positively middle-aged in its stodgy approach, with a cast that looks far too old and a script mouldering with aged clichés.

w Ed Waters story Leo Lieberman d Roger Corman ph Monroe P. Askins m Ronald Stein
ed Charles Gross Jnr

Susan Cabot, Dick Miller, Barboura O'Neill, June Kenney, Barbara Crane, Fay Baker, Jeanne Wood, Joan Lora

Sorrell and Son
GB 1933 97m bw
B and D/Herbert Wilcox

When his wife leaves them, a man devotes his life to his worthless son.

Fair picturization of a popular novel.

w Lydia Hayward novel Warwick Deeping d Jack Raymond

H. B. Warner, Hugh Williams, Winifred Shotter, Margot Grahame, Donald Calthrop, Louis Hayward

'Insufficient in action for the average American screen devotee.' – Variety

† H. B. Warner played the same role in the silent version of 1927.

Sorrowful Jones
US 1949 88m bw
Paramount (Robert L. Welch)
V*, L

A racetrack tout unofficially adopts an orphan girl.

Heavy-going sentimental comedy peopled by comic gangsters, a remake of Little Miss Marker with the emphasis changed.

w Melville Shavelson, Edmund Hartmann, Jack Rose story Damon Runyon d Sidney Lanfield
ph Daniel L. Fapp m Robert Emmett Dolan

Bob Hope, Lucille Ball, William Demarest, Bruce Cabot, Thomas Gomez, Tom Pedi, Houseley Stevenson, Mary Jane Saunders

The Sorrows of Satan *
US 1926 115m approx bw silent
Famous Players/Paramount

A struggling writer accepts success in the form of a fortune offered to him by a prince who is in fact Satan.

Smooth Faust derivative with a few choice scenes of special effects.

w Forrest Halsey, John Russell, George Hull
novel Marie Corelli d D. W. Griffith (who didn't want to do it)

Adolphe Menjou, Ricardo Cortez, Lya de Putti, Carol Dempster, Ivan Lebedeff

Sorry Wrong Number **
US 1948 89m bw
Paramount (Hal B. Wallis, Anatole Litvak)
V*

A bedridden neurotic woman discovers she is marked for murder and tries to summon help.

Artificial but effective suspenser, extended from a radio play.

w Lucille Fletcher play Lucille Fletcher d Anatole Litvak ph Sol Polito m Franz Waxman
ed Warren Low

Barbara Stanwyck, Burt Lancaster, Ann Richards, Wendell Corey, Ed Begley, Harold Vermilyea, Leif Erickson, William Conrad

'The people who made it . . . have tried to do just one thing – to thrill. This they have triumphantly done.' – James Monahan

AAN: Barbara Stanwyck

Soshun: see Early Spring

Le Souffle au Coeur **
France/Italy/West Germany 1971 118m colour
NEF/Marianne Films/Video Films/Seitz (Maurice Urbain)
V, V*, L
US title: Murmur of the Heart; aka: Dearest Love

Recovering from an illness at a spa, a 15-year-old boy

overcomes his sexual problems after sleeping, almost inadvertently, with his mother.

A witty and observant study of middle-class attitudes to love, sex and adolescent traumas, with incest forming a minor theme.

wd Louis Malle ph Ricardo Aronovich m Gaston Frèche, Sidney Bechet, Henri Renaud, Charlie Parker
pd Jean-Jacques Caziot, Philippe Turlure
ed Suzanne Baron

Léa Massari, Benoit Ferreux, Daniel Gelin, Michel Lonsdale, Ave Ninchi, Gila von Weitershausen

The Soul Kiss: see A Lady's Morals

Soul Man
US 1986 101m Technicolor Panavision
New World (Steve Tisch)
V, V*, L

A white student tans his skin to win a black scholarship to law school.

Despite its premise, basically a farce of mistaken identities rather than a treatment of racism.

w Carol Black d Steve Miner ph Jeffrey Jur
m Tom Scott pd Greg Fonseca ed David Finfer

C. Thomas Howell, Rae Dawn Chong, Arye Gross, Melora Hardin, James B. Sikking, Leslie Nielsen, James Earl Jones

The Soul of a Monster
US 1944 61m bw
Ted Richmond/Columbia

A rich man is saved from death by a female hypnotist, who keeps him under her spell.

Unusual but not very interesting thriller.

w Edward Dein d Will Jason

Rose Hobart, George Macready, Jim Bannon, Jeanne Bates

'Out of the secret annals of the sea comes the strangest story ever told!'
Souls at Sea *
US 1937 93m bw
Paramount (Henry Hathaway)

In a 19th-century shipwreck an intelligence officer must save himself, and his mission, at the cost of other lives, and is courtmartialled.

A lively seafaring melodrama produced on a fairly impressive scale.

w Grover Jones, Dale Van Every d Henry Hathaway ph Charles Lang Jnr md Boris Morros
m Milan Roder, W. Franke Harling ad Hans Dreier, Roland Anderson

Gary Cooper, George Raft, Frances Dee, Henry Wilcoxon, Harry Carey, Olympe Bradna, Robert Cummings, Porter Hall, George Zucco, Virginia Weidler, Joseph Schildkraut, Gilbert Emery

'First rate slave ship adventure.' – Variety

AAN: Milan Roder, W. Franke Harling; art direction

The Sound and the Fury
US 1959 117m Eastmancolor Cinemascope
TCF/Jerry Wald
S

A once proud Southern family has sunk low in finance and moral stature, and a stern elder son tries to do something about it.

Heavy melodrama with performances to match.

w Irving Ravetch, Harriet Frank Jnr novel William Faulkner d Martin Ritt ph Charles G. Clarke
m Alex North

Yul Brynner, Joanne Woodward, Margaret Leighton, Stuart Whitman, Ethel Waters, Jack Warden, Françoise Rosay, John Beal, Albert Dekker

'A fourth carbon copy of Chekhov in Dixie.' – *Stanley Kauffmann*

The Sound Barrier **

GB   1952   118m   bw
London Films (David Lean)
V
US title: *Breaking the Sound Barrier*

An aircraft manufacturer takes risks with the lives of his family and friends to prove that the sound barrier can be broken.

Riveting, then topical, melodrama with splendid air sequences; a bit upper crust, but with well-drawn characters.

w Terence Rattigan   d David Lean   ph Jack Hildyard   m Malcolm Arnold

Ralph Richardson, Nigel Patrick, Ann Todd, John Justin, Dinah Sheridan, Joseph Tomelty, Denholm Elliott

'The most exciting film about the air that has ever been produced anywhere.' – *Daily Express*

'A peacetime film as exciting as any wartime one.' – *Sunday Dispatch*

AAN: Terence Rattigan

The Sound of Fury: see *Try and Get Me*

The Sound of Music ***

US   1965   172m   DeLuxe   Todd-AO
TCF/Argyle (Robert Wise)
V, V (W), V*, L, S

In 1938 Austria, a trainee nun becomes governess to the Trapp family, falls in love with the widower father, and helps them all escape from the Nazis.

Slightly muted, very handsome version of an enjoyably old-fashioned stage musical with splendid tunes.

w Ernest Lehman   book Howard Lindsay, Russel Crouse   d Robert Wise   ph Ted McCord   md Irwin Kostal   pd Boris Leven   m/y Richard Rodgers, Oscar Hammerstein II

Julie Andrews, Christopher Plummer, Richard Haydn, Eleanor Parker, Peggy Wood, Anna Lee, Marni Nixon

'The success of a movie like *The Sound of Music* makes it even more difficult for anyone to try to do anything worth doing, anything relevant to the modern world, anything inventive or expressive.' – *Pauline Kael, New Yorker*

'This last, most remunerative and least inspired, let alone sophisticated, of the Rodgers and Hammerstein collaborations is square and solid sugar. Calorie-counters, diabetics and grown-ups from eight to eighty had best beware.' – *Judith Crist*

'. . . sufficient warning to those allergic to singing nuns and sweetly innocent children.' – *John Gillett*

AA: best picture; Robert Wise; Irwin Kostal

AAN: Ted McCord; Julie Andrews; Peggy Wood

Sound Off

US   1952   83m   Supercinecolor
Columbia (Jonie Taps)

An entertainer is recruited into the army and has predictable difficulties.

Dishevelled service farce with funny moments.

w Blake Edwards, Richard Quine   d Richard Quine   ph Ellis Carter   md Morris Stoloff   m George Duning

Mickey Rooney, Anne James, Sammy White, John Asher, Gordon Jones

Sounder *

US   1972   105m   DeLuxe   Panavision
TCF/Radnitz-Mattel (Robert B. Radnitz)
V*, L

During the 30s Depression, black sharecroppers in the deep South endure various tribulations.

Well made liberated family movie . . . but not very exciting.

w Lonnie Elder III   novel William H. Armstrong   d Martin Ritt   ph John Alonzo   m Taj Mahal

Paul Winfield, Cicely Tyson, Kevin Hooks, Carmen Mathews, James Best, Taj Mahal

AAN: best picture; Lonnie Elder III; Paul Winfield; Cicely Tyson

Le Soupirant: see *The Suitor*

Soursweet **

GB   1988   111m   colour
Curzon/First Film/British Screen/Zenith/Film Four International (Roger Randall-Cutler)

A Chinese couple living in London start their own small restaurant.

Affecting drama of immigrant life.

w Ian McEwan   novel Timothy Mo   d Mike Newell   ph Michael Garfath   m Richard Hartley   pd Adrian Smith   ed Mick Audsley

Sylvia Chang, Danny An-Ning, Jodi Long, Speedy Choo, Han Tan, Soon-Tek Oh, William Chow

Sous le Ciel de Paris Coule la Seine

France   1951   111m   bw
Regina Filmsonor (Pierre O'Connell and Arys Nisotti)

The adventures of a variety of characters during a day in Paris.

The director is back on his multi-story band wagon, but in this case the stories are undeveloped and the handling less than interesting.

w René Lefèvre, Julien Duvivier   d Julien Duvivier   ph Nicholas Hayer   m Jean Winer

Brigitte Auber, Jean Brochard, René Blancard, Paul Frankeur, Sylvie

'A hotchpotch of familiar story devices, camera tricks and picturesque characterizations and settings, bundled together with an old hand's facility.' – *MFB*

Sous le Soleil de Satan: see *Under Satan's Sun*

Sous les Toits de Paris *

France   1930   92m   bw
Tobis (Frank Clifford)

A Parisian street singer falls in love with a girl, fights her lover, and proves himself innocent of theft.

Surprisingly serious and darkly lit little comedy-drama which, while well enough directed, hardly seems to merit its classic status.

wd René Clair   ph Georges Périnal   m Armand Bernard   pd Lazare Meerson

Albert Préjean, Pola Illery, Gaston Modot, Edmond Gréville

'Real film fare of quality . . . a talker which is intelligible to any country.' – *Variety*

'It is far more movie than talkie, which exercises the imagination and rests the ear.' – *National Board of Review*

The South **

Spain/France   1983   94m   colour
Connoisseur/Television EspanolaChloe/Elias Querejeta
original title: *El Sur*

A woman recalls her childhood in the late 1950s and her relationship with her unhappy father.

Delicate, poetic account of a child's view of adult experience.

w Jose Luis Lopez Linares   story Adelaida Garcia Morales   d Victor Erice   ph Jose Luis Alcaine   ad Antonio Belizon   ed Pablo G. Del Amo

Omero Antonutti, Lola Cardona, Aurore Clement, Sonsoles Arangueren, Iciar Bollan, Rafaela Aparicio, Germaine Montero, Maria Caro

South **

Argentina/France   1988   127m   colour
Cinesur/Pacific/Canal+ (Sabina Sigler)
original title: *Sur*

Released after five years, a political prisoner wanders the streets of his home town accompanied by the ghosts of his past.

Dream, fantasy, past and present merge into a powerful, elegaic account of tyranny and oppression, hope and despair.

wd Fernando Solanas   ph Felix Monti   m Astor Piazzolla   pd Fernando Solanas   ed Juan Carlos Macias, Pablo Mari

Susu Pecoraro, Miguel Angel Sola, Philippe Leotard, Lito Cruz, Ulises Dumont

† The film won Solanas the award for best director at the Cannes Film Festival in 1988.

South American George

GB   1941   93m   bw
Ben Henry/Columbia

An unsuccessful singer poses as a South American opera star.

Not among the star's best.

w Leslie Arliss, Norman Lee and Austin Melford   d Marcel Varnel

George Formby, Linden Travers, Enid Stamp-Taylor, Jacques Brown, Felix Aylmer

South Central *

US   1992   99m   DeLuxe
Ixtlan/Monument/Enchantment (Janet Yang, William B. Steakley)
V, V*, S
GB title: *South Central L.A.*

A black hoodlum, imprisoned for murder, discovers that his 10-year-old son has joined his old gang.

A well-acted but over-earnest account of a man's attempt to redeem his violent past.

wd Steve Anderson   book Crips by Donald Bakeer   ph Charlie Lieberman   m Tim Truman   pd David Brian Miller, Marina Kieser   ed Steve Nevius

Glenn Plummer, Byron Keith Minns, LaRita Shelby, Kevin Best, Christian Coleman, Starletta Dupois, Ivory Ocean, Carl Lumbly

'Speaks eloquently to black kids desperately in need of straight talk. A profoundly moving story . . . It has the power to save lives.' – *Variety*

South of Algiers

GB   1952   95m   Technicolor
ABP/Mayflower (Aubrey Baring, Maxwell Setton)
US title: *The Golden Mask*

Archaeologists and thieves search the Sahara for a priceless mask.

Schoolboy adventure story with a straightforward plot and plenty of local colour.

w Robert Westerby   d Jack Lee   ph Oswald Morris   m Robert Gill

Van Heflin, Wanda Hendrix, Eric Portman, Charles Goldner, Jacques François, Jacques Brunius, Alec Mango, Marne Maitland

'A thousand thundering terrific thrills in a fight-swept tropic paradise!'

South of Pago Pago

US   1940   96m   bw
(UA) Edward Small (Erle C. Kenton)

Greedy white men seek riches in pearls by cheating and overworking the natives.

Slightly unfamiliar backgrounds and a fair supply of two-fisted action gave this romantic adventure drama plenty of box-office pull.

w George Bruce   d Alfred E. Green   ph John Mescall   m Edward Ward

Victor McLaglen, Jon Hall, Frances Farmer, Olympe Bradna, Gene Lockhart, Douglass Dumbrille, Francis Ford

South of St Louis

US 1948 88m Technicolor
Milton Sperling/Warner

Before the Civil War starts, Southern farmers are plagued by Union guerrillas.

Pretty good Western with plenty of action.

w Zachary Gold and James R. Webb d Ray Enright

Joel McCrea, Zachary Scott, Victor Jory, Douglas Kennedy, Dorothy Malone, Alexis Smith, Alan Hale

'Distinguished by the fact that all the good men wear bells on their spurs in contradistinction to the bad men. This determines character without benefit of acting, as well as making a jolly noise.' – C. A. Lejeune

South of Suez

US 1940 85m bw
Warner

A diamond miner falls for the daughter of a man he is accused of murdering.

Watchable melodrama with pleasing actors.

w Barry Triver d Lewis Seiler

George Brent, Brenda Marshall, George Tobias, James Stephenson, Lee Patrick, Eric Blore, Cecil Kellaway

South of Tahiti

US 1941 75m bw
Universal
GB title: White Savage

Four adventurers drift ashore on a tropical island.

Penny-pinching hokum without even the colour to make it watchable.

w Gerald Geraghty d George Waggner

Brian Donlevy, Maria Montez, Broderick Crawford, Andy Devine, Henry Wilcoxon, H. B. Warner

South Pacific **

US 1958 170m Technicolor Todd-AO
Magna/S. P. Enterprises (Buddy Adler)
V, V (W), V*, L, S

In 1943 an American navy nurse on a South Pacific island falls in love with a middle-aged French planter who becomes a war hero.

Overlong, solidly produced film of the musical stage hit, with great locations, action climaxes and lush photography (also a regrettable tendency to use alarming colour filters for dramatic emphasis).

w Paul Osborn, Richard Rodgers, Oscar Hammerstein II, Joshua Logan stories Tales of the South Pacific by James A. Michener d Joshua Logan ph Leon Shamroy md Alfred Newman, Ken Darby ch Le Roy Prinz m/ly Richard Rodgers, Oscar Hammerstein II

Mitzi Gaynor, Rossano Brazzi, Ray Walston, John Kerr, France Nuyen, Juanita Hall

'What a monstrous visual riot! What a din!' – C. A. Lejeune

AAN: Leon Shamroy; Alfred Newman, Ken Darby

South Riding **

GB 1937 91m bw
London Films (Alexander Korda, Victor Saville)

A schoolmistress in a quiet Yorkshire dale exposes crooked councillors and falls for the depressed local squire.

Dated but engrossing multi-drama from a famous novel; a good compact piece of film-making.

w Ian Dalrymple, Donald Bull, novel Winifred Holtby d Victor Saville ph Harry Stradling m Richard Addinsell

Ralph Richardson, Edna Best, Edmund Gwenn, Ann Todd, Glynis Johns, John Clements, Marie Lohr, Milton Rosmer, Edward Lexy

'Another artistic Korda film . . . lacking in a story of popular appeal.' – Variety

'A convincing and dramatic picture of English provincial life.' – Film Weekly

South Sea Sinner

US 1949 88m bw
Universal-International
GB title: East of Java

On a South Sea island, a fugitive from justice is blackmailed by a café owner.

Hackneyed elements are strung together without much flair in this routine melodrama.

w Joel Malone, Oscar Brodney d Bruce Humberstone

Macdonald Carey, Shelley Winters, Luther Adler, Helena Carter, Frank Lovejoy, Art Smith, Liberace

South Sea Woman

US 1953 99m bw
Warner (Sam Bischoff)

Adventures of a fight-loving marine in the Pacific war.

Unlovable mixture of brawling, romancing and war-winning.

w Edwin Blum play William M. Rankin d Arthur Lubin ph Ted McCord m David Buttolph

Burt Lancaster, Virginia Mayo, Chuck Connors, Arthur Shields, Barry Kelley, Leon Askin

Southern Comfort ****

US 1981 106m DeLuxe
EMI/Phoenix/Cinema Group Venture (David Giler)
V, V*, L

National Guardsmen on a routine exercise into swampland find themselves involved in a life-and-death struggle with the Cajun inhabitants.

Brilliant, compelling, tightly-constructed thriller that manages also to be an allegory of American involvement in Vietnam.

w Michael Kane, Walter Hill, David Giler d Walter Hill ph Andrew Laszlo m Ry Cooder

Keith Carradine, Powers Boothe, Fred Ward, Franklyn Seales, T. K. Carter, Lewis Smith

'As an action director Walter Hill has a dazzling competence. Southern Comfort comes across with such immediacy that it had a near-hypnotic hold on me and I felt startled – brought up short – when it ended.' – Pauline Kael, New Yorker

'Africa explodes with a thousand surprises!'
The Southern Star *

GB/France 1968 105m Techniscope
Columbia/Eurofrance/Capitole (Roger Duchet)

In French West Africa in 1912, a penniless American finds a huge diamond which several crooks are after.

Quite a likeable adventure romp, with good suspense sequences and convincing jungle settings.

w David Pursall, Jack Seddon novel Jules Verne d Sidney Hayers ph Raoul Coutard m Georges Garvarentz

George Segal, Ursula Andress, Orson Welles, Ian Hendry, Michael Constantine, Johnny Sekka, Harry Andrews

A Southern Yankee *

US 1948 90m bw
MGM (Paul Jones)
V*
GB title: My Hero

During the Civil War a Southern bellboy masquerades as a spy and finds himself behind enemy lines.

A rather feeble reworking of Buster Keaton's The General, with some excellent gags supervised by the master himself.

w Harry Tugend d Edward Sedgwick ph Ray June m David Snell

Red Skelton, Brian Donlevy, Arlene Dahl, George Coulouris, Lloyd Gough, John Ireland, Minor Watson, Charles Dingle

'She was his woman! And he was her man! That's all they had to fight with – against the world, the flesh, and the devil!'
The Southerner ***

US 1945 91m bw
(UA) David Loew, Robert Hakim
V*

Problems of penniless farmers in the deep South.

Impressive, highly pictorial outdoor drama, more poetic than The Grapes of Wrath and lacking the acting strength.

wd Jean Renoir novel Hold Autumn in Your Hand by George Sessions Perry ph Lucien Andriot m Werner Janssen

Zachary Scott, Betty Field, Beulah Bondi, J. Carrol Naish, Percy Kilbride, Blanche Yurka, Norman Lloyd

'I cannot imagine anybody failing to be spellbound by this first successful essay in Franco-American screen collaboration.' – Richard Winnington

'You can smell the earth as the plough turns it up; you can sense the winter and the rain and the sunshine.' – C. A. Lejeune

† Some sources state that the script was by William Faulkner.

AAN: Jean Renoir (as director); Werner Janssen

Southwest to Sonora: see The Appaloosa

Souvenir

GB 1987 93m Technicolor
Curzon/Fancy Free/Geoff Reeve Pictures (Tom Reeve, James Reeve)

An elderly German living in New York returns to the French town where he was involved in a massacre of the inhabitants during the Second World War.

Unsuccessful and heavy-handed, it never comes close to exploring the themes of guilt and individual responsibility that it raises.

w Paul Wheeler novel The Pork Butcher by David Hughes d Geoffrey Reeve ph Fred Tammes m Tony Kinsey pd Morley Smith ed Bob Morgan

Christopher Plummer, Catherine Hicks, Michael Lonsdale, Christopher Cazenove, Lisa Daniely, Jean Badin, Patrick Bailey

'Could be a bad joke about the type of international co-production which is made because the money, rather than the audience, can be found for it.' – MFB

Soylent Green *

US 1973 97m Metrocolor Panavision
MGM (Walter Seltzer, Russell Thatcher)
V*, L

In 2022, the population of New York exists in perpetual heat on synthetic foods; a policeman hears from his elderly friend about an earlier time when things were better.

Lively futuristic yarn with a splendid climax revealing the nature of the artificial food; marred by narrative incoherence and by direction which fails to put plot points clearly across.

w Stanley R. Greenberg novel Make Room, Make Room by Harry Harrison d Richard Fleischer ph Richard H. Kline m Fred Myrow

Charlton Heston, Edward G. Robinson, Leigh Taylor-Young, Chuck Connors, Brock Peters, Joseph Cotten

The Space Children

US 1958 71m bw VistaVision
Paramount (William Alland)

Children at a rocket testing site sabotage equipment on the instructions of a strange pulsating object.

Naïve moral fable, not badly done on its level.

w Bernard Schoenfeld d Jack Arnold

Adam Williams, Peggy Webber, Michel Ray, Jackie Coogan

Space Raiders

US 1983 82m colour
Millennium (Roger Corman)
V*

A space mercenary promises to help return a 10-year-old stowaway to his home planet.

Low-budget Star Wars rip-off for juvenile audiences, incorporating footage from Battle beyond the Stars.

wd Howard R. Cohen ph Alec Hirschfeld

Vince Edwards, David Mendenhall, Patsy Pease, Thom Christopher, Dick Miller

Spaceballs

US 1987 96m Metrocolor
MGM/UA (Mel Brooks, Ezra Swerdlow)
V, V*, L

A ruthless race is out to steal the air supply from the planet Druidia.

Flabby spoof of Star Wars, without any funny ideas.

w Mel Brooks, Thomas Meehan, Ronny Graham d Mel Brooks ph Nick McLean m John Morris pd Terence Marsh ed Conrad Buff IV

Mel Brooks, John Candy, Rick Moranis, Bill Pullman, Daphne Zuniga, Dom DeLuise, John Hurt

'At its worst, it displays a colossal ego at work and humour better left to home movies.' – Daily Variety

Spaced Invaders

US 1989 100m CFI
Medusa/Smart Egg Pictures (Luigi Cingolani)
V, V*, L

A spaceship load of inept Martians mistakenly try to conquer the Earth.

Inane spoof of the current cycle of science fiction films.

w Patrick Read Johnson, Scott Alexander d Patrick Read Johnson ph James L. Carter m David Russo pd Tony Tremblay ed Seth Gaven, Daniel Bross

Douglas Barr, Royal Dano, Ariana Richards, J. J. Anderson, Gregg Berger, Fred Applegate, Patrika Darbo

Spacehunter: Adventures in the Forbidden Zone

US 1983 90m Metrocolor 3-D
Columbia/Delphi (Don Carmody, Andre Link, John Dunning)
V, V*, L

In the 22nd century, a spaceship salvage expert lands on a long-forgotten planet to rescue three Earthwomen from the tyrants of Graveyard City.

Mindless and rather unattractive space fantasy, far less likeable than Flash Gordon.

w David Preston, Edith Rey, Dan Goldbert, Len Blum d Lamont Johnson ph Frank Tidy m Elmer Bernstein pd Jackson de Govia

Peter Strauss, Molly Ringwald, Ernie Hudson, Andrea Marcovicci, Michael Ironside

The Spaceman and King Arthur

GB 1979 93m Technicolor
Walt Disney
US title: Unidentified Flying Oddball

An astronaut and his robot accidentally land themselves back at the court of King Arthur.

Mindless but occasionally funny rewrite of Mark Twain's A Connecticut Yankee.

w Don Tait d Russ Mayberry

Dennis Dugan, Jim Dale, Ron Moody, Kenneth More, John Le Mesurier, Rodney Bewes, Robert Beatty

Spaceways

GB 1953 76m bw
Exclusive/Hammer (Michael Carreras)

A scientist is suspected of killing his wife and her lover and sending their bodies into space in Britain's first satellite.

Trite marital drama in a science-fiction setting, interesting only for its belief that the 1960s would bring the first manned space station.

w Paul Tabori, Richard Landau play Charles Eric Maine d Terence Fisher ph Reginald Wyer md Ivor Slaney ad J. Elder Wills sp The Trading Post ed Maurice Rootes

Howard Duff, Eva Bartok, Alan Wheatley, Philip Leaver, Michael Medwin, Andrew Osborn, Cecile Chevreau

The Spaniard's Curse

GB 1958 74m bw
Independent Film Distributors/Wentworth (Roger Proudlock)

A man wrongly convicted of murder pronounces an old Spanish death curse on the judge, prosecuting counsel, foreman of the jury and the killer.

A neat, well-plotted little thriller.

w Kenneth Hyde, Ralph Kemplen, Roger Proudlock story Edith Pargeter d Ralph Kemplen ph Arthur Grant d Lambert Williamson pd Tony Masters ed Stanley Hawkes

Tony Wright, Lee Patterson, Michael Hordern, Susan Beaumont, Ralph Truman, Henry Oscar, Brian Oulton, Olga Dickie, Roddy Hughes, Joe Gibbons

Spanish Affair

US 1958 92m Technicolor Vistavision
Paramount/Nomad (Bruce Odlum)

An American architect in Madrid falls in love with his interpreter and is pursued by her lover.

Curiously plotless excuse for a travelogue, lushly photographed but not exactly gripping.

w Richard Collins d Don Siegel ph Sam Leavitt m Daniele Amfitheatrof

Richard Kiley, Carmen Sevilla, Jose Guardiola

Spanish Fly

GB 1975 86m Technicolor
EMI (Peter James, Gerald Flint-Shipman)
V

An Englishman in Majorca tries to improve a purchase of local wine by putting an aphrodisiac in it, with predictable results.

Crude, tatty comedy by people who should know better.

w Robert Ryerson d Bob Kellett

Terry-Thomas, Leslie Phillips, Graham Armitage, Frank Thornton, Sue Lloyd

The Spanish Gardener

GB 1956 97m Technicolor Vistavision
Rank (John Bryan)

The British consul in Spain is annoyed when his young son develops a strong friendship with the gardener.

Slow, understated study in human relationships which doesn't come off; any sexual relevance is well concealed.

w Lesley Storm, John Bryan novel A. J. Cronin d Philip Leacock ph Christopher Challis m John Veale

Dirk Bogarde, Michael Hordern, Jon Whiteley, Cyril Cusack, Geoffrey Keen, Maureen Swanson, Lyndon Brook, Josephine Griffin, Bernard Lee, Rosalie Crutchley

The Spanish Main *

US 1945 101m Technicolor
RKO (Robert Fellows)
L

In the Caribbean, the fiancée of the Spanish viceroy is kidnapped by a pirate who determines to tame her before marrying her.

Slightly tongue-in-cheek pirate hokum; generally good value for the easily amused.

w George Worthing Yates, Herman J. Mankiewicz d Frank Borzage ph George Barnes md Constantin Bakaleinikoff m Hanns Eisler

Paul Henreid, Maureen O'Hara, Binnie Barnes, Walter Slezak, John Emery, Barton MacLane, J. M. Kerrigan, Nancy Gates, Fritz Leiber, Jack La Rue, Mike Mazurki, Victor Kilian

AAN: George Barnes

Spare a Copper *

GB 1940 77m bw
Ealing

A police war reservist catches saboteurs.

One of the last good Formby comedies, with everything percolating as it should.

w Roger MacDougall, Austin Melford, Basil Dearden d John Paddy Carstairs

George Formby, Dorothy Hyson, Bernard Lee, John Warwick, John Turnbull, George Merritt

Spare the Rod

GB 1961 93m bw
British Lion/Bryanston/Weyland (Victor Lyndon)

At an East End school, a novice master wins the confidence of tough pupils.

A British Blackboard Jungle, paving the way for To Sir with Love; not exciting on its own account.

w John Cresswell novel Michael Croft d Leslie Norman ph Paul Beeson m Laurie Johnson

Max Bygraves, Geoffrey Keen, Donald Pleasence, Richard O'Sullivan, Betty McDowall, Eleanor Summerfield, Mary Merrall

Sparrows Can't Sing

GB 1962 94m bw
Elstree/Carthage (Donald Taylor)
V

Returning after two years at sea, a sailor searches for his wife and threatens vengeance on her lover.

Relentlessly caricatured cockney comedy melodrama, too self-conscious to be effective, and not at all likeable anyway.

w Stephen Lewis, Joan Littlewood d Joan Littlewood ph Max Greene m James Stevens

James Booth, Barbara Windsor, Roy Kinnear, Avis Bunnage, George Sewell, Barbara Ferris, Murray Melvin, Arthur Mullard

Spartacus **

US 1960 196m Super Technirama 70
U-I/Bryna (Edward Lewis)
V, V (W), V*, L, S

The slaves of ancient Rome revolt and are quashed.

Long, well-made, downbeat epic with deeper than usual characterization and several bravura sequences.

w Dalton Trumbo novel Howard Fast d Stanley Kubrick ph Russell Metty m Alex North pd Alexander Golitzen ed Robert Lawrence

Kirk Douglas, Laurence Olivier, Charles Laughton, Tony Curtis, Jean Simmons, Peter Ustinov, John

Gavin, Nina Foch, Herbert Lom, John Ireland, John Dall, Charles McGraw, Woody Strode

'Everything is depicted with a lack of imagination that is truly Marxian.' – *Anne Grayson*

'A lot of first-rate professionals have pooled their abilities to make a first-rate circus.' – *Stanley Kauffmann*

'One comes away feeling rather revolted and not at all ennobled.' – *Alan Dent, Illustrated London News*

AA: Russell Metty; Peter Ustinov; art direction

AAN: Alex North; editing

Spartacus the Gladiator
Italy 1953 103m bw
Consorzio Spartacus

Action-oriented remake of a familiar story.

w Jean Ferry, Mario Bori *d* Riccardo Freda
ph Gabor Pigany *m* Renzo Rossellini

Massimo Girotti, Ludmilla Tcherina, Maria Canala

'A love story stormy as raging Arctic seas!'
Spawn of the North **
US 1938 110m bw
Paramount (Albert Lewin)

In 1890s Alaska, American fishermen combat Russian poachers.

Solidly carpentered all-star action melodrama, a sizzler of its day. Remade 1953 as *Alaska Seas*.

w Talbot Jennings, Jules Furthman *d* Henry Hathaway *ph* Charles Lang *m* Dimitri Tiomkin

George Raft, Henry Fonda, Dorothy Lamour, *John Barrymore*, Akim Tamiroff, Louise Platt, Lynne Overman, Fuzzy Knight, Vladimir Sokoloff, Duncan Renaldo, John Wray

'The visual features are so realistic and terrifying that audiences will find complete satisfaction in the production.' – *Variety*

'This film has something which the cinema of bygone days used to supply as a matter of course – action and thrills, the quickened pulse and the lump in the throat.' – *Basil Wright*

'Rousing old-fashioned spectacle.' – *New York Times*

AA: Special Award for special effects

Speak Easily *
US 1932 83m bw
MGM (Lawrence Weingarten)

A professor inherits a Broadway musical and falls for the lure of the bright lights.

Interesting Keaton talkie at the point of his decline.

w Ralph Spence, Lawrence E. Johnson
novel *Footlights* by Clarence Budington Kelland
d Edward Sedgwick *ph* Harold Wentstrom

Buster Keaton, Jimmy Durante, Hedda Hopper

Speaking Parts
Canada 1989 92m colour
Recorded Releasing/Ego Film Arts/Telefilm Canada/Ontario
Film Development Company/Academy Pictures/Film Four International
V*, L

A screenwriter and a hotel maid both fall in love with a gigolo who wants to be an actor.

Curious and ultimately unsatisfactory triangular drama of personalities who connect with each other mainly through the medium of video.

wd Atom Egoyan *ph* Paul Sarossy *m* Mychael Danna *ad* Linda Del Rosario *ed* Bruce McDonald

Michael McManus, Arsinee Khanjian, Gabrielle Rose, Tony Nardi, David Hemblen, Patricia Collins

Special Agent
US 1935 74m bw
Cosmopolitan/Warner

A special investigator pretends to be a newspaperman.

Routine rough stuff, quite watchable.

w Laird Doyle, Abem Finkel *d* William Keighley

Bette Davis, George Brent, Ricardo Cortez, Jack La Rue, Henry O'Neill, J. Carrol Naish

'Indifferent entertainment but Bette Davis may help.' – *Variety*

Special Delivery
US 1976 99m DeLuxe
TCF/Bing Crosby Productions (Richard Berg)

Three disabled Vietnam veterans rob a bank, and the consequences are complicated.

Unremarkable suspenser which takes itself too seriously.

w Don Gazzaniga *d* Paul Wendkos *ph* Harry Stradling Jnr *m* Lalo Schifrin

Bo Svenson, Cybill Shepherd, Michael C. Gwynne, Vic Tayback, Sorrell Booke

The Speckled Band
GB 1931 80m bw
Herbert Wilcox/B and D
V*

Sherlock Holmes saves an heiress from a horrible death.

Limp and overstretched version of Conan Doyle's story, interesting only for the actors.

w W. P. Lipscomb *d* Jack Raymond

Raymond Massey, Athole Stewart (as Watson), Lyn Harding (as Roylott), Angela Baddeley, Nancy Price

The Specter of the Rose *
US 1946 90m bw
Republic (Ben Hecht)
V*

A schizophrenic ballet dancer lives his role and nearly murders his wife.

A rather hilarious bid for culture: hard to sit through without laughing, but unique.

wd Ben Hecht *ph* Lee Garmes *m* Georges Antheil

Viola Essen, Ivan Kirov, Michael Chekhov

The Spectre of Edgar Allan Poe
US 1972 86m Eastmancolor
Doverton/Cintel (Mohy Quandour)
V*

Poe visits an asylum where his beloved Lenore has been taken to recover from being buried alive and finds himself in a nightmare world of murder and monsters.

An intriguing notion is quickly done to death in an unimaginative production.

wd Mohy Quandour *story* Kenneth Hartford, Denton Foxx *ph* Robert Birchall *m* Allen D. Allen *sp* Byrd Holland *ed* Abbas Amin

Robert Walker, Mary Grover, Cesar Romero, Tom Drake, Carol Ohmart

Speedy **
US 1928 90m approx bw silent
Paramount (Harold Lloyd)

A young man saves his girl's grandfather's trolley car business.

One of its star's most stylish comedies, and his last silent film, with a trolley car ride for climax.

w John Grey, Lex Neal, Howard Emmett Rogers, Jay Howe *d* Ted Wilde

Harold Lloyd, Ann Christy, Bert Woodruff, Brooks Benedict, Babe Ruth

AAN: Ted Wilde

The Spell of Amy Nugent: see *Spellbound* (1940)

Spell of the Circus
US 1931 bw serial: 10 eps
Universal

A scheming circus manager wants to marry the owner's daughter, but she loves the cowboy star.

Slight basis for a serial.

d Robert F. Hill

Francis X. Bushman Jnr, Alberta Vaughn, Tom London, Walter Shumway

The Spellbinder
US 1939 68m bw
RKO

A criminal lawyer full of tricks finds himself on trial for murder.

Contrived courtroom drama tailored to its star.

w Thomas Lennon, Joseph A. Fields *d* Jack Hively

Lee Tracy, Barbara Read, Patric Knowles, Allan Lane, Morgan Conway

'Average supporter for duals.' – *Variety*

Spellbound
GB 1940 82m bw
Pyramid Amalgamated (R. Murray Leslie)
aka: *Passing Clouds*; US title: *The Spell of Amy Nugent*

A young man is in despair when his fiancée dies, and nearly goes mad when a medium materializes her from the dead.

Very odd, very naïve, but somehow rather winning.

w Miles Malleson *novel* *The Necromancers* by Robert Benson *d* John Harlow *ph* Walter Harvey

Derek Farr, Vera Lindsay, Frederick Leister, Hay Petrie, Diana King, Felix Aylmer

Spellbound **
US 1945 111m bw
David O. Selznick
V*, L, S

The new head of a mental institution is an impostor and an amnesiac; a staff member falls in love with him and helps him recall the fate of the real Dr Edwardes.

Enthralling and rather infuriating psychological mystery; the Hitchcock touches are splendid, and the stars shine magically, but the plot could have stood a little more attention.

w Ben Hecht, Angus MacPhail *novel* *The House of Dr Edwardes* by Francis Beeding *d* Alfred Hitchcock *ph* George Barnes *dream sequence* Salvador Dali *m* Miklos Rozsa *ad* James Basevi

Ingrid Bergman, Gregory Peck, Leo G. Carroll, Michael Chekhov, Rhonda Fleming, John Emery, Norman Lloyd, Steve Geray

'Just about as much of the id as could be safely displayed in a Bergdorf Goodman window.' – *James Agee*

'Glossily produced and wildly improbable.' – *George Perry, 1965*

'Bergman's apple-cheeked sincerity has rarely been so out of place as in this confection whipped up by jaded chefs.' – *New Yorker, 1976*

AA: Miklos Rozsa

AAN: best picture; Alfred Hitchcock; George Barnes; Michael Chekhov

Spencer's Mountain *
US 1963 121m Technicolor Panavision
Warner (Delmer Daves)
L

Life in rural America in the thirties with a poor quarry worker and his family of nine.

Sentimental rose-tinted hokum which later became TV's *The Waltons*. Expertly concocted, Hollywood style.

wd Delmer Daves   *novel* Earl Hanmer Jnr
ph Charles Lawton, H. F. Koenekamp   *m* Max Steiner

Henry Fonda, Maureen O'Hara, James MacArthur, Donald Crisp, Wally Cox, Mimsy Farmer, Lilian Bronson

'Outstanding for its smirking sexuality, its glorification of the vulgar, its patronizing tone, its mealymouthed piety.' – *Judith Crist*

Spendthrift
US   1936   80m   bw
Paramount

A millionaire playboy runs out of cash.

Mild romantic comedy.

w Raoul Walsh, Bert Hanlon   *d* Raoul Walsh

Henry Fonda, Pat Paterson, Mary Brian, George Barbier, Ed Brophy

Speriamo Che Sia Femmina: see *Let's Hope It's A Girl*

Spetters **
Netherlands   1980   115m   Eastmancolor
Embassy/VSE (Joop Van Den Ende)
V*

In a small town, three young men, two of them hoping to win a motor-cross biking championship, are all involved with a blonde sex siren who serves food from a mobile canteen.

High energy melodrama, full of sex and violence, but eminently watchable.

w Gerard Soeteman   *d* Paul Verhoeven   *ph* Jöst Vacano   *m* Ton Scherpenzeel   *ad* Dick Schillemans   *ed* Ine Schenkkan

Hans Van Tongeren, Renee Soutendijk, Toon Agterberg, Maarten Spanjer, Marianne Boyer, Hugo Metsjers, Kittye Courbois, Rutger Hauer, Jeroen Krabbé

The Sphinx
US   1933   63m   bw
Monogram
V*

A murderer uses his deaf mute brother as an alibi.

Mildly ingenious low-budget thriller.

w Albert DeMond   *d* Phil Rosen

Lionel Atwill, Sheila Terry, Theodore Newton, Paul Hurst, Luis Alberni

'Fair returns are probable if dated properly.' – *Variety*

Sphinx
US   1980   118m   Technicolor   Panavision
Warner/Orion (Stanley O'Toole)
V*

Archaeologists in modern Cairo find clues to an ancient treasure.

Expensive penny dreadful which lurches about from comedy to horror but is often well worth looking at.

w John Byrum   *novel* Robin Cook   *d* Franklin J. Schaffner   *ph* Ernest Day   *m* Michael J. Lewis   *pd* Terence Marsh

Lesley-Anne Down, Frank Langella, Maurice Ronet, John Gielgud, Vic Tablian, Martin Benson, John Rhys-Davies

'A glossily-packaged exercise in random-selection box-office formulae.' – *Jo Imeson, MFB*

Spicy Rice: see *Dragon's Food*

The Spider
US   1931   65m   bw
Fox

A theatre magician traps a killer.

Rather flat transcription of a play which in its original form took every advantage of the audience and other elements.

play Fulton Oursler, Lowell Brentano   *d* William Cameron Menzies, Kenneth MacKenna

Edmund Lowe, Howard Philips, Lois Moran, George E. Stone, El Brendel

The Spider
GB   1940   81m   bw
Victor M. Greene/Admiral Films

A theatrical agent kills his partner on a train.

Barely competent murder thriller.

w Kenneth Horne, Reginald Long   *novel* Henry Holt   *d* Maurice Elvey

Derrick de Marney, Diana Churchill, Cecil Parker, Jean Gillie, Frank Cellier, Allan Jeayes

The Spider and the Fly
GB   1949   95m   bw
GFD/Maxwell Setton, Aubrey Baring

In 1913 a Parisian safecracker constantly outwits an inspector of the Sûreté, but war brings changes.

Coldly ironic comedy drama which really, regrettably, doesn't work.

w Robert Westerby   *d* Robert Hamer   *ph* Geoffrey Unsworth   *m* Georges Auric

Eric Portman, Guy Rolfe, Nadia Gray, George Cole, Edward Chapman, John Carol, Maurice Denham

'Not sufficiently exciting for a thriller, not quite sharp enough for a real drama of character.' – *Gavin Lambert, MFB*

The Spider Returns
US   1941   bw   serial: 15 eps
Columbia

A wealthy socialite dons disguises to fight the underworld.

Enjoyable comic strip hokum; a feature version was also released.

d James W. Horne

Warren Hull, Mary Ainslee, Dave O'Brien, Joe Girard

† Sequel to *The Spider's Web*.

Spider Woman **
US   1944   62m   bw
Universal (Roy William Neill)
V*
aka: *Sherlock Holmes and the Spider Woman*

A female Moriarty kills her victims with spiders so that she can collect on their insurance policies.

Lively episode in the modernized series, which packs in several suspenseful episodes borrowed from a variety of Conan Doyle originals.

w Bertram Millhauser   *d* Roy William Neill   *ph* Charles Van Enger   *m* Hans Salter

Basil Rathbone, Nigel Bruce, Gale Sondergaard, Dennis Hoey, Vernon Downing, Alec Craig, Mary Gordon

The Spider Woman Strikes Back
US   1946   59m   bw
Universal (Howard Welsch)

An innocent girl is used as decoy by a conniving female criminal.

Boring crime filler, scarcely a worthy sequel to *Spider Woman*.

w Eric Taylor   *d* Arthur Lubin

Gale Sondergaard, Brenda Joyce, Rondo Hatton, Milburn Stone, Kirby Grant, Hobart Cavanaugh

The Spider's Stratagem *
Italy   1970   97m   Eastmancolor
Radiotelevisione Italiana/Red Film (Giovanni Bertolucci)
V, V*
original title: *Strategia del Ragno*

Revisiting the village in the Po valley where his father was murdered by fascists in 1936, our gradually disillusioned hero learns that his father was really a traitor executed by his own men.

Elaborately mysterious puzzle play for intellectuals, with infinite shades of meaning which few will bother to explore. The atmosphere, however, is superbly caught.

w Bernardo Bertolucci, Eduardo de Gregorio, Marilu Parolini   *story The Theme of the Traitor and the Hero* by Jorge Luis Borges   *d* Bernardo Bertolucci   *ph* Vittorio Storaro, Franco di Giacomo

Giulio Brogi, Alida Valli, Tino Scotti, Pino Campanini

The Spider's Web
US   1938   bw   serial: 15 eps
Columbia

The Spider (see *The Spider Returns*) fights The Octopus, an outlaw demoralizing the nation's transport system.

Predictable adventures, less lively than the sequel.

d Ray Taylor and James W. Horne

Warren Hull, Iris Meredith, Richard Fiske, Marc Lawrence

The Spider's Web
GB   1960   89m   colour
Danzigers

A diplomat's wife has an unwanted corpse on her hands.

Fairly standard who-done-it played unwisely for comedy.

w Albert G. Miller, Eldon Howard   *play* Agatha Christie   *d* Godfrey Grayson

Glynis Johns, John Justin, Cicely Courtneidge, Jack Hulbert, Ronald Howard, David Nixon

Der Spiegel Ayna: see *The Mirror*

The Spies: see *Les Espions*

Spies Like Us
US   1985   109m   Technicolor
Warner (Brian Grazer, George Folsey Jnr)
V, V*, L

Bumbling bureaucrats are mistakenly chosen for a spy mission.

Inept attempts at humour fall flat throughout this dreary venture, which is as though Hope and Crosby had set out on the road to Morocco without a script.

w Dan Aykroyd, Lowell Ganz, Babaloo Mandel   *d* John Landis   *ph* Robert Paynter   *m* Elmer Bernstein   *pd* Peter Murton   *ed* Malcolm Campbell

Chevy Chase, Dan Aykroyd, Steve Forrest, Donna Dixon, Bruce Davison, William Prince, Bernie Casey

Spies of the Air
GB   1939   77m   bw
British National (John Corfield)

A test pilot turns out to be an enemy agent.

Moderate programmer with an engaging cast.

w A. R. Rawlinson, Bridget Boland   *play Official Secrets* by Jeffrey Dell   *d* David MacDonald

Barry K. Barnes, Roger Livesey, Joan Marion, Basil Radford, Felix Aylmer, John Turnbull, Henry Oscar

The Spikes Gang

US   1974   96m   DeLuxe
UA/Mirisch/Duo/Sanford (Walter Mirisch)

Three boys shelter a bank robber and join his gang.

Doom-laden, violent Western with a few comic lines.

w Irving Ravetch, Harriet Frank Jnr   novel The Bank
Robber by Giles Tippette   d Richard Fleischer
ph Brian West   m Fred Karlin

Lee Marvin, Gary Grimes, Ron Howard, Charles
Martin Smith, Arthur Hunnicutt, Noah Beery Jnr

Spin of a Coin: see The George Raft Story

Spinout

US   1966   93m   Metrocolor   Panavision
MGM/Euterpe (Joe Pasternak)
V, V*, L
GB title: California Holiday

A carefree touring singer agrees to drive an
experimental car in a road race.

Mild star musical which at least stays in the open air.

w Theodore J. Flicker, George Kirgo   d Norman
Taurog   ph Daniel L. Fapp   md Georgie Stoll

Elvis Presley, Shelley Fabares, Carl Betz, Cecil
Kellaway, Diane McBain, Deborah Walley, Jack
Mullaney, Will Hutchins, Una Merkel

La Spina Dorsale del Diavolo: see The Deserter

Spinster: see Two Loves

The Spiral Road

US   1962   145m   Eastmancolor
U-I (Robert Arthur)

In 1936 Java, an atheist medical man fights a leprosy
epidemic and eventually becomes a missionary.

A long slog through jungle/religious clichés, with a
hilariously miscast star and an almost Victorian script.

w John Lee Mahin, Neil Paterson   novel Jan de
Hartog   d Robert Mulligan   ph Russell Harlan
m Jerry Goldsmith

Rock Hudson, Burl Ives, Geoffrey Keen, Gena
Rowlands, Will Kuluva, Neva Patterson, Philip
Abbott

The Spiral Staircase ***

US   1945   83m   bw
RKO (Dore Schary)
V*, L

A small town in 1906 New England is terrorized by a
psychopathic killer of deformed girls.

Archetypal old dark house thriller, superbly detailed
and set during a most convincing thunderstorm. Even
though the identity of the villain is pretty obvious,
this is a superior Hollywood product.

w Mel Dinelli,   novel Some Must Watch by Ethel Lina
White   d Robert Siodmak   ph Nicholas Musuraca
m Roy Webb   ad Albert S. D'Agostino, Jack Okey

Dorothy McGuire, George Brent, Kent Smith, Ethel
Barrymore, Rhys Williams, Rhonda Fleming, Gordon
Oliver, Sara Allgood, James Bell

'A nice, cosy and well-sustained atmosphere of
horror.' – C. A. Lejeune

AAN: Ethel Barrymore

The Spiral Staircase

GB   1975   89m   Technicolor
Warner/Raven (Peter Shaw)
V*

Modernized remake of the above using virtually the
same script, and apparently determined to prove how
badly it can be presented.

w Andrew Meredith   d Peter Collinson   ph Ken
Hodges   m David Lindup

Jacqueline Bisset, Christopher Plummer, Sam
Wanamaker, Mildred Dunnock, Gayle Hunnicutt,
Sheila Brennan, Elaine Stritch, John Ronane, Ronald
Radd, John Phillip Law

'I don't think this needless remake is going to set
anyone's flesh creeping, except at the vulgar
flashiness of the whole enterprise.' – Michael Billington,
Illustrated London News

The Spirit Is Willing

US   1966   100m   Technicolor
Paramount/William Castle

A family finds that its holiday home is haunted by the
ghosts of a crime passionel.

Overlong, overplayed and witless farce with virtually
no opportunity well taken.

w Ben Starr   novel The Visitors by Nathaniel Benchley
d William Castle   ph Hal Stine   m Vic Mizzy

Sid Caesar, Vera Miles, John McGiver, Cass Daley,
John Astin, Mary Wickes, Jesse White

Spirit of Culver

US   1939   89m   bw
Universal

A boy grows up at Culver Military Academy.

Very humdrum flagwaver combined with a last
attempt to maintain stardom for two child performers.

w Nathaniel West, Whitney Bolton   d Joseph
Santley

Jackie Cooper, Freddie Bartholomew, Tim Holt,
Henry Hull, Andy Devine, Gene Reynolds

'Mild entertainment for duals and kids.' – Variety

The Spirit of St Louis *

US   1957   135m   Warnercolor   Cinemascope
Warner (Leyland Hayward)
V, V*, L, S

In 1927 Charles Lindbergh flies a specially
constructed plane 3,600 miles nonstop New York to
Paris in 33½ hours.

Impeccably in its period, this needlessly
Cinemascoped reconstruction can scarcely avoid dull
patches since for long stretches its hero is on screen
solo apart from a fly, and his monologues become
soporific.

w Billy Wilder, Wendell Mayes   book Charles
Lindbergh   d Billy Wilder   ph Robert Burks,
Peverell Marley   m Franz Waxman

James Stewart, Murray Hamilton, Marc Connelly

The Spirit of the Beehive *

Spain   1973   98m   Eastmancolor
Elias Querejeta
V*
original title: El Espíritu de la Colmene

In 1940 in a remote village, two children see a
travelling film show of Frankenstein, and their
imaginations run riot; or do they?

Sensitive story of childish imagination, reminiscent of
Jeux Interdits and yet very much its own vision.

w Francisco J. Querejeta   d Victor Erice   ph Luis
Cuadrado   m Luis de Pablo

Fernando Fernan Gomez, Teresa Gimpera, Ana
Torrent, Isabel Telleria

Spirit of the People: see Abe Lincoln in Illinois

Spirits of the Dead: see Histoires Extraordinaires

The Spiritualist: see The Amazing Dr X

Spite Marriage *

US   1929   77m (24 fps)   bw   silent
MGM/Buster Keaton (Lawrence Weingarten)

A tailor's assistant loves an actress, who marries him
to spite someone else.

For a Keaton comedy from his great period, this is
remarkably thin on invention, and its pleasures,
though undeniable, are minor.

w Richard Schayer, Lew Lipton   d Edward
Sedgwick   ph Reggie Lanning

Buster Keaton, Dorothy Sebastian, Edward Earle,
Leila Hyams

Spitfire *

US   1934   88m   bw
RKO (Pandro S. Berman)
V*

An Ozark mountain girl believes herself to be a faith
healer and is driven from the community.

Curious star melodrama with effective moments.

w Jane Murfin   play Trigger by Lula Vollmer
d John Cromwell   ph Edward Cronjager   m Max
Steiner

Katharine Hepburn, Robert Young, Ralph Bellamy,
Martha Sleeper, Louis Mason

'The veins of the story carry thin milk rather than
heavy corpuscles.' – Variety

'The picture would suggest that Katharine Hepburn is
condemned to elegance, doomed to be a lady for the
rest of her natural life, and that her artistry does not
extend to the interpretation of the primitive or the
uncouth. That her producers have not bothered to give
her a scenario of any interest or quality is another
aspect of the situation.' – New Yorker

Spitfire (1942): see The First of the Few

Spivs: see I Vitelloni

Splash! *

'She was the woman of his dreams. She had large dark
eyes, a beautiful smile, and a great pair of fins.'
US   1984   110m   Technicolor
Touchstone/Buena Vista (Brian Grazer)
V, V*, L

A New York wholesaler on holiday off Cape Cod falls
in love with a mermaid.

A kind of updated and mildly sexed-up Miranda:
occasionally funny but far too long.

w Lowell Ganz, Babaloo Mandel, Bruce Jay
Friedman, Brian Grazer   d Ron Howard   ph Don
Peterman   m Lee Holdridge

Tom Hanks, Daryl Hannah, Eugene Levy, John
Candy, Dody Goodman, Shecky Greene, Richard B.
Shull, Howard Morris

'A typically Disney subject trying to be grown up.' –
Kim Newman, MFB

'The picture is frequently on the verge of being more
wonderful than it is . . . more lyrical, a little wilder.' –
Pauline Kael, New Yorker

AAN: screenplay

Splendor

US   1935   77m   bw
Samuel Goldwyn

The son of a once-wealthy Park Avenue family
marries a poor girl.

Dated romantic drama.

w Rachel Crothers   play Rachel Crothers   d Elliott
Nugent   ph Gregg Toland   md Alfred Newman

Joel McCrea, Miriam Hopkins, Helen Westley,
Katherine Alexander, David Niven, Paul Cavanagh,
Billie Burke, Arthur Treacher

'An unusually good production, but probably too
quiet for the lesser spots.' – Variety

'A model of dramatic exposition, but it suffers from inaction and its theme is too commonplace.' – *New York Times*

Splendor **

Italy/France 1988 99m Cinecitta
Warner/Cecchi Gori/Tiger Cinematografica/Studio El/
   Gaumont/Generale d'Images/RAI (Mario Cecchi Gori,
   Vittorio Cecchi Gori)

A bankrupt small-town cinema owner remembers past glories.

Charming, gently nostalgic lament for movies as a communal experience.

wd Ettore Scola *ph* Luciano Tovoli *m* Armando Trovaioli *ad* Luciano Ricceri *ed* Francesco Malvestito

Marcello Mastroianni, Massimo Troisi, Marina Vlady, Paolo Panelli, Pamela Villoresi, Giacomo Piperno, Massimo Bartocini

Splendor in the Grass *

US 1961 124m Technicolor
Warner/NBI (Elia Kazan)
V*, L

Adolescent love in a small Kansas town in the twenties.

Impressive though curiously unmemorable addition to a nostalgic young sex cycle which was already played out; production and performances well up to scratch.

w William Inge *d* Elia Kazan *ph* Boris Kaufman *m* David Amram

Natalie Wood, Warren Beatty, Pat Hingle, Audrey Christie, Barbara Loden, Zohra Lampert, Sandy Dennis

'Less like a high-school version of *Summer and Smoke* than [like] an Andy Hardy story with glands.' – *Stanley Kauffmann*

AA: William Inge

AAN: Natalie Wood

Splinters

GB 1929 82m bw
Herbert Wilcox/B and D

Soldiers at the front in 1915 form a concert party.

Easy-going crowd-pleaser of its time.

w W. P. Lipscomb *d* Jack Raymond

Nelson Keys, Sidney Howard, Lew Lake, Hal Jones

† Sequels, of roughly the same standard, included *Splinters in the Navy*, 1931, and *Splinters in the Air*, 1937; both with Sidney Howard.

The Split

US 1968 90m Metrocolor Panavision
MGM/Spectrum (Robert Chartoff, Irwin Winkler)

A black criminal plans to rob the Los Angeles Coliseum during a football match.

Busy, brutal crime thriller, well enough done but totally unsympathetic.

w Robert Sabaroff *novel* The Seventh by Richard Stark *d* Gordon Flemyng *ph* Burnett Guffey *m* Quincy Jones

Jim Brown, Diahann Carroll, Ernest Borgnine, Julie Harris, Gene Hackman, Jack Klugman, Warren Oates, James Whitmore, Donald Sutherland

Split Image *

US 1982 111m Metrocolor Panavision
Polygram Pictures (Ted Kotcheff)

A normal middle-class college athlete becomes involved with a religious cult.

Effective melodrama about brainwashing.

w Scott Spencer, Robert Kaufman, Robert Mark Kamen *d* Ted Kotcheff *ph* Robert Jessup *m* Bill Conti *pd* Wolf Kroeger *ed* Jay Kamen

Michael O'Keefe, Karen Allen, James Woods, Elizabeth Ashley, Brian Dennehy, Ronnie Scribner, Michael Sacks, Peter Fonda

Split Second

US 1953 85m bw
RKO (Edmund Grainger)

An escaped convict hides out with four hostages in an Arizona ghost town which has been cleared in preparation for an atom bomb test.

Routine suspenser.

w William Bowers, Irving Wallace *d* Dick Powell *ph* Nicholas Musuraca *m* Roy Webb

Stephen McNally, Alexis Smith, Jan Sterling, Keith Andes, Arthur Hunnicutt, Paul Kelly, Richard Egan, Robert Paige

Split Second

GB 1991 90m Eastmancolor
Entertainment/Challenge/Muse (Laura Gregory)
V, V*, L

In 2008, in a flooded London, a cop goes after a serial killer who turns out to be a monster.

A gallant, if misguided, attempt to revive the man-in-a-rubber-suit school of horror movies.

w Gary Scott Thompson *d* Tony Maylam *ph* Clive Tickner *m* Stephen Parsons, Francis Haines *pd* Chris Edwards *ed* Dan Rae

Rutger Hauer, Kim Cattrall, Neil Duncan, Michael J. Pollard, Alun Armstrong, Peter Postlethwaite, Ian Dury, Roberta Eaton, Tony Steedman

'An extremely stupid monster film, boasting enough violence and special effects to satisfy less discriminating vid fans.' – *Variety*

Splitface: see Dick Tracy

Splitting Heirs

GB 1993 87m Technicolor
UIP/Prominent Features (Simon Bosanquet, Redmond Morris)

A city businessman, adopted by a Pakistani family, discovering that he, and not his best friend, is really the heir to the Dukedom of Bournemouth, decides to murder his rival.

Sad and trivial comedy, consisting of ineptly performed knockabout routines.

w Eric Idle *d* Robert Young *ph* Tony Pierce-Roberts *m* Michael Kamen *pd* John Beard *ed* John Jympson

Eric Idle, Rick Moranis, Barbara Hershey, Catherine Zeta Jones, John Cleese, Sadie Frost, Stratford Johns, Brenda Bruce, William Franklyn, Jeremy Clyde, Eric Sykes

'Breezy but lightweight comedy.' – *Variety*

'The pace and cheerful inanity of the picture may go some way to excusing its lack of wit and subtlety.' – *Geoffrey Macnab, Sight and Sound*

The Spoilers *

US 1930 86m bw
Paramount (Lloyd Sheldon)

In Alaska during the gold rush, crooked government officials begin despoiling the richest claims.

Early talkie version of a famous brawling saga.

w Bartlett Cormack, Agnes Brand Leahy *novel* Rex Beach *d* Edward Carewe *ph* Harry Fischbeck

Gary Cooper, William 'Stage' Boyd, Betty Compson, Kay Johnson, Harry Green, Slim Summerville

'Fair for a week in the de luxers, but made to order for the neighbourhoods and grinds everywhere.' – *Variety*

The Spoilers **

US 1942 87m bw
Universal (Frank Lloyd)
V*, L

Two adventurers in the Yukon quarrel over land rights and a saloon entertainer.

Well-packaged mixture of saloon brawls, romance and adventure, much filmed as a silent.

w Lawrence Hazard, Tom Reed *d* Ray Enright *ph* Milton Krasner *m* Hans Salter *ad* Jack Otterson, John B. Goodman

Marlene Dietrich, Randolph Scott, John Wayne, Margaret Lindsay, Harry Carey, Richard Barthelmess, George Cleveland, Samuel S. Hinds

'All concerned have kept their tongues firmly in their cheeks.' – *New York Times*

AAN: art direction

The Spoilers *

US 1955 82m Technicolor
U-I (Ross Hunter)

Adequate, unmemorable remake of the above.

w Oscar Brodney, Charles Hoffman *d* Jesse Hibbs *ph* Maury Gertsman *m* Joseph Gershenson

Anne Baxter, Jeff Chandler, Rory Calhoun, Barbara Britton, Carl Benton Reid, Ray Danton, John McIntire, Raymond Walburn, Wallace Ford

Spontaneous Combustion

US 1990 108m colour
Taurus (Jim Rogers)
V*, L

The son of parents subjected to nuclear experiments discovers that he can set people on fire.

Direly ridiculous horror, a wet blanket of a movie, depressing and unimaginative.

w Tobe Hooper, Howard Goldberg *d* Tobe Hooper *ph* Levie Isaacks *m* Graeme Revell *ed* David Kern

Brad Dourif, Cynthia Bain, Jon Cypher, William Prince, Dey Young, Melinda Dillon, John Landis

'Silly beyond belief . . . a horror pic that literally goes up in flames.' – *Variety*

Spoorloos: see The Vanishing

Sport of a Nation: see The All-American

The Sport of Kings

GB 1931 98m bw
Gainsborough

A strict JP inherits a bookie business.

Heavy-going adaptation of a stage comedy warhorse, which nevertheless paved the way for many screen farces of the thirties.

w Angus MacPhail *play* Ian Hay *d* Victor Saville

Leslie Henson, Gordon Harker, Hugh Wakefield, Dorothy Boyd

Sporting Blood

US 1931 80m bw
MGM

A horse passes through various hands and finally wins the Kentucky Derby.

Unremarkable programme fodder.

w Charles Brabin, Wanda Tuchock, Willard Mack *story* Horseflesh by Frederick Hazlitt Brennan *d* Charles Brabin

Clark Gable, Ernest Torrence, Madge Evans, Lew Cody, Marie Prevost

'Racetrack romance with a different twist and only name Clark Gable.' – *Variety*

Sporting Love
GB   1937   68m   bw
British Lion/Hammer

Two owners of a bankrupt racing stable try to kidnap their prize horse which has been mortgaged.

Thin musical farce from a stage success.

w Fenn Sherie, Ingram D'Abbern   play Stanley Lupino   d J. Elder Wills   ph Eric Cross

Stanley Lupino, Laddie Cliff, Henry Carlisle, Edna Peel, Bobby Comber

Spot: see *Dogpound Shuffle*

'It's the business.'
Spotswood *
Australia   1991   95m   colour
Feature/Meridian/Smiley (Richard Brennan, Timothy White)
S

An English time-and-motion expert investigates a ramshackle shoe factory.

Pleasant comedy in the Ealing tradition of the little man against uncaring bureaucracy.

w Max Dann, Andrew Knight   d Mark Joffe ph Ellery Ryan   m Ricky Fataar   pd Chris Kennedy   ed Nicholas Beauman

Anthony Hopkins, Ben Mendelsohn, Alwyn Kurts, Bruno Lawrence, Angela Punch McGregor, Russell Crowe, Toni Colette

'Glides along with a dry wit, a keen visual sense and a kindly heart.' – *Geoff Brown, The Times*

Spring and Port Wine
GB   1970   101m   Technicolor
EMI/Memorial (Michael Medwin)
V

A Lancashire family runs into trouble when stern father insists that teenage daughter should eat a meal she refuses.

A popular old-fashioned stage comedy which simply doesn't work on film, partly from being set in a too-real town (Bolton) and partly because of a miscast lead.

w Bill Naughton   play Bill Naughton   d Peter Hammond   ph Norman Warwick   m Douglas Gamley   pd Reece Pemberton

James Mason, Diana Coupland, Susan George, Rodney Bewes, Hannah Gordon, Adrienne Posta, Arthur Lowe

Spring in Park Lane **
GB   1948   92m   bw
Imperadio/Herbert Wilcox

A diamond merchant's niece falls for a footman who just happens to be an impoverished lord in disguise.

Flimsy but highly successful romantic comedy which managed to get its balance right and is still pretty entertaining, much more so than its sequel *Maytime in Mayfair*.

w Nicholas Phipps,   play *Come Out of the Kitchen* by Alice Duer Miller   d Herbert Wilcox   ph Max Greene m Robert Farnon

Anna Neagle, Michael Wilding, Tom Walls, Nicholas Phipps, Peter Graves, Marjorie Fielding, *Nigel Patrick*, Lana Morris

'A never-failing dream of Olde Mayfaire and its eternally funny butlers and maids, its disguised lords and ladies.' – *Richard Winnington*

'A gag comedy which absolutely sparkles.' – *Picture Show*

'The best comedy any British studio has produced for more years than I care to remember.' – *News of the World*

Spring Madness
US   1938   66m   bw
MGM

The romance of a Harvard man and a student in the nearby women's college.

Very thin comedy material, stretched to its tearing point.

w Edward Chodorov   play *Spring Dance* by Philip Barry   d S. Sylvan Simon

Maureen O'Sullivan, Lew Ayres, Ruth Hussey, Burgess Meredith, Joyce Compton

Spring Meeting
GB   1940   93m   bw
ABPC

In Ireland, an impecunious widow wants her son to marry the daughter of an old flame.

Staid film version of a comedy whose characters turned up again in *Treasure Hunt*.

w Walter C. Mycroft, Norman Lee   play M. J. Farrell, John Perry   d Walter C. Mycroft

Nova Pilbeam, Basil Sydney, Henry Edwards, Sarah Churchill, Michael Wilding, *Margaret Rutherford*, Enid Stamp Taylor, Hugh McDermott

Spring Parade *
US   1940   89m   bw
Universal (Joe Pasternak)

A single baker's assistant falls for a prince.

Pleasing, artificial Austrian frou-frou with star and support in good escapist form.

w Bruce Manning, Felix Jackson   story Ernst Marischka   d Henry Koster   ph Joseph Valentine md Charles Previn   m Robert Stolz

Deanna Durbin, Robert Cummings, S. Z. Sakall, Mischa Auer, Henry Stephenson, Anne Gwynne, Butch and Buddy

AAN: Joseph Valentine; Charles Previn; song 'Waltzing in the Clouds' (m Robert Stolz, ly Gus Kahn)

Spring Reunion
US   1956   79m   bw
UA/Bryna (Jerry Bresler)

College classmates fall in love all over again at a reunion fifteen years later.

Romantic fiction for the middle-aged, performed with bare competence.

wd Robert Pirosh   ph Harold Lipstein   m Herbert Spencer, Earle Hagen

Betty Hutton, Dana Andrews, Jean Hagen, Robert Simon, James Gleason, Laura La Plante, Irene Ryan

Spring Symphony
West Germany   1983   103m   colour
Blue Dolphin/Allianz Filmproduktion/Peter Schamoni
original title: *Frühlingssinfonie*

Biopic of the love affair between the composer Robert Schumann and the pianist Clara Wieck.

Glossy and stolid plod through a decade that relies on the music to maintain interest.

wd Peter Schamoni   ph Gerard Vandenberg m Schumann   pd Alfred Hirschmeier   ed Elfi Tillack

Nastassja Kinski, Herbert Grönemeyer, Rolf Hoppe, André Heller, Bernhard Wicki, Gidon Kremer, Edda Seippel

Spring Tonic
US   1935   55m   bw
Fox

An escaped tigress causes various farcical episodes.

Comedy extravaganza on modest lines, like a stretched-out two-reeler.

w Patterson McNutt, H. W. Hanemann   play *Man Eating Tiger* by Ben Hecht, Rose Caylor   d S. Sylvan Simon

Lew Ayres, Claire Trevor, Walter Woolf King, ZaSu Pitts, Jack Haley, Tala Birell, Sig Rumann

'Hodge-podge of hokum that offers no hope to distraught exhibitors.' – *Variety*

'The gun … the girl … they made one man the equal of five!'
Springfield Rifle
US   1952   93m   Warnercolor
Warner (Louis E. Edelman)
V

A Union officer gets himself cashiered, joins the Confederates as a spy, and unmasks a traitor.

Stolid Civil War Western with Grade-A production but not much individuality.

w Charles Marquis Warren, Frank Davis   d André de Toth   ph Edwin DuPar   m Max Steiner

Gary Cooper, Phyllis Thaxter, David Brian, Lon Chaney Jnr, Paul Kelly, Phil Carey, James Millican, Guinn Williams

Springtime for Henry
US   1935   73m   bw
Fox (Jesse L. Lasky)

A rich man makes a vocation of woman chasing.

Modest version of a play which was toured for many years with Edward Everett Horton in the lead.

w Keene Thompson, Frank Tuttle   play Benn W. Levy   d Frank Tuttle

Otto Kruger, Nancy Carroll, Nigel Bruce, Heather Angel, Herbert Mundin

'Farcical intent, but only a few snickers.' – *Variety*

Springtime in the Rockies
US   1942   91m   Technicolor
TCF (Darryl F. Zanuck)
V, V*, L

Romances blossom on a mountain holiday.

Flimsily-plotted, studio-bound, absolutely routine musical.

w Walter Bullock, Ken Englund   d Irving Cummings   ph Ernest Palmer   m Alfred Newman songs Mack Gordon, Harry Warren

Betty Grable, John Payne, Carmen Miranda, Edward Everett Horton, Cesar Romero, Charlotte Greenwood, Frank Orth, Harry James and his Music Makers

Spy for a Day
GB   1939   71m   bw
Two Cities

A farm hand is discovered to be the exact double of a spy.

The only screen vehicle for this 'gormless' comedian, and not a bad one.

w Anatole de Grunwald, Hans Wilhelm, Emeric Pressburger, Ralph Block, Tommy Thompson story Stacy Aumonier   d Mario Zampi

Duggie Wakefield, Paddy Browne, Jack Allen, Albert Lieven, Nicholas Hannen, Gibb McLaughlin

Spy Hunt *
US   1950   74m   bw
Universal (Ralph Dietrich)
GB title: *Panther's Moon*

Secret microfilm is stowed in the collar of one of two panthers being transported out of Europe by train for circus use.

Slick minor espionage thriller.

w George Zuckerman, Leonard Lee   novel *Panther's Moon* by Victor Canning   d George Sherman

ph Irving Glassberg   *md* Joseph Gershenson
m Walter Scharf

Howard Duff, Marta Toren, Philip Friend, Robert
Douglas, Philip Dorn, Walter Slezak, Kurt Kreuger

The Spy in Black **
GB   1939   82m   bw
Harefield/Alexander Korda (Irving Asher)
V*, L
US title: *U-Boat 29*

In the Orkneys in 1917, German spies don't trust each
other.

Unusual romantic melodrama which provided an
unexpectedly interesting romantic team.

w Emeric Pressburger, Roland Pertwee,   novel J. Storer
Clouston   *d* Michael Powell   *ph* Bernard Browne
m Miklos Rozsa

Conrad Veidt, Valerie Hobson, Hay Petrie, Helen Haye,
Sebastian Shaw, Marius Goring, June Duprez, Athole
Stewart, Cyril Raymond

Spy in the Pantry: see *Ten Days in Paris*

The Spy in White: see *The Secret of Stamboul*

Spy of Napoleon
GB   1936   101m   bw
JH Productions

A dancer saves Louis Napoleon from assassination.

Solidly mounted period piece without much sense of
humour.

w L. DuGarde Peach, Frederick Merrick, Harold
Simpson   *d* Maurice Elvey

Richard Barthelmess, Dolly Haas, Frank Vosper,
Francis L. Sullivan, Lyn Harding, Henry Oscar

Spy Smasher
US   1942   bw   serial: 12 eps
Republic

An American agent in occupied France is captured by
Nazis while trying to unmask The Mask.

Busy, peripatetic serial adventures.

d William Witney

Kane Richmond, Sam Flint, Marguerite Chapman,
Tristram Coffin

Spy 13: see *Operator 13*

'Brace yourself for greatness!'
The Spy Who Came in from the Cold **
GB   1965   112m   bw
Paramount/Salem (Martin Ritt)
V*, L

A British master spy is offered a chance to get even
with his East German opponent by being apparently
sacked, disillusioned, and open for recruitment.

The old undercover yarn with trimmings of such
sixties malaises as death wish, anti-establishmentism
and racial problems. As a yarn, quite gripping till it
gets too downbeat, but very harshly photographed.

w Paul Dehn, Guy Trosper   novel John Le Carré
d Martin Ritt   *ph* Oswald Morris   *m* Sol Kaplan
pd Tambi Larsen

Richard Burton, Claire Bloom, *Oskar Werner*, Peter Van
Eyck, Sam Wanamaker, Rupert Davies, George
Voskovec, Cyril Cusack, Michael Hordern, Robert
Hardy, Bernard Lee, Beatrix Lehmann

AAN: Richard Burton

The Spy Who Loved Me
GB   1977   125m   Eastmancolor   Panavision
UA/Eon (Albert R. Broccoli)
V, V*, L, S

James Bond and a glamorous Russian spy combine

forces to track down and eliminate a megalomaniac
shipping magnate with an undersea missile base.

Witless spy extravaganza in muddy colour, with the
usual tired chases and pussyfoot violence but no new
gimmicks except a seven-foot villain with steel teeth.

w Christopher Wood, Richard Maibaum   novel Ian
Fleming   *d* Lewis Gilbert   *ph* Claude Renoir
m Marvin Hamlisch   *pd* Ken Adam

Roger Moore, Barbara Bach, Curt Jurgens, Richard
Kiel, Caroline Munro, Walter Gotell, Bernard Lee,
Lois Maxwell, George Baker, Desmond Llewellyn,
Edward de Souza, Sydney Tafler

'The film, bearing no relation to its nominal source,
seems to do nothing more than anthologize its
forerunners.' – *Tim Pulleine, MFB*

AAN: Marvin Hamlisch; song 'Nobody Does It Better'
(*m* Marvin Hamlisch, *ly* Carole Bayer Sager)

The Spy with a Cold Nose
GB   1966   93m   Eastmancolor
Paramount/Associated London/Embassy (Robert Porter)

A fashionable vet is blackmailed by MI5 into
inserting a radio transmitter into a bulldog.

Rather painful, overacted and overwritten farce full of
obvious jokes masquerading as satire.

w Ray Galton, Alan Simpson   *d* Daniel Petrie
ph Kenneth Higgins   *m* Riz Ortolani

Lionel Jeffries, Laurence Harvey, Daliah Lavi, Eric
Sykes, Eric Portman, Colin Blakely, Denholm Elliott,
Robert Flemyng, Paul Ford, Bernard Lee, June
Whitfield, Bernard Archard

The Spy with My Face
US   1966   86m   Metrocolor
MGM/Arena (Sam Rolfe)

Enemy spies use a double of Napoleon Solo in an
attempt to take over the world.

An extended version of an episode from the television
series *The Man from U.N.C.L.E.*, no better than the
others in the series and more confusing than most.

w Clyde Ware, Joseph Calvelli   *ph* Fred
Koenekamp   *m* Morton Stevens   *ad* George W.
Davis, Merrill Pye   *ed* Joseph Dervin

Robert Vaughn, David McCallum, Leo G. Carroll,
Michael Evans, Sharon Farrell

Spylarks: see *The Intelligence Men*

S*P*Y*S
GB   1974   100m   Technicolor
Dymphana/C-W/American Film Properties (Irwin Winkler,
Robert Chartoff)
V

Clumsy CIA agents in Paris come across a list of KGB
agents in China.

Surprisingly dull and unfashionable parade of comic
spy clichés; the talents involved obviously intended
something closer to *M*A*S*H*.

w Malcolm Marmorstein, Lawrence J. Cohen, Fred
Freeman   *d* Irwin Kershner   *ph* Gerry Fisher
m John Scott

Elliott Gould, Donald Sutherland, Zouzou, Joss
Ackland, Kenneth Griffith, Vladek Sheybal

'Seems to have arrived several years too late to find its
true niche.' – *Sight and Sound*

Squadron Leader X
GB   1942   100m   bw
RKO (Victor Hanbury)

A Nazi hero poses as a British pilot but has difficulty
getting back home.

Tall war story with dreary romantic trimmings.

w Wolfgang Wilhelm, Miles Malleson   *d* Lance
Comfort   *ph* Mutz Greenbaum (Max Greene)

Eric Portman, Ann Dvorak, Walter Fitzgerald, Barry
Jones, Henry Oscar, Beatrice Varley

The Squall
US   1929   105m   bw
First National

A Hungarian gypsy girl attracts all the male members
of a farming family, and causes trouble.

Perfectly awful melodrama made worse by early
sound techniques.

w Bradley King   play Jean Bart   *d* Alexander
Korda

Myrna Loy, Alice Joyce, Loretta Young, Richard
Ticker, Carroll Nye, ZaSu Pitts, Harry Cording

Square Dance *
GB   1986   112m   Metrocolor
NBC/Michael Nesmith/Island (Daniel Petrie)
V*, L

An awkward 13-year-old girl in rural Texas leaves her
gruff grandfather for a visit to the mother she dislikes.

Unremarkable but cohesive family drama which most
will feel they have seen before.

w Alan Hines   novel Alan Hines   *d* Daniel Petrie
ph Jacek Laskus   *m* Bruce Broughton   *pd* Jan Scott
ed Bruce Green

Jason Robards, Jane Alexander, Winona Ryder, Rob
Lowe, Deborah Richter

The Square Jungle
US   1955   85m   bw
U-I (Albert Zugsmith)

A conceited boxer gets his come-uppance.

Tailor-made studio co-feature.

w George Zuckerman   *d* Jerry Hopper   *ph* George
Robinson   *m* Heinz Roemheld

Tony Curtis, Ernest Borgnine, Pat Crowley, Jim
Backus, Paul Kelly

The Square Peg *
GB   1958   89m   bw
Rank (Hugh Stewart)
V

An army recruit finds he is the double of a German
general.

Slam-bang star slapstick, shorter than usual and with
a few jokes that can't fail.

w Jack Davies   *d* John Paddy Carstairs   *ph* Jack
Cox   *m* Philip Green

Norman Wisdom, Honor Blackman, Edward Chapman,
Campbell Singer, Hattie Jacques, Brian Worth,
Terence Alexander

The Square Ring *
GB   1953   83m   bw
Ealing/Relph-Dearden

One night at a boxing stadium.

An assortment of anecdotes does not constitute one of
Ealing's best films, but the competence level is high.

w Robert Westerby, Peter Myers, Alec Grahame
play Ralph Peterson   *d* Basil Dearden

Jack Warner, Robert Beatty, Maxwell Reed, Bill
Owen, Joan Collins, Kay Kendall, Bernadette
O'Farrell, Eddie Byrne, Sid James, Alfie Bass

The Squaw Man
US   1931   106m   bw
MGM (Cecil B. de Mille)
GB title: *The White Man*

An Indian maiden saves the life of a British aristocrat,
bears his child and commits suicide.

Third outing for a hoary miscegenation drama filmed
in 1914 with Dustin Farnum and Red Wing, and in

1918 with Elliott Dexter and Ann Little. This talkie version sank without trace.

w Lucien Hubbard, Lenore Coffee   *play* Edwin Milton Royle   *d* Cecil B. de Mille   *ph* Harold Rosson   *m* Herbert Stothart

Warner Baxter, Lupe Velez, Charles Bickford, Eleanor Boardman, Roland Young, Paul Cavanagh, Raymond Hatton

'Should be generally fair b.o. in the smaller localities and perhaps not so hot for the diffident big-town show shoppers.' – *Variety*

The Squeaker *
GB   1937   77m   bw
UA/Denham Productions (Alexander Korda)
V*
US title: *Murder on Diamond Row*

A dangerous diamond fence is unmasked by a discredited policeman.

Typical Edgar Wallace who-is-it, performed with old-fashioned bravura.

w Edward O. Berkman, Bryan Wallace   *novel* Edgar Wallace   *d* William K. Howard   *ph* Georges Périnal   *m* Miklos Rozsa   *ad* Vincent Korda   *ed* Russell Lloyd

Edmund Lowe, Sebastian Shaw, Ann Todd, Tamara Desni, Alastair Sim, Robert Newton, Allan Jeayes, Stewart Rome

† Previously filmed in 1930, directed by Edgar Wallace for British Lion; with Percy Marmont, Eric Maturin, Anne Grey and Nigel Bruce.

The Squeeze
GB   1977   107m   Technicolor
Warner/ Martinat (Stanley O'Toole)

An alcoholic ex-cop rescues his ex-wife from kidnappers.

Sleazy action thriller which despite efficient production goes over the top in its search for unpleasant detail.

w Leon Griffiths   *novel* David Craig   *d* Michael Apted   *ph* Dennis Lewiston   *m* David Hentschel

Stacy Keach, David Hemmings, Stephen Boyd, Edward Fox, Carol White, Freddie Starr

'It provides action and moral ambiguity enough to stock a Don Siegel thriller.' – *Richard Combs, MFB*

Squibs *
GB   1935   77m   bw
Twickenham

A cockney flowergirl wins a sweepstake.

Acceptable sound version of a series of rather naïve silents which pleased the crowds in the early twenties with the same star: they were *Squibs, Squibs MP, Squibs' Honeymoon* and *Squibs Wins the Calcutta Sweep*.

w Michael Hogan, H. Fowler Mear   *d* Clifford Seyler, George Pearson   *d* Henry Edwards

Betty Balfour, Gordon Harker, Stanley Holloway, Margaret Yarde, Michael Shepley

Squirm
US   1976   92m   Movielab
AIP/The Squirm Company (Edgar Lansbury, Joseph Beruh)
V*

A power cable cut in a storm turns worms into maneaters.

Revolting shocker with a few funny moments for those who can take it.

wd Jeff Lieberman   *ph* Joseph Mangine   *m* Robert Prince

John Scardino, Patricia Pearcy, R. A. Dow, Jean Sullivan

Stablemates
US   1938   89m   bw
MGM

A broken-down vet saves a stableboy's racehorse.

Sentimental comedy vehicle for two masters of the surreptitious tear.

w Reginald Owen, William Thiele   *d* Sam Wood

Wallace Beery, Mickey Rooney, Margaret Hamilton, Minor Watson, Marjorie Gateson

Stage Door ***
US   1937   93m   bw
RKO (Pandro S. Berman)
V*, L

Life in a New York theatrical boarding house for girls.

Melodramatic, sharply comedic, always fascinating slice of stagey life from a Broadway hit; the performances alone make it worth preserving.

w Morrie Ryskind, Anthony Veiller   *play* Edna Ferber, George S. Kaufman   *d* Gregory La Cava   *ph* Robert de Grasse   *m* Roy Webb   *ad* Van Nest Polglase

Katharine Hepburn, Ginger Rogers, Adolphe Menjou, Gail Patrick, Constance Collier, Andrea Leeds, Lucille Ball, Samuel S. Hinds, Jack Carson, Franklin Pangborn, Eve Arden

'It is a long time since we have seen so much feminine talent so deftly handled.' – *Otis Ferguson*

'Zest and pace and photographic eloquence.' – *Frank S. Nugent, New York Times*

'A rare example of a film substantially improving on a stage original and a remarkably satisfying film on all levels.' – *NFT, 1973*

'One of the flashiest, most entertaining comedies of the 30s, even with its tremolos and touches of heartbreak.' – *Pauline Kael, 70s*

AAN: best picture; script; Gregory La Cava; Andrea Leeds

'48 stars plus a great love story!'
Stage Door Canteen *
US   1943   132m   bw
Sol Lesser (Barnett Briskin)
V*, L

How the stars in New York entertained the armed forces during World War II.

Nothing as a film, mildly interesting as sociology and for some rarish appearances.

w Delmer Daves   *d* Frank Borzage   *ph* Harry Wild   *m* Freddie Rich   *pd* Harry Horner

Cheryl Walker, Lon McCallister, Judith Anderson, Tallulah Bankhead, Ray Bolger, Katherine Cornell, Helen Hayes, George Jessel, Alfred Lunt, Harpo Marx, Yehudi Menuhin, Elliott Nugent, Cornelia Otis Skinner, Ethel Waters, May Whitty, William Demarest, Gracie Fields, Katharine Hepburn, Gertrude Lawrence, Ethel Merman, Merle Oberon, Johnny Weissmuller, Edgar Bergen, Jane Cowl, Lynn Fontanne, Paul Muni, Gypsy Rose Lee, George Raft, etc; Count Basie, Benny Goodman, Xavier Cugat, Guy Lombardo, Kay Kyser and their bands

'A nice harmless picture for the whole family, and a goldmine for those who are willing to go to it in the wrong spirit.' – *James Agee*

AAN: Freddie Rich; song 'We Mustn't Say Goodbye' (*m* James V. Monaco, *ly* Al Dubin)

Stage Fright *
GB   1950   110m   bw
Warner/ABPC (Alfred Hitchcock)
V*, L

A man is on the run for a backstage murder, and his girlfriend takes a job as maid to the great star he says is responsible.

Creaky Hitchcock thriller in which you can see all the joins and the stars seem stuck in treacle; but a few of the set-pieces work well enough.

w Whitfield Cook   *novel Man Running* by Selwyn Jepson   *d* Alfred Hitchcock   *ph* Wilkie Cooper   *m* Leighton Lucas

Marlene Dietrich, Jane Wyman, Richard Todd, Alastair Sim, Michael Wilding, Sybil Thorndike, Kay Walsh, Miles Malleson

Stage Mother
US   1933   85m   bw
MGM

The mother of a young actress is not above sacrificing her daughter for financial gain.

Wisecracking comedy-romance, rather similar to the later *Gypsy*.

w John Meehan, Bradford Ropes   *novel* Bradford Ropes   *d* Charles Brabin

Alice Brady, Maureen O'Sullivan, Franchot Tone, Phillips Holmes, Ted Healy, C. Henry Gordon

'Packed with colour, not a little s.a., and certain of adequate b.o. attention.' – *Variety*

Stage Struck
US   1936   95m   bw
Warner (Robert Lord)

Young people put on a show and become instant hits.

Dim musical oddly shorn of production numbers.

w Tom Buckinham, Pat C. Flick, Robert Lord   *d/ch* Busby Berkeley   *ph* Byron Haskin   *m* Leo F. Forbstein   *songs* Harold Arlen, E. Y. Harburg

Dick Powell, Joan Blondell, Jeanne Madden, the Yacht Club Boys, Warren William, Frank McHugh

Stage Struck **
US   1957   95m   Technicolor
RKO (Stuart Millar)
V*, L

A young actress comes to New York intent on stardom . . .

Careful, slightly arid remake of *Morning Glory* marred by a tiresome central performance; good theatrical detail.

w Ruth and Augustus Goetz   *play* Zoe Akins   *d* Sidney Lumet   *ph* Franz Planer   *m* Alex North   *ad* Kim Edgar Swados

Susan Strasberg, Henry Fonda, Herbert Marshall, *Joan Greenwood*, Christopher Plummer

Stage to Thunder Rock
US   1964   89m   Techniscope
Paramount/A.C. Lyles

An ageing sheriff takes a bank robber back to jail by stagecoach.

Acceptable lower-berth Western with the producer's usual roster of half-forgotten character actors.

w Charles Wallace   *d* William F. Claxton   *ph* W. Wallace Kelley   *m* Paul Dunlap

Barry Sullivan, Marilyn Maxwell, Scott Brady, Keenan Wynn, Allan Jones, Lon Chaney Jnr, John Agar, Wanda Hendrix, Anne Seymour, Robert Lowery

Stagecoach ****
US   1939   99m   bw
(UA) Walter Wanger
V, V*, L

Various Western characters board a stagecoach in danger from an Indian war party.

What looked like a minor Western with a plot borrowed from Maupassant's *Boule de suif*, became a classic by virtue of the firm characterization, restrained writing, exciting climax and the scenery of Monument Valley. Whatever the reasons, it damn well works.

w Dudley Nichols,　story Stage to Lordsburg by Ernest Haycox　*d* John Ford　*ph* Bert Glennon　*md* Boris Morros　*m* Richard Hageman, W. Frank Harling, John Leopold, Leo Shuken, Louis Gruenberg　*ad* Alexander Toluboff　*ed* Otho Lovering, Dorothy Spencer

Claire Trevor, John Wayne, Thomas Mitchell, George Bancroft, Andy Devine, Berton Churchill, Louise Platt, John Carradine, Donald Meek, Tim Holt, Chris-Pin Martin

'It displays potentialities that can easily drive it through as one of the surprise big grossers of the year.' – *Variety*

'The basic western, a template for everything that followed.' – *John Baxter, 1968*

'*Grand Hotel* on wheels.' – *New Yorker, 1975*

'A motion picture that sings a song of camera.' – *Frank S. Nugent, New York Times*

AA: music; Thomas Mitchell

AAN: best picture; John Ford; Bert Glennon; art direction; editing

Stagecoach

US　1966　114m　DeLuxe　Cinemascope
TCF/Martin Rackin
S

Absolutely awful remake of the above; costly but totally spiritless, miscast and uninteresting.

w Joseph Landon　*d* Gordon Douglas　*ph* William H. Clothier　*m* Jerry Goldsmith

Ann-Margret, Alex Cord, Bing Crosby, Van Heflin, Slim Pickens, Robert Cummings, Stefanie Powers, Michael Connors, Red Buttons, Keenan Wynn

The Stagecoach Kid

US　1949　63m　bw
RKO (Herman Schlom)

In order to escape to the big city, a rancher's daughter disguises herself as a cowboy but then falls in love with a stagecoach owner.

Light-hearted Western, a pleasant if unmemorable programme-filler.

w Norman Hutson　*d* Lew Landers　*ph* Nicholas Musuraca　*m* Paul Sawtell　*ad* Albert D'Agostino, Feild Gray　*ed* Les Millbrook

Tim Holt, Richard Martin, Jeff Donnell, Joe Sawyer, Thurston Hall, Carol Hughes, Robert Bray

Staircase *

US/France　1969　101m　DeLuxe　Panavision
TCF/Stanley Donen

The problems of two ageing homosexual hairdressers.

Unsatisfactorily opened-out and over-acted version of an effective two-handler play. Oddly made in France, so that the London detail seems all wrong.

w Charles Dyer　*play* Charles Dyer　*d* Stanley Donen　*ph* Christopher Challis　*m* Dudley Moore

Richard Burton, Rex Harrison, Cathleen Nesbitt, Beatrix Lehmann

'The shape is smashed . . . no longer a graceful duet, it becomes a waddling tale, spattered with ugliness, that falls into the biggest sentimental trap for homosexual material: it pleads for pity.' – *Stanley Kauffmann*

Stairway to Heaven: see *A Matter of Life and Death*

Stakeout

US　1987　115m　DeLuxe
Touchstone (Jim Kouf, Cathleen Summers)
V*, L

One of two Seattle cops engaged in a long stakeout falls in love with a suspect.

Ho-hum *policier* with insufficient plot for its length.

w Jim Kouf　*d* John Badham　*ph* John Seale　*m* Arthur B. Rubinstein　*pd* Philip Harrison　*ed* Tom Rolf, Michael Ripps

Richard Dreyfuss, Emilio Estevez, Madeleine Stowe, Aidan Quinn, Dan Lauria

Stakeout on Dope Street *

US　1958　83m　bw
Warner (Andrew J. Fenady)

Three young men find a briefcase containing heroin and are attacked by the gangsters who lost it.

Lively little crime morality, uneven but worth a look.

w Irwin Schwartz, Irvin Kershner, Andrew J. Fenady　*d* Irvin Kershner　*ph* Mark Jeffrey　*m* Richard Markowitz

Yale Wexler, Jonathon Haze, Morris Miller, Abby Dalton

Stalag 17 **

US　1953　120m　bw
Paramount (Billy Wilder)
V, V*, L

Comedy and tragedy for American servicemen in a Nazi prisoner-of-war camp.

High jinks, violence and mystery in a sharply calculated mixture; an atmosphere quite different from the understated British films on the subject.

w Billy Wilder, Edwin Blum　*play* Donald Bevan, Edmund Trzinski　*d* Billy Wilder　*ph* Ernest Laszlo　*m* Franz Waxman

William Holden, Don Taylor, Otto Preminger, *Robert Strauss*, Harvey Lembeck, Richard Erdman, Peter Graves, Neville Brand, Sig Rumann

'A facility for continuous rapid-fire action which alternately brings forth the laughs and tingles the spine.' – *Otis L. Guernsey Jnr*

'Raucous and tense, heartless and sentimental, always fast-paced, it has already been assigned by critics to places on their lists of the year's ten best movies.' – *Life*

AA: William Holden

AAN: Billy Wilder (as director), Robert Strauss

Stalker *

USSR　1979　161m　colour
Mosfilm Unit 2
V, V*

In the centre of an industrial wasteland there appears a mysterious zone where all normal laws of life are suspended.

Part political allegory, part personal fantasy, all very fascinating but rather hard tack for anybody in search of entertainment.

w Arkady Strugatsky, Boris Strugatsky　*story* Arkady Strugatsky, Boris Strugatsky　*d/ph* Andrei Tarkovsky　*m* Eduard Artemyev

Aleksandr Kaidanovsky, Anatoly Solonitsin, Nikolai Grinko, Alisa Freindlikh

The Stalking Moon *

US　1968　109m　Technicolor　Panavision
National General/Stalking Moon Company (Alan J. Pakula)
V*

An ageing scout escorts home a white woman who has escaped from the Indians, and kills a murderous Apache.

Slow, thoughtful Western with effective moments.

w Alvin Sargent　*novel* Theodore V. Olsen　*d* Robert Mulligan　*ph* Charles Lang　*m* Fred Karlin

Gregory Peck, Eva Marie Saint, Robert Forster, Frank Silvera

Stallion Road

US　1947　97m　bw
Warner (Alex Gottlieb)

An outbreak of anthrax threatens a racing stable.

Routine romantic drama with sporting background.

w Stephen Longstreed　*d* James V. Kern　*ph* Arthur Edeson　*m* Frederick Hollander

Ronald Reagan, Alexis Smith, Zachary Scott, Peggy Knudsen, Patti Brady, Harry Davenport, Frank Puglia

'The film, so free and fluent as long as it is talking horses, becomes curiously trite and turgid over the business of mating humans.' – *C. A. Lejeune, Observer*

Stamboul Quest

US　1934　88m　bw
MGM (Walter Wanger)

During World War I, Germany's most notorious lady spy falls for an American medical student.

Modest variation on the true story twice filmed as *Fraülein Doktor;* standard Hollywood values.

w Herman J. Mankiewicz　*d* Sam Wood　*ph* James Wong Howe　*m* Herbert Stothart

Myrna Loy, George Brent, Lionel Atwill, C. Henry Gordon, Douglass Dumbrille, Mischa Auer

Stampeded: see *The Big Land*

Stand and Deliver **

US　1988　104m　Foto-Kem
Warner/American Playhouse (Tom Musca)
V*, L

A maths teacher at a tough high school persuades his class of violent pupils that education is an asset.

Based on facts, the engaging story wins out over the rudimentary cinematic style.

w Ramon Menendez, Tom Musca　*d* Ramon Menendez　*ph* Tom Richmond　*m* Craig Safan　*ad* Milo　*ed* Nancy Richardson

Edward James Olmos, Lou Diamond Phillips, Rosana de Soto, Andy Garcia, Ingrid Oliu, Karla Montana, Vanessa Marquez, Mark Eliot

AAN: Edward James Olmos

The Stand at Apache River

US　1953　77m　Technicolor
Universal-International

Apaches attack a reservation when the army won't listen to reason.

Conventional Western with sympathy for the Indians.

w Arthur Ross　*d* Lee Sholem

Stephen McNally, Julie Adams, Hugh Marlowe, Hugh O'Brian, Jack Kelly

Stand by for Action

US　1943　109m　bw
MGM (Robert Z. Leonard, Orville O. Dull)
GB title: *Cargo of Innocents*

A Harvard graduate learns the realities of war on an old destroyer.

Studio-bound war heroics slurping into sentiment.

w George Bruce, Herman J. Mankiewicz, John L. Balderston　*d* Robert Z. Leonard　*ph* Charles Rosher　*m* Lennie Hayton

Robert Taylor, Charles Laughton, Brian Donlevy, Walter Brennan, Marilyn Maxwell, Henry O'Neill

Stand by Me *

US　1986　89m　Technicolor/DeLuxe
Columbia/Act III
V, V*, L, S

A boys' gang finds the body of a missing teenager.

Less macabre than its source would suggest, the film is mostly concerned with the friendships and tensions within the group; nostalgia for 50s childhood is nicely conveyed.

w Raynold Gideon and others   story The Body by Stephen King   d Rob Reiner   ph Thomas Del Ruth   m Jack Nitzsche   pd Dennis Washington

Wil Wheaton, River Phoenix, Corey Feldman, Jerry O'Connell, Kiefer Sutherland, Richard Dreyfuss

Der Stand Der Dinge: see The State of Things

Stand In *
US   1937   90m   bw
Walter Wanger
V*

An efficiency expert is sent to save a Hollywood studio from bankruptcy.

Amusing satire which could have done with sharper scripting and firmer control but is pleasantly remembered.

w Gene Towne, Graham Baker   serial Clarence Budington Kelland   d Tay Garnett   ph Charles G. Clarke   m Heinz Roemheld

Leslie Howard, Joan Blondell, Humphrey Bogart, Alan Mowbray, Marla Shelton, C. Henry Gordon, Jack Carson, Tully Marshall

'A joyous and nonsensical Hollywood fantasia.' – Spectator

Stand Up and Be Counted *
US   1971   99m   Eastmancolor
Columbia/Mike Frankovich

An international woman journalist returns to Denver and becomes involved in women's lib.

A glamoured-up flirtation with a fashionable theme, quite nicely done but instantly dated – and sociologically interesting.

w Bernard Slade   d Jackie Cooper   ph Fred Koenekamp   m Ernie Wilkins

Jacqueline Bisset, Stella Stevens, Steve Lawrence, Gary Lockwood, Loretta Swit, Lee Purcell, Madlyn Rhue

Stand Up and Cheer *
US   1934   80m   bw
Fox (Winfield Sheehan)
V*

The new US Secretary of Amusement attempts to shake the country's Depression blues by staging a mammoth revue.

Naïve propaganda, but the whole world was swept away to cloud nine – by Shirley Temple.

w Ralph Spence, Will Rogers, Philip Klein   d Hamilton McFadden   ph Ernest Palmer   md Arthur Lange

Warner Baxter, Madge Evans, Nigel Bruce, Stepin Fetchit, Frank Melton, Lila Lee, Ralph Morgan, James Dunn, Shirley Temple, John Boles, George K. Arthur

'Its intrinsic merits do not quite match its pretentiousness.' – Variety

'Impossible to file it away in an ordinary drawer marked "Stinkers". This one is extra, it is super, and it butters itself very thickly with the most obvious sort of topical significance.' – Otis Ferguson

† The original title was Fox Follies.

Stand Up and Fight *
US   1938   99m   bw
MGM (Mervyn Le Roy)

A Southern aristocrat comes into conflict with a stagecoach operator used as transportation for stolen slaves.

Superior star action piece with plenty of vigorous brawls.

w James M. Cain, Jane Murfin, Harvey Ferguson   d W. S. Van Dyke II   ph Leonard Smith   m William Axt

Wallace Beery, Robert Taylor, Florence Rice, Helen Broderick, Charles Bickford, Barton MacLane, Charley Grapewin, John Qualen

'An action thriller that will please the muggs more than the dames . . . should prove strong at the b.o.' – Variety

Stand Up Virgin Soldiers
GB   1977   90m   Technicolor
Warner/Greg Smith/Maidenhead

More sexual adventures of National Servicemen in Singapore in 1950.

The Virgin Soldiers had a certain authenticity behind the fooling; this is a bawdy romp, and not a very efficient one.

w Leslie Thomas   novel Leslie Thomas   d Norman Cohen   ph Ken Hodges   m Ed Welch

Nigel Davenport, Robin Askwith, George Layton, Robin Nedwell, Warren Mitchell, John Le Mesurier, Edward Woodward, Irene Handl

'The hilarious story of what a girl will do to get her boss a bed in Washington!'

Standing Room Only *
US   1944   83m   bw
Paramount (Paul Jones)

Hotel rooms being hard to find in wartime Washington, a resourceful secretary hires out herself and her boss as a servant couple.

Moderate romantic farce with a few good laughs.

w Darrell Ware, Karl Tunberg   d Sidney Lanfield   ph Charles Lang   m Robert Emmett Dolan

Paulette Goddard, Fred MacMurray, Edward Arnold, Roland Young, Hillary Brooke, Porter Hall, Clarence Kolb, Anne Revere

Stanley & Iris
US   1989   105m   DuArt
UIP/MGM/Star Partners II (Arlene Sellers, Alex Winitsky)
V, V*, L, S

A cook who loses his job because he is illiterate is taught to read by a sympathetic widow.

Dull, heavy-handed and sentimental, not even its stars can save it from tedium.

w Harriet Frank Jnr, Irving Ravetch   novel Union Street by Pat Barker   d Martin Ritt   ph Donald McAlpine   m John Williams   pd Joel Schiller   ed Sidney Levin

Jane Fonda, Robert de Niro, Swoosie Kurtz, Martha Plimpton, Harley Cross, Jamey Sheridan, Feodor Chaliapin

Stanley and Livingstone ***
US   1939   101m   bw
TCF (Kenneth MacGowan)
V*

An American journalist goes to Africa to find a lost Victorian explorer.

A prestige picture which played reasonably fair with history and still managed to please the masses.

w Philip Dunne, Julien Josephson   d Henry King   ph George Barnes   m David Raksin, David Buttolph, Cyril Mockridge, Alfred Newman   ad Thomas Little

Spencer Tracy, Cedric Hardwicke, Richard Greene, Nancy Kelly, Walter Brennan, Charles Coburn, Henry Hull, Henry Travers, Miles Mander, Holmes Herbert

'Sound, worthy, interesting.' – Richard Mallett, Punch

'Most of the film consists of long shots of stand-ins moving across undistinguished scenery . . . Mr Tracy is always a human being, but Sir Cedric is an elocution lesson, a handclasp.' – Graham Greene

'Holds box office promise for socko biz . . . it's absorbing and adventurous drama.' – Variety

Stanno Tutti Bene **
Italy   1990   125m   colour
Erre/Ariane (Angelo Rizzoli)
V, V*, S
aka: Everybody's Fine

An elderly Sicilian decides to visit his five adult children living in various parts of Italy and finds that the reality does not live up to his expectations for them.

Bitter-sweet tale of muddling through life, elegantly acted and directed.

w Giuseppe Tornatore, Tonino Guerra   d Giuseppe Tornatore   ph Blasco Giurato   m Ennio Morricone   ad Andrea Crisanti   ed Mario Morra

Marcello Mastroianni, Michele Morgan, Marino Cenna, Roberto Nobile, Valeria Cavali, Norma Martelli

'Liberally sprinkled with ideas that provide the viewer with periodic payoffs and laughs.' – Variety

'When the star fades, the woman is born!'
'The story of every woman who ever climbed the stairway to the stars – and found herself at the bottom looking up!'

The Star *
US   1952   91m   bw
TCF/Bert E. Friedlob
V*

A once famous Hollywood star is financially and psychologically on her uppers.

A movie apparently tailor-made for its star turns out to be a disappointingly plotless wallow.

w Katherine Albert, Dale Eunson   d Stuart Heisler   ph Ernest Laszlo   m Victor Young

Bette Davis, Sterling Hayden, Natalie Wood, Warner Anderson, Minor Watson

† The role was originally designed for Joan Crawford.

AAN: Bette Davis

Star! **
US   1968   194m   DeLuxe   Todd-AO
TCF/Robert Wise (Saul Chaplin)
V*, L, S

Revue artist Gertrude Lawrence rises from poverty to international stardom and a measure of happiness.

Elephantiasis finally ruins this patient, detached, generally likeable recreation of a past theatrical era. In the old Hollywood style, it would probably have been even better on a smaller budget; but alas the star would still have been ill at ease with the drunken termagant scenes.

w William Fairchild   d Robert Wise   ph Ernest Laszlo   md Lennie Hayton   ch Michael Kidd   pd Boris Leven

Julie Andrews, Richard Crenna, Michael Craig, Daniel Massey (as Noël Coward), John Collin, Robert Reed, Bruce Forsyth, Beryl Reid, Jenny Agutter

† Short version: Those Were the Happy Days.
†† The film cost 14 million and took four.

AAN: Ernest Laszlo; Lennie Hayton; title song (m James Van Heusen, ly Sammy Cahn); Daniel Massey

The Star Chamber
US   1983   109m   DeLuxe   Panavision
TCF/Frank Yablans
V*, L

Judges get together to retry defendants who have been unjustly freed, and then have them executed by hired assassins.

A bit hard to swallow; also overlong and rather unpleasant.

w Roderick Taylor, Peter Hyams   d Peter Hyams
ph Richard Hannah   m Michael Small   pd Bill
Malley

Michael Douglas, Hal Holbrook, Yaphet Kotto,
Sharon Gless, James B. Sikking, Joe Regalbuto

'Michael Winner territory with a veneer of
conscience.' – *Sight and Sound*

'Small-screen material suffering from crippling
inflation.' – *Steve Jenkins, MFB*

Star Dust *
US   1940   85m   bw
TCF (Kenneth MacGowan)

A talent scout discovers a new Hollywood star.

Light, amusing studio comedy, a pleasing addition to
Hollywood mythology.

w Robert Ellis, Helen Logan   d Walter Lang
ph Peverell Marley   m David Buttolph

Linda Darnell, John Payne, Roland Young, Charlotte
Greenwood, William Gargan, Mary Beth Hughes,
Donald Meek, Jessie Ralph

Star 80
US   1983   103m   Technicolor
Warner/Ladd (Wolfgang Glattes, Kenneth Utt)
V*, L

The murder by her husband of Dorothy Stratten, the
Playboy centrefold model.

Unappetizing recounting, made less palatable by
flashy direction, of a story with no possible moral.

wd Bob Fosse   ph Sven Nykvist   m Ralph Burns
pd Tony Walton

Mariel Hemingway, Eric Roberts, Cliff Robertson (as
Hugh Hefner), Carroll Baker, Roger Rees

'A mishmash of embarrassments.' – *Tom Milne, MFB*

'Obviously intended as a cautionary tale for our times,
with the beautiful dreamers and ruthless schemers
peopling a colour supplement world of success.' –
Sight and Sound

A Star Is Born ***
US   1937   111m   Technicolor
David O. Selznick
V*, L

A young actress meets Hollywood success and marries
a famous leading man, whose star wanes as hers
shines brighter.

Abrasive romantic melodrama which is also the most
accurate study of Hollywood ever put on film.

w Dorothy Parker, Alan Campbell, Robert Carson,
story William A. Wellman, based partly on *What Price
Hollywood* (1932) (qv)   d William A. Wellman   ph W.
Howard Greene   m Max Steiner

Janet Gaynor, Fredric March, Adolphe Menjou, Lionel
Stander, Andy Devine, May Robson, Owen Moore,
Franklin Pangborn

'One of those rare ones which everyone will want to
see and talk about . . . disproves the tradition that
good pictures can't be made with a Hollywood
background.' – *Variety*

'Good entertainment by any standards.' – *Frank
S. Nugent, New York Times*

'A peculiar sort of masochistic self-congratulatory
Hollywood orgy.' – *New Yorker, 1975*

'The first colour job that gets close to what colour
must eventually come to: it keeps the thing in its
place, underlining the mood and situation of the story
rather than dimming everything else out in an
iridescent razzle-dazzle.' – *Otis Ferguson*

AA: original story; Special Award to W. Howard
Greene for colour photography

AAN: best picture; script; William A. Wellman; Janet
Gaynor; Fredric March

'Fate raised her to fame – and killed the man she loved!'
A Star Is Born **
US   1954   181m   Technicolor   Cinemascope
Warner/Transcona (Sidney Luft)
V, V*, L, S

Musical version of the above which begins very
strongly and has two splendid performances, but
suffers in the second half from a lack of writing
strength and heavy post-production cutting. The
numbers add very little except length.

w Moss Hart   d George Cukor   ph Sam Leavitt
md Ray Heindorf   ad Malcolm Bert, Gene Allen, Irene
Sharaff

Judy Garland, James Mason, Charles Bickford, Jack
Carson, Tommy Noonan, Amanda Blake, Lucy
Marlow

'Maintains a skilful balance between the musical and
the tear jerker.' – *Penelope Houston*

'By far the best of all the films about life behind the
cameras, the lights, the wind-machines, and the
cocktail bars of Hollywood.' – *Dilys Powell*

† Cary Grant and Humphrey Bogart were both sought
before James Mason was signed

AAN: Ray Heindorf; song 'The Man that Got Away'
(m Harold Arlen, ly Ira Gershwin); Judy Garland;
James Mason; art direction

A Star Is Born *
US   1976   140m   Metrocolor
Warner/Barwood/First Artists (Barbra Streisand, Jon Peters)
V, V*, L, S

Interminable remake set in the pop world amid
screaming crowds and songs at high decibel level;
also an insufferable piece of showing off by the star.
But some of the handling has style.

w John Gregory Dunne, Joan Didion, Frank Pierson
d Frank Pierson   ph Robert Surtees   md Paul
Williams   pd Polly Platt

Barbra Streisand, Kris Kristofferson, Paul Mazursky,
Gary Busey

'A clear case for the monopolies commission.' –
Michael Billington, Illustrated London News

'A bore is starred.' – *Village Voice*

AA: song 'Evergreen' (m Barbra Streisand, ly Paul
Williams)

AAN: Robert Surtees; Roger Kellaway (music
underscoring)

The Star Maker *
US   1939   94m   bw
Paramount (Charles R. Rodgers)

A songwriter makes the big time by organizing kid
acts.

Pleasant minor musical based on the career of Gus
Edwards.

w Frank Butler, Don Hartman, Arthur Caesar   d Roy
del Ruth   ph Karl Struss

Bing Crosby, Louise Campbell, Linda Ware, Ned
Sparks, Laura Hope Crews, Janet Waldo, Walter
Damrosch

'A rollicking filmusical, first-class entertainment.' –
Variety

Star of Midnight *
US   1935   90m   bw
RKO (Pandro S. Berman)
V*, L

A New York attorney solves the disappearance of a
leading lady.

Wisecracking, debonair murder mystery modelled on
The Thin Man.

w Howard J. Green, Anthony Veiller, Edward
Kaufman   d Stephen Roberts   ph J. Roy Hunt
m Max Steiner

William Powell, Ginger Rogers, Paul Kelly, Gene
Lockhart, Ralph Morgan, Leslie Fenton, J. Farrell
MacDonald

'Too bad the title isn't more attractive, but the picture
is excellent otherwise and should be a snappy
grosser.' – *Variety*

'It is all suavity and amusement, pistol shots and
cocktails.' – *Graham Greene*

'One of the best sophisticated comedy-mysteries in a
period full of such films.' – *NFT, 1973*

The Star Packer
US   1934   60m   bw
Monogram/Lone Star (Paul Malvern)
V*

Investigating the murders of his three predecessors, a
new sheriff and his Indian aide uncover the identity
of an outlaw known as The Shadow.

Wayne as usual gets his man and the girl in a low-
budget Western full of action and some novel stunts.

wd Robert N. Bradbury   ph Archie Stout   ed Carl
Pierson

John Wayne, Verna Hillie, George Hayes, Yakima
Canutt, Billy Franey, Ed Parker, Earl Dwire, Tom
Lingham

The Star Said No: see *Callaway Went Thataway*

The Star Spangled Girl
US   1971   92m   colour
Paramount (Howard W. Koch)

A sweet old-fashioned girl is fought for by two young
radicals.

Unamusingly 'with it' comedy from an unsuccessful
play.

w Arnold Margolin, Jim Parker   play Neil Simon
d Jerry Paris   ph Sam Leavitt   m Charles Fox

Sandy Duncan, Tony Roberts, Todd Susman,
Elizabeth Allen

Star Spangled Rhythm ***
US   1942   99m   bw
Paramount (Joseph Sistrom)
S

The doorman of Paramount Studios pretends to his
sailor son that he is a big producer.

Frenetic farce involving most of the talent on
Paramount's payroll and culminating in an
'impromptu' show staged for the navy. A good
lighthearted glimpse of wartime Hollywood.

w Harry Tugend   d George Marshall   ph Leo
Tover, Theodor Sparkuhl   md Robert Emmett Dolan
songs Johnny Mercer, Harold Arlen

Betty Hutton, Eddie Bracken, Victor Moore, Walter Abel,
Anne Revere, Cass Daley, Gil Lamb, Macdonald
Carey, Bob Hope, Bing Crosby, Paulette Goddard,
Veronica Lake, Dorothy Lamour, Vera Zorina, Fred
MacMurray, Ray Milland, Lynne Overman, Franchot
Tone, Dick Powell, Walter Dare Wahl and Co, Cecil B. de
Mille, Preston Sturges, Alan Ladd, Rochester, Katherine
Dunham, Susan Hayward

AAN: Robert Emmett Dolan; song 'That Old Black
Magic' (m Harold Arlen, ly Johnny Mercer)

'The human adventure is just beginning!'
Star Trek: The Motion Picture
US   1979   132m   Metrocolor   Panavision
Paramount (Gene Roddenberry)
V, V (W), V*, L, S

In the 23rd century, Admiral Kirk resumes command
of the *Enterprise* to combat an alien force.

And a surprisingly boring one. Vast sets and big-
screen solemnity hardly make this more enjoyable
than some of the TV episodes which got more tricks
and philosophical fun into one-third of the length.

w Harold Livingstone, Alan Dean Foster   d Robert
Wise   ph Richard H. Kline, Richard Yuricich
m Jerry Goldsmith   pd Harold Michelson   ed Todd
Ramsey

William Shatner, Leonard Nimoy, DeForest Kelley,
Stephen Collins, Persis Khambatta

AAN: Jerry Goldsmith; visual effects (Douglas
Trumbull, John Dykstra and others); art direction

'At the end of the universe lies the beginning of
vengeance!'

Star Trek: The Wrath of Khan
US   1982   114m   Movielab   Panavision
Paramount (Harve Bennett)
V, V (W), V*, L, S

The crew of the starship *Enterprise* counter the wiles of
an evil genius on a distant planet.

Comic strip capers a long way from the controlled
intelligence of some episodes of the TV series; but
more entertaining than the first movie.

w Jack B. Sowards   d Nicholas Meyer   ph Gayne
Rescher   m James Horner   pd Joseph R. Jennings

William Shatner, Leonard Nimoy, Ricardo
Montalban, DeForest Kelley, Ike Eisenmann

'A pitiful snack for the eyes with some unappetizing
crumbs left over for the mind to chew on.' – *Philip
Strick, MFB*

Star Trek III: The Search for Spock
US   1984   105m   Metrocolor   Panavision
Paramount/Cinema Group Venture (Harve Bennett)
V, V (W), V*, L, S

Admiral Kirk discovers that Spock is not dead but has
been reborn as a Vulcan child . . .

Very silly, empty and unamusing follow-up.

w Harve Bennett   d Leonard Nimoy   ph Charles
Correll   m James Horner

William Shatner, DeForest Kelley, James Doohan,
Walter Koenig, Michelle Nichols, Robert Hooks,
Leonard Nimoy

Star Trek IV: The Voyage Home *
US   1986   119m   Technicolor   Panavision
Paramount/Harve Bennett
V, V (W), V*, L, S
GB title: *The Voyage Home: Star Trek IV*

The *Enterprise* crew is called home to face trial for
mutiny: they find a very alien world.

The best of the series: it isn't saying much, but at least
there are shreds of wit in the script.

w Harve Bennett, Steve Meerson, Peter Krikes,
Nicholas Meyer   d Leonard Nimoy   ph Don
Peterman   m Leonard Rosenman   pd Jack T. Collis
ed Peter E. Berger

William Shatner, Leonard Nimoy, DeForest Kelley,
James Doohan, George Takei, Walter Koenig, Jane
Wyatt, Catherine Hicks

AAN: Don Peterman; Leonard Rosenman

Star Trek V: The Final Frontier
US   1989   107m   Technicolor   Panavision
UIP/Paramount (Harve Bennett)
V, V (W), V*, L

Captain Kirk goes in search of a legendary planet,
said to be inhabited by God.

Mystic moments, tamely rendered, that indicate it is
long after the time when the series should have been
laid to rest.

w David Loughery   story William Shatner, Harve
Bennett, David Loughery   d William Shatner
ph Andrew Laszlo   m Jerry Goldsmith
pd Herman Zimmerman   ed Peter Berger

William Shatner, Leonard Nimoy, DeForest Kelley,
James Doohan, Walter Koenig, Nichelle Nichols,
George Takei, David Warner, Laurence Luckinbill

'The battle for peace has begun.'

Star Trek VI: The Undiscovered Country **
US   1991   110m   Technicolor
UIP/Paramount (Ralph Winter, Steven-Charles Jaffe)
V, V*, L, CD, S

Mr Spock attempts to solve the murder of a Klingon
peace delegate after Captain Kirk and Dr McCoy are
convicted of the crime.

The last voyage of the original crew of the Starship
Enterprise turns out to be their finest hour and fifty
minutes.

w Nicholas Meyer, Denny Martin Flynn
story Leonard Nimoy, Lawrence Konner, Mark
Rosenthal   d Nicholas Meyer   ph Hiro Narita
m Cliff Eidelman   pd Herman Zimmerman
sp Industrial Light and Magic   ed Ronald Roose,
William Hoy

William Shatner, Leonard Nimoy, DeForest Kelley,
James Doohan, Walter Koenig, George Takei,
Christian Slater, Kim Cattrall, Mark Lenard,
Christopher Plummer, David Warner

'A lumbering and self-indulgent picture, dragged
down at every turn by the weight of twenty-five years
of illogical mediocrity, as if the series' notional
science-fiction aspects pre-empted the need for
characters, stories or a universe that made any
dramatic sense.' —*Kim Newman, Sight and Sound*

'There are no signs of waning energy here, not even in
an *Enterprise* crew that looks ever more ready for
intergalactic rocking chairs.' – *Janet Maslin, New York
Times*

Star Wars ****
US   1977   121m   Technicolor   Panavision
TCF/Lucasfilm (Gary Kurtz)
V, V (W), V*, L, S

A rebel princess in a distant galaxy escapes, and with
the help of her robots and a young farmer overcomes
the threatening forces of evil.

Flash Gordon rides again, but with timing so
impeccably right that the movie became a
phenomenon and one of the top grossers of all time.
Good harmless fun, put together with style and
imagination.

wd George Lucas   ph Gilbert Taylor   m John
Williams   pd John Barry   sp many and various
ed Paul Hirsch, Marcia Lucas, Richard Chew

Mark Hamill, Harrison Ford, Carrie Fisher, Peter
Cushing, Alec Guinness, Anthony Daniels (See
Threepio), Kenny Baker (Artoo Detoo), Dave Prowse
(Darth Vader)

'A great work of popular art, fully deserving the riches
it has reaped.' – *Time*

'Acting in this movie I felt like a raisin in a giant fruit
salad. And I didn't even know who the coconuts or
the canteloups were.' – *Mark Hamill*

'He intended his film, Lucas confesses, for a
generation growing up without fairy tales. His target
audience was fourteen years and younger . . . It was a
celebration, a social affair, a collective dream, and
people came again and again, dragging their friends
and families with them.' – *Les Keyser, Hollywood in the
Seventies*

'The loudness, the smash and grab editing and the
relentless pacing drive every idea from your head, and
even if you've been entertained you may feel cheated
of some dimension – a sense of wonder, perhaps.' –
New Yorker, 1982

'Heartless fireworks ignited by a permanently
retarded director with too much clout and cash.' –
Time Out, 1984

AA: John Williams; John Barry; editing; costumes
(John Mollo); visual effects (John Stears, John
Dykstra and others); sound

AAN: best picture; script; direction; Alec Guinness

The Star Witness *
US   1931   68m   bw
Warner

An old man witnesses a crime and is threatened by
gangsters.

Pacy melodrama with good performances.

w Lucien Hubbard   d William Wellman   ph James
Van Trees

Walter Huston, Chic Sale, Grant Mitchell, Frances
Starr, Sally Blane

'Plenty of action, laughs, and a tear.' – *Variety*

AAN: Lucien Hubbard

'Show me a boy who never wanted to be a rock star –
and I'll show you a liar'

Stardust
GB   1974   111m   Technicolor
EMI/Goodtimes (David Puttnam, Sandy Lieberson)
V

The rise and fall of a pop singer.

Unappetizing rehash of the road to ruin, pop music
style.

w Ray Connolly   d Michael Apted   ph Tony
Richmond   md Dave Edmunds, David Puttnam

David Essex, Adam Faith, Larry Hagman, Marty
Wilde, Rosalind Ayres

Stardust Memories *
US   1980   88m   bw
UA/Jack Rollins, Charles H. Joffe
V*, L

An increasingly melancholy comedian attends a
retrospective of his work and is plagued by real and
imaginary fears.

A plainly autobiographical work which, while
amusing and moving in spots, makes it doubtful that
the writer/director/star can even now shake off his
obsessions.

wd Woody Allen   ph Gordon Willis   m Dick Hyman

Woody Allen, Charlotte Rampling, Jessica Harper,
Marie-Christine Barrault, Tony Roberts, Helen Hanft

'Its posturing pyrotechnics seem more the symptom of
a crisis than its controlled expression.' – *Gilbert Adair,
MFB*

Starlift
US   1951   102m   bw
Warner (Robert Arthur)

Movie stars entertain at Travis Air Base, where the
boys are constantly leaving for Korea.

Insipid musical with even more insipid romantic
interludes.

w John Klorer, Karl Kamb   d Roy del Ruth
ph Ted McCord   md Ray Heindorf

Janice Rule, Dick Wesson, Richard Webb, Howard St
John; and guest stars Doris Day, Gordon MacRae,
Virginia Mayo, Gene Nelson, Ruth Roman, James
Cagney, Gary Cooper, Phil Harris, Louella Parsons,
Randolph Scott, Jane Wyman

Starlight Hotel *
New Zealand   1987   90m
Recorded Releasing/Challenge Film Corp/NZ Film Commission
   (Finola Dwyer, Larry Parr)
V*, L

Two runaways – one a rebellious child, the other a
suspected murderer – team up on the road.

Slight but engaging story, with good period detail.

w Grant Hinden-Miller   novel The Dream Monger
d Sam Pillsbury   ph Warrick Attewell   m Andrew
Hayes, Morton Wilson   pd Mike Becroft   ad Roger
Guise   ed Michael Horton

Peter Phelps, Greer Robson, Marshall Napier, Alice
Fraser

Starman

US 1984 115m MGM color
Columbia/Delphi (Larry J. Franco)
V, V*, L, S

An alien arrives in Wisconsin and takes human form, falling in love with the widow of the man he impersonates.

Derivative but eccentric science-fiction fantasy with lapses of narrative and a general attempt to make the love story predominant over the hardware.

w Bruce A. Evans, Raynold Gideon   d John Carpenter   ph Donald M. Morgan   m Jack Nitzsche   pd Daniel Lomino   ed Marion Rothman

Jeff Bridges, Karen Allen, Charles Martin Smith, Richard Jaeckel, Robert Phalen, Tony Edwards

AAN: Jeff Bridges

Staroye i Novoye: see The General Line

Stars and Bars

US 1988 94m DuArt/DeLuxe
Columbia (Sandy Lieberson)
V, V*, L

Cliché Englishman's encounters with stereotyped Americans in search for long-lost Renoir painting.

w William Boyd   novel William Boyd   d Pat O'Connor   ph Jerzy Zielinski   m Stanley Myers   pd Leslie Dilley, Stuart Craig   ed Michael Bradsell

Daniel Day-Lewis, Harry Dean Stanton, Martha Plimpton, Joan Cusack

'Unhappy mixture of farce and misdirected satire.' – Variety

Stars and Stripes Forever *

US 1952 89m Technicolor
TCF (Lamar Trotti)
V*
GB title: Marching Along

In the 1890s John Philip Sousa, a bandmaster who wants to write ballads, finds success as a writer of marches.

Low-key musical biopic with predictably noisy numbers.

w Lamar Trotti   autobiography John Philip Sousa   d Henry Koster   ph Charles G. Clarke   md Alfred Newman

Clifton Webb, Debra Paget, Robert Wagner, Ruth Hussey, Finlay Currie, Roy Roberts, Lester Matthews

The Stars Are Singing

US 1952 99m Technicolor
Paramount (Irving Asher)

A Polish refugee girl illegally enters the US and becomes an opera star.

Painless Cinderella fantasy in which everybody sings.

w Liam O'Brien   d Norman Taurog   ph Lionel Lindon   md Victor Young

Anna Maria Alberghetti, Lauritz Melchior, Rosemary Clooney, Fred Clark, Mikhail Rasumny

Stars in My Crown *

US 1950 89m bw
MGM (William H. Wright)

A two-gun parson brings peace to a Tennessee town after the Civil War.

Sentimental family Western, quite pleasantly made and performed.

w Margaret Fitts   novel Joe David Brown   d Jacques Tourneur   ph Charles Schoenbaum   m Adolph Deutsch

Joel McCrea, Ellen Drew, Dean Stockwell, Juano Hernandez, James Mitchell, Lewis Stone, Alan Hale, Amanda Blake

The Stars Look Down **

GB 1939 110m bw
Grafton (Isadore Goldsmidt)
V, V*

The son of a coal miner struggles to become an MP.

Economically but well made social drama from a popular novel, with good pace and backgrounds.

w J. B. Williams, A. J. Cronin   novel A. J. Cronin   d Carol Reed   ph Max Greene   m Hans May

Michael Redgrave, Margaret Lockwood, Edward Rigby, Emlyn Williams, Nancy Price, Allan Jeayes, Cecil Parker, Linden Travers

'Dr Cronin's mining novel has produced a very good film – I doubt whether in England we have ever produced a better.' – Graham Greene

'A splendidly directed portrait of those who burrow for the black diamond in England's northland . . . the picture is mounted with exactness of detail and technique.' – Variety

Stars over Broadway

US 1935 89m bw
Warner (Sam Bischoff)

Agent turns hotel porter into radio star.

Unremarkable musical, with unusual talent.

w Jerry Wald, Julius J. Epstein, Pat C. Flick   d William Keighley   ph George Barnes   md Leo F. Forbstein   ch Busby Berkeley, Bobby Connolly   songs Harry Warren, Al Dubin

James Melton, Jane Froman, Pat O'Brien, Jean Muir, Frank McHugh, Marie Wilson, Frank Fay

'A far from inspired backstage yarn with pleasant dialogue and fancy trimmings.' – Variety

Starstruck

Australia 1982 102m colour
Palm Beach Pictures (David Elfick, Richard Brennan)
V*, L

In a bid to keep open the family pub, a teenage boy makes a star of his young cousin.

Youth musical that does no more than transfer the usual backstage clichés to a punk and working-class setting.

w Stephen MacLean   d Gillian Armstrong   ph Russell Boyd   md Mark Moffat   pd Brian Thomson   ed Nicholas Beauman

Jo Kennedy, Ross O'Donovan, Margo Lee, Max Cullen, Pat Evison, John O'May, Ned Lander

Start Cheering

US 1938 78m bw
Columbia
V*

An actor's agent has problems when his potential star decides to go to college.

Fairly amusing low-budget musical with some surprises.

w Eugene Solow, Richard E. Wormser, Philip Rapp, Corey Ford   d Albert S. Rogell

Jimmy Durante, Walter Connolly, Joan Perry, Charles Starrett, the Three Stooges, Hal Leroy, Ernest Truex, Gertrude Niesen, Raymond Walburn, Broderick Crawford

'Longer on entertainment satisfaction than many of the more formidable pricers.' – Variety

Start the Revolution without Me *

US 1969 90m Technicolor
Warner/Norbud (Norman Lear)
V*

Two sets of twins get mixed up at the court of Louis XVI.

Historical spoof of the kind subsequently made familiar by Mel Brooks; the script might have suited Abbott and Costello better than these two actors.

w Fred Freeman, Lawrence J. Cohen   d Bud Yorkin   ph Jean Tournier   m John Addison

Donald Sutherland, Gene Wilder, Hugh Griffith, Jack McGowran, Billie Whitelaw, Victor Spinetti, Ewa Aulin

Starting Over *

US 1979 106m Movielab
Paramount/Century Associates (Alan J. Pakula, James L. Brooks)
V*, L

A divorced man nearly goes back to his wife but finally plumps for a nursery school teacher.

Plain-speaking sex comedy-drama with accomplished stars giving rather more than the script is worth.

w James L. Brooks   novel Dan Wakefield   d Alan J. Pakula   ph Sven Nykvist   m Marvin Hamlisch   pd George Jenkins

Burt Reynolds, Jill Clayburgh, Candice Bergen, Charles Durning, Austin Pendleton

AAN: Jill Clayburgh, Candice Bergen

State Fair **

US 1933 98m bw
Fox (Winfield Sheehan)

Dad wants his prize pig to win at the fair, but the younger members of his family have romance in mind.

Archetypal family film, much remade but never quite so pleasantly performed.

w Paul Green, Sonya Levien   novel Phil Stong   d Henry King   ph Hal Mohr   md Louis de Francesco

Will Rogers, Janet Gaynor, Lew Ayres, Sally Eilers, Norman Foster, Louise Dresser, Frank Craven, Victor Jory, Hobart Cavanaugh

'A pungent, good-humoured motion picture.' – Pare Lorentz

'Vigour, freshness and sympathy abound in its admittedly idealized fantasy treatment of small-town life.' – Charles Higham, 1972

AAN: best picture; script

State Fair **

US 1945 100m Technicolor
TCF (William Perlberg)
V, V*, L
TV title: It Happened One Summer

Musical remake with an amiable cast and a rousing score.

w/ly Oscar Hammerstein II   d Walter Lang   ph Leon Shamroy   md Alfred Newman   m Richard Rodgers

Charles Winninger, Jeanne Crain, Dana Andrews, Vivian Blaine, Dick Haymes, Fay Bainter, Frank McHugh, Percy Kilbride, Donald Meek

'Surely the sort of theme that clamours for movie treatment. But no, say Twentieth Century Fox: let's make the fair look like a night club. Let's look around for stars of pristine nonentity. Let's screw the camera down to the studio floor. The result, "an epic that sings to the skies . . . with glorious, glamorous new songs".' – Richard Winnington

'Comes pretty close to being another Oklahoma.' – Motion Picture Herald

AA: song 'It Might As Well Be Spring'

AAN: Alfred Newman

State Fair

US 1962 118m DeLuxe Cinemascope
TCF (Charles Brackett)
V*

Dullsville modernized version, condescending

towards the rurals and peopled by unattractive youngsters.

w Richard Breen d José Ferrer ph William C. Mellor md Alfred Newman

Pat Boone, Alice Faye, Tom Ewell, Pamela Tiffin, Ann-Margret, Bobby Darin, Wally Cox

State of Grace
US   1990   134m   DeLuxe   Panavision
Rank/Cinehaus/Orion (Ned Dowd, Randy Ostrow, Ron Rotholz)
V, V*, L, S

In New York, an undercover cop returns to the district where he grew up in order to infiltrate an Irish gang that is about to make a deal with the Mafia.

Dull and plodding gangster movie.

w Dennis McIntyre d Phil Joanou ph Jordan Cronenweth m Ennio Morricone pd Patrizia von Brandenstein, Doug Kraner ed Claire Simpson

Sean Penn, Ed Harris, Gary Oldman, Robin Wright, John Turturro, John C. Reilly, R. D. Call, Joe Vitorelli, Burgess Meredith, Deirdre O'Connell

'One of the more intriguing American thrillers of the year if only because it turns out to be dripping with old-fashioned romanticism as well as new-fangled violence.' – *Derek Malcolm, Guardian*

State of the Union ***
US   1948   110m   bw
MGM/Liberty Films (Frank Capra)
V*, L
GB title: *The World and His Wife*

An estranged wife rejoins her husband when he is running for president.

Brilliantly scripted political comedy which unfortunately goes soft at the end but offers stimulating entertainment most of the way.

w Anthony Veiller, Myles Connelly *play Howard Lindsay, Russel Crouse* d Frank Capra ph George J. Folsey m Victor Young

Spencer Tracy, Katharine Hepburn, Adolphe Menjou, Van Johnson, Angela Lansbury, Lewis Stone, Howard Smith, Raymond Walburn, Charles Dingle

'A triumphant film, marked all over by Frank Capra's artistry.' – *Howard Barnes*

The State of Things *
US/Portugal   1982   120m   bw
Artificial Eye/Road Movies/Pro-Ject/ZDF/Musidora/Film International (Chris Sievernich)
V*, L
original title: *Der Stand Der Dinge*

A film director tracks down in Los Angeles the producer who abandoned him and his film crew in Portugal.

A sort of B movie about the making of a B movie and a reflection on the meaning of cinema, within the loose format of a thriller.

w Wim Wenders, Robert Kramer d Wim Wenders ph Henri Alekan, Martin Schafer, Fred Murphy m Jurgen Knieper ad Ze Branco ed Barbara von Weitershausen, Peter Przygodda

Isabelle Weingarten, Rebecca Pauly, Patrick Bauchau, Paul Getty III, Samuel Fuller, Roger Corman, Allen Goorwitz

State Secret **
GB   1950   104m   bw
British Lion/London (Frank Launder, Sidney Gilliat)
US title: *The Great Manhunt*

In a Ruritanian country, spies pursue a surgeon, the only man who knows that the dictator is dead.

Hitchcockian chase comedy-thriller which is well detailed and rises to the heights on occasion.

wd Sidney Gilliat *novel Appointment with Fear* by Roy Huggins ph Robert Krasker m William Alwyn ed Thelma Myers

Douglas Fairbanks Jnr, Glynis Johns, Herbert Lom, Jack Hawkins, Walter Rilla, Karel Stepanek, Carl Jaffe

'An admirably fast-moving diversion in the Hitchcock tradition.' – *Richard Mallett, Punch*

'One of the best thrillers a British studio (any studio, for that matter) has made for years.' – *Leonard Mosley*

State's Attorney *
US   1932   79m   bw
RKO
V*
GB title: *Cardigan's Last Case*

A prosecuting counsel nearly pays the penalty for arrogance.

Good star melodrama.

w Rowland Brown and Gene Fowler d George Archainbaud

John Barrymore, Jill Esmond, William Boyd, Helen Twelvetrees

'Good programme box office stuff if not particularly smashing.' – *Variety*

Static
US   1986   93m   colour
Necessity Films (Amy Ness)
V*, L

An unemployed young man invents a device for displaying images of heaven on a television set, but he is the only one able to see them.

A desultory variation on the fable of the Emperor's new clothes, in which it is assumed that eccentricity is interesting and amusing; here, it isn't.

w Keith Gordon, Mark Romanek d Mark Romanek ph Jeff Jur pd Cynthia Sowder ed Emily Paine

Keith Gordon, Amanda Plummer, Bob Gunton, Lily Knight, Barton Heyman, Reathel Bean

Station Six Sahara
GB   1962   101m   bw
British Lion/CCC/Artur Brauner (Victor Lyndon)

Five men working on a remote Saharan pipeline quarrel over the favours of an American girl whose car crashes nearby.

Raging old-fashioned melodrama with the courage of its lack of convictions.

w Bryan Forbes, Brian Clemens d Seth Holt ph Gerald Gibbs m Ron Grainer

Carroll Baker, Ian Bannen, Peter Van Eyck, Denholm Elliott, Mario Adorf, Jorg Felmy, Biff McGuire

Station West
US   1948   91m   bw
RKO (Robert Sparks)

A saloon queen is the secret head of a gang of gold robbers.

Predictable but well-made Western patterned after *Destry Rides Again*.

w Frank Fenton, Winston Miller *novel Luke Short* d Sidney Lanfield ph Harry J. Wild m Heinz Roemheld

Dick Powell, Jane Greer, Agnes Moorehead, Burl Ives, Tom Powers, Gordon Oliver, Steve Brodie, Guinn Williams, Raymond Burr, Regis Toomey

'The face was his . . . the body was his . . . but suddenly, Hello, Charlie!'
The Statue
GB   1970   89m   Eastmancolor
Cinerama/Josef Shaftel (Anis Nohra)
V*

A languages professor is embarrassed when his

sculptress wife makes an immense nude statue of him – with someone else's private parts.

Strained phallic comedy which doesn't even make the most of its one joke.

w Alec Coppel, Denis Norden d Rod Amateau ph Piero Portalupi m Riz Ortolani

David Niven, Virna Lisi, Robert Vaughn, Ann Bell, John Cleese, Hugh Burden

Stay Away Joe
US   1968   102m   Metrocolor   Panavision
MGM (Douglas Lawrence)
V, V*, L

An Indian rodeo rider returns to his reservation, makes several romantic conquests, and helps a government rehabilitation scheme.

Thin if surprising vehicle for a singing star; all rather tedious.

w Michael A. Hoey *novel Dan Cushman* d Peter Tewkesbury ph Fred Koenekamp m Jack Marshall

Elvis Presley, Burgess Meredith, Joan Blondell, Katy Jurado, Thomas Gomez, Henry Jones, L. Q. Jones

Stay Hungry
US   1976   102m   DeLuxe
UA/Outov (Harold Schneider, Bob Rafaelson)
V*

The heir to an Alabama estate annoys the locality by assembling a curious bunch of friends and making unexpected use of his money.

Rather obvious and pointless fable; well made but not very stimulating.

w Charles Gaines, Bob Rafaelson *novel Charles Gaines* d Bob Rafaelson ph Victor Kemper m Bruce Langhorne, Byron Berline

Jeff Bridges, Sally Field, Arnold Schwarzenegger, R. G. Armstrong, Robert Englund, Roger E. Mosley

'The picture isn't just unsatisfying, it's a mess.' – *Stanley Kauffmann*

Stay Tuned
US   1992   87m   Technicolor
Warner/Morgan Creek (James G. Robinson)
V, V*, L, S

A couple are trapped in a cable television system run by the Devil.

An unsuccessful send-up of obsessive television viewing, mainly because it picks targets, such as *Wayne's World*, that are beyond parody.

w Tom S. Parker, Jim Jennewein d Peter Hyams ph Peter Hyams m Bruce Broughton pd Philip Harrison sp Rhythm and Hues Inc. ed Peter E. Berger

John Ritter, Pam Dawber, Jeffrey Jones, David Thom, Heather McComb, Bob Dishy

'High class trash . . . redeemed by a manic script, good special effects and production values.' – *Sheila Johnston, Independent*

'A picture with nothing for everybody.' – *Variety*

'It's five years later for Tony Manero. The fever still burns!'
Staying Alive
US   1983   96m   Metrocolor
Paramount/Robert Stigwood/Cinema Group Venture (Sylvester Stallone)
V, V*, L, S

Tony Manero becomes a Broadway dancer.

Fragile sequel to *Saturday Night Fever*, with some of its frenetic quality but none of its impact.

w Sylvester Stallone, Norman Wexler d Sylvester Stallone ph Nick McLean m Johnny Mandel, Robin Garb, others pd Robert Boyle

John Travolta, Cynthia Rhodes, Finola Hughes, Steve Inwood, Julie Bovasso

'By turns exhilarating and absurd.' – *Nick Roddick, MFB*

'Stallone doesn't bother much with character, scenes or dialogue. He just puts the newly muscle-plated Travolta in front of the camera, covers him with what looks like oil slick, and goes for the whambams.' – *Pauline Kael, New Yorker*

Staying Together
US   1989   91m   CFI
Hemdale (Joseph Fuery)
V, V*, L

Three brothers growing up in a small town experience the pangs of requited love.

Exuberant but corny tale of family relationships.

w Monte Merrick   d Lee Grant   ph Dick Bush
m Miles Goodman   pd Stuart Wurtzel
ed Katherine Wenning

Sean Astin, Stockard Channing, Melinda Dillon, Jim Haynie, Levon Helm, Dinah Manoff, Dermot Mulroney, Tim Quill

'Whips up the clichés and homilies of American small-town melodrama without adding the slightest spice.' – *Geoff Brown, MFB*

Stealing Heaven
GB/Yugoslavia   1988   115m   colour
Rank/Amy International/Jadran (Simon McCorkindale)
V*, L, S

The dying Heloise recalls her love-affair with Abelard.

Pasteboard reproduction of medieval life and love.

w Chris Bryant   novel Marion Meade   d Clive Donner   ph Mikael Salomon   m Nick Bicar
pd Voytek Roman   ed Michael Ellis

Derek de Lint, Kim Thompson, Denholm Elliott, Bernard Hepton, Kenneth Cranham, Patsy Byrne, Cassie Stuart, Philip Locke, Rachel Kempson, Angela Pleasence, Yvonne Bryceland, Mark Jax

Steamboat Bill Jnr *
US   1928   71m (24 fps)   bw   silent
UA/Buster Keaton/Joseph Schenck
V*, L

A student takes over his father's old Mississippi steamboat, and wins the daughter of his rival.

Rather flat comedy redeemed by a magnificent cyclone climax.

w Carl Harbaugh, Buster Keaton   d Charles Riesner
ph J. Devereaux Jennings, Bert Haines

Buster Keaton, Ernest Torrence, Marion Byron

Steamboat round the Bend *
US   1935   80m   bw
TCF (Sol M. Wurtzel)

A Mississippi steamboat captain defeats his rival and finds evidence to clear his nephew of a murder charge.

Rather heavily-scripted star vehicle which sacrifices fun for atmosphere but is often good to look at.

w Dudley Nichols, Lamar Trotti   novel Ben Lucien Berman   d John Ford   ph George Schneiderman
m Samuel Kaylin

Will Rogers, Anne Shirley, Eugene Pallette, John McGuire, Irvin S. Cobb, Berton Churchill, Stepin Fetchit, Roger Imhof, Raymond Hatton

'Will Rogers' final picture . . . in the money despite a drab theme.' – *Variety*

Steaming
GB   1985   95m   colour
Paul Mills/World Film Services/Columbia
V*

Women in a rundown steam bath confide in each other.

Excessively dreary talk piece which apparently seemed crisper on the stage.

w Patricia Losey   play Nell Dunn   d Joseph Losey (his last film)   ph Chris Challis

Vanessa Redgrave, Sarah Miles, Diana Dors, Patti Love, Brenda Bruce

'It cannot be denied that it is very British. The humor is coarse and the outlook grim. It is the work of Nell Dunn and is a shameless feminist and socialist treatise. Whether these qualities rank as vices or virtues is, of course, a matter of taste.' – *Quentin Crisp*

Steel
US   1979   101m   Movielab
Columbia/Panzer/Davis/Fawcett-Majors (Lee Majors)
V*

When a construction boss is killed, his daughter vows to complete his last project.

Flashy, foul-mouthed, but basically old-fashioned hokum climaxing in a race to complete before foreclosure.

w Leigh Chapman   d Steve Carver   ph Roger Shearman   m Michael Colombier   pd Ward Preston

Lee Majors, Jennifer O'Neill, Art Carney, George Kennedy, Harris Yulin, Terry Kiser, Richard Lynch, Albert Salmi

The Steel Bayonet
GB   1957   85m   bw   Hammerscope
UA/Hammer (Michael Carreras)

During the assault on Tunis a battle-weary platoon holds a farm against enemy attack.

Dreary cliché-ridden war melodrama, peopled by all the usual types.

w Howard Clewes   d Michael Carreras   ph Jack Asher   m Leonard Salzedo   ad Ted Marshall
ed Bill Lenny

Leo Genn, Kieron Moore, Michael Medwin, Robert Brown, Michael Ripper, John Paul, Bernard Horsfall

Steel Magnolias *
US   1989   117m   Technicolor
Columbia TriStar/Rastar/Ray Stark
V, V*, L, S

A group of women, who gather in a small-town beauty parlour, face up to life's vicissitudes.

Slickly made, sentimental account of marriage and motherhood that provides some meaty roles for the assembled actresses.

w Robert Harling   play Robert Harling   d Herbert Ross   ph John A. Alonzo   m Georges Delerue
pd Gene Callahan, Edward Pisoni   ed Paul Hirsch

Sally Field, Dolly Parton, Shirley Maclaine, Daryl Hannah, Olympia Dukakis, Julia Roberts, Tom Skerrit, Sam Shepard

'A lush, excruciatingly elongated emotional wallow.' – *Tom Milne, MFB*

AAN: Julia Roberts

Steel Town
US   1952   84m   Technicolor
U-I (Leonard Goldstein)

A steel president's nephew joins the company as a furnace hand.

Routine drama with an unusual background.

w Gerald Drayson Adams, Lou Breslow   d George Sherman   ph Charles P. Boyle   m Joseph Gershenson

Ann Sheridan, John Lund, Howard Duff, James Best, Nancy Kulp

The Steel Trap *
US   1952   85m   bw
TCF/Thor (Bert E. Friedlob)

An assistant bank manager steals half a million dollars from the vault but is troubled by conscience and manages to put it back before the loss is discovered.

Solidly competent little suspenser with plenty of movement.

wd Andrew Stone   ph Ernest Laszlo   m Dimitri Tiomkin

Joseph Cotten, Teresa Wright, Jonathan Hale, Walter Sande

Steelyard Blues
US   1972   92m   Technicolor
Warner/S. B. Productions (Tony Bill, Michael and Julia Phillips)
V*

An ex-con and his call-girl friend are an embarrassment to his DA brother.

Bits and pieces of anti-establishment comedy are tacked on to a thin plot; a few of them work.

w David S. Ward   d Alan Myerson   ph Laszlo Kovacs, Steven Larner   m Nick Gravenites

Donald Sutherland, Jane Fonda, Peter Boyle, Howard Hesseman

Stella
US   1990   109m   colour
Rank/Samuel Goldwyn Company/Touchstone (David V. Picker)
V, V*, L

A waitress makes sacrifices so that her illegitimate daughter can escape from the working class.

Outmoded soap opera that fails to achieve the tears provoked by the two earlier film versions.

w Robert Getchell   novel Stella Dallas by Olive Higgins Prouty   d John Erman   ph Billy Williams
m John Morris   pd James Hulsey   ed Jerrold L. Ludwig, Bud Molin, Lisa M. Citron

Bette Midler, John Goodman, Trini Alvarado, Stephen Collins, Marsha Mason, Eileen Brennan, Linda Hart

'Bette Midler deserves better than this heap of cornball slush.' – *John Coldstream, Daily Telegraph*

Stella Dallas *
US   1925   110m approx (24 fps)   bw   silent
Samuel Goldwyn

An uncouth woman loses both husband and daughter.

Standard weepie complete with 'out into the cold cold snow' ending, but handled here with tact and discretion. A seminal film of its time.

w Frances Marion   novel Olive Higgins Prouty
d Henry King   ph Arthur Edeson

Belle Bennett, Ronald Colman, Lois Moran, Jean Hersholt, Douglas Fairbanks Jnr, Alice Joyce

'A sad film, but sad with the curious quality of sadness that leaves only happiness in its train. We, watching it, are happy to be so sad. We find here a vicarious courage; a fidelity and a generous understanding that by proxy become ours.' – *C. A. Lejeune*

Stella Dallas *
US   1937   106m   bw
Samuel Goldwyn
V*, L

Fashionable remake with excellent talent; 1937 audiences came to sneer and stayed to weep.

w Victor Heerman, Sara Y. Mason   d King Vidor
ph Rudolph Maté   m Alfred Newman

Barbara Stanwyck, John Boles, Anne Shirley, Barbara O'Neil, Alan Hale, Marjorie Main, Tim Holt

'A tear-jerker of A ranking. There are things about the story that will not appeal to some men, but no one will be annoyed or offended by it. And the wallop is inescapably there for femmes.' – *Variety*

† Goldwyn's premier choices for the lead were Ruth Chatterton and Gladys George.

AAN: Barbara Stanwyck; Anne Shirley

Step by Step *
US   1946   62m   bw
Sid Rogell/RKO

The FBI gives chase to a young couple who may or may not have stolen government plans.

Trim second feature melodrama with nice touches.

w Stuart Palmer   d Phil Rosen

Lawrence Tierney, Anne Jeffreys, Lowell Gilmore, George Cleveland, Jason Robards

Step Down to Terror
US   1959   76m   bw
U-I (Joseph Gershenson)
GB title: The Silent Stranger

A man returns to his home town and is discovered to be a psychopathic killer on the run.

Dismal reworking of Shadow of a Doubt; strictly second feature stuff.

w Mel Dinelli, Czenzi Ormonde, Chris Cooper
d Harry Keller   ph Russell Metty   m Joseph Gershenson

Charles Drake, Coleen Miller, Rod Taylor, Josephine Hutchinson, Jocelyn Brando

Step Lively *
US   1944   88m   bw
RKO (Robert Fellows)
V*, L

Gleaming musical remake of Room Service (qv); all very efficient if witless.

w Warren Duff, Peter Milne   d Tim Whelan
ph Robert de Grasse   md Constantin Bakaleinikoff
songs Jule Styne, Sammy Cahn   ad Albert S. D'Agostino, Carroll Clark

Frank Sinatra, George Murphy, Adolphe Menjou, Gloria de Haven, Anne Jeffreys, Walter Slezak, Eugene Pallette

AAN: art direction

The Stepfather
US   1986   88m   CFI colour
Jay Benson/Vista/New World
V, V*, L

A teenage girl discovers that her new stepfather is a psychopath who may make her his victim.

Well enough done but rather obvious suspenser on the lines of Love from a Stranger.

w Donald E. Westlake   d Joseph Ruben

Terry O'Quinn, Jill Schoelen, Shelley Hack, Charles Lanyer

'A one-joke movie, but the joke is wonderfully subversive . . . It's not the culture's violence that drives people mad, but its fake harmony – especially the sunny world of TV sitcoms, where every crisis is handily resolved.' – David Edelstein, Village Voice

'There's Something You Should Know About My Past.'
Stepfather II
US   1989   86m   colour
ITC (Darin Scott, William Burr)
V, V*, L

A mass murderer escapes from an asylum and sets up as a psychiatrist so that he can discover a ready-made family to take over.

A limp sequel that lacks suspense and offers no more than a predictable re-run of the original.

w John Auerbach   d Jeff Burr   ph Jacek Laskus
m Jim Manzie, Pat Regan   pd Byrnadette Disanto
ed Pasquale A. Buba

Terry O'Quinn, Meg Foster, Caroline Williams, Jonathan Brandis, Henry Brown, Mitchell Laurance

† It was followed by a made-for-TV movie, Stepfather III, which provided little variation on the original plot.

The Stepford Wives *
US   1974   115m   TVC
Fadsin/Palomar (Edgar J. Sherick)
V*

A new wife in a commuter village outside New York finds all her female friends too good to be true . . . because their husbands have had them replaced by computerized models.

An attractive idea which needs a much lighter and pacier touch but entertains in patches and shows agreeable sophistication.

w William Goldman   novel Ira Levin   d Bryan Forbes   ph Owen Roizman   m Michael Small
pd Gene Callahan

Katharine Ross, Paula Prentiss, Nanette Newman, Peter Masterson, Patrick O'Neal, Tina Louise, William Prince

'It was hard to tell Katharine Ross playing a robot from Katharine Ross playing a normal housewife.' – Les Keyser, Hollywood in the Seventies

'The first women's lib gothic – hardly the landmark the world had been waiting for.' – Pauline Kael, New Yorker

Stephen King's IT
US   1990   180m   colour
Lorimar (Matthew O'Connor)
V

Childhood friends gather after 30 years to rid their home town of a murderous evil spirit.

Overlong, indifferently acted, predictably scripted TV mini-series transferred to video.

w Lawrence D. Cohen, Tommy Lee Wallace   novel IT by Stephen King   d Tommy Lee Wallace
ph Richard Leiterman   m Richard Bellis
pd Douglas Higgins   ed Robert F. Shugrue, David Blangsted

Harry Anderson, Dennis Christopher, Richard Masur, Annette O'Toole, Tim Reid, John Ritter, Richard Thomas, Tim Curry, Olivia Hussey

Stepkids: see Big Girls Don't Cry . . . They Get Even

Steppin' in Society
US   1945   72m   bw
Republic (Joseph Bercholtz)

A judge is caught in a storm and takes refuge in a low club frequented by criminals.

Uncertain comedy which never really works.

w Bradford Ropes   novel Marcel Arnac
d Alexandre Esway

Edward Everett Horton, Gladys George, Ruth Terry, Robert Livingston, Jack La Rue, Lola Lane

'Your dreams are just a step away.'
Stepping Out
US   1991   110m   Technicolor
UIP/Paramount (Lewis Gilbert)
V, V*, L, S

A tap-dance teacher attempts to prepare a class of amateurs for a charity performance.

Mundane and old-fashioned drama that lacks precision.

w Richard Harris   play Richard Harris   d Lewis Gilbert   ph Alan Hume   m Peter Matz   pd Peter Mullins   ch Danny Daniels   ed Humphrey Dixon

Liza Minelli, Shelley Winters, Robyn Stevan, Jane Krakowski, Bill Irwin, Ellen Greene, Sheila

McCarthy, Andrea Martin, Julie Walters, Carol Woods, Luke Reilly

'The man, the music, the murder.'
Stepping Razor Red X *
Canada   1992   92m   Fuji colour
Feature Film/SC Entertainment (Edgar Egger)
V

Documentary on the life and violent death, in 1987, of Jamaican Rastafarian reggae singer Peter Tosh, using some concert performances and tapes he recorded, which he intended to use as the basis of his autobiography, to be called Red X, after the cross in red ink he saw after his name on official documents, showing where he should put his signature, but which he interpreted as indicating that he was being singled out.

Interesting, if inconclusive, investigation of the reasons for Tosh's murder: was it a robbery or a politically motivated hit? Tosh's own, often bitter, paranoid and rambling commentary, couched in apocalyptical language, adds another layer of mystification.

wd Nicholas Campbell   ph Edgar Egger   ed Trevor Ambrose

'For all the stridency of his ideas and of his music, Peter Tosh remains a phantom beyond this film's grasp.' – Sight and Sound

Steptoe and Son
GB   1972   98m   Technicolor
EMI/Associated London Films (Aida Young)
V

Harold gets married, mislays his wife but thinks he is a father.

Strained attempt to transfer the TV rag-and-bone comedy (which in the US became Sanford and Son) to the big screen. Not the same thing at all.

w Ray Galton, Alan Simpson   d Cliff Owen
ph John Wilcox   m Roy Budd, Jack Fishman

Wilfrid Brambell, Harry H. Corbett, Carolyn Seymour, Arthur Howard, Victor Maddern

† Steptoe and Son Ride Again, which followed in 1973, was even more crude and out of character.

The Sterile Cuckoo
US   1969   107m   Technicolor
Paramount/Boardwalk (Alan J. Pakula)
V*, L
GB title: Pookie

A talkative but insecure college girl has her first sexual adventures.

Rather tiresome comedy drama with good scenes; general handling far too restrained.

w Alvin Sargent   novel John Nicholson   d Alan J. Pakula   ph Milton Krasner   m Fred Karlin

Liza Minnelli, Tim McIntire, Wendell Burton, Austin Green, Sandra Faison

AAN: song 'Come Saturday Morning' (m Fred Karlin, ly Dory Previn); Liza Minnelli

Stevie *
US/GB   1978   102m   Technicolor
First Artists/Grand Metropolitan (Robert Enders)
V*

An account of the uneventful life of poetess Stevie Smith, lived out mainly in a London suburb under the fear of death.

Claustrophobic showcase for a whimsical lady; interesting for some specialized audiences.

w Hugh Whitemore   play Hugh Whitemore
d Robert Enders   ph Freddie Young   m Marcus Gowers

Glenda Jackson, Mona Washbourne, Trevor Howard, Alec McCowen

Stick

US 1985 109m Technicolor
Universal/Jennings Lang (Robert Daley)
V*, L

A hardboiled ex-con goes to Miami's low-life district in search of the man who killed his friend.

Wearisome crime melodrama with too many pauses for the hero's self-examination.

w Elmore Leonard, Joseph C. Stinson *novel* Elmore Leonard *d* Burt Reynolds *ph* Nick McLean *m* Barry de Vorzon, Joseph Conlan

Burt Reynolds, Candice Bergen, George Segal, Charles Durning

'Plot is of the convoluted kind beloved by exhibitors since patrons can wander out for popcorn and come back without missing anything.' – *Variety*

The Stick Up

GB 1977 101m colour
Backstage (Elliott Kastner, Danny O'Donovan)

In Devon in 1935, an American gives a lift to a café waitress and finds she is a thief on the run.

Numbingly peculiar comedy melodrama which tries too hard to have any chance of succeeding.

wd Jeffrey Bloom *ph* Michael Reed *m* Michael J. Lewis

David Soul, Pamela McMyler, Johnny Wade, Michael Balfour

'The worst film of this or possibly any year.' – *Barry Took, Punch*

Sticky Fingers

US 1988 88m DuArt
Virgin/Hightop/Spectrafilm (Catlin Adams, Melanie Mayron)
V*, L

Two struggling musicians spend a fortune left with them for safe keeping by a drug dealer.

Lacklustre comedy without enough wit to keep it alive.

w Catlin Adams, Melanie Mayron *d* Catlin Adams *ph* Gary Thieltges *m* Gary Chang *ed* Bob Reitano

Helen Slater, Melanie Mayron, Danitra Vance, Eileen Brennan, Carol Kane, Loretta Devine, Stephen McHattie, Christopher Guest

Stiletto

US 1969 99m Berkeley-Pathé
Avco/Harold Robbins (Norman Rosemont)

A wealthy playboy racing driver is in fact a Mafia executioner.

Dreary, violent, fashionable Mafioso melodrama with international jet set trimmings.

w A. J. Russell *novel* Harold Robbins *d* Bernard Kowalski *ph* Jack Priestly *m* Sid Ramin

Alex Cord, Britt Ekland, Barbara McNair, Patrick O'Neal, Joseph Wiseman, John Dehner, Eduardo Ciannelli, Roy Scheider

'Cardboard characters crumpled by a script which deals exclusively in clichés.' – *Sight and Sound*

Still of the Night *

US 1982 91m Technicolor
MGM/UA (Arlene Donovan)
V*, L

A psychiatrist finds himself in danger when one of his patients is murdered.

Hitchcock-style mystery melodrama with the villain fairly well concealed . . . but somehow not very entertaining. The actors all take their characters too seriously.

w Robert Benton, David Newman *d* Robert Benton *ph* Nestor Almendros *m* John Gibson *pd* Mel Bourne

Roy Scheider, Meryl Streep, Jessica Tandy, Sara Botsford, Josef Somner, Joe Grifasi

'A lifeless and frustrating muddle.' – *Steve Jenkins, MFB*

De Stilte Rond Christine M: see *A Question of Silence*

'All it takes is a little confidence!'
The Sting **

US 1973 129m Technicolor
Universal/Richard Zanuck, David Brown (Tony Bill, Michael S. Phillips)
V, V*, L, S

In twenties Chicago, two con men stage an elaborate revenge on a big time gangster who caused the death of a friend.

Bright, likeable, but overlong, unconvincingly studio-set and casually developed comedy suspenser cashing in on star charisma but riding to enormous success chiefly on its tinkly music and the general lack of simple entertainment.

w David S. Ward *d* George Roy Hill *ph* Robert Surtees *m* Scott Joplin (arranged by Marvin Hamlisch) *ad* Henry Bumstead

Paul Newman, *Robert Redford*, Robert Shaw, Charles Durning, Ray Walston, Eileen Brennan

'A visually claustrophobic, mechanically plotted movie that's meant to be a roguishly charming entertainment.' – *New Yorker*

'It demonstrates what can happen when a gifted young screenwriter has the good fortune to fall among professionals his second time out.' – *Judith Crist*

'A testament to the value of blue eyes and bright smiles.' – *Les Keyser, Hollywood in the Seventies*

AA: best picture; David S. Ward; George Roy Hill; Marvin Hamlisch

AAN: Robert Surtees; Robert Redford

'The con is on – place your bets!'
The Sting 2

US 1983 102m Technicolor
Universal (Jennings Lang)
V*, L

Lonnegan plots his revenge on the two who stung him in twenties Chicago.

Boring reprise of an overrated movie: though efficiently made, it never catches fire, and the cast is indisputably a second team.

w David S. Ward *d* Jeremy Paul Kagan *ph* Bill Butler *m* Lalo Schifrin *pd* Edward C. Carfagno

Jackie Gleason, Mac Davis, Karl Malden, Oliver Reed, Bert Remsen, Teri Garr

'The vivid minor characters have been squeezed into lifelessness by the python-like plot.' – *Tom Milne, MFB*

AAN: Lalo Schifrin

Stingaree

US 1934 76m bw (colour sequence)
RKO (Pandro S. Berman)

An Australian outlaw of the eighties falls for a rancher's daughter.

Unexciting but unobjectionable piece of Robin Hoodery.

w Becky Gardiner *stories* E. W. Hornung *d* William A. Wellman *ph* James Van Trees *m* Max Steiner

Irene Dunne, Richard Dix, Mary Boland, Conway Tearle, Andy Devine, Henry Stephenson, Una O'Connor, Reginald Owen, Snub Pollard, George Barraud

'Should bring medium results. It does not promise to rise to greater heights.' – *Variety*

Stir Crazy

US 1980 111m Metrocolor
Columbia/Hannah Weinstein
V, V*, L

Two New Yorkers heading for California to try their luck are wrongly convicted of a bank robbery but plan escape from prison.

Extended farce giving rather too free rein to its stars' potential for mugging, and polishing up every prison gag in the book.

w Bruce Jay Friedman *d* Sidney Poitier *ph* Fred Schuler *m* Tom Scott *pd* Alfred Sweeney

Gene Wilder, Richard Pryor, George Stanford Brown, Jobeth Williams

A Stitch in Time

GB 1963 94m bw
Rank (Hugh Stewart)

A butcher's boy goes into hospital and falls for a nurse.

Thin star slapstick; all one can say is that it's marginally preferable to Jerry Lewis.

w Jack Davies *d* Robert Asher *ph* Jack Asher *m* Philip Green

Norman Wisdom, Edward Chapman, Jerry Desmonde, Jeanette Sterke, Jill Melford

Stockade

US 1990 97m colour
Entertainment/Movie Group/Northern Lights Media Corporation (Richard Davis)
V, V*, L
US title: *Count a Lonely Cadence*

A young soldier, sent to the stockade for brawling, is persecuted by a bigoted sergeant in charge.

Uninvolving prison drama.

w Dennis Schyrack, Martin Sheen *novel* Count a Lonely Cadence by Gordon Weaver *d* Martin Sheen *ph* Richard Leiterman *m* Georges Delerue *pd* Ian Thomas *ed* Martin Hunter

Charlie Sheen, Martin Sheen, F. Murray Abraham, Larry Fishburne, Blu Mankuma, Michael Beach, Harry Stewart

'Predictably staged, glossily performed, erratically edited, and seems unable to conceal a mood of smug optimism.' – *Philip Strick, MFB*

The Stolen Children **

Italy/France 1992 114m Technicolor
Mayfair/Erre/Alia/RAIDUE/Arena/Vega (Angelo Rizzoli, Stefano Munafo)
original title: *Il Ladro di Bambini*

A young cop travels across Italy to a children's home with an 11-year-old girl, forced to become a prostitute by her mother, and her younger brother.

Tough and compassionate movie that refuses to sensationalize its subject-matter, of adult and official indifference to the sufferings of the young.

w Sandro Petraglia, Stefano Rulli, Gianni Amelio *d* Gianni Amelio *ph* Tonino Nardi, Renato Tafuri *m* Franco Piersanti *pd* Andrea Crisanti *ed* Simona Paggi

Enrico Lo Verso, Valentina Scalici, Giuseppe Ieracitano, Renato Carpentieri, Vitalba Andrea, Grignani, Massimo de Lorenzo

'Classical humanist cinema, almost in the neo-realist tradition.' – *Derek Malcolm, Guardian*

'Quiet, honest, admirably acted.' – *Philip French, Observer*

Stolen Face

GB 1952 72m bw
Exclusive/Hammer (Michael Hinds)

Via plastic surgery a girl criminal is given another face, which produces a different kind of trouble.

Quickie melodrama which proved fairly popular because of its Hollywood stars.

w Martin Berkeley, Richard Landau d Terence Fisher ph Walter Harvey m Malcolm Arnold

Paul Henreid, Lizabeth Scott, André Morell, John Wood, Susan Stephen, Mary Mackenzie, Arnold Ridley

Stolen Harmony

US 1935 79m bw
Paramount

An ex-con becomes a saxophonist with a band and is suspected of a robbery.

Tedious mix-up of mayhem and music.

w Leon Gordon, Harry Ruskin, Claude Binyon, Lewis Foster d Alfred Werker

George Raft, Ben Bernie, Grace Bradley, Iris Adrian, Lloyd Nolan, Ralf Harolde

'Once under way it provides some exciting entertainment; but the poor beginning isn't easily tossed off.' – Variety

'Its surprise finish will lift you to amazing emotional peaks!'

Stolen Heaven

US 1931 72m bw
Paramount

A boy and girl decide to commit suicide after spending the twenty thousand dollars they've stolen, but neither can go through with it.

A very silly idea, ineptly presented.

w Dana Burnet d George Abbott

Nancy Carroll, Phillips Holmes, Louis Calhern, Edward Keane

'It will range down from moderate figures.' – Variety

Stolen Heaven

US 1938 88m bw
Paramount

Two jewel thieves in love are harboured on the run by an old concert pianist.

Sentimental melodrama which almost works, with its backing of classical piano pieces.

w Eve Greene, Frederick Jackson, Andrew L. Stone d Andrew L. Stone

Gene Raymond, Olympe Bradna, Lewis Stone, Glenda Farrell, Porter Hall, Douglass Dumbrille

'Pleasing entertainment all the way.' – Variety

Stolen Holiday

US 1937 82m bw
Warner

A model marries a fortune hunter to protect him from the law.

Slightly unusual romantic drama based on the career of Alexander Stavisky.

w Casey Robinson d Michael Curtiz

Claude Rains, Kay Francis, Ian Hunter, Alison Skipworth, Charles Halton, Alex D'Arcy

Stolen Hours

GB 1963 97m DeLuxe
UA/Mirisch/Barbican (Denis Holt)

An American divorcee with only a year to live falls in love with her surgeon.

Tired remake of Dark Victory; pleasant Cornish backgrounds.

w Jessamyn West d Daniel Petrie ph Harry Waxman m Mort Lindsey

Susan Hayward, Michael Craig, Diane Baker, Edward Judd, Paul Rogers

Stolen Kisses *

France 1968 91m Eastmancolor
Films du Carrosse/Artistes Associés (Marcel Berbert)
original title: Baisers Volés

An ineffective young man can find neither work nor love.

A pleasing, rather sad little comedy which has almost the feel of a Keaton; but one is not quite sure at the end what its creator intended.

w François Truffaut, Claude de Givray, Bernard Revon d François Truffaut ph Denys Clerval m Antoine Duhamel

Jean-Pierre Léaud, Delphine Seyrig, Michel Lonsdale, Claude Jade

AAN: best foreign film

A Stolen Life *

GB 1939 91m bw
(Paramount) Orion (Anthony Havelock-Allan)

In Brittany, a woman deceives her husband by exchanging identities with her dead twin.

An actress's showcase, quite satisfactorily mounted.

w Margaret Kennedy, George Barraud novel Karel J. Benes d Paul Czinner ph Philip Tannura m William Walton

Elisabeth Bergner, Michael Redgrave, Wilfrid Lawson, Richard Ainley, Mabel Terry-Lewis, Clement McCallin

A Stolen Life *

US 1946 107m bw
Warner (Bette Davis)
V*, L

Enjoyable if slightly disappointing remake with New England backgrounds.

w Catherine Turney d Curtis Bernhardt ph Sol Polito, Sid Hickox m Max Steiner

Bette Davis, Glenn Ford, Dane Clark, Walter Brennan, Charles Ruggles, Bruce Bennett, Peggy Knudsen, Esther Dale

'A distressingly empty piece of show-off.' – Bosley Crowther

'What I'm waiting for is a film about beautiful identical quintuplets who all love the same man.' – Richard Winnington

'Drugs, Sex And Murder.'

Stone Cold

US 1992 92m DeLuxe
Columbia TriStar/Stone Group/Mace Neufeld/Yoram Ben Ami/ Walter Doniger
V, V*, L

A cop goes undercover in Mississippi to investigate a gang of violent bikers who have gone on a killing spree.

Standard action-movie stuff, but done with a little flair, despite its overblown climax.

w Walter Doniger d Craig R. Baxley ph Alexander Gruszynski m Sylvester Levay pd John Mansbridge, Richard Johnson ed Mark Helfrich, Larry Bock, Edward A. Warschilka Jnr

Brian Bosworth, Lance Henriksen, William Forsythe, Arabella Holzbog, Sam McMurray, Richard Gant, David Tress

'Strictly six-pack fodder.' – Empire

Stone Cold Dead

Canada 1979 97m Bellevue Pathé colour
Ko-Zak (George Mendeluk, John Ryan)
V*

A tough cop investigates the serial murders of prostitutes.

Beginning with a death, by gunshot in a shower, by a killer who photographs his victims, it attempts a few variations on very familiar themes but fails to

establish any rhythm of its own; it also takes much suspension of disbelief to accept Paul Williams as a successful pimp.

wd George Menduluk novel The Sin Sniper by Hugh Garner ph Dennis Miller m Paul James Zaza ed Martin Pepler

Richard Crenna, Paul Williams, Linda Sorensen, Belinda J. Montgomery, Monique Mercure, George Chuvalo, Jennifer Dale, Frank Moore

'Take away his badge and he'd top the Ten Most Wanted list!'

The Stone Killer *

US 1973 96m Technicolor
Columbia/Dino de Laurentiis (Michael Winner)
V, V*, L, S

A brutal Los Angeles police detective takes on the Mafia.

Fast-moving amalgam of chases and violence with a downbeat hero.

w Gerald Wilson novel A Complete State of Death by John Gardner d Michael Winner ph Richard Moore m Roy Budd

Charles Bronson, Martin Balsam, Ralph Waite, David Sheiner, Norman Fell

'Film-making as painting by numbers.' – Sight and Sound

'Keeps turning into exciting cinema, crude, often funny and sometimes quite brilliantly idiomatic. It may come as close to inspired primitivism as we are likely to get in the movies these days.' – Roger Greenspun, New York Times

The Stooge

US 1952 100m bw
Paramount/Hal B. Wallis

In 1930 a conceited song and dance man fails to realize that his moronic stooge is the act's real attraction.

Typical, and particularly resistible, Martin and Lewis concoction: whenever one thinks of laughing, a dollop of sentimentality comes along and promptly quashes the idea.

w Fred Finkelhoffe, Martin Rackin d Norman Taurog ph Daniel L. Fapp m Joseph J. Lilley

Dean Martin, Jerry Lewis, Polly Bergen, Marie McDonald, Eddie Mayehoff, Marion Marshall, Richard Erdman

Stop Me Before I Kill: see The Full Treatment

Stop! Or My Mom Will Shoot

US 1992 87m DeLuxe
UIP/Universal/Northern Lights (Ivan Reitman, Joe Medjuck, Michael C. Gross)
V, V*, L

The mother of a Los Angeles cop helps him solve a murder and get back together with his girlfriend.

Lamentable comedy, a failed attempt to extend Stallone's narrow range.

w Blake Snyder, William Osborne, William Davies d Roger Spottiswoode ph Frank Tidy m Alan Silvestri pd Charles Rosen ed Mark Conte, Lois Freeman-Fox

Sylvester Stallone, Estelle Getty, JoBeth Williams, Roger Rees, Martin Ferrero, Gailard Sartain, Dennis Burkley

'One of those Hollywood films in which the flimsiest of plots buckles under the most obvious of concepts.' – Lizzie Franke, Sight and Sound

Stop Press Girl

GB 1949 78m bw
Rank/Aquila

A girl finds she has the unconscious power to bring all machinery to a halt.

Weary comedy which has nowhere to go after its first silly idea.

w Basil Thomas, T. J. Morrison   d Michael Barry

Sally Ann Howes, Gordon Jackson, Basil Radford, Naunton Wayne, James Robertson Justice, Sonia Holm, Nigel Buchanan, Kenneth More

Stop You're Killing Me
US   1953   86m   Warnercolor
Warner (Louis F. Edelman)

At the end of prohibition a beer baron decides to go straight, but finds his house filled with the corpses of rival gangsters.

Frantic remake of *A Slight Case of Murder* with a few musical numbers added; all rather messy.

w James O'Hanlon   d Roy del Ruth   ph Ted McCord   md Ray Heindorf

Broderick Crawford, Claire Trevor, Virginia Gibson, Bill Hayes, Sheldon Leonard, Joe Vitale, Howard St John, Henry Morgan, Margaret Dumont

Stopover Forever
GB   1964   59m   bw
Associated British Pathé

An air hostess on holiday in Sicily believes that someone wants to murder her.

Mundane thriller with an unsympathetic heroine and nothing else to engage the attention.

w David Osborne   d Frederick Goode   ph William Jordan   m Edwin Astley   ed Ronald Glenister

Ann Bell, Anthony Bate, Conrad Phillips, Bruce Boa, Julian Sherrier

Stopover Tokyo
US   1957   100m   Eastmancolor   Cinemascope
TCF (Walter Reisch)
V, V*

An American spy in Tokyo seeks to capture a communist undercover man.

Sprawling espionage stuff with frequent halts for scenic tours.

w Richard L. Breen, Walter Reisch   novel John P. Marquand   d Richard L. Breen   ph Charles G. Clarke   m Paul Sawtell

Robert Wagner, Joan Collins, Edmond O'Brien, Ken Scott, Larry Keating

Stories from a Flying Trunk
GB   1979   88m   Technicolor
EMI/Sands (John Brabourne, Richard Goodwin)

Three Hans Andersen stories are performed by stop frame animation and by ballet dancers dressed as vegetables.

Lugubrious attempt to repeat the success of *Tales of Beatrix Potter*; moments to make one smile, but on the whole a depressing experience.

wd Christine Edzard   ph Robin Browne, Brian West   m Gioacchino Rossini

Murray Melvin, Ann Firbank, Johanna Sonnex, Tasneem Maqsood

Stork Bites Man
US   1948   67m   bw
Ralph Cohn/Buddy Rogers

An apartment house manager has a pregnant wife and a baby-hating boss.

Threadbare farce, not enlivened by wit or pacing.

wd Cyril Endfield

Jackie Cooper, Gene Roberts, Gus Schilling, Emory Parnell

The Stork Club
US   1945   98m   bw
Paramount (B. G. de Sylva)

A night-club hat-check girl saves an elderly millionaire from drowning.

Very light comedy with music, a great ad for a once famous night haunt.

w B. G. de Sylva, John McGowan   d Hal Walker   ph Charles Lang Jnr   md Robert Emmett Dolan

Betty Hutton, Barry Fitzgerald, Don Defore, Robert Benchley, Bill Goodwin, Iris Adrian, Mary Young, Mikhail Rasumny

The Storm
US   1930   76m   bw
Universal

An orphan girl left with a trapper becomes an object of jealousy between him and his partner.

Old-fashioned outdoor melodrama, previously filmed in 1916 and 1922. Not really talkie material.

w Wells Root   play Langdon McCormick   d William Wyler

Lupe Velez, Paul Cavanagh, William Boyd, Alphonse Ethier

'A fairly good programmer . . . the fight is a pip.' – *Variety*

The Storm
US   1938   79m   bw
Universal (Ken Goldsmith)

Tensions lead to violence among shipboard radio operators.

Lively action melodrama culminating in a storm at sea.

w Daniel Moore, Hugh King, Theodore Reeves   d Harold Young

Charles Bickford, Barton MacLane, Preston Foster, Tom Brown, Nan Grey, Andy Devine, Frank Jenks

'Good enough for the duals, but too weak for solo billing.' – *Variety*

Storm at Daybreak
US   1932   80m   bw
MGM

A fanciful reconstruction of events leading up to the Sarajevo assassination which precipitated World War I.

Unlikely melodrama with stars forced to overact; still, a rich and historically interesting slice of ham.

w Bertram Millhauser   play Sandor Hunyady   d Richard Boleslawski

Walter Huston, Kay Francis, Nils Asther, Phillips Holmes, Eugene Pallette, C. Henry Gordon, Jean Parker

'A good cast unwisely spent on weak material: doubtful as a grosser.' – *Variety*

'Who really set the town aflame?'
Storm Center
US   1956   87m   bw
Columbia/Phoenix (Julian Blaustein)

A small-town librarian is dismissed when she refuses to remove a communist book from the shelves.

Formula anti-McCarthy melodrama originally designed for Mary Pickford's comeback; not very absorbing and rather dingily produced.

w Daniel Taradash, Elick Moll   d Daniel Taradash   ph Burnett Guffey   m George Duning

Bette Davis, Brian Keith, Kim Hunter, Paul Kelly, Joe Mantell

Storm Fear
US   1955   88m   bw
UA/Theodora (Cornel Wilde)

Three fugitives from justice hide in a mountain cabin, but all meet violent deaths.

Gloomy, strenuous melodrama, partly shot outdoors.

w Horton Foote   novel Clinton Seeley   d Cornel Wilde   ph Joseph LaShelle   m Elmer Bernstein

Cornel Wilde, Jean Wallace, Dan Duryea, Lee Grant, Steven Hill, Dennis Weaver

Storm in a Teacup *
GB   1937   87m   bw
Alexander Korda/Victor Saville
V*

A national sensation ensues when a Scottish provost fines an old lady for not licensing her dog, and she refuses to pay.

Early Ealing-type comedy, a bit emaciated by later standards.

w Ian Dalrymple, Donald Bull   play Sturm im Wasserglass by Bruno Frank   d Ian Dalrymple, Victor Saville   ph Max Greene   m Frederic Lewis

Vivien Leigh, Rex Harrison, Cecil Parker, Sara Allgood, Ursula Jeans, Gus McNaughton, Arthur Wontner

Storm over Africa: see Royal African Rifles

Storm over Asia *
USSR   1928   93m approx (24 fps)   bw   silent
Mezhrabpomfilm
V, V*
original title: *Potomok Chingis-Khana*; aka: *The Heir to Genghis Khan*

A Mongolian trapper is discovered to be descended from Genghis Khan and made puppet emperor of a Soviet province.

Curious yarn without much discernible point though with the usual patches of propagandizing. It certainly looks good.

w Osip Brik   d V. I. Pudovkin   ph A. L. Golovnya

I. Inkizhinov, Valeri Inkizhinov, A. Dedintsev

'Fetid with propaganda and thematically ridiculous to any semi-intelligent audience. The more illiterate a man is in these Russian blurbs, the better his chances to make a name for himself in the Red World.' – *Variety*

Storm over Lisbon
US   1944   86m   bw
Republic (George Sherman)

An international spy mastermind runs a Lisbon night-club and sells documents to the highest bidder.

Feeble copy of *Casablanca*.

w Doris Gilbert, Dane Lussier   d George Sherman   ph John Alton   m Walter Scharf

Vera Hruba Ralston, Erich von Stroheim, Richard Arlen, Eduardo Ciannelli, Otto Kruger, Robert Livingston, Mona Barrie, Frank Orth

Storm over the Andes
US   1935   82m   bw
Maurice Pivar/Universal

An American flyer helps Bolivia against Paraguay.

Thick-ear melodrama about a forgotten local war; soundly made of its kind.

w Eliot Gibbons, Laclede Christy, Frank Wead, Al de Mond, Eva Greene   d Christy Cabanne

Jack Holt, Antonio Moreno, Mona Barrie, Gene Lockhart, Grant Withers

Storm over the Nile
GB   1955   107m   Technicolor   Cinemascope
Independent/London (Zoltan Korda)

Feeble remake of *The Four Feathers* (qv), using most of that film's action highlights stretched out to fit the wide screen.

w R. C. Sherriff   d Terence Young   ph Ted Scaife, Osmond Borradaile   m Benjamin Frankel

Anthony Steel, Laurence Harvey, Ronald Lewis, Ian Carmichael, James Robertson Justice, Mary Ure, Geoffrey Keen, Jack Lambert, Ferdy Mayne, Michael Hordern

'The material appears not so much dated as fossilized within its period.' – *Penelope Houston*

Storm over Tibet

US 1951 87m bw
Columbia/Summit (Ivan Tors, Laslo Benedek)

An explorer steals a holy mask which brings bad luck.

Slight adventure yarn ingeniously built around an old German documentary.

w Ivan Tors, Sam Mayer d Andrew Marton ph George E. Diskant, Richard Angst m Arthur Honegger

Rex Reason, Diana Douglas, Myron Healey

Storm over Wyoming

US 1950 60m bw
RKO (Herman Schlom)
V*

Two cowboys intervene in a range war between a rancher and a sheepman.

Fast-moving but standard stuff, with an over-familiar, no-surprises plot.

w Ed Earl Repp d Lesley Selander ph J. Roy Hunt m Paul Sawtell ad Albert S. D'Agostino, Feild Gray ed Robert Swink

Tim Holt, Richard Martin, Noreen Nash, Richard Powers (Tom Keene), Betty Underwood, Bill Kennedy

Storm Warning *

US 1950 93m bw
Warner (Jerry Wald)

A New York model goes south to visit her sister, and finds that her brother-in-law is an oversexed brute and a Ku Klux Klan killer.

Heavy melodrama disguised as a social document; sufficiently arresting for its purposes.

w Daniel Fuchs, Richard Brooks d Stuart Heisler ph Carl Guthrie m Daniele Amfitheatrof

Ginger Rogers, Doris Day, *Steve Cochran*, Ronald Reagan, Hugh Sanders, Raymond Greenleaf, Ned Glass

Stormy Monday

GB 1987 93m colour
Palace/Moving Picture Company/Film Four International/
Atlantic Entertainment/British Screen (Nigel Stafford-Clark)
V, V*, L, S

An American gangster tries to put a Newcastle club-owner out of business.

Dull and implausible thriller of uninteresting characters.

wd Mike Figgis ph Roger Deakins m Mike Figgis pd Andrew McAlpine ed Dave Martin

Melanie Griffith, Tommy Lee Jones, Sting, Sean Bean, James Cosmo, Mark Long, Brian Lewis

'An obscure, uninvolving and lethargic movie.' – *Kim Newman, MFB*

Stormy Waters: see *Remorques*

Stormy Weather

GB 1935 74m bw
Gainsborough

A top executive foils a blackmail racket in Chinatown.

Very presentable vehicle for the Aldwych team of farceurs.

w Ben Travers play Ben Travers d Tom Walls

Tom Walls, Ralph Lynn, Robertson Hare, Yvonne Arnaud, Gordon James, Graham Moffatt

Stormy Weather ***

US 1943 77m bw
TCF (Irving Mills)
V*, L

A backstage success story lightly based on the career of Bill Robinson.

Virtually a high-speed revue with all-black talent, and what talent! The production is pretty slick too.

w Frederick Jackson, Ted Koehler d Andrew Stone ph Leon Shamroy, Fred Sersen md Benny Carter ch Clarence Robinson

Bill Robinson, Lena Horne, Fats Waller, Ada Brown, Cab Calloway, Katherine Dunham and her Dancers, Eddie Anderson, Flournoy Miller, The Nicholas Brothers, Dooley Wilson

'A first-rate show, a spirited divertissement . . . a joy to the ear.' – *New York Times*

The Story of a Cheat: see *Le Roman d'un Tricheur*

The Story of a Woman

US/Italy 1969 101m Technicolor
Universal/Westward (Leonardo Bercovici)

A Swedish girl pianist in Rome falls in love with a fashionable doctor, then back in Sweden meets an American diplomat.

Intermezzo-type romantic drama with colour supplement trappings. Tolerable of its kind.

wd Leonardo Bercovici ph Piero Portalupi m John Williams

Robert Stack, Bibi Andersson, James Farentino, Annie Girardot, Frank Sundstrom

The Story of Adèle H *

France 1975 98m Eastmancolor
Films du Carrosse/Artistes Associés (Marcel Berbert, Claude Miller)
V*, L

In 1863, the daughter of Victor Hugo follows her lover to Nova Scotia.

Surprisingly slow and stilted version of a true story, though with a few of the expected subtleties.

w François Truffaut, Jean Gruault, Suzanne Schiffman d François Truffaut ph Nestor Almendros m Maurice Jaubert

Isabelle Adjani, Bruce Robinson, Sylvia Marriott

AAN: Isabelle Adjani

'America's most thrilling story! Of love so great and faith so strong that it inspired this man to endure ridicule, privation and hunger – to achieve the miracle of wings for the human voice!'

The Story of Alexander Graham Bell **

US 1939 97m bw
TCF (Kenneth MacGowan)
GB title: *The Modern Miracle*

The inventor of the telephone marries a deaf girl.

Acceptable history lesson with dullish principals but excellent production.

w Lamar Trotti d Irving Cummings ph Leon Shamroy m Louis Silvers

Don Ameche, Henry Fonda, Loretta Young, Charles Coburn, Gene Lockhart, Spring Byington, Bobs Watson

'Production will need teasing to get the women.' – *Variety*

The Story of Dr Ehrlich's Magic Bullet: see *Dr Ehrlich's Magic Bullet*

The Story of Dr Wassell *

US 1944 140m Technicolor
Paramount/Cecil B. de Mille

The adventures of a naval doctor who heroically saved men during the Pacific war.

Long, slogging, glamorized account of real events which is typical de Mille and very unconvincing physically, but keeps one watching simply as a story.

w Alan le May, Charles Bennett book James Hilton d Cecil B. de Mille ph Victor Milner, William Snyder m Victor Young

Gary Cooper, Laraine Day, Signe Hasso, Dennis O'Keefe, Carol Thurston, Carl Esmond, Paul Kelly, Stanley Ridges

'The director has taken a true story of heroism . . . and jangled it into a cacophony of dancing girls, phoney self-sacrifice and melodramatic romance.' – *Howard Barnes*

'To be regretted beyond qualification. It whips the story into a nacreous foam of lies whose speciousness is only the more painful because Mr de Mille is so obviously free from any desire to alter the truth except for what he considers to be its own advantage.' – *James Agee*

'Close to the last word in honest understanding and convincing production.' – *Motion Picture Herald*

The Story of Esther Costello *

GB 1957 103m bw
Columbia/Romulus (James Woolf)
US title: *The Golden Virgin*

A blind Irish deaf mute girl is adopted by an American socialite and her plight becomes an international cause.

Rich melodrama develops from this unlikely premise and the star enjoys it hugely.

w Charles Kaufman novel Nicholas Monsarrat d David Miller ph Robert Krasker m Georges Auric

Joan Crawford, Heather Sears, Rossano Brazzi, Ron Randell, Lee Patterson, Fay Compton, John Loder, Denis O'Dea, Sidney James, Maureen Delany

'A regular little *Titus Andronicus*, it abounds in fraud, embezzlement, suicide, murder and rape; all it wants is somebody baked in a pie.' – *Dilys Powell*

The Story of GI Joe **

US 1945 108m bw
(UA) Lester Cowan (David Hall)
aka: *War Correspondent*

Journalist Ernie Pyle follows fighting men into the Italian campaign.

Slow, convincing, sympathetic war film with good script and performances; not by any means the usual action saga.

w Leopold Atlas, Guy Endore, Philip Stevenson book Ernie Pyle d William A. Wellman ph Russell Metty m Ann Ronell, Louis Applebaum

Burgess Meredith, Robert Mitchum, Freddie Steele, Wally Cassell, Jimmy Lloyd, Jack Reilly

'It is humorous, poignant and tragic, an earnestly human reflection of a stern life and the dignity of man.' – *Thomas M. Pryor*

'A tragic and eternal work of art.' – *James Agee*

'One of the best films of the war.' – *Richard Mallett, Punch*

AAN: script; music score; song 'Linda' (m/ly Ann Ronell); Robert Mitchum

The Story of Gilbert and Sullivan *

GB 1953 109m Technicolor
British Lion/London Films (Frank Launder, Sidney Gilliat)
US title: *The Great Gilbert and Sullivan*

In 1875 a young composer named Arthur Sullivan and a librettist named William Gilbert come together under the auspices of Rupert D'Oyly Carte and write the Savoy Operas.

Light, accurate, well-cast and well-produced Victorian musical which somehow fails to ignite despite the immense talent at hand.

w Sidney Gilliat, Leslie Baily   *d* Sidney Gilliat   *ph* Christopher Challis   *md* Sir Malcolm Sargent   *pd* Hein Heckroth

Robert Morley, Maurice Evans, Peter Finch, Eileen Herlie, Dinah Sheridan, Isabel Dean, Wilfrid Hyde-White, Muriel Aked

'It is like a sound radio scrapbook, combined with a television passing show. It is bright, swift and bitty; faintly sentimental, enormously good-natured.' – *C. A. Lejeune*

The Story of Louis Pasteur ***
US   1936   85m   bw
Warner/Cosmopolitan (Henry Blanke)
V*

How the eminent 19th-century French scientist overcomes obstacles in finding cures for various diseases.

Adequate biopic which caused a sensation and started a trend; some of the others were better but this was the first example of Hollywood bringing schoolbook history to box-office life.

w Sheridan Gibney, Pierre Collings   *d* William Dieterle   *ph* Tony Gaudio   *m* Bernhard Kaun, Heinz Roemheld

Paul Muni, Josephine Hutchinson, Anita Louise, Donald Woods, Fritz Leiber, Henry O'Neill, Porter Hall, Akim Tamiroff, Walter Kingsford

'Probably limited b.o. but a creditable prestige picture.' – *Variety*

'What should be vital and arresting has been made hollow and dull . . . we are tendered something that is bright and stagey for something out of life.' – *Otis Ferguson*

'More exciting than any gangster melodrama.' – *C. A. Lejeune*

AA: original story; screenplay; Paul Muni

AAN: best picture

'Men and their women from the beginning of creation! Never so vast an undertaking!'
The Story of Mankind
US   1957   100m   Technicolor
Warner/Cambridge (Irwin Allen)

A heavenly tribunal debates whether to allow man to destroy himself, and both the Devil and the Spirit of Man cite instances from history.

Hilarious charade, one of the worst films ever made, but full of surprises, bad performances, and a wide range of stock shots.

w Irwin Allen, Charles Bennett   *book* Henrik Van Loon   *d* Irwin Allen   *ph* Nicholas Musuraca   *m* Paul Sawtell

Ronald Colman, Vincent Price, Cedric Hardwicke, the Marx Brothers, Hedy Lamarr, Agnes Moorehead, Reginald Gardiner, Peter Lorre, Virginia Mayo, Charles Coburn, Francis X. Bushman

'A poor excuse to use a batch of available actors in some of the weirdest casting ever committed.' – *Newsweek*

The Story of Molly X
US   1949   82m   bw
Universal/International

When a criminal is killed, his wife masterminds the gang to find out who killed him.

Silly melodrama, generally ineptly presented.

wd Crane Wilbur

June Havoc, John Russell, Dorothy Hart, Elliott Lewis, Connie Gilchrist

The Story of Qiu Ju ***
China/Hong Kong   1992   100m   colour
Sil-Metropole/Beijing Film Academy Youth Film Studio (Ma Fung Kwok)
V, V*, L

The pregnant wife of a peasant appeals to higher authorities to force the village headman to apologize for injuring her husband.

Less flamboyant than the director's previous films, this takes a documentary-style approach to the story of a woman determined that principles must be upheld whatever the cost.

w Liu Heng   *novel* Chen Yuanbin   *d* Zhang Yimou   *ph* Chi Xiaoning, Yu Xiaoqun   *m* Zhao Jiping   *ad* Cao Jiuping   *ed* Du Yuan

Gong Li, Lei Laosheng, Liu Peiqi, Yang Liuchun

'This simple, repetitive tale has a mesmerizing quality able to hook audiences from beginning to end.' – *Variety*

† The film won the Golden Lion award for best film and Gong Li won the award for best actress at the 1992 Venice Film Festival.

The Story of Robin Hood and his Merrie Men
GB   1952   84m   Technicolor
Walt Disney (Perce Pearce)
V*, L

When Prince John starts a ruthless taxation campaign, Robert Fitzooth turns outlaw.

Fairly competent but quite forgettable version of the legend, softened for children.

w Laurence E. Watkin   *d* Ken Annakin   *ph* Guy Green   *m* Clifton Parker

Richard Todd, Joan Rice, James Hayter, Hubert Gregg, James Robertson Justice, Martita Hunt, Peter Finch

The Story of Ruth
US   1960   132m   DeLuxe   Cinemascope
TCF (Samuel G. Engel)
V*

Ruth becomes the favourite of a pagan king but eventually flees to Israel.

Tedious, portentous bible-in-pictures, of virtually no interest or entertainment value.

w Norman Corwin   *d* Henry Koster   *ph* Arthur E. Arling   *m* Franz Waxman

Elana Eden, Peggy Wood, Viveca Lindfors, Stuart Whitman, Tom Tryon, Jeff Morrow, Thayer David, Eduard Franz

The Story of Seabiscuit
US   1949   98m   Technicolor
Warner (William Jacobs)
V*
GB title: *Pride of Kentucky*

The success story of a racehorse.

Blue grass vapidities, the kind of family entertainment that drove the families away.

w John Taintor Foote   *d* David Butler   *ph* Wilfrid Cline   *md* David Buttolph

Shirley Temple, Barry Fitzgerald, Lon McCallister, Rosemary de Camp, Donald McBride, Pierre Watkin

The Story of Shirley Yorke
GB   1948   92m   bw
Nettlefold

A nobleman tries to blame his wife's nurse for her death by poison.

Lethargic version of a play previously filmed as *Lord Camber's Ladies* (qv).

w A. R. Rawlinson, Maclean Rogers and Kathleen Butler   *play* *The Case of Lady Camber* by H. A. Vachell   *d* Maclean Rogers

Derek Farr, Dinah Sheridan, Margaretta Scott, John Robinson, Barbara Couper, Valentine Dyall

The Story of Temple Drake *
US   1933   71m   bw
Paramount (Ben Glazer)

A neurotic Southern flapper is abducted by gangsters, and likes it.

Deliberately shocking melodrama of its time, restructured from a notorious book later filmed under its own title. Very dated, but interesting.

w Oliver H. P. Garrett   *novel* *Sanctuary* by William Faulkner   *d* Stephen Roberts   *ph* Karl Struss

Miriam Hopkins, Jack La Rue, William Gargan, William Collier Jnr, Irving Pichel, Guy Standing, Elizabeth Patterson, Florence Eldridge

'Under Haysian ban the title of the novel can't be ballyhooed, but any whispering campaign about this is the picture's best b.o. asset. It has little else to commend it.' – *Variety*

The Story of Three Loves
US   1953   122m   Technicolor
MGM (Sidney Franklin)

Three love stories concerning the passengers on a transatlantic liner.

Three bits of old-fashioned kitsch, one tragic, one whimsical, one melodramatic, all rather slow and dull though well produced.

w John Collier, Jan Lustig, George Froeschel   *d* Gottfried Reinhardt, Vincente Minnelli   *ph* Charles Rosher, Harold Rosson   *m* Miklos Rozsa   *ad* Cedric Gibbons, Preston Ames, Edward Carfagno, Gabriel Scognamillo

Ethel Barrymore, James Mason, Moira Shearer, Pier Angeli, Leslie Caron, Kirk Douglas, Farley Granger, Agnes Moorehead, Zsa Zsa Gabor

AAN: art direction

The Story of Vernon and Irene Castle **
US   1939   93m   bw
RKO (George Haight, Pandro S. Berman)
V*, L

The story of a husband and wife dance team who had their first success in Paris and became influential international celebrities before he was killed as a flyer in World War I.

Pleasant understated musical with very agreeable dance sequences and a firm overall style. The last of the main stream of Astaire-Rogers musicals.

w Richard Sherman, Oscar Hammerstein II, Dorothy Yost   *books* Irene Castle   *d* H. C. Potter   *ph* Robert de Grasse   *md* Victor Baravalle   *ch* Hermes Pan   *ad* Van Nest Polglase

Fred Astaire, Ginger Rogers, Edna May Oliver, Walter Brennan, Lew Fields, Etienne Girardot, Donald MacBride

'One of the best Astaire-Rogers musicals . . . a wealth of nostalgic appeal.' – *Variety*

† The title was devised and insisted on by Mrs Castle.

The Story of Will Rogers
US   1950   109m   Technicolor
Warner (Robert Arthur)

A wild west performer becomes a Ziegfeld star and pop philosopher.

Bland, unshaped biopic of one of American show business's best loved figures, who died in an air crash in 1935.

w Frank Davis, Stanley Roberts   *d* Michael Curtiz   *ph* Wilfrid M. Cline   *md* Victor Young

Will Rogers Jnr, Jane Wyman, James Gleason, Eddie
Cantor (as himself), Carl Benton Reid

The Story on Page One
US   1960   123m   bw   Cinemascope
TCF/Company of Artists (Jerry Wald)

A lawyer undertakes the defence of a woman who
with her lover is charged with the murder of her
husband.

Long-drawn-out and not very interesting courtroom
drama, performed and presented with some style.

wd Clifford Odets   ph James Wong Howe
m Elmer Bernstein

Rita Hayworth, Tony Franciosa, Gig Young, Mildred
Dunnock, Hugh Griffith, Sanford Meisner, Alfred
Ryder

'A candidate's private moment can all too quickly become
  public record.'
Storyville
US   1992   113m   CFI colour
Spelling/Davis (David Roe, Edward R. Pressman)
V, V*, S

A rich young lawyer running for Congress and trying
to discover why his father killed himself finds himself
caught up in scandal and murder.

Overheated and muddled story of corruption with a
narrative that depends on its central character
behaving extremely stupidly throughout; an audience
with any sense will keep well away.

w Mark Frost, Lee Reynolds   novel Juryman by
Frank Galbally and Robert Macklin   d Mark Frost
ph Ron Garcia   m Carter Burwell   pd Richard
Hoover   ed B. J. Sears

James Spader, Joanne Whalley-Kilmer, Jason
Robards, Charlotte Lewis, Michael Warren, Michael
Parks, Chuck McCann, Charlie Haid, Chino Fats
Williams, Woody Strode, Jeff Perry, Piper Laurie

'A straightforward and lacklustre potboiler, composed
of disparate elements with little dynamic coherence.' –
Sight and Sound

Stowaway *
US   1936   86m   bw
TCF (Earl Carroll, Harold Wilson)
V

The orphan daughter of a Shanghai missionary stows
away on an American pleasure ship.

Very good star vehicle in which Shirley performs
some of her best musical numbers.

w William Conselman, Arthur Sheekman, Nat Perrin
d William A. Seiter   ph Arthur Miller   md Louis
Silvers   songs Mack Gordon, Harry Revel

Shirley Temple, Robert Young, Alice Faye, Eugene
Pallette, Helen Westley, Arthur Treacher, J. Edward
Bromberg, Astrid Allwyn

'No exhib worrying necessary for this one.' – Variety

Stowaway Girl: see Manuela

La Strada ***
Italy   1954   94m   bw
Ponti/de Laurentiis
V, S
aka: The Road

A half-witted peasant girl is sold to an itinerant strong
man and ill-used by him.

Curious attempt at a kind of poetic neo-realism, saved
by style and performances.

w Federico Fellini, Ennio Flaiano, Tullio Pinelli
d Federico Fellini   ph Otello Martelli   m Nino Rota

Giulietta Masina, Anthony Quinn, Richard Basehart

AA: best foreign film

AAN: script

Straight on Till Morning
GB   1972   96m   Technicolor
EMI/Hammer (Roy Skeggs)
V*

A Liverpool girl in London meets a dangerous
psychotic.

Unattractive suspenser, wildly directed.

w Michael Peacock   d Peter Collinson   ph Brian
Probyn   m Roland Shaw

Rita Tushingham, Shane Briant, Tom Bell, Annie
Ross, James Bolam

Straight out of Brooklyn
US   1991   83m   colour
Artificial Eye/Blacks N'Progress/American Playhouse (Matty
Rich)
V, V*, L

Determined to escape the poverty that has engulfed
his hard-working mother and drunken father, a
young black man persuades his friends to rob some
local hoodlums.

Interesting first feature of ghetto life from a teenaged
director.

wd Matty Rich   ph John Rosnell   m Harold
Wheeler   ad Walter Meade   ed Jack Haigis

George T. Odom, Ann D. Sanders, Lawrence Gilliard
Jnr, Barbara Sanon, Reana E. Drummond, Matty Rich,
Mark Malone

'Not a glittering debut, but it does have a low-budget,
first-time energy which sets it apart from much
mainstream work.' – Michael O'Pray, Sight and Sound

'Rudimentary in every way, from writing to acting to
camerawork, and covers all-too-familiar ground with
no particular flair.' – Variety

Straight, Place and Show *
US   1938   66m   bw
TCF
GB title: They're Off

Three pony-ride proprietors impersonate Russian
jockeys to save a race.

Lively, unpretentious vehicle for three zanies, with a
further bonus in its lead singer.

w M. M. Musselman, Allen Rivkin   play Damon
Runyon, Irving Caesar   d David Butler

The Ritz Brothers, Ethel Merman, Richard Arlen,
Phyllis Brooks, George Barbier, Sidney Blackmer

'Dreams do come true . . . sometimes.'
Straight Talk
US   1992   91m   Technicolor
Warner/Hollywood/Sandollar (Robert Chartoff, Fred Berner)
V, V*, L, S

An Arkansas dance teacher goes to Chicago to become
a TV agony aunt.

Mundane romantic comedy tailored to the personality
of Dolly Parton.

w Craig Bolotin, Patricia Resnick   d Barnet Kellman
ph Peter Sova   m Brad Fiedel   pd Jeffrey
Townsend   ed Michael Tronick

Dolly Parton, James Woods, Griffin Dunne, Michael
Madsen, Deirdre O'Connell, John Sayles, Teri
Hatcher, Spalding Gray, Jerry Orbach, Philip Bosco

'Glib but sunny romantic comedy . . . should be a B.O.
winner.' – Variety

Straight Time
US   1978   114m   Technicolor
Warner/First Artist/Sweetwall (Stanley Beck, Tim Zinnemann)
V*

A psychotic parolee fails to go straight.

Unappetizing social melodrama with an irresolute
leading performance.

w Alvin Sargent, Edward Bunker, Jeffrey Boam
novel No Beast So Fierce by Edward Bunker   d Ulu
Grosbard   ph Owen Roizman   m David Shire

Dustin Hoffman, Theresa Russell, Gary Busey, Harry
Dean Stanton

'One leaves the theatre hoping the character will die
painfully and slowly in a hail of bullets.' – Variety

'Just keep saying to yourself – it's only a film, it's only a film!'
Strait Jacket
US   1963   92m   bw
Columbia/William Castle
V*

A woman who murdered her faithless husband with
an axe is released twenty years later, and more axe
murders occur.

Dull and unattractive shocker in which all concerned
lean over backwards to conceal the trick ending.

w Robert Bloch   d William Castle   ph Arthur E.
Arling   m Van Alexander

Joan Crawford, Diane Baker, Leif Erickson, Howard
St John, Rochelle Hudson, George Kennedy

Stranded
US   1936   73m   bw
Warner

A woman working for Traveller's Aid meets an old
school beau.

Much ado about nothing, the kind of movie that loses
stars their reputations.

w Delmer Daves, Carl Erickson, Frank Wead,
Ferdinand Reyher   d Frank Borzage

Kay Francis, George Brent, Patricia Ellis, Donald
Woods, Robert Barrat, Barton MacLane

'Limited chances.' – Variety

Stranded in Paris: see Artists and Models Abroad

The Strange Adventure of David Gray: see
  Vampyr

The Strange Affair
GB   1968   106m   Techniscope
Paramount (Howard Harrison, Stanley Mann)

A young London policeman finds that his superiors
are almost as corrupt as the villains.

Stylishly made melodrama of despair, with a sexy
nymphet heroine straight from swinging London. It
all leaves a sour taste in the mouth.

w Stanley Mann   novel Bernard Toms   d David
Greene   ph Alex Thompson   m Basil Kirchin

Michael York, Jeremy Kemp, Susan George, Jack
Watson, George A. Cooper

The Strange Affair of Uncle Harry
US   1945   82m   bw
Universal (Joan Harrison)
V*, L
aka: Uncle Harry

A man henpecked by his two sisters plans to murder
one of them.

Stilted melodrama from an uninspired stage original,
with a cop-out dream ending tacked on.

w Stephen Longstreet, Keith Winter   play Thomas
Job   d Robert Siodmak   ph Woody Bredell
m Hans Salter

George Sanders, Geraldine Fitzgerald, Ella Raines,
Sara Allgood, Moyna MacGill, Samuel S. Hinds,
Harry von Zell, Ethel Griffies

Strange Bargain
US   1949   68m   bw
Sid Rogell/RKO
V*

A lowly bookkeeper finds himself accomplice in an insurance swindle.

Watchable second feature suspenser.

w Lillie Hayward d Will Price

Jeffrey Lynn, Henry Morgan, Martha Scott, Katherine Emery, Richard Gaines, Henry O'Neill

Strange Bedfellows

US 1965 99m Technicolor
U-I/Panama-Frank (Melvin Frank)

An American executive in London nearly divorces his fiery Italian wife.

Frantic sex comedy with picture postcard background; fatiguing rather than funny, but with minor compensations.

w Melvin Frank, Michael Pertwee d Melvin Frank
ph Leo Tover m Leigh Harline

Rock Hudson, Gina Lollobrigida, Gig Young, Edward Judd, Howard St John, Arthur Haynes, Dave King, Terry-Thomas

'The grind of predictable situations is further afflicted by considerable lapses in taste.' – MFB

Strange Boarders *

GB 1938 79m bw
GFD/Gainsborough (Edward Black)

A police detective postpones his honeymoon to book into a boarding house and discover which of the guests is a spy.

Quite engaging comedy-thriller in the Hitchcock mould, with entertaining performances and incidents.

w A. R. Rawlinson, Sidney Gilliat novel The Strange Boarders of Paradise Crescent by E. Phillips Oppenheim
d Herbert Mason ph Jack Cox

Tom Walls, Renee Saint-Cyr, Leon M. Lion, Googie Withers, C. V. France, Ronald Adam, Irene Handl, George Curzon, Martita Hunt

Strange Brew

US 1983 90m colour
MGM (Louis M. Silverstein)
V*, L

Two dim-witted, beer-swilling Canadian brothers visit the Elsinore brewery in search of free drinks and, with the aid of some lunatics, thwart a plan to take over the world.

Offbeat but unamusing comedy, based on two characters from the SCTV Network television comedy series and borrowing much of its plot from Hamlet.

w Rick Moranis, Dave Thomas, Steven de Jarnatt
d Dave Thomas, Rick Moranis ph Steven Poster
m Charles Fox pd David L. Snyder ed Patrick McMahon

Dave Thomas, Rick Moranis, Max von Sydow, Paul Dooley, Lynne Griffin, Angus MacInnes, Tom Harvey, Douglas Campbell

Strange Cargo *

US 1940 105m bw
MGM (Joseph L. Mankiewicz)
V*

Eight convicts escape from Devil's Island and are influenced by a Christ-like fugitive.

One of Hollywood's occasional lunacies; one doubts whether even the author knew the point of this cockamamy parable, but it was well produced and acted.

w Lawrence Hazard novel Not Too Narrow, Not Too Deep by Richard Sale d Frank Borzage ph Robert Planck m Franz Waxman

Clark Gable, Joan Crawford, Ian Hunter, Peter Lorre, Paul Lukas, Albert Dekker, J. Edward Bromberg, Eduardo Ciannelli, Frederick Worlock

'Even the most hardened mystics may blush.' – New Yorker, 1978

The Strange Case of Clara Deane

US 1932 60m bw
Paramount

A young mother is unjustly convicted of a crime which she didn't commit and bids a tearful farewell to her child . . .

Hilariously inept and theatrical rendering of a very outmoded play.

w Max Marcin play Arthur M. Brillant d Louis Gasnier, Max Marcin

Wynne Gibson, Pat O'Brien, Frances Dee, Dudley Digges

'Strictly for the minors where the clientele is elderly and naive.' – Variety

The Strange Case of Doctor RX

US 1942 66m bw
Universal

A mysterious murderer eliminates criminals whom the law can't touch.

Inept semi-horror which wastes a good cast, as did the same author's Night Monster.

w Clarence Upson Young d William Nigh

Lionel Atwill, Patric Knowles, Anne Gwynne, Samuel S. Hinds, Shemp Howard, Mona Barrie, Paul Cavanagh, Mantan Moreland

Strange Confession: see The Imposter

Strange Conquest: see The Crime of Dr Hallet

Strange Conspiracy: see The President Vanishes

The Strange Death of Adolf Hitler *

US 1943 74m bw
Universal (Ben Pivar)

A stage impressionist murders the Führer and takes his place, steering Germany deliberately into losing the war.

One of the more eccentric curios of World War II, especially from a mundane studio like Universal. Once one recovers from the shock of its existence, the thing is moderately well done. See also The Magic Face.

w Fritz Kortner d James Hogan m Hans Salter

Ludwig Donath, Gale Sondergaard, Fritz Kortner, George Dolenz

The Strange Door *

US 1951 81m bw
U-I (Ted Richmond)

A young nobleman, passing through the one-way door of a castle, finds himself the prisoner of a madman.

Torture-chamber suspenser, adequately if rather tediously developed, with most of its interest reposing in the cast.

w Jerry Sackheim story The Sire de Maletroit's Door by Robert Louis Stevenson d Joseph Pevney
ph Irving Glassberg m Hans Salter

Charles Laughton, Boris Karloff, Michael Pate, Sally Forrest, Richard Stapley, Alan Napier

Strange Evidence

GB 1932 71m bw
Paramount/London Films (Alexander Korda)

When an invalid dies, his adulterous wife is suspected.

Mildly interesting quickie whodunnit.

w Miles Malleson story Lajos Biro d Robert Milton ph Robert Martineau Stephen Harrison

Leslie Banks, Carol Goodner, George Curzon, Frank Vosper, Norah Baring, Diana Napier

Strange Holiday

US 1945 61m bw
General Motors (Arch Oboler)

A man back from holiday discovers that American Nazis have taken over the country.

Over-talkative fantasy which barely scraped a release, especially since it was made in 1940 but not offered until five years later.

wd Arch Oboler

Claude Rains, Gloria Holden, Milton Kibbee

Strange Incident: see The Ox Bow Incident

'A woman suspected! A woman desired! A woman possessed!'
'The film in which you hear the characters think!'

Strange Interlude **

US 1932 110m bw
MGM (Irving Thalberg)
V*
GB title: Strange Interval

Problems of an unfulfilled wife and her lover.

Surprising film version of a very heavy modern classic, complete with asides to the audience; very dated now, but a small milestone in Hollywood's development.

w Bess Meredyth, C. Gardner Sullivan play Eugene O'Neill d Robert Z. Leonard ph Lee Garmes

Norma Shearer, Clark Gable, May Robson, Alexander Kirkland, Ralph Morgan, Robert Young, Maureen O'Sullivan, Henry B. Walthall

'Chiefly a reserved seat attraction, dubious for general release appeal' – Variety

'A cinematic novelty to be seen by discerning audiences.' – Film Weekly

'More exciting than a thousand "action" movies.' – Pare Lorentz

Strange Interval: see Strange Interlude

Strange Intruder

US 1957 78m bw
AA (Lindsley Parsons)

A psychopathic ex-POW menaces the children of his dead friend's wife.

Gloomy second feature melodrama, rather well presented.

w David Evans, Warren Douglas novel Helen Fowler d Irving Rapper ph Ernest Haller
m Paul Dunlap

Edmund Purdom, Ida Lupino, Ann Harding, Jacques Bergerac, Carl Benton Reid

Strange Invaders *

US 1983 93m DeLuxe
EMI/Orion/Michael Laughlin (Walter Coblenz)
V, V*, L

An Illinois town is taken over by beings from outer space.

Patchy but often amusing take-off of the Invasion of the Body Snatchers genre.

w William Condon, Michael Laughlin d Michael Laughlin ph Louis Horvath, Zoltan Vidor m John Addison pd Susanna Moore

Paul Le Mat, Nancy Allen, Diana Scarwid, Michael Lerner, Louise Fletcher, Fiona Lewis, Kenneth Tobey

'Isn't so much a spoof of '50s sci-fi formulae as it is a running commentary on styles of cultural awareness.' – Richard T. Jameson, Seattle Weekly

Strange Lady in Town

US 1955 118m Warnercolor Cinemascope
Warner (Mervyn Le Roy)

Adventures of a woman doctor in 1880 Santa Fe.

Quaint Western drama which is never any more convincing than its star.

w Frank Butler *d* Mervyn Le Roy *ph* Harold Rosson *m* Dimitri Tiomkin

Greer Garson, Dana Andrews, Cameron Mitchell, Lois Smith, Walter Hampden

'Fate drew them together and only murder can part them!' 'Whisper her name!'
The Strange Love of Martha Ivers **
US 1946 116m bw
Paramount/Hal B. Wallis
V*

A murderous child becomes a wealthy woman with a spineless lawyer husband; the melodrama starts when an ex-boyfriend returns to town.

Irresistible star melodrama which leaves no stone unturned; compulsive entertainment of the old school.

w Robert Rossen *d* Lewis Milestone *ph* Victor Milner *m* Miklos Rozsa

Barbara Stanwyck, Van Heflin, Kirk Douglas, Lizabeth Scott, Judith Anderson, Roman Bohnen

AAN: original story (Jack Patrick)

The Strange Love of Molly Louvain
US 1932 72m bw
Warner

A young mother has gone to the bad through men.

Hoary melodrama which the cast seem forever on the point of sending up.

w Maurine Watkins, Erwin Gelsey *play The Tinsel Girl* by Maurine Watkins *d* Michael Curtiz

Lee Tracy, Ann Dvorak, Richard Cromwell, Guy Kibbee, Leslie Fenton, Frank McHugh

'A lightweight yarn which never takes a toehold to deliver a sock.' – *Variety*

The Strange Mr Gregory
US 1945 63m bw
Louis Berkoff/Monogram

In pursuit of a murder fraud, a magician feigns his own death and poses as his brother.

Complex but watchable little crime thriller.

w Myles Connelly, Charles S. Belden *d* Phil Rosen

Edmund Lowe, Jean Rogers, Don Douglas, Frank Reicher, Robert Emmett Keane

The Strange One *
US 1957 99m bw
Columbia/Sam Spiegel
GB title: *End as a Man*

A sadistic cadet causes trouble at a Southern military college.

A weird and unsavoury but rather compelling melodrama which unreels like a senior version of *Tom Brown's Schooldays*.

w Calder Willingham *novel End as a Man* by Calder Willingham *d* Jack Garfein *ph* Burnett Guffey *m* Kenyon Hopkins

Ben Gazzara, George Peppard, Mark Richman, Pat Hingle, Arthur Storch, Paul Richards, Geoffrey Horne, James Olson

'The film's brilliance is in its persuasive depiction of a highly controversial, artificially organized world; its failure is to make any dramatic statement about it.' – *MFB*

The Strange Ones: see *Les Enfants Terribles*

A Strange Place to Meet: see *Drôle D'Endroit pour une Rencontre*

The Strange Woman
US 1946 100m bw
UA/Hunt Stromberg (Jack Chertok)
V*

A scheming woman plays with the lives of three men.

Star wish-fulfilment; otherwise a hammy costume piece.

w Herb Meadows *novel* Ben Ames Williams *d* Edgar G. Ulmer *ph* Lucien Andriot *m* Carmen Dragon

Hedy Lamarr, George Sanders, Louis Hayward, Gene Lockhart, Hillary Brooke

'Shock by incredible shock this ravaging death overruns the earth ... menacing mankind with overwhelming chaos.' 'When men of different planets unite to combat the most loathsome peril the universe has ever known!'
Strange World of Planet X
GB 1957 bw
Eros Films (George Maynard)
V*
US title: *Cosmic Monsters*

A mad scientist's experiments with magnetic fields cause insects to mutate into huge creatures with a taste for human flesh.

Risible science fiction with a great deal too much talk and the feeblest monsters to be found in any of the giant insect movies of the period.

w Paul Ryder *novel* Rene Ray *d* Gilbert Gunn *ph* Joe Ambor *m* Robert Sharples *ad* Bernard Sarron *ed* Francis Bieber

Forrest Tucker, Gaby André, Martin Benson, Alec Mango, Wyndham Goldie, Hugh Latimer

The Stranger *
US 1946 95m bw
International (Sam Spiegel)
V*, L

An escaped Nazi criminal marries an American woman and settles in a Connecticut village.

Highly unconvincing and artificial melodrama enhanced by directorial touches, splendid photography and no-holds-barred climax involving a church clock.

w Anthony Veiller *story* Victor Trivas, Decia Dunning *d* Orson Welles *ph* Russell Metty *m* Bronislau Kaper

Edward G. Robinson, Orson Welles, Loretta Young, Philip Merivale, Richard Long, Konstantin Shayne

'Some striking effects, with lighting and interesting angles much relied on.' – *Bosley Crowther*

'A film of confused motivations and clumsy effects.' – *Basil Wright, 1972*

AAN: original story

The Stranger: see *The Intruder* (1961)

The Stranger (1991): see *Agantuk*

Stranger at My Door
US 1956 85m bw
Republic (Sidney Picker)

A gunman takes refuge in the house of a preacher who tries to convert him.

Odd, sentimental little Western morality play, not badly presented.

w Barry Shipman *d* William Witney *ph* Bud Thackery *m* Dale Butts

Macdonald Carey, Skip Homeier, Patricia Medina, Louis Jean Heydt

The Stranger Came Home
GB 1954 80m bw
Exclusive/Hammer (Michael Carreras)
US title: *The Unholy Four*

After being assaulted in the Far East, a financier loses his memory and does not return home until three years later, when murder ensues.

Muddled mystery quickie, only notable as the film which persuaded its star to retire.

w Michael Carreras *novel Stranger at Home* by George Sanders *d* Terence Fisher *ph* James Harvey *m* Ivor Slaney *ed* Bill Lenney

Paulette Goddard, William Sylvester, Patrick Holt, Paul Carpenter, Russell Napier, Alvys Maben

The Stranger In Between: see *Hunted*

A Stranger in My Arms
US 1958 88m bw Cinemascope
U-I (Ross Hunter)

A test pilot falls in love with his dead friend's widow and helps her face up to her in-laws.

Dreary romantic drama.

w Peter Berneis *novel And Ride a Tiger* by Robert Wilder *d* Helmut Kautner *ph* William Daniels *m* Joseph Gershenson

June Allyson, Jeff Chandler, *Mary Astor*, Sandra Dee, Charles Coburn, Conrad Nagel, Peter Graves

A Stranger in Town
US 1943 67m bw
MGM (Robert Sisk)

A supreme court judge on vacation finds himself sorting out crooked local politicians.

Interesting second feature with good cast and production values.

w Isobel Lennart, William Koslenko *d* Roy Rowland

Frank Morgan, Richard Carlson, Jean Rogers, Porter Hall, Robert Barrat, Donald MacBride, Andrew Tombes, John Hodiak

A Stranger Is Watching
US 1981 92m Metrocolor
MGM-UA (Sidney Beckerman)

A small girl is terrified by the psychopath who raped and murdered her mother.

Unpleasant thriller in the modern manner.

w Earl MacRaugh, Victor Miller *novel* Mary Higgins Clark *d* Sean S. Cunningham

Kate Mulgrew, Rip Torn, James Naughton, Shawn Van Schreiber

The Stranger Left no Card **
GB 1952 23m bw
British Lion/Meteor (George Arthur)

A weirdly dressed eccentric comes to a small town and is accepted by the townspeople; but his real purpose is murder.

Smart little trick film which as a novelty has not been surpassed.

w Sidney Carroll *d* Wendy Toye

Alan Badel, Cameron Hall, Eileen Way

Stranger on the Prowl
Italy/US 1952 82m (100m in Italy) bw
UA/CPCT (Noel Calef)
Italian title: *Imbarco a Mezzanotte*; GB title: *Encounter*

In an Italian port, a stranger helps a boy but is shot by the police.

Ineffective melodrama, a sad comedown for its star.

w Andrea Forzano (Ben Barzman) *story* Noel Calef *d* Andrea Forzano (Joseph Losey) *ph* Henri Alekan *m* G. C. Sonzogno *ad* Antonio Valente *ed* Thelma Connell

Paul Muni, Joan Lorring, Vittorio Manunta, Aldo Silvani

† Both director and scriptwriter worked under a pseudonym owing to Hollywood's black-listing.

Stranger on the Third Floor *

US   1940   64m   bw
RKO (Lee Marcus)
V*, L

A reporter finds that he was wrong in the well-intentioned testimony which helps convict an innocent man for murder.

Stylish B feature with a striking dream scene and a curious fleeting performance by Lorre as the real murderer.

w Frank Partos   d Boris Ingster   ph Nicholas Musuraca   m Roy Webb

Margaret Tallichet, Peter Lorre, John McGuire, Charles Waldron, Elisha Cook Jnr, Charles Halton, Ethel Griffies

Stranger than Paradise *

US/Germany   1984   90m   bw
Grokenberger/Cinesthesia/ZDF (Sara Driver)
V, V*, L

The small adventures in America of a young Hungarian immigrant, her cousin and his friend.

Filmed in bleached-out black and white and not edited in the conventional sense – each take is shown complete and followed by a brief blackout before the next shot is shown – it focuses upon grungey lives in which nothing happens – and if it should, no one would notice; but it exerts a slight charm by its very waywardness.

wd Jim Jarmusch   ph Tom DiCillo   m John Lurie   ed Jim Jarmusch, Melody London

John Lurie, Eszter Balint, Richard Edson, Cecillia Stark

'To think Stranger than Paradise was a knockout of a movie you'd have to tune in to its minimalism so passively that you lowered your expectations. The film is so hemmed in that it has the feel of a mousy East European comedy; it's like a comedy of sensory deprivation.' – Pauline Kael, New Yorker

'Full of a quirky character and irony that makes its central theme of American alienation seem extremely entertaining.' – Derek Malcolm, Guardian

A Stranger Walked In: see Love from a Stranger

'For him death has two faces – and he faces them both, alone!'
The Stranger Wore a Gun

US   1953   83m   Technicolor   3-D
Columbia
V*

An honest adventurer finds that the man who once saved his life has become a stagecoach robber.

Routine Western with many objects hurled at the audience to show off the 3-D process.

w Kenneth Gamet   d André de Toth

Randolph Scott, George Macready, Claire Trevor, Joan Weldon, Lee Marvin, Ernest Borgnine, Alfonso Bedoya

Strangers: see Voyage to Italy

Strangers All

US   1935   70m   bw
RKO

A mother tries to keep the peace while her three unsuccessful sons – a shopkeeper, an actor and a political activist – quarrel about the worth of their callings and her daughter abandons her wealthy fiancé to marry a lawyer.

Sentimental family comedy-drama, enjoyable enough in its old-fashioned way if somewhat abrupt in its sudden ending.

w Milton Krims   play Marie M. Bercovici   d Charles Vidor   ph John W. Boyle   md Roy Webb   ad Van Nest Polglase   ed Jack Hively

May Robson, Preston Foster, Florine McKinney, William Bakewell, James Bush, Samuel Hinds, Leon Ames

The Stranger's Hand

GB   1953   85m   bw
Independent Film Producers/John Stafford, Peter Moore
aka: Mano della Straniero

A schoolboy is due to meet his father in Venice, but the father is kidnapped by enemy agents.

Rather tentative suspense thriller with a vague plot which seems to defeat an excellent cast.

w Guy Elmes, Giorgio Bassani   story Graham Greene   d Mario Soldati   ph Enzo Serafin   m Nino Rota

Trevor Howard, Richard O'Sullivan, Francis L. Sullivan, Alida Valli, Eduardo Ciannelli, Richard Basehart, Stephen Murray

Strangers in Good Company: see The Company of Strangers

Strangers in Love

US   1932   68m   bw
Paramount
V*

A ne'er-do-well has some difficulties when he tries to step into his dead twin's shoes.

Predictable comedy-melodrama, quite well acted.

w Grover Jones, William Slavens McNutt   play The Shorn Lamb by William J. Locke   d Lothar Mendes

Fredric March, Kay Francis, Stuart Erwin, Juliette Compton, George Barbier, Sidney Toler

'All the qualities that bespeak wide appeal.' – Variety

Strangers May Kiss

US   1931   82m   bw
MGM

A sophisticated wife takes love and fidelity lightly.

Dated romantic drama.

w John Meehan   novel Ursula Parrott   d George Fitzmaurice   ph William Daniels

Norma Shearer, Robert Montgomery, Neil Hamilton, Marjorie Rambeau, Irene Rich

'Outstanding money picture. It'll sell itself.' – Variety

'It begins with the scream of a train whistle – and ends with screaming excitement!'
Strangers on a Train ***

US   1951   101m   bw
Warner (Alfred Hitchcock)
V, V*, L

A tennis star is pestered on a train by a psychotic who wants to swap murders, and proceeds to carry out his part of the bargain.

This quirky melodrama has the director at his best, sequence by sequence, but the story is basically unsatisfactory. It makes superior suspense entertainment, however.

w Raymond Chandler, Czenzi Ormonde   novel Patricia Highsmith   d Alfred Hitchcock   ph Robert Burks   md Ray Heindorf   m Dimitri Tiomkin

Farley Granger, Robert Walker, Ruth Roman, Leo G. Carroll, Patricia Hitchcock, Marion Lorne, Howard St John, Jonathan Hale, Laura Elliott

BRUNO (Robert Walker): 'Some people are better off dead – like your wife and my father, for instance.'

'You may not take it seriously, but you certainly don't have time to think about anything else.' – Richard Mallett, Punch

'The construction seems a little lame, but Hitch takes delight in the set pieces.' – Time Out, 1985

† Remade 1970 as Once You Kiss A Stranger.

AAN: Robert Burks

The Stranger's Return

US   1933   89m   bw
MGM

An old farmer disapproves of his granddaughter's affair with a married man.

An American view of Cold Comfort Farm country, too heavy to click at the box-office.

w Brown Holmes, Phil Stong   d King Vidor

Lionel Barrymore, Miriam Hopkins, Franchot Tone, Beulah Bondi, Stuart Erwin, Irene Hervey

Strangers When We Meet *

US   1960   117m   Technicolor   Cinemascope
Columbia/Bryna (Richard Quine)
V*

A successful architect starts an affair with a beautiful married neighbour.

Beverly Hills soap opera with lots of romantic suffering in luxury. Lumpy but generally palatable.

w Evan Hunter   novel Evan Hunter   d Richard Quine   ph Charles Lang Jnr   m George Duning

Kirk Douglas, Kim Novak, Ernie Kovacs, Walter Matthau, Barbara Rush, Virginia Bruce, Helen Gallagher, Kent Smith

The Strangler (1940): see East of Piccadilly

The Strangler

US   1963   80m   bw
AA
V*

An obese lab technician murders nurses who help his hated mother.

Modest, lively shocker.

w Bill S. Ballinger   d Burt Topper   ph Jacques Marquette   m Marlin Skiles

Victor Buono, David McLean, Ellen Corby, Diane Sayer

The Stranglers of Bombay

GB   1960   80m   bw   MegaScope
Columbia/Hammer (Anthony Nelson-Keys)

In 1826 travellers are waylaid and sacrificially killed by a cult of stranglers.

Semi-historical parade of atrocities, repellent but scarcely exciting.

w David Z. Goodman   d Terence Fisher   ph Arthur Grant   m James Bernard   ad Bernard Robinson, Don Mingaye   ed James Needs, Alfred Cox

Guy Rolfe, Allan Cuthbertson, Andrew Cruickshank, Marne Maitland, Jan Holden, George Pastell, Paul Stassino

Strapless

GB   1988   100m   Technicolor
Virgin/Granada/Film Four International (Rick McCallum)
V, V*, L

Two sisters assert their independence after unsatisfactory relationships with men.

Uneasy blend of unbelievable romance and politics.

wd David Hare   ph Andrew Dunn   m Nick Bicat   pd Roger Hall   ed Edward Marnier

Blair Brown, Bruno Ganz, Bridget Fonda, Alan Howard, Michael Gough, Hugh Laurie, Suzanne Burden, Rohan McCullough

Strategic Air Command
US   1955   114m   Technicolor   Vistavision
Paramount (Samuel J. Briskin)
V*, L

A baseball player is recalled to air force duty.

Sentimental flagwaver featuring the newest jets of the fifties.

w Valentine Davies, Beirne Lay Jnr   d Anthony Mann   ph William Daniels   m Victor Young

James Stewart, June Allyson, Frank Lovejoy, Barry Sullivan, Alex Nicol, Bruce Bennett, Jay C. Flippen, James Millican, James Bell

AAN: original story (Beirne Lay Jnr)

The Stratton Story
US   1949   106m   bw
MGM (Jack Cummings)

An amateur baseball enthusiast becomes a famous professional, but suffers an accident which involves the amputation of a leg.

Mild sentimental biopic, well made but not very interesting.

w Douglas Morrow, Guy Trosper   d Sam Wood   ph Harold Rosson   m Adolph Deutsch

James Stewart, June Allyson, Frank Morgan, Agnes Moorehead, Bill Williams

AA: original story (Douglas Morrow)

Strauss's Great Waltz: see *Waltzes from Vienna*

'The knock at the door meant the birth of one man and the death of seven others!'
Straw Dogs
GB   1971   118m   Eastmancolor
Talent Associates/Amerbroco (Daniel Melnick)
V*, L

In a Cornish village, a mild American university researcher erupts into violence when taunted by drunken villagers who commit sustained assaults on himself and his wife.

Totally absurd, poorly contrived, hilariously overwritten *Cold Comfort Farm* melodrama with farcical violence.

w David Zelag Goodman, Sam Peckinpah   novel *The Siege of Trencher's Farm* by Gordon M. Williams   d Sam Peckinpah   ph John Coquillon   m Jerry Fielding

Dustin Hoffman, Susan George, Peter Vaughan, David Warner, T. P. McKenna, Colin Welland

'Before the end you will have gasped and shuddered through an orgy of detailed rape, slaughter, arson and wanton destruction.' – *Cecil Wilson, Daily Mail*

'A magnificent piece of red-raw, meaty entertainment.' – *Ernest Betts, The People*

AAN: Jerry Fielding

The Strawberry Blonde **
US   1941   97m   bw
Warner (William Cagney)
V*

A dentist in turn-of-the-century Brooklyn wonders whether he married the right woman.

Pleasant period comedy drama, a remake of *One Sunday Afternoon* (qv).

w Julius J. and Philip G. Epstein   d Raoul Walsh   ph James Wong Howe   m Heinz Roemheld

James Cagney, Olivia de Havilland, *Rita Hayworth*, Alan Hale, George Tobias, Jack Carson, Una O'Connor, George Reeves

'It not only tells a very human story, it also creates an atmosphere, recreates a period.' – *New York Sun*

'A blithe, sentimental, turn-of-the-century buggy ride.' – *Time*

AAN: Heinz Roemheld

Strawberry Roan
GB   1944   84m   bw
British National

A farmer weds a showgirl who ruins his life.

Rather glum rural drama with some style but little entertainment value.

w Elizabeth Baron   novel A. G. Street   d Maurice Elvey

William Hartnell, Carol Raye, Walter Fitzgerald, Sophie Stewart, John Ruddock, Wylie Watson, Petula Clark

The Strawberry Statement
US   1970   109m   Metrocolor
MGM/Robert Chartoff, Irwin Winkler
V*, S

Student rebels occupy a university administration building.

One of a short-lived group of student anti-discipline films of the early seventies, and about the most boring.

w Israel Horowitz   novel James Simon Kunen   d Stuart Hagmann   ph Ralph Woolsey   m Ian Freebairn Smith

Bruce Davison, Kim Darby, Bud Cort, Murray MacLeod

Streamers
US   1983   118m   Movielab
Rank/Streamers International (Robert Altman, Nick J. Mileti)
V, V*, L

Tensions mount at a training camp for the 83rd Airborne Division.

Claustrophobic photographed play about generally worthless people.

w David Rabe   play David Rabe   d Robert Altman   ph Pierre Mignot   pd Wolf Kroeger   ed Norman Smith

Matthew Modine, Michael Wright, Mitchell Lichtenstein, David Alan Grier, Guy Boyd, George Dzundza

'A thing of beauty is a joy for ever ...'
Street Angel *
US   1928   101m   bw   part-talkie
Fox

An unwilling prostitute becomes a circus artiste.

A sentimental and tawdry tale becomes a vehicle for good typical work by director and stars.

w Marion Orth   play *Lady Cristallinda* by Monckton Hoffe   d Frank Borzage   ph Ernest Palmer, Paul Ivano   ad Harry Oliver

Janet Gaynor, Charles Farrell, Henry Armetta, Guido Trento

AA: Janet Gaynor

AAN: Ernest Palmer; Harry Oliver

Street Corner
GB   1953   94m   bw
Rank/LIP/Sydney Box (William MacQuitty)
US title: *Both Sides of the Law*

Days in the lives of the women police of Chelsea.

Patter-plotted female *Blue Lamp*; just about watchable.

w Muriel and Sydney Box   d Muriel Box   ph Reg Wyer   m Temple Abady

Rosamund John, Anne Crawford, Peggy Cummins, Terence Morgan, Barbara Murray, Sarah Lawson,

Ronald Howard, Eleanor Summerfield, Michael Medwin

Street Fleet: see *D. C. Cab*

Street of Chance
US   1930   78m   bw
Paramount (David O. Selznick)

A New York gambler gets his come-uppance.

Dullish family melodrama with gangsters as *dei ex machina*.

w Howard Estabrook, Lenore Coffee   d John Cromwell   ph Charles Lang

William Powell, Kay Francis, Regis Toomey, Jean Arthur

'Strong exploitation can cinch this one. Strongly hints at recent murder of well-known gambler.' – *Variety*

AAN: script

'Where women came to forget – one man came to remember!'
Street of Chance *
US   1942   74m   bw
Burt Skelly/Sol C. Siegel/Paramount

An amnesia case discovers that he is wanted for murder.

The plot was fairly original at the time, and the treatment maintains interest.

w Garrett Fort   story Cornell Woolrich   d Jack Hively

Burgess Meredith, Claire Trevor, Sheldon Leonard, Jerome Cowan, Frieda Inescort, Louise Platt

Street of Shame *
Japan   1956   85m   bw
Daiei (Masaichi Nagata)
V*
original title: *Akasen Chitai*

Stories of women in a Tokyo brothel.

Unremarkable material executed with the style expected of the director.

w Masashige Narusawa   d Kenji Mizoguchi   ph Kazuo Miyagawa   m Toshiro Mayazumi

Machiko Kyo, Ayako Wakao, Aiko Mimasu

Street of Women
US   1932   59m   bw
Warner

A property developer is torn between his wife and his mistress.

Choppily developed drama which starts haltingly and gets nowhere.

w Mary McCall Jnr   novel Polan Banks   d Archie Mayo

Kay Francis, Alan Dinehart, Roland Young, Marjorie Gateson, Gloria Stuart

'Just a programme picture.' – *Variety*

Street People: see *Sicilian Cross*

Street Scene *
US   1931   80m   bw
Samuel Goldwyn
V*

In a New York slum street on a hot summer night, an adulterous woman is shot by her husband.

Slice-of-life drama from an influential play; never much of a film, and very dated.

w Elmer Rice   play Elmer Rice   d King Vidor   ph George Barnes   m Alfred Newman

Sylvia Sidney, William Collier Jnr, Max Mantor, David Landau, Estelle Taylor, Russell Hopton

'Whenever the camera starts to focus on two or three characters, the plot thickens and *Street Scene* flies out the window; petty domestic tragedy supplants the original slice-of-life conception.' – *National Board of Review*

'As a commercial proposition it will cause talk and reap honours, but whether it will prove an exceptional box office attraction remains to be seen.' – *Variety*

The Street Singer
GB   1937   85m   bw
British National

A musical comedy star is mistaken for a beggar by a girl with whom he falls in love.

Rather tiresome star vehicle.

w Reginald Arkell   *d* Jean de Marguenat

Arthur Tracy, Margaret Lockwood, Arthur Riscoe, Hugh Wakefield

Street Smart
US   1987   95m   TVC
Cannon (Menahem Golan, Yoram Globus)
V*, L

A top journalist turns in a story that gets him involved with pimps and prostitutes.

Unpersuasive crime melodrama in which the star seems surprised to find himself.

w David Freeman   *d* Jerry Schatzberg   *ph* Adam Holender   *m* Robert Irving   *pd* Dan Leigh   *ed* Priscilla Nedd

Christopher Reeve, Kathy Baker, Mimi Rogers, Jay Patterson, Andre Gregory, Morgan Freeman

AAN: Morgan Freeman

The Street with No Name *
US   1948   93m   bw
TCF (Samuel G. Engel)

An FBI man goes undercover to unmask a criminal gang.

The oldest crime plot in the world, applied with vigour to the documentary realism of *The House on 92nd Street* and built around the *Kiss of Death* psychopathic character created by Richard Widmark.

w Harry Kleiner   *d* William Keighley   *ph* Joe MacDonald   *m* Lionel Newman

Richard Widmark, Mark Stevens, Lloyd Nolan, Barbara Lawrence, Ed Begley

† Remade 1955 as *House of Bamboo.*

A Streetcar Named Desire **
US   1951   122m   bw
Charles K. Feldman/Elia Kazan
V*, L, S

A repressed Southern widow is raped and driven mad by her brutal brother-in-law.

Reasonably successful, decorative picture from a highly theatrical but influential play; unreal sets and atmospheric photography vaguely Sternbergian.

w Tennessee Williams   *play* Tennessee Williams   *d* Elia Kazan   *ph* Harry Stradling   *m* Alex North   *ad* Richard Day

Vivien Leigh, Marlon Brando, Kim Hunter, Karl Malden

AA: Vivien Leigh; Kim Hunter; Karl Malden

AAN: best picture; Tennessee Williams; Elia Kazan; Harry Stradling; Alex North; Marlon Brando; Richard Day

The Streetfighter: see *Hard Times*

Streets of Fire
US   1984   94m   Technicolor
Universal/RKO/Hill-Gordon-Silver (Lawrence Gordon, Joel Silver)
V*, L, S

A rock singer is kidnapped and a professional trouble shooter takes on the job of recovery.

Violent melodrama with an unsuccessful comic strip approach which fails to raise the material into the realm of myth.

w Walter Hill, Larry Gross   *d* Walter Hill   *ph* Andrew Laszlo   *m* Ry Cooder   *pd* John Vallone   *ed* Freeman Davies, Michael Ripps

Michael Paré, Diane Lane, Rick Moranis, Amy Madigan, Willem Dafoe

Streets of Gold *
US   1986   95m   DeLuxe
TCF/James G. Robinson/Ufland-Roth
V*, L

A disenchanted immigrant finds an unexpected road to success as a boxing coach for two streetwise kids.

Unappealing variation on the Rocky movies, good to look at but devoid of content.

w Heywood Gould, Richard Price, Tom Cole   *d* Joe Roth   *ph* Arthur Albert   *m* Jack Nitzsche   *pd* Marcos Flaksman   *ed* Richard Chew

Klaus Maria Brandauer, Adrian Pasdar, Wesley Snipes, Angela Molina

Streets of Laredo
US   1949   92m   Technicolor
Paramount (Robert Fellows)

Two of three bandit friends become Texas Rangers.

Adequate star Western, a remake of *The Texas Rangers.*

w Charles Marquis Warren   *d* Leslie Fenton   *ph* Ray Rennahan   *m* Victor Young

William Holden, William Bendix, Macdonald Carey, Mona Freeman

Streets of New York
US   1939   72m   bw
Monogram
V*

The teenage owner of a newsstand studies law at night school.

Unconvincing street-life drama, an obvious vehicle for a boy star.

w Robert Andrews   *d* William Nigh

Jackie Cooper, Martin Spellman, George Cleveland, Dick Purcell

'Should do all right if not pointed too high.' – *Variety*

Strictly Ballroom ***
Australia   1992   94m   Eastmancolor
Rank/M&A/Australian Film Finance Corp. (Tristram Miall)
V, V*, L, S

A would-be champion ballroom dancer, who incurs the wrath of the establishment by improvising his own steps, searches for a new partner in tune with his ideas.

Exuberant, charming, witty romance acted and directed with style and verve.

w Baz Luhrmann, Craig Pearce   *play* N.I.D.A. stage production devised by its original cast   *story* Baz Luhrmann, Andrew Bovell   *d* Baz Luhrmann   *ph* Steve Mason   *m* David Hirschfelder   *pd* Catherine Martin   *ch* John 'Cha Cha' O'Connell, Paul Mercurio   *ed* Jill Bilcock

Paul Mercurio, Tara Morice, Bill Hunter, Pat Thomson, Gia Carides, Peter Whitford, Barry Otto, John Hannan, Sonia Kruger, Kris McQuade, Antonio Vargas, Armonia Benedito

'Bright, breezy and immensely likable musical-comedy.' – *Variety*

Strictly Confidential: see *Broadway Bill*

Strictly Dishonourable
US   1951   94m   bw
MGM (Melvin Frank, Norman Panama)

A young girl falls in love with a rakish Italian opera star; he is such a sentimentalist that he marries her.

Emasculated sentimental version of the sharp Preston Sturges comedy.

wd Norman Panama, Melvin Frank   *ph* Ray June   *m* Lennie Hayton

Ezio Pinza, Janet Leigh, Millard Mitchell, Maria Palmer

† Previously filmed in 1931 by Universal, with Paul Lukas, Sidney Fox and Lewis Stone.

Strictly for Pleasure: see *The Perfect Furlough*

Strictly Unconventional: see *The Circle*

Strike ***
USSR   1924   70m approx (24 fps)   bw   silent
Goskino/Proletkult
V, V*

A 1912 strike of factory workers is brutally put down by the authorities.

Brilliant propaganda piece with superbly cinematic sequences.

wd Sergei M. Eisenstein   *ph* Edouard Tissé, Vassili Khvatov

Grigori Alexandrov, Maxim Strauch, Mikhail Gomarov

Strike Me Pink *
US   1935   104m   bw
Samuel Goldwyn

A timid amusement park owner is threatened by crooks.

Acceptable star comedy with music.

w Frank Butler, Walter de Leon, Francis Martin   *d* Norman Taurog   *ph* Gregg Toland, Merritt Gerstad   *m* Alfred Newman   *songs* Harold Arlen, Lew Brown

Eddie Cantor, Sally Eilers, Ethel Merman, William Frawley, Parkyakarkus

'At the box office both here and abroad the take will be big.' – *Variety*

Strike Up the Band *
US   1940   120m   bw
MGM (Arthur Freed)
V*, L

A high-school band takes part in a nationwide radio contest.

Rather tiresomely high-spirited musical with the stars at the top of their young form.

w Fred Finklehoffe, John Monks Jnr   *d/ch* Busby Berkeley   *ph* Ray June   *m* Roger Edens   *ly* Arthur Freed

Judy Garland, Mickey Rooney, Paul Whiteman and his Orchestra, June Preisser, William Tracy, Larry Nunn

AAN: Georgie Stoll, Roger Edens; song 'Our Love Affair' (*m/ly* Roger Edens, Georgie Stoll)

The Strip *
US   1951   85m   bw
MGM (Joe Pasternak)

A band drummer is accused of the murder of a racketeer.

Minor mystery melodrama intriguingly set on Sunset Strip, with jazz accompaniment.

w Allen Rivkin   *d* Leslie Kardos   *ph* Robert Surtees   *m* George Stoll

Mickey Rooney, Sally Forrest, William Demarest, James Craig, Kay Brown; and Louis Armstrong, Earl Hines, Jack Teagarden

AAN: song 'A Kiss To Build a Dream On (*m/ly* Bert Kalmar, Harry Ruby, Oscar Hammerstein II)

'Today's army needs men of courage – honesty – integrity – ambition. Instead, they got John Winger . . .'

Stripes

US   1981   106m   Metrocolor
Columbia (Ivan Reitman, Dan Goldberg)
V, V*, L

Sergeant Hulka tries to train a platoon of misfit volunteers.

Ancient army wheezes dressed up with fashionable black comedy and sex, but no funnier than *Carry On Sergeant.*

w Len Blum, Dan Goldberg, Harold Ramis   d Ivan Reitman   ph Bill Butler   m Elmer Bernstein

Bill Murray, Harold Ramis, Warren Oates, P. J. Soles, John Larroquette, Sean Young

The Stripper *

US   1963   95m   bw   Cinemascope
TCF (Jerry Wald)
GB title: *Woman of Summer*

An ageing beauty queen returns to her Kansas hometown and has an affair with a 19-year-old garage hand.

Downbeat character melodrama typical of its time and its author; competent but sterile and rather tedious.

w Meade Roberts   play *A Loss of Roses* by William Inge   d Franklin Schaffner   ph Ellsworth Fredericks   m Jerry Goldsmith

Joanne Woodward, Richard Beymer, *Claire Trevor*, Carol Lynley, Robert Webber, Louis Nye, Gypsy Rose Lee, Michael J. Pollard

Striptease Lady: see *Lady of Burlesque*

Stroker Ace

US   1983   96m   Technicolor   Panavision
Universal/Warner (Hank Moonjean)
V*

A top racing car driver is sponsored by the owner of a chain of fast-food restaurants.

Tediously leering comedy, with Reynolds repeating his over-familiar role as a macho ladies' man.

w Hugh Wilson, Hal Needham   novel *Stand On It* by William Neely, Robert K. Ottum   d Hal Needham   ph Nick McLean   m Al Capps   ad Paul Peters   ed Carl Kress, William Gordean

Burt Reynolds, Ned Beatty, Jim Nabors, Parker Stevenson, Loni Anderson

Stromboli

Italy   1949   107m   bw
RKO/Be-Ro (Roberto Rossellini)
V*

A Lithuanian refugee accepts the protection of marriage to an Italian fisherman, but resents the barrenness and hostility of her life, especially when the local volcano erupts.

Sloppy melodrama with pretensions, interesting but not even attractive to the eye.

w Roberto Rossellini and others   d Roberto Rossellini   ph Otello Martelli   m Renzo Rossellini

Ingrid Bergman, Mario Vitale, Renzo Cesana

† The international version was cut to 81m.

The Strong Man *

US   1926   75m approx (24 fps)   bw (colour sequence)   silent
First National/Harry Langdon
V*, L

A war veteran returns and searches the city for his female penfriend.

Quite charming star comedy, probably Langdon's best.

w Frank Capra, Arthur Ripley, Hal Conklin, Robert Eddy   d Frank Capra   ph Elgin Lessley, Glenn Kershner

Harry Langdon, Gertrude Astor, Tay Garnett

Stronger than Desire

US   1939   82m   bw
MGM

A lawyer's wife gets into trouble and lets him try an innocent man for her crime.

Fast remake of *Evelyn Prentice;* a good half-bill.

w David Hertz, William Ludwig   d Leslie Fenton

Walter Pidgeon, Virginia Bruce, Ann Dvorak, Lee Bowman, Rita Johnson, Ilka Chase

Stronger than Fear: see *Edge of Doom*

The Strongest Man in the World

US   1976   92m   Technicolor
Walt Disney (Bill Anderson)

An accident in a science lab gives a student superhuman strength.

Formula comedy for older children.

w Joseph L. McEveety, Herman Groves   d Vincent McEveety   ph Andrew Jackson   m Robert F. Brunner

Kurt Russell, Joe Flynn, Eve Arden, Cesar Romero, Phil Silvers, Dick Van Patten, Harold Gould, William Schallert, James Gregory, Roy Roberts, Fritz Feld, Raymond Bailey, Eddie Quillan, Burt Mustin

Strongroom *

GB   1961   80m   bw
Bryanston/Theatrecraft (Guido Coen)

Two car breakers plan a once-for-all bank robbery but get involved with potential murder when their hostages get locked in.

Suspenseful second feature with gloss and pace.

w Max Marquis, René Harris   d Vernon Sewell   ph Basil Emmott   m Johnny Gregory

Colin Gordon, Ann Lynn, Derren Nesbitt, Keith Faulkner

Stroszeck *

West Germany   1977   108m   colour
Werner Herzog/ZDF
V*

A crook, a prostitute and a friend move from Germany to what they hope will be the freedom of a mobile home in the United States; but everything goes wrong and they part company.

A simple narrative – described as 'a ballad' by its director – of a failed search for individuality and the exchange of one prison for another.

wd Werner Herzog   ph Thomas Mauch, Ed Lachmann, Wolfgang Knigge, Stefano Guidi   m Chet Atkins, Sonny Terry   ed Beate Mainka-Jellinghaus

Bruno S, Eva Mattes, Clemens Scheitz, Burkhard Driest, Alfred Edel, Norbert Grupe

The Struggle *

US   1931   88m   bw
UA/D. W. Griffith

A New Yorker goes to the bad on bootleg liquor.

The director's last film reveals many of his old skills allied to a Victorian tract.

w Anita Loos, John Emerson   d D. W. Griffith   ph Joseph Ruttenberg

Hal Skelly, Zita Johann, Charlotte Wynters, Jackson Halliday

'A dull and sodden rendering with old-time ranting and little drama . . . just dull when it isn't in the highest degree maudlin.' – *Dwight MacDonald*

† It was based on *The Drunkard* by Émile Zola.
†† The picture failed and was re-released as *Ten Nights in a Bar-room.*

The Stud

GB   1978   90m   colour
Brent Walker/Artoc (Edward D. Simons)
V*

A millionaire's wife installs her lover as manager of a discotheque, but he becomes bored and wants a place of his own.

Life among the unpleasant rich. A surprise box-office success, richly undeserved.

w Jackie Collins   novel Jackie Collins   d Quentin Masters   ph Peter Hannan   m Biddu

Joan Collins, Oliver Tobias, Sue Lloyd, Mark Burns, Doug Fisher, Walter Gotell

'Watching it is rather like being buried alive in a coffin stuffed with back numbers of *Men Only*.' – *Alan Brien*

The Student Prince

US   1954   107m   Anscocolor   Cinemascope
MGM (Joe Pasternak)
V*, L

A prince studies in Heidelberg and falls for a barmaid.

Ruritanian operetta, lumpishly filmed, with Mario Lanza providing only the voice of the hero as he got too fat to play the part.

w William Ludwig, Sonya Levien   play *Old Heidelberg* by Wilhelm Meyer-Foerster   operetta Dorothy Donnelly   d Richard Thorpe   ph Paul C. Vogel   md George Stoll   m Sigmund Romberg

Edmund Purdom, Ann Blyth, John Williams, Edmund Gwenn, S. Z. Sakall, John Ericson, Louis Calhern, Betta St John, Evelyn Varden

† Without the music, the play had been filmed at MGM in 1926, with Ramon Novarro and Norma Shearer under Ernst Lubitsch's direction.

Student Tour

US   1934   80m   bw
MGM

A professor of philosophy chaperones a world tour by collegiates.

Very thin comedy yarn with songs.

w Ralph Spence, Philip Dunne   d Charles F. Reisner

Jimmy Durante, Charles Butterworth, Maxine Doyle, Phil Regan, Douglas Fowley, Betty Grable, Nelson Eddy

'Long, slow, and of mild entertainment appeal.' – *Variety*

The Studio Murder Mystery

US   1929   62m   bw
Paramount

An actor is murdered on a film set.

Primitive talkie comedy mystery now interesting only for its studio backgrounds.

w Frank Tuttle   serial the Edingtons   d Frank Tuttle

Neil Hamilton, Florence Eldridge, Warner Oland, Eugene Pallette, Fredric March, Doris Hill, Chester Conklin

Studs Lonigan

US   1960   95m   bw
Philip Yordan
V*

The growing up of an unlettered Chicago Irishman in the twenties.

Rough-and-ready version of a celebrated novel, not a bad try but insufficiently detailed to be any kind of classic.

w Philip Yordan   *novel* James T. Farrell   *d* Irving Lerner

Christopher Knight, Jack Nicholson, Frank Gorshin

A Study in Scarlet
US   1933   71m   bw
KBS
V*

Sherlock Holmes solves a mysterious murder.

Rather emaciated version of a spirited yarn.

w Robert Florey   *story* Sir Arthur Conan Doyle
d Edwin L. Marin

Reginald Owen, Warburton Gamble, Anna May Wong, June Clyde, Alan Dinehart, Alan Mowbray

'Okay for secondary houses.' – *Variety*

A Study in Terror *
GB   1965   95m   Eastmancolor
Compton-Tekli/Sir Nigel (Henry E. Lester)
V*, L

Sherlock Holmes discovers the identity of Jack the Ripper.

A reasonably good Holmes pastiche marred by a surfeit of horror and over-riotous local colour; quite literate, but schizophrenic.

w Donald and Derek Ford   *novel* Ellery Queen
d James Hill   *ph* Desmond Dickinson   *m* John Scott   *ad* Alex Vetchinsky

John Neville, Donald Houston, John Fraser, Robert Morley, Cecil Parker, Anthony Quayle, Barbara Windsor, Adrienne Corri, Judi Dench, Frank Finlay, Barry Jones, Kay Walsh, Georgia Brown

The Stuff
US   1985   93m   Technicolor
New World
V, V*

A monstrous yogurt-like goo eats people from the inside out.

Messy comedy-horror without benefit of much plotline.

wd Larry Cohen

Michael Moriarty, Andrea Marcovicci, Paul Sorvino, Scott Bloom, Danny Aiello, Alexander Scourby

The Stunt Man *
US   1980   129m   Metrocolor
Melvin Simon (Richard Rush)
V, V*, L

A Vietnam veteran on the run from the police finds refuge as a star stunt man for a sinister film director.

Overlong, curious, but sometimes compelling melodrama which entertains on the surface while its actual aims are harder to fathom.

w Lawrence B. Marcus   *novel* Paul Brodeur
d Richard Rush   *ph* Mario Tosi   *m* Dominic Frontière

Peter O'Toole, Steve Railsback, Barbara Hershey, Allen Goorwitz, Alex Rocco, Sharon Farrell

'It's like one of those sets of Chinese boxes, each one with another box inside, growing smaller and smaller until finally there is nothing left at all.' – *Roger Ebert*

AAN: screenplay; Richard Rush; Peter O'Toole

Stunts *
US   1977   90m   colour
New Line (Raymond Lafaro, William Panzer)
V*

The brother of a murdered stuntman takes his place in order to investigate the death.

Slick action thriller which capitalizes on the attraction of daring stunts.

w Barney Chen, Dennis Johnson   *story* Michael Harpster, Raymond Lafaro, Robert Shaye   *d* Mark L. Lester   *ph* Bruce Logan   *m* Michael Kamen
ed Corky Ehlers

Robert Forster, Fiona Lewis, Joanna Cassidy, Darrell Fetty, Bruce Glover, Jim Luisi

The Subject Was Roses *
US   1968   107m   Metrocolor
MGM (Edgar Lansbury)

A young war veteran finds he can't communicate with his parents, and vice versa.

Photographed play notable for its performances.

w Frank D. Gilroy   *play* Frank D. Gilroy   *d* Ulu Grosbard   *ph* Jack Priestley

Patricia Neal, Jack Albertson, Martin Sheen, Don Saxon, Elaine Williams

AA: Jack Albertson

AAN: Patricia Neal

Submarine Command
US   1951   87m   bw
Paramount (John Farrow, Joseph Sistrom)

A submarine officer who considers himself a coward becomes a hero in Korea.

Very routine soul-searching actioner.

w Jonathan Latimer   *d* John Farrow   *ph* Lionel Lindon   *m* David Buttolph

William Holden, Don Taylor, Nancy Olsen, William Bendix, Moroni Olsen, Peggy Webber

Submarine D1
US   1937   93m   bw
Cosmopolitan/Warner

Adventures of recruits to the naval submarine service.

Standard flagwaver of no intrinsic interest.

w Frank Wead, Warren Duff, Lawrence Kimble
d Lloyd Bacon

Pat O'Brien, George Brent, Wayne Morris, Frank McHugh, Doris Weston, Ronald Reagan, Henry O'Neill, Regis Toomey, Broderick Crawford

'An instructive and illuminating document . . . film waves its own flag, the best on earth, and with some exhibitor push it should do business.' – *Variety*

Submarine Patrol
US   1938   93m   bw
TCF (Darryl Zanuck)

Recruits learn to handle sub-chasing boats at Annapolis.

Cheerful propaganda comedy-drama with familiar faces on hand and some good thrill sequences.

w Rian James, Darrell Ware, Jack Yellen   *book* Ray Milholland   *d* John Ford

Richard Greene, Nancy Kelly, Preston Foster, George Bancroft, Slim Summerville, John Carradine, Henry Armetta, Warren Hymes, Elisha Cook Jnr, E. E. Clive, Ward Bond, George E. Stone

'Surefire film entertainment directed by a veteran who knows all the tricks.' – *Variety*

Submarine Raider
US   1942   65m   bw
Wallace MacDonald/Columbia

An American sub learns too late about the attack on Pearl Harbor.

Stodgy wartime filler with unconvincing action sequences.

w Aubrey Wisberg   *d* Lew Landers

John Howard, Marguerite Chapman, Bruce Bennett, Warren Ashe

Submarine X-1
GB   1967   90m   Eastmancolor
UA/Mirisch (John C. Champion)

A submarine commander in World War II trains men to attack the *Lindendorf* in midget submarines.

Belated quota quickie, routine in every department.

w Donald S. Sanford, Guy Elmes   *d* William Graham   *ph* Paul Beeson

James Caan, Norman Bowler, David Sumner

Submarine Zone: see *Escape to Glory*

Subterfuge
GB   1968   86m   Eastmancolor
Rank/Intertel (Peter Snell)

In London a CIA agent becomes involved with the wife of a British double-agent.

A routine retread of standard spy stories, crippled by its inexplicable narrative.

w David Whitaker   *d* Peter Graham Scott   *ph* Roy Garner, Albert Tolley   *m* Cyril Ornadel   *ad* Ron Fouracre   *ed* Bill Lewthwaite

Gene Barry, Joan Collins, Richard Todd, Tom Adams, Suzanna Leigh, Michael Rennie, Marius Goring, Colin Gordon

'A sad waste of several very capable players.' – *Brenda Davies, MFB*

'We are the new Bohemians!'
The Subterraneans
US   1960   89m   Metrocolor   Cinemascope
MGM (Arthur Freed)

The love affairs of San Francisco bohemians.

A boring oddity with lashings of eccentric behaviour and sexual hang-ups; MGM venturing very timidly outside its field.

w Robert Thom   *novel* Jack Kerouac   *d* Ranald MacDougall   *ph* Joseph Ruttenberg   *m* André Previn

George Peppard, Leslie Caron, Janice Rule, Roddy McDowall, Anne Seymour, Jim Hutton

'He's an intergalactic Super Hero whose quest is to rid the Universe of evil-doers and combat the forces of darkness . . . But sometimes you gotta come down to Earth.'
Suburban Commando
US   1991   DeLuxe
Entertainment/New Line (Howard Gottfried)
V, V*, L

An alien bounty-hunter takes a holiday on Earth and lodges with a suburban family.

Amiable, juvenile, low-brow comedy of no particular originality or distinction.

w Frank Capello   *d* Burt Kennedy   *ph* Patrick J. Swovelin   *pd* Ivo Cristante, C. J. Strawn
sp creature effects: Steve Johnson's XFX Productions
ed Sonny Baskin

Hulk Hogan, Christopher Lloyd, Shelley Duvall

'A sort of sickly lovechild of *Star Wars* (whose effects are reproduced on the cheap, and whose music is repeatedly plagiarized) and *Kindergarten Cop*.' – *Adam Mars-Jones, Independent*

Suburbia *
US   1983   99m   colour
Suburbia Productions (Bert Dragin)
V*

A gang of rebellious teenagers leave home to set up their own community, arousing the antagonism of their parents.

Uncompromising account of unlovely LA punks and unlovelier adults that makes something personal out of standard teen-rebellion material.

wd Penelope Spheeris   *ph* Timothy Suhrstedt
m Alex Gibson   *ad* Randy Moore   *ed* Ross Albert

Chris Pederson, Bill Coyne, Jennifer Clay, Timothy Eric O'Brien, Wade Walston, Mike B. The Flea, Maggie Ehrig, Grant Miner, Christina Beck

Subway

France   1985   104m   colour   CinemaScope
Gaumont/Films du Loup/TSF/TFI
V, V*, L, S

An eccentric hero on the run from thugs takes refuge overnight in the Paris Metro.

Oddball melodrama with more style than substance.

w Luc Besson and others   *d* Luc Besson

Christophe Lambert, Isabelle Adjani, Richard Bohringer

Subway in the Sky

GB   1958   87m   bw
Orbit (John Temple-Smith, Patrick Filmer-Sankey)

A Berlin cabaret star finds her landlady's ex-husband, a deserter, hiding in her apartment and sets out to prove his innocence of drug smuggling.

Tedious photographed play with precious few points of dramatic interest.

w Jack Andrews   *play* Ian Main   *d* Muriel Box
ph Wilkie Cooper   *m* Mario Nascimbene

Hildegarde Neff, Van Johnson, Katherine Kath, Cec Linder, Albert Lieven, Edward Judd

Success at Any Price

US   1934   74m   bw
RKO

A young man climbs to great business heights by crushing those around him, then attempts suicide when the crash comes.

Slackly handled drama with an unsympathetic hero.

w John Howard Lawson, Howard J. Green   *d* J. Walter Ruben

Douglas Fairbanks Jnr, Genevieve Tobin, Frank Morgan, Colleen Moore, Edward Everett Horton, Nydia Westman, Henry Kolker

'Episodic, unreasonable and anything but audience proof.' – *Variety*

Success Is the Best Revenge

GB/France   1984   91m   Technicolor
De Vere/Gaumont (Jerzy Skolimowski)
V*, L

A Polish theatre director in London stages a symbolic show but alienates his son.

Another study of Polish exiles to follow *Moonlighting*, but this time with surrealist elements.

w Jerzy Skolimowski, Michael Lyndon   *d* Jerzy Skolimowski   *ph* Mike Fash   *m* Stanley Myers, Hans Zimmer

Michael York, Joanna Szczerbic, Michael Lyndon, Jerry Skol, Michel Piccoli, John Hurt, Anouk Aimée, Jane Asher

A Successful Calamity

US   1931   75m   bw
Warner

A millionaire discovers the true worth of his family when he pretends to be poor.

Good star vehicle which pleases despite its predictability.

w Maude Howell, Julien Josephson and Austin Parker   *play* Clare Kummer   *d* John G. Adolfi

George Arliss, Mary Astor, Evalyn Knapp, Grant Mitchell, William Janney

Succubus (dubbed)

West Germany   1967   91m   colour
Border/Trans American/Aquila (Adrian Hoven)
V

original title: *Necronomicon – Geträumte Stünden*; aka: *Necronomicon*

A mysterious woman, who performs a night-club act that involves sex and sadism, is haunted by a past she cannot quite remember and fantasizes scenes of love-making and death.

An unholy mix of cut-rate surrealism, pretentious dialogue and incomprehensible narrative which has a vague connection with the legend of Faust; it will not bear close examination.

w Pier A. Caminneci   *d* Jess (Jesús) Franco
ph Robert Gaffron   *md* Jerry Van Rooyen
m Friedrich Gulda   *ad* Karl Heinz Mannchen
ed Frizzi Schmidt

Janine Reynaud, Jack Taylor, Howard Varnon, Nathalie Nort, Michel Lemoine, Pier A. Caminneci, Adrian Hoven

'An absurdly hit-or-miss affair, with scenes that have a certain bizarre appeal (shop window dummies coming to life) juxtaposed with others of crushing banality.' – *David McGillivray, MFB*

† The British release was cut to 81m.

Such a Gorgeous Kid Like Me: see *Une Belle Fille Comme Moi*

Such a Pretty Little Beach: see *Une Si Jolie Petite Plage*

Such Good Friends *

US   1971   102m   Movielab
Paramount/Sigma (Otto Preminger)

A successful man has a mysterious illness and his wife enlists help from her friends.

Satirical parable which alternates between sex comedy and medical exposé; generally heavy-going but with good moments.

w Elaine May   *novel* Lois Gould   *d* Otto Preminger   *ph* Gayne Rescher   *m* Thomas Z. Shepherd

Dyan Cannon, James Coco, Jennifer O'Neil, Nina Foch, Laurence Luckinbill, Ken Howard, Burgess Meredith, Louise Lasser, Sam Levene, Rita Gam, Nancy Guild

Such Men Are Dangerous

US   1930   83m   bw
Fox

A crooked financier undergoes plastic surgery and leads a new life.

Phoney melodrama with slow pace and unconvincing details.

w Ernest Vajda, Elinor Glyn   *d* Kenneth Hawks

Warner Baxter, Catherine Dale Owen, Albert Conti, Hedda Hopper, Claud Allister, Bela Lugosi

'Will bore intelligent fans and impress even the gullible with its implausibilities.' – *Variety*

Such Men Are Dangerous (1955): see *The Racers*

Such Women Are Dangerous

US   1934   81m   bw
Fox

Through circumstances an innocent man about town is accused of murder.

Mild drama which fails through slack handling.

w Jane Storm, Oscar M. Sheridan   *story* Odd Thursday by Vera Caspary   *d* James Flood

Warner Baxter, Rosemary Ames, Rochelle Hudson, Mona Barrie, Herbert Mundin, Henrietta Crosman

'Just fair screen amusement.' – *Variety*

Sudba Cheloveka: see *Destiny of a Man*

Sudden Fear **

US   1952   111m   bw
RKO/Joseph Kaufman

A playwright heiress finds that her husband is plotting to kill her.

Archetypal star suspenser, glossy and effectively climaxed.

w Lenore Coffee, Robert Smith   *d* David Miller
ph Charles Lang Jnr   *m* Elmer Bernstein

Joan Crawford, Jack Palance, Gloria Grahame, Bruce Bennett, Mike Connors

AAN: Charles Lang Jnr; Joan Crawford; Jack Palance

'Go on – make his day!'

Sudden Impact

US   1983   117m   Technicolor
Warner/Malpaso (Clint Eastwood)
V, V*, L

San Francisco detective Harry Callahan goes after a lady killer of men who raped her.

Unattractive and overlong cop show featuring an increasingly tired Dirty Harry.

w Joseph C. Stinson   *d* Clint Eastwood   *ph* Bruce Surtees   *m* Lalo Schifrin   *pd* Edward Carfagno

Clint Eastwood, Sondra Locke, Pat Hingle, Bradford Dillman, Paul Drake

'Eastwood presumably takes credit for such gems of authorial self-awareness as replacing the orang-outang of the *Which Way* films, with a farting dog.' – *Paul Taylor, MFB*

'To all those cowboy movies we saw in our youth, all those TV westerns and cop dramas and war movies, Dirty Harry has brought a great simplification: A big man, a big gun, a bad guy, and instant justice.' – *Roger Ebert*

Suddenly *

US   1954   75m   bw
UA/Robert Bassler
V, V*

Gunmen take over a suburban house and plan to assassinate the President who is due to pass by.

Moderately effective minor suspenser with rather too much psychological chat.

w Richard Sale   *d* Lewis Allen   *ph* Charles G. Clarke   *m* David Raksin

Frank Sinatra, Sterling Hayden, James Gleason, Nancy Gates, Kim Charney

'What she doesn't know about spring – neither does Cupid!'

Suddenly It's Spring

US   1947   87m   bw
Paramount (Claude Binyon)

A WAC captain comes home to find that her husband wants a divorce.

Tired romantic comedy with no fizz at all.

w Claude Binyon   *d* Mitchell Leisen   *ph* Daniel L. Fapp   *m* Victor Young

Paulette Goddard, Macdonald Carey, Fred MacMurray, Arleen Whelan, Lillian Fontaine, Frank Faylen, Victoria Horne

Suddenly Last Summer *

GB   1959   114m   bw
Columbia/Horizon (Sam Spiegel)
V, V*, L

A homosexual poet's young cousin goes mad when she sees him raped and murdered by beach boys.

Arty flashback talk-piece from a one-act play, padded out with much sub-poetic mumbo jumbo; it takes too long to get to the revelation, which is ambiguously presented anyway.

w Gore Vidal   play Tennessee Williams   d Joseph L. Mankiewicz   ph Jack Hildyard   m Buxton Orr, Malcolm Arnold   pd Oliver Messel

Katharine Hepburn, Elizabeth Taylor, Montgomery Clift, Albert Dekker, Mercedes McCambridge, Gary Raymond

'A short play turns into a ludicrous, lumbering horror movie.' – New Yorker, 1978

'I loathe this film, I say so candidly. To my mind it is a decadent piece of work, sensational, barbarous and ridiculous.' – C. A. Lejeune, Observer

'A wholly admirable rendering into film of a work at once fascinating and nauseating, brilliant and immoral.' – Arthur Knight

AAN: Katharine Hepburn; Elizabeth Taylor; art direction

Suez *
US   1938   104m   bw
TCF (Gene Markey)

The career of French engineer Ferdinand de Lesseps, who built the Suez Canal.

Superbly mounted but rather undramatic fictionalized biopic.

w Philip Dunne, Julien Josephson   d Allan Dwan   ph Peverell Marley   md Louis Silvers   m David Raksin, David Buttolph, Cyril Mockridge

Tyrone Power, Annabella, Loretta Young, J. Edward Bromberg, Joseph Schildkraut, Henry Stephenson, Sidney Blackmer, Maurice Moscovitch, Sig Rumann, Nigel Bruce, Miles Mander, George Zucco, Leon Ames, Rafaela Ottiano

'It's a big film in its attempt, but it misses out on its epic aims.' – Variety

AAN: Peverell Marley; Louis Silvers

Sugar Cane Alley: see Rue Cases Nègres

Sugarbaby **
West Germany   1984   87m   colour
Electric/Pelemele film/BMI/Bayerischen Rundfunks (Eleonore Adlon)
V*
original title: Zuckerbaby

A fat woman pursues a handsome, married train driver whom she loves.

Enjoyable and witty romantic comedy.

wd Percy Adlon   ph Johanna Heer   m Dreier, Franz Erlmeier, Fritz Köstler, Paul Würges Combo   pd Matthias Heller   ed Jean-Claude Piroue

Marianne Sägebrecht, Eisi Gulp, Toni Berger, Manuela Denz, Will Spindler, Hans Stadlbauer

Sugarfoot
US   1951   80m   Technicolor
Warner
TV title: Swirl of Glory

Two men meet on a train for Prescott, Arizona, and each determines to make the town his own.

Unusual but fatally sluggish Western.

w Russell Hughes   novel Clarence Budington Kelland   d Edwin L. Marin

Randolph Scott, Raymond Massey, Adele Jergens, S. Z. Sakall, Robert Warwick, Arthur Hunnicutt

'The true story of a girl who took on all of Texas ... and almost won.'

Sugarland Express *
US   1974   110m   Technicolor   Panavision
Universal (Richard Zanuck, David Brown)
V*, L

A convict's wife persuades him to escape because their baby is being adopted, and they inadvertently

leave behind them a trail of destruction, ending in tragedy.

Mainly comic adventures with a bitter aftertaste, very stylishly handled.

w Hal Barwood, Matthew Robbins   d Steven Spielberg   ph Vilmos Zsigmond   m John Williams

Goldie Hawn, Ben Johnson, Michael Sacks, William Atherton

'Ace in the Hole meets Vanishing Point.' – Sight and Sound

The Suicide Club: see Trouble for Two

Suicide Squadron: see Dangerous Moonlight

The Suitor *
France   1962   85m   bw
CAPAC
original title: Le Soupirant

A nervous young man makes several attempts to get married.

The most successful feature of Pierre Etaix, a student of Tati: his jokes are more polished but in the end his own personality seems rather lacking.

w Pierre Etaix, Jean-Claude Carrière   d Pierre Etaix   ph Pierre Levant   m Jean Paillaud

Pierre Etaix, Laurence Lignères, France Arnell

The Sullivans *
US   1944   111m   bw
TCF (Sam Jaffe)
reissue title: The Fighting Sullivans

Five sons of the same family are killed in World War II.

Inspirational true story which had a wide appeal.

w Mary C. McCall Jnr   d Lloyd Bacon   ph Lucien Andriot   m Alfred Newman

Anne Baxter, Thomas Mitchell, Selena Royle, Edward Ryan, Trudy Marshall, John Campbell, James Cardwell, John Alvin, George Offerman Jnr, Roy Roberts

AAN: original story (Jules Schermer, Edward Doherty)

'There's no speed limit and no brake
When Sullivan travels with Veronica Lake!'
Sullivan's Travels ****
US   1941   90m   bw
Paramount (Paul Jones)
V*, L

A Hollywood director tires of comedy and goes out to find real life.

Marvellously sustained tragi-comedy which ranges from pratfalls to the chain gang and never loses its grip or balance.

wd Preston Sturges   ph John Seitz   m Leo Shuken

Joel McCrea, Veronica Lake, Robert Warwick, William Demarest, Franklin Pangborn, Porter Hall, Byron Foulger, Eric Blore, Robert Greig, Torben Meyer, Jimmy Conlin, Margaret Hayes

DEDICATION: 'To all the funny men and clowns who have made people laugh.'

'A brilliant fantasy in two keys – slapstick farce and the tragedy of human misery.' – James Agee

'The most witty and knowing spoof of Hollywood movie-making of all time.' – Film Society Review

'A deftly sardonic apologia for Hollywood make-believe.' – New York Times

'Reflecting to perfection the mood of wartime Hollywood, it danced on the grave of thirties social cinema.' – Eileen Bowser, 1969

Summer: see The Green Ray

A Summer Affair *
France   1977   84m   Eastmancolor   Panavision
Gala/Renn Productions/Société Française de Production (Pierre Grunstein)
original title: Un Moment D'Égarement; aka: One Wild Moment

A middle-aged man begins an affair with his best friend's teenage daughter when the two families go on holiday together.

Occasionally witty examination of the generation gap.

wd Claude Berri   ph André Neau   m Michel Stelio   ed Jacques Witta

Jean-Pierre Marielle, Victor Lanoux, Christine Dejoux, Arnes Soral, Martine Sarcey

† In 1984, the film was remade by Stanley Donen as Blame It On Rio.

'Bold ideas ... bolder people!'
Summer and Smoke
US   1961   118m   Technicolor   Panavision
Paramount/Hal B. Wallis
V*, L

In a small Mississippi town in 1916, the minister's spinster daughter nurses an unrequited love for the local rebel.

Wearisome screen version, in hothouse settings, of a pattern play about earthly and spiritual love.

w James Poe, Meade Roberts   play Tennessee Williams   d Peter Glenville   ph Charles Lang Jnr   m Elmer Bernstein   ad Walter Tyler

Geraldine Page, Laurence Harvey, Una Merkel, John McIntire, Pamela Tiffin, Rita Moreno, Thomas Gomez, Casey Adams, Earl Holliman, Lee Patrick, Malcolm Atterbury

AAN: Elmer Bernstein; Geraldine Page; Una Merkel

A Summer at Grandpa's **
Taiwan   1984   102m   colour
Marble Road (Chang Hwa-Kuen)
original title: Tung-Tung-te chia-ch'i

When his mother becomes seriously ill, a 12-year-old boy is sent with his small sister to stay with his grandfather in the country.

An episodic film of some charm, in part nostalgic for the idle pleasures of a holiday, and in part a comment on the world of adults as seen through the eyes of the disinterested young. The family is the bedrock of society, remarks a notary marrying a reluctant couple, but the family depicted here seems on the point of disintegration, surviving only by absorbing some antisocial behaviour.

w Chu Tien-Wen, Hou Hsiao-Hsien   d Hou Hsiao-Hsien   ph Chen K'un'hou   m Edward Yang

Wang Qiguang, Zhou Shengli, Gu Jun, Mei Fang, Lin Xiuling

Summer Holiday **
US   1948   92m   Technicolor
MGM (Arthur Freed)
V*, L

Life for a small-town family at the turn of the century.

Musical version of a famous play: excellent individual numbers, warm playing and sympathetic scenes, but a surprising lack of overall style.

w Frances Goodrich, Albert Hackett, Ralph Blane   play Ah Wilderness by Eugene O'Neill   d Rouben Mamoulian   ph Charles Schoenbaum   md Lennie Hayton   songs Harry Warren, Ralph Blane   ch Charles Walters

Walter Huston, Mickey Rooney, Frank Morgan, Agnes Moorehead, Butch Jenkins, Selena Royle, Marilyn Maxwell, Gloria de Haven, Anne Francis

† The film was finished in 1946 and held back because it seemed unlikely to succeed.

Summer Holiday *

GB 1962 109m Technicolor Cinemascope
ABP/Ivy (Kenneth Harper)
V, V*

Four young London Transport mechanics borrow a
double-decker bus for a continental holiday.

Pacy, location-filmed youth musical with plenty of
general appeal.

w Peter Myers, Ronnie Cass   d Peter Yates   ph John
Wilcox   md Stanley Black

Cliff Richard, Lauri Peters, Melvyn Hayes, Una Stubbs,
Teddy Green, Ron Moody, Lionel Murton, David
Kossoff

Summer Interlude *

Sweden 1950 97m bw
Svensk Filmindustri (Alan Ekelund)
V*
original title: *Sommarlek*

A prima ballerina remembers a happy summer she
spent with a boy who was tragically killed.

Melancholy romance quite typical of its creator but
with less density of meaning than usual.

w Ingmar Bergman, Herbert Grevenius   d Ingmar
Bergman   ph Gunnar Fischer, Bengt Jarnmark
m Erik Nordgren

Maj-Britt Nilsson, Birger Malmsten, Alf Kjellin

Summer Lightning: see *Scudda Hoo, Scudda Hay*

Summer Madness: see *Summertime*

Summer Magic *

US 1963 104m Technicolor
Walt Disney (Ron Miller)
V*

Children help their widowed mother in 1912 Boston.

Amiable remake of *Mother Carey's Chickens*,
irreproachably presented.

w Sally Benson   d James Neilson   ph William
Snyder   m Buddy Baker   songs the Sherman
Brothers

Hayley Mills, Burl Ives, Dorothy McGuire, Darren
McGavin, Deborah Walley, Una Merkel, Eddie
Hodges, Michael J. Pollard

Summer Manoeuvres: see *Les Grandes
Manoeuvres*

The Summer of Aviya *

Israel 1988 95m colour
Mutual/HSA (Eitan Evan, Gila Almagor)
original title: *Hakayitz Shel Aviya*

A young girl's unhappy relationship with her
disturbed mother comes to a head during a summer
holiday.

Affecting, semi-autobiographical account of suffering
in the aftermath of the Second World War.

w Eli Cohen, Gila Almagor, Chaim Buzaglo
novel Gila Almagor   d Eli Cohen   ph David
Gurfinkel   m Shem-Tov Levi   ad Yoram Shayer
ed Tova Ne'eman

Gila Almagor, Kaipo Cohen, Eli Cohen, Marina
Rosetti, Avital Dicker, Dina Avrech

'Eli Cohen transforms the horror and trauma of the
past and its excesses into a measured, assured and
humane expression of what can be achieved in the
face of evil.' – *MFB*

Summer of '42 *

US 1971 103m Technicolor
Warner/Mulligan-Roth (Richard Alan Roth)
V, V*, L

Adolescents make sexual explorations on a New
England island in 1942.

Well-observed indulgence in the new permissiveness.

w Herman Raucher   d Robert Mulligan   ph Robert
Surtees   m Michel Legrand

Jennifer O'Neill, Gary Grimes, Jerry Houser, Oliver
Conant, Lou Frizell

AA: Michel Legrand

AAN: Herman Raucher; Robert Surtees

Summer of the Seventeenth Doll

US/Australia 1959 94m bw
UA/Hecht-Hill-Lancaster (Leslie Norman)
US title: *Season of Passion*

Two cane-cutters on their annual city lay-off have
woman trouble.

Miscast and unsatisfactory rendering of a good play;
the humour has evaporated.

w John Dighton   play Ray Lawler   d Leslie
Norman   ph Paul Beeson   m Benjamin Frankel

Ernest Borgnine, John Mills, Angela Lansbury, Anne
Baxter, Vincent Ball

A Summer Place

US 1959 130m Technicolor
Warner (Delmer Daves)
V*, L

Romantic summer adventures of teenagers and their
elders on an island off the coast of Maine.

Sex among the idle rich: a routine piece of Hollywood
gloss, bowdlerized from a bestseller.

wd Delmer Daves   novel Sloan Wilson   ph Harry
Stradling   m Max Steiner

Richard Egan, Dorothy McGuire, Sandra Dee, Arthur
Kennedy, Troy Donahue, Constance Ford, Beulah
Bondi

Summer Stock *

US 1950 109m Technicolor
MGM (Joe Pasternak)
V*, L, S
GB title: *If You Feel Like Singing*

A theatre troupe takes over a farm for rehearsals, and
the lady owner gets the bug.

Likeable but halting musical with the star's weight
problems very obvious.

w George Wells, Sy Gomberg   d Charles Walters
ph Robert Planck   md Johnny Green   ch Nick
Castle

Judy Garland, Gene Kelly, Gloria de Haven, Carleton
Carpenter, Eddie Bracken, Phil Silvers, Hans Conried

† June Allyson was to have starred, but became
pregnant.

Summer Storm *

US 1944 106m bw
(UA) Angelus

In 1912 Russia, a provincial judge falls for a local
mancatcher.

One of Hollywood's occasional aberrations, an
attempt to do something very European in typical
west coast style. An interesting failure.

w Rowland Leigh   story *The Shooting Party* by Anton
Chekhov   d Douglas Sirk   ph Archie Stout
md Karl Hajos

George Sanders, Linda Darnell, *Edward Everett Horton*,
Anna Lee, Hugo Haas, John Philiber, Sig Rumann,
André Charlot

'There are bits of acting and photography which put it
as far outside the run of American movies as it
laudably tries to be. But most of it had for me the
sporty speciousness of an illustrated drugstore
classic.' – *James Agee*

AAN: Karl Hajos

A Summer Story

GB 1988 97m colour
Warner/ITC (Danton Rissner)
V*

A lawyer recalls his love for a working-class country
girl.

Stiff upper lip romance, pretty to look at but
providing little else.

w Penelope Mortimer   story *The Apple Cart* by John
Galsworthy   d Piers Haggard   ph Kenneth
MacMillan   m Georges Delerue   pd Leo Austin
ed Ralph Sheldon

James Wilby, Imogen Stubbs, Ken Colley, Sophie
Ward, Susannah York, Jerome Flynn

Summer Vacation 1999

Japan 1988 90m Eastmancolor
New Century/CBS-Sony (Yutaka Okada, Eiji Kishi)
original title: *1999 – Nen No Natsu Yasumi*

Three adolescent boys spending the summer at an
otherwise deserted school think their friend has
returned from the dead when they are joined by a
fourth boy who exactly resembles him.

Slow-moving, self-consciously poetic and finally
ridiculous tale of repressed love and teenage angst,
not helped by the fact that the boys are played by
girls.

w Rio Kishida   d Shusuke Kaneko   ph Kenji
Takama   m Yuriko Nakamura   ad Shu Yamaguchi

Eri Miyajima, Tomoko Otakara, Miyuki Nakano, Rie
Mizuhara

Summer Wishes, Winter Dreams *

US 1973 88m Technicolor
Columbia/Rastar (Jack Brodsky)
V*

A neurotic New York housewife goes to pieces when
her mother dies but finds a new understanding of her
husband when she accompanies him on a trip to the
World War II battlefields.

Menopausal melodrama, well observed but
disappointingly wispy and underdeveloped.

w Stewart Stern   d Gilbert Cates   ph Gerald
Hirschfeld   m Johnny Mandel

Joanne Woodward, Martin Balsam, Sylvia Sidney, Dori
Brenner, Win Forman

AAN: Joanne Woodward; Sylvia Sidney

Summer with Monika *

Sweden 1952 97m bw
Svensk Filmindustri (Allan Ekelund)
V*

A wild, restless girl defies her parents and goes off
with her boyfriend for an island holiday. Her
subsequent pregnancy and motherhood don't in the
least suit her, and the father is left alone with the
baby.

Probably truthful but rather glum and
unsophisticated drama of young love; not among
Bergman's most interesting films.

wd Ingmar Bergman   novel Per Anders Fogelstrom
ph Gunnar Fischer   m Erik Nordgren

Harriet Andersson, Lars Ekborg

Summertime ***

US 1955 99m Eastmancolor
London Films/Lopert Productions (Ilya Lopert)
V*, L
GB title: *Summer Madness*

An American spinster has a holiday in Venice and
becomes romantically involved.

Delightful, sympathetic travelogue with dramatic
asides, great to look at and hinging on a single superb
performance.

w David Lean, H. E. Bates *play The Time of the Cuckoo*
by Arthur Laurents *d* David Lean *ph* Jack Hildyard
m Sandro Cicognini

Katharine Hepburn, Rossano Brazzi, Isa Miranda,
Darren McGavin, Mari Aldon, André Morell

'The eye is endlessly ravished.' – *Dilys Powell*

AAN: David Lean; Katharine Hepburn

Summertree

US 1971 88m Eastmancolor
Warner/Bryna (Kirk Douglas)
V*

A bored student learns about life and becomes a
Vietnam casualty.

Well-made, rather tedious character study; good social
observation.

w Edward Hume, Stephen Yafa *play* Ron Cowen
d Anthony Newley *ph* Richard C. Glouner
m David Shire

Michael Douglas, Brenda Vaccaro, Jack Warden,
Barbara Bel Geddes

The Sun Also Rises **

US 1957 129m Eastmancolor Cinemascope
TCF (Darryl F. Zanuck)

In Paris after World War I an impotent journalist
meets a nymphomaniac lady of title, and they and
their odd group of friends have various saddening
adventures around Europe.

Not a bad attempt to film a difficult novel, though
Cinemascope doesn't help and the last half hour
becomes turgid. *The Last Flight* (qv) conveyed the same
atmosphere rather more sharply.

w Peter Viertel *novel* Ernest Hemingway *d* Henry
King *ph* Leo Tover *m* Hugo Friedhofer

Tyrone Power, Ava Gardner, *Errol Flynn*, Eddie Albert,
Mel Ferrer, Robert Evans, Juliette Greco, Gregory
Ratoff, Marcel Dalio, Henry Daniell

The Sun Never Sets

US 1939 98m bw
Universal (Rowland V. Lee)

Two brothers in the African colonial service prevent a
munitions baron from plunging the world into war.

Stiff upper lip melodrama, very dated.

w W. P. Lipscomb *d* Rowland V. Lee *ph* George
Robinson *md* Charles Previn *m* Frank Skinner

Basil Rathbone, Douglas Fairbanks Jnr, Virginia
Field, Lionel Atwill, Barbara O'Neil, C. Aubrey
Smith, Melville Cooper

'Confusing script and poor direction relegate this to
lower duals . . . brightest thing is the title.' – *Variety*

The Sun Shines Bright **

US 1953 92m bw
Republic/Argosy (John Ford, Merian C. Cooper)

Forty years after the Civil War, the judge of a
Kentucky town still has trouble quelling the
Confederate spirit.

Mellow anecdotes of time gone by, scrappily linked
but lovingly polished; a remake of a Will Rogers
vehicle *Judge Priest*.

w Lawrence Stallings *stories* Irwin S. Cobb
d John Ford *ph* Archie Stout *m* Victor Young

Charles Winninger, Arleen Whelan, John Russell,
Stepin Fetchit, Milburn Stone, Grant Withers, Russell
Simpson

'Passages of quite remarkable poetic feeling . . . alive
with affection and truthful observation.' – *Lindsay
Anderson*

Sun Valley Serenade *

US 1941 86m bw
TCF (Milton Sperling)
V*, L

The band manager at an Idaho ice resort takes care of
a Norwegian refugee.

Simple-minded musical which still pleases because of
the talent involved.

w Robert Ellis, Helen Logan *d* H. Bruce
Humberstone *ph* Edward Cronjager *songs* Mack
Gordon, Harry Warren *m* Emil Newman

Sonja Henie, *Glenn Miller and his Orchestra*, John Payne,
Milton Berle, Lynn Bari, Joan Davis, *The Nicholas
Brothers*, Dorothy Dandridge

AAN: Edward Cronjager; Emil Newman; song
'Chattanooga Choo-Choo' (*m* Harry Warren, *ly* Mack
Gordon)

Suna no Onna: see *Woman of the Dunes*

Sunbonnet Sue

US 1945 89m bw
Monogram/Scott R. Dunlap

In the 1890s, a Park Avenue matron objects to her
niece singing in a Bowery saloon.

Old-fashioned family movie for the innocent-minded.

w Paul Gerard Smith, Bradford Ropes *d* Ralph
Murphy

Gale Storm, Phil Regan, Minna Gombell, George
Cleveland, Raymond Hatton, Alan Mowbray

AAN: Edward J. Kay (music)

Sunburn

GB/US 1979 98m Technicolor
Hemdale/Bind Films (David Korda)
V*

An insurance investigator hires a model to act as his
wife while he trails a suspected murderer in
Acapulco.

All sun and skin and swirling cameras, this entire
movie is a seventies cliché, but it provides some fitful
amusement.

w John Daly, Stephen Oliver, James Booth
novel The Bind by Stanley Ellin *d* Richard
C. Sarafian *ph* Alex Phillips Jnr *m* John Cameron

Farrah Fawcett, Charles Grodin, Art Carney, Joan
Collins, William Daniels, John Hillerman, Eleanor
Parker, Keenan Wynn

'It's about three decent people. They will break your
heart!'

Sunday, Bloody Sunday ***

GB 1971 110m DeLuxe
UA/Vectia (Joseph Janni)
V*, L

A young designer shares his sexual favours equally
between two loves of different sexes, a Jewish doctor
and a lady executive.

Stylishly made character study with melodramatic
leanings, rather self-conscious about its risky subject
but, scene by scene, both adult and absorbing, with
an overpowering mass of sociological detail about the
way we live.

w Penelope Gilliatt *d* John Schlesinger *ph* Billy
Williams *m* Ron Geesin *pd* Luciana Arrighi

Glenda Jackson, Peter Finch, Murray Head, Peggy
Ashcroft, Maurice Denham, Vivian Pickles, Frank
Windsor, Tony Britton, Harold Goldblatt

'This is not a story about the loss of love, but about its
absence.' – *Roger Ebert*

AAN: Penelope Gilliatt; John Schlesinger; Glenda
Jackson; Peter Finch

'Their eyes met! Their lips questioned! Their arms
answered!'

Sunday Dinner for a Soldier *

US 1944 86m bw
TCF (Walter Morosco)

A poor family living on a derelict Florida houseboat

scrape together enough money to invite a soldier for a
meal.

Sentimental little flagwaving romance, quite
sympathetically presented and agreeably underacted.

w Wanda Tuchock, Melvin Levy *d* Lloyd Bacon
ph Joe MacDonald *m* Alfred Newman

Anne Baxter, John Hodiak, Charles Winninger, Anne
Revere, Connie Marshall, Chill Wills, Bobby Driscoll,
Jane Darwell

'Simple, true and tender, the best propaganda
America has put out in the current year.' – *Richard
Winnington*

Sunday in August: see *Domenico d'Agosto*

Sunday in New York *

US 1963 105m Metrocolor
MGM/Seven Arts (Everett Freeman)

Complications in the love life of a brother and sister,
each of whom thinks the other is very moral.

Fresh, fairly adult sex comedy with New York
backgrounds.

w Norman Krasna *play* Norman Krasna *d* Peter
Tewkesbury *ph* Leo Tover *m* Peter Nero

Cliff Robertson, Rod Taylor, Jane Fonda, Robert Culp,
Jo Morrow, Jim Backus

Sunday in the Country **

France 1984 94m Eastmancolor
Sara Films/Films A2/Little Bear (Alain Sarde)
V, V*

original title: *Un Dimanche à la Campagne*

An elderly artist enjoys a Sunday visit from his
family.

Delightful, slight and moving sketch for a drama,
which gives nothing but pleasure yet is hard to
recapture.

w Bertrand and Colo Tavernier *novella* Pierre Bost
d Bertrand Tavernier *ph* Bruno de Keyzer *m* Gabriel
Fauré

Louis Ducreux, Sabine Azema, Michel Aumont,
Geneviève Mnich, Monique Chaumette, Claude
Winter

Sunday Too Far Away

Australia 1977 94m colour
South Australian Film Corporation
V*

Itinerant sheep shearers become involved in an
industrial dispute.

Almost the archetypal Australian outback movie,
good to look at but hard to care about.

w John Dingwall *d* Ken Hannam

Jack Thompson, Max Cullen, Reg Lye, John Ewart

Sundays and Cybèle *

France 1962 110m bw Franscope
Terra/Fides/Orsa/Trocadéro (Romain Pinès)
V*

original title: *Cybèle ou les Dimanches de Ville d'Avray*

An amnesiac ex-pilot strikes up a friendship with an
abandoned 12-year-old girl, but the relationship is
misunderstood and ends in tragedy.

A fashionable film of its time which now has little to
offer: its director's reputation sagged alarmingly when
he went to Hollywood.

w Serge Bourguignon, Antoine Tudal *novel* Bernard
Echasseriaux *d* Serge Bourguignon *ph* Henri
Decaë *m* Maurice Jarre

Hardy Kruger, Nicole Courcel, Patricia Gozzi, Daniel
Ivernel

'Studied charm and a creakingly melodramatic
dénouement take the place of any serious attempt to
probe the characters or situation . . . the film is so
busily preoccupied with being as attractive, visually

and sentimentally, as it possibly can, that it never has time to consider what it is being attractive about.' – *Tom Milne, MFB*

'Uneven but highly meritorious . . . a near-triumph of the intelligently mobile camera.' – *John Simon*

AA: best foreign film

AAN: script; Maurice Jarre

Sundown
US   1941   91m   bw
Walter Wanger
V*

The adopted daughter of an Arab trader assists British troops in Africa during World War II.

Artificial-looking romantic actioner with good cast.

w Barre Lyndon   *d* Henry Hathaway   *ph* Charles Lang   *m* Miklos Rozsa   *ad* Alexander Golitzen

Gene Tierney, Bruce Cabot, George Sanders, Harry Carey, Joseph Calleia, Cedric Hardwicke, Carl Esmond, Reginald Gardiner

AAN: Charles Lang; Miklos Rozsa; Alexander Golitzen

The Sundowners **
GB/Australia   1960   133m   Technicolor
Warner (Gerry Blatner)
V*, L

In the twenties an Irish sheepdrover and his family travel from job to job in the Australian bush.

Easygoing, often amusing but lethargically developed family film with major stars somewhat ill at ease. Memorable sequences.

w Isobel Lennart   *novel* Jon Cleary   *d* Fred Zinnemann   *ph* Jack Hildyard   *m* Dimitri Tiomkin

Robert Mitchum, Deborah Kerr, *Glynis Johns, Peter Ustinov,* Michael Anderson Jnr, Dina Merrill, *Wylie Watson,* Chips Rafferty

'For all Zinnemann's generous attention to character, the hints of longing, despair and indomitable spirit, the overall impression remains one of sheer length and repetition and synthetic naturalism.' – *Richard Winnington*

AAN: best picture; Isobel Lennart; Fred Zinnemann; Deborah Kerr; Glynis Johns

'In a world gone mad – a love story!'
Sunflower
France/Italy   1970   101m   Technicolor
Champion/Concordia
V*, S

A man and wife are separated during World War II.

Sudsy romantic drama, partly shot in Moscow but with no other redeeming feature.

w Tonino Guerra, Cesare Zavattini, Georgiy Mdivani   *d* Vittorio de Sica   *m* Henry Mancini

Sophia Loren, Marcello Mastroianni, Lyudmyla Savelyeva

AAN: Henry Mancini

Sunny *
US   1930   81m   bw
Warner

A showgirl falls for a rich young man.

Tinny early musical notable for its star.

w Humphrey Pearson, Henry McCarthy   *musical play* Otto Harbach, Oscar Hammerstein II, Jerome Kern   *d* William A. Seiter   *ph* Ernest Haller

Marilyn Miller, Lawrence Grey, Jack Donahue, Mackenzie Ward, O. P. Heggie

Sunny *
US   1941   97m   bw
RKO/Imperator (Herbert Wilcox)

Adequate remake of the above.

w Sig Herzig   *d* Herbert Wilcox   *ph* Russell Metty   *m* Anthony Collins

Anna Neagle, Ray Bolger, John Carroll, Edward Everett Horton, Frieda Inescort, Grace and Paul Hartman

AAN: Anthony Collins

Sunny Side Up *
US   1929   80m   bw   ('Multicolor' sequence)
Fox
V*, L

A slum girl falls for the son of a rich Southampton family.

Typical early musical of the softer kind; rewarding for those who can project themselves back.

w/m/ly B. G. de Sylva, Lew Brown, Ray Henderson   *d* David Butler   *ph* Ernest Palmer

Janet Gaynor, Charles Farrell, El Brendel, Marjorie White, Sharon Lynn

Sunnyside *
US   1919   27m approx (24 fps)   bw   silent
First National/Charles Chaplin

The overworked odd job man at a country hotel has a pastoral dream.

Very mildly funny star comedy which was intended as a satire on the D. W. Griffith/Charles Ray type of rural drama then popular. It doesn't work in this vein either.

wd Charles Chaplin   *ph* Rollie Totheroh

Charles Chaplin, Edna Purviance, Tom Wilson, Albert Austin, Henry Bergman

Sunrise **
US   1927   97m (24 fps)   bw   silent
Fox
V*

A villager in love with a city woman tries to kill his wife but then repents and spends a happy day with her.

Lyrical melodrama, superbly handled: generally considered among the finest Hollywood productions of the twenties.

w Carl Meyer   *novel* A Trip to Tilsit by Hermann Sudermann   *d* F. W. Murnau   *ph* Karl Struss, Charles Rosher   *m* (sound version) Hugo Riesenfeld   *ad* Rochas Gliese

Janet Gaynor, George O'Brien, Margaret Livingston

OPENING TITLE: 'This story of a man and his wife is of nowhere and everywhere, you might hear it anywhere and at any time.'

'It is filled with intense feeling and in it is embodied an underlying subtlety . . . exotic in many ways for it is a mixture of Russian gloom and Berlin brightness.' – *Mordaunt Hall, New York Times*

'Not since the earliest, simplest moving pictures, when locomotives, fire engines and crowds in streets were transposed to the screen artlessly and endearingly, when the entranced eye was rushed through tunnels and over precipices on runaway trains, has there been such joy in motion as under Murnau's direction.' – *Louise Bogan, The New Republic*

'The story is told in a flowing, lyrical German manner that is extraordinarily sensual, yet perhaps too self-conscious, too fable-like, for American audiences.' – *Pauline Kael, 70s*

AA: Karl Struss, Charles Rosher; Janet Gaynor; Unique and Artistic Picture

AAN: Rochas Gliese

Sunrise at Campobello *
US   1960   143m   Technicolor
Warner/Dore Schary
V*, L

The early life of Franklin Roosevelt, including his battle against polio and return to politics.

Static filming of a rather interesting Broadway success and of a memorable performance.

w Dore Schary   *play* Dore Schary   *d* Vincent J. Donehue   *ph* Russell Harlan   *m* Franz Waxman   *ad* Edward Carrere

Ralph Bellamy, Greer Garson, Ann Shoemaker, Hume Cronyn, Jean Hagen

AAN: Greer Garson; art direction

Sunset
US   1988   107m   Technicolor   Panavision
Columbia/Tri-Star/ML Delphi (Tony Adams)
V*, L

In Hollywood as an adviser to a studio making a film of his life, Wyatt Earp teams up with cowboy star Tom Mix to solve a murder.

A comedy-thriller that misfires.

wd Blake Edwards   *story* Rod Amateau   *ph* Anthony B. Richmond   *m* Henry Mancini   *pd* Rodger Maus   *ed* Robert Pergament

Bruce Willis, James Garner, Malcolm McDowell, Mariel Hemingway, Kathleen Quinlan, Jennifer Edwards, Patricia Hodge, Richard Bradford, M. Emmet Walsh, Joe Dallesandro

'It happened in Hollywood . . . a love story . . . a drama real and ruthless, tender and terrifying!'
Sunset Boulevard ***
US   1950   110m   bw
Paramount (Charles Brackett)
V*, L

A luckless Hollywood scriptwriter goes to live with a wealthy older woman, a slightly dotty and extremely possessive relic of the silent screen.

Incisive melodrama with marvellous moments but a tendency to overstay its welcome; the first reels are certainly the best, though the last scene is worth waiting for and the malicious observation throughout is a treat.

w Charles Brackett, Billy Wilder, D. M. Marshman Jnr   *d* Billy Wilder   *ph* John F. Seitz   *m* Franz Waxman   *ed* Arthur Schmidt, Doane Harrison

Gloria Swanson, William Holden, Erich von Stroheim, Fred Clark, Nancy Olson, Jack Webb, Lloyd Gough, *Cecil B. de Mille,* H. B. Warner, Anna Q. Nilsson, Buster Keaton, Hedda Hopper

'That rare blend of pungent writing, expert acting, masterly direction and unobtrusively artistic photography which quickly casts a spell over an audience and holds it enthralled to a shattering climax.' – *New York Times (T.M.P.)*

'Miss Swanson's performance takes her at one bound into the class of Boris Karloff and Tod Slaughter.' – *Richard Mallett, Punch*

'A weird, fascinating motion picture about an art form which, new as it is, is already haunted by ghosts.' – *Otis L. Guernsey Jnr, New York Herald Tribune*

'The most intelligent film to come out of Hollywood for years; lest the idea of intelligence in the cinema should lack allure, let me say that it is also one of the most exciting.' – *Dilys Powell*

AA: script; Franz Waxman

AAN: best picture; Billy Wilder (as director); John F. Seitz; Gloria Swanson; William Holden; Erich von Stroheim; Nancy Olson; editing

Sunset in Vienna
GB   1937   73m   bw
Herbert Wilcox
US title: *Suicide Legion*

An Italian cavalry officer finds that his wife's brother is a spy, and shoots him.

Dated romantic melodrama with music.

w Florence Tranter *d* Norman Walker

Lilli Palmer, Tullio Carminati, John Garrick, Geraldine Hislop

'For the price of a movie, you'll feel like a million!'
The Sunshine Boys *

US   1975   111m   Metrocolor
MGM/Rastar (Ray Stark)
V, V*, L

Two feuding old vaudeville comedians come together for a television spot, and ruin it.

Over-extended sketch in which one main role is beautifully underplayed, the other hammed up, and the production lacks any kind of style. The one-liners are good, though.

w Neil Simon *play* Neil Simon *d* Herbert Ross
ph David M. Walsh *md* Harry V. Lojewski

Walter Matthau, *George Burns*, Richard Benjamin, Carol Arthur

'It's just shouting, when it needs to be beautifully timed routines.' – *New Yorker*

'They feud with ill-matched resources, and the movie's visual delights vanish with the title sequence.' – *Sight and Sound*

† George Burns stepped in when Jack Benny became ill and died.

AA: George Burns

AAN: Neil Simon; Walter Matthau

Sunshine Susie
GB   1931   87m   bw
Gainsborough

A banker pretends to be a clerk in order to court a typist.

Viennese-set comedy which worked at the time but quickly dated.

w Angus MacPhail, Robert Stevenson, Victor Saville, Noel Wood-Smith *play The Private Secretary* by Franz Schultz *d* Victor Saville

Renate Muller, Jack Hulbert, Owen Nares, Morris Harvey, Sybil Grove

Sunstruck
Australia   1972   92m   Eastmancolor
Immigrant (Jack Neary, James Grafton)

A shy Welsh schoolmaster emigrates to the Australian outback.

Simple-minded, uninspired, predictable family comedy for star fans.

w Stan Mars *d* James Gilbert *ph* Brian West
m Peter Knight

Harry Secombe, Maggie Fitzgibbon, John Meillon, Dawn Lake

Il Suo Modo di Fari: see *The Girl Who Couldn't Say No*

Suor Omicidi: see *Killer Nun*

'The judge sentenced slumlord Louis Kritski to six months in his own building. He would have been better off in jail.'
The Super
US   1991   85m   colour
Largo/JVC (Charles Gordon)
V, V*, L

A New York landlord is forced to live in one of his slum properties.

A misfiring movie, comic when it should be serious, and sentimental the rest of the time.

w Sam Simon *d* Rod Daniel *ph* Bruce Surtees
m Miles Goodman *pd* Kristi Zea *ed* Jack Hofstra

Joe Pesci, Vincent Gardenia, Madolyn Smith-Osborne, Ruben Blades, Stacey Travis, Carole Shelley, Paul Benjamin

'A lesson, perhaps, that those movies that fail to get a theatrical release do, with the occasional exception, deserve the direct-to-video treatment.' – *Empire*

† The film was released direct to video in Britain.

The Super Cops
US   1974   94m   Metrocolor
St Regis Films/UA

Two New York cops are suspended for breaking too many rules, but wage their private war on crime.

Low-life crime melodrama which plays effectively enough as a lighter-hearted *Serpico*.

w Lorenzo Semple Jnr *book* L. H. Whittemore
d Gordon Parks Jnr

Ron Leibman, David Selby, Sheila Frazier, Pat Hingle, Dan Frazer

Super Fuzz: see *Supersnooper*

'This Ain't No Game.'
Super Mario Brothers
US   1993   104m   Technicolor
Entertainment/Lightmotive/Allied/Cinergi (Jake Eberts, Roland Joffé)
V, V*, S

The Mario brothers, two plumbers, rescue a princess from a universe in another dimension, where reptilian humanoids, descended from dinosaurs, plan to rule both worlds.

An attempt to transfer a best-selling Nintendo video game to the screen; it doesn't work.

w Parker Bennett, Terry Runté, Ed Solomon, based on characters and concept created by Shigeru Miyamato, Takashi Tezuka *d* Rocky Morton, Annabel Jankel *ph* Dean Semler *m* Alan Silvestri *pd* David L. Snyder *sp* Christopher Francis Woods, Patrick Tatopoulos *ed* Caroline Ross

Bob Hoskins, John Leguizamo, Dennis Hopper, Samantha Mathis, Fisher Stevens, Richard Edson, Rona Shaw, Dana Kaminski, Lance Henrikson

'There are plenty of gags, but not one laugh.' – *Variety*

'One and a half square miles of plywood went into the making of *Super Mario Brothers*, and that was just for the performances.' – *Sight and Sound*

Superdad
US   1974   95m   Technicolor
Walt Disney
V*

A lawyer is determined to rule the life of his teenage daughter.

Bumbling farce with frenzied and unattractive characters.

w Joseph L. McEveety *d* Vincent McEveety

Bob Crane, Barbara Rush, Kurt Russell, Joe Flynn, Kathleen Cody

Superfly
US   1972   98m   Technicolor
Warner (Sig Shore)
V*, S

The New York adventures of black cocaine peddlers.

'Sensational' comedy with violence in which the pushers exit laughing. Tedious and deplorable.

w Philip Fenty *d* Gordon Parks *ph* James Signorelli *m* Curtis Mayfield

Ron O'Neal, Carl Lee, Sheila Frazier

'It suggests that New York is now nothing more than a concrete junkieyard.' – *Philip Strick*

Supergirl *
GB   1984   124m   colour   Panavision
Cantharus/Ilya Salkind (Pierre Spengler, Timothy Burrill)
V, V*, L, S

A Krypton power source falls into the hands of a power-hungry witch, and Supergirl is sent to retrieve it.

Playful comic strip spectacular which entertains in *Wizard of Oz* style for most of its way but was savaged by the critics.

w David Odell *d* Jeannot Szwarc *ph* Alan Hume
m Jerry Goldsmith *pd* Richard MacDonald

Helen Slater, Faye Dunaway, Peter O'Toole, Mia Farrow, Brenda Vaccaro, Peter Cook, Simon Ward, Marc McClure, Hart Bochner, David Healy

The Supergrass
GB   1985   105m   colour
Recorded Releasing
V, V*

The police unwisely believe that a boaster can lead them to a drug ring.

For those who enjoy the somewhat remote satirical humour of Channel 4's *The Comic Strip*.

w Pete Richens, Peter Richardson *d* Peter Richardson

Adrian Edmondson, Jennifer Saunders, Peter Richardson, Dawn French

Superman
US   1948   bw   serial: 15 eps
Columbia
V*, L

The man from Krypton who poses as mild-mannered Clark Kent combats The Spider Lady.

The subject makes this serial fairly lively – livelier in fact than the multi-million-dollar 1978 film.

d Spencer Bennet, Thomas Carr

Kirk Alyn, Noel Neill, Tommy Bond, Carol Forman, George Meeker

'You'll believe a man can fly!'
Superman
US/GB   1978   142m   colour   Panavision
Warner/Alexander Salkind (Pierre Spengler)
V, V*, L, S

A baby saved from the planet Krypton when it explodes grows up as a newspaperman and uses his tremendous powers to fight evil and support the American way.

Long, lugubrious and only patchily entertaining version of the famous comic strip, with far too many irrelevant preliminaries and a misguided sense of its own importance.

w Mario Puzo, David Newman, Robert Benton, Leslie Newman *d* Richard Donner *ph* Geoffrey Unsworth *m* John Williams *pd* John Barry
sp various *ed* Stuart Baird

Christopher Reeve, Marlon Brando, Margot Kidder, Jackie Cooper, Glenn Ford, Phyllis Thaxter, Trevor Howard, Gene Hackman, Ned Beatty, Susannah York, Valerie Perrine

'Though one of the two or three most expensive movies made to date, it's cheesy-looking, and the plotting is so hit or miss that the story never seems to get started; the special effects are far from wizardly and the editing often seems hurried and jerky just at the crucial points.' – *New Yorker*

'It gives the impression of having been made in panic – in fear that style or too much imagination might endanger its approach to the literal-minded.' – *Pauline Kael, New Yorker*

'The epitome of supersell.' – *Les Keyser, Hollywood in the Seventies*

† Reprehensible records were set by Brando getting three million dollars for a ten-minute performance (and then suing for a share of the gross); and by the incredible 7½-minute credit roll at the end.
†† Tiny roles were played by Noel Neill, who was Lois Lane in the TV series, and by Kirk Alyn, who was Superman in two serials.

AAN: John Williams; editing; sound; visual effects

Superman 2
US   1980   127m   Technicolor   Panavision
Warner/Alexander Salkind (Pierre Spengler)
V, V*, L

Three renegade Kryptonians threaten Earth with a space bomb.

Half the first episode was devoted to a creaky and unnecessary setting up of plot and characters. This sequel is all the better for diving straight into action, but a classic it isn't, even of the comic strip kind.

w Mario Puzo, David Newman, Leslie Newman
d Richard Lester   ph Geoffrey Unsworth, Robert Paynter   m Ken Thorne

Christopher Reeve, Gene Hackman, Ned Beatty, Jackie Cooper, Sarah Douglas, Margot Kidder, Valerie Perrine, Susannah York, Terence Stamp, Jack O'Halloran, E. G. Marshall

Superman 3
GB   1983   125m   colour   Panavision
Dovemead/Cantharus (Pierre Spengler)
V*, L

Synthetic Kryptonite warps Superman's character, but his conscience is reawakened by a plea from a small boy.

Sometimes humorous but overwritten and overacted variation on a tired theme. The special effects are the thing, but there's too much padding in between.

w David Newman, Leslie Newman   d Richard Lester   ph Robert Paynter   m Ken Thorne
pd Peter Murton

Christopher Reeve, Richard Pryor, Jackie Cooper, Marc McClure, Annette O'Toole, Annie Ross, Pamela Stephenson, Robert Vaughn, Margot Kidder

Superman 4: The Quest for Peace
GB   1987   89m   colour   JDC widescreen
Cannon
V, V*, L

Superman determines that the world shall lay down its nuclear arms.

Stolid dialogue and poor technicalities are evident throughout what will surely be the last of the series.

w Lawrence Konner, Mark Rosenthal, Christopher Reeve   d Sidney J. Furie

Christopher Reeve, Gene Hackman, Jackie Cooper, Marc McClure, Sam Wanamaker, Mariel Hemingway, Margot Kidder

'Her heart cried out for love – yet her hands reached out to destroy!'
Supernatural *
US   1933   67m   bw
Paramount (Victor and Edward Halperin)

A girl is possessed by the soul of a dead murderess.

Mad doctor nonsense, interestingly but not very successfully styled.

w Harvey Thew, Brian Marlow   d Victor Halperin
ph Arthur Martinelli

Carole Lombard, H. B. Warner, Randolph Scott, Vivienne Osborne, Alan Dinehart

'A 65-minute ghost story that dies after the first half-hour.' – Variety

Supersnooper
Italy/US   1981   94m   Technicolor
Columbia/Trans-Cinema TV (Maximilian Wolkoff)
V*
aka: Super Fuzz

A Miami cop develops superhuman powers after being exposed to radiation.

Stolid comedy with poor special effects.

w Sergio Corbucci, Sabatino Giuffini   d Sergio Corbucci   ph Silvano Ippoliti   m La Bionda
pd Marco Dentici   ed Eugene Ballaby

Terence Hill, Ernest Borgnine, Joanne Dru, Marc Lawrence, Julie Gordon, Lee Sandman

Support Your Local Gunfighter
US   1971   92m   DeLuxe
UA/Cherokee/Brigade (Burt Kennedy)
V, V*

A con man jumps a train at a small mining town and is mistaken for a dreaded gunfighter.

Disappointing sequel to the following; just a couple of good jokes.

w James Edward Grant   d Burt Kennedy
ph Harry Stradling Jnr   m Jack Elliott, Allyn Ferguson

James Garner, Suzanne Pleshette, Joan Blondell, Jack Elam, Chuck Connors, Harry Morgan, Marie Windsor, Henry Jones, John Dehner

Support Your Local Sheriff **
US   1968   92m   Technicolor
UA/Cherokee (William Bowers)
V, V*

Gold is found near a Western village, and the resulting influx of desperate characters causes problems for the sheriff.

Amusing comedy, drawing on many Western clichés.

w William Bowers   d Burt Kennedy   ph Harry Stradling Jnr   m Jeff Alexander

James Garner, Joan Hackett, Walter Brennan, Jack Elam, Henry Morgan, Bruce Dern, Henry Jones

'It rejuvenates a stagnating genre by combining just the right doses of parody and affectionate nostalgia.' – Jan Dawson

Suppose They Gave a War and Nobody Came
US   1969   114m   DeLuxe
Engel – Auerbach/ABC (Fred Engel)
V*

Three accident-prone PROs try to give the army a good name in a town which wishes it would go away; they eventually cause panic by arriving at a dance in a tank.

Muddled farce which may have hoped to be satire.

w Don McGuire, Hal Captain   d Hy Averback
ph Burnett Guffey   m Jerry Fielding

Tony Curtis, Brian Keith, Ernest Borgnine, Ivan Dixon, Suzanne Pleshette, Tom Ewell, Bradford Dillman, Arthur O'Connell, Robert Emhardt, John Fiedler, Don Ameche

El Sur: see The South

The Sure Thing
US   1985   94m   DeLuxe
Roger Birnbaum/Monument/Embassy
V, V*, L

Two uneasy couples travel west to California for Christmas.

Slightly unsettling youth comedy which, in the form of It Happened One Night, seems to be saying that friendship is more important than sex.

w Steven L. Bloom, Jonathan Roberts   d Rob Reiner

John Cusack, Daphne Zuniga, Anthony Edwards, Boyd Gaines, Tim Robbins, Lisa Jane Persky, Viveca Lindfors

'Two sounds clash: old wine being poured into new bottles, and familiar barrels being scraped.' – Philip French, Observer

Surf Ninjas
US   1993   87m   DeLuxe
Entertainment/New Line (Ezven Kolar)
V, V*

Two Californian surfers discover that they are the rightful heirs to an island kingdom in the South China Sea, ruled by an evil dictator.

Jokey action film aimed at an audience too young to enjoy the real thing.

w Dan Gordon   d Neal Israel   m David Kitay
pd Michael Novotny   ed Tom Walls

Leslie Nielsen, Ernie Reyes Jnr, Rob Schneider, Tone Loc, John Karlen, Ernie Reyes Snr, Kelly Hu

'Brain-dead though this film is, it has a certain goofy charm that's almost endearing.' – Sight and Sound

Surprise Package
GB   1960   100m   bw
Columbia/Stanley Donen

An American gangster is deported to the same Mediterranean island as an exiled European king, whose crown gets stolen.

Flat and feeble comedy which defeats its stars.

w Harry Kurnitz   novel Art Buchwald   d Stanley Donen   ph Christopher Challis   m Benjamin Frankel

Yul Brynner, Noël Coward, Mitzi Gaynor, Bill Nagy, Eric Pohlmann, George Coulouris, Warren Mitchell

Sur: see South

Surrender
US   1931   69m   bw
Fox

A French soldier in a German prison camp falls in love with a German girl at the nearby castle.

Flabby drama which seems constantly about to make symbolic points.

w S. N. Behrman, Sonya Levien   play Axelle by Pierre Benoit   d William K. Howard

Warner Baxter, Leila Hyams, Ralph Bellamy, C. Aubrey Smith, William Pawley, Alexander Kirkland

'Anaemic picture product, not for A houses in big towns.' – Variety

Surrender
US   1987   95m   TVC colour
Cannon (Aaron Spelling, Alan Greisman)
V*, L, S

A writer with a history of unsatisfactory relationships with women falls for an artist who has had similar experiences with men.

Lacklustre attempt at a romantic comedy, taken at a snail's pace and with dialogue that fails to sparkle.

wd Jerry Belson   ph Juan-Ruiz Anchia   m Michel Colombier   pd Lily Kilvert   ed Wendy Greene Bricmont

Sally Field, Michael Caine, Steve Guttenberg, Peter Boyle, Jackie Cooper, Julie Kavner, Louise Lasser

Surrounded by Women: see Between Two Women

Survive
Mexico/US   1976   86m   Technicolor
EMI/Robert Stigwood-Allan Carr/Conacine/Productora Filmica (Rene Cardona Jnr)

After a plane crash high in the Andes, surviving members of a rugby team resort to cannibalism in order to survive.

Unpleasant low-budget film, based on a true story and concentrating on the grislier aspects.

wd Rene Cardona Snr (English adaptation Martin Sherman) *book* Clay Blair Jnr *ph* Luis Medina *m* Gerald Fried *ad* A. L. de Guevara *ed* Marshall M. Borden

Hugo Sitlitz, Norma Lazareno, Luzma Aguilar, Fernando Larranaga, Lorenzo de Rodas, Luz Ma

'In its original form this low budget Mexican production clearly had little to offer: a sketchy script, feeble performances and scenes cloaked in fog which conveniently disguised polystyrene snow. Having been doctored in America for universal consumption, and fitted out with Dragnet-style commentary and limply banal dialogue, it is quite unbearable.' – *David McGillivray, MFB*

† The event was also the basis of the 1992 Hollywood movie *Alive* (qv).

The Survivors
US   1983   102m   Metrocolor
Columbia-Delphi-Rastar-William Sackheim
V*, L

An executive and a gas station attendant, both potential victims of a hit man, take refuge in the snowy mountains of Vermont.

Bewilderingly unfocused black comedy with some pleasant barbs along the way.

w Michael Leeson *d* Michael Ritchie *ph* Billy Williams *m* Paul Chihara *pd* Gene Callahan *ed* Richard A. Harris

Walter Matthau, Robin Williams, Jerry Reed, James Wainwright, Kristen Vigard, Annie McEnroe

Susan and God *
US   1940   117m   bw
MGM (Hunt Stromberg)
V*
GB title: *The Gay Mrs Trexel*

A flighty society woman gets religion but fails to practise what she preaches.

Unusual comedy-drama for MGM to tackle, but a fairly successful one for high-class audiences.

w Anita Loos *play* Rachel Crothers *d* George Cukor *ph* Robert Plack *m* Herbert Stothart

Joan Crawford, Fredric March, Ruth Hussey, John Carroll, Rita Hayworth, Nigel Bruce, Bruce Cabot, Rita Quigley, Rose Hobart, Constance Collier, Gloria de Haven, Marjorie Main

'It's not a good comedy, but it has a certain fascination, because the theme is such an odd one for Hollywood to have attempted at all.' – *Pauline Kael, 70s*

'Thrill to them together!'
Susan Lenox, Her Fall and Rise *
US   1931   76m   bw
MGM (Paul Bern)
V*
GB title: *The Rise of Helga*

A farm girl flees to the city when her father tries to marry her off to a brute.

Moderate star melodrama with the star somewhat miscast.

w Wanda Tuchock *novel* David Graham Phillips *d* Robert Z. Leonard *ph* William Daniels

Greta Garbo, Clark Gable, Jean Hersholt, John Miljan, Alan Hale

'A torrid romance that will fascinate the femmes.' – *Variety*

'If you like your romance spread thick, your passions strong and your Garbo hot, don't miss this.' – *Photoplay*

---

† The author of the book had been shot by a crank who disapproved of his treatment of women.

Susan Slade
US   1961   116m   Technicolor
Warner (Delmer Daves)

An engineer brings his family back to San Francisco from Chile, and his teenage daughter runs into problems of the heart.

Stilted, busy sudser.

wd Delmer Daves *novel* Doris Hume *ph* Lucien Ballard *m* Max Steiner

Connie Stevens, Troy Donahue, Dorothy McGuire, Lloyd Nolan, Brian Aherne, Natalie Schaefer, Grant Williams, Bert Convy, Kent Smith

Susan Slept Here
US   1954   98m   Technicolor
RKO (Harriet Parsons)
V*, L

The Hollywood scriptwriter of a film about youth problems agrees to look after a delinquent teenage girl.

Skittish, would-be piquant comedy; quite unattractive.

w Alex Gottlieb *d* Frank Tashlin *ph* Nicholas Musuraca *md* Leigh Harline *songs* Jack Lawrence, Richard Myers

Dick Powell, Debbie Reynolds, Anne Francis, Glenda Farrell, Alvy Moore, Horace MacMahon

AAN: song 'Hold My Hand'

Susannah of the Mounties *
US   1939   78m   bw
TCF (Kenneth MacGowan)
V*

A little girl who is the only survivor of a wagon train massacre is looked after by the Canadian Mounties.

Adequate star action romance, Shirley's last real success.

w Robert Ellis, Helen Logan *d* William A. Seiter *ph* Arthur Miller *md* Louis Silvers

Shirley Temple, Randolph Scott, Margaret Lockwood, J. Farrell MacDonald, Maurice Moscovitch, Moroni Olsen, Victor Jory

'Strictly for the juvenile trade . . . illogical situations make it no more than a moderate fairy tale.' – *Variety*

'His was a strange secret! Hers was a strange love!'
The Suspect *
US   1944   84m   bw
Universal (Islin Auster)

A henpecked husband kills his wife and is blackmailed.

Efficient studio-bound suspenser with theatrically effective acting.

w Bertram Millhauser *novel* James Ronald *d* Robert Siodmak *ph* Paul Ivano *m* Frank Skinner

Charles Laughton, Henry Daniell, Rosalind Ivan, Ella Raines, Molly Lamont, Dean Harens

'High marks for tension, local colour, story.' – *William Whitebait*

Suspect *
GB   1960   81m   bw
British Lion/The Boulting Brothers

Government research chemists find a traitor in their midst.

Entertaining but fairly routine spy melodrama, shot on an experimental low budget but confined to lower berth bookings.

---

w Nigel Balchin *novel Sort of Traitors* by Nigel Balchin *d* Roy and John Boulting *ph* Max Greene *m* John Wilkes

Tony Britton, Virginia Maskell, Peter Cushing, Ian Bannen, Raymond Huntley, Donald Pleasence, Thorley Walters, Spike Milligan, Kenneth Griffith

'A better standard of second feature film is badly needed, but the way to do it is not by making pictures which look as though they have strayed from TV.' – *Penelope Houston*

Suspect *
US   1987   121m   colour
Columbia/Tri-Star (John Veitch)
V, V*, L, S

A public defender, with the aid of a member of the jury, uncovers high-level corruption when she defends a deaf-mute tramp accused of murder.

Despite its many implausibilities, a thriller that engages the attention.

w Eric Roth *d* Peter Yates *ph* Billy Williams *m* Michael Kamen *pd* Stuart Wurtzel *ed* Ray Lovejoy

Cher, Dennis Quaid, Liam Neeson, John Mahoney, Joe Mantegna, Philip Bosco, E. Katherine Kerr, Fred Melamed, Lisbeth Bartlett, Paul D'Amato

Suspected Person
GB   1943   78m   bw
Associated British

Thieves fall out and are tracked by police.

Slightly bitter crime drama which adequately filled half a bill.

wd Lawrence Huntington

Clifford Evans, Patricia Roc, David Farrar, Robert Beatty

'Unmasking a beautiful woman's secret and unholy desires!'
Suspense
US   1946   103m   bw
Monogram (Maurice and Frank King)

A tough guy crashes an ice palace and makes a play for the boss's skating star wife.

Heavy melodrama with skating interludes; remarkably similar in plot to the more famous *Gilda*. Chiefly remarkable as Monogram's most expensive film.

w Philip Yordan *d* Frank Tuttle *ph* Karl Struss

Belita, Barry Sullivan, Albert Dekker, Bonita Granville, Eugene Pallette, George E. Stone, Leon Belasco

Suspicion **
US   1941   99m   bw
RKO (Alfred Hitchcock)
V, V*, L

A sedate young girl marries a playboy, and comes to suspect that he is trying to murder her.

Rather artificial and stiff Hitchcock suspenser, further marred by an ending suddenly switched to please the front office. Full of the interesting touches one would expect.

w Samson Raphaelson, Alma Reville, Joan Harrison *novel Before the Fact* by Francis Iles *d Alfred Hitchcock* *ph* Harry Stradling *m* Franz Waxman

Joan Fontaine, Cary Grant, Nigel Bruce, Cedric Hardwicke, May Whitty, Isabel Jeans, Heather Angel, Leo G. Carroll

'The fact that Hitchcock throws in a happy end during the last five minutes, like a conjuror explaining his tricks, seems to me a pity; but it spoils the film only in retrospect, and we have already had our thrills.' – *William Whitebait, New Statesman*

AA: Joan Fontaine

AAN: best picture; Franz Waxman

'The only thing more terrifying than the last twelve minutes of this film is the first eighty!'

'Once you've seen it you will never again feel safe in the dark!'

Suspiria **

Italy 1976 97m Eastmancolor Technovision
Seda Spettacoli (Claudio Argento)
V, V*, L

A young American dance student arrives at dead of night at a continental academy where murder is the order of the day.

Psycho meets *The Exorcist*, with no holds barred: a genuinely scary thriller with gaudy visuals and a screaming sound track. A pyrotechnic display for those who can take it.

w Dario Argento, Daria Nicolodi d Dario Argento ph Luciano Tovoli m Dario Argento Goblin

Jessica Harper, Alida Valli, Joan Bennett, Stefania Casini, Udo Kier

'Thunderstorms and explicitly grotesque murders pile up as Argento happily abandons plot mechanics to provide a bravura display of his technical skill.' – *Time Out*

Sutter's Gold

US 1936 75m bw
Universal

During the California gold rush an immigrant has to fight for his rights when a strike starts on his land.

Patchily arresting Western which by costing much more than it should started the exit of Carl Laemmle from the chairman's office.

w Jack Kirkland, Walter Woods and George O'Neil d James Cruze

Edward Arnold, Lee Tracy, Binnie Barnes, Katherine Alexander, Addison Richards, Montagu Love, John Miljan

† Most of the action footage was reused in a 1939 quickie, *Mutiny on the Blackhawk*.

Suzy *

US 1936 95m bw
MGM (Maurice Revnes)
V*

A French air ace of World War I marries an American showgirl; they then find that her former husband, thought dead, is still alive.

Proficient star comedy-drama with romance, action, comedy and a complex plot. A showcase for its stars.

w Dorothy Parker, Alan Campbell, Horace Jackson, Lenore Coffee novel Herbert Gorman d George Fitzmaurice ph Ray June m William Axt

Jean Harlow, Cary Grant, Franchot Tone, Benita Hume, Lewis Stone

AAN: song 'Did I Remember' (*m* Walter Donaldson, *ly* Harold Adamson)

Svengali **

US 1931 81m bw
Warner

In 1890s Paris, a hypnotist turns a girl into a great opera singer but she does not reciprocate his love.

Victorian fantasy melodrama with a great grotesque part for the star and interesting artwork.

w J. Grubb Alexander novel *Trilby* by George du Maurier d Archie Mayo ph Barney McGill ad Anton Grot

John Barrymore, Marian Marsh, Luis Alberni, Lumsden Hare, Donald Crisp, Paul Porcasi

'A slow and old-fashioned melodrama.' – *Variety*

'Barrymore never needed occult powers to be magnetic, but interest flags when he's offscreen.' – *New Yorker, 1978*

AAN: Barney McGill; Anton Grot

Svengali

GB 1954 82m Eastmancolor
Renown/Alderdale (Douglas Pierce)
V*

Flatulent remake which does have the virtue of following the original book illustrations but is otherwise unpersuasive.

wd Noel Langley ph Wilkie Cooper m William Alwyn ad Fred Pusey

Donald Wolfit, Hildegarde Neff, Terence Morgan, Derek Bond, Paul Rogers, David Kossoff, Hubert Gregg, Noel Purcell, Alfie Bass, Harry Secombe

S.W.A.L.K.: see *Melody*

Swallows and Amazons

GB 1974 92m Eastmancolor
EMI/Theatre Projects (Richard Pilbrow)

In the twenties four children have adventures in the Lake District.

Mild family film, great to look at but lacking in real excitement or style.

w David Wood novel Arthur Ransome d Claude Whatham ph Denis Lewiston m Wilfred Josephs

Virginia McKenna, Ronald Fraser, Simon West, Sophie Neville, Zanna Hamilton, Stephen Grenville

Swamp Fire

US 1946 68m bw
Pine-Thomas/Paramount

The rehabilitation of a war veteran bar pilot in the treacherous waters at the mouth of the Mississippi.

Routine romantic melo, notable only as its star's only screen appearance in long trousers.

w Geoffrey Homes d William Pine

Johnny Weissmuller, Buster Crabbe, Virginia Grey, Carol Thurston, Edwain Maxwell, Pedro de Cordoba

Swamp Thing

US 1981 91m Technicolor
UA/Swamp Films (Benjamin Melniker, Michael E. Uslan)
V*, L

A scientist, turned by accident into a cross between a man and a plant, battles against an evil colleague who wants to take over the world.

Less a horror pic, or a big-screen comic strip, more a sentimental story of vegetable love, it is about as interesting as watching grass grow.

wd Wes Craven ph Robin Goodwin m Harry Manfredini ad David Nichols, Robb Wilson King sp William Munns ed Richard Bracken

Louis Jourdan, Adrienne Barbeau, Ray Wise, David Hess, Nicholas Worth, Don Knight

† It was followed by a sequel, *Return of The Swamp Thing* (qv).

Swamp Water **

US 1941 90m bw
TCF (Irving Pichel)
GB title: *The Man Who Came Back*

A fugitive holds out for years in the Okefenokee swamp, and affects the lives of the local township.

A strange little story, not very compelling as drama but with striking photography and atmosphere. Remade more straightforwardly as *Lure of the Wilderness* (qv).

w Dudley Nichols story Vereen Bell d Jean Renoir ph Peverell Marley m David Buttolph

Walter Huston, Walter Brennan, Anne Baxter, Dana Andrews, Virginia Gilmore, John Carradine, Eugene Pallette, Ward Bond, Guinn Williams

'So bad it's terrific.' – *Otis Ferguson*

The Swan *

US 1956 108m Eastmancolor Cinemascope
MGM (Dore Schary)
V*, L

In 1910 Hungary, a girl of noble stock is groomed to marry the crown prince.

Interesting chiefly for a typical Hollywood reaction to a news event; about to lose their top star to a real life prince, MGM dusted off this old and creaky property for her last film. The star cast can't make much of it and the treatment is very heavy.

w John Dighton play Ferenc Molnar d Charles Vidor ph Robert Surtees m Bronislau Kaper ad Cedric Gibbons, Randall Duell

Grace Kelly, Alec Guinness, Louis Jourdan, Agnes Moorehead, Jessie Royce Landis, Brian Aherne, Leo G. Carroll, Estelle Winwood, Robert Coote

'Balancing between artificial comedy and a no less artificial romantic theme, the film ultimately requires considerably greater finesse and subtlety in the handling.' – *Penelope Houston*

Swanee River **

US 1939 84m Technicolor
TCF (Darryl F. Zanuck)

The life and loves of Stephen Foster.

Attractive, unsurprising family film in rich early colour, sparked by Jolson as E. P. Christy.

w John Taintor Foote, Philip Dunne d Sidney Lanfield ph Bert Glennon md Louis Silvers

Don Ameche, *Al Jolson*, Andrea Leeds, Felix Bressart, Russell Hicks

'An unimpressive story: will hit profitable but not big b.o.' – *Variety*

AAN: Louis Silvers

Swann in Love **

France 1983 111m colour
Gaumont/FR3/SFPC/Bioskop/Films du Losange (Margaret Menegoz)
V, V*
original title: *Un Amour de Swann*

An elegant Jew in 19th-century Paris society becomes obsessed by a beautiful demi-mondaine.

Reasonably successful attempt to film part of an unfilmable book. Comparisons with *Letter from an Unknown Woman* are inevitable.

w Peter Brook, Jean-Claude Carrière, Marie-Hélène Estienne, from the works of Marcel Proust d Volker Schlöndorff ph Sven Nykvist m Hans Werner Henze

Jeremy Irons, Ornella Muti, Alain Delon, Fanny Ardant, Marie-Christine Barrault, Anne Bennent

'A film of more taste than vision.' – *Gilbert Adair, MFB*

'If you've read the original, forget it.' – *Volker Schlöndorff*

'A failure, maybe, but one that deserves to be seen.' – *Observer*

The Swarm

US 1978 116m Technicolor Panavision
Warner (Irwin Allen)
V*, L

African killer bees menace the US.

Very obvious all-star disaster movie with risible dialogue. A box-office flop, probably because several TV movies had already tackled the same subject.

w Stirling Silliphant novel Arthur Herzog d Irwin Allen ph Fred J. Koenekamp m Jerry Goldsmith sp L. B. Abbott, Van Der Veer, Howard Jensen

Michael Caine, Katharine Ross, Richard Widmark, Richard Chamberlain, Olivia de Havilland, Fred MacMurray, Ben Johnson, Lee Grant, José Ferrer,

Patty Duke Astin, Slim Pickens, Bradford Dillman, Henry Fonda, Cameron Mitchell

'You could pass it all off as a sick joke, except that it cost twelve million dollars, twenty-two million bees, and several years of someone's life.' – *Guardian*

'The story is of a banality matched only by the woodenness of the acting.' – *Barry Took, Punch*

Swashbuckler *
US 1976 101m Technicolor Panavision
Universal/Elliott Kastner (Jennings Lang)
V*, L
GB title: *The Scarlet Buccaneer*

Rival pirates help a wronged lady.

Uninspired reworking of some old Errol Flynn ideas; the idea was pleasant, but the old style is sadly lacking.

w Jeffrey Bloom d James Goldstone ph Philip Lathrop m John Addison pd John Lloyd

Robert Shaw, James Earl Jones, Peter Boyle, Geneviève Bujold, Beau Bridges, Geoffrey Holder

'This tacky pastepot job can't make up its mind whether it's serious, tongue-in-cheek, satirical, slapstick, burlesque, parody or travesty; but be assured it is all of the above.' – *Variety*

'The talented cast is left to play living statues, immobilized by dumb dialogue and awkward action.' – *Judith Crist*

Sweeney! *
GB 1976 89m Technicolor
EMI/Euston (Ted Childs)

Scotland Yard's Flying Squad investigates a suicide and uncovers an elaborate political blackmail scheme.

Enjoyable big screen version of a pacy, violent TV cop show.

w Ranald Graham d David Wickes ph Dusty Miller m Denis King

John Thaw, Denis Waterman, Barry Foster, Ian Bannen, Colin Welland, Michael Coles, Joe Melia

Sweeney 2
GB 1978 108m Technicolor
Euston Films (Ted Childs)

The flying squad discovers that a series of armed bank robberies is being committed by a gang of expatriates who return from a luxurious Malta development for each caper.

Silly, sluggish and violent extension of thin material which would scarcely have made a good one-hour TV episode. There isn't even an exciting climax.

w Troy Kennedy Martin d Tom Clegg ph Dusty Miller m Tony Hatch

John Thaw, Dennis Waterman, Barry Stanton, Denholm Elliott, Nigel Hawthorne, John Flanagan, David Casey

Sweeney Todd, the Demon Barber of Fleet Street *
GB 1936 68m bw
George King
V*

A barber kills his customers and makes them into 'mutton pies' for sale at the shop next door.

Decent version of a famous old melodrama; stilted as film-making, but preserving a swaggering star performance.

w Frederick Hayward, H. F. Maltby play George Dibdin-Pitt d George King ph Jack Parker

Tod Slaughter, Bruce Seton, Eve Lister, Stella Rho, Ben Soutten

Sweepings *
US 1933 77m bw
RKO

An ambitious Chicago merchant finds that his sons do not wish to emulate him.

Curious family melodrama based on fact; interesting but not exactly inspiring.

w Lester Cohen novel Lester Cohen d John Cromwell

Lionel Barrymore, Alan Dinehart, Eric Linden, William Gargan, Gloria Stuart, Gregory Ratoff

'Nothing to interest the women and a subject too sombre to interest the men.' – *Variety*

Sweet Adeline
US 1934 85m bw
Warner (Edward Chodorov)
V*

In the 1890s, the daughter of a beer garden owner attracts the attention of a composer and becomes a Broadway star.

Unexceptionable, and quite forgotten, adaptation of a pleasant, old-fashioned Broadway musical.

w Erwin S. Gelsey play Jerome Kern, Oscar Hammerstein II, Harry Armstrong, Dick Gerard d Mervyn Le Roy ph Sol Polito ch Bobby Connolly m/ly Jerome Kern, Oscar Hammerstein II ad Robert Haas

Irene Dunne, Donald Woods, Ned Sparks, Hugh Herbert, Wini Shaw, Louis Calhern, Nydia Westman, Joseph Cawthorn

'As a production in the bigtime musical class, but strictly on merit it rates no better than fair.' – *Variety*

Sweet Aloes: see Give Me Your Heart

'He used love like most men use money!'
Sweet Bird of Youth *
US 1962 120m Metrocolor Cinemascope
MGM/Roxbury (Pandro S. Berman)
V*, L

A Hollywood drifter brings an ageing glamour star back to his home town, but runs into revenge from the father of a girl he had seduced.

Emasculated version of an overwrought play with the author's usual poetic squalor; comatose patches alternate with flashes of good acting and diverting dialogue, but the wide screen and heavy colour don't direct the attention.

wd Richard Brooks play Tennessee Williams ph Milton Krasner md Robert Armbruster m Harold Gellman

Paul Newman, Geraldine Page, *Ed Begley*, Mildred Dunnock, Rip Torn, Shirley Knight, Madeleine Sherwood

AA: Ed Begley

AAN: Geraldine Page; Shirley Knight

'Love is what it's all about!'
Sweet Charity *
US 1969 149m Technicolor Panavision 70
Universal (Robert Arthur)
V*, L

A New York taxi dancer dreams of love.

A revue-type musical bowdlerized from Fellini's *Le notti di Cabiria* accords ill with real New York locations, especially as its threads of plot come to nothing; but behind the camera are sufficient stylists to ensure striking success with individual numbers.

w Peter Stone play Neil Simon d Robert Fosse ph Robert Surtees md Joseph Gershenson m Cy Coleman ly Dorothy Fields

Shirley Maclaine, Ricardo Montalban, John McMartin, *Chita Rivera*, Paula Kelly, Stubby Kaye, Sammy Davis Jnr

'The kind of platinum clinker designed to send audiences flying towards the safety of their television sets.' – *Rex Reed*

AAN: Cy Coleman (as music director)

Sweet Dreams
US 1985 115m Technicolor
Tri-Star/HBO/Silver Screen (Bernard Schwartz)
V*, L, S

The effect on her marriage of the rise to success of folk singer Patsy Cline.

Pleasant, muted, unremarkable modern biopic.

w Robert Getchell d Karel Reisz ph Robbie Greenberg m Charles Gross

Jessica Lange, Ed Harris, Ann Wedgeworth, David Clennon, James Staley

AAN: Jessica Lange

'The Story Of Two Women's Struggle For Survival, Self-Respect And Hard Currency.'
Sweet Emma, Dear Böbe *
Hungary 1992 78m Eastmancolor
Objektiv/Manfred Durniok Filmproduktion (Lajos Ovari, Gabriella Groz)
V
original title: *Édes Emma, Drága Böbe – Vazlatok, Aktok*

Two young female teachers move to Budapest to work, sharing a tatty room together.

A well-made, engrossing study of glum lives.

w István Szabó, Andrea Veszits d István Szabó ph Lajos Koltai m Richard Schumann pd Attila Kovacs ed Eszter Kovacs

Johanna Ter Steege, Eniko Börcsök, Peter Andorai

'The realities of day-to-day life in post-Communist Hungary are vividly brought to life in this compassionate, memorable film. Though the settings and narrative are understandably bleak, the treatment throbs with life and love, resulting in a most satisfying film.' – *Variety*

'The best movie to date about the way ordinary Central Europeans are experiencing the cataclysmic changes following the collapse of Communism.' – *Philip French, Observer*

Sweet Hearts Dance
US 1988 101m Technicolor
Columbia TriStar/Bright Star/Tri-Star ML Delphi Premier Productions (Jeffrey Lurie)
V*, L

A small-town couple experience marital problems.

A drama of small incidents that never builds into a coherent whole.

w Ernest Thompson d Robert Greenwald ph Tak Fujimoto m Richard Gibbs pd James Allen ed Robert Florio, Janet Bartells

Don Johnson, Susan Sarandon, Jeff Daniels, Elizabeth Perkins, Kate Reid, Justin Henry, Holly Marie Combs, Heather Coleman

Sweet Kitty Bellairs
US 1930 60m Technicolor
Warner

A romance of stagecoach days set in Bath.

A decided curiosity to come from this studio in *Little Caesar* days, and not a successful one.

w Hermann Harrison play David Belasco novel Agnes and Egerton Castle d Alfred E. Green

Claudia Dell, Ernest Torrence, Walter Pidgeon, June Collyer, Perry Askam, Lionel Belmore, Flora Finch

'Artistic achievement, but weak on fan pull.' – *Variety*

Sweet Liberty
US 1986 107m colour
Universal/Martin Bregman
V*, L

A college professor is disgusted as he watches the Hollywood filming of his historical novel.

A good idea surprisingly wasted: the plot turns to tedium before the half-way mark.

wd Alan Alda   *ph* Frank Tidy   *m* Bruce Broughton *pd* Ben Edwards   *ed* Michael Economou

Alan Alda, Michael Caine, Michelle Pfeiffer, Lillian Gish, Bob Hoskins, Saul Rubinek, Lois Chiles, Lise Hilboldt

The Sweet Life: see *La Dolce Vita*

Sweet Lorraine *
US   1987   91m   colour
Autumn Pictures (Steve Gomer)
V*

The owner of a rundown hotel in the Catskills has her granddaughter spend the summer working for her.

Gentle and charming film, strong on character.

w Michael Zettler, Shelly Altman   *d* Steve Gomer *ph* Rene Ohashi   *m* Richard Robbins   *pd* David Gropman   *ed* Laurence Solomon

Maureen Stapleton, Trini Alvarado, Lee Richardson, John Bedford Lloyd, Freddie Roman

Sweet Music
US   1934   100m   bw
Warner

An orchestra leader and a girl singer spar a lot but finally make it up.

The slimmest of stories stretches over a few good numbers and some snappy dialogue; but it's all too long.

w Jerry Wald, Carl Erickson and Warren Duff
d Alfred E. Green

Rudy Vallee, Ann Dvorak, Ned Sparks, Helen Morgan, Allen Jenkins, Alice White, Robert Armstrong

Sweet November
US   1968   113m   Technicolor
Warner Seven Arts/Jerry Gershwin, Elliott Kastner

An English tycoon in New York meets a girl who takes a new lover every month because she hasn't long to live.

Irritating exercise in eccentric sentimentality, not helped by twitchy stars.

w Herman Raucher   *d* Robert Ellis Miller *ph* Daniel L. Fapp   *m* Michel Legrand

Anthony Newley, Sandy Dennis, Theodore Bikel, Burr de Benning

Sweet Revenge: see *Dandy the All-American Girl*

The Sweet Ride
US   1967   110m   DeLuxe   Panavision
TCF (Joe Pasternak)

Surfers and drop-outs on a California beach have woman trouble.

Teenage melodrama, well produced but abysmal of content.

w Tom Mankiewicz   *novel* William Murray *d* Harvey Hart   *ph* Robert B. Hauser   *m* Pete Rugolo

Jacqueline Bisset, Tony Franciosa, Michael Sarrazin, Bob Denver, Michael Wilding

Sweet Rosie O'Grady *
US   1943   79m   Technicolor
TCF (William Perlberg)

A *Police Gazette* reporter tries to uncover the past of a musical comedy star.

Pleasant 1890s musical with plenty of zest but a lack of good numbers. A typical success of the war years.

w Ken Englund   *d* Irving Cummings   *ph* Ernest Palmer   *ch* Hermes Pan   *songs* Mack Gordon, Harry Warren   *ad* James Basevi, Joseph C. Wright

Betty Grable, Robert Young, Adolphe Menjou, Reginald Gardiner, Virginia Grey, Phil Regan, Sig Rumann, Hobart Cavanaugh, Alan Dinehart

† Remake of *Love Is News;* remade as *That Wonderful Urge.*

'This is the story of J.J. – but not the way he wants it told!'
Sweet Smell of Success ****
US   1957   96m   bw
UA/Norma/Curtleigh (James Hill)
V, V*, L

A crooked press agent helps a megalomaniac New York columnist break up his sister's marriage.

Moody, brilliant, Wellesian melodrama put together with great artificial style; the plot matters less than the photographic detail and the skilful manipulation of decadent characters, bigger than life-size.

w Clifford Odets, Ernest Lehman   *d* Alexander Mackendrick   *ph* James Wong Howe   *m* Elmer Bernstein *ad* Edward Carrere

Burt Lancaster, *Tony Curtis*, Martin Milner, Sam Levene, Susan Harrison, Barbara Nichols, *Emile Meyer*

'A sweet slice of perversity, a study of dollar and power worship.' – *Pauline Kael*

Sweet William
GB   1980   90m   Eastmancolor
Kendon
V*

A London girl discovers that her American lover is constantly unfaithful.

A situation in search of a story makes this slight piece with its wry observations rather less memorable than the average TV play.

w Beryl Bainbridge   *novel* Beryl Bainbridge *d* Claude Whatham

Sam Waterston, Jenny Agutter, Anna Massey, Daphne Oxenford, Arthur Lowe, Geraldine James

Sweetheart of the Campus
US   1941   64m   bw
Jack Fier/Columbia
GB title: *Broadway Ahead*

A college principal objects to Ozzie Nelson's band playing at a nearby night spot.

Evanescent musical filler.

w Robert D. Andrews, Edmund Hartmann *d* Edward Dmytryk

Ruby Keeler, Ozzie Nelson, Harriet Hilliard, Gordon Oliver, Don Beddoe, Kathleen Howard

Sweethearts **
US   1938   120m   Technicolor
MGM (Hunt Stromberg)
V*, L

Two stars of the musical stage never stop fighting each other.

The lightest and most successful of the MacDonald/Eddy musicals, with an excellent script, production and cast.

w Dorothy Parker, Alan Campbell   *d* W. S. Van Dyke *ph* Oliver Marsh, Allen Davey   *md* Herbert Stothart *m* Victor Herbert

Jeanette MacDonald, Nelson Eddy, Frank Morgan, Ray Bolger, Florence Rice, Mischa Auer, Fay Holden, Reginald Gardiner, Herman Bing, Allyn Joslyn, Raymond Walburn, Lucile Watson, Gene Lockhart

'It will disappoint because of length, and general lethargy and sameness of production values.' – *Variety*

AA: Special Award to Oliver Marsh and Allen Davey for 'colour photography'

AAN: Herbert Stothart

Sweetie **
Australia   1989   100m   colour
Electric/Arena Film (John Maynard)
V, V*, L

A woman with marital problems is visited by her unbalanced but exuberant sister.

Deliberately off-balance movie that explores the dynamic of family relationships and stifled lives.

w Gerard Lee, Jane Campion   *d* Jane Campion *ph* Sally Bongers   *m* Martin Armiger   *ad* Peter Harris   *ed* Veronika Haussler

Genevieve Lemon, Karen Colston, Tom Lycos, Jon Darling, Dorothy Barry, Michael Lake, Andre Pataczek, Jean Hadgraft

Swell Guy
US   1946   86m   bw
Mark Hellinger/Universal-International

A war correspondent comes home to visit his family but turns out to be something of a heel.

Ironical drama which deserved better casting and handling.

w Richard Brooks   *play The Hero* by Gilbert Emery *d* Frank Tuttle

Sonny Tufts, Ann Blyth, Ruth Warrick, William Gargan, John Litel, Thomas Gomez, Millard Mitchell, Mary Nash

'They had the pools – but he had their wives!'
The Swimmer *
US   1968   94m   Technicolor
Columbia/Horizon/Dover (Frank Perry, Roger Lewis)
V*, L

A man clad only in trunks swims his way home via the pools of his rich friends, and arrives home to find that his success is a fantasy.

Strange but compelling fable, too mystifying for popular success, about the failure of the American dream. Annoyingly inexplicit, but well made and sumptuously photographed in a variety of Connecticut estates.

w Eleanor Perry,   *short stories* John Cheever   *d* Frank Perry, Sydney Pollack   *ph* David L. Quaid *m* Marvin Hamlisch

Burt Lancaster, Janice Rule, Kim Hunter, Diana Muldaur, Cornelia Otis Skinner, Marge Champion

The Swimmer **
USSR   1981   105m   bw/colour
Gruzia Film
original title: *Plovec*

A middle-aged man invades a film set to recount the exploits of his father and grandfather, famous swimmers who were cheated of their success.

The film's subtitle provides an indication of the contents: 'Twenty-two little stories from the life of three swimmers', but not the charm. It was banned by the Soviets for a time, presumably because of its celebration of individuality.

wd Irakli Kvirikadze   *ph* Turam Tugshi *m* Teimuraz Bakuradze

Elgudza Burduli, Ruslan Mikaberidze, Baadur Tsuladze, Guram Pirtskhalava, Nana Kvachantiradze, Gia Lezhava, Imedo Kahkiani

Swimming to Cambodia **
US   1987   87m   colour   Panavision
Mainline/Cinecom International/The Swimming Co (R. A. Shafransky)
V, V*, L

An actor who played a bit part in *The Killing Fields* reminisces about his experiences in Thailand.

Witty and fascinating one-man show, skilfully filmed.

w Spalding Gray *d* Jonathan Demme *ph* John Bailey *m* Laurie Anderson *pd* Sandy McLeod *ed* Carol Littleton

Spalding Gray

The Swindlers: see *Il Bidone*

The Swing **

West Germany 1983 133m colour
Pelemele Film/Roxy/Pro-Ject (Percy Adlon)
original title: *Die Schaukel*

In the 1930s an elderly novelist recalls her childhood with her exuberant brothers and sisters and improvident mother and father.

Charming and humorous evocation of family life.

wd Percy Adlon *novel* Annette Kolb *d* Percy Adlon *ph* Jürgen Martin *m* Peer Raben

Anja Jaenicke, Rolf Illig, Christine Kaufmann, Lena Stolze, Joachim Bernhard, Susanne Herlet

Swing Fever

US 1943 80m bw
MGM

A bandleader uses hypnotism to train a boxer.

Witless farrago with sprightly musical numbers.

w Nat Perrin, Warren Wilson *d* Tim Whelan

Kay Kyser and his band, Marilyn Maxwell, Nat Pendleton, William Gargan, Lena Horne

Swing High Swing Low **

US 1937 97m bw
Paramount (Arthur Hornblow Jnr)
V*

A talented trumpeter goes on a bender but is rescued by his wife.

Backstage comedy-drama, a beautifully cinematic version of a very tedious story also filmed as *Dance of Life* (1929) and *When My Baby Smiles at Me* (1948).

w Virginia Van Upp, Oscar Hammerstein II *play Burlesque* by George Manker Walters, Arthur Hopkins *d* Mitchell Leisen *ph* Ted Tetzlaff *md* Boris Morros *m* Victor Young

Carole Lombard, Fred MacMurray, Charles Butterworth, Jean Dixon, Dorothy Lamour, Harvey Stephens, Franklin Pangborn, Anthony Quinn

'No reason to believe it won't jam 'em at the gate . . . it's a cinch for the younger trade, and will satisfy general audience standards.' – *Variety*

'Enough concentrated filmcraft to fit out half a dozen of those gentlemen who are always dashing around in an independent capacity making just the greatest piece of cinema ever.' – *Otis Ferguson*

Swing Kids

US 1993 114m Technicolor
Buena Vista/Hollywood (Mark Gordon, John Bard Manulis)
V, V*, S

In Germany during the rise of the Nazis, a group of young men is trapped between the attractions of American swing music and the Hitler Youth.

An extremely peculiar movie, which makes little attempt at a period authenticity, apart from its music, and seems unlikely to appeal to any audience, least of all the young.

w Jonathan Marc Feldman *d* Thomas Carter *ph* Jerzy Zielinski *m* James Horner *pd* Allan Cameron *ed* Michael R. Miller

Robert Sean Leonard, Christian Bale, Frank Whaley, Barbara Hershey, Kenneth Branagh, Tushka Bergen, David Tom, Julia Stemberger

'Apart from its appealing young cast and period score, it has precious little to entice audiences.' – *Variety*

Swing Shift

US 1984 100m Technicolor
Warner/Lantana/Hawn-Sylbert/Jerry Bick
V, V*, L

During World War II, in her husband's absence at war, a woman factory hand has an affair with a co-worker.

Surprisingly dreary romantic drama on a subject which could at least have had a livelier surface despite the lack of surprise in what passes for plot.

w 'Rob Morton' (Ron Nyswaner, Bo Goldman, Nancy Dowd) *d* Jonathan Demme *ph* Tak Fujimoto *m* Patrick Williams *pd* Peter Jamison *ed* Craig McKay

Goldie Hawn, Kurt Russell, Christine Lahti, Fred Ward, Ed Harris

'Bland, muddled and inconclusive.' – *Steve Jenkins, MFB*

AAN: Christine Lahti (supporting actress)

Swing, Teacher, Swing: see *College Swing*

Swing Time **

US 1936 103m bw
RKO (Pandro S. Berman)
V, V*, L

A dance team can't get together romantically because he has a commitment to a girl back home.

Satisfactory but unexciting musical vehicle for two stars at the top of their professional and box-office form.

w Howard Lindsay, Allan Scott *d* George Stevens *ph* David Abel *md* Nathaniel Shilkret *songs* Jerome Kern, Dorothy Fields *ch* Hermes Pan

Fred Astaire, Ginger Rogers, Victor Moore, Helen Broderick, Eric Blore, Betty Furness, Georges Metaxa

AA: song 'The Way You Look Tonight'

AAN: Hermes Pan

Swing Your Lady *

US 1937 77m bw
Warner (Sam Bischoff)

A promoter gets involved in the problems of a hillbilly wrestler.

Minor comedy with some laughs.

w Joseph Schrank, Maurice Leo *story Toehold on Artemus* by H. R. Marsh *d* Ray Enright *ph* Arthur Edeson *m* Adolph Deutsch

Humphrey Bogart, Louise Fazenda, Nat Pendleton, Frank McHugh, Penny Singleton, Allen Jenkins, Ronald Reagan, The Weaver Brothers and Elviry

'A comedy of not immense proportions, it is nevertheless a rollicking, considerably different laugh-piece which should do from average to good business everywhere.' – *Variety*

The Swinger

US 1966 81m Technicolor
Paramount/George Sidney

When a girl writer's wholesome stories are rejected, she pretends to have a naughty past.

With-it comedy which audiences preferred to be without.

w Lawrence Roman *d* George Sidney *ph* Joseph Biroc *m* Marty Paich

Ann-Margret, Tony Franciosa, Robert Coote, Yvonne Romain, Horace MacMahon, Nydia Westman

'A hectically saucy mixture of lechery, depravity, perversion, voyeurism and girlie magazines . . . a heavy, witless pudding.' – *MFB*

The Swinging Maiden: see *The Iron Maiden*

Swirl of Glory: see *Sugarfoot*

The Swiss Family Robinson

US 1940 93m bw
(RKO) Gene Towne, Graham Baker

A shipwrecked family builds a new home on a desert island.

Pleasing low-budgeter.

w Gene Towne, Graham Baker, Walter Ferris *novel* Johann Wyss *d* Edward Ludwig *ph* Nicholas Musuraca

Thomas Mitchell, Edna Best, Freddie Bartholomew, Tim Holt, Terry Kilburn

'In outlook, dialogue and manner it is frankly old-fashioned.' – *MFB*

The Swiss Family Robinson *

GB 1960 126m Technicolor Panavision
Walt Disney (Bill Anderson, Basil Keys)
V*, L

Quite pleasing comedy adventure from the children's classic.

w Lowell S. Hawley *d* Ken Annakin *ph* Harry Waxman *m* William Alwyn

John Mills, Dorothy McGuire, James MacArthur, Tommy Kirk, Kevin Corcoran, Janet Munro, Sessue Hayakawa, Cecil Parker

Swiss Miss *

US 1938 73m bw
(MGM) Hal Roach
V, V (C), V*

Two mousetrap salesmen in Switzerland run into trouble with a cook, a gorilla and two opera singers.

Operetta style vehicle which constrains its stars, since their material is somewhat below vintage anyway. Not painful to watch, but disappointing.

w James Parrott, Felix Adler, Charles Nelson *d* John G. Blystone *ph* Norbert Brodine

Stan Laurel, Oliver Hardy, Walter Woolf King, Della Lind, Eric Blore

'Story, production, acting and direction suggest a revival of early sound filmusicals presented with stage technique.' – *Variety*

The Swissmakers

Switzerland 1978 108m Eastmancolor
Lyssy/Rex/Willora/Schoch/Ecco

Cases of a department investigating applicants for naturalization.

Amusing satirical comedy which presumably has more bite in its home territory.

w Rolf Lyssy and Christa Maerker *d* Rolf Lyssy

Walo Luond, Emil Steinberger, Beatrice Kessler

'For a ladykiller like Steve there was a fate worse than death: when he got to heaven they sent him back . . . with some modifications . . . It's tough being a woman in a man's world.'

Switch

US 1991 103m Technicolor Panavision
Columbia TriStar/Odyssey-Regency/HBO/Cinema Plus/LP/Beco (Tony Adams)
V, V*, L, S

Murdered by old flames, a male chauvinist is sent back to Earth as a woman and told that he can live again if he can find a woman who likes him.

Bizarre farce that relies on the most obvious of sex-change jokes.

wd Blake Edwards *ph* Dick Bush *m* Henry Mancini *pd* Rodger Maus *ed* Robert Pergament

Ellen Barkin, Jimmy Smits, JoBeth Williams, Lorraine Bracco, Tony Roberts, Perry King, Bruce Martin Payne, Lysette Anthony, Victoria Mahoney

'A talented cast is wasted on a witless script.' – *Sunday Telegraph*

Switching Channels *
US 1988 105m colour
Rank (Martin Ransohoff)
V, V*, L

A television reporter, leaving to be married, agrees to undertake one last assignment.

The third remake of *The Front Page*, this does not match the classic *His Girl Friday*, which, like this version, changed the sex of the hero, but it provides some amusement.

w Jonathan Reynolds   play *The Front Page* by Ben Hecht, Charles MacArthur   d Ted Kotcheff
ph François Protat   m Michel Legrand   pd Anne Pritchard   ed Thom Noble

Kathleen Turner, Burt Reynolds, Christopher Reeve, Ned Beatty, Henry Gibson, George Newbern, Al Waxman, Ken James

'Leopold and Loeb. The Perfect Crime. A Deadly Love Affair.'

Swoon *
US 1992 80m bw
Argos Films (Tom Kalin, Christine Vachon)
V, V*

In Chicago in 1924, two young middle-class homosexual Jews kidnap and kill a young boy as a demonstration of their criminal abilities.

An undeniably stylish account of the murders and murderers which may be closer to the real events and the couple's motivations than either of the other movie versions, *Rope* or *Compulsion*, but which is less effective as a film.

w Tom Kalin, Hilton Als   d Tom Kalin   ph Ellen Kuras   m James Bennett   ed Tom Kalin

Daniel Schlachet, Craig Chester, Ron Vawter, Michael Kirby, Michael Stumm, Valda Z. Drabla, Natalie Stanford

'Kalin suggests that the couple internalised the homophobia and anti-Semitism around them into a pathological self-loathing but he doesn't show that process: his heroes seem simply born to be bad.' – *Sheila Johnston, Independent.*

'A determined attempt to reclaim a pair of notorious murderers on behalf of the gay community.' – *Philip French, Observer*

'Tom Kalin's brilliant debut feature presents history as you've always dreamed it might be: with personal, social and political perspectives all refracted through each other, and with a burning sense of the need to know and understand more, and better.' – *Tony Rayns*

The Sword and the Rose
GB 1952 91m Technicolor
Walt Disney (Perce Pearce)
V*, L

The romantic problems of young Mary Tudor.

Unhistorical charade not quite in the usual Disney vein, and not very good.

w Laurence E. Watkin   novel *When Knighthood Was in Flower* by Charles Major   d Ken Annakin
ph Geoffrey Unsworth   m Clifton Parker

Richard Todd, Glynis Johns, James Robertson Justice, Michael Gough, Jane Barrett, Peter Copley, Rosalie Crutchley, Jean Mercure, D. A. Clarke-Smith

The Sword and the Sorcerer
US 1982 99m DeLuxe
Sorcerer Productions/Group One/Brandon Chase
V, V*, L

A tyrant wins an idyllic kingdom with the help of an evil sorcerer; young Prince Talon gets it back.

Medieval magic and violence, laid on with a shovel; hopefully the last attempt to start an ill-fated cycle.

w Tom Karnowski, Albert Pyun, John Stuckmeyer
d Albert Pyun   ph Joseph Mangine   m David Whitaker

Lee Horsley, Kathleen Beller, Simon MacCorkindale, George Maharis, Richard Lynch

Sword in the Desert
US 1949 100m bw
Robert Arthur/Universal

During World War II, Jewish refugees are smuggled to the Palestine coast.

Dim topical melodrama with an anti-British slant which caused international embarrassment.

w Robert Buckner   d George Sherman

Dana Andrews, Marta Toren, Jeff Chandler, Stephen McNally, Philip Friend

The Sword in the Stone **
US 1963 80m Technicolor
Walt Disney (Ken Peterson)
V, V*, L

In the Dark Ages, a young forest boy named Wart becomes King Arthur.

Feature cartoon with goodish sequences but disappointingly showing a flatness and economy of draughtsmanship.

w Bill Peet   novel *The Once and Future King* by T. H. White   d Wolfgang Reitherman   m George Bruns   songs The Sherman Brothers

AAN: George Bruns

Sword of Ali Baba
US 1965 81m Technicolor
Universal

Ali Baba is forced from the royal court to become a king of thieves.

Cut-rate programme filler utilizing great chunks of *Ali Baba and the Forty Thieves* (twenty-one years older), with one actor, Frank Puglia, playing the same role in both films.

w Edmund Hartmann, Oscar Brodney   d Virgil Vogel

Peter Mann, Jocelyn Lane, Peter Whitney, Gavin McLeod

Sword of Lancelot: see *Lancelot and Guinevere*

Sword of Monte Cristo
US 1951 80m Supercinecolor
Edward L. Alperson
V*

Virtuous rebels and a villainous minister all seek the fabulous treasure of Monte Cristo.

Rubbishy sequel apparently shot in somebody's back garden by people only recently acquainted with film techniques.

wd Maurice Geraghty

George Montgomery, Paula Corday, Berry Kroeger, Robert Warwick, William Conrad

Sword of Sherwood Forest
GB 1960 80m Technicolor Megascope
Columbia/Hammer/Yeoman (Richard Greene, Sidney Cole)
V, V*

Robin Hood reveals the villainy of the Sheriff of Nottingham and the Earl of Newark.

This big-screen version of a popular TV series makes a rather feeble addition to the legend, but the actors try hard.

w Alan Hackney   d Terence Fisher   ph Ken Hodges   m Alan Hoddinott

Richard Greene, Peter Cushing, Richard Pasco, Niall MacGinnis, Jack Gwyllim, Sarah Branch, Nigel Green

Sword of the Valiant
GB 1984 101m Fujicolor JDC Wide Screen
Cannon (Michael Kagan, Philip M. Breen)
V*

In the mythical middle ages, squire Gawain takes on a challenge from the magical Green Knight.

An unsatisfactory mixture of realism, fantasy and deadly seriousness. Spoofing might have worked better.

w Stephen Weeks, Philip M. Breen, Howard C. Pen
d Stephen Weeks   ph Freddie Young, Peter Hurst
m Ron Geesin   pd Maurice Fowler, Derek Nice
ed Richard Marden, Barry Peters

Miles O'Keeffe, Sean Connery, Trevor Howard, Leigh Lawson, Cyrielle Claire, Peter Cushing, Ronald Lacey, Lila Kedrova, John Rhys Davies, Douglas Wilmer, Wilfred Brambell

Swords of Blood: see *Cartouche*

The Swordsman
US 1947 80m Technicolor
Columbia

A young 18th-century Scot tries to end a family feud so that he can marry the girl of his choice.

Amiable costume programmer, quite forgettable but mostly enjoyable while it's on.

w Wilfred Petitt   d Joseph H. Lewis   ph William Snyder   m Hugo Friedhofer

Larry Parks, Ellen Drew, George Macready

Sylvia
US 1964 115m bw
Paramount/Joseph E. Levine (Martin H. Poll)

A millionaire with a mysterious fiancée hires a detective to discover the truth about her past.

Improbable story of a high-minded prostitute, sluggishly narrated and variably acted.

w Sidney Boehm   novel E. V. Cunningham
d Gordon Douglas   ph Joseph Ruttenberg
m David Raksin

Carroll Baker, George Maharis, Peter Lawford, Joanne Dru, Ann Sothern, Viveca Lindfors, Edmond O'Brien, Aldo Ray

'Maharis manages to suggest that he might be worth watching in a role worth acting in a movie worth making. Sylvia wasn't.' – *Judith Crist*

Sylvia **
New Zealand 1985 98m colour
Southern Light/Cinepro (Don Reynolds, Michael Firth)
V*

In New Zealand, a wife of a headmaster at a village school encounters official opposition to her innovative methods of teaching Maori children to read.

An effective and moving low-key account, though full of repressed sexual feelings, based on the life and autobiographical books of writer Sylvia Ashton Warner.

w Michael Quill, F. Fairfax, Michael Firth
books *Teacher* and *I Passed This Way* by Sylvia Ashton Warner   d Michael Firth   ph Ian Paul   m Leonard Rosenman   pd Gary Hansen   ed Michael Horton

Eleanor David, Nigel Terry, Tom Wilkinson, Mary Regan, Martyn Sanderson, Terence Cooper, David Letch, Sarah Peirce

Sylvia and the Ghost *
France 1944 93m bw
Ecran Français/André Paulvé
original title: *Sylvie et la Fantôme*

A sixteen-year-old girl lives in her father's castle and is friendly with the ghost of a man killed in a duel fought for love of her grandmother.

Melancholy comedy which despite some charming moments somehow misses the expected style which would have made it a minor classic.

w Jean Aurenche   play Alfred Adam   d Claude Autant-Lara   ph Philippe Agostini   m René Cloerc

Odette Joyeux, François Périer, Jacques Tati, Louis Salou, Jean Desailly

'A charming film, written, handled and acted with wit, feeling and a beautiful lightness of touch.' – *Gavin Lambert*

'She's a boy! It's Mr Hepburn to you!'
Sylvia Scarlett *
US 1935 94m bw
RKO (Pandro S. Berman)
V*, L

A girl masquerades as a boy in order to escape to France with her crooked father.

Strange, peripatetic English comedy-adventure which failed to ring any bells but preserves aspects of interest.

w Gladys Unger, John Collier, Mortimer Offner *novel* Compton Mackenzie d George Cukor ph Joseph August m Roy Webb

Katharine Hepburn, Cary Grant, Edmund Gwenn, Brian Aherne, Lennox Pawle

'A story that's hard to believe. Dubious entertainment for the public.' – *Variety*

'It seems to go wrong in a million directions, but it has unusually affecting qualities.' – *New Yorker, 1978*

'A sprawling and ineffective essay in dramatic chaos.' – *Richard Watts Jnr, New York Herald Tribune*

'A tragic waste of time and screen talent.' – *Eileen Creelman, New York Sun*

'A much more polished comedy than most, and consistently engaging.' – *Winston Burdett, Brooklyn Daily Eagle*

Sylvie et la Fântome: see *Sylvia and the Ghost*

La Symphonie Fantastique *
France 1947 90m bw
L'Atelier Français

The life of Hector Berlioz.

Stately but uninspired biopic chiefly notable for its leading performance.

w J. P. Feydeau, H. A. Legrand d Christian-Jaque

Jean-Louis Barrault, Renée Saint-Cyr, Jules Berry, Bernard Blier

La Symphonie Pastorale *
France 1946 105m bw
Les Films Gibe

A Swiss pastor takes in an orphan child who grows up to be a beautiful girl and causes jealousy between himself and his son.

Curious mountain tragedy, a great visual pleasure with its symbolic use of snow and water.

w Jean Delannoy, Jean Aurenche *novel* André Gide d Jean Delannoy ph Armand Thirard m Georges Auric

Pierre Blanchar, Michèle Morgan

Symphony of Six Million
US 1932 94m bw
RKO (Pandro S. Berman)
GB title: *Melody of Life*

A doctor drags himself from New York's slums to Park Avenue, but feels guilty and demoralized when he can't save the life of his own father.

Monumental tearjerker, not badly done.

w Bernard Schubert, J. Walter Ruben *novel* Fannie Hurst d Gregory La Cava ph Leo Tover m Max Steiner

Irene Dunne, Ricardo Cortez, Gregory Ratoff, Anna Appel, Noel Madison, Julie Haydon

'Picture of Jewish home life in the familiar Hurst style . . . a good-looking picture without strongly marked cast names.' – *Variety*

Symptoms *
GB 1974 91m Eastmancolor
SF/Finiton (Jean Dupuis)

A woman living in a remote and decaying mansion begins to show signs of madness.

Creepy thriller with lesbian undertones, stylishly directed.

w Joseph Larraz, Stanley Miller d Joseph Larraz (José Larraz) ph Trevor Mann m John Scott ad Kenneth Bridgeman ed Brian Smedley-Aston

Angela Pleasence, Peter Vaughan, Lorna Heilbron, Nancy Nevinson, Ronald O'Neil, Raymond Huntley

'Works more on the level of atmosphere than of ideas, but its psychological perceptions are unusually sophisticated for genre cinema.' – *David Pirie, MFB*

† The film was cut to 80m on its British cinema release.

Synanon
US 1965 106m bw
Columbia/Richard Quine
GB title: *Get Off My Back*

Stories of the inmates of a voluntary Californian institution for the rehabilitation of drug addicts.

Well-intentioned but rather dreary case histories, unconvincingly dramatized. The house and its leader subsequently came in for much press criticism.

w Ian Bernard, S. Lee Pogostin d Richard Quine ph Harry Stradling m Neal Hefti

Edmond O'Brien (as Chuck Dederich), Chuck Connors, Stella Stevens, Alex Cord, Eartha Kitt, Richard Conte, Barbara Luna

'The real drug addicts who appear in the background are plumpish, greyish and utterly ordinary; but the fictional ones are glamorously handsome, and lead lives which are full of throbbing emotion and upset.' – *Tom Milne, MFB*

Syncopation *
US 1942 88m bw
RKO/William Dieterle (Charles F. Glett)

The career of a young trumpeter parallels the development of jazz.

Somewhat disappointing musical considering the talents involved.

w Philip Yordan, Frank Cavett, Valentine Davies d William Dieterle

Jackie Cooper, Adolphe Menjou, Bonita Granville, Connee Boswell, the Hall Johnson Choir, Benny Goodman, Harry James, Gene Krupa, Charlie Barnet

The System
US 1953 90m bw
Warner (Sam Bischoff)

A crime leader is softened by love, and allows himself to be convicted.

Strange nonsense inspired by the Kefauver investigations into American society; neither edifying nor entertaining.

w Jo Eisinger d Lewis Seiler ph Edwin DuPar m David Buttolph

Frank Lovejoy, Joan Weldon, Bob Arthur, Paul Picerni, Don Beddoe

The System
GB 1964 90m bw
British Lion/Bryanston/Kenneth Shipman
US title: *The Girl-Getters*

Seaside layabouts have a system for collecting and sharing rich girl visitors, but one of the latter traps the leader at his own game.

Adequate sexy showcase for some looming talents; all very unattractive, but smoothly directed in a number of imitated styles.

w Peter Draper d Michael Winner ph Nicolas Roeg m Stanley Black

Oliver Reed, Jane Merrow, Barbara Ferris, Julia Foster, Ann Lynn, Guy Doleman, Andrew Ray, David Hemmings, John Alderton, Derek Nimmo, Harry Andrews

'A modest, skilful, charming, inconsequential, and fairly dishonest little picture, to be enjoyed and deprecated in roughly equal measure.' – *John Simon*

'The year is 2020. He's mostly human. He's totally invincible . . . until now.'

TC 2000
Canada 1993 90m colour
Shapiro Glickenhaus/Film One (Jalal Merhi)
V, V*

In the future, when criminal gangs control a polluted world and the rich live in a heavily protected underground environment, a former cop saves the world for more dumb movies like this.

A dim rip-off of *Robocop* with elements of *Blade Runner*, done without wit or style, featuring a scantily clad female cyborg and an illogical narrative; even when outnumbered, the cops' preferred method of law enforcement is kick-boxing.

wd T. J. Scott *story* J. Stephen Maunder, Richard M. Samuels *ph* Curtis Petersen *m* Varouje *ad* Jasna Stefanovic *ed* Reid Dennison

Bolo Yeung, Jalal Merhi, Billy Blanks, Bobbie Phillips, Matthias Hues, Ramsay Smith, Gregory Philpott, Harry Mok, Kelly Gallant

T. R. Baskin
US 1971 89m Technicolor
Paramount (Peter Hyams)
V*
GB title: *A Date with a Lonely Girl*

A businessman in Chicago meets an unhappy girl who tells him her story of loneliness and lack of communication.

Intolerable self-pitying mishmash with no place to go.

w Peter Hyams *d* Herbert Ross *ph* Gerald Hirschfeld *m* Jack Elliott

Candice Bergen, Peter Boyle, James Caan, Marcia Rodd, Erin O'Reilly

Table for Five
US 1983 124m DeLuxe
CBS/Voight-Schaffel (Robert Schaffel)
V, V*, L

A divorced husband takes his children on a European holiday and has to tell them that their mother has been killed.

Slow, sentimental domestic drama with attractive travel backgrounds, like a TV movie writ large.

w David Seltzer *d* Robert Lieberman *ph* Vilmos Zsigmond *m* John Morris *pd* Robert F. Boyle

Jon Voight, Richard Crenna, Marie-Christine Barrault, Millie Perkins, Roxana Zal, Robby Kiger, Son Hoang Bui, Maria O'Brien

'A family problem picture resolutely updated for the eighties.' – *Robert Brown, MFB*

Tabu *
US 1931 80m bw
Colorart Synchrotone
V*, L

The life of a young Tahitian pearl fisherman.

The plot is used only to bring together the elements of a superb travelogue, but the conflicts between the aims of the two directors are clearly seen.

wd F. W. Murnau, Robert Flaherty *ph* Floyd Crosby, Robert Flaherty *m* Hugo Riesenfeld

'Never more than interesting . . . it is not going to set anything on fire.' – *Variety*

AA: Floyd Crosby

Tacones Lejanos: see *High Heels*

Ta'Det Som En Mand, Frue!: see *Take It Like a Man, Ma'am*

Taffin
GB 1988 96m colour
Vestron (Peter Shaw)
V*, L

A debt collector battles with crooked developers who want to build a chemical plant in an Irish village.

Dull thriller that never rises above the mundane.

w David Ambrose *d* Francis Megahy *ph* Paul Beeson *m* Stanley Myers, Hans Zimmer *pd* William Alexander *ed* Rodney Holland, Peter Tanner

Pierce Brosnan, Alison Doody, Ray McAnally, Jeremy Child, Patrick Bergan, Alan Stanford

Tagebuch einer Verliebten: see *The Diary of a Married Woman*

Tagebuch einer Verlorenen: see *Diary of a Lost Girl*

Taggart
US 1965 85m Technicolor print
Universal

A young Western squatter avenges his parents' murder but finds himself pursued by three professional gunslingers.

Tough adult Western, quite well made.

w Robert Creighton Williams *novel* Louis L'Amour *d* R. G. Springsteen

Tony Young, Dan Duryea, Dick Foran, Emile Meyer, Elsa Cardenas, Jean Hale, David Carradine

Taiheiyo Hitoribochi: see *Alone on the Pacific*

Tail Spin
US 1938 83m bw
TCF (Harry Joe Brown)

The interwoven private lives of lady civilian air pilots.

Predictable romantic goings on; a tear, a smile, a song, etc.

w Frank Wead *d* Roy del Ruth *ph* Karl Freund *m* Louis Silvers

Alice Faye, Constance Bennett, Joan Davis, Nancy Kelly, Charles Farrell, Jane Wyman, Kane Richmond, Wally Vernon, Harry Davenport

'Story zooms and flutters to create many slow spots in between the spectacular flying sequences.' – *Variety*

Tailspin Tommy
US 1934 bw serial: 12 eps
Universal

A young auto mechanic learns to fly and battles aerial pirates.

Juvenile serial comic strip.

d Louis Friedlander

Maurice Murphy, Patricia Farr, Noah Beery Jnr, Grant Withers

Tailspin Tommy in the Great Air Mystery
US 1935 bw serial: 12 eps
Universal

Our heroes prevent a villainous plan to steal oil reserves.

More of the above.

d Ray Taylor

Clark Williams, Noah Beery Jnr, Jean Rogers, Bryant Washburn

Tainted Money: see *Show Them No Mercy*

Tai-Pan
US 1986 127m Technicolor JDC Widescreen
Dino de Laurentiis (Rafaella de Laurentiis)
V*, L

Various problems afflict the leader of the European community in Canton and Hong Kong.

19th-century soap opera with 18th-century plotting and dialogue.

w John Briley, Stanley Mann *novel* James Clavell *d* Daryl Duke *ph* Jack Cardiff *m* Maurice Jarre *pd* Tony Masters

Bryan Brown, Joan Chen, John Stanton, Tom Guinee, Bill Leadbitter, Russell Wong

'Underneath all the gloss the film isn't really about anything.' – *Variety*

With some movies, you're forever checking your watch. With *Tai-Pan*, you'll be checking your calendar.' – *People*

'Miniseries kitsch which shortchanges on dramatic spectacle.' – *Sight and Sound*

Take a Giant Step
US 1958 100m bw
UA/Sheila/Hecht-Hill-Lancaster (Julius J. Epstein)

A young black person brought up in a white town feels ill at ease and runs into adolescent troubles.

Well-meaning racial drama with good detail but no real feeling.

w Louis S. Peterson, Julius J. Epstein *d* Philip Leacock *ph* Arthur Arling *m* Jack Marshall

Johnny Nash, Estelle Hemsley, Ruby Dee, Frederick O'Neal

Take a Girl Like You
GB 1970 101m Eastmancolor
Columbia/Albion (Hal E. Chester)
V*

A north country girl comes to teach in London and has man trouble.

Old-fashioned novelette with sex trimmings and neither zest nor humour.

w George Melly *novel* Kingsley Amis *d* Jonathan Miller *ph* Dick Bush *m* Stanley Myers

Hayley Mills, Oliver Reed, Noel Harrison, Sheila Hancock, John Bird, Aimi MacDonald

Take a Letter, Darling **
US 1942 94m bw
Paramount (Fred Kohlmar)
GB title: Green-Eyed Woman

A woman executive hires a male secretary.

Smartish romantic comedy.

w Claude Binyon d Mitchell Leisen ph John Mescall
m Victor Young ad Hans Dreier, Roland Anderson

Rosalind Russell, Fred MacMurray, MacDonald
Carey, Constance Moore, Cecil Kellaway, Charles
Arnt, Kathleen Howard, Dooley Wilson

AAN: John Mescall; Victor Young; art direction

Take Care of My Little Girl
US 1951 93m Technicolor
TCF (Julian Blaustein)

A university freshwoman gets into trouble with her
sorority.

Ho-hum exposé of college conventions, of routine
interest at best.

w Julius J. and Philip G. Epstein novel Peggy
Goodwin d Jean Negulesco ph Harry Jackson
m Alfred Newman

Jeanne Crain, Mitzi Gaynor, Dale Robertson, Jean
Peters, Jeffrey Hunter

'As is customary in college pictures, it appears that Tri
U recruits most of its strength from the chorus.' –
Penelope Houston

Take Her, She's Mine *
US 1963 98m DeLuxe Cinemascope
TCF (Henry Koster)

A lawyer protects his teenage daughter from boys and
causes.

Routine Hollywood family comedy with some laughs
and an agreeable cast.

w Nunnally Johnson play Phoebe and Henry
Ephron d Henry Koster ph Lucien Ballard
m Jerry Goldsmith

James Stewart, Sandra Dee, Robert Morley, Audrey
Meadows, Philippe Forquet, John McGiver

Take It Easy
1971 90m colour
Adel Productions (Alain Delon)
original title: Doucement les Basses

A Catholic priest, a former organist, living in an
isolated village, is visited by his wife, who he thought
had died eight years earlier, and discovers she is now
running a bordello.

A broad comedy that fails to extract much fun from its
situation.

w Pascal Jardin d Jacques Deray ph Jean-
Jacques Tarbes m Claude Bolling ad François de
Lamotne ed Paul Cayatte

Alain Delon, Paul Meurisse, Nathalie Delon, Julien
Guiomar, Paul Préboist, André Bollet, Serge Davri

Take It Like a Man, Ma'am *
Denmark 1975 96m colour
Røde Søster (Ilse M. Haugaard, Trine Hedman, Annelise
   Hovinand)
original title: Ta'Det Som En Mand, Frue!

A bored middle-aged housewife dreams of the sexual
roles being reversed.

Mildly enjoyable feminist movie.

wd Elisabeth Rygard, Mette Knudsen, Li Vilstrup
ph Katia Forbert Petersen, Judy Irola, Lene Fog-
Moller, Leni Schou m Nina Larsen, Gudrun Steen-
Andersen, Maria Marcus ed Ann-Lis Lund

Tove Maës, Bertha Quistgard, Asta Esper Andersen,
Birgit Brüel, Alf Lassen

Take It or Leave It
US 1944 68m bw
TCF

A sailor enters a quiz show to raise money for his
expectant wife.

Thin link for a string of old movie clips which form
the questions; all from Fox films of course.

w Harold Buchman, Snag Werris, Mac Benoff
d Ben Stoloff

Phil Baker, Phil Silvers, Edward Ryan, Marjorie
Massow; with clips of Shirley Temple, the Ritz
Brothers, Betty Grable, Alice Faye, Sonja Henie, Al
Jolson, etc

Take Me High
GB 1973 90m Technicolor
EMI (Kenneth Harper)
V

A bank manager helps an unsuccessful restaurant to
launch a new hamburger.

Jaded youth musical with no dancing but some zip
and bounce to commend it to mums and dads if not to
its intended young audience.

w Christopher Penfold d David Askey
ph Norman Warwick m/songs Tony Cole

Cliff Richard, Debbie Watling, Hugh Griffith, George
Cole, Anthony Andrews, Richard Wattis

Take Me Out to the Ball Game **
US 1949 93m Technicolor
MGM (Arthur Freed)
V, V*, L
GB title: Everybody's Cheering

A woman takes over a baseball team and the players
are antagonistic.

Lively, likeable 1890s comedy musical which served
as a trial run for On the Town and in its own right is a
fast-moving, funny, tuneful delight with no
pretensions.

w Harry Tugend, George Wells d Busby Berkeley
ph George Folsey md Adolph Deutsch songs Betty
Comden, Adolph Green, Roger Edens

Gene Kelly, Frank Sinatra, Esther Williams, Betty
Garrett, Jules Munshin, Edward Arnold, Richard
Lane, Tom Dugan

Take Me to Town
US 1953 81m Technicolor
U-I (Ross Hunter)

The three sons of a backwoods widower import a
vaudeville artiste as their new mother.

Old-fashioned family schmaltz containing every
known cliché professionally stitched into the plot.

w Richard Morris d Douglas Sirk ph Russell
Metty m Joseph Gershenson

Ann Sheridan, Sterling Hayden, Philip Reed, Lee
Patrick, Lee Aaker, Harvey Grant, Dusty Henley

Take My Life **
GB 1947 79m bw
GFD/Cineguild (Anthony Havelock-Allan)

A man is suspected of murdering an ex-girlfriend, and
his wife journeys to Scotland to prove him innocent.

Hitchcock-style thriller with excellent detail and
performances.

w Winston Graham, Valerie Taylor d Ronald Neame
ph Guy Green m William Alwyn

Hugh Williams, Greta Gynt, Marius Goring, Francis L.
Sullivan, Rosalie Crutchley, Henry Edwards, Ronald
Adam

'An extremely confident and exciting British thriller,
with a story no less plausible than the average made
infinitely more plausible by the smooth narrative
style.' – Dilys Powell, Sunday Times

Take My Tip
GB 1937 74m bw
Gaumont-British (Michael Balcon)

Lord Pilkington gets his revenge on a confidence
trickster when they meet at a Dalmatian hotel.

Reasonably lively comedy musical adapted for the
stars.

w Sidney Gilliat, Michael Hogan, Jack Hulbert
d Herbert Mason ph Bernard Knowles songs Sam
Lerner, Al Goodhart, Al Hoffman

Jack Hulbert, Cicely Courtneidge, Frank Cellier,
Harold Huth, Frank Pettingell, Robb Wilton, H. F.
Maltby

Take One False Step *
US 1949 94m bw
U-I (Chester Erskine)

An innocent middle-aged man who has befriended a
girl is hunted by the police when she is murdered.

Fairly absorbing and well-cast chase thriller in a
minor key.

w Irwin Shaw, Chester Erskine story Night Call by
Irwin and David Shaw d Chester Erskine
ph Franz Planer m Walter Scharf

William Powell, Shelley Winters, Marsha Hunt,
Dorothy Hart, James Gleason, Felix Bressart, Art
Baker, Sheldon Leonard

Take the High Ground
US 1953 101m Anscocolor
MGM (Dore Schary)

A tough sergeant trains army conscripts for action in
Korea.

Very routine flagwaver.

w Millard Kaufman d Richard Brooks ph John
Alton m Dimitri Tiomkin

Richard Widmark, Karl Malden, Carleton Carpenter,
Elaine Stewart, Russ Tamblyn, Jerome Courtland,
Steve Forrest, Robert Arthur

AAN: Millard Kaufman

Take the Money and Run
US 1968 85m Technicolor
Palomar (Charles H. Joffe)
V, V*, L

A social misfit becomes a bungling crook.

A torrent of middling visual gags, not the star's best
vehicle.

wd Woody Allen ph Lester Shorr m Marvin
Hamlisch

Woody Allen, Janet Margolin, Marcel Hillaire

Take the Stage: see Curtain Call at Cactus Creek

Take This Job and Shove It
US 1981 106m colour
Avco Embassy/Cinema Group (Greg Blackwell)

A thrusting business executive discovers his social
conscience when he returns to his home town to take
over a run-down brewery.

Unoriginal but affable corn-belt comedy affirming
small-town values.

w Barry Schneider story Jeffrey Bernini, Barry
Schneider, from a song by David Allan Coe d Gus
Trikonis ph James Devis m Billy Sherrill
ad Jim Dultz ed Richard Belding

Robert Hays, Barbara Hershey, David Keith, Art
Carney, Tim Thomerson, Eddie Albert, Penelope
Milford, Charlie Rich, Martin Mull

Taking Care of Business

US 1990 108m Technicolor
Warner/Hollywood Pictures/Silver Screen Partners IV (Geoffrey Taylor)
V, V*, L
GB title: Filofax

A thief assumes the identity of an advertising executive whose Filofax he acquires.

Slow-moving comedy that fails to get much mileage from its tired central idea.

w Jill Mazursky, Jeffrey Abrams d Arthur Hiller ph David M. Walsh m Stewart Copeland pd Jon Hutman ed William Reynolds

James Belushi, Charles Grodin, Anne DeSalvo, Loryn Locklin, Stephen Elliott, Hector Elizondo, Veronica Hamel

'Hiller brings his usual dogged persistence to bear, but it would take an alchemist's touch to turn Filofax into comic gold.' – Geoff Brown, Sight and Sound

The Taking of Pelham 123 *

US 1974 104m Technicolor Panavision
UA/Palomar/Palladium (Gabriel Katzka)
V, V*, L

Four ruthless gunmen hold a New York subway train to ransom and have an ingenious plan for escape.

Entertaining crime caper made less enjoyable by all the fashionable faults – the script is deliberately hard to follow and full of four letter words, the sound track hard to hear, and the visuals ugly.

w Peter Stone novel John Godey d Joseph Sargent ph Owen Roizman m David Shire

Walter Matthau, Robert Shaw, Martin Balsam, Hector Elizondo, Earl Hindman, James Broderick

'Full of noise and squalling and dirty words used for giggly shock effects.' – New Yorker

Taking Off **

US 1971 92m Movielab
Universal (Alfred W. Crown, Michael Hausman)

Suburban parents seek their errant daughter among the hippies, and gradually lose their own inhibitions.

Slight, formless, but amusing revue-style comment by a Czech director on the American scene.

w Milos Forman, John Guare, Jean-Claude Carrière, John Klein d Milos Forman ph Miroslav Ondricek

Lynn Carlin, Buck Henry, Linnea Heacock

Tale of a Vampire

GB/Japan 1992 102m colour
State Screen/Tsuburaya Ezio/Furama (Simon Johnson)
V

A vampire in London is tracked down by the husband of his lost lover.

Slow-moving and gory account of an obsessive love.

w Shimako Sato, Jane Corbett d Shimako Sato ph Zubin Mistry m Julian Joseph pd Alice Normington sp Dave Watkins ed Chris Wright

Julian Sands, Suzanna Hamilton, Kenneth Cranham, Marian Diamond, Michael Kenton, Catherine Blake, Mark Kempner, Nik Myers

'A flawed but impressive debut from a talent which deserves to be nurtured.' – Mark Kermode, Sight and Sound

'Is nailed to the floor by anaemic perfs from its two leads and a script that's all tease and no bite. Pic may build a small cult following among genre buffs but won't score many general converts.' – Variety

A Tale of Five Cities

GB 1951 99m bw
Grand National (Alexander Paal)
US title: A Tale of Five Women

An amnesiac American seeks clues to his past in Rome, Vienna, Paris, Berlin and London.

Tedious pattern drama remarkable only for its then untried cast.

w Patrick Kirwan, Maurice J. Wilson d Montgomery Tully ph Gordon Lang m Hans May

Bonar Colleano, Gina Lollobrigida, Barbara Kelly, Lana Morris, Anne Vernon, Eva Bartok

A Tale of Five Women: see A Tale of Five Cities

A Tale of Springtime: see Conte de Printemps

The Tale of the Fox ***

France 1931 65m bw
BFI/Wladyslaw Starewicz (Louis Nalpas, Roger Richebé)
original title: Le Roman de Renard

A cunning fox defeats all the other animals that unite to attack him.

A brilliant animated film, which with its British release in 1994 helped bring belated recognition to a master of the art.

w Wladyslaw Starewicz, Irène Starewicz, Jean Nohain, Antoinette Nordmann d Wladyslaw Starewicz m Vincent Scotto pd Wladyslaw Starewicz ed Laura Séjourné

voices of Claude Dauphin, Romain Bouquet, Sylvain Itkine, Léon Larive, Robert Seller, Edy Debray, Nicolas Amato

'His love challenged the flames of revolution!'

A Tale of Two Cities **

US 1935 121m bw
MGM (David O. Selznick)
V, V*, L

A British lawyer sacrifices himself to save another man from the guillotine.

Richly detailed version of the classic melodrama, with production values counting more than the acting.

w W. P. Lipscomb, S. N. Behrman novel Charles Dickens d Jack Conway ph Oliver T. Marsh m Herbert Stothart ed Conrad A. Nervig

Ronald Colman, Elizabeth Allan, Basil Rathbone, Edna May Oliver, Blanche Yurka, Reginald Owen, Henry B. Walthall, Donald Woods, Walter Catlett, H. B. Warner, Claude Gillingwater, Fritz Leiber

'A screen classic . . . technically it is about as flawless as possible . . . it has been made with respectful and loving care.' – Variety

'A prodigiously stirring production . . . for more than two hours it crowds the screen with beauty and excitement.' – New York Times

† Originally prepared at Warner for Leslie Howard.

AAN: best picture; editing

A Tale of Two Cities *

GB 1958 117m bw
Rank (Betty E. Box)
V, V*

Modest but still costly remake with good moments but a rather slow pace.

w T. E. B. Clarke d Ralph Thomas ph Ernest Steward m Richard Addinsell

Dirk Bogarde, Dorothy Tutin, Christopher Lee, Athene Seyler, Rosalie Crutchley, Ernest Clark, Stephen Murray, Paul Guers, Donald Pleasence, Ian Bannen, Cecil Parker, Alfie Bass

'Serviceable rather than imaginative.' – MFB

A Talent for Loving

US 1969 101m colour
Paramount (Walter Shenson)
V*

Two generations of an international jet-setting family have woman trouble.

Little-seen melodrama apparently disowned by those who made it.

novel Richard Condon d Richard Quine

Richard Widmark, Cesar Romero, Topol, Genevieve Page

Tales from the Crypt *

GB 1972 92m Eastmancolor
Metromedia/Amicus (Milton Subotsky)
V*

Five people get lost in catacombs and are shown the future by a sinister monk who turns out to be Satan.

Fair ghoulish fun; a quintet of stories with a recognizable Amicus link.

w Milton Subotsky comic strips William Gaines d Freddie Francis ph Norman Warwick m Douglas Gamley

Ralph Richardson, Geoffrey Bayldon, Peter Cushing, Joan Collins, Ian Hendry, Robin Phillips, Richard Greene, Barbara Murray, Roy Dotrice, Nigel Patrick, Patrick Magee

Tales from the Darkside: The Movie

US 1991 93m Technicolor
Columbia TriStar/Paramount (Richard P. Rubinstein, Mitchell Galin)
V, V*, L

Facing being roasted in an oven for dinner, a small boy postpones the event by telling stories.

Bloody anthology of horrific anecdotes that fails to cohere.

w Michael McDowell ('Wraparound Story', 'Lover's Vow', 'Lot 249'); George Romero ('Cat From Hell')

story Lot 249 by Arthur Conan Doyle; Cat From Hell by Stephen King d John Harrison ph Robert Draper m Donald A. Rubinstein ('Wraparound Story'); Jim Manzie, Pat Regan ('Lot 249'); Chaz Jankel ('Cat From Hell'); John Harrison ('Lover's Vow') pd Ruth Ammon sp Dick Smith ed Harry B. Miller III

'Wraparound Story': Deborah Harry, Matthew Lawrence. 'Lot 249': Christian Slater, Robert Sedgwick, Steve Buscemi, Donald Van Horn, Michael Deak. 'Cat From Hell': David Johansen, Paul Greene, William Hickey. 'Lover's Vow': James Remar, Ashton Wise, Philip Lenkowsky, Rae Dawn Chong

'The rending of flesh that punctuates each episode is so extravagantly disgusting that the senses are quickly stirred not to admiration but to apathy.' – Philip Strick, Sight and Sound

Tales of Beatrix Potter **

GB 1971 90m Technicolor
EMI (Richard Goodwin)
V*
US title: Peter Rabbit and the Tales of Beatrix Potter

Children's stories danced by the Royal Ballet in animal masks.

A charming entertainment for those who can appreciate it, though hardly the most direct way to tell these stories.

w Richard Goodwin, Christine Edward d Reginald Mills ph Austin Dempster m John Lanchbery ch Frederick Ashton masks Rotislav Doboujinsky pd Christine Edward

The Tales of Hoffman **

GB 1951 127m Technicolor
British Lion/London/Michael Powell, Emeric Pressburger
V*, L

The poet Hoffman, in three adventures, seeks the eternal woman and is beset by eternal evil.

Overwhelming combination of opera, ballet, and rich production design, an indigestible hodgepodge with flashes of superior talent.

wd Michael Powell, Emeric Pressburger
ph Christopher Challis   *m* *Jacques Offenbach*
pd Hein Heckroth

Robert Rounseville, Robert Helpmann, Pamela
Brown, Moira Shearer, Frederick Ashton, Leonide
Massine, Ludmilla Tcherina, Ann Ayars, Mogens
Wieth; music conducted by Sir Thomas Beecham with
the Royal Philharmonic Orchestra

'The most spectacular failure yet achieved by Powell
and Pressburger, who seem increasingly to dissipate
their gifts in a welter of aimless ingenuity.' – *Gavin
Lambert*

'An art director's picnic: I marvelled without being
enthralled.' – *Richard Mallett, Punch*

'Enchanting, a labour of love.' – *Sunday Telegraph*

'It echoes the peak of the Victorian spirit.' – *Time*

AAN: art direction

Tales of Manhattan **
US   1942   118m   bw
TCF (Boris Morros, Sam Spiegel)

Separate stories of a tail coat, which passes from
owner to owner.

The stories are all rather disappointing in their
different veins, but production standards are high and
a few of the stars shine. A sequence starring W.
C. Fields was deleted before release.

w Ben Hecht, Ferenc Molnar, Donald Ogden Stewart,
Samuel Hoffenstein, Alan Campbell, Ladislas Fodor,
Laslo Vadnay, Laszlo Gorog, Lamar Trotti, Henry
Blankfort   *d* Julien Duvivier   *ph* Joseph Walker
m Sol Kaplan

Charles Boyer, Rita Hayworth, Thomas Mitchell,
Eugene Pallette; Ginger Rogers, Henry Fonda, Cesar
Romero, Gail Patrick, Roland Young; *Charles Laughton,*
Elsa Lanchester, Victor Francen, Christian Rub;
Edward G. Robinson, George Sanders, James
Gleason, Harry Davenport; Paul Robeson, Ethel
Waters, Eddie Anderson

† Duvivier was clearly chosen to make this film
because of his success with the similar *Carnet de Bal*;
he and Boyer went on to make the less successful *Flesh
and Fantasy* on similar lines.

Tales of Mystery and Imagination: see *Histoires
Extraordinaires*

Tales of Ordinary Madness
Italy/France   1981   108m   Eastmancolor   English
   version
23 Giugno/Ginis (Jacqueline Ferreri)
V, V*

A drunken poet is obsessed by sex but can't find a
happy relationship with his women.

Outlandish, episodic wallow, mostly on Venice beach
in California. Not for maiden aunts, and probably not
for anyone else either.

w Marco Ferreri and others   *book* Erections,
Ejaculations, Exhibitions and Tales of Ordinary Madness *by*
Charles Bukowski   *d* Marco Ferreri   *ph* Tonino
Delli Colli   *m* Philippe Sarde

Ben Gazzara, Ornella Muti, Susan Tyrrell, Tanya
Lopert, Katia Berger

'By turns repellent, naive and risible.' – *Sight and
Sound*

Tales of Terror *
US   1962   90m   Pathecolor   Panavision
AIP (Roger Corman)
V*

'Morella': a dying girl discovers the mummified body
of her mother. 'The Black Cat': a henpecked husband
kills his wife and walls up the body. 'The Facts in the
Case of M Valdemar': an old man is hypnotized at the
moment of death.

Tolerable short story compendium, rather short on
subtlety and style.

w Richard Matheson   *stories* Edgar Allan Poe
d Roger Corman   *ph* Floyd Crosby   *m* Les Baxter

Vincent Price, Peter Lorre, Basil Rathbone, Debra
Paget

'An orgy of the damned!'

Tales That Witness Madness
GB   1973   90m   colour
Paramount/Amicus (Milton Subotsky, Norman Priggen)

Five ghostly tales linked by an old bookshop.

Extreme example of the Amicus compendiums.

w Jay Fairbank   *d* Freddie Francis   *ph* Norman
Warwick   *m* Bernard Ebbinghouse

Jack Hawkins, Donald Pleasence, Georgia Brown,
Donald Houston, Suzy Kendall, Peter McEnery, Joan
Collins, Michael Jayston, Kim Novak, Michael
Petrovitch, Mary Tamm

Talk About a Lady
US   1946   71m   bw
Columbia

A country cousin comes to town and makes good.

Easy-going musical filler, better than some.

w Richard Weil, Ted Thomas   *d* George Sherman

Jinx Falkenburg, Forrest Tucker, Joe Besser, Trudy
Marshall, Richard Lane, Stan Kenton and his
orchestra

Talk About a Stranger *
US   1952   65m   bw
MGM (Richard Goldstone)

In a small town, gossip is unjustly aroused over a
mysterious stranger who is suspected of various
crimes.

Unusual though rather naïve second feature, directed
for more than its worth.

w Margaret Fitts   *novel* Charlotte Armstrong
d David Bradley   *ph* John Alton   *m* David
Buttolph

George Murphy, Nancy Davis, Lewis Stone, Billy
Gray, Kurt Kasznar

Talk About Jacqueline
GB   1942   84m   bw
Excelsior/Marcel Hellman

A girl is mistaken for her naughtier sister.

Thin, very British comedy with nowhere to go.

w Roland Pertwee, Marjorie Deans   *novel* Katherine
Holland   *d* Harold French

Hugh Williams, Carla Lehmann, Joyce Howard,
Roland Culver, John Warwick, Mary Jerrold, Guy
Middleton, Max Adrian

Talk of the Devil
GB   1936   78m   bw
B and D

An impersonator pins a crooked deal on a magnate,
who kills himself.

Glum drama chiefly notable as the first film to be shot
at Pinewood Studios.

w Carol Reed, George Barraud, Anthony Kimmins
d Carol Reed

Ricardo Cortez, Sally Eilers, Basil Sydney, Randle
Ayrton, Charles Carson

The Talk of the Town ***
US   1942   118m   bw
Columbia (George Stevens, Fred Guiol)
V, V*, L

A girl loves both a suspected murderer and the lawyer
who defends him.

Unusual mixture of comedy and drama, delightfully
handled by three sympathetic stars.

w Irwin Shaw, Sidney Buchman   *d* George Stevens
ph Ted Tetzlaff   *m* Frederick Hollander   *ad* Lionel
Banks, Rudolph Sternad   *ed* Otto Meyer

Ronald Colman, Cary Grant, Jean Arthur, Edgar
Buchanan, Glenda Farrell, Charles Dingle, Emma
Dunn, Rex Ingram

'A rip-roaring, knock-down-and-drag-out comedy
about civil liberties.' – *John T. McManus*

'Well tuned and witty, at its best when it sticks to the
middle ground between farce and melodrama. The
chief fault of the script is its excessive length and the
fact that a standard lynching mob climax is followed
by a prolonged anti-climax.' – *Newsweek*

'I can't take my lynching so lightly, even in a
screwball. Still, I am all for this kind of comedy and
for players like Arthur and Grant, who can mug more
amusingly than most scriptwriters can write.' – *Manny
Farber*

'Did the authors think they were writing a Shavian
comedy of ideas? The ideas are garbled and silly, but
the people are so pleasant that the picture manages to
be quite amiable and high-spirited.' – *Pauline Kael, 70s*

'I knew it was going to come off all along: it didn't
have that element of hazard in it. It was more of an
understood flight with a take-off time and an arrival
time and not too much headwind.' – *George Stevens*

† Two endings were filmed: the eventual choice of
mate for Miss Arthur was determined by audience
reaction at previews.

AAN: best picture; original story (Sidney Harmon);
script; Ted Tetzlaff; Frederick Hollander; art direction;
Otto Meyer

Talk Radio **
US   1988   109m   DeLuxe
Fox/Cineplex Odeon/Ten-Four Productions (Edward
   R. Pressman, Kitman Ho)
V, V*, L, S

Billed as 'the man you love to hate', the host of a radio
talk-show, whose private life is a mess, courts trouble
by abusing his listeners.

Powerful, virulent near-monologue of a mind at the
end of its tether, filmed in an appropriately restless
style.

w Eric Bogosian, Oliver Stone   *play* Eric Bogosian,
Ted Savinar   *book* Talked to Death: The Life and Murder
of Alan Berg *by* Stephen Singular   *d* Oliver Stone
ph Robert Richardson   *m* Stewart Copeland
pd Bruno Rubeo   *ed* David Brenner, Joe Hutshing

Eric Bogosian, Alec Baldwin, Ellen Greene, Leslie
Hope, John C. McGinley, John Pankow, Michael
Wincott

The Tall Blond Man with One Black Shoe: see
Le Grand Blond avec une Chaussure Noire

Tall, Dark and Handsome
US   1941   78m   bw
TCF

In 1929 Chicago, a gangster aspires to be a gentleman.

Moderate crime comedy.

w Karl Tunberg, Darrell Ware   *d* H. Bruce
Humberstone

Cesar Romero, Virginia Gilmore, Charlotte
Greenwood, Milton Berle, Sheldon Leonard

AAN: Karl Tunberg, Darrell Ware

The Tall Guy
GB   1989   92m   Eastmancolor
Virgin/LWT/Working Title (Tim Bevan)
V, V*, L

The stooge to a sadistic comedian tries for stardom on
his own.

Lamentably unfunny comedy, ponderously directed.

w Richard Curtis d Mel Smith ph Adrian Biddle
m Peter Brewis pd Grant Hicks ed Dan Rae

Jeff Goldblum, Emma Thompson, Rowan Atkinson,
Geraldine James, Emil Wolk, Kim Thomson, Harold
Innocent, Anna Massey

The Tall Headlines
GB 1952 100m bw
Grand National/Raymond Stross
aka: The Frightened Bride

A family is affected when the eldest son is executed
for murder.

Glum, boring, badly cast, badly written and generally
inept melodrama.

w Audrey Erskine Lindop, Dudley Leslie
novel Audrey Erskine Lindop d Terence Young
ph C. M. Pennington-Richards m Hans May

Flora Robson, Michael Denison, Mai Zetterling, Jane
Hylton, André Morell, Dennis Price, Mervyn Johns,
Naunton Wayne

'A falsity which will surely surprise even those
familiar with the conventions of British middle-class
cinema.' – Lindsay Anderson

Tall in the Saddle
US 1944 87m bw
RKO (Robert Fellows)
V*, L

The newly-arrived ranch foreman finds that his boss
has been murdered.

Quite a watchable, and forgettable, mystery Western.

w Michael Hogan, Paul J. Fix d Edwin L. Marin
ph Robert de Grasse md Constantin Bakaleinikoff
m Roy Webb

John Wayne, Ella Raines, Ward Bond, George
'Gabby' Hayes, Audrey Long, Elizabeth Risdon, Don
Douglas, Paul Fix, Russell Wade

Tall Man Riding
US 1955 83m Warnercolor
Warner

An adventurer feuds with a rancher but in the end
marries his daughter.

Unremarkable star Western.

w Joseph Hoffman d Lesley Selander

Randolph Scott, Robert Barrat, Dorothy Malone,
Peggie Castle, John Dehner

The Tall Men *
US 1955 122m DeLuxe Cinemascope
TCF (William A. Bacher, William B. Hawks)
V*

After the Civil War, two Texans head north for the
Montana goldfields.

Solid star Western.

w Sidney Boehm, Frank Nugent novel Clay Fisher
d Raoul Walsh ph Leo Tover m Victor Young

Clark Gable, Jane Russell, Robert Ryan, Cameron
Mitchell, Juan Garcia, Harry Shannon, Emile Meyer

'A big action feast and value for anyone's money.' –
Newsweek

Tall Story
US 1960 91m bw
Warner/Mansfield (Joshua Logan)
V*, L

A college basketball player faces various kinds of
trouble when he marries.

Dislikeable campus comedy with leading players
miscast.

w Julius J. Epstein novel The Homecoming Game by
Howard Nemoor d Joshua Logan ph Ellsworth
Fredericks m Cyril Mockridge

Anthony Perkins, Jane Fonda, Ray Walston, Anne
Jackson, Marc Connelly, Murray Hamilton, Elizabeth
Patterson

The Tall Stranger
US 1957 83m DeLuxe Cinemascope
Allied Artists

Cared for by wagon train pioneers after being
mysteriously shot, a rancher tries to help them settle.

Fair star Western with some tough action.

w Christopher Knopf story Louis L'Amour
d Thomas Carr

Joel McCrea, Virginia Mayo, Barry Kelley, Michael
Ansara, Whit Bissell

The Tall T *
US 1957 78m Technicolor
Columbia/Scott-Brown (Harry Joe Brown)
V*

Three bandits hold up a stagecoach and take a
hostage, but are outwitted by a rancher.

Good small-scale suspense Western with plenty of
action and a blood-spattered finale.

w Burt Kennedy d Budd Boetticher ph Charles
Lawton Jnr m Heinz Roemheld

Randolph Scott, Richard Boone, Maureen O'Sullivan,
Arthur Hunnicutt, Skip Homeier, John Hubbard,
Henry Silva

The Tall Target **
US 1951 78m bw
MGM (Richard Goldstone)

A discredited police officer tries to stop the
assassination of Abraham Lincoln on a train to
Washington.

Lively period suspenser with excellent attention to
detail and much of the attraction of The Lady Vanishes.
The plot slightly relaxes its hold before the end.

w George Worthing Yates, Art Cohn d Anthony Mann
ph Paul C. Vogel ad Cedric Gibbons, Eddie Imazu

Dick Powell, Adolphe Menjou, Paula Raymond, Marshall
Thompson, Ruby Dee, Richard Rober, Will Geer,
Florence Bates

'An intelligent minor picture which makes good use
of its material.' – MFB

Tamahine
GB 1962 95m Technicolor Cinemascope
ABP (John Bryan)

The headmaster of a boys' school is visited by his
glamorous half-caste Polynesian cousin.

Simple-minded school comedy with predictable
situations.

w Denis Cannan novel Thelma Niklaus d Philip
Leacock ph Geoffrey Unsworth m Malcolm
Arnold

John Fraser, Nancy Kwan, Dennis Price, Derek
Nimmo, Justine Lord, James Fox, Coral Browne,
Michael Gough, Allan Cuthbertson

The Tamarind Seed *
GB 1974 125m Eastmancolor Panavision
Jewel/Lorimar/Pimlico (Ken Wales)
V*

While holidaying in Barbados, a British widow falls
for a Russian military attaché.

Old-fashioned romance which turns into a mild spy
caper. A well-heeled time-passer.

wd Blake Edwards novel Evelyn Anthony
ph Frederick A. Young m John Barry

Julie Andrews, Omar Sharif, Sylvia Syms, Dan
O'Herlihy, Anthony Quayle, Oscar Homolka

'A painless timekiller, but one wishes Miss Andrews
didn't always give the impression that she had just

left her horse in the hallway.' – Michael Billington,
Illustrated London News

The Taming of the Shrew *
US 1929 68m bw
United Artists/Pickford/Elton
V*, L

A condensed version of the play which did not do
much in its day for its stars' then declining
reputations, but can now be watched with a fair
measure of enjoyment.

w William Shakespeare, 'with additional dialogue by
Sam Taylor' d Sam Taylor ph Karl Struss
pd William Cameron Menzies, Laurence Irving

Douglas Fairbanks, Mary Pickford, Edwin Maxwell,
Joseph Cawthorn, Clyde Cook, Dorothy Jordan

† A 'widescreen' version was issued in 1976.

'In the war between the sexes, there always comes a time
to surrender unconditionally!'

The Taming of the Shrew *
US 1967 122m Technicolor Panavision
Columbia/Royal/FAI (Richard McWhorter)
V*, L

Petruchio violently tames his shrewish wife.

Busy version of one of Shakespeare's more proletarian
comedies; the words in this case take second place to
violent action and rioting colour.

w Suso Cecchi d'Amico, Paul Dehn, Franco Zeffirelli
d Franco Zeffirelli ph Oswald Morris, Luciano
Trasatti m Nino Rota

Richard Burton, Elizabeth Taylor, Michael York, Michael
Hordern, Cyril Cusack, Alfred Lynch, Natasha Pyne,
Alan Webb, Victor Spinetti

'As entertainment Kiss Me Kate is infinitely better but
then Cole Porter was a real artist and Burton is a
culture vulture.' – Wilfrid Sheed

'The old warhorse of a comedy has been spanked into
uproarious life.' – Hollis Alpert

Tam-Lin
GB 1971 106m Technicolor Panavision
Winkast (Jerry Gershwin, Elliott Kastner)/Commonwealth
United
aka: The Devil's Widow; The Ballad of Tam-Lin

A sinister, beautiful, middle-aged widow has a
diabolic influence on the bright young people she
gathers around her.

Self-indulgent melodrama which might have worked
with a shorter running time and a tighter script; as it
was, it sank almost without trace.

w William Spier poem Robert Burns d Roddy
McDowall ph Willy Williams m Stanley Myers

Ava Gardner, Ian MacShane, Richard Wattis, Cyril
Cusack, Stephanie Beacham, David Whitman, Fabia
Drake, Sinead Cusack, Joanna Lumley, Jenny Hanley

Tammy: see Tammy and the Bachelor

Tammy and the Bachelor *
US 1957 89m Technicolor Cinemascope
U-I (Ross Hunter)
V*
GB title: Tammy

A backwoods tomboy falls for a stranded flyer.

Whimsical romance for middle America, which
started Hollywood's last series of proletarian family
appeal before the family was entirely forsaken for four
letter words.

w Oscar Brodney stories Cid Ricketts Summer
d Joseph Pevney ph Arthur E. Arling md Joseph
Gershenson m Frank Skinner

Debbie Reynolds, Walter Brennan, Leslie Nielsen,
Mala Powers, Fay Wray, Sidney Blackmer, Mildred
Natwick

AAN: song 'Tammy' (m/y Ray Evans, Jay Livingstone)

Tammy and the Doctor

US   1963   88m   Eastmancolor
U-I/Ross Hunter
V*

Tammy leaves her riverboat to accompany an old lady who needs an operation in the big city.

More artless family fodder.

w Oscar Brodney   d Harry Keller   ph Russell Metty   m Frank Skinner

Sandra Dee, Peter Fonda, Macdonald Carey, Beulah Bondi, Margaret Lindsay, Reginald Owen, Adam West

'The aura of simple religion and naïve philosophy remains singularly charmless.' – MFB

Tammy and the Millionaire

US   1967   88m   Technicolor
Universal

Tammy becomes a private secretary in the big city.

A re-edit from four half-hour TV shows; not at all watchable.

w George Tibbles   d Sidney Miller, Leslie Goodwins and Ezra Stone

Debbie Watson, Donald Woods, Dorothy Green, Denver Pyle, Frank McGrath

Tammy Tell Me True

US   1961   97m   Eastmancolor
U-I (Ross Hunter)

Tammy gets a college education and charms all comers.

Sugar-coated sequel to the original.

w Oscar Brodney   d Harry Keller   ph Clifford Stine   m Percy Faith

Sandra Dee, John Gavin, Charles Drake, Virginia Grey, *Beulah Bondi*, Julia Meade, Cecil Kellaway, Edgar Buchanan

'The heroine appears to be not so much old-fashioned as positively retarded.' – MFB

Tampico

US   1944   75m   bw
TCF (Robert Bassler)

A tanker captain picks up survivors from a torpedoed ship and finds himself involved with spies.

Very minor action melodrama, efficiently made.

w Kenneth Gamet, Fred Niblo Jnr, Richard Macaulay   d Lothar Mendes   ph Charles G. Clarke   m David Raksin

Edward G. Robinson, Lynn Bari, Victor McLaglen, Marc Lawrence, E. J. Ballentine, Mona Maris

Tampopo **

Japan   1986   117m   colour   Panavision
Itami Productions/New Century Producers (Juzo Itami, Yashushi Tamaoki, Seigo Hosogoe)
V, V*, L

Encouraged by a truck driver, a woman learns to become the best of noodle cooks.

Witty, affectionate, episodic celebration of food as nourishment, pleasure and aid to sexual enjoyment, contained within a parody of film genres, notably the Western.

wd Juzo Itami   ph Masaki Tamura   m Kinihiko Murai   ad Takeo Kimura   ed Akira Suzuki

Tsutomu Yamazaki, Nobuko Miyamoto, Koji Yakuso, Ken Watanabe, Rikiya Yasouka

Tanganyika

US   1954   81m   Technicolor
Universal-International

A 1900 settler finds that the African colony of his choice is terrorized by a murderer.

Curious blend of outdoor action and who-is-it; not at all bad.

w Richard Alan Simmons and William Sackheim   d André de Toth

Van Heflin, Howard Duff, Ruth Roman, Jeff Morrow, Joe Comadaore

Tangier

US   1946   74m   bw
Universal-International

A dancer hunts for the Nazi war criminal responsible for her father's death.

You can tell returns had been bad from the fact that the queen of Technicolor was sentenced to monochrome, and in a two-bit *Casablanca.*

w M. M. Musselman, Monty Collins   d George Waggner

Maria Montez, Kent Taylor, Robert Paige, Sabu, Preston Foster, Louise Albritton, Reginald Denny, J. Edward Bromberg

'A comedy that keeps women hopping.'

Tango ***

France   1993   90m   colour
Cinea/Hachette Premiere/TF1/Zoulou (Henri Brichetti)
V

A woman-hating judge arranges the murder of his nephew's wife by a husband he acquitted of killing his wife and her lover.

An outrageous black comedy and a witty examination of masculine and feminine attitudes to life. Style, and sprightly acting, carry the day.

w Patrice Leconte, Patrick Dewolf   d Patrice Leconte   ph Eduardo Serra   m Angelique and Jean-Claude Nachon   ad Ivan Maussion   ed Genevieve Winding

Philippe Noiret, Richard Bohringer, Thierry Lhermitte, Miou Miou, Judith Godreche, Carole Bouquet, Jean Rochefort

'A deliciously dark comedy.' – *Variety*

Tango & Cash

US   1989   101m   Technicolor   Panavision
Warner/John Peters, Peter Guber
V, V*, L

Two cops, one suave, the other dishevelled, are jailed on a false murder charge but escape to get their revenge.

Deliberately stylized, over-the-top action movie that never touches reality at any point and provides some unintentional amusement.

w Randy Feldman   d Andrei Konchalovsky   ph Donald E. Thorin   m Harold Faltermeyer   pd J. Michael Riva   ed Hubert de La Bouillerie, Robert Ferretti

Sylvester Stallone, Kurt Russell, Jack Palance, Teri Hatcher, Michael J. Pollard, Brion James, Geoffrey Lewis, James Hong, Robert Z'Dar

Tank

US   1984   113m   Metrocolor
Lorimar/Universal (Irwin Yablans)
V*, L

A retired army sergeant lovingly restores an old tank and uses it to secure justice for his wrongly imprisoned son.

Fairly lively if predictable American fantasy in which one just man stands up against the uncaring and/or corrupt mob.

w Dan Gordon   d Marvin Chomsky   ph Don Birnkrant   m Lalo Schifrin   pd Bill Kenney

James Garner, Shirley Jones, C. Thomas Howell, Mark Herrier, Dorian Harewood, G. D. Spradlin

'Further dispiriting evidence of the new reactionary spirit of Reagan's America.' – *Tom Milne, MFB*

Tank Malling

GB   1988   109m   Metrocolor
Cineplex/Parkfield Pictures/Pointlane Films (Glen Murphy, Jamie Foreman)

An investigative reporter is framed for murder.

Trivial thriller with a confusing plot and a silly denouement.

w James Marcus, Mick Southworth   d James Marcus   ph Jason Lehel   m Rick Fenn, Nick Mason   pd Geoffrey Sharpe, Chris Cook   ed Brian Peachey

Ray Winstone, Jason Connery, Amanda Donohue, Glen Murphy, Marsha Hunt, Peter Wyngarde, John Conteh, Terry Marsh, Nick Berry

Tanks a Million

US   1941   50m   bw
Hal Roach

An army recruit has a freak memory which keeps him out of trouble.

Acceptable programme filler.

w Paul Gerard Smith, Warren Wilson, Edward E. Seabrook   d Fred Guiol

William Tracy, James Gleason, Noah Beery Jnr, Joe Sawyer, Elyse Knox, Douglas Fowley

AAN: Edward Ward (music)

The Tanks Are Coming

US   1951   90m   bw
Warner

A tough sergeant learns humility during the race to Berlin.

Tedious war drama which tries in vain to interest us in non-characters.

w Robert Hardy Andrews   d D. Ross Lederman and Lewis Seiler

Steve Cochran, Paul Picerni, Mari Aldon, Harry Bellaver, Philip Carey

Tap *

US   1989   101m   Technicolor   Panavision
Braveworld/Fox/Morgan Creek/BECO (Tony Adams)
V*, L, S

A tap-dancer turned jewel-thief is persuaded to put on his dancing shoes again.

Its slight narrative is bolstered by an enjoyable celebration of the dying art of tap.

wd Nick Castle   ph David Gribble   m James Newton Howard   pd Patricia Norris   ed Patrick Kennedy

Gregory Hines, Suzzanne Douglas, Sammy Davis Jnr, Savion Glover, Joe Morton, Dick Anthony Williams, Sandman Sims, Bunny Briggs, Steve Condos

Tap Roots

US   1948   109m   Technicolor
Universal-International (Walter Wanger)

A Southern family tries to remain neutral in the Civil War.

Minor *Gone with the Wind* saga, quite expensively produced but not very exciting.

w Alan le May   novel James Street   d George Marshall   ph Winton C. Hoch, Lionel Lindon   m Frank Skinner

Susan Hayward, Van Heflin, Boris Karloff, Julie London, Whitfield Connor

Taps

US   1981   126m   DeLuxe
TCF/Stanley Jaffe
V, V*

Cadets at a military academy go on strike when the site is sold for development, and violence ensues.

Rather uninteresting moral fable, comparable with the British *If*. The moral attitudes are worked out on entirely predictable lines.

w Darryl Ponicsan, Robert Mark Kamen *novel* *Father Sky* by Devery Freeman   *d* Harold Becker   *ph* Owen Roizman   *m* Maurice Jarre

Timothy Hutton, George C. Scott, Ronny Cox, Sean Penn, Tom Cruise, Brendan Ward

'Even science was stunned!'
Tarantula
US   1955   80m   bw
U-I (William Alland)
V*, L

Scientists working on an artificial food become grossly misshapen, and an infected spider escapes and grows to giant size.

Moderate monster hokum with the desert setting which became a cliché; the grotesque faces are more horrific than the spider, which seldom seems to touch the ground.

w Robert M. Fresco, Martin Berkeley   *d* Jack Arnold   *ph* George Robinson   *md* Joseph Gershenson

Leo G. Carroll, John Agar, Mara Corday, Nestor Paiva

'It's a great children's picture . . . particularly for bad children. It'll scare hell out of the little monsters.' – *Hollywood Reporter*

'Now! add a motion picture to the wonders of the world!'
Taras Bulba *
US   1962   124m   Eastmancolor   Panavision
UA/H-H/Avala (Harold Hecht)
V*, L

A cossack leader has bitter disagreements with his rebellious son.

Violent action epic based on a well-worn story; plenty of spectacular highlights.

w Waldo Salt, Karl Tunberg   *novel* Nicolai Gogol   *d* J. Lee-Thompson   *ph* Joe MacDonald   *m* Franz Waxman   *pd* Edward Carrere

Yul Brynner, Tony Curtis, Christine Kaufmann, Sam Wanamaker, Guy Rolfe, George Macready, Vladimir Sokoloff, Abraham Sofaer

AAN: Franz Waxman

La Tarea
Mexico   1990   85m   colour
Metro/Clasa Films Mundiales (Pablo Barbachano, Francisco Barbachano)
V
aka: *Homework*

A husband and wife indulge in a sexual fantasy with the aid of a video camera.

Curiously uninvolving, voyeuristic movie that fails to illuminate its theme of sex in the cinema.

wd Jaime Humberto Hermosillo   *ph* Toni Kuhn   *m* Luis Arcaraz   *ad* Laura Santa Cruz

Maria Rojo, José Alonso, Xanic Zepeda, Christopher

Target
US   1985   117m   Technicolor
CBS/Richard Zanuck, David Brown
V, V*, L

When his wife is kidnapped, an ex-spy goes back into action.

Lethargic, simple-minded, and often ludicrous melodrama: the intent seems to be to pile up as many clichés of the genre as the writers can remember.

w Howard Berk, Don Petersen   *d* Arthur Penn   *ph* Jean Tournier   *m* Michael Small

Gene Hackman, Matt Dillon, Gayle Hunnicutt, Josef Sommer, Guy Boyd, Herbert Berghof

Target for Scandal: see *Washington Story*

Target for Tonight ****
GB   1941   48m   bw
The Crown Film Unit
V

The story of a bombing raid over Germany.

Classic RAF semi-documentary, not quite so genuine as it seems since many scenes were re-created in the studio.

w Harry Watt, B. Cooper   *d* Harry Watt

'It looks like a sure grosser . . . one of the must-see films of 1941.' – *Variety*

AA: Special AA

Target Harry
US   1969   81m   colour
ABC/Corman Company (Gene Corman)
aka: *How to Make It*

Various criminals try to discover the whereabouts of printing plates for banknotes that have gone missing from the Royal Mint.

Low budget variation on *The Maltese Falcon* with an uncharismatic cast. The director's name hides the identity of Roger Corman.

w Bob Barbash   *d* Henry Neill   *ph* Patrice Pouget   *m* Les Baxter   *pd* Sharon Compton   *ed* Monte Hellman

Vic Morrow, Suzanne Pleshette, Victor Buono, Cesar Romero, Stanley Holloway, Charlotte Rampling, Michael Ansara, Katy Fraysse, Fikret Hakan

Target Zero
US   1955   93m   bw
Warner (David Weisbart)

An infantry patrol in Korea is cut off behind enemy lines.

Routine battle exploits with a highly unlikely superimposed romance.

w Sam Rolfe   *d* Harmon Jones   *ph* Edwin DuPar   *m* David Buttolph

Richard Conte, Charles Bronson, Richard Stapley, Chuck Connors, L. Q. Jones, Peggie Castle

Targets *
US   1967   90m   Pathecolor
(Paramount) Peter Bogdanovich
V*

An elderly horror film star confronts and disarms a mad sniper at a drive-in movie.

Oddball melodrama apparently meant to contrast real and fantasy violence; it doesn't quite work despite effective moments, and the low budget shows.

wd Peter Bogdanovich   *ph* Laszlo Kovacs

Boris Karloff, Tim O'Kelly, James Brown, Sandy Baron

The Tarnished Angels
US   1957   91m   bw   Cinemascope
U-I (Albert Zugsmith)

A reporter falls in with a self-torturing family of circus air aces.

Unsatisfactory attempt to reunite the talents of *Written on the Wind*; a dull story, very boringly presented.

w George Zuckerman   *novel* *Pylon* by William Faulkner   *d* Douglas Sirk   *ph* Irving Glassberg   *md* Joseph Gershenson   *m* Frank Skinner

Rock Hudson, Robert Stack, Dorothy Malone, Jack Carson, Robert Middleton

'Married to a man she doesn't love! Loving a man she can't have! What does life hold for this pampered beauty of the drawing rooms?'
Tarnished Lady
US   1931   80m   bw
Paramount

Two society women and their lovers cross each other's paths.

Exaggerated melodrama which failed to justify the London stage reputation of its American star.

w Donald Ogden Stewart   *d* George Cukor

Tallulah Bankhead, Clive Brook, Phoebe Foster, Alexander Kirkland, Osgood Perkins, Elizabeth Patterson

'A poor picture that fits the straight grinds best. Heavy production but too ponderous to mean anything.' – *Variety*

Tars and Spars
US   1945   86m   bw
Columbia (Milton H. Bren)

Adventures of members of the Coast Guard's touring wartime revue.

Limp musical with interesting talent.

w John Jacoby, Sarett Tobias, Decla Dunning, Barry Trivers   *d* Alfred E. Green

Alfred Drake, Sid Caesar, Janet Blair, Marc Platt, Jeff Donnell

The Tartars
Italy   1960   105m   Technicolor   Totalscope
Lux (Riccardo Gualino)

Viking settlers on the Russian steppes fight Tartar invaders.

Action-packed comic strip.

d Richard Thorpe   *ph* Amerigo Genarelli   *m* Renzo Rossellini

Orson Welles, Victor Mature, Folco Lulli, Arnoldo Foa

Tartu: see *The Adventures of Tartu*

Tarzan

The talkie *Tarzans* began with Johnny Weissmuller and tailed off from there. (See *Filmgoer's Companion* for the silents.) The 1932 version more or less followed the original Edgar Rice Burroughs novel, and all the MGM entries had a special vivid quality about them, but subsequently the productions, usually produced under the aegis of Sol Lesser, tailed off towards the standard of the TV series of the sixties starring Ron Ely.

1929: TARZAN THE TIGER (qv)
1932: TARZAN THE APE MAN** (MGM: V*, L: Weissmuller with Maureen O'Sullivan: *d* W. S. Van Dyke: 99m). Publicity line: 'Mothered by an ape – he knew the law of the jungle – to seize what he wanted!'
1933: TARZAN THE FEARLESS (qv)
1934: TARZAN AND HIS MATE*** (MGM: V*, L: Weissmuller with Maureen O'Sullivan: *d* Cedric Gibbons: 105m). 'Certainly one of the funniest things you'll ever see.' – *Otis Ferguson*
1935: THE NEW ADVENTURES OF TARZAN (qv)
1936: TARZAN ESCAPES** (MGM: V*, L: Weissmuller with Maureen O'Sullivan: *d* Richard Thorpe: 95m)
1938: TARZAN'S REVENGE (Sol Lesser: V*: Glenn Morris: *d* D. Ross Lederman: 70m); TARZAN AND THE GREEN GODDESS (Principal: Herman Brix (Bruce Bennett): *d* Edward Kull: 72m: largely a re-edit of NEW ADVENTURES)
1939: TARZAN FINDS A SON (MGM: V*, L: Weissmuller with O'Sullivan: *d* Richard Thorpe: 90m)
1941: TARZAN'S SECRET TREASURE (MGM: V*, L: Weissmuller with O'Sullivan: *d* Richard Thorpe: 81m)

1942: TARZAN'S NEW YORK ADVENTURE (MGM: V*, L: Weissmuller with O'Sullivan: *d* Richard Thorpe: 71m)

1943: TARZAN TRIUMPHS (RKO: Weissmuller: *d* William Thiele: 78m); TARZAN'S DESERT MYSTERY (RKO: Weissmuller: *d* William Thiele: 70m)

1945: TARZAN AND THE AMAZONS (RKO: Weissmuller: *d* Kurt Neumann: 76m)

1946: TARZAN AND THE LEOPARD WOMAN (RKO: Weissmuller: *d* Kurt Neumann: 72m)

1947: TARZAN AND THE HUNTRESS (RKO: Weissmuller: *d* Kurt Neumann: 72m)

1948: TARZAN AND THE MERMAIDS (RKO: *d* Robert Florey: Weissmuller: 68m)

1949: TARZAN'S MAGIC FOUNTAIN (RKO: Lex Barker: *d* Lee Sholem: 73m)

1950: TARZAN AND THE SLAVE GIRL (RKO: Lex Barker: *d* Lee Sholem: 74m)

1951: TARZAN'S PERIL (RKO: Lex Barker: *d* Byron Haskin: 79m)

1952: TARZAN'S SAVAGE FURY (RKO: Lex Barker: *d* Cy Endfield: 80m)

1953: TARZAN AND THE SHE-DEVIL (aka: *Tarzan Meets the Vampire*) (RKO: Lex Barker: *d* Kurt Neumann: 76m)

1955: TARZAN'S HIDDEN JUNGLE (RKO: Gordon Scott: *d* Harold Schuster: 73m)

1957: TARZAN AND THE LOST SAFARI (colour) (Solar: Gordon Scott: *d* Bruce Humberstone: 84m)

1958: TARZAN'S FIGHT FOR LIFE (colour) (MGM: Gordon Scott: *d* Bruce Humberstone: 86m)

1959: TARZAN'S GREATEST ADVENTURE (colour) (Solar: Gordon Scott: *d* John Guillermin: 90m)

1959: TARZAN THE APE MAN (colour: remake of the original story) (MGM: Denny Miller: *d* Joseph Newman: 82m)

1960: TARZAN THE MAGNIFICENT (colour) (Paramount: Gordon Scott: *d* Robert Day: 88m)

1962: TARZAN GOES TO INDIA (colour) (MGM: Jock Mahoney: *d* John Guillermin: 86m)

1963: TARZAN'S THREE CHALLENGES (colour) (MGM: Jock Mahoney: *d* Robert Day: 92m)

1966: TARZAN AND THE VALLEY OF GOLD (colour) (NatGen: Mike Henry: *d* Robert Day: 90m)

1967: TARZAN AND THE GREAT RIVER (colour) (Paramount: Mike Henry: *d* Robert Day: 88m)

1968: TARZAN AND THE JUNGLE BOY (colour) (Paramount: Mike Henry: *d* Robert Day: 90m)

1981: TARZAN THE APE MAN (colour) (MGM: Miles O'Keefe: *d* John Derek; 112m). A debased version with the emphasis on the undressed Jane played by Bo Derek. Publicity line: 'The most exciting pair in the jungle!'

1984: GREYSTOKE: THE LEGEND OF TARZAN, LORD OF THE APES (qv). A pretentious retelling of the original story.

Tarzan the Fearless
US   1933   bw   serial: 15 eps
Principal

Tarzan rescues explorers from the lost city of Zar, God of the Jewelled Fingers.

Lively serial version of a production also released as a feature.

d Robert Hill

Buster Crabbe, Jacqueline Wells, E. Alyn Warren, Edward Woods, Mischa Auer (as high priest)

Tarzan the Tiger
US   1929   bw   serial: 10 eps
Universal

Tarzan rescues Jane from slave traders.

Primitive talkie serial.

d Henry McRae

Frank Merrill, Natalie Kingston, Lillian Worth, Al Ferguson

'It's that rare kind of movie that lights the spark that lights the heart!'
Task Force
US   1949   116m   bw (Technicolor sequences)
Warner (Jerry Wald)

An admiral about to retire recalls his struggle to promote the cause of aircraft carriers.

Stilted and long-drawn-out flagwaver with too much chat and action highlights borrowed from wartime newsreel.

wd Delmer Daves   *ph* Robert Burks, Wilfrid M. Cline   *m* Franz Waxman

Gary Cooper, Walter Brennan, Jane Wyatt, Wayne Morris, Julie London, Bruce Bennett, Stanley Ridges, Jack Holt

A Taste of Excitement
GB   1968   99m   Eastmancolor
Trio Films (George Willoughby)

An English girl holidaying on the Riviera suspects that someone is trying to kill her.

Standard frightened lady/'they won't believe me' mystery with enough twists to satisfy addicts.

w Brian Carton, Don Sharp   *novel* *Waiting for a Tiger* by Ben Healey   *d* Don Sharp   *ph* Paul Beeson   *m* Keith Mansfield

Eva Renzi, David Buck, Peter Vaughan, Sophie Hardy, Paul Hubschmid, Kay Walsh

Taste of Fear **
GB   1961   82m   bw
Columbia/Hammer (Jimmy Sangster)
US title: *Scream of Fear*

A crippled heiress visits her long-lost father and is haunted by his corpse.

Smartly tricked-out sub-Hitchcock screamer with sudden shocks among the Riviera settings and a plot which Hammer borrowed from *Les Diaboliques* and used again and again.

w Jimmy Sangster   *d* Seth Holt   *ph* Douglas Slocombe   *m* Clifton Parker   *ad* Tom Goswell   *ed* James Needs, Eric Boyd Perkins

Susan Strasberg, Ann Todd, Ronald Lewis, Christopher Lee, Leonard Sachs

'All those creaking shutters, flickering candles, wavering shadows and pianos playing in empty rooms still yield a tiny frisson.' – *Penelope Houston*

'It plays its particular brand of the three-card trick with ingenuity and without scruple.' – *The Times*

A Taste of Honey ***
GB   1961   100m   bw
British Lion/Bryanston/Woodfall (Tony Richardson)
V, V*

Adventures of a pregnant Salford teenager, her sluttish mother, black lover and homosexual friend.

Fascinating offbeat comedy drama with memorable characters and sharply etched backgrounds.

w Shelagh Delaney, Tony Richardson   *play* Shelagh Delaney   *d* Tony Richardson   *ph* Walter Lassally   *m* John Addison

Rita Tushingham, Dora Bryan, Murray Melvin, Robert Stephens, Paul Danquah

'Tart and lively around the edges and bitter at the core.' – *Peter John Dyer*

'Rich, full work, directed with an unerring sense of rightness.' – *New Yorker*

Taste the Blood of Dracula
GB   1970   95m   Technicolor
Warner/Hammer (Aida Young)
V, V*

A depraved peer involves three Victorian businessmen in the reactivation of Dracula.

Latterday vampire saga, initially lively but mainly dreary.

w John Elder (Anthony Hinds)   *d* Peter Sasdy   *ph* Arthur Grant   *m* James Bernard   *ad* Scott MacGregor   *ed* Chris Barnes

Christopher Lee, Geoffrey Keen, Gwen Watford, Linda Hayden, Peter Sallis, Anthony Corlan, John Carson, Ralph Bates

'You haven't met her yet and she already hates you.'
Tatie Danielle **
France   1990   112m   colour
Palace/Téléma/FR3/Les Productions du Champ Poirer/Sofica (Charles Gassot)
V, V*, L

A malicious elderly woman creates problems when she moves in with her nephew's family.

Sharp and enjoyable black comedy.

w Florence Quentin   *d* Etienne Chatillez   *ph* Philippe Welt   *m* Gabriel Yared   *pd* Geoffroy Larcher   *ed* Catherine Renault

Tsilla Chelton, Catherine Jacob, Isabelle Nanty, Neige Dolsky, Eric Pratt, Laurence Février, Virgine Pradal

'A tart comedy providing welcome Gallic relief to the saccharine Hollywood-endorsed stereotypes of the elderly as armchair dispensers of love and bromides.' – *Variety*

The Tattered Dress
US   1957   93m   bw   Cinemascope
U-I (Albert Zugsmith)

While conducting a murder defence, a criminal lawyer annoys a vindictive small-town sheriff, who plots revenge.

Silly melodrama which rapidly loses interest after a promising start.

w George Zuckerman   *d* Jack Arnold   *ph* Carl Guthrie   *m* Frank Skinner

Jeff Chandler, Jack Carson, Jeanne Crain, Gail Russell, George Tobias, Edward Andrews, Philip Reed

'Every great love leaves its mark!'
Tattoo
US   1980   103m   Technicolor
Joseph E. Levine (Robert F. Colesberry)
V, V*

A mad tattooist kidnaps a cover girl and tattoos her all over before forcing her to have sex. She kills him.

And not before time.

w Joyce Bunuel   *d* Bob Brooks   *ph* Arthur Ornitz   *m* Barry de Vorzon   *pd* Stuart Wurtzel

Bruce Dern, Maud Adams, Leonard Frey, Rikke Borge

'*The Collector* crossed with *Ai No Corrida* . . . a sensational package for the eighties confected from ideas half remembered from other films.' – *Mark Lefanu, MFB*

Tawny Pipit *
GB   1944   85m   bw
GFD/Two Cities (Bernard Miles)

The life of a village in wartime is disrupted when two rare birds nest in a local meadow.

Pleasant, thin little comedy, a precursor of the Ealing school.

wd Bernard Miles, Charles Saunders   *ph* Eric Cross   *m* Noel Mewton-Wood

Bernard Miles, Rosamund John, Niall MacGinnis, Jean Gillie, Christopher Steele, Lucie Mannheim, Brefni O'Rourke, Marjorie Rhodes

'Almost unimaginably genteel.' – *James Agee*

'Not quite dry enough for the epicures nor sweet enough for the addicts.' – *C. A. Lejeune*

'Seldom does such a piece of unsophisticated charm and humour reach the screen.' – *New York Times*

Taxi!
US   1931   68m   bw
Warner (Robert Lord)

Independent cab drivers defy a powerful trust.

Sassy comedy drama with plenty going on.

w Kubec Glasmon, John Bright   *play The Blind Spot* by Kenyon Nicholson   d Roy del Ruth   ph James Van Trees   md Leo Forbstein

James Cagney, Loretta Young, George E. Stone, Guy Kibbee, David Landau, Leila Bennett, Matt McHugh

'As a deese, dem and dose, chip-on-the-shoulder, on-the-make example of young America the audience knows no better interpretation on the screen than that which Cagney gives it. The populace are now expectant of this player socking all and sundry including all the women in the cast.' – *Variety*

'A sordid but amusing observation on minor metropolitan endeavours.' – *Time*

Taxi
US   1952   77m   bw
TCF (Samuel G. Engel)

A taxi driver helps a young mother find her husband, and falls for her himself.

Practised sentimental guff, Hollywoodized from the French film *Sans Laisser d'Adresse*.

w D. M. Marshman Jnr, Daniel Fuchs   d Gregory Ratoff   ph Milton Krasner   m Leigh Harline

Dan Dailey, Constance Smith, Neva Patterson, Blanche Yurka, Walter Woolf King

The Taxi Dancer
US   1926   64m at 24 fps   bw   silent
MGM

A Virginia girl in the big city rises from dime-a-dance joints to the big time.

Mildly suggestive star melodrama which promises more than it gives.

w A. P. Younger and Robert Terry Shannon   d Harry Millarde

Joan Crawford, Owen Moore, Douglas Gilmore, Marc McDermott, Gertrude Astor

Taxi Driver ****
US   1976   114m   Metrocolor
Columbia/Italo-Judeo (Michael and Julia Philips)
V, V*, L, S

A lonely Vietnam veteran becomes a New York taxi driver and allows the violence and squalor around him to explode in his mind.

The epitome of the sordid realism of the 70s, this unlovely but brilliantly made film haunts the mind and paints a most vivid picture of a hell on earth.

w Paul Schrader   d Martin Scorsese   ph Michael Chapman   m Bernard Herrmann

Robert de Niro, Jodie Foster, Cybill Shepherd, Peter Boyle, Leonard Harris, Harvey Keitel

'I don't question the truth of this material. I question Scorsese's ability to lift it out of the movie gutters into which less truthful directors have trampled it.' – *Stanley Kauffmann*

† Schrader says the story was modelled after the diaries of would-be assassin Arthur Bremer.

AAN: best picture; Bernard Herrmann; Robert de Niro; Jodie Foster

Taxi to the Toilet: see *Taxi Zum Klo*

Taxi Zum Klo *
West Germany   1981   92m   colour
Laurens Straub, Frank Ripploh, Horst Schier
V, V*
aka: *Taxi to the Toilet*

A homosexual schoolteacher, at odds with his home-loving partner, spends his spare time cruising lavatories, bars and parks in search of sex.

A semi-autobiographical film, saved from unpleasantness by its sense of humour. Its scenes of homosexual activity in grubby lavatories, seedy apartments and at a tacky drag ball may turn off all but the similarly inclined.

wd Frank Ripploh   ph Horst Schier   m Hans Wittstatt   ed Marina Runne, Mathias von Gunten

Frank Ripploh, Bernd Broaderup, Orpha Termin, Peter Fahrni, Dieter Godde

'An admirable film, not least for tackling its subject with a warm sense of humour.' – *Films and Filming*

A Taxing Woman **
Japan   1987   130m   colour   Panavision
Itami Productions (Juzo Itami)
V*, L
original title: *Marusa no onna*

A dedicated female tax inspector investigates the financial affairs of a crooked hotelier

Quirky, slyly observant comedy of greed that was a big hit in Japan.

wd Juzo Itami   ph Yonezo Maeda

Nobuko Miyamoto, Tsutomu Yamazaki, Masahiko Tsugawa, Hideo Murota, Mitsuko Sugino

Taza, Son of Cochise
US   1954   79m   Technicolor
Universal-International

Peace-loving Taza succeeds his dad and tries not to be influenced by Geronimo.

Routine pro-Indian Western.

w George Zuckerman and Gerald Drayson Adams   d Douglas Sirk

Rock Hudson (as Taza), Barbara Rush, Gregg Palmer, Bart Roberts, Morris Ankrum

'Years from now, when you talk about this – and you will – be kind!'
'Even the most daring story can be brought onto the screen when done with courage, honesty and good taste.'

Tea and Sympathy
US   1956   122m   Metrocolor   Cinemascope
MGM (Pandro S. Berman)
V*, L

A sensitive teenage schoolboy is scorned by his tougher classmates, but his housemaster's wife takes him in hand . . .

Overblown and bowdlerized version of a quiet little Broadway play; impeccable production values, but no spark.

w Robert Anderson (and the Hays office)   play Robert Anderson   d Vincente Minnelli   ph John Alton   m Adolph Deutsch

Deborah Kerr, *John Kerr*, Leif Erickson, Edward Andrews, Darryl Hickman

'. . . mounted for the screen as if it were a precious objet d'art in danger from rioting but miraculously saved. Besides being archaic, the film is a prodigiously silly fable, pulling the realities with which it deals dishonestly, systematically out of whack.' – *Parker Tyler*

Tea for Two *
US   1950   97m   Technicolor
Warner (William Jacobs)
V*, L

A nearly bankrupt financier promises his niece 25,000

dollars for her new musical show if she can say no to every question for twenty-four hours.

Tinkly, quite amusing light musical which has little to do with *No No Nanette* on which it is allegedly based.

w Harry Clork   d David Butler   ph Wilfrid Cline   md Ray Heindorf   ch Le Roy Prinz

Doris Day, Gordon Macrae, Gene Nelson, Eve Arden, Billy de Wolfe, S. Z. Sakall, Bill Goodwin, Patrice Wymore

Teachers
US   1984   106m   Metrocolor
MGM-UA (Aaron Russo)

A burnt-out teacher is drawn back to his ideas despite, or because of, apparent lunacy in the administration.

Wildly unconsidered black comedy which takes stabs at everything and hits nothing.

w W. R. McKinney   d Arthur Hiller   ph David M. Walsh   m Sandy Gibson   pd Richard MacDonald   ed Don Zimmermann

Nick Nolte, JoBeth Williams, Judd Hirsch, Ralph Macchio, Richard Mulligan, Allen Garfield, Royal Dano

Teacher's Pet *
US   1958   120m   bw   Vistavision
Paramount/Perlberg-Seaton (William Perlberg)
V*, L

A tough city editor falls for a lady professor of journalism and enrols as a student.

Overlong one-joke comedy which quickly reneges on its early promise; but the principals play up divertingly.

w Fay and Michael Kanin   d George Seaton   ph Haskell Boggs   m Roy Webb

Clark Gable, Doris Day, Gig Young, Mamie Van Doren, Nick Adams

AAN: Fay and Michael Kanin; Gig Young

The Teahouse of the August Moon *
US   1956   123m   Metrocolor   Cinemascope
MGM (Jack Cummings)
V*, L

Okinawa 1944: a wily interpreter helps American troops succumb to the oriental way of life.

Adequate, well-acted screen version of a Broadway comedy which succeeded largely because of its theatricality. A few good jokes remain.

w John Patrick   play John Patrick   d Daniel Mann   ph John Alton   m Saul Chaplin

Marlon Brando, Glenn Ford, Eddie Albert, *Paul Ford,* Michiko Kyo, Henry Morgan

Tears for Simon: see *Lost*

The Teckman Mystery
GB   1954   90m   bw
British Lion/London Films/Corona (Josef Somlo)

An author commissioned to write the biography of a dead airman finds him very much alive and his own life in danger.

Peripatetic spy story with the twists expected of this author; all quite enjoyable.

w Francis Durbridge, James Matthews   BBC serial Francis Durbridge   d Wendy Toye   ph Jack Hilyard   m Clifton Parker

Margaret Leighton, John Justin, Michael Medwin, Meier Tzelniker, Roland Culver, George Coulouris, Raymond Huntley, Duncan Lamont

Teen Agent

US 1991 88m Technicolor
Warner (Craig Zadan, Neil Meron)
V, V*, L
aka: *If Looks Could Kill*

A student is mistaken for a CIA undercover agent and assigned to guard a top European politician.

Tired teenage copy of the James Bond formula of gags and gadgetry.

w Darren Star story Fred Dekker d William Dear
ph Doug Milsome m David Foster pd Guy J.
Comtois ed John F. Link, Mark Stevens

Richard Grieco, Linda Hunt, Roger Rees, Robin Bartlett, Gabrielle Anwar, Geraldine James, Roger Daltrey

Teen Wolf

US 1985 91m United Color Lab Color
Entertainment/Atlantic (Mark Levinson, Scott Rosenfelt)
V, V*, L

An ineffective college basketball player finds he is a hereditary werewolf, and in his altered form becomes a star.

Bewilderingly silly teenage variation on a famous legend, good-natured but totally empty.

w Joseph Loeb III, Matthew Weisman d Rod
Daniel ph Tim Suhrstedt m Miles Goodman
ed Lois Freeman-Fox

Michael J. Fox, James Hampton, Scott Paulin, Susan Ursitti

Teen Wolf Too

US 1987 94m colour
Entertainment/Atlantic (Kent Bateman)
V, V*, L

A college student with a talent for boxing makes the most of the fact that he is a werewolf.

Drear comedy sequel that attempts to reprise the original with a leaden touch.

w R. Timothy Kring story Joseph Loeb III, Matthew
Weisman d Christopher Leitch ph Jules Brenner
m Mark Goldenberg ad Peg McClellan ed Steven
Polivka, Kim Secrist, Harvey Rosenstock, Raja
Gosnell

Jason Bateman, Kim Darby, John Astin, Paul Sand, James Hampton, Mark Holton, Estee Chandler

Teenage Bad Girl: see *My Teenage Daughter*

Teenage Frankenstein: see *I Was a Teenage Frankenstein*

Teenage Monster

US 1957 65m bw
Marquette Productions

A meteor turns a home-loving teenager into a hairy rampaging monster.

Ridiculous monster movie, inept in every respect.

w Ray Buffum d Jacques Marquette ph Taylor
Byars

Anne Gwynne, Gloria Castillo, Stuart Wade, Gilbert Perkins, Steven Parker, Charles Courtney

'Mean. Green. And on the screen'
Teenage Mutant Ninja Turtles *

US 1990 93m Technicolor
Virgin/Golden Harvest/Limelight (Kim Dawson, Simon Fields, David Chan)
V, V*, L, S

Pizza-loving, sewer-dwelling turtles and their rat guru, mutated into half-human creatures by radioactivity, battle against a gang of teenage martial arts experts led by an evil Japanese ninja.

Comic-book mayhem brought to the screen in the frenetic style of rock videos, it took more money at the box-office than any other independent film has ever done.

w Todd W. Langen, Bobby Herbeck, from comic-book characters created by Kevin Eastman and Peter Laird
d Steve Barron ph John Fenner m John Du Prez
pd Roy Forge Smith sp creatures designed by Jim
Henson's Creature Shop ed William Gordean, Sally
Menke, James Symons

Judith Hoag, Elias Koteas, Josh Pais, Michelan Sisti, Leif Tilden, David Forman, James Sato

Teenage Mutant Ninja Turtles II: The Secret of the Ooze

US 1991 87m colour
TCF/Golden Harvest (Thomas K. Gray, Kim Dawson, David Chan)
V, V*, L, S

The four mutant ninja turtles go into battle against their arch-enemy Shredder and his two new monsters, a mutant dog and tortoise.

A tame sequel, seemingly aimed at the young audience that watches the anodyne animated TV cartoon versions of the four sewer-dwelling heroes.

w Todd W. Langen d Michael Pressman
ph Shelly Johnson m John Du Prez pd Ray Forge
Smith ed John Wright, Steve Mirkovich

Paige Turco, David Warner, Michelan Sisti, Leif Tilden, Kenn Troum, Mark Caso, Kevin Clash, Ernie Reyes Jnr, François Chau

'If watching the first Turtles film was like chewing a good pizza, watching II is more like munching on the cardboard packaging, but – as fast food goes – even that can taste good enough in parts.' – *David Lusted, Sight and Sound*

Teenage Mutant Ninja Turtles III: The Turtles Are Back . . . in Time

US 1992 96m Technicolor
TCF/Golden Harvest/Clearwater (Thomas K. Gray, Kim Dawson, David Chan)

The turtles travel back to 17th-century Japan to rescue their friend.

The least of the adventures, a tired and aimless movie lacking in fun.

wd Stuart Gillard ph David Gurfinkel m John Du
Prez pd Roy Forge Smith ed William D. Gordean,
James R. Symons

Elias Koteas, Paige Turco, Stuart Wilson, Sab Shimono, Vivian Wu, Mark Caso, Matt Hill, Jim Raposa, David Fraser, James Murray, Henry Hayashi

'A decided case of diminishing returns.' – *Variety*

Teenage Rebel

US 1956 94m bw Cinemascope
TCF (Charles Brackett)

A wealthy California woman is visited by her teenage daughter from a former marriage; the girl proceeds to make difficulties for everyone.

The first film in black-and-white Cinemascope is a tedious drama of unreal people.

w Walter Reisch, Charles Brackett play Edith
Sommer d Edmund Goulding ph Joe MacDonald
m Leigh Harline ad Lyle Wheeler, Jack Martin
Smith

Ginger Rogers, Michael Rennie, Mildred Natwick, Betty Lou Keim, Warren Berlinger, Louise Beavers, Irene Hervey

AAN: art direction

Teheran

GB 1947 86m bw
Pendennis
US title: *The Plot to Kill Roosevelt*

A correspondent in Iran foils an assassination plot.

Low-key blood and thunder; passable time-filler.

w Akos Tolnay, William Freshman d William
Freshman, Giacomo Gentilomo

Derek Farr, Marta Labarr, Manning Whiley, John Slater, John Warwick

'Your next phone call may be your last!'
Telefon *

US 1977 103m Metrocolor Panavision
MGM (James B. Harris)
V*

A Russian agent is instructed to seek out and destroy a ring of hard liners who are opposing detente with the west.

Moderately watchable espionage capers with a slightly new twist.

w Peter Hyams, Stirling Silliphant novel Walter
Wager d Don Siegel ph Michael Butler m Lalo
Schifrin

Charles Bronson, Lee Remick, Donald Pleasence, Tyne Daly, Alan Badel, Patrick Magee, Sheree North

Le Téléphone Rose: see *The Pink Telephone*

Television Spy

US 1939 58m bw
Paramount

Enemy agents compete for the secret of long-range television transmission.

Watchable pocket thriller, with the hero and heroine getting acquainted only by television from a 3000-mile distance.

w Horace McCoy, William R. Lipman, Lillie Hayward
d Edward Dmytryk

William Henry, Judith Barrett, William Collier Snr, Anthony Quinn, Richard Denning, John Eldredge

'It may move slowly, but it does avoid the absurdity that goes with the average film crack at television.' – *Variety*

Tell England

GB 1931 88m bw
British Instructional
US title: *The Battle of Gallipoli*

In 1914, school chums join up and mostly die at Gallipoli.

Even the most patriotic audiences ended up roaring with laughter at this stiff-upper-lip charade.

w Anthony Asquith novel Ernest Raymond
d Anthony Asquith, Gerald Barkas

Carl Harbord, Fay Compton, Tony Bruce, Dennis Hoey, Gerald Rawlinson, Wally Patch

'Not likely to bring in any money.' – *Variety*

Tell It to a Star

US 1945 67m bw
Republic (Walter H. Goetz)

A cigarette girl in a Florida hotel aspires to be a vocalist.

The plot sets the level: minor musical.

w John K. Butler d Frank McDonald

Ruth Terry, Robert Livingston, Alan Mowbray, Franklin Pangborn, Isabel Randolph

Tell It to the Judge

US 1949 87m bw
Columbia (Buddy Adler)
V*

A female candidate for judicial honours is suddenly re-attracted to her divorced husband.

Leaden farce, relying entirely on its stars.

w Nat Perrin, Devery Freeman, Roland Kibbee
d Norman Foster ph Joseph Walker m Werner
Heyman

Rosalind Russell, Robert Cummings, Gig Young, Marie McDonald, Harry Davenport

Tell It to the Marines
US   1926   75m at 24 fps   bw   silent
MGM

A marine sergeant has an eventful time during training and in the Philippines.

Lively war action piece with a more or less straight role for its star.

w Richard Schayer   *d* George Hill

Lon Chaney, William Haines, Eleanor Boardman, Carmel Myers, Warner Oland

Tell Me a Riddle
US   1980   90m   CFI color
Godmother/Filmways
V*

A dying old woman, long a recluse, is reconciled with her family.

Adequate if not exciting treatment of a very downbeat subject.

w Joyce Eliason, Alev Lytle   *novel* Tillie Olsen
d Lee Grant

Lila Kedrova, Melvyn Douglas, Brooke Adams, Dolores Dorn, Lili Valenty, Zalman King

Tell Me That You Love Me, Junie Moon
US   1969   113m   Technicolor
Paramount/Sigma (Otto Preminger)

A disfigured girl, a homosexual paraplegic and an introvert epileptic set up house together.

Absurd tragicomedy which remains disturbingly icky in conception and execution.

w Marjorie Kellogg   *novel* Marjorie Kellogg
d Otto Preminger   *ph* Boris Kaufman   *m* Philip Springer

Liza Minnelli, Ken Howard, Robert Moore, Kay Thompson, Leonard Frey, James Coco, Fred Williamson

'Like seeing a venerated senior citizen desperately trying to show he's in love with today by donning see-through clothes.' – *Michael Billington, Illustrated London News*

'It slushes us with sentimentality to the point past compassion.' – *Judith Crist*

Tell Me Tonight
GB/Germany   1932   91m   bw
Herman Fellner-Josef Somlo/Cine Alliance
US title: *Be Mine Tonight*

An Italian tenor falls in love with a Swiss mayor's daughter, but complicates matters by pretending to be someone else.

Bilingual operetta, fondly remembered for its singing star.

w John Orton   *d* Anatole Litvak

Jan Kiepura, Sonnie Hale, Magda Schneider, Edmund Gwenn, Athene Seyler

Tell No Tales **
US   1939   68m   bw
MGM (Edward Chodorov)

A managing editor seeks a big scoop to save his newspaper, and solves a kidnap-murder case.

Intriguingly written and handled second feature, with excellent pace, performance and entertainment value.

w Lionel Houser   *d* Leslie Fenton   *ph* Joseph Ruttenberg   *m* William Axt

Melvyn Douglas, Louise Platt, Gene Lockhart, Douglass Dumbrille, Zeffie Tilbury, Halliwell Hobbes

'Full of excellent detail, and the smallest part is a genuine character. Add these qualities to its pace and

excitement and you have something well worth seeing.' – *Richard Mallett, Punch*

Tell Them Willie Boy is Here *
US   1969   97m   Technicolor
Universal/Jennings Lang (Philip A. Waxman)
V, V*, L

In 1909 an Indian turned cowboy comes up against old prejudices and is pursued into the desert after an accidental death.

Boringly predictable story of white man's guilt, very professionally made.

wd Abraham Polonsky,   *novel* Willie Boy by Harry Lawton   *ph* Conrad Hall   *m* Dave Grusin

Robert Redford, Robert Blake, Katharine Ross, Susan Clark, Barry Sullivan, Charles McGraw, Charles Aidman, John Vernon

The Temp
US   1993   95m   DeLuxe
Paramount/Columbus Circle (David Permut, Tom Engelman)
V, V*

A temporary secretary works her way up the executive ladder.

A feeble and forgettable drama of office life.

w Kevin Falls   *d* Tom Holland   *ph* Steve Yaconelli   *m* Frederic Talgorn   *pd* Joel Schiller   *ed* Scott Conrad

Timothy Hutton, Lara Flynn Boyle, Dwight Schultz, Oliver Platt, Steven Weber, Colleen Flynn, Faye Dunaway

'Derivative, artificial and moronic are the first adjectives that come to mind to describe this concoction.' – *Variety*

The Tempest
GB   1980   95m   Eastmancolor
Boyd's Company

A punk version of Shakespeare's play; less horrendous than might be supposed, but far from interesting in its own right.

wd Derek Jarman   *ph* Peter Middleton
m Wavemaker

Heathcote Williams, Karl Johnson, Toyah Wilcox, Peter Bull, Richard Warwick, Elisabeth Welch

Tempest
Italy/France/Yugoslavia   1958   123m   Technirama
(Paramount) Dino de Laurentiis/Gray/S. N Pathé/Bosnia

Adventures of a Russian ensign banished by Catherine the Great.

Expensive but sloppy epic which fails to generate much interest.

w Louis Peterson, Alberto Lattuada, Ivo Perelli
novel The Captain's Daughter by Alexander Pushkin
d Alberto Lattuada   *ph* Aldo Tonti   *m* Piero Piccioni

Van Heflin, Geoffrey Horne, Silvana Mangano, Oscar Homolka, Viveca Lindfors, Robert Keith, Vittorio Gassman, Finlay Currie, Agnes Moorehead, Helmut Dantine, Laurence Naismith

'Most men dream their fantasies. Philip decided to live his!'
Tempest
US   1982   142m   DeLuxe
Columbia (Paul Mazursky)
V*

An architect leaves his unfaithful wife and takes his daughter to live on a Greek island attended only by a half-witted shepherd.

Absurd attempt to update Shakespeare; any initial amusement quickly gives way to abject boredom.

w Paul Mazursky, Leon Capetanos   *d* Paul Mazursky   *ph* Don McAlpine   *m* Stomu Yamashta   *pd* Pato Guzman

John Cassavetes, Gena Rowlands, Susan Sarandon, Vittorio Gassman, Raul Julia, Jerry Hardin, Molly Ringwald, Paul Stewart

'An aura of dottiness hangs over it . . . the fact remains that it is handsomely visualized and, within the limits of the material, excellently played.' – *Tim Pulleine, MFB*

Tempos dificeis, este tempo: see *Hard Times*

Temptation
US   1946   92m   bw
Universal (Edward Small)

An archaeologist's wife takes to poisoning both her husband and her blackmailing lover.

Hoary Edwardian melodrama, unpersuasively restaged.

w Robert Thoeren   *novel* Bella Donna by Robert Hichens   *d* Irving Pichel   *ph* Lucien Ballard   *m* Daniele Amfitheatrof

Merle Oberon, George Brent, Charles Korvin, Paul Lukas, Lenore Ulric, Arnold Moss, Ludwig Stossel, Gavin Muir, Ilka Gruning, André Charlot

Temptation Harbour
GB   1946   104m   bw
ABP (Victor Skutezky)

A railway signalman finds and keeps stolen money.

Well-presented but boringly predictable melodrama with an overwrought leading performance set against yards of studio fog.

w Victor Skutezky, Frederic Gotfurt, Rodney Ackland   *novel* Newhaven/Dieppe by Georges Simenon   *d* Lance Comfort

Robert Newton, Simone Simon, William Hartnell, Marcel Dalio, Margaret Barton, Edward Rigby, Joan Hopkins, Charles Victor, Kathleen Harrison

The Temptress *
US   1927   80m (24 fps)   bw   silent
MGM

An immoral woman drives men to disgrace, murder and suicide.

No-holds-barred melodrama which, being Garbo's second American film, fully confirmed her stardom.

w Dorothy Farnum   *d* Mauritz Stiller, Fred Niblo

Greta Garbo, Antonio Moreno, Lionel Barrymore, Roy D'Arcy, Marc McDermott

'Just when he thought it was safe to go back in the water . . .'
'10'
US   1979   122m   Metrocolor   Panavision
Warner/Orion/Geoffrey (Blake Edwards, Tony Adams)
V, V*, L

A sex-mad middle-aged composer marks his girls from one to ten according to their performance.

Randy farce which struck some, but not all, audiences as the funniest thing since sliced bread.

wd Blake Edwards   *ph* Frank Stanley   *m* Henry Mancini   *pd* Rodger Maus

Dudley Moore, Julie Andrews, Bo Derek, Robert Webber, Dee Wallace, Sam Jones

AAN: Henry Mancini; song 'It's Easy to Say' (*m* Henry Mancini, *ly* Robert Wells)

Ten Cents a Dance
US   1931   75m   bw
Columbia

A dance hostess is desired by a rich man but marries a ne'er-do-well.

Rubbishy story inspired by a then-popular song.

w Jo Swerling   *d* Lionel Barrymore

Barbara Stanwyck, Monroe Owsley, Ricardo Cortez, Sally Blane, Blanche Friderici

'It lacks the magic of fancy that makes for universal entertainment.' – *Variety*

'The mightiest dramatic spectacle of all the ages!'
The Ten Commandments **
US   1923   150m approx (24 fps)   part Technicolor silent
Paramount/Famous Players-Lasky (Cecil B. de Mille)
V*, L, S

Moses leads the Israelites into the promised land in modern San Francisco; a story of two brothers shows the power of prayer and truth.

The two halves in fact are totally disconnected; but this is a de Mille spectacular and therefore beyond reproach, while as a Hollywood milestone it cannot be denied a place in the Hall of Fame.

w Jeanie MacPherson   *d* Cecil B. de Mille   *ph* Bert Glennon and others (colour, Ray Rennahan)

Theodore Roberts, Richard Dix, Rod la Rocque, Edythe Chapman, Leatrice Joy, Nita Naldi

'It will last as long as the film on which it is recorded.' – *James R. Quirk, Photoplay*

'What a story it tells! What majesty it encompasses! What loves it unveils! What drama it unfolds!'
The Ten Commandments *
US   1956   219m   Technicolor   Vistavision
Paramount/Cecil B. de Mille (Henry Wilcoxon)
V, V (W), V*, L

The life of Moses and his leading of the Israelites to the Promised Land.

Popular but incredibly stilted and verbose bible-in-pictures spectacle. A very long haul along a monotonous route, with the director at his pedestrian worst.

w Aeneas Mackenzie, Jesse L. Lasky Jnr, Jack Gariss, Frederic M. Frank   *d* Cecil B. de Mille   *ph* Loyal Griggs   *m* Elmer Bernstein   *ad* Hal Pereira, Walter H. Tyler, Albert Nozaki   *ed* Anne Bauchens

Charlton Heston, Yul Brynner, Edward G. Robinson, Anne Baxter, Nina Foch, Yvonne de Carlo, John Derek, H. B. Warner, Henry Wilcoxon, Judith Anderson, John Carradine, Douglass Dumbrille, Cedric Hardwicke, Martha Scott, Vincent Price, Debra Paget

'De Mille not only moulds religion into a set pattern of Hollywood conventions; he has also become an expert at making entertainment out of it.' – *Gordon Gow, Films and Filming*

'The result of all these stupendous efforts? Something roughly comparable to an eight-foot chorus girl – pretty well put together, but much too big and much too flashy. . . . What de Mille has really done is to throw sex and sand into the moviegoers' eyes for almost twice as long as anyone else has ever dared to.' – *Time*

AA: special effects (John Fulton)

AAN: best picture; Loyal Griggs; art direction; editing; sound; costumes (Edith Head and others)

Ten Days in Paris
GB   1939   82m   bw
Columbia/Irving Asher (Jerome J. Jackson)
US titles: Missing Ten Days; Spy in the Pantry

An amnesiac wakes up in Paris and finds he has been involved in espionage activities.

Modest, quite likeable little comedy suspenser.

w John Meehan Jnr, James Curtis   *novel The Disappearance of Roger Tremayne* by Bruce Graeme   *d* Tim Whelan   *ph* Otto Kanturek   *m* Miklos Rozsa

Rex Harrison, Karen Verne, Leo Genn, Joan Marion, Anthony Holles, John Abbott, Hay Petrie

Ten Days That Shook the World: see October

Ten Gentlemen from West Point **
US   1942   104m   bw
TCF (William Perlberg)

Adventures in Indian territory, and back at West Point, of the first recruits to that military academy in the early 1800s.

Likeable mixture of comedy and flagwaving adventure, with excellent production values and a dominating performance.

w Richard Maibaum, George Seaton   *d* Henry Hathaway   *ph* Leon Shamroy   *m* Alfred Newman

Laird Cregar, George Montgomery, Maureen O'Hara, John Sutton, Shepperd Strudwick, Victor Francen, Harry Davenport, Ward Bond, Douglass Dumbrille, Ralph Byrd, Louis Jean Heydt

AAN: Leon Shamroy

Ten Little Indians *
GB   1966   91m   bw
Tenlit (Harry Alan Towers)
V*

Ten people, including two servants, invited to a remote house in the Austrian Alps are murdered one by one.

Fair copy of a classic whodunnit.

w Peter Yeldham, Harry Alan Towers   *novel* Agatha Christie   *d* George Pollock   *ph* Ernest Steward   *m* Malcolm Lockyer

Wilfrid Hyde-White, Dennis Price, Stanley Holloway, Leo Genn, Shirley Eaton, Hugh O'Brian, Daliah Lavi, Fabian, Mario Adorf, Marianne Hoppe

† Made also in 1945 and 1975, as *And Then There Were None* (qv).

Ten Little Niggers: see And Then There Were None (1945)

Ten North Frederick *
US   1958   102m   bw   Cinemascope
TCF (Charles Brackett)
V*

At the funeral of a local politico, his family and friends think back to the events of his life.

Small beer, but a generally adult and entertaining family drama despite a miscast lead.

wd Philip Dunne,   *novel* John O'Hara   *ph* Joe MacDonald   *m* Leigh Harline

Gary Cooper, Geraldine Fitzgerald, Diane Varsi, Stuart Whitman, Suzy Parker, Tom Tully, Ray Stricklyn, John Emery

Ten Rillington Place **
GB   1971   111m   Eastmancolor
Columbia/Filmways (Basil Appleby)
V, V*, L

An account of London's sordid Christie murders of the forties.

Agreeably seedy reconstruction of a *cause célèbre*, carefully built around the star part of a murderous aberrant landlord. Too long, however, and finally too lacking in detail.

w Clive Exton   *book* Ludovic Kennedy   *d* Richard Fleischer   *ph* Denys Coop   *m* Johnny Dankworth

Richard Attenborough, *John Hurt*, Judy Geeson, Pat Heywood, Isobel Black, Geoffrey Chater, André Morell, Robert Hardy

Ten Seconds to Hell
US   1959   93m   bw
UA/Hammer/Seven Arts (Michael Carreras)

Bomb disposal experts in post-war Berlin quarrel over a girl.

Boring, harsh, hollow melodrama, so artificially constructed that no one can possibly care who gets exploded.

w Robert Aldrich, Teddi Sherman   *novel The Phoenix* by Lawrence Bachmann   *d* Robert Aldrich   *ph* Ernest Laszlo   *m* Kenneth V. Jones   *ed* James Needs, Henry Richardson

Jack Palance, Jeff Chandler, Martine Carol, Robert Cornthwaite, Dave Willock, Wesley Addy

Ten Tall Men
US   1951   97m   Technicolor
Columbia/Norma (Harold Hecht)

A Foreign Legion patrol prevents a Riff attack.

Comic strip adventures, efficiently handled.

w Roland Kibbee, Frank Davis   *d* Willis Goldbeck   *ph* William Snyder   *m* David Buttolph

Burt Lancaster, Gilbert Roland, Kieron Moore, John Dehner, Jody Lawrance, George Tobias, Mike Mazurki

10.30 pm Summer
US/Spain   1966   85m   Technicolor
UA/Jorill/Argos (Jules Dassin, Anatole Litvak)

The neurotic Greek wife of an Englishman travelling in Spain becomes obsessed with a murderer on the run.

Preposterously overwrought romantic melodrama.

w Jules Dassin, Marguerite Duras   *novel* Marguerite Duras   *d* Jules Dassin   *ph* Gabor Pogany   *m* Christobel Hallfter

Peter Finch, Melina Mercouri, Romy Schneider, Julian Mateos

Ten Thousand Bedrooms
US   1956   114m   Metrocolor   Cinemascope
MGM (Joe Pasternak)

An American millionaire finds romance when he buys a Rome hotel.

Old-fashioned, unfunny comedy sadly lacking pace and style.

w Laslo Vadnay, Art Cohn, William Ludwig, Leonard Spigelgass   *d* Richard Thorpe   *ph* Robert Bronner   *m* George Stoll   *songs* Nicholas Brodszky, Sammy Cahn

Dean Martin, Eva Bartok, Anna Maria Alberghetti, Walter Slezak, Paul Henreid, Jules Munchin, Marcel Dalio

10 to Midnight
US   1983   102m   Metrocolor
Cannon/Golan-Globus (Pancho Kohner, Lance Hool)
V*, L

A sexual deficient kills girls who reject him, but is tracked down and shot by a cop who is the father of one of the threatened girls.

Crude and rather nasty vigilante melodrama.

w William Roberts   *d* J. Lee-Thompson   *ph* Adam Greenberg   *m* Robert O. Ragland   *ad* Jim Freiburger   *ed* Peter Lee-Thompson

Charles Bronson, Lisa Eilbacher, Andrew Stevens, Gene Davis, Geoffrey Lewis

'Too slow, slick and semi-respectable to live down to its inspirations.' – *Kim Newman, MFB*

Ten Wanted Men
US   1955   80m   Technicolor
Columbia/Scott-Brown (Harry Joe Brown)
V*, L

A rancher and his family are besieged by bandits in a lady's house.

Rather elementary but efficient and good-looking Western programmer.

w Kenneth Gamet   *story* Irving Ravetch, Harriet Frank Jnr   *d* Bruce Humberstone

Randolph Scott, Jocelyn Brando, Richard Boone, Alfonso Bedoya, Donna Martell, Skip Homeier

Ten Who Dared

US 1960 92m Technicolor
Walt Disney (James Algar)
V*

In 1869 a scientific expedition sets out to chart the Colorado River.

Tedious and unconvincing adventures.

w Lawrence E. Watkin journal Major John Wesley Powell d William Beaudine ph Gordon Avil m Oliver Wallace

Brian Keith, John Beal, James Drury, R. G. Armstrong, Ben Johnson, L. Q. Jones

The Tenant

France 1976 126m Eastmancolor
Paramount/Marianne (Andrew Braunsberg)
original title: Le Locataire

A displaced person becomes convinced that his fellow lodgers are out to murder him.

Rather like a male version of the same director's Repulsion, this wearisome case history shows the total dissipation of whatever talent he once had.

w Gerard Brach, Roman Polanski novel Roland Topor d Roman Polanski ph Sven Nykvist m Philippe Sarde

Roman Polanski, Melvyn Douglas, Isabelle Adjani, Shelley Winters, Jo Van Fleet, Lila Kedrova, Claude Dauphin

'It does not seem to have been designed as self-parody, but it certainly comes across that way.' – Janet Maslin, Newsweek

'A long-winded exercise in tedium and morbidity.' – Kevin Thomas, LA Times

Tender Comrade

US 1943 101m bw
RKO (David Hempstead)
V*

Lady welders whose husbands are fighting men keep their chins up during World War II.

Dim tearjerker.

w Dalton Trumbo d Edward Dmytryk ph Russell Metty m Leigh Harline

Ginger Rogers, Robert Ryan, Ruth Hussey, Patricia Collinge, Mady Christians, Kim Hunter, Jane Darwell

Tender Is the Night *

US 1961 146m DeLuxe Cinemascope
TCF (Henry T. Weinstein)

Adventures around Europe between the wars of a rich American psychiatrist who has married his patient.

Patchy, fairly literal transcription of a patently unfilmable novel about defiantly unreal people in what would now be the jet set. About half the result is superficially entertaining.

w Ivan Moffat novel F. Scott Fitzgerald d Henry King ph Leon Shamroy m Bernard Herrmann

Jennifer Jones, Jason Robards Jnr, Joan Fontaine, Tom Ewell, Cesare Danova, Jill St John, Paul Lukas

AAN: title song (m Sammy Fain, ly Paul Francis Webster)

Tender Flesh: see Welcome to Arrow Beach

Tender Mercies *

US 1982 92m Movielab
EMI/Antron Media (Horton Foote, Robert Duvall)
V, V*, L

An ex-alcoholic resumes his former career as a country and western singer.

Quiet, downbeat character study with scenic Texas backgrounds. Mildly impressive, but no real reason to go to the cinema.

w Horton Foote d Bruce Beresford ph Russell Boyd m George Dreyfus

Robert Duvall (who sang his own songs), Tess Harper, Betty Buckley, Wilford Brimley, Ellen Barkin

'It conceals its deficiencies behind heartfelt performances . . . the construction is so rickety that it seems at times entirely to lack a plot.' – Kim Newman, MFB

AA: Robert Duvall; Horton Foote

AAN: best picture; Bruce Beresford; song 'Over You' (Austin Roberts, Bobby Hart)

The Tender Trap *

US 1955 111m Eastmancolor Cinemascope
MGM (Lawrence Weingarten)
V*, L

A smart New York agent has a way with women which annoys his friend; but Casanova gets his come-uppance when he sets his sights on an apparently naïve young actress.

Thin comedy with agreeable moments, not helped by the wide screen.

w Julius J. Epstein play Max Shulman, Robert Paul Smith d Charles Walters ph Paul Vogel m Jeff Alexander

Frank Sinatra, Debbie Reynolds, David Wayne, Celeste Holm, Lola Albright, Carolyn Jones

AAN: title song (m James Van Heusen, ly Sammy Cahn)

The Tender Years

US 1947 81m bw
TCF (Edward L. Alperson)
V*

A minister's son befriends a mistreated runaway dog.

Excessively sentimental tear-jerker that is mercifully short.

w Jack Jungmeyer Jnr, Arnold Belgaard d Harold Schuster ph Henry Freulich m Dr Edward Kilenyi ad Arthur Lonergen ed Richard Farrell

Joe E. Brown, Richard Lyon, Noreen Nash, Charles Drake, Josephine Hutchinson, James Millican, Griff Barnett

The Tenderfoot

US 1931 73m bw
Warner

Adventures of a cowboy in New York.

Slapstick version of George Kaufman's often-remade comedy The Butter and Egg Man; not remarkable in any way.

w Arthur Caesar, Monty Banks, Earl Baldwin d Ray Enright

Joe E. Brown, Ginger Rogers, Lew Cody, Vivian Oakland, Robert Greig

'It ought to do well where they like lowdown comedy.' – Variety

Tenderloin

US 1928 88m bw
Warner

A dancer is accused of stealing a fortune and finds gangsters suddenly interested in her.

Primitive part-talkie (15 minutes of dialogue), unspeakably hammy to listen to though visually it had some inventiveness.

w Edward T. Lowe story Darryl Zanuck d Michael Curtiz

Dolores Costello, Conrad Nagel, Mitchell Lewis, George E. Stone, Dan Wolheim

Tenderness of Wolves *

West Germany 1973 83m colour
Cinegate/Tango (Rainer Werner Fassbinder)
original title: Zärtlichkeit der Wölfe

In Hanover, a petty criminal seduces and kills young

boys, drinking their blood and selling their bodies as meat.

A blackly comic re-telling of the true story of serial killer Fritz Haarmann, showing the influence of the company's mentor, Rainer Werner Fassbinder.

w Kurt Raab d Ulli Lommel ph Jürgen Jürges m Bach ad Kurt Raab ed Thea Eymèsz

Kurt Raab, Jeff Roden, Margit Carstensen, Hannelore Tiefenbrunner, Wolfgang Schenck, Rainer Hauer, Rainer Werner Fassbinder, Jürgen Prochnow

Tendre Ennemie *

France 1938 66m bw
World Pictures

A woman's three dead lovers return to prevent her daughter from making a romantic mistake.

Decorative whimsy which is not among its director's best, but mildly amusing none the less.

w Max Ophuls, Kurt Alexander play L'Ennemie by A. P. Antoine d Max Ophuls

Simone Berriau, Jacqueline Daix, Georges Vitray, Marc Valbel, Lucien Nat

'Story is sacrificed for camera angles . . . weak even for the arties.' – Variety

Tendre Poulet: see Dear Inspector

Teni Zabytykh Predkov: see Shadows of Our Forgotten Ancestors

Tennessee Champ

US 1954 75m Anscocolor
MGM

The Lord helps a religious boxer to win a few fights.

Tedious sentimental square ring melodrama.

w Art Cohn d Fred M. Wilcox

Earl Holliman, Dewey Martin, Keenan Wynn, Shelley Winters, Yvette Dugay

Tennessee Johnson *

US 1943 102m bw
MGM (J. Walter Ruben)
GB title: The Man on America's Conscience

The rise and the problems of President Andrew Johnson.

Sincere, straightforward, well-produced historical drama which failed to set the Thames – or the Hudson – on fire.

w John Balderston, Wells Root d William Dieterle ph Harold Rosson m Herbert Stothart

Van Heflin, Ruth Hussey, Lionel Barrymore, Marjorie Main, Regis Toomey, Montagu Love, Porter Hall, Charles Dingle, J. Edward Bromberg

'Dieterle's customary high-minded, high-polished mélange of heavy touches and intelligent performances.' – James Agee

Tennessee's Partner

US 1955 87m Technicolor Superscope
RKO
V*

A gambling queen and a tenderfoot are involved in a double cross which leads to murder.

Predictable Western.

w Milton Krims, D. D. Beauchamp, Graham Baker and Teddi Sherman story Bret Harte d Allan Dwan

Ronald Reagan, John Payne, Rhonda Fleming, Colleen Gray

Tension

US 1950 91m bw
MGM (Robert Sisk)

A chemist plans the perfect murder of his wife's lover,

loses his nerve, then finds himself suspected when the man is murdered after all.

Disappointing suspenser which starts well but outstays its welcome.

w Allen Rivkin   *d* John Berry   *ph* Harry Stradling   *m* André Previn

Richard Basehart, Audrey Totter, Barry Sullivan, Cyd Charisse, Lloyd Gough, Tom d'Andrea

Tension at Table Rock
US   1956   93m   Technicolor
RKO

When a stagecoach station owner is killed, a gunman takes care of his small son and at the same time rids a town of outlaws.

All the clichés are in this one, fairly neatly amassed in corners labelled *High Noon, Hondo* and *Shane.*

w Winston Miller   *novel* Frank Gruber   *d* Charles Marquis Warren

Richard Egan, Dorothy Malone, Cameron Mitchell, Angie Dickinson

Tentacles
Italy   1976   102m   Technicolor   Technovision
Esse Cinematografica (E. F. Doria)
V*

A deadly menace which leaves its victims as skeletons washed up on the California beach turns out to be a giant octopus . . .

Dreary *Jaws* rehash. Sadly there is no element of spoofing, it's all deadly serious.

w Jerome Max, Tito Carpi, Steve Carabatsos, Sonia Molteni   *d* Oliver Hellman (Sonia Assonitis)   *ph* Roberto d'Ettore Piazzoli   *m* S. W. Cipriani

Shelley Winters, John Huston, Bo Hopkins, Henry Fonda, Claude Akins, Cesare Danova, Delia Boccardo

Tenth Avenue Angel
US   1948   74m   bw
MGM (Ralph Wheelwright)

The little daughter of poor parents loses her faith in life.

Icky sentimental piece for a waning child star.

w Angna Enters, Craig Rice, Harry Ruskin, Eleanore Griffin   *d* Roy Rowland   *ph* Robert Surtees   *m* Rudolph G. Kopp

Margaret O'Brien, Angela Lansbury, George Murphy, Phyllis Thaxter, Rhys Williams, Warner Anderson, Audrey Totter, Connie Gilchrist

The Tenth Man
GB   1936   68m   bw
BIP

A wife shows faith in her husband even though she knows him to be a crook.

Stock film version of one of Somerset Maugham's less pungent plays.

w Geoffrey Kerr, Dudley Leslie, Marjorie Deans, Jack Davies   *d* Brian Desmond Hurst

John Lodge, Antoinette Cellier, Aileen Marson, Clifford Evans, George Graves

The Tenth Victim
Italy/France   1965   92m   Technicolor
Avco/CC Champion/Concordia (Carlo Ponti)
V*

In the 21st century murder is legalized to avoid birth control and war, and ten killings bring a fabulous prize.

Science fiction satire which just about gets by.

w Tonina Guerra, Giorgio Salvioni, Ennio Flaiano, Elio Petri   *story The Seventh Victim* by Robert Sheckley   *d* Elio Petri   *ph* Gianni di Venanzo   *m* Piero Piccioni

Ursula Andress, Marcello Mastroianni, Elsa Martinelli, Massimo Serato

Tenue de Soirée *
France   1986   85m   Eastmancolor   Panavision
Hachette Premiere/DD Productions/Cine Valse/Philippe Dussart
V*
GB title: *Evening Dress*; aka: *Menage*

A husky burglar seduces the puny husband of a couple he involves in his criminal activities.

Anti-bourgeois comedy that tries too hard to be outrageous. Michel Blanc won the award for best actor at the Cannes Film Festival in 1986 for his performance as the timid husband.

wd Bertrand Blier   *ph* Jean Penzer   *m* Serge Gainsbourg   *pd* Theobald Meurisse   *ed* Claudine Merlin

Gérard Depardieu, Michel Blanc, Miou-Miou, Michel Creton, Jean-François Stevenin, Mylène Demongeot, Caroline Sihol, Jean-Yves Berteloot, Bruno Cremer

'Never has there been a picture that made it more hideously clear that, even without the intervention of the police, crime does not pay and that sexual experimentation does not reward its practitioners with happiness.' – *Quentin Crisp*

'A business on the line. A friendship on the edge. A woman caught in the middle.'
Tequila Sunrise
US   1988   115m   DeLuxe
Warner/Mount Company (Tom Shaw)
V, V*, L, S

A former drug-dealer, who is being tempted to get involved in one last major deal, and his friend, an undercover narcotics cop, compete for the same girl.

Wordy thriller in which everyone goes through the motions without much enthusiasm.

wd Robert Towne   *ph* Conrad L. Hall   *m* Dave Grusin   *pd* Richard Sylbert   *ed* Claire Simpson

Mel Gibson, Michelle Pfeiffer, Kurt Russell, Raul Julia, J. T. Walsh, Arliss Howard, Ayre Gross, Gabriel Damon

AAN: Conrad L. Hall

Teresa **
US   1951   101m   bw
MGM (Arthur M. Loew)

A soldier with mother problems brings home an Italian bride.

Careful, sensitive, intelligent variation on a problem frequently considered by films of this period (*Frieda, Fräulein, Japanese War Bride*).

w Stewart Stern   *d* Fred Zinnemann   *ph* William J. Miller   *m* Louis Applebaum

Pier Angeli, John Ericson, Patricia Collinge, Richard Bishop, Peggy Ann Garner, Ralph Meeker, Bill Mauldin

AAN: original story (Arthur Hayes, Stewart Stern)

Term of Trial *
GB   1962   130m   bw
Romulus (James Woolf)

An unsuccessful schoolmaster is accused of rape by a nymphomaniac schoolgirl he has scorned.

Rather flabby 'adult' drama, too schematic to be really interesting despite the best that acting can do.

wd Peter Glenville   *novel The Burden of Proof* by James Barlow   *ph* Oswald Morris   *m* Jean-Michel Demase   *ad* Antony Woolard

Laurence Olivier, Sarah Miles, Simone Signoret, Hugh Griffith, Terence Stamp, Roland Culver, Frank Pettingell, Thora Hird, Dudley Foster, Norman Bird

'Harry Benson is a brilliant computer scientist. For three minutes a day, he is violently homicidal.'
The Terminal Man *
US   1974   104m   colour
Warner (Mike Hodges)
V, V*

A man, who has a computer implanted in his brain to control his murderous tendencies, discovers he enjoys the aftermath of his violent outbursts.

A moderately intriguing, modern variation on Frankenstein, done with a clinical style, in which scientists create a human monster that they cannot control.

wd Mike Hodges   *novel* Michael Crichton   *ph* Richard H. Kline   *ad* Fred Harpman   *ed* Robert Wolfe

George Segal, Joan Hackett, Richard Dysart, Jill Clayburgh, Donald Moffat, Matt Clark

'Of all the bad sci-fi movies of the 70s, this one probably has the least charm.' – *Pauline Kael, New Yorker*

The Terminator *
US   1984   108m   CFI colour
Orion/Hemdale/Pacific Western (Gale Anne Hurd)
V, V*, L, S

A man from the future is sent back on a mission of extermination.

Slick rather nasty but undeniably compelling comic book adventures.

w James Cameron, Gale Anne Hurd   *d* James Cameron   *ph* Adam Greenberg   *m* Brad Fiedel   *ed* Mark Goldblatt

Arnold Schwarzenegger, Michael Biehn, Linda Hamilton, Paul Winfield, Rick Rossovich, Lance Henriksen

'It's Nothing Personal.'
Terminator 2: Judgement Day **
US   1991   135m   CFI colour
Guild/Carolco/Pacific Western/Lightstorm (James Cameron)
V, V*, L, S

An android returns from the future to save a boy and his mother from a murderous shape-changing robot.

Thunderous, high-voltage action movie with dazzling special effects that provide a distraction from the often silly narrative.

w James Cameron, William Wisher   *d* James Cameron   *ph* Adam Greenberg   *m* Brad Fiedel   *pd* Joseph Nemec III   *sp* Fantasy II Film Effects, Industrial Light and Magic   *ed* Richard A. Harris, Mark Goldblatt, Conrad Buff

Arnold Schwarzenegger, Linda Hamilton, Edward Furlong, Robert Patrick, Earl Boen, Joe Morton, S. Epatha Merkerson, Castulo Guerra

'A science-fiction film with verve, imagination and even a little wit.' – *Derek Malcolm, Guardian*

'A humongous, visionary parable that intermittently enthralls and ultimately disappoints. T2 is half of a terrific movie – the wrong half. For a breathless first hour, the film zips along in a textbook display of plot planting and showmanship. But then it stumbles over its own ambitions before settling for a conventional climax with a long fuse.' – *Richard Corliss, Time*

† Reportedly the most expensive film so far made, at a cost of $80–$100 million, it was the biggest box-office success of 1991, taking $112m in rentals in North America alone.

AA: visual effects (Dennis Murren, Stan Winstone, Gene Warren Jnr, Robert Skotak); make-up (Stan Winstone, Jeff Dawn)

AAN: Adam Greenberg; editing

Terminus ***
GB   1961   30m   bw
British Transport Films

Twenty-four hours in the life of Waterloo Station.

An excellent 'fly-on-the-wall' documentary which launched the feature film career of its director and is still both funny and moving.

wd John Schlesinger   *ph* Ken Phipps, Robert Paynter   *m* Ron Grainer

Terminus
France/West Germany   1986   83m   colour
Fox/CAT/Films du Cheval de Fer/Initial Groupe/CLB/A2 (Anne François)

In the future, a driver takes over a computer-programmed truck from its dead owner in a dangerous race.

Virtually incomprehensible science fiction, cut from its original length of 110 minutes; even when it is understandable, it fails to grip.

w Pierre-William Glenn, Patrice Duvic   *story* Alain Gillot   *d* Pierre-William Glenn   *ph* Jean-Claude Vicquery   *m* David Cunningham   *ad* Alain Challier   *ed* Thierry Derocles

Johnny Hallyday, Karen Allen, Jurgen Prochnow, Gabriel Damon, Julie Glenn, Louise Vincent

Terminus Station: see *Indiscretion of an American Wife*

'Come To Laugh. Come To Cry. Come To Care. Come To Terms.'
Terms of Endearment **
US   1983   132m   Metrocolor
Paramount (James L. Brooks)
V, L, S

An eccentric widow fends off suitors while interfering with her daughter's marriage; but all is forgiven when the daughter dies.

This shapeless film is little more than an excuse for actors and writer to show off, which they do to great excess; but parts of it are entertaining enough and it certainly impressed the Academy Award committee.

wd James L. Brooks   *novel* Larry McMurtry   *ph* Andrzej Bartkowiak   *m* Michael Gore   *pd* Polly Platt

Shirley Maclaine, Jack Nicholson, Debra Winger, Danny de Vito, Jeff Daniels, John Lithgow

'An outsize sitcom and a crassly constructed slice of anti-feminism that contrives to rub liberal amounts of soap in the viewer's eyes.' – *Sight and Sound*

'There isn't a thing I would change.' – *Roger Ebert*

AA: best picture; Shirley Maclaine; Jack Nicholson; direction; adaptation

AAN: John Lithgow; editing (Richard Marks); Michael Gore; art direction; Debra Winger

La Terra Trema *
Italy   1948   160m   bw
Universalia

The life of a Sicilian fisherman and his family.

Seriously intended, carefully composed semi-documentary stressing the economic problems of the simple life. A commercial disaster: even the Italians couldn't understand the accents of the local actors.

wd Luchino Visconti   *ph* G. R. Aldo   *m* Luchino Visconti, Willy Ferrero

† The cast was drawn from the inhabitants of Aci Trezza, Sicily.

The Terra-Cotta Warrior *
Hong Kong   1990   111m   Eastmancolor
Panavision
Art & Talent Group (Hon Pou Chu)

A soldier encased in clay and buried with his emperor comes back to life 3,000 years later to be re-united with his lover, reincarnated as an actress.

A familiar mix of the supernatural and martial arts, performed with verve.

w Lee Bik Wah   *d* Ching Tung Yee   *ph* Peter Pau   *m* Joseph Koo   *pd* Yee Chung Man   *sp* Tsui Hark   *ed* Mak Chi Shin

Zhang Yimou, Gong Li, Yu Yung Kang

A Terrible Beauty
GB   1960   90m   bw
UA/Raymond Stross
US title: *Night Fighters*

In a north Irish village, the IRA revive their activities on the outbreak of World War II.

Heavily Oirish melodrama with a muddled message.

w Robert Wright Campbell   *novel* Arthur Roth   *d* Tay Garnett   *ph* Stephen Dade   *m* Cedric Thorpe Davie

Robert Mitchum, Anne Heywood, Dan O'Herlihy, Cyril Cusack, Richard Harris, Marianne Benet

The Terror
US   1928   82m approx   bw
Warner

A mysterious killer lurks in the cellars of a country house.

Primitive talkie which attempted a few new styles but showed that more were needed, also that some silent actors could not make the transfer.

w Harvey Gates   *play* Edgar Wallace   *novel* Edgar Wallace   *d* Roy del Ruth   *ph* Barney McGill

May McAvoy, Edward Everett Horton, Louise Fazenda, Alec B. Francis, John Miljan, Frank Austin

'The only terrible thing about this talkie Terror is its unnatural slowness . . . the characters speak as if they were dictating important letters.' – A. P. Herbert, *Punch*

'May be crude, but it is a maker of history. Something has been achieved here. A new chapter of film evolution is beginning. Today it is as foolish to argue that talking films cannot be successful as to declare that a man in London cannot possibly speak by telephone to a man in New York.' – C. A. Lejeune

† The first film without a single subtitle: all the credits were spoken.

†† *Return of the Terror* (US 1934) has little to do with it.

The Terror
GB   1938   73m   bw
Associated British

Stilted remake of the above.

w William Freshman   *d* Richard Bird

Wilfrid Lawson, Arthur Wontner, Alastair Sim, Linden Travers, Bernard Lee, Henry Oscar

The Terror
US   1963   81m   Pathecolor
AIP/Filmgroup (Roger Corman, Francis Ford Coppola)
V*

A baron lives for twenty years in a creepy castle, mourning the death of his wife . . .

Shoddy horror improvised over a weekend on the set of *The Raven*. It looks it.

w Leo Gordon, Jack Hill   *d* Roger Corman   *ph* John Nickolaus   *m* Ronald Stein

Boris Karloff, Jack Nicholson, Sandra Knight, Dorothy Neumann

Terror Aboard
US   1933   70m   bw
Paramount

Gruesome murders occur during a pleasure cruise.

Fair murder mystery.

w Harvey Thew, Manuel Seff   *d* Paul Sloane

Charles Ruggles, John Halliday, Shirley Grey, Neil Hamilton, Verree Teasdale, Jack La Rue

---

Terror by Night *
US   1946   60m   bw
Universal (Howard Benedict)
V, V*, L

Sherlock Holmes recovers a stolen jewel and solves a murder or two aboard a speeding train.

An amusing entry in the modernized series despite some bad support acting and hilarious interposed shots of the supposed scenery between London and Edinburgh.

w Frank Gruber   *d* Roy William Neill   *ph* Maury Gertsman   *m* Hans Salter

Basil Rathbone, Nigel Bruce, Dennis Hoey, Alan Mowbray, Renee Godfrey, Bill Bevan, Mary Forbes, Frederic Worlock

Terror from the Year 5000
US   1958   74m   bw
AIP (Robert J. Gurney Jnr)
V*
GB title: *Cage of Doom*

A brash young entrepreneur who has invested in an experimental time machine inadvertently brings back a woman, disfigured by radiation, from the future.

A mix of sex and science fiction with a moral, effective enough in its low-budget way, though audiences have to wait a long time for the terror to arrive.

wd Robert J. Gurney Jnr   *ph* Arthur Florman   *ed* Dede Allen

Ward Costello, Joyce Holden, Frederick Downs, John Stratton, Salome Jens, Fred Herrick

Terror House: see *The Night Has Eyes*

Terror in a Texas Town *
US   1958   81m   bw
UA/Frank N. Seltzer

A Swedish seaman arrives in a small Western town and avenges the death of his father.

Stylish second-feature Western, a genuine sleeper which holds the interest throughout.

w Ben L. Perry   *d* Joseph H. Lewis   *ph* Ray Rennahan   *m* Gerald Fried

Sterling Hayden, Sebastian Cabot, Carol Kelly, Eugene Martin, Ned Young

Terror in the Aisles
US   1984   82m   CFI color
TEM/Kaleidoscope/Universal

A compilation of fragments from mainly shock films, of no great interest even to film buffs because in most cases the scenes are wrenched out of context to fit a fatuous commentary.

w Margery Doppelt   *d* Andrew Kuehn

Terror in the Haunted House
US   1958   81m   bw
Howco
aka: *My World Dies Screaming*

A bride finds that her honeymoon mansion is one about which she has been having recurring nightmares.

The plot has everything, even an axe murderer, but the treatment is soporific.

w Robert C. Dennis   *d* Harold Daniels

Gerald Mohr, Cathy O'Donnell, William Ching, John Qualen, Barry Bernard

Terror in the Wax Museum
US   1973   94m   DeLuxe
Bing Crosby Productions/Fenady Associates (Andrew J. Fenady)

In Victorian London a waxworks owner is murdered . . .

Cheaply produced murder mystery (even the waxworks can't stand still) with horror asides and a cast of elderly hams.

w Jameson Brewer d George Fenady ph William Jurgensen m George Duning

Ray Milland, Broderick Crawford, Elsa Lanchester, Louis Hayward, John Carradine, Shani Wallis, Maurice Evans, Patric Knowles

Terror of Mechagodzilla: see *Monsters from an Unknown Planet*

'Drug-crazed assassins carrying out their hate-filled ritual murders!'

The Terror of the Tongs
GB 1961 79m Technicolor
BLC/Hammer/Merlin (Kenneth Hyman)

In 1910 Hong Kong a merchant avenges the death of his daughter at the hands of a villainous secret society.

Gory melodrama with dollops of screams, torture and vaguely orgiastic goings-on.

w Jimmy Sangster d Anthony Bushell ph Arthur Grant m James Bernard ad Bernard Robinson, Thomas Goswell ed Jim Needs, Eric Boyd-Perkins

Geoffrey Toone, Christopher Lee, Yvonne Monlaur, Brian Worth, Richard Leech

The Terror of the Vampires: see *Le Frisson des Vampires*

Terror on a Train: see *Time Bomb*

Terror Train
Canada 1980 97m DeLuxe
Fox/Triple T (Harold Greenberg)
V, V*, L

Participants in a wild party aboard a train are decimated by a mysterious psychotic.

Shocks and blood in the Carpenter tradition, adequately mounted.

w T. Y. Drake d Roger Spottiswoode ph John Alcott m John Mills-Cockle pd Glenn Bydwell ed Anne Henderson

Ben Johnson, Jamie Lee Curtis, David Copperfield, Hart Bochner

The Terroriser
Taiwan/Hong Kong 1986 109m colour
ICA/Sunny Overseas Corporation/Golden Harvest (Lin Dengfei, Raymond Chow)
original title: *Kongbufenzi*; aka: *The Terrorizers*

A writer, whose marriage is going wrong, finds that life is beginning to resemble her latest novel.

Unconvincing melodrama with intellectual pretensions that makes little sense.

w Xiao Ye, Edward Yang d Edward Yang ph Zhang Zhan m Weng Xiaoliang ad Lai Mingtang ed Liao Qingsong

Cora Miao, Li Liqun, Jin Shijie, Gu Baoming, Wang An, Liu Ming, You Anshun

The Terrorists: see *Ransom* (1975)

The Terrorizers: see *The Terroriser*

Terry and the Pirates
US 1940 bw serial: 15 eps
Columbia

The son of an American archaeologist in Asia fights Fang and the Tiger Men.

Colourful nonsense for the kiddies.

d James W. Horne

William Tracy, Granville Owen, Joyce Bryan, Allen Jung

The Terry Fox Story
Canada 1983 97m colour
ITC/CTV (Robert Cooper)
V*

A young man dying of cancer has a leg amputated, but still runs across Canada in aid of research.

True it may be, but dramatically this is a one-note film with endless pretty pictures of countryside and in the foreground signs of failing health.

w Edward Hume d Ralph L. Thomas ph Richard Ciupka m Bill Conti ad Gavin Mitchell ed Ron Wisman

Eric Fryer, Robert Duvall, Christopher Makepeace, Rosalind Chao

Terry of the Times
US 1930 bw serial: 10 eps
Universal

The son of a newspaper publisher overthrows a criminal league called The Mystic Mendicants.

Early talkie serial which fulfilled its purpose.

d Henry McRae

Reed Howes, Lotus Thompson, Sheldon Lewis, John Oscar, Will Hays

Tess *
France-GB 1979 180m colour
Renn-Burrill (Claude Berri)
V*, L

A peasant girl tries to prove her noble heritage but finds herself with an illegitimate child.

Solid, unexciting version of the classic Wessex novel; a hard sell for 1980 audiences.

w Roman Polanski, Gerard Brach, John Brownjohn novel *Tess of the D'Urbervilles* by Thomas Hardy d Roman Polanski ph Geoffrey Unsworth, Ghislain Cloquet m Philippe Sarde pd Pierre Guffroy, Jack Stevens

Nastassja Kinski, Leigh Lawson, Peter Firth, John Collin, David Markham, Richard Pearson

'It emerges without a hint of what might have drawn Polanski to the material.' – *Sight and Sound*

AA: Geoffrey Unsworth, Ghislain Cloquet; art direction; costume design (Anthony Powell)

AAN: best film; Roman Polanski; Philippe Sarde

BFA: best photography

Tess of the Storm Country
US 1932 80m bw
Fox

A retired sea captain's daughter loves the lord of the manor.

Antiquated tushery first filmed as a Mary Pickford silent.

w S. N. Behrman, Sonya Levien, Rupert Hughes novel Grace Miller White d Alfred Santell ph Hal Mohr

Janet Gaynor, Charles Farrell, Dudley Digges, June Clyde, George Meeker

Test Pilot **
US 1938 118m bw
MGM (Louis D. Lighton)
V*

A brilliant but unpredictable test pilot is helped by his wife and his self-sacrificing friend.

A big box-office star vehicle of its time, still interesting as a highly efficient product.

w Waldemar Young, Vincent Lawrence story Frank Wead d Victor Fleming ph Ray June m Franz Waxman ed Tom Held

Clark Gable, Myrna Loy, Spencer Tracy, Lionel Barrymore, Samuel S. Hinds, Marjorie Main, Gloria Holden

'B.o. potential of above-average calibre . . . could have been cut 10–15 minutes without spoiling.' – *Variety*

'The picture is so noisy with sure-fire elements – box office cast, violent excitement, glycerine tears and such – that it may be hard to keep the ear attuned to the quieter, more authentically human things in it.' – *James Shelley Hamilton*

AAN: best picture; Frank Wead; Tom Held

Testament *
US 1983 90m CFI
Entertainment Events/American Playhouse
V*, L

A small California town is hit by a nuclear attack.

Probably better than the TV movie *The Day After*, this was less well publicized and therefore lost out.

w John Sacret Young story Carol Amen d Lynne Littman

Jane Alexander, William Devane, Ross Harris, Roxana Zal, Lukas Haas, Lilia Skala, Leon Ames

'After thirty years of learning to live with the Bomb, we still lack ways of conceiving the Unthinkable.' – *Sheila Johnston, MFB*

AAN: Jane Alexander

Testament
GB 1988 80m Technicolor
Black Audio Film Collective/Channel 4 (Avril Johnson, Lina Gopaul)

Twenty years after the military coup that overthrew Nkrumah's government, a television interviewer returns to Ghana to try to interview Werner Herzog and to make sense of the past.

Part documentary, part fiction, it is too personal a film to mean much to the uncommitted.

wd John Akomfrah ph David Scott m Trevor Mathison ed Brand Thumin

Tania Rogers, Evans Hunter, Emma Francis Wilson, Frank Parkes, Errol Shaker

'A richly allusive, evocative meditation on memory, history and identity, both national and personal.' – *MFB*

Le Testament d'Orphée *
France 1959 83m bw
Editions Cinégraphiques (Jean Thuillier)
aka: *The Testament of Orpheus*

The poet, as an 18th-century man, dies, enters spacetime, is revived, and seeks his identity.

Rather like a melancholy madman's *Alice in Wonderland*, this bizarre jumble has its fascinations but misses by a mile the arresting qualities of *Orphée*.

wd Jean Cocteau ph Roland Pointoizeau m Georges Auric and others

Jean Cocteau, Edouard Dermithe, Maria Casarès, François Périer, Henri Crémieux, Yul Brynner, Jean-Pierre Léaud, Daniel Gélin, Jean Marais, Pablo Picasso, Charles Aznavour

The Testament of Dr Mabuse **
Germany 1933 122m bw
Nero (Fritz Lang)
V*

A sequel to *Dr Mabuse the Gambler*: the criminal mastermind dies in an asylum, and his assistant takes over his identity.

Fast-moving penny dreadful, alleged by its director to be a denouncing of the doctrines of Hitler, but showing little evidence of being more than a very slick entertainment.

w Thea von Harbou, Fritz Lang d Fritz Lang ph Fritz Arno Wagner m Hans Erdmann ad Karl Vollbrecht, Emil Hassler

Rudolf Klein-Rogge, Otto Wernicke, Gustav Diesl

† On arrival in America Lang claimed that 'slogans of the Third Reich have been put into the mouths of criminals in the film'. Yet his wife, who co-scripted it, stayed behind as a confirmed Nazi.

The Testament of Orpheus: see *Le Testament d'Orphée*

Tetsuo: The Iron Man *
Japan   1991   67m   bw
Kaijyu
V, V*

After a metal fetishist is hit by a car, the driver begins to turn into a metallic man.

Weird science-fiction fantasy, by turns surreal and nasty, but displaying an unusual visual flair by its writer-director.

wd Shinya Tsukamoto   *ph* Shinya Tsukamoto, Kei Fujiwara   *m* Chu Ishikawa   *ed* Shinya Tsukamoto

Tomoroh Taguchi, Kei Fujiwara, Nobu Kanaoko, Shinya Tsukamoto, Naomasa Musaka, Renji Ishibashi

'For most viewers it will be the cinematic equivalent of being run over by a car and turning into a metal blob.' – *Variety*

'Bizarre, Beautiful, Horrific . . .'
Tetsuo II: Bodyhammer **
Japan   1991   83m   colour
ICA/Kaiju Theatre/Toshiba EMI (Fuminori Shisido, Fumio Kurokawa)
V

A clerk, pursuing punks who have killed his son, mutates into a metallic man with built-in weaponry.

Bizarre but eminently watchable science-fiction fable.

wd Shinya Tsukamoto   *ph* Shinya Tsukamoto, Fumikazu Oda, Katsunori Yokoyama   *ad* Shinya Tsukamoto   *ed* Shinya Tsukamoto

Tomoroh Taguchi, Nobu Kanaoka, Shinya Tsukamoto, Keinosuke Tomioka, Sujin Kim, Min Tanaka

'Brain-blowing . . . this gruesome gore fest looks to be a solid click with the midnight crowd and metal fetishists.' – *Variety*

Tevya the Milkman *
US   1939   93m   bw
Henry Ziskin

A Russian village milkman watches with awe as the pogroms begin to affect his people.

One of the best Yiddish films with the best Yiddish actor, this pleasing comedy-drama was the basis for the musical *Fiddler on the Roof*.

wd Maurice Schwarz   *story* Sholem Aleichem

Maurice Schwarz, Miriam Riselle, Rebecca Weintraub, Paula Lubelska

Tex and The Lord of the Deep
Italy   1985   96m   colour
Sacis/RAI (Giocchino Marano, José M. Rodriguez, Paola Bistolfi)

Tex Willer defeats an attempt to revive the Aztec empire in Mexico.

Last decadent gasp of the spaghetti Western, managing to combine cowboys and Indians with Kit Carson, a comic book hero, a scantily clad priestess, a fat man in a fez, a mummifying weapon and a volcanic eruption.

w Giorgio Bonelli, Gianfranco Clerici, Marcello Coscia, Duccio Tessari   *story* Giovanni L. Bonelli   *d* Duccio Tessari   *ph* Pietro Morbidelli   *m* Gianni Ferrio   *ad* Antonello Geleng, Walter Patriarca   *ed* Mirella Mercio, Lidia Bordi

Giuliano Gemma, William Berger, Carlo Mucari, Isabel Russinova, Peter Berling, Flavio Bucci

Tex Granger
US   1948   bw   serial: 15 eps
Columbia

A wandering Western hero buys a newspaper and vanquishes various villains.

Unremarkable sagebrush serial.

d Derwin Abrahams

Robert Kellard, Peggy Stewart, Buzz Henry, Smith Ballew, I. Stanford Jolley

The Texan
US   1930   79m   bw
Paramount (Hector Turnbull)

The Llano Kid absolves his bandit past.

Early sound Western, an interesting curiosity.

w Daniel Nathan Rubin   *story The Double-Dyed Deceiver* by O. Henry   *d* John Cromwell   *ph* Victor Milner

Gary Cooper, Fay Wray, Emma Dunn, Oscar Apfel

'Few westerns are as well made and rate as high in every particular.' – *Variety*

'Love and glory on America's last frontier!'
The Texans
US   1938   92m   bw
Paramount (Lucien Hubbard)

Problems of the post-Civil War years include new railroads, the Ku Klux Klan, and the new cattle drive routes.

Formula Western with fairly well staged excitements backing a routine romantic triangle.

w Bertram Millhauser, Paul Sloane, William Wister Haines   *d* James Hogan   *ph* Theodor Sparkuhl   *m* Gerard Carbonara

Joan Bennett, Randolph Scott, May Robson, Walter Brennan, Robert Cummings, Raymond Halton, Robert Barrat, Francis Ford

'Enough sweep and thrills to justify generally good business.' – *Variety*

Texas
US   1941   94m   bw (released in sepia)
Columbia (Sam Bischoff)
V*

Two veteran Civil War Southerners head for Texas to set up a cattle business.

Western vehicle for two young stars, now very ordinary-looking.

w Horace McCoy, Lewis Meltzer, Michael Blankfort   *d* George Marshall   *ph* George Meehan

William Holden, Glenn Ford, Claire Trevor, George Bancroft, Edgar Buchanan, Don Beddoe, Andrew Tombes, Addison Richards

'While spoofing a little along the way, it observes the etiquette and tradition of an accepted cinema form. It has rough riding, cattle rustling, shooting and a story that leaves out only the Indian raid and the rescue by the US Cavalry.' – *Christian Science Monitor*

Texas across the River
US   1966   101m   Techniscope
Universal (Harry Keller)

A Texan, an Indian and a Spanish nobleman on the run from jealous rivals have various adventures.

Sloppy Western which seems to have had jokes added when someone realized it wasn't good enough to be taken seriously.

w Wells Root, Harold Greene, Ben Starr   *d* Michael Gordon   *ph* Russell Metty   *md* Joseph Gershenson   *m* Frank de Vol

Dean Martin, Alain Delon, Joey Bishop, Rosemary Forsyth, Tina Marquand, Peter Graves, Andrew Prine, Michael Ansara

Texas, Brooklyn and Heaven
US   1948   76m   bw
Robert S. Golden/United Artists
GB title: *The Girl from Texas*

A Texas boy meets a Texas girl in New York; after various eccentric encounters, they end up riding the range again.

Would-be Saroyanesque dalliance with odd characters which never begins to come off and has been abruptly edited into the bargain.

w Lewis Meltzer   *story* Barry Benefield   *d* William Castle

Guy Madison, Diana Lynn, James Dunn, Lionel Stander, Florence Bates, Michael Chekov, Margaret Hamilton, Moyna McGill, Irene Ryan, Roscoe Karns, William Frawley

Texas Carnival
US   1951   77m   Technicolor
MGM (Jack Cummings)
V*, L

A fairground showman is mistaken for a millionaire and runs up debts.

Very thin comedy musical relying entirely on its stars.

w Dorothy Kingsley   *d* Charles Walters   *ph* Robert Planck   *m* Harry Warren   *ly* Dorothy Fields   *ch* Hermes Pan

Esther Williams, Red Skelton, Howard Keel, Ann Miller, Paula Raymond, Keenan Wynn, Tom Tully

The Texas Chainsaw Massacre
US   1974   81m   CFI Color
Vortex (Tobe Hooper)
V*, L

Visitors to a cemetery in rural Texas find their house occupied by a homicidal maniac.

Cheapjack horror thriller adapted from real events which also inspired *Psycho*. Nothing but shocks and gore, but the beginning of the wave of such deplorable movies which flooded the world's screens towards the end of the decade.

w Kim Henkel, Tobe Hooper   *d* Tobe Hooper   *ph* Daniel Pearl   *m* Tobe Hooper, Wayne Bell

Marilyn Burns, Allen Danziger, Paul A. Partain, William Vail

'An absolute must for all maniacs and blood drinkers in need of a few tips.' – *Benny Green, Punch*

'It's without any apparent purpose, unless the creation of disgust and fright is a purpose.' – *Roger Ebert*

The Texas Chainsaw Massacre Part 2
US   1986   95m   TVC colour
Cannon (Menahem Golan, Yoram Globus)
V*, L

A family of Sweeney Todds lives in an abandoned Alamo theme park, and woe betide the stray visitor.

Splatter shocker on predictable lines.

w L. M. Kit Carson   *d* Tobe Hooper   *ph* Richard Kooris   *m* Tobe Hooper, Jerry Lambert   *pd* Cary White   *ed* Alain Jakubowicz

Dennis Hopper, Caroline Williams, Bill Johnson, Jim Siedow

Texas Lady
US   1955   85m   Technicolor   Superscope
RKO (Nat Holt)
V*

A lady newspaper owner runs an anti-corruption campaign.

Mild family Western.

w Horace McCoy   *d* Tim Whelan   *ph* Ray Rennahan   *m* Paul Sawtell

Claudette Colbert, Barry Sullivan, Grey Walcott, James Bell, Horace MacMahon, Ray Collins, Walter Sande, Douglas Fowley

'They wrote their story in words of fire!'
The Texas Rangers *
US   1936   95m   bw
Paramount (King Vidor)

Three wandering ne'er-do-wells break up; two join the Texas Rangers and hunt down the third, who is an outlaw.

Pleasantly remembered star Western, later remade as *The Streets of Laredo* (qv).

w Louis Stevens   d King Vidor   ph Edward Cronjager

Fred MacMurray, Jack Oakie, Lloyd Nolan, Jean Parker, Edward Ellis

† Another film called *The Texas Rangers* came from Columbia in 1952 and had a similar plot to the original; otherwise it was a shoddy piece of work in Supercinecolor, with George Montgomery and Jerome Courtland.

Texas Rangers Ride Again
US   1940   67m   bw
Paramount

Modern Rangers capture cattle rustlers.

Second-feature 'sequel' with no relation to the original.

w William R. Lipman, Horace McCoy   d James Hogan

John Howard, Ellen Drew, Akim Tamiroff, May Robson, Broderick Crawford, Charley Grapewin, John Miljan, Anthony Quinn

Texas Terror
US   1935   58m   bw
Monogram/Lone Star (Paul Malvern)
V*

A sheriff who believes he was responsible for the death of an old friend discovers the real culprit.

Mediocre Western, one of the least interesting of Wayne's early efforts, lacking the action and stunts that usually raised Malvern's productions above his low-budget rivals.

wd Robert N. Bradbury   ph William Hyer   ed Carl Pierson

John Wayne, Lucille Browne, Leroy Mason, Fern Emmett, George Hayes, Buffalo Bill Jnr, John Ince

Texas to Tokyo: see We've Never Been Licked

'It's not a place ... it's a state of mind'
Texasville
US   1990   125m   DeLuxe
Guild/Nelson Films/Cine-Source (Barry Spikings, Peter Bogdanovich)
V, V*, L

A middle-aged oil man faces difficulties with his wife and family and in his business.

A downbeat sequel, lacking in magic, to *The Last Picture Show*, with its characters now much older and more miserable.

wd Peter Bogdanovich   novel Larry McMurtry   ph Nicholas von Sternberg   pd Phedon Papamichael   ed Richard Fields

Jeff Bridges, Cybill Shepherd, Annie Potts, Cloris Leachman, Timothy Bottoms, Eileen Brennan, Randy Quaid, Harvey Christiansen, Pearl Jones, Loyd Catlett

'Making a hash of trying to adapt McMurtry's extremely long and dense novel, Bogdanovich has simply thrown away the flesh and kept the bones.' – Tom Milne, MFB

Thank God It's Friday
US   1978   89m   Metrocolor
Columbia/Motown/Casablanca (Rob Cohen)
V, V*

Problems of a disc jockey in a Hollywood disco.

Routine youth programmer, rather like *Rock Around the Clock* twenty years after.

w Barry Armyan Bernstein   d Robert Klane   ph James Crabe   m various   pd Tom H. John

Valerie Landsburg, Terri Nunn, Chick Vennera, Donna Summer, The Commodores

AA: song 'Last Dance' (m/ly Paul Jabara)

Thank You All Very Much: see A Touch of Love

Thank You, Jeeves *
US   1936   57m   bw
TCF (Sol M. Wurtzel)

A valet helps prevent his master from becoming involved in gun-running.

Competent second feature notable as Niven's first leading role; also one of the very few attempts to film Wodehouse.

w Joseph Hoffman, Stephen Gross   story P. G. Wodehouse   d Arthur Greville Collins   ph Barney McGill   m Samuel Kaylin

David Niven, Arthur Treacher, Virginia Field, Lester Matthews, Colin Tapley

Thank You, Mr Moto
US   1938   67m   bw
TCF

Mr Moto protects the tomb of Genghis Khan from unscrupulous treasure-hunters.

Slick and enjoyable small-scale thriller.

w Willis Cooper, Norman Foster   story John P. Marquand   d Norman Foster   ph Virgil Miller   md Samuel Kaylin   ad Bernard Herzbrun, Albert Hogsett   ed Irene Morra, Nick DeMaggio

Peter Lorre, Thomas Beck, Pauline Frederick, Jayne Regan, Sidney Blackmer, Sig Rugmann, John Carradine

Thank Your Lucky Stars ***
US   1943   127m   bw
Warner (Mark Hellinger)
V, V*, L, S

Eddie Cantor and his double get involved in planning a patriotic show.

All-star wartime musical with some unexpected turns and a generally funny script.

w Norman Panama, Melvin Frank, James V. Kern   d David Butler   ph Arthur Edeson   md Leo F. Forbstein   ch Le Roy Prinz   songs Frank Loesser, Arthur Schwartz

Eddie Cantor, Dennis Morgan, Joan Leslie, Edward Everett Horton, S. Z. Sakall, Humphrey Bogart, Jack Carson, Bette Davis, Olivia de Havilland, Errol Flynn, John Garfield, Alan Hale, Ida Lupino, Ann Sheridan, Dinah Shore, George Tobias, Spike Jones and his City Slickers, Willie Best, Hattie McDaniel

'The loudest and most vulgar of the current musicals, it is also the most fun, if you are amused when show people kid their own idiom.' – James Agee

'An all-star show with the conspicuous flavour of amateur night at the studio.' – New York Times

'Everyone had a good time making it.' – Motion Picture Herald

AAN: song 'They're Either Too Young or Too Old'

Thanks a Million **
US   1935   87m   bw
TCF (Darryl F. Zanuck)
V*

A crooner runs for governor.

Smart, amusing political musical.

w Nunnally Johnson   d Roy del Ruth   ph Peverell Marley   songs Arthur Johnston, Gus Kahn   m Arthur Lange

Dick Powell, Fred Allen, Ann Dvorak, Patsy Kelly, Phil Baker, Paul Whiteman and his band, the Yacht Club Boys, Benny Baker, Raymond Walburn, Alan Dinehart

'Socko filmusical for big grosses . . . an example of canny showmanship and presentation.' – Variety

Thanks for Everything *
US   1938   70m   bw
TCF (Darryl F. Zanuck)

Mr Average American is discovered, promoted and merchandized.

Very acceptable satirical comedy of the advertising world.

w Harry Tugend   d William A. Seiter   ph George Meehan   m Abe Meyer

Adolphe Menjou, Jack Haley, Jack Oakie, Arleen Whelan, Tony Martin, Binnie Barnes, George Barbier

'Light and breezy, a cinch for popular audience appeal.' – Variety

'The funniest film I can remember seeing for many months, with something of the old Kaufman touch.' – Graham Greene

Thanks for the Memory *
US   1938   75m   bw
Paramount (Mel Shaver)

A smart novelist has trouble with his marriage.

Light, agreeable domestic comedy on familiar lines.

w Lynn Starling   play Up Pops the Devil by Frances Goodrich, Albert Hackett   d George Archainbaud   ph Karl Struss   m Boris Morros

Bob Hope, Shirley Ross

'Although lightweight, it will please if not exactly boff them.' – Variety

Thark *
GB   1932   79m   bw
British and Dominion (Herbert Wilcox)

The heir to an old mansion spends a night in it to prove it is not haunted.

Very funny Aldwych farce, plainly transferred to the screen with the original stage team intact. One's only regret is that it peters out at the end.

w Ben Travers   play Ben Travers   d Tom Walls   ph F. A. Young

Ralph Lynn, Tom Walls, Robertson Hare, Mary Brough, Claude Hulbert, Gordon James

'Scream after scream of laughter of the wobbling midriff variety.' – Variety

That Brennan Girl
US   1946   97m   bw
Republic

A young mother neglects her baby for the sake of a good time.

Absurdly padded-out moral tract.

w Doris Anderson   d Alfred Santell

Mona Freeman, James Dunn, William Marshall, June Duprez

That Certain Age *
US   1938   100m   bw
Universal (Joe Pasternak)

A girl gets a crush on an older man.

Pleasant, well-cast star musical for the family.

w Bruce Manning   d Edward Ludwig   ph Joseph Valentine   songs Jimmy McHugh, Harold Adamson

Deanna Durbin, Melvyn Douglas, Jackie Cooper, Irene Rich, Nancy Carroll, John Halliday, Juanita Quigley, Jackie Searl, Charles Coleman

'Certain for top grosses and extended runs.' – *Variety*

AAN: song 'My Own'

That Certain Feeling

US 1956 102m Technicolor Vistavision
Paramount (Melvin Frank, Norman Panama)

An arrogant comic strip artist loses his touch and hires a 'ghost' – the ex-husband of his secretary/fiancée.

Arid comedy from a mild Broadway play, totally miscast and lacking any kind of interest.

w Norman Panama, Melvin Frank, I. A. L. Diamond, William Altman *play King of Hearts* by Jean Kerr, Eleanor Brooke *d* Norman Panama, Melvin Frank *ph* Loyal Griggs *m* Joseph J. Lilley

Bob Hope, George Sanders, Eva Marie Saint, Pearl Bailey, Al Capp

'She got all the breaks – in her heart!'
That Certain Woman *

US 1937 91m bw
Warner (Hal B. Wallis)
V*

A gangster's widow goes straight but runs into complex marriage trouble.

Self-sacrifice and mother love are rewarded by two convenient deaths and a happy ending in this routine romantic melodrama remade from a silent success.

wd Edmund Goulding *original screenplay The Trespasser* by Edmund Goulding *ph* Ernest Haller *m* Max Steiner

Bette Davis, Henry Fonda, Ian Hunter, Anita Louise, Donald Crisp, Katherine Alexander, Mary Philips, Minor Watson

'Big-time cast in a well-made first run film.' – *Variety*

That Championship Season *

US 1982 108m Metrocolor
Cannon-Golan-Globus (Menahem Golan, Yoram Globus)
V*

Five rather unlikeable middle-aged men live by recreating the glory of a team basketball victory 25 years ago.

Unimaginative film version of a play which had dramatic strength but very limited general appeal. Rather less can be said of the film, as the acting shows a lack of team spirit.

wd Jason Miller *play* Jason Miller *ph* John Bailey *m* Bill Conti *pd* Ward Preston *ed* Richard Halsey

Bruce Dern, Stacy Keach, Robert Mitchum, Martin Sheen, Paul Sorvino, Arthur Franz

That Cold Day in the Park

Canada 1969 115m Eastmancolor
(Commonwealth United) Donald Factor/Robert Altman/Leon Mirrell
V*

A spinster invites a lonely wandering boy into her home, makes him a prisoner and becomes possessively jealous.

A companion piece to *The Collector*, rather better done for those who like morbid psychology.

w Gillian Freeman *novel* Richard Miles *d* Robert Altman *ph* Laszlo Kovacs *m* Johnny Mandel

Sandy Dennis, Michael Burns, Suzanne Benton, Luana Anders, John Garfield Jnr

'About as pretentious, loathsome and stupid as a film can get.' – *John Simon*

That Dangerous Age

GB 1949 98m bw
London Films (Gregory Ratoff)
US title: *If This Be Sin*

Recovering from a breakdown, a KC discovers that his daughter wants to marry a man with whom his wife once had an affair.

Purple patch melodrama which sympathetic actors can't quite freshen up.

w Gene Markey *play Autumn* by Margaret Kennedy, Ilya Surgutchoff *d* Gregory Ratoff *ph* Georges Périnal *m* Mischa Spoliansky

Roger Livesey, Myrna Loy, Peggy Cummins, Richard Greene, Elizabeth Allan, Gerard Heinz, Jean Cadell, G. H. Mulcaster

That Darn Cat! *

US 1965 116m Technicolor
Walt Disney (Bill Walsh, Ron Miller)
V*

A troublesome cat inadvertently helps to trail bank robbers.

Overlong but generally pleasing small-town comedy with well-paced sequences and a fascinating feline hero.

w The Gordons, Bill Walsh *novel Undercover Cat* by The Gordons *d* Robert Stevenson *ph* Edward Colman *m* Bob Brunner

Hayley Mills, Dean Jones, Dorothy Provine, Roddy McDowall, Neville Brand, Elsa Lanchester, William Demarest, Frank Gorshin, Grayson Hall, Ed Wynn

That Forsyte Woman *

US 1949 114m Technicolor
MGM (Leon Gordon)
V*
GB title: *The Forsyte Saga*

The wife of an Edwardian man of property falls in love with her niece's fiancé.

Moderately successful American attempt to film the first part of a very British novel sequence; so genteel, however, that it becomes dull.

w Jan Lustig, Ivan Tors, James B. Williams *novel A Man of Property* by John Galsworthy *d* Compton Bennett *ph* Joseph Ruttenberg *m* Bronislau Kaper

Greer Garson, *Errol Flynn*, Robert Young, Janet Leigh, Walter Pidgeon, Harry Davenport, Aubrey Mather

That Funny Feeling

US 1965 92m Technicolor
U-I (Harry Keller)

A maid pretends she lives in her boss's apartment.

Makeshift romantic comedy which barely takes the attention even while it's on.

w David R. Schwarz *d* Richard Thorpe *ph* Clifford Stine *m* Joseph Gershenson

Sandra Dee, Bobby Darin, Donald O'Connor, Nita Talbot, Larry Storch, Leo G. Carroll, James Westerfield

That Girl from Paris

US 1936 105m bw
RKO (Pandro S. Berman)
V*

A Paris opera singer falls for a swing band leader and stows away on a transatlantic liner to be near him.

Comedy-accented musical romance: not bad but not memorable.

w P. J. Wolfson, Dorothy Yost, Jane Murfin *d* Leigh Jason *ph* J. Roy Hunt *md* Nathaniel Shilkret *m* Edward Heyman

Lily Pons, Gene Raymond, Jack Oakie, Herman Bing, Lucille Ball, Mischa Auer, Frank Jenks

'When it's good it's very good, and when it's bad it's pretty awful.' – *Variety*

'Around her young heart she wore the scarlet letter of another woman's shame!'
That Hagen Girl

US 1947 83m bw
Warner (Alex Gottlieb)

A girl is convinced she is the illegitimate daughter of her teacher.

Stale teenage drama with odd anti-establishment overtones.

w Charles Hoffman *novel* Edith Kneipple Roberts *d* Peter Godfrey *ph* Karl Freund *m* Franz Waxman

Shirley Temple, Ronald Reagan, Rory Calhoun, Lois Maxwell, Dorothy Peterson, Charles Kemper, Conrad Janis, Harry Davenport

'Less a film than a series of false situations.' – *MFB*

'They shouldn't do such things to Shirley.' – *Bosley Crowther, New York Times*

That Hamilton Woman **

US 1941 128m bw
Alexander Korda Films
V, V*, L
GB title: *Lady Hamilton*

The affair of Lord Nelson and Emma Hamilton.

Bowdlerized version of a famous misalliance; coldly made but quite effective scene by scene, with notable performances.

w Walter Reisch, R. C. Sherriff *d* Alexander Korda *ph* Rudolph Maté *m* Miklos Rozsa *ad* Vincent Korda

Laurence Olivier, Vivien Leigh, Gladys Cooper, Alan Mowbray, Sara Allgood, Henry Wilcoxon, Halliwell Hobbes

'All its minor graces don't somehow add up to a major achievement . . . It is my impression that the film would have been a better job if it had stuck more to this man Nelson and bothered less about that woman Hamilton. These are not days when we have much patience for looking at history through the eyes of a trollop. And I am not at all sure that English people, who have been fighting for two years for something they like to call an ideal, will very much care for the implication that the future died with Nelson.' – *C. A. Lejeune*

AAN: Rudolph Maté; Vincent Korda

That Kind of Woman

US 1959 92m bw
Paramount/Ponti-Girosi

World War II remake of *Shopworn Angel* (qv); rather well made but basically dated and dull.

w Walter Bernstein *d* Sidney Lumet *ph* Boris Kaufman *m* Daniele Amfitheatrof

Sophia Loren, Tab Hunter, George Sanders, Jack Warden, Barbara Nichols, Keenan Wynn

'The romantic reunion of Tab Hunter and Sophia Loren resembles nothing so much as a sea scout given a luxury liner for Christmas.' – *Peter John Dyer*

That Lady

GB 1955 100m Eastmancolor Cinemascope
TCF/Atlanta (Sy Bartlett)

A noble widow at the court of Philip II of Spain loves a minister but incurs the king's jealous hatred.

Tepid historical romance which never flows as a film should.

w Anthony Veiller, Sy Bartlett *novel* Kate O'Brien *d* Terence Young *ph* Robert Krasker *m* John Addison

Olivia de Havilland, Gilbert Roland, *Paul Scofield*, Françoise Rosay, Dennis Price, Anthony Dawson, Robert Harris, Peter Illing, Christopher Lee

'Somehow, somewhere, one feels, something went very wrong.' – *MFB*

That Lady in Ermine

US   1948   89m   Technicolor
TCF (Ernst Lubitsch)

Two generations of European noblewomen learn to repel invaders.

Cheerless musical comedy which never gets started, what with the director dying during production and unsuitable stars lost in tinselly sets; the result can have appealed to no one.

w Samson Raphaelson   *d* Ernst Lubitsch, Otto Preminger   *ph* Leon Shamroy   *songs* Leo Robin, Frederick Hollander   *m* Alfred Newman

Betty Grable, Douglas Fairbanks Jnr, Cesar Romero, Walter Abel, Reginald Gardiner, Harry Davenport

AAN: song 'This is the Moment' (*m* Frederick Hollander, *ly* Leo Robin)

'When A No No Girl Meets A Go Go Man – Wham!!!'
That Lucky Touch

GB   1975   93m   Technicolor
Rank/Gloria (Dimitri de Grunwald)

During NATO war games in Brussels, a lady correspondent falls for an arms dealer.

Dim romantic farce which gives the impression of emanating from a dog-eared script written for the kind of stars who no longer shine.

w John Briley   *story* Moss Hart   *d* Christopher Miles   *ph* Douglas Slocombe   *m* John Scott

Roger Moore, Susannah York, Lee J. Cobb, Shelley Winters, Jean-Pierre Cassel, Raf Vallone, Sydne Rome, Donald Sinden

That Mad Mr Jones: see *The Fuller Brush Man*

That Man Bolt

US   1973   103m   Technicolor
Universal (Bernard Schwarz)

Adventures of a professional black courier skilled in the martial arts.

Black Kung Fu hokum from a major company; tolerable of its debased kind.

w Quentin Werty, Charles Johnson   *d* Henry Levin, David Lowell Rich   *ph* Gerald Perry Finnerman   *m* Charles Bernstein

Fred Williamson, Bryon Webster, Miko Mayama, Teresa Graves

'Gives every indication of having been devised by a computer fed with a variety of ingredients currently thought to guarantee box office success.' – *John Raisbeck, MFB*

That Man from Rio

France/Italy   1964   120m   Eastmancolor
Ariane/Artistes Associés/Dear Film/Vides (Alexander Mnouchkine, Georges Danciger)
original title: *L'Homme de Rio*

An airforce pilot finds himself helping his girlfriend in a worldwide search for stolen statuettes.

Elaborate mock thriller which is never quite as much fun as those involved seem to think. It provoked several inferior sequels.

w J. P. Rappeneau, Ariane Mnouchkine, Daniel Boulanger, Philippe de Broca   *d* Philippe de Broca   *ph* Edmond Séchan   *m* Georges Delerue

Jean-Paul Belmondo, Jean Servais, Françoise Dorléac, Adolfo Celi, Simone Renant

'Fantasy takes over, with Belmondo outdoing Fairbanks in agility, Lloyd in cliffhanging, and Bond in indestructibility.' – *Brenda Davies, MFB*

AAN: script

That Midnight Kiss

US   1949   98m   Technicolor
MGM (Joe Pasternak)
V*

An unknown becomes a great singing star.

Simple-minded vehicle for the first appearance of Mario Lanza.

w Bruce Manning, Tamara Hovey   *d* Norman Taurog   *ph* Robert Surtees   *m* Bronislau Kaper

Kathryn Grayson, Ethel Barrymore, Jose Iturbi, Mario Lanza, Keenan Wynn, J. Carrol Naish, Jules Munshin, Thomas Gomez, Marjorie Reynolds

That Night *

US   1957   88m   bw
Galahad (Himan Brown)

An overwhelmed TV writer has a heart attack, and recovers after a series of medical setbacks.

Impressive minor case history, hardly entertainment but quite arresting.

w Robert Wallace, Burton J. Rowles   *d* John Newland   *ph* Maurice Hartzband   *m* Mario Nascimbene

John Beal, Augusta Dabney, Shepperd Strudwick, Ralph Murphy

That Night in London

GB   1933   78m   bw
Paramount/London Films (Alexander Korda)
US title: *Overnight*

A bank clerk decides to steal money to have one final fling before he commits suicide.

Dim low-budget drama that wastes its star.

w Dorothy Greenhill, Arthur Wimperis   *d* Rowland V. Lee   *ph* Robert Martin   *m* Peter Mendoza   *ed* Stephen Harrison

Robert Donat, Pearl Argyle, Miles Mander, Lawrence Hanray, Roy Emmerton, Graham Soutten

That Night in Rio *

US   1941   90m   Technicolor
TCF (Fred Kohlmar)

A night-club entertainer is paid to impersonate a lookalike count, but this causes complications with the countess.

Zippy musical based on a story first used in *Folies Bergère* (qv) and later in *On the Riviera* (qv).

w George Seaton, Bess Meredyth, Hal Long   *play* Rudolph Lothar, Hans Adler   *d* Irving Cummings   *ph* Leon Shamroy   *songs* Mack Gordon, Harry Warren   *md* Alfred Newman

Don Ameche, Alice Faye, Carmen Miranda, S. Z. Sakall, J. Carrol Naish, Curt Bois, Leonid Kinskey, Maria Montez

'An eye-filling and ear-filling musical comedy extravaganza.' – *Motion Picture Herald*

That Night in Varennes: see *La Nuit de Varennes*

That Night with You

US   1945   84m   bw
Universal (Michael Fessier, Ernest Pagano)

A girl singer anxious to get on tells a producer that she is his illegitimate daughter.

Mindless farce with music, its gimmick being that all the songs are set to Tchaikovsky's music. Otherwise very dull.

w Michael Fessier, Ernest Pagano   *d* William A. Seiter   *ph* Woody Bredell

Franchot Tone, Susanna Foster, David Bruce, Louise Allbritton, Buster Keaton, Irene Ryan, Jacqueline de Wit

That Obscure Object of Desire **

France/Spain   1977   103m   Eastmancolor
Greenwich/Galaxie/In Cine (Serge Silberman)
V, V*, L

A middle-aged gentleman suffers continual humiliations from the girl he loves.

Unrecognizable remake of a novel previously filmed as a vehicle for Dietrich and Bardot. Despite the tricking out with surrealist touches (the girl is played by two different actresses) it is not one of Buñuel's best, and amuses only on the surface.

w Luis Buñuel, Jean-Claude Carrière   *novel La Femme et le Pantin* by Pierre Louys   *d* Luis Buñuel   *ph* Edmond Richard   *m* from Richard Wagner

Fernando Rey, Carole Bouquet, Angela Molina, Julien Bertheau

AAN: best foreign film; script

That Riviera Touch

GB   1966   98m   Eastmancolor
Rank (Hugh Stewart)

Two tourists in the south of France get mixed up with jewel thieves.

Disappointing star comedy ending in a surfboard chase.

w S. C. Green, R. M. Hills, Peter Blackmore   *d* Cliff Owen   *ph* Otto Heller   *m* Ron Goodwin

Eric Morecambe, Ernie Wise, Suzanne Lloyd, Paul Stassino, Armand Mestral

That Touch of Mink **

US   1962   99m   Eastmancolor   Panavision
U-I/Granley/Arwin/Nob Hill (Stanley Shapiro, Martin Melcher)
V, V*

Bachelor tycoon pursues virginal secretary.

Jaded sex comedy (or what passed for it in nudge-nudge 1962) enlivened by practised star performances and smart timing.

w Stanley Shapiro, Nate Monaster   *d* Delbert Mann   *ph* Russell Metty   *m* George Duning

Cary Grant, Doris Day, Gig Young, Audrey Meadows, Dick Sargent, *John Astin*

'Too often there's a hampering second-hand air about situation and joke. Throughout, the determination is to keep faith with the American sex mythology at all costs.' – *Jack Pitman, Variety*

AAN: script

That Uncertain Feeling *

US   1941   84m   bw
UA/Sol Lesser (Ernst Lubitsch)
V*

A wife with insomnia and hiccups befriends a wacky concert pianist who proceeds to move into her home.

Although Lubitsch had made this story before, as the silent *Kiss Me Again*, the elements didn't really jell in this version, which seemed silly rather than funny.

w Donald Ogden Stewart, Walter Reisch   *play Divorçons* by Victorien Sardou, Emile de Najac   *d* Ernst Lubitsch   *ph* George Barnes   *m* Werner Heymann   *pd* Alexander Golitzen

Merle Oberon, Melvyn Douglas, Burgess Meredith, Alan Mowbray, Olive Blakeney, Harry Davenport, Eve Arden, Sig Rumann

'Gay entertainment.' – *Picture Show*

AAN: Werner Heymann

That Was Then . . . This Is Now

US   1985   102m   TVC colour
Paramount/Media Ventures (Gary R. Lindberg, John M. Ondov)
V*, L

Urban youths growing into manhood find the world a gloomy place.

Highly resistible chunk of pessimistic philosophizing with a few fights thrown in.

w Emilio Estevez *novel* S. E. Hinton
d Christopher Cain *ph* Juan Ruiz-Anchia
m Keith Olsen *ad* Chester Kaczenski *ed* Ken Johnson

Emilio Estevez, Craig Sheffer, Kim Delaney, Jill Schoelen, Barbara Babcock, Morgan Freeman

'God save the kids who live in an S. E. Hinton novel. They're firecrackers waiting to go off.' – *Variety*

That Way With Women

US 1947 84m bw
Warner (Charles Hoffman)

A millionaire amuses himself by playing Cupid to a young couple.

Routine remake of *The Millionaire*: just about watchable.

w Leo Townsend *d* Frederick de Cordova *ph* Ted McCord *m* Frederick Hollander

Sidney Greenstreet, Dane Clark, Martha Vickers, Alan Hale, Craig Stevens, Barbara Brown

That Woman Opposite

GB 1957 83m bw
Monarch (William Gell)
US title: *City after Midnight*

In a small French town, a killer returns to silence a witness.

Slow-paced semi-mystery, reasonably well done.

wd Compton Bennett *story The Emperor's Snuff Box* by John Dickson Carr *ph* Lionel Banes
m Stanley Black

Phyllis Kirk, Dan O'Herlihy, Wilfrid Hyde-White, Petula Clark, Jack Watling, William Franklyn, Margaret Withers

That Wonderful Urge

US 1948 82m bw
TCF (Fred Kohlmar)

A newspaperman is forced into marriage with a publicity-shy heiress.

Tepid romantic comedy, a remake of *Love Is News* (qv).

w Jay Dratler *d* Robert B. Sinclair *ph* Charles Clarke *m* Cyril Mockridge

Gene Tierney, Tyrone Power, Reginald Gardiner, Arleen Whelan, Lucile Watson, Gene Lockhart, Porter Hall, Taylor Holmes

That'll Be the Day *

GB 1973 91m Technicolor
EMI/Goodtimes (David Puttnam, Sanford Lieberson)
V, V*, L

In 1958, a young drifter becomes a fairground worker, and eventually walks out on his wife and family to become a pop star.

Spirited return to British realism, with well-sketched cameos, a likeable dour viewpoint, and a cheerful pop music background.

w Ray Connolly *d* Claude Whatham *ph* Peter Suschitzky *md* Neil Aspinall, Keith Moon

David Essex, Ringo Starr, Rosemary Leach, James Booth, Billy Fury, Keith Moon, Rosalind Ayres

'As insubstantial as one of its own attempts at a statement.' – *Tony Rayns*

That's a Good Girl *

GB 1933 83m bw
Herbert Wilcox/British and Dominions

A man about town seeks ways of making money.

Archetypal vehicle for a debonair song and dance man.

w Douglas Furber, Donovan Pedelty, Jack Buchanan
d Jack Buchanan

Jack Buchanan, Elsie Randolph, Dorothy Hyson, Garry Marsh, Vera Pearce, William Kendall

That's Dancin'! **

US 1985 105m Metrocolor
MGM–UA/David Niven Jnr, Jack Haley Jnr
V, L

Selections from the golden age of the movie musical, featuring the likes of Fred Astaire, Gene Kelly, Eleanor Powell, Busby Berkeley.

Fascinating compilation which made little impact at the box-office.

narrators Gene Kelly, Sammy Davis Jnr, Mikhail Baryshnikov, Liza Minnelli, Ray Bolger

'Boy! do we need it now!'

That's Entertainment **

US 1974 137m Metrocolor 70mm (blown up)/ scope
MGM (Daniel Melnick, Jack Haley Jnr)
V, V*, L

Fred Astaire, Gene Kelly, Elizabeth Taylor, James Stewart, Bing Crosby, Liza Minnelli, Donald O'Connor, Debbie Reynolds, Mickey Rooney and Frank Sinatra introduce highlights from MGM's musical past.

A slapdash compilation which was generally very big at the box-office and obviously has fascinating sequences, though the narration is sloppily sentimental and the later wide-screen sequences let down the rest.

wd Jack Haley Jnr *ph* various *m* various

Principal stars as above plus Judy Garland, Esther Williams, Eleanor Powell, Clark Gable, Ray Bolger

'While many ponder the future of MGM, none can deny that it has one hell of a past.' – *Variety*

'It is particularly gratifying to get the key sequences from certain movies without having to sit through a fatuous storyline.' – *Michael Billington, Illustrated London News*

'No other film in town offers such a harvest of undiluted joy.' – *Sunday Express*

That's Entertainment Part Two **

US 1976 133m Metrocolor 70mm (blown up)/ scope
MGM (Saul Chaplin, Daniel Melnick)
V, V*, L

More of the above, introduced by Fred Astaire and Gene Kelly, with comedy and drama sequences as well as musical.

d Gene Kelly *titles* Saul Bass *ph* various

Principal stars as above plus Jeanette MacDonald, Nelson Eddy, the Marx Brothers, Laurel and Hardy, Jack Buchanan, Judy Garland, Ann Miller, Mickey Rooney, Oscar Levant, Louis Armstrong, etc

That's Life!

US 1986 102m DeLuxe Panavision
Columbia/Paradise Cove/Ubilam (Tony Adams)
V*, L

An architect touching sixty, with a sick wife, pours out all his fears of old age and mortality.

Blake Edwards exposing himself again; the movie was even shot in his own house. Somewhat embarrassing to watch, and overwrought, it does have a few good moments.

w Milton Wexler, Blake Edwards *d* Blake Edwards
ph Anthony Richmond *m* Henry Mancini

Jack Lemmon, Julie Andrews, Sally Kellerman, Robert Loggia, Jennifer Edwards

AAN: song 'Life in a Looking Glass' (Mancini, Leslie Bricusse)

That's My Boy

US 1951 98m bw
Paramount/Hal B. Wallis (Cy Howard)

An athletic father tries to press his hypochondriac teenage son into the same mould.

American college comedy of no international interest.

w Cy Howard *d* Hal Walker *ph* Lee Garmes
m Leigh Harline

Dean Martin, Jerry Lewis, Eddie Mayehoff, Ruth Hussey, Polly Bergen, John McIntire

That's My Man

US 1946 98m bw
Republic (Frank Borzage)
GB title: *Will Tomorrow Ever Come?*

A racing man is reunited with his wife when their son has pneumonia.

A compendium of clichés, with everything but a title card reading *Came the Dawn*. Of no real interest.

w Steve Fisher, Bradley King *d* Frank Borzage
ph Tony Gaudio *m* Cy Feuer

Don Ameche, Catherine McLeod, Roscoe Karns, John Ridgely

That's My Wife *

US 1929 20m bw silent
Hal Roach

Stan dresses up as Ollie's wife to impress his rich uncle.

Lesser-known star comedy which well sustains its basic joke and includes some splendidly timed farce in a restaurant.

w Leo McCarey, H. M. Walker *d* Lloyd French

Laurel and Hardy, Vivien Oakland, William Courtright

That's Right, You're Wrong *

US 1939 91m bw
RKO (David Butler)
L

A band leader gets a Hollywood contract but is hated by the studio head.

Typical of the nonsense musicals featuring Kay Kyser and his radio Kollege of Musical Knowledge. The movie background and self-spoofing made this first attempt one of the best.

w William Conselman, James V. Kern *d* David Butler *ph* Russell Metty *m* George Duning
songs various

Kay Kyser, Adolphe Menjou, Lucille Ball, Dennis O'Keefe, May Robson, Edward Everett Horton, Ish Kabibble, Ginny Simms, Roscoe Karns, Moroni Olsen, Hobart Cavanaugh, Sheilah Graham, Hedda Hopper

'Moderate entertainment which will satisfy as a bill-topper.' – *Variety*

That's the Spirit

US 1945 87m bw
Universal

A ghost comes back to tell his actress wife he didn't desert her as she thought.

Rather heavy comedy of the *Here Comes Mr Jordan* school.

w Michael Fessier, Ernest Pagano *d* Charles Lamont

Jack Oakie, Peggy Ryan, June Vincent, Gene Lockhart, Andy Devine, Arthur Treacher, Irene Ryan, Buster Keaton

Theatre of Blood *

GB 1973 102m DeLuxe
UA/Cineman (John Kohn, Stanley Mann)
V*, L

A Shakespearean actor uses appropriate murder

methods on the various critics who have ridiculed his performances.

Spoof horror picture which goes too far with some sick visuals; the idea and some of the performances are fine.

w Anthony Greville-Bell d Douglas Hickox
ph Wolfgang Suschitzky m Michael J. Lewis
pd Michael Seymour

Vincent Price, Diana Rigg, Ian Hendry, Harry Andrews, Coral Browne, Robert Coote, Jack Hawkins, Michael Hordern, Arthur Lowe, Robert Morley, Dennis Price, Diana Dors, Joan Hickson, Renée Asherson, Milo O'Shea, Eric Sykes

Theatre of Death

GB 1966 91m Techniscope
Pennea (Michael Smedley-Aston)
V*
US title: Blood Fiend

Vampire-like murders in Paris are eventually connected with a Grand Guignol theatre.

Dreary backstage shocker with inadequate production values.

w Roger Marshall, Ellis Kadison d Sam Gallu

Christopher Lee, Jenny Till, Lelia Goldoni, Julian Glover, Ivor Dean, Evelyn Laye

Theatre Royal (1930): see The Royal Family of Broadway

Theatre Royal

GB 1943 92m bw
British National

A revue and a theatre are saved by a sentimental prop man.

Shapeless star comedy with music; not their best.

w Bud Flanagan, Austin Melford, Geoffrey Orme d John Baxter

Bud Flanagan and Chesney Allen, Peggy Dexter, Lydia Sherwood, Horace Kenney, Marjorie Rhodes, Finlay Currie

Their Big Moment

US 1934 68m bw
RKO

Phoney mindreaders solve a murder mystery in a spooky house.

Quite good, well-organized fun of its type.

w Arthur Caesar, Marian Dix, Walter Hackett d James Cruze

ZaSu Pitts, Slim Summerville, William Gaxton, Ralph Morgan, Bruce Cabot, Julie Haydon, Kay Johnson

'Should have fairly good audience strength.' – Variety

Their First Mistake **

US 1932 20m bw
Hal Roach
V

Ollie decides to improve his marriage by adopting a baby, only to find that his wife has left him.

Sublimely silly but endearing star comedy with brilliant passages of imbecilic conversation followed by well-timed farce.

w H. M. Walker d George Marshall (who also plays a bit)

Laurel and Hardy, Mae Busch

Their Purple Moment

US 1928 20m bw silent
Hal Roach

Stan and Ollie go out on the town, only to discover that Stan's wife has replaced his money with grocery coupons.

Minor star comedy with efficient but predictable restaurant scenes ending in a pie fight.

w H. M. Walker d James Parrott

Laurel and Hardy, Anita Garvin, Kay Deslys

Their Secret Affair: see Top Secret Affair

Thelma and Louise ***

US 1991 129m DeLuxe Panavision
UIP/Pathé Entertainment (Ridley Scott, Mimi Polk)
V, V*, L, S

Two women, off together on a weekend spree, go on the run after one of them kills a man who tries to rape the other.

Timely, exuberant and off-beat feminist road movie that manages to say something interesting about the relationship between the sexes.

w Callie Khouri d Ridley Scott ph Adrian Biddle m Hans Zimmer pd Norris Spencer ed Thom Noble

Susan Sarandon, Geena Davis, Harvey Keitel, Michael Madsen, Christopher McDonald, Stephen Tobolowsky, Brad Pitt

'An exhilarating feminist movie . . . that's designed to appeal to the outlaw lurking in all of us.' – Philip French, Observer

'The first important American movie to plop two women in a car and send them careering down open Western roads with the cops in wheel-spinning pursuit. And it is the first to use sexism as the motivating force for their misdeeds.' – Richard Schickel, Time

AA: Callie Khouri

AAN: Ridley Scott; Geena Davis; Susan Sarandon; Adrian Biddle; editing

Thelma Jordan: see The File on Thelma Jordan

'Kill one and two others take its place! Don't turn your back or you're doomed! And don't tell anyone what Them are!'

Them! **

US 1954 94m bw
Warner (David Weisbart)
V*, L

Atomic bomb radiation causes giant ants to breed in the New Mexico desert.

Among the first, and certainly the best, of the post-atomic monster animal cycle, this durable thriller starts with several eerie desert sequences and builds up to a shattering climax in the Los Angeles sewers. A general air of understatement helps a lot.

w Ted Sherdeman story George Worthing Yates d Gordon Douglas ph Sid Hickox m Bronislau Kaper

Edmund Gwenn, James Whitmore, Joan Weldon, James Arness, Onslow Stevens

'I asked the editor: How does it look? And he said: Fine. I said: Does it look honest? He said: As honest as twelve foot ants can look.' – Gordon Douglas

Them Thar Hills **

US 1934 20m bw
Hal Roach

Stan and Ollie go camping, drink from a well full of moonshine whisky, and get drunk with another camper's wife.

Consistently funny star comedy culminating in a tit-for-tat routine which was reprised in Tit for Tat the following year.

w Stan Laurel, H. M. Walker d Charles Rogers

Laurel and Hardy, Charlie Hall, Mae Busch, Billy Gilbert

Themroc **

France 1972 110m Eastmancolor
The Other Cinema/Filmanthrope/FDL (Jean-Claude Bourlat)

A depressed worker in a dead-end job suddenly breaks free of all his restrictions, making love to his sister and demolishing the walls of his apartment.

An exuberant anti-authoritarian comedy, in which normal dialogue is replaced by an invented language of grunts and whistles.

wd Claude Faraldo ph Jean-Marc Ripert ad C. Lamarque ed Noun Serra

Michel Piccoli, Béatrice Romand, Marilu Tolo, Francesca R. Coluzzi, Patrick Dewaere, Miou-Miou

'Succeeds in being poetic without being arty and, by using laughter as a critical tactic, in suggesting that revolution in a puritanical society ought to take a hedonistic form.' – Jan Dawson, MFB

Theodora Goes Wild *

US 1936 94m bw
Columbia (Everett Riskin)

A small-town girl writes a titillating bestseller.

Mildly crazy comedy which helped develop the trend for stars performing undignified antics but today seems rather slow and dated.

w Sidney Buchman story Mary McCarthy d Richard Boleslawski ph Joseph Walker m Morris Stoloff ed Otto Meyer

Irene Dunne, Melvyn Douglas, Thomas Mitchell, Thurston Hall, Rosalind Keith, Spring Byington, Elizabeth Risdon, Nana Bryant

AAN: Irene Dunne; Otto Meyer

Theorem *

Italy 1968 98m Eastmancolor
Aetos Film
V, V*

A handsome young man arrives unexpectedly to stay with a Milan industrialist and his family, gratifying their desires but leaving them tragically unhappy.

Moderately amusing fable with the presumed intent of decrying all universal panaceas, including Christianity.

wd Pier Paolo Pasolini novel Pier Paolo Pasolini ph Giuseppe Ruzzolini m Ennio Morricone

Terence Stamp, Silvana Mangano, Massimo Girotti, Anne Wiazemsky, Laura Betti

There Ain't No Justice

GB 1939 83m bw
Ealing

A young boxer refuses to throw a fight.

Minor sporting drama, well praised at the time but later forgotten.

w Pen Tennyson, James Curtis, Sergei Nolbandov d Pen Tennyson

Jimmy Hanley, Edward Rigby, Mary Clare, Edward Chapman, Phyllis Stanley, Michael Wilding

There Goes My Heart

US 1938 81m bw
Hal Roach

A reporter is assigned to track down a runaway heiress.

Very pale imitation of It Happened One Night.

w Jack Jevne, Eddie Moran d Norman Z. McLeod ph Norbert Brodine m Marvin Hatley

Fredric March, Virginia Bruce, Patsy Kelly, Nancy Carroll, Eugene Pallette, Claude Gillingwater, Arthur Lake, Harry Langdon, Etienne Girardot

'A comedy clicko . . . plenty of zip and zing.' – Variety

AAN: Marvin Hatley

There Goes the Bride

GB 1980 91m Eastmancolor
Lonsdale (Martin Schute, Ray Cooney)
V

A harassed advertising executive suffers

hallucinations about a lifesize cardboard cut-out of a twenties flapper.

Embarrassingly witless and plotless revamp of innumerable better comedies in the Topper tradition; it has to be seen to be believed.

w Terence Marcel, Ray Cooney play Ray Cooney, John Chapman d Terence Marcel ph James Devis m Harry Robinson pd Peter Mullins

Tom Smothers, Twiggy, Sylvia Syms, Martin Balsam, Michael Whitney, Geoffrey Sumner, Hermione Baddeley, Phil Silvers, Broderick Crawford, Jim Backus

'The whole thing would be laughable if it weren't so unfunny.' – Gilbert Adair, MFB

There Goes the Groom
US 1937 64m bw
Albert Lewis/RKO

A young man comes back rich from the Alaskan gold fields and reminds an old girlfriend of her promise to marry him.

A well-played comedy which can't conceal its threadbare situations.

w S. K. Lauren, Dorothy Yost, Harold Kusell, David Garth d Joseph Santley

Ann Sothern, Burgess Meredith, Mary Boland, Onslow Stevens, Louise Henry

There Goes the Neighborhood
US 1992 89m DeLuxe Panavision
Rank/Kings Road (Stephen Friedman)
V, V*
aka: Paydirt

A prison psychologist and a gang of convicts go in search of a stolen fortune buried in a suburban basement.

Laboured farce with heavy-handed acting and direction which fails to raise a laugh.

wd Bill Phillips ph Walt Lloyd m David Bell pd Dean Tschetter ed Sharyn L. Ross

Jeff Daniels, Catherine O'Hara, Hector Elizondo, Rhea Perlman, Judith Ivey, Harris Yulin, Jonathan Banks, Chazz Palminteri, Dabney Coleman

'A TV-inspired high concept and inept production values combine for an unappealing film sans redeeming qualities.' – Variety

† The film was released direct to video in Britain.

There Is Another Sun
GB 1951 95m bw
Nettlefold
US title: Wall of Death

A fairground wall of death rider turns to crime.

Glum quickie which was oddly popular.

w Guy Morgan d Lewis Gilbert

Maxwell Reed, Susan Shaw, Laurence Harvey, Hermione Baddeley, Leslie Dwyer

There Was a Crooked Man *
GB 1960 107m bw
UA/Knightsbridge (John Bryan)

An ex-safecracker outwits the crooked mayor of an industrial town.

Semi-happy attempt to humanize a knockabout clown; good supporting performances and production.

w Reuben Ship d Stuart Burge ph Arthur Ibbetson m Kenneth V. Jones

Norman Wisdom, Andrew Cruickshank, Alfred Marks, Susannah York, Reginald Beckwith

There Was a Crooked Man *
US 1970 126m Technicolor Panavision
Warner Seven Arts (Joseph L. Mankiewicz)
V*, L

In 1883 Arizona a murderer tries to escape from jail and recover hidden loot but is constantly thwarted by the sheriff who arrested him, now a warden.

Curious black comedy melodrama with lots of talent going nowhere in particular; hard to endure as a whole but with entertaining scenes.

w David Newman, Robert Benton d Joseph L. Mankiewicz ph Harry Stradling Jnr m Charles Strouse ad Edward Carrere

Kirk Douglas, Henry Fonda, Hume Cronyn, Warren Oates, Burgess Meredith, John Randolph, Arthur O'Connell, Martin Gabel, Alan Hale

'This example of commercialized black comedy nihilism seems to have been an evil two-year-old, and it has been directed in the Grand Rapids style of moviemaking.' – Pauline Kael, New Yorker

There's a Girl in my Heart
US 1949 82m bw
Allied Artists (Arthur Dreifuss)

The attractive widow who owns a music hall finds the site in demand.

Slight, artificial but mildly pleasing musical extravaganza of the gay nineties.

w Arthur Hoerl, John Eugene Hasty d Arthur Dreifuss

Lee Bowman, Elyse Knox, Lon Chaney Jnr, Gloria Jean, Peggy Ryan, Ludwig Donath, Ray McDonald, Irene Ryan

There's a Girl in My Soup *
GB 1970 96m Eastmancolor
Columbia/Ascot (John Boulting)
V, V*

A randy TV personality finds himself outplotted by a waif he picks up.

Flimsy screen version of a long-running sex comedy; some laughs, but the star is uncomfortably miscast.

w Terence Frisby play Terence Frisby d Roy Boulting ph Harry Waxman m Mike D'Abo

Peter Sellers, Goldie Hawn, Tony Britton, Nicky Henson, John Comer, Diana Dors, Judy Campbell

There's Always a Woman *
US 1938 81m bw
Columbia

A private detective's wife beats him to the solution of a murder.

Amiably scatty crime comedy in the Thin Man tradition.

w Gladys Lehman, Wilson Collison d Alexander Hall

Joan Blondell, Melvyn Douglas, Mary Astor, Frances Drake, Jerome Cowan, Robert Paige, Thurston Hall, Pierre Watkin

'Will provide general satisfaction as entertainment and as a grosser.' – Variety

There's Always Tomorrow
US 1934 86m bw
Universal

A depressed family man is cheered up by a former sweetheart.

Basically rather a dull drama, but with sincere performances which lift it.

w William Hurlbut novel Ursula Parrott d Edward Sloman

Frank Morgan, Binnie Barnes, Lois Wilson, Louise Latimer, Alan Hale, Robert Taylor

'Attractive screen material, it weighs in for what looks like a favourable sprint for coin.' – Variety.

† Remade 1956 as These Wilder Years, with James Cagney and Barbara Stanwyck.

There's Always Tomorrow
US 1956 84m bw
Universal (Ross Hunter)

A married man falls for another woman.

Very flat variation on Brief Encounter, with stars going through mechanical paces.

w Bernard Schoenfeld story Ursula Parrott d Douglas Sirk ph Russell Metty m Herman Stein, Heinz Roemheld

Barbara Stanwyck, Fred MacMurray, Joan Bennett, Pat Crowley, William Reynolds, Gigi Perreau, Jane Darwell

† Previously made by Universal in 1934 with Frank Morgan and Binnie Barnes.

There's No Business like Show Business **
US 1954 117m DeLuxe Cinemascope
TCF (Sol C. Siegel)
V, V*, L, S

The life and times of a family of vaudevillians.

Mainly entertaining events and marvellous tunes make up this very Cinemascoped musical, in which the screen is usually filled with six people side by side.

w Phoebe and Henry Ephron d Walter Lang ph Leon Shamroy m Lionel Newman, Alfred Newman m/ly Irving Berlin ad John DeCuir, Lyle Wheeler

Ethel Merman, Dan Dailey, Marilyn Monroe, Donald O'Connor, Johnny Ray, Mitzi Gaynor, Hugh O'Brian, Frank McHugh

'One of the saddening films which only occasionally live up to their huge promise.' – Dilys Powell

AAN: original story (Lamar Trotti); Lionel Newman, Alfred Newman

There's Nothing Out There *
US 1991 90m colour
Valkhn (Victor Kanefsky)

Teenagers staying in an isolated mountain cabin are threatened by an alien monster.

Mildly amusing spoof of horror and science-fiction exploitation movies.

wd Rolfe Kanefsky ph Ed Hershberger m Christopher Thomas sp Scott Hart; creature design: Ken Quinn ed Victor Kanefsky

Craig Peck, Wendy Bednarz, Mark Collver, Bonnie Bowers, John Carhart III, Claudia Flores, Jeff Dachis, Lisa Grant

'Tongue-in-cheeky thriller which takes dead aim at the clichés abounding in B and C list titles.' – Variety

There's Something about a Soldier
US 1943 81m bw
Columbia (Samuel Bischoff)

The destinies of five officer candidates at the Anti-Aircraft Training School.

Transparent recruiting poster dramatics.

w Horace McCoy, Barry Trivers d Alfred E. Green

Tom Neal, Evelyn Keyes, Bruce Bennett, John Hubbard, Jeff Donnell, Frank Sully

There's That Woman Again
US 1938 75m bw
Columbia

A district attorney is hampered by his meddlesome spouse.

Half-hearted follow-up to There's Always a Woman; the McMillan and Wife of its day.

w Philip G. Epstein, James Edward Grant, Ken Englund d Alexander Hall

Melvyn Douglas, Virginia Bruce, Margaret Lindsay, Stanley Ridges, Gordon Oliver, Tom Dugan, Don Beddoe

Therese *

France 1986 91m colour
AFC/Films AZ/CNC

A 19th-century Normandy girl becomes a nun, dies at 24, and is canonized.

Straightforward, austere biographical account which weaves a curious spell.

wd Alain Cavalier *ph* Philippe Rousselot
m Offenbach, Fauré

Catherine Mouchet, Aurore Prieto, Sylvie Habault

These Are the Damned: see *The Damned*

These Dangerous Years

GB 1957 92m bw
Everest/Anna Neagle
US title: *Dangerous Youth*

A Liverpool teenage gang leader is called up and becomes a better guy.

Dim drama with music marking the debut of a singing star.

w John Trevor Story *d* Herbert Wilcox
ph Gordon Dines *m* Stanley Black

Frankie Vaughan, George Baker, Carole Lesley, Jackie Lane, Katherine Kath, Eddie Byrne, Kenneth Cope

These Foolish Things: see *Daddy Nostalgie*

These Glamour Girls

US 1939 78m bw
MGM

A drunken college student invites a dime-a-dance girl for a festive weekend with his snobbish friends.

Wincingly predictable romantic comedy-drama with no outstanding talent displayed from any quarter.

w Marion Parsonnet, Jane Hall *d* S. Sylvan Simon

Lew Ayres, Lana Turner, Tom Brown, Richard Carlson, Jane Bryan, Anita Louise, Ann Rutherford, Marsha Hunt

'Silly situations and mawkish lines. A dualler.' – *Variety*

These Things Happen: see *Les Choses de la Vie*

These Thousand Hills

US 1958 96m Eastmancolor Cinemascope
TCF (David Weisbart)

A successful cattle rancher finds that his best friend is a rustler.

Large-scale but somehow unimpressive Western variant on *The Virginian*, cluttered with sub-plots.

w Alfred Hayes *novel* A. B. Guthrie Jnr *d* Richard Fleischer *ph* Charles G. Clarke *m* Leigh Harline

Richard Egan, Stuart Whitman, Don Murray, Lee Remick, Albert Dekker, Harold J. Stone, Patricia Owens

These Three **

US 1936 93m bw
Samuel Goldwyn
V, V*, L

A lying schoolgirl accuses two schoolmistresses of scandalous behaviour.

Bowdlerized version of a famous play (instead of lesbianism we have extra-marital affairs). It worked well enough at the time but now seems dated; oddly enough when the play was filmed full strength in 1962 it didn't work at all.

w Lillian Hellman *play* The Children's Hour by Lillian Hellman *d* William Wyler *ph* Gregg Toland *m* Alfred Newman

Merle Oberon, Miriam Hopkins, Joel McCrea, *Bonita Granville*, Catherine Doucet, Alma Kruger, Marcia Mae Jones, Margaret Hamilton, Walter Brennan

AAN: Bonita Granville

These Wilder Years

US 1956 91m bw
MGM (Jules Schermer)

A wealthy industrialist returns to his home town to trace his illegitimate son.

Modest sentimental drama with practised stars.

w Frank Fenton *d* Roy Rowland *ph* George Folsey *m* Jeff Alexander

James Cagney, Barbara Stanwyck, Walter Pidgeon, Betty Lou Keim, Don Dubbins, Edward Andrews

They All Died Laughing: see *A Jolly Bad Fellow*

They All Kissed the Bride

US 1942 86m bw
Columbia (Edward Kaufman)

A woman executive falls in love with the crusading writer who is out to expose working conditions in her company.

No surprises are expected or provided in this very ho-hum romantic comedy.

w P. J. Wolfson *d* Alexander Hall *ph* Joseph Walker *md* Morris Stoloff *m* Werner Heyman

Joan Crawford, Melvyn Douglas, Roland Young, Billie Burke, Allen Jenkins, Andrew Tombes, Helen Parrish, Mary Treen

They All Laughed *

US 1982 115m Movielab
Time-Life/Moon (George Morfogen, Blaine Novak)
V*, L

Three agency detectives fall in and out of love in the course of their duties.

It has the air of a somewhat misshapen and Americanized *La Ronde*, with added suggestions of *On the Town*, but it adds up to very little and provides only a few laughs on the way.

wd Peter Bogdanovich *ph* Robby Muller *m* various

Audrey Hepburn, Ben Gazzara, John Ritter, Dorothy Stratten, Colleen Camp, Patti Hansen, George Morfogen, Blaine Novak

'One tires of long looks that speak volumes, of endless successions of meeting cute.' – *John Pym, MFB*

They Call It Sin

US 1932 68m bw
First National
GB title: *The Way of Life*

A Kansas girl joins a New York chorus and needs to be rescued from a villainous producer.

Ho-hum romantic drama without much substance.

w Lillie Hayward, Howard Green *novel* Alberta Steadman Eagan *d* Thornton Freeland

Loretta Young, George Brent, Louis Calhern, David Manners, Una Merkel

'It needs the sexy title to bolster a just so-so flicker.' – *Variety*

They Call Me Mister Tibbs!

US 1970 108m DeLuxe
UA/Mirisch (Herbert Hirshman)
V*

A San Francisco police lieutenant suspects a crusading local minister of murder.

Flat, dispirited police melodrama with irrelevant domestic asides, a long way after *In the Heat of the Night* which introduced the main character. (*The Organization* was the third and last in the so-called series.)

w Alan R. Trustman, James R. Webb *d* Gordon Douglas *ph* Gerald Finnerman *m* Quincy Jones

Sidney Poitier, Martin Landau, Barbara McNair, Anthony Zerbe, Jeff Corey, Juano Hernandez, Ed Asner

They Came by Night

GB 1939 72m bw
TCF

A jeweller pretends to be a crook in order to lure the men who killed his brother.

Smart little suspense yarn.

w Frank Launder, Sidney Gilliat, Michael Hogan, Roland Pertwee *d* Harry Lachman

Will Fyffe, Phyllis Calvert, Anthony Hulme, George Merritt, Athole Stewart, John Glyn Jones

They Came from beyond Space

GB 1967 85m Eastmancolor
Amicus (Max J. Rosenberg, Milton Subotsky)
V*

Disembodied aliens take over a team of scientists investigating a mysterious fall of meteors.

Implausible science fiction, lacking flair in acting, direction and writing and not helped by the change in locale from the original to an olde-worlde English setting.

w Milton Subotsky *novel* The Gods Hate Kansas by Joseph Millard *d* Freddie Francis *ph* Norman Warwick *m* James Stevens *pd* Bill Constable *ed* Peter Musgrave

Robert Hutton, Jennifer Jayne, Zia Mohyeddin, Bernard Kay, Michael Gough, Geoffrey Wallace

They Came from Within: see *Shivers*

They Came to a City *

GB 1944 77m bw
Ealing (Sidney Cole)

Assorted people find themselves outside the gates of a mysterious city.

The *Outward Bound* format applied to postwar reconstruction, with characters deciding what kind of a world they want. Good talk and good acting, but not quite cinema.

w Basil Dearden, Sidney Cole *play* J. B. Priestley *d* Basil Dearden *ph* Stan Pavey

Googie Withers, John Clements, Raymond Huntley, Renée Gadd, A. E. Matthews, Mabel Terry-Lewis, *Ada Reeve*, Norman Shelley, Frances Rowe

They Came to Blow Up America

US 1943 73m bw
TCF

An FBI man of German parentage goes to Nazi Germany and trains with a group of saboteurs, who are arrested when they set foot in the US.

Tolerable propaganda potboiler.

w Aubrey Wisberg *d* Edward Ludwig

George Sanders, Anna Sten, Ward Bond, Dennis Hoey, Sig Rumann, Ludwig Stossel

They Came to Cordura *

US 1959 123m Technicolor Cinemascope
Columbia/Goetz-Baroda (William Goetz)
V*, L

In 1916 Mexico, six American military heroes are recalled to base, but the hardships of the journey reveal their true colours.

Watchable adventure epic, not so arresting as was intended but quite professional.

w Ivan Moffat, Robert Rossen *novel* Glendon Swarthout *d* Robert Rossen *ph* Burnett Guffey *m* Elie Siegmeister

Gary Cooper, Rita Hayworth, Van Heflin, Richard Conte, Tab Hunter, Michael Callan, Dick York, Robert Keith

They Came to Rob Las Vegas *

Spain/France/Germany/Italy   1969   128m
Techniscope
Warner/Isasi/Capitoli/Eichberg/Franca

Criminals ambush a security truck in the Nevada desert.

Long-winded, flashily directed, gleamingly photographed, occasionally lively, frequently violent, finally tedious caper melodrama with a multi-lingual cast.

w Antonio Isasi, Jo Eisinger   d Antonio Isasi
ph Juan Gelpi   m Georges Gavarentz

Jack Palance, Lee J. Cobb, Elke Sommer, Gary Lockwood, Georges Geret, Jean Servais

They Dare Not Love

US   1941   76m   bw
Columbia (Sam Bischoff)

An Austrian prince flees the Nazis, but they force him to return and he has to leave his fiancée in America.

Curiously naïve romantic propaganda from this director; not at all memorable.

w Charles Bennett, Ernest Vajda   d James Whale
ph Franz Planer   m Morris Stoloff

George Brent, Martha Scott, Paul Lukas, Egon Brecher, Roman Bohnen, Edgar Barrier, Frank Reicher

They Died with Their Boots On **

US   1941   140m   bw
Warner (Robert Fellows)
V, V*, L

The life of General Custer and his death at Little Big Horn.

It seems it all happened because of an evil cadet who finished up selling guns to the Indians. Oh, well! The first half is romantic comedy, the second steels itself for the inevitable tragic outcome, but it's all expertly mounted and played in the best old Hollywood style.

w Wally Kline, Aeneas Mackenzie   d Raoul Walsh
ph Bert Glennon   m Max Steiner

Errol Flynn, Olivia de Havilland, Arthur Kennedy, Charles Grapewin, Anthony Quinn, Sidney Greenstreet, Gene Lockhart, Stanley Ridges, John Litel, Walter Hampden, Regis Toomey, Hattie McDaniel

They Drive by Night **

GB   1938   84m   bw
Warner (Jerome Jackson)

An ex-convict is helped by lorry drivers to solve the silk stocking murders of which he is suspected.

Excellent, little-seen British suspenser of the Hitchcock school.

w Derek Twist   novel James Curtis   d Arthur Woods
ph Basil Emmott

Emlyn Williams, Ernest Thesiger, Anna Konstam, Allan Jeayes, Antony Holles, Ronald Shiner

'Dialogue, acting and direction put this picture on a level with the French cinema.' – Graham Greene

They Drive by Night **

US   1940   97m   bw
Warner (Mark Hellinger)
V*, L
GB title: The Road to Frisco

A truck driver loses his brother in an accident, and in an attempt to improve his lot becomes involved with a scheming murderess.

Solid melodramatic entertainment which borrows the second half of its plot from Bordertown.

w Jerry Wald, Richard Macaulay   novel Long Haul by A. I. Bezzerides   d Raoul Walsh   ph Arthur Edeson
md Adolph Deutsch

George Raft, Humphrey Bogart, Ann Sheridan, Ida Lupino, Gale Page, Alan Hale, Roscoe Karns, John Litel, Henry O'Neill, George Tobias

They Flew Alone *

GB   1941   103m   bw
RKO/Imperator (Herbert Wilcox)
US title: Wings and the Woman

The story of Amy Johnson and Jim Mollison, married flying pioneers of the thirties.

Adequate fictionalized history with interesting historical detail.

w Miles Malleson   d Herbert Wilcox   ph Frederick A. Young

Anna Neagle, Robert Newton, Edward Chapman, Nora Swinburne, Joan Kemp-Welch, Charles Carson, Brefni O'Rourke

They Gave Him a Gun

US   1937   94m   bw
MGM (Harry Rapf)

Despite the efforts of his friend, a war-hardened veteran turns to crime and comes to a sticky end.

Dullish moral melodrama with its stars looking as though stuck in glue.

w Cyril Hume, Richard Maibaum, Maurice Rapf
novel William Joyce Cowan   d W. S. Van Dyke II
ph Harold Rosson

Spencer Tracy, Franchot Tone, Gladys George, Edgar Dearing, Mary Treen, Cliff Edwards

'Meller overboard on grief. Does not sum up as having b.o. punch.' – Variety

They Go Boom

US   1929   20m   bw
Hal Roach

Stan's nocturnal efforts to cure Ollie's cold nearly bring down the house about their ears.

Average, rather protracted star comedy.

w Leo McCarey, H. M. Walker   d James Parrott

Laurel and Hardy, Charlie Hall

They Got Me Covered *

US   1943   93m   bw
Samuel Goldwyn
V*, L

An incompetent foreign correspondent inadvertently breaks up a spy ring in Washington.

One of Hope's better and most typical comedy-thriller vehicles.

w Harry Kurnitz   d David Butler   ph Rudolph Maté   m Leigh Harline

Bob Hope, Dorothy Lamour, Otto Preminger, Lenore Aubert, Eduardo Ciannelli, Marion Martin, Donald Meek, Donald MacBride, Walter Catlett, John Abbott, Florence Bates, Philip Ahn

They Just Had to Get Married

US   1933   69m   bw
Universal

A butler and maid come into money and rise in the social scale.

Rather muddled comedy for star fans.

w Gladys Lehman, H. M. Walker   play Syril Harcourt   d Edward Ludwig

ZaSu Pitts, Slim Summerville, C. Aubrey Smith, Roland Young, Verree Teasdale, Fifi D'Orsay, Robert Greig, David Landau, Elizabeth Patterson

'Not for big town first runs, but a booker's selection for B houses or less.' – Variety

They Knew Mr Knight

GB   1945   93m   bw
JP/GHW

A clerk and his family become rich, then poor, through listening to a speculator.

Slightly oddball domestic drama reminiscent of Priestley's Angel Pavement.

w Norman Walker, Victor MacClure   novel Dorothy Whipple   d Norman Walker

Mervyn Johns, Alfred Drayton, Nora Swinburne, Joyce Howard, Joan Greenwood, Olive Sloane, Peter Hammond

They Knew What They Wanted **

US   1940   96m   bw
RKO (Erich Pommer)
V*

A waitress agrees by mail to marry a California-Italian vineyard owner, but is aghast when she arrives to discover that he sent his handsome foreman's photograph.

First-rate minor drama, expertly handled by stars and production team alike.

w Robert Ardrey   play Sidney Howard   d Garson Kanin   ph Harry Stradling   m Alfred Newman

Charles Laughton, Carole Lombard, William Gargan, Harry Carey, Frank Fay

'For dialogue, acting, background and film creation it's a honey.' – Otis Ferguson

† Previous versions include The Secret Love (1928) with Pola Negri and A Lady to Love (1930) with Vilma Banky (and Edward G. Robinson).

AAN: William Gargan

They Live

US   1988   94m   DeLuxe   Panavision
Guild/Alive Films (Larry Franco)
V, V*, L, S

A labourer discovers that aliens are taking over the world, using subliminal advertising.

A standard action film with an uncertain tone, as if it started out to be something more interesting.

w Frank Armitage   story Eight O'Clock in the Morning by Ray Nelson   d John Carpenter   ph Gary B. Kibbe   m John Carpenter, Alan Howarth
ad William J. Durrell Jnr, Daniel Lomino   ed Gib Jaffe, Frank E. Jiminez

Roddy Piper, Keith David, Meg Foster, George 'Buck' Flower, Peter Jason, Raymond St. Jacques, Jason Robards III

They Live by Night *

US   1948   96m   bw
RKO (Dore Schary)

A young man imprisoned for an accidental killing escapes with two hardened criminals and is forced to take part in their crimes.

Well-made if basically uninteresting melodrama with a draggy romantic interest; its 'realistic' yet impressionist style drew attention on its first release, and it was remade in the seventies as Thieves Like Us (qv).

w Charles Schnee   novel Edward Anderson
d Nicholas Ray   ph George E. Diskant   m Leigh Harline   ed Sherman Todd

Farley Granger, Cathy O'Donnell, Howard da Silva, Helen Craig

'I recommend this film for the manner in which this love-story threads its way through the criminal scene like a white line on a dark road, and for the two wonderfully tender performances by the young principal players.' – Paul Dehn

They Loved Life: see Kanal

They Made Me a Criminal *

US   1939   92m   bw
Warner (Benjamin Glazer)
V, V*, L

When he thinks he has killed a boxing opponent, a young man flees to the west and settles on a farm.

Competent remake of *The Life of Jimmy Dolan*, a tribute to the American way.

w Sig Herzig   *d* Busby Berkeley   *ph* James Wong Howe   *m* Max Steiner

John Garfield, Claude Rains, Gloria Dickson, May Robson, Billy Halop, Bobby Jordan, Leo Gorcey, Huntz Hall, Gabriel Dell, Ann Sheridan

'Handsomely mounted and printed on sepia stock – all of which helps.' – *Variety*

They Made Me a Fugitive *
GB   1947   104m   bw
Warner/Alliance (Nat Bronsten, James Carter)
US title: *I Became a Criminal*

An ex-RAF pilot is drawn into black marketeering. Framed for a killing, he escapes from Dartmoor and takes revenge on the gang leader.

Deliberately squalid thriller which began a fashion for British realism, but now seems only momentarily entertaining.

w Noel Langley   *novel* *A Convict Has Escaped* by Jackson Budd   *d* Alberto Cavalcanti   *ph* Otto Heller

Trevor Howard, Sally Gray, *Griffith Jones*, René Ray, Mary Merrall, Vida Hope, Ballard Berkeley, Phyllis Robins

'The direction and cutting, in a word, are masterly and must set up in anyone – even in one like myself who is inclined to be impatient with depravity unredeemed – an alert, uneasy, tingling excitement.' – *Alan Dent, News Chronicle*

They Made Me a Killer
US   1946   65m   bw
Pine-Thomas/Paramount

A young man framed by bank robbers proves his innocence.

Elementary cops-and-robbers, not too badly presented for a second feature.

w Geoffrey Homes, Winston Miller, Kae Salkow, Owen Francis   *d* William C. Thomas

Robert Lowery, Barbara Britton, Frank Albertson, Lola Lane, James Bush

They Met in Argentina
US   1941   76m   bw
RKO (Lou Brock)

A Texas oil millionaire sends his representative to buy a horse which has been winning races in Buenos Aires.

Thin romantic comedy in pursuance of the good neighbour policy.

w Jerry Cady, Lou Brock, Harold Daniels   *d* Leslie Goodwins, Jack Hively

Maureen O'Hara, James Ellison, Alberto Vila, Buddy Ebsen, Robert Barrat, Joseph Buloff

They Met in Bombay *
US   1941   86m   bw
MGM (Hunt Stromberg)

Jewel thieves on the run in the East fall in love.

A rather unusual romantic comedy chase which provides pretty satisfactory star entertainment.

w Edwin Justus Mayer, Anita Loos, Leon Gordon   *d* *Clarence Brown*   *ph* William Daniels   *m* Herbert Stothart

Clark Gable, Rosalind Russell, Peter Lorre, Reginald Owen, Jessie Ralph, Matthew Boulton, Eduardo Ciannelli, Luis Alberni

They Met in the Dark
GB   1943   104m   bw
Rank (Marcel Hellman)

A Blackpool theatrical agent is really a master spy.

Elementary spy romance with a richly villainous performance from Tom Walls.

w Anatole de Grunwald, Miles Malleson, Basil Bartlett, Victor MacClure, James Seymour   *novel* *The Vanishing Corpse* by Anthony Gilbert   *d* Karel Lamac

Tom Walls, Joyce Howard, James Mason, Phyllis Stanley, Edward Rigby, Ronald Ward, David Farrar

They Might be Giants *
US   1972   88m   Technicolor
Universal/Paul Newman, John Foreman
V*

A lawyer imagines he is Sherlock Holmes, and is taken in hand by Dr Mildred Watson.

Curious fantasy comedy which rather tentatively satirizes modern life and the need to retreat into unreality. Mildly pleasing entertainment for intellectuals.

w James Goldman   *play* James Goldman   *d* Anthony Harvey   *ph* Victor Kemper   *m* John Barry

George C. Scott, Joanne Woodward, Jack Gilford, Lester Rawlins

They Only Kill Their Masters *
US   1972   98m   Metrocolor
MGM (William Belasco)
V*

A village police chief doggedly solves a series of murders.

Atmospheric, serio-comic murder mystery with a cast of old hands.

w Lane Slate   *d* James Goldstone   *ph* Michel Hugo   *m* Perry Botkin Jnr

James Garner, Katharine Ross, Hal Holbrook, June Allyson, Harry Guardino, Tom Ewell, Peter Lawford, Ann Rutherford, Chris Connelly, Edmond O'Brien, Art Metrano, Arthur O'Connell

They Passed This Way: see Four Faces West

'The lovers of *The Caine Mutiny* have a picture all their own!'
They Rode West
US   1954   84m   Technicolor
Columbia

A cavalry doctor at a frontier fort gets into trouble by trying to help the Indians.

Western programmer whose sights are higher than its achievement.

w De Vallon Scott, Frank Nugent   *d* Phil Karlson

Robert Francis, Donna Reed, May Wynn, Phil Carey, Onslow Stevens, Jack Kelly

They Shall Have Music
US   1939   105m   bw
Samuel Goldwyn
V*
GB title: *Melody of Youth*

Jascha Heifetz conducts a charity concert to help a music school for slum children.

Formula family film given the best possible production.

w John Howard Lawson, Irmgard von Cube   *d* Archie Mayo   *ph* Gregg Toland   *md* Alfred Newman

Joel McCrea, Jascha Heifetz, Andrea Leeds, Gene Reynolds, Walter Brennan, Porter Hall, Terry Kilburn, Diana Lynn (Dolly Loehr)

'A natural for the musically minded . . . elemental and surefire audience appeal.' – *Variety*

AAN: Alfred Newman

They Shoot Horses, Don't They? ***
US   1969   129m   DeLuxe   Panavision
Palomar/Chartoff-Winkler-Pollack
V, V*

Tragedy during a six-day marathon dance contest in the early thirties.

An unrelievedly harrowing melodrama about dreary people, confused by 'flashforwards' but full of skilled technique, entertaining detail, and one brilliant performance.

w James Poe, Robert E. Thompson   *novel* Horace McCoy   *d* Sydney Pollack   *ph* Philip Lathrop   *md* John Green, Albert Woodbury   *m* John Green   *pd* Harry Horner

Gig Young, Jane Fonda, Susannah York, Michael Sarrazin, Red Buttons, Bonnie Bedelia, Bruce Dern

COMPÈRE (Gig Young): 'There can only be one winner, folks, but isn't that the American way?'

'Although *They Shoot Horses, Don't They?* does not, as a whole, reach the domain of art, many of its aspects and an aura that lingers on establish it as a true and eminent cinematic achievement.' – *John Simon*

AA: Gig Young

AAN: script; John Green, Albert Woodbury; Sydney Pollack; Jane Fonda; Susannah York

They Were Expendable *
US   1945   135m   bw
MGM (John Ford, Cliff Reid)
V*, L

Life in and around motor torpedo boats in the Pacific War.

Long drawn out flagwaver with some nice moments.

w Frank Wead   *book* William L. White   *d* John Ford   *ph* Joseph H. August   *m* Herbert Stothart

John Wayne, Robert Montgomery, Donna Reed, Jack Holt, Ward Bond, Marshall Thompson, Leon Ames, Cameron Mitchell, Jeff York

'For what seems at least half its dogged, devoted length all you have to watch is men getting on or off PT boats and other men watching them do so. But this is made so beautiful and so real that I could not feel one foot of the film was wasted.' – *James Agee*

They Were Not Divided *
GB   1950   102m   bw
Rank/Two Cities (Earl St. John)

The life of a Guards officer is paralleled with that of his American friend; they both die on a reconnaissance during the advance on Berlin.

Odd mixture of barrack room comedy, semi-documentary action, propaganda and the most appalling sentimentality. No one questioned it at the box-office, though.

wd Terence Young   *ph* Harry Waxman   *m* Lambert Williamson   *ed* Ralph Kemplen, Vera Campbell

Edward Underdown, Ralph Clanton, Helen Cherry, Stella Andrews, Michael Brennan, Michael Trubshaw, R.S.M. Brittain

'It is a rather curious experience to see a film made with all the best trappings of realism containing so many of the clichés of the studio.' – *Gavin Lambert*

'Rides off in so many directions as to be beyond toleration . . . an empty, fumbling and evasive film.' – *Richard Winnington*

They Were Sisters
GB   1945   115m   bw
GFD/Gainsborough (Harold Huth)

The problems of three married sisters.

Flatly handled multi-melodrama, the chief attraction being 'wicked' James Mason as a sadist.

w Roland Pertwee   *novel* Dorothy Whipple   *d* Arthur Crabtree   *ph* Jack Cox   *m* Louis Levy

James Mason, Phyllis Calvert, Dulcie Gray, Hugh Sinclair, Anne Crawford, Peter Murray Hill, Pamela Kellino

They Who Dare
GB 1953 107m Technicolor
British Lion/Mayflower (Aubrey Baring, Maxwell Setton)

During World War II a group of British soldiers are sent on a raiding expedition to Rhodes.

Grimmish war actioner with plenty of noise but not much holding power.

w Robert Westerby   d Lewis Milestone   ph Wilkie Cooper   m Robert Gill

Dirk Bogarde, Denholm Elliott, Akim Tamiroff, Gérard Oury, Eric Pohlmann, Alec Mango

They Won't Believe Me *
US 1947 95m bw
RKO (Joan Harrison)
V*, L

A playboy finds himself on trial for murder because of his philandering with three women.

Unusual suspenser with Hitchcock touches; quite neatly packaged, complete with twist ending.

w Jonathan Latimer   d Irving Pichel   ph Harry J. Wild   m Roy Webb

Robert Young, Susan Hayward, Rita Johnson, Jane Greer, Tom Powers, Don Beddoe, Frank Ferguson

'Talk and die! Until now their lips were frozen with fear!'
They Won't Forget ***
US 1937 94m bw
Warner (Mervyn Le Roy)
V*

The murder of a girl in a Southern town leads to a lynching.

Finely detailed social drama, a classic of American realism; harrowing to watch.

w Robert Rossen, Aben Kandel   novel Death in the Deep South by Ward Greene   d Mervyn Le Roy   ph Arthur Edeson, Warren Lynch   md Leo F. Forbstein   m Adolph Deutsch

Claude Rains, Gloria Dickson, Edward Norris, Otto Kruger, Allyn Joslyn, Linda Perry, Elisha Cook Jnr, Lana Turner, Cy Kendall, Elizabeth Risdon

'Not only an honest picture, but an example of real movie-making.' – Pare Lorenz

They're a Weird Mob
Australia 1966 112m colour
Williamson-Powell

An Italian journalist goes to Australia and doesn't get on at first.

Patchy comedy from a local best-seller.

w Richard Imrie   novel Nino Culotta (John O'Grady)   d Michael Powell

Walter Chiari, Clare Dunne, Chips Rafferty, Alida Chelli, Ed Devereaux, John Meillon

They're Off: see Straight, Place and Show

Thicker than Water
US 1935 20m bw
Hal Roach
V

Ollie spends his savings on a grandfather clock which is promptly destroyed by a passing truck.

Well made but slightly tiresome star comedy, the last short ever made featuring Stan and Ollie.

w Stan Laurel   d James W. Horne

Laurel and Hardy, Daphne Pollard, James Finlayson

The Thief *
US 1952 86m bw
Harry M. Popkin (Clarence Greene)
V*

A nuclear physicist is on the run from the FBI, who suspect him of being a spy.

Curious attempt to produce a thriller with no dialogue whatever; parts are well done, but the strain eventually shows, as the makers are not quite clever enough to flesh out the trickery with human interest.

w Clarence Greene, Russel Rouse   d Russel Rouse   ph Sam Leavitt   m Herschel Gilbert

Ray Milland, Martin Gabel, Rita Gam, Harry Bronson, John McKutcheon

AAN: Herschel Gilbert

Thief
US 1981 123m Astrocolor
United Artists/Michael Mann/Caan Productions
V*, L, S
GB title: Violent Streets

A high-class thief's professional life is contrasted with his personal problems.

And at far too great a length, with the additional problem that few people are really interested. A slick but empty melodrama.

wd Michael Mann   novel The Home Invaders by Frank Hohimer   ph Donald Thorin   m Tangerine Dream   pd Mel Bourne

James Caan, Tuesday Weld, Willie Nelson, James Belushi

'It promises too much and delivers too little.' – Richard Combs, MFB

The Thief of Bagdad ***
US 1924 approx 135m (24 fps) bw silent
Douglas Fairbanks
V (C), V*, L

In old Bagdad, a thief uses magic to outwit the evil Caliph.

Celebrated silent version of the old fable, its camera tricks a little timeworn now but nevertheless maintaining the air of a true classic by virtue of its leading performance and driving narrative energy.

w Lotta Woods, Douglas Fairbanks   d Raoul Walsh   ph Arthur Edeson   m Mortimer Wilson   ad William Cameron Menzies

Douglas Fairbanks, Snitz Edwards, Charles Belcher, Anna May Wong, Julanne Johnston, Etta Lee, Brandon Hurst, Sojin

'An entrancing picture, wholesome and compelling, deliberate and beautiful, a feat of motion picture art which has never been equalled.' – New York Times

'Here is magic. Here is beauty. Here is the answer to cynics who give the motion picture no place in the family of the arts . . . a work of rare genius.' – James Quirk, Photoplay

The Thief of Baghdad ****
GB 1940 109m Technicolor
London Films (Alexander Korda)
V*, L, S

A boy thief helps a deposed king thwart an evil usurper.

Marvellous blend of magic, action and music, the only film to catch on celluloid the overpowering atmosphere of the Arabian Nights.

w Miles Malleson, Lajos Biro   d Michael Powell, Ludwig Berger, Tim Whelan   ph Georges Périnal, Osmond Borradaile   m Miklos Rozsa   ad Vincent Korda   sp Lawrence Butler

Conrad Veidt, Sabu, John Justin, June Duprez, Morton Selten, Miles Malleson, Rex Ingram, Mary Morris

ABU (Sabu): 'I'm Abu the thief, son of Abu the thief, grandson of Abu the thief, most unfortunate of ten sons with a hunger that yearns day and night . . .'
AGED KING (Morton Selten): 'This is the Land of Legend, where everything is possible when seen through the eyes of youth.'

'The true stuff of fairy tale.' – Basil Wright

'Both spectacular and highly inventive.' – NFT, 1969

'Magical, highly entertaining, and now revalued by Hollywood moguls Lucas and Coppola.' – Time Out, 1980

AA: Georges Périnal; Vincent Korda

AAN: Miklos Rozsa

The Thief of Baghdad
Italy/France 1960 100m Eastmancolor Cinemascope
Titanus/Lux
V*

A very moderate remake in the form of an action star vehicle.

w Augusto Frassinetti, Filippo Sanjust, Bruno Vailati   d Arthur Lubin

Steve Reeves, Georgia Moll, Arturo Dominici

Thief of Damascus
US 1952 78m Technicolor
Columbia/Sam Katzman

The wicked ruler of Damascus is deposed by his own general, in league with Sinbad, Aladdin, and Scheherezade.

Mindless bosh, interesting only for its liberal use of scenes from Joan of Arc; the mind boggles at the costume compromise.

w Robert E. Kent   d Will Jason   ph Ellis W. Carter   m Mischa Bakaleinikoff

Paul Henreid, Lon Chaney Jnr, Jeff Donnell, John Sutton, Elena Verdugo

Thief of Hearts
US 1984 100m Metrocolor Panavision
Paramount (Don Simpson, Jerry Bruckheimer)
V*, L

A burglar begins an obsessive affair with a woman whose intimate diary he steals.

Plodding, glossily vacuous thriller with an over-obtrusive disco score.

wd Douglas Day Stewart   ph Andrew Laszlo   m Giorgio Moroder   ad Edward Richardson   ed Tom Rolf

Steven Bauer, Barbara Williams, John Getz, George Wendt, David Caruso, Christine Ebersole

The Thief Who Came to Dinner
US 1973 105m DeLuxe
Warner/Tandem (Bud Yorkin)
V*

A computer analyst determines to become a jewel thief.

Tedious comedy aping the Raffles school but saddled with a complex plot and listless script.

w Walter Hill   novel Terence L. Smith   d Bud Yorkin   ph Philip Lathrop   m Henry Mancini

Ryan O'Neal, Jacqueline Bisset, Warren Oates, Jill Clayburgh, Charles Cioffi

Thieves Fall Out
US 1941 72m bw
First National/Warner

An old lady lends her grandson money to start his business, but he has to rescue her when she's kidnapped.

Fairly amusing goings-on to fill the lower half of a bill.

w Charles Grayson, Ben Markson play Irving
Gaumont, Jack Sobel d Ray Enright

Jane Darwell, Eddie Albert, Joan Leslie, Alan Hale,
William T. Orr, John Litel, Anthony Quinn, Edward
Brophy

Thieves' Highway **
US 1949 94m bw
TCF (Robert Bassler)

A truck driver tracks down the racketeers who
cheated and maimed his father.

Glossy, highly professional thick ear shedding a
convincing light into one of America's less salubrious
corners.

w A. I. Bezzerides novel Thieves' Market by A. I.
Bezzerides d Jules Dassin ph Norbert Brodine
m Alfred Newman

Richard Conte, Valentina Cortesa, Lee J. Cobb, Jack
Oakie, Millard Mitchell, Joseph Pevney, Barbara
Lawrence, Hope Emerson

'You will never be able to eat an apple again without
calling up visions of trickery, mayhem, vandalism and
violent death.' – New York Times

'The action sequences are brilliantly done.' – Daily
Mail

Thieves' Holiday: see A Scandal in Paris

Thieves Like Us *
US 1974 123m DeLuxe
United Artists/Jerry Bick-George Litto (Robert Eggenwiler)

Three convicts break jail, and the youngest is attracted
to the daughter of the farmer who helps them escape.

Gloomy romantic melodrama, agreeably set in the
thirties and feelingly acted, but otherwise inferior to
the much shorter version released in the forties as They
Live by Night.

w Calder Willingham, Joan Tewkesbury, Robert
Altman novel Edward Anderson d Robert Altman
ph Jean Boffety m various songs ed Lou
Lombardo

Keith Carradine, Shelley Duvall, John Schuck, Bert
Remsen, Louise Fletcher, Tom Skerritt

The Thin Blue Line **
US 1988 101m DuArt
BFI/Third Floor/American Playhouse (Mark Lipson)
V, V*, L, S

Documentary that set out, successfully, to prove the
innocence of a man found guilty of the murder of a
Dallas policeman in 1976.

Gripping, excellently structured investigative
journalism.

d Errol Morris ph Stefan Czapsky, Robert Chappell
m Philip Glass ed Paul Barnes

Thin Ice *
US 1937 78m bw
TCF (Raymond Griffith)
GB title: Lovely to Look At

A skating instructress at an Alpine resort falls in love
with a visiting prince.

Light-hearted musical vehicle for Hollywood's newest
novelty – a skating star.

w Boris Ingster, Milton Sperling novel Der Komet by
Attilla Orbok d Sidney Lanfield ph Robert
Planck, Edward Cronjager md Louis Silvers
songs Lew Pollack, Sidney Mitchell ch Harry Losee

Sonja Henie, Tyrone Power, Arthur Treacher, Raymond
Walburn, Joan Davis, Sig Rumann, Alan Hale,
Melville Cooper

'She's a flash of winter lightning, a great combination
of muscle and music, a Pavlova on ice . . . production

wallop is the staging of three elaborate ice ballets.' –
Variety

AAN: Harry Losee

'A laugh tops every thrilling moment!'
The Thin Man ***
US 1934 93m bw
MGM/Cosmopolitan (Hunt Stromberg)
V*, L

In New York over Christmas, a tipsy detective with
his wife and dog solves the murder of an eccentric
inventor.

Fast-moving, alternately comic and suspenseful
mystery drama developed in brief scenes and fast
wipes. It set a sparkling comedy career for two stars
previously known for heavy drama, it was frequently
imitated, and it showed a wisecracking, affectionate
married relationship almost for the first time.

w Frances Goodrich, Albert Hackett novel Dashiell
Hammett d W. S. Van Dyke ph James Wong Howe
m William Axt

William Powell, Myrna Loy, Maureen O'Sullivan, Nat
Pendleton, Minna Gombell, Edward Ellis, Porter Hall,
Henry Wadsworth, William Henry, Harold Huber,
Cesar Romero, Edward Brophy

'A strange mixture of excitement, quips and hard-
boiled sentiment . . . full of the special touches that
can come from nowhere but the studio, that really
make the feet a movie walks on.' – Otis Ferguson

† Sequels, on the whole of descending merit,
included the following, all made at MGM with the
same star duo: 1936: After the Thin Man (V*, L; 110m).
1939: Another Thin Man (V*, L; 102m). 1941: Shadow of
the Thin Man (V*, L; 97m). 1944: The Thin Man Goes
Home (V*, L; 100m). 1947: Song of the Thin Man (V*, L;
86m).

AAN: best picture; script; W. S. Van Dyke; William
Powell

The Thin Red Line
US 1964 99m bw Cinemascope
Security/ACE (Sidney Harmon)

Raw recruits land on Guadalcanal and most of them
are killed.

Weary, routine, realistic war drama.

w Bernard Gordon novel James Jones d Andrew
Marton ph Manuel Berenguer m Malcolm Arnold

Keir Dullea, Jack Warden, James Philbrook, Kieron
Moore

The Thing **
US 1951 87m bw
RKO/Winchester (Howard Hawks)
V*, L
GB title: The Thing from Another World

A US scientific expedition in the Arctic is menaced by
a ferocious being they inadvertently thaw out from a
spaceship.

Curiously drab suspense shocker mainly set in
corridors, with insufficient surprises to sustain its
length. It does, however, contain the first space
monster on film, and is quite nimbly made, though it
fails to use the central gimmick from its original story.

w Charles Lederer story Who Goes There by J. W.
Campbell Jnr d Christian Nyby (with mysterious
help, either Hawks or Orson Welles) ph Russell
Harlan m Dimitri Tiomkin

Robert Cornthwaite, Kenneth Tobey, Margaret
Sheridan, Bill Self, Dewey Martin, James Arness (as
the thing)

LAST SPEECH OF FILM: 'I bring you warning – to
every one of you listening to the sound of my voice.
Tell the world, tell this to everyone wherever they are:
watch the skies, watch everywhere, keep looking –
watch the skies!'

'There seems little point in creating a monster of such
original characteristics if he is to be allowed only to
prowl about the North Pole, waiting to be destroyed
by the superior ingenuity of the US Air Force.' –
Penelope Houston

'A monster movie with pace, humour and a collection
of beautifully timed jabs of pure horror.' – NFT, 1967

'Man is the warmest place to hide!'
The Thing
US 1982 109m Technicolor Panavision
Universal/Lawrence Turman, David Foster
V, V*, L, S

A remake using the basis of the original story (the
thing conceals itself within each of the characters in
turn) but filled with revolting detail which alienated
many audiences.

w Bill Lancaster d John Carpenter ph Dean
Cundey m Ennio Morricone sp Albert Whitlock

Kurt Russell, A. Wilford Brimley, T. K. Carter, David
Clennon, Richard Dysart, Richard Masur

The Thing Called Love
US 1993 110m DeLuxe
Paramount (John Davis)
V, V*, L, S

A young New York woman goes to Nashville to join
other hopefuls trying to become country and western
stars.

An insipid failure of a film, a thin drama strung out
long after it has ceased to entertain.

w Carol Heikkinen d Peter Bogdanovich
ph Peter James pd Michael Seymour ed Terry
Stokes

River Phoenix, Samantha Mathis, Dermot Mulroney,
Sandra Bullock, K. T. Oslin, Trisha Yearwood,
Anthony Clark, Webb Wilder, Earl Poole Ball

'It's like a home movie in more ways than one;
Phoenix looks drunk or tranquillised most of the
time, and shows none of the gifts he once had to burn
. . . The film is quite stupendously aimless, with a
lousy plot and even worse dialogue.' – Sunday Times

'Phoenix's performance is perceivably off-kilter – at
best strange in a Methody mumbo-jumbo kind of
way, at worst downright creepy. Camouflaged as a
greasy-haired wreck with a cobra-lidded gaze, he
lurches from lucidity to functionally impaired,
mumbling throughout. All of this, however, is unfair
baggage with which to saddle Bogdanovich's
formulaic musical drama, a film which otherwise
registers as a wispy but mostly enjoyable romantic
fable.' – Matt Mueller, Empire

† The film was released direct to video in Britain,
although it also received a brief showing at the
National Film Theatre. It was River Phoenix's last film
to be released, though he later made Dark Blood, which
was abandoned following his death. Bogdanovich
joined the film at a relatively late stage, replacing the
original director.

The Thing from Another World: see The Thing
(1951)

'The doctor blew it – he transplanted a white bigot's head
onto a soul brother's body!'
The Thing with Two Heads
US 1972 89m colour
AIP

A racist brain surgeon with terminal cancer arranges
to have his head transplanted on to the body of a
convict; but the convict turns out to be black.

Bad taste comedy-horror with a great many frantic
action sequences. Beyond criticism.

w Lee Frost, Wes Bishop, James Gordon White
d Lee Frost

Ray Milland, Rosey Grier, Roger Perry, William Smith

'Every bit as preposterous as it sounds.' – *LA Times*

Things Are Looking Up
GB   1935   78m   bw
Gaumont

A circus horsewoman has to pose as her schoolmistress sister.

Lively star vehicle for an oddly matched team.

w Stafford Davies, Con West   d Albert de Courville

Cicely Courtneidge, William Gargan, Max Miller, Mary Lawson, Dick Henderson, Dick Henderson Jnr, Judy Kelly, Suzanne Lenglen, Vivien Leigh

Things Are Tough All Over
US   1982   92m   Metrocolor   Panavision
Columbia/C & C Brown (Howard Brown)
V, V*, L

Two layabouts are hired by Arabs to drive a limousine containing five million dollars to Las Vegas.

Dire and inane comedy, full of racist jokes.

w Cheech Marin, Tommy Chong   d Thomas K. Avildsen   ph Bobby Byrne   m Gaye Delorme   pd Richard Tom Sawyer   ed Dennis Dolan

Richard 'Cheech' Marin, Tommy Chong, Shelby Fields, Rikki Marin, Evelyn Guerrero, John Steadman, Rip Taylor

Things Change **
US   1988   100m   DuArt
Columbia TriStar/Filmhaus (Michael Hausman)
V, V*, L

An incompetent crook is given the task of guarding for a week an elderly shoemaker who has agreed to go to jail in place of the leading gangster he resembles.

Gently comic anecdote, delicately played.

w David Mamet, Shel Silverstein   d David Mamet   ph Juan Ruiz Anchia   m Alaric Jans   pd Michael Merritt   ed Trudy Ship

Don Ameche, Joe Mantegna, Robert Prosky, J. J. Johnston, Ricky Jay, Mike Nussbaum, Jack Wallace, Dan Conway

The Things of Life: see Les Choses de la Vie

Things to Come ****
GB   1936   113m   bw
London Films (Alexander Korda)
V*

War in 1940 is followed by plague, rebellion, a new glass-based society, and the first rocketship to the moon.

Fascinating, chilling and dynamically well-staged vignettes tracing mankind's future. Bits of the script and acting may be wobbly, but the sets and music are magnificent, the first part of the prophecy chillingly accurate, and the whole mammoth undertaking almost unique in film history.

w H. G. Wells   book The Shape of Things to Come by H. G. Wells   d/pd William Cameron Menzies   ph Georges Périnal   m Arthur Bliss   ad Vincent Korda   sp Harry Zech, Ned Mann

Raymond Massey, Edward Chapman, Ralph Richardson, Margaretta Scott, Cedric Hardwicke, Sophie Stewart, Derrick de Marney, John Clements

CABAL (Raymond Massey): 'It is this or that – all the universe or nothing. Which shall it be, Passworthy? Which shall it be?'
THEOTOCOPULOS (Cedric Hardwicke): 'What is this progress? What is the good of all this progress onward and onward? We demand a halt. We demand a rest . . . an end to progress! Make an end to this progress now! Let this be the last day of the scientific age!'

'Successful in every department except emotionally. For heart interest Mr Wells hands you an electric switch . . . It's too bad present-day film distribution isn't on a Wells 2040 basis, when the negative cost could be retrieved by button pushing. It's going to be harder than that. It's going to be almost impossible.' – *Variety*

'An amazingly ingenious technical accomplishment, even if it does hold out small hope for our race . . . the existence pictured is as joyless as a squeezed grapefruit.' – *Don Herold*

'A leviathan among films . . . a stupendous spectacle, an overwhelming, Dorean, Jules Vernesque, elaborated Metropolis, staggering to eye, mind and spirit, the like of which has never been seen and never will be seen again.' – *Sunday Times*

Think Fast, Mr Moto *
US   1937   66m   bw
TCF

Mr Moto goes on a long cruise from San Francisco to Shanghai to solve a case of diamond smuggling.

Enjoyable, quick-moving comedy thriller, the first in the series featuring Peter Lorre as the mild-mannered Japanese detective skilled in disguises and at judo.

w Norman Ellis Smith, Norman Foster   story J. P. Marquand   d Norman Foster   ph Harry Jackson   md Samuel Kaylin   ad Lewis Creber   ed Alex Troffey

Peter Lorre, Virginia Field, Thomas Beck, Sig Rumann, Murray Kinnell, John Rogers, Lotus Long, George Cooper, J. Carrol Naish

The Third Day
US   1965   119m   Technicolor   Panavision
Warner (Jack Smight)

An amnesiac learns that he is a rich unpopular tycoon facing a major crisis.

Glum melodrama which suggests domestic mystery but provides only interminable chat.

w Burton Wohl, Robert Presnell Jnr   novel Joseph Hayes   d Jack Smight   ph Robert Surtees   m Percy Faith

George Peppard, Elizabeth Ashley, Roddy McDowall, Herbert Marshall, Mona Washbourne, Robert Webber, Charles Drake, Sally Kellerman, Arte Johnson, Vincent Gardenia

Third Finger Left Hand
US   1940   96m   bw
MGM (John W. Considine Jnr)

A lady fashion editor fends off unwanted suitors by saying she is already married, but a commercial artist trumps this card by claiming to be the long lost husband of her invention.

Cheerful but overstretched romantic comedy.

w Lionel Houser   d Robert Z. Leonard   ph George Folsey   m David Snell

Myrna Loy, Melvyn Douglas, Lee Bowman, Bonita Granville, Raymond Walburn, Felix Bressart, Sidney Blackmer

The Third Generation
West Germany   1979   111m   colour
Tango/Pro-Ject/FDA (Harry Baer)
original title: Die dritte Generation

A Berlin executive becomes the victim of a gang of terrorists.

Realistic melodrama, curiously muted in its satire and its anger, watchable more as an entertainment than as a polemic.

wd Rainer Werner Fassbinder   ph Rainer Werner Fassbinder   m Peer Raben   ed Juliane Lorenz

Volker Spengler, Bulle Ogier, Harry Baer, Eddie Constantine, Udo Kier, Hanna Schygulla

The Third Key: see The Long Arm

The Third Man ****
GB   1949   100m   bw
British Lion/London Films/David O. Selznick/Alexander Korda (Carol Reed)
V*, L

An unintelligent but tenacious writer of Westerns arrives in post-war Vienna to join his old friend Harry Lime, who seems to have met with an accident . . . or has he?

Totally memorable and irresistible romantic thriller. Stylish from the first to the last, with inimitable backgrounds of zither music and war-torn buildings pointing up a then-topical black market story full of cynical characters but not without humour. Hitchcock with feeling, if you like.

w Graham Greene   d Carol Reed   ph Robert Krasker   m Anton Karas   ed Oswald Hafenrichter

Joseph Cotten, Trevor Howard, Alida Valli, Orson Welles, Bernard Lee, Wilfrid Hyde-White, Ernst Deutsch, Siegfried Breuer, Erich Ponto, Paul Hoerbiger

HARRY LIME (Orson Welles): 'Look down there. Would you really feel any pity if one of those dots stopped moving for ever? If I offered you twenty thousand pounds for every dot that stopped, would you really, old man, tell me to keep my money, or would you calculate how many dots you could afford to spare? Free of income tax, old man, free of income tax. It's the only way to save money nowadays.'
LIME: 'In Italy for thirty years under the Borgias they had warfare, terror, murder and bloodshed, but they produced Michelangelo, Leonardo da Vinci and the Renaissance. In Switzerland, they had brotherly love; they had five hundred years of democracy and peace – and what did that produce? The cuckoo clock.'

'Sensitive and humane and dedicated, [Reed] would seem to be enclosed from life with no specially strong feelings about the stories that come his way other than that they should be something he can perfect and polish with a craftsman's love.' – *Richard Winnington*

'Reaffirms Carol Reed as our foremost film-maker and one of the best three or four in the world' – *Fred Majdalany*

'Crammed with cinematic plums which could do the early Hitchcock proud.' – *Time*

AA: Robert Krasker

AAN: Carol Reed; editing

Third Man on the Mountain
GB   1959   103m   Technicolor
Walt Disney (Bill Anderson)
V*

In 1865 a Swiss dishwasher dreams of conquering the local mountain, and befriends a distinguished mountaineer.

Handsomely photographed boys' adventure story.

w Eleanore Griffin   novel Banner in the Sky by James Ramsay Ullman   d Ken Annakin   ph Harry Waxman, George Tairraz   m William Alwyn

James MacArthur, Michael Rennie, Janet Munro, James Donald, Herbert Lom, Laurence Naismith, Walter Fitzgerald, Nora Swinburne

'The story of a man searching for a killer – who might even be himself!'

The Third Secret
GB   1964   103m   bw   Cinemascope
TCF/Hubris (Robert L. Joseph)

A psychiatrist apparently commits suicide; a patient who has relied on his strength finds the truth by interviewing other patients.

Pretentious package of short stories, only one of which is relevant to the frame (yet another one featuring Patricia Neal was shot but discarded); full of philosophical conversations on a Thames mudbank and other absurdities, but well enough put together.

w *Robert L. Joseph* *d* *Charles Crichton* *ph* Douglas Slocombe *m* Richard Arnell

Stephen Boyd, *Pamela Franklin*, Jack Hawkins, Richard Attenborough, Rachel Kempson, Diane Cilento, Paul Rogers, Freda Jackson

'An unappealing and irritatingly muddled scribble of a film, thoroughly lacking in suspense, veracity and justification.' – *MFB*

The Third Voice **
US 1959 80m bw Cinemascope
TCF (Maury Dexter, Hubert Cornfield)

A woman kills her wealthy lover and an accomplice impersonates him through a series of complex negotiations.

Superstylish minor thriller, with a plot fascinating as it unfolds and a climax which is only a slight letdown.

wd Hubert Cornfield, *novel* *All the Way* by Charles Williams *ph* Ernest Haller *m* Johnny Mandel

Edmond O'Brien, Laraine Day, Julie London

Thirst: see *Three Strange Loves*

The Thirst of Baron Blood: see *Baron Blood*

Thirteen *
USSR 1937 90m approx bw
Mosfilm

Red Army soldiers are trekking from well to well through the desert. When help arrives only one is left.

Russian adventure film which was supposedly copied from *The Lost Patrol* but itself inspired *Sahara*. Good stuff, anyway.

w L. Prout, Mikhail Romm *d* Mikhail Romm

Thirteen Ghosts
US 1960 88m bw (colour sequence)
Columbia/William Castle
V*

A penniless scholar inherits a haunted house.

Childish thriller for which the audience was issued with a 'ghost viewer' (anaglyph spectacles) so that they could see the 'spirits'. The gimmick was called Illusion-O.

w Robb White *d* William Castle *ph* Joseph Biroc *m* Von Dexter

Charles Herbert, Jo Morrow, Martin Milner, Rosemary de Camp, Donald Woods, Margaret Hamilton

'Hurtling through space, eight people live fifteen dangerous, unforgettable hours!'
Thirteen Hours by Air *
US 1936 80m bw
Paramount (E. Lloyd Sheldon)

A transcontinental plane is hijacked by an ex-convict.

Solidly carpentered minor thriller which is also an interesting record of the early days of commercial aviation.

w Bogart Rogers, Kenyon Nicholson *d* Mitchell Leisen *ph* Theodor Sparkuhl

Fred MacMurray, Joan Bennett, ZaSu Pitts, Alan Baxter, Fred Keating, Brian Donlevy, John Howard, Ruth Donnelly, Dean Jagger

13 Rue Madeleine *
US 1946 95m bw
TCF (Louis de Rochemont)
V, V*

Four trained American espionage agents locate a Nazi rocket site in France.

Semi-documentary spy stuff in the tradition of *The House on 92nd Street* but rather less satisfactory despite excellent technique.

w John Monks Jnr, Sy Bartlett *d* Henry Hathaway *ph* Norbert Brodine *md* Alfred Newman *m* David Buttolph

James Cagney, Annabella, Richard Conte, Frank Latimore, Walter Abel, Melville Cooper, Sam Jaffe, Blanche Yurka

'Far and away the roughest, toughest spy chase yet gleaned from the bulging files of the OSS.' – *Time*

'I stole the plot of *The Virginian* and used it. I'd always wanted to make that story anyway.' – *Henry Hathaway*

'It carries the kick of a mule.' – *Kine Weekly*

† Rex Harrison rejected the role taken by Cagney.

'This is where evil lurks!'
13 West Street *
US 1962 80m bw
Columbia/Ladd Enterprises (William Bloom)

An engineer is attacked on the street by teenage hoodlums and becomes obsessed by revenge.

Competent, darkly photographed, rather dislikeable little thriller, a kind of trial run for *Death Wish*.

w Bernard Schoenfeld, Robert Presnell Jnr *d* Philip Leacock *ph* Charles Lawton Jnr *m* George Duning

Alan Ladd, Rod Steiger, Dolores Dorn, Michael Callan, Kenneth MacKenna, Margaret Hayes

Thirteen Women
US 1932 73m bw
RKO

One of thirteen boarding school graduates is trying to murder the others.

Thin mystery which wastes its cast.

w Bartlett Cormack *novel* Tiffany Thayer *d* George Archainbaud

Ricardo Cortez, Irene Dunne, Myrna Loy, Jill Esmond, Florence Eldridge, Julie Haydon, Marjorie Gateson, C. Henry Gordon

The Thirteenth Chair
US 1929 85m bw
MGM

A medium holds a seance to unmask a murderer.

Effective though now very dated chiller from a Broadway hit.

w Elliott Clawson *play* Bayard Veiller *d* Tod Browning

Margaret Wycherly, Bela Lugosi, Holmes Herbert, Conrad Nagel, Leila Hyams

'Playgoer type will get more enjoyment from it than the moviegoer.' – *Variety*

† The same studio remade the vehicle in 1936 with Dame May Whitty, Henry Daniell, Holmes Herbert – again – Elissa Landi and Lewis Stone; the director was George B. Seitz.

The Thirteenth Guest
US 1932 70m bw
Monogram (M. H. Hoffman)
V*

A haunted house, a will at midnight, and a frightened lady.

Archetypal comedy thriller, shot on Poverty Row but still watchable.

w Francis Hyland, Arthur Hoerl *novel* Armitage Traill *d* Albert Ray *ph* Harry Neumann, Tom Galligan

Ginger Rogers, Lyle Talbot, J. Farrell MacDonald, James Eagles, Eddie Phillips, Erville Alderson

'For all classes of houses a positive money maker.' – *Variety*

The Thirteenth Letter *
US 1951 85m bw
TCF (Otto Preminger)

A small French-Canadian town suffers from an outbreak of poison pen letters.

Moderate transcription of a memorable French film, *Le Corbeau;* in this version the events seem all too predictable and the performances dull.

w Howard Koch *d* Otto Preminger *ph* Joseph LaShelle *m* Alex North

Charles Boyer, Linda Darnell, Constance Smith, Michael Rennie, Françoise Rosay, Judith Evelyn

—30—
US 1959 96m bw
Warner/Mark VII (Jack Webb)
GB title: *Deadline Midnight*

A night in the newsroom of a paper preoccupied with scoops.

Not very dramatic, oddly titled and rather pretentious newspaper melodrama confined largely to one set.

w William Bowers *d* Jack Webb *ph* Edward Colman *m* Ray Heindorf

Jack Webb, William Conrad, David Nelson, Whitney Blake, James Bell, Nancy Valentine

Thirty Day Princess *
US 1934 74m bw
Paramount (B. P. Schulberg)

An actress is hired to impersonate a princess who gets mumps while visiting New York in hope of a loan.

Modest comedy which needed a wittier script but is stylishly played.

w Preston Sturges, Frank Partos *novel* Clarence Budington Kelland *d* Marion Gering *ph* Leon Shamroy

Sylvia Sidney, Cary Grant, Edward Arnold, Henry Stephenson, Vince Barnett, Edgar Norton, Lucien Littlewood

'A compact little picture which will entertain generally.' – *Variety*

Thirty Is a Dangerous Age, Cynthia
GB 1967 84m Technicolor
Columbia/Walter Shenson
V*

A timid night-club pianist has trouble with women but sells his first musical.

Mild star vehicle for a very mild star, basically a few thin sketches, frantically overdirected.

w Dudley Moore, Joe McGrath, John Wells *d* Joe McGrath *ph* Billy Williams *m* Dudley Moore *titles* Richard Williams

Dudley Moore, Eddie Foy Jnr, Suzy Kendall, John Bird, Duncan Macrae, Patricia Routledge, John Wells

The Thirty-Nine Steps ****
GB 1935 81m bw
Gaumont British (Ivor Montagu)
V*, L

A spy is murdered; the man who has befriended her is suspected, but eludes the police until a chase across Scotland produces the real villains.

Marvellous comedy thriller with most of the gimmicks found not only in Hitchcock's later work but in anyone else's who has tried the same vein. It has little to do with the original novel, and barely sets foot outside the studio, but it makes every second count, and is unparalleled in its use of timing, atmosphere and comedy relief.

w *Charles Bennett, Alma Reville, novel* John Buchan *d* Alfred Hitchcock *ph* Bernard Knowles *md* Louis Levy *m* Hubert Bath, Jack Beaver

Robert Donat, Madeleine Carroll, Godfrey Tearle, Lucie Mannheim, Peggy Ashcroft, John Laurie, Wylie Watson, Helen Haye, Frank Cellier

'A narrative of the unexpected – a humorous, exciting, dramatic, entertaining, pictorial, vivid and novel tale told with a fine sense of character and a keen grasp of the cinematic idea.' – *Sydney W. Carroll*

'A miracle of speed and light.' – *Otis Ferguson*

'Such is the zest of the Hitchcock plot that the original point of the title was totally forgotten, and half a line had to be added at the end by way of explanation.' – *George Perry, 1965*

The Thirty-Nine Steps
GB 1959 93m Eastmancolor
Rank (Betty E. Box)
V*

Just to show that stars and story aren't everything, this scene-for-scene remake muffs every opportunity for suspense or general effectiveness, and is practically a manual on how not to make a thriller.

w Frank Harvey *d* Ralph Thomas *ph* Ernest Steward *m* Clifton Parker

Kenneth More, Taina Elg, Barry Jones, Faith Brook, Brenda de Banzie, Duncan Lamont, James Hayter, Michael Goodliffe, Reginald Beckwith

The Thirty-Nine Steps *
GB 1978 102m Eastmancolor
Rank/Norfolk International (James Kenelm Clarke)
V*, L

Eager-to-please remake which goes back to the original period and more or less the original story, but rather spoils itself by a cliffhanger climax on the face of Big Ben, absurdly borrowed from Will Hay's *My Learned Friend*.

w Michael Robson *d* Don Sharp *ph* John Coquillon *m* Ed Welch *pd* Harry Pottle

Robert Powell, Karen Dotrice, John Mills, Eric Porter, David Warner, George Baker, Ronald Pickup, Timothy West, Donald Pickering, Andrew Keir, Robert Flemyng, Miles Anderson

Thirty Seconds over Tokyo **
US 1944 138m bw
MGM (Sam Zimbalist)
V*, L

How the first American attack on Japan was planned.

Sturdy World War II action flagwaver, with Tracy guesting as Colonel Doolittle.

w Dalton Trumbo *d* Mervyn Le Roy *ph* Harold Rosson, Robert Surtees *m* Herbert Stothart

Spencer Tracy, Van Johnson, Robert Walker, Phyllis Thaxter, Tim Murdock, Don Defore, Robert Mitchum

'All of the production involving planes and technical action is so fine that the film has the tough and literal quality of an air force documentary.' – *Bosley Crowther, New York Times*

'A big studio, big scale film, free of artistic pretensions, it is transformed by its not very imaginative but very dogged sincerity into something forceful, simple and thoroughly sympathetic.' – *James Agee*

AAN: Harold Rosson, Robert Surtees

36 Chowringhee Lane
India 1981 122m colour
Shashi Kapoor

A repressed, elderly Anglo-Indian teacher suffers a life of disappointments and defeats.

Downbeat film, made watchable by Jennifer Kendal's performance.

wd Aparna Sen *ph* Ashok Mehta *md* Vanraj Bhatia *ad* Bansi Chandragupta *ed* Bhanudas Divkar

Jennifer Kendal, Dhritiman Chatterjee, Debashree Roy, Geoffrey Kendal, Soni Razdan

Thirty-Six Hours *
US 1964 115m bw Panavision
MGM/Perlberg-Seaton/Cherokee (William Perlberg)

In 1944 an American major is kidnapped by the Nazis and after drugging is made to think that the war is over.

Well-detailed spy suspenser.

wd George Seaton *stories* Roald Dahl, Carl K. Hittleman *ph* Philip Lathrop *m* Dimitri Tiomkin

James Garner, Rod Taylor, Eva Marie Saint, Werner Peters, John Banner

Thirty Years of Fun **
US 1962 85m bw
Robert Youngson Productions

A compilation of silent comedy, including Chaplin's *The Floorwalker, Easy Street, The Pawnshop* and *The Rink*; Keaton's *The Balloonatic* and *Daydreams*; Langdon's *Smile Please*; and Laurel and Hardy's first meeting in *Lucky Dog*.

Not the most hilarious of the compilations, but historically important, with the usual high quality prints which Youngson alone seemed able to provide.

wd *Robert Youngson film quality control* Paul Guffanti

'What we're fighting for is bigger than you or me!'
This Above All *
US 1942 110m bw
TCF (Darryl F. Zanuck)

A surgeon's daughter on active service during World War II falls in love with a conscientious objector who is also an army deserter: he proves his bravery during an air raid.

Superior studio-set war romance.

w R. C. Sherriff *novel* Eric Knight *d* Anatole Litvak *ph* Arthur Miller *m* Alfred Newman *ad* Richard Day, Joseph Wright *ed* Walter Thompson

Tyrone Power, Joan Fontaine, Thomas Mitchell, Henry Stephenson, Nigel Bruce, Gladys Cooper, Philip Merivale, Alexander Knox, Melville Cooper

'Beautiful, stimulating and occasionally powerful.' – *New York Herald Tribune*

'One of the truly great pictures to come out of this war.' – *Motion Picture Herald*

AA: Richard Day, Joseph Wright

AAN: Arthur Miller; Walter Thompson

This Angry Age
Italy 1957 104m Technirama
Dino de Laurentiis
aka: *The Sea Wall*; original title: *La Diga sul Pacifico*

A French widow in Indo-China struggles to keep her rice fields going despite her family's waning interest.

Curious international production which suffers from the audience's lack of interest in the central situation. Moments of interest and even beauty, though.

w Irwin Shaw, René Clément, Ivo Perelli and Diego Fabbri *novel Barrage Contre le Pacifique* by Marguerite Duras *d* René Clément

Silvana Mangano, Jo Van Fleet, Anthony Perkins, Alida Valli, Richard Conte, Nehemiah Persoff

This Boy's Life
US 1993 115m Technicolor
Warner (Art Linson)

In the 1950s, a teenaged boy finds life hard when his mother settles down with a violent new husband.

An escapist drama, in which a series of dramatic confrontations fail to carry the power they should.

w Robert Getchell *book* Tobias Wolff *d* Michael Caton-Jones *ph* David Watkin *m* Carter Burwell *pd* Stephen J. Lineweaver *ed* Jim Clark, Peter N. Lonsdale

Robert de Niro, Ellen Barkin, Leonardo DiCaprio, Jonah Blechman, Eliza Dushku, Chris Cooper, Carla Gugino, Zack Ansley

'Despite its admirable strengths and the fact of it being a true story, there is somehow a failure to completely connect with the fierce boy, giving his unhappy and alienating youth an unfortunate air of reality.' – *Angie Errigo, Empire*

This Could Be the Night
US 1957 104m bw Cinemascope
MGM (Joe Pasternak)
V*, L

A schoolteacher becomes secretary to a gangster in his Broadway night-club.

Unlikely romantic melodrama with music, like a more solemn *Guys and Dolls*.

w Isobel Lennart *story* Cornelia Baird Gross *d* Robert Wise *ph* Russell Harlan *m* George Stoll

Jean Simmons, Paul Douglas, Tony Franciosa, Julie Wilson, Joan Blondell, J. Carrol Naish, ZaSu Pitts

'The master of inspiring spectacle makes his first great spectacle of modern times!'
This Day and Age *
US 1933 98m bw
Paramount/Cecil B. de Mille

During a youth week, boys put a gangster on trial and by his own methods force him to confess to murder.

A curious aberration for de Mille, this fairly powerful movie was condemned in some quarters as an incitement to fascism.

w Bartlett Cormack *d* Cecil B. de Mille *ph* Peverell Marley *m* Howard Jackson, L. W. Gilbert, Abel Baer

Charles Bickford, Richard Cromwell, Judith Allen, Harry Green, Ben Alexander

'A highly improbable and fantastic story but, as done by de Mille, carries more than average audience appeal.' – *Variety*

'Loaded with that power which excites emotional hysteria . . . should stimulate audiences to the same pitch of enthusiasm as it did the preview crowd.' – *Motion Picture Herald*

'A strange tale from the Hollywood hills . . . the technical work is beyond reproach, but the story is excessively melodramatic.' – *Mordaunt Hall, New York Times*

This Earth Is Mine
US 1959 124m Technicolor Cinemascope
U-I/Vintage (Casey Robinson, Claude Heilman)
S

A French-American vineyard owner in California brings out his granddaughter from England in the hope that she will consolidate his dynasty.

Solidly efficient film of a solidly efficient novel.

w Casey Robinson *novel The Cup and the Sword* by Alice Tisdale Hobart *d* Henry King *ph* Winton Hoch, Russell Metty *m* Hugo Friedhofer

Jean Simmons, *Claude Rains*, Rock Hudson, Dorothy McGuire, Kent Smith, Anna Lee, Ken Scott

This England
GB 1941 84m bw
British National

Landowner and labourer express contrary views through five periods of English history.

Unintentionally hilarious charade with all concerned left with egg on their faces. With propaganda like this, it's a wonder we still won the war.

w Emlyn Williams, A. R. Rawlinson, Bridget Boland   *d* David MacDonald

John Clements, Emlyn Williams, Constance Cummings, Frank Pettingell, Roland Culver, Esmond Knight, Morland Graham, Leslie French

† In Scotland the film was known as *Our Heritage*.

This Gun for Hire ***
US   1942   81m   bw
Paramount (Richard M. Blumenthal)
V*, L

A professional killer becomes involved in a fifth columnist plot.

Efficient Americanization of one of its author's more sombre entertainments. The melodrama has an authentic edge and strangeness to it, and it established the star images of both Ladd and Lake, as well as being oddly downbeat for a Hollywood product of this jingoistic time.

w Albert Maltz, W. R. Burnett   *novel* A Gun for Sale by Graham Greene   *d* Frank Tuttle   *ph* John Seitz   *m* David Buttolph

Alan Ladd, Veronica Lake, Robert Preston, *Laird Cregar*, Tully Marshall, Mikhail Rasumny, Marc Lawrence

This Happy Breed **
GB   1944   114m   Technicolor
GFD/Two Cities/Cineguild (Noël Coward, Anthony Havelock-Allan)
V*

Life between the wars for a London suburban family.

Coward's domestic epic is unconvincingly written and largely miscast, but sheer professionalism gets it through, and the decor is historically interesting.

w David Lean, Ronald Neame, Anthony Havelock-Allan   *play* Noël Coward   *d* David Lean   *ph* Ronald Neame

Robert Newton, Celia Johnson, Stanley Holloway, John Mills, Kay Walsh, Amy Veness, Alison Leggatt

'Nearly two hours of the pleasure of recognition, which does not come very far up the scale of aesthetic values.' – *Richard Mallett, Punch*

This Happy Feeling
US   1958   92m   Eastmancolor   Cinemascope
U-I (Ross Hunter)
V*

An ageing actor is invigorated by a mild affair with his secretary.

Flat romantic comedy: the bubbles obstinately refuse to rise.

wd Blake Edwards   *play* For Love or Money by F. Hugh Herbert   *ph* Arthur E. Arling   *m* Frank Skinner

Curt Jurgens, Debbie Reynolds, John Saxon, Alexis Smith, *Mary Astor*, Estelle Winwood

This is Dynamite!: see *The Turning Point*

This Is My Affair **
US   1937   102m   bw
TCF (Kenneth MacGowan)
GB title: *His Affair*

When President McKinley is assassinated, one of his top undercover agents is suspected of being a criminal, and threatened with execution.

Jolly good romantic melodrama with excellent period trappings; Hollywood of the thirties at its routine best.

w Allen Rivkin, Lamar Trotti   *d* William A. Seiter   *ph* Robert Planck   *md* Arthur Lange

Robert Taylor, Barbara Stanwyck, Victor McLaglen, Brian Donlevy, Sidney Blackmer, John Carradine, Sig Rumann, Alan Dinehart, Douglas Fowley

'Something of a G-man story in a costume setting.' – *Variety*

'The best American melodrama of the year . . . admirable acting, quick and cunning direction . . . a sense of doom, of almost classic suspense.' – *Graham Greene*

This Is My Affair (1951): see *I Can Get It for You Wholesale*

'It's 10 p.m. Do you know where your mother is?'
This Is My Life **
US   1992   94m   DeLuxe
TCF (Lynda Obst)
V, V*, L, S

A mother with two young daughters tries to make it as a stand-up comedian.

Sharply observed movie with a tough comic edge about the problems and conflicts between daughters and a working mother.

w Nora Ephron, Delia Ephron   *novel* This Is Your Life by Meg Wolitzer   *d* Nora Ephron   *ph* Bobby Byrne   *m* Carly Simon   *pd* David Chapman   *ed* Robert Reitano

Julie Kavner, Samantha Mathis, Gaby Hoffman, Carrie Fisher, Dan Aykroyd, Bob Nelson, Marita Geraghty

'Intimate, honestly rendered film looks likely to score some emotional points with the working parents it speaks to, but a funny but frank teen sex scene may somewhat erode its potential as family fare.' – *Variety*

'Woefully unfunny. If comedy is all about timing then Ephron's directorial watch needs winding.' – *Stephen Amidon, Financial Times*

This Is My Love
US   1954   91m   Technicolor
RKO

A sensitive young writer gives up everything to help her sister and crippled husband run a restaurant.

Weird, miscast melodrama which ends with Cinderella murdering the ugly sister.

w Hagar Wilde, Hugh Brooke   *d* Stuart Heisler

Linda Darnell, Faith Domergue, Dan Duryea, Rick Jason

This Is My Street
GB   1963   94m   bw
Anglo-Amalgamated/Adder (Jack Hanbury)

A Battersea wife has a fling with her mother's lodger.

Unremarkable low-life drama.

w Bill MacIlwraith   *novel* Nan Maynard   *d* Sidney Hayers   *ph* Alan Hume   *m* Eric Rogers

June Ritchie, Ian Hendry, Avice Landon, Meredith Edwards, Madge Ryan, John Hurt, Mike Pratt, Tom Adams

This Is Spinal Tap ****
US   1984   82m   CFI colour
Mainline/Embassy (Karen Murphy)
V, V*, L, S

Adventures of a British heavy metal rock group on tour in America.

Witty, wickedly accurate satire that skewers the pretensions of rock musicians and their hangers-on, done in documentary style. It hits its target with total precision.

w Christopher Guest, Michael McKean, Harry Shearer, Rob Reiner   *d* Rob Reiner   *ph* Peter Smokler   *m* Christopher Guest, Michael McKean, Harry Shearer, Rob Reiner   *pd* Dryan Jones   *ed* Robert Leighton

Christopher Guest, Michael McKean, Harry Shearer, Rob Reiner, R. J. Parnell, David Kaff, Tony Hendra, Bruno Kirby

This Is the Army **
US   1943   121m   Technicolor
Warner (Jack L. Warner, Hal B. Wallis)
V*

Army recruits put on a musical revue.

Mammoth musical flagwaver.

w Casey Robinson, Claude Binyon   *d* Michael Curtiz   *ph* Bert Glennon, Sol Polito   *songs* Irving Berlin   *m* Ray Heindorf   *ad* John Hughes, Lt. John Koenig

George Murphy, Joan Leslie, Irving Berlin, George Tobias, Alan Hale, Charles Butterworth, Rosemary de Camp, Dolores Costello, Una Merkel, Stanley Ridges, Ruth Donnelly, Kate Smith, Frances Langford, Gertrude Niesen, Ronald Reagan, Joe Louis

AA: Ray Heindorf

AAN: art direction

This Is the Life
US   1943   87m   bw
Universal

A young girl singer gets a crush on an older man.

Lively youth musical from better-mannered days.

w Wanda Tuchock   *play* Angela Is 22 by Fay Wray, Sinclair Lewis   *d* Felix Feist

Donald O'Connor, Susanna Foster, Peggy Ryan, Patric Knowles, Louise Allbritton, Dorothy Peterson, Jonathan Hale

This Is the Night *
US   1932   73m   bw
Paramount

A married lady with an eye for other men has an unfortunate habit of getting her dress caught in doors.

Forgotten high comedy in the Lubitsch style, but without his command.

w George Marion Jnr   *play* Naughty Cinderella by Avery Hopwood   *d* Frank Tuttle

Lili Damita, Charles Ruggles, Roland Young, Thelma Todd, Cary Grant

'The supreme entertainment of our time! Two and a half years in the making!'
This Island Earth **
US   1955   86m   Technicolor
U-I (William Alland)
V*, L

Scientists at a mysterious research station are really visitors from a planet in outer space, to which they kidnap brilliant minds who they hope can help them.

Absorbing science fiction mystery with splendid special effects and only one mutant monster to liven the last reels.

w Franklin Coen, Edward G. O'Callaghan, *novel* Raymond F. Jones   *d* Joseph Newman   *ph/sp* Clifford Stine, David S. Horsley   *m* Joseph Gershenson   *m* Henry Mancini, Herman Stein, Hans Salter   *ad* Alexander Golitzen, Richard H. Riedel

Jeff Morrow, Faith Domergue, Rex Reason, Lance Fuller, Russell Johnson, Robert Nicholas, Karl Lindt

'We women who have known love – have learned how to hate!'
This Land Is Mine *
US   1943   103m   bw
RKO (Jean Renoir, Dudley Nichols)
V*, L

A European village fights for freedom under occupying Nazis, and a schoolmaster becomes a hero.

Rather superfluous flagwaver with good performances wasted in a totally predictable and rather uninspiring script which gives the director little scope.

w Dudley Nichols *d* Jean Renoir *ph* Frank Redman *m* Lothar Perl

Charles Laughton, Maureen O'Hara, George Sanders, Walter Slezak, Una O'Connor, Kent Smith, Philip Merivale, Thurston Hall, George Couleuris

'Directed with the same Zolaesque intensity, the same excited obsession with locomotives, the same exquisite pictorial sense, that informed La Bête Humaine.' – *Guardian*

'Dull, prolix and unamusing.' – *James Agate*

'You cannot afford to dislocate or internationalize your occupied country; or to try to sell it to Americans by making your citizens as well fed, well dressed and comfortably idiomatic as Americans; or to treat the show to the corrupted virtuosities of studio lighting and heavy ballet composition.' – *James Agee*

This Love of Ours
US 1945 90m bw
U-I (Edward Dodds)

A jealous doctor leaves his wife but years later saves her from an unhappy second marriage.

Stupid romantic melodrama with characters in whose idiotic behaviour one can take no interest. Remade as *Never Say Goodbye* (qv).

w Bruce Manning, John Klorer, Leonard Lee *play* Come Meglio di Prima by Luigi Pirandello *d* William Dieterle *ph* Lucien Ballard *m* Hans Salter

Merle Oberon, Charles Korvin, Claude Rains, Carl Esmond, Jess Barker, Harry Davenport, Ralph Morgan, Fritz Leiber

'About as captivating as a funeral dirge.' – *Thomas M. Pryor, New York Times*

'A juicy example of masochistic team work . . . my favourite bad film in two years.' – *Richard Winnington*

AAN: Hans Salter

This Man in Paris
GB 1939 86m bw
Pinebrook

A London reporter in Paris exposes a counterfeiting gang.

Slightly disappointing sequel to the spruce *This Man Is News;* no more were made.

w Allan McKinnon, Roger MacDougall *d* David MacDonald

Barry K. Barnes, Valerie Hobson, Alastair Sim, Edward Lexy, Garry Marsh

'Five years have passed since *The Thin Man*, and this particular uxorious relationship of loving insults, hygienic sex, and raillery from twin beds is period enough for *Punch*.' – *Graham Greene*

This Man Is Dangerous
GB 1941 82m bw
Rialto
aka: *The Patient Vanishes*

A police inspector's son solves the case of a fake doctor and a mysterious nursing home.

Nostalgically innocent crime caper; still quite entertaining.

w John Argyle, Edward Dryhurst *novel* They Called Him Death by David Hume *d* Lawrence Huntington

James Mason, Mary Clare, Margaret Vyner, Gordon McLeod, Frederick Valk

This Man Is Mine
US 1934 76m bw
RKO

A woman wins back her wandering playboy husband.

Tedious marital drama which might have fared better as farce.

w Jane Murfin *play* Love Flies in the Window by Anne Morrison Chapin *d* John Cromwell

Irene Dunne, Ralph Bellamy, Constance Cummings, Kay Johnson, Sidney Blackmer, Charles Starrett

This Man Is Mine
GB 1946 103m bw
Columbia

A family invites a Canadian soldier for Christmas.

Moderate heartwarmer which still exudes a patriotic sentimental glow.

w Doreen Montgomery, Nicholas Phipps, Reginald Beckwith, Mabel Constanduros, Val Valentine, David Evans *play* A Soldier for Christmas by Reginald Beckwith *d* Marcel Varnel

Tom Walls, Glynis Johns, Jeanne de Casalis, Hugh McDermott, Nova Pilbeam, Barry Morse

This Man Is News **
GB 1938 77m bw
Paramount/Pinebrook (Anthony Havelock-Allan)

A reporter tracks down jewel thieves.

Thoroughly brisk and lively comedy-thriller on *Thin Man* lines. (See *This Man in Paris*.)

w Allan MacKinnon, Roger Macdougall, Basil Dearden *d* David MacDonald *ph* Henry Harris *md* Percival Mackey

Barry K. Barnes, Valerie Hobson, Alastair Sim, John Warwick, Garry Marsh

This Man Reuter: see *A Dispatch from Reuter's*

This Man's Navy
US 1945 100m bw
MGM

Two old navy men compare their sons' exploits, especially in the matter of how many submarines destroyed.

Easy-going star flagwaver.

w Borden Chase *d* William Wellman

Wallace Beery, James Gleason, Tom Drake, Noah Beery, Selena Royle

This Modern Age
US 1931 68m bw
MGM

The socialite child of divorced parents goes to Paris to stay with her sophisticated mother.

Mildly daring melodrama typical of its star and year.

w Sylvia Thalberg, Frank Butler *story* Mildred Cram *d* Nick Grinde *ph* Charles Rosher

Joan Crawford, Pauline Frederick, Monroe Owsley, Neil Hamilton, Hobart Bosworth, Emma Dunn

'Alva was growing up the only way she knew how!'
This Property Is Condemned *
US 1966 110m Technicolor
Paramount/Seven Arts/Ray Stark (John Houseman)
V*, L

Sexual adventures of a tubercular but beautiful girl in her mother's boarding house in a Mississippi town.

The Tennessee Williams mixture as before, quite well done but almost entirely resistible.

w Francis Ford Coppola, Fred Coe, Edith Sommer *play* Tennessee Williams *d* Sydney Pollack *ph* James Wong Howe *m* Kenyon Hopkins

Natalie Wood, Robert Redford, Mary Badham, Kate Reid, Charles Bronson, Jon Provost, John Harding, Alan Baxter, Robert Blake

This Rebel Age: see *The Beat Generation*

This Side of Heaven
US 1934 78m bw
MGM

A slightly whacky family gets together when father is accused of embezzlement.

Unmemorable but enjoyable domestic comedy drama.

w Zelda Sears, Eve Greene *novel* Marjorie Paradis *d* William K. Howard

Lionel Barrymore, Fay Bainter, Mae Clarke, Tom Brown, Una Merkel, Mary Carlisle, Onslow Stevens

'The type of clean picture Will Hays has been telling Hollywood about.' – *Variety*

This Sporting Life **
GB 1963 134m bw
Rank/Independent Artists (Karel Reisz)
V*

A tough miner becomes a successful rugby player, but his inner crudeness and violence keep contentment at bay.

Skilful movie-making around an unattractive hero in dismal settings; for all the excellent detail, we do not care sufficiently for the film to become any kind of classic.

w David Storey *novel* David Storey *d* Lindsay Anderson *ph* Denys Coop *m* Roberto Gerhard

Richard Harris, Rachel Roberts, Alan Badel, William Hartnell, Colin Blakely, Vanda Godsell, Arthur Lowe

AAN: Richard Harris; Rachel Roberts

This Strange Passion: see *El*

This Thing Called Love *
US 1941 98m bw
Columbia (William Perlberg)
GB title: *Married But Single*

A lady executive insists on proving that marriage is best if the partners start out just good friends.

Amusing comedy which at the time seemed a little saucy, and got itself banned by the Legion of Decency.

w George Seaton, Ken Englund, P. J. Wolfson *d* Alexander Hall *ph* Joseph Walker *md* Morris Stoloff *m* Werner Heyman

Rosalind Russell, Melvyn Douglas, Binnie Barnes, Allyn Joslyn, Gloria Dickson, Lee J. Cobb, Gloria Holden, Don Beddoe

'One of those laborious forties comedies in which the independent-minded woman has no common sense.' – *New Yorker, 1979*

This Time for Keeps
US 1947 105m Technicolor
MGM (Joe Pasternak)

The son of a famous singer falls in love with a swimming star.

Dim star musical with no outstanding sequences.

w Gladys Lehman *d* Richard Thorpe *ph* Karl Freund *songs* various

Esther Williams, Jimmy Durante, Lauritz Melchior, Johnnie Johnston, Xavier Cugat and his Orchestra

'The money spent on this production might easily have kept Mozart and Schubert alive and busy to the age of sixty, with enough left over to finance five of the best movies ever made. It might even have been invested in a good movie musical.' – *James Agee*

This Was a Woman
GB 1948 104m bw
Excelsior

A paranoid wife, prevented from running the lives of her offspring, tries to poison her husband.

Intolerable, interminable melodrama; a stage event makes a very stagey film.

w Val Valentine   *play* Joan Morgan   *d* Tim Whelan

Sonia Dresdel, Barbara White, Walter Fitzgerald, Cyril Raymond, Marjorie Rhodes, Emrys Jones

This Was Paris

GB 1941 88m bw
Warner

Spies suspect each other in Paris just before the Nazi occupation.

Unpersuasive studio-bound potboiler.

w Brock Williams, Edward Dryhurst   *d* John Harlow

Ben Lyon, Ann Dvorak, Griffith Jones, Robert Morley, Harold Huth, Mary Maguire

This Way Please

US 1937 72m bw
Paramount (Mel Shauer)

Romance backstage at a cine-variety theatre.

Uninspired musical now interesting for its sociological detail.

w Maxwell Shane, Bill Thomas, Grant Garret, Seena Owen, Howard J. Green   *d* Robert Florey

Charles Buddy Rogers, Betty Grable, Ned Sparks, Jim and Marion Jordan, Porter Hall, Lee Bowman, Wally Vernon

This Week of Grace

GB 1933 92m bw
Real Art

An unemployed factory girl goes into service.

Very typical but underproduced star vehicle.

w H. Fowler Mear, Jack Marks   *d* Maurice Elvey

Gracie Fields, Frank Pettingell, Henry Kendall, John Stuart, Douglas Wakefield, Minnie Rayner

'Every inch a lady – till you look at the record!'
This Woman Is Dangerous

US 1952 97m bw
Warner (Robert Sisk)

A woman gangster goes blind and falls in love with her doctor.

Glossy hokum without much dramatic movement; strictly for star fans.

w Geoffrey Homes, George Worthing Yates   *d* Felix Feist   *ph* Ted McCord   *m* David Buttolph

Joan Crawford, David Brian, Dennis Morgan, Mari Aldon, Phil Carey

This Woman Is Mine

US 1941 92m bw
Universal

Fur traders fall out over a beautiful stowaway.

Fairly well-produced but unexciting period drama.

w Seton I. Miller   *novel* I, James Lewis by Gilbert Wolff Gabriel   *d* Frank Lloyd   *m* Richard Hageman

Franchot Tone, John Carroll, Walter Brennan, Carol Bruce, Nigel Bruce, Leo G. Carroll, Sig Rumann

AAN: Richard Hageman

This'll Make You Whistle *

GB 1936 78m bw
Herbert Wilcox Productions

A playboy pretends to be a crook so as to shock his unwanted fiancée's guardian.

Rather flat comedy from a stage musical; all depends on the star.

w Guy Bolton, Fred Thompson   *d* Herbert Wilcox

Jack Buchanan, Elsie Randolph, Jean Gillie, William Kendall, David Hutcheson, Anthony Holles

The Thomas Crown Affair **

US 1968 102m DeLuxe Panavision
UA/Mirisch/Simkoe/Solar (Norman Jewison)
V, V*, L

A bored property tycoon masterminds a bank robbery and is chased by a glamorous insurance investigator.

Not so much a movie as an animated colour supplement, this glossy entertainment makes style its prime virtue, plays cute tricks with multiple images and has a famous sexy chess game, but is not above being boring for the rest of the way.

w Alan R. Trustman   *d* Norman Jewison   *ph* Haskell Wexler   *m* Michel Legrand   *ad* Robert Boyle

Steve McQueen, Faye Dunaway, Paul Burke, Jack Weston, Yaphet Kotto

'Jewison and Wexler seem to have gone slightly berserk, piling up tricks and mannerisms until the film itself sinks out of sight, forlorn and forgotten.' – *Tom Milne*

'A glimmering, empty film reminiscent of an haute couture model – stunning on the surface, concave and undernourished beneath.' – *Stefan Kanter*

AA: song 'The Windmills of Your Mind' (*m* Michel Legrand, *ly* Alan and Marilyn Bergman)

AAN: Michel Legrand

Thoroughbreds Don't Cry

US 1937 80m bw
MGM
V*

Jockeys fight for the chance to ride a valuable English horse.

Ho-hum racetrack yarn significant as the first teaming of two young stars.

w Lawrence Hazard, J. Walter Ruben, Eleanor Griffin   *d* Alfred E. Green

Mickey Rooney, Judy Garland, Ronald Sinclair, Sophie Tucker, C. Aubrey Smith

Thoroughly Modern Millie *

US 1967 138m Technicolor
Universal (Ross Hunter)
V*, L, S

In the twenties, a young girl comes to New York, becomes thoroughly modern, falls for her boss, and has various adventures unmasking a white slave racket centring on a Chinese laundry.

Initially most agreeable but subsequently very patchy spoof of twenties fads and films, including a Harold Lloyd thrill sequence which just doesn't work and a comedy performance from Beatrice Lillie which does. Tunes and performances are alike variable.

w Richard Morris   *d* George Roy Hill   *ph* Russell Metty   *md* André Previn, Joseph Gershenson   *ch* Joe Layton   *songs* various   *m* Elmer Bernstein   *ad* Alexander Golitzen, George Webb

Julie Andrews, Mary Tyler Moore, *John Gavin,* James Fox, Carol Channing, *Beatrice Lillie,* Jack Soo, Pat Morita, Anthony Dexter

'What a nice 65-minute movie is buried therein!' – *Judith Crist*

AA: Elmer Bernstein

AAN: André Previn, Joseph Gershenson; title song (*m* James Van Heusen, *ly* Sammy Cahn); Carol Channing

Those Calloways

US 1964 131m Technicolor
Walt Disney (Winston Hibler)
V*

Adventures of a marsh trapper and his family who live near a Maine village and try to protect wild geese from hunters.

Predictable family saga with pleasant backgrounds.

w Louis Pelletier   *novel* Swift Water by Paul Annixter   *d* Norman Tokar   *ph* Edward Colman   *m* Max Steiner

Brian Keith, Vera Miles, Brandon de Wilde, Walter Brennan, Ed Wynn, Linda Evans, Philip Abbott, John Larkin, John Qualen

Those Daring Young Men in Their Jaunty Jalopies

US/Italy/France 1969 125m Technicolor Panavision
Paramount/Dino de Laurentiis/Marianne (Ken Annakin, Basil Keys)
V, V*
GB title: *Monte Carlo or Bust*

Accidents befall various competitors in the Monte Carlo Rally.

Rough-edged imitation of *The Great Race* and *Those Magnificent Men in Their Flying Machines,* much feebler than either but with the waste of a big budget well in evidence.

w Jack Davies, Ken Annakin   *d* Ken Annakin   *ph* Gabor Pogany   *m* Ron Goodwin

Peter Cook, Dudley Moore, Tony Curtis, Bourvil, Walter Chiari, Terry-Thomas, Gert Frobe, Susan Hampshire, Jack Hawkins, Eric Sykes

Those Endearing Young Charms

US 1945 81m bw
RKO

An air corps mechanic loves a shopgirl.

Nothing to remember about this light star time-passer.

w Jerome Chodorov   *play* Edward Chodorov   *d* Lewis Allen

Robert Young, Laraine Day, Bill Williams, Ann Harding, Marc Cramer, Anne Jeffries

'Well played, well directed, and not quite interesting enough to be worth the time it takes.' – *James Agee*

Those Eyes, That Mouth

France/Italy 1982 100m colour
Triumph/Columbia/Odissya/Gaumont/RAI/Enca Ferrario (Enzo Porcelli)
original title: *Gli Occhi, La Bocca*

Returning home for the funeral of his suicidal brother, a failing actor begins an affair with the dead man's pregnant fiancée.

Intense family melodrama that refers back to the director's first film, *Fists in the Pocket,* but lacks the same impact.

w Marco Bellochio, Vincenzo Cerami   *d* Marco Bellochio   *ph* Giuseppe Lanci   *m* Nicola Piovani   *ed* Sergio Nuti

Lou Castel, Angela Molina, Emmanuelle Riva, Antonio Piovanelli, Michel Piccoli

Those High Grey Walls

US 1939 80m bw
Columbia

A doctor is convicted for aiding a criminal.

Modest variation on a plot used for *Prisoner of Shark Island, Devil's Island,* and so on.

w William A. Ullman, Lewis Meltzer   *d* Charles Vidor

Walter Connolly, Onslow Stevens, Iris Meredith, Paul Fix, Bernard Nedell, Don Beddoe

'Effective prison melodrama . . . will do all right where properly booked.' – *Variety*

Those Kids from Town

GB 1941 82m bw
British National

An earl takes in a group of noisy cockney kids evacuated from the city.

Sentimental wartime crowdpleaser, not especially good but a fairly rare record of one aspect of the war.

w Adrian Arlington   novel *These Our Strangers* by Adrian Arlington   d Lance Comfort

Shirley Lenner, Jeanne de Casalis, Percy Marmont, Maire O'Neill, George Cole, Charles Victor

Those Magnificent Men in Their Flying Machines, or How I Flew from London to Paris in 25 hours and 11 Minutes **
GB   1965   133m   Technicolor   Todd-AO
TCF (Stan Margulies, Jack Davies)
V, V*, L

In 1910, a newspaper owner sponsors a London to Paris air race.

Long-winded, generally agreeable knockabout comedy with plenty to look at but far too few jokes to sustain it.

w Jack Davies, Ken Annakin   d Ken Annakin
ph Christopher Challis   m Ron Goodwin   pd Tom Morahan

Sarah Miles, Stuart Whitman, Robert Morley, Eric Sykes, Terry-Thomas, James Fox, Alberto Sordi, Gert Frobe, Jean-Pierre Cassel, Karl Michael Vogler, Irina Demich, Benny Hill, Flora Robson, Sam Wanamaker, Red Skelton, Fred Emney, Cicely Courtneidge, Gordon Jackson, John Le Mesurier, Tony Hancock, William Rushton

'There is many a likely gag, but none that survives the second or third reprise. It could have been a good bit funnier by being shorter: the winning time is 25 hours 11 minutes, and by observing some kind of neo-Aristotelian unity the film seems to last exactly as long.' – *John Simon*

AAN: script

Those Marvellous Benchley Shorts: see
Benchley

Those Were the Days *
GB   1934   80m   bw
BIP (Walter C. Mycroft)

In the 1890s, a magistrate seeks out his teenage stepson in a music hall.

Lively comedy which is valuable as giving the screen's best re-creation of an old-time music hall.

w Fred Thompson, Frank Miller, Frank Launder, Jack Jordan   play *The Magistrate* by Arthur Wing Pinero   d Thomas Bentley   ph Otto Kanturek
md Idris Lewis

Will Hay, John Mills, Iris Hoey, Angela Baddeley, Claud Allister, George Graves, Jane Carr, H. F. Maltby

† Music hall acts include Gaston and Andrée, Lily Morris, G. H. Elliott, Sam Curtis, Frank Boston and Betty

Those Were the Days
US   1940   74m   bw
Paramount (J. Theodore Reed)
GB title: *Good Old Schooldays*

During their 40th anniversary celebrations, a married couple look back to their courtship days at college.

Pleasant, light, nostalgic escapades.

w Don Hartman   stories George Fitch
d J. Theodore Reed   ph Victor Milner

William Holden, Bonita Granville, Ezra Stone, Judith Barrett, Vaughan Glazer, Lucien Littlefield, Richard Denning

Those Wonderful Movie Cranks *
Czechoslovakia   1978   88m   colour
Barrandov (Jan Suster)

A travelling conjuror at the turn of the century introduces short cinema films into his act, and solves his woman trouble meanwhile.

Charming melancholy comedy which adds a little to art as well as to history.

w Oldrich Vlcek, Jiri Menzel   d Jiri Menzel
ph Jaromir Sofr   m Jiri Sust

Rudolf Hrusinsky, Vlasta Fabianova, Blazena Holisova

A Thousand and One Nights *
US   1945   92m   Technicolor
Columbia (Samuel Bischoff)

Aladdin seeks his princess.

Amusing take-off on the Arabian Nights, with good jokes and music.

w Wilfrid H. Pettitt, Richard English, Jack Henley
d Alfred E. Green   ad Stephen Goosson, Rudolph Sternad

Cornel Wilde, Phil Silvers, Evelyn Keyes, Adele Jergens, Dusty Anderson, Dennis Hoey

AAN: art direction

A Thousand Clowns *
US   1965   115m   bw
UA/Harell (Fred Coe)
V*

A New Yorker who has abdicated from work leads a cheerful, useless life with his young nephew, but the school board have their doubts.

Imitative nonconformist comedy with frequent reminiscences of older, better plays such as *You Can't Take It with You*. Good lines occasionally make themselves felt, but the overall effect is patchy, the lead is miscast, and the location montages only emphasize the basic one-room set.

w Herb Gardner,   play Herb Gardner   d Fred Coe
ph Arthur J. Ornitz   m Don Walker

Jason Robards, Martin Balsam, Barry Gordon, Barbara Harris, *William Daniels*, Gene Saks

'A broad and joyous comment on the rebellions and concessions of our daily life, a mature comedy that mixes its compassion with hilarity.' – *Judith Crist*

AA: Martin Balsam

AAN: best picture; Herb Gardner; Don Walker

The Thousand Eyes of Dr Mabuse *
France/Italy/Germany   1960   103m   bw
CCC/Filmkunst/Incom Criterion/Ajay
V*

Murders in a Berlin hotel are attributed to a reincarnation of the evil Dr Mabuse.

Lively if belated sequel to the director's silent films.

w Fritz Lang, Jeinz Oskar Wuttig   d Fritz Lang

Dawn Addams, Peter Van Eyck, Gert Frobe, Wolfgang Preiss, Werner Peters

Thousands Cheer *
US   1943   126m   Technicolor
MGM (Joe Pasternak)
V*, L

An army base stages an all-star variety show.

Ho-hum studio extravaganza with some good numbers.

w Paul Jarrico, Richard Collins   d George Sidney
ph George Folsey   md Herbert Stothart
songs various   ad Cedric Gibbons, Daniel Cathcart

Kathryn Grayson, Gene Kelly, John Boles, Mary Astor, Jose Iturbi, Kay Kyser and his Orchestra, Lionel Barrymore, Margaret O'Brien, June Allyson, Mickey Rooney, Judy Garland, Red Skelton, Eleanor Powell, Bob Crosby and his Orchestra, Lena Horne, Frank Morgan

'A thoroughly routine musical distinguished only by Gene Kelly with nothing to use his talents on, a terrible piece of trash by Shostakovich, and the unpleasant sight of Jose Iturbi proving he is a real guy

by playing the sort of boogie woogie anyone ought to be able to learn through a correspondence course.' – *James Agee*

AAN: George Folsey; Herbert Stothart; art direction

Three
GB   1969   105m   DeLuxe
UA/Obelisk (Bruce Becker)

Two American students on holiday in Europe pick up an English girl to show them the sights.

An aimless road movie.

wd James Salter   story *Then We Were Three* by Irwin Shaw   ph Etienne Becker   m Laurence Rosenthal
ad Guy Littaye   ed Edward Nielson

Charlotte Rampling, Robie Porter, Sam Waterston, Pascale Roberts, Edina Ronay, Gillian Hills

'Ambiguous action, coolly inscrutable characters, dialogue that is little more than half-heard clichés.' – *Richard Combs, MFB*

† The film was cut to 95m on its British release.

The Three Ages *
US   1923   80m approx   bw   silent
Joseph Schenck/Metro

Three stories parodying Griffith's *Intolerance*.

The star's first feature film, not his strongest, is saved by the final chases.

w Clyde Bruckman, Jean Havez, Joseph Mitchell
d Buster Keaton, Eddie Cline

Buster Keaton, Wallace Beery, Margaret Leahy, Joe Roberts

Three Amigos
US   1986   105m   Technicolor
Orion (Lorne Michaels, George Folsey Jnr)
V, V*, L

Three wimpish cowboy stars find themselves hired to defend a desert town from a bandit.

Weak take-off of *The Magnificent Seven*, with performances that grate.

w Steve Martin, Lorne Michaels, Randy Newman
d John Landis   ph Ronald W. Browne   m Elmer Bernstein   pd Richard Sawyer   ed Malcolm Campbell

Chevy Chase, Steve Martin, Martin Short, Patrice Martinez, Alfonso Arau

Three Bites of the Apple
US   1966   98m   Metrocolor   Panavision
MGM (Alvin Ganzer)

An English travel courier wins a lot of money in a Rome casino, and nearly loses it all.

Very dull comedy perked up by attractive locations.

w George Wells   d Alvin Ganzer   ph Gabor Pogany   m Eddy Manson

David McCallum, Sylva Koscina, Tammy Grimes, Harvey Korman, Aldo Fabrizi

Three Blind Mice *
US   1938   75m   bw
TCF (Raymond Griffith)

Three Kansas girls in the big city seek rich husbands.

Mild comedy remade as *Three Little Girls in Blue* and *How to Marry a Millionaire*, and not all that different from any of the *Gold Diggers* comedy musicals.

w Brown Holmes, Lynn Starling   d William A. Seiter   ph Ernest Palmer   m Charles Maxwell

Loretta Young, Joel McCrea, David Niven, Stuart Erwin, Marjorie Weaver, Pauline Moore, Binnie Barnes, Jane Darwell, Leonid Kinskey

'More names than can be handled on the marquee . . . good summer entertainment.' – *Variety*

Three Brave Men *

US   1956   88m   bw   Cinemascope
TCF (Herbert B. Swope Jnr)

A civilian employee in the US Navy is suspended as a security risk and it takes a lawsuit to set things straight.

Semi-factual anti-McCarthy drama proving that America is a great place to live – when you're winning. Good courtroom scenes.

wd Philip Dunne   articles Anthony Lewis
ph Charles G. Clarke   m Hans Salter

Ray Milland, Ernest Borgnine, Nina Foch, Dean Jagger, Frank Lovejoy, Edward Andrews, Frank Faylen, James Westerfield, Joseph Wiseman

The Three Caballeros ***

US   1945   70m   Technicolor
Walt Disney (Norman Ferguson)
V*, L

A programme of shorts about South America, linked by Donald Duck as a tourist.

Rapid-fire mélange of fragments supporting the good neighbour policy, following the shorter Saludos Amigos of 1943. The kaleidoscopic sequences and the combination of live action with cartoon remain of absorbing interest.

w various   d various   m Edward Plumb, Paul J. Smith, Charles Wolcott

† Stories include Pablo the Penguin, Little Gauchito, a Mexican sequence and some adventures with Joe Carioca

AAN: Edward Plumb, Paul J. Smith, Charles Wolcott

Three Came Home **

US   1950   106m   bw
TCF (Nunnally Johnson)
V*

In 1941 writer Agnes Newton Keith tries to escape from Borneo but is interned and ill-used by the Japanese.

Well-made, harrowing war adventure.

w Nunnally Johnson   book Agnes Newton Keith
d Jean Negulesco   ph Milton Krasner   md Lionel Newman   m Hugo Friedhofer

Claudette Colbert, Patric Knowles, Sessue Hayakawa, Florence Desmond, Sylvia Andrew, Phyllis Morris

'It will shock you, disturb you, tear your heart out. But it will fill you with great respect for a heroic soul.' – New York Times

Three Cases of Murder *

GB   1954   99m   bw
British Lion/Wessex/London Films (Ian Dalrymple, Hugh Perceval)

'In the Picture': a painting comes to life. 'You Killed Elizabeth': a man suspects himself of his faithless fiancée's murder. 'Lord Mountdrago': the foreign secretary dreams of killing an MP he hates.

Unlinked compendium, in which the first and third stories are quite interesting and well done, the second very commonplace.

w Donald Wilson, Sidney Caroll, Ian Dalrymple (original stories Roderick Wilkinson, Brett Halliday, W. Somerset Maugham)   d Wendy Toye, David Eady, George More O'Ferrall   ph Georges Périnal   m Doreen Carwithen

Alan Badel, Hugh Pryse, Leueen MacGrath, Elizabeth Sellars, John Gregson, Emrys Jones, Orson Welles, André Morell

Three Cheers for the Irish

US   1940   100m   bw
Warner (Sam Bischoff)

An Irishman's daughter causes family trouble when she falls for a Scot.

Pleasant, unpretentious but overlong romantic comedy.

w Richard Macaulay, Jerry Wald   d Lloyd Bacon
ph Charles Rosher   m Adolph Deutsch

Thomas Mitchell, Priscilla Lane, Dennis Morgan, Alan Hale, Virginia Grey, Irene Hervey, William Lundigan

Three Cockeyed Sailors: see Sailors Three

Three Coins in the Fountain **

US   1954   102m   DeLuxe   Cinemascope
TCF (Sol C. Siegel)
V, V*, L

Three American girls find romance in Rome.

An enormous box-office hit, the pattern of which was frequently repeated against various backgrounds; it was actually remade in Madrid as The Pleasure Seekers. In itself a thin entertainment, but the title song carried it.

w John Patrick   novel John H. Secondari   d Jean Negulesco   ph Milton Krasner   m Victor Young

Clifton Webb, Dorothy McGuire, Louis Jourdan, Jean Peters, Rossano Brazzi, Maggie McNamara, Howard St John, Kathryn Givney, Cathleen Nesbitt

AA: Milton Krasner; title song (m Jule Styne, ly Sammy Cahn)

AAN: best picture

Three Colours: Blue ***

France   1993   98m   Eastmancolor
Artificial Eye/MK2/CED/France 3/CAB/TOR/Canal+ (Marin Karmitz)
V, S

original title: Trois Couleurs: Bleu

A secretive woman, whose husband, a composer, and child are killed in a car crash, destroys his final work, sells all their possessions and sets out to remake her life.

The first part of a trilogy, based on the colours of the French tricolour and dealing with the theme of liberty, as experienced from the viewpoint of its enigmatic central character, for whom liberty often means a refusal to engage with the world, in order to avoid pain.

w Krzysztof Pisiewicz, Krzysztof Kieslowski
d Krzysztof Kieslowski   ph Slawomir Idziak   m Zbigniew Preisner   ad Claude Lenoir   ed Jacques Witta

Juliette Binoche, Benoît Régent, Florence Pernel, Charlotte Véry, Hélène Vincent, Philippe Volter, Claude Duneton, Hugues Quester, Emmanuelle Riva

'What lifts it out of the doldrums is Kieslowski's fascinating use of reflections, focusing techniques and camera angles to give the somewhat pedestrian material a profound and otherwordly East European feel.' – Kim Newman, Empire

† The music for the film was written first and the action was filmed to match its rhythms.

'Out of the inferno of war came three men and a woman – to live their lives, to strive for happiness, to seek love!'

Three Comrades **

US   1938   98m   bw
MGM (Joseph L. Mankiewicz)
V*

In twenties Germany, three friends find life hard but derive some joy from their love for a high-spirited girl who is dying of tuberculosis.

Despairing romance becomes a sentimental tearjerker with all the stops out; immaculately produced and very appealing to the masses, but prevented by censorship from being the intended indictment of Nazi Germany. The final scene in which the two surviving comrades are joined in the churchyard by their ghostly friends still packs a wallop.

w F. Scott Fitzgerald, Edward A. Paramore,   novel Erich Maria Remarque   d Frank Borzage   ph Joseph Ruttenberg   m Franz Waxman

Margaret Sullavan, Robert Taylor, Robert Young, Franchot Tone, Guy Kibbee, Lionel Atwill, Henry Hull, Charley Grapewin

'Just what Frank Borzage is trying to prove is very difficult to fathom . . . there must have been some reason for making this picture, but it certainly isn't in the name of entertainment.' – Variety

'A remarkably high combination of talents has made it all very impressive and moving – good writing, a good man at the camera, good actors, and presiding over them a good director . . . such unforgettable bits as the pursuit of the boy who shot Gottfried, a glimpse from under the muffling blanket of the girl's stricken face, the startling downswoop of the camera's eye upon the girl getting up from bed to remove the burden of her illness from those who love her. These are high moments in a film full of beauty.' – National Board of Review

'A love story, beautifully told and consummately acted, but so drenched in hopelessness and heavy with the aroma of death, of wasted youth in a world of foggy shapes and nameless menaces, that its beauty and strength are often clouded and betrayed.' – Time

AAN: Margaret Sullavan

'They might be the family next door – but if they were, you'd move!'

Three Cornered Moon *

US   1933   72m   bw
Paramount

A newly-poor Depression family has trouble finding work.

Slightly screwball romantic comedy, a predecessor of You Can't Take It with You; the humour now seems very faded, but it was a signpost of its day.

w S. K. Lauren, Ray Harris   play Gertrude Tonkonogy   d Elliott Nugent   ph Leon Shamroy

Claudette Colbert, Mary Boland, Richard Arlen, Wallace Ford, Lyda Roberti, Tom Brown, Hardie Albright

Three Daring Daughters

US   1948   115m   Technicolor
MGM (Joe Pasternak)
GB title: The Birds and the Bees

Three girls are dismayed to hear that their mother is remarrying.

Cheerful comedy with music, but nothing to write home about.

w Albert Mannheimer, Frederick Kohner, Sonya Levien, John Meehan   d Fred M. Wilcox   ph Ray June   md Georgie Stoll

Jeanette MacDonald, Jose Iturbi, Jane Powell, Ann E. Todd, Mary Elinor Donahue, Larry Adler, Edward Arnold, Harry Davenport, Moyna MacGill

'His code name is Condor. In the next twenty-four hours everyone he trusts will try to kill him.'

Three Days of the Condor **

US   1975   118m   Technicolor   Panavision
Paramount/Dino de Laurentiis/Wildwood (Stanley Schneider)
V*, L, S

An innocent researcher for a branch of the CIA finds himself marked for death by assassins employed by another branch.

Entertaining New York-based thriller which shamelessly follows most of the twists of The 39 Steps. It is just possible to follow its complexities, and the dialogue is smart.

w Lorenzo Semple Jnr, David Rayfiel,   novel Six Days of the Condor by James Grady   d Sydney Pollack   ph Owen Roizman   m Dave Grusin

Robert Redford, Faye Dunaway, Cliff Robertson, Max von Sydow, John Houseman, Walter McGinn

Three Faces East *
US 1930 71m bw
Warner (Darryl F. Zanuck)

The butler to the British war minister is a German spy, and the German nurse sent to help him is really a British agent . . .

Slow, melodramatic remake of 1926 silent, later turned into a Karloff vehicle, *British Intelligence* (qv).

w Oliver H. P. Garrett, Arthur Caesar *play* Anthony Paul Kelly *d* Roy del Ruth *ph* Chick McGill

Constance Bennett, Erich von Stroheim, Anthony Bushell, William Holden

'Bennett and von Stroheim guarantee a better than average week.' – *Variety*

The Three Faces of Eve **
US 1957 95m bw Cinemascope
TCF (Nunnally Johnson)
V, V*, L

A psychiatrist discovers that a female patient has three distinct personalities: a drab housewife, a good time girl and a mature sophisticated woman.

Alistair Cooke introduces this tall tale as if he believed it; as presented, it is entertaining but not very convincing. Its box-office success was sufficient to start a schizophrenia cycle.

w Nunnally Johnson *book* Corbett H. Thigpen MD, Hervey M. Cleckley MD *d* Nunnally Johnson *ph* Stanley Cortez *m* Robert Emmett Dolan

Joanne Woodward, Lee J. Cobb, David Wayne, Nancy Kulp, Edwin Jerome

AA: Joanne Woodward

Three Faces West
US 1940 79m bw
Republic (Sol C. Siegel)
V*

A dust bowl community is helped by an Austrian doctor fleeing from the Nazis, but his daughter is followed by a Nazi suitor.

Unusual modern Western, blandly told.

w F. Hugh Herbert, Joseph Moncure March, Samuel Ornitz *d* Bernard Vorhaus *ph* John Alton *m* Victor Young

John Wayne, Charles Coburn, Sigrid Gurie, Roland Varno, Spencer Charters, Sonny Bupp

Three for Bedroom C
US 1952 74m Natural Color
Brenco (Edward L. Alperson Jnr)
V*

Confusion reigns on a train when a film star takes a compartment booked for a Harvard scientist.

Inept farce which never rises above mediocrity and coasts along well below it.

wd Milton H. Bren *ph* Ernest Laszlo *m* Heinz Roemheld

Gloria Swanson, Fred Clark, James Warren, Hans Conried, Steve Brodie, Margaret Dumont

Three for Jamie Dawn
US 1956 81m bw
AA (Hayes Goetz)

A crooked lawyer bribes three members of a murder jury.

Minor courtroom melodrama, limply developed.

w John Klempner *d* Thomas Carr *ph* Duke Green *m* Walter Scharf

Laraine Day, Ricardo Montalban, Richard Carlson, June Havoc

Three for the Show *
US 1955 93m Technicolor Cinemascope
Columbia (Jonie Taps)
L

A married Broadway star finds that her first husband is still alive.

Adequate musical remake of *Too Many Husbands* (qv); not bad, not good.

w Edward Hope, Leonard Stern *play Too Many Husbands* by W. Somerset Maugham *d* H. C. Potter *ph* Arthur E. Arling *ch* Jack Cole *songs* various *md* George Duning

Betty Grable, Jack Lemmon, Marge Champion, Gower Champion, Myron McCormick, Paul Harvey

Three Fugitives *
US 1989 96m Metrocolor
Warner/Touchstone/Silver Screen Partners IV (Lauren Shuler-Donner)
V, V*, L, S

An ex-convict, trying to reform, is forced to go on the run with an inept bank robber and his small daughter.

A chase farce that piles up the absurdities with diminishing effect.

wd Francis Veber *ph* Haskell Wexler *m* David McHugh *pd* Rick Carter *ed* Bruce Green

Nick Nolte, Martin Short, Sarah Rowland Doroff, James Earl Jones, Alan Ruck, Kenneth McMillan, David Arnott, Bruce McGill

Three Girls about Town *
US 1942 71m bw
Columbia

Three sisters in New York find a corpse in their hotel bedroom.

A funny 'B' picture: fast paced and lively from start to finish.

w Richard Carroll *d* Leigh Jason *ph* Franz Planer

Joan Blondell, Binnie Barnes, Janet Blair, John Howard, Robert Benchley, Eric Blore, Una O'Connor

Three Godfathers *
US 1948 106m Technicolor
MGM/Argosy (John Ford)
V*, L

Three outlaws escaping across the desert take charge of an orphan baby.

'Orrible sentimental parable partly redeemed by splendid scenery.

w Laurence Stallings, Frank S. Nugent *story* Frank B. Kyne *d* John Ford *ph* Winton Hoch *m* Richard Hageman

John Wayne, Pedro Armendariz, Harry Carey Jnr, Ward Bond

† The story also appeared in 1909 as *Bronco Billy and the Baby*; in 1916 as *Three Godfathers*, with Harry Carey; in 1920 as *Marked Men*, with Harry Carey; in 1929 as *Hell's Heroes*, with Charles Bickford; in 1936 as *Three Godfathers*, with Chester Morris; and in 1975 as a TV movie, *The Godchild*, with Jack Palance.
†† The film is dedicated 'to the memory of Harry Carey, bright star of the early western sky'.

Three Guys Named Mike
US 1951 90m bw
MGM (Armand Deutsch)
V*

An accident-prone air hostess has three suitors.

Inconsequential romantic comedy which shows the effort of stretching its thin material to feature length.

w Sidney Sheldon *story* Ruth Brooks Flippen *d* Charles Walters *ph* Paul Vogel *m* Bronislau Kaper

Jane Wyman, Barry Sullivan, Van Johnson, Howard Keel, Phyllis Kirk, Jeff Donnell

Three Hats for Lisa *
GB 1965 99m Eastmancolor
Seven Hills/Jack Hanbury

A docker and a taxi driver help a foreign film star to steal three typically English hats.

Minor musical, silly but good to look at.

w Leslie Bricusse, Talbot Rothwell *d* Sidney Hayers

Joe Brown, Sid James, Sophie Hardy, Una Stubbs, Dave Nelson, Peter Bowles

Three Hearts for Julia
US 1943 90m bw
MGM

A reporter courts his wife all over again when she threatens to divorce him.

One of those thin romantic comedies which sent its male lead back to the theatre.

w Lionel Houser *d* Richard Thorpe

Melvyn Douglas, Ann Sothern, Lee Bowman, Felix Bressart, Reginald Owen, Richard Ainley

365 Nights in Hollywood
US 1934 77m bw
Sol M. Wurtzel/Fox

A down-and-out becomes a director of a fake school of acting.

Slight and casually developed comedy-romance, with comedy interludes by Mitchell and Durant.

w William Conselman, Henry Johnson *d* George Marshall

James Dunn, Alice Faye, John Bradford, Grant Mitchell

'A picture with no punch and little appeal.' – *Variety*

The 300 Spartans *
US 1962 114m DeLuxe Cinemascope
TCF (Rudolph Maté, George St George)

Sparta leads the ancient Greek states against Persia's attack at Thermopylae.

Quite a lively epic with some dignity.

w George St George *d* Rudolph Maté *ph* Geoffrey Unsworth *m* Manos Hadjikakis

Richard Egan, Ralph Richardson, David Farrar, Diane Baker, Barry Coe, Donald Houston, Kieron Moore, John Crawford, Robert Brown

Three Husbands
US 1950 76m bw
UA/Gloria (I. G. Goldsmith)
V*

Three husbands receive letters from a dead friend claiming that he had affairs with each of their wives.

Silly copy of *A Letter to Three Wives*, with neither style nor sophistication.

w Vera Caspary, Edward Eliscu *d* Irving Reis *ph* Franz Planer *m* Herschel Burke Gilbert

Emlyn Williams, Eve Arden, Howard da Silva, Ruth Warrick, Shepperd Strudwick, Vanessa Brown, Billie Burke, Jonathan Hale

Three in the Attic
US 1968 90m Pathecolor
AIP-Hermes (Richard Wilson)
V*

A college Casanova is locked in an attic by three girls who seduce him by rota until he cries for mercy.

One of the first outspoken comedies of the sexual revolution, but not a particularly funny one.

w Stephen Yafa *novel Paxton Quigley's Had the Course* by Stephen Yafa *d* Richard Wilson *ph* J. Burgi Contner *m* Chad Stuart

Chris Jones, Yvette Mimieux, Judy Pace, Maggie Turett, Nan Martin

Three in the Cellar: see *Up in the Cellar*

'Hello, Mrs Howard, I'm a friend of Mr Howard!'
Three into Two Won't Go *
GB   1969   100m   Technicolor
Universal (Julian Blaustein)

An executive has an affair with a girl hitch-hiker who later moves into his house to his wife's astonishment.

Palatable sex drama with good performances, rather flabbily written and directed.

w Edna O'Brien   *novel* Andrea Newman   *d* Peter Hall   *ph* Walter Lassally   *m* Francis Lai

Rod Steiger, Claire Bloom, Judy Geeson, Peggy Ashcroft, Paul Rogers

Three is a Family *
US   1944   81m   bw
Sol Lesser/United Artists

A henpecked husband having made some unwise investments is relegated by his wife to the spouse position.

Quite amusing comedy on a familiar theme.

w Harry Chandlee, Marjorie L. Pfaelzer   *play* Phoebe and Henry Ephron   *d* Edward Ludaig

Charles Ruggles, Fay Bainter, Marjorie Reynolds, Helen Broderick, Arthur Lake, Hattie McDaniel, John Philliber, Jeff Donnell, Walter Catlett, Clarence Kolb, Warren Hymer

Three Kids and a Queen
US   1935   85m   bw
Universal

Three boys decide to kidnap a rich old lady, but are dismayed to find that she enjoys the experience.

Sentimental comedy which seemed to hit the right note.

w Barry Trivers, Samuel Ornitz, Harry Poppe, Chester Beecroft   *d* Edward Ludwig

May Robson, Frankie Darro, Billy Burrud, Billy Benedict, Charlotte Henry, Herman Bing, Henry Armetta, John Miljan, Hedda Hopper

'A cinch for box office satisfaction.' – *Variety*

Three Little Girls in Blue
US   1946   90m   Technicolor
TCF (Mack Gordon)

Musical remake of *Three Blind Mice* (qv); adequate and quite forgettable.

w Valentine Davies   *d* Bruce Humberstone   *ph* Ernest Palmer   *songs* Mack Gordon, Joseph Myrow

June Haver, George Montgomery, Vivian Blaine, Celeste Holm, Vera-Ellen, Frank Latimore, Charles Smith, Charles Halton

Three Little Words *
US   1950   102m   Technicolor
MGM (Jack Cummings)
V*, L

The careers of songwriters Bert Kalmar and Harry Ruby.

Disappointingly ordinary musical in which two witty people are made to seem dull, and the plot allows Fred Astaire only one dance.

w George Wells   *d* Richard Thorpe   *ph* Harry Jackson   *md* André Previn   *ch* Hermes Pan   *songs* Bert Kalmar, Harry Ruby and various collaborators

Fred Astaire, Red Skelton, Vera-Ellen, Arlene Dahl, Keenan Wynn, Gale Robbins, Gloria de Haven, Phil Regan, *Debbie Reynolds*

AAN: André Previn

The Three Lives of Thomasina
GB   1963   97m   Technicolor
Walt Disney
V*, L

In a Scottish village in 1912, a vet finds that his methods are no match for a local girl who treats animals by giving them love.

Syrupy film for children: the animals are the main interest and one of them narrates . . .

w Robert Westerby   *novel* Thomasina by Paul Gallico   *d* Don Chaffey   *ph* Paul Beeson   *m* Paul Smith

Susan Hampshire, Patrick McGoohan, Karen Dotrice, Vincent Winter, Laurence Naismith, Finlay Currie, Wilfrid Brambell

Three Loves Has Nancy
US   1938   69m   bw
MGM (Norman Krasna)

A jilted bride takes her time about her next selection.

Adequate star comedy.

w Bella and Sam Spewack, George Oppenheimer, David Hertz   *d* Richard Thorpe   *ph* William Daniels

Janet Gaynor, Robert Montgomery, Franchot Tone, Guy Kibbee, Claire Dodd, Reginald Owen, Charley Grapewin, Emma Dunn, Cora Witherspoon

'This may not be the funniest picture of the season, but it's certainly one of the wackiest.' – *Variety*

The Three Maxims
GB   1937   87m   bw
GFD/Pathé Consortium (Herbert Wilcox)

Two trapezists love the girl member of the team, and the situation leads to attempted murder.

Effective Paris-set treatment of a well worn theme (see *Trapeze*).

w Herman Mankiewicz   *d* Herbert Wilcox   *ph* Frederick A. Young, Jack Cox

Anna Neagle, Tullio Carminati, Leslie Banks, Horace Hodges

'They changed her diapers – she changed their lives!'
Three Men and a Baby
US   1987   102m   DeLuxe
Touchstone/Silver Screen III (Ted Field, Robert W. Cort)
V, V*, L

Three swinging bachelors find a baby on their doorstep.

Slight comedy, given some momentum by a heroin-dealing subplot, which proved surprisingly successful with audiences thanks to energetic playing.

w James Orr, Jim Cruickshank   *d* Leonard Nimoy   *ph* Adam Greenberg   *m* Marvin Hamlisch   *pd* Peter Larkin

Tom Selleck, Steve Guttenberg, Ted Danson, Nancy Travis

† Remake of the more thoughtful and elegant *Trois Hommes et un Couffin* of 1985, whose director Coline Serreau was to have directed the US version but backed out.

Three Men and a Cradle *
France   1985   107m   colour
UKFD/Floch Film/Soprofilm/TF1 Films (Jean-François Lepetit)
V*, L
original title: *Trois Hommes et un Couffin*

Three bachelors fall for a baby left on their doorstep by a former girl-friend.

Amusing comedy of role reversal which was remade by Hollywood as the glossier *Three Men and a Baby*.

wd Coline Serreau   *ph* Jean-Yves Éscoffier, Jean-Jacques Bouhon   *pd* Yvan Maussion   *ed* Catherine Renault

Roland Giraud, Michel Boujenah, André Dussollier, Philippine Leroy Beaulieu

Three Men and a Girl: see *Golden Arrow* (1949)

Three Men and a Little Lady
US   1990   100m
Touchstone/Jean François LePetit-Interscope Communications (Ted Field, Robert W. Cort)
V, V*, L

Three bachelors prevent the mother of the child they 'adopted' marrying an Englishman.

Dire sequel to *Three Men and a Baby*, notably silly in its depiction of England as a backward rural country inhabited entirely by eccentrics.

w Charlie Peters   *story* Sara Parriott, Josann McGibbon   *d* Emilio Ardolino   *ph* Adam Greenberg   *m* James Newton Howard   *pd* Stuart Wurtzel   *ad* David M. Haber   *ed* Michael A. Stevenson

Tom Selleck, Steve Guttenberg, Ted Danson, Nancy Travis, Robin Weisman, Christopher Cazenove, Sheila Hancock, Fiona Shaw

'Thinking people will be hard-pressed to find a single interesting moment in this relentlessly predictable fantasy.' – *Variety*

Three Men in a Boat
GB   1956   94m   Eastmancolor   Cinemascope
Romulus (Jack Clayton)
V*

In the 1890s, misadventures befall three men holidaying on the Thames.

Flabby burlesque of a celebrated comic novel whose style is never even approached.

w Hubert Gregg, Vernon Harris   *novel* Jerome K. Jerome   *d* Ken Annakin   *ph* Eric Cross   *m* John Addison   *ad* John Howell

David Tomlinson, Jimmy Edwards, Laurence Harvey, Shirley Eaton, Robertson Hare, Jill Ireland, Lisa Gastoni, Martita Hunt, A. E. Matthews, Ernest Thesiger, Adrienne Corri

† A previous version in 1933 starred William Austin, Edmond Breon and Billy Milton; directed by Graham Cutts for ATP.

Three Men on a Horse *
US   1936   85m   bw
Warner (Sam Bischoff)
V*

A timid Brooklynite finds he can always pick winners, and gangsters get interested.

Smooth New Yorkish comedy which pleased at the time.

w Laird Doyle   *play* John Cecil Holm, George Abbott   *d* Mervyn Le Roy   *ph* Sol Polito

Frank McHugh, Sam Levene, Joan Blondell, Guy Kibbee, Carol Hughes, Allen Jenkins, Edgar Kennedy, Eddie Anderson, Harry Davenport

The Three Mesquiteers

A three-man cowboy team who operated in popular B features at the Hopalong Cassidy level. The make-up of the team varied: the actors most often found in it were John Wayne, Max Terhune, Bob Livingston, Ray Corrigan, Bob Steele, Rufe Davis, Tom Tyler, Raymond Hatton, Duncan Renaldo and Jimmy Dodd. The first film was made for RKO, all the rest for Republic: most frequent directors were George Sherman, Mack V. Wright, Joseph Kane, John English and Lester Orlebeck.

1935: POWDERSMOKE RANGE, THE THREE MESQUITEERS
1936: GHOST TOWN, GOLD, ROARIN' LEAD
1937: RIDERS OF THE WHISTLING SKULL, HIT THE SADDLE, GUNSMOKE RANCH, COME

ON COWBOYS, RANGE DEFENDERS, HEART OF THE ROCKIES, THE TRIGGER TRIO, WILD HORSE RODEO
1938: THE PURPLE VIGILANTES, CALL THE MESQUITEERS, CALL OF THE MESQUITEERS, OUTLAWS OF SONORA, RIDERS OF THE BLACK HILLS, HEROES OF THE HILLS, PALS OF THE SADDLE, OVERLAND STAGE RAIDERS, SANTA FE STAMPEDE, RED RIVER RANGE
1939: THE NIGHT RIDERS, THREE TEXAS STEERS, WYOMING OUTLAW, NEW FRONTIER, THE KANSAS TERRORS, COWBOYS FROM TEXAS
1940: HEROES OF THE SADDLE, PIONEERS OF THE WEST, COVERED WAGON DAYS, ROCKY MOUNTAIN RANGERS, OKLAHOMA RENEGADES, UNDER TEXAS SKIES, THE TRAIL BLAZERS, LONE STAR RAIDERS
1941: PRAIRIE PIONEERS, PALS OF THE PECOS, SADDLEMATES, GANGS OF SONORA, OUTLAWS OF THE CHEROKEE TRAIL, GAUCHOS OF EL DORADO, WEST OF CIMARRON
1942: CODE OF THE OUTLAW, RIDERS OF THE RANGE, WESTWARD HO, THE PHANTOM PLAINSMAN, SHADOWS ON THE SAGE, VALLEY OF HUNTED MEN
1943: THUNDERING TRAILS, THE BLOCKED TRAIL, SANTA FE SCOUTS, RIDERS OF THE RIO GRANDE

The Three Musketeers

US   1933   bw   serial: 12 eps
Mascot

Three Foreign Legionnaires defy the Devil of the Desert.

Adequate serial with interesting cast.

d Armand Schaefer and Colbert Clark

John Wayne, Ruth Hall, Jack Mulhall, Raymond Hatton, Francis X. Bushman Jnr, Lon Chaney Jnr, Noah Beery Jnr

The Three Musketeers

US   1935   97m   bw
RKO
V*, L

See below for synopsis.

A thin and poorly handled version.

w Dudley Nichols, Rowland V. Lee   *d* Rowland V. Lee

Walter Abel (D'Artagnan), Paul Lukas (Athos), Moroni Olsen (Porthos), Onslow Stevens (Aramis), Margot Grahame (Milady), Heather Angel (Constance), Ian Keith (de Rochefort), Miles Mander (King), Nigel de Brulier (Richelieu)

'Ineffective and disappointing adaptation . . . dull entertainment.' – *Variety*

The Three Musketeers **

US   1939   73m   bw
TCF (Raymond Griffith)
V*
GB title: *The Singing Musketeer*

A burlesque of the familiar story with pauses for song.

A very satisfactory entertainment with all concerned in top form.

w M. M. Musselman, William A. Drake, Sam Hellman   *d* Allan Dwan   *ph* Peverell Marley   *songs* Samuel Pokrass, Walter Bullock

Don Ameche, the Ritz Brothers, Binnie Barnes, *Joseph Schildkraut*, Lionel Atwill, Miles Mander, Gloria Stuart, Pauline Moore, John Carradine

'Whenever the action lags, the trio take the rostrum for a slapstick specialty . . . moderate b.o., a topper for the key duals.' – *Variety*

The Three Musketeers ***

US   1948   125m   Technicolor
MGM (Pandro S. Berman)
V, V*, L

High-spirited version of the famous story, with duels and fights presented like musical numbers.

Its vigour and inventiveness is a pleasure to behold.

w Robert Ardrey   *d* George Sidney   *ph* Robert Planck   *m* Herbert Stothart

Gene Kelly, Lana Turner, June Allyson, Frank Morgan, Van Heflin, Angela Lansbury, Vincent Price, Keenan Wynn, John Sutton, Gig Young, Robert Coote, Reginald Owen, Ian Keith, Patricia Medina

'A heavy, rough-housing mess. As Lady de Winter, Lana Turner sounds like a drive-in waitress exchanging quips with hotrodders, and as Richelieu, Vincent Price might be an especially crooked used car dealer. Angela Lansbury wears the crown of France as though she had won it at a county fair.' – *New Yorker*, 1980

AAN: Robert Planck

'A Place Of Betrayal. The Fate Of A King. A Time For Heroes.'
Three Musketeers

US   1993   105m   Technicolor   Panavision
Buena Vista/Walt Disney/One For All/Caravan (Joe Roth, Roger Birnbaum)
V, V*, L

D'Artagnan and the three musketeers save the throne of France through the machinations of Cardinal Richelieu.

A half-hearted romp by a group of actors to whom swashbuckling is a lost art, this is simply *Young Guns* with swords, no more than a feeble adventure with little sense of period.

w David Loughery   *novel* Alexandre Dumas   *d* Stephen Herek   *ph* Dean Semler   *m* Michael Kamen   *pd* Wolf Kroeger   *ed* John F. Link

Charlie Sheen, Kiefer Sutherland, Chris O'Donnell, Oliver Platt, Tim Curry, Rebecca de Mornay, Gabrielle Anwar, Paul McGann, Julie Delphy

'There should be a better reason for re-making *The Three Musketeers* than to provide a vehicle for whiskery Brat-packers whose careers are on the slide.' – *Sheila Johnston, Independent*

The Three Musketeers (The Queen's Diamonds) **

Panama   1973   107m   Technicolor
Film Trust (Alex Salkind)
V, V*, S

Jokey version with realistic blood; despite very lively highlights it wastes most of its high production cost by not giving its plot a chance; but money was saved by issuing the second half separately as *The Four Musketeers (The Revenge of Milady)*. The latter section was less attractive.

w George MacDonald Fraser   *d* Richard Lester   *ph* David Watkin   *m* Michel Legrand   *pd* Brian Eatwell

Michael York, Oliver Reed, Richard Chamberlain, Frank Finlay, Raquel Welch, Geraldine Chaplin, Spike Milligan, Faye Dunaway, Charlton Heston, Christopher Lee, Jean-Pierre Cassel

'It's one dragged-out forced laugh. No sweep, no romance, no convincing chivalric tradition to mock.' – *Stanley Kauffmann*

3 Ninjas *

US   1992   84m   Technicolor
Buena Vista/Touchstone/Global Venture Hollywood (Martha Chang)
V*, L

The sons of an FBI agent, taught martial arts by their grandfather, defeat an evil arms dealer.

Amiable martial arts caper that should please the pre-teens.

w Edward Emanuel   *story* Kenny Kim   *d* John Turtletaub   *ph* Richard Michalak   *m* Rick Marvin   *pd* Kirk Petruccelli   *ed* David Rennie

Victor Wong, Michael Treanor, Max Elliott Slade, Chad Power, Rand Kingsley, Alan McRae, Margarita Franco, Toru Tanaka

'The gracefully choreographed spectacle of three little boys fighting hordes of evil adult ninjas is a surefire juve crowd-pleaser.' – *Variety*

'Just your average Girl meets Girl. Girl loses Girl. Girl hires Boy to get Girl back story. With a twist.'
Three of Hearts

US   1992   110m   DeLuxe
Guild/Three of Hearts/New Line (Joel B. Michaels, Matthew Irmas)

A gigolo is hired by a lesbian to break the heart of her bisexual lover so that she will return to her.

Trite tale of sexual role-playing that pussyfoots around before coming to a predictable conclusion.

w Adam Greenman, Mitch Glazer   *d* Yurek Bogayevicz   *ph* Andrzej Sekula   *m* Richard Gibbs   *pd* Nelson Coates   *ed* Dennis M. Hill, Suzanne Hines

William Baldwin, Kelly Lynch, Sherilyn Fenn, Joe Pantoliano, Gail Strickland, Cec Verrell, Claire Callaway, Marek Johnson

'Shallow, contrived and less than credible. But marvellously exploiting New York's downtown world, it is a commercially slick and appealing film.' – *Variety*

The Three of Us: see *Noi Tre*

'Move over, Casanova!'
Three on a Couch

US   1966   109m   Technicolor
Columbia/Jerry Lewis Productions (Jerry Lewis)

An artist tries to cure the sexual hang-ups of his psychiatrist fiancée's three female patients.

Intolerably lengthy and witless comedy.

w Bob Ross, Samuel A. Taylor, Arne Sultan, Marvin Worth   *d* Jerry Lewis

Jerry Lewis, Janet Leigh, James Best, Mary Ann Mobley, Gila Golan, Leslie Parrish, Kathleen Freeman, Fritz Feld

'A long drag through stock situations.' – *MFB*

'Unintentionally unfunny.' – *Leonard Maltin*

'Stay on your own couch and don't bother with Jerry's.' – *Steven Scheuer*

Three on a Match *

US   1932   63m   bw
Warner (Sam Bischoff)
V*

Three schoolgirl friends meet again in the big city, after which their paths cross melodramatically.

Predictable, watchable multi-story dramatics with an ironic twist: remade in 1938 as *Broadway Musketeers*.

w Lucien Hubbard   *d* Mervyn Le Roy   *ph* Sol Polito

Joan Blondell, Bette Davis, Ann Dvorak, Warren William, Grant Mitchell, Lyle Talbot, Humphrey Bogart, Glenda Farrell, Clara Blandick

'A nice picture descending to mediocrity in its final two reels.' – *Variety*

Three on a Weekend: see *Bank Holiday*

Three Ring Circus

US   1954   103m   Technicolor   Vistavision
Paramount/Hal B. Wallis

Ex-army veterans join a circus.

The mixture as before from Martin and Lewis: variety acts interspersed with sentiment and heavy mugging.

w Don McGuire, Joseph Pevney *d* Joseph Pevney *ph* Loyal Griggs *m* Walter Scharf

Dean Martin, Jerry Lewis, Joanne Dru, Zsa Zsa Gabor, Wallace Ford, Sig Rumann, Gene Sheldon, Nick Cravat, Elsa Lanchester

Three Russian Girls

US 1943 80m bw
United Artists (Gregor Rabinovitch)
GB title: *She Who Dares*

A remake of the Russian film *Girl from Stalingrad*, about a nurse called for duty at the front.

Sheer propaganda, almost unwatchable now.

w Maurice Clark, Victor Trivas, Aben Kandel, Dan James *d* Fedor Ozep, Henry Kesler *m* W. Franke Harling

Anna Sten, Kent Smith, Mimi Forsythe, Alexander Granach, Kathy Frye, Paul Guilfoyle, Feodor Chaliapin

AAN: W. Franke Harling

Three Sailors and a Girl

US 1953 95m Technicolor
Warner (Sammy Cahn)

A ship's funds are unofficially invested in a musical show.

Undernourished comedy musical.

w Roland Kibbee, Devery Freeman *play The Butter and Egg Man* by George S. Kaufman *d* Roy del Ruth *ph* Carl Guthrie *songs* Sammy Fain, Sammy Cahn

Jane Powell, Gordon Macrae, Gene Nelson, Sam Levene, George Givot, Veda Ann Borg

Three Secrets *

US 1949 98m bw
Warner/US Pictures (Milton Sperling)
V*

Three women wait anxiously to find out whose child survived a plane crash.

Well-made, formula woman's picture.

w Martin Rackin, Gina Kaus *d* Robert Wise *ph* Sid Hickox *m* David Buttolph

Eleanor Parker, Patricia Neal, Ruth Roman, Frank Lovejoy, Leif Erickson, Ted de Corsia, Edmon Ryan, Larry Keating

The Three Sisters *

GB 1970 165m Eastmancolor
Alan Clore Films
V

At the turn of the century, three fatherless sisters dream of abandoning Russian provincial life for the big city.

Filmed Chekhov, better than most but still lacking cinematic vigour.

translator Moura Budberg *d* Laurence Olivier *ph* Geoffrey Unsworth *m* William Walton

Laurence Olivier, Joan Plowright, Jeanne Watts, Louise Purnell, Derek Jacobi, Alan Bates, Ronald Pickup

Three Sisters

Italy/France/Germany 1990 112m Eastmancolor
Curzon/Erre Produzioni/Reteitalia/Cinemax/Generale d'Images/
    Bioskop (Angelo Rizzoli)
original title: *Paura E Amore*

Three Italian sisters suffer for love.

More intelligent than the average soap opera, but not far removed from one with its emphasis on romantic entanglements.

w Dacia Maraini, Margarethe von Trotta *d* Margarethe von Trotta *ph* Giuseppe Lanci *m* Franco Piersanti *ed* Enzo Meniconi

Fanny Ardant, Greta Scacchi, Valeria Golino, Peter Simonischek, Sergio Castellitto, Agnes Soral, Paolo Hendel

Three Smart Girls **

US 1936 86m bw
Universal (Joe Pasternak)

Three sisters bring their parents back together.

Pleasant, efficient family film which made a world star of Deanna Durbin.

w Adele Commandini, Austin Parker *story* Adele Commandini *d* Henry Koster *ph* Joseph Valentine *md* Charles Previn

Deanna Durbin, Barbara Read, Nan Grey, Charles Winninger, Binnie Barnes, Ray Milland, Alice Brady, Mischa Auer, Ernest Cossart, Hobart Cavanaugh

'Surefire entertainment for any and all types of audiences. It also has that rare quality of making an audience feel better for having seen it.' – *Variety*

'Idiotically tuned in to happiness, but it isn't boring.' – *New Yorker, 1978*

'Clever, intelligent and witty, this delightful bit of entertainment has a genuineness which is rare.' – *Photoplay*

† Remade as *Three Daring Daughters*.

AAN: best picture; original story

Three Smart Girls Grow Up *

US 1939 87m bw
Universal (Joe Pasternak)

A girl helps her sisters to find beaus.

More of the above, quite palatable but inevitably warmed over.

w Bruce Manning, Felix Jackson *d* Henry Koster *ph* Joe Valentine

Deanna Durbin, Helen Parrish, Nan Grey, Charles Winninger, Robert Cummings, William Lundigan, Ernest Cossart, Nella Walker

'The white feminine room which the three sisters share, the quilted beds, the little furry jackets over the pajamas – the whole upholstery is so virginal that it evokes little twitters of nostalgia from the stalls. Pillow fights and first love and being sent to bed without any dinner – the awkward age has never been so laundered and lavendered and laid away.' – *Graham Greene*

Three Strange Loves *

Sweden 1949 84m bw
Svensk Filmindustri
original title: *Törst*; aka: *Thirst*

A married couple tear each other apart on a train journey from Switzerland through Germany to Sweden, while the husband's former lover suffers a breakdown and commits suicide.

Gloomy domestic drama, reminiscent of Strindberg in its depiction of a couple locked together in a struggle neither can win without destroying them both.

w Herbert Grevenius *novel* Birgit Tengroth *d* Ingmar Bergman *ph* Gunnar Fischer *m* Erik Nordgren *ad* Nils Svenwall *ed* Oscar Rosander

Eva Henning, Birger Malmsten, Birgit Tengroth, Mimmi Nelson, Hasse Ekman, Bengt Eklund, Gaby Stenberg, Naima Wifstrand

Three Strangers *

US 1946 92m bw
Warner (Wolfgang Reinhardt)

A sweepstake ticket brings fortune and tragedy to three ill-assorted people.

Humdrum pattern play: the stars work hard to bring a little magic to it.

w John Huston, Howard Koch *d* Jean Negulesco *ph* Arthur Edeson *m* Adolph Deutsch

Sidney Greenstreet, Peter Lorre, Geraldine Fitzgerald, Joan Lorring, Robert Shayne, Marjorie Riordan, Arthur Shields

Three Stripes in the Sun

US 1955 93m bw
Columbia (Fred Kohlmar)
GB title: *The Gentle Sergeant*

After World War II, a Japanese-hating sergeant in the US occupation forces helps a poverty-stricken orphanage.

Predictable sentimentality based on fact, with good background detail.

wd Richard Murphy *articles* E. J. Kelly *ph* Burnett Guffey *m* George Duning

Aldo Ray, Phil Carey, Dick York, Chuck Connors, Mitsuko Kimura

3.10 to Yuma **

US 1957 92m bw
Columbia (David Heilwell)
V*, L

A sheriff has to get his prisoner on to a train despite the threatening presence of the prisoner's outlaw friends.

Tense, well-directed but rather talky low-budget Western: excellent performances and atmosphere flesh out an unconvincing physical situation.

w Halsted Welles *d* Delmer Daves *ph* Charles Lawton Jnr *m* George Duning

Glenn Ford, Van Heflin, Felicia Farr, Leora Dana, Henry Jones, Richard Jaeckel, Robert Emhardt

'A vivid, tense and intelligent story about probable people, enhanced by economical writing and supremely efficient direction and playing.' – *Guardian*

'We experimented by not filling the shadows with reflected light.' – *Delmer Daves*

Three Violent People

US 1956 100m Eastmancolor Vistavision
Paramount (Hugh Brown)
V*

Brother ranchers quarrel over the wife of one of them, an ex-saloon hostess.

Characterless 'character' Western, a long way after *Duel in the Sun*.

w James Edward Grant *d* Rudolph Maté *ph* Loyal Griggs *m* Walter Scharf

Charlton Heston, Anne Baxter, *Gilbert Roland*, Tom Tryon, Bruce Bennett, Forrest Tucker, Elaine Stritch, Barton MacLane

The Three Weird Sisters

GB 1948 82m bw
British National (Louis H. Jackson)

Three old maids in a Welsh village plot to kill their rich half-brother but are swept away by a flood.

All-stops-out melodrama which doesn't quite work and is generally remembered, if at all, for the last third of its writing team.

w Louise Birt, David Evans, Dylan Thomas *novel* Charlotte Armstrong *d* Dan Birt *ph* Ernest Palmer

Nancy Price, Mary Clare, Mary Merrall, Nova Pilbeam, Raymond Lovell, Anthony Hulme

Three Wise Fools

US 1946 90m bw
MGM (William Wright)

Three crusty old gents adopt an orphan, who softens them.

Antediluvian whimsy without the expected fun, remade from a silent.

w John McDermott, James O'Hanlon *play* Austin Strong *d* Edward Buzzell *m* Bronislau Kaper

Margaret O'Brien, Lionel Barrymore, Thomas Mitchell, Edward Arnold, Lewis Stone, Jane Darwell, Harry Davenport, Cyd Charisse

Three Wise Girls

US   1932   80m approx   bw
Columbia

Three small-town girls gain wisdom in New York.

Three millgirls' romances for the price of one. Adequate, predictable romantic fodder of its time.

w Robert Riskin, Agnes C. Johnson   d William Beaudine   ph Ted Tetzlaff

Jean Harlow, Mae Clarke, Walter Byron, Marie Prevost, Andy Devine, Natalie Moorhead, Jameson Thomas

'Should turn in a respectable score . . . Miss Harlow fails to be convincing.' – Variety

Three Women *

US   1924   60m approx (24 fps)   bw   silent
Warner

A rake charms three women, each for a different purpose.

Subtle satirical comedy; not one of the director's masterpieces, but with enough barbs to keep one watching.

w Ernst Lubitsch, Hans Kraly   novel The Lilie by Yolanthe Marees   d Ernst Lubitsch   ph Charles Van Enger

Lew Cody, Pauline Frederick, May McAvoy, Marie Prevost

Three Women

US   1977   123m   DeLuxe   Panavision
TCF/Lion's Gate (Robert Altman)

Three women come to California for different reasons; when their problems become insurmountable they rely on each other.

Tiresomely somnambulistic multi-character drama, half a satire, half a wallow, and never an entertainment.

wd Robert Altman   ph Charles Rosher   m Gerald Busby

Sissy Spacek, Janice Rule, Shelley Duvall, Robert Fortier, Ruth Nelson, John Cromwell, Sierra Pecheur

Three Women in Love: see Der Philosoph

The Three Worlds of Gulliver

US/Spain   1959   100m   Technicolor
Columbia/Morningside (Charles Schneer)
V, V*, L

Gulliver's adventures in Lilliput and Brobdingnag.

Flat treatment of marvellous material, with all the excitement squeezed out of it and not even much pizazz in the trick photography.

w Arthur Ross, Jack Sher   d Jack Sher   ph Wilkie Cooper   m Bernard Herrmann   sp Ray Harryhausen

Kerwin Mathews, Basil Sydney, Mary Ellis, Jo Morrow, June Thorburn, Grégoire Aslan, Charles Lloyd Pack, Martin Benson

The Threepenny Opera: see Die Dreigroschenoper

Thrill of a Lifetime

US   1937   72m   bw
Paramount

Summer campers put on a show which goes to Broadway.

Stereotyped lower-case musical with agreeable acts.

w Seena Owen, Grant Garrett, Paul Gerard Smith   d George Archainbaud

Judy Canova, Ben Blue, the Yacht Club Boys, Eleanore Whitney, Betty Grable, Johnny Downs, Dorothy Lamour (guest), Larry Crabbe

'Lightweight but pleasant.' – Variety

Thrill of a Romance

US   1945   105m   Technicolor
MGM (Joe Pasternak)
V*

A lady swimmer falls for a returning serviceman.

Empty musical vehicle with nothing memorable about it except the waste of time and money.

w Richard Connell, Gladys Lehmann   d Richard Thorpe   ph Harry Stradling   md George Stoll

Esther Williams, Van Johnson, Lauritz Melchior, Frances Gifford, Henry Travers, Spring Byington, Tommy Dorsey

The Thrill of Brazil

US   1946   90m   bw
Columbia (Sidney Biddell)

An American impresario in Brazil tries to win back his estranged wife.

Efficient but unpersuasive musical, another result of the good neighbour policy.

w Allen Rivkin, Harry Clork, Devery Freeman   d S. Sylvan Simon

Evelyn Keyes, Keenan Wynn, Ann Miller, Allyn Joslyn, Tito Guizar, Veloz and Yolanda, Felix Bressart

The Thrill of It All *

US   1963   104m   Eastmancolor
U-I/Ross Hunter/Arwin (Ross Hunter, Marty Melcher)
V*

The wife of a gynaecologist becomes an advertising model, and work pressures disrupt her marriage.

Glossy matrimonial farce which starts brightly but eventually flags and becomes exhausting. Its better jokes linger in the memory.

w Carl Reiner   d Norman Jewison   ph Russell Metty   m Frank de Vol

Doris Day, James Garner, Arlene Francis, Edward Andrews, Reginald Owen, ZaSu Pitts, Elliot Reid

'Pleasantly reminiscent of some of the screwball comedies of the thirties.' – MFB

Throne of Blood ****

Japan   1957   105m   bw
Toho (Akira Kurosawa, Sojiro Motoki)
V, V*, L
original title: Kumonosu-Jo

A samurai, spurred on by his wife and an old witch, murders his lord at Cobweb Castle.

A Japanese version of Macbeth with a savage and horrifying final sequence. The whole film is a treat to look at.

w Hideo Oguni, Shinobu Hashimoto, Ryuzo Kikushima, Akira Kurosawa   play William Shakespeare   d Akira Kurosawa   ph Asaichi Nakai   m Masaru Sato

Toshiro Mifune, Isuzu Yamada

'Its final impression is of a man who storms into a room with an impassioned speech to deliver and then discovers that he has forgotten what he came to say.' – Kenneth Cavander, MFB

Through a Glass Darkly *

Sweden   1961   91m   bw
Svensk Filmindustri
V, V*

Four unfulfilled people on a remote island fail to communicate with each other or to understand what God is.

It sounds like a parody Bergman film, and it almost is. The same themes were carried through in Winter Light and The Silence.

wd Ingmar Bergman   ph Sven Nykvist   m Bach

Harriet Andersson, Gunnar Bjornstrand, Max von Sydow, Lars Passgard

AA: best foreign film
AAN: Ingmar Bergman (as writer)

Through Different Eyes

US   1943   65m   bw
TCF

A veteran DA cites an old murder case to illustrate the dangers of circumstantial evidence.

Neat and peppy crime programme filler.

w Samuel G. Engel   d Thomas Z. Loring

Frank Craven, Donald Woods, Vivian Blaine, Mary Howard, Jerome Cowan

Throw Momma from the Train *

US   1987   88m   DeLuxe
Orion (Larry Brezner)
V, V*, L

After seeing Strangers on a Train, a student tries to persuade his professor to 'swap' murders.

Cheerful black comedy-cum-homage to Hitchcock.

w Stu Silver   d Danny DeVito   ph Barry Sonnenfeld   m David Newman   pd Ida Random

Danny DeVito, Billy Crystal, Anne Ramsey, Kim Greist, Kate Mulgrew

'Very clever and engaging from beginning to end.' – Variety

AAN: Anne Ramsey

Thumb Tripping *

US   1972   94m   DeLuxe
Avco (Robert Chartoff, Irwin Winkler)
V*

A boy and a girl hitch-hiker in California have a variety of violent adventures.

Tail end of the Easy Rider fashion, with odd moments of interesting detail.

w Don Mitchell   novel Don Mitchell   d Quentin Masters   ph Harry Stradling Jnr   m Bob Thompson

Michael Burns, Meg Foster, Marianna Hill, Bruce Dern

Thumbs Up

US   1943   67m   bw
Republic (Albert J. Cohen)

An American singing star in London is passed over in favour of talent from the war factories.

Curious hands-across-the-sea filler which gives the weirdest impression of Britain at war.

w Frank Gill Jnr   d Joseph Santley

Brenda Joyce, Richard Fraser, Elsa Lanchester, Arthur Margetson, J. Pat O'Malley, Gertrude Niesen, Andre Charlot

Thunder

US   1929   90m at 24 fps   bw   silent
MGM

A train driver has trouble with his sons.

Almost forgotten star melodrama, his last silent one, made when his health was already failing.

w Byron Morgan, Ann Price   d William Nigh

Lon Chaney, James Murray, George Duryea, Phyllis Haver

Thunder Across the Pacific: see The Wild Blue Yonder

Thunder Afloat

US 1939 95m bw
MGM

Rival boat owners vie for a 1918 navy contract, and the winner finds he has been trapped into enlisting.

Rumbustious Flagg-and-Quirt style comedy, good enough value for the undemanding.

w Ralph Wheelwright, Wells Root, Harvey Haislip d George B. Seitz

Wallace Beery, Chester Morris, Virginia Grey, Douglass Dumbrille, Regis Toomey, Henry Victor, Jonathan Hale

'Timely actioner, cinch for exploitation.' – *Variety*

Thunder and Lightning

US 1977 93m DeLuxe
TCF (Roger Corman)
V*

An independent maker of moonshine whiskey finds himself in competition with his girlfriend's father.

Action-filled comedy, mainly consisting of car and boat chases and crashes.

w William Hjortsberg d Corey Allen ph James Pergola m Andy Stein ed Anthony Redman

David Carradine, Kate Jackson, Roger C. Carmel, Sterling Holloway, Ed Barth

Thunder Bay *

US 1953 102m Technicolor
U-I (Aaron Rosenberg)

An engineer is convinced that oil can be raised from the Louisiana sea-bed.

Well-produced outdoor actioner.

w Gil Doud, John Michael Hayes d Anthony Mann ph William Daniels m Frank Skinner

James Stewart, Joanne Dru, Dan Duryea, Jay C. Flippen, Anthony Moreno, Gilbert Roland, Marcia Henderson

Thunder Below

US 1932 71m bw
Paramount

A wife loves her husband's best friend.

Dreary melodrama with a star already seen to be box-office poison.

novel Thomas Rourke d Richard Wallace

Tallulah Bankhead, Charles Bickford, Paul Lukas

'Star as weak as story . . . dull and uneventful.' – *Variety*

Thunder Birds: see *Thunderbirds*

Thunder in the City

GB 1937 88m bw
Atlantic (Akos Tolnay, Alexander Esway)

An American salesman in London helps a penniless duke promote a non-existent metal.

Mild satire on British and American idiosyncrasies, now very faded.

w Robert Sherwood, Abem Kandel, Akos Tolnay d Marion Gering ph Al Gilks m Miklos Rozsa

Edward G. Robinson, Lulu Deste, Ralph Richardson, Nigel Bruce, Constance Collier, Arthur Wontner

'Cinch to be an important feature and satisfactory booking.' – *Variety*

Thunder in the East (1934): see *The Battle*

Thunder in the East

US 1951 98m bw
Paramount (Everett Riskin)

When India becomes independent in 1947, an American wanting to sell arms clashes with the peace-loving chief of a principality, but the arms are needed when rebels attack.

Artificial and boring action melodrama with platitudinous conversations.

w Jo Swerling novel *Rage of the Vulture* by Alan Moorehead d Charles Vidor ph Lee Garmes m Hugo Friedhofer

Alan Ladd, Charles Boyer, Deborah Kerr, Corinne Calvet, Cecil Kellaway

Thunder in the Night

US 1935 69m bw
Fox

A police captain solves the murder of a blackmailer.

Reasonably snappy mystery set in Budapest.

w Frances Hyland, Eugene Solow play *A Woman Lies* by Ladislas Fodor d George Archainbaud

Edmund Lowe, Karen Morley, Paul Cavanagh, Una O'Connor, Gene Lockhart, John Qualen, Russell Hicks

'Tops average: deserves to do fairly well.' – *Variety*

Thunder in the Sun

US 1958 81m Technicolor
Seven Arts/Carollton (Clarence Greene)

In 1847 an Indian scout guides a group of Basques to California with their vines.

Overwritten and melodramatic wagon train story.

wd Russel Rouse ph Stanley Cortez m Cyril Mockridge

Susan Hayward, Jeff Chandler, Jacques Bergerac, Blanche Yurka, Carl Esmond

Thunder of Battle: see *Coriolanus – Hero without a Country*

'I'll make a soldier of you, Mr McQuade – if you don't break first!'

A Thunder of Drums *

US 1961 97m Metrocolor Cinemascope
MGM (Robert J. Enders)

Trouble with Apaches at a frontier post in 1870.

Solid, unexciting first-feature Western, some way after Ford.

w James Warner Bellah d Joseph Newman ph William Spencer m Harry Sukman

Richard Boone, George Hamilton, Arthur O'Connell, Luana Patten, Richard Chamberlain, Charles Bronson

Thunder on the Hill

US 1951 84m bw
U-I (Michael Kraike)
GB title: *Bonaventure*

In Norfolk, a nun solves a murder mystery during a flood.

Modest whodunnit with an unusual background but not much suspense.

w Oscar Saul, André Solt play *Bonaventure* by Charlotte Hastings d Douglas Sirk ph William Daniels m Hans Salter

Claudette Colbert, Ann Blyth, Robert Douglas, Anne Crawford, Philip Friend, Gladys Cooper, John Abbott, Connie Gilchrist, Gavin Muir

Thunder over Mexico **

US 1933 60m bw silent (with music score)
Principal Pictures

The Upton Sinclair version of the troubled Eisenstein travelogue.

Packed with moments of genius, but not really a finished film in any sense.

m Hugo Reisenfeld

'It will not get to first base either as a critic's picture, or in straight box office parlance . . . beautiful, slow and dull.' – *Variety*

† See also *Time in the Sun*.

Thunder over the Plains

US 1953 82m Warnercolor
Warner

After the Civil War, a Union officer is posted with his family to the southwest territory, and finds tension.

Busy but uninvolving Western programmer with a reliable star.

w Russell Hughes d André de Toth

Randolph Scott, Phyllis Kirk, Lex Barker, Charles McGraw, Elisha Cook Jnr, Fess Parker

Thunder Road *

US 1958 92m bw
UA/DRM (Robert Mitchum)
V*

Hillbilly bootleggers defy a Chicago gangster.

Downbeat but actionful crime melodrama with an unusual background and plenty of car chases.

w James Arlee Philips, Walter Wise d Arthur Ripley ph Alan Stensvold m Jack Marshall

Robert Mitchum, Gene Barry, Jacques Aubuchon, Keely Smith

Thunder Rock ***

GB 1942 112m bw
Charter Films (John Boulting)
V*

A journalist disgusted with the world of the thirties retires to a lighthouse on Lake Michigan and is haunted by the ghosts of immigrants drowned a century before.

Subtle adaptation of an impressive and topical anti-isolationist play, very well acted and presented.

w Jeffrey Dell, Bernard Miles play *Robert Ardrey* d Roy Boulting ph Mutz Greenbaum (Max Greene) m Hans May

Michael Redgrave, Lilli Palmer, Barbara Mullen, James Mason, Frederick Valk, Frederick Cooper, Finlay Currie, Sybilla Binder

'Boldly imaginative in theme and treatment.' – *Sunday Express*

'More interesting technically than anything since *Citizen Kane.*' – *Manchester Guardian*

'If I thought it wouldn't keep too many people away, I'd call it a work of art.' – *Daily Express*

'What a stimulus to thought it is, this good, brave, outspoken, unfettered picture.' – *Observer*

Thunderball **

GB 1965 132m Technicolor Panavision
UA/Eon/Kevin McClory
V, V (W), V*, L, S

James Bond goes underwater.

Commercially the most successful Bond, but certainly not the best despite a plethora of action sequences.

w Richard Maibaum, John Hopkins novel Ian Fleming d Terence Young ph Ted Moore m John Barry

Sean Connery, Adolfo Celi, Claudine Auger, Luciana Paluzzi, Rik Van Nutter, Bernard Lee, Lois Maxwell, Martine Beswick

'The screenplay stands on tiptoe at the outermost edge of the suggestive and gazes yearningly down into the obscene.' – *John Simon*

AA: special visual effects (John Stears)

Thunderbird Six

GB 1968 90m Technicolor Techniscope
UA/AP/Century 21 (Gerry and Sylvia Anderson)

International Rescue combats the Black Phantom.

Bright, suspenseful puppetoon based on the TV series.

w Gerry and Sylvia Anderson   d David Lane
ph Harry Oakes   m Barry Gray   ad Bob Bell

'Holds some charm for adults, or at least for those who enjoy playing with miniature trains.' – *MFB*

Thunderbirds
US   1942   79m   Technicolor
TCF (Lamar Trotti)

Problems of Arizona flight instructors during World War II.

Very minor flagwaver.

w Lamar Trotti   d William A. Wellman   ph Ernest Palmer   m David Buttolph

Gene Tierney, Preston Foster, John Sutton, Jack Holt, May Whitty, George Barbier, Richard Haydn, Reginald Denny, Ted North

Thunderbirds
US   1952   99m   bw
Republic (John H. Auer)

An Oklahoma unit covers itself in glory during World War II.

Scrappy, noisy war actioner with much newsreel footage.

w Mary McCall Jnr   d John H. Auer   ph Reggie Lanning   m Victor Young

John Derek, John Barrymore Jnr, Mona Freeman, Ward Bond, Gene Evans

Thunderbolt **
US   1929   94m   bw
Paramount

A gangster is caught, tried, and repents.

Gloomy melodrama with interesting style and credits.

w Jules Furthman, Herman J. Mankiewicz   d Josef von Sternberg   ph Henry Gerrard

George Bancroft, Fay Wray, Richard Arlen, Tully Marshall, Eugénie Besserer

AAN: George Bancroft

Thunderbolt and Lightfoot *
US   1974   115m   DeLuxe   Panavision
UA/Malpaso (Robert Daley)
V, V*, L

A bank robber escapes prison, disguises himself as a preacher, befriends a young drifter, and discovers that a new building stands on the spot where the loot is hidden.

Violent melodrama reworking an ancient comedy situation; well made on its level.

wd Michael Cimino   ph Frank Stanley   m Dee Barton

Clint Eastwood, Jeff Bridges, George Kennedy, Geoffrey Lewis, Catherine Bach

AAN: Jeff Bridges

Thundercloud: see *Colt 45*

Thunderhead, Son of Flicka *
US   1945   78m   Technicolor
TCF (Robert Bassler)

More where *My Friend Flicka* came from.

Unexceptional family film with excellent outdoor photography.

w Dwight Cummins, Dorothy Yost   novel Mary O'Hara   d Louis King   ph Charles Clarke   m Cyril Mockridge

Roddy McDowall, Preston Foster, Rita Johnson, James Bell, Carleton Young

'Two Men From Different Worlds. Two Cops After The Same Killer. Together They Must Uncover The Secrets. Together They Must Discover The Truth.'

Thunderheart **
US   1992   119m   DuArt
Columbia TriStar/Tribeca/Waterhorse (Robert de Niro, Jane Rosenthal, John Fusco)
V, V*, L, S

A young FBI agent, assigned to help with a murder investigation in a Sioux reservation, discovers official connivance behind the killing.

An enjoyable thriller that manages to deal with questions of identity and self-discovery along the way.

w John Fusco   d Michael Apted   ph Roger Deakins   m James Horner   pd Dan Bishop   ed Ian Crafford

Val Kilmer, Sam Shepard, Graham Greene, Fred Ward, Fred Dalton Thompson, Sheila Tousey, Chief Ted Thin Elk, John Trudell, Julius Drum, Sarah Brave

'Reasonably engrossing as a mystery-thriller despite its overburdened plot, Thunderheart succeeds most in its captivating portrayal of mystical Native American ways.' – *Variety*

Thunderstorm
GB   1955   88m   bw
Hemisphere/Binnie Barnes

A Spanish fisherman rescues a mysterious girl from a derelict yacht and falls in love with her although the villagers regard her as a witch.

Heady stuff on a low budget, quite smoothly done for lovers of peasant drama.

w George St George, Geoffrey Holmes   d John Guillermin   ph Manuel Berenguer   m Paul Misraki

Linda Christian, Carlos Thompson, Charles Korvin

Thursday's Child
GB   1942   81m   bw
ABPC
V*

A child from an ordinary family has success in films and it goes to her head.

Predictable domestic drama with some good moments, but rather overpraised at the time.

w Donald Macardle and Rodney Ackland   novel Donald Macardle   d Rodney Ackland

Sally Ann Howes, Wilfrid Lawson, Kathleen O'Regan, Eileen Bennett, Stewart Granger, Felix Aylmer

'Visit the future where love is the ultimate crime!'

THX 1138 *
US   1970   95m   Technicolor/scope
Warner/American Zoetrope (Francis Ford Coppola, Lawrence Sturhahn)
V (W), V*, L

In a future society, computer programmed and emotionless, an automated human begins to break the rules.

Orwellian science fiction; a thoughtful, rather cold affair which is always good to look at.

w George Lucas, Walter Murch   d George Lucas   ph Dave Meyers, Albert Kihn   m Lalo Schifrin

Robert Duvall, Donald Pleasence, Pedro Colley, Maggie McOmie, Ian Wolfe

Thy Soul Shall Bear Witness *
Sweden   1920   70m approx (24 fps)   bw   silent
Svensk Filmindustri
original title: *Korkarlen*; aka: *The Phantom Carriage*

A drunkard is knocked senseless, retraces his misspent life, hears the carriage of death approaching and returns to his family.

Old-fashioned moralistic saga which hit the right note at the time and has scenes which still impress.

wd Victor Sjostrom,   novel Selma Lagerlöf   ph J. Julius Jaenzon

Victor Sjostrom, Hilda Borgstrom, Astrid Holm

† Remade in France in 1939 by Julien Duvivier, as *La Charette Fantôme*, with Pierre Fresnay and Louis Jouvet; and again in Sweden in 1958 as *Korkarlen*, by Arne Mattson.

Tiara Tahiti *
GB   1962   100m   Eastmancolor
Rank/Ivan Foxwell
V*

An up-from-the-ranks colonel and an aristocratic smoothie captain continue their antipathy in peacetime Tahiti, where one is nearly murdered and the other gets his come-uppance.

Uneasy mixture of light comedy and character drama; enjoyable in parts, but flabbily assembled and muddily photographed.

w Geoffrey Cotterell, Ivan Foxwell   novel Geoffrey Cotterell   d William T. Kotcheff   ph Otto Heller   m Philip Green

John Mills, James Mason, Herbert Lom, Claude Dauphin, Rosenda Monteros

Tick, Tick, Tick . . . *
US   1969   100m   Metrocolor   Panavision
MGM/Nelson-Barrett (Ralph Nelson, James Lee Barrett)

The first black sheriff in a Southern community has trouble with murder and rape cases.

Socially conscious suspenser, well enough made from predictable elements and leading surprisingly to an upbeat ending.

w James Lee Barrett   d Ralph Nelson   ph Loyal Griggs   m Jerry Stynes

Jim Brown, George Kennedy, Fredric March, Lynn Carlin, Don Stroud, Clifton James

Ticket of Leave Man
GB   1937   71m   bw
George King Productions (E. M. Smedley-Ashton)

The Tiger, 'the most dangerous killer in London', falls in love with a singer.

A ponderous mid-Victorian melodrama complete with barnstorming acting, and interesting mainly as an example of an earlier form of popular entertainment faithfully translated to the screen.

w H. F. Maltby, A. R. Rawlinson   play Tom Taylor   d George King   ph H. M. Glendining   md Jack Beaver   ad Philip Bawcombe, Jack Hallward   ed Robert Walters

Tod Slaughter, John Warwick, Marjorie Taylor, Frank Cochran, Robert Adair

† The play was first produced in 1863. A typical line of dialogue from the film preserves the flavour of the original. A policeman gloats over the grave of his adversary: 'You are avenged. And so shall perish all who fall foul of Hawkshaw the detective.'

Ticket to Heaven *
Canada   1981   108m   colour
Ronald Cohen Productions
V*

A rootless young man is taken over by a religious co-operative.

Thinly veiled attack on the Moonies, quite well handled but perhaps better as a straight documentary.

w Ralph L. Thomas, Anne Cameron   book *Moonwebs* by Josh Freed   d Ralph L. Thomas

Nick Mancuso, Saul Rubinek, Meg Foster, Kim Cattrall

A Ticket to Tomahawk *
US 1950 90m Technicolor
TCF (Robert Bassler)
V*

A stagecoach line defies the new Western railroad.

Would-be satirical Western which doesn't quite have the stamina and after some pleasing touches settles for dullness.

w Mary Loos d Richard Sale ph Harry Jackson
m Cyril Mockridge

Anne Baxter, Dan Dailey, Rory Calhoun, Walter Brennan, Charles Kemper, Connie Gilchrist, Arthur Hunnicutt, Sen Yung

Tickle Me
US 1965 90m DeLuxe Panavision
AA (Ben Schwalb)
V, V*

An unemployed rodeo star accepts a job at a health ranch and helps a girl escape from villains after hidden treasure.

Wispy star vehicle with an unexpected haunted ghost town climax.

w Elwood Ullman, Edward Bernds d Norman Taurog ph Loyal Griggs m Walter Scharf

Elvis Presley, Julia Adams, Jocelyn Lane, Jack Mullaney, Merry Anders, Connie Gilchrist

A Ticklish Affair
US 1963 95m Metrocolor Panavision
MGM/Euterpe (Joe Pasternak)

A naval commander in San Diego falls for a widow with several children.

Thin romantic comedy with too many juvenile antics.

w Ruth Brooks Flippen d George Sidney
ph Milton Krasner m George Stoll, Robert Van Eyps

Shirley Jones, Gig Young, Red Buttons, Carolyn Jones, Edgar Buchanan

'A highly strung love story …'
Tie Me Up! Tie Me Down!
Spain 1989 102m colour
Enterprise/El Deseo (Agustin Almodóvar)
V, V*, L, S
original title: ¡Atame!

A man just released from a psychiatric hospital kidnaps a drug-addicted pornographic film actress and threatens to keep her tied up until she falls in love with him.

Shallow and glib, all surface and no substance, poorly constructed and flashily photographed, it nevertheless found some vociferous admirers.

wd Pedro Almodóvar ph José Luis Alcaine
m Ennio Morricone ed Jose Salcedo

Victoria Abril, Antonio Banderas, Loles Leon, Francisco Rabal, Julieta Serrano, Maria Barranco, Rossy de Palma, Lola Cardona

'The film never stops surprising, moving with fluid momentum toward a tear-jerker ending that verges on the comic but – at least the night I saw it – left most viewers in tears.' – David Leavitt, New York Times

Tiempo de Morir: see Time to Die

Tiffany Jones
GB 1973 90m Eastmancolor
Hemdale/Peter Walker

A model helps a prince overthrow the dictator who deposed his father.

Comic romp in the style of a Carry On movie with some sex appeal.

w Alfred Shaughnessy comic-strip Pat Tourret, Jenny Butterworth d Peter Walker ph Peter Jessop m Cyril Ornadel ed Alan Brett

Anouska Hempel, Ray Brooks, Susan Sheers, Damien Thomas, Eric Pohlmann, Lynda Baron, Bill Kerr

'In the place of humour, the production has recourse to some of the more lethal devices of British farce – funny foreigners and inflated third-form puns.' – Gareth Jones, MFB

Tiger Bay **
GB 1959 105m bw
Rank/Wintle-Parkyn (John Hawkesworth)
V, V*

A Polish seaman in Cardiff kills his faithless girlfriend and kidnaps a child who proves more than a match for him.

Generally very proficient police chase melodrama with strong characterizations: a considerable box-office success of its time.

w John Hawkesworth, Shelley Smith d J. Lee-Thompson ph Eric Cross m Laurie Johnson

Hayley Mills, John Mills, Horst Buchholz, Megs Jenkins, Anthony Dawson, Yvonne Mitchell

Tiger in the Sky: see The McConnell Story

Tiger in the Smoke *
GB 1956 94m bw
Rank (Leslie Parkyn)

Ex-commando criminals comb London for hidden loot and threaten a young girl.

Odd little melodrama with a complex plot and a different, Graham Greene-like atmosphere.

w Anthony Pelissier novel Marjorie Allingham
d Roy Baker ph Geoffrey Unsworth m Malcolm Arnold

Tony Wright, Muriel Pavlow, Donald Sinden, Bernard Miles, Alec Clunes, Laurence Naismith, Christopher Rhodes, Kenneth Griffith, Beatrice Varley

The Tiger Makes Out *
US 1967 94m Technicolor
Columbia/Elan (George Justin)

A middle-aged New York postman takes revenge on society by kidnapping a young girl – who rather enjoys the experience.

Semi-surrealist comedy misguidedly extended from a two-character play; frantic pace prevents more than a few effective moments.

w Murray Shisgal play Murray Shisgal d Arthur Hiller ph Arthur J. Ornitz m Milton Rogers

Eli Wallach, Anne Jackson, Bob Dishy, David Burns, Charles Nelson Reilly

'An attractive and bemusing piece of costume jewelry – but not comparable to the real thing.' – Judith Crist

Tiger of the Seven Seas
Italy/France 1963 90m colour
Liber Film/Euro International (Ottavio Poggi)
V*
aka: La Tigre de Sette Mari

A pirate's daughter takes over his command to revenge herself on his killer.

Mundane swashbuckler with a heroine who lacks the panache of Errol Flynn.

d Luigi Capuano ph Alvaro Mancori

Gianna Maria Canale, Anthony Steel, Grazia Maria Spina, Andrea Aureli

Tiger Man: see The Lady and the Monster

Tiger Shark *
US 1932 80m bw
Warner

A tuna fisherman who has lost a hand to a shark marries the daughter of an old friend, finds she loves someone else, and is conveniently killed by another shark.

Vivid melodrama with a plot partly borrowed from Moby Dick and itself partly borrowed by innumerable other Warner films including Kid Galahad, The Wagons Roll at Night, Slim and Manpower.

w Wells Root story Tuna by Houston Branch
d Howard Hawks ph Tony Gaudio

Edward G. Robinson, J. Carrol Naish, Zita Johann

'Strong and exceedingly well played and directed sea drama.' – Variety

A Tiger Walks *
US 1963 91m Technicolor
Walt Disney (Ron Miller)
V*

In a small Western town, a tiger escapes from the circus.

A splendid animal and a happy ending help to make this a pretty good film for children.

w Lowell S. Hawley novel Ian Niall d Norman Tokar ph William Snyder m Buddy Baker

Sabu, Brian Keith, Vera Miles, Pamela Franklin, Kevin Corcoran, Edward Andrews, Una Merkel, Frank McHugh

'The Disney message runs true to form – grown-ups should practise what they preach and children are right about animals.' – MFB

Tiger Warsaw
US 1988 90m colour
Recorded Releasing/Continental Film Group/Cineplex (Amin Q. Chaudhri)
V, V*, L

After fifteen years away, a former drug-addict, who shot his father, returns home.

Predictable and ponderous melodrama.

w Roy London d Amin Q. Chaudhri ph Robert Draper m Ernest Troost pd Tom Targownik
ed Brian Smedley-Aston

Patrick Swayze, Barbara Williams, Piper Laurie, Lee Richardson, Mary McDonnell, Bobby DiCicco

The Tiger Woman
US 1944 bw serial: 12 eps
Republic
V*

Oil drillers are delayed by jungle people led by a strange white woman who proves to be an heiress lost as a child in a plane crash.

Ho-hum hokum.

d Spencer Bennet, Wallace Grissell

Allan Lane, Linda Stirling, Duncan Renaldo, George J. Lewis, LeRoy Mason

A Tiger's Tale
US 1987 97m colour
Entertainment/Atlantic (Peter Douglas)
V*, L

A middle-aged woman becomes pregnant as a result of an affair with a high-school student.

Dire comedy with no visible or audible wit.

wd Peter Douglas novel Love and Other Natural Disasters by Allen Hanney III ph Tony Pierce-Roberts m Lee Holdridge pd Shay Austin
ed David Campling

Ann-Margret, C. Thomas Howell, Charles Durning, Kelly Preston, William Zabka, Ann Wedgeworth, James Noble

Tight Little Island: see Whisky Galore

Tight Shoes
US 1941 67m bw
Universal/Mayfair (Jules Levey)

A political grafter buys tight shoes which have a series of dramatic consequences.

Moderately witty little comedy which conveyed the Runyon flavour as well as any.

w Leonard Spigelgass, Art Arthur story Damon Runyon d Albert S. Rogell

Broderick Crawford, Binnie Barnes, John Howard, Anne Gwynne, Leo Carrillo, Samuel S. Hinds, Shemp Howard

Tight Spot
US 1955 97m bw
Columbia (Lewis J. Rachmil)
V

A material witness in the trial of a gangster is released from prison in the custody of an attorney.

Fairly routine crime melodrama with unexciting star performances.

w William Bowers play Dead Pigeon by Leonard Kantor d Phil Karlson ph Burnett Guffey m Morris Stoloff

Edward G. Robinson, Ginger Rogers, Brian Keith, Lorne Greene, Lucy Marlow, Katherine Anderson

Tightrope
US 1984 114m Technicolor
Warner/Malpaso (Clint Eastwood, Fritz Manes)
V, V*, L

A New Orleans detective investigating a series of sex murders finds that his own impulses are none too healthy.

Boring, dimly lit and generally unappealing low life thriller.

wd Richard Tuggle ph Billy Bragg m Lennie Niehaus

Clint Eastwood, Geneviève Bujold, Dan Hedaya, Alison Eastwood, Jennifer Beck

'Til We Meet Again
US 1940 99m bw
Warner (David Lewis)

On a ship bound from Hong Kong to San Francisco, a dying woman falls for a crook about to be executed.

Stolid remake of One Way Passage (qv).

w Warren Duff story Robert Lord d Edmund Goulding ph Tony Gaudio m Ray Heindorf

Merle Oberon, George Brent, Frank McHugh, Pat O'Brien, Geraldine Fitzgerald, Eric Blore, Binnie Barnes, Henry O'Neill, George Reeves

† Marlene Dietrich was originally scheduled for the lead.

Tilai **
Burkina Faso/Switzerland/France 1990 81m colour
Artificial Eye/Les Films de L'Avenir/Waka Films/Rhea Films (Idrissa Ouedraogo)
V

Returning home after being away for two years, a man discovers that his father has married his fiancée.

An African tragedy of domestic conflicts and broken promises, told with an uncomplicated directness.

wd Idrissa Ouedraogo ph Jean Monsigny, Pierre Laurent Chenieux m Abdullah Ibrahim ed Luc Barnier

Rasmane Ouedraogo, Ina Cisse, Roukietou Barry, Assane Ouedraogo, Sibidou Sidibe, Moumouni Ouedraogo, Mariam Barry, Seydou Ouedraogo

'There is no doubt about Idrissa Ouedraogo's cinematic mastery.' – MFB

Till Death Us Do Part *
GB 1968 100m Eastmancolor
British Lion/Associated London Films (Jon Pennington)
V

From the thirties to the sixties with loud-mouthed, bigoted Londoner Alf Garnett.

Unremarkable and frequently misguided opening-up of a phenomenally successful TV series, adapted for the US as All in the Family. The original cast wades cheerfully enough through a bitty script; the sequel, The Alf Garnett Saga, defeated them.

w Johnny Speight d Norman Cohen ph Harry Waxman m Wilfrid Burns

Warren Mitchell, Dandy Nichols, Anthony Booth, Una Stubbs, Liam Redmond, Bill Maynard, Sam Kydd, Brian Blessed

Till the Clouds Roll By **
US 1946 137m Technicolor
MGM (Arthur Freed)
V*, L, S

The life and times of composer Jerome Kern.

Better-than-average biopic with better-than-average tunes and stars.

w Myles Connolly, Jean Holloway d Richard Whorf ph Harry Stradling, George J. Folsey md Lennie Hayton

Robert Walker, Judy Garland, Lucille Bremer, Van Heflin, Mary Nash, Dinah Shore, Van Johnson, June Allyson, Tony Martin, Kathryn Grayson, Lena Horne, Frank Sinatra, Virginia O'Brien

'A little like sitting down to a soda fountain de luxe atomic special of maple walnut on vanilla on burnt almond on strawberry on butter pecan on coffee on raspberry sherbert on tutti frutti with hot fudge, butterscotch, marshmallow, filberts, pistachios, shredded pineapple, and rainbow sprills on top, go double on the whipped cream.' – James Agee

Till the End of Time *
US 1946 105m bw
RKO (Dore Schary)
V*, L

Three returning GIs find romance and problems in their small town.

Downbeat variation on The Best Years of Our Lives with a theme tune which puts words to a Chopin Polonaise.

w Allen Rivkin d Edward Dmytryk ph Harry J. Wild m Leigh Harline

Dorothy McGuire, Guy Madison, Robert Mitchum

Till There Was You
Australia 1990 95m colour
Rank/Five Arrows/Ayer/Southern Star (Jim McElroy)
V*

An American barman investigates the mysterious death of his brother in the South Pacific state of Vanuatu.

An unconvincing thriller that offers nothing but occasionally spectacular photography.

w Michael Thomas d John Seale ph Geoffrey Simpson, Robert Primes m Graeme Revell pd George Liddle, Susan Emshwiller ed Jill Bilcock

Mark Harmon, Deborah Unger, Jeroen Krabbé, Shane Briant, Ivan Kesa

Till We Meet Again
US 1936 87m bw
Paramount

Former sweethearts find themselves both spies, but on opposing sides.

Unconvincing but climactically suspenseful romantic drama.

w Edwin Justus Mayer, Franklin Coen, Brian Marlow play Alfred Davis d Robert Florey

Herbert Marshall, Gertrude Michael, Lionel Atwill

'She came from a woman's world – into his world of men – and danger!'
Till We Meet Again
US 1944 88m bw
Paramount (David Lewis)

A French nun helps an American aviator escape from the Nazis.

Very moderate, nicely photographed, romantic war actioner.

w Lenore Coffee play Alfred Maury d Frank Borzage ph Theodor Sparkuhl m David Buttolph

Ray Milland, Barbara Britton, Walter Slezak, Lucile Watson, Konstantin Shayne, Vladimir Sokoloff, Mona Freeman

Tillie and Gus *
US 1933 61m bw
Paramount (Douglas MacLean)

Two middle-aged cardsharps return home, help their niece and nephew win an inheritance, and come first in a paddleboat race.

Jumbled comedy with good moments and a rousing climax.

w Walter de Leon, Francis Martin d Francis Martin ph Benjamin Reynolds

W. C. Fields, Alison Skipworth, Baby Le Roy, Jacqueline Wells, Clifford Jones, Clarence Wilson, Edgar Kennedy, Barton MacLane

'Very funny in spots, but not enough spots.' – Variety

Tillie's Punctured Romance *
US 1914 60m approx (24 fps) bw silent
Keystone/Mack Sennett
V*, L

A country maid falls for a con man who steals her money; but she finally gets her revenge.

Museum piece comedy which no longer irritates the funny bone but has clear historical interest.

w Hampton Del Ruth play Tillie's Nightmare by Edgar Smith d Mack Sennett ph Frank D. Williams

Marie Dressler, Charles Chaplin, Mabel Normand, Mack Swain

Tilly of Bloomsbury
GB 1940 83m bw
Hammersmith

The daughter of a boarding house keeper falls for a rich young man.

Basically a millgirl's romance, remembered for one final drunk scene for the star comedian.

w Nils Hostius, Jack Marks play Ian Hay d Leslie Hiscott

Sydney Howard, Jean Gillie, Henry Oscar, Athene Seyler, Michael Wilding, Kathleen Harrison, Michael Denison, Martita Hunt, Athole Stewart

† Previous versions: 1921, with Tom Reynolds and Edna Best, for Samuelson; 1931, with Sydney Howard and Phyllis Konstam, for Sterling.

Tim
Australia 1979 98m colour
Pisces Productions (Michael Pate)
V, V*

A romance develops between a wealthy middle-aged spinster and a young, simple-minded builder.

Sentimental melodrama, notable only as the film that launched the career of Mel Gibson.

wd Michael Pate novel Colleen McCullough ph Paul Onorato m Eric Jupp ad John Carroll ed David Stiven

Piper Laurie, Mel Gibson, Alwyn Kurts, Pat Evison, Peter Gwynne, Deborah Kennedy

Tim Burton's The Nightmare before Christmas: see The Nightmare before Christmas

Tim Tyler's Luck

US   1937   bw   serial: 12 eps
Universal

Tim goes to gorilla country in search of his father, and finds a criminal who steals ivory and diamonds.

Standard thick ear from the Hollywood jungle.

d Ford Beebe

Frankie Thomas, Al Shean, Frances Robinson, Norman Willis

Timberjack

US   1954   94m   Trucolor
Republic

A young man seeks his father's killer among forest lumberjacks.

Resiliently cast action story of no great interest.

w Allen Rivkin   novel Dan Cushman   d Joe Kane

Sterling Hayden, Vera Ralston, Adolphe Menjou, David Brian, Hoagy Carmichael, Chill Wills, Jim Davis, Elisha Cook Jnr

Timbuktu

US   1958   92m   bw
Edward Small

A gun runner quells a desert revolt in the French Sudan during World War II.

Leaden-footed melodrama full of stock characters despite its complex plot.

w Anthony Veiller   d Jacques Tourneur

Yvonne de Carlo, Victor Mature, George Dolenz, John Dehner, Marcia Henderson

Time after Time *

US   1980   112m   Metrocolor   Panavision
Warner/Orion (Herb Jaffe)
V, V*, L

Jack the Ripper escapes via H. G. Wells's time machine from Victorian London to modern San Francisco; Wells gives chase and eventually projects him into limbo.

Amusing fantasy for those with light literary inclinations, marred by too much gore and a wandering middle section.

wd Nicholas Meyer   story Karl Alexander, Steve Hayes   ph Paul Lohmann   m Miklos Rozsa
pd Edward Carfagno

Malcolm McDowell, David Warner, Mary Steenburgen, Charles Cioffi, Kent Williams

Time Bandits *

GB   1981   113m   Technicolor
HandMade Films (Terry Gilliam)
V, V*, L

A schoolboy is taken through time by a group of demonic dwarfs.

Curious tall tale in which schoolboy fantasy alternates with violence and black comedy. In general, much less funny than it intended to be, but with some hilarious moments.

w Michael Palin, Terry Gilliam   d Terry Gilliam
ph Peter Biziou   m Mike Moran   pd Millie Burns

John Cleese (as Robin Hood), Sean Connery (as Agamemnon), Ian Holm (as Napoleon), Ralph Richardson (as God), David Warner (as Satan), Shelley Duvall, Katherine Helmond, Michael Palin, Peter Vaughan, David Rappaport

Time Bomb *

GB   1952   72m   bw
MGM (Richard Goldstone)
US title: Terror on a Train

A saboteur places a bomb on a goods train travelling from the north of England to Portsmouth.

Tolerable suspenser padded out with domestic asides.

w Ken Bennett   novel Death at Attention by Ken Bennett   d Ted Tetzlaff   ph Frederick A. Young
m John Addison

Glenn Ford, Anne Vernon, Maurice Denham, Harcourt Williams, Harold Warrender, Bill Fraser, John Horsley, Victor Maddern

Time Flies *

GB   1944   88m   bw
GFD/Gainsborough (Edward Black)

A professor invents a time machine and takes his friends back to the court of Good Queen Bess.

Very passable star farce.

w J. O. C. Orton, Ted Kavanaugh, Howard Irving Young   d Walter Forde   ph Basil Emmott
md Louis Levy

Tommy Handley, Felix Aylmer, Evelyn Dall, George Moon, Moore Marriott, Graham Moffatt, John Salew, Olga Lindo, Stephane Grappelly

Time for Action: see Tip on a Dead Jockey

A Time for Giving: see Generation

A Time for Killing

US   1967   83m   Pathecolor   Panavision
Columbia/Sage Western (Harry Joe Brown)
GB title: The Long Ride Home

Confederate prisoners escape from a Union fort and the commander sets off in pursuit.

Fairly savage Western with Something to Say about the corruption of war.

w Halsted Welles   novel Southern Blade by Nelson and Shirley Wolford   d Phil Karlson   ph Kenneth Peach   m Mundell Lowe

Glenn Ford, George Hamilton, Inger Stevens, Max Baer, Paul Petersen, Timothy Carey, Todd Armstrong

A Time for Loving

GB   1971   104m   colour
London Screen Plays/Mel Ferrer

Short romantic comedies set at different times in the same Paris flat.

Portmanteau ooh-la-la, quite neat but pitifully undernourished; certainly no Plaza Suite.

w Jean Anouilh   d Christopher Miles   ph Andreas Winding   m Michel Legrand   pd Theo Meurisse

Joanna Shimkus, Mel Ferrer, Britt Ekland, Philippe Noiret, Lila Kedrova, Robert Dhery, Mark Burns, Susan Hampshire

Time Gentlemen Please

GB   1952   83m   bw
Group Three (Herbert Mason)

A lazy tramp is the one blot on a prize-winning English village.

Artificial, thinly scripted and overlit sub-Ealing comedy with familiar characters and situations.

w Peter Blackmore   novel Nothing to Lose by R. J. Minney   d Lewis Gilbert   ph Wilkie Cooper
m Antony Hopkins

Eddie Byrne, Hermione Baddeley, Jane Barrett, Robert Brown, Raymond Lovell, Marjorie Rhodes, Dora Bryan, Thora Hird, Sidney James, Edie Martin, Ivor Barnard, Sidney Tafler

'Quite a nice little picture.' – Karel Reisz

Time in the Sun ***

Mexico   1933   60m   bw
Marie Seton
V

Unfinished fragments of Eisenstein's incomplete Que

Viva Mexico, snippets from which were later released in various forms.

This is the longest and presumably best version, with splendidly pictorial sequences of peasant and Indian life culminating with Death Day, all skulls and fireworks. Clearly the work of a master, though if completed the film might well have been a bore.

w Marie Seton, Paul Burnford   d Sergei Eisenstein
ph Edouard Tissé

Time Limit *

US   1957   95m   bw
UA/Richard Widmark, William Reynolds

During the Korean war an officer is courtmartialled for suspected collaboration.

Suspenseful talk piece from a somewhat intellectualized play.

w Henry Denker   play Henry Denker, Ralph Berkey
d Karl Malden   ph Sam Leavitt   m Fred Steiner

Richard Widmark, Richard Basehart, Dolores Michaels, June Lockhart, Carl Benton Reid, Martin Balsam, Rip Torn

'The tightly constructed story leads logically and unfalteringly to a tense climax.' – Lindsay Anderson

Time Lock *

GB   1957   73m   bw
Romulus (Peter Rogers)

A small boy is trapped in a bank vault just as it is being locked for the weekend.

Acceptable expansion of a Canadian TV suspenser.

w Peter Rogers   play Arthur Hailey   d Gerald Thomas   ph Peter Hennessy   m Stanley Black

Robert Beatty, Betty McDowall, Vincent Winter, Lee Patterson, Alan Gifford, Robert Ayres

Time Lost and Time Remembered: see I Was Happy Here

The Time Machine *

US   1960   103m   Metrocolor
MGM/Galaxy (George Pal)
V, V*, L, S

A Victorian scientist builds a machine which after some trial and error transports him into the year 802701.

Surprisingly careful recreation of a period, and an undeniably charming machine, go for little when the future, including the villainous Morlocks, is so dull.

w David Duncan   novel H. G. Wells   d George Pal
ph Paul C. Vogel   m Russell Garcia   ad George W. Davis, William Ferrari

Rod Taylor, Yvette Mimieux, Alan Young, Sebastian Cabot, Tom Helmore, Whit Bissell, Doris Lloyd

AA: special effects (Gene Warren, Tim Baar)

A Time of Destiny

US   1988   118m   colour
Rank/Columbia/Nelson Entertainment/Alive Films (Anna Thomas)
V*, L

An immigrant's son swears vengeance on the GI who married his sister and inadvertently caused the death of his father.

Dull revenge drama set in the 1940s.

w Gregory Nava, Anna Thomas   d Gregory Nava
ph James Glennon   m Ennio Morricone   pd Henry Bumstead   ed Betsy Blankett

William Hurt, Timothy Hutton, Melissa Leo, Franciso Rabal, Concha Hidalgo, Stockard Channing, Megan Follows, Frederick Coffin

Time of Miracles *

Yugoslavia   1990   100m   colour
Singidunum/Television Belgrad/Channel 4/Metropolitan (Goran
Paskaljevic)
original title: *Vrema Cuda*

In September 1945, after the village school burns
down, the victorious Communists commandeer the
church and whitewash over its religious murals; but
the paintings reappear and a stranger arrives who
apparently can raise the dead.

Intriguing, if sometimes ponderous, account of faith,
belief and their interactions with reality.

w Borislav Pekic, Goran Paskaljevic   *novel* Borislav
Pekic   *d* Goran Paskaljevic   *ph* Radoslav Vladic
m Zoran Simjanovic   *ad* Miodrag Nikolic   *ed* Olga
Skrigin, Olga Obradov

Predrag Miki Manojlovic, Dragan Maksimovic,
Svetozar Cvetkovic, Mirjana Karanovic, Danilo Bata
Stojkovic, Mirjana Jokovic, Ljuba Tadic

Time of the Gypsies *

Yugoslavia   1989   142m   colour
Enterprise/Forum Film/Sarajevo TV (Mirza Pasic)
V, V*, L
original title: *Dom Za Vesanje*

A young gypsy with magic powers is forced to work
with a band of itinerant thieves and beggars.

Cut from a six-part television series, the film, despite
some lively episodes, suffers from a disjointed
narrative, though that did not prevent Kusturica being
voted best director at the Cannes Film Festival.

w Emir Kusturica, Gordon Mihic   *d* Emir Kusturica
ph Vilko Filac   *m* Goran Bregovic   *pd* Miljen
Kljakovic   *ed* Andrija Zafranovic

Davor Dujmovic, Bora Todorovic, Ljubica Adzovic,
Husnija Hasmovic, Sinolicka Trpkova, Zabit
Memedov

The Time of Their Lives *

US   1946   82m   bw
Universal (Val Burton)
V*

Revolutionary ghosts haunt a country estate.

Unusual, quite effective Abbott and Costello vehicle
with the comedians not playing as a team.

w Val Burton, Walter de Leon, Bradford Ropes, John
Grant   *d* Charles Barton   *ph* Charles Van Enger
m Milton Rosen

Bud Abbott, Lou Costello, Marjorie Reynolds, Binnie
Barnes, Gale Sondergaard, John Shelton

The Time of Your Life *

US   1948   109m   bw
Cagney Productions (William Cagney)
V*

A group of lovable eccentrics spend much of their
time philosophizing in a San Francisco bar.

Not really a film at all, this essence of Saroyan
contains much to enjoy or to annoy. The performances
are pretty good.

w Nathaniel Curtis   *play* William Saroyan   *d* H.
C. Potter   *ph* James Wong Howe   *m* Carmen
Dragon

James Cagney, William Bendix, Wayne Morris, Jeanne
Cagney, Gale Page, Broderick Crawford, *James Barton,*
Ward Bond, Paul Draper, James Lydon, Richard
Erdman, Natalie Schaefer

'They have done so handsomely by Saroyan that in
the long run everything depends on how much of
Saroyan you can take.' – *Time*

Time Out for Romance

US   1937   75m   bw
TCF

A millionairess runs from the altar and teams up with
a car factory driver.

Weakish rehash of *It Happened One Night,* but the script
isn't up to the intention.

w Lou Breslow, John Patrick, Eleanore Griffin,
William Rankin   *d* Malcolm St Clair

Claire Trevor, Michael Whalen, Joan Davis, Chick
Chandler, Douglas Fowley, William Demarest,
Andrew Tombes

'Just misses being able to stand on its own legs as a
solo performer.' – *Variety*

Time out of Mind

US   1947   88m   bw
Universal-International (Robert Siodmak)

The housekeeper's daughter finances music studies
for the master's ungrateful son.

Silly romantic melodrama with few visible
compensations.

w Abem Finkel, Arnold Phillips   *novel* Rachel Field
d Robert Siodmak   *ph* Maury Gertsman
m Miklos Rozsa

Phyllis Calvert, Robert Hutton, Ella Raines, Eddie
Albert, Leo G. Carroll

A Time out of War *

US   1954   20m   bw
Terry and Denis Sanders

Two men on opposite sides of a river during the
American Civil War strike up a brief friendship.

Interesting but overpraised student piece.

wd Denis Sanders   *story* Pickets by Robert W.
Chambers

Barry Atwater, Robert Sherry, Alan Cohen

The Time, the Place and the Girl

US   1946   105m   Technicolor
Warner (Alex Gottlieb)

Two night-club owners have problems.

Lightweight musical, indistinguishable from a dozen
others.

w Francis Swann, Agnes Christine Johnston, Lynn
Starling   *d* David Butler   *ph* William V. Skall
m Arthur Schwartz

Dennis Morgan, Jack Carson, Janis Paige, Martha
Vickers, S. Z. Sakall, Alan Hale, Donald Woods,
Angela Greene, Florence Bates

AAN: song 'A Gal in Calico' (*m* Arthur Schwartz, *ly*
Leo Robin)

Time to Die **

Columbia/Cuba   1985   94m   colour
Artificial Eye/Focine/ICIAC (Gabriel García Marquez)
original title: *Tiempo de Morir*

After serving an eighteen-year sentence for murder, a
man returns home to find that the victim's sons are
waiting to exact revenge.

Basically a Latin American Western, it grips the
attention in its exploration of masculine codes of
honour and duty.

w Gabriel García Marquez   *d* Jorge Ali Triana
ph Mario Garcia Joya   *m* Leo Brower, Nafer Duran
pd Patricia Bonilla   *ed* Nelson Rodriquez

Gustavo Angarita, Sebastian Ospina, Jorge Emilio
Salazar, Maria Eugenia Davila, Lina Botero, Enrique
Almirante

A Time to Live and a Time to Die: see *Le Feu Follet*

The Time to Live and the Time to Die **

Taiwan   1985   137m   colour
Central Motion Pictures
original title: *Tongnian Wangshi*

A Chinese man remembers growing up in Taiwan in
the 1950s and 60s as one of a large family headed by
his consumptive, intellectual father and his doting,

rambling grandmother who dreams of returning to the
mainland.

An episodic, semi-autobiographical film of family life,
reaching few conclusions, other than those brought
about by death, but affording insight into the tensions
of everyday living.

w Zu Tianwen, Hou Hsiao-hsien   *d* Hou Hsiao-
hsien   *ph* Li Pingbin   *m* Wu Chuchu

You Anshun, Tian Feng, Mei Fang, Tang Ruyun, Xiao
Ai, Xin Shufen, Hu Xiangping

A Time to Love and a Time to Die *

US   1958   132m   Eastmancolor   Cinemascope
U-I (Robert Arthur)
V*

During World War II, a German officer on his last
leave solves problems at home but is killed on his
return to the front.

Interesting but preachy and generally misguided
attempt, by the studio which made *All Quiet on the
Western Front* and *The Road Back,* to repeat the dose in
colour and wide screen.

w Orin Jannings   *novel* Erich Maria Remarque
d Douglas Sirk   *ph* Russell Metty   *m* Miklos
Rozsa

John Gavin, Lilo Pulver, Keenan Wynn, Jock
Mahoney, Thayer David, Agnes Windeck, Erich Maria
Remarque

The Time Travelers *

US   1964   84m   Pathecolor
AIP/Dobie (William Redlin)
V*

Scientists venture 107 years into the future, and on
escaping find themselves in a time trap.

Ingenious and lively low-budget science fiction with
a sobering ending.

wd Ib Melchior   *ph* William Zsigismond   *m* Richard
La Salle

Preston Foster, Phil Carey, Merry Anders, John Hoyt,
Joan Woodbury

Time without Pity *

GB   1957   88m   bw
Harlequin (John Arnold, Anthony Simmons)

An alcoholic arrives in London to seek new evidence
which will prevent his son from being executed for
murder.

Heavy-going, introspective, hysterical, downbeat
melodrama which takes itself with a seriousness
which is almost deadly.

w Ben Barzman   *play* Someone Waiting by Emlyn
Williams   *d* Joseph Losey   *ph* Freddie Francis
m Tristam Cary

Michael Redgrave, Alec McCowen, Leo McKern,
Renée Houston, Ann Todd, Peter Cushing, Paul
Daneman, Lois Maxwell, George Devine, Richard
Wordsworth, Joan Plowright

'It hammers home its effects with the concentration of
a heavyweight out for the kill.' – *Philip Oakes*

Timebomb

US   1991   96m   colour
MGM/Raffaella (Raffaella de Laurentiis)
V, V*, L

A watchmaker and former hitman prevents a CIA plot
to assassinate a liberal politician.

Confused action adventure that updates *The
Manchurian Candidate* to no great effect.

wd Avi Nesher   *ph* Anthony B. Richmond
m Patrick Leonard   *pd* Greg Pruss, Curtis A. Schnell
ed Isaac Sehayek

Michael Biehn, Patsy Kensit, Tracy Scoggins, Robert
Culp, Richard Jordan, Raymond St Jacques

'A throwaway B-picture.' – *Empire*

Times Square

US   1980   113m   Technicolor
EMI/Robert Stigwood
V*

Two ill-matched teenage girls form a shabby night-club act and soon have New York by its ears.

Sometimes sharply made but generally unpleasant urban fairy story with suicide as the end, like a cross between *Saturday Night Fever* and *Midnight Cowboy*. Among a number of forgettable songs is one called 'Pissing in the River'.

w Jacob Brackman   *story* Alan Moyle and Leanne Unger   *d* Alan Moyle   *ph* James A. Contner   *m* Blue Weaver

Tim Curry, Trini Alvarado, Robin Johnson, Peter Coffield, Herbert Berghof, David Margulies

Times Square Lady

US   1935   69m   bw
MGM

The daughter of a Broadway hustler, being chiselled by her father's attorney, is helped by one of his employees.

Flat romantic drama designed as a test for young stars.

w Albert Cohen, Robert Shannon   *d* George B. Seitz

Robert Taylor, Virginia Bruce, Pinky Tomlin, Helen Twelvetrees, Isabel Jewell, Nat Pendleton, Henry Kolker, Jack La Rue

'Not sufficient heft to be important.' – *Variety*

Times Square Playboy: see *The Home Towners*

Timetable *

US   1955   79m   bw
UA (Mark Stevens)

An insurance investigator is assigned to a train robbery which he actually committed himself.

Concise suspenser with good script and treatment.

w Aben Kandel   *d* Mark Stevens   *ph* Charles Van Enger   *m* Walter Scharf

Mark Stevens, Felicia Farr, King Calder, Wesley Addy

The Tin Drum ****

West Germany/France   1979   142m   Eastmancolor
UA/Franz Seitz/Bioskop/GGB 14 KG/Hallelujah/Artemis/Argos/Jadran/Film Polski
V*, S
original title: *Die Blechtrommel*

Not caring for the world he is growing up in, a small boy determines to remain a child.

Brilliantly made version of a labyrinthine satire on German nationalism and the rise of the Nazis; the emphasis is sometimes on sex and scatological detail, for it is intended to be disturbing viewing, succeeding in its aim of depicting a frightening world where reason is overthrown.

w Jean-Claude Carrière, Franz Seitz, Volker Schlöndorff   *novel* Günter Grass   *d* Volker Schlöndorff   *ph* Igor Luther   *m* Maurice Jarre   *pd* Nicos Perakis

David Bennent, Mario Adorf, Angela Winkler, Daniel Olbrychski

AA: best foreign film

Tin Men **

US   1987   112m   DeLuxe
Touchstone/Silver Screen Partners II (Mark Johnson)
V*, L

In 1960s Baltimore, two aluminium salesmen have a series of feuds.

A comedy enjoyable not for its plot but for its authentic period backgrounds and characters.

wd Barry Levinson   *ph* Peter Sova   *m* David Steele   *pd* Peter Jamison   *ed* Stu Linder

Richard Dreyfuss, Danny DeVito, Barbara Hershey, John Mahoney, Jackie Gayle, Stanley Brock

Tin Pan Alley ***

US   1940   95m   bw
TCF (Kenneth MacGowan)

During World War I and after, two dancing girls love the same composer.

Archetypal musical, full of Broadway clichés, razzmatazz and zip. Remade 1950 as *I'll Get By*, not to such peppy effect.

w Robert Ellis, Helen Logan   *d* Walter Lang   *ph* Leon Shamroy   *ch* Seymour Felix   *songs* Mack Gordon, Harry Warren   *m* Alfred Newman

Alice Faye, Betty Grable, John Payne, Jack Oakie, Allen Jenkins, Esther Ralston, The Nicholas Brothers, John Loder, Elisha Cook Jnr

AA: Alfred Newman

The Tin Star *

US   1957   93m   bw   Vistavision
Paramount/Perlberg-Seaton
V*

An ex-sheriff turned bounty hunter helps a new young sheriff to catch bandits.

Dignified and well-characterized Western with customary pleasures.

w Dudley Nichols   *story* Barney Slater, Joel Kane   *d* Anthony Mann   *ph* Loyal Griggs   *m* Elmer Bernstein

Henry Fonda, Anthony Perkins, Betsy Palmer, Michel Ray, Neville Brand, John McIntire

AAN: Barney Slater, Joel Kane, Dudley Nichols

Tina: What's Love Got to Do with It: see *What's Love Got to Do with It*

'Do you have the guts to sit in this chair?'

The Tingler

US   1959   82m   bw
Columbia/William Castle

Fear (it says here) can create on the spinal column a parasite removable only by screaming. A scientist isolates it and it runs amok in a silent cinema.

Ridiculous shocker with generally dull handling but effective moments.

w Robb White   *d* William Castle   *ph* Wilfrid Cline   *m* Von Dexter

Vincent Price, Judith Evelyn, Darryl Hickman, Patricia Cutts

'The sheer effrontery of this piece of hokum is enjoyable in itself.' – *MFB*

Tinpis Run

France/Belgium/Papua New Guinea   1990   94m   colour
JBA/Tinpis/La Sept/RTBF/Femis/Varan/Skul Bilong Wokim Piksa (Jacques Bidou)

A tribal chief who runs a taxi service with his daughter and her boyfriend returns to his village to take part in a war against a neighbouring tribe.

Moderately entertaining anecdotal account of an unusual generation clash – between the peace-loving young and their elders.

w John Barre, Severin Blanchet, Martin Maden, Pengau Nengo   *d* Pengau Nengo   *ph* Martin Maden   *m* Severin Blanchet, Mick Giani   *ad* Thomas Gawi   *ed* Andrée Davanture

Rhoda Selan, Leo Konga, Oscar Wanu, Gerard Gabud

'More a travelog of the island country than a wholly satisfying dramatic film.' – *Variety*

Tip-off Girls *

US   1938   61m   bw
Paramount

Gangsters use girl employees to get tips on merchandise shipments.

Routine but watchable G-man second.

w Maxwell Shane, Robert Yost, Stuart Anthony   *d* Louis King

Lloyd Nolan, Mary Carlisle, J. Carrol Naish, Harvey Stephens, Roscoe Karns, Larry Crabbe, Anthony Quinn

'Excellent meller . . . bristles with action, tensity and suspense.' – *Variety*

Tip on a Dead Jockey

US   1957   99m   bw
MGM (Edwin H. Knopf)
GB title: *Time for Action*

A flyer loses his nerve and turns international smuggler, but reforms.

Gloomy, pedestrian star melodrama, dully cast.

w Charles Lederer   *novel* Irwin Shaw   *d* Richard Thorpe   *ph* George J. Folsey   *m* Miklos Rozsa

Robert Taylor, Dorothy Malone, Gia Scala, Martin Gabel, Marcel Dalio, Jack Lord

Tirez sur le Pianiste: see *Shoot the Pianist*

'Tis Pity She's a Whore **

Italy   1971   109m   Technicolor
Miracle/Clesi (Silvio Clementelli)
V
original title: *Addio, Fratello Crudele*

A husband seeks revenge when he discovers that his wife is pregnant by her brother.

A gripping version of a Jacobean tragedy on the themes of obsessive love and jealousy.

w Giuseppe Patroni Griffi, Alfio Valdarnini, Carlo Carunchio   *play* John Ford   *d* Giuseppe Patroni Griffi   *ph* Vittorio Storaro   *m* Ennio Morricone   *ad* Mario Ceroli   *ed* Franco Arcalli

Charlotte Rampling, Oliver Tobias, Fabio Testi, Antonio Falsi, Rik Battaglia, Angela Luce, Rino Imperio

'Magnificently expressive, as sensitive a transposition of the play as *Throne of Blood* was of *Macbeth*.' – *Tony Rayns, MFB*

'Too inclined to soft-focus ramblings through pretty countryside with characters' dubbed voices failing to match their lip movements. Odd but worthwhile.' – *Empire*

† The film was cut to 102m in its English version.

Tish

US   1942   84m   bw
Orville O. Dull/MGM

A maiden aunt tries to guide her family's life.

Boring domestic taradiddles which waste a good cast.

w Harry Ruskin   *stories* Mary Roberts Rinehart   *d* S. Sylvan Simon

Marjorie Main, ZaSu Pitts, Aline MacMahon, Susan Peters, Lee Bowman, Guy Kibbee, Virginia Grey, Richard Quine, Al Shean

Tit for Tat *

US   1934   20m   bw
Hal Roach

Adjoining shopkeepers violently settle an old difference.

Archetypal late star comedy: brilliant timing, but the warmth and sympathy have begun to ebb.

w Stan Laurel   *d* Charles Rogers

Laurel and Hardy, Charlie Hall, Mae Busch

AAN: best short

Titanic *

US   1953   98m   bw
TCF (Charles Brackett)

Personal dramas aboard the *Titanic* in 1912 come to a head as the ship hits an iceberg.

An excellent example of studio production is squandered on a dim script which arouses no excitement.

w Charles Brackett, Walter Reisch, Richard Breen d Jean Negulesco ph Joe MacDonald m Sol Kaplan ad Lyle Wheeler, Maurice Ransford

Clifton Webb, Barbara Stanwyck, Robert Wagner, Audrey Dalton, Thelma Ritter, Brian Aherne, Richard Basehart, Allyn Joslyn

AA: script

AAN: art direction

The Titfield Thunderbolt ***
GB   1952   84m   Technicolor
Ealing (Michael Truman)
V

When a branch railway line is threatened with closure, the villagers take it over as a private concern.

Undervalued on its release in the wake of other Ealing comedies, this now seems among the best of them as well as an immaculate colour production showing the England that is no more; the script has pace, the whole thing is brightly polished and the action works up to a fine climactic frenzy.

w T. E. B. Clarke   d Charles Crichton   ph Douglas Slocombe   m Georges Auric

Stanley Holloway, George Relph, John Gregson, Godfrey Tearle, Edie Martin, Naunton Wayne, Gabrielle Brune, Hugh Griffith, Sidney James, Jack McGowran, Ewan Roberts, Reginald Beckwith

T-Men *
US   1947   96m   bw
Eagle Lion (Aubrey Schenck)
V*

Treasury Department detectives trail a gang of counterfeiters.

Tough, well-made crime melodrama which still packs a punch in the traditional vein.

w John C. Higgins   d Anthony Mann   ph John Alton   m Paul Sawtell

Dennis O'Keefe, Alfred Ryder, Mary Meade, Wallace Ford, June Lockhart, Charles McGraw, Jane Randolph, Art Smith

To Be or Not to Be ****
US   1942   99m   bw
Alexander Korda/Ernst Lubitsch
V*

Warsaw actors get involved in an underground plot and an impersonation of invading Nazis, including Hitler.

Marvellous free-wheeling entertainment which starts as drama and descends through romantic comedy and suspense into farce; accused of bad taste at the time, but now seen as an outstanding example of Hollywood moonshine, kept alight through sheer talent and expertise.

w Edwin Justus Mayer,   story Ernst Lubitsch, Melchior Lengyel   d Ernst Lubitsch   ph Rudolph Maté m Werner Heymann   ad Vincent Korda

Jack Benny, Carole Lombard, Robert Stack, Stanley Ridges, Felix Bressart, Lionel Atwill, Sig Rumann, Tom Dugan, Charles Halton

TURA in disguise (Jack Benny): 'That great, great Polish actor Joseph Tura – you must have heard of him.'
ERHARDT (Sig Rumann): 'Ah, yes . . . what he did to Shakespeare, we are now doing to Poland!'
ERHARDT (and others): 'So they call me Concentration Camp Erhardt!'

'The comedy is hilarious, even when it is hysterically thrilling.' – Commonweal

'As effective an example of comic propaganda as The Great Dictator and far better directed.' – Charles Higham, 1972

'Based on an indiscretion, but undoubtedly a work of art.' – James Agee

'In any other medium it would be acknowledged as a classic to rank with The Alchemist or A Modest Proposal.' – Peter Barnes

'Lubitsch's comic genius and corrosive wit are displayed at every turn.' – John Baxter

'The actual business at hand . . . is nothing less than providing a good time at the expense of Nazi myth . . . Lubitsch distinguishes the film's zanier moments with his customary mastery of sly humour and innuendo, and when the story calls for outright melodrama he is more than equal to the occasion.' – Newsweek

AAN: Werner Heymann

To Be or Not to Be
US   1983   107m   DeLuxe
TCF/Brooksfilms (Mel Brooks)
V, V*, L

Flat-footed remake of the above, with stagey sets, unconvincing acting (including the unnecessary addition of a gay dresser) and a leading comedian who won't stay still in case his lack of style should be noticed.

w Thomas Meehan, Ronnie Graham   d Alan Johnson   ph Gerald Hirschfeld   m John Morris pd Terence Marsh

Mel Brooks, Anne Bancroft, Tim Matheson, Charles Durning, José Ferrer, George Gaynes, Christopher Lloyd, James Haake

AAN: Charles Durning

To Catch a Thief *
US   1955   97m   Technicolor   Vistavision
Paramount/Alfred Hitchcock
V, V*, L

A famous cat burglar who has retired to the Riviera catches a thief who is imitating his old style.

Very slow, floppy and rather boring entertainment enlivened by the scenery and the odd Hitchcock touch.

w John Michael Hayes   novel David Dodge d Alfred Hitchcock   ph Robert Burks   m Lyn Murray   md Hal Pereira, Joseph McMillan Johnson

Cary Grant, Grace Kelly, Jessie Royce Landis, John Williams, Charles Vanel, Brigitte Auber

'Why should I steal? I'm rich.'
— 'How did you get rich?'
'By stealing.'

'Billed as a comedy-mystery, it stacks up as a drawn-out pretentious piece that seldom hits the comedy level.' – Variety

AA: Robert Burks

AAN: art direction

'Don't let the frilly shirt fool you. This man can kill without stirring a ruffle.'

To Commit a Murder (dubbed)
France/West Germany/Italy   1967   91m
   Eastmancolor
Cinerama/SNEG/Gaumont/Waterview/Eichberg/Franca (Alan Poiré)
original title: Peau d'Espion

A writer becomes involved in a plot to kidnap a nuclear scientist and take him to China.

Confused and confusing thriller, long on talk and short on action.

w Edouard Molinaro, Jacques Robert   novel Peau d'Espion by Jacques Robert   d Eduardo Molinaro ph Raymond Le Moigne   m José Berghmans ad Robert Clavel, Olivier Girard   ed Robert Isnardon, Monique Isnardon

Louis Jourdan, Senta Berger, Edmond O'Brien, Bernard Blier

'A sleepy espionage yarn which almost grinds to a halt at the halfway mark.' – David McGillivray, Films and Filming

'As long as there are lovers – this picture will live!' 'Paramount proudly brings to the screens of America one of the three great love stories of all time!'

To Each His Own **
US   1946   100m   bw
Paramount (Charles Brackett)

During World War II, a middle-aged woman in London meets the soldier who is her own illegitimate and long-since-adopted son.

The woman's picture par excellence, put together with tremendous Hollywood flair and extremely enjoyable to watch.

w Charles Brackett, Jacques Théry   d Mitchell Leisen   ph Daniel L. Fapp   m Victor Young   ad Hans Dreier, Roland Anderson

Olivia de Havilland, John Lund, Roland Culver, Mary Anderson, Philip Terry, Bill Goodwin, Virginia Welles, Virginia Horne

AA: Olivia de Havilland

AAN: original story (Charles Brackett)

To Find a Man *
US   1971   93m   Eastmancolor
Columbia/Rastar (Irving Pincus)

The spoiled daughter of a rich family becomes pregnant and is helped by a young chemist.

Quiet, well-made minor drama about maturity, with good small-town atmosphere.

w Arnold Schulman,   novel S. J. Wilson   d Buzz Kulik   ph Andy Laszlo   m David Shire

Pamela Martin, Darrell O'Connor, Lloyd Bridges, Phyllis Newman, Tom Ewell, Tom Bosley

To Have and Have Not **
US   1945   100m   bw
Warner (Howard Hawks)
V, V*, L

An American charter boat captain in Martinique gets involved with Nazis.

Fairly routinely made studio adventure notable for first pairing of Bogart and Bacall, as an imitation of Casablanca, and for its consistent though not outstanding entertainment value. Remade later as The Breaking Point (qv) and The Gun Runners (qv), and not dissimilar from Key Largo (qv).

w Jules Furthman, William Faulkner,   novel Ernest Hemingway   d Howard Hawks   ph Sid Hickox md Leo F. Forbstein   m Franz Waxman (uncredited)

Humphrey Bogart, Lauren Bacall, Walter Brennan, Hoagy Carmichael, Dolores Moran, Sheldon Leonard, Dan Seymour, Marcel Dalio

'Remarkable for the ingenuity and industry with which the original story and the individualities of Ernest Hemingway have been rendered down into Hollywood basic.' – Richard Winnington

'Sunlight on the lattice, sex in the corridors, a new pianist at the café, pistol shots, the fat sureté man coming round after dark.' – William Whitebait

To Hell and Back
US   1955   106m   Technicolor   Cinemascope
U-I (Aaron Rosenberg)
V (W), V*

The war career of America's most decorated infantryman.

Routine war story which happens to be about a fellow who later became a film star.

w Gil Doud   book Audie Murphy   d Jesse Hibbs ph Maury Gertsman   m Joseph Gershenson

Audie Murphy, Marshall Thompson, Charles Drake, Gregg Palmer, Jack Kelly, Paul Picerni, Susan Kohner

'The emotion is congealed and there is no real personal response to the anguish of war.' – *John Gillett*

To Kill a Clown

GB   1971   104m   DeLuxe
Palomar (Theodore Sills)
V*

A painter and his wife move to a New England isle and are menaced by a crippled Vietnam veteran and his vicious dogs.

Pretentious, politically oriented rehash of *The Most Dangerous Game* (qv), carefully made but too slow for suspense.

w George Bloomfield, I. C. Rapoport   *novel Master of the Hounds* by Algis Budrys   d George Bloomfield   ph Walter Lassally   m Richard Hill, John Hawkins

Alan Alda, Blythe Danner, Heath Lamberts, Eric Clavering

To Kill a Mockingbird **

US   1962   129m   bw
U-I (Alan Pakula)
V, V*, L, S

A lawyer in a small Southern town defends a black man accused of rape.

Familiar dollops of social conscience, very well presented with a child interest and excellent atmosphere, but a mite overlong.

w Horton Foote   *novel* Harper Lee   d Robert Mulligan   ph Russell Harlan   m Elmer Bernstein

Gregory Peck, Mary Badham, Philip Alford, John Megna, Frank Overton, Rosemary Murphy, Ruth White, Brock Peters

† The narrator is Kim Stanley

AA: script; Gregory Peck

AAN: best picture; Robert Mulligan; Russell Harlan; Elmer Bernstein; Mary Badham

To Kill a Priest

France/US   1988   113m   colour
J. P. Productions/FR3/Sofica Valor (Jean-Pierre Alessandri)
V*, L

A militant Polish priest runs foul of the local police chief.

Vaguely based on the life and death of Father Jerzy Popieluszko, a proponent of trade unions, it fails to make explicit the political and ideological events it attempts to portray.

w Agnieszka Holland, Jean-Yves Pitoun   d Agnieszka Holland   ph Adam Holender   pd Emile Ghigo   ed Herve de Luze

Christophe Lambert, Ed Harris, Joss Ackland, Tim Roth, Timothy Spall, Peter Postlethwaite, Cherie Lunghi, Joanne Whalley, David Suchet

To Live and Die in L.A.

US   1985   116m   Technicolor
MGM-UA/New Century/SLM/Irving H. Levin
V, V*, L, S

A secret service agent nails the counterfeiter who killed his partner.

High-gloss, foul-mouthed, hysterical crime melo, a kind of west coast *French Connection*.

w William Friedkin, Gerald Petievich   *novel* Gerald Petievich   d William Friedkin   ph Robby Muller   m Wang Chung   pd Lilly Kilvert   ed Scott Smith

William L. Petersen, William Dafoe, John Pankow, Debra Feuer, Dean Stockwell, John Turturro, Darlanne Fluegel

'The intense vulgarity of the characters and virtuoso stylistic overkill will turn off mainstream audiences.' – *Variety*

To Mary with Love

US   1936   87m   bw
TCF

A businessman thinks back affectionately over ten years of married life.

Harmless romantic comedy-drama.

w Richard Sherman, Howard Ellis Smith   d John Cromwell

Warner Baxter, Myrna Loy, Ian Hunter, Claire Trevor, Jean Dixon

To Our Loves *

France   1983   102m   colour
Les Films Du Livradois/Gaumont/FR3 (Micheline Pialat)
V*

A teenage girl, whose parents are splitting up, looks for love and settles for promiscuity.

Domestic misery from a specialist in teenage angst.

w Arlette Langman, Maurice Pialat   d Maurice Pialat   ph Jacques Loiseleux   ed Yann Dedet

Sandrine Bonnaire, Evelyne Ker, Dominique Besnehard, Maurice Pialat, Christopher Odent

To Paris with Love

GB   1954   78m   Technicolor
GFD/Two Cities (Anthony Darnborough)

A middle-aged widower and his son go to Paris on holiday and devise matrimonial plans for each other.

Thin, disappointing taradiddle which is short but seems long.

w Robert Buckner   d Robert Hamer   ph Reg Wyer   m Edwin Astley

Alec Guinness, Vernon Gray, Odile Versois, Jacques François, Elina Labourdette, Austin Trevor

'The general impression is somehow too aimless, too muted.' – *Gavin Lambert*

'John Davis came on the set one day and said: Give us some pratfalls, Alec, give us some laughs. I realized there and then that I was not going to fit in.' – *Alec Guinness*

To Please a Lady *

US   1950   91m   bw
MGM (Clarence Brown)

A ruthless midget-car racer falls for the lady journalist who is hounding him.

Good action programmer with no frills.

w Barre Lyndon, Marge Decker   d Clarence Brown   ph Harold Rosson   m Bronislau Kaper

Clark Gable, Barbara Stanwyck, Adolphe Menjou, Will Geer, Roland Winters, Emory Parnell, Frank Jenks

'A story as fresh as the girls in their minis!'

To Sir with Love

GB   1967   105m   Technicolor
Columbia (James Clavell)
V, V*

A West Indian teacher comes to a tough East End school.

Sentimental non-realism patterned after *The Blackboard Jungle* but much softer; its influence led to a TV situation comedy, *Please Sir*.

wd James Clavell   *novel* E. R. Braithwaite   ph Paul Beeson   m Ron Grainer

Sidney Poitier, Christian Roberts, Judy Geeson, Suzy Kendall, Lulu, Faith Brook, Geoffrey Bayldon, Patricia Routledge

'The sententious script sounds as if it has been written by a zealous Sunday school teacher after a particularly exhilarating boycott of South African oranges.' – *MFB*

To Sleep with Anger **

US   1990   102m   CFI
Metro/SVS Films (Caldecott Chubb, Thomas S. Byrnes, Darin Scott)
V*

A black family which has moved from the South to Los Angeles finds itself in trouble when an old friend visits with stories of the past.

Engrossing drama of social disintegration.

wd Charles Burnett   ph Walt Lloyd   m Stephen James Taylor   pd Penny Barrett   ed Nancy Richardson

Danny Glover, Paul Butler, Mary Alice, Carl Lumbly, Vonetta McGee, Richard Brooks, Sheryl Lee Ralph, Ethel Ayler, Julius Harris

'With a whole string of superb performances, dialogue that manages the difficult trick of hitting notes both lyrical and earthy, and a magical gospel and blues score, it demonstrates Burnett's instinct for cinema every inch of the way.' – *Tom Milne, MFB*

To Telefteo Psemma: see *A Matter of Dignity*

'It's more than just a sport. It's survival.'
To the Death

US   1991   86m   Agfa colour
Cannon/Distant Horizon/Tangent (Anant Singh)
V, V*

A retired kick-boxing champion is lured back into the ring by a corrupt gambler who organizes private fights in which the loser is shot.

Numbingly predictable nonsense, acted and directed with the sensitivity of a boot in the face. The dialogue seems to have strayed from a Victorian melodrama.

w Greg Latter   *story* Darrell James Roodt, Greg Latter   d Darrell James Roodt   ph Mark Vicente   m Frank Becker   pd David Barkham   ed Davedd Heitner

John Barrett, Michel Qissi, Robert Whitehead, Michèle Bestbier, Greg Latter

Husband to wife surprised in bed with another man: 'Why? Why? Why? Oh God! I give you everything your heart desires and this is how you repay me!'

To the Devil a Daughter

GB/Germany   1976   93m   Technicolor
EMI/Hammer-Terra Filmkunst (Roy Skeggs)
V, V*

An occult novelist is asked to take care of a girl who has been 'promised' to a group of Satanists.

Confusingly told, high camp diabolic thriller.

w Chris Wicking   *novel* Dennis Wheatley   d Peter Sykes   ph David Watkin   m Paul Glass   ad Don Picton   sp Les Bowie   ed John Trumper

Richard Widmark, Christopher Lee, Denholm Elliott, Honor Blackman, Michael Goodliffe, Anthony Valentine, Derek Francis, Nastassja Kinski

To the Ends of the Earth **

US   1948   107m   bw
Columbia (Sidney Buchman)

A government agent follows a world-wide trail after a narcotics gang.

Thoroughly riveting conventional thriller, nicely made and photographed.

w Jay Richard Kennedy   d Robert Stevenson   ph Burnett Guffey   m George Duning

Dick Powell, Signe Hasso, Ludwig Donath, Vladimir Sokoloff, Edgar Barrier

To the Shores of Tripoli

US   1942   82m   Technicolor
TCF (Milton Sperling)
V*

A cocky playboy becomes a tough marine.

Despite the title, this modest flagwaver with romantic trimmings never moves out of the San Diego training grounds.

w Lamar Trotti   d Bruce Humberstone   ph Edward Cronjager   m Alfred Newman

Maureen O'Hara, John Payne, Randolph Scott, Nancy Kelly, William Tracy, Maxie Rosenbloom, Henry Morgan, Russell Hicks, Minor Watson

AAN: cinematography

To the Victor (1938): see Owd Bob

To the Victor
US   1948   100m   bw
Warner (Jerry Wald)

French collaborators stand trial for war crimes.

Glum melodrama with inadequate cast.

w Richard Brooks   d Delmer Daves   ph Robert Burks   m David Buttolph

Dennis Morgan, Viveca Lindfors, Bruce Bennett, Victor Francen, Dorothy Malone, Tom d'Andrea, Eduardo Ciannelli, Joseph Buloff, Luis Van Rooten, William Conrad

To Trap a Spy
US   1966   92m   Metrocolor
MGM (Norman Felton)

American secret agents protect an African diplomat from being killed.

An extended version of the pilot for the television series The Man from U.N.C.L.E.; despite it, they still went ahead with more episodes.

w Sam Rolfe   d Don Medford   ph Joseph Biroc   m Jerry Goldsmith   ad George W. Davis, Merrill Pye   ed Henry Berman

Robert Vaughn, David McCallum, Luciana Paluzzi, Patricia Crowley, Fritz Weaver, Will Kuluva, Leo G. Carroll

To What Red Hell
GB   1929   100m   bw
Strand/Twickenham

A young epileptic kills a prostitute and is protected by his mother.

Unpalatable melodrama which failed to be as significant as it wished.

w Leslie Hiscott   play Percy Robinson   d Edwin Greenwood

Sybil Thorndike, John Hamilton, Bramwell Fletcher, Janice Adair

The Toast of New Orleans
US   1950   97m   Technicolor
MGM (Joe Pasternak)
V*

A Bayou villager becomes a star of the New Orleans opera.

Very ordinary setting for a new singing star.

w Sy Gomberg, George Wells   d Norman Taurog   ph William Snyder   md George Stoll   ch Eugene Loring

Kathryn Grayson, David Niven, Mario Lanza, J. Carrol Naish, James Mitchell, Richard Hageman, Clinton Sundberg, Sig Arno

'Sheer excruciation.' – Pauline Kael, New Yorker

AAN: song 'Be My Love' (m Nicholas Brodszky, ly Sammy Cahn)

'The screen sensation of a decade, played by a galaxy of stars in a hell-bent world of wine and women!'
The Toast of New York **
US   1937   109m   bw
RKO (Edward Small)
V*, L

A 19th-century medicine showman becomes a notorious Wall Street financier.

Smart biopic of Jim Fisk; good entertainment with accomplished production.

w Dudley Nichols, John Twist, Joel Sayre   d Rowland V. Lee   ph Peverell Marley   m Nathaniel Shilkret

Edward Arnold, Cary Grant, Frances Farmer, Jack Oakie, Donald Meek, Clarence Kolb, Thelma Leeds

'Making no pretence for serious consideration as a faithful and accurate reflection of life and manners in the period it depicts, it rates as a piece of hokum aimed at the box office. It will do business.' – Variety

Toast of the Legion: see Kiss Me Again (1931)

Tobacco Road ***
US   1941   84m   bw
TCF (Jack Kirkland, Harry H. Oshrin)

Poor whites in Georgia are turned off their land.

This bowdlerized version of a sensational book and play has superbly orchestrated farcical scenes separated by delightfully pictorial quieter moments: it isn't what was intended, but in its own way it's quite marvellous.

w Nunnally Johnson,   play Jack Kirkland   novel Erskine Caldwell   d John Ford   ph Arthur Miller   m David Buttolph

Charley Grapewin, Elizabeth Patterson, Dana Andrews, Gene Tierney, Marjorie Rambeau, Ward Bond, William Tracy, Zeffie Tilbury, Slim Summerville, Grant Mitchell, Russell Simpson, Spencer Charters

Tobruk
US   1967   110m   Techniscope
Universal/Corman/Gibraltar (Gene Corman)
V*

During the North African war, a British major and some German Jews try to blow up the Nazi fuel bunkers.

Routine war adventure, quite tough and spectacular but undistinguished.

w Leo V. Gordon   d Arthur Hiller   ph Russell Harlan   m Bronislau Kaper   ad Alexander Golitzen, Henry Bumstead   ed Robert C. Jones

Rock Hudson, George Peppard, Nigel Green, Guy Stockwell, Jack Watson, Liam Redmond, Leo Gordon, Norman Rossington, Percy Herbert

AAN: special effects

Toby Tyler *
US   1959   96m   Technicolor
Walt Disney (Bill Walsh)
V*

In 1910, a young orphan runs away to join a travelling circus in the midwest, and with the help of a chimp becomes a famous star.

Acceptable, predictable family fare.

w Bill Walsh, Lillie Hayward   novel James Otis Kaler   d Charles Barton   ph William Snyder   m Buddy Baker

Kevin Corcoran, Henry Calvin, Gene Sheldon, Bob Sweeney, James Drury

Today We Live *
US   1933   113m   bw
MGM (Howard Hawks)

During World War I, an aristocratic English girl and her three lovers all find themselves at the front, and two fail to return.

Stilted romantic melodrama with imposing credentials.

w Edith Fitzgerald, Dwight Taylor, William Faulkner   story Turnabout by William Faulkner   d Howard Hawks   ph Oliver T. Marsh

Joan Crawford, Gary Cooper, Robert Young, Franchot Tone, Roscoe Karns, Louise Closser Hale, Rollo Lloyd

'One of those overly long features which would serve the purpose better in 2000 or more less feet . . . but the action, the men and the Crawford name should translate into satisfying figures.' – Variety

† Much of the flying footage was taken from the Hell's Angels stock.

The Todd Killings *
US   1970   93m   Technicolor   Panavision
National General (Barry Shear)
V*

In a small American town, a 23-year-old boy starts out on a rampage of rape and murder.

Violent psychological melodrama, based on fact, with inventive direction.

w Dennis Murphy, Joe L. Oliansky   d Barry Shear   ph Harold E. Stine   m Leonard Rosenman

Robert F. Lyons, Richard Thomas, Belinda Montgomery, Barbara Bel Geddes, Gloria Grahame

'The most striking of the many recent film versions of the souring of the American dream.' – Tony Rayns

Together Again
US   1944   93m   bw
Columbia (Virginia Van Upp)

The widow of a New England mayor commissions a statue in his honour. The title refers to the reteaming of the stars who were so popular in Love Affair and When Tomorrow Comes, which is a sign of the lack of invention elsewhere.

A comedy without laughs.

w Virginia Van Upp, F. Hugh Herbert   d Charles Vidor   ph Joseph Walker   m Werner Heymann

Charles Boyer, Irene Dunne, Charles Coburn, Mona Freeman, Jerome Courtland, Elizabeth Patterson, Charles Dingle, Walter Baldwin

Tokyo Drifter **
Japan   1966   83m   colour   Nikkatsu-Scope
Nikkatsu (Nakagawa Tetsuro)
original title: Tokyo Nagaremono; aka: The Man from Tokyo

A hitman goes on the run around Japan, followed by killers hired by his former boss.

An enjoyably delirious thriller in which virtually anything goes, including a parody of a bar brawl straight out of a John Wayne Western. It has an exotic appeal, together with a flamboyant visual style.

w Kawauchi Yasunori   novel Kawauchi Yasunori   d Suzuki Seijun   ph Mine Shigeyoshi   m Kaburagi So   ad Kimura Takeo   ed Inoue Shinya

Watari Tetsuya, Matsubara Chieko, Nitani Hideaki, Kita Ryuji, Yoshida Tsuyoshi, Esumi Hideaki, Kawachi Tamio, Cho Hiroshi

'A barrage of aestheticised violence, visual gags, incongruous songs and hairdryers and mind-warping colour effects. This is a reckless reduction of the yazuka genre to its most fundamental elements, strung together with only the most minimal regard for logic or even narrative coherence.' – Tony Rayns

Tokyo Joe
US   1949   88m   bw
Columbia/Santana (Robert Lord)
V*, L

A former night-club owner returns to postwar Japan to reclaim his fortune and his ex-wife.

Dispirited star melodrama.

w Cyril Hume, Bertram Millhauser   d Stuart Heisler   ph Charles Lawton Jnr   m George Antheil

Humphrey Bogart, Florence Marly, Alexander Knox, Sessue Hayakawa, Lora Lee Michel, Jerome Courtland

Tokyo Monogatari: see *Tokyo Story*

Tokyo Nagaremono: see *Tokyo Drifter*

Tokyo Pop
US   1988   99m   TVC colour
Fries/Spectrafilm/Lorimar/Kuzui (Kaz Kuzui, Joel Tuber)
V*, L

A backing singer in a New York punk rock group goes to Tokyo in search of fame.

Mildly entertaining tale of cultural cross-over.

w Fran Rubel Kuzui, Lynn Grossman   d Fran Rubel Kuzui   ph James Hayman   m Alan Brewer
pd Terumi Hosoishi   ed Camilla Toniolo

Carrie Hamilton, Yutaka Tadokoro, Daisuke Oyama, Hiroshi Kabayashi, Hiroshi Sugita, Satoshi Kanai.

Tokyo Story **
Japan   1953   135m   bw
Shochiku
V, V*
original title: *Tokyo Monogatari*

An elderly couple, who travel to Tokyo to visit their married son and daughter, discover that their children have little time for them.

Bleak, austere and moving family drama of life's disappointments.

w Kogo Noda, Yasujiro Ozu   d *Yasujiro Ozu*
ph Yuharu Atsuta   m Kojun Saito   ad Tatsuo Hamada   ed Yoshiyasu Hamamura

Chishu Ryu, Chieko Higashiyama, Setsuko Hara, Haruko Sugimura, Nobuo Nakamura, So Yamamura, Kuniko Miyaki, Eijiro Tono

Tol'able David *
US   1921   80m approx (24 fps)   bw   silent
First National/Inspiration
V*

A quiet farming community is disrupted by three marauding convicts, who are finally despatched by the peace-loving youngest son.

Fresh, sympathetic David-and-Goliath story which was a huge popular success on its release.

w Edmund Goulding, Henry King   novel Joseph Hergesheimer   d *Henry King*   ph Henry Cronjager

Richard Barthelmess, Gladys Hulette, Ernest Torrence, Warner Richmond

'It is sentimental in places, but not sloppy. It is bucolic, but its rusticity is not rubbed in . . . it is restrained, imaginatively suggestive when not briefly literal. For all these reasons it is stimulating.' – *New York Times*

† Columbia remade the story in 1930 with Richard Cromwell, but its time had passed.

Tom and Jerry: The Movie
US   1992   84m   CFI colour
First Independent/Turner/WMG (Phil Roman)
V, V*

Tom and Jerry, left homeless, become the best of friends.

A lacklustre cartoon, which replaces the inspired mayhem of the classic shorts with sickly sweetness.

w Dennis Marks   d Phil Roman   m Henry Mancini
ed Julie Ann Gustafson

voices of Richard Kind, Dana Hill, Anndi McAfee, Henry Gibson, Tony Jay

'Though slickly animated, this first full-length pic featuring the vintage cat and mouse is misconceived from start to finish. Full of gooey sentimentality in a banal melodramatic plot.' – *Variety*

Tom Brown of Culver
US   1932   79m   bw
Universal

Life at a military cadet school.

Idealized propaganda, with the hero a boy subsidized by the local legion because his dead father was a war hero.

w Tom Beckingham   d William Wyler

Tom Brown, H. B. Warner, Slim Summerville, Richard Cromwell, Ben Alexander, Sidney Toler, Betty Blythe

'It will probably make acceptable film fare to other than irritated cadets.' – *Variety*

Tom Brown's Schooldays *
US   1940   86m   bw
(RKO) The Play's the Thing (Gene Towne, Graham Baker)
V*

Tom Brown finds life at Rugby brutal, but helps to become a civilizing influence.

Pretty lively Hollywood version of a rather unattractive semi-classic.

w Walter Ferris, Frank Cavell   novel Thomas Hughes   d Robert Stevenson   ph Nicholas Musuraca   m Anthony Collins

Jimmy Lydon, Cedric Hardwicke, Billy Halop, Freddie Bartholomew, Gale Storm, Josephine Hutchinson

Tom Brown's Schooldays
GB   1951   96m   bw
Talisman (George Minter)
V*

Unexciting remake featuring one surprisingly strong performance.

w Noel Langley   d Gordon Parry   ph C. Pennington-Richards   m Richard Addinsell

Robert Newton, John Howard Davies, Diana Wynyard, Francis de Wolff, Kathleen Byron, Hermione Baddeley, James Hayter, Rachel Gurney, Amy Veness, Max Bygraves, Michael Hordern, John Charlesworth, John Forrest

'An odd mixture of the brutal and the solemnly improving.' – *Richard Mallett, Punch*

Tom, Dick and Harry **
US   1941   86m   bw
RKO (Robert Sisk)
V*, L

A girl daydreams about her three boyfriends, but can't make up her mind.

Brightly-handled comedy which became a minor classic but does seem to have faded a little. Remade as *The Girl Most Likely* (qv).

w Paul Jarrico   d Garson Kanin   ph Merrit Gerstad   m Roy Webb

Ginger Rogers, Burgess Meredith, Alan Marshal, George Murphy, *Phil Silvers,* Joe Cunningham, Jane Seymour, Lenore Lonergan

'Foot by foot the best made picture of this year.' – *Otis Ferguson*

AAN: Paul Jarrico

Tom Horn
US   1979   97m   Technicolor   Panavision
Warner/Solar/First Artists (Fred Weintraub)
V, V*

An ex-cavalry scout gets a job as a stock detective, is framed for murder, and allows himself to be hanged.

Curious pessimistic and unsatisfactory semi-Western in which the star was found to have lost his old charisma after being too long away.

w Thomas McGuane, Bid Shrake, from the alleged autobiography of Tom Horn   d William Wiard
ph John Alonzo   m Ernest Gold

Steve McQueen, Linda Evans, Richard Farnsworth, Billy Green Bush, Slim Pickens, Elisha Cook Jnr
'Imagine a film that opens up with dialogue that can't

be heard at all, then proceeds to build up to a fist fight that's never seen, that cuts away to sunsets to fill in other scenes that have no dramatic point, that presents a meal where the sound of knives and forks drowns out what's being said, and you have just the beginning of what's wrong with *Tom Horn.*' – *Variety*

'The whole world loves him!'
Tom Jones **
GB   1963   129m   Eastmancolor
UA/Woodfall (Tony Richardson)
V, V*, L

In 18th-century England a foundling is brought up by the squire and marries his daughter after many adventures.

Fantasia on Old England, at some distance from the original novel, with the director trying every possible jokey approach against a meticulously realistic physical background. Despite trade fears, the *Hellzapoppin* style made it an astonishing box-office success (the sex helped), though it quickly lost its freshness and was much imitated.

w *John Osborne,*   novel Henry Fielding   d Tony Richardson   ph Walter Lassally, Manny Wynn   m John Addison   pd Ralph Brinton

Albert Finney, Susannah York, Hugh Griffith, Edith Evans, Joan Greenwood, Diane Cilento, George Devine, Joyce Redman, David Warner, Wilfrid Lawson, Freda Jackson, Rachel Kempson

'Uncertainty, nervousness, muddled method . . . desperation is writ large over it.' – *Stanley Kauffmann*

'Much of the time it looks like a home movie, made with sporadic talent by a group with more enthusiasm than discipline.' – *Tom Milne*

'It is as though the camera had become a method actor: there are times when you wish you could buy, as on certain juke boxes, five minutes' silence . . . Obviously a film which elicits such lyric ejaculations from the reviewers cannot be all good.' – *John Simon*

'I just felt I was being used. I wasn't involved . . . I was bored most of the time.' – *Albert Finney*

† The narrator was Michael MacLiammoir.

AA: best picture; John Osborne; Tony Richardson; John Addison

AAN: Albert Finney; Hugh Griffith; Edith Evans; Diane Cilento; Joyce Redman

Tom Sawyer
US   1973   103m   DeLuxe   Panavision
UA/Readers Digest (Arthur P. Jacobs)
V*

Reverential, rather tediously over-produced version for family audiences of the seventies, with brief songs and real Mississippi locations.

w/m/ly Richard and Robert Sherman   d Don Taylor
ph Frank Stanley   md John Williams   pd Philip Jefferies

Johnnie Whitaker, Celeste Holm, Warren Oates, Jeff East, Jodie Foster

† There had been a version with Jackie Coogan in 1930. Selznick's *The Adventures of Tom Sawyer* followed in 1937. In 1939 Billy Cook was Tom Sawyer, Detective, with Donald O'Connor as Huckleberry Finn.

AAN: Richard and Robert Sherman; John Williams

Tom Thumb *
GB   1958   98m   Eastmancolor
MGM/Galaxy (George Pal)
V*, L

A tiny forest boy outwits a couple of thieves.

Slight musical built round the legend of a two-inch boy; good trickwork and songs make it a delightful film for children.

w Ladislas Fodor *d* George Pal *ph* Georges Périnal *m* Douglas Gamley, Kenneth V. Jones *sp* Tom Howard

Russ Tamblyn, Jessie Matthews, Peter Sellers, Terry-Thomas, Alan Young, June Thorburn, Bernard Miles, Ian Wallace

† Donald O'Connor badly wanted the role, but it went to the MGM contractee.

AA: special effects

Tomahawk
US   1951   82m   Technicolor
Universal-International
GB title: *Battle of Powder River*

An Indian scout helps the Sioux to get their territory rights.

Competent small-scale Western.

w Silvia Richards, Maurice Geraghty *d* George Sherman

Van Heflin, Yvonne de Carlo, Alex Nicol, Preston Foster, Jack Oakie, Tom Tully, Rock Hudson

The Tomahawk and the Cross: see *Pillars of the Sky*

The Tomb of Ligeia **
GB   1964   81m   Eastmancolor   Cinemascope
American International (Roger Corman)
V*, L

A brooding Victorian metamorphoses his dead wife into a cat, then into the beautiful Lady Rowena.

Complex but rather fascinating horror suspenser which rejogs familiar elements into something new; the best of the Corman Poes.

w Robert Towne story Edgar Allan Poe *d* Roger Corman *ph* Arthur Grant *m* Kenneth V. Jones

Vincent Price, Elizabeth Shepherd, John Westbrook, Oliver Johnston, Richard Johnson, Derek Francis

Tomb of the Living Dead: see *The Mad Doctor of Blood Island*

Tombs of the Blind Dead (dubbed)
Spain/Portugal   1972   86m   Eastmancolor
Plata/Interfilme
V, V*
original title: *La Noche del Terror Ciego*; aka: *The Blind Dead*

Devil-worshipping Knights Templar, killed at the time of the Crusades, rise from their graves to kill all they encounter.

Gruesome, low-budget horror with a few original touches; it proved popular enough to spawn a few sequels.

wd Amando de Ossorio *ph* Pablo Ripoli *ad* Jaime Duarte de Brito *ed* José Antonio Rojo

Cesar Burner, Lone Fleming, Joseph Thelman, Helen Harp, Rufino Ingles, Veronica Llimera, Maria Sylva

† It was followed by *The Return of the Evil Dead* (qv).

'Justice is coming.'
Tombstone *
US   1993   129m   Technicolor   Panavision
Entertainment/Cinergi (James Jacks, Sean Daniel, Bob Misiorowski)
S

After his brother is killed in Tombstone, Wyatt Earp and his friend Doc Holliday take on the lawless Clanton gang.

Vigorous retelling of the incidents that led up to the famous gunfight at the OK Corral, celebrating Earp as the archetypal Western hero.

w Kevin Jarre *d* George P. Cosmatos *ph* William A. Fraker *m* Bruce Broughton *pd* Catherine Hardwicke *ed* Frank J. Urioste, Roberto Silvi, Harvey Rosenstock

Kurt Russell, Val Kilmer, Sam Elliott, Bill Paxton, Powers Boothe, Michael Biehn, Charlton Heston, Jason Priestley, Jon Tenney, Stephen Lang, Robert Mitchum (narrator)

'A tough-talking but soft-hearted tale that is entertaining in a sprawling, old-fashioned manner.' – *Variety*

† Kevin Jarre was replaced as director during shooting.

'Good men (and women) live in Tombstone – but not for long!'
Tombstone (The Town Too Tough to Die)
US   1942   80m   bw
Paramount

How Wyatt Earp cleaned up the town.

Lacklustre low-budget version of a famous story.

w Albert Shelby Le Vino, Edward E. Paramore *d* William McGann

Richard Dix, Frances Gifford, Kent Taylor, Edgar Buchanan, Don Castle, Victor Jory

Tommy *
GB   1975   108m   colour
Hemdale/Robert Stigwood
V, V*, L

A deaf, dumb and blind child is eventually cured and becomes a rock celebrity.

Mystical rock opera screened with the director's usual barrage of effects and an ear-splitting score. Of occasional interest.

w Ken Russell opera Pete Townshend and the Who *d* Ken Russell *ph* Dick Bush, Ronnie Taylor *m* Pete Townshend and the Who

Roger Daltrey, Ann-Margret, Oliver Reed, Elton John, Eric Clapton, Keith Moon

AAN: Ann-Margret; score

Tommy the Toreador
GB   1959   86m   Technicolor
Fanfare/AB
V

A seaman takes the place of a bullfighter framed for smuggling.

Acceptable star comedy of its time.

w Nicholas Phipps, Sid Colin, Talbot Rothwell *d* John Paddy Carstairs

Tommy Steele, Sid James, Janet Munro, Pepe Nieto, Noel Purcell, Kenneth Williams, Eric Sykes

Tomorrow and Tomorrow
US   1932   73m   bw
Paramount

A happily married woman suddenly falls for a foreign scientist.

Sturdy woman's picture of its day.

w Josephine Lovett play Philip Barry *d* Richard Wallace

Ruth Chatterton, Paul Lukas, Robert Ames, Harold Minjir, Tad Alexander

'A screen play of the first grade . . . reflects credit on everybody concerned in its making.' – *Variety*

Tomorrow at Ten *
GB   1962   80m   bw
Mancunian (Tom Blakeley)

A crook kidnaps a small boy and locks him up with a time bomb while he makes his demands in person. When the kidnapper is killed, the police have to hunt against time.

Tense second feature, well acted and efficiently done.

w Peter Millar, James Kelly *d* Lance Comfort *ph* Basil Emmott *m* Bernie Fenton

Robert Shaw, John Gregson, Alec Clunes, Alan Wheatley, Ernest Clark, Kenneth Cope

Tomorrow Is Another Day
US   1951   90m   bw
Warner

An ex-convict is soon on the run for a crime he didn't commit.

Miserable melodrama apparently left over from John Garfield days.

w Guy Endore, Art Cohn *d* Felix Feist

Steve Cochran, Ruth Roman, Lurene Tuttle, Bobby Hyatt, Ray Teal

Tomorrow Is Forever *
US   1945   105m   bw
RKO-International (David Lewis)
V*

A man supposed dead in the war returns with an altered face to find his wife has remarried.

Enoch Arden rides again in a rampant woman's picture which is well enough made to be generally entertaining.

w Lenore Coffee *d* Irving Pichel *ph* Joe Valentine *m* Max Steiner

Orson Welles, Claudette Colbert, George Brent, Lucile Watson, Richard Long, Natalie Wood

Tomorrow is Too Late: see *Domani è Troppo Tardi*

Tomorrow Never Comes
Canada/GB   1977   109m   colour
Rank/Classic/Montreal Trust/Neffbourne (Michael Klinger, Julian Melzack)
V, V*

A jealous lover shoots a caller at his girl's beach cabana and a police siege begins.

Far from the class of *Le Jour Se Lève*, this is an exploitative and violent melodrama which need never have been made.

w David Pursall, Jack Seddon, Sydney Banks *d* Peter Collinson *ph* François Protat *m* Roy Budd

Oliver Reed, Susan George, Raymond Burr, Stephen McHattie, John Ireland, Donald Pleasence, John Osborne, Cec Linder

Tomorrow the World *
US   1944   86m   bw
UA/Lester Cowan

A college professor adopts his orphaned German nephew, who turns out to be an ardent 12-year-old Nazi.

Adequate, predictable screen version of a once-topical play.

w Ring Lardner Jnr, Leopold Atlas play James Gow, Armand D'Usseau *d* Leslie Fenton *ph* Henry Sharp *m* Louis Applebaum

Fredric March, Betty Field, *Skip Homeier*, Agnes Moorehead, Joan Carroll

Tomorrow We Live
GB   1942   85m   bw
British Aviation (George King)
US title: *At Dawn We Die*

French villagers help a spy escape to Britain.

Minor flagwaver marred by cheap sets.

w Anatole de Grunwald, Katherine Strueby *d* George King

John Clements, Greta Gynt, Hugh Sinclair, Judy Kelly, Godfrey Tearle, Yvonne Arnaud, Bransby Williams

Tongnian Wangshi: see *The Time to Live and the Time to Die*

Tonight and Every Night
US 1945 92m Technicolor
Columbia (Victor Saville)
V*

The lives and loves of London showgirls during the blitz.

Ludicrous concoction looking nothing like London and certainly nothing like the Windmill, the theatre to which it allegedly pays tribute. There are some tolerable numbers along the way.

w Lesser Samuels, Abem Finkel play *Heart of a City* by Lesley Storm d Victor Saville ph Rudolph Maté md Morris Stoloff, Marlin Skiles

Rita Hayworth, Lee Bowman, Janet Blair, Marc Platt, Leslie Brooks, Dusty Anderson, Florence Bates, Ernest Cossart

AAN: Morris Stoloff, Marlin Skiles; song 'Anywhere' (*m* Jule Styne, *ly* Sammy Cahn)

Tonight Is Ours
US 1932 76m bw
Paramount

A Balkan princess falls for a commoner in Paris.

One of the master's less sparkling plays gets the heavy Hollywood treatment.

w Edwin Justus Mayer play Noël Coward d Stuart Walker

Fredric March, Claudette Colbert, Alison Skipworth, Paul Cavanagh, Arthur Byron, Ethel Griffies

'Slow and talky flicker, better for the class houses.' – *Variety*

Tonight or Never
US 1931 80m bw
Samuel Goldwyn

A prima donna falls for a man she thinks is a Venetian gigolo, but he turns out to be an impresario from New York.

Flimsy comedy which turned out to be its star's last vehicle of any consequence for twenty years.

w Ernest Vajda play Lily Hatvany d Mervyn Le Roy ph Gregg Toland md Alfred Newman

Gloria Swanson, Melvyn Douglas (debut), Ferdinand Gottschalk, Robert Greig, Alison Skipworth, Boris Karloff

Tonight We Raid Calais
US 1943 70m bw
TCF

A British agent lands in occupied France to pave the way for a bombing raid.

Adequate low-budget morale booster.

w Waldo Salt d John Brahm

John Sutton, Annabella, Lee J. Cobb, Beulah Bondi, Blanche Yurka, Howard Da Silva, Marcel Dalio

Tonight We Sing *
US 1953 109m Technicolor
TCF (George Jessel)

Sol Hurok stifles his own talent to become a great musical impresario.

Blameless uppercrust biopic, with plenty of well-staged guest talent.

w Harry Kurnitz, George Oppenheimer d Mitchell Leisen ph Leon Shamroy md Alfred Newman ch David Lichine

David Wayne, Anne Bancroft, Ezio Pinza (Chaliapin), Roberta Peters, Tamara Toumanova (Pavlova), Isaac Stern (Eugene Ysaye), Jan Peerce

Tonight's the Night: see *Happy Ever After* (1954)

Tonka
US 1958 97m Technicolor
Walt Disney
V*

A Sioux Indian tames a magnificent white horse, and after many adventures is reunited with him at Little Big Horn.

Unremarkable and overlong adventure story.

w Lewis R. Foster, Lillie Hayward novel *Comanche* by David Appel d Lewis R. Foster ph Loyal Griggs

Sal Mineo, Phil Carey, Jerome Courtland, Rafael Campos, H. M. Wynant

Tons of Money
GB 1930 97m bw
Herbert Wilcox/B and D

An inventor poses as his own cousin, and in this guise achieves instant success.

A long-running stage farce makes a grimly overlong movie.

w Herbert Wilcox, Ralph Lynn play Will Evans, Arthur Valentine d Tom Walls

Ralph Lynn, Yvonne Arnaud, Mary Brough, Robertson Hare, Gordon James, Madge Saunders

Tony Draws a Horse
GB 1950 91m bw
Pinnacle/GFD

How to deal with a naughty boy causes mounting disagreement in the family.

Very theatrical farce which on screen seems merely silly.

w Brock Williams play Leslie Storm d John Paddy Carstairs

Cecil Parker, Anne Crawford, Derek Bond, Barbara Murray, Mervyn Johns, Edward Rigby

Tony Rome *
US 1967 111m DeLuxe Panavision
TCF/Arcola/Millfield (Aaron Rosenberg)
V*, L

A seedy Miami private eye runs into murder when he guards a millionaire's daughter.

Complex old-fashioned murder mystery decorated with the new amorality and fashionable violence. Tolerable for its backgrounds and professional expertise. Sequel: *Lady in Cement* (qv).

w Richard L. Breen novel *Miami Mayhem* by Marvin H. Albert d Gordon Douglas ph Joe Biroc m Billy May

Frank Sinatra, Jill St John, Richard Conte, Gena Rowlands, Simon Oakland, Jeffrey Lynn, Lloyd Bochner, Sue Lyon

Too Beautiful For You: see *Trop Belle Pour Toi!*

Too Busy to Work
US 1932 76m bw
Fox

A tramp goes looking for his long lost wife.

Amiable remake of one of the star's most successful silents.

w Barry Conners, Philip Klein story *Jubilo* by Ben Ames Williams d John Blystone

Will Rogers, Marian Nixon, Dick Powell, Frederick Burton, Louise Beavers

'A homey story of programmer weight . . . better than average business should be figured on.' – *Variety*

Too Dangerous to Love: see *Perfect Strangers* (1950)

Too Hot to Handle *
US 1938 105m bw
MGM (Lawrence Weingarten)
V, V*

Adventures of a scoop-seeking newsreel cameraman.

Boisterous comedy-melodrama with as many sags as highlights but generally making a cheerful star entertainment.

w Laurence Stallings, John Lee Mahin d Jack Conway ph Harold Rosson m Franz Waxman

Clark Gable, Myrna Loy, Walter Connolly, Walter Pidgeon, Leo Carrillo, Johnny Hines, Virginia Weidler

'Even more than *Test Pilot* it's hoked beyond the level of credibility. But it has a driving excitement, crackling dialogue, glittering performances and inescapable romantic pull. So it's a socko audience picture and should make a parachuteful of money.' – *Variety*

'It's like an old-fashioned serial . . . no one can call it dull.' – *Howard Barnes*

'Breathlessly paced, witty, and violent, this is one of the more acid comedies to have been produced by the Thirties.' – *John Baxter*

Too Hot to Handle
GB 1960 100m Eastmancolor
ABP/Wigmore (Selim Cattan)
V*
aka: *Playgirl After Dark*

Two Soho strip club owners join forces to hunt down a blackmailer.

Rotten, hilarious British gangster film set in a totally unreal underworld and very uncomfortably cast.

w Herbert Kretzmer d Terence Young ph Otto Heller m Eric Spear

Leo Genn, Jayne Mansfield, Karl Boehm, Danik Patisson, Christopher Lee, Patrick Holt

Too Hot to Handle: see *The Marrying Man*

Too Late Blues
US 1961 100m bw
Paramount (John Cassavetes)

A jazz musician falls for a neurotic girl and has fears of going commercial.

Uninteresting professional feature from a director whose reputation was made with the amateur *Shadows*.

w John Cassavetes, Richard Carr d John Cassavetes ph Lionel Lindon m David Raksin

Stella Stevens, Bobby Darin, John Cassavetes, Everett Chambers, Nick Dennis, Rupert Crosse, Vince Edwards

Too Late for Tears
US 1949 99m bw
UA/Hunt Stromberg
V*

A lady bluebeard disposes of both husbands and boyfriends.

Silly melodrama, poorly cast.

w Roy Huggins d Byron Haskin ph William Mellor m Dale Butts

Lizabeth Scott, Don Defore, Arthur Kennedy, Dan Duryea, Kristine Miller, Barry Kelley

Too Late the Hero *
US 1969 144m Technicolor 70mm
Associates and Aldrich/Palomar
V, V*

In World War II the Japanese hold one end of a small Pacific island, British and Americans the other.

Semi-cynical, long and bloody war adventure of competence but no great merit.

w Robert Aldrich, Lukas Heller   *d* Robert Aldrich
ph Joseph Biroc   *m* Gerald Fried

Michael Caine, Cliff Robertson, Ian Bannen, Henry
Fonda, Harry Andrews, Denholm Elliott, Ronald
Fraser, Percy Herbert

Too Many Crooks *
GB   1958   87m   bw
Rank/Mario Zampi
V*

Incompetent crooks plot a kidnapping.

Agreeable farce with black edges and an excellent
chase sequence.

w Michael Pertwee   *d* Mario Zampi   *ph* Stan
Pavey   *m* Stanley Black

Terry-Thomas, George Cole, Brenda de Banzie,
Bernard Bresslaw, Sidney James, Joe Melia, Vera
Day, John Le Mesurier

Too Many Girls
US   1940   85m   bw
RKO (Harry Edgington, George Abbott)
V*, L

The father of a wealthy co-ed hires four football
heroes to protect her.

Witless nonsense, flabbily derived from a Broadway
show.

w John Twist   *play* George Marion Jnr, Richard
Rodgers, Lorenz Hart   *d* George Abbott   *ph* Frank
Redman   *songs* Rodgers and Hart

Lucille Ball, Desi Arnaz, Richard Carlson, Ann Miller,
Eddie Bracken, Frances Langford, Harry Shannon

† The film on which Ball and Arnaz first met.

Too Many Husbands *
US   1940   84m   bw
Columbia (Wesley Ruggles)
GB title: *My Two Husbands*

Allegedly drowned on a boat cruise, a man turns up
again after his wife has remarried.

Modest variation on a familiar theme, professional but
unexciting; later remade as *Three for the Show* (qv).

w Claude Binyon   *play* Home and Beauty by W.
Somerset Maugham   *d* Wesley Ruggles   *ph* Joseph
Walker   *m* Frederick Hollander

Jean Arthur, Melvyn Douglas, Fred MacMurray,
Harry Davenport, Dorothy Peterson, Melville Cooper,
Edgar Buchanan

Too Many Lovers
France   1958   102m   Eastmancolor
Sirius (Jacques Roitfeld)
original title: *Charmants Garçons*

A dancer is pursued by a jewel thief, a gigolo, a boxer,
a wealthy businessman and several husbands.

Light romantic comedy that offers occasional
amusement, as well as a couple of dances by its star.

w Charles Spaak, Dominique Fabre, Etienne Perier
d Henri Decoin   *ph* Pierre Montazel   *m* Georges
Van Parys   *ch* Roland Petit   *ad* Robert Clavel
ed Claude Durand

Zizi Jeanmaire, Daniel Gelin, Henri Vidal, François
Perier, Gert Frobe

Too Much Harmony
US   1933   76m   bw
Paramount

A star singer helps a promising girl to the top.

Routine light musical which filled a need.

w Harry Ruskin, Joseph L. Mankiewicz   *d* Eddie
Sutherland

Bing Crosby, Jack Oakie, Judith Allen, Skeets
Gallagher, Lilyan Tashman, Harry Green, Ned Sparks

'Should be an easy pleaser.' – *Variety*

'Always a man! Almost any man!'

Too Much Too Soon *
US   1958   121m   bw
Warner (Henry Blanke)

Young actress Diana Barrymore goes to Hollywood to
look after her alcoholic father John, but mild success
goes to her head and she too turns to drink.

Rather dismal and murkily photographed account of
an absorbing real-life situation; one performance
holds the first half together.

wd Art Napoleon   *memoirs* Diana Barrymore
ph Nicholas Musuraca, Carl Guthrie   *m* Ernest Gold
ad George James Hopkins

Dorothy Malone, *Errol Flynn*, Efrem Zimbalist Jnr,
Neva Patterson, Martin Milner, Ray Danton, Murray
Hamilton

Too Young to Kiss
US   1951   89m   bw
MGM (Sam Zimbalist)

A girl pianist poses as an infant prodigy, and falls for
the impresario who wants to adopt her.

Dull conveyor belt comedy.

w Frances Goodrich, Albert Hackett   *d* Robert Z.
Leonard   *ph* Joseph Ruttenberg   *m* Johnny Green
ad Cedric Gibbons, Paul Groesse

June Allyson, Van Johnson, Gig Young, Paula
Corday, Larry Keating, Hans Conried

AAN: art direction

'If this happened to your daughter, would you be to
blame?'

Too Young to Love
GB   1959   89m   bw
Rank/Welbeck (Herbert Smith)

A 15-year-old prostitute is brought before a Brooklyn
juvenile court.

Tepid filming of a popular exploitation play of the
fifties, mysteriously made in England.

w Sydney and Muriel Box   *play* Pick Up Girl by Elsa
Shelley   *d* Muriel Box   *ph* Gerald Gibbs
m Bruce Montgomery

Thomas Mitchell, Pauline Hahn, Joan Miller, Austin
Willis, Jess Conrad, Bessie Love, Alan Gifford

Tootsie ****
US   1982   116m   colour
Columbia/Mirage/Punch (Sydney Pollack)
V, V*, L, S

An out-of-work actor pretends to be a woman in order
to get a job in a soap opera.

As with *Genevieve* and *Whisky Galore*, an unlikely
comedy subject makes an instant classic. It's all in the
handling.

w Larry Gelbart, Murray Shisgal   *story* Don McGuire
d Sydney Pollack   *ph* Owen Roizman   *m* Dave
Grusin   *pd* Peter Larkin   *ed* Frederick and William
Steinkamp

Dustin Hoffman, Jessica Lange, Teri Garr, Dabney
Coleman, Charles Durning, Sydney Pollack, George
Gaynes

AA: Jessica Lange

AAN: best picture; Dustin Hoffman; Teri Garr;
Sydney Pollack as director; original screenplay;
cinematography; editing; song, 'It Might Be You' (*m*
Dave Grusin, *ly* Alan Bergman, Marilyn Bergman);
sound

BFA: Dustin Hoffman

Top Banana *
US   1953   100m   Color Corporation
Roadshow/Harry M. Popkin
V*

A TV comedian invites an attractive salesgirl to join
his show.

A wisp of plot is the excuse for a revue, and the
interest is in the old-time burlesque acts, some of
which survive the generally shoddy treatment.

w Gene Towne   *d* Alfred E. Green   *ph* William
Bradford   *m/ly* Johnny Mercer

Phil Silvers, Rose Marie, Danny Scholl, Jack Albertson

Top Gun
US   1986   110m   Metrocolor
Paramount/Don Simpson, Jerry Bruckheimer
V, V*, L, CD, S

Adventures of naval fighter pilots.

A feast of hardware and noisy music; not much story.

w Jim Cash, Jack Epps Jnr   *d* Tony Scott
ph Jeffrey Kimball   *m* Harold Faltermeyer
pd John F. DeCuir Jnr   *ed* Billy Weber, Chris
Lebenzon

Tom Cruise, Kelly McGillis, Val Kilmer, Anthony
Edwards, Tom Skerritt

'Audiences prepared to go with it will be taken for a
thrilling ride in the wild blue yonder.' – *Variety*

AA: song 'Take My Breath Away' (Giorgio Moroder,
Tom Whitlock)

AAN: editors

Top Hat ****
US   1935   100m   bw
RKO (Pandro S. Berman)
V, V*, L

The path of true love is roughened by mistaken
identities.

Marvellous Astaire-Rogers musical, with a more or
less realistic London supplanted by a totally artificial
Venice, and show stopping numbers in a style which
is no more, separated by amusing plot complications
lightly handled by a team of deft *farceurs*.

w Dwight Taylor, Allan Scott   *d* Mark Sandrich
ph David Abel, Vernon Walker   *m/ly* Irving Berlin
ch Hermes Pan   *ad* Van Nest Polglase, Carroll Clark

Fred Astaire, Ginger Rogers, Edward Everett Horton, Helen
Broderick, Eric Blore, Erik Rhodes

'The theatres will hold their own world series with
this one. It can't miss.' – *Variety*

'In 25 years *Top Hat* has lost nothing of its gaiety and
charm.' – *Dilys Powell, 1960*

AAN: best picture; song 'Cheek to Cheek'; Hermes
Pan; art direction

Top Man
US   1943   74m   bw
Universal

When an officer is recalled to active duty his teenage
son becomes head of the family.

Lively little putting-on-a-show comedy musical
which established a new young star.

w Zachary Gold   *d* Charles Lamont

Donald O'Connor, Richard Dix, Peggy Ryan, Lillian
Gish, Susanna Foster, Anne Gwynne

Top o' the Morning
US   1949   100m   bw
Paramount (Robert L. Welch)

Investigations follow the theft of the Blarney Stone.

More Irish whimsy from the *Going My Way* stars.

w Edmund Beloin, Richard Breen   *d* David Miller
ph Lionel Lindon   *m* James Van Heusen

Bing Crosby, Barry Fitzgerald, Ann Blyth, Hume
Cronyn, Eileen Crowe, John McIntire

The Top of His Head
Canada   1989   110m   colour
Rhombus Media/Grimthorpe Film (Niv Fichman)

A satellite-dish salesman falls in love with a

performance artist who is being investigated by the police.

Disastrously pretentious romantic thriller that uses experimental effects to little purpose.

wd Peter Mettler   ph Peter Mettler   m Fred Frith
ad Valanne Ridgeway, Angela Murphy   ed Peter Mettler, Margaret Van Eerdewijk

Stephen Ouimette, Gary Reineke, Christie MacFadyen, David Main, Julie Wildman, Diane Barrington, David Fox

Top of the Town
US   1937   86m   bw
Universal

The daughter of the owner of the Moonbeam Room wants to oust the swing band and stage a symbolic ballet.

A wisp of plot supports some expensive but not especially attractive numbers in a musical variety show that was supposed to be Universal's answer to other studios' biggies.

w Brown Holmes, Charles Grayson, Lou Brock
d Ralph Murphy

George Murphy, Doris Nolan, Hugh Herbert, Gregory Ratoff, Ella Logan, Gertrude Niesen, Henry Armetta, Mischa Auer, Samuel S. Hinds, Peggy Ryan

'A bundle of mediocrity . . . it neither goes nor gets anywhere.' – Variety

Top Secret *
GB   1952   94m   bw
ABP (Mario Zampi)
US title: Mr Potts Goes to Moscow

A sanitary engineer, mistaken for a spy, is kidnapped to Moscow when his blueprints are taken for atomic secrets.

Farcical satire full of chases and lavatory humour; much of it comes off nicely.

w Jack Davies, Michael Pertwee   d Mario Zampi
ph Stan Pavey   m Stanley Black

George Cole, Oscar Homolka, Nadia Gray, Frederick Valk, Wilfrid Hyde-White, Geoffrey Sumner, Ronald Adam

Top Secret!
US   1984   90m   Metrocolor
Paramount/Kingsmere (Jon Davison, Hunt Lowry)
V, V*, L

An American rock star in Germany gets involved with spies of both sides.

Dull spoof from the folks who gave us Airplane! A very few sight gags stand out among the dross.

w Jim Abrahams, David Zucker, Jerry Zucker, Martyn Burke   d Jim Abrahams, David Zucker, Jerry Zucker   ph Christopher Challis   m Maurice Jarre   pd Peter Lamont

Val Kilmer, Lucy Gutteridge, Peter Cushing, Jeremy Kemp, Warren Clarke, Michael Gough, Omar Sharif, Christopher Villiers

'Too far over the top to retain any comic sense of the targets it sets out to lampoon. The overwhelming impression is of a Mad magazine strip in a particularly poor week.' – Martyn Auty, MFB

Top Secret Affair *
US   1956   100m   bw
Warner/United States (Martin Rackin)
GB title: Their Secret Affair

A female news publisher tries to discredit a military diplomat but falls in love with him.

Curious comedy adaptation of a rather heavy novel, moderately skilled in all departments.

w Roland Kibbee, Allan Scott   novel Melville Goodwin USA by John P. Marquand   d H. C. Potter
ph Stanley Cortez   m Roy Webb

Kirk Douglas, Susan Hayward, Jim Backus, Paul Stewart, John Cromwell, Roland Winters

Topaz *
US   1969   124m   Technicolor
Universal/Alfred Hitchcock
V*, L

In 1962 the CIA enlists a French agent to break up a Russian spy ring.

Oddly halting, desultory and unconvincing spy thriller shot mainly in flat TV style, with just a few short sequences in its director's better manner. A measure of its unsatisfactoriness is that three different endings were shot and actually used at various points of release.

w Samuel Taylor   novel Leon Uris   d Alfred Hitchcock   ph Jack Hildyard   m Maurice Jarre

Frederick Stafford, John Forsythe, John Vernon, Roscoe Lee Browne, Dany Robin, Karin Dor, Michel Piccoli, Philippe Noiret

'A larger, slower, duller version of the spy thrillers he used to make in the thirties.' – New Yorker, 1975

Topaze *
US   1933   78m   bw
(RKO) David O. Selznick
V*, L

A simple schoolmaster allows himself to be exploited.

Interesting little comedy with the star playing against type: remade as Mr Topaze (qv).

w Ben Hecht   play Marcel Pagnol   d Harry d'Abbadie d'Arrast   ph Lucien Andriot   m Max Steiner

John Barrymore, Myrna Loy, Jobyna Howland, Jackie Searl

'Okay, for metropolitan spots, but scarcely for the subsequents . . . there haven't been half a dozen foreign dramas that have clicked on the screen.' – Variety

† In 1952 Howard Hughes announced a remake with Vincent Price, but it never happened.

Topio Stin Omichli: see Landscape in a Mist

Topkapi *
US   1964   119m   Technicolor
UA/Filmways (Jules Dassin)
V, V*, L

International thieves try to rob the Istanbul museum.

Light-hearted caper story which gets out of control because of the variety of styles and accents, the director's impression that his wife can do no wrong, and the general slowness and lack of wit; but there are bright moments, colourful backgrounds, and a final suspense sequence in the Rififi manner.

w Monja Danischewsky   novel The Light of Day by Eric Ambler   d Jules Dassin   ph Henri Alekan
m Manos Hadjidakis

Melina Mercouri, Maximilian Schell, Peter Ustinov, Robert Morley, Akim Tamiroff, Gilles Segal, Jess Hahn

AA: Peter Ustinov

Topper **
US   1937   96m   bw
(MGM) Hal Roach (Milton H. Bren)
V*, L

A stuffy banker is haunted by the ghosts of his sophisticated friends the Kirbys, who are visible only to him.

Influential supernatural farce, still pretty funny and deftly acted though a shade slow to get going.

w Jack Jevne, Eric Hatch, Eddie Moran   novel The Jovial Ghosts by Thorne Smith   d Norman Z. McLeod
ph Norbert Brodine   md Arthur Morton

Cary Grant, Constance Bennett, Roland Young, Billie Burke, Alan Mowbray, Eugene Pallette, Arthur Lake, Hedda Hopper

'How substantial the fan support will be is difficult to anticipate . . . None of the other films of similar theme aroused more than mild enthusiasm among a small group who patronize the arty theatres and talk about pictures in terms of art expression . . . Effort to excuse the story's absurdities on the theory that the intent is farce comedy does not entirely excuse the production from severe rebuke. Fact also that the living dead are always facetious may be shocking to sensibilities. Some of the situations and dialogue offend conventional good taste.' – Variety

AAN: Roland Young

Topper Returns **
US   1941   87m   bw
Hal Roach
V*, L

A girl ghost helps Topper solve her own murder.

Spirited supernatural farce which spoofs murder mysteries, spooky houses, frightened servants, dumb cops, etc, in a pacy, accomplished and generally delightful manner.

w Jonathan Latimer, Gordon Douglas, with additional dialogue by Paul Gerard Smith   d Roy del Ruth   ph Norbert Brodine   m Werner Heyman

Roland Young, Joan Blondell, Eddie Anderson, Carole Landis, Dennis O'Keefe, H. B. Warner, Billie Burke, Donald McBride, Rafaela Ottiano

'Ectoplasm runs riot and blazes a trail of hilarity from 5th Avenue to the French Riviera!'

Topper Takes a Trip *
US   1939   85m   bw
Hal Roach
V*

Ghostly Mrs Kirby helps Topper to save his wife from a Riviera philanderer.

Mildly pleasant follow-up, with a dog replacing Cary Grant who had become too expensive.

w Eddie Moran, Jack Jevne, Corey Ford   d Norman Z. McLeod   ph Norbert Brodine   m Hugo Friedhofer

Constance Bennett, Roland Young, Billie Burke, Alan Mowbray, Verree Teasdale, Franklin Pangborn, Alexander D'Arcy

'Dandy comedy sequel . . . can't miss at the b.o. . . . the original ended up a fine money-maker . . . no doubt one a year about Topper would be welcomed by exhibitors.' – Variety

Tops is the Limit: see Anything Goes

Tora! Tora! Tora! *
US   1970   144m   DeLuxe   Panavision
TCF (Elmo Williams)
V, V (W), V*, L

A reconstruction from both sides of the events leading up to Pearl Harbor.

Immense, largely studio-bound, calcified war spectacle with much fidelity to the record but no villains and no hero, therefore no drama and no suspense.

w Larry Forrester, Hideo Oguni, Ryuzo Kikushima
d Richard Fleischer, Ray Kellogg, Toshio Masuda, Kinji Fukasaku   ph Charles F. Wheeler and Japanese crews   m Jerry Goldsmith   ad Jack Martin Smith, Yoshiro Muraki, Richard Day, Taizoh Kawashima   sp L. B. Abbott, Art Cruickshank
ed James E. Newcomb, Pembroke J. Herring, Innoue Chikaya

Martin Balsam, Joseph Cotten, James Whitmore, Jason Robards, Edward Andrews, Leon Ames, George Macready, Soh Yamamura, Takahiro Tamura

'One of the least stirring and least photogenic historical epics ever perpetrated on the screen.' – *Gary Arnold*

AA: special visual effects (A. D. Flowers, L. B. Abbott)

AAN: Charles F. Wheeler, Osami Furuya, Sinsaku Himeda, Masamichi Satoh; art direction; sound; editing

'She sings torch songs to daddies and lullabies to babies!'
Torch Singer
US   1933   72m   bw
Paramount (Albert Lewis)
aka: *Broadway Singer*

An unwed mother supports her child by singing in night-clubs.

Banal melodrama.

w Lenore Coffee, Lynn Starling   *play Mike* by Grace Perkins   d Alexander Hall   ph Karl Struss

Claudette Colbert, Ricardo Cortez, David Manners, Lyda Roberti, Baby LeRoy, Florence Roberts, Ethel Griffies, Helen Jerome Eddy

'Unwed mother film not so forte.' – *Variety*

Torch Song
US   1953   90m   Technicolor
MGM (Henry Berman, Sidney Franklin Jnr)
V*, L

A temperamental musical comedy star falls for a blind pianist.

Ossified star vehicle which looks great but is too often unintentionally funny.

w John Michael Hayes, Jan Lustig   *story Why Should I Cry?* by I. A. R. Wylie   d Charles Walters   ph Robert Planck   m Adolph Deutsch

Joan Crawford, Michael Wilding, Gig Young, Marjorie Rambeau, Henry Morgan, Dorothy Patrick

'Here is Joan Crawford all over the screen, in command, in love and in color.' – *Otis L. Guernsey Jnr*

AAN: Marjorie Rambeau

Torch Song Trilogy *
US   1988   119m   Metrocolor
Palace/New Line (Howard Gottfried)
V, V*, L

Three incidents in the life of a drag artiste: in 1971, there is an on-and-off affair with a school teacher; in 1973, a young man comes to live with him; in 1980, his mother discovers his homosexuality as an old lover moves back in.

A truncated version of a successful Broadway show, the film loses the theatricality of the original and transforms the material into a dated melodrama.

w Harvey Fierstein   *play* Harvey Fierstein   d Paul Bogart   ph Mikael Salomon   m Peter Matz   pd Richard Hoover   ed Nicholas C. Smith

Harvey Fierstein, Anne Bancroft, Matthew Broderick, Brian Kerwin, Karen Young, Eddie Castrodad, Ken Page, Charles Pierce, Axel Vera

Torchy Blane
Glenda Farrell played the hard-boiled girl reporter and Barton MacLane the tough police inspector who puts up with her in seven out of the nine second features made by Warner in the late 30s. The characters were created in short stories by Frederick Nebel, and the films were mostly directed by William Beaudine or Frank McDonald.

1936: SMART BLONDE
1937: FLY AWAY BABY, THE ADVENTUROUS BLONDE
1938: BLONDES AT WORK, TORCHY BLANE IN PANAMA (with Lola Lane, Paul Kelly), TORCHY GETS HER MAN

1939: TORCHY BLANE IN CHINATOWN, TORCHY RUNS FOR MAYOR, TORCHY PLAYS WITH DYNAMITE (with Jane Wyman, Allen Jenkins)

Torment: see *Frenzy*

Torments: see *El*

Torn Curtain **
US   1966   119m   Technicolor
Universal/Alfred Hitchcock
V*, L, S

A defector who is really a double agent is embarrassed when his girlfriend follows him into East Germany.

Patchy Hitchcock with some mechanically effective suspense sequences, a couple of efforts at something new, a few miscalculations, some evidence of carelessness, and a little enjoyable repetition of old situations.

w Brian Moore   d Alfred Hitchcock   ph John F. Warren   m John Addison

Paul Newman, Julie Andrews, *Wolfgang Kieling*, Ludwig Donath, Lila Kedrova, Hans-Joerg Felmy, Tamara Toumanova

'The pace is plodding, the political background trite, and the actors stranded by their director's customary lack of concern with performance.' – *Time Out, 1984*

Torpedo Run *
US   1958   98m   Metrocolor   Cinemascope
MGM (Edmund S. Grainger)
V*

A US submarine in World War II destroys a Japanese aircraft carrier in Tokyo Bay.

Well-staged potboiler with excellent action sequences marred slightly by excessive platitudinizing.

w Richard Sale, William Wister Haines   d Joseph Pevney   ph George J. Folsey

Glenn Ford, Ernest Borgnine, Diane Brewster, Dean Jones

Torpedoed: see *Our Fighting Navy*

The Torrent *
US   1925   75m (24 fps)   bw   silent
MGM (Hunt Stromberg)

Spanish sweethearts are parted by a domineering mother, and the girl consoles herself by becoming a Paris prima donna.

Adequate emotional vehicle of its day which happened to be Garbo's first American film.

w Dorothy Farnum   *novel* Vicente Blasco Ibáñez   d Monta Bell   ph William Daniels

Ricardo Cortez, Greta Garbo, Gertrude Olmsted, Edward Connelly, Lucien Littlefield

Torrents of Spring **
Italy/France   1989   101m   Technicolor
Hobo/Erre Produzione/Reteitalia/Les Films Ariane/Films A2/Curzon (Angelo Rizzoli)
V*, L

A young Russian aristocrat is unfaithful to the beautiful Italian pastrycook he plans to marry.

Charming and evocative treatment of a tragic romance.

w Jerzy Skolimowski, Arcangelo Bonaccorso   *novel* Ivan Turgenev   d Jerzy Skolimowski   ph Dante Spinotti, Witold Sobocinski   m Stanley Myers   pd Francesco Bronzi   ed Cesare D'Amico, Andrzej Kostenko

Timothy Hutton, Nastassja Kinski, Valeria Golino, William Forsythe, Urbano Barberini, Francesca de Sapio, Jacques Herlin

'Immensely beguiling.' – *Tom Milne, MFB*

Torrid Zone **
US   1940   88m   bw
Warner (Mark Hellinger)

In Central America, a banana plantation manager is tricked by his boss into staying on, and helps a wandering showgirl as well as foiling bandits.

Enjoyable, fast-paced hokum with a plot borrowed from both *The Front Page* and *Red Dust*.

w Richard Macaulay, Jerry Wald   d William Keighley   ph James Wong Howe   m Adolph Deutsch

James Cagney, Pat O'Brien, Ann Sheridan, Helen Vinson, Andy Devine, Jerome Cowan, George Tobias, George Reeves

Törst: see *Three Strange Loves*

Tortilla Flat *
US   1942   106m   bw
MGM (Sam Zimbalist)
V*

The problems of poor Mexican half-breeds in California.

Expensive but unappealing variation on *The Grapes of Wrath*, with none of the cast quite getting under the skin of their parts, and no sense of reality, rather that of a musical without music.

w John Lee Mahin, Benjamin Glazier   *novel* John Steinbeck   d Victor Fleming   ph Sidney Wagner   m Franz Waxman

Spencer Tracy, Hedy Lamarr, John Garfield, Frank Morgan, Akim Tamiroff, Connie Gilchrist, John Qualen, Sheldon Leonard, Donald Meek, Allen Jenkins, Henry O'Neill

AAN: Frank Morgan

The Torture Chamber of Baron Blood: see *Baron Blood*

The Torture Chamber of Dr Sadism: see *The Blood Demon*

Torture Garden *
GB   1967   93m   Technicolor
Columbia/Amicus (Milton Subotsky)
V, V*, L

Five fairground visitors are told their future by the mysterious Dr Diablo.

Crude but effective horror portmanteau including one story about the resurrection of Edgar Allan Poe.

w Robert Bloch   d Freddie Francis   ph Norman Warwick   m Don Banks, James Bernard

Burgess Meredith, Jack Palance, Peter Cushing, Beverly Adams, Michael Bryant, John Standing

'They stole his mind. Now he wants it back.'
Total Recall **
US   1990   109m   Technicolor
Guild/Carolco (Buzz Feitshans, Ronald Shusett)
V, V*, L, S

Following an artificially-induced dream, a labourer remembers his previous existence as a secret agent on Mars.

An over-violent, paranoid and engrossing fantasy, with more than enough twists of plot to dizzy the mind.

w Ronald Shusett, Dan O'Bannon, Gary Goldman   *story We Can Remember It For You Wholesale* by Philip K. Dick   d Paul Verhoeven   ph Jost Vacano   m Jerry Goldsmith   pd William Sandell   ed Frank J. Urioste

Arnold Schwarzenegger, Rachel Ticotin, Sharon Stone, Ronny Cox, Michael Ironside, Marshall Bell, Mel Johnson Jnr, Michael Champion, Roy Brocksmith, Ray Baker, Rosemary Dunsmore, Priscilla Allen

'While the temptation is just to shrug off *Total Recall* as an excessive but exciting "no brainer", enough intelligence and artistry lie behind the numbing spectacle to also make one regret its heedless contribution to the accelerating brutality of its time.' – *Variety*

AA: best visual effects

Toto le Héros **

Belgium/France/Germany 1991 91m colour
Electric/Ibis/Metropolis/RTBF/FRZ/ZDF/CanalPlus (Philippe Dussart, Luciano Gloor)
V, V*, S
aka: *Toto the Hero*

A bitter old man recalls the past as he plots the murder of his childhood enemy who married the woman he loved.

Strange but largely successful mix of childhood fantasy and black and bitter comedy.

w Jaco van Dormael, Laurette Vankeerberghen, Pascal Lonhay, Didier de Neck   *d* Jaco van Dormael   *ph* Walther van den Ende   *m* Pierre van Dormael   *ad* Herbert Pouille   *ed* Susana Rossberg

Michel Bouquet, Jo de Backer, Thomas Godet, Gisela Uhlen, Mireille Perrier, Sandrine Blancke, Peter Böhlke, Didier Ferney, Hugo Harold Harrisson

The Touch *

Sweden/US 1970 112m Eastmancolor
ABC/Cinematograph AB (Lars/Owe Carlburg)

The wife of a provincial surgeon falls in love with an archaeologist.

Freedom versus security; the Bergman treatment is given to a familiar love story, but the expected finesse is lacking.

wd Ingmar Bergman   *ph* Sven Nykvist   *m* Jan Johansson

Bibi Andersson, Elliott Gould, Max von Sydow

Touch and Go

GB 1955 85m Technicolor
Ealing (Seth Holt)
L
US title: *The Light Touch*

A family has doubts about its decision to emigrate to Australia.

Very mild comedy which fails to engage sympathy because the characters don't seem real.

w William Rose   *ph* Michael Truman   *ph* Douglas Slocombe   *m* John Addison

Jack Hawkins, Margaret Johnston, June Thorburn, John Fraser, Roland Culver, Alison Leggatt, James Hayter

'They had the perfect love affair. Until they fell in love!'
A Touch of Class **

GB 1973 106m Technicolor Panavision
Avco/Brut/Gordon Films (Melvin Frank)
V*

A married American businessman in London has a hectic affair with a dress designer.

Amiable and very physical sex farce with hilarious highlights and a few longueurs between; the playing keeps it above water.

w Melvin Frank, Jack Rose   *d* Melvin Frank   *ph* Austin Dempster   *m* John Cameron

Glenda Jackson, George Segal, Paul Sorvino, Hildegarde Neil

'Machine-tooled junk.' – *William S. Pechter*

'Brightly performed and quite engaging until it fades into vapid variations on a one-joke theme.' – *Sight and Sound*

AA: Glenda Jackson

AAN: best picture; script; John Cameron; song 'All That Love Went to Waste' (*m* George Barrie, *ly* Sammy Cahn)

Touch of Evil ****

US 1958 95m or 114m bw
U-I (Albert Zugsmith)
V*, L, S

A Mexican narcotics investigator honeymooning in a border town clashes with the local police chief over a murder.

Overpoweringly atmospheric melodrama crammed with Wellesian touches, but very cold and unsympathetic, with rather restrained performances (especially his) and a plot which takes some following. Hardly the most auspicious return to Hollywood for a wanderer, but now a cult classic.

wd Orson Welles,   *novel Badge of Evil* by Whit Masterson   *ph* Russell Metty   *m* Henry Mancini

Charlton Heston, Orson Welles, Janet Leigh, Marlene Dietrich, Akim Tamiroff, Joseph Calleia, Ray Collins, Dennis Weaver

'Pure Orson Welles and impure balderdash, which may be the same thing.' – *Gerald Weales, Reporter*

A Touch of Larceny *

GB 1959 92m bw
Paramount/Ivan Foxwell

A naval commander mysteriously disappears in the hope that he will be branded a traitor and can sue for libel.

Fairly amusing light comedy with lively performances.

w Roger MacDougall, Guy Hamilton, Ivan Foxwell *novel The Megstone Plot* by Andrew Garve   *d* Guy Hamilton   *ph* John Wilcox   *m* Philip Green

James Mason, Vera Miles, George Sanders, Robert Flemyng, Ernest Clark, Duncan Lamont, Peter Barkworth

'A beguilingly polished comedy, reminiscent in its style, urbanity and sheen of the sort of thing Lubitsch was doing in the 30s.' – *Daily Mail*

A Touch of Love

GB 1969 107m Eastmancolor
Amicus/Palomar (Milton Subotsky)
US title: *Thank You All Very Much*

A pregnant London student tries to get an abortion but later decides against it.

Curious bid for serious drama by horror producers; all very conscientious but rather dreary.

w Margaret Drabble   *novel The Millstone* by Margaret Drabble   *d* Waris Hussein   *ph* Peter Suschitzky   *m* Michael Dress

Sandy Dennis, Ian McKellen, Michael Coles, John Standing, Eleanor Bron

A Touch of the Sun

GB 1956 80m bw
Eros/Raystro (Raymond Stross)

A hall porter is left a fortune but after living it up for a while returns to his old hotel which is on the rocks.

Limp comedy vehicle.

w Alfred Shaughnessy   *d* Gordon Parry   *ph* Arthur Grant   *m* Eric Spear

Frankie Howerd, Ruby Murray, Dorothy Bromiley, Gordon Harker, Reginald Beckwith, Richard Wattis, Dennis Price, Alfie Bass, Willoughby Goddard

Touchez pas au Grisbi *

France/Italy 1953 90m approx bw
Del Duca/Antares
aka: *Honour among Thieves; Hands Off the Loot*

Two crooks succeed in stealing a consignment of gold, but that's only the start of their worries.

Smooth underworld hokum, with a slightly comic attitude implied if not stated.

w Jacques Becker, Maurice Griffe   *novel* Albert Simonin   *d* Jacques Becker   *ph* Pierre Montazel   *m* Jean Wiener

Jean Gabin, Jeanne Moreau, Gaby Basset, Daniel Cauchy, Marilyn Buferd, Lino Ventura, René Dary

Tough Guys

US 1986 104m DeLuxe Panavision
Touchstone/Silver Screen/Brynal (Joe Wizan)
V*, L

The last train robbers are released from prison after 30 years, and, finding that an old people's home is not for them, return to their old ways.

Slackly written caper comedy with two former stars in their seventh teaming.

w James Orr, Jim Cruickshank   *d* Jeff Kanew   *ph* King Baggot   *m* James Newton Howard

Burt Lancaster, Kirk Douglas, Charles Durning, Alexis Smith, Eli Wallach

Tough Guys Don't Dance

US 1987 108m TVC colour
Zoetrope/Cannon (Menahem Golan, Yoram Globus)
V*, L

A small businessman in Massachusetts gets involved in a drugs deal.

Would-be parody of the Chandler style which works only fitfully and long outstays its welcome.

wd Norman Mailer   *novel* Norman Mailer   *ph* Michael Moyer, Danny Dukovny   *m* Paula Erickson   *pd* Armin Ganz   *ed* Debra McDermot

Ryan O'Neal, Isabella Rossellini, Debra Sandlund, Wings Hauser, Lawrence Tierney

Toughest Man in Arizona

US 1952 90m Trucolor
Republic (Sidney Picker)

In 1861 a US marshal falls in love with the wife of an outlaw.

Easy-going, pleasant Western aimed at the top half of a double bill.

w John K. Butler   *d* R. G. Springsteen   *ph* Reggie Lanning   *m* Dale Butts

Vaughn Monroe, Joan Leslie, Edgar Buchanan, Victor Jory, Jean Parker, Henry Morgan

Tous les matins du monde *

France 1992 115m colour
Electric/FilmParFilm/D.D./Divali/Sedif/FR3/C.N.C./Canal+/Paravision (Jean-Louis Livi)
V, S

Marin Marais, a French musician and composer at the court of Louis XIV, recalls the man who taught him musical values, the austere Monsieur de Sainte Colombe, and an unhappy love affair with his teacher's daughter.

Glossy period drama, often delightful to look at and hear, but hollow-centred.

w Pascal Quignard, Alain Corneau   *novel* Pascal Quignard   *d* Alain Corneau   *ph* Yves Angelo   *m* Jordi Savall   *ad* Bernard Vezat   *ed* Marie-Josephe Yoyotte

Gérard Depardieu, Jean-Pierre Marielle, Anne Brochet, Guillaume Depardieu, Caroline Sihol, Carole Richert, Violaine Lacroix, Nadege Teron

'A memorably audacious parable, performed with understanding and set out before us with no evident compromise. But you just have to listen to the music to realise exactly what it's about.' – *Derek Malcolm, Guardian*

Toute une Vie: see *And Now My Love*

'The most exciting screen event of all time!'
Tovarich **
US   1937   98m   bw
Warner (Robert Lord)

A royal Russian husband and wife flee the revolution to Paris and take jobs as servants in an eccentric household.

A lively comedy of its time; though many of the jokes now seem obvious, the playing preserves its essential quality.

w Casey Robinson   *play adaptation Robert E. Sherwood original* Jacques Deval   *d* Anatole Litvak   *ph* Charles Lang   *m* Max Steiner

Claudette Colbert, Charles Boyer, Basil Rathbone, Anita Louise, Melville Cooper, Isabel Jeans, Maurice Murphy, Morris Carnovsky, Gregory Gaye, Montagu Love, Fritz Feld

'A yarn of charming and finely shaded characterizations. Both humour and heart appeal spring from intimate acquaintance with the background and motives of each player. Class production, magnet for first runs.' – *Variety*

Toward the Unknown
US   1956   115m   Warnercolor   Warnerscope
Warner/Toluca (Mervyn Le Roy)
GB title: *Brink of Hell*

An over-age officer takes part in the X2 experiments with rocket-firing aircraft.

Humourless flagwaver, very forgettable.

w Beirne Lay Jnr   *d* Mervyn Le Roy   *ph* Harold Rosson   *m* Paul Baron

William Holden, Lloyd Nolan, Virginia Leith, Charles McGraw, Murray Hamilton, L. Q. Jones, James Garner, Paul Fix, Karen Steele

Towed in a Hole ***
US   1932   20m   bw
Hal Roach

Two would-be fishermen wreck the boat they have just bought.

Brilliant star farce, filled with wonderfully lunatic dialogues and freshly conceived slapstick.

w Stan Laurel   *d* George Marshall

Laurel and Hardy

Tower of Evil
GB/US   1972   89m   Technicolor
MGM-EMI/Grenadier/Fanfare (Richard Gordon)
V
US title: *Horror of Snape Island*

A private investigator takes his family to an island lighthouse to discover the truth about three mysterious deaths.

An unoriginal little shocker.

wd Jim O'Connolly   *story* George Baxt
ph Desmond Dickinson   *m* Kenneth V. Jones
ad Disley Jones   *ed* Henry Richardson

Bryant Halliday, Jill Haworth, Anna Palk, William Lucas, Anthony Valentine, Jack Watson, Derek Fowlds, Dennis Price, George Coulouris

'As much energy is expended on the self-conscious nudity and violence as on the suspense, but the dialogue and performances are anyway equally unconvincing.' – *David McGillivray, MFB*

Tower of London **
US   1939   92m   bw
Universal (Rowland V. Lee)
V*

With the help of Mord the executioner, Richard Crookback kills his way to the throne but is destroyed at Bosworth.

The Shakespearean view of history played as a horror comic: despite an overall lack of pace, spirited scenes and good performances win the day.

w Robert N. Lee   *d* Rowland V. Lee   *ph* George Robinson   *m* Charles Previn

Basil Rathbone, Boris Karloff, Barbara O'Neil, Ian Hunter, Vincent Price, Nan Grey, John Sutton, Leo G. Carroll, Miles Mander

'Spine-tingling horror picture . . . so strong that it may provide disturbing nightmares as aftermath.' – *Variety*

Tower of London *
US   1962   79m   bw
AIP/Admiral (Gene Corman)
V*

A variation on the same events, with Price graduating from Clarence to Crookback, and the addition of ghostly visions.

All very cheap, but occasionally vivid melodrama, despite intrusive American accents.

w Leo V. Gordon, Amos Powell, James B. Gordon   *d* Roger Corman   *ph* Arch Dalzell   *m* Michael Anderson

Vincent Price, Michael Pate, Joan Freeman, Robert Brown, Justice Eatson, Sara Salby, Richard McCauly, Bruce Gordon

The Tower of Terror
GB   1941   78m   bw
ABPC
V*

British and German agents clash in a lighthouse tended by a mad keeper.

Lurid penny-dreadful, quite amusing in its way.

w John Argyle, John Reinhart   *d* Lawrence Huntington

Wilfrid Lawson, Movita, Michael Rennie, Morland Graham, George Woodbridge

'One tiny spark becomes a night of towering suspense!'
The Towering Inferno ***
US   1974   165m   DeLuxe   Panavision
TCF/Warner (Irwin Allen)
V, V*, L

The world's tallest building is destroyed by fire on the night of its inauguration.

Showmanlike but relentlessly padded disaster spectacular, worth seeing for its cast of stars, its sheer old-fashioned expertise, and its special effects.

w Stirling Silliphant   *novels The Tower* by Richard Martin Stern, *The Glass Inferno* by Thomas M. Scortia, Frank M. Robinson   *d* John Guillermin, Irwin Allen   *ph* Fred Koenekamp, Joseph Biroc   *m* John Williams   *pd* William Creber   *sp* Bill Abbott   *ed* Harold F. Kress, Carl Kress

Paul Newman, Steve McQueen, William Holden, Faye Dunaway, Fred Astaire, Susan Blakely, Richard Chamberlain, Robert Vaughn, Jennifer Jones, O. J. Simpson, Robert Wagner

'Several generations of blue-eyed charmers act their roles as if each were under a separate bell jar.' – *Verina Glaessner*

'Each scene of someone horribly in flames is presented as a feat for the audience's delectation.' – *New Yorker*

'The combination of Grade A spectacle and B-picture characters induces a feeling of sideline detachment.' – *Michael Billington, Illustrated London News*

AA: photography; song 'We May Never Love Like This Again' (*m/ly* Al Kasha, Joel Hirschhorn); editing

AAN: best picture; John Williams; Fred Astaire; art direction; sound

A Town Called Bastard
GB   1971   97m   Technicolor   Franscope
Benmar/Zurbano (Ben Fisz)
aka: *A Town Like Hell*

Mexican revolutionaries massacre a priest and his congregation and take over the town. Ten years later a widow arrives seeking vengeance.

Sadistic Western with an opening massacre followed by twenty-two killings (count 'em). Pretty dull otherwise.

w Richard Aubrey   *d* Robert Parrish   *ph* Manuel Berenguer   *m* Waldo de Los Rios

Robert Shaw, Stella Stevens, Telly Savalas, Martin Landau, Michael Craig, Fernando Rey, Dudley Sutton

A Town Called Hell: see *A Town Called Bastard*

A Town like Alice **
GB   1956   117m   bw
Rank/Vic Films (Joseph Janni)
L
US title: *The Rape of Malaya*

Life among women prisoners of the Japanese in Malaya, especially one who is finally reunited with her Australian lover.

Genteelly harrowing war film, formlessly adapted from the first part of a popular novel; a big commercial success of its day.

w W. P. Lipscomb, Richard Mason   *novel* Nevil Shute   *d* Jack Lee   *ph* Geoffrey Unsworth   *m* Matyas Seiber

Virginia McKenna, Peter Finch, Takagi, Marie Lohr, Maureen Swanson, Jean Anderson, Renée Houston, Nora Nicholson

'There she lay, wearing her nylons – right around her neck!'
Town *
GB   1956   96m   bw
Columbia/Marksman (Maxwell Setton)

A police inspector solves the murder of a girl after a tennis club dance in a British country town.

Straightforward murder mystery shot in Weybridge, with a wide variety of suspects having something to hide; settings and characters are quite realistic and also a little dreary.

w Ken Hughes, Robert Westerby   *d* John Guillermin   *ph* Basil Emmott   *m* Tristam Cary

John Mills, Charles Coburn, Derek Farr, Barbara Bates, Alec McCowen, Geoffrey Keen, Elizabeth Seal, Margaretta Scott, Fay Compton

The Town Went Wild
US   1945   78m   bw
PRC

Feuding next-door neighbours have children in love.

Romeo and Juliet in small-town America, and none of it sharp enough.

w Bernard R. Roth, Clarence Greene, Russel Rouse   *d* Ralph Murphy

Freddie Bartholomew, Edward Everett Horton, James Lydon, Tom Tully, Jill Browning, Minna Gombell, Maude Eburne, Charles Halton

Town without Pity *
US/Switzerland/Germany   1961   103m   bw
UA/Mirisch/Osweg/Gloria (Gottfried Reinhardt)
V

A German girl is raped and four American soldiers are accused; the defence counsel's wiles lead to the girl's suicide.

Dour drama with overpowering expressionist technique but not much real sympathy, interest or surprise.

w Silvia Reinhardt, George Hurdalek   *novel The Verdict* by Manfred Gregor   *d* Gottfried Reinhardt   *ph* Kurt Hasse   *m* Dimitri Tiomkin

Kirk Douglas, E. G. Marshall, Christine Kaufmann, Barbara Rutting, Robert Blake, Richard Jaeckel

AAN: title song (*m* Dimitri Tiomkin, *ly* Ned Washington)

The Toxic Avenger
US   1985   76m   colour
Blue Dolphin/Troma/Lloyd Kaufman, Michael Herz
V*, L

A retarded weakling falls into a vat of radioactive chemicals and is transformed into a monstrously ugly super-hero.

A spoof of the horror genre, but so crudely made and acted as to be even more offensive than the worst of what it mocks.

w Joe Ritter   *story* Lloyd Kaufman   *d* Michael Herz, Samuel Weil   *ph* James London, Michael Kaufma*ned* Richard W. Haines

Andree Maranda, Mitchell Cohen, Pat Ryan Jnr, Jennifer Babtist, Cindy Manion, Robert Prichard, Gary Schneider, Mark Torgl

The Toxic Avenger, Part II
US   1989   95m   TVC
Troma/Lloyd Kaufman, Michael Herz
V, V*, L

A chemical company wanting to dump its dangerous waste products attempts to kill the Toxic Avenger.

A marginal improvement on the first film, but only because it could hardly be worse.

w Gay Partington Terry, Lloyd Kaufman   *d* Michael Herz, Lloyd Kaufman   *ph* James London   *m* Christopher Demarco   *ad* Alexis Grey   *ed* Joseph McGirr

Ron Fazio, John Altamura, Phoebe Legere, Rich Collins, Rikiya Yasuoka, Tsutomu Sekine, Mayako Katsuragi, Jessica Dublin

The Toxic Avenger Part III: The Last Temptation Of Toxie
US   1989   89m   TVC
Troma/Lloyd Kaufman, Michael Herz
V

The Toxic Avenger is momentarily transformed into an upwardly mobile monster before reverting to type.

Violence, crude humour and deliberately inept acting and directing create a cinematic pollution of their own.

w Gay Partington Terry   *story* Lloyd Kaufman   *d* Lloyd Kaufman, Michael Herz   *ph* James London   *m* Barrie Guard   *ad* Alex Grey   *ed* Michael Schweitzer

Ron Fazio, John Altamura, Phoebe Legere, Rick Collins, Lisa Gaye, Jessica Dublin, Tsutomu Sekine

The Toy
US   1983   102m   colour
Columbia/Rastar (Phil Feldman)
V*, L

A black janitor is hired as a toy for a millionaire's nine-year-old son.

Feeble attempt to translate a 1976 French film by Francis Veber. The few laughs are laughs of embarrassment.

w Carol Sobieski   *d* Richard Donner   *ph* Laszlo Kovacs   *m* Patrick Williams   *pd* Charles Rosen

Richard Pryor, Jackie Gleason, Ned Beatty, Scott Schwarz, Teresa Ganzel, Wilfrid Hyde-White, Tony King

'Tasteless in implication, flavourless in execution.' – *Sight and Sound*

The Toy Maker
US   1991   Foto-Kem colour
Still Silent (Brian Yuzna, Richard N. Gladstein)
V

The son of a sweet old alcoholic toy-maker creates toys with a difference: they kill.

A nasty little gory horror movie.

w Martin Kitrosser, Brian Yuzna   *d* Martin Kitrosser   *ph* James Mathers   *m* Matthew Morse   *pd* W. Brooke Wheeler   *sp* Screaming Mad George, Ken Tarallo   *ed* Norman Buckley

Jane Higginson, Tracy Fraim, Brian Bremer, William Thorne, Neith Hunter, Mickey Rooney

Toy Soldiers
US   1991   112m   Continental colour
Columbia TriStar/Island World (Jack E. Freedman, Wayne S. Williams, Patricia Herskovic)
V, V*, L, S

Wealthy teenage American schoolkids turn the tables on a group of mercenaries, hired by a South American drug dealer, who take them hostage.

Silly, violent action movie presumably aimed at a teen audience that likes plenty of blood and gore.

w Daniel Petrie Jnr, David Koepp   *novel* William P. Kennedy   *d* Daniel Petrie Jnr   *ph* Thomas Burstyn   *m* Robert Folk   *pd* Chester Kaczenski   *ed* Michael Kahn

Sean Astin, Wil Wheaton, Keith Coogan, Andrew Divoff, R. Lee Ermey, Mason Adams, Denholm Elliott, Louis Gosset Jnr, George Perez

'Incompetent botch-up of a potentially good if unlikely story.' – *Derek Malcolm, Guardian*

Toy Tiger
US   1956   88m   Technicolor   Cinemascope
U-I (Howard Christie)

The imaginative small son of a widow 'adopts' her business friend as his father.

Flat sentimental comedy off the studio's conveyor belt, a remake of *Mad about Music.*

w Ted Sherdeman   *d* Jerry Hopper   *ph* George Robinson   *m* Joseph Gershenson

Jeff Chandler, Laraine Day, Tim Hovey, Cecil Kellaway, Richard Haydn, David Janssen

The Toy Wife *
US   1938   95m   bw
MGM (Merian C. Cooper)
GB title: *Frou Frou*

In the early 19th century in Louisiana, a flirtatious girl causes jealousy and tragedy.

Another bid in the *Jezebel/Gone with the Wind* stakes, this handsome production proved a commercial misfire and hastened the end of its star's career.

w Zoe Akins   *d* Richard Thorpe   *ph* Oliver T. Marsh   *m* Edward Ward

Luise Rainer, Melvyn Douglas, Robert Young, Barbara O'Neil, H. B. Warner, Alma Kruger, Walter Kingsford

'Old-fashioned melodrama, beautifully produced but creaky.' – *Variety*

'Laughter Is A State of Mind.'
Toys
US   1992   121m   CFI colour
TCF (Mark Johnson, Barry Levinson)
V, V*, L, S

An uptight army officer inherits a toy factory and switches production from cuddly toys to increasingly aggressive ones.

Visually splendid but otherwise totally incoherent movie.

w Valerie Curtin, Barry Levinson   *d* Barry Levinson   *ph* Adam Greenberg   *m* Hans Zimmer, Trevor Horn   *pd* Ferdinando Scarfiotti   *ed* Stu Linder

Robin Williams, Michael Gambon, Joan Cusack, Robin Wright, LL Cool J, Donald O'Connor, Jack Warden

'Only a filmmaker with Barry Levinson's clout would have been so indulged to create such a sprawling, seemingly unsupervised mess . . . It will be hard to top as the season's major clunker.' – *Variety*

'A disaster . . . It is quite unlike anything Levinson has done before, and it is sincerely to be hoped that he never does anything like it again.' – *Derek Malcolm, Guardian*

AAN: Ferdinando Scarfiotti; Albert Wolsky (costume design)

Toys in the Attic *
US   1963   90m   bw   Panavision
UA/Claude/Mirisch
V*

In a shabby New Orleans home, two ageing spinsters struggle to look after their ne'er-do-well brother.

Play into film doesn't go in this case, but the script and acting are interesting.

w James Poe   *play* Lillian Hellman   *d* George Roy Hill   *ph* Joseph Biroc   *m* George Duning   *ad* Cary Odell

Geraldine Page, Wendy Hiller, Dean Martin, Yvette Mimieux, Gene Tierney, Larry Gates

Traces of Red
US   1992   105m   colour
Entertainment/Samuel Goldwyn Company (Mark Gordon)
V, V*, L

A cop attempts to solve a series of killings of women with whom he has been involved and for which he is chief suspect.

Deadly dull thriller, of no interest whatsoever.

w Jim Piddock   *d* Andy Wolk   *ph* Tim Suhrstedt   *m* Graeme Revel   *pd* Dan Bishop, Dianna Freas   *ed* Trudy Ship

James Belushi, Lorraine Bracco, Tony Goldwyn, William Russ, Faye Grant, Michelle Joyner, Joe Lisi, Victoria Bass, Jim Piddock

'What could have been, and perhaps was intended to be, a fetching latterday film noir, is constantly stymied by a wooden script, a cast that is at a loss to deal with it, and direction that gives nobody any help.' – *Derek Malcolm, Guardian*

'A dramatic failure but an entertaining exercise in camp.' – *Variety*

'A story of how men and women act when they think nobody is looking!'
Track of the Cat *
US   1954   102m   Warnercolor   Cinemascope
Warner/Wayne-Fellows/Batjac (Robert Fellows)

In the northern California backwoods one winter in the 1880s a farming family is menaced by a marauding mountain lion.

With the lion a symbol of evil, this is real *Cold Comfort Farm* country and despite good intentions all round becomes irresistibly funny before the end, largely because everyone moves and speaks so s-l-o-w-l-y. The bleached colour is interesting but would suit only snowy settings.

w A. I. Bezzerides   *novel* Walter Van Tilburg Clark   *d* William A. Wellman   *ph* William H: Clothier   *m* Roy Webb

Robert Mitchum, Diana Lynn, Beulah Bondi, Teresa Wright, Tab Hunter, Philip Tonge, William Hopper, Carl Switzer

'Cinemascope's first genuine weirdie . . . the script is redolent of Eugene O'Neill, and to its presentation the director brings a touch of Poe . . . Despair hangs in the air like a curse . . . unfortunately ambition overreaches itself, and the film topples over into barnstorming melodrama.' – *MFB*

'Bill Wellman had the idea: he wanted to make a colour picture with very little colour.' – *William Clothier*

Track 29

GB 1988 91m colour
Recorded Releasing/Handmade (Rick McCullum)
V*

A sensual woman, whose husband prefers playing
with his electric train-set, is attracted to a mysterious
stranger who claims to be her long-lost son.

Offbeat but unsatisfactory psychological drama that
loses its way in thickets of sexuality.

w Dennis Potter d Nicolas Roeg ph Alex
Thomson m Stanley Myers ad David Brockhurst
ed Tony Lawson

Theresa Russell, Gary Oldham, Christopher Lloyd,
Sarah Bernhard, Colleen Camp, Seymour Cassell

Trackdown

US 1976 98m DeLuxe
UA/Essaness (Bernard Schwarz)

A Montana rancher follows his sister to Los Angeles
and avenges her ill-treatment there by gangsters.

Routine action thriller with fashionable realism and
violence.

w Paul Edwards d Richard T. Heffron ph Gene
Polito m Charles Bernstein

Jim Mitchum, Karen Lamm, Anne Archer, Erik
Estrada, Cathy Lee Crosby, Vince Cannon

Trade Winds

US 1939 93m bw
Walter Wanger

A girl who thinks she has committed murder flees to
the Far East, and a cynical detective is sent to bring
her back. Guess what happens.

Smartly written mixture of comedy, drama, mystery
and travelogue which comes off only in spots; it
needed a firmer hand.

w Dorothy Parker, Alan Campbell, Frank R. Adams
d Tay Garnett ph Rudolph Maté m Alfred
Newman

Fredric March, Joan Bennett, Ralph Bellamy, Ann
Sothern, Sidney Blackmer, Thomas Mitchell, Robert
Elliott

'All the elements that provide broad entertainment
are present in this picture, and it should reap healthy
grosses.' – Variety

Trader Horn *

US 1930 120m bw
MGM (Irving Thalberg)

An experienced African trader overcomes tribal
hostility.

Primitive talkie for which second units were sent to
Africa amid much publicity hoo-ha. After fifty years,
nothing of interest remains to be seen.

w Richard Schayer, Dale Van Every, Thomas Neville
novel Alfred Aloysius Horn, Etheldreda Lewis d W.
S. Van Dyke ph Clyde de Vinna

Harry Carey, Edwina Booth, Duncan Renaldo, Mutia
Omoolu, C. Aubrey Smith

'Sure money-getter. Outstanding animal stuff, great
sound effects, and thin story, which has good-looking
white girl romping around scantily clad.' – Variety

'A movie that contains all the best features of a zoo, a
cannibal dance, and a big yarn by Rider Haggard.' –
National Board of Review

AAN: best picture

Trader Horn

US 1973 105m Metrocolor
MGM (Lewis J. Rachmil)

Pitiful remake patched together largely from stock
footage.

w William Norton, Edward Harper d Reza Badiyi
ph Ronald W. Browne m Shelly Manne

Rod Taylor, Anne Heywood, Jean Sorel

'Laughably inept . . . it cannot face word of mouth for
long.' – Variety

Trader Tom of the China Seas

US 1954 bw serial: 12 eps
Republic

A young trader scotches a plot to spread revolution in
Sumatra.

Among the last half dozen serials made, but far from
the best.

d Franklin Adreon

Harry Lauter, Aline Towne, Lyle Talbot, Robert
Shayne, Victor Sen Yung

Trading Places **

US 1983 116m Technicolor
Paramount/Landis-Folsey (Aaron Russo)
V, V*, L

Two rich men arrange a wager on the effects of
environment over heredity, and arrange for a con man
and a stockbroker to change places.

Surprisingly witty comedy, which while not aspiring
to great heights, and marred by a few excesses,
brought a refreshing breath of air to a declining genre.

w Timothy Harris, Herschel Weingrod d John Landis
ph Robert Paynter m Elmer Bernstein pd Gene
Rudolf

Dan Aykroyd, Eddie Murphy, Ralph Bellamy, Don
Ameche, Denholm Elliott, Jamie Lee Curtis, Kristin
Holby

'Proof positive that the genuine American populist
comedy can still attract attention.' – John Pym, MFB

BFA: Jamie Lee Curtis, Denholm Elliott

AAN: Elmer Bernstein

Traffic *

France/Italy 1970 96m Eastmancolor
Corona/Gibe/Selenia (Robert Dorfman)

The designer of a camping car has various little
accidents on the way from the works to a show.

Rambling comedy with understated jokes and an
almost invisible star.

w Jacques Tati, Jacques Legrange d Jacques Tati
(with Bert Haanstra) ph Edouard Van Den Enden,
Marcel Weiss m Charles Dumont

Jacques Tati

The Tragedy of a Ridiculous Man **

Italy 1981 116m Technicolor
Warner/Ladd Company (Giovanni Bertolucci)
V*

original title: La Tragedia Di Un Uomo Ridicolo

A dairy farmer is faced with losing his livelihood in
order to pay a ransom demanded by terrorists who
have kidnapped his son.

Engrossing study of contemporary terrorism and
individual responsibility, though its refusal to explain
everything alienated many audiences.

wd Bernardo Bertolucci ph Carlo Di Palma
m Ennio Morricone pd Gianni Silvestri
ed Gabriella Cristani

Ugo Tognazzi, Anouk Aimee, Laura Morante, Victor
Cavallo, Olympia Carlisi, Riccardo Tognazzi, Vittorio
Caprioli

The Tragic Pursuit: see Caccia Tragica

The Trail Beyond

US 1934 57m bw
Monogram/Lone Star (Paul Malvern)
V*

A cowboy goes to Canada to find missing relatives of
his father's best friend and helps an old college friend
along the way.

A routine Western, with rather more plot and less
action than usual.

w Lindsley Parsons story The Wolf Hunters by James
Oliver Curwood d Robert N. Bradbury ph Archie
Stout ad E. R. Hickson ed Charles Hunt

John Wayne, Verna Hillie, Noah Beery Snr, Noah
Beery Jnr, Robert Frazer, Iris Lancaster, James Marcus

The Trail of '98 *

US 1928 90m at 24 fps bw silent
MGM

San Franciscans leave their homes for the Klondike
gold rush.

Impressive spectacular while it stays outdoors; not so
good when the plot takes over.

w Waldmar Young, Ben Glazer novel Robert W.
Service d Clarence Brown

Dolores Del Rio, Ralph Forbes, Harry Carey, Karl
Dane, Tully Marshall

'The surging drama of love in the Kentucky hills springs to
thrilling life as the first outdoor action romance filmed in
colour!'

The Trail of the Lonesome Pine *

US 1936 102m Technicolor
Paramount (Walter Wanger)

A hillbilly girl goes back home when her brother is
killed in a family feud.

Antediluvian Ozarkian melodrama, notable as the
first outdoor film to be shot in three-colour
Technicolor.

w Grover Jones, Horace McCoy, Harvey Thew
novel John Fox Jnr d Henry Hathaway ph Howard
Green m Hugo Friedhofer, Gerrard Carbonara

Sylvia Sidney, Fred MacMurray, Henry Fonda, Fred
Stone, Nigel Bruce, Beulah Bondi, Robert Barrat,
Spanky McFarland, Fuzzy Knight

'A good show saleable for big grosses, a flicker the
ballyhoo boys can and will do tricks with.' – Variety

'Unnatural as it is, the colour does no serious damage
to the picture. This moldy bit of hokum . . . takes
movies back to the days of their childhood.' –
Newsweek

† The story was first filmed in 1915 by Cecil B. de
Mille.

AAN: song 'A Melody from the Sky' (m Louis Alter,
ly Sidney Mitchell)

Trail of the Pink Panther

GB 1982 97m Technicolor Panavision
MGM-UA/Titan (Blake Edwards, Tony Adams)
V, V*, L, S

Inspector Clouseau is reported missing at sea and a
television reporter interviews those who had known
him.

Flimsy, necrophiliac excuse for a movie, with a star
cast clearly failing to make bricks without straw two
years after the nominal star's death.

w Frank and Tom Waldman, Blake Edwards,
Geoffrey Edwards d Blake Edwards ph Dick
Bush m Henry Mancini pd Peter Mullins
ed Alan Jones

Peter Sellers, Joanna Lumley, Herbert Lom, David
Niven, Richard Mulligan, Capucine, Robert Loggia,
Harvey Korman, Burt Kwouk, Graham Stark, Leonard
Rossiter, Peter Arne, Ronald Fraser

Trail of the Vigilantes *

US 1940 78m bw
Universal

In the old west, a reporter sets out to break up a band
of outlaws.

A mild Western which at the time had some
reputation as a wild comedy; the fact was that it

turned out badly and the editors did the best they could.

w Harold Shumate d Allan Dwan

Franchot Tone, Warren William, Broderick Crawford, Andy Devine, Mischa Auer, Porter Hall, Peggy Moran

'As light amusement it does all right, but it is amusement in confusion.' – *Otis Ferguson*

Trail Street

US 1947 84m bw
Nat Holt/RKO
V*

Wheat is planted in Kansas by the early settlers.

Pretty good, unpretentious Western.

w Norman Houston, Gene Lewis d Ray Enright

Randolph Scott, Robert Ryan, Anne Jeffreys, Billy House, George 'Gabby' Hayes

'It carried their hopes, their nation's honour!'
The Train **
US 1964 140m bw
UA/Ariane/Dear (Jules Bricken)
V*

In 1944, the French resistance tries to prevent the Nazis from taking art treasures back to Germany on a special train.

Proficient but longwinded suspense actioner with spectacular sequences; a safe bet for train enthusiasts.

w Franklin Coen, Frank Davis, Walter Bernstein d John Frankenheimer ph Jean Tournier, Walter Wottiz m Maurice Jarre

Burt Lancaster, *Paul Scofield*, Jeanne Moreau, Michael Simon, Wolfgang Preiss, Suzanne Flon

'Extraordinarily good in many of its parts but rather disappointing as a whole . . . its greatest virtue is an almost overpowering physical realism.' – *Moira Walsh, America*

AAN: script

Train of Events
GB 1949 89m bw
Ealing (Michael Relph)

Portmanteau of stories à la *Friday the 13th* or *Dead of Night*, linked by a train disaster.

A rather mechanical entertainment, proficiently made.

w Basil Dearden, T. E. B. Clarke, Ronald Millar, Angus MacPhail d Basil Dearden, Charles Crichton, Sidney Cole ph Lionel Banes, Gordon Dines m Leslie Bridgewater

Valerie Hobson, John Clements, Jack Warner, Gladys Henson, Peter Finch, Irina Baronova, Susan Shaw, Patric Doonan, Joan Dowling, Laurence Payne, Mary Morris

The Train Robbers
US 1973 92m Technicolor Panavision
Warner/Batjac (Michael Wayne)
V*, L

A widow asks three gunmen to help her clear her husband's name by retrieving gold he had stolen.

Shaggy-dog Western, sadly lacking in comic situation and detail.

wd Burt Kennedy ph William Clothier m Dominic Frontière

John Wayne, Ann-Margret, Rod Taylor, Ben Johnson, Bobby Vinton, Christopher George

The Traitor *
GB 1957 88m bw
Fantur (E. J. Fancey)
US title: *The Accused*

At the annual reunion of a resistance group, the host announces that one of their number was a traitor.

Heavy-handed theatrical melodrama, helped by a stout plot and some directional flair.

wd Michael McCarthy ph Bert Mason m Jackie Brown

Donald Wolfit, Robert Bray, Jane Griffiths, Carl Jaffe, Anton Diffring, Oscar Quitak, Rupert Davies, John Van Eyssen

The Traitors *
GB 1962 69m bw
Ello (Jim O'Connelly)

A top scientist is killed and MI5 springs into action.

Commendable second feature with narrative virtues absent in most big films.

w Jim O'Connelly d Robert Tronson ph Michael Reed m Johnny Douglas

Patrick Allen, James Maxwell, Ewan Roberts, Zena Walker

Traitor's Gate
GB 1965 80m bw
Columbia/Summit (Ted Lloyd)

A London businessman organizes a gang to steal the Crown Jewels.

Modest caper melodrama, routine but watchable.

w John Sansom novel Edgar Wallace d Freddie Francis ph Denys Coop

Albert Lieven, Gary Raymond, Margot Trooger, Klaus Kinski, Catherina von Schell, Edward Underdown

The Tramp *
US 1915 20m approx (24 fps) bw silent
Mutual

A tramp saves a girl from crooks, is wounded and cared for by her, deliriously happy – until her lover arrives.

Fairly funny star comedy, the first with sentimental touches and the origin of the into-the-sunset fade-out.

wd Charles Chaplin ph Rollie Totheroh

Charles Chaplin, Edna Purviance, Bud Jamison, Leo White, Lloyd Bacon

Tramp Tramp Tramp *
US 1926 65m approx (24 fps) bw silent
Harry Langdon

Harry enters a cross-country walking contest in order to impress his girl.

Well-staged peripatetic comedy, the star's first feature.

w Frank Capra, Tim Whelan, Hal Conklin, Gerald Duffy, Murray Roth, J. Frank Holliday d Harry Edwards

Harry Langdon, Joan Crawford, Alec B. Francis

'Jack Deth is back . . . and he's never been here before!'
Trancers *
US 1985 85m DeLuxe
Empire Pictures (Charles Band)
V
aka: *Future Cop*

A tough policeman, Jack Deth, is sent from the future into the present day to hunt down a villain who wants to take over the world by creating Trancers, weak-willed and violent individuals under his psychic influence.

Engaging and occasionally witty low-budget science-fiction action movie, featuring a hero with the manner of a world-weary private eye of the 1930s.

w Paul de Meo, Danny Bilson d Charles Band ph Mac Ahlberg m Mark Ryder, Phil Davies pd Jeff Staggs sp John Buechler ed Ted Nicolaou

Tim Thomerson, Helen Hunt, Michael Stefani, Art Le Fleur, Telma Hopkins, Richard Herd, Anne Seymour, Miguel Fernandez, Biff Manard

Trancers II
US 1991 87m colour
Full Moon (Charles Band)
V
aka: *Trancers II: The Return of Jack Deth*

Jack Deth protects the father of a future high official against attacks from Trancers.

Abysmal sequel in which little happens and nothing matters, made, by the look of it, on an even more infinitesimal budget.

w Jackson Barr story Jackson Barr, Charles Band d Charles Band ph Adolfo Bartoli m Mark Ryder, Phil Davies pd Kathleen Coates sp Palah Sandling, Kevin McCarthy ed Ted Nicolaou, Andy Hornitch

Tim Thomerson, Helen Hunt, Megan Ward, Biff Manard, Richard Lynch, Martine Beswick, Jeffrey Combs, Telma Hopkins

'Some unintentional humor doesn't save this unnecessary sequel, a quickie that's all talk and no action.' – *Variety*

Trancers III
US 1992 83m Foto-Kem colour
Paramount/Full Moon (Albert Band)
V
aka: *Trancers III: Deth Lives*

While working as a detective in Los Angeles in 1992, Jack Deth is transported to 2352, when the Trancers are destroying the world, to be ordered back to 2005 to kill their creator.

A low-budget variation on the familiar theme of one man single-handedly overcoming a highly trained army; it is also low on skill and imagination.

wd C. Courtney Joyner ph Adolfo Bartoli m Mark Ryder, Phil Davies, Richard Band pd Milo sp Kurtzman, Nicotero, Berger EFX Group ed Lauren Schaffer, Margaret-Anne Smith

Tim Thomerson, Melanie Smith, Andrew Robinson, Tony Pierce, Ed Beechner, Dawn Ann Billings, Helen Hunt, Megan Ward, Stephan Macht, Telma Hopkins

'This has some funny lines, smart science fiction riffs, hateworthy villains and, most valuable of all, Thomerson's hard-bitten but hilarious leading performance, to make it worth checking out.' – *Empire*

† The film was cut to 72m on its British video release.

Transatlantic *
US 1931 74m bw
Fox

Various personal stories come to a climax aboard a transatlantic liner.

Early attempt at what has now become a very worn format; quite lively it must have seemed then.

w Guy Bolton, Lynn Starling d William K. Howard ad Gordon Wiles

Edmund Lowe, Lois Moran, John Halliday, Greta Nissen, Jean Hersholt, Myrna Loy, Earle Foxe, Billy Bevan

'An aquatic Grand Hotel; should prosper.' – *Variety*

AAN: Gordon Wiles

Transatlantic Merry Go Round
US 1934 92m bw
Reliance
V*

Romantic misunderstandings on an ocean liner.

Patchy comedy with some good scenes.

w Joseph Moncure March, Harry W. Conn and Leon Gordon d Ben Stoloff

Jack Benny, Nancy Carroll, Gene Raymond, Sydney Howard

'Good, popular screen entertainment; certain box office fodder.' – *Variety*

Transatlantic Tunnel: see *The Tunnel*

Trans-Europe Express *
France   1966   90m   bw
Como Film (Samy Halfon)

Film-makers on a train invent a violent plot and then find life aping it.

A theme beloved of Hollywood is treated intellectually, and almost succeeds in attracting all classes.

wd Alain Robbe-Grillet   *ph* Willy Kurant   *m* Verdi

Jean-Louis Trintignant, Marie-France Pisier, Nadine Verdier, Christian Barbier, Charles Millot, Alain Robbe-Grillet

Transgression
US   1931   70m   bw
RKO

During a Paris vacation, a man forgives his wife for her affair with a Spanish gigolo.

Very routine, matinée drama.

w Elizabeth Meehan   *novel* Kate Jordan   *d* Herbert Brenon

Kay Francis, Ricardo Cortez, Paul Cavanagh, Nance O'Neil

'Doubtful de luxe subject, principally because its story lacks conviction.' – *Variety*

The Transvestite: see *Glen or Glenda*

The Trap *
US   1958   84m   Technicolor
Paramount/Parkwood-Heath (Melvin Frank, Norman Panama)
V*
GB title: *The Baited Trap*

A lawyer helps a vicious killer to escape into Mexico, but the plan backfires.

Reasonably tense action thriller with desert backgrounds.

w Richard Alan Simmons, Norman Panama   *d* Norman Panama   *ph* Daniel L. Fapp   *m* Irvin Talbot

Richard Widmark, Lee J. Cobb, Earl Holliman, Tina Louise, Carl Benton Reid, Lorne Green

The Trap
GB/Canada   1966   106m   Eastmancolor
Panavision
Parallel (George H. Brown)
V*

In 19th-century British Columbia a rough trapper takes a wife, who at first is terrified of him but nurses him when he is hurt . . .

Primitive open air melodrama with good action sequences; well made but hardly endearing.

w David Osborn   *d* Sidney Hayers   *ph* Robert Krasker   *m* Ron Goodwin

Oliver Reed, Rita Tushingham, Rex Sevenoaks, Barbara Chilcott

'The Wonder Show Of The World!'
Trapeze **
US   1956   105m   DeLuxe   Cinemascope
UA/Hecht-Lancaster (James Hill)
V*

A circus partnership almost breaks up when a voluptuous third member is engaged.

Concentrated, intense melodrama filmed almost entirely within a French winter circus and giving a very effective feel, almost a smell, of the life therein. Despite great skill in the making, however, the length is too great for a wisp of plot that goes back to *The Three Maxims* and doubtless beyond.

w James R. Webb   *d* Carol Reed   *ph* Robert Krasker   *m* Malcolm Arnold

Burt Lancaster, Tony Curtis, Gina Lollobrigida, Thomas Gomez, Johnny Puleo, Katy Jurado, Sidney James

† This version was supposedly adapted from a Max Catto novel, *The Killing Frost*, but in 1932 Harmonie of Germany issued a film with the title *Trapeze* and a remarkably similar story. It had a scenario by Alfred Machard and was directed by E. A. Dupont. The Anna Neagle film *The Three Maxims* (qv) was also very similar, but that was supposedly an original by Herman Mankiewicz.

Trash *
US   1970   103m   colour
Vaughn/Andy Warhol
V
aka: *Andy's Warhol's Trash*

A drug addict finds that the women he knows are anxious to cure him of his impotence.

Casually filmed and acted, with casual sexual encounters and moments of comedy along the way.

wd Paul Morrissey

Joe Dallesandro, Geri Miller, Holly Woodlawn, Bruce Pecheur, Jane Forth, Michael Sklar

Trauma
US   1993   105m   Technicolor
Overseas Filmgroup/ADC (Dario Argento)
V, V*

A couple track down a serial killer who is decapitating his victims.

Argento's first American film has little of the visual flair of the best of his Italian shockers; its predictability soon becomes wearing.

w Dario Argento, T. E. D. Klein, Franco Ferrini, Giovanni Romoli   *d* Dario Argento   *ph* Raffaele Mertes   *m* Pino Donaggio   *pd* Billy Jett   *sp* Tom Savini   *ed* Conrad Gonzalez

Christopher Rydell, Asia Argento, Piper Laurie, Frederic Forrest, James Russo, Brad Dourif, Laura Johnson

'A by-the-numbers stalker thriller for undemanding genre fans only.' – *Variety*

The Traveling Executioner *
US   1970   95m   Metrocolor   Panavision
MGM (Jack Smight)

In 1918 an ex-carnival showman travels the American South with his portable electric chair and charges a hundred dollars per execution, but falls for one of his proposed victims.

Oddball fable without apparent moral; neither fantastic nor funny enough.

w Garrie Bateson   *d* Jack Smight   *ph* Philip Lathrop   *m* Jerry Goldsmith

Stacy Keach, Mariana Hill, Bud Cort, Graham Jarvis

Traveling Saleslady
US   1935   75m   bw
Warner

A toothpaste manufacturer's daughter shows her father the value of advertising.

Warner stock company comedy which hits no heights but provided reliable entertainment.

w Hugh Herbert, Manuel Seff, Benny Rubin, Frank Howard Clark   *d* Ray Enright

Joan Blondell, Hugh Herbert, Glenda Farrell, William Gargan, Al Shean, Grant Mitchell, Ruth Donnelly, Bert Roach

'It will please and should do all right at the wicket.' – *Variety*

Traveller's Joy
GB   1949   78m   bw
Gainsborough/Rank

A divorced couple, stranded in Sweden by lack of funds, have to take joint action.

Mild topical comedy from a popular play.

w Allan MacKinnon, Bernard Quayle   *play* Arthur Macrae   *d* Ralph Thomas

Googie Withers, John McCallum, Yolande Donlan, Maurice Denham, Geoffrey Sumner, Colin Gordon, Dora Bryan

Travelling North *
Australia   1986   96m   Eastmancolor
View Pictures/CEL (Ben Gannon)
V*

A vigorous 70-year-old leaves Melbourne for sub-tropical Queensland, but his health gives out.

Moving Australian mirror image of *On Golden Pond*, with good acting and direction.

w David Williamson   *play* David Williamson   *d* Carl Schultz   *ph* Julian Penney   *md* Alan John   *pd* Owen Paterson   *ed* Henry Dangar

Leo McKern, Julia Blake, Graham Kennedy, Henri Szeps

Travels with My Aunt *
US   1972   109m   Metrocolor   Panavision
MGM (Robert Fryer, James Cresson)
V*, L

A staid bank accountant is landed in a series of continental adventures by his eccentric life-loving aunt.

Busy but fairly disastrous adaptation of a delightful novel, ruined by ceaseless chatter, lack of characterization, shapeless incident and an absurdly caricatured central performance.

w Jay Presson Allen, Hugh Wheeler   *novel* Graham Greene   *d* George Cukor   *ph* Douglas Slocombe   *m* Tony Hatch   *pd* John Box

Maggie Smith, *Alec McCowen*, Lou Gossett, Robert Stephens, Cindy Williams

'It seems to run down before it gets started.' – *New Yorker, 1977*

AAN: Douglas Slocombe; Maggie Smith

La Traviata **
Italy   1982   109m   colour
Accent Films/RAI (Tarak Ben Ammar)
V*, L

A much-acclaimed version of an opera which had previously defied transcription to the screen.

w Francesco Maria Piave, Franco Zeffirelli   *opera* Verdi   *d* and designed by *Franco Zeffirelli*   *ph* Ennio Guarnieri *ed* Peter Taylor, Franca Sylvi

Placido Domingo, Teresa Stratas, Cornell MacNeil, Allan Monk, Axell Gall

'Décors so opulent as on occasion to resemble a three-ring circus.' – *Sight and Sound*

AAN: costume design; art direction

Tread Softly Stranger *
GB   1958   91m   bw
Alderdale (George Minter)

In a north country town, two brothers in love with the same girl rob a safe.

Hilarious murky melodrama full of glum faces, with a well-worn trick ending; rather well photographed.

w George Minter, Denis O'Dell   *play* Jack Popplewell   *d* Gordon Parry   *ph* Douglas Slocombe   *m* Tristam Cary

George Baker, Terence Morgan, Diana Dors, Wilfrid Lawson, Patrick Allen, Jane Griffith, Joseph Tomelty, Norman Macowan

Treason: see *Guilty of Treason*

Treasure Hunt

GB 1952 79m bw
Romulus (Anatole de Grunwald)

The eccentric middle-aged members of an Irish family find their father's fortune is missing.

Theatrical comedy with some charm and humour, but very much a photographed play.

w Anatole de Grunwald play M. J. Perry d John Paddy Carstairs ph C. Pennington-Richards m Mischa Spoliansky

Jimmy Edwards, *Martita Hunt, Athene Seyler,* Naunton Wayne, June Clyde, Susan Stephen, Brian Worth

Treasure Island **

US 1934 105m bw
MGM (Hunt Stromberg)
V*

An old pirate map leads to a long sea voyage, a mutiny, and buried treasure.

Nicely mounted Hollywood version of a classic adventure story, a little slow in development but meticulously produced.

w John Lee Mahin novel Robert Louis Stevenson d Victor Fleming ph Ray June, Clyde de Vinna, Harold Rosson m Herbert Stothart

Wallace Beery, Jackie Cooper, Lewis Stone, *Lionel Barrymore,* Otto Kruger, Douglass Dumbrille, Nigel Bruce, Chic Sale

'While much of it entrances, the whole is somewhat tiring.' – *Variety*

'The first three-quarters is so lively and well established in its mood as to make the whole quite worth going to.' – *Otis Ferguson*

Treasure Island *

GB 1950 96m Technicolor
RKO/Walt Disney (Perce Pearce)
V*, L

Cheerful Disney remake, poor on detail but transfixed by a swaggeringly overplayed and unforgettable leading performance.

w Lawrence Edward Watkin d Byron Haskin ph F. A. Young m Clifton Parker pd Thomas Morahan ed Alan Jaggs

Robert Newton, Bobby Driscoll, Walter Fitzgerald, Basil Sydney, Denis O'Dea, Geoffrey Wilkinson, Ralph Truman

'Serviceable rather than imaginative.' – *Lindsay Anderson*

'The result is an absolutely super party, but not "the world's greatest adventure story". Walt Disney may have, as Synopsis suggests, "much in common with Stevenson". But not this; shiver my timbers, not *Treasure Island.'* – *C. A. Lejeune.*

'The Long John Silver of Robert Newton . . . is the finest I ever saw . . . as succulent as peach-fed ham, as sweet as a spoonful of sugar held high over the porridge plate, as darkly oily as a car sump, as tricky as an ageing jockey.' – *Paul Holt*

Treasure Island

GB/France/Germany/Spain 1971 95m colour
Massfilms/FDL/CCC/Eguiluz (Harry Alan Towers)
V*

Spiritless and characterless international remake with poor acting, production and dubbing.

w Wolf Mankowitz, O. W. Jeeves (Welles) d John Hough ph Cicilio Paniagua m Natal Massara

Orson Welles, Kim Burfield, Lionel Stander, Walter Slezak, Rik Battaglia

'Sail the high seas. Battle the pirates. Live the adventure.'
Treasure Island

US 1990 132m colour
Warner/Agamemnon/British Lion (Fraser C. Heston)
V, V*, L

Faithful to the original, but a version lacking in panache, and plodding when it should be exciting.

wd Fraser C. Heston novel Robert Louis Stevenson ph Robert Steadman m Paddy Maloney pd Tony Woollard ed Eric Boyd-Perkins, Bill Parnell, Gregory Gontz

Charlton Heston, Christian Bale, Oliver Reed, Christopher Lee, Richard Johnson, Julian Glover, Clive Wood, John Benfield, Isla Blair

Treasure Island

France/USA 1991 115m colour
BFI/Les Films du Passage/Cannon (Paolo Branco)
French title: *L'Ile au trésor*

A boy dreams, or perhaps lives, a series of events that bear some resemblance to Stevenson's tale of pirates and buried treasure.

A delirious modern-day version, in which events are repeated with variations from different viewpoints, and nothing is what it seems. And nothing is what it amounts to.

wd Raúl Ruiz novel *Treasure Island* by Robert Louis Stevenson ph Acacio de Almeida m Georges Arriagada ad Maria-José Branco ed Rodolfo Wedeles

Melvil Poupaud, Martin Landau, Vic Tayback, Lou Castel, Jeffrey Kime, Anna Karina, Jean-Pierre Léaud

'One of Ruiz's most seductive films because it so evidently falls short of the grandiose completeness to which it aspires. A richly messy narrative bricolage, it is finally revealed as a game that the viewer is invited to play. It may finally be about very little of serious substance – or indeed about something as trivial as the "future of Western Civilisation", to which the dying Captain portentously alludes – but that in itself makes it all the more worth playing.' – *Jonathan Romney, Sight and Sound*

The Treasure of Lost Canyon

US 1952 82m Technicolor
U-I (Leonard Goldstein)

A small boy robbed of his inheritance finds it with the help of a country doctor who turns out to be his uncle.

Modest juvenile adventure, rather boringly narrated.

w Brainerd Duffield, Emerson Crocker story Robert Louis Stevenson d Ted Tetzlaff ph Russell Metty m Joseph Gershenson

William Powell, Julia Adams, Charles Drake, Rosemary de Camp, Henry Hull, Tommy Ivo

Treasure of Matecumbe

US 1976 116m Technicolor
Walt Disney (Bill Anderson)
V*

Two boys seek buried gold in the Florida keys.

Cheerful adventure tale with a few nods to *Treasure Island;* all very competent in the Disney fashion.

w Don Tait d Vincent McEveety ph Frank Phillips m Buddy Baker

Robert Foxworth, Joan Hackett, Peter Ustinov, Vic Morrow, Jane Wyatt, Johnny Duran, Billy Attmore

Treasure of Monte Cristo

US 1949 76m bw
Lippert/Screen Guild

In modern San Francisco, a descendant of Monte Cristo is framed for murder.

Mildly amusing but slackly made variant on a familiar theme.

w Aubrey Wisberg, Jack Pollexfen d William Berke

Glenn Langan, Adele Jergens, Steve Brodie, Robert Jordan, Michael Whalen

The Treasure of Pancho Villa

US 1955 96m Technicolor Superscope
RKO/Edmund Grainger
V*

Mexico 1915: an American adventurer becomes involved with the revolutionary Pancho Villa; both seek a gold consignment but it is buried in an avalanche.

Modestly well made, routine action drama.

w Niven Busch d George Sherman ph William Snyder m Leith Stevens

Rory Calhoun, Shelley Winters, *Gilbert Roland,* Joseph Calleia

Treasure of San Teresa

GB 1959 81m bw
Orbit (John Nasht, Patrick Filmer-Sankey)

An American secret service agent finds Nazi loot in a Czech convent.

Roughly-made, watchable actioner.

w Jack Andrews, Jeffrey Dell d Alvin Rakoff ph Wilkie Cooper m Philip Martell

Eddie Constantine, Dawn Addams, Marius Goring, Christopher Lee, Walter Gotell

Treasure of the Golden Condor

US 1952 93m Technicolor
TCF (Jules Buck)
V*

A young Frenchman flees to the South Seas but returns to discredit his wicked uncle.

Ineffectual remake of *Son of Fury* (qv) with Guatemalan backgrounds and no punch at all.

wd Delmer Daves ph Edward Cronjager m Sol Kaplan

Cornel Wilde, Finlay Currie, Constance Smith, George Macready, Walter Hampden, Anne Bancroft, Fay Wray, Leo G. Carroll

'Greed, gold and gunplay on a Mexican mountain of malice!'
'The nearer they got to their treasure the further they got from the law!'
The Treasure of the Sierra Madre **

US 1948 126m bw
Warner (Henry Blanke)
V, V*, L

Three gold prospectors come to grief through greed.

Well-acted but partly miscast action fable on the oldest theme in the world; rather tedious and studio-bound for a film with such a high reputation.

wd John Huston novel B. Traven ph Ted McCord md Leo F. Forbstein m Max Steiner

Humphrey Bogart, *Walter Huston,* Tim Holt, Alfonso Bedoya, John Huston, Bruce Bennett, Barton MacLane

'This bitter fable is told with cinematic integrity and considerable skill.' – *Henry Hart*

'The faces of the men, in close-up or in a group, achieve a kind of formal pattern and always dominate the screen.' – *Peter Ericsson*

'One of the very few movies made since 1927 which I am sure will stand up in the memory and esteem of qualified people alongside the best of the silent movies.' – *James Agee*

AA: John Huston (as writer and director); Walter Huston

AAN: best picture

The Treasure Seekers

US 1977 88m colour
Halart (Sam Manners)

Two old friends search for Henry Morgan's pirate treasure on Jamaica.

Dull thriller, in which very little happens and nothing to catch one's interest or attention.

w Rod Taylor story Walter Brough d Henry Levin ph Richard Kelly, Joe Jackman m Byron Lee ed Keith Stafford

Rod Taylor, Stuart Whitman, Elke Sommer, Jeremy Kemp, Keenan Wynn, Bob Phillips, Jennie Sherman

A Tree Grows in Brooklyn ***
US 1945 128m bw
TCF (Louis D. Lighton)
V*, L

Life for an Irish family with a drunken father in New York's teeming slums at the turn of the century.

A superbly-detailed studio production of the type they don't make any more: a family drama with interest for everybody.

w Tess Slesinger, Frank Davis novel Betty Smith d Elia Kazan ph Leon Shamroy m Alfred Newman

Peggy Ann Garner, James Dunn, Dorothy McGuire, Joan Blondell, Lloyd Nolan, Ted Donaldson, James Gleason, Ruth Nelson, John Alexander, Adeline de Walt Reynolds, Charles Halton

'He tells a maximum amount of story with a minimum of film. Little touches of humour and human understanding crop up throughout.' – Frank Ward, NBR

'An artistically satisfying and emotionally quickening tearjerker.' – Kine Weekly

'Its drabness is softened by a glow of love and hope.' – Picture Show

AA: James Dunn; Peggy Ann Garner (Special Award as outstanding child actress)

AAN: script

Tree of Hands
GB 1988 89m Eastmancolor
Pathé/Granada/British Screen/Film Four International/
   Greenpoint (Ann Scott)

After her young son dies, an American writer gives a home to an abused boy kidnapped by her mother.

Turgid and downbeat thriller that offers few pleasures.

w Gordon Williams novel Ruth Rendell d Giles Foster ph Kenneth MacMillan m Richard Hartley pd Adrian Smith ed David Martin

Helen Shaver, Lauren Bacall, Malcolm Stoddard, Peter Firth, Paul McGann, Kate Hardie, Tony Haygarth, Phyllida Law

'The film remains essentially comic-strip in its description of the various milieux and its treatment of the theme of who, in this chaotic selfish world, is best suited to care for the innocent.' – Louise Sweet, MFB

The Tree of Liberty: see The Howards of Virginia

The Tree of Wooden Clogs *
Italy 1978 186m Gevacolor
Curzon Films/RAI/GPC (Giulio Mandelli)
V*, L

In 19th-century Lombardy the lives of four peasant families are interwined.

Sensitive, novel-like investigation of times gone by; never very exciting but certainly never dull, despite the limits of 16mm and a non-professional cast.

wd Ermanno Olmi ph Carlo Petriocioli md Fernando Germani m Bach pd Franco Gambarana

Trelawny of the Wells: see The Actress

Tremors **
US 1989 96m DeLuxe
UIP/Universal/No Frills/Brent Maddock, S. S. Wilson
V*, L

Giant man-eating worms threaten a small Western town.

Enjoyable monster movie in the style of 50s films, which manages to be both funny and suspenseful.

w S. S. Wilson, Brent Maddock, Ron Underwood d Ron Underwood ph Alexander Gruszynski m Ernest Troost pd Ivo Cristante ed O. Nicholas Brown

Kevin Bacon, Fred Ward, Finn Carter, Michael Gross, Reba McEntire, Bobby Jacoby, Charlotte Stewart, Tony Genaro

'Shrewdly, unpretentiously written, energetically directed and played with high comic conviction, Tremors is bound to become a cult classic.' – Richard Schickel, Time

Trent's Last Case
GB 1952 90m bw
Wilcox-Neagle (Herbert Wilcox)

A journalist suspects that the death of a tycoon was murder.

Desultory version of a famous novel, with none of the original style and a few naïveties of its own.

w Pamela Bower novel E. C. Bentley d Herbert Wilcox ph Max Greene m Anthony Collins

Michael Wilding, Margaret Lockwood, Orson Welles, John McCallum, Miles Malleson

Trespass **
US 1993 101m DeLuxe
Universal (Neil Canton)
V, V*, L

Two firemen go on a treasure hunt for a gold cross, which turns out to be hidden in a deserted factory, used as a headquarters by a heavily armed black gang.

Tense and violent thriller, like a modernized, interior, technological version of The Treasure of the Sierra Madre.

w Bob Gale, Robert Zemeckis d Walter Hill ph Lloyd Ahern m Ry Cooder pd Jon Hutman ed Freeman Davies

Bill Paxton, Ice T, William Sadler, Ice Cube, Art Evans, De'Voreaux White, Bruce A. Young, Glenn Plummer

'Fizzles like a Molotov cocktail with a soggy fuse.' – Kim Newman, Empire

Trial *
US 1955 109m bw
MGM (Charles Schnee)

A young lawyer defends a Mexican boy accused of rape and murder.

Stereotyped but pacy and watchable racial drama with political overtones, Our Hero having to resist bigots, Commies and McCarthyites.

w Don M. Mankiewicz novel Don M. Mankiewicz d Mark Robson ph Robert Surtees m Daniele Amfitheatrof

Glenn Ford, Dorothy McGuire, Arthur Kennedy, John Hodiak, Katy Jurado, Rafael Campos, Juano Hernandez, Robert Middleton, John Hoyt

AAN: Arthur Kennedy

The Trial *
France/Italy/West Germany 1962 120m bw
Paris Europe/Ficit/Hisa (Alexander Salkind)
V, V*
original title: Le Procès

Joseph K is tried and condemned for an unspecified crime.

Kafka's nightmares tend to go on too long, and this film of one of them is no exception, despite its pin-screen prologue by Alexeieff and its inventive setting in the old Gare d'Orsay. Once again Welles the

magician badly needs a Hollywood studio behind him.

wd/ed Orson Welles ph Edmond Richard m Jean Ledrut pd Jean Mandarut

Orson Welles, Jeanne Moreau, Anthony Perkins, Madeleine Robinson, Elsa Martinelli, Suzanne Flon, Akim Tamiroff, Romy Schneider

'The elaboration of scale and decor is as boring as in any biblical spectacular and for the same reason: because it is used without mind or feeling, not to bring out meaning but to distract us from asking for it.' – Dwight MacDonald

The Trial
GB 1992 120m colour
BBC/Europanda (Louis Marks)
V

In Prague, Joseph K is arrested, tried and condemned without being able to discover his crime.

Plodding and uninteresting version, with a vacuous central performance and listless direction.

w Harold Pinter novel Franz Kafka d David Jones ph Phil Meheux m Carl Davis pd Don Taylor ed John Stothart

Kyle MacLachlan, Anthony Hopkins, Jason Robards, Juliet Stevenson, Polly Walker, Alfred Molina, Michael Kitchen

'Dull, lifeless and strictly TV-bound in its aesthetics.' – Variety

'The result is like a translation of a translation of a translation; it has zero vitality.' – Michael Sragow, New Yorker

Trial and Error: see The Dock Brief

Trial by Combat
GB 1976 90m Technicolor
Warner/Combat (Fred Weintraub, Paul Heller)
V*
aka: Choice of Weapons

An apparently harmless secret society of 'medieval knights' rededicates itself to the ritual execution of criminals who have escaped the law.

A rare specimen of comic macabre apparently inspired by the TV series The Avengers. Sadly, not much of it really works.

w Julian Bond, Steven Rossen, Mitchell Smith d Kevin Conner ph Alan Hume m Frank Cordell pd Edward Marshall

John Mills, Donald Pleasence, Peter Cushing, Barbara Hershey, David Birney, Margaret Leighton, Brian Glover

The Trial of Mary Dugan
US 1929 120m bw
MGM

Prosecution and defence counsel both change their feelings towards the girl on trial for murder.

A cast-iron audience pleaser, this adapted stage play was the studio's first all-talking picture. It wouldn't stand the test of time.

w Bayard Veiller, Becky Gardner play Bayard Veiller d Bayard Veiller

Norma Shearer, H. B. Warner, Raymond Hackett, Lewis Stone, Lilyan Tashman

† A 1940 remake directed by Norman Z. McLeod starred Laraine Day, Tom Conway, Robert Young, John Litel and Frieda Inescort, but was not a particular success.

The Trial of Vivienne Ware
US 1932 56m bw
Fox

An attempt is made to kill a woman witness during a murder trial.

Fast, complex courtroom murder mystery which even finds time for frequent bouts of comic relief.

w Philip Klein, Barry Connors novel Kenneth M. Ellis d William K. Howard

Joan Bennett, Donald Cook, Skeets Gallagher, ZaSu Pitts, Lillian Bond, Alan Dinehart, Herbert Mundin, Noel Madison

'A skilful bit of claptrap melodrama.' – Variety

Trial on the Road **
Russia 1985 (produced 1971) 98m bw
Lenfilm
original title: Proverka Na Dorogakh

A former Red Army sergeant fighting for the Germans in Russia deserts to join the partisans.

Banned for 14 years, a stark, unheroic account of war and its effect on the human spirit, set in a bleak winter landscape.

w Eduard Volodarksy story Yuri Gherman d Alexei Gherman ph L. Kolganov, B. Alexsandrovsky, V. Mironov m I. Shvarts ad V. Yurkevich

Rolan Bykov, Anatoly Solonitsin, Vladimir Zamansky, Oleg Borisov, Fedor Odinokov, Gennady Dindoyev

Trial Run
New Zealand 1984 89m colour
Cinema and Television/Double Feature (Don Reynolds)

An amateur photographer finds her metier photographing penguins, but in her remote retreat finds herself terrorized by a mysterious prowler.

Suspenseful but overlong thriller with a weak ending and too much psychological probing.

wd Melanie Read ph Allen Guilford m Jan Preston, Blair Greenberg pd Judith Crozier ed Finola Dwyer

Annie Whittle, Judith Gibson, Christopher Broun, Philippa Mayne, Stephen Tozer

The Trials of Oscar Wilde **
GB 1960 123m Super Technirama 70
Warwick/Viceroy (Harold Huth)
US title: The Man with the Green Carnation

Oscar Wilde fatally sues the Marquis of Queensberry for libel, and loses; he is then prosecuted for sodomy.

Plush account of a fascinating event; narrative drive is unfortunately lacking, but one is left with interesting performances.

wd Ken Hughes ph Ted Moore m Ron Goodwin ad Ken Adam, Bill Constable

Peter Finch, Yvonne Mitchell, John Fraser, Lionel Jeffries, Nigel Patrick, James Mason, Emrys Jones, Maxine Audley, Paul Rogers, James Booth

Tribute *
Canada 1980 122m colour
TCF/Joel B. Michaels, Garth B. Drabinsky
V*, L

A Broadway press agent comes to know his son by his divorced wife just as he comes to know of his own fatal illness.

Satisfactory screen treatment of a play which is really a vehicle for a charismatic star.

w Bernard Slade play Bernard Slade d Bob Clark ph Reginald H. Morris m various

Jack Lemmon, Lee Remick, Robby Benson, Colleen Dewhurst, Kim Cattrall, John Marley

AAN: Jack Lemmon

Tribute to a Bad Man
US 1956 95m Eastmancolor Cinemascope
MGM (Sam Zimbalist)

A Wyoming horse breeder is callous in his treatment

of rustlers, and wins the woman he wants when he becomes more understanding.

Somewhere behind an unsympathetic story and hesitant development lies a convincing picture of life in the old west.

w Michael Blankfort story Jack Schaefer d Robert Wise ph Robert Surtees m Miklos Rozsa

James Cagney, Irene Papas, Don Dubbins, Stephen McNally, Vic Morrow, Royal Dano, Lee Van Cleef

Trinity Is Still My Name (dubbed)
Italy 1971 90m DeLuxe Scope
Avco Embassy/West Film (Italo Zingarelli)
V*, L
original title: Continuavamo a Chiamarlo Trinity

Two brothers set out for a life of crime but are sidetracked in rescuing some monks from a gun-runner.

Amiable parody of spaghetti Westerns, high-spirited rather than funny.

wd E. B. Clucher (Enzo Barboni) ph Aldo Giordani m Guido de Angelis, Maurizio de Angelis Enzo Bulgarelli ed Antonio Siciliano

Terence Hill, Bud Spencer, Harry Carey Jnr, Jessica Dublin, Yanti Somer, Enzo Tarascio

† The film was originally released in Italy at 121m.

Trio *
GB 1950 91m bw
Rank/Gainsborough (Antony Darnborough)
V*

Following Quartet (qv), three more stories from Somerset Maugham: 'The Verger', 'Mr Knowall', and 'Sanatorium'.

An enjoyable package, unpretentiously handled but with full weight to the content.

w W. Somerset Maugham, R. C. Sherriff, Noel Langley stories W. Somerset Maugham d Ken Annakin, Harold French ph Reg Wyer, Geoffrey Unsworth m John Greenwood ad Maurice Carter ed Alfred Roome

James Hayter, Kathleen Harrison, Michael Hordern, Felix Aylmer; Nigel Patrick, Anne Crawford, Naunton Wayne, Wilfrid Hyde-White; Michael Rennie, Jean Simmons, John Laurie, Finlay Currie, Roland Culver, Betty Ann Davies, Raymond Huntley, André Morell

'The casting of all three films with stars and near stars is equally happy. Excellent entertainment.' – Joan Lester

'Listen to the sound of love! Feel people! Taste green!'

The Trip *
US 1967 85m Pathecolor
AIP (Roger Corman)

A director of TV commercials tries LSD and has hallucinations.

Much-banned plotless wallow, the ultimate opt-out movie; well done for those who can take it.

w Jack Nicholson d Roger Corman ph Arch Dalzell psychedelic effects Peter Gardiner, montage Dennis Jakob

Peter Fonda, Susan Strasberg, Bruce Dern, Salli Sachse, Dennis Hopper

The Trip to Bountiful *
US 1985 106m Allied and WBS colour
Island/Film Dallas/Bountiful Film Partners (Sterling Vanwagenen, Horton Foote)
V*, L

An old woman leaves her tiresome family to return by bus to the town where she was raised.

A relic of the fifties, when writers were mystical about mid-America, this oddity survives as an acting tour de force.

w Horton Foote play Horton Foote d Peter Masterson ph Fred Murphy m J. A. C. Redford

Geraldine Page, John Heard, Carlin Glynn, Richard Bradford, Rebecca de Mornay

'A wistful tale made for people old enough to appreciate that there is no going back – that the present, however wretched, is all we have.' – Quentin Crisp

AA: Geraldine Page

AAN: adapted screenplay

Triple Bogey on a Par 5 Hole
US 1991 85m colour/bw
ICA/Poe/Island World (Amos Poe)

A researcher questions three rich and spoiled children about the violent deaths of their parents on a golf course 13 years earlier.

Introspective navel-gazing movie that combines many of the least attractive aspects of underground cinema.

wd Amos Poe ph Joe Desalvo m Anna Domino, Michel Delory, Mader, Chic Streetman pd Jocelyne Beaudoin ed Dana Congdon

Eric Mitchell, Daisy Hall, Angela Goethals, Jesse McBride, Alba Clemente, Robbie Coltrane, Olga Bagnasco

'Deeply minimalist, deeply minimal.' – Nigel Andrews, Financial Times

'Deliberately repetitious, funny and slightly threatening at the same time.' – Derek Malcolm, Guardian

Triple Cross
GB 1967 140m colour
Warner/Cineurop (Fred Feldkamp)
V*

A small-time crook imprisoned on Jersey at the start of World War II offers to spy for the Nazis but reports to the English.

Ho-hum biopic of double agent Eddie Chapman; effective scenes merely interrupt the general incoherence.

w René Hardy book The Eddie Chapman Story by Frank Owen d Terence Young ph Henri Alekan m Georges Garvarentz

Christopher Plummer, Yul Brynner, Trevor Howard, Romy Schneider, Gert Frobe, Claudine Auger

Triple Cross
Hong Kong 1991 81m colour
Rapi Films (Gope T. Samtani)
V

Rival gangs trying to steal a computer in a suitcase are outwitted by a female security chief.

Car and boat chases, gun and fist fights, and martial arts action with an occasional spectacular stunt take most of the running time so that viewers will have little time to attend to the silly, confused narrative and unsubtle acting, or wonder why so many would kill, or die, for a portable computer.

w Christopher Mitchum story Deddy Armand d Ackyl Anwary ph H. Asmawi m Embie C. Noor ad Hendro Tangkilisan ed Amin Kertaraharia

Cynthia Rothrock, Chris Barnes, Peter O'Brian, Jurek Kylne, Roy Marten, Tanaka, Agust Melasz, Fei Lung, Jack Maland

Triple Echo *
GB 1972 94m colour
Hemdale/Senta (Graham Cottle)
V*

In 1942, a soldier's wife welcomes another soldier to her farm for tea; he deserts and poses as her sister.

Foolish story which would possibly have worked as a TV play but hardly justifies a film despite the talent on hand.

w Robin Chapman *novel* H. E. Bates *d* Michael Apted *ph* John Coquillon *m* Marc Wilkinson

Glenda Jackson, Brian Deacon, Oliver Reed

Triple Trouble: see *Kentucky Kernels*

Tripoli *
US 1950 95m Technicolor
Pine-Thomas/Paramount

In 1805 the United States sends marines to rout the Barbary pirates.

Not a superior actioner, but it passed the time.

w Winston Miller *d* Will Price

John Payne, Maureen O'Hara, Howard Da Silva, Philip Reed, Grant Withers, Lowell Gilmore

Tristana ****
Spain/Italy/France 1970 105m Eastmancolor
Academy/Connoisseur/Epoca/Talia/Selenia/Les Films Corona
(Juan Estelrich)
V, V*

An impoverished, womanizing aristocrat seduces his young ward and pays the price for his action.

Complex black comedy of obsessive behaviour which also mocks religion and other forms of consolation.

w Luis Buñuel, Julio Alejandro *novel* Benito Pérez Galdós *d* Luis Buñuel *ph* José F. Aguayo *ad* Enrique Alarcón *ed* Pedro Del Rey

Catherine Deneuve, Fernando Rey, Franco Nero, Lola Gaos, Antonio Casas, Jesús Fernández

'It is Buñuel at his most majestic.' – *Tom Milne, MFB*

The Triumph of Sherlock Holmes *
GB 1935 84m bw
Real Art
V*

Sherlock Holmes solves a murder stemming from enmity between Pennsylvania coal miners.

Solidly satisfying adaptation of Conan Doyle's *The Valley of Fear*, with more of Moriarty added.

w H. Fowler Mear *d* Leslie Hiscott

Arthur Wontner, Ian Fleming, Lyn Harding, Jane Carr, Leslie Perrins, Michael Shepley

Triumph of the Spirit *
US 1989 120m Eastmancolor
Guild/Nova International (Arnold Kopelson, Shimon Arama)
V, V*, L

A Jewish boxer is forced by the Nazis to fight for his life in a series of boxing matches in Auschwitz.

Tough, sincere but not always convincing drama, based on fact.

w Andrzej Krakowski, Laurence Heath
story Shimon Arama, Zion Haen *d* Robert M. Young *ph* Curtis Clark *m* Cliff Eidelman *pd* Jerzy Maslowska *ed* Arthur Coburn, Norman Buckley

Willem Dafoe, Edward James Olmos, Robert Loggia, Wendy Gazelle, Kelly Wolf, Costas Mandylor, Kario Salem, Edward Zentara, Hartmut Becker

Triumph of the Will ****
Germany 1936 120m bw
Leni Riefenstahl/Nazi Party
V, V*

The official record of the Nazi party congress held at Nuremberg in 1934.

A devastatingly brilliant piece of filmmaking – right from the opening sequence of Hitler descending from the skies, his plane shadowed against the clouds. The rally scenes are a terrifying example of the camera's power of propaganda. After World War II it was banned for many years because of general fears that it might inspire a new Nazi party.

d/ed Leni Riefenstahl *ph* Sepp Allgeier and 36 assistants *m* Herbert Windt

Triumphs of a Man Called Horse
Spain 1982 89m CFI
Sandy Howard/Redwing/Transpacific/Hesperia
V*

Third in a dispensable series (*A Man Called Horse, Return of a Man Called Horse*) of dour Westerns.

In this scrappy item the man dies early on, but his son upholds the tradition.

w Ken Blackwell, Carlos Aured, Jack de Witt *d* John Hough

Richard Harris, Michael Beck, Ana de Sade, Vaughn Armstrong, Buck Taylor

'From a million years back – horror explodes into today!'
Trog
GB 1970 91m Technicolor
Warner/Herman Cohen

A man-ape is discovered in a pothole and trained by a lady scientist.

Ridiculous semi-horror film which degrades its star.

w Aben Kandel *d* Freddie Francis *ph* Desmond Dickinson *m* John Scott

Joan Crawford, Michael Gough, Bernard Kay, David Griffin

Trois Couleurs: Bleu: see *Three Colours: Blue*

Trois Hommes et un Couffin: see *Three Men and a Cradle*

The Trojan Horse: see *The Trojan War*

The Trojan War
Italy/France 1961 105m Technicolor
Techniscope
Europa Cinematografica/CICC/Les Films Modernes (Gian Paolo Bigazzi)
original title: La Guerra di Troia; *aka:* The Wooden Horse of Troy, The Trojan Horse

Aeneas performs heroic deeds before fleeing his doomed city with his new-born son.

Good-looking, if stolid, epic which is one of the better efforts of its muscular star.

w Ugo Liberatore, Giorgio Stegani, Federico Zardi, Giorgio Ferroni *d* Giorgio Ferroni *ph* Rino Filippini *m* Giovanni Fusco *pd* Pier Vittorio Marchi *ed* Antonietta Zita

Steve Reeves, John Drew Barrymore, Juliette Mayniel, Hedy Vessel, Lydia Alfonsi

'The strength of mankind has always been its women'
The Trojan Women *
US 1971 111m Eastmancolor
Josef Shaftel (Michael Cacoyannis, Anis Nohra)
V*

Troy has fallen to the Greeks and its women bemoan their fate.

And oh, how they bemoan! Even with this cast, Greek tragedy does not fill the big screen.

w Michael Cacoyannis *play* Euripides *d* Michael Cacoyannis *ph* Alfio Contini *m* Mikis Theodorakis

Katharine Hepburn, Vanessa Redgrave, Geneviève Bujold, Irene Papas, Patrick Magee, Brian Blessed, Pauline Letts

The Trollenberg Terror
GB 1958 84m bw
Tempean
US title: The Crawling Eye

Extraterrestrials invade Switzerland.

Tolerable low-budget sci-fi from a BBC serial.

w Jimmy Sangster *story* Peter Key *d* Quentin Lawrence

Forrest Tucker, Laurence Payne, Janet Munro, Jennifer Jayne, Warren Mitchell

Tron *
US 1982 96m Technicolor Super Panavision 70mm
Walt Disney/Lisberger-Kushner
V*, L

A computer games designer gets his revenge on an enemy by fighting things out in the computer world he has created.

Complicated science fantasy chiefly interesting for its computerized blend of live action and animation, which isn't always successful.

wd Steven Lisberger *ph* Bruce Logan *m* Michael Femer *associate producer (animation)* Harrison Ellenshaw *pd* Dean Edward Mitzner

Bruce Boxleitner, Jeff Bridges, David Warner, Barnard Hughes

'Loaded with the expected visual delights, but falls way short of the mark in story and viewer involvement.' – *Variety*

AAN: costume design; sound

Troop Beverly Hills *
US 1989 106m Metrocolor
Columbia TriStar/Weintraub Entertainment/Fries Entertainment (Ava Ostern Fries, Martin Mickelson, Peter MacGregor-Scott)
V, V*, L

A wealthy mother transforms her daughter's disintegrating Girl Scout troop by giving them badges in shopping and other consumer activities.

A broad and far from sparkling comedy which emphasises that it is best to be born rich.

w Pamela Norris, Margaret Grieco Oberman *story* Ava Ostern Fries *d* Jeff Kanew *ph* Donald E. Thorin *m* Randy Edelman, Lou Hemsey *pd* Robert F. Boyle *ed* Mark Melnick

Shelley Long, Craig T. Nelson, Betty Thomas, Mary Gross, Stephanie Beacham, David Gautreaux, Karen Kopins, Dinah Lacey, Shelley Morrison

Trooper Hook *
US 1957 92m bw
UA/Sol Baer Fielding

A woman prisoner of the Indians has a half-breed son and becomes an outcast when returned to her people.

Peculiar Western with good moments, but generally very slow and downbeat.

w Charles Marquis Warren, David Victor, Herbert Little Jnr *story* Jack Schaefer *d* Charles Marquis Warren *ph* Ellsworth Fredericks *m* Gerald Fried

Barbara Stanwyck, Joel McCrea, Earl Holliman, Edward Andrews, John Dehner, Susan Kohner, Royal Dano

Troopship: see *Farewell Again*

Trop Belle pour Toi! *
France 1989 91m colour
Artificial Eye/Cine Valse/DD Productions/Orly Films/SEDIF/TF1 (Bernard Marescot)
V (W), V*, L
aka: Too Beautiful for You

A successful car salesman with a beautiful wife begins an affair with his homely secretary.

Mildly amusing romantic comedy, for all that it seems no more than a heterosexual variation on Blier's *Tenue de Soirée*.

wd Bertrand Blier *ph* Philippe Rousselot *m* Schubert *ad* Theobald Meurisse *ed* Claudine Merlin

Gérard Depardieu, Josiane Balasko, Carole Bouquet, Roland Blanche, François Cluzet, Didier Benureau, Philippe Loffredo

'Estupendo! Magnifico! Esplendido!'
Tropic Holiday
US   1938   78m   bw
Paramount

A Hollywood scriptwriter finds romance in Mexico.

Musical time-filler with a bit of everything and not much of anything.

w Don Hartman, Frank Butler, John C. Moffett and Duke Atteberry   d Theodore Reed

Ray Milland, Dorothy Lamour, Bob Burns, Martha Raye, Binnie Barnes, Tito Guizar

'Will need strong selling to top average business.' – *Variety*

AAN: Boris Morros (music direction)

Tropic of Cancer
US   1970   88m   Eastmancolor
Paramount/Tropic (Joseph Strick)

The sexual exploits of an American writer in Paris.

An adaptation that fails to capture the raw energy of the original, despite, or possibly owing to, quoting from it at great length.

w Joseph Strick, Betty Botley   *novel* Henry Miller   d Joseph Strick   ph Alain Derobe   m Stanley Myers

Rip Torn, James Callahan, Ellen Burstyn, David Bauer, Laurence Ligneres, Phil Brown

'The cinema here pays unfortunate tribute to literary achievement – by erecting a blank and ugly monument with the work itself firmly interred beneath.' – *Richard Coombs, MFB*

'A trivial but entertaining sex comedy.' – *Pauline Kael*

Tropic Zone
US   1953   94m   Technicolor
Paramount/Pine-Thomas

In a banana port a man wanted by the police saves a plantation from being taken over by crooks.

Tropical thick ear, not entirely unendurable.

wd Lewis R. Foster   *novel* Tom Gill

Ronald Reagan, Rhonda Fleming, Noah Beery Jnr, Estelita, Grant Withers, John Wengraf

Tropicana: see *The Heat's On*

Trottie True *
GB   1949   98m   Technicolor
GFD/Two Cities (Hugh Stewart)
V*
US title: *The Gay Lady*

Adventures of a Gaiety girl who married a lord.

Self-conscious period comedy which could have been highly diverting but manages only to be sporadically charming in a whimsically amateurish way.

w C. Denis Freeman   *novel* Caryl Brahms, S. J. Simon   d Brian Desmond Hurst   ph Harry Waxman   m Benjamin Frankel   ad Ralph Brinton

Jean Kent, James Donald, Hugh Sinclair, Bill Owen, Andrew Crawford, Lana Morris

Le Trou: see *The Hole*

Trouble along the Way
US   1953   110m   bw
Warner (Melville Shavelson)
V*, L

A famous football coach is co-opted to help a bankrupt college but some of his methods are not quite above board.

American college comedy with dollops of religiosity – a double threat.

w Melville Shavelson, Jack Rose   d Michael Curtiz   ph Archie Stout   m Max Steiner

John Wayne, Donna Reed, Charles Coburn, Tom Tully, Sherry Jackson, Marie Windsor

'No opportunities for a laugh or a tear are missed by the entire cast.' – *MFB*

Trouble Bound
US   1993   89m   CFI colour
ITC (Tom Kuhn, Fred Weintraub)
V

A gullible small-time crook finds himself in the middle of a gang war after he picks up a girl on the run from her Mafia family.

Routine road movie that takes the fast lane to clichéville.

w Darrell Fetty, Francis Delia   d Jeffrey Reiner   ph Janusz Kaminski   m Vinny Golia   pd Richard Sherman   ed Neil Grieve

Michael Madsen, Patricia Arquette, Florence Stanley, Seymour Cassel, Sal Jenco, Paul Ben-Victor

'A likeable road movie with a couple of decent central performances but few original ideas.' – *Empire*

Trouble Brewing *
GB   1939   87m   bw
ATP

A newspaper printer catches counterfeiters.

Lively star comedy.

w Anthony Kimmins, Angus MacPhail and Michael Hogan   d Anthony Kimmins

George Formby, Googie Withers, Gus MacNaughton, Joss Ambler, Martita Hunt, Garry Marsh, Ronald Shiner, C. Denier Warren, Basil Radford

Trouble for Two *
US   1936   75m   bw
MGM (Louis D. Lighton)
L
GB title: *The Suicide Club*

A European prince in London for an arranged wedding gets involved with an ingenious organization for murder.

Light-hearted, black-edged Victorian literary spoof which starts nicely but can't quite keep up the pace.

w Manuel Seff, Edward Paramore Jnr   *stories New Arabian Nights* by Robert Louis Stevenson   d J. Walter Rubin   ph Charles G. Clarke   m Franz Waxman

Robert Montgomery, Rosalind Russell, *Reginald Owen*, Frank Morgan, *Louis Hayward*, E. E. Clive, Walter Kingsford

Trouble in Paradise **
US   1932   86m   bw
Paramount (Ernst Lubitsch)
V

Jewel thieves insinuate themselves into the household of a rich Parisienne, and one falls in love with her.

A masterpiece of light comedy, with sparkling dialogue, innuendo, great performances and masterly cinematic narrative. For connoisseurs, it can't be faulted, and is the masterpiece of American sophisticated cinema.

w *Samson Raphaelson, Grover Jones   play The Honest Finder* by Laszlo Aladar   d *Ernst Lubitsch*   ph Victor Milner   m W. Franke Harling

Herbert Marshall, Miriam Hopkins, Kay Francis, Edward Everett Horton, Charles Ruggles, C. Aubrey Smith, Robert Greig, Leonid Kinskey

'Swell title, poor picture. Better for the class houses than the subsequents.' – *Variety*

'One of the gossamer creations of Lubitsch's narrative art . . . it would be impossible in this brief notice to describe the innumerable touches of wit and of

narrative skill with which it is unfolded.' – *Alexander Bakshy*

'A shimmering, engaging piece of work . . . in virtually every scene a lively imagination shines forth.' – *New York Times*

'An almost continuous musical background pointed up and commented on the action. The settings were the last word in modernistic design.' – *Theodor Huff, 1948*

Trouble in Store *
GB   1953   85m   bw
GFD/Two Cities (Maurice Cowan)
V, V*

A stock assistant causes chaos in a department store.

First, simplest and best of the Wisdom farces.

w John Paddy Carstairs, Maurice Cowan, Ted Willis   d John Paddy Carstairs   ph Ernest Steward   m Mischa Spoliansky

Norman Wisdom, Jerry Desmonde, Margaret Rutherford, Moira Lister, Derek Bond, Lana Morris, Megs Jenkins, Joan Sims

Trouble in the Glen
GB   1954   91m   Trucolor
Republic/Wilcox-Neagle (Stuart Robertson)
V*

An Argentinian laird in a Scottish glen causes ill-feeling.

Heavy-handed Celtic comedy whose predictability and sentimentality could have been forgiven were it not for the most garish colour ever seen.

w Frank S. Nugent   *novel* Maurice Walsh   d Herbert Wilcox   ph Max Greene   m Victor Young

Margaret Lockwood, Orson Welles, Forrest Tucker, Victor McLaglen, John McCallum, Eddie Byrne, Archie Duncan, Moultrie Kelsall

Trouble in the Sky: see *Cone of Silence*

The Trouble Shooter: see *The Man with the Gun*

The Trouble with Angels
US   1966   112m   Pathecolor
Columbia/William Frye
V*, L, S

Two mischievous new pupils cause trouble at a convent school.

Fun with the nuns, for addicts only.

w Blanche Hanalis   *novel Life with Mother Superior* by Jane Trahey   d Ida Lupino   ph Lionel Lindon   m Jerry Goldsmith

Rosalind Russell, Hayley Mills, June Harding, Marge Redmond, Binnie Barnes, Gypsy Rose Lee, Camilla Sparv, Mary Wickes, Margalo Gillmore

'A relentless series of prankish escapades.' – *MFB*

The Trouble with Girls
US   1969   105m   Metrocolor   Panavision
MGM (Lester Welch)
V*, L

In the twenties the manager of a travelling chautauqua (educational medicine show) gets involved in a small-town murder.

Curious vehicle for a very bored singing star, with some interesting background detail.

w Arnold and Lois Peyser   *novel The Chautauqua* by Day Keene, Dwight Babcock   d Peter Tewksbury   ph Jacques Marquette   m Billy Strange

Elvis Presley, Marlyn Mason, Nicole Jaffe, Sheree North, Edward Andrews, John Carradine, Vincent Price, Joyce Van Patten

The Trouble with Harry **

US   1955   99m   Technicolor   Vistavision
Paramount (Alfred Hitchcock)
V, V*, L

In the New England woods, various reasons cause various people to find and bury the same body.

Black comedy which never quite, despite bright moments, catches the style of the book; however, it is finely performed and the autumnal backgrounds are splendid.

w John Michael Hayes   novel Jack Trevor Story   d Alfred Hitchcock   ph Robert Burks   m Bernard Herrmann

Edmund Gwenn, Mildred Natwick, John Forsythe, Shirley Maclaine, Mildred Dunnock

'Has, I fear, neither the desperation which makes the predicament of its characters wryly enjoyable nor the urbanity which would make their actions sympathetic.' – Dilys Powell

The Trouble with Women

US   1947   80m   bw
Paramount

A psychology professor thinks women enjoy being treated rough; a lady reporter tests his theories.

Silly romantic comedy.

w Arthur Sheekman   story Ruth McKenney   d Sidney Lanfield

Ray Milland, Brian Donlevy, Teresa Wright, Rose Hobart, Charles Smith, Iris Adrian, Lloyd Bridges

† The film was completed in 1945, but held from release for two years because of overstock.

True as a Turtle

GB   1956   96m   Eastmancolor
Rank (Peter de Sarigny)

Honeymooners join a variety of friends on a yacht crossing the Channel, and get involved in smuggling.

Artless, undemanding comedy for those who like messing about in boats.

w Jack Davies, John Coates, Nicholas Phipps   d Wendy Toye   ph Reg Wyer   m Robert Farnon

John Gregson, June Thorburn, Cecil Parker, Elvi Hale, Keith Michell, Avice Landone

True Believer *

US   1989   103m   DeLuxe
Columbia (Walter F. Parkes, Lawrence Lasker)
V*, L

A tough, once idealistic lawyer is persuaded to take on the case of an Asian-American who may have been wrongfully imprisoned.

Entertaining thriller, though it would have been as effective on television and, indeed, led to a TV series, Eddie Dodd, based on its central character.

w Wesley Strick   d Joseph Ruben   ph John W. Lindley   m Brad Fiedel   pd Lawrence Miller   ed George Bowers

James Woods, Robert Downey Jnr, Margaret Colin, Yuji Okumoto, Kurtwood Smith, Tom Bower, Miguel Fernandes, Charles Hallahan

True Confession **

US   1937   85m   bw
Paramount (Albert Lewin)

A fantasy-prone girl confesses to a murder she didn't commit, and her upright lawyer husband defends her.

Archetypal crazy comedy with fine moments despite longueurs and a lack of cinematic inventiveness. Remade as Cross My Heart (qv).

w Claude Binyon   play Mon Crime by Louis Verneuil, George Berr   d Wesley Ruggles   ph Ted Tetzlaff   m Frederick Hollander

Carole Lombard, Fred MacMurray, John Barrymore, Una Merkel, Porter Hall, Edgar Kennedy, Lynne Overman, Fritz Feld, Irving Bacon

'Not a big bet but a favourable enough one . . . it just falls short of being a smash.' – Variety

'The best comedy of the year.' – Graham Greene

True Confessions *

US   1981   108m   colour
United Artists/Chartoff-Winkler (James D. Brubaker)
V*, L

A policeman working on a murder case finds that his brother, a priest, is involved.

Unnecessary fictional elaboration on a real Los Angeles murder case of the forties (the 'Black Dahlia'); chiefly notable for performances.

w John Gregory Dunne, Joan Didion   novel John Gregory Dunne   d Ulu Grosbard   ph Owen Roizman   m Georges Delerue   pd Stephen S. Grimes

Robert Duvall, Robert de Niro, Charles Durning, Kenneth McMillan, Ed Flanders, Cyril Cusack, Burgess Meredith

'The Victory You Helped To Make . . . Now on the screen in all its glory!'
The True Glory ****

GB/US   1945   90m   bw
Ministry of Information/Office of War Information
V

The last year of the war, retold by edited newsreels: D-Day to the Fall of Berlin.

A magnificent piece of reportage, worth a dozen fiction films in its exhilarating Shakespearean fervour, though the poetic commentary does occasionally go over the top. One of the finest of all compilations.

w Eric Maschwitz, Arthur Macrae, Jenny Nicholson, Gerald Kersh, Guy Trosper   d Carol Reed, Garson Kanin   research Peter Cusick   m William Alwyn

'Dwarfs all the fiction pictures of the year.' – Richard Mallett, Punch

'Bold, welcome but inadequate use of blank verse; much more successful use of many bits of individualized vernacular narration, unusually free of falseness. Very jab-paced, energetic cutting; intelligent selection of shots, of which several hundred are magnificent.' – James Agee

'An inspiring recital of human endeavour which all the world will want to see.' – The Cinema

AA: best documentary

True Grit *

US   1969   128m   Technicolor
Paramount/Hal B. Wallis (Paul Nathan)
V, V*, L

In the Old West, a young girl wanting to avenge her murdered father seeks the aid of a hard-drinking old marshal.

Disappointingly slow-moving and uninventive semi-spoof Western with a roistering performance from a veteran star, who won a sentimental Oscar for daring to look fat and old.

w Marguerite Roberts   novel Charles Portis   d Henry Hathaway   ph Lucien Ballard   m Elmer Bernstein

John Wayne, Kim Darby, Glen Campbell, Dennis Hopper, Jeremy Slate, Robert Duvall, Strother Martin, Jeff Corey

'Readers may remember it as a book about a girl, but it's a film about John Wayne.' – Stanley Kauffmann

'There is a slight consistent heightening or lowering into absurdity, but there is also a strong feeling for the unvarnished preposterousness of everyday existence.' – John Simon

† Rooster Cogburn featured more adventures of the Wayne character, who also showed up on TV in 1978 in the guise of Warren Oates.

AA: John Wayne

AAN: title song (m Elmer Bernstein, ly Don Black)

True Heart Susie *

US   1919   62m approx (24 fps)   bw   silent
D. W. Griffith/Artcraft

A country girl sells her cow to send her boyfriend to college, but he is ungrateful.

Lavender-flavoured rustic romance, with the director at his most sentimental. But of its kind it is carefully done.

wd D. W. Griffith   story Marion Fremont   ph Billy Bitzer

Lillian Gish, Robert Harron, Clarine Seymour

True Identity

USA   1991   93m   Technicolor
Warner/Touchstone/Silver Screen Partners IV/Sandollar (Carol Baum, Teri Schwartz)
V, V*, L

On the run from the Mafia, a black actor disguises himself as a white man.

A star vehicle that, despite an engaging central performance, failed, due to a weak script.

w Andy Breckman   d Charles Lane   ph Tom Ackerman   m Marc Marder   pd John DeCuir Jnr   ed Kent Beyda

Lenny Henry, Frank Langella, Charles Lane, J. T. Walsh, Anne-Marie Johnson, Andreas Katsulas, Michael McKean, Peggy Lipton

'Mild comedy that works best as a showcase for Lenny Henry.' – New York Times

'If All You Want To Do Is Have A Good Time . . . Why Get Married?'
True Love **

US   1989   100m   DuArt
Oasis/UA (Richard Guay, Shelley Houis)
V*, L

A young Italian-American couple in the Bronx prepare for their marriage, she with determination, he with reluctance.

Well-observed, low-budget comedy with a ring of truth about it.

w Nancy Savoca, Richard Guay   d Nancy Savoca   ph Lisa Rinzler   pd Lester W. Cohen   ed John Tintori

Annabella Sciorra, Ron Eldard, Aida Turturro, Roger Rignack, Star Jasper, Michael J. Wolfe, Kelly Cinnante, Rick Shapiro

'. . . Stealing . . . Cheating . . . Killing . . . who says romance is dead?'
True Romance **

US   1993   119m   colour   Panvision
Warner/Morgan Creek/Davis (Bill Unger, Steve Perry, Samuel Hadida)
V, V*, L

A shop assistant and a callgirl go on the run with a suitcase full of cocaine, chased by gangsters.

A clever, very violent, high-energy thriller, providing opportunity for striking cameos by a variety of actors as well as narrative twists that owe much to farce; the conclusion, a three-way stand-off, brings to mind a minor 30s screwball comedy, The Housekeeper's Daughter, but then the film is stuffed with references to other movies.

w Quentin Tarantino   d Tony Scott   ph Jeffrey L. Kimball   m Hans Zimmer   pd Benjamin Fernandez   ed Michael Tronick, Christian Wagner

Christian Slater, Patricia Arquette, Dennis Hopper, Val Kilmer, Gary Oldman, Brad Pitt, Christopher Walken

'Creates a new genre: screwball violence.' – *Tom Hutchinson*

'Provides some amazing encounters, bravura acting turns and gruesome carnage. But it doesn't add up to enough, as preposterous plotting and graphic violence ultimately prove an audience turnoff.' – *Variety*

'Looks like a piece of designer chic searching but unable to find any kind of holding centre.' – *Derek Malcolm, Guardian*

True Stories *

US 1986 89m DuArt
Warner/Edward R. Pressman/Gary Kurfirst
V, V*, L

A narrator introduces people from the town of Virgil, Texas.

A curious entertainment which plays like a whimsical update of Thornton Wilder's *Our Town*, though without the subtlety.

w Stephen Tobolowsky, Beth Henley, David Byrne
d David Byrne ph Ed Lachman m David Byrne

David Byrne, John Goodman, Annie McEnroe, Jo Harvey Allen, Spalding Gray, Alix Elias, Swoosie Kurtz

'The story is just a trick to get your attention. It opens the door and lets the real movie in.' – *David Byrne*

The True Story of Jesse James

US 1956 92m Eastmancolor Cinemascope
TCF (Herbert Swope Jnr)
GB title: *The James Brothers*

After the Civil War, Jesse and Frank James become outlaws and train robbers.

Fairly slavish remake of *Jesse James*, without the style.

w Walter Newman d Nicholas Ray ph Joe MacDonald m Leigh Harline

Robert Wagner, Jeffrey Hunter, Hope Lange, Agnes Moorehead, John Carradine, Alan Hale Jnr, Alan Baxter

True to Life *

US 1943 93m Technicolor
Paramount (Paul Jones)

The writer of a radio soap opera moves in with an average family to get the right atmosphere.

Quite a percipient comedy of its day, though it does not forgo the customary romantic entanglements.

w Don Hartman, Harry Tugend d George Marshall
ph Charles Lang m Victor Young

Mary Martin, Dick Powell, Franchot Tone, Victor Moore, Mabel Paige, William Demarest, Clarence Kolb, Ernest Truex

True to the Navy

US 1930 70m bw
Paramount

A drug store girl has too many sailor sweethearts for comfort.

Very ordinary star vehicle, with little about it worth remembering next day.

w Keene Thompson, Doris Anderson, Herman Mankiewicz d Frank Tuttle

Clara Bow, Fredric March, Harry Green, Rex Bell, Eddie Fetherston

'Hardly better than fair. Slow in tempo, sappy in story, and bearing the stamp of perfunctory production.' – *Variety*

Truly, Madly, Deeply **

GB 1990 106m colour
Samuel Goldwyn Company/Winston/BBC/Lionheart (Robert Cooper)
V, V*, L

A woman grieving for the death of her husband is visited by his ghost.

Unusual story of coming to terms with loss, combining wit, insight and excellent acting.

wd Anthony Minghella ph Remi Adefarasin
m Barrington Pheloung pd Barbara Gasnold
ed John Stothart

Juliet Stevenson, Alan Rickman, Bill Paterson, Michael Maloney, Jenny Howe, Carolyn Choa, Christopher Rozycki, Keith Bartlett, David Ryall

'Intelligent, charming, ironic and exceptionally well played.' – *Derek Malcolm, Guardian*

The Trumpet Blows

US 1934 68m bw
Paramount

A matador comes home to Mexico and quarrels with his bandit brother.

Tedious melodrama with bullring scenes.

w Bartlett Cormack, Wallace Smith, Porter Emerson Browne, J. Parker Read Jnr d Stephen Roberts

George Raft, Adolphe Menjou, Frances Drake, Sidney Toler, Edward Ellis, Nydia Westman

'Story weak, dialogue bad, casting hopeless.' – *Variety*

Trunk Crime

GB 1939 51m bw
Charter (John Boulting)

A student goes mad and tries to bury his enemy alive.

Now dated, but at the time a smart little programme-filler by an enterprising young producer-director team.

w Francis Miller play Edward Percy, Reginald Denham d Roy Boulting

Manning Whiley, Barbara Everest, Hay Petrie, Thorley Walters

The Trunk Mystery: see *One New York Night*

'A slightly twisted comedy.'

Trust **

GB/USA 1990 106m colour
Palace/Zenith/True Fiction/Film Four (Bruce Weiss)
V, V*, L

A pregnant teenager meets a moody, grenade-carrying electronics expert and takes him home with her.

Off-beat film that examines motherhood and marriage with a beady eye.

wd Hal Hartley ph Michael Spiller m Phillip Reed pd Dan Ouellette ed Nick Gomez

Adrienne Shelly, Martin Donovan, Marritt Nelson, John MacKay, Edie Falco, Gary Sauer, Matt Malloy

The Truth about Spring *

GB 1964 102m Technicolor
U-I /Quota Rentals (Alan Brown)

The bored nephew of a millionaire cruising in the Caribbean jumps at the chance to join friends on a scruffy yacht, but they all get involved with pirates.

Pleasing family film with good scenery and a friendly cast.

w James Lee Barrett novel H. de Vere Stacpoole d Richard Thorpe ph Ted Scaife m Robert Farnon

Hayley Mills, James MacArthur, David Tomlinson, Lionel Jeffries, John Mills, Harry Andrews, Niall MacGinnis

The Truth about Women

GB 1957 107m Eastmancolor
British Lion/Beaconsfield (Sydney Box)
V*

An old roué recounts to his son-in-law his early amorous adventures.

Tedious charade with neither wit nor grace.

w Muriel and Sydney Box d Muriel Box
ph Otto Heller m Bruce Montgomery

Laurence Harvey, Julie Harris, Diane Cilento, Mai Zetterling, Eva Gabor, Michael Denison, Derek Farr, Roland Culver, Wilfrid Hyde-White, Christopher Lee, Marius Goring, Thorley Walters, Ernest Thesiger, Griffith Jones

'It's amazing that with all those talented people nothing happens on the screen.' – *Pauline Kael, 70s*

Truth or Dare *

US 1991 119m colour/bw
Rank/Propaganda/Boy Toy (Tim Clawson, Jay Roewe)
V, V*, L
GB title: *In Bed with Madonna*

Documentary of Madonna's international concert tour of 1990.

Fascinating, if manipulative, look at a current phenomenon, made under the control of Madonna and carefully projecting an image of wild sexuality.

d Alex Keshishian ph Robert Leacock md Jai Winding ad Christopher Ciccone ed Barry Alexander Brown, Anne B. Erikson, John Murray

'An ace manipulator's self-portrait, unmediated by interviewers or pundits. Raw, raunchy and epically entertaining, this is pure, unadulterated Madonna.' – *Richard Corliss, Time*

Try and Find It: see *Hi Diddle Diddle*

Try and Get Me *

US 1951 92m bw
(UA) Robert Stillman
V*
GB title: *The Sound of Fury*

Two men are arrested for kidnapping and murder, and a journalist stirs the small town to lynch fury.

Harrowing, relentless melodrama, possibly the best on this subject.

w Jo Pagano novel *The Condemned* by Jo Pagano
d Cyril Endfield ph Guy Roe m Hugo Friedhofer

Frank Lovejoy, Lloyd Bridges, Kathleen Ryan, Richard Carlson, Katherine Locke, Adele Jergens, Art Smith

'The characterization and the handling of the drama are remarkable, at times reaching a complexity rare in films of this type.' – *Gavin Lambert*

'A strange, uncomfortable, sometimes brutal and depressing picture.' – *Richard Mallett, Punch*

The Trygon Factor *

GB 1966 88m Technicolor
Rank/Rialto Film/Preben Phillipsen (Ian Warren)

Bogus nuns plan a million pound bank raid.

When you get used to its mixture of styles, this Anglo-German production is pretty good imitation Edgar Wallace, with bags of mystery and melodramatic goings-on involving larger than life characters most of whom come to sticky ends.

w Derry Quinn, Stanley Munro, Kingsley Amis
d Cyril Frankel ph Harry Waxman m Peter Thomas

Stewart Granger, Susan Hampshire, Cathleen Nesbitt, Robert Morley, James Culliford, Brigitte Horney, Sophie Hardy, James Robertson Justice

Tsareubiitsa: see *Assassin of the Tsar*

Tsubaki Sanjuro: see *Sanjuro*

Tsvet Granata: see *The Colour of Pomegranates*

Tucker: The Man and His Dream **

US 1988 115m colour
UIP/Lucasfilm (Fred Roos, Fred Fuchs)
V, V*, L, S

A designer is put out of business after he creates a revolutionary new car.

Slick, engaging, well-crafted story, based on fact.

w Arnold Schulman, David Seidler d Francis Ford Coppola ph Vittorio Storaro m Joe Jackson pd Dean Tavoularis ad Armin Ganz ed Priscilla Nedd

Jeff Bridges, Joan Allen, Martin Landau, Frederic Forrest, Mako, Elias Koteas, Christian Slater, Lloyd Bridges, Dean Stockwell

AAN: Martin Landau; Dean Tavoularis, Armin Ganz; best costume design

Tudor Rose *
GB 1936 78m bw
GFD/Gainsborough (Michael Balcon)
US title: Nine Days a Queen

The brief life and reign of Lady Jane Grey.

Modestly well made historical textbook.

w Robert Stevenson, Miles Malleson d Robert Stevenson ph Max Greene m Louis Levy

Cedric Hardwicke, Nova Pilbeam, John Mills, Felix Aylmer, Leslie Perrins, Frank Cellier, Desmond Tester, Gwen Frangcon Davies, Sybil Thorndike, Martita Hunt, Miles Malleson, John Laurie

'There is not a character, not an incident in which history has not been altered for the cheapest of reasons.' – Graham Greene

Tuff Turf
US 1985 112m CFI colour
Blue Dolphin/New World (Donald P. Borchers)
V*

A street rebel and his moll have trouble understanding themselves and their world.

Audiences had trouble getting interested.

w Jette Rinck story Greg Collins O'Neill, Murray Michaels d Fritz Kiersch ph Willy Kurant m Jonathan Elias ad Craig Stearns ed Marc Grossman

James Spader, Kim Richards, Paul Mones, Robert Downey, Matt Clark

Tugboat Annie **
US 1933 88m bw
MGM (Harry Rapf)

An elderly waterfront lady and her boozy friend smooth out the path of young love.

Hilarious and well-loved comedy vehicle for two great stars of the period.

w Zelda Sears, Eve Greene stories Norman Reilly Raine d Mervyn Le Roy ph Gregg Toland

Marie Dressler, Wallace Beery, Robert Young, Maureen O'Sullivan, Willard Robertson, Paul Hurst

'One of those rare naturals in the picture business – a flicker that sells itself immediately the stars' names go into the lights.' – Variety

'A bare outline of the story cannot convey the note of mother love that runs through it, the laughs, the pathos.' – Picturegoer

Tugboat Annie Sails Again
US 1940 75m bw
Edmund Grainger/Warner

The river lady defeats all comers in her efforts to whip up trade.

Badly developed sequel which isn't badly acted but gets nowhere.

w Walter DeLeon d Lewis Seiler

Marjorie Rambeau, Alan Hale, Jane Wyman, Ronald Reagan, Clarence Kolb, Charles Halton, Victor Kilian

Tulitikkutehtaan Tytto: see The Match Factory Girl

'Meet Cherokee Lansing . . . half wildcat . . . half angel . . . all woman!'
Tulsa *
US 1949 88m Technicolor
Eagle-Lion (Walter Wanger)
V*

The daughter of a cattle owner builds an oil empire.

Splendid Hollywood hokum of the second grade, very predictable but well-oiled.

w Frank Nugent, Curtis Kenyon d Stuart Heisler ph Winton Hoch m Frank Skinner

Susan Hayward, Robert Preston, Pedro Armendariz, Lloyd Gough, Chill Wills, Ed Begley

'Like a damp fuse, it produces a loud bang at the end of a long splutter.' – Time

Tumbleweeds **
US 1925 80m (24 fps) bw silent
United Artists/William S. Hart
V*, L

A wandering cowboy helps a family of settlers.

The same plot as Shane works wonders in the last film of William S. Hart, which has the apparently authentic flavour of the old west.

w C. Gardner Sullivan story Hal G. Evarts d King Baggott ph Joseph August

William S. Hart, Barbara Bedford, Lucien Littlefield, Monte Collins

† Reissued in 1939 with an added eight-minute introduction by Hart, showing how the west has changed.

'They're having a secret love affair. Only fifty thousand listeners know about it.'
Tune In Tomorrow *
US 1990 104m colour
Hobo/Polar/Odyssey/Cinecom (John Fielder, Mark Tarlov)
V, V*, L, S
GB title: Aunt Julia and The Scriptwriter

A writer of a daily radio serial manipulates an affair between a young journalist and his older aunt to provide material for his scripts.

A comedy at the expense of soap operas and the original novel.

w William Boyd novel Aunt Julia and The Scriptwriter by Mario Vargas Llosa d Jon Amiel ph Robert Stevens m Wynton Marsalis pd Jim Clay, James L. Schoppe ed Peter Boyle

Barbara Hershey, Keanu Reeves, Peter Falk, Bill McCutheon, Patricia Clarkson, Richard Portnow, Jerome Dempsey

'A sharp-fanged novel has been turned into an ingratiating puppy walking on its hind legs.' – Philip French, Observer

Tunes of Glory **
GB 1960 107m Technicolor
UA/Knightsbridge (Albert Fennell)
V*, L

The new disciplinarian CO of a highland regiment crosses swords with his lax, hard drinking predecessor.

Wintry barracks melodrama, finely acted and well made with memorable confrontation scenes compensating for a somewhat underdeveloped script.

w James Kennaway novel James Kennaway d Ronald Neame ph Arthur Ibbetson

Alec Guinness, John Mills, Susannah York, Dennis Price, Kay Walsh, Duncan Macrae, Gordon Jackson, John Fraser, Allan Cuthbertson

'The picture is persuasive. But I daresay one does it wrong by looking too hard for social reflections. Lucky enough to find a film which has life in it.' – Dilys Powell

AAN: James Kennaway

Tung-Tung-te chia-ch'i: see A Summer at Grandpa's

The Tunnel *
GB 1935 94m bw
Gaumont (Michael Balcon)
V*
US title: Transatlantic Tunnel

Crooked finances mar the completion of an undersea tunnel to America.

A rare example of British science fiction from this period, though the film was in fact first made in German and French versions, the latter with Jean Gabin.

w Curt Siodmak, L. DuGarde Peach, Clemence Dane novel Bernard Kellerman d Maurice Elvey ph Gunther Krampf m Louis Levy

Richard Dix, Leslie Banks, Madge Evans, Helen Vinson, C. Aubrey Smith, George Arliss, Walter Huston, Basil Sydney, Jimmy Hanley

The Tunnel of Love
US 1958 98m bw Cinemascope
MGM/Joseph Fields
V*, L

A husband applying to adopt an orphan thinks he may, while drunk, have seduced the glamorous orphan agency official.

Tasteless and not very funny comedy, somewhat miscast.

w Joseph Fields play Joseph Fields, Peter de Vries novel Peter de Vries d Gene Kelly ph Robert Bronner

Richard Widmark, Doris Day, Gig Young, Gia Scala, Elizabeth Fraser, Elizabeth Wilson

Tunnel 28: see Escape from East Berlin

Turk 182 *
US 1985 98m TVC colour
TCF (Ted Field, Rene DuPont)
V, V*

A mystery do-gooder embarrasses the city bureaucracy into doing right by citizens with a grievance.

Interesting urban drama with a non-violent vigilante.

w James Gregory Kingston, Denis and John Hamill d Bob Clark ph Reginald H. Morris m Paul Zaza pd Harry Pottle ed Stan Cole

Timothy Hutton, Robert Urich, Kim Cattrall, Robert Culp, Darren McGavin, Steven Keats, Peter Boyle, Paul Sorvino

Turkey Time
GB 1933 73m bw
Gaumont

Family indiscretions come out at Christmas time.

Vehicle for fruity characterizations by the popular Aldwych team, but not very strong as a farce.

w Ben Travers play Ben Travers d Tom Walls

Tom Walls, Ralph Lynn, Robertson Hare, Dorothy Hyson, Mary Brough, Norma Varden

Turkish Delight *
Netherlands 1973 106m colour
Columbia-Warner/Rob Houwer (Mia van't Hof)
original title: Turks Fruit

A promiscuous young sculptor marries unhappily but falls in love with his wife again during her terminal illness.

Scabrous satire on Dutch middle-class attitudes combined with shock tactics and as much sex as the director could get past the censor; undeniably displaying talent of a not very likeable kind, it was a box-office success in Holland.

w Gerard Soeteman *novel* Jan Wolkers *d* Paul Verhoeven *ph* Jan de Bont *m* Rogier van Otterloo *ad* Ralf van der Elst *ed* Jan Bosdriess

Monqiue van de Ven, Rutger Hauer, Tonny Huurdeman, Wim van den Brink, Dolf de Vries

'Repulsive and meaningless' – *Clyde Jeavons, MFB*

'Underscored by a romanticism which slowly accumulates as time goes by. The difficulties of combining scatology and tenderness are neatly handled.' – *Derek Elley, Films and Filming*

Turks Fruit: see *Turkish Delight*

Turksib *
USSR 1929 60m approx (24 fps) bw silent
Vostok Kino

The making of the Turkestan–Siberia railway.

A highly fluent and pictorial documentary with an especially famous climax as the men struggle to lay the last rails and meet a deadline.

w Victor Turin and others *d* Victor Turin *ph* Yevgeni Slavinsky, Boris Frantzisson

Turn Back the Clock *
US 1933 80m bw
MGM

A man dreams of changing places with his rich friend.

Unusual, quite pleasing comedy-drama.

w Edgar Selwyn, Ben Hecht *d* Edgar Selwyn

Lee Tracy, Otto Kruger, Mae Clarke, C. Henry Gordon, George Barbier

'Neatly turned domestic comedy with a dramatic touch that will please all round.' – *Variety*

Turn of the Tide *
GB 1935 80m bw
British National (John Corfield)
V

A feud between two fishing families ends in marriage.

Low-key, location-set action drama with a moral. The film which brought J. Arthur Rank into the business, which he saw had religious possibilities.

w L. DuGarde Peach, J. O. C. Orton *novel Three Fevers* by Leo Walmsley *d* Norman Walker

Geraldine Fitzgerald, John Garrick, Niall MacGinnis, J. Fisher White, Joan Maude, Sam Livesey, Wilfrid Lawson, Moore Marriott

'Cut to an hour, it should make an acceptable second feature.' – *Variety*

'An unpretentious and truthful film.' – *Graham Greene*

† The film has been released on video together with *The Man at the Gate.*

Turn Off the Moon
US 1937 79m bw
Paramount/Fanchon

The proprietor of a department store is persuaded by an astrologer to stage a big show in celebration of his 25th anniversary.

Thinly structured musical with some acceptable gags and turns.

w Marguerite Roberts, Harlan Ware, Paul Gerard Smith, Mildred Harrington *d* Lewis Seiler

Charles Ruggles, Eleanore Whitney, Johnny Downs, Kenny Baker, Phil Harris and his Orchestra, Ben Blue, Andrew Tombes, Marjorie Gateson, Grady Sutton, Franklin Pangborn

'B from title to climax.' – *Variety*

Turn the Key Softly
GB 1953 81m bw
GFD/Chiltern (Maurice Cowan)

The problems of three women released from prison.

Soppy formula multi-drama with contrived and uninteresting plots and characters.

w Jack Lee, Maurice Cowan *novel* John Brophy *d* Jack Lee *ph* Geoffrey Unsworth *m* Mischa Spoliansky

Yvonne Mitchell, Terence Morgan, Joan Collins, Kathleen Harrison, Thora Hird, Dorothy Alison, Glyn Houston, Geoffrey Keen, Clive Morton

'Pardon my error, the stork meekly smiled, I've overlooked wifey, gave hubby the child!'

Turnabout *
US 1940 83m bw
Hal Roach

A benevolent god enables a quarrelsome couple to change bodies and see how they like it.

'The man's had a baby instead of the lady', said the ads. Well, not quite, but it did seem pretty daring at the time, and it still provides a hilarious moment or two.

w Mickell Novak, Berne Giler, John McLain *novel* Thorne Smith *d* Hal Roach *ph* Norbert Brodine *m* Arthur Morton

Adolphe Menjou, John Hubbard, Carole Landis, Mary Astor, Verree Teasdale, Donald Meek, William Gargan, Joyce Compton

Turned Out Nice Again
GB 1941 81m bw
ATP

An employee teaches an underwear firm to move with the times.

Tolerable star comedy from his late period.

w Austin Melford, John Dighton, Basil Dearden *play As You Are* by Hugh Mills, Wells Root *d* Marcel Varnel

George Formby, Peggy Bryan, Edward Chapman, Elliot Mason, Mackenzie Ward, O. B. Clarence

Turner & Hooch
US 1989 99m Metrocolor
Warner/Touchstone/Silver Screen Partners IV (Raymond Wagner)
V, V*, L

In order to solve a murder, a cop teams up with the only witness, a large dog.

The cycle of police buddy-buddy movies reaches its nadir in this strenuously unfunny release.

w Dennis Shryack, Michael Blodgett, Daniel Petrie Jnr, Jim Cash, Jack Epps Jnr *d* Roger Spottiswoode *ph* Adam Greenberg *m* Charles Gross *pd* John DeCuir Jnr *ed* Paul Seydor, Mark Conte, Kenneth Morrisey, Lois Freeman-Fox

Tom Hanks, Mare Winningham, Craig T. Nelson, Reginald VelJohnson, Scott Paulin, J. C. Quinn, John McIntire

The Turners of Prospect Road
GB 1947 88m bw
Grand National

A taxi driver's family greyhound wins a big race.

Uneasily cast domestic comedy drama.

w Victor Katona, Patrick Kirwan *d* Maurice J. Wilson

Wilfrid Lawson, Jeanne de Casalis, Maureen Glynne, Helena Pickard, Leslie Perrins, Peter Bull

The Turning Point *
US 1952 85m bw
Paramount (Irving Asher)
original title: *This is Dynamite!*

A young lawyer is appointed by the state governor to smash a crime syndicate.

Familiar exposé drama of its time, quite crisply done.

w Warren Duff *d* William Dieterle *ph* Lionel Lindon *md* Irwin Talbot

William Holden, Alexis Smith, Edmond O'Brien, Tom Tully, Ray Teal

'A story of envy, hatred, friendship, triumph and love!'
The Turning Point *
US 1977 119m DeLuxe
TCF/Hera (Nora Kaye)
V*

The American Ballet Theatre visits Oklahoma City, and its ageing star revisits an ex-colleague, now a housewife.

Posh person's soap opera, rather boringly made and interesting only for its performances, which are certainly vivid.

w Arthur Laurents *d* Herbert Ross *ph* Robert Surtees *m* John Lanchbery *pd* Albert Brenner *ed* William Reynolds

Anne Bancroft, Shirley Maclaine, Mikhail Baryshnikov, Leslie Browne, Tom Skerritt, Martha Scott, Marshall Thompson

'A backstage musical dressed up with smart cultural trimmings.' – *Alan Brien*

'We get a glimpse of something great in the movie – Mikhail Baryshnikov dancing – and these two harpies out of the soaps block the view.' – *New Yorker, 1978*

AAN: best picture; Herbert Ross; Robert Surtees; Anne Bancroft; Shirley Maclaine; Mikhail Baryshnikov; Leslie Browne; Arthur Laurents; art direction; editing

Turtle Beach
Australia 1992 88m colour
Warner/Roadshow/Coote & Carroll
V, S

A reporter leaves her husband and children to go to Malaysia to cover the story of the problems of Vietnamese boat people and witnesses a massacre.

An apparent attempt to expose racism and corruption in Malaysia and Australia, but too muddled to make much sense.

w Ann Turner *novel* Blanche d'Alpuget *d* Stephen Wallace *ph* Russell Boyd *m* Chris Neal *pd* Brian Thomson *ed* Lee Smith, Louise Innes

Greta Scacchi, Joan Chen, Jack Thompson, Art Malik, Norman Kaye, Victoria Longley, Martin Jacobs, William McInnes, George Whaley

'Rarely has such an interesting story resulted in such drab fare.' – *Variety*

Turtle Diary *
GB 1985 97m Technicolor
CBS/United British Artists/Britannic (Richard Johnson)
V*, L

Two self-admitted eccentrics take it upon themselves to release turtles from captivity in the London Zoo.

Mainly ineffective character comedy, memorable only for fragments of dialogue and acting.

w Harold Pinter *novel* Russell Hoban *d* John Irvin *ph* Peter Hannan *m* Geoffrey Burgon *pd* Leo Austin *ed* Peter Tanner

Glenda Jackson, Ben Kingsley, Richard Johnson, Michael Gambon, Rosemary Leach, Eleanor Bron, Harriet Walter, Nigel Hawthorne, Michael Aldridge

The Tuttles of Tahiti
US 1942 91m bw
RKO (Sol Lesser)
V*, L

The Tuttles have one ambition: to do no work.

A negative prospect even for a light comedy, and this one rapidly sinks under a welter of flat dialogue.

w S. Lewis Meltzer, Robert Carson, James Hilton *novel No More Gas* by Charles Noordhof, James Norman Hall   *d* Charles Vidor

Charles Laughton, Jon Hall, Victor Francen, Peggy Drake, Florence Bates

Twelve Angry Men ****
US   1957   95m   bw
(UA) Orion-Nova (Henry Fonda, Reginald Rose)
V, V*, L

A murder case jury about to vote guilty is convinced otherwise by one doubting member.

Though unconvincing in detail, this is a brilliantly tight character melodrama which is never less than absorbing to experience. Acting and direction are superlatively right, and the film was important in helping to establish television talents in Hollywood.

w Reginald Rose   *play* Reginald Rose   *d* Sidney Lumet   *ph* Boris Kaufman   *m* Kenyon Hopkins

Henry Fonda, Lee J. Cobb, E. G. Marshall, Jack Warden, Ed Begley, Martin Balsam, John Fiedler, Jack Klugman, George Voskovec, Robert Webber, Edward Binns, Joseph Sweeney

'Holds the attention unquestioning. It is one of the most exciting films for months.' – *Dilys Powell*

'Generates more suspense than most thrillers.' – *New Yorker*

AAN: best picture; Reginald Rose; Sidney Lumet

The Twelve Chairs: see *Twelve Plus One*

The Twelve Chairs
US   1970   93m   Movielab
UMC/Crossbow (Michael Hertzberg)
V*, L

A Russian bureaucrat chases twelve dining chairs, in one of which is hidden the family jewels.

Tedious Mel Brooks romp with not too many laughs, from a yarn better handled in *Keep Your Seats Please* and *It's in the Bag,* from both of which he might have learned something about comedy timing.

w Mel Brooks   *novel* Ilya Ilf, Evgeny Petrov   *d* Mel Brooks   *ph* Dorde Nikolic   *m* John Morris

Ron Moody, Frank Langella, Dom de Luise, Bridget Brice, Diana Coupland, Mel Brooks

'In the end it runs out of both steam and jokes.' – *Michael Billington, Illustrated London News*

Twelve Good Men
GB   1936   64m   bw
Warner

A convict escapes to murder the jury who convicted him.

Solidly carpentered suspenser.

w Sidney Gilliat, Frank Launder   *novel Murders in Praed Street* by John Rhode   *d* Ralph Ince

Henry Kendall, Nancy O'Neill, Percy Parsons, Morland Graham, Bernard Miles

'A story of twelve men as their women never knew them!'

Twelve O'Clock High **
US   1949   132m   bw
TCF (Darryl F. Zanuck)
V, V*, L

During World War II, the commander of a US bomber unit in Britain begins to crack under the strain.

Absorbing character drama, justifiably a big box-office success of its day, later revived as a TV series. All production values are excellent.

w Sy Bartlett, Beirne Lay Jnr   *d* Henry King   *ph* Leon Shamroy   *m* Alfred Newman

Gregory Peck, Hugh Marlowe, Gary Merrill, Millard Mitchell, Dean Jagger, Robert Arthur, Paul Stewart, John Kellogg

'The best war film since the fighting stopped.' – *Daily Mirror*

'Integrity all the way down the line.' – *New York Times*

AA: Dean Jagger

AAN: best picture; Gregory Peck

Twelve Plus One
Italy/France   1969   108m   Technicolor
CEF/COFCI (Claude Giroux, Edward J. Pope)
original title: *Una su 13*; aka: *The Twelve Chairs*

After he sells some chairs inherited from his aunt, a barber discovers that one of them contains a fortune and sets out to retrieve it.

Broad farce that wastes the talents of its cast, though it contains a bizarrely enjoyable moment by Welles as a barnstorming actor giving a ham performance of *Dr Jekyll and Mr Hyde.*

w Marc Behm, Dennis Norden, Nicolas Gessner   *novel Twelve Chairs* by Ilf and Petrov   *d* Nicolas Gessner   *ph* Giuseppe Ruzzolini   *m* Stelvio Cipriani   *ed* Giancarlo Cappelli

Sharon Tate, Vittorio Gassman, Orson Welles, Vittoria de Sica, Terry-Thomas, Mylene Demongeot, Grégoire Aslan, Tim Brooke-Taylor, Lionel Jeffries

Twentieth Century **
US   1934   91m   bw
Columbia (Howard Hawks)
V, V*

A temperamental Broadway producer trains an untutored actress, but when a star she proves a match for him.

Though slightly lacking in pace, this is a marvellously sharp and memorable theatrical burlesque, and the second half, set on the train of the title, reaches highly agreeable peaks of insanity.

w Ben Hecht, Charles MacArthur   *play Napoleon of Broadway* by Charles Bruce Millholland   *d* Howard Hawks   *ph* Joseph August

John Barrymore, Carole Lombard, Roscoe Karns, Walter Connolly, Ralph Forbes, *Etienne Girardot,* Charles Lane, Edgar Kennedy

'Probably too smart for general consumption . . . a long shot for grosses outside the large cities that boast a cosmopolitan clientele.' – *Variety*

'Notable as the first comedy in which sexually attractive, sophisticated stars indulged in their own slapstick instead of delegating it to their inferiors.' – *Andrew Sarris, 1963*

'In the role of Jaffe John Barrymore fits as wholly and smoothly as a banana in a skin.' – *Otis Ferguson*

The Twenty-Fifth Hour
France/Italy/Yugoslavia   1967   133m   Eastmancolor Franscope
Concordia/CCC/Avala/Carlo Ponti

When the Nazis deport Rumanian Jews, a simple-minded farmer is sent with them because the officer desires his wife.

Peripatetic adventure with the storm-tossed hero flitting from one symbolic situation to another. All a bit much.

w Henri Verneuil, Wolf Mankowitz, François Boyer   *novel* C. Virgil Gheorghiu   *d* Henri Verneuil   *ph* Andreas Winding   *m* Georges Delerue

Anthony Quinn, Virna Lisi, Grégoire Aslan, Michael Redgrave, Serge Reggiani, Marcel Dalio, Marius Goring, Alexander Knox, Liam Redmond, Meier Tzelniker, John Le Mesurier, Françoise Rosay

24 Hours
US   1931   65m   bw
Paramount

A day in the life of an ultra-rich couple whose marriage has gone sour.

Fairly slick matrimonial drama with an attempt at filmic treatment.

w Louis Witzenkorn   *novel* Louis Bromfield   *d* Marion Gering

Clive Brook, Kay Francis, Miriam Hopkins, Regis Toomey, George Barbier, Adrienne Ames

'An absorbing bit of fiction that should engage the attention of the fan regulars and register abundantly at the box office.' – *Variety*

Twenty-Four Hours of a Woman's Life
GB   1952   90m   Technicolor
ABPC (Ivan Foxwell)
US title: *Affair in Monte Carlo*

A young widow tries to reform an inveterate gambler, but he kills himself.

Stilted, over-literary romantic melodrama with philosophical dialogue, flashback framing and Riviera settings.

w Warren Chetham Strode   *novel* Stefan Zweig   *d* Victor Saville   *ph* Christopher Challis   *m* Robert Gill, Philip Green

Merle Oberon, Leo Genn, Richard Todd, Stephen Murray, Peter Illing, Isabel Dean

Twenty Million Miles to Earth
US   1957   82m   bw
Columbia/Morningside (Charles Schneer)
V, V*, L

An American rocket ship returning from Venus breaks open and a scaly monster escapes into the Mediterranean and is cornered in the Roman coliseum.

Cheeseparing monster fiction which doesn't wake up till the last five minutes, and looks pretty silly even then.

w Bob Williams, Chris Knopf   *d* Nathan Juran   *ph* Irving Lippmann   *m* Mischa Bakaleinikoff   *sp* Ray Harryhausen

William Hopper, Joan Taylor, Frank Puglia, John Zaremba

Twenty Million Sweethearts
US   1934   89m   bw
Warner

Singing radio sweethearts are kept apart because of their images.

Thin musical with moderate numbers, remade as *My Dream Is Yours.*

w Warren Duff, Harry Sauber   *d* Ray Enright   *ph* Sid Hickox   *songs* Harry Warren, Al Dubin

Dick Powell, Ginger Rogers, Pat O'Brien, the Mills Brothers, Ted Fio Rito and his band, the Radio Rogues, Allen Jenkins, Grant Mitchell

'An entry the theatre boys won't have to worry about.' – *Variety*

Twenty Mule Team *
US   1940   84m   bw
MGM (J. Walter Ruben)

Rivalry among the borax miners in Death Valley.

Adequate semi-Western with an unusual theme and setting.

w Robert C. DuSoe, Owen Atkinson   *d* Richard Thorpe   *ph* Clyde de Vinna   *m* David Snell

Wallace Beery, Leo Carrillo, Marjorie Rambeau, Anne Baxter, Douglas Fowley, Berton Churchill, Noah Beery Jnr, Arthur Hohl, Clem Bevans, Charles Halton, Minor Watson

29 Acacia Avenue
GB   1945   83m   bw
Boca/Columbia

Young people are having a good time when their parents return unexpectedly from holiday.

Popular domestic comedy of its day.

w Muriel and Sydney Box *play* Mabel and Denis Constanduros *d* Henry Cass

Gordon Harker, Betty Balfour, Carla Lehmann, Jimmy Hanley, Jill Evans, Hubert Gregg, Dinah Sheridan, Henry Kendall, Guy Middleton

'Old enough to know better, young enough not to care.'
Twenty-One
GB 1991 101m colour
Entertainment/Anglo International (Morgan Mason, John Hardy)
V, V*, L

A 21-year-old English girl living in New York recalls her past lovers.

Tedious semi-comedy, full of unconvincing monologues delivered direct to the camera.

w Zoe Heller, Don Boyd *d* Don Boyd *ph* Keith Goddard *m* Michael Berkeley *ed* David Spiers

Patsy Kensit, Jack Shepherd, Patrick Ryecart, Maynard Eziashi, Rufus Sewell, Sophie Thompson, Susan Wooldridge

'A movie that is vulgarly flawed, often made like it was improvised fast on the spot but still managing to contain not only a holding central performance but a certain honesty you can't ignore.' – *Derek Malcolm, Guardian*

Twenty-One Days *
GB 1937 75m bw
London Films (Alexander Korda)
aka: *The First and the Last*

A barrister's brother accidentally kills a man and lets an old eccentric take the blame.

Watchable but very stilted melodrama with interesting early performances by Olivier and Leigh and a few good moments.

w Graham Greene *play* The First and the Last by John Galsworthy *d* Basil Dean *ph* Jan Stallich *m* John Greenwood

Laurence Olivier, Vivien Leigh, Leslie Banks, Hay Petrie, Francis L. Sullivan, Esmé Percy, Robert Newton, Victor Rietti

'I wish I could tell the extraordinary story that lies behind this shelved and resurrected picture, a story involving a theme song, and a bottle of whisky, and camels in Wales. Meanwhile let one guilty man, at any rate, stand in the dock, swearing never to do it again . . .' – *Graham Greene*

† The film was not shown until 1940.

The Twenty Questions Murder Mystery
GB 1949 95m bw
Pax-Pendennis

A killer taunts the police with clues sent to a radio quiz show.

Somewhat heavy comedy mystery with interest arising from the broadcasting background.

w Patrick Kirwan, Victor Katona *d* Paul Stein

Robert Beatty, Rona Anderson, Clifford Evans, Edward Lexy, Olga Lindo, Richard Dimbleby, Jack Train, Stewart MacPherson, Daphne Padel, Norman Hackforth, Jeanne de Casalis

Twenty Thousand Leagues under the Sea **
US 1954 122m Technicolor Cinemascope
Walt Disney
V*, L

Victorian scientists at sea are wrecked and captured by the mysterious captain of a futuristic submarine.

Pretty full-blooded adaptation of a famous yarn, with strong performances and convincing art and trick work.

w Earl Felton *novel* Jules Verne *d* Richard Fleischer *ph* Franz Planer, Franz Lehy, Ralph Hammeras, Till Gabbani *m* Paul Smith *ad* John Meehan *ed* Elmo Williams

Kirk Douglas, James Mason, Paul Lukas, Peter Lorre, Robert J. Wilke, Carlton Young, Ted de Corsia

AA: art direction; special effects

AAN: editing

Twenty Thousand Men a Year
US 1939 83m bw
Cosmopolitan/TCF (Sol M. Wurtzel)

Experiences of recruits to college student aviation training.

Very threadbare flagwaver.

w Lou Breslow, Owen Francis, Frank Wead *d* Alfred E. Green

Randolph Scott, Preston Foster, Margaret Lindsay, Robert Shaw, Mary Healy, Kane Richmond, Maxie Rosenbloom, Sen Yung

'Needs exploitation as upper-bracket attraction.' – *Variety*

Twenty Thousand Years in Sing Sing **
US 1933 77m bw
Warner (Robert Lord)

A tough criminal escapes from prison but his girl kills a man during the attempt, and he takes the blame.

Dated but fast-moving and still-powerful crime melodrama, remade to less effect as *Castle on the Hudson* (qv).

w Wilson Mizner, Brown Holmes *book* Lewis E. Lawes *d* Michael Curtiz *ph* Barney McGill *m* Bernhard Kaun

Spencer Tracy, Bette Davis, Arthur Byron, Lyle Talbot, Louis Calhern, Warren Hymer, Sheila Terry, Edward McNamara

'Good entertainment and good box office with that inside prison routine touch . . . Finally, it begins to appear Sing Sing wouldn't be a bad place at all to spend a vacation during the depression.' – *Variety*

'Somewhere in the fog there is a voice, a perfume, a glove, a knife – and a victim!'
Twenty-Three Paces to Baker Street *
US 1956 103m Eastmancolor Cinemascope
TCF (Henry Ephron)
V*

A blind playwright in a pub overhears a murder plot and follows the trail to the bitter end despite attacks on his life.

Sufficiently engrossing murder mystery with a weird idea of London's geography: the hero's Portman Square apartment has a balcony overlooking the Thames two miles away. Perhaps this is part of the script's light touch.

w Nigel Balchin *novel* Philip MacDonald *d* Henry Hathaway *ph* Milton Krasner *m* Leigh Harline

Van Johnson, Vera Miles, Cecil Parker, Patricia Laffan, Maurice Denham, Estelle Winwood, Liam Redmond

Twice Blessed
US 1945 76m bw
MGM (Arthur L. Field)

Twin daughters of a divorced couple deliberately confuse their parents into a reconciliation.

Paper-thin comedy without much wit.

w Ethel Hill *d* Harry Beaumont

Preston Foster, Gail Patrick, Lee and Lyn Wilde, Richard Gaines, Jean Porter, Ethel Smith at the organ

Twice in a Lifetime
US 1985 117m colour
Yorkin Company/Bud Yorkin
V, V*, L

A man turns fifty and decides to make a clean break with his family.

Comedy drama of the mid-life crisis: nothing new.

w Colin Welland *play* Kisses at 50 by Colin Welland *d* Bud Yorkin *ph* Nick McLean *m* Pat Metheny, Paul McCartney *pd* William Creber *ed* Robert Jones

Gene Hackman, Ellen Burstyn, Ann-Margret, Amy Madigan, Ally Sheedy

AAN: Amy Madigan (supporting actress)

Twice round the Daffodils
GB 1962 89m bw
Anglo Amalgamated/GHW (Peter Rogers)

Comic and serious episodes in the lives of male patients at a TB sanatorium.

Acceptable broadening, almost in *Carry On* style, of a modestly successful play.

w Norman Hudis *play* Ring for Catty by Patrick Cargill, Jack Beale *d* Gerald Thomas *ph* Alan Hume *m* Bruce Montgomery

Juliet Mills, Donald Sinden, Donald Houston, Kenneth Williams, Ronald Lewis, Joan Sims, Andrew Ray, Lance Percival, Jill Ireland, Sheila Hancock, Nanette Newman

Twice Two
US 1933 20m bw
Hal Roach
V, V (C)

Stan and Ollie have each married the other's twin sister . . .

Strained and laboured trick comedy in which neither the double exposures nor the gags quite come off.

w Stan Laurel *d* James Parrott

Laurel and Hardy

Twilight for the Gods
US 1958 120m Eastmancolor
U-I (Gordon Kay)

The captain of an old sailing ship takes her for a last voyage from Mexico to Tahiti.

Dull and miscast adventure story lacking the spark of the original novel; watchable only for the travelogue elements.

w Ernest K. Gann *novel* Ernest K. Gann *d* Joseph Pevney *ph* Irving Glassberg *md* Joseph Gershenson *m* David Raksin

Rock Hudson, Cyd Charisse, Arthur Kennedy, Leif Erickson, Charles McGraw, Ernest Truex, Richard Haydn, Wallace Ford, Celia Lovsky, Vladimir Sokoloff

'Rock Hudson has difficulty in suggesting a dedicated seaman who has served under sail for thirty years.' – *MFB*

The Twilight Hour
GB 1944 85m bw
British National

A nobleman's gardener turns out to be the amnesiac father of the girl about to marry into the family.

Plodding and very predictable drama with popular cast.

w Jack Whittingham *novel* Arthur Valentine *d* Paul Stein

Mervyn Johns, Basil Radford, Marie Lohr, A. E. Matthews, Lesley Brook, Grey Blake

Twilight of Honor
US 1963 115m bw Panavision
MGM/Perlsea
GB title: *The Charge Is Murder*

A young small-town lawyer defends a neurotic no-good on a murder charge.

Modest courtroom melodrama in which the detail is better than the main plot.

w Henry Denker *novel* Al Dewlen *d* Boris Sagal *ph* Philip Lathrop *m* John Green

Richard Chamberlain, *Claude Rains*, Joey Heatherton, Nick Adams, Joan Blackman, James Gregory, Pat Buttram, Jeanette Nolan

AAN: Nick Adams

Twilight of The Dead: see *City of The Living Dead*

'You're travelling through another dimension into a wondrous land whose only boundaries are those of the imagination'

Twilight Zone: The Movie *
US 1983 101m Technicolor
Warner (Steven Spielberg, John Landis)
V*, L

Four supernatural stories in the tradition of Rod Serling's long-running TV series of the fifties.

A disappointing collection on the whole, though with these talents what's on the screen is never quite boring.

w John Landis, George Clayton Johnson, Richard Matheson, Josh Rogan, Rod Serling *d* John Landis, Steven Spielberg, Joe Dante, George Miller *ph* Stevan Larner, Allen Daviau, John Hora *m* Jerry Goldsmith

Dan Aykroyd, Vic Morrow, Scatman Crothers, Bill Quinn, Kathleen Quinlan, Kevin McCarthy, John Lithgow

'If there is an overriding irony to this catalogue of misfortunes, it is that the desire of four up-and-coming directors to honour TV as an imaginative source should have rebounded so disastrously on their cinematic reputations.' – *Richard Combs, MFB*

Twilight's Last Gleaming *
US/West Germany 1977 146m Technicolor
Lorimar/Bavaria Studios (Helmut Jedele)
V*, L, S

An ex-general commandeers an atomic missile plant and blackmails the president into telling some political truths.

Suspense thriller, fairly incompetent on its level and with ideas above its station. A distinctly overlong and unlikeable entertainment.

w Ronald M. Cohen, Edward Huebsch *novel Viper Three* by Walter Wager *d* Robert Aldrich *ph* Robert Hauser *m* Jerry Goldsmith

Burt Lancaster, Richard Widmark, Charles Durning, Melvyn Douglas, Paul Winfield, Burt Young, Joseph Cotten, Roscoe Lee Brown, Gerald S. O'Loughlin, Charles Aidman

'It suggests an overextended episode of a TV series, and the attempts at wit are pathetically gross.' – *New Yorker*

Twin Beds *
US 1942 84m bw
Edward Small

A married couple are embarrassed by the antics of a drunken neighbour.

Slight pretext for a pretty funny old-fashioned farce.

w Curtis Kenyon, Kenneth Earl, E. Edwin Moran *play* Margaret Mayo, Edward Salisbury Field *d* Tim Whelan *ph* Hal Mohr *m* Dimitri Tiomkin

George Brent, Joan Bennett, *Mischa Auer*, Una Merkel, Glenda Farrell, Ernest Truex, Margaret Hamilton, Charles Coleman

Twin Peaks *
US 1989 113m colour Panavision
Lynch-Frost Productions/Propaganda Films (David J. Latt)
V, S

An FBI agent is sent to a small town to investigate the murder of a young girl.

The pilot for what became a controversial and cult TV series was released on video in Europe as a surrealist parody of soap opera, full of deliberately over-the-top performances.

w Mark Frost, David Lynch *d* David Lynch *ph* Ron Garcia *m* Angelo Badalamenti *pd* Patricia Norris *ed* Duwayne R. Dunham

Kyle MacLachlan, Michael Ontkean, Madchen Amick, Dana Ashbrook, Richard Beymer, Lara Flynn Boyle, Sherilyn Fenn, Warren Frost, Joan Chen, Piper Laurie

'In a town like Twin Peaks, no one is innocent.'
'These are the last seven days of Laura Palmer.'
Twin Peaks: Fire Walk with Me
US 1992 134m CFI colour Panavision
Guild/Twin Peaks (Gregg Fienberg)
V, V*, L, S

Events leading up to the murder of the teenage Laura Palmer.

Mystifyingly obscure and dull prequel to the TV series *Twin Peaks* which tries one's patience with its visions and precognitions.

w David Lynch, Robert Engels *d* David Lynch *ph* Ron Garcia *m* Angelo Badalamenti *pd* Patricia Norris *ed* Mark Sweeney

Sheryl Lee, Ray Wise, Mädchen Amick, Dana Ashbrook, Phoebe Augustine, Eric DaRue, Miguel Ferrer, Chris Isaak, Kyle MacLachlan, James Marshall, Jürgen Prochnow, Harry Dean Stanton, Kiefer Sutherland, David Lynch

'Pic will inevitably attract die-hard fans but is too weird and not very meaningful for general audiences.' – *Variety*

'It looks, in fact, like a very bad movie made by a very good director, tired of fooling around for a television audience.' – *Derek Malcolm, Guardian*

The Twinkle in God's Eye
US 1955 73m bw
Republic (Mickey Rooney)

A parson rebuilds a church in a Western town where his father was killed by Indians.

Amiable if unlikely Western drama with the star more convincing than one might expect.

w P. J. Wolfson *d* George Blair *ph* Bud Thackery *m* Van Alexander

Mickey Rooney, Hugh O'Brian, Colleen Gray, Michael Connors, Don Barry

Twinkle Twinkle Lucky Stars (dubbed)
Hong Kong 1985 90m colour
Golden Harvest/Paragon (Eric Tsang)
V

Cops protect an actress from assassination.

Comic martial arts, more under the influence of the Three Stooges than of Bruce Lee. There are, however, some splendidly choreographed fight sequences to compensate for the laborious slapstick.

w Barry Wong *story* Barry Wong, Szeto Cheuk Hon, Lo Kin *d* Samo Hung *ph* Arthur Wong, Johnny Koo *m* Anders Nelson *ad* Eddie Ma *ed* Peter Cheung

Jackie Chan, Samo Hung, Yuen Biao, Richard Ng, Eric Tsang, Fung Shui Fan, Miu Kiu Wai, John Shum, Sibelle Hu, Rosamund Kwan, Richard Norton

Twinky
GB 1969 98m Technicolor
Rank/World Film Services (Clive Sharp)
US title: *Lola*

A 16-year-old London schoolgirl marries a dissolute 40-year-old American author.

Dreary sex comedy drama, the fag end of London's swinging sixties.

w Norman Thaddeus Vane *d* Richard Donner *ph* Walter Lassally *m* John Scott

Charles Bronson, Susan George, Trevor Howard, Michael Craig, Honor Blackman, Robert Morley, Jack Hawkins

Twins *
US 1988 107m DeLuxe
UIP/Universal (Ivan Reitman)
V, V*, L, S

A 36-year-old man, bred in a genetic experiment as the perfect man, discovers that he has a less-than-perfect twin brother.

Amusing, if sometimes ponderous, comedy with the joke depending on the physical disparity of its two protagonists.

w William Davies, William Osborne, Timothy Harris, Herschel Weingrod *d* Ivan Reitman *ph* Andrzej Bartkowiak *m* Georges Delerue, Randy Edelman *pd* James D. Bissel *ed* Sheldon Kahn, Donn Cambern

Arnold Schwarzenegger, Danny DeVito, Kelly Preston, Chloe Webb, Bonnie Bartlett, Marshall Bell, Trey Wilson, David Caruso, Hugh O'Brien

'They use the satanic power of their bodies to turn men and women into their blood slaves!'
Twins of Evil
GB 1971 87m Eastmancolor
Rank/Hammer (Harry Fine, Michael Style)
V, V*

Identical Austrian twins become devotees of a vampire cult.

Vampire-chasing Puritans add a little flavour to a routine Hammer horror.

w Tudor Gates *d* John Hough *ph* Dick Bush *m* Harry Robinson *ad* Roy Stannard *ed* Spencer Reeve

Madeleine and Mary Collinson, Peter Cushing, Kathleen Byron, Dennis Price, Isobel Black

Twist around the Clock
US 1961 83m bw
Columbia/Sam Katzman
V*

An astute manager discovers a small-town dance called the twist and promotes it nationally.

Rock around the Clock revisited, with an even lower budget and fewer shreds of talent.

w James B. Gordon *d* Oscar Rudolph *ph* Gordon Avil *md* Fred Karger

Chubby Checker, the Marcels, Dion, John Cronin, Mary Mitchell

Twist of Fate: see *Beautiful Stranger*

A Twist of Sand
GB 1968 91m DeLuxe
UA/Christina (Fred Engel)

An ill-matched set of criminals seek hidden diamonds on Africa's skeleton coast.

Pattern melodrama of thieves falling out, quite nicely put together but with performances too high pitched.

w Marvin H. Albert *novel* Geoffrey Jenkins *d* Don Chaffey *ph* John Wilcox *m* Tristam Cary

Richard Johnson, Honor Blackman, Roy Dotrice, Peter Vaughan, Jeremy Kemp

'Enough to make even Hitchcock jump!'
Twisted Nerve
GB 1968 118m Eastmancolor
British Lion/Charter (John Boulting)

A rich, disturbed young man disguises himself as a retarded teenager in order to kill his hated stepfather.

Absurd, unpleasant, longwinded and naïvely scripted shocker, rightly attacked because it asserted that brothers of mongoloids are apt to become murderers. A long way behind the worst Hitchcock.

w Leo Marks, Roy Boulting *d* Roy Boulting *ph* Harry Waxman *m* Bernard Herrmann

Hayley Mills, Hywel Bennett, Phyllis Calvert, Billie Whitelaw, Frank Finlay, *Barry Foster*, Salmaan Peer

'Curious and in some respects disagreeable . . . never thrilling enough to reach the Hitchcock level and without sufficient medical credibility to be taken seriously as a case history.' – *Michael Billington, Illustrated London News*

Twitch of the Death Nerve: see *A Bay of Blood*

Two a Penny
GB   1967   98m   Eastmancolor
World Wide (Frank R. Jacobson)

An idle art student becomes involved in the drug racket but finally sees the light.

Naïve religious propaganda sponsored by the Billy Graham movement and featuring the evangelist in a cameo. A curiosity.

w Stella Linden   d James F. Collier   ph Michael Reed   m Mike Leander

Cliff Richard, Dora Bryan, Ann Holloway, Avril Angers, Geoffrey Bayldon, Peter Barkworth

Two against the World
US   1936   64m   bw
Warner (Bryan Foy)
GB title: *The Case of Mrs Pembroke*

A gutter newspaper unnecessarily digs up a sordid murder case and causes the suicide of two people involved.

Remake of *Five Star Final* with the interest boringly shifted to the do-gooders who *don't* want to publish the story.

w Michel Jacoby   *play* Louis Weitzenkorn   d William McGann   ph Sid Hickox   m Heinz Roemheld

Humphrey Bogart, Beverly Roberts, Helen MacKellar, Henry O'Neill, Linda Perry, Virginia Brissac

Two Alone
US   1934   72m   bw
RKO

The orphanage drudge on a remote farm gets herself pregnant.

Heavy-going *Cold Comfort Farm* melodrama, with virtually no light relief in sight.

w Josephine Lovett, Joseph Moncure March   *play* Wild Birds by Dan Totheroh   d Elliott Nugent

Jean Parker, Tom Brown, Arthur Byron, ZaSu Pitts, Beulah Bondi, Nydia Westman

Two and Two Make Six
GB   1961   89m   bw
Bryanston/Prometheus (Monja Danischewsky)

Two motor cycling couples almost accidentally swap partners.

Reasonably fresh little romantic comedy.

w Monja Danischewsky   d Freddie Francis   ph Desmond Dickinson, Ronnie Taylor   m Norrie Paramor

George Chakiris, Janette Scott, Alfred Lynch, Jackie Lane, Malcolm Keen, Ambrosine Philpotts, Bernard Braden

Two Bright Boys
US   1939   69m   bw
Universal (Burt Kelly)

A British boy and his father help an American boy save his oil ranch from a foreclosing villain.

Traditional action stuff, quite pleasantly done for undemanding audiences.

w Val Burton, Edmund L. Hartman   d Joseph Santley

Jackie Cooper, Freddie Bartholomew, Melville Cooper, Dorothy Peterson, Alan Dinehart, Willard Robertson

'Adequate support for the duals.' – *Variety*

Two English Girls: see *Anne And Muriel*

The Two Faces of Dr Jekyll
GB   1960   88m   Technicolor   Megascope
Hammer (Michael Carreras, Anthony Nelson-Keys)
US title: *House of Fright*

A variation on the much-filmed story: the schizo's evil half is the more handsome.

Surprisingly flat and tedious remake.

w Wolf Mankowitz   *novel* Robert Louis Stevenson   d Terence Fisher   ph Jack Asher   m David Heneker, Monty Norman   ad Bernard Robinson   ed Jim Needs, Eric Boyd-Perkins

Paul Massie, Dawn Addams, Christopher Lee, David Kossoff, Francis de Wolff

Two-Faced Woman *
US   1941   90m   bw
MGM (Gottfried Reinhardt)
V*

A ski instructress, who fears she may be losing her publisher husband to another woman, poses as her own more vivacious twin sister.

The failure of this scatterbrained comedy is alleged to be the reason for Garbo's premature retirement. Looked at half a century later, it is no great shakes but harmless and eager to please; what sabotages it is a shoddy production and flagging pace.

w S. N. Behrman, Salka Viertel, George Oppenheimer   *play* Ludwig Fulda   d George Cukor   ph Joseph Ruttenberg   m Bronislau Kaper

Greta Garbo, Melvyn Douglas, *Constance Bennett*, Roland Young, Robert Sterling, Ruth Gordon, George Cleveland

'It is almost as shocking as seeing your mother drunk.' – *Time*

Two Fisted
US   1935   60m   bw
Paramount (Harold Hurley)

A prizefighter and his manager join a socialite's household as bodyguards.

Flat comedy which doesn't get very far in any direction; a remake of the silent *Is Zat So?*

w Sam Hellman, Francis Martin, Eddie Moran   *play* James Gleason, Richard Taber   d James Cruze

Lee Tracy, Roscoe Karns, Grace Bradley, Kent Taylor, Gail Patrick

'Some periods of hilarity.' – *Variety*

Two Flags West *
US   1950   92m   bw
TCF (Casey Robinson)

Sixty Confederate prisoners of war are granted an amnesty and go west to fight the Indians.

Laboured but good-looking Civil War Western.

w Casey Robinson   d Robert Wise   ph Leon Shamroy   m Hugo Friedhofer

Joseph Cotten, Jeff Chandler, Linda Darnell, Cornel Wilde, Dale Robertson, Jay C. Flippen, Noah Beery Jnr, Harry von Zell

'Its period reconstruction is remarkable.' – *Gavin Lambert*

Two for the Road *
GB   1966   113m   DeLuxe   Panavision
TCF/Stanley Donen
V*, L, S

An architect and his wife motoring through France recall the first twelve years of their relationship.

Fractured, fashionable light romantic comedy dressed up to seem of more significance than the gossamer thing it really is; and some of the gossamer has a Woolworth look.

w Frederic Raphael   d Stanley Donen   ph Christopher Challis   m Henry Mancini

Albert Finney, Audrey Hepburn, Eleanor Bron, William Daniels, Claude Dauphin

'The facile, comic bits set off audience expectations which are then betrayed, and the clever, bitter stuff just seems sour.' – *Pauline Kael, New Yorker*

AAN: Frederic Raphael

Two for the Seesaw
US   1962   120m   bw   Panavision
UA/Seesaw/Mirisch/Argyle/Talbot (Robert Wise)
V*, L

A New York dance instructress has a tempestuous affair with an Omaha attorney on the verge of divorce.

Serious comedy or light drama, meticulously detailed but immensely long for its content and too revealing of its stage origins.

w Isobel Lennart   *play* William Gibson   d Robert Wise   ph Ted McCord   m André Previn   ad Boris Leven

Robert Mitchum, Shirley Maclaine

AAN: Ted McCord; song 'Second Chance' (*m* André Previn, *ly* Dory Langdon)

Two for Tonight
US   1935   60m   bw
Paramount (Douglas MacLean)

Three half-brothers write a play for a temperamental star.

Much ado about nothing, but not an unpleasant way of passing an hour.

w George Marion Jnr, Jane Storm   *play* Max and J. O. Lief   d Frank Tuttle

Bing Crosby, Joan Bennett, Mary Boland, Lynne Overman, Thelma Todd, Ernest Cossart

'No wow . . . the songs, the fetching title, the competent cast and mostly Crosby will have to offset the other deficiencies.' – *Variety*

'A very amusing and well-written entertainment.' – *Graham Greene*

Two Girls and a Sailor **
US   1944   124m   bw
MGM (Joe Pasternak)
V*, L

The title says it all.

Loosely-linked wartime musical jamboree with first-class talent; a lively entertainment of its type.

w Richard Connell, Gladys Lehman   d Richard Thorpe   ph Robert Surtees   m George Stoll   *songs* various

June Allyson, Gloria de Haven, Van Johnson, Xavier Cugat and his Orchestra, *Jimmy Durante*, Tom Drake, Lena Horne, Carlos Ramirez, Harry James and his Orchestra, Jose Iturbi, *Gracie Allen*, Virginia O'Brien, Albert Coates

AAN: script

Two Girls on Broadway
US   1940   73m   bw
MGM
GB title: *Choose Your Partner*

A song and dance man breaks up a sister act.

Acceptable lower-case vaudeville musical which rewrites the already wispy plot of *Broadway Melody*.

w Joseph Fields, Jerome Chodorov   d S. Sylvan Simon

George Murphy, Joan Blondell, Lana Turner, Kent Taylor, Wallace Ford, Lloyd Corrigan

Two Guys from Milwaukee

US   1946   90m   bw
Warner
GB title: *Royal Flush*

A young Balkan prince goes incognito in Brooklyn
and befriends a cab driver.

Rumbustious comedy with an amiable cast and gag
guest appearances.

w I. A. L. Diamond, Charles Hoffman   *d* David
Butler

Dennis Morgan, Jack Carson, Joan Leslie, Janis Paige,
S. Z. Sakall, Franklin Pangborn

Two Guys from Texas

US   1948   86m   Technicolor
Warner
GB title: *Two Texas Knights*

Two vaudevillians find themselves on the run from
crooks.

Little more than a peg on which to hang some
clowning and a few musical numbers.

w I. A. L. Diamond, Allen Boretz   *d* David Butler

Dennis Morgan, Jack Carson, Dorothy Malone, Penny
Edwards, Fred Clark, Gerald Mohr, Forrest Tucker

The Two-Headed Spy *

GB   1958   93m   bw
Columbia (Hal E. Chester)

A bogus Nazi worms his way into the Gestapo
hierarchy.

Adequate, not too exciting biopic of Colonel Alex
Schottland; standard production values.

w James O'Donnell   *d* André de Toth   *ph* Ted
Scaife   *m* Bernard Schurmann

Jack Hawkins, Gia Scala, Alexander Knox, Erik
Schumann, Felix Aylmer, Laurence Naismith, Donald
Pleasence, Kenneth Griffith

200 Motels *

US   1971   98m   Technicolor
United Artists/Murakami Wolf/Bizarre (Jerry Good, Herb
    Cohen)
V, V*, S

Concert footage of Zappa and The Mothers of
Invention is intercut with jokes, sketches and
animation, derived from the life of a band on the road
– 'touring can make you crazy', as Zappa comments.

A minor cult movie, an often inventive and witty
surrealist montage and a notable influence on later
rock videos.

wd Frank Zappa, Tony Palmer   *m* Frank Zappa
pd Cal Schenkel   *ch* Gillian Lynne   *ed* Rich
Harrison

The Mothers of Invention (Mark Volman, Howard
Kaylan, Ian Underwood, Aynsley Dunbar, George
Duke), Theodore Bikel, Keith Moon, Ringo Starr

† The film was shot on videotape in England at
Pinewood Studios. Zappa had intended it as a live
concert, but turned to video after it was cancelled on
the grounds that the libretto was obscene.

Two in the Dark

US   1936   72m   bw
RKO

An amnesiac tries to find out whether he was
involved in the murder of a theatrical producer.

Mildly intriguing mystery.

w Seton I. Miller   *novel* Gelett Burgess   *d* Ben
Stoloff

Walter Abel, Margot Grahame, Wallace Ford, Gail
Patrick, Alan Hale, Leslie Fenton, Eric Blore

'A programmer that'll suit both audiences and b.o.
outside of larger first runs.' – *Variety*

The Two Jakes *

US   1990   138m   Technicolor
Blue Dolphin/Paramount (Robert Evans, Harold Schneider)
V, V*, L

A private eye, hired by a real-estate developer to
investigate his wife's adultery, tape-records a murder
that is part of a complex conspiracy.

Convoluted thriller of small-scale corruption that
overstays its welcome.

w Robert Towne   *d* Jack Nicholson   *ph* Vilmos
Zsigmond   *m* Van Dyke Parks   *pd* Jeremy Railton,
Richard Sawyer   *ed* Anne Goursaud

Jack Nicholson, Harvey Keitel, Meg Tilly, Madeleine
Stowe, Eli Wallach, Rubén Blades, Frederic Forrest,
David Keith, Richard Farnsworth

'A jumbled, obtuse yet not entirely unsatisfying
follow-up.' – *Variety*

† A sequel to *Chinatown* (qv), it was originally to have
been made in 1985 with Robert Towne directing and
producer Robert Evans in the role played by Harvey
Keitel.

Two Lane Blacktop

US   1971   103m   Technicolor   scope
Universal/Michael S. Laughlin

In the American southwest, the aimless owners of two
souped-up cars have an interminable race.

Occasionally arresting, generally boring eccentricity
by a big studio looking for another *Easy Rider*.

w Rudolph Wurlitzer, Will Corry   *d* Monte Hellman
ph Jack Deerson   *m* Billy James

James Taylor, Warren Oates, Laurie Bird, Dennis
Wilson

Two Left Feet

GB   1963   93m   bw
British Lion/Roy Baker (Leslie Gilliat)

A callow 19-year-old has girl trouble.

Ponderous sex comedy with no apparent purpose but
some well observed scenes.

w Roy Baker, John Hopkins   *novel* In My Solitude by
David Stuart Leslie   *d* Roy Baker   *ph* Wilkie
Cooper   *m* Philip Green

Michael Crawford, Nyree Dawn Porter, Julia Foster,
David Hemmings, Dilys Watling, David Lodge,
Bernard Lee

The Two Lives of Mattia Pascal **

Italy/West Germany   1984   118m   colour
RAI/Excelsior Cinematografica/Cinecitta/Antenne 2/
    Telemunchen/RTVE/RTS1/Channel 4 (Silvia D'Amico
    Bendico, Carlo Cucci)
original title: *Le Due Vite di Mattia Pascal*

Cheated out of his inheritance and humiliated by his
wife, a man adopts a new identity.

Witty, dark comedy of a personality crisis.

w Suso Cecchi D'Amico, Ennio de Concini, Amanzo
Todini, Mario Monicelli   *novel* Il Fu Mattia Pascal by
Luigi Pirandello   *d* Mario Monicelli   *ph* Camillo
Bazzoni   *m* Nicola Piovani   *ad* Lorenzo Baraldi
ed Ruggero Mastroianni

Marcello Mastroianni, Flavio Bucci, Laura Morante,
Laura Del Sol, Nestor Garay, Alessandro Haber, Carlo
Bagno, Rosalia Maggio, Senta Berger, Bernard Blier

Two Loves

US   1961   100m   Metrocolor   Cinemascope
MGM/Julian Blaustein
GB title: *Spinster*

An American teacher in New Zealand teaches Maoris
and whites and falls for two men.

Pretentious romantic drama with unspeakable
dialogue and eccentric characters.

w Ben Maddow   *novel* Sylvia Ashton Warner
d Charles Walters   *ph* Joseph Ruttenberg
m Bronislau Kaper

Shirley Maclaine, Jack Hawkins, Laurence Harvey,
Nobu McCarthy

Two Men and a Girl: see *Honeymoon*

Two Minds for Murder: see *Someone Behind the
Door*

'91,000 people . . . 33 exit gates . . . one sniper!'

Two Minute Warning

US   1976   115m   Technicolor   Panavision
Universal/Filmways (Edward S. Feldman)
V*, L

A sniper terrifies the crowd at a championship
football game.

Smartly directed but weakly plotted and scripted
disaster movie: the mystery gunman remains a
mystery at the end.

w Edward Hume   *novel* George LaFountaine
d Larry Peerce   *ph* Gerald Hirschfeld   *m* Charles
Fox

Charlton Heston, John Cassavetes, Martin Balsam,
Beau Bridges, David Janssen, Marilyn Hassett, Jack
Klugman, Gena Rowlands, Walter Pidgeon, Brock
Peters, Mitch Ryan

'Even by the standards of exploitation movies, this
film is an unusually dehumanizing experience. Not
only does it exist solely for its gore, but it reduces the
victims to the dimensions of plastic ducks at a
shooting gallery.' – *Frank Rich, New York Post*

The Two Mrs Carrolls

US   1945 (released 1947)   99m   bw
Warner (Mark Hellinger)
V*

A psychopathic artist paints his wives as the Angel of
Death, then murders them with poisoned milk.

Stilted film of an old warhorse of a play, unhappily
cast but working up some last-minute tension.

w Thomas Job   *play* Martin Vale   *d* Peter Godfrey
ph Peverell Marley   *m* Franz Waxman

Barbara Stanwyck, Humphrey Bogart, Alexis Smith,
Nigel Bruce, Isobel Elsom, Pat O'Moore, Peter
Godfrey

'Most of the show is a clutter of entrance and exit,
about as dramatically arresting as a game in and out of
the window. Miss Stanwyck, who does well enough
with a tough worldly kind of part, is baffled by the
sleight of hand required for this one. Humphrey
Bogart also appears uncomfortable.' – *Time*

Two Moon Junction

US   1988   105m   CFI
Recorded Releasing/DDM/Samuel Goldwyn Company (Donald
    P. Borchers)
V, V*, L

Despite her approaching marriage, a rich Southern
woman begins an affair with a handsome carnival
worker.

Ludicrously overwrought romantic melodrama.

wd Zalman King   *story* Zalman King, MacGregor
Douglas   *ph* Mark Plummer   *m* Jonathan Elias
pd Michelle Minch   *ed* Marc Grossman

Sherilyn Fenn, Richard Tyson, Louise Fletcher, Burl
Ives, Kristy McNichol, Martin Hewitt, Juanita Moore,
Don Galloway, Millie Perkins

Two Mules for Sister Sara

US   1969   116m   Technicolor   Panavision
Universal/Malpaso (Martin Rackin)
V, V*

A wandering cowboy kills three men trying to rape a
nun, but she is not what she seems.

Vaguely unsatisfactory Western with patches of nasty brutality leading to an action-packed climax.

w Albert Maltz, Budd Boetticher *d* Don Siegel *ph* Gabriel Figueroa, Gabriel Torres *m* Ennio Morricone

Clint Eastwood, Shirley Maclaine, Manolo Fabregas, Alberto Morin

Two O'Clock Courage
US 1945 66m bw
Ben Stoloff/RKO

An amnesia victim is suspected of killing a Broadway producer.

Tepid murder mystery.

w Robert E. Kent *story* Gelett Burgess *d* Anthony Mann

Tom Conway, Ann Rutherford, Richard Lane, Roland Drew, Emory Parnell, Jane Greer

Two of a Kind
US 1951 75m bw
Columbia (William Dozier)

A man is picked up by a glamorous girl who involves him in an elaborate scheme to defraud an elderly couple.

Modest suspenser.

w Lawrence Kimble, James Grunn *d* Henry Levin *ph* Burnett Guffey *m* George Duning

Edmond O'Brien, Lizabeth Scott, Terry Moore, Alexander Knox, Griff Barnett, Virginia Brissac

Two of a Kind
US 1983 87m DeLuxe
TCF (Roger M. Rothstein, Joe Wizan)
V*, L

Four angels propose that Earth be spared from a second flood if two arbitrarily chosen human beings can be seen to perform a great sacrifice for each other.

Curious reversion to angelic comedies of the thirties and forties. Lacking the right measures of wit and whimsy, it is totally unsuccessful.

wd John Herzfeld *ph* Fred Koenekamp, Warren Rothenberger *md* Patrick Williams *pd* Albert Brenner

John Travolta, Olivia Newton-John, Charles Durning, Oliver Reed, Beatrice Straight, Scatman Crothers

'It feels as if it must be a remake of something . . .' – *Sheila Johnston, MFB*

Two on a Guillotine *
US 1965 107m bw Panavision
Warner (William Conrad)

An illusionist arranges to be chained into his coffin at his funeral but promises to return from the dead.

Longwinded and unconvincing shocker with some effectively scary sequences.

w Henry Slesar, John Kneubuhl *d* William Conrad *ph* Sam Leavitt *m* Max Steiner

Connie Stevens, Dean Jones, Cesar Romero, Parley Baer, Virginia Gregg, Connie Gilchrist, John Hoyt

Two or Three Things I Know about Her **
France 1967 95m Eastmancolor Techniscope
Contemporary/Anouchka/Argos/Les Films du Carrosse/Parc Film (Philippe Senné)
V
original title: *Deux ou trois choses que je sais d'elle*

A mother of two spends her day window-shopping and working as a prostitute to maintain her middle-class way of life.

An episodic and critical look at city life – the title refers to Paris, not the central character – and the constraints it puts upon individuals. Godard at his most polemic, by turns infuriating and fascinating.

wd Jean-Luc Godard *ph* Raoul Coutard *m* Beethoven *ed* Françoise Collin, Chantal Delattre

Jean-Luc Godard (narrator), Marina Vlady, Anny Duperey, Roger Montsoret, Jean Narboni, Christophe Bourseiller, Marie Bourseiller

'A bit of pontifical journalism, a column and a half, interviews and all, about housing estates, the cost of living and the decay of family life.' – *Dilys Powell*

Two Pennyworth of Hope: see *Due Soldi de Speranza*

'They had just 36 hours to share the love of a lifetime!'
Two People
US 1973 100m Technicolor
Universal (Robert Wise)

An army deserter returns home and falls for a fashion photographer.

Solemn, inconsequential topical drama which made no impact whatever.

w Richard de Roy *d* Robert Wise *ph* Gerald Hirschfeld *m* David Shire

Peter Fonda, Lindsay Wagner, Estelle Parsons, Alan Fudge

'Sluggish pacing, lifeless looping and terminally ludicrous dialogue eventually turn the film into a travesty of its own form.' – *Variety*

Two Rode Together
US 1961 109m Technicolor
Columbia/John Ford/Shpetner
V, V*, L

An army commander and a tough marshal negotiate with Comanches for the return of prisoners.

Substandard Ford, moderately good-looking but uninteresting of plot and dreary of development.

w Frank Nugent *novel* Will Cook *d* John Ford *ph* Charles Lawton Jnr *m* George Duning

James Stewart, Richard Widmark, Shirley Jones, Linda Cristal, Andy Devine, John McIntire

Two Seconds *
US 1932 68m bw
Warner

In the last two seconds of his life a criminal reviews the events leading up to his execution.

Competent, pacy crime melodrama.

w Harvey Thew *play* Elliott Lester *d* Mervyn Le Roy *ph* Sol Polito *m* W. Franke Harling

Edward G. Robinson, Preston Foster, Vivienne Osborne, J. Carrol Naish, Guy Kibbee, Adrienne Dare

'General slowness and stodgy overdramatics won't draw the flaps, nor will a tragic finale help.' – *Variety*

'A film that compels attention.' – *Mordaunt Hall, New York Times*

Two Sinners
US 1935 71m bw
Republic

A man jailed for shooting his wife's lover makes a fresh start.

Curious but tedious romantic drama.

w Jefferson Parker *story* Two Black Sheep by Warwick Deeping *d* Arthur Lubin

Otto Kruger, Martha Sleeper, Minna Gombell, Cora Sue Collins

Two Sisters from Boston *
US 1946 112m bw
MGM (Joe Pasternak)

Two girls visiting New York find work in a Bowery saloon.

Nicely-detailed turn-of-the-century musical with pleasant talent.

w Myles Connolly *d* Henry Koster *ph* Robert Surtees *md* Charles Previn *songs* Sammy Fain, Ralph Freed

June Allyson, Kathryn Grayson, Lauritz Melchior, Jimmy Durante, Peter Lawford, Ben Blue

Two Smart People
US 1946 93m bw
MGM (Ralph Wheelwright)

A con man on parole in New Orleans is chased by a lady crook in search of his hidden loot.

Dog-eared comedy drama.

w Ethel Hill, Leslie Charteris *d* Jules Dassin *ph* Karl Freund *m* George Bassman

Lucille Ball, John Hodiak, Lloyd Nolan, Hugo Haas, Lenore Ulric, Elisha Cook Jnr, Lloyd Corrigan, Vladimir Sokoloff

Two Tars ****
US 1928 20m bw silent
Hal Roach
V

Two sailors in an old banger cause a traffic jam and a consequent escalation of violence.

Marvellous elaboration of a tit-for-tat situation, with the stars already at their technical best.

w Leo McCarey, H. M. Walker *d* James Parrott

Laurel and Hardy, Edgar Kennedy, Charley Rogers

Two Texas Knights: see *Two Guys from Texas*

2001: A Space Odyssey ****
GB 1968 141m Metrocolor Panavision
MGM/Stanley Kubrick (Victor Lyndon)
V, V*, L, S

From ape to modern space scientist, mankind has striven to reach the unattainable.

A lengthy montage of brilliant model work and obscure symbolism, this curiosity slowly gathered commercial momentum and came to be cherished by longhairs who used it as a trip without LSD.

w Stanley Kubrick, Arthur C. Clarke *story* The Sentinel by Arthur C. Clarke *d* Stanley Kubrick *ph* Geoffrey Unsworth, John Alcott *m* various classics *pd* Tony Masters, Harry Lange, Ernie Archer *ad* John Hoesli

Gary Lockwood, Keir Dullea, William Sylvester, Leonard Rossiter, Robert Beatty, Daniel Richter, Douglas Rain (voice of HAL)

'Somewhere between hypnotic and immensely boring.' – *Renata Adler*

'Morally pretentious, intellectually obscure and inordinately long . . . intensely exciting visually, with that peculiar artistic power which comes from obsession . . . a film out of control, an infuriating combination of exactitude on small points and incoherence on large ones.' – *Arthur Schlesinger Jnr*

'The satire throughout is tepid and half-hearted, and tends to look like unintended stupidity.' – *John Simon*

† Alex North's rejected score for the film has also been released on compact disc.

AA: special effects

AAN: script; Stanley Kubrick; art direction

2010
US 1984 114m Metrocolor Panavision
MGM-UA (Peter Hyams)
V, V*, L, S

With Earth on the brink of war, scientists return to Jupiter to decide on the fate of *Discovery* and the meaning of the black monolith.

Tame, almost flatfooted sequel to *2001: A Space Odyssey*, with none of the supposed significance and not much else to offer.

wd Peter Hyams   *novel* Arthur C. Clarke   *m* David Shire   *pd* Albert Brenner   *ed* James Mitchell

Roy Scheider, John Lithgow, Helen Mirren, Bob Balaban, Keir Dullea, Dana Elcar, Madolyn Smith

AAN: art direction

Two Thousand Women
GB   1944   97m   bw
GFD/Gainsborough (Edward Black)
V

Two pilots try to rescue British women from a French concentration camp.

Routine mix of laughter and tears; hardly an outstanding film of its time, but mildly entertaining.

wd Frank Launder   *ph* Jack Cox   *md* Louis Levy

Phyllis Calvert, Flora Robson, Patricia Roc, Renée Houston, Anne Crawford, Jean Kent, James McKechnie, Reginald Purdell, Robert Arden, Thora Hird, Dulcie Gray, Carl Jaffe, Muriel Aked

Two Tickets to Broadway
US   1951   106m   Technicolor
RKO (Jerry Wald)
V*

Small-town college girl finds romance and success in the big city.

Very mild musical with TV studio backdrop.

w Sid Silvers, Hal Kanter   *d* James V. Kern
ph Edward Cronjager, Harry J. Wild   *m* Walter Scharf

Janet Leigh, Eddie Bracken, Gloria de Haven, Tony Martin, Barbara Lawrence, *Joe Smith, Charlie Dale*

Two Tickets to London
US   1943   78m   bw
Universal

A sailor accused of aiding an enemy submarine escapes and finds the true villain.

Routine wartime thick ear.

w Tom Reed   *d* Edwin L. Marin

Alan Curtis, Michele Morgan, C. Aubrey Smith, Barry Fitzgerald, Dooley Wilson, Mary Gordon

Two Way Stretch **
GB   1960   87m   bw
British Lion/Shepperton (M. Smedley Aston)
V*

Three convicts break jail to rob a maharajah.

Amusing comedy with good performances and situations, unofficially borrowed in part from *Convict 99*.

w John Warren, Len Heath   *d* Robert Day   *ph* Geoffrey Faithfull   *m* Ken Jones

Peter Sellers, *Lionel Jeffries*, Wilfrid Hyde-White, Bernard Cribbins, David Lodge, Maurice Denham, Beryl Reid, Liz Fraser, Irene Handl, George Woodbridge

Two Weeks in Another Town *
US   1962   107m   Metrocolor   Cinemascope
MGM (John Houseman)
L

An ex-alcoholic film director gets his comeback chance in Rome but is plagued by old memories.

Self-indulgent melodrama with entertaining patches for *cinéastes*, especially those who saw *The Bad and the Beautiful*.

w Charles Schnee   *novel* Irwin Shaw   *d* Vincente Minnelli   *ph* Milton Krasner   *m* David Raksin

Kirk Douglas, Edward G. Robinson, Cyd Charisse, Daliah Lavi, George Hamilton, Claire Trevor, Rosanna Schiaffino, James Gregory, George Macready

'The result may be a fantasy world, but it is a fantasy which this director understands and makes his own and into which he can breathe an intense, feverish life.' – *Dilys Powell*

Two Weeks with Love *
US   1950   92m   Technicolor
MGM (Jack Cummings)
V*

Adventures on a family summer holiday at the turn of the century.

Pleasant family musical.

w John Larkin, Dorothy Kingsley   *d* Roy Rowland
ph Al Gilks   *m* Georgie Stoll

Jane Powell, Ricardo Montalban, Louis Calhern, Ann Harding, Phyllis Kirk, Debbie Reynolds, Carleton Carpenter, Clinton Sundberg

Two Who Dared: see A Woman Alone

Two Women *
Italy/France   1960   110m   bw
Champion/Marceau/Cocinor/SGC (Carlo Ponti)
V*
original title: *La Ciociara*

During the Allied bombing of Rome a woman and her daughter travel arduously south and have a hard time at the hands of invading soldiers.

Rather hysterical character drama allowing for a splendid top-note performance from its star.

w Cesare Zavattini, Vittorio de Sica   *novel* Alberto Moravia   *d* Vittorio de Sica   *ph* Gabor Pogany   *m* Armando Trovaioli

Sophia Loren, Eleonora Brown, Jean-Paul Belmondo, Raf Vallone

AA: Sophia Loren

Two Yanks in Trinidad
US   1942   82m   bw
Samuel Bischoff/Columbia

Minor racketeers join the army and capture a German agent.

One of the many variations on the Flagg and Quirt formula, and not a bad one.

w Sy Bartlett, Richard Carroll, Harry Segal
d Gregory Ratoff

Pat O'Brien, Brian Donlevy, Janet Blair, Roger Clark, Donald MacBride, John Emery

Two Years before the Mast *
US   1946   98m   bw
Paramount (Seton I. Miller)

In the mid-19th century, a writer becomes a sailor to expose bad conditions.

Well-made but unconvincing-looking picturization of a famous book.

w Seton I. Miller, George Bruce   *book* Richard Henry Dana   *d* John Farrow   *ph* Ernest Laszlo   *m* Victor Young

Alan Ladd, Brian Donlevy, William Bendix, Barry Fitzgerald, Howard da Silva, Albert Dekker, Luis Van Rooten, Darryl Hickman

Two's Company
GB   1936   74m   bw
B and D/Paul Soskin

An earl's son loves the daughter of an American millionaire.

Not particularly successful hands-across-the-sea comedy.

w Tom Geraghty. Roland Pertwee, J. B. Morton, John Paddy Carstairs, Tim Whelan   *novel* Romeo and Julia by Sidney Horler   *d* Tim Whelan

Gordon Harker, Ned Sparks, Mary Brian, Patric Knowles, Robb Wilton, Morton Selten

Tycoon
US   1947   129m   Technicolor
RKO

An engineer is hired to drive a tunnel through the Andes, and starts a feud with his boss when he falls in love with his daughter.

Boring, studio-set action saga with too many stops for romance.

w Borden Chase, John Twist   *d* Richard Wallace   *ph* Harry J. Wild   *m* Leigh Harline

John Wayne, Cedric Hardwicke, Laraine Day, James Gleason, Judith Anderson, Anthony Quinn, Grant Withers

Typhoon
US   1940   70m   Technicolor
Paramount (Anthony Veiller)

On a Dutch Guianan island, two sailors find a girl who has been a castaway since childhood.

One of Lamour's several sarongers, quite entertaining in its way and commendably brisk.

w Allen Rivkin   *d* Louis King   *ph* William Mellor   *m* Frederick Hollander

Dorothy Lamour, Robert Preston, Lynne Overman, J. Carrol Naish, Frank Reicher

'One of the most emphatically silly pictures I ever saw in my life.' – *Richard Mallet, Punch*

'The gem of pure, pellucid silliness.' – *James Agate*

Tystnaden: see The Silence

U

U Boat 29: see *The Spy in Black*

U.F.O.
GB 1993 79m colour
Feature Film/Polygram/George Foster (Simon Wright)

Feminists from outer space kidnap comedian Roy 'Chubby' Brown so that they can try him for telling offensive jokes.

Witless, cheap and nasty movie, starring the self-styled 'rudest, crudest, filthiest comedian in the world'; it is certainly crudely made and performed.

w Richard Hall, Simon Wright, Roy 'Chubby' Brown *d* Tony Dow *ph* Paul Wheeler *m* Clever Music *pd* David McHenry *ed* Geoff Hogg

Roy 'Chubby' Brown, Sara Stockbridge, Amanda Symonds, Roger Lloyd Pack, Shirley Anne Field, Sue Lloyd, Kenny Baker

'Wildly uneven, often offensive, but with a cheerful inanity which goes some way to compensate for its grosser shortcomings.' – *Sight and Sound*

USS Teakettle: see *You're in the Navy Now*

U2 Rattle and Hum *
US 1988 99m colour/bw
Paramount/Midnight (Michael Hamlyn)
V, V*

Documentary on the Irish rock group recording a new album and performing at home and in the States, described by its participants as 'a musical journey'. Blues guitarist and singer B. B. King joins them for one number.

Fans will enjoy this celebration of one of the most successful groups of the period, which alternates between coarse-toned black and white and colour photography for no apparent reason; those looking for some deeper insight into the business and art of rock will need to go elsewhere.

d Phil Joanou *ph* Jordan Cronenweth (colour), Robert Brinkman (bw) *ed* Phil Joanou

Ugetsu Monogatari *
Japan 1953 94m bw
Daiei (Masaichi Nagata)
V*

During a 16th-century civil war two potters find a way of profiteering, but their ambitions bring disaster on their families.

Unique mixture of action, comedy and the supernatural, with strong, believable characters participating and a delightfully delicate touch in script and direction. On its first release it began to figure in many best ten lists, but quickly seemed to fade from public approbation.

w Matsutaro Kawaguchi, from 17th-century collection by Akinara Ueda, *Tales of a Pale and Mysterious Moon after the Rain* *d* Kenji Mizoguchi *ph* Kazuo Miyagawa *m* Fumio Hayasaka

Masayuki Mori, Machiko Kyo, Sakae Ozawa, Mitsuko Mito

'Heavy going in spots, but with marvellous passages that are worth a bit of patience.' – *New Yorker*

The Ugly American
US 1962 120m Eastmancolor
U-I/George Englund
V, V*

A publisher is made ambassador to a southeast Asian state.

Self-dating anti-communist drama which was muddled and boring when new.

w Stewart Stern *novel* William J. Lederer, Eugene Burdick *d* George Englund *ph* Clifford Stine *m* Frank Skinner

Marlon Brando, Eiji Okada, Sandra Church, Pat Hingle, Arthur Hill, Jocelyn Brando, *Kukrit Pramoj*

The Ugly Dachshund *
US 1965 93m Technicolor
Walt Disney (Winston Hibler)
V*

A dachshund bitch fosters among its puppies an orphan Great Dane.

Cheerful, fast-moving animal farce.

w Albert Aley *novel* G. B. Stern *d* Norman Tokar *ph* Edward Colman *m* George Bruns

Dean Jones, Suzanne Pleshette, Charles Ruggles, Kelly Thordsen, Parley Baer, Mako, Charles Lane

'In his world, brute force isn't enough.'

Ulterior Motives
US 1991 92m DeLuxe
Den Music/Elk/Ian Page (J. Max Kirishima, Thomas Ian Griffith)
V, V*

A *New York Times* journalist hires a high-kicking private eye to help her expose a Japanese research scientist in America who is selling classified information.

Unpleasant paranoid thriller with unsympathetic characters and a little martial arts action thrown in for bad measure. *wd* James Becket *story* James Becket, Thomas Ian Griffith *ph* Stephen M. Katz *m* Parmer Fuller *pd* Michael Helmy *ed* Virginia Katz

Thomas Ian Griffith, Mary Page Keller, Joe Yamanaka, Ellen Crawford, Tyra Ferrell, M. C. Gainey, Ken Howard

'Spoilt only by the weak ending which negates our hero's most despicable act of violence.' – *Sight and Sound*

'The fight sequences are fair only.' – *Empire*

La Ultima Cena: see *The Last Supper*

La Ultima Siembra: see *The Last Harvest*

Ultimas Imagenes del Naufragio: see *Last Images of the Shipwreck*

The Ultimate Solution of Grace Quigley: see *Grace Quigley*

The Ultimate Warrior
US 1975 94m Technicolor
Warner (Fred Weintraub, Paul Heller)
V*

In AD 2012 New York is ruled by a gangster, the atmosphere is poisoned, and the only hope is a new community on an island off North Carolina.

Curious pretentious fantasy without the courage of its convictions or much entertainment value.

wd Robert Clouse *ph* Gerald Hirschfeld *m* Gil Melle

Yul Brynner, Max von Sydow, Joanna Miles, William Smith, Richard Kelton, Stephen McHattie

'Less a prophetic vision than a kind of thick-ear West Side Story.' – *Richard Combs*

'Actually filmed along the route he travelled 3000 years ago!'

Ulysses *
Italy 1954 103m Technicolor
Lux Film/Ponti-de Laurentiis (Fernando Cinquini)
V*, S

Ulysses and his crew sail under the curse of Cassandra, and encounter Circe, the sirens and the cyclops.

Peripatetic adventure yarn not too far after Homer; narrative style uncertain but highlights good.

w Franco Brusati, Mario Camerini, Ennio de Concini, Hugh Gray, Ben Hecht, Ivo Perelli, Irwin Shaw *poem* The Odyssey by Homer *d* Mario Camerini *ph* Harold Rosson *m* Alessandro Cicognini

Kirk Douglas, Silvana Mangano, Anthony Quinn, Rosanna Podesta

Ulysses *
GB 1967 132m bw Panavision
Walter Reade (Joseph Strick)

Twenty-four hours in Dublin with a young poet and a Jewish newspaper man.

A pleasant enough literary exercise, a decent précis of an unmanageably prolix classic novel, this specialized offering would have passed unnoticed were it not for its language, which got it banned in many places but now seems mild indeed.

w Joseph Strick, Fred Haines *novel* James Joyce *d* Joseph Strick *ph* Wolfgang Suschitsky *m* Stanley Myers

Maurice Roeves, Milo O'Shea, Barbara Jefford, T. P. McKenna, Anna Manahan, Maureen Potter

'No amount of pious invoking of Joyce's name can disguise the fact that a cheaply produced film is being sold at exorbitant prices so that someone can make his boodle off "culture".' – *John Simon*

'An act of homage in the form of readings from the book plus illustrated slides.' – *Pauline Kael*

'A facile and ludicrous reduction.' – *Stanley Kauffmann*

AAN: script

'Only one man understood the savagery of the early American west!'

Ulzana's Raid
US 1972 103m Technicolor
Universal/Carter de Haven/Robert Aldrich
V, V*, L

An ageing Indian fighter and a tenderfoot officer lead a platoon sent out to counter a murderous Apache attack.

Bloodthirsty, reactionary Western with unpleasant shock moments.

w Alan Sharp   d Robert Aldrich   ph Joseph Biroc
m Frank de Vol

Burt Lancaster, Bruce Davison, Jorge Luke, Richard
Jaeckel, Lloyd Bochner

Umberto D **
Italy   1952   89m   bw
Dear Films
V*, L

A retired civil servant can barely afford his rent but
won't part with his dog.

Downbeat, immensely moving study of old age in a
society which fails to provide for it.

w Cesare Zavattini, Vittorio de Sica   d Vittorio de Sica
ph G. R. Aldo   m Alessandro Cicognini

Carlo Battista, Maria Pia Casilio, Lina Gennari

'There isn't a minute of banality in this simple, direct
film.' – New Yorker

AAN: Cesare Zavattini (original story)

The Umbrellas of Cherbourg: see Les Parapluies
de Cherbourg

Un Homme et une Femme: see A Man and a
Woman

Una su 13: see Twelve Plus One

Unaccustomed as We Are
US   1929   20m   bw   silent
Hal Roach
V (C)

Ollie takes a friend home to dinner, but his wife
walks out, leaving him to get into all kinds of trouble.

The team's first sound comedy, rather hesitant in its
use of the new medium. The story was later reworked
as the last half hour of Blockheads.

w Leo McCarey and H. M. Walker   d Lewis
R. Foster

Laurel and Hardy, Edgar Kennedy, Mae Busch,
Thelma Todd

The Unbearable Lightness of Being **
US   1987   172m   Technicolor/DeLuxe
Saul Zaentz
V, V*, L, S

A womanizing brain surgeon and his two lovers
painfully achieve maturity after the putting down of
the Prague Spring by Soviet troops.

Brave and largely successful attempt to transfer a
complex, ironic Czech novel to the screen.

w Jean-Claude Carrière, Philip Kaufman
novel Milan Kundera   d Philip Kaufman   ph Sven
Nykvist   m Leos Janáček   pd Pierre Guffroy

Daniel Day-Lewis, Juliette Binoche, Lena Olin,
Erland Josephson, Daniel Olbrychski

'It's a prankish sex comedy that treats modern
political events with a delicate – yet almost sly – sense
of tragedy. It's touching in sophisticated ways that
you don't expect from an American director.' – Pauline
Kael, New Yorker

AAN: Sven Nykvist; best adapted screenplay

Unbelievable Truth *
US   1989   90m   colour
Electric/Contemporary/Action (Bruce Weiss, Hal Hartley)
V, V*

A convicted murderer returns to his home town and
attracts the intellectual daughter of his employer, a
garage owner.

Clever low-budget first feature of an unlikely
romance.

wd Hal Hartley   ph Michael Spiller   m Jim
Coleman   pd Carla Gerona   ed Hal Hartley

Adrienne Shelly, Robert Burke, Christopher Cooke,
Julia McNeal, Mark Bailey, Gary Sauer, Katherine
Mayfield

The Uncanny
Canada/GB   1977   85m   colour
Rank/Cinevideo/Tor (Claude Héroux, Milton Subotsky)
V*

An author tells his publisher three stories about evil
cats.

Below-par horror compendium with crude effects
failing to bolster a sagging script.

w Michael Parry   d Denis Héroux   ph Harry
Waxman, James Bawden   m Wilfred Josephs

Peter Cushing, Ray Milland, Susan Penhaligon, Joan
Greenwood, Simon Williams, Roland Culver,
Alexandra Stewart, Donald Pleasence, Samantha
Eggar, John Vernon

Uncensored
GB   1942   108m   bw
GFD/Gainsborough (Edward Black)

In Brussels during the Nazi occupation, the leader of a
toe-the-line paper secretly leads the patriots.

Unconvincing underground melodrama with stilted
presentation and performances.

w Wolfgang Wilhelm, Terence Rattigan, Rodney
Ackland   novel Oscar Millard   d Anthony Asquith
ph Arthur Crabtree   m Hans May

Eric Portman, Phyllis Calvert, Griffith Jones,
Raymond Lovell, Peter Glenville, Irene Handl, Carl
Jaffe, Felix Aylmer

Uncertain Glory
US   1944   102m   bw
Warner (Robert Buckner)
V

During World War II, a French playboy sacrifices
himself for his country.

Tame star vehicle needing more action and less
philosophy.

w Laszlo Vadnay, Max Brand   d Raoul Walsh
ph Sid Hickox   m Adolph Deutsch

Errol Flynn, Paul Lukas, Jean Sullivan, Lucile
Watson, Faye Emerson, James Flavin, Douglass ·
Dumbrille, Dennis Hoey

Uncertain Lady
US   1934   63m   bw
Universal

An executive wife recovers her husband from the
clutches of another woman.

Transparent comedy with the principals ill cast.

w Daniel Evena, Martin Brown   play Harry Segal
d Karl Freund

Edward Everett Horton, Genevieve Tobin, Renee
Gadd, Paul Cavanagh, Mary Nash

Unchained
US   1955   75m   bw
Warner/Hall Bartlett

A new governor experiments with a prison without
bars.

Decent documentary drama which reaches no great
heights.

wd Hall Bartlett   book Prisoners Are People by Kenyon
J. Scudder   ph Virgil Miller   m Alex North

Chester Morris, Elroy Hirsch, Barbara Hale, Todd
Duncan, Johnny Johnston, Peggy Knudsen, Jerry
Paris, John Qualen

AAN: title song (m Alex North, ly Hy Zaret)

The Uncle
GB   1964   87m   bw
Play-Pix

A 7-year-old boy finds he is uncle to a boy the same
age.

Comedy-drama about the first stirrings of maturity; its
failure to find a release got it championed by some
critics, but it's essentially a thin piece of work.

w Margaret Abrams, Desmond Davis
novel Margaret Abrams   d Desmond Davis

Rupert Davies, Brenda Bruce, Maurice Denham,
Christopher Ariss

Uncle Benjamin
France   1969   90m   Eastmancolor
Gaumont International (Robert Sussfeld, Roger Debelmas)
original title: Mon Oncle Benjamin

A rakish country doctor tries to seduce the virginal
daughter of the local innkeeper.

A Gallic attempt at the bawdy zest of Tom Jones, often
coarse in tone and closer to the Carry On films in style.

André Couteaux, Jean-François Hauduro, Edouard
Molinaro   d Edouard Molinaro   ph Alain Levent
m Jacques Brel, François Rauber   ed Robert and
Monique Isnardon

Jacques Brel, Claude Jade, Rosy Varte, Bernard
Alane, Paul Frankeur, Alfred Adam, Bernard Blier

Uncle Buck *
US   1989   100m   DeLuxe
UIP/Universal (John Hughes, Tom Jacobson)
V, V*, L

A good-natured but slobbish layabout straightens out
his sister's warring children and learns to love
domesticity.

Rambling, moderately enjoyable comedy, although it
is not far removed from a television sit-com.

wd John Hughes   ph Ralph Bode   m Ira Newborn
pd John W. Corso   ed Lou Lombardo, Tom
Lombardo, Peck Prior

John Candy, Jean Louisa Kelly, Gaby Hoffman,
Macaulay Culkin, Amy Madigan, Elaine Bromka,
Garrett M. Brown

Uncle Harry: see The Strange Affair of Uncle Harry

Uncle Silas *
GB   1947   103m   bw
GFD/Two Cities (Josef Somlo, Laurence Irving)
V
US title: The Inheritance

A young Victorian heiress finds herself menaced by
her uncle and his housekeeper.

Slow-starting but superbly made period suspenser;
unfortunately the characters are all sticks.

w Ben Travers   novel Sheridan Le Fanu   d Charles
Frank

Jean Simmons, Derrick de Marney, Katina Paxinou,
Derek Bond, Esmond Knight, Sophie Stewart,
Manning Whiley, Reginald Tate, Marjorie Rhodes

Uncommon Valor
US   1983   105m   Movielab
Paramount/Ted Kotcheff (John Milius, Buzz Feitshans)
V, V*, L

A retired colonel goes looking for his son, declared
missing in action in Vietnam, and is helped by a
similarly placed industrialist who backs a rescue raid.

Slam-bang action piece with the customary patriotic
and personal sentiment.

w Joe Gayton   d Ted Kotcheff   ph Stephen H.
Burum   m James Horner   pd James L. Schoppe

Gene Hackman, Robert Stack, Fred Ward, Reb Brown,
Randall Cobb, Patrick Swayze

'Plunging over the falls – lashed at the stake – trapped by savages in the mightiest love-spectacle de Mille ever filmed!'

'I bought this woman for my own ... and I'll kill the man who touches her!'

Unconquered
US 1947 146m Technicolor
Paramount/Cecil B. de Mille
V

An 18th-century English convict girl is deported to the American colonies and suffers various adventures before marrying a Virginia militiaman.

Cardboard epic, expensive and noisy but totally unpersuasive despite cannon, arrows, fire and dynamite.

w Charles Bennett, Frederic M. Frank, Jesse Lasky Jnr novel Neil H. Swanson d Cecil B. de Mille ph Ray Rennahan m Victor Young

Paulette Goddard, Gary Cooper, Boris Karloff, Howard da Silva, Cecil Kellaway, Ward Bond, Katherine de Mille, Henry Wilcoxon, C. Aubrey Smith, Victor Varconi, Virginia Grey, Porter Hall, Mike Mazurki

'De Mille bangs the drum as loudly as ever but his sideshow has gone cold on us.' – Richard Winnington

'A five-million dollar celebration of Gary Cooper's virility, Paulette Goddard's femininity, and the American frontier spirit.' – Time

Unconventional Linda: see Holiday (1938)

The Undead
US 1956 75m bw
Balboa Productions (Roger Corman)
V*

A psychic researcher hypnotizes a prostitute, sending her back to a past life in a medieval world of witchcraft and magic.

A tale told by the devil, but signifying no more than the usual ineptly acted fantasy.

w Charles Griffith, Mark Hanna d Roger Corman ph William Sickner m Ronald Stein ed Frank Sullivan

Pamela Duncan, Richard Garland, Allison Hayes, Val Dufour, Mel Welles, Dorothy Neumann, Billy Barty

The Undefeated
US 1969 119m DeLuxe Panavision
TCF (Robert L. Jacks)
V, V*, L

After the Civil War, two colonels from opposite sides meet on the Rio Grande.

Sprawling, lethargic star Western with moments of glory.

w James Lee Barrett d Andrew V. McLaglen ph William H. Clothier m Hugo Montenegro

John Wayne, Rock Hudson, Lee Meriwether, Tony Aguilar, Roman Gabriel

Under a Texas Moon
US 1930 70m Technicolor
Warner

A rancher of the Don Juan type makes hay with the ladies but also rounds up cattle rustlers.

Lightweight early talkie outdoor spectacle with music, not at all memorable.

w Gordon Rigby, Stewart Edward White d Michael Curtiz ph Bill Rees song Ray Perkins

Frank Fay, Myrna Loy, Raquel Torres, Armida, Noah Beery, George E. Stone, Fred Kohler

'Unusually pleasing western ... de luxe programmer of its kind.' – Variety

Under California Stars
US 1948 70m Trucolor
Republic (Edward J. White)

After celebrating his 10th anniversary as a film star, Roy Rogers rides out to deal with the crooks who have kidnapped Trigger, 'the smartest horse in the West', an activity that does not prevent him singing songs at the drop of a stetson.

Amiably daft Western in Rogers' usual mode of music, comedy and occasional mayhem.

w Sloan Nibley, Paul Gangelin d William Witney ph Jack Marta m Morton Scott ad Frank Hotaling ed Tony Martinelli

Roy Rogers, Jane Frazee, Andy Devine, Bob Nolan and the Sons of the Pioneers.

Under Capricorn
GB 1949 117m Technicolor
Transatlantic (Sidney Bernstein, Alfred Hitchcock)
V*, L

In Australia in 1830 an English immigrant stays with his cousin Henrietta, who has become a dipsomaniac because of her husband's cruelty.

Cardboard 'woman's picture' with elements of Rebecca, shot with vestiges of Hitch's ten-minute take. A pretty fair disaster.

w James Bridie novel Helen Simpson d Alfred Hitchcock ph Jack Cardiff, Paul Beeson, Ian Craig m Richard Addinsell

Ingrid Bergman, Joseph Cotten, Michael Wilding, Margaret Leighton, Jack Watling, Cecil Parker, Denis O'Dea

'A lengthy, unhurried, and generally quiet picture, directed by Hitchcock with the dreamy contemplation of one embarked on a long sea voyage ... I can't feel that the choice of subject is a very happy one, for either Hitchcock or his actors.' – C. A. Lejeune

Under Cover of Night
US 1937 70m bw
MGM (Lucien Hubbard)

A city detective and his wife nab a murderer.

One of many to which this plot might be applied in the wake of The Thin Man, and not a good example.

w Bertram Millhauser d George B. Seitz

Edmund Lowe, Florence Rice, Henry Daniell, Nat Pendleton, Sara Haden, Dean Jagger, Frank Reicher

Under Fire *
US 1983 127m Technicolor
Orion/Lion's Gate/Greenberg Brothers (Jonathan Taplin)
V, V*, L, S

War correspondents in Nicaragua become involved in the dirty politics on both sides.

A thinking man's action piece, but no help to anybody in finding the true facts.

w Ron Shelton, Clayton Frohman d Roger Spottiswoode ph John Alcott m Jerry Goldsmith

Gene Hackman, Nick Nolte, Joanna Cassidy, Jean-Louis Trintignant, Ed Harris, Richard Masur, Rene Enriquez

'A complex, genuinely thrilling drama of commitment, the mercenary mentality and the tortuous ironies of history.' – Sight and Sound

AAN: Jerry Goldsmith

Under Milk Wood *
GB 1971 88m Technicolor
Timon (Hugo French, Jules Buck)
V*

Life in the Welsh village of Llareggub, as seen by the poet's eye.

Attractive but vaguely unsatisfactory screen rendering of an essentially theatrical event (originally a radio play); everything is much too literal, a real place instead of a fantasy.

wd Andrew Sinclair play Dylan Thomas ph Bob Huke m Brian Gascoigne

Richard Burton, Elizabeth Taylor, Peter O'Toole, Glynis Johns, Vivien Merchant, Sian Phillips, Victor Spinetti, Rachel Thomas, Angharad Rees, Ann Beach

Under My Skin
US 1949 86m bw
TCF (Casey Robinson)

A crooked jockey is idolized by his son and finally reforms rather than disillusion the boy.

Hokey sentimental melodrama with racetrack backgrounds.

w Casey Robinson short story My Old Man by Ernest Hemingway d Jean Negulesco ph Joseph LaShelle m Daniele Amfitheatrof

John Garfield, Micheline Presle, Luther Adler, Orley Lindgren, Ann Codee

Under Satan's Sun *
France 1987 98m colour
Cannon/Erato films/A2/Action Films (Daniel Toscan du Plantier)
V*

original title: Sous le Soleil du Satan

A rural priest begins to believe that Satan is controlling mankind.

Austere examination of the nature of religious belief that won the Palme d'Or for best film at the 1987 Cannes Film Festival.

w Sylvie Danton novel Georges Bernanos d Maurice Pialat ph Willy Kurant m Henri Dutilleux ad Katia Vischkof ed Yann Dedet

Gérard Depardieu, Sandrine Bonnaire, Maurice Pialat, Alain Artur, Yann Dedet, Brigitte Legendre

'1992 ... Stop ... Battleship Besieged By Terrorists ... Stop ... Nuclear Warheads Stolen ... Stop ... Crew Helpless ... Stop ... Lone Man Fighting To Save Ship ...'

Under Siege
US 1992 102m Technicolor
Warner (Amon Milchan, Steven Seagal, Steven Reuther)
V, V*, L, S

A ship's cook, aided by a stripper, saves the day after a battleship is hijacked by a force of highly trained killers intent on stealing its nuclear weapons.

Often risible, always predictable action movie in which one man conquers all, and consisting of a succession of slickly done martial arts combats and gun battles. For diehard fans of the star, or fans of Die Hard.

w J. F. Lawton d Andrew Davis ph Frank Tidy m Gary Chang pd Bill Kenney ed Robert A. Ferretti

Steven Seagal, Tommy Lee Jones, Gary Busey, Erika Eleniak, Patrick O'Neal, Damian Chapa, Troy Evans, David McKnight, Lee Hinton

'An immensely slick, if also old-fashioned and formulaic, entertainment. Steven Seagal fans and action buffs should eat this up.' – Variety

'This delivers lean, suspenseful, he-man heroics with all the whizz-bang aplomb you could wish for.' – Matt Mueller, Empire

AAN: Sound; sound effects editing

Under Suspicion *
GB 1991 100m colour
Rank/Carnival/Columbia/LWT (Brian Eastman)
V, V*, L

In the 1950s, a private detective specializing in divorce is accused of murdering his client and his wife when they are found dead in a hotel room.

Moody attempt at a film noir that looks clumsy when set against the classics of the genre.

wd Simon Moore ph Vernon Layton, Ivan Strasberg m Christopher Gunning pd Tim Hutchinson ed Tariq Anwar

Liam Neeson, Kenneth Cranham, Laura San Giacomo, Maggie O'Neil, Alan Talbot, Malcolm Storry, Martin Grace, Kevin Moore

'Displays most of the virtues of a well-constructed seaside roller-coaster. Twists, switchbacks, lots of flashing lights and gaudy paintwork: no great emotional significance but a thoroughly exhilarating ride.' – *Philip Kemp, Sight and Sound*

'A taut and entertaining mystery melodrama.' – *Vincent Canby, New York Times*

Under Ten Flags
US 1960 92m bw
Paramount/Dino de Laurentiis

In World War II, a German surface raider in disguise menaces British shipping.

Muddled naval epic with too many allegiances.

w Vittorio Petrilli, Duilio Coletti, Ulrich Mohr, William Douglas Home *d* Duilio Coletti, Silvio Narizzano *ph* Aldo Tonti *m* Nino Rota

Van Heflin, Charles Laughton, John Ericson, Mylène Demongeot, Cecil Parker, Folco Lulli, Alex Nicol, Liam Redmond

Under the Clock: see *The Clock*

Under the Gun
US 1950 83m bw
Universal-International

A racketeer is jailed and tries to escape.

Lower-case prison adventure without much conviction.

w George Zuckerman *d* Ted Tetzlaff

Richard Conte, Audrey Totter, John McIntire, Sam Jaffe, Shepperd Strudwick

Under the Pampas Moon
US 1935 78m bw
Fox

A gaucho leader recovers his stolen horse.

Amiable modern adventure set in Argentina.

w Ernest Pascal, Bradley King *d* James Tinling

Warner Baxter, Ketti Gallian, Rita Hayworth, Jack La Rue, J. Carrol Naish

Under the Rainbow
US 1981 95m colour
Orion/Warner
V*

Nazis and midgets mingle backstage while *The Wizard of Oz* is being filmed.

Zany fantasy which someone must have thought was a good idea. Wrong.

w Pat McCormick, Harry Hurwitz, Martin Smith, Pat Bradley, Fred Bauer *d* Steve Rash

Chevy Chase, Carrie Fisher, Billy Barty, Eve Arden, Joseph Maher

† The film allegedly cost 20 million dollars and took eight.

Under the Red Robe *
GB 1937 82m bw
New World (Robert T. Kane)
V*

A hell-raising nobleman is persuaded by Cardinal Richelieu to unmask the ringleader of an anti-monarchist conspiracy.

Smart, unusual swashbuckler on the lines of *The Prisoner of Zenda*, modestly but quite effectively made.

w Lajos Biro, Philip Lindsay, J. L. Hodson *novel* Stanley J. Weyman *d* Victor Sjostrom *ph* Georges Périnal

Conrad Veidt, Raymond Massey, Annabella, Romney Brent, Sophie Stewart, Wyndham Goldie, Lawrence Grant

'Gripping meller of swashbuckling era . . . surprisingly fine entertainment.' – *Variety*

Under the Roofs of Paris: see *Sous les Toits de Paris*

Under the Volcano *
US 1984 111m Technicolor
TCF/Ithaca/Michael and Kathy Fitzgerald (Moritz Borman, Wieland Schulz-Keil)
V*, L

Mexico 1938: the ex-British consul, drinking himself to death, is surprised by a visit from his ex-wife.

A subtle novel has on film become a drunken monologue, fascinating as a *tour de force* but scarcely tolerable after the first half-hour.

w Guy Gallo *novel* Malcolm Lowry *d* John Huston *ph* Gabriel Figueroa *m* Alex North *pd* Gunther Gerzso

Albert Finney, Jacqueline Bisset, Anthony Andrews, Katy Jurado, James Villiers

'Ultimately one is left not, as in the novel, with a man destroyed by the apocalypse of his own imagination, but with little more than another world-weary cuckold following in the wake of Greene's whisky priest and all those other drunkards who have mooned in Mexico.' – *Tom Milne, MFB*

AAN: Albert Finney; music

Under the Yum Yum Tree
US 1963 110m Eastmancolor
Columbia/Sonnis/Swift (Frederick Brisson)

Two college students have a trial marriage in an apartment block with a lecherous landlord.

Coy, non-erotic and extremely tedious comedy which runs out of jokes after reel one.

w Lawrence Roman, David Swift *d* David Swift *ph* Joseph Biroc *m* Frank de Vol

Jack Lemmon, Carol Lynley, Dean Jones, Imogene Coca, Edie Adams, Paul Lynde, Robert Lansing

'Love as burning as Sahara's sands!'
Under Two Flags *
US 1936 111m bw
TCF (Raymond Griffith)

A dashing French Foreign Legionnaire is helped by a café girl.

Despite a highly predictable plot (of *Destry Rides Again*) this was a solidly-produced epic with a nice deployment of star talent.

w W. P. Lipscomb, Walter Ferris *novel* 'Ouida' *d* Frank Lloyd *ph* Ernest Palmer *m* Louis Silvers

Ronald Colman, Claudette Colbert, Rosalind Russell, Victor McLaglen, J. Edward Bromberg, Nigel Bruce, Herbert Mundin, Gregory Ratoff, C. Henry Gordon, John Carradine, Onslow Stevens

'How Ouida would have loved the abandon of this picture, the thirty-two thousand rounds of ammunition shot off into the Arizona desert, the cast of more than ten thousand, the five thousand pounds which insured the stars against camel bites . . . and, in the words of the programme, a fort two hundred feet square, an Arabian oasis with eight full-sized buildings, a forest of transplanted date palms, two Arabian cities, a horse market and a smaller fort.' – *Graham Greene*

Under Your Hat *
GB 1940 79m bw
Grand National (Jack Hulbert)

Film stars chase spies and recover a stolen carburettor.

Light-hearted adaptation of a stage musical, showing the stars in their best film form.

w Rodney Ackland, Anthony Kimmins *play* Jack Hulbert, Archie Menzies, Geoffrey Kerr, Arthur Macrae *d* Maurice Elvey *ph* Mutz Greenbaum (Max Greene)

Jack Hulbert, Cicely Courtneidge, Austin Trevor, Leonora Corbett, Cecil Parker, H. F. Maltby, Glynis Johns, Charles Oliver

Undercover
GB 1943 80m bw
Ealing

Yugoslavian partisans fight the Nazis.

A rather obviously English cast doesn't help to make this flagwaver convincing.

w John Dighton, Monja Danischewsky, Sergei Nolbandov, Sergei Sokulich *d* Sergei Nolbandov

Tom Walls, Michael Wilding, Mary Morris, John Clements, Godfrey Tearle, Robert Harris, Rachel Thomas

Undercover Blues
US 1993 90m DuArt color
MGM (Mike Lobell)

A married couple who are also FBI agents have trouble with a vengeful mugger while trying to capture an arms dealer.

A comedy that desperately strains for laughs without delivering any; it is almost a throwback to the spy spoofs of the 60s.

w Ian Abrams *d* Herbert Ross *ph* Donald E. Thorin *m* David Newman *pd* Ken Adam *ed* Patricia Nedd-Friendly, Gregg London

Kathleen Turner, Dennis Quaid, Fiona Shaw, Stanley Tucci, Larry Miller, Obba Babatunde, Tom Arnold, Park Overall

'Plays like a big-screen, big-budget pilot for a TV series.' – *Variety*

'Virtually incomprehensible and unfunny to boot. A waste of two good talents.' – *Derek Malcolm*

Undercover Girl (1939): see *Maisie (Undercover Maisie)*

Undercover Girl
US 1950 80m bw
Universal-International

A New York policewoman goes undercover to avenge her father's murder.

Rather tedious crime programmer.

w Harry Essex *d* Joseph Pevney

Alexis Smith, Scott Brady, Richard Egan, Gladys George, Edmon Ryan, Gerald Mohr

Undercover Man
US 1932 74m bw
Paramount

A man avenges his father's death by going undercover for the FBI and nabbing a bond-stealing gang.

Routine gangster thriller with situations well worn even in 1932.

w Garrett Fort, Francis Faragoh *d* James Flood

George Raft, Nancy Carroll, Roscoe Karns, Gregory Ratoff, Lew Cody

Undercover Man *
US 1949 89m bw
Columbia (Robert Rossen)

US treasury agents indict a gang leader for tax evasion.

Good semi-documentary crime melodrama based on the Al Capone case.

w Sidney Boehm, Malvin Wald *d* Joseph H. Lewis *ph* Burnett Guffey *m* George Duning

Glenn Ford, Nina Foch, Barry Kelley, James Whitmore, David Wolf, Esther Minciotti

Undercovers Hero: see *Soft Beds, Hard Battles*

Undercurrent *
US 1946 116m bw
MGM (Pandro S. Berman)
V*

A professor's daughter marries an industrialist and is frightened and finally endangered by the mystery surrounding his brother.

Overlong suspenser with solid performances and production values; a variation on *Gaslight*.

w Edward Chodorov story Thelma Strabel d Vincente Minnelli ph Karl Freund m Herbert Stothart

Katharine Hepburn, Robert Taylor, Robert Mitchum, Edmund Gwenn, Marjorie Main, Jayne Meadows, Clinton Sundberg, Dan Tobin

'The indigestible plot, full of false leads and unkept promises, is like a woman's magazine serial consumed at one gulp.' – *Time*

Underground
US 1941 95m bw
Warner (William Jacobs)

Underground leaders in Germany during World War II send out radio messages under the noses of the Nazis.

Forgotten actioner, quite solidly made.

w Charles Grayson d Vincent Sherman ph Sid Hickox m Adolph Deutsch

Jeffrey Lynn, Philip Dorn, Karen Verne, Mona Maris, Frank Reicher, Martin Kosleck, Ilka Gruning

Underground
US 1970 100m DeLuxe
UA/Levy-Gardner-Laven

An American paratrooper joins a French resistance group to kidnap a Nazi general.

Routine war actioner.

w Ron Bishop, Andy Lewis d Arthur H. Nader ph Ken Talbot m Stanley Myers

Robert Goulet, Danièle Gaubert, Laurence Dobkin, Carl Duering

Underneath the Arches
US 1937 71m bw
Julius Hagen/Twickenham

Ship stowaways help to prevent a peace gas from getting into the wrong hands.

Moderate star comedy with music.

w H. Fowler Mear d Redd David

Flanagan and Allen, Stella Moya, Enid Stamp Taylor, Lyn Harding, Edmund Willard, Edward Ashley

The Underpup
US 1939 81m bw
Joe Pasternak/Universal

A slum girl wins a country holiday among rich folk who ignore her.

Light comedy-drama with music which seemed about to launch a rival to Deanna Durbin.

w Grover Jones d Richard Wallace

Gloria Jean, Robert Cummings, Nan Grey, C. Aubrey Smith, Beulah Bondi, Virginia Weidler, Raymond Walburn, Margaret Lindsay

Undersea Kingdom
US 1936 bw serial: 12 eps
Republic

At the bottom of the ocean lies Atlantis, where the White Robes are in constant battle with the Black Robes.

Slightly hilarious chapter play.

d B. Reeves Eason, Joseph Kane

Ray 'Crash' Corrigan, Lois Wilde, Monte Blue, William Farnum, Smiley Burnette, Lon Chaney Jnr, Raymond Hatton

Undertow
US 1949 70m bw
Universal-International

An ex-racketeer proves his innocence when a big-time gambler is murdered.

Stock suspense crime story, not at all memorable.

w Arthur T. Horman, Lee Loeb d William Castle

Scott Brady, John Russell, Dorothy Hart, Peggy Dow, Bruce Bennett

Underwater
US 1955 99m Technicolor SuperScope
RKO/Howard Hughes
V*, L

Treasure hunters dive in the Caribbean for sunken pirate treasure.

Flabby adventure yarn, badly designed for the purpose of showing off its star in a variety of dress and undress.

w Walter Newman, Hugh King, Robert B. Bailey d John Sturges ph Harry J. Wild, Lamar Boren m Roy Webb

Jane Russell, Gilbert Roland, Richard Egan, Lori Nelson, Robert Keith, Joseph Calleia

'This presentation of Miss Russell is like one of those fountain pens guaranteed to write under water – novel, but impractical.' – *Bosley Crowther, New York Times*

Underwater Warrior
US 1958 91m bw Cinemascope
MGM (Ivan Tors)

A naval reserve commander trains frogmen.

Dry semi-documentary drama, unlikely to win any recruits.

w Gene Levitt d Andrew Marton

Dan Dailey, Ross Martin, James Gregory, Claire Kelly

'Revolvers bark! Figures steal slowly among the shadows of the night! Then all is still … That's just a bit of the underworld!'
'It takes you to the haunts of the human birds of prey, to the refuge of the hunted!'

Underworld *
US 1927 82m (24 fps) bw silent
Paramount (Hector Turnbull)
GB title: *Paying the Penalty*

A gangster is rescued from prison by his moll and his lieutenant, and when he realizes they are in love he allows them to escape when the law closes in.

An innovative film in its time, this melodrama was the first to look at crime from the gangsters' point of view. Its main appeal now lies in its lush direction.

w Ben Hecht, Robert N. Lee, Josef von Sternberg d Josef von Sternberg ph Bert Glennon ad Hans Dreier

George Bancroft, Evelyn Brent, Clive Brook, Larry Semon

† The film was a great international success and had an influence on the pessimistic French school of the thirties.

AA: Ben Hecht

Underworld
GB 1985 100m colour
Limehouse/Green Man
V*

A mad doctor keeps his mutants underground.

H. G. Wells up to date, but none the better for it.

w Clive Barker, James Caplin d George Pavlou

Denholm Elliott, Steven Berkoff, Larry Lamb, Miranda Richardson, Art Malik, Ingrid Pitt

Underworld Informers: see *The Informers*

The Underworld Story **
US 1950 90m bw
UA (Hal E. Chester)
V*

An unscrupulous reporter buys a half-share in a small-town newspaper and brings his slick city methods with him when he covers a murder.

Very effective, moodily atmospheric and unpretentious thriller.

w Henry Blankfort, Cyril Endfield story Craig Rice d Cyril Endfield ph Stanley Cortez m David Rose ad Gordon Wiles ed Richard Heermance

Dan Duryea, Herbert Marshall, Gale Storm, Howard Da Silva, Michael O'Shea, Mary Anderson, Gar Moore, Melville Cooper, Frieda Inescort, Art Baker

'A sensational film that puts the finger on today's biggest business – crime.'

Underworld USA *
US 1960 99m bw
Columbia/Globe (Samuel Fuller)
V*

A young gangster takes elaborate revenge for the killing of his father.

Violent syndicate melodrama with a semi-documentary veneer and some brutal scenes. Well done but heavy going.

wd Samuel Fuller ph Hal Mohr m Harry Sukman ad Robert Peterson ed Jerome Thoms

Cliff Robertson, Beatrice Kay, Larry Gates, Dolores Dorn, *Robert Emhardt*, Paul Dubov, Richard Rust

'Savage! Sinister! Supernatural! The black fury of a werewolf – sacrificing life and love to the maddening evil that drove him to the most monstrous murders man ever committed!'

The Undying Monster *
US 1943 63m bw
TCF
V*
GB title: *The Hammond Mystery*

A curse hangs over the English ancestral home of the Hammonds.

Silly but well-photographed and directed minor horror on wolf man lines.

w Lillie Hayward, Michel Jacoby novel Jessie D. Kerruish d John Brahm ph Lucien Ballard m Emil Newman, David Raksin

James Ellison, John Howard, Heather Angel, Bramwell Fletcher, Heather Thatcher, Eily Malyon, Halliwell Hobbes, Aubrey Mather

THE FAMILY CURSE:
When stars are bright
On a frosty night
Beware thy bane
On the rocky lane.

Unearthly Stranger *
GB 1963 75m bw
Independent Artists (Julian Wintle, Leslie Parkyn, Albert Fennell)

Scientists working on a time-space formula find that the bride of one of them is an alien in search of their secret.

Surprisingly effective minor science fiction, in some ways all the better for its modest, TV-style production values.

w *Rex Carlton*   d *John Krish*   ph *Reg Wyer*   m *Edward Williams*

John Neville, Gabriella Licudi, Philip Stone, Jean Marsh, Patrick Newell, Warren Mitchell

Uneasy Terms
GB   1948   91m   bw
British National

Detective Slim Callaghan proves that a blackmail victim is not a murderer.

The film which proved that the British simply can't make crime movies on the American model.

w *Peter Cheyney*   novel *Peter Cheyney*   d *Vernon Sewell*

Michael Rennie, Moira Lister, Faith Brook, Joy Shelton, Nigel Patrick, Paul Carpenter, Barry Jones

Unexpected Father
US   1939   78m   bw
Universal
GB title: *Sandy Takes a Bow*

A dancer looks after his late partner's baby.

Genial comedy introducing a baby star who was popular until she got out of diapers.

w *Leonard Spigelgass and Charles Grayson*   d *Charles Lamont*

Baby Sandy, Mischa Auer, Dennis O'Keefe, Shirley Ross, Mayo Methot

Unexpected Uncle
US   1941   67m   bw
RKO

An elderly steel tycoon gives everything up to become a tramp and play Cupid.

Money-is-not-everything fable, entirely dependent on amiable performances.

w *Delmer Daves, Noel Langley*   novel *Eric Hatch*   d *Peter Godfrey*

Charles Coburn, Anne Shirley, James Craig, Ernest Truex, Russell Gleason, Jed Prouty

'If she were yours, would you forgive?'
The Unfaithful *
US   1947   109m   bw
Warner (Jerry Wald)

A wife gets involved in a murder while her husband is out of town.

Glossy romantic melodrama, an unofficial remake of *The Letter*.

w *David Goodis, James Gunn*   d *Vincent Sherman*   ph *Ernest Haller*   m *Max Steiner*

Ann Sheridan, Zachary Scott, Lew Ayres, Eve Arden, Steve Geray, Jerome Cowan, John Hoyt

The Unfaithful Wife: see *La Femme Infidèle*

Unfaithfully Yours **
US   1948   105m   bw
TCF (Preston Sturges)
V*, L

An orchestral conductor believes his wife is unfaithful, and while conducting a concert thinks of three different ways of dealing with the situation.

A not entirely happy mixture of romance, farce, melodrama and wit, but in general a pretty entertaining concoction and the last major film of its talented writer-director.

wd *Preston Sturges*   ph *Victor Milner*   m *Alfred Newman*

Rex Harrison, Linda Darnell, Barbara Lawrence, Rudy Vallee, Kurt Kreuger, Lionel Stander, *Edgar Kennedy, Al Bridge*, Julius Tannen, Torben Meyer, Robert Greig

'Harrison discovers more ways of tripping over a telephone cable than one can count, and his efforts to falsify evidence through a recalcitrant tape recorder are as funny as anything thought up by Clair in *A Nous La Liberté* or by Chaplin in *Modern Times*.' – *Basil Wright, 1972*

† The Rex Harrison character is named Sir Alfred de Carter and is meant to be Sir Thomas Beecham. (In America the equivalent of Beecham's Pills is Carter's Little Liver Pills.)
†† The pieces of music played are as follows:

For murder: the *Semiramide Overture* by Rossini

For surrender: the *Venusberg* music from *Tannhäuser*, by Wagner

For Russian roulette: *Francesca da Rimini* by Tchaikovsky

Unfaithfully Yours
US   1983   96m   DeLuxe
TCF (Marvin Worth, Joe Wizan)
V*, L

Modernized and simplified version of the above, with only one plot instead of three.

This proves to be an advantage, and the film does deliver some laughs.

w *Valerie Curtin, Barry Levinson, Robert Klane*   d *Howard Zieff*   ph *David M. Walsh*   m *Bill Conti*   pd *Albert Brenner*

Dudley Moore, Nastassja Kinski, Armand Assante, Albert Brooks, Cassie Yates, Richard Libertini, Richard B. Shull

Unfinished Business
US   1941   95m   bw
Universal (Gregory La Cava)

A wife has thoughts that she should have married her husband's brother.

Smooth but disappointing romantic comedy; the detail is good enough, but it sadly lacks drive.

w *Eugene Thackery*   d *Gregory La Cava*   ph *Joseph Valentine*   m *Franz Waxman*

Irene Dunne, Robert Montgomery, Eugene Pallette, Preston Foster, Walter Catlett, June Clyde, Phyllis Barry, Esther Dale, Samuel S. Hinds

'Once sentiment gets the upper hand, reach for the exit.' – *Otis Ferguson*

The Unfinished Dance
US   1947   101m   Technicolor
MGM (Joe Pasternak)

The young star of a ballet school becomes jealous of a talented newcomer, and causes her injury in an accident.

The delicacies of the French original, *La Mort du Cygne*, give way to standard Hollywood hokum and produce an accomplished but totally uninteresting film.

w *Myles Connolly*   story *Paul Morand*   d *Henry Koster*   ph *Robert Surtees*   md *Herbert Stothart*

Margaret O'Brien, Cyd Charisse, Karin Booth, Danny Thomas, Esther Dale

'The same old story, with pathos, humour and ballet substituted for pathos, humour and chorus girls.' – *MFB*

The Unforgiven *
US   1960   125m   Technicolor   Panavision
UA/James Productions/Hecht-Hill-Lancaster (James Hill)
V*, L

A rancher's daughter is suspected of being an Indian orphan, and violence results.

Good-looking, expensive but muddled racist Western, hard to enjoy.

w *Ben Maddow*   novel *Alan le May*   d *John Huston*   ph *Franz Planer*   m *Dimitri Tiomkin*

Burt Lancaster, Audrey Hepburn, Audie Murphy, Lillian Gish, Charles Bickford, Doug McClure, John Saxon, Joseph Wiseman, Albert Salmi

'How much strain can a director's reputation take? Of late, John Huston seems to have been trying to find out. I think he has carried the experiment too far with *The Unforgiven* . . . a work of profound phoniness, part adult western, part that *Oklahoma!* kind of folksy Americana.' – *Dwight MacDonald*

'Ludicrous . . . a hodgepodge of crudely stitched sententiousness and lame story-conference inspirations.' – *Stanley Kauffmann*

Unforgiven ****
US   1992   131m   Technicolor   Panavision
Warner (Clint Eastwood)
V, V*, L, S

A former hired killer turned unsuccessful farmer, together with a young would-be gunfighter and an old friend, set out to collect a thousand-dollar reward for killing the cowboys who slashed the face of a prostitute.

Harsh Western of revenge and needless slaughter that re-invents and revives the genre to spectacular effect.

w *David Webb Peoples*   d *Clint Eastwood*   ph *Jack N. Green*   m *Lennie Niehaus*   pd *Henry Bumstead*   ed *Joel Cox*

Clint Eastwood, Gene Hackman, Morgan Freeman, Richard Harris, Jaimz Woolvett, Saul Rubinek, Frances Fisher, Anna Thomson, David Mucci, Rod Campbell, Anthony James

'The movie's grizzled male ensemble, its gradual build, and its juxtaposition of brutality and sardonic humor testify to its disdain for box-office conventions.' – *Michael Sragow, New Yorker*

'Eastwood climbs back into the saddle to make a classic western.' – *Ian Johnstone, Sunday Times*

'A tense, hard-edged, superbly dramatic yarn that is also an exceedingly intelligent meditation on the West, its myths and its heroes.' – *Variety*

AA: best picture; Clint Eastwood (as director); Gene Hackman; Joel Cox

AAN: Clint Eastwood (as actor); Henry Bumstead; Jack N. Green; David Webb Peoples; best sound

The Unguarded Hour *
US   1936   87m   bw
MGM

A blackmailed woman has evidence to free a man accused of murder, but dare not reveal it.

Twisty suspense thriller with a rather splendid cast.

w *Howard Emmett Rogers, Leon Gordon*   play *Ladislas Fodor, Bernard Merivale*   d *Sam Wood*

Franchot Tone, Loretta Young, Roland Young, Henry Daniell, Jessie Ralph, Lewis Stone, Dudley Digges, E. E. Clive, Robert Greig, Aileen Pringle

The Unguarded Moment
US   1956   85m   Technicolor
U-I (Gordon Kay)

A schoolmistress who receives anonymous love notes from a psychotic pupil is discredited by his even more unbalanced father.

Well-meaning but boring melodrama with the star attractively out of her usual element.

w *Herb Meadow, Larry Marcus*   story *Rosalind Russell*   d *Harry Keller*   ph *William Daniels*   m *Herman Stein*

Esther Williams, George Nader, John Saxon, *Edward Andrews*, Jack Albertson

The Unholy

US   1987   102m   CFI
Vestron/Limelight Studios/Team Effort (Matthew Hayden)
V*, L

A new priest is sent to a demon-haunted church.

Routine horror, in which evil seems to be equated with sexual desire.

w Philip Yordan, Fernando Fonseca   d Camilo Vilo   ph Henry Vargas   m Roger Bellon, Fernando Fonseca   pd Fernando Fonseca, Jim Darfus, Cathy Carlisle   ed Mark Melnick

Ben Cross, Ned Beatty, William Russ, Jill Carroll, Hal Holbrook, Trevor Howard, Peter Frechette, Claudia Robinson

'A particularly routine effort in an already overcrowded horror sub-genre.' – *Julian Petley, MFB*

The Unholy Four: see *The Stranger Came Home*

The Unholy Garden

US   1931   75m   bw
Samuel Goldwyn

A gentleman thief hides out in a North African den of misfits.

Would-be romantic nonsense, much less interesting than its credits.

w Ben Hecht, Charles MacArthur   d George Fitzmaurice   ph Gregg Toland, George Barnes   m Alfred Newman

Ronald Colman, Fay Wray, Estelle Taylor, Tully Marshall, Warren Hymer, Mischa Auer, Henry Armetta, Lawrence Grant

'Splendid presentation of an ordinary story.' – *Variety*

The Unholy Night

US   1929   94m   bw
MGM

A strangler is caught in the London fog.

Clumsy and talkative early talkie, chiefly interesting for its cast.

w Ben Hecht   d Lionel Barrymore

Lionel Barrymore, Roland Young, Boris Karloff, John Loder, Natalie Moorhead, Ernest Torrence, Polly Moran, John Miljan

Unholy Partners *

US   1941   95m   bw
MGM (Samuel Marx)

The editor of a sensational newspaper has to accept finance from a gangster, but friction results when the newspaper exposes some of the gangster's activities.

Agreeable twenties melodrama with two solid stars battling it out.

w Earl Baldwin, Lesser Samuels, Bartlett Cormack   d Mervyn Le Roy   ph George Barnes   m David Snell

Edward G. Robinson, Edward Arnold, Laraine Day, Marsha Hunt, William T. Orr, Don Beddoe, Charles Dingle, Walter Kingsford, Marcel Dalio

The Unholy Three *

US   1925   76m approx (24 fps)   bw   silent
MGM
V*

A ventriloquist, a dwarf and a strong man carry out a series of crimes which end in murder.

Curious melodrama which set its star and director off on a series of seven more and even weirder eccentricities.

w Waldemar Young   story Clarence Robbins   d Tod Browning   ph David Kesson

Lon Chaney, Harry Earles, Victor McLaglen, Mae Busch, Matt Moore

The Unholy Three *

US   1930   74m   bw
MGM
V*, L

Remake of the above.

The star's only talkie – he died before it was released – is less effective than the silent version.

w J. C. and Elliott Nugent   novel Clarence Robbins   d Jack Conway

Lon Chaney, Lila Lee, Harry Earles, Ivan Linow, Elliott Nugent, John Miljan

The Unholy Wife

US   1957   94m   Technicolor   RKOscope
RKO/Treasure
V*

A bored wife shoots a friend in mistake for her husband but is sentenced for the accidental death of her mother-in-law.

Totally uninteresting melodrama in the *Double Indemnity* style, professionally made but turgid.

w Jonathan Latimer   d John Farrow   ph Lucien Ballard   m Daniele Amfitheatrof

Diana Dors, Rod Steiger, Tom Tryon, Beulah Bondi, Marie Windsor, Arthur Franz, Luis Van Rooten

Unidentified Flying Oddball: see *The Spaceman and King Arthur*

'A love haunted by nameless evil which fought to live in their hearts!'

The Uninvited **

US   1944   98m   bw
Paramount (Charles Brackett)
V*, L

A girl returns to her family house and is haunted by her mother's spirit, which seems to be evil.

One of the cinema's few genuine ghost stories, and a good one, though encased in a rather stiff production; it works up to a fine pitch of frenzy.

w Dodie Smith   novel Uneasy Freehold by Dorothy Macardle   d Lewis Allen   ph Charles Lang   m Victor Young

Ray Milland, Ruth Hussey, *Gail Russell,* Donald Crisp, Cornelia Otis Skinner, Dorothy Stickney, Barbara Everest, Alan Napier

'It will hold audiences glued to their seats.' – *Variety*

'It sets out to give you the shivers – and will do so, if you're readily disposed.' – *New York Times*

'I experienced thirty-five first class jolts, not to mention a well calculated texture of minor frissons.' – *Nation*

'Still manages to ice the blood with its implied horrors . . . you can almost smell the ghostly mimosa.' – *Peter John Dyer, 1966*

'A superior and satisfying shocker.' – *Newsweek*

† British critics of the time congratulated the director on not showing the ghosts; in fact the visible manifestations had been cut by the British censor.

AAN: Charles Lang

Union Depot

US   1932   68m   bw
Warner
GB title: *Gentleman for a Day*

The fortunes of several people clash in a railway station.

Pale but moderately interesting imitation of *Grand Hotel.*

w Kenyon Nicholson, Walter de Leon   play Gene Fowler, Douglas Durkin, Joe Laurie   d Alfred E. Green

Douglas Fairbanks Jnr, Joan Blondell, Alan Hale, Frank McHugh, George Rosener, Guy Kibbee, David Landau

Union Pacific **

US   1939   133m   bw
Paramount/Cecil B. de Mille

Indians and others cause problems for the railroad builders.

Standard big-scale Western climaxing in a spectacular wreck; not exactly exciting, but very watchable.

w Walter de Leon, C. Gardner Sullivan, Jesse Lasky Jnr   d Cecil B. de Mille   ph Victor Milner, Dewey Wrigley   m John Leipold, Sigmund Krumgold   ad Hans Dreier, Roland Anderson

Barbara Stanwyck, Joel McCrea, Akim Tamiroff, Robert Preston, Lynne Overman, Brian Donlevy, Robert Barrat, Anthony Quinn, Stanley Ridges, Henry Kolker, Evelyn Keyes, Regis Toomey

'A socko spectacular, surefire for big grosses right down the line.' – *Variety*

'This latest de Mille epic contains all the excelsior qualities we expect of his work – that sense of a Salvationist drum beating round the next corner – but it is never as funny as *The Crusades* and he has lost his touch with crowds.' – *Graham Greene*

'Excitement is the dominant emotion, with swift succession of contrasting materials and episodes, grim and gay, often furious, sometimes funny. The narrative and action take hold at the start and never let go.' – *Motion Picture Herald*

'The largest conglomeration of thrills and cold-blooded murder since Pauline was in peril.' – *Brooklyn Daily Eagle*

'A movie in the old tradition, melodramatic and breathtaking and altogether wonderful.' – *Photoplay*

† De Mille's last picture in black and white.

Union Station **

US   1950   80m   bw
Paramount (Jules Schermer)

Kidnappers nominate a crowded railroad station as their ransom collection point.

Compelling little thriller modelled after *Naked City,* with real locations and plenty of excitement.

w Sidney Boehm   novel Thomas Walsh   d Rudolph Maté   ph Daniel L. Fapp   md Irvin Talbot   m David Buttolph, Heinz Roemheld

William Holden, *Barry Fitzgerald,* Nancy Olson, *Lyle Bettger,* Jan Sterling, Allene Roberts

Universal Soldier

GB   1971   96m   colour
Appaloosa/Ionian (Frank J. Schwarz, Donald L. Factor)

A mercenary returns to London but can't escape his past.

Solemnly meaningful melodrama on a tight budget.

wd Cy Endfield   ph Tony Imi   m Philip Goodhand-Tait

George Lazenby, Edward Judd, Benito Carruthers, Germaine Greer, Rudolph Walker

'The future has a bad attitude.'

Universal Soldier

US   1992   103m   Technicolor   Panavision
Guild/Carolco (Allen Shapiro, Craig Baumgarten, Joel B. Michaels)
V, V*, L, S

Two soldiers who killed each other in Vietnam are resurrected as androids to form part of an élite group of soldiers for special missions; but one of them goes out of control.

Science-fiction hokum intended to boost the appeal of its two action stars, done with enough energy and containing more than enough mayhem to appeal to fans of action movies.

w Richard Rothstein, Christopher Leitch, Dean Devlin d Roland Emmerich ph Karl Walter Lindenlaub md Brynmor Jones m Christopher Franke pd Holger Gross ed Michael J. Duthie

Jean-Claude Van Damme, Dolph Lundgren, Ally Walker, Ed O'Ross, Jerry Orbach, Leon Rippy, Tico Wells

'To get through the garish mayhem, you need a high vicarious-pain threshold.' – *Michael Sragow, New Yorker*

'A classy rollercoaster ride through the clichés of modern fantasy cinema.' – *Mark Kermode, Sight and Sound*

The Unknown

US   1927   65m   bw   silent
MGM

A fake armless wonder has his arms amputated to please a girl who can't stand the touch of a man's hand. (She then changes her mind.)

Weird melodrama which even this contortionist star can't save.

w Waldemar Young d Tod Browning

Lon Chaney, Joan Crawford, Norman Kerry

The Unknown

US   1946   70m   bw
Columbia

An amnesiac heiress returns to her family mansion.

Twisty creeper in the *I Love a Mystery* series; not bad for a second feature.

w Malcolm Stuart Boylan, Julian Harmon d Henry Levin

Karen Morley, Jeff Donnell, Jim Bannon

Unknown Chaplin ***

GB   1986   157m   colour/bw
Thames Television
V

A three-part documentary on Chaplin's early years including excerpts from films, out-takes and on-camera rehearsals never seen in public before, much of it taken from Chaplin's own archives, which he had ordered to be destroyed.

First shown as three television programmes, this is by far the finest examination available of Chaplin's genius, which is shown to be due to constant hard work as well as to improvisation.

wd Kevin Brownlow, David Gill ph Ted Adcock m Carl Davis ed Trevor Waite

narrator: James Mason

The Unknown Guest

US   1943   61m   bw
Monogram (Maurice King)

A supposedly no-good young man is suspected of murdering his aunt and uncle.

Rather tedious and silly mystery with little happening.

w Philip Yordan d Kurt Neumann

Victor Jory, Pamela Blake, Harry Hayden, Veda Ann Borg, Nora Cecil

The Unknown Man

US   1951   86m   bw
MGM (Robert Thomsen)

A civil court lawyer of high principles successfully undertakes a criminal case, finds his client was really guilty, and sets matters straight.

Contrived but entertaining morality with standard production and performances.

w Ronald Millar, George Froeschel d Richard Thorpe ph William Mellor m Conrad Salinger

Walter Pidgeon, Ann Harding, Lewis Stone, Barry Sullivan, Keefe Brasselle, Eduard Franz, Richard Anderson, Dawn Addams

Unlawful Entry *

US   1992   111m   DeLuxe
TCF/Largo/JVC (Charles Gordon)
V, V*, L, S

A Los Angeles policeman who befriends a young couple turns out to be a psychopath.

Moderate thriller of a now very familiar kind that deals with a flatmate, tenant, nanny, and, in this instance, a cop from hell.

w Lewis Colick story George D. Putnam, John Katchmer, Lewis Colick d Jonathan Kaplan ph Jamie Anderson m James Horner pd Lawrence G. Paull ed Curtiss Clayton

Kurt Russell, Ray Liotta, Madeleine Stowe, Roger E. Mosley, Ken Lerner, Deborah Offner, Carmen Argenziano, Andy Romano, Johnny Ray McGhee

'The film's main achievement is to fit its trenchant social critique into conventional thriller form . . . The film catches the fear and paranoia of the couple "home alone".' – *Geoffrey Macnab, Sight and Sound*

Unman, Wittering and Zigo

GB   1971   102m   colour
Paramount/Mediarts (Gareth Wigan)

A nervous schoolmaster discovers that his predecessor was murdered by the boys.

Macabre school story which overreaches itself and peters out.

w Simon Raven TV play Giles Cooper d John Mackenzie ph Geoffrey Unsworth m Michael J. Lewis

David Hemmings, Douglas Wilmer, Hamilton Dyce, Carolyn Seymour

Unmarried

US   1939   66m   bw
Paramount
GB title: *Night Club Hostess*

An ex-boxer, shy of marriage, raises an orphan boy.

Modest domestic drama notable as one of the rare non-Western appearances of its star.

w Lillie Hayward, Brian Marlow, Grover Jones d Kurt Neumann

Buck Jones, Donald O'Connor, Helen Twelvetrees

An Unmarried Woman *

US   1978   124m   Movielab
TCF (Paul Mazursky, Tony Ray)
V*

A sophisticated New York woman is deserted by her husband, fights with her daughter, and takes up with two men.

Frank, well-observed depiction of one woman in New York's new society; as modern as all get out but not very attractive.

wd Paul Mazursky ph Arthur J. Ornitz m Bill Conti pd Pato Guzman

Jill Clayburgh, Alan Bates, Michael Murphy, Cliff Gorman, Pat Quinn, Kelly Bishop

'The motions of the story are not what cripple it – it's the low level of insight and the pervasive sense of exploitation . . . It's what once would have been called woman's-magazine fiction.' – *Stanley Kauffmann*

AAN: best picture; script; Jill Clayburgh

The Unnamable

Canada   1988   87m   Foto-Kem colour
Yankee Classic/KP (Dean Ramser, Jean-Paul Oullette)
V

Students explore a deserted house and discover a monster that has been imprisoned there for 200 years.

Unexceptional, low-budget, gory rendition of Lovecraft's short stories, padded out with a great deal of irrelevance.

wd Jean-Paul Oullette story The Statement of Randolph Carter and The Unnamable by H. P. Lovecraft ph Tom Fraser m David Bergeaud pd Gene Abel sp R. Christopher Biggs ed Wendy J. Plump

Charles King, Mark Kinsey Stephenson, Alexandra Durrell, Laura Albert, Katrin Alexandre, Eben Ham, Blane Wheatley, Mark Parra

The Unnamable Returns

Canada   1992   92m   Foto-Kem colour
Yankee Classic/AM East/Prism/New Age (Jean-Paul Ouellette)
V
aka: *H. P. Lovecraft's The Unnamable Returns*

Students dabbling in black magic unleash a murderous demon on the Miskatonic university campus in Arkham.

Supernatural variation on the usual low-budget slasher movie, featuring a cut-price monster.

wd Jean-Paul Ouellette story The Statement of Randolph Carter and The Unnamable by H. P. Lovecraft ph Greg Gardener, Roger Olkowski m David Bergeaud pd Tim Keating sp R. Christopher Biggs ed William C. Williams

John Rhys-Davies, Mark Kinsey Stephenson, Charles Klausmeyer, Maria Ford, Julie Strain, Peter Breck, David Warner

Unpublished Story

GB   1942   91m   bw
Columbia/Two Cities (Anthony Havelock-Allan)

A reporter exposes the Nazis behind a pacifist organization.

Ho-hum formula flagwaver with generally stilted production.

w Anatole de Grunwald, Patrick Kirwan d Harold French ph Bernard Knowles m Nicholas Brodzky

Valerie Hobson, Richard Greene, Basil Radford, Roland Culver, Brefni O'Rourke, Miles Malleson, George Carney, André Morell

The Unseen

US   1945   82m   bw
Paramount

A London governess comes to suspect that dark deeds have taken place in the empty house next door.

Period suspenser with good atmosphere but an insubstantial plot.

w Hagar Wilde, Raymond Chandler d Lewis Allen ph John Seitz m Ernst Toch

Joel McCrea, Gail Russell, Herbert Marshall, Richard Lyon, Nona Griffith

† The film seems to have been a hurried attempt to repeat and combine the previous year's successes, *Gaslight* and *The Uninvited*.

Unseen Heroes: see *The Battle of the V1*

Unsichtbare Gegner: see *Invisible Adversaries*

The Unsinkable Molly Brown *

US   1964   128m   Metrocolor   Panavision
MGM/Marten (Lawrence Weingarten)
V, V*, L, S

Western orphan Molly Brown grows up determined to become a member of Denver society.

Semi-Western comedy-musical about a real lady who wound up surviving the *Titanic*. Bouncy and likeable but not at all memorable.

w Helen Deutsch musical play Richard Morris d Charles Walters ph Daniel L. Fapp md Robert Armbruster ad George W. Davis, Preston Ames

Debbie Reynolds, Harve Presnell, *Ed Begley*, Jack Kruschen, Hermione Baddeley, Martita Hunt

AAN: Daniel L. Fapp; Robert Armbruster; Debbie Reynolds

An Unsuitable Job for a Woman
GB   1982   90m   Gevacolor
Gold Crest/NFFC/Boyd's Co (Michael Relph, Peter McKay)
V*

A young woman, hired to discover why the son of a wealthy businessman killed himself, becomes obsessed by the dead youth.

Tepid and murky thriller that irons out the ambiguities of a convoluted plot.

w Elizabeth McKay, Brian Scobie, Christopher Petit *novel* P. D. James   d Christopher Petit   ph Martin Schäfer   m Chaz Jankel, Philip Bagenal, Pete Van-Hooke   pd Anton Furst   ed Mick Audsley

Billie Whitelaw, Paul Freeman, Pippa Guard, Dominic Guard, Elizabeth Spriggs, David Horovitch, Dawn Archibald

The Unsuspected *
US   1947   103m   bw
Warner (Charles Hoffman)

A writer-producer of radio crime shows commits a murder and is forced to follow the clues on air.

Sleek, new look mystery thriller with a disappointing plot which gives its interesting cast little to do, and allows itself to peter out in chases.

w Ranald MacDougall   *novel* Charlotte Armstrong   d Michael Curtiz   ph Woody Bredell   m Franz Waxman   ad Anton Grot

Claude Rains, Joan Caulfield, Audrey Totter, Constance Bennett, Michael North, Hurd Hatfield, Fred Clark

Untamed
US   1940   83m   Technicolor
Paramount (Paul Jones)

A doctor in the frozen north is beset by an epidemic as well as natural hazards.

Old-fashioned melodrama which found an eager audience.

w Frederick Hazlitt Brennan, Frank Butler *novel* Mantrap by Sinclair Lewis   d George Archainbaud   ph Leo Tover, W. Howard Greene   m Victor Young

Ray Milland, Patricia Morison, Akim Tamiroff, William Frawley, Jane Darwell, Esther Dale, J. M. Kerrigan, Eily Malyon

† A remake of Clara Bow's 1926 film *Mantrap*.

Untamed
US   1955   109m   Technicolor   Cinemascope
TCF (Bert E. Friedlob, William A. Bacher)

A Dutchman and an Irish girl meet again on a Boer trek to South Africa, and survive Zulu attacks.

A long and involved epic-style plot provides standard excitements and predictable romantic complications.

w Talbot Jennings, Michael Blankfort, Frank Fenton *novel* Helga Moray   d Henry King   ph Leo Tover   m Franz Waxman

Tyrone Power, Susan Hayward, Richard Egan, John Justin, Agnes Moorehead, Rita Moreno, Hope Emerson, Brad Dexter, Henry O'Neill

'A not unenjoyable essay in hokum.' – *MFB*

Untamed Frontier
US   1952   78m   Technicolor
U-I (Leonard Goldstein)

The son of an unpopular Texan landowner commits murder.

Stolid minor Western.

w Gerald Drayson Adams, Gwen and John Bagni   d Hugo Fregonese   ph Charles P. Boyle   m Hans Salter

Joseph Cotten, Shelley Winters, Scott Brady, Suzan Ball, Minor Watson

'He doesn't make sense. She doesn't make sense. Together they make sense.'

Untamed Heart
US   1993   102m   DeLuxe
MGM (Tony Bill, Helen Buck Bartlett)
V, V*, S

A young man with a heart condition begins a tentative love affair with a waitress.

Sickly romantic sob-story, a teenage fantasy of idealized passion which is remote from real life.

w Tom Sierchio   d Tony Bill   ph Jost Vacano   m Cliff Eidelman   pd Steven Jordan   ed Mia Goldman

'The movie largely works on its own terms, particularly for those looking for a traditional "good cry".' – *Variety*

'Has the kind of sympathetic handling that isn't totally destroyed by the American propensity for weepie but upbeat endings, and slurpy music to enable even people as silly as ourselves to pinpoint its more dramatic moments.' – *Derek Malcolm, Guardian*

Until the End of the World *
Germany/France/Australia   1991   158m   colour
Warner/Road Movies/Argos/Village Roadshow (Anatole Dauman, Jonathan Taplin)
V, V*, L, S
original title: *Bis ans Ende der Welt*

As a rogue nuclear satellite threatens to explode, a woman tracks a man with multiple identities across Europe to Japan, China and Australia, where she meets his blind mother and his father, who has invented a camera enabling the blind to see.

Rambling, often confusing, sometimes boring road movie with moments of brilliance.

w Peter Carey, Wim Wenders   d Wim Wenders   ph Robby Müller   m Graeme Revell   pd Thierry Flamand, Sally Campbell   ed Peter Przygodda

William Hurt, Solveig Dommartin, Sam Neill, Max von Sydow, Rüdiger Vogler, Ernie Dingo, Jeanne Moreau, Chick Ortega, David Gulpilil, Ryu Chishu

'A dream still partly realised and partly still in the head of the director.' – *Variety*

'Comes across as heavy-handed, chaotic and immensely cluttered, finally leaving one with an overwhelming sense of bewilderment.' – *Julia Knight, Sight and Sound*

† Wenders has announced his intention of releasing a five-hour version of the film on video.

Until They Sail
US   1957   95m   bw   Cinemascope
MGM (Charles Schnee)
V*

Four New Zealand sisters have wartime romances.

Solid 'woman's picture', well enough presented.

w Robert Anderson   *novel* James A. Michener   d Robert Wise   ph Joseph Ruttenberg   m David Raksin

Jean Simmons, Joan Fontaine, Paul Newman, Piper Laurie, Charles Drake, Wally Cassell, Sandra Dee

The Untouchables **
US   1987   119m   Technicolor
Paramount/Art Linson
V, V*, L

Law enforcers in 20s Chicago go after Al Capone and other mobsters.

The long-running TV show is given a new polish in this showy, violent gangster picture, which seemed to please all classes.

w David Mamet   d Brian de Palma   ph Stephen H. Burum   m Ennio Morricone   pd Patrizia von Brandenstein   ad Hal Gausman   ed Jerry Greenberg, Bill Pankow

Kevin Costner, Sean Connery, Robert de Niro, Charles Martin Smith, Andy Garcia, Richard Bradford

'Time honoured mayhem in the windy city.' – *Time Out*

'The picture is more like an attempt to visualize the public's collective dream of Chicago gangsters; our movie-fed imagination of the past is enlarged and given new vividness.' – *Pauline Kael, New Yorker*

AA: Sean Connery

AAN: Ennio Morricone; art direction; costume design (Marilyn Vance-Straker)

The Unvanquished: see *Aparajito*

Up for the Cup
GB   1931   76m   bw
B & D (Herbert Wilcox)

A Yorkshireman gets into trouble when he comes to London for the Cup Final.

Slap-happy star farce which pleased the public.

w Con West, R. P. Weston, Bert Lee   d Jack Raymond

Sydney Howard, Joan Wyndham, Stanley Kirk, Sam Livesey, Moore Marriott

† The same star appeared in *Up for the Derby* in the following year; and in 1950 the original, with much the same script, was refashioned for Albert Modley; it was also directed by Jack Raymond.

'A lone American sergeant on the most impossible mission of the war!'

Up from the Beach *
US   1965   98m   bw   Cinemascope
TCF/Panoramic (Christian Ferry)

Just after D-Day, GIs have trouble in a Normandy village.

A kind of subdued sequel to *The Longest Day*, well made for war action addicts, but barely memorable.

w Stanley Mann, Claude Brule   *novel* Epitaph for an Enemy by George Barr   d Robert Parrish   ph Walter Wottiz   m Edgar Cosma

Cliff Robertson, Red Buttons, Françoise Rosay, Marius Goring, Irina Demick, Broderick Crawford, James Robertson Justice, Slim Pickens

Up in Arms **
US   1944   106m   Technicolor
Samuel Goldwyn
V*

A hypochondriac joins the army.

Loose, generally pleasant introductory vehicle for Danny Kaye.

w Don Hartman, Robert Pirosh, Allen Boretz   d Elliott Nugent   ph Ray Rennahan   md Ray Heindorf, Louis Forbes

Danny Kaye, Dinah Shore, Constance Dowling, Dana Andrews, Louis Calhern, Lyle Talbot

'Not since Greta Garbo made her bow has there been anything so terrific as the inimitable Danny, one of the most exhilarating and spontaneous personalities in film history.' – *New York Daily Mirror*

AAN: song 'Now I Know' (m Harold Arlen, ly Ted Koehler); Ray Heindorf, Louis Forbes

Up in Central Park
US   1948   88m   bw
U-I (Karl Tunberg)

In turn-of-the-century New York, an Irish girl becomes involved in a crooked political set up.

Stiff and unyielding star musical.

w Karl Tunberg d William A. Seiter ph Milton Krasner songs Sigmund Romberg, Dorothy Fields md John Green

Deanna Durbin, Vincent Price, Dick Haymes, Albert Sharpe, Tom Powers

'A misery.' – New Yorker

Up in Mabel's Room
US 1944 77m bw
Edward Small

A flustered professor has to retrieve incriminating evidence from an old flame's room.

Antediluvian bedroom farce which keeps several ardent practitioners working happily.

w Tom Reed play Wilson Collinson, Otto Harbach d Allan Dwan m Edward Paul

Dennis O'Keefe, Mischa Auer, Marjorie Reynolds, Gail Patrick

'As horrible, and wonderful, as watching a Gopher Prairie dramatic club play a mail order farce (6m, 6f).' – James Agee

AAN: Edward Paul

Up in Smoke
US 1978 86m colour
Paramount (Lou Adler, Lou Lombardo)
V*, L

Two dopeheads from a rock band go in search of pot so that they can play.

Direly unamusing; the slapstick is badly timed and the humour infantile. Stoned or sober, Cheech and Chong are the least funny comedy team since The Three Stooges.

w Tommy Chong, Cheech Marin d Lou Adler ph Gene Polito ad Leon Ericksen ed Scott Conrad, Lou Lombardo

Cheech Marin, Tommy Chong, Strother Martin, Edie Adams, Stacy Keach, Tom Skerritt

'The humor is like dogface underclass humor – but without the resentment of the officers. And Cheech and Chong are so gracefully dumb-assed that if you're in a relaxed mood you can't help laughing at them.' – Pauline Kael, New Yorker

Up in the Cellar
US 1970 94m Movielab
AIP (William J. Immerman)
V*

A dejected freshman tries various schemes to revenge himself on the college president.

Youth satire aimed at a number of targets which quickly became obsolete; mildly interesting sociologically.

wd Theodore J. Flicker novel The Late Boy Wonder by Angus Hall ph Earl Roth m Don Randi

Wes Stern, Joan Collins, Larry Hagman, Judy Pace

Up in the World
GB 1956 91m bw
Rank (Hugh Stewart)

A window cleaner becomes friendly with a boy millionaire.

Slow and unattractive comedy star vehicle.

w Jack Davies, Henry Blyth, Peter Blackmore d John Paddy Carstairs ph Jack Cox m Philip Green

Norman Wisdom, Martin Caridia, Jerry Desmonde, Maureen Swanson, Ambrosine Philpotts, Colin Gordon

Up Periscope
US 1959 111m Technicolor Warnerscope
Warner/Lakeside (Aubrey Schenck)
V*, L

During World War II a submarine frogman is landed on a Pacific island to steal a Japanese code book.

Stock adventure story given stock presentation.

w Richard Landau novel Robb White d Gordon Douglas ph Carl Guthrie m Ray Heindorf

James Garner, Edmond O'Brien, Alan Hale Jnr, Carleton Carpenter

Up Pompeii
GB 1971 90m Technicolor
EMI/Associated London Films (Ned Sherrin)
V

A wily slave outwits Nero and escapes the eruption of Vesuvius.

Yawnmaking spinoff of a lively TV comedy series: the jokes just lie there, and die there.

w Sid Colin d Bob Kellett ph Ian Wilson m Carl Davis

Frankie Howerd, Patrick Cargill, Michael Hordern, Barbara Murray, Lance Percival, Bill Fraser, Adrienne Posta

† Sequels: Up the Front, Up the Chastity Belt (qv).

Up Pops the Devil
US 1931 74m bw
Paramount

A wife supports her husband so that he can write novels.

Odd little comedy-drama which struck most people as rather half-hearted.

w Arthur Kober, Eve Unsell play Frances Goodrich, Albert Hackett d A. Edward Sutherland

Carole Lombard, Norman Foster, Skeets Gallagher, Stuart Erwin, Lilyan Tashman

'Here's a plenty satisfying strip of celluloid but it won't do any drawing unless it's by word-of-mouth advertising.' – Variety

Up She Goes: see Maisie (Up Goes Maisie)

Up the Chastity Belt *
GB 1971 94m Technicolor
EMI/Associated London Films (Ned Sherrin)
V

Medieval adventures of the serf Lurkalot and his master Sir Coward de Custard.

Patchy pantomime which doesn't always have the courage of its own slapdash vulgarity.

w Sid Colin, Ray Galton, Alan Simpson d Bob Kellett ph Ian Wilson m Carl Davis

Frankie Howerd, Graham Crowden, Bill Fraser, Roy Hudd, Hugh Paddick, Anna Quayle, Eartha Kitt, Dave King, Fred Emney

Up the Creek *
GB 1958 83m bw HammerScope
Byron (Henry Halsted)
V*

A none-too-bright naval lieutenant is assigned command of a broken-down shore establishment.

Cheeky remake of Oh Mr Porter. Jokes fair, atmosphere cheerful and easy-going.

wd Val Guest ph Arthur Grant

David Tomlinson, Peter Sellers, Wilfrid Hyde-White, Vera Day, Tom Gill, Michael Goodliffe, Reginald Beckwith, Lionel Jeffries

† Sequel: Further Up the Creek.

Up the Down Staircase *
US 1967 124m Technicolor
Warner/Pakula-Mulligan
V*

Problems of a schoolteacher in one of New York's tough sections.

Earnest, well-acted, not very likeable melodrama.

w Tad Mosel novel Bel Kaufman d Robert Mulligan ph Joseph Coffey m Fred Karlin

Sandy Dennis, Patrick Bedford, Eileen Heckart, Ruth White, Jean Stapleton, Sorrel Booke, Roy Poole

'Sandy Dennis, blinking as if she'd taken pills and been awakened in the middle of the night . . . She reacts confusedly before the situations even develop, but the audience is ahead of her anyway.' – Pauline Kael, New Yorker

Up the Front
GB 1972 89m Technicolor
EMI/Associated London Films (Ned Sherrin)
V

A footman is hypnotized into enlisting in World War I and has an enemy 'plan' tattooed on his buttocks.

Threadbare end-of-the-pier romp.

w Sid Colin, Eddie Braben d Bob Kellett ph Tony Spratling m Patrick Greenwell ad Seamus Flannery

Frankie Howerd, Bill Fraser, Zsa Zsa Gabor, Stanley Holloway, Hermione Baddeley, Robert Coote, Lance Percival, Dora Bryan

'Don't get caught is what she wasn't taught!'
Up the Junction
GB 1967 119m Techniscope
Paramount/BHE (Anthony Havelock-Allan, John Brabourne)

A well-off girl crosses London's river to live among the workers of Clapham.

Socially obsolete sensationalism based on a television semi-documentary. An irritating heroine moves hygienically among motorbikes.

w Roger Smith book Nell Dunn d Peter Collinson ph Arthur Lavis m Mike Hugg, Manfred Mann

Suzy Kendall, Dennis Waterman, Adrienne Posta, Maureen Lipman, Michael Gothard, Liz Fraser, Hylda Baker, Alfie Bass

Up the River
US 1930 80m bw
Fox

An ex-convict is threatened with exposure, but his two pals escape to help him.

Very minor comedy with interesting credits.

w Maurine Watkins d John Ford ph Joseph August

Spencer Tracy, Warren Hymer, Claire Luce, Humphrey Bogart, William Collier Snr

'No cast names to draw, but if the exploitation can make 'em attend, the film will meet its entertainment obligations.' – Variety

† In 1938 TCF released a remake directed by Alfred Werker, with Preston Foster, Tony Martin, Slim Summerville and Arthur Treacher.

Up the Sandbox
US 1972 98m Technicolor
Barwood/First Artists (Robert Chartoff, Irwin Winkler)
V*, L

A professor's wife finds she is pregnant again and fantasizes about her future life.

Muddled comedy-drama with little point and less entertainment value.

w Paul Zindel novel Anne Richardson Roiphe d Irwin Kershner ph Gordon Willis, Andy Marton m Billy Goldenberg ad Harry Horner

Barbra Streisand, David Selby, Ariane Heller, Jane Hoffman

'A magical mystery tour through the picture book mind of one Manhattan housewife.' – *Richard Combs*

Up Tight
US 1968 104m Technicolor
Paramount/Marlukin (Jules Dassin)

A black street cleaner betrays his criminal pals for money and is hunted down by them.

Ponderous black remake of *The Informer*, too schematic to make any dramatic or human impression.

w Jules Dassin, Ruby Dee, Julian Mayfield d Jules Dassin ph Boris Kaufman m Booker T. Jones pd Alexander Trauner

Raymond St Jacques, Ruby Dee, Julian Mayfield, Frank Silvera, Roscoe Lee Browne, Juanita Moore

Upperworld
US 1934 75m bw
Warner

A society-conscious wife drives her husband into the arms of a girl from the Bronx.

Smooth romantic melodrama with a murder angle; dated but enjoyable.

w Ben Markson story Ben Hecht d Roy del Ruth

Warren William, Mary Astor, Ginger Rogers, Andy Devine, J. Carrol Naish, Henry O'Neill

Upstairs and Downstairs
GB 1959 101m Eastmancolor
Rank (Betty E. Box)

Newlyweds have trouble with maids and au pair girls.

Glossy, cheerful, empty-headed domestic comedy.

w Frank Harvey novel Ronald Scott Thorn d Ralph Thomas ph Ernest Steward

Michael Craig, Anne Heywood, Mylène Demongeot, James Robertson Justice, Sidney James, Daniel Massey, Claudia Cardinale, Joan Hickson, Joan Sims

Uptown Saturday Night *
US 1974 104m Technicolor
Warner/Verdon/First Artists (Melville Tucker)
V, V*

Three friends pursue crooks who have inadvertently stolen a winning lottery ticket.

Witless but high-spirited star comedy for blacks, with a variety of sordid backgrounds.

w Richard Wesley d Sidney Poitier ph Fred J. Koenekamp m Tom Scott

Sidney Poitier, Bill Cosby, Harry Belafonte, Flip Wilson, Roscoe Lee Browne, Richard Pryor, Rosalind Cash, Paula Kelly

'If it had been filmed with a white cast this collection of atrophied comedy routines would have been indistinguishable from a Monogram farce of the forties.' – *David McGillivray*

The Upturned Glass *
GB 1947 86m bw
GFD/Triton (Sydney Box, James Mason)

A Harley Street surgeon murders the woman responsible for the death of the girl he loved.

Rather pointless psychopathology with an ill-explained title; an interesting example of a top star not knowing what's best for him.

w Jon P. Monaghan, Pamela Kellino d Lawrence Huntington ph Reg Wyer m Bernard Stevens

James Mason, Pamela Kellino, Rosamund John, Ann Stephens, Henry Oscar, Morland Graham, Brefni O'Rourke

'The psychology is genuine; so too is the tension; the camera plays some good quiet tricks.' – *William Whitebait*

Uranus **
France 1990 99m colour
Artificial Eye/Renn/DD/Sofica (Patrick Bordier)
V, V*, S

In the aftermath of the Second World War, political rivalries between Communists and Fascists, Resistance fighters and collaborators, tear apart the inhabitants of a small French town.

Excellently acted and engaging, though wordy, account of postwar witch hunts.

w Claude Berri, Arlette Langmann novel Marcel Aymé d Claude Berri ph Renato Berta m Jean-Claude Petit ad Bernard Vezat ed Hervé de Luze

Philippe Noiret, Gérard Depardieu, Jean-Pierre Marielle, Michel Blanc, Gérard Desarthe, Michel Galabru, Fabrice Luchini

'The intrinsic interest of the subject matter holds us for a while, which is just as well, because this dull, talkative film is dramatically barren.' – *Philip French, Observer*

'The film makes the case against the totalitarian intolerance of empowered Stalinism – in French practice it often amounted to a settling of personal scores – with persuasive force.' – *Richard Schickel, Time*

Urban Cowboy
US 1980 135m Movielab Panavision
Paramount (Robert Evans, Irving Azoff)
V*, L

A rural Texan finds it difficult to succeed in the big city.

Unpleasant and uninteresting star melodrama with a plot vaguely reminiscent of the first part of *An American Tragedy*.

w James Bridges novel Aaron Latham d James Bridges ph Ray Villalobos m various songs pd Stephen Grimes

John Travolta, Debra Winger, Scott Glenn, Madolyn Smith

'A fatuous vehicle for John Travolta, requiring him to stride (stiffly and expressionlessly) through various macho torments . . . the two-hour-plus running time, incorporating a wealth of cliché characters, is excruciatingly protracted.' – *Tom Milne, MFB*

Urga **
France/USSR 1991 120m colour
Hachette Première/Studio Trite (Michel Seydoux)
V, V*, L
US title: *Close to Eden*

A Mongolian herdsman rescues a Russian lorry-driver who crashes into a river and takes him home to his family.

Delightful and exuberant fable of a clash between urban and rural ways of life.

w Nikita Mikhalkov, Roustam Ibraguimbekov d Nikita Mikhalkov ph Villenn Kaluta m Eduard Artemiev pd Alexei Levchenko ed Joelle Hache

Bayaertu, Badema, Vladimir Gostukhin, Babushka

'It hardly advances cinematic art, but story and characters resonate with life.' – *Geoff Brown, The Times*

AAN: foreign language film

Urotsukidōji: see *Legend of the Overfiend*

Urotsukidōji II: see *Legend of the Demon Womb*

Urotsukidōji III: see *Legend of the Demon Womb*

Ursus (dubbed)
Italy/Spain 1961 95m Eastmancolor Totalscope
UA/Ciné Italia/Atenea (Italo Zingarelli)
S
aka: *Mighty Ursus*

Ursus returns from the wars to discover that the woman he loves has been kidnapped.

Mundane muscle-man epic, with a dreary narrative and very little action.

w Giuseppe Mangione, Sergio Sollima, Giuliano Carnimeo d Carlo Campogalliani ph Eloy Mella m Roman Vlad ad Romoloa Girolami ed Jolanda Benvenuti, Julia Pena

Ed Fury, Cristina Gajoni, Moira Orfei, Mary Marlon, Mario Scaccia

'The stiff performances and excruciating dialogue come as no surprise, but even the spectacle is gracelessly mounted.' – *David McGillivray*

Ursus and the Tartar Princess (dubbed)
France/Italy 1961 80m Technicolor Techniscope
Explorer Film '58/CFFP (Nino Battiferri)
S

In 17th-century Poland, a captured nobleman falls in love with the daughter of the leader of an invading Tartar army.

A romantic epic, with strongman Ursus's role reduced to a walk-on; it is a little different from the usual Italian spectacles in preaching a gospel of peace between scenes of swordplay and bloodshed.

w Remigio Del Grosso (English dialogue John Hart) d Remigo Del Grosso (d English-language version Richard McNamara) ph Anchise Brizzi m A. F. Lavagnino ad Antonio Visone ed Antonietta Zita

Yoko Tani, Ettore Manni, Joe Robinson, Akim Tamiroff, Roland Lesaffre, Maria Grazia Spina

Used Cars *
US 1980 111m Metrocolor
Columbia (Bob Gale)
V*, L

For the love of his boss's daughter, a fast-talking car salesman saves a used-car lot from being taken over by a mean-spirited rival.

Vigorous broad comedy, amusing enough if you're feeling indulgent.

w Robert Zemeckis, Bob Gale d Robert Zemeckis ph Donald M. Morgan m Patrick Williams pd Peter M. Jamison ed Michael Kahn

Kurt Russell, Gerrit Graham, Frank McRae, Deborah Harmon, Jack Russell

'A classic screwball fantasy – a neglected modern comedy that's like a more restless and visually high-spirited version of the W. C. Fields pictures.' – *Pauline Kael, New Yorker*

Used People *
US 1992 116m DeLuxe
TCF/Largo (Peggy Rajski)
V, V*

An Italian widower courts a Jewish widow whom he has loved from a distance for more than 20 years.

A romantic comedy for the middle-aged, leisurely in pace, giving its cast room to display their skills.

w Todd Graff play The Grandma Plays by Todd Graff d Beeban Kidron ph David Watkin m Rachel Portman pd Stuart Wurtzel ed John Tintori

Shirley Maclaine, Marcello Mastroianni, Bob Dishy, Kathy Bates, Jessica Tandy, Marcia Gay Harden, Lee Wallace, Louis Guss

'An actors' showcase, with heightened performances

by the ensemble eschewing the naturalism favored by mainstream fare.' – *Variety*

'Funny, touching and very well-observed . . . But it finally exposes itself as clichéd, a little shapeless and too long.' – *Derek Malcolm, Guardian*

Utopia: see *Robinson Crusoeland*

Utu ***
New Zealand   1983   118m   Fujicolor
Glitteron (Geoff Murphy, Don Blakeney)
V, V*, S

In New Zealand in the 1870s, a Maori, whose family is massacred by the army, and a farmer, whose wife is killed by the Maoris, are both obsessed by revenge.

Powerful and absorbing drama of imperialistic and colonial attitudes, set against wild, open spaces.

w Geoff Murphy, Keith Aberdein   *d* Geoff Murphy
ph Graeme Cowley   *m* John Charles   *pd* Ron Highfield   *ed* Michael Horton, Ian John

Anzac Wallace, Bruno Lawrence, Wi Kuki Kaa, Kelly Johnson, Tim Elliott, Tanya Bristowe, Ilona Rodgers, Merata Mita, Tom Polan

Utvandrarna: see *The Emigrants*

Utz *
GB/Germany/Italy   1992   colour
BBC/NDR/Academy/Cine Electric/Viva (John Goldschmidt)
V

An American art dealer tries to discover what has happened to a priceless collection of porcelain figures.

Gently civilized entertainment on acquisitive and obsessive pleasures, although one lacking much popular appeal.

w Hugh Whitemore   *novel* Bruce Chatwin
d George Sluizer   *ph* Gerard Vandenberg
m Nicola Piovani   *pd* Karel Vacek   *ed* Lin Friedman

Armin Mueller-Stahl, Brenda Fricker, Peter Riegert, Paul Scofield, Gaye Brown, Miriam Karlin, Pauline Melville, Vera Soukupova

'The polyglot cast and crew can't provide a cohesive basis on which to pin a frustratingly fragmented screenplay.' – *Variety*

V

V. I. Warshawski
US 1991 89m Technicolor
Warner/Hollywood Pictures/Silver Screen Partners IV/Chestnut
Hill (Jeffrey Lurie)
V, V*, L

A female private eye is hired to investigate the murder of a businessman.

Exceedingly dull thriller intended to introduce to film a tough feminist detective from fiction. Its failure to find an audience is likely to mean that the planned sequels will not appear.

w Edward Taylor, David Aaron Cohen, Nick Thiel
novel Indemnity Only by Sara Paretsky   d Jeff Kanew
ph Jan Kiesser   m Randy Edelman   pd Barbara
Ling   ed C. Timothy O'Meara, Debra Neil

Kathleen Turner, Jay O. Sanders, Charles Durning, Angela Goethals, Nancy Paul, Frederick Coffin, Charles McCaughan, Stephen Meadows, Wayne Knight

'The feebly-plotted movie comes over as a padded-out 90-minute episode of a routine private eye series, or more accurately the black box from a TV pilot that crashed shortly after take-off. It could be shown in film schools as an example of how not to adapt a novel for the screen.' – Philip French, Observer

Les Vacances de Monsieur Hulot: see *Monsieur Hulot's Holiday*

'A tale of violence, romance and madness.'
Vacas *
Spain 1992 96m colour
ICA/Sogetel (Ricardo Garcia Arrojos)
V

Rivalry and love between two families, linked by children, continue over three generations.

An intricate, enjoyable story of family feuds and affairs, agreeably tinged with fantasy.

w Julio Medem, Michael Gaztambide   d Julio
Medem   ph Carles Gusi   m Alberto Iglesias
ed Maria Elena Sainz de Rozas

Emma Suárez, Carmelo Gómez, Ana Torrent, Karra Elejalde, Klara Badiola, Txema Blasco

'With lush cinematography, energetic performances and a strong sense of the mystery and terror to be found in the Great Outdoors, pic lingers in the memory as impressive and unusual.' – Variety

'A poetic, boldly directed first film that serves notice of a promising talent.' – Sheila Johnston, Independent

Vacation from Marriage: see *Perfect Strangers* (GB)

La Vache et le Prisonnier: see *The Cow and I*

The Vagabond King
US 1956 88m Technicolor Vistavision
Paramount (Pat Duggan)

The life and loves of French medieval poet and rebel François Villon.

Shiny, antiseptic studio-set remake of an old musical warhorse.

w Ken Englund, Noel Langley   operetta Rudolf
Friml   d Michael Curtiz   ph Robert Burks

md Victor Young   m/y Rudolf Friml, Brian Hooker,
Johnny Burke   ad Hans Dreier

Oreste, Kathryn Grayson, Rita Moreno, Walter Hampden, Leslie Nielsen, Cedric Hardwicke, William Prince

† A 1930 version with Dennis King is lost. Non-musical versions of the story include *If I Were King*, in 1920 with William Farnum, 1928's *The Beloved Rogue* with John Barrymore, and in 1938 with Ronald Colman.

AAN: Hans Dreier

Vagabond Lady
US 1935 72m bw
MGM

The two sons of a department store owner fall for their father's secretary.

Medium romantic comedy which didn't seem to stick in anyone's memory.

w Frank Butler   d Sam Taylor

Robert Young, Reginald Denny, Evelyn Venable, Frank Craven, Berton Churchill

'This just misses being a charm picture, the kind they hold over or bring back for repeat dates.' – Variety

Vagabonde ***
France 1985 104m colour
Cine-Tamaris/A2/Ministère de la Culture
V*, L
French title: Sans Toit ni Loi; aka: Vagabond

After a young woman is found frozen to death in a ditch, people tell of their experiences of her in the last weeks of her life, and of how she abandoned conventional living to become a tramp.

Disturbingly chill movie of the accidental collisions of people's lives, and the changes they cause, with an enigma at its centre.

wd Agnès Varda   ph Patrick Blossier   m Joanna
Bruzdowicz   ed Agnès Varda, Patricia Mazuy

Sandrine Bonnaire, Macha Meril, Stéphane Freiss, Laurence Cortadellas, Marthe Jarnais, Yolande Moreau, Joel Fosse

† It won the Golden Lion award for best film at the Venice Film Festival in 1985.

The Valachi Papers
France/Italy 1972 127m Technicolor
Euro France/de Laurentiis Intermarco (Dino de Laurentiis)
V, V*

A convicted gangster talks to an FBI agent about his life in the Mafia.

Rough, violent gangster melodrama, none the better for being based on actual events.

w Stephen Geller   book Peter Maas   d Terence
Young   ph Aldo Tonti   m Riz Ortolani

Charles Bronson, Fred Valleca, Gerald S. O'Loughlin, Lino Ventura, Walter Chiari, Amedeo Nazzari, Joseph Wiseman

Valdez Is Coming
US 1970 90m DeLuxe
UA/Norlan/Ira Steiner
V*

A Mexican confronts a rancher who has double-crossed him.

Simply conceived Western which doesn't quite manage to be the classic intended.

w Roland Kibbee, David Rayfiel   d Edwin Sherin
ph Gabor Pogany   m Charles Gross

Burt Lancaster, Susan Clark, Jon Cypher, Barton Heyman, Frank Silvera

Valentino
US 1951 105m Technicolor
Columbia (Edward Small)

An Italian immigrant to the US becomes a world-famous romantic film star but dies young.

Disastrously flat attempt to recapture the feel of Hollywood in the twenties as a background to a flatulent romance.

w George Bruce   d Lewis Allen   ph Harry
Stradling   m Heinz Roemheld

Anthony Dexter, Eleanor Parker, Richard Carlson, Patricia Medina, Joseph Calleia, Dona Drake, Lloyd Gough, Otto Kruger

'One can almost see the decorated border round the words . . . it mixes fact, speculation, needless inaccuracy and bathos.' – Gavin Lambert

'The dialogue is unbelievably ham, the "entirely imaginary" story commonplace; the players deserve sympathy.' – Richard Mallett, Punch

Valentino *
GB 1977 127m DeLuxe
UA/Aperture/Chartoff-Winkler (Harry Benn)
V

Reporters quiz celebrities at a star's funeral, and his eccentric life unfolds.

Sensationalist 'exposé' of Valentino's rise to fame, with excellent period detail but no sympathy for its subject.

w Ken Russell, Mardik Martin   book Brad Steiger,
Chaw Mank   d Ken Russell   ph Peter Suschitzky
m Ferde Grofe, Stanley Black   ad Philip Harrison

Rudolf Nureyev, Leslie Caron, Michelle Phillips, Carol Kane, Felicity Kendal, Huntz Hall, David de Keyser, Alfred Marks, Anton Diffring, Jennie Linden, John Justin

'By attaching the names of actual people to his sadomasochistic fantasies, the director, Ken Russell, gives the picture a nasty inside-joke appeal.' – Pauline Kael

Valentino Returns
US 1989 90m Alpha Cine colour
Owl/Vidmark (Peter Hoffman, David Wisnievitz)
V*, L

The adolescent son of a mismatched couple buys a pink Cadillac in order to impress his girlfriend.

Low-key, lacklustre drama stuck in a familiar groove.

w Leonard Gardner   story Christ Has Returned to Earth
and Preaches Here Nightly by Leonard Gardner   d Peter
Hoffman   ph Jerzy Zielinski   ad Woody Romine
ed Denine Rowan

Barry Tubb, Frederic Forrest, Veronica Cartwright, Jenny Wright, Macon McCalman, Kit McDonough, Seth Isler, Miguel Ferrer, Leonard Gardner

Valerie

US   1957   80m   bw
UA/Hal R. Makelim

A Western rancher is accused of wounding his wife and murdering her parents.

Curious little *Rashomon*-like courtroom melodrama, quite well made and acted.

w Leonard Heidemann, Emmett Murphy   d Gerd Oswald   ph Ernest Laszlo   m Albert Glasser

Anita Ekberg, Sterling Hayden, Anthony Steel, John Wengraf

Valerie A Týden Divu: see *Valerie and Her Week of Wonders*

Valerie and Her Week of Wonders **

Czechoslovakia   1970   77m   Eastmancolor
Contemporary/Ceskoslovensky/Barrandov
V

original title: *Valerie A Týden Divu*

A young girl on the verge of puberty dreams of vampires and her own death, burned as a witch by a priest who tried to rape her.

A surrealist vision of the awakening of sexuality, full of startling images drawn from myth and religious ritual, somewhat like a more explicitly Freudian version of *Alice in Wonderland*.

w Jaromil Jires, Ester Krumbachová   story Vitezlav Nezval   *Jaromil Jires*   ph Jan Curik   m Jan Klusák   ad Jan Oliva   ed Josef Valusiak

Jaroslava Schallerová, Helena Anýzová, Petr Kopriva, Jüiri Prymek, Jan Klusák, Libuse Komancová, Karel Engel, Alena Stojáková

'The real and the unreal are disturbingly fused, while the images are continually eloquent.' – *Gordon Gow, Films and Filming*

The Valiant

GB/Italy   1961   89m   bw
(UA) BHP/Euro International (Jon Penington)

During World War II, a battleship in Alexandria harbour is mined, and the captain tries desperately to avert disaster.

Ill-made war fodder, of no interest at any level.

w Keith Waterhouse, Willis Hall   d Roy Baker   ph Wilkie Cooper, Egil Woxholt   m Christopher Whelen

John Mills, Ettore Manni, Robert Shaw, Liam Redmond, Ralph Michael, Colin Douglas, Dinsdale Landen

'I who have laughed at love, have fallen in love at last!'

Valiant Is the Word for Carrie

US   1936   110m   bw
RKO (Wesley Ruggles)

A childless woman devotes her life to orphan children.

Tedious soap opera.

w Claude Binyon   novel Barry Benefield   d Wesley Ruggles   ph Leo Tover   m Frederick Hollander

Gladys George, John Howard, Dudley Digges, Arline Judge, Harry Carey, Isabel Jewell

AAN: Gladys George

The Valley of Decision *

US   1945   119m   bw
MGM (Edwin H. Knopf)

In old Pittsburgh, an Irish housemaid marries the master's son.

Trouble at t' mill epic romance, American style; starrily cast but not excitingly made.

w John Meehan, Sonya Levien   novel Marcia Davenport   d Tay Garnett   ph Joseph Ruttenberg   m Herbert Stothart

Greer Garson, Gregory Peck, Lionel Barrymore, Donald Crisp, Preston Foster, Gladys Cooper, Marsha Hunt, Reginald Owen, Dan Duryea, Jessica Tandy, Barbara Everest, Marshall Thompson

AAN: Herbert Stothart, Greer Garson

Valley of Eagles

GB   1951   86m   bw
Independent Sovereign/GFD
V*

A Swedish scientist chases into Lapland after his wife and her lover who have stolen an important formula.

Unconvincing scenery mars what might have been an unusual adventure drama.

w Paul Tabori, Nat Bronsten, Terence Young   d Terence Young

Jack Warner, John McCallum, Nadia Gray, Anthony Dawson, Mary Laura Wood, Christopher Lee

Valley of Fury: see *Chief Crazy Horse*

The Valley of Gwangi

US   1968   95m   Technicolor
Warner/Morningside (Charles H. Schneer)
V*, L

Cowboys and scientists discover prehistoric monsters in a 'forbidden' Mexican Valley.

Tedious adventure yarn enhanced by good special effects.

w William E. Best   d James O'Connelly   ph Erwin Hillier   m Jerome Moross   sp Ray Harryhausen

Richard Carlson, Laurence Naismith, James Franciscus, Gila Golan, Freda Jackson

Valley of Song

GB   1953   74m   bw
ABPC
US title: *Men Are Children Twice*

Members of a Welsh valley choir nearly come to blows over the interpretation of *The Messiah*.

Neat, Ealing-style comedy from a well-known radio play.

w Cliff Gordon, Phil Park   play *Choir Practice* by Cliff Gordon   d Gilbert Gunn

Mervyn Johns, Clifford Evans, Maureen Swanson, John Fraser, Rachel Thomas, Rachel Roberts, Kenneth Williams

Valley of the Dolls *

US   1967   123m   DeLuxe   Panavision
TCF/Red Lion (David Weisbart)
V*, L

An innocent young actress is corrupted by Broadway and Hollywood, and takes to drugs.

Cliché-ridden but good-looking road-to-ruin melodrama from a bitchy bestseller; production values high, but the whole thing goes over the top at the end.

w Helen Deutsch, Dorothy Kingsley   novel Jacqueline Susann   d Mark Robson   ph William H. Daniels   md John Williams   m André Previn   ad Jack Martin Smith, Richard Day

Barbara Parkins, Patty Duke, Susan Hayward, Paul Burke, Sharon Tate, Martin Milner, Tony Scotti, Charles Drake, Alex Davion, Lee Grant, Robert H. Harris

'What kind of pills do you take to sit through a film like this?' – *The Golden Turkey Awards*

'A skilfully deceptive imitation of a real drama . . . on a closer look the characters turn out to be images that have almost nothing to do with people.' – *Christian Science Monitor*

'One of the most stupefyingly clumsy films ever made by alleged professionals.' – *Joseph Morgenstern, Newsweek*

† Judy Garland was originally slated to play the Susan Hayward part.

AAN: John Williams

Valley of the Giants

US   1938   79m   Technicolor
Warner

A lumberman fights pirates to preserve his beloved redwoods.

Routine outdoor thick ear to which colour lent the semblance of freshness.

w Seton I. Miller, Michael Fessier   novel Peter B. Kyne   d William Keighley

Wayne Morris, Claire Trevor, Frank McHugh, Alan Hale, Donald Crisp, Charles Bickford

'A yarn which contains nearly all the proven surefire elements of the successful outdoor picture.' – *Variety*

† This was the third version of the story; the first, in 1919, starred Wallace Reid; the second, in 1927, starred Milton Sills. The 1952 movie *The Big Trees*, with Kirk Douglas, had a suspiciously similar storyline.

Valley of the Kings

US   1954   86m   Eastmancolor
MGM

Archaeologists fight looters in the tomb of a Pharaoh.

Thin as drama, with little action or suspense and dispirited acting, this hokum piece nevertheless benefits from splendid locations.

w Robert Pirosh, Karl Tunberg   d Robert Pirosh   ph Robert Surtees   m Miklos Rozsa

Robert Taylor, Eleanor Parker, Carlos Thompson, Kurt Kasznar, Victor Jory

Valley of the Sun

US   1942   79m   bw
RKO (Graham Baker)
V*

A government spy in old Arizona outwits a crooked Indian agent.

Cheapjack Western with nothing to commend it.

w Horace McCoy   story Clarence Budington Kelland   d George Marshall   ph Harry J. Wild   m Paul Sawtell

James Craig, Lucille Ball, Dean Jagger, Billy Gilbert, Cedric Hardwicke, Peter Whitney, Tom Tyler, Antonio Moreno, George Cleveland

Valley of the Zombies

US   1946   56m   bw
Republic

A big city zombie goes on a murder spree.

Entirely unpersuasive hokum which wouldn't chill a baby. No valley is apparent.

w The McGowans   d Philip Ford

Ian Keith, Robert Livingston, Adrian Booth, Thomas Jackson, Charles Trowbridge

The Valley of Vanishing Men

US   1942   bw   serial: 15 eps
Columbia

Adventurers in New Mexico trap a renegade European general who uses captive patriots as slaves.

Less than eventful serial.

d Spencer G. Bennet

Bill Elliott, Slim Summerville, Carmen Morales, Kenneth MacDonald

Valmont

France/GB   1989   137m   colour
Orion/Claude Berri/Renn (Paul Rassam, Michael Hausman)
V*, L

In the 1780s, two aristocrats conspire in the seduction of a young and virginal bride-to-be.

A playful adaptation and one that suggests a fancy dress party rather than a period film, with the tragic ending of the original being altered into something more upbeat and cynical.

w Jean-Claude Carrière   novel Les Liaisons Dangereuses by Choderlos de Laclos   d Milos Forman
ph Miroslav Ondricek   m Christopher Palmer
pd Pierre Guffroy   ed Alan Heim, Nena Danevic

Colin Firth, Annette Bening, Meg Tilly, Fairuza Balk, Sian Phillips, Jeffery Jones, Henry Thomas, Fabia Drake, T. P. McKenna, Isla Blair, Ronald Lacey

† A rival, and better, version of the novel was filmed almost simultaneously as Dangerous Liaisons (qv).

Les Valseuses **
France   1974   118m   Eastmancolor
CAPAC/UPF/SN (Paul Claudon)
V, V*
GB title: Making it; US title: Going Places

Two young layabouts indulge in petty crime and inconsequential sex.

High-spirited and occasionally charming, despite its sometimes unpleasant content and general amorality; adolescents are likely to respond most favourably to it.

w Bertrand Blier, Philippe Dumarcay
novel Bertrand Blier   d Bertrand Blier   ph Bruno Nuyten   m Stéphane Grappelli   ed Kénout Peltier

Gérard Depardieu, Miou-Miou, Patrick Dewaere, Christian Alers, Brigitte Fossey, Michel Peyrelon, Isabelle Huppert, Jeanne Moreau

Value for Money
GB   1955   93m   Technicolor   Vistavision
Rank/Group Films (Sergei Nolbandov)

A Yorkshire businessman determines to broaden his outlook, and falls in love with a London showgirl.

Highly undistinguished north country romantic farce which wastes a good production and cast.

w R. F. Delderfield, William Fairchild   novel Derick Boothroyd   d Ken Annakin   ph Geoffrey Unsworth   m Malcolm Arnold

John Gregson, Diana Dors, Susan Stephen, Derek Farr, Frank Pettingell, Jill Adams, Ernest Thesiger, Charles Victor, Joan Hickson

Vamp
US   1986   94m   Metrocolor
New World/Balcor (Donald P. Borchers)
V, V*, L

Three college boys in search of a stripper find themselves in a den of vampires.

A cheap and gory horror flick, luridly photographed, and most likely to be enjoyed by colour-blind teenagers.

wd Richard Wenk   story Donald P. Borchers,
Richard Wenk   ph Elliot Davis   m Jonathan Elias
pd Alan Roderick-Jones   sp Greg Cannom
ed Marc Grossman

Grace Jones, Chris Makepeace, Sandy Baron, Robert Rusler, Dedee Pfeiffer, Gedde Watanabe, Billy Drago

Vampira
GB   1974   88m   colour
Columbia/World Film Services (Jack H. Wiener)
US title: Old Dracula

A vampire count lures beauty-contest winners to his castle and uses their blood to revive his dead wife.

Would-be spoof which falls flat on its fangs.

w Jeremy Lloyd   d Clive Donner   ph Tony Richmond   m David Whitaker

David Niven, Teresa Graves, Peter Bayliss, Jennie Linden, Linda Hayden, Nicky Henson, Bernard Bresslaw, Veronica Carlson

The Vampire
US   1957   74m   bw
UA/Gardner-Levy
V*

A research scientist takes bat essence and becomes a vampire.

Silly attempt to turn a legend into science fiction: more risible than sinister.

w Pat Fielder   d Paul Landres   ph Jack Mackenzie
m Gerald Fried

John Beal, Colleen Gray, Kenneth Tobey, Lydia Reed

'Mad? I, who have solved the secret of life, you call me mad?'

The Vampire Bat
US   1932   71m   bw
Majestic (Phil Goldstone)
V, V*

A mad doctor kills townsfolk in search of 'blood substitute'.

Primitive but vigorous low budget chiller.

w Edward Lowe   d Frank Strayer   ph Ira Morgan

Lionel Atwill, Fay Wray, Melvyn Douglas, Maude Eburne, George E. Stone, Dwight Frye, Lionel Belmore

'Shiver picture, well enough done but coming too late in the cycle to take any money.' – Variety

Vampire Circus
GB   1971   87m   colour
Rank/Hammer (Wilbur Stark)
V

In 1825 a plague-ridden village is visited by a circus of animal vampires.

Silly but quite inventive horror thriller.

w Judson Kinberg   d Robert Young   ph Moray Grant   m David Whittaker   ad Scott MacGregor
ed Peter Musgrave

Adrienne Corri, Laurence Payne, Thorley Walters, John Moulder Brown, Elizabeth Seal, Lynne Frederick, Robin Hunter

Vampire in Venice: see Vampires in Venice

The Vampire Lovers
GB   1970   91m (88m US)   Technicolor
MGM-EMI/Hammer/AIP (Harry Fine, Michael Style)
V*

A lady vampire worms her way into several noble households.

Reasonably close retelling of Sheridan Le Fanu's Carmilla, complete with lesbian love scenes. Adequate production but not much spirit.

w Tudor Gates, Harry Fine, Michael Styles
story Carmilla by Sheridan Le Fanu   d Roy Ward Baker   ph Moray Grant   m Harry Robinson
ad Scott MacGregor   ed James Needs

Ingrid Pitt, Peter Cushing, Pippa Steele, Madeleine Smith, George Cole, Dawn Addams, Douglas Wilmer, Kate O'Mara

La Vampire Nue (dubbed)
France   1969   90m   colour
Tigon/Films ABC (Jean Lavie)
V
aka: The Naked Vampire

A son discovers that his father is a member of a private club given over to investigations of ritual suicide, sex and vampirism.

A perversely unconventional horror movie, more concerned with surrealist ornament, nudity and

fetishistic costumes than narrative; the director's interest rarely strays beyond striking images and interior decor, but you may be amused by his pretension.

wd Jean Rollin   ph Jean-Jacques Renon   m Yvon Serault   ad Jio Berk

Christine François, Olivier Martin, Maurice Lemaître, Bernard Musson, Jean Aron, Ursule Pauly, Michel Delahaye

'The essential thinness of the script is reinforced by Rollin's tendency to strive for a sustained mood of mystery by holding shots for several seconds after the action has been completed. Unfortunately, the cumulative effect of these delays is a deadeningly slow pace which appears more contrived than supernatural.' – David McGillivray, MFB

'One of Rollin's most enjoyable films.' – Peter Tombs and Cathal Tohill, NFT

The British video release runs for 82m. The film was cut to 79m on its British cinema release in 1973.

Vampire Thrills: see Le Frisson des Vampires

Vampire Woman: see Crypt of the Living Dead

The Vampire's Ghost
US   1945   59m   bw
Republic (Rudolph E. Abel)

A vampire takes control of a West African plantation.

Unconvincing horror comic with no horror.

w John K. Butler, Leigh Brackett   d Lesley Selander

John Abbott, Charles Gordon, Peggy Stewart, Grant Withers

Vampires in Venice
Italy   1988   90m   colour
Scena/Reteitalia (Augusto Caminito)
original title: Nosferatu a Venezia; aka: Vampire in Venice

In Venice, where Nosferatu was last seen 200 years earlier, a princess summons the vampire during a seance.

Despite an atmospheric opening, a muddled and unenticing addition to the endless round of vampire movies, with Kinski reprising his role without visible enthusiasm.

wd Augusto Caminito   story Alberto Alfieri, Leandro Luchetti   ph Antonio Nardi   m Luigi Ceccarelli, Vangelis   pd Joseph Teichner, Luca Antonucci
ed Claudio Cutry

Klaus Kinski, Donald Pleasence, Christopher Plummer, Barbara de Rossi, Yorgo Voyagis, Anne Knecht

The film was a sequel of sorts to Kinski's Nosferatu the Vampyre (qv).

'Seduction. Romance. Murder. The things one does for love.'
Vampire's Kiss
US   1989   103m   colour
Hemdale/Magellan Pictures (Barry Shils, Barbara Zitwer)
V, V*, L

A literary agent begins to fantasize that he is a vampire and behaves accordingly.

Over-heated film of urban disquiet, too tame for die-hard horror fans and too incoherent to interest any other audience.

w Joseph Minion   d Robert Bierman   ph Stefan Czapsky   m Colin Towns   pd Christopher Nowak
ed Angus Newton

Nicolas Cage, Maria Conchita Alonso, Jennifer Beals, Elizabeth Ashley, Kasi Lemmons, Bob Lujan, Jessica Lundy, John Walker

Vampyr **

Germany/France   1932   83m   bw
Tobis Klangfilm/Carl Dreyer
V, V*, L
US title: Castle of Doom; aka: The Strange Adventure of
David Gray

A young man staying in a remote inn suspects that he
is surrounded by vampires and has a dream of his
own death.

Vague, misty, virtually plotless but occasionally
frightening and always interesting to look at, this
semi-professional film long since joined the list of
minor classics for two scenes: the hero dreaming of his
own death and the villain finally buried by flour in a
mill.

w Christen Jul, Carl Dreyer   story Carmilla by
Sheridan Le Fanu   d Carl Dreyer   ph Rudolph Maté,
Louis Née   m Wolfgang Zeller

Julian West, Sybille Schmitz, Maurice Schutz, Jan
Hieronimko

'It makes our contemporary, explicit Draculas look
like advertisements for false teeth.' – Sunday Times,
1976

'It is intensely a film of hints, of eerie non sequiturs,
of barely perceivable yet striking images . . . evil
wafts off the screen like a smell of bad breath.' – New
Statesman, 1976

'Imagine we are sitting in an ordinary room.
Suddenly we are told there is a corpse behind the
door. In an instant, the room is completely altered;
everything in it has taken another look; the light, the
atmosphere have changed, though they are physically
the same. This is because we have changed, and the
objects are as we perceive them. That is the effect I
meant to get in my film.' – Carl Dreyer

† 'Julian West' was really Baron Nicholas de
Gunsberg, who financed the project.

Vampyres *

GB   1974   84m   Eastmancolor
Fox-Rank/Essay (Brian Smedley-Aston)

Two murdered lesbian lovers become vampires after
their deaths and lure men to a deserted mansion so
that they can suck their blood.

Cheaply made, single-minded horror that manages to
generate a relentless tension.

w D. Daubeney   d Joseph Larraz (José Larraz)
ph Harry Waxman   m James Clarke   ad Ken
Bridgeman   ed Geoff R. Brown

Marianne Morris, Anulka, Murray Brown, Brian
Deacon, Sally Faulkner, Michael Byrne, Karl
Lanchberry, Bessie Love

'A sex-horror film about lesbian vampires for which
the budget and schedule were insignificant, even by
British exploitation standards.' – David Pirie, MFB

'A minor masterpiece of erotic fantasy.' – Peter Tombs
and Cathal Tohill, NFT

Van Gogh *

France   1991   158m   colour
Artificial Eye/Erato/Canal+/A2/Livradois (Daniel Toscan du
Plantier)

In the final three months of his life, Vincent Van Gogh
goes to live in Auvers, where he begins an affair with
the young daughter of the local doctor, a collector of
paintings, quarrels with his brother and kills himself.

Fictionalized biopic that adds little to an
understanding of the artist, even if it sets him in an
everyday context as one man among many.

wd Maurice Pialat   ph Gilles Henry   m A. Bernot,
J. M. Bourget, J. Dutronc, P. Revedy

Jacques Dutronc, Alexandra London, Bernard Le Coq,
Gerard Sety, Corinne Bourdon, Elsa Zylberstein,
Leslie Azoulai, Jacques Vidal, Chantal Barbarit

'The punitive running time and unlovely hero mean
that this will hardly be embraced by all cinemagoers,
but Van Gogh is certainly the best of the Van Gogh
movies to date.' – Kim Newman, Empire

Vanessa, Her Love Story

US   1935   76m   bw
MGM (David O. Selznick)

When her husband becomes insane, a Victorian lady
falls for a gypsy.

Very dated romance which finished Helen Hayes's
star career, for thirty years at least.

w Lenore Coffee   novel Hugh Walpole   d William
K. Howard   ph Ray June   m Herbert Stothart

Helen Hayes, Robert Montgomery, May Robson, Otto
Kruger, Lewis Stone, Henry Stephenson, Violet
Kemble-Cooper, Jessie Ralph

'It drips with agony and dullness.' – Variety

Il Vangelo Secondo Matteo: see The Gospel
According to St Matthew

The Vanishing *

Netherlands/France   1988   106m   colour
Metro/Golden Egg Film/Ingrid Productions/MGS Film (Anne
Lordo, George Sluizer)
V, V*
original title: Spoorloos

After spending three years searching for his girlfriend
who suddenly disappeared while they were on
holiday, a man is approached by her kidnapper.

Black thriller with a shock ending.

w Tim Krabbé   novel The Golden Egg by Tim Krabbé
d George Sluizer   ph Toni Kuhn   m Henry
Vrienten   ad Santiago Isidro Pin, Cor Spijk
ed George Sluizer, Lin Friedman

Bernard-Pierre Donnadieu, Gene Bervoets, Johanna
Ter Steege, Gwen Eckhaus, Bernadette Le Sache,
Tania Latarjet

'A consistently bewildering and surprising thriller,
chillingly unsentimental and expertly constructed.' –
Kim Newman, MFB

The Vanishing

US   1993   110m   DeLuxe
TCF/Morra, Brezner, Steinberg and Tenenbaum (Larry Brezner,
Paul Schiff)
V, V*

A teacher searches for his kidnapped girlfriend for
three years without success; then he gets a call from
the kidnapper.

A disastrous remake of a chilling original, so softened
and given such a happy Hollywood ending that the
narrative loses all point.

w Todd Graff   novel The Golden Egg by Tim Krabbé
d George Sluizer   ph Peter Suschitzky   m Jerry
Goldsmith   pd Jeannine C. Oppewall   ed Bruce
Green

Jeff Bridges, Kiefer Sutherland, Nancy Travis, Sandra
Bullock, Park Overall, Lisa Eichhorn, Maggie
Linderman

'This is one remake that sacrifices much of what made
the original work so well.' – Variety

'Has been systematically and often laughably divested
of its subtler moments.' – Derek Malcolm, Guardian

The Vanishing American

US   1925   110m at 24 fps   bw   silent
Paramount

A history of the American Indian.

Solid Western epic, now of historical interest only.
story Zane Grey   d George B. Seitz

Richard Dix, Lois Wilson, Noah Beery, Malcolm
McGregor, Charles Stevens

The Vanishing Corporal *

France   1962   106m   bw
Films du Cyclope (J. W. Beyer)
original title: Le Caporal Epinglé

After several attempts, three Frenchmen succeed in
escaping from a detention camp.

Symbolic World War II drama told in mainly comic
terms. Not one of its director's great films, but a warm
and assured one.

w Jean Renoir, Guy Lefranc   d Jean Renoir
ph Georges Leclerc   m Joseph Kosma

Jean-Pierre Cassel, Claude Brasseur, Claude Rich, O.
E. Hasse

'A comedy which shades sometimes into farce and
once into tragedy . . . The mood, except in two or three
scenes, is deliberately light.' – Dilys Powell

The Vanishing Legion

US   1931   bw   serial: 12 eps
Mascot

A Western adventurer finds the reason for Indian
raids on Milesburg.

Modest Western serial.   d B. Reeves Eason

Harry Carey, Edwina Booth, Rex the wild horse,
Frankie Darro, William Desmond

Vanishing Point *

US   1971   107m   DeLuxe
TCF/ Cupid (Norman Spencer)
V*, L

An ex-racing driver who delivers cars for a living
becomes hepped up on benzedrine and leads police a
rare chase through the Nevada desert.

Strange, fashionable action suspenser which is better
to look at than to understand.

w Guillermo Cain   d Richard Sarafin   ph John A.
Alonzo   md Jimmy Brown

Barry Newman, Cleavon Little, Dean Jagger, Victoria
Medlin, Paul Koslo, Bob Donner

'Uncomfortably reminiscent of Easy Rider as an
odyssey through an unknown America in its
discovery of strange alliances and unpredictable
hostilities.' – Tom Milne

The Vanishing Shadow

US   1934   bw   serial: 12 eps
Universal

A man sworn to revenge uses an array of scientific
weapons against his father's enemies.

Absurd chapter play with many unintentional laughs,
especially at the gadgets.   d Louis Friedlander

Onslow Stevens, Ada Ince, Walter Miller, James
Durkin

The Vanishing Virginian

US   1941   97m   bw
MGM (Edwin H. Knopf)

A conservative Virginian finds that he harbours
suffragettes in his household.

Life with Father in another setting; rather yawn-
provoking.

w Jan Fortune   novel Rebecca Yancey Williams
d Frank Borzage   ph Charles Lawton Jnr   m David
Snell

Frank Morgan, Spring Byington, Kathryn Grayson,
Elizabeth Patterson, Louise Beavers

Vanity Fair

US   1932   78m   bw
Hoffman/Allied

The story of Becky Sharp is told in modern dress.

A poorly made independent venture which rapidly
dropped from sight.

w F. Hugh Herbert   *novel* W. M. Thackeray
d Chester M. Franklin

Myrna Loy, Conway Tearle, Barbara Kent, Walter Byron, Anthony Bushell

'Poor photography, tepid direction, poor dialogue.' – *Variety*

The Vanquished
US   1953   84m   Technicolor
Paramount/Pine-Thomas

After the Civil War, a returning Confederate officer finds corruption in his home town.

Uninspiring semi-Western.

w Winston Miller, Frank Moss, Lewis R. Foster *novel* Karl Brown   *d* Edward Ludwig

John Payne, Jan Sterling, Colleen Gray, Lyle Bettger, Willard Parker, Roy Gordon

Vargtimmen: see *The Hour of the Wolf*

Variety **
Germany   1925   104m (24 fps)   bw   silent
UFA
aka: *Vaudeville*

An ageing acrobat seduces a young girl and later kills another man who is interested in her.

Crude, vivid backstage story, inventively presented to overcome the dullness and tawdriness of the plot.

w E. A. Dupont, Leo Birinsky   *novel* Frederick Hollander   *d* E. A. Dupont   *ph* Karl Freund

Emil Jannings, Lya de Putti, Maly Delschaft, Warwick Ward

'A continually roving lens seizes the best angle for every detail, expression and scene.' – *Leon Moussinac*

'The enduring power of the movie is not in its far from original story but in the restless, subjective camera and the fast editing which make it an almost voluptuous experience.' – *Pauline Kael, 70s*

'It was my aim to show a single childish grown-up, devoted, lovable, and his reaction to betrayal and duplicity.' – *E. A. Dupont*

Variety Girl
US   1947   83m   bw
Paramount (Daniel Dare)

Of all the young hopefuls arriving in Hollywood, one girl becomes a star.

The slightest of excuses for a tour of the Paramount studios, with all the contract stars doing bits. It doesn't add up to much.

w Edmund Hartmann, Frank Tashlin, Monte Brice, Robert Welch   *d* George Marshall   *ph* Lionel Lindon, Stuart Thompson   *md* Joseph J. Lilley, Troy Saunders

Mary Hatcher, Olga San Juan, De Forrest Kelley, Glenn Tryon; and Bob Hope, Bing Crosby, Gary Cooper, Ray Milland, Alan Ladd, Barbara Stanwyck, Paulette Goddard, Dorothy Lamour, Veronica Lake, Sonny Tufts, Joan Caulfield, William Holden, Lizabeth Scott, Burt Lancaster, Gail Russell, Diana Lynn, Sterling Hayden, Robert Preston, William Bendix, Barry Fitzgerald, Billy de Wolfe, George Pal Puppetoons, Cecil B. de Mille, Mitchell Leisen, George Marshall, Spike Jones and his City Slickers, etc

Variety Jubilee
GB   1942   92m   bw
Butcher's

Two generations in the life of a music hall.

Naïve romance with fascinating appearances by some famous names of variety.

w Kathleen Butler   *d* Maclean Rogers

Lesley Brook, Ellis Irving, Reginald Purdell, George Robey, Charles Coburn, Ella Retford, Wilson Keppel and Betty, The Ganjou Brothers and Juanita, Slim Rhyder, Betty Warren as Florrie Forde; Marie Lloyd Jnr as Marie Lloyd; Tom Finglass as Eugene Stratton; John Rorke as Gus Elen

Variety Lights: see *Lights of Variety*

Varsity Show
US   1937   120m   bw
Warner (Louis F. Edelman)

Collegians stage a revue.

Mild musical.

w Warren Duff, Richard Macaulay, Jerry Wald, Sig Herzig   *d* William Keighley   *ph* Sol Polito, George Barnes   *ch* Busby Berkeley   *m/ly* Richard Whiting, Johnny Mercer

Dick Powell, Priscilla Lane, Rosemary Lane, Fred Waring and his Pennsylvanians, Buck and Bubbles, Johnny 'Scat' Davis, Ted Healy, Walter Catlett

'A rah-rah musical entertainment made to order for early autumn business when college boys start pegging out the pigskin.' – *Variety*

AAN: Busby Berkeley

Vaudeville: see *Variety*

'Everything that makes life worth leaving!'
Vault of Horror *
GB   1973   86m   Eastmancolor
Metromedia/Amicus (Milton Subotsky)
V, V*

Five men trapped in the basement of a skyscraper tell of their recurring dreams.

All-star horror omnibus, plainly but well staged.

w Milton Subotsky   *stories* William Gaines   *d* Roy Ward Baker   *ph* Denys Coop   *m* Douglas Gamley

Daniel Massey, Anna Massey, Terry-Thomas, Glynis Johns, Curt Jurgens, Dawn Addams, Michael Craig, Edward Judd, Tom Baker, Denholm Elliott

The Velvet Touch *
US   1948   97m   bw
RKO/Independent Artists (Frederick Brisson)
V*, L

A famous actress murders her producer and is struck by conscience but allows a detective to find his own way to the truth.

Solid murder melodrama with an excellent theatrical atmosphere.

w Leo Rosten   *d* John Gage   *ph* Joseph Walker   *m* Leigh Harline

Rosalind Russell, Leo Genn, Sidney Greenstreet, Claire Trevor, Leon Ames, Frank McHugh

'Child of the devil, she lives by a secret code!'
Vendetta
US   1950   84m   bw
RKO/Howard Hughes

The daughter of an esteemed Corsican family takes vengeance on her father's enemies.

Outmoded ethnic melodrama with nothing to recommend it.

w W. R. Burnett   *novel Columba* by Prosper Mérimée   *d* Mel Ferrer   *ph* Franz Planer, Al Gilks   *md* Constantin Bakaleinikoff   *m* Roy Webb

Faith Domergue, George Dolenz, Donald Buka, Hilary Brooke, Nigel Bruce, Joseph Calleia, Hugo Haas

Vendetta
Italy   1990   120m   Fujicolor
Reteitalia/Titanus (Ciro Ippolito)
V, V*

An Irish hit-man working for the Mafia falls in love with the daughter of a man he shot by mistake.

Interminable and predictable movie, with too little action to work as a thriller and too shallow and stereotypical to be a character study. It also requires the viewer to be sympathetic to the problems of hoodlums and murderers.

w Ennio de Concini, Stuart Margolin, Alan Di Fiore *novel Woman of Honor* by Svena Casati Modignani   *d* Stuart Margolin   *ph* Ennio Guarnieri   *m* Bruce Ruddel, Stuart Margolin, Riz Ortolani   *pd* Danilo Donati   *ed* Mario Morra

Eric Roberts, Carol Alt, Burt Young, Nick Mancuso, Thomas Calabro, Marcie Leeds, Serena Grandi, Billy Barty, Stuart Margolin, Eli Wallach

† There is also a version, made for TV, that lasts 200m.

La vendetta di Ursus: see *The Vengeance of Ursus*

The Venetian Affair
US   1966   92m   Metrocolor   Panavision
MGM/Jerry Thorpe

A reporter investigates the death in Venice of an American diplomat.

Uninteresting and complicated spy thriller with pleasant locations.

w E. Jack Neuman   *novel* Helen MacInnes   *d* Jerry Thorpe   *ph* Milton Krasner, Enzo Serafin   *m* Lalo Schifrin

Robert Vaughn, Karl Boehm, Elke Sommer, Ed Asner, Boris Karloff, Felicia Farr, Roger C. Carmel, Luciana Paluzzi, Joe de Santis

Venetian Bird *
GB   1952   95m   bw
Rank/British Film Makers (Betty E. Box)
US title: *The Assassin*

A private detective goes to Venice to reward a wartime partisan, who turns out to have become a notorious criminal.

Standard action fare with a nod to *The Third Man* but not much excitement or sense of place.

w Victor Canning   *novel* Victor Canning   *d* Ralph Thomas   *ph* Ernest Steward   *m* Nino Rota

Richard Todd, Eva Bartok, John Gregson, George Coulouris, Margot Grahame, Walter Rilla, Sidney James

Vengeance
GB/Germany   1962   83m   bw
CCC/Raymond Stross
aka: *The Brain*

After a fatal accident, the brain of a tycoon is kept alive and persuades a doctor to find his murderer.

Twisty remake of *Donovan's Brain* (qv), not too badly done.

w Robert Stewart, Philip Mackie   *d* Freddie Francis   *ph* Bob Hulke   *m* Ken Jones

Anne Heywood, Peter Van Eyck, Cecil Parker, Bernard Lee, Maxine Audley, Jeremy Spenser, Miles Malleson

Vengeance (dubbed) *
Italy/West Germany   1968   100m   Eastmancolor   Cromoscope
MGM-EMI/Super International/Top (Renato Savino)
V
original title: *Joko, Invoca Dio ... e Muori*

An outlaw takes revenge on the five men who tortured and killed his friend after a bungled bullion robbery.

A bravura and baroque, if violent, spaghetti Western, in which style triumphs over substance.

w Renato Savino, Antonio Margheriti   *d* Anthony Dawson (Antonio Margheriti)   *ph* Riccardo Pallottini   *m* Carlo Savina   *ed* Otello Colangeli

Richard Harrison, Claudio Camaso, Werner Pochat, Paolo Gozlino

'An immensely enjoyable mix of Gothic horror, thriller and Western motifs, the deaths in particular are unusually imaginative.' – *Sight and Sound*

The British release was cut to 81m.

The Vengeance of Fu Manchu
GB   1967   92m   Eastmancolor
Anglo Amalgamated/Harry Alan Towers

The Yellow Peril plans a crime syndicate to counter Interpol, and creates a double for Nayland Smith . . .

Limp addition to a series which started well, but was subsequently robbed of period flavour.

w Harry Alan Towers   *novel* Sax Rohmer
d Jeremy Summers   *ph* John von Kotze
m Malcolm Lockyer

Christopher Lee, Douglas Wilmer, Tony Ferrer, Tsai Chin, Howard Marion Crawford, Wolfgang Kieling

The Vengeance of She
GB   1968   101m   Technicolor
Warner-Pathé/Hammer (Aida Young)

A girl is possessed by the spirit of long-dead Queen Ayesha.

Grotesquely unpersuasive reincarnation melodrama, a long long way from its inspiration.

w Peter O'Donnell   *d* Cliff Owen   *ph* Wolfgang Suschitsky   *m* Mario Nascimbene   *pd* Lionel Couch   *ed* Raymond Poulton

John Richardson, Olinka Berova, Edward Judd, Colin Blakely, Derek Godfrey, Noel Willman, André Morell, Jill Melford

The Vengeance of Ursus (dubbed)
Italy   1962   90m   Eastmancolor   Techniscope
Jonia/Splendor
original title: *La vendetta di Ursus*; aka: *The Mighty Warrior*

Ursus overthrows a tyrant who plans to marry the princess he loves.

Standard Italian muscleman stuff, following a familiar narrative and with little to distinguish it from similar movies featuring Hercules and Maciste.

w Marcello Ciorciolini, Nino Scolaro, Roberto Gianviti (English dialogue: John Hart)   *d* Luigi Capuano (English-language version *d* Richard McNamara)   *ph* Oberdan Troiani   *m* Carlo Innocenzi   *ad* Alfredo Montiori   *ed* Antonietta Zita

Samson Burke, Wandisa Guida, Livio Lorenzon, Nadine Sanders, Nerio Bernardi, Gianni Rizzo, Franco Fantasia, Roberto Chevalier, Gina Rovere

Vengeance Valley
US   1951   82m   Technicolor
MGM (Nicholas Nayfack)
V*

A Western rancher keeps his foster-brother's misdeeds from their father.

Well-made character Western, a little short on action.

w Irving Ravetch   *novel* Luke Short   *d* Richard Thorpe   *ph* George Folsey   *m* Rudolph G. Kopp

Burt Lancaster, Robert Walker, Ray Collins, Joanne Dru, Sally Forrest, John Ireland, Carleton Carpenter, Ted de Corsia

Venom
GB   1981   92m   Technicolor
Aribage/Morison (Martin Bregman)
V*

A kidnap plan goes awry when a deadly snake is let loose in a besieged house.

Hoary melodrama which veers between dullness, artificial suspense and unpleasant detail.

w Robert Carrington   *novel* Alan Scholefield
d Piers Haggard   *ph* Gilbert Taylor   *m* Michael Kamen

Sterling Hayden, Klaus Kinski, Oliver Reed, Sarah Miles, Cornelia Sharpe, Nicol Williamson, Susan George

'Woefully archaic in its British B-picture reliance on very cheap thrills, and without any self-parodic saving grace.' – *Time Out*

Venus in Furs (dubbed)
Italy   1970   81m   colour
VIP/Roxy
V

While on holiday, a writer falls in love with, and marries, a woman staying in the next room, believing that she can satisfy his masochistic and voyeuristic sexual fantasies.

Trite, poorly dubbed would-be erotic thriller, updating the original to the swinging 60s and transforming the unreadable into the unwatchable.

w Fabio Massimo   *novel* Leopold Sacher-Masoch
d Massimo Dallamano   *ph* Sergio D'Offizi   *m* Gian Franco Reverberi   *ad* Alida Cappellini

Laura Antonelli, Régis Vallée, Ewing Loren, Renate Kasche

Venus Peter **
GB   1989   94m   Fujicolor
Recorded Releasing/BFI/Channel 4/British Screen (Christopher Young)

A young boy grows up in a Scottish fishing village in the 1950s.

Nostalgic and enjoyable account of a community on the point of disintegration.

w Ian Sellar, Christopher Rush   *book A Twelve-month and a Day* by Christopher Rush   *d* Ian Sellar   *ph* Gabriel Beristain   *m* Jonathan Dove   *pd* Andy Harris   *ed* David Spiers

Ray McAnally, David Hayman, Sinead Cusack, Gordon R. Strachan, Sam Hayman, Caroline Paterson, Alex McAvoy

Vera Cruz **
US   1953   94m   Technicolor   Superscope
UA/Hecht-Lancaster (James Hill)
V*, L

Adventurers in 1860 Mexico become involved in a plot against Emperor Maximilian.

Terse, lively Western melodrama with unusual locations and comedy and suspense touches. Great outdoor entertainment.

w Roland Kibbee, James R. Webb, Borden Chase   *d* Robert Aldrich   *ph* Ernest Laszlo   *m* Hugo Friedhofer

Gary Cooper, Burt Lancaster, Denise Darcel, Cesar Romero, George Macready, Sarita Montiel, Ernest Borgnine, Morris Ankrum, Charles Bronson

'A Mad Generation Spawned In Lust . . . Consumed By Hate. Where Everything Decent Is . . .'
Verboten! *
US   1959   93m   bw
Columbia/Globe (Samuel Fuller)
V, V*, L

In Germany at the end of the Second World War, an American soldier marries a German girl and faces trouble from people of both nationalities and a secret Nazi organization.

An effective mix of thriller and romance which gives some sense of the messy aftermath and confusions of war.

wd Samuel Fuller   *ph* Joseph Biroc   *m* Harry Sukman, Wagner, Beethoven   *ad* John Mansbridge   *ed* Philip Cahn

James Best, Susan Cummings, Tom Pittman, Paul Dubov, Harold Daye, Dick Kallman, Stuart Randall

The Verdict *
US   1946   86m   bw
Warner (William Jacobs)

A retired Scotland Yard inspector continues to work on a case which vexes him.

Victorian murder mystery with very unconvincing Hollywood sets and curious casting, but rather nicely detailed.

w Peter Milne   *novel The Big Bow Mystery* by Israel Zangwill   *d* Don Siegel   *ph* Ernest Haller   *m* Frederick Hollander

Sidney Greenstreet, Peter Lorre, Joan Lorring, George Coulouris, Rosalind Ivan, Paul Cavanagh, Arthur Shields

Verdict *
France/Italy   1974   97m   Eastmancolor
Concordia/CCC (Carlo Ponti)

A gangster's widow kidnaps the judge who is trying her son for rape and murder.

Tortuous but watchable melodrama with star performances and the director's usual eagerness to exploit legal morality.

w Andre Cayatte, Henri Coupon   *novel* Henri Coupon   *d* Andre Cayatte   *ph* Jean Badal   *m* Louiguy

Sophia Loren, Jean Gabin, Henri Garcin, Julien Bertheau

'Not exciting enough to qualify as a thriller nor penetrating enough to make you support Gallic penal reform.' – *Michael Billington, Illustrated London News*

'Frank Galvin has one last chance to do something right'
The Verdict *
US   1982   128m   Technicolor
TCF/Zanuck-Brown (Richard D. Zanuck, David Brown)
V, V*, L

An ageing and failed attorney is unexpectedly handed a case of medical malpractice and successfully sues a hospital.

Complex and interesting but rather sombrely handled exposé of legal and medical ethics.

w David Mamet   *novel* Barry Reed   *d* Sidney Lumet   *ph* Andrzej Bartkowiak   *m* Johnny Mandel   *pd* Edward Pisoni

Paul Newman, James Mason, Charlotte Rampling, Jack Warden, Milo O'Shea, Lindsay Crouse, Edward Binns, Wesley Addy

AAN: best picture; Paul Newman; James Mason; Sidney Lumet; screenplay (adaptation)

Vérités et Mensonges: see *F for Fake*

Veronika Voss **
West Germany   1982   104m   bw
Maura/Tango/Rialto/Trio/Maran (Thomas Schühly)
V*

In the fifties, a distraught star of the previous decade flees from her own image, but finds that her psychiatrist is her own worst enemy.

Fascinatingly convoluted puzzle play with enough to say for a year of late-night discussions; but the bleached-out black and white photography is an unnecessary strain.

w Peter Märthesheimer, Pea Fröhlich, Rainer Werner Fassbinder   *d* Rainer Werner Fassbinder   *ph* Xaver Schwarzenberger   *m* Peer Raben

Rosel Zech, Hilmar Thate, Annemarie Düringer, Doris Schade, Cornelia Froboess

'A dazzling parable of all cinema, of the penalties of living out one another's fantasies.' – *Sight and Sound*

Vertigo ****

US   1958   128m   Technicolor   Vistavision
Paramount (Alfred Hitchcock)
V, V*, L, S

A detective with a fear of heights is drawn into a complex plot in which a girl he loves apparently falls to her death. Then he meets her double . . .

Double identity thriller which has many sequences in Hitchcock's best style. A film as unsettling as the phobia it deals with, keeping its audience dizzy and off balance throughout.

w Alec Coppel, Samuel Taylor   novel D'entre les Morts by Pierre Boileau, Thomas Narcejac   d Alfred Hitchcock ph Robert Burks   m Bernard Herrmann   ad Hal Pereira, Henry Bumstead

James Stewart, Kim Novak, Barbara Bel Geddes, Tom Helmore, Henry Jones

AAN: art direction

'No woman should see this film without a man!'

The Very Edge

GB   1962   89m   bw   Cinevision
British Lion/Garrick/Raymond Stross
V*

An obsessive young man menaces a mother-to-be.

Rather unpleasant suspenser, adequately presented.

w E. J. Howard   d Cyril Frankel   ph Bob Huke m David Lee

Anne Heywood, Richard Todd, Jack Hedley, Jeremy Brett, Nicole Maurey, Barbara Mullen, Maurice Denham, William Lucas

Very Important Person **

GB   1961   98m   bw
Rank/Independent Artists (Julian Wintle, Leslie Parkyn)
US title: A Coming-Out Party

A senior British scientist is caught by the Nazis and has to be rescued.

Very satisfactory British comedy with a few suspense scenes; POW fare with a difference.

w Jack Davies   d Ken Annakin   ph Ernest Steward m Reg Owen

James Robertson Justice, Stanley Baxter, Leslie Phillips, Eric Sykes, Richard Wattis, Colin Gordon

A Very Private Affair: see Vie Privée

A Very Special Favor *

US   1965   105m   Technicolor
Universal/Lankershim (Robert Arthur)

A Frenchman with a spinster daughter asks an American lawyer to 'initiate' her.

Tasteless, smirking comedy with several funny scenes, glossily photographed in the lap of luxury and interesting in its early use of homosexuality as a comedy subject.

w Nate Monaster, Stanley Shapiro   d Michael Gordon   ph Leo Tover   m Vic Mizzy

Rock Hudson, Charles Boyer, Leslie Caron, Nita Talbot, Dick Shawn, Walter Slezak, Larry Storch

The Very Thought of You

US   1944   99m   bw
Warner (Jerry Wald)

Problems of a wartime marriage.

Tepid romantic potboiler.

w Alvah Bessie, Delmer Daves   d Delmer Daves ph Bert Glennon   m Franz Waxman

Dennis Morgan, Eleanor Parker, Dane Clark, Faye Emerson, Beulah Bondi, Henry Travers, William Prince, Andrea King

A Very Young Lady

US   1941   80m   bw
TCF (Robert T. Kane)

A tomboy develops a crush on her headmaster.

Remake of Girls' Dormitory, used as a vehicle for an ageing child star. Predictable comedy, neatly made.

w Ladislas Fodor, Elaine Ryan   play Ladislas Fodor d Harold Schuster

Jane Withers, John Sutton, Nancy Kelly, Janet Beecher, Cecil Kellaway

Vesnicko Ma Strediskova: see My Sweet Little Village

Vesolye Rebyata: see Jazz Comedy

Vessel of Wrath **

GB   1938   93m   bw
Mayflower (Erich Pommer)
US title: The Beachcomber

In the Dutch East Indies, the missionary's spinster sister falls for a drunken beachcomber.

First-rate character comedy, remade as The Beachcomber (qv).

w Bartlett Cormack, B. Van Thal   story W. Somerset Maugham   d Erich Pommer   ph Jules Kruger m Richard Addinsell

Charles Laughton, Elsa Lanchester, Robert Newton, Tyrone Guthrie, Dolly Mollinger, Eliot Makeham

'The moment this film starts you recognize the master touch.' – Variety

Viaggio in Italia: see Voyage to Italy

El Viaje: see The Voyage

Vibes

US   1988   99m   DeLuxe
Imagine (Deborah Blum, Tony Ganz)
V*

A psychic couple go to Ecuador to find a lost city of gold.

Dim comedy that had no future at the box-office.

w Lowell Ganz, Babaloo Mandell   d Ken Kwapis ph John Bailey   m James Horner   pd Richard Sawyer   ed Carol Littleton

Cindi Lauper, Jeff Goldblum, Julian Sands, Peter Falk, Karen Akers, Michael Lerner, Ramon Bieri, Elizabeth Pena

The Vicar of Bray

GB   1937   68m   bw
JH Productions

The ex-tutor of Charles I persuades him to pardon a traitor.

Mild historical fable with song; in its way quite refreshing.

w H. Fowler Mear   d Henry Edwards

Stanley Holloway, Hugh Miller, Margaret Vyner, Felix Aylmer, Esmond Knight, Garry Marsh

The Vice Squad *

US   1931   78m   bw
Paramount

Stool pigeons account for many arrests of supposed prostitutes.

Rather draggy exposé of police methods, allegedly torn from the headlines.

w Oliver H. P. Garrett   d John Cromwell

Kay Francis, Paul Lukas, Judith Wood, William B. Davidson, Rockcliffe Fellowes, Esther Howard

'Should draw adult attention in the large cities.' – Variety

Vice Squad

US   1953   88m   bw
UA/Jules Levy, Arthur Gardner
GB title: The Girl in Room 17

A police captain tracks down two bank robbers who have killed a cop.

A day in the life of a police captain, quite watchable but scarcely engrossing.

w Lawrence Roman   novel Harness Bull by Leslie T. White   d Arnold Laven   ph Joseph C. Biroc m Herschel Burke Gilbert

Edward G. Robinson, Paulette Goddard, K. T. Stevens, Porter Hall, Adam Williams, Edward Binns, Lee Van Cleef

Vice Versa *

GB   1947   111m   bw
Rank/Two Cities (Peter Ustinov, George H. Brown)

A magic stone enables an unhappy Victorian boy to change places with his pompous father.

Funny moments can't disguise the fact that this overlong comedy is a bit of a fizzle, its talented creator not being a film-maker. A pity, as British films have so rarely entered the realms of fancy.

wd Peter Ustinov   novel F. Anstey

Roger Livesey, Kay Walsh, Anthony Newley, James Robertson Justice, David Hutcheson, Petula Clark, Joan Young

'A repository of English oddities.' – John Russell Taylor

Vice Versa

US   1988   98m   colour
Columbia (Dick Clement, Ian La Frenais)
V, V*, L

A father and his 11-year-old son find their minds transplanted into the other's body by a magic skull.

One of the last and certainly the least of the mid-1980s cycle of role swapping movies.

w Dick Clement, Ian La Frenais   d Brian Gilbert ph King Baggott   m David Shire   pd Jim Schoppe ed David Garfield

Judge Reinhold, Fred Savage, Corinne Bohrer, Swoosie Kurtz, David Profal, Jane Kaczmerek, Gloria Gifford

The Vicious Circle

US   1948   77m   bw
United Artist (W. Lee Wilder)
GB title: The Woman in Brown

Five Jewish farmers in Hungary are framed for murder.

Well-meaning but tedious and very static melodrama.

w Heinz Herald, Guy Endore   play The Burning Bush by Herald and Geza Herczeg   d W. Lee Wilder

Conrad Nagel, Fritz Kortner, Reinhold Schunzel, Philip Van Zandt, Edwin Maxwell, Lyle Talbot

The Vicious Circle *

GB   1957   84m   bw
Romulus (Peter Rogers)
US title: The Circle

An actress is found dead in Dr Latimer's flat and the weapon turns up in the boot of his car . . .

Entertaining whodunnit from a TV serial.

w Francis Durbridge,   serial The Brass Candlestick by Francis Durbridge   d Gerald Thomas   ph Otto Heller   m Stanley Black

John Mills, Derek Farr, Noelle Middleton, Roland Culver, Wilfrid Hyde-White, Mervyn Johns, René Ray, Lionel Jeffries, Lisa Daniely

Vicki *

US   1953   85m   bw
TCF (Leonard Goldstein)

A girl model is murdered, and her sister proves that her boyfriend is innocent, despite the efforts of a brutal detective.

Very competent if uninspired remake of *I Wake Up Screaming* (qv).

w Dwight Taylor   *d* Harry Horner   *ph* Milton Krasner   *m* Leigh Harline

Jeanne Crain, Jean Peters, Richard Boone, Elliott Reid, Casey Adams, Alex D'Arcy, Carl Betz, Aaron Spelling

'Fear is the oxygen of blackmail. If Barrett was paying, others are. Find me one!'

Victim ***
GB   1961   100m   bw
Rank/Allied Filmmakers/Parkway (Michael Relph)
V*

A barrister with homosexual inclinations tracks down a blackmailer despite the risk to his own reputation.

A plea for a change in the law is very smartly wrapped up as a murder mystery which allows all aspects to be aired, and the London locations are vivid.

w Janet Green, John McCormick   *d* Basil Dearden   *ph* Otto Heller   *m* Philip Green

Dirk Bogarde, Sylvia Syms, John Barrie, Norman Bird, Peter McEnery, Anthony Nicholls, Dennis Price, *Charles Lloyd Pack*, Derren Nesbitt, John Cairney, Hilton Edwards, Peter Copley, Donald Churchill, Nigel Stock

'Ingenious, moralistic, and moderately amusing.' – *Pauline Kael, 70s*

La Victoire en Chantant: see *Black and White in Colour*

Victor/Victoria *
GB   1982   134m   Technicolor   Panavision
MGM/Peerford/Ladbroke Entertainments/Blake Edwards
V, V*, L

In 1934 Paris, a girl singer becomes successful when she poses as a female impersonator, but it causes complications in her love life.

The story was previously filmed more innocuously as a Jessie Matthews vehicle, *First a Girl*; Edwards makes it a sexually harping, grotesque low comedy, but there are pleasurable moments.

wd Blake Edwards, from the German film of 1933 *Viktor und Viktoria* (*wd* Reinhold Schunzel)   *ph* Dick Bush   *m* Henry Mancini   *pd* Rodger Maus

Julie Andrews, James Garner, *Robert Preston*, Lesley Anne Warren, Alex Karras, John Rhys-Davies, Graham Stark

'An audience pleaser in the worst sense.' – *New Yorker*

'Edwards' idea of European sophistication and Gallic naughtiness is seen throughout to be depressingly crude, parochial and second-hand, based on old American farces and reprises of his own Clouseau routines.' – *Sunday Times*

AA: original song score (Henry Mancini, Leslie Bricusse)

AAN: Julie Andrews; Robert Preston; Lesley Ann Warren; screenplay (adaptation); costume design; art direction

Victoria the Great ***
GB   1937   112m   bw (Technicolor sequence)
British Lion/Imperator/Herbert Wilcox
V

Episodes in the life of Queen Victoria.

A decent film with all the British virtues, and a milestone in the cinema of its time. Script and performances are excellent; production sometimes falters a little.

w Robert Vansittart, Miles Malleson,   play *Victoria Regina* by Laurence Housman   *d* Herbert Wilcox   *ph* F. A. Young, William V. Skall   *m* Anthony Collins

Anna Neagle, Anton Walbrook, H. B. Warner, Walter Rilla, Mary Morris, C. V. France, Charles Carson, Felix Aylmer, Derrick de Marney

'The effect of the final colour reel is to make the picture look like something enamelled on pottery and labelled "A Present from Blackpool".' – *James Agate*

'The six most exciting women in the world – in the most expensive entertainment you have ever seen!'

The Victors *
GB   1963   175m   bw   Panavision
Columbia/Open Road (Carl Foreman)

World War II adventures of an American infantry platoon.

Patchy compendium with moral too heavily stressed but plenty of impressive scenes and performances along the way. The mixture of realism and irony, though, doesn't really mix.

w Carl Foreman   *novel* The Human Kind by Alexander Baron & Carl Foreman   *ph* Christopher Challis   *m* Sol Kaplan

George Peppard, George Hamilton, Albert Finney, Melina Mercouri, Eli Wallach, Vince Edwards, Rosanna Schiaffino, James Mitchum, *Jeanne Moreau*, Elke Sommer, Senta Berger, Peter Fonda, Michael Callan

'Doggerel epic.' – *John Coleman*

'War has revealed Mr Foreman as a pompous bore.' – *John Simon*

'Having made a point through an image it continually feels the need to state it all over again by way of dialogue.' – *Penelope Houston*

Victory *
US   1940   77m   bw
Paramount (Anthony Veiller)

A Dutch East Indies recluse rescues a girl and is menaced by three villains who think he is wealthy.

Curious, ineffective but occasionally compelling attempt to translate the untranslatable to the screen.

w John L. Balderston   *novel* Joseph Conrad   *d* John Cromwell   *ph* Leo Tover   *m* Frederick Hollander

Fredric March, Betty Field, *Cedric Hardwicke*, Sig Rumann, Margaret Wycherly, Jerome Cowan, Fritz Feld, Rafaela Ottiano

'There is achieved a combination of amateur theatricals and earnest emptiness of motive and motion that will throw a blanket of reminiscent affection around this solemn, unusual and exotic buffoonery.' – *Otis Ferguson*

'A mood of impending doom and horror more than makes up for its slow and deliberate action . . . a fine and penetrating motion picture melodrama.' – *New York World Telegram*

'This is an unusual film at almost every level, yet it's unusual and disturbing, too.' – *Pauline Kael, 70s*

'Not a film of flamboyant hues . . . but it has quality, weight, and above all, compelling drama.' – *Philadelphia Record*

† The story was previously filmed in 1919 by Maurice Tourneur (with Jack Holt) and in 1930 by William Wellman (with Richard Arlen).

Victory
US   1981   117m   Metrocolor   Panavision
Lorimar/Victory Company/Tom Stern (Freddie Fields)
V*
alternative and GB release title: *Escape to Victory*

A German POW camp in 1943 houses many international football stars. A Nazi officer sees propaganda in a game against a German side, but the allies make it an opportunity for escape.

Flabby and unconvincing POW story with agreeably old-fashioned values sacrificed to trendy casting and a silly ending.

w Evan Jones, Yabo Yablonsky   *d* John Huston   *ph* Gerry Fisher   *m* Bill Conti   *pd* J. Dennis Washington

Sylvester Stallone, Michael Caine, Pele, Bobby Moore, Max von Sydow, George Mikell, Daniel Massey

'Even readers of the Boy's Own Paper might have blenched . . . ludicrous beyond belief.' – *Tom Milne, MFB*

Victory through Air Power **
US   1943   65m   Technicolor
Walt Disney

The history of aviation and the theories of Major Alexander de Seversky.

What was thought by many to be propaganda was in fact a demonstration of Disney's own fascination with the theories of a controversial figure. The cartoon segments are put together with the studio's accustomed brilliance.

w various   *d* H. C. Potter (live action), various   *m* Edward H. Plumb, Paul J. Smith, Oliver G. Wallace

AAN: Edward H. Plumb, Paul J. Smith, Oliver G. Wallace

Videodrome
Canada   1982   89m   colour
Filmplan International
V, V*

A videodrome TV channel induces pornographic hallucinations in the viewer.

Dangerous when it is not risible, this thoroughly tawdry concept is made worse by being slickly done.

wd David Cronenberg

James Woods, Sonja Smits, Deborah Harry, Peter Dvorsky

'Almost as incoherent as it is speculative.' – *Sight and Sound*

La Vie à l'Envers: see *Life Upside Down*

La Vie Devant Soi: see *Madame Rosa*

La Vie Est un Long Fleuve Tranquille
France   1988   91m   colour
Electric/Contemporary/Téléma/MK2/FR3 (Charles Gassot)
V, V*
GB title: *Life is a Long Quiet River*

Wealthy and respectable parents discover that their child was switched at its birth twelve years before with the baby of a poor and feckless family.

Glossy comedy at the expense of class, demonstrating that environment is more important than breeding in creating character.

w Florence Quentin, Etienne Chatiliez   *d* Etienne Chatiliez   *ph* Pascal Lebegue   *m* Gérard Kawczynski   *pd* Geoffroy Larcher   *ed* Chantal Delattre

Benoît Magimel, Valerie Lalande, Tara Romer, Jérôme Floc'h, Sylvie Cubertafon, Emmanuel Cendrier

La Vie Est Un Roman: see *Life Is a Bed of Roses*

La Vie et Rien D'Autre: see *Life and Nothing But*

Vie Privée *
France   1961   103m   Eastmancolor
Progefi/Cipra/CCM (Christine Gouze-Rénal)
V*
aka: *A Very Private Affair*

A promiscuous movie star who retreats from fame to

her home town of Geneva falls again for the theatre director who was her first love.

An unsatisfactory movie given to melodrama, but interesting for its insights into the universe of an actress much like Bardot herself in her strong-willed refusal to conform.

w Jean-Paul Rappeneau, Louis Malle, Jean Ferry *d* Louis Malle *ph* Henri Decaë *m* Fiorenzo Carpi *ad* Bernard Evein *ed* Kenout Peltier

Brigitte Bardot, Marcello Mastroianni, Eleonore Hirt, Grégoire von Rezzori, Dirk Sanders

The production was troubled, with Bardot and Mastroianni, who played lovers, not hiding their dislike for one another. A dubbed version was cut to 94m by MGM for its American release, despite Malle's protests.

La vieille qui marchait dans la mer: see *The Old Lady Who Walked in the Sea*

De Vierde Man: see *The Fourth Man*

The View from Pompey's Head *
US   1955   97m   Eastmancolor   Cinemascope
TCF (Philip Dunne)
GB title: *Secret Interlude*

A New York lawyer returns on a case to the small town of his youth, and falls in love again with his old sweetheart.

Routine Marquand-type novelette, long on atmosphere and short on plot.

wd Philip Dunne   *novel* Hamilton Basso   *ph* Joe MacDonald   *m* Elmer Bernstein

Richard Egan, Dana Wynter, Cameron Mitchell, *Sidney Blackmer, Marjorie Rambeau*

A View from the Bridge
France   1961   117m   bw
Transcontinental (Paul Graetz)
original title: *Vu du Pont*

A longshoreman on the New York waterfront has passionate feelings for his wife's niece, and these erupt when she announces her engagement.

Solemn, self-examining melodrama, poorly adapted from the stage.

w Norman Rosten   *play* Arthur Miller   *d* Sidney Lumet   *ph* Michel Kelber   *m* Maurice Leroux

Raf Vallone, Maureen Stapleton, Carol Lawrence, Jean Sorel, Raymond Péllégrin, Morris Carnovsky, Harvey Lembeck, Vincent Gardenia

† The film was shot in several languages.

A View to a Kill
GB   1985   121m   Metrocolor   Panavision
MGM-UA/Albert R. Broccoli
V, V*, L, S

James Bond tangles with a ruthless international industrialist.

A tedious Bond adventure in which even the expensive highlights are unmemorable.

w Richard Maibaum, Michael G. Wilson   *d* John Glen   *ph* Alan Hume   *m* John Barry   *pd* Peter Lamont   *ed* Peter Davies

Roger Moore, Christopher Walken, Grace Jones, Tanya Roberts, Patrick MacNee, David Yip, Fiona Fullerton

Vigil *
New Zealand   1984   90m   Eastmancolor
First Blood/Last Rites/John Maynard
V, V*

On a remote farm, a teenage girl learns about life after her father is killed.

Austere but vaguely impressive drama; one is pleased however when it ends.

w Vincent Ward, Graeme Tetley   *d* Vincent Ward

Bill Kerr, Fiona Kay, Gordon Shields, Penelope Stewart, Frank Whitten

Vigil in the Night
US   1940   96m   bw
RKO (George Stevens)

Two nurses are attracted to the same doctor; one dies during an epidemic.

Dull, downbeat romantic melodrama with a miscast lead.

w Fred Guiol, P. J. Wolfson, Rowland Leigh *novel* A. J. Cronin   *d* George Stevens   *ph* Robert de Grasse   *m* Alfred Newman

Carole Lombard, Anne Shirley, Brian Aherne, Julien Mitchell, Robert Coote, Peter Cushing, Ethel Griffies

The Vigilante
US   1947   bw   serial: 15 eps
Columbia

A government undercover agent calls himself The Vigilante in his bid to protect a priceless string of pearls.

The usual cliffhangers are spliced into an artless plot.
d Wallace Fox

Ralph Byrd, Ransay Ames, Lyle Talbot, Hugh Prosser

Vigilante Force
US   1976   89m   DeLuxe
United Artists/Corman Company (Gene Corman)

A Vietnam veteran goes too far in using his wartime skills to crush lawlessness in a small town.

Standard action movie, full of mindless mayhem.

wd George Armitage   *ph* William Cronjager *m* Gerald Fried   *ad* Jack Fisk   *ed* Morton Tubor

Kris Kristofferson, Jan-Michael Vincent, Victoria Principal, Bernadette Peters, Brad Dexter, Judson Pratt

'Sharp, bright, and not averse to exploitation bandwagons.' – *Tom Milne, MFB*

The Vigilantes are Coming
US   1936   bw   serial: 12 eps
Republic

In 1940 a wealthy California settler makes himself dictator, but is dislodged by a masked man called The Eagle.

No credit given to *The Mark of Zorro*, but that's what it is.

d Mack V. Wright and Ray Taylor

Bob Livingston, Kay Hughes, William Farnum, Guinn 'Big Boy' Williams, Raymond Hatton

The Viking Queen
GB   1967   91m   Technicolor
Warner/Hammer (John Temple-Smith)

During the first century AD, the queen of the Iceni tries to keep peace with the occupying Romans but has trouble with hot-headed Druids.

Stuff and nonsense from the Dark Ages; light should not have been shed upon it.

w Clarke Reynolds   *story* John Temple-Smith *d* Don Chaffey   *ph* Stephen Dade   *m* Gary Hughes *pd* George Provis   *ed* James Needs, Peter Boita

Don Murray, Carita, Donald Houston, Andrew Keir, Patrick Troughton, Adrienne Corri, Niall MacGinnis, Wilfrid Lawson, Nicola Pagett

'Mightiest Of Men … Mightiest Of Spectacles … Mightiest Of Motion Pictures!'
The Vikings ***
US   1958   116m   Technirama
UA/KD Productions (Jerry Bresler)
V*, S

Two Viking half-brothers quarrel over the throne of Northumbria.

Slightly unpleasant and brutal but extremely well-staged and good-looking epic in which you can almost feel the harsh climate. Fine colour, strong performances, natural settings, vivid action, and all production values as they should be.

w Calder Willingham   *novel The Viking* by Edison Marshall   *d* Richard Fleischer   *ph* Jack Cardiff *m* Mario Nascimbene   *sp* credit titles United Productions of America

narrator Orson Welles, *Kirk Douglas, Tony Curtis*, Ernest Borgnine, Janet Leigh, Alexander Knox, Frank Thring, James Donald, Maxine Audley, Eileen Way

Villa Rides!
US   1968   125m   Technicolor   Panavision
Paramount (Ted Richmond)

1912 Mexico: an American pilot who has been gun-running for the rebels is pressed into more active service.

Bang-bang actioner which pauses too often for reflection and local colour.

w Robert Towne, Sam Peckinpah   *d* Buzz Kulik *ph* Jack Hildyard   *m* Maurice Jarre   *ad* Ted Howarth

Yul Brynner, Robert Mitchum, Charles Bronson, Grazia Bucetta, Herbert Lom, Alexander Knox, Fernando Rey, Jill Ireland

Village of Daughters
GB   1961   86m   bw
MGM (George H. Brown)

An unemployed commercial traveller in an Italian village finds himself choosing a bride for a successful émigré.

Voluble, gesticulating minor comedy.

w David Pursall, Jack Seddon   *d* George Pollock *ph* Geoffrey Faithfull   *m* Ron Goodwin

Eric Sykes, Warren Mitchell, Scilla Gabel, Carol White, Grégoire Aslan, John Le Mesurier

Village of the Damned **
GB   1960   78m   bw
MGM (Ronald Kinnoch)
V*, L

Children born simultaneously in an English village prove to be super-intelligent and deadly beings from another planet.

Modestly made but absorbing and logical science fiction, cleanly presented.

w Stirling Silliphant, Wolf Rilla, Geoffrey Barclay *novel The Midwich Cuckoos* by *John Wyndham   d* Wolf Rilla   *ph* Geoffrey Faithfull   *m* Ron Goodwin

George Sanders, Barbara Shelley, Michael Gwynn, Martin Stephens, Laurence Naismith

† Sequel: *Children of the Damned* (qv).

A Village Tale *
US   1935   79m   bw
RKO (David Hempstead)

Envy leads to a clash between two rural landowners.

Unusual but very interesting attempt by Hollywood to film with integrity an old-fashioned country novel. Very dated, but pleasant to watch.

w Allan Scott   *novel* Phil Strong   *d* John Cromwell *ph* Nicholas Musuraca   *m* Alberto Columbo

Randolph Scott, Robert Barrat, Kay Johnson, Arthur Hohl, Janet Beecher, Edward Ellis, Donald Meek, Dorothy Burgess, Andy Clyde, Guinn Williams

'Depressing story without marquee strength. Restricted in appeal.' – *Variety*

Villain

GB 1971 98m Technicolor Panavision
EMI/Kastner/Ladd/Kanter

The come-uppance of a cowardly, sadistic,
homosexual East End gang boss with a mother
fixation.

Very unpleasant and unentertaining British low life
shocker, plainly inspired by *White Heat*.

w Dick Clement, Ian La Frenais   novel *The Burden of
Proof* by James Barlow   d Michael Tuchner
ph Christopher Challis   m Jonathan Hodge

Richard Burton, Ian MacShane, Nigel Davenport, Joss
Ackland, Cathleen Nesbitt, Donald Sinden, T. P.
McKenna, Fiona Lewis

The Villain

US 1979 89m Metrocolor
Columbia/Rastar (Paul Maslansky, Mort Engelberg)
V*
GB title: *Cactus Jack*

An incompetent outlaw rides from one disaster to
another.

No doubt amusing in conception, this attempt to put
the cartoon character Wile E. Coyote into human form
lamentably misfires, six minutes being an ideal length
for that kind of comedy.

w Robert G. Kane   d Hal Needham   ph Bobby
Byrne   m Bill Justis

Kirk Douglas, Arnold Schwarzenegger, Ann-Margret,
Paul Lynde, Ruth Buzzi, Jack Elam, Strother Martin

'Timing is entirely absent from this limp, laughless
fiasco, as is any evidence of imagination . . .
desperation is the keynote.' – Paul Taylor, MFB

The Villain Still Pursued Her *

US 1940 66m bw
RKO (Harold B. Franklin)
V*

An innocent family suffers at the hands of a villainous
landlord.

Clumsy burlesque of old time melodrama, interesting
that it was done at all and with this cast.

w Elbert Franklin   d Edward Cline   ph Lucien
Ballard   m Frank Tours

Buster Keaton, Alan Mowbray, Anita Louise, Hugh
Herbert, Joyce Compton, Margaret Hamilton, Billy
Gilbert

Vincent and Theo *

France/GB 1990 140m colour
Blue Dolphin/Belbo Films/Central Films (Ludi Boeken, David
Conroy, Emma Hayter)
V, V*, L
original title: *Vincent et Theo*

Biopic of Van Gogh and his supportive, but equally
tortured, brother.

Interesting, unsensational account of the brothers'
lives, though not particularly illuminating.

w Julian Mitchell   d Robert Altman   ph Jean
Lepine   m Gabriel Yared   pd Stephen Altman
ed Françoise Coispeau, Geraldine Peroni

Tim Roth, Paul Rhys, Johanna Ter Steege, Wladimir
Yordanoff, Jip Wijngaarden, Anne Canovas

Vincent: The Life and Death of Vincent van Gogh **

Australia 1987 99m colour
Illumination/Look/Daska (Tony Llewellyn-Jones)
V*

The life and suicide of the artist is recalled in his
letters to his brother Theo.

Intriguing documentary, beautifully filmed and much
helped by the passion and urgency of John Hurt's
readings.

d Paul Cox
voice of John Hurt

The Vintage

US 1957 92m Metrocolor Cinemascope
MGM (Edwin H. Knopf)

Two fugitives from justice cause trouble when they
become grape pickers.

Steamy drama with an unconvincing French setting; a
Hollywood aberration.

w Michael Blankfort   novel *Ursula Keir*   d Jeffrey
Hayden   ph Joseph Ruttenberg   m David Raksin

Mel Ferrer, John Kerr, Michèle Morgan, Pier Angeli,
Theodore Bikel, Leif Erickson

Vintage Wine

GB 1935 90m bw
Gaumont-British/Real Art (Julius Hagen)

A 62-year-old widower upsets his family by marrying
a young girl.

Amiable boulevard comedy transferred to the screen
in a stagey fashion but providing a vehicle for the
well-honed comic skills of Seymour Hicks.

w H. Fowler Mear, Seymour Hicks, Ashley Dukes
play *Der Ewige Jüngling* by Alexander Engel   d Henry
Edwards   ph Sydney Blyth   md W. L. Trytel
ad James A. Carter   ed Ralph Kemplen

Seymour Hicks, Claire Luce, Eva Moore, Judy Gunn,
Miles Malleson, Kynaston Reeves, A. Bromley
Davenport, Michael Shepley

Violence

US 1947 72m bw
Monogram

War veterans fall victim to a group spreading civil
discord.

Propaganda thick ear.

w Stanley Rubin, Louis Lantz   d Jack Bernhard

Nancy Coleman, Michael O'Shea, Sheldon Leonard,
Peter Whitney, Emory Parnell

Violent City

Italy/France 1970 100m Technicolor
Techniscope
Rank/Fono Roma/Unidis/Universal France (Harry Colombo,
George Papi)
original title: *Città Violenta*; aka: *The Family*

Released from prison, a hitman goes after the man
who betrayed him and stole his girlfriend.

Fast-moving, body-strewn melodrama that rarely
strays from the obvious.

wd Sauro Scavolini, Gianfranco Calligarich, Lina
Wertmüller, Sergio Sollima   story Dino Maiuri,
Massimo de Rita   d Sergio Sollima   ph Aldo Tonti
m Ennio Morricone   ad Francesco Bronzi   ed Nino
Baragli

Charles Bronson, Jill Ireland, Michael Constantin,
Telly Savalas, Umberto Orsini, George Savalas

The film was cut to 91m for its British release.

Violent Cop *

Japan 1989 103m colour
ICA/Bandai/Shochiku-Fuji (Hisao Nabeshima, Takio Yoshida,
Shozo Ichoyama)
original title: *Sono Otoko Kyobo ni Tsuki*; aka: *Warning,
This Man Is Wild*

A maverick homicide cop, while teaching his new
partner the tricks of the trade, discovers that his
crooked colleagues are involved in drug dealing.

A violent story of revenge and casual brutality, which
resembles *Dirty Harry* translated to Tokyo.

w Hisashi Nozawa   d Takeshi Kitano   ph Yasushi
Sakakibara   m Daisaku, Kume, Eric Satie
ad Masuteru Mochizuki   ed Nobutake Kamiya

'Beat' Takeshi (Takeshi Kitano), Maiko Kawakami,
Makoto Ashigawa, Haku Ryu, Ken Yoshizawa, Shiro
Sano, Ittoku Kishibe, Shigeru Hiraizumi

'Slow tempo and arty look suits it for film festival
dates.' – *Variety*

The Violent Enemy

GB 1968 98m Eastmancolor
Trio/Group W. (Wilfrid Eades)

An IRA explosives expert escapes from a British jail
but quarrels with his leaders.

Dullish political melodrama needlessly rubbing salt
in old wounds.

w Edmund Ward   novel *A Candle for the Dead* by
Hugh Marlowe   d Don Sharp   ph Alan Hume
m John Scott

Tom Bell, Ed Begley, Susan Hampshire, Noel Purcell,
Michael Standing

The Violent Hour: see *Dial 1119*

The Violent Men *

US 1955 96m Technicolor Cinemascope
Columbia (Lewis J. Rachmil)
L
GB title: *Rough Company*

A crippled cattle baron drives small landowners from
his valley, while his wife has an affair with his
younger brother.

So much snarling goes on that this seems like a
gangster film in fancy dress, but it does hold the
attention.

w Harry Kleiner   novel Donald Hamilton
d Rudolph Maté   ph Burnett Guffey, W. Howard
Greene   m Max Steiner

Edward G. Robinson, Barbara Stanwyck, Glenn Ford,
Brian Keith, Dianne Foster, May Wynn, Warner
Anderson, Basil Ruysdael

The Violent Ones *

US 1967 90m Eastmancolor
Madison/Harold Goldman
V*

In a small Mexican town, three American hobos are
interrogated after the rape and murder of a local girl.

Rather well-shot murder mystery with emphasis on
character, leading to a desert chase climax.

w Doug Wilson, Charles Davis   d Fernando Lamas
ph Fleet Southcott   m Martin Skiles

Fernando Lamas, Aldo Ray, David Carradine, Tommy
Sands

Violent Playground

GB 1958 108m bw
Rank (Michael Relph)

A junior liaison officer in the Liverpool slums falls in
love with the sister of a fire-raiser.

'Realistic' melodrama sabotaged by an entirely
schematic and predictable plot; enervatingly dull
until the siege climax.

w James Kennaway   d Basil Dearden   ph Reg
Wyer   m Philip Green

Stanley Baker, Anne Heywood, David McCallum,
Peter Cushing, John Slater, Clifford Evans

'The bank robbers that caught a town with its morals
down!'

Violent Saturday *

US 1955 90m DeLuxe Cinemascope
TCF (Buddy Adler)

Crooks move quietly into a small town with the
intention of robbing the bank.

Interesting little melodrama which the wide screen
robs of its proper tension. Adequate presentation and
performance.

w Sidney Boehm   d Richard Fleischer   ph Charles G. Clarke   m Hugo Friedhofer

Richard Egan, Victor Mature, Stephen McNally, Sylvia Sidney, Virginia Leith, Tommy Noonan, Lee Marvin, Margaret Hayes, J. Carrol Naish, Ernest Borgnine

Violent Streets: see *The Thief*

Violette Nozière *
France/Canada   1977   122m   Eastmancolor
Filmel/Cinevideo (Roger Morand)
V*

In 1933 Paris, an eighteen-year-old girl leads a double life, gets syphilis, poisons her parents and is convicted of murder.

Oddly erratic but interesting recapitulation of a famous French murder case, not quite typical of its director.

w Odile Barski, Herve Bromberger, Frederic Grendel   d Claude Chabrol   ph Jean Rabier   m Pierre Jansen   pd Jacques Brizzio

Isabelle Huppert, Jean Carmier, Stephane Audran, Bernadette Lafont

The VIPs **
GB   1963   119m   Metrocolor   Panavision
MGM (Anatole de Grunwald)
V*

Passengers at London Airport are delayed by fog and spend the night at a hotel.

Multi-story compendium cunningly designed to exploit the real-life Burton-Taylor romance. In itself, competent rather than stimulating.

w Terence Rattigan   d Anthony Asquith   ph Jack Hildyard   m Miklos Rozsa

Richard Burton, Elizabeth Taylor, Maggie Smith, Rod Taylor, *Margaret Rutherford*, Louis Jourdan, Elsa Martinelli, Orson Welles, Linda Christian, Dennis Price, Richard Wattis, David Frost, Robert Coote, Joan Benham, Michael Hordern, Lance Percival, Martin Miller

'If Mr Rattigan's Aunt Edna still goes to the pictures she should like his latest offering, especially if she has a good lunch first.' – *Brenda Davies*

AA: Margaret Rutherford

The Virgin and the Gypsy *
GB   1970   95m   colour
Kenwood/Dimitri de Grunwald (Kenneth Harper)
V*

A Midlands clergyman's daughter falls in love with a gypsy fortune teller.

Slow, sensitive, stylish picturization of a Lawrence novella, with generally good performances.

w Alan Plater   story D. H. Lawrence   d Christopher Miles   ph Robert Huke   m Patrick Gowers   pd Terence Knight

Joanna Shimkus, Franco Nero, Honor Blackman, Mark Burns, Maurice Denham, Fay Compton, Kay Walsh, Norman Bird

'A minor but lively pleasure.' – *John Simon*

Virgin Island
GB   1958   94m   Eastmancolor
British Lion/Countryman (Leon Clore, Graham Tharp)
US title: *Our Virgin Island*

A young couple set up house on a tiny Caribbean island.

Pleasant comedy slowed down by lack of plot and too much conversation.

w Philip Rush, Pat Jackson   book *Our Virgin Island* by Robb White   d Pat Jackson   ph Freddie Francis   m Clifton Parker

Virginia Maskell, John Cassavetes, Sidney Poitier, Isabel Dean, Colin Gordon

'Twentieth Century Fox spectacularly spreads before you the violent age and velvet cape of Sir Walter Raleigh!'
The Virgin Queen *
US   1955   92m   DeLuxe   Cinemascope
TCF (Charles Brackett)
V

The relationship of Queen Elizabeth I and Sir Walter Raleigh.

Unhistorical charade, quite pleasantly made and worth noting for its star performance.

w Harry Brown, Mindret Lord   d Henry Koster   ph Charles G. Clarke   m Franz Waxman

Bette Davis, Richard Todd, Joan Collins, Herbert Marshall, Jay Robinson, Dan O'Herlihy, Robert Douglas, Romney Brent

'Sooner or later they're going to get it!'
The Virgin Soldiers **
GB   1969   96m   Technicolor
Columbia/Carl Foreman (Leslie Gilliat, Ned Sherrin)
V, V*

Serio-comic adventures of recruits in the British army in 1960 Singapore.

Autobiographical fragments, mostly from below the belt, sharply observed and often very funny.

w John Hopkins   novel Leslie Thomas   d John Dexter   ph Ken Higgins   m Peter Greenwell

Hywel Bennett, Nigel Patrick, *Lynn Redgrave*, Nigel Davenport, *Rachel Kempson*, Michael Gwynn, Tsai Chin

'A kind of monstrous mating of *Private's Progress* and *The Family Way*, with bits of *The Long and the Short and the Tall* thrown in for good measure.' – *David Pirie*

† Sequel 1977: *Stand Up Virgin Soldiers*.

The Virgin Spring *
Sweden   1959   87m   bw
Svensk Filmindustri (Allan Ekelund)
original title: *Jungfrukällan*

When her murderers are killed, a spring bubbles up from the spot where a young maiden met her death.

Stark and rather lovely filming of a medieval legend, with heavy symbolism and a strong pictorial sense.

w Ulla Isaakson   d Ingmar Bergman   ph Sven Nykvist   m Erik Nordgren

Max von Sydow, Brigitta Valberg, Gunnel Lindblom, Brigitta Pettersson

'When I first saw the film I thought it merely nauseous. At a second view I find it generally tedious, occasionally absurd, and always retrograde.' – *Dilys Powell*

AA: best foreign film

Virgin Witch
GB   1971   89m   colour
Univista (Ralph Solomons)
V

Two sisters run away to London and become involved with the lesbian head of a modelling agency who persuades them to take part in satanic rituals.

Cheaply and ineptly shot horror movie, with script and acting to match, in which the cast shed their clothes at the slightest opportunity.

w Klaus Vogel   d Ray Austin   ph Gerald Moss   m Ted Dicks   ed Philip Barnikel

Patricia Haines, Neil Hallett, Keith Buckley, James Chase, Vicki Michelle, Ann Michelle

Virginia
US   1940   107m   Technicolor
Paramount (Edward H. Griffith)

A showgirl goes home to claim her inheritance, but thinks of marrying a rich Yankee.

Languid post-Civil War romantic melodrama, only memorable for its colour.

w Virginia Van Upp   d Edward H. Griffith   ph Bert Glennon, William V. Skall

Madeleine Carroll, Fred MacMurray, Sterling Hayden, Helen Broderick, Paul Hurst, Marie Wilson, Carolyn Lee, Louise Beavers

Virginia City *
US   1940   121m   bw
Warner (Robert Fellows)
V*

A dance hall girl is really a Southern spy helping a rebel colonel to steal a gold shipment from her Yankee boyfriend.

Lumpy Western in Warner's best budget but worst manner: the stars look unhappy and the plot progresses in fits and starts.

w Robert Buckner   d Michael Curtiz   ph Sol Polito   m Max Steiner

Errol Flynn, Randolph Scott, Miriam Hopkins, Humphrey Bogart, Frank McHugh, Alan Hale, Guinn Williams, John Litel, Moroni Olsen, Russell Hicks, Douglass Dumbrille

The Virginia Judge
US   1935   70m   bw
Paramount (Charles R. Rogers)

A Southern judge's ne'er-do-well son gets deeper into trouble.

Homely vehicle for a star whose 'judge' was for many years the centre of a vaudeville monologue.

w Henry Johnson, Frank Adams, Inez Lopez   d Edward Sedgwick

Walter C. Kelly, Marsha Hunt, Stepin Fetchit, Johnny Downs, Robert Cummings

The Virginian *
US   1929   95m   bw
Paramount (Louis D. Lighton)
V*

A stalwart ranch foreman has to see his best friend hanged for rustling, and defeats the local bad man.

Standard Western with famous clichés, e.g. 'Smile when you say that . . .'

w Edward E. Paramore Jnr, Howard Estabrook   novel Owen Wister   d Victor Fleming   ph J. Roy Hunt

Gary Cooper, Walter Huston, Richard Arlen, Mary Brian, Chester Conklin, Eugene Pallette

The Virginian
US   1946   90m   Technicolor
Paramount (Paul Jones)

Forgettable remake of the above.

w Frances Goodrich, Albert Hackett   d Stuart Gilmore   ph Harry Hallenberger   m Daniele Amfitheatrof

Joel McCrea, Brian Donlevy, Sonny Tufts, Barbara Britton, William Frawley, Henry O'Neill, Fay Bainter

Virgins and Vampires: see *Requiem for a Vampire*

Viridiana ****
Spain/Mexico   1961   91m   bw
Uninci/Films 59/Gustavo Alatriste (Munoz Suay)
V*

A novice about to take her vows is corrupted by her wicked uncle and installs a load of beggars in his house.

Often hilarious surrealist melodrama packed with shades of meaning, most of them sacrilegious. A fascinating film to watch.

w Luis Buñuel, Julio Alajandro   d Luis Buñuel   ph José F. Agayo

Silvia Pinal, Francisco Rabal, Fernando Rey

'One of the cinema's few major philosophical works.'
– *Robert Vas*

'An extraordinary film, a superb film.' – *Dilys Powell*

Virtue
US 1932 68m bw
Columbia

A woman of the streets is regenerated through marriage.

Routine matinée programmer.

w Robert Riskin *story* Ethel Hill *d* Eddie Buzzell

Carole Lombard, Pat O'Brien, Mayo Methot, Jack La Rue, Ward Bond

'A lot of plot is squeezed into the running time . . . the picture will be liked.' – *Variety*

The Virtuous Bigamist: see *Four Steps in the Clouds*

The Virtuous Sin
US 1930 81m bw
Paramount
GB title: *Cast Iron*

A girl tries to help her student husband when war takes him away from bacteriology.

Stilted romantic drama.

w Martin Brown, Louise Long *novel* Lajos Zilahy
d George Cukor, Louis Gasnier *ph* David Abel

Walter Huston, Kay Francis, Kenneth MacKenna, Paul Cavanagh

'Average programme flicker . . . cast names all from legit . . . nor is there much excuse for the picture running 80 minutes when 70 would have been better.' – *Variety*

Visions of Light ***
US/Japan 1992 92m bw/colour
City Screen/American Film Institute/NHK (Stuart Samuels)

Documentary tracing the development of cinematography from *The Birth of a Nation* in 1915 through to the present day.

An engrossing look at the contribution to film of the often unsung cinematographers, with excerpts from 125 feature films and interviews with 27 practitioners, from Nestor Almendros to Vilmos Zsigmond.

w Todd McCarthy *d* Arnold Glassman, Todd McCarthy, Stuart Samuels *ph* Nancy Schreiber *ed* Arnold Glassman

Todd McCarthy (interviewer)

The Visit
West Germany/France/Italy/US 1964 100m bw
Cinemascope
TCF/Deutschefox/Cinecittà/Dear Film/Films du Siècle/PECF (Julien Derode, Anthony Quinn)

A millionairess offers a fortune to her home town, providing someone will kill her ex-lover.

A realistic production ill befits an essentially theatrical play, and all the effort goes for nothing.

w Ben Barzman *play* Friedrich Durrenmatt
d Bernhard Wicki *ph* Armando Nannuzzi
m Hans-Martin Majewski

Ingrid Bergman, Anthony Quinn, Paolo Stoppa, Hans-Christian Blech, Valentina Cortesa, Irina Demick, Claude Dauphin, Eduardo Ciannelli

Visit to a Chief's Son
US 1974 92m DeLuxe Panavision
UA/Robert Halmi

An American anthropologist and his son hope to film the rituals of an African tribe.

Minor adventure film with a happy resolution, based on a photomontage by the producer, a *Life* photographer.

w Albert Ruben *d* Lamont Johnson *ph* Ernest Day
m Francis Lai

Robert Mulligan, Johnny Sekka, John Philip Hodgdon

Visit to a Small Planet
US 1960 101m bw
Paramount/Wallis-Hazen
V*

A young man from outer space takes a look at Earth and falls in love.

A satirical play disastrously adapted for the moronic comedy of an unsuitable star.

w Edmund Beloin, Henry Garson *play* Gore Vidal
d Norman Taurog *ph* Loyal Griggs *m* Leigh Harline

Jerry Lewis, Joan Blackman, Earl Holliman, Fred Clark, John Williams, Jerome Cowan, Gavin Gordon, Lee Patrick

AAN: *ad* Hal Pereira, Walter Tyler

'They Weren't Born Yesterday!'
Les Visiteurs *
France 1993 107m colour
Arrow/Gaumont/France 3/Alpilles/Amigo (Alain Terzian)
S

A knight and his servant are transported from the 12th century to the modern day.

Broad farce that will appeal to lovers of *Carry On* films.

w Christian Claiver, Jean-Marie Poiré *d* Jean-Marie Poiré *ph* Jean-Yves Le Mener *m* Eric Lévi *pd* Hugues Tissandier *ed* Catherine Kelber

Christian Clavier, Jean Reno, Valérie Lemercier, Marie-Anne Chazel, Christian Bujeau, Isabelle Nanty, Didier Pain

'The French tradition doesn't always recognise the distinction between high and low comedy, and there is certainly a boisterousness about the proceedings which some viewers will find wearing.' – *Adam Mars-Jones*

'People fall over a lot, or hit each other, or shout very loud.' – *Sight and Sound*

The film was the biggest box-office success of 1993 in France, taking twice as much at the box-office as the No. 2 film, *Jurassic Park*.

Les Visiteurs du Soir *
France 1942 110m bw
André Paulvé
aka: *The Devil's Envoys*

The devil sends messengers to Earth to corrupt two lovers, but he fails: even though he turns them to stone, their hearts still beat.

Made during the Occupation, this stately medieval fable was intended to be significant: the devil was Hitler, and the heartbeat that of France. Perhaps because it is so conscious of hidden meanings, it moves rather stiffly but is often beautiful to behold.

w Jacques Prévert, Pierre Laroche *d* Marcel Carné
ph Roger Hubert *m* Joseph Kosma, Maurice Thiriet
ad Alexandre Trauner, Georges Wakhevitch

Arletty, *Jules Berry*, Marie Déa, Alain Cuny, Fernand Ledoux, Marcel Herrand

'There are wonderful images, but the movie is heavy on the allegorical and becomes rather slow and stylized.' – *Pauline Kael, 70s*

Visiting Hours
Canada 1981 105m colour Panavision
Filmplan International (Claude Héroux)
V*

A homicidal maniac is at large in a hospital.

Tedious shocker wasting a reliable idea.

w Brian Taggert *d* Jean Claude Lord *ph* René Verzier *m* Jonathan Goldsmith

Michael Ironside, Lee Grant, Linda Purl, William Shatner, Lenore Zann, Harvey Atkin

The Visitor
Italy 1979 90m colour
Ovidio Assonitis
V*

Creatures from another world come to Earth to deal with a child who is the offspring of an evil mutant alien.

Fussy direction, minimal acting and a plot that makes little sense combine to create an incoherent movie.

w Lou Comici, Robert Mundy *story* Michael J. Paradise, Ovidio Assonitis *d* Michael J. Paradise (Giulio Paradisi) *ph* Ennio Guarnieri *m* Franco Micalizzi *ad* Frank Vanorio *ed* Robert Curi

Mel Ferrer, Glenn Ford, Lance Henriksen, John Huston, Joanne Nail, Sam Peckinpah, Shelley Winters, Paige Conner

Viskingar och Rop: see *Cries and Whispers*

Visszaesök: see *Forbidden Relations*

I Vitelloni
Italy/France 1953 109m bw
Peg/Cité (Lorenzo Pegoraro)
aka: *Spivs*

In a small Italian resort, aimless young people get into various kinds of trouble.

Interesting in its realistic detail, this sharply observed slice of life is long enough for its basic purposelessness to become apparent.

w Federico Fellini, Ennio Flaiano, Tullio Pinelli
d Federico Fellini *ph* Otello Martelli, Tasatti, Carlini *m* Nino Rota

Franco Fabrizi, Franco Interlenghi, Eleonora Ruffo, Alberto Sordi

AAN: script

Viva Knievel
US 1977 104m Technicolor Panavision
Warner
V*

Evel Knievel becomes involved with drug smugglers.

Abysmal attempt to turn a stuntman into an actor; a most ramshackle vehicle.

w Antonio Santillan, Norman Katkov *d* Gordon Douglas

Evel Knievel, Gene Kelly, Lauren Hutton, Leslie Nielsen, Red Buttons, Cameron Mitchell, Marjoe Gortner

'A paste-and-scissors B picture of quite breathtaking inanity.' – *Financial Times*

Viva Las Vegas! (1956): see *Meet Me in Las Vegas*

Viva Las Vegas
US 1964 85m Metrocolor Panavision
MGM (Jack Cummins, George Sidney)
V*, L, S
GB title: *Love in Las Vegas*

A sports car racer has fun in the gambling city.

Tolerable star musical.

w Sally Benson *d* George Sidney *ph* Joseph Biroc *md* George Stoll

Elvis Presley, Ann-Margret, Cesare Danova, William Demarest, Nicky Blair, Jack Carter

Viva Maria!

France/Italy 1965 120m Eastmancolor
Panavision
Nouvelles Editions/Artistes Associés/Vides (Oscar Dancigers,
Louis Malle)

An Irish anarchist girl arrives in Central America and
joins a group of strolling players.

All show and no substance, this is a colour
supplement of a film, neither fish, flesh nor good red
herring.

w Louis Malle, Jean-Claude Carrière d Louis Malle
ph Henri Decaë m Georges Delerue ad Bernard
Evein

Jeanne Moreau, Brigitte Bardot, George Hamilton,
Paulette Dubost, Claudio Brook

Viva Max

US 1969 93m Eastmancolor
Commonwealth United/Mark Carliner
V*

A Mexican general marches his troops into Texas and
seizes the Alamo.

Flat comedy with mildly amusing passages but too
much noise, bluster and sentiment.

w Elliott Baker novel James Lehrer d Jerry Paris
ph Jack Richards m Hugo Montenegro

Peter Ustinov, John Astin, Pamela Tiffin, Jonathan
Winters, Keenan Wynn, Henry Morgan, Alice
Ghostley

'1001 nights of glorious romantic adventure!'
Viva Villa **

US 1934 110m bw
MGM (David O. Selznick)
V*, L

The career of a Mexican rebel.

Gutsy action drama with some smoothing over of fact
in the name of entertainment. A big, highly competent
production of its year.

w Ben Hecht d Jack Conway ph James Wong Howe,
Charles G. Clarke m Herbert Stothart

Wallace Beery, Fay Wray, Leo Carrillo, Donald Cook,
Stuart Erwin, George E. Stone, Joseph Schildkraut,
Henry B. Walthall, Katherine de Mille

'Glorified western . . . strong b.o. fodder, handicapped
a bit perhaps by its abnormal masculine appeal.' –
Variety

'A strange poem of violence.' – John Baxter, 1968

'A glorified horse opera . . . the spectator's excitement
is incited by the purely physical impact of the furious
riding and war sequences, by the frequent sadism,
and by the lively musical score.' – Irving Lerner

AAN: best picture; script

Viva Zapata **

US 1952 113m bw
TCF (Darryl F. Zanuck)
V, V*, L

A Mexican revolutionary is finally betrayed by a
friend.

Moody, good-looking star vehicle taking a
romanticized but glum view of history.

w John Steinbeck d Elia Kazan ph Joe MacDonald
md Alfred Newman m Alex North ad Lyle
Wheeler, Leland Fuller

Marlon Brando, Jean Peters, Joseph Wiseman,
Anthony Quinn, Arnold Moss, Margo, Frank Silvera

AA: Anthony Quinn

AAN: John Steinbeck; Alex North; Marlon Brando;
art direction

Vivacious Lady *

US 1938 90m bw
RKO (George Stevens)
V*

A night-club singer marries a botany professor and
has trouble with his parents.

Pleasant romantic comedy for two popular stars.

w P. J. Wolfson, Ernest Pagano d George Stevens
ph Robert de Grasse m Roy Webb

Ginger Rogers, James Stewart, Charles Coburn, Beulah
Bondi, James Ellison, Frances Mercer, Franklin
Pangborn, Grady Sutton, Jack Carson

'A good-natured, unpretentiously entertaining
comedy.' – New Yorker

AAN: Robert de Grasse

Vivement Dimanche!: see Finally, Sunday

Vivre pour Vivre: see Live for Life

Vixen

US 1968 71m Eastmancolor
Cinecenta/Eve/Coldstream (Russ Meyer)

A nymphomaniac seduces every passing stranger of
either sex.

Comic exploitation film in which the cast, at least,
appear to be enjoying themselves.

w Robert Rudelson story Russ Meyer, Anthony
James Ryan d Russ Meyer ph Russ Meyer
ad Wilfred Kues ed Russ Meyer, Richard Brummer

Erica Gavin, Harrison Page, Garth Pillsbury, Michael
Donovan O'Donnell, Vincene Wallace

The film was cut to 47m for its British release.

Vogues of 1938 *

US 1937 108m Technicolor
Walter Wanger
reissue title: All This and Glamour Too

Rival fashion houses compete at the Seven Arts Ball.

A fashion show with threads of plot, interesting for
clothes and cast, all working hard.

w Bella and Samuel Spewack d Irving Cummings
ph Ray Rennahan md Boris Morros ch Seymour
Felix m Victor Young ad Alexander Toluboff

Joan Bennett, Walter Baxter, Helen Vinson, Mischa
Auer, Alan Mowbray, Jerome Cowan, Alma Kruger,
Marjorie Gateson, Penny Singleton, Hedda Hopper

AAN: song 'That Old Feeling' (m Sammy Fain, ly
Lew Brown); Alexander Toluboff

The Voice in the Mirror

US 1958 102m bw Cinemascope
Universal-International

A reformed alcoholic thinks back on his past life.

Glum case history of no particular point or
persuasiveness.

w Larry Marcus d Harry Keller

Richard Egan, Julie London, Walter Matthau, Arthur
O'Connell, Troy Donahue, Mae Clarke, Ann Doran

A Voice in the Night: see Freedom Radio

A Voice in the Wind

US 1944 85m bw
UA/Arthur Ripley

Two refugees from the Nazis meet again and die on a
remote island.

Pretentious romantic claptrap, fascinating only for a
few of the impressionist effects it contrives on the
lowest of budgets.

w Frederick Torberg d Arthur Ripley m Michel
Michelet

Francis Lederer, Sigrid Gurie, J. Carrol Naish

Like a mid-thirties French melodrama drenched in the
Rembrandt-and-molasses manner of German films of
the early to middle twenties. Even within those terms
it is much less good than it might be, solemn,
unimaginative, thinly detailed; but it is also richly
nostalgic if you have any feeling for bad period art.' –
James Agee

AAN: Michel Michelet

The Voice of Bugle Ann *

US 1936 70m bw
MGM (John Considine Jnr)

When a dog is killed its embittered owner seeks
revenge.

Old-fashioned country tale, rather heavy-going but
emotionally strong.

w Harvey Gates, Samuel Hoffenstein
novel Mackinlay Kantor d Richard Thorpe
ph Ernest Haller

Lionel Barrymore, Maureen O'Sullivan, Eric Linden,
Dudley Digges, Spring Byington, Charley Grapewin

'A very fine movie indeed.' – Pare Lorentz

The Voice of Merrill

GB 1952 84m bw
Tempean (Robert Baker, Monty Berman)
US title: Murder Will Out

Three men are suspected of murder but one becomes a
potential victim.

Complicated murder thriller which intrigues but
hardly satisfies.

wd John Gilling ph Monty Berman m Frank
Cordell

Valerie Hobson, James Robertson Justice, Edward
Underdown, Henry Kendall, Garry Marsh, Sam Kydd

The Voice of the Turtle **

US 1948 103m bw
Warner (Charles Hoffman)
aka: One for the Book

A girl shares her apartment with a soldier on leave.

A three-character play is smoothly filmed, slightly
broadened, and burnished till its pale wit glows
nicely.

w John Van Druten play John Van Druten d Irving
Rapper ph Sol Polito m Max Steiner

Eleanor Parker, Ronald Reagan, Eve Arden, Wayne
Morris, Kent Smith

'A light and lovely comedy.' – People

Voices

GB 1973 91m Technicolor
Hemdale/Warden (Robert Enders)
V*

A young couple in an old country house are haunted
by the voice of their dead son.

Twisty little ghost story which would have been more
effective at one third of its length.

w George Kirgo, Robert Enders play Richard Lortz
d Kevin Billington ph Geoffrey Unsworth
m Richard Rodney Bennett

Gayle Hunnicutt, David Hemmings

La Voie Lactée: see The Milky Way

Volcano: see Les Rendezvous du Diable

Volere Volare *

Italy 1991 92m colour
Metro/Italtoons (Ernesto di Sarro, Mario Cecchi Gori, Vittorio
Cecchi Gori)
V, V*, L

A sound engineer who dubs animated films finds
himself changing into a cartoon character as he
becomes involved with a psycho-sexual prostitute.

Witty and inventive comedy that mixes live action and animation to amusing effect. *wd* Maurizio Nichetti, Guido Manuli *ph* Mario Battistoni *ad* Maria Pio Angelini *ed* Rita Rossi

Maurizio Nichetti, Angela Finocchiaro, Mariella Valentina, Patrizio Roversi

'An offbeat fable for adults. Pic's expensive technical bravura is more impressive than the comedy.' – *Variety*

Voltaire *
US 1933 72m bw
Warner (Ray Griffith)

The life and times of the 18th-century French wit.

One of the better Arliss charades, because the film is as stagey as his performance.

w Paul Green, Maude T. Howell *novel* George Gibbs, E. Laurence Dudley *d* John Adolfi *ph* Tony Gaudio

George Arliss, Doris Kenyon, Margaret Lindsay, Reginald Owen, Alan Mowbray, David Torrence, Douglass Dumbrille, Theodore Newton

'Sumptuously staged and photographed . . . sufficiently modern story to get interest.' – *Variety*

Volunteers
US 1985 106m Metrocolor
EMI/HBO/Tri-Star/Silver Screen (Richard Shepherd, Walter F. Parkes)

High jinks in the 1962 Peace Corps.

Tawdry comedy about the exploits of a young Home Guard.

w Ken Levine, David Isaacs *story* Keith Critchlow *d* Nicholas Meyer *ph* Ric Waite *m* James Horner *pd* James Schoppe, Delia Castaneda *ed* Ronald Roose, Steven Polivka

Tom Hanks, John Candy, Rita Wilson, Tim Thomerson

Von Richthofen and Brown
US 1971 97m DeLuxe
UA/Roger Corman (Gene Corman)
GB title: *The Red Baron*

During World War I, a Canadian pilot takes on Germany's air ace.

The airplanes are nice, but the film is grounded by plot and dialogue.

w John and Joyce Corrington *d* Roger Corman *ph* Michael Reed *m* Hugo Friedhofer

John Phillip Law, Don Stroud, Barry Primus, Karen Huston, Corin Redgrave, Hurd Hatfield

Von Ryan's Express **
US 1965 117m DeLuxe Cinemascope
TCF (Saul David)
V, V*

In an Italian POW camp during World War II, an unpopular American captain leads English prisoners in a train escape.

Exhilarating action thriller with slow spots atoned for by nail-biting finale, though the downbeat curtain mars the general effect.

w Wendell Mayes, Joseph Landon *novel* Davis Westheimer *d* Mark Robson *ph* William H. Daniels, Harold Lipstein *m* Jerry Goldsmith

Frank Sinatra, Trevor Howard, Sergio Fantoni, Edward Mulhare, Brad Dexter, John Leyton, Wolfgang Preiss, James Brolin, Adolfo Celi, Rafaela Cara

Voodoo Man
US 1944 62m bw
Monogram (Sam Katzman)

A mad scientist kidnaps young girls and reduces them to zombies.

Hopeless chiller wasting three stars.

w Robert Charles *d* William Beaudine

Bela Lugosi, John Carradine, George Zucco, Michael Ames, Wanda McKay

Voodoo Woman
US 1956 77m bw
AIP/Carmel (Alex Gordon)

A domineering woman and her weak boyfriend go in search of treasure in the jungle, where a mad scientist in a silly hat has created an indestructible beastlike woman with the aid of voodoo rituals.

Ridiculous horror, with clichéd dialogue and situations; the monster looks like Mighty Joe Young in drag.

w Russell Bender, V. I. Voss *d* Edward L. Cahn *ph* Frederick E. West *m* Darrell Calker *ad* Don Ament *sp* Harry Thomas *ed* Ronald Sinclair

Marla English, Tom Conway, Touch Connors, Lance Fuller, Mary Ellen Kaye

> Wife: 'You're insane.'
> Husband: 'Never say that! Never say that to me again!'

The Voyage **
Argentina/France 1991 150m colour
Metro/Cinesur/Du Sud (Fernando E. Solanas)

An isolated and unhappy student sets out on a long journey to find his father, a comic-book artist last heard of in Buenos Aires.

An acerbic, always engaging trip through South American consciousness, part fantasy but never far from being real, as an innocent gains experience of the world.

wd Fernando E. Solanas *ph* Felix Monti *m* Egberto Gismonti, Astor Piazzolla, Fernando E. Solanas *pd* Fernando E. Solanas *ed* Alberto Borello, Jacqueline Meppiel, Jacques Gaillard

Walter Quiroz, Soledad Alfaro, Ricardo Bartis, Cristina Becerra, Marc Berman, Chiquinho Brandao, Franklin Caicedo

'A smooth mixture of stunningly beautiful camerawork and bitter two-fingers-to-them-all political satire.' – *Marcus Trower, Empire*

Solanas survived an attempt to assassinate him during his post-production work on the film.

Voyage of the Damned *
GB 1976 155m Eastmancolor
ITC/Associated General (Robert Fryer)
V*

In 1939, a ship leaves Hamburg for Cuba with Jewish refugees; but Cuba won't take them.

High-minded, expensive, but poorly devised rehash of *Ship of Fools*, with too many stars in cameos and not enough central plot.

w Steve Shagan, David Butler *book* Gordon Thomas, Max Morgan-Witts *d* Stuart Rosenberg *ph* Billy Williams *m* Lalo Schifrin

Faye Dunaway, Max von Sydow, Oskar Werner, Malcolm McDowell, James Mason, Orson Welles, Katharine Ross, Ben Gazzara, Lee Grant, Sam Wanamaker, Julie Harris, Helmut Griem, Luther Adler, Wendy Hiller, Nehemiah Persoff, Maria Schell, Fernando Rey, Donald Houston, José Ferrer, Denholm Elliott, Janet Suzman

'Not a single moment carries any conviction.' – *New Yorker*

'The movie stays surprisingly distanced and impersonal, like a panning shot that moves too quickly for all the details to register.' – *Charles Champlin, Los Angeles Times*

'With a story that is true (or thereabouts), tragic in its detail and implications, and about which it is impossible to take a neutral attitude, you feel an

absolute bounder unless you give it the thumbs up.' – *Barry Took, Punch*

AAN: script; Lalo Schifrin; Lee Grant

Voyage to Italy **
Italy/France 1953 100m bw
Titanus/Sveva/Junior/Italiafilm (Mario Del Papa, Marcello D'Amico)
V, V*
original title: *Viaggio in Italia*; aka: *Journey to Italy*; *The Lonely Woman*; *Strangers* (US)

During a trip to Italy to sell a property they have inherited, an English couple realize that their marriage is empty and sterile.

Understated narrative of two repressed Northerners failing to respond to the warmth and fecundity of Italians and their landscape. As a portrait of an unhappy marriage it has its moments, but they do not include the film's unsatisfactory resolution. Undervalued on its first release, it later featured in lists of the top ten films compiled by Italian and French critics.

w Vitaliano Brancati, Roberto Rossellini *d* Roberto Rossellini *ph* Enzo Serafin *m* Renzo Rossellini *ad* Piero Filippone *ed* Jolanda Benvenuti

Ingrid Bergman, George Sanders, Maria Mauban, Anna Proclemer, Paul Muller, Leslie Daniels, Natalia Rai, Jackie Frost

'It seems impossible to me to see *Viaggio in Italia* without experiencing, like a whip, the fact that this film opens a breach that the entire cinema must pass through under the pain of death.' – *Jacques Rivette, Cahiers du Cinema*

'An influential film . . . marred by banality and clumsiness.' – *Pauline Kael*

The film was cut to 80m in its English-language version, which is the one released on video. The filming itself was fraught, with both the leads unhappy. Sanders was sometimes in tears over Rossellini's habit of giving him his lines at the last moment.

Voyage to the Bottom of the Sea *
US 1961 105m DeLuxe Cinemascope
TCF/Windsor (Irwin Allen)
V, V*

USN Admiral Nelson takes scientists in his futuristic atomic submarine to explode a belt of radiation.

Childish but sometimes entertaining science fiction which spawned a long-running TV series.

w Irwin Allen, Charles Bennett *d* Irwin Allen *ph* Winton Hoch, John Lamb *m* Paul Sawtell, Bert Shefter *ad* J. M. Smith, Herman A. Blumenthal

Walter Pidgeon, Robert Sterling, Joan Fontaine, Peter Lorre, Barbara Eden, Michael Ansara, Henry Daniell, Regis Toomey, Frankie Avalon

Voyager
Germany/France 1991 100m colour
Palace/Bioskop/Action/Stefi 2/Hellas (Eberhard Junkersdorf)
V, S

A middle-aged engineer begins an affair with a teenage girl, only to discover that she is the daughter of his former mistress.

Involved drama, depending upon a series of coincidences, that never fully engages its audience.

w Rudy Wurlitzer *novel* Homo Faber by Max Frisch *d* Volker Schlöndorff *ph* Yorgos Arvanitis, Pierre L'homme *m* Stanley Myers *pd* Nicos Perakis *ed* Dagmar Hirtz

Sam Shepard, Julie Delphy, Julie Delphy, Barbara Sukowa, Dieter Kirchlechner, Traci Lind, Deborah Lee-Furness, August Zirner, Thomas Heinze

'The film's knowing slickness, especially in an array of visually stunning locations and masterfully choreographed crowd scenes, may leave cinema-goers feeling strangely dissatisfied with the whole enterprise.' – *Screen International*

Le Voyou **

France/Italy   1970   120m   Eastmancolor
UA/Les Films Ariane/Les Films 13/Artistes Associés/P.E.A.
   (Alexandre Mnouchkine)
aka: *Simon the Swiss*; US title: *The Crook*

A crooked lawyer escapes from prison so that he can see his daughter, implicate the accomplice who put him behind bars and flee the country with his swag.

Entertaining, light-hearted thriller, done with great style.

w Claude Lelouch, Pierre Uytterhoeven, Claude Pinoteau   *d* Claude Lelouch   *ph* Claude Lelouch   *m* Francis Lai   *ad* Albert Volper   *ed* Marie-Claude Lacambre

Jean-Louis Trintignant, Christine Lelouch, Charles Gérard, Danièle Delorme, Yves Robert, Amidou, Sacha Distel

'It is all much too good-tempered to be taken seriously. It is strictly for fun, and on that level it works very well.' – *Brenda Davies, MFB*

Vredens Dag: see *Day of Wrath*

Vrema Cuda: see *Time of Miracles*

Všichni Dobřri Rodáci: see *All My Good Countrymen*

Vu du Pont: see *A View from the Bridge*

The Vulture

GB   1967   92m   bw
Lawrence Huntington Productions
V*

A family curse transforms a scientist into a giant vulture.

Incredible nonsense – incredible that anyone should try to get away with it. Fun for those who like to watch actors in trouble.

wd Lawrence Huntington

Robert Hutton, Akim Tamiroff, Broderick Crawford, Diane Clare

Vzlomshchik: see *The Burglar*

W

W
US 1973 95m DeLuxe
Bing Crosby Productions (Mel Ferrer)
V*

A young wife is threatened by her psychotic first husband.

Tedious rehash of several frightened lady themes, all rather sick.

w Gerald di Pego, James Kelly   d Richard Quine
ph Gerry Hirschfeld   m Johnny Mandell

Twiggy, Michael Witney, Eugene Roche, Dirk Benedict, John Vernon

'On screen he played the child-hating, dog-hating, acid-tongued old swindler. It was no act!'

W. C. Fields and Me
US 1976 112m Technicolor Panavision
Universal (Jay Weston)

The rise to Hollywood fame of alcoholic comedian W. C. Fields.

Untruthful and rather boring biopic, with minor compensations.

w Bob Merrill   book Carlotta Monti   d Arthur Hiller   ph David M. Walsh   m Henry Mancini
pd Robert Boyle

Rod Steiger, Valerie Perrine, John Marley, Jack Cassidy (as John Barrymore), Paul Stewart (as Ziegfeld), Billy Barty, Bernadette Peters

'Steiger's impersonation largely keeps pace with the overriding vulgarity of the enterprise.' – *Sight and Sound*

'A stupid and pointless slander.' – *Judith Crist*

'Just the sort of memorial Fields might have wished for Baby Leroy.' – *Les Keyser, Hollywood in the Seventies*

The W Plan *
GB 1930 105m bw
BIP/Burlington (Victor Saville)

A British spy helps destroy Germany's secret tunnels.

Slightly fantasticated spy/war action which was a big popular success at the time.

w Victor Saville, Miles Malleson, Frank Launder
novel Graham Seton   d Victor Saville   ph F. A. Young, Werner Brandes

Brian Aherne, Madeleine Carroll, Gordon Harker, Gibb McLaughlin, George Merritt, Mary Jerrold

'One of the best pictures yet from England, but unconvincing b.o. for the US. Lacks punch.' – *Variety*

'Fast, spectacular action, fine acting and notably realistic war scenes.' – *NFT, 1971*

WUSA *
US 1970 117m Technicolor Panavision
Paramount/Mirror/Coleytown/Stuart Rosenberg (Paul Newman, John Foreman)

A penniless wanderer causes chaos when he becomes the announcer for a right-wing radio station.

A farcical melodrama for the intelligentsia, and for the most part a thoroughgoing bore. The last part offers a compensation or two.

w Robert Stone   novel Hall of Mirrors by Robert Stone
d Stuart Rosenberg   ph Richard Moore   m Lalo Schifrin

Paul Newman, Joanne Woodward, Laurence Harvey, Anthony Perkins, Pat Hingle, Cloris Leachman, Don Gordon, Robert Quarry, Bruce Cabot, Moses Gunn, Wayne Rogers

'The most significant film I've ever made and the best.' – *Paul Newman*

WW and the Dixie Dancekings
US 1975 94m TVC
TCF (Stanley S. Canter)

In a Southern state in the 1950s, a crook uses a travelling band as an alibi and stays to promote them.

Combination of *American Graffiti* and *Easy Rider*, either tiresome or tolerable according to one's mood. Very flashy, anyway.

w Thomas Rickman   d John G. Avildsen   ph Jim Crabe   m Dave Grusin

Burt Reynolds, Art Carney, Conny Van Dyke, Jerry Reed, Ned Beatty

Wabash Avenue *
US 1950 92m Technicolor
TCF (William Perlberg)

During the Chicago World's Fair of 1892, a shimmy dancer is pursued by two men.

Bright rehash of *Coney Island* (qv), with solid tunes and performances.

w Harry Tugend, Charles Lederer   d Henry Koster
ph Arthur E. Arling   md Lionel Newman

Betty Grable, Victor Mature, Phil Harris, Reginald Gardiner, Margaret Hamilton, James Barton, Barry Kelley

AAN: song 'Wilhelmina' (m Josef Myrow, ly Mack Gordon)

Das Wachsfigurenkabinett: see *Waxworks*

The Wackiest Ship in the Army
US 1960 99m Technicolor Cinemascope
Columbia/Fred Kohlmar
V*, L

In the South Pacific during World War II a decrepit sailing ship with an inexperienced crew manages to confuse Japanese patrols and land a scout behind enemy lines.

Slapstick war comedy with fragments of action; effect rather muddled.

wd Richard Murphy   story Herbert Carlson
ph Charles Lawton   m George Duning

Jack Lemmon, Ricky Nelson, John Lund, Chips Rafferty, Tom Tully, Joby Baker, Warren Berlinger, Richard Anderson

Wacko
US 1981 90m Movielab colour
OSM (Greydon Clark)

A slobbish cop tracks down a Halloween killer armed with a lawn mower.

Dire parody of slasher and horror movies, lacking anything resembling a joke.

w Dana Olsen, Michael Spound, M. James Kouf Jnr, David Greenwalt   d Greydon Clark   ph Nicholas J. von Sternberg   m Arthur Kempel   ad Chester Kaczenski   ed Earl Watson, Curtis Burch

Joe Don Baker, Stella Stevens, George Kennedy, Julia Duffy, Scott McGinnis, Andrew Clay

Waco
US 1966 85m Technicolor
Paramount (A. C. Lyles)

A gunfighter is hired to straighten out a corrupt town.

Routine Western programmer with familiar faces in cameo parts.

w Steve Fisher   novel Emporia by Harry Sanford and Max Lamb   d R. G. Springsteen

Howard Keel, Jane Russell, Wendell Corey, Brian Donlevy, John Smith, Gene Evans, DeForest Kelley, Terry Moore, John Agar, Richard Arlen, Robert Lowery, Willard Parker, Fuzzy Knight

The Wages of Fear ***
France/Italy 1953 140m bw
Filmsonor/CICC/Vera
V, V*, L
original title: *Le Salaire de la Peur*

The manager of a Central American oilfield offers big money to drivers who will take nitro-glycerine into the jungle to put out an oil well fire.

After too extended an introduction to the less than admirable characters, this fascinating film resolves itself into a suspense shocker with one craftily managed bad moment after another.

wd Henri-Georges Clouzot   novel Georges Arnaud
ph Armand Thirard   m Georges Auric

Yves Montand, Folco Lulli, Peter Van Eyck, Charles Vanel, Vera Clouzot, William Tubbs

'As skilful as, in its preoccupation with violence and its unrelieved pessimism, it is unlikeable.' – *Penelope Houston, Sight and Sound*

'It has some claim to be the greatest suspense thriller of all time; it is the suspense not of mystery but of Damocles' sword.' – *Basil Wright, 1972*

† See *Sorcerer*, a lamentable remake.

Wages of Fear (1977): see *Sorcerer*

Wagonmaster **
US 1950 86m bw
RKO/Argosy (John Ford, Merian C. Cooper)
V*, L

Adventures of a Mormon wagon train journeying towards Utah in 1879.

Low-key Ford Western, essentially a collection of incidents, fondly and enjoyably presented.

w Frank Nugent, Patrick Ford   d John Ford   ph Bert Glennon   m Richard Hageman

Ben Johnson, Joanne Dru, Harry Carey Jnr, Ward Bond, Charles Kemper, Alan Mowbray, Jane Darwell, Russell Simpson

'The feel of the period, the poetry of space and of endeavour, is splendidly communicated.' – *Lindsay Anderson*

'What emerges at the end is nothing less than a view of life itself, the view of a poet.' – *Patrick Gibbs, 1965*

The Wagons Roll at Night
US 1941 83m bw
Warner (Harlan Thompson)

The sweetheart of a circus owner makes a pass at the new young lion-tamer.

Dull remake of *Kid Galahad* (qv), whose plot was borrowed from *Tiger Shark* (qv). Warner were good at this kind of retreading, but gradually poor quality began to show.

w Fred Niblo Jnr, Barry Trivers   *d* Ray Enright   *ph* Sid Hickox   *m* Heinz Roemheld

Humphrey Bogart, Sylvia Sidney, Eddie Albert, Joan Leslie, Sig Rumann, Cliff Clark, Frank Wilcox

Waikiki Wedding *
US   1937   89m   bw
Paramount (Arthur Hornblow Jnr)

A press agent in Hawaii promotes a Pineapple Queen contest.

Light-hearted, empty-headed musical very typical of this studio . . . except that this one is quite good.

w Frank Butler, Walter de Leon, Don Hartman, Francis Martin   *d* Frank Tuttle   *ph* Karl Struss   *md* Boris Morros   *m* Leo Shukin   *ch* Leroy Prinz

Bing Crosby, Shirley Ross, Bob Burns, Martha Raye, George Barbier, Leif Erickson, Grady Sutton, Granville Bates, Anthony Quinn

'Shouldn't have any trouble getting by . . . it's saccharine celluloid, sugar-coated.' – *Variety*

AA: song 'Sweet Leilani' (*m/y* Harry Owens)

AAN: Leroy Prinz

Wait 'Til the Sun Shines, Nellie *
US   1952   108m   Technicolor
TCF (George Jessel)

The life of a small-town barber, from marriage through tragedy to retirement.

Amiable, leisurely family drama with pleasant settings; small beer, but oddly compulsive.

w Allan Scott   *novel* Ferdinand Reyher   *d* Henry King   *ph* Leon Shamroy   *m* Alfred Newman

David Wayne, Jean Peters, Hugh Marlowe, Albert Dekker, Alan Hale Jnr, Helene Stanley

Wait until Dark **
US   1967   108m   Technicolor
Warner Seven Arts (Mel Ferrer)
V*, L

A photographer unwittingly smuggles a drug-filled doll into New York, and his blind wife, alone in their flat, is terrorized by murderous crooks in search of it.

Sharp suspenser with shock moments, from a successful play; in this case the claustrophobic atmosphere helps, though a lack of light relief makes itself felt.

w Robert and Jane Howard-Carrington   *play* Frederick Knott   *d* Terence Young   *ph* Charles Lang   *m* Henry Mancini   *ad* George Jenkins

Audrey Hepburn, Alan Arkin, Richard Crenna, Efrem Zimbalist Jnr, Jack Weston

AAN: Audrey Hepburn

Waiting *
Australia   1990   94m   colour
Contemporary/Filmside/ABC/Film Four (Ross Matthews)

A group of friends gather in a remote farmhouse as one of their number, an artist who has agreed to bear a baby for a friend, goes into labour.

Interesting and ironic film about surrogate motherhood and doctors' attitudes to childbirth.

wd Jackie McKimmie   *ph* Steve Mason   *m* Martin Armiger   *pd* Murray Picknett   *ed* Michael Honey

Noni Hazelhurst, Deborra-Lee Furness, Frank Whitten, Helen Jones, Denis Moore, Fiona Press, Ray Barrett

Waiting for the Light *
US   1989   94m   DeLuxe
Entertainment/Epic Productions/Sarlui/Diamant (Caledecot Chubb, Ron Bozman)
V

Business at a rundown diner is boosted by fake religious visions.

Ramshackle comedy of character that yields a succession of small pleasures.

wd Christopher Monger   *ph* Gabriel Beristain   *m* Michael Storey   *pd* Phil Peters   *ed* Eva Gardos

Colin Baumgartner, Clancy Brown, Vincent Schiavelli, John Bedford Lloyd, Jeff McCracken, Jack McGee, Louis Guzzo, William Dore

'A wholly appealing confection that crumbles at the first critical touch.' – *Philip Strick, MFB*

Wake in Fright: see *Outback*

'It thrills the women!'
'To the last gun – to the last plane – to the last man!'
Wake Island *
US   1942   78m   bw
Paramount (Joseph Sistrom)
V*

During World War II, marines fight to hold an American base on a small Pacific island.

Terse, violent flagwaver, well done within its limits.

w W. R. Burnett, Frank Butler   *d* John Farrow   *ph* Theodor Sparkuhl, William C. Mellor   *m* David Buttolph

Brian Donlevy, Macdonald Carey, Robert Preston, William Bendix, Albert Dekker, Walter Abel, Mikhail Rasumny, Rod Cameron, Barbara Britton

'Hollywood's first intelligent, honest and completely successful attempt to dramatize the deeds of an American force on a fighting front.' – *Newsweek*

AAN: best picture; script; John Farrow; William Bendix

Wake Me When It's Over
US   1960   126m   DeLuxe   Cinemascope
TCF/Mervyn Le Roy

Soldiers holding a Pacific island build a de luxe hotel from surplus war material.

Aptly-titled army farce on the lines of *The Teahouse of the August Moon* but constructed from inferior material. Yawningly tedious.

w Richard Breen   *novel* Howard Singer   *d* Mervyn Le Roy   *ph* Leon Shamroy   *m* Cyril Mockridge

Ernie Kovacs, Dick Shawn, Jack Warden, Margo Moore, Nobu McCarthy, Don Knotts, Robert Emhardt

Wake of the Red Witch **
US   1948   106m   bw
Republic (Edmund Grainger)
V*

The owner and captain of a ship settle their differences to seek treasure on an East Indian island.

Rattling good action yarn told in flashback, with adequate production and performances.

w Harry Brown, Kenneth Gamet   *novel* Garland Roark   *d* Edward Ludwig   *ph* Reggie Lanning   *m* Nathan Scott

John Wayne, *Luther Adler*, Gail Russell, Gig Young, Adele Mara, Eduard Franz, Grant Withers, Henry Daniell, Paul Fix, Dennis Hoey

Wake Up and Dream
US   1946   92m   Technicolor
TCF (Walter Morosco)

A little girl is determined to find her brother who is missing in action in World War II.

Ambitious but unappealing whimsy which descends into sentimentality; either way it bewildered audiences and critics.

w Elick Moll   *novel* The Enchanted Voyage by Robert Nathan   *d* Lloyd Bacon   *ph* Harry Jackson   *md* Emil Newman   *m* Cyril Mockridge

June Haver, John Payne, Connie Marshall, Charlotte Greenwood, John Ireland, Clem Bevans, Lee Patrick

Wake Up and Live *
US   1937   91m   bw
TCF (Kenneth MacGowan)

Success and failure in the radio world as a commentator and a bandleader fight a verbal duel in public.

Fast-moving spoof in which something is always happening, and usually something funny.

w Harry Tugend, Jack Yellen   *book* Dorothea Brande   *d* Sidney Lanfield   *ph* Edward Cronjager   *m* Louis Silvers   *songs* Mack Gordon, Harry Revel

Walter Winchell, Ben Bernie and his band, Alice Faye, Jack Haley, Patsy Kelly, Ned Sparks, Grace Bradley, Walter Catlett, Joan Davis, Douglas Fowley, Miles Mander, Etienne Girardot

'Thoroughly satisfying film entertainment.' – *Variety*

Walk a Crooked Mile
US   1948   91m   bw
Columbia (Edward Small)

British and American agents investigate the leakage of atomic secrets.

Moderate semi-documentary spy thriller.

w George Bruce   *d* Gordon Douglas   *ph* George Robinson   *m* Paul Sawtell

Louis Hayward, Dennis O'Keefe, Louise Allbritton, Carl Esmond, Raymond Burr, Onslow Stevens

Walk a Crooked Path
GB   1969   88m   Eastmancolor
Hanover (John Brason)

A housemaster at a boys' school is accused of homosexuality.

Po-faced melodrama in a minor key; reasonably effective but not exciting.

w Barry Perowne   *d* John Brason   *ph* John Taylor   *m* Leslie Bridgewater

Tenniel Evans, Faith Brook, Christopher Coll, Patricia Haines, Pat Endersby, Margery Mason, Peter Copley

Walk, Don't Run *
US   1966   114m   Technicolor   Panavision
Columbia/Granley (Sol C. Siegel)
V*

In Tokyo during the Olympics accommodation is hard to find, and two men move in with a girl.

Witless reprise of *The More the Merrier*, notable only for the Tokyo backgrounds and for Cary Grant's farewell appearance.

w Sol Saks   *d* Charles Walters   *ph* Harry Stradling   *m* Quincy Jones

Cary Grant, Samantha Eggar, Jim Hutton, *John Standing*, Miiko Taka

'Too long as are most comedies today, it seems to take its title far too literally; but there are several very funny sequences, a jaunty score, and the unflawed elegance of Mr Grant.' – *Arthur Knight*

Walk East on Beacon *
US   1952   98m   bw
Columbia (Louis de Rochemont)
GB title: *The Crime of the Century*

The FBI exposes communist spies in the US.

Fast-moving semi-documentary spy thriller modelled on the same producer's *The House on 92nd Street*.

w Leo Rosten   *d* Alfred Werker   *ph* Joseph Brun
m Louis Applebaum

George Murphy, Finlay Currie, Virginia Gilmore,
Karel Stepanek, Louisa Horton

'There weren't supposed to be any more surprises in their
lives. And then they met each other!'
A Walk in the Spring Rain
US   1969   98m   Technicolor   Panavision
Columbia/Pingee (Stirling Silliphant)
V*

A college lecturer's wife, on holiday in the mountains,
falls in love with a local man.

Romance for the middle-aged, nicely done if lacking
in surprise.

w Stirling Silliphant   *novel* Rachel Maddox   *d* Guy
Green   *ph* Charles B. Lang   *m* Elmer Bernstein

Ingrid Bergman, Anthony Quinn, Fritz Weaver,
Katherine Crawford

'Not one line or scene is believably written or acted
and the direction is so lazy it appears to have been
mailed in during the postal strike.' – *Richard Roud*

A Walk in the Sun ***
US   1946   117m   bw
Lewis Milestone Productions
V*, L

The exploits of a single army patrol during the
Salerno landings of 1943, on one vital morning.

Vivid war film in a minor key, superbly disciplined
and keenly acted.

w Robert Rossen   *novel* Harry Brown   *d* Lewis
Milestone   *ph* Russell Harlan   *m* Fredric Efrem Rich

Dana Andrews, Richard Conte, Sterling Holloway,
John Ireland, George Tyne, Herbert Rudley, Richard
Benedict, Norman Lloyd, Lloyd Bridges, Huntz Hall

'Concerned with the individual rather than the
battlefield, the film is finely perceptive, exciting, and
very moving.' – *Penelope Houston*

'A swiftly overpowering piece of work.' – *Bosley
Crowther*

'A notable war film, if not the most notable war film
to come from America.' – *Richard Winnington*

'After nearly two hours one is sorry when it ends.' –
Richard Mallett, Punch

Walk like a Dragon
US   1960   95m   bw
Paramount/James Clavell

In 1870 San Francisco, a cowboy sets free a Chinese
slave girl but incurs racial intolerance when he takes
her home.

Curious 'liberated' Western which gets itself in a
muddle and doesn't come off at all.

w James Clavell, Dan Mainwaring   *d* James Clavell
ph Loyal Griggs   *m* Paul Dunlap

Jack Lord, James Shigeta, Nobu McCarthy, Mel
Tormé, Josephine Hutchinson, Rodolfo Acosta

'A side of life you never expected to see on the screen!'
Walk on the Wild Side
US   1962   114m   bw
Columbia/Famous Artists (Charles K. Feldman)
V*

In the thirties, a penniless farmer finds the girl he
once loved working in a New Orleans brothel.

A brilliant title sequence heralds the dreariest and
most verbose of self-conscious melodramas, quite
missing the sensational effect promised by the
advertising.

w John Fante, Edmund Morris   *novel* Nelson Algren
d Edward Dmytryk   *ph* Joe MacDonald   *m* Elmer
Bernstein   *credits* Saul Bass

Jane Fonda, Capucine, Barbara Stanwyck, Laurence
Harvey, Anne Baxter, Richard Rust

'Since the film prides itself in calling a spade a spade,
it is surprising to find all concerned reacting to their
material as though they were up to their waists in a
quagmire.' – *MFB*

AAN: title song (*m* Elmer Bernstein, *ly* Mack David)

Walk Softly Stranger
US   1950   81m   bw
RKO (Robert Sparks)
V*

A crook on the run falls for a crippled girl, who
promises to wait for him.

Dismal love-conquers-all melodrama.

w Frank Fenton   *d* Robert Stevenson   *ph* Harry J.
Wild   *m* Frederick Hollander

Alida Valli, Joseph Cotten, Spring Byington, Paul
Stewart, Jack Paar, Jeff Donnell, John McIntire

Walk the Proud Land
US   1956   88m   Technicolor   Cinemascope
U-I (Aaron Rosenberg)

An Indian agent persuades the army to use less
violent methods.

Fair standard Western with a thoughtful and
sympathetic attitude.

w Gil Doud, Jack Sher   *d* Jesse Hibbs   *ph* Harold
Lipstein   *m* Hans Salter

Audie Murphy, Anne Bancroft, Pat Crowley, Robert
Warwick, Charles Drake, Tommy Rall, Jay Silverheels

'In a strange and horrifying playground the innocents act
out their game of life and death . . .'
Walkabout ****
Australia   1970   100m   DeLuxe
Max L. Raab/Si Litvinoff

A man kills himself in the desert and his small
children trek among the aborigines to safety.

Eerily effective contrast of city with native life, a
director's and photographer's experimental success.

w Edward Bond   *novel* James Vance Marshall   *d/
ph* Nicolas Roeg   *m* John Barry

Jenny Agutter, Lucien John, David Gulpilil

'The film is rich enough, especially at a second look,
to make you forget the flaws. You are left with the
impression of a fresh, powerful and humane
imagination.' – *Dilys Powell*

Walker
US   1987   94m   colour
Recorded Releasing/Walker Film/Incine (Lorenzo O'Brien,
   Angel Flores Marini)
V*

In the 1850s, an American adventurer invades
Nicaragua and sets himself up as the country's
dictator.

Based on fact, it fails to develop its fascinating theme
in a satisfactory way, relying on anachronistic details
such as helicopters to point its message.

w Rudy Wurlitzer   *d* Alex Cox   *ph* David Bridges
m Joe Strummer   *pd* Bruno Rubeo, J. Rae Fox
ed Carlos Puente, Alex Cox

Ed Harris, Richard Masur, Rene Auberjonois, Keith
Szarabajka, Sy Richardson, Xander Berkeley, John
Diehl, Peter Boyle

The Walking Dead *
US   1936   66m   bw
Warner (Louis F. Edelman)

A man is revived after electrocution and takes revenge
on his enemies.

Dour but well-mounted horror thriller in a shadowy
style very typical of its director.

w Ewart Adamson, Peter Milne, Robert Andrews,
Lillie Hayward   *d* Michael Curtiz   *ph* Hal Mohr

Boris Karloff, Edmund Gwenn, Marguerite Churchill,
Ricardo Cortez, Barton MacLane, Warren Hull, Henry
O'Neill

'Weak story and haphazardly interpolated assortment
of scientific abadaba prevent Karloff from making
much of a shocker out of this one.' – *Variety*

Walking Down Broadway: see *Hello Sister*

The Walking Hills *
US   1949   78m   bw
Columbia (Harry Joe Brown)

Various interests combine to locate gold bullion
hidden in Death Valley . . . then thieves fall out.

Elementary but fairly satisfying Western.

w Alan LeMay   *d* John Sturges

Randolph Scott, Ella Raines, William Bishop, Edgar
Buchanan, Arthur Kennedy, John Ireland, Jerome
Courtland, Josh White

Walking My Baby Back Home *
US   1953   95m   Technicolor
U-I (Ted Richmond)

Ex-army musicians hit on a combination of
symphonic and dixieland jazz.

The lightest of light musicals, this highly polished
offering remains mildly pleasing though thinly
written throughout.

w Don McGuire, Oscar Brodney   *d* Lloyd Bacon
ph Irving Glassberg   *md* Joseph Gershenson

Donald O'Connor, Janet Leigh, Buddy Hackett, Lori
Nelson, Scatman Crothers, Kathleen Lockhart, George
Cleveland, John Hubbard

The Walking Stick *
GB   1970   101m   Metrocolor   Panavision
MGM/Winkast (Alan Ladd Jnr)

A repressed girl polio victim falls reluctantly in love
with a painter who involves her in his criminal
schemes.

Slow moving character romance which has its heart in
the right place but too often promises suspense which
never comes, and is made in a chintzy cigarette
commercial style.

w George Bluestone   *novel* Winston Graham
d Eric Till   *ph* Arthur Ibbetson   *m* Stanley Myers

David Hemmings, Samantha Eggar, Phyllis Calvert, Ferdy
Mayne, Emlyn Williams, Francesca Annis, Dudley
Sutton

Walking Tall *
US   1973   125m   DeLuxe
Bing Crosby Productions (Mort Briskin)
V*, L

A Tennessee farmer-sheriff meets violence with
violence and becomes a local hero.

True story of an American vigilante, made with
modest competence; its great commercial success may
have been due to the support of the righteous, or of
those who revel in violence.

w Mort Briskin   *d* Phil Karlson   *ph* Jack Marta
m Walter Scharf

Joe Don Baker, Elizabeth Hartman, Gene Evans, Noah
Beery Jnr

'A terrifying image of Nixon's silent majority at work.'
– *Gareth Jones*

'It generates a primitive, atavistic sort of power: it
awakens more apprehension and dredges up more
complicated and contradictory emotions than one
anticipates.' – *Gary Arnold*

† Sequel 1976: *Part Two Walking Tall*. (GB title: *Legend
of the Lawman*.) 1977: *Walking Tall: Final Chapter*.

The Wall *

France 1983 117m Fujicolor
Contemporary/Guney Productions/MK2 Productions/TFI Films
(Marin Karmitz)
original title: *Le Mur*; aka: *Guney's The Wall*

Boys in a Turkish prison revolt against their persecutors.

Powerfully filmed indictment of brutality, based on a true incident and made a year before the director's death. **wd** Yilmaz Guney **ph** Izzet Akay **m** Ozan Garip Sahin, Setrak Bakirel, Ali Dede Altuntas, Robert Kempler **ed** Sabine Mamou

Tuncel Kurtiz, Ayse Emel Mesci, Saban, Sisko, Ziya, Garip, Zapata, Mankafa, Malik Berrichi, Nicolas Hossein, Habes Bounabi

Wall of Noise

US 1963 112m bw
Warner (Joseph Landon)

A racehorse trainer falls for the boss's wife.

Complex but predictable melodrama of the old school, adequately presented and performed.

w Joseph Landon **novel** Daniel Michael Stein **d** Richard Wilson **ph** Lucien Ballard **m** William Lava

Suzanne Pleshette, Ty Hardin, Dorothy Provine, Ralph Meeker, Simon Oakland, Murray Matheson, Robert F. Simon

Wall Street **

US 1987 124m DeLuxe
Edward R. Pressman/American Entertainment
V, V*, L

An ambitious young financial broker is forced to choose between the values of his Wall Street hero and his own father, an aircraft mechanic.

Almost documentary in its detailed account of financial skulduggery but slipping ultimately into sentimentality, the film is marked by a brilliant performance from Michael Douglas as the scheming megalomaniac Gordon Gekko.

w Stanley Weiser, Oliver Stone **d** Oliver Stone **ph** Robert Richardson **m** Stewart Copeland **pd** Stephen Hendrickson

Charlie Sheen, *Michael Douglas,* Martin Sheen, Daryl Hannah, Terence Stamp

AA: Michael Douglas

Wallflower

US 1948 77m bw
Warner

Two sisters chase the same man; the less aggressive gets him.

So-so comedy on familiar lines.

w Phoebe and Henry Ephron **play** Reginald Denham, Mary Orr **d** Frederick de Cordova

Joyce Reynolds, Janis Paige, Robert Hutton, Edward Arnold, Jerome Cowan, Barbara Brown

The Walls Came Tumbling Down *

US 1946 81m bw
Columbia (Albert J. Cohen)

A Broadway columnist tracks down the murderer of a priest.

Very acceptable whodunnit with familiar cast.

w Wilfrid H. Pettitt **novel** Jo Eisinger **d** Lothar Mendes

Lee Bowman, Marguerite Chapman, George Macready, Edgar Buchanan, Lee Patrick, Jonathan Hale, J. Edward Bromberg, Elizabeth Risdon, Miles Mander, Moroni Olsen, Robert Ryan

Walls of Glass

US 1985 86m colour
Tenth Muse (Scott Goldstein, Mark Slater)

A Shakespeare-loving taxi-driver tries to cope with his life's frustrations and return to his first love, the stage.

An engaging character study with a strong central performance.

w Edmond Collins, Scott Goldstein **d** Scott Goldstein **ph** Ivan Strasburg **m** Scott Goldstein **pd** Ruth Ammon **ed** Scott Vickrey

Philip Bosco, Geraldine Page, Olympia Dukakis, Brian Bloom, Steven Weber, Louis Zorich, Linda Thorsen

The Walls of Jericho

US 1948 106m bw
TCF (Lamar Trotti)

An influential small-town newspaperman is undermined by his vindictive wife.

Filmed novel of standard competence but minimum interest, ending in a courtroom scene.

w Lamar Trotti **novel** Paul Wellman **d** John M. Stahl **ph** Arthur Miller **m** Cyril Mockridge

Cornel Wilde, Linda Darnell, Anne Baxter, Kirk Douglas, Ann Dvorak, Marjorie Rambeau, Henry Hull, Colleen Townsend

Waltz across Texas

US 1982 99m colour
Aster (Martin Jurow)
V*

Love blossoms when an uptight female geologist agrees to help a laid-back Texan search for oil.

Folksy, sentimental, romantic drama, pleasant without being in any way memorable.

w Bill Svanoe **d** Ernest Day **ph** Robert Elswit **m** Steve Dorff **ed** Jay Lash Cassidy

Anne Archer, Terry Jastrow, Noah Beery, Richard Farnsworth, Mary Kay Place, Josh Taylor, Ben Piazza

The Waltz King

US 1963 95m Technicolor
Walt Disney (Peter V. Herald)
V*

The life of young Johann Strauss in 1850s Vienna.

Medium-budget international family musical, tolerably well done.

w Maurice Tombragel **d** Steve Previn **ph** Gunther Anders **md** Helmuth Froschauer

Kerwin Mathews, Brian Aherne, Senta Berger, Peter Kraus, Fritz Eckhardt

The Waltz of the Toreadors *

GB 1962 105m Technicolor
Rank Wintle-Parkyn (Peter de Sarigny)
V*

A lecherous retired general finds his past creeping up on him and loses his young mistress to his son.

Lukewarm adaptation of a semi-classic comedy, disastrously translated to English setting and characters.

w Wolf Mankowitz **play** Jean Anouilh **d** John Guillermin **ph** John Wilcox **m** Richard Addinsell **pd** Wilfrid Shingleton

Peter Sellers, Margaret Leighton, Dany Robin, John Fraser, Cyril Cusack, Prunella Scales

Waltz Time

GB 1933 82m bw
Gaumont

Things are not what they seem to be at a Viennese masked ball.

Pleasant but slight musical comedy vaguely derived from *Die Fledermaus.*

w A. P. Herbert **d** William Thiele

Evelyn Laye, Fritz Schultz, Gina Malo, Jay Laurier, Frank Titterton

Waltz Time

GB 1945 100m bw
British National

At a Viennese ball, an Empress poses as her masked friend to win a philandering count.

Rather plodding operetta which also has an unattributed allegiance to *Die Fledermaus.*

w Montgomery Tully, Jack Whittingham, Henry C. James, Karl Rossier **d** Paul Stein

Carol Raye, Peter Graves, Patricia Medina, Thorley Walters, Richard Tauber, Harry Welchman, George Robey, Anne Ziegler, Webster Booth

Waltzes from Vienna

GB 1933 80m bw
Gaumont (Tom Arnold)
US title: *Strauss's Great Waltz*

A romance of the Strausses.

There is very little music and very little Hitchcock in this extremely mild romantic comedy.

w Alma Reville, Guy Bolton **play** Guy Bolton **d** Alfred Hitchcock **ph** Glen MacWilliams

Jessie Matthews, Esmond Knight, Frank Vosper, Fay Compton, Edmund Gwenn, Robert Hale, Hindle Edgar

'I hate this sort of thing. Melodrama is the only thing I can do.' – *Alfred Hitchcock*

The Wanderers

US/Netherlands 1979 117m Technicolor
GTO/PSO/Poly International (Martin Ransohoff)
V, V*

In 1963, teenage street gangs fight in the Bronx.

A bad boys' *American Graffiti,* all violence and unpleasantness.

w Rose and Philip Kaufman **novel** Richard Price **d** Philip Kaufman **ph** Michael Chapman **ad** Jay Moore **ed** Ronald Roose, Stuart H. Pappe

Ken Wahl, John Friedrich, Karen Allen, Toni Kalem, Linda Manz

The Wandering Jew *

GB 1933 111m bw
Gaumont/Twickenham (Julius Hagen)

A Jew is condemned to live forever, but dies in the Spanish Inquisition.

Ambitious fantasy which comes off pretty well for those in the mood, but was a curious choice for a British studio at the time.

w H. Fowler Mear **play** E. Temple Thurston **d** Maurice Elvey **ph** Sydney Blythe

Conrad Veidt, Marie Ney, Basil Gill, Anne Grey, Dennis Hoey, John Stuart, Peggy Ashcroft, Francis L. Sullivan, Felix Aylmer, Abraham Sofaer

'A beautiful production, a historic triumph – and most likely a commercial error.' – *Variety*

The Wannsee Conference *

Germany/Austria 1987 87m colour
Infafilm/Austrian TV/ORF/Bavarian Broadcasting (Manfred Korytowski)
V*, L
original title: *Die Wannseekonferenz*

A group of Nazi officials gather for a conference to discuss Hitler's 'final solution' to exterminate the Jewish people.

Careful re-creation of an historic event, which lasted for 85 minutes, demonstrating the banality of evil. It was originally made for television, to which medium it is better suited.

w Paul Mommertz *d* Heinz Schirk *ph* Horst Schier *ad* Robert Hofer-Ach, Barbara Siebner *ed* Ursula Mollinger

Robert Artzorn, Friedrich Beckhaus, Gerd Bochmann, Jochen Busse, Hans W. Bussinger, Harald Dietl, Peter Fitz, Reinhard Glemnitz, Dieter Groest, Martin Luttge

Wanted for Murder *
GB 1946 103m bw
Marcel Hellman

A man, obsessed with the fact that his father was the public hangman, becomes a murderer himself.

Curiously stagey melodrama with intermittent use of London backgrounds; an interesting curiosity.

w Emeric Pressburger, Rodney Ackland, Maurice Cowan *d* Lawrence Huntington *ph* Max Greene *m* Mischa Spoliansky

Eric Portman, Dulcie Gray, Derek Farr, Roland Culver, Stanley Holloway, Barbara Everest, Bonar Colleano, Kathleen Harrison

'A pleasant and unpretentious thriller of the second or third grade.' – *James Agee*

Wanted: Jane Turner
US 1936 64m bw
Cliff Reid/RKO

The postal service tracks down mail van crooks.

Familiar but lively action support.

w John Twist *d* Edward Killy

Lee Tracy, Gloria Stuart, Judith Blake, John McGuire, Frank M. Thomas

The Wanton: see *Manèges*

The Wanton Countess: see *Senso*

The War against Mrs Hadley *
US 1942 86m bw
MGM (Irving Asher)

A Washington matron tries to ignore the war and preserve her social life.

Efficient little propaganda piece with a middle-aged heroine.

w George Oppenheimer *d* Harold S. Bucquet *ph* Karl Freund *m* David Snell

Fay Bainter, Edward Arnold, Richard Ney, Jean Rogers, Sara Allgood, Spring Byington, Van Johnson, Isobel Elsom, Halliwell Hobbes, Miles Mander, Frances Rafferty, Connie Gilchrist

'If this film is, as some have labelled it, the American Mrs Miniver, then some of us must have grave illusions about our own (or the English) way of life.' – *Bosley Crowther*

AAN: George Oppenheimer

War and Peace **
US/Italy 1956 208m Technicolor Vistavision
Carlo Ponti/Dino de Laurentiis
V*, L, S

A Russian family's adventures at the time of Napoleon's invasion.

Despite miscasting and heavy dubbing, the pictorial parts of this précis of a gargantuan novel are powerful and exciting enough; the human side drags a little.

w Bridget Boland, Robert Westerby, King Vidor, Mario Camerini, Ennio de Concini, Ivo Perelli *novel* Leo Tolstoy *d* King Vidor, (battle scenes) *Mario Soldati* *ph* Jack Cardiff, (battle scenes) *Aldo Tonti* *m* Nino Rota *ad* Mario Chiari

Audrey Hepburn, Henry Fonda, Mel Ferrer, *Herbert Lom*, John Mills, Oscar Homolka, Wilfrid Lawson, Vittorio Gassman, Anita Ekberg, Helmut Dantine, Milly Vitale, Barry Jones

'The film has no more warmth than pictures in an art gallery.' – *Philip T. Hartung*

'When I first agreed to do it the screenplay by Irwin Shaw was fine, but what happened? King Vidor used to go home nights with his wife and rewrite it. All the genius of Tolstoy went out the window.' – *Henry Fonda*

AAN: King Vidor; Jack Cardiff

War and Peace ***
USSR 1967 507m Sovcolor 'Scope 70mm
Mosfilm
V, V*

An immensely long Russian version with some of the most magnificently spectacular battle scenes ever filmed.

A treat for the eyes throughout, and perhaps less taxing than reading the novel, which it follows punctiliously.

w Sergei Bondarchuk, Vasili Solovyov *d* Sergei Bondarchuk *ph* Anatoli Petritsky *m* Vyacheslav Ovchinnikov

Lyudmila Savelyeva, Sergei Bondarchuk, Vyacheslav Tikhonov

† The film was five years in production and cost between 50 and 70 million dollars.

AA: best foreign film

The War between Men and Women
US 1972 105m Technicolor Panavision
National General/Jalem/Llenroc/4D (Danny Arnold)

A half-blind cartoonist marries a divorcee and is troubled by her ex-husband.

Semi-serious comedy vaguely based on Thurber, but not so that you'd notice, apart from the blind hero; generally neither funny nor affecting.

w Mel Shavelson, Danny Arnold, based on the writings of James Thurber *d* Melville Shavelson *ph* Charles F. Wheeler *m* Marvin Hamlisch *pd* Stan Jolley

Jack Lemmon, Barbara Harris, Jason Robards Jnr, Herb Edelman, Lisa Gerritsen

War Correspondent: see *The Story of GI Joe*

War Games *
US 1983 113m Metrocolor
MGM-UA/Sherwood (Leonard Goldberg, Harold Schneider)
V, L

A teenager unwittingly taps his home computer into the Pentagon and pretends to be Russia on the point of launching missiles.

Mildly intriguing science fantasy which becomes uncomfortable and finally boring because of the excess of jargon and flashing lights.

w Lawrence Lasker, Walter F. Parkes *d* John Badham *ph* William A. Fraker *m* Arthur B. Rubenstein *pd* Angelo P. Graham

Matthew Broderick, Dabney Coleman, John Wood, Ally Sheedy, Barry Corbin, Kent Williams

'All the film's adventure and suspense is inevitably at odds with its ostensible sentiments . . . [but] the result has a kind of seamless efficiency.' – *Steve Jenkins, MFB*

AAN: screenplay; cinematography

War Gods of the Deep: see *City under the Sea*

War Hunt
US 1961 83m bw
TD Enterprises (Terry Sanders)

Korea 1953: a kill-crazy private is befriended by a war orphan but finally has to be shot.

Vaguely commendable but not very expert indictment of the realities of war.

w Stanford Whitmore *d* Denis Sanders *ph* Ted McCord *m* Bud Shank

John Saxon, Robert Redford, Sidney Pollack, Charles Aidman, Tommy Matsuda

The War Is Over: see *La Guerre Est Finie*

The War Lord **
US 1965 121m Technicolor Panavision
Universal/Court (Walter Seltzer)

An officer of the Duke of Normandy has trouble with Druids and the law of *droit de seigneur.*

Complex medieval melodrama with an air of fantasy about it; generally likeably strange, but the production should have been more stylized and fanciful.

w John Collier, Millard Kaufman *play The Lovers* by Leslie Stevens *d* Franklin Schaffner *ph* Russell Metty *m* Jerome Moross *ad* Alexander Golitzen, Henry Bumstead

Charlton Heston, Richard Boone, Rosemary Forsyth, Maurice Evans, Guy Stockwell, Niall MacGinnis, Henry Wilcoxon, James Farentino

The War Lover
GB 1962 105m bw
Columbia/Arthur Hornblow Jnr
V, L

In 1943, a Flying Fortress commander based in East Anglia has the wrong ideas about women and war.

Solemn character drama punctuated by aerial battles.

w Howard Koch *novel* John Hersey *d* Philip Leacock *ph* Bob Huke *m* Richard Addinsell

Steve McQueen, Shirley Anne Field, Robert Wagner, Gary Cockrell, Michael Crawford

War Nurse
US 1930 79m bw
MGM

Problems of a nurse behind the lines in World War I.

Ambitious but unsuccessful attempt to do another *Big Parade*; a lack of style and story kills it.

w Becky Gardner, Joe Farnham, from an anonymous autobiography *d* Edgar Selwyn

Robert Montgomery, Anita Page, June Walker, Robert Ames, ZaSu Pitts, Marie Prevost, Helen Jerome Eddy, Hedda Hopper

'Won't get anywhere in the major houses; too filled with audible suffering to class as entertainment.' – *Variety*

'Once in a lifetime comes a motion picture that makes you feel like falling in love all over again. This is not that movie.'

The War of the Roses *
US 1989 116m DeLuxe
Fox/Gracie Films (James L. Brooks, Arnon Milchan)
V, V*, L

A couple who decide to divorce fight to the death over who gets the house.

Rancorous comedy, sometimes amusing but too mean-spirited for many laughs.

w Michael Leeson *novel* Warren Adler *d* Danny DeVito *ph* Stephen H. Burum *m* David Newman *pd* Ida Random *ed* Lynzee Klingman

Michael Douglas, Kathleen Turner, Danny DeVito, Marianne Sägebrecht, Sean Astin, Heather Fairfield, G. D. Spradlin, Trenton Teigen, Bethany McKinney

War of the Wildcats
US 1943 102m bw
Republic (Robert North)
V*
aka: *In Old Oklahoma*

A lady writer causes friction between an oil operator and a cowboy.

Action potboiler which once passed an hour and three-quarters quite painlessly.

w Ethel Hill, Eleanore Griffith, Thomson Burtis d Albert S. Rogell ph Jack Marta m Walter Scharf

John Wayne, Martha Scott, Albert Dekker, George 'Gabby' Hayes, Marjorie Rambeau, Dale Evans, Grant Withers, Sidney Blackmer

AAN: Walter Scharf

The War of the Worlds *
US 1953 85m Technicolor
Paramount/George Pal
V*, L

Terrifying aliens invade Earth via the American midwest.

Spectacular battle scenes are the mainstay of this violent fantasy, which goes to pieces once the cardboard aliens open their mouths.

w Barre Lyndon novel H. G. Wells d Byron Haskin ph George Barnes m Leith Stevens ad Hal Pereira, Albert Nozaki ed Everett Douglas

Gene Barry, Ann Robinson, Les Tremayne, Bob Cornthwaite, Sandra Giglio

AA: special effects
AAN: editing

War Party
US 1989 97m CFI colour
Hemdale (John Daly, Derek Gibson)
V, V*, L

The centennial re-enactment of a massacre by the US Cavalry of the local Blackfoot Indians leads to a real battle after a white youth murders one of the Indians.

A mundane excuse for a not very interesting modern-day Western.

w Spencer Eastman d Franc Roddam ph Brian Tufano m Chaz Jankel pd Michael Bingham ed Sean Barton

Billy Wirth, Kevin Dillon, Tim Sampson, Jimmie Ray Weeks, Kevyn Major Howard, M. Emmet Walsh, Jerry Hardin, Bill McKinney

'Its message is that it takes danger and excitement to release the pent-up, dulled emotions of both the Indians on the reservation and the white men in town. The result is a straightforward celebration of action-movie clichés.' – Julian Stringer, MFB

War Requiem *
GB 1988 93m bw/colour
Anglo International/BBC (Don Boyd)

Images of war, and of the poet Wilfred Owen in the trenches, accompany the music of Benjamin Britten's War Requiem.

A series of tableaux, some savagely comic but most tragic, intensify the experience of the music.

d Derek Jarman ph Richard Greatrex m Benjamin Britten pd Lucy Morahan ed Rick Elgood

Nathaniel Parker, Tilda Swinton, Laurence Olivier, Patricia Hayes, Rohan McCillough, Nigel Terry, Owen Teale, Sean Bean, Alex Jennings

The War Wagon **
US 1967 99m Technicolor Panavision
Universal/Batjac (Marvin Schwartz)
V*, L

Two cowboys and an Indian plan to ambush the gold wagon of a crooked mining contractor.

Exhilarating but simply-plotted action Western with strong comedy elements and a cast of old reliables.

w Clair Huffaker novel Badman by Clair Huffaker d Burt Kennedy ph William H. Clothier m Dimitri Tiomkin

John Wayne, Kirk Douglas, Howard Keel, Robert Walker, Keenan Wynn, Bruce Cabot, Gene Evans, Bruce Dern

'It all works splendidly.' – MFB

The Ware Case *
GB 1938 79m bw
Ealing/Capad (S. C. Balcon)

A nobleman is suspected of murdering his wife's rich brother.

Courtroom melodrama twice filmed as a silent; stagey but reasonably compelling in its way.

w Robert Stevenson, Roland Pertwee, E. V. H. Emmett play G. P. Bancroft d Robert Stevenson ph Ronald Neame m Ernest Irving

Clive Brook, Jane Baxter, Barry K. Barnes, C. V. France, Francis L. Sullivan, Frank Cellier, Edward Rigby, Peter Bull, Athene Seyler, Ernest Thesiger

† Previous versions had been made in 1917 (with Matheson Lang) and 1930 (with Stewart Rome).

Warlock *
US 1959 123m DeLuxe Cinemascope
TCF (Edward Dmytryk)
V*

The cowardly citizens of a small Western town hire a gunman as their unofficial marshal.

Overlong, talkative and somewhat pretentious star Western with good sequences.

w Robert Alan Aurthur novel Oakley Hall d Edward Dmytryk ph Joe MacDonald m Leigh Harline

Henry Fonda, Richard Widmark, Anthony Quinn, Dorothy Malone, Dolores Michaels, Wallace Ford, Tom Drake, Richard Arlen, Regis Toomey, Don Beddoe, De Forrest Kelley

Warlock
US 1988 102m DeLuxe
Medusa/New World (Steve Miner)
V, V*, L, S

A witchfinder and the warlock he is hunting are translated from the 17th century to modern-day Los Angeles.

Enjoyable chase film, energetically performed.

w David T. Twohy d Steve Miner ph David Eggby m Jerry Goldsmith pd Roy Forge Smith ed David Finfer

Richard E. Grant, Julian Sands, Lori Singer, Kevin O'Brien, Mary Woronov, Richard Kuss, Juli Burkhart, Harry Johnson, David Carpenter

Warlords of Atlantis
GB 1978 96m Technicolor
EMI/John Dark, Kevin Connor

Victorian sea scientists discover a lost land under the Mediterranean.

Predictable compote of monsters and unwearable costumes, without a trace of wit in the script. For infants only.

w Brian Hayles d Kevin Connor ph Alan Hume m Mike Vickers pd Elliot Scott

Doug McClure, Peter Gilmore, Shane Rimmer, Lea Brodie, Michael Gothard

A Warm December
GB/US 1972 101m Technicolor
First Artists/Verdon (Melville Tucker)

A widowed American doctor in London falls for a mysterious African girl who turns out to be the dying niece of a diplomat.

Weird mishmash of Love Story, Brief Encounter and Dark Victory, getting the worst of all worlds.

w Lawrence Roman d Sidney Poitier ph Paul Beeson m Coleridge-Taylor Parkinson

Sidney Poitier, Esther Anderson, George Baker, Johnny Sekka, Earl Cameron

Warn London
GB 1934 74m bw
British Lion

A London policeman who is the double of a well-known burglar replaces him and infiltrates an international gang.

Exuberant minor thriller which made a good novelty booking at the time.

w Charles Bennett, Billie Bristow novel Denison Clift d T. Hayes Hunter ph Alex Bryce ad Norman Arnold

Edmund Gwenn, John Loder, Leonora Corbett, D. A. Clarke-Smith

Warn That Man
GB 1943 82m bw
ABPC

German spies pose as an English nobleman and his staff but are routed by an unexpected guest.

On the stage this must have been an effective comedy-thriller, but the film is stymied by stiff handling.

w Vernon Sylvaine, Lawrence Huntington play Vernon Sylvaine d Lawrence Huntington

Gordon Harker, Raymond Lovell, Jean Kent, Finlay Currie, Philip Friend, Frederick Cooper

'Slick drama, mounting success, and spectacular military enterprise.' – The Cinema

'What's a little bullet between friends?'
Warning Shot *
US 1966 100m Technicolor
Paramount/Bob Banner (Buzz Kulik)

While looking for a psychopathic killer, a cop shoots dead a man who draws a gun on him. But the dead man's gun cannot be found, and the officer is suspended . . .

Watchable mystery decked out with guest stars; possibly intended as a TV movie.

w Mann Rubin novel 711—Officer Needs Help by Whit Masterson d Buzz Kulik ph Joseph Biroc m Jerry Goldsmith

David Janssen, Lillian Gish, Ed Begley, Keenan Wynn, Sam Wanamaker, Eleanor Parker, Stefanie Powers, Walter Pidgeon, George Sanders, George Grizzard, Steve Allen, Carroll O'Connor, Joan Collins

Warning Sign
US 1985 100m DeLuxe
TCF/Barwood-Robbins (Jim Bloom)
V*, S

A solitary cop combats scientists who may unwittingly unleash a deadly plague.

Unimpressive as propaganda and tedious as suspense.

w Hal Barwood, Matthew Robbins d Hal Barwood ph Dean Cundey m Craig Safan pd Henry Bumstead ed Robert Lawrence

Sam Waterston, Kathleen Quinlan, Yaphet Kotto, Richard Dysart, Jeffrey de Munn

Warning, This Man Is Wild: see Violent Cop

Warning to Wantons
GB 1948 104m bw
Aquila/GFD

A nobleman takes in a flirtatious girl and finds she causes trouble for him and his family.

Interminable comedy-drama made even duller by the Independent Frame production method, which cut costs but restricted movement.

w Donald B. Wilson, James Laver   *novel* Mary Mitchell   *d* Donald B. Wilson

Harold Warrender, Anne Vernon, David Tomlinson, Sonia Holm, Marie Burke, Judy Kelly

Warpath
US   1951   93m   Technicolor
Paramount (Nat Holt)

An ex-army captain tracks down the outlaws who murdered his girl.

Goodish standard Western.

w Frank Gruber   *d* Byron Haskin   *ph* Ray Rennahan   *m* Paul Sawtell

Edmond O'Brien, Dean Jagger, Forrest Tucker, Harry Carey Jnr, Wallace Ford, Polly Bergen

The Warriors (1955): see The Dark Avenger

'These are the armies of the night ...'
The Warriors
US   1979   94m   Movielab
Paramount (Laurence Gordon)
V*, L

A New York street gang runs into trouble when making a cross-city journey.

A sick exploitation movie about urban violence, poorly made into the bargain.

w David Shaber, Walter Hill   *novel* Sol Yurick   *d* Walter Hill   *ph* Andrew Laszlo   *m* Barry de Vorzon

Michael Beck, James Remar, Thomas Waites, Dorsey Wright, Brian Tyler, David Harris

The Warrior's Husband
US   1933   75m   bw
Fox (Jesse L. Lasky)

The Greeks break into Amazonia and conquer the women, provoking a worm to turn.

A weird attempt by Hollywood to film a whimsical comedy which belonged only on Broadway, where the Greeks no doubt have a word for it.

w Sonya Levien   *play* Julian Thompson   *d* Walter Lang

Elissa Landi, Marjorie Rambeau, Ernest Truex, David Manners, Helen Ware, Maude Eburne

'Novel farce will need astute exploitation aid.' – *Variety*

Warui Yatsu Yoku Nemuru: see The Bad Sleep Well

Washington Masquerade
US   1932   92m   bw
MGM
GB title: *Mad Masquerade*

A high-minded senator is corrupted by a worthless girl.

Solid star melodrama.

w John Meehan, Samuel Blythe   *play The Claw* by Henri Bernstein   *d* Charles Brabin

Lionel Barrymore, Karen Morley, Nils Asther, C. Henry Gordon, William Collier Snr

Washington Merry-go-round *
US   1932   75m   bw
Columbia

A crusading young congressman attacks the crooks in the government.

Naïve comedy-drama with a miscast star.

w Jo Swerling from an original by Maxwell Anderson   *d* James Cruze

Lee Tracy, Constance Cummings, Alan Dinehart, Walter Connolly, Clarence Muse, Arthur Vinton

'Lots of flagwaving and political timeliness the chief appeal.' – *Variety*

Washington Story
US   1952   82m   bw
MGM (Dore Schary)
GB title: *Target for Scandal*

A lady reporter goes to Washington to expose corruption, but falls for an honest congressman.

Standard flagwaver which takes itself a shade too seriously.

wd Robert Pirosh   *ph* John Alton   *m* Conrad Salinger

Van Johnson, Patricia Neal, Louis Calhern, Sidney Blackmer, Philip Ober, Patricia Collinge, Elizabeth Patterson, Moroni Olsen

Watch It, Sailor
GB   1961   81m   bw
Columbia/Cormorant/Hammer (Maurice Cowan)

A sailor about to be married receives a paternity accusation.

Glum farce with wasted talent.

w Falkland Cary, Phillip King   *play* Falkland Cary, Phillip King   *d* Wolf Rilla   *ph* Arthur Grant   *m* Douglas Gamley   *ad* Bernard Robinson, Don Mingaye   *ed* James Needs, Alfred Cox

Dennis Price, Marjorie Rhodes, Irene Handl, Liz Fraser, Vera Day, John Meillon, Cyril Smith

Watch on the Rhine **
US   1943   114m   bw
Warner (Hal B. Wallis)
V, V*

A German refugee and his family are pursued by Nazi agents in Washington.

Talky play doesn't make much of a film, though the talk is good talk and the performances outstanding; but it made a prestige point or two for Hollywood.

w Dashiell Hammett   *play* Lillian Hellman   *d* Herman Shumlin   *ph* Merritt Gerstad, Hal Mohr   *m* Max Steiner

Paul Lukas, Bette Davis, Lucile Watson, *George Coulouris*, Donald Woods, Geraldine Fitzgerald, Beulah Bondi, Henry Daniell

AA: Paul Lukas
AAN: best picture; script; Lucile Watson

Watch the Birdie
US   1950   71m   bw
MGM (Harry Ruskin)
V*

A photographer meets a rich girl and saves her from a crook.

Unhappy remake of Buster Keaton's *The Cameraman*, enlivened by a chase finale, but not helped by the star playing three members of the same family.

w Ivan Tors, Devery Freeman, Harry Ruskin   *d* Jack Donohue   *ph* Paul C. Vogel   *m* George Stoll

Red Skelton, Arlene Dahl, Ann Miller, Leon Ames, Pamela Britton, Richard Rober

The Watcher in the Woods
US   1980/82   100m or 83m   Technicolor
Walt Disney (Tom Leetch)
V*, L

The teenage daughter of an American composer has strange and apparently supernatural experiences in the British countryside.

Unsatisfactory attempt by the Disney people to aim at a wider audience than is expected of them. The mixture of cuteness, menace and the supernatural simply doesn't gel, and the film was much re-edited between its two appearances.

w Brian Clemens, Harry Spaulding, Rosemary Anne Sisson   *novel* Florence Engel Randall   *d* John Hough (and Vincent McEveety)   *ph* Alan Hume   *m* Stanley Myers

Bette Davis, Carroll Baker, David McCallum, Lynn-Holly Johnson, Kyle Richards, Ian Bannen, Richard Pasco

Watchers
Canada   1988   91m   colour
Guild/Concorde/Centaur/Carolco (Damian Lee, David Mitchell)
V*, L

Two experimental animals, an intelligent dog and an ape-like killer, escape from a top secret government research laboratory.

Dogged horror movie, with plentiful gore but little suspense.

w Bill Freed, Damian Lee   *novel* Dean R. Koontz   *d* Jon Hess   *ph* Richard Leiterman   *m* Joel Goldsmith   *pd* Richard Wilcox   *ed* Bill Freda, Carolle Alain, Rick Fields

Michael Ironside, Christopher Carey, Graeme Campbell, Dan O'Dowd, Lala, Corey Haim, Dale Wilson, Blu Mankuma, Colleen Winton

The Watchmaker of St Paul *
France   1973   105m   Eastmancolor
Lira (Raymond Danon)
V
original title: *L'Horloger de St Paul*

A watchmaker's tranquil life is shattered when he learns that his son is wanted for murder.

Solid character drama with careful writing and acting.

w Jean Aurenche, Pierre Bost, Bertrand Tavernier   *novel L'Horloger d'Everton* by Georges Simenon   *d* Bertrand Tavernier   *ph* Pierre William Glenn   *m* Philippe Sarde

Philippe Noiret, Jean Rochefort, Sylvain Rougerie, Christine Pascal

Water *
GB   1985   95m   colour
HandMade (Ian La Frenais)
V*

Chaos comes to a Caribbean island when industrialists check it for mineral springs.

Hysterical comedy which never develops a single line for long, and quickly wears out its welcome.

w Dick Clement, Ian La Frenais, Bill Bersky   *d* Dick Clement   *ph* Douglas Slocombe   *m* Mike Moran

Michael Caine, Valerie Perrine, Brenda Vaccaro, Leonard Rossiter, Billy Connolly, Fred Gwynne, Maureen Lipman

The Water Babies
GB/Poland   1978   92m   colour
Ariadne/Studio Miniatur Filmowych (Peter Shaw)
V*

An 1850 chimney sweep evades his pursuers by jumping into a pool, where he becomes involved in an underwater adventure.

The live action bookends are strangely subdued, the animated middle totally characterless and seeming to bear little relation to the rest. A considerable disappointment.

w Michael Robson   *novel* Charles Kingsley   *d* Lionel Jeffries   *ph* Ted Scaife   *m* Phil Coulter

James Mason, Billie Whitelaw, Bernard Cribbins, Joan Greenwood, David Tomlinson, Tommy Pender

Water Birds: see The Living Desert

The Water Gypsies
GB   1932   80m   bw
ATP

Adventures of two girls who live on a Thames barge.

Rather naïve and ordinary version of a successful book which many years later emerged as a stage musical; the film production has a stagey look throughout.

w Basil Dean, Miles Malleson, Alma Reville, John Paddy Carstairs *novel* A. P. Herbert *d* Maurice Elvey

Ann Todd, Sari Maritza, Richard Bird, Frances Doble, Ian Hunter, Anthony Ireland

'Should do business in the best type of places.' – *Variety*

The Waterdance **
US 1991 107m colour
Samuel Goldwyn/No Frills (Gale Anne Hurd)
V, V*

Three paraplegics in a rehabilitation centre attempt to come to terms with their condition and each other.

Graceful, perceptive, quietly effective movie on the pain of adjustment and the pleasures of friendship.

w Neil Jiminez *d* Neil Jiminez, Michael Steinberg *ph* Mark Plummer *m* Michael Convertino *pd* Robert Ziembicki *ed* Jeff Freeman

Eric Stoltz, Wesley Snipes, William Forsythe, Helen Hunt, Elizabeth Pena, William Allen Young, Henry Harris, Tony Genaro, Eva Rodriguez, Grace Zabriskie

'An honest, unsentimental, deeply moving, often extremely funny account of an adjustment to a new way of living, of confronting overnight the deprivations that time will visit on us should we live into old age, of facing up to the injustices and misfortunes of life.' – *Philip French, Observer*

'A smashing success if great performances and a deftly told, thoroughly absorbing tale mean anything.' – *Variety*

'The desires and loneliness of seafaring men and their women!'
Waterfront
GB 1950 80m bw
GFD/Conqueror/Paul Soskin
V*
US title: *Waterfront Women*

A drunken ship's fireman comes back to Liverpool after many years and causes trouble.

Unintentionally funny melodrama which gives the actors a lot of trouble.

w John Brophy, Paul Soskin *novel* John Brophy *d* Michael Anderson *ph* Harry Waxman *md* Muir Mathieson

Robert Newton, Richard Burton, Kathleen Harrison, Susan Shaw, Avis Scott, Kenneth Griffith

Waterfront Women: see *Waterfront*

Waterhole Three
US 1967 100m Techniscope
Paramount
V*

Sheriff, crooks and a gambler seek buried loot.

Rather irritatingly immoral Western with a hero who defines rape as assault with a friendly weapon; in between it tries hard for the ballad style.

w Joseph Steck, Robert R. Young *d* William Graham *ph* Robert Burks *m* Dave Grusin

James Coburn, Carroll O'Connor, Margaret Blye, Claude Akins, Joan Blondell, Timothy Carey

Waterland
GB 1992 95m colour Scope
Mayfair/Palace/Pandora/Channel 4 Films/British Screen (Katy McGuinness, Patrick Cassavetti)
V, V*, L

In the 1970s an English history teacher working in Pittsburgh tells his class of his own difficult past growing up in East Anglia.

A domestic saga of marital difficulties, incest and murder that soon slides into glum melodrama.

w Peter Prince *novel* Graham Swift *d* Stephen Gyllenhaal *ph* Robert Elswit *m* Carter Burwell *pd* Hugo Luczyc-Whyowski *ed* Lesley Walker

Jeremy Irons, Sinead Cusack, Ethan Hawke, Grant Warnock, Lena Headey, David Morrissey, John Heard

'A talented but terminally parched piece of literary cinema. Decorous, academic treatment of bizarre and traumatic material makes for a merely unpleasant film rather than an insightful or genuinely disturbing one.' – *Variety*

'The men, the battle, the glory the world will remember forever!'
Waterloo *
Italy/USSR 1970 132m Technicolor Panavision
Columbia/DDL/Mosfilm (Dino de Laurentiis)
V, V*, S

Historical events leading up to the 1815 battle.

The battle forms the last hour of this historical charade, and looks both exciting and splendid, though confusion is not avoided. The rest is a mixed blessing.

w H. A. L. Craig, Sergei Bondarchuk *d* Sergei Bondarchuk *ph* Armando Nannuzzi *m* Nino Rota *pd* Mario Garbuglia

Rod Steiger, Christopher Plummer, Orson Welles, Jack Hawkins, Virginia McKenna, Dan O'Herlihy, Rupert Davies, Ian Ogilvy, Michael Wilding

Waterloo Bridge *
US 1931 72m bw
Universal (Carl Laemmle Jnr)

An army officer marries a ballerina; when he is reported missing his family ignore her and she sinks into prostitution.

One for the ladies, who lapped it up.

w Tom Reed, Benn W. Levy *play* Robert E. Sherwood *d* James Whale *ph* Arthur Edeson

Mae Clarke, Kent Douglass, Doris Lloyd, Ethel Griffies, Enid Bennett, Frederick Kerr, Bette Davis

'Just fair programme fodder, and it ought to be better. Not helped by an uninspiring sad ending.' – *Variety*

Waterloo Bridge **
US 1940 103m bw
MGM (Sidney Franklin)
V*, L

Lush, all-stops-out remake of the above; for yet another version see *Gaby*.

w S. N. Behrman, Hans Rameau, George Froeschel *d* Mervyn Le Roy *ph* Joseph Ruttenberg *m* Herbert Stothart

Vivien Leigh, Robert Taylor, Lucile Watson, Virginia Field, Maria Ouspenskaya, C. Aubrey Smith, Steffi Duna

'The director uses candlelight and rain more effectively than he does the actors.' – *New Yorker, 1977*

AAN: Joseph Ruttenberg; Herbert Stothart

The Waterloo Bridge Handicap *
GB 1978 21m colour
Paramount/Fetter

Commuters enjoy a daily race across Westminster Bridge.

Amusing trifle, well shot and edited. *wd* Ross Cramer *ed* Sean Barton

Leonard Rossiter, Lynda Bellingham, John Quentin, Gordon Laye

Waterloo Road
GB 1944 76m bw
GFD/Gainsborough (Edward Black)

A soldier whose wife is enamoured of a petty crook absents himself to settle matters.

What at the time seemed cheerful realism now seems chronically forced, but amusing moments can still be found.

wd Sidney Gilliat *story* Val Valentine *ph* Arthur Crabtree *md* Louis Levy

John Mills, Stewart Granger, Joy Shelton, Alastair Sim, Beatrice Varley, Alison Leggatt, *Jean Kent*

'The harsh rattle of trains over a viaduct, the clamour of the street market, the wailing of sirens and the crash of bombs are the accompaniment of this wartime love story.' – *Richard Winnington*

'Unpretentious, credible, continuously entertaining and just the right length.' – *Richard Mallett, Punch*

Watermelon Man
US 1970 100m Technicolor
Columbia/Johanna (John B. Bennett)
V*, L

A bigoted insurance salesman wakes up one morning to find he has turned into a black man.

Spasmodically funny racial comedy, compromised by the impossibility of a black man playing white even with heavy make-up.

w Herman Raucher *d* Melvin Van Peebles *ph* W. Wallace Kelley *m* Melvin Van Peebles

Godfrey Cambridge, Estelle Parsons, Howard Caine, Mantan Moreland

Waters of Time *
GB 1951 37m bw
Port of London Authority

A poetic impression of the Port of London, from the mouth of the Thames to Kingston.

Notably stylish documentary, made to coincide with the Festival of Britain.

wd Basil Wright, Bill Launder *ed* Basil Wright, Bill Launder

Watership Down
GB 1978 92m Technicolor
Nepenthe (Martin Rosen)
V, V*

A colony of rabbits seek a new home following a vision of the destruction of their warren.

A brilliantly written if somewhat pretentious parable becomes a rather flatly made cartoon in which it is difficult to distinguish one rabbit from another; the whole thing becomes a bit doomladen for family audiences, while adults will presumably prefer to re-read the novel.

wd Martin Rosen *novel* Richard Adams *animation director* Tony Guy *m* Angela Morley *voices* John Hurt, Richard Briers, Ralph Richardson, Zero Mostel, Roy Kinnear, Denholm Elliott, John Bennett, Simon Cadell

Watusi
US 1959 85m Technicolor
MGM (Al Zimbalist)

Harry Quartermain retraces his father's footsteps to King Solomon's Mines.

Skilful re-use of *King Solomon's Mines* footage; acceptable *Boy's Own Paper* stuff.

w James Clavell *d* Kurt Neumann *ph* Harold E. Wellman

George Montgomery, Taina Elg, David Farrar, Rex Ingram, Dan Seymour

Waxwork

US 1988 96m colour
Vestron/Palla Pictures/Filmrullen (Staffen Ahrenberg)
V*, L

Students visit a waxworks' chamber of horrors in an old dark house, where the figures come to life.

Direly unimaginative, hammily acted horror movie.

wd Anthony Hickox *ph* Gerry Lively *m* Roger Bellon *pd* Gianni Quaranta *ed* Christopher Cibelli

Zach Galligan, Deborah Freeman, Michelle Johnson, Dana Ashbrook, Miles O'Keefe, Charles McCaughlin, J. Kenneth Campbell, John Rhys Davies, Patrick McNee, David Warner

'Film-making by numbers.' – *MFB*

Waxwork II: Lost in Time

'An eye popping, teeth chattering, mind blowing movie!!!'
US 1991 100m Foto-Kem
Electric Pictures (Nancy Paloian)
V
aka: *Lost in Time*

Having destroyed a wax museum where monsters came to life, a couple travel into a parallel universe of 'God's Nintendo game' where the battle between good and evil is fought as scenarios from horror movies.

From *Nosferatu* to Godzilla and *Alien*, taking in *Frankenstein, Jekyll and Hyde*, Edgar Allen Poe and *The Haunting* along the way, classic horrors are parodied in a clever low-budget style with cut-rate wit, ham acting and a lot of blood-letting. The result may entertain fans of the genre in an indulgent mood.

wd Anthony Hickox *ph* Gerry Lively *m* Steve Schiff *pd* Steve Hardie *sp* Bob Keen *ed* Christopher Cibelli

Zach Galligan, Monika Schnarre, Martin Kemp, Bruce Campbell, Michael Des Barres, Jim Metzler, Sophie Ward, Bill Kane, Juliet Mills, John Ireland, Patrick Macnee, David Carradine, Alexander Godunov

'A loopy gags-and-gore fest striving a mite too self-consciously for cult status.' – *Variety*

'A profound lack of style that confirms just because Hickox loves good horror movies doesn't necessarily mean he knows how to make them.' – *Shivers*

Waxworks *

Germany 1924 62m approx (24 fps) bw silent
Neptun-Film
original title: *Das Wachsfigurenkabinett*

A young poet in a fairground waxwork museum concocts stories about Haroun al Raschid, Ivan the Terrible and Jack the Ripper.

The form later became familiar in such horror films as *Torture Garden* and *Tales from the Crypt*, but here the emphasis is not on horror but on grotesquerie, and indeed the idea is somewhat more entertaining than the rather plodding execution.

w Henrik Galeen *d* Paul Leni *ph* Helmar Lerski *ad* Paul Leni, Ernst Stern, Alfred Junge

William Dieterle, Emil Jannings, Conrad Veidt, Werner Krauss

The Way: see *Yol*

The Way Ahead ***

GB 1944 115m bw
GFD/Two Cities (John Sutro, Norman Walker)
V*
US title: *Immortal Battalion*

Adventures of a platoon of raw recruits during World War II.

Memorable semi-documentary originally intended as a training film; the warm humour of the early scenes, however, never leads quite naturally into the final action and tragedy.

w Eric Ambler, Peter Ustinov *d* Carol Reed *ph* Guy Green *m* William Alwyn

David Niven, Stanley Holloway, Raymond Huntley, William Hartnell, James Donald, John Laurie, Leslie Dwyer, Hugh Burden, Jimmy Hanley, Renée Asherson, Penelope Dudley Ward, Reginald Tate, Leo Genn, Mary Jerrold, Peter Ustinov

'Is to be admired and recommended for its direction, its writing and its playing.' – *Dilys Powell*

Way Back Home

US 1932 81m bw
RKO

Problems of a Maine preacher.

Unintentionally hilarious farrago of dark deeds in a small town, from a radio serial.

w Jane Murfin *d* William A. Seiter

Phillips Lord, Bette Davis, Effie Palmer, Bennett Kilpack, Frank Albertson, Mrs Phillips Lord

Way Down East **

US 1920 110m approx (24 fps) bw with colour sequence silent
D. W. Griffith
V*

A country girl is seduced; her baby dies; her shame is revealed; but a kindly farmer rescues her from drowning and marries her.

Old-fashioned tearjerker impeccably mounted and very typical of its director in its sentimental mood. The ice floe sequence is famous for its excitement and realism.

w Anthony Paul Kelly, Joseph R. Grismer, D. W. Griffith *play* Lottie Blair Parker *d* D. W. Griffith *ph* Billy Bitzer, Henrik Sortov

Lillian Gish, Richard Barthelmess, Lowell Sherman, Creighton Hale

'Griffith took a creaking, dated stage melodrama and turned it into a melodramatic epic.' – *Pauline Kael, 70s*

Way Down East

US 1935 85m bw
TCF (Winfield Sheehan)

Tedious and unwise remake.

w Howard Estabrook, William Hurlbut *d* Henry King

Rochelle Hudson, Henry Fonda, Slim Summerville, Edward Trevor, Margaret Hamilton, Andy Devine, Spring Byington, Russell Simpson, Sara Haden

Way for a Sailor

US 1930 83m bw
MGM

Adventures of a tough seafarer and a pet seal.

Thin vehicle for a declining star whose talkie voice was at odds with his image.

w Laurence Stallings, W. L. River *novel* Albert Richard Wetjen *d* Sam Wood *ph* Percy Hilburn

John Gilbert, Wallace Beery, Leila Hyams, Jim Tully, Polly Moran, Doris Lloyd

'It throws John Gilbert for a loss, and it's not his fault. His voice is okay.' – *Variety*

Way of a Gaucho

US 1952 91m Technicolor
TCF (Philip Dunne)

An Argentine gaucho joins the militia and fights Indians.

Mildly interesting Western-in-disguise.

w Philip Dunne *novel* Herbert Childs *d* Jacques Tourneur *ph* Harry Jackson *m* Sol Kaplan

Rory Calhoun, Gene Tierney, Richard Boone, Hugh Marlowe, Everett Sloane, Enrique Chaico

The Way of All Flesh *

US 1928 94m (24 fps) bw silent
Paramount
(Adolph Zukor, Jesse L. Lasky)

A respectable man leaves his wife, goes to the dogs, and is too ashamed to come back.

Star character drama, most watchable now when it goes over the top.

d Victor Fleming

Emil Jannings, Belle Bennett, Phyllis Haver

AA: Emil Jannings

The Way of All Flesh

'He left his heart behind when he took it!'
US 1940 82m bw
Paramount (Eugene Zukor)

Remake of the above, well enough done but clearly outmoded.

w Lenore Coffee *story* Jules Furthman, Lajos Biro *novel* Perley Poore Sheehan *d* Louis King *ph* Theodor Sparkuhl

Akim Tamiroff, Gladys George, Muriel Angelus, Berton Churchill, Fritz Leiber

The Way of the Dragon (dubbed)

Hong Kong 1973 99m Cine Art colour Scope
Cathay/Concord/Golden Harvest (Raymond Chow)

A martial arts expert goes to Rome to help a friend save her restaurant which is threatened by gangsters.

A kung fu movie incongruously shifted from the East to Italy, where it seems silly, although the fight sequences are well done.

wd Bruce Lee *ph* Ho Lan Shan *m* Joseph Koo *ad* Chien Hsin *ed* Chang Yao Ching

Bruce Lee, Nora Miao, Chuck Norris, Wei Ping Ao, Wang Chung Hsin

'At once deeply flawed and the most personal film to have come out of Hong Kong.' – *Tony Rayns, MFB*

† The film was cut to 91m on its British release.

Way Out West ****

US 1937 66m bw
Hal Roach (Stan Laurel)
V, V (C), V*, L

Laurel and Hardy come to Brushwood Gulch to deliver the deed to a gold mine.

Seven reels of perfect joy, with the comedians at their very best in brilliantly-timed routines, plus two song numbers as a bonus.

w Jack Jevne, Charles Rogers, James Parrott, Felix Adler *d* James Horne *ph* Art Lloyd, Walter Lundin *m* Marvin Hatley

Stan Laurel, Oliver Hardy, James Finlayson, Sharon Lynne, Rosina Lawrence

'Thin returns indicated . . . for added feature on duallers.' – *Variety*

'Not only one of their most perfect films, it ranks with the best screen comedy anywhere.' – *David Robinson, 1962*

'The film is leisurely in the best sense; you adjust to a different rhythm and come out feeling relaxed as if you'd had a vacation.' – *New Yorker, 1980*

AAN: Marvin Hatley

The Way to Love

'Of course he's naughty! But that's the way you love him best!'
US 1933 80m bw
Paramount (Benjamin Glazer)

A would-be Paris tourist guide works as a pavement hawker and helps a showgirl evade her knife-thrower partner.

Thin star vehicle with a few pleasant moments.

w Gene Fowler, Benjamin Glazer   *d* Norman Taurog
ph Charles Lang   *m/y* Ralph Rainger, Leo Robin

Maurice Chevalier, Edward Everett Horton, Ann
Dvorak, Arthur Pierson, Minna Gombell, Blanche
Frederici, Douglass Dumbrille, John Miljan

'The poorest of the Chevaliers but poor entertainment
which will get by on the strength of the star.' – *Variety*

The Way to the Gold

US   1957   94m   bw
TCF (David Weisbart)

An ex-convict seeks hidden loot but is pursued by
competitors.

Gloomy, self-pitying melodrama.

w Wendell Mayes   *novel* Wilber Steele   *d* Robert
D. Webb   *ph* Leo Tover   *m* Lionel Newman

Jeffrey Hunter, Sheree North, Barry Sullivan, Walter
Brennan, Ruth Donnelly, Neville Brand

The Way to the Stars ****

GB   1945   109m   bw
Two Cities (Anatole de Grunwald)
V
US title: *Johnny in the Clouds*

World War II as seen by the guests at a small hotel
near an airfield.

Generally delightful comedy drama suffused with
tragic atmosphere but with very few flying shots, one
of the few films which instantly bring back the
atmosphere of the war in Britain for anyone who was
involved.

w Terence Rattigan, Anatole de Grunwald   *poem* John
Pudney   *d* Anthony Asquith   *ph* Derrick Williams
m Nicholas Brodszky

*John Mills, Rosamund John, Michael Redgrave, Douglass
Montgomery,* Basil Radford, Stanley Holloway, Joyce
Carey, Renée Asherson, Felix Aylmer, Bonar
Colleano, Trevor Howard, Jean Simmons

'Not for a long time have I seen a film so satisfying, so
memorable, or so successful in evoking the precise
mood and atmosphere of the recent past.' – *Richard
Mallett, Punch*

'Humour, humanity, and not a sign of mawkishness
. . . a classic opening sequence, with the camera
wandering through an abandoned air base, peering in
at each detail in the nissen huts, the sleeping quarters,
the canteens, noting all the time a procession of
objects each of which will have its own special
significance in the action of the film.' – *Basil Wright,
1972*

Way Way Out

US   1966   105m   DeLuxe   Cinemascope
TCF/Coldwater/Jerry Lewis (Malcolm Stuart)

In 1994 a weather expert on the moon has woman
trouble.

Dismal sex farce with an unusual backdrop; painful to
sit through.

w William Bowers, Laslo Vadnay   *d* Gordon
Douglas   *ph* William H. Clothier   *m* Lalo Schifrin

Jerry Lewis, Connie Stevens, Robert Morley, Dick
Shawn, Anita Ekberg, Dennis Weaver, Howard
Morris, Brian Keith

'Everything seemed so important then – even love!'
The Way We Were **

US   1973   118m   Eastmancolor   Panavision
Columbia/Rastar (Ray Stark)
V, V*, L, S

The romance and marriage of an upper-crust young
novelist and a Jewish bluestocking girl, from college
to Hollywood in the thirties, forties and fifties.

Instant nostalgia for Americans, some fun and a lot of
boredom for everybody is provided by this very
patchy star vehicle which makes a particular mess of

the McCarthy witch hunt sequence but has
undeniable moments of vitality.

w Arthur Laurents   *novel* Arthur Laurents
d Sydney Pollack   *ph* Harry Stradling Jnr
m Marvin Hamlisch

Barbra Streisand, Robert Redford, Patrick O'Neal, Viveca
Lindfors, Bradford Dillman, Lois Chiles, Allyn Ann
McLerie, Herb Edelman, Murray Hamilton

'Not one moment of the picture is anything but
garbage under the gravy of false honesty.' – *Stanley
Kauffmann*

'A real curate's egg of a movie, composed of so many
disparate parts as to put you in mind of Leacock's
knight, who got on his horse and rode off furiously in
all directions.' – *Benny Green, Punch*

AA: Marvin Hamlisch; title song (*m* Marvin
Hamlisch, *ly* Alan and Marilyn Bergman)

AAN: Harry Stradling Jnr; Barbra Streisand

The Way West *

US   1967   122m   DeLuxe   Panavision
UA/Harold Hecht
V*

Hazards of a wagon train between Missouri and
Oregon in 1843.

Semi-spectacular Western which looks good but falls
apart dramatically, especially in its insistence on a
sub-plot about a most unlikely nymphet.

w Ben Maddow, Mitch Lindemann   *novel* A. B.
Guthrie Jnr   *d* Andrew V. McLaglen   *ph* William
H. Clothier   *m* Bronislau Kaper

Kirk Douglas, Robert Mitchum, Richard Widmark,
Lola Albright, Michael Witney, Sally Field, Stubby
Kaye, Jack Elam

'A jerk's idea of an epic; big stars, big landscapes, bad
jokes, folksy-heroic music to plug up the holes, and
messy hang-ups.' – *Pauline Kael*

'You'll laugh. You'll cry. You'll hurl.'
Wayne's World

US   1992   95m   Technicolor
UIP/Paramount (Lorne Michaels)
V, V*, L, CD, S

A ramshackle cable TV show, put together by two
girl- and rock-obsessed teenagers, is given big-time
exposure by a sleazy TV executive.

Tedious teen comedy, based on characters developed
for the *Saturday Night Live* TV show, which long
outstays its welcome. It was, though, one of 1992's
surprise hits, ranking sixth at the US box-office and
doing well in Europe.

w Mike Myers, Bonnie Turner, Terry Turner
d Penelope Spheeris   *ph* Theo Van de Sande
m J. Peter Robinson   *pd* Gregg Fonseca
ed Malcolm Campbell

Mike Myers, Dana Carvey, Rob Lowe, Tia Carrere,
Brian Doyle-Murray, Lara Flynn Boyle, Michael
DeLuise, Dan Bell

'Aggressively pitched at a young white male
audience, feature is unlikely to appeal to mainstream
moviegoers . . . Even for fans of the TV comics, the
laugh-to-running-time ratio is extremely low.' –
Variety

Wayne's World 2 *

US   1993   95m   DeLuxe
Paramount (Lorne Michaels)
S

In a dream, Wayne is told to organize Waynestock, the
ultimate rock concert.

The mixture is much the same as the first film, but this
time around the jokes are slightly better.

w Mike Myers, Bonnie Turner, Terry Turner
d Stephen Surjik   *ph* Francis Kenny   *m* Carter
Burwell   *pd* Gregg Fonseca   *ed* Malcolm Campbell

Mike Myers, Dana Carvey, Christopher Walken, Tia
Carrere, Ralph Brown, Kim Basinger, Drew
Barrymore, Michael Nickles (as Jim Morrison),
Aerosmith

'A puerile, misguided and loathsome effort . . . NOT!'
– *Variety*

'Something of a disappointment, though that is not to
say that a lot of people won't enjoy it – especially if
drunk or on drugs.' – *Ben Thompson, Sight and Sound*

The Wayward Bus

US   1957   89m   bw   Cinemascope
TCF (Charles Brackett)

A landslide strands an assortment of bus passengers
in a lonely farmhouse . . .

. . . but not the old dark house, unfortunately: this lot
does nothing but talk, and the plot never really forms.

w Ivan Moffat   *novel* John Steinbeck   *d* Victor
Vicas   *ph* Charles G. Clarke   *m* Leigh Harline

Dan Dailey, Jayne Mansfield, Joan Collins, Rick
Jason, Dolores Michaels, Larry Keating, Betty Lou
Keim

We Are Not Alone *

US   1939   112m   bw
Warner (Henry Blanke)

A man having an innocent affair is accused of
murdering his wife.

Gloomy, well-acted drama with a rather uneasy
English setting.

w James Hilton, Milton Krims   *novel* James Hilton
d Edmund Goulding   *ph* Tony Gaudio   *m* Max
Steiner

Paul Muni, Jane Bryan, Flora Robson, Raymond
Severn, Una O'Connor, Henry Daniell, Montagu Love,
James Stephenson, Cecil Kellaway

'It has dignity and warmth and is genuinely moving
. . . handsomely produced, skilfully directed, and
eloquently played.' – *Variety*

'An extraordinarily moving story, beautifully told and
perfectly acted.' – *MFB*

We Dive at Dawn

GB   1943   98m   bw
GFD/Gainsborough (Edward Black)
V*

World War II adventures of a British submarine
disabled in the Baltic.

Fairly routine war suspenser.

w J. P. Williams, Val Valentine, Frank Launder
d Anthony Asquith   *ph* Jack Cox   *md* Louis Levy

John Mills, Eric Portman, Reginald Purdell, Niall
MacGinnis, Joan Hopkins, Josephine Wilson, Jack
Watling

We Faw Down

US   1928   20m   bw   silent
Hal Roach

Stan and Ollie have an evening out, but their lies to
their wives become apparent.

Moderate star comedy, later elaborated in *Sons of the
Desert.*

w H. M. Walker   *d* Leo McCarey

Laurel and Hardy, Bess Flowers, Vivien Oakland

We Have Our Moments

US   1937   63m   bw
Edmund Grainger/Universal

Gangsters hide their loot in the trunk of a
schoolteacher going to Europe on a vacation.

Rather slackly handled comedy with amusing bits.

w Bruce Manning, Charles Grayson, David Belden,
Frederick Stephani   *d* Alfred Werker

James Dunn, Sally Eilers, Mischa Auer, David Niven, Warren Hymer, Marjorie Gateson, Thurston Hall

'As the number two feature on doubles it will manage to get by.' – *Variety*

We Humans: see *Young America*

We Joined the Navy

GB　1962　105m　Eastmancolor　Cinemascope
Dial/Daniel M. Angel

A carefree naval commander and three cadets get involved in the affairs of a small Mediterranean country.

Desperate naval farce which sinks from script malnutrition in reel two.

w Arthur Dales　*novel* John Winton　d Wendy Toye　ph Otto Heller　m Ron Grainer

Kenneth More, Lloyd Nolan, Mischa Auer, Joan O'Brien, Jeremy Lloyd, Dinsdale Landen, Derek Fowlds

We Live Again *

US　1934　85m　bw
Samuel Goldwyn

A Russian prince is brought up in the country and falls in love with a servant girl whose life later takes a downward path.

Beautifully made but dramatically uninteresting version of a Russian classic.

w Preston Sturges, Maxwell Anderson, Leonard Praskins　*novel Resurrection* by Leo Tolstoy
d *Rouben Mamoulian*　ph *Gregg Toland*　m Alfred Newman

Fredric March, Anna Sten, Jane Baxter, C. Aubrey Smith, Ethel Griffies, Jessie Ralph, Sam Jaffe

'It's a class picture basically. That limits its mass b.o. appeal.' – *Variety*

We of the Never Never *

Australia　1982　134m　Eastmancolor
Technovision
Adams Packer/Film Corporation of Western Australia/GTC (Greg Tepper)
V*

Around 1900, a city girl marries the owner of an isolated cattle station.

Longwinded but attractively photographed recollections of another time and another place. Not really very memorable despite a plethora of incident.

w Peter Schreck　*book* Mrs Aeneas Gunn　d Igor Auzins　ph *Gary Hansen*　m Peter Best

Angela Punch-McGregor, Arthur Dignam, Tony Barry, Martin Vaughan

'Tasteful period re-creation, choked-back emotionalism, a *Men of Two Worlds* attempt at assuaging colonial guilt, and the kind of tidily suffering heroine Deborah Kerr used to play.' – *Kim Newman, MFB*

We Think the World of You *

GB　1988　94m　Technicolor
Recorded Releasing/Gold Screen/Film Four International/British Screen (Tommaso Jandelli)
V*, L

A middle-aged homosexual becomes devoted to his lover's dog.

Understated and reticent drama, enjoyable mainly for its acting.

w Hugh Stoddart　*novel* J. R. Ackerley　d Colin Gregg　ph Mike Garfath　m Julian Jacobson
pd Jamie Leonard　ed Peter Delfgou

Alan Bates, Max Wall, Liz Smith, Frances Barber, Gary Oldman, Ryan Batt, Kerry Wise, Sheila Ballantine

We Were Dancing

US　1942　93m　bw
MGM (Robert Z. Leonard, Orville Dull)

A Polish princess elopes from her engagement party with a gigolo.

Leaden romantic comedy produced in high style.

w Claudine West, Hans Rameau, George Froeschel
play (partly based on) *Tonight at 8.30* by Noël Coward
d Robert Z. Leonard　ph Robert Planck
m Bronislau Kaper

Norma Shearer, Melvyn Douglas, Gail Patrick, Lee Bowman, Marjorie Main, Reginald Owen, Alan Mowbray, Florence Bates, Sig Rumann, Dennis Hoey, Heather Thatcher, Connie Gilchrist

We Were Strangers *

US　1949　105m　bw
Columbia/Horizon (Sam Spiegel)

Cuban rebels in the thirties plan to assassinate a politician and have to build a tunnel through a cemetery.

Well-made but very downbeat adventure story, too cheerless to be exciting.

w Peter Viertel, John Huston　*novel Rough Sketch* by Robert Sylvester　d John Huston　ph Russell Metty
m Georges Antheil

John Garfield, Jennifer Jones, Pedro Armendariz, Gilbert Roland, Wally Cassell, Ramon Novarro, David Bond, Jose Perez

'There is so much about this film I cannot swallow – the implausibilities of detail, the convention of broken accents, the literary conversaziones, the naïve doctrines of revolution . . . [but] it continues to haunt the mind and has therefore had its say.' – *Richard Winnington*

We Who Are About to Die

US　1937　82m　bw
RKO

Life on Death Row.

Modest prison melodrama with a lot of opportunity for character actors to display hysteria.

w John Twist, David Lamson　d Christy Cabanne

Preston Foster, Ann Dvorak, John Beal, Ray Mayer, Gordon Jones, Russel Hopton, J. Carrol Naish, Willie Fung, Paul Hurst, Frank Jenks, Barnett Parker, John Wray, John Carroll

'An action drama of considerable tension that should please the general run of fans with plenty of special charm for the kids and the menfolk.' – *Variety*

The Weak and the Wicked

GB　1953　88m　bw
ABPC/Marble Arch (Victor Skutezky)

Flashbacks show how various women came to find themselves in prison.

Predictable portmanteau drama with stalwart performances.

w J. Lee-Thompson, Anne Burnaby　*book Who Lie in Gaol* by Joan Henry　d J. Lee-Thompson
ph Gilbert Taylor　m Leighton Lucas

Glynis Johns, John Gregson, Diana Dors, Jane Hylton, Sidney James, Olive Sloane, Eliot Makeham, A. E. Matthews, Athene Seyler, Sybil Thorndike, Anthony Nicholls, Joan Haythorne

The Weaker Sex

GB　1948　84m　bw
Two Cities (Paul Soskin)

Day-to-day problems of a well-to-do war widow.

Mild suburban comedy which sparkled more on stage, with such curtain lines as: 'Quick, the fishmonger's got fish!'

w Esther McCracken, Paul Soskin　*play No Medals* by Esther McCracken　d Roy Baker

Ursula Jeans, Cecil Parker, Joan Hopkins, Derek Bond, Lana Morris, Thora Hird, John Stone

The Weapon

GB　1956　81m　bw　Superscope 235
Periclean (Frank Bevis)

A boy finds a loaded revolver on a bomb site and mistakenly thinks he has killed someone with it.

Standard suspenser with a cast worthy of something more interesting.

w Fred Freiburger　d Val Guest　ph Reg Wyer
m James Stevens

Lizabeth Scott, Steve Cochran, George Cole, Herbert Marshall, Nicole Maurey, Jon Whiteley, Laurence Naismith

The Web *

US　1947　87m　bw
Universal (Jerry Bresler)

A financier hires a young lawyer as his bodyguard and lures him into committing murder.

Modestly well staged and glossy thriller.

w William Bowers, Bertram Millhauser　d Michael Gordon　ph Irving Glassberg　m Hans Salter

Edmond O'Brien, Vincent Price, Ella Raines, William Bendix

Web of Evidence: see *Beyond This Place*

Web of Passion: see *À Double Tour*

The Webster Boy

GB　1961　83m　bw
Emmet Dalton
US title: *Middle of Nowhere*

A teenager suffers at the hands of a sadistic schoolmaster.

Curious, totally unbelievable melodrama.

w Ted Allen　d Don Chaffey　ph Gerald Gibbs
m Wilfrid Joseph

Richard O'Sullivan, John Cassavetes, David Farrar, Elizabeth Sellars, Niall MacGinnis

A Wedding *

US　1978　125m　DeLuxe
TCF/Lion's Gate (Thommy Thompson, Robert Altman)
V*

Two families converge for a fashionable wedding, but the day is beset by calamities.

Wide-ranging satirical comedy which despite excellent moments goes on far too long, is rather too black, and is sabotaged by the director's *penchant* for having fourteen people talking at the same time. An exhausting experience.

w John Considine, Patricia Resnick, Allan Nicholls, Robert Altman　d Robert Altman　ph Charles Rosher　md Tom Walls

Carol Burnett, Paul Dooley, Amy Stryker, Mia Farrow, Peggy Ann Garner, Lillian Gish, Nina Van Pallandt, Vittorio Gassman, Howard Duff, Desi Arnaz Jnr, Dina Merrill, Geraldine Chaplin, Viveca Lindfors, Lauren Hutton, John Cromwell

'Altman has become our leading silky utilizer of film styles. This time it's quick-sale ugliness. Just because he is so technically accomplished, so vacuously smooth and smart, he is depressing: he seems a kind of walking death sentence on the prospects of American film, much more menacing than clumsy or arrantly sentimental film-makers.' – *Stanley Kauffmann*

'Everyone Wants To Kiss The Bride . . . Except The Groom.'

The Wedding Banquet ***
Taiwan/US   1993   108m   DuArt color
Māinline/Central Motion Picture/Good Machine (Ang Lee, Ted Hope, James Schamus)
S
original title: *Xiyan*

A homosexual American-Taiwanese businessman has to conceal his sexual preferences and his lover when his staid mother and father arrive in New York to celebrate his arranged marriage to a Chinese woman.

A delightful comedy of culture clashes, racial and generational differences and the problems of living up to your parents' expectations; it makes light of situations without concealing their truth and occasional pain.

w Ang Lee, Neil Peng, James Schamus   d Ang Lee   ph Jong Lin   m Mader   pd Steve Rosenzweig   ed Tim Squyres

Mitchell Lichtenstein, Winston Chao, May Chin, Sihung Lung, Ah-Leh Gua, Dion Birney, Jeanne Kuo Chang

'Canny mix of feelgood elements and ethnic color.' – *Variety*

'A wish-fulfilment fantasy on a par with the equally crowd-pleasing *Strictly Ballroom*.' – *Tony Rayns, Sight and Sound*

AAN: best foreign-language film

Wedding Bells: see *Royal Wedding*

Wedding Breakfast: see *The Catered Affair*

The Wedding March **
US   1928   196m approx (24 fps)   bw   silent
Paramount/Celebrity
V*

A Habsburg prince loves a poor girl but is forced to marry a crippled princess, who dies; he is then murdered by the poor girl's enraged defender.

A marathon dose of Stroheim's favourite subject, sex, with some violence and a few fetishes thrown in. Full of fascinating touches, but desperately overlong, it was originally released in two parts, but failed to draw.

w Harry Carr, Erich von Stroheim   d Erich von Stroheim   ph Hal Mohr, Ben Reynolds   ad Erich von Stroheim, Richard Day

Erich von Stroheim, Fay Wray, ZaSu Pitts, Matthew Betz, Maude George, Cesare Gravina, George Fawcett

'A pitilessly authentic portrait of decadent Imperialist Austria.' – *Georges Sadoul*

'The slowness, heaviness, mindlessness of this temple of unnaturalness through which man passes as through a forest of clichés defied description.' – *John Simon, 1967*

† In 1975 there was published a pictorial record, *The Complete Wedding March*, by Herman G. Weinberg

The Wedding Night *
US   1935   83m   bw
Samuel Goldwyn

A Connecticut author causes tragedy when he takes an interest in the local Polish immigrant farmers and especially in the daughter of one of them.

Interesting and unusual but slightly tediously told drama.

w Edith Fitzgerald   d King Vidor   ph Gregg Toland   m Alfred Newman

Gary Cooper, Anna Sten, Sig Rumann, Helen Vinson, Ralph Bellamy, Esther Dale

'Fine artistic film, possibly too artistic.' – *Variety*

'Convincing and curiously powerful.' – *New York Herald Tribune*

The Wedding of Lilli Marlene
GB   1953   87m   bw
Monarch

The heroine of World War II becomes a success in show business.

Poorly confected programme filler, an unnecessary sequel if ever there was one.

w John Baines   d Arthur Crabtree

Lisa Daniely, Hugh McDermott, Sid James, Gabrielle Brune, Robert Ayres

'He gave her something to remember him by!'
Wedding Present *
US   1936   81m   bw
Paramount (B. P. Schulberg)

A pair of crack newspaper reporters take their jobs and themselves lightly.

Whimsical star comedy with some funny scenes.

w Joseph Anthony   story Paul Gallico   d Richard Wallace   ph Leon Shamroy

Cary Grant, Joan Bennett, George Bancroft, Conrad Nagel, Gene Lockhart, William Demarest, Edward Brophy

'Grant and Bennett try hard, but the combination of story, direction and whatnot is pretty much against them.' – *Variety*

Wedding Rehearsal
GB   1932   84m   bw
Ideal/London Films/Alexander Korda

A Guards officer foils his grandmother's plans to get him married by finding suitors for all the young ladies offered.

Frail comedy with unsure technique.

w Helen Gardom   story Lajos Biro, George Grossmith   d Alexander Korda   ph Leslie Rowson   m Kurt Schroeder   ad O. F. Werndorff, Vincent Korda   ed Harold Young

Roland Young, George Grossmith, John Loder, Lady Tree, Wendy Barrie, Maurice Evans, Joan Gardner, Merle Oberon, Kate Cutler, Edmund Breon

'If I were Korda, I would get up in the night, steal the negative, and quietly drop it in the Thames.' – *Marcel Ermans, World Film News*

Wedlock
US   1991   98m   CFI colour
Spectacor (Branko Lustig)
V, V*, S
aka: *Deadlock*

Two convicts go on the run linked by electronic collars that will explode if they are more than a hundred yards apart.

Plodding, violent thriller which reaches the conclusion that it's acceptable to steal providing you can get away with it.

w Broderick Miller   d Lewis Teague   ph Dietrich Lohmann   m Richard Gibbs   pd Veronica Hadfield   ed Carl Kress

Rutger Hauer, Mimi Rogers, Joan Chen, James Remar

'Nice idea, unsatisfying results.' – *Sight and Sound*

Wee Geordie: see *Geordie*

Wee Willie Winkie **
US   1937   99m   bw
TCF (Gene Markey)
V*

A small girl becomes the mascot of a British regiment in India.

Vaguely based on a Kipling tale, this was the most expensive Temple vehicle and a first-rate family action picture with sentimental asides.

w Ernest Pascal, Julien Josephson   story Rudyard Kipling   d John Ford   ph Arthur Miller   m Alfred Newman   ad William S. Darling, David Hall

Shirley Temple, Victor McLaglen, C. Aubrey Smith, June Lang, Michael Whalen, Cesar Romero, Constance Collier, Gavin Muir

'Will add another clean-up to her cycle, but those knees are losing their contour . . . a pretentiously produced melodrama which launches the leading feminine box office star into a distinctly new phase of her career and story material.' – *Variety*

AAN: art direction

Weekend ****
France/Italy   1968   103m   Eastmancolor
Comacico/Copernic/Lira/Ascot
V, V*

A bourgeois couple leave Paris for the weekend and are caught in an endless traffic jam, where cars crash, tempers fray and savagery takes over.

A brilliant black satire at the expense of consumerism and conventional values.

wd Jean-Luc Godard   ph Raoul Coutard   m Antoine Duhamel, Mozart   ed Agnes Guillemot

Mireille Darc, Jean Yanne, Jean-Pierre Kalfon, Valerie Lagrange, Jean-Pierre Léaud, Yves Beneyton, Paul Gegauff

'Though deeply flawed, this film has more depth than any of Godard's earlier work. It's his vision of Hell and it ranks with the greatest.' – *Pauline Kael, New Yorker*

Weekend at Bernie's
US   1989   99m   DuArt
Fox/Gladden (Victor Drai)
V, V*, S

Two minor executives, fearing that they will be blamed when they discover the murdered body of their boss on a weekend visit to his beach house, pretend that he is still alive.

Black farce that manages occasionally to amuse.

w Robert Klane   d Ted Kotcheff   ph François Protat   m Andy Summers   pd Peter Jamison   ed Joan E. Chapman

Andrew McCarthy, Jonathan Silverman, Catherine Mary Stewart, Terry Kiser, Don Calfa, Catherine Parks, Eloise Broady, Ted Kotcheff

Weekend at the Waldorf *
US   1945   130m   bw
MGM (Arthur Hornblow Jnr)
V*

Four stories about guests at New York's largest hotel.

Disguised version of *Grand Hotel*, with the same stories twisted; the talent at hand, however, is serviceable rather than inspiring.

w Sam and Bella Spewack   d Robert Z. Leonard   ph Robert Planck   md Johnny Green

Ginger Rogers, Walter Pidgeon, Van Johnson, Lana Turner, Robert Benchley, Edward Arnold, Constance Collier, Leon Ames, Warner Anderson, Phyllis Thaxter, Keenan Wynn, Porter Hall, Samuel S. Hinds, George Zucco, Xavier Cugat

Weekend for Three
US   1941   66m   bw
RKO (Tay Garnett)

A wife uses a male guest's attentions to excite her husband's jealousy.

Fairly ordinary comedy with moments of wit in the script.

w Dorothy Parker, Alan Campbell   d Irving Reis

Dennis O'Keefe, Jane Wyatt, Philip Reed, Edward Everett Horton, ZaSu Pitts, Franklin Pangborn

Weekend in Havana

US 1941 80m Technicolor
TCF (William Le Baron)

A shopgirl in Havana falls for a shipping executive.

Routine Fox musical showcasing familiar talents: adequate wartime escapist fare.

w Karl Tunberg, Darrell Ware d Walter Lang
ph Ernest Palmer md Alfred Newman

Alice Faye, John Payne, Carmen Miranda, Cesar Romero, Cobina Wright Jnr, George Barbier, Sheldon Leonard, Leonid Kinskey

Weekend Marriage

US 1932 64m bw
First National
GB title: *Weekend Lives*

A wife wants to remain independent.

Comedy drama with nothing new to say about a familiar subject.

w Sheridan Gibney novel *Part-Time Wives* by Faith Baldwin d Thornton Freeland

Loretta Young, Norman Foster, George Brent, Aline MacMahon, Vivienne Osborne

'Unimportant rewrite on familiar theme minus necessary key strength.' – *Variety*

Weekend with Father

US 1951 83m bw
U-I (Ted Richmond)

A widow and a widower fall in love when taking their respective children to a summer camp.

Mechanical comedy of upsets and embarrassments.

w Joseph Hoffman d Douglas Sirk ph Clifford Stine m Frank Skinner

Van Heflin, Patricia Neal, Gigi Perreau, Virginia Field, Richard Denning

Weird Science

US 1985 94m Technicolor
Universal (Joel Silver)
V, V*, L

Teenage science students create a woman from a computer.

Sex-obsessed frolics which go nowhere.

wd John Hughes ph Matthew F. Leonetti, Joseph Calloway m Ira Newborn pd John W. Corso ed Mark Warner, Christopher Lebenzon, Scott Wallace

Anthony Michael Hall, Kelly Le Brock, Ilan Mitchell-Smith, Bill Paxton, Robert Downey

'She strikes with the curse of voodoo!'
Weird Woman

US 1944 64m bw
Universal

A professor brings home from the South Seas a wife who seems to bring murder in her wake.

Stiff and stilted thriller from an interesting original; one of the disappointing *Inner Sanctum* series.

w Brenda Weisberg novel *Conjure Wife* by Fritz Leiber d Reginald Le Borg

Lon Chaney, Evelyn Ankers, Anne Gwynne, Ralph Morgan, Elizabeth Risdon

Welcome Danger *

US 1929 110m bw
Harold Lloyd

The meek son of a police chief gets involved in a tong war.

Moderate early talkie comedy showing the star in some trouble with pace and dialogue.

w Clyde Bruckman, Lex Neal, Felix Adler, Paul Gerard Smith d Clyde Bruckman ph Walter Lundin, Henry Kohler

Harold Lloyd, Barbara Kent, Noah Young, Charles Middleton

Welcome Home: see SNAFU

Welcome Home

US 1989 92m Eastmancolor
Rank (Martin Ransohoff)
V*, L

Presumed dead in the Vietnamese war, a pilot who has acquired a Cambodian wife and two children returns after a 17-year absence to his American wife, who has remarried, and their teenage son.

Mundane, slow-moving drama that raises more questions than it answers.

w Maggie Kleinman d Franklin J. Schaffner ph Fred J. Koenekamp pd Dan Yarhi, Dennis Davenport ed Bob Swink

Kris Kristofferson, JoBeth Williams, Brian Keith, Sam Waterston, Trey Wilson

Welcome Home Roxy Carmichael

US 1991 96m Technicolor
Castle Premier/ITC (Penney Finkelman Cox)
V, V*, L, S

An adopted teenage girl, who is unhappy at home, convinces herself that she is the illegitimate daughter of her small town's only celebrity.

Limp and unconvincing drama of fame and teenage angst.

w Karen Leigh Hopkins d Jim Abrahams ph Paul Elliott m Thomas Newman pd Dena Roth ed Bruce Green

Winona Ryder, Jeff Daniels, Laila Robins, Thomas Wilson Brown, Joan McMurtrey, Graham Beckel, Frances Fisher, Robby Kiger

'Just another tale about a girl who discovers she's pretty in pink.' – *Sight and Sound*

Welcome Home Soldier Boys

US 1972 92m DeLuxe
TCF

Four war veterans go home and start a wave of violence.

Clumsily brutal anti-war tract which merely repels.

w Guerdon Trueblood d Richard Compton

Joe Don Baker, Paul Koslo, Alan Vint, Billy Green Bush

Welcome Mr Washington

GB 1944 90m bw
British National/Shaftesbury

A US sergeant in an English village falls for a local lady.

Mild plea for harmony between allies; rather embarrassing to watch even at the time.

w Jack Whittingham novel Noel Streatfeild d Leslie Hiscott

Barbara Mullen, Donald Stewart, Peggy Cummins, Graham Moffatt, Martita Hunt

Welcome Stranger

US 1947 107m bw
Paramount (Sol C. Siegel)

A genial young doctor fills in for a crusty old one on vacation in a small town.

Formula sentimental comedy, one of several reuniting the stars of *Going My Way*.

w Arthur Sheekman d Elliott Nugent ph Lionel Lindon m Robert Emmett Dolan

Bing Crosby, Barry Fitzgerald, Joan Caulfield, Wanda Hendrix, Frank Faylen, Elizabeth Patterson, Robert Shayne, Percy Kilbride

Welcome to Arrow Beach

US 1973 99m colour
Brut (Jack Cushingham)
V*
aka: *Tender Flesh*

A photographer living in a California beach community has become a cannibal after his experiences in the Korean War.

Abysmal horror movie with insufficient plot.

w Wallace C. Bennett, Jack Gross Jnr d Laurence Harvey ph Gerald Perry Finnerman m Tony Camillo

Laurence Harvey, Joanna Pettet, Stuart Whitman, John Ireland, Meg Foster

Welcome to Hard Times *

US 1967 103m Metrocolor
MGM/Max E. Youngstein, David Carr
GB title: *Killer on a Horse*

A small Western town arms itself against a mysterious bandit.

Curiously likeable, almost symbolic suspense Western which has a good start and middle but not much idea how to end.

wd Burt Kennedy novel E. L. Doctorow ph Harry Stradling Jnr m Harry Sukman

Henry Fonda, Janice Rule, Keenan Wynn, Janis Paige, John Anderson, Warren Oates, Fay Spain, Edgar Buchanan, Aldo Ray, Lon Chaney Jnr, Elisha Cook Jnr

Welcome to LA *

US 1976 106m DeLuxe
Lion's Gate/Robert Altman
V*

A young composer in Los Angeles has a varied sex life.

Fragmentary, vaguely mystical, momentarily interesting, frequently confusing slice of life as seen through misty glasses.

wd Alan Rudolph ph Dave Myers m Richard Baskin

Keith Carradine, Sally Kellerman, Geraldine Chaplin, Harvey Keitel, Lauren Hutton, Viveca Lindfors, Sissy Spacek, Denver Pyle

'The supposedly free-form, improvisational dynamics of an Altman movie have here become a strictly choreographed ballet.' – *Richard Combs, MFB*

Welcome to the Club

GB 1970 88m bw
Welcome (Sam Lomberg)

Hiroshima 1945; an American Quaker sergeant upsets military protocol.

Pale satirical comedy shot in Copenhagen.

w Clement Biddle Wood novel Clement Biddle Wood d Walter Shenson ph Mikael Salomon m Ken Thomas

Brian Foley, Jack Warden, Lee Meredith, Andy Jarrett

The Well *

US 1951 85m bw
Cardinal/Harry M. Popkin (Clarence Greene, Leo Popkin)
V*

A black child falls down a well, and the town unites to save her.

Forceful high-pitched melodrama, cut to a do-gooder pattern which became very familiar.

w Russel Rouse, Clarence Greene d Leo Popkin, Russel Rouse ph Ernest Laszlo m Dimitri Tiomkin ed Chester Schaeffer

Richard Rober, Henry Morgan, Barry Kelley, Christine Larson

AAN: script; editing

The Well Groomed Bride *
US 1946 75m bw
Paramount (Fred Kohlmar)

A naval officer searches San Francisco for a magnum of champagne with which to launch a ship.

Thin but cheerful star comedy.

w Claude Binyon, Robert Russell   d Sidney Lanfield   ph John F. Seitz   m Roy Webb

Ray Milland, Olivia de Havilland, Sonny Tufts, James Gleason, Constance Dowling, Percy Kilbride, Jean Heather

We'll Meet Again
GB 1942 84m bw
Columbia

A girl singer suffers while her boyfriend loves another.

Unassuming star vehicle for the Forces' Sweetheart.

w James Seymour, Howard Thomas   d Phil Brandon

Vera Lynn, Geraldo, Patricia Roc, Ronald Ward, Donald Gray, Frederick Leister

The Well-Digger's Daughter: see La Fille du Puisatier

'Paramount's thundering romance of the winning of the west!'

Wells Fargo *
US 1937 115m bw
Paramount (Frank Lloyd)

How the express delivery service was built up.

Large-scale, entertaining Western with overmuch emphasis on domestic issues.

w Paul Schofield, Gerald Geraghty, John Boland   story Stuart N. Lake   d Frank Lloyd   ph Theodor Sparkuhl   m Victor Young

Joel McCrea, Bob Burns, Frances Dee, Lloyd Nolan, Henry O'Neill, Mary Nash, Ralph Morgan, John Mack Brown, Porter Hall, Clarence Kolb

'Big b.o. right across the playdate board.' – Variety

Went the Day Well? ***
GB 1942 92m bw
Ealing (S. C. Balcon)
US title: Forty-eight Hours

Villagers resist when German paratroopers invade an English village and the squire proves to be a quisling.

Could-it-happen melodrama which made excellent wartime propaganda; generally well staged.

w Angus MacPhail, John Dighton, Diana Morgan   story Graham Greene   d Alberto Cavalcanti   ph Wilkie Cooper   m William Walton

Leslie Banks, Elizabeth Allan, Frank Lawton, Basil Sydney, Valerie Taylor, Mervyn Johns, Edward Rigby, Marie Lohr, C. V. France, David Farrar

'At last, it seems, we are learning to make films with our own native material.' – Sunday Times

'It has the sinister, freezing beauty of an Auden prophecy come true.' – James Agee

'A refreshing, an exciting and an excellent film.' – Documentary News Letter

We're Going to Be Rich
GB 1938 80m bw
TCF

In the South African goldfields in 1880, a singer leaves her worthless husband for a publican.

First American attempt to take over Our Gracie; it didn't work, but the damage was done.

w Monty Banks, James Edward Grant, Rohama Siegel, Sam Hellman   d Monty Banks

Gracie Fields, Victor McLaglen, Brian Donlevy, Coral Browne, Gus McNaughton

'Will do well in England. In the States, will slide into the duals.' – Variety

We're in the Army Now: see Pack Up Your Troubles

We're in the Money
US 1935 65m bw
Warner

Adventures of female process servers working for a dizzy lawyer.

Minor comedy using up contract artistes.

w F. Hugh Herbert, Brown Holmes, Erwin Gelsey, George Bilson   d Ray Enright

Joan Blondell, Glenda Farrell, Hugh Herbert, Ross Alexander, Hobart Cavanaugh

'Only those exhibitors whose clients get hysterical on short notice will profit from it.' – Variety

We're No Angels *
US 1954 106m Technicolor Vistavision
Paramount (Pat Duggan)
V, V*, L

Three escaped Devil's Island convicts help a downtrodden storekeeper and his family to outwit a scheming relative.

Whimsical, overstretched period comedy suffering from miscasting but with some pleasantries along the way.

w Ranald MacDougall   play La Cuisine des Anges by Albert Husson   d Michael Curtiz   ph Loyal Griggs   m Frederick Hollander

Humphrey Bogart, Peter Ustinov, Aldo Ray, Joan Bennett, Basil Rathbone, Leo G. Carroll, John Smith

We're No Angels
US 1989 106m Technicolor Panavision
UIP/Paramount (Art Linson)
V, V*, L, S

Convicts on the run disguise themselves as priests and take refuge in a monastery.

Dismal remake that suggests its stars have little talent for comedy.

w David Mamet   play La Cuisine des Anges by Albert Husson   d Neil Jordan   ph Philippe Rousselot   m George Fenton   pd Wolf Kroeger   ed Mick Audsley, Joke Van Wijk

Robert de Niro, Sean Penn, Demi Moore, Hoyt Axton, Bruno Kirby, Ray McAnally, James Russo, Wallace Shawn, John C. Reilly, Jay Brazeau

'It's a circus! Something doing every minute!'
We're Not Dressing *
US 1934 77m bw
Paramount (Benjamin Glazer)

A spoiled heiress shipwrecked on a Pacific island is tamed by an easy-going sailor.

Pleasant, madly dated, light-hearted variation on a much-filmed play, resolving itself into a series of comic turns.

w Horace Jackson, Francis Martin, George Marion Jnr   play The Admirable Crichton by J. M. Barrie   d Norman Taurog   ph Charles Lang   songs Harry Revel, Mack Gordon

Bing Crosby, Carole Lombard, George Burns, Gracie Allen, Leon Errol, Ethel Merman, Jay Henry, Ray Milland

'Tiptop audience appeal musical.' – Variety

We're Not Married *
US 1952 85m bw
TCF (Nunnally Johnson)
V*

Six couples find that they were never legally married.

Amiable, smartly-played compendium of sketches on a familiar theme.

w Nunnally Johnson   d Edmund Goulding   ph Leo Tover   m Cyril Mockridge

Ginger Rogers, Fred Allen, Victor Moore, Paul Douglas, Eve Arden, Marilyn Monroe, David Wayne, Louis Calhern, Zsa Zsa Gabor, Mitzi Gaynor, Eddie Bracken, James Gleason, Jane Darwell

We're on the Jury
US 1937 71m bw
RKO

Disagreements break out in the jury room after a murder trial.

More comedy than drama, a modest remake of Ladies of the Jury (qv).

w Franklin Coen   play John Frederick Ballard   d Ben Holmes

Helen Broderick, Victor Moore, Philip Huston, Louise Latimer, Robert McWade

'Good secondary b.o. value.' – Variety

We're Only Human
US 1936 67m bw
RKO (Edward Kaufman)

A police sergeant loses a convicted prisoner and catches him again.

Routine bang-bang melodrama with unconvincing dialogue.

w Rian James   story Thomas Walsh   d James Flood

Preston Foster, Jane Wyatt, James Gleason, Arthur Hohl, Jane Darwell, Christian Rub, Moroni Olsen, Mischa Auer

'Nothing which will raise it above double-feature standards.' – Variety

The Werewolf
US 1956 80m bw
Columbia/Clover (Sam Katzman)

In a small mountain town, a victim of radiation exposure periodically becomes a werewolf and is hounded down.

Absurd and tedious thriller which wastes an interesting background.

w Robert E. Kent, James B. Gordon   d Fred F. Sears   ph Edwin Linden   m Mischa Bakaleinikoff

Steven Ritch, Don McGowan, Joyce Holden

Werewolf of London *
US 1935 75m bw
Universal (Stanley Bergerman)
V*, L

Werewolves fight for a rare Tibetan flower with curative properties.

Patchy horror film which lurches from excellent suspense scenes to tedious chunks of superfluous dialogue. In many ways a milestone in the history of its kind.

w Robert Harris   d Stuart Walker   ph Charles Stumar   m Karl Hajos

Henry Hull, Warner Oland, Valerie Hobson, Spring Byington, Lester Matthews, Zeffie Tilbury, Ethel Griffies

'Horror attempt that doesn't horrify sufficiently. Requires a build-up and may disappoint.' – Variety

The Werewolf of Washington
US   1973   90m   colour
Millco (Nina Schulman)
V, V*

The US President attempts to cover up the fact that a White House press secretary has turned werewolf and is running amok.

A political satire in the aftermath of Watergate that lacks bite and fails as a horror spoof.

wd Milton Moses Ginsberg   ph Bob Baldwin
m Arnold Freed   ad Nancy Miller-Corwin   sp Bob Obradovich

Dean Stockwell, Biff McGuire, Clifton James, Michael Dunn, Beeson Carroll, Thayer David

West Eleven
GB   1963   93m   bw
ABP/Daniel M. Angel (Vivian Cox)

A young London drifter is offered £10,000 to commit murder.

Dingy but not very convincing 'realist' melodrama with a jazzy style which induces weariness.

w Keith Waterhouse, Willis Hall   novel The Furnished Room by Laura del Rivo   d Michael Winner
ph Otto Heller   m Stanley Black, Acker Bilk

Alfred Lynch, Eric Portman, Kathleen Harrison, Diana Dors, Kathleen Breck, Freda Jackson, Finlay Currie, Harold Lang

West of Broadway
US   1932   68m   bw
MGM

A millionaire gets married while drunk and regrets it the next day.

Unappetizing light drama which did no good to anyone concerned with it.

w Gene Markey, J. K. McGuinness, Ralph Graves, Bess Meredyth   d Harry Beaumont

John Gilbert, El Brendel, Lois Moran, Madge Evans, Ralph Bellamy, Frank Conroy, Hedda Hopper

'Rates neighbourhood and grind spotting only.' – Variety

West of Montana: see Mail Order Bride

West of Shanghai
US   1937   64m   bw
Warner

Fugitives in the Far East are saved by the self-sacrifice of a Chinese war lord.

Unpersuasive melodrama remade from The Bad Man (1930), heavily depending on a star performance.

w Crane Wilbur   d John Farrow

Boris Karloff, Beverly Roberts, Ricardo Cortez, Gordon Oliver, Vladimir Sokoloff

† First released as Warlord.

West of the Divide
US   1933   54m   bw
Monogram/Lone Star (Paul Malvern)
V*

A cowboy who is searching for his long-lost brother impersonates a killer in order to expose a crooked rancher.

John Wayne gets the girl, the boy and a ranch in this otherwise routine Western.

wd Robert N. Bradbury   ph Archie Stout   ed Carl Pierson

John Wayne, Virginia Faire Brown, George Hayes, Loyd Whitlock, Yakima Canutt, Lafe McKee, Billie O'Brien

West of the Pecos
US   1934   70m   bw
RKO

In Texas after the Civil War a girl masquerades as a boy in order to get things done.

Moderate Western.

w Milton Krims, John Twist   novel Zane Grey
d Phil Rosen

Richard Dix, Martha Sleeper, Samuel S. Hinds, Fred Kohler, Louise Beavers, Willie Best ('Sleep 'n Eat')

'Superior entertainment of the horse opera type.' – Variety

West of Zanzibar
US   1928   70m at 24 fps   bw   silent
MGM
V*, L

A paralysed magician turned ivory trader settles an old score.

Corny star vehicle remade in 1932 as Kongo, with Walter Huston.

w Waldemar Young, Elliott Clawson   d Tod Browning

Lon Chaney, Lionel Barrymore, Jacqueline Gadsden, Mary Nolan

West of Zanzibar
GB   1954   94m   Technicolor
Ealing (Leslie Norman)
V*

Native tribesmen move towards Mombasa and are drawn into ivory smuggling.

Fairly feeble follow-up to Where No Vultures Fly; quite good to look at but clearly not an original.

w Max Catto, Jack Whittingham   d Harry Watt
ph Paul Beeson   m Alan Rawsthorne

Anthony Steel, Sheila Sim, William Simons, Orlando Martins, Martin Benson, Edric Connor, Howard Marion Crawford

West Point of the Air
US   1935   90m   bw
MGM (Monta Bell)

The army sergeant father of an air cadet has great hopes for him.

Routine sentimental flagwaver.

w James J. McGuinness, John Monk Saunders, Frank Wead, Arthur J. Beckhard   d Richard Rosson
ph Clyde de Vinna, Charles A. Marshall, Elmer Dyer
m Charles Maxwell

Wallace Beery, Robert Young, Maureen O'Sullivan, Lewis Stone, James Gleason, Rosalind Russell, Russell Hardie, Henry Wadsworth, Robert Taylor

'Trite story holds it down to just moderate entertainment rating.' – Variety

West Point Story *
US   1950   107m   bw
Warner (Louis F. Edelman)
V*
GB title: Fine and Dandy

A Broadway producer stages a show at the military academy.

Thin and rather tedious musical saved by its irrepressible star.

w John Monks Jnr, Charles Hoffman, Irving Wallace
d Roy del Ruth   ph Sid Hickox   md Ray Heindorf
songs Sammy Cahn, Jule Styne

James Cagney, Virginia Mayo, Doris Day, Gordon Macrae, Gene Nelson, Alan Hale Jnr, Roland Winters, Jerome Cowan

AAN: Ray Heindorf

West Side Story ****
US   1961   155m   Technicolor   Panavision 70
(UA) Mirisch/Seven Arts (Robert Wise)
V, V*, L, S

The Romeo and Juliet story in a New York dockland setting.

The essentially theatrical conception of this entertainment is nullified by determinedly realistic settings, but production values are fine and the song numbers electrifying.

w Ernest Lehman   play Arthur Laurents, after William Shakespeare   d Robert Wise, Jerome Robbins
ph Daniel L. Fapp   m Leonard Bernstein   ly Stephen Sondheim   pd Boris Leven

Natalie Wood (sung by Marni Nixon), Richard Beymer (sung by Jimmy Bryant), Russ Tamblyn, Rita Moreno, George Chakiris

AA: best picture; Robert Wise, Jerome Robbins; Daniel L. Fapp; Rita Moreno; George Chakiris; Saul Chaplin; musical direction (Saul Chaplin, Johnny Green, Sid Ramin, Irwin Kostal); art direction; sound; costume design

AAN: Ernest Lehman

Westbound
US   1959   69m   Warnercolor
Warner

A stagecoach manager is entrusted with Californian gold, which attracts assorted villains.

Stalwart star Western which served its purpose.

w Berne Giler   d Budd Boetticher

Randolph Scott, Virginia Mayo, Karen Steele, Andrew Duggan, Michael Pate

Western Approaches ***
GB   1944   83m   Technicolor
Crown Film Unit
US title: The Raider

Torpedoed merchantmen in the Atlantic are used by a U-boat as a decoy.

A fictional story is played to great documentary effect by men of the allied navies. One of the outstanding 'factual' films of the war years.

wd Pat Jackson   ph Jack Cardiff   m Clifton Parker

'Without a doubt the best sea film in existence.' – Daily Mail

Western Union **
US   1941   94m   Technicolor
TCF (Harry Joe Brown)
V*

Politicians and crooks hamper the laying of cross-country cables.

First-rate Western with familiar excitements.

w Robert Carson   novel Zane Grey   d Fritz Lang
ph Edward Cronjager   m David Buttolph

Randolph Scott, Robert Young, Dean Jagger, Virginia Gilmore, Slim Summerville, John Carradine, Chill Wills, Barton MacLane

'It is impossible to know what clichés the director may have prevented, but it is enough and too much to see those he left in.' – Otis Ferguson

'Two women helped him overthrow the most ruthless power in the west!'
The Westerner **
US   1940   99m   bw
Samuel Goldwyn
V, V*, L

Judge Roy Bean comes to grief through his love for Lily Langtry.

Moody, melodramatic Western with comedy touches; generally entertaining, the villain more so than the hero.

w Jo Swerling, Niven Busch *story* Stuart N. Lake *d* William Wyler *ph* Gregg Toland *m* Dimitri Tiomkin *ad* James Basevi

Gary Cooper, *Walter Brennan*, Doris Davenport, Fred Stone, Paul Hurst, Chill Wills, Charles Halton, Forrest Tucker, Dana Andrews, Lilian Bond, Tom Tyler

AA: Walter Brennan

AAN: Stuart N. Lake; James Basevi

Westward Ho the Wagons
US 1956 85m Technicolor Cinemascope
Walt Disney (Bill Walsh)
V*

A wagon train defends itself against Indians.

Slow and simple-minded family Western.

w Tom Blackburn *d* William Beaudine *ph* Charles Boyle *m* Paul Smith

Fess Parker, Kathleen Crowley, Jeff York, David Stollery, Sebastian Cabot, George Reeves

Westward Passage
US 1932 73m bw
RKO (David O. Selznick)

A wealthy girl weds a poor novelist but wants the rich full life for their children.

Dogged romantic drama with only the casting of interest.

w Bradley and Humphrey King *novel* Margaret Ayer Barnes *d* Robert Milton *ph* Lucien Andriot *m* Max Steiner

Ann Harding, Laurence Olivier, ZaSu Pitts, Irving Pichel, Juliette Compton, Florence Roberts

'Slow, prone to be dull, and hardly warm weather theatre inducement.' – *Variety*

Westward the Women *
US 1951 118m bw
MGM (Dore Schary)

In the 1850s an Indian scout leads 150 Chicago women to meet husbands in California.

Good-looking episodic Western, apparently intended mainly to amuse but seldom rising to the occasion.

w Charles Schnee *d* William Wellman *ph* William Mellor *m* Jeff Alexander

Robert Taylor, Denise Darcel, John McIntire, Marilyn Erskine, Hope Emerson, Lenore Lonergan, Julie Bishop

'Where nothing can possibly go worng...'
Westworld **
US 1973 89m Metrocolor Panavision
MGM (Paul N. Lazarus III)
V, V(W), V*, L

In a millionaire holiday resort which recreates the past, a Western badman robot goes berserk and relentlessly attacks two visitors.

Unusual and amusing but under-produced melodrama with slipshod story development and continuity, atoned for by memorable moments and underlying excitement.

wd Michael Crichton *ph* Gene Polito *m* Fred Karlin *ad* Herman Blumenthal

Yul Brynner, Richard Benjamin, James Brolin, Norman Bartold, Alan Oppenheimer

The Wet Parade *
US 1932 122m bw
MGM (Hunt Stromberg)

A politician points to the corruption caused by prohibition.

Sociologically interesting melodrama.

w John Lee Mahin *novel* Upton Sinclair *d* Victor Fleming *ph* George Barnes *m* William Axt

Walter Huston, Myrna Loy, Neil Hamilton, Lewis Stone, Jimmy Durante, Wallace Ford, Dorothy Jordan, John Miljan, Robert Young

'Final impression strongly anti-liquor, but outside of reaction that may bring, picture hasn't much chance. What it lacks as entertainment isn't covered by propaganda possibilities.' – *Variety*

Wetherby *
GB 1985 97m Technicolor
Greenpoint/Film Four/Zenith (Simon Relph)
V*

After a party at the home of a lonely and frustrated woman, a young man shoots himself.

Interesting if rather irritating drama which leaves as many puzzles as it solves.

wd David Hare *ph* Stuart Harris *m* Nick Bicat *pd* Hayden Griffin

Vanessa Redgrave, Ian Holm, Judi Dench, Tim McInnery, Stuart Wilson

We've Never Been Licked
US 1943 103m bw
Universal (Walter Wanger)
GB title: *Texas to Tokyo*

A young American raised in Japan finds himself on the wrong side after Pearl Harbor.

Shoddy flagwaver, low on talent and inspiration.

w Norman Reilly Raine, Nick Grinde *d* John Rawlins

Richard Quine, Anne Gwynne, Noah Beery Jnr, Harry Davenport, Martha O'Driscoll, William Frawley, Robert Mitchum

The Whales of August *
US 1987 90m TVC colour
Circle/Nelson (Carolyn Pfeiffer, Mike Kaplan)
V, V*, L, S

Two elderly sisters live on the Maine coast and think of the past.

Edgy, sympathetic talk-piece in which old ladies prove that they are still stars.

w David Berry *novel* David Berry *d* Lindsay Anderson *ph* Mike Fash *m* Alan Price *pd* Joselyn Herbert

Bette Davis, Lillian Gish, Vincent Price, Ann Sothern, Harry Carey Jnr, Mary Steenburgen, Tisha Stirling

'Lovely on all counts.' – *Daily Variety*

AAN: Ann Sothern

'He had a price on his head ... she had a price on her heart!'
Wharf Angel
US 1934 65m bw
Paramount

To quote *Variety*, prostie goes softie for sailor with murder rap hanging over his head.

Dim little fogbound melodrama.

w Sam Hoffenstein, Frank Partos, Steve Avery, Frederick Schlick *d* William Cameron Menzies, George Somnes

Victor McLaglen, Dorothy Dell, Preston Foster, Alison Skipworth

'Poor stuff for de luxe audiences: old-fashioned, drab, lacking in box office draw.' – *Variety*

What?
Italy/France/West Germany 1972 113m
Eastmancolor Todd-AO 35
Gala/C.C. Champion/Concordia/Dieter Geissler (Carlo Ponti)
V*
original title: *Che?*

An American hitch-hiker, who is forever losing her clothes, seeks refuge in the home of an Italian millionaire full of curious and lecherous guests.

Eccentric comedy of innocence and experience that works only fitfully.

w Gerard Brach, Roman Polanski *d* Roman Polanski *ph* Marcello Gatti, Giuseppe Ruzzolini *md* Claudio Gizzi *m* Schubert, Mozart, Beethoven *pd* Aurelio Crugnola *ed* Alastair McIntyre

Sydne Rome, Marcello Mastroianni, Hugh Griffith, Romolo Valli, Guido Alberti, Roman Polanski

'Despite its erratic moments of brilliance, the overall impression left by the film is of a rather puerile graffito scrawled in the margins of its literary antecedants.' – *Jan Dawson, MFB*

'Far from being a masterpiece and several notches below being even a good film, but it does stand in danger of being seriously underrated – not to say dismissed – by virtue of its gaudy wrapping.' – *Derek Elley, Films and Filming*

What a Carve Up
GB 1961 88m bw
New World/Baker-Berman
V*

A madman fakes his own death in order to murder his relatives.

Spooky house farce, allegedly a remake of *The Ghoul* but bearing little resemblance to it.

w Ray Cooney, Tony Hilton *novel* The Ghoul by Frank King *d* Pat Jackson

Sid James, Kenneth Connor, Shirley Eaton, Dennis Price, Donald Pleasence, Michael Gough, Valerie Taylor

What a Chassis: see *La Belle Américaine*

What a Crazy World
GB 1963 88m bw
Capricorn/AB Pathé (Michael Carreras)

A working-class London boy sets out to be a rock-and-roller.

Unsurprising star musical, quite lively of its kind.

w Alan Klein *play* Alan Klein *d* Michael Carreras

Joe Brown, Susan Maughan, Marty Wilde, Harry H. Corbett, Avis Bunnage

What a Life
US 1939 75m bw
Paramount

Henry Aldrich has difficulties in high school.

First of the domestic comedy series (see under *Henry*) which became more farcical and had a different cast; this episode closely followed the Broadway success.

w Charles Brackett, Billy Wilder *play* Clifford Goldsmith *d* Theodore Reed

Jackie Cooper, Betty Field, John Howard, Janice Logan, Lionel Stander, Hedda Hopper, Dorothy Stickney

'A fine comedy drama, excellent for family trade.' – *Variety*

What a Man: see *Never Give a Sucker an Even Break*

What a Way to Go *
US 1964 111m DeLuxe Cinemascope
TCF/APJAC/Orchard (Arthur P. Jacobs)

An immensely rich girl tells her psychiatrist how all her husbands proved not only successful but accident-prone.

Wild, mainly agreeable, star-and-gag-laden black comedy which starts on too high a note and fails to sustain.

w Betty Comden, Adolph Green *d* J. Lee-Thompson *ph* Leon Shamroy *md* Nelson Riddle *ly* Betty Comden, Adolph Green *songs* Jule Styne

Shirley Maclaine, Bob Cummings, Dick Van Dyke, Robert Mitchum, Gene Kelly, Dean Martin, Paul Newman, Reginald Gardiner, Margaret Dumont

What a Woman
US   1943   90m   bw
Columbia
aka: *The Beautiful Cheat*

An author's agent gets into romantic escapades with her writers.

Ho-hum romantic comedy, quickly forgotten.

w Therese Lewis, Barry Trivers   *d* Irving Cummings

Rosalind Russell, Brian Aherne, Willard Parker, Ann Savage, Alan Dinehart

What about Bob? *
US   1991   99m   Technicolor
Warner/Touchstone/Touchwood Pacific Partners I (Laura Ziskin)
V, V*, L

A disturbed patient moves in on holidaying psychiatrist and his equally disturbed family.

Intermittently amusing black comedy.

w Tom Schulman   *story* Alvin Sargent, Laura Ziskin   *d* Frank Oz   *ph* Michael Ballhaus   *m* Miles Goodman   *pd* Les Dilley   *ed* Anne V. Coates

Bill Murray, Richard Dreyfuss, Julie Hagerty, Charlie Korsmo, Kathryn Erbe, Tom Aldredge, Susan Willis

'Frank Oz proves that he's a director with just the mean sense of humor these bland times desperately need.' – *Richard Schickel, Time*

'Off to grandmother's house they go, For love in the attic and death down below!'
What Became of Jack and Jill?
GB   1971   90m   DeLuxe
Palomar/Amicus (Milton Subotsky)

A young man tries to hasten his grandmother's death but she has the last laugh.

Feeble suspenser with a dim ending.

w Roger Marshall   *novel* The Ruthless Ones by Laurence Moody   *d* Bill Bain   *ph* Gerry Turpin   *m* Carl Davis

Vanessa Howard, Paul Nicholas, Mona Washbourne, Peter Copley, Peter Jeffrey

What Changed Charley Farthing
GB   1975   101m   Eastmancolor
Patina-Hidalgo (Tristam Cones)
V*

A philandering sailor has adventures in Cuba.

Weirdly ineffective comedy actioner which never gets started and should never have been thought of.

w David Pursall, Jack Seddon   *novel* Mark Hebdon   *d* Sidney Hayers   *ph* Graham Edgar   *m* Angela Arteaga

Doug McClure, Lionel Jeffries, Warren Mitchell, Hayley Mills, Dilys Hamlett, Fernando Sancho

What Did You Do in the War, Daddy?
US   1966   115m   DeLuxe   Panavision
UA/Mirisch/Geoffrey (Owen Crump, Blake Edwards)
V*

In 1943, an Italian town surrenders readily to the Americans providing its wine festival and football match can take place.

Silly war comedy with insufficient jokes for its wearisome length. The performances are bright enough.

w William Peter Blatty   *d* Blake Edwards   *ph* Philip Lathrop   *m* Henry Mancini

James Coburn, Dick Shawn, Sergio Fantoni, Giovanni Ralli, Aldo Ray, Harry Morgan, Carroll O'Connor, Leon Askin

What Every Woman Knows *
US   1934   90m   bw
MGM

A quiet little wife encourages her husband into parliament.

Adequate version of the sentimental play, very pleasantly acted.

w Monckton Hoffe, John Meehan, James Kevin McGuinness   *play* J. M. Barrie   *d* Gregory La Cava

Helen Hayes, Brian Aherne, Madge Evans, Lucile Watson, Dudley Digges, Henry Stephenson, Donald Crisp, David Torrence

'Cinch b.o., a swell woman's picture.' – *Variety*

What Happened to Santiago *
Puerto Rico   1989   100m   colour
Dios Los Cria (Pedro Muñiz)
original title: *Lo que le pasó de Santiago*

An accountant retires and falls for a woman with a mysterious past.

A gently charming domestic drama, most likely to appeal to the over-50s.

wd Jacobo Morales   *ph* Augustin Cubano   *m* Pedro Rivera Toledo   *ad* Ivonne Torres   *ed* Alfonso Borrell

Tommy Muñiz, Gladys Rodriguez, Johanna Rosaly, René Monclova, Pedro Javier Muñiz, Jacobo Morales

AAN: Best foreign language film

What Have I Done to Deserve This? *
Spain   1984   101m   colour
Metro/Tesauro/Kaktus (Tadeo Villabla)
V, V*, L
original title: *¿Que He Hecho Yo Para Merecer Esto?*

A slum family falls apart, to the indifference of the busy mother, who takes drugs to keep her awake as she works hard as a cleaner.

Fast-paced inconsequential black comedy, lacking any internal coherence as it rushes from one tasteless joke to another.

wd Pedro Almodóvar   *ph* Angel Luis Fernandez   *m* Bernardo Bonezzi   *ed* Jose Solcedo

Carmen Maura, Luis Hostalot, Angel de Andres-Lopez, Gonzalo Suarez, Veronica Forque, Juan Martinez, Miguel Angel Harranz

'Almodóvar is an underground theatre clown. He may not know how to make anything stay with you – he may not even care to. He just likes to put on a show. Some of the vignettes might be comedy classics if their timing weren't so sloppy.' – *Pauline Kael, New Yorker*

What Lola Wants: see *Damn Yankees*

What, No Beer?
US   1933   65m   bw
MGM
V*

A barber rushes to be first on the market with beer after its legalization, but finds himself premature and at odds with gangsters.

Topical farce ending in a slapstick mêlée.

w Carey Wilson, Jack Cluett, Robert E. Hopkins   *d* Edward Sedgwick

Buster Keaton, Jimmy Durante, Rosco Ates, Phyllis Barry, John Miljan, Henry Armetta

'A commercial little laugh picture.' – *Variety*

What Price Glory? *
US   1952   111m   Technicolor
TCF (Sol C. Siegel)
V, V*

In 1917 France Captain Flagg and Sergeant Quirt spar for the same girl.

Stagey remake of the celebrated silent film and play; watchable if not exactly inspired.

w Phoebe and Henry Ephron   *play* Maxwell Anderson, Lawrence Stallings   *d* John Ford   *ph* Joe MacDonald   *m* Alfred Newman

James Cagney, Dan Dailey, Corinne Calvet, William Demarest, Robert Wagner, Marisa Pavan, James Gleason

'A heart-touching drama of the world, the flesh and the movies!'
What Price Hollywood? *
US   1932   87m   bw
RKO (Pandro S. Berman)
V*, L

A waitress becomes a film star with the help of a drunken director who later commits suicide.

Fairly trenchant early study of the mores of the film city, later revamped as *A Star Is Born*.

w Ben Markson, Gene Fowler, Rowland Brown   *story* Adela Rogers St John, Jane Murfin   *d* George Cukor   *ph* Charles Rosher   *m* Max Steiner   *montage* Slavko Vorkapich

Constance Bennett, Lowell Sherman, Neil Hamilton, Gregory Ratoff, Brooks Benedict, Louise Beavers, Eddie Anderson

'Many of the scenes are like sketches for the later versions, but this film has its own interest, especially because of its glimpses into the studio life of the time.' – *New Yorker, 1977*

AAN: Adela Rogers St John, Jane Murfin

What Shall It Profit: see *Hard Steel*

Whatever Happened to Aunt Alice? *
US   1969   101m   Metrocolor
Palomar/Associates and Aldrich (Robert Aldrich)
V*

A genteel widow murders her housekeepers for their private incomes.

Ladylike shocker with some black humour and good performances.

w Theodore Apstein   *novel* The Forbidden Garden by Ursula Curtiss   *d* Lee H. Katzin   *ph* Joseph Biroc   *m* Gerald Fried

Geraldine Page, Ruth Gordon, Rosemary Forsyth, Robert Fuller, Mildred Dunnock

'Sister, sister, oh so fair, why is there blood all over your hair?'
Whatever Happened to Baby Jane? *
US   1962   132m   bw
Warner Seven Arts/Associates and Aldrich (Robert Aldrich)
V, V*, L

In middle age, a demented ex-child star lives in an old Hollywood mansion with her invalid sister, and tension leads to murder.

Famous for marking the first time Hollywood's ageing first ladies stooped to horror, and followed by *Hush Hush Sweet Charlotte* and the other *Whatevers*, this dreary looking melodrama only occasionally grabs the attention and has enough plot for about half its length. The performances, however, are striking.

w Lukas Heller   *novel* Henry Farrell   *d* Robert Aldrich   *ph* Ernest Haller   *m* Frank de Vol

Bette Davis, Joan Crawford, Victor Buono, Anna Lee

'It goes on and on, in a light much dimmer than necessary, and the climax, when it belatedly arrives, is a bungled, languid mingling of pursuers and pursued . . .' – *New Yorker*

AAN: Ernest Haller; Bette Davis; Victor Buono

What's a Nice Girl Like You Doing in a Place Like This? *
US   1963   10m   bw   16mm
Contemporary/New York University Department of Television, Motion Picture and Radio Presentation Summer Motion Picture Workshop
V

A would-be writer tries various ways to overcome his hang-ups.

An exuberant and amusing short, much influenced by the style of the French New Wave.

wd Martin Scorsese   ph James Newman
m Richard H. Cole   ed Robert Hunsicker

Zeph Michaelis, Mimi Stark, Sarah Braveman, Fred Sica, Robert Uricola

It was released on video with three other shorts under the title *Scorsese x 4*.

What's Buzzin', Cousin?
US   1943   75m   bw
Columbia (Jack Fier)

An attorney turns band singer and helps revive a droopy hotel.

Listless musical with a few good numbers.

w Harry Sauber   d Charles Barton

Ann Miller, John Hubbard, Eddie Anderson, Leslie Brooks, Jeff Donnell

'A film about the love you find … in the last place you look.'

What's Eating Gilbert Grape?
US   1993   118m   DeLuxe
Paramount (Meir Teper, Bertil Ohlsson, David Matalon)

A small-town grocery clerk is the main support of his family: obese, stay-at-home mother, two disturbed sisters and a brain-damaged brother.

Gentle, unsentimental drama, but so low-key that it does not always engage the interest.

w Peter Hedges   novel Peter Hedges   d Lassie Hallstrom   ph Sven Nykvist   m Alan Parker
pd Bernt Capra   ed Andrew Monshein

Johnny Depp, Juliette Lewis, Mary Steenburgen, Leonardo DiCaprio, Darlene Cates, Laura Harrington, Mary Kate Schellhardt, Crispin Glover, Kevin Tighe

'An offbeat middleweight charmer that is lent a measure of substance by its astute performances and observational insight.' – *Variety*

'The film is still implicitly condescending since almost all the characters (including the afflicted ones) function as tests of Gilbert's patience.' – *Michael Sragow, New Yorker*

AAN: Leonardo DiCaprio

What's Good for the Goose
GB   1969   104m   Eastmancolor
Tigon (Tony Tenser, Norman Wisdom)

An assistant bank manager falls for a girl hitch-hiker and tries to recover his youth.

Embarrassing attempt to build a sexy vehicle for a star whose sentimental mugging always appealed mainly to children.

w Norman Wisdom   d Menahem Golan
ph William Brayne   m Reg Tilsley

Norman Wisdom, Sally Geeson, Sally Bazely, Derek Francis, Terence Alexander

'Who needs a heart when a heart can be broken?'

What's Love Got to Do with It *
US   1993   118m   Technicolor
Buena Vista/Touchstone (Doug Chapin, Barry Krost)
V*, L, S
aka: *Tina: What's Love Got to Do with It*

Biopic of the rock singer Tina Turner, from her violent relationship with, and marriage to, Ike Turner to her successful emergence as a solo artist.

Excellent performances by the two leads, some well-staged musical numbers and marital rows and lusty singing by Tina Turner herself make this a better than average picture of its kind.

w Kate Lanier   book *I, Tina* by Tina Turner, Kurt Loder   d Brian Gibson   ph Jamie Anderson
m Stanley Clarke   pd Stephen Altman   ed Stuart Pappé

Angela Bassett, Laurence Fishburne, Vanessa Bell Calloway, Jenifer Lewis, Phyllis Yvonne Stickney, Khandi Alexander, Rae'ven Kelly

'A passionate personal and professional drama that hits both the high and low notes of an extraordinary life and career. An immensely enjoyable saga.' – *Variety*

AAN: Laurence Fishburne; Angela Bassett

What's New Pussycat?
US/France   1965   108m   Technicolor
UA/Famous Artists (Charles K. Feldman)
V*, L

A fashion editor is distracted by beautiful girls.

Zany sex comedy with many more misses than hits, a product of the wildly swinging sixties when it was thought that a big budget and stars making fools of themselves would automatically ensure a success.

w Woody Allen   d Clive Donner   ph Jean Badal
m Burt Bacharach

Peter O'Toole, Peter Sellers, Woody Allen, Ursula Andress, Romy Schneider, Capucine, Paula Prentiss

'Unfortunately for all concerned, to make something enjoyably dirty a lot of taste is required.' – *John Simon*

AAN: title song (m Burt Bacharach, ly Hal David)

What's So Bad about Feeling Good?
US   1965   94m   Technicolor
Universal (George Seaton)

A 'happy virus' is carried into New York by a toucan, and affects the lives of various people.

Flimsy pretext for a comedy, further hampered by a less than sparkling script. The actors have their moments.

w George Seaton, Robert Pirosh   d George Seaton
ph Ernesto Caparros   m Frank de Vol

George Peppard, Mary Tyler Moore, Dom de Luise, John McMartin, Susan St James, Don Stroud, Charles Lane

What's the Matter with Helen? *
US   1971   101m   DeLuxe
Filmways/Raymax (George Edwards, James C. Pratt)
V*

In 1934 Hollywood, two women run a dancing school for child stars; one of them is a killer.

More *Baby Jane* melodramatics, quite lively and with interesting period detail.

w Henry Farrell   d Curtis Harrington   ph Lucien Ballard   m David Raksin   pd Eugene Lourié

Debbie Reynolds, Shelley Winters, Michael MacLiammoir, Dennis Weaver, Agnes Moorehead

'A cast of seasoned troupers cannot quite alter the impression that they are all working to revive a stiff.' – *Bruce Williamson*

What's Up, Doc? **
US   1972   94m   Technicolor
Warner/Saticoy (Peter Bogdanovich)
V, V*, L

In San Francisco, an absent-minded young musicologist is troubled by the attentions of a dotty girl who gets him involved with crooks and a series of accidents.

Madcap comedy, a pastiche of several thirties originals. Spectacular slapstick and willing players

are somewhat let down by exhausted patches and a tame final reel.

w Buck Henry, David Newman, Robert Benton
d Peter Bogdanovich   ph Laszlo Kovacs   m Artie Butler   pd Polly Pratt

Barbra Streisand, Ryan O'Neal, Kenneth Mars, Austin Pendleton, Madeleine Kahn, Mabel Albertson, Sorrell Booke

'A comedy made by a man who has seen a lot of movies, knows all the mechanics, and has absolutely no sense of humour. Seeing it is like shaking hands with a joker holding a joy buzzer: the effect is both presumptuous and unpleasant.' – *Jay Cocks*

'It's all rather like a 19th-century imitation of Elizabethan blank verse drama.' – *Stanley Kauffmann*

'It freely borrows from the best screen comedy down the ages but has no discernible style of its own.' – *Michael Billington, Illustrated London News*

What's Up, Tiger Lily? *
US   1966   80m   Eastmancolor   Tohoscope
Benedict/Toho (Woody Allen)
V, V*, L

A Japanese agent searches for the world's greatest egg salad recipe.

Woody Allen and his American cast re-dub a Japanese spy film to create an off-beat comedy that is amusing in fits and starts.

w Kazuo Yamada, Woody Allen and others
d Senkichi Taniguchi   m Jack Lewis, The Lovin' Spoonful   ed Richard Krown

Tatsua Mihashi, Mie Hama, Akiko Wakabayashi, Tadeo Nakamuru, Susumu Kurobe, Woody Allen, Frank Buxton, Len Maxwell, Louise Lasser, Mickey Rose

'The jokes get rather desperate, but there are enough wildly sophomoric ones to keep this pop stunt fairly amusing until about midway.' – *Pauline Kael, New Yorker*

The Wheeler Dealers
US   1963   106m   Metrocolor   Panavision
MGM/Filmways (Martin Ransohoff)
V*
GB title: *Separate Beds*

A Texas tycoon with a flair for the stock market sets Wall Street agog by manipulating a mysterious and non-existent new product.

Fun for financiers, but barely worth following for the rest. A slick, loud, hollow show.

w G. J. W. Goodman, Ira Wallach   d Arthur Hiller
ph Charles Lang Jnr   m Frank de Vol

James Garner, Lee Remick, Phil Harris, Chill Wills, Jim Backus, Louis Nye, John Astin

Wheels on Meals
Hong Kong   1984   102m   colour
Paragon Films (Leonard K. C. Ho)

Two Chinese fast-food operatives working in Spain bring fortune to a local girl.

Bizarre kung-fu comedy with a little romance on the side. Too slow and with not enough action to interest fans of the genre, even if it does include a parody of *The Three Musketeers*.

d Samo Hung

Jackie Chan, Benny Urquidez, Keith Vitali, Herb Edelman, Samo Hung

When a Man Loves
US   1927   83m at 24 fps   bw   silent with synchronized music
Warner

A hero escapes from a prison ship and gives his all for love of a worthless woman.

Freely adapted version of *Manon Lescaut*, successful because of the real-life romance of the stars.

w Bess Meredyth *d* Alan Crosland

John Barrymore, Dolores Costello, Warner Oland, Stuart Holmes, Holmes Herbert

'Every baby sitter's nightmare becomes real!'

When a Stranger Calls

US   1979   97m   colour
UA/Melvin Simon (Doug Chapin, Steve Feke)
V, V*, L

A policeman determinedly chases a baby-murdering maniac.

Middling screamer extended from a short, *The Sitter;* a passive midsection separates a suspenseful start and finish.

w Steve Feke, Fred Walton *d* Fred Walton
ph Don Peterman *m* Dana Kaproff *pd* Elayne Barbara Ceder *ed* Sam Vitale

Charles Durning, Tony Beckley, Carol Kane, Colleen Dewhurst, Rachel Roberts

When Boys Leave Home: see *Downhill*

When Comedy Was King ***

US   1959   84m   bw
Robert Youngson Productions
V*, L

Valuable compilation of silent comedy sequences, with the high print quality and poor commentary to be expected from this source. Extracts include Buster Keaton in *Cops*, Laurel and Hardy in *Big Business*, and a Fatty Arbuckle comedy.

ed Robert Youngson

When Dinosaurs Ruled the Earth

GB   1969   100m (96m US)   Technicolor
Warner/Hammer (Aida Young)
V*, L

In prehistoric times, a girl is swept out to sea by a cyclone and adopted by a dinosaur.

Sequel to *One Million Years BC*, all very silly but tolerably well done.

wd Val Guest, from a treatment by J. G. Ballard
ph Dick Bush *m* Mario Nascimbene *ad* John Blezard *sp* Jim Danforth *ed* Peter Curran

Victoria Vetri, Patrick Allen, Robin Hawdon, Patrick Holt, Imogen Hassall

'I'm very proud that my first screen credit was for what is, without doubt, the worst film ever made.' – *J. G. Ballard*

AAN: special visual effects (Jim Danforth, Roger Dicken)

When Eight Bells Toll *

GB   1971   94m   Eastmancolor   Panavision
Winkast (Elliott Kastner)

A naval secret service agent investigates the pirating of gold bullion ships off the Scottish coast.

Acceptable kill-happy thriller: humourless James Bondery graced by splendid Scottish landscapes.

w Alistair MacLean *novel* Alistair Maclean
d Etienne Perier *ph* Arthur Ibbetson *m* Wally Stott

Anthony Hopkins, Robert Morley, Corin Redgrave, Jack Hawkins, Ferdy Mayne, Derek Bond, Nathalie Delon

When Father Was Away on Business **

Yugoslavia   1985   136m   colour   Cannon/Forum/
Sarajevo Film (Vera Mihic-Jolic)

V, V*
original title: *Otac Na Službenom Putu*

Family life in Yugoslavia in the 1950s, as seen through the eyes of a young boy whose father is sent to the mines after being betrayed by his mistress and brother-in-law.

Well-observed study of politics seen from a child's perspective, which adds charm and humour. It won the Palme d'Or for best film at the Cannes Film Festival in 1985.

w Abdulah Sidran *d* Emir Kusturica *ph* Vilko Filaň *m* Zoran Simjanović *pd* Predrag Lukovac *ed* Andrija Zafranovic

Moreno de Bartoli, Miki Manojlović, Mirjana Karanović, Mustafa Nadarević, Mira Furlan, Zoran Radmilovic, Jelena Covic, Tomislav Gelić, Davor Dujmović, Amir Kapetanović

When Harry Met Sally ****

US   1989   95m   DuArt
Palace/Castle Rock/Nelson Entertainment (Rob Reiner, Andrew Scheinman)
V, V*, L

Over a period of 12 years, a couple meet occasionally to debate whether there can be friendship without sex between a man and a woman.

Deft, witty romantic comedy, as good of its kind as we're likely to get these days.

w Nora Ephron *d* Rob Reiner *ph* Barry Sonnenfeld *m* Harry Connick Jnr and others *pd* Jane Musky *ed* Robert Leighton

Billy Crystal, *Meg Ryan*, Carrie Fisher, Bruno Kirby, Steven Ford, Lisa Jane Persky, Michelle Nicastro

AAN: Nora Ephron

When I Fall In Love

US   1988   127m   Technicolor
Warner/New Visions (Taylor Hackford, Laura Ziskin, Ian Sander)
V*, L
US title: *Everybody's All-American*

A star football player and his beauty queen wife survive 25 years of married life.

A lengthy soap opera, sentimentally indulging in an emotional switchback as its protagonists go from happiness to grief and back.

w Tom Rickman *novel* Frank Deford *d* Taylor Hackford *ph* Stephen Goldblatt *m* James Newton Howard *pd* Joe Alves *ed* Don Zimmerman

Dennis Quaid, Jessica Lange, Timothy Hutton, John Goodman, Carl Lumbly, Raymond Baker, Savannah Smith Boucher, Patricia Clarkson

When I Grow Up *

US   1951   90m   bw
Horizon (S. P. Eagle)

A boy about to run away changes his mind after reading his grandfather's diaries.

Pleasant, sentimental family film with an unusual approach.

wd Michael Kanin *ph* Ernest Laszlo *m* Jerome Moross

Bobby Driscoll, Robert Preston, Charley Grapewin, Martha Scott, Ralph Dumke

When in Rome

US   1952   78m   bw
MGM (Clarence Brown)

A gangster in Rome steals a priest's clothes and is accepted in his place.

Typically American religious comedy, nicely made but straying somewhat over the top when the gangster reforms and becomes a monk.

w Charles Schnee, Dorothy Kingsley, Robert Buckner *d* Clarence Brown *ph* William Daniels *m* Carmen Dragon

Van Johnson, Paul Douglas, Joseph Calleia, Carlo Rizzo, Tudor Owen, Aldo Silvani, Dono Nardi

When Johnny Comes Marching Home

US   1942   73m   bw
Universal (Bernard W. Burton)

A war hero on leave escapes formalities and returns to the theatrical boarding house he remembers.

And so to the puttin'-on-a-show finale: not bad of its kind.

w Oscar Brodney, Dorothy Bennett *d* Charles Lamont

Allan Jones, Jane Frazee, Gloria Jean, Donald O'Connor, Peggy Ryan, Phil Spitalny and his all-girl orchestra

When Knights Were Bold

GB   1929   80m at 24 fps   bw   silent
Herbert Wilcox

An incompetent heir dreams that he lives in medieval times.

Naïve romp which pleased at the time.

w Tim Whelan, Herbert Wilcox *play* Charles Marlow *d* Tim Whelan

Nelson Keys, Miriam Seeger, Eric Bransby Williams

† Remade in 1936 with Jack Buchanan, Fay Wray and Garry Marsh; directed by Jack Raymond; for Max Schach.

When Ladies Meet *

US   1933   73m   bw
MGM

A successful lady novelist falls in love with her married publisher.

Smartish comedy of manners which still has a sting.

w John Meehan, Leon Gordon *play* Rachel Crothers *d* Harry Beaumont *ph* Ray June *ad* Cedric Gibbons

Ann Harding, Robert Montgomery, *Myrna Loy, Alice Brady*, Frank Morgan, Martin Burton, Luis Alberni

'Nice production. Well-spaced comedy helps, and picture should be an outstander.' – *Variety*

AAN: Cedric Gibbons

When Ladies Meet

US   1941   108m   bw
MGM (Robert Z. Leonard, Orville O. Dull)
V*, L

Over-produced and very talkative remake of the above.

w S. K. Lauren, Anita Loos *d* Robert Z. Leonard *ph* Robert Planck *m* Bronislau Kaper *ad* Cedric Gibbons, Randall Duell

Joan Crawford, Robert Taylor, Greer Garson, Spring Byington, Herbert Marshall, Rafael Storm, Olaf Hytten

AAN: Cedric Gibbons, Randall Duell

When Love Is Young

US   1937   75m   bw
Universal (Robert Presnell)

A Broadway stage star returns to her home town in hopes of marrying her old beau, but he is found wanting.

Very moderate comedy to fill a programme.

w Eve Greene, Joseph Fields *story Class Prophecy* by Eleanore Griffin *d* Hal Mohr

Virginia Bruce, Kent Taylor, Walter Brennan, Greta Meyer, Christian Rub, Sterling Holloway, Nydia Westman

'Will provide average filmgoers with averagely good amusement.' – *Variety*

When My Baby Smiles at Me

US   1948   98m   Technicolor
TCF (George Jessel)

A vaudevillian goes on the skids but is saved by his wife.

Routine musical handling of a dreary drama previously filmed as *Dance of Life* (1929) and *Swing High Swing Low* (qv).

w Lamar Trotti   *play* Burlesque by George Manker Walters, Arthur Hopkins   d Walter Lang   ph Harry Jackson   md Alfred Newman

Betty Grable, Dan Dailey, Jack Oakie, June Havoc, Richard Arlen, James Gleason, Jean Wallace

AAN: Alfred Newman; Dan Dailey

When New York Sleeps: see *Now I'll Tell*

When Strangers Marry *
US   1944   67m   bw
Monogram (Maurice King)
aka: *Betrayed*

A young bride in New York discovers that she may have married a murderer.

Much-praised second feature: a bit stodgy now, but still entertaining.

w Philip Yordan, Dennis Cooper   d William Castle   ph Ira Morgan   m Dimitri Tiomkin

Dean Jagger, Kim Hunter, Robert Mitchum, Neil Hamilton, Lou Lubin, Milt Kibbee, Dewey Robinson

'The obviousness of the low budget is completely overcome by the solid craftsmanship of the direction, script, music, editing and performances.' – *Don Miller*

'Taking it as a whole I have seldom for years now seen one hour so energetically and sensibly used in a film.' – *James Agee*

When the Bough Breaks
GB   1947   81m   bw
GFD/Gainsborough (Betty Box)

The bewildered wife of a bigamist allows her child to be adopted and then regrets it.

Peg's Paper stuff in the then-accepted Gainsborough tradition.

w Peter Rogers   *story* Moie Charles, Herbert Victor   d Lawrence Huntington   ph Bryan Langley   m Clifton Parker   ad George Provis   ed Gordon Hales

Patricia Roc, Rosamund John, Bill Owen, Patrick Holt, Brenda Bruce, Leslie Dwyer, Jane Hylton

When the Daltons Rode *
US   1940   80m   bw
Universal

Adventures of the Dalton Gang.

Good standard Western with whitewashed bad men for heroes.

w Harold Shumate, Stuart Anthony, Lester Cole   d George Marshall   ph Hal Mohr   m Frank Skinner

Randolph Scott, Kay Francis, Brian Donlevy, Andy Devine, George Bancroft, Stuart Erwin

When the Door Opened: see *Escape* (1940)

When the Legends Die **
US   1972   105m   DeLuxe
Fox-Rank/Sagaponack (Stuart Miller)
V*

An ageing rodeo rider befriends a young Indian and teaches him the tricks of the trade.

Downbeat tale of the souring of the American dream, with fine performances from the two leads.

w Robert Dozier   *novel* Hal Borland   d Stuart Miller   ph Richard H. Kline   md Lionel Newman   m Glenn Paxton   ad Angelo Graham   ed Louis San Andres

Richard Widmark, Frederic Forrest, Luana Anders, Vito Scotti, Herbert Nelson, John War Eagle

When the Lights go on Again
US   1944   70m   bw
PRC (Leon Fromkess)

An ex-marine comes home with shell shock.

One of the first films to deal with the problems of war veterans: a modest effort, but sincere.

w Milton Lazarus   *story* Frank Craven   d William K. Howard

James Lydon, Barbara Belden, Grant Mitchell, Dorothy Peterson, Regis Toomey

When the Whales Came
GB   1989   100m   Fujicolor
Fox/Golden Swan/Central Television (Simon Channing Williams)
V, V*, L, S

In 1914, fishermen on one of the Scilly Isles are persuaded by a recluse and a boy to save a beached whale, an act which brings them luck.

Ecologically sound, dramatically dull story, not helped by its insistently soft focus photography.

w Michael Morpurgo   *novel* Why the Whales Came by Michael Morpurgo   d Clive Rees   ph Robert Paynter   m Christopher Gunning   pd Bruce Grimes   ed Andrew Boulton

Helen Mirren, Paul Scofield, David Suchet, Barbara Jefford, David Threlfall, Barbara Ewing, John Hallan, Jeremy Kemp, Max Rennie, Helen Pearce

When the Wind Blows *
GB   1987   85m   TVC colour
Film Four/Penguin/TVC/NFFC (John Coates)

An elderly man and wife fail to cope with nuclear destruction.

Cartoon picturization of a popular book; the film was less likely, despite its merits, to find an audience.

w Raymond Briggs   *book* Raymond Briggs   d Jimmy Murakami   m Roger Waters   ed John Cary   *voices* John Mills, Peggy Ashcroft

When Thief Meets Thief: see *Jump for Glory*

When Time Ran Out
US   1980   109m   Technicolor   Panavision
Warner/Irwin Allen
V*

Inhabitants of a South Sea island are threatened by a volcano.

Incredibly inept disaster movie, with all clichés on hand in the characters of some downcast actors.

w Carl Foreman, Stirling Silliphant   *novel* The Day the World Ended by Max Morgan Witts and Gordon Thomas   d James Goldstone   ph Fred J. Koenekamp   m Lalo Schifrin

Paul Newman, Jacqueline Bisset, William Holden, Edward Albert, Burgess Meredith, Valentina Cortesa, Red Buttons, Alex Carras, Ernest Borgnine, James Franciscus

'Disaster movies don't come any more disastrous than this.' – *Tom Milne, MFB*

† Said to have cost 22 million dollars and taken less than two.

AAN: costumes (Paul Zastupnevich)

When Tomorrow Comes **
US   1939   82m   bw
Universal (John M. Stahl)

A waitress falls for a concert pianist with a mad wife.

Fascinating star romantic drama, a successful follow-up to *Love Affair*; full of clichés, but impeccably set and acted. The stuff that Hollywood dreams were made of.

w Dwight Taylor   *story* James M. Cain   d John M. Stahl   ph John Mescall   m Charles Previn

Charles Boyer, Irene Dunne, Barbara O'Neil, Nydia Westman, Onslow Stevens

'A persuasive love story . . . a director's achievement.' – *Variety*

† The same story was remade twice in 1956, as *Serenade* and *Interlude,* and in 1968 as *Interlude* (all qv).

When We Are Married *
GB   1942   98m   bw
British National (John Baxter)

In 1890s Yorkshire, three couples celebrating their silver wedding are told they were never legally married.

A very funny play smartly filmed with a superb cast of character actors.

w Austin Melford, Barbara K. Emery   *play* J. B. Priestley   d Lance Comfort   ph James Wilson

Raymond Huntley, Marian Spencer, Lloyd Pearson, Olga Lindo, Ernest Butcher, Ethel Coleridge, Sydney Howard, Barry Morse, Lesley Brook, Marjorie Rhodes, Charles Victor, Cyril Smith, George Carney

When Willie Comes Marching Home *
US   1950   82m   bw
TCF (Fred Kohlmar)

During World War II, events suddenly transform a small-town air training instructor into a war hero.

Awkwardly paced comedy which could have been much funnier but does amuse in fits and starts.

w Mary Loos, Richard Sale   d John Ford   ph Leo Tover   m Alfred Newman

Dan Dailey, Colleen Townshend, Corinne Calvet, William Demarest, Evelyn Varden, James Lydon, Mae Marsh, Lloyd Corrigan

AAN: original story (Sy Gomberg)

When Worlds Collide
US   1951   82m   Technicolor
Paramount (George Pal)
V*, L

Another planet is found to be rushing inevitably towards Earth, but before the collision a few people escape in a space ship.

Stolid science fiction with a spectacular but not marvellous climax following seventy minutes of inept talk.

w Sidney Boehm   *novel* Philip Wylie, Edwin Balmer   d Rudolph Maté   ph John Seitz, W. Howard Greene   m Leith Stevens

Richard Derr, Barbara Rush, Larry Keating, Peter Hanson, John Hoyt

AA: special effects

AAN: John Seitz, W. Howard Greene

When You're in Love *
US   1937   110m   bw
Columbia (Everett Riskin)
GB title: *For You Alone*

A European opera singer takes on a husband in order to get into the United States.

Pleasing musical star vehicle with comedy touches.

wd Robert Riskin   ph Joseph Walker   md Alfred Newman

Grace Moore, Cary Grant, Aline MacMahon, Henry Stephenson, Thomas Mitchell, Catherine Doucet, Luis Alberni, Emma Dunn

'Nice musical with fair quota of giggles . . . should do nice biz.' – *Variety*

'Two lovers caught between convention and passion ...'

Where Angels Fear to Tread

GB   1991   112m   Eastmancolor
Rank/Sovereign/LWT/Stagescreen/Compact (Derek Granger)
V, V*, S

A brother and sister travel to Italy to bring back the baby of their sister-in-law who defied family opposition to marry a young Italian and died in childbirth.

Vapid and disjointed adaptation, glossily made but not helped by mannered performances.

w Tim Sullivan, Derek Granger, Charles Sturridge
d Charles Sturridge   ph Michael Coulter
m Rachel Portman   pd Simon Holland   ed Peter Coulson

Helena Bonham Carter, Judy Davis, Rupert Graves, Giovanni Guidelli, Barbara Jefford, Helen Mirren, Thomas Wheatley, Sophie Kullman

'A story about fine ironies and "fine" behaviour becomes a genre exercise in fine acting and even finer linen.' – MFB

Where Angels Go, Trouble Follows

US   1968   95m   Eastmancolor
Columbia/William Frye
V*

Nuns from a convent school take pupils to a California youth rally, and learn a thing or two.

Peripatetic comedy, rather frantically assembled; a sequel to The Trouble with Angels.

w Blanche Hanalis   d James Neilson   ph Sam Leavitt   m Lalo Schifrin

Rosalind Russell, Stella Stevens, Binnie Barnes, Mary Wickes, Milton Berle, Arthur Godfrey, Robert Taylor, Van Johnson, Susan St James

Where are your Children?

US   1943   78m   bw
Monogram (Jeffrey Bernerd)

A wandering rich boy takes up with a hash slinger, and they wind up suspected of murder ...

An 'awful warning' melodrama, risible now.

w Hilary Lynn, George W. Syre   d William Nigh

Jackie Cooper, Gale Storm, Patricia Morison, John Litel, Gertrude Michael, Addison Richards, Betty Blythe

Where Danger Lives

US   1950   84m   bw
RKO (Irving Cummings Jnr)

A doctor falls in love with a murderous patient and is drawn into her schemes.

Standard film noir of its time, competent enough in its depressing way.

w Charles Bennett   d John Farrow   ph Nicholas Musuraca   m Roy Webb

Faith Domergue, Robert Mitchum, Claude Rains, Maureen O'Sullivan, Charles Kemper

Where Do We Go from Here? *

US   1945   77m   Technicolor
TCF (William Perlberg)

A writer stumbles on a genie who takes him through periods of American history, including a voyage with Christopher Columbus.

Well-staged and rather funny charade with at least one memorable song.

w Morrie Ryskind   d Gregory Ratoff   ph Leon Shamroy   songs Kurt Weill, Ira Gershwin   m David Raksin

Fred MacMurray, June Haver, Joan Leslie, Gene Sheldon, Anthony Quinn, Carlos Ramirez, Fortunio Bonanova, Alan Mowbray, Herman Bing, Otto Preminger

'Nine parts heavy facetiousness to one part very good fun.' – James Agee

'Don't tell your doctor about this film – it could give him ideas!'

Where Does it Hurt?

US   1971   88m   colour
Josef Shaftel (Rod Amateau, William Schwarz)

Adventures of a profiteering hospital administrator.

Dislikeable, plodding smut in the form of black comedy.

wd Rod Amateau   novel The Operator by Budd Robinson, Rod Amateau   ph Brick Marquard   m Keith Allison

Peter Sellers, Jo Ann Pflug, Rick Lenz, Eve Druce

Where Eagles Dare **

GB   1969   155m   Metrocolor   Panavision 70
MGM/Winkast (Elliott Kastner)
V, V*, L

During World War II, seven British paratroopers land in the Bavarian Alps to rescue a high-ranking officer from an impregnable castle.

Archetypal schoolboy adventure, rather unattractively photographed but containing a sufficient variety of excitements.

w Alistair MacLean   novel Alistair MacLean
d Brian G. Hutton   ph Arthur Ibbetson, H. A. R. Thompson   m Ron Goodwin

Richard Burton, Clint Eastwood, Mary Ure, Patrick Wymark, Michael Hordern, Donald Houston, Peter Barkworth, Robert Beatty

Where It's At

US   1969   106m   DeLuxe
UA/Frank Ross

The owner of a Las Vegas gambling hotel tries to make his son take an interest in the business.

Flaccid comedy drama which belies its credits.
wd Garson Kanin   ph Burnett Guffey   m Benny Olsen

David Janssen, Rosemary Forsyth, Robert Drivas, Brenda Vaccaro

Where Love Has Gone *

US   1964   114m   Techniscope
Paramount/Embassy (Joseph E. Levine)
V*

A middle-aged man is appalled to hear that his teenage daughter has killed her mother's lover.

Squalid, glossy pulp fiction lightly based on the Lana Turner case, distinguished only by the game performances of its leading ladies.

w John Michael Hayes   novel Harold Robbins
d Edward Dmytryk   ph Joe MacDonald   m Walter Scharf

Susan Hayward, Bette Davis, Mike Connors, Joey Heatherton, Jane Greer, George Macready

'A typical Robbins pastiche of newspaper clippings liberally shellacked with sentiment and glued with sex.' – Newsweek

AAN: title song (m James Van Heusen, ly Sammy Cahn)

Where No Vultures Fly *

GB   1951   107m   Technicolor
Ealing (Leslie Norman)
US title: Ivory Hunter

Adventures of an East African game warden.

Pleasantly improving family film, nicely shot on location; a sequel, West of Zanzibar, was less impressive.

w W. P. Lipscomb, Ralph Smart, Leslie Norman
d Harry Watt   ph Geoffrey Unsworth   m Alan Rawsthorne

Anthony Steele, Dinah Sheridan, Harold Warrender, Meredith Edwards

'These expeditionary films are really journalistic jobs. You get sent out to a country by the studio, stay as long as you can without getting fired, and a story generally crops up.' – Harry Watt

'No one will wonder why it was chosen for this year's royal film show. It is not sordid, as so many new films are; it has a theme that almost everyone will find appealing; and the corner of the Empire where it is set is fresh, beautiful and exciting to look at.' – Daily Telegraph

Where Sinners Meet

US   1934   68m   bw
RKO
GB title: The Dover Road

A millionaire eccentric kidnaps eloping couples to find out whether they are making a mistake.

Stagebound whimsy saddled with an absurd American title.

w H. W. Hanemann   play The Dover Road by A. A. Milne   d J. Walter Ruben

Diana Wynyard, Clive Brook, Billie Burke, Reginald Owen, Alan Mowbray, Gilbert Emery, Phyllis Barry

'Despite fine performances and good production, very dubious.' – Variety

Where the Boys Are

US   1960   99m   Metrocolor   Cinemascope
MGM/Euterpe (Joe Pasternak)
V*, L

Four college girls spend the Easter vacation near a Florida military post in search of conquests.

Mindless, frothy youth musical, quite smoothly done.

w George Wells   novel Glendon Swarthout
d Henry Levin   ph Robert Bronner   m George Stoll

George Hamilton, Dolores Hart, Paula Prentiss, Jim Hutton, Yvette Mimieux, Connie Francis, Frank Gorshin, Chill Wills, Barbara Nichols

Where the Boys Are

US   1984   94m   colour
ITC/TriStar (Allan Carr)
V*, L

The 1960 musical becomes a teenage sex movie.

Neither version has much to do with the original novel.

w Stu Krieger, Jeff Burkhart   d Hy Averback
ph James A. Contner   m Sylvester Levay
ed Melvin Shapiro, Bobbie Shapiro

Lisa Hartman, Lorna Luft, Wendy Schaal, Lynn-Holly Johnson, Russel Todd, Howard McGillin

'A travesty . . . insufferably coy.' – Tom Milne, MFB

Where the Buffalo Roam

US   1980   98m   Technicolor   Panavision
Universal (Art Linson)
V*

A drug-crazed journalist takes a trip through Nixon's America.

Frenetic, rarely funny comedy, based on the work of self-styled 'gonzo journalist' Hunter S. Thompson.

w John Kaye   d Art Linson   ph Tak Fujimoto
m Mal Young   pd Richard Sawyer   ed Christopher Greenburg

Peter Boyle, Bill Murray, Bruno Kirby, Rene Auberjonois, R. G. Armstrong, Rafael Campos, Leonard Frey

Where the Green Ants Dream

West Germany   1984   100m   colour
Werner Herzog Filmproduktion/ZDF (Lucki Stipetić)
V*

original title: Wo die grünen Ameisen träumen

Aborigines object to a mining company developing one of their sacred sites.

Dull drama that engages its subject matter only in a desultory way.

w Werner Herzog, Bob Ellis *d* Werner Herzog *ph* Jörg Schmidt-Reitwein *m* Fauré, Wagner and others *pd* Ulrich Bergfelder *ed* Beate Mainka-Jellinghaus

Bruce Spence, Wandjuk Marika, Roy Marika, Ray Barrett, Norman Kaye, Colleen Clifford

Where the Heart Is *

US   1990   94m   Technicolor
Buena Vista/Touchstone (John Boorman)
V, V*, L

A tycoon orders his children to leave their life of luxury and live in a slum tenement.

Domestic comedy with some heavy-handed humour that is never funny enough to be entertaining.

w John Boorman, Telsche Boorman *d* John Boorman *ph* Peter Suschitzky *m* Peter Martin *pd* Carol Spier *ed* Ian Crafford

Dabney Coleman, Uma Thurman, Joanna Cassidy, Crispin Glover, Suzy Amis, Christopher Plummer

Where the Hot Wind Blows

France/Italy   1958   125m   bw
MGM/Cité Films/Groupe des Quatre/Titanus (Jacques Bar)
V*

original title: *La Loi*

In an Adriatic port, a voluptuous young girl is pursued by the aged local squire, a racketeer, her brother-in-law and a young agriculturist. Guess who wins her.

Hoary melodrama with the emphasis on virility and illicit passion. Long and tiresome, it failed to justify the pretensions with which it announced itself at the time.

w Jules Dassin, Diego Fabbri *novel* Roger Vailland *d* Jules Dassin *ph* Otello Martelli *m* Roman Vlad

Gina Lollobrigida, Yves Montand, Marcello Mastroianni, Pierre Brasseur, Melina Mercouri, Paolo Stoppa

† An English version was generally available.

Where the Lilies Bloom

US   1974   96m   DeLuxe
Radnitz/Mattel Productions (Robert B. Radnitz)
V*

Fearful of being sent to an institution, four children living in the Appalachians keep secret the death of their father and fend for themselves.

Slight but charming domestic drama which keeps sentimentality at bay for the most part.

w Earl Hamner Jnr *book* Vera and Bill Cleaver *d* William A. Graham *ph* Urs Furrer *m* Earl Scruggs *ad* Tambi Larsen *ed* O. Nicholas Brown

Julie Gholson, Harry Dean Stanton, Jan Smithers, Matthew Burril, Helen Harmon, Sudie Bond, Rance Howard, Tom Spratley, Alice Beardsley, Helen Bragdon

Where the River Bends: see *Bend of the River*

Where the River Runs Black

US   1986   92m   colour
MGM/IPI (Joe Roth, Harry Ufland)
V*

In Brazil a Catholic priest tries to care for the wild, orphaned son of an Indian woman and a priest working in the rain forest.

Slight, sentimental, ecological fable, given over to lyrical nature photography rather than to story-telling.

w Peter Silverman, Neal Jimenez *book* David Kendall *d* Christopher Cain *ph* Juan-Ruiz

Anchia *m* James Horner *pd* Marcos Flaksman *ed* Richard Chew

Charles Durning, Peter Horton, Ajay Naidu, Conchata Ferrell, Castulo Guerra, Alessandro Rabelo

Where the Sidewalk Ends

US   1950   95m   bw
TCF (Otto Preminger)

A tough policeman accidentally kills a suspect and tries to implicate a gang leader.

Gloomy *policier* with curious moral values.

w Rex Connor (Ben Hecht) *novel* William L. Stuart *d* Otto Preminger *ph* Joseph LaShelle *m* Cyril Mockridge

Dana Andrews, Gene Tierney, Gary Merrill, Bert Freed, Tom Tully, Karl Malden, Ruth Donnelly, Craig Stevens, Robert Simon

Where the Spies Are

GB   1965   113m   Metrocolor   Panavision
MGM/Val Guest

A country doctor is bribed to become a spy by the promise of a car he greatly covets.

Patchy spy adventure which never settles into a comfortable style but provides occasional entertainment along its bumpy way.

w Wolf Mankowitz, Val Guest *novel* Passport to Oblivion *by* James Leasor *d* Val Guest *ph* Arthur Grant *m* Mario Nascimbene

David Niven, Françoise Dorléac, Nigel Davenport, John Le Mesurier, Ronald Radd, Cyril Cusack, Eric Pohlmann

Where There's a Will *

GB   1936   81m   bw
Gainsborough (Edward Black, Sidney Gilliat)

A seedy education expert sponges on his rich relations but redeems himself by rounding up gangsters at a Christmas party.

Rather slapdash star comedy with very good scenes along the way.

w Will Hay, Robert Edmunds, Ralph Spence *d* William Beaudine *ph* Charles Van Enger *md* Louis Levy

Will Hay, Hartley Power, Gibb McLaughlin, Graham Moffatt, Norma Varden, Gina Malo

Where There's a Will

GB   1955   79m   bw
Film Locations/Eros

A London family inherits a dilapidated Devon farm and makes a go of it.

Slight comedy with pleasant players.

w R. F. Delderfield *play* R. F. Delderfield *d* Vernon Sewell

Kathleen Harrison, George Cole, Leslie Dwyer, Dandy Nichols, Ann Hanslip, Michael Shepley

'If you laugh yourself sick at this picture – sue Bob Hope!'

Where There's Life

US   1947   75m   bw
Paramount (Paul Jones)

A timid New Yorker turns out to be heir to the throne of a Ruritanian country, and is harassed by spies of both sides.

Mild star comedy with slow patches.

w Allen Boretz, Melville Shavelson *d* Sidney Lanfield *ph* Charles Lang Jnr *m* Irwin Talbot

Bob Hope, Signe Hasso, William Bendix, George Coulouris

Where Were You When the Lights Went Out? *

US   1968   94m   Metrocolor   Panavision
MGM (Everett Freeman, Martin Melcher)

New York's famous electrical blackout in 1965 has its effect on the life of a musical comedy star.

Cheerful sex farce with intriguing beginnings; the later confinement to one set is just a bit harmful.

w Everett Freeman, Karl Tunberg *play* Claude Magnier *d* Hy Averback *ph* Ellsworth Fredericks *m* Dave Grusin

Doris Day, Terry-Thomas, Patrick O'Neal, Robert Morse, Lola Albright, Jim Backus, Ben Blue

Where's Charley? *

GB   1952   97m   Technicolor
Warner

An Oxford undergraduate impersonates the rich aunt of his best friend.

Slow and rather stately musical version of the famous farce *Charley's Aunt*, unsatisfactorily shot on a mixture of poor sets and sunlit Oxford locations; worth cherishing for the ebullient performance of its over-age star.

w John Monks Jnr *play* Brandon Thomas (via stage musical) *book* George Abbott *d* David Butler *ph* Erwin Hillier *ch* Michael Kidd *m* Frank Loesser

Ray Bolger, Robert Shackleton, Mary Germaine, Allyn McLerie, Margaretta Scott, Horace Cooper

Where's Jack? *

GB   1968   119m   Eastmancolor
Paramount/Oakhurst (Stanley Baker)

In 18th-century London Jack Sheppard becomes a romantic highwayman at the behest of underworld leader Jonathan Wild.

Deliberately unromantic, squalid and 'realistic' period piece which takes no hold on the fancy despite the considerable care which was obviously taken in all departments.

w Rafe and David Newhouse *d* James Clavell *ph* John Wilcox *m* Elmer Bernstein *pd* Cedric Dawe

Tommy Steele, Stanley Baker, Fiona Lewis, Alan Badel, Dudley Foster, Sue Lloyd, Noel Purcell

Where's Poppa? *

US   1970   82m   DeLuxe
Jerry Tokovsky/Marvin Worth
V*, L

A Jewish lawyer's aged mother constantly harms his love life, and he considers various means of getting rid of her.

Much-censored black comedy which might have been funnier in a complete form. Even so, it has its moments.

w Robert Klane *novel* Robert Klane *d* Carl Reiner *ph* Jack Priestly *m* Jack Elliott

George Segal, Ruth Gordon, Trish Van Devere, Ron Leibman

Where's That Fire? *

GB   1939   73m   bw
TCF (Edward Black)

An incompetent village fire brigade accidentally saves the crown jewels from thieves.

Routine but not despicable star comedy, long thought lost; flat patches are well separated by hilarious sequences.

w Marriott Edgar, Val Guest, J. O. C. Orton *d* Marcel Varnel *ph* Arthur Crabtree

Will Hay, Moore Marriott, Graham Moffatt, Peter Gawthorne, Eric Clavering, Charles Hawtrey

W.H.I.F.F.S.

US   1975   92m   Technicolor   Panavision
Brut (C. O. Erickson)
V, V*
GB title: *C.A.S.H.*

An impotent army veteran finds that a criminal career, helped by stolen army gas, helps his sex life.

Over-the-top comedy with vaguely anti-war and anti-pollution leanings.

w Malcolm Marmorstein d Ted Post ph David M. Walsh m John Cameron

Elliott Gould, Eddie Albert, Harry Guardino, Godfrey Cambridge, Jennifer O'Neill

† Rather typical of the film was its ambiguous catch line: 'The biggest bang in history!'

AAN: song 'Now That We're in Love' (m George Barrie, ly Sammy Cahn)

While I Live
GB   1947   85m   bw
Edward Dryhurst
reissue title: The Dream of Olwen

A Cornishwoman believes an amnesiac girl to be the reincarnation of her dead sister.

Silly melodrama which achieved phenomenal popularity, despite poor production, because of its haunting theme tune The Dream of Olwen by Charles Williams.

w John Harlow, Doreen Montgomery play This Same Garden by Robert Bell d John Harlow ph F. A. Young m Charles Williams

Tom Walls, Sonia Dresdel, Carol Raye, Clifford Evans, Patricia Burke, John Warwick, Edward Lexy

'A Girl leaves her door open … A Stranger tiptoes in … A big city newspaper blazes with murder headlines! Then the chase as newsmen and women feud with each other … to be the first to find the killer!'

While the City Sleeps
US   1956   100m   bw   Superscope
RKO (Bert Friedlob)
V, V*, L

Three chief executives of a newspaper empire are pitted against each other in a search for a murder scoop.

Star-packed but leaden-paced news bureau melodrama; a major disappointment considering the talent.

w Casey Robinson novel The Bloody Spur by Charles Einstein d Fritz Lang ph Ernest Laszlo m Herschel Burke Gilbert

Dana Andrews, George Sanders, Ida Lupino, Sally Forrest, Thomas Mitchell, Rhonda Fleming, Vincent Price, Howard Duff, James Craig, Robert Warwick, John Barrymore Jnr

While the Patient Slept
US   1935   65m   bw
First National

A nurse hired to look after a stricken millionaire finds herself in the middle of a murder case.

Announced as the first of a series of Clue Club Mysteries, this was derived from a source similar to, or possibly the same as, Miss Pinkerton (qv). It sufficed.

w Robert N. Lee novel Mignon G. Eberhart d Ray Enright

Aline MacMahon, Guy Kibbee, Lyle Talbot, Patricia Ellis, Allen Jenkins, Gene Solow, Brown Holmes, Robert Barrat, Hobart Cavanaugh

'Seems probable that it will please wherever mysteries are liked.' – Variety

While the Sun Shines
GB   1946   81m   bw
ABPC/International Screenplays (Anatole de Grunwald)

An American soldier and a young Frenchman seek to woo Lady Elizabeth away from her intended.

Mild wartime comedy, rather stagey and considerably undercast.

w Anatole de Grunwald, Terence Rattigan play Terence Rattigan d Anthony Asquith ph Jack Hildyard m Nicholas Brodszky

Brenda Bruce, Ronald Howard, Bonar Colleano, Ronald Squire, Barbara White, Margaret Rutherford, Miles Malleson, Joyce Grenfell

The Whip Hand
US   1951   82m   bw
RKO (Lewis J. Rachmil)

A fisherman finds himself unwelcome in a lonely town run by ex-Nazi, now communist, bacteriologists.

Preposterous, pretentious anti-communist low-budgeter, mildly enjoyable for its sheer gall.

w George Bricker, Frank L. Moss d/pd William Cameron Menzies ph Nicholas Musuraca m Paul Sawtell

Elliott Reid, Carla Balenda, Edgar Barrier, Raymond Burr

Whiplash
US   1948   90m   bw
Warner (William Jacobs)

A painter becomes a prizefighter.

Hokey, unpersuasive romantic melodrama.

w Maurice Geraghty, Harriet Frank Jnr d Lewis Seiler ph Peverell Marley m Franz Waxman

Dane Clark, Alexis Smith, Zachary Scott, Eve Arden, Jeffrey Lynn, S. Z. Sakall, Alan Hale, Douglas Kennedy

Whipsaw *
US   1935   88m   bw
MGM (Harry Rapf)

A G-man infiltrates a gang by wooing its girl member.

Fairly snappy romantic drama which further established both its stars.

w Howard Emmett Rogers d Sam Wood ph James Wong Howe m William Axt

Spencer Tracy, Myrna Loy, Harvey Stephens, Clay Clements, William Harrigan

'Should do okay biz . . . romance and sex angles mingling with the light touch of sophistication so popular nowadays carries events along at a speedy pace that is unabated until the fadeout.' – Variety

Whirlpool
US   1934   69m   bw
Columbia

A convict is released and makes contact with the daughter who never knew him.

Heavily plotted melodrama with an unhappy ending; technically quite proficient.

w Dorothy Howell, Ethel Hill, Howard Emmett Rogers d Roy William Neill

Jack Holt, Jean Arthur, Allen Jenkins, Donald Cook, Lila Lee, John Miljan, Ward Bond

'One of the most surefire father and daughter stories ever screened, with heart interest running high throughout . . . well above fair in entertainment appeal.' – Variety

Whirlpool *
US   1950   98m   bw
TCF (Otto Preminger)

A girl is accused of a murder committed by her hypnotist, who has willed himself out of a hospital bed.

Silly murder melodrama; glossy production makes it entertaining.

w Lester Barstow, Andrew Solt novel Guy Endore d Otto Preminger ph Arthur Miller m David Raksin

Gene Tierney, José Ferrer, Richard Conte, Charles Bickford, Barbara O'Neil, Eduard Franz, Fortunio Bonanova

'It is sometimes difficult to discover from Miss Tierney's playing whether she is or is not under hypnosis.' – MFB

† Lester Barstow = Ben Hecht.

Whirlpool
GB   1959   95m   Eastmancolor
Rank (George Pitcher)

A killer escapes in Cologne; his girlfriend separates from him and gets a lift down the Rhine in a barge; the trip reforms her and she betrays her lover.

Modestly attractive travelogue with the burden of a very boring melodrama.

w Lawrence P. Bachmann novel The Lorelei by Lawrence P. Bachmann d Lewis Allen ph Geoffrey Unsworth m Ron Goodwin

Juliette Greco, O. W. Fischer, William Sylvester, Marius Goring, Muriel Pavlow

Whisky Galore ****
GB   1948   82m   bw
Ealing (Monja Danischewsky)
V, V*
US title: Tight Little Island

During World War II, a ship full of whisky is wrecked on a small Hebridean island, and the local customs and excise man has his hands full.

Marvellously detailed, fast-moving, well-played and attractively photographed comedy which firmly established the richest Ealing vein.

w Compton Mackenzie, Angus Macphail novel Compton Mackenzie d Alexander Mackendrick ph Gerald Gibbs m Ernest Irving

Basil Radford, Joan Greenwood, Jean Cadell, Gordon Jackson, James Robertson Justice, Wylie Watson, John Gregson, Morland Graham, Duncan Macrae, Catherine Lacey, Bruce Seton, Henry Mollinson, Compton Mackenzie, A. E. Matthews

'Brilliantly witty and fantastic, but wholly plausible.' – Sunday Chronicle

† Fourteen whisky bottles, said to be the last surviving from the wreck of the SS Politician, the real-life shipwreck that inspired the film, were sold in 1993 at a Glasgow auction for £12,012, with a bottle of Haig Dimple fetching £1,210.

The Whisperers
GB   1966   106m   bw
UA/Seven Pines (Michael S. Laughlin, Ronald Shedlo)

An old lady hears voices and is put upon by her son, her wandering husband, and various others.

Interesting but cold and finally unsatisfactory character melodrama; even the acting, though in a sense admirable, is too genteel.

w Bryan Forbes novel Robert Nicolson d Bryan Forbes ph Gerry Turpin m John Barry

Edith Evans, Eric Portman, Avis Bunnage, Nanette Newman, Gerald Sim, Ronald Fraser

AAN: Edith Evans

Whispering City
Canada   1947   95m   bw
Quebec/Eagle Lion

A girl reporter has dangerous information.

Fairly watchable mystery, all Canadian apart from the three leads.

w Rian James Leonard Lee d Fedor Ozep

Paul Lukas, Mary Anderson, Helmut Dantine, John Pratt, George Alexander

Whispering Ghosts

US 1942 75m bw
TCF (Sol M. Wurtzel)

A radio detective tackles the unsolved murder of an old sea captain.

No ghosts are evident, and not much plot, in this slow mystery comedy which failed to do for Berle what *The Cat and the Canary* did for Hope.

w Lou Breslow *d* Alfred Werker

Milton Berle, Brenda Joyce, John Carradine, John Shelton, Willie Best

Whispering Shadows

US 1933 bw serial: 12 eps
Mascot

A waxworks owner makes figures which speak and move; but he and they are prey to The Whispering Shadow.

Quaint melodramatic serial, still good for a few laughs.

d Albert Herman, Colbert Clark

Bela Lugosi, Henry B. Walthall, Karl Dane, Viva Tattersall, Robert Warwick

'The epic spectacle of America's most flaming era!'
Whispering Smith

US 1948 88m Technicolor
Paramount (Mel Epstein)

A government agent investigating robberies finds his friend is implicated.

Fairly entertaining detective Western.

w Frank Butler, Karl Lamb *novel* Frank H. Spearman *d* Leslie Fenton *ph* Ray Rennahan *m* Adolph Deutsch

Alan Ladd, Robert Preston, Brenda Marshall, Donald Crisp, William Demarest, Fay Holden, Murvyn Vye, Frank Faylen

Whispering Smith Hits London

GB 1951 82m (77m US) bw
Exclusive/Hammer (Anthony Hinds)
US title: *Whispering Smith vs. Scotland Yard*

An American detective in London investigates the case of a suicide which may be murder.

Tolerable programmer of its time: competence without inspiration.

w John Gilling *story* Frank H. Spearman *d* Francis Searle *ph* Walter Harvey *m* Frank Spencer *ed* James Needs

Richard Carlson, Greta Gynt, Herbert Lom, Rona Anderson, Alan Wheatley, Dora Bryan, Reginald Beckwith

Whispers in the Dark

US 1992 98m DeLuxe
Paramount (Martin Bregman, Michael S. Bregman)
V, V*, S

A New York psychiatrist is disturbed to discover that her new and apparently gentle boyfriend seems also to be the sadistic lover who acts out dangerous fantasies with one of her patients.

Mindlessly entertaining thriller that makes few demands on its audience and concludes that psychiatrists need their heads examining.

wd Christopher Crowe *ph* Michael Chapman *m* Thomas Newman *pd* John Jay Moore *ed* Bill Pankow

Annabella Sciorra, Jamey Sheridan, Anthony LaPaglia, Jill Clayburgh, John Leguizamo, Deborah Unger, Alan Alda, Anthony Heald

'An entertaining pot-boiler, this bypassed the cinemas, but is certainly better value for your rental money than many another upmarket sex slasher.' – *Kim Newman, Empire*

The Whistle at Eaton Falls *

US 1951 96m bw
Columbia (Louis de Rochemont)
GB title: *Richer than the Earth*

The story of a strike at a small-town plastics factory.

Reasonably absorbing semi-documentary with a final 'solution' which rather evades the issues.

w Lemist Esler, Virginia Shaler *d* Robert Siodmak *ph* Joseph Brun *m* Louis Applebaum

Lloyd Bridges, Dorothy Gish, Carleton Carpenter, Murray Hamilton, James Westerfield, Lenore Lonergan

Whistle Down the Wind *

GB 1961 99m bw
Rank/Allied Film Makers/Beaver (Richard Attenborough)
V*

Three north country children think a murderer on the run is Jesus Christ.

Charming allegorical study of childhood innocence, extremely well made, amusing, and avoiding sentimentality.

w Keith Waterhouse, Willis Hall *novel* Mary Hayley Bell *d* Bryan Forbes *ph* Arthur Ibbetson *m* Malcolm Arnold

Hayley Mills, Bernard Lee, Alan Bates, Norman Bird, Elsie Wagstaff, Alan Barnes

Whistle Stop

US 1946 84m bw
United Artists/Nero/Seymour Nebenzal
V*

A city girl returns to her small-town home and finds herself torn between a night-club proprietor and an indolent charmer.

Would-be *film noir*, miscast and rather glum when it isn't unintentionally funny.

w Philip Yordan *novel* Maritta M. Wolff *d* Leonide Moguy *ph* Russell Metty *m* Dimitri Tiomkin

George Raft, Ava Gardner, Tom Conway, Victor McLaglen

The Whistler

Originally a radio series of suspense stories introduced by someone whistling the theme tune, this was turned by Columbia into a fairly workmanlike series of second features quite unrelated to each other except for the leading actor, Richard Dix, who alternated as hero and villain, and William Castle, who directed or produced most of them.

1944: THE WHISTLER, THE MARK OF THE WHISTLER
1945: THE POWER OF THE WHISTLER
1946: THE VOICE OF THE WHISTLER
1947: MYSTERIOUS INTRUDER, THE SECRET OF THE WHISTLER, THE 12TH HOUR
1948: THE RETURN OF THE WHISTLER

Whistling in the Dark *

US 1941 77m bw
MGM (George Haight)
V*

A radio detective is kidnapped by a criminal who wants him to devise a perfect murder which will then be pinned on him.

Scatty comedy-thriller which, though it now seems slow to start, was popular enough to warrant two sequels (*Whistling in Brooklyn, Whistling in Dixie*).

w Robert MacGunigle, Harry Clork, Albert Mannheimer *play* Laurence Gross, Edward Childs Carpenter *d* S. Sylvan Simon *ph* Sidney Wagner *m* Bronislau Kaper

Red Skelton, Conrad Veidt, Ann Rutherford, Virginia Grey, Eve Arden, Rags Ragland, Don Douglas, Lloyd Corrigan

† The play was previously filmed in 1933 with Ernest Truex, and this version is now shown on TV as *Scared*.

The White Angel *

US 1936 91m bw
Warner (Henry Blanke)

The life of Florence Nightingale.

Starchy biopic; the Victorian atmosphere is never quite caught.

w Mordaunt Sharp, Michael Jacoby *d* William Dieterle *ph* Tony Gaudio

Kay Francis, Ian Hunter, Donald Woods, Nigel Bruce, Donald Crisp, Henry O'Neill, Billy Mauch, Halliwell Hobbes

White Banners *

US 1938 88m bw
Warner (Henry Blanke)

A social worker tries to solve the problems of a troubled family among whom is her own son, a fact unknown to him.

Moderate middle-class drama.

w Lenore Coffee, Cameron Rogers, Abem Finkel *novel* Lloyd C. Douglas *d* Edmund Goulding *ph* Charles Rosher *m* Max Steiner

Fay Bainter, Claude Rains, Jackie Cooper, Bonita Granville, Henry O'Neill, James Stephenson, Kay Johnson

'Emotional drama, okay for the family trade . . . there is something fine and tender about it.' – *Variety*

AAN: Fay Bainter

White Blood: see *The Planter's Wife*

The White Buffalo

US 1977 97m Technicolor
Dino de Laurentiis (Pancho Kohner)
V, V*

Wild Bill Hickok and Chief Crazy Horse join forces to kill a marauding white buffalo.

Ridiculous symbolic Western, not helped by the very artificial looking beast of the title.

w Richard Sale *novel* Richard Sale *d* J. Lee-Thompson *ph* Paul Lohmann *m* John Barry

Charles Bronson, Jack Warden, Will Sampson, Kim Novak, Clint Walker, Stuart Whitman, John Carradine, Slim Pickens, Cara Williams, Douglas Fowley

'The dried husk of a *Moby Dick* allegory seems to be rattling around here amidst all the other dead wood.' – *Jonathan Rosenbaum, MFB*

White Captive: see *White Savage*

White Cargo *

US 1942 90m bw
MGM (Victor Saville)

White rubber planters are driven mad with desire for a scheming native girl.

Antediluvian melodrama previously filmed in 1930. Good for laughing at, and the star looked great as Tondelayo.

w Leon Gordon *play* Leon Gordon *novel* Hell's Playground by Vera Simonton *d* Richard Thorpe *m* Bronislau Kaper

Hedy Lamarr, Walter Pidgeon, Richard Carlson, Frank Morgan, Bramwell Fletcher, Richard Ainley, Reginald Owen

† There was also a British version in 1929 (silent) with Leslie Faber and Gypsy Rhouma; and a few months later it emerged with added dialogue.

White Cargo

GB 1973 62m Eastmancolor
Border/Negus-Fancey (Mervyn Collard)

A dim-witted civil servant becomes involved in rescuing some Soho strippers who are being sold to an Arab harem.

Limp comedy that mixes poor slapstick and coy sex to no effect.

w Ray Selfe, David McGillivray d Ray Selfe ph John Barnard m David Lindup ad Jack Shampan ed Peter Austen-Hunt

David Jason, Hugh Lloyd, Imogen Hassall, Tim Barrett, Dave Prowse, Raymond Cross, John Barber

'Mercifully, there is every sign that the film has been heavily cut.' – Tony Rayns, MFB

White Christmas *

US 1954 120m Technicolor Vistavision
Paramount (Robert Emmett Dolan)
V, V (W), V*, L, S

Two entertainers boost the popularity of a winter resort run by an old army buddy.

Humdrum musical lifted only by its stars; a revamp of Holiday Inn, which was much better.

w Norman Krasna, Norman Panama, Melvin Frank d Michael Curtiz ph Loyal Griggs songs Irving Berlin

Bing Crosby, Danny Kaye, Rosemary Clooney, Vera-Ellen, Dean Jagger, Mary Wickes, Sig Rumann, Grady Sutton

AAN: 'Count Your Blessings Instead of Sheep'

The White Cliffs of Dover *

US 1944 126m bw
MGM (Sidney Franklin)
V*

An American girl who marries into the British aristocracy loses a husband in World War I and a son in World War II.

Tearful flagwaver with some entertaining scenes in the first half and the general sense of an all-stops-out production.

w Claudine West, Jan Lustig, George Froeschel poem Alice Duer Miller d Clarence Brown ph George Folsey m Herbert Stothart

Irene Dunne, Alan Marshal, Frank Morgan, May Whitty, Roddy McDowall, C. Aubrey Smith, Gladys Cooper, Peter Lawford, Van Johnson

'A long, earnest, well-intentioned, over-emotionalized cliché.' – Richard Mallett, Punch

'This sterling silver picture . . . is such a tribute to English gentility as only an American studio would dare to make.' – New York Times

'Sentimental patriotism . . . a truly monstrous cultural artifact.' – Pauline Kael, 70s

AAN: George Folsey

The White Cockatoo

US 1935 72m bw
Warner

Male and female heirs to a will suffer death threats.

Bland transcription of a popular mystery book.

w Ben Markson, Lillie Hayward novel Mignon G. Eberhart d Alan Crosland

Ricardo Cortez, Jean Muir, Ruth Donnelly, Minna Gombell, Walter Kingsford, John Eldredge

White Comanche

Spain/US 1968 92m Eastmancolor
Rank/International Producers/Cinematográficas A.B. (Sam White)
aka: Comancho Blanco

A renegade Comanche is challenged to a duel to the death by his law-abiding twin brother.

Uninteresting, unconvincing and unoriginal Western.

w José Briz, Manuel G. Rivera story Robert I. Holt, Frank Gruber d Gilbert Lee Kay (José Briz) ph Francisco Fraile m Jean Ledut

William Shatner, Joseph Cotten, Rossana Yani, Perla Cristal

'The story rambles through stock routines accommodating stock characters.' – MFB

† The film was cut to 83m on its British release.

White Corridors *

GB 1951 102m bw
GFD/Vic (Joseph Janni, John Croydon)

Life in a small Midlands hospital.

Competent multi-drama which found a big audience.

w Jan Read, Pat Jackson novel Yeoman's Hospital by Helen Ashton d Pat Jackson ph C. Pennington-Richards

James Donald, Googie Withers, Godfrey Tearle, Petula Clark, Jack Watling, Moira Lister, Barry Jones, Megs Jenkins, Basil Radford

'This quality of professionalism is comparatively rare in British films.' – Gavin Lambert

White Cradle Inn

GB 1947 83m bw
British Lion/Peak (Ivor McLaren, A. G. Hardman)
US title: High Fury

A Swiss hotel owner adopts a refugee boy and is menaced by her ne'er-do-well husband, who finally sacrifices himself for the boy.

Unimpressive little drama which wastes its cast, but provides beautiful scenery.

w Harold French, Lesley Storm d Harold French ph Deric Williams m Bernard Green

Madeleine Carroll, Michael Rennie, Ian Hunter, Anne Marie Blanc, Michael McKeag

The White Dawn

US 1976 110m Movielab
Paramount/American Film Properties (Martin Ransohoff)
V*, L

In 1900, survivors from a whaling ship are cared for by Eskimos, who turn on them when nature proves unkind.

Unpleasant fable with lots of bitter weather and subtitled Eskimos. Scarcely an entertainment, and its message is mumbled.

w James Houston, Tom Rickman d Philip Kaufman ph Michael Chapman m Henry Mancini

Warren Oates, Timothy Bottoms, Lou Gossett, Eskimo cast

'Chief among the pleasures the film offers us is the sensation of having gained insight into a distant, primitive culture.' – Wall Street Journal

White Dog *

US 1982 90m Metrocolor
Paramount/Edgar J. Scherick

An actress unknowingly acquires a dog that has been trained to attack blacks only.

Oddball thriller that attracted unjustified criticism as a racist work, which prevented it from obtaining a proper release.

w Samuel Fuller, Curtis Hanson book Romain Gary d Samuel Fuller ph Bruce Surtees m Ennio Morricone

Kristy McNichol, Paul Winfield, Burl Ives, Jameson Parker, Lynne Moody, Marshall Thompson

White Eagle

US 1941 bw serial: 15 eps
Columbia

A pony express rider is threatened by revengeful crooks.

Solid Western serial with an Indian hero.

d James W. Horne

Buck Jones, Raymond Hatton, Dorothy Fay, James Craven

White Fang

US 1990 109m Eastmancolor
Warner/Hybrid/Disney/Silver Screen Partners IV (Marykay Powell)
V, V*, L

A youth, who goes to the Klondike to take over his dead father's gold-mining claim, befriends a dog that is half-wolf.

Tame, youth-oriented version, far closer to Lassie than to Jack London's original.

w Jeanne Rosenberg, Nick Thiel, David Fallon novel Jack London d Randal Kleiser ph Tony Pierce-Roberts m Basil Poledouris pd Michael Bolton ed Lisa Day

Klaus Maria Brandauer, Ethan Hawke, Seymour Cassel, Susan Hogan, James Remar, Bill Moseley, Clint B. Younggreen

White Feather *

US 1955 100m Technicolor Cinemascope
TCF/Panoramic (Robert L. Jacks)

A cavalry colonel tries to hold back gold prospectors until the Cheyenne have moved on to their new reservations.

Old-fashioned cowboys and (sympathetic) Indians, very efficiently done.

w Delmer Daves, Leo Townsend d Robert Webb ph Lucien Ballard m Hugo Friedhofer

Robert Wagner, John Lund, Jeffrey Hunter, Debra Paget, Eduard Franz, Noah Beery Jnr, Hugh O'Brian, Virginia Leith, Emile Meyer

'Pick up the pieces, folks, Jimmy's in action again!'

White Heat ***

US 1949 114m bw
Warner (Louis F. Edelman)
V, V*, L

A violent, mother-fixated gangster gets his come-uppance when a government agent is infiltrated into his gang.

This searing melodrama reintroduced the old Cagney and then some: spellbinding suspense sequences complemented his vivid and hypnotic portrayal.

w Ivan Goff, Ben Roberts story Virginia Kellogg d Raoul Walsh ph Sid Hickox m Max Steiner

James Cagney, Edmond O'Brien, Margaret Wycherly, Virginia Mayo, Steve Cochran, John Archer

'The most gruesome aggregation of brutalities ever presented under the guise of entertainment.' – Cue

'In the hurtling tabloid traditions of the gangster movies of the thirties, but its matter-of-fact violence is a new post-war style.' – Time

'A wild and exciting picture of mayhem and madness.' – Life

AAN: Virginia Kellogg

The White Hell of Pitz Palu *

Germany 1929 approx 90m bw
UFA

Mountaineers have a difficult ascent of Pitz Palu.

Classic semi-documentary, noted for its pictorial compositions more than its dramatic qualities.

wd G. W. Pabst, Dr Arnold Fank

'An astonishing and, to me, wildly terrifying film.' – James Agate

White Hunter

US   1936   65m   bw
TCF/Darryl F. Zanuck

An African hunter is hired by an old enemy.

Extremely predictable melodrama with poor technical work.

w Sam Duncan, Kenneth Earl, Gene Markey
d Irving Cummings

Warner Baxter, Wilfrid Lawson, June Lang, Gail Patrick, Alison Skipworth

'An adventure in obsession . . . '

White Hunter Black Heart **

US   1990   112m   Technicolor
Warner/Malpaso/Rastar (Clint Eastwood)
V, V*, L

A film director goes to Africa ostensibly to make a film but primarily to shoot an elephant.

Based on a novel about John Huston making *The African Queen*, by a writer involved in that film, it emerges as an entertaining account of Hollywood egotism.

w Peter Viertel, James Bridges, Burt Kennedy
novel Peter Viertel   d Clint Eastwood   ph Jack N. Green   m Lennie Niehaus   pd John Graysmark
ed Joel Cox

Clint Eastwood, Jeff Fahey, Charlotte Cornwell, Norman Lumsden, George Dzundza, Edward Tudor Pole, Roddy Maude-Roxby

'Its chief strength is that it is one of those increasingly rare Hollywood entertainments that treats its audience as adults.' – *Derek Malcolm, Guardian*

'Trapped unhappily between fact and fiction, the film builds up not to a bang but a whimper, leaving one wondering bemusedly what it is trying to say, and about whom.' – *Tom Milne, MFB*

White Lightning

US   1973   101m   DeLuxe
United Artists/Levy-Gardner-Laven
V*

A convict escapes to wreak vengeance on the corrupt sheriff who had killed his brother.

Heavy-going Southern melodrama which comes to life only during its occasional fits of violence. *Gator* was a kind of sequel.

w William Norton   d Joseph Sargent   ph Edward Rosson   m Charles Bernstein

Burt Reynolds, Jennifer Billingsley, Ned Beatty, Matt Clark, Bo Hopkins, Louise Latham, Diane Ladd

White Line Fever

US/Canada   1975   89m   Metrocolor
Columbia-Warner/White Line Fever Syndicate/International Cinemedia (John Kemeny)
V*, L

A poor but honest trucker riles the powerful by refusing to haul stolen goods.

A predictably violent action thriller with little to recommend it.

w Ken Friedman, Jonathan Kaplan   d Jonathan Kaplan   ph Fred Koenekamp   m David Nichtern
ad Sydney Litwak   ed O. Nicholas Brown

Jan-Michael Vincent, Kay Lenz, Slim Pickens, L. Q. Jones, Don Porter, Sam Laws, Dick Miller

The White Man: see *The Squaw Man*

'It Ain't Easy Being This Good.'

White Men Can't Jump **

US   1992   DeLuxe
TCF (Don Miller, David Lester)
V, V*, L, S

Two baseball hustlers – one white, one black – team up to part the unwary from their money.

Crisply performed, enjoyable caper with something to say about relationships between races.

wd Ron Shelton   ph Russell Boyd   m Bennie Wallace   pd Dennis Washington   ed Paul Seydor

Wesley Snipes, Woody Harrelson, Rosie Perez, Tyra Ferrell, Cylk Cozart, Kadeem Hardison, Ernest Harden Jnr

'As fast, buoyant and full of feinting rubato as basketball itself.' – *Nigel Andrews, Financial Times*

'With a remarkable lack of soap-box oratory, Shelton's film manages to catch the prevailing tone of American race relations, to show us what urban America really looks like, and to depict the moral quandaries that poverty inevitably forces on its victims.' – *Henry Sheehan, Sight and Sound*

White Mischief

GB   1987   107m   Agfa-Gevaert
Umbrella (Michael White)
V, V*, L, S

Real-life unsolved murder of Lord Erroll in Kenya's Happy Valley.

Starry cast and slick direction fail to engage interest in the sybaritic lifestyle of white settlers in colonial Africa.

w Michael Radford, Jonathan Gems   book James Fox   d Michael Radford   ph Roger Deakins
m George Fenton   pd Roger Hall

Charles Dance, Greta Scacchi, Joss Ackland, Sarah Miles, John Hurt, Trevor Howard

White Nights

US   1985   135m   Metrocolor
Columbia/New Visions/Delphi V (Taylor Hackford, William S. Gilmore)
V, V*, L, S

After a plane crash, a Russian emigré ballet star finds himself a prisoner in Leningrad.

Basically an escape story with silly details, this tries also to be a dance film about relationships. Despite the star's powerful presence, it fails on most counts.

w James Goldman, Eric Hughes   d Taylor Hackford
ph David Watkin   m Michel Colombier   pd Philip Harrison   ed Fredric and William Steinkamp

Mikhail Baryshnikov, Gregory Hines, Jerzy Skolimowski, Helen Mirren, Geraldine Page, Isabella Rossellini

'Good looks but no style . . . neither fish nor fowl, good nor bad, box office gold nor poison.' – *Variety*

AA: song 'Say You, Say Me' (Lionel Richie)

'Love is the last thing on their minds.'

White Palace

US   1990   103m   colour
UIP/Universal/Mirage/Double Play (Mark Rosenberg, Amy Robinson, Griffin Dunne)
V, V*, L, S

A successful young advertising executive begins an affair with a fortyish waitress in a hamburger joint.

Soft-centred romance in which love conquers social differences and aspirations.

w Ted Tally, Alvin Sargent   novel Glenn Savan
d Luis Mondoki   ph Lajos Koltai   m George Fenton   pd Jeannine C. Oppewall   ed Carol Fischer

Susan Sarandon, James Spader, Jason Alexander, Kathy Bates, Eileen Brennan, Steven Hill, Rachel Levin

'One of the best films of its kind since *The Graduate*. Rave word-of-mouth should help warm up the box-office grill.' – *Variety*

The White Parade

US   1934   80m   bw
TCF (Jesse L. Lasky)

Incidents at the nurses' training school of a midwestern hospital.

Smooth but very predictable semi-documentary.

w Sonya Levien, Ernest Pascal   novel Rian James
d Irving Cummings

Loretta Young, John Boles, Dorothy Wilson, Muriel Kirkland, Sara Haden, Astrid Allwyn, Jane Darwell, Frank Conroy

'Sympathetic comedy drama with strong *femme* draw value.' – *Variety*

AAN: best picture

'The most dangerous way to solve a murder . . . become the victim.'

White Sands

US   1992   101m   colour
Warner/Morgan Creek (William Sackheim, Scott Rudin)
V, V*, L, S

Investigating a murder in New Mexico, a deputy sheriff finds himself involved with the FBI, the CIA and arms dealers.

Confusing thriller of cross and double-cross that fails to sustain an interest in its many twists and turns.

w Daniel Pyne   d Roger Donaldson   ph Peter Menzies Jnr   m Patrick O'Hearn   pd John Graysmark   ed Nicholas Beauman, Sue Blainey

Willem Dafoe, Mary Elizabeth Mastrantonio, Mickey Rourke, M. Emmet Walsh, Mimi Rogers, James Rebhorn, Maura Tierney

'An absorbing, tightly coiled thriller not always easy to follow.' – *Variety*

'Initially intriguing, ultimately disappointing, but fun for much of the way.' – *Philip French, Observer*

White Savage (1941): see *South of Tahiti*

White Savage

US   1943   75m   Technicolor
Universal (George Waggner)
GB title: *White Captive*

The queen of a beautiful South Sea island has trouble with shark hunters and crooks after her mineral deposits.

Self-admitted hokum strung loosely and colourfully around its star: big box-office in the middle of the war.

w Richard Brooks   d Arthur Lubin   ph Lester White, William Snyder   m Frank Skinner

Maria Montez, Jon Hall, Sabu, Thomas Gomez, Sidney Toler, Paul Guilfoyle, Turhan Bey, Don Terry

'It may be that these semi-burlesques were more fun to make than to watch.' – *Pauline Kael, 70s*

White Shadows in the South Seas *

US   1928   88m (sound version)   bw
MGM

An alcoholic doctor in Tahiti finds happiness with a native girl until he is killed by white colonials.

Rather boring melodrama illuminated by superb photography.

w John Colton, Jack Cunningham   book Frederick J. O'Brien   d W. S. Van Dyke (and Robert Flaherty)
ph Clyde DeVinna and others (including Flaherty)

Monte Blue, Raquel Torres

AA: Clyde DeVinna

The White Sheik **

Italy   1952   88m   bw
PDC/OFI (Luigi Rovere)
V, V*
original title: *Lo Sceicco Bianco*

A provincial couple come to Rome on their honeymoon, where the wife is infatuated with a common actor who portrays a dashing, aristocratic lover in a photo-novel.

A gently comic, ironic drama of illusion and reality, based on an idea of Michelangelo Antonioni's.

w Federico Fellini, Tullio Pinelli, Ennio Flaiano *d* Federico Fellini *ph* Arturo Gallea *m* Nino Rota *ad* Raffaello Tolfo *ed* Rolando Bebedetti

Brunello Bovo, Leopoldo Trieste, *Alberto Sordi,* Giulietta Masina

'This affectionate satire on glamour and delusion is probably the most gentle and naturalistic of Fellini's films, but it was not a success, maybe because it is a little flat in places.' – *Pauline Kael*

The White Sister
US 1933 110m bw
MGM (Hunt Stromberg)
V*

When her lover is reported killed in the war, an Italian noblewoman takes the veil . . . but he comes back.

Tiresome romantic drama from another age, a big prestige production of its time.

w Donald Ogden Stewart *novel* F. Marion Crawford, Walter Hackett *d* Victor Fleming *ph* William Daniels *m* Herbert Stothart

Helen Hayes, Clark Gable, Lewis Stone, Louise Closser Hale, May Robson, Edward Arnold

'An eloquent yoking of marquee names . . . certain money maker for general release.' – *Variety*

† The silent version of 1923 starred Lillian Gish and Ronald Colman, and bore the tagline: 'A love that outlived passion!'

White Tie and Tails
US 1946 81m bw
Universal

A butler left in charge of the house gets ideas above his station.

Modest comedy which lacks the required high style.

w Bertram Millhauser *novel The Victoria Docks at Eight* by Rufus King, Charles Leakon *d* Charles Barton

Dan Duryea, Ella Raines, William Bendix, Richard Gaines, Clarence Kolb, Frank Jenks

The White Tower
US 1950 98m Technicolor
RKO (Sid Rogell)
V*

Various people have personal reasons for climbing an Alpine mountain.

Pretentiously symbolic melodrama with some good action sequences and curiously stilted performances.

w Paul Jarrico *novel* James Ramsay Ullman *d* Ted Tetzlaff *ph* Ray Rennahan *m* Roy Webb

Glenn Ford, Claude Rains, Alida Valli, Oscar Homolka, Cedric Hardwicke, Lloyd Bridges, June Clayworth

'The main interest is a curiosity as to who will fall over which precipice when.' – *Penelope Houston*

The White Unicorn
GB 1947 97m bw
GFD/John Corfield (Harold Huth)
US title: *Bad Sister*

In a home for delinquent girls, the worst offender exchanges reminiscences with the warden.

Peg's Paper melodrama in complex flashback form.

w Robert Westerby, A. R. Rawlinson, Moie Charles *novel* Flora Sandstrom *d* Bernard Knowles *ph* Reginald Wyer *m* Bretton Byrd

Margaret Lockwood, Joan Greenwood, Ian Hunter, Dennis Price, Guy Middleton, Catherine Lacey, Mabel Constanduros, Paul Dupuis

White Witch Doctor
US 1953 96m Technicolor
TCF (Otto Lang)

A nurse in the Congo converts a gold-seeking adventurer.

Stale hokum in which the animals are the most interesting feature.

w Ivan Goff, Ben Roberts *novel* Louise A. Stinetorf *d* Henry Hathaway *ph* Leon Shamroy *m* Bernard Herrmann

Susan Hayward, Robert Mitchum, Walter Slezak, Timothy Carey

'Alone among outcasts who hadn't seen a white woman in ten years!'
White Woman
US 1933 68m bw
Paramount

A cockney overseer in the Malaysian jungle takes back a cabaret singer as his bride.

Risible melodrama with an obvious outcome.

w Samuel Hoffenstein, Gladys Lehman *story* Norman Reilly Raine, Frank Butler *d* Stuart Walker *ph* Harry Fischbeck

Charles Laughton, Carole Lombard, Kent Taylor, Charles Bickford, Percy Kilbride, Charles Middleton, James Bell

'Bromidic South Sea stuff . . . seems best for dual bills.' – *Variety*

† Remade as *Island of Lost Men.*

White Zombie **
US 1932 74m bw
American Securities Corporation (Edward Halperin)
V, V*

Haitian zombies work a sugar mill for a white schemer.

Genuinely eerie horror film with a slow, stagey, out-of-this world quality coupled with an interesting sense of composition.

w Garnett Weston *d* Victor Halperin *ph* Arthur Martinelli *md* Abe Meyer

Bela Lugosi, Madge Bellamy, John Harron, Joseph Cawthorn

'Fine work of Lugosi is backed by good cast and bizarre staging . . . not quite up to Broadway.' – *Variety*

'A Gothic fairy tale filled with dreamlike imagery, traditional symbols, echoes of Romanticism, and (probably unintentional) psychosexual overtones.' – *Carlos Clarens*

'For those absolutely dedicated to gothic silliness.' – *New Yorker, 1977*

Who?
GB 1974 93m Eastmancolor
British Lion/Hemisphere/Maclean
V*

An American scientist is captured by the Russians after a car crash and returned six months later as a somewhat suspect android.

So-what mixture of character drama and James Bondery; aiming clearly at no particular audience, it failed to get a release.

w John Gould *novel* Algis Budrys *d* Jack Gold *ph* Petrus Schloemp *m* John Cameron

Elliott Gould, Trevor Howard, Joseph Bova, Ed Grover, James Noble, Lyndon Brook

'The Closest You'll Ever Get To Knowing The Secrets Of The Legendary S.A.S.'
Who Dares Wins
GB 1982 125m colour
Rank/Richmond Light Horse/Euan Lloyd (Raymond Menmuir)
V, V*
US title: *The Final Option*

An SAS captain infiltrates a ruthless antinuclear group which finally holds the American Secretary of State to ransom.

Crude exploitation of the SAS's successful relief of the Iranian Embassy. The entertainment is thick ear at best, and some of the dialogue and performances have to be seen to be believed.

w Reginald Rose *d* Ian Sharp *ph* Phil Meheux *m* Roy Budd, Jerry and Marc Donahue *pd* Syd Cain

Lewis Collins, Judy Davis, Ingrid Pitt, Richard Widmark, Edward Woodward, Robert Webber, Kenneth Griffith, Norman Rodway

'It should manage to offend anybody – punk, pacifist or policeman – inclined to take seriously the subject of global security.' – *Philip Strick, MFB*

'Cinematically antiquated and with hawkish politics poking unappealingly through the thin cloak of fiction.' – *Sight and Sound*

Who Done It?
US 1942 77m bw
Universal (Alex Gottlieb)
V*

Soda jerks in a New York radio station catch a murderer.

So-so comedy thriller, fatally lacking atmosphere (and good jokes).

w Stanley Roberts, Edmund Joseph, John Grant *d* Erle C. Kenton *ph* Charles Van Enger *m* Frank Skinner

Bud Abbott, Lou Costello, William Gargan, Louise Allbritton, Patric Knowles, Don Porter, Jerome Cowan, William Bendix, Mary Wickes, Thomas Gomez

Who Done It?
GB 1956 85m bw
Ealing (Michael Relph, Basil Dearden)
V, V*

An ice-rink sweeper sets up as a private eye and captures a ring of spies.

Lively but disappointing film debut for a star comic whose screen personality proved too bland.

w T. E. B. Clarke *d* Basil Dearden *ph* Otto Heller *m* Philip Green

Benny Hill, Belinda Lee, David Kossoff, Garry Marsh, Ernest Thesiger, Thorley Walters

Who Framed Roger Rabbit ****
US 1988 103m Rank Color/Metrocolor/DeLuxe
Warner/Touchstone/Amblin (Robert Watts, Frank Marshall)
V, V*, L, S

Cartoon characters become involved in Dashiel Hammett-style whodunnit.

Criticisms of thin plotting are irrelevant: the seamless integration of animation and live-action enchanted audiences.

w Jeffrey Price, Peter S. Seaman *book Who Censored Roger Rabbit?* by Gary K. Wold *d* Robert Zemeckis *ph* Dean Cundey *m* Alan Silvestri *pd* Elliot Scott *animation* Richard Williams *ed* Arthur Schmidt

Bob Hoskins, Christopher Lloyd, Joanna Cassidy, Stubby Kaye *voices* Charles Fleischer, Kathleen Turner, Amy Irving, Lou Hirsch, Mel Blanc

'A deplorable development in the possibilities of animation – and a melancholy waste of the gifts of one of our most gifted actors.' – *Dilys Powell*

AA: Arthur Schmidt; visual effects

AAN: Dean Cundey; art direction

Who Goes There?

GB   1952   85m   bw
British Lion/London Films (Anthony Kimmins)
US title: *The Passionate Sentry*

In a Grace and Favour house near St James's Palace, a guardsman is involved in a trail of romantic intrigue.

Very British romantic farce, dully and quickly filmed from a West End success.

w John Dighton   *play* John Dighton   d Anthony Kimmins   ph John Wilcox, Ted Scaife   m Muir Mathieson

Peggy Cummins, Valerie Hobson, George Cole, Nigel Patrick, A. E. Matthews, Anthony Bushell

Who Is Harry Kellerman and Why Is He Saying These Terrible Things About Me?

US   1971   108m   DeLuxe
Cinema Center (Ulu Grosbard, Herb Gardner)

A New York composer is persecuted by a mysterious figure who turns out to be himself.

Wild, shapeless, satirical psycho-comedy-melodrama. Not very good.

w Herb Gardner   d Ulu Grosbard   ph Victor Kemper   pd Harry Horner

Dustin Hoffman, Barbara Harris, Jack Warden, David Burns, Gabriel Dell, Dom de Luise

AAN: Barbara Harris

Who Is Killing the Great Chefs of Europe? *

US   1978   112m   Metrocolor
Warner/Aldrich/Lorimar (Merv Adelson, Lee Rich, William Aldrich)
V*
GB title: *Too Many Chefs*

A fast food entrepreneur in London finds himself at the centre of a series of grisly murders.

Unusual and lighthearted black comedy against the background of international gastronomy.

w Peter Stone   *novel* Nan and Ivan Lyons   d Ted Kotcheff   ph John Alcott   m Henry Mancini

George Segal, Jacqueline Bisset, *Robert Morley*, Jean-Pierre Cassel, Philippe Noiret, Jean Rochefort, Madge Ryan

Who Killed Doc Robbin?

US   1948   55m   Cinecolor
Hal Roach

Local kids prowl a supposedly haunted mansion.

Hesitant revival of the Our Gang comedy style in a semi-feature format; it had only mild success.

w Maurice Geraghty, Dorothy Reid   d Bernard Carr

George Zucco, Virginia Grey, Don Castle

Who Killed Mary What's Her Name?

US   1971   90m   DeLuxe
Cannon (George Manasse)
V*

An ex-boxer determines to solve the murder of a prostitute.

Old-fashioned whodunnit with something to say grafted on every five minutes: an unsatisfactory mix.

w John O'Toole   d Ernest Pintoff   ph Greg Sandor   m Gary McFarland

Red Buttons, Alice Playten, Sylvia Miles, Sam Waterston

Who Was That Lady? *

US   1960   115m   bw
Columbia/Ansark/George Sidney (Norman Krasna)

A professor seen kissing a student persuades a friend

to tell his wife that they are both FBI agents on duty. Foreign spies believe them . . .

Agreeably wacky comedy with a strained and prolonged middle section leading to a totally zany climax.

w Norman Krasna   *play* Norman Krasna   d George Sidney   ph Harry Stradling   m André Previn

Tony Curtis, Dean Martin, Janet Leigh, James Whitmore, John McIntire, Barbara Nichols, Larry Keating

'The hand that rocks the cradle has no flesh on it!'
Whoever Slew Auntie Roo?

GB   1972   91m   Movielab
EMI-MGM/AIP/Hemdale (Louis M. Heyward)
V*
US title: *Who Slew Auntie Roo?*

A madwoman menaces two orphan children.

Pointless and slenderly plotted adaptation of *Hansel and Gretel*, crude in all departments.

w Robert Blees, Jimmy Sangster   d Curtis Harrington   ph Desmond Dickinson   m Ken Jones

Shelley Winters, Ralph Richardson, Mark Lester, Lionel Jeffries, Chloe Franks, Hugh Griffith, Rosalie Crutchley, Pat Heywood

'Not content with being a delicate fantasy of childish nightmare, it tries to add a totally inappropriate seasoning of Grand Guignol.' – *Tom Milne*

The Whole Town's Talking *

US   1935   86m   bw
Columbia (Lester Cowan)
GB title: *Passport to Fame*

A gangster finds it convenient occasionally to pose as his double, a meek little clerk.

Pleasingly neat comedy, well staged and acted.

w Jo Swerling, Robert Riskin   *novel* W. R. Burnett   d John Ford   ph Joseph August

Edward G. Robinson, Jean Arthur, Arthur Hohl, Wallace Ford, Arthur Byron, Donald Meek, Edward Brophy, Etienne Girardot

'Wow comedy-melodrama . . . swell entertainment.' – *Variety*

'A lively and satisfactory combination of farce and melodrama.' – *Richard Watts Jnr*

The Whole Truth *

GB   1958   84m   bw
Columbia/Romulus (Jack Clayton)

A jealous husband poses as a detective in order to murder his wife and incriminate a film producer.

A filmed play, but quite a solidly carpentered murder thriller with a couple of neat twists.

w Jonathan Latimer   *play* Philip Mackie   d John Guillermin   ph Wilkie Cooper   m Mischa Spoliansky

Stewart Granger, George Sanders, Donna Reed, Gianna Maria Canale

Who'll Stop the Rain? *

US   1978   125m   colour
UA/Gabriel Katzka, Herb Jaffe
V*, L
GB title: *Dog Soldiers*

A Vietnam veteran takes to smuggling heroin into the US, but gets his wife and friend involved with gangsters.

Heavy-going, downbeat character drama with action sequences.

w Judith Roscoe   *novel* Dog Soldiers by Robert Stone   d Karel Reisz   ph Richard H. Kline   m Laurence Rosenthal

Nick Nolte, Tuesday Weld, Michael Moriarty,

Anthony Zerbe, Richard Masur, David Opatoshu, Roy Sharkey, Gail Strickland

'Just another ambition-downer, a wasted effort to make something meaningful out of wasted lives.' – *Richard Schickel, Time*

Wholly Moses

US   1980   109m   Metrocolor   Panavision
Columbia/David Begelman
V*, L

A shepherd hears God talking to Moses, and thinks he himself has been ordained to set his people free.

Inept and tasteless biblical spoof which must set back by about ten years the reputations of all connected with it.

w Guy Thomas   d Gary Weis

Dudley Moore, James Coco, Paul Sand, Jack Gilford, Dom DeLuise, John Houseman, Madeleine Kahn

'Deadly dullness of both writing and execution render pointless any attempt to single out blame for misfire, which leaves many talented performers flailing about in desperate attempts to generate laughs.' – *Variety*

Whoopee *

US   1930   94m   Technicolor
Samuel Goldwyn, Florenz Ziegfeld
V*

A timid young man is catapulted into various adventures.

Early sound musical from a popular Broadway show, later remade as *Up in Arms* (qv).

w William Conselman   *musical play* William Anthony McGuire   *play* The Nervous Wreck by Owen Davis   d Thornton Freeland   ph Lee Garmes, Ray Rennahan, Gregg Toland   ch Busby Berkeley   *songs* Walter Donaldson, Gus Kahn   ad Richard Day

Eddie Cantor, Eleanor Hunt, Paul Gregory, Jack Rutherford, Ethel Shutta

'Dandiest of screen musicals and okay dough-getter.' – *Variety*

AAN: Richard Day

Whoops Apocalypse

GB   1986   91m   Eastmancolor
ITC (Brian Eastman)
V

First woman president of the US tries to avert nuclear attack.

Frenetic but pathetic attempt at *Dr Strangelove* for the 80s.

w Andrew Marshall, David Renwick   d Tom Bussmann   ph Ron Robson   m Patrick Gowers   pd Tony Noble   ed Peter Boyle

Loretta Swit, Peter Cook, Rik Mayall, Ian Richardson, Alexei Sayle, Herbert Lom

Whore

US   1991   85m   colour
Palace/Trimark (Dan Ireland, Ronaldo Vasconcellos)
V, V*, L

A prostitute, hiding from her vicious pimp, recalls good customers and bad.

Dispiriting account of sexual exploitation, not helped by transferring the original's specifically London setting to the United States.

w Ken Russell, Deborah Dalton   *play* Bondage by David Hines   d Ken Russell   ph Amir Mokri   m Michael Gibbs   pd Richard Lewis   ed Brian Tagg

Theresa Russell, Benjamin Mouton, Antonio Fargas, Sanjay, Elizabeth Moorehead, Michael Crabtree

'You are cordially invited to George and Martha's for an evening of fun and games!'

Who's Afraid of Virginia Woolf? ****

US   1966   129m   bw
Warner (Ernest Lehman)
V, V*, L

A college professor and his wife have an all-night shouting match and embarrass their guests.

As a film of a play, fair to middling; as a milestone in cinematic permissiveness, very important; as an entertainment, sensational for those in the mood.

w Ernest Lehman   play Edward Albee   d Mike Nichols   ph Haskell Wexler   m Alex North

Richard Burton, Elizabeth Taylor, George Segal, Sandy Dennis

'A magnificent triumph of determined audacity.' – Bosley Crowther

'One of the most scathingly honest American films ever made.' – Stanley Kauffmann

AA: Haskell Wexler; Elizabeth Taylor; Sandy Dennis

AAN: best picture; Ernest Lehman; Mike Nichols; Alex North; Richard Burton; George Segal

Who's Been Sleeping in My Bed?

US   1963   103m   Technicolor   Panavision
Paramount/Amro (Jack Rose)

A TV matinee idol finds he is a sex symbol also in his private life.

Coy bedroom farce with no real action but a smattering of jokes.

w Jack Rose   d Daniel Mann   ph Joseph Ruttenberg   m George Duning

Dean Martin, Elizabeth Montgomery, Martin Balsam, Jill St John, Richard Conte, Carol Burnett, Louis Nye, Yoko Tani, Elizabeth Fraser

'The most riotous bedtime story ever!'

Who's Got the Action?

US   1962   93m   Technicolor   Panavision
Paramount/Amro (Jack Rose)

A bored wife and her law partner husband have remarkable success betting on horses.

Badly cast and rather slow comedy with flashes of wit.

w Jack Rose   novel Four Horse Players Are Missing by Alexander Rose   d Daniel Mann   ph Joseph Ruttenberg   m George Duning

Dean Martin, Lana Turner, Eddie Albert, Walter Matthau, Nita Talbot, Margo, Paul Ford, John McGiver

Who's Guilty?

US   1945   bw   serial: 15 eps
Columbia

Eerie happenings in a spooky house.

Lively clutching hand serial.

d Howard Bretherton, Wallace Grissell

Robert Kent, Amelita Ward, Tim Ryan, Jayne Hazard, Minerva Urecal, Charles Middleton

Who's Harry Crumb?

US   1989   90m   Technicolor
Columbia TriStar/NBC (Arnon Milchan)
V, V*, L

An incompetent, accident-prone private detective investigates the kidnapping of a millionaire's daughter.

Broad, slapstick comedy that offers occasional pleasures.

w Robert Conte, Peter Martin Wortmann   d Paul Flaherty   ph Stephen M. Katz   m Michel Colombier   pd Trevor Williams   ed Danford B. Greene, Scott Conrad

John Candy, Jeffrey Jones, Annie Potts, Tim Thomerson, Barry Corbin, Shawnee Smith, Valri Bromfield, Doug Steckler, Renee Coleman

Who's Minding the Mint? *

US   1967   97m   Technicolor
Columbia/Norman Maurer
V*

An employee of the US mint and his friends find a means of printing bills at night.

Smartly-made action comedy with good performances.

w R. S. Allen, Harvey Bullock   d Howard Morris   ph Joseph Biroc   m Lalo Schifrin

Jim Hutton, Dorothy Provine, Milton Berle, Joey Bishop, Bob Denver, Walter Brennan, Victor Buono, Jack Gilford

Who's Minding the Store? *

US   1963   90m   Technicolor
Paramount/York/Jerry Lewis (Paul Jones)

An accident-prone young man gets a job in a department store.

Better-than-average star comedy, slapstick being allowed precedence over sentimentality.

w Frank Tashlin, Harry Tugend   d Frank Tashlin   ph W. Wallace Kelley   m Joseph J. Lilley

Jerry Lewis, Jill St John, Agnes Moorehead, John McGiver, Ray Walston, Nancy Kulp

Who's That Girl?

US   1987   94m   Technicolor
Warner/Peter Guber, Jon Peters, Roger Birnbaum
V, V*, L

A mild lawyer finds an ex-jailbird starlet his hardest client to handle.

Muddled 'realistic' comedy which starts at screaming pitch and stays there.

w Andrew Smith, Ken Finkleman   d James Foley   ph Jan DeBont   ed Pembroke J. Herring

Madonna, Griffin Dunne, Haviland Morris, John McMartin, Robert Swan, Drew Pilsbury

'What's lacking is pure and simple good humour.' – Variety

Who's That Knocking at My Door *

US   1968   90m   bw
Cinegate/Tri-Mod (Joseph Weill, Haig Manoogian, Betzi Manoogian)
aka: I Call First; J. R.

An Italian-American's relationship with a more sophisticated woman is ruined by his working-class Catholic upbringing.

Scorsese's first and an intriguing film, a groping towards the subject-matter that found assured expression in Mean Streets.

wd Martin Scorsese   ph Michael Wadleigh, Richard Coll   ad Vic Magnotta   ed Thelma Schoonmaker

Harvey Keitel, Zina Bethune, Lennard Kuras, Ann Collette, Michael Scala, Harry Northup, Catherine Scorsese, Phil Carlson

† The film was first shown under the title I Call First at the Chicago Film Festival in 1967. It was later released under its present title with the addition of a nude scene.

Whose Life Is It Anyway?

US   1981   118m   Metrocolor
MGM/Martin C. Schute, Ray Cooney (Lawrence P. Bachmann)
V, V*

Totally paralysed after a car crash, a young sculptor lies in hospital wanting to die.

Ill-advised film of a very static play which was a freak success on account of various very good leading performances. It makes a very uneasy movie.

w Brian Clark, Reginald Rose   play Brian Clark   d John Badham   ph Mario Tosi   m Arthur B. Rubenstein

Richard Dreyfuss, John Cassavetes, Christine Lahti, Bob Balaban, Kenneth McMillan

Why Bother to Knock: see Don't Bother to Knock

Why Did Bodhi-Dharma Leave for the East? *

South Korea   1989   135m   colour
ICA/Bae Yong-Kyun
original title: Dharmaga Tongjoguro Kan Kkadalgun?

In a remote monastery an old monk prepares for his death, a younger one feels guilt about abandoning his family and his blind mother, and an orphaned child grieves for a moment over a bird he kills accidentally.

A leisurely Zen Buddhist meditation on death and enlightenment that offers few of the usual pleasures of movies, such as narrative and character development.

wd Bae Yong-Kyun   ph Bae Yong-Kyun   m Chin Kyn-Yong   ed Bae Yong-Kyun

Yi Pan-Yong, Sin Won-Sop, Huang Hae-Jin, Ko Su Myoung

† The film won the Golden Leopard award at the 1990 Locarno Film Festival.

Why Me?

US   1989   87m   colour
Entertainment/Epic Productions/Sarlui/Diamant (Marjorie Israel)
V, L

Two jewel thieves, who inadvertently steal a famous ruby ring, double-cross the authorities who demand its return.

Weakly acted, limp comedy-thriller that fails to sparkle.

w Donald E. Westlake, Leonard Maas Jnr   novel Donald E. Westlake   d Gene Quintano   ph Peter Deming   m Phil Marshall   pd Woody Crocker   ed Alan Balsam

Christopher Lambert, Kim Greist, Christopher Lloyd, J. T. Walsh, Gregory Millar, Wendel Meldrum, Michael J. Pollard, John Plana, Tony Plana

Why Shoot the Teacher?

Canada   1976   99m   colour
WSTT/Fraser Films (Lawrence Hertzog)
V*

In 1935 a school teacher finds a chilly reception when he settles in a Saskatchewan village.

Unsatisfactory but occasionally quite entertaining comedy-drama which hovers around the Cold Comfort Farm mark.

w James Defilice   novel Max Braithwaite   d Silvio Narizzano   ph Marc Champion   m Ricky Hyslop

Bud Cort, Samantha Eggar, Chris Wiggins, Gary Reineke

Why We Fight ****

US War Office   1942–5   bw
Frank Capra

A series of feature-length compilations for primary showing to the armed forces, these were superbly vigorous documentaries which later fascinated the public at large.

Editing, music and diagrams were all used to punch home the message.Individual titles were:

'Prelude to War' (53m)
   w Eric Knight, Anthony Veiller   d Frank Capra
   AA: best documentary
'The Nazis Strike' (42m)
   w as above, d as above
'Divide and Conquer' (58m)
   w Anthony Veiller, Robert Heller   d Frank Capra, Anatole Litvak
'The Battle of Britain' (54m)
   wd Anthony Veiller

'The Battle of Russia' (80m)
 w Anthony Veiller, Robert Heller, Anatole Litvak d Anatole Litvak
 AAN: best documentary
'The Battle of China' (60m)
 w Eric Knight, Anthony Veiller d Frank Capra, Anatole Litvak
'War Comes to America' (70m)
 w Anthony Veiller d Anatole Litvak
 † All had editing by *William Hornbeck*, music by *Dimitri Tiomkin* and commentary by *Walter Huston*.

Why Worry? *
US 1923 60m approx (24 fps) bw silent
Hal Roach-Harold Lloyd

A hypochondriac is cured when he gets mixed up in a South American revolution.

Moderate star comedy with highlights well spaced out.

d Sam Taylor, Fred Newmeyer

Harold Lloyd, Jobyna Ralston, Leo White

Wichita
US 1955 81m Technicolor Cinemascope
Walter Mirisch/AA
V*

Wyatt Earp is hired to bring law and order to a wide-open cow town.

Standard, i.e. romanticized, version of Earp's exploits: quite entertaining to watch.

w Daniel Ullman *d* Jacques Tourneur

Joel McCrea, Vera Miles, Lloyd Bridges, Wallace Ford, Edgar Buchanan, Peter Graves, Keith Larsen, Carl Benton Reid

Wicked
US 1931 57m bw
Fox

A woman is innocently sent to prison and when she comes out sets about finding the child she had to sign away.

Woman's picture, packed with predictable incident.

w anonymous hands *d* Allan Dwan

Elissa Landi, Victor McLaglen, Theodore von Eltz, Alan Dinehart, Una Merkel, Oscar Apfel, Irene Rich

'Old-fashioned tearjerker now too old to jerk tears or grosses.' – *Variety*

'If every woman has her price . . . there's a reason!'
Wicked As They Come
GB 1956 94m bw
Columbia/Film Locations (Maxwell Setton)
US title: *Portrait in Smoke*

A beauty contest winner from the slums makes money and luxury her goal.

Busy melodrama which interests without edifying.

wd Ken Hughes *co-w* Robert Westerby, Sigmund Miller *ph* Basil Emmott *m* Malcolm Arnold

Arlene Dahl, Herbert Marshall, Phil Carey, Michael Goodliffe, David Kossoff, Sidney James, Ralph Truman, Faith Brook

Wicked City (dubbed)
Japan 1993 81m colour
Hideyuki Kikuchi/Tokuma Shoten/Video Art/Japan Home Video/Manga (Kenji Kurada, Makoto Sedani)
V

A human bodyguard and a woman from the dark world of monsters are assigned to guard from assassins a doctor essential to the signing of a peace treaty between the two worlds.

A well-animated saga of exotic sex, violence and sentimentality.

w Maretoshi Naga *novel* Hideyuki Kikuchi *d* Yoshiaki Kawajiri *ph* Kinichi Ishikawa

m Yoshimasa Tokai *ad* Kazuo Oga *ed* Nobuyuki Ogata

voices of Stuart Miller, Tammy Holloway, George Littlewood, Bill Richards, Ronald Baker, Lisa Robinson, Philip Gough

The Wicked Lady *
GB 1945 104m bw
GFD/Gainsborough (R. J. Minney)
V*

In the days of Charles II, Lady Skelton befriends a highwayman and takes to crime.

The most commercially successful of the Gainsborough costume charades because of its atmosphere of gloomy sin. Dramatically turgid and surprisingly poorly acted and directed, but with good period detail. It had to be reshot for America because of the ladies' décolletage.

wd Leslie Arliss *novel The Life and Death of the Wicked Lady Skelton* by Magdalen King-Hall *ph* Jack Cox *md* Louis Levy *m* Hans May

Margaret Lockwood, James Mason, Griffith Jones, Patricia Roc, Michael Rennie, Enid Stamp-Taylor, Felix Aylmer, Martita Hunt, David Horne

'A mixture of hot passion and cold suet pudding.' – *Manchester Guardian*

'Rather dull and juvenile in its determination to be daring.' – *Richard Mallett, Punch*

The Wicked Lady
GB 1983 99m colour
Columbia/Cannon (Menahem Golan, Yoram Globus)
V*

A remake with colour, sex and violence.

Pictorially quite attractive, but that's about all. It caused controversy when the British censor tried to cut a scene showing Faye Dunaway lashing another woman with a horse-whip but retracted after Winner protested. (The fight owed much to a similar scene in *Idol of Paris* [qv], directed by Leslie Arliss in 1948.)

w Leslie Arliss, Michael Winner *d* Michael Winner *ph* Jack Cardiff *m* Tony Banks *ad* John Blezard *ed* Arnold Crust

Faye Dunaway, Alan Bates, John Gielgud, Denholm Elliott, Prunella Scales, Oliver Tobias, Glynis Barber, Joan Hickson

'The images look as cheap as expensive greetings cards.' – *Sunday Times*

'A first-class piece of popular entertainment.' – *Lindsay Anderson*

The Wicked Wife: see Grand National Night

A Wicked Woman
US 1934 71m bw
MGM (Harry Rapf)

A woman kills her drunken husband to protect her children, later confesses and is exonerated.

The tail end of the mother love saga, better made than most.

w Florence Ryerson, Zelda Sears *novel* Anne Austin *d* Charles Brabin *ph* Lester White *m* William Axt

Mady Christians, Charles Bickford, Betty Furness, William Henry, Jackie Searle, Robert Taylor, Paul Harvey

The Wicker Man *
GB 1973 86m Eastmancolor
British Lion (Peter Snell)
V, V*

A policeman flies to a remote Scottish isle to investigate the death of a child, and finds himself in the hands of diabolists.

Old-fashioned but remarkably well made scare story, with effective shock moments.

w Anthony Shaffer *d* Robin Hardy *ph* Harry Waxman *m* Paul Giovanni *ad* Seamus Flannery

Edward Woodward, Britt Ekland, Christopher Lee, Ingrid Pitt, Diane Cilento

'An encouraging achievement for those who had begun to despair of the British cinema.' – *David McGillivray*

Wide Open Faces
US 1938 67m bw
Columbia (David L. Loew)

Public enemies congregate in a wayside inn where missing loot is supposedly buried.

Moderately amusing slapstick farce.

w Earle Snell, Clarence Marks, Joe Bigelow, Richard Flournoy *d* Kurt Neumann

Joe E. Brown, Jane Wyman, Alison Skipworth, Lyda Roberti, Alan Baxter, Lucien Littlefield, Sidney Toler, Berton Churchill

'On the corny side, strictly for dual bills.' – *Variety*

'An erotic tale of beauty and bewitchment.'
Wide Sargasso Sea
Australia 1992 98m colour
Rank/Sargasso/New Line/Laughing Kookaburra (Jan Sharp)
V, V*, L

In Jamaica in the mid-1800s, as her marriage to an English gentleman disintegrates, a plantation owner fears that, like her mother, she may go mad.

A prequel to *Jane Eyre*, concentrating on the fate of the mad Mrs Rochester, this is a lush and overblown saga of sex and revenge, bordering on the risible.

w Jan Sharp, Carole Angier, John Duigan *novel* Jean Rhys *d* John Duigan *ph* Geoff Burton *m* Stewart Copeland *pd* Franckie D *ed* Anne Goursaud

Karina Lombard, Nathaniel Parker, Claudia Robinson, Michael York, Rachel Ward, Martine Beswick, Huw Christie Williams

'A faintly absurd erotic melodrama whose protagonists must have been cast for their looks and their eagerness to sweat through copious bed scenes rather than for acting ability.' – *Sheila Johnston, Independent*

† The same theme was explored in an earlier film, *I Walked with a Zombie* (qv).

The Widow from Chicago
US 1930 63m bw
First National

A woman mixes with a gang to avenge her brother's murder.

Bottom-of-the-barrel gangster drama, presented with little flair.

w Earl Baldwin *d* Edward Cline

Alice White, Edward G. Robinson, Neil Hamilton, Frank McHugh, E. H. Calvert

'Barely makes programme grade . . . will have to struggle to break even.' – *Variety*

Widow from Monte Carlo
US 1935 60m bw
Warner

The theft of an indiscreet letter causes much embarrassment in an English country house.

Society comedy-drama with curious farcical asides: not an obvious success.

w F. Hugh Herbert, Charles Belden *play* Ian Hunter, A. E. W. Mason *d* Arthur G. Collins

Warren William, Dolores del Rio, Louise Fazenda, Colin Clive, Herbert Mundin, Warren Hymer

'Behind the eight ball where big-time dates are concerned.' – *Variety*

Wife, Doctor and Nurse *

US 1937 84m bw
TCF (Raymond Griffith)

A romantic triangle as the title suggests.

Agreeable fluff with a mildly surprising end (for 1937) suggesting a *ménage à trois*.

w Kathryn Scola, Darrell Ware, Lamar Trotti
d Walter Lang ph Edward Cronjager m Arthur Lange

Loretta Young, Warner Baxter, Virginia Bruce, Jane Darwell, Sidney Blackmer, Maurice Cass, Minna Gombell, Elisha Cook Jnr, Lon Chaney Jnr

'A smart comedy that will please all.' – *Variety*

Wife, Husband and Friend *

US 1939 80m bw
TCF (Nunnally Johnson)

A man sabotages his wife's efforts to become a professional singer.

Modestly agreeable romantic comedy later remade as *Everybody Does It* (qv).

w Nunnally Johnson story James M. Cain
d Gregory Ratoff ph Ernest Palmer m David Buttolph

Loretta Young, Warner Baxter, Binnie Barnes, Cesar Romero, George Barbier, J. Edward Bromberg, Eugene Pallette, Helen Westley

'Diverting farce comedy with appeal pointed to class audiences.' – *Variety*

The Wife of General Ling

GB 1937 72m bw
John Stafford/Premier

In China, a merchant's white wife unmasks him as a criminal.

Stilted melodrama.

w Akos Tolnay, Reginald Long, Peter Cheyney, Dorothy Hope d Ladislas Vajda

Griffith Jones, Inkijinoff, Adrianne Renn, Alan Napier, Anthony Eustrel, Hugh McDermott, Gibson Gowland

'Hardly up to West End level.' – *Variety*

Wife of Monte Cristo

US 1946 83m bw
PRC (Leon Fromkess)

In 1832 Paris, the Count leads an underground movement against racketeers.

And the film plays like a Brooklyn melodrama in fancy dress; as such, not too bad.

w Dorcas Cochran d Edgar G. Ulmer

John Loder, Lenore Aubert, Charles Dingle, Fritz Kortner, Martin Kosleck (as the Count!), Eduardo Ciannelli, Fritz Feld, Eva Gabor

The Wife Takes a Flyer

US 1942 86m bw
Columbia (B. P. Schulberg)
GB title: *A Yank in Dutch*

A Dutchwoman whose husband is in the asylum takes in a fugitive USAF pilot in his place although a Nazi officer is billeted on the household.

Downright peculiar World War II comedy which at the time seemed the height of bad taste – and no laughs.

w Gina Kaus, Jay Dratler d Richard Wallace
ph Franz Planer m Werner Heyman

Joan Bennett, Franchot Tone, Allyn Joslyn, Cecil Cunningham, Lloyd Corrigan, Georgia Caine

'Kicks in the pants, belching, and exaggerated face-making are lifted from burlesque to decorate this feeble attempt.' – *New York Post*

Wife versus Secretary *

US 1936 88m bw
MGM (Hunt Stromberg)

A publisher's wife starts to believe rumours about his attention to his secretary.

Practised star comedy drama which provided thoroughly satisfactory entertainment of a kind the cinema seems to have forgotten.

w Norman Krasna, Alice Duer Miller, John Lee Mahin novel Faith Baldwin d Clarence Brown
ph Ray June m Herbert Stothart, Edward Ward

Clark Gable, Myrna Loy, Jean Harlow, May Robson, George Barbier, James Stewart, Hobart Cavanaugh

'A real box office picture for the sticks and the stems.' – *Variety*

'See this picture if you enjoy the spectacle of three clever stars shining for all they are worth.' – *Film Weekly*

The Wilby Conspiracy *

GB 1975 105m DeLuxe
UA/Optimus/Baum-Dantine (Stanley Sopel)
V*

A British mining engineer is persuaded to help a black revolutionary in his flight from Cape Town to Johannesburg.

Reasonably exciting political chase thriller with a sufficiency of twists and action sequences; philosophy is present but secondary.

w Rod Amateau, Harold Nebenzal novel Peter Driscoll d Ralph Nelson ph John Coquillon
m Stanley Myers

Sidney Poitier, Michael Caine, Nicol Williamson, Prunella Gee, Saeed Jaffrey, Persis Khambatta

The Wild Affair *

GB 1965 87m bw
Seven Arts (Richard Patterson)

An office Christmas party nearly turns into an orgy.

Curious little comedy drama which plays almost like the *Road to Ruin* and has an attractive but miscast leading lady. Interesting elements.

wd John Krish novel *The Last Hours of Sandra Lee* by William Sansom ph Arthur Ibbetson m Martin Slavin

Nancy Kwan, Terry-Thomas, Jimmy Logan, Bud Flanagan, Betty Marsden, Gladys Morgan, Paul Whitsun-Jones, Donald Churchill, Victor Spinetti

The Wild and the Innocent

US 1959 85m Eastmancolor Cinemascope
Universal-International

A trapper is torn between a mountain girl and a city tart.

Oddly old-fashioned Western, like *The Gold Rush* without laughs.

w Sy Gomberg, Jack Sher d Jack Sher

Audie Murphy, Joanne Dru, Gilbert Roland, Sandra Dee, Jim Backus, Peter Breck

The Wild and the Willing

GB 1962 112m bw
Rank/Box-Thomas (Betty E. Box)
US title: *Young and Willing*

A troublesome student at a provincial university seduces the wife of his professor.

Watchable sex melodrama with an interesting background on which no one seems to have quite enough grip; 'realism' is simply there to be exploited.

w Nicholas Phipps, Mordecai Richler play *The Tinker* by Laurence Dobie, Robert Sloman d Ralph Thomas ph Ernest Steward m Norrie Paramor

Virginia Maskell, Paul Rogers, Ian McShane, Samantha Eggar, John Hurt, Catherine Woodville, John Standing, Jeremy Brett

Wild and Wonderful

US 1963 88m Eastmancolor
U-I/Harold Hecht

A French film star poodle makes friends with an American gambler.

Amiable zany comedy in a set-bound Gay Paree.

w Larry Markes, Michael Morris, Waldo Salt
d Michael Anderson ph Joseph LaShelle
m Morton Stevens

Tony Curtis, Christine Kaufmann, Larry Storch, Marty Ingels, Jacques Aubuchon, Jules Munshin

Wild and Woolly

US 1937 90m bw
TCF (John Stone)

During a small-town frontier celebration an attempt to rob the bank is thwarted.

Pleasant family Western with music.

w Lynn Root, Frank Fenton d Alfred Werker

Jane Withers, Walter Brennan, Pauline Moore, Alfalfa Switzer, Jack Searl, Berton Churchill, Lon Chaney Jnr

'Whatever its companion feature happens to be, this is the one the audience talks about on the way home.' – *Variety*

The Wild Angels *

US 1966 85m Pathecolor Panavision
AIP (Roger Corman)
V, V*

A Californian motorcycle gang is run on semi-religious, ritualistic, Nazi lines.

Much-banned melodrama, cheaply made but vigorously handled and of some interest on social and historical levels.

w Charles B. Griffith d Roger Corman
ph Richard Moore m Mike Curb ad Leon Ericksen ed Monte Hellman

Peter Fonda, Nancy Sinatra, Bruce Dern, Michael J. Pollard, Gayle Hunnicut

'Roger Corman's color-film account of the orgiastic raping, looting, brawling, pot-smoking, corpse-desecrating, church-wrecking, parson-torturing, swastika-swaddled activities of a gang of motorcyclists. After we've feasted our eyes on the detailing thereof by, incidentally, a thoroughly inept cast, without even the context of good cycling sequences, we're given a one-line moral by the suddenly regenerate gang leader: "There's no place to go," he mumbles. Yes, indeed, there's still room at the bottom.' – *Judith Crist*

Wild at Heart **

US 1990 127m
Palace/Polygram/Propaganda (Monty Montgomery, Steve Golin, Joni Sighvatsson)
V, V*, L

A petty criminal is redeemed by the love of a histrionic woman.

Over-ripe acting, violent action, and a melodramatic plot combine to produce the cinematic equivalent of *Grand Guignol*. It won the Palme d'Or at the Cannes Film Festival in 1990.

wd David Lynch novel Barry Gifford ph Fred Elmes m Angelo Badalamenti ed Duwayne Dunham

Nicolas Cage, Laura Dern, Diane Ladd, Willem Dafoe, Isabella Rossellini, Harry Dean Stanton, Crispin Glover, J. E. Freeman, W. Morgan Shephard

'Joltingly violent, wickedly funny and rivetingly erotic.' – *Variety*

'The picture is packed with so much deranged energy, so many bravura images, that it's hard not to be seduced by the sick wonder of it all.' – *Richard Corliss, Time*

AAN: Diane Ladd

Wild Bill Hickok Rides

US 1941 81m bw
Warner

Wild Bill helps a homesteader keep his land.

Oddly cast, rather naïve little Western.

w Charles Grayson, Paul Gerard Smith and Raymond Schrock   d Ray Enright

Constance Bennett, Bruce Cabot, Warren William, Ward Bond, Howard da Silva

The Wild Blue Yonder

US 1952 98m bw
Republic (Herbert J. Yates)
GB title: *Thunder Across the Pacific*

Incidents in the lives of bomber pilots in the Pacific during World War II.

Routine action flagwaver.

w Richard Tregaskis   d Allan Dwan   ph Reggie Lanning   m Victor Young

Wendell Corey, Vera Hruba Ralston, Forrest Tucker, Phil Harris, Walter Brennan, Ruth Donnelly

Wild Boys of the Road *

US 1933 88m bw
Warner (Robert Presnell)
GB title: *Dangerous Days*

Boys of poor families take to the road in gangs.

Vivid social melodrama of its day, now rather overstated.

w Earl Baldwin   d William Wellman   ph Arthur Todd

Frankie Darro, Rochelle Hudson, Edwin Philips, Arthur Hohl

'A depressing evening in the theatre, one which the general fan public will gladly avoid.' – *Variety*

Wild Brian Kent

US 1936 57m bw
TCF (Sol Lesser)

An amiable Western con man helps a town to rid itself of a villain.

Mild comedy drama.

w Earle Snell, Don Swift   novel *The Recreation of Brian Kent* by Harold Bell Wright   d Howard Bretherton

Ralph Bellamy, Mae Clarke, Helen Lowell, Stanley Andrews, Lew Kelly

'Little to commend it.' – *Variety*

'Nine men who came too late and stayed too long!'
'The land had changed. They hadn't. The earth had changed. They couldn't!'

The Wild Bunch ****

US 1969 145m Technicolor Panavision
Warner Seven Arts/Phil Feldman
V, V*, L, S

In 1914, Texas bandits are ambushed by an old enemy and die bloodily in defence of one of their number against a ruthless Mexican revolutionary.

Arguably the director's best film, and one which set a fashion for blood-spurting violence in Westerns. Undeniably stylish, thoughtful, and in places very exciting.

w Walon Green, Sam Peckinpah   d Sam Peckinpah   ph Lucien Ballard   m Jerry Fielding   ad Edward Carrere

William Holden, Ernest Borgnine, Robert Ryan, Edmond O'Brien, Warren Oates, Jaime Sanchez, Ben Johnson, Strother Martin, L. Q. Jones, Albert Dekker

'A western that enlarged the form aesthetically, thematically, demonically.' – *Stanley Kauffmann, 1972*

'We watch endless violence to assure us that violence is not good.' – *Judith Crist, 1976*

'The bloody deaths are voluptuous, frightening, beautiful. Pouring new wine into the bottle of the western, Peckinpah explodes the bottle; his story is too simple for this imagist epic.' – *Pauline Kael, New Yorker*

'One of the most moving elegies for a vanished age ever created within the genre.' – *Time Out, 1984*

AAN: script; Jerry Fielding

The Wild Child: see *L'Enfant Sauvage*

The Wild Country

US 1970 100m Technicolor
Walt Disney (Ron Miller)
V*

In the late 1880s a farmer buys a dilapidated Wyoming ranch and falls foul of a local rancher who controls the water supply.

Predictable family Western in the familiar Disney style.

w Calvin Clements Jnr, Paul Savage   novel *Little Britches* by Ralph Moody   d Robert Totten   ph Frank Phillips   m Robert Bronner

Steve Forrest, Vera Miles, Jack Elam, Ronny Howard, Morgan Woodward

'The best ******* mercenaries in the business!'

The Wild Geese

GB 1978 134m Eastmancolor Panavision
Rank/Richmond (Euan Lloyd)
V*, L

Adventures of four British mercenaries in a central African state.

All-star blood and guts with a few breezy touches in the script.

w Reginald Rose   novel *Daniel Carney*   d Andrew V. McLaglen   ph Jack Hildyard   m Roy Budd

Roger Moore, Richard Burton, Richard Harris, Hardy Kruger, Stewart Granger, Jack Watson, Frank Finlay, Kenneth Griffith, Barry Foster, Jeff Corey, Ronald Fraser, Percy Herbert, Patrick Allen, Jane Hylton

Wild Geese II

GB 1985 125m Technicolor
Thorn EMI/Frontier/Euan Lloyd
V, V*

A mercenary is commissioned by an American TV station to kidnap Rudolf Hess from Spandau jail.

Ingenious if unlikely premise for another tough adventure; it largely fails because of silly plotting.

w Reginald Rose   novel *The Square Circle* by Daniel Carney   d Peter Hunt   ph Michael Reed   m Roy Budd   pd Syd Cain   ed Keith Palmer

Scott Glenn, Barbara Carrera, Edward Fox, Laurence Olivier, Robert Webber, Kenneth Haigh, Stratford Johns

Wild Geese Calling

US 1941 77m bw
TCF (Harry Joe Brown)

A young adventurer in Oregon weds the girlfriend of a conniving gambler.

Minor semi-Western which never really finds a style.

w Horace McCoy   novel *Stewart Edward White*   d John Brahm   ph Lucien Ballard   m Alfred Newman

Joan Bennett, Henry Fonda, Warren William, Ona Munson, Barton MacLane, Russell Simpson, Iris Adrian

Wild Harvest

US 1947 92m bw
Paramount (Robert Fellows)

A romantic triangle develops among wheat harvesters on the Western plains.

Standard star hokum.

w John Monks Jnr   d Tay Garnett   ph John F. Seitz   m Hugo Friedhofer

Alan Ladd, Dorothy Lamour, Robert Preston, Lloyd Nolan, Dick Erdman, Allen Jenkins, Will Wright

The Wild Heart: see *Gone to Earth*

Wild in the Country

US 1961 114m DeLuxe Cinemascope
TCF/Company of Artists (Jerry Wald)
V, V*

A rebellious hillbilly is involved with three women.

Weird confection designed to show the star in all his facets.

w Clifford Odets   novel *The Lost Country* by J. R. Salamanca   d Philip Dunne   ph William C. Mellor   m Kenyon Hopkins

Elvis Presley, Hope Lange, Tuesday Weld, Millie Perkins, John Ireland, Gary Lockwood

'One can't help feeling he was better off prior to this misguided bid for class.' – *MFB*

Wild in the Sky

US 1971 83m colour
AIP/Bald Eagle (William T. Naud, Dick Gautier)

Three young offenders skyjack a B52 jet bomber.

Black comedy melodrama, uncontrolled but with some engaging absurdities.

w William T. Naud, Dick Gautier   d William T. Naud   ph Thomas E. Spalding   m Jerry Styner

Brandon de Wilde, Keenan Wynn, Dick Gautier, Tim O'Connor, James Daly, Robert Lansing

Wild in the Streets *

US 1968 97m Perfectcolor
AIP (Jack Cash)
V*, L

In the imminent future, a pop singer becomes president and launches a campaign for teenage emancipation.

Satirical melodrama with a profusion of wild gags, some of which hit the target.

w Robert Thom   d Barry Shear   ph Richard Moore   m Les Baxter   ad Fred Feitshans, Eve Newman

Shelley Winters, Chris Jones, Diane Varsi, Hal Holbrook, Millie Perkins

'Blatant, insensitive, crummy-looking . . . enjoyable at a pop, comic-strip level.' – *New Yorker, 1977*

'It is no less timely a parable today than Orwell's *1984* was 20 years ago.' – *Daily Telegraph*

AAN: editing

Wild Is the Wind

US 1957 114m bw Vistavision
Paramount/Hal B. Wallis

A widowed Italian sheep rancher in Nevada marries his wife's sister from Italy, but she falls for his adopted son.

Intense *Cold Comfort Farm* melodrama with a strong similarity to *They Knew What They Wanted;* the strain shows, and the performances are tiresomely noisy.

w Arnold Schulman   d George Cukor   ph Charles Lang Jnr   m Dimitri Tiomkin

Anna Magnani, Anthony Quinn, Tony Franciosa, Dolores Hart, Joseph Calleia

AAN: title song (m Dimitri Tiomkin, ly Ned Washington); Anna Magnani; Anthony Quinn

The Wild Man of Borneo
US   1941   78m   bw
MGM (Joseph L. Mankiewicz)

An unsuccessful braggart comes to live with his daughter in a Manhattan boarding house.

Mildly likeable though very predictable sentimental comedy from an old Broadway warhorse.

w Waldo Scott, John McClain   play Herman J. Mankiewicz, Marc Connelly   d Robert B. Sinclair   ph Oliver T. Marsh   m David Snell

Frank Morgan, Mary Howard, Dan Dailey, Billie Burke, Donald Meek, Bonita Granville, Marjorie Main, Connie Gilchrist, Walter Catlett, Andrew Tombes, Phil Silvers, Joe Yule

The Wild North
US   1951   97m   Anscocolor
MGM (Stephen Ames)

A mountie gets his man but needs his help getting back to base.

Standard adventure story with avalanche and wolf attacks.

w Frank Fenton   d Andrew Marton   ph Robert Surtees   m Bronislau Kaper

Stewart Granger, Wendell Corey, Cyd Charisse

'That streetcar man has a new desire!'
**The Wild One ** **
US   1954   79m   bw
Columbia/Stanley Kramer
V, V*, L

Hoodlum motorcyclists terrorize a small town.

Brooding, compulsive, well-made little melodrama which was much banned because there was no retribution. As a narrative it does somewhat lack dramatic point.

w John Paxton   story The Cyclists' Raid by Frank Rooney   d Laslo Benedek   ph Hal Mohr   m Leith Stevens

Marlon Brando, Lee Marvin, Mary Murphy, Robert Keith, Jay C. Flippen

'A picture that tries to grasp an idea, even though the reach falls short.' – New York Times

† 'What are you rebelling against?' 'What've you got?' – sample dialogue.

† Sharpness of photography was achieved by the Garutso lens.

Wild Orchid
US   1989   111m   DeLuxe
Entertainment/Vision (Mark Damon, Tony Anthony)
V, V*, L, S

An American businessman in Rio plays sexual games with two female lawyers in a struggle over the ownership of an hotel.

Voyeuristic thriller that is less than watchable.

w Patricia Louisianna Knop, Zalman King   d Zalman King   ph Gale Tattersal   m Geoff MacCormack, Simon Goldenberg   pd Carlos Conti   ed Marc Grossman, Glenn A. Morgan

Mickey Rourke, Jacqueline Bisset, Carre Otis, Assumpta Serna, Bruce Greenwood, Jens Peter, Oleg Vidov

The Wild Party
US   1956   81m   bw
UA/Security (Sidney Harmon)

An ex-football player and some Los Angeles layabouts plot a kidnap.

Unpleasant melodrama laced with sex, violence and loud music.

w John McPartland   d Harry Horner   ph Sam Leavitt   m Buddy Bregman

Anthony Quinn, Carol Ohmart, Jay Robinson, Arthur Franz, Nehemiah Persoff, Kathryn Grant, Paul Stewart

The Wild Party
US   1974   91m   Movielab
AIP/Edgar Lansbury, Joseph Beruh (Ismail Merchant)
V*

In 1929, a silent film comedian on the skids throws a party to show his latest movie.

Evocative of its period but virtually confined to a single set which becomes boring, this collection of unlikely events and tedious people has only obvious points to make and its final descent into tragedy is not compelling.

w Walter Marks   poem Joseph Moncure March   d James Ivory   ph Walter Lassally   m Larry Rosenthal

James Coco, Raquel Welch, Perry King, Tiffany Bolling, Royal Dano, David Dukes, Dena Dietrich

'Seems to promise a pointillist precision about its characters and milieu which it never quite delivers.' – Jonathan Rosenbaum

Wild River *
US   1960   115m   DeLuxe   Cinemascope
TCF (Elia Kazan)

In 1933 a Tennessee Valley Authority inspector incurs the wrath of a local matriarch who will not leave her valley even though it is to be flooded.

Interesting liberal-minded sociological drama marred by an added love story, as the similar Last Days of Dolwyn was marred by melodrama. Well made but somehow unmemorable.

w Paul Osborn   novels Borden Deal, William Bradford Huie   d Elia Kazan   ph Ellsworth Fredericks   m Kenyon Hopkins

Montgomery Clift, Jo Van Fleet, Lee Remick, Albert Salmi, Jay C. Flippen, James Westerfield, Bruce Dern

Wild Rovers
US   1971   132m   Metrocolor   Panavision 70
MGM/Geoffrey (Blake Edwards, Ken Wales)
V*, L

A middle-aged cowboy, depressed with the state of his life, joins with a younger man to become a bank robber.

Fashionable, derivative, quite unsuccessful Western tragi-comedy mixing in shades of every director from Ford to Peckinpah.

wd Blake Edwards   ph Philip Lathrop   m Jerry Goldsmith

William Holden, Ryan O'Neal, Karl Malden, Lynn Carlin, Tom Skerritt, Joe Don Baker, Rachel Roberts, Leora Dana, Moses Gunn

'An existentialist western which will not do much for existentialism, the western, or the box office.' – Charles Champlin, Los Angeles Times

Wild Search *
Hong Kong   1989   95m
Borntop International (Ringo Lam)
original title: Bun Ngo Tsong Tinngai

A city policeman, on the trail of a Triad gang, falls in love with a country girl.

Odd mix of sentimental romance and fierce action.

w Nam Yin   d Ringo Lam   ph Lau Wai-keung   m Lowell Lo   pd Luk Tze-fung   ed Tony Chow

Chow Yun-fat, Cherie Chung, Paul Chin, Chan Chuek-yan

'Several notches above the usual Hong Kong crime actioner.' – Variety

Wild Seed: see Fargo

Wild Stallion: see Crin Blanc

Wild Strawberries **
Sweden   1957   93m   bw
Svensk Filmindustri (Allan Ekelund)
V, V*, L
original title: Smultronstället

An elderly professor has a nightmare and thinks back over his long life.

A beautifully paced and acted, but somewhat obscure piece of probing symbolism.

wd Ingmar Bergman   ph Gunnar Fischer   m Erik Nordgren

Victor Sjostrom, Ingrid Thulin, Gunnar Bjornstrand, Bibi Andersson, Naima Wifstrand, Jullan Kindahl

'The work of a man obsessed by cruelty, especially spiritual cruelty, trying to find some resolution.' – Kenneth Cavander, MFB

AAN: script

Wild West *
GB   1992   100m   Metrocolor
Initial/Channel 4/British Screen (Eric Fellner)
V, S

Young Asians, living in London and dreaming of stardom, form a country and western band.

Engagingly energetic comedy of cultural misunderstandings and fantasies.

w Harwant Bains   d David Attwood   ph Nic Knowland   m Dominic Miller   pd Caroline Hanania   ed Martin Walsh

Naveen Andrews, Sarita Choudhury, Ronny Jhutti, Ravi Kapoor, Ameet Chana, Bhasker, Lalita Ahmed, Shaun Scott

'Mangy and artless, this boisterous low-budgeter generates plenty of good laughs and gets lots of mileage from its comic, knowing observations about a vibrant British sub-culture.' – Variety

Wild West Days
US   1937   bw   serial: 13 eps
Universal

Three Western friends outwit the scheming owner of The Brimstone News.

Elementary but harmless Western serial.

d Ford Beebe, Cliff Smith

Johnny Mack Brown, George Shelley, Robert Kortman, Russell Simpson, Frank Yaconelli

Wildcat: see The Great Scout and Cathouse Thursday

Wildcats
US   1986   107m   Technicolor
Warner (Anthea Sylbert)
V, V*, L

A girl is appointed football coach at a ghetto school, and of course works wonders.

Silly comedy with few laughs and not much plot development.

w Ezra Sacks   d Michael Ritchie   ph Donald E. Thorin   m Hawk Wolinski, James Newton Howard   pd Boris Leven   ed Richard A. Harris

Goldie Hawn, Swoosie Kurtz, Robyn Lively, Brandy Gold, James Keach, Bruce McGill, M. Emmet Walsh

The Wildcats of St Trinian's
GB   1980   91m   Technicolor
Wildcat (E. M. Smedley-Aston)

The awful schoolgirls get unionized, and kidnap an Arab's daughter to gain attention.

Crude and belated tailpiece to a series which was never very satisfactory. (See The Belles of . . ., Blue Murder at . . ., The Pure Hell of . . ., The Great St Trinian's Train Robbery)

wd Frank Launder   ph Ernest Steward   m James Kenelm Clarke

Sheila Hancock, Michael Hordern, Joe Melia, Thorley Walters, Rodney Bewes, Maureen Lipman, Ambrosine Philpotts

Will Any Gentleman?

GB   1953   84m   Technicolor
ABPC
V

A meek bank clerk is hypnotized and becomes a ladies' man.

Efficient comedy from a stage success.

w Vernon Sylvaine   *play* Vernon Sylvaine
d Michael Anderson

George Cole, Veronica Hurst, Jon Pertwee, Heather Thatcher, James Hayter, William Hartnell, Diana Decker, Joan Sims, Alan Badel

'Will heats up slow, but when he gets there, he's hell with the hide off!'

Will Penny *

US   1967   109m   Technicolor
Paramount/Fred Engel/Walter Seltzer/Tom Gries
V*, L

A middle-aged cowpuncher falls foul of a family of maniacal cut-throats.

Realistically spare, laconic, uncomforting Western with a curiously melodramatic set of villains.

wd Tom Gries   *ph* Lucien Ballard   *m* David Raksin

Charlton Heston, Joan Hackett, Donald Pleasence, Lee Majors, Bruce Dern, Anthony Zerbe, Clifton James, Ben Johnson

Will Success Spoil Rock Hunter?

US   1957   95m   Eastmancolor   Cinemascope
TCF (Frank Tashlin)
GB title: *Oh! For a Man!*

A timid advertising executive is touted for a publicity stunt as the world's greatest lover.

A too-wild satire on TV commercials: less frenzied direction and gag-writing would have prised more humour from the situations.

w Frank Tashlin   *play* George Axelrod   *d* Frank Tashlin   *ph* Joe MacDonald   *m* Cyril Mockridge

Jayne Mansfield, Tony Randall, Betsy Drake, Joan Blondell, John Williams, Henry Jones, Mickey Hargitay

Will Tomorrow Ever Come?: see *That's My Man*

'The one film you should not see alone! Where your nightmare ends, Willard *begins!*'

Willard *

US   1971   95m   DeLuxe
Cinerama/Bing Crosby (Mort Briskin)
V*, L

A shy, withdrawn young man breeds and trains rats to kill his enemies.

Modest, rather unusual suspenser which builds well after a slow start; only horrifying to people who can't stand rats. A sequel, *Ben* (qv), later appeared.

w Gilbert Ralston   *novel Ratman's Notebooks* by Stephen Gilbert   *d* Daniel Mann   *m* Robert B. Hauser   *m* Alex North   *rat trainer* Moe de Sesso

Bruce Davison, Elsa Lanchester, Ernest Borgnine, Sondra Locke, Michael Dante, J. Pat O'Malley

William at the Circus

GB   1948   89m   bw
A. R. Shipman & David Coplan (John R. Sloan)
aka: *William Comes to Town*

William achieves national notoriety and overcomes parental obstacles in his determination to see a circus.

Tired and miscast comedy, with much documentary footage of fun-fair and circus to pad out its trite narrative.

wd Val Guest   *novel* Richmal Crompton   *ph* Bert Mason   *m* Robert Farnon   *ad* Harry Moore   *ed* Carmen Beliaeff

William Graham, Garry Marsh, Jane Walsh, Hugh Cross, Kathleen Stuart, Muriel Aked, A. E. Matthews, Michael Medwin, Michael Balfour, Jon Pertwee

† It was a sequel to *Just William's Luck* (qv).

William Comes to Town: see *William at the Circus*

Willie and Phil

US   1980   116m   DeLuxe
TCF (Paul Mazursky, Tony Ray)
V*

Two men and a woman enjoy a variable *ménage à trois* throughout the seventies.

Curious attempt at an American *Jules et Jim;* not badly done if you have to do it, but why do it?

wd Paul Mazursky   *ph* Sven Nykvist   *m* Claude Bolling

Michael Ontkean, Margot Kidder, Ray Sharkey

'Truffaut's film existed both in the real world and in a world of the imagination. Mazursky's has no imagination and doesn't even touch a passable form of reality.' – *Sunday Times*

Will-O'-The-Wisp: see *Le Feu Follet*

Willow *

US   1988   126m   colour
UIP/MGM (Nigel Wooll)
V, V*, L, S

In a time of magic, two heroes set out to bring a baby to safety and fulfil a prophecy that will overthrow an evil empire.

Spectacular jaunt around familiar material, plundered from mythology, fairy-tales and old movies, that relies on special effects to maintain interest.

w Bob Dolman   *story* George Lucas   *d* Ron Howard   *ph* Adrian Biddle   *m* James Horner   *pd* Allan Cameron   *sp* John Richardson   *ed* Daniel Hanley, Michael Hill

Val Kilmer, Joanne Whalley, Warwick Davies, Jean Marsh, Patricia Hayes, Billy Barty, Pat Roach, Gavan O'Herlihy, David Steinberg

'It's doubtful if any action-adventure director has a strong enough style to give this script a tone and a shape, and Ron Howard, who's got the job, is lost.' – *Pauline Kael, New Yorker*

Willy Wonka and the Chocolate Factory *

US   1971   100m   Technicolor
David Wolper
V, V*, L

A boy wins a tour of the local chocolate factory and finds himself in the power of a magician.

Semi-satiric Grimms Fairy Tale pastiche which looks good but never seems quite happy with itself.

w Roald Dahl   *novel* Roald Dahl   *d* Mel Stuart   *ph* Arthur Ibbetson   *songs* Leslie Bricusse, Anthony Newley   *md* Walter Scharf   *ad* Harper Goff

Gene Wilder, Jack Albertson, Peter Ostrum, Roy Kinnear, Aubrey Woods

AAN: Walter Scharf

Wilson **

US   1944   154m   Technicolor
TCF (Darryl F. Zanuck)
V*

The rise and fall of an American president.

Admirably careful biopic which raises no particular excitement but entertains and instructs on various levels.

w Lamar Trotti   *d* Henry King   *ph* Leon Shamroy   *m* Alfred Newman   *ad* James Basevi, Wiard Ihnen   *ed* Barbara McLean

Alexander Knox, Charles Coburn, Cedric Hardwicke, Geraldine Fitzgerald, Thomas Mitchell, Ruth Nelson, William Eythe, Vincent Price, Mary Anderson, Ruth Ford, Sidney Blackmer, Stanley Ridges, Eddie Foy Jnr, Charles Halton, Thurston Hall, J. M. Kerrigan, Francis X. Bushman

'Not without tedium, but worth seeing as an enormous expensive curiosity.' – *Richard Mallett, Punch*

'Rich with the sense of movement and multitude.' – *Daily Sketch*

'Absorbing, significant and entertaining.' – *Time*

† Alexander Knox had 1194 lines in 294 scenes.

AA: Lamar Trotti; Leon Shamroy; art direction; editing

AAN: best picture; Henry King; Alfred Newman; Alexander Knox

Wilt

GB   1989   93m   Eastmancolor
Rank/LWT/Picture Partnership (Brian Eastman)
V

A polytechnic lecturer is suspected of having murdered his wife by an inept police inspector.

A low farce which, briskly directed, affords moderate amusement.

w Andrew Marshall, David Renwick   *novel* Tom Sharpe   *d* Michael Tuchner   *ph* Norman Langley   *m* Anne Dudley   *pd* Leo Austin   *ed* Chris Blunden

Griff Rhys Jones, Mel Smith, Alison Steadman, Diana Quick, Jeremy Clyde, Roger Allam, David Ryall, Roger Lloyd Pack, Dermot Crowley, John Normington

Winchester 73 **

US   1950   92m   bw
U-I (Aaron Rosenberg)
V, V*, L

Long-time enemies settle an old grudge.

Entertaining, popular, hard-riding, hard-shooting Western of the old school.

w Robert L. Richards, Borden Chase   *story* Stuart N. Lake   *d* Anthony Mann   *ph* William Daniels   *md* Joseph Gershenson   *m* Frank Skinner

James Stewart, Shelley Winters, Dan Duryea, Stephen McNally, Millard Mitchell, Charles Drake, John McIntire, Will Geer, Jay C. Flippen, Rock Hudson, Tony Curtis, John Alexander, Steve Brodie

The Wind ***

US   1927   75m (sound version 1928)   bw
MGM
V*, L

A sheltered Virginia girl goes to live on the rough and windy Texas prairie, marries a man she doesn't love and kills a would-be rapist.

Heavy melodrama with a strong visual sense.

w Frances Marion   *novel* Dorothy Scarborough   *d* Victor Sjostrom   *ph* John Arnold

Lillian Gish, Lars Hanson, Montagu Love, Dorothy Cummings

'So penetrating is the atmosphere that one can almost feel the wind itself and taste the endless dust.' – *Georges Sadoul*

'Unrelieved by the ghost of a smile . . . but its relentlessness is gripping . . . a fine and dignified achievement.' – *Pictureplay*

† New version by Thames Silents 1984.

The Wind

Mali   1982   100m   colour
Les Films Cissé
original title: *Finyé*

The daughter of a military governor becomes involved in political demonstrations against army rule after falling in love with a poor student.

Episodic account of romance and repression in Africa.

wd Souleymane Cissé   *ph* Etienne Carton de Grammont   *m* Pierre Gorse

Fousseyni Sossoko, Guondo Guisse, Balla Moussa Keita, Ismaila Sarr, Oumou Diarra, Ismaila Cissé, Massitan Ballo, Dioncounda Kone

Wind

US   1992   125m   Technicolor
Filmlink International/American Zoetrope (Mata Yamamoto, Tom Luddy)
V, V*, S

A young sailor, who loses the America's Cup to the Australians, persuades a designer to create a new yacht to win back the title.

Uninteresting and water-logged drama.

w Rudy Wurlitzer, Mac Gudgeon   *story* Jeff Benjamin, Roger Vaughan, Kimball Livingston   *d* Carroll Ballard   *ph* John Toll   *m* Basil Poledouris   *pd* Laurence Eastwood   *ed* Michael Chandler

Matthew Modine, Jennifer Grey, Stellan Skarsgard, Rebecca Miller, Ned Vaughn, Cliff Robertson, Jack Thompson

'Despite the sometimes striking images of expert crews guiding their beautiful boats through challenging waters, predictable story trajectory and bland human element will keep this physically ambitious picture in a b.o. stall.' – *Variety*

Wind across the Everglades *

US   1958   93m   Technicolor
(Warner) Schulberg Productions (Stuart Schulberg)

Florida 1900: a young schoolteacher tracks down those responsible for hunting rare birds for their feathers, and becomes a game warden.

Meandering adventure story with a purpose, relying heavily on violence and eccentric characters.

w Budd Schulberg   *d* Nicholas Ray   *ph* Joseph Brun

Christopher Plummer, Burl Ives, Gypsy Rose Lee, Emmett Kelly, George Voskovec, Tony Galento, Mackinlay Kantor

The Wind and the Lion

US   1975   119m   Metrocolor   Panavision
Columbia/MGM (Herb Jaffe, Phil Rawlins)
V*, L, S

In 1904 Tangier, an American widow and her children are kidnapped by a Riffian chief, and the eyes of the world are focused on the incident.

Basing itself very lightly on an actual event, this adventure story is both confused as a narrative and unexciting as an action piece: the camera stops too often to look at sunsets, the plot stops too often for philosophizing, and there are too many underexplained characters and incidents fitting into the international jigsaw.

wd John Milius   *ph* Billy Williams   *m* Jerry Goldsmith

Sean Connery, Candice Bergen, Brian Keith, John Huston, Geoffrey Lewis, Steve Kanaly, Vladek Sheybal

'When the actors begin to talk (which they do incessantly) the flat-footed dialogue and the amateurish acting take one back to the low-budget

buffoonery of Maria Montez and Turhan Bey.' – *Pauline Kael, New Yorker*

AAN: Jerry Goldsmith

The Wind Cannot Read

GB   1958   115m   Eastmancolor
Rank (Betty E. Box)

In India and Burma during World War II, a flying officer falls in love with a Japanese language instructor suffering from a brain disease.

Or, love is a many-splendoured dark victory. Old-fashioned romance for addicts, well enough produced.

w Richard Mason   *novel* Richard Mason   *d* Ralph Thomas   *ph* Ernest Steward   *m* Angelo Lavagnino

Dirk Bogarde, Yoko Tani, Ronald Lewis, John Fraser, Anthony Bushell, Michael Medwin

Wind in the Willows: see *Ichabod and Mr Toad*

Windbag the Sailor

GB   1936   85m   bw
Gainsborough (Edward Black)

An incompetent seaman is washed away on an old ketch and lands on a South Sea isle.

Rather uninventive star comedy with inevitable pleasing moments.

w Marriott Edgar, Stafford Dickens, Will Hay   *d* William Beaudine   *ph* Jack Cox   *md* Louis Levy

Will Hay, Moore Marriott, Graham Moffatt, Norma Varden

Windom's Way *

GB   1957   108m   Technicolor
Rank (John Bryan)
V*

A doctor on a Far Eastern island tries to quell a native uprising.

Tolerably well intentioned action melodrama, topical because of Malaya; dramatically rather sober and predictable.

w Jill Craigie   *novel* James Ramsay Ullman   *d* Ronald Neame   *ph* Christopher Challis   *m* James Bernard

Peter Finch, Mary Ure, Natasha Parry, Robert Flemyng, Michael Hordern

The Window ***

US   1949   73m   bw
RKO (Frederick Ullman)
V*

A New York slum boy is always telling tall tales, so no one believes him when he actually witnesses a murder . . . except the murderer.

Classic little second feature, entertaining and suspenseful; unfortunately it had few successful imitators.

w Mel Dinelli   *d* Ted Tetzlaff   *ph* William Steiner   *m* Roy Webb   *ed* Frederic Knudtson

Bobby Driscoll, Barbara Hale, Arthur Kennedy, Paul Stewart, Ruth Roman

'Logical, well-shaped, cohesive, admirably acted, beautifully photographed and cut to a nicety.' – *Richard Winnington*

AAN: editing

A Window in London *

GB   1939   77m   bw
G and S/GFD
V*
US title: *Lady in Distress*

A *crime passionel* is witnessed from a passing train.

Modest Anglo-Saxon remake of the French film *Metropolitan*.

w Ian Dalrymple, Brigid Cooper   *d* Herbert Mason

Michael Redgrave, Sally Gray, Paul Lukas, Hartley Power, Patricia Roc

A Window to the Sky: see *The Other Side of the Mountain*

Windprints

GB   1989   99m   colour
Virgin/Apex Motion Pictures/United British Artists (Michael L. Games, Raymond Day)
V

A British journalist and a South African cameraman go in search of a black poet and murderer in Namibia.

Confusing thriller that deals ineffectually with apartheid and its aftermath.

w David Wicht, Johann Potgieter, Heinrich Dahms   *d* David Wicht   *ph* Brian Tufano   *m* John Keane   *pd* Michael Phillips   *ed* Robin Sales

John Hurt, Sean Bean, Marius Weyers, Eric Nobbs, Lesley Fong, Kurt Egelhof, Dana Niehaus, Trudie Taljaard, Goliath Davids

Wing and a Prayer *

US   1944   97m   bw
TCF (William Becker, William Morosco)
V*

Life aboard an aircraft carrier.

Standard action flagwaver.

w Jerome Cady   *d* Henry Hathaway   *ph* Glen MacWilliams   *m* Hugo Friedhofer

Don Ameche, Cedric Hardwicke, Dana Andrews, Charles Bickford, Richard Jaeckel, Henry Morgan

AAN: Jerome Cady

The Winged Serpent: see *Q, The Winged Serpent*

Winged Victory **

US   1944   130m   bw
TCF (Darryl F. Zanuck)

During World War II, pilots are inducted, trained and sent on dangerous missions.

Solid, competent, best-foot-forward flagwaver of the highest inspirational intention.

w Moss Hart   *play* Moss Hart   *d* George Cukor   *ph* Glen MacWilliams   *m* David Rose

Lon McCallister, Jeanne Crain, Edmond O'Brien, Jane Ball, Mark Daniels, Don Taylor, Lee J. Cobb, Judy Holliday, Peter Lind Hayes, Alan Baxter, Red Buttons, Barry Nelson, Gary Merrill, Karl Malden, Martin Ritt, Jo-Carroll Dennison

'I suppose it is all right, but I don't enjoy having anyone tell me, so cheerfully and energetically, that the Air Force personnel is without exception composed of boy scouts old enough to shave.' – *James Agee*

'There is no question that Mr Hart captured much of the gallantry and pathos of youth rushing towards dangerous adventures with surface enthusiasm and inner dread.' – *Bosley Crowther, New York Times*

Wings *

US   1927   136m (24 fps)   bw   silent
Paramount (B. P. Schulberg)
V*, L

Two young men join the Air Service during World War I, and one eventually shoots down the other by accident.

An epic of early aviation, still stirring in its action sequences.

w Hope Loring, Harry D. Lighton   *d* William Wellman   *ph* Harry Perry

Clara Bow, Charles Buddy Rogers, Richard Arlen, Gary Cooper, Jobyna Ralston, El Brendel

'Air battles are photographed from every conceivable angle, producing many bold cinematic effects . . . so much in fact happens in the air that it is impossible to take it all in.' – *National Board of Review*

AA: best picture; best engineering effects (Roy Pomeroy)

Wings and the Woman: see *They Flew Alone*

Wings for the Eagle
US   1942   85m   bw
Warner (Robert Lord)

Aircraft workers do their bit during World War II.

Home Front propaganda, well enough produced.

w Byron Morgan, Harrison Orkow   d Lloyd Bacon
ph Tony Gaudio   m Frederick Hollander

Ann Sheridan, Dennis Morgan, Jack Carson, George Tobias, Don Defore

Wings in the Dark *
US   1935   75m   bw
Paramount (Arthur Hornblow Jnr)

Embittered after being blinded in an accident, a research flyer finally leaps into action when his stranded girlfriend needs help.

Satisfactory romantic melodrama.

w Jack Kirkland, Frank Partos   d James Flood
ph William C. Mellor

Cary Grant, Myrna Loy, Roscoe Karns, Hobart Cavanaugh, Dean Jagger, Bert Hanlon, Samuel S. Hinds

'Unconvincing and improbable story, but handled so deftly that it may nose through to moderate grosses.' – *Variety*

Wings of Desire ****
France/West Germany   1987   127m   bw/colour
Road Movies/Argos films
V, V*, L, S
original title: *Der Himmel über Berlin*

One of a pair of angels, visiting Berlin, decides he wants to be human after falling in love with a circus performer.

Marvellously photographed encounter with humanity and recent German history, full of a quiet joy.

w Wim Wenders, Peter Handke   d Wim Wenders
ph Henri Alekan   m Jürgen Knieper   ad Heidi Ludi   ed Peter Przygodda

Bruno Ganz, Solveig Dommartin, Otto Sander, Curt Bois, Peter Falk

'A friend of mine says that he loved every second of this movie and he couldn't wait to leave. To put it simply, *Wings of Desire* has a visual fascination but no animating force – that's part of why it's being acclaimed as art.' – *Pauline Kael, New Yorker*

The Wings of Eagles *
US   1957   110m   Metrocolor
MGM (Charles Schnee)
V*

A navy flyer breaks his neck in an accident and on recovery becomes a Hollywood writer.

Sentimental biopic of Frank 'Spig' Wead, a routine, easy-going assignment for its director (who is caricatured by Ward Bond as John Dodge).

w Frank Fenton, William Wister Haines   d John Ford   ph Paul C. Vogel   m Jeff Alexander

John Wayne, Maureen O'Hara, Ward Bond, Dan Dailey, Ken Curtis, Edmund Lowe, Kenneth Tobey, Sig Rumann, Henry O'Neill

Wings of Fame
Netherlands   1990   109m   Agfacolor
Gala/First Floor Features (Laurens Geels, Dick Maas)

After a writer kills a film star, both find themselves in a luxury hotel where they can stay for as long as they are remembered.

Unsuccessful entry in the current cycle of revenant movies.

w Otakar Votoček, Herman Koch   d Otakar Votoček
ph Alex Thomson   m Paul van Brugge   pd Dick Schillemans   ed Hans van Dongen

Peter O'Toole, Colin Firth, Marie Trintignant, Ellen Umlauf, Andréa Ferréol, Maria Becker, Gottfried John

Wings of the Apache
US   1990   85m
Medusa/Inter-Ocean Films (William Badalato)
V, V*, L
US title: *Fire Birds*

US pilots go into action against drug barons.

Top Gun with helicopters, but even less interesting.

w Nick Thiel, Paul F. Edwards   story Step Tyner, John K. Swensson, Dale Dye   d David Green
ph Tony Imi   m David Newman   pd Joseph T. Garrity   ed Jon Poll, Norman Buckley, Dennis O'Connor

Nicolas Cage, Tommy Lee Jones, Sean Young, Bryan Kestner, Dale Dye, Mary Ellen Trainor, J. A. Preston, Peter Onorati, Charles Lanyer, Bert Rhine

'Enjoyable, old-fashioned aerial adventure pic.' – *Variety*

Wings of the Hawk
US   1953   81m   Technicolor   3-D
U-I (Aaron Rosenberg)

Mexico 1911: a gold miner falls into the hands of revolutionaries.

Routine bang-bang, rather sloppily produced.

w James E. Moser   d Budd Boetticher   ph Clifford Stine   m Frank Skinner

Van Heflin, Julie Adams, George Dolenz, Pedro Gonzales-Gonzales, Rodolfo Acosta, Antonio Moreno, Abbe Lane

Wings of the Morning *
GB   1937   89m   Technicolor
New World (Robert T. Kane)

In 1899, a gypsy princess marries an Irish nobleman; in 1937, romance again blooms between their descendants.

Britain's first Technicolor film was great to look at and quite charming, though slight; its major attractions being horse races, songs from John McCormack, and a heroine dressed for plot purposes as a boy.

w Tom Geraghty   story Donn Byrne   d Harold Schuster   ph Ray Rennahan, Jack Cardiff
m Arthur Benjamin

Henry Fonda, Annabella, Stewart Rome, John McCormack, Leslie Banks, Irene Vanbrugh, Harry Tate, Edward Underdown, Helen Haye

'A wholesome, refreshing and altogether likeable little romance.' – *Frank S. Nugent*

Wings of the Navy
US   1938   89m   bw
Warner (Lou Edelman)

The loves and careers of navy pilots.

Competent animated recruiting poster.

w Michael Fessier   d Lloyd Bacon   ph Arthur Edeson, Elmer Dyer

George Brent, Olivia de Havilland, John Payne, Frank McHugh, John Litel, Victor Jory, Henry O'Neill, John Ridgely

'A convincer to mould public opinion and support in favour of current government plans for wide expansion of American air defence forces.' – *Variety*

Wings over Honolulu
US   1937   78m   bw
Universal

A young naval airman is posted to Hawaii and followed by his bride.

Lightweight flagwaver, all smiles at the end.

w Isabel Dawn, Boyce DeGaw, Mildred Cram
d H. C. Potter   ph Joseph Valentine

Ray Milland, Wendy Barrie, William Gargan, Kent Taylor, Polly Knowles, Samuel S. Hinds

AAN: Joseph Valentine

Winner Take All *
US   1932   76m   bw
Warner

A prizefighter rises to fame and helps a sick girl and her child.

Slightly-plotted comedy-drama allowing its star full rein.

w Wilson Mizner, Robert Lord, Gerald Beaumont
d Roy del Ruth

James Cagney, Marian Nixon, Guy Kibbee, Clarence Muse, Virginia Bruce, Dickie Moore

'Enjoyable prizefight talker: sprightly gags and bits bolster conventional story.' – *Variety*

Winners of the West
US   1940   bw   serial: 13 eps
Universal

A self-styled ruler of the prairies tries to block the advance of the railroads.

Predictable serial exploits.

d Ford Beebe and Ray Taylor

Dick Foran, Anne Nagel, James Craig, Tom Fadden, Trevor Bardette

Winning *
US   1969   123m   Technicolor   Panavision 70
Universal/Newman-Foreman (John Foreman)
V*, L

A racing driver's professional problems strain his relationship with his wife.

Cliché track melodrama with pretensions, well but needlessly made.

w Howard Rodman   d James Goldstone
ph Richard Moore   m Dave Grusin

Paul Newman, Joanne Woodward, Richard Thomas, Robert Wagner, David Sheiner, Clu Gulager

The Winning of Barbara Worth *
US   1926   97m (24 fps)   bw   silent
Samuel Goldwyn

Desert engineers vie for the daughter of a landowner.

Forgettable action romance, a big hit in its day because of the climactic flood sequence, which still thrills.

w Frances Marion   novel Harold Bell Wright
d Henry King   ph George Barnes   m Ted Henkel

Ronald Colman, Vilma Banky, Charles Lane, Gary Cooper, Paul McAllister

The Winning Team
US   1952   98m   bw
Warner (Bryan Foy)
V*, L

A telephone linesman becomes a great baseball player despite trouble with his vision after an accident.

Standard biopic of Grover Cleveland Alexander; all very pleasant but no surprises.

w Ted Sherdeman, Seeleg Lester, Merwin Gerard
d Lewis Seiler   ph Sid Hickox   m David Buttolph

Doris Day, Ronald Reagan, Frank Lovejoy, Eve Miller, James Millican, Russ Tamblyn

The Winning Ticket

US   1935   69m   bw
MGM

An Italian barber wins a sweepstake but can't find his ticket.

Modest, lively comedy which pleased at the time.

w Ralph Spence, Richard Shayer, Robert Pirosh, George Seaton   d Charles F. Reisner

Leo Carrillo, Louise Fazenda, Ted Healy, Irene Hervey, James Ellison, Luis Alberni, Akim Tamiroff

The Winning Way: see The All-American

The Winslow Boy ***

GB   1948   117m   bw
British Lion/London Films (Anatole de Grunwald)
V, V*

A naval cadet is expelled for stealing a postal order; his father spends all he has on proving his innocence.

Highly enjoyable middle-class British entertainment based on an actual case; performances and period settings are alike excellent, though the film is a trifle overlong.

w Terence Rattigan, Anatole de Grunwald   play Terence Rattigan   d Anthony Asquith   ph Frederick Young   m William Alwyn

Robert Donat, Cedric Hardwicke, Margaret Leighton, Frank Lawton, Jack Watling, Basil Radford, Kathleen Harrison, Francis L. Sullivan, Marie Lohr, Neil North, Wilfrid Hyde-White, Ernest Thesiger

'Only a clod could see this film without excitement, laughter and some slight moisture about the eyes.' – Daily Telegraph

Winter Carnival

US   1939   89m   bw
UA (Walter Wanger)

College romances over a holiday weekend.

Nondescript romantic comedy.

w Lester Cole, Budd Schulberg   d Charles Riesner   ph Merrit Gerstad   m Werner Janssen

Ann Sheridan, Richard Carlson, Helen Parrish, Virginia Gilmore, Robert Walker

'Slick production of an undistinguished yarn about the annual Dartmouth winter sports.' – Variety

Winter Kills

US   1979   97m   colour   Panavision
Avco Embassy/Winter Gold (Fred Caruso)
V*, L

The brother of an assassinated president tracks down the killers, but finds that his tycoon father is involved.

Heavy-going and confusing melodrama with much flashy editing. Despite its cast, it was never satisfactorily released.

wd William Richert   novel Richard Condon   ph Vilmos Zsigmond   pd Robert Boyle   ed David Bretherton

Jeff Bridges, John Huston, Anthony Perkins, Elizabeth Taylor, Sterling Hayden, Eli Wallach, Dorothy Malone, Tomas Milian, Richard Boone, Toshiro Mifune

Winter Light *

Sweden   1962   80m   bw
Svensk Filmindustri (Allan Ekelund)
V, V*
original title: Nattvardsgästerna

A widowed village pastor loses his vocation.

In a sense almost parody Bergman; in another, one of his clearest statements of despair. The middle section of a pessimistic trilogy which also included Through a Glass Darkly and The Silence.

wd Ingmar Bergman   ph Sven Nykvist   m none

Max von Sydow, Ingrid Thulin, Gunnar Bjornstrand, Gunnel Lindblom

'The film-maker's mastery alone does not guarantee a great film. Winter Light is scarcely even a good one.' – John Simon, 1967

Winter Meeting

US   1948   104m   bw
Warner (Henry Blanke)
V*

A repressed spinster falls for a naval hero intent on becoming a priest.

Dreary talk marathon which did its star's career no good at all.

w Catherine Turney   novel Ethel Vance   d Bretaigne Windust   ph Ernest Haller   m Max Steiner

Bette Davis, James Davis, Janis Paige, John Hoyt, Florence Bates, Walter Baldwin

Winter of Our Dreams *

Australia   1981   90m   Eastmancolor
Vega Films (Richard Mason)
V*

A bookseller investigates the suicide of an old girlfriend, and becomes involved with an unhappy prostitute.

Intriguing character drama with a tendency to haunt the mind, though its effectiveness depends largely on its acting.

wd John Duigan   ph Tom Cowan   m Sharyn Calcraft

Judy Davis, Bryan Brown, Cathy Downes, Baz Luhrmann

Winter People

US   1988   111m   DeLuxe
Rank/Nelson Entertainment/Castle Rock (Robert H. Solo)
V, V*, L

In the 1930s, a wandering clockmaker becomes involved in a feud between two families in a backwoods community.

Frenzied old-fashioned melodrama guaranteed to chill the interest of its audience.

w Carol Sobieski   novel John Ehle   d Ted Kotcheff   ph François Protat   m John Scott   pd Ron Foreman   ed Thomas Noble

Kurt Russell, Kelly McGillis, Lloyd Bridges, Mitchell Ryan, Amelia Burnette, Eileen Ryan, Lanny Flaherty

A Winter's Tale: see Conte d'hiver

'Like a thunderbolt of naked light it struck Broadway – now it tears at your heart on the screen!'

Winterset **

US   1936   78m   bw
RKO
V*

On the New York waterfront, a drifter determines to avenge his father's death.

Very dated poetic melodrama, here given a talky, artificial production which at the time impressed many critics but is now fairly difficult to endure.

w Anthony Veiller   play Maxwell Anderson   d Alfred Santell   ph Peverell Marley   m Nathaniel Shilkret   ad Perry Ferguson

Burgess Meredith, Eduardo Ciannelli, Margo, Paul Guilfoyle, John Carradine, Edward Ellis, Stanley Ridges, Maurice Moscovitch, Myron McCormick, Mischa Auer

'Not big box office . . . in certain locales they may even wonder what it's all about.' – Variety

'Still in a grand manner that just won't do on the screen . . . but there are fine moments in the performances, and there's something childishly

touching in the florid dramatic effects.' – New Yorker, 1978

AAN: Nathaniel Shilkret; Perry Ferguson

Wintertime

US   1943   82m   bw
TCF (William Le Baron)

A Norwegian skating star comes to Canada where her uncle's winter resort is on its uppers.

The last of the star's Fox musicals is pure routine.

w Edward Moran, Jack Jevne, Lynn Starling   d John Brahm   ph Glen MacWilliams   md Charles Henderson   m Alfred Newman

Sonja Henie, Jack Oakie, Cesar Romero, S. Z. Sakall, Carole Landis, Cornel Wilde, Woody Herman and his Band

Wired

US   1989   109m   colour
Entertainment/Lion Screen Entertainment (Edward S. Feldman, Charles R. Meeker)
V, V*, L, S

The ghost of comedian John Belushi, dead from a drug overdose, relives his life, while a journalist interviews his friends.

Fantasy substitutes for the harder, documented facts in a frenetic film that fails to capture Belushi's comic talents.

w Earl MacRauch   book Wired: The Short Life and Fast Times of John Belushi by Bob Woodward   d Larry Peerce   ph Tony Imi   m Michael Ruff   pd Brian Eatwell   ed Eric Sears

Michael Chiklist, Patti D'Arbanville, J. T. Walsh, Lucinda Jenney, Gary Groomes, Ray Sharkey, Alex Rocco, Jerre Burns

Wise Blood *

US/Germany   1979   108m   colour
Artificial Eye/Anthea/Ithaca (Michael Fitzgerald, Kathy Fitzgerald)
V*

In the deep South, a war veteran with no beliefs becomes a travelling preacher.

Odd story, not easy to like but with many impressive moments.

w Benedict Fitzgerald   novel Flannery O'Connor   d John Huston   ph Gerry Fisher   m Alex North   ad Sarah Fitzgerald   ed Roberto Silver

Brad Dourif, Ned Beatty, Harry Dean Stanton, Daniel Shor, Amy Wright, John Huston

Wise Girl

US   1937   70m   bw
RKO (Edward Kaufman)

A rich girl goes bohemian in Greenwich village.

Pretty absurd romantic comedy which strains the patience.

w Allan Scott, Charles Norman   d Leigh Jason

Miriam Hopkins, Ray Milland, Walter Abel, Henry Stephenson, Alec Craig, Guinn Williams, Margaret Dumont

'Slow-moving narrative, considerable silliness, lack of convincing plot.' – Variety

Wise Guys

US   1986   91m   Technicolor
MGM-UA (Aaron Russo)
V*

Two small-time hoods unwittingly heist Mafia funds.

Haven't we seen this somewhere before? And done better?

w George Gallo   d Brian de Palma   ph Fred Schuler   m Ira Newborn   pd Edward Pisoni   ed Jerry Greenberg

Danny DeVito, Joe Piscopo, Harvey Keitel, Ray Sharkey, Patti LuPone

The Wiser Sex

US 1932 72m bw
Paramount

A society girl goes undercover to save her public prosecutor boyfriend from smears.

Unattractive comedy-melodrama which never seems to get going.

w Harry Hervey, Caroline Franke play Her Confessions by Clyde Fitch d Berthold Viertel

Claudette Colbert, Melvyn Douglas, Lilyan Tashman, William Boyd, Ross Alexander, Douglass Dumbrille

'Story a handicap: picture suffers accordingly.' – Variety

Wish You Were Here **

GB 1987 92m colour
Zenith/Film Four (Sarah Radclyffe)
V, V*, L, S

The growing pains of a teenage girl in a seaside town.

Noted chiefly for its central performance, this is a film full of telling detail and compassion, despite its apparently defiant mood.

wd David Leland ph Ian Wilson m Stanley Myers
pd Caroline Amies ed George Akers

Emily Lloyd, Tom Bell, Clare Clifford, Barbara Durkin, Geoffrey Hutchings

The Wistful Widow of Wagon Gap *

US 1947 78m bw
U-I (Robert Arthur)
V*

In old Montana, an accident-prone wayfarer accidentally kills a man and has to look after his family.

Tame and disappointing comedy vehicle.

w D. D. Beauchamp, William Bowers d Charles T. Barton, Robert Lees, Frederic I. Rinaldo, John Grant
ph Charles Van Enger m Walter Shumann

Bud Abbott, Lou Costello, Marjorie Main, Audrey Young, George Cleveland

Witch Doctor: see Men of Two Worlds

Witchcraft *

GB 1964 79m bw
TCF/Lippert (Robert Lippert, Jack Parsons)

A family of witches take revenge on their longtime enemies.

Spasmodically arresting horror film spoiled by too complex a plot line and some variable acting.

w Harry Spaulding d Don Sharp ph Arthur Lavis
m Carlo Martelli

Jack Hedley, Lon Chaney Jnr, Marie Ney, Jill Dixon, David Weston

'Unpretentious and uncommonly gripping.' – MFB

Witchcraft through the Ages **

Sweden 1922 83m approx (24 fps) bw silent
Svensk Filmindustri
original title: Häxan

A 'documentary' investigation of the history of witchcraft, with acted examples.

Fascinating reconstruction of ancient rituals, still maintaining its power to frighten.

wd Benjamin Christensen ph Johan Ankarstjerne

Oscar Stribolt, Clara Pontoppidan, Karen Winther

The Witches

GB 1966 91m Technicolor
Warner/Hammer (Anthony Nelson-Keys)
US title: The Devil's Own

A schoolmistress finds witchcraft in an English village.

Chintzy horror with predictable development and risible climax.

w Nigel Kneale novel The Devil's Own by Peter Curtis
d Cyril Frankel ph Arthur Grant m Richard Rodney Bennett pd Bernard Robinson ed James Needs, Chris Barnes

Joan Fontaine, Kay Walsh, Alec McCowen, Gwen Ffrangcon Davies, Ingrid Brett, John Collin, Michèle Dotrice, Leonard Rossiter, Martin Stephens, Carmel McSharry

The Witches **

US 1990 91m Eastmancolor
Warner/Lorimar (Mark Shivas)
V, V*, L

A small boy, who has been turned into a mouse, schemes with his granny to thwart witches' plans to poison all the children in Britain.

Superior entertainment, intended for children, but as likely to be enjoyed by adults.

w Allan Scott novel Roald Dahl d Nicolas Roeg
ph Harvey Harrison m Stanley Myers pd Voytek, Andrew Sanders ed Tony Lawson

Anjelica Huston, Mai Zetterling, Jasen Fisher, Rowan Atkinson, Bill Patterson, Brenda Blethyn, Charlie Potter, Anne Lambton, Jane Horrocks

'A controlled and suitably dark piece of filmmaking.' – Variety

The Witches of Eastwick **

US 1987 118m Technicolor
Warner/Guber-Peters/Kennedy Miller
V, V*, L

Three divorcees on the make are seduced by the devil.

Horny fantasy, impeccably played, though it could have been shorter.

w Michael Cristofer novel John Updike d George Miller ph Vilmos Zsigmond m John Williams
pd Polly Platt

Jack Nicholson, Cher, Susan Sarandon, Michelle Pfeiffer, Veronica Cartwright, Richard Jenkins

AAN: John Williams

The Witches of Salem *

France/East Germany 1957 143m bw
Borderie/CICC/DEFA/Pathé (Raymond Borderie)
original title: Les Sorcières de Salem

In 1692 Massachusetts, jealousies lead to accusations of witchcraft and multiple trials and executions.

An account of a horrifying historical fact which was also intended to reflect on the McCarthy witch hunts of the fifties; but the film, despite splendid acting, is too literal and slow-moving.

w Jean-Paul Sartre play The Crucible by Arthur Miller d Raymond Rouleau ph Claude Renoir
m Georges Auric

Simone Signoret, Yves Montand, Mylène Demongeot, Jean Debucourt

'Keep the children home! And if you're squeamish, stay home with them!'

Witchfinder General *

GB 1968 87m Eastmancolor
Tigon/American International (Arnold Miller, Philip Waddilove, Louis M. Heyward)
V, V*
US title: The Conqueror Worm

In 1645 a villainous lawyer finds it profitable to travel the country instigating witch hunts.

Savage, stylish minor horror melodrama with a growing reputation as the best work of its young director. Not for the squeamish despite its pleasing countryside photography.

w Michael Reeves, Tom Baker novel Ronald Bassett
d Michael Reeves ph John Coquillon m Paul Ferris, Jim Morahan

Vincent Price, Rupert Davies, Ian Ogilvy, Patrick Wymark, Hilary Dwyer, Wilfred Brambell

'He made a murderer of the boy who was to marry his own daughter!'

The Witching Hour

US 1934 65m bw
Paramount (Bayard Veiller)

A gambler hypnotizes a young man into taking the blame for a murder.

Stalwart melodrama, reasonably well done.

w Anthony Veiller, Salisbury Field play Augustus Thomas d Henry Hathaway

John Halliday, Guy Standing, Judith Allen, Tom Brown, William Frawley

† There was a previous (silent) version in 1921.

With a Song in My Heart *

US 1952 117m Technicolor
TCF (Lamar Trotti)

Singer Jane Froman is crippled in a plane crash but finally makes a comeback.

Romanticized showbiz biopic with the singer providing voice only. Adequate production and plenty of familiar tunes made this a successful mass appeal sob story.

w Lamar Trotti d Walter Lang ph Leon Shamroy
md Alfred Newman

Susan Hayward, David Wayne, Rory Calhoun, Thelma Ritter, Una Merkel, Robert Wagner, Helen Westcott

AA: Alfred Newman

AAN: Susan Hayward; Thelma Ritter

With Six You Get Egg Roll

US 1968 99m DeLuxe Panavision
Cinema Center/Arwin (Martin Melcher)
V*

A widow with three sons marries a widower with one daughter.

Quite a bright and inventive family comedy.

w Gwen Bagni, Paul Dubov d Howard Morris
ph Ellsworth Fredericks, Harry Stradling Jnr
m Robert Mersey

Doris Day, Brian Keith, Pat Carroll, Barbara Hershey

Within the Law (1930): see Paid

Within the Law

US 1939 66m bw
MGM

A girl wrongly convicted studies law in prison and later takes her revenge on the real culprit.

Reasonably interesting melodrama, filmed several times previously: in 1912, 1917, 1923 and in 1930 as Paid.

w Charles Lederer, Edith Fitzgerald play Bayard Veiller d Gustav Machaty

Ruth Hussey, Tom Neal, Paul Kelly, William Gargan, Paul Cavanagh, Samuel S. Hinds, Rita Johnson, Sidney Blackmer

'Certain of appeal where cops and robbers click.' – Variety

Within These Walls

US 1945 71m bw
TCF (Ben Silvey)

A stern prison governor makes no exceptions when his son becomes a convict.

Formula penitentiary drama with no surprises.

w Charles Trapnell, James R. Fisher, Eugene Ling, Wanda Tuchock   *d* Bruce Humberstone

Thomas Mitchell, Mary Anderson, Edward Ryan, Mark Stevens, Roy Roberts

Withnail and I *
GB   1987   108m   colour
Recorded Releasing/HandMade Films (Paul M. Heller)
V, V*, L, S

In the 60s in Britain two out-of-work actors settle in a dilapidated country cottage.

Deliberately seedy comedy which settles down as a study of character and contrives to be hard to forget.

wd Bruce Robinson   *ph* Peter Hannan   *m* David Dundas   *pd* Michael Pickwoad   *ed* Alan Strachan

Richard E. Grant, Paul McGann, Richard Griffiths, Ralph Brown, Michael Elphick

Without a Clue
US   1988   107m   CFI
Rank/ITC (Marc Stirdivant)
V, V*, L

Dr Watson hires a failed actor to impersonate Sherlock Holmes, a fictional character he has invented to hide his own abilities as a detective.

The mystery is that anyone should have released this witless spoof.

w Gary Murphy, Larry Strawther   *d* Thom Eberhardt   *ph* Alan Hume   *m* Henry Mancini   *pd* Brian Ackland-Snow, Martyn Hebert   *ed* Peter Tanner

Michael Caine, Ben Kingsley, Jeffrey Jones, Lysette Anthony, Paul Freeman, Nigel Davenport, Pat Keen, Peter Cook, Tim Killick

Without a Trace
US   1983   120m   DeLuxe
TCF (Stanley R. Jaffe)
V*

A mother solves the mystery of her missing child.

Fairly interesting modern melodrama with emphasis on character rather than the somewhat arbitrarily resolved plot.

w Beth Gutcheon   *novel* Still Missing by Beth Gutcheon   *d* Stanley R. Jaffe   *ph* John Bailey   *m* Jack Nitzsche   *pd* Paul Sylbert

Kate Nelligan, Judd Hirsch, David Dukes, Stockard Channing, Jacqueline Brookes, Keith McDermott, Kathleen Widdoes

'Dignified understatement is the keynote.' – *Tom Milne, MFB*

Without Love *
US   1945   111m   bw
MGM (Lawrence Weingarten)
V*, L

The housing shortage in wartime Washington causes a widow to allow a scientist to move in with her, quite platonically.

Altered version of a popular play; rather long-drawn-out and disappointing considering the talent on hand.

w Donald Ogden Stewart   *play* Philip Barry   *d* Harold S. Bucquet   *ph* Karl Freund   *m* Bronislau Kaper

Spencer Tracy, Katharine Hepburn, Lucille Ball, Keenan Wynn, Carl Esmond, Patricia Morison, Felix Bressart, Gloria Grahame

'One of those glossy conversation pieces that MGM does up so handsomely.' – *Rose Pelswick*

Without Reservations
US   1946   101m   bw
RKO/Jesse L. Lasky
V*, L

A famous woman writer heads for Hollywood by train

and meets a marine who seems ideal for her male lead.

Would-be zany romantic comedy à la *It Happened One Night;* doesn't quite come off.

w Andrew Solt   *d* Mervyn Le Roy   *ph* Milton Krasner   *m* Roy Webb

Claudette Colbert, John Wayne, Don Defore, Phil Brown, Frank Puglia

Without Warning
US   1952   70m   bw
UA/Allart

A sex maniac murders a succession of blondes.

Semi-documentary, low-budget police thriller with all elements adequate for their purpose.

w Bill Raynor   *d* Arnold Laven   *ph* Joseph Biroc   *m* Herschel Burke Gilbert

Adam Williams, Edward Binns, Meg Randall

Without Witnesses: see *A Private Conversation*

Without You I'm Nothing
US   1990   89m   Technicolor
Electric/MCEG (Jonathan D. Krane)
V*, L

Stand-up comedian Sandra Bernhard performs her one-woman show.

A self-indulgent ramble through the performer's past, interspersed with a few deft but uninteresting recreations of popular musical styles.

w Sandra Bernhard, John Boscovich   *d* John Boscovich   *ph* Joseph Yacoe   *m* Patrice Rushen   *pd* Kevin Rupnik   *ed* Pamela Malouf-Cundy

Sandra Bernhard, John Doe, Steve Antin, Lu Leonard, Ken Foree, Cynthia Bailey

'It aims for the spin-off thrills of a transgressive act in which much is suggested but nothing really is said.' – *Cynthia Rose, Sight and Sound*

'One of the sharpest and original comic talents of the past decade.' – *Empire*

'A big city cop who knows too much. His only witness – a small boy who's seen too much!'

Witness ****
US   1985   112m   Technicolor
Paramount/Edward S. Feldman
V, V*, L, S

A young Amish boy witnesses a murder, and a big-city detective hides out in the community to protect him.

As much about the meeting of cultures as about cops and robbers, this is one of those lucky movies which works out well on all counts and shows that there are still craftsmen lurking in Hollywood.

w Earl W. Wallace, William Kelley   *d* Peter Weir   *ph* John Seale   *m* Maurice Jarre   *pd* Stan Jolley   *ed* Thom Noble

Harrison Ford, Kelly McGillis, Josef Sommer, Lukas Haas, Jan Rubes, Alexander Godunov

AA: editing; original screenplay

AAN: best picture; direction; Harrison Ford; photography; music; art direction

BFA: music

The Witness Chair
US   1936   64m   bw
RKO

A secretary accidentally kills her nasty employer and almost allows an associate to take the blame.

Stiff, old-fashioned melodrama that served its purpose.

w Rian James, Gertrude Purcell   *story* Rita Weiman   *d* George Nicholls Jnr

Ann Harding, Walter Abel, Douglass Dumbrille, Frances Sage, Moroni Olsen, Margaret Hamilton

Witness for the Prosecution ***
US   1957   114m   bw
UA/Theme/Edward Small (Arthur Hornblow Jnr)
V, V*, L

A convalescent QC takes on a murder defence and finds himself in a web of trickery.

Thoroughly likeable though relentlessly over-expanded movie version of a clever stage thriller. Some miscasting and artificiality is condoned by smart dialogue and handling, one celebrated performance, and a handful of surprises.

w Billy Wilder, Harry Kurnitz   *play* Agatha Christie   *d* Billy Wilder   *ph* Russell Harlan   *m* Matty Melneck   *ed* Daniel Mandell

Charles Laughton, Tyrone Power, Marlene Dietrich, John Williams, Henry Daniell, Elsa Lanchester, Norma Varden, Una O'Connor, Ian Wolfe

AAN: best picture; Billy Wilder; Charles Laughton; Elsa Lanchester; Daniel Mandell

Witness to Murder *
US   1954   81m   bw
UA (Chester Erskine)

A lonely woman sees a strangling in the flat across the street; the police don't believe her but the murderer does.

Predictable but quite effective screamer with a nick-of-time dénouement.

w Chester Erskine   *d* Roy Rowland   *ph* John Alton   *m* Herschel Burke Gilbert

Barbara Stanwyck, George Sanders, Gary Merrill, Jesse White, Harry Shannon, Claire Carleton

Wittgenstein **
GB   1993   75m   colour
BFI/Channel 4/Uplink/Bandung (Tariq Ali)
V

Biopic of the linguistic philosopher Ludwig Wittgenstein, from his birth in Austria to his death in Cambridge in 1951.

Made on a tiny budget and shot as a series of scenes, using a minimum of props, against a black background, this is nevertheless a colourful and intriguing work, interested both in Wittgenstein as a person and in what he had to say; inevitably, its appeal will be limited to those interested in philosophy and in the inventive use of film

w Derek Jarman, Terry Eagleton, Ken Butler   *d* Derek Jarman   *ph* James Welland   *m* Jan Latham-Koenig   *ad* Annie Lapaz   *ed* Budge Tremlett

Karl Johnson, Michael Gough, Tilda Swinton, John Quentin, Kevin Collins, Clancy Chassay, Jill Balcon

'Wonderfully theatrical in its execution, this is Jarman pared down to basics – actors, stage, lighting – allowing the script, the real strength of the film, with its equal measures of wit and weight (and surprisingly little pretension) to take centre stage.' – *Philippa Bloom, Empire*

'You can't tell them apart without a scorecard!'
Wives and Lovers
US   1963   103m   bw
Paramount/Hal B. Wallis

A successful author moves his family into Connecticut, where sex rears its ugly head.

Would-be sophisticated comedy with insufficient bubbles.

w Edward Anhalt   *play* The First Wife by Jay Presson Allen   *d* John Rich   *ph* Lucien Ballard   *m* Lyn Murray

Van Johnson, Janet Leigh, Ray Walston, Shelley Winters, Martha Hyer, Jeremy Slate

Wives under Suspicion

US 1938 68m bw
Universal
V*

A district attorney involved in a love-triangle murder discovers a similar situation developing in his own life.

Flat remake of the same director's *The Kiss Before the Mirror;* of little interest.

w Myles Connelly *d* James Whale

Warren William, Gail Patrick, Ralph Morgan, William Lundigan, Constance Moore

The Wiz *

US 1978 134m Technicolor
Universal/Motown (Robert Cohen)
V, V*, L

A black version of *The Wizard of Oz,* set in New York.

Glossy version of the Broadway musical hit; it offers some rewards, but on the whole the first is the best.

w Joel Schumacher *play* Charlie Smalls (*m/y*) *book* William Brown *d* Sidney Lumet *ph* Oswald Morris *md* Quincy Jones *m* Quincy Jones *pd* Tony Walton *songs* Charlie Smalls

Diana Ross, Michael Jackson, Nipsey Russell, Ted Ross, Lena Horne, Richard Pryor, Mabel King, Theresa Merritt

AAN: Oswald Morris; Quincy Jones

The Wizard

US 1989 97m DeLuxe
UIP/Universal (David Chisholm, Ken Topolsky)
V*, L

A young boy runs away with his almost-mute even younger brother in order to compete in a video-game championship.

Uninteresting pre-teen road movie, which has no other purpose than to sell video games.

w David Chisholm *d* Todd Holland *ph* Robert Yeoman *m* J. Peter Robinson *pd* Michael Mayer *ed* Tom Finan

Fred Savage, Luke Edwards, Christian Slater, Beau Bridges, Vincent Leahr, Wendy Phillips, Dea McAllister, Sam McMurray, Will Seltzer

The Wizard of Oz

US 1925 70m bw silent
Larry Semon
V, V*, L

On her 18th birthday a girl abandoned as a small baby at a Kansas farm discovers that she is the Queen of Oz and, after deposing its dictator, lives there happily ever after.

The emphasis is on farmyard slapstick comedy, mainly executed with a heavy hand, which makes it hard to appreciate why Semon was once almost as popular as Chaplin and Keaton, but it has its moments – particularly a chase sequence in wooden boxes.

w L. Frank Baum Jnr, Leon Lee, Larry Semon *novel* L. Frank Baum *d* Larry Semon *ph* H. F. Koenenkamp, Frank Good, Leonard Smith *ad* Robert Stevens *ed* Sam Zimbalist

Larry Semon (as the Scarecrow), Oliver N. Hardy (as the Tin Woodsman), Dorothy Dwan, Mary Carr, Virginia Pearson, Bryant Washburn, Josef Swickard, Otto Lederer, Charles Murray

† The film is available on video with a musical accompaniment.

The Wizard of Oz ***

US 1939 102m Technicolor
MGM (Mervyn Le Roy)
V, V*, L

Unhappy Dorothy runs away from home, has adventures in a fantasy land, but finally decides that happiness was in her own back yard all the time.

Classic fairy tale given vigorous straightforward treatment, made memorable by performances, art direction and hummable tunes.

w Noel Langley, Florence Ryerson, Edgar Allan Wolfe *book* Frank L. Baum *d* Victor Fleming *ph* Harold Rosson *songs* E. Y. Harburg, Harold Arlen *md* Herbert Stothart *ad* Cedric Gibbons, William A. Horning

Judy Garland, Frank Morgan, Ray Bolger, Jack Haley, Bert Lahr, Margaret Hamilton, Billie Burke, Charley Grapewin, Clara Blandick

SCARECROW (Ray Bolger):
'I could while away the hours
Conversin' with the flowers
Consultin' with the rain.
And perhaps I'd deserve you
And be even worthy erv you
If I only had a brain . . . '
COWARDLY LION (Bert Lahr):
'Oh, it's sad to be admittin'
I'm as vicious as a kitten
Widout de vim and voive;
I could show off my prowess
Be a lion, not a mowess
If I only had de noive.'
GLINDA, the good witch (Billie Burke): 'Close your eyes and tap your heels together three times. And think to yourself, there's no place like home.'
DOROTHY (Judy Garland): 'If I ever go looking for my heart's desire again, I won't look any further than my own back yard, because if it isn't there, I never really lost it to begin with.'
DOROTHY, LION, SCARECROW, TIN MAN:
'We're off to see the Wizard
The wonderful Wizard of Oz.
We hear he is a whiz of a wiz
If ever a wiz there was.
If ever a wever a wiz there was
The Wizard of Oz is one because
Because of the wonderful things he does . . .'

'There's an audience for it wherever there's a projection machine and a screen.' – *Variety*

'I don't see why children shouldn't like it, but for adults there isn't very much except Bert Lahr.' – *Richard Mallett, Punch*

'As for the light touch of fantasy, it weighs like a pound of fruitcake soaking wet.' – *Otis Ferguson*

† Ray Bolger was originally cast as the tin man but swapped roles with Buddy Ebsen who was to have been the scarecrow. Ebsen then got sick from the metal paint and was replaced by Jack Haley. Edna May Oliver was originally cast as the wicked witch. For Dorothy MGM wanted Shirley Temple, but Twentieth Century Fox wouldn't loan her.
†† The sepia scenes at beginning and end were directed by King Vidor.

AA: song 'Over the Rainbow'; Herbert Stothart

AAN: best picture; art direction

Wo die Grünen Ameisen Träumen: see *Where the Green Ants Dream*

The Wolf Dog

US 1933 bw serial: 12 eps
Mascot

An intelligent dog protects the inventor of an electric ray.

Simple-minded action adventures.

d Harry Frazer and Colbert Clark

Rin Tin Tin Jnr, Frankie Darro, George Lewis, Boots Mallory, Henry B. Walthall, Fred Kohler

Wolf Larsen

US 1958 83m bw
AA (Lindsley Parsons)
V*

Serviceable remake of *The Sea Wolf* (qv) without the Nietzschean overtones.

w Jack de Witt, Turnley Walker *d* Harmon Jones *ph* Floyd Crosby *m* Paul Dunlap

Barry Sullivan, Peter Graves, Thayer David, Gita Hall

'His hideous howl a dirge of death!'
'Night monster with the blood lust of a savage beast!'
The Wolf Man *

US 1940 70m bw
Universal (George Waggner)
V*, L

The son of an English squire comes home, is bitten by a gypsy werewolf, and becomes one himself.

Dazzlingly cast, moderately well staged, but dramatically very disappointing horror piece which established a new Universal monster who later met Frankenstein, Abbott and Costello, and several other eccentrics.

w Curt Siodmak *d* George Waggner *ph* Joseph Valentine *md* Charles Previn *m* Hans Salter, Frank Skinner

Lon Chaney Jnr, Claude Rains, Warren William, Ralph Bellamy, Bela Lugosi, *Maria Ouspenskaya,* Patric Knowles, Evelyn Ankers, Fay Helm

MALEVA (Maria Ouspenskaya):
'Even the man who is pure in heart
And says his prayers by night
May become a wolf when the wolf bane blooms
And the moon is pure and bright . . .'

'It will tear the scream from your throat!'
Wolfen

US 1981 115m Technicolor Panavision
Warner/Orion (Rupert Hitzig)
V*, L

Mutilation murders in New York turn out to be the work of savage beasts descended from Indian hunters who went underground in despair at the future of mankind.

Nuthatch horror movie with a message, though providing little of either commodity. Clearly a waste of money.

w David Eyre, Michael Wadleigh *novel* Whitley Strieber *d* Michael Wadleigh *ph* Gerry Fisher, Fred Abeles *m* James Horner *pd* Paul Sylbert

Albert Finney, Diane Venora, Edward James Olmos, Gregory Hines, Tom Noonan

'A thriller so slow, complicated and frankly rather dull that one's sympathy is all on the side of the predators.' – *Daily Mail*

The Wolves of Willoughby Chase

GB 1988 93m colour
Entertainment/Subatomnic/Zenith (Mark Forstater)
V, S

Two girls discover that their wicked governess is attempting to steal the family estate.

Lively children's film with relishable villains.

w William M. Akers *novel* Joan Aiken *d* Stuart Orme *ph* Paul Beeson *m* Colin Towns *pd* Christopher Hobbs *ed* Martin Walsh

Stephanie Beacham, Mel Smith, Geraldine James, Richard O'Brien, Emily Hudson, Aleks Darowska, Jane Horrocks, Eleanor David, Jonathan Coy

Woman Accused *

US 1933 73m bw
Paramount

A woman kills her ex-lover in a struggle and goes on the run.

Intriguing rigmarole written as a magazine serial by ten well-known authors contributing a chapter each. The result confirms the method.

w Bayard Veiller   *serial* Rupert Hughes, Vicki Baum, Zane Grey, Vina Delmar, Irvin S. Cobb, Gertrude Atherton, J. P. McEvoy, Ursula Parrott, Polan Banks, Sophie Kerr   *d* Paul Sloane   *ph* Karl Struss

Nancy Carroll, Cary Grant, John Halliday, Irving Pichel, Louis Calhern, Jack La Rue, John Lodge

'It may convince producers and exhibitors that new writing talent should be encouraged . . . business possibilities anything but bright on so-so cast names.' – *Variety*

A Woman Alone

GB   1936   78m   bw
Garrett-Klement
US title: *Two Who Dared*

In 19th-century Russia, a captain falls for a peasant girl.

Uninteresting melodrama with stilted actors.

w Leo Lania, Warren Chetham Strode   *novel* Fedor Ozep   *d* Eugene Frenke

Anna Sten, Henry Wilcoxon, Viola Keats, John Garrick, Rimilly Lunge

A Woman Alone (1936): see *Sabotage*

The Woman Between: see *The Woman I Love*

Woman Chases Man

US   1937   71m   bw
Samuel Goldwyn
V

A lady architect persuades a millionaire to help his land developer father.

Thin, lame comedy which constantly amazes by its lack of success.

w Joseph Anthony, Mannie Seff, David Hertz   *story* Lynn Root, Frank Fenton   *d* John G. Blystone   *ph* Gregg Toland   *m* Alfred Newman

Miriam Hopkins, Joel McCrea, Charles Winninger, Erik Rhodes, Broderick Crawford, Leona Maricle, Ella Logan, Charles Halton

'Laughs stopped at the Music Hall when the action on the screen became so insanely illogical, and dull, that the amazed disappointment of the house expressed itself in chilly silence.' – *Variety*

'A pleasant warm weather fabrication – lightweight, attractively tailored and not meant to withstand the rigours of wear or the chill blasts of the critics.' – *Frank S. Nugent*

† The unhappy production began as a vehicle for Miss Hopkins. Writers who worked on it include Ben Hecht, Sam and Bella Spewack, and Dorothy Parker. Directors involved were Edward Ludwig, William Wyler and Gregory La Cava.

A Woman Commands

US   1932   85m   bw
RKO Pathé

A cabaret entertainer rejects her lover for a king, but regains him when the king is murdered.

Romantic melodrama of the silent school, quite unrevivable.

w Thilde Forster   *d* Paul Stein

Pola Negri, Basil Rathbone, Roland Young, H. B. Warner, Anthony Bushell, Reginald Owen

A Woman Destroyed: see *Smash-Up, The Story of a Woman*

A Woman Disappeared, Portrait of a Woman: see *Une Femme Disparait*

Woman Doctor

US   1939   65m   bw
Republic (Sol C. Siegel)

Her career prospers, her marriage suffers.

Old hat domestic drama, tolerably put over.

w Joseph Moncure March   *d* Sidney Salkow

Frieda Inescort, Henry Wilcoxon, Claire Dodd, Sybil Jason, Cora Witherspoon

The Woman from Monte Carlo

US   1931   68m   bw
Warner

The wife of a naval officer is suspected of adultery.

Stiff marital melodrama based on a silent film *The Night Watch*; it worked no wonders for its German star.

w Harvey Thew   *d* Michael Curtiz

Lil Dagover, Walter Huston, Warren William, Robert Warwick, John Wray

'Looks a light draw at best.' – *Variety*

The Woman from Nowhere: see *La Femme de Nulle Part*

Woman Hater

GB   1948   105m   bw
GFD/Two Cities (William Sistrom)
V*

An English nobleman tries to disprove a film star's statement that she hates men and loves solitude.

Incredibly slight material is interminably stretched out, well beyond an excellent cast's ability to help.

w Robert Westerby, Nicholas Phipps   *d* Terence Young   *ph* André Thomas   *m* Lambert Williamson

Stewart Granger, Edwige Feuillère, Ronald Squire, Mary Jerrold, Jeanne de Casalis

Woman Hunt: see *Au Royaume des Cieux*

The Woman I Love *

US   1937   85m   bw
RKO (Albert Lewis)
GB title: *The Woman Between*

In World War I France, a pilot loves his superior officer's wife.

Well-made romantic action melodrama from a well-praised original.

w Mary Borden   *novel* L'Equipage by Joseph Kessel   *d* Anatole Litvak   *ph* Charles Rosher   *m* Arthur Honegger, Maurice Thiriet

Paul Muni, Miriam Hopkins, Louis Hayward, Colin Clive, Minor Watson, Elizabeth Risdon, Paul Guilfoyle, Mady Christians

'Needs all the marquee help it can get . . . spotty business indicated.' – *Variety*

Woman in a Dressing Gown *

GB   1957   94m   bw
Godwin/Willis/J. Lee-Thompson

After twenty years of marriage, a wife's slatternly ways alienate her once devoted husband, and he asks for a divorce.

Classic British TV play adequately filmed but now rather dated and irritating.

w Ted Willis   *play* Ted Willis   *d* J. Lee-Thompson   *ph* Gilbert Taylor   *m* Louis Levy

Yvonne Mitchell, Anthony Quayle, Sylvia Syms, Andrew Ray, Carole Lesley

A Woman in Her Thirties: see *Side Streets*

Woman in Hiding

US   1949   92m   bw
U-I (Michael Kraike)

After escaping her husband's attempts to murder her, a woman goes into hiding while evidence is being accumulated against him.

Modest suspenser with too many near escapes and not much else.

w Oscar Saul   *d* Michael Gordon   *ph* William Daniels   *m* Frank Skinner

Ida Lupino, Howard Duff, Stephen McNally, John Litel, Taylor Holmes, Irving Bacon, Peggy Dow, Joe Besser, Don Beddoe

'The detail is full of things interesting and amusing at the time and pleasant to remember afterwards.' – *Richard Mallett, Punch*

The Woman in His House: see *The Animal Kingdom*

The Woman in Question *

GB   1949   88m   bw
GFD/Javelin (Teddy Baird)
US title: *Five Angles on Murder*

Police investigating a woman's death build up several different impressions of her.

Multi-flashback melodrama which somehow doesn't quite come off despite effort all round.

w John Cresswell   *d* Anthony Asquith   *ph* Desmond Dickinson   *m* John Wooldridge

Jean Kent, Dirk Bogarde, Susan Shaw, John McCallum, Hermione Baddeley, Charles Victor, Duncan Macrae, Lana Morris, Vida Hope

The Woman in Red

US   1935   68m   bw
Warner

A professional horsewoman marries into society and is ill received.

Stiff class melodrama partly redeemed by its star.

w Mary McCall Jnr, Peter Milne   *novel* North Shore by Wallace Irwin   *d* Robert Florey

Barbara Stanwyck, Genevieve Tobin, John Eldredge, Gene Raymond, Philip Reed

The Woman in Red *

US   1984   86m   DeLuxe
Orion (Victor Drai)
V, V*, L

A middle-aged married man has fantasies of infidelity.

Moderately successful transfer to America of a French comedy success.

wd Gene Wilder, from the film *Un Eléphant Ça Trompe Enormement* by Jean-Loup Dabadie, Yves Robert   *ph* Fred Schuler   *m* John Morris   *pd* David L. Snyder   *ed* Christopher Greenbury

Gene Wilder, Charles Grodin, Joseph Bologna, Judith Ivey, Gilda Radner

AA: song 'I Just Called to Say I Love You' (Stevie Wonder)

The Woman in Room 13

US   1932   58m   bw
Fox

The wife of an innocent convict tricks the real culprit into a confession.

Stagey melodrama which just about fills an hour.

w Guy Bolton   *play* Sam Shipman, Max Marcin, Percival Wilde   *d* Henry King

Elissa Landi, Ralph Bellamy, Neil Hamilton, Myrna Loy, Gilbert Roland

'Just another factory-made release.' – *Variety*

Woman in the Dark

US   1935   68m   bw
Select/RKO

A man convicted of manslaughter gets himself on his release into another awkward situation.

Moderate semi-crime melodrama.

w Sada Cowan   *story* Dashiell Hammett   *d* Phil Rosen

Fay Wray, Melvyn Douglas, Ralph Bellamy, Roscoe Ates

'Marquee weakness only thing that may keep it out of single-feature houses . . . murder mystery fare of sufficient relish to keep 'em from leaving the table.' – *Variety*

The Woman in the Hall

GB　1947　93m　bw
GFD/IP/Wessex (Ian Dalrymple)

A well-intentioned woman takes to begging and becomes a bad influence on her daughter.

Finger-wagging novelette makes an unrewarding film.

w G. B. Stern, Ian Dalrymple, Jack Lee　*novel* G. B. Stern　d Jack Lee　ph C. Pennington-Richards, H. E. Fowle　m Temple Abady　pd Peter Proud

Ursula Jeans, Cecil Parker, Jean Simmons, Jill Raymond, Edward Underdown, Joan Miller, Susan Hampshire

The Woman in the Moon *

Germany　1929　125m (24 fps)　bw　silent
UFA
V*

original title: *Frau im Mond*

Two scientists are forced to journey to the moon by criminals anxious to mine its gold deposits.

Heavy-handed fantasy which is not among its director's best work.

w Thea von Harbou　d Fritz Lang

Willy Fritsch, Gerda Maurus, Gusti Stark-Gatettenbaur

'Half of it could be removed; as it is, it winds ponderously on.' – *Variety*

'It was the look in her eyes that did it. How could he resist? How could he know it meant murder?'
The Woman in the Window ***

US　1944　95m　bw
International (Nunnally Johnson)
V

A grass widow professor befriends a girl who gets him involved with murder.

A refreshingly intelligent little thriller which was criticized at the time for a cop-out ending; this can now be seen as a decorative extra to a story which had already ended satisfactorily. Good middlebrow entertainment.

w *Nunnally Johnson*　*novel Once Off Guard* by J. H. Wallis　d *Fritz Lang*　ph *Milton Krasner*　m Arthur Lange, Hugo Friedhofer

Edward G. Robinson, Joan Bennett, *Raymond Massey*, Dan Duryea, Edmund Breon, Thomas Jackson, Dorothy Peterson, Arthur Loft

'A perfect example of its kind, and a very good kind too.' – *James Shelley Hamilton*

'The accumulation of tiny details enlarged as though under a district attorney's magnifying glass gives reality a fantastic and anguishing appearance.' – *Jacques Bourgeois*

'In its rather artificial, club library style an effective and well made piece, absorbing, diverting and full of often painful suspense.' – *Richard Mallett, Punch*

'Art and Mammon, it seems to me, have been very prettily served.' – *Spectator*

AAN: Arthur Lange, Hugo Friedhofer

'Born in shame – living in mystery – what is her sinister secret?'
The Woman in White *

US　1948　109m　bw
Warner (Henry Blanke)

The new tutor of a strange household finds himself among eccentrics, villains and ill-used ladies.

A Victorian thriller which is long on atmosphere but not so hot on suspense or plot development. The cast helps a lot.

w Stephen Morehouse Avery　*novel* Wilkie Collins　d Peter Godfrey　ph Carl Guthrie　m Max Steiner

Gig Young, Eleanor Parker, *Sidney Greenstreet*, Alexis Smith, Agnes Moorehead, John Emery, *John Abbott*, Curt Bois

'The Wilkie Collins novel is given the studious, stolid treatment ordinarily reserved for the ritual assassination of a great classic. This is not intended as a recommendation.' – *James Agee*

'Greenstreet and others move through the murky passages of the story like visitors in some massive Gothic museum, and they move, on the whole, with stately discretion, and do not scribble on the objects or show anything but the greatest veneration for them.' – *C. A. Lejeune*

A Woman Is a Woman **

France　1961　85m　Eastmancolor　Scope
V, V*

original title: *Une Femme est une Femme*

A stripper quarrels with her boyfriend because she wants to have a baby and he doesn't.

Exuberantly playful tribute to the high spirits of MGM's classic musicals, even though there is little actual singing and dancing. It has a lovers' bicycle ride that was imitated much later in *Butch Cassidy and The Sundance Kid*.　wd Jean-Luc Godard　ph Raoul Coutard　m Michel Legrand

Jean-Paul Belmondo, Jean-Claude Brialy, Anna Karina, Marie Dubois, Jeanne Moreau

The Woman Next Door

France　1981　106m　Fujicolor
Les Films du Carrosse/TF1
V*

An engineer is embarrassed when an old flame, now married, comes to live next door; their love rekindles but ends in tragedy.

Rather uninteresting melodrama with a failure to communicate its apparent personal importance for the director.

w François Truffaut, Suzanne Schiffman, Jean Aurel　d François Truffaut　ph William Lubtchansky　m Georges Delerue

Gérard Depardieu, Fanny Ardant, Henri Garcin, Michele Baumgarner

Woman Obsessed

US　1959　102m　DeLuxe　Cinemascope
TCF (Sidney Boehm)

In the Canadian Rockies, a pioneer woman's small son does not take to his new stepfather.

Antediluvian pulp fiction with quicksand and a forest fire for highlights. Shades of D. W. Griffith, and badly done into the bargain.

w Sidney Boehm　*novel* John Mantley　d Henry Hathaway　ph William C. Mellor　m Hugo Friedhofer

Susan Hayward, Stephen Boyd, Dennis Holmes, Theodore Bikel, Barbara Nichols, Ken Scott, Arthur Franz

A Woman of Affairs

US　1928　90m (24 fps)　bw　silent
MGM
V*, L

A wild rich girl goes from man to man and finally kills herself in a car crash.

Romantic star tosh from a fashionable novel of the time.

w Bess Meredyth　*novel The Green Hat* by Michael Arlen　d Clarence Brown　ph William Daniels

Greta Garbo, Lewis Stone, John Gilbert, John Mack Brown, Douglas Fairbanks Jnr, Hobart Bosworth

AAN: Bess Meredyth

Woman of Antwerp: see *Dédée d'Anvers*

A Woman of Distinction

US　1950　85m　bw
Columbia (Buddy Adler)
V*, L

The lady dean of a New England school falls for a British astronomer.

Pratfall farce for ageing stars. No go.

w Charles Hoffman　d Edward Buzzell　ph Joseph Walker　md Morris Stoloff　m Werner Heymann

Rosalind Russell, Ray Milland, Edmund Gwenn, Janis Carter, Mary Jane Saunders, Francis Lederer, Jerome Courtland

Woman of Dolwyn: see *The Last Days of Dolwyn*

A Woman of Paris **

US　1923　85m (24 fps)　bw　silent (music track added 1976)
Charles Chaplin
V*

A country girl goes to the city, becomes a demi-mondaine, and inadvertently causes the death of the one man she loves.

Remarkably simply-handled 'road to ruin' melodrama; its subtleties of treatment make it still very watchable for those so inclined.

wd Charles Chaplin　ph Rollie Totheroh, Jack Wilson

Edna Purviance, Adolphe Menjou, Carl Miller, Lydia Knott

'A thoroughly workmanlike entertainment and a candidate for honours and dollars entirely independent of the drawing power built up by Chaplin in other fields.' – *Variety*

'After five minutes of watching the sparkling new print, the spell begins to work. Chaplin is neatly turning the clichés inside out, like a glove.' – *Alan Brien, Sunday Times, 1980*

'Mr Chaplin as writer and director has not done anything radical or anything esoteric; he has merely used his intelligence to the highest degree, an act which for many years has ceased to be expected of motion picture people.' – *Robert E. Sherwood*

'The plot is desperately simple, but played with a control, a complete absence of histrionic vehemence, rare in the early twenties.' – *Dilys Powell, Punch, 1980*

† Chaplin appeared unbilled as a railway porter. The film was not a commercial success and he withdrew it for fifty years.

Woman of Straw *

GB　1964　114m　Eastmancolor
UA/Novus (Michael Relph)

A rich old man's nurse conspires with his nephew in a murder plot.

Rather half-hearted but good-looking star melodrama which ventures into Hitchcock territory.

w Robert Muller, Stanley Mann, Michael Relph　*novel* Catherine Arley　d Basil Dearden　ph Otto Heller　m Muir Mathieson　pd Ken Adam

Gina Lollobrigida, Sean Connery, *Ralph Richardson*, Johnny Sekka, Laurence Hardy, Alexander Knox

Woman of Summer: see *The Stripper*

Woman of the Dunes *

Japan　1964　127m　bw
Teshigahara (Kiichi Ichikawa)
V

original title: *Suna no Onna*

An entomologist on a deserted beach finds an attractive young widow living in a shack at the bottom of a huge sand pit, spends the night with her, can't escape, and finally doesn't want to.

Unique sex melodrama, all shifting sand and picturesque angles, with a clear meaning; but far too long.

w Kobo Abe *d* Hiroshi Teshigahara *ph* Hiroshi Segawa

Eiji Okada, Kyoko Kishoda

'Teasingly opaque, broodingly erotic.' – *MFB*

AAN: Hiroshi Teshigahara; best foreign film

Woman of the North Country
US 1952 90m Trucolor
Republic (Joseph Kane)

Minnesota 1890: rivalry over an iron ore mine erupts between a young engineer and an ambitious woman.

Standard Western.

w Norman Reilly Raine *d* Joseph Kane *ph* Jack Marta *m* R. Dale Butts

Ruth Hussey, Rod Cameron, John Agar, Gale Storm, Jim Davis, J. Carrol Naish

Woman of the River *
Italy/France 1955 95m Technicolor
Ponti/de Laurentiis/Films du Centaure

A peasant girl has nothing but trouble after falling for a handsome smuggler.

Lively melodrama whose primary purpose was to demonstrate the physical charms of its new star. It succeeded well enough in the *Bitter Rice* tradition.

w Basilio Franchina, Giorgio Bassani, Pier Paolo Pasolini, Florestano Vancini, Antonio Antoviti, Mario Soldati *story* Alberto Moravia, Ennio Flainio *d* Mario Soldati *ph* Otello Martelli *m* Angelo Lavagnini, Armando Trovaioli

Sophia Loren, Gerard Oury, Rik Battaglia, Lise Bourdin

The Woman of the Town *
US 1943 87m bw
United Artists (Harry Sherman)
V*

Bat Masterson becomes marshal of Dodge and falls for a saloon singer.

Busy, old-fashioned urban Western with good entertainment values.

w Aeneas Mackenzie *d* George Archainbaud *m* Miklos Rozsa

Albert Dekker, Claire Trevor, Barry Sullivan, Henry Hull, Marion Martin, Porter Hall, Percy Kilbride

AAN: Miklos Rozsa

A Woman of the World: see *Outcast Lady*

Woman of the Year ***
US 1942 114m bw
MGM (Joseph L. Mankiewicz)
V*, L

A sports columnist marries a lady politician; they have nothing in common but love.

Simple, effective, mildly sophisticated comedy which allows two splendid stars, in harness for the first time, to do their thing to the general benefit.

w Ring Lardner Jnr, Michael Kanin *d* George Stevens *ph* Joseph Ruttenberg *m* Franz Waxman

Spencer Tracy, Katharine Hepburn, Fay Bainter, Reginald Owen, William Bendix, Dan Tobin, Minor Watson, Roscoe Karns

'Between them they have enough charm to keep any ball rolling.' – *William Whitebait*

AA: script
AAN: Katharine Hepburn

The Woman on Pier 13
US 1949 73m bw
RKO (Jack J. Gross)
aka: *I Married a Communist*

A shipping executive is blackmailed by communists, who know of a youthful crime, into helping them spy.

Laboured witch-hunt melodrama.

w Charles Grayson, Robert Hardy Andrews *d* Robert Stevenson *ph* Nicholas Musuraca *m* Leigh Harline

Laraine Day, Robert Ryan, John Agar, Thomas Gomez, Janis Carter, Richard Rober, William Talman

The Woman on the Beach
US 1947 71m bw
RKO (Jack J. Gross)

A mentally ailing coastguard meets a *femme fatale* and comes between her and her sadistic husband.

Nuthouse melodrama which neither convinces nor compels for a moment.

w Frank Davis, Jean Renoir *novel* None So Blind by Mitchell Wilson *d* Jean Renoir *ph* Leo Tover, Harry Wild *m* Hanns Eisler

Joan Bennett, Robert Ryan, Charles Bickford, Nan Leslie, Walter Sande

'One may have to strain to see it as more than an over-aestheticized, interesting failure.' – *Pauline Kael, 70s*

Woman on the Run
US 1950 77m bw
Universal-International/Fidelity (Howard Welsch)
V*

A man runs away after witnessing a murder; his wife is menaced by the killer.

Slightly unusual thriller which alas fails to thrill.

w Norman Foster, Alan Campbell *d* Norman Foster *ph* Hal Mohr *m* Emil Newman

Ann Sheridan, Dennis O'Keefe, Robert Keith, Ross Elliott

A Woman Rebels *
US 1936 88m bw
RKO (Pandro S. Berman)

A Victorian miss fights for women's rights and has an illegitimate baby.

Interesting, half-forgotten star drama.

w Anthony Veiller, Ernest Vajda *novel* Portrait of a Rebel by Netta Syrett *d* Mark Sandrich *ph* Robert de Grasse *m* Roy Webb *ad* Van Nest Polglase

Katharine Hepburn, Herbert Marshall, Elizabeth Allan, Donald Crisp, Doris Dudley, David Manners, Van Heflin, Lucile Watson, Eily Malyon

'Delving into the fascinating ugliness of Victorian England, RKO Radio have found material that is picturesque, humorous and tragic.' – *Frank Nugent, New York Times*

The Woman They Almost Lynched
US 1952 90m bw
Republic

An innocent girl out west is blamed for a crime wave and almost executed as a spy.

Incredible, random-plotted Western with a few entertaining moments.

w Steve Fisher *story* Michael Fessier *d* Allan Dwan

Joan Leslie, Audrey Totter, John Lund, Brian Donlevy, Ben Cooper

'As naughty as a black lace nightgown!'

Woman Times Seven
US/France 1967 99m DeLuxe
TCF/Embassy (Arthur Cohn)

Seven sketches, in each of which a woman behaves typically of her sex.

Humourless after-dinner entertainment.

w Cesare Zavattini *d* Vittorio de Sica *ph* Christian Matras *m* Riz Ortolani

Shirley Maclaine, Peter Sellers, Rossano Brazzi, Vittorio Gassman, Lex Barker, Elsa Martinelli, Robert Morley, Adrienne Corri, Patrick Wymark, Alan Arkin, Michael Caine, Anita Ekberg, Philippe Noiret

Woman to Woman
GB 1923 83m at 24 fps bw silent
Balcon, Freedman and Saville

A shell-shocked officer marries into society and later adopts his son by a French ballerina.

Far-fetched melodrama in what later became the *Random Harvest* style; a great box-office hit of its time.

w Alfred Hitchcock *play* Michael Morton *d* Graham Cutts

Betty Compson, Clive Brook, Josephine Earle, Marie Ault

† Victor Saville directed a sound remake in 1929, with Betty Compson and George Barraud; and in 1946 Maclean Rogers had another shot with Adele Dixon and Douglass Montgomery.

A Woman under the Influence *
US 1974 155m colour
Faces International (Sam Shaw)
V, V*

A Los Angeles housewife and mother suffers a mental breakdown as she increasingly feels at odds with society.

Fine acting from Rowlands and Falk lifts an otherwise overlong domestic drama.

wd John Cassavetes *ph* Mitch Breit, Caleb Deschanel *m* Bo Harwood *ad* Phedon Papamichael *ed* Tom Cornwell

Peter Falk, Gena Rowlands, Matthew Cassel, Matthew Laborteaux, Christina Grisanti, Katherine Cassavetes

'Though some in the audience will once again accept what is going on as raw, anguishing truth, most people will – rightly, I think – take their embarrassment as evidence of Cassavetes' self-righteous ineptitude.' – *Pauline Kael, New Yorker*

AAN: John Cassavetes (as director); Gena Rowlands

Woman Wanted
US 1935 65m bw
MGM

A girl accused of murder is helped by an attorney.

Initially appealing comedy-thriller which moves fast enough but has a very muddled plotline.

w Leonard Fields, Dave Silverstein, Wilson Collison *d* George B. Seitz

Maureen O'Sullivan, Joel McCrea, Lewis Stone, Louis Calhern, Edgar Kennedy, Adrienne Ames, Robert Greig, Noel Madison

The Woman Who Came Back *
US 1945 68m bw
Republic (Walter Colmes)
V*

A girl returning to her home village in New England is made to think she is a witch.

Quite an agreeably spooky second feature.

w Dennis Cooper, Lee Willis *d* Walter Colmes

Nancy Kelly, John Loder, Otto Kruger, Ruth Ford, Harry Tyler

The Woman with No Name
GB   1950   83m   bw
IFP/ABP
US title: *Her Panelled Door*

An amnesiac wife finds herself threatened from all sides.

Hoary melodrama with some unintentional laughs.

w Ladislas Vajda, Guy Morgan   *novel* *Happy Now I Go* by Theresa Charles   *d* Ladislas Vajda, George More O'Ferrall

Phyllis Calvert, Edward Underdown, Helen Cherry, Richard Burton, Anthony Nicholls, James Hayter, Betty Ann Davies

Woman Without a Face: see *Mister Buddwing*

The Woman's Angle
GB   1952   86m   bw
ABP/Leslie Arliss/Bow Belles (Walter Mycroft)

In a divorce court three flashbacks tell of the life of a composer.

Damp little formula drama for matinée audiences, refashioned from a successful silent film.

wd Leslie Arliss   *novel* *Three Cups of Coffee* by Ruth Feiner   *ph* Erwin Hillier   *m* Robert Gill; the Mansell Concerto by Kenneth Leslie Smith

Edward Underdown, Cathy O'Donnell, Lois Maxwell, Claude Farrell, Peter Reynolds, Marjorie Fielding

'Whatever I am, men made me!'
A Woman's Face **
US   1941   105m   bw
MGM (Victor Saville)
V*, L

A scarred and embittered woman turns to crime but jibs at murder.

Curious, unexpected but very entertaining melodrama with a courtroom frame, Swedish settings, an excellent cast and some bravura sequences.

w Donald Ogden Stewart   *play* *Il Était une Fois* by François de Croisset   *d* George Cukor   *ph* Robert Planck   *m* Bronislau Kaper

Joan Crawford, Melvyn Douglas, *Conrad Veidt*, Osa Massen, Reginald Owen, Albert Basserman, Marjorie Main, Donald Meek, Connie Gilchrist

† Also involved in the script were Elliott Paul and Christopher Isherwood.

A Woman's Secret
US   1949   85m   bw
RKO (Herman J. Mankiewicz)
V*

An ex-singer grooms a girl as her successor but lives to regret it.

Downright peculiar little *film noir* by the co-author of *Citizen Kane* (though not so that you'd notice).

w Herman J. Mankiewicz   *novel* *Mortgage on Life* by Vicki Baum   *d* Nicholas Ray   *ph* George Diskant   *md* Constantin Bakaleinikoff   *m* Frederick Hollander

Maureen O'Hara, Gloria Grahame, Melvyn Douglas, Bill Williams, Victor Jory, Mary Phillips

A Woman's Vengeance *
US   1948   96m   bw
Universal-International (Zoltan Korda)

A man is convicted for the murder of his invalid wife, actually committed by a jealous woman in love with him but later spurned.

Interesting but very stagey melodrama from one of its author's more commercial ventures.

w Aldous Huxley   *story and play* *The Gioconda Smile* by Aldous Huxley   *d* Zoltan Korda   *ph* Russell Metty   *m* Miklos Rozsa

Charles Boyer, Jessica Tandy, Ann Blyth, Cedric Hardwicke, Mildred Natwick

'A rather literary movie, but most movies aren't even that; much less are they real movies.' – *James Agee*

'It's a great big wonderful woman's world because men are in it!'
Woman's World **
US   1954   94m   Technicolor   Cinemascope
TCF (Charles Brackett)

Three top salesmen and their wives are summoned to New York by the boss, who seeks to choose a new general manager.

Amusing, superficial pattern comedy-drama for an all-star cast, backed by all-round technical competence.

w Claude Binyon, Mary Loos, Richard Sale   *d* Jean Negulesco   *ph* Joe MacDonald   *m* Cyril Mockridge

Clifton Webb, Lauren Bacall, Van Heflin, June Allyson, Fred MacMurray, Arlene Dahl, Cornel Wilde, Elliott Reid, Margalo Gillmore

Wombling Free
GB   1977   96m   Eastmancolor
Rank/Ian Shand
V, V*

The furry creatures who live under Wimbledon Common at last make contact with humans.

Disastrous attempt to film a popular TV series for children. The series came in five-minute chunks; this elephantine transcription leaves several talents high and dry.

wd Lionel Jeffries, from characters created by Elizabeth Beresford   *ph* Alan Hume   *m* Mike Batt

David Tomlinson, Frances de la Tour, Bonnie Langford, Bernard Spear

'A fiasco. If you really must take your kids, it would be less of a pain to go shopping at the same time.' – *Derek Malcolm, Guardian*

'135 women with men on their minds!'
The Women ***
US   1939   132m   bw   (Technicolor sequence)
MGM (Hunt Stromberg)
V*, L

A New York socialite gets a divorce but later thinks better of it.

Bitchy comedy drama distinguished by an all-girl cast ('135 women with men on their minds'). An over-generous slice of real theatre, skilfully adapted, with rich sets, plenty of laughs, and some memorable scenes between the fighting ladies.

w Anita Loos, Jane Murfin   *play* *Clare Boothe*   *d* George Cukor   *ph* Oliver T. Marsh, Joseph Ruttenberg   *m* Edward Ward, David Snell

Norma Shearer, Joan Crawford, *Rosalind Russell*, Mary Boland, Paulette Goddard, Joan Fontaine, Lucile Watson, Phyllis Povah, Virginia Weidler, Ruth Hussey, Margaret Dumont, Marjorie Main, Hedda Hopper

'Smash hit of solid proportions for extended runs and heavy profits . . . a strong woman entry but still has plenty of spicy lines and situations for the men.' – *Variety*

'A mordant, mature description of the social decay of one corner of the American middle class.' – *Time*

'So marvellous that we believe every Hollywood studio should make at least one thoroughly nasty picture a year.' – *New York Times*

'Whether you go or not depends on whether you can stand Miss Shearer with tears flowing steadily in all directions at once, and such an endless damn back fence of cats.' – *Otis Ferguson*

Women Are Like That
US   1938   78m   bw
Warner

A separated couple meet again years later and find each other changed.

Witless elaboration of a good idea: far too slow and talky.

w Horace Jackson, Albert Z. Carr   *d* Stanley Logan

Kay Francis, Pat O'Brien, Ralph Forbes, Melville Cooper, Thurston Hall, Grant Mitchell

'Terribly tiresome, slow and talky.' – *Variety*

Women in Bondage
US   1943   72m   bw
Monogram (Herman Millakowsky)

How the Nazis treat their women.

Cheap but vigorous exploitation piece, not quite so sensational as it now sounds.

w Houston Branch, Frank Wisbar   *d* Steve Sekely

Gail Patrick, Nancy Kelly, Gertrude Michael, Anne Nagel, Tala Birell, Maris Wrixon, William Henry, H. B. Warner, Alan Baxter

Women in Love ***
GB   1969   130m   DeLuxe
UA/Brandywine (Larry Kramer)
V, V*, L

Two girls have their first sexual encounters in the Midlands during the twenties.

Satisfactory rendering of a celebrated novel, with excellent period detail atoning for rather irritating characters. The nude wrestling scene was a famous first.

w Larry Kramer   *novel* *D. H. Lawrence*   *d* Ken Russell   *ph* Billy Williams   *m* Georges Delerue

Glenda Jackson, Jennie Linden, Alan Bates, Oliver Reed, Michael Gough, Alan Webb

'They should take all the pretentious dialogue off the soundtrack and call it Women in Heat.' – *Rex Reed*

'Two-thirds success, one-third ambitious failure.' – *Michael Billington, Illustrated London News*

AA: Glenda Jackson

AAN: Larry Kramer; Ken Russell; Billy Williams

Women in the Wind
US   1939   63m   bw
Warner (Mark Hellinger)

Conflict arises between contestants in the Women's Air Derby.

Formula multi-character picture, only moderately watchable.

w Lee Katz, Albert DeMond   *novel* *Francis Walton*   *d* John Farrow

Kay Francis, William Gargan, Victor Jory, Maxie Rosenbloom, Eddie Foy Jnr, Eve Arden

'Good programmer for duals and cinch for action spots.' – *Variety*

Women in War
US   1942   71m   bw
Republic (Sol C. Siegel)

A socialite playgirl is recruited into war nursing in order to escape a prison sentence.

Early World War II exploitation piece; lowish marks in its own right.

w F. Hugh Herbert, Doris Anderson   *d* John H. Auer

Elsie Janis, Wendy Barrie, Patric Knowles, Mae Clarke, Dorothy Peterson, Billy Gilbert

Women of All Nations
US   1931   72m   bw
Fox

Flagg and Quirt, back in the Marines, have amorous adventures in Sweden, Nicaragua and Egypt.

Routine fun and games with the heroes of *What Price Glory* (qv).

w Barry Connors d Raoul Walsh ph Lucien Andriot m Reginald H. Bassett

Edmund Lowe, Victor McLaglen, Greta Nissen, El Brendel, Fifi D'Orsay, Bela Lugosi, Humphrey Bogart

Women of Glamour
US   1937   65m   bw
Columbia

A man is loved by a society flower and a gold-digger, and chooses the latter.

Minor woman's picture.

w Lynn Starling, Mary McCall Jnr story Milton Herbert Gropper d Gordon Wiles

Melvyn Douglas, Virginia Bruce, Reginald Denny, Leona Maricle, Pert Kelton

'Featherweight triangle headed for the dual round-up.' – *Variety*

Women of Twilight
GB   1952   89m   bw
Romulus (Daniel M. Angel)

Unmarried mothers are victimized by a professional baby farmer.

Sordid, claustrophobic and ham-handed version of an exploitation play designed to provide another monstrous part for its star.

w Anatole de Grunwald novel Sylvia Rayman d Gordon Parry ph Jack Asher m Alan Gray

Freda Jackson, René Ray, Lois Maxwell, Joan Dowling, Dora Bryan, Vida Hope, Mary Germaine, Laurence Harvey

Women on the Verge of a Nervous Breakdown **
Spain   1988   89m   Eastmancolor
Rank/El Deseo/Lauren Film/Orion (Agustin Almodóvar)
V, V*, L
original title: *Mujeres al borde de un ataque de nervios*

Three women approach crack-up as their lives entangle: a demented wife whose husband has abandoned her, her husband's estranged mistress, a temperamental actress, and the actress's friend, who has fallen in love with a terrorist.

Frenetic, fashionable farce that manages to amuse most of the time.

wd Pedro Almodóvar ph Jose Luis Alcaine m Bernardo Bonezzi ed Jose Salcedo

Carmen Maura, Antonio Banderas, Julieta Serrano, Maria Barranco, Rossy de Palma, Guillermo Montesinos, Kiti Manver

'The best to be said for *Women on the Verge* is that Almodóvar makes a good interior decorator.' – *Mark Finch, MFB*

AAN: best foreign film

Women without Men
GB   1956   73m   bw
Exclusive/Hammer (Anthony Hinds)

An actress breaks out of prison in order to keep a rendezvous with the man she loves.

Standard programme-filler of a thriller.

w Richard Landau d Elmo Williams ph Walter Harvey md John Hollingsworth m Leonard Salzedo ad John Elphick ed James Needs

Beverley Michaels, Joan Rice, Thora Hird, Avril Angers, Paul Carpenter, Hermione Baddeley, Gordon Jackson, Ralph Michael, Maurice Kaufmann, David Lodge

'Caged emotions, yearning for love!'
Women without Names
US   1940   62m   bw
Paramount (Eugene Zukor)

An innocent girl is accused of murder, is sent to prison, but saves her boyfriend from the gallows.

Eventful second feature; no one would complain.

w William H. Lipman, Horace McCoy d Robert Florey

Ellen Drew, Robert Paige, Judith Barrett, John Miljan, Fay Helm, Louise Beavers, Marjorie Main, Esther Dale

Won Ton Ton, the Dog Who Saved Hollywood
US   1976   92m   colour
Paramount/David V. Picker, Arnold Schulman, Michael Winner

In twenties Hollywood, a lost Alsatian dog becomes a movie star but later suffers some ups and downs before being reunited with his mistress.

Scatty, unlikeable comedy with too frantic a pace, apparently in desperation at the dearth of funny lines and situations. The sixty 'guest stars' barely get a look in; the director seems to think (erroneously) that their appearance makes some kind of point even though they have nothing to do. Altogether, an embarrassment.

w Arnold Schulman, Cy Howard d Michael Winner ph Richard H. Kline m Neal Hefti

Madeleine Kahn, Art Carney, Bruce Dern, Ron Leibman; and Dennis Morgan, William Demarest, Virginia Mayo, Rory Calhoun, Henry Wilcoxon, Ricardo Montalban, Jackie Coogan, Johnny Weissmuller, Aldo Ray, Ethel Merman, Joan Blondell, Yvonne de Carlo, Andy Devine, Broderick Crawford, Richard Arlen, Jack La Rue, Dorothy Lamour, Phil Silvers, Gloria de Haven, Stepin Fetchit, Rudy Vallee, George Jessel, Ann Miller, Janet Blair, the Ritz Brothers, Victor Mature, Fernando Lamas, Cyd Charisse, Huntz Hall, Edgar Bergen, Peter Lawford, Regis Toomey, Alice Faye, Milton Berle, John Carradine, Walter Pidgeon, etc

'The film tries to conceal its deficiencies in comic ideas and comic skill by doing everything at the pace of a clockwork toy with a too-tight spring.' – *Dave Robinson, Times*

Wonder Bar **
US   1934   84m   bw
Warner (Robert Lord)
L

Love and hate backstage at a Paris night-club.

Curious musical drama with an interesting cast and fairly stunning numbers.

w Earl Baldwin play Geza Herczeg, Karl Farkas, Robert Katscher d Lloyd Bacon ph Sol Polito ch Busby Berkeley songs Harry Warren, Al Dubin ad Jack Okey

Al Jolson, Kay Francis, Dolores del Rio, Ricardo Cortez, Dick Powell, Guy Kibbee, Ruth Donnelly, Hugh Herbert, Louise Fazenda, Fifi D'Orsay

'Romance, flash, dash, colour, songs, star-studded talent, and almost every known requisite to ensure sturdy attention and attendance.' – *Variety*

'A tip-top musical.' – *Variety*

Wonder Man **
US   1945   97m   Technicolor
Samuel Goldwyn
V*

A mild-mannered student is persuaded by the ghost of his dead twin to avenge his murder.

Smooth, successful mixture of *Topper*, a night-club musical, a gangster drama and the star's own brand of fooling; this is possibly his best vehicle after *The Court Jester*.

w Don Hartman, Melville Shavelson, Philip Rapp story Arthur Sheekman d Bruce Humberstone ph Victor Milner, William Snyder md Louis Forbes, Ray Heindorf sp John Fulton

Danny Kaye, Vera-Ellen, Virginia Mayo, Steve Cochran, S. Z. Sakall, Allen Jenkins, Ed Brophy, Donald Woods, Otto Kruger, Richard Lane, Natalie Schaefer

AAN: Louis Forbes, Ray Heindorf; song 'So in Love' (m David Rose, ly Leo Robin)

The Wonderful Country
US   1959   96m   Technicolor
UA/DRM (Chester Erskine)

A wandering gunman is offered a job by the Texas Rangers.

Complexly plotted Western offering a range of familiar exploits.

w Robert Ardrey novel Tom Lea d Robert Parrish ph Floyd Crosby, Alex Phillips m Alex North

Robert Mitchum, Julie London, Pedro Armendariz, Gary Merrill, Jack Oakie, Albert Dekker, Charles McGraw, John Banner, Jay Novello

Wonderful Life *
GB   1964   113m   Techniscope
EMI/Elstree Distributors/Ivy (Kenneth Harper)

Four entertainers on a luxury liner are hired by a film crew in Africa.

Slight but zestful youth musical with highly illogical detail; the highlight is a ten-minute spoof history of the movies.

w Peter Myers, Ronald Cass d Sidney J. Furie ph Ken Higgins pd Stanley Dorfman

Cliff Richard, Walter Slezak, Susan Hampshire, Melvyn Hayes, Richard O'Sullivan, Una Stubbs, Derek Bond, Gerald Harper, the Shadows

Wonderful to Be Young: see *The Young Ones*

The Wonderful World of Dogs
Australia   1990   60m   colour
Radio Pictures/Australian Film Commission/ABC/Channel 4 (Mark Lewis)
V

A documentary on dogs and their effect on people's lives in an Australian suburb.

Witty and bizarre account of man's best, or worst, friend, one that even cat-lovers should enjoy.

wd Mark Lewis ph Tony Wilson, Steve Windon m Martin Armiger ed Lindsay Frazer

The Wonderful World of the Brothers Grimm *
US   1962   134m   Technicolor   Cinerama
MGM/Cinerama/George Pal
V*, L

An account of the lives of the German fairy tale writers is supplemented by three of their stories, *The Dancing Princess*, *The Cobbler and the Elves* and *The Singing Bone*.

Saccharine, heavy-handed pantomime with insufficient comedy, menace or spectacle.

w David P. Harmon, Charles Beaumont, William Roberts d Henry Levin, George Pal ph Paul C. Vogel m Leigh Harline songs Bob Merrill ad George W. Davis, Edward Carfagno

Laurence Harvey, Karl Boehm, Claire Bloom, Barbara Eden, Walter Slezak, Oscar Homolka, *Martita Hunt*, Russ Tamblyn, Yvette Mimieux, *Jim Backus*, Beulah Bondi, Terry-Thomas, Buddy Hackett, Otto Kruger

AAN: Paul C. Vogel; Leigh Harline

The Wonders of Aladdin
Italy   1961   92m   Technicolor   Cinemascope
Embassy/Lux
V*

With the help of a genie, Aladdin defeats a usurper and wins the princess's hand.

Flat and disappointing pantomime with virtually no charm.

w Luther Davis   *d* Henry Levin, Mario Bava
ph Tonino Delli Colli   *m* Angelo Lavagnino

Donald O'Connor, Vittorio de Sica, Aldo Fabrizi, Michèle Mercier

The Woo Woo Kid *
US   1987   100m   CFI   Guild/Lorimar/Kings Road
    Entertainment (Gary Adelson, Karen Mack)
V, V*, L
US title: *In the Mood*

A 15-year-old boy marries an older woman and, after the marriage is annulled, runs away with a soldier's wife.

Based on a true story from the 1940s, the comedy has a bizarre period charm.

wd Phil Alden Robinson   *story* Bob Kosberg, David Simon, Phil Alden Robinson   *ph* John Lindley
m Ralph Burns   *pd* Dennis Gassner   *ed* Patrick Kennedy

Patrick Dempsey, Talia Balsam, Beverly D'Angelo, Michael Constantine, Betty Jinnette, Kathleen Freeman, Peter Hobbs, Tony Longo, Douglas Rowe

The Wooden Horse **
GB   1950   101m   bw
British Lion/Wessex/London Films (Ian Dalrymple)
V, V*

During World War II, British prisoners escape from Stalag Luft III by tunnelling under a vaulting horse.

Standard, solid POW drama with predictable but exciting and occasionally moving developments.

w Eric Williams   *novel* Eric Williams   *d* Jack Lee
ph C. Pennington-Richards   *m* Clifton Parker

Leo Genn, David Tomlinson, Anthony Steele, David Greene, Michael Goodliffe, Bryan Forbes, Jacques Brunius

'All the suspense I care to take.' – *Sunday Chronicle*

The Wooden Horse of Troy: see *The Trojan War*

Wooden Soldiers: see *Babes in Toyland* (1934)

'This time the whole world is watching...'
Woodstock ****
US   1970   184m   Technicolor
Warner/Wadleigh-Maurice (Bob Maurice)
V, V(W), V*, L, S

A documentary on the three-day festival ('of peace, music... and love') that attracted an audience of around 500,000 young people.

A definitive moment of the 60s, with the mood and music brilliantly captured on film. To do it took a team of 20 cameramen, who shot 120 hours of film, as well as eight camera assistants, 20 sound-men and engineers, six still photographers and 30 production assistants.

d Michael Wadleigh   *ph* Michael Wadleigh and others
ed Thelma Schoonmaker, Martin Scorsese

Joan Baez, Canned Heat, Joe Cocker, Country Joe and The Fish, Crosby, Stills, Nash & Young, Arlo Guthrie, Richie Havens, Jimi Hendrix, Santana, John Sebastian, Sha-Na-Na, Sly & The Family Stone, Ten Years After, The Who

'A joyous, volcanic new film that will make those who missed the festival feel as if they were there. But *Woodstock* is far more than a sound-and-light souvenir of a long weekend concert. Purely as a piece of cinema, it is one of the finest documentaries ever made in the U.S.' – *Time*

'What is distressing about most of the performers at this mammoth mud-in, apart from their obvious lack of musical talent, is, in most cases, their equally obvious hostility. I mean not just laudable hostility to the war, but also profound neurotic hostility.' – *John Simon*

AA: best documentary

† A 'director's cut' lasting 220m was released in cinemas and on video in 1994.

Words and Music **
US   1948   121m   Technicolor
MGM (Arthur Freed)
V*, L, S

The songwriting collaboration of Richard Rodgers and Lorenz Hart.

Musical biopic which packs in a lot of good numbers and manages a script which is neither too offensive nor too prominent.

w Fred Finklehoffe   *d* Norman Taurog   *ph* Charles Rosher, Harry Stradling   *md* Lennie Hayton
ch Robert Alton, Gene Kelly

Tom Drake, Mickey Rooney, Perry Como, *Mel Tormé*, Betty Garrett, *June Allyson*, Lena Horne, Ann Sothern, Allyn McLerie, *Gene Kelly*, Vera-Ellen, Cyd Charisse, Janet Leigh, Marshall Thompson

Work Is a Four-Letter Word
GB   1968   93m   Technicolor
Universal/Cavalcade (Thomas Clyde)

A power station attendant is interested only in growing mushrooms, which have a chaotic effect on his private life.

Weakly futuristic industrial fantasy which the author would probably claim to be about lack of communication. Bored audiences might have a similar view.

w Jeremy Brooks   *play Eh?* by Henry Livings
d Peter Hall   *ph* Gilbert Taylor   *m* Guy Woolfenden

David Warner, Cilla Black, Elizabeth Spriggs, Zia Mohyeddin, Joe Gladwin

Working Girl **
US   1988   113m   DuArt
Fox (Douglas Wick)
V, V*, L, S

A secretary outsmarts her female boss in business and love.

Glossy comedy that owes much to the performances of its leading actors.

w Kevin Wade   *d* Mike Nichols   *ph* Michael Ballhaus   *m* Carly Simon   *pd* Patrizia von Brandenstein   *ed* Sam O'Steen, Richard Nord

Harrison Ford, Sigourney Weaver, Melanie Griffith, Alec Baldwin, Joan Cusack, Philip Bosco, Nora Dunn, Oliver Platt, James Lally, Olympia Dukakis

AA: best song

AAN: best picture; Mike Nicholls; Melanie Griffith; Joan Cusack

Working Girls **
US   1986   90m   colour
Lizzie Borden/Alternate Current (Lizzie Borden, Andi Gladstone)
V*

After a hard day's work and overtime, a prostitute decides to quit working in a New York brothel.

A near-documentary style enlivens an account of workaday prostitutes, an upwardly mobile madame, and their rather sad male clients.

w Lizzie Borden, Sandra Kay   *d* Lizzie Borden
ph Judy Irola   *m* David Van Tieghen   *pd* Kurt Ossenfort   *ed* Lizzie Borden

Louise Smith, Ellen McElduff, Amanda Goodwin, Marusia Zach, Janne Peters, Helen Nicholas

The Working Man
US   1933   78m   bw
Warner

A wealthy shoe manufacturer hands over his business, goes on holiday, and finds himself helping his bitterest rival.

Palatable star parable.

w Maude T. Howell, Charles Kenyon   *novel* Edgar Franklin   *d* John Adolfi

George Arliss, Bette Davis, Theodore Newton, J. Farrell MacDonald

The World According to Garp *
US   1982   136m   Technicolor
Warner/Pan Arts (George Roy Hill, Robert L. Crawford)
V, V*, L

A young man grows up with a determination to become a writer.

Unlikely and uneasy film version of a somewhat cerebral novel; any drama there might have been in the original got lost in the transition, but at least the intention is to be applauded.

w Steve Tesich   *novel* John Irving   *d* George Roy Hill   *ph* Miroslav Ondricek   *md* David Shire
pd Henry Bumstead   *ed* Stephen A. Rotter

Robin Williams, Mary Beth Hurt, Glenn Close, John Lithgow, Hume Cronyn, Jessica Tandy, Swoosie Kurtz

'Rather like watching a puppy chasing its own tail: engaging, touching, but pointless.' – *Margaret Hinxman, Daily Mail*

'When the movie was over, all I could find to ask myself was: What the hell was all that about?' – *Roger Ebert*

AAN: John Lithgow; Glenn Close (supporting actress)

The World and His Wife: see *State of the Union*

A World Apart **
GB   1987   110m   colour
Palace/British Screen/Atlantic/Working Title (Sarah Radclyffe)
V, V*, L, S

Anti-apartheid struggles in the 1960s seen through the eyes of a 13-year-old South African girl whose mother is imprisoned for her support of the African National Congress.

Excellently acted and moving mix of political and domestic drama.

w Shawn Slovo   *d* Chris Menges   *ph* Peter Biziou
m Hans Zimmer   *pd* Brian Morris   *ed* Nicolas Gaster

Johdi May, Jeroen Krabbé, Barbara Hershey, Linda Mvusi, David Suchet, Pau Freeman, Tim Roth, Yvonne Bryceland, Albee Lesotho, Rosalie Crutchley

† Shawn Slovo is the daughter of Ruth First, on whose life the story is based.

The World Changes *
US   1933   91m   bw
Warner (Robert Lord)

A simple farmer becomes a powerful executive, and success goes to his head.

Adequate moral drama of its time, well staged and acted.

w Edward Chodorov   *d* Mervyn Le Roy   *ph* Tony Gaudio

Paul Muni, Aline MacMahon, Mary Astor, Donald Cook, Patricia Ellis, Jean Muir, Margaret Lindsay, Guy Kibbee, Alan Dinehart

'It won't appeal to the hotsy-totsy type of fan, but the parents will bring the youngsters, which should sort of balance things.' – *Variety*

World Gone Wild

US   1987   90m   colour
Apollo Pictures (Robert L. Rosen)
V*

In 2087, a small desert community seeks help against an attack from a messianic killer and his disciples.

Inept combination of *The Magnificent Seven* and *Mad Max*, lacking in style and substance.

w Jorge Zamacona   *d* Lee H. Katzin   *ph* Don Burgess   *m* Laurence Juber   *pd* Donald L. Harris   *ed* Gary A. Griffin

Bruce Dern, Michael Pare, Catherine Mary Stewart, Anthony James, Rick Podell, Julius J. Carry III, Alan Autry, Mindy McEnnan, Adam Ant

World in Flames *

US   1940   62m   bw
Paramount (Albert J. Richard)

A newsreel account of the rise to power of dictators during the thirties.

Effective propaganda at the time, and a neat editing job.

The World in His Arms *

US   1952   104m   Technicolor
Universal (Aaron Rosenberg)

In old San Francisco, a seal-poaching sea captain meets a Russian countess.

Romantic melodrama with plushy period backgrounds and a fair measure of action, climaxing in a boat race.

w Borden Chase   *d* Raoul Walsh   *ph* Russell Metty   *m* Frank Skinner

Gregory Peck, Ann Blyth, Anthony Quinn, John McIntire, Andrea King, Carl Esmond, Eugenie Leontovitch

World in My Corner *

US   1955   85m   bw
U-I (Aaron Rosenberg)

A penniless would-be prizefighter becomes the protégé of a millionaire and wins his daughter but not the crucial fight.

Well-done minor melodrama.

w Jack Sher   *d* Jesse Hibbs   *ph* Maury Gertsman   *m* Joseph Gershenson

Audie Murphy, Barbara Rush, Jeff Morrow, John McIntire, Tommy Rall, Howard St John

The World in My Pocket: see On Friday at Eleven

The World Is Full of Married Men

GB   1979   106m   Eastmancolor
New Realm/Married Men Productions (Adrienne Fancey)
V*

The wife of an advertising executive tries to pay him out in kind for his infidelity.

Tedious jet-setting morality play which shows in great detail all the vices it wags a finger at.

w Jackie Collins   *novel* Jackie Collins   *d* Robert Young   *ph* Ray Parslow   *m* Frank Musker, Dominic Bugatti

Carroll Baker, Anthony Franciosa, Sherrie Cronn, Paul Nicholas, Gareth Hunt, Georgina Hale, Anthony Steel

The World Moves On *

US   1934   104m   bw
Fox (Winfield Sheehan)

The saga of a Louisiana family up to World War I.

Careful, good-looking general entertainment.

w Reginald C. Berkeley   *d* John Ford   *ph* George Schneiderman   *m* Louis de Francesco

Madeleine Carroll, Franchot Tone, Reginald Denny, Stepin Fetchit, Lumsden Hare, Louise Dresser, Sig Rumann

'Pacifistic picture inviting endorsement from all bodies. Big on production and cast with six minutes of superb war stuff.' – *Variety*

The World of Apu ****

India   1959   106m   bw
Satyajit Ray Productions
V*

original title: *Apur Sansar*

An impoverished writer, working as a clerk, who agrees to an arranged marriage, is devastated by the death of his wife in childbirth and rejects his son.

An emotional and satisfyingly moving conclusion to a great artistic experience.

wd Satyajit Ray   *novel* Aparajita by Bibhutibhushan Banerjee   *ph* Subrata Mitra   *m* Ravi Shankar   *ad* Bansi Chandragupta   *ed* Dulal Dutta

Soumitra Chatterjee, Sarmila Tagore, Alok Chakravarti, Swapan Mukherjee, Dhiresh Majumdar, Sefalika Devi, Dhires Ghosh

'Rich and contemplative, and a great, convincing affirmation.' – *Pauline Kael, New Yorker*

† The film is the final part of a trilogy that began with *Pather Panchali* and continued with *Aparajito* (qqv).

The World of Henry Orient **

US   1964   106m   DeLuxe   Panavision
UA/Pan Arts (Jerome Hellman)
V*, L

Two rich 14-year-old New York girls build fantasies around a concert pianist.

Charming, immaculately mounted, refreshingly unusual but overlong comedy.

w Nora and Nunnally Johnson   *novel* Nora Johnson   *d* George Roy Hill   *ph* Boris Kaufman, Arthur J. Ornitz   *m* Elmer Bernstein   *pd* James Sullivan

Tippy Walker, Merri Spaeth, Peter Sellers, Angela Lansbury, Paula Prentiss, Phyllis Thaxter, Tom Bosley, Bibi Osterwald

World of Plenty ***

GB   1943   45m   bw
The Ministry of Information

How the distribution of food should be handled after the war.

Classic documentary with many new film-making insights, including the use of statistical diagrams.

w Paul Rotha, Eric Knight, Miles Malleson   *d* Paul Rotha

'Any theatre audience will be grateful for seeing it. It is the epitome of educational picture-making.' – *Variety*

The World of Suzie Wong

GB   1960   129m   Technicolor
Paramount/Ray Stark (Hugh Perceval)
V*, L

A Hong Kong prostitute falls in love with the artist for whom she poses.

Dull, set-bound romantic melodrama without much gusto.

w John Patrick   *play* Paul Osborn   *d* Richard Quine   *ph* Geoffrey Unsworth   *m* George Duning

William Holden, Nancy Kwan, Sylvia Syms, Michael Wilding, Laurence Naismith, Jackie Chan

'Maybe one day it will all make the grade as a musical.' – *MFB*

The World Owes Me a Living

GB   1944   91m   bw
British National

A man gets his memory back and recalls his air force career.

Pointless flagwaving farrago.

w Vernon Sewell, Erwin Reiner   *novel* John Llewellyn Rhys   *d* Vernon Sewell

David Farrar, Judy Campbell, Sonia Dresdel, Jack Livesey, John Laurie, Wylie Watson

World Premiere *

US   1940   70m   bw
Paramount (Sol C. Siegel)

A zany film producer thinks up some wild publicity schemes for his new film and accidentally traps some Nazi spies.

Occasionally amusing farce mainly notable for its star.

w Earl Felton   *d* Ted Tetzlaff   *ph* Daniel Fapp

John Barrymore, Ricardo Cortez, Frances Farmer, Sig Rumann, Fritz Feld, Eugene Pallette, Luis Alberni, Virginia Dale, Don Castle

The World Ten Times Over

GB   1963   93m   bw
Cyclops (Michael Luke)
US title: *Pussycat Alley*

Two semi-prostitutes try to improve their lot.

Dreary, derivative low-life drama with flashy technique.

wd Wolf Rilla   *ph* Larry Pizer   *m* Edwin Astley

Sylvia Syms, June Ritchie, Edward Judd, William Hartnell, Francis de Wolff

The World, the Flesh and the Devil *

US   1959   95m   bw   Cinemascope
MGM/Sol C. Siegel/Harbel

Trapped for five days in a mine cave-in, a man struggles to the surface to find a dead world devastated by atomic war; but still alive are the elements of an eternal triangle . . .

Enterprising but rather disappointing fantasy tends to become merely glum and rather self-consciously carries a panic button message.

wd Ranald MacDougall   *ph* Harold J. Marzorati   *m* Miklos Rozsa   *ad* William A. Horning, Paul Groesse

Harry Belafonte, Inger Stevens, Mel Ferrer

World without End

US   1956   80m   Technicolor   Cinemascope
AA (Richard Heermance)

A space ship breaks the time barrier and returns to Earth in 2508, to find that intelligent humans have been driven underground by mutants.

Reasonably lively sci-fi with horror elements, and a plot borrowed from H. G. Wells.

wd Edward Bernds   *ph* Ellsworth Fredericks   *m* Leith Stevens

Hugh Marlowe, Nancy Gates, Rod Taylor

A World without Pity

France   1989   88m   colour
Artificial Eye/Les Productions Lazennec (Alain Rocca)
V, S

A poker-playing youth, living with his young drug-dealing brother, falls in love with a clever student.

A thin romance, whose appeal will depend on how much sympathy can be summoned up for its shiftless, egocentric central character.

wd Eric Rochant   *ph* Pierre Novion   *m* Gerard Torikian   *ad* Thierry François   *ed* Michele Darmon

Hippolyte Girardot, Mireille Perrier, Yvan Attal, Jean-Marie Rollin, Cecile Mazan, Aline Still, Paul Pavel

The World's Greatest Athlete

US 1973 92m Technicolor
Walt Disney (Bill Walsh)
V*

An American sports coach on an African holiday finds a young Tarzan with amazing powers.

Simple-minded comedy with lame tomfoolery and trickwork.

w Gerald Gardiner, Dee Caruso d Robert Scheerer
ph Frank Phillips m Marvin Hamlisch

Tim Conway, Jan-Michael Vincent, John Amos, Roscoe Lee Browne

The World's Greatest Lover

US 1977 89m DeLuxe
TCF (Gene Wilder)
V*

In the twenties, a rival studio starts a search for a man to surpass Valentino.

Imitative slapstick extravaganza in which anything goes but hardly anything pleases.

wd Gene Wilder ph Gerald Hirschfeld m John Morris

Gene Wilder, Carol Kane, Dom DeLuise, Fritz Feld

'Infantile humour for young, slow kids who want everything pounded at them.' – Pauline Kael, New Yorker

† The film carries a credit to Federico Fellini, 'for encouragement at the right time'.

Worm's Eye View

GB 1951 77m bw
ABFD/Byron (Henry Halsted)

Incidents in the lives of a group of RAF billetees.

Plotless comedy from a highly successful stage romp; plainly made and empty-headed but not disagreeable.

w R. F. Delderfield play R. F. Delderfield d Jack Raymond ph James Wilson m Tony Lowry, Tony Fones

Ronald Shiner, Garry Marsh, Diana Dors, Eric Davis, John Blythe

The Worst Woman in Paris

US 1933 75m bw
Jesse L. Lasky/Fox

An American girl unfairly gets a bad reputation in Paris and on her way home becomes a heroine in Kansas.

Silly, pointless story on which good production values are wasted.

w Marion Dix, Monta Bell, Martin Brown d Monta Bell

Benita Hume, Adolphe Menjou, Harvey Stephens, Helen Chandler, Margaret Seddon

'Does not give promise of scoring in any placement.' – Variety

The Wrath of God

US 1972 111m Metrocolor Panavision
MGM/Rainbow/Cineman (William S. Gilmore Jnr)

During a twenties Central American revolution, a bootlegger joins forces with a defrocked priest.

Noisy, violent adventure yarn which works up to a gory climax but does not take itself too seriously.

wd Ralph Nelson novel James Graham ph Alex Phillips Jnr m Lalo Schifrin

Robert Mitchum, Frank Langella, Rita Hayworth, Victor Buono, John Colicos

The Wreck of the Mary Deare *

US 1959 108m Metrocolor Cinemascope
MGM/Blaustein-Baroda (Julian Blaustein)
V*, L

An insurance fraud comes to light when a salvage boat is rescued from high seas.

Curious, star-studded amalgam of seafaring action and courtroom melodrama, originally intended for Hitchcock.

w Eric Ambler novel Hammond Innes d Michael Anderson ph Joseph Ruttenberg, F. A. Young m George Duning

Charlton Heston, Gary Cooper, Michael Redgrave, Emlyn Williams, Cecil Parker, Alexander Knox, Virginia McKenna, Richard Harris

The Wrecking Crew

US 1968 104m Technicolor
Columbia/Meadway/Claude (Irving Allen)

Special agent Matt Helm recovers bullion stolen from a Danish train.

Camped-up spy buffoonery with the usual nubile ladies and a production which seeks to be flashy but succeeds only in being tatty.

w William McGivern novel Donald Hamilton d Phil Karlson ph Sam Leavitt m Hugo Montenegro

Dean Martin, Elke Sommer, Sharon Tate, Nancy Kwan, Nigel Green, Tina Louise

'The story of a family's ugly secret and the stark moment that thrust their private lives into public view!'

Written on the Wind **

US 1956 99m Technicolor
U-I (Albert Zugsmith)
V*

A secretary marries her oil tycoon boss and finds herself the steadying force in a very rocky family.

The sheerest Hollywood moonshine: high-flying melodramatic hokum which moves fast enough to be very entertaining.

w George Zuckerman novel Robert Wilder d Douglas Sirk ph Russell Metty m Frank Skinner

Lauren Bacall, Robert Stack, Dorothy Malone, Rock Hudson, Robert Keith, Grant Williams

AA: Dorothy Malone
AAN: title song (m Victor Young, ly Sammy Cahn); Robert Stack

Wrong Again

US 1929 20m bw silent
Hal Roach

A horse instead of a painting is delivered to a rich man's house.

Pleasing but not very inventive star comedy.

w Lewis R. Foster, Leo McCarey, H. M. Walker d Leo McCarey

Laurel and Hardy, Del Henderson

The Wrong Arm of the Law *

GB 1962 94m bw
Romulus/Robert Velaise (Aubrey Baring, E. M. Smedley Aston)
V, V*

London gangsters plan retaliation against Australian interlopers, and offer Scotland Yard a temporary truce.

Forgettable but pretty funny crook comedy in the British vein, with pacy script and excellent comedy timing.

w Ray Galton, Alan Simpson, John Antrobus screenplay Len Heath, John Warren d Cliff Owen ph Ernest Steward m Richard Rodney Bennett

Peter Sellers, Lionel Jeffries, Bernard Cribbins, Davy Kaye, Nanette Newman, Bill Kerr, John Le Mesurier

Wrong Bet: see A.W.O.L.

The Wrong Box *

GB 1966 110m Technicolor
Columbia/Salamander (Bryan Forbes)
V*

Two elderly Victorian brothers are the last survivors of a tontine (an involved form of lottery) and try to murder each other.

Well-intentioned and star-studded black farce in which the excellent period trappings and stray jokes completely overwhelm the plot.

w Larry Gelbart, Burt Shevelove novel Robert Louis Stevenson, Lloyd Osbourne d Bryan Forbes ph Gerry Turpin m John Barry ad Ray Simm

Ralph Richardson, John Mills, Michael Caine, Wilfrid Lawson, Nanette Newman, Peter Cook, Dudley Moore, Peter Sellers, Tony Hancock, Thorley Walters, Cicely Courtneidge, Irene Handl, John Le Mesurier, Gerald Sim, Norman Bird, Tutte Lemkow

'A slapdash affair in which anything goes, irrespective of whether or not it fits.' – Tom Milne

'Only Patrick Hale Can Prevent A Desperate President, The Head Of The CIA, A Trigger-Happy General, Terrorists, An Arms Dealer, And Religious Fanatics From Destroying The World. But He Has Other Things On His Mind.'

Wrong Is Right

US 1982 117m Metrocolor
Columbia/Richard Brooks
V*, L
GB title: The Man with the Deadly Lens

An international TV commentator discovers that the world is being manipulated by the CIA.

Wild satiric melodrama which takes potshots at everything and usually misses.

wd Richard Brooks novel The Deadly Angels by Charles McCarry ph Fred J. Koenekamp m Artie Kane pd Edward Carfagno ed George Grenville

Sean Connery, George Grizzard, Katharine Ross, Robert Conrad, G. D. Spradlin, John Saxon, Henry Silva, Leslie Nielsen, Robert Webber, Rosalind Cash, Hardy Kruger, Dean Stockwell, Ron Moody

'Intended as a sharply cynical overview of the current political scene, it emerges as a drearily murky thriller.' – Sight and Sound

The Wrong Kind of Girl: see Bus Stop

The Wrong Man *

US 1957 105m bw
Warner (Herbert Coleman)
V*, L

A New York musician is mistaken by police for an armed bandit, and both witnesses and circumstances prevent the truth from emerging.

True but downbeat story from the headlines, filmed with remarkably little persuasion; not its director's métier despite evidence of his usual thoroughness.

w Maxwell Anderson, Angus MacPhail d Alfred Hitchcock ph Robert Burks m Bernard Herrmann

Henry Fonda, Vera Miles, Anthony Quayle, Harold J. Stone, Esther Minciotti

'Torn with desire ... twisted with hate!'

Wuthering Heights ***

US 1939 104m bw
Samuel Goldwyn
V, V*, L, S

The daughter of an unhappy middle-class Yorkshire family falls passionately in love with a gypsy who has been brought up with her.

Despite American script and settings, this wildly romantic film makes a pretty fair stab at capturing the power of at least the first half of a classic Victorian novel, and in all respects it's a superb Hollywood production of its day and a typical one, complete with ghostly finale and a first-rate cast.

w Ben Hecht, Charles MacArthur   novel Emily Brontë
d William Wyler   ph Gregg Toland   m Alfred Newman
ad James Basevi

Laurence Olivier, Merle Oberon, David Niven, Hugh
Williams, Flora Robson, Geraldine Fitzgerald, Donald
Crisp, Leo G. Carroll, Cecil Kellaway, *Miles Mander*

CATHY (Merle Oberon): 'I don't think I belong in
heaven, Ellen. I dreamt once I was there. I dreamt I
went to heaven and that heaven didn't seem to be my
home and I broke my heart with weeping to come
back to earth and the angels were so angry they flung
me out in the middle of the heath on top of Wuthering
Heights and I woke up sobbing with joy.'
HEATHCLIFF (Laurence Olivier): 'What do they
know of heaven or hell, Cathy, who know nothing of
life? Oh, they're praying for you, Cathy. I'll pray one
prayer with them. I'll repeat till my tongue stiffens:
Catherine Earnshaw, may you not rest while I live on.
I killed you. Haunt me, then! Haunt your murderer! I
know that ghosts have wandered on the earth. Be
with me always – take any form – drive me mad! Only
do not leave me in this dark alone where I cannot find
you. I cannot live without my life! I cannot die
without my soul . . .'

'Sombre dramatic tragedy, productionally fine, but
with limited appeal.' – *Variety*

'Unquestionably one of the most distinguished
pictures of the year.' – *Frank S. Nugent, New York Times*

'A pattern of constant forward motion, with overtones
maintained throughout the rise of interest and
suspense.' – *Otis Ferguson*

'A strong and sombre film, poetically written as the
novel not always was, sinister and wild as it was
meant to be, far more compact dramatically than Miss
Brontë had made it.' – *Richard Mallett, Punch*

AA: Gregg Toland

AAN: best picture; script; William Wyler; Alfred
Newman; Laurence Olivier; Geraldine Fitzgerald; art
direction

'The power, the passion, the terror!'
Wuthering Heights *
GB   1970   105m   Movielab
AIP (John Pellatt)
V*, L

Somewhat rewritten and overkeen to find a 1970
mood and interpretation for what can only be a period
piece, this disappointing version marks a Z-film
company's first determined effort to enter the big-
time.

w Patrick Tilley   *d* Robert Fuest   ph *John Coquillon*
m Michel Legrand

Anna Calder-Marshall, Timothy Dalton, Harry
Andrews, Pamela Brown, Judy Cornwell, James
Cossins, Rosalie Crutchley, Julian Glover, Hugh
Griffith, Ian Ogilvy, Aubrey Woods

Wuthering Heights
US   1992   106m   colour
UIP/Paramount (Mary Selway)
S

Heathcliff, an orphaned gypsy, seeks revenge on those
who humiliated him despite his passionate love for
the girl with whom he was brought up.

Unimaginative version, hampered by Binoche's
unconvincing English and the lack of any spark
between her and Fiennes.

w Anne Devlin   novel Emily Brontë   *d* Peter
Kosminsky   ph Mike Southon   m Ryuichi
Sakamoto   pd Brian Morris   ed Tony Lawson

Juliette Binoche, Ralph Fiennes, Janet McTeer,
Sophie Ward, Simon Shepherd, Jeremy Northam,
Jason Riddington, Simon Ward, John Woodvine

'A by-the-numbers telling of the Emily Brontë classic
that's as cool as a Yorkshire moor.' – *Variety*

Wuya Yu Maque: see *Crows And Sparrows*

Wyoming
US   1940   88m   bw
MGM
GB title: *Bad Man of Wyoming*

A Missouri badman is persuaded to try an honest life.

Well-liked minor Western responsible for the first
teaming of its inelegant stars.

w Jack Jevne, Hugo Butler   *d* Richard Thorpe

Wallace Beery, Marjorie Main, Leo Carrillo, Ann
Rutherford, Joseph Calleia, Lee Bowman, Henry
Travers

Wyoming
US   1947   84m   bw
Republic
V*

Early settlers in the west meet trouble from
government squatters.

Minor Western for undemanding audiences.

w Lawrence Hazard and Gerald Geraghty   *d* Joe
Kane

Bill Elliott, Vera Ralston, John Carroll, George
'Gabby' Hayes, Albert Dekker

The Wyoming Kid: see *Cheyenne*

X

'If thine eye offends thee, pluck it out!'

X – The Man with X-Ray Eyes
US 1963 80m Pathecolor 'Spectarama'
AIP (Roger Corman)
V*
GB title: *The Man with the X-Ray Eyes*

A scientist gives himself X-ray vision and goes mad.

Interesting but rather unpleasant horror story with moments of cleverness but a general air of disappointment.

w Robert Dillon, Ray Russell   d Roger Corman
ph Floyd Crosby   m Les Baxter

Ray Milland, Diana Van Der Vlis, Harold J. Stone, John Hoyt, Don Rickles, John Dierkes

'When the dialogue suggests that Xavier is being driven insane by strange and satanic visions, what one actually sees is rather a comedown.' – *MFB*

'Concise, confident, and not an ounce overweight.' – *NFT, 1967*

X the Unknown *
GB 1956 78m bw
Exclusive/Hammer (Anthony Hinds)

A mysterious force feeds on radiation from a research station on a Scottish moor, and becomes a seeping mass.

Minor sci-fi horror with a monster-like liquid lino, rushed into release to cash in on *The Quatermass Experiment*.

w Jimmy Sangster   d Leslie Norman   ph Gerald Gibbs   m James Bernard   ed James Needs

Dean Jagger, Edward Chapman, Leo McKern, William Lucas, John Harvey, Peter Hammond, Michael Ripper, Anthony Newley

X, Y and Zee: see *Zee and Co*

Xala *
Senegal 1974 123m colour
Filmi Domireew/Société Nationale Cinématographique (Paulin Soumanou Vieyra)
GB title: *The Curse*

A leading businessman is humiliated when he finds that he is unable to consummate his marriage to his third wife.

Exuberant satire on corruption and a clash of cultures: tribal and urban, African and European, revolutionary and colonial, feminine and masculine, rich and poor.

wd Ousmane Sembène   novel Ousmane Sembène
ph Georges Caristan, Orlando R. Lopez, Seydina D. Gaye, Farba Seck   m Samba Diabare Samb
ed Florence Eymon

Thierno Lege, Miriam Niang, Seune Samb, Fatim Diagne, Younouss Seye, Moustapha Toure, Dieynaba Niang

Xanadu
US 1980 93m Technicolor
Universal/Lawrence Gordon
V, V*, L, S

The muse Terpsichore comes to Earth and becomes involved in the opening of a roller-derby disco.

Misguided attempt at a clean nostalgic musical, apparently conceived in a nightmare after somebody saw *Down to Earth* on the late show.

w Richard Christian Danus, Marc Reid Rubel
d Robert Greenwald   ph Victor J. Kemper
m Barry de Vorzon   songs Jeff Lynne, John Farrar
pd John W. Corso

Olivia Newton-John, Gene Kelly, Michael Beck

'Truly a stupendously bad film whose only salvage is the music.' – *Variety*

'A forties musical submerged by contemporary tat.' – *Guardian*

'Mushy and limp, so insubstantial it evaporates before our eyes.' – *Roger Ebert*

† Gene Kelly uses the same character name, Danny McGuire, as he did in *Cover Girl*.

Xiyan: see *The Wedding Banquet*

Xtro
GB 1982 86m colour
New Realm/Ashley/Amalgamated Film Enterprises (Mark Forstater)
V

An alien on the rampage rapes a woman who gives birth to a man – the clone of one who was abducted by a flying saucer three years earlier.

Weird but not wonderful low-budget horror that is a succession of odd moments rather than a conventional narrative.

w Iain Cassie, Robert Smith, Jo Ann Kaplan, Michel Parry, Harry Bromley Davenport   d Harry Bromley Davenport   ph John Metcalfe   m Harry Bromley Davenport   ad Andrew Mollo   ed Nicolas Gaster

Bernice Stegers, Philip Sayer, Danny Brainin, Simon Nash, Maryam D'Abo, David Cardy, Anna Wing, Peter Mandell

Yaaba **
Burkina Faso/France/Switzerland 1989 90m colour
Oasis/Les Films de l'Avenir/Thelma Film/Arcadia Films (Pierre
    Alain Meier, Freddy Denaës, Idrissa Ouedraogo)

A young boy befriends an old woman, ostracized by
the villagers and regarded as a witch.

Riveting account of African village life and a child's
growing to maturity, told with directness and
humour.

wd Idrissa Ouedraogo   ph Matthias Kalin
m Francis Bebey   ed Loredana Cristelli

Fatima Sanga, Noufou Ouedraogo, Barry Roukietou,
Adama Ouedraogo, Amade Toure, Sibidou
Ouedraogo, Adame Sidibe

The Yakuza
US 1975 112m Technicolor Panavision
Warner (Sydney Pollack, Michael Hamilburg)
V*, L

Japanese gangsters kidnap the daughter of a Los
Angeles shipping magnate.

Violent thriller roughly exploiting an ancient
Japanese genre.

w Paul Schrader, Robert Towne   d Sydney Pollack
ph Okazaki Kozo, Duke Callaghan   m Dave Grusin

Robert Mitchum, Takakura Ken, Brian Keith, Kishi
Keilo, Okada Eiji

'No more than a curious footnote to the western
exploitation of oriental action movies.' – Tony Rayns

Yam Daabo: see *The Choice*

Yangtse Incident *
GB 1957 113m bw
British Lion/Wilcox/Neagle (Herbert Wilcox)
US title: *Battle Hell*; aka: *Escape of the Amethyst*

In 1949 a British frigate is shelled and held captive by
communist shore batteries in the Yangtse.

Stalwart but not very exciting British war heroics.

w Eric Ambler   book Franklin Gollings   d Michael
Anderson   ph Gordon Dines   m Leighton Lucas

Richard Todd, William Hartnell, Akim Tamiroff,
Donald Houston, Keye Luke, Sophie Stewart, Robert
Urquhart, James Kenney, Barry Foster

A Yank at Eton
US 1942 88m bw
MGM (John Considine Jnr)

A rich, wild American boy is sent to Eton to cool
down.

Tame, tasteless imitation of *A Yank at Oxford* with
younger participants.

w George Oppenheimer, Lionel Houser, Thomas
Phipps   d Norman Taurog   ph Karl Freund,
Charles Lawton   m Bronislau Kaper

Mickey Rooney, Freddie Bartholomew, Ian Hunter,
Edmund Gwenn, Alan Mowbray, Tina Thayer, Marta
Linden, Alan Napier, Terry Kilburn

A Yank at Oxford **
GB 1937 105m bw
MGM (Michael Balcon)

A cocky young American student comes to Oxford
and meets all kinds of trouble.

A huge pre-war success which now seems naïve, this
was the first big Anglo-American production from a
team which went on to make *The Citadel* and *Goodbye
Mr Chips* before war stymied them.

w Malcolm Stuart Boylan, Walter Ferris, George
Oppenheimer, Leon Gordon, Roland Pertwee, John
Monk Saunders, Sidney Gilliat, Michael Hogan
d Jack Conway   ph Harold Rosson   m Edward
Ward

Robert Taylor, Vivien Leigh, Maureen O'Sullivan,
Lionel Barrymore, Robert Coote, Edmund Gwenn,
C. V. France, Griffith Jones, Morton Selten

'A draw picture for Taylor at a critical moment in his
meteoric bid for fame.' – *Variety*

† A total of 31 writers are alleged to have worked
without credit.

A Yank in Dutch: see *The Wife Takes a Flyer*

A Yank in Ermine
GB 1955 85m colour
Monarch

An American finds that he is really an English earl.

Thin comedy, thinly developed.

w John Paddy Carstairs   novel *Solid Said the Earl* by
John Paddy Carstairs   d Gordon Parry

Peter Thompson, Noelle Middleton, Harold Lloyd Jnr,
Diana Decker, Jon Pertwee, Reginald Beckwith,
Edward Chapman, Richard Wattis

A Yank in London: see *I Live in Grosvenor Square*

A Yank in the RAF *
US 1941 98m bw
TCF (Lou Edelman)
V*

An American chorine stranded in London falls for the
titular gentleman.

Silly but entertaining wartime flagwaver.

w Karl Tunberg, Darrell Ware   story Melville
Crossman (Zanuck)   d Henry King   ph Leon
Shamroy   m Alfred Newman

Tyrone Power, Betty Grable, John Sutton, Reginald
Gardiner, Donald Stuart, Morton Lowry, Richard
Fraser, Bruce Lester

A Yank on the Burma Road
US 1941 66m bw
MGM (Samuel Marx)
GB title: *China Caravan*

A tough truck driver in the Far East abandons profit
for heroism when he hears of Pearl Harbor.

Crass action flagwaver.

w George Kahn, Hugo Butler, David Lang   d George
B. Seitz   ph Lester White

Barry Nelson, Laraine Day, Stuart Crawford, Keye
Luke, Sen Yung

'Glib humbug, playing tiddleywinks with high
stakes.' – *Theodore Strauss*

Yankee Doodle Dandy ***
US 1942 126m bw
Warner (Hal B. Wallis, William Cagney)
V, V*, L, S

The life story of dancing vaudevillian George M.
Cohan.

Outstanding showbiz biopic, with unassuming but
effective production, deft patriotic backdrops and a
marvellous, strutting, magnetic star performance.

w Robert Buckner, Edmund Joseph   d Michael Curtiz
ph James Wong Howe   md Heinz Roemheld, Ray
Heindorf   songs George M. Cohan   m Heinz
Roemheld   ed George Amy

James Cagney, Joan Leslie, *Walter Huston*, Rosemary de
Camp, Richard Whorf, George Tobias, Jeanne
Cagney, Irene Manning, S. Z. Sakall, George Barbier,
Frances Langford, Walter Catlett, Eddie Foy Jnr

COHAN (James Cagney) at end of vaudeville act:
'My mother thanks you. My father thanks you. My
sister thanks you. And I thank you.'
COHAN: 'Where else in the world could a plain guy
like me sit down and talk things over with the head
man?'
ROOSEVELT (Captain Jack Young): 'Well now,
you know, Mr Cohan, that's as good a description of
America as I've ever heard.'

'Possibly the most genial screen biography ever
made.' – *Time*

AA: music direction; James Cagney

AAN: best picture; original story (Robert Buckner);
Michael Curtiz; Walter Huston; George Amy

A Yankee in King Arthur's Court: see *A
Connecticut Yankee in King Arthur's Court*

Yankee Pasha
US 1954 84m Technicolor
Universal-International (Howard Christie)

An American adventurer in 19th-century Marseilles
saves his girlfriend from pirates.

Studio-bound hokum for double-featuring.

w Joseph Hoffman   novel Edison Marshall
d Joseph Pevney

Jeff Chandler, Rhonda Fleming, Mamie Van Doren,
Lee J. Cobb, Bart Roberts, Hal March

Yanks **
GB 1979 141m Technicolor
United Artists/CIP/Joe Janni-Lester Persky
V, V*, L

Romances of American GIs billeted on a Lancashire
town during World War II.

Not an entirely promising subject, this overlong piece
maintains its interest by sheer skill of dramaturgy and
cinematic narrative.

w Colin Welland, Walter Bernstein   d John
Schlesinger   ph Dick Bush   m Richard Rodney
Bennett   pd Brian Morris

Vanessa Redgrave, Richard Gere, William Devane,
Lisa Eichhorn, Rachel Roberts, Chick Vennera

Yanzhi Kou: see *Rouge*

The Year My Voice Broke *
Australia 1987 105m colour
Palace/Kennedy Miller Productions (Terry Hayes, Doug
    Mitchell, George Miller)
V, V*, L

A 15-year-old boy, who is having a troubled

relationship with an orphaned girl, discovers the shameful secret behind a haunted house in his small town.

An engaging account of growing up that avoids nostalgia and easy sentiment. *wd* John Duigan *ph* Geoff Burton *pd* Roger Ford *ed* Neil Thumpston

Noah Taylor, Loene Carmen, Ben Mendelsohn, Graeme Blundell, Lynette Curran, Malcolm Robertson, Judi Farr

'Risking it was all part of the job!'
The Year of Living Dangerously *
Australia 1982 114m Eastmancolor
MGM/McElroy and McElroy/Peter Weir
V, V*, L, S

A young Australian journalist takes his first international assignment in Indonesia.

Freshly observed but ultimately pointless political parable which undoubtedly means more to its maker than it will to audiences.

w David Williamson, Peter Weir, C. J. Koch *novel* C. J. Koch *d* Peter Weir *ph* Russell Boyd *m* Maurice Jarre *ed* Bill Anderson

Mel Gibson, Sigourney Weaver, Linda Hunt, Michael Murphy, Bill Kerr, Noel Ferrier

'I was held by it and had had a very good time, though I didn't believe any of it. And I was held despite my aversion to its gusts of wind about destiny, truth versus appearance and so on.' – *Pauline Kael*

AA: Linda Hunt

Year of the Comet
US 1992 89m colour
Columbia/Castle Rock/New Line (Peter Yates, Nigel Wooll)
V, V*, L

Various people scramble to obtain a 150-year-old bottle of wine, found in a Scottish castle.

A disappointing romantic comedy, given the talents involved, which fails to sparkle.

w William Goldman *d* Peter Yates *ph* Roger Pratt *m* Hummie Mann *pd* Anthony Pratt *ed* Ray Lovejoy

Penelope Ann Miller, Tim Daly, Louis Jourdan, Art Malik, Ian Richardson, Ian McNiece, Timothy Bentinck, Julia McCarthy, Jacques Mathou

'This wine-soaked comedy-adventure never really ferments, in part due to a lack of chemistry between its romantic leads.' – *Variety*

'It's Chinatown – and it's about to explode!'
The Year of the Dragon
US 1985 136m Technicolor Panavision
MGM-UA/Dino de Laurentiis
V, V*, L, S

A tough cop clears Chinatown of a group of murderous youth gangs.

Extremely violent and convoluted thriller with an unpleasant hero.

w Oliver Stone, Michael Cimino *novel* Robert Daley *d* Michael Cimino *ph* Alex Thomson *m* David Mansfield *pd* Wolf Kroeger *ed* Noelle Boisson

Mickey Rourke, John Lone, Ariane, Leonard Termo, Ray Barry

'Never as important as the director thinks it is . . . nothing is clearly resolved beyond the last dead body.' – *Variety*

'In A City Bathed In Blood . . . Who Can You Trust?'
Year of the Gun
US 1991 111m DeLuxe
First Independent/J & M Entertainment/Initial (Edward R. Pressman)
V, V*, L

In the 1970s an American journalist working in Rome becomes a target for the terrorist Red Brigades.

Dull political thriller with a bland and uninteresting hero.

w David Ambrose *novel* Michael Mewshaw *d* John Frankenheimer *ph* Blasco Giurato *m* Bill Conti *pd* Aurelio Crugnola *ed* Lee Percy

Andrew McCarthy, Valeria Golino, Sharon Stone, John Pankow, George Murcell, Mattia Sbragia, Roberto Posse

'How can a thriller so stacked with gunfire, chases, twists and red herrings send one to sleep?' – *Geoff Brown, The Times*

'They tamed a tropic wilderness!'
The Yearling **
US 1946 134m Technicolor
MGM (Sidney Franklin)
V*, L

The son of an old-time country farmer is attached to a stray deer.

Excellent family film for four-handkerchief patrons.

w Paul Osborn *novel* Marjorie Kinnan Rawlings *d* Clarence Brown *ph* Charles Rosher, Leonard Smith *m* Herbert Stothart *ad* Cedric Gibbons, Paul Groesse *ed* Harold Kress

Gregory Peck, Jane Wyman, Claude Jarman Jnr, Chill Wills, Clem Bevans, Margaret Wycherly, Henry Travers, Forrest Tucker

'An unspoilt and simple story of human dignity, patience, struggle, and love, and its appeal should be universal.' – *Fred Majdalany, Daily Mail*

AA: Claude Jarman Jnr (Special Award as outstanding child actor); Charles Rosher, Leonard Smith (and Arthur Arling); art direction

AAN: best picture; Clarence Brown; Gregory Peck; Jane Wyman; editing

The Years Between
GB 1946 100m bw
GFD/Sydney Box

An MP returns after being presumed dead in the war and finds his wife has been elected in his place.

Stilted variation on the *Enoch Arden* theme; plot and performances alike unpersuasive.

w Muriel and Sydney Box *play* Daphne du Maurier *d* Compton Bennett *ph* Reg Wyer

Michael Redgrave, Valerie Hobson, Flora Robson, Felix Aylmer, James McKechnie, Dulcie Gray, Edward Rigby

Years without Days: see *Castle on the Hudson*

Yeelen *
Mali 1987 105m colour
Artificial Eye/Les Films Cissé/Souleymane Cissé
US title: *Brightness*

A son struggles to destroy his father, a black magician.

Engrossing and lively mythic tale that holds the attention even when the significance of certain rituals is hard to grasp.

wd Souleymane Cissé *ph* Jean-Noel Ferragut, Jean-Michel Humeau *m* Michel Portal, Salif Keita *ad* Kossa Mody Keita *ed* Dounamba Coulibaly, Andree Davanture, Marie-Catherine Mique

Issiaka Kane, Niamanto Sanogo, Aoua Sangare, Balla Moussa Keita, Soumba Traore, Ismaila Sarr, Youssouf Cissé, Koke Sangare

The Yellow Balloon
GB 1952 80m bw
ABP (Victor Skutezky)

A small boy who thinks he has killed his friend is terrorized by a murderer.

Tense but not especially rewarding suspenser, clearly borrowed from *The Window*.

w Anne Burnaby, J. Lee-Thompson *d* J. Lee-Thompson *ph* Gilbert Taylor *m* Philip Green

Kenneth More, William Sylvester, Kathleen Ryan, Andrew Ray, Bernard Lee, Veronica Hurst

The Yellow Cab Man
US 1950 84m bw
MGM (Richard Goldstone)

A taxi-driving inventor is pursued by crooks after his secret formula.

Moderate star comedy.

w Devery Freeman, Albert Beich *d* Jack Donohue *ph* Harry Stradling *m* Scott Bradley

Red Skelton, Gloria de Haven, Walter Slezak, Edward Arnold, James Gleason, Paul Harvey, Jay C. Flippen

Yellow Canary *
GB 1943 98m bw
RKO/Imperator (Herbert Wilcox)

A socialite suspected of being a Nazi sympathizer is really a British spy.

Mild wartime melodrama chiefly notable for allotting an apparently unsympathetic part to the beloved Miss Neagle.

w De Witt Bodeen, Miles Malleson *story* Pamela Bower *d* Herbert Wilcox *ph* Max Greene

Anna Neagle, Richard Greene, Nova Pilbeam, Lucie Mannheim, Cyril Fletcher, Albert Lieven, Margaret Rutherford, Marjorie Fielding

Yellow Canary
US 1963 93m bw Cinemascope
TCF/Cooga Mooga (Maury Dexter)

The baby son of a singing idol is kidnapped.

Rather dreary suspenser with too much dialogue.

w Rod Serling *novel* Evil Come, Evil Go by Whit Masterson *d* Buzz Kulik *ph* Floyd Crosby *m* Kenyon Hopkins

Pat Boone, Barbara Eden, Steve Forrest, Jack Klugman, Jesse White, John Banner, Jeff Corey

Yellow Dog
GB 1973 101m Eastmancolor
Scotia-Barber/Akari (Terence Donovan)

A Japanese agent in London keeps watch on a mysterious scientist.

Incoherent spy thriller with a few hybrid oddities.

w Shinobu Hashimoto *d* Terence Donovan *ph* David Watkin *m* Ron Grainer

Jiro Tamiya, Robert Hardy, Carolyn Seymour, Joseph O'Conor

Yellow Earth **
China 1984 89m colour
Guangxi Film Studio
Huang Tudi

In 1939, a communist soldier collecting folk songs tries to persuade a peasant family to abandon their traditional ways.

Lyrically photographed against a vast and barren landscape, it celebrates folk traditions in a modern and colourful way.

w Zhang Ziliang *novel* Echo in the Deep Valley by Ke Lan *d* Chen Kaige *ph* Zhang Yimou *m* Zhao Jiping *ad* He Qun *ed* Wan Liu, Pei Xiaonan

Xue Bai, Wang Xueqi, Tan Tuo, Liu Qiang

Yellow Jack *
US 1938 83m bw
MGM (Jack Cummings)

In 1899 Cuba a marine offers himself as a guinea pig to combat yellow fever.

Solid, unsurprising, period medical melodrama with conventional romantic sidelights.

w Edward Chodorov   *play* Sidney Howard, Paul de Kruif   *d* George B. Seitz   *ph* Lester White   *m* William Axt

Robert Montgomery, Virginia Bruce, Lewis Stone, Andy Devine, Henry Hull, Charles Coburn, Buddy Ebsen, Henry O'Neill, Janet Beecher

'Okay for single billing, but no wow.' – *Variety*

The Yellow Passport: see *The Yellow Ticket*

The Yellow Rolls Royce *
GB 1964 122m Metrocolor Panavision
MGM (Anatole de Grunwald)
V*, L

Three stories about the owners of an expensive car: an aristocrat, a gangster, and a wandering millionairess.

Lukewarm all-star concoction lacking either good stories or a connecting thread.

w Terence Rattigan   *d* Anthony Asquith   *ph* Jack Hildyard   *m* Riz Ortolani   *pd* Vincent Korda

Rex Harrison, Jeanne Moreau, Edmund Purdom, Moira Lister, Roland Culver, Shirley Maclaine, George C. Scott, Alain Delon, Art Carney, Ingrid Bergman, Omar Sharif, Joyce Grenfell

'Tame, bloodless, smothered in elegance and the worst kind of discreetly daring good taste.' – *Peter John Dyer*

Yellow Sands
GB 1938 68m bw
ABPC

A Cornish family sets to bickering over a will.

Reliable comedy from a popular stage original.

w Michael Barringer, Rodney Ackland   *play* Eden and Adelaide Phillpotts   *d* Herbert Brenon

Marie Tempest, Wilfrid Lawson, Belle Chrystall, Robert Newton, Patrick Barr, Edward Rigby

'It was a moment for being a woman . . . for only a woman's revenge could keep her alive – now!'
Yellow Sky **
US 1948 98m bw
TCF (Lamar Trotti)

Outlaws on the run take over a desert ghost town.

Gleaming, stylish Western melodrama which benefits from its unusual and confined setting.

w Lamar Trotti   *story* W. R. Burnett   *d* William Wellman   *ph* Joe MacDonald   *m* Alfred Newman

Gregory Peck, Anne Baxter, Richard Widmark, Robert Arthur, John Russell, Henry Morgan, James Barton

Yellow Submarine *
GB 1968 87m DeLuxe
King Features/Apple (Al Brodax)
V*, L

The happy kingdom of Pepperland is attacked by the Blue Meanies.

Way-out cartoon fantasia influenced by Beatlemania and the swinging sixties; hard to watch for non-addicts.

w Lee Minoff, Al Brodax, Jack Mendelsohn, Erich Segal   *d* George Duning   *m* John Lennon, Paul McCartney

'The film is fun, and an animated feature that holds the interest of adults of all ages (I don't think there are children of any age left) is not to be sneezed at.' – *John Simon*

The Yellow Ticket *
US 1931 76m bw
Fox
GB title: *The Yellow Passport*

In Russia during the pogroms, a Jewish girl pretends

to be a prostitute in order to get a travel permit to see her dying father.

Curious anti-Russian melodrama deriving its plot from *La Tosca*.

w Jules Furthman, Guy Bolton,   *play* Michael Morton   *d* Raoul Walsh   *ph* James Wong Howe

Elissa Landi, Laurence Olivier, Lionel Barrymore, Walter Byron, Sarah Padden, Mischa Auer, Boris Karloff

'A picture filled with swashbucklers, privateers, public floggings, saucy tarts, looney lords, beggars, queens, and even a very jolly Roger!'
Yellowbeard
US 1983 96m DeLuxe
Orion/Seagoat (Carter de Haven Jnr)
V, V*, L

Farcical adventures of a 17th-century pirate captain.

A spoofy saga in deliberately bad taste, this ragbag of old gags and new unpleasantness sank rapidly to the bottom of the box-office barrel.

w Graham Chapman, Peter Cook, Bernard McKenna   *d* Mel Damski   *ph* Gerry Fisher   *m* John Morris   *pd* Joseph R. Jennings

Graham Chapman, Peter Boyle, Cheech and Chong, Peter Cook, Marty Feldman, Michael Hordern, Eric Idle, Madeline Kahn, James Mason, John Cleese, Kenneth Mars, Spike Milligan, Susannah York, Beryl Reid, Ferdy Mayne, Peter Bull

'The atrocious script and haphazard direction elicit generally embarrassing performances from all concerned.' – *Kim Newman, MFB*

Yellowstone Kelly
US 1959 91m Technicolor
Warner

A fur trapper prevents war between Indians and whites.

Standard Western with routine excitements and a cast of TV faces.

w Burt Kennedy   *d* Gordon Douglas   *ph* Carl Guthrie   *m* Howard Jackson

Clint Walker, Edd Byrnes, John Russell, Ray Danton, Claude Akins

Yentl *
GB 1983 133m Technicolor
MGM-UA/Barwood/Ladbroke (Barbra Streisand, Rusty Lemorande)
V, V*, L

Many years ago in Poland, a Jewish girl tries to get on in the world by dressing as a boy.

A personal and some would say megalomaniac extravagance by its producer-director-writer-star, who before embarking should have learned the value of brevity. Nevertheless there is about the enterprise a certain heavy style which may appeal strongly to Jews while precluding the interest and understanding of others.

w Jack Rosenthal, Barbra Streisand   *story* Isaac Bashevis Singer   *d* Barbra Streisand   *ph* David Watkin   *m* Michel Legrand   *pd* Roy Walker   *ed* Terry Rawlings

Barbra Streisand, Mandy Patinkin, Amy Irving, Nehemiah Persoff, Steven Hill, David de Keyser, Bernard Spear

AA: music

AAN: Amy Irving; songs 'Papa, Can You Hear Me?', 'The Way He Makes Me Feel' (*m* Michel Legrand, *ly* Alan Bergman, Marilyn Bergman); art director

'A glorious uproarious love story!'
Yes, Giorgio *
US 1982 110m Metrocolor
MGM-UA/Peter Fetterman
V, V*, L

A top international tenor falls for the lady throat specialist who cures his ailment.

Nostalgic musical romance, fine in its way but out of key with the modern film business. A treat for television viewers.

w Norman Steinberg   *novel* Anne Piper   *d* Franklin J. Schaffner   *ph* Fred J. Koenekamp   *m* John Williams   *pd* William D. Creber

Luciano Pavarotti, Kathryn Harrold, Eddie Albert, Paola Borboni

† The film allegedly cost 19 million and took only one.

AAN: original song 'If We Were In Love' (*m* John Williams, *ly* Alan and Marilyn Bergman)

Yes, Madam
GB 1938 77m bw
ABPC

Heirs to a fortune are obliged to act as servants for three months.

Agreeable minor comedy.

w Clifford Grey, Bert Lee and William Freshman   *novel* K. R. G. Browne   *d* Norman Lee

Bobby Howes, Diana Churchill, Billy Milton, Fred Emney, Bertha Belmore, Wylie Watson, Vera Pearce

† Previously filmed in 1933 with Frank Pettingell and Kay Hammond.

Yes Mr Brown *
GB 1933 90m bw
British and Dominions/Herbert Wilcox

A businessman's secretary pretends to be his wife after the latter has walked out on him.

One of its star's most fondly remembered musical farces, a thin thing but his own.

w Douglas Furber   *play* *Business with America* by Paul Frank, Ludwig Hershfield   *d* Herbert Wilcox, Jack Buchanan

Jack Buchanan, Elsie Randolph, Hartley Power, Clifford Heatherley, Vera Pearce

Yes My Darling Daughter
US 1939 86m bw
Warner (Ben Glazer)

Lovers elope and are pursued by her family.

Mildly amusing domestic comedy.

w Casey Robinson   *play* Mark Reed   *d* William Keighley   *ph* Charles Rosher

Priscilla Lane, Jeffrey Lynn, Roland Young, Fay Bainter, May Robson, Genevieve Tobin, Ian Hunter

Yes Sir, That's My Baby
US 1949 82m Technicolor
U-I (Leonard Goldstein)

Ex-service undergraduates and their wives have trouble settling down to studies.

Witless and exhausting college comedy.

w Oscar Brodney   *d* George Sherman   *ph* Irving Glassberg   *m* Walter Scharf

Donald O'Connor, Gloria de Haven, Charles Coburn, Barbara Brown, Joshua Shelley

Yesterday Girl: see *Abschied von Gestern*

Yesterday, Today and Tomorrow
Italy/France 1963 119m Techniscope
CCC/Concordia/Joseph E. Levine (Carlo Ponti)
V, V*

Three stories of naughty ladies.

A relentlessly boring compendium with everybody shouting at once.

w Eduardo de Filippo, Cesare Zavattini, others
d Vittorio de Sica *ph* Giuseppe Rotunno
m Armando Trovajoli

Marcello Mastroianni, Sophia Loren

'A sad intimation of the sort of rainy day the Italian cinema is currently having.' – *MFB*

'One begins to see, amid the sunsets and sunrises and Roman rooftops, the sheer venality of the creation, the cynical circus thrust upon us on the assumption that breasts and bodies and fornication are all that these leading lights of the Italian cinema need provide to keep us from baying at the moon.' – *Judith Crist*

AA: best foreign film

Yesterday's Enemy

GB 1959 95m bw Megascope
Columbia/Hammer (T. S. Lyndon-Haynes)

In 1942 Burma, a British unit violently takes over a village and finds an unsolved puzzle.

Would-be ironic war suspenser, economically made but quite effective in putting its message across.

w Peter R. Newman *TV play* Peter R. Newman
d Val Guest *ph* Arthur Grant *m* none
ad Bernard Robinson *ed* James Needs, Alfred Cox

Stanley Baker, Guy Rolfe, Leo McKern, Philip Ahn, Gordon Jackson, David Oxley, Richard Pasco, Russell Waters, Bryan Forbes, David Lodge, Percy Herbert

Yesterday's Hero

GB 1979 95m colour
Columbia/CinemaSeven (Elliott Kastner)

A successful footballer goes to the bad but redeems himself.

Totally uninteresting sporting version of the Road to Ruin.

w Jackie Collins *d* Neil Leifer *ph* Brian West
md Stanley Myers *pd* Keith Wilson

Ian McShane, Suzanne Somers, Adam Faith, Paul Nicholas, Sam Kydd

Les Yeux sans Visage: see *Eyes without a Face*

Yield to the Night *

GB 1956 99m bw
ABP (Kenneth Harper)
US title: *Blonde Sinner*

A condemned murderess relives the events which led to her arrest.

Gloomy prison melodrama vaguely based on the Ruth Ellis case and making an emotional plea against capital punishment.

w John Cresswell, Joan Henry *novel* Joan Henry
d J. Lee-Thompson *ph* Gilbert Taylor *m* Ray Martin

Diana Dors, Yvonne Mitchell, Michael Craig, Marie Ney, Athene Seyler, Geoffrey Keen

Yo, la peor de todas: see *I, The Worst of All*

Yoidore Tenshi: see *Drunken Angel*

Yojimbo ****

Japan 1961 110m bw
Toho
V, V*, L

A wandering samurai tricks two rival gangs of cutthroats into destroying one other.

Masterful, beautifully composed, witty movie that inspired the 'spaghetti Western' cycle when it was remade by Sergio Leone as *A Fistful Of Dollars*.

w Ryuzo Kikushima, Akira Kurosawa *d* Akira Kurosawa *ph* Kazuo Miyagawa *m* Masuru Sato

Toshiro Mifune, Eijiro Tono, Kamatari Fujiwara, Takashi Shimura, Seizaburo Kawazu, Isuzu Yamada, Hiroshi Tachikawa

'One of the rare Japanese movies that is both great and funny to American audiences.' – *New Yorker*

Yokel Boy

US 1942 69m bw
Republic (Robert North)
GB title: *Hitting the Headlines*

A film buff from the sticks comes to Hollywood and gets involved with production.

Spoofy comedy which doesn't come off despite the talent around.

w Isabel Dawn *story* Russel Rouse (the legit musical by Lew Brown was thrown away, together with the songs) *d* Joseph Santley

Eddie Foy Jnr, Joan Davis, Albert Dekker, Alan Mowbray, Roscoe Karns, Mikhail Rasumny, Marc Lawrence, Tom Dugan

Yol **

Switzerland 1982 114m Fujicolor
Cactus/Maran/Antenne 2/Swiss Television/Güney (Edi Hubschmid, K. L. Puldi)
V, V*

Five convicts are released on a week's leave, and their various circumstances lead them to tragedy.

Rewarding if heavy-going Turkish saga which exhausts the spectator almost as much as its long-suffering characters. It feels and looks like an epic.

w Yilmaz Güney *d* Serif Gören *ph* Erdogan Engin *m* Sebastian Argol *ed* Yilmaz Güney, Elisabeth Waelchli

Tarik Akan, Halil Ergün, Necmettin Cobanoglu, Serif Sezer

Yolanda and the Thief *

US 1945 108m Technicolor
MGM (Arthur Freed)
V*, L

A con man poses as the guardian angel of a naïve heiress.

Laboured musical fantasy with arty Mexican settings; not a success in any way, but with a few effective moments.

w Irving Brecher *story* Ludwig Bemelmans, Jacques Théry *d* Vincente Minnelli *ph* Charles Rosher
m Lennie Hayton *songs* Harry Warren, Arthur Freed

Fred Astaire, Lucille Bremer, Frank Morgan, Leon Ames, Mildred Natwick

'The most extreme of the big musical mistakes.' – *New Yorker, 1979*

'It perhaps needs to be seen by anyone who wants to know what killed the MGM musicals.' – *New Yorker*

'Every time she says I love you, she breaks the law!'

You and Me

US 1938 90m bw
Paramount (Fritz Lang)

A department store owner employs ex-convicts, one of whom has not quite reformed.

Curious comedy drama which never has a hope of coming off.

w Virginia Van Upp *story* Norman Krasna *d* Fritz Lang *ph* Charles Lang Jnr *m* Kurt Weill

Sylvia Sidney, George Raft, Harry Carey, Barton MacLane, Warren Hymer, Roscoe Karns, George E. Stone, Adrian Morris

'Lang's individual touch is visible everywhere . . . but for the ordinary George Raft fan it will not only be unappreciated but will be actually confusing.' – *National Board of Review*

'Given proper control over story and scenario, Lang couldn't have made so bad a film as *You and Me*; the whole picture is like an elegant and expensive gesture of despair.' – *Graham Greene*

You Belong to Me

US 1934 67m bw
Paramount (Louis D. Lighton)

An alcoholic vaudeville comic plays father to an orphan.

Muddled backstage melodrama which would be enjoyed by fans of the star.

w Walter DeLeon, Elizabeth Alexander *d* Alfred Werker

Lee Tracy, Helen Mack, Helen Morgan, Lynne Overman, David Holt

'Should gain attention in the nabe spots.' – *Variety*

You Belong to Me *

US 1941 94m bw
Columbia (Wesley Ruggles)
GB title: *Good Morning, Doctor*

A playboy becomes jealous of the male patients of his doctor wife.

Mild comedy for two stars who are well capable of keeping it afloat.

w Claude Binyon, Dalton Trumbo *d* Wesley Ruggles *ph* Joseph Walker *m* Frederick Hollander

Barbara Stanwyck, Henry Fonda, Edgar Buchanan, Roger Clark, Ruth Donnelly, Melville Cooper, Maude Eburne

You Belong to My Heart: see *Mr Imperium*

You Came Along

US 1945 103m bw
Paramount (Hal B. Wallis)

A girl from the treasury department falls in love with one of three GIs she takes on a war bond tour, but he dies of leukaemia.

Weird mishmash of farce and sentimentality; quite watchable in its way, but an odd showcase for a new female star.

w Robert Smith, Ayn Rand *d* John Farrow
ph Daniel L. Fapp *m* Victor Young

Lizabeth Scott, Robert Cummings, Don Defore, Charles Drake, Julie Bishop, Kim Hunter, Rhys Williams, Franklin Pangborn, Minor Watson

You Can't Buy Everything *

US 1934 72m bw
MGM

A woman obsessed by her mounting bank balance almost ruins the lives of her family.

Unusual and rather well-acted period melodrama with a pleasing cast.

w Dudley Nichols, Lamar Trotti *d* Charles F. Reisner

May Robson, Jean Parker, Lewis Stone, Mary Forbes, Reginald Mason

You Can't Cheat an Honest Man *

US 1939 79m bw
Universal (Lester Cowan)

Trials and tribulations of a circus owner.

Flat, desultory and generally disappointing comedy vehicle for an irresistible star combination.

w George Marion Jnr, Richard Mack, Everett Freeman *story* Charles Bogle (W. C. Fields)
d George Marshall *ph* Milton Krasner *m* Charles Previn

W. C. Fields, Edgar Bergen (with Charlie McCarthy and Mortimer Snerd), Constance Moore, Mary Forbes, Thurston Hall, Charles Coleman, Edward Brophy

'Fairly amusing but lacks sustained overall interest.' – *Variety*

You Can't Do That to Me: see *Maisie (Maisie Goes to Reno)*

You Can't Escape Forever
US   1942   77m   bw
Warner

A girl reporter demoted to the lovelorn column exposes a racket boss.

Untidy remake of *Hi Nellie;* tolerable on a double bill, but not for close criticism.

w Fred Niblo Jnr and Hector Chevigny   d Jo Graham

George Brent, Brenda Marshall, Gene Lockhart, Roscoe Karns, Eduardo Ciannelli, Paul Harvey

You Can't Get Away with Murder
US   1939   78m   bw
Warner (Sam Bischoff)

A juvenile delinquent teams up with a gangster and takes a prison rap for him.

Standard post-Dead End crime melodrama with no surprises.

w Robert Buckner, Don Ryan, Kenneth Gamet   play *Chalked Out* by Lewis Lawes, Jonathan Finn   d Lewis Seiler   ph Sol Polito   m Heinz Roemheld

Humphrey Bogart, Billy Halop, Gale Page, John Litel, Henry Travers, Harvey Stephens, Harold Huber

'Strictly a filler for the duals . . . ponderous and slow moving.' – *Variety*

You Can't Have Everything *
US   1937   99m   bw
TCF (Lawrence Schwab)
V*

A failed play is turned into a musical.

Lively backstage comedy with good moments.

w Harry Tugend, Jack Yellen, Karl Tunberg   d Norman Taurog   ph Lucien Andriot   md David Buttolph   songs Mack Gordon, Harry Revel

Alice Faye, *the Ritz Brothers,* Don Ameche, Charles Winninger, Gypsy Rose Lee, Tony Martin, Arthur Treacher, Louis Prima, Tip Tap and Toe, Wally Vernon

'An expert piecing together of story, melody, blackouts, night club specialties and production numbers.' – *Variety*

You Can't Have Everything
US   1970   90m   Eastmancolor
Koala (Lou Brandt)
aka: *Cactus in the Snow*

An 18-year-old virgin GI is about to leave for Vietnam when he picks up a girl and spends a happy but platonic twenty-four hours.

An agreeably understated little love story for those absorbed by teenage sex problems.

wd Martin Zweibach   ph David M. Walsh   m Joe Parnello

Richard Thomas, Mary Layne, Lucille Benson, Oscar Beregi

You Can't Ration Love
US   1944   78m   bw
Michel Kraike/Paramount

It's wartime at college, and dates are rationed.

Silly idea for a forgettable musical.

w Val Burton, Hal Fimberg, Muriel Roy Bolton   d Lester Fuller

Betty Jane Rhodes, Johnnie Johnston, Bill Edwards, Marjorie Weaver, Marie Wilson, Mabel Paige

You Can't Run Away from It
US   1956   96m   Technicolor   Cinemascope
Columbia (Dick Powell)

An heiress runs away from a marriage arranged by her father, and falls for an amiable reporter.

Flat remake of *It Happened One Night,* with practically no comic sense or talent.

w Claude Binyon, Robert Riskin   d Dick Powell   ph Charles Lawton Jnr   md Morris Stoloff   m George Duning

June Allyson, Jack Lemmon, Charles Bickford, Jim Backus, Stubby Kaye, Paul Gilbert, Allyn Joslyn

You Can't Sleep Here: see *I Was a Male War Bride*

You Can't Take It with You **
US   1938   127m   bw
Columbia (Frank Capra)
V*, L

The daughter of a highly eccentric New York family falls for a rich man's son.

A hilarious, warm and witty play is largely changed into a tirade against big business, but the Capra expertise is here in good measure and the stars all pull their weight.

w Robert Riskin   play George S. Kaufman, Moss Hart   d Frank Capra   ph Joseph Walker   m Dimitri Tiomkin   ed Gene Havlik

Jean Arthur, Lionel Barrymore, James Stewart, Edward Arnold, Spring Byington, Mischa Auer, Ann Miller, Samuel S. Hinds, Donald Meek, H. B. Warner, Halliwell Hobbes, Mary Forbes, Dub Taylor, Lillian Yarbo, Eddie Anderson, *Harry Davenport*

GRANDPA VANDERHOF (Lionel Barrymore) offering a prayer: 'Well, sir, here we are again. We had a little trouble, but that's not your fault. You spread the milk of human kindness, and if some of it gets curdled, that's our look-out. Anyway, things have turned out fine. Alice is going to marry Tony. The Kirbys are going to live with us for a while. And everybody on the block is happy. We've all got our health – and as far as anything else is concerned, we'll leave it up to you. Thank you.'

'The comedy is wholly American, wholesome, homespun, human, appealing, and touching in turn.' – *Variety*

'Shangri-La in a frame house.' – *Otis Ferguson*

AA: best picture; Frank Capra

AAN: Robert Riskin; Joseph Walker; Spring Byington; Gene Havlik

You Can't Take Money: see *Internes Can't Take Money*

'It's bedlam in Islam!'
You Can't Win 'em All
GB   1970   99m   Technicolor   Panavision
Columbia/SRO (Gene Corman)

In 1922, two rival American mercenaries have adventures in the Mediterranean.

Hectic, overplotted comedy actioner.

w Leo V. Gordon   d Peter Collinson   ph Ken Higgins   m Bert Kaempfert

Tony Curtis, Charles Bronson, Michèle Mercier, Grégoire Aslan, Patrick Magee

You Don't Need Pajamas at Rosie's: see *The First Time*

You for Me
US   1952   71m   bw
MGM (Henry Berman)

A millionaire patient is courted by a needy hospital and falls for a popular nurse.

Cheerful but thin little programme-filler.

w William Roberts   d Don Weis   ph Paul Vogel   m Alberto Columbo

Peter Lawford, Jane Greer, Gig Young, Paula Corday, Elaine Stewart

You Gotta Stay Happy
US   1948   100m   bw
Universal (Karl Tunberg)

A runaway heiress joins cargo pilots on a transcontinental hop with some very queer passengers.

Ho-hum imitation of a Capra comedy; the effort shows.

w Karl Tunberg   story Robert Carson   d H. C. Potter   ph Russell Metty   m Daniele Amfitheatrof

Joan Fontaine, James Stewart, Eddie Albert, Roland Young, Willard Parker, Percy Kilbride, Porter Hall, Paul Cavanagh, Halliwell Hobbes

You Light Up My Life
US   1977   90m   Technicolor
Columbia/Mondial International (Joseph Brooks)

A comedian's daughter tries for success as a composer and singer.

Commonplace showbiz schmaltz, ineptly presented.

wd Joseph Brooks   ph Eric Saarinen   m Joseph Brooks   pd Tom Rasmussen   m/y Joseph Brooks   ed Lynzee Klingman

Didi Conn, Joe Silver, Michael Zaslow, Stephan Nathan, Melanie Mayron, Amy Letterman, Jerry Keller

'The movie is both amateurish and slick – it oozes heart. The scenes go on too long and there isn't enough in them.' – *Pauline Kael*

AA: song 'You Light Up My Life' (m/y Joseph Brooks)

You Live and Learn
GB   1937   80m   bw
Warner

American night-club dancers are stranded in Paris and helped by a nitwit Englishman who turns out to be not what he seems.

Rather flat comedy which gets flatter as it goes along.

w Brock Williams, Tom Phipps   story Norma Petterson   d Arthur Woods

Glenda Farrell, Claude Hulbert, Glen Alyn, John Carol, James Stephenson, George Galleon

You Made Me Love You
GB   1934   69m   bw
British International

A temperamental heiress is tamed by an amorous songwriter.

Flimsy comedy with amusing moments.

w Frank Launder   story Stanley Lupino   d Monty Banks

Thelma Todd, Stanley Lupino, John Loder, James Carew, Gerald Rawlinson

You, Me & Marley **
GB   1992   90m   colour
BBC

Three friends on a West Belfast estate persist in joy-riding in stolen cars to the annoyance of residents and the IRA.

Excellent drama, tough and authentic in feeling, which deals on a small scale with the complexities of the Irish situation.

w Graham Reid   story Richard Spence   d Graham Veevers   m Stephen Warbeck   pd David Wilson   ed Greg Miller

Marc O'Shea, Bronagh Gallagher, Michael Liebmann, Michael Gregory, Emma Moylan, Marie Jones, Frank Grimes

† The film was made for TV, but was shown at the 1992 Edinburgh Film Festival, where it won an award.

You Must Be Joking *
GB 1965 100m bw
Columbia/Ameran (Charles H. Schneer)

Assorted army personnel vie in an extended initiative test.

Slam-bang location comedy with more hits than misses: cheerful entertainment.

w Alan Hackney d Michael Winner ph Geoffrey Unsworth m Laurie Johnson

Terry-Thomas, Lionel Jeffries, Michael Callan, Gabriella Licudi, *Denholm Elliott*, Lee Montague, Bernard Cribbins, Wilfrid Hyde-White, James Robertson Justice, Richard Wattis, James Villiers

You Never Can Tell *
US 1951 78m bw
U-I (Leonard Goldstein)
GB title: You Never Know

An Alsatian dog is murdered and is sent back from heaven in the guise of a private detective to expose his killer.

Self-confidently outrageous comedy fantasy in the wake of *Here Comes Mr Jordan*; not badly done if you accept the premise.

w Lou Breslow, David Chandler d Lou Breslow ph Maury Gertsman m Hans Salter

Dick Powell, Peggy Dow, Charles Drake, Joyce Holden, Albert Sharpe, Sara Taft

You Never Know: see You Never Can Tell

'Living, loving – as though any moment a vengeful world might tear her from his arms!'
You Only Live Once **
US 1937 85m bw
Walter Wanger
V*

A petty crook framed for murder breaks out of prison and tries to escape to Canada with his wife.

Gloomy melodrama partly based on Bonnie and Clyde and incorporating a plea for justice; very well made and acted.

w Graham Baker story Gene Towne d Fritz Lang ph Leon Shamroy m Alfred Newman

Sylvia Sidney, Henry Fonda, Barton MacLane, Jean Dixon, William Gargan, Jerome Cowan, Chic Sale, Margaret Hamilton, Warren Hymer

'Crack blend of spectacular drama and romance . . . good direction, strong scripting and an arresting production.' – *Variety*

'Again and again in this film we find what can only be described as camera style, the use of the pictorial image to narrate with the maximum of emotional impact.' – *Dilys Powell*

You Only Live Twice **
GB 1967 117m Technicolor Panavision
UA/Eon (Harry Saltzman, Albert R. Broccoli)
V, V (W), V*, L, S

James Bond goes to Japan.

The Bond saga at its most expensive and expansive, full of local colour and in-jokes, with an enormously impressive set for the climactic action.

w Roald Dahl novel Ian Fleming d Lewis Gilbert ph Freddie Young, Bob Huke m John Barry pd Ken Adam

Sean Connery, Tetsuro Tamba, Akiko Wakabayashi, Mie Hama, Karin Dor, Bernard Lee, Lois Maxwell, Desmond Llewellyn, *Charles Gray, Donald Pleasence*

You Said a Mouthful
US 1932 75m bw
Warner

The inventor of an unsinkable bathing suit is mistaken for a champion swimmer.

Tepid star comedy.

w Robert Lord and Bolton Mallory d Lloyd Bacon

Joe E. Brown, Ginger Rogers, Sheila Terry, Guinn Williams, Oscar Apfel

You Were Meant for Me
US 1948 92m bw
TCF (Fred Kohlmar)

A small-town girl marries a bandleader.

Mildly pleasing, muted, musical romance, with good twenties atmosphere.

w Elick Moll, Valentine Davies d Lloyd Bacon ph Victor Milner md Lionel Newman m/y various

Jeanne Crain, Dan Dailey, Oscar Levant, Barbara Lawrence, Selena Royle, Percy Kilbride, Herbert Anderson

You Were Never Lovelier *
US 1942 97m bw
Columbia (Louis F. Edelman)
V, V*, L

An Argentinian hotel tycoon tries to interest his daughter in marriage by creating a mysterious admirer.

Pleasing musical, a follow-up for the stars of *You'll Never Get Rich*.

w Michael Fessier, Ernest Pagano, Delmer Daves d William A. Seiter ph Ted Tetzlaff m Leigh Harline m/y Jerome Kern, Johnny Mercer

Fred Astaire, Rita Hayworth, Adolphe Menjou, Leslie Brooks, Adele Mara, Isobel Elsom, Gus Schilling, Xavier Cugat and his Orchestra, Larry Parks

AAN: Leigh Harline; song 'Dearly Beloved'

You Will Remember
GB 1940 86m bw
Jack Raymond Productions

The life of the late Victorian songwriter Leslie Stuart.

Pleasant, rather surprising, minor British biopic.

w Lydia Hayward d Jack Raymond

Robert Morley, Emlyn Williams, Dorothy Hyson, Tom E. Finglass, Nicholas Phipps, Allan Jeayes

You'll Find Out *
US 1940 97m bw
RKO (David Butler)
V*, L

Kay Kyser's band is hired to play for a 21st birthday party at a gloomy mansion; they help save the life of the girl concerned.

Cheerful if slow-starting spooky house send-up with a splendid trio of villains.

w James V. Kern, David Butler d David Butler ph Frank Redman m Roy Webb m/y Jimmy McHugh, Johnny Mercer

Kay Kyser, Boris Karloff, Peter Lorre, Bela Lugosi, Dennis O'Keefe, Ginny Simms, Helen Parrish, Alma Kruger, Ish Kabibble

AAN: song 'I'd Know You Anywhere'

You'll Like My Mother
US 1972 92m Technicolor
Universal/Bing Crosby Productions (Mort Briskin)

Pregnant widow visits neurotic mother-in-law in a snowbound mansion.

Predictable frightened lady shocker aiming somewhere between *Psycho* and *Fanatic*; of strictly routine interest.

w Jo Heims novel Naomi Hintze d Lamont Johnson ph Jack Marta m Gil Melle

Rosemary Murphy, Patty Duke, Richard Thomas, Sian Barbara Allen

You'll Never Get Rich *
US 1941 88m bw
Columbia (Sam Bischoff)
V, V*, L

A Broadway dance director helps his philandering producer by taking a romantically-inclined showgirl off his hands.

Smart comedy-musical which set its female lead as a top star.

w Michael Fessier, Ernest Pagano d Sidney Lanfield ph Philip Tannura ch Robert Alton m Morris Stoloff m/y Cole Porter

Fred Astaire, Rita Hayworth, Robert Benchley, John Hubbard, Osa Massen, Frieda Inescort, Guinn Williams, Donald MacBride

AAN: Morris Stoloff; song 'Since I Kissed My Baby Goodbye'

Young America
US 1932 74m bw
Fox
GB title: We Humans

Two young boys get into trouble with the law.

Dog-eared domestic flagwaver.

w William Conselman play John Frederick Ballard d Frank Borzage ph George Schneiderman md George Lipschultz

Spencer Tracy, Doris Kenyon, Tommy Conlon, Ralph Bellamy, Beryl Mercer, Sarah Padden

'Hokey propaganda for juvenile courts. Not for smart houses and doubtful elsewhere unless there is a preponderance of mothers.' – *Variety*

'American Drug Wars Come To Britain . . . And It Takes A Special Cop To Infiltrate Their World Of Violence.'
The Young Americans *
GB 1993 103m Rank Film Panavision
Rank/Polygram/Live Entertainment (Paul Trijbits)
S

An American cop comes to London to help local police investigate drug-related killings.

Loud, frenetic attempt to make an English imitation of an American gangster movie; it is partially successful, though the more it resembles an American film, the more it becomes a lurid fantasy.

wd Danny Cannon, David Hilton d Danny Cannon ph Vernon Layton m David Arnold pd Laurence Dorman ed Alex Mackie

Harvey Keitel, Iain Glen, John Wood, Terence Rigby, Keith Allen, Craig Kelly, Thandie Newton, Viggo Mortensen

'A high-octane, in-your-face cop thriller that's got everything going for it except a well-rounded script.' – *Variety*

Young and Eager: see Claudelle Inglish

Young and Innocent ***
GB 1937 80m bw
GFD/Gainsborough (Edward Black)
V*, L
US title: A Girl Was Young

A girl goes on the run with her boyfriend when he is suspected of murder.

Pleasant, unassuming chase melodrama with a rather weak cast but plenty of its director's touches.

w Charles Bennett, Alma Reville   *novel A Shilling for Candles* by Josephine Tey   *d* Alfred Hitchcock   *ph* Bernard Knowles   *m* Louis Levy

Nova Pilbeam, Derrick de Marney, Mary Clare, Edward Rigby, Basil Radford, George Curzon, Percy Marmont, John Longden

'I like it best of all his pictures. It may not be, academically speaking, the cleverest. The adepts who go to a Hitchcock film to grub out bits of montage may be disappointed.' – *C. A. Lejeune*

The Young and the Damned: see *Los Olvidados*

Young and Willing
US   1942   83m   bw
UA (made by Paramount) (Edward H. Griffith)
V*

Impecunious actors in a New York boarding house hit on a great play.

Very mild, innocuous comedy which passed quickly from the public memory.

w Virginia Van Upp   *play* Francis Swann   *d* Edward H. Griffith   *ph* Leo Tover   *m* Victor Young

William Holden, Susan Hayward, Eddie Bracken, Robert Benchley, Martha O'Driscoll, Barbara Britton, James Brown, Mabel Paige

Young and Willing (1962): see *The Wild and the Willing*

Young as you Feel *
US   1931   78m   bw
Fox

In order to reform his family a father pretends to be as irresponsible as they are.

Medium star vehicle.

w Edwin Burke   *play Father and the Boys* by George Ade   *d* Frank Borzage

Will Rogers, Fifi D'Orsay, Lucien Littlefield, Donald Dillaway

'Looks fair b.o. due to star.' – *Variety*

Young at Heart **
US   1954   117m   Warnercolor
Warner/Arwin (Henry Blanke)
V, V*

The daughters of a small-town music teacher have romantic problems.

Softened, musicalized remake of *Four Daughters* (qv), an old-fashioned treat with roses round the door and a high standard of proficiency in all departments.

w Julius J. Epstein, Lenore Coffee   *novel* Fannie Hurst   *d* Gordon Douglas   *ph* Ted McCord   *md* Ray Heindorf

Doris Day, Frank Sinatra, Ethel Barrymore, Gig Young, Dorothy Malone, Robert Keith, Elizabeth Fraser, Alan Hale Jnr

Young Bess *
US   1953   112m   Technicolor
MGM (Sidney Franklin)

The early years of Elizabeth I and her romance with Tom Seymour.

Historical fiction, wildly unreliable as to fact and dramatically not very rewarding. The character actors have the best of it.

w Arthur Wimperis, Jan Lustig   *novel* Margaret Irwin   *d* George Sidney   *ph* Charles Rosher   *m* Miklos Rozsa   *ad* Cedric Gibbons, Urie McCleary

Jean Simmons, Stewart Granger, Charles Laughton (as Henry VIII), Kay Walsh, Deborah Kerr, Guy Rolfe, Kathleen Byron, Cecil Kellaway, Robert Arthur, Leo

G. Carroll, Elaine Stewart, Dawn Addams, Rex Thompson

AAN: art direction

Young Billy Young
US   1969   89m   DeLuxe
UA/Talbot-Youngstein (Max Youngstein)

A young Western gunman is helped out of scrapes by a mysterious stranger bent on revenge.

Good-looking but rather ineffective Western which throws away good production values.

wd Burt Kennedy   *novel Who Rides with Wyatt* by Will Henry   *ph* Harry Stradling Jnr   *m* Shelly Manne

Robert Mitchum, Angie Dickinson, Robert Walker Jnr, David Carradine, John Anderson, Paul Fix

Young Cassidy *
GB   1964   110m   Technicolor
MGM/Sextant (Robert D. Graff, Robert Emmett Ginna)

A romantic view of the early Dublin life of writer Sean O'Casey.

Ambling, unconvincing but generally interesting picture of a past time.

w John Whiting, from the writings of Sean O'Casey   *d* Jack Cardiff, John Ford   *ph* Ted Scaife   *m* Sean O'Riada

Rod Taylor, Maggie Smith, Edith Evans, Flora Robson, Michael Redgrave, Julie Christie, Jack MacGowran, Sian Phillips, T. P. McKenna

Young Dillinger
US   1964   102m   bw
Alfred Zimbalist
V*

An embittered young convict becomes Public Enemy Number One.

Fantasized forgettable biopic with violent moments.

w Arthur Hoerl, Don Zimbalist   *d* Terry Morse   *ph* Stanley Cortez   *m* Shorty Rogers

Nick Adams, John Ashley, Robert Conrad, Mary Ann Mobley, Victor Buono, John Hoyt, Reed Hadley

The Young Doctors *
US   1961   102m   bw
UA/Drexel/Stuart Millar/Laurence Turman

Old Dr Pearson resents his modern young assistant and almost causes a tragedy.

Routine medical melo of the Kildare/Gillespie kind, given a Grade A production and cast.

w Joseph Hayes   *novel The Final Diagnosis* by Arthur Hailey   *d* Phil Karlson   *ph* Arthur J. Ornitz   *m* Elmer Bernstein

Fredric March, Ben Gazzara, Dick Clark, Eddie Albert, Ina Balin, Aline MacMahon, Edward Andrews, Arthur Hill, George Segal, Rosemary Murphy

Young Doctors in Love
US   1982   95m   Metrocolor
TCF/ABC (Jerry Bruckheimer)
V*, L

Goings-on in a modern hospital.

Spoof soap opera in the wake of *Airplane* but seeming more like a flat edition of *Carry On.*

w Michael Elias, Rich Eustis   *d* Garry Marshall   *ph* Don Peterman   *m* Maurice Jarre

Michael McKean, Sean Young, Harry Dean Stanton, Patrick MacNee, Hector Elizondo, Dabney Coleman

Young Eagles *
US   1930   71m   bw
Paramount

The adventures of American aviators in World War I.

Spirited early sound actioner.

w William McNutt, Grover Jones   *d* William Wellman   *ph* Archie Stout

Charles Rogers, Jean Arthur, Paul Lukas, Stuart Erwin, Virginia Bruce, James Finlayson

'Pint-sized version of *Wings.* Comedy and production almost square silly plot.' – *Variety*

Young Eagles
US   1934   bw   serial: 12 eps
First Division

Two Eagle Scouts are awarded trips to South America and stumble across treasure.

Unremarkable juvenile serial dedicated by the scout movement to President Roosevelt.

Bobbie Cox, Jim Vance

Young Einstein
Australia   1988   91m   colour
Warner/Serious Productions (Yahoo Serious, Warwick Ross, David Roach)
V, V*, L, S

Einstein discovers the theory of relativity, falls in love with Marie Curie, and then invents the surfboard, the electric guitar and rock 'n' roll.

A smash-hit in its native land, it is a ramshackle, slapstick comedy that, relatively speaking, does not travel well.

w Yahoo Serious, David Roach   *d* Yahoo Serious   *ph* Jeff Darling   *m* William Motzing, Martin Armiger, Tommy Tycho   *ad* Steve Marr, Laurie Faen, Colin Gibson, Ron Highfield   *ed* Yahoo Serious

Yahoo Serious, Odile Le Clezio, John Howard, Peewee Wilson, Su Cruikshank

'A film which manages to be innocuous and appalling at the same time.' – *MFB*

Young Frankenstein **
US   1974   108m   bw
TCF/Gruskoff/Venture/Jouer/Crossbow (Michael Gruskoff)
V, V*, L

Young Frederick Frankenstein, a brain surgeon, goes back to Transylvania and pores over his grandfather's notebooks.

The most successful of Mel Brooks's parodies, *Mad Magazine* style; the gleamingly reminiscent photography is the best of it, the script being far from consistently funny, but there are splendid moments.

w Gene Wilder, Mel Brooks   *d* Mel Brooks   *ph* Gerald Hirschfeld   *m* John Morris   *ad* Dale Hennesy

Gene Wilder, Marty Feldman, Madeleine Kahn, *Peter Boyle,* Cloris Leachman, Kenneth Mars, Gene Hackman, Richard Haydn

'Like a sketch from the old Sid Caesar show, for which Brooks wrote, spun out ten times as long. Ten times too long. Brooks is a sprinter, and there aren't enough good sprints here.' – *Stanley Kauffmann*

AAN: script

Young Giants
US   1983   97m   DeLuxe   Panavision
Entertainment Enterprises (Tom Moyer, Megan Moyer)

A San Diego priest helps a boys' home by re-organizing a football team so that an old priest can die happy.

Shades of *Going My Way,* but somewhat ineptly done, with a guest appearance from Pele as *deus ex machina.*

w Tom Moyer, Terrill Tannen, Mike Lammers   *d* Terrill Tannen   *ph* Raoul Lomas   *m* Rick Patterson   *ad* Daniel R. Webster   *ed* Denine Rowan, Marion W. Cronin, Daniel Gross

Peter Fox, John Huston, Lisa Wills, F. William Parker, Severn Darden

'At least it has the courage of its throwback convictions.' – *Kim Newman, MFB*

The Young Girls of Rochefort

France 1967 126m Eastmancolor Franscope
Parc Film/Madeleine/Seven Arts (Mag Bodard, Gilbert de Goldschmidt)
S
original title: *Les Demoiselles de Rochefort*

Two country girls join a travelling dancing troupe, and find love on the day of the fair.

Flat, empty tribute to the Hollywood musical, which never inspires despite the presence of one of its greatest stars.

wd Jacques Demy *ph* Ghislain Cloquet *m* Michel Legrand

Catherine Deneuve, François Dorléac, George Chakiris, Gene Kelly, Danielle Darrieux, Grover Dale, Michel Piccoli

AAN: Michel Legrand

Young Guns

US 1988 107m DeLuxe
Vestron/Morgan Creek Productions (Joe Roth, Christopher Cain)
V, V*, L

Billy Bonney joins a group of young ranch hands and they are quickly transformed into Billy the Kid and a gang of outlaws.

Teenage Western, with a background authenticity that does not extend to the characterization.

w John Fusco *d* Christopher Cain *ph* Dean Semler *m* Anthony Marinelli, Brian Banks *pd* Jane Musky *ed* Jack Hofstra

Emilio Estevez, Kiefer Sutherland, Lou Diamond Phillips, Charlie Sheen, Dermot Mulroney, Casey Siemaszko, Terence Stamp, Jack Palance, Patrick Wayne

Young Guns II

US 1990 103m DeLuxe
Fox/Morgan Creek (Paul Schiff, Irby Smith)
V, V*, L

Billy the Kid and his gang, on the run from justice, face death as they begin to squabble among themselves.

Continuing from where the first film ended, it provides a similar modern treatment of its youthful anti-heroes.

w John Fusco *d* Geoff Murphy *ph* Dean Semler *m* Alan Silvestri *pd* Gene Rudolph *m/y* Jon Bon Jovi *ad* Christa Munro *ed* Bruce Green

Emilio Estevez, Kiefer Sutherland, Lou Diamond Phillips, Christian Slater, William Peterson, Alan Ruck, R. D. Call, James Coburn, Balthazar Getty, Jack Kehoe

Young Guns of Texas

US 1962 78m DeLuxe Cinemascope
TCF (Maury Dexter)

An Easterner, accompanied by two cowboys and a runaway heiress, rides into Indian territory in search of stolen gold.

Dull, routine Western featuring the untalented offspring of the famous.

w Henry Cross *d* Maury Dexter *ph* John Nickolaus Jnr *m* Paul Sawtell, Bert Shefter *ed* Jodie Copelan, Richard Einfeld

James Mitchum, Alana Ladd, Jody McCrea, Chill Wills, Gary Conway, Barbara Mansell, Robert Lowery

Young Ideas

US 1943 75m bw
Robert Sisk/MGM

The proposed marriage of two academics is interrupted by the protests of their children.

Predictable light concoction with practised players.

w Ian McLellan Hunter, Bill Noble *d* Jules Dassin

Mary Astor, Herbert Marshall, Susan Peters, Elliott Reid, Richard Carlson, Allyn Joslyn

The Young in Heart ***

US 1938 91m bw
David O. Selznick
V*

A family of charming confidence tricksters move in on a rich old lady but she brings out the best in them.

Delightful, roguish romantic comedy, perfectly cast and pacily handled.

w Paul Osborn, Charles Bennett *novel* The Gay Banditti by I. A. R. Wylie *d* Richard Wallace *ph* Leon Shamroy *m* Franz Waxman

Douglas Fairbanks Jnr, Janet Gaynor, Roland Young, Billie Burke, Minnie Dupree, Paulette Goddard, Richard Carlson, Henry Stephenson

'Sentimental drama, vastly touching and entertaining . . . has everything to ensure box office success.' – *Variety*

'It comes as a gentle breeze in the hurricane of hurly burly comedies that have hurtled across the screen of late.' – *Motion Picture Herald*

AAN: Leon Shamroy; Franz Waxman

The Young Invaders: see *Darby's Rangers*

The Young Land

US 1957 89m Technicolor
Columbia/C. V. Whitney (Patrick Ford)

A young sheriff arrests a gunman and after the trial has to save him from lynching.

Rather stiff attempt at a youth Western.

w Norman Shannon Hall *d* Ted Tetzlaff *ph* Winton C. Hoch, Henry Sharp *m* Dimitri Tiomkin

Dan O'Herlihy, Patrick Wayne, Yvonne Craig, Dennis Hopper

AAN: song 'Strange Are the Ways of Love' (*m* Dimitri Tiomkin, *ly* Ned Washington)

The Young Lions **

US 1958 167m bw Cinemascope
TCF (Al Lichtman)
V, V*, L, S

World War II adventures of two Americans and a German skiing instructor.

Three strands are loosely interwoven into a would-be modern epic; the result is well mounted and generally absorbing but uneven and decidedly overlong.

w Edward Anhalt *novel* Irwin Shaw *d* Edward Dmytryk *ph* Joe MacDonald *m* Hugo Friedhofer

Marlon Brando, Montgomery Clift, Dean Martin, Hope Lange, Barbara Rush, May Britt, Maximilian Schell, Lee Van Cleef

'Episodic and overproduced, like a wartime *Grand Hotel*.' – *Pauline Kael, 70s*

AAN: Joe MacDonald; Hugo Friedhofer

The Young Lovers *

GB 1954 96m bw
GFD/Group Films (Anthony Havelock-Allan)
US title: *Chance Meeting*

A US Embassy man in London falls in love with the daughter of an Iron Curtain minister.

Romeo and Juliet, cold war style, quite nicely put together with a thriller climax.

w Robin Estridge *story* George Tabori *d* Anthony Asquith *ph* Jack Asher *m* Tchaikovsky

Odile Versois, David Knight, David Kossoff, Joseph Tomelty, Paul Carpenter, Theodore Bikel, Jill Adams

Young Man of Music: see *Young Man with a Horn*

'Put down your trumpet, jazz man – I'm in the mood for love'

Young Man with a Horn *

US 1950 112m bw
Warner (Jerry Wald)
V*, L
GB title: *Young Man of Music*

The professional and romantic tribulations of a trumpet player.

Overwrought character melodrama based on the life of Bix Beiderbecke; quite absorbing though occasionally risible.

w Carl Foreman, Edmund H. North *novel* Dorothy Baker *d* Michael Curtiz *ph* Ted McCord *m* Ray Heindorf (trumpet dubbed by Harry James)

Kirk Douglas, Lauren Bacall, Doris Day, Hoagy Carmichael, Juano Hernandez, Jerome Cowan, Mary Beth Hughes, Nestor Paiva

Young Man with Ideas *

US 1952 84m bw
MGM (Gottfried Reinhardt, William H. Wright)

A small-town lawyer tries to better himself in Los Angeles.

Modestly likeable comedy which doesn't add up to much.

w Arthur Sheekman *d* Mitchell Leisen *ph* Joseph Ruttenberg *m* David Rose

Glenn Ford, Ruth Roman, Nina Foch, Denise Darcel, Donna Corcoran, Mary Wickes, Sheldon Leonard

Young Man's Fancy

GB 1939 77m bw
Ealing

A young Victorian lord avoids an unsuitable match by eloping to Paris.

Rather pallid romantic comedy with likeable period detail.

w Roland Pertwee, Rodney Ackland, E. V. H. Emmett *d* Robert Stevenson

Griffith Jones, Anna Lee, Seymour Hicks, Billy Bennett, Edward Rigby, Francis L. Sullivan

Young Mr Lincoln ***

US 1939 100m bw
TCF (Kenneth MacGowan)
V*, L

Abraham Lincoln as a young country lawyer stops a lynching and proves a young man innocent of murder.

Splendid performances and period atmosphere are rather nipped in the bud by second-feature courtroom twists, but this is a marvellous old-fashioned entertainment with its heart in the right place.

w Lamar Trotti *d* John Ford *ph* Bert Glennon *m* Alfred Newman

Henry Fonda, Alice Brady, Marjorie Weaver, Arleen Whelan, Eddie Collins, Richard Cromwell, Donald Meek, Eddie Quillan, Spencer Charters

'A dignified saga of early Lincolniana, paced rather slowly . . . lack of romance interest is one of the prime factors which deter the film from interpreting itself into big box office.' – *Variety*

'Its simple good faith and understanding are an expression of the country's best life that says as much as forty epics.' – *Otis Ferguson*

'Period details are lovingly sketched in – a log splitting contest, a tug of war, a tar barrel rolling match . . .' – *Charles Higham*

'Its source is a womb of popular and national spirit. This could account for its unity, its artistry, its genuine beauty.' – *Sergei Eisenstein*

'A film which indisputably has the right to be called Americana.' – *New York Times*

'In spite of the excitements of a murder, a near-lynching and a crackerjack trial, it remains a character study.' – *New York Sun*

'One of John Ford's most memorable films.' – *Pauline Kael, 70s*

AAN: Lamar Trotti

The Young Mr Pitt *
GB 1942 118m bw
TCF (Edward Black)

Britain's youngest prime minister quells the threat of invasion by Napoleon.

Shapeless and overlong but generally diverting historical pastiche timed as wartime propaganda against Hitler.

w Frank Launder, Sidney Gilliat d Carol Reed
ph Frederick A. Young m Charles Williams
ad Vetchinsky

Robert Donat, Robert Morley, Phyllis Calvert, John Mills, Raymond Lovell, Max Adrian, Felix Aylmer, Albert Lieven

The Young Ones *
GB 1961 108m Technicolor Cinemascope
ABP (Kenneth Harper)
V
US title: *Wonderful to be Young*

The son of a tycoon starts a youth club and puts on a musical to raise funds.

A shopworn idea is the springboard for a brave try in a field where Britain was presumed to have failed; despite the enthusiasm with which it was greeted at the time, it has dated badly.

w Peter Myers, Ronald Cass d Sidney J. Furie
ph Douglas Slocombe m Stanley Black

Cliff Richard, Robert Morley, Carole Grey, Richard O'Sullivan, Melvyn Hayes, Gerald Harper, Robertson Hare

Young People
US 1940 78m bw
TCF (Harry Joe Brown)

Vaudevillians retire to give their daughter a proper upbringing, but find that showbiz is in her blood.

Pleasant but unremarkable comedy-drama with music, marking the end of its star's association with the studio.

w Edwin Blum, Don Ettlinger d Allan Dwan
ph Edward Cronjager md Alfred Newman

Shirley Temple, Jack Oakie, Charlotte Greenwood, Arleen Whelan, George Montgomery, Kathleen Howard, Mae Marsh

The Young Philadelphians *
US 1959 136m bw
Warner (producer not credited)
V*
GB title: *The City Jungle*

A forceful young lawyer pushes his way to the top of the snobbish Philadelphia heap despite threats to expose his illegitimacy.

Novel on film, gleamingly done and acted with assurance.

w James Gunn novel *The Philadelphian* by Richard Powell d Vincent Sherman ph Harry Stradling
m Ernest Gold

Paul Newman, Barbara Rush, Alexis Smith, Brian Keith, Billie Burke, John Williams, Otto Kruger,

Diane Brewster, Robert Vaughn, Paul Picerni, Robert Douglas

AAN: Harry Stradling; Robert Vaughn

The Young Savages *
US 1961 103m bw
UA/Contemporary (Pat Duggan)

An assistant DA prosecutes three hoodlums for murder but begins to feel that one is not guilty.

Tough, realistic melodrama of the New York slums, with roughhouse climaxes and a political conscience.

w Edward Anhalt, J. P. Miller novel *A Matter of Conviction* by Evan Hunter d John Frankenheimer
ph Lionel Lindon m David Amram

Burt Lancaster, Shelley Winters, John David Chandler, Dina Merrill, Edward Andrews, Telly Savalas

Young Scarface: see *Brighton Rock*

Young Sherlock Holmes
US 1985 109m Technicolor
Paramount/Amblin (Mark Johnson)
V, V*, L
GB title: *Young Sherlock Holmes and the Pyramid of Fear*

Holmes and Watson meet as teenage students, and trace some mysterious murders to an eastern cult.

More expensive gimmickry with acres of tedium in between the technical highlights. Nothing for Holmes buffs.

w Chris Columbus d Barry Levinson ph Stephen Goldblatt m Bruce Broughton pd Norman Reynolds ed Stu Linder

Nicholas Rowe, Alan Cox, Sophie Ward, Anthony Higgins, Freddie Jones, Nigel Stock

'Another Steven Spielberg version of those lamps made from driftwood and coffee tables from redwood burl. It's not art but they all serve their purpose and sell by millions.' – *Variety* (This one was a box-office disappointment.)

AAN: visual effects

Young Soul Rebels *
GB 1991 105m colour
BFI/Film Four/Sankofa/La Sept/Kinowelt/Iberoamericana (Nadine Marsh-Edwards)
V

In the mid-1970s, two pirate radio disc jockeys specializing in soul music solve the murder of a friend.

Examining black and gay culture in Britain, the movie tries to pack in too much, losing focus as a result.

w Paul Hallam, Derrick Saldaan McClintock, Isaac Julien d Isaac Julien ph Nina Kellgren
m Simon Boswell pd Derek Brown ed John Wilson

Valentine Nonyela, Mo Sesay, Dorian Healy, Frances Barber, Sophie Okonedo, Jason Durr, Gary McDonald, Debra Gillet

'It ultimately suffers from trying to say too many things too fast to too many people, the penalty, one suspects, from working in a British film industry where your first film so easily doubles up as your last.' – *Empire*

The Young Stranger *
US 1957 84m bw
RKO (Stuart Millar)
V, L

The 16-year-old son of a film executive gets into trouble with the police.

Reasonably stimulating film of a TV play about the kind of causeless rebel who quickly became a cliché.

w Robert Dozier d John Frankenheimer
ph Robert Planck m Leonard Rosenman

James MacArthur, Kim Hunter, James Daly, James Gregory, Whit Bissell

Young Tom Edison *
US 1940 82m bw
MGM (John Considine Jnr)
V*, L

First of a two-parter (see *Edison the Man*) tracing Edison's first experiments.

Reasonably factual and absorbing junior biopic.

w Bradbury Foote, Dore Schary, Hugo Butler
d Norman Taurog ph Sidney Wagner m Edward Ward

Mickey Rooney, Eugene Pallette, George Bancroft, Fay Bainter, Virginia Weidler, Victor Kilian, Lloyd Corrigan

'A picture for all of the people in all of the places.' – *Motion Picture Herald*

Young Warriors
US 1983 103m colour
Cannon
V*

After the sister of one of them dies after being raped, high-school graduates set themselves up as vigilantes.

Dangerous rubbish.

w Lawrence D. Foldes, Russell W. Colgin
d Lawrence D. Foldes

Ernest Borgnine, Richard Roundtree, Lynda Day George, James Van Patten, Anne Lockhart, Tom Reilly, Dick Shawn

'A lurid mishmash.' – *Jo Imeson, MFB*

The Young Widow
US 1946 100m bw
UA/Hunt Stromberg

The widow of a World War II flyer returns to the Virginia farm where they had spent happy hours.

Glum sudser with talent all at sea.

w Richard Macaulay, Margaret Buell Wilder
novel Clarissa Fairchild Cushman d Edwin L. Marin ph Lee Garmes m Carmen Dragon
pd Nicolai Remisoff

Jane Russell, Louis Hayward, Faith Domergue, Marie Wilson, Kent Taylor, Penny Singleton, Connie Gilchrist, Cora Witherspoon

Young Winston **
GB 1972 157m Eastmancolor Panavision
Columbia/Open Road/Hugh French (Carl Foreman)
V, V*

The adventurous life of Winston Churchill up to his becoming an MP.

Generally engaging if lumpy film which switches too frequently from action to family drama to politics to character study and is not helped by irritating directorial tricks.

w Carl Foreman book My Early Life by Winston Churchill d Richard Attenborough ph Gerry Turpin m Alfred Ralston pd Don Ashton, Geoffrey Drake

Simon Ward, Robert Shaw, Anne Bancroft, Jack Hawkins, Ian Holm, *Anthony Hopkins*, John Mills, Patrick Magee, Edward Woodward

AAN: Carl Foreman

Young Wives' Tale
GB 1951 79m bw
ABPC

A playwright and his slaphappy wife share a house with a super-efficient couple.

Very mild but palatable comedy set 'at the wrong end of St John's Wood'.

w Anne Burnaby   *play* Ronald Jeans   *d* Henry Cass

Joan Greenwood, Nigel Patrick, Derek Farr, Guy Middleton, Athene Seyler, Helen Cherry, Audrey Hepburn, Irene Handl

Young Woodley
GB 1929 79m bw
BIP

A schoolboy falls in love with his teacher's wife.

Modest early talkie version of a play thought mildly shocking at the time.

w John Van Druten, Victor Kendall   *play* John Van Druten   *d* Thomas Bentley

Madeleine Carroll, Frank Lawton, Sam Livesey, Gerald Rawlinson, Billy Milton

† A silent version made earlier in the same year, with Marjorie Hume and Robin Irvine, was never released.

Youngblood
US 1985 109m Metrocolor
United Artists/Guber-Peters (Peter Bart, Patrick Wells)
V, V*, L

Romances of a young hockey star, for those interested; it turned out that there weren't many.

wd Peter Markle   *story* Peter Markle, Patrick Wells   *ph* Mark Irwin   *m* William Orbit   *ad* Alicia Keywan   *ed* Stephen E. Rivkin, Jack Hofstra

Rob Lowe, Cynthia Gibb, Patrick Swayze, Ed Lauter, Jim Youngs

Youngblood Hawke
US 1964 137m bw
Warner (Delmer Daves)

A Kentucky truck driver becomes a successful novelist and is spoiled by New York success.

Absurdly archetypal soap opera from a bestseller, spilling over with every imaginable cliché; some of its excesses are glossily entertaining.

wd Delmer Daves   *novel* Herman Wouk   *ph* Charles Lawton   *m* Max Steiner

James Franciscus, Genevieve Page, Suzanne Pleshette, Eva Gabor, *Mary Astor*, Lee Bowman, Edward Andrews, John Emery, Don Porter

The Younger Brothers
US 1949 76m Technicolor
Warner (Saul Elkins)

A whitewashed version of the career of the legendary outlaws, who wind up expecting pardons; otherwise routine sagebrush stuff.

w Edna Anhalt   *d* Edwin L. Marin

Wayne Morris, Janis Paige, Bruce Bennett, Geraldine Brooks, Robert Hutton, Alan Hale, Fred Clark

The Youngest Profession
US 1943 82m bw
MGM (B. F. Ziedman)

Teenage autograph hounds cause trouble at the MGM studio.

Innocuous comedy with guest stars.

w George Oppenheimer, Charles Lederer, Leonard Spigelgass   *book* Lillian Day   *d* Edward Buzzell   *ph* Charles Lawton   *m* David Snell

Virginia Weidler, Jean Porter, Edward Arnold, John Carroll, Agnes Moorehead, Greer Garson, William Powell, Lana Turner, Walter Pidgeon, Robert Taylor

Your Past is Showing: see *The Naked Truth*

Your Witness *
GB 1950 100m bw
Warner/Coronado (Joan Harrison)
US title: *Eye Witness*

An American lawyer comes to an English village to defend a war buddy on a murder charge.

Interesting but ineffective blend of comedy and courtroom procedure intended to contrast English and American ways.

w Hugo Butler, Ian Hunter, William Douglas Home   *d* Robert Montgomery   *ph* Gerald Gibbs   *m* Malcolm Arnold

Robert Montgomery, Leslie Banks, Patricia Cutts, Felix Aylmer, Andrew Cruickshank, Harcourt Williams, Jenny Laird, Michael Ripper

You're a Big Boy Now *
US 1967 96m Eastmancolor
Warner Seven Arts (William Fadiman)
V*

A young assistant librarian discovers girls.

Freewheeling semi-surrealist comedy with exhilarating moments and the inevitable letdowns associated with this kind of campy high style.
wd Francis Ford Coppola   *novel* David Benedictus   *ph* Andy Laszlo   *m* Bob Prince

Peter Kastner, Elizabeth Hartman, Geraldine Page, Julie Harris, Rip Torn, Tony Bill, Karen Black, Michael Dunn

'A half-kooky, half-sweetly-innocent comedy . . . which is wonderfully photogenic from a young director's point of view.' – *Judith Crist*

AAN: Geraldine Page

You're a Lucky Fellow, Mr Smith
US 1943 63m bw
Edward Lilley/Universal

A girl must marry quickly in order to secure her inheritance.

Very light musical support.

w Lawrence Riley, Ben Barzman, Louis Lantz   *d* Felix Feist

Allan Jones, Evelyn Ankers, Billie Burke, David Bruce, Patsy O'Connor, Stanley Clements

You're a Sweetheart
US 1937 96m bw
Universal (B. G. de Sylva)

A Broadway star suffers from her press agent's bright ideas.

Muffed musical with all concerned ill at ease with below par material.

w Monte Brice, Charles Grayson   *d* David Butler   *ph* George Robinson   *md* Charles Previn   *songs* various   *ad* Jack Otterson

Alice Faye, George Murphy, Ken Murray, William Gargan, Frances Hunt, Frank Jenks, Andy Devine, Charles Winninger, Donald Meek

'Just what the doctor ordered for the holiday first runs . . . enough entertainers for two shows.' – *Variety*

You're Darn Tootin' ***
US 1929 20m bw silent
Hal Roach

Two musicians get into trouble at work, in their digs and in the street.

Star comedy which though early in their teaming shows Stan and Ollie at their best in a salt shaker routine and in a surreal pants-ripping contest.

w H. M. Walker   *d* Edgar Kennedy

Laurel and Hardy, Agnes Steele

You're in the Army Now (1936): see *O.H.M.S.*

You're in the Army Now **
US 1941 79m bw
Warner (Ben Stoloff)

Two incompetent vacuum cleaner salesmen accidentally join the army.

An excellent vehicle for two star comedians who have often suffered from poor material, with a silent-comedy-style climax involving a house on wheels.

w Paul Gerard Smith, George Beatty   *d* Lewis Seiler   *ph* James Van Trees   *m* Howard Jackson

Jimmy Durante, Phil Silvers, Donald MacBride, Jane Wyman, Regis Toomey

You're in the Navy Now *
US 1951 93m bw
TCF (Fred Kohlmar)
aka: *USS Teakettle*

Trouble results when the navy instals steam turbines in an experimental patrol craft.

Amusing service comedy with good script touches and capable performances.

w Richard Murphy   *d* Henry Hathaway   *ph* Joe MacDonald   *m* Cyril Mockridge

Gary Cooper, Millard Mitchell, Jane Greer, Eddie Albert, John McIntire, Ray Collins, Harry von Zell, Jack Webb, Richard Erdman

You're My Everything *
US 1949 94m Technicolor
TCF (Lamar Trotti)

A Boston socialite marries a hoofer and becomes a movie star.

Pleasant twenties comedy with good period detail and lively performances.

w Lamar Trotti, Will Hays Jnr   *d* Walter Lang   *ph* Arthur E. Arling   *m* Alfred Newman

Anne Baxter, Dan Dailey, Anne Revere, Stanley Ridges, Shari Robinson, Henry O'Neill, Selena Royle, Alan Mowbray, Buster Keaton

You're Never Too Young
US 1955 103m Technicolor Vistavision
Paramount/Hal B. Wallis (Paul Jones)

An apprentice barber on the run from a murderer poses as a 12-year-old child to travel half fare.

Unattractive revamping of *The Major and the Minor* (qv), with the star team trying too obviously to make bricks with inferior straw.

w Sidney Sheldon   *d* Norman Taurog   *ph* Daniel L. Fapp   *m* Arthur Schwartz

Dean Martin, Jerry Lewis, Diana Lynn, Nina Foch, Raymond Burr, Veda Ann Borg

You're Only Young Once: see *The Hardy Family*

You're Only Young Twice
GB 1952 81m bw
Group Three (Terry Bishop)

The puritanical head of a Scottish university is laid low by circumstance and his own folly.

Misfire eccentric comedy which deserves marks for trying but fails to amuse.

w Reginald Beckwith, Lindsay Galloway, Terry Bishop   *play What Say They* by James Bridie   *d* Terry Bishop   *ph* Jo Jago

Duncan Macrae, Charles Hawtrey, Joseph Tomelty, Patrick Barr, Diane Hart, Robert Urquhart

You're Telling Me *
US 1934 66m bw
Paramount

A small-town inventor meets a princess and makes the social grade.

Meaninglessly-titled star vehicle which is often defiantly unamusing but does include the famous golf routine.

w Walter de Leon, Paul M. Jones *d* Erle C. Kenton
ph Alfred Gilks *m* Arthur Johnston

W. C. Fields, Larry 'Buster' Crabbe, Joan Marsh,
Adrienne Ames, Louise Carter

'The kind of comedy that Chaplin used to do in two
reels, but stretched out like Carnera's suspenders to
run an even six.' – *Variety*

Yours Mine and Ours *
US   1968   111m   Technicolor
UA/Desilu/Walden (Robert F. Blumofe)

A widower with nine children marries a widow with
eight, and they settle in an old San Francisco house.

Generally appealing comedy, based on fact and well
suited to its stars.

w Mel Shavelson, Mort Lachman *d* Mel Shavelson
ph Charles Wheeler *m* Fred Karlin

Lucille Ball, Henry Fonda, Van Johnson

Youth Runs Wild
US   1944   67m   bw
RKO (Val Lewton)

Indifferent parents are responsible for the problems of
teenagers.

Dreary little sermon from the unit which produced
semi-classic horrors.

w John Fante, Herbert Kline *d* Mark Robson

Bonita Granville, Kent Smith, Jean Brooks, Glenn
Vernon, Arthur Shields

Youth Takes a Fling
US   1938   77m   bw
Universal (Joe Pasternak)

A reluctant truck driver is chased by a department
store salesgirl.

Mildly scatty comedy which failed to ring the bell.

w Myles Connelly *d* Archie Mayo

Joel McCrea, Andrea Leeds, Frank Jenks, Dorothea
Kent, Isabel Jeans, Virginia Grey, Grant Mitchell,
Willie Best

'Good standard entertainment with many light and
diverting passages.' – *Variety*

You've Got to Live Dangerously: see *Il Faut Vivre
Dangereusement*

Yukinojo Henge: see *An Actor's Revenge*

Z

Z ****

France/Algeria 1968 125m Eastmancolor
Reggane/ONCIC/Jacques Pérrin
V*, L, S

A leading opposition MP is murdered at a rally. The police are anxious to establish the event as an accident, but the examining magistrate proves otherwise.

An exciting police suspense drama which also recalls events under the Greek colonels and was therefore highly fashionable for a while both as entertainment and as a political *roman à clef*.

w Costa-Gavras, Jorge Semprun *novel* Vassili Vassilikos *d* Costa-Gavras *ph* Raoul Coutard *m* Mikis Theodorakis

Jean-Louis Trintignant, Jacques Pérrin, Yves Montand, François Périer, Irene Papas, Charles Denner

AA: best foreign film

AAN: best picture; director; script

'It will blow your mind!'
Zabriskie Point

US 1969 112m Metrocolor Panavision
MGM/Carlo Ponti
V*, L, S

A rebellious Los Angeles student steals a private airplane, meets an aimless girl, and finds a revelation in Death Valley . . .

Highly self-indulgent and unattractive fantasy about escape from the crudities of our over-civilized world. An expensive failure and an awful warning of what happens if you give an arty director carte blanche.

w Michelangelo Antonioni, Fred Gardner, Sam Shepard, Tonino Guerra, Clare Peploe
d Michelangelo Antonioni *ph* Alfio Contini
m pop songs

Mark Frechette, Daria Halprin, Rod Taylor, Paul Fix

'Not even a good tourist's notebook . . . from the choice of Death Valley as a symbol of American civilization to the inclusion of gag signs on bar-room walls to the shots of garish billboards, this film sticks to the surface, stranded.' – *Stanley Kauffmann*

'A huge, jerry-built, crumbling ruin of a movie.' – *Pauline Kael, New Yorker*

'A small, sad shambles of a film that has obviously been salvaged from a larger shambles. Bad enough to give anti-Americanism a bad name.' – *Joseph Morgenstern, Newsweek*

'He has tried to make a serious movie and hasn't even achieved a beach party level of insight.' – *Roger Ebert*

'The First Electric Western.'
Zachariah

1971 93m Metrocolor
Cinerama/ABC (George Englund)
V*

A youth leaves home to become a gunfighter but learns that pacificism is best.

Bizarre rock Western that is never sure whether it's satirical or serious; an audience is likely to be as confused. It was not only the first of its kind, but also the last.

w Joe Massot, The Firesign Theatre (Philip Austin, Peter Bergman, David Ossman, Philip Proctor)
d George Englund *ph* Jorge Shahl *m* Jimmie Haskell *pd* Assheton Gorton *ed* Gary Griffen

John Rubinstein, Pat Quinn, Don Johnson, Country Joe and the Fish, Elvin Jones, Doug Kershaw, William Challee, Dick Van Patten, The James Gang

'Nothing quite works, yet it's a relaxed and generally inoffensive movie.' – *Pauline Kael*

Zamri, Umri, Voskresni! **

USSR 1989 103m bw
Artificial Eye/Lenfilm/Trinity Bridge/First Film Creative Studio (Valentina Tarasova)
aka: *Don't Move, Die and Rise Again!*

In the 1940s in a grim Soviet town, the 12-year-old son of a prostitute is befriended by a girl of his own age.

Supposedly autobiographical film of a depressingly violent semi-criminal childhood marked by tragedy.

wd Vitaly Kanevsky *ph* Vladimir Bryliakov
m Sergei Banevich *pd* Yury Pashigorev *ed* G. Kornilova

Dinara Drukarova, Pavel Nazarov, Elena Popova

'It makes a compulsive, unpredictable, unreliable, contradictory, and often remarkably beautiful autobiographical memoir from a powerful and refreshingly undisciplined voice.' – *Philip Strick, Sight and Sound*

'One of those autobiographical first features which suddenly arrives out of nowhere and surprises us with its freshness, power and rough-hewn skill.' – *Derek Malcolm, Guardian*

† The film won the Camera d'Or for best first feature at the Cannes Film Festival in 1990.

'One woman . . . two men . . . one driven by desire. The other driven to the edge.'
Zandalee

US 1990 104m colour
Rank/Electric (William Blaycock, Eyal Rimmon)
V, V*, L

A hard-drinking artist makes love to the wife of his increasingly unhappy childhood friend.

Appalling dialogue and a ludicrous narrative are combined with lubricious sexual encounters to create a wholly unlovely experience.

w Mari Kornhauser *d* Sam Pillsbury *ph* Walt Lloyd *m* Pray For Rain *pd* Michael Corenblith
ed Michael Horton

Nicolas Cage, Judge Reinhold, Erika Anderson, Viveca Lindfors, Aaron Neville, Joe Pantoliano, Steve Buscemi

'Ill-written, pretentious trash.' – *Philip French, Observer*

Zandy's Bride

US 1974 116m Technicolor Panavision
Warner (Harry Matofsky)
V*

Life for a frontier family.

Dour semi-Western.

w Marc Norman *novel* The Stranger by Lillian Bos Ross *d* Joan Troell *ph* Jordan Cronenweth
m Fred Karlin

Gene Hackman, Liv Ullmann, Eileen Heckart, Harry Dean Stanton, Joe Santos, Frank Cady

Zanzibar

US 1940 69m bw
Universal (Warren Douglas)

European powers both want the sacred skull of an African chieftain, but so does a local tribe.

Adventure nonsense patched together with stock shots, including a volcanic finale.

w Maurice Tombragel, Maurice Wright *d* Harold Schuster

Lola Lane, James Craig, Eduardo Ciannelli, Tom Fadden, Henry Victor, Samuel S. Hinds

Zapped!

US 1982 98m CFI
Thunder Associates
V*, L

A high-school boffin discovers his own telekinetic powers, by which he is able to tear everyone's clothes off at the senior prom.

Mild adolescent smut, half-way between *Porky's* and the unbearable Disney comedies of the sixties.

w Bruce Rubin, Robert J. Rosenthal *d* Robert J. Rosenthal

Scott Baio, Willie Aames, Robert Mandan, Scatman Crothers

Zarak *

GB 1956 99m Technicolor Cinemascope
Columbia/Warwick (Phil C. Samuel)

An Afghan outlaw finally saves a British officer at the cost of his own life.

Box-office actioner, shot in Morocco with a weird cast and the help of old movie clips.

w Richard Maibaum *d* Terence Young *second unit* Yakima Canutt *ph* John Wilcox, Ted Moore, Cyril Knowles *m* William Alwyn *ad* John Box

Victor Mature, Michael Wilding, Anita Ekberg, Bonar Colleano, Finlay Currie, Bernard Miles, Eunice Gayson, Peter Illing, Frederick Valk, André Morell

Zardoz

GB 1973 105m DeLuxe Panavision
TCF/John Boorman
V*, L

Life in 2293, when the Earth has become wasteland and a mass of Brutals are ruled by a few Exterminators who have both memory and intelligence.

Pompous, boring fantasy for the so-called intelligentsia.

wd John Boorman *ph* Geoffrey Unsworth
m David Munrow *pd* Anthony Pratt

Sean Connery, Charlotte Rampling, John Alderton

'A glittering cultural trash pile . . . the most gloriously fatuous movie since *The Oscar*.' – *New Yorker*

Zärtlichkeit der Wölfe: see *Tenderness of Wolves*

Zateriannyi v Sibiri: see *Lost in Siberia*

Zaza

US   1938   83m   bw
Paramount (Albert Lewin)

A 1904 French chanteuse is in love with a married aristocrat.

Rather flat period romantic drama with interesting credits.

w Zoe Atkins   *play* Pierre Berton, Charles Simon   *d* George Cukor   *ph* Charles Lang   *songs* Frank Loesser, Frederick Hollander

Claudette Colbert, Herbert Marshall, Bert Lahr, Constance Collier, Helen Westley, Genevieve Tobin, Walter Catlett, Rex O'Malley

'Fine production with hefty woman-appeal.' – *Variety*

† The original David Belasco stage production made Mrs Leslie Carter famous. Silent film versions starred Pauline Frederick in 1915 and Gloria Swanson in 1923.

Zazie dans le Métro **

France   1960   88m   Eastmancolor
Nouvelles Editions (Irène Leriche)
V, V*

A naughty little girl has a day in Paris and causes chaos.

Inventive little comedy which almost turns into a French *Hellzapoppin*, with everybody chasing or fighting everybody else.

wd Louis Malle   *novel* Raymond Queneau   *ph* Henri Raichi   *m* Fiorenzo Capri

Catherine Demongeot, Philippe Noiret, Vittorio Caprioli

'There is something not quite innocent or healthy about this film.' – *Bosley Crowther*

Zebra in the Kitchen

US   1965   93m   Metrocolor
MGM/Ivan Tors
V*

A young boy tries to improve the lot of zoo animals.

Pleasing family film.

w Art Arthur   *d* Ivan Tors   *ph* Lamar Boren

Jay North, Martin Milner, Andy Devine, Joyce Meadows, Jim Davis

A Zed and Two Noughts **

GB   1985   115m   colour
Artificial Eye/BFI/Allarts Enterprises/Film Four International (Peter Sainsbury, Kees Kasander)
V, V*, S

An assemblage of images of loss and decay decorate a slim narrative about twin husbands, whose wives are killed in a car crash with a swan, and their relationship with the survivor, a woman whose leg is amputated.

Intriguing, visually compelling and witty, although it may not appeal to those expecting a traditional narrative.

wd Peter Greenaway   *ph* Sacha Vierny   *m* Michael Nyman   *pd* Ben Van Os, Jan Roelfs   *ed* John Wilson

Andrea Ferreol, Eric Deacon, Brian Deacon, Frances Barber, Joss Ackland

Zee and Co *

GB   1971   109m   colour
Columbia/Zee Films (Kastner-Ladd-Kanter)
V*
US title: *X, Y and Zee*

A successful architect battles with his termagant wife and seeks an affair.

Overwritten but entertaining sexual melodrama about an absolute bitch. The flow of bad language was new at the time.

w Edna O'Brien   *d* Brian G. Hutton   *ph* Billy Williams   *m* Stanley Myers   *ad* Peter Mullins

Elizabeth Taylor, Michael Caine, Susannah York, Margaret Leighton, John Standing

'Miss Taylor is rapidly turning into a latterday Marie Dressler.' – *Tom Milne*

'A slice-of-jet-set-life nightmare far beyond the dreams of the piggiest male chauvinist . . . the distinction of this film is that its characters are repulsive, its style vulgar, its situations beyond belief and its dialogue moronic.' – *Judith Crist*

Zelig **

US   1983   79m (including about 5m of credits)   bw/colour
Orion/Rollins-Joffe (Robert Greenhut)
V, V*, L

A parody documentary tracing a chameleon-like nonentity who contrives to have been associated with all the major events of the 20th century.

The central idea is more elusive than appealing, and the mid-section of psychiatric consultation is downright dull, but considerable amusement derives from the technical trickery which puts Woody Allen in pictorial association with Hitler, Roosevelt and Eugene O'Neill. In all, an after-dinner treat for the intellectuals.

wd Woody Allen   *ph* Gordon Willis   *m* Dick Hyman   *pd* Mel Bourne

Woody Allen, Mia Farrow

'We can all admire the brilliance and economy with which it is made. But is it funny enough? I take leave to doubt it.' – *Derek Malcolm, Guardian*

'*Citizen Kane* miraculously transformed into side-splitting comedy.' – *New York Times*

'The movie is a technical masterpiece, but in artistic and comic terms, only pretty good.' – *Roger Ebert*

AAN: cinematography; costume design

Zelly and Me *

US   1988   87m   Technicolor
Columbia/Cypress Films/Tony Mark/Sue Jett
V, V*, L

A poor little rich girl, who lives with a grandmother greedy for love, is comforted by her governess.

Unusual in its depiction of the psychological damage an adult can inflict on a child, it handles sympathetically its themes of the failure of love and the need to develop individual strength.

wd Tina Rathbone   *ph* Mikael Salomon   *m* Pino Donaggio   *pd* David Morong   *ed* Cindy Kaplan Rooney

Isabella Rossellini, Glynis Johns, Kaivlani Lee, David Lynch, Joe Morton, Alexandra Johnes

Zemlya: see *Earth*

Zenobia

US   1939   83m   bw
Hal Roach
V
GB title: *Elephants Never Forget*

A small-town doctor finds himself looking after a performing elephant.

Very mild small-town comedy made during a break-up in the Laurel and Hardy contract.

w Corey Ford, Arnold Belgard, Walter de Leon   *d* Gordon Douglas   *ph* Karl Struss   *m* Marvin Hatley

Oliver Hardy, Harry Langdon, Jean Parker, Billie Burke, Alice Brady, James Ellison, Stepin Fetchit, Hattie McDaniel

Zeppelin *

GB   1971   97m   Technicolor   Panavision
Warner/Getty and Fromkess (Owen Crump)
V*

In 1915, the British need to steal secrets from the zeppelin works at Friedrichshafen.

Undistinguished but entertaining period actioner with adequate spectacle but wooden performances.

w Arthur Rowe, Donald Churchill   *d* Etienne Périer   *ph* Alan Hume   *m* Roy Budd   *sp* Wally Veevers

Michael York, Elke Sommer, Peter Carsten, Marius Goring, Anton Diffring, Andrew Keir, Rupert Davies

Zéro de Conduite **

France   1933   45m approx   bw
Gaumont/Franco Film/Aubert
V, V*

Boys return from the holiday to a nasty little boarding school, where the headmaster is an unpleasant dwarf and all the staff are hateful. A revolution breaks out . . .

A clear forerunner of *If . . .* and one of the most famous of surrealist films, though it pales beside Buñuel and is chiefly valuable for being funny.

wd Jean Vigo   *ph* Boris Kaufman   *m* Maurice Jaubert

Jean Dasté, Louis Lefébvre, Gilbert Pruchon, le nain Delphin

'One of the most poetic films ever made and one of the most influential.' – *New Yorker, 1978*

Zero Hour!

US   1957   83m   bw
Paramount/Bartlett/Champion (John Champion)

Half the passengers and all the crew of a jet plane are stricken with food poisoning and a shell-shocked ex-fighter pilot has to land the plane.

Adequate air melodrama with a premise which later served for *Terror in the Sky* (TV) and *Airport 75*.

w Arthur Hailey, John Champion, Hall Bartlett   *teleplay Flight into Danger* by Arthur Hailey   *d* Hall Bartlett   *ph* John F. Warren   *m* Ted Dale

Dana Andrews, Linda Darnell, Sterling Hayden, Elroy Hirsch, Jerry Paris

Zero Population Growth

US   1971   96m   Eastmancolor
Sagittarius (Thomas F. Madigan)

In the 21st century there is a death penalty for having children, but a young couple defy the authorities.

Good sci-fi quickly develops into sticky sentimentality.

w Max Ehrlich, Frank de Felita   *d* Michael Campus   *ph* Michael Reed   *m* Jonathan Hodge   *pd* Tony Masters

Oliver Reed, Geraldine Chaplin, Diane Cilento, Don Gordon, Bill Nagy, Aubrey Woods

Zhivoi Trup: see *The Living Corpse*

Ziegfeld Follies **

US   1944 (released 1946)   110m   Technicolor
MGM (Arthur Freed)
V, V*, L

In heaven, Florenz Ziegfeld dreams up one last spectacular revue.

A rather airless all-star entertainment in which the comedy suffers from the lack of an audience but some of the production numbers are magnificently stylish.

w various   *d* Vincente Minnelli   *ph* George Folsey, Charles Rosher   *md* Lennie Hayton   *m* various   *ad* Cedric Gibbons, Merrill Pye, Jack Martin Smith

Fred Astaire, Lucille Ball, Bunin's Puppets, William Powell, Jimmy Durante, Edward Arnold, *Fannie Brice*, Lena Horne, Lucille Bremer, Esther Williams, Judy

Garland, *Red Skelton, Gene Kelly,* James Melton, Hume Cronyn, Victor Moore, Marion Bell

'Between opening and closing is packed a prodigious amount of material, some of which is frankly not deserving of the lavish treatment accorded it.' – *Film Daily*

'The fastidious are advised to head for the lobby while Kathryn Grayson sings "There's Beauty Everywhere" against magenta foam skies.' – *Pauline Kael, 70s*

Ziegfeld Girl *
US 1941 131m bw
MGM (Pandro S. Berman)
V*, L

The professional and romantic problems of Ziegfeld chorus girls.

Adequate big-budget drama with music.

w Marguerite Roberts, Sonya Levien *d* Robert Z. Leonard *ph* Ray June *m* Herbert Stothart *ch* Busby Berkeley *songs* various

James Stewart, Judy Garland, Hedy Lamarr, Lana Turner, Tony Martin, Jackie Cooper, Ian Hunter, *Charles Winninger, Al Shean,* Edward Everett Horton, Philip Dorn, Paul Kelly, Eve Arden, Dan Dailey, Fay Holden, Felix Bressart

'Heaping portions of show life in the opulent days of Flo Ziegfeld, the man who wanted bigger and better staircases.' – *C. A. Lejeune*

Zigzag *
US 1970 104m Metrocolor Panavision
MGM/Freeman-Enders
GB title: *False Witness*

A dying man frames himself for an unsolved murder so that the reward money, claimed under another name, will go to his wife.

Complex thriller which sustains itself pretty well most of the way, but lacks humour and character.

w John T. Kelley *d* Richard A. Colla *ph* James A. Crabe *m* Oliver Nelson

George Kennedy, Anne Jackson, Eli Wallach, Steve Ihnat, William Marshall, Joe Maross

Zoltan, Hound of Dracula: see *Dracula's Dog*

Zombi 2: see *Zombie Flesh Eaters*

Zombie: see *Zombie Flesh Eaters*

'When The Earth Spits Out The Dead.'
Zombie Flesh Eaters
Italy 1979 93m Technicolor
Variety Film (Ugo Tucci, Fabrizio de Angelis)
V*, L
original title: *Zombi 2;* aka: *Zombie; Island of The Living Dead*

After a yacht with a zombie aboard is found floating off New York, a journalist discovers that it originated on a small Caribbean island where a mad scientist's experiments result in the dead, including Spanish conquistadores, rising from their graves.

Visceral, gore-filled horror movie, owing much to the example of George Romero but made by a director who does not understand that less can be more.

w Elisa Briganti *d* Lucio Fulci *ph* Sergio Salvati *m* Fabio Frizzi, Giorgio Tucci *pd* Walter Patriarca

Ian McCulloch, Tisa Farrow, Richard Johnson, Al Cliver, Auretta Gay

† The film was cut to 85m for its British video release.

Zombies: see *Dawn of the Dead*

The Zombies of Mora Tau
US 1957 71m bw
Columbia (Sam Katzman)
V*
GB title: *The Dead that Walk*

A diver plans to salvage a subterranean West African treasure: but it is guarded by zombies.

Modest addition to the walking dead cycle.

w Raymond T. Marcus *d* Edward Cahn

Gregg Palmer, Allison Hayes, Autumn Russell, Morris Ankrum

Zombies of the Stratosphere
US 1952 bw serial: 12 eps
Republic

Invading rockets are intercepted by the Interplanetary Patrol and turn out to contain supernatural beings.

Lively serial antics.

d Fred Brannon

Judd Holdren, Aline Towne; Wilson Wood, Lane Bradford, Leonard Nimoy

Zombies on Broadway
US 1945 70m bw
Ben Stoloff/RKO
V*, L

Press agents seek a real zombie for the opening of a new night-club . . . and a mad professor provides one.

Knockabout comedy-thriller, just tolerable for addicts of the genre.

w Lawrence Kimble *d* Gordon Douglas

Wally Brown, Alan Carney, Bela Lugosi, Anne Jeffreys, Sheldon Leonard

Zoo in Budapest *
US 1933 83m bw
Fox (Jesse Lasky)

An orphan waif runs away to live with a zookeeper.

Curious little romance remembered for its luminescent photography.

w Dan Totheroh, Louise Long, Rowland V. Lee *d* Rowland V. Lee *ph* Lee Garmes

Loretta Young, Gene Raymond, O. P. Heggie, Wally Albright, Paul Fix

'Appeal for all classes . . . a subject of great photographic and pictorial beauty.' – *Variety*

'Richly composed impressionistic images, assisted by highly imaginative use of sound and background music, create a poem that Murnau himself would have envied.' – *NFT, 1971*

Un Zoo La Nuit: see *Night Zoo*

Zorba the Greek **
GB 1964 142m bw
TCF/Rockley/Cacoyannis
V, V*, L, S

A young English writer in Crete is befriended by a huge gregarious Greek who comes to dominate his life.

A mainly enjoyable character study of a larger-than-life character, this film made famous by its music does not really hang together dramatically and has several melodramatic excrescences.

wd Michael Cacoyannis *novel* Nikos Kazantzakis *ph* Walter Lassally *m* Mikis Theodorakis

Anthony Quinn, Alan Bates, Lila Kedrova, Irene Papas

'For all its immense length, the film never gets down to a clear statement of its theme, or comes within measuring distance of its vast pretensions.' – *Brenda Davies*

AA: Walter Lassally; Lila Kedrova

AAN: best picture; Michael Cacoyannis (as writer and director); Anthony Quinn

Zorro (dubbed)
Italy/France 1975 100m colour
Mondial/Artistes Associés (Vittorio Galiano)

After his friend is assassinated, Zorro takes his place as governor of a Spanish colony where a corrupt colonel and his friends are terrorizing and exploiting the locals.

Swashbuckling, tongue-in-cheek adventure done with some style and very little bloodshed.

w Giorgio Arlorio *d* Duccio Tessari *ph* Giulio Albonico *m* Guido and Maurizio de Angelis *ad* Enzo Bulgarelli *ed* Mario Morra

Alain Delon, Stanley Baker, Ottavia Piccolo, Enzo Cerusico, Moustache, Adriana Asti, Giacomo Rossi Stuart, Giampiero Albertini, Marino Mase, Rajka Jurcec

Zorro Rides Again
US 1937 bw serial: 12 eps
Republic

A masked stranger helps the California – Yucatan railroad against the predations of a ruthless industrialist.

Solidly carpentered serial.

d William Witney and John English

John Carroll, Helen Christian, Noah Beery, Duncan Renaldo, Nigel de Brulier

'Zany! Zexy! Zensational!'
Zorro the Gay Blade
US 1981 93m DeLuxe
Melvin Simon (George Hamilton, C. O. Erickson)
V*

Zorro, the masked avenger, not only pretends to be a fop but is one. Luckily he has a twin brother.

Abysmal attempt to do for Zorro what *Love at First Bite* did for Dracula.

w Hal Dresner *d* Peter Medak *ph* John A. Alonzo *m* Max Steiner themes

George Hamilton, Lauren Hutton, Brenda Vaccaro, Ron Leibman, James Booth

'A wonderful giddy farce.' – *Pauline Kael*

Zorro's Black Whip
US 1944 bw serial: 12 eps
Republic

In 1889 Idaho, sinister forces are opposed to the coming of law and order.

Saturday morning serial adventures, quite adequate to their purpose.

d Spencer Bennet and Wallace Grissell

George J. Lewis, Linda Stirling, Lucien Littlefield, Francis McDonald

Zorro's Fighting Legion
US 1939 bw serial: 12 eps
Republic

While Don Diego masquerades as Zorro, his adversary in the San Mendolita Mines masquerades as a god named Don-deoro.

Serial with most of the expected elements.

d William Witney and John English

Reed Hadley, Sheila Darcy, William Corson, Leander de Cordova

Zotz!
US 1962 87m bw
Columbia/William Castle
V*

A professor finds a rare coin with occult powers.

Footling farce patterned after *The Absent-Minded Professor*. Poor, to say the least.

w Ray Russell *novel* Walter Karig *d* William Castle *ph* Gordon Avil *m* Bernard Green

Tom Poston, Fred Clark, Jim Backus, Cecil Kellaway, Margaret Dumont

Zuckerbaby: see *Sugarbaby*

Zulu *
GB 1964 135m Technirama
Paramount/Diamond (Stanley Baker, Cyril Endfield)
V, V*, L

In 1879 British soldiers stand fast against the Zulus at Rorke's Drift.

Standard period heroics, well presented and acted.

w John Prebble, Cy Endfield *d* Cy Endfield
ph Stephen Dade *m* John Barry

Stanley Baker, Jack Hawkins, *Michael Caine,* Ulla Jacobsson, James Booth, Nigel Green, Ivor Emmanuel, Paul Daneman

Zulu Dawn
US/Netherlands 1979 117m Technicolor Panavision
Samarkand/Zulu Dawn NV (Barrie Saint Clair)
V*, L, S

In 1878, 1,300 British troops are massacred at Isandlwhana.

Confusing historical action adventure, very similar to *Zulu* but failing in its cross-cut attempt to show both sides.

w Cy Endfield, Anthony Storey *d* Douglas Hickox
ph Ousama Rawi *m* Elmer Bernstein *pd* John Rosewarne

Burt Lancaster, Denholm Elliott, Peter O'Toole, John Mills, Simon Ward, Nigel Davenport, Michael Jayston, Ronald Lacey, Freddie Jones, Christopher Cazenove, Ronald Pickup, Anna Calder-Marshall

Academy Award-winners

1927/28
Picture: Wings
Director: Frank Borzage (*Seventh Heaven*)
Comedy Director: Lewis Milestone (*Two Arabian Knights*)
Actor: Emil Jannings (*The Last Command, The Way of All Flesh*)
Actress: Janet Gaynor (*Seventh Heaven, Street Angel, Sunrise*)
Original Screenplay: Ben Hecht (*Underworld*)
Adapted Screenplay: Benjamin Glazer (*Seventh Heaven*)
Title Writing: Joseph Farnham (*Telling the World*)

1928/29
Picture: Broadway Melody
Director: Frank Lloyd (*The Divine Lady, Weary River, Drag*)
Actor: Warner Baxter (*Old Arizona*)
Actress: Mary Pickford (*Coquette*)
Writing Achievement: Hans Kraly (*The Patriot*)

1929/30
Picture: All Quiet on the Western Front
Director: Lewis Milestone (*All Quiet on the Western Front*)
Actor: George Arliss (*Disraeli*)
Actress: Norma Shearer (*The Divorcee*)
Writing Achievement: Frances Marion (*The Big House*)

1930/31
Picture: Cimarron
Director: Norman Taurog (*Skippy*)
Actor: Lionel Barrymore (*A Free Soul*)
Actress: Marie Dressler (*Min and Bill*)
Original Screenplay: John Monk Saunders (*The Dawn Patrol*)
Adapted Screenplay: Howard Eastabrook (*Cimarron*)

1931/32
Picture: Grand Hotel
Director: Frank Borzage (*Bad Girl*)
Actor: Wallace Beery (*The Champ*)
Actress: Helen Hayes (*The Sin of Madelon Claudet*)
Original Screenplay: Francis Marion (*The Champ*)
Adapted Screenplay: Edwin Burke (*Bad Girl*)

1932/33
Picture: Cavalcade
Director: Frank Lloyd (*Cavalcade*)
Actor: Charles Laughton (*The Private Life of Henry VIII*)
Actress: Katharine Hepburn (*Morning Glory*)
Original Screenplay: Robert Lord (*One Way Passage*)
Adapted Screenplay: Victor Heerman, Sarah Y. Mason (*Little Women*)

1934
Picture: It Happened One Night
Director: Frank Capra (*It Happened One Night*)
Actor: Clark Gable (*It Happened One Night*)
Actress: Claudette Colbert (*It Happened One Night*)
Original Screenplay: Arthur Caesar (*Manhattan Melodrama*)
Adapted Screenplay: Robert Riskin (*It Happened One Night*)

1935
Picture: Mutiny on the Bounty
Director: John Ford (*The Informer*)
Actor: Victor McLaglen (*The Informer*)
Actress: Bette Davis (*Dangerous*)
Original Screenplay: Ben Hecht, Charles MacArthur (*The Scoundrel*)
Adapted Screenplay: Dudley Nichols (*The Informer*)

1936
Picture: The Great Ziegfeld
Director: Frank Capra (*Mr Deeds Goes to Town*)
Actor: Paul Muni (*The Story of Louis Pasteur*)
Actress: Luise Rainer (*The Great Ziegfeld*)
Supporting Actor: Walter Brenna (*Come and Get It*)
Supporting Actress: Gale Sondergaard (*Anthony Adverse*)
Original Screenplay: Pierre Collings, Sheridan Gibney (*The Story of Louis Pasteur*)

1937
Picture: The Life of Emile Zola
Director: Leo McCarey (*The Awful Truth*)
Actor: Spencer Tracy (*Captains Courageous*)
Actress: Luise Rainer (*The Good Earth*)
Supporting Actor: Joseph Schildkraut (*The Life of Emile Zola*)
Supporting Actress: Alice Brady (*In Old Chicago*)
Original Story: William A. Wellman, Robert Carson (*A Star Is Born*)
Original Screenplay: Heinz Herald, Geza Herczeg, Norman Reilly Raine (*The Life of Emile Zola*)

1938
Picture: You Can't Take It with You
Director: Frank Capra (*You Can't Take It with You*)
Actor: Spencer Tracy (*Boys' Town*)
Actress: Bette Davis (*Jezebel*)
Supporting Actor: Walter Brennan (*Kentucky*)
Supporting Actress: Fay Bainter (*Jezebel*)
Original Story: Eleanore Griffin, Dore Schary (*Boys' Town*)
Screenplay: George Bernard Shaw, adapted by Ian Dalrymple, Cecil Lewis, W. P. Liscomb (*Pygmalion*)

1939
Picture: Gone with the Wind
Director: Victor Fleming (*Gone with the Wind*)
Actor: Robert Donat (*Goodbye Mr Chips*)
Actress: Vivien Leigh (*Gone with the Wind*)
Supporting Actor: Thomas Mitchell (*Stagecoach*)
Supporting Actress: Hattie McDaniel (*Gone with the Wind*)
Original Story: Lewis R. Foster (*Mr Smith Goes to Washington*)
Screenplay: Sidney Howard (*Gone with the Wind*)

1940
Picture: Rebecca
Director: John Ford (*The Grapes of Wrath*)
Actor: James Stewart (*The Philadelphia Story*)
Actress: Ginger Rogers (*Kitty Foyle*)
Supporting Actor: Walter Brennan (*The Westerner*)
Supporting Actress: Jane Darwell (*The Grapes of Wrath*)
Original Story: Benjamin Glazer, John S. Toldy (*Arise My Love*)
Original Screenplay: Preston Sturges (*The Great McGinty*)
Screenplay: Donald Ogden Stewart (*The Philadelphia Story*)

1941
Picture: How Green Was My Valley
Director: John Ford (*How Green Was My Valley*)
Actor: Gary Cooper (*Sergeant York*)
Actress: Joan Fontaine (*Suspicion*)
Supporting Actor: Donald Crisp (*How Green Was My Valley*)
Supporting Actress: Mary Astor (*The Great Lie*)
Original Story: Harry Segall (*Here Comes Mr Jordan*)
Original Screenplay: Herman J. Mankiewicz, Orson Welles (*Citizen Kane*)
Screenplay: Sidney Buchman, Seton I. Miller (*Here Comes Mr Jordan*)

1942
Picture: Mrs Miniver
Director: William Wyler (*Mrs Miniver*)
Actor: James Cagney (*Yankee Doodle Dandy*)
Actress: Greer Garson (*Mrs Miniver*)
Supporting Actor: Van Heflin (*Johnny Eager*)
Supporting Actress: Teresa Wright (*Mrs Miniver*)
Original Story: Emeric Pressburger (*Forty-ninth Parallel;* US title: *The Invaders*)
Original Screenplay: Michael Kanin, Ring Lardner Jnr (*Woman of the Year*)
Screenplay: George Froeschel, James Hilton, Claudine West, Arthur Wimperis (*Mrs Miniver*)

1943
Picture: Casablanca
Director: Michael Curtiz (*Casablanca*)
Actor: Paul Lukas (*Watch on the Rhine*)
Actress: Jennifer Jones (*Song of Bernadette*)
Supporting Actor: Charles Coburn (*The More the Merrier*)
Supporting Actress: Katina Paxinou (*For Whom the Bell Tolls*)
Original Story: William Saroyan (*The Human Comedy*)
Original Screenplay: Norman Krasna (*Princess O'Rourke*)

Screenplay: Julius J. Epstein, Philip G. Epstein, Howard Koch (*Casablanca*)

1944
Picture: Going My Way
Director: Leo McCarey (*Going My Way*)
Actor: Bing Crosby (*Going My Way*)
Actress: Ingrid Bergman (*Gaslight*)
Supporting Actor: Barry Fitzgerald (*Going My Way*)
Supporting Actress: Ethel Barrymore (*None but the Lonely Heart*)
Original Story: Leo McCarey (*Going My Way*)
Original Screenplay: Lamar Trotti (*Wilson*)
Screenplay: Frank Butler, Frank Cavett (*Going My Way*)

1945
Picture: The Lost Weekend
Director: Billy Wilder (*The Lost Weekend*)
Actor: Ray Milland (*The Lost Weekend*)
Actress: Joan Crawford (*Mildred Pierce*)
Supporting Actor: James Dunn (*A Tree Grows in Brooklyn*)
Supporting Actress: Anne Revere (*National Velvet*)
Original Story: Charles G. Booth (*The House on 92nd Street*)
Original Screenplay: Richard Schweizer (*Marie-Louise*)
Screenplay: Charles Brackett, Billy Wilder (*The Lost Weekend*)

1946
Picture: The Best Years of Our Lives
Director: William Wyler (*The Best Years of Our Lives*)
Actor: Fredric March (*The Best Years of Our Lives*)
Actress: Olivia de Havilland (*To Each His Own*)
Supporting Actor: Harold Russell (*The Best Years of Our Lives*)
Supporting Actress: Anne Baxter (*The Razor's Edge*)
Original Story: Clemence Dane (*Perfect Strangers;* US title: *Vacation from Marriage*)
Original Screenplay: Muriel Box, Sydney Box (*The Seventh Veil*)
Screenplay: Robert E. Sherwood (*The Best Years of Our Lives*)

1947
Picture: Gentleman's Agreement
Director: Elia Kazan (*Gentleman's Agreement*)
Actor: Ronald Colman (*A Double Life*)
Actress: Loretta Young (*The Farmer's Daughter*)
Supporting Actor: Edmund Gwenn (*Miracle on 34th Street*)
Supporting Actress: Celeste Hom (*Gentleman's Agreement*)
Original Story: Valentine Davies (*Miracle on 34th Street*)
Original Screenplay: Sidney Sheldon (*The Bachelor and the Bobby-Soxer*)
Screenplay: George Seaton (*Miracle on 34th Street*)

1948
Picture: Hamlet
Director: John Huston (*The Treasure of the Sierra Madre*)
Actor: Laurence Olivier (*Hamlet*)
Actress: Jane Wyman (*Johnny Belinda*)
Supporting Actor: Walter Huston (*The Treasure of the Sierra Madre*)
Supporting Actress: Claire Trevor (*Key Largo*)

Motion Picture Story: Richard Sweizer, David Wechsler (*The Search*)

Screenplay: John Huston (*The Treasure of the Sierra Madre*)

1949

Picture: All the King's Men

Director: Joseph L. Mankiewicz (*A Letter to Three Wives*)

Actor: Broderick Crawford (*All the King's Men*)

Actress: Olivia de Havilland (*The Heiress*)

Supporting Actor: Dean Jagger (*Twelve O'Clock High*)

Supporting Actress: Mercedes McCambridge (*All the King's Men*)

Motion Picture Story: Douglas Morrow (*The Stratton Story*)

Screenplay: Joseph L. Mankiewicz (*A Letter to Three Wives*)

Story & Screenplay: Robert Pirosh (*Battleground*)

1950

Picture: All About Eve

Director: Joseph L. Mankiewicz (*All About Eve*)

Actor: José Ferrer (*Cyrano de Bergerac*)

Actress; Judy Holliday (*Born Yesterday*)

Supporting Actor: George Sanders (*All About Eve*)

Supporting Actress: Josephine Hull (*Harvey*)

Motion Picture Story: Edna Anhalt, Edward Anhalt (*Panic in the Streets*)

Screenplay: Joseph L. Mankiewicz (*All About Eve*)

Story & Screenplay: Charles Brackett, Billy Wilder, D. M. Marshman Jnr (*Sunset Boulevard*)

1951

Picture: An American in Paris

Director: George Stevens (*A Place in the Sun*)

Actor: Humphrey Bogart (*The African Queen*)

Actress: Vivien Leigh (*A Streetcar Named Desire*)

Supporting Actor: Karl Malden (*A Streetcar Named Desire*)

Supporting Actress: Kim Hunter (*A Streetcar Named Desire*)

Motion Picture Story: Paul Dehn, James Bernard (*Seven Days to Noon*)

Screenplay: Michael Wilson, Harry Brown (*A Place in the Sun*)

Story & Screenplay: Alan Jay Lerner (*An American in Paris*)

1952

Picture: The Greatest Show on Earth

Director: John Ford (*The Quiet Man*)

Actor: Gary Cooper (*High Noon*)

Actress: Shirley Booth (*Come Back Little Sheba*)

Supporting Actor: Anthony Quinn (*Viva Zapata!*)

Supporting Actress: Gloria Grahame (*The Bad and the Beautiful*)

Motion Picture Story: Frederic M. Frank, Theodore St John, Frank Cavett (*The Greatest Show on Earth*)

Screenplay: Charles Schnee (*The Bad and the Beautiful*)

Story & Screenplay: T. E. B. Clarke (*The Lavender Hill Mob*)

1953

Picture: From Here to Eternity

Director: Fred Zinnemann (*From Here to Eternity*)

Actor: William Holden (*Stalag 17*)

Actress: Audrey Hepburn (*Roman Holiday*)

Supporting Actor: Frank Sinatra (*From Here to Eternity*)

Supporting Actress: Donna Reed (*From Here to Eternity*)

Motion Picture Story: Ian McLellan Hunter, fronting for the blacklisted Dalton Trumbo (*Roman Holiday*)

Screenplay: Daniel Taradash (*From Here to Eternity*)

Story & Screenplay: Charles Brackett, Walter Reisch, Richard Breen (*Titanic*)

1954

Picture: On the Waterfront

Director: Elia Kazan (*On the Waterfront*)

Actor: Marlon Brando (*On the Waterfront*)

Actress: Grace Kelly (*The Country Girl*)

Supporting Actor: Edmond O'Brien (*The Barefoot Contessa*)

Supporting Actress: Eva Marie Saint (*On the Waterfront*)

Motion Picture Story: Philip Yordan (*Broken Lance*)

Screenplay: George Seaton (*The Country Girl*)

Story & Screenplay: Budd Schulberg (*On the Waterfront*)

1955

Picture: Marty

Director: Delbert Mann (*Marty*)

Actor: Ernest Borgnine (*Marty*)

Actress: Anna Magnani (*The Rose Tattoo*)

Supporting Actor: Jack Lemmon (*Mister Roberts*)

Supporting Actress: Jo Van Fleet (*East of Eden*)

Motion Picture Story: Daniel Fuchs (*Love Me or Leave Me*)

Screenplay: Paddy Chayevsky (*Marty*)

Story & Screenplay: William Ludwig, Sonya Levien (*Interrupted Melody*)

1956

Picture: Around the World in Eighty Days

Director: George Stevens (*Giant*)

Actor: Yul Brynner (*The King and I*)

Actress: Ingrid Bergman (*Anastasia*)

Supporting Actor: Anthony Quinn (*Lust for Life*)

Supporting Actress: Dorothy Malone (*Written on the Wind*)

Motion Picture Story: Dalton Trumbo (as Robert Rich) (*The Brave One*)

Original Screenplay: Albert Lamorisse (*The Red Balloon*)

Adapted Screenplay: James Poe, John Farrow, S. J. Perelman (*Around the World in Eighty Days*)

1957

Picture: The Bridge on the River Kwai

Director: David Lean (*The Bridge on the River Kwai*)

Actor: Alec Guinness (*The Bridge on the River Kwai*)

Actress: Joanne Woodward (*The Three Faces of Eve*)

Supporting Actor: Red Buttons (*Sayonara*)

Supporting Actress: Miyoshi Umeki (*Sayonara*)

Original Story & Screenplay: George Wells (*Designing Woman*)

Adapted Screenplay: Pierre Boulle, Michael Wilson, Carl Foreman (*The Bridge on the River Kwai*)

1958

Picture: Gigi

Director: Vincente Minnelli (*Gigi*)

Actor: David Niven (*Separate Tables*)

Actress: Susan Hayward (*I Want to Live*)
Supporting Actor: Burl Ives (*The Big Country*)
Supporting Actress: Wendy Hiller (*Separate Tables*)
Original Story & Screenplay: Nathan E. Douglas (the blacklisted Ned Young), Harold Jacob Smith (*The Defiant Ones*)
Adapted Screenplay: Alan Jay Lerner (*Gigi*)

1959
Picture: Ben-Hur
Director: William Wyler (*Ben-Hur*)
Actor: Charlton Heston (*Ben-Hur*)
Actress: Simone Signoret (*Room at the Top*)
Supporting Actor: Hugh Griffith (*Ben-Hur*)
Supporting Actress: Shelley Winters (*The Diary of Anne Frank*)
Original Story & Screenplay: Russell Rouse, Clarence Greene, Stanley Shapiro, Maurice Richlin (*Pillow Talk*)
Adapted Screenplay: Neil Paterson (*Room at the Top*)

1960
Picture: The Apartment
Director: Billy Wilder (*The Apartment*)
Actor: Burt Lancaster (*Elmer Gantry*)
Actress: Elizabeth Taylor (*Butterfield 8*)
Supporting Actor: Peter Ustinov (*Spartacus*)
Supporting Actress: Shirley Jones (*Elmer Gantry*)
Original Story & Screenplay: Billy Wilder, I. A. L. Diamond (*The Apartment*)
Adapted Screenplay: Richard Brooks (*Elmer Gantry*)

1961
Picture: West Side Story
Director: Jerome Robbins, Robert Wise (*West Side Story*)
Actor: Maximilian Schell (*Judgment at Nuremberg*)
Actress: Sophia Loren (*Two Women*)
Supporting Actor: George Chakiris (*West Side Story*)
Supporting Actress: Rita Moreno (*West Side Story*)
Original Story & Screenplay: William Inge (*Splendor in the Grass*)
Adapted Screenplay: Abby Mann (*Judgment at Nuremberg*)

1962
Picture: Lawrence of Arabia
Director: David Lean (*Lawrence of Arabia*)
Actor: Gregory Peck (*To Kill a Mockingbird*)
Actress: Anne Bancroft (*The Miracle Worker*)
Supporting Actor: Ed Begley (*Sweet Bird of Youth*)
Supporting Actress: Patty Duke (*The Miracle Worker*)
Original Story & Screenplay: Ennio de Concini, Alfredo Gianetti, Pietro Germi (*Divorce Italian Style*)
Adapted Screenplay: Horton Foote (*To Kill a Mockingbird*)

1963
Picture: Tom Jones
Director: Tony Richardson (*Tom Jones*)
Actor: Sidney Poitier (*Lilies of the Field*)
Actress: Patricia Neal (*Hud*)
Supporting Actor: Melvyn Douglas (*Hud*)
Supporting Actress: Margaret Rutherford (*The VIPs*)

Original Story & Screenplay: James R. Webb (*How the West Was Won*)
Adapted Screenplay: John Osborne (*Tom Jones*)

1964
Picture: My Fair Lady
Director: George Cukor (*My Fair Lady*)
Actor: Rex Harrison (*My Fair Lady*)
Actress: Julie Andrews (*Mary Poppins*)
Supporting Actor: Peter Ustinov (*Topkapi*)
Supporting Actress: Lila Kedrova (*Zorba the Greek*)
Original Story & Screenplay: S. H. Barnett, Peter Stone, Frank Tarloff (*Father Goose*)
Adapted Screenplay: Edward Anhalt (*Becket*)

1965
Picture: The Sound of Music
Director: Robert Wise (*The Sound of Music*)
Actor: Lee Marvin (*Cat Ballou*)
Actress: Julie Christie (*Darling*)
Supporting Actor: Martin Balsam (*A Thousand Clowns*)
Supporting Actress: Shelley Winters (*A Patch of Blue*)
Original Story & Screenplay: Frederic Raphael (*Darling*)
Adapted Screenplay: Robert Bolt (*Dr Zhivago*)

1966
Picture: A Man for All Seasons
Director: Fred Zinnemann (*A Man for All Seasons*)
Actor: Paul Scofield (*A Man for All Seasons*)
Actress: Elizabeth Taylor (*Who's Afraid of Virginia Woolf?*)
Supporting Actor: Walter Matthau (*The Fortune Cookie*)
Supporting Actress: Sandy Dennis (*Who's Afraid of Virginia Woolf?*)
Original Story & Screenplay: Claude Lelouch, Pierre Uytterhoeven (*A Man and a Woman*)
Adapted Screenplay: Robert Bolt (*A Man for All Seasons*)

1967
Picture: In the Heat of the Night
Director: Mike Nichols (*The Graduate*)
Actor: Rod Steiger (*In the Heat of the Night*)
Actress: Katharine Hepburn (*Guess Who's Coming to Dinner*)
Supporting Actor: George Kennedy (*Cool Hand Luke*)
Supporting Actress: Estelle Parsons (*Bonnie and Clyde*)
Original Story & Screenplay: William Rose (*Guess Who's Coming to Dinner*)
Adapted Screenplay: Sterling Silliphant (*In the Heat of the Night*)

1968
Picture: Oliver!
Director: Carol Reed (*Oliver!*)
Actor: Cliff Robertson (*Charly*)
Actress: Katharine Hepburn (*The Lion in Winter*)
Supporting Actor: Jack Albertson (*The Subject Was Roses*)
Supporting Actress: Ruth Gordon (*Rosemary's Baby*)
Original Story & Screenplay: Mel Brooks (*The Producers*)
Adapted Screenplay: James Goldman (*The Lion in Winter*)

1969
Picture: Midnight Cowboy
Director: John Schlesinger (*Midnight Cowboy*)
Actor: John Wayne (*True Grit*)
Actress: Maggie Smith (*The Prime of Miss Jean Brodie*)
Supporting Actor: Gig Young (*They Shoot Horses, Don't They?*)
Supporting Actress: Goldie Hawn (*Cactus Flower*)
Original Story & Screenplay: William Goldman (*Butch Cassidy and the Sundance Kid*)
Adapted Screenplay: Waldo Salt (*Midnight Cowboy*)

1970
Picture: Patton
Director: Franklin J. Schaffner (*Patton*)
Actor: George C. Scott (*Patton*)
Actress: Glenda Jackson (*Women in Love*)
Supporting Actor: John Mills (*Ryan's Daughter*)
Supporting Actress: Helen Hayes (*Airport*)
Original Story & Screenplay: Francis Ford Coppola, Edmund H. North (*Patton*)
Adapted Screenplay: Ring Lardner Jnr (*M*A*S*H*)

1971
Picture: The French Connection
Director: William Friedkin (*The French Connection*)
Actor: Gene Hackman (*The French Connection*)
Actress: Jane Fonda (*Klute*)
Supporting Actor: Ben Johnson (*The Last Picture Show*)
Supporting Actress: Cloris Leachman (*The Last Picture Show*)
Original Story & Screenplay: Paddy Chayevsky (*The Hospital*)
Adapted Screenplay: Ernest Tidyman (*The French Connection*)

1972
Picture: The Godfather
Director: Bob Fosse (*Cabaret*)
Actor: Marlon Brando (*The Godfather*)
Actress: Liza Minnelli (*Cabaret*)
Supporting Actor: Joel Grey (*Cabaret*)
Supporting Actress: Eileen Heckart (*Butterflies Are Free*)
Original Story & Screenplay: Jeremy Larner (*The Candidate*)
Adapted Screenplay: Mario Puzo, Francis Ford Coppola (*The Godfather*)

1973
Picture: The Sting
Director: George Roy Hill (*The Sting*)
Actor: Jack Lemmon (*Save the Tiger*)
Actress: Glenda Jackson (*A Touch of Class*)
Supporting Actor: John Houseman (*The Paper Chase*)
Supporting Actress: Tatum O'Neal (*Paper Moon*)
Original Story & Screenplay: David S. Ward (*The Sting*)
Adapted Screenplay: William Peter Blatty (*The Exorcist*)

1974
Picture: The Godfather Part II
Director: Francis Ford Coppola (*The Godfather Part II*)
Actor: Art Carney (*Harry and Tonto*)
Actress: Ellen Burstyn (*Alice Doesn't Live Here Any More*)

Supporting Actor: Robert de Niro (*The Godfather Part II*)
Supporting Actress: Ingrid Bergman (*Murder on the Orient Express*)
Original Story & Screenplay: Robert Towne (*Chinatown*)
Adapted Screenplay: Francis Ford Coppola, Mario Puzo (*The Godfather Part II*)

1975
Picture: One Flew over the Cuckoo's Nest
Director: Milos Forman (*One Flew over the Cuckoo's Nest*)
Actor: Jack Nicholson (*One Flew over the Cuckoo's Nest*)
Actress: Louise Fletcher (*One Flew over the Cuckoo's Nest*)
Supporting Actor: George Burns (*The Sunshine Boys*)
Supporting Actress: Lee Grant (*Shampoo*)
Original Screenplay: Frank Pierson (*Dog Day Afternoon*)
Adapted Screenplay: Lawrence Hauben, Bo Goldman (*One Flew over the Cuckoo's Nest*)

1976
Picture: Rocky
Director: John G. Avildsen (*Rocky*)
Actor: Peter Finch (*Network*)
Actress: Faye Dunaway (*Network*)
Supporting Actor: Jason Robards (*All the President's Men*)
Supporting Actress: Beatrice Straight (*Network*)
Original Screenplay: Paddy Chayevsky (*Network*)
Adapted Screenplay: William Goldman (*All the President's Men*)

1977
Picture: Annie Hall
Director: Woody Allen (*Annie Hall*)
Actor: Richard Dreyfuss (*The Goodbye Girl*)
Actress: Diane Keaton (*Annie Hall*)
Supporting Actor: Jason Robards (*Julia*)
Supporting Actress: Vanessa Redgrave (*Julia*)
Original Screenplay: Woody Allen, Marshall Brickman (*Annie Hall*)
Adapted Screenplay: Alvin Sargent (*Julia*)

1978
Picture: The Deer Hunter
Director: Michael Cimino (*The Deer Hunter*)
Actor: Jon Voight (*Coming Home*)
Actress: Jane Fonda (*Coming Home*)
Supporting Actor: Christopher Walken (*The Deer Hunter*)
Supporting Actress: Maggie Smith (*California Suite*)
Original Screenplay: Nancy Dowd, Waldo Salt, Robert C. Jones (*Coming Home*)
Adapted Screenplay: Oliver Stone (*Midnight Express*)

1979
Picture: Kramer versus Kramer
Director: Robert Benton (*Kramer versus Kramer*)
Actor: Dustin Hoffman (*Kramer versus Kramer*)
Actress: Sally Field (*Norma Rae*)
Supporting Actor: Melvyn Douglas (*Being There*)
Supporting Actress: Meryl Streep (*Kramer versus Kramer*)

Original Screenplay: Steve Tesich (*Breaking Away*)
Adapted Screenplay: Robert Benton (*Kramer versus Kramer*)

1980
Picture: Ordinary People
Director: Robert Redford (*Ordinary People*)
Actor: Robert de Niro (*Raging Bull*)
Actress: Sissy Spacek (*Coal Miner's Daughter*)
Supporting Actor: Timothy Hutton (*Ordinary People*)
Supporting Actress: Mary Steenburgen (*Melvin and Howard*)
Original Screenplay: Bo Goldman (*Melvin and Howard*)
Adapted Screenplay: Alvin Sargent (*Ordinary People*)

1981
Picture: Chariots of Fire
Director: Warren Beatty (*Reds*)
Actor: Henry Fonda (*On Golden Pond*)
Actress: Katharine Hepburn (*On Golden Pond*)
Supporting Actor: John Gielgud (*Arthur*)
Supporting Actress: Maureen Stapleton (*Reds*)
Original Screenplay: Colin Welland (*Chariots of Fire*)
Adapted Screenplay: Ernest Thompson (*On Golden Pond*)

1982
Picture: Gandhi
Director: Richard Attenborough (*Gandhi*)
Actor: Ben Kingsley (*Gandhi*)
Actress: Meryl Streep (*Sophie's Choice*)
Supporting Actor: Louis Gossett Jnr (*An Officer and a Gentleman*)
Supporting Actress: Jessica Lange (*Tootsie*)
Original Screenplay: John Briley (*Gandhi*)
Adapted Screenplay: Costa-Gavras, Donald Stewart (*Missing*)

1983
Picture: Terms of Endearment
Director: James L. Brooks (*Terms of Endearment*)
Actor: Robert Duvall (*Tender Mercies*)
Actress: Shirley Maclaine (*Terms of Endearment*)
Supporting Actor: Jack Nicholson (*Terms of Endearment*)
Supporting Actress: Linda Hunt (*The Year of Living Dangerously*)
Original Screenplay: Horton Foote (*Tender Mercies*)
Adapted Screenplay: James L. Brooks (*Terms of Endearment*)

1984
Picture: Amadeus
Director: Milos Forman (*Amadeus*)
Actor: F. Murray Abraham (*Amadeus*)
Actress: Sally Field (*Places in the Heart*)
Supporting Actor: Haing S. Ngor (*The Killing Fields*)
Supporting Actress: Peggy Ashcroft (*A Passage to India*)
Original Screenplay: Robert Benton (*Places in the Heart*)
Adapted Screenplay: Peter Shaffer (*Amadeus*)

1985
Picture: Out of Africa
Director: Sydney Pollack (*Out of Africa*)
Actor: William Hurt (*Kiss of the Spider Woman*)
Actress: Geraldine Page (*The Trip to Bountiful*)

Supporting Actor: Don Ameche (*Cocoon*)
Supporting Actress: Anjelica Huston (*Prizzi's Honor*)
Original Screenplay: William Kelley, Pamela Wallace, Earl W. Wallace (*Witness*)
Adapted Screenplay: Kurt Luedtke (*Out of Africa*)

1986
Picture: Platoon
Director: Oliver Stone (*Platoon*)
Actor: Paul Newman (*The Color of Money*)
Actress: Marlee Matlin (*Children of a Lesser God*)
Supporting Actor: Michael Caine (*Hannah and Her Sisters*)
Supporting Actress: Dianne Wiest (*Hannah and Her Sisters*)
Original Screenplay: Woody Allen (*Hannah and Her Sisters*)
Adapted Screenplay: Ruth Prawer Jhabvala (*A Room with a View*)

1987
Picture: The Last Emperor
Director: Bernardo Bertolucci (*The Last Emperor*)
Actor: Michael Douglas (*Wall Street*)
Actress: Cher (*Moonstruck*)
Supporting Actor: Sean Connery (*The Untouchables*)
Supporting Actress: Olympia Dukakis (*Moonstruck*)
Original Screenplay: John Patrick Shanley (*Moonstruck*)
Adapted Screenplay: Mark Peploe, Bernardo Bertolucci (*The Last Emperor*)

1988
Picture: Rain Man
Director: Barry Levinson (*Rain Man*)
Actor: Dustin Hoffman (*Rain Man*)
Actress: Jodie Foster (*The Accused*)
Supporting Actor: Kevin Kline (*A Fish Called Wanda*)
Supporting Actress: Geena Davis (*The Accidental Tourist*)
Original Screenplay: Ronald Bass, Barry Morrow (*Rain Man*)
Adapted Screenplay: Christopher Hampton (*Dangerous Liaisons*)

1989
Picture: Driving Miss Daisy
Director: Oliver Stone (*Born on the Fourth of July*)
Actor: Daniel Day-Lewis (*My Left Foot*)
Actress: Jessica Tandy (*Driving Miss Daisy*)
Supporting Actor: Denzel Washington (*Glory*)
Supporting Actress: Brenda Fricker (*My Left Foot*)
Original Screenplay: Tom Schulman (*Dead Poets Society*)
Adapted Screenplay: Alfred Uhry (*Driving Miss Daisy*)

1990
Picture: Dances with Wolves
Director: Kevin Costner (*Dances with Wolves*)
Actor: Jeremy Irons (*Reversal of Fortune*)
Actress: Kathy Bates (*Misery*)
Supporting Actor: Joe Pesci (*GoodFellas*)
Supporting Actress: Whoopi Goldberg (*Ghost*)
Original Screenplay: Bruce Joel Rubin (*Ghost*)
Adapted Screenplay: Michael Blake (*Dances with Wolves*)

1991
Picture: Silence of the Lambs
Director: Jonathan Demme (*Silence of the Lambs*)
Actor: Anthony Hopkins (*Silence of the Lambs*)
Actress: Jodie Foster (*Silence of the Lambs*)
Supporting Actor: Jack Palance (*City Slickers*)
Supporting Actress: Mercedes Ruehl (*The Fisher King*)
Original Screenplay: Callie Khouri (*Thelma and Louise*)
Adapted Screenplay: Ted Tally (*Silence of the Lambs*)

1992
Picture: Unforgiven
Director: Clint Eastwood (*Unforgiven*)
Actor: Al Pacino (*Scent of a Woman*)
Actress: Emma Thompson (*Howards End*)

Supporting Actor: Gene Hackman (*Unforgiven*)
Supporting Actress: Marisa Tomei (*My Cousin Vinny*)
Original Screenplay: Neil Jordan (*The Crying Game*)
Adapted Screenplay: Ruth Prawer Jhabvala (*Howards End*)

1993
Picture: Schindler's List
Director: Steven Spielberg (*Schindler's List*)
Actor: Tom Hanks (*Philadelphia*)
Actress: Holly Hunter (*The Piano*)
Supporting Actor: Tommy Lee Jones (*The Fugitive*)
Supporting Actress: Anna Paquin (*The Piano*)
Original Screenplay: Jane Campion (*The Piano*)
Adapted Screenplay: Steven Zaillian (*Schindler's List*)

Four-Star Films – By Title

À Bout de Souffle (Breathless)
À Nous la Liberté
The Adventures of Robin Hood
Aguirre, Wrath of God
Aladdin
Alexander Nevsky
Alien
All Quiet on the Western Front
All That Money Can Buy
All the President's Men
An American in Paris
And Then There Were None
Andrei Rublev
Angels with Dirty Faces
Annie Hall
Aparajito
Ashes and Diamonds
Au Revoir Les Enfants
Bad Day at Black Rock
Badlands
Bambi
The Band Wagon
Battle of Algiers
The Battleship Potemkin
Begone Dull Care
Belle de Jour
The Best Years of Our Lives
Big Business
The Birth of a Nation
The Blue Angel
Bonnie and Clyde
The Bride of Frankenstein
The Bridge on the River Kwai
Brief Encounter
Butch Cassidy and the Sundance Kid
Cabaret
The Cabinet of Dr Caligari
Casablanca
The Chant of Jimmy Blacksmith
Chinatown
Cinema Paradiso
Citizen Kane
Cries and Whispers
Crossfire
The Cure
David Copperfield
A Day at the Races
Day for Night
Days of Heaven
The Dead

Dead of Night
Deliverance
Destry Rides Again
The Discreet Charm of the Bourgeoisie
Doctor Jekyll and Mr Hyde
Dr Strangelove
La Dolce Vita (The Sweet Life)
Don't Look Now
Double Indemnity
The Driver
Duck Soup
Dumbo
E.T.
Easy Rider
Easy Street
Eight and a Half
Les Enfants du Paradis (Children of
    Paradise)
The Enigma of Kaspar Hauser
Face to Face
Fanny and Alexander
Fantasia
Fitzcarraldo
Foreign Correspondent
The Four Feathers
Frankenstein
The French Connection
Gaslight
The Gay Divorcee
The General
Genevieve
The Godfather
The Godfather Part II
The Golden Age of Comedy
    (compilation)
Gone with the Wind
GoodFellas
The Graduate
The Grapes of Wrath
Great Expectations
A Hard Day's Night
Harold Lloyd's World of Comedy
    (compilation)
Henry V
High Noon
His Girl Friday
Hud
The Hunchback of Notre Dame
The Hustler
I Am a Fugitive from a Chain Gang

If . . .
In the Heat of the Night
In Which We Serve
Intolerance
Invasion of the Body Snatchers
The Invisible Man
It's a Wonderful Life
The Jazz Singer
The Jolson Story
Jules et Jim
Kes
The Kid Brother
A Kind of Loving
King Kong
King of Comedy
King's Row
The Knack
Kwaidan
Lacombe, Lucien
The Lady Vanishes
Last Metro
The Last Picture Show
The Lavender Hill Mob
Lawrence of Arabia
The Leopard
The Letter
Listen to Britain
Little Caesar
London Can Take It
Lost Horizon
The Lost Weekend
Love Me Tonight
The Magnificent Ambersons
The Maltese Falcon
A Man for All Seasons
The Man in the White Suit
The Manchurian Candidate
Manhattan
Marty
M*A*S*H
A Matter of Life and Death
Mean Streets
Mephisto
Midnight Cowboy
Le Million
Les Misérables
Mr Smith Goes to Washington
Monsieur Hulot's Holiday
The Music Box
The Naked City

Napoleon
Network
A Night at the Opera
North by Northwest
Oh Mr Porter
The Old Dark House
Oliver Twist
On the Town
On the Waterfront
Once Upon a Time in America
One Flew over the Cuckoo's Nest
The Passion of Joan of Arc
Passport to Pimlico
Pather Panchali
Paths of Glory
Pelle the Conqueror
Persona
The Philadelphia Story
The Piano
Picnic at Hanging Rock
Pinocchio
The Player
The Prisoner of Zenda
Psycho
Pygmalion
Raging Bull
Ran
Rashomon
Rear Window
Rebecca
The Red Shoes

Rembrandt
San Francisco
Saturday Night and Sunday Morning
Scarface
Schindler's List
The Searchers
The Seven Samurai
The Seventh Seal
A Short Film about Killing
Singin' in the Rain
Snow White and the Seven Dwarfs
Some Like It Hot
Sons of the Desert
Southern Comfort
Stagecoach
Star Wars
Sullivan's Travels
Sweet Smell of Success
Target for Tonight
Taxi Driver
The Thief of Baghdad
Things to Come
The Third Man
The Thirty-Nine Steps
This Is Spinal Tap
Throne of Blood
The Tin Drum
To Be or Not to Be
Tokyo Story
Tom Jones
Tootsie

Top Hat
Touch of Evil
Tristana
Triumph of the Will
Trouble in Paradise
The True Glory
Twelve Angry Men
Two Tars
2001: A Space Odyssey
Unforgiven
Vertigo
Viridiana
Walkabout
Way Out West
The Way to the Stars
Weekend
West Side Story
When Harry Met Sally
Whisky Galore
Who Framed Roger Rabbit
Who's Afraid of Virginia Woolf?
Why We Fight (compilations)
The Wild Bunch
Wild Strawberries
Wings of Desire
Witness
Woodstock
The World of Apu
Yojimbo
Z

Four-Star Films – Year by Year

1915
The Birth of a Nation

1916
Intolerance

1917
The Cure
Easy Street

1919
The Cabinet of Dr Caligari

1925
The Battleship Potemkin

1926
The General

1927
The Jazz Singer
The Kid Brother
Napoleon

1928
The Passion of Joan of Arc
Two Tars

1929
Big Business

1930
All Quiet on the Western Front
The Blue Angel

1931
À Nous la Liberté
Doctor Jekyll and Mr Hyde
Frankenstein
Little Caesar
Le Million

1932
I Am a Fugitive from a Chain Gang
Love Me Tonight
The Music Box
The Old Dark House
Scarface
Trouble in Paradise

1933
Duck Soup
The Invisible Man
King Kong

1934
David Copperfield
The Gay Divorcee
Sons of the Desert

1935
The Bride of Frankenstein
Les Misérables
A Night at the Opera
The Thirty-Nine Steps
Top Hat

1936
Rembrandt
San Francisco
Things to Come
Triumph of the Will

1937
A Day at the Races
Lost Horizon
Oh Mr Porter
The Prisoner of Zenda
Snow White and the Seven Dwarfs
Way Out West

1938
The Adventures of Robin Hood
Alexander Nevsky
Angels with Dirty Faces
The Lady Vanishes
Pygmalion

1939
Destry Rides Again
The Four Feathers
Gone with the Wind
The Hunchback of Notre Dame
Mr Smith Goes to Washington
Stagecoach

1940
Fantasia
Foreign Correspondent
Gaslight
The Grapes of Wrath
His Girl Friday
The Letter
London Can Take It
The Philadelphia Story
Pinocchio
Rebecca
The Thief of Baghdad

1941
All That Money Can Buy
Citizen Kane
Dumbo
Listen to Britain
The Maltese Falcon
Sullivan's Travels
Target for Tonight

1942
Bambi
Casablanca
King's Row
The Magnificent Ambersons
To Be or Not to Be

1944
Double Indemnity
Henry V

1945
And Then There Were None
Brief Encounter
Dead of Night
Les Enfants du Paradis (Children of
    Paradise)
The Lost Weekend
The True Glory
The Way to the Stars

1946
The Best Years of Our Lives
Great Expectations
It's a Wonderful Life
The Jolson Story
A Matter of Life and Death

1947
Crossfire
In Which We Serve

1948
The Naked City
Oliver Twist
The Red Shoes
Whisky Galore

1949
On the Town
Passport to Pimlico
The Third Man

1951
An American in Paris
The Lavender Hill Mob
The Man in the White Suit
Rashomon

1952
High Noon
Singin' in the Rain

1953
The Band Wagon
Begone Dull Care
Genevieve
Monsieur Hulot's Holiday
Tokyo Story

1954
On the Waterfront
Rear Window
The Seven Samurai

1955
Bad Day at Black Rock
Marty
Pather Panchali

1956
Aparajito
The Searchers

1957
The Bridge on the River Kwai
Invasion of the Body Snatchers
Paths of Glory
The Seventh Seal
Sweet Smell of Success
Throne of Blood
Twelve Angry Men
Wild Strawberries

1958
Ashes and Diamonds
Touch of Evil
Vertigo

1959
North by Northwest
Some Like It Hot
The World of Apu

1960
À Bout de Souffle (Breathless)
La Dolce Vita (The Sweet Life)
Psycho
Saturday Night and Sunday Morning

1961
The Hustler
West Side Story
Viridiana
Yojimbo

1962
A Kind of Loving
Lawrence of Arabia
The Manchurian Candidate
Jules et Jim

1963
Dr Strangelove
Eight and a Half
Hud
The Leopard
Tom Jones

1964
A Hard Day's Night
Kwaidan

1965
Battle of Algiers
The Knack

1966
Andrei Rublev
A Man for All Seasons
Persona
Who's Afraid of Virginia Woolf?

1967
Belle de Jour
Bonnie and Clyde
The Graduate
In the Heat of the Night

1968
If . . .
2001: A Space Odyssey
Weekend
Z

1969
Butch Cassidy and the Sundance Kid
Easy Rider

Kes
Midnight Cowboy
The Wild Bunch

1970
M*A*S*H
Tristana
Walkabout
Woodstock

1971
The French Connection
The Last Picture Show

1972
Aguirre, Wrath of God
Cabaret
Cries and Whispers
Deliverance
The Discreet Charm of the Bourgeoisie
The Godfather

1973
Badlands
Day for Night
Don't Look Now
Mean Streets

1974
Chinatown
The Enigma of Kaspar Hauser
The Godfather Part II
Lacombe, Lucien

1975
One Flew over the Cuckoo's Nest
Picnic at Hanging Rock

1976
All the President's Men
Face to Face
Network
Taxi Driver

1977
Annie Hall
Star Wars

1978
The Chant of Jimmy Blacksmith
Days of Heaven
The Driver

1979
Alien
Manhattan
The Tin Drum

1980
Last Metro
Raging Bull

1981
Mephisto
Southern Comfort

1982
E.T.
Fanny and Alexander
Fitzcarraldo
Tootsie

1983
King of Comedy

1984
Once Upon a Time in America
This Is Spinal Tap

1985
Ran
Witness

1987
The Dead
Pelle the Conqueror
Wings of Desire

1988
Au Revoir Les Enfants
A Short Film about Killing
Who Framed Roger Rabbit

1989
Cinema Paradiso
When Harry Met Sally

1990
GoodFellas

1992
Aladdin
The Player
Unforgiven

1993
The Piano
Schindler's List